2003 BASEBALL CARD PRICE GUIDE

• 17TH EDITION •

PRICE GUIDE
EDITORS OF

Published by

700 East State Street • Iola, WI 54990-0001
715-445-2214 • 888-457-2873
www.krause.com

Please call or write for our free catalog of publications.
Our toll-free number to place an order or obtain a free catalog is 800-258-0929
or please use our regular business telephone, 715-445-2214.

Library of Congress Catalog Number: 87-80033
ISBN: 0-87349-587-X

Printed in the United States of America

TABLE OF CONTENTS

B

C

D

E

F

L

M

P

S

T

U

Z

HOW TO USE THIS CATALOG

This catalog has been uniquely designed to serve the needs of collectors and dealers at all levels from beginning to advanced. It provides a comprehensive guide to more than 21 years of baseball card issues, arranged so that even the most novice hobbyist can consult it with confidence and ease.

The following explanations summarize the general practices used in preparing this catalog's listings. However, because of specialized requirements which may vary from card set to card set, these must not be considered ironclad. Where these standards have been set aside, appropriate notations are usually incorporated.

ARRANGEMENT

The most important feature in identifying and pricing a baseball card is its set of origin. Therefore, the main body of this catalog, covering cards issued from 1981-date, has been alphabetically arranged within specific eras of issue according to the name by which the set is most popularly known to collectors, or by which it can be most easily identified by a person examining a card.

Among those card issuers who produced sets for more than a single year, their sets are then listed chronologically, from earliest to most recent, again within specific eras.

Within each set, the cards are listed by their designated card number, or in the absence of card numbers, alphabetically according to the last name of the player pictured. Listing numbers found in parentheses indicate the number does not appear on the card. Certain cards which fall outside the parameters of the normal card numbering for a specific set may be found at the beginning or end of the listings for that set.

VINTAGE-MODERN ISSUES

The main body of the book details modern major league baseball card issues from 1981-2003, as produced by the major national card companies. In general, prior to about 1990, this will include issues which picture one or more baseball players, usually contemporary with their playing days, printed on paper or cardboard in a variety of shapes and sizes and given away as a premium with the purchase of another product or service. After 1990 or so the definition is broadened to remove the restriction of the card as an ancillary product and to include those printed on plastic, wood, metal, etc.

IDENTIFICATION

While most modern baseball cards are well identified on front, back or both, as to date and issue, such has not always been the case. In general, the back of the card is more useful in identifying the set of origin than the front. The issuer or sponsor's name will usually appear on the back since, after all, baseball cards were first produced as a promotional item to stimulate sales of other products. As often as not, that issuer's name is the name by which the set is known to collectors and under which it will be found listed in this catalog.

In some difficult cases, identifying a baseball card's general age, if not specific year of issue, can usually be accomplished by studying the biological or statistical information on the back of the card. The last year mentioned in either the biography or stats is usually the year which preceded the year of issue.

PHOTOGRAPHS

A photograph of the front and (prior to 1981) back of at least one representative card from virtually every set listed in this catalog has been incorporated into the listings to aid in identification.

Photographs have been printed in reduced size. The actual size of cards in each set is given in the introductory text preceding its listing, unless the card is the standard size (2.5" by 3.5").

DATING

The dating of baseball cards by year of issue on the front or back of the card itself is a relatively new phenomenon. In most cases, to accurately determine a date of issue for an unidentified card, it must be studied for clues. As mentioned, the biography, career summary or statistics on the back of the card are the best way to pinpoint a year of issue. In most cases, the year of issue will be the year after the last season mentioned on the card.

In some cases, particular card sets were issued over a period of more than one calendar year, but since they are collected together as a single set, their specific year of issue is not important. Such sets will be listed with their complete known range of issue years.

NUMBERING

While many baseball card issues as far back as the 1880s have contained card numbers assigned by the issuer to facilitate the collecting of a complete set, the practice has by no means been universal. Even today, not every set bears card numbers.

Logically, those baseball cards which were numbered by their manufacturer are presented in that numerical order within the listings of this catalog whenever possible. In a few cases, complete player checklists were obtained from earlier published sources which did not note card numbers, and so numbers have been arbitrarily assigned. Many other unnumbered issues have been assigned catalog numbers to facilitate their universal identification within the hobby, especially when buying and selling by mail.

In all cases, numbers which have been assigned, or which otherwise do not appear on the card through error or by design, are shown in this catalog within parentheses. In virtually all cases, unless a more natural system suggested itself by the unique matter of a particular set, the assignment of numbers by the cataloging staff has been done by alphabetical arrangement of the players' last names or the card's principal title.

Significant collectible variations for any particular card are noted within the listings by the application of a suffix letter. In instances of variations, the suffix "a" is assigned to the variation which was created first, when it can be so identified.

NAMES

The identification of a player by full name on the front of his baseball card has been a common practice only since the 1920s. Prior to that, the player's last name and team were the usual information found on the card front.

As a general -- though not universally applied -- practice, the listings in this volume present the player's name exactly as it appears on the front of the card. If the player's full name only appears on the back, rather than on the front of the card, the listing may correspond to that designation.

A player's name checklisted in italic type indicates a rookie card.

Cards which contain misspelled first or last names, or even wrong initials, will have included in their listings the incorrect information, with a correction accompanying in parentheses. This extends, also, to cases where the name on the card does not correspond to the player actually pictured.

In some cases, to facilitate efficient presentations, to maintain ease of use for the reader, or to allow for proper computer sorting of data, a player's name or card title may be listed other than as it appears on the card.

GRADING

It is necessary that some sort of card grading standard be used so that buyer and seller (especially when dealing by mail) may reach an informed agreement on the value of a card.

Modern issues, which have been preserved in top condition in considerable number, are listed only in grade of Mint (MT), reflective of the fact that there exists in the current market little or no demand for cards of the recent past in lower grades.

Values for lower-grade cards from 1981-date may be generally figured by using a figure of 75% of the Mint price for Near Mint specimens, and 40% of the Mint price for Excellent cards.

For the benefit of the reader, we present herewith the grading guide which was originally formulated in 1981 by Baseball Cards magazine (now SportsCards magazine) and Sports Collectors Digest, and has been continually refined since that time.

These grading definitions have been used in the pricing of cards in this book, but they are by no means a universally-accepted grading standard.

The potential buyer of a baseball card should keep that in mind when encountering cards of nominally the same grade, but at a price which differs widely from that quoted in this book.

Ultimately, the collector himself must formulate his own personal grading standards in deciding whether cards available for purchase meet the needs of his own collection.

Mint (MT): A perfect card. Well-centered, with parallel borders which appear equal to the naked eye. Four sharp, square corners. No creases, edge dents, surface scratches, paper flaws, loss of luster, yellowing or fading, regardless of age. No imperfectly printed card -- out of register, badly cut or ink flawed -- or card stained by contact with gum, wax or other substances can be considered truly Mint, even if new out of the pack. Generally, to be considered in Mint condition, a card's borders must exist in a ratio of 60/40 side to side and top to bottom.

Near Mint (NR MT): A nearly perfectly card. At first glance, a Near Mint card appears perfect; upon closer examination, however, a minor flaw will be discovered. On well-centered cards, three of the four corners must be perfectly sharp; only one corner shows a minor imperfection upon close inspection. A slightly off-center card with one or more borders being noticeably unequal -- but no worse than in a ratio of 70/30 S/S or T/B -- would also fit this grade.

Excellent (EX): Corners are still fairly sharp with only moderate wear. Card borders may be off center as much as 80/20. No creases. May have very minor gum, wax or product stains, front or back. Surfaces may show slight loss of luster from rubbing across other cards.

Very Good (VG): Show obvious handling. Corners rounded and/or perhaps showing minor creases. Other minor creases may be visible. Surfaces may exhibit loss of luster, but all printing is intact. May show major gum, wax or other packaging stains. No major creases, tape marks or extraneous markings or writing. All four borders visible, though the ratio may be as poor as 95/5. Exhibits honest wear.

Good (G): A well-worn card, but exhibits no intentional damage or abuse. May have major or multiple creases. Corners rounded well beyond the border. A good card will generally sell for about 50% the value of a card in Very Good condition.

Fair (F or Fr.): Shows excessive wear, along with damage or abuse. Will show all the wear characteristics of a Good card, along with such damage as thumb tack holes in or near margins, evidence of having been taped or pasted, perhaps small tears around the edges, or creases so heavy as to break the cardboard. Backs may show minor added pen or pencil writing, or be missing small bits of paper. Still, basically a complete card. A Fair card will generally for 50% the value of a Good specimen.

Poor (P): A card that has been tortured to death. Corners or other areas may be torn off. Card may have been trimmed, show holes from a paper punch or have been used for BB gun practice. Front may have extraneous pen or pencil writing, or other defacement. Major portions of front or back design may be missing. Not a pretty sight.

In addition to these terms, collectors may encounter intermediate grades, such as NM-MT or EX-MT. These cards usually have characteristics of both the lower and higher grades, and are generally priced midway between those two values.

Grading and pricing reflected in this book are for cards which have not been authenticated, graded and encapsulated by one of the third-party certification services. Cards which have been "slabbed" by these services generally sell for a premium above the price which a "raw" card will bring.

ROOKIE CARDS

While the status (and automatic premium value) which a player's rookie card carries has fallen and risen in recent years, and though the hobby still has not reached a universal definition of a rookie card, many significant rookie cards are noted in this catalog's listings by the use of italic type. For purposes of this catalog, a player's rookie card is considered to be any card in a licensed set from a major manufacturer in the first year in which that player appears on a card.

VALUATIONS

Values quoted in this book represent the current retail market at the time of compilation (January, 2003). The quoted values are the result of a unique system of evaluation and verification created by the catalog's editors. Utilizing specialized computer analysis and drawing upon recommendations provided through their daily involvement in the publication of the hobby's leading sports collectors' periodicals, as well as the input of consultants, dealers and collectors, each listing is, in the final analysis, the interpretation of that data by one or more of the editors.

It should be stressed, however, that this book is intended to serve only as an aid in evaluating cards; actual market conditions are constantly changing. This is especially true of the cards of current players, whose on-field performance during the course of a season can greatly affect the value of their cards -- upwards or downwards. Because of the extremely volatile nature of new card prices, especially high-end issues, we have chosen not to include the very latest releases such as premium-price brands from the major companies, feeling it is better to have no listings at all for those cards than to have inaccurate values in print.

Because this volume is intended to reflect the national market, users will find regional price variances caused by demand differences. Cards of Astros slugger Jeff Bagwell will, for instance, often sell at prices greater than quoted herein at shops and shows in the Houston area. Conversely, his cards may be acquired at a discount from these valuations when purchased on the East or West Coast.

Publication of this book is not intended as a solicitation to buy or sell the listed cards by the editors, publishers or contributors.

Again, the values here are retail prices -- what a collector can expect to pay when buying a card from a dealer. The wholesale price, that which a collector can expect to receive from a dealer when selling cards, will be significantly lower.

SETS

Collectors may note that the complete set prices for newer issues quoted in these listings are usually significantly lower than the total of the value of the individual cards which comprise the set. This reflects two factors in the baseball card market. First, a seller is often willing to take a lower composite price for a complete set as a "volume discount" and to avoid carrying in inventory a large number of common player or other lower-demand cards.

Some set prices shown, especially for old cards in top condition, are merely theoretical in that it is unlikely that a complete set exists in that condition. In general among older cards the range of conditions found in even the most painstakingly assembled complete set make the set values quoted useful only as a starting point for price negotiations.

ERRORS/VARIATIONS

It is often hard for the beginning collector to understand that an error on a baseball card, in and of itself, does not usually add premium value to that card. It is usually only when the correcting of an error in the subsequent printing creates a variation that premium value attaches to an error.

Minor errors, such as wrong stats or personal data, misspellings, inconsistencies, etc. -- usually affecting the back of the card -- are very common, especially in recent years. Unless a corrected variation was also printed, these errors are not noted in the listings of this book because they are not generally perceived by collectors to have premium value.

On the other hand, major effort has been expended to include the most complete listings ever for collectible variation cards. Many scarce and valuable variations are included in these listings because they are widely collected and often have significant premium value.

Beginning in the early 1990s, some card companies began production of their basic sets at more than one printing facility. This frequently resulted in numerous minor variations in photo cropping and back data presentation. Combined with a general decline in quality control from the mid-1980s through the early 1990s, which allowed unprecedented numbers of uncorrected error cards to be released, this caused a general softening of collector interest in errors and variations. Despite the fact most of these modern variations have no premium value, they are listed here as a matter of record.

COUNTERFEITS/REPRINTS

As the value of baseball cards has risen, certain cards and sets have become too expensive for the average collector to obtain. This, along with changes in the technology of color printing, has given rise to increasing numbers of counterfeit and reprint cards.

While both terms describe essentially the same thing -- a modern day copy which attempts to duplicate as closely as possible an original baseball card -- there are differences which are important to the collector.

Generally, a counterfeit is made with the intention of deceiving somebody into believing it is genuine, and thus paying large amounts of money for it. The counterfeiter takes every pain to try to make his fakes look as authentic as possible. In recent years, the 1963 Pete Rose, 1984 Donruss Don Mattingly and more than 100 superstar cards of the late 1960s-early 1990s have been counterfeited - many of which were quickly detected because of the differences in quality of cardboard on which they were printed.

A reprint, on the other hand, while it may have been made to look as close as possible to an original card, is made with the intention of allowing collectors to buy them as substitutes for cards they may never be otherwise able to afford. The big difference is that a reprint is generally marked as such, usually on the back of the card.

A collector's best defense against reprints and counterfeits is to acquire a knowledge of the look and feel of genuine baseball cards of various eras and issues.

MODERN MAJOR LEAGUE CARDS (1981-2002)

The vast majority of cards listed in this section were issued between 1981 and late-2002 and feature major league players only. The term "card" is used rather loosely as in this context it is construed to include virtually any series of cardboard or paper product, of whatever size and/or shape, depicting baseball players. Further, "cards" printed on wood, metal, plastic and other materials are either by their association with other issues or by their compatibility in size with the current 2-1/2" x 3-1/2" card standard also listed here.

Because modern cards are generally not popularly collected in lower grades, cards in this section carry only a Mint (MT) value quote. In general, post-1980 cards which grade Near Mint (NM) will retail at about 75% of the Mint price, while Excellent (EX) condition cards bring 40%.

B

1988 Bazooka

This 22-card set from Topps marks the first Bazooka issue since 1971. Full-color player photos are bordered in white, with the player name printed on a red, white and blue bubble gum box in the lower right corner. Flip sides are also red, white and blue, printed vertically. A large, but faint, Bazooka logo backs the Topps baseball logo team name, card number, player's name and position, followed by batting records, personal information and brief career highlights. Cards were sold inside specially marked 59Û and 79Û Bazooka gum and candy boxes, one card per box.

		MT
Complete Set (22):		6.00
Common Player:		.20
1	George Bell	.20
2	Wade Boggs	.60
3	Jose Canseco	.35
4	Roger Clemens	.60
5	Vince Coleman	.20
6	Eric Davis	.20
7	Tony Fernandez	.20
8	Dwight Gooden	.20
9	Tony Gwynn	.60
10	Wally Joyner	.20
11	Don Mattingly	1.00
12	Willie McGee	.20
13	Mark McGwire	2.00
14	Kirby Puckett	.75
15	Tim Raines	.20
16	Dave Righetti	.20
17	Cal Ripken, Jr.	2.00
18	Juan Samuel	.20
19	Ryne Sandberg	.50
20	Benny Santiago	.20
21	Darryl Strawberry	.20
22	Todd Worrell	.20

1989 Bazooka

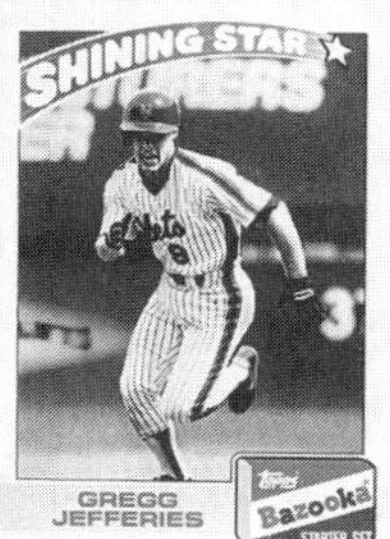

Topps produced this 22-card set in 1989 to be included (one card per box) in specially-marked boxes of its Bazooka brand bubblegum. The player photos have the words "Shining Star" along the top, while the player's name appears along the bottom of the card, along with the Topps Bazooka logo in the lower right corner. The cards are numbered alphabetically.

		MT
Complete Set (22):		4.00
Common Player:		.15
1	Tim Belcher	.15
2	Damon Berryhill	.15
3	Wade Boggs	.50
4	Jay Buhner	.15
5	Jose Canseco	.35
6	Vince Coleman	.15
7	Cecil Espy	.15
8	Dave Gallagher	.15
9	Ron Gant	.15
10	Kirk Gibson	.15
11	Paul Gibson	.15
12	Mark Grace	.50
13	Tony Gwynn	.75
14	Rickey Henderson	.50
15	Orel Hershiser	.15
16	Gregg Jefferies	.15
17	Ricky Jordan	.15
18	Chris Sabo	.15
19	Gary Sheffield	.30
20	Darryl Strawberry	.15
21	Frank Viola	.15
22	Walt Weiss	.15

1990 Bazooka

For the second consecutive year, Bazooka entitled its set "Shining Stars." Full color action and posed player shots are featured on the card fronts. The flip sides feature player statistics in a style much like the cards from the previous two Bazooka issues. Unlike the past two releases, the cards are not numbered alphabetically. The cards measure 2-1/2" x 3-1/2" in size and 22 cards complete the set.

		MT
Complete Set (22):		4.00
Common Player:		.15
1	Kevin Mitchell	.15
2	Robin Yount	.35
3	Mark Davis	.15
4	Bret Saberhagen	.15
5	Fred McGriff	.15
6	Tony Gwynn	.50
7	Kirby Puckett	.50
8	Vince Coleman	.15
9	Rickey Henderson	.35
10	Ben McDonald	.15
11	Gregg Olson	.15
12	Todd Zeile	.15
13	Carlos Martinez	.15
14	Gregg Jefferies	.15
15	Craig Worthington	.15
16	Gary Sheffield	.20
17	Greg Briley	.15
18	Ken Griffey, Jr.	2.00
19	Jerome Walton	.15
20	Bob Geren	.15
21	Tom Gordon	.15
22	Jim Abbott	.15

1991 Bazooka

For the third consecutive year Bazooka entitled its set "Shining Stars." The cards are styled like the 1990 issue, but include the Topps "40th Anniversary" logo. The 1991 issue is considered much scarcer than the previous releases. The cards measure 2-1/2" x 3-1/2" in size and 22 cards complete the set.

		MT
Complete Set (22):		10.00
Common Player:		.30
1	Barry Bonds	1.50
2	Rickey Henderson	.45
3	Bob Welch	.30
4	Doug Drabek	.30

5	Alex Fernandez	.30
6	Jose Offerman	.30
7	Frank Thomas	1.25
8	Cecil Fielder	.30
9	Ryne Sandberg	.75
10	George Brett	.75
11	Willie McGee	.30
12	Vince Coleman	.30
13	Hal Morris	.30
14	Delino DeShields	.30
15	Robin Ventura	.30
16	Jeff Huson	.30
17	Felix Jose	.30
18	Dave Justice	.30
19	Larry Walker	.50
20	Sandy Alomar, Jr.	.30
21	Kevin Appier	.30
22	Scott Radinsky	.30

1992 Bazooka

This set of 22 cards features miniature versions of the 1953 Topps Archives issue. The mini-cards are set against a blue background on front and back. Besides reproductions of issued 1953 Topps cards, these "Quadracards" include miniature versions of many of the special cards created for the Archives set. Cards feature the Bazooka logo on back, and were distributed in boxes of that bubble gum. They are readily available in complete set form.

		MT
Complete Set (22):		17.50
Common Player:		.50
1	Joe Adcock, Bob Lemon, Willie Mays, Vic Wertz	3.00
2	Carl Furillo, Don Newcombe, Phil Rizzuto, Hank Sauer	.50
3	Ferris Fain, John Logan, Ed Mathews, Bobby Shantz	.50
4	Yogi Berra, Del Crandall, Howie Pollett, Gene Woodling	.50
5	Richie Ashburn, Leo Durocher, Allie Reynolds, Early Wynn	.50
6	Hank Aaron, Ray Boone, Luke Easter, Dick Williams	3.00
7	Ralph Branca, Bob Feller, Rogers Hornsby, Bobby Thomson	.50
8	Jim Gilliam, Billy Martin, Orestes Minoso, Hal Newhouser	.50
9	Smoky Burgess, John Mize, Preacher Roe, Warren Spahn	.50
10	Monte Irvin, Bobo Newsom, Duke Snider, Wes Westrum	.50
11	Carl Erskine, Jackie Jensen, George Kell, Al Schoendienst	.50
12	Bill Bruton, Whitey Ford, Ed Lopat, Mickey Vernon	.50
13	Joe Black, Lew Burdette, Johnny Pesky, Enos Slaughter	.50
14	Gus Bell, Mike Garcia, Mel Parnell, Jackie Robinson	2.50
15	Alvin Dark, Dick Groat, Pee Wee Reese, John Sain	.50
16	Gil Hodges, Sal Maglie, Wilmer Mizell, Billy Pierce	1.00
17	Nellie Fox, Ralph Kiner, Ted Kluszewski, Eddie Stanky	.50
18	Ewell Blackwell, Vern Law, Satchell Paige, Jim Wilson	1.00
19	Lou Boudreau, Roy Face, Harvey Haddix, Bill Rigney	.50
20	Roy Campanella, Walt Dropo, Harvey Kuenn, Al Rosen	1.00
21	Joe Garagiola, Robin Roberts, Casey Stengel, Hoyt Wilhelm	.50
22	John Antonelli, Bob Friend, Dixie Walker, Ted Williams	2.00

1993 Bazooka Team USA

The members of Team USA are featured on this boxed set. The 2-1/2" x 3-1/2" cards feature the same basic design as 1993 Topps baseball, except for a Bazooka gum logo in one of the upper corners. Both front and back feature posed player photos. Backs have a design simulating the U.S. flag and include amateur stats, biographical details and career highlights. The cards are virtually identical to the same players' cards in the 1993 Topps Traded set, with the addition of the Bazooka logo on front and the differences in card numbers.

		MT
Complete Set (22):		12.00
Common Player:		.25
1	Terry Harvey	.25
2	Dante Powell	.50
3	Andy Barkett	.25
4	Steve Reich	.25
5	Charlie Nelson	.25
6	Todd Walker	1.00
7	Dustin Hermanson	1.00
8	Pat Clougherty	.25
9	Danny Graves	.25
10	Paul Wilson	.75
11	Todd Helton	3.00
12	Russ Johnson	.50
13	Darren Grass	.25
14	A.J. Hinch	.35
15	Mark Merila	.25
16	John Powell	.25
17	Bob Scafa	.25
18	Matt Beaumont	.25
19	Todd Dunn	.25
20	Mike Martin	.25
21	Carlton Loewer	.25
22	Bret Wagner	.25

1995 Bazooka

Topps returned to the beginner's level baseball card niche in 1995 by resurrecting its Bazooka brand name. The set was unabashedly aimed at the younger collector, offering five cards and a Bazooka Joe cartoon-wrapped chunk of bubble-gum for 50 cents. Cards feature on their backs a "roulette" wheel design based on the player's 1994 stats, to be used to play a game of spinner baseball. A game instruction card and cardboard spinner was included in each pack. Limiting the set to 132 cards allowed for a concentration of established stars and hot rookies. A 22-card Red Hot insert set is found at the rate of one card per six packs, on average.

		MT
Complete Set (132):		7.50
Common Player:		.05
Pack (5):		.50
Wax Box (36):		12.00
1	Greg Maddux	.65
2	Cal Ripken Jr.	1.50
3	Lee Smith	.05
4	Sammy Sosa	.75
5	Jason Bere	.05
6	Dave Justice	.05
7	Kevin Mitchell	.05
8	Ozzie Guillen	.05
9	Roger Clemens	.65
10	Mike Mussina	.40
11	Sandy Alomar	.05
12	Cecil Fielder	.05
13	Dennis Martinez	.05
14	Randy Myers	.05
15	Jay Buhner	.05
16	Ivan Rodriguez	.45
17	Mo Vaughn	.35
18	Ryan Klesko	.05
19	Chuck Finley	.05
20	Barry Bonds	.75
21	Dennis Eckersley	.05
22	Kenny Lofton	.05
23	Rafael Palmeiro	.15
24	Mike Stanley	.05
25	Gregg Jefferies	.05
26	Robin Ventura	.05
27	Mark McGwire	1.50
28	Ozzie Smith	.65
29	Troy Neel	.05
30	Tony Gwynn	.65
31	Ken Griffey Jr.	1.25
32	Will Clark	.15
33	Craig Biggio	.10
34	Shawon Dunston	.05
35	Wilson Alvarez	.05
36	Bobby Bonilla	.05
37	Marquis Grissom	.05
38	Ben McDonald	.05
39	Delino DeShields	.05
40	Barry Larkin	.10
41	John Olerud	.05
42	Jose Canseco	.35
43	Greg Vaughn	.05
44	Gary Sheffield	.20
45	Paul O'Neill	.05
46	Bob Hamelin	.05
47	Don Mattingly	.75
48	John Franco	.05
49	Bret Boone	.05
50	Rick Aguilera	.05
51	Tim Wallach	.05
52	Roberto Kelly	.05
53	Danny Tartabull	.05
54	Randy Johnson	.35
55	Greg McMichael	.05
56	Bip Roberts	.05
57	David Cone	.05
58	Raul Mondesi	.05
59	Travis Fryman	.05
60	Jeff Conine	.05
61	Jeff Bagwell	.50
62	Rickey Henderson	.40
63	Fred McGriff	.05
64	Matt Williams	.15
65	Rick Wilkins	.05
66	Eric Karros	.05
67	Mel Rojas	.05
68	Juan Gonzalez	.50
69	Chuck Carr	.05
70	Moises Alou	.10
71	Mark Grace	.20
72	Alex Fernandez	.05
73	Rod Beck	.05
74	Ray Lankford	.05
75	Dean Palmer	.05
76	Joe Carter	.05
77	Mike Piazza	1.00
78	Eddie Murray	.45
79	Dave Nilsson	.05
80	Brett Butler	.05
81	Roberto Alomar	.20
82	Jeff Kent	.05
83	Andres Galarraga	.05
84	Brady Anderson	.05
85	Jimmy Key	.05
86	Bret Saberhagen	.05
87	Chili Davis	.05
88	Jose Rijo	.05
89	Wade Boggs	.45
90	Len Dykstra	.05
91	Steve Howe	.05
92	Hal Morris	.05
93	Larry Walker	.15
94	Jeff Montgomery	.05
95	Wil Cordero	.05
96	Jay Bell	.05
97	Tom Glavine	.10
98	Chris Hoiles	.05
99	Steve Avery	.05
100	Ruben Sierra	.05
101	Mickey Tettleton	.05
102	Paul Molitor	.40
103	Carlos Baerga	.05
104	Walt Weiss	.05
105	Darren Daulton	.05
106	Jack McDowell	.05
107	Doug Drabek	.05
108	Mark Langston	.05
109	Manny Ramirez	.50
110	Kevin Appier	.05
111	Andy Benes	.05
112	Chuck Knoblauch	.05
113	Kirby Puckett	.65
114	Dante Bichette	.05
115	Deion Sanders	.10
116	Albert Belle	.15
117	Todd Zeile	.05
118	Devon White	.05
119	Tim Salmon	.05
120	Frank Thomas	.75
121	John Wetteland	.05

122	James Mouton	.05
123	Javy Lopez	.05
124	Carlos Delgado	.15
125	Cliff Floyd	.05
126	Alex Gonzalez	.05
127	Billy Ashley	.05
128	Rondell White	.05
129	Rico Brogna	.05
130	Melvin Nieves	.05
131	Jose Oliva	.05
132	J.R. Phillips	.05

1995 Bazooka Red Hot Inserts

Twenty-two of the game's biggest stars were chosen for inclusion in 1995 Bazooka's only insert set - Red Hots. The chase cards are found at an average rate of one per six packs. Red Hots are identical to the players' cards in the regular set except that the background has been rendered in shades of red, and the player name printed in gold foil. Card numbers have an "RH" prefix.

		MT
Complete Set (22):		12.00
Common Player:		.25
1	Greg Maddux	1.50
2	Cal Ripken Jr.	3.00
3	Barry Bonds	2.00
4	Kenny Lofton	.25
5	Mike Stanley	.25
6	Tony Gwynn	1.50
7	Ken Griffey Jr.	3.00
8	Barry Larkin	.30
9	Jose Canseco	.50
10	Paul O'Neill	.25
11	Randy Johnson	.75
12	David Cone	.25
13	Jeff Bagwell	1.00
14	Matt Williams	.35
15	Mike Piazza	2.00
16	Roberto Alomar	.35
17	Jimmy Key	.25
18	Wade Boggs	.60
19	Paul Molitor	.60
20	Carlos Baerga	.25
21	Albert Belle	.35
22	Frank Thomas	1.25

1996 Bazooka

Using a simple, yet nostalgic design, Topps' 1996 Bazooka set offers collectors a source of fun with its cards geared for a flipping game. Each front has a full-color action photo of the player. The back contains one of five different Bazooka Joe characters, along with the Bazooka Ball game, the player's biographical data, and 1995 and career stats. Each card also contains a Funny Fortune, which predicts the fate of a player on a particular date. Cards were available five per pack for 50 cents. The complete set of all 132 cards is also offered in a factory set, packaged in an attractive gift box. All the top veterans, rookies and rising stars are included, as well as a Bazooka Ball info card containing all the rules to play the flipping game. As an exclusive bonus, one 1959 Bazooka Mickey Mantle reprint card can be found in every factory set. This card was originally found on boxes of Bazooka gum sold that year. Ten pieces of Mega Bazooka Gum are also included with the set.

		MT
Unopened Factory Set (133):		16.00
Complete Set (132):		12.00
Common Player:		.05
Pack (5):		.50
Wax Box (36):		15.00
1	Ken Griffey Jr.	1.25
2	J.T. Snow	.05
3	Rondell White	.05
4	Reggie Sanders	.05
5	Jeff Montgomery	.05
6	Mike Stanley	.05
7	Bernie Williams	.15
8	Mike Piazza	1.00
9	Brian Hunter	.05
10	Len Dykstra	.05
11	Ray Lankford	.05
12	Kenny Lofton	.05
13	Robin Ventura	.05
14	Devon White	.05
15	Cal Ripken Jr.	1.50
16	Heathcliff Slocumb	.05
17	Ryan Klesko	.05
18	Terry Steinbach	.05
19	Travis Fryman	.05
20	Sammy Sosa	.75
21	Jim Thome	.05
22	Kenny Rogers	.05
23	Don Mattingly	.75
24	Kirby Puckett	.65
25	Matt Williams	.15
26	Larry Walker	.15
27	Tim Wakefield	.05
28	Greg Vaughn	.05
29	Denny Neagle	.05
30	Ken Caminiti	.05
31	Garret Anderson	.05
32	Brady Anderson	.05
33	Carlos Baerga	.05
34	Wade Boggs	.35
35	Roberto Alomar	.20
36	Eric Karros	.05
37	Jay Buhner	.05
38	Dante Bichette	.05
39	Darren Daulton	.05
40	Jeff Bagwell	.50
41	Jay Bell	.05
42	Dennis Eckersley	.05
43	Will Clark	.15
44	Tom Glavine	.15
45	Rick Aguilera	.05
46	Kevin Seitzer	.05
47	Bret Boone	.05
48	Mark Grace	.30
49	Ray Durham	.05
50	Rico Brogna	.05
51	Kevin Appier	.05
52	Moises Alou	.10
53	Jeff Conine	.05
54	Marty Cordova	.05
55	Jose Mesa	.05
56	Rod Beck	.05
57	Marquis Grissom	.05
58	David Cone	.05
59	Albert Belle	.15
60	Lee Smith	.05
61	Frank Thomas	.75
62	Roger Clemens	.65
63	Bobby Bonilla	.05
64	Paul Molitor	.35
65	Chuck Knoblauch	.05
66	Steve Finley	.05
67	Craig Biggio	.10
68	Ramon Martinez	.05
69	Jason Isringhausen	.05
70	Mark Wohlers	.05
71	Vinny Castilla	.05
72	Ron Gant	.05
73	Juan Gonzalez	.50
74	Mark McGwire	1.50
75	Jeff King	.05
76	Pedro Martinez	.40
77	Chad Curtis	.05
78	John Olerud	.05
79	Greg Maddux	.65
80	Derek Jeter	1.00
81	Mike Mussina	.40
82	Gregg Jefferies	.05
83	Jim Edmonds	.05
84	Carlos Perez	.05
85	Mo Vaughn	.20
86	Todd Hundley	.05
87	Roberto Hernandez	.05
88	Derek Bell	.05
89	Andres Galarraga	.05
90	Brian McRae	.05
91	Joe Carter	.05
92	Orlando Merced	.05
93	Cecil Fielder	.05
94	Dean Palmer	.05
95	Randy Johnson	.35
96	Chipper Jones	1.00
97	Barry Larkin	.10
98	Hideo Nomo	.45
99	Gary Gaetti	.05
100	Edgar Martinez	.05
101	John Wetteland	.05
102	Rafael Palmeiro	.20
103	Chuck Finley	.05
104	Ivan Rodriguez	.35
105	Shawn Green	.20
106	Manny Ramirez	.50
107	Lance Johnson	.05
108	Jose Canseco	.25
109	Fred McGriff	.05
110	David Segui	.05
111	Tim Salmon	.05
112	Hal Morris	.05
113	Tino Martinez	.05
114	Bret Saberhagen	.05
115	Brian Jordan	.05
116	David Justice	.05
117	Jack McDowell	.05
118	Barry Bonds	.75
119	Mark Langston	.05
120	John Valentin	.05
121	Raul Mondesi	.05
122	Quilvio Veras	.05
123	Randy Myers	.05
124	Tony Gwynn	.65
125	Johnny Damon	.10
126	Doug Drabek	.05
127	Bill Pulsipher	.05
128	Paul O'Neill	.05
129	Rickey Henderson	.40
130	Deion Sanders	.10
131	Orel Hershiser	.05
132	Gary Sheffield	.15

1996 Bazooka Mickey Mantle 1959 Reprint

Continuing its tribute to the late Mickey Mantle across all of its product lines, Topps produced a special reprint of the 1959 Bazooka Mantle card exclusively for inclusion in factory sets of its 1996 Bazooka cards. While the original '59 Mantle was printed in nearly 3" x 5" size on the bottom of gum boxes, the reprint is in the current 2-1/2" x 3-1/2" size.

	MT
Mickey Mantle	9.00

1989 Bowman

Topps, which purchased Bowman in 1955, revived the brand name in 1989, issuing a 484-card set. The 2-1/2" x 3-3/4" cards are slightly taller than current standard. Fronts contain a full-color player photo, with facsimile autograph and the Bowman logo in an upper corner. Backs include a breakdown of the player's stats against each team in his league. A series of "Hot Rookie Stars" highlights the set. The cards were distributed in both wax packs and rack packs. Each pack included a special reproduction of a classic Bowman card with a sweepstakes on the back.

	MT
Complete Set (484):	25.00
Common Player:	.05

No.	Player	Price
	Pack (12+1):	2.00
	Wax Box (36):	30.00
1	Oswald Peraza	.05
2	Brian Holton	.05
3	Jose Bautista	.05
4	*Pete Harnisch*	.20
5	Dave Schmidt	.05
6	Gregg Olson	.05
7	Jeff Ballard	.05
8	Bob Melvin	.05
9	Cal Ripken, Jr.	.75
10	Randy Milligan	.05
11	*Juan Bell*	.05
12	Billy Ripken	.05
13	Jim Trabor	.05
14	Pete Stanicek	.05
15	*Steve Finley*	.25
16	Larry Sheets	.05
17	Phil Bradley	.05
18	Brady Anderson	.05
19	Lee Smith	.05
20	Tom Fischer	.05
21	Mike Boddicker	.05
22	Rob Murphy	.05
23	Wes Gardner	.05
24	John Dopson	.05
25	Bob Stanley	.05
26	Roger Clemens	.50
27	Rich Gedman	.05
28	Marty Barrett	.05
29	Luis Rivera	.05
30	Jody Reed	.05
31	Nick Esasky	.05
32	Wade Boggs	.40
33	Jim Rice	.10
34	Mike Greenwell	.05
35	Dwight Evans	.05
36	Ellis Burks	.05
37	Chuck Finley	.05
38	Kirk McCaskill	.05
39	Jim Abbott	.05
40	*Bryan Harvey*	.05
41	Bert Blyleven	.05
42	Mike Witt	.05
43	Bob McClure	.05
44	Bill Schroeder	.05
45	Lance Parrish	.05
46	Dick Schofield	.05
47	Wally Joyner	.05
48	Jack Howell	.05
49	Johnny Ray	.05
50	Chili Davis	.05
51	Tony Armas	.05
52	Claudell Washington	.05
53	Brian Downing	.05
54	Devon White	.05
55	Bobby Thigpen	.05
56	Bill Long	.05
57	Jerry Reuss	.05
58	Shawn Hillegas	.05
59	Melido Perez	.05
60	Jeff Bittiger	.05
61	Jack McDowell	.05
62	Carlton Fisk	.35
63	Steve Lyons	.05
64	Ozzie Guillen	.05
65	Robin Ventura	.05
66	Fred Manrique	.05
67	Dan Pasqua	.05
68	Ivan Calderon	.05
69	Ron Kittle	.05
70	Daryl Boston	.05
71	Dave Gallagher	.05
72	Harold Baines	.05
73	*Charles Nagy*	.25
74	John Farrell	.05
75	Kevin Wickander	.05
76	Greg Swindell	.05
77	Mike Walker	.05
78	Doug Jones	.05
79	Rich Yett	.05
80	Tom Candiotti	.05
81	Jesse Orosco	.05
82	Bud Black	.05
83	Andy Allanson	.05
84	Pete O'Brien	.05
85	Jerry Browne	.05
86	Brook Jacoby	.05
87	*Mark Lewis*	.05
88	Luis Aguayo	.05
89	Cory Snyder	.05
90	Oddibe McDowell	.05
91	Joe Carter	.05
92	Frank Tanana	.05
93	Jack Morris	.05
94	Doyle Alexander	.05
95	Steve Searcy	.05
96	Randy Bockus	.05
97	Jeff Robinson	.05
98	Mike Henneman	.05
99	Paul Gibson	.05
100	Frank Williams	.05
101	Matt Nokes	.05
102	Rico Brogna	.05
103	Lou Whitaker	.05
104	Al Pedrique	.05
105	Alan Trammell	.05
106	Chris Brown	.05
107	Pat Sheridan	.05
108	Gary Pettis	.05
109	Keith Moreland	.05
110	Mel Stottlemyre, Jr.	.05
111	Bret Saberhagen	.05
112	Floyd Bannister	.05
113	Jeff Montgomery	.05
114	Steve Farr	.05
115	Tom Gordon	.05
116	Charlie Leibrandt	.05
117	Mark Gubicza	.05
118	Mike MacFarlane	.05
119	Bob Boone	.05
120	Kurt Stillwell	.05
121	George Brett	.50
122	Frank White	.05
123	Kevin Seitzer	.05
124	Willie Wilson	.05
125	Pat Tabler	.05
126	Bo Jackson	.10
127	Hugh Walker	.05
128	Danny Tartabull	.05
129	Teddy Higuera	.05
130	Don August	.05
131	Juan Nieves	.05
132	Mike Birkbeck	.05
133	Dan Plesac	.05
134	Chris Bosio	.05
135	Bill Wegman	.05
136	Chuck Crim	.05
137	B.J. Surhoff	.05
138	Joey Meyer	.05
139	Dale Sveum	.05
140	Paul Molitor	.40
141	Jim Gantner	.05
142	*Gary Sheffield*	1.50
143	Greg Brock	.05
144	Robin Yount	.40
145	Glenn Braggs	.05
146	Rob Deer	.05
147	Fred Toliver	.05
148	Jeff Reardon	.05
149	Allan Anderson	.05
150	Frank Viola	.05
151	Shane Rawley	.05
152	Juan Berenguer	.05
153	Johnny Ard	.05
154	Tim Laudner	.05
155	Brian Harper	.05
156	Al Newman	.05
157	Kent Hrbek	.05
158	Gary Gaetti	.05
159	Wally Backman	.05
160	Gene Larkin	.05
161	Greg Gagne	.05
162	Kirby Puckett	.50
163	Danny Gladden	.05
164	Randy Bush	.05
165	Dave LaPoint	.05
166	Andy Hawkins	.05
167	Dave Righetti	.05
168	Lance McCullers	.05
169	Jimmy Jones	.05
170	Al Leiter	.05
171	John Candelaria	.05
172	Don Slaught	.05
173	Jamie Quirk	.05
174	Rafael Santana	.05
175	Mike Pagliarulo	.05
176	Don Mattingly	.65
177	Ken Phelps	.05
178	Steve Sax	.05
179	Dave Winfield	.40
180	Stan Jefferson	.05
181	Rickey Henderson	.45
182	Bob Brower	.05
183	Roberto Kelly	.05
184	Curt Young	.05
185	Gene Nelson	.05
186	Bob Welch	.05
187	Rick Honeycutt	.05
188	Dave Stewart	.05
189	Mike Moore	.05
190	Dennis Eckersley	.05
191	Eric Plunk	.05
192	Storm Davis	.05
193	Terry Steinbach	.05
194	Ron Hassey	.05
195	Stan Royer	.05
196	Walt Weiss	.05
197	Mark McGwire	.75
198	Carney Lansford	.05
199	Glenn Hubbard	.05
200	Dave Henderson	.05
201	Jose Canseco	.35
202	Dave Parker	.05
203	Scott Bankhead	.05
204	Tom Niedenfuer	.05
205	Mark Langston	.05
206	*Erik Hanson*	.05
207	Mike Jackson	.05
208	Dave Valle	.05
209	Scott Bradley	.05
210	Harold Reynolds	.05
211	Tino Martinez	.05
212	Rich Renteria	.05
213	Rey Quinones	.05
214	Jim Presley	.05
215	Alvin Davis	.05
216	Edgar Martinez	.05
217	Darnell Coles	.05
218	Jeffrey Leonard	.05
219	Jay Buhner	.05
220	*Ken Griffey, Jr.*	15.00
221	Drew Hall	.05
222	Bobby Witt	.05
223	Jamie Moyer	.05
224	Charlie Hough	.05
225	Nolan Ryan	.75
226	Jeff Russell	.05
227	Jim Sundberg	.05
228	Julio Franco	.05
229	Buddy Bell	.05
230	Scott Fletcher	.05
231	Jeff Kunkel	.05
232	Steve Buechele	.05
233	Monty Fariss	.05
234	Rick Leach	.05
235	Ruben Sierra	.05
236	Cecil Espy	.05
237	Rafael Palmeiro	.15
238	Pete Incaviglia	.05
239	Dave Steib	.05
240	Jeff Musselman	.05
241	Mike Flanagan	.05
242	Todd Stottlemyre	.05
243	Jimmy Key	.05
244	Tony Castillo	.05
245	Alex Sanchez	.05
246	Tom Henke	.05
247	John Cerutti	.05
248	Ernie Whitt	.05
249	Bob Brenly	.05
250	Rance Mulliniks	.05
251	Kelly Gruber	.05
252	Ed Sprague	.05
253	Fred McGriff	.05
254	Tony Fernandez	.05
255	Tom Lawless	.05
256	George Bell	.05
257	Jesse Barfield	.05
258	Sandy Alomar, Sr.	.05
259	Ken Griffey (with Ken Griffey, Jr.)	1.00
260	Cal Ripken, Sr.	.05
261	Mel Stottlemyre, Sr.	.05
262	Zane Smith	.05
263	Charlie Puleo	.05
264	Derek Lilliquist	.05
265	Paul Assenmacher	.05
266	John Smoltz	.10
267	Tom Glavine	.10
268	*Steve Avery*	.05
269	*Pete Smith*	.05
270	Jody Davis	.05
271	Bruce Benedict	.05
272	Andres Thomas	.05
273	Gerald Perry	.05
274	Ron Gant	.05
275	Darrell Evans	.05
276	Dale Murphy	.20
277	Dion James	.05
278	Lonnie Smith	.05
279	Geronimo Berroa	.05
280	Steve Wilson	.05
281	Rick Sutcliffe	.05
282	Kevin Coffman	.05
283	Mitch Williams	.05
284	Greg Maddux	.50
285	Paul Kilgus	.05
286	Mike Harkey	.05
287	Lloyd McClendon	.05
288	Damon Berryhill	.05
289	Ty Griffin	.05
290	Ryne Sandberg	.45
291	Mark Grace	.25
292	Curt Wilkerson	.05
293	Vance Law	.05
294	Shawon Dunston	.05
295	Jerome Walton	.05
296	Mitch Webster	.05
297	Dwight Smith	.05
298	Andre Dawson	.15
299	Jeff Sellers	.05
300	Jose Rijo	.05
301	John Franco	.05
302	Rick Mahler	.05
303	Ron Robinson	.05
304	Danny Jackson	.05
305	Rob Dibble	.05
306	Tom Browning	.05
307	Bo Diaz	.05
308	Manny Trillo	.05
309	Chris Sabo	.05
310	Ron Oester	.05
311	Barry Larkin	.10
312	Todd Benzinger	.05
313	Paul O'Neill	.05
314	Kal Daniels	.05
315	Joel Youngblood	.05
316	Eric Davis	.05
317	Dave Smith	.05
318	Mark Portugal	.05
319	Brian Meyer	.05
320	Jim Deshaies	.05
321	Juan Agosto	.05
322	Mike Scott	.05
323	Rick Rhoden	.05
324	Jim Clancy	.05
325	Larry Andersen	.05
326	Alex Trevino	.05
327	Alan Ashby	.05
328	Craig Reynolds	.05
329	Bill Doran	.05
330	Rafael Ramirez	.05
331	Glenn Davis	.05
332	*Willie Ansley*	.05
333	Gerald Young	.05
334	Cameron Drew	.05
335	Jay Howell	.05
336	Tim Belcher	.05
337	Fernando Valenzuela	.05
338	Ricky Horton	.05
339	Tim Leary	.05
340	Bill Bene	.05
341	Orel Hershiser	.05
342	Mike Scioscia	.05
343	Rick Dempsey	.05
344	Willie Randolph	.05
345	Alfredo Griffin	.05
346	Eddie Murray	.35
347	Mickey Hatcher	.05
348	Mike Sharperson	.05
349	John Shelby	.05
350	Mike Marshall	.05
351	Kirk Gibson	.05
352	Mike Davis	.05
353	Bryn Smith	.05
354	Pascual Perez	.05
355	Kevin Gross	.05
356	Andy McGaffigan	.05
357	Brian Holman	.05
358	Dave Wainhouse	.05
359	Denny Martinez	.05
360	Tim Burke	.05
361	Nelson Santovenia	.05
362	Tim Wallach	.05
363	Spike Owen	.05
364	Rex Hudler	.05
365	Andres Galarraga	.05
366	Otis Nixon	.05
367	Hubie Brooks	.05
368	Mike Aldrete	.05
369	Rock Raines	.05
370	Dave Martinez	.05
371	Bob Ojeda	.05
372	Ron Darling	.05
373	Wally Whitehurst	.05
374	Randy Myers	.05
375	David Cone	.05
376	Dwight Gooden	.05
377	Sid Fernandez	.05
378	Dave Proctor	.05
379	Gary Carter	.15
380	Keith Miller	.05

No.	Player	MT
381	Gregg Jefferies	.05
382	Tim Teufel	.05
383	Kevin Elster	.05
384	Dave Magadan	.05
385	Keith Hernandez	.05
386	Mookie Wilson	.05
387	Darryl Strawberry	.05
388	Kevin McReynolds	.05
389	Mark Carreon	.05
390	Jeff Parrett	.05
391	Mike Maddux	.05
392	Don Carman	.05
393	Bruce Ruffin	.05
394	Ken Howell	.05
395	Steve Bedrosian	.05
396	Floyd Youmans	.05
397	Larry McWilliams	.05
398	Pat Combs	.05
399	Steve Lake	.05
400	Dickie Thon	.05
401	Ricky Jordan	.05
402	Mike Schmidt	.50
403	Tom Herr	.05
404	Chris James	.05
405	Juan Samuel	.05
406	Von Hayes	.05
407	Ron Jones	.05
408	Curt Ford	.05
409	Bob Walk	.05
410	Jeff Robinson	.05
411	Jim Gott	.05
412	Scott Medvin	.05
413	John Smiley	.05
414	Bob Kipper	.05
415	Brian Fisher	.05
416	Doug Drabek	.05
417	Mike Lavalliere	.05
418	Ken Oberkfell	.05
419	Sid Bream	.05
420	Austin Manahan	.05
421	Jose Lind	.05
422	Bobby Bonilla	.05
423	Glenn Wilson	.05
424	Andy Van Slyke	.05
425	Gary Redus	.05
426	Barry Bonds	.65
427	Don Heinkel	.05
428	Ken Dayley	.05
429	Todd Worrell	.05
430	Brad DuVall	.05
431	Jose DeLeon	.05
432	Joe Magrane	.05
433	John Ericks	.05
434	Frank DiPino	.05
435	Tony Pena	.05
436	Ozzie Smith	.50
437	Terry Pendleton	.05
438	Jose Oquendo	.05
439	Tim Jones	.05
440	Pedro Guerrero	.05
441	Milt Thompson	.05
442	Willie McGee	.05
443	Vince Coleman	.05
444	Tom Brunansky	.05
445	Walt Terrell	.05
446	Eric Show	.05
447	Mark Davis	.05
448	*Andy Benes*	.20
449	Eddie Whitson	.05
450	Dennis Rasmussen	.05
451	Bruce Hurst	.05
452	Pat Clements	.05
453	Benito Santiago	.05
454	Sandy Alomar, Jr.	.05
455	Garry Templeton	.05
456	Jack Clark	.05
457	Tim Flannery	.05
458	Roberto Alomar	.35
459	Camelo Martinez	.05
460	John Kruk	.05
461	Tony Gwynn	.50
462	Jerald Clark	.05
463	Don Robinson	.05
464	Craig Lefferts	.05
465	Kelly Downs	.05
466	Rick Rueschel	.05
467	Scott Garrelts	.05
468	Wil Tejada	.05
469	Kirt Manwaring	.05
470	Terry Kennedy	.05
471	Jose Uribe	.05
472	*Royce Clayton*	.10
473	Robby Thompson	.05
474	Kevin Mitchell	.05
475	Ernie Riles	.05
476	Will Clark	.15
477	Donnell Nixon	.05
478	Candy Maldonado	.05
479	Tracy Jones	.05
480	Brett Butler	.05
481	Checklist 1-121	.05
482	Checklist 122-242	.05
483	Checklist 243-363	.05
484	Checklist 364-484	.05

1989 Bowman Tiffany

A special collectors' version of the revitalized Bowman cards was produced in 1989, differing from the regular-issue cards in the application of a high-gloss finish to the front and the use of a white cardboard stock. The "Tiffany" version (as the glossies are known to collectors), was sold only in complete boxed sets, with an estimated production of 6,000 sets.

	MT
Complete (Sealed) Set (495):	800.00
Complete (Opened) Set (495):	150.00
Common Player:	.25

(Star/rookie cards valued at 4-5X regular-issue 1989 Bowman.)

1989 Bowman Inserts

Bowman inserted sweepstakes cards in its 1989 packs. Each sweepstakes card reproduces a classic Bowman card on the front, with a prominent "REPRINT" notice. With one card in each pack, they are by no means scarce. A "Tiffany" version of the reprints was produced for inclusion in the factory set of 1989 Bowman cards. The glossy-front inserts are valued at 10X the standard version.

		MT
Complete Set (11):		6.00
Common Player:		.10
(1)	Richie Ashburn	.10
(2)	Yogi Berra	.15
(3)	Whitey Ford	.10
(4)	Gil Hodges	.10
(5)	Mickey Mantle (1951)	4.00
(6)	Mickey Mantle (1953)	2.00
(7)	Willie Mays	.50
(8)	Satchel Paige	.25
(9)	Jackie Robinson	1.00
(10)	Duke Snider	.15
(11)	Ted Williams	1.00

1990 Bowman

Bowman followed its 1989 rebirth with a 528-card set in 1990. The 1990 cards follow the classic Bowman style featuring a full-color photo bordered in white. The Bowman logo appears in the upper-left corner. The player's team nickname and name appear on the bottom border of the card photo. Unlike the 1989 set, the 1990 cards are standard 2-1/2" x 3-1/2". Backs are horizontal and display the player's statistics against the teams in his league. Included in the set are special insert cards featuring a painted image of a modern-day superstar done in the style of the 1951 Bowman cards. The paintings were produced for Bowman by artist Craig Pursley. Insert backs contain a sweepstakes offer with a chance to win a complete set of 11 lithographs made from these paintings.

		MT
Factory (Sealed) Set (528):		100.00
Complete (Opened) Set (528):		20.00
Common Player:		.05
Wax Pack (14+1):		1.50
Wax Box (36):		25.00
1	*Tommy Greene*	.05
2	Tom Glavine	.10
3	Andy Nezelek	.05
4	Mike Stanton	.05
5	Rick Lueken	.05
6	Kent Mercker	.05
7	Derek Lilliquist	.05
8	Charlie Liebrandt	.05
9	Steve Avery	.05
10	John Smoltz	.10
11	Mark Lemke	.05
12	Lonnie Smith	.05
13	Oddibe McDowell	.05
14	*Tyler Houston*	.10
15	Jeff Blauser	.05
16	Ernie Whitt	.05
17	Alexis Infante	.05
18	Jim Presley	.05
19	Dale Murphy	.15
20	Nick Esasky	.05
21	Rick Sutcliffe	.05
22	Mike Bielecki	.05
23	Steve Wilson	.05
24	Kevin Blankenship	.05
25	Mitch Williams	.05
26	Dean Wilkins	.05
27	Greg Maddux	.60
28	Mike Harkey	.05
29	Mark Grace	.25
30	Ryne Sandberg	.50
31	Greg Smith	.05
32	Dwight Smith	.05
33	Damon Berryhill	.05
34	Earl Cunningham	.05
35	Jerome Walton	.05
36	Lloyd McClendon	.05
37	Ty Griffin	.05
38	Shawon Dunston	.05
39	Andre Dawson	.15
40	Luis Salazar	.05
41	Tim Layana	.05
42	Rob Dibble	.05
43	Tom Browning	.05
44	Danny Jackson	.05
45	Jose Rijo	.05
46	Scott Scudder	.05
47	Randy Myers	.05
48	Brian Lane	.05
49	Paul O'Neill	.05
50	Barry Larkin	.10
51	Reggie Jefferson	.05
52	Jeff Branson	.05
53	Chris Sabo	.05
54	Joe Oliver	.05
55	Todd Benzinger	.05
56	Rolando Roomes	.05
57	Hal Morris	.05
58	Eric Davis	.05
59	Scott Bryant	.05
60	Ken Griffey	.05
61	*Darryl Kile*	.50
62	Dave Smith	.05
63	Mark Portugal	.05
64	*Jeff Juden*	.15
65	Bill Gullickson	.05
66	Danny Darwin	.05
67	Larry Andersen	.05
68	Jose Cano	.05
69	Dan Schatzeder	.05
70	Jim Deshaies	.05
71	Mike Scott	.05
72	Gerald Young	.05
73	Ken Caminiti	.05
74	Ken Oberkfell	.05
75	Dave Rhode	.05
76	Bill Doran	.05
77	Andujar Cedeno	.05
78	Craig Biggio	.10
79	Karl Rhodes	.05
80	Glenn Davis	.05
81	*Eric Anthony*	.15
82	John Wetteland	.05
83	Jay Howell	.05
84	Orel Hershiser	.05
85	Tim Belcher	.05
86	Kiki Jones	.05
87	Mike Hartley	.05
88	Ramon Martinez	.05
89	Mike Scioscia	.05
90	Willie Randolph	.05
91	Juan Samuel	.05
92	*Jose Offerman*	.15
93	Dave Hansen	.05
94	Jeff Hamilton	.05
95	Alfredo Griffin	.05
96	Tom Goodwin	.05
97	Kirk Gibson	.05
98	Jose Vizcaino	.05
99	Kal Daniels	.05
100	Hubie Brooks	.05
101	Eddie Murray	.30
102	Dennis Boyd	.05
103	Tim Burke	.05
104	Bill Sampen	.05
105	Brett Gideon	.05
106	Mark Gardner	.05
107	Howard Farmer	.05
108	Mel Rojas	.05
109	Kevin Gross	.05
110	Dave Schmidt	.05
111	Denny Martinez	.05
112	Jerry Goff	.05
113	Andres Galarraga	.05
114	Tim Welch	.05
115	*Marquis Grissom*	.50
116	Spike Owen	.05
117	*Larry Walker*	1.50
118	Rock Raines	.05
119	*Delino DeShields*	.20
120	Tom Foley	.05

121 Dave Martinez .05
122 Frank Viola .05
123 Julio Valera .05
124 Alejandro Pena .05
125 David Cone .05
126 Dwight Gooden .05
127 Kevin Brown .15
128 John Franco .05
129 Terry Bross .05
130 Blaine Beatty .05
131 Sid Fernandez .05
132 Mike Marshall .05
133 Howard Johnson .05
134 Jaime Roseboro .05
135 Alan Zinter .05
136 Keith Miller .05
137 Kevin Elster .05
138 Kevin McReynolds .05
139 Barry Lyons .05
140 Gregg Jefferies .05
141 Darryl Strawberry .05
142 *Todd Hundley* .50
143 Scott Service .05
144 Chuck Malone .05
145 Steve Ontiveros .05
146 Roger McDowell .05
147 Ken Howell .05
148 Pat Combs .05
149 Jeff Parrett .05
150 Chuck McElroy .05
151 Jason Grimsley .05
152 Len Dykstra .05
153 Mickey Morandini .05
154 John Kruk .05
155 Dickie Thon .05
156 Ricky Jordan .05
157 Jeff Jackson .05
158 Darren Daulton .05
159 Tom Herr .05
160 Von Hayes .05
161 *Dave Hollins* .10
162 Carmelo Martinez .05
163 Bob Walk .05
164 Doug Drabek .05
165 Walt Terrell .05
166 Bill Landrum .05
167 Scott Ruskin .05
168 Bob Patterson .05
169 Bobby Bonilla .05
170 Jose Lind .05
171 Andy Van Slyke .05
172 Mike LaValliere .05
173 *Willie Greene* .05
174 Jay Bell .05
175 Sid Bream .05
176 Tom Prince .05
177 Wally Backman .05
178 *Moises Alou* .50
179 Steve Carter .05
180 Gary Redus .05
181 Barry Bonds .75
182 Don Slaught .05
183 Joe Magrane .05
184 Bryn Smith .05
185 Todd Worrell .05
186 Jose Deleon .05
187 Frank DiPino .05
188 John Tudor .05
189 Howard Hilton .05
190 John Ericks .05
191 Ken Dayley .05
192 *Ray Lankford* .40
193 Todd Zeile .05
194 Willie McGee .05
195 Ozzie Smith .60
196 Milt Thompson .05
197 Terry Pendleton .05
198 Vince Coleman .05
199 Paul Coleman .05
200 Jose Oquendo .05
201 Pedro Guerrero .05
202 Tom Brunansky .05
203 Roger Smithberg .05
204 Eddie Whitson .05
205 Dennis Rasmussen .05
206 Craig Lefferts .05
207 Andy Benes .05
208 Bruce Hurst .05
209 Eric Show .05
210 Rafael Valdez .05
211 Joey Cora .05
212 Thomas Howard .05
213 Rob Nelson .05
214 Jack Clark .05
215 Garry Templeton .05
216 Fred Lynn .05
217 Tony Gwynn .60
218 Benny Santiago .05
219 Mike Pagliarulo .05
220 Joe Carter .05
221 Roberto Alomar .35
222 Bip Roberts .05
223 Rick Reuschel .05
224 Russ Swan .05
225 Eric Gunderson .05
226 Steve Bedrosian .05
227 Mike Remlinger .05
228 Scott Garrelts .05
229 Ernie Camacho .05
230 Andres Santana .05
231 Will Clark .15
232 Kevin Mitchell .05
233 Robby Thompson .05
234 Bill Bathe .05
235 Tony Perezchica .05
236 Gary Carter .20
237 Brett Butler .05
238 Matt Williams .15
239 Ernie Riles .05
240 Kevin Bass .05
241 Terry Kennedy .05
242 *Steve Hosey* .05
243 *Ben McDonald* .15
244 Jeff Ballard .05
245 Joe Price .05
246 Curt Schilling .20
247 Pete Harnisch .05
248 Mark Williamson .05
249 Gregg Olson .05
250 Chris Myers .05
251 David Segui .05
252 Joe Orsulak .05
253 Craig Worthington .05
254 Mickey Tettleton .05
255 Cal Ripken, Jr. 1.00
256 Billy Ripken .05
257 Randy Milligan .05
258 Brady Anderson .05
259 *Chris Hoiles* .05
260 Mike Devereaux .05
261 Phil Bradley .05
262 *Leo Gomez* .05
263 Lee Smith .05
264 Mike Rochford .05
265 Jeff Reardon .05
266 Wes Gardner .05
267 Mike Boddicker .05
268 Roger Clemens .60
269 Rob Murphy .05
270 Mickey Pina .05
271 Tony Pena .05
272 Jody Reed .05
273 Kevin Romine .05
274 Mike Greenwell .05
275 *Mo Vaughn* .75
276 Danny Heep .05
277 Scott Cooper .05
278 *Greg Blosser* .05
279 Dwight Evans .05
280 Ellis Burks .05
281 Wade Boggs .40
282 Marty Barrett .05
283 Kirk McCaskill .05
284 Mark Langston .05
285 Bert Blyleven .05
286 Mike Fetters .05
287 Kyle Abbott .05
288 Jim Abbott .05
289 Chuck Finley .05
290 Gary DiSarcina .05
291 Dick Schofield .05
292 Devon White .05
293 Bobby Rose .05
294 Brian Downing .05
295 Lance Parrish .05
296 Jack Howell .05
297 Claudell Washington .05
298 John Orton .05
299 Wally Joyner .05
300 Lee Stevens .05
301 Chili Davis .05
302 Johnny Ray .05
303 Greg Hibbard .05
304 Eric King .05
305 Jack McDowell .05
306 Bobby Thigpen .05
307 Adam Peterson .05
308 *Scott Radinsky* .10
309 Wayne Edwards .05
310 Melido Perez .05
311 Robin Ventura .05
312 *Sammy Sosa* 6.00
313 Dan Pasqua .05
314 Carlton Fisk .35
315 Ozzie Guillen .05
316 Ivan Calderon .05
317 Daryl Boston .05
318 Craig Grebeck .05
319 Scott Fletcher .05
320 *Frank Thomas* 4.00
321 Steve Lyons .05
322 Carlos Martinez .05
323 Joe Skalski .05
324 Tom Candiotti .05
325 Greg Swindell .05
326 Steve Olin .05
327 Kevin Wickander .05
328 Doug Jones .05
329 Jeff Shaw .05
330 Kevin Bearse .05
331 Dion James .05
332 Jerry Browne .05
333 Albert Belle .20
334 Felix Fermin .05
335 Candy Maldonado .05
336 Cory Snyder .05
337 Sandy Alomar .05
338 Mark Lewis .05
339 *Carlos Baerga* .15
340 Chris James .05
341 Brook Jacoby .05
342 Keith Hernandez .05
343 Frank Tanana .05
344 Scott Aldred .05
345 Mike Henneman .05
346 Steve Wapnick .05
347 Greg Gohr .05
348 Eric Stone .05
349 Brian DuBois .05
350 Kevin Ritz .05
351 Rico Brogna .05
352 Mike Heath .05
353 Alan Trammell .05
354 Chet Lemon .05
355 Dave Bergman .05
356 Lou Whitaker .05
357 Cecil Fielder .05
358 Milt Cuyler .05
359 Tony Phillips .05
360 *Travis Fryman* .40
361 Ed Romero .05
362 Lloyd Moseby .05
363 Mark Gubicza .05
364 Bret Saberhagen .05
365 Tom Gordon .05
366 Steve Farr .05
367 Kevin Appier .05
368 Storm Davis .05
369 Mark Davis .05
370 Jeff Montgomery .05
371 Frank White .05
372 Brent Mayne .05
373 Bob Boone .05
374 Jim Eisenreich .05
375 Danny Tartabull .05
376 Kurt Stillwell .05
377 Bill Pecota .05
378 Bo Jackson .10
379 *Bob Hamelin* .05
380 Kevin Seitzer .05
381 Rey Palacios .05
382 George Brett .60
383 Gerald Perry .05
384 Teddy Higuera .05
385 Tom Filer .05
386 Dan Plesac .05
387 *Cal Eldred* .10
388 Jaime Navarro .05
389 Chris Bosio .05
390 Randy Veres .05
391 Gary Sheffield .20
392 George Canale .05
393 B.J. Surhoff .05
394 Tim McIntosh .05
395 Greg Brock .05
396 Greg Vaughn .05
397 Darryl Hamilton .05
398 Dave Parker .05
399 Paul Molitor .40
400 Jim Gantner .05
401 Rob Deer .05
402 Billy Spiers .05
403 Glenn Braggs .05
404 Robin Yount .35
405 Rick Aguilera .05
406 Johnny Ard .05
407 *Kevin Tapani* .10
408 Park Pittman .05
409 Allan Anderson .05
410 Juan Berenguer .05
411 Willie Banks .05
412 Rich Yett .05
413 Dave West .05
414 Greg Gagne .05
415 *Chuck Knoblauch* .75
416 Randy Bush .05
417 Gary Gaetti .05
418 Kent Hrbek .05
419 Al Newman .05
420 Danny Gladden .05
421 Paul Sorrento .05
422 Derek Parks .05
423 Scott Leius .05
424 Kirby Puckett .60
425 Willie Smith .05
426 Dave Righetti .05
427 Jeff Robinson .05
428 Alan Mills .05
429 Tim Leary .05
430 Pascual Perez .05
431 Alvaro Espinoza .05
432 Dave Winfield .35
433 Jesse Barfield .05
434 Randy Velarde .05
435 Rick Cerone .05
436 Steve Balboni .05
437 Mel Hall .05
438 Bob Geren .05
439 *Bernie Williams* 1.50
440 Kevin Maas .05
441 Mike Blowers .05
442 Steve Sax .05
443 Don Mattingly .75
444 Roberto Kelly .05
445 Mike Moore .05
446 Reggie Harris .05
447 Scott Sanderson .05
448 Dave Otto .05
449 Dave Stewart .05
450 Rick Honeycutt .05
451 Dennis Eckersley .05
452 Carney Lansford .05
453 Scott Hemond .05
454 Mark McGwire 1.00
455 Felix Jose .05
456 Terry Steinbach .05
457 Rickey Henderson .40
458 Dave Henderson .05
459 Mike Gallego .05
460 Jose Canseco .35
461 Walt Weiss .05
462 Ken Phelps .05
463 *Darren Lewis* .10
464 Ron Hassey .05
465 *Roger Salkeld* .10
466 Scott Bankhead .05
467 Keith Comstock .05
468 Randy Johnson .35
469 Erik Hanson .05
470 Mike Schooler .05
471 Gary Eave .05
472 Jeffrey Leonard .05
473 Dave Valle .05
474 Omar Vizquel .05
475 Pete O'Brien .05
476 Henry Cotto .05
477 Jay Buhner .05
478 Harold Reynolds .05
479 Alvin Davis .05
480 Darnell Coles .05
481 Ken Griffey, Jr. 1.00
482 Greg Briley .05
483 Scott Bradley .05
484 Tino Martinez .05
485 Jeff Russell .05
486 Nolan Ryan 1.00
487 Robb Nen .05
488 Kevin Brown .05
489 Brian Bohanon .05
490 Ruben Sierra .05
491 Pete Incaviglia .05
492 *Juan Gonzalez* 2.00
493 Steve Buechele .05
494 Scott Coolbaugh .05
495 Geno Petralli .05
496 Rafael Palmeiro .15
497 Julio Franco .05
498 Gary Pettis .05
499 Donald Harris .05
500 Monty Fariss .05
501 Harold Baines .05
502 Cecil Espy .05
503 Jack Daugherty .05
504 Willie Blair .05

505 Dave Steib .05
506 Tom Henke .05
507 John Cerutti .05
508 Paul Kilgus .05
509 Jimmy Key .05
510 *John Olerud* .60
511 Ed Sprague .05
512 Manny Lee .05
513 Fred McGriff .05
514 Glenallen Hill .05
515 George Bell .05
516 Mookie Wilson .05
517 Luis Sojo .05
518 Nelson Liriano .05
519 Kelly Gruber .05
520 Greg Myers .05
521 Pat Borders .05
522 Junior Felix .05
523 Eddie Zosky .05
524 Tony Fernandez .05
525 Checklist .05
526 Checklist .05
527 Checklist .05
528 Checklist .05

1990 Bowman Tiffany

Reported production of fewer than 10,000 sets has created a significant premium for these glossy "Tiffany" versions of Bowman's 1990 baseball card set. The use of white cardboard stock and high-gloss front finish distinguishes these cards from regular-issue Bowmans.

MT
Complete (Sealed) Set (539): 375.00
Complete (Opened) Set (539): 100.00
Common Player: .25
(Star/rookie cards valued about 4-5X regular-issue 1990 Bowman.)

1990 Bowman Inserts

Bowman inserted sweepstakes cards in its 1990 packs, much like in 1989. This 11-card set features current players displayed in drawings by Craig Pursley.

MT
Complete Set (11): 1.25
Common Player: .05
(1) Will Clark .10
(2) Mark Davis .05
(3) Dwight Gooden .10
(4) Bo Jackson .10
(5) Don Mattingly .25
(6) Kevin Mitchell .05
(7) Gregg Olson .05
(8) Nolan Ryan .50
(9) Bret Saberhagen .05
(10) Jerome Walton .05
(11) Robin Yount .15

1991 Bowman

The 1991 Bowman set features 704 cards compared to 528 cards in the 1990 issue. The cards imitate the 1953 Bowman style. Special Rod Carew cards and gold foil-stamped cards are included. The set is numbered by teams. Like the 1989 and 1990 issues, the card backs feature a breakdown of performance against each other team in the league.

MT
Complete Set (704): 30.00
Factory Set (704): 35.00
Common Player: .05
Green Cello Pack (14): 2.00
Green Cello Wax Box (36): 35.00
1 Rod Carew-I .10
2 Rod Carew-II .10
3 Rod Carew-III .10
4 Rod Carew-IV .10
5 Rod Carew-V .10
6 Willie Fraser .05
7 John Olerud .05
8 William Suero .05
9 Roberto Alomar .35
10 Todd Stottlemyre .05
11 Joe Carter .05
12 *Steve Karsay* .15
13 Mark Whiten .05
14 Pat Borders .05
15 Mike Timlin .05
16 Tom Henke .05
17 Eddie Zosky .05
18 Kelly Gruber .05
19 Jimmy Key .05
20 Jerry Schunk .05
21 Manny Lee .05
22 Dave Steib .05
23 Pat Hentgen .05
24 Glenallen Hill .05
25 Rene Gonzales .05
26 Ed Sprague .05
27 Ken Dayley .05
28 Pat Tabler .05
29 *Denis Boucher* .05
30 Devon White .05
31 Dante Bichette .05
32 Paul Molitor .35
33 Greg Vaughn .05
34 Dan Plesac .05
35 Chris George .05
36 Tim McIntosh .05
37 Franklin Stubbs .05
38 Bo Dodson .05
39 Ron Robinson .05
40 Ed Nunez .05
41 Greg Brock .05
42 Jaime Navarro .05
43 Chris Bosio .05
44 B.J. Surhoff .05
45 Chris Johnson .05
46 Willie Randolph .05
47 Narciso Elvira .05
48 Jim Gantner .05
49 Kevin Brown .05
50 Julio Machado .05
51 Chuck Crim .05
52 Gary Sheffield .20
53 Angel Miranda .05
54 Teddy Higuera .05
55 Robin Yount .35
56 Cal Eldred .05
57 Sandy Alomar .05
58 Greg Swindell .05
59 Brook Jacoby .05
60 Efrain Valdez .05
61 Ever Magallanes .05
62 Tom Candiotti .05
63 Eric King .05
64 Alex Cole .05
65 Charles Nagy .05
66 Mitch Webster .05
67 Chris James .05
68 *Jim Thome* 1.00
69 Carlos Baerga .05
70 Mark Lewis .05
71 Jerry Browne .05
72 Jesse Orosco .05
73 Mike Huff .05
74 Jose Escobar .05
75 Jeff Manto .05
76 *Turner Ward* .05
77 Doug Jones .05
78 *Bruce Egloff* .05
79 Tim Costo .05
80 Beau Allred .05
81 Albert Belle .20
82 John Farrell .05
83 Glenn Davis .05
84 Joe Orsulak .05
85 Mark Williamson .05
86 Ben McDonald .05
87 Billy Ripken .05
88 Leo Gomez .05
89 Bob Melvin .05
90 Jeff Robinson .05
91 Jose Mesa .05
92 Gregg Olson .05
93 Mike Devereaux .05
94 Luis Mercedes .05
95 *Arthur Rhodes* .20
96 Juan Bell .05
97 *Mike Mussina* 3.00
98 Jeff Ballard .05
99 Chris Hoiles .05
100 Brady Anderson .05
101 Bob Milacki .05
102 David Segui .05
103 Dwight Evans .05
104 Cal Ripken, Jr. 1.50
105 Mike Linskey .05
106 *Jeff Tackett* .05
107 Jeff Reardon .05
108 Dana Kiecker .05
109 Ellis Burks .05
110 Dave Owen .05
111 Danny Darwin .05
112 Mo Vaughn .25
113 Jeff McNeely .05
114 Tom Bolton .05
115 Greg Blosser .05
116 Mike Greenwell .05
117 *Phil Plantier* .05
118 Roger Clemens .60
119 John Marzano .05
120 Jody Reed .05
121 Scott Taylor .05
122 Jack Clark .05
123 Derek Livernois .05
124 Tony Pena .05
125 Tom Brunansky .05
126 Carlos Quintana .05
127 Tim Naehring .05
128 Matt Young .05
129 Wade Boggs .50
130 Kevin Morton .05
131 Pete Incaviglia .05
132 Rob Deer .05
133 Bill Gullickson .05
134 Rico Brogna .05
135 Lloyd Moseby .05
136 Cecil Fielder .05
137 Tony Phillips .05
138 Mark Leiter .05
139 John Cerutti .05
140 Mickey Tettleton .05
141 Milt Cuyler .05
142 Greg Gohr .05
143 Tony Bernazard .05
144 Dan Gakeler .05
145 Travis Fryman .05
146 Dan Petry .05
147 Scott Aldred .05
148 John DeSilva .05
149 Rusty Meacham .05
150 Lou Whitaker .05
151 Dave Haas .05
152 Luis de los Santos .05
153 Ivan Cruz .05
154 Alan Trammell .05
155 Pat Kelly .05
156 *Carl Everett* 1.50
157 Greg Cadaret .05
158 Kevin Maas .05
159 Jeff Johnson .05
160 Willie Smith .05
161 Gerald Williams .05
162 Mike Humphreys .05
163 Alvaro Espinoza .05
164 Matt Nokes .05
165 Wade Taylor .05
166 Roberto Kelly .05
167 John Habyan .05
168 Steve Farr .05
169 Jesse Barfield .05
170 Steve Sax .05
171 Jim Leyritz .05
172 Robert Eenhoorn .05
173 Bernie Williams .25
174 Scott Lusader .05
175 Torey Lovullo .05
176 Chuck Cary .05
177 Scott Sanderson .05
178 Don Mattingly 1.00
179 Mel Hall .05
180 Juan Gonzalez .40
181 Hensley Meulens .05
182 Jose Offerman .05
183 *Jeff Bagwell* 5.00
184 *Jeff Conine* .25
185 *Henry Rodriguez* .50
186 Jimmie Reese .05
187 Kyle Abbott .05
188 Lance Parrish .05
189 Rafael Montalvo .05
190 Floyd Bannister .05
191 Dick Schofield .05
192 Scott Lewis .05
193 Jeff Robinson .05
194 Kent Anderson .05
195 Wally Joyner .05
196 Chuck Finley .05
197 Luis Sojo .05
198 Jeff Richardson .05
199 Dave Parker .05
200 Jim Abbott .05
201 Junior Felix .05
202 Mark Langston .05
203 *Tim Salmon* 1.00
204 Cliff Young .05
205 Scott Bailes .05
206 Bobby Rose .05
207 Gary Gaetti .05
208 Ruben Amaro .05
209 Luis Polonia .05
210 Dave Winfield .50
211 Bryan Harvey .05
212 Mike Moore .05
213 Rickey Henderson .40
214 Steve Chitren .05
215 Bob Welch .05
216 Terry Steinbach .05
217 Ernie Riles .05
218 *Todd Van Poppel* .10
219 Mike Gallego .05
220 Curt Young .05
221 Todd Burns .05
222 Vance Law .05
223 Eric Show .05
224 *Don Peters* .05
225 Dave Stewart .05
226 Dave Henderson .05
227 Jose Canseco .35
228 Walt Weiss .05
229 Dann Howitt .05
230 Willie Wilson .05
231 Harold Baines .05
232 Scott Hemond .05
233 Joe Slusarski .05
234 Mark McGwire 1.50
235 *Kirk Dressendorfer* .05
236 *Craig Paquette* .10
237 Dennis Eckersley .05
238 Dana Allison .05
239 Scott Bradley .05

No.	Player	Price
240	Brian Holman	.05
241	Mike Schooler	.05
242	Rich Delucia	.05
243	Edgar Martinez	.05
244	Henry Cotto	.05
245	Omar Vizquel	.05
246a	Ken Griffey, Jr.	1.25
246b	Ken Griffey Sr. (should be #255)	.10
247	Jay Buhner	.05
248	Bill Krueger	.05
249	*Dave Fleming*	.05
250	*Patrick Lennon*	.05
251	Dave Valle	.05
252	Harold Reynolds	.05
253	Randy Johnson	.35
254	Scott Bankhead	.05
255	(Not issued, see #246b)	
256	Greg Briley	.05
257	Tino Martinez	.05
258	Alvin Davis	.05
259	Pete O'Brien	.05
260	Erik Hanson	.05
261	*Bret Boone*	1.50
262	Roger Salkeld	.05
263	Dave Burba	.05
264	*Kerry Woodson*	.05
265	Julio Franco	.05
266	Dan Peltier	.05
267	Jeff Russell	.05
268	Steve Buechele	.05
269	Donald Harris	.05
270	Robb Nen	.05
271	Rich Gossage	.05
272	*Ivan Rodriguez*	4.00
273	Jeff Huson	.05
274	Kevin Brown	.10
275	*Dan Smith*	.10
276	Gary Pettis	.05
277	Jack Daugherty	.05
278	Mike Jeffcoat	.05
279	Brad Arnsberg	.05
280	Nolan Ryan	1.50
281	Eric McCray	.05
282	Scott Chiamparino	.05
283	Ruben Sierra	.05
284	Geno Petralli	.05
285	Monty Fariss	.05
286	Rafael Palmeiro	.20
287	Bobby Witt	.05
288	Dean Palmer	.05
289	Tony Scruggs	.05
290	Kenny Rogers	.05
291	Bret Saberhagen	.05
292	*Brian McRae*	.10
293	Storm Davis	.05
294	Danny Tartabull	.05
295	David Howard	.05
296	Mike Boddicker	.05
297	Joel Johnston	.05
298	Tim Spehr	.05
299	Hector Wagner	.05
300	George Brett	.65
301	Mike Macfarlane	.05
302	Kirk Gibson	.05
303	Harvey Pulliam	.05
304	Jim Eisenreich	.05
305	Kevin Seitzer	.05
306	Mark Davis	.05
307	Kurt Stillwell	.05
308	Jeff Montgomery	.05
309	Kevin Appier	.05
310	Bob Hamelin	.05
311	Tom Gordon	.05
312	*Kerwin Moore*	.05
313	Hugh Walker	.05
314	Terry Shumpert	.05
315	Warren Cromartie	.05
316	Gary Thurman	.05
317	Steve Bedrosian	.05
318	Danny Gladden	.05
319	Jack Morris	.05
320	Kirby Puckett	.65
321	Kent Hrbek	.05
322	Kevin Tapani	.05
323	Denny Neagle	.05
324	Rich Garces	.05
325	Larry Casian	.05
326	Shane Mack	.05
327	Allan Anderson	.05
328	Junior Ortiz	.05
329	*Paul Abbott*	.05
330	Chuck Knoblauch	.05
331	Chili Davis	.05
332	*Todd Ritchie*	.05
333	Brian Harper	.05
334	Rick Aguilera	.05
335	Scott Erickson	.05
336	Pedro Munoz	.05
337	Scott Leuis	.05
338	Greg Gagne	.05
339	Mike Pagliarulo	.05
340	Terry Leach	.05
341	Willie Banks	.05
342	Bobby Thigpen	.05
343	*Roberto Hernandez*	.50
344	Melido Perez	.05
345	Carlton Fisk	.40
346	*Norberto Martin*	.05
347	*Johnny Ruffin*	.05
348	*Jeff Carter*	.05
349	Lance Johnson	.05
350	Sammy Sosa	1.00
351	Alex Fernandez	.05
352	Jack McDowell	.05
353	Bob Wickman	.05
354	Wilson Alvarez	.05
355	Charlie Hough	.05
356	Ozzie Guillen	.05
357	Cory Snyder	.05
358	Robin Ventura	.05
359	Scott Fletcher	.05
360	Cesar Bernhardt	.05
361	Dan Pasqua	.05
362	Tim Raines	.05
363	Brian Drahman	.05
364	Wayne Edwards	.05
365	Scott Radinsky	.05
366	Frank Thomas	1.00
367	Cecil Fielder	.05
368	Julio Franco	.05
369	Kelly Gruber	.05
370	Alan Trammell	.05
371	Rickey Henderson	.40
372	Jose Canseco	.30
373	Ellis Burks	.05
374	Lance Parrish	.05
375	Dave Parker	.05
376	Eddie Murray	.35
377	Ryne Sandberg	.50
378	Matt Williams	.15
379	Barry Larkin	.10
380	Barry Bonds	1.00
381	Bobby Bonilla	.05
382	Darryl Strawberry	.05
383	Benny Santiago	.05
384	Don Robinson	.05
385	Paul Coleman	.05
386	Milt Thompson	.05
387	Lee Smith	.05
388	Ray Lankford	.05
389	Tom Pagnozzi	.05
390	Ken Hill	.05
391	Jamie Moyer	.05
392	*Greg Carmona*	.05
393	John Ericks	.05
394	Bob Tewksbury	.05
395	Jose Oquendo	.05
396	Rheal Cormier	.05
397	*Mike Milchin*	.05
398	Ozzie Smith	.65
399	*Aaron Holbert*	.05
400	Jose DeLeon	.05
401	Felix Jose	.05
402	Juan Agosto	.05
403	Pedro Guerrero	.05
404	Todd Zeile	.05
405	Gerald Perry	.05
406	Not issued	
407	Bryn Smith	.05
408	Bernard Gilkey	.05
409	Rex Hudler	.05
410a	Ralph Branca, Bobby Thomson	.10
410b	Donovan Osborne	.05
411	Lance Dickson	.05
412	Danny Jackson	.05
413	Jerome Walton	.05
414	Sean Cheetham	.05
415	Joe Girardi	.05
416	Ryne Sandberg	.35
417	Mike Harkey	.05
418	George Bell	.05
419	*Rick Wilkins*	.25
420	Earl Cunningham	.05
421	Heathcliff Slocumb	.05
422	Mike Bielecki	.05
423	*Jessie Hollins*	.05
424	Shawon Dunston	.05
425	Dave Smith	.05
426	Greg Maddux	.60
427	Jose Vizcaino	.05
428	Luis Salazar	.05
429	Andre Dawson	.15
430	Rick Sutcliffe	.05
431	Paul Assenmacher	.05
432	Erik Pappas	.05
433	Mark Grace	.25
434	Denny Martinez	.05
435	Marquis Grissom	.05
436	*Wil Cordero*	.10
437	Tim Wallach	.05
438	*Brian Barnes*	.05
439	Barry Jones	.05
440	Ivan Calderon	.05
441	*Stan Spencer*	.05
442	Larry Walker	.25
443	*Chris Haney*	.05
444	Hector Rivera	.05
445	Delino DeShields	.05
446	Andres Galarraga	.05
447	Gilberto Reyes	.05
448	Willie Greene	.05
449	Greg Colbrunn	.05
450	*Rondell White*	1.50
451	Steve Frey	.05
452	*Shane Andrews*	.10
453	Mike Fitzgerald	.05
454	Spike Owen	.05
455	Dave Martinez	.05
456	Dennis Boyd	.05
457	Eric Bullock	.05
458	*Reid Cornelius*	.05
459	Chris Nabholz	.05
460	David Cone	.05
461	Hubie Brooks	.05
462	Sid Fernandez	.05
463	*Doug Simons*	.05
464	Howard Johnson	.05
465	Chris Donnels	.05
466	Anthony Young	.05
467	Todd Hundley	.05
468	Rick Cerone	.05
469	Kevin Elster	.05
470	Wally Whitehurst	.05
471	Vince Coleman	.05
472	Dwight Gooden	.05
473	Charlie O'Brien	.05
474	*Jeromy Burnitz*	1.00
475	John Franco	.05
476	Daryl Boston	.05
477	Frank Viola	.05
478	D.J. Dozier	.05
479	Kevin McReynolds	.05
480	Tom Herr	.05
481	Gregg Jefferies	.05
482	Pete Schourek	.05
483	Ron Darling	.05
484	Dave Magadan	.05
485	*Andy Ashby*	.10
486	Dale Murphy	.20
487	Von Hayes	.05
488	*Kim Batiste*	.05
489	*Tony Longmire*	.10
490	Wally Backman	.05
491	Jeff Jackson	.05
492	Mickey Morandini	.05
493	Darrel Akerfelds	.05
494	Ricky Jordan	.05
495	Randy Ready	.05
496	Darrin Fletcher	.05
497	Chuck Malone	.05
498	Pat Combs	.05
499	Dickie Thon	.05
500	Roger McDowell	.05
501	Len Dykstra	.05
502	Joe Boever	.05
503	John Kruk	.05
504	Terry Mulholland	.05
505	Wes Chamberlain	.05
506	*Mike Lieberthal*	.75
507	Darren Daulton	.05
508	Charlie Hayes	.05
509	John Smiley	.05
510	Gary Varsho	.05
511	Curt Wilkerson	.05
512	*Orlando Merced*	.20
513	Barry Bonds	.75
514	Mike Lavalliere	.05
515	Doug Drabek	.05
516	Gary Redus	.05
517	*William Pennyfeather*	.05
518	Randy Tomlin	.05
519	*Mike Zimmerman*	.05
520	Jeff King	.05
521	*Kurt Miller*	.10
522	Jay Bell	.05
523	Bill Landrum	.05
524	Zane Smith	.05
525	Bobby Bonilla	.05
526	Bob Walk	.05
527	Austin Manahan	.05
528	*Joe Ausanio*	.05
529	Andy Van Slyke	.05
530	Jose Lind	.05
531	*Carlos Garcia*	.15
532	Don Slaught	.05
533	Colin Powell	.25
534	*Frank Bolick*	.05
535	*Gary Scott*	.05
536	Nikco Riesgo	.05
537	*Reggie Sanders*	.40
538	*Tim Howard*	.05
539	*Ryan Bowen*	.10
540	Eric Anthony	.05
541	Jim Deshaies	.05
542	Tom Nevers	.05
543	Ken Caminiti	.05
544	Karl Rhodes	.05
545	Xavier Hernandez	.05
546	Mike Scott	.05
547	Jeff Juden	.05
548	Darryl Kile	.05
549	Willie Ansley	.05
550	*Luis Gonzalez*	3.00
551	*Mike Simms*	.05
552	Mark Portugal	.05
553	Jimmy Jones	.05
554	Jim Clancy	.05
555	Pete Harnisch	.05
556	Craig Biggio	.10
557	Eric Yelding	.05
558	Dave Rohde	.05
559	Casey Candaele	.05
560	Curt Schilling	.15
561	Steve Finley	.05
562	Javier Ortiz	.05
563	Andujar Cedeno	.05
564	Rafael Ramirez	.05
565	*Kenny Lofton*	1.00
566	Steve Avery	.05
567	Lonnie Smith	.05
568	Kent Mercker	.05
569	*Chipper Jones*	7.00
570	Terry Pendleton	.05
571	Otis Nixon	.05
572	Juan Berenguer	.05
573	Charlie Leibrandt	.05
574	Dave Justice	.20
575	Keith Mitchell	.05
576	Tom Glavine	.10
577	Greg Olson	.05
578	Rafael Belliard	.05
579	Ben Rivera	.05
580	John Smoltz	.10
581	Tyler Houston	.05
582	*Mark Wohlers*	.05
583	Ron Gant	.05
584	Ramon Caraballo	.05
585	Sid Bream	.05
586	Jeff Treadway	.05
587	*Javier Lopez*	1.00
588	Deion Sanders	.10
589	Mike Heath	.05
590	*Ryan Klesko*	.75
591	Bob Ojeda	.05
592	Alfredo Griffin	.05
593	*Raul Mondesi*	1.00
594	Greg Smith	.05
595	Orel Hershiser	.05
596	Juan Samuel	.05
597	Brett Butler	.05
598	Gary Carter	.20
599	Stan Javier	.05
600	Kal Daniels	.05
601	*Jamie McAndrew*	.05
602	Mike Sharperson	.05
603	Jay Howell	.05
604	*Eric Karros*	.75
605	Tim Belcher	.05
606	Dan Opperman	.05
607	Lenny Harris	.05
608	Tom Goodwin	.05
609	Darryl Strawberry	.05
610	Ramon Martinez	.05
611	Kevin Gross	.05
612	Zakary Shinall	.05
613	Mike Scioscia	.05
614	Eddie Murray	.35
615	Ronnie Walden	.05
616	Will Clark	.15
617	Adam Hyzdu	.05
618	Matt Williams	.15
619	Don Robinson	.05

620	Jeff Brantley	.05
621	Greg Litton	.05
622	Steve Decker	.05
623	Robby Thompson	.05
624	*Mark Leonard*	.05
625	Kevin Bass	.05
626	Scott Garrelts	.05
627	Jose Uribe	.05
628	Eric Gunderson	.05
629	Steve Hosey	.05
630	Trevor Wilson	.05
631	Terry Kennedy	.05
632	Dave Righetti	.05
633	Kelly Downs	.05
634	Johnny Ard	.05
635	*Eric Christopherson*	.05
636	Kevin Mitchell	.05
637	John Burkett	.05
638	*Kevin Rogers*	.10
639	Bud Black	.05
640	Willie McGee	.05
641	Royce Clayton	.05
642	Tony Fernandez	.05
643	Ricky Bones	.05
644	Thomas Howard	.05
645	Dave Staton	.05
646	Jim Presley	.05
647	Tony Gwynn	.60
648	Marty Barrett	.05
649	Scott Coolbaugh	.05
650	Craig Lefferts	.05
651	Eddie Whitson	.05
652	Oscar Azocar	.05
653	Wes Gardner	.05
654	Bip Roberts	.05
655	*Robbie Beckett*	.05
656	Benny Santiago	.05
657	Greg W. Harris	.05
658	Jerald Clark	.05
659	Fred McGriff	.05
660	Larry Andersen	.05
661	Bruce Hurst	.05
662	Steve Martin	.05
663	Rafael Valdez	.05
664	*Paul Faries*	.05
665	Andy Benes	.05
666	Randy Myers	.05
667	Rob Dibble	.05
668	Glenn Sutko	.05
669	Glenn Braggs	.05
670	Billy Hatcher	.05
671	Joe Oliver	.05
672	Freddie Benavides	.05
673	Barry Larkin	.10
674	Chris Sabo	.05
675	Mariano Duncan	.05
676	*Chris Jones*	.05
677	*Gino Minutelli*	.05
678	Reggie Jefferson	.05
679	Jack Armstrong	.05
680	Chris Hammond	.05
681	Jose Rijo	.05
682	Bill Doran	.05
683	Terry Lee	.05
684	Tom Browning	.05
685	Paul O'Neill	.05
686	Eric Davis	.05
687	*Dan Wilson*	.15
688	Ted Power	.05
689	Tim Layana	.05
690	Norm Charlton	.05
691	Hal Morris	.05
692	Rickey Henderson	.40
693	*Sam Militello*	.05
694	*Matt Mieske*	.10
695	*Paul Russo*	.05
696	*Domingo Mota*	.05
697	*Todd Guggiana*	.05
698	Marc Newfield	.05
699	Checklist	.05
700	Checklist	.05
701	Checklist	.05
702	Checklist	.05
703	Checklist	.05
704	Checklist	.05

1992 Bowman

Topps introduced several changes with the release of its 1992 Bowman set. The 705-card set features 45 special insert cards stamped with gold foil. The cards are printed with a premium UV coated glossy card stock. Several players without major league experience are featured in the set. Included in this group are 1991 MVP's of the minor leagues and first round draft choices. Eighteen of the gold-foil enchanced cards have been identified as short-prints (designated SP in the listings), printed in quantities one-half the other foils.

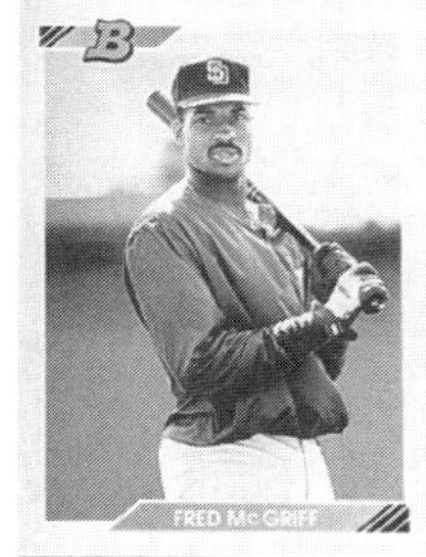

	MT
Complete Set (705):	250.00
Common Player:	.20
Pack (15):	10.00
Wax Box (36):	325.00

1	Ivan Rodriguez	2.00
2	Kirk McCaskill	.20
3	Scott Livingstone	.20
4	*Salomon Torres*	.20
5	Carlos Hernandez	.20
6	Dave Hollins	.20
7	Scott Fletcher	.20
8	Jorge Fabregas	.20
9	Andujar Cedeno	.20
10	Howard Johnson	.20
11	*Trevor Hoffman*	2.00
12	Roberto Kelly	.20
13	Gregg Jefferies	.20
14	Marquis Grissom	.20
15	Mike Ignasiak	.20
16	Jack Morris	.20
17	William Pennyfeather	.20
18	Todd Stottlemyre	.20
19	Chito Martinez	.20
20	Roberto Alomar	1.50
21	Sam Militello	.20
22	Hector Fajardo	.20
23	*Paul Quantrill*	.40
24	Chuck Knoblauch	.20
25	Reggie Jefferson	.20
26	Jeremy McGarity	.20
27	Jerome Walton	.20
28	Chipper Jones	20.00
29	*Brian Barber*	.20
30	Ron Darling	.20
31	*Roberto Petagine*	.20
32	Chuck Finley	.20
33	Edgar Martinez	.20
34	Napolean Robinson	.20
35	Andy Van Slyke	.20
36	Bobby Thigpen	.20
37	Travis Fryman	.20
38	Eric Christopherson	.20
39	Terry Mulholland	.20
40	Darryl Strawberry	.20
41	*Manny Alexander*	.50
42	*Tracey Sanders*	.20
43	Pete Incaviglia	.20
44	Kim Batiste	.20
45	Frank Rodriguez	.20
46	Greg Swindell	.20
47	Delino DeShields	.20
48	John Ericks	.20
49	Franklin Stubbs	.20
50	Tony Gwynn	3.00
51	*Clifton Garrett*	.20
52	Mike Gardella	.20
53	Scott Erickson	.20
54	Gary Caballo	.20
55	*Jose Oliva*	.20
56	Brook Fordyce	.20
57	Mark Whiten	.20
58	Joe Slusarski	.20
59	*J.R. Phillips*	.20
60	Barry Bonds	4.00
61	Bob Milacki	.20
62	Keith Mitchell	.20
63	Angel Miranda	.20
64	Raul Mondesi	.75
65	Brian Koelling	.20
66	Brian McRae	.20
67	John Patterson	.20
68	John Wetteland	.20
69	Wilson Alvarez	.20
70	Wade Boggs	1.50
71	Darryl Ratliff	.20
72	Jeff Jackson	.20
73	Jeremy Hernandez	.20
74	Darryl Hamilton	.20
75	Rafael Belliard	.20
76	Ricky Trilcek	.20
77	*Felipe Crespo*	.40
78	Carney Lansford	.20
79	Ryan Long	.20
80	Kirby Puckett	3.00
81	Earl Cunningham	.20
82	Pedro Martinez	20.00
83	Scott Hatteberg	.20
84	Juan Gonzalez	2.50
85	Robert Nutting	.20
86	*Calvin Reese*	1.00
87	Dave Silvestri	.20
88	*Scott Ruffcorn*	.40
89	Rick Aguilera	.20
90	Cecil Fielder	.20
91	Kirk Dressendorfer	.20
92	Jerry DiPoto	.20
93	Mike Felder	.20
94	Craig Paquette	.20
95	Elvin Paulino	.20
96	Donovan Osborne	.20
97	Hubie Brooks	.20
98	*Derek Lowe*	6.00
99	David Zancanaro	.20
100	Ken Griffey, Jr.	5.00
101	Todd Hundley	.20
102	Mike Trombley	.20
103	*Ricky Gutierrez*	.50
104	Braulio Castillo	.20
105	Craig Lefferts	.20
106	Rick Sutcliffe	.20
107	Dean Palmer	.20
108	Henry Rodriguez	.20
109	*Mark Clark*	.20
110	Kenny Lofton	.20
111	Mark Carreon	.20
112	*J.T. Bruett*	.20
113	Gerald Williams	.20
114	Frank Thomas	3.00
115	Kevin Reimer	.20
116	Sammy Sosa	4.00
117	Mickey Tettleton	.20
118	Reggie Sanders	.20
119	Trevor Wilson	.20
120	Cliff Brantley	.20
121	Spike Owen	.20
122	Jeff Montgomery	.20
123	Alex Sutherland	.20
124	*Brien Taylor*	.20
125	Brian Williams	.20
126	Kevin Seitzer	.20
127	*Carlos Delgado*	15.00
128	Gary Scott	.20
129	Scott Cooper	.20
130	*Domingo Jean*	.20
131	*Pat Mahomes*	.20
132	Mike Boddicker	.20
133	Roberto Hernandez	.20
134	Dave Valle	.20
135	Kurt Stillwell	.20
136	*Brad Pennington*	.50
137	Jermaine Swifton	.20
138	Ryan Hawblitzel	.20
139	Tito Navarro	.20
140	Sandy Alomar	.20
141	Todd Benzinger	.20
142	Danny Jackson	.20
143	*Melvin Nieves*	.50
144	Jim Campanis	.20
145	Luis Gonzalez	1.00
146	Dave Doorneweerd	.20
147	Charlie Hayes	.20
148	Greg Maddux	3.00
149	Brian Harper	.20
150	Brent Miller	.20
151	*Shawn Estes*	1.00
152	Mike Williams	.20
153	Charlie Hough	.20
154	Randy Myers	.20
155	*Kevin Young*	1.00
156	Rick Wilkins	.20
157	Terry Schumpert	.20
158	Steve Karsay	.20
159	Gary DiSarcina	.20
160	Deion Sanders	.35
161	Tom Browning	.20
162	Dickie Thon	.20
163	Luis Mercedes	.20
164	Ricardo Ingram	.20
165	*Tavo Alavarez*	.20
166	Rickey Henderson	.75
167	Jaime Navarro	.20
168	*Billy Ashley*	.20
169	Phil Dauphin	.20
170	Ivan Cruz	.20
171	Harold Baines	.20
172	Bryan Harvey	.20
173	Alex Cole	.20
174	Curtis Shaw	.20
175	Matt Williams	.40
176	Felix Jose	.20
177	Sam Horn	.20
178	Randy Johnson	1.50
179	Ivan Calderon	.20
180	Steve Avery	.20
181	William Suero	.20
182	Bill Swift	.20
183	*Howard Battle*	.20
184	Ruben Amaro	.20
185	Jim Abbott	.20
186	Mike Fitzgerald	.20
187	Bruce Hurst	.20
188	Jeff Juden	.20
189	Jeromy Burnitz	.20
190	Dave Burba	.20
191	Kevin Brown	.20
192	Patrick Lennon	.20
193	Jeffrey McNeely	.20
194	Wil Cordero	.20
195	Chili Davis	.20
196	Milt Cuyler	.20
197	Von Hayes	.20
198	*Todd Revening*	.20
199	Joel Johnson	.20
200	Jeff Bagwell	2.50
201	Alex Fernandez	.20
202	Todd Jones	.20
203	Charles Nagy	.20
204	Tim Raines	.20
205	Kevin Maas	.20
206	Julio Franco	.20
207	Randy Velarde	.20
208	Lance Johnson	.20
209	Scott Leius	.20
210	Derek Lee	.20
211	Joe Sondrini	.20
212	Royce Clayton	.20
213	Chris George	.20
214	Gary Sheffield	.60
215	Mark Gubicza	.20
216	Mike Moore	.20
217	Rick Huisman	.20
218	Jeff Russell	.20
219	D.J. Dozier	.20
220	Dave Martinez	.20
221	Al Newman	.20
222	Nolan Ryan	6.00
223	Teddy Higuera	.20
224	*Damon Buford*	.40
225	Ruben Sierra	.20
226	Tom Nevers	.20
227	Tommy Greene	.20
228	*Nigel Wilson*	.20
229	John DeSilva	.20
230	Bobby Witt	.20
231	Greg Cadaret	.20
232	John VanderWal	.20
233	Jack Clark	.20
234	Bill Doran	.20
235	Bobby Bonilla	.20
236	Steve Olin	.20
237	Derek Bell	.20
238	David Cone	.20
239	Victor Cole	.20
240	Rod Bolton	.20
241	Tom Pagnozzi	.20
242	Rob Dibble	.20
243	Michael Carter	.20
244	Don Peters	.20

No.	Player	Value
245	Mike LaValliere	.20
246	Joe Perona	.20
247	Mitch Williams	.20
248	Jay Buhner	.20
249	Andy Benes	.20
250	*Alex Ochoa*	.50
251	Greg Blosser	.20
252	Jack Armstrong	.20
253	Juan Samuel	.20
254	Terry Pendleton	.20
255	Ramon Martinez	.20
256	Rico Brogna	.20
257	John Smiley	.20
258	Carl Everett	.30
259	Tim Salmon	.75
260	Will Clark	.35
261	*Ugueth Urbina*	.50
262	Jason Wood	.20
263	Dave Magadan	.20
264	Dante Bichette	.20
265	Jose DeLeon	.20
266	*Mike Neill*	.20
267	Paul O'Neill	.20
268	Anthony Young	.20
269	Greg Harris	.20
270	Todd Van Poppel	.20
271	Pete Castellano	.20
272	Tony Phillips	.20
273	Mike Gallego	.20
274	*Steve Cooke*	.20
275	Robin Ventura	.20
276	Kevin Mitchell	.20
277	Doug Linton	.20
278	Robert Eenhorn	.20
279	*Gabe White*	.50
280	Dave Stewart	.20
281	Mo Sanford	.20
282	Greg Perschke	.20
283	Kevin Flora	.20
284	Jeff Williams	.20
285	Keith Miller	.20
286	Andy Ashby	.20
287	Doug Dascenzo	.20
288	Eric Karros	.20
289	*Glenn Murray*	.20
290	*Troy Percival*	.50
291	Orlando Merced	.20
292	Peter Hoy	.20
293	Tony Fernandez	.20
294	Juan Guzman	.20
295	Jesse Barfield	.20
296	Sid Fernandez	.20
297	Scott Cepicky	.20
298	*Garret Anderson*	6.00
299	Cal Eldred	.20
300	Ryne Sandberg	2.00
301	Jim Gantner	.20
302	*Mariano Rivera*	10.00
303	Ron Lockett	.20
304	Jose Offerman	.20
305	Denny Martinez	.20
306	*Luis Ortiz*	.20
307	David Howard	.20
308	Russ Springer	.20
309	Chris Howard	.20
310	Kyle Abbott	.20
311	*Aaron Sele*	2.00
312	Dave Justice	.40
313	Pete O'Brien	.20
314	Greg Hansell	.20
315	Dave Winfield	1.00
316	Lance Dickson	.20
317	Eric King	.20
318	Vaughn Eshelman	.20
319	Tim Belcher	.20
320	Andres Galarraga	.20
321	Scott Bullett	.20
322	Doug Strange	.20
323	Jerald Clark	.20
324	Dave Righetti	.20
325	Greg Hibbard	.20
326	Eric Dillman	.20
327	*Shane Reynolds*	.50
328	Chris Hammond	.20
329	Albert Belle	.40
330	*Rich Becker*	.50
331	Eddie Williams	.20
332	Donald Harris	.20
333	Dave Smith	.20
334	Steve Fireovid	.20
335	Steve Buechele	.20
336	Mike Schooler	.20
337	Kevin McReynolds	.20
338	Hensley Meulens	.20
339	*Benji Gil*	.50
340	Don Mattingly	3.00
341	Alvin Davis	.20
342	Alan Mills	.20
343	Kelly Downs	.20
344	Leo Gomez	.20
345	*Tarrik Brock*	.20
346	Ryan Turner	.20
347	John Smoltz	.35
348	Bill Sampen	.20
349	Paul Byrd	.20
350	Mike Bordick	.20
351	Jose Lind	.20
352	David Wells	.25
353	Barry Larkin	.35
354	Bruce Ruffin	.20
355	Luis Rivera	.20
356	Sid Bream	.20
357	Julian Vasquez	.20
358	*Jason Bere*	.50
359	Ben McDonald	.20
360	Scott Stahoviak	.20
361	Kirt Manwaring	.20
362	Jeff Johnson	.20
363	Rob Deer	.20
364	Tony Pena	.20
365	Melido Perez	.20
366	Clay Parker	.20
367	Dale Sveum	.20
368	Mike Scioscia	.20
369	Roger Salkeld	.20
370	Mike Stanley	.20
371	Jack McDowell	.20
372	Tim Wallach	.20
373	Billy Ripken	.20
374	Mike Christopher	.20
375	Paul Molitor	1.00
376	Dave Stieb	.20
377	Pedro Guerrero	.20
378	Russ Swan	.20
379	Bob Ojeda	.20
380	Donn Pall	.20
381	Eddie Zosky	.20
382	Darnell Coles	.20
383	Tom Smith	.20
384	Mark McGwire	6.00
385	Gary Carter	.35
386	Rich Amaral	.20
387	Alan Embree	.20
388	Jonathan Hurst	.20
389	*Bobby Jones*	1.00
390	Rico Rossy	.20
391	Dan Smith	.20
392	Terry Steinbach	.20
393	Jon Farrell	.20
394	Dave Anderson	.20
395	Benito Santiago	.20
396	Mark Wohlers	.20
397	Mo Vaughn	.60
398	Randy Kramer	.20
399	*John Jaha*	.20
400	Cal Ripken, Jr.	6.00
401	Ryan Bowen	.20
402	Tim McIntosh	.20
403	Bernard Gilkey	.20
404	Junior Felix	.20
405	Cris Colon	.20
406	Marc Newfield	.20
407	Bernie Williams	1.00
408	Jay Howell	.20
409	Zane Smith	.20
410	Jeff Shaw	.20
411	Kerry Woodson	.20
412	Wes Chamberlain	.20
413	Dave Mlicki	.20
414	Benny Distefano	.20
415	Kevin Rogers	.20
416	Tim Naehring	.20
417	Clemente Nunez	.20
418	Luis Sojo	.20
419	Kevin Ritz	.20
420	Omar Oliveras	.20
421	Manuel Lee	.20
422	Julio Valera	.20
423	Omar Vizquel	.20
424	Darren Burton	.20
425	Mel Hall	.20
426	Dennis Powell	.20
427	Lee Stevens	.20
428	Glenn Davis	.20
429	Willie Greene	.20
430	Kevin Wickander	.20
431	Dennis Eckersley	.20
432	Joe Orsulak	.20
433	Eddie Murray	1.00
434	*Matt Stairs*	1.00
435	Wally Joyner	.20
436	Rondell White	1.00
437	Rob Mauer	.20
438	Joe Redfield	.20
439	Mark Lewis	.20
440	Darren Daulton	.20
441	Mike Henneman	.20
442	John Cangelosi	.20
443	*Vince Moore*	.20
444	John Wehner	.20
445	Kent Hrbek	.20
446	Mark McLemore	.20
447	Bill Wegman	.20
448	Robby Thompson	.20
449	Mark Anthony	.20
450	Archi Cianfrocco	.20
451	Johnny Ruffin	.20
452	Javier Lopez	.20
453	Greg Gohr	.20
454	Tim Scott	.20
455	Stan Belinda	.20
456	Darrin Jackson	.20
457	Chris Gardner	.20
458	Esteban Beltre	.20
459	Phil Plantier	.20
460	Jim Thome	3.00
461	*Mike Piazza*	50.00
462	Matt Sinatro	.20
463	Scott Servais	.20
464	*Brian Jordan*	4.00
465	Doug Drabek	.20
466	Carl Willis	.20
467	Bret Barbarie	.20
468	Hal Morris	.20
469	Steve Sax	.20
470	Jerry Willard	.20
471	Dan Wilson	.20
472	Chris Hoiles	.20
473	Rheal Cormier	.20
474	John Morris	.20
475	Jeff Reardon	.20
476	Mark Leiter	.20
477	Tom Gordon	.20
478	*Kent Bottenfield*	.50
479	Gene Larkin	.20
480	Dwight Gooden	.20
481	B.J. Surhoff	.20
482	Andy Stankiewicz	.20
483	Tino Martinez	.20
484	Craig Biggio	.35
485	Denny Neagle	.20
486	Rusty Meacham	.20
487	Kal Daniels	.20
488	Dave Henderson	.20
489	Tim Costo	.20
490	Doug Davis	.20
491	Frank Viola	.20
492	Cory Snyder	.20
493	Chris Martin	.20
494	Dion James	.20
495	Randy Tomlin	.20
496	Greg Vaughn	.20
497	Dennis Cook	.20
498	Rosario Rodriguez	.20
499	Dave Staton	.20
500	George Brett	3.00
501	Brian Barnes	.20
502	Butch Henry	.20
503	Harold Reynolds	.20
504	*David Nied*	.20
505	Lee Smith	.20
506	Steve Chitren	.20
507	Ken Hill	.20
508	Robbie Beckett	.20
509	Troy Afenir	.20
510	Kelly Gruber	.20
511	Bret Boone	.35
512	Jeff Branson	.20
513	Mike Jackson	.20
514	Pete Harnisch	.20
515	Chad Kreuter	.20
516	Joe Vitko	.20
517	Orel Hershiser	.20
518	*John Doherty*	.20
519	Jay Bell	.20
520	Mark Langston	.20
521	Dann Howitt	.20
522	Bobby Reed	.20
523	Roberto Munoz	.20
524	Todd Ritchie	.20
525	Bip Roberts	.20
526	*Pat Listach*	.20
527	*Scott Brosius*	1.00
528	*John Roper*	.20
529	*Phil Hiatt*	.40
530	Denny Walling	.20
531	Carlos Baerga	.20
532	*Manny Ramirez*	40.00
533	Pat Clements	.20
534	Ron Gant	.20
535	Pat Kelly	.20
536	Billy Spiers	.20
537	Darren Reed	.20
538	Ken Caminiti	.20
539	*Butch Huskey*	1.00
540	Matt Nokes	.20
541	John Kruk	.20
542	John Jaha (Foil, SP)	.50
543	*Justin Thompson*	.25
544	Steve Hosey	.20
545	Joe Kmak	.20
546	John Franco	.20
547	Devon White	.20
548	Elston Hansen (Foil, SP)	.35
549	Ryan Klesko	1.00
550	Danny Tartabull	.20
551	Frank Thomas (Foil, SP)	2.50
552	Kevin Tapani	.20
553a	Willie Banks	.20
553b	Pat Clements	.20
554	*B.J. Wallace* (Foil, SP)	.50
555	*Orlando Miller*	.20
556	*Mark Smith*	.25
557	Tim Wallach (Foil)	.35
558	Bill Gullickson	.20
559	Derek Bell (Foil)	.35
560	Joe Randa (Foil)	.35
561	Frank Seminara	.20
562	Mark Gardner	.20
563	Rick Greene (Foil)	.35
564	Gary Gaetti	.20
565	Ozzie Guillen	.20
566	Charles Nagy (Foil)	.45
567	Mike Milchin	.20
568	Ben Shelton (Foil)	.35
569	Chris Roberts (Foil)	.35
570	Ellis Burks	.20
571	Scott Scudder	.20
572	Jim Abbott (Foil)	.35
573	Joe Carter	.20
574	Steve Finley	.20
575	Jim Olander (Foil)	.35
576	Carlos Garcia	.20
577	Greg Olson	.20
578	Greg Swindell (Foil)	.35
579	Matt Williams (Foil)	.50
580	Mark Grace	.40
581	Howard House (Foil)	.20
582	Luis Polonia	.20
583	Erik Hanson	.20
584	Salomon Torres (Foil)	.35
585	Carlton Fisk	.75
586	Bret Saberhagen	.20
587	*Chad McDonnell* (Foil)	.35
588	Jimmy Key	.20
589	Mike MacFarlane	.20
590	Barry Bonds (Foil)	2.00
591	Jamie McAndrew	.20
592	Shane Mack	.20
593	Kerwin Moore	.20
594	Joe Oliver	.20
595	Chris Sabo	.20
596	*Alex Gonzalez*	1.50
597	Brett Butler	.20
598	Mark Hutton	.20
599	Andy Benes (Foil)	.35
600	Jose Canseco	1.00
601	Darryl Kile	.20
602	Matt Stairs (Foil, SP)	.50
603	Rob Butler (Foil)	.35
604	Willie McGee	.20
605	Jack McDowell	.20
606	Tom Candiotti	.20
607	Ed Martel	.20
608	Matt Mieske (Foil)	.35
609	Darrin Fletcher	.20
610	Rafael Palmeiro	.40
611	Bill Swift (Foil)	.35
612	Mike Mussina	2.00
613	Vince Coleman	.20
614	Scott Cepicky (Foil)	.35
615	Mike Greenwell	.20
616	Kevin McGehee	.20
617	Jeffrey Hammonds (Foil)	.35
618	Scott Taylor	.20
619	Dave Otto	.20
620	Mark McGwire (Foil)	4.00
621	Kevin Tatar	.20
622	Steve Farr	.20
623	Ryan Klesko (Foil)	.75

625	Andre Dawson	.40
626	Tino Martinez (Foil, SP)	.50
627	*Chad Curtis*	.75
628	Mickey Morandini	.20
629	Gregg Olson (Foil, SP)	.50
630	Lou Whitaker	.20
631	Arthur Rhodes	.20
632	Brandon Wilson	.20
633	*Lance Jennings*	.20
634	*Allen Watson*	.20
635	Len Dykstra	.20
636	Joe Girardi	.20
637	Kiki Hernandez (Foil, SP)	.50
638	*Mike Hampton*	4.00
639	Al Osuna	.20
640	Kevin Appier	.20
641	Rick Helling (Foil, SP)	.50
642	Jody Reed	.20
643	Ray Lankford	.20
644	John Olerud	.20
645	Paul Molitor (Foil, SP)	1.00
646	Pat Borders	.20
647	Mike Morgan	.20
648	Larry Walker	.75
649	Pete Castellano (Foil, SP)	.50
650	Fred McGriff	.20
651	Walt Weiss	.20
652	*Calvin Murray* (Foil, SP)	.50
653	Dave Nilsson	.20
654	Greg Pirkl	.20
655	Robin Ventura (Foil, SP)	.50
656	Mark Portugal	.20
657	Roger McDowell	.20
658	Rick Hirtensteiner (Foil, SP)	.50
659	Glenallen Hill	.20
660	Greg Gagne	.20
661	Charles Johnson (Foil, SP)	.50
662	Brian Hunter	.20
663	Mark Lemke	.20
664	Tim Belcher (Foil, SP)	.35
665	Rich DeLucia	.20
666	Bob Walk	.20
667	Joe Carter (Foil, SP)	.50
668	Jose Guzman	.20
669	Otis Nixon	.20
670	Phil Nevin (Foil)	.35
671	Eric Davis	.20
672	*Damion Easley*	1.00
673	Will Clark (Foil)	.50
674	Mark Kiefer	.20
675	Ozzie Smith	2.00
676	Manny Ramirez (Foil)	5.00
677	Gregg Olson	.20
678	*Cliff Floyd*	8.00
679	Duane Singleton	.20
680	Jose Rijo	.20
681	Willie Randolph	.20
682	*Michael Tucker* (Foil)	1.00
683	Darren Lewis	.20
684	Dale Murphy	.35
685	Mike Pagliarulo	.20
686	Paul Miller	.20
687	Mike Robertson	.20
688	Mike Devereaux	.20
689	Pedro Astacio	.20
690	Alan Trammell	.20
691	Roger Clemens	3.00
692	Bud Black	.20
693	Turk Wendell	.20
694	Barry Larkin (Foil, SP)	.50
695	Todd Zeile	.20
696	Pat Hentgen	.20
697	*Eddie Taubensee*	.40
698	Guillermo Vasquez	.20
699	Tom Glavine	.35
700	Robin Yount	1.00
701	Checklist	.20
702	Checklist	.20
703	Checklist	.20
704	Checklist	.20
705	Checklist	.20

1993 Bowman

Bowman's 708-card 1993 set once again features a premium UV-coated glossy stock. There are also 48 special insert cards, with gold foil stamping, randomly inserted one per pack or two per jumbo pack. The foil cards, numbered 339-374 and 693-704, feature top prospects and rookie-of-the-year candidates, as do several regular cards in the set. Cards are standard size.

		MT
Complete Set (708):		50.00
Common Player:		.10
Pack (15):		2.50
Wax Box (24):		50.00
1	Glenn Davis	.10
2	*Hector Roa*	.10
3	*Ken Ryan*	.10
4	*Derek Wallace*	.10
5	Jorge Fabregas	.10
6	Joe Oliver	.10
7	Brandon Wilson	.10
8	*Mark Thompson*	.30
9	Tracy Sanders	.10
10	Rich Renteria	.10
11	Lou Whitaker	.10
12	*Brian Hunter*	.75
13	Joe Vitiello	.10
14	Eric Karros	.10
15	Joe Kmak	.10
16	Tavo Alvarez	.10
17	*Steve Dunn*	.30
18	Tony Fernandez	.10
19	Melido Perez	.10
20	Mike Lieberthal	.20
21	Terry Steinbach	.10
22	Stan Belinda	.10
23	Jay Buhner	.10
24	Allen Watson	.10
25	*Daryl Henderson*	.10
26	*Ray McDavid*	.30
27	Shawn Green	1.50
28	Bud Black	.10
29	*Sherman Obando*	.10
30	*Mike Hostetler*	.10
31	*Nate Hinchey*	.10
32	Randy Myers	.10
33	*Brian Grebeck*	.10
34	John Roper	.10
35	Larry Thomas	.10
36	Alex Cole	.10
37	*Tom Kramer*	.10
38	*Matt Whisenant*	.25
39	*Chris Gomez*	.40
40	Luis Gonzalez	.35
41	Kevin Appier	.10
42	*Omar Daal*	.75
43	Duane Singleton	.10
44	Bill Risley	.10
45	*Pat Meares*	.25
46	Butch Huskey	.10
47	Bobby Munoz	.10
48	Juan Bell	.10
49	*Scott Lydy*	.10
50	Dennis Moeller	.10
51	Marc Newfield	.10
52	*Tripp Cromer*	.10
53	Kurt Miller	.10
54	Jim Pena	.10
55	Juan Guzman	.10
56	Matt Williams	.25
57	Harold Reynolds	.10
58	*Donnie Elliott*	.10
59	*Jon Shave*	.10
60	*Kevin Roberson*	.10
61	*Hilly Hathaway*	.10
62	Jose Rijo	.10
63	*Kerry Taylor*	.10
64	Ryan Hawblitzel	.10
65	Glenallen Hill	.10
66	*Ramon D. Martinez*	.20
67	Travis Fryman	.10
68	Tom Nevers	.10
69	Phil Hiatt	.10
70	Tim Wallach	.10
71	B.J. Surhoff	.10
72	Rondell White	.30
73	*Denny Hocking*	.20
74	*Mike Oquist*	.10
75	Paul O'Neill	.10
76	Willie Banks	.10
77	Bob Welch	.10
78	*Jose Sandoval*	.10
79	Bill Haselman	.10
80	Rheal Cormier	.10
81	Dean Palmer	.10
82	*Pat Gomez*	.10
83	Steve Karsay	.10
84	*Carl Hanselman*	.10
85	*T.R. Lewis*	.10
86	Chipper Jones	4.00
87	Scott Hatteberg	.10
88	Greg Hibbard	.10
89	*Lance Painter*	.20
90	*Chad Mottola*	.40
91	Jason Bere	.10
92	Dante Bichette	.10
93	Sandy Alomar	.10
94	Carl Everett	.15
95	*Danny Bautista*	.10
96	Steve Finley	.10
97	David Cone	.10
98	Todd Hollandsworth	.10
99	Matt Mieske	.10
100	Larry Walker	.75
101	Shane Mack	.10
102	*Aaron Ledesma*	.10
103	*Andy Pettitte*	4.00
104	Kevin Stocker	.10
105	Mike Mobler	.10
106	Tony Menedez	.10
107	Derek Lowe	.10
108	Basil Shabazz	.10
109	Dan Smith	.10
110	*Scott Sanders*	.10
111	Todd Stottlemyre	.10
112	*Benji Sikonton*	.10
113	Rick Sutcliffe	.10
114	*Lee Heath*	.10
115	Jeff Russell	.10
116	*Dave Stevens*	.10
117	*Mark Holzemer*	.10
118	Tim Belcher	.10
119	Bobby Thigpen	.10
120	*Roger Bailey*	.10
121	*Tony Mitchell*	.10
122	Junior Felix	.10
123	*Rich Robertson*	.10
124	*Andy Cook*	.10
125	*Brian Bevil*	.10
126	Darryl Strawberry	.10
127	Cal Eldred	.10
128	Cliff Floyd	.10
129	Alan Newman	.10
130	Howard Johnson	.10
131	Jim Abbott	.10
132	Chad McConnell	.10
133	*Miguel Jimenez*	.10
134	*Brett Backlund*	.10
135	*John Cummings*	.30
136	Brian Barber	.10
137	Rafael Palmeiro	.25
138	*Tim Worrell*	.10
139	*Jose Pett*	.10
140	Barry Bonds	1.50
141	Damon Buford	.10
142	Jeff Blauser	.10
143	Frankie Rodriguez	.10
144	Mike Morgan	.10
145	Gary DeSarcina	.10
146	Calvin Reese	.10
147	Johnny Ruffin	.10
148	David Nied	.10
149	Charles Nagy	.10
150	*Mike Myers*	.10
151	*Kenny Carlyle*	.10
152	Eric Anthony	.10
153	Jose Lind	.10
154	Pedro Martinez	3.00
155	Mark Kiefer	.10
156	*Tim Laker*	.10
157	Pat Mahomes	.10
158	Bobby Bonilla	.10
159	Domingo Jean	.10
160	Darren Daulton	.10
161	Mark McGwire	5.00
162	*Jason Kendall*	4.00
163	Desi Relaford	.10
164	Ozzie Canseco	.10
165	Rick Helling	.10
166	*Steve Pegues*	.10
167	Paul Molitor	.45
168	*Larry Carter*	.10
169	Arthur Rhodes	.10
170	*Damon Hollins*	.35
171	Frank Viola	.10
172	*Steve Trachsel*	.40
173	*J.T. Snow*	1.50
174	*Keith Gordon*	.10
175	Carlton Fisk	.30
176	*Jason Bates*	.10
177	*Mike Crosby*	.10
178	Benny Santiago	.10
179	Mike Moore	.10
180	Jeff Juden	.10
181	Darren Burton	.10
182	*Todd Williams*	.10
183	John Jaha	.10
184	*Mike Lansing*	.75
185	*Pedro Grifol*	.10
186	Vince Coleman	.10
187	Pat Kelly	.10
188	*Clemente Alvarez*	.10
189	Ron Darling	.10
190	Orlando Merced	.10
191	Chris Bosio	.10
192	*Steve Dixon*	.10
193	Doug Dascenzo	.10
194	*Ray Holbert*	.10
195	Howard Battle	.10
196	Willie McGee	.10
197	*John O'Donoghue*	.10
198	Steve Avery	.10
199	Greg Blosser	.10
200	Ryne Sandberg	.75
201	Joe Grahe	.10
202	Dan Wilson	.10
203	*Domingo Martinez*	.10
204	Andres Galarraga	.10
205	*Jamie Taylor*	.10
206	*Darrell Whitmore*	.10
207	*Ben Blomdahl*	.10
208	Doug Drabek	.10
209	Keith Miller	.10
210	Billy Ashley	.10
211	*Mike Farrell*	.10
212	John Wetteland	.10
213	Randy Tomlin	.10
214	Sid Fernandez	.10
215	*Quilvio Veras*	.60
216	Dave Hollins	.10
217	Mike Neill	.10
218	Andy Van Slyke	.10
219	Bret Boone	.15
220	Tom Pagnozzi	.10
221	*Mike Welch*	.10
222	Frank Seminara	.10
223	Ron Villone	.10
224	*D.J. Thielen*	.10
225	Cal Ripken, Jr.	4.00
226	*Pedro Borbon*	.10
227	Carlos Quintana	.10
228	*Tommy Shields*	.10
229	Tim Salmon	.60
230	John Smiley	.10
231	Ellis Burks	.10
232	Pedro Castellano	.10
233	Paul Byrd	.10
234	Bryan Harvey	.10
235	Scott Livingstone	.10
236	*James Mouton*	.35
237	Joe Randa	.10
238	Pedro Astacio	.10
239	Darryl Hamilton	.10
240	*Joey Eischen*	.40
241	*Edgar Herrera*	.10
242	Dwight Gooden	.10
243	Sam Militello	.10

244 *Ron Blazier* .10
245 Ruben Sierra .10
246 Al Martin .10
247 Mike Felder .10
248 Bob Tewksbury .10
249 Craig Lefferts .10
250 Luis Lopez .10
251 Devon White .10
252 Will Clark .30
253 Mark Smith .10
254 Terry Pendleton .10
255 Aaron Sele .10
256 *Jose Viera* .10
257 Damion Easley .10
258 *Rod Lofton* .10
259 *Chris Snopek* .40
260 *Quinton McCracken* .50
261 *Mike Matthews* .10
262 *Hector Carrasco* .40
263 Rick Greene .10
264 *Chris Bolt* .10
265 George Brett 1.00
266 *Rick Gorecki* .10
267 *Francisco Gamez* .10
268 Marquis Grissom .10
269 Kevin Tapani .10
270 Ryan Thompson .10
271 Gerald Williams .10
272 *Paul Fletcher* .10
273 Lance Blankenship .10
274 *Marty Heff* .10
275 Shawn Estes .30
276 *Rene Arocha* .10
277 *Scott Evre* .10
278 Phil Plantier .10
279 *Paul Spoljaric* .30
280 Chris Gahbs .10
281 Harold Baines .10
282 *Jose Oliva* .10
283 Matt Whiteside .10
284 *Brant Brown* .75
285 Russ Springer .10
286 Chris Sabo .10
287 Ozzie Guillen .10
288 *Marcus Moore* .10
289 Chad Ogea .10
290 Walt Weiss .10
291 Brian Edmondson .10
292 Jimmy Gonzalez .10
293 *Danny Miceli* .30
294 Jose Offerman .10
295 Greg Vaughn .10
296 Frank Bolick .10
297 *Mike Maksudian* .10
298 John Franco .10
299 Danny Tartabull .10
300 Len Dykstra .10
301 Bobby Witt .10
302 *Trey Beamon* .40
303 Tino Martinez .10
304 Aaron Holbert .10
305 Juan Gonzalez 1.00
306 *Billy Hall* .10
307 Duane Ward .10
308 Rod Beck .10
309 *Jose Mercedes* .10
310 Otis Nixon .10
311 *Gettys Glaze* .10
312 Candy Maldonado .10
313 Chad Curtis .10
314 Tim Costo .10
315 Mike Robertson .10
316 Nigel Wilson .10
317 *Greg McMichael* .10
318 *Scott Pose* .10
319 Ivan Cruz .10
320 Greg Swindell .10
321 Kevin McReynolds .10
322 Tom Candiotti .10
323 *Bob Wishnevski* .10
324 Ken Hill .10
325 Kirby Puckett 1.00
326 *Tim Bogar* .30
327 Mariano Rivera .45
328 Mitch Williams .10
329 Craig Paquette .10
330 Jay Bell .10
331 *Jose Martinez* .10
332 Rob Deer .10
333 Brook Fordyce .10
334 Matt Nokes .10
335 Derek Lee .10
336 *Paul Ellis* .10
337 *Desi Wilson* .10
338 Roberto Alomar .75
339 Jim Tatum (Foil) .10
340 J.T. Snow (Foil) .30
341 Tim Salmon (Foil) .75
342 *Russ Davis* (Foil) 1.00
343 Javier Lopez (Foil) .60
344 *Troy O'Leary* (Foil) 1.00
345 *Marty Cordova* (Foil) .50
346 *Bubba Smith* (Foil) .10
347 Chipper Jones (Foil) 4.00
348 Jessie Hollins (Foil) .10
349 Willie Greene (Foil) .10
350 Mark Thompson (Foil) .10
351 Nigel Wilson (Foil) .10
352 Todd Jones (Foil) .10
353 Raul Mondesi (Foil) .35
354 Cliff Floyd (Foil) .50
355 Bobby Jones (Foil) .30
356 Kevin Stocker (Foil) .10
357 Midre Cummings (Foil) .35
358 Allen Watson (Foil) .10
359 Ray McDavid (Foil) .10
360 Steve Hosey (Foil) .10
361 Brad Pennington (Foil) .10
362 Frankie Rodriguez (Foil) .10
363 Troy Percival (Foil) .10
364 Jason Bere (Foil) .10
365 Manny Ramirez (Foil) 3.00
366 Justin Thompson (Foil) .10
367 Joe Vitello (Foil) .10
368 Tyrone Hill (Foil) .10
369 David McCarty (Foil) .10
370 Brien Taylor (Foil) .10
371 Todd Van Poppel (Foil) .10
372 Marc Newfield (Foil) .10
373 *Terrell Lowery* (Foil) .10
374 Alex Gonzalez (Foil) .15
375 Ken Griffey, Jr. 3.00
376 Donovan Osborne .10
377 *Ritchie Moody* .10
378 Shane Andrews .10
379 Carlos Delgado 1.00
380 Bill Swift .10
381 Leo Gomez .10
382 Ron Gant .10
383 Scott Fletcher .10
384 *Matt Walbeck* .10
385 Chuck Finley .10
386 Kevin Mitchell .10
387 Wilson Alvarez .10
388 *John Burke* .10
389 Alan Embree .10
390 Trevor Hoffman .10
391 Alan Trammell .10
392 Todd Jones .10
393 Felix Jose .10
394 Orel Hershiser .10
395 Pat Listach .10
396 Gabe White .10
397 *Dan Serafini* .30
398 Todd Hundley .10
399 Wade Boggs .50
400 Tyler Green .10
401 Mike Bordick .10
402 Scott Bullett .10
403 *Lagrande Russell* .10
404 Ray Lankford .10
405 Nolan Ryan 3.00
406 Robbie Beckett .10
407 *Brent Bowers* .10
408 *Adell Davenport* .10
409 Brady Anderson .10
410 Tom Glavine .15
411 *Doug Hecker* .10
412 Jose Guzman .10
413 Luis Polonia .10
414 Brian Williams .10
415 Bo Jackson .15
416 Eric Young .10
417 Kenny Lofton .10
418 Orestes Destrade .10
419 Tony Phillips .10
420 Jeff Bagwell 1.00
421 Hark Gardner .10
422 Brett Butler .10
423 *Graeme Lloyd* .10
424 Delino DeShields .10
425 Scott Erickson .10
426 Jeff Kent .10
427 Jimmy Key .10
428 Mickey Morandini .10
429 *Marcos Arkas* .10
430 Don Slaught .10
431 Randy Johnson .45
432 Omar Olivares .10
433 Charlie Leibrandt .10
434 Kurt Stillwell .10
435 *Scott Brow* .10
436 Robby Thompson .10
437 Ben McDonald .10
438 Deion Sanders .15
439 Tony Pena .10
440 Mark Grace .35
441 Eduardo Perez .10
442 *Tim Pugh* .10
443 Scott Ruffcorn .10
444 *Jay Gainer* .10
445 Albert Belle .40
446 Bret Barberie .10
447 Justin Mashore .10
448 Pete Harnisch .10
449 Greg Gagne .10
450 Eric Davis .10
451 Dave Mlicki .10
452 Moises Alou .15
453 Rick Aguilera .10
454 Eddie Murray .50
455 Bob Wickman .10
456 Wes Chamberlain .10
457 Brent Gates .10
458 Paul Weber .10
459 Mike Hampton .10
460 Ozzie Smith .50
461 Tom Henke .10
462 Ricky Gutuerrez .10
463 Jack Morris .10
464 *Joel Chimelis* .10
465 Gregg Olson .10
466 Javier Lopez .10
467 Scott Cooper .10
468 Willie Wilson .10
469 Mark Langston .10
470 Barry Larkin .15
471 Rod Bolton .10
472 Freddie Benavides .10
473 *Ken Ramos* .10
474 Chuck Carr .10
475 Cecil Fielder .10
476 Eddie Taubensee .10
477 *Chris Eddy* .10
478 Greg Hansell .10
479 Kevin Reimer .10
480 Denny Martinez .10
481 Chuck Knoblauch .10
482 Mike Draper .10
483 Spike Owen .10
484 Terry Mulholland .10
485 Dennis Eckersley .10
486 Blas Minor .10
487 Dave Fleming .10
488 Dan Cholonsky .10
489 Ivan Rodriguez .75
490 Gary Sheffield .30
491 Ed Sprague .10
492 Steve Hosey .10
493 *Jimmy Haynes* .50
494 John Smoltz .15
495 Andre Dawson .25
496 Rey Sanchez .10
497 *Ty Van Burkleo* .10
498 *Bobby Ayala* .40
499 Tim Raines .10
500 Charlie Hayes .10
501 Paul Sorrento .10
502 *Richie Lewis* .10
503 *Jason Pfaff* .10
504 Ken Caminiti .10
505 Mike Macfarlane .10
506 Jody Reed .10
507 *Bobby Hughes* .75
508 Wil Cordero .10
509 *George Tsanis* .10
510 Bret Saberhagen .10
511 *Derek Jeter* 35.00
512 Gene Schall .10
513 Curtis Shaw .10
514 Steve Cooke .10
515 Edgar Martinez .10
516 Mike Milchin .10
517 Billy Ripken .10
518 Andy Benes .10
519 *Juan de la Rosa* .10
520 John Burkett .10
521 Alex Ochoa .10
522 *Tony Tarasco* .10
523 Luis Ortiz .10
524 Rick Williams .10
525 *Chris Turner* .10
526 Rob Dibble .10
527 Jack McDowell .10
528 Daryl Boston .10
529 *Bill Wertz* .10
530 Charlie Hough .10
531 Sean Bergman .10
532 Doug Jones .10
533 Jeff Montgomery .10
534 *Roger Cedeno* 1.50
535 Robin Yount .50
536 Mo Vaughn .40
537 Brian Harper .10
538 Juan Castillo .10
539 Steve Farr .10
540 John Kruk .10
541 Troy Neel .10
542 *Danny Clyburn* .30
543 *Jim Converse* .10
544 Gregg Jefferies .10
545 Jose Canseco .40
546 *Julio Bruno* .10
547 Rob Butler .10
548 Royce Clayton .10
549 Chris Hoiles .10
550 Greg Maddux 1.50
551 *Joe Ciccarella* .10
552 Ozzie Timmons .10
553 Chili Davis .10
554 Brian Koelling .10
555 Frank Thomas 1.50
556 Vinny Castilla .30
557 Reggie Jefferson .10
558 Rob Natal .10
559 Mike Henneman .10
560 Craig Biggio .15
561 *Billy Brewer* .10
562 Dan Melendez .10
563 *Kenny Felder* .40
564 *Miguel Batista* .10
565 Dave Winfield .45
566 Al Shirley .10
567 Robert Eenhoorn .10
568 Mike Williams .10
569 *Tanyon Sturtze* .10
570 Tim Wakefield .10
571 Greg Pirkl .10
572 *Sean Lowe* .30
573 *Terry Burows* .10
574 *Kevin Higgins* .10
575 Joe Carter .10
576 Kevin Rogers .10
577 Manny Alexander .10
578 Dave Justice .30
579 *Brian Conroy* .10
580 *Jessie Hollins* .10
581 *Ron Watson* .10
582 Bip Roberts .10
583 *Tom Urbani* .10
584 *Jason Hutchins* .10
585 Carlos Baerga .10
586 Jeff Mutis .10
587 Justin Thompson .30
588 Orlando Miller .10
589 Brian McRae .10
590 Ramon Martinez .10
591 Dave Nilsson .10
592 *Jose Vidro* 6.00
593 Rich Becker .10
594 *Preston Wilson* 3.00
595 Don Mattingly 1.50
596 Tony Longmire .10
597 Kevin Seitzer .10
598 *Midre Cummings* .45
599 Omar Vizquel .10
600 Lee Smith .10
601 *David Hulse* .15
602 *Darrell Sherman* .10
603 Alex Gonzalez .10
604 Geronimo Pena .10
605 Mike Devereaux .10
606 *Sterling Hitchcock* .50
607 Mike Greenwell .10
608 Steve Buechele .10
609 Troy Percival .10
610 Bobby Kelly .10
611 *James Baldwin* 3.00
612 Jerald Clark .10
613 *Albie Lopez* .15
614 Dave Magadan .10
615 Mickey Tettleton .10
616 *Sean Runyan* .10
617 Bob Hamelin .10
618 Raul Mondesi .30
619 Tyrone Hill .10
620 Darrin Fletcher .10

621 Mike Trombley .10
622 Jeromy Burnitz .10
623 Bernie Williams .30
624 *Mike Farmer* .10
625 Rickey Henderson .45
626 Carlos Garcia .10
627 *Jeff Darwin* .10
628 Todd Zeile .10
629 Benji Gil .10
630 Tony Gwynn 2.00
631 *Aaron Small* .10
632 *Joe Rosselli* .10
633 Mike Mussina .50
634 Ryan Klesko .10
635 Roger Clemens 2.00
636 Sammy Sosa 2.00
637 *Orlando Palmeiro* .10
638 Willie Greene .10
639 George Bell .10
640 *Garvin Alston* .10
641 *Pete Janicki* .10
642 *Chris Sheff* .10
643 *Felipe Lira* .10
644 Roberto Petagine .10
645 Wally Joyner .10
646 Mike Piazza 3.00
647 Jaime Navarro .10
648 *Jeff Hartsock* .10
649 David McCarty .10
650 Bobby Jones .10
651 Mark Hutton .10
652 Kyle Abbott .10
653 *Steve Cox* .50
654 Jeff King .10
655 Norm Charlton .10
656 *Mike Gulan* .10
657 Julio Franco .10
658 *Cameron Cairncross* .10
659 John Olerud .10
660 Salomon Torres .10
661 Brad Pennington .10
662 Melvin Nieves .10
663 Ivan Calderon .10
664 Turk Wendell .10
665 Chris Pritchett .10
666 Reggie Sanders .10
667 Robin Ventura .10
668 Joe Girardi .10
669 Manny Ramirez 3.00
670 Jeff Conine .10
671 Greg Gohr .10
672 Andujar Cedeno .10
673 *Les Norman* .10
674 *Mike James* .10
675 *Marshall Boze* .10
676 B.J. Wallace .10
677 Kent Hrbek .10
678 Jack Voight .10
679 Brien Taylor .10
680 Curt Schilling .30
681 Todd Van Poppel .10
682 Kevin Young .10
683 Tommy Adams .10
684 Bernard Gilkey .10
685 Kevin Brown .10
686 Fred McGriff .10
687 Pat Borders .10
688 Kirt Manwaring .10
689 Sid Bream .10
690 John Valentin .10
691 *Steve Olsen* .10
692 *Roberto Mejia* .10
693 Carlos Delgado (Foil) 1.00
694 *Steve Gibralter* (Foil) .40
695 Gary Mota (Foil) .10
696 *Jose Malave* (Foil) .50
697 *Larry Sutton* (Foil) .50
698 *Dan Frye* (Foil) .10
699 *Tim Clark* (Foil) .10
700 *Brian Rupp* (Foil) .10
701 Felipe Alou, Moises Alou (Foil) .20
702 Bobby Bonds, Barry Bonds (Foil) 1.00
703 Ken Griffey Sr., Ken Griffey Jr. (Foil) 1.00
704 Hal McRae, Brian McRae (Foil) .20
705 Checklist 1 .10
706 Checklist 2 .10
707 Checklist 3 .10
708 Checklist 4 .10

1994 Bowman Previews

Bowman Preview cards were randomly inserted into Stadium Club 1994 Baseball Series II at a rate of one every 24 packs. This 10-card set featured several proven major league stars, as well as minor league players. Card number 10, James Mouton, is designed as a special MVP foil card.

		MT
Complete Set (10):		27.50
Common Player:		2.00
1	Frank Thomas	6.00
2	Mike Piazza	8.00
3	Albert Belle	2.00
4	Javier Lopez	2.50
5	Cliff Floyd	2.50
6	Alex Gonzalez	2.50
7	Ricky Bottalico	2.50
8	Tony Clark	3.00
9	Mac Suzuki	2.00
10	James Mouton (Foil)	2.00

1994 Bowman

Bowman baseball for 1994 was a 682-card set issued all in one series, including a 52-card foil subset. There were 11 regular cards plus one foil card in each pack, with a suggested retail price of $2. The cards have a full-bleed design, with gold-foil stamping on every card. As in the past, the set includes numerous rookies and prospects, along with the game's biggest stars. The 52-card foil subset features 28 Top Prospects, with the player's team logo in the background; 17 Minor League MVPs, with a stadium in the background; and seven Diamonds in the Rough, with, you guessed it, a diamond as a backdrop.

		MT
Complete Set (682):		80.00
Common Player:		.10
Pack (12):		2.50
Wax Box (24):		50.00

1 Joe Carter .10
2 Marcus Moore .10
3 *Doug Creek* .10
4 Pedro Martinez 1.25
5 Ken Griffey, Jr. 3.50
6 Greg Swindell .10
7 J.J. Johnson .10
8 *Homer Bush* .75
9 *Arquimedez Pozo* .10
10 Bryan Harvey .10
11 J.T. Snow .10
12 *Alan Benes* 1.00
13 Chad Kreuter .10
14 Eric Karros .10
15 Frank Thomas 2.00
16 Bret Saberhagen .10
17 Terrell Lowery .10
18 Rod Bolton .10
19 Harold Baines .10
20 Matt Walbeck .10
21 Tom Glavine .15
22 Todd Jones .10
23 Alberto Castillo .10
24 Ruben Sierra .10
25 Don Mattingly 2.00
26 Mike Morgan .10
27 *Jim Musselwhite* .10
28 *Matt Brunson* .10
29 *Adam Meinershagen* .10
30 Joe Girardi .10
31 Shane Halter .10
32 *Jose Paniagua* .10
33 Paul Perkins .10
34 *John Hudek* .10
35 Frank Viola .10
36 *David Lamb* .15
37 Marshall Boze .10
38 *Jorge Posada* 4.00
39 *Brian Anderson* 1.00
40 Mark Whiten .10
41 Sean Bergman .10
42 *Jose Parra* .10
43 Mike Robertson .10
44 *Pete Walker* .10
45 Juan Gonzalez 1.00
46 *Cleveland Ladell* .10
47 Mark Smith .10
48 *Kevin Jarvis* .10
49 *Amaury Telemaco* .15
50 Andy Van Slyke .10
51 *Rikkert Faneyte* .10
52 Curtis Shaw .10
53 *Matt Drews* .10
54 Wilson Alvarez .10
55 Manny Ramirez 1.00
56 Bobby Munoz .10
57 Ed Sprague .10
58 *Jamey Wright* .75
59 Jeff Montgomery .10
60 Kirk Rueter .10
61 Edgar Martinez .10
62 Luis Gonzalez .35
63 *Tim Vanegmond* .10
64 Bip Roberts .10
65 John Jaha .10
66 Chuck Carr .10
67 Chuck Finley .10
68 Aaron Holbert .10
69 Cecil Fielder .10
70 *Tom Engle* .10
71 Ron Karkovice .10
72 Joe Orsulak .10
73 *Duff Brumley* .10
74 *Craig Clayton* .10
75 Cal Ripken, Jr. 4.00
76 *Brad Fullmer* 4.00
77 Tony Tarasco .10
78 *Terry Farrar* .10
79 Matt Williams .30
80 Rickey Henderson .75
81 Terry Mulholland .10
82 Sammy Sosa 2.00
83 Paul Sorrento .10
84 Pete Incaviglia .10
85 *Darren Hall* .10
86 Scott Klingenbeck .10
87 *Dario Perez* .10
88 Ugueth Urbina .10
89 *Dave Vanhof* .10
90 Domingo Jean .10
91 Otis Nixon .10
92 Andres Berumen .10
93 Jose Valentin .10
94 *Edgar Renteria* 2.50
95 Chris Turner .10
96 Ray Lankford .10
97 Danny Bautista .10
98 *Chan Ho Park* 5.00
99 *Glenn DiSarcina* .10
100 Butch Huskey .10
101 Ivan Rodriguez 1.00
102 Johnny Ruffin .10
103 Alex Ochoa .10
104 *Torii Hunter* 12.00
105 Ryan Klesko .10
106 Jay Bell .10
107 *Kurt Peltzer* .10
108 Miguel Jimenez .10
109 Russ Davis .10
110 Derek Wallace .10
111 *Keith Lockhart* .15
112 Mike Lieberthal .10
113 Dave Stewart .10
114 Tom Schmidt .10
115 Brian McRae .10
116 Moises Alou .20
117 Dave Fleming .10
118 Jeff Bagwell 1.25
119 Luis Ortiz .10
120 Tony Gwynn 1.50
121 Jaime Navarro .10
122 Benny Santiago .10
123 Darrel Whitmore .10
124 *John Mabry* .15
125 Mickey Tettleton .10
126 Tom Candiotti .10
127 Tim Raines .10
128 Bobby Bonilla .10
129 John Dettmer .10
130 Hector Carrasco .10
131 Chris Hoiles .10
132 Rick Aguilera .10
133 Dave Justice .35
134 *Esteban Loaiza* .20
135 Barry Bonds 2.00
136 Bob Welch .10
137 Mike Stanley .10
138 Roberto Hernandez .10
139 Sandy Alomar .10
140 Darren Daulton .10
141 *Angel Martinez* .10
142 Howard Johnson .10
143 Bob Hamelin .10
144 *J.J. Thobe* .10
145 Roger Salkeld .10
146 Orlando Miller .10
147 Dmitri Young .10
148 *Tim Hyers* .10
149 *Mark Loretta* .25
150 Chris Hammond .10
151 *Joel Moore* .10
152 Todd Zeile .10
153 Wil Cordero .10
154 Chris Smith .10
155 James Baldwin .10
156 *Edgardo Alfonzo* 12.00
157 *Kym Ashworth* .10
158 *Paul Bako* .10
159 *Rick Krivda* .10
160 Pat Mahomes .10
161 Damon Hollins .10
162 *Felix Martinez* .10
163 *Jason Myers* .10
164 *Izzy Molina* .10
165 Brien Taylor .10
166 *Kevin Orie* .75
167 *Casey Whitten* .10
168 Tony Longmire .10
169 John Olerud .10
170 Mark Thompson .10
171 Jorge Fabregas .10
172 John Wetteland .10
173 Dan Wilson .10
174 Doug Drabek .10
175 Jeffrey McNeely .10
176 Melvin Nieves .10
177 *Doug Glanville* 2.50
178 *Javier De La Hoya* .10
179 Chad Curtis .10
180 Brian Barber .10

No.	Player	Price
181	Mike Henneman	.10
182	Jose Offerman	.10
183	*Robert Ellis*	.10
184	John Franco	.10
185	Benji Gil	.10
186	Hal Morris	.10
187	Chris Sabo	.10
188	*Blaise Ilsley*	.10
189	Steve Avery	.10
190	*Rick White*	.15
191	Rod Beck	.10
(192)	Mark McGwire (no card number)	4.00
193	Jim Abbott	.10
194	Randy Myers	.10
195	Kenny Lofton	.10
196	Mariano Duncan	.10
197	*Lee Daniels*	.10
198	Armando Reynoso	.10
199	Joe Randa	.10
200	Cliff Floyd	.10
201	*Tim Harkrider*	.10
202	*Kevin Gallaher*	.10
203	Scott Cooper	.10
204	*Phil Stidham*	.10
205	*Jeff D'Amico*	2.00
206	Matt Whisenant	.10
207	De Shawn Warren	.10
208	Rene Arocha	.10
209	*Tony Clark*	2.50
210	*Jason Jacome*	.10
211	*Scott Christman*	.10
212	Bill Pulsipher	.10
213	Dean Palmer	.10
214	Chad Mottola	.10
215	Manny Alexander	.10
216	Rich Becker	.10
217	*Andre King*	.10
218	Carlos Garcia	.10
219	*Ron Pezzoni*	.10
220	Steve Karsay	.10
221	*Jose Musset*	.10
222	Karl Rhodes	.10
223	*Frank Cimorelli*	.10
224	*Kevin Jordan*	.15
225	Duane Ward	.10
226	John Burke	.10
227	Mike MacFarlane	.10
228	Mike Lansing	.10
229	Chuck Knoblauch	.10
230	Ken Caminiti	.10
231	*Gar Finnvold*	.10
232	*Derrek Lee*	2.00
233	Brady Anderson	.10
234	*Vic Darensbourg*	.10
235	Mark Langston	.10
236	*T.J. Mathews*	.10
237	Lou Whitaker	.10
238	Roger Cedeno	.15
239	Alex Fernandez	.10
240	Ryan Thompson	.10
241	*Kerry Lacy*	.10
242	Reggie Sanders	.10
243	Brad Pennington	.10
244	*Bryan Eversgerd*	.10
245	Greg Maddux	1.50
246	Jason Kendall	.10
247	J.R. Phillips	.10
248	Bobby Witt	.10
249	Paul O'Neill	.10
250	Ryne Sandberg	1.00
251	Charles Nagy	.10
252	Kevin Stocker	.10
253	Shawn Green	.30
254	Charlie Hayes	.10
255	Donnie Elliott	.10
256	*Rob Fitzpatrick*	.10
257	Tim Davis	.10
258	James Mouton	.10
259	Mike Greenwell	.10
260	Ray McDavid	.10
261	Mike Kelly	.10
262	*Andy Larkin*	.10
(263)	Marquis Riley (no card number)	.10
264	Bob Tewksbury	.10
265	Brian Edmondson	.10
266	*Eduardo Lantigua*	.10
267	Brandon Wilson	.10
268	Mike Welch	.10
269	Tom Henke	.10
270	Calvin Reese	.10
271	*Greg Zaun*	.10
272	Todd Ritchie	.10
273	Javier Lopez	.10
274	Kevin Young	.10
275	Kirt Manwaring	.10
276	*Bill Taylor*	.10
277	Robert Eenhoorn	.10
278	Jessie Hollins	.10
279	*Julian Tavarez*	.35
280	Gene Schall	.10
281	Paul Molitor	.75
282	*Neifi Perez*	2.00
283	Greg Gagne	.10
284	Marquis Grissom	.10
285	Randy Johnson	.50
286	Pete Harnisch	.10
287	*Joel Bennett*	.10
288	Derek Bell	.10
289	Darryl Hamilton	.10
290	Gary Sheffield	.30
291	Eduardo Perez	.10
292	Basil Shabazz	.10
293	Eric Davis	.10
294	Pedro Astacio	.10
295	Robin Ventura	.10
296	Jeff Kent	.10
297	Rick Helling	.10
298	Joe Oliver	.10
299	Lee Smith	.10
300	Dave Winfield	.65
301	Deion Sanders	.15
302	*Ravelo Manzanillo*	.10
303	Mark Portugal	.10
304	Brent Gates	.10
305	Wade Boggs	.50
306	Rick Wilkins	.10
307	Carlos Baerga	.10
308	Curt Schilling	.25
309	Shannon Stewart	.25
310	Darren Holmes	.10
311	*Robert Toth*	.10
312	Gabe White	.10
313	*Mac Suzuki*	.25
314	*Alvin Morman*	.10
315	Mo Vaughn	.50
316	*Bryce Florie*	.10
317	*Gabby Martinez*	.10
318	Carl Everett	.15
319	Kerwin Moore	.10
320	Tom Pagnozzi	.10
321	Chris Gomez	.10
322	Todd Williams	.10
323	Pat Hentgen	.10
324	*Kirk Presley*	.10
325	Kevin Brown	.10
326	*Jason Isringhausen*	1.50
327	*Rick Forney*	.10
328	*Carlos Pulido*	.10
329	*Terrell Wade*	.10
330	Al Martin	.10
331	*Dan Carlson*	.10
332	*Mark Acre*	.10
333	Sterling Hitchcock	.10
334	*Jon Ratliff*	.10
335	*Alex Ramirez*	.10
336	*Phil Geisler*	.10
337	*Eddie Zambrano* (Foil)	.10
338	Jim Thome (Foil)	.10
339	James Mouton (Foil)	.10
340	Cliff Floyd (Foil)	.10
341	Carlos Delgado (Foil)	.20
342	Roberto Petagine (Foil)	.10
343	Tim Clark (Foil)	.10
344	Bubba Smith (Foil)	.10
345	*Randy Curtis* (Foil)	.10
346	*Joe Biasucci* (Foil)	.10
347	*D.J. Boston* (Foil)	.10
348	*Ruben Rivera* (Foil)	2.00
349	*Bryan Link* (Foil)	.10
350	*Mike Bell* (Foil)	.25
351	*Marty Watson* (Foil)	.10
352	Jason Myers (Foil)	.10
353	Chipper Jones (Foil)	1.50
354	Brooks Kieschnick (Foil)	.10
355	Calvin Reese (Foil)	.10
356	John Burke (Foil)	.10
357	Kurt Miller (Foil)	.10
358	Orlando Miller (Foil)	.10
359	Todd Hollandsworth (Foil)	.10
360	Rondell White (Foil)	.25
361	Bill Pulsipher (Foil)	.10
362	Tyler Green (Foil)	.10
363	Midre Cummings (Foil)	.10
364	Brian Barber (Foil)	.10
365	Melvin Nieves (Foil)	.10
366	Salomon Torres (Foil)	.10
367	Alex Ochoa (Foil)	.10
368	Frank Rodriguez (Foil)	.10
369	Brian Anderson (Foil)	.10
370	James Baldwin (Foil)	.10
371	Manny Ramirez (Foil)	.75
372	Justin Thompson (Foil)	.10
373	Johnny Damon (Foil)	.25
374	Jeff D'Amico (Foil)	.75
375	Rich Becker (Foil)	.10
376	Derek Jeter (Foil)	3.00
377	Steve Karsay (Foil)	.10
378	Mac Suzuki (Foil)	.10
379	Benji Gil (Foil)	.10
380	Alex Gonzalez (Foil)	.15
381	Jason Bere (Foil)	.10
382	Brett Butler (Foil)	.10
383	Jeff Conine (Foil)	.10
384	Darren Daulton (Foil)	.10
385	Jeff Kent (Foil)	.10
386	Don Mattingly (Foil)	1.00
387	Mike Piazza (Foil)	1.50
388	Ryne Sandberg (Foil)	.60
389	Rich Amaral	.10
390	Craig Biggio	.15
391	*Jeff Suppan*	.75
392	Andy Benes	.10
393	Cal Eldred	.10
394	Jeff Conine	.10
395	Tim Salmon	.35
396	*Ray Suplee*	.10
397	Tony Phillips	.10
398	Ramon Martinez	.10
399	Julio Franco	.10
400	Dwight Gooden	.10
401	*Kevin Lomon*	.10
402	Jose Rijo	.10
403	Mike Devereaux	.10
404	*Mike Zolecki*	.10
405	Fred McGriff	.10
406	Danny Clyburn	.10
407	Robby Thompson	.10
408	Terry Steinbach	.10
409	Luis Polonia	.10
410	Mark Grace	.35
411	Albert Belle	.30
412	John Kruk	.10
413	*Scott Spiezio*	2.00
414	Ellis Burks	.10
415	Joe Vitiello	.10
416	Tim Costo	.10
417	Marc Newfield	.10
418	*Oscar Henriquez*	.10
419	*Matt Perisho*	.15
420	Julio Bruno	.10
421	Kenny Felder	.10
422	Tyler Green	.10
423	Jim Edmonds	.15
424	Ozzie Smith	1.25
425	Rick Greene	.10
426	Todd Hollandsworth	.10
427	*Eddie Pearson*	.10
428	Quilvio Veras	.10
429	Kenny Rogers	.10
430	Willie Greene	.10
431	Vaughn Eshelman	.10
432	Pat Meares	.10
433	*Jermaine Dye*	10.00
434	Steve Cooke	.10
435	Bill Swift	.10
436	*Fausto Cruz*	.10
437	Mark Hutton	.10
438	*Brooks Kieschnick*	.15
439	Yorkis Perez	.10
440	Len Dykstra	.10
441	Pat Borders	.10
442	*Doug Walls*	.10
443	Wally Joyner	.10
444	Ken Hill	.10
445	Eric Anthony	.10
446	Mitch Williams	.10
447	*Cory Bailey*	.25
448	Dave Staton	.10
449	Greg Vaughn	.10
450	Dave Magadan	.10
451	Chili Davis	.10
452	*Gerald Santos*	.10
453	Joe Perona	.10
454	Delino DeShields	.10
455	Jack McDowell	.10
456	Todd Hundley	.10
457	Ritchie Moody	.10
458	Bret Boone	.15
459	Ben McDonald	.10
460	Kirby Puckett	1.50
461	Gregg Olson	.10
462	*Rich Aude*	.10
463	John Burkett	.10
464	Troy Neel	.10
465	Jimmy Key	.10
466	Ozzie Timmons	.10
467	Eddie Murray	.50
468	*Mark Tranberg*	.10
469	Alex Gonzalez	.20
470	David Nied	.10
471	Barry Larkin	.15
472	*Brian Looney*	.15
473	Shawn Estes	.10
474	*A.J. Sager*	.10
475	Roger Clemens	1.50
476	Vince Moore	.10
477	*Scott Karl*	.10
478	Kurt Miller	.10
479	Garret Anderson	.10
480	Allen Watson	.10
481	*Jose Lima*	1.00
482	Rick Gorecki	.10
483	*Jimmy Hurst*	.10
484	Preston Wilson	.10
485	Will Clark	.30
486	*Mike Ferry*	.10
487	*Curtis Goodwin*	.10
488	Mike Myers	.10
489	Chipper Jones	2.50
490	Jeff King	.10
491	*Bill Van Landingham*	.50
492	*Carlos Reyes*	.20
493	Andy Pettitte	1.00
494	Brant Brown	.10
495	Daron Kirkreit	.10
496	*Ricky Bottalico*	.25
497	Devon White	.10
498	*Jason Johnson*	.10
499	Vince Coleman	.10
500	Larry Walker	.50
501	Bobby Ayala	.10
502	Steve Finley	.10
503	Scott Fletcher	.10
504	Brad Ausmus	.10
505	*Scott Talanoa*	.10
506	Orestes Destrade	.10
507	Gary DiSarcina	.10
508	*Willie Smith*	.10
509	Alan Trammell	.10
510	Mike Piazza	2.50
511	Ozzie Guillen	.10
512	Jeromy Burnitz	.10
513	Darren Oliver	.10
514	Kevin Mitchell	.10
515	Rafael Palmeiro	.30
516	David McCarty	.10
517	Jeff Blauser	.10
518	Trey Beamon	.10
519	Royce Clayton	.10
520	Dennis Eckersley	.10
521	Bernie Williams	.30
522	Steve Buechele	.10
523	Denny Martinez	.10
524	Dave Hollins	.10
525	Joey Hamilton	.10
526	Andres Galarraga	.10
527	Jeff Granger	.10
528	Joey Eischen	.10
529	Desi Relaford	.10
530	Roberto Petagine	.10
531	Andre Dawson	.20
532	Ray Holbert	.10
533	Duane Singleton	.10
534	*Kurt Abbott*	.20
535	Bo Jackson	.15
536	Gregg Jefferies	.10
537	David Mysel	.10
538	Raul Mondesi	.30
539	Chris Snopek	.10
540	Brook Fordyce	.10
541	*Ron Frazier*	.10
542	Brian Koelling	.10
543	Jimmy Haynes	.10
544	Marty Cordova	.10
545	*Jason Green*	.10
546	Orlando Merced	.10
547	*Lou Pote*	.10
548	Todd Van Poppel	.10
549	Pat Kelly	.10
550	Turk Wendell	.10
551	*Herb Perry*	.10
552	*Ryan Karp*	.10
553	Juan Guzman	.10

554	*Bryan Rekar*	.15
555	Kevin Appier	.10
556	*Chris Schwab*	.10
557	Jay Buhner	.10
558	Andujar Cedeno	.10
559	*Ryan McGuire*	.10
560	Ricky Gutierrez	.10
561	*Keith Kimsey*	.10
562	Tim Clark	.10
563	Damion Easley	.10
564	*Clint Davis*	.10
565	Mike Moore	.10
566	Orel Hershiser	.10
567	Jason Bere	.10
568	Kevin McReynolds	.10
569	*Leland Macon*	.10
570	*John Courtright*	.10
571	Sid Fernandez	.10
572	Chad Roper	.10
573	Terry Pendleton	.10
574	Danny Miceli	.10
575	Joe Rosselli	.10
576	Mike Bordick	.10
577	Danny Tartabull	.10
578	Jose Guzman	.10
579	Omar Vizquel	.10
580	Tommy Greene	.10
581	Paul Spoljaric	.10
582	Walt Weiss	.10
583	*Oscar Jimenez*	.10
584	Rod Henderson	.10
585	Derek Lowe	.10
586	*Richard Hidalgo*	15.00
587	*Shayne Bennett*	.10
588	*Tim Belk*	.10
589	Matt Mieske	.10
590	Nigel Wilson	.10
591	*Jeff Knox*	.10
592	Bernard Gilkey	.10
593	David Cone	.10
594	*Paul LoDuca*	12.00
595	Scott Ruffcorn	.10
596	Chris Roberts	.10
597	*Oscar Munoz*	.10
598	*Scott Sullivan*	.10
599	*Matt Jarvis*	.10
600	Jose Canseco	.45
601	*Tony Graffanino*	.10
602	Don Slaught	.10
603	*Brett King*	.10
604	*Jose Herrera*	.10
605	Melido Perez	.10
606	*Mike Hubbard*	.10
607	Chad Ogea	.10
608	*Wayne Gomes*	.25
609	Roberto Alomar	.40
610	*Angel Echevarria*	.10
611	Jose Lind	.10
612	Darrin Fletcher	.10
613	Chris Bosio	.10
614	Darryl Kile	.10
615	Frank Rodriguez	.10
616	Phil Plantier	.10
617	Pat Listach	.10
618	Charlie Hough	.10
619	*Ryan Hancock*	.10
620	*Darrel Deak*	.10
621	Travis Fryman	.10
622	Brett Butler	.10
623	Lance Johnson	.10
624	Pete Smith	.10
625	James Hurst	.10
626	Roberto Kelly	.10
627	Mike Mussina	.65
628	Kevin Tapani	.10
629	John Smoltz	.15
630	Midre Cummings	.10
631	Salomon Torres	.10
632	Willie Adams	.10
633	Derek Jeter	3.00
634	Steve Trachsel	.10
635	Albie Lopez	.10
636	Jason Moler	.10
637	Carlos Delgado	.30
638	Roberto Mejia	.10
639	Darren Burton	.10
640	B.J. Wallace	.10
641	*Brad Clontz*	.10
642	*Billy Wagner*	1.00
643	Aaron Sele	.10
644	Cameron Cairncross	.10
645	Brian Harper	.10
(646)	Marc Valdes (no card number)	.15
647	Mark Ratekin	.10
648	*Terry Bradshaw*	.10
649	Justin Thompson	.10
650	*Mike Busch*	.10
651	*Joe Hall*	.10
652	Bobby Jones	.10
653	*Kelly Stinnett*	.15
654	*Rod Steph*	.10
655	*Jay Powell*	.25
(656)	*Keith Garagozzo* (no card number)	.15
657	Todd Dunn	.10
658	*Charles Peterson*	.10
659	Darren Lewis	.10
660	*John Wasdin*	.25
661	*Tate Seefried*	.10
662	*Hector Trinidad*	.10
663	*John Carter*	.10
664	Larry Mitchell	.10
665	*David Catlett*	.10
666	Dante Bichette	.10
667	Felix Jose	.10
668	Rondell White	.25
669	Tino Martinez	.10
670	Brian Hunter	.10
671	Jose Malave	.10
672	Archi Cianfrocco	.10
673	*Mike Matheny*	.25
674	Bret Barberie	.10
675	*Andrew Lorraine*	.25
676	Brian Jordan	.10
677	Tim Belcher	.10
678	*Antonio Osuna*	.10
679	Checklist I	.10
680	Checklist II	.10
681	Checklist III	.10
682	Checklist IV	.10

1994 Bowman Superstar Sampler

As an insert in 1994 Topps retail factory sets, three-card cello packs of "Superstar Sampler" cards were included. The packs contained special versions of the same player's 1994 Bowman, Finest and Stadium Club cards. Forty-five of the game's top stars are represented in the issue. The Bowman cards in this issue are identical to the cards in the regular set except for the appearance of a round "Topps Superstar Sampler" logo on back.

		MT
Complete Set (45):		145.00
Common Player:		2.00
1	Joe Carter	2.00
5	Ken Griffey Jr.	20.00
15	Frank Thomas	16.00
21	Tom Glavine	2.50
25	Don Mattingly	16.00
45	Juan Gonzalez	6.00
50	Andy Van Slyke	2.00
55	Manny Ramirez	6.00
69	Cecil Fielder	2.00
75	Cal Ripken Jr.	24.00
79	Matt Williams	2.00
118	Jeff Bagwell	6.00
120	Tony Gwynn	10.00
128	Bobby Bonilla	2.00
133	Dave Justice	2.50
135	Barry Bonds	16.00
140	Darren Daulton	2.00
169	John Olerud	2.00
200	Cliff Floyd	2.00
245	Greg Maddux	10.00
250	Ryne Sandberg	7.50
281	Paul Molitor	5.00
284	Marquis Grissom	2.00
285	Randy Johnson	5.00
290	Gary Sheffield	2.50
307	Carlos Baerga	2.00
315	Mo Vaughn	3.00
395	Tim Salmon	2.50
405	Fred McGriff	2.00
410	Mark Grace	3.50
411	Albert Belle	2.50
440	Len Dykstra	2.00
455	Jack McDowell	2.00
460	Kirby Puckett	10.00
471	Barry Larkin	2.00
475	Roger Clemens	10.00
485	Will Clark	2.00
500	Larry Walker	2.50
510	Mike Piazza	18.00
515	Rafael Palmeiro	2.50
526	Andres Galarraga	2.00
536	Gregg Jefferies	2.00
538	Raul Mondesi	2.50
600	Jose Canseco	4.00
609	Roberto Alomar	5.00

1994 Bowman's Best

The first ever set of Bowman's Best consisted of 90 Blue cards, 90 Red cards and 20 Mirror Images, featuring a Red veteran and a Blue prospect player matched by position on each card. This 200-card set utilized Topps Finest technology and includes full-color photos front and back with a high-gloss finish. Bowman's Best was available in eight-card wax packs, with each pack containing seven cards and a Mirror Image card. There is also a 200-card parallel set officially titled "Special Effects," which uses Topps' refractor technology. Both the Red and Blue set are numbered 1-90, with the Mirror Image cards numbered 91-110.

		MT
Complete Set (200):		50.00
Common Player:		.25
Red Set		
1	Paul Molitor	.75
2	Eddie Murray	.75
3	Ozzie Smith	2.00
4	Rickey Henderson	.75
5	Lee Smith	.25
6	Dave Winfield	1.00
7	Roberto Alomar	.75
8	Matt Williams	.40
9	Mark Grace	.40
10	Lance Johnson	.25
11	Darren Daulton	.25
12	Tom Glavine	.35
13	Gary Sheffield	.35
14	Rod Beck	.25
15	Fred McGriff	.25
16	Joe Carter	.25
17	Dante Bichette	.25
18	Danny Tartabull	.25
19	Juan Gonzalez	1.50
20	Steve Avery	.25
21	John Wetteland	.25
22	Ben McDonald	.25
23	Jack McDowell	.25
24	Jose Canseco	.65
25	Tim Salmon	.35
26	Wilson Alvarez	.25
27	Gregg Jefferies	.25
28	John Burkett	.25
29	Greg Vaughn	.25
30	Robin Ventura	.25
31	Paul O'Neill	.25
32	Cecil Fielder	.25
33	Kevin Mitchell	.25
34	Jeff Conine	.25
35	Carlos Baerga	.25
36	Greg Maddux	2.00
37	Roger Clemens	2.00
38	Deion Sanders	.35
39	Delino DeShields	.25
40	Ken Griffey, Jr.	3.50
41	Albert Belle	.40
42	Wade Boggs	1.00
43	Andres Galarraga	.25
44	Aaron Sele	.25
45	Don Mattingly	2.50
46	David Cone	.25
47	Len Dykstra	.25
48	Brett Butler	.25
49	Bill Swift	.25
50	Bobby Bonilla	.25
51	Rafael Palmeiro	.35
52	Moises Alou	.35
53	Jeff Bagwell	1.50
54	Mike Mussina	.75
55	Frank Thomas	2.50
56	Jose Rijo	.25
57	Ruben Sierra	.25
58	Randy Myers	.25
59	Barry Bonds	2.50
60	Jimmy Key	.25
61	Travis Fryman	.25
62	John Olerud	.25
63	Dave Justice	.35
64	Ray Lankford	.25
65	Bob Tewksbury	.25
66	Chuck Carr	.25
67	Jay Buhner	.25
68	Kenny Lofton	.25
69	Marquis Grissom	.25
70	Sammy Sosa	2.50
71	Cal Ripken, Jr.	4.00
72	Ellis Burks	.25
73	Jeff Montgomery	.25
74	Julio Franco	.25
75	Kirby Puckett	2.00
76	Larry Walker	.35
77	Andy Van Slyke	.25
78	Tony Gwynn	2.00
79	Will Clark	.35
80	Mo Vaughn	.45
81	Mike Piazza	3.00
82	James Mouton	.25
83	Carlos Delgado	.50
84	Ryan Klesko	.25
85	Javier Lopez	.25
86	Raul Mondesi	.35
87	Cliff Floyd	.25
88	Manny Ramirez	1.50
89	Hector Carrasco	.25
90	Jeff Granger	.25
Blue Set		
1	Chipper Jones	3.00
2	Derek Jeter	4.00
3	Bill Pulsipher	.25
4	James Baldwin	.25
5	*Brooks Kieschnick*	.25
6	Justin Thompson	.25
7	Midre Cummings	.25
8	Joey Hamilton	.25
9	Calvin Reese	.25
10	Brian Barber	.25
11	John Burke	.25
12	De Shawn Warren	.25

13	*Edgardo Alfonzo*	10.00
14	*Eddie Pearson*	.25
15	Jimmy Haynes	.25
16	Danny Bautista	.25
17	Roger Cedeno	.25
18	Jon Lieber	.25
19	*Billy Wagner*	1.00
20	*Tate Seefried*	.25
21	Chad Mottola	.25
22	Jose Malave	.25
23	*Terrell Wade*	.25
24	Shane Andrews	.25
25	*Chan Ho Park*	4.00
26	*Kirk Presley*	.25
27	Robbie Beckett	.25
28	Orlando Miller	.25
29	*Jorge Posada*	4.00
30	Frank Rodriguez	.25
31	Brian Hunter	.25
32	Billy Ashley	.25
33	Rondell White	.35
34	John Roper	.25
35	Marc Valdes	.25
36	Scott Ruffcorn	.25
37	Rod Henderson	.25
38	Curt Goodwin	.25
39	Russ Davis	.25
40	Rick Gorecki	.25
41	Johnny Damon	.35
42	Roberto Petagine	.25
43	Chris Snopek	.25
44	Mark Acre	.25
45	Todd Hollandsworth	.25
46	Shawn Green	.75
47	John Carter	.25
48	Jim Pittsley	.25
49	*John Wasdin*	.25
50	D.J. Boston	.25
51	Tim Clark	.25
52	Alex Ochoa	.25
53	Chad Roper	.25
54	Mike Kelly	.25
55	*Brad Fullmer*	4.00
56	Carl Everett	.35
57	*Tim Belk*	.25
58	*Jimmy Hurst*	.25
59	*Mac Suzuki*	.25
60	Michael Moore	.25
61	*Alan Benes*	.50
62	*Tony Clark*	2.50
63	*Edgar Renteria*	3.00
64	Trey Beamon	.25
65	*LaTroy Hawkins*	.50
66	*Wayne Gomes*	.75
67	Ray McDavid	.25
68	John Dettmer	.25
69	Willie Greene	.25
70	Dave Stevens	.25
71	*Kevin Orie*	.25
72	Chad Ogea	.25
73	Ben Van Ryn	.25
74	Kym Ashworth	.25
75	Dmitri Young	.25
76	Herb Perry	.25
77	Joey Eischen	.25
78	*Arquimedez Pozo*	.25
79	Ugueth Urbina	.25
80	Keith Williams	.25
81	*John Frascatore*	.25
82	Garey Ingram	.25
83	Aaron Small	.25
84	*Olmedo Saenz*	.25
85	Jesus Tavarez	.25
86	*Jose Silva*	.25
87	*Gerald Witasick, Jr.*	.25
88	Jay Maldonado	.25
89	Keith Heberling	.25
90	*Rusty Greer*	2.00

Mirror Images

Pack (7):	4.50
Wax Box (24):	60.00

91	Frank Thomas, Kevin Young	1.50
92	Fred McGriff, Brooks Kieschnick	.40
93	Matt Williams, Shane Andrews	.50
94	Cal Ripken, Jr., Kevin Orie	2.50
95	Barry Larkin, Derek Jeter	2.00
96	Ken Griffey, Jr., Johnny Damon	2.25
97	Barry Bonds, Rondell White	1.50
98	Albert Belle, Jimmy Hurst	.50
99	Raul Mondesi, *Ruben Rivera*	1.00
100	Roger Clemens, Scott Ruffcorn	1.25
101	Greg Maddux, John Wasdin	1.25
102	Tim Salmon, Chad Mottola	.50
103	Carlos Baerga, Arquimedez Pozo	.40
104	Mike Piazza, Buddy Hughes	2.00
105	Carlos Delgado, Melvin Nieves	.75
106	Javier Lopez, Jorge Posada	.60
107	Manny Ramirez, Jose Malave	1.25
108	Travis Fryman, Chipper Jones	2.00
109	Steve Avery, Bill Pulsipher	.40
110	John Olerud, Shawn Green	1.00

1994 Bowman's Best Refractors

This 200-card parallel set, officially titled "Special Effects," uses Topps' refractor technology. The refractors were packed at the rate of three per wax box of Bowman's Best, but are very difficult to differentiate from the regular high-tech cards.

	MT
Complete Set (200):	450.00
Common Player:	1.00
Superstars:	4-8X
Stars:	3-6X

(See 1994 Bowman's Best for checklist and base card values.)

1995 Bowman

Large numbers of rookie cards and a lengthy run of etched-foil cards distinguishes the 1995 Bowman set. The set's basic cards share a design with a large color photo flanked at left by a severely horizontally compressed mirror image in green, and at bottom by a similar version in brown. Most of the bottom image is covered by the player's last name printed in silver (cards #1-220, rookies) or gold (cards #275-439, veterans) foil. A color team logo is in the lower-left corner of all cards, and the Bowman logo is in red foil at top. In between are the foil-etched subsets of "Minor League MVPs," "1st Impressions," and "Prime Prospects." Each of these cards, seeded one per regular pack and two per jumbo, has the player photo set against a background of textured color foil, with a prismatic silver border. Each of the foil cards can also be found in a gold-toned version, in a ratio of six silver to one gold. Backs of the rookies' cards have a portrait photo at right and a scouting report at left. Veterans' cards have either a scouting report for younger players, or a chart of stats versus each team played in 1994. Backs of all the foil cards have a scouting report.

	MT
Complete Set (439):	225.00
Common Player:	.15
Pack (10):	15.00
Wax Box (24):	300.00

1	Billy Wagner	.15
2	Chris Widger	.15
3	Brent Bowers	.15
4	*Bob Abreu*	10.00
5	*Lou Collier*	.15
6	*Juan Acevedo*	.25
7	*Jason Kelley*	.15
8	Brian Sackinsky	.15
9	Scott Christman	.15
10	Damon Hollins	.15
11	*Willis Otanez*	.15
12	*Jason Ryan*	.15
13	Jason Giambi	1.00
14	*Andy Taulbee*	.15
15	Mark Thompson	.15
16	*Hugo Pivaral*	.15
17	Brien Taylor	.15
18	Antonio Osuna	.15
19	Edgardo Alfonzo	.15
20	Carl Everett	.25
21	Matt Drews	.15
22	*Bartolo Colon*	8.00
23	*Andruw Jones*	35.00
24	*Robert Person*	.25
25	Derrek Lee	.15
26	*John Ambrose*	.15
27	*Eric Knowles*	.15
28	Chris Roberts	.15
29	Don Wengert	.15
30	*Marcus Jensen*	.15
31	Brian Barber	.15
32	Kevin Brown	.15
33	Benji Gil	.15
34	Mike Hubbard	.15
35	*Bart Evans*	.15
36	*Enrique Wilson*	.50
37	*Brian Buchanan*	.15
38	*Ken Ray*	.15
39	*Micah Franklin*	.15
40	*Ricky Otero*	.15
41	Jason Kendall	.15
42	Jimmy Hurst	.15
43	*Jerry Wolak*	.15
44	*Jayson Peterson*	.15
45	*Allen Battle*	.15
46	Scott Stahoviak	.15
47	*Steve Schrenk*	.15
48	*Travis Miller*	.25
49	*Eddie Rios*	.15
50	Mike Hampton	.15
51	*Chad Frontera*	.15
52	*Tom Evans*	.15
53	C.J. Nitkowski	.15
54	*Clay Caruthers*	.15
55	Shannon Stewart	.20
56	Jorge Posada	.15
57	Aaron Holbert	.15
58	*Harry Berrios*	.15
59	Steve Rodriguez	.15
60	Shane Andrews	.15
61	*Will Cunnane*	.15
62	Richard Hidalgo	.45
63	*Bill Selby*	.15
64	*Jay Cranford*	.15
65	Jeff Suppan	.15
66	Curtis Goodwin	.15
67	*John Thomson*	.15
68	Justin Thompson	.15
69	Troy Percival	.15
70	*Matt Wagner*	.15
71	Terry Bradshaw	.15
72	Greg Hansell	.15
73	John Burke	.15
74	Jeff D'Amico	.15
75	Ernie Young	.15
76	Jason Bates	.15
77	Chris Stynes	.15
78	*Cade Gaspar*	.15
79	Melvin Nieves	.15
80	Rick Gorecki	.15
81	*Felix Rodriguez*	.50
82	Ryan Hancock	.15
83	*Chris Carpenter*	.75
84	Ray McDavid	.15
85	Chris Wimmer	.15
86	Doug Glanville	.15
87	DeShawn Warren	.15
88	*Damian Moss*	.50
89	*Rafael Orellano*	.15
90	*Vladimir Guerrero*	60.00
91	*Raul Casanova*	.50
92	*Karim Garcia*	1.00
93	Bryce Florie	.15
94	Kevin Orie	.15
95	*Ryan Nye*	.15
96	*Matt Sachse*	.15
97	*Ivan Arteaga*	.15
98	Glenn Murray	.15
99	*Stacy Hollins*	.15
100	Jim Pittsley	.15
101	*Craig Mattson*	.15
102	Neifi Perez	.15
103	Keith Williams	.15
104	Roger Cedeno	.15
105	*Tony Terry*	.15
106	Jose Malave	.15
107	Joe Rosselli	.15
108	Kevin Jordan	.15
109	*Sid Roberson*	.15
110	Alan Embree	.15
111	Terrell Wade	.15
112	Bob Wolcott	.15
113	*Carlos Perez*	.15
114	*Mike Bovee*	.15
115	*Tommy Davis*	.15
116	*Jeremey Kendall*	.15
117	Rich Aude	.15
118	Rick Huisman	.15
119	Tim Belk	.15
120	Edgar Renteria	.15
121	*Calvin Maduro*	.15
122	*Jerry Martin*	.15
123	*Ramon Fermin*	.15
124	*Kimera Bartee*	.15
125	Mark Farris	.25
126	Frank Rodriguez	.15
127	*Bobby Higginson*	4.00
128	Bret Wagner	.15
129	*Edwin Diaz*	.15
130	Jimmy Haynes	.15
131	*Chris Weinke*	5.00
132	*Damian Jackson*	.15
133	Felix Martinez	.15
134	*Edwin Hurtado*	.25
135	*Matt Raleigh*	.15
136	Paul Wilson	.15

137 Ron Villone .15
138 *Eric Stuckenschneider* .15
139 Tate Seefried .15
140 *Rey Ordonez* 2.00
141 Eddie Pearson .15
142 Kevin Gallaher .15
143 Torii Hunter .15
144 Daron Kirkreit .15
145 Craig Wilson .15
146 Ugueth Urbina .15
147 Chris Snopek .15
148 Kym Ashworth .15
149 Wayne Gomes .15
150 Mark Loretta .15
151 *Ramon Morel* .15
152 Trot Nixon .15
153 Desi Relaford .15
154 Scott Sullivan .15
155 Marc Barcelo .15
156 Willie Adams .15
157 *Derrick Gibson* .15
158 *Brian Meadows* .15
159 Julian Tavarez .15
160 Bryan Rekar .15
161 Steve Gibralter .15
162 Esteban Loaiza .15
163 John Wasdin .15
164 Kirk Presley .15
165 Mariano Rivera .65
166 Andy Larkin .15
167 *Sean Whiteside* .15
168 *Matt Apana* .15
169 *Shawn Senior* .15
170 Scott Gentile .15
171 Quilvio Veras .15
172 *Elieser Marrero* 1.50
173 *Mendy Lopez* .15
174 Homer Bush .15
175 *Brian Stephenson* .15
176 Jon Nunnally .15
177 Jose Herrera .15
178 *Corey Avrard* .15
179 David Bell .15
180 Jason Isringhausen .15
181 Jamey Wright .15
182 *Lonell Roberts* .15
183 Marty Cordova .15
185 Amaury Telemaco .15
185 John Mabry .15
186 *Andrew Vessel* .15
187 *Jim Cole* .15
188 Marquis Riley .15
189 Todd Dunn .15
190 John Carter .15
191 *Donnie Sadler* .25
192 Mike Bell .15
193 *Chris Cumberland* .15
194 Jason Schmidt .15
195 Matt Brunson .15
196 James Baldwin .15
197 *Bill Simas* .15
198 Gus Gandarillas .15
199 Mac Suzuki .15
200 *Rick Holifield* .15
201 *Fernando Lunar* .15
202 Kevin Jarvis .15
203 *Everett Stull* .15
204 Steve Wojciechowski .15
205 Shawn Estes .15
206 Jermaine Dye .15
207 Marc Kroon .15
208 *Peter Munro* .15
209 Pat Watkins .15
210 Matt Smith .15
211 Joe Vitiello .15
212 Gerald Witasick, Jr. .15
213 *Freddy Garcia* .15
214 *Glenn Dishman* .15
215 *Jay Canizaro* .15
216 Angel Martinez .15
217 *Yamil Benitez* .25
218 *Fausto Macey* .15
219 Eric Owens .15
220 Checklist .15
221 *Dwayne Hosey* (Minor League MVPs) .15
222 *Brad Woodall* (Minor League MVPs) .25
223 Billy Ashley (Minor League MVPs) .15
224 *Mark Grudzielanek* (Minor League MVPs) 1.00
225 *Mark Johnson* (Minor League MVPs) .15
226 *Tim Unroe* (Minor League MVPs) .15
227 Todd Greene (Minor League MVPs) .15
228 Larry Sutton (Minor League MVPs) .15
229 Derek Jeter (Minor League MVPs) 3.00
230 *Sal Fasano* (Minor League MVPs) .15
231 Ruben Rivera (Minor League MVPs) .15
232 *Chris Truby* (Minor League MVPs) 1.00
233 John Donati (Minor League MVPs) .15
234 *Decomba Conner* (Minor League MVPs) .15
235 *Sergio Nunez* (Minor League MVPs) .15
236 *Ray Brown* (Minor League MVPs) .15
237 *Juan Melo* (Minor League MVPs) .15
238 *Hideo Nomo* (First Impressions) 6.00
239 *Jaime Bluma* (First Impressions) .15
240 *Jay Payton* (First Impressions) 4.00
241 Paul Konerko (First Impressions) .25
242 *Scott Elarton* (First Impressions) 2.00
243 *Jeff Abbott* (First Impressions) .25
244 *Jim Brower* (First Impressions) .15
245 *Geoff Blum* (First Impressions) .45
246 *Aaron Boone* (First Impressions) .75
247 J.R. Phillips (Top Prospects) .15
248 Alex Ochoa (Top Prospects) .15
249 Nomar Garciaparra (Top Prospects) 5.00
250 Garret Anderson (Top Prospects) .15
251 Ray Durham (Top Prospects) .15
252 Paul Shuey (Top Prospects) .15
253 Tony Clark (Top Prospects) .15
254 Johnny Damon (Top Prospects) .30
255 Duane Singleton (Top Prospects) .15
256 LaTroy Hawkins (Top Prospects) .15
257 Andy Pettitte (Top Prospects) .50
258 Ben Grieve (Top Prospects) 1.00
259 Marc Newfield (Top Prospects) .15
260 Terrell Lowery (Top Prospects) .15
261 Shawn Green (Top Prospects) .50
262 Chipper Jones (Top Prospects) 3.00
263 Brooks Kieschnick (Top Prospects) .15
264 Calvin Reese (Top Prospects) .15
265 Doug Million (Top Prospects) .15
266 Marc Valdes (Top Prospects) .15
267 Brian Hunter (Top Prospects) .15
268 Todd Hollandsworth (Top Prospects) .15
269 Rod Henderson (Top Prospects) .15
270 Bill Pulsipher (Top Prospects) .15
271 *Scott Rolen* (Top Prospects) 15.00
272 Trey Beamon (Top Prospects) .15
273 Alan Benes (Top Prospects) .15
274 Dustin Hermanson (Top Prospects) .25
275 Ricky Bottalico .15
276 Albert Belle .40
277 Deion Sanders .20
278 Matt Williams .30
279 Jeff Bagwell 1.50
280 Kirby Puckett 2.00
281 Dave Hollins .15
282 Don Mattingly 2.00
283 Joey Hamilton .15
284 Bobby Bonilla .15
285 Moises Alou .25
286 Tom Glavine .25
287 Brett Butler .15
288 Chris Hoiles .15
289 Kenny Rogers .15
290 Larry Walker .40
291 Tim Raines .15
292 Kevin Appier .15
293 Roger Clemens 2.00
294a Chuck Carr .15
294b Cliff Floyd (Should be #394) .20
295 Randy Myers .15
296 Dave Nilsson .15
297 Joe Carter .15
298 Chuck Finley .15
299 Ray Lankford .15
300 Roberto Kelly .15
301 Jon Lieber .15
302 Travis Fryman .15
303 Mark McGwire 3.00
304 Tony Gwynn 2.00
305 Kenny Lofton .15
306 Mark Whiten .15
307 Doug Drabek .15
308 Terry Steinbach .15
309 Ryan Klesko .15
310 Mike Piazza 3.00
311 Ben McDonald .15
312 Reggie Sanders .15
313 Alex Fernandez .15
314 Aaron Sele .15
315 Gregg Jefferies .15
316 Rickey Henderson .50
317 Brian Anderson .15
318 Jose Valentin .15
319 Rod Beck .15
320 Marquis Grissom .15
321 Ken Griffey Jr. 3.00
322 Bret Saberhagen .15
323 Juan Gonzalez 1.50
324 Paul Molitor .50
325 Gary Sheffield .35
326 Darren Daulton .15
327 Bill Swift .15
328 Brian McRae .15
329 Robin Ventura .15
330 Lee Smith .15
331 Fred McGriff .15
332 Delino DeShields .15
333 Edgar Martinez .15
334 Mike Mussina .75
335 Orlando Merced .15
336 Carlos Baerga .15
337 Wil Cordero .15
338 Tom Pagnozzi .15
339 Pat Hentgen .15
340 Chad Curtis .15
341 Darren Lewis .15
342 Jeff Kent .15
343 Bip Roberts .15
344 Ivan Rodriguez 1.25
345 Jeff Montgomery .15
346 Hal Morris .15
347 Danny Tartabull .15
348 Raul Mondesi .30
349 Ken Hill .15
350 Pedro Martinez 1.25
351 Frank Thomas 2.50
352 Manny Ramirez 1.25
353 Tim Salmon .30
354 William Van Landingham .15
355 Andres Galarraga .15
356 Paul O'Neill .15
357 Brady Anderson .15
358 Ramon Martinez .15
359 John Olerud .15
360 Ruben Sierra .15
361 Cal Eldred .15
362 Jay Buhner .15
363 Jay Bell .15
364 Wally Joyner .15
365 Chuck Knoblauch .15
366 Len Dykstra .15
367 John Wetteland .15
368 Roberto Alomar .40
369 Craig Biggio .20
370 Ozzie Smith 1.50
371 Terry Pendleton .15
372 Sammy Sosa 2.50
373 Carlos Garcia .15
374 Jose Rijo .15
375 Chris Gomez .15
376 Barry Bonds 2.00
377 Steve Avery .15
378 Rick Wilkins .15
379 Pete Harnisch .15
380 Dean Palmer .15
381 Bob Hamelin .15
382 Jason Bere .15
383 Jimmy Key .15
384 Dante Bichette .15
385 Rafael Palmeiro .30
386 David Justice .40
387 Chili Davis .15
388 Mike Greenwell .15
389 Todd Zeile .15
390 Jeff Conine .15
391 Rick Aguilera .15
392 Eddie Murray .50
393 Mike Stanley .15
394 (NOT ISSUED, SEE #294)
395 Randy Johnson .75
396 David Nied .15
397 Devon White .15
398 Royce Clayton .15
399 Andy Benes .15
400 John Hudek .15
401 Bobby Jones .15
402 Eric Karros .15
403 Will Clark .30
404 Mark Langston .15
405 Kevin Brown .25
406 Greg Maddux 2.00
407 David Cone .15
408 Wade Boggs .50
409 Steve Trachsel .15
410 Greg Vaughn .15
411 Mo Vaughn .45
412 Wilson Alvarez .15
413 Cal Ripken Jr. 3.50
414 Rico Brogna .15
415 Barry Larkin .25
416 Cecil Fielder .15
417 Jose Canseco .40
418 Jack McDowell .15
419 Mike Lieberthal .15
420 Andrew Lorraine .15
421 Rich Becker .15
422 Tony Phillips .15
423 Scott Ruffcorn .15
424 Jeff Granger .15
425 Greg Pirkl .15
426 Dennis Eckersley .15
427 Jose Lima .15
428 Russ Davis .15
429 Armando Benitez .15
430 Alex Gonzalez .25
431 Carlos Delgado .45
432 Chan Ho Park .25
433 Mickey Tettleton .15
434 Dave Winfield .65
435 John Burkett .15
436 Orlando Miller .15
437 Rondell White .25
438 Jose Oliva .15
439 Checklist .15

1995 Bowman Gold

The only chase cards in the '95 Bowman set are gold versions of the foil-etched

"Minor League MVPs," "1st Impressions" and "Prime Prospects." The gold cards are found in every 6th (regular) or 12th (jumbo) pack, on average, in place of the silver versions.

	MT
Complete Set (54):	100.00
Common Player:	.50
Superstars:	1-1.5X
Stars:	1.5-2X

(See 1995 Bowman #221-274 for checklist and base card values.)

1995 Bowman's Best

Actually made up of three subsets, all cards feature a player photo set against a silver foil background. The 90 veterans' cards have a broad red-foil stripe in the background beneath the team logo; the 90 rookies' cards have a similar stripe in tones of blue. All of those cards are printed in Topps' Finest technology. The 15 Mirror Image cards are in horizontal format, printed more conventionally on metallic foil, and have a rookie and veteran sharing the card. Backs of each card continue the color theme, have '94 and career stats and a highlight or two. Standard packaging was seven-card foil packs with inserts consisting of higher-tech parallel sets of the regular issue.

		MT
Complete Set (195):		300.00
Common Player:		.25
Pack (7):		22.00
Wax Box (24):		500.00
Complete Set Red (90):		50.00
1	Randy Johnson	1.25
2	Joe Carter	.25
3	Chili Davis	.25
4	Moises Alou	.35
5	Gary Sheffield	.40
6	Kevin Appier	.25
7	Denny Neagle	.25
8	Ruben Sierra	.25
9	Darren Daulton	.25
10	Cal Ripken Jr.	4.00
11	Bobby Bonilla	.25
12	Manny Ramirez	1.50
13	Barry Bonds	2.25
14	Eric Karros	.25
15	Greg Maddux	2.00
16	Jeff Bagwell	1.50
17	Paul Molitor	.75
18	Ray Lankford	.25
19	Mark Grace	.50
20	Kenny Lofton	.25
21	Tony Gwynn	2.00
22	Will Clark	.40
23	Roger Clemens	2.00
24	Dante Bichette	.25
25	Barry Larkin	.30
26	Wade Boggs	.75
27	Kirby Puckett	2.00
28	Cecil Fielder	.25
29	Jose Canseco	.50
30	Juan Gonzalez	1.50
31	David Cone	.25
32	Craig Biggio	.35
33	Tim Salmon	.40
34	David Justice	.40
35	Sammy Sosa	2.50
36	Mike Piazza	3.00
37	Carlos Baerga	.25
38	Jeff Conine	.25
39	Rafael Palmeiro	.40
40	Bret Saberhagen	.25
41	Len Dykstra	.25
42	Mo Vaughn	.50
43	Wally Joyner	.25
44	Chuck Knoblauch	.25
45	Robin Ventura	.25
46	Don Mattingly	2.25
47	Dave Hollins	.25
48	Andy Benes	.25
49	Ken Griffey Jr.	3.50
50	Albert Belle	.40
51	Matt Williams	.40
52	Rondell White	.35
53	Raul Mondesi	.35
54	Brian Jordan	.25
55	Greg Vaughn	.25
56	Fred McGriff	.25
57	Roberto Alomar	.50
58	Dennis Eckersley	.25
59	Lee Smith	.25
60	Eddie Murray	.50
61	Kenny Rogers	.25
62	Ron Gant	.25
63	Larry Walker	.40
64	Chad Curtis	.25
65	Frank Thomas	2.50
66	Paul O'Neill	.25
67	Kevin Seitzer	.25
68	Marquis Grissom	.25
69	Mark McGwire	4.00
70	Travis Fryman	.25
71	Andres Galarraga	.25
72	*Carlos Perez*	.25
73	Tyler Green	.25
74	Marty Cordova	.25
75	Shawn Green	.50
76	Vaughn Eshelman	.25
77	John Mabry	.25
78	Jason Bates	.25
79	Jon Nunnally	.25
80	Ray Durham	.25
81	Edgardo Alfonzo	.25
82	Esteban Loaiza	.25
83	*Hideo Nomo*	10.00
84	Orlando Miller	.25
85	Alex Gonzalez	.35
86	*Mark Grudzielanek*	1.00
87	Julian Tavarez	.25
88	Benji Gil	.25
89	Quilvio Veras	.25
90	Ricky Bottalico	.25
Complete Set Blue (90):		265.00
1	Derek Jeter	3.00
2	*Vladimir Guerrero*	80.00
3	*Bob Abreu*	15.00
4	Chan Ho Park	.75
5	Paul Wilson	.25
6	Chad Ogea	.25
7	*Andruw Jones*	40.00
8	Brian Barber	.25
9	Andy Larkin	.25
10	*Richie Sexson*	10.00
11	*Everett Stull*	.25
12	Brooks Kieschnick	.25
13	Matt Murray	.25
14	John Wasdin	.25
15	Shannon Stewart	.45
16	Luis Ortiz	.25
17	Marc Kroon	.25
18	Todd Greene	.25
19	Juan Acevedo	.25
20	Tony Clark	.25
21	Jermaine Dye	.25
22	Derrek Lee	.25
23	Pat Watkins	.25
24	Calvin Reese	.25
25	Ben Grieve	.75
26	*Julio Santana*	.25
27	*Felix Rodriguez*	.25
28	Paul Konerko	.25
29	Nomar Garciaparra	8.00
30	Pat Ahearne	.25
31	Jason Schmidt	.25
32	Billy Wagner	.25
33	*Rey Ordonez*	3.00
34	Curtis Goodwin	.25
35	*Sergio Nunez*	.25
36	Tim Belk	.25
37	*Scott Elarton*	3.00
38	Jason Isringhausen	.25
39	Trot Nixon	.25
40	Sid Roberson	.25
41	Ron Villone	.25
42	Ruben Rivera	.25
43	Rick Huisman	.25
44	Todd Hollandsworth	.25
45	Johnny Damon	.45
46	Garret Anderson	.25
47	Jeff D'Amico	.25
48	Dustin Hermanson	.25
49	*Juan Encarnacion*	8.00
50	Andy Pettitte	.60
51	Chris Stynes	.25
52	Troy Percival	.25
53	LaTroy Hawkins	.25
54	Roger Cedeno	.25
55	Alan Benes	.25
56	*Karim Garcia*	.75
57	Andrew Lorraine	.25
58	*Gary Rath*	.25
59	Bret Wagner	.25
60	Jeff Suppan	.25
61	Bill Pulsipher	.25
62	*Jay Payton*	6.00
63	Alex Ochoa	.25
64	Ugueth Urbina	.25
65	Armando Benitez	.25
66	George Arias	.25
67	*Raul Casanova*	.50
68	Matt Drews	.25
69	Jimmy Haynes	.25
70	Jimmy Hurst	.25
71	C.J. Nitkowski	.25
72	*Tommy Davis*	.25
73	*Bartolo Colon*	10.00
74	*Chris Carpenter*	1.00
75	Trey Beamon	.25
76	Bryan Rekar	.25
77	James Baldwin	.25
78	Marc Valdes	.25
79	*Tom Fordham*	.25
80	Marc Newfield	.25
81	Angel Martinez	.25
82	Brian Hunter	.25
83	Jose Herrera	.25
84	*Glenn Dishman*	.25
85	*Jacob Cruz*	.25
86	Paul Shuey	.25
87	*Scott Rolen*	20.00
88	Doug Million	.25
89	Desi Relaford	.25
90	Michael Tucker	.25
Mirror Image:		.50
1	*Ben Davis*, Ivan Rodriguez	2.00
2	*Mark Redman*, Manny Ramirez	2.00
3	*Reggie Taylor*, Deion Sanders	.60
4	Ryan Jaroncyk, Shawn Green	.60
5	Juan LeBron, Juan Gonzalez	1.25
6	Toby McKnight, Craig Biggio	.50
7	*Michael Barrett*, Travis Fryman	2.00
8	Corey Jenkins, Mo Vaughn	.65
9	Ruben Rivera, Frank Thomas	1.50
10	Curtis Goodwin, Kenny Lofton	.50
11	Brian Hunter, Tony Gwynn	1.50
12	Todd Greene, Ken Griffey Jr.	2.50
13	Karim Garcia, Matt Williams	.85
14	Billy Wagner, Randy Johnson	1.00
15	Pat Watkins, Jeff Bagwell	1.50

1995 Bowman's Best Refractors

The large volume of silver foil in the background of the red and blue subsets in '95 Best make the Refractor technology much easier to see than in past issues. The chase cards, found one per six packs on average, also have a small "REFRACTOR" printed near the lower-left corner on back. The 15-card Mirror Image subset was not paralleled in Refractor technology, but in a process Topps calls "diffraction-foil" which creates a strong vertical-stripe rainbow effect in the background. Cards #72 (Carlos Perez) and 84 (Orlando Miller) can be found both with and without the "REFRACTOR" notice on back; neither version commands a premium.

	MT
Complete Set (195):	1900.
Common Player:	1.00
Stars:	3-6X
Rookies:	2-3X

(See 1995 Bowman's Best for checklist and base card values.)

1995 Bowman's Best Refractors - Jumbo

These super-size versions of Bowman's Best Refractors were produced exclusively for inclusion as a one-per-box insert in retail boxes of the product distributed by ANCO to large retail chains. The 4-1/4" x 5-3/4" cards are identical in all ways except size to the regular refractors. The jumbo inserts were not produced in equal quantities, with the most popular players being printed in greater numbers.

		MT
Complete Set (10):		75.00
Common Player:		2.50
10	Cal Ripken Jr.	15.00
15	Greg Maddux	6.00
21	Tony Gwynn	6.00
35	Sammy Sosa	7.50
36	Mike Piazza	12.00
42	Mo Vaughn	2.50
49	Ken Griffey Jr.	13.50
50	Albert Belle	2.50
65	Frank Thomas	7.50
83	Hideo Nomo	5.00

1996 Bowman

In a "Guaranteed Value Program," Topps stated it would pay $100 for this set in 1999, if collectors mail in a request form (one per three packs), a $5 fee and the complete set in numerical order (only one per person). Every set redeemed was destroyed. The 385-card set has 110 veteran stars and 275 prospects. Backs of the prospects' cards provide a detailed scouting report. A "1st Bowman Card" gold-foil stamped logo was included on the card front for 156 players making their first appearance in a Bowman set. Insert sets include Bowman's Best Previews (along with Refractor and Atomic Refractor versions), a 1952 Mickey Mantle Bowman reprint (1 in 48 packs) and Minor League Player of the Year candidates. A 385-card parallel version of the entire base set was also produced on 18-point foilboard; seeded one per pack.

		MT
Complete Set (385):		90.00
Common Player:		.15
Foils:		1.5X
Pack (11):		4.00
Wax Box (24):		70.00
1	Cal Ripken Jr.	3.00
2	Ray Durham	.15
3	Ivan Rodriguez	1.50
4	Fred McGriff	.15
5	Hideo Nomo	1.25
6	Troy Percival	.15
7	Moises Alou	.25
8	Mike Stanley	.15
9	Jay Buhner	.15
10	Shawn Green	.30
11	Ryan Klesko	.15
12	Andres Galarraga	.15
13	Dean Palmer	.15
14	Jeff Conine	.15
15	Brian Hunter	.15
16	J.T. Snow	.15
17	Larry Walker	.50
18	Barry Larkin	.20
19	Alex Gonzalez	.25
20	Edgar Martinez	.15
21	Mo Vaughn	.50
22	Mark McGwire	3.00
23	Jose Canseco	.50
24	Jack McDowell	.15
25	Dante Bichette	.15
26	Wade Boggs	.75
27	Mike Piazza	2.50
28	Ray Lankford	.15
29	Craig Biggio	.20
30	Rafael Palmeiro	.30
31	Ron Gant	.15
32	Javy Lopez	.15
33	Brian Jordan	.15
34	Paul O'Neill	.15
35	Mark Grace	.40
36	Matt Williams	.30
37	Pedro Martinez	1.50
38	Rickey Henderson	.50
39	Bobby Bonilla	.15
40	Todd Hollandsworth	.15
41	Jim Thome	.15
42	Gary Sheffield	.45
43	Tim Salmon	.30
44	Gregg Jefferies	.15
45	Roberto Alomar	1.25
45p	Roberto Alomar (unmarked promo card, fielding photo on front)	10.00
46	Carlos Baerga	.15
47	Mark Grudzielanek	.15
48	Randy Johnson	1.00
49	Tino Martinez	.15
50	Robin Ventura	.15
51	Ryne Sandberg	1.25
52	Jay Bell	.15
53	Jason Schmidt	.15
54	Frank Thomas	1.00
55	Kenny Lofton	.15
56	Ariel Prieto	.15
57	David Cone	.15
58	Reggie Sanders	.15
59	Michael Tucker	.15
60	Vinny Castilla	.15
61	Lenny Dykstra	.15
62	Todd Hundley	.15
63	Brian McRae	.15
64	Dennis Eckersley	.15
65	Rondell White	.35
66	Eric Karros	.15
67	Greg Maddux	2.00
68	Kevin Appier	.15
69	Eddie Murray	.50
70	John Olerud	.15
71	Tony Gwynn	2.00
72	David Justice	.30
73	Ken Caminiti	.15
74	Terry Steinbach	.15
75	Alan Benes	.15
76	Chipper Jones	2.50
77	Jeff Bagwell	1.50
77p	Jeff Bagwell (unmarked promo card, name in gold)	12.50
78	Barry Bonds	2.50
79	Ken Griffey Jr.	2.75
80	Roger Cedeno	.15
81	Joe Carter	.15
82	Henry Rodriguez	.15
83	Jason Isringhausen	.15
84	Chuck Knoblauch	.15
85	Manny Ramirez	1.50
86	Tom Glavine	.25
87	Jeffrey Hammonds	.15
88	Paul Molitor	.50
89	Roger Clemens	2.00
90	Greg Vaughn	.15
91	Marty Cordova	.15
92	Albert Belle	.40
93	Mike Mussina	1.25
94	Garret Anderson	.15
95	Juan Gonzalez	1.50
96	John Valentin	.15
97	Jason Giambi	.60
98	Kirby Puckett	2.00
99	Jim Edmonds	.15
100	Cecil Fielder	.15
101	Mike Aldrete	.15
102	Marquis Grissom	.15
103	Derek Bell	.15
104	Raul Mondesi	.30
105	Sammy Sosa	2.25
106	Travis Fryman	.15
107	Rico Brogna	.15
108	Will Clark	.35
109	Bernie Williams	.30
110	Brady Anderson	.15
111	Torii Hunter	.15
112	Derek Jeter	3.00
113	*Mike Kusiewicz*	.15
114	Scott Rolen	1.25
115	Ramon Castro	.15
116	*Jose Guillen*	1.00
117	*Wade Walker*	.15
118	Shawn Senior	.15
119	*Onan Masaoka*	.15
120	*Marlon Anderson*	1.00
121	*Katsuhiro Maeda*	.50
122	*Garrett Stephenson*	2.00
123	Butch Huskey	.15
124	*D'Angelo Jimenez*	1.00
125	*Tony Mounce*	.15
126	Jay Canizaro	.15
127	Juan Melo	.15
128	Steve Gibralter	.15
129	Freddy Garcia	.15
130	Julio Santana	.15
131	Richard Hidalgo	.25
132	Jermaine Dye	.15
133	Willie Adams	.15
134	Everett Stull	.15
135	Ramon Morel	.15
136	Chan Ho Park	.25
137	Jamey Wright	.15
138	*Luis Garcia*	.15
139	Dan Serafini	.15
140	*Ryan Dempster*	3.00
141	Tate Seefried	.15
142	Jimmy Hurst	.15
143	Travis Miller	.15
144	Curtis Goodwin	.15
145	*Rocky Coppinger*	.15
146	Enrique Wilson	.15
147	Jaime Bluma	.15
148	Andrew Vessel	.15
149	Damian Moss	.15
150	*Shawn Gallagher*	.15
151	Pat Watkins	.15
152	Jose Paniagua	.15
153	Danny Graves	.15
154	*Bryon Gainey*	.15
155	Steve Soderstrom	.15
156	*Cliff Brumbaugh*	.15
157	*Eugene Kingsale*	.15
158	Lou Collier	.15
159	Todd Walker	.15
160	*Kris Detmers*	.15
161	*Josh Booty*	.35
162	*Greg Whiteman*	.15
163	Damian Jackson	.15
164	Tony Clark	.15
165	Jeff D'Amico	.15
166	Johnny Damon	.25
167	Rafael Orellano	.15
168	Ruben Rivera	.15
169	Alex Ochoa	.15
170	Jay Powell	.15
171	Tom Evans	.15
172	Ron Villone	.15
173	Shawn Estes	.15
174	John Wasdin	.15
175	Bill Simas	.15
176	Kevin Brown	.25
177	Shannon Stewart	.25
178	Todd Greene	.15
179	Bob Wolcott	.15
180	Chris Snopek	.15
181	Nomar Garciaparra	2.00
182	*Cameron Smith*	.15
183	Matt Drews	.15
184	Jimmy Haynes	.15
185	Chris Carpenter	.15
186	Desi Relaford	.15
187	Ben Grieve	.45
188	Mike Bell	.15
189	*Luis Castillo*	2.00
190	Ugueth Urbina	.15
191	Paul Wilson	.15
191p	Paul Wilson (unmarked promo card, name in gold)	4.50
192	Andruw Jones	1.50
193	Wayne Gomes	.15
194	*Craig Counsell*	.40
195	Jim Cole	.15
196	Brooks Kieshnick	.15
197	Trey Beamon	.15
198	*Marino Santana*	.15
199	Bob Abreu	.50
200	Calvin Reese	.15
201	Dante Powell	.15
202	George Arias	.15
202p	George Arias (unmarked promo card, name in gold)	2.50
203	*Jorge Velandia*	.15
204	*George Lombard*	2.00
205	*Byron Browne*	.15
206	John Frascatore	.15
207	Terry Adams	.15
208	*Wilson Delgado*	.15
209	Billy McMillon	.15
210	Jeff Abbott	.15
211	Trot Nixon	.15
212	Amaury Telemaco	.15
213	Scott Sullivan	.15
214	Justin Thompson	.15
215	Decomba Conner	.15
216	Ryan McGuire	.15
217	*Matt Luke*	.15
218	Doug Million	.15
219	*Jason Dickson*	.50
220	*Ramon Hernandez*	1.50
221	*Mark Bellhorn*	.15
222	*Eric Ludwick*	.15
223	*Luke Wilcox*	.15
224	*Marty Malloy*	.15
225	*Gary Coffee*	.15
226	*Wendell Magee*	.15
227	*Brett Tomko*	.50
228	Derek Lowe	.15
229	*Jose Rosado*	.25
230	*Steve Bourgeois*	.15
231	*Neil Weber*	.15
232	Jeff Ware	.15
233	Edwin Diaz	.15
234	Greg Norton	.15
235	Aaron Boone	.15
236	Jeff Suppan	.15
237	Bret Wagner	.15
238	Elieser Marrero	.15
239	Will Cunnane	.15
240	*Brian Barkley*	.15
241	Jay Payton	.15
242	Marcus Jensen	.15
243	Ryan Nye	.15
244	Chad Mottola	.15
245	*Scott McClain*	.15
246	*Jesse Ibarra*	.15
247	*Mike Darr*	1.00
248	*Bobby Estalella*	2.00
249	Michael Barrett	.15
250	*Jamie Lopiccolo*	.15
251	*Shane Spencer*	2.00
252	*Ben Petrick*	3.00
253	*Jason Bell*	.15
254	*Arnold Gooch*	.15
255	T.J. Mathews	.15
256	Jason Ryan	.15
257	*Pat Cline*	.15
258	*Rafael Carmona*	.15
259	*Carl Pavano*	1.50
260	Ben Davis	.15
261	*Matt Lawton*	1.00
262	*Kevin Sefcik*	.20
263	*Chris Fussell*	.15
264	*Mike Cameron*	2.50
265	*Marty Janzen*	.15
266	*Livan Hernandez*	1.25
267	*Raul Ibanez*	.15
268	Juan Encarnacion	.15
269	*David Yocum*	.15
270	*Jonathan Johnson*	.15
271	Reggie Taylor	.15
272	*Danny Buxbaum*	.15
273	Jacob Cruz	.15
274	*Bobby Morris*	.15
275	*Andy Fox*	.15
276	Greg Keagle	.15
277	Charles Peterson	.15
278	Derrek Lee	.15
279	*Bryant Nelson*	.15
280	Antone Williamson	.15
281	Scott Elarton	.15
282	*Shad Williams*	.15

283	*Rich Hunter*	.15
284	Chris Sheff	.15
285	Derrick Gibson	.15
286	Felix Rodriguez	.15
287	*Brian Banks*	.25
288	Jason McDonald	.15
289	*Glendon Rusch*	.75
290	Gary Rath	.15
291	Peter Munro	.15
292	Tom Fordham	.15
293	Jason Kendall	.15
294	Russ Johnson	.15
295	*Joe Long*	.15
296	*Robert Smith*	.15
297	*Jarrod Washburn*	5.00
298	*Dave Coggin*	.15
299	*Jeff Yoder*	.15
300	*Jed Hansen*	.15
301	*Matt Morris*	4.00
302	*Josh Bishop*	.15
303	Dustin Hermanson	.15
304	Mike Gulan	.15
305	Felipe Crespo	.15
306	Quinton McCracken	.15
307	*Jim Bonnici*	.15
308	Sal Fasano	.15
309	*Gabe Alvarez*	.15
310	*Heath Murray*	.15
311	*Jose Valentin*	.15
312	Bartolo Colon	.15
313	Olmedo Saenz	.15
314	*Norm Hutchins*	.15
315	*Chris Holt*	.15
316	*David Doster*	.15
317	Robert Person	.15
318	*Donne Wall*	.25
319	*Adam Riggs*	.15
320	Homer Bush	.15
321	*Brad Rigby*	.15
322	*Lou Merloni*	.50
323	Neifi Perez	.15
324	Chris Cumberland	.15
325	*Alvie Shepherd*	.15
326	*Jarrod Patterson*	.15
327	*Ray Ricken*	.15
328	*Danny Klassen*	.15
329	*David Miller*	.15
330	*Chad Alexander*	.15
331	Matt Beaumont	.15
332	Damon Hollins	.15
333	Todd Dunn	.15
334	*Mike Sweeney*	6.00
335	Richie Sexson	.15
336	Billy Wagner	.15
337	*Ron Wright*	.15
338	Paul Konerko	.15
339	*Tommy Phelps*	.15
340	Karim Garcia	.15
341	*Mike Grace*	.15
342	*Russell Branyan*	4.00
343	*Randy Winn*	.15
344	*A.J. Pierzynski*	.15
345	*Mike Busby*	.15
346	*Matt Beech*	.15
347	*Jose Cepeda*	.15
348	Brian Stephenson	.15
349	Rey Ordonez	.15
350	*Rich Aurilia*	3.00
351	*Edgard Velazquez*	.75
352	Raul Casanova	.15
353	*Carlos Guillen*	1.50
354	*Bruce Aven*	.15
355	*Ryan Jones*	.15
356	*Derek Aucoin*	.15
357	*Brian Rose*	.25
358	*Richard Almanzar*	.15
359	*Fletcher Bates*	.15
360	*Russ Ortiz*	2.00
361	*Wilton Guerrero*	.50
362	*Geoff Jenkins*	5.00
363	Pete Janicki	.15
364	Yamil Benitez	.15
365	Aaron Holbert	.15
366	Tim Belk	.15
367	Terrell Wade	.15
368	Terrence Long	.15
369	Brad Fullmer	.15
370	Matt Wagner	.15
371	Craig Wilson	.15
372	Mark Loretta	.15
373	Eric Owens	.15
374	Vladimir Guerrero	1.50
375	Tommy Davis	.15
376	Donnie Sadler	.15
377	Edgar Renteria	.15
378	Todd Helton	1.50
379	*Ralph Milliard*	.15
380	*Darin Blood*	.15
381	Shayne Bennett	.15
382	Mark Redman	.15
383	Felix Martinez	.15
384	*Sean Watkins*	.15
385	Oscar Henriquez	.15

1996 Bowman's Best Preview

These cards use Topps' Finest technology. The cards were seeded one per every 12 packs of 1996 Bowman baseball. Fifteen veterans and 15 prospects are featured in the set. Refractor versions are found one per 24 packs, with Atomic Refractors a 1:48 pick.

		MT
Complete Set (30):		20.00
Common Player:		.25
Refractors:		2X
Atomic Refractors:		3X
1	Chipper Jones	2.00
2	Alan Benes	.25
3	Brooks Kieshnick	.25
4	Barry Bonds	1.50
5	Rey Ordonez	.25
6	Tim Salmon	.35
7	Mike Piazza	2.50
8	Billy Wagner	.25
9	Andruw Jones	1.00
10	Tony Gwynn	1.00
11	Paul Wilson	.25
12	Calvin Reese	.25
13	Frank Thomas	1.00
14	Greg Maddux	1.25
15	Derek Jeter	3.00
16	Jeff Bagwell	1.00
17	Barry Larkin	.25
18	Todd Greene	.25
19	Ruben Rivera	.25
20	Richard Hidalgo	.25
21	Larry Walker	.50
22	Carlos Baerga	.25
23	Derrick Gibson	.25
24	Richie Sexson	.25
25	Mo Vaughn	.65
26	Hideo Nomo	1.00
27	Nomar Garciaparra	1.50
28	Cal Ripken Jr.	3.00
29	Karim Garcia	.25
30	Ken Griffey Jr.	2.50

1996 Bowman Minor League Player of the Year

Fifteen prospects who were candidates for Minor League Player of the Year are featured in this 1996 Bowman baseball insert set. Cards were seeded one per every 12 packs.

		MT
Complete Set (15):		17.50
Common Player:		.50
1	Andruw Jones	5.00
2	Derrick Gibson	.50
3	Bob Abreu	1.50
4	Todd Walker	1.00
5	Jamey Wright	.50
6	Wes Helms	.50
7	Karim Garcia	2.00
8	Bartolo Colon	.50
9	Alex Ochoa	.50
10	Mike Sweeney	1.00
11	Ruben Rivera	.50
12	Gabe Alvarez	.50
13	Billy Wagner	1.50
14	Vladimir Guerrero	5.00
15	Edgard Velazquez	2.50

1996 Bowman 1952 Mickey Mantle Reprints

Reprints of Mickey Mantle's 1952 Bowman baseball card were created for insertion in Bowman and Bowman's Best products for 1996. The 2-1/2" x 3-1/2" card can be found in regular (gold seal on front), Finest, Finest Refractor and Atomic Refractor versions.

		MT
Complete Set (4):		30.00
Common Card:		4.00
20	Mickey Mantle/ Reprint	4.00
20	Mickey Mantle/ Finest	6.00
20	Mickey Mantle/ Refractor	9.00
20	Mickey Mantle/ Atomic Refractor	15.00

1996 Bowman's Best

Bowman's Best returns in its traditional format of 180 cards: 90 established stars and 90 up-and-coming prospects and rookies. Three types of insert sets are found in Bowman's Best - Mirror Image, Bowman's Best Cuts and the 1952 Bowman Mickey Mantle reprints. There are also parallel sets of Refractors and Atomic Refractors randomly seeded in packs. Refractors are found on average of one per 12 packs; Atomic Refractors are seeded one per 48 packs. Mirror Image Refractors are found one per 96 packs, while Mirror Image Atomic Refractors are seeded one per 192 packs. Refractor versions of the Mantle reprint are seeded one per every 96 packs; Atomic Refractor Mantle reprints are seeded in every 192nd pack.

		MT
Complete Set (180):		50.00
Common Player:		.25
Refractors:		4X
Atomics:		30X
1952 Mickey Mantle:		4.00
1952 Mantle Finest:		6.00
1952 Mantle Refractor:		9.00
1952 Mantle Atomic:		15.00
Pack (6):		4.00
Wax Box (24):		80.00
1	Hideo Nomo	.75
2	Edgar Martinez	.25
3	Cal Ripken Jr.	4.00
4	Wade Boggs	.75
5	Cecil Fielder	.25
6	Albert Belle	.45
7	Chipper Jones	3.00
8	Ryne Sandberg	1.00
9	Tim Salmon	.40
10	Barry Bonds	2.50
11	Ken Caminiti	.25
12	Ron Gant	.25
13	Frank Thomas	2.00
14	Dante Bichette	.25
15	Jason Kendall	.25
16	Mo Vaughn	.50
17	Rey Ordonez	.25
18	Henry Rodriguez	.25
19	Ryan Klesko	.25
20	Jeff Bagwell	1.00
21	Randy Johnson	1.00
22	Jim Edmonds	.25
23	Kenny Lofton	.25
24	Andy Pettitte	.40
25	Brady Anderson	.25
26	Mike Piazza	3.00
27	Greg Vaughn	.25
28	Joe Carter	.25
29	Jason Giambi	1.00
30	Ivan Rodriguez	1.00
31	Jeff Conine	.25
32	Rafael Palmeiro	.35
33	Roger Clemens	1.50
34	Chuck Knoblauch	.25

35 Reggie Sanders .25
36 Andres Galarraga .25
37 Paul O'Neill .25
38 Tony Gwynn 1.50
39 Paul Wilson .25
40 Garret Anderson .25
41 David Justice .40
42 Eddie Murray .50
43 *Mike Grace* .25
44 Marty Cordova .25
45 Kevin Appier .25
46 Raul Mondesi .35
47 Jim Thome .25
48 Sammy Sosa 2.00
49 Craig Biggio .35
50 Marquis Grissom .25
51 Alan Benes .25
52 Manny Ramirez 1.00
53 Gary Sheffield .50
54 Mike Mussina .75
55 Robin Ventura .25
56 Johnny Damon .30
57 Jose Canseco .60
58 Juan Gonzalez 1.00
59 Tino Martinez .25
60 Brian Hunter .25
61 Fred McGriff .25
62 Jay Buhner .25
63 Carlos Delgado .50
64 Moises Alou .30
65 Roberto Alomar .75
66 Barry Larkin .25
67 Vinny Castilla .25
68 Ray Durham .25
69 Travis Fryman .25
70 Jason Isringhausen .25
71 Ken Griffey Jr. 3.50
72 John Smoltz .25
73 Matt Williams .40
74 Chan Ho Park .50
75 Mark McGwire 4.00
76 Jeffrey Hammonds .25
77 Will Clark .40
78 Kirby Puckett 1.50
79 Derek Jeter 3.00
80 Derek Bell .25
81 Eric Karros .25
82 Lenny Dykstra .25
83 Larry Walker .40
84 Mark Grudzielanek .25
85 Greg Maddux 1.50
86 Carlos Baerga .25
87 Paul Molitor .65
88 John Valentin .25
89 Mark Grace .40
90 Ray Lankford .25
91 Andruw Jones 1.00
92 Nomar Garciaparra 2.50
93 Alex Ochoa .25
94 Derrick Gibson .25
95 Jeff D'Amico .25
96 Ruben Rivera .25
97 Vladimir Guerrero 1.00
98 Calvin Reese .25
99 Richard Hidalgo .35
100 Bartolo Colon .25
101 Karim Garcia .25
102 Ben Davis .25
103 Jay Powell .25
104 Chris Snopek .25
105 *Glendon Rusch* 1.50
106 Enrique Wilson .25
107 *Antonio Alfonseca* 1.50
108 *Wilton Guerrero* .50
109 *Jose Guillen* 1.50
110 *Miguel Mejia* .25
111 Jay Payton .25
112 Scott Elarton .25
113 Brooks Kieschnick .25
114 Dustin Hermanson .25
115 Roger Cedeno .25
116 Matt Wagner .25
117 Lee Daniels .25
118 Ben Grieve .40
119 Ugueth Urbina .25
120 Danny Graves .25
121 *Dan Donato* .25
122 *Matt Ruebel* .25
123 *Mark Sievert* .25
124 Chris Stynes .25
125 Jeff Abbott .25
126 *Rocky Coppinger* .25
127 Jermaine Dye .25
128 Todd Greene .15
129 Chris Carpenter .25
130 Edgar Renteria .25
131 Matt Drews .25
132 *Edgard Velazquez* 1.50
133 Casey Whitten .25
134 *Ryan Jones* .25
135 Todd Walker .20
136 *Geoff Jenkins* 5.00
137 *Matt Morris* 6.00
138 Richie Sexson .25
139 *Todd Dunwoody* 1.00
140 *Gabe Alvarez* 1.00
141 J.J. Johnson .25
142 Shannon Stewart .25
143 Brad Fullmer .25
144 Julio Santana .25
145 Scott Rolen .75
146 Amaury Telemaco .25
147 Trey Beamon .25
148 Billy Wagner .20
149 Todd Hollandsworth .25
150 Doug Million .25
151 *Jose Valentin* .25
152 *Wes Helms* .25
153 Jeff Suppan .25
154 *Luis Castillo* 3.00
155 Bob Abreu .40
156 Paul Konerko .25
157 Jamey Wright .25
158 Eddie Pearson .25
159 Jimmy Haynes .25
160 Derrek Lee .15
161 Damian Moss .15
162 *Carlos Guillen* 1.00
163 *Chris Fussell* .25
164 *Mike Sweeney* 10.00
165 Donnie Sadler .15
166 Desi Relaford .15
167 Steve Gibralter .15
168 Neifi Perez .25
169 Antone Williamson .15
170 *Marty Janzen* .25
171 Todd Helton 2.50
172 *Raul Ibanez* .25
173 Bill Selby .25
174 *Shane Monahan* .35
175 *Robin Jennings* .25
176 *Bobby Chouinard* .25
177 Einar Diaz .25
178 Jason Thompson .15
179 *Rafael Medina* .25
180 Kevin Orie .15

1996 Bowman's Best Mirror Image

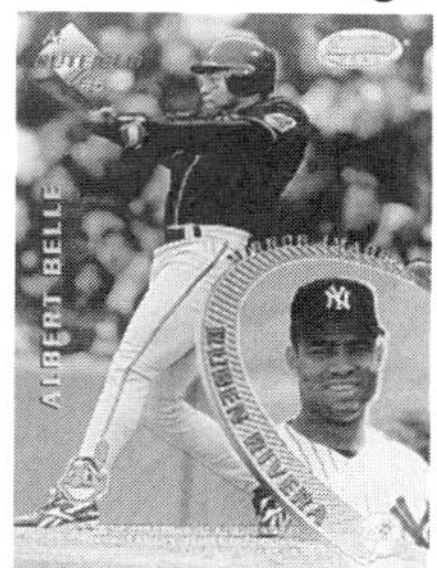

Mirror Image inserts feature four top players at 10 different positions, pairing an American League veteran and a prospect on one side and a National League veteran and prospect on the other. These cards are seeded one per every 48 packs. Mirror Image Refractors (one in every 96 packs) and Mirror Image Atomic Refractors (one in every 192 packs) were also produced.

	MT
Complete Set (10):	25.00
Common Player:	1.25
Refractors:	1.5X
Atomics:	2X
1 Jeff Bagwell, Todd Helton, Frank Thomas, Richie Sexson	3.00
2 Craig Biggio, Luis Castillo, Roberto Alomar, Desi Relaford	1.25
3 Chipper Jones, Scott Rolen, Wade Boggs, George Arias	3.00
4 Barry Larkin, Neifi Perez, Cal Ripken Jr., Mark Bellhorn	4.00
5 Larry Walker, Karim Garcia, Albert Belle, Ruben Rivera	1.25
6 Barry Bonds, Andruw Jones, Kenny Lofton, Donnie Sadler	3.00
7 Tony Gwynn, Vladimir Guerrero, Ken Griffey Jr., Ben Grieve	5.00
8 Mike Piazza, Ben Davis, Ivan Rodriguez, Jose Valentin	3.00
9 Greg Maddux, Jamey Wright, Mike Mussina, Bartolo Colon	3.00
10 Tom Glavine, Billy Wagner, Randy Johnson, Jarrod Washburn	1.50

1996 Bowman's Best Cuts

Bowman's Best Cuts gave collectors the first die-cut chromium cards in a 15-card set of top stars. The cards were seeded one per 24 packs. Refractor versions are inserted on average of one per 48 packs; Atomic Refractor versions are found one per 96 packs.

	MT
Complete Set (15):	15.00
Common Player:	.25
Refractors:	3X
Atomic Refractors:	4X
1 Ken Griffey Jr.	3.00
2 Jason Isringhausen	.25
3 Derek Jeter	2.50
4 Andruw Jones	1.00
5 Chipper Jones	2.50
6 Ryan Klesko	.25
7 Raul Mondesi	.35
8 Hideo Nomo	.75
9 Mike Piazza	2.50
10 Manny Ramirez	1.00
11 Cal Ripken Jr.	3.50
12 Ruben Rivera	.25
13 Tim Salmon	.35
14 Frank Thomas	1.00
15 Jim Thome	.25

1997 Bowman Pre-production

The format for 1997 Bowman's base set was previewed in this sample issue distributed to card dealers and the hobby press. The samples are virtually identical to the issued versions of the same players' cards, except they carry a "PP" prefix to the number on back.

	MT
Complete Set (4):	12.00
Common Player:	2.00
PP1 Jose Cruz, Jr.	2.00
PP2 Andruw Jones	3.00
PP3 Derek Jeter	5.00
PP4 Sammy Sosa	6.00

1997 Bowman

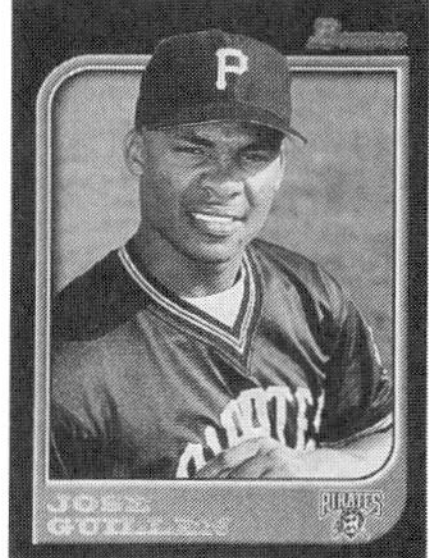

The 1997 Bowman set consists of 440 base cards, an increase of 55 cards from the '96 set. Fronts have a player photo within a red or blue frame with black borders. Backs feature another color photo, along with 1996 statistics broken down by opponent. Players making their first appearance in a Bowman set have a "1st Bowman Card" designation on the card. Prospects' cards have red foil on front; veterans have blue. Inserts include International parallels, Certified Autographs, Scout's Honor Roll and Bowman's Best Previews. Cards were sold in 10-card packs with a suggested retail price of $2.50. Topps offered collectors a $125 guarantee on the value of the set through the year 2000.

		MT
Complete Set (440):		80.00
Complete Series 1 Set (221):		40.00
Complete Series 2 Set (219):		40.00
Common Player:		.15
Series 1 Pack (10):		2.50
Series 1 Wax Box (24):		50.00
Series 2 Pack (10):		2.50
Series 2 Wax Box (24):		50.00
1	Derek Jeter	3.00
2	Edgar Renteria	.15
3	Chipper Jones	2.50
4	Hideo Nomo	.65
5	Tim Salmon	.30
6	Jason Giambi	.40
7	Robin Ventura	.15
8	Tony Clark	.15
9	Barry Larkin	.20
10	Paul Molitor	.75
11	Bernard Gilkey	.15
12	Jack McDowell	.15
13	Andy Benes	.15
14	Ryan Klesko	.15
15	Mark McGwire	3.00
16	Ken Griffey Jr.	2.75
17	Robb Nen	.15
18	Cal Ripken Jr.	3.00
19	John Valentin	.15
20	Ricky Bottalico	.15
21	Mike Lansing	.15
22	Ryne Sandberg	.75
23	Carlos Delgado	.35
24	Craig Biggio	.20
25	Eric Karros	.15
26	Kevin Appier	.15
27	Mariano Rivera	.40
28	Vinny Castilla	.15
29	Juan Gonzalez	1.00
30	Al Martin	.15
31	Jeff Cirillo	.15
32	Eddie Murray	.75
33	Ray Lankford	.15
34	Manny Ramirez	1.00
35	Roberto Alomar	.75
36	Will Clark	.30
37	Chuck Knoblauch	.15
38	Harold Baines	.15
39	Trevor Hoffman	.15
40	Edgar Martinez	.15
41	Geronimo Berroa	.15
42	Rey Ordonez	.15
43	Mike Stanley	.15
44	Mike Mussina	.75
45	Kevin Brown	.25
46	Dennis Eckersley	.15
47	Henry Rodriguez	.15
48	Tino Martinez	.15
49	Eric Young	.15
50	Bret Boone	.20
51	Raul Mondesi	.25
52	Sammy Sosa	2.00
53	John Smoltz	.20
54	Billy Wagner	.15
55	Jeff D'Amico	.15
56	Ken Caminiti	.15
57	Jason Kendall	.15
58	Wade Boggs	.75
59	Andres Galarraga	.15
60	Jeff Brantley	.15
61	Mel Rojas	.15
62	Brian Hunter	.15
63	Bobby Bonilla	.15
64	Roger Clemens	1.50
65	Jeff Kent	.15
66	Matt Williams	.30
67	Albert Belle	.35
68	Jeff King	.15
69	John Wetteland	.15
70	Deion Sanders	.20
71	*Bubba Trammell*	.35
72	*Felix Heredia*	.40
73	*Billy Koch*	.50
74	*Sidney Ponson*	.50
75	*Ricky Ledee*	.25
76	Brett Tomko	.15
77	*Braden Looper*	.40
78	Damian Jackson	.15
79	Jason Dickson	.15
80	*Chad Green*	.15
81	*R.A. Dickey*	.15
82	Jeff Liefer	.15
83	Matt Wagner	.15
84	Richard Hidalgo	.25
85	Adam Riggs	.15
86	Robert Smith	.15
87	*Chad Hermansen*	.15
88	Felix Martinez	.15
89	J.J. Johnson	.15
90	Todd Dunwoody	.15
91	Katsuhiro Maeda	.15
92	Darin Erstad	.50
93	Elieser Marrero	.15
94	Bartolo Colon	.15
95	Chris Fussell	.15
96	Ugueth Urbina	.15
97	*Josh Paul*	.15
98	Jaime Bluma	.15
99	*Seth Greisinger*	.15
100	*Jose Cruz*	2.50
101	Todd Dunn	.15
102	*Joe Young*	.15
103	Jonathan Johnson	.15
104	*Justin Towle*	.15
105	Brian Rose	.15
106	Jose Guillen	.15
107	Andruw Jones	1.00
108	*Mark Kotsay*	1.00
109	Wilton Guerrero	.15
110	Jacob Cruz	.15
111	Mike Sweeney	.15
112	Julio Mosquera	.15
113	Matt Morris	.15
114	Wendell Magee	.15
115	John Thomson	.15
116	*Javier Valentin*	.15
117	Tom Fordham	.15
118	Ruben Rivera	.15
119	*Mike Drumright*	.15
120	Chris Holt	.15
121	*Sean Maloney*	.15
122	Michael Barrett	.15
123	*Tony Saunders*	.15
124	Kevin Brown	.25
125	Richard Almanzar	.15
126	Mark Redman	.15
127	*Anthony Sanders*	.15
128	Jeff Abbott	.15
129	Eugene Kingsale	.15
130	Paul Konerko	.25
131	*Randall Simon*	.15
132	Andy Larkin	.15
133	Rafael Medina	.15
134	Mendy Lopez	.15
135	Freddy Garcia	.15
136	Karim Garcia	.25
137	*Larry Rodriguez*	.15
138	Carlos Guillen	.15
139	Aaron Boone	.15
140	Donnie Sadler	.15
141	Brooks Kieschnick	.15
142	Scott Spiezio	.15
143	Everett Stull	.15
144	Enrique Wilson	.15
145	*Milton Bradley*	1.00
146	Kevin Orie	.15
147	Derek Wallace	.15
148	Russ Johnson	.15
149	*Joe Lagarde*	.15
150	Luis Castillo	.15
151	Jay Payton	.15
152	Joe Long	.15
153	Livan Hernandez	.15
154	*Vladimir Nunez*	.25
155	Not issued	
156a	George Arias	.15
156b	Calvin Reese (Should be #155)	.15
157	Homer Bush	.15
158	Not issued	
159a	*Eric Milton*	.50
159b	Chris Carpenter (Should be #158)	.15
160	Richie Sexson	.15
161	Carl Pavano	.15
162	*Chris Gissell*	.15
163	Mac Suzuki	.15
164	Pat Cline	.15
165	Ron Wright	.15
166	Dante Powell	.15
167	Mark Bellhorn	.15
168	George Lombard	.15
169	*Pee Wee Lopez*	.15
170	*Paul Wilder*	.15
171	Brad Fullmer	.15
172	*Willie Martinez*	.15
173	*Dario Veras*	.15
174	Dave Coggin	.15
175	*Kris Benson*	.15
176	Torii Hunter	.15
177	*D.T. Cromer*	.15
178	*Nelson Figueroa*	.15
179	*Hiram Bocachica*	.50
180	Shane Monahan	.15
181	*Jimmy Anderson*	.15
182	Juan Melo	.15
183	*Pablo Ortega*	.25
184	*Calvin Pickering*	.25
185	Reggie Taylor	.15
186	*Jeff Farnsworth*	.15
187	Terrence Long	.15
188	Geoff Jenkins	.15
189	*Steve Rain*	.15
190	*Nerio Rodriguez*	.15
191	Derrick Gibson	.15
192	Darin Blood	.15
193	Ben Davis	.15
194	*Adrian Beltre*	4.00
195	*Damian Sapp*	.15
196	*Kerry Wood*	4.00
197	*Nate Rolison*	.15
198	*Fernando Tatis*	.75
199	*Brad Penny*	1.00
200	*Jake Westbrook*	.25
201	Edwin Diaz	.15
202	*Joe Fontenot*	.15
203	*Matt Halloran*	.40
204	*Blake Stein*	.25
205	Onan Masaoka	.15
206	Ben Petrick	.15
207	*Matt Clement*	1.00
208	Todd Greene	.15
209	Ray Ricken	.15
210	*Eric Chavez*	3.00
211	Edgard Velazquez	.15
212	*Bruce Chen*	.25
213	*Danny Patterson*	.25
214	Jeff Yoder	.15
215	*Luis Ordaz*	.25
216	Chris Widger	.15
217	Jason Brester	.15
218	Carlton Loewer	.15
219	*Chris Reitsma*	.15
220	Neifi Perez	.15
221	*Hideki Irabu*	.40
222	Ellis Burks	.15
223	Pedro Martinez	1.00
224	Kenny Lofton	.15
225	Randy Johnson	.75
226	Terry Steinbach	.15
227	Bernie Williams	.35
228	Dean Palmer	.15
229	Alan Benes	.15
230	Marquis Grissom	.15
231	Gary Sheffield	.40
232	Curt Schilling	.30
233	Reggie Sanders	.15
234	Bobby Higginson	.20
235	Moises Alou	.25
236	Tom Glavine	.20
237	Mark Grace	.30
238	Ramon Martinez	.15
239	Rafael Palmeiro	.30
240	John Olerud	.15
241	Dante Bichette	.15
242	Greg Vaughn	.15
243	Jeff Bagwell	1.00
244	Barry Bonds	2.00
245	Pat Hentgen	.15
246	Jim Thome	.15
247	Jermaine Allensworth	.15
248	Andy Pettitte	.40
249	Jay Bell	.15
250	John Jaha	.15
251	Jim Edmonds	.15
252	Ron Gant	.15
253	David Cone	.15
254	Jose Canseco	.45
255	Jay Buhner	.15
256	Greg Maddux	1.50
257	Brian McRae	.15
258	Lance Johnson	.15
259	Travis Fryman	.15
260	Paul O'Neill	.15
261	Ivan Rodriguez	.75
262	Gregg Jefferies	.15
263	Fred McGriff	.15
264	Derek Bell	.15
265	Jeff Conine	.15
266	Mike Piazza	2.50
267	Mark Grudzielanek	.15
268	Brady Anderson	.15
269	Marty Cordova	.15
270	Ray Durham	.15
271	Joe Carter	.15
272	Brian Jordan	.15
273	David Justice	.40
274	Tony Gwynn	1.50
275	Larry Walker	.35
276	Cecil Fielder	.15
277	Mo Vaughn	.35
278	Alex Fernandez	.15
279	Michael Tucker	.15
280	Jose Valentin	.15
281	Sandy Alomar	.15
282	Todd Hollandsworth	.15
283	Rico Brogna	.15
284	Rusty Greer	.15
285	Roberto Hernandez	.15
286	Hal Morris	.15
287	Johnny Damon	.20
288	Todd Hundley	.15
289	Rondell White	.25
290	Frank Thomas	2.00
291	*Don Denbow*	.15
292	Derrek Lee	.15
293	Todd Walker	.15
294	Scott Rolen	.75
295	Wes Helms	.15
296	Bob Abreu	.20
297	*John Patterson*	.25
298	*Alex Gonzalez*	.25
299	*Grant Roberts*	.50
300	Jeff Suppan	.15
301	Luke Wilcox	.15
302	Marlon Anderson	.15
303	Ray Brown	.15
304	*Mike Caruso*	.50
305	*Sam Marsonek*	.15
306	*Brady Raggio*	.15
307	*Kevin McGlinchy*	.25
308	*Roy Halladay*	1.00
309	*Jeremi Gonzalez*	.25
310	*Aramis Ramirez*	3.00
311	*Dermal Brown*	.15
312	Justin Thompson	.15
313	*Jay Tessmer*	.15
314	Mike Johnson	.15
315	Danny Clyburn	.15
316	Bruce Aven	.15
317	*Keith Foulke*	.15
318	*Jimmy Osting*	.15
319	*Valerio DeLosSantos*	.15
320	Shannon Stewart	.20
321	Willie Adams	.15
322	Larry Barnes	.15
323	Mark Johnson	.15
324	*Chris Stowers*	.15
325	Brandon Reed	.15
326	Randy Winn	.15
327	Steven Chavez	.15
328	Nomar Garciaparra	2.00
329	*Jacque Jones*	1.50
330	Chris Clemons	.15
331	Todd Helton	1.00
332	*Ryan Brannan*	.15
333	*Alex Sanchez*	.25
334	Arnold Gooch	.15
335	Russell Branyan	.15
336	Daryle Ward	.15
337	*John LeRoy*	.15
338	Steve Cox	.15
339	Kevin Witt	.15
340	Norm Hutchins	.15
341	Gabby Martinez	.15
342	Kris Detmers	.15
343	*Mike Villano*	.15
344	Preston Wilson	.15
345	*Jim Manias*	.15
346	*Deivi Cruz*	1.00
347	*Donzell McDonald*	.15
348	*Rod Myers*	.15
349	*Shawn Chacon*	.15
350	*Elvin Hernandez*	.15
351	*Orlando Cabrera*	.75
352	Brian Banks	.15
353	Robbie Bell	.15
354	Brad Rigby	.15
355	Scott Elarton	.15
356	*Kevin Sweeney*	.15
357	Steve Soderstrom	.15
358	Ryan Nye	.15
359	*Marlon Allen*	.15
360	*Donny Leon*	.15
361	*Garrett Neubart*	.15
362	*Abraham Nunez*	.75
363	*Adam Eaton*	1.00
364	*Octavio Dotel*	1.00
365	*Dean Crow*	.15
366	*Jason Baker*	.15
367	Sean Casey	.50
368	*Joe Lawrence*	.15
369	*Adam Johnson*	.15

370	*Scott Schoeneweis*	.15
371	Gerald Witasick, Jr.	.15
372	*Ronnie Belliard*	.50
373	Russ Ortiz	.15
374	*Robert Stratton*	.15
375	Bobby Estalella	.15
376	*Corey Lee*	.15
377	Carlos Beltran	.20
378	Mike Cameron	.15
379	*Scott Randall*	.15
380	*Corey Erickson*	.15
381	Jay Canizaro	.15
382	*Kerry Robinson*	.15
383	*Todd Noel*	.15
384	*A.J. Zapp*	.25
385	Jarrod Washburn	.15
386	Ben Grieve	.40
387	*Javier Vazquez*	3.00
388	Tony Graffanino	.15
389	*Travis Lee*	1.00
390	DaRond Stovall	.15
391	*Dennis Reyes*	.25
392	Danny Buxbaum	.15
393	*Marc Lewis*	.15
394	*Kelvim Escobar*	.50
395	Danny Klassen	.15
396	*Ken Cloude*	.25
397	Gabe Alvarez	.15
398	*Jaret Wright*	.75
399	Raul Casanova	.15
400	*Clayton Brunner*	.15
401	*Jason Marquis*	1.00
402	Marc Kroon	.15
403	Jamey Wright	.15
404	*Matt Snyder*	.15
405	*Josh Garrett*	.25
406	Juan Encarnacion	.15
407	Heath Murray	.15
408	*Brett Herbison*	.15
409	*Brent Butler*	.25
410	*Danny Peoples*	.25
411	*Miguel Tejada*	5.00
412	Damian Moss	.15
413	Jim Pittsley	.15
414	Dmitri Young	.15
415	Glendon Rusch	.15
416	Vladimir Guerrero	1.00
417	*Cole Liniak*	.15
418	Ramon Hernandez	.15
419	*Cliff Politte*	.25
420	*Mel Rosario*	.15
421	*Jorge Carrion*	.15
422	*John Barnes*	.15
423	*Chris Stowe*	.15
424	*Vernon Wells*	2.00
425	*Brett Caradonna*	.15
426	*Scott Hodges*	.15
427	*Jon Garland*	.50
428	*Nathan Haynes*	.25
429	*Geoff Goetz*	.25
430	*Adam Kennedy*	1.00
431	*T.J. Tucker*	.15
432	*Aaron Akin*	.15
433	*Jayson Werth*	.25
434	*Glenn Davis*	.25
435	*Mark Mangum*	.15
436	*Troy Cameron*	.15
437	*J.J. Davis*	.15
438	*Lance Berkman*	14.00
439	*Jason Standridge*	.25
440	*Jason Dellaero*	.15
441	*Hideki Irabu*	.40

1997 Bowman International

Inserted at the rate of one per pack, the International parallel set replaces the regular photo background on front and back with the flag of the player's native land. Card #441 from the regular-issue version does not exist as an International parallel.

	MT
Complete Set (440):	100.00
Complete Series 1 (221):	50.00
Complete Series 2 (219):	50.00
Common Player:	.25
Stars and Rookies:	1.5X

(See 1997 Bowman for checklist and base card values.)

1997 Bowman Scout's Honor Roll

This insert features 15 prospects deemed to have the most potential by Topps' scouts. Each card features a double-etched foil design and is inserted 1:12 packs.

		MT
Complete Set (15):		12.50
Common Player:		.50
1	Dmitri Young	.50
2	Bob Abreu	.75
3	Vladimir Guerrero	2.00
4	Paul Konerko	1.00
5	Kevin Orie	.50
6	Todd Walker	1.00
7	Ben Grieve	1.00
8	Darin Erstad	1.75
9	Derrek Lee	.50
10	Jose Cruz	.50
11	Scott Rolen	1.75
12	Travis Lee	.50
13	Andruw Jones	1.75
14	Wilton Guerrero	.50
15	Nomar Garciaparra	2.50

1997 Bowman Certified Autographs

Ninety players signed autographs for inclusion in Series 1 and 2 packs. Each autograph card features a gold-foil Certified Autograph stamp on front and can be found in one of three versions: Blue, 1:96 packs; black, 1:503 packs and gold, 1:1,509 packs. Derek Jeter's card can also be found in a green-ink autographed version, inserted one per 1,928 packs. Card numbers have a "CA" prefix.

		MT
Complete Set (90):		500.00
Complete Series 1 Set (46):		225.00
Complete Series 2 Set (44):		300.00
Common Blue:		2.00
Black:		1.5X
Gold:		2X
Derek Jeter Green:		1.5X
1	Jeff Abbott	2.00
2	Bob Abreu	12.00
3	Willie Adams	2.00
4	Brian Banks	2.00
5	Kris Benson	18.00
6	Darin Blood	2.00
7	Jaime Bluma	2.00
8	Kevin Brown	2.00
9	Ray Brown	2.00
10	Homer Bush	4.00
11	Mike Cameron	7.50
12	Jay Canizaro	4.00
13	Luis Castillo	5.00
14	Dave Coggin	2.00
15	Bartolo Colon	7.50
16	Rocky Coppinger	3.00
17	Jacob Cruz	7.50
18	Jose Cruz	12.00
19	Jeff D'Amico	7.50
20	Ben Davis	7.50
21	Mike Drumbright	2.00
22	Scott Elarton	7.50
23	Darin Erstad	12.00
24	Bobby Estalella	7.50
25	Joe Fontenot	4.00
26	Tom Fordham	2.00
27	Brad Fullmer	6.00
28	Chris Fussell	2.00
29	Karim Garcia	5.00
30	Kris Detmers	2.00
31	Todd Greene	4.00
32	Ben Grieve	15.00
33	Vladimir Guerrero	30.00
34	Jose Guillen	5.00
35	Roy Halladay	10.00
36	Wes Helms	6.00
37	Chad Hermansen	4.00
38	Richard Hidalgo	12.50
39	Todd Hollandsworth	3.00
40	Damian Jackson	3.00
41	Derek Jeter	65.00
42	Andruw Jones	20.00
43	Brooks Kieschnick	3.00
44	Eugene Kingsale	2.00
45	Paul Konerko	6.00
46	Marc Kroon	2.00
47	Derrek Lee	7.50
48	Travis Lee	15.00
49	Terrence Long	4.00
50	Curt Lyons	2.00
51	Elieser Marrero	3.00
52	Rafael Medina	2.00
53	Juan Melo	3.00
54	Shane Monahan	2.00
55	Julio Mosquera	2.00
56	Heath Murray	2.00
57	Ryan Nye	2.00
58	Kevin Orie	4.00
59	Russ Ortiz	2.00
60	Carl Pavano	3.00
61	Jay Payton	7.50
62	Neifi Perez	4.00
63	Sidney Ponson	5.00
64	Calvin Reese	5.00
65	Ray Ricken	3.00
66	Brad Rigby	3.00
67	Adam Riggs	3.00
68	Ruben Rivera	4.00
69	J.J. Johnson	2.00
70	Scott Rolen	20.00
71	Tony Saunders	4.00
72	Donnie Sadler	5.00
73	Richie Sexson	15.00
74	Scott Spiezio	6.00
75	Everett Stull	2.00
76	Mike Sweeney	5.00
77	Fernando Tatis	7.50
78	Miguel Tejada	20.00
79	Justin Thompson	5.00
80	Justin Towle	3.00
81	Billy Wagner	5.00
82	Todd Walker	5.00
83	Luke Wilcox	2.00
84	Paul Wilder	4.00
85	Enrique Wilson	5.00
86	Kerry Wood	20.00
87	Jamey Wright	5.00
88	Ron Wright	5.00
89	Dmitri Young	5.00
90	Nelson Figueroa	2.00

1997 Bowman Rookie of the Year Candidates

This 15-card insert was inserted in one per 12 packs of Bowman Series 2. Fronts feature a color shot of the player over a textured foil background, with the player's name across the bottom and the words "Rookie of the Year Favorites" across the top with the word "Rookie" in large script letters. Card numbers have a "ROY" prefix.

		MT
Complete Set (15):		10.00
Common Player:		.50
1	Jeff Abbott	.50
2	Karim Garcia	1.00
3	Todd Helton	2.00
4	Richard Hidalgo	1.00
5	Geoff Jenkins	.50
6	Russ Johnson	.50
7	Paul Konerko	1.25
8	Mark Kotsay	1.00
9	Ricky Ledee	.50
10	Travis Lee	1.00
11	Derrek Lee	.50
12	Elieser Marrero	.50
13	Juan Melo	.50
14	Brian Rose	.50
15	Fernando Tatis	1.25

1997 Bowman International Best

This Series 2 insert set features a flag design in the background of each card front depicting the player's country of origin. On back is another color photo, player personal data, a record of his best season and colored flags representing 14 nations which have sent players to the major leagues. One International Best card was inserted in every second series pack. Card numbers carry a "BBI" prefix. Refractor versions are a 1:48 parallel with Atomic Refractors found 1:96.

		MT
Complete Set (20):		30.00
Common Player:		1.00
Refractors:		1.5X
Atomic Refractors:		2X
1	Frank Thomas	2.50
2	Ken Griffey Jr.	6.00
3	Juan Gonzalez	2.50
4	Bernie Williams	1.50
5	Hideo Nomo	2.00
6	Sammy Sosa	4.00
7	Larry Walker	1.25
8	Vinny Castilla	1.00
9	Mariano Rivera	2.00
10	Rafael Palmeiro	1.25
11	Nomar Garciaparra	4.00
12	Todd Walker	1.00
13	Andruw Jones	2.50
14	Vladimir Guerrero	2.50
15	Ruben Rivera	1.00
16	Bob Abreu	1.50
17	Karim Garcia	1.00
18	Katsuhiro Maeda	1.00
19	Jose Cruz Jr.	1.50
20	Damian Moss	1.00

1997 Bowman Chrome

Bowman Chrome was released in one 300-card series following the conclusion of the 1997 season. Four-card foil packs carried an SRP of $3. Each card reprints one of the regular Bowman set, utilizing chromium technology on front. Inserts include: International parallels, Rookie of the Year Favorites and Scout's Honor Roll.

		MT
Complete Set (300):		200.00
Common Player:		.25
Internationals:		2X
Pack (3):		9.00
Wax Box (24):		170.00
1	Derek Jeter	4.00
2	Chipper Jones	3.00
3	Hideo Nomo	.75
4	Tim Salmon	.35
5	Robin Ventura	.25
6	Tony Clark	.25
7	Barry Larkin	.30
8	Paul Molitor	1.25
9	Andy Benes	.25
10	Ryan Klesko	.25
11	Mark McGwire	4.00
12	Ken Griffey Jr.	3.50
13	Robb Nen	.25
14	Cal Ripken Jr.	4.00
15	John Valentin	.25
16	Ricky Bottalico	.25
17	Mike Lansing	.25
18	Ryne Sandberg	1.50
19	Carlos Delgado	.50
20	Craig Biggio	.30
21	Eric Karros	.25
22	Kevin Appier	.25
23	Mariano Rivera	.60
24	Vinny Castilla	.25
25	Juan Gonzalez	1.50
26	Al Martin	.25
27	Jeff Cirillo	.25
28	Ray Lankford	.25
29	Manny Ramirez	1.50
30	Roberto Alomar	1.00
31	Will Clark	.40
32	Chuck Knoblauch	.25
33	Harold Baines	.25
34	Edgar Martinez	.25
35	Mike Mussina	1.25
36	Kevin Brown	.40
37	Dennis Eckersley	.25
38	Tino Martinez	.25
39	Raul Mondesi	.40
40	Sammy Sosa	2.50
41	John Smoltz	.30
42	Billy Wagner	.25
43	Ken Caminiti	.25
44	Wade Boggs	1.00
45	Andres Galarraga	.25
46	Roger Clemens	2.00
47	Matt Williams	.40
48	Albert Belle	.45
49	Jeff King	.25
50	John Wetteland	.25
51	Deion Sanders	.30
52	Ellis Burks	.25
53	Pedro Martinez	1.50
54	Kenny Lofton	.25
55	Randy Johnson	1.25
56	Bernie Williams	.40
57	Marquis Grissom	.25
58	Gary Sheffield	.50
59	Curt Schilling	.50
60	Reggie Sanders	.25
61	Bobby Higginson	.30
62	Moises Alou	.35
63	Tom Glavine	.35
64	Mark Grace	.50
65	Rafael Palmeiro	.35
66	John Olerud	.25
67	Dante Bichette	.25
68	Jeff Bagwell	1.50
69	Barry Bonds	2.50
70	Pat Hentgen	.25
71	Jim Thome	.25
72	Andy Pettitte	.75
73	Jay Bell	.25
74	Jim Edmonds	.25
75	Ron Gant	.25
76	David Cone	.25
77	Jose Canseco	.50
78	Jay Buhner	.25
79	Greg Maddux	2.00
80	Lance Johnson	.25
81	Travis Fryman	.25
82	Paul O'Neill	.25
83	Ivan Rodriguez	1.25
84	Fred McGriff	.25
85	Mike Piazza	3.00
86	Brady Anderson	.25
87	Marty Cordova	.25
88	Joe Carter	.25
89	Brian Jordan	.25
90	David Justice	.45
91	Tony Gwynn	2.00
92	Larry Walker	.50
93	Mo Vaughn	.50
94	Sandy Alomar	.25
95	Rusty Greer	.25
96	Roberto Hernandez	.25
97	Hal Morris	.25
98	Todd Hundley	.25
99	Rondell White	.35
100	Frank Thomas	2.50
101	*Bubba Trammell*	.75
102	*Sidney Ponson*	2.50
103	*Ricky Ledee*	.50
104	Brett Tomko	.25
105	*Braden Looper*	.50
106	Jason Dickson	.25
107	*Chad Green*	.50
108	*R.A. Dickey*	.50
109	Jeff Liefer	.25
110	Richard Hidalgo	.30
111	*Chad Hermansen*	.50
112	Felix Martinez	.25
113	J.J. Johnson	.25
114	Todd Dunwoody	.25
115	Katsuhiro Maeda	.25
116	Darin Erstad	.50
117	Elieser Marrero	.25
118	Bartolo Colon	.25
119	Ugueth Urbina	.25
120	Jaime Bluma	.25
121	*Seth Greisinger*	.50
122	*Jose Cruz Jr.*	5.00
123	Todd Dunn	.25
124	*Justin Towle*	.25
125	Brian Rose	.25
126	Jose Guillen	.25
127	Andruw Jones	1.50
128	*Mark Kotsay*	4.00
129	Wilton Guerrero	.25
130	Jacob Cruz	.25
131	Mike Sweeney	.25
132	Matt Morris	.25
133	John Thomson	.25
134	*Javier Valentin*	.25
135	*Mike Drumright*	.25
136	Michael Barrett	.25
137	*Tony Saunders*	.25
138	Kevin Brown	.25
139	*Anthony Sanders*	.25
140	Jeff Abbott	.25
141	Eugene Kingsale	.25
142	Paul Konerko	.25
143	*Randall Simon*	.25
144	Freddy Garcia	.25
145	Karim Garcia	.25
146	Carlos Guillen	.25
147	Aaron Boone	.25
148	Donnie Sadler	.25
149	Brooks Kieschnick	.25
150	Scott Spiezio	.25
151	Kevin Orie	.25
152	Russ Johnson	.25
153	Livan Hernandez	.25
154	*Vladimir Nunez*	.50
155	Calvin Reese	.25
156	Chris Carpenter	.25
157	*Eric Milton*	4.00
158	Richie Sexson	.25
159	Carl Pavano	.25
160	Pat Cline	.25
161	Ron Wright	.25
162	Dante Powell	.25
163	Mark Bellhorn	.25
164	George Lombard	.25
165	*Paul Wilder*	.50
166	Brad Fullmer	.25
167	*Kris Benson*	4.00
168	Torii Hunter	.25
169	D.T. Cromer	.25
170	*Nelson Figueroa*	.50
171	*Hiram Bocachica*	.50
172	Shane Monahan	.25
173	Juan Melo	.25
174	*Calvin Pickering*	.50
175	Reggie Taylor	.25
176	Geoff Jenkins	.25
177	*Steve Rain*	.25
178	Nerio Rodriguez	.25
179	Derrick Gibson	.25
180	Darin Blood	.25
181	Ben Davis	.25
182	*Adrian Beltre*	12.00
183	*Kerry Wood*	15.00
184	Nate Rolison	.25
185	*Fernando Tatis*	1.50
186	Jake Westbrook	.25
187	Edwin Diaz	.25
188	*Joe Fontenot*	.25
189	*Matt Halloran*	.50
190	*Matt Clement*	5.00
191	Todd Greene	.25
192	*Eric Chavez*	20.00
193	Edgard Velazquez	.25
194	*Bruce Chen*	.75
195	Jason Brester	.25
196	*Chris Reitsma*	.50
197	Neifi Perez	.25
198	*Hideki Irabu*	.75
199	*Don Denbow*	.25
200	Derrek Lee	.25
201	Todd Walker	.25
202	Scott Rolen	1.25
203	Wes Helms	.25
204	Bob Abreu	.40
205	*John Patterson*	2.50
206	*Alex Gonzalez*	.75
207	*Grant Roberts*	1.00
208	Jeff Suppan	.25
209	Luke Wilcox	.25
210	Marlon Anderson	.25
211	*Mike Caruso*	.75
212	*Roy Halladay*	4.00
213	*Jeremi Gonzalez*	.50
214	*Aramis Ramirez*	8.00
215	*Dermal Brown*	.25
216	Justin Thompson	.25
217	Danny Clyburn	.25
218	Bruce Aven	.25
219	Keith Foulke	.25
220	Shannon Stewart	.25
221	Larry Barnes	.25
222	*Mark Johnson*	.50
223	Randy Winn	.25
224	Nomar Garciaparra	2.50
225	*Jacque Jones*	6.00
226	Chris Clemons	.25
227	Todd Helton	2.00
228	*Ryan Brannan*	.25
229	*Alex Sanchez*	.25
230	Russell Branyan	.25
231	Daryle Ward	.25
232	Kevin Witt	.25
233	Gabby Martinez	.25
234	Preston Wilson	.25
235	*Donzell McDonald*	.25
236	*Orlando Cabrera*	2.50
237	Brian Banks	.25
238	Robbie Bell	.25
239	Brad Rigby	.25
240	Scott Elarton	.25
241	*Donny Leon*	.25
242	*Abraham Nunez*	2.00
243	*Adam Eaton*	6.00
244	*Octavio Dotel*	2.00
245	Sean Casey	3.00
246	*Joe Lawrence*	.25
247	*Adam Johnson*	.50
248	*Ronnie Belliard*	2.00
249	Bobby Estalella	.25
250	*Corey Lee*	.25
251	Mike Cameron	.25
252	*Kerry Robinson*	.50
253	*A.J. Zapp*	1.00
254	Jarrod Washburn	.25
255	Ben Grieve	.40
256	*Javier Vazquez*	6.00
257	*Travis Lee*	5.00
258	*Dennis Reyes*	.75
259	Danny Buxbaum	.25
260	*Kelvim Escobar*	1.00
261	Danny Klassen	.25
262	*Ken Cloude*	.25
263	Gabe Alvarez	.25
264	*Clayton Brunner*	.25
265	*Jason Marquis*	5.00
266	Jamey Wright	.25
267	*Matt Snyder*	.25
268	*Josh Garrett*	1.00
269	Juan Encarnacion	.25
270	Heath Murray	.25
271	*Brent Butler*	.50
272	*Danny Peoples*	.50
273	*Miguel Tejada*	30.00
274	Jim Pittsley	.25
275	Dmitri Young	.25
276	Vladimir Guerrero	1.50
277	*Cole Liniak*	.40
278	Ramon Hernandez	.25
279	*Cliff Politte*	.50
280	*Mel Rosario*	.25
281	*Jorge Carrion*	.25
282	*John Barnes*	.25
283	*Chris Stowe*	.25
284	*Vernon Wells*	6.00
285	*Brett Caradonna*	.25
286	*Scott Hodges*	.25
287	*Jon Garland*	4.00
288	*Nathan Haynes*	.50
289	*Geoff Goetz*	1.00
290	*Adam Kennedy*	4.00
291	*T.J. Tucker*	.50
292	*Aaron Akin*	.50
293	*Jayson Werth*	.50
294	*Glenn Davis*	.50
295	*Mark Mangum*	.25
296	*Troy Cameron*	.50

297	*J.J. Davis*	.25
298	*Lance Berkman*	40.00
299	*Jason Standridge*	.50
300	*Jason Dellaero*	.25

1997 Bowman Chrome Refractors

All 300 cards in Bowman Chrome were reprinted in Refractor versions and inserted one per 12 packs. The cards are very similar to the base cards, but feature a refractive foil finish on front.

	MT
Complete Set (300):	500.00
Common Player:	1.00
Stars:	4X

(See 1997 Bowman Chrome for checklist and base card values.)

1997 Bowman Chrome International Refractors

Each International parallel card was also reprinted in a Refractor version. International Refractors were seeded one per 24 packs.

	MT
Common Player:	2.00
Stars:	6X

(See 1997 Bowman Chrome for checklist and base card values.)

1997 Bowman Chrome Scout's Honor Roll

This 15-card set features top prospects and rookies as selected by the Topps' scouts. These chromium cards are numbered with a "SHR" prefix and are inserted one per 12 packs, while Refractor versions are seeded one per 36 packs.

		MT
Complete Set (15):		18.00
Common Player:		.50
Refractors:		1.5X
1	Dmitri Young	.50
2	Bob Abreu	1.00
3	Vladimir Guerrero	3.75
4	Paul Konerko	1.50
5	Kevin Orie	.50
6	Todd Walker	1.00
7	Ben Grieve	1.75
8	Darin Erstad	1.50
9	Derrek Lee	.50
10	Jose Cruz, Jr.	1.00
11	Scott Rolen	2.50
12	Travis Lee	1.50
13	Andruw Jones	2.50
14	Wilton Guerrero	.50
15	Nomar Garciaparra	4.50

1997 Bowman Chrome ROY Candidates

This 15-card insert set features color action photos of 1998 Rookie of the Year candidates printed on chromium finish cards. Card backs are numbered with a "ROY" prefix and were inserted one per 24 packs of Bowman Chrome. Refractor versions are seeded one per 72 packs.

		MT
Complete Set (15):		17.50
Common Player:		1.00
Refractors:		1.5X
1	Jeff Abbott	1.00
2	Karim Garcia	1.50
3	Todd Helton	4.00
4	Richard Hidalgo	2.00
5	Geoff Jenkins	1.00
6	Russ Johnson	1.00
7	Paul Konerko	2.00
8	Mark Kotsay	2.00
9	Ricky Ledee	1.00
10	Travis Lee	2.00
11	Derrek Lee	1.00
12	Elieser Marrero	1.00
13	Juan Melo	1.00
14	Brian Rose	1.00
15	Fernando Tatis	2.00

1997 Bowman's Best Preview

This 20-card set, featuring 10 veterans and 10 prospects, is a preview of the format used in the Bowman's Best product. Three different versions of the Preview cards were available: Regular (1:12 packs), Refractors (1:48) and Atomic Refractors (1:96).

		MT
Complete Set (20):		35.00
Common Player:		.75
Refractors:		2X
Atomic Refractors:		3-4X
1	Frank Thomas	2.00
2	Ken Griffey Jr.	5.00
3	Barry Bonds	2.50
4	Derek Jeter	5.00
5	Chipper Jones	3.00
6	Mark McGwire	6.00
7	Cal Ripken Jr.	6.00
8	Kenny Lofton	.75
9	Gary Sheffield	1.00
10	Jeff Bagwell	2.00
11	Wilton Guerrero	.75
12	Scott Rolen	1.50
13	Todd Walker	1.00
14	Ruben Rivera	.75
15	Andruw Jones	2.00
16	Nomar Garciaparra	3.00
17	Vladimir Guerrero	2.00
18	Miguel Tejada	1.50
19	Bartolo Colon	1.00
20	Katsuhiro Maeda	.75

1997 Bowman's Best

The 200-card base set is divided into a 100-card subset featuring current stars on a gold-chromium stock, and 100 cards of top prospects in silver chromium. Packs contain six cards and were issued with a suggested retail price of $5. Autographed cards of 10 different players were randomly inserted into packs, with each player signing regular, Refractor and Atomic Refractor versions of their cards. Bowman's Best Laser Cuts and Mirror Image are the two other inserts, each with Refractor and Atomic Refractor editions.

		MT
Complete Set (200):		35.00
Common Player:		.25
Star Refractors:		4X
Star Atomics:		6X
Pack (6):		3.00
Wax Box (24):		60.00
1	Ken Griffey Jr.	3.50
2	Cecil Fielder	.25
3	Albert Belle	.40
4	Todd Hundley	.25
5	Mike Piazza	3.00
6	Matt Williams	.40
7	Mo Vaughn	.40
8	Ryne Sandberg	1.00
9	Chipper Jones	3.00
10	Edgar Martinez	.25
11	Kenny Lofton	.25
12	Ron Gant	.25
13	Moises Alou	.35
14	Pat Hentgen	.25
15	Steve Finley	.25
16	Mark Grace	.50
17	Jay Buhner	.25
18	Jeff Conine	.25
19	Jim Edmonds	.25
20	Todd Hollandsworth	.25
21	Andy Petitte	.45
22	Jim Thome	.25
23	Eric Young	.25
24	Ray Lankford	.25
25	Marquis Grissom	.25
26	Tony Clark	.25
27	Jermaine Allensworth	.25
28	Ellis Burks	.25
29	Tony Gwynn	2.00
30	Barry Larkin	.30
31	John Olerud	.25
32	Mariano Rivera	.50
33	Paul Molitor	.75
34	Ken Caminiti	.25
35	Gary Sheffield	.45
36	Al Martin	.25
37	John Valentin	.25
38	Frank Thomas	2.50
39	John Jaha	.25
40	Greg Maddux	2.00
41	Alex Fernandez	.25
42	Dean Palmer	.25
43	Bernie Williams	.45
44	Deion Sanders	.30
45	Mark McGwire	4.00
46	Brian Jordan	.25
47	Bernard Gilkey	.25
48	Will Clark	.40
49	Kevin Appier	.25
50	Tom Glavine	.35
51	Chuck Knoblauch	.25
52	Rondell White	.35
53	Greg Vaughn	.25
54	Mike Mussina	1.00
55	Brian McRae	.25
56	Chili Davis	.25
57	Wade Boggs	.75
58	Jeff Bagwell	1.50
59	Roberto Alomar	.60
60	Dennis Eckersley	.25
61	Ryan Klesko	.25
62	Manny Ramirez	1.50
63	John Wetteland	.25
64	Cal Ripken Jr.	4.00
65	Edgar Renteria	.25
66	Tino Martinez	.25
67	Larry Walker	.45
68	Gregg Jefferies	.25
69	Lance Johnson	.25
70	Carlos Delgado	.40
71	Craig Biggio	.35
72	Jose Canseco	.50
73	Barry Bonds	2.50
74	Juan Gonzalez	1.50
75	Eric Karros	.25
76	Reggie Sanders	.25
77	Robin Ventura	.25
78	Hideo Nomo	.75
79	David Justice	.40
80	Vinny Castilla	.25
81	Travis Fryman	.25
82	Derek Jeter	3.00
83	Sammy Sosa	2.50
84	Ivan Rodriguez	1.00
85	Rafael Palmeiro	.35
86	Roger Clemens	2.00
87	Jason Giambi	.75
88	Andres Galarraga	.25
89	Jermaine Dye	.25
90	Joe Carter	.25
91	Brady Anderson	.25
92	Derek Bell	.25
93	Randy Johnson	1.00
94	Fred McGriff	.25
95	John Smoltz	.30
96	Harold Baines	.25
97	Raul Mondesi	.35
98	Tim Salmon	.35
99	Carlos Baerga	.25
100	Dante Bichette	.25
101	Vladimir Guerrero	1.50
102	Richard Hidalgo	.35
103	Paul Konerko	.25

104 *Alex Gonzalez* .35
105 Jason Dickson .25
106 Jose Rosado .25
107 Todd Walker .25
108 *Seth Greisinger* .40
109 Todd Helton 1.25
110 Ben Davis .25
111 Bartolo Colon .25
112 Elieser Marrero .25
113 Jeff D'Amico .25
114 *Miguel Tejada* 5.00
115 Darin Erstad .75
116 *Kris Benson* 1.00
117 *Adrian Beltre* 5.00
118 Neifi Perez .25
119 Calvin Reese .25
120 Carl Pavano .25
121 Juan Melo .25
122 *Kevin McGlinchy* .40
123 Pat Cline .25
124 *Felix Heredia* .40
125 Aaron Boone .25
126 Glendon Rusch .25
127 Mike Cameron .25
128 Justin Thompson .25
129 *Chad Hermansen* .50
130 *Sidney Ponson* 1.00
131 *Willie Martinez* .25
132 *Paul Wilder* .25
133 Geoff Jenkins .25
134 *Roy Halladay* 1.50
135 Carlos Guillen .25
136 Tony Batista .25
137 Todd Greene .25
138 Luis Castillo .25
139 *Jimmy Anderson* .25
140 Edgard Velazquez .25
141 Chris Snopek .25
142 Ruben Rivera .25
143 *Javier Valentin* .25
144 Brian Rose .25
145 *Fernando Tatis* 1.00
146 *Dean Crow* .25
147 Karim Garcia .25
148 Dante Powell .25
149 *Hideki Irabu* .40
150 Matt Morris .25
151 Wes Helms .25
152 Russ Johnson .25
153 Jarrod Washburn .25
154 *Kerry Wood* 5.00
155 *Joe Fontenot* .25
156 Eugene Kingsale .25
157 Terrence Long .25
158 Calvin Maduro .25
159 Jeff Suppan .25
160 DaRond Stovall .25
161 Mark Redman .25
162 *Ken Cloude* .25
163 Bobby Estalella .25
164 *Abraham Nunez* 1.00
165 Derrick Gibson .25
166 *Mike Drumright* .25
167 Katsuhiro Maeda .25
168 Jeff Liefer .25
169 Ben Grieve .40
170 Bob Abreu .40
171 Shannon Stewart .25
172 *Braden Looper* .40
173 Brant Brown .25
174 Marlon Anderson .25
175 Brad Fullmer .25
176 Carlos Beltran .25
177 Nomar Garciaparra 2.50
178 Derrek Lee .25
179 *Valerio DeLosSantos* .25
180 Dmitri Young .25
181 Jamey Wright .25
182 *Hiram Bocachica* .40
183 Wilton Guerrero .25
184 Chris Carpenter .25
185 Scott Spiezio .25
186 Andruw Jones 1.50
187 *Travis Lee* 1.50
188 *Jose Cruz Jr.* 2.00
189 Jose Guillen .25
190 Jeff Abbott .25
191 *Ricky Ledee* .50
192 Mike Sweeney .25
193 Donnie Sadler .25
194 Scott Rolen 1.00
195 Kevin Orie .25
196 *Jason Conti* .25
197 *Mark Kotsay* 1.00
198 *Eric Milton* 1.50
199 Russell Branyan .25
200 *Alex Sanchez* .25

1997 Bowman's Best Autographs

Ten different players each signed 10 regular versions of their respective Bowman's Best cards (1:170 packs), 10 of their Bowman's Best Refractors (1:2,036 packs) and 10 of their Bowman's Best Atomic Refractors (1:6,107 packs). Each autograph card features a special Certified Autograph stamp on the front.

MT
Complete Set (10): 150.00
Common Player: 5.00
Refractors: 1.5X
Atomics: 2X
29 Tony Gwynn 25.00
33 Paul Molitor 25.00
82 Derek Jeter 75.00
91 Brady Anderson 12.50
98 Tim Salmon 10.00
107 Todd Walker 6.00
183 Wilton Guerrero 5.00
185 Scott Spiezio 5.00
188 Jose Cruz Jr. 6.00
194 Scott Rolen 15.00

1997 Bowman's Best Cuts

Each of these 20-card inserts features a laser-cut pattern in the chromium stock. Backs have another color photo and list several of the player's career "Bests". Three different versions of each card are available: Regular (1:24 packs), Refractor (1:48) and Atomic Refractor (1:96). Cards are numbered with a "BC" prefix.

MT
Complete Set (20): 15.00
Common Player: .50
Refractors: 1.5X
Atomic Refractors: 2X
1 Derek Jeter 4.00
2 Chipper Jones 3.00
3 Frank Thomas 2.50
4 Cal Ripken Jr. 5.00
5 Mark McGwire 5.00
6 Ken Griffey Jr. 4.50
7 Jeff Bagwell 1.50
8 Mike Piazza 3.00
9 Ken Caminiti .50
10 Albert Belle .75
11 Jose Cruz Jr. .50
12 Wilton Guerrero .50
13 Darin Erstad 1.00
14 Andruw Jones 2.00
15 Scott Rolen 1.25
16 Jose Guillen .50
17 Bob Abreu .75
18 Vladimir Guerrero 2.00
19 Todd Walker .50
20 Nomar Garciaparra 2.50

1997 Bowman's Best Mirror Image

This 10-card insert features four players on each double-sided card - two veterans and two rookies - utilizing Finest technology. Regular Mirror Image cards are found 1:48 packs, while Refractor versions are seeded 1:96 packs and Atomic Refractors are found 1:192 packs. Cards are numbered with an "MI" prefix.

MT
Complete Set (10): 50.00
Common Card: 3.00
Refractors: 1.5X
Atomic Refractors: 2-3X
1 Nomar Garciaparra, Derek Jeter, Hiram Bocachica, Barry Larkin 10.00
2 Travis Lee, Frank Thomas, Derrek Lee, Jeff Bagwell 6.00
3 Kerry Wood, Greg Maddux, Kris Benson, John Smoltz 5.00
4 Kevin Brown, Ivan Rodriguez, Elieser Marrero, Mike Piazza 8.00
5 Jose Cruz Jr., Ken Griffey Jr., Andruw Jones, Barry Bonds 8.00
6 Jose Guillen, Juan Gonzalez, Richard Hidalgo, Gary Sheffield 3.00
7 Paul Konerko, Mark McGwire, Todd Helton, Rafael Palmeiro 9.00
8 Wilton Guerrero, Craig Biggio, Donnie Sadler, Chuck Knoblauch 3.00
9 Russell Branyan, Matt Williams, Adrian Beltre, Chipper Jones 6.00
10 Bob Abreu, Kenny Lofton, Vladimir Guerrero, Albert Belle 4.00

1997 Bowman's Best Jumbos

This large-format (4" x 5-5/8") version of 1997 Bowman's Best features 16 of the season's top stars and hottest rookies. Utilizing chromium, Refractor and Atomic Refractor technologies, the cards are identical in every way except size to the regular-issue Bowman's Best. The jumbos were sold only through Topps Stadium Club. Each of the sets consists of 12 chromium cards, plus three randomly packaged Refractors and one Atomic Refractor. About 900 sets were produced according to Topps sales literature, which breaks down to 700 regular cards, 170 Refractors and 60 Atomic Refractors of each player.

MT
Complete Set (16): 100.00
Common Player: 6.00
Refractor: 3X
Atomic Refractor: 5X
1 Ken Griffey Jr. 10.00
5 Mike Piazza 8.00
9 Chipper Jones 8.00
11 Kenny Lofton 5.00
29 Tony Gwynn 6.00
33 Paul Molitor 5.00
38 Frank Thomas 6.00
45 Mark McGwire 10.00
64 Cal Ripken Jr. 10.00
73 Barry Bonds 7.50
74 Juan Gonzalez 6.00
82 Derek Jeter 8.00
101 Vladimir Guerrero 6.00
177 Nomar Garciaparra 8.00
186 Andruw Jones 6.00
188 Jose Cruz, Jr. 5.00

1998 Bowman

Bowman was a 441-card set released in a pair of 220-card series in 1998 (Orlando Hernandez, #221, was a late Series 1 addition.) Within each series are 150 prospects printed in a silver and blue design and 70 veterans printed in silver and red. Cards feature a Bowman seal, and in cases of a player's first Bowman card, a "Bowman Rookie Card" stamp is applied. The player's facsimile signature from his first contract runs down the side. The entire set was paralleled twice in Bowman International (one per pack) and Golden Anniversary (serially numbered to 50). Inserts in Series 1 include Autographs, Scout's Choice, and Japanese Rookies. Inserts in Series 2 include Autographs, 1999 Rookie of the Year Favorites, Minor League MVPs and Japanese Rookies.

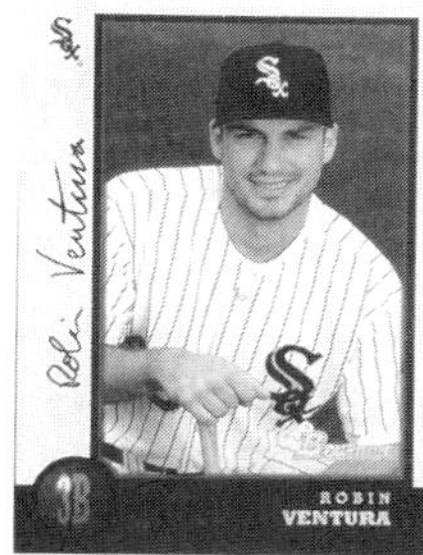

	MT
Complete Set (441):	90.00
Series 1 (221):	50.00
Series 2 (220):	40.00
Common Player:	.15
Inserted 1:1	
Series 1 Pack (10):	3.50
Series 1 Wax Box (24):	60.00
Series 2 Pack (10):	2.50
Series 2 Wax Box (24):	45.00

1 Nomar Garciaparra 2.00
2 Scott Rolen .75
3 Andy Pettitte .40
4 Ivan Rodriguez .75
5 Mark McGwire 3.00
6 Jason Dickson .15
7 Jose Cruz Jr. .25
8 Jeff Kent .15
9 Mike Mussina .60
10 Jason Kendall .15
11 Brett Tomko .15
12 Jeff King .15
13 Brad Radke .15
14 Robin Ventura .15
15 Jeff Bagwell .75
16 Greg Maddux 1.50
17 John Jaha .15
18 Mike Piazza 2.50
19 Edgar Martinez .15
20 David Justice .40
21 Todd Hundley .15
22 Tony Gwynn 1.50
23 Larry Walker .40
24 Bernie Williams .35
25 Edgar Renteria .15
26 Rafael Palmeiro .35
27 Tim Salmon .35
28 Matt Morris .15
29 Shawn Estes .15
30 Vladimir Guerrero 1.00
31 Fernando Tatis .15
32 Justin Thompson .15
33 Ken Griffey Jr. 2.75
34 Edgardo Alfonzo .15
35 Mo Vaughn .35
36 Marty Cordova .15
37 Craig Biggio .20
38 Roger Clemens 1.50
39 Mark Grace .40
40 Ken Caminiti .15
41 Tony Womack .15
42 Albert Belle .35
43 Tino Martinez .15
44 Sandy Alomar .15
45 Jeff Cirillo .15
46 Jason Giambi .50
47 Darin Erstad .50
48 Livan Hernandez .15
49 Mark Grudzielanek .15
50 Sammy Sosa 2.00
51 Curt Schilling .30
52 Brian Hunter .15
53 Neifi Perez .15
54 Todd Walker .15
55 Jose Guillen .15
56 Jim Thome .15
57 Tom Glavine .20
58 Todd Greene .15
59 Rondell White .25
60 Roberto Alomar .40
61 Tony Clark .15
62 Vinny Castilla .15
63 Barry Larkin .20
64 Hideki Irabu .15
65 Johnny Damon .20
66 Juan Gonzalez .75
67 John Olerud .15
68 Gary Sheffield .40
69 Raul Mondesi .30
70 Chipper Jones 2.50
71 David Ortiz .15
72 *Warren Morris* .50
73 Alex Gonzalez .25
74 Nick Bierbrodt .15
75 Roy Halladay .15
76 Danny Buxbaum .15
77 Adam Kennedy .15
78 *Jared Sandberg* .75
79 Michael Barrett .15
80 Gil Meche .15
81 Jayson Werth .15
82 Abraham Nunez .15
83 Ben Petrick .15
84 Brett Caradonna .15
85 *Mike Lowell* 1.50
86 *Clay Bruner* .15
87 *John Curtice* .25
88 Bobby Estalella .15
89 Juan Melo .15
90 Arnold Gooch .15
91 *Kevin Millwood* 2.00
92 Richie Sexson .15
93 Orlando Cabrera .15
94 Pat Cline .15
95 Anthony Sanders .15
96 Russ Johnson .15
97 Ben Grieve .40
98 Kevin McGlinchy .15
99 Paul Wilder .15
100 Russ Ortiz .15
101 *Ryan Jackson* .25
102 Heath Murray .15
103 Brian Rose .15
104 *Ryan Radmanovich* .15
105 Ricky Ledee .15
106 *Jeff Wallace* .25
107 *Ryan Minor* .15
108 Dennis Reyes .15
109 *James Manias* .25
110 Chris Carpenter .15
111 Daryle Ward .15
112 Vernon Wells .15
113 Chad Green .15
114 *Mike Stoner* .25
115 Brad Fullmer .15
116 Adam Eaton .15
117 Jeff Liefer .15
118 *Corey Koskie* 1.50
119 Todd Helton .75
120 *Jaime Jones* .15
121 Mel Rosario .15
122 Geoff Goetz .15
123 Adrian Beltre .40
124 Jason Dellaero .15
125 *Gabe Kapler* 2.50
126 Scott Schoeneweis .15
127 Ryan Brannan .15
128 Aaron Akin .15
129 *Ryan Anderson* 2.00
130 Brad Penny .15
131 Bruce Chen .15
132 Eli Marrero .15
133 Eric Chavez .40
134 *Troy Glaus* 8.00
135 Troy Cameron .15
136 *Brian Sikorski* .25
137 *Mike Kinkade* .25
138 Braden Looper .15
139 Mark Mangum .15
140 Danny Peoples .15
141 J.J. Davis .15
142 Ben Davis .15
143 Jacque Jones .25
144 Derrick Gibson .15
145 Bronson Arroyo .15
146 *Cristian Guzman* .50
147 Jeff Abbott .15
148 *Mike Cuddyer* 2.00
149 Jason Romano .15
150 Shane Monahan .15
151 *Ntema Ndungidi* .15
152 Alex Sanchez .15
153 *Jack Cust* 2.00
154 Brent Butler .15
155 Ramon Hernandez .15
156 Norm Hutchins .15
157 Jason Marquis .15
158 Jacob Cruz .15
159 *Rob Burger* .15
160 Eric Milton .10
161 Preston Wilson .15
162 *Jason Fitzgerald* .15
163 Dan Serafini .15
164 Peter Munro .15
165 Trot Nixon .15
166 Homer Bush .15
167 Dermal Brown .15
168 Chad Hermansen .10
169 *Julio Moreno* .15
170 *John Roskos* .15
171 Grant Roberts .15
172 Ken Cloude .15
173 Jason Brester .15
174 Jason Conti .15
175 Jon Garland .15
176 Robbie Bell .15
177 Nathan Haynes .15
178 *Ramon Ortiz* 1.00
179 Shannon Stewart .20
180 Pablo Ortega .15
181 *Jimmy Rollins* 2.50
182 Sean Casey .40
183 *Ted Lilly* .15
184 *Chris Enochs* .15
185 *Magglio Ordonez* 4.00
186 Mike Drumright .15
187 Aaron Boone .15
188 Matt Clement .15
189 Todd Dunwoody .15
190 Larry Rodriguez .15
191 Todd Noel .15
192 Geoff Jenkins .15
193 George Lombard .15
194 Lance Berkman .35
195 *Marcus McCain* .15
196 Ryan McGuire .15
197 *Jhensy Sandoval* .15
198 Corey Lee .15
199 Mario Valdez .15
200 *Robert Fick* .50
201 Donnie Sadler .15
202 Marc Kroon .15
203 David Miller .15
204 Jarrod Washburn .15
205 Miguel Tejada .40
206 Raul Ibanez .15
207 John Patterson .15
208 Calvin Pickering .15
209 Felix Martinez .15
210 Mark Redman .15
211 Scott Elarton .15
212 *Jose Amado* .25
213 Kerry Wood .40
214 Dante Powell .15
215 Aramis Ramirez .15
216 A.J. Hinch .15
217 *Dustin Carr* .15
218 Mark Kotsay .15
219 Jason Standridge .15
220 Luis Ordaz .15
221 *Orlando Hernandez* 1.50
222 Cal Ripken Jr. 3.00
223 Paul Molitor .60
224 Derek Jeter 3.00
225 Barry Bonds 2.00
226 Jim Edmonds .15
227 John Smoltz .20
228 Eric Karros .15
229 Ray Lankford .15
230 Rey Ordonez .15
231 Kenny Lofton .15
232 Alex Rodriguez 2.75
233 Dante Bichette .15
234 Pedro Martinez .75
235 Carlos Delgado .35
236 Rod Beck .15
237 Matt Williams .35
238 Charles Johnson .15
239 Rico Brogna .15
240 Frank Thomas 1.00
241 Paul O'Neill .15
242 Jaret Wright .15
243 Brant Brown .15
244 Ryan Klesko .15
245 Chuck Finley .15
246 Derek Bell .15
247 Delino DeShields .15
248 Chan Ho Park .25
249 Wade Boggs .65
250 Jay Buhner .15
251 Butch Huskey .15
252 Steve Finley .15
253 Will Clark .35
254 John Valentin .15
255 Bobby Higginson .20
256 Darryl Strawberry .15
257 Randy Johnson .75
258 Al Martin .15
259 Travis Fryman .15
260 Fred McGriff .15
261 Jose Valentin .15
262 Andruw Jones .75
263 Kenny Rogers .15
264 Moises Alou .25
265 Denny Neagle .15
266 Ugueth Urbina .15
267 Derrek Lee .15
268 Ellis Burks .15
269 Mariano Rivera .45
270 Dean Palmer .15
271 Eddie Taubensee .15
272 Brady Anderson .15
273 Brian Giles .15
274 Quinton McCracken .15
275 Henry Rodriguez .15
276 Andres Galarraga .15
277 Jose Canseco .45
278 David Segui .15
279 Bret Saberhagen .15
280 Kevin Brown .25
281 Chuck Knoblauch .15
282 Jeromy Burnitz .15
283 Jay Bell .15
284 Manny Ramirez .75
285 Rick Helling .15
286 Francisco Cordova .15
287 Bob Abreu .20
288 J.T. Snow Jr. .15
289 Hideo Nomo .65
290 Brian Jordan .15
291 Javy Lopez .15
292 Travis Lee .15
293 Russell Branyan .15
294 Paul Konerko .15
295 *Masato Yoshii* 1.00
296 Kris Benson .15
297 Juan Encarnacion .15
298 Eric Milton .15
299 Mike Caruso .15
300 *Ricardo Aramboles* .50
301 Bobby Smith .15
302 Billy Koch .15
303 Richard Hidalgo .20
304 *Justin Baughman* .25
305 Chris Gissell .15
306 *Donnie Bridges* .15
307 *Nelson Lara* .15
308 *Randy Wolf* .75
309 *Jason LaRue* .25
310 *Jason Gooding* .25
311 *Edgar Clemente* .50
312 Andrew Vessel .15
313 Chris Reitsma .15
314 *Jesus Sanchez* .15
315 *Buddy Carlyle* .25
316 Randy Winn .15
317 Luis Rivera .15
318 *Marcus Thames* .15
319 A.J. Pierzynski .15
320 Scott Randall .15
321 Damian Sapp .15
322 *Eddie Yarnell* .15
323 *Luke Allen* .25
324 J.D. Smart .15
325 Willie Martinez .15
326 Alex Ramirez .15
327 *Eric DuBose* .15
328 Kevin Witt .15

329 *Dan McKinley* .25
330 Cliff Politte .15
331 Vladimir Nunez .15
332 *John Halama* .50
333 Nerio Rodriguez .15
334 Desi Relaford .15
335 Robinson Checo .15
336 *John Nicholson* .15
337 *Tom LaRosa* .15
338 *Kevin Nicholson* .15
339 Javier Vazquez .30
340 A.J. Zapp .15
341 Tom Evans .15
342 Kerry Robinson .15
343 *Gabe Gonzalez* .15
344 Ralph Milliard .15
345 Enrique Wilson .15
346 Elvin Hernandez .15
347 *Mike Lincoln* .25
348 *Cesar King* .15
349 *Cristian Guzman* 2.00
350 Donzell McDonald .15
351 *Jim Parque* 1.00
352 *Mike Saipe* .15
353 *Carlos Febles* .75
354 *Dernell Stenson* .50
355 *Mark Osborne* .15
356 *Odalis Perez* .75
357 *Jason Dewey* .25
358 Joe Fontenot .15
359 *Jason Grilli* .50
360 *Kevin Haverbusch* .75
361 *Jay Yennaco* .15
362 Brian Buchanan .15
363 John Barnes .15
364 Chris Fussell .15
365 *Kevin Gibbs* .15
366 Joe Lawrence .15
367 DaRond Stovall .15
368 *Brian Fuentes* .15
369 Jimmy Anderson .15
370 *Laril Gonzalez* .15
371 *Scott Williamson* .50
372 Milton Bradley .15
373 *Jason Halper* .15
374 *Brent Billingsley* .15
375 *Joe DePastino* .15
376 Jake Westbrook .15
377 Octavio Dotel .15
378 *Jason Williams* .15
379 *Julio Ramirez* .15
380 Seth Greisinger .15
381 *Mike Judd* .15
382 *Ben Ford* .15
383 Tom Bennett .15
384 *Adam Butler* .15
385 *Wade Miller* 2.50
386 *Kyle Peterson* .15
387 *Tommy Peterman* .25
388 Onan Masaoka .15
389 *Jason Rakers* .25
390 Rafael Medina .15
391 Luis Lopez .15
392 Jeff Yoder .15
393 *Vance Wilson* .15
394 *Fernando Seguignol* .75
395 Ron Wright .15
396 *Ruben Mateo* 1.00
397 *Steve Lomasney* .15
398 Damian Jackson .15
399 *Mike Jerzembeck* .15
400 *Luis Rivas* 1.00
401 *Kevin Burford* .15
402 Glenn Davis .15
403 *Robert Luce* .15
404 Cole Liniak .15
405 *Matthew LeCroy* .25
406 *Jeremy Giambi* 1.00
407 Shawn Chacon .15
408 *Dewayne Wise* .15
409 *Steve Woodard* .25
410 *Francisco Cordero* .15
411 *Damon Minor* .25
412 Lou Collier .15
413 Justin Towle .15
414 Juan LeBron .15
415 Michael Coleman .15
416 Felix Rodriguez .15
417 *Paul Ah Yat* .50
418 *Kevin Barker* .25
419 Brian Meadows .15
420 *Darnell McDonald* .15
421 *Matt Kinney* .40
422 *Mike Vavrek* .15
423 *Courtney Duncan* .15
424 *Kevin Millar* .50
425 Ruben Rivera .15
426 *Steve Shoemaker* .15
427 *Dan Reichert* .15
428 *Carlos Lee* 3.00
429 Rod Barajas .15
430 *Pablo Ozuna* 1.00
431 *Todd Belitz* .15
432 Sidney Ponson .15
433 *Steve Carver* .15
434 Esteban Yan .15
435 *Cedrick Bowers* .15
436 Marlon Anderson .15
437 Carl Pavano .15
438 *Jae Weong Seo* .50
439 *Jose Taveras* .15
440 *Matt Anderson* .50
441 *Darron Ingram* .25

1998 Bowman International

All 441 cards in Bowman Series 1 and 2 are paralleled in an International version, with the player's native country highlighted. Background map designs and vital information were translated into the player's native language on these one per pack parallel cards.

	MT
Complete Set (441):	200.00
Common Player:	.25
Stars:	1.5-3X
Inserted 1:1	

(See 1998 Bowman for checklist and base card values.)

1998 Bowman Golden Anniversary

This 441-card parallel set celebrates Bowman's 50th anniversary with a gold, rather than black, facsimile autograph on each card. Golden Anniversary cards were inserted in both Series 1 (1:237) and Series 2 (1:194) packs and are sequentially numbered to 50.

	MT
Common Player:	7.50
Veteran Stars:	40-80X
Young Stars:	20-40X
Rookie Cards:	6-12X

(See 1998 Bowman for checklist and base card values.)

1998 Bowman Autographs

Rookies and prospects are featured on the certified autograph cards found as '98 Bowman inserts. Each player signed cards in blue, silver and gold ink. The front of each autographed card bears a certification seal. Relative values in the current market come nowhere near reflecting those scarcities.

		MT
Complete Set, Blue (70):		400.00
Common Player:		4.00
Inserted 1:149		
Silvers (1:992):		1.5-2.5X
Golds (1:2,976):		2-4X
1	Adrian Beltre	10.00
2	Brad Fullmer	6.00
3	Ricky Ledee	6.00
4	David Ortiz	4.00
5	Fernando Tatis	6.00
6	Kerry Wood	20.00
7	Mel Rosario	4.00
8	Cole Liniak	5.00
9	A.J. Hinch	5.00
10	Jhensy Sandoval	4.00
11	Jose Cruz Jr.	6.00
12	Richard Hidalgo	8.00
13	Geoff Jenkins	8.00
14	Carl Pavano	5.00
15	Richie Sexson	12.00
16	Tony Womack	5.00
17	Scott Rolen	15.00
18	Ryan Minor	5.00
19	Elieser Marrero	5.00
20	Jason Marquis	5.00
21	Mike Lowell	15.00
22	Todd Helton	20.00
23	Chad Green	4.00
24	Scott Elarton	4.00
25	Russell Branyan	6.00
26	Mike Drumright	4.00
27	Ben Grieve	10.00
28	Jacque Jones	8.00
29	Jared Sandberg	5.00
30	Grant Roberts	6.00
31	Mike Stoner	5.00
32	Brian Rose	4.00
33	Randy Winn	4.00
34	Justin Towle	5.00
35	Anthony Sanders	4.00
36	Rafael Medina	4.00
37	Corey Lee	4.00
38	Mike Kinkade	4.00
39	Norm Hutchins	4.00
40	Jason Brester	4.00
41	Ben Davis	5.00
42	Nomar Garciaparra	60.00
43	Jeff Liefer	4.00
44	Eric Milton	6.00
45	Preston Wilson	6.00
46	Miguel Tejada	15.00
47	Luis Ordaz	4.00
48	Travis Lee	6.00
49	Kris Benson	5.00
50	Jacob Cruz	5.00
51	Dermal Brown	4.00
52	Marc Kroon	4.00
53	Chad Hermansen	5.00
54	Roy Halladay	8.00
55	Eric Chavez	10.00
56	Jason Conti	4.00
57	Juan Encarnacion	5.00
58	Paul Wilder	5.00
59	Aramis Ramirez	6.00
60	Cliff Politte	4.00
61	Todd Dunwoody	5.00
62	Paul Konerko	10.00
63	Shane Monahan	4.00
64	Alex Sanchez	4.00
65	Jeff Abbott	4.00
66	John Patterson	4.00
67	Peter Munro	4.00
68	Jarrod Washburn	10.00
69	Derrek Lee	5.00
70	Ramon Hernandez	5.00

1998 Bowman Japanese Rookies

Bowman offered collectors a chance to receive original 1991 BBM-brand Japanese rookie cards of three players. Series 1 had rookie cards of Hideo Nomo and Shigetoshi Hasegawa inserted in one per 2,685 packs, while Series 2 offered Hideki Irabu seeded one per 4,411 packs. Card numbers have a "BBM" prefix.

		MT
Complete Set (3):		20.00
Common Player:		5.00
11	Hideo Nomo	10.00
17	Shigetosi Hasegawa	5.00
	Hideki Irabu	7.50

1998 Bowman Minor League MVP

This 11-card insert set features players who are former Minor League MVPs who had graduated to the majors. Minor League MVPs are seeded one per 12 packs of Series 2 and are numbered with a "MVP" prefix.

		MT
Complete Set (11):		10.00
Common Player:		.50
1	Jeff Bagwell	1.50
2	Andres Galarraga	.50
3	Juan Gonzalez	1.50
4	Tony Gwynn	2.00
5	Vladimir Guerrero	1.00
6	Derek Jeter	2.50
7	Andruw Jones	1.00
8	Tino Martinez	.50
9	Manny Ramirez	1.50
10	Gary Sheffield	.75
11	Jim Thome	.50

1998 Bowman Rookie of the Year Favorites

Rookie of the Year Favorites displays 10 players who had a legitimate shot at the 1999 ROY award in the opinion of the Bowman scouts. The insert was seeded one per 12 packs of Series 2 and numbered with an "ROY" prefix.

		MT
Complete Set (10):		10.00
Common Player:		.50
1	Adrian Beltre	1.00
2	Troy Glaus	5.00
3	Chad Hermansen	.50
4	Matt Clement	.50
5	Eric Chavez	2.50
6	Kris Benson	.50
7	Richie Sexson	.50
8	Randy Wolf	.50
9	Ryan Minor	.50
10	Alex Gonzalez	.50

1998 Bowman Scout's Choice

This Series 1 insert has players with potential for Major League stardom. Fronts have action photos with gold-foil highlights. Backs have a portrait photo and an assessment of the player's skills in the traditional five areas of raw talent. Cards are numbered with an "SC" prefix.

		MT
Complete Set (21):		21.00
Common Player:		.50
Inserted 1:12		
1	Paul Konerko	1.50
2	Richard Hidalgo	1.50
3	Mark Kotsay	1.25
4	Ben Grieve	2.00
5	Chad Hermansen	.75
6	Matt Clement	.75
7	Brad Fullmer	1.50
8	Eli Marrero	.75
9	Kerry Wood	2.00
10	Adrian Beltre	2.00
11	Ricky Ledee	1.00
12	Travis Lee	1.25
13	Abraham Nunez	.75
14	Ryan Anderson	1.50
15	Dermal Brown	.50
16	Juan Encarnacion	.75
17	Aramis Ramirez	1.25
18	Todd Helton	3.00
19	Kris Benson	1.00
20	Russell Branyan	1.25
21	Mike Stoner	.75

1998 Bowman Chrome

All 441 cards in Bowman 1 and 2 were reprinted with a chromium finish for Bowman Chrome. Chrome contains International and Golden Anniversary parallels, like Bowman. Internationals are seeded one per four packs, with Refractor versions every 24 packs. Golden Anniversary parallels are exclusive to hobby packs and inserted one per 164 packs and sequentially numbered to 50 sets. Refractor versions are seeded one per 1,279 packs and numbered to just five sets. In addition, 50 Bowman Chrome Reprints were inserted with 25 in each series.

		MT
Complete Set (441):		160.00
Complete Series 1 (221):		100.00
Complete Series 2 (220):		70.00
Common Player:		.20
Series 1 Pack (4):		6.00
Series 2 Pack (4):		3.00
Series 1 Box (24):		125.00
Series 2 Box (24):		50.00
1	Nomar Garciaparra	2.50
2	Scott Rolen	1.00
3	Andy Pettitte	.50
4	Ivan Rodriguez	1.00
5	Mark McGwire	4.00
6	Jason Dickson	.20
7	Jose Cruz Jr.	.35
8	Jeff Kent	.20
9	Mike Mussina	.75
10	Jason Kendall	.20
11	Brett Tomko	.20
12	Jeff King	.20
13	Brad Radke	.20
14	Robin Ventura	.20
15	Jeff Bagwell	1.50
16	Greg Maddux	2.00
17	John Jaha	.20
18	Mike Piazza	3.00
19	Edgar Martinez	.20
20	David Justice	.40
21	Todd Hundley	.20
22	Tony Gwynn	2.00
23	Larry Walker	.50
24	Bernie Williams	.40
25	Edgar Renteria	.20
26	Rafael Palmeiro	.40
27	Tim Salmon	.40
28	Matt Morris	.20
29	Shawn Estes	.20
30	Vladimir Guerrero	1.50
31	Fernando Tatis	.20
32	Justin Thompson	.20
33	Ken Griffey Jr.	3.50
34	Edgardo Alfonzo	.20
35	Mo Vaughn	.50
36	Marty Cordova	.20
37	Craig Biggio	.25
38	Roger Clemens	2.00
39	Mark Grace	.50
40	Ken Caminiti	.20
41	Tony Womack	.20
42	Albert Belle	.40
43	Tino Martinez	.20
44	Sandy Alomar	.20
45	Jeff Cirillo	.20
46	Jason Giambi	.75
47	Darin Erstad	.75
48	Livan Hernandez	.20
49	Mark Grudzielanek	.20
50	Sammy Sosa	2.50
51	Curt Schilling	.40
52	Brian Hunter	.20
53	Neifi Perez	.20
54	Todd Walker	.20
55	Jose Guillen	.20
56	Jim Thome	.20
57	Tom Glavine	.25
58	Todd Greene	.20
59	Rondell White	.35
60	Roberto Alomar	.50
61	Tony Clark	.20
62	Vinny Castilla	.20
63	Barry Larkin	.25
64	Hideki Irabu	.20
65	Johnny Damon	.35
66	Juan Gonzalez	1.00
67	John Olerud	.20
68	Gary Sheffield	.40
69	Raul Mondesi	.35
70	Chipper Jones	3.00
71	David Ortiz	.20
72	*Warren Morris*	1.00
73	Alex Gonzalez	.35
74	Nick Bierbrodt	.20
75	Roy Halladay	.20
76	Danny Buxbaum	.20
77	Adam Kennedy	.20
78	*Jared Sandberg*	1.00
79	Michael Barrett	.20
80	Gil Meche	.20
81	Jayson Werth	.20
82	Abraham Nunez	.20
83	Ben Petrick	.20
84	Brett Caradonna	.20
85	*Mike Lowell*	6.00
86	*Clay Bruner*	.20
87	*John Curtice*	.50
88	Bobby Estalella	.20
89	Juan Melo	.20
90	Arnold Gooch	.20
91	*Kevin Millwood*	4.00
92	Richie Sexson	.20
93	Orlando Cabrera	.20
94	Pat Cline	.20
95	Anthony Sanders	.20
96	Russ Johnson	.20
97	Ben Grieve	.75
98	Kevin McGlinchy	.20
99	Paul Wilder	.20
100	Russ Ortiz	.20
101	*Ryan Jackson*	.50
102	Heath Murray	.20
103	Brian Rose	.20
104	*Ryan Radmanovich*	.20
105	Ricky Ledee	.20
106	*Jeff Wallace*	.50
107	*Ryan Minor*	.75
108	Dennis Reyes	.20
109	*James Manias*	.50
110	Chris Carpenter	.20
111	Daryle Ward	.20
112	Vernon Wells	.20
113	Chad Green	.20
114	*Mike Stoner*	1.00
115	Brad Fullmer	.20
116	Adam Eaton	.20
117	Jeff Liefer	.20
118	*Corey Koskie*	4.00
119	Todd Helton	1.50
120	*Jaime Jones*	.75
121	Mel Rosario	.20
122	Geoff Goetz	.20
123	Adrian Beltre	.50
124	Jason Dellaero	.20
125	*Gabe Kapler*	5.00
126	Scott Schoeneweis	.20
127	Ryan Brannan	.20
128	Aaron Akin	.20
129	*Ryan Anderson*	8.00
130	Brad Penny	.20
131	Bruce Chen	.20
132	Eli Marrero	.20
133	Eric Chavez	1.00
134	*Troy Glaus*	30.00
135	Troy Cameron	.20
136	*Brian Sikorski*	1.00
137	*Mike Kinkade*	1.50
138	Braden Looper	.20
139	Mark Mangum	.20
140	Danny Peoples	.20
141	J.J. Davis	.20
142	Ben Davis	.20
143	Jacque Jones	.50
144	Derrick Gibson	.20
145	Bronson Arroyo	.20
146	*Luis DeLosSantos*	.20
147	Jeff Abbott	.20
148	*Mike Cuddyer*	8.00
149	Jason Romano	.20
150	Shane Monahan	.20
151	*Ntema Ndungidi*	.40
152	Alex Sanchez	.20
153	*Jack Cust*	8.00
154	Brent Butler	.20
155	Ramon Hernandez	.20
156	Norm Hutchins	.20
157	Jason Marquis	.30
158	Jacob Cruz	.20
159	*Rob Burger*	.20
160	Eric Milton	.30
161	Preston Wilson	.20
162	*Jason Fitzgerald*	.20
163	Dan Serafini	.20
164	Peter Munro	.20
165	Trot Nixon	.20
166	Homer Bush	.20
167	Dermal Brown	.20
168	Chad Hermansen	.20
169	*Julio Moreno*	.20
170	*John Roskos*	.20
171	Grant Roberts	.20
172	Ken Cloude	.20
173	Jason Brester	.20
174	Jason Conti	.20
175	Jon Garland	.20
176	Robbie Bell	.20
177	Nathan Haynes	.20
178	*Ramon Ortiz*	4.00
179	Shannon Stewart	.35
180	Pablo Ortega	.20
181	*Jimmy Rollins*	10.00
182	Sean Casey	.75
183	*Ted Lilly*	.20
184	*Chris Enochs*	.20
185	*Magglio Ordonez*	15.00
186	Mike Drumright	.20
187	Aaron Boone	.20
188	Matt Clement	.20
189	Todd Dunwoody	.20
190	Larry Rodriguez	.20
191	Todd Noel	.20
192	Geoff Jenkins	.20
193	George Lombard	.20
194	Lance Berkman	.50
195	*Marcus McCain*	.20
196	Ryan McGuire	.20
197	*Jhensy Sandoval*	.20
198	Corey Lee	.20
199	Mario Valdez	.20
200	*Robert Fick*	1.00
201	Donnie Sadler	.20
202	Marc Kroon	.20
203	David Miller	.20
204	Jarrod Washburn	.20
205	Miguel Tejada	.75
206	Raul Ibanez	.20
207	John Patterson	.20
208	Calvin Pickering	.20
209	Felix Martinez	.20
210	Mark Redman	.20
211	Scott Elarton	.20
212	*Jose Amado*	.20
213	Kerry Wood	.75
214	Dante Powell	.20
215	Aramis Ramirez	.20
216	A.J. Hinch	.20
217	*Dustin Carr*	.50
218	Mark Kotsay	.20
219	Jason Standridge	.20
220	Luis Ordaz	.20
221	*Orlando Hernandez*	4.00
222	Cal Ripken Jr.	4.00
223	Paul Molitor	.75

224 Derek Jeter 3.00
225 Barry Bonds 2.50
226 Jim Edmonds .20
227 John Smoltz .25
228 Eric Karros .20
229 Ray Lankford .20
230 Rey Ordonez .20
231 Kenny Lofton .20
232 Alex Rodriguez 3.50
233 Dante Bichette .20
234 Pedro Martinez 1.00
235 Carlos Delgado .50
236 Rod Beck .20
237 Matt Williams .40
238 Charles Johnson .20
239 Rico Brogna .20
240 Frank Thomas 2.50
241 Paul O'Neill .20
242 Jaret Wright .20
243 Brant Brown .20
244 Ryan Klesko .20
245 Chuck Finley .20
246 Derek Bell .20
247 Delino DeShields .20
248 Chan Ho Park .40
249 Wade Boggs .75
250 Jay Buhner .20
251 Butch Huskey .20
252 Steve Finley .20
253 Will Clark .40
254 John Valentin .20
255 Bobby Higginson .25
256 Darryl Strawberry .20
257 Randy Johnson 1.00
258 Al Martin .20
259 Travis Fryman .20
260 Fred McGriff .20
261 Jose Valentin .20
262 Andruw Jones 1.50
263 Kenny Rogers .20
264 Moises Alou .30
265 Denny Neagle .20
266 Ugueth Urbina .20
267 Derrek Lee .20
268 Ellis Burks .20
269 Mariano Rivera .40
270 Dean Palmer .20
271 Eddie Taubensee .20
272 Brady Anderson .20
273 Brian Giles .20
274 Quinton McCracken .20
275 Henry Rodriguez .20
276 Andres Galarraga .20
277 Jose Canseco .50
278 David Segui .20
279 Bret Saberhagen .20
280 Kevin Brown .40
281 Chuck Knoblauch .20
282 Jeromy Burnitz .20
283 Jay Bell .20
284 Manny Ramirez 1.00
285 Rick Helling .20
286 Francisco Cordova .20
287 Bob Abreu .25
288 J.T. Snow Jr. .20
289 Hideo Nomo .75
290 Brian Jordan .20
291 Javy Lopez .20
292 *Aaron Akin* .20
293 Russell Branyan .20
294 Paul Konerko .20
295 *Masato Yoshii* 3.00
296 Kris Benson .20
297 Juan Encarnacion .20
298 Eric Milton .25
299 Mike Caruso .20
300 *Ricardo Aramboles* 1.50
301 Bobby Smith .20
302 Billy Koch .20
303 Richard Hidalgo .25
304 *Justin Baughman* .50
305 Chris Gissell .20
306 *Donnie Bridges* .50
307 *Nelson Lara* .20
308 *Randy Wolf* .50
309 *Jason LaRue* .75
310 *Jason Gooding* .20
311 *Edgar Clemente* .75
312 Andrew Vessel .20
313 Chris Reitsma .20
314 *Jesus Sanchez* .20
315 *Buddy Carlyle* .20
316 Randy Winn .20
317 Luis Rivera .20
318 *Marcus Thames* .20
319 A.J. Pierzynski .20
320 Scott Randall .20
321 Damian Sapp .20
322 *Eddie Yarnell* .20
323 *Luke Allen* 1.00
324 J.D. Smart .20
325 Willie Martinez .20
326 Alex Ramirez .20
327 *Eric DuBose* .20
328 Kevin Witt .20
329 *Dan McKinley* .20
330 Cliff Politte .20
331 Vladimir Nunez .20
332 *John Halama* .75
333 Nerio Rodriguez .20
334 Desi Relaford .20
335 Robinson Checo .20
336 *John Nicholson* .20
337 *Tom LaRosa* .20
338 *Kevin Nicholson* .20
339 Javier Vazquez .40
340 A.J. Zapp .20
341 Tom Evans .20
342 Kerry Robinson .20
343 *Gabe Gonzalez* .20
344 Ralph Milliard .20
345 Enrique Wilson .20
346 Elvin Hernandez .20
347 *Mike Lincoln* .40
348 *Cesar King* .20
349 *Cristian Guzman* 6.00
350 Donzell McDonald .20
351 *Jim Parque* 1.50
352 *Mike Saipe* .20
353 *Carlos Febles* .50
354 *Dernell Stenson* .75
355 *Mark Osborne* .20
356 *Odalis Perez* 3.00
357 *Jason Dewey* .50
358 Joe Fontenot .20
359 *Jason Grilli* .50
360 *Kevin Haverbusch* 1.00
361 *Jay Yennaco* .20
362 Brian Buchanan .20
363 John Barnes .20
364 Chris Fussell .20
365 *Kevin Gibbs* .20
366 Joe Lawrence .20
367 DaRond Stovall .20
368 *Brian Fuentes* .20
369 Jimmy Anderson .20
370 *Laril Gonzalez* .20
371 *Scott Williamson* 1.00
372 Milton Bradley .20
373 *Jason Halper* .20
374 *Brent Billingsley* .50
375 *Joe DePastino* .20
376 Jake Westbrook .20
377 Octavio Dotel .20
378 *Jason Williams* .50
379 *Julio Ramirez* .50
380 Seth Greisinger .20
381 *Mike Judd* .50
382 *Ben Ford* .20
383 *Tom Bennett* .20
384 *Adam Butler* .50
385 *Wade Miller* 6.00
386 *Kyle Peterson* .50
387 *Tommy Peterman* .50
388 Onan Masaoka .20
389 *Jason Rakers* .20
390 Rafael Medina .20
391 Luis Lopez .20
392 Jeff Yoder .20
393 *Vance Wilson* .20
394 *Fernando Seguignol* .50
395 Ron Wright .20
396 *Ruben Mateo* 1.00
397 *Steve Lomasney* .50
398 Damian Jackson .20
399 *Mike Jerzembeck* .20
400 *Luis Rivas* .50
401 *Kevin Burford* .50
402 Glenn Davis .20
403 *Robert Luce* .75
404 Cole Liniak .20
405 *Matthew LeCroy* .50
406 *Jeremy Giambi* 3.00
407 Shawn Chacon .20
408 *Dewayne Wise* .20
409 *Steve Woodard* .50
410 *Francisco Cordero* .20
411 *Damon Minor* .50
412 Lou Collier .20
413 Justin Towle .20
414 Juan LeBron .20
415 Michael Coleman .20
416 Felix Rodriguez .20
417 *Paul Ah Yat* .75
418 *Kevin Barker* .20
419 Brian Meadows .20
420 *Darnell McDonald* .50
421 *Matt Kinney* .50
422 *Mike Vavrek* .20
423 *Courtney Duncan* .20
424 *Kevin Millar* 1.50
425 Ruben Rivera .20
426 *Steve Shoemaker* .20
427 *Dan Reichert* .20
428 *Carlos Lee* 8.00
429 *Rod Barajas* .20
430 *Pablo Ozuna* 1.00
431 *Todd Belitz* .20
432 Sidney Ponson .20
433 *Steve Carver* .20
434 *Esteban Yan* .50
435 *Cedrick Bowers* .20
436 Marlon Anderson .20
437 Carl Pavano .20
438 *Jae Weong Seo* 1.50
439 *Jose Taveras* .20
440 *Matt Anderson* .75
441 *Darron Ingram* .20

1998 Bowman Chrome Refractors

Refractor versions for all 441 cards in Bowman Chrome Series 1 and 2 were created. The cards contained the word "Refractor" on the back in black letters directly under the card number.

	MT
Common Player:	2.00
Stars:	3X
Inserted 1:12	
Int'l Refractors:	6X
Inserted 1:24	

(See 1998 Bowman Chrome for checklist and base card values.)

1998 Bowman Chrome International

All 441 cards throughout Bowman Chrome Series 1 and 2 were paralleled in International versions. Cards fronts have the regular background replaced by a map denoting the player's birthplace. Backs are written in the player's native language.

	MT
Common Player:	.50
Stars and rookies:	1.5X
Inserted	1:4
Refractors:	3X
Inserted 1:24	

(See 1998 Bowman Chrome for checklist and base card values.)

1998 Bowman Chrome Golden Anniversary

Golden Anniversary parallels were printed for all 441 cards in Bowman Chrome. They are exclusive to hobby packs, seeded one per 164 packs and sequentially numbered to 50 sets. Refractor versions were also available, numbered to just five sets and inserted one per 1,279 packs.

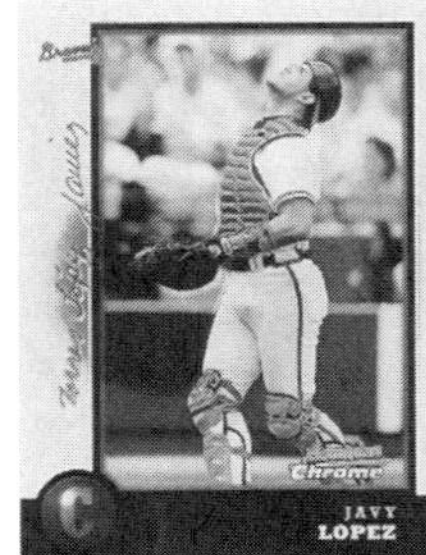

	MT
Common Player:	5.00
Stars:	20X

(See 1998 Bowman Chrome for checklist and base card values. Golden Anniversary Refractors cannot be accurately priced due to their rarity (five each).)

1998 Bowman Chrome Reprints

Bowman Chrome Reprints showcas 50 of the most popular rookie cards to appear in the brand since 1948. The 25 odd-numbered cards are found in Series 1; the evens in Series 2. The Reprints are numbered with a "BC" prefix.

		MT
Complete Set (50):		40.00
Common Player:		.35
Inserted 1:12		
Refractors:		1.5X
Inserted 1:36		
1	Yogi Berra	1.50
2	Jackie Robinson	4.00
3	Don Newcombe	.35
4	Satchel Paige	2.00
5	Willie Mays	3.00
6	Gil McDougald	.35
7	Don Larsen	.75
8	Elston Howard	.35
9	Robin Ventura	.35
10	Brady Anderson	.35
11	Gary Sheffield	.35
12	Tino Martinez	.35
13	Ken Griffey Jr.	3.00
14	John Smoltz	.35
15	Sandy Alomar Jr.	.35
16	Larry Walker	.35
17	Todd Hundley	.35
18	Mo Vaughn	.35
19	Sammy Sosa	2.50
20	Frank Thomas	1.50
21	Chuck Knoblauch	.35
22	Bernie Williams	.35

23 Juan Gonzalez 1.00
24 Mike Mussina .75
25 Jeff Bagwell 1.00
26 Tim Salmon .35
27 Ivan Rodriguez .75
28 Kenny Lofton .35
29 Chipper Jones 2.50
30 Javier Lopez .35
31 Ryan Klesko .35
32 Raul Mondesi .35
33 Jim Thome .35
34 Carlos Delgado .35
35 Mike Piazza 2.75
36 Manny Ramirez 1.00
37 Andy Pettitte .45
38 Derek Jeter 2.50
39 Brad Fullmer .35
40 Richard Hidalgo .35
41 Tony Clark .35
42 Andruw Jones 1.00
43 Vladimir Guerrero 1.00
44 Nomar Garciaparra 2.50
45 Paul Konerko .35
46 Ben Grieve .35
47 Hideo Nomo .75
48 Scott Rolen .50
49 Jose Guillen .35
50 Livan Hernandez .35

1998 Bowman's Best

Bowman's Best was issued in a single 200-card series comprised of 100 prospects and 100 veterans. Prospects are shown on a silver background, while the veterans are showcased on gold. The set was paralleled twice: A Refractor version is seeded one per 20 packs and sequentially numbered to 400, while an Atomic Refractor version is a 1:82 find and numbered to 100 sets. Inserts include regular, Refractor and Atomic Refractor versions of: Autographs, Mirror Image and Performers.

	MT
Complete Set (200):	40.00
Common Player:	.25
Pack (6):	2.75
Wax Box (24):	55.00

1 Mark McGwire 3.00
2 Hideo Nomo .65
3 Barry Bonds 2.00
4 Dante Bichette .25
5 Chipper Jones 2.50
6 Frank Thomas 2.00
7 Kevin Brown .30
8 Juan Gonzalez 1.00
9 Jay Buhner .25
10 Chuck Knoblauch .25
11 Cal Ripken Jr. 3.00
12 Matt Williams .40
13 Jim Edmonds .25
14 Manny Ramirez .75
15 Tony Clark .25
16 Mo Vaughn .50
17 Bernie Williams .50
18 Scott Rolen .75
19 Gary Sheffield .40
20 Albert Belle .40
21 Mike Piazza 2.50
22 John Olerud .25
23 Tony Gwynn 1.50
24 Jay Bell .25
25 Jose Cruz Jr. .35
26 Justin Thompson .25
27 Ken Griffey Jr. 2.75
28 Sandy Alomar .25
29 Mark Grudzielanek .25
30 Mark Grace .40
31 Ron Gant .25
32 Javy Lopez .25
33 Jeff Bagwell .75
34 Fred McGriff .25
35 Rafael Palmeiro .40
36 Vinny Castilla .25
37 Andy Benes .25
38 Pedro Martinez .75
39 Andy Pettitte .40
40 Marty Cordova .25
41 Rusty Greer .25
42 Kevin Orie .25
43 Chan Ho Park .35
44 Ryan Klesko .25
45 Alex Rodriguez 2.75
46 Travis Fryman .25
47 Jeff King .25
48 Roger Clemens 1.50
49 Darin Erstad .60
50 Brady Anderson .25
51 Jason Kendall .25
52 John Valentin .25
53 Ellis Burks .25
54 Brian Hunter .25
55 Paul O'Neill .25
56 Ken Caminiti .25
57 David Justice .40
58 Eric Karros .25
59 Pat Hentgen .25
60 Greg Maddux 1.50
61 Craig Biggio .30
62 Edgar Martinez .25
63 Mike Mussina .65
64 Larry Walker .40
65 Tino Martinez .25
66 Jim Thome .25
67 Tom Glavine .30
68 Raul Mondesi .35
69 Marquis Grissom .25
70 Randy Johnson .75
71 Steve Finley .25
72 Jose Guillen .25
73 Nomar Garciaparra 2.00
74 Wade Boggs .75
75 Bobby Higginson .30
76 Robin Ventura .25
77 Derek Jeter 2.50
78 Andruw Jones .75
79 Ray Lankford .25
80 Vladimir Guerrero 1.00
81 Kenny Lofton .25
82 Ivan Rodriguez .65
83 Neifi Perez .25
84 John Smoltz .30
85 Tim Salmon .40
86 Carlos Delgado .40
87 Sammy Sosa 2.00
88 Jaret Wright .25
89 Roberto Alomar .65
90 Paul Molitor .60
91 Dean Palmer .25
92 Barry Larkin .30
93 Jason Giambi .75
94 Curt Schilling .35
95 Eric Young .25
96 Denny Neagle .25
97 Moises Alou .35
98 Livan Hernandez .25
99 Todd Hundley .25
100 Andres Galarraga .25
101 Travis Lee .35
102 Lance Berkman .35
103 Orlando Cabrera .25
104 *Mike Lowell* 1.50
105 Ben Grieve .40
106 *Jae Weong Seo* 1.00
107 Richie Sexson .25
108 Eli Marrero .25
109 Aramis Ramirez .25
110 Paul Konerko .25
111 Carl Pavano .25
112 Brad Fullmer .25
113 Matt Clement .25
114 Donzell McDonald .25
115 Todd Helton 1.00
116 Mike Caruso .25
117 Donnie Sadler .25
118 Bruce Chen .25
119 Jarrod Washburn .25
120 Adrian Beltre .50
121 *Ryan Jackson* .50
122 *Kevin Millar* .75
123 *Corey Koskie* 1.00
124 Dermal Brown .25
125 Kerry Wood .50
126 Juan Melo .25
127 Ramon Hernandez .25
128 Roy Halladay .25
129 Ron Wright .25
130 *Darnell McDonald* .50
131 *Odalis Perez* .50
132 *Alex Cora* .25
133 Justin Towle .25
134 Juan Encarnacion .25
135 Brian Rose .25
136 Russell Branyan .25
137 *Cesar King* .25
138 Ruben Rivera .25
139 Ricky Ledee .25
140 Vernon Wells .30
141 *Luis Rivas* 1.00
142 Brent Butler .25
143 Karim Garcia .25
144 George Lombard .25
145 *Masato Yoshii* 1.00
146 Braden Looper .25
147 Alex Sanchez .25
148 Kris Benson .25
149 Mark Kotsay .25
150 Richard Hidalgo .30
151 Scott Elarton .25
152 *Ryan Minor* .25
153 *Troy Glaus* 10.00
154 *Carlos Lee* 4.00
155 Michael Coleman .25
156 *Jason Grilli* .50
157 *Julio Ramirez* .50
158 *Randy Wolf* .50
159 Ryan Brannan .25
160 *Edgar Clemente* .50
161 Miguel Tejada .40
162 Chad Hermansen .25
163 *Ryan Anderson* 3.00
164 Ben Petrick .25
165 Alex Gonzalez .35
166 Ben Davis .25
167 John Patterson .25
168 Cliff Politte .25
169 Randall Simon .25
170 Javier Vazquez .35
171 Kevin Witt .25
172 Geoff Jenkins .25
173 David Ortiz .25
174 Derrick Gibson .25
175 Abraham Nunez .25
176 A.J. Hinch .25
177 *Ruben Mateo* 1.00
178 *Magglio Ordonez* 6.00
179 Todd Dunwoody .25
180 Daryle Ward .25
181 *Mike Kinkade* .50
182 Willie Martinez .25
183 *Orlando Hernandez* 1.50
184 Eric Milton .25
185 Eric Chavez .40
186 Damian Jackson .25
187 *Jim Parque* .50
188 *Dan Reichert* .25
189 Mike Drumright .25
190 Todd Walker .25
191 Shane Monahan .25
192 Derrek Lee .25
193 *Jeremy Giambi* 1.00
194 *Dan McKinley* .25
195 *Tony Armas* 3.00
196 *Matt Anderson* .50
197 *Jim Chamblee* .25
198 *Francisco Cordero* .25
199 Calvin Pickering .25
200 Reggie Taylor .25

1998 Bowman's Best Refractors

Refractor versions for all 200 cards in Bowman's Best were available. Fronts featured a reflective finish, while backs were numbered to 400 and inserted one per 20 packs.

	MT
Common Player:	4.00
Stars: 10X	
Production 400 sets	

(See 1998 Bowman's Best for checklist and base card values.)

1998 Bowman's Best Atomic Refractors

Atomic Refractor versions were available for all 200 cards in Bowman's Best. The cards were printed in a prismatic foil on the front, sequentially numbered to 100 sets on the back and inserted one per 82 packs.

	MT
Common Player:	10.00
Stars:	10X
Production 100 sets	

(See 1998 Bowman's Best for checklist and base card values.)

1998 Bowman's Best Autographs

This 10-card set offers autographs from five prospects and five veteran stars. Each card has on front the Topps "Certified Autograph Issue" logo for authentication.

	MT
Complete Set (10):	75.00
Common Player:	5.00
Inserted 1:180	
Refractors:	1.5X
Inserted 1:2,158	
Atomics:	2X
Inserted 1:6,437	

5 Chipper Jones 30.00
10 Chuck Knoblauch 7.50
15 Tony Clark 5.00
20 Albert Belle 10.00
25 Jose Cruz Jr. 5.00
105 Ben Grieve 6.00
110 Paul Konerko 5.00
115 Todd Helton 20.00
120 Adrian Beltre 5.00
125 Kerry Wood 10.00

1998 Bowman's Best Mirror Image Fusion

This 20-card die-cut insert features a veteran star on one side and a young player at the same position on the other. Regular versions are seeded one per 12 packs, while Refractors are found 1:809 packs and numbered within an edition of 100, and Atomic Refractors are a 1:3237 find numbered to 25. All have a "MI" prefix to the card number.

		MT
Complete Set (20):		60.00
Common Player (1:12):		.75
Refractor (1:809):		6X
Atomic Refractor (1:3237):		12X
1	Frank Thomas, David Ortiz	5.00
2	Chuck Knoblauch, Enrique Wilson	.75
3	Nomar Garciaparra, Miguel Tejada	5.00
4	Alex Rodriguez, Mike Caruso	5.00
5	Cal Ripken Jr., Ryan Minor	8.50
6	Ken Griffey Jr., Ben Grieve	8.50
7	Juan Gonzalez, Juan Encarnacion	2.75
8	Jose Cruz Jr., Ruben Mateo	2.00
9	Randy Johnson, Ryan Anderson	1.50
10	Ivan Rodriguez, A.J. Hinch	2.25
11	Jeff Bagwell, Paul Konerko	2.25
12	Mark McGwire, Travis Lee	13.50
13	Craig Biggio, Chad Hermanson	.75
14	Mark Grudzielanek, Alex Gonzalez	.75
15	Chipper Jones, Adrian Beltre	5.00
16	Larry Walker, Mark Kotsay	1.00
17	Tony Gwynn, Preston Wilson	5.00
18	Barry Bonds, Richard Hidalgo	4.00
19	Greg Maddux, Kerry Wood	5.00
20	Mike Piazza, Ben Petrick	7.50

1998 Bowman's Best Performers

Performers are 10 players who had the best minor league seasons in 1997. Regular versions were inserted one per six packs, while Refractors are seeded 1:809 and serially numbered to 200, and Atomic Refractors are 1:3237 and numbered to 50 sets. All versions have card numbers with a "BP" prefix.

		MT
Complete Set (10):		5.00
Common Player:		.35
Refractor (1:309):		3X
Atomic Refractor (1:3237):		5X
1	Ben Grieve	.75
2	Travis Lee	1.00
3	Ryan Minor	.35
4	Todd Helton	.75
5	Brad Fullmer	.50
6	Paul Konerko	.35
7	Adrian Beltre	.75
8	Richie Sexson	.35
9	Aramis Ramirez	.35
10	Russell Branyan	.35

1999 Bowman Pre-Production

Bowman's 1999 issue was introduced with this group of sample cards. Format is nearly identical to the issued cards, except for the use of a "PP" prefix to the card number on back.

		MT
Complete Set (6):		8.00
Common Player:		1.25
1	Andres Galarraga	1.25
2	Raul Mondesi	1.75
3	Vinny Castilla	1.25
4	Corey Koskie	2.00
5	Octavio Dotel	2.00
6	Dernell Stenson	2.50

1999 Bowman

The set was issued in two 220-card series, each comprised of 70 veterans and 150 rookies and prospects. Rookie/prospect cards have blue metallic foil highlights; veteran cards are highlighted with red foil. On each card is the player's facsimile autograph, reproduced from their initial Topps contract.

		MT
Complete Set (440):		100.00
Complete Series 1 (220):		45.00
Complete Series 2 (220):		55.00
Common Player:		.15
Series 1 Pack (10):		2.50
Series 1 Box (24):		45.00
Series 2 Pack (10):		3.50
Series 2 Box (24):		75.00
1	Ben Grieve	.25
2	Kerry Wood	.25
3	Ruben Rivera	.15
4	Sandy Alomar	.15
5	Cal Ripken Jr.	3.00
6	Mark McGwire	3.00
7	Vladimir Guerrero	1.00
8	Moises Alou	.25
9	Jim Edmonds	.15
10	Greg Maddux	1.50
11	Gary Sheffield	.40
12	John Valentin	.15
13	Chuck Knoblauch	.15
14	Tony Clark	.15
15	Rusty Greer	.15
16	Al Leiter	.25
17	Travis Lee	.15
18	Jose Cruz Jr.	.25
19	Pedro Martinez	.75
20	Paul O'Neill	.25
21	Todd Walker	.15
22	Vinny Castilla	.15
23	Barry Larkin	.25
24	Curt Schilling	.25
25	Jason Kendall	.15
26	Scott Erickson	.15
27	Andres Galarraga	.25
28	Jeff Shaw	.15
29	John Olerud	.25
30	Orlando Hernandez	.40
31	Larry Walker	.35
32	Andruw Jones	.75
33	Jeff Cirillo	.15
34	Barry Bonds	1.75
35	Manny Ramirez	1.00
36	Mark Kotsay	.15
37	Ivan Rodriguez	.75
38	Jeff King	.15
39	Brian Hunter	.15
40	Ray Durham	.15
41	Bernie Williams	.50
42	Darin Erstad	.40
43	Chipper Jones	2.00
44	Pat Hentgen	.15
45	Eric Young	.15
46	Jaret Wright	.15
47	Juan Guzman	.15
48	Jorge Posada	.25
49	Bobby Higginson	.20
50	Jose Guillen	.15
51	Trevor Hoffman	.15
52	Ken Griffey Jr.	2.50
53	David Justice	.40
54	Matt Williams	.35
55	Eric Karros	.15
56	Derek Bell	.15
57	Ray Lankford	.15
58	Mariano Rivera	.25
59	Brett Tomko	.15
60	Mike Mussina	.65
61	Kenny Lofton	.20
62	Chuck Finley	.15
63	Alex Gonzalez	.20
64	Mark Grace	.40
65	Raul Mondesi	.25
66	David Cone	.15
67	Brad Fullmer	.15
68	Andy Benes	.15
69	John Smoltz	.20
70	Shane Reynolds	.15
71	Bruce Chen	.15
72	Adam Kennedy	.15
73	Jack Cust	.15
74	Matt Clement	.15
75	Derrick Gibson	.15
76	Darnell McDonald	.15
77	*Adam Everett*	.50
78	Ricardo Aramboles	.15
79	*Mark Quinn*	1.00
80	Jason Rakers	.15
81	*Seth Etherton*	.50
82	*Jeff Urban*	.50
83	Manny Aybar	.15
84	*Mike Nannini*	1.00
85	Onan Masaoka	.15
86	Rod Barajas	.15
87	Mike Frank	.15
88	Scott Randall	.15
89	*Justin Bowles*	.50
90	Chris Haas	.15
91	*Arturo McDowell*	.50
92	*Matt Belisle*	.50
93	Scott Elarton	.15
94	Vernon Wells	.20
95	Pat Cline	.15
96	Ryan Anderson	.35
97	Kevin Barker	.15
98	Ruben Mateo	.15
99	Robert Fick	.15
100	Corey Koskie	.15
101	Ricky Ledee	.15
102	*Rick Elder*	.75
103	*Jack Cressend*	.50
104	Joe Lawrence	.15
105	Mike Lincoln	.15
106	*Kit Pellow*	1.00
107	*Matt Burch*	.50
108	Brent Butler	.15
109	Jason Dewey	.15
110	Cesar King	.15
111	Julio Ramirez	.15
112	Jake Westbrook	.15
113	*Eric Valent*	1.50
114	*Roosevelt Brown*	.75
115	*Choo Freeman*	.75
116	Juan Melo	.15
117	Jason Grilli	.15
118	Jared Sandberg	.15
119	Glenn Davis	.15
120	*David Riske*	.50
121	Jacque Jones	.15
122	Corey Lee	.15
123	Michael Barrett	.15
124	Lariel Gonzalez	.15
125	Mitch Meluskey	.15
126	Freddy Garcia	.25
127	*Tony Torcato*	1.00
128	Jeff Liefer	.15
129	Ntema Ndungidi	.15
130	*Andy Brown*	.50
131	*Ryan Mills*	.75
132	*Andy Abad*	.50
133	Carlos Febles	.15
134	*Jason Tyner*	.50
135	Mark Osborne	.15
136	*Phil Norton*	.50
137	Nathan Haynes	.15
138	Roy Halladay	.15
139	Juan Encarnacion	.15
140	Brad Penny	.15
141	Grant Roberts	.15
142	Aramis Ramirez	.15
143	Cristian Guzman	.15
144	*Mamon Tucker*	.50
145	Ryan Bradley	.15
146	Brian Simmons	.15
147	Dan Reichert	.15
148	Russ Branyon	.15
149	*Victor Valencia*	.40
150	Scott Schoeneweis	.15
151	*Sean Spencer*	.40
152	Odalis Perez	.15
153	Joe Fontenot	.15
154	Milton Bradley	.15
155	*Josh McKinley*	.25
156	Terrence Long	.15
157	Danny Klassen	.15
158	*Paul Hoover*	.25
159	Ron Belliard	.15
160	Armando Rios	.15
161	Ramon Hernandez	.15
162	Jason Conti	.15
163	Chad Hermansen	.15
164	Jason Standridge	.15
165	Jason Dellaero	.15
166	John Curtice	.15
167	*Clayton Andrews*	.25
168	Jeremy Giambi	.15
169	Alex Ramirez	.15
170	*Gabe Molina*	.25
171	*Mario Encarnacion*	.25
172	*Mike Zywica*	.25
173	*Chip Ambres*	.50
174	Trot Nixon	.15
175	*Pat Burrell*	4.00
176	Jeff Yoder	.15
177	*Chris Jones*	.50

No.	Player	Value
178	Kevin Witt	.15
179	*Keith Luuloa*	.25
180	Billy Koch	.15
181	*Damaso Marte*	.25
182	*Ryan Glynn*	.25
183	Calvin Pickering	.15
184	Michael Cuddyer	.15
185	*Nick Johnson*	5.00
186	*Doug Mientkiewicz*	1.50
187	*Nate Cornejo*	.50
188	Octavio Dotel	.15
189	Wes Helms	.15
190	Nelson Lara	.15
191	*Chuck Abbott*	.25
192	Tony Armas Jr.	.15
193	Gil Meche	.15
194	Ben Petrick	.15
195	*Chris George*	.25
196	*Scott Hunter*	.50
197	Ryan Brannan	.15
198	*Amaury Garcia*	.25
199	Chris Gissell	.15
200	*Austin Kearns*	7.00
201	Alex Gonzalez	.15
202	Wade Miller	.15
203	Scott Williamson	.15
204	Chris Enochs	.15
205	Fernando Seguignol	.15
206	Marlon Anderson	.15
207	*Todd Sears*	.50
208	*Nate Bump*	.25
209	*J.M. Gold*	.25
210	Matt LeCroy	.15
211	Alex Hernandez	.15
212	Luis Rivera	.15
213	Troy Cameron	.15
214	*Alex Escobar*	1.50
215	Jason LaRue	.15
216	Kyle Peterson	.15
217	Brent Butler	.15
218	Dernell Stenson	.15
219	Adrian Beltre	.30
220	Daryle Ward	.15
----	Series 1 Checklist Folder	.10
221	Jim Thome	.15
222	Cliff Floyd	.15
223	Rickey Henderson	.60
224	Garret Anderson	.15
225	Ken Caminiti	.15
226	Bret Boone	.25
227	Jeromy Burnitz	.15
228	Steve Finley	.15
229	Miguel Tejada	.25
230	Greg Vaughn	.15
231	Jose Offerman	.15
232	Andy Ashby	.15
233	Albert Belle	.35
234	Fernando Tatis	.15
235	Todd Helton	.75
236	Sean Casey	.25
237	Brian Giles	.15
238	Andy Pettitte	.25
239	Fred McGriff	.15
240	Roberto Alomar	.60
241	Edgar Martinez	.15
242	Lee Stevens	.15
243	Shawn Green	.30
244	Ryan Klesko	.15
245	Sammy Sosa	1.75
246	Todd Hundley	.15
247	Shannon Stewart	.20
248	Randy Johnson	.75
249	Rondell White	.25
250	Mike Piazza	2.00
251	Craig Biggio	.20
252	David Wells	.20
253	Brian Jordan	.15
254	Edgar Renteria	.15
255	Bartolo Colon	.15
256	Frank Thomas	2.00
257	Will Clark	.35
258	Dean Palmer	.15
259	Dmitri Young	.15
260	Scott Rolen	.75
261	Jeff Kent	.15
262	Dante Bichette	.15
263	Nomar Garciaparra	1.75
264	Tony Gwynn	1.50
265	Alex Rodriguez	2.50
266	Jose Canseco	.45
267	Jason Giambi	.50
268	Jeff Bagwell	.75
269	Carlos Delgado	.35
270	Tom Glavine	.20
271	Eric Davis	.15
272	Edgardo Alfonzo	.15
273	Tim Salmon	.25
274	Johnny Damon	.20
275	Rafael Palmeiro	.35
276	Denny Neagle	.15
277	Neifi Perez	.15
278	Roger Clemens	1.50
279	Brant Brown	.15
280	Kevin Brown	.25
281	Jay Bell	.15
282	Jay Buhner	.15
283	Matt Lawton	.15
284	Robin Ventura	.15
285	Juan Gonzalez	.75
286	Mo Vaughn	.45
287	Kevin Millwood	.15
288	Tino Martinez	.15
289	Justin Thompson	.15
290	Derek Jeter	2.00
291	Ben Davis	.15
292	Mike Lowell	.15
293	*Joe Crede*	2.00
294	*Micah Bowie*	.25
295	Lance Berkman	.25
296	Jason Marquis	.15
297	Chad Green	.15
298	Dee Brown	.15
299	Jerry Hairston Jr.	.15
300	Gabe Kapler	.15
301	*Brent Stentz*	.50
302	*Scott Mullen*	.50
303	Brandon Reed	.15
304	*Shea Hillenbrand*	4.00
305	*J.D. Closser*	.50
306	Gary Matthews Jr.	.15
307	*Toby Hall*	1.50
308	*Jason Phillips*	.25
309	*Jose Macias*	.50
310	*Jung Bong*	.50
311	*Ramon Soler*	.50
312	*Kelly Dransfeldt*	.25
313	*Carlos Hernandez*	.25
314	Kevin Haverbusch	.15
315	*Aaron Myette*	.50
316	*Chad Harville*	.75
317	*Kyle Farnsworth*	1.00
318	*Travis Dawkins*	.50
319	Willie Martinez	.15
320	Carlos Lee	.15
321	*Carlos Pena*	2.50
322	*Peter Bergeron*	.50
323	*A.J. Burnett*	.75
324	*Bucky Jacobsen*	.25
325	*Mo Bruce*	.25
326	Reggie Taylor	.15
327	Jackie Rexrode	.15
328	*Alvin Morrow*	.25
329	Carlos Beltran	.25
330	Eric Chavez	.25
331	John Patterson	.15
332	Jayson Werth	.15
333	Richie Sexson	.15
334	Randy Wolf	.15
335	Eli Marrero	.15
336	Paul LoDuca	.15
337	J.D. Smart	.15
338	Ryan Minor	.15
339	Kris Benson	.15
340	George Lombard	.15
341	Troy Glaus	1.00
342	Eddie Yarnell	.15
343	*Kip Wells*	.75
344	*C.C. Sabathia*	3.00
345	*Sean Burroughs*	5.00
346	*Felipe Lopez*	1.50
347	*Ryan Rupe*	.50
348	*Orber Moreno*	.25
349	*Rafael Roque*	.25
350	*Alfonso Soriano*	12.00
351	Pablo Ozuna	.15
352	*Corey Patterson*	3.00
353	Braden Looper	.15
354	Robbie Bell	.15
355	*Mark Mulder*	4.00
356	Angel Pena	.15
357	Kevin McGlinchy	.15
358	*Michael Restovich*	1.00
359	Eric DuBose	.15
360	Geoff Jenkins	.15
361	*Mark Harriger*	.60
362	*Junior Herndon*	.25
363	*Tim Raines Jr.*	.25
364	*Rafael Furcal*	2.00
365	*Marcus Giles*	2.00
366	Ted Lilly	.15
367	*Jorge Toca*	.50
368	*David Kelton*	.75
369	*Adam Dunn*	10.00
370	*Guillermo Mota*	.50
371	*Brett Laxton*	.25
372	*Travis Harper*	.25
373	*Tom Davey*	.25
374	*Darren Blakely*	.50
375	*Tim Hudson*	4.00
376	Jason Romano	.15
377	Dan Reichert	.15
378	*Julio Lugo*	.75
379	*Jose Garcia*	.25
380	*Erubiel Durazo*	1.50
381	Jose Jimenez	.15
382	Chris Fussell	.15
383	Steve Lomasney	.15
384	*Juan Pena*	.50
385	*Allen Levrault*	.25
386	*Juan Rivera*	1.50
387	*Steve Colyer*	.25
388	*Joe Nathan*	.75
389	*Ron Walker*	.15
390	Nick Bierbrodt	.15
391	*Luke Prokopec*	.50
392	*Dave Roberts*	.50
393	Mike Darr	.15
394	*Abraham Nunez*	1.50
395	*Giuseppe Chiaramonte*	.75
396	*Jermaine Van Buren*	.25
397	Mike Kusiewicz	.15
398	*Matt Wise*	.25
399	*Joe McEwing*	.50
400	*Matt Holliday*	.50
401	*Willi Mo Pena*	1.50
402	*Ruben Quevedo*	.25
403	*Rob Ryan*	.25
404	*Freddy Garcia*	4.00
405	*Kevin Eberwein*	.25
406	*Jesus Colome*	.75
407	*Chris Singleton*	.50
408	*Bubba Crosby*	.25
409	*Jesus Cordero*	.25
410	Donny Leon	.15
411	*Goefrey Tomlinson*	.15
412	*Jeff Winchester*	.25
413	*Adam Piatt*	1.50
414	Robert Stratton	.15
415	T.J. Tucker	.15
416	*Ryan Langerhans*	.25
417	*Anthony Shumaker*	.25
418	*Matt Miller*	.25
419	*Doug Clark*	.25
420	*Kory DeHaan*	.15
421	*David Eckstein*	1.50
422	*Brian Cooper*	.50
423	*Brady Clark*	.25
424	*Chris Magruder*	.25
425	*Bobby Seay*	.25
426	*Aubrey Huff*	.75
427	Mike Jerzembeck	.15
428	*Matt Blank*	.50
429	*Benny Agbayani*	.75
430	*Kevin Beirne*	.15
431	*Josh Hamilton*	6.00
432	*Josh Girdley*	.75
433	*Kyle Snyder*	.15
434	*Mike Paradis*	.25
435	*Jason Jennings*	.75
436	*David Walling*	.75
437	*Omar Ortiz*	.25
438	*Jay Gehrke*	.25
439	*Casey Burns*	.25
440	*Carl Crawford*	2.00

1999 Bowman International

International parallels are a one-per-pack insert. Fronts are printed in metallic silver on which the photo's background has been replaced with a scenic picture supposed to be indicative of the player's native land. That location is spelled out at the lower-left corner of the photo. Backs of the Internationals are printed in the player's native language.

	MT
Complete Set (220):	150.00
Common Player:	.25
Int'l Stars:	1.5X

(See 1999 Bowman for checklist and base card values.)

1999 Bowman Gold

Gold, rather than black, ink for the facsimile autograph, Bowman logo and player name on front, and a serial number on back from within an edition of 99, designate these parallels. Stated odds of finding the Gold cards were one per 111 packs of Series 1, and 1:59 in Series 2.

	MT
Common Player:	3.00
Gold Stars:	10X

(See 1999 Bowman for checklist and base card values.)

1999 Bowman Autographs

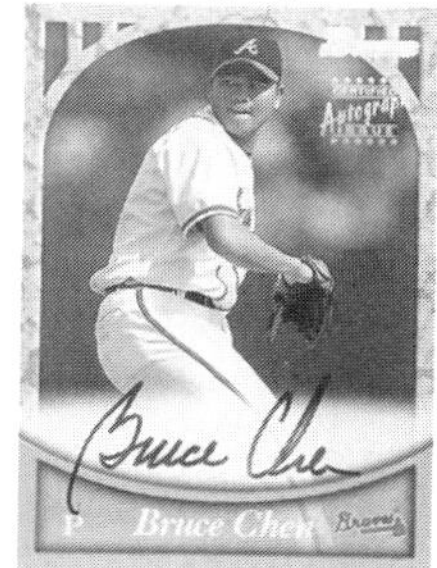

Autographs were randomly seeded in Series 1 and 2 packs, with each card bearing a Topps Certified Autograph seal on the front and numbered with a "BA" prefix on back. Levels of scarcity are color coded by the metallic-foil highlights on front: Golds are the most difficult to find at 1:1941 Series 1 packs and 1:1024 Series 2. Silvers are seeded 1:485 in Series 1, 1:256 Series 2. Blues are found at an average rate of 1:162 in first series and 1:85 in second series.

		MT
Common Player:		3.00
Blues inserted 1:162 or 1:85		
Silvers inserted 1:485 or 1:256		
Golds inserted 1:1954 or 1:1024		
1	Ruben Mateo B	7.50
2	Troy Glaus G	100.00
3	Ben Davis G	15.00
4	Jayson Werth B	10.00
5	Jerry Hairston Jr. S	10.00
6	Darnell McDonald B	7.50
7	Calvin Pickering S	10.00
8	Ryan Minor S	7.50
9	Alex Escobar B	10.00
10	Grant Roberts B	7.50
11	Carlos Guillen B	7.50
12	Ryan Anderson S	20.00
13	Gil Meche S	15.00
14	Russell Branyan S	6.50
15	Alex Ramirez S	15.00
16	Jason Rakers S	7.50
17	Eddie Yarnall B	7.50
18	Freddy Garcia B	20.00
19	Jason Conti B	3.00
20	Corey Koskie B	8.00
21	Roosevelt Brown B	8.00
22	Willie Martinez B	3.00
23	Mike Jerzembeck B	3.00
24	Lariel Gonzalez B	3.00
25	Fernando Seguignol B	5.00
26	Robert Fick S	10.00
27	J.D. Smart B	3.00
28	Ryan Mills B	3.00
29	Chad Hermansen G	10.00
30	Jason Grilli B	8.00
31	Michael Cuddyer B	7.50
32	Jacque Jones S	15.00
33	Reggie Taylor B	3.00
34	Richie Sexson G	20.00
35	Michael Barrett B	12.00
36	Paul LoDuca B	12.00
37	Adrian Beltre G	20.00
38	Peter Bergeron B	10.00
39	Joe Fontenot B	4.00
40	Randy Wolf B	10.00
41	Nick Johnson B	20.00
42	Ryan Bradley B	10.00
43	Mike Lowell S	10.00
44	Ricky Ledee B	10.00
45	Mike Lincoln S	6.50
46	Jeremy Giambi B	10.00
47	Dermal Brown S	3.00
48	Derrick Gibson B	5.00
49	Scott Randall B	3.00
50	Ben Petrick S	10.00
51	Jason LaRue B	3.00
52	Cole Liniak B	5.00
53	John Curtice B	3.00
54	Jackie Rexrode B	3.00
55	John Patterson B	10.00
56	Brad Penny S	10.00
57	Jared Sandberg B	8.00
58	Kerry Wood G	35.00
59	Eli Marrero B	7.00
60	Jason Marquis B	15.00
61	George Lombard S	7.50
62	Bruce Chen S	5.00
63	Kevin Witt S	6.00
64	Vernon Wells B	15.00
65	Billy Koch B	3.00
66	Roy Halladay B	20.00
67	Nathan Haynes B	3.00
68	Ben Grieve G	15.00
69	Eric Chavez G	15.00
70	Lance Berkman S	25.00

1999 Bowman Late Bloomers

This 10-card set features late-round picks from previous drafts who have emerged as bona fide stars. These inserts are numbered with an "LB" prefix.

		MT
Complete Set (10):		6.00
Common Player:		.25
Inserted 1:12		
LB1	Mike Piazza	3.00
LB2	Jim Thome	.25
LB3	Larry Walker	.75
LB4	Vinny Castilla	.25
LB5	Andy Pettitte	.75
LB6	Jim Edmonds	.50
LB7	Kenny Lofton	.25
LB8	John Smoltz	.40
LB9	Mark Grace	.75
LB10	Trevor Hoffman	.25

1999 Bowman Scout's Choice

Scout's Choice inserts were randomly inserted in Series 1 packs and feature a borderless, double-etched design. The 21-card set focuses on prospects who have potential to win a future Rookie of the Year award.

		MT
Complete Set (21):		20.00
Common Player:		.50
Inserted 1:12		
SC1	Ruben Mateo	1.00
SC2	Ryan Anderson	2.00
SC3	Pat Burrell	4.00
SC4	Troy Glaus	5.00
SC5	Eric Chavez	2.50
SC6	Adrian Beltre	1.25
SC7	Bruce Chen	.50
SC8	Carlos Beltran	.75
SC9	Alex Gonzalez	.50
SC10	Carlos Lee	1.00
SC11	George Lombard	.50
SC12	Matt Clement	.50
SC13	Calvin Pickering	.50
SC14	Marlon Anderson	.50
SC15	Chad Hermansen	.50
SC16	Russell Branyan	.50
SC17	Jeremy Giambi	.50
SC18	Ricky Ledee	.50
SC19	John Patterson	.50
SC20	Roy Halladay	1.00
SC21	Michael Barrett	.75

1999 Bowman 2000 Rookie of the Year

Randomly inserted in Series 2 packs, these cards have a borderless, double-etched foil design. The 10-card set focuses on players that have potential to win the 2000 Rookie of the Year award.

		MT
Complete Set (10):		10.00
Common Player:		.50
Inserted 1:12		
1	Ryan Anderson	1.00
2	Pat Burrell	2.00
3	A.J. Burnett	.50
4	Ruben Mateo	.75
5	Alex Escobar	1.25
6	Pablo Ozuna	.50
7	Mark Mulder	1.00
8	Corey Patterson	1.75
9	George Lombard	.50
10	Nick Johnson	2.50

1999 Bowman Early Risers

This insert set features 11 current baseball superstars who have already won a Rookie of the Year award and who continue to excel. Cards have an "ER" prefix to the number on back.

		MT
Complete Set (11):		11.00
Common Player:		.50
Inserted 1:12		
1	Mike Piazza	2.00
2	Cal Ripken Jr.	2.50
3	Jeff Bagwell	1.00
4	Ben Grieve	.50
5	Kerry Wood	.50
6	Mark McGwire	2.50
7	Nomar Garciaparra	1.50
8	Derek Jeter	2.00
9	Scott Rolen	.60
10	Jose Canseco	.50
11	Raul Mondesi	.50

1999 Bowman Chrome

Bowman Chrome was released in two 220-card series as an upscale chromium parallel version of Bowman Baseball. Like Bowman, each series has 150 prospect cards with blue foil, while 70 veteran cards have red foil. Packs contain four cards with an original SRP of $3.

		MT
Complete Set (440):		325.00
Complete Series 1 (220):		100.00
Complete Series 2 (220):		250.00
Common Player:		.25
Series 1 Pack (4):		4.00
Series 1 Wax Box (24):		80.00
Series 2 Pack (4):		12.00
Series 2 Wax Box (24):		275.00
1	Ben Grieve	.50
2	Kerry Wood	.45
3	Ruben Rivera	.25
4	Sandy Alomar	.25
5	Cal Ripken Jr.	4.00
6	Mark McGwire	4.00
7	Vladimir Guerrero	1.50
8	Moises Alou	.35
9	Jim Edmonds	.25
10	Greg Maddux	2.00
11	Gary Sheffield	.45
12	John Valentin	.25
13	Chuck Knoblauch	.25
14	Tony Clark	.25
15	Rusty Greer	.25
16	Al Leiter	.25
17	Travis Lee	.25
18	Jose Cruz Jr.	.35
19	Pedro Martinez	1.00
20	Paul O'Neill	.25
21	Todd Walker	.25
22	Vinny Castilla	.25
23	Barry Larkin	.30
24	Curt Schilling	.40
25	Jason Kendall	.25
26	Scott Erickson	.25
27	Andres Galarraga	.25
28	Jeff Shaw	.25
29	John Olerud	.25
30	Orlando Hernandez	.50
31	Larry Walker	.45
32	Andruw Jones	1.50
33	Jeff Cirillo	.25

No.	Player	Price
34	Barry Bonds	2.50
35	Manny Ramirez	1.50
36	Mark Kotsay	.25
37	Ivan Rodriguez	1.25
38	Jeff King	.25
39	Brian Hunter	.25
40	Ray Durham	.25
41	Bernie Williams	.40
42	Darin Erstad	1.00
43	Chipper Jones	3.00
44	Pat Hentgen	.25
45	Eric Young	.25
46	Jaret Wright	.25
47	Juan Guzman	.25
48	Jorge Posada	.25
49	Bobby Higginson	.25
50	Jose Guillen	.25
51	Trevor Hoffman	.25
52	Ken Griffey Jr.	3.50
53	David Justice	.45
54	Matt Williams	.40
55	Eric Karros	.25
56	Derek Bell	.25
57	Ray Lankford	.25
58	Mariano Rivera	.50
59	Brett Tomko	.25
60	Mike Mussina	.75
61	Kenny Lofton	.25
62	Chuck Finley	.25
63	Alex Gonzalez	.25
64	Mark Grace	.50
65	Raul Mondesi	.30
66	David Cone	.25
67	Brad Fullmer	.30
68	Andy Benes	.25
69	John Smoltz	.30
70	Shane Reynolds	.25
71	Bruce Chen	.25
72	Adam Kennedy	.25
73	Jack Cust	.25
74	Matt Clement	.25
75	Derrick Gibson	.25
76	Darnell McDonald	.25
77	*Adam Everett*	1.00
78	Ricardo Aramboles	.25
79	*Mark Quinn*	2.00
80	Jason Rakers	.25
81	*Seth Etherton*	.75
82	*Jeff Urban*	.75
83	Manny Aybar	.25
84	*Mike Nannini*	1.75
85	Onan Masaoka	.25
86	Rod Barajas	.25
87	Mike Frank	.25
88	Scott Randall	.25
89	*Justin Bowles*	.50
90	Chris Haas	.25
91	*Arturo McDowell*	.50
92	*Matt Belisle*	.50
93	Scott Elarton	.25
94	Vernon Wells	.30
95	Pat Cline	.25
96	Ryan Anderson	.50
97	Kevin Barker	.25
98	Ruben Mateo	.25
99	Robert Fick	.25
100	Corey Koskie	.25
101	Ricky Ledee	.25
102	*Rick Elder*	2.00
103	*Jack Cressend*	.75
104	Joe Lawrence	.25
105	Mike Lincoln	.25
106	*Kit Pellow*	1.50
107	*Matt Burch*	.50
108	Brent Butler	.25
109	Jason Dewey	.25
110	Cesar King	.25
111	Julio Ramirez	.25
112	Jake Westbrook	.25
113	*Eric Valent*	1.50
114	*Roosevelt Brown*	.50
115	*Choo Freeman*	2.50
116	Juan Melo	.25
117	Jason Grilli	.25
118	Jared Sandberg	.25
119	Glenn Davis	.25
120	*David Riske*	.75
121	Jacque Jones	.25
122	Corey Lee	.25
123	Michael Barrett	.25
124	Lariel Gonzalez	.25
125	Mitch Meluskey	.25
126	*Freddy Garcia*	.25
127	*Tony Torcato*	2.00
128	Jeff Liefer	.25
129	Ntema Ndungidi	.25
130	*Andy Brown*	1.25
131	*Ryan Mills*	.50
132	*Andy Abad*	.75
133	Carlos Febles	.25
134	*Jason Tyner*	.75
135	Mark Osborne	.25
136	*Phil Norton*	.50
137	Nathan Haynes	.25
138	Roy Halladay	.25
139	Juan Encarnacion	.35
140	Brad Penny	.25
141	Grant Roberts	.25
142	Aramis Ramirez	.25
143	Cristian Guzman	.25
144	*Mamon Tucker*	.50
145	Ryan Bradley	.25
146	Brian Simmons	.25
147	Dan Reichert	.25
148	Russ Branyon	.25
149	*Victor Valencia*	.50
150	Scott Schoeneweis	.25
151	*Sean Spencer*	.50
152	Odalis Perez	.25
153	Joe Fontenot	.25
154	Milton Bradley	.25
155	*Josh McKinley*	.50
156	Terrence Long	.25
157	Danny Klassen	.25
158	*Paul Hoover*	.50
159	Ron Belliard	.25
160	Armando Rios	.25
161	Ramon Hernandez	.25
162	Jason Conti	.25
163	Chad Hermansen	.25
164	Jason Standridge	.25
165	Jason Dellaero	.25
166	John Curtice	.25
167	*Clayton Andrews*	.50
168	Jeremy Giambi	.25
169	Alex Ramirez	.25
170	*Gabe Molina*	.50
171	*Mario Encarnacion*	.50
172	*Mike Zywica*	.25
173	*Chip Ambres*	.75
174	Trot Nixon	.25
175	*Pat Burrell*	20.00
176	Jeff Yoder	.25
177	*Chris Jones*	.85
178	Kevin Witt	.25
179	*Keith Luuloa*	.50
180	Billy Koch	.25
181	*Damaso Marte*	.50
182	*Ryan Glynn*	.50
183	Calvin Pickering	.25
184	Michael Cuddyer	.25
185	*Nick Johnson*	15.00
186	*Doug Mientkiewicz*	2.50
187	*Nate Cornejo*	2.50
188	Octavio Dotel	.25
189	Wes Helms	.25
190	Nelson Lara	.25
191	*Chuck Abbott*	.50
192	Tony Armas Jr.	.25
193	Gil Meche	.25
194	Ben Petrick	.25
195	*Chris George*	3.00
196	*Scott Hunter*	.85
197	Ryan Brannan	.25
198	*Amaury Garcia*	.50
199	Chris Gissell	.25
200	*Austin Kearns*	25.00
201	Alex Gonzalez	.25
202	Wade Miller	.25
203	Scott Williamson	.25
204	Chris Enochs	.25
205	Fernando Seguignol	.25
206	Marlon Anderson	.25
207	*Todd Sears*	1.50
208	*Nate Bump*	.50
209	*J.M. Gold*	.50
210	*Matt LeCroy*	.25
211	Alex Hernandez	.25
212	Luis Rivera	.25
213	Troy Cameron	.25
214	*Alex Escobar*	2.00
215	Jason LaRue	.25
216	Kyle Peterson	.25
217	Brent Butler	.25
218	Dernell Stenson	.25
219	Adrian Beltre	.50
220	Daryle Ward	.25
221	Jim Thome	.25
222	Cliff Floyd	.25
223	Rickey Henderson	.75
224	Garret Anderson	.25
225	Ken Caminiti	.25
226	Bret Boone	.30
227	Jeromy Burnitz	.25
228	Steve Finley	.25
229	Miguel Tejada	.25
230	Greg Vaughn	.25
231	Jose Offerman	.25
232	Andy Ashby	.25
233	Albert Belle	.40
234	Fernando Tatis	.25
235	Todd Helton	1.00
236	Sean Casey	.75
237	Brian Giles	.25
238	Andy Pettitte	.40
239	Fred McGriff	.25
240	Roberto Alomar	.75
241	Edgar Martinez	.25
242	Lee Stevens	.25
243	Shawn Green	.35
244	Ryan Klesko	.25
245	Sammy Sosa	2.50
246	Todd Hundley	.25
247	Shannon Stewart	.35
248	Randy Johnson	1.00
249	Rondell White	.35
250	Mike Piazza	3.00
251	Craig Biggio	.30
252	David Wells	.25
253	Brian Jordan	.25
254	Edgar Renteria	.25
255	Bartolo Colon	.25
256	Frank Thomas	2.50
257	Will Clark	.40
258	Dean Palmer	.25
259	Dmitri Young	.25
260	Scott Rolen	1.00
261	Jeff Kent	.25
262	Dante Bichette	.25
263	Nomar Garciaparra	2.50
264	Tony Gwynn	2.00
265	Alex Rodriguez	3.50
266	Jose Canseco	.45
267	Jason Giambi	1.00
268	Jeff Bagwell	1.50
269	Carlos Delgado	.50
270	Tom Glavine	.30
271	Eric Davis	.25
272	Edgardo Alfonzo	.25
273	Tim Salmon	.40
274	Johnny Damon	.35
275	Rafael Palmeiro	.40
276	Denny Neagle	.25
277	Neifi Perez	.25
278	Roger Clemens	2.00
279	Brant Brown	.25
280	Kevin Brown	.35
281	Jay Bell	.25
282	Jay Buhner	.25
283	Matt Lawton	.25
284	Robin Ventura	.25
285	Juan Gonzalez	1.50
286	Mo Vaughn	.50
287	Kevin Millwood	.25
288	Tino Martinez	.25
289	Justin Thompson	.25
290	Derek Jeter	4.00
291	Ben Davis	.25
292	Mike Lowell	.25
293	*Joe Crede*	5.00
294	*Micah Bowie*	.50
295	Lance Berkman	.35
296	Jason Marquis	.25
297	Chad Green	.25
298	Dee Brown	.25
299	Jerry Hairston Jr.	.25
300	Gabe Kapler	.35
301	*Brent Stentz*	.85
302	*Scott Mullen*	.85
303	Brandon Reed	.25
304	*Shea Hillenbrand*	15.00
305	*J.D. Closser*	2.00
306	Gary Matthews Jr.	.25
307	*Toby Hall*	4.00
308	*Jason Phillips*	.50
309	*Jose Macias*	.85
310	*Jung Bong*	2.00
311	*Ramon Soler*	.75
312	*Kelly Dransfeldt*	.75
313	*Carlos Hernandez*	.50
314	Kevin Haverbusch	.25
315	*Aaron Myette*	.85
316	*Chad Harville*	.75
317	*Kyle Farnsworth*	2.00
318	*Travis Dawkins*	.85
319	Willie Martinez	.25
320	Carlos Lee	.25
321	*Carlos Pena*	10.00
322	*Peter Bergeron*	1.00
323	*A.J. Burnett*	5.00
324	*Bucky Jacobsen*	.50
325	*Mo Bruce*	.50
326	Reggie Taylor	.25
327	Jackie Rexrode	.25
328	*Alvin Morrow*	.50
329	Carlos Beltran	.25
330	Eric Chavez	.50
331	John Patterson	.25
332	Jayson Werth	.25
333	Richie Sexson	.25
334	Randy Wolf	.25
335	Eli Marrero	.25
336	Paul LoDuca	.25
337	J.D. Smart	.25
338	Ryan Minor	.25
339	Kris Benson	.25
340	George Lombard	.25
341	Troy Glaus	2.00
342	Eddie Yarnell	.25
343	*Kip Wells*	2.00
344	*C.C. Sabathia*	8.00
345	*Sean Burroughs*	15.00
346	*Felipe Lopez*	6.00
347	*Ryan Rupe*	.75
348	*Orber Moreno*	.50
349	*Rafael Roque*	.50
350	*Alfonso Soriano*	55.00
351	Pablo Ozuna	.25
352	*Corey Patterson*	15.00
353	Braden Looper	.25
354	Robbie Bell	.25
355	*Mark Mulder*	12.00
356	Angel Pena	.25
357	Kevin McGlinchy	.25
358	*Michael Restovich*	4.00
359	Eric DuBose	.25
360	Geoff Jenkins	.25
361	*Mark Harriger*	.50
362	*Junior Herndon*	.50
363	*Tim Raines Jr.*	.50
364	*Rafael Furcal*	4.00
365	*Marcus Giles*	4.00
366	Ted Lilly	.25
367	*Jorge Toca*	.85
368	*David Kelton*	4.00
369	*Adam Dunn*	40.00
370	*Guillermo Mota*	.50
371	*Brett Laxton*	.50
372	*Travis Harper*	.50
373	*Tom Davey*	.50
374	*Darren Blakely*	.85
375	*Tim Hudson*	15.00
376	Jason Romano	.25
377	Dan Reichert	.25
378	*Julio Lugo*	1.00
379	*Jose Garcia*	.50
380	*Erubiel Durazo*	6.00
381	Jose Jimenez	.25
382	Chris Fussell	.25
383	Steve Lomasney	.25
384	*Juan Pena*	.85
385	*Allen Levrault*	2.00
386	*Juan Rivera*	6.00
387	*Steve Colyer*	.50
388	*Joe Nathan*	1.00
389	*Ron Walker*	.50
390	Nick Bierbrodt	.25
391	*Luke Prokopec*	1.00
392	*Dave Roberts*	.75
393	Mike Darr	.25
394	*Abraham Nunez*	5.00
395	*Giuseppe Chiaramonte*	1.00
396	*Jermaine Van Buren*	.50
397	Mike Kusiewicz	.25
398	*Matt Wise*	.50
399	*Joe McEwing*	.85
400	*Matt Holliday*	1.50
401	*Willi Mo Pena*	8.00
402	*Ruben Quevedo*	2.00
403	*Rob Ryan*	.50
404	*Freddy Garcia*	8.00
405	*Kevin Eberwein*	.50
406	*Jesus Colome*	1.25
407	*Chris Singleton*	.85
408	*Bubba Crosby*	.50
409	*Jesus Cordero*	.50
410	Donny Leon	.25
411	*Goefrey Tomlinson*	.25
412	*Jeff Winchester*	.50
413	*Adam Piatt*	2.50
414	Robert Stratton	.25
415	T.J. Tucker	.25
416	*Ryan Langerhans*	.50
417	*Chris Wakeland*	.50
418	*Matt Miller*	.50
419	*Doug Clark*	.50
420	*Kory DeHaan*	.25
421	*David Eckstein*	4.00

422	*Brian Cooper*	.50
423	*Brady Clark*	.50
424	*Chris Magruder*	.50
425	*Bobby Seay*	.50
426	*Aubrey Huff*	1.25
427	Mike Jerzembeck	.25
428	*Matt Blank*	.85
429	*Benny Agbayani*	1.25
430	*Kevin Beirne*	.25
431	*Josh Hamilton*	15.00
432	*Josh Girdley*	1.25
433	*Kyle Snyder*	.25
434	*Mike Paradis*	.50
435	*Jason Jennings*	2.50
436	*David Walling*	1.25
437	*Omar Ortiz*	.50
438	*Jay Gehrke*	.50
439	*Casey Burns*	.50
440	*Carl Crawford*	7.00

1999 Bowman Chrome Refractors

Refractor versions of all Bowman Chrome base cards and inserts were also created. Base card Refractors are found at the average rate of one per 12 packs. Scout's Choice Refractors are a 1:48 find; International Refractors (serially numbered within an edition of 100 each) are 1:76 and Diamond Aces Refractors are 1:84.

	MT
Common Player:	1.00
Refractor Stars:	5X

(See 1999 Bowman Chrome for checklist and base card values.)

1999 Bowman Chrome International

Replacing the regular-card background with a scene from the player's native land gives this parallel issue an international flavor. For the geographically challenged, the place of birth is spelled out in the lower-left corner of the photo. In addition, the card backs are printed in the player's native language. Series 1 Internationals are found on the average of one per four packs, while the scarcer Series 2 Internationals are a 1:12 pick. Conversely, the Refractor version, individually numbered within an edition of 100 each is scarcer in Series 1 (1:76) than in Series 2 (1:50).

	MT
Complete Set (440):	600.00
Complete Series 1 (220):	200.00
Complete Series 2 (220):	400.00
Common Player, Series 1:	.25
Common Player, Series 2:	.50
Stars:	1.5X
Common Refractor:	5.00
Refractors:	12X

(See 1999 Bowman Chrome for checklist and base card values.)

1999 Bowman Chrome Gold

A gold, rather than black, facsimile signature differentiates this parallel from the base-card issue. At an average insertion rate of 1:12, the Series 1 Golds are twice as easy as the Series 2 (1:24). Conversely, a Refractor version which is limited to 25 serially numbered sets, is an easier pull in Series 2 (1:200) than in Series 1 (1:305).

	MT
Complete Set (440):	1000.
Complete Series 1 (220):	400.00
Complete Series 2 (220):	650.00
Common Player, Series 1:	1.50
Common Player, Series 2:	2.00
Stars:	3X
Gold Refractors:	30X

(See 1999 Bowman Chrome for checklist and base card values.)

1999 Bowman Chrome Diamond Aces

This 18-card set features nine emerging stars along with nine proven veterans. The cards have a prismatic look with "Diamond Aces" across the top. They are inserted in Series 1 packs. A parallel Refractor version is also randomly inserted.

		MT
Complete Set (18):		50.00
Common Player:		1.50
Inserted 1:21		
Refractors:		1.5X
Inserted 1:84		
DA1	Troy Glaus	4.00
DA2	Eric Chavez	2.00
DA3	Fernando Seguignol	1.50
DA4	Ryan Anderson	2.50
DA5	Ruben Mateo	1.50
DA6	Carlos Beltran	1.50
DA7	Adrian Beltre	2.00
DA8	Bruce Chen	1.50
DA9	Pat Burrell	4.00
DA10	Mike Piazza	5.00
DA11	Ken Griffey Jr.	6.00
DA12	Chipper Jones	5.00
DA13	Derek Jeter	5.00
DA14	Mark McGwire	7.50
DA15	Nomar Garciaparra	4.50
DA16	Sammy Sosa	4.00
DA17	Juan Gonzalez	2.00
DA18	Alex Rodriguez	6.00

1999 Bowman Chrome Scout's Choice

This is a chromium parallel of the inserts found in Series 1 Bowman. The 21-card set showcases prospects that have potential to win a future Rookie of the Year award. Refractor parallels are also randomly inserted.

		MT
Complete Set (21):		37.50
Common Player:		1.00
Inserted 1:12		
Refractors:		1.5X
Inserted 1:48		
SC1	Ruben Mateo	1.50
SC2	Ryan Anderson	2.00
SC3	Pat Burrell	5.00
SC4	Troy Glaus	6.00
SC5	Eric Chavez	4.00
SC6	Adrian Beltre	2.00
SC7	Bruce Chen	1.00
SC8	Carlos Beltran	1.50
SC9	Alex Gonzalez	1.00
SC10	Carlos Lee	1.00
SC11	George Lombard	1.00
SC12	Matt Clement	1.00
SC13	Calvin Pickering	1.00
SC14	Marlon Anderson	1.00
SC15	Chad Hermansen	1.00
SC16	Russell Branyan	1.00
SC17	Jeremy Giambi	1.00
SC18	Ricky Ledee	1.00
SC19	John Patterson	1.00
SC20	Roy Halladay	1.50
SC21	Michael Barrett	1.50

1999 Bowman Chrome 2000 Rookie of the Year

This is a chromium parallel of the inserts found in Series 2 Bowman. The 10-card set is inserted in Series 2 Chrome packs and showcases prospects that have potential to win the 2000 Rookie of the Year award. Refractor parallels are also randomly inserted.

		MT
Complete Set (10):		15.00
Common Player:		1.00
Inserted 1:20		
Refractors:		1.5-3X
Inserted 1:100		
1	Ryan Anderson	1.50
2	Pat Burrell	4.00
3	A.J. Burnett	1.00
4	Ruben Mateo	1.50
5	Alex Escobar	1.00
6	Pablo Ozuna	1.00
7	Mark Mulder	1.50
8	Corey Patterson	2.50
9	George Lombard	1.00
10	Nick Johnson	4.00

1999 Bowman Chrome Early Impact

The checklist of this Series 2 insert mixes a dozen youngsters - labeled "Early Impact" on front - who are already making a mark in the majors with eight veteran stars, whose cards are labeled "Lasting Impact". A Refractor version is a parallel.

		MT
Complete Set (20):		37.50
Common Player:		.75
Inserted 1:15		
Refractor:		1.5X
Inserted 1:75		
1	Alfonso Soriano	2.50
2	Pat Burrell	2.00
3	Ruben Mateo	.75
4	A.J. Burnett	.75
5	Corey Patterson	2.00
6	Daryle Ward	.75
7	Eric Chavez	1.50

8	Troy Glaus	2.50
9	Sean Casey	1.50
10	Joe McEwing	.75
11	Gabe Kapler	1.00
12	Michael Barrett	.75
13	Sammy Sosa	3.00
14	Alex Rodriguez	4.00
15	Mark McGwire	5.00
16	Derek Jeter	3.50
17	Nomar Garciaparra	3.00
18	Mike Piazza	3.50
19	Chipper Jones	3.50
20	Ken Griffey Jr.	4.00

1999 Bowman's Best Pre-production

These cards were issued to draw interest to the '99 Bowman's Best issue. The promos are virtually identical to the issued version of each player's card except for the card number which is preceeded by a "PP" prefix.

	MT
Complete Set (3):	5.00
Common Player:	2.00
PP1 Javy Lopez	2.00
PP2 Marlon Anderson	2.00
PP3 J.M. Gold	2.00

1999 Bowman's Best

Bowman's Best consists of 200 cards printed on thick 27-point stock. Within the base set are 85 veteran stars printed on gold foil, 15 Best Performers on bronze foil, 50 Prospects on silver foil and 50 rookies on blue foil. The rookies are seeded one per pack. There are also two parallel versions: Refractors and Atomic Refractors. Refractors are inserted 1:15 packs and are sequentially numbered to 400, while Atomic Refractors are found 1:62 packs and are sequentially numbered to 100.

		MT
Complete Set (200):		75.00
Common Player:		.25
Pack (6):		4.00
Wax Box (24):		75.00
1	Chipper Jones	2.50
2	Brian Jordan	.25
3	David Justice	.40
4	Jason Kendall	.25
5	Mo Vaughn	.50
6	Jim Edmonds	.25
7	Wade Boggs	.65
8	Jeromy Burnitz	.25
9	Todd Hundley	.25
10	Rondell White	.35
11	Cliff Floyd	.25
12	Sean Casey	.40
13	Bernie Williams	.50
14	Dante Bichette	.25
15	Greg Vaughn	.25
16	Andres Galarraga	.25
17	Ray Durham	.25
18	Jim Thome	.25
19	Gary Sheffield	.45
20	Frank Thomas	2.00
21	Orlando Hernandez	.50
22	Ivan Rodriguez	.75
23	Jose Cruz Jr.	.35
24	Jason Giambi	.75
25	Craig Biggio	.30
26	Kerry Wood	.40
27	Manny Ramirez	1.00
28	Curt Schilling	.40
29	Mike Mussina	.65
30	Tim Salmon	.35
31	Mike Piazza	2.50
32	Roberto Alomar	.60
33	Larry Walker	.40
34	Barry Larkin	.30
35	Nomar Garciaparra	2.00
36	Paul O'Neill	.25
37	Todd Walker	.25
38	Eric Karros	.25
39	Brad Fullmer	.25
40	John Olerud	.25
41	Todd Helton	1.00
42	Raul Mondesi	.35
43	Jose Canseco	.50
44	Matt Williams	.35
45	Ray Lankford	.25
46	Carlos Delgado	.45
47	Darin Erstad	.75
48	Vladimir Guerrero	1.00
49	Robin Ventura	.25
50	Alex Rodriguez	2.75
51	Vinny Castilla	.25
52	Tony Clark	.25
53	Pedro Martinez	.75
54	Rafael Palmeiro	.40
55	Scott Rolen	.75
56	Tino Martinez	.25
57	Tony Gwynn	1.00
58	Barry Bonds	2.00
59	Kenny Lofton	.25
60	Javy Lopez	.25
61	Mark Grace	.40
62	Travis Lee	.25
63	Kevin Brown	.35
64	Al Leiter	.25
65	Albert Belle	.35
66	Sammy Sosa	2.00
67	Greg Maddux	1.50
68	Mark Kotsay	.25
69	Dmitri Young	.25
70	Mark McGwire	3.00
71	Juan Gonzalez	1.00
72	Andruw Jones	1.00
73	Derek Jeter	2.50
74	Randy Johnson	.75
75	Cal Ripken Jr.	3.00
76	Shawn Green	.35
77	Moises Alou	.35
78	Tom Glavine	.30
79	Sandy Alomar	.25
80	Ken Griffey Jr.	2.75
81	Ryan Klesko	.25
82	Jeff Bagwell	1.00
83	Ben Grieve	.40
84	John Smoltz	.30
85	Roger Clemens	1.50
86	Ken Griffey Jr.	1.25
87	Roger Clemens	.75
88	Derek Jeter	1.25
89	Nomar Garciaparra	1.00
90	Mark McGwire	1.50
91	Sammy Sosa	1.00
92	Alex Rodriguez	1.50
93	Greg Maddux	.75
94	Vladimir Guerrero	.50
95	Chipper Jones	1.25
96	Kerry Wood	.35
97	Ben Grieve	.35
98	Tony Gwynn	.75
99	Juan Gonzalez	.50
100	Mike Piazza	1.25
101	Eric Chavez	.40
102	Billy Koch	.25
103	Dernell Stenson	.25
104	Marlon Anderson	.25
105	Ron Belliard	.25
106	Bruce Chen	.25
107	Carlos Beltran	.25
108	Chad Hermansen	.25
109	Ryan Anderson	.50
110	Michael Barrett	.25
111	Matt Clement	.25
112	Ben Davis	.25
113	Calvin Pickering	.25
114	Brad Penny	.25
115	Paul Konerko	.25
116	Alex Gonzalez	.25
117	George Lombard	.25
118	John Patterson	.25
119	Rob Bell	.25
120	Ruben Mateo	.35
121	*Peter Bergeron*	1.00
122	Ryan Bradley	.25
123	Carlos Lee	.25
124	Gabe Kapler	.35
125	Ramon Hernandez	.25
126	Carlos Febles	.35
127	Mitch Meluskey	.25
128	Michael Cuddyer	.25
129	Pablo Ozuna	.25
130	Jayson Werth	.25
131	Ricky Ledee	.25
132	Jeremy Giambi	.25
133	Danny Klassen	.25
134	Mark DeRosa	.25
135	Randy Wolf	.25
136	Roy Halladay	.35
137	Derrick Gibson	.25
138	Ben Petrick	.25
139	Warren Morris	.25
140	Lance Berkman	.35
141	Russell Branyan	.25
142	Adrian Beltre	.75
143	Juan Encarnacion	.35
144	Fernando Seguignol	.25
145	Corey Koskie	.25
146	Preston Wilson	.25
147	Homer Bush	.25
148	Daryle Ward	.25
149	*Joe McEwing*	.50
150	*Peter Bergeron*	1.00
151	*Pat Burrell*	6.00
152	*Choo Freeman*	.50
153	*Matt Belisle*	.50
154	*Carlos Pena*	6.00
155	*A.J. Burnett*	1.50
156	*Doug Mientkiewicz*	1.50
157	*Sean Burroughs*	6.00
158	*Mike Zywica*	.50
159	*Corey Patterson*	4.00
160	*Austin Kearns*	8.00
161	*Chip Ambres*	.50
162	*Kelly Dransfeldt*	.50
163	*Mike Nannini*	.75
164	*Mark Mulder*	5.00
165	*Jason Tyner*	.50
166	*Bobby Seay*	.50
167	*Alex Escobar*	1.00
168	*Nick Johnson*	6.00
169	*Alfonso Soriano*	12.00
170	*Clayton Andrews*	.25
171	*C.C. Sabathia*	3.00
172	*Matt Holliday*	.50
173	*Brad Lidge*	.75
174	*Kit Pellow*	.75
175	*J.M. Gold*	.50
176	*Roosevelt Brown*	.50
177	*Eric Valent*	1.00
178	*Adam Everett*	1.00
179	*Jorge Toca*	.75
180	*Matt Roney*	.50
181	*Andy Brown*	.50
182	*Phil Norton*	.50
183	*Mickey Lopez*	.50
184	*Chris George*	.75
185	*Arturo McDowell*	.50
186	*Jose Fernandez*	.25
187	*Seth Etherton*	.50
188	*Josh McKinley*	.50
189	*Nate Cornejo*	1.50
190	*Giuseppe Chiaramonte*	.50
191	*Mamon Tucker*	.50
192	*Ryan Mills*	.50
193	*Chad Moeller*	.50
194	*Tony Torcato*	1.00
195	*Jeff Winchester*	.50
196	*Rick Elder*	1.00
197	*Matt Burch*	.50
198	*Jeff Urban*	.50
199	*Chris Jones*	.50
200	*Masao Kida*	.50

1999 Bowman's Best Refractors

Inserted at an average rate of about one per 15 packs, Best Refractor's are so marked on the back in the card-number box at upper-right. Also found on back is a serial numbered stamped in gold-foil from within an edition of 400.

	MT
Complete Set (200):	450.00
Common Player:	1.00
Stars:	8X

(See 1999 Bowman's Best for checklist and base card values.)

1999 Bowman's Best Atomic Refractors

The vibrant refractive background on front announces these parallels which are found on average of about once per 62 packs. Backs identify the variation in the card-number box at upper-right and with a serial number from within an edition of 100 per card.

	MT
Common Player:	3.00
Stars:	15X

(See 1999 Bowman's Best for checklist and base card values.)

1999 Bowman's Best Franchise Best

Ten league leaders are featured in this insert set on three different technologies: Mach I, Mach II and Mach III. Mach I feature die-cut Serillusion stock and is numbered to 3,000. Mach II features die-cut refractive styrene stock, numbered to 1,000; and, Mach III features die-cut polycarbonate stock and is limited to 500 numbered sets. All cards numbers have an "FB" prefix.

		MT
Complete Set (10):		20.00
Common Player:		1.00
Production 3,000 sets		
Mach II (1,000):		1.5X
Mach III (500):		2.5X
1	Mark McGwire	3.00
2	Ken Griffey Jr.	3.00
3	Sammy Sosa	2.00
4	Nomar Garciaparra	2.00
5	Alex Rodriguez	3.00
6	Derek Jeter	4.00
7	Mike Piazza	2.50
8	Frank Thomas	1.25
9	Chipper Jones	2.50
10	Juan Gonzalez	1.00

1999 Bowman's Best Franchise Favorites

This six-card set features retired legends and current stars in three versions. Version A features a current star, Version B features a retired player and Version C pairs the current star with the retired player. Cards have an "FR" prefix to the number on back.

		MT
Complete Set (6):		25.00
Common Player:		1.00
Inserted 1:75		
1A	Derek Jeter	10.00
1B	Don Mattingly	4.00
1C	Derek Jeter, Don Mattingly	10.00
2A	Scott Rolen	1.00
2B	Mike Schmidt	3.00
2C	Scott Rolen, Mike Schmidt	2.00

1999 Bowman's Best Franchise Favorites Autographs

This is a parallel autographed version of the regular Franchise Favorites inserts.

		MT
Common Player:		15.00
Version A & B 1:1548		
Version C 1:6191		
1A	Derek Jeter	125.00
1B	Don Mattingly	125.00
1C	Derek Jeter, Don Mattingly	350.00
2A	Scott Rolen	15.00
2B	Mike Schmidt	50.00
2C	Scott Rolen, Mike Schmidt	150.00

1999 Bowman's Best Future Foundations

Ten up-and-coming players are featured in this set that has the same technologies as the Franchise Best inserts and broken down the same way. The insert rates are 1:41 packs for Mach I, 1:124 for Mach II and 1:248 for Mach III.

		MT
Complete Set (10):		25.00
Common Player:		1.50
Production 3,000 sets		
Mach II (1,000):		1.5X
Mach III (500):		2.5X
1	Ruben Mateo	2.00
2	Troy Glaus	6.00
3	Eric Chavez	3.00
4	Pat Burrell	6.00
5	Adrian Beltre	2.50
6	Ryan Anderson	2.50
7	Alfonso Soriano	5.00
8	Brad Penny	1.50
9	Derrick Gibson	1.50
10	Bruce Chen	1.50

1999 Bowman's Best Mirror Image

These inserts feature a veteran player on one side and a prospect on the other side for a total of 10 double-sided cards featuring 20 players. There are also parallel Refractor and Atomic Refractor versions.

		MT
Complete Set (10):		30.00
Common Player:		2.00
Inserted 1:24		
Refractors (1:96):		1.5X
Atomic Refractors (1:192):		2X
1	Alex Rodriguez, Alex Gonzalez	4.00
2	Ken Griffey Jr., Ruben Mateo	3.00
3	Derek Jeter, Alfonso Soriano	5.00
4	Sammy Sosa, Corey Patterson	3.00
5	Greg Maddux, Bruce Chen	2.00
6	Chipper Jones, Eric Chavez	3.00
7	Vladimir Guerrero, Carlos Beltran	2.00
8	Frank Thomas, Nick Johnson	3.00
9	Nomar Garciaparra, Pablo Ozuna	3.00
10	Mark McGwire, Pat Burrell	6.00

1999 Bowman's Best Rookie of the Year

This set salutes 1998 AL and NL Rookie of Year award winners Kerry Wood and Ben Grieve. They are inserted 1:95 packs and are numbered with a ROY prefix. Ben Grieve also autographed some of the inserts which feature a "Topps Certified Autograph Issue" stamp. Autographs are seeded 1:1,241 packs.

		MT
Complete Set (2):		4.00
1	Ben Grieve	2.00
2	Kerry Wood	2.00
A1	Ben Grieve (Auto.)	20.00

1999 Bowman's Best Rookie Locker Room Autographs

This five-card set features autographs of baseball's current hot prospects. Each card is branded with a "Topps Certified Autograph Issue" stamp.

		MT
Complete Set (5):		90.00
Common Player:		15.00
Inserted 1:248		
1	Pat Burrell	35.00
2	Michael Barrett	15.00
3	Troy Glaus	30.00
4	Gabe Kapler	15.00
5	Eric Chavez	15.00

1999 Bowman's Best Rookie Locker Room Game-Used Lumber

This six-card set features actual pieces of each player's game-used bat embedded into the cards.

		MT
Complete Set (6):		100.00
Common Player:		10.00
Inserted 1:258		
1	Pat Burrell	40.00
2	Michael Barrett	10.00
3	Troy Glaus	40.00
4	Gabe Kapler	15.00
5	Eric Chavez	15.00
6	Richie Sexson	10.00

1999 Bowman's Best Rookie Locker Room Game-Worn Jerseys

This four-card set spotlights hot prospects and has a swatch of game-used jersey from the featured player embedded into the card.

	MT
Complete Set (4):	60.00
Common Player:	10.00

Inserted 1:270

1	Richie Sexson	15.00
2	Michael Barrett	10.00
3	Troy Glaus	40.00
4	Eric Chavez	20.00

2000 Bowman

Released in one 440-card series. The card fronts are foil stamped to differentiate Veterans (gold foil) from Rookies and Prospects (silver). All card fronts feature facsimile signatures from the players' original Topps contracts. All bona fide rookie cards also exhibit the "Bowman Rookie Card" stamped under the 2000 Bowman logo.

		MT
Complete Set (440):		125.00
Common Player:		.15
Common Rookie:		.50
Pack (10):		3.00
Wax Box:		65.00
1	Vladimir Guerrero	1.50
2	Chipper Jones	1.50
3	Todd Walker	.15
4	Barry Larkin	.40
5	Bernie Williams	.50
6	Todd Helton	.75
7	Jermaine Dye	.15
8	Brian Giles	.25
9	Freddy Garcia	.15
10	Greg Vaughn	.25
11	Alex Gonzalez	.15
12	Luis Gonzalez	.15
13	Ron Belliard	.15
14	Ben Grieve	.30
15	Carlos Delgado	.50
16	Brian Jordan	.15
17	Fernando Tatis	.25
18	Ryan Rupe	.15
19	Miguel Tejada	.15
20	Mark Grace	.30
21	Kenny Lofton	.50
22	Eric Karros	.25
23	Cliff Floyd	.15
24	John Halama	.15
25	Cristian Guzman	.15
26	Scott Williamson	.15
27	Mike Lieberthal	.15
28	Tim Hudson	.25
29	Warren Morris	.15
30	Pedro Martinez	1.00
31	John Smoltz	.15
32	Ray Durham	.15
33	Chad Allen	.15
34	Tony Clark	.25
35	Tino Martinez	.40
36	J.T. Snow Jr.	.15
37	Kevin Brown	.25
38	Bartolo Colon	.15
39	Rey Ordonez	.15
40	Jeff Bagwell	.75
41	Ivan Rodriguez	.75
42	Eric Chavez	.25
43	Eric Milton	.15
44	Jose Canseco	.75
45	Shawn Green	.50
46	Rich Aurilia	.15
47	Roberto Alomar	.50
48	Brian Daubach	.15
49	Magglio Ordonez	.15
50	Derek Jeter	3.00
51	Kris Benson	.15
52	Albert Belle	.50
53	Rondell White	.25
54	Justin Thompson	.15
55	Nomar Garciaparra	2.00
56	Chuck Finley	.15
57	Omar Vizquel	.25
58	Luis Castillo	.15
59	Richard Hidalgo	.15
60	Barry Bonds	1.00
61	Craig Biggio	.40
62	Doug Glanville	.15
63	Gabe Kapler	.30
64	Johnny Damon	.15
65	Pokey Reese	.15
66	Andy Pettitte	.25
67	B.J. Surhoff	.15
68	Richie Sexson	.15
69	Javy Lopez	.25
70	Raul Mondesi	.25
71	Darin Erstad	.30
72	Kevin Millwood	.25
73	Ricky Ledee	.15
74	John Olerud	.25
75	Sean Casey	.40
76	Carlos Febles	.15
77	Paul O'Neill	.40
78	Bob Abreu	.25
79	Neifi Perez	.15
80	Tony Gwynn	1.50
81	Russ Ortiz	.15
82	Matt Williams	.40
83	Chris Carpenter	.15
84	Roger Cedeno	.15
85	Tim Salmon	.30
86	Billy Koch	.15
87	Jeromy Burnitz	.25
88	Edgardo Alfonzo	.25
89	Jay Bell	.15
90	Manny Ramirez	.75
91	Frank Thomas	1.00
92	Mike Mussina	.50
93	J.D. Drew	.40
94	Adrian Beltre	.30
95	Alex Rodriguez	2.50
96	Larry Walker	.50
97	Juan Encarnacion	.15
98	Mike Sweeney	.15
99	Rusty Greer	.15
100	Randy Johnson	.50
101	Jose Vidro	.15
102	Preston Wilson	.15
103	Greg Maddux	1.50
104	Jason Giambi	.25
105	Cal Ripken Jr.	2.50
106	Carlos Beltran	.25
107	Vinny Castilla	.25
108	Mariano Rivera	.25
109	Mo Vaughn	.25
110	Rafael Palmeiro	.50
111	Shannon Stewart	.15
112	Mike Hampton	.15
113	Joe Nathan	.15
114	Ben Davis	.15
115	Andruw Jones	.50
116	Robin Ventura	.25
117	Damion Easley	.15
118	Jeff Cirillo	.25
119	Kerry Wood	.40
120	Scott Rolen	.75
121	Sammy Sosa	2.00
122	Ken Griffey Jr.	2.50
123	Shane Reynolds	.15
124	Troy Glaus	.75
125	Tom Glavine	.30
126	Michael Barrett	.15
127	Al Leiter	.25
128	Jason Kendall	.25
129	Roger Clemens	1.00
130	Juan Gonzalez	.75
131	Corey Koskie	.15
132	Curt Schilling	.25
133	Mike Piazza	2.00
134	Gary Sheffield	.30
135	Jim Thome	.40
136	Orlando Hernandez	.40
137	Ray Lankford	.15
138	Geoff Jenkins	.25
139	Jose Lima	.15
140	Mark McGwire	3.00
141	Adam Piatt	.15
142	*Pat Manning*	1.50
143	*Marcos Castillo*	.50
144	*Lesli Brea*	.50
145	*Humberto Cota*	1.00
146	Ben Petrick	.15
147	Kip Wells	.15
148	Willi Mo Pena	.75
149	Chris Wakeland	.50
150	*Brad Baker*	1.50
151	*Robbie Morrison*	.50
152	Reggie Taylor	.15
153	*Brian Cole*	.15
154	Peter Bergeron	.15
155	Roosevelt Brown	.15
156	*Matt Cepicky*	.50
157	Ramon Castro	.15
158	*Brad Baisley*	1.00
159	*Jeff Goldbach*	1.50
160	Mitch Meluskey	.15
161	Chad Harville	.15
162	Brian Cooper	.15
163	Marcus Giles	.15
164	Jim Morris	.15
165	Geoff Goetz	.15
166	*Bobby Bradley*	2.00
167	Rob Bell	.15
168	Joe Crede	.15
169	Michael Restovich	.15
170	*Quincy Foster*	.50
171	*Enrique Cruz*	.75
172	Mark Quinn	.15
173	Nick Johnson	.15
174	Jeff Liefer	.15
175	*Kevin Mench*	3.00
176	Steve Lomasney	.15
177	Jayson Werth	.15
178	Tim Drew	.15
179	Chip Ambres	.15
180	Ryan Anderson	.40
181	Matt Blank	.15
182	Giuseppe Chiaramonte	.15
183	*Corey Myers*	1.50
184	Jeff Yoder	.15
185	*Craig Dingman*	.50
186	*Jon Hamilton*	.50
187	Toby Hall	.15
188	Russell Branyan	.15
189	*Brian Falkenborg*	.50
190	*Aaron Harang*	.50
191	Juan Pena	.15
192	*Travis Thompson*	.50
193	Alfonso Soriano	.50
194	*Alejandro Diaz*	1.00
195	Carlos Pena	.15
196	Kevin Nicholson	.15
197	Mo Bruce	.15
198	C.C. Sabathia	.15
199	Carl Crawford	.15
200	Rafael Furcal	.25
201	*Andrew Beinbrink*	.50
202	Jimmy Osting	.15
203	*Aaron McNeal*	1.00
204	Brett Laxton	.15
205	Chris George	.15
206	Felipe Lopez	.15
207	*Ben Sheets*	2.00
208	*Mike Meyers*	2.00
209	Jason Conti	.15
210	Milton Bradley	.15
211	*Chris Mears*	.50
212	*David Tavarez*	.50
213	Jason Romano	.15
214	Goefrey Tomlinson	.15
215	Jimmy Rollins	.15
216	Pablo Ozuna	.15
217	Steve Cox	.15
218	Terrence Long	.15
219	*Jeff DaVanon*	.50
220	Rick Ankiel	.40
221	Jason Standridge	.15
222	Tony Armas	.15
223	Jason Tyner	.15
224	Ramon Ortiz	.15
225	Daryle Ward	.15
226	*Enger Veras*	.50
227	*Chris Jones*	.75
228	*Eric Cammack*	.50
229	Ruben Mateo	.15
230	*Ken Harvey*	1.00
231	Jake Westbrook	.15
232	*Rob Purvis*	.50
233	Choo Freeman	.15
234	Aramis Ramirez	.15
235	A.J. Burnett	.15
236	Kevin Barker	.15
237	*Chance Caple*	.75
238	Jarrod Washburn	.15
239	Lance Berkman	.15
240	*Michael Wenner*	.50
241	Alex Sanchez	.15
242	*Jake Esteves*	.50
243	Grant Roberts	.15
244	*Mark Ellis*	1.50
245	Donny Leon	.15
246	David Eckstein	.15
247	*Dicky Gonzalez*	.50
248	John Patterson	.15
249	Chad Green	.15
250	*Scot Shields*	.50
251	Troy Cameron	.15
252	Jose Molina	.15
253	*Rob Pugmire*	.50
254	Rick Elder	.15
255	Sean Burroughs	.75
256	*Josh Kalinowski*	.50
257	Matt LeCroy	.15
258	*Alex Graman*	1.00
259	*Tomokazu Ohka*	1.00
260	Brady Clark	.15
261	*Rico Washington*	.75
262	Gary Matthews Jr.	.15
263	Matt Wise	.15
264	*Keith Reed*	1.00
265	*Santiago Ramirez*	.50
266	*Ben Broussard*	5.00
267	Ryan Langerhans	.15
268	Juan Rivera	.15
269	Shawn Gallagher	.15
270	Jorge Toca	.15
271	Brad Lidge	.15
272	*Leo Estrella*	.50
273	Ruben Quevedo	.15
274	Jack Cust	.15
275	T.J. Tucker	.15
276	Mike Colangelo	.15
277	Brian Schneider	.15
278	Calvin Murray	.15
279	Josh Girdley	.15
280	Mike Paradis	.15
281	Chad Hermansen	.15
282	*Ty Howington*	.75
283	Aaron Myette	.15
284	D'Angelo Jimenez	.15
285	Dernell Stenson	.15
286	Jerry Hairston Jr.	.15
287	*Gary Majewski*	.50
288	*Derrin Ebert*	.50
289	*Steve Fish*	.50
290	Carlos Hernandez	.15
291	Allen Levrault	.15
292	*Sean McNally*	.50
293	*Randey Dorame*	.75
294	*Wes Anderson*	1.00
295	B.J. Ryan	.15
296	*Alan Webb*	.50
297	*Brandon Inge*	.75
298	David Walling	.15
299	*Sun-Woo Kim*	1.00
300	Pat Burrell	.50
301	*Rick Guttormson*	.50
302	Gil Meche	.15
303	*Carlos Zambrano*	1.00
304	*Eric Byrnes* (photo actually Bo Porter)	.50
305	*Robb Quinlan*	.50
306	Jackie Rexrode	.15
307	Nate Bump	.15
308	*Sean DePaula*	.50
309	Matt Riley	.15
310	Ryan Minor	.15
311	J.J. Davis	.15
312	Randy Wolf	.15
313	Jason Jennings	.15
314	*Scott Seabol*	.50
315	Doug Davis	.15
316	*Todd Moser*	.50
317	Rob Ryan	.15
318	Bubba Crosby	.15
319	*Lyle Overbay*	1.50
320	Mario Encarnacion	.15
321	*Francisco Rodriguez*	2.00
322	Michael Cuddyer	.15
323	Eddie Yarnall	.15
324	*Cesar Saba*	.75
325	Travis Dawkins	.15
326	Alex Escobar	.25
327	*Julio Zuleta*	.50
328	Josh Hamilton	1.00
329	*Nick Neugebauer*	1.50
330	Matt Belisle	.15
331	*Kurt Ainsworth*	1.50
332	Tim Raines Jr.	.15
333	Eric Munson	.40

334	Donzell McDonald	.15
335	*Larry Bigbie*	.15
336	Matt Watson	.15
337	Aubrey Huff	.15
338	Julio Ramirez	.15
339	*Jason Grabowski*	.75
340	Jon Garland	.15
341	Austin Kearns	.15
342	Josh Pressley	.15
343	*Miguel Olivo*	.50
344	Julio Lugo	.15
345	Roberto Vaz	.15
346	Ramon Soler	.15
347	*Brandon Phillips*	.75
348	*Vince Faison*	1.50
349	Mike Venafro	.15
350	*Rick Asadoorian*	1.50
351	*B.J. Garbe*	2.00
352	Dan Reichert	.15
353	*Jason Stumm*	2.00
354	*Ruben Salazar*	.75
355	Francisco Cordero	.15
356	*Juan Guzman*	.50
357	*Mike Bacsik*	.50
358	Jared Sandberg	.15
359	Rod Barajas	.15
360	*Junior Brignac*	.75
361	J.M. Gold	.15
362	Octavio Dotel	.15
363	David Kelton	.15
364	*Scott Morgan*	.50
365	*Wascar Serrano*	1.00
366	Wilton Veras	.15
367	Eugene Kingsale	.15
368	Ted Lilly	.15
369	George Lombard	.15
370	Chris Haas	.15
371	*Wilton Pena*	.75
372	Vernon Wells	.15
373	*Lyle Overbay*	.75
374	*Jeff Heaverlo*	.75
375	Calvin Pickering	.15
376	*Mike Lamb*	1.25
377	Kyle Snyder	.15
378	*Javier Cardona*	.50
379	*Aaron Rowand*	1.00
380	Dee Brown	.15
381	*Brett Myers*	2.50
382	Abraham Nunez	.50
383	Eric Valent	.15
384	*Jody Gerut*	.50
385	Adam Dunn	.40
386	Jay Gehrke	.15
387	Omar Ortiz	.15
388	Darnell McDonald	.15
389	Chad Alexander	.15
390	J.D. Closser	.15
391	*Ben Christensen*	1.00
392	Adam Kennedy	.15
393	*Nick Green*	.50
394	Ramon Hernandez	.15
395	*Roy Oswalt*	4.00
396	*Andy Tracy*	.50
397	Eric Gagne	.15
398	*Michael Tejera*	.50
399	Adam Everett	.15
400	Corey Patterson	.50
401	*Gary Knotts*	.50
402	*Ryan Christianson*	2.00
403	*Eric Ireland*	.50
404	*Andrew Good*	.50
405	Brad Penny	.15
406	Jason LaRue	.15
407	Kit Pellow	.15
408	Kevin Beirne	.15
409	Kelly Dransfeldt	.15
410	Jason Grilli	.15
411	*Scott Downs*	.75
412	Jesus Colome	.15
413	*John Sneed*	.50
414	*Tony McKnight*	.50
415	Luis Rivera	.15
416	Adam Eaton	.15
417	*Mike MacDougal*	.50
418	Mike Nannini	.15
419	*Barry Zito*	4.00
420	Dewayne Wise	.15
421	Jason Dellaero	.15
422	Chad Moeller	.15
423	Jason Marquis	.15
424	*Tim Redding*	.50
425	Mark Mulder	.15
426	Josh Paul	.15
427	Chris Enochs	.15
428	*Wilfredo Rodriguez*	1.00
429	Kevin Witt	.15
430	*Scott Sobkowiak*	.50
431	McKay Christensen	.15
432	Jung Bong	.15
433	*Keith Evans*	.15
434	Garry Maddox Jr.	.15
435	*Ramon Santiago*	1.00
436	Alex Cora	.15
437	Carlos Lee	.15
438	*Jason Repko*	1.50
439	Matt Burch	.15
440	*Shawn Sonnier*	.50

2000 Bowman Retro/Future

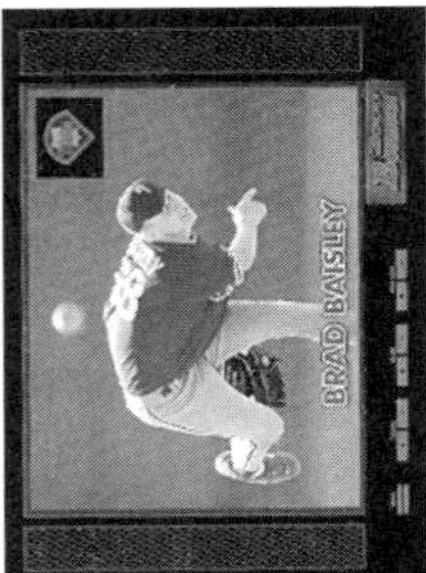

These inserts are a parallel to the 440-card base set. The foiled card fronts have a horizontal format and a design reminiscent of the 1955 Bowman "television set" design. They were seeded one per pack.

	MT
Common Player:	.25
Stars:	2-3X
Rookies:	1-2X
Inserted 1:1	

(See 2000 Bowman for checklist and base card values.)

2000 Bowman Gold

Golds are a 440-card parallel to the base set and are highlighted by gold-stamped facsimile autographs on the card front. Golds are limited to 99 serial numbered sets.

	MT
Stars:	20-40X
Rookies:	5-10X
Production 99 sets	

(See 2000 Bowman for checklist and base card values.)

2000 Bowman Autographs

This set consists of 40 players with card rarity differentiated by either a Blue, Silver or Gold foil Topps "Certified Autograph Issue" stamp. Card backs are numbered using the player initials and have a Topps serial numbered foil hologram to ensure the authenticity of the autograph.

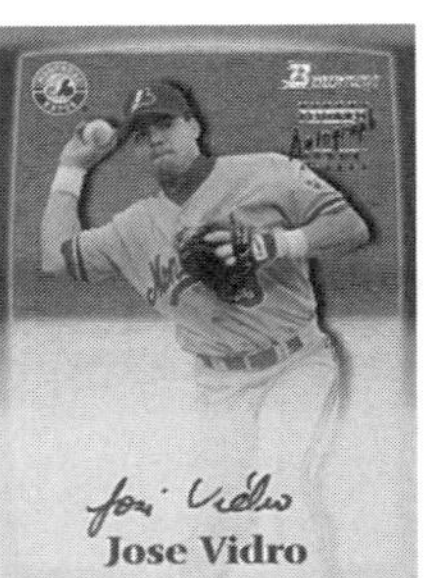

		MT
Common Player:		10.00
Blue Inserted 1:144		
Silver 1:312		
Gold 1:1,604		
CA	Chip Ambres B	10.00
RA	Rick Ankiel G	35.00
CB	Carlos Beltran G	25.00
LB	Lance Berkman S	15.00
DB	Dee Brown S	15.00
SB	Sean Burroughs S	30.00
JDC	J.D. Closser B	10.00
SC	Steve Cox B	10.00
MC	Michael Cuddyer S	20.00
JC	Jack Cust S	20.00
SD	Scott Downs S	15.00
JDD	J.D. Drew G	40.00
AD	Adam Dunn B	40.00
CF	Choo Freeman B	10.00
RF	Rafael Furcal S	25.00
AH	Aubrey Huff B	10.00
JJ	Jason Jennings B	10.00
NJ	Nick Johnson S	30.00
AK	Austin Kearns B	30.00
DK	David Kelton B	10.00
RM	Ruben Mateo G	30.00
MM	Mike Meyers B	10.00
CP	Corey Patterson S	30.00
BWP	Brad Penny B	10.00
BP	Ben Petrick G	20.00
AP	Adam Piatt S	20.00
MQ	Mark Quinn S	20.00
MR	Mike Restovich B	15.00
MR	Matt Riley S	25.00
JR	Jason Romano B	10.00
BS	Ben Sheets B	25.00
AS	Alfonso Soriano S	30.00
EV	Eric Valent B	10.00
JV	Jose Vidro S	20.00
VW	Vernon Wells G	30.00
SW	Scott Williamson G	20.00
KJW	Kevin Witt S	15.00
KLW	Kerry Wood S	30.00
EY	Eddie Yarnall S	15.00
JZ	Julio Zuleta B	10.00

2000 Bowman Bowman's Best Previews

This 10-card insert set is identical in design to 2000 Bowman's Best. The card fronts have a Refractor like sheen and the card backs are numbered with a "BBP" prefix.

		MT
Complete Set (10):		40.00
Common Player:		1.50
Inserted 1:18		
1	Derek Jeter	8.00
2	Ken Griffey Jr.	6.00
3	Nomar Garciaparra	5.00
4	Mike Piazza	5.00
5	Alex Rodriguez	6.00
6	Sammy Sosa	5.00
7	Mark McGwire	8.00
8	Pat Burrell	2.50
9	Josh Hamilton	3.00
10	Adam Piatt	1.50

2000 Bowman Early Indications

This 10-card set has a blue foiled card front with red foil stamping. Card backs are numbered with an "E" prefix.

		MT
Complete Set (10):		50.00
Common Player:		2.00
Inserted 1:24		
1	Nomar Garciaparra	6.00
2	Cal Ripken Jr.	8.00
3	Derek Jeter	10.00
4	Mark McGwire	10.00
5	Alex Rodriguez	8.00
6	Chipper Jones	5.00
7	Todd Helton	2.50
8	Vladimir Guerrero	5.00
9	Mike Piazza	6.00
10	Jose Canseco	2.50

2000 Bowman Major Power

This 10-card set spotlights the top home run hitters. Card fronts have a red border on a full foiled card front. These are numbered with an "MP" prefix on the card back.

		MT
Complete Set (10):		50.00
Common Player:		2.00
Inserted 1:24		
1	Mark McGwire	10.00
2	Chipper Jones	5.00
3	Alex Rodriguez	8.00
4	Sammy Sosa	6.00
5	Rafael Palmeiro	2.00
6	Ken Griffey Jr.	8.00
7	Nomar Garciaparra	6.00
8	Barry Bonds	3.00
9	Derek Jeter	10.00
10	Jeff Bagwell	2.50

2000 Bowman Tool Time

This 20-card set focuses on the top minor league Prospects in five different categories: batting, power, speed, arm strength and defense. These are seeded 1:8 packs. Backs are numbered with a "TT" prefix.

		MT
Complete Set (20):		25.00
Common Player:		1.00
Inserted 1:8		
1	Pat Burrell	2.00
2	Aaron Rowand	1.00
3	Chris Wakeland	1.00
4	Ruben Mateo	1.00
5	Pat Burrell	2.00
6	Adam Piatt	1.50
7	Nick Johnson	2.00
8	Jack Cust	1.00
9	Rafael Furcal	1.50
10	Julio Ramirez	1.00
11	Travis Dawkins	1.00
12	Corey Patterson	2.00
13	Ruben Mateo	1.00
14	Jason Dellaero	1.00
15	Sean Burroughs	1.50
16	Ryan Langerhans	1.00
17	D'Angelo Jimenez	1.00
18	Corey Patterson	2.00
19	Troy Cameron	1.00
20	Michael Cuddyer	1.00

2000 Bowman Chrome

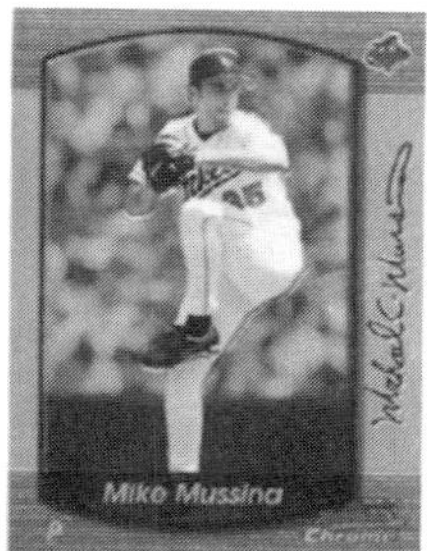

Released as a single series 440-card set, Bowman Chrome is identical in design to 2000 Bowman besides the Chromium finish on all cards. Foil highlights differentiate rookies and prospects (blue) from veterans (red). Three parallels to the base set are randomly seeded: Refractors, Retro/Future and Retro/Future Refractors.

		MT
Complete Set (440):		280.00
Common Player:		.25
Common Rookie:		1.00
Pack (4):		3.50
Box (24):		80.00
1	Vladimir Guerrero	1.50
2	Chipper Jones	2.00
3	Todd Walker	.25
4	Barry Larkin	.60
5	Bernie Williams	.75
6	Todd Helton	1.00
7	Jermaine Dye	.25
8	Brian Giles	.40
9	Freddy Garcia	.25
10	Greg Vaughn	.40
11	Alex Gonzalez	.25
12	Luis Gonzalez	.25
13	Ron Belliard	.25
14	Ben Grieve	.50
15	Carlos Delgado	1.00
16	Brian Jordan	.25
17	Fernando Tatis	.40
18	Ryan Rupe	.25
19	Miguel Tejada	.25
20	Mark Grace	.40
21	Kenny Lofton	.60
22	Eric Karros	.40
23	Cliff Floyd	.25
24	John Halama	.25
25	Cristian Guzman	.25
26	Scott Williamson	.25
27	Mike Lieberthal	.25
28	Tim Hudson	.40
29	Warren Morris	.25
30	Pedro Martinez	1.50
31	John Smoltz	.25
32	Ray Durham	.25
33	Chad Allen	.25
34	Tony Clark	.30
35	Tino Martinez	.40
36	J.T. Snow Jr.	.25
37	Kevin Brown	.30
38	Bartolo Colon	.25
39	Rey Ordonez	.25
40	Jeff Bagwell	1.00
41	Ivan Rodriguez	1.00
42	Eric Chavez	.40
43	Eric Milton	.25
44	Jose Canseco	.75
45	Shawn Green	.75
46	Rich Aurilia	.25
47	Roberto Alomar	.75
48	Brian Daubach	.25
49	Magglio Ordonez	.25
50	Derek Jeter	4.00
51	Kris Benson	.25
52	Albert Belle	.75
53	Rondell White	.40
54	Justin Thompson	.25
55	Nomar Garciaparra	2.50
56	Chuck Finley	.25
57	Omar Vizquel	.35
58	Luis Castillo	.25
59	Richard Hidalgo	.25
60	Barry Bonds	1.50
61	Craig Biggio	.50
62	Doug Glanville	.25
63	Gabe Kapler	.40
64	Johnny Damon	.25
65	Pokey Reese	.25
66	Andy Pettitte	.40
67	B.J. Surhoff	.25
68	Richie Sexson	.25
69	Javy Lopez	.25
70	Raul Mondesi	.40
71	Darin Erstad	.50
72	Kevin Millwood	.25
73	Ricky Ledee	.25
74	John Olerud	.40
75	Sean Casey	.40
76	Carlos Febles	.25
77	Paul O'Neill	.50
78	Bob Abreu	.40
79	Neifi Perez	.25
80	Tony Gwynn	1.50
81	Russ Ortiz	.25
82	Matt Williams	.50
83	Chris Carpenter	.25
84	Roger Cedeno	.25
85	Tim Salmon	.40
86	Billy Koch	.25
87	Jeromy Burnitz	.25
88	Edgardo Alfonzo	.40
89	Jay Bell	.15
90	Manny Ramirez	1.00
91	Frank Thomas	1.50
92	Mike Mussina	.75
93	J.D. Drew	.50
94	Adrian Beltre	.40
95	Alex Rodriguez	3.00
96	Larry Walker	.50
97	Juan Encarnacion	.25
98	Mike Sweeney	.25
99	Rusty Greer	.25
100	Randy Johnson	.75
101	Jose Vidro	.25
102	Preston Wilson	.25
103	Greg Maddux	2.00
104	Jason Giambi	.40
105	Cal Ripken Jr.	3.00
106	Carlos Beltran	.25
107	Vinny Castilla	.25
108	Mariano Rivera	.40
109	Mo Vaughn	.50
110	Rafael Palmeiro	.50
111	Shannon Stewart	.25
112	Mike Hampton	.25
113	Joe Nathan	.25
114	Ben Davis	.25
115	Andruw Jones	.75
116	Robin Ventura	.40
117	Damion Easley	.25
118	Jeff Cirillo	.40
119	Kerry Wood	.50
120	Scott Rolen	.75
121	Sammy Sosa	2.50
122	Ken Griffey Jr.	3.00
123	Shane Reynolds	.25
124	Troy Glaus	1.00
125	Tom Glavine	.40
126	Michael Barrett	.25
127	Al Leiter	.25
128	Jason Kendall	.25
129	Roger Clemens	1.50
130	Juan Gonzalez	1.00
131	Corey Koskie	.25
132	Curt Schilling	.35
133	Mike Piazza	2.50
134	Gary Sheffield	.40
135	Jim Thome	.50
136	Orlando Hernandez	.50
137	Ray Lankford	.25
138	Geoff Jenkins	.40
139	Jose Lima	.25
140	Mark McGwire	4.00
141	Adam Piatt	.25
142	*Pat Manning*	4.00
143	*Marcos Castillo*	1.00
144	*Lesli Brea*	1.00
145	*Humberto Cota*	3.00
146	Ben Petrick	.25
147	Kip Wells	.25
148	Willi Mo Pena	1.00
149	Chris Wakeland	1.00
150	*Brad Baker*	5.00
151	*Robbie Morrison*	1.00
152	Reggie Taylor	.25
153	*Matt Ginter*	2.00
154	Peter Bergeron	.25
155	Roosevelt Brown	.25
156	*Matt Cepicky*	1.00
157	Ramon Castro	.25
158	*Brad Baisley*	3.00
159	*Jason Hart*	5.00
160	Mitch Meluskey	.25
161	Chad Harville	.25
162	Brian Cooper	.25
163	Marcus Giles	.25
164	Jim Morris	.25
165	Geoff Goetz	.25
166	*Bobby Bradley*	6.00
167	Rob Bell	.25
168	Joe Crede	.25
169	Michael Restovich	.25
170	*Quincy Foster*	1.00
171	*Enrique Cruz*	2.00
172	Mark Quinn	.25
173	Nick Johnson	.25
174	Jeff Liefer	.25
175	*Kevin Mench*	8.00
176	Steve Lomasney	.25
177	Jayson Werth	.25
178	Tim Drew	.25
179	Chip Ambres	.25
180	Ryan Anderson	.50
181	Matt Blank	.25
182	Giuseppe Chiaramonte	.25
183	*Corey Myers*	3.00
184	Jeff Yoder	.25
185	*Craig Dingman*	1.00
186	*Jon Hamilton*	1.00
187	Toby Hall	.25
188	Russell Branyan	.25
189	*Brian Falkenborg*	1.00
190	*Aaron Harang*	1.00
191	Juan Pena	.25
192	*Chin-Hui Tsao*	5.00
193	Alfonso Soriano	.50
194	*Alejandro Diaz*	3.00
195	Carlos Pena	.25
196	Kevin Nicholson	.25
197	Mo Bruce	.25
198	C.C. Sabathia	.25
199	Carl Crawford	.25
200	Rafael Furcal	.50
201	*Andrew Beinbrink*	1.00
202	Jimmy Osting	.25
203	*Aaron McNeal*	2.50
204	Brett Laxton	.25
205	Chris George	.25
206	Felipe Lopez	.25
207	*Ben Sheets*	5.00
208	*Mike Meyers*	6.00
209	Jason Conti	.25
210	Milton Bradley	.25
211	*Chris Mears*	1.00
212	*David Tavarez*	1.00
213	Jason Romano	.25
214	Goefrey Tomlinson	.25
215	Jimmy Rollins	.25
216	Pablo Ozuna	.25
217	Steve Cox	.25
218	Terrence Long	.25
219	*Jeff DaVanon*	1.00
220	Rick Ankiel	.50
221	Jason Standridge	.25
222	Tony Armas	.25
223	Jason Tyner	.25
224	Ramon Ortiz	.25
225	Daryle Ward	.25
226	*Enger Veras*	1.00
227	*Chris Jones*	1.50
228	*Eric Cammack*	1.00
229	Ruben Mateo	.25
230	*Ken Harvey*	3.00
231	Jake Westbrook	.25
232	*Rob Purvis*	1.00
233	Choo Freeman	.25
234	Aramis Ramirez	.25
235	A.J. Burnett	.25
236	Kevin Barker	.25
237	*Chance Caple*	2.50
238	Jarrod Washburn	.25
239	Lance Berkman	.25
240	*Michael Wenner*	1.00
241	Alex Sanchez	.25
242	*Jake Esteves*	1.00
243	Grant Roberts	.25
244	*Mark Ellis*	4.00
245	Donny Leon	.25
246	David Eckstein	.25
247	*Dicky Gonzalez*	1.00
248	John Patterson	.25
249	Chad Green	.25
250	*Scot Shields*	1.00
251	Troy Cameron	.25
252	Jose Molina	.25
253	*Rob Pugmire*	1.00
254	Rick Elder	.25
255	Sean Burroughs	.75
256	*Josh Kalinowski*	1.50
257	Matt LeCroy	.25
258	*Alex Graman*	3.00
259	*Juan Silvestre*	4.00
260	Brady Clark	.25
261	*Rico Washington*	2.00
262	Gary Matthews Jr.	.25
263	Matt Wise	.25
264	*Keith Reed*	4.00
265	*Santiago Ramirez*	1.00
266	*Ben Broussard*	5.00
267	Ryan Langerhans	.25
268	Juan Rivera	.25
269	Shawn Gallagher	.25
270	Jorge Toca	.25
271	Brad Lidge	.25
272	*Leo Estrella*	1.00
273	Ruben Quevedo	.25
274	Jack Cust	.25
275	T.J. Tucker	.25
276	Mike Colangelo	.25
277	Brian Schneider	.25
278	Calvin Murray	.25
279	Josh Girdley	.25
280	Mike Paradis	.25
281	Chad Hermansen	.25
282	*Ty Howington*	2.00
283	Aaron Myette	.25
284	D'Angelo Jimenez	.25
285	Dernell Stenson	.25
286	Jerry Hairston Jr.	.25
287	*Gary Majewski*	2.00
288	*Derrin Ebert*	1.00
289	*Steve Fish*	1.00
290	Carlos Hernandez	.25
291	Allen Levrault	.25
292	*Sean McNally*	1.00
293	*Randey Dorame*	2.50
294	*Wes Anderson*	3.00
295	B.J. Ryan	.25
296	*Alan Webb*	1.00
297	*Brandon Inge*	3.00
298	David Walling	.25
299	*Sun-Woo Kim*	3.00
300	Pat Burrell	.75
301	*Rick Guttormson*	1.00
302	Gil Meche	.25
303	*Carlos Zambrano*	3.00
304	*Eric Byrnes* (photo actually Bo Porter)	1.00
305	*Robb Quinlan*	1.00

306	Jackie Rexrode	.25
307	Nate Bump	.25
308	*Sean DePaula*	1.00
309	Matt Riley	.25
310	Ryan Minor	.25
311	J.J. Davis	.25
312	Randy Wolf	.25
313	Jason Jennings	.25
314	*Scott Seabol*	1.00
315	Doug Davis	.25
316	*Todd Moser*	1.00
317	Rob Ryan	.25
318	Bubba Crosby	.25
319	*Lyle Overbay*	4.00
320	Mario Encarnacion	.25
321	*Francisco Rodriguez*	8.00
322	Michael Cuddyer	.25
323	Eddie Yarnall	.25
324	*Cesar Saba*	3.00
325	Travis Dawkins	.25
326	Alex Escobar	.25
327	*Julio Zuleta*	1.00
328	Josh Hamilton	1.50
329	*Carlos Urquiola*	3.00
330	Matt Belisle	.25
331	*Kurt Ainsworth*	4.00
332	Tim Raines Jr.	.25
333	Eric Munson	.60
334	Donzell McDonald	.25
335	*Larry Bigbie*	2.00
336	Matt Watson	.25
337	Aubrey Huff	.25
338	Julio Ramirez	.25
339	*Jason Grabowski*	2.50
340	Jon Garland	.25
341	Austin Kearns	.25
342	Josh Pressley	.25
343	*Miguel Olivo*	1.00
344	Julio Lugo	.25
345	Roberto Vaz	.25
346	Ramon Soler	.25
347	*Brandon Phillips*	2.50
348	*Vince Faison*	4.00
349	Mike Venafro	.25
350	*Rick Asadoorian*	4.00
351	*B.J. Garbe*	5.00
352	Dan Reichert	.25
353	*Jason Stumm*	3.00
354	*Ruben Salazar*	3.00
355	Francisco Cordero	.25
356	*Juan Guzman*	1.00
357	*Mike Bacsik*	1.00
358	Jared Sandberg	.25
359	Rod Barajas	.25
360	*Junior Brignac*	2.50
361	J.M. Gold	.25
362	Octavio Dotel	.25
363	David Kelton	.25
364	*Scott Morgan*	1.00
365	*Wascar Serrano*	3.00
366	Wilton Veras	.25
367	Eugene Kingsale	.25
368	Ted Lilly	.25
369	George Lombard	.25
370	Chris Haas	.25
371	*Wilton Pena*	2.50
372	Vernon Wells	.25
373	*Keith Ginter*	5.00
374	*Jeff Heaverlo*	2.50
375	Calvin Pickering	.25
376	*Mike Lamb*	4.00
377	Kyle Snyder	.25
378	*Javier Cardona*	1.00
379	*Aaron Rowand*	4.00
380	Dee Brown	.25
381	*Brett Myers*	12.00
382	Abraham Nunez	.75
383	Eric Valent	.25
384	*Jody Gerut*	1.00
385	Adam Dunn	.50
386	Jay Gehrke	.25
387	Omar Ortiz	.25
388	Darnell McDonald	.25
389	Chad Alexander	.25
390	J.D. Closser	.25
391	*Ben Christensen*	3.00
392	Adam Kennedy	.25
393	*Nick Green*	1.00
394	Ramon Hernandez	.25
395	*Roy Oswalt*	15.00
396	*Andy Tracy*	1.00
397	Eric Gagne	.25
398	*Michael Tejera*	1.00
399	Adam Everett	.25
400	Corey Patterson	.50
401	*Gary Knotts*	1.00
402	*Ryan Christianson*	4.00
403	*Eric Ireland*	1.00
404	*Andrew Good*	1.00
405	Brad Penny	.25
406	Jason LaRue	.25
407	Kit Pellow	.25
408	Kevin Beirne	.25
409	Kelly Dransfeldt	.25
410	Jason Grilli	.25
411	*Scott Downs*	1.50
412	Jesus Colome	.25
413	*John Sneed*	1.00
414	*Tony McKnight*	1.00
415	Luis Rivera	.25
416	Adam Eaton	.25
417	*Mike MacDougal*	1.00
418	Mike Nannini	.25
419	*Barry Zito*	12.00
420	Dewayne Wise	.25
421	Jason Dellaero	.25
422	Chad Moeller	.25
423	Jason Marquis	.25
424	*Tim Redding*	2.00
425	Mark Mulder	.25
426	Josh Paul	.25
427	Chris Enochs	.25
428	*Wilfredo Rodriguez*	3.00
429	Kevin Witt	.25
430	*Scott Sobkowiak*	1.50
431	McKay Christensen	.25
432	Jung Bong	.25
433	*Keith Evans*	1.00
434	Garry Maddox Jr.	.25
435	*Ramon Santiago*	3.00
436	Alex Cora	.25
437	Carlos Lee	.25
438	*Jason Repko*	3.00
439	Matt Burch	.25
440	*Shawn Sonnier*	1.00

2000 Bowman Chrome Refractors

A parallel to the 440-card base set, these inserts have a mirror like sheen to them on the card front and are listed Refractor underneath the card number on the back. These were seeded 1:12 packs.

	MT
Stars:	4-8X
Rookies:	2-4X
Inserted 1:12	

(See 2000 Bowman Chrome for checklist and base card values.)

2000 Bowman Chrome Retro/Future

This 440-card parallel to the base set is modeled after the 1955 Bowman "television set" design and are seeded 1:6 packs, with Refractors seeded 1:60 packs.

	MT
Stars:	2-3X
Rookies:	1X
Inserted 1:6	
Refractors:	6-8X
Rookies:	1-3X
Inserted 1:60	

(See 2000 Bowman Chrome for checklist and base values.)

2000 Bowman Chrome Oversize

		MT
Complete Set (8):		15.00
Common Player:		1.00
Inserted 1:box		
1	Pat Burrell	4.00
2	Josh Hamilton	4.00
3	Rafael Furcal	1.00
4	Corey Patterson	1.50
5	A.J. Burnett	1.00
6	Eric Munson	1.00
7	Nick Johnson	1.50
8	Alfonso Soriano	2.00

2000 Bowman Chrome Bidding for the Call

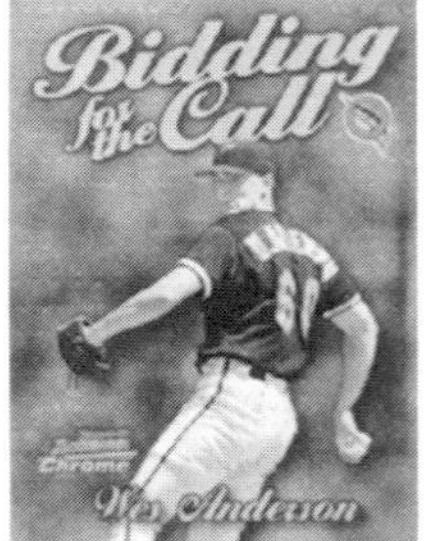

Top minor league prospects are highlighted on a design with gold foil background on an all chromium finish. Card backs are numbered with a "BC" prefix. A Refractor parallel version was also produced.

		MT
Complete Set (15):		20.00
Common Player:		1.00
Inserted 1:16		
Refractors:		2-4X
Inserted 1:160		
1	Adam Piatt	1.00
2	Pat Burrell	3.00
3	Mark Mulder	1.50
4	Nick Johnson	2.00
5	Alfonso Soriano	4.00
6	Chin-Feng Chen	4.00
7	Scott Sobkowiak	1.00
8	Corey Patterson	2.00
9	Jack Cust	1.00
10	Sean Burroughs	2.00
11	Josh Hamilton	2.00
12	Corey Myers	1.00
13	Eric Munson	1.00
14	Wes Anderson	1.00
15	Lyle Overbay	1.50

2000 Bowman Chrome Rookie Class 2000

This set highlighted 10 prospects who were thought to contend for the 2000 Rookie of the Year awards. Backs are numbered with a "RC" prefix. A Refractor parallel version was also issued.

		MT
Complete Set (10):		25.00
Common Player:		1.50
Inserted 1:24		
Refractors:		2-4X
Inserted 1:240		
1	Pat Burrell	4.00
2	Rick Ankiel	2.00
3	Ruben Mateo	1.50
4	Vernon Wells	1.50
5	Mark Mulder	1.50
6	A.J. Burnett	1.50
7	Chad Hermansen	1.50
8	Corey Patterson	2.00
9	Rafael Furcal	2.00
10	Mike Lamb	1.50

2000 Bowman Chrome Teen Idols

This 15-card set highlights top teenagers who are predicted to emerge as major league standouts.

		MT
Complete Set (15):		40.00
Common Player:		1.50
Inserted 1:16		
Refractors:		2-4X
Inserted 1:160		
1	Alex Rodriguez	8.00
2	Andruw Jones	2.00
3	Juan Gonzalez	2.50
4	Ivan Rodriguez	2.50

5	Ken Griffey Jr.	8.00
6	Bobby Bradley	2.00
7	Brett Myers	1.50
8	C.C. Sabathia	1.50
9	Ty Howington	1.50
10	Brandon Phillips	1.50
11	Rick Asadoorian	5.00
12	Wily Pena	2.50
13	Sean Burroughs	2.00
14	Josh Hamilton	4.00
15	Rafael Furcal	2.00

2000 Bowman Chrome Meteoric Rise

This 10-card set spotlights players who all made their first All-Star team within their first two years. Card fronts have a futuristic background, with the player in an intergalactic setting. Card backs are numbered with a "MR" prefix. A Refractor parallel version also exists.

		MT
Complete Set (10):		40.00
Common Player:		1.50
Inserted 1:24		
Refractors:		2-4X
Inserted 1:240		
1	Nomar Garciaparra	5.00
2	Mark McGwire	6.00
3	Ken Griffey Jr.	6.00
4	Chipper Jones	5.00
5	Manny Ramirez	2.50
6	Mike Piazza	6.00
7	Cal Ripken Jr.	8.00
8	Ivan Rodriguez	2.00
9	Greg Maddux	5.00
10	Randy Johnson	2.00

2000 Bowman Chrome Draft Picks and Prospects

		MT
Complete Set (110):		45.00
Common Player:		.25
1	Pat Burrell	2.00
2	Rafael Furcal	.50
3	Grant Roberts	.25
4	Barry Zito	3.00
5	Julio Zuleta	1.00
6	Mark Mulder	.25
7	Rob Bell	.25
8	Adam Piatt	1.00
9	Mike Lamb	.75
10	Pablo Ozuna	.25
11	Jason Tyner	.25
12	Jason Marquis	.25
13	Eric Munson	.50
14	Seth Etherton	.25
15	Milton Bradley	.25
16	Nick Green	.25
17	*Chin-Feng Chen*	5.00
18	*Matt Boone*	2.00
19	*Kevin Gregg*	1.00
20	*Eddy Garabito*	1.50
21	*Aaron Capista*	1.00
22	*Esteban German*	1.00
23	*Derek Thompson*	1.00
24	*Phil Merrell*	1.00
25	*Brian O'Connor*	1.00
26	Yamid Haad	.25
27	*Hector Mercado*	1.00
28	*Jason Woolf*	1.00
29	*Eddie Furniss*	1.00
30	*Cha Sueng Baek*	1.50
31	*Colby Lewis*	1.00
32	*Pasqual Coco*	1.00
33	*Jorge Cantu*	1.00
34	*Erasmo Ramirez*	1.50
35	*Bobby Kielty*	3.00
36	*Joaquin Benoit*	2.50
37	*Brian Esposito*	2.00
38	Michael Wenner	.25
39	*Juan Rincon*	1.00
40	*Yorvit Torrealba*	1.00
41	*Chad Durham*	1.00
42	*Jim Mann*	1.00
43	*Shane Loux*	1.00
44	Luis Rivas	.25
45	*Ken Chenard*	1.00
46	*Mike Lockwood*	1.00
47	*Giovanni Lara*	1.00
48	*Bubba Carpenter*	1.00
49	*Ryan Dittfurth*	.75
50	*John Stephens*	1.00
51	*Pedro Feliz*	2.00
52	*Kenny Kelly*	2.00
53	*Neil Jenkins*	1.50
54	*Mike Glendenning*	1.00
55	Bo Porter	.25
56	Eric Byrnes	.25
57	*Tony Alvarez*	1.50
58	*Kazuhiro Sasaki*	4.00
59	*Chad Durbin*	1.00
60	*Mike Bynum*	1.00
61	*Travis Wilson*	1.00
62	*Jose Leon*	1.00
63	*Ryan Vogelsong*	1.00
64	*Geraldo Guzman*	1.00
65	*Craig Anderson*	1.00
66	*Carlos Silva*	1.00
67	*Brad Thomas*	1.00
68	*Chin-Hui Tsao*	2.00
69	*Mark Buehrle*	4.00
70	*Juan Salas*	1.00
71	*Denny Abreu*	1.00
72	*Keith McDonald*	1.00
73	*Chris Richard*	3.00
74	*Tomas de la Rosa*	1.00
75	Vicente Padilla	.25
76	*Justin Brunette*	1.00
77	*Scott Linebrink*	1.00
78	*Jeff Sparks*	1.00
79	*Tike Redman*	1.00
80	*John Lackey*	2.00
81	*Joe Strong*	1.00
82	*Brian Tollberg*	1.50
83	*Steve Sisco*	1.00
84	Chris Clapinski	.25
85	*Augie Ojeda*	1.00
86	*Adrian Gonzalez* (Draft Picks)	12.00
87	*Mike Stodolka* (Draft Picks)	2.00
88	*(Adam Johnson)* (Draft Picks)	3.00
89	*(Matt Wheatland)* (Draft Picks)	2.00
90	*Corey Smith* (Draft Picks)	4.00
91	*Rocco Baldelli* (Draft Picks)	6.00
92	*Keith Bucktrot* (Draft Picks)	1.00
93	*Adam Wainwright* (Draft Picks)	4.00
94	*Blaine Boyer* (Draft Picks)	1.00
95	*Aaron Herr* (Draft Picks)	1.00
96	*Scott Thorman* (Draft Picks)	2.00
97	*Brian Digby* (Draft Picks)	1.00
98	*Josh Shortslef* (Draft Picks)	1.00
99	*Sean Smith* (Draft Picks)	1.00
100	*Alex Cruz* (Draft Picks)	1.00
101	*Marc Love* (Draft Picks)	1.00
102	*Kevin Lee* (Draft Picks)	1.00
103	*Timoniel Perez* (Draft Picks)	2.00
104	*Alex Cabrera* (Draft Picks)	2.00
105	*Shane Heams* (Draft Picks)	1.50
106	*Tripper Johnson* (Draft Picks)	2.00
107	*Brent Abernathy* (Draft Picks)	2.00
108	*John Cotton* (Draft Picks)	.75
109	*Brad Wilkerson* (Draft Picks)	1.50
110	*Jon Rauch* (Draft Picks)	5.00

2000 Bowman Draft Picks and Prospects

		MT
Complete Set (110):		25.00
Common Player:		.15
1	Pat Burrell	.75
2	Rafael Furcal	.25
3	Grant Roberts	.15
4	Barry Zito	1.00
5	Julio Zuleta	.40
6	Mark Mulder	.15
7	Rob Bell	.15
8	Adam Piatt	.40
9	Mike Lamb	.40
10	Pablo Ozuna	.15
11	Jason Tyner	.15
12	Jason Marquis	.15
13	Eric Munson	.25
14	Seth Etherton	.15
15	Milton Bradley	.15
16	Nick Green	.15
17	*Chin-Feng Chen*	2.50
18	*Matt Boone*	.40
19	*Kevin Gregg*	.15
20	*Eddy Garabito*	.25
21	*Aaron Capista*	.25
22	*Esteban German*	.25
23	*Derek Thompson*	.25
24	*Phil Merrell*	.25
25	*Brian O'Connor*	.25
26	Yamid Haad	.15
27	*Hector Mercado*	.25
28	*Jason Woolf*	.25
29	*Eddie Furniss*	.25
30	*Cha Sueng Baek*	.75
31	*Colby Lewis*	.25
32	*Pasqual Coco*	.25
33	*Jorge Cantu*	.15
34	*Erasmo Ramirez*	.50
35	*Bobby Kielty*	.50
36	*Joaquin Benoit*	.50
37	*Brian Esposito*	.40
38	Michael Wenner	.15
39	*Juan Rincon*	.25
40	*Yorvit Torrealba*	.25
41	*Chad Durham*	.25
42	*Jim Mann*	.25
43	*Shane Loux*	.15
44	Luis Rivas	.15
45	*Ken Chenard*	.25
46	*Mike Lockwood*	.25
47	*Yovanny Lara*	.25
48	*Bubba Carpenter*	.25
49	*Jeremy Griffiths*	.15
50	*John Stephens*	.25
51	*Pedro Feliz*	2.00
52	*Kenny Kelly*	.50
53	*Neil Jenkins*	1.00
54	*Mike Glendenning*	.25
55	Bo Porter	.15
56	Eric Byrnes	.15
57	*Tony Alvarez*	.50
58	*Kazuhiro Sasaki*	1.50
59	*Chad Durbin*	.25
60	*Mike Bynum*	.75
61	*Travis Wilson*	.25
62	*Jose Leon*	.40
63	*Bill Ortega*	.50
64	*Geraldo Guzman*	.25
65	*Craig Anderson*	.25
66	*Carlos Silva*	.25
67	*Brad Thomas*	.25
68	*Chin-Hui Tsao*	2.50
69	*Mark Buehrle*	.50
70	*Juan Salas*	.25
71	*Denny Abreu*	.25
72	*Keith McDonald*	.25
73	*Chris Richard*	1.00
74	*Tomas de la Rosa*	.25
75	Vicente Padilla	.15
76	*Justin Brunette*	.40
77	*Scott Linebrink*	.25
78	*Jeff Sparks*	.25
79	*Tike Redman*	.25
80	*John Lackey*	.40
81	*Joe Strong*	.25
82	*Brian Tollberg*	.40
83	*Steve Sisco*	.25
84	Chris Clapinski	.15
85	*Augie Ojeda*	.25
86	*Adrian Gonzalez* (Draft Picks)	3.00
87	*Mike Stodolka* (Draft Picks)	.50
88	*(Adam Johnson)* (Draft Picks)	.75
89	*(Matt Wheatland)* (Draft Picks)	.75
90	*Corey Smith* (Draft Picks)	.75
91	*Rocco Baldelli* (Draft Picks)	2.50
92	*Keith Bucktrot* (Draft Picks)	.40
93	*Adam Wainwright* (Draft Picks)	1.00
94	*Blaine Boyer* (Draft Picks)	.25
95	*Aaron Herr* (Draft Picks)	1.00
96	*Scott Thorman* (Draft Picks)	1.00
97	*Brian Digby* (Draft Picks)	.25
98	*Josh Shortslef* (Draft Picks)	.25
99	*Sean Smith* (Draft Picks)	.25
100	*Alex Cruz* (Draft Picks)	.40
101	*Marc Love* (Draft Picks)	.40
102	*Kevin Lee* (Draft Picks)	.25
103	*Victor Ramos* (Draft Picks)	.25
104	*Jason Kanoi* (Draft Picks)	.25
105	*Luis Escobar* (Draft Picks)	.25
106	*Tripper Johnson* (Draft Picks)	1.00
107	*Phil Dumatrait* (Draft Picks)	.50

108	*Bryan Edwards* (Draft Picks)	.25
109	*Grady Sizemore* (Draft Picks)	4.00
110	*Thomas Mitchell* (Draft Picks)	.25

2000 Bowman Draft Picks and Prospects Autograph

		MT
Common Player:		8.00
Inserted 1:set		
1	Pat Burrell	25.00
2	Rafael Furcal	20.00
3	Grant Roberts	8.00
4	Barry Zito	25.00
5	Julio Zuleta	8.00
6	Mark Mulder	20.00
7	Bob Bell	8.00
8	Adam Piatt	15.00
9	Mike Lamb	10.00
10	Pablo Ozuna	8.00
11	Jason Tyner	8.00
12	Jason Marquis	8.00
13	Eric Munson	15.00
14	Seth Etherton	8.00
15	Milton Bradley	10.00
16	NOT ISSUED	
17	Michael Wenner	8.00
18	Mike Glendenning	8.00
19	Tony Alvarez	15.00
20	Adrian Gonzalez	35.00
21	Corey Smith	15.00
22	Matt Wheatland	15.00
23	Adam Johnson	15.00
24	Mike Stodolka	15.00
25	Rocco Baldelli	25.00
26	Juan Rincon	8.00
27	Chad Durbin	10.00
28	Yorvit Torrealba	8.00
29	Nick Green	8.00
30	Derek Thompson	8.00
31	John Lackey	8.00
32	NOT ISSUED	
33	Kevin Gregg	8.00
34	NOT ISSUED	
35	Denny Abreu	10.00
36	Brian Tollberg	8.00
37	Yamid Haad	8.00
38	Grady Sizemore	35.00
39	Carlos Silva	10.00
40	Jorge Cantu	8.00
41	Bobby Kielty	12.00
42	Scott Thorman	15.00
43	Juan Salas	8.00
44	Phil Dumatrait	15.00
45	NOT ISSUED	
46	Mike Lockwood	8.00
47	Yovanny Lara	8.00
48	Tripper Johnson	12.00
49	Colby Lewis	8.00
50	Neil Jenkins	12.00
51	Keith Bucktrot	10.00
52	Eric Byrnes	15.00
53	Aaron Herr	15.00
54	Erasmo Ramirez	10.00
55	Chris Richard	20.00
56	NOT ISSUED	
57	Mike Bynum	15.00
58	Brian Esposito	8.00
59	Chris Clapinski	8.00
60	Augie Ojeda	8.00

2000 Bowman's Best Pre-Production

Three-card cello packs of promotional cards introduced the Bowman's Best issue for 2000. The cards are virtually identical to the regularly issued version except for the numbering on the back which includes a "PP" prefix.

		MT
Complete Set (3):		6.00
Common Player:		2.00
PP1	Larry Walker	2.00
PP2	Adam Dunn	2.00
PP3	Brett Myers	2.00

2000 Bowman's Best

The base set consists of 200-cards on a mirror like sheen, reminiscent of Refractors. Veteran cards have gold highlights while rookies and prospects have blue highlights. There are three subsets: Best Performers (86-100), Prospects (101-150) and Rookies (151-200). Rookies are serially numbered to 2,999 on the card back and are randomly inserted on the average of 1:7 packs.

		MT
Complete Set (200):		500.00
Common Player:		.20
Common Rookie (151-200):		8.00
Production 2,999 sets		
Pack (4):		6.00
Box (24):		120.00
1	Nomar Garciaparra	2.50
2	Chipper Jones	1.50
3	Damion Easley	.20
4	Bernie Williams	.75
5	Barry Bonds	1.00
6	Jermaine Dye	.20
7	John Olerud	.40
8	Mike Hampton	.20
9	Cal Ripken Jr.	3.00
10	Jeff Bagwell	1.00
11	Troy Glaus	.75
12	J.D. Drew	.40
13	Jeromy Burnitz	.20
14	Carlos Delgado	.75
15	Shawn Green	.40
16	Kevin Millwood	.20
17	Rondell White	.40
18	Scott Rolen	.75
19	Jeff Cirillo	.20
20	Barry Larkin	.50
21	Brian Giles	.20
22	Roger Clemens	1.50
23	Manny Ramirez	1.00
24	Alex Gonzalez	.20
25	Mark Grace	.40
26	Fernando Tatis	.40
27	Randy Johnson	.75
28	Roger Cedeno	.20
29	Brian Jordan	.20
30	Kevin Brown	.40
31	Greg Vaughn	.20
32	Roberto Alomar	.75
33	Larry Walker	.40
34	Rafael Palmeiro	.50
35	Curt Schilling	.30
36	Orlando Hernandez	.30
37	Todd Walker	.20
38	Juan Gonzalez	1.00
39	Sean Casey	.30
40	Tony Gwynn	1.00
41	Albert Belle	.30
42	Gary Sheffield	.50
43	Michael Barrett	.20
44	Preston Wilson	.20
45	Jim Thome	.50
46	Shannon Stewart	.20
47	Mo Vaughn	.40
48	Ben Grieve	.40
49	Adrian Beltre	.20
50	Sammy Sosa	2.00
51	Bob Abreu	.40
52	Edgardo Alfonzo	.40
53	Carlos Febles	.20
54	Frank Thomas	1.00
55	Alex Rodriguez	2.50
56	Cliff Floyd	.20
57	Jose Canseco	.60
58	Erubiel Durazo	.20
59	Tim Hudson	.40
60	Craig Biggio	.40
61	Eric Karros	.20
62	Mike Mussina	.50
63	Robin Ventura	.30
64	Carlos Beltran	.20
65	Pedro Martinez	1.00
66	Gabe Kapler	.40
67	Jason Kendall	.30
68	Derek Jeter	3.00
69	Magglio Ordonez	.40
70	Mike Piazza	2.50
71	Mike Lieberthal	.20
72	Andres Galarraga	.50
73	Raul Mondesi	.30
74	Eric Chavez	.30
75	Greg Maddux	2.00
76	Matt Williams	.50
77	Kris Benson	.20
78	Ivan Rodriguez	1.00
79	Pokey Reese	.20
80	Vladimir Guerrero	1.00
81	Mark McGwire	3.00
82	Vinny Castilla	.20
83	Todd Helton	1.00
84	Andruw Jones	.50
85	Ken Griffey Jr.	2.50
86	Mark McGwire (Best Performers)	1.50
87	Derek Jeter (Best Performers)	1.50
88	Chipper Jones (Best Performers)	1.00
89	Nomar Garciaparra (Best Performers)	1.00
90	Sammy Sosa (Best Performers)	1.00
91	Cal Ripken Jr. (Best Performers)	1.50
92	Juan Gonzalez (Best Performers)	.50
93	Alex Rodriguez (Best Performers)	1.50
94	Barry Bonds (Best Performers)	.50
95	Sean Casey (Best Performers)	.20
96	Vladimir Guerrero (Best Performers)	.50
97	Mike Piazza (Best Performers)	1.25
98	Shawn Green (Best Performers)	.20
99	Jeff Bagwell (Best Performers)	.50
100	Ken Griffey Jr. (Best Performers)	1.50
101	Rick Ankiel (Prospects)	.40
102	John Patterson (Prospects)	.20
103	David Walling (Prospects)	.20
104	Michael Restovich (Prospects)	.20
105	A.J. Burnett (Prospects)	.20
106	Matt Riley (Prospects)	.20
107	Chad Hermansen (Prospects)	.20
108	Choo Freeman (Prospects)	.20
109	Mark Quinn (Prospects)	.20
110	Corey Patterson (Prospects)	.50
111	Ramon Ortiz (Prospects)	.20
112	Vernon Wells (Prospects)	.20
113	Milton Bradley (Prospects)	.20
114	Travis Dawkins (Prospects)	.20
115	Sean Burroughs (Prospects)	.50
116	Willi Mo Pena (Prospects)	1.00
117	Dee Brown (Prospects)	.20
118	C.C. Sabathia (Prospects)	.20
119	*Larry Bigbie* (Prospects)	.20
120	Octavio Dotel (Prospects)	.20
121	Kip Wells (Prospects)	.20
122	Ben Petrick (Prospects)	.20
123	Mark Mulder (Prospects)	.20
124	Jason Standridge (Prospects)	.20
125	Adam Piatt (Prospects)	.20
126	Steve Lomasney (Prospects)	.20
127	Jayson Werth (Prospects)	.20
128	Alex Escobar (Prospects)	.20
129	Ryan Anderson (Prospects)	.40
130	Adam Dunn (Prospects)	.20
131	Omar Ortiz (Prospects)	.20
132	Brad Penny (Prospects)	.20
133	Daryle Ward (Prospects)	.20
134	Eric Munson (Prospects)	.50
135	Nick Johnson (Prospects)	.50
136	Jason Jennings (Prospects)	.20
137	Tim Raines Jr. (Prospects)	.20
138	Ruben Mateo (Prospects)	.20
139	Jack Cust (Prospects)	.20
140	Rafael Furcal (Prospects)	.40
141	Eric Gagne (Prospects)	.20
142	Tony Armas (Prospects)	.20

143	Mike Paradis (Prospects)	.20
144	Chris George (Prospects)	.20
145	Alfonso Soriano (Prospects)	.50
146	Josh Hamilton (Prospects)	1.00
147	Michael Cuddyer (Prospects)	.20
148	Jay Gehrke (Prospects)	.20
149	Josh Girdley (Prospects)	.20
150	Pat Burrell (Prospects)	1.00
151	*Brett Myers*	25.00
152	*Scott Seabol*	8.00
153	*Keith Reed*	15.00
154	*Francisco Rodriguez*	30.00
155	*Barry Zito*	40.00
156	*Pat Manning*	12.00
157	*Ben Christensen*	8.00
158	*Corey Myers*	10.00
159	*Wascar Serrano*	10.00
160	*Wes Anderson*	10.00
161	*Andy Tracy*	8.00
162	*Cesar Saba*	8.00
163	*Mike Lamb*	10.00
164	*Bobby Bradley*	15.00
165	*Vince Faison*	8.00
166	*Ty Howington*	15.00
167	*Ken Harvey*	25.00
168	*Josh Kalinowski*	8.00
169	*Ruben Salazar*	12.00
170	*Aaron Rowand*	15.00
171	*Ramon Santiago*	8.00
172	*Scott Sobkowiak*	8.00
173	*Lyle Overbay*	15.00
174	*Rico Washington*	8.00
175	*Rick Asadoorian*	12.00
176	*Matt Ginter*	8.00
177	*Jason Stumm*	10.00
178	*B.J. Garbe*	15.00
179	*Mike MacDougal*	8.00
180	*Ryan Christianson*	12.00
181	*Kurt Ainsworth*	15.00
182	*Brad Baisley*	8.00
183	*Ben Broussard*	20.00
184	*Aaron McNeal*	10.00
185	*John Sneed*	8.00
186	*Junior Brignac*	8.00
187	*Chance Caple*	10.00
188	*Scott Downs*	8.00
189	*Matt Cepicky*	8.00
190	*Chin-Feng Chen*	25.00
191	*Johan Santana*	8.00
192	*Brad Baker*	10.00
193	*Jason Repko*	8.00
194	*Craig Dingman*	8.00
195	Chris Wakeland	10.00
196	*Rogelio Arias*	8.00
197	*Luis Matos*	10.00
198	*Robert Ramsay*	8.00
199	*Willie Bloomquist*	15.00
200	*Tony Pena Jr.*	10.00

2000 Bowman's Best Bets

This 10-card set highlighted prospects who had the best chance of making the big league. The upper left corner and bottom right corner are die-cut. An small action photo is super imposed over a larger background shot of the featured player. Backs are numbered with a "BBB" prefix.

		MT
Complete Set (10):		25.00
Common Player:		1.50
Inserted 1:15		
1	Pat Burrell	4.00
2	Alfonso Soriano	2.00
3	Corey Patterson	1.50
4	Eric Munson	2.00
5	Sean Burroughs	2.00
6	Rafael Furcal	1.50
7	Rick Ankiel	2.00
8	Nick Johnson	2.00
9	Ruben Mateo	1.50
10	Josh Hamilton	4.00

2000 Bowman's Best Franchise 2000

Each of the 25-cards in this set have rounded corners on a holographic silver design. Backs are numbered with a "F" prefix.

		MT
Complete Set (25):		150.00
Common Player:		2.00
Inserted 1:18		
1	Cal Ripken Jr.	15.00
2	Nomar Garciaparra	12.00
3	Frank Thomas	8.00
4	Manny Ramirez	5.00
5	Juan Gonzalez	5.00
6	Carlos Beltran	2.00
7	Derek Jeter	15.00
8	Alex Rodriguez	15.00
9	Ben Grieve	3.00
10	Jose Canseco	3.00
11	Ivan Rodriguez	5.00
12	Mo Vaughn	3.00
13	Randy Johnson	4.00
14	Chipper Jones	10.00
15	Sammy Sosa	12.00
16	Ken Griffey Jr.	15.00
17	Larry Walker	3.00
18	Preston Wilson	2.00
19	Jeff Bagwell	5.00
20	Shawn Green	3.00
21	Vladimir Guerrero	8.00
22	Mike Piazza	12.00
23	Scott Rolen	4.00
24	Tony Gwynn	8.00
25	Barry Bonds	6.00

2000 Bowman's Best Franchise Favorites

Two current players and two retired stars are featured in this six-card set. Card backs are numbered with a "FR" prefix.

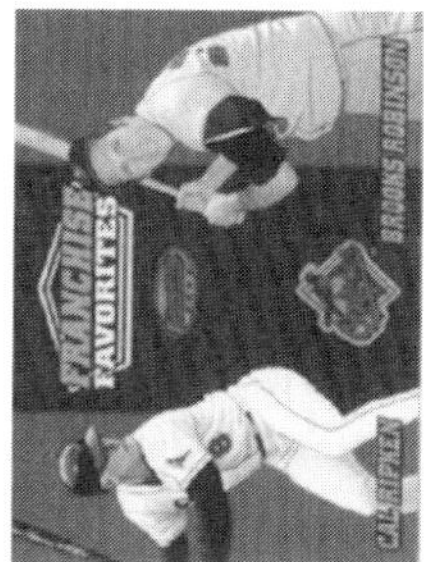

		MT
Complete Set (6):		25.00
Common Player:		1.50
Inserted 1:17		
1A	Sean Casey	1.50
1B	Johnny Bench	4.00
1C	Sean Casey, Johnny Bench	4.00
2A	Cal Ripken Jr.	8.00
2B	Brooks Robinson	3.00
2C	Cal Ripken Jr., Brooks Robinson	8.00

2000 Bowman's Best Franchise Favorites Autograph

These autographs are seeded 1:1,291 packs, while the two dual autographed versions are inserted 1:5,153 packs.

		MT
Common Player:		30.00
Version A & B 1:1,291		
Version C 1:5,153		
1A	Sean Casey	25.00
1B	Johnny Bench	100.00
1C	Sean Casey, Johnny Bench	125.00
2A	Cal Ripken Jr.	180.00
2B	Brooks Robinson	50.00
2C	Cal Ripken Jr., Brooks Robinson	250.00

2000 Bowman's Best Locker Room Collection Autographs

Part of the Locker Room Collection, these autographs feature 19 players. Backs are numbered with a "LRCA" prefix.

		MT
Complete Set (19):		360.00
Common Player:		15.00
Inserted 1:57		
1	Carlos Beltran	15.00
2	Rick Ankiel	20.00
3	Vernon Wells	15.00
4	Ruben Mateo	15.00
5	Ben Petrick	15.00
6	Adam Piatt	25.00
7	Eric Munson	25.00
8	Alfonso Soriano	25.00
9	Kerry Wood	30.00
10	Jack Cust	20.00
11	Rafael Furcal	25.00
12	Josh Hamilton	40.00
13	Brad Penny	15.00
14	Dee Brown	15.00
15	Milton Bradley	20.00
16	Ryan Anderson	20.00
17	John Patterson	15.00
18	Nick Johnson	20.00
19	Peter Bergeron	15.00

2000 Bowman's Best Locker Room Collection Lumber

These inserts have a piece of game-used bat embedded into them. They are numbered with a "LRCL" prefix on the back.

		MT
Complete Set (11):		
Common Player:		25.00
Inserted 1:376		
1	Carlos Beltran	25.00
2	Rick Ankiel	25.00
3	Vernon Wells	25.00
4	Adam Kennedy	25.00
5	Ben Petrick	25.00
6	Adam Piatt	30.00
7	Eric Munson	30.00
8	Rafael Furcal	25.00
9	J.D. Drew	40.00
10	Pat Burrell	50.00

2000 Bowman's Best Locker Room Collection Jerseys

These inserts have a piece of game-worn jersey embedded into them and are numbered with a "LRCJ" prefix.

		MT
Complete Set (5):		160.00
Common Player:		25.00
Inserted 1:206		
1	Carlos Beltran	25.00
2	Rick Ankiel	25.00
3	Adam Kennedy	25.00
4	Ben Petrick	25.00
5	Adam Piatt	30.00

2000 Bowman's Best Rookie Signed Baseballs

Redemption inserts, redeemable for Rookie Signed Baseballs, were randomly inserted. signed baseball displays the Bowman "Rookie Autograph" logo and the Topps "Genuine Issue" sticker.

		MT
Complete Set (5):		160.00
Common Player:		25.00
Inserted 1:688		
1	Josh Hamilton	50.00
2	Rick Ankiel	30.00
3	Alfonso Soriano	35.00
4	Nick Johnson	25.00
5	Corey Patterson	40.00

2000 Bowman's Best Selections

This 15-card set is printed on a luminescent, die-cut design. The set features former Rookies of the Year and former No. 1 overall Draft Picks. These are seeded 1:30 packs. Backs are numbered with a "BBS" prefix.

		MT
Complete Set (15):		120.00
Common Player:		2.50
Inserted 1:30		
1	Alex Rodriguez	15.00
2	Ken Griffey Jr.	15.00
3	Pat Burrell	5.00
4	Mark McGwire	20.00
5	Derek Jeter	20.00
6	Nomar Garciaparra	12.00
7	Mike Piazza	12.00
8	Josh Hamilton	5.00
9	Cal Ripken Jr.	15.00
10	Jeff Bagwell	5.00
11	Chipper Jones	10.00
12	Jose Canseco	3.00
13	Carlos Beltran	2.50
14	Kerry Wood	3.00
15	Ben Grieve	3.00

2000 Bowman's Best Year By Year

This 10-card set highlights 10 duos who began their careers in the same year. They have a horizontal format on a mirror foiled card front. Backs are numbered with a "YY" prefix.

		MT
Complete Set (10):		75.00
Common Player:		4.00
Inserted 1:23		
1	Sammy Sosa, Ken Griffey Jr.	12.00
2	Nomar Garciaparra, Vladimir Guerrero	10.00
3	Alex Rodriguez, Jeff Cirillo	12.00
4	Mike Piazza, Pedro Martinez	10.00
5	Derek Jeter, Edgardo Alfonzo	12.00
6	Alfonso Soriano, Rick Ankiel	3.00
7	Mark McGwire, Barry Bonds	15.00
8	Juan Gonzalez, Larry Walker	4.00
9	Ivan Rodriguez, Jeff Bagwell	4.00
10	Shawn Green, Manny Ramirez	4.00

A card number in parentheses ( ) indicates the set is unnumbered.

2001 Bowman

		MT
Complete Set (440):		120.00
Common Player:		.15
Common Rookie:		.50
Golds:		1-2X
Inserted 1:1		
Pack (10):		3.50
Box (24):		75.00
1	Jason Giambi	.40
2	Rafael Furcal	.25
3	Rick Ankiel	.15
4	Freddy Garcia	.15
5	Magglio Ordonez	.25
6	Bernie Williams	.50
7	Kenny Lofton	.25
8	Al Leiter	.25
9	Albert Belle	.15
10	Craig Biggio	.25
11	Mark Mulder	.15
12	Carlos Delgado	.60
13	Darin Erstad	.40
14	Richie Sexson	.15
15	Randy Johnson	.75
16	Greg Maddux	1.50
17	Cliff Floyd	.15
18	Mark Buehrle	.15
19	Chris Singleton	.15
20	Orlando Hernandez	.25
21	Javier Vazquez	.15
22	Jeff Kent	.25
23	Jim Thome	.25
24	John Olerud	.25
25	Jason Kendall	.15
26	Scott Rolen	.40
27	Tony Gwynn	1.00
28	Edgardo Alfonzo	.15
29	Pokey Reese	.15
30	Todd Helton	.75
31	Mark Quinn	.15
32	*Dan Tosca*	.50
33	Dean Palmer	.15
34	Jacque Jones	.15
35	Ray Durham	.15
36	Rafael Palmeiro	.40
37	Carl Everett	.15
38	Ryan Dempster	.15
39	Randy Wolf	.15
40	Vladimir Guerrero	1.00
41	Livan Hernandez	.15
42	Mo Vaughn	.25
43	Shannon Stewart	.15
44	Preston Wilson	.15
45	Jose Vidro	.15
46	Fred McGriff	.20
47	Kevin Brown	.25
48	Peter Bergeron	.15
49	Miguel Tejada	.25
50	Chipper Jones	1.50
51	Edgar Martinez	.15
52	Tony Batista	.15
53	Jorge Posada	.25
54	Rickey Ledee	.15
55	Sammy Sosa	1.50
56	Steve Cox	.15
57	Tony Armas Jr.	.15
58	Gary Sheffield	.25
59	Bartolo Colon	.15
60	Pat Burrell	.40
61	Jay Payton	.15
62	Sean Casey	.25
63	Larry Walker	.25
64	Mike Mussina	.40
65	Nomar Garciaparra	2.00
66	Darren Dreifort	.15
67	Richard Hidalgo	.25
68	Troy Glaus	.75
69	Ben Grieve	.25
70	Jim Edmonds	.25
71	Raul Mondesi	.25
72	Andruw Jones	.60
73	Luis Castillo	.15
74	Mike Sweeney	.15
75	Derek Jeter	2.50
76	Ruben Mateo	.15
77	Carlos Lee	.15
78	Cristian Guzman	.15
79	Mike Hampton	.25
80	J.D. Drew	.25
81	Matt Lawton	.15
82	Moises Alou	.25
83	Terrence Long	.15
84	Geoff Jenkins	.25
85	Manny Ramirez	1.00
86	Johnny Damon	.15
87	Barry Larkin	.40
88	Pedro Martinez	1.00
89	Juan Gonzalez	.75
90	Roger Clemens	1.00
91	Carlos Beltran	.15
92	Brad Radke	.15
93	Orlando Cabrera	.15
94	Roberto Alomar	.60
95	Barry Bonds	1.25
96	Tim Hudson	.25
97	Tom Glavine	.25
98	Jeromy Burnitz	.15
99	Adrian Beltre	.15
100	Mike Piazza	2.00
101	Kerry Wood	.25
102	Steve Finley	.15
103	Alex Cora	.15
104	Bob Abreu	.15
105	Neifi Perez	.15
106	Mark Redman	.15
107	Paul Konerko	.15
108	Jermaine Dye	.15
109	Brian Giles	.25
110	Ivan Rodriguez	.75
111	Vinny Castilla	.15
112	Adam Kennedy	.15
113	Eric Chavez	.25
114	Billy Koch	.15
115	Shawn Green	.25
116	Matt Williams	.25
117	Greg Vaughn	.15
118	Gabe Kapler	.25
119	Jeff Cirillo	.15
120	Frank Thomas	1.00
121	David Justice	.30
122	Cal Ripken Jr.	2.50
123	Rich Aurilia	.15
124	Curt Schilling	.25
125	Barry Zito	.25
126	Brian Jordan	.15
127	Chan Ho Park	.25
128	J.T. Snow Jr.	.15
129	Kazuhiro Sasaki	.15
130	Alex Rodriguez	2.00
131	Mariano Rivera	.25
132	Eric Milton	.15
133	Andy Pettite	.25
134	Scott Elarton	.15
135	Ken Griffey Jr.	2.00
136	Bengie Molina	.15
137	Jeff Bagwell	.75
138	Kevin Millwood	.15
139	Tino Martinez	.15
140	Mark McGwire	2.50
141	Larry Barnes	.15
142	*John Buck*	.75
143	*Freddie Bynum*	.75
144	Abraham Nunez	.15
145	*Felix Diaz*	.50
146	*Horatio Estrada*	.50
147	Ben Diggins	.15
148	*Tsuyoshi Shinjo*	2.00
149	Rocco Baldelli	.15
150	Rod Barajas	.15
151	Luis Terrero	.15
152	Milton Bradley	.15
153	Kurt Ainsworth	.15
154	Russell Branyan	.15
155	Ryan Anderson	.15
156	*Mitch Jones*	.50
157	Chip Ambres	.15
158	*Steve Bennett*	1.50
159	Ivanon Coffie	.15
160	Sean Burroughs	.15
161	Keith Bucktrot	.15
162	Tony Alvarez	.15
163	Joaquin Benoit	.15
164	Rick Asadoorian	.25
165	Ben Broussard	.15
166	*Ryan Madson*	.75
167	Dee Brown	.15
168	*Sergio Contreras*	.75
169	John Barnes	.15
170	*Ben Washburn*	1.00
171	*Erick Almonte*	.50
172	*Shawn Fagan*	.50
173	*Gary Johnson*	.75
174	Brady Clark	.15
175	Grant Roberts	.15
176	Tony Torcato	.15
177	Ramon Castro	.15
178	Esteban German	.15
179	*Joe Hamer*	.50
180	Nick Neugebauer	.50
181	Dernell Stenson	.15
182	*Yhency Brazoban*	1.00
183	Aaron Myette	.15
184	Juan Sosa	.15
185	Brandon Inge	.15
186	*Domingo Guante*	.50
187	Adrian Brown	.15
188	*Deivi Mendez*	1.00
189	Luis Matos	.15
190	*Pedro Liriano*	.50
191	Donnie Bridges	.15
192	Alex Cintron	.15
193	Jace Brewer	.15
194	*Ron Davenport*	.50
195	*Jason Belcher*	1.00
196	*Adrian Hernandez*	1.00
197	Bobby Kielty	.15
198	*Reggie Griggs*	.75
199	*Reggie Abercrombie*	.50
200	*Troy Farnsworth*	.50
201	Matt Belisle	.15
202	*Miguel Villilo*	.50
203	Adam Everett	.15
204	John Lackey	.15
205	Pasqual Coco	.15
206	Adam Wainwright	.15
207	*Matt White*	1.00
208	Chin-Feng Chen	.25
209	*Jeff Andra*	.50
210	Willie Bloomquist	.15
211	Wes Anderson	.15
212	Enrique Cruz	.15
213	Jerry Hairston Jr.	.15
214	Mike Bynum	.15
215	*Brian Hitchcox*	.50
216	Ryan Christianson	.15
217	J.J. Davis	.15
218	Jovanny Cedeno	.15
219	Elvin Nina	.15
220	Alex Graman	.15
221	Arturo McDowell	.15
222	*Deivi Santos*	1.00
223	Jody Gerut	.15
224	Sun-Woo Kim	.15
225	Jimmy Rollins	.15
226	Pappy Ndungidi	.15
227	Ruben Salazar	.15
228	Josh Girdley	.15
229	Carl Crawford	.15
230	*Luis Montanez*	1.50
231	*Ramon Carvajal*	.50
232	Matt Riley	.15
233	Ben Davis	.15
234	Jason Grabowski	.15
235	Chris George	.15
236	*Hank Blalock*	4.00
237	Roy Oswalt	.15
238	*Eric Reynolds*	1.00
239	Brian Cole	.15
240	*Denny Bautista*	.75
241	*Hector Garcia*	.50
242	*Joe Thurston*	1.00
243	Brad Cresse	.75
244	Corey Patterson	.25
245	*Brett Evert*	.50
246	*Elpidio Guzman*	.50
247	Vernon Wells	.15
248	*Roberto Miniel*	.50
249	*Brian Bass*	.50
250	*Mark Burnett*	.50
251	Juan Silvestre	.15
252	Pablo Ozuna	.15
253	Jayson Werth	.15
254	*Russ Jacobsen*	.50
255	Chad Hermansen	.15
256	*Travis Hafner*	.50
257	Bradley Baker	.15
258	Gookie Dawkins	.15
259	Michael Cuddyer	.15
260	Mark Buehrle	.15
261	Ricardo Aramboles	.15
262	*Esix Snead*	.50

263 *Wilson Betemit* 3.00
264 *Albert Pujols* 12.00
265 Joe Lawrence .15
266 Ramon Ortiz .15
267 Ben Sheets .50
268 *Luke Lockwood* .50
269 Toby Hall .15
270 Jack Cust .15
271 Pedro Feliz .15
272 *Noel Devarez* .50
273 Josh Beckett .15
274 Alex Escobar .15
275 *Doug Gredvig* .75
276 Marcus Giles .15
277 Jon Rauch .15
278 *Brian Schmitt* .50
279 *Seung Song* 1.00
280 Kevin Mench .15
281 Adam Eaton .15
282 Shawn Sonnier .15
283 *Andy Van Hekken* 3.00
284 Aaron Rowand .15
285 *Tony Blanco* 3.00
286 Ryan Kohlmeier .15
287 C.C. Sabathia .15
288 Bubba Crosby .15
289 Josh Hamilton .25
290 *Dee Haynes* .50
291 Jason Marquis .15
292 Julio Zuleta .15
293 Carlos Hernandez .15
294 Matt LeCroy .15
295 *Andy Beal* .50
296 Carlos Pena .15
297 Reggie Taylor .15
298 *Bob Keppel* .50
299 Miguel Cabrera .15
300 Ryan Franklin .15
301 Brandon Phillips .15
302 *Victor Hall* 1.00
303 Tony Pena Jr. .15
304 *Jim Journell* .50
305 Cristian Guerrero .40
306 Miguel Olivo .15
307 Jin Ho Cho .15
308 Choo Freeman .15
309 *Danny Borrell* .75
310 Doug Mientkiewicz .15
311 Aaron Herr .15
312 Keith Ginter .15
313 Felipe Lopez .15
314 *Jeff Goldbach* .50
315 Travis Harper .15
316 Paul Loduca .15
317 Joe Torres .15
318 Eric Byrnes .15
319 George Lombard .15
320 David Krynzel .15
321 Ben Christensen .15
322 Aubrey Huff .15
323 Lyle Overbay .15
324 Sean McGowan .15
325 Jeff Heaverlo .15
326 Timo Perez .15
327 *Octavio Martinez* .50
328 Vince Faison .15
329 *David Parrish* .75
330 Bobby Bradley .15
331 *Jason Miller* .50
332 *Corey Spencer* .50
333 Craig House .15
334 *Maxim St. Pierre* .50
335 Adam Johnson .15
336 Joe Crede .15
337 *Greg Nash* 1.00
338 Chad Durbin .15
339 *Pat Magness* .75
340 Matt Wheatland .15
341 Julio Lugo .15
342 Grady Sizemore .15
343 Adrian Gonzalez .40
344 Tim Raines Jr. .15
345 *Rainier Olmedo* .50
346 Phil Dumatrait .15
347 *Brandon Mims* .75
348 Jason Jennings .15
349 *Phil Wilson* .50
350 Jason Hart .25
351 Cesar Izturis .15
352 *Matt Butler* .50
353 David Kelton .15
354 Luke Prokopec .15
355 Corey Smith .15
356 *Joel Piniero* .50
357 Ken Chenard .15
358 Keith Reed .15
359 David Walling .15
360 *Alexis Gomez* .75
361 *Justin Morneau* 1.00
362 *Josh Fogg* 1.00
363 J.R. House .40
364 Andy Tracy .15
365 Kenny Kelly .15
366 Aaron McNeal .15
367 Nick Johnson .15
368 Brian Esposito .15
369 *Charles Frazier* .50
370 Scott Heard .15
371 Patrick Strange .15
372 Mike Meyers .15
373 *Ryan Ludwick* 1.50
374 Brad Wilkerson .15
375 Allen Levrault .15
376 *Seth McClung* .50
377 Joe Nathan .15
378 *Rafael Soriano* .50
379 Chris Richard .15
380 Xavier Nady .15
381 Tike Redman .15
382 Adam Dunn .15
383 *Jared Abruzzo* .75
384 *Jason Richardson* .50
385 Matt Holliday .15
386 *Darwin Cubillian* .50
387 Mike Nannini .15
388 *Blake Williams* .50
389 *Valentino Pascucci* .75
390 Jon Garland .15
391 Josh Pressley .15
392 Jose Ortiz .40
393 *Ryan Hannaman* .50
394 *Steve Smyth* .50
395 John Patterson .15
396 *Chad Petty* 1.00
397 *Jake Peavey* 1.00
398 *Onix Mercado* .50
399 Jason Romano .15
400 *Luis Torres* .50
401 *Casey Fossum* .75
402 *Eduardo Figueroa* .50
403 *Bryan Barnowski* .50
404 Tim Redding .15
405 Jason Standridge .15
406 *Marvin Seale* .50
407 Todd Moser .15
408 Alex Gordon .15
409 *Steve Smitherman* .75
410 Ben Petrick .15
411 Eric Munson .15
412 Luis Rivas .15
413 Matt Ginter .15
414 Alfonso Soriano .40
415 *Rafael Boitel* .50
416 *Dany Morban* .50
417 *Justin Woodrowc* .75
418 Wilfredo Rodriguez .15
419 *Derrick Van Dusen* .75
420 *Josh Spoerl* .50
421 Juan Pierre .15
422 J.C. Romero .15
423 *Ed Rogers* .75
424 Tomokazu Ohka .25
425 *Ben Hendrickson* .50
426 Carlos Zambrano .15
427 Brett Myers .15
428 Scott Seabol .15
429 Thomas Mitchell .15
430 *Jose Reyes* 1.00
431 Kip Wells .15
432 Willi Mo Pena .15
433 *Adam Pettyjohn* .50
434 Austin Kearns .15
435 Rico Washington .15
436 *Doug Nickle* .50
437 Steve Lomasney .15
438 *Jason Jones* .50
439 Bobby Seay .15
440 *Justin Wayne* 1.00

2001 Bowman Autographed Game-Used Bat Rookie Reprints

MT

1 Willie Mays
2 Duke Snider
3 Minnie Minoso
4 Hank Bauer
5 Al Rosen

2001 Bowman Autographs

MT

Common Player: 10.00
Inserted 1:74
BA-BBBrian Barnowski 15.00
BA-WBWilson Betemit 25.00
BA-JBJason Botts 15.00
BA-SBSean Burroughs 15.00
BA-FBFreddie Bynum 10.00
BA-NDNoel Devarez 10.00
BA-JDJose Diaz 10.00
BA-BDBen Diggins 10.00
BA-AEAlex Escobar 15.00
BA-RFRafael Furcal 20.00
BA-AGAdrian Gonzalez 20.00
BA-AKGAlex Gordon 10.00
BA-AJGAlex Graman 10.00
BA-CGCristian Guerrero 20.00
BA-THTravis Hafner 10.00
BA-JHJosh Hamilton 25.00
BA-JWHJason Hart 15.00
BA-JRHJ.R. House 25.00
BA-RJRuss Jacobson 10.00
BA-AJAdam Johnson 10.00
BA-TJTripper Johnson 10.00
BA-DWKDavid Kelton 10.00
BA-DKDavid Krynzel 15.00
BA-PLPedro Liriano 10.00
BA-SMSean McGowan 10.00
BA-KMKevin Mench 15.00
BA-LMLuis Montanez 20.00
BA-JMJustin Morneau 25.00
BA-LOLyle Overbay 10.00
BA-ADPAdam Piatt 10.00
BA-JPJosh Pressley 10.00
BA-APAlbert Pujols 125.00
BA-KSKazuhiro Sasaki
BA-BSBen Sheets 20.00
BA-SDSSteve Smyth 10.00
BA-SSShawn Sonnier 10.00
BA-SUSixto Urena 10.00
BA-MVMiguel Villilo 10.00
BA-BWBrad Wilkerson 10.00
BA-BZBarry Zito 25.00

2001 Bowman Autoproofs

MT

Inserted 1:18,259
Hank Bauer/50 Redemp
Carlos Delgado/ 92 Redemp
Carl Erskine/51
Chipper Jones/ 91 Redemp
Ralph Kiner/48 Redemp
Don Larsen/54
Gil McDougald/ 52 Redemp
Ivan Rodriguez/ 91 Redemp
Pat Burrell/99 Redemp
Rafael Furcal/99

2001 Bowman Futures Game-Worn Jersey

MT

Common Player: 10.00
Inserted 1:82
FGR-KAKurt Ainsworth 15.00
FGR-CACraig Anderson 10.00
FGR-RARyan Anderson 20.00
FGR-BBBobby Bradley 20.00
FGR-MBMike Bynum 10.00
FGR-RCRamon Castro 10.00
FGR-CCChin-Feng Chen 30.00
FGR-JCJack Cust 15.00
FGR-TDTravis Dawkins 10.00
FGR-RDRandey Dorame 10.00
FGR-AEAlex Escobar 20.00
FGR-CGChris George 15.00
FGR-MGMarcus Giles 20.00
FGR-JHJosh Hamilton 30.00
FGR-CHCarlos Hernandez 15.00
FGR-SKSun-Woo Kim 20.00
FGR-FLFelipe Lopez 15.00
FGR-EMEric Munson 20.00
FGR-AMAaron Myette 10.00
FGR-NNNtema Ndungidi 10.00
FGR-TOTomokazu Ohka 40.00
FGR-RORamon Ortiz 15.00
FGR-DCPCorey Patterson 25.00
FGR-CPCarlos Pena 25.00
FGR-BPBen Petrick 15.00
FGR-GRGrant Roberts 10.00
FGR-JRJason Romano 10.00
FGR-BSBen Sheets 30.00
FGR-CTChin-Hui Tsao 30.00
FGR-VWVernon Wells 15.00
FGR-BWBrad Wilkerson 10.00
FGR-TWTravis Wilson 10.00
FGR-BZBarry Zito 25.00
FGR-JZJulio Zuleta 20.00

2001 Bowman Futures Game Three-Piece Game-Used

MT

Common Player: 30.00
MGR-RCRamon Castro 35.00
MGR-CCChin-Feng Chen 80.00
MGR-JCJack Cust 35.00
MGR-TDTravis Dawkins 30.00
MGR-AEAlex Escobar 60.00
MGR-MGMarcus Giles 60.00
MGR-JHJosh Hamilton 80.00
MGR-FLFelipe Lopez 40.00
MGR-EMEric Munson
MGR-NNNtema Ndungidi 35.00
MGR-DCPCorey Patterson 70.00
MGR-CPCarlos Pena 50.00
MGR-BPBen Petrick 40.00
MGR-JRJason Romano 35.00
MGR-VWVernon Wells
MGR-BWBrad Wilkerson
MGR-TWTravis Wilson 35.00
MGR-JZJulio Zuleta 40.00

2001 Bowman Autographed Three-Piece Game-Used

MT

Complete Set (5):
Common Player:
AMGR-AEAlex Escobar
AMGR-JHJosh Hamilton
AMGR-EMEric Munson
AMGR-CPCorey Patterson
AMGR-BWBrad Wilkerson

2001 Bowman Rookie of the Year Dual Jersey

MT

Inserted 1:2,202
ROYRKazuhiro Sasaki, Rafael Furcal 90.00

2001 Bowman Rookie Reprints

		MT
Complete Set (25):		60.00
Common Player:		1.50
Inserted 1:12		
1	Yogi Berra	8.00
2	Ralph Kiner	2.00
3	Stan Musial	6.00
4	Warren Spahn	5.00
5	Roy Campanella	5.00
6	Bob Lemon	1.50
7	Robin Roberts	2.00
8	Duke Snider	4.00
9	Early Wynn	1.50
10	Richie Ashburn	1.50
11	Gil Hodges	2.00
12	Hank Bauer	2.00
13	Don Newcombe	1.50
14	Al Rosen	1.50
15	Willie Mays	10.00
16	Joe Garagiola	2.00
17	Whitey Ford	4.00
18	Lew Burdette	1.50
19	Gil McDougald	1.50
20	Minnie Minoso	1.50
21	Eddie Mathews	5.00
22	Harvey Kuenn	2.00
23	Don Larsen	3.00
24	Elston Howard	2.00
25	Don Zimmer	1.50

2001 Bowman Autographed Rookie Reprints

		MT
Common Player:		25.00
Inserted 1:2,467		
1	Yogi Berra	100.00
2	Willie Mays	250.00
3	Stan Musial	140.00
4	Duke Snider	75.00
5	Warren Spahn	75.00
6	Ralph Kiner	40.00
7	Eddie Mathews	
8	Don Larsen	40.00
9	Don Zimmer	25.00
10	Minnie Minoso	30.00

2001 Bowman Game-Used Bat Rookie Reprints

		MT
Common Player:		25.00
Inserted 1:1,954		
1	Willie Mays	125.00
2	Duke Snider	65.00
3	Minnie Minoso	25.00
4	Hank Bauer	25.00
5	Al Rosen	

2001 Bowman Chrome

		MT
Complete Set (351):		
Common (1-110, 201-310):		.20
Common Ref. (111-200, 311-330):		4.00
Inserted 1:4		
Common Ref. Auto. (331-350):		40.00
Production 500		
Pack (4):		7.00
Box (24):		150.00
1	Jason Giambi	.60
2	Rafael Furcal	.40
3	Bernie Williams	.75
4	Kenny Lofton	.40
5	Al Leiter	.20
6	Albert Belle	.20
7	Craig Biggio	.40
8	Mark Mulder	.20
9	Carlos Delgado	.75
10	Darin Erstad	.60
11	Richie Sexson	.20
12	Randy Johnson	1.00
13	Greg Maddux	2.00
14	Orlando Hernandez	.20
15	Javier Vazquez	.20
16	Jeff Kent	.40
17	Jim Thome	.50
18	John Olerud	.50
19	Jason Kendall	.20
20	Scott Rolen	.50
21	Tony Gwynn	1.25
22	Edgardo Alfonzo	.20
23	Pokey Reese	.20
24	Todd Helton	1.00
25	Mark Quinn	.20
26	Dean Palmer	.20
27	Ray Durham	.20
28	Rafael Palmeiro	.75
29	Carl Everett	.20
30	Vladimir Guerrero	1.25
31	Livan Hernandez	.20
32	Preston Wilson	.20
33	Jose Vidro	.20
34	Fred McGriff	.40
35	Kevin Brown	.20
36	Miguel Tejada	.40
37	Chipper Jones	2.00
38	Edgar Martinez	.20
39	Tony Batista	.20
40	Jorge Posada	.40
41	Sammy Sosa	2.00
42	Gary Sheffield	.50
43	Bartolo Colon	.20
44	Pat Burrell	.75
45	Jay Payton	.20
46	Mike Mussina	.60
47	Nomar Garciaparra	2.50
48	Darren Dreifort	.20
49	Richard Hidalgo	.40
50	Troy Glaus	1.00
51	Ben Grieve	.20
52	Jim Edmonds	.40
53	Raul Mondesi	.20
54	Andruw Jones	.75
55	Mike Sweeney	.20
56	Derek Jeter	3.00
57	Ruben Mateo	.20
58	Cristian Guzman	.20
59	Mike Hampton	.20
60	J.D. Drew	.50
61	Matt Lawton	.20
62	Moises Alou	.40
63	Terrence Long	.20
64	Geoff Jenkins	.40
65	Manny Ramirez	1.00
66	Johnny Damon	.20
67	Pedro Martinez	1.00
68	Juan Gonzalez	1.00
69	Roger Clemens	1.50
70	Carlos Beltran	.20
71	Roberto Alomar	.75
72	Barry Bonds	1.50
73	Tim Hudson	.50
74	Tom Glavine	.50
75	Jeromy Burnitz	.20
76	Adrian Beltre	.40
77	Mike Piazza	2.50
78	Kerry Wood	.50
79	Steve Finley	.20
80	Bobby Abreu	.40
81	Neifi Perez	.20
82	Mark Redman	.20
83	Paul Konerko	.20
84	Jermaine Dye	.20
85	Brian Giles	.40
86	Ivan Rodriguez	1.00
87	Adam Kennedy	.20
88	Eric Chavez	.40
89	Billy Koch	.20
90	Shawn Green	.40
91	Matt Williams	.40
92	Greg Vaughn	.20
93	Jeff Cirillo	.20
94	Frank Thomas	1.25
95	David Justice	.50
96	Cal Ripken Jr.	3.00
97	Curt Schilling	.20
98	Barry Zito	.40
99	Brian Jordan	.20
100	Chan Ho Park	.20
101	J.T. Snow Jr.	.20
102	Kazuhiro Sasaki	.20
103	Alex Rodriguez	2.50
104	Mariano Rivera	.40
105	Eric Milton	.20
106	Andy Pettitte	.50
107	Ken Griffey Jr.	2.50
108	Bengie Molina	.20
109	Jeff Bagwell	1.00
110	Mark McGwire	3.00
111	*Dan Tosca*	6.00
112	*Sergio Contreras*	6.00
113	*Mitch Jones*	6.00
114	*Ramon Carvajal*	6.00
115	*Ryan Madson*	6.00
116	*Hank Blalock*	60.00
117	*Ben Washburn*	8.00
118	*Erick Almonte*	5.00
119	*Shawn Fagan*	4.00
120	*Gary Johnson*	4.00
121	*Brett Evert*	6.00
122	*Joe Hamer*	6.00
123	*Yhency Brazoban*	6.00
124	*Domingo Guante*	6.00
125	*Deivi Mendez*	10.00
126	*Adrian Hernandez*	8.00
127	*Reggie Abercrombie*	6.00
128	*Steve Bennett*	4.00
129	*Matt White*	8.00
130	*Brian Hitchcox*	4.00
131	*Deivis Santos*	6.00
132	*Luis Montanez*	15.00
133	*Eric Reynolds*	8.00
134	*Denny Bautista*	6.00
135	*Hector Garcia*	8.00
136	*Joe Thurston*	6.00
137	*Tsuyoshi Shinjo*	12.00
138	*Elpidio Guzman*	5.00
139	*Brian Bass*	8.00
140	*Mark Burnett*	5.00
141	*Russ Jacobsen*	4.00
142	*Travis Hafner*	8.00
143	*Wilson Betemit*	20.00
144	*Luke Lockwood*	6.00
145	*Noel Devarez*	5.00
146	*Doug Gredvig*	8.00
147	*Seung Jun Song*	8.00
148	*Andy Van Hekken*	6.00
149	Ryan Kohlmeier	4.00
150	*Dee Haynes*	5.00
151	*Jim Journell*	4.00
152	*Chad Petty*	6.00
153	*Danny Borrell*	6.00
154	David Krynzel	5.00
155	*Octavio Martinez*	6.00
156	*David Parrish*	8.00
157	*Jason Miller*	6.00
158	*Corey Spencer*	4.00
159	*Maxim St. Pierre*	6.00
160	*Pat Magness*	8.00
161	*Rainier Olmedo*	6.00
162	*Brandon Mims*	6.00
163	*Phil Wilson*	6.00
164	*Jose Reyes*	6.00
165	*Matt Butler*	6.00
166	Joel Pineiro	25.00
167	Ken Chenard	4.00
168	*Alexis Gomez*	6.00
169	*Justin Morneau*	20.00
170	*Josh Fogg*	8.00
171	*Charles Frazier*	6.00
172	*Ryan Ludwick*	15.00
173	*Seth McClung*	6.00
174	*Justin Wayne*	8.00
175	*Rafael Soriano*	8.00
176	*Jared Abruzzo*	6.00
177	*Jason Richardson*	6.00
178	*Darwin Cubillan*	4.00
179	*Blake Williams*	6.00
180	*Valentino Pascucci*	6.00
181	*Ryan Hannaman*	6.00
182	*Steve Smyth*	5.00
183	*Jake Peavy*	8.00
184	*Onix Mercado*	6.00
185	*Luis Torres*	6.00
186	*Casey Fossum*	8.00
187	*Eduardo Figueroa*	6.00
188	*Bryan Barnowski*	6.00
189	Jason Standridge	4.00
190	*Marvin Seale*	6.00
191	*Steve Smitherman*	6.00
192	*Rafael Boitel*	6.00
193	*Dany Morban*	6.00
194	*Justin Woodrowc*	6.00
195	*Ed Rogers*	8.00
196	*Ben Hendrickson*	6.00
197	Thomas Mitchell	4.00
198	*Adam Pettyjohn*	5.00
199	*Doug Nickle*	4.00
200	*Jason Jones*	6.00
201	Larry Barnes	.20
202	Ben Diggins	.20
203	Dee Brown	.20
204	Rocco Baldelli	.20
205	Luis Terrero	.20
206	Milton Bradley	.20
207	Kurt Ainsworth	.20
208	Sean Burroughs	.40
209	Rick Asadoorian	.20
210	Ramon Castro	.20
211	Nick Neugebauer	.50
212	Aaron Myette	.20
213	Luis Matos	.20
214	Donnie Bridges	.20
215	Alex Cintron	.20
216	Bobby Kielty	.20
217	Matt Belisle	.20
218	Adam Everett	.20
219	John Lackey	.20
220	Adam Wainwright	.20
221	Jerry Hairston Jr.	.20
222	Mike Bynum	.20
223	Ryan Christianson	.20
224	J.J. Davis	.20
225	Alex Graman	.20
226	Abraham Nunez	.20
227	Sun-Woo Kim	.20
228	Jimmy Rollins	.20
229	Ruben Salazar	.20
230	Josh Girdley	.20
231	Carl Crawford	.20
232	Ben Davis	.20
233	Jason Grabowski	.20
234	Chris George	.20
235	Roy Oswalt	.75
236	Brian Cole	.20
237	Corey Patterson	.40
238	Vernon Wells	.20
239	Bradley Baker	.20
240	Gookie Dawkins	.20
241	Michael Cuddyer	.20
242	Ricardo Aramboles	.20
243	Ben Sheets	1.00
244	Toby Hall	.20
245	Jack Cust	.20
246	Pedro Feliz	.20
247	Josh Beckett	.50
248	Alex Escobar	.20
249	Marcus Giles	.20
250	Jon Rauch	.40
251	Kevin Mench	.20
252	Shawn Sonnier	.20

253 Aaron Rowand .20
254 C.C. Sabathia .20
255 Bubba Crosby .20
256 Josh Hamilton 1.00
257 Carlos Hernandez .20
258 Carlos Pena .20
259 Miguel Cabrera .20
260 Brandon Phillips .20
261 Tony Pena Jr. .20
262 Cristian Guerrero .75
263 Jin Ho Cho .20
264 Aaron Herr .20
265 Keith Ginter .20
266 Felipe Lopez .20
267 Travis Harper .20
268 Joe Torres .20
269 Eric Byrnes .20
270 Ben Christensen .20
271 Aubrey Huff .20
272 Lyle Overbay .20
273 Vince Faison .20
274 Bobby Bradley .20
275 Joe Crede .20
276 Matt Wheatland .20
277 Grady Sizemore .20
278 Adrian Gonzalez 1.00
279 Timothy Raines Jr. .20
280 Phil Dumatrait .20
281 Jason Hart .50
282 David Kelton .20
283 David Walling .20
284 J.R. House .75
285 Kenny Kelly .20
286 Aaron McNeal .20
287 Nick Johnson .20
288 Scott Heard .20
289 Brad Wilkerson .20
290 Allen Levrault .20
291 Chris Richard .20
292 Jared Sandberg .20
293 Tike Redman .20
294 Adam Dunn 5.00
295 Josh Pressley .20
296 Jose Ortiz .20
297 Jason Romano .20
298 Tim Redding .20
299 Alex Gordon .20
300 Ben Petrick .20
301 Eric Munson .20
302 Luis Rivas .20
303 Matt Ginter .20
304 Alfonso Soriano .50
305 Wilfredo Rodriguez .20
306 Brett Myers .20
307 Scott Seabol .20
308 Tony Alvarez .20
309 Donzell McDonald .20
310 Austin Kearns .20
311 *Will Ohman* 6.00
312 *Ryan Soules* 4.00
313 *Cody Ross* 5.00
314 *Bill Whitecotton* 6.00
315 *Mike Burns* 4.00
316 *Manuel Acosta* 6.00
317 *Lance Niekro* 10.00
318 *Travis Thompson* 6.00
319 *Zach Sorensen* 8.00
320 *Austin Evans* 4.00
321 *Brad Stiles* 6.00
322 *Joe Kennedy* 10.00
323 *Luke Martin* 5.00
324 *Juan Diaz* 5.00
325 *Pat Hallmark* 4.00
326 *Christian Parker* 4.00
327 *Ronny Corona* 6.00
328 *Jermaine Clark* 4.00
329 *Scott Dunn* 6.00
330 *Scott Chiasson* 6.00
331 *Greg Nash Auto* 50.00
332 Brad Cresse Auto 60.00
333 *John Buck Auto* 50.00
334 *Freddie Bynum Auto* 50.00
335 *Felix Diaz Auto* 50.00
336 *Jason Belcher Auto* 50.00
337 *Troy Farnsworth* 50.00
338 *Roberto Miniel* 60.00
339 *Esix Snead* 50.00
340 *Albert Pujols* 350.00
341 *Jeff Andra* 60.00
342 *Victor Hall* 50.00
343 *Pedro Liriano* 60.00
344 *Andy Beal* 50.00
345 *Bob Keppel* 50.00
346 *Brian Schmitt* 50.00
347 *Ron Davenport* 65.00
348 *Tony Blanco* 90.00
349 *Reggie Griggs* 50.00
350 *Derrick Van Dusen* 60.00
351a *Ichiro Suzuki Eng.* 60.00
351b *Ichiro Suzuki japanese* 50.00

2001 Bowman Chrome Gold Refractors

MT
Stars: 8-15X
Rookies: 2-4X
Production 99 sets
(See 2001 Bowman Chrome for checklist and base card values.)

2001 Bowman Chrome X-Fractors

MT
Stars: 4-8X
Rookies: 1-1.5X
Inserted 1:23

2001 Bowman Chrome Futures Game Memorabilia

MT
Common Player: 12.00
Inserted 1:460
FGR-KAKurt Ainsworth 20.00
FGR-CACraig Anderson 12.00
FGR-RARyan Anderson 20.00
FGR-BBBobby Bradley 15.00
FGR-MBMike Bynum 15.00
FGR-RCRamon Castro 12.00
FGR-CCChin-Feng Chen 40.00
FGR-JCJack Cust 12.00
FGR-RDRandey Dorame 12.00
FGR-AEAlex Escobar 20.00
FGR-CGChris George 15.00
FGR-MGMarcus Giles 15.00
FGR-JHJosh Hamilton 50.00
FGR-CHCarlos Hernandez 15.00
FGR-SKSun-Woo Kim 20.00
FGR-FLFelipe Lopez 12.00
FGR-EMEric Munson 15.00
FGR-AMAaron Myette 12.00
FGR-NNNtema Ndungidi 12.00
FGR-TOTomokazu Ohka 30.00
FGR-DCPCorey Patterson 20.00
FGR-CPCarlos Pena 15.00
FGR-BPBen Petrick 12.00
FGR-JRJason Romano 12.00
FGR-BSBen Sheets 30.00
FGR-CTChin-Hui Tsao 40.00
FGR-BWBrad Wilkerson 15.00
FGR-TWTravis Wilson 12.00
FGR-BZBarry Zito 40.00
FGR-JZJulio Zuleta 12.00

2001 Bowman Chrome Rookie Reprints

MT
Complete Set (25): 70.00
Common Player: 2.00
Inserted 1:12
Refractors: 2-4X
Production 299 sets
1 Yogi Berra 6.00
2 Ralph Kiner 2.00
3 Stan Musial 8.00
4 Warren Spahn 5.00
5 Roy Campanella 5.00
6 Bob Lemon 2.00
7 Robin Roberts 2.00
8 Duke Snider 4.00
9 Early Wynn 2.00
10 Richie Ashburn 3.00
11 Gil Hodges 3.00
12 Hank Bauer 2.00
13 Don Newcombe 2.00
14 Al Rosen 2.00
15 Willie Mays 10.00
16 Joe Garagiola 3.00
17 Whitey Ford 5.00
18 Lew Burdette 2.00
19 Gil McDougald 2.00
20 Minnie Minoso 2.00
21 Eddie Mathews 5.00
22 Harvey Kuenn 2.00
23 Don Larsen 4.00
24 Elston Howard 2.00
25 Don Zimmer 2.00

2001 Bowman Chrome Rookie Reprint Relics

MT
Common Player: 15.00
Inserted 1:244
1 David Justice 20.00
2 Richie Sexson 15.00
3 Sean Casey 20.00
4 Mike Piazza 75.00
5 Carlos Delgado 30.00
6 Chipper Jones 40.00

2001 Bowman Draft Picks & Prospects

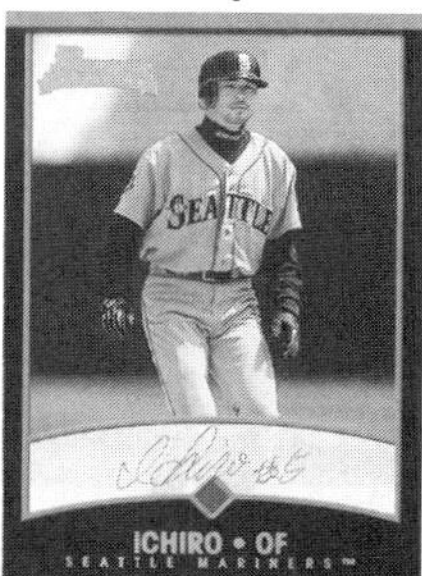

MT
Complete Set (110): 40.00
Common Player: .10
1 *Alfredo Amezaga* .50
2 Andrew Good .10
3 *Kelly Johnson* 1.50
4 Larry Bigbie .10
5 *Matt Thompson* .40
6 *Wilton Chavez* .40
7 *Joe Borchard* 3.00
8 David Espinosa .10
9 *Zach Day* .10
10 *Brad Hawpe* 2.00
11 Nate Cornejo .10
12 *Jim Kavourias* .10
13 Brad Lidge .10
14 *Angel Berroa* .10
15 *Lamont Matthews* .10
16 Jose Garcia .10
17 *Grant Balfour* .10
18 *Ron Chiavacci* .10
19 Jae Seo .10
20 Juan Rivera .10
21 D'Angelo Jimenez .10
22 Aaron Harang .10
23 *Marlon Byrd* 2.00
24 Sean Burnett .10
25 *Josh Pearce* .10
26 *Brandon Duckworth* 1.50
27 *Jack Taschner* .10
28 *Bo Robinson* .10
29 Brent Abernathy .10
30 *David Elder* .10
31 *Scott Cassidy* .10
32 *Dennis Tankersley* 1.50
33 Denny Stark .10
34 *Dave Williams* .10
35 *Boof Bonser* 1.00
36 *Kris Foster* .10
37 *Neal Musser* .10
38 Shawn Chacon .10
39 *Mike Rivera* 1.00
40 *Will Smith* 1.00
41 *Morgan Ensberg* .75
42 Ken Harvey .10
43 *Ricardo Rodriguez* .75
44 *Jose Mieses* .10
45 *Luis Maza* .10
46 *Julio Perez* .10
47 *Billy Traber* .10
48 *David Martinez* .10
49 *Covelli Crisp* .10
50 *Mario Ramos* .10
51 *Matt Thornton* .20
52 Xavier Nady .10
53 Ryan Vogelsong .10
54 *Jim Magrane* .10
55 *Domingo Valdez* .10
56 Brent Butler .10
57 *Brian Tallet* .10
58 *Brian Reith* .10
59 *Mario Valenzuela* .10
60 *Bobby Hill* .75
61 *Rich Rundles* .10
62 Rick Elder .10
63 J.D. Closser .10
64 Scot Shields .10
65 Miguel Olivo .10
66 *Stubby Clapp* .10
67 *Jerome Williams* 1.50
68 *Jason Lane* 1.50
69 *Chase Utley* .75
70 *Erik Bedard* .10
71 *Alex Herrera* .10
72 *Juan Cruz* 2.00
73 *Billy Martin* .10
74 *Ronnie Merrill* .10
75 *Jason Kinchen* .10
76 *Wilken Ruan* .10
77 *Cody Ransom* .10
78 *Bud Smith* 3.00
79 Wily Mo Pena .10
80 *Jeff Nettles* .10
81 *Jamal Strong* .10
82 Bill Ortega .10
83 Junior Zamora .10
84 *Ichiro Suzuki* 8.00
85 *Fernando Rodney* .10
86 *Chris Smith* .50
87 *John VanBenschoten* 1.00
88 *Bobby Crosby* .50
89 *Kenny Baugh* .50
90 *Jake Gautreau* 1.00
91 *Gabe Gross* 1.00
92 *Kris Honel* .50
93 *Daniel Denham* .75
94 *Aaron Heilman* .50
95 *Irvin Guzman* 1.00
96 *Mike Jones* .50
97 *John-Ford Griffin* 1.00
98 *MaCay McBride* .50

99	*John Rheinecker*	.50
100	*Bronson Sardinha*	1.00
101	*Jason Weintraub*	.75
102	*J.D. Martin*	1.00
103	*Jayson Nix*	.50
104	*Noah Lowry*	.40
105	*Richard Lewis*	.40
106	*Brad Hennessey*	.50
107	*Jeff Mathis*	.60
108	*Jon Skaggs*	.50
109	*Justin Pope*	.50
110	*Josh Burrus*	.50

2001 Bowman Draft Picks & Prospects Autographs

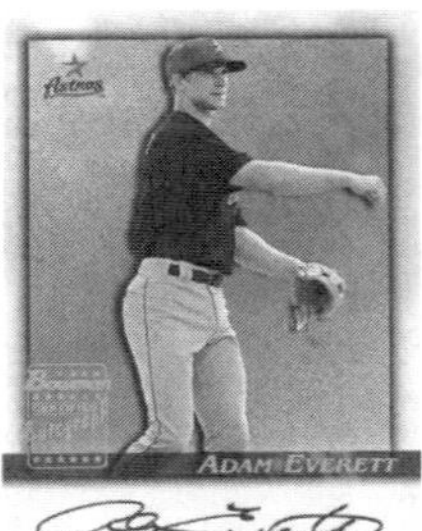

	MT
Common Autograph:	8.00
Inserted 1:set	
BDPA-JAJared Abruzzo	8.00
BDPA-AAAlfredo Amezaga	8.00
BDPA-GAGarrett Atkins	8.00
BDPA-KBKenny Baugh	8.00
BDPA-BBBobby Bradley	8.00
BDPA-CBChris Burke	8.00
BDPAANCAntoine Cameron	8.00
BDPAROCRamon Carvajal	8.00
BDPA-RCRyan Church	8.00
BDPA-ACAlex Cintron	8.00
BDPA-DDDanier Denham	8.00
BDPA-RDRyan Dittfurth	8.00
BDPA-AEAdam Everett	8.00
BDPA-AFAlex Fernandez	8.00
BDPA-JGJake Gautreau	8.00
BDPA-AGAlexis Gomez	8.00
BDPA-GGGabe Gross	8.00
BDPA-CGCristian Guerrero	8.00
BDPA-BHBeau Hale	8.00
BDPA-SHScott Heard	8.00
BDPAAAHAaron Heilman	8.00
BDPABRHBrad Hennessey	8.00
BDPA-AHAaron Herr	8.00
BDPA-KHKris Honel	8.00
BDPA-CICesar Izturis	8.00
BDPA-FJForrest Johnson	8.00
BDPA-GJGary Johnson	8.00
BDPA-NJNick Johnson	12.00
BDPA-AKAustin Kearns	15.00
BDPA-DKDanny Kelly	8.00
BDPA-JKJoe Kennedy	8.00
BDPA-JLJohn Lackey	8.00
BDPA-FLFelipe Lopez	8.00
BDPA-RIRyan Ludwick	8.00
BDPARMMRyan Madson	8.00
BDPA-TOTomo Ohka	12.00
BDPA-RORoy Oswalt	25.00
BDPA-CPChristian Parra	8.00
BDPA-BPBrandon Phillips	8.00
BDPA-JPJoel Pineiro	15.00
BDPA-NRNick Regilio	8.00
BDPA-EREd Rogers	8.00
BDPA-SSScott Seabol	8.00
BDPA-BSBud Smith	25.00
BDPA-CSChris Smith	8.00
BDPABJSBrian Specht	8.00
BDPA-JTJoe Torres	8.00
BDPA-JVJohn VanBenschotten	8.00
BDPAJMWJustin Wayne	12.00
BDPA-JWJerome Williams	8.00

2001 Bowman Draft Picks & Prospects Draft Pick Relics

		MT
Common Player:		8.00
One Relic:Factory Set		
CI	Cesar Izturis	8.00
GJ	Gary Johnson	8.00
NR	Nick Regillo	8.00
RC	Ryan Church	8.00
BJS	Brian Specht	8.00
JRH	J.R. House	15.00

2001 Bowman Draft Picks & Prospects Futures Game Relics

		MT
Common Player:		8.00
Inserted 1:set		
AA	Alfredo Amezaga	8.00
AD	Adam Dunn	30.00
AG	Adrian Gonzalez	8.00
AH	Alex Herrera	8.00
BM	Brett Myers	8.00
CD	Cody Ransom	8.00
CG	Chris George	8.00
CH	Carlos Hernandez	8.00
CU	Chase Utley	10.00
EB	Eric Bedard	8.00
GB	Grant Balfour	8.00
HB	Hank Blalock	20.00
JB	Joe Borchard	25.00
JC	Juan Cruz	20.00
JP	Josh Pearce	8.00
JR	Juan Rivera	8.00
LG	Luis Garcia	8.00
MC	Miguel Cabrera	8.00
MR	Mike Rivera	10.00
RR	Ricardo Rodriguez	8.00
SC	Scott Chiasson	8.00
SS	Seung Jun Song	10.00
TB	Toby Hall	8.00
WB	Wilson Betemit	20.00
WP	Wily Mo Pena	10.00
JAP	Juan Pena	8.00

2001 Bowman's Best

		MT
Complete Set (200):		
Common Player:		.20
Common SP (151-200):		6.00
Production 2,999		
Pack (5):		5.00
Box (24):		110.00
1	Vladimir Guerrero	1.25
2	Miguel Tejada	.40
3	Geoff Jenkins	.40
4	Jeff Bagwell	1.00
5	Todd Helton	1.00
6	Ken Griffey Jr.	2.50
7	Nomar Garciaparra	2.50
8	Chipper Jones	2.00
9	Darin Erstad	.40
10	Frank Thomas	1.25
11	Jim Thome	.50
12	Preston Wison	.20
13	Kevin Brown	.40
14	Derek Jeter	3.00
15	Scott Rolen	.50
16	Ryan Klesko	.20
17	Jeff Kent	.40
18	Raul Mondesi	.20
19	Greg Vaughn	.20
20	Bernie Williams	.75
21	Mike Piazza	2.50
22	Richard Hidalgo	.40
23	Dean Palmer	.20
24	Roberto Alomar	.75
25	Sammy Sosa	2.50
26	Randy Johnson	1.00
27	Manny Ramirez	1.25
28	Roger Clemens	1.50
29	Terrence Long	.20
30	Jason Kendall	.20
31	Richie Sexson	.20
32	David Wells	.20
33	Andruw Jones	.75
34	Pokey Reese	.20
35	Juan Gonzalez	1.00
36	Carlos Beltran	.20
37	Shawn Green	.40
38	Mariano Rivera	.40
39	John Olerud	.40
40	Jim Edmonds	.40
41	Andres Galarraga	.40
42	Carlos Delgado	.75
43	Kris Benson	.20
44	Andy Pettite	.40
45	Jeff Cirillo	.20
46	Magglio Ordonez	.40
47	Tom Glavine	.50
48	Garret Anderson	.20
49	Cal Ripken Jr.	3.00
50	Pedro Martinez	1.25
51	Barry Bonds	1.50
52	Alex Rodriguez	2.50
53	Ben Grieve	.20
54	Edgar Martinez	.20
55	Jason Giambi	.50
56	Jeromy Burnitz	.20
57	Mike Mussina	.60
58	Moises Alou	.40
59	Sean Casey	.40
60	Greg Maddux	2.00
61	Tim Hudson	.40
62	Mark McGwire	3.00
63	Rafael Palmeiro	.50
64	Tony Batista	.20
65	Kazuhiro Sasaki	.20
66	Jorge Posada	.40
67	Johnny Damon	.20
68	Brian Giles	.40
69	Jose Vidro	.20
70	Jermaine Dye	.20
71	Craig Biggio	.40
72	Larry Walker	.50
73	Eric Chavez	.40
74	David Segui	.20
75	Tim Salmon	.40
76	Javy Lopez	.20
77	Paul Konerko	.20
78	Barry Larkin	.40
79	Mike Hampton	.40
80	Bobby Higginson	.20
81	Mark Mulder	.20
82	Pat Burrell	.50
83	Kerry Wood	.40
84	J.T. Snow	.20
85	Ivan Rodriguez	1.00
86	Edgardo Alfonzo	.20
87	Orlando Hernandez	.20
88	Gary Sheffield	.40
89	Mike Sweeney	.20
90	Carlos Lee	.20
91	Rafael Furcal	.40
92	Troy Glaus	1.00
93	Bartolo Colon	.20
94	Cliff Floyd	.20
95	Barry Zito	.40
96	J.D. Drew	.50
97	Eric Karros	.20
98	Jose Valentin	.20
99	Ellis Burks	.20
100	David Justice	.50
101	Larry Barnes	.20
102	Rod Barajas	.20
103	Tony Pena	.20
104	Jerry Hairston Jr.	.20
105	Keith Ginter	.20
106	Corey Patterson	.50
107	Aaron Rowand	.20
108	Miguel Olivo	.20
109	Gookie Dawkins	.20
110	C.C. Sabathia	.50
111	Ben Petrick	.20
112	Eric Munson	.20
113	Ramon Castro	.20
114	Alex Escobar	.20
115	Josh Hamilton	.75
116	Jason Marquis	.20
117	Ben Davis	.20
118	Alex Cintron	.20
119	Julio Zuleta	.20
120	Ben Broussard	.20
121	Adam Everett	.20
122	*Ramon Carvajal*	1.00
123	Felipe Lopez	.20
124	Alfonso Soriano	.50
125	Jayson Werth	.20
126	Donzell McDonald	.20
127	Jason Hart	.50
128	Joe Crede	.20
129	Sean Burroughs	.20
130	Jack Cust	.20
131	Corey Smith	.20
132	Adrian Gonzalez	.75
133	J.R. House	.50
134	Steve Lomasney	.20
135	Tim Raines Jr.	.20
136	Tony Alvarez	.20
137	Doug Mientkiewicz	.20
138	Rocco Baldelli	.20
139	Jason Romano	.20
140	Vernon Wells	.20
141	Mike Bynum	.20
142	Xavier Nady	.50
143	Brad Wilkerson	.20
144	Ben Diggins	.20
145	Aubrey Huff	.20
146	Eric Byrnes	.20
147	Alex Gordon	.20
148	Roy Oswalt	.50
149	Brian Esposito	.20
150	Scott Seabol	.20
151	*Erick Almonte*	6.00
152	*Gary Johnson*	6.00
153	*Pedro Liriano*	8.00
154	*Matt White*	10.00
155	*Luis Montanez*	12.00
156	Brad Cresse	6.00
157	*Wilson Betemit*	20.00
158	*Octavio Martinez*	8.00
159	*Adam Pettyjohn*	6.00
160	*Corey Spencer*	6.00

161	*Mark Burnett*	6.00
162	*Ichiro Suzuki*	60.00
163	*Alexis Gomez*	8.00
164	*Greg "Toe" Nash*	20.00
165	*Roberto Miniel*	8.00
166	*Justin Morneau*	20.00
167	*Ben Washburn*	10.00
168	*Bob Keppel*	6.00
169	*Deivi Mendez*	12.00
170	*Tsuyoshi Shinjo*	15.00
171	*Jared Abruzzo*	8.00
172	*Derrick Van Dusen*	10.00
173	*Hee Seop Choi*	25.00
174	*Albert Pujols*	50.00
175	*Travis Hafner*	8.00
176	*Ron Davenport*	12.00
177	*Luis Torres*	8.00
178	*Jake Peavey*	15.00
179	*Elvis Corporan*	12.00
180	David Krynzel	6.00
181	*Tony Blanco*	20.00
182	*Elpidio Guzman*	6.00
183	*Matt Butler*	8.00
184	*Joe Thurston*	8.00
185	*Andy Beal*	8.00
186	*Kevin Nulton*	12.00
187	*Sneideer Santos*	8.00
188	*Joe Dillon*	10.00
189	*Jeremy Blevins*	8.00
190	*Chris Amador*	10.00
191	*Mark Hendrickson*	8.00
192	*Willy Aybar*	20.00
193	*Antoine Cameron*	10.00
194	*Jonathan Johnson*	6.00
195	*Ryan Ketchner*	8.00
196	*Bjorn Ivy*	8.00
197	*Josh Kroeger*	15.00
198	*Ty Wigginton*	15.00
199	*Stubby Clapp*	10.00
200	*Jerrod Riggan*	8.00

2001 Bowman's Best Autographs

		MT
Common Player:		10.00
Inserted 1:95		
SB	Sean Burroughs	15.00
BC	Brad Cresse	20.00
AG	Adrian Gonzalez	20.00
JH	Josh Hamilton	25.00
JRH	J.R. House	25.00
TL	Terrence Long	10.00
JR	Jon Rauch	15.00

2001 Bowman's Best Exclusive Rookie Autographs

		MT
Common Player:		10.00
Inserted 1:50		
WA	Willy Aybar	15.00
SC	Stubby Clapp	15.00
BI	Bjorn Ivy	25.00
JJ	Jonathan Johnson	10.00
TW	Ty Wigginton	20.00
JR	Jerrod Riggan	10.00
SS	Sneideer Santos	15.00
JB	Jeremy Blevins	10.00
SC	Stubby Clapp	15.00
MH	Mark Hendrickson	15.00

2001 Bowman's Best Franchise Favorites

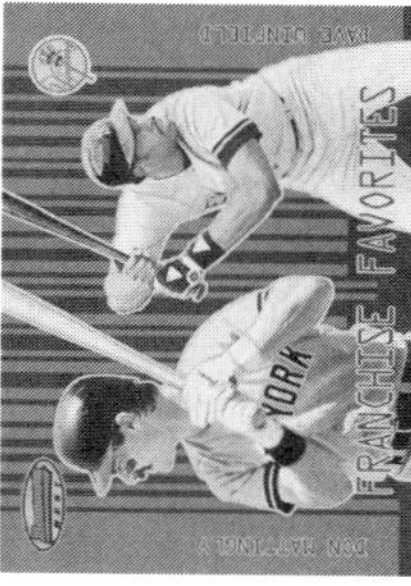

		MT
Complete Set (8):		40.00
Common Player:		1.50
Inserted 1:16		
DM	Don Mattingly	8.00
AR	Alex Rodriguez	8.00
DE	Darin Erstad	1.50
DW	Dave Winfield	1.50
NR	Nolan Ryan	10.00
RJ	Reggie Jackson	3.00
MW	Don Mattingly, Dave Winfield	5.00
RR	Nolan Ryan, Alex Rodriguez	8.00
EJ	Darin Erstad, Reggie Jackson	3.00

2001 Bowman's Best Franchise Favorites Autographs

		MT
Common Player:		25.00
Inserted 1:556		
Combo 1:4,436		
DE	Darin Erstad	30.00
RJ	Reggie Jackson	50.00
DM	Don Mattingly	150.00
MW	Don Mattingly, Dave Winfield	
AR	Alex Rodriguez	80.00
NR	Nolan Ryan	200.00
RR	Nolan Ryan, Alex Rodriguez	
DW	Dave Winfield	40.00

2001 Bowman's Best Franchise Favorites Relics

		MT
Common Player:		20.00
Jersey 1:139		
Pants 1:307		
Combo Relic 1:1,114		
JB	Jeff Bagwell	30.00
CB	Craig Biggio	20.00
BB	Craig Biggio, Jeff Bagwell	50.00
DE	Darin Erstad	20.00
RJ	Reggie Jackson	30.00
EJ	Reggie Jackson, Darin Erstad	50.00
DM	Don Mattingly	75.00
MW	Don Mattingly, Nolan Ryan	150.00
AR	Alex Rodriguez	35.00
NR	Nolan Ryan	75.00
RR	Nolan Ryan, Alex Rodriguez	150.00
DW	Dave Winfield	25.00

2001 Bowman's Best Franchise Futures

		MT
Complete Set (12):		40.00
Common Player:		1.50
Inserted 1:24		
FF1	Josh Hamilton	8.00
FF2	Wes Helms	1.50
FF3	Alfonso Soriano	6.00
FF4	Nick Johnson	2.00
FF5	Jose Ortiz	2.00
FF6	Ben Sheets	5.00
FF7	Sean Burroughs	3.00
FF8	Ben Petrick	1.50
FF9	Corey Patterson	2.00
FF10	J.R. House	8.00
FF11	Alex Escobar	1.50
FF12	Travis Hafner	1.50

2001 Bowman's Best Game-Used Bats

		MT
Common Player:		15.00
Inserted 1:267		
PB	Pat Burrell	25.00
SB	Sean Burroughs	15.00
AG	Adrian Gonzalez	20.00
EM	Eric Munson	15.00
CP	Corey Patterson	20.00

2001 Bowman's Best Game-Worn Jerseys

		MT
Common Player:		10.00
Inserted 1:133		
EC	Eric Chavez	15.00
MM	Mark Mulder	20.00
JP	Jay Payton	15.00
PR	Pokey Reese	10.00
PW	Preston Wilson	10.00

A card number in parentheses ( ) indicates the set is unnumbered.

2001 Bowman's Best Impact Players

		MT
Complete Set (20):		40.00
Common Player:		1.00
Inserted 1:7		
IP1	Mark McGwire	8.00
IP2	Sammy Sosa	5.00
IP3	Manny Ramirez	2.50
IP4	Troy Glaus	2.50
IP5	Ken Griffey Jr.	6.00
IP6	Gary Sheffield	1.00
IP7	Vladimir Guerrero	3.00
IP8	Carlos Delgado	2.00
IP9	Jason Giambi	1.50
IP10	Frank Thomas	2.50
IP11	Vernon Wells	1.00
IP12	Carlos Pena	1.00
IP13	Joe Crede	1.00
IP14	Keith Ginter	1.00
IP15	Aubrey Huff	1.00
IP16	Brad Cresse	1.00
IP17	Austin Kearns	1.00
IP18	Nick Johnson	1.50
IP19	Josh Hamilton	3.00
IP20	Corey Patterson	1.50

2001 Bowman's Best Rookie Fever

		MT
Complete Set (10):		20.00
Common Player:		1.00
Inserted 1:10		
RF1	Chipper Jones	5.00
RF2	Preston Wilson	1.00
RF3	Todd Helton	2.50
RF4	Jay Payton	1.00
RF5	Ivan Rodriguez	2.50
RF6	Manny Ramirez	2.50
RF7	Derek Jeter	8.00
RF8	Orlando Hernandez	1.00
RF9	Marcus Quinn	1.00
RF10	Terrence Long	1.00

2001 Bowman's Best Team Topps

		MT
Common Player:		10.00
Overall odds 1:71		
13R	Warren Spahn	40.00
37R	Tug McGraw	10.00
48R	Bobby Richardson	25.00

25R	Luis Tiant	15.00
31R	Clete Boyer	15.00
23R	Gil McDougald	20.00
27R	Andy Pafko	15.00
28R	Herb Score	15.00
18R	Bob Gibson	40.00
29R	Moose Skowron	15.00
37F	Tug McGraw	15.00
28F	Herb Score	15.00

2001 Bowman Heritage

	MT
Complete Set (440):	200.00
Common Player:	.15
Common (331-440):	1.00
Inserted 1:2	

1	Chipper Jones	1.25
2	Pete Harnisch	.15
3	Brian Giles	.25
4	J.T. Snow	.15
5	Bartolo Colon	.15
6	Jorge Posada	.30
7	Shawn Green	.25
8	Derek Jeter	2.50
9	Benito Santiago	.15
10	Ramon Hernandez	.15
11	Bernie Williams	.50
12	Greg Maddux	1.25
13	Barry Bonds	1.25
14	Roger Clemens	1.00
15	Miguel Tejada	.15
16	Pedro Feliz	.15
17	Jim Edmonds	.25
18	Tom Glavine	.30
19	David Justice	.25
20	Rich Aurilia	.15
21	Jason Giambi	.40
22	Orlando Hernandez	.15
23	Shawn Estes	.15
24	Nelson Figueroa	.15
25	Terrence Long	.15
26	Mike Mussina	.50
27	Eric Davis	.15
28	Jimmy Rollins	.15
29	Andy Pettitte	.30
30	Shawon Dunston	.15
31	Tim Hudson	.25
32	Jeff Kent	.20
33	Scott Brosius	.15
34	Livian Hernandez	.15
35	Alfonso Soriano	.25
36	Mark McGwire	2.00
37	Russ Ortiz	.15
38	Fernando Vina	.15
39	Ken Griffey Jr.	1.50
40	Edgar Renteria	.15
41	Kevin Brown	.15
42	Robb Nen	.15
43	Paul Loduca	.15
44	Bobby Abreu	.15
45	Adam Dunn	.50
46	Osvaldo Fernandez	.15
47	Marvin Benard	.15
48	Mark Gardner	.15
49	Alex Rodriguez	.15
50	Preston Wilson	.15
51	Roberto Alomar	.50
52	Ben Davis	.15
53	Derek Bell	.15
54	Ken Caminiti	.15
55	Barry Zito	.15
56	Scott Rolen	.30
57	Geoff Jenkins	.25
58	Mike Cameron	.15
59	Ben Grieve	.15
60	Chuck Knoblauch	.25
61	Matt Lawton	.15
62	Chan Ho Park	.15
63	Lance Berkman	.25
64	Carlos Beltran	.15
65	Dean Palmer	.15
66	Alex Gonzalez	.15
67	Larry Walker	.25
68	Magglio Ordonez	.15
69	Ellis Burks	.15
70	Mark Mulder	.25
71	Randy Johnson	.60
72	John Smoltz	.15
73	Jerry Hairston Jr.	.15
74	Pedro Martinez	.60
75	Fred McGriff	.25
76	Sean Casey	.25
77	C.C. Sabathia	.15
78	Todd Helton	.60
79	Brad Penny	.15
80	Mike Sweeney	.15
81	Billy Wagner	.15
82	Mark Buehrle	.15
83	Cristian Guzman	.15
84	Jose Vidro	.15
85	Pat Burrell	.40
86	Jermaine Dye	.15
87	Brandon Inge	.15
88	David Wells	.15
89	Mike Piazza	1.50
90	Jose Cabrera	.15
91	Cliff Floyd	.15
92	Matt Morris	.15
93	Raul Mondesi	.15
94	*Joe Kennedy*	.25
95	*Jack Wilson*	.25
96	Andruw Jones	.50
97	Mariano Rivera	.25
98	Mike Hampton	.15
99	Roger Cedeno	.15
100	Jose Cruz	.15
101	Mike Lowell	.15
102	Pedro Astacio	.15
103	Joe Mays	.15
104	John Franco	.15
105	Tim Redding	.15
106	Sandy Alomar	.15
107	Bret Boone	.15
108	*Josh Towers*	.50
109	Matt Stairs	.15
110	Chris Truby	.15
111	Jeff Suppan	.15
112	J.C. Romero	.15
113	Felipe Lopez	.15
114	Ben Sheets	.25
115	Frank Thomas	.60
116	A.J. Burnett	.15
117	Tony Clark	.15
118	Mac Suzuki	.15
119	Brad Radke	.15
120	Jeff Shaw	.15
121	Nick Neugebauer	.15
122	Kenny Lofton	.25
123	Jacque Jones	.15
124	Brent Mayne	.15
125	Carlos Hernandez	.15
126	Shane Spencer	.15
127	John Lackey	.15
128	Sterling Hitchcock	.15
129	Darren Dreifort	.15
130	Rusty Greer	.15
131	Michael Cuddyer	.15
132	Tyler Houston	.15
133	Chin-Feng Chen	.15
134	Ken Harvey	.15
135	Marquis Grissom	.15
136	Russell Branyan	.15
137	Eric Karros	.15
138	Josh Beckett	.15
139	Todd Zeile	.15
140	Corey Koskie	.15
141	Steve Sparks	.15
142	Bobby Seay	.15
143	Tim Raines	.15
144	Julio Zuleta	.15
145	Jose Lima	.15
146	Dante Bichette	.15
147	Randy Keisler	.15
148	Brent Butler	.15
149	Antonio Alfonseca	.15
150	Bryan Rekar	.15
151	Jeffrey Hammonds	.15
152	Larry Bigbie	.15
153	Blake Stein	.15
154	Robin Ventura	.25
155	Rondell White	.25
156	Juan Silvestre	.15
157	Marcus Thames	.15
158	Sidney Ponson	.15
159	Juan Pena	.15
160	Charles Johnson	.15
161	Adam Everett	.15
162	Eric Munson	.15
163	Jason Isringhausen	.15
164	Brad Fullmer	.15
165	Miguel Olivo	.15
166	Fernando Tatis	.15
167	Freddy Garcia	.15
168	Tom Goodwin	.15
169	Armando Benitez	.15
170	Paul Konerko	.15
171	Jeff Cirillo	.15
172	Shane Reynolds	.15
173	Kevin Tapani	.15
174	Joe Crede	.15
175	*Ben Hendrickson*	.25
176	*Jake Peavy*	.25
177	Corey Patterson	.15
178	*Alfredo Amezaga*	.25
179	Jeromy Burnitz	.15
180	David Segui	.15
181	Marcus Giles	.15
182	Paul O'Neill	.30
183	John Olerud	.25
184	Andy Benes	.15
185	*Brad Cresse*	.25
186	Ricky Ledee	.15
187	Allen Levrault	.25
188	Royce Clayton	.15
189	*Kelly Johnson*	.25
190	Quilvio Veras	.15
191	Mike Williams	.15
192	*Jason Lane*	.25
193	Rick Helling	.15
194	Tim Wakefield	.15
195	James Baldwin	.15
196	*Cody Ransom*	.25
197	Bobby Kielty	.15
198	Bobby Jones	.15
199	Steve Cox	.15
200	*Jamal Strong*	.25
201	Steve Lomasney	.15
202	Bill Ortega	.25
203	Mike Matheny	.15
204	*Jeff Randazzo*	.25
205	Aubrey Huff	.15
206	Chuck Finley	.15
207	*Denny Bautista*	.25
208	Terry Mulholland	.15
209	Rey Ordonez	.15
210	*Jason Belcher*	.25
211	Orlando Cabrera	.15
212	Juan Encarnacion	.15
213	Dustin Hermanson	.15
214	Luis Rivas	.15
215	Mark Quinn	.15
216	Randy Velarde	.15
217	Billy Koch	.15
218	Ryan Rupe	.15
219	Keith Ginter	.15
220	Woody Williams	.15
221	*Blake Williams*	.25
222	Aaron Myette	.15
223	*Joe Borchard*	.25
224	Nate Cornejo	.15
225	Julian Tavarez	.15
226	Kevin Millwood	.15
227	*Travis Hafner*	.50
228	Charles Nagy	.15
229	Mike Lieberthal	.15
230	Jeff Nelson	.15
231	Ryan Dempster	.15
232	Andres Galarraga	.25
233	Chad Durbin	.15
234	Timoniel Perez	.15
235	Troy O'Leary	.15
236	Kevin Young	.15
237	Gabe Kapler	.15
238	*Juan Cruz*	2.00
239	Masato Yoshii	.15
240	Aramis Ramirez	.15
241	*Matt Cooper*	.25
242	*Randy Flores*	.25
243	Rafael Furcal	.25
244	David Eckstein	.15
245	Matt Clement	.15
246	Craig Biggio	.25
247	Rick Reed	.15
248	Jose Macias	.15
249	Alex Escobar	.15
250	Roberto Hernandez	.15
251	Andy Ashby	.15
252	Tony Armas	.15
253	Jamie Moyer	.15
254	Jason Tyner	.15
255	*Ryan Ludwick*	.25
256	Jeff Conine	.15
257	Francisco Cordova	.15
258	Ted Lilly	.15
259	Joe Randa	.15
260	Jeff D'Amico	.15
261	Albie Lopez	.15
262	Kevin Appier	.15
263	Richard Hidalgo	.15
264	Omar Daal	.15
265	Ricky Gutierrez	.15
266	John Rocker	.15
267	Ray Lankford	.15
268	*Beau Hale*	.25
269	*Tony Blanco*	.25
270	Derrick Lee	.15
271	Jamey Wright	.15
272	Alex Gordon	.15
273	Jeff Weaver	.15
274	Jaret Wright	.15
275	Jose Hernandez	.15
276	Bruce Chen	.15
277	Todd Hollandsworth	.15
278	Wade Miller	.15
279	Luke Prokopec	.15
280	*Rafael Soriano*	.25
281	Damion Easley	.15
282	Darren Oliver	.15
283	*Brandon Duckworth*	.75
284	Aaron Herr	.15
285	Ray Durham	.15
286	*Adrian Hernandez*	.50
287	Ugueth Urbina	.15
288	Scott Seabol	.15
289	*Lance Niekro*	.25
290	Trot Nixon	.15
291	Adam Kennedy	.15
292	*Brian Schmitt*	.25
293	Grant Roberts	.15
294	Benny Agbayani	.15
295	Travis Lee	.15
296	*Erick Almonte*	.40
297	Jim Thome	.40
298	Eric Young	.15
299	*Daniel Denham*	.25
300	*Boof Bonser*	.25
301	Denny Neagle	.15
302	Kenny Rogers	.15
303	J.D. Closser	.15
304	*Chase Utley*	.25
305	Rey Sanchez	.15
306	Sean McGowan	.15
307	*Justin Pope*	.25
308	Torii Hunter	.15
309	B.J. Surhoff	.15
310	*Aaron Heilman*	.25
311	*Gabe Gross*	.25
312	Lee Stevens	.15
313	Todd Hundley	.15
314	*MaCay McBride*	.25
315	Edgar Martinez	.15
316	Omar Vizquel	.25
317	Reggie Sanders	.15
318	*John-Ford Griffin*	.25
319	Tim Salmon	.30
320	Pokey Reese	.15
321	Jay Payton	.15
322	Doug Glanville	.15
323	Greg Vaughn	.15
324	Ruben Sierra	.15
325	Kip Wells	.15
326	Carl Everett	.15
327	Garret Anderson	.15
328	Jay Bell	.15
329	Barry Larkin	.40
330	*Jeff Mathis*	.25
331	Adrian Gonzalez	2.50
332	Juan Rivera	1.00
333	Tony Alvarez	1.00
334	Xavier Nady	1.00
335	Josh Hamilton	3.00
336	*Will Smith*	2.50
337	Israel Alcantara	1.00
338	Chris George	1.00
339	Sean Burroughs	2.00
340	Jack Cust	1.00
341	Eric Byrnes	1.00
342	Carlos Pena	1.00
343	J.R. House	3.00
344	Carlos Silva	1.00
345	*Mike Rivera*	2.50
346	Adam Johnson	1.00

347	Scott Heard	1.00
348	Alex Cintron	1.00
349	Miguel Cabrera	1.00
350	Nick Johnson	1.00
351	*Albert Pujols*	20.00
352	*Ichiro Suzuki*	30.00
353	Carlos Delgado	2.00
354	Troy Glaus	3.00
355	Sammy Sosa	6.00
356	Ivan Rodriguez	3.00
357	Vladimir Guerrero	3.00
358	Manny Ramirez	3.00
359	Luis Gonzalez	2.50
360	Roy Oswalt	1.00
361	Moises Alou	1.00
362	Juan Gonzalez	3.00
363	Tony Gwynn	3.00
364	Hideo Nomo	2.00
365	*Tsuyoshi Shinjo*	8.00
366	Kazuhiro Sasaki	1.00
367	Cal Ripken Jr.	12.00
368	Rafael Palmeiro	2.00
369	J.D. Drew	1.50
370	Doug Mientkiewicz	1.00
371	Jeff Bagwell	3.00
372	Darin Erstad	1.50
373	Tom Gordon	1.00
374	Ben Petrick	1.00
375	Eric Milton	1.00
376	Nomar Garciaparra	10.00
377	Julio Lugo	1.00
378	Tino Martinez	1.50
379	Javier Vazquez	1.00
380	Jeremy Giambi	1.00
381	Marty Cordova	1.00
382	Adrian Beltre	1.00
383	John Burkett	1.00
384	Aaron Boone	1.00
385	Eric Chavez	1.00
386	Curt Schilling	2.00
387	Cory Lidle	1.00
388	Jason Schmidt	1.00
389	Johnny Damon	1.00
390	Steve Finley	1.00
391	Edgardo Alfonzo	1.00
392	Jose Valentin	1.00
393	Jose Canseco	1.50
394	Ryan Klesko	1.00
395	David Cone	1.00
396	Jason Kendall	1.00
397	Placido Polanco	1.00
398	Glendon Rusch	1.00
399	Aaron Sele	1.00
400	D'Angelo Jimenez	1.00
401	Mark Grace	2.00
402	Al Leiter	1.50
403	Brian Jordan	1.00
404	Phil Nevin	1.00
405	Brent Abernathy	1.00
406	Kerry Wood	2.00
407	Alex Gonzalez	1.00
408	Robert Fick	1.00
409	Dmitri Young	1.00
410	Wes Helms	1.00
411	Trevor Hoffman	1.00
412	Rickey Henderson	2.00
413	Bobby Higginson	1.00
414	Gary Sheffield	1.50
415	Darryl Kile	1.00
416	Richie Sexson	1.00
417	Frank Menechino	1.00
418	Javy Lopez	1.00
419	Carlos Lee	1.00
420	Jon Lieber	1.00
421	*Hank Blalock*	10.00
422	*Marlon Byrd*	12.00
423	*Jason Kinchen*	1.50
424	*Morgan Ensberg*	5.00
425	*Greg "Toe" Nash*	12.00
426	*Dennis Tankersley*	6.00
427	Joel Pineiro	1.00
428	*Chris Smith*	1.50
429	*Jake Gautreau*	6.00
430	John Van Benschoten	5.00
431	Travis Thompson	1.00
432	*Billy Martin*	2.00
433	*Jerome Williams*	5.00
434	Kevin Reese	1.00
435	*Ed Rogers*	4.00
436	*Grant Balfour*	1.00
437	*Adam Pettyjohn*	1.00
438	*Hee Seop Choi*	8.00
439	Justin Morneau	8.00
440	*Mitch Jones*	5.00

2001 Bowman Heritage Chrome

	MT
Stars:	4-8X
SPs:	2-4X

Inserted 1:12

(See 2001 Bowman Heritage for checklist and base card values.)

2001 Bowman Heritage 1948 Bowman Reprints

		MT
Complete Set (13):		10.00
Common Player:		.75
Inserted 1:2		
1	Ralph Kiner	.75
2	Johnny Mize	.75
3	Bobby Thomson	.75
4	Yogi Berra	1.50
5	Phil Rizzuto	1.00
6	Bob Feller	1.00
7	Enos Slaughter	.75
8	Stan Musial	2.00
9	Hank Sauer	.75
10	Ferris Fain	.75
11	Red Schoendienst	.75
12	Allie Reynolds	.75
13	Johnny Sain	.75

2001 Bowman Heritage 1948 Reprint Relics

		MT
Common Player:		10.00
Inserted 1:44		
YB1	Yogi Berra	25.00
YB2	Yogi Berra	60.00
FF	Ferris Fain	10.00
BF	Bob Feller	20.00
RK	Ralph Kiner	15.00
JM	Johnny Mize	20.00
SM1	Stan Musial	35.00
PR	Phil Rizzuto	20.00
HS	Hank Sauer	10.00
RS	Red Schoendienst	20.00
ES	Enos Slaughter	20.00
BT	Bobby Thomson	15.00

Figure values of lower-grade cards from 1981-date as:
Near Mint (NM) 75%
Excellent (EX) 40%
of the listed Mint price

For cards through 1980, values should be figured as:
Excellent (EX) 50%
Very Good (VG) 30%
of the listed Near Mint price

2001 Bowman Heritage 1948 Bowman Reprint Autographs

		MT
Common Autograph:		50.00
1	Warren Spahn	50.00
2	Bob Feller	50.00

2001 Bowman Heritage Bowman Heritage Autographs

	MT
BHA-BB Barry Bonds	
BHA-RC Roger Clemens	
BHA-NG Nomar Garciaparra	
BHA-AR Alex Rodriguez	

2001 Bowman Heritage Team Topps Legends Autographs

	MT
Common Autograph:	50.00
Inserted 1:332	
TT13R Warren Spahn	40.00
TT21R Bob Feller	30.00

2002 Bowman

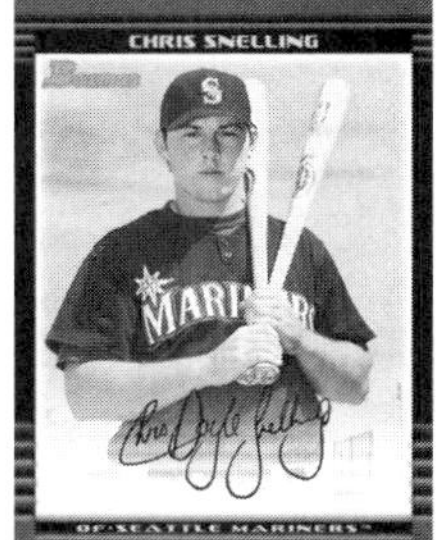

		MT
Complete Set (440):		100.00
Common Player:		.20
Common Rookie:		.40
Pack (10):		3.00
Box (24):		55.00
1	Adam Dunn	.50
2	Derek Jeter	2.00
3	Alex Rodriguez	1.50
4	Miguel Tejada	.30
5	Nomar Garciaparra	1.25
6	Toby Hall	.20
7	Brandon Duckworth	.20
8	Paul LoDuca	.20
9	Brian Giles	.30
10	C.C. Sabathia	.20
11	Curt Schilling	.50
12	Tsuyoshi Shinjo	.40
13	Ramon Hernandez	.20
14	Jose Cruz Jr.	.20
15	Albert Pujols	.75
16	Joe Mays	.20
17	Javy Lopez	.20
18	J.T. Snow	.20
19	David Segui	.20
20	Jorge Posada	.40
21	Doug Mientkiewicz	.20
22	Jerry Hairston Jr.	.20
23	Bernie Williams	.40
24	Mike Sweeney	.20
25	Jason Giambi	.60
26	Ryan Dempster	.20
27	Ryan Klesko	.20
28	Mark Quinn	.20
29	Jeff Kent	.20
30	Eric Chavez	.30
31	Adrian Beltre	.20
32	Andruw Jones	.40
33	Alfonso Soriano	.50
34	Aramis Ramirez	.20
35	Greg Maddux	1.00
36	Andy Pettitte	.40
37	Bartolo Colon	.30
38	Ben Sheets	.40
39	Bobby Higginson	.20
40	Ivan Rodriguez	.40
41	Brad Penny	.20
42	Carlos Lee	.20
43	Damion Easley	.20
44	Preston Wilson	.20
45	Jeff Bagwell	.50
46	Eric Milton	.20
47	Rafael Palmeiro	.40
48	Gary Sheffield	.30
49	J.D. Drew	.40
50	Jim Thome	.50
51	Ichiro Suzuki	2.00
52	Bud Smith	.20
53	Chan Ho Park	.20
54	D'Angelo Jimenez	.20
55	Ken Griffey Jr.	1.25
56	Wade Miller	.20
57	Vladimir Guerrero	.50
58	Troy Glaus	.50
59	Shawn Green	.40
60	Kerry Wood	.40
61	Jack Wilson	.20
62	Kevin Brown	.30
63	Marcus Giles	.20
64	Pat Burrell	.40
65	Larry Walker	.30
66	Sammy Sosa	1.25
67	Raul Mondesi	.20
68	Tim Hudson	.40
69	Lance Berkman	.40
70	Mike Mussina	.40
71	Barry Zito	.40
72	Jimmy Rollins	.20
73	Barry Bonds	1.50
74	Craig Biggio	.30
75	Todd Helton	.40
76	Roger Clemens	.75
77	Frank Catalanotto	.20
78	Josh Towers	.20
79	Roy Oswalt	.40
80	Chipper Jones	1.00
81	Cristian Guzman	.20
82	Darin Erstad	.30
83	Freddy Garcia	.20
84	Jason Tyner	.20
85	Carlos Delgado	.40
86	Jon Lieber	.20
87	Juan Pierre	.20
88	Matt Morris	.20
89	Phil Nevin	.20
90	Jim Edmonds	.30
91	Magglio Ordonez	.30
92	Mike Hampton	.20
93	Rafael Furcal	.20
94	Richie Sexson	.40
95	Luis Gonzalez	.40
96	Scott Rolen	.40
97	Tim Redding	.20
98	Moises Alou	.25
99	Jose Vidro	.20
100	Mike Piazza	1.50
101	Pedro Martinez	.50
102	Geoff Jenkins	.20
103	Johnny Damon	.20
104	Mike Cameron	.20
105	Randy Johnson	.50
106	David Eckstein	.20
107	Javier Vazquez	.20
108	Mark Mulder	.20
109	Robert Fick	.20
110	Roberto Alomar	.40

111 Wilson Betemit .20
112 *Chris Tritle* 1.00
113 Ed Rogers .20
114 Juan Pena .20
115 Josh Beckett .50
116 Juan Cruz .20
117 *Noochie Varner* .50
118 *Taylor Buchholz* .50
119 Mike Rivera .20
120 Hank Blalock .40
121 *Hansel Izquierdo* .50
122 Orlando Hudson .20
123 Bill Hall .20
124 Jose Reyes .20
125 Juan Rivera .20
126 Eric Valent .20
127 *Scotty Layfield* .40
128 Austin Kearns .50
129 *Nic Jackson* .20
130 *Chris Baker* .50
131 *Chad Qualls* .40
132 Marcus Thames .20
133 Nathan Haynes .20
134 Brett Evert .20
135 Joe Borchard .20
136 Ryan Christianson .20
137 Josh Hamilton .20
138 Corey Patterson .20
139 Travis Wilson .20
140 Alex Escobar .20
141 Alexis Gomez .20
142 Nick Johnson .20
143 Kenny Kelly .20
144 Marlon Byrd .20
145 Kory DeHaan .20
146 Matt Belisle .20
147 Carlos Hernandez .20
148 Sean Burroughs .20
149 Angel Berroa .20
150 Aubrey Huff .20
151 Travis Hafner .20
152 Brandon Berger .20
153 David Krynzel .20
154 Ruben Salazar .20
155 J.R. House .20
156 Juan Silvestre .20
157 Dewon Brazelton .20
158 Jayson Werth .20
159 Larry Barnes .20
160 Elvis Pena .20
161 *Ruben Gotay* .40
162 *Tommy Marx* .50
163 *John Suomi* .40
164 Javier Colina .20
165 *Greg Sain* .20
166 *Robert Cosby* .20
167 *Angel Pagan* .20
168 *Ralph Santana* .50
169 *Joe Orloski* .40
170 *Shayne Wright* .50
171 *Jay Caligiuri* .20
172 *Greg Montalbano* 1.50
173 *James Harden* .50
174 *Rich Thompson* 1.00
175 *Fred Bastardo* .40
176 *Alejandro Giron* .40
177 *Jesus Medrano* .40
178 *Kevin Deaton* .75
179 *Mike Rosamond* .50
180 *Jon Guzman* .40
181 *Gerard Oakes* .40
182 *Francisco Liriano* .40
183 *Matt Allegra* .40
184 *Mike Snyder* .40
185 *James Shanks* .40
186 *Anderson Hernandez* .40
187 *Dan Trumble* .40
188 *Luis DePaula* .40
189 *Randall Shelley* .40
190 *Richard Lane* .40
191 *Antwon Rollins* .75
192 *Ryan Bukvich* .40
193 Derrick Lewis .20
194 *Eric Miller* .40
195 *Justin Schuda* .40
196 *Brian West* .75
197 *Adam Roller* .40
198 *Neal Frendling* .40
199 *Jeremy Hill* .40
200 *James Barrett* 2.00
201 *Brett Kay* .75
202 *Ryan Mottl* .50
203 *Brad Nelson* 1.50
204 Juan Gonzalez .20
205 *Curtis Legendre* .40
206 *Ronald Acuna* .40
207 *Chris Flinn* .40
208 *Nick Alvarez* .40
209 *Jason Ellison* .40
210 *Blake McGinley* .40
211 *Dan Phillips* .75
212 *Demetrius Heath* .40
213 *Eric Bruntlett* .40
214 *Joe Jiannetti* .40
215 *Mike Hill* .40
216 *Ricardo Cordova* .40
217 *Mark Hamilton* .50
218 *David Mattox* .40
219 *Jose Morban* .50
220 *Scott Wiggins* .75
221 Steve Green .20
222 Brian Rogers .20
223 Chin-Hui Tsao .40
224 Kenny Baugh .20
225 Nate Teut .20
226 *Josh Wilson* .40
227 Christian Parker .20
228 Tim Raines Jr. .20
229 *Anastacio Martinez* .40
230 Richard Lewis .20
231 *Tim Kalita* .40
232 *Edwin Almonte* .40
233 Hee Seop Choi .50
234 Ty Howington .20
235 *Victor Alvarez* .40
236 Morgan Ensberg .20
237 *Jeff Austin* 3.00
238 Luis Terrero .20
239 Adam Wainwright .20
240 *Clint Weibl* .40
241 *Eric Cyr* 1.00
242 *Marlyn Tisdale* .40
243 John VanBenschoten .20
244 *Ryan Raburn* .75
245 Miguel Cabrera .20
246 Jung Bong .20
247 *Raul Chavez* .75
248 Erik Bedard .20
249 *Chris Snelling* 4.00
250 *Joe Rogers* .40
251 *Nate Field* .40
252 Matt Herges .20
253 *Matt Childers* .50
254 Erick Almonte .20
255 Nick Neugebauer .20
256 *Ron Calloway* .40
257 Seung Jun Song .20
258 Brandon Phillips .20
259 Cole Barthel .20
260 Jason Lane .20
261 Jae Weong Seo .20
262 Randy Flores .20
263 Scott Chiasson .20
264 Chase Utley .20
265 Tony Alvarez .20
266 *Ben Howard* 1.50
267 *Nelson Castro* .40
268 Mark Lukasiewicz .20
269 *Eric Glaser* .75
270 *Rob Henkel* 1.00
271 *Jose Valverde* .40
272 Ricardo Rodriguez .20
273 Chris Smith .20
274 Mark Prior 2.00
275 Miguel Olivo .20
276 Ben Broussard .20
277 Zach Sorensen .20
278 *Brian Mallette* .40
279 Brad Wilkerson .20
280 Carl Crawford .20
281 *Chone Figgins* .40
282 *Jimmy Alvarez* .40
283 Gavin Floyd 3.00
284 *Josh Bonifay* 1.50
285 *Garrett Guzman* 1.00
286 Blake Williams .20
287 Matt Holliday .20
288 Ryan Madson .20
289 Luis Torres .20
290 *Jeff Verplancke* .40
291 *Nate Espy* 1.00
292 *Jeff Lincoln* .40
293 *Ryan Snare* .40
294 Jose Ortiz .20
295 Eric Munson .20
296 Denny Bautista .20
297 Willy Aybar .20
298 Kelly Johnson .20
299 Justin Morneau .20
300 Derrick Van Dusen .20
301 Chad Petty .20
302 Mike Restovich .20
303 Shawn Fagan .20
304 *Yurendell DeCaster* .40
305 Justin Wayne .20
306 *Mike Peeples* .40
307 *Joel Guzman* .40
308 Ryan Vogelsong .20
309 *Jorge Padilla* 1.00
310 Grady Sizemore .20
311 *Joe Jester* .40
312 Jim Journell .20
313 Bobby Seay .20
314 *Ryan Church* .75
315 Grant Balfour .20
316 Mitch Jones .20
317 Travis Foley 1.00
318 Bobby Crosby .20
319 Adrian Gonzalez .20
320 Ronnie Merrill .20
321 Joel Pineiro .20
322 John-Ford Griffin .20
323 *Brian Forystek* .40
324 Sean Douglass .20
325 *Manny Delcarmen* .40
326 Donnie Bridges .20
327 Jim Kavourias .20
328 Gabe Gross .20
329 Greg "Toe" Nash .20
330 Bill Ortega .20
331 *Joey Hammond* .40
332 *Ramon Moreta* .40
333 Ron Davenport .20
334 Brett Myers .20
335 Carlos Pena .20
336 *Ezequiel Astacio* .40
337 *Edwin Yan* .50
338 Josh Girdley .20
339 Shaun Boyd .20
340 Juan Rincon .20
341 *Chris Duffy* .75
342 Jason Kinchen .20
343 Brad Thomas .20
344 David Kelton .20
345 Rafael Soriano .20
346 *Colin Young* .50
347 Eric Byrnes .20
348 *Chris Narveson* .50
349 *John Rheinecker* .40
350 *Mike Wilson* .40
351 *Justin Sherrod* 1.50
352 Deivi Mendez .20
353 Wily Mo Pena .20
354 *Brett Roneberg* .75
355 *Trey Lunsford* .40
356 *Jimmy Gobble* 1.50
357 Brent Butler .20
358 Aaron Heilman .20
359 Wilkin Ruan .20
360 *Brian Wolfe* .40
361 Cody Ransom .20
362 Koyie Hill .75
363 Scott Cassidy .20
364 *Tony Fontana* .60
365 Mark Teixeira .40
366 *Doug Sessions* .40
367 Victor Hall .20
368 *Josh Cisneros* .40
369 Kevin Mench .20
370 Tike Redman .20
371 Jeff Heaverlo .20
372 *Carlos Brackley* .40
373 Brad Hawpe .20
374 Jesus Colome .20
375 David Espinosa .20
376 Jesse Foppert .75
377 *Ross Peeples* .40
378 *Alexander Requena* .40
379 *Joe Mauer* 6.00
380 Carlos Silva .20
381 George Perez .20
382 *Craig Kuzmic* .75
383 *Peter Zamora* .40
384 *Matt Parker* .40
385 Ricardo Rodriguez .20
386 *Gary Cates Jr.* .40
387 *Justin Reid* .50
388 *Jake Mauer* .75
389 John-Ford Griffin .20
390 Josh Barfield .20
391 Luis Maza .20
392 *Henry Pichardo* .40
393 *Michael Floyd* .40
394 *Clint Nageotte* 1.00
395 Jim Warden .20
396 *Mauricio Lara* .75
397 *Alejandro Cadena* .40
398 *Jonny Gomes* 2.00
399 *Jason Bulger* 1.00
400 *Bobby Jenks* .40
401 *David Gil* .40
402 *Joel Crump* .40
403 *Kazuhisa Ishii* 6.00
404 *So Taguchi* .75
405 *Ryan Doumit* .40
406 MaCay McBride .20
407 Brandon Claussen .20
408 Chin-Feng Chen .20
409 Josh Phelps .40
410 *Freddie Money* .40
411 *Clifford Bartosh* .75
412 Josh Pearce .20
413 Lyle Overbay .20
414 Ryan Anderson .20
415 *Terrance Hill* .40
416 *John Rodriguez* .40
417 *Richard Stahl* .40
418 Brian Specht .20
419 *Chris Latham* .50
420 *Carlos Cabrera* .40
421 *Jose Bautista* .40
422 *Kevin Frederick* .40
423 Jerome Williams .20
424 *Napoleon Calzado* .50
425 Benito Baez .20
426 Xavier Nady .20
427 *Jason Botts* .40
428 *Steve Bechler* 1.00
429 *Reed Johnson* .40
430 *Mark Outlaw* .40
431 Billy Sylvester .20
432 Luke Lockwood .20
433 Jake Peavy .20
434 Alfredo Amezega .20
435 *Aaron Cook* .40
436 *Josh Shaffer* .40
437 Dan Wright .20
438 *Ryan Gripp* .75
439 Alex Herrera .20
440 *Jason Bay* .40

2002 Bowman Gold

MT

Stars: 1-2.5X
Rookies: 1-2X
Inserted 1:1

2002 Bowman Uncirculated

MT

Common Player: 8.00
Production 1,000 sets

112 Chris Tritle 10.00
113 Ed Rogers 8.00
114 Juan Pena 8.00
115 Josh Beckett 10.00
116 Juan Cruz 8.00
117 Noochie Varner 8.00
118 Taylor Buchholz 8.00
119 Mike Rivera 8.00
120 Hank Blalock 8.00
121 Hansel Izquierdo 8.00
122 Orlando Hudson 8.00
123 Bill Hall 8.00
124 Jose Reyes 8.00
125 Juan Rivera 8.00
126 Eric Valent 8.00
127 Scotty Layfield 8.00
128 Austin Kearns 10.00
129 Nic Jackson 8.00
130 Chris Baker 8.00
131 Chad Qualls 8.00

2002 Bowman Autographs

MT

Common Autograph: 8.00
Inserted 1:37

AA Alfredo Amezaga 8.00
GA Garrett Atkins 8.00
JB Josh Beckett 20.00
WB Wilson Betemit 10.00
LB Larry Bigbie 8.00
HB Hank Blalock 25.00
TB Tony Blanco 8.00
JAB Jason Botts 10.00
MB Marlon Byrd 15.00
BDC Brian Cardwell 8.00
BC Ben Christensen 8.00
BAC Brandon Claussen 12.00
JD Jeff Davanon 8.00
MD Manny Delcarmen 8.00
RF Randy Flores 8.00
RF Ryan Franklin 8.00
KG Keith Ginter 8.00
TH Toby Hall 8.00
AH Aubrey Huff 8.00
GJ Gary Johnson 8.00

NJ Nick Johnson 20.00
CK Charles Kegley 8.00
JL Jason Lane 10.00
NN Nick Neugebauer 8.00
RO Roy Oswalt 20.00
JP Juan Pena 8.00
MP Mark Prior 60.00
CR Cody Ransom 8.00
JS Juan Silvestre 8.00
TS Terrmel Sledge 8.00
BS Bud Smith 12.00
CS Chris Smith 8.00
WS Will Smith 12.00
BJS Brian Specht 8.00
CT Chris Tritle 15.00
CU Chase Utley 12.00
DV Domingo Valdez 8.00
NV Noochie Varner 8.00
RV Ryan Vogelsong 8.00
JLW Jerome Williams 12.00
DW Dan Wright 10.00

2002 Bowman Autographed Futures Game Game-Worn Jersey

MT
Common Player: 15.00
Inserted 1:193
WB Wilson Betemit 20.00
CH Carlos Hernandez 18.00
JRH J.R. House 20.00
NJ Nick Johnson 35.00
RL Ryan Ludwick 15.00
CP Carlos Pena 20.00
DT Dennis Tankersley 15.00
JW Jerome Williams 15.00

2002 Bowman Autographed Futures Game Game-Used Base

MT
Randomly inserted
TB Toby Hall 15.00

2002 Bowman Game-Used Relics

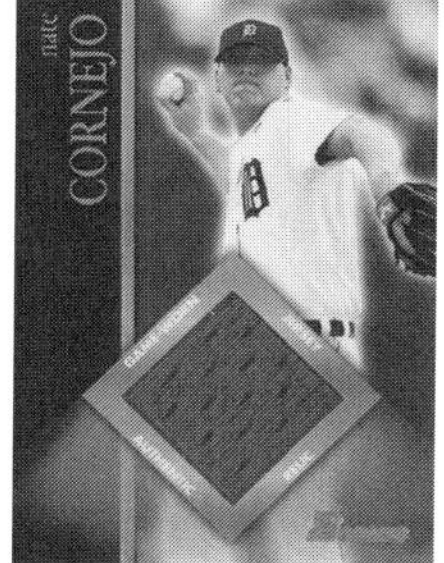

MT
Common Player: 6.00
Inserted 1:165

JA1 Jared Abruzzo 6.00
JA2 Jared Abruzzo 6.00
GA Garrett Atkins 6.00
AB Angel Berroa 8.00
AC Antoine Cameron 6.00
RC Ryan Church 12.00
ALC Alex Cintron 6.00
NC Nate Cornejo 6.00
RD Ryan Dittfurth 6.00
AE Adam Everett 6.00
AF1 Alex Fernandez 6.00
AF2 Alex Fernandez 6.00
AG Alexis Gomez 10.00
CG Cristian Guerrero 6.00
CI Cesar Izturis 8.00
DJ D'Angelo Jimenez 6.00
FJ Forrest Johnson 6.00
AK Austin Kearns 20.00
JL Jason Lane 10.00
RM Ryan Madson 6.00
NN Nick Neugebauer 8.00
CP Corey Patterson 10.00
RS Ruben Salazar 6.00
RST Richard Stahl 6.00
JS Jamal Strong 6.00
CY Colin Young 10.00

2002 Bowman Chrome

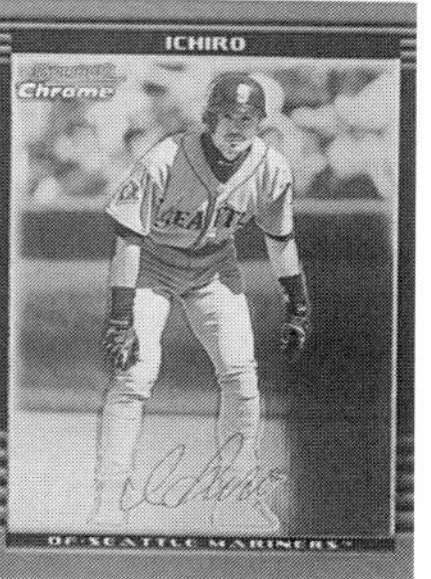

MT
Complete Set (405):
Common Player: .25
Common SP: 3.00
Inserted 1:3
Common Auto
(384-402, 405) 15.00
Inserted 1:18
Pack (4): 5.00
Box (18): 80.00
1 Adam Dunn .75
2 Derek Jeter 3.00
3 Alex Rodriguez 2.50
4 Miguel Tejada .50
5 Nomar Garciaparra 2.00
6 Toby Hall .25
7 Brandon Duckworth .25
8 Paul LoDuca .25
9 Brian Giles .50
10 C.C. Sabathia .25
11 Curt Schilling .75
12 Tsuyoshi Shinjo .50
13 Ramon Hernandez .25
14 Jose Cruz Jr. .25
15 Albert Pujols 1.50
16 Joe Mays .25
17 Javy Lopez .25
18 J.T. Snow .25
19 David Segui .25
20 Jorge Posada .50
21 Doug Mientkiewicz .25
22 Jerry Hairston Jr. .25
23 Bernie Williams .50
24 Mike Sweeney .25
25 Jason Giambi 1.00
26 Ryan Dempster .25
27 Ryan Klesko .25
28 Mark Quinn .25
29 Jeff Kent .25
30 Eric Chavez .40
31 Adrian Beltre .40
32 Andruw Jones .50
33 Alfonso Soriano 1.50
34 Aramis Ramirez .25
35 Greg Maddux 1.50
36 Andy Pettitte .50
37 Bartolo Colon .25
38 Ben Sheets .25
39 Bobby Higginson .25
40 Ivan Rodriguez .50
41 Brad Penny .25
42 Carlos Lee .25
43 Damion Easley .25
44 Preston Wilson .25
45 Jeff Bagwell .75
46 Eric Milton .25
47 Rafael Palmeiro .50
48 Gary Sheffield .50
49 J.D. Drew .50
50 Jim Thome .50
51 Ichiro Suzuki 2.50
52 Bud Smith .25
53 Chan Ho Park .25
54 D'Angelo Jimenez .25
55 Ken Griffey Jr. 2.00
56 Wade Miller .25
57 Vladimir Guerrero .75
58 Troy Glaus .50
59 Shawn Green .40
60 Kerry Wood .50
61 Jack Wilson .25
62 Kevin Brown .25
63 Marcus Giles .25
64 Pat Burrell .50
65 Larry Walker .40
66 Sammy Sosa 1.50
67 Raul Mondesi .25
68 Tim Hudson .40
69 Lance Berkman .75
70 Mike Mussina .50
71 Barry Zito .50
72 Jimmy Rollins .25
73 Barry Bonds 2.00
74 Craig Biggio .25
75 Todd Helton .75
76 Roger Clemens 1.00
77 Frank Catalanotto .25
78 Josh Towers .25
79 Roy Oswalt .50
80 Chipper Jones 1.50
81 Cristian Guzman .25
82 Darin Erstad .50
83 Freddy Garcia .25
84 Jason Tyner .25
85 Carlos Delgado .50
86 Jon Lieber .25
87 Juan Pierre .25
88 Matt Morris .25
89 Phil Nevin .25
90 Jim Edmonds .50
91 Magglio Ordonez .50
92 Mike Hampton .25
93 Rafael Furcal .25
94 Richie Sexson .50
95 Luis Gonzalez .50
96 Scott Rolen .50
97 Tim Redding .25
98 Moises Alou .25
99 Jose Vidro .25
100 Mike Piazza 2.00
101 Pedro Martinez 1.00
102 Geoff Jenkins .25
103 Johnny Damon .25
104 Mike Cameron .25
105 Randy Johnson 1.00
106 David Eckstein .25
107 Javier Vazquez .25
108 Mark Mulder .50
109 Robert Fick .25
110 Roberto Alomar .50
111 Wilson Betemit .25
112 *Chris Tritle/SP* 8.00
113 Ed Rogers .25
114 Juan Pena .25
115 Josh Beckett .50
116 Juan Cruz .25
117 *Noochie Varner/SP* 8.00
118 Blake Williams .25
119 Mike Rivera .25
120 Hank Blalock .50
121 *Hansel Izquierdo/SP* 5.00
122 Orlando Hudson .25
123 Bill Hall .25
124 Jose Reyes .25
125 Juan Rivera .25
126 Eric Valent .25
127 *Scotty Layfield/SP* 3.00
128 Austin Kearns 1.00
129 *Nic Jackson/SP* 6.00
130 Scott Chiasson .25
131 *Chad Qualls/SP* 5.00
132 Marcus Thames .25
133 Nathan Haynes .25
134 Joe Borchard .25
135 Josh Hamilton .25
136 Corey Patterson .25
137 Travis Wilson .25
138 Alex Escobar .25
139 Alexis Gomez .25
140 Nick Johnson .50
141 Marlon Byrd .50
142 Kory DeHaan .25
143 Carlos Hernandez .25
144 Sean Burroughs .50
145 Angel Berroa .25
146 Aubrey Huff .25
147 Travis Hafner .25
148 Brandon Berger .25
149 J.R. House .25
150 Dewon Brazelton .25
151 Jayson Werth .25
152 Larry Barnes .25
153 *Ruben Gotay/SP* 5.00
154 *Tommy Marx/SP* 3.00
155 *John Suomi/SP* 5.00
156 Javier Colina/SP 3.00
157 *Greg Sain* 3.00
158 *Robert Cosby* 5.00
159 *Angel Pagan* 3.00
160 *Ralph Santana* 3.00
161 *Joe Orloski* 3.00
162 *Shayne Wright* 3.00
163 *Jay Caligiuri* 4.00
164 *Greg Montalbano* 3.00
165 *James Harden* 3.00
166 *Rich Thompson* 3.00
167 *Fred Bastardo* 3.00
168 *Alejandro Giron* 3.00
169 *Jesus Medrano* 3.00
170 *Kevin Deaton* 8.00
171 *Mike Rosamond* 2.00
172 *Jon Guzman* 3.00
173 *Gerard Oakes* 5.00
174 *Francisco Liriano* 4.00
175 *Matt Allegra* 6.00
176 *Mike Snyder* 8.00
177 *James Shanks* 3.00
178 *Anderson Hernandez* 3.00
179 *Dan Trumble* 3.00
180 *Luis DePaula* 4.00
181 *Randall Shelley* 3.00
182 *Richard Lane* 3.00
183 *Antwon Rollins* 3.00
184 *Ryan Bukvich* 3.00
185 Derrick Lewis .25
186 *Eric Miller* 3.00
187 *Justin Schuda* 3.00
188 *Brian West* 5.00
189 Brad Wilkerson .25
190 *Neal Frendling* 3.00
191 *Jeremy Hill* 3.00
192 *James Barrett* 3.00
193 *Brett Kay* 3.00
194 *Ryan Mottl* 3.00
195 *Brad Nelson* 25.00
196 Juan Gonzalez .25
197 *Curtis Legendre* 3.00
198 *Ronald Acuna* 3.00
199 *Chris Flinn* 3.00
200 *Nick Alvarez* 3.00
201 *Jason Ellison* 4.00
202 *Blake McGinley* 3.00
203 *Dan Phillips* 3.00
204 *Demetrius Heath* 3.00
205 *Eric Bruntlett* 3.00
206 *Joe Jiannetti* 3.00
207 *Mike Hill* 3.00
208 *Ricardo Cordova* 3.00
209 *Mark Hamilton* 3.00
210 *David Mattox* 3.00
211 *Jose Morban* 3.00
212 *Scott Wiggins* 3.00
213 Steve Green .25
214 Brian Rogers .25
215 Kenny Baugh .25
216 *Anastacio Martinez* 3.00
217 Richard Lewis .25
218 *Tim Kalita* 3.00
219 *Edwin Almonte* 3.00
220 Hee Seop Choi .25
221 Ty Howington .25
222 *Victor Alvarez* 3.00
223 Morgan Ensberg .25
224 *Jeff Austin* 3.00
225 *Clint Weibl* 4.00
226 *Eric Cyr* 4.00
227 *Marlyn Tisdale* 3.00

228 John VanBenschoten .25
229 Ruben Salazar .25
230 *Raul Chavez* 4.00
231 Brett Evert .25
232 *Joe Rogers* 6.00
233 Adam Wainwright .25
234 Matt Herges .25
235 *Matt Childers* 4.00
236 Nick Neugebauer .25
237 Carl Crawford .25
238 Seung Jun Song .25
239 Randy Flores .25
240 Jason Lane .25
241 Chase Utley .25
242 *Ben Howard* 8.00
243 *Eric Glaser* 4.00
244 *Josh Wilson* 3.00
245 *Jose Valverde* 3.00
246 Chris Smith .25
247 Mark Prior 10.00
248 *Brian Mallette* 3.00
249 *Chone Figgins* 3.00
250 *Jimmy Alvarez* 3.00
251 Luis Terrero .25
252 *Josh Bonifay* 8.00
253 *Garrett Guzman* 5.00
254 *Jeff Verplancke* 3.00
255 *Nate Espy* 5.00
256 *Jeff Lincoln* 3.00
257 *Ryan Snare* 3.00
258 Jose Ortiz .25
259 Denny Bautista .25
260 Willy Aybar .25
261 Kelly Johnson .25
262 Shawn Fagan .25
263 *Yurendell DeCaster* 3.00
264 *Mike Peeples* 3.00
265 *Joel Guzman* 4.00
266 Ryan Vogelsong .25
267 *Jorge Padilla* 5.00
268 *Joe Jester* 5.00
269 *Ryan Church* 5.00
270 Mitch Jones .25
271 Travis Foley 6.00
272 Bobby Crosby .25
273 Adrian Gonzalez .25
274 Ronnie Merrill .25
275 Joel Pineiro .25
276 John-Ford Griffin .25
277 *Brian Forystek* 4.00
278 Sean Douglass .25
279 *Manny Delcarmen* 3.00
280 Jim Kavourias 3.00
281 Gabe Gross .25
282 Bill Ortega .25
283 *Joey Hammond* 3.00
284 Brett Myers .25
285 Carlos Pena .25
286 *Ezequiel Astacio* 3.00
287 *Edwin Yan* 3.00
288 *Chris Duffy* 5.00
289 Jason Kinchen .25
290 Rafael Soriano .25
291 *Colin Young* .25
292 Eric Byrnes .25
293 *Chris Narveson* 5.00
294 *John Rheinecker* 3.00
295 *Mike Wilson* 5.00
296 *Justin Sherrod* 8.00
297 Deivi Mendez .25
298 Wily Mo Pena .25
299 *Brett Roneberg* 5.00
300 *Trey Lunsford* 3.00
301 Christian Parker .25
302 Brent Butler .25
303 Aaron Heilman .25
304 Wilkin Ruan .25
305 Kenny Kelly .25
306 Cody Ransom .25
307 Koyie Hill .25
308 *Tony Fontana* 4.00
309 Mark Teixeira .75
310 *Doug Sessions* 3.00
311 *Josh Cisneros* 3.00
312 *Carlos Brackley* 3.00
313 Tim Raines Jr. .25
314 *Ross Peeples* 3.00
315 *Alexander Requena* 3.00
316 Chin-Hui Tsao .25
317 Tony Alvarez .25
318 *Craig Kuzmic* 5.00
319 *Peter Zamora* 3.00
320 *Matt Parker* 3.00
321 Keith Ginter .25
322 *Gary Cates Jr.* 3.00
323 Matt Belisle .25
324 Ben Broussard .25
325 Dennis Tankersley .25
326 Juan Silvestre .25
327 *Henry Pichardo* 3.00
328 *Michael Floyd* 3.00
329 *Clint Nageotte* 6.00
330 *Raymond Cabrera* 5.00
331 *Mauricio Lara* 4.00
332 *Alejandro Cadena* 3.00
333 *Jonny Gomes* 10.00
334 *Jason Bulger* 8.00
335 Nate Teut .25
336 *David Gil* 3.00
337 *Joel Crump* 3.00
338 Brandon Phillips .25
339 MaCay McBride .25
340 Brandon Claussen .25
341 Josh Phelps .25
342 *Freddie Money* 4.00
343 *Clifford Bartosh* 3.00
344 *Terrance Hill* 3.00
345 *John Rodriguez* 4.00
346 *Chris Latham* 5.00
347 *Carlos Cabrera* 3.00
348 *Jose Bautista* 3.00
349 *Kevin Frederick* 3.00
350 Jerome Williams .25
351 *Napoleon Calzado* 4.00
352 Benito Baez 3.00
353 Xavier Nady .25
354 *Jason Botts* 6.00
355 *Steve Bechler* 5.00
356 *Reed Johnson* 4.00
357 *Mark Outlaw* 4.00
358 Jake Peavy .25
359 *Josh Shaffer* 3.00
360 Dan Wright 3.00
361 *Ryan Gripp* 4.00
362 *Nelson Castro* 3.00
363 *Jason Bay* 3.00
364 *Franklin German* 5.00
365 Corwin Malone 8.00
366 *Kelly Ramos* 5.00
367 *John Ennis* 5.00
368 George Perez 3.00
369 *Rene Reyes* 3.00
370 *Rolando Viera* 3.00
371 *Earl Snyder* 5.00
372 *Kyle Kane* 4.00
373 Mario Ramos 3.00
374 *Tyler Yates* 3.00
375 *Jason Young* 5.00
376 *Chris Bootcheck* 4.00
377 *Jesus Cota* 20.00
378 Corky Miller 3.00
379 *Matt Erickson* 3.00
380 *Justin Huber* 15.00
381 *Felix Escalona* 3.00
382 *Kevin Cash* 5.00
383 *J.J. Putz* 3.00
384 *Chris Snelling* 35.00
385 David Wright 25.00
386 *Brian Wolfe* 15.00
387 *Justin Reid* 15.00
388 *Jake Mauer* 20.00
389 *Ryan Raburn* 20.00
390 Josh Barfield 20.00
391 *Joe Mauer* 65.00
392 *Bobby Jenks* 20.00
393 *Rob Henkel* 20.00
394 *Jimmy Gobble* 25.00
395 Jesse Foppert 25.00
396 Gavin Floyd 45.00
397 *Nate Field* 15.00
398 *Ryan Doumit* 15.00
399 *Ron Calloway* 20.00
400 *Taylor Buchholz* 15.00
401 *Adam Roller* 25.00
402 Cole Barthel 20.00
403 *Kazuhisa Ishii* 15.00
404 *So Taguchi* 8.00
405 *Chris Baker* 15.00

2002 Bowman Chrome Refractors

	MT
Star Refractors (1-220):	2-5X
SP Refractors:	.5-1.5X
Production 500	
X-Fractors (1-220):	4-8X
SP X-Fractors:	.75-2X
Production 250:	
Gold Refractors (1-220):	10-20X
SP Gold Refractors:	3-5X
Production 50	
Refractor Autos. (384-402,405)	.75-1.5X
Production 500	
X-Fractor Autos.:	.75-2X
Production 250	
Gold Autographs:	2-5X
Production 50	

2002 Bowman Chrome Uncirculated

	MT
Cards:	1-3X
Production 350	
Autos. 10 cards of each player	

2002 Bowman Chrome Rookie Reprints

		MT
Complete Set (20):		25.00
Common Player:		1.00
Inserted 1:6		
Refractors:		1.5-2X
Inserted 1:18		
JB	Jeff Bagwell	1.50
BC	Bartolo Colon	1.00
CD	Carlos Delgado	1.00
JG	Juan Gonzalez	1.50
LG	Luis Gonzalez	1.50
KG	Ken Griffey Jr.	3.00
VG	Vladimir Guerrero	2.00
DJ	Derek Jeter	5.00
AJ	Andruw Jones	1.50
CJ	Chipper Jones	3.00
JK	Jason Kendall	1.00
MP	Mike Piazza	3.00
JP	Jorge Posada	1.00
IR	Ivan Rodriguez	1.00
SR	Scott Rolen	1.00
GS	Gary Sheffield	1.00
MS	Mike Sweeney	1.00
FT	Frank Thomas	1.50
LW	Larry Walker	1.00
BW	Bernie Williams	1.50

2002 Bowman Chrome Ishii & Taguchi Autographs

		MT
Refractors:		.75-1.5X
Production 100		
X-Fractors:		2-4X
Production 50		
Golds: production 10		
403	Kazuhisa Ishii	120.00
404	So Taguchi	60.00

2002 Bowman Heritage

		MT
Complete Set (439):		190.00
Common Player:		.25
Common SP:		1.00
Inserted 1:2		
Black Box variations:		2-3X
Inserted 1:2		
Pack (10):		3.00
Box (24):		60.00
1	Brent Abernathy	.25
2	Jermaine Dye	.25
3	*James Shanks*	.40
4	*Chris Flinn*	.40
5	*Mike Peeples/SP*	1.50
6	Gary Sheffield	.50
7	Livan Hernandez/SP	1.00
8	*Jeff Austin*	.40
9	Jeremy Giambi	.25
10	*Adam Roller*	.50
11	Sandy Alomar Jr/SP	1.00
12	Matt Williams/SP	1.50
13	Hee Seop Choi	.25
14	Jose Offerman	.25
15	Robin Ventura	.50
16	Craig Biggio	.50
17	*Boomer Wells*	.40
18	*Rob Henkel*	.40
19	Edgar Martinez	.25
20	Matt Morris/SP	2.00
21	Jose Valentin	.25
22	Barry Bonds	2.00
23	*Justin Schuda*	.50
24	Josh Phelps	.25
25	*John Rodriguez*	.50
26	*Angel Pagan*	.50
27	Aramis Ramirez	.25
28	Jack Wilson	.25
29	Roger Clemens	1.50
30	*Kazuhisa Ishii*	3.00
31	Carlos Beltran	.25
32	Drew Henson/SP	2.00
33	Kevin Young/SP	1.00
34	Juan Cruz	.25
35	*Curtis Legendre*	.40
36	*Jose Morban*	.40
37	*Ricardo Cordova/SP*	1.50

No.	Player	Value
38	Adam Everett	.25
39	Mark Prior	1.50
40	*Jose Bautista*	.40
41	Travis Foley	.25
42	Kerry Wood	.50
43	B.J. Surhoff	.25
44	Moises Alou	.25
45	*Joey Hammond*	.50
46	*Eric Bruntlett*	.50
47	Carlos Guillen	.25
48	Joe Crede	.25
49	*Dan Phillips*	.50
50	Jason LaRue	.25
51	Javy Lopez	.25
52	Larry Bigbie/SP	1.00
53	*Chris Baker*	.75
54	Marty Cordova	.25
55	C.C. Sabathia	.25
56	Mike Piazza	1.50
57	Brian Giles	.50
58	Mike Bordick/SP	1.00
59	Tyler Houston/SP	1.00
60	Gabe Kapler	.25
61	Ben Broussard	.25
62	Steve Finley/SP	1.50
63	Koyie Hill	.25
64	Jeff D'Amico	.25
65	*Edwin Almonte*	.50
66	Pedro J. Martinez	1.00
67	Travis Fryman/SP	1.50
68	Brady Clark	.25
69	*Reed Johnson/SP*	1.50
70	Mark Grace/SP	4.00
71	Tony Batista/SP	1.00
72	Roy Oswalt	.50
73	Pat Burrell	.75
74	Dennis Tankersley	.25
75	Ramon Ortiz	.25
76	*Neal Frendling/SP*	1.50
77	Omar Vizquel/SP	2.00
78	Hideo Nomo	.50
79	Orlando Hernandez/SP	1.50
80	Andy Pettitte	.50
81	Cole Barthel	.25
82	Bret Boone	.25
83	Alfonso Soriano	2.00
84	Brandon Duckworth	.25
85	Ben Grieve	.25
86	*Mike Rosamond/SP*	1.50
87	Luke Prokopec	.25
88	*Chone Figgins*	.40
89	Rick Ankiel/SP	1.50
90	David Eckstein	.25
91	Corey Koskie	.25
92	David Justice	.50
93	*Jimmy Alvarez*	.40
94	Jason Schmidt	.25
95	Reggie Sanders	.25
96	*Victor Alvarez*	.40
97	*Brett Roneberg*	.40
98	D'Angelo Jimenez	.25
99	Hank Blalock	.50
100	Juan Rivera	.25
101	Mark Buehrle/SP	1.50
102	Juan Uribe	.25
103	Royce Clayton/SP	1.00
104	*Brett Kay*	.50
105	John Olerud	.50
106	Richie Sexson	.50
107	Chipper Jones	1.50
108	Adam Dunn	.75
109	Tim Salmon/SP	1.50
110	Eric Karros	.25
111	Jose Vidro	.25
112	Jerry Hairston Jr.	.25
113	*Anastacio Martinez*	.50
114	Robert Fick/SP	1.50
115	Randy Johnson	1.00
116	Trot Nixon/SP	2.00
117	Nick Bierbrodt/SP	1.00
118	Jim Edmonds	.50
119	Rafael Palmeiro	.50
120	Jose Macias	.25
121	Josh Beckett	.25
122	Sean Douglass	.25
123	Jeff Kent	.40
124	Tim Redding	.25
125	Xavier Nady	.25
126	Carl Everett	.25
127	Joe Randa	.25
128	Luke Hudson/SP	1.00
129	*Eric Miller*	.40
130	Melvin Mora	.25
131	Adrian Gonzalez	.25
132	Larry Walker/SP	2.50
133	*Nic Jackson/SP*	3.00
134	Mike Lowell/SP	1.00
135	Jim Thome	.75
136	Eric Milton	.25
137	*Rich Thompson/SP*	1.50
138	Placido Polanco/SP	1.00
139	Juan Pierre	.25
140	David Segui	.25
141	Chuck Finley	.25
142	Felipe Lopez	.25
143	Toby Hall	.25
144	*Fred Bastardo*	.50
145	Troy Glaus	.50
146	Todd Helton	.75
147	*Ruben Gotay/SP*	1.50
148	Darin Erstad	.50
149	*Ryan Gripp/SP*	1.50
150	Orlando Cabrera	.25
151	*Jason Young*	.50
152	Sterling Hitchcock/SP	1.00
153	Miguel Tejada	.50
154	Al Leiter	.40
155	*Taylor Buchholz*	.40
156	Juan Gonzalez	.50
157	Damion Easley	.25
158	*Jimmy Gobble*	1.00
159	Dennis Ulacia/SP	1.00
160	Shane Reynolds/SP	1.00
161	Javier Colina	.25
162	Frank Thomas	.75
163	Chuck Knoblauch	.25
164	Sean Burroughs	.25
165	Greg Maddux	1.50
166	*Jason Ellison*	.50
167	Tony Womack	.25
168	*Randall Shelley/SP*	1.50
169	Jason Marquis	.25
170	Brian Jordan	.25
171	Darryl Kile	.25
172	Barry Zito	.50
173	*Matt Allegra/SP*	1.50
174	*Ralph Santana/SP*	1.50
175	Carlos Lee	.25
176	Richard Hidalgo/SP	1.00
177	*Kevin Deaton*	.50
178	Juan Encarnacion	.25
179	Mark Quinn	.25
180	Rafael Furcal	.25
181	Garret Anderson	.25
182	David Wright	.25
183	Jose Reyes	.25
184	Mario Ramos/SP	1.00
185	J.D. Drew	.50
186	Juan Gonzalez	.50
187	Nick Neugebauer	.25
188	*Alejandro Giron*	.50
189	John Burkett	.25
190	Ben Sheets	.50
191	Vinny Castilla/SP	1.00
192	Cory Lidle	.25
193	Fernando Vina	.25
194	Russell Branyan/SP	2.00
195	Ben Davis	.25
196	Angel Berroa	.25
197	Alex Gonzalez	.25
198	Jared Sandberg	.25
199	Travis Lee/SP	2.50
200	*Luis DePaula/SP*	1.50
201	Ramon Hernandez/SP	1.00
202	Brandon Inge	.25
203	Aubrey Huff	.25
204	Mike Rivera	.25
205	*Brad Nelson*	.50
206	Colt Griffin/SP	1.00
207	Joel Pineiro	.25
208	Adam Pettyjohn	.25
209	Mark Redman	.25
210	Roberto Alomar/SP	3.00
211	Denny Neagle	.25
212	Adam Kennedy	.25
213	Jason Arnold/SP	1.50
214	Jaime Moyer	.25
215	Aaron Boone	.25
216	Doug Glanville	.25
217	Nick Johnson/SP	3.00
218	Mike Cameron/SP	1.50
219	Tim Wakefield/SP	2.00
220	Todd Stottlemyre/SP	2.00
221	Mo Vaughn	.50
222	Vladimir Guerrero	1.00
223	Bill Ortega	.25
224	Kevin Brown	.25
225	Peter Bergeron/SP	1.00
226	Shannon Stewart/SP	1.50
227	Eric Chavez	.50
228	*Clint Weibl*	.40
229	Todd Hollandsworth/SP	1.00
230	Jeff Bagwell	.75
231	*Chad Qualls*	.40
232	*Ben Howard*	1.00
233	Rondell White/SP	2.00
234	Fred McGriff	.40
235	Steve Cox/SP	1.00
236	*Chris Tritle*	1.50
237	Eric Valent	.25
238	*Joe Mauer*	3.00
239	Shawn Green	.50
240	Jimmy Rollins	.25
241	Edgar Renteria	.25
242	*Edwin Yan*	.40
243	*Noochie Varner*	.40
244	Kris Benson/SP	1.50
245	Mike Hampton	.25
246	*So Taguchi*	1.00
247	Sammy Sosa	1.50
248	Terrence Long	.25
249	*Jason Bay*	.40
250	Kevin Millar/SP	1.00
251	Albert Pujols	1.50
252	*Chris Latham*	.40
253	Eric Byrnes	.25
254	*Napoleon Calzado/SP*	1.50
255	Bobby Higginson	.25
256	Ben Molina	.25
257	Torii Hunter/SP	3.00
258	Jason Giambi	1.50
259	Bartolo Colon	.25
260	Benito Baez	.25
261	Ichiro Suzuki	2.00
262	Mike Sweeney	.25
263	*Brian West*	.40
264	Brad Penny	.25
265	Kevin Millwood/SP	2.00
266	Orlando Hudson	.25
267	Doug Mientkiewicz	.25
268	Luis Gonzalez/SP	2.50
269	*Jay Caligiuri*	.40
270	Nate Cornejo/SP	1.00
271	Lee Stevens	.25
272	Eric Hinske	.40
273	*Antwon Rollins*	.50
274	*Bobby Jenks*	.50
275	Joe Mays	.25
276	*Josh Shaffer*	.40
277	*Jonny Gomes*	.40
278	Bernie Williams	.50
279	Ed Rogers	.25
280	Carlos Delgado	.50
281	Raul Mondesi/SP	2.00
282	Jose Ortiz	.25
283	Cesar Izturis	.25
284	Ryan Dempster/SP	1.00
285	Brian Daubach	.25
286	*Hansel Izquierdo*	.40
287	Mike Lieberthal/SP	1.00
288	Marcus Thames	.25
289	Nomar Garciaparra	2.00
290	Brad Fullmer	.25
291	Tino Martinez	.40
292	*James Barrett*	.40
293	Jacque Jones	.25
294	*Nick Alvarez/SP*	1.50
295	*Jason Grove/SP*	1.50
296	*Mike Wilson/SP*	1.50
297	J.T. Snow	.25
298	Cliff Floyd	.25
299	Todd Hundley/SP	1.00
300	Tony Clark/SP	1.00
301	*Demetrius Heath*	.40
302	Morgan Ensberg	.25
303	Cristian Guzman	.25
304	Frank Catalanotto	.25
305	Jeff Weaver	.25
306	Tim Hudson	.50
307	*Scott Wiggins/SP*	1.50
308	Shea Hillenbrand/SP	4.00
309	Todd Walker/SP	1.00
310	Tsuyoshi Shinjo	.40
311	Adrian Beltre	.40
312	*Craig Kuzmic*	.40
313	Paul Konerko	.50
314	Scott Hairston	.25
315	Chan Ho Park	.25
316	Jorge Posada	.50
317	*Chris Snelling*	.75
318	Keith Foulke	.25
319	John Smoltz	.25
320	*Ryan Church/SP*	1.50
321	Mike Mussina	.75
322	Tony Armas Jr/SP	1.00
323	Craig Counsell	.25
324	Marcus Giles	.25
325	Greg Vaughn	.25
326	Curt Schilling	.75
327	Jeromy Burnitz	.25
328	Eric Byrnes	.25
329	Johnny Damon	.25
330	*Michael Floyd/SP*	1.50
331	Edgardo Alfonzo	.25
332	*Jeremy Hill*	.40
333	*Josh Bonifay*	.40
334	Byung-Hyun Kim	.25
335	Keith Ginter	.25
336	*Ronald Acuna/SP*	1.50
337	*Mike Hill/SP*	1.50
338	Sean Casey	.25
339	Matt Anderson/SP	1.00
340	Dan Wright	.25
341	Ben Petrick	.25
342	Mike Sirotka/SP	1.00
343	Alex Rodriguez	2.00
344	Einar Diaz	.25
345	Derek Jeter	2.50
346	Jeff Conine	.25
347	Ray Durham/SP	1.00
348	Wilson Betemit/SP	1.50
349	Jeffrey Hammonds	.25
350	*Dan Trumble*	.40
351	Phil Nevin/SP	1.50
352	A.J. Burnett	.25
353	Bill Mueller	.25
354	Charles Nagy	.25
355	Rusty Greer/SP	1.00
356	*Jason Botts*	.25
357	Magglio Ordonez	.50
358	Kevin Appier	.25
359	Brad Radke	.25
360	Chris George	.25
361	*Chris Piersoll*	.25
362	Ivan Rodriguez	.50
363	Jim Kavourias	.25
364	Rick Helling/SP	1.00
365	Dean Palmer	.25
366	Rich Aurilia/SP	1.00
367	Ryan Vogelsong	.25
368	Matt Lawton	.25
369	Wade Miller	.25
370	Dustin Hermanson	.25
371	Craig Wilson	.25
372	Todd Zeile/SP	1.00
373	*Jon Guzman*	.40
374	Ellis Burks	.25
375	*Robert Cosby/SP*	1.50
376	Jason Kendall	.25
377	Scott Rolen/SP	4.00
378	Andruw Jones	.50
379	*Greg Sain*	.40
380	Paul LoDuca	.25
381	*Scotty Layfield*	.40
382	Drew Henson	.50
383	*Garrett Guzman*	.40
384	Jack Cust	.25
385	*Shayne Wright*	.40
386	Derrek Lee	.25
387	*Jesus Medrano*	.40
388	Javier Vazquez	.25
389	Preston Wilson/SP	1.50
390	Gavin Floyd	.25
391	Sidney Ponson/SP	1.00
392	Jose Hernandez	.25
393	Scott Erickson/SP	1.00
394	*Jose Valverde*	.40
395	*Mark Hamilton/SP*	1.50
396	Brad Cresse	.25
397	Danny Bautista	.25
398	Ray Lankford/SP	1.00
399	Miguel Batista/SP	1.00
400	Brent Butler	.25
401	*Manny Delcarmen/SP*	1.50
402	Kyle Farnsworth/SP	1.00
403	Freddy Garcia	.25
404	*Joe Jiannetti*	.40
405	Josh Barfield	.25
406	Corey Patterson	.25
407	Josh Towers	.25
408	Carlos Pena	.25
409	Jeff Cirillo	.25
410	Jon Lieber	.25
411	Woody Williams/SP	1.00
412	*Richard Lane/SP*	1.50

413	Alex Gonzalez	.25
414	Wilkin Ruan	.25
415	Geoff Jenkins	.25
416	Carlos Hernandez	.25
417	Matt Clement/SP	1.50
418	Jose Cruz Jr.	.25
419	*Jake Mauer*	.75
420	*Matt Childers*	.50
421	Tom Glavine/SP	2.50
422	Ken Griffey Jr.	1.50
423	*Anderson Hernandez*	.40
424	*John Suomi*	.40
425	*Doug Sessions*	.40
426	Jaret Wright	.25
427	*Rolando Viera/SP*	1.50
428	Aaron Sele	.25
429	Dmitri Young	.25
430	Ryan Klesko	.25
431	Kevin Tapani/SP	1.00
432	Joe Kennedy	.25
433	Austin Kearns	.50
434	Roger Cedeno	.25
435	Lance Berkman	.75
436	Frank Menechino	.25
437	Brett Myers	.25
438	Bobby Abreu	.25
439	Shawn Estes	.25

2002 Bowman Heritage Chrome Refractor

	MT
Stars:	3-6X
SP's:	1.5-3X
Inserted 1:16	
Gold Refractors:	4-8X
SP's	2-4X
Inserted 1:32	

2002 Bowman Heritage Autographs

		MT
Common Player:		8.00
Inserted 1:45		
LB	Lance Berkman	20.00
HB	Hank Blalock	15.00
KG	Keith Ginter	8.00
TH	Toby Hall	8.00
DH	Drew Henson	20.00
KI	Kazuhisa Ishii	35.00
CI	Cesar Izturis	10.00
PL	Paul LoDuca	15.00
JM	Joe Mauer	30.00
RO	Roy Oswalt	15.00
MP	Mark Prior	45.00
AP	Albert Pujols	50.00
JR	Juan Rivera	12.00

2002 Bowman Heritage 1954 Bowman Reprints

		MT
Complete Set (20):		40.00
Common Player:		2.00
Inserted 1:12		
RA	Richie Ashburn	2.00
YB	Yogi Berra	4.00
DC	Del Crandell	2.00
BF	Bob Feller	2.50
WF	Whitey Ford	4.00
NF	Nellie Fox	2.00
CL	Clem Labine	2.00
DL	Don Larsen	3.00
JL	Johnny Logan	2.00
WM	Willie Mays	6.00
GM	Gil McDougald	2.00
DM	Don Mueller	2.00
JP	Jimmy Piersall	2.00
AR	Allie Reynolds	2.00
PR	Phil Rizzuto	3.00
ES	Enos Slaughter	2.00
DS	Duke Snider	4.00
WW	Wes Westrum	2.00
HW	Hoyt Wilhelm	2.00
DW	Davey Williams	2.00

2002 Bowman Heritage 1954 Bowman Reprint Autographs

		MT
Common Player:		10.00
Inserted 1:118		
YB	Yogi Berra	40.00
DC	Del Crandell	15.00
CL	Clem Labine	15.00
JL	Johnny Logan	12.00
DM	Don Mueller	10.00
DW	Davey Williams	10.00

2002 Bowman Heritage Relics

		MT
Common Player:		5.00
Inserted 1:47		
EA	Edgardo Alfonzo	5.00
JB	Josh Beckett	5.00
BB	Barry Bonds	20.00
EC	Eric Chavez	8.00
CD	Carlos Delgado	5.00
JE	Jim Edmonds	8.00
DE	Darin Erstad	5.00
NG	Nomar Garciaparra	30.00
TG	Tony Gwynn	10.00
TH	Todd Helton	8.00
CJ	Chipper Jones	15.00
PK	Paul Konerko	8.00
GM	Greg Maddux	15.00
EM	Edgar Martinez	8.00
MP	Mike Piazza	15.00
AP	Albert Pujols	15.00
MR	Mariano Rivera	8.00
IR	Ivan Rodriguez	8.00
SR	Scott Rolen	10.00
TS	Tim Salmon	5.00
KS	Kazuhiro Sasaki	8.00
JS	John Smoltz	8.00
FT	Frank Thomas	8.00
JT	Jim Thome	10.00
LW	Larry Walker	5.00
PW	Preston Wilson	5.00

2002 Bowman Heritage Team Topps Legends Autographs

MT
Gil McDougald
Joe Pepitone
Bobby Richardson
Robin Roberts
Warren Spahn
Luis Tiant
Carl Yastrzemski

2002 Bowman's Best

		MT
Complete Set (181):		NA
Common Player:		.40
Common (91-181):		8.00
Inserted 1:pack		
Blue (1-90):		3-5X
Production 300		
Red (1-90):		4-6X
Production 200		
Gold (1-90):		8-15X
Production 50		
Blue (91-181):		.75-1.5X
Production 500		
Red (91-181):		1-2X
Production 150		
Gold (91-181):		-4X
Production 50		
Pack (5):		15.00
Box (10):		120.00
1	Josh Beckett	.40
2	Derek Jeter	4.00
3	Alex Rodriguez	3.00
4	Miguel Tejada	.75
5	Nomar Garciaparra	3.00
6	Aramis Ramirez	.40
7	Jeremy Giambi	.40
8	Bernie Williams	.75
9	Juan Pierre	.40
10	Chipper Jones	2.00
11	Jimmy Rollins	.40
12	Alfonso Soriano	3.00
13	Daryle Ward	.40
14	Paul Konerko	.40
15	Tim Hudson	.75
16	Doug Mientkiewicz	.40
17	Todd Helton	.75
18	Moises Alou	.40
19	Juan Gonzalez	.75
20	Jorge Posada	.75
21	Jeff Kent	.60
22	Roger Clemens	2.00
23	Phil Nevin	.40
24	Brian Giles	.75
25	Carlos Delgado	.75
26	Jason Giambi	2.00
27	Vladimir Guerrero	1.25
28	Cliff Floyd	.40
29	Shea Hillenbrand	.40
30	Ken Griffey Jr.	2.50
31	Mike Piazza	3.00
32	Carlos Pena	.40
33	Larry Walker	.60
34	Magglio Ordonez	.60
35	Mike Mussina	.75
36	Andruw Jones	.75
37	Mark Teixeira	.60
38	Curt Schilling	.75
39	Eric Chavez	.75
40	Bartolo Colon	.40
41	Eric Hinske	.40
42	Sean Burroughs	.40
43	Randy Johnson	1.00
44	Adam Dunn	1.00
45	Pedro Martinez	1.50
46	Garret Anderson	.60
47	Jim Thome	1.00
48	Gary Sheffield	.75
49	Tsuyoshi Shinjo	.40
50	Albert Pujols	2.00
51	Ichiro Suzuki	3.00
52	C.C. Sabathia	.40
53	Bobby Abreu	.40
54	Ivan Rodriguez	.75
55	J.D. Drew	.60
56	Jacque Jones	.40
57	Jason Kendall	.40
58	Javier Vazquez	.40
59	Jeff Bagwell	1.00
60	Greg Maddux	2.00
61	Jim Edmonds	.60
62	Austin Kearns	.75
63	Jose Vidro	.40
64	Kevin Brown	.40
65	Preston Wilson	.40
66	Sammy Sosa	2.00
67	Lance Berkman	.75
68	Mark Mulder	.75
69	Marty Cordova	.40
70	Frank Thomas	.75
71	Mike Cameron	.40
72	Mike Sweeney	.40
73	Barry Bonds	3.00
74	Troy Glaus	.75
75	Barry Zito	.75
76	Pat Burrell	.75
77	Paul LoDuca	.40
78	Rafael Palmeiro	.75
79	Mark Prior	.75
80	Darin Erstad	.75
81	Richie Sexson	.75
82	Roberto Alomar	.75
83	Roy Oswalt	.75
84	Ryan Klesko	.40
85	Luis Gonzalez	.75
86	Scott Rolen	.75
87	Shannon Stewart	.40
88	Shawn Green	.60
89	Toby Hall	.40
90	Bret Boone	.40
91	Casey Kotchman/bat	30.00
92	*Jose Valverde/auto*	10.00
93	Cole Barthel/bat	8.00
94	*Brad Nelson/auto*	40.00
95	*Mauricio Lara/auto*	8.00
96	*Ryan Gripp/bat*	8.00
97	*Brian West/auto.*	10.00
98	*Chris Piersoll/auto.*	8.00
99	*Ryan Church/auto.*	18.00
100	Javier Colina/auto.	8.00
101	Juan Gonzalez/auto.	8.00
102	Benito Baez/auto.	8.00
103	*Mike Hill/bat*	8.00
104	*Jason Grove/auto.*	10.00
105	Koyie Hill/auto.	10.00
106	*Mark Outlaw/auto.*	8.00
107	*Jason Bay/bat*	10.00
108	*Jorge Padilla/auto.*	15.00
109	*Peter Zamora/auto.*	12.00
110	*Joe Mauer/auto.*	45.00
111	*Franklyn German/auto.*	12.00
112	*Chris Flinn/auto.*	8.00
113	David Wright/bat	10.00
114	*Anastacio Martinez/auto.*	8.00
115	*Nic Jackson/bat*	10.00
116	*Rene Reyes/auto.*	8.00
117	*Colin Young/auto.*	8.00
118	*Joe Orloski/auto.*	10.00

119 *Mike Wilson/auto.* 10.00
120 *Rich Thompson/auto.* 10.00
121 *Jake Mauer/auto.* 15.00
122 Mario Ramos/auto. 10.00
123 *Doug Sessions/auto.* 10.00
124 *Doug Devore/bat* 8.00
125 Travis Foley/auto. 20.00
126 *Chris Baker/auto.* 10.00
127 *Michael Floyd/auto.* 12.00
128 Josh Barfield/bat 10.00
129 *Jose Bautista/bat* 8.00
130 Gavin Floyd/auto. 30.00
131 *Jason Botts/bat* 8.00
132 *Clint Nageotte/auto.* 15.00
133 *Jesus Cota/auto.* 30.00
134 *Ron Calloway/bat* 8.00
135 *Kevin Cash/bat* 8.00
136 *Jonny Gomes/auto.* 30.00
137 Dennis Ulacia/auto. 10.00
138 *Joe Mauer/auto.* 50.00
139 *Kevin Deaton/auto.* 15.00
140 *Bobby Jenks/auto.* 8.00
141 Casey Kotchman/auto. 40.00
142 *Adam Walker/auto.* 8.00
143 *Mike Gonzalez/auto.* 10.00
144 *Ruben Gotay/bat* 10.00
145 *Jason Grove/bat* 8.00
146 *Freddy Sanchez/auto.* 10.00
147 Jason Arnold/auto. 15.00
148 Scott Hairston/auto. 25.00
149 *Jason St. Clair/auto.* 15.00
150 *Chris Tritle/bat* 8.00
151 *Edwin Yan/bat* 8.00
152 *Freddy Sanchez/bat* 8.00
153 *Greg Sain/bat* 8.00
154 *Yurendell DeCaster/bat* 8.00
155 *Noochie Varner/bat* 15.00
156 *Nelson Castro/auto.* 8.00
157 *Randall Shelley/bat* 8.00
158 *Reed Johnson/bat* 8.00
159 *Ryan Raburn/auto.* 8.00
160 *Jose Morban/bat* 8.00
161 *Justin Schuda/auto.* 8.00
162 *Henry Pichardo/auto.* 8.00
163 *Josh Bard/auto.* 15.00
164 *Josh Bonifay/auto.* 20.00
165 Brandon League/auto. 10.00
166 *Julio DePaula/auto.* 8.00
167 *Todd Linden/auto.* 25.00
168 *Francisco Liriano/auto.* 8.00
169 *Chris Snelling/auto.* 25.00
170 *Blake McGinley/auto.* 8.00
171 *Cody McKay/auto.* 12.00
172 *Jason Stanford/auto.* 8.00
173 *Lenny Dinardo/auto.* 8.00
174 *Greg Montalbano/auto.* 8.00
175 *Earl Snyder/auto.* 15.00
176 *Justin Huber/auto.* 20.00
177 *Chris Narveson/auto.* 8.00
178 Jon Switzer/auto. 8.00
179 *Ronald Acuna/auto.* 8.00
180 *Chris Duffy/bat* 8.00
181 *Kazuhisa Ishii/bat* 15.00

Values quoted in this guide reflect the retail price of a card — the price a collector can expect to pay when buying a card from a dealer.

The wholesale price — that which a collector can expect to receive from a dealer when selling cards — will be significantly lower, depending on desirability and condition.

C

1996 Circa

This hobby-exclusive product was limited to 2,000 sequentially numbered cases. The regular-issue set has 196 player cards, including 18 top prospects and four prospects. Circa also has a 200-card parallel set called Rave which is limited to 150 sets. Each Rave card is sequentially numbered from 1-150. Two other insert sets were also produced - Access and Boss.

	MT
Complete Set (200):	15.00
Common Player:	.10
Raves:	35X
Pack (8):	1.50
Wax Box (24):	30.00

1 Roberto Alomar .40
2 Brady Anderson .10
3 *Rocky Coppinger* .10
4 Eddie Murray .45
5 Mike Mussina .40
6 Randy Myers .10
7 Rafael Palmeiro .25
8 Cal Ripken Jr. 2.00
9 Jose Canseco .40
10 Roger Clemens 1.00
11 Mike Greenwell .10
12 Tim Naehring .10
13 John Valentin .10
14 Mo Vaughn .40
15 Tim Wakefield .10
16 Jim Abbott .10
17 Garret Anderson .10
18 Jim Edmonds .10
19 *Darin Erstad* 2.00
20 Chuck Finley .10
21 Troy Percival .10
22 Tim Salmon .20
23 J.T. Snow .10
24 Wilson Alvarez .10
25 Harold Baines .10
26 Ray Durham .10
27 Alex Fernandez .10
28 Tony Phillips .10
29 Frank Thomas 1.25
30 Robin Ventura .10
31 Sandy Alomar Jr. .10
32 Albert Belle .35
33 Kenny Lofton .10
34 Dennis Martinez .10
35 Jose Mesa .10
36 Charles Nagy .10
37 Manny Ramirez .75
37p Manny Ramirez (overprinted "PROMOTIONAL SAMPLE") 2.00
38 Jim Thome .10
39 Travis Fryman .10
40 Bob Higginson .15
41 Melvin Nieves .10
42 Alan Trammell .10
43 Kevin Appier .10
44 Johnny Damon .15
45 Keith Lockhart .10
46 Jeff Montgomery .10
47 Joe Randa .10
48 Bip Roberts .10
49 Ricky Bones .10
50 Jeff Cirillo .10
51 Marc Newfield .10
52 Dave Nilsson .10
53 Kevin Seitzer .10
54 Ron Coomer .10
55 Marty Cordova .10
56 Roberto Kelly .10
57 Chuck Knoblauch .10
58 Paul Molitor .40
59 Kirby Puckett 1.00
60 Scott Stahoviak .10
61 Wade Boggs .40
62 David Cone .10
63 Cecil Fielder .10
64 Dwight Gooden .10
65 Derek Jeter 1.50
66 Tino Martinez .10
67 Paul O'Neill .10
68 Andy Pettitte .25
69 Ruben Rivera .10
70 Bernie Williams .30
71 Geronimo Berroa .10
72 Jason Giambi .35
73 Mark McGwire 2.00
74 Terry Steinbach .10
75 Todd Van Poppel .10
76 Jay Buhner .10
77 Norm Charlton .10
78 Ken Griffey Jr. 1.75
79 Randy Johnson .65
80 Edgar Martinez .10
81 Alex Rodriguez 1.50
82 Paul Sorrento .10
83 Dan Wilson .10
84 Will Clark .30
85 Kevin Elster .10
86 Juan Gonzalez .75
87 Rusty Greer .10
88 Ken Hill .10
89 Mark McLemore .10
90 Dean Palmer .10
91 Roger Pavlik .10
92 Ivan Rodriguez .65
93 Joe Carter .10
94 Carlos Delgado .30
95 Juan Guzman .10
96 John Olerud .10
97 Ed Sprague .10
98 Jermaine Dye .10
99 Tom Glavine .15
100 Marquis Grissom .10
101 Andruw Jones .75
102 Chipper Jones 1.25
103 David Justice .35
104 Ryan Klesko .10
105 Greg Maddux 1.00
106 Fred McGriff .10
107 John Smoltz .15
108 Brant Brown .10
109 Mark Grace .30
110 Brian McRae .10
111 Ryne Sandberg .65
112 Sammy Sosa 1.25
113 Steve Trachsel .10
114 Bret Boone .15
115 Eric Davis .10
116 Steve Gibralter .10
117 Barry Larkin .15
118 Reggie Sanders .10
119 John Smiley .10
120 Dante Bichette .10
121 Ellis Burks .10
122 Vinny Castilla .10
123 Andres Galarraga .10
124 Larry Walker .30
125 Eric Young .10
126 Kevin Brown .15
127 Greg Colbrunn .10
128 Jeff Conine .10
129 Charles Johnson .10
130 Al Leiter .10
131 Gary Sheffield .40
132 Devon White .10
133 Jeff Bagwell .75
134 Derek Bell .10
135 Craig Biggio .15
136 Doug Drabek .10
137 Brian Hunter .10
138 Darryl Kile .10
139 Shane Reynolds .10
140 Brett Butler .10
141 Eric Karros .10
142 Ramon Martinez .10
143 Raul Mondesi .25
144 Hideo Nomo .50
145 Chan Ho Park .25
146 Mike Piazza 1.25
147 Moises Alou .20
148 Yamil Benitez .10
149 Mark Grudzielanek .10
150 Pedro Martinez .50
151 Henry Rodriguez .10
152 David Segui .10
153 Rondell White .25
154 Carlos Baerga .10
155 John Franco .10
156 Bernard Gilkey .10
157 Todd Hundley .10
158 Jason Isringhausen .10
159 Lance Johnson .10
160 Alex Ochoa .10
161 Rey Ordonez .10
162 Paul Wilson .10
163 Ron Blazier .10
164 Ricky Bottalico .10
165 Jim Eisenreich .10
166 Pete Incaviglia .10
167 Mickey Morandini .10
168 Ricky Otero .10
169 Curt Schilling .25
170 Jay Bell .10
171 Charlie Hayes .10
172 Jason Kendall .10
173 Jeff King .10
174 Al Martin .10
175 Alan Benes .10
176 Royce Clayton .10
177 Brian Jordan .10
178 Ray Lankford .10
179 John Mabry .10
180 Willie McGee .10
181 Ozzie Smith 1.00
182 Todd Stottlemyre .10
183 Andy Ashby .10
184 Ken Caminiti .10
185 Steve Finley .10
186 Tony Gwynn 1.00
187 Rickey Henderson .45
188 Wally Joyner .10
189 Fernando Valenzuela .10
190 Greg Vaughn .10
191 Rod Beck .10
192 Barry Bonds 1.25
193 Shawon Dunston .10
194 Chris Singleton .10
195 Robby Thompson .10
196 Matt Williams .25
197 Checklist (Barry Bonds) .30
198 Checklist (Ken Griffey Jr.) .40
199 Checklist (Cal Ripken Jr.) .50
200 Checklist (Frank Thomas) .25

1996 Circa Rave

Rainbow metallic foil highlights on front and a serial number on back from within an edition of 150 of each card differentiate this parallel issue from the Circa base cards. Announced insertion rate for Raves was one per 60 packs.

	MT
Complete Set (200):	500.00
Common Player:	2.00
Stars:	35X

(See 1996 Circa for checklist and base card values.)

1996 Circa Access

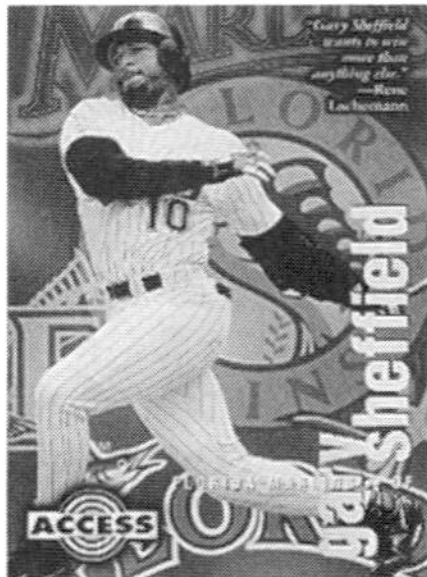

This 1996 Fleer Circa insert set highlights 30 players on a three-panel foldout design that includes multiple photographs, personal information and statistics. The cards were seeded about one every 12 packs.

		MT
Complete Set (30):		60.00
Common Player:		.75
1	Cal Ripken Jr.	7.50
2	Mo Vaughn	2.00
3	Tim Salmon	1.00
4	Frank Thomas	4.00
5	Albert Belle	2.00
6	Kenny Lofton	.75
7	Manny Ramirez	3.00
8	Paul Molitor	2.00
9	Kirby Puckett	3.50
10	Paul O'Neill	.75
11	Mark McGwire	7.50
12	Ken Griffey Jr.	6.00
13	Randy Johnson	2.50
14	Greg Maddux	3.50
15	John Smoltz	.75
16	Sammy Sosa	4.00
17	Barry Larkin	.75
18	Gary Sheffield	1.50
19	Jeff Bagwell	3.00
20	Hideo Nomo	2.00
21	Mike Piazza	5.00
22	Moises Alou	.75
23	Henry Rodriguez	.75
24	Rey Ordonez	.75
25	Jay Bell	.75
26	Ozzie Smith	3.50
27	Tony Gwynn	3.50
28	Rickey Henderson	1.25
29	Barry Bonds	3.50
30	Matt Williams	1.25
30p	Matt Williams (overprinted "PROMOTIONAL SAMPLE")	1.25

1996 Circa Boss

This insert set showcases the game's top stars on an embossed design. Cards were seeded one per six packs.

		MT
Complete Set (50):		60.00
Common Player:		.50
1	Roberto Alomar	1.50
2	Cal Ripken Jr.	6.00
2p	Cal Ripken Jr. (overprinted "PROMOTIONAL SAMPLE")	3.00
3	Jose Canseco	1.00
4	Mo Vaughn	2.00
5	Tim Salmon	.75
6	Frank Thomas	3.50
7	Robin Ventura	.50
8	Albert Belle	2.00
9	Kenny Lofton	.50
10	Manny Ramirez	2.50
11	Dave Nilsson	.50
12	Chuck Knoblauch	.50
13	Paul Molitor	1.50
14	Kirby Puckett	3.00
15	Wade Boggs	1.50
16	Dwight Gooden	.50
17	Paul O'Neill	.50
18	Mark McGwire	6.00
19	Jay Buhner	.50
20	Ken Griffey Jr.	5.00
21	Randy Johnson	1.50
22	Will Clark	.75
23	Juan Gonzalez	2.00
24	Joe Carter	.50
25	Tom Glavine	.50
26	Ryan Klesko	.50
27	Greg Maddux	3.00
28	John Smoltz	.50
29	Ryne Sandberg	2.50
30	Sammy Sosa	3.50
31	Barry Larkin	.50
32	Reggie Sanders	.50
33	Dante Bichette	.50
34	Andres Galarraga	.50
35	Charles Johnson	.50
36	Gary Sheffield	1.00
37	Jeff Bagwell	2.50
38	Hideo Nomo	1.50
39	Mike Piazza	4.00
40	Moises Alou	.50
41	Henry Rodriguez	.50
42	Rey Ordonez	.50
43	Ricky Otero	.50
44	Jay Bell	.50
45	Royce Clayton	.50
46	Ozzie Smith	3.00
47	Tony Gwynn	3.00
48	Rickey Henderson	1.00
49	Barry Bonds	3.50
50	Matt Williams	1.00

1997 Circa

Circa baseball returned for the second year in 1997, with a 400-card set, including 393 player cards and seven checklists. Cards feature action photos on a dynamic graphic arts background, and arrived in eight-card packs. The set was paralelled in a Rave insert and was accompanied by five inserts: Boss, Fast Track, Icons, Limited Access and Rave Reviews.

		MT
Complete Set (400):		25.00
Common Player:		.10
Pack (8):		1.25
Retail Wax Box (18):		20.00
Hobby Wax Box (36):		40.00
1	Kenny Lofton	.10
2	Ray Durham	.10
3	Mariano Rivera	.30
4	Jon Lieber	.10
5	Tim Salmon	.20
6	Mark Grudzielanek	.10
7	Neifi Perez	.10
8	Cal Ripken Jr.	2.50
9	John Olerud	.10
10	Edgar Renteria	.10
11	Jose Rosado	.10
12	Mickey Morandini	.10
13	Orlando Miller	.10
14	Ben McDonald	.10
15	Hideo Nomo	.65
16	Fred McGriff	.10
17	Sean Berry	.10
18	Roger Pavlik	.10
19	Aaron Sele	.10
20	Joey Hamilton	.10
21	Roger Clemens	1.50
22	Jose Herrera	.10
23	Ryne Sandberg	.75
24	Ken Griffey Jr.	2.50
25	Barry Bonds	1.75
26	Dan Naulty	.10
27	Wade Boggs	.50
28	Ray Lankford	.10
29	Rico Brogna	.10
30	Wally Joyner	.10
31	F.P. Santangelo	.10
32	Vinny Castilla	.10
33	Eddie Murray	.50
34	Kevin Elster	.10
35	Mike Macfarlane	.10
36	Jeff Kent	.10
37	Orlando Merced	.10
38	Jason Isringhausen	.10
39	Chad Ogea	.10
40	Greg Gagne	.10
41	Curt Lyons	.10
42	Mo Vaughn	.60
43	Rusty Greer	.10
44	Shane Reynolds	.10
45	Frank Thomas	1.75
46	Chris Hoiles	.10
47	Scott Sanders	.10
48	Mark Lemke	.10
49	Fernando Vina	.10
50	Mark McGwire	3.00
51	Bernie Williams	.35
52	Bobby Higginson	.15
53	Kevin Tapani	.10
54	Rich Becker	.10
55	*Felix Heredia*	.30
56	Delino DeShields	.10
57	Rick Wilkins	.10
58	Edgardo Alfonzo	.10
59	Brett Butler	.10
60	Ed Sprague	.10
61	Joe Randa	.10
62	Ugueth Urbina	.10
63	Todd Greene	.10
64	Devon White	.10
65	Bruce Ruffin	.10
66	Mark Gardner	.10
67	Omar Vizquel	.10
68	Luis Gonzalez	.30
69	Tom Glavine	.15
70	Cal Eldred	.10
71	William VanLandingham	.10
72	Jay Buhner	.10
73	James Baldwin	.10
74	Robin Jennings	.10
75	Terry Steinbach	.10
76	Billy Taylor	.10
77	Armando Benitez	.10
78	Joe Girardi	.10
79	Jay Bell	.10
80	Damon Buford	.10
81	Deion Sanders	.15
82	Bill Haselman	.10
83	John Flaherty	.10
84	Todd Stottlemyre	.10
85	J.T. Snow	.10
86	Felipe Lira	.10
87	Steve Avery	.10
88	Trey Beamon	.10
89	Alex Gonzalez	.15
90	Mark Clark	.10
91	Shane Andrews	.10
92	Randy Myers	.10
93	Gary Gaetti	.10
94	Jeff Blauser	.10
95	Tony Batista	.10
96	Todd Worrell	.10
97	Jim Edmonds	.10
98	Eric Young	.10
99	Roberto Kelly	.10
100	Alex Rodriguez	2.50
100p	Alex Rodriguez (overprinted "PROMOTIONAL SAMPLE")	2.50
101	Julio Franco	.10
102	Jeff Bagwell	1.00
103	Bobby Witt	.10
104	Tino Martinez	.10
105	Shannon Stewart	.15
106	Brian Banks	.10
107	Eddie Taubensee	.10
108	Terry Mulholland	.10
109	Lyle Mouton	.10
110	Jeff Conine	.10
111	Johnny Damon	.15
112	Quilvio Veras	.10
113	Wilton Guerrero	.10
114	Dmitri Young	.10
115	Garret Anderson	.10
116	Bill Pulsipher	.10
117	Jacob Brumfield	.10
118	Mike Lansing	.10
119	Jose Canseco	.35
120	Mike Bordick	.10
121	Kevin Stocker	.10
122	Frank Rodriguez	.10
123	Mike Cameron	.10
124	*Tony Womack*	.40
125	Bret Boone	.15
126	Moises Alou	.15
127	Tim Naehring	.10
128	Brant Brown	.10
129	Todd Zeile	.10
130	Dave Nilsson	.10
131	Donne Wall	.10
132	Jose Mesa	.10
133	Mark McLemore	.10
134	Mike Stanton	.10
135	Dan Wilson	.10
136	Jose Offerman	.10
137	David Justice	.35
138	Kirt Manwaring	.10
139	Raul Casanova	.10
140	Ron Coomer	.10
141	Dave Hollins	.10
142	Shawn Estes	.10
143	Darren Daulton	.10
144	Turk Wendell	.10
145	Darrin Fletcher	.10
146	Marquis Grissom	.10
147	Andy Benes	.10
148	Nomar Garciaparra	1.50
149	Andy Pettitte	.35
150	Tony Gwynn	1.50
151	Robb Nen	.10
152	Kevin Seitzer	.10
153	Ariel Prieto	.10
154	Scott Karl	.10
155	Carlos Baerga	.10
156	Wilson Alvarez	.10
157	Thomas Howard	.10
158	Kevin Appier	.10
159	Russ Davis	.10
160	Justin Thompson	.10
161	Pete Schourek	.10
162	John Burkett	.10

163	Roberto Alomar	.75
164	Darren Holmes	.10
165	Travis Miller	.10
166	Mark Langston	.10
167	Juan Guzman	.10
168	Pedro Astacio	.10
169	Mark Johnson	.10
170	Mark Leiter	.10
171	Heathcliff Slocumb	.10
172	Dante Bichette	.10
173	*Brian Giles*	1.50
174	Paul Wilson	.10
175	Eric Davis	.10
176	Charles Johnson	.10
177	Willie Greene	.10
178	Geronimo Berroa	.10
179	Mariano Duncan	.10
180	Robert Person	.10
181	David Segui	.10
182	Ozzie Guillen	.10
183	Osvaldo Fernandez	.10
184	Dean Palmer	.10
185	Bob Wickman	.10
186	Eric Karros	.10
187	Travis Fryman	.10
188	Andy Ashby	.10
189	Scott Stahoviak	.10
190	Norm Charlton	.10
191	Craig Paquette	.10
192	John Smoltz	.15
193	Orel Hershiser	.10
194	Glenallen Hill	.10
195	George Arias	.10
196	Brian Jordan	.10
197	Greg Vaughn	.10
198	Rafael Palmeiro	.25
199	Darryl Kile	.10
200	Derek Jeter	2.00
201	Jose Vizcaino	.10
202	Rick Aguilera	.10
203	Jason Schmidt	.10
204	Trot Nixon	.10
205	Tom Pagnozzi	.10
206	Mark Wohlers	.10
207	Lance Johnson	.10
208	Carlos Delgado	.25
209	Cliff Floyd	.10
210	Kent Mercker	.10
211	Matt Mieske	.10
212	Ismael Valdes	.10
213	Shawon Dunston	.10
214	Melvin Nieves	.10
215	Tony Phillips	.10
216	Scott Spiezio	.10
217	Michael Tucker	.10
218	Matt Williams	.25
219	Ricky Otero	.10
220	Kevin Ritz	.10
221	Darryl Strawberry	.10
222	Troy Percival	.10
223	Eugene Kingsale	.10
224	Julian Tavarez	.10
225	Jermaine Dye	.10
226	Jason Kendall	.10
227	Sterling Hitchcock	.10
228	Jeff Cirillo	.10
229	Roberto Hernandez	.10
230	Ricky Bottalico	.10
231	Bobby Bonilla	.10
232	Edgar Martinez	.10
233	John Valentin	.10
234	Ellis Burks	.10
235	Benito Santiago	.10
236	Terrell Wade	.10
237	Armando Reynoso	.10
238	Danny Graves	.10
239	Ken Hill	.10
240	Dennis Eckersley	.10
241	Darin Erstad	1.00
242	Lee Smith	.10
243	Cecil Fielder	.10
244	Tony Clark	.10
245	Scott Erickson	.10
246	Bob Abreu	.15
247	Ruben Sierra	.10
248	Chili Davis	.10
249	Darryl Hamilton	.10
250	Albert Belle	.50
251	Todd Hollandsworth	.10
252	Terry Adams	.10
253	Rey Ordonez	.10
254	Steve Finley	.10
255	Jose Valentin	.10
256	Royce Clayton	.10
257	Sandy Alomar	.10
258	Mike Lieberthal	.10
259	Ivan Rodriguez	.65
260	Rod Beck	.10
261	Ron Karkovice	.10
262	Mark Gubicza	.10
263	Chris Holt	.10
264	Jaime Bluma	.10
265	Francisco Cordova	.10
266	Javy Lopez	.10
267	Reggie Jefferson	.10
268	Kevin Brown	.10
269	Scott Brosius	.10
270	Dwight Gooden	.10
271	Marty Cordova	.10
272	Jeff Brantley	.10
273	Joe Carter	.10
274	Todd Jones	.10
275	Sammy Sosa	1.75
276	Randy Johnson	.75
277	B.J. Surhoff	.10
278	Chan Ho Park	.20
279	Jamey Wright	.10
280	Manny Ramirez	1.00
281	John Franco	.10
282	Tim Worrell	.10
283	Scott Rolen	.75
284	Reggie Sanders	.10
285	Mike Fetters	.10
286	Tim Wakefield	.10
287	Trevor Hoffman	.10
288	Donovan Osborne	.10
289	Phil Nevin	.10
290	Jermaine Allensworth	.10
291	Rocky Coppinger	.10
292	Tim Raines	.10
293	Henry Rodriguez	.10
294	Paul Sorrento	.10
295	Tom Goodwin	.10
296	Raul Mondesi	.25
297	Allen Watson	.10
298	Derek Bell	.10
299	Gary Sheffield	.40
300	Paul Molitor	.50
301	Shawn Green	.15
302	Darren Oliver	.10
303	Jack McDowell	.10
304	Denny Neagle	.10
305	Doug Drabek	.10
306	Mel Rojas	.10
307	Andres Galarraga	.10
308	Alex Ochoa	.10
309	Gary DiSarcina	.10
310	Ron Gant	.10
311	Gregg Jefferies	.10
312	Ruben Rivera	.10
313	Vladimir Guerrero	1.00
314	Willie Adams	.10
315	Bip Roberts	.10
326	Mark Grace	.25
317	Bernard Gilkey	.10
318	Marc Newfield	.10
319	Al Leiter	.10
320	Otis Nixon	.10
321	Tom Candiotti	.10
322	Mike Stanley	.10
323	Jeff Fassero	.10
324	Billy Wagner	.10
325	Todd Walker	.25
326	Chad Curtis	.10
327	Quinton McCracken	.10
328	Will Clark	.25
329	Andruw Jones	1.00
330	Robin Ventura	.10
331	Curtis Pride	.10
332	Barry Larkin	.15
333	Jimmy Key	.10
334	David Wells	.10
335	Mike Holtz	.10
336	Paul Wagner	.10
337	Greg Maddux	1.50
338	Curt Schilling	.25
339	Steve Trachsel	.10
340	John Wetteland	.10
341	Rickey Henderson	.40
342	Ernie Young	.10
343	Harold Baines	.10
344	Bobby Jones	.10
345	Jeff D'Amico	.10
346	John Mabry	.10
347	Pedro Martinez	.25
348	Mark Lewis	.10
349	Dan Miceli	.10
350	Chuck Knoblauch	.10
351	John Smiley	.10
352	Brady Anderson	.10
353	Jim Leyritz	.10
354	Al Martin	.10
355	Pat Hentgen	.10
356	Mike Piazza	2.00
357	Charles Nagy	.10
358	Luis Castillo	.10
359	Paul O'Neill	.10
360	Steve Reed	.10
361	Tom Gordon	.10
362	Craig Biggio	.15
363	Jeff Montgomery	.10
364	Jamie Moyer	.10
365	Ryan Klesko	.10
366	Todd Hundley	.10
367	Bobby Estalella	.10
368	Jason Giambi	.30
369	Brian Hunter	.10
370	Ramon Martinez	.10
371	Carlos Garcia	.10
372	Hal Morris	.10
373	Juan Gonzalez	1.00
374	Brian McRae	.10
375	Mike Mussina	.75
376	John Ericks	.10
377	Larry Walker	.35
378	Chris Gomez	.10
379	John Jaha	.10
380	Rondell White	.20
381	Chipper Jones	2.00
382	David Cone	.10
383	Alan Benes	.10
384	Troy O'Leary	.10
385	Ken Caminiti	.10
386	Jeff King	.10
387	Mike Hampton	.10
388	Jaime Navarro	.10
389	Brad Radke	.10
390	Joey Cora	.10
391	Jim Thome	.10
392	Alex Fernandez	.10
393	Chuck Finley	.10
394	Andruw Jones CL	.40
395	Ken Griffey Jr. CL	1.00
396	Frank Thomas CL	.50
397	Alex Rodriguez CL	1.00
398	Cal Ripken Jr. CL	1.25
399	Mike Piazza CL	.75
400	Greg Maddux CL	.50

1997 Circa Rave

In its second year, Circa Rave parallel inserts were limited to inclusion only in hobby packs at the stated. rate of one card per "30 to 40" packs. Raves are distinguished from regular-edition Circa cards by the use of purple metallic foil for the brand name and player identification on front. Rave backs carry a silver-foil serial number detailing its position within a production of 150 for each card.

	MT
Complete Set (400):	600.00
Common Player:	5.00
Veteran Stars:	25-40X
Young Stars:	15-30X

(See 1997 Circa for checklist and base card values.)

1997 Circa Boss

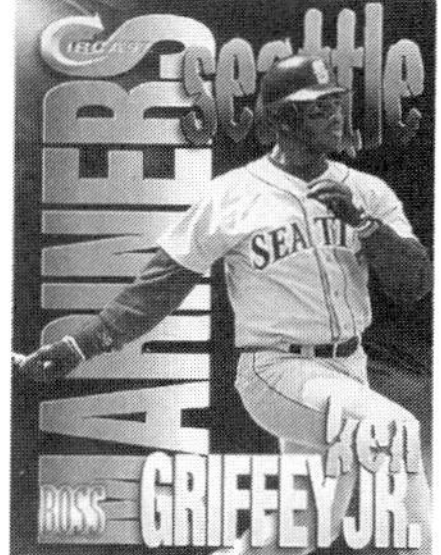

Boss was Circa's most common insert series. Twenty embossed cards were seeded one per six packs, displaying some of baseball's best players. A Super Boss parallel insert features metallic-foil background and graphics on front, and is inserted at a rate of one per 36 packs.

		MT
Complete Set (20):		20.00
Common Player:		.25
Super Boss:		1.5X
1	Jeff Bagwell	1.00
2	Albert Belle	.60
3	Barry Bonds	1.75
4	Ken Caminiti	.25
5	Juan Gonzalez	1.00
6	Ken Griffey Jr.	2.50
7	Tony Gwynn	1.50
8	Derek Jeter	2.00
9	Andruw Jones	1.00
10	Chipper Jones	2.00
11	Greg Maddux	1.50
12	Mark McGwire	3.00
13	Mike Piazza	2.00
14	Manny Ramirez	1.00
15	Cal Ripken Jr.	3.00
16	Alex Rodriguez	2.50
17	John Smoltz	.35
18	Frank Thomas	1.75
19	Mo Vaughn	.75
20	Bernie Williams	.45

1997 Circa Emerald Autograph Redemption Cards

These box-topper cards were a hobby exclusive redeemable until May 31, 1998, for autographed special cards of six young stars. Fronts have a green-foil enhanced player action photo. Backs provide details of the redemption program.

		MT
Complete Set (6):		6.50
Common Player:		.50
(1)	Darin Erstad	1.25
(2)	Todd Hollandsworth	.50
(3)	Alex Ochoa	.50
(4)	Alex Rodriguez	4.50
(5)	Scott Rolen	1.25
(6)	Todd Walker	.75

1997 Circa Emerald Autographs

Special green-foil enhanced cards of six top young stars were available via a mail-in redemption. The cards feature authentic player signatures on front and an embossed authentication seal. Backs are identical to the regular card of each featured player.

		MT
Complete Set (6):		100.00
Common Player:		7.50
100	Alex Rodriguez	45.00
241	Darin Erstad	20.00
251	Todd Hollandsworth	7.50
283	Scott Rolen	20.00
308	Alex Ochoa	7.50
325	Todd Walker	10.00

1997 Circa Fast Track

Fast Track highlights 10 top rookies and young stars on a flocked background simulating grass. Cards were inserted every 24 packs.

		MT
Complete Set (10):		20.00
Common Player:		.75
1	Vladimir Guerrero	2.50
2	Todd Hollandsworth	.75
3	Derek Jeter	5.00
4	Andruw Jones	2.00
5	Chipper Jones	4.00
6	Andy Pettitte	1.50
7	Mariano Rivera	1.50
8	Alex Rodriguez	5.00
9	Scott Rolen	2.00
10	Todd Walker	1.50

1997 Circa Icons

Twelve of baseball's top sluggers were displayed on 100-percent holofoil cards in Icons. Icons were found at a rate of one per 36 packs.

		MT
Complete Set (12):		55.00
Common Player:		2.00
1	Juan Gonzalez	4.00
2	Ken Griffey Jr.	8.00
3	Tony Gwynn	5.00
4	Derek Jeter	6.00
5	Chipper Jones	6.00
6	Greg Maddux	5.00
7	Mark McGwire	10.00
8	Mike Piazza	6.00
9	Cal Ripken Jr.	10.00
10	Alex Rodriguez	8.00
11	Frank Thomas	5.00
12	Matt Williams	2.00

1997 Circa Limited Access

Limited Access was a retail-only insert found every 18 packs. Cards feature an in-depth, statistical analysis including the player's favorite pitcher to hit and each pitcher's least favorite hitter to face. Limited Access is formatted as a die-cut, bi-fold design resembling a book.

		MT
Complete Set (15):		45.00
Common Player:		1.50
1	Jeff Bagwell	2.50
2	Albert Belle	1.50
3	Barry Bonds	3.50
4	Juan Gonzalez	2.50
5	Ken Griffey Jr.	5.00
6	Tony Gwynn	3.00
7	Derek Jeter	6.00
8	Chipper Jones	4.00
9	Greg Maddux	3.00
10	Mark McGwire	6.00
11	Mike Piazza	4.00
12	Cal Ripken Jr.	6.00
13	Alex Rodriguez	5.00
14	Frank Thomas	2.50
15	Mo Vaughn	1.50

1997 Circa Rave Reviews

Hitters that continually put up great numbers were selected for Rave Reviews. The insert was found every 288 packs and was printed on 100-percent holofoil.

		MT
Complete Set (12):		80.00
Common Player:		3.00
1	Albert Belle	3.00
2	Barry Bonds	8.00
3	Juan Gonzalez	5.00
4	Ken Griffey Jr.	12.00
5	Tony Gwynn	8.00
6	Greg Maddux	8.00
7	Mark McGwire	15.00
8	Eddie Murray	4.00
9	Mike Piazza	10.00
10	Cal Ripken Jr.	15.00
11	Alex Rodriguez	12.00
12	Frank Thomas	6.00

1998 Circa Thunder

Circa Thunder was issued as one series of 300 cards, sold in packs of eight for $1.59. The set marked SkyBox's brand transition from Circa to Thunder so the cards are labeled with both names. Inserts include: Rave and Super Rave parallels, Boss, Fast Track, Quick Strike, Limited Access, Rave Review and Thunder Boomers.

		MT
Complete Set (300):		25.00
Common Player:		.15
Pack (8):		1.25
Wax Box (36):		30.00
1	Ben Grieve	.40
2	Derek Jeter	2.00
3	Alex Rodriguez	2.50
4	Paul Molitor	.60
5	Nomar Garciaparra	1.75
6	Fred McGriff	.15
7	Kenny Lofton	.15
8a	Cal Ripken Jr.	3.00
8b	Marquis Grissom (should be #280)	.15
8s	Cal Ripken Jr. ("PROMOTIONAL SAMPLE" on back)	3.00
9	Matt Williams	.30
10	Chipper Jones	2.00
11	Barry Larkin	.20
12	Steve Finley	.15
13	Billy Wagner	.15
14	Rico Brogna	.15
15	Tim Salmon	.30
16	Hideo Nomo	.65
17	Tony Clark	.15
18	Jason Kendall	.15
19	Juan Gonzalez	1.00
20	Jeromy Burnitz	.15
21	Roger Clemens	1.50
22	Mark Grace	.30
23	Robin Ventura	.15
24	Manny Ramirez	1.00
25	Mark McGwire	3.00
26	Gary Sheffield	.40
27	Vladimir Guerrero	1.00
28	Butch Huskey	.15
29	Cecil Fielder	.15
30	Roderick Myers	.15
31	Greg Maddux	1.50
32	Bill Mueller	.15
33	Larry Walker	.30
34	Henry Rodriguez	.15
35	Mike Mussina	.65
36	Ricky Ledee	.15
37	Bobby Bonilla	.15
38	Curt Schilling	.30
39	Luis Gonzalez	.35
40	Troy Percival	.15
41	Eric Milton	.20
42	Mo Vaughn	.50
43	Raul Mondesi	.25
44	Kenny Rogers	.15
45	Frank Thomas	1.75
46	Jose Canseco	.40
47	Tom Glavine	.20
48	*Rich Butler*	.40
49	Jay Buhner	.15
50	Jose Cruz Jr.	.20
51	Bernie Williams	.45
52	Doug Glanville	.15
53	Travis Fryman	.15
54	Rey Ordonez	.15
55	Jeff Conine	.15
56	Trevor Hoffman	.15
57	Kirk Rueter	.15
58	Ron Gant	.15
59	Carl Everett	.20
60	Joe Carter	.15
61	Livan Hernandez	.15
62	John Jaha	.15
63	Ivan Rodriguez	.75
64	Willie Blair	.15
65	Todd Helton	.75
66	Kevin Young	.15
67	Mike Caruso	.15
68	Steve Trachsel	.15
69	Marty Cordova	.15
70	Alex Fernandez	.15
71	Eric Karros	.15
72	Reggie Sanders	.15
73	Russ Davis	.15
74	Roberto Hernandez	.15
75	Barry Bonds	1.75
76	Alex Gonzalez	.20
77	Roberto Alomar	.60
78	Troy O'Leary	.15
79	Bernard Gilkey	.15
80	Ismael Valdes	.15
81	Travis Lee	.15
82	Brant Brown	.15
83	Gary DiSarcina	.15
84	Joe Randa	.15
85	Jaret Wright	.25
86	Quilvio Veras	.15

87	Rickey Henderson	.40
88	Randall Simon	.15
89	Mariano Rivera	.25
90	Ugueth Urbina	.15
91	Fernando Vina	.15
92	Alan Benes	.15
93	Dante Bichette	.15
94	Karim Garcia	.15
95	A.J. Hinch	.15
96	Shane Reynolds	.15
97	Kevin Stocker	.15
98	John Wetteland	.15
99	Terry Steinbach	.15
100	Ken Griffey Jr.	2.50
101	Mike Cameron	.15
102	Damion Easley	.15
103	Randy Myers	.15
104	Jason Schmidt	.15
105	Jeff King	.15
106	Gregg Jefferies	.15
107	Sean Casey	.40
108	Mark Kotsay	.15
109	Brad Fullmer	.15
110	Wilson Alvarez	.15
111	Sandy Alomar Jr.	.15
112	Walt Weiss	.15
113	Doug Jones	.15
114	Andy Benes	.15
115	Paul O'Neill	.15
116	Dennis Eckersley	.15
117	Todd Greene	.15
118	Bobby Jones	.15
119	Darrin Fletcher	.15
120	Eric Young	.15
121	Jeffrey Hammonds	.15
122	Mickey Morandini	.15
123	Chuck Knoblauch	.15
124	Moises Alou	.25
125	Miguel Tejada	.30
126	Brian Anderson	.15
127	Edgar Renteria	.15
128	Mike Lansing	.15
129	Quinton McCracken	.15
130	Ray Lankford	.15
131	Andy Ashby	.15
132	Kelvim Escobar	.15
133	*Mike Lowell*	.40
134	Randy Johnson	.60
135	Andres Galarraga	.15
136	Armando Benitez	.15
137	Rusty Greer	.15
138	Jose Guillen	.15
139	Paul Konerko	.15
140	Edgardo Alfonzo	.15
141	Jim Leyritz	.15
142	Mark Clark	.15
143	Brian Johnson	.15
144	Scott Rolen	.75
145	David Cone	.15
146	Jeff Shaw	.15
147	Shannon Stewart	.20
148	Brian Hunter	.15
149	Garret Anderson	.15
150	Jeff Bagwell	1.00
151	James Baldwin	.15
152	Devon White	.15
153	Jim Thome	.15
154	Wally Joyner	.15
155	Mark Wohlers	.15
156	Jeff Cirillo	.15
157	Jason Giambi	.40
158	Royce Clayton	.15
159	Dennis Reyes	.15
160	Raul Casanova	.15
161	Pedro Astacio	.15
162	Todd Dunwoody	.15
163	Sammy Sosa	1.75
164	Todd Hundley	.15
165	Wade Boggs	.45
166	Robb Nen	.15
167	Dan Wilson	.15
168	Hideki Irabu	.15
169	B.J. Surhoff	.15
170	Carlos Delgado	.25
171	Fernando Tatis	.15
172	Bob Abreu	.20
173	David Ortiz	.15
174	Tony Womack	.15
175	*Magglio Ordonez*	2.00
176	Aaron Boone	.15
177	Brian Giles	.15
178	Kevin Appier	.15
179	Chuck Finley	.15
180	Brian Rose	.15
181	Ryan Klesko	.15
182	Mike Stanley	.15
183	Dave Nilsson	.15
184	Carlos Perez	.15
185	Jeff Blauser	.15
186	Richard Hidalgo	.15
187	Charles Johnson	.15
188	Vinny Castilla	.15
189	Joey Hamilton	.15
190	Bubba Trammell	.15
191	Eli Marrero	.15
192	Scott Erickson	.15
193	Pat Hentgen	.15
194	Jorge Fabregas	.15
195	Tino Martinez	.15
196	Bobby Higginson	.20
197	Dave Hollins	.15
198	*Rolando Arrojo*	.40
199	Joey Cora	.15
200	Mike Piazza	2.00
201	Reggie Jefferson	.15
202	John Smoltz	.20
203	Bobby Smith	.15
204	Tom Goodwin	.15
205	Omar Vizquel	.15
206	John Olerud	.15
207	Matt Stairs	.15
208	Bobby Estalella	.15
209	Miguel Cairo	.15
210	Shawn Green	.20
211	Jon Nunnally	.15
212	Al Leiter	.15
213	Matt Lawton	.15
214	Brady Anderson	.15
215	Jeff Kent	.15
216	Ray Durham	.15
217	Al Martin	.15
218	Jeff D'Amico	.15
219	Kevin Tapani	.15
220	Jim Edmonds	.15
221	Jose Vizcaino	.15
222	Jay Bell	.15
223	Ken Caminiti	.15
224	Craig Biggio	.20
225	Bartolo Colon	.15
226	Neifi Perez	.15
227	Delino DeShields	.15
228	Javier Lopez	.15
229	David Wells	.15
230	Brad Rigby	.15
231	John Franco	.15
232	Michael Coleman	.15
233	Edgar Martinez	.15
234	Francisco Cordova	.15
235	Johnny Damon	.20
236	Deivi Cruz	.15
237	J.T. Snow	.15
238	Enrique Wilson	.15
239	Rondell White	.25
240	Aaron Sele	.15
241	Tony Saunders	.15
242	Ricky Bottalico	.15
243	Cliff Floyd	.15
244	Chili Davis	.15
245	Brian McRae	.15
246	Brad Radke	.15
247	Chan Ho Park	.25
248	Lance Johnson	.15
249	Rafael Palmeiro	.30
250	Tony Gwynn	1.50
251	Denny Neagle	.15
252	Dean Palmer	.15
253	Jose Valentin	.15
254	Matt Morris	.15
255	Ellis Burks	.15
256	Jeff Suppan	.15
257	Jimmy Key	.15
258	Justin Thompson	.15
259	Brett Tomko	.15
260	Mark Grudzielanek	.15
261	Mike Hampton	.15
262	Jeff Fassero	.15
263	Charles Nagy	.15
264	Pedro Martinez	.60
265	Todd Zeile	.15
266	Will Clark	.30
267	Abraham Nunez	.15
268	Dave Martinez	.15
269	Jason Dickson	.15
270	Eric Davis	.15
271	Kevin Orie	.15
272	Derrek Lee	.15
273	Andruw Jones	.75
274	Juan Encarnacion	.15
275	Carlos Baerga	.15
276	Andy Pettitte	.40
277	Brent Brede	.15
278	Paul Sorrento	.15
279	Mike Lieberthal	.15
280	(Not issued, see #8)	
281	Darin Erstad	.75
282	Willie Greene	.15
283	Derek Bell	.15
284	Scott Spiezio	.15
285	David Segui	.15
286	Albert Belle	.50
287	Ramon Martinez	.15
288	Jeremi Gonzalez	.15
289	Shawn Estes	.15
290	Ron Coomer	.15
291	John Valentin	.15
292	Kevin Brown	.15
293	Michael Tucker	.15
294	Brian Jordan	.15
295	Darryl Kile	.15
296	David Justice	.40
297	Jose Cruz Jr. CL	.20
298	Alex Rodriguez CL	1.00
299	Ken Griffey Jr. CL	1.00
300	Frank Thomas CL	.65

1998 Circa Thunder Rave

Rave parallels each card in Circa Thunder except for the four checklist cards. A special silver sparkling foil is used on the player's name and the Thunder logo on front. This 296-card set was inserted approximately one per 36 packs and sequentially numbered to 150 sets on the back.

	MT
Common Player:	2.00
Stars:	35X

(See 1998 Circa Thunder for checklist and base card values.)

1998 Circa Thunder Super Rave

Only 25 Super Rave parallel sets were printed and they were inserted approximately one per 216 packs. The set contains 296 player cards (no checklist cards). Fronts are identified by sparkling gold foil on the player's name and the Thunder logo, with sequential numbering on the back to 25.

	MT
Common Player:	9.00
Stars:	85X

(See 1998 Circa Thunder for checklist and base card values.)

1998 Circa Thunder Boss

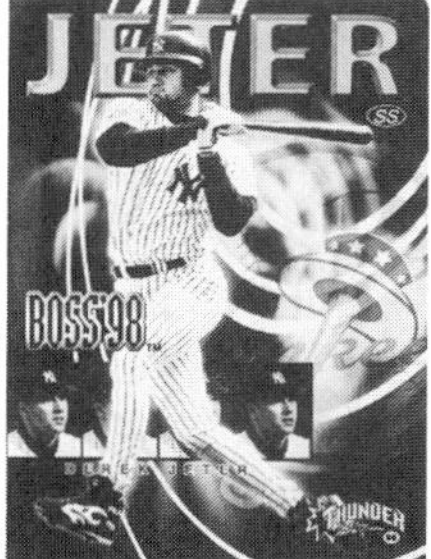

This 20-card insert, seeded one per six packs, has cards embossed with the player's last name in large letters across the top.

		MT
Complete Set (20):		15.00
Common Player:		.30
Inserted 1:6		
1B	Jeff Bagwell	.75
2B	Barry Bonds	1.00
3B	Roger Clemens	1.00
4B	Jose Cruz Jr.	.30
5B	Nomar Garciaparra	1.00
6B	Juan Gonzalez	.75
7B	Ken Griffey Jr.	1.50
8B	Tony Gwynn	1.00
9B	Derek Jeter	1.25
10B	Chipper Jones	1.25
11B	Travis Lee	.30
12B	Greg Maddux	1.00
13B	Pedro Martinez	.60
14B	Mark McGwire	2.00
15B	Mike Piazza	1.25
16B	Cal Ripken Jr.	2.00
17B	Alex Rodriguez	1.50
18B	Scott Rolen	.60
19B	Frank Thomas	1.00
20B	Larry Walker	.30

1998 Circa Thunder Fast Track

This 10-card insert showcases some of the top young stars in baseball. Fronts picture the player over a closeup of a gold foil baseball on the left. The right side has smaller head shots of all 10 players with the featured player's head in gold foil.

		MT
Complete Set (10):		12.00
Common Player:		.75
Inserted 1:24		
1FT	Jose Cruz Jr.	1.00
2FT	Juan Encarnacion	.75

3FT	Brad Fullmer	1.50
4FT	Nomar Garciaparra	4.50
5FT	Todd Helton	2.50
6FT	Livan Hernandez	.75
7FT	Travis Lee	.75
8FT	Neifi Perez	.75
9FT	Scott Rolen	2.50
10FT	Jaret Wright	.75

1998 Circa Thunder Limited Access

These retail-exclusive insert cards are bi-fold and die-cut with foil stamping on front. The theme of the insert was to provide an in-depth statistical scouting analysis of each player.

		MT
Complete Set (15):		60.00
Common Player:		1.50
Inserted 1:18		
1LA	Jeff Bagwell	4.00
2LA	Roger Clemens	5.00
3LA	Jose Cruz Jr.	1.50
4LA	Nomar Garciaparra	6.00
5LA	Juan Gonzalez	4.00
6LA	Ken Griffey Jr.	8.00
7LA	Tony Gwynn	5.00
8LA	Derek Jeter	10.00
9LA	Greg Maddux	5.00
10LA	Pedro Martinez	3.50
11LA	Mark McGwire	10.00
12LA	Mike Piazza	7.00
13LA	Alex Rodriguez	8.00
14LA	Frank Thomas	4.00
15LA	Larry Walker	1.50

1998 Circa Thunder Quick Strike

This insert pictures players over a colorful die-cut foil-board front.

		MT
Complete Set (12):		37.50
Common Player:		1.00
Inserted 1:36		
1QS	Jeff Bagwell	2.50
2QS	Roger Clemens	4.00
3QS	Jose Cruz Jr.	1.00
4QS	Nomar Garciaparra	4.50
5QS	Ken Griffey Jr.	6.00
6QS	Greg Maddux	4.00
7QS	Pedro Martinez	2.00
8QS	Mark McGwire	8.00
9QS	Mike Piazza	5.00
10QS	Alex Rodriguez	6.00
11QS	Frank Thomas	4.50
12QS	Larry Walker	1.00

1998 Circa Thunder Rave Reviews

Rave Reviews cards are die-cut in a horizontal design with bronze foil etching and the image of a ballfield in the background.

		MT
Complete Set (15):		120.00
Common Player:		2.00
Inserted 1:288		
1RR	Jeff Bagwell	5.00
2RR	Barry Bonds	10.00
3RR	Roger Clemens	6.00
4RR	Jose Cruz Jr.	2.00
5RR	Nomar Garciaparra	12.00
6RR	Juan Gonzalez	5.00
7RR	Ken Griffey Jr.	20.00
8RR	Tony Gwynn	6.00
9RR	Derek Jeter	20.00
10RR	Greg Maddux	8.00
11RR	Mark McGwire	20.00
12RR	Mike Piazza	12.00
13RR	Alex Rodriguez	15.00
14RR	Frank Thomas	6.00
15RR	Larry Walker	2.00

1998 Circa Thunder Thunder Boomers

Thunder Boomers feature top power hitters imposed over a see-through cloud-like plastic center with the imagery of a wooden fence with a large hole blasted through the middle of it.

		MT
Complete Set (12):		60.00
Common Player:		2.00
Inserted 1:96		
1TB	Jeff Bagwell	5.00
2TB	Barry Bonds	8.00
3TB	Jay Buhner	2.00
4TB	Andres Galarraga	2.00
5TB	Juan Gonzalez	5.00
6TB	Ken Griffey Jr.	12.50
7TB	Tino Martinez	2.00
8TB	Mark McGwire	15.00
9TB	Mike Piazza	10.00
10TB	Frank Thomas	5.00
11TB	Jim Thome	2.00
12TB	Larry Walker	2.00

1987 Classic Major League Baseball Game

The "Classic Major League Baseball Board Game" set consists of 100 full-color cards used to play the game in which participants answer trivia questions found on the card backs. Cards measure 2-1/2" x 3-1/2" and are printed on semi-gloss stock. Backs carry the player's career stats besides the trivia questions. The game was produced by Game Time, Ltd. of Marietta, Ga., and sold for $19.95 in most retail outlets. In 1991-92 the set was selling for $200 or more, with the Bo Jackson card advertised as high as $80.

		MT
Complete Set (100):		25.00
Common Player:		.10
1	Pete Rose	2.50
2	Len Dykstra	.10
3	Darryl Strawberry	.10
4	Keith Hernandez	.10
5	Gary Carter	.35
6	Wally Joyner	.10
7	Andres Thomas	.10
8	Pat Dodson	.10
9	Kirk Gibson	.10
10	Don Mattingly	1.50
11	Dave Winfield	.75
12	Rickey Henderson	.60
13	Dan Pasqua	.10
14	Don Baylor	.10
15	Bo Jackson	1.50
16	Pete Incaviglia	.10
17	Kevin Bass	.10
18	Barry Larkin	.15
19	Dave Magadan	.10
20	Steve Sax	.10
21	Eric Davis	.10
22	Mike Pagliarulo	.10
23	Fred Lynn	.10
24	Reggie Jackson	1.00
25	Larry Parrish	.10
26	Tony Gwynn	1.00
27	Steve Garvey	.25
28	Glenn Davis	.10
29	Tim Raines	.10
30	Vince Coleman	.10
31	Willie McGee	.10
32	Ozzie Smith	.75
33	Dave Parker	.10
34	Tony Pena	.10
35	Ryne Sandberg	1.00
36	Brett Butler	.10
37	Dale Murphy	.30
38	Bob Horner	.10
39	Pedro Guerrero	.10
40	Brook Jacoby	.10
41	Carlton Fisk	.60
42	Harold Baines	.10
43	Rob Deer	.10
44	Robin Yount	.60
45	Paul Molitor	.60
46	Jose Canseco	.75
47	George Brett	1.00
48	Jim Presley	.10
49	Rich Gedman	.10
50	Lance Parrish	.10
51	Eddie Murray	.60
52	Cal Ripken, Jr.	4.00
53	Kent Hrbek	.10
54	Gary Gaetti	.10
55	Kirby Puckett	1.00
56	George Bell	.10
57	Tony Fernandez	.10
58	Jesse Barfield	.10
59	Jim Rice	.15
60	Wade Boggs	.60
61	Marty Barrett	.10
62	Mike Schmidt	1.00
63	Von Hayes	.10
64	Jeff Leonard	.10
65	Chris Brown	.10
66	Dave Smith	.10
67	Mike Krukow	.10
68	Ron Guidry	.10
69	Rob Woodward (photo actually Pat Dodson)	.10
70	Rob Murphy	.10
71	Andres Galarraga	.10
72	Dwight Gooden	.10
73	Bob Ojeda	.10
74	Sid Fernandez	.10
75	Jesse Orosco	.10
76	Roger McDowell	.10
77	John Tutor (Tudor)	.10
78	Tom Browning	.10
79	Rick Aguilera	.10
80	Lance McCullers	.10
81	Mike Scott	.10
82	Nolan Ryan	4.00
83	Bruce Hurst	.10
84	Roger Clemens	1.00
85	Oil Can Boyd	.10
86	Dave Righetti	.10
87	Dennis Rasmussen	.10
88	Bret Saberhagan (Saberhagen)	.10
89	Mark Langston	.10
90	Jack Morris	.10
91	Fernando Valenzuela	.10
92	Orel Hershiser	.10
93	Rick Honeycutt	.10
94	Jeff Reardon	.10
95	John Habyan	.10
96	Goose Gossage	.10
97	Todd Worrell	.10
98	Floyd Youmans	.10
99	Don Aase	.10
100	John Franco	.10

1987 Classic Travel Update (Yellow)

Game Time, Ltd. of Marietta, Ga., issued as an update to its Classic Baseball Board Game a 50-card set entitled "Travel Edition." Cards measure 2-1/2" x 3-1/2" in the same format as the first release, though with yellow, rather than green, borders. Numbered from 101 to 150, the "Travel Edition," besides updating player trades and showcasing rookies, offers several highlights from the 1987 season. All new trivia questions are found on the card backs.

		MT
Complete Set (50):		15.00
Common Player:		.10
101	Mike Schmidt	.60
102	Eric Davis	.10
103	Pete Rose	1.50
104	Don Mattingly	.75
105	Wade Boggs	.50
106	Dale Murphy	.20
107	Glenn Davis	.10
108	Wally Joyner	.10
109	Bo Jackson	.15
110	Cory Snyder	.10
111	Jim Lindeman	.10
112	Kirby Puckett	.60
113	Barry Bonds	5.00
114	Roger Clemens	.60
115	Oddibe McDowell	.10
116	Bret Saberhagen	.10
117	Joe Magrane	.10
118	Scott Fletcher	.10
119	Mark McLemore	.10
120	Who Me? (Joe Niekro)	.25
121	Mark McGwire	2.00
122	Darryl Strawberry	.10
123	Mike Scott	.10
124	Andre Dawson	.20
125	Jose Canseco	.40
126	Kevin McReynolds	.10
127	Joe Carter	.10
128	Casey Candaele	.10
129	Matt Nokes	.10
130	Kal Daniels	.10
131	Pete Incaviglia	.10
132	Benito Santiago	.10
133	Barry Larkin	.15
134	Gary Pettis	.10
135	B.J. Surhoff	.15
136	Juan Nieves	.10
137	Jim Deshaies	.10
138	Pete O'Brien	.10
139	Kevin Seitzer	.10
140	Devon White	.15
141	Rob Deer	.10
142	Kurt Stillwell	.10
143	Edwin Correa	.10
144	Dion James	.10
145	Danny Tartabull	.10
146	Jerry Browne	.10
147	Ted Higuera	.10
148	Jack Clark	.10
149	Ruben Sierra	.10
150	Mark McGwire, Eric Davis	1.00

1988 Classic Travel Update 1 (Red)

This set was produced for use with the travel edition of Game Time's Classic Baseball Board Game. Special cards in the set include a McGwire/Mattingly, an instruction card with McGwire/Canseco and three different cards featuring Phil Niekro (in different uniforms). Update I card fronts have red borders, a yellow Classic logo in the upper-left corner and a black and beige name banner beneath the photo. Backs are printed in red and pink on white and include the player name, personal info, major league records, a baseball question and space for the player autograph. Classic card series sold via hobby dealers and retail toy stores nationwide. Game Time Ltd., the set's producer, was purchased by Scoreboard of Cherry Hill, N.J. in 1988.

		MT
Complete Set (50):		8.00
Common Player:		.05
151	Don Mattingly, Mark McGwire	1.00
152	Don Mattingly	.75
153	Mark McGwire	2.00
154	Eric Davis	.05
155	Wade Boggs	.45
156	Dale Murphy	.15
157	Andre Dawson	.15
158	Roger Clemens	.60
159	Kevin Seitzer	.05
160	Benito Santiago	.05
161	Kal Daniels	.05
162	John Kruk	.05
163	Bill Ripken	.05
164	Kirby Puckett	.60
165	Jose Canseco	.40
166	Matt Nokes	.05
167	Mike Schmidt	.60
168	Tim Raines	.05
169	Ryne Sandberg	.45
170	Dave Winfield	.50
171	Dwight Gooden	.05
172	Bret Saberhagen	.05
173	Willie McGee	.05
174	Jack Morris	.05
175	Jeff Leonard	.05
176	Cal Ripken, Jr.	2.00
177	Pete Incaviglia	.05
178	Devon White	.05
179	Nolan Ryan	2.00
180	Ruben Sierra	.05
181	Todd Worrell	.05
182	Glenn Davis	.05
183	Frank Viola	.05
184	Cory Snyder	.05
185	Tracy Jones	.05
186	Terry Steinbach	.05
187	Julio Franco	.05
188	Larry Sheets	.05
189	John Marzano	.05
190	Kevin Elster	.05
191	Vincente Palacios	.05
192	Kent Hrbek	.05
193	Eric Bell	.05
194	Kelly Downs	.05
195	Jose Lind	.05
196	Dave Stewart	.05
197	Jose Canseco, Mark McGwire	1.00
198	Phil Niekro	.20
199	Phil Niekro	.20
200	Phil Niekro	.20

1988 Classic Travel Update 2 (Blue)

This set was produced for use with the travel edition of Game Time's Classic Baseball Board Game. Fronts have blue borders, a yellow Classic logo in the upper-left corner and a black and beige name banner beneath the photo. Backs are printed in blue on white and include the player name, personal info, major league records, a baseball question and space for the player autograph. Classic card series are sold via hobby dealers and retail toy stores nationwide. Game Time Ltd., the set's producer, was purchased by Scoreboard of Cherry Hill, N.J. in 1988.

		MT
Complete Set (50):		6.00
Common Player:		.05
201	Dale Murphy, Eric Davis	.15
202	B.J. Surhoff	.05
203	John Kruk	.05
204	Sam Horn	.05
205	Jack Clark	.05
206	Wally Joyner	.05
207	Matt Nokes	.05
208	Bo Jackson	.10
209	Darryl Strawberry	.05
210	Ozzie Smith	.60
211	Don Mattingly	.75
212	Mark McGwire	1.50
213	Eric Davis	.05
214	Wade Boggs	.50
215	Dale Murphy	.25
216	Andre Dawson	.25
217	Roger Clemens	.60
218	Kevin Seitzer	.05
219	Benito Santiago	.05
220	Tony Gwynn	.60
221	Mike Scott	.05
222	Steve Bedrosian	.05
223	Vince Coleman	.05
224	Rick Sutcliffe	.05
225	Will Clark	.15
226	Pete Rose	1.00
227	Mike Greenwell	.05
228	Ken Caminiti	.05
229	Ellis Burks	.05
230	Dave Magadan	.05
231	Alan Trammell	.05
232	Paul Molitor	.40
233	Gary Gaetti	.05
234	Rickey Henderson	.40
235	Danny Tartabull	.05
236	Bobby Bonilla	.05
237	Mike Dunne	.05
238	Al Leiter	.05
239	John Farrell	.05
240	Joe Magrane	.05
241	Mike Henneman	.05
242	George Bell	.05
243	Gregg Jefferies	.15
244	Jay Buhner	.05
245	Todd Benzinger	.05
246	Matt Williams	.15
(247)	Don Mattingly, Mark McGwire (No card number on back)	1.50
248	George Brett	.60
249	Jimmy Key	.05
250	Mark Langston	.05

1989 Classic

This 100-card set was released by The Score Board to accompany trivia board games. Fronts have a wide border which graduates from pink at the top to blue at the bottom. Card backs are printed in blue. The flip side includes personal information, and major league record in a boxed area. Another boxed area below the record presents five trivia questions. The lower border on back provides an autograph space. The Classic card series was sold by retail stores and hobby dealers nationwide.

		MT
Complete Set (100):		9.00
Common Player:		.05
1	Orel Hershiser	.05
2	Wade Boggs	.50
3	Jose Canseco	.45
4	Mark McGwire	1.50
5	Don Mattingly	.75
6	Gregg Jefferies	.05
7	Dwight Gooden	.05
8	Darryl Strawberry	.05
9	Eric Davis	.05
10	Joey Meyer	.05
11	Joe Carter	.05
12	Paul Molitor	.45
13	Mark Grace	.35
14	Kurt Stillwell	.05
15	Kirby Puckett	.60
16	Keith Miller	.05
17	Glenn Davis	.05
18	Will Clark	.15
19	Cory Snyder	.05
20	Jose Lind	.05
21	Andres Thomas	.05
22	Dave Smith	.05
23	Mike Scott	.05
24	Kevin McReynolds	.05

25	B.J. Surhoff	.05
26	Mackey Sasser	.05
27	Chad Kreuter	.05
28	Hal Morris	.05
29	Wally Joyner	.05
30	Tony Gwynn	.60
31	Kevin Mitchell	.05
32	Dave Winfield	.50
33	Billy Bean	.05
34	Steve Bedrosian	.05
35	Ron Gant	.05
36	Len Dykstra	.05
37	Andre Dawson	.20
38	Brett Butler	.05
39	Rob Deer	.05
40	Tommy John	.05
41	Gary Gaetti	.05
42	Tim Raines	.05
43	George Bell	.05
44	Dwight Evans	.05
45	Denny Martinez	.05
46	Andres Galarraga	.05
47	George Brett	.60
48	Mike Schmidt	.60
49	Dave Steib	.05
50	Rickey Henderson	.40
51	Craig Biggio	.10
52	Mark Lemke	.05
53	Chris Sabo	.05
54	Jeff Treadway	.05
55	Kent Hrbek	.05
56	Cal Ripken, Jr.	1.50
57	Tim Belcher	.05
58	Ozzie Smith	.60
59	Keith Hernandez	.05
60	Pedro Guerrero	.05
61	Greg Swindell	.05
62	Bret Saberhagen	.05
63	John Tudor	.05
64	Gary Carter	.20
65	Kevin Seitzer	.05
66	Jesse Barfield	.05
67	Luis Medina	.05
68	Walt Weiss	.05
69	Terry Steinbach	.05
70	Barry Larkin	.10
71	Pete Rose	1.00
72	Luis Salazar	.05
73	Benito Santiago	.05
74	Kal Daniels	.05
75	Kevin Elster	.05
76	Rob Dibble	.05
77	Bobby Witt	.05
78	Steve Searcy	.05
79	Sandy Alomar	.05
80	Chili Davis	.05
81	Alvin Davis	.05
82	Charlie Leibrandt	.05
83	Robin Yount	.50
84	Mark Carreon	.05
85	Pascual Perez	.05
86	Dennis Rasmussen	.05
87	Ernie Riles	.05
88	Melido Perez	.05
89	Doug Jones	.05
90	Dennis Eckersley	.05
91	Bob Welch	.05
92	Bob Milacki	.05
93	Jeff Robinson	.05
94	Mike Henneman	.05
95	Randy Johnson	.75
96	Ron Jones	.05
97	Jack Armstrong	.05
98	Willie McGee	.05
99	Ryne Sandberg	.45
100	David Cone, Danny Jackson	.05

1989 Classic Travel Update 1 (Orange)

Sold only as a 50-card complete set under the official name of "Travel Update I," these cards are identical in format to the 1989 Classic 100-card set with the exception that the borders are orange at the top, graduating to maroon at the bottom. Backs are maroon.

		MT
Complete Set (50):		10.00
Common Player:		.05
101	Gary Sheffield	.25
102	Wade Boggs	.45
103	Jose Canseco	.45
104	Mark McGwire	1.00
105	Orel Hershiser	.05
106	Don Mattingly	.75
107	Dwight Gooden	.05
108	Darryl Strawberry	.05
109	Eric Davis	.05
110	Bam Bam Meulens	.05
111	Andy Van Slyke	.05
112	Al Leiter	.05
113	Matt Nokes	.05
114	Mike Krukow	.05
115	Tony Fernandez	.05
116	Fred McGriff	.05
117	Barry Bonds	.75
118	Gerald Perry	.05
119	Roger Clemens	.60
120	Kirk Gibson	.05
121	Greg Maddux	.60
122	Bo Jackson	.10
123	Danny Jackson	.05
124	Dale Murphy	.20
125	David Cone	.05
126	Tom Browning	.05
127	Roberto Alomar	.35
128	Alan Trammell	.05
129	Ricky Jordan	.05
130	Ramon Martinez	.05
131	Ken Griffey, Jr.	6.00
132	Gregg Olson	.05
133	Carlos Quintana	.05
134	Dave West	.05
135	Cameron Drew	.05
136	Ted Higuera	.05
137	Sil Campusano	.05
138	Mark Gubicza	.05
139	Mike Boddicker	.05
140	Paul Gibson	.05
141	Jose Rijo	.05
142	John Costello	.05
143	Cecil Espy	.05
144	Frank Viola	.05
145	Erik Hanson	.05
146	Juan Samuel	.05
147	Harold Reynolds	.05
148	Joe Magrane	.05
149	Mike Greenwell	.05
150	Darryl Strawberry, Will Clark	.10

1989 Classic Travel Update 2 (Purple)

Numbered from 151-200, this set features rookies and traded players with their new teams. The cards are purple and gray and were sold as part of a board game with baseball trivia questions.

		MT
Complete Set (50):		7.50
Common Player:		.05
151	Jim Abbott	.05
152	Ellis Burks	.05
153	Mike Schmidt	.75
154	Gregg Jefferies	.05
155	Mark Grace	.25
156	Jerome Walton	.05
157	Bo Jackson	.10
158	Jack Clark	.05
159	Tom Glavine	.10
160	Eddie Murray	.35
161	John Dopson	.05
162	Ruben Sierra	.05
163	Rafael Palmeiro	.20
164	Nolan Ryan	1.50
165	Barry Larkin	.10
166	Tommy Herr	.05
167	Roberto Kelly	.05
168	Glenn Davis	.05
169	Glenn Braggs	.05
170	Juan Bell	.05
171	Todd Burns	.05
172	Derek Lilliquist	.05
173	Orel Hershiser	.05
174	John Smoltz	.10
175	Ozzie Guillen, Ellis Burks	.05
176	Kirby Puckett	.75
177	Robin Ventura	.05
178	Allan Anderson	.05
179	Steve Sax	.05
180	Will Clark	.15
181	Mike Devereaux	.05
182	Tom Gordon	.05
183	Rob Murphy	.05
184	Pete O'Brien	.05
185	Cris Carpenter	.05
186	Tom Brunansky	.05
187	Bob Boone	.05
188	Lou Whitaker	.05
189	Dwight Gooden	.05
190	Mark McGwire	1.50
191	John Smiley	.05
192	Tommy Gregg	.05
193	Ken Griffey, Jr.	4.00
194	Bruce Hurst	.05
195	Greg Swindell	.05
196	Nelson Liriano	.05
197	Randy Myers	.05
198	Kevin Mitchell	.05
199	Dante Bichette	.05
200	Deion Sanders	.10

1990 Classic

Classic baseball returned in 1990 with a 150-card set. Cards have a blue border on front, with splashes of pink. The cards were again sold as part of a baseball trivia game.

		MT
Complete Set (150):		5.50
Common Player:		.05
1	Nolan Ryan	1.00
2	Bo Jackson	.15
3	Gregg Olson	.05
4	Tom Gordon	.05
5	Robin Ventura	.05
6	Will Clark	.15
7	Ruben Sierra	.05
8	Mark Grace	.25
9	Luis de los Santos	.05
10	Bernie Williams	.20
11	Eric Davis	.05
12	Carney Lansford	.05
13	John Smoltz	.10
14	Gary Sheffield	.20
15	Kent Merker	.05
16	Don Mattingly	.75
17	Tony Gwynn	.60
18	Ozzie Smith	.60
19	Fred McGriff	.05
20	Ken Griffey, Jr.	1.00
21a	Deion Sanders ("Prime Time")	.30
21b	Deion Sanders (Deion "Prime Time" Sanders)	.15
22	Jose Canseco	.35
23	Mitch Williams	.05
24	Cal Ripken, Jr.	1.00
25	Bob Geren	.05
26	Wade Boggs	.35
27	Ryne Sandberg	.50
28	Kirby Puckett	.60
29	Mike Scott	.05
30	Dwight Smith	.05
31	Craig Worthington	.05
32	Ricky Jordan	.05
33	Darryl Strawberry	.05
34	Jerome Walton	.05
35	John Olerud	.05
36	Tom Glavine	.10
37	Rickey Henderson	.40
38	Rolando Roomes	.05
39	Mickey Tettleton	.05
40	Jim Abbott	.05
41	Dave Righetti	.05
42	Mike LaValliere	.05
43	Rob Dibble	.05
44	Pete Harnisch	.05
45	Jose Offerman	.05
46	Walt Weiss	.05
47	Mike Greenwell	.05
48	Barry Larkin	.10
49	Dave Gallagher	.05
50	Junior Felix	.05
51	Roger Clemens	.60
52	Lonnie Smith	.05
53	Jerry Browne	.05
54	Greg Briley	.05
55	Delino DeShields	.05
56	Carmelo Martinez	.05
57	Craig Biggio	.10
58	Dwight Gooden	.05
59a	Bo, Ruben, Mark (Bo Jackson, Ruben Sierra, Mark McGwire)	.50
59b	A.L. Fence Busters (Bo Jackson, Ruben Sierra, Mark McGwire)	.50
60	Greg Vaughn	.05
61	Roberto Alomar	.25
62	Steve Bedrosian	.05
63	Devon White	.05
64	Kevin Mitchell	.05
65	Marquis Grissom	.05
66	Brian Holman	.05
67	Julio Franco	.05
68	Dave West	.05
69	Harold Baines	.05
70	Eric Anthony	.05
71	Glenn Davis	.05
72	Mark Langston	.05
73	Matt Williams	.15
74	Rafael Palmeiro	.20
75	Pete Rose, Jr.	.25
76	Ramon Martinez	.05

No.	Player	MT
77	Dwight Evans	.05
78	Mackey Sasser	.05
79	Mike Schooler	.05
80	Dennis Cook	.05
81	Orel Hershiser	.05
82	Barry Bonds	.75
83	Geronimo Berroa	.05
84	George Bell	.05
85	Andre Dawson	.20
86	John Franco	.05
87a	Clark/Gwynn (Will Clark, Tony Gwynn)	.25
87b	N.L. Hit Kings (Will Clark, Tony Gwynn)	.25
88	Glenallen Hill	.05
89	Jeff Ballard	.05
90	Todd Zeile	.05
91	Frank Viola	.05
92	Ozzie Guillen	.05
93	Jeff Leonard	.05
94	Dave Smith	.05
95	Dave Parker	.05
96	Jose Gonzalez	.05
97	Dave Steib	.05
98	Charlie Hayes	.05
99	Jesse Barfield	.05
100	Joey Belle	.25
101	Jeff Reardon	.05
102	Bruce Hurst	.05
103	Luis Medina	.05
104	Mike Moore	.05
105	Vince Coleman	.05
106	Alan Trammell	.05
107	Randy Myers	.05
108	Frank Tanana	.05
109	Craig Lefferts	.05
110	John Wetteland	.05
111	Chris Gwynn	.05
112	Mark Carreon	.05
113	Von Hayes	.05
114	Doug Jones	.05
115	Andres Galarraga	.05
116	Carlton Fisk	.40
117	Paul O'Neill	.05
118	Tim Raines	.05
119	Tom Brunansky	.05
120	Andy Benes	.05
121	Mark Portugal	.05
122	Willie Randolph	.05
123	Jeff Blauser	.05
124	Don August	.05
125	Chuck Cary	.05
126	John Smiley	.05
127	Terry Mullholland	.05
128	Harold Reynolds	.05
129	Hubie Brooks	.05
130	Ben McDonald	.05
131	Kevin Ritz	.05
132	Luis Quinones	.05
133a	Bam Bam Muelens (last name incorrect)	.25
133b	Bam Bam Meulens (last name correct)	.05
134	Bill Spiers	.05
135	Andy Hawkins	.05
136	Alvin Davis	.05
137	Lee Smith	.05
138	Joe Carter	.05
139	Bret Saberhagen	.05
140	Sammy Sosa	.75
141	Matt Nokes	.05
142	Bert Blyleven	.05
143	Bobby Bonilla	.05
144	Howard Johnson	.05
145	Joe Magrane	.05
146	Pedro Guerrero	.05
147	Robin Yount	.40
148	Dan Gladden	.05
149	Steve Sax	.05
150a	Clark/Mitchell (Will Clark, Kevin Mitchell)	.25
150b	Bay Bombers (Will Clark, Kevin Mitchell)	.25

1990 Classic Series 2

As in previous years, Classic released a 50-card second series set for use with its trivia board game. Unlike earlier update sets, the 1990 Series II set is numbered 1-50 with a "T" designation accompanying the card number. Cards measure 2-1/2" x 3-1/2" and share the format of the original 1990 Classic cards; Series II cards have pink borders with blue highlights. The cards were issued only in complete set form.

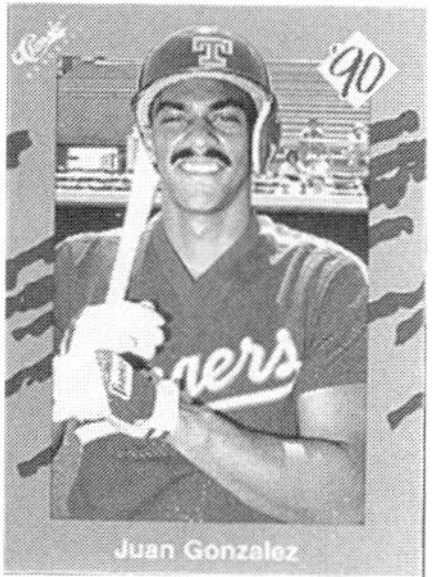

Juan Gonzalez

		MT
Complete Set (50):		3.50
Common Player:		.05
1	Gregg Jefferies	.05
2	Steve Adkins	.05
3	Sandy Alomar, Jr.	.05
4	Steve Avery	.05
5	Mike Blowers	.05
6	George Brett	.75
7	Tom Browning	.05
8	Ellis Burks	.05
9	Joe Carter	.05
10	Jerald Clark	.05
11	"Hot Corners" (Matt Williams, Will Clark)	.15
12	Pat Combs	.05
13	Scott Cooper	.05
14	Mark Davis	.05
15	Storm Davis	.05
16	Larry Walker	.20
17	Brian DuBois	.05
18	Len Dykstra	.05
19	John Franco	.05
20	Kirk Gibson	.05
21	Juan Gonzalez	.50
22	Tommy Greene	.05
23	Kent Hrbek	.05
24	Mike Huff	.05
25	Bo Jackson	.10
26	Nolan Knows Bo (Bo Jackson, Nolan Ryan)	1.50
27	Roberto Kelly	.05
28	Mark Langston	.05
29	Ray Lankford	.05
30	Kevin Maas	.05
31	Julio Machado	.05
32	Greg Maddux	.75
33	Mark McGwire	1.00
34	Paul Molitor	.40
35	Hal Morris	.05
36	Dale Murphy	.15
37	Eddie Murray	.40
38	Jaime Navarro	.05
39	Dean Palmer	.05
40	Derek Parks	.05
41	Bobby Rose	.05
42	Wally Joyner	.05
43	Chris Sabo	.05
44	Benito Santiago	.05
45	Mike Stanton	.05
46	Terry Steinbach	.05
47	Dave Stewart	.05
48	Greg Swindell	.05
49	Jose Vizcaino	.05
---	"Royal Flush" (Bret Saberhagen, Mark Davis)	.05

1990 Classic Series 3

Classic's third series of 1990 features the same format as the previous two releases. Series III borders are yellow with blue accents. The cards have trivia questions on back and are numbered 1T-100T. No card 51T or 57T exists. Two cards in the set are unnumbered. Like other Classic issues, the cards are designed for use with the trivia board game and were sold only as complete sets.

Scott Coolbaugh

		MT
Complete Set (100):		7.50
Common Player:		.05
1	Ken Griffey, Jr.	1.00
2	John Tudor	.05
3	John Kruk	.05
4	Mark Gardner	.05
5	Scott Radinsky	.05
6	John Burkett	.05
7	Will Clark	.15
8	Gary Carter	.25
9	Ted Higuera	.05
10	Dave Parker	.05
11	Dante Bichette	.05
12	Don Mattingly	.75
13	Greg Harris	.05
14	David Hollins	.05
15	Matt Nokes	.05
16	Kevin Tapani	.05
17	Shane Mack	.05
18	Randy Myers	.05
19	Greg Olson	.05
20	Shawn Abner	.05
21	Jim Presley	.05
22	Randy Johnson	.40
23	Edgar Martinez	.05
24	Scott Coolbaugh	.05
25	Jeff Treadway	.05
26	Joe Klink	.05
27	Rickey Henderson	.40
28	Sam Horn	.05
29	Kurt Stillwell	.05
30	Andy Van Slyke	.05
31	Willie Banks	.05
32	Jose Canseco	.40
33	Felix Jose	.05
34	Candy Maldonado	.05
35	Carlos Baerga	.05
36	Keith Hernandez	.05
37	Frank Viola	.05
38	Pete O'Brien	.05
39	Pat Borders	.05
40	Mike Heath	.05
41	Kevin Brown	.15
42	Chris Bosio	.05
43	Shawn Boskie	.05
44	Carlos Quintana	.05
45	Juan Samuel	.05
46	Tim Layana	.05
47	Mike Harkey	.05
48	Gerald Perry	.05
49	Mike Witt	.05
50	Joe Orsulak	.05
51	(Not issued)	
52	Willie Blair	.05
53	Gene Larkin	.05
54	Jody Reed	.05
55	Jeff Reardon	.05
56	Kevin McReynolds	.05
57	(Not issued)	
58	Eric Yelding	.05
59	Fred Lynn	.05
60	Jim Leyritz	.05
61	John Orton	.05
62	Mike Lieberthal	.05
63	Mike Hartley	.05
64	Kal Daniels	.05
65	Terry Shumpert	.05
66	Sil Campusano	.05
67	Tony Pena	.05
68	Barry Bonds	.75
69	Oddibe McDowell	.05
70	Kelly Gruber	.05
71	Willie Randolph	.05
72	Rick Parker	.05
73	Bobby Bonilla	.05
74	Jack Armstrong	.05
75	Hubie Brooks	.05
76	Sandy Alomar, Jr.	.05
77	Ruben Sierra	.05
78	Erik Hanson	.05
79	Tony Phillips	.05
80	Rondell White	.25
81	Bobby Thigpen	.05
82	Ron Walden	.05
83	Don Peters	.05
84	#6 (Nolan Ryan)	1.00
85	Lance Dickson	.05
86	Ryne Sandberg	.40
87	Eric Christopherson	.05
88	Shane Andrews	.05
89	Marc Newfield	.05
90	Adam Hyzdu	.05
91	"Texas Heat" (Nolan Ryan, Reid Ryan)	1.00
92	Chipper Jones	1.00
93	Frank Thomas	.75
94	Cecil Fielder	.05
95	Delino DeShields	.05
96	John Olerud	.05
97	Dave Justice	.25
98	Joe Oliver	.05
99	Alex Fernandez	.05
100	Todd Hundley	.05
---	Mike Marshall (Game instructions on back)	.05
---	4 in 1 (Frank Viola, Nolan/Reid Ryan, Chipper Jones, Don Mattingly)	.50

1991 Classic

Kirby Puckett

Top rookies and draft picks highlight this set from Classic. The cards come with a trivia board game and accessories. Fronts have fading blue borders with a touch of red. A blank-back "4-in-1" micro-player card is included with each game set.

		MT
Complete Set (99):		5.50
Common Player:		.05
1	John Olerud	.05
2	Tino Martinez	.05
3	Ken Griffey, Jr.	1.00
4	Jeromy Burnitz	.05
5	Ron Gant	.05
6	Mike Benjamin	.05
7	Steve Decker	.05

8 Matt Williams .15
9 Rafael Novoa .05
10 Kevin Mitchell .05
11 Dave Justice .25
12 Leo Gomez .05
13 Chris Hoiles .05
14 Ben McDonald .05
15 David Segui .05
16 Anthony Telford .05
17 Mike Mussina .35
18 Roger Clemens .60
19 Wade Boggs .45
20 Tim Naehring .05
21 Joe Carter .05
22 Phil Plantier .05
23 Rob Dibble .05
24 Mo Vaughn .45
25 Lee Stevens .05
26 Chris Sabo .05
27 Mark Grace .20
28 Derrick May .05
29 Ryne Sandberg .45
30 Matt Stark .05
31 Bobby Thigpen .05
32 Frank Thomas .75
33 Don Mattingly .75
34 Eric Davis .05
35 Reggie Jefferson .05
36 Alex Cole .05
37 Mark Lewis .05
38 Tim Costo .05
39 Sandy Alomar, Jr. .05
40 Travis Fryman .05
41 Cecil Fielder .05
42 Milt Cuyler .05
43 Andujar Cedeno .05
44 Danny Darwin .05
45 Randy Henis .05
46 George Brett .60
47 Jeff Conine .05
48 Bo Jackson .15
49 Brian McRae .05
50 Brent Mayne .05
51 Eddie Murray .40
52 Ramon Martinez .05
53 Jim Neidlinger .05
54 Jim Poole .05
55 Tim McIntosh .05
56 Randy Veres .05
57 Kirby Puckett .60
58 Todd Ritchie .05
59 Rich Garces .05
60 Moises Alou .15
61 Delino DeShields .05
62 Oscar Azocar .05
63 Kevin Maas .05
64 Alan Mills .05
65 John Franco .05
66 Chris Jelic .05
67 Dave Magadan .05
68 Darryl Strawberry .05
69 Hensley Meulens .05
70 Juan Gonzalez .50
71 Reggie Harris .05
72 Rickey Henderson .45
73 Mark McGwire 1.00
74 Willie McGee .05
75 Todd Van Poppel .05
76 Bob Welch .05
77 "Future Aces" (Todd Van Poppel, Don Peters, David Zancanaro, Kirk Dressendorfer) .05
78 Lenny Dykstra .05
79 Mickey Morandini .05
80 Wes Chamberlain .05
81 Barry Bonds .75
82 Doug Drabek .05
83 Randy Tomlin .05
84 Scott Chiamparino .05
85 Rafael Palmeiro .20
86 Nolan Ryan 1.00
87 Bobby Witt .05
88 Fred McGriff .05
89 Dave Steib .05
90 Ed Sprague .05
91 Vince Coleman .05
92 Rod Brewer .05
93 Bernard Gilkey .05
94 Roberto Alomar .30
95 Chuck Finley .05
96 Dale Murphy .20
97 Jose Rijo .05
98 Hal Morris .05
99 "Friendly Foes" (Dwight Gooden, Darryl Strawberry) .05
--- John Olerud, Dwight Gooden, Jose Canseco, Darryl Strawberry .10

1991 Classic Series 2

Classic released a 100-card second series in 1991. Cards feature the same format as the first series, with the exception of border color; Series II features maroon borders. The cards are designed for trivia game use. Series II includes several players with new teams and top rookies. Special Four-In-One, 300 Game Winner and Strikout Kings cards are included with each set.

MT
Complete Set (100): 4.50
Common Player: .05
1 Ken Griffey, Jr. 1.00
2 Wilfredo Cordero .05
3 Cal Ripken, Jr. 1.00
4 D.J. Dozier .05
5 Darrin Fletcher .05
6 Glenn Davis .05
7 Alex Fernandez .05
8 Cory Snyder .05
9 Tim Raines .05
10 Greg Swindell .05
11 Mark Lewis .05
12 Rico Brogna .05
13 Gary Sheffield .20
14 Paul Molitor .45
15 Kent Hrbek .05
16 Scott Erickson .05
17 Steve Sax .05
18 Dennis Eckersley .05
19 Jose Canseco .40
20 Kirk Dressendorfer .05
21 Ken Griffey, Sr. .05
22 Erik Hanson .05
23 Dan Peltier .05
24 John Olerud .05
25 Eddie Zosky .05
26 Steve Avery .05
27 John Smoltz .10
28 Frank Thomas .75
29 Jerome Walton .05
30 George Bell .05
31 Jose Rijo .05
32 Randy Myers .05
33 Barry Larkin .10
34 Eric Anthony .05
35 Dave Hansen .05
36 Eric Karros .05
37 Jose Offerman .05
38 Marquis Grissom .05
39 Dwight Gooden .05
40 Gregg Jefferies .05
41 Pat Combs .05
42 Todd Zeile .05
43 Benito Santiago .05
44 Dave Staton .05
45 Tony Fernandez .05
46 Fred McGriff .05
47 Jeff Brantley .05
48 Junior Felix .05
49 Jack Morris .05
50 Chris George .05
51 Henry Rodriguez .05
52 Paul Marak .05
53 Ryan Klesko .05
54 Darren Lewis .05
55 Lance Dickson .05
56 Anthony Young .05
57 Willie Banks .05
58 Mike Bordick .05
59 Roger Salkeld .05
60 Steve Karsay .05
61 Bernie Williams .25
62 Mickey Tettleton .05
63 Dave Justice .20
64 Steve Decker .05
65 Roger Clemens .60
66 Phil Plantier .05
67 Ryne Sandberg .45
68 Sandy Alomar,Jr. .05
69 Cecil Fielder .05
70 George Brett .60
71 Delino DeShields .05
72 Dave Magadan .05
73 Darryl Strawberry .05
74 Juan Gonzalez .45
75 Rickey Henderson .45
76 Willie McGee .05
77 Todd Van Poppel .05
78 Barry Bonds .75
79 Doug Drabek .05
80 Nolan Ryan (300 games) 1.00
81 Roberto Alomar .30
82 Ivan Rodriguez .35
83 Dan Opperman .05
84 Jeff Bagwell .45
85 Braulio Castillo .05
86 Doug Simons .05
87 Wade Taylor .05
88 Gary Scott .05
89 Dave Stewart .05
90 Mike Simms .05
91 Luis Gonzalez .25
92 Bobby Bonilla .05
93 Tony Gwynn .60
94 Will Clark .10
95 Rich Rowland .05
96 Alan Trammell .05
97 "Strikeout Kings" (Nolan Ryan, Roger Clemens) .50
98 Joe Carter .05
99 Jack Clark .05
100 Four-In-One .25

1991 Classic Series 3

Green borders highlight Classic's third series of cards for 1991. The set includes a gameboard and player cards featuring trivia questions on the back. Statistics and biographical information are also found on back.

MT
Complete Set (100): 5.00
Common Player: .05
1 Jim Abbott .05
2 Craig Biggio .10
3 Wade Boggs .45
4 Bobby Bonilla .05
5 Ivan Calderon .05
6 Jose Canseco .40
7 Andy Benes .05
8 Wes Chamberlain .05
9 Will Clark .15
10 Royce Clayton .05
11 Gerald Alexander .05
12 Chili Davis .05
13 Eric Davis .05
14 Andre Dawson .20
15 Rob Dibble .05
16 Chris Donnels .05
17 Scott Erickson .05
18 Monty Fariss .05
19 Ruben Amaro, Jr. .05
20 Chuck Finley .05
21 Carlton Fisk .45
22 Carlos Baerga .05
23 Ron Gant .05
24 Dave Justice, Ron Gant .25
25 Mike Gardiner .05
26 Tom Glavine .10
27 Joe Grahe .05
28 Derek Bell .05
29 Mike Greenwell .05
30 Ken Griffey, Jr. 1.00
31 Leo Gomez .05
32 Tom Goodwin .05
33 Tony Gwynn .60
34 Mel Hall .05
35 Brian Harper .05
36 Dave Henderson .05
37 Albert Belle .25
38 Orel Hershiser .05
39 Brian Hunter .05
40 Howard Johnson .05
41 Felix Jose .05
42 Wally Joyner .05
43 Jeff Juden .05
44 Pat Kelly .05
45 Jimmy Key .05
46 Chuck Knoblauch .05
47 John Kruk .05
48 Ray Lankford .05
49 Ced Landrum .05
50 Scott Livingstone .05
51 Kevin Maas .05
52 Greg Maddux .60
53 Dennis Martinez .05
54 Edgar Martinez .05
55 Pedro Martinez .50
56 Don Mattingly .75
57 Orlando Merced .05
58 Keith Mitchell .05
59 Kevin Mitchell .05
60 Paul Molitor .40
61 Jack Morris .05
62 Hal Morris .05
63 Kevin Morton .05
64 Pedro Munoz .05
65 Eddie Murray .35
66 Jack McDowell .05
67 Jeff McNeely .05
68 Brian McRae .05
69 Kevin McReynolds .05
70 Gregg Olson .05
71 Rafael Palmeiro .20
72 Dean Palmer .05
73 Tony Phillips .05
74 Kirby Puckett .60
75 Carlos Quintana .05
76 Pat Rice .05
77 Cal Ripken, Jr. 1.00
78 Ivan Rodriguez .35
79 Nolan Ryan 1.00
80 Bret Saberhagen .05
81 Tim Salmon .15
82 Juan Samuel .05
83 Ruben Sierra .05
84 Heathcliff Slocumb .05
85 Joe Slusarski .05
86 John Smiley .05
87 Dave Smith .05
88 Ed Sprague .05
89 Todd Stottlemyre .05
90 Mike Timlin .05
91 Greg Vaughn .05
92 Frank Viola .05
93 John Wehner .05
94 Devon White .05
95 Matt Williams .15

96	Rick Wilkins	.05
97	Bernie Williams	.20
98	Starter & Stopper (Goose Gossage, Nolan Ryan)	.20
99	Gerald Williams	.05
----	4-in-1 (Bobby Bonilla, Will Clark, Cal Ripken Jr., Scott Erickson)	.25

1991 Classic Collector's Edition

The Classic Collector's edition made its debut in 1991. This package includes a board game, trivia baseball player cards, a baseball tips booklet and a certificate of authenticity, all packaged in a collector's edition box. Each box is individually and sequentially numbered on the outside, with a reported 100,000 available.

		MT
Complete Set (200):		10.00
Common Player:		.05
1	Frank Viola	.05
2	Tim Wallach	.05
3	Lou Whitaker	.05
4	Brett Butler	.05
5	Jim Abbott	.05
6	Jack Armstrong	.05
7	Craig Biggio	.10
8	Brian Barnes	.05
9	Dennis "Oil Can" Boyd	.05
10	Tom Browning	.05
11	Tom Brunansky	.05
12	Ellis Burks	.05
13	Harold Baines	.05
14	Kal Daniels	.05
15	Mark Davis	.05
16	Storm Davis	.05
17	Tom Glavine	.10
18	Mike Greenwell	.05
19	Kelly Gruber	.05
20	Mark Gubicza	.05
21	Pedro Guerrero	.05
22	Mike Harkey	.05
23	Orel Hershiser	.05
24	Ted Higuera	.05
25	Von Hayes	.05
26	Andre Dawson	.20
27	Shawon Dunston	.05
28	Roberto Kelly	.05
29	Joe Magrane	.05
30	Dennis Martinez	.05
31	Kevin McReynolds	.05
32	Matt Nokes	.05
33	Dan Plesac	.05
34	Dave Parker	.05
35	Randy Johnson	.20
36	Bret Saberhagen	.05
37	Mackey Sasser	.05
38	Mike Scott	.05
39	Ozzie Smith	.60
40	Kevin Seitzer	.05
41	Ruben Sierra	.05
42	Kevin Tapani	.05
43	Danny Tartabull	.05
44	Robby Thompson	.05
45	Andy Van Slyke	.05
46	Greg Vaughn	.05
47	Harold Reynolds	.05
48	Will Clark	.15
49	Gary Gaetti	.05
50	Joe Grahe	.05
51	Carlton Fisk	.40
52	Robin Ventura	.05
53	Ozzie Guillen	.05
54	Tom Candiotti	.05
55	Doug Jones	.05
56	Eric King	.05
57	Kirk Gibson	.05
58	Tim Costo	.05
59	Robin Yount	.40
60	Sammy Sosa	.75
61	Jesse Barfield	.05
62	Marc Newfield	.05
63	Jimmy Key	.05
64	Felix Jose	.05
65	Mark Whiten	.05
66	Tommy Greene	.05
67	Kent Mercker	.05
68	Greg Maddux	.60
69	Danny Jackson	.05
70	Reggie Sanders	.05
71	Eric Yelding	.05
72	Karl Rhodes	.05
73	Fernando Valenzuela	.05
74	Chris Nabholz	.05
75	Andres Galarraga	.05
76	Howard Johnson	.05
77	Hubie Brooks	.05
78	Terry Mulholland	.05
79	Paul Molitor	.45
80	Roger McDowell	.05
81	Darren Daulton	.05
82	Zane Smith	.05
83	Ray Lankford	.05
84	Bruce Hurst	.05
85	Andy Benes	.05
86	John Burkett	.05
87	Dave Righetti	.05
88	Steve Karsay	.05
89	D.J. Dozier	.05
90	Jeff Bagwell	.45
91	Joe Carter	.05
92	Wes Chamberlain	.05
93	Vince Coleman	.05
94	Pat Combs	.05
95	Jerome Walton	.05
96	Jeff Conine	.05
97	Alan Trammell	.05
98	Don Mattingly	.75
99	Ramon Martinez	.05
100	Dave Magadan	.05
101	Greg Swindell	.05
102	Dave Stewart	.05
103	Gary Sheffield	.25
104	George Bell	.05
105	Mark Grace	.20
106	Steve Sax	.05
107	Ryne Sandberg	.45
108	Chris Sabo	.05
109	Jose Rijo	.05
110	Cal Ripken, Jr.	1.00
111	Kirby Puckett	.60
112	Eddie Murray	.40
113	Roberto Alomar	.25
114	Randy Myers	.05
115	Rafael Palmeiro	.20
116	John Olerud	.05
117	Gregg Jefferies	.05
118	Kent Hrbek	.05
119	Marquis Grissom	.05
120	Ken Griffey, Jr.	1.00
121	Dwight Gooden	.05
122	Juan Gonzalez	.45
123	Ron Gant	.05
124	Travis Fryman	.05
125	John Franco	.05
126	Dennis Eckersley	.05
127	Cecil Fielder	.05
128	Phil Plantier	.05
129	Kevin Mitchell	.05
130	Kevin Maas	.05
131	Mark McGwire	1.00
132	Ben McDonald	.05
133	Lenny Dykstra	.05
134	Delino DeShields	.05
135	Jose Canseco	.40
136	Eric Davis	.05
137	George Brett	.60
138	Steve Avery	.05
139	Eric Anthony	.05
140	Bobby Thigpen	.05
141	Ken Griffey, Sr.	.05
142	Barry Larkin	.10
143	Jeff Brantley	.05
144	Bobby Bonilla	.05
145	Jose Offerman	.05
146	Mike Mussina	.25
147	Erik Hanson	.05
148	Dale Murphy	.15
149	Roger Clemens	.60
150	Tino Martinez	.05
151	Todd Van Poppel	.05
152	Mo Vaughn	.25
153	Derrick May	.05
154	Jack Clark	.05
155	Dave Hansen	.05
156	Tony Gwynn	.60
157	Brian McRae	.05
158	Matt Williams	.15
159	Kirk Dressendorfer	.05
160	Scott Erickson	.05
161	Tony Fernandez	.05
162	Willie McGee	.05
163	Fred McGriff	.05
164	Leo Gomez	.05
165	Bernard Gilkey	.05
166	Bobby Witt	.05
167	Doug Drabek	.05
168	Rob Dibble	.05
169	Glenn Davis	.05
170	Danny Darwin	.05
171	Eric Karros	.05
172	Eddie Zosky	.05
173	Todd Zeile	.05
174	Tim Raines	.05
175	Benito Santiago	.05
176	Dan Peltier	.05
177	Darryl Strawberry	.05
178	Hal Morris	.05
179	Hensley Meulens	.05
180	John Smoltz	.10
181	Frank Thomas	.75
182	Dave Staton	.05
183	Scott Chiamparino	.05
184	Alex Fernandez	.05
185	Mark Lewis	.05
186	Bo Jackson	.10
187	Mickey Morandini (photo actually Darren Daulton)	.10
188	Cory Snyder	.05
189	Rickey Henderson	.45
190	Junior Felix	.05
191	Milt Cuyler	.05
192	Wade Boggs	.45
193	"Justice Prevails" (David Justice)	.25
194	Sandy Alomar, Jr.	.05
195	Barry Bonds	.75
196	Nolan Ryan	1.00
197	Rico Brogna	.05
198	Steve Decker	.05
199	Bob Welch	.05
200	Andujar Cedeno	.05

1992 Classic Series 1

Classic introduced an innovative design with the release of its 1992 set. Fronts feature full-color photos bordered in white, while backs feature statistics, biographical information and trivia questions accented by a fading stadium shot. The cards were released with a gameboard and are numbered on back with a "T" prefix.

		MT
Complete Set (100):		5.00
Common Player:		.05
1	Jim Abbott	.05
2	Kyle Abbott	.05
3	Scott Aldred	.05
4	Roberto Alomar	.35
5	Wilson Alvarez	.05
6	Andy Ashby	.05
7	Steve Avery	.05
8	Jeff Bagwell	.40
9	Bret Barberie	.05
10	Kim Batiste	.05
11	Derek Bell	.05
12	Jay Bell	.05
13	Albert Belle	.15
14	Andy Benes	.05
15	Sean Berry	.05
16	Barry Bonds	.75
17	Ryan Bowen	.05
18	Trifecta (Alejandro Pena, Mark Wohlers, Kent Mercker)	.05
19	Scott Brosius	.05
20	Jay Buhner	.05
21	David Burba	.05
22	Jose Canseco	.45
23	Andujar Cedeno	.05
24	Will Clark	.15
25	Royce Clayton	.05
26	Roger Clemens	.50
27	David Cone	.05
28	Scott Cooper	.05
29	Chris Cron	.05
30	Len Dykstra	.05
31	Cal Eldred	.05
32	Hector Fajardo	.05
33	Cecil Fielder	.05
34	Dave Fleming	.05
35	Steve Foster	.05
36	Julio Franco	.05
37	Carlos Garcia	.05
38	Tom Glavine	.10
39	Tom Goodwin	.05
40	Ken Griffey, Jr.	1.00
41	Chris Haney	.05
42	Bryan Harvey	.05
43	Rickey Henderson	.45
44	Carlos Hernandez	.05
45	Roberto Hernandez	.05
46	Brook Jacoby	.05
47	Howard Johnson	.05
48	Pat Kelly	.05
49	Darryl Kile	.05
50	Chuck Knoblauch	.05
51	Ray Lankford	.05
52	Mark Leiter	.05
53	Darren Lewis	.05
54	Scott Livingstone	.05
55	Shane Mack	.05
56	Chito Martinez	.05
57	Dennis Martinez	.05
58	Don Mattingly	.75
59	Paul McClellan	.05
60	Chuck McElroy	.05
61	Fred McGriff	.05
62	Orlando Merced	.05
63	Luis Mercedes	.05
64	Kevin Mitchell	.05
65	Hal Morris	.05
66	Jack Morris	.05
67	Mike Mussina	.35
68	Denny Neagle	.05
69	Tom Pagnozzi	.05
70	Terry Pendleton	.05
71	Phil Plantier	.05
72	Kirby Puckett	.50
73	Carlos Quintana	.05
74	Willie Randolph	.05
75	Arthur Rhodes	.05
76	Cal Ripken	1.00
77	Ivan Rodriguez	.30
78	Nolan Ryan	1.00
79	Ryne Sandberg	.45
80	Deion Sanders	.10
81	Reggie Sanders	.05
82	Mo Sanford	.05

83 Terry Shumpert .05
84 Tim Spehr .05
85 Lee Stevens .05
86 Darryl Strawberry .05
87 Kevin Tapani .05
88 Danny Tartabull .05
89 Frank Thomas .75
90 Jim Thome .05
91 Todd Van Poppel .05
92 Andy Van Slyke .05
93 John Wehner .05
94 John Wetteland .05
95 Devon White .05
96 Brian Williams .05
97 Mark Wohlers .05
98 Robin Yount .40
99 Eddie Zosky .05
--- 4-in-1 (Barry Bonds, Roger Clemens, Steve Avery, Nolan Ryan) .50

1992 Classic Series 2

The 100-cards in Classic's 1992 Series II came packaged with a gameboard and spinner. In a completely different format from Classic's other '92 issues, Series II features player photos bordered at left and right with red or blue color bars which fade toward top and bottom. Backs have biographical data, previous-year and career statistics and five trivia questions, along with a color representation of the team's uniform. Cards, except the 4-In-1, are numbered with a "T" prefix.

		MT
Complete Set (100):		5.00
Common Player:		.05
1	Jim Abbott	.05
2	Jeff Bagwell	.35
3	Jose Canseco	.35
4	Julio Valera	.05
5	Scott Brosius	.05
6	Mark Langston	.05
7	Andy Stankiewicz	.05
8	Gary DiSarcina	.05
9	Pete Harnisch	.05
10	Mark McGwire	1.00
11	Ricky Bones	.05
12	Steve Avery	.05
13	Deion Sanders	.10
14	Mike Mussina	.35
15	Dave Justice	.25
16	Pat Hentgen	.05
17	Tom Glavine	.10
18	Juan Guzman	.05
19	Ron Gant	.05
20	Kelly Gruber	.05
21	Eric Karros	.05
22	Derrick May	.05
23	Dave Hansen	.05
24	Andre Dawson	.25
25	Eric Davis	.05
26	Ozzie Smith	.50
27	Sammy Sosa	.75
28	Lee Smith	.05
29	Ryne Sandberg	.35
30	Robin Yount	.25
31	Matt Williams	.15
32	John Vander Wal	.05
33	Bill Swift	.05
34	Delino DeShields	.05
35	Royce Clayton	.05
36	Moises Alou	.15
37	Will Clark	.15
38	Darryl Strawberry	.05
39	Larry Walker	.25
40	Ramon Martinez	.05
41	Howard Johnson	.05
42	Tino Martinez	.05
43	Dwight Gooden	.05
44	Ken Griffey, Jr.	1.00
45	David Cone	.05
46	Kenny Lofton	.05
47	Bobby Bonilla	.05
48	Carlos Baerga	.05
49	Don Mattingly	.75
50	Sandy Alomar, Jr.	.05
51	Lenny Dykstra	.05
52	Tony Gwynn	.50
53	Felix Jose	.05
54	Rick Sutcliffe	.05
55	Wes Chamberlain	.05
56	Cal Ripken, Jr.	1.00
57	Kyle Abbott	.05
58	Leo Gomez	.05
59	Gary Sheffield	.30
60	Anthony Young	.05
61	Roger Clemens	.50
62	Rafael Palmeiro	.20
63	Wade Boggs	.35
64	Andy Van Slyke	.05
65	Ruben Sierra	.05
66	Denny Neagle	.05
67	Nolan Ryan	1.00
68	Doug Drabek	.05
69	Ivan Rodriguez	.35
70	Barry Bonds	.75
71	Chuck Knoblauch	.05
72	Reggie Sanders	.05
73	Cecil Fielder	.05
74	Barry Larkin	.10
75	Scott Aldred	.05
76	Rob Dibble	.05
77	Brian McRae	.05
78	Tim Belcher	.05
79	George Brett	.50
80	Frank Viola	.05
81	Roberto Kelly	.05
82	Jack McDowell	.05
83	Mel Hall	.05
84	Esteban Beltre	.05
85	Robin Ventura	.05
86	George Bell	.05
87	Frank Thomas	.75
88	John Smiley	.05
89	Bobby Thigpen	.05
90	Kirby Puckett	.50
91	Kevin Mitchell	.05
92	Peter Hoy	.05
93	Russ Springer	.05
94	Donovan Osborne	.05
95	Dave Silvestri	.05
96	Chad Curtis	.05
97	Pat Mahomes	.05
98	Danny Tartabull	.05
99	John Doherty	.05
---	4-in-1 (Ryne Sandberg, Mike Mussina, Reggie Sanders, Jose Canseco)	.25

1992 Classic Collector's Edition

The second annual 200-card "Collector's Edition" set was packaged with a gameboard, spinner, generic player pieces, a mechanical scoreboard and a book of tips from star players. The UV-coated card fronts feature color player photos against a deep purple border. Backs have a few biographical details, previous season and career stats, plus five trivia questions in case anyone actually wanted to play the game.

		MT
Complete Set (200):		11.00
Common Player:		.05
1	Chuck Finley	.05
2	Craig Biggio	.10
3	Luis Gonzalez	.25
4	Pete Harnisch	.05
5	Jeff Juden	.05
6	Harold Baines	.05
7	Kirk Dressendorfer	.05
8	Dennis Eckersley	.05
9	Dave Henderson	.05
10	Dave Stewart	.05
11	Joe Carter	.05
12	Juan Guzman	.05
13	Dave Stieb	.05
14	Todd Stottlemyre	.05
15	Ron Gant	.05
16	Brian Hunter	.05
17	Dave Justice	.25
18	John Smoltz	.10
19	Mike Stanton	.05
20	Chris George	.05
21	Paul Molitor	.40
22	Omar Olivares	.05
23	Lee Smith	.05
24	Ozzie Smith	.60
25	Todd Zeile	.05
26	George Bell	.05
27	Andre Dawson	.25
28	Shawon Dunston	.05
29	Mark Grace	.35
30	Greg Maddux	.60
31	Dave Smith	.05
32	Brett Butler	.05
33	Orel Hershiser	.05
34	Eric Karros	.05
35	Ramon Martinez	.05
36	Jose Offerman	.05
37	Juan Samuel	.05
38	Delino DeShields	.05
39	Marquis Grissom	.05
40	Tim Wallach	.05
41	Eric Gunderson	.05
42	Willie McGee	.05
43	Dave Righetti	.05
44	Robby Thompson	.05
45	Matt Williams	.15
46	Sandy Alomar, Jr.	.05
47	Reggie Jefferson	.05
48	Mark Lewis	.05
49	Robin Ventura	.05
50	Tino Martinez	.05
51	Roberto Kelly	.05
52	Vince Coleman	.05
53	Dwight Gooden	.05
54	Todd Hundley	.05
55	Kevin Maas	.05
56	Wade Taylor	.05
57	Bryan Harvey	.05
58	Leo Gomez	.05
59	Ben McDonald	.05
60	Ricky Bones	.05
61	Tony Gwynn	.60
62	Benito Santiago	.05
63	Wes Chamberlain	.05
64	Tommy Greene	.05
65	Dale Murphy	.15
66	Steve Buechele	.05
67	Doug Drabek	.05
68	Joe Grahe	.05
69	Rafael Palmeiro	.20
70	Wade Boggs	.45
71	Ellis Burks	.05
72	Mike Greenwell	.05
73	Mo Vaughn	.30
74	Derek Bell	.05
75	Rob Dibble	.05
76	Barry Larkin	.10
77	Jose Rijo	.05
78	Doug Henry	.05
79	Chris Sabo	.05
80	Pedro Guerrero	.05
81	George Brett	.60
82	Tom Gordon	.05
83	Mark Gubicza	.05
84	Mark Whiten	.05
85	Brian McRae	.05
86	Danny Jackson	.05
87	Milt Cuyler	.05
88	Travis Fryman	.05
89	Mickey Tettleton	.05
90	Alan Trammell	.05
91	Lou Whitaker	.05
92	Chili Davis	.05
93	Scott Erickson	.05
94	Kent Hrbek	.05
95	Alex Fernandez	.05
96	Carlton Fisk	.45
97	Ramon Garcia	.05
98	Ozzie Guillen	.05
99	Tim Raines	.05
100	Bobby Thigpen	.05
101	Kirby Puckett	.60
102	Bernie Williams	.25
103	Dave Hansen	.05
104	Kevin Tapani	.05
105	Don Mattingly	.75
106	Frank Thomas	.75
107	Monty Fariss	.05
108	Bo Jackson	.10
109	Jim Abbott	.05
110	Jose Canseco	.45
111	Phil Plantier	.05
112	Brian Williams	.05
113	Mark Langston	.05
114	Wilson Alvarez	.05
115	Roberto Hernandez	.05
116	Darryl Kile	.05
117	Ryan Bowen	.05
118	Rickey Henderson	.45
119	Mark McGwire	1.50
120	Devon White	.05
121	Roberto Alomar	.35
122	Kelly Gruber	.05
123	Eddie Zosky	.05
124	Tom Glavine	.10
125	Kal Daniels	.05
126	Cal Eldred	.05
127	Deion Sanders	.10
128	Robin Yount	.40
129	Cecil Fielder	.05
130	Ray Lankford	.05
131	Ryne Sandberg	.45
132	Darryl Strawberry	.05
133	Chris Haney	.05
134	Dennis Martinez	.05
135	Bryan Hickerson	.05
136	Will Clark	.15
137	Hal Morris	.05
138	Charles Nagy	.05
139	Jim Thome	.05
140	Albert Belle	.25
141	Reggie Sanders	.05
142	Scott Cooper	.05
143	David Cone	.05
144	Anthony Young	.05
145	Howard Johnson	.05
146	Arthur Rhodes	.05
147	Scott Aldred	.05
148	Mike Mussina	.40
149	Fred McGriff	.05
150	Andy Benes	.05
151	Ruben Sierra	.05
152	Len Dykstra	.05
153	Andy Van Slyke	.05
154	Orlando Merced	.05
155	Barry Bonds	.75
156	John Smiley	.05
157	Julio Franco	.05
158	Juan Gonzalez	.45
159	Ivan Rodriguez	.35
160	Willie Banks	.05
161	Eric Davis	.05

162 Eddie Murray .40
163 Dave Fleming .05
164 Wally Joyner .05
165 Kevin Mitchell .05
166 Ed Taubensee .05
167 Danny Tartabull .05
168 Ken Hill .05
169 Willie Randolph .05
170 Kevin McReynolds .05
171 Gregg Jefferies .05
172 Patrick Lennon .05
173 Luis Mercedes .05
174 Glenn Davis .05
175 Bret Saberhagen .05
176 Bobby Bonilla .05
177 Kenny Lofton .05
178 Jose Lind .05
179 Royce Clayton .05
180 Scott Scudder .05
181 Chuck Knoblauch .05
182 Terry Pendleton .05
183 Nolan Ryan 1.50
184 Rob Maurer .05
185 Brian Bohanon .05
186 Ken Griffey, Jr. 1.00
187 Jeff Bagwell .45
188 Steve Avery .05
189 Roger Clemens .60
190 Cal Ripken, Jr. 1.00
191 Kim Batiste .05
192 Bip Roberts .05
193 Greg Swindell .05
194 Dave Winfield .60
195 Steve Sax .05
196 Frank Viola .05
197 Mo Sanford .05
198 Kyle Abbott .05
199 Jack Morris .05
200 Andy Ashby .05

1993 Classic

A 100-card travel edition of Classic's baseball trivia cards was produced for 1993. Cards feature game-action player photos with dark blue borders. Backs have previous season and career stats along with five trivia questions. Card numbers have a "T" prefix.

MT
Complete Set (100): 6.00
Common Player: .05
1 Jim Abbott .05
2 Roberto Alomar .30
3 Moises Alou .15
4 Brady Anderson .05
5 Eric Anthony .05
6 Alex Arias .05
7 Pedro Astacio .05
8 Steve Avery .05
9 Carlos Baerga .05
10 Jeff Bagwell .40
11 George Bell .05
12 Albert Belle .15
13 Craig Biggio .10
14 Barry Bonds .65
15 Bobby Bonilla .05
16 Mike Bordick .05
17 George Brett .50
18 Jose Canseco .35
19 Joe Carter .05
20 Royce Clayton .05
21 Roger Clemens .50
22 Greg Colbrunn .05
23 David Cone .05
24 Darren Daulton .05
25 Delino DeShields .05
26 Rob Dibble .05
27 Dennis Eckersley .05
28 Cal Eldred .05
29 Scott Erickson .05
30 Junior Felix .05
31 Tony Fernandez .05
32 Cecil Fielder .05
33 Steve Finley .05
34 Dave Fleming .05
35 Travis Fryman .05
36 Tom Glavine .10
37 Juan Gonzalez .40
38 Ken Griffey, Jr. 1.00
39 Marquis Grissom .05
40 Juan Guzman .05
41 Tony Gwynn .50
42 Rickey Henderson .35
43 Felix Jose .05
44 Wally Joyner .05
45 David Justice .25
46 Eric Karros .05
47 Roberto Kelly .05
48 Ryan Klesko .05
49 Chuck Knoblauch .05
50 John Kruk .05
51 Ray Lankford .05
52 Barry Larkin .10
53 Pat Listach .05
54 Kenny Lofton .05
55 Shane Mack .05
56 Greg Maddux .50
57 Dave Magadan .05
58 Edgar Martinez .05
59 Don Mattingly .65
60 Ben McDonald .05
61 Jack McDowell .05
62 Fred McGriff .05
63 Mark McGwire 1.00
64 Kevin McReynolds .05
65 Sam Militello .05
66 Paul Molitor .40
67 Jeff Montgomery .05
68 Jack Morris .05
69 Eddie Murray .35
70 Mike Mussina .30
71 Otis Nixon .05
72 Donovan Osborne .05
73 Terry Pendleton .05
74 Mike Piazza .75
75 Kirby Puckett .50
76 Cal Ripken, Jr. 1.00
77 Bip Roberts .05
78 Ivan Rodriguez .30
79 Nolan Ryan 1.00
80 Ryne Sandberg .40
81 Deion Sanders .10
82 Reggie Sanders .05
83 Frank Seminara .05
84 Gary Sheffield .25
85 Ruben Sierra .05
86 John Smiley .05
87 Lee Smith .05
88 Ozzie Smith .50
89 John Smoltz .10
90 Danny Tartabull .05
91 Bob Tewksbury .05
92 Frank Thomas .65
93 Andy Van Slyke .05
94 Mo Vaughn .25
95 Robin Ventura .05
96 Tim Wakefield .05
97 Larry Walker .25
98 Dave Winfield .50
99 Robin Yount .35
--- 4-in-1 (Mark McGwire, Sam Militello, Ryan Klesko, Greg Maddux) .50

1994 Collector's Choice Promos

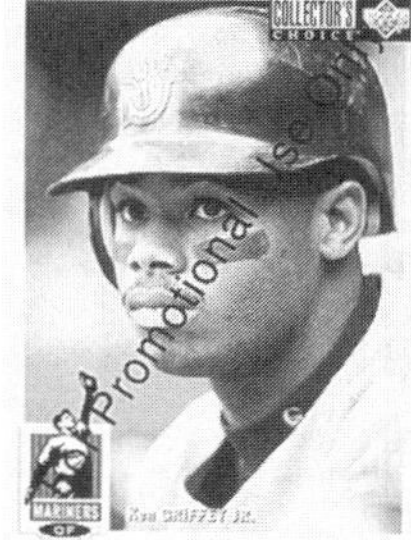

Upper Deck used a pair of promo cards to preview its new 1994 Collector's Choice brand. Ken Griffey, Jr. was featured on the promos, though the photos differ from those which appear on his regular-issue card, as does the card number. "For Promotional Use Only" is printed diagonally in black on both the front and back of the regular-size card. The 5" x 7-3/8" promo card uses the same front photo as the smaller promo and has advertising on the back describing the Collector's Choice issue.

MT
50 Ken Griffey, Jr. 5.00
--- Ken Griffey, Jr. (jumbo) 5.00

1994 Collector's Choice

This base-brand set, released in two series, was more widely available than the regular 1994 Upper Deck issue. Cards feature UD production staples such as UV coating and hologram and have large photos with a narrow pinstripe border. Backs have stats and a color photo. Series 1 has 320 cards and subsets titled Rookie Class, Draft Picks and Top Performers. Series 2 subsets are Up Close and Personal, Future Foundation and Rookie Class. Each of the set's player cards can also be found with either a gold- (1 in 36 packs) or silver-foil replica-autograph card; one silver-signature card appears in every pack. Factory sets include five randomly selected gold-signature cards.

MT
Complete Set (670): 20.00
Unopened Factory Set (675): 25.00
Common Player: .05
Pack (12): 1.00
Wax Box (36): 20.00
1 *Rich Becker* .05
2 Greg Blosser .05
3 Midre Cummings .05
4 Carlos Delgado .20
5 *Steve Dreyer* .05
6 *Carl Everett* .50
7 Cliff Floyd .05
8 Alex Gonzalez .10
9 Shawn Green .20
10 Butch Huskey .05
11 Mark Hutton .05
12 Miguel Jimenez .05
13 Steve Karsay .05
14 Marc Newfield .05
15 Luis Ortiz .05
16 Manny Ramirez .60
17 Johnny Ruffin .05
18 *Scott Stahoviak* .05
19 Salomon Torres .05
20 *Gabe White* .10
21 *Brian Anderson* .10
22 *Wayne Gomes* .10
23 Jeff Granger .05
24 *Steve Soderstrom* .05
25 *Trot Nixon* .25
26 *Kirk Presley* .05
27 *Matt Brunson* .05
28 *Brooks Kieschnick* .05
29 *Billy Wagner* .25
30 *Matt Drews* .05
31 *Kurt Abbott* .10
32 Luis Alicea .05
33 Roberto Alomar .30
34 Sandy Alomar Jr. .05
35 Moises Alou .10
36 Wilson Alvarez .05
37 Rich Amaral .05
38 Eric Anthony .05
39 Luis Aquino .05
40 Jack Armstrong .05
41 Rene Arocha .05
42 *Rich Aude* .05
43 Brad Ausmus .05
44 Steve Avery .05
45 Bob Ayrault .05
46 Willie Banks .05
47 Bret Barberie .05
48 Kim Batiste .05
49 Rod Beck .05
50 Jason Bere .05
51 Sean Berry .05
52 Dante Bichette .05
53 Jeff Blauser .05
54 Mike Blowers .05
55 Tim Bogar .05
56 Tom Bolton .05
57 Ricky Bones .05
58 Bobby Bonilla .05
59 Bret Boone .10
60 Pat Borders .05
61 Mike Bordick .05
62 Daryl Boston .05
63 Ryan Bowen .05
64 Jeff Branson .05
65 George Brett .75
66 Steve Buechele .05
67 Dave Burba .05
68 John Burkett .05
69 Jeromy Burnitz .05
70 Brett Butler .05
71 Rob Butler .05
72 Ken Caminiti .05
73 Cris Carpenter .05
74 Vinny Castilla .05
75 Andujar Cedeno .05
76 Wes Chamberlain .05
77 Archi Cianfrocco .05
78 Dave Clark .05

No.	Player	Price
79	Jerald Clark	.05
80	Royce Clayton	.05
81	David Cone	.05
82	Jeff Conine	.05
83	Steve Cooke	.05
84	Scott Cooper	.05
85	Joey Cora	.05
86	Tim Costa	.05
87	Chad Curtis	.05
88	Ron Darling	.05
89	Danny Darwin	.05
90	Rob Deer	.05
91	Jim Deshaies	.05
92	Delino DeShields	.05
93	Rob Dibble	.05
94	Gary DiSarcina	.05
95	Doug Drabek	.05
96	Scott Erickson	.05
97	*Rikkert Faneyte*	.05
98	Jeff Fassero	.05
99	Alex Fernandez	.05
100	Cecil Fielder	.05
101	Dave Fleming	.05
102	Darrin Fletcher	.05
103	Scott Fletcher	.05
104	Mike Gallego	.05
105	Carlos Garcia	.05
106	Jeff Gardner	.05
107	Brent Gates	.05
108	Benji Gil	.05
109	Bernard Gilkey	.05
110	Chris Gomez	.05
111	Luis Gonzalez	.25
112	Tom Gordon	.05
113	Jim Gott	.05
114	Mark Grace	.25
115	Tommy Greene	.05
116	Willie Greene	.05
117	Ken Griffey, Jr.	1.50
118	Bill Gullickson	.05
119	Ricky Gutierrez	.05
120	Juan Guzman	.05
121	Chris Gwynn	.05
122	Tony Gwynn	.75
123	Jeffrey Hammonds	.05
124	Erik Hanson	.05
125	Gene Harris	.05
126	Greg Harris	.05
127	Bryan Harvey	.05
128	Billy Hatcher	.05
129	Hilly Hathaway	.05
130	Charlie Hayes	.05
131	Rickey Henderson	.40
132	Mike Henneman	.05
133	Pat Hentgen	.05
134	Roberto Hernandez	.05
135	Orel Hershiser	.05
136	Phil Hiatt	.05
137	Glenallen Hill	.05
138	Ken Hill	.05
139	Eric Hillman	.05
140	Chris Hoiles	.05
141	Dave Hollins	.05
142	David Hulse	.05
143	Todd Hundley	.05
144	Pete Incaviglia	.05
145	Danny Jackson	.05
146	John Jaha	.05
147	Domingo Jean	.05
148	Gregg Jefferies	.05
149	Reggie Jefferson	.05
150	Lance Johnson	.05
151	Bobby Jones	.05
152	Chipper Jones	1.00
153	Todd Jones	.05
154	Brian Jordan	.05
155	Wally Joyner	.05
156	Dave Justice	.25
157	Ron Karkovice	.05
158	Eric Karros	.05
159	Jeff Kent	.05
160	Jimmy Key	.05
161	Mark Kiefer	.05
162	Darryl Kile	.05
163	Jeff King	.05
164	Wayne Kirby	.05
165	Ryan Klesko	.05
166	Chuck Knoblauch	.05
167	Chad Kreuter	.05
168	John Kruk	.05
169	Mark Langston	.05
170	Mike Lansing	.05
171	Barry Larkin	.10
172	Manuel Lee	.05
173	*Phil Leftwich*	.05
174	Darren Lewis	.05
175	Derek Lilliquist	.05
176	Jose Lind	.05
177	Albie Lopez	.05
178	Javier Lopez	.05
179	Torey Lovullo	.05
180	Scott Lydy	.05
181	Mike Macfarlane	.05
182	Shane Mack	.05
183	Greg Maddux	.75
184	Dave Magadan	.05
185	Joe Magrane	.05
186	Kirt Manwaring	.05
187	Al Martin	.05
188	*Pedro A. Martinez*	.10
189	Pedro J. Martinez	.30
190	Ramon Martinez	.05
191	Tino Martinez	.05
192	Don Mattingly	1.00
193	Derrick May	.05
194	David McCarty	.05
195	Ben McDonald	.05
196	Roger McDowell	.05
197	Fred McGriff	.05
198	Mark McLemore	.05
199	Greg McMichael	.05
200	Jeff McNeely	.05
201	Brian McRae	.05
202	Pat Meares	.05
203	Roberto Mejia	.05
204	Orlando Merced	.05
205	Jose Mesa	.05
206	Blas Minor	.05
207	Angel Miranda	.05
208	Paul Molitor	.40
209	Raul Mondesi	.15
210	Jeff Montgomery	.05
211	Mickey Morandini	.05
212	Mike Morgan	.05
213	Jamie Moyer	.05
214	Bobby Munoz	.05
215	Troy Neel	.05
216	Dave Nilsson	.05
217	John O'Donoghue	.05
218	Paul O'Neill	.05
219	Jose Offerman	.05
220	Joe Oliver	.05
221	Greg Olson	.05
222	Donovan Osborne	.05
223	Jayhawk Owens	.05
224	Mike Pagliarulo	.05
225	Craig Paquette	.05
226	Roger Pavlik	.05
227	Brad Pennington	.05
228	Eduardo Perez	.05
229	Mike Perez	.05
230	Tony Phillips	.05
231	Hipolito Pichardo	.05
232	Phil Plantier	.05
233	*Curtis Pride*	.05
234	Tim Pugh	.05
235	Scott Radinsky	.05
236	Pat Rapp	.05
237	Kevin Reimer	.05
238	Armando Reynoso	.05
239	Jose Rijo	.05
240	Cal Ripken, Jr.	2.00
241	Kevin Roberson	.05
242	Kenny Rogers	.05
243	Kevin Rogers	.05
244	Mel Rojas	.05
245	John Roper	.05
246	Kirk Rueter	.05
247	Scott Ruffcorn	.05
248	Ken Ryan	.05
249	Nolan Ryan	2.00
250	Bret Saberhagen	.05
251	Tim Salmon	.15
252	Reggie Sanders	.05
253	Curt Schilling	.15
254	David Segui	.05
255	Aaron Sele	.05
256	Scott Servais	.05
257	Gary Sheffield	.25
258	Ruben Sierra	.05
259	Don Slaught	.05
260	Lee Smith	.05
261	Cory Snyder	.05
262	Paul Sorrento	.05
263	Sammy Sosa	1.25
264	Bill Spiers	.05
265	Mike Stanley	.05
266	Dave Staton	.05
267	Terry Steinbach	.05
268	Kevin Stocker	.05
269	Todd Stottlemyre	.05
270	Doug Strange	.05
271	Bill Swift	.05
272	Kevin Tapani	.05
273	Tony Tarasco	.05
274	*Julian Tavarez*	.05
275	Mickey Tettleton	.05
276	Ryan Thompson	.05
277	Chris Turner	.05
278	John Valentin	.05
279	Todd Van Poppel	.05
280	Andy Van Slyke	.05
281	Mo Vaughn	.25
282	Robin Ventura	.05
283	Frank Viola	.05
284	Jose Vizcaino	.05
285	Omar Vizquel	.05
286	Larry Walker	.20
287	Duane Ware	.05
288	Allen Watson	.05
289	Bill Wegman	.05
290	Turk Wendell	.05
291	Lou Whitaker	.05
292	Devon White	.05
293	Rondell White	.15
294	Mark Whiten	.05
295	Darrell Whitmore	.05
296	Bob Wickman	.05
297	Rick Wilkins	.05
298	Bernie Williams	.20
299	Matt Williams	.15
300	Woody Williams	.05
301	Nigel Wilson	.05
302	Dave Winfield	.75
303	Anthony Young	.05
304	Eric Young	.05
305	Todd Zeile	.05
306	Jack McDowell, John Burkett, Tom Glavine (Top Performers)	.05
307	Randy Johnson (Top Performers)	.15
308	Randy Myers (Top Performers)	.05
309	Jack McDowell (Top Performers)	.05
310	Mike Piazza (Top Performers)	.50
311	Barry Bonds (Top Performers)	.40
312	Andres Galarraga (Top Performers)	.05
313	Juan Gonzalez, Barry Bonds (Top Performers)	.40
314	Albert Belle (Top Performers)	.15
315	Kenny Lofton (Top Performers)	.05
316	Checklist 1-64 (Barry Bonds)	.15
317	Checklist 65-128 (Ken Griffey, Jr.)	.35
318	Checklist 129-192 (Mike Piazza)	.15
319	Checklist 193-256 (Kirby Puckett)	.15
320	Checklist 257-320 (Nolan Ryan)	.25
321	Checklist 321-370 (Roberto Alomar)	.10
322	Checklist 371-420 (Roger Clemens)	.15
323	Checklist 421-470 (Juan Gonzalez)	.15
324	Checklist 471-520 (Ken Griffey, Jr.)	.25
325	Checklist 521-570 (David Justice)	.10
326	Checklist 571-620 (John Kruk)	.05
327	Checklist 621-670 (Frank Thomas)	.20
328	Angels Checklist (Tim Salmon)	.10
329	Astros Checklist (Jeff Bagwell)	.15
330	Athletics Checklist (Mark McGwire)	.50
331	Blue Jays Checklist (Roberto Alomar)	.15
332	Braves Checklist (David Justice)	.10
333	Brewers Checklist (Pat Listach)	.05
334	Cardinals Checklist (Ozzie Smith)	.25
335	Cubs Checklist (Ryne Sandberg)	.25
336	Dodgers Checklist (Mike Piazza)	.25
337	Expos Checklist (Cliff Floyd)	.05
338	Giants Checklist (Barry Bonds)	.25
339	Indians Checklist (Albert Belle)	.10
340	Mariners Checklist (Ken Griffey, Jr.)	.45
341	Marlins Checklist (Gary Sheffield)	.10
342	Mets Checklist (Dwight Gooden)	.05
343	Orioles Checklist (Cal Ripken, Jr.)	.50
344	Padres Checklist (Tony Gwynn)	.20
345	Phillies Checklist (Lenny Dykstra)	.05
346	Pirates Checklists (Andy Van Slyke)	.05
347	Rangers Checklist (Juan Gonzalez)	.15
348	Red Sox Checklist (Roger Clemens)	.25
349	Reds Checklist (Barry Larkin)	.05
350	Rockies Checklist (Andres Galarraga)	.05
351	Royals Checklist (Kevin Appier)	.05
352	Tigers Checklist (Cecil Fielder)	.05
353	Twins Checklist (Kirby Puckett)	.25
354	White Sox Checklist (Frank Thomas)	.35
355	Yankees Checklist (Don Mattingly)	.40
356	Bo Jackson	.10
357	Randy Johnson	.30
358	Darren Daulton	.05
359	Charlie Hough	.05
360	Andres Galarraga	.05
361	Mike Felder	.05
362	Chris Hammond	.05
363	Shawon Dunston	.05
364	Junior Felix	.05
365	Ray Lankford	.05
366	Darryl Strawberry	.05
367	Dave Magadan	.05
368	Gregg Olson	.05
369	Len Dykstra	.05
370	Darrin Jackson	.05
371	Dave Stewart	.05
372	Terry Pendleton	.05
373	Arthur Rhodes	.05
374	Benito Santiago	.05
375	Travis Fryman	.05
376	Scott Brosius	.05
377	Stan Belinda	.05
378	Derek Parks	.05
379	Kevin Seitzer	.05
380	Wade Boggs	.40
381	Wally Whitehurst	.05
382	Scott Leius	.05
383	Danny Tartabull	.05
384	Harold Reynolds	.05
385	Tim Raines	.05
386	Darryl Hamilton	.05
387	Felix Fermin	.05
388	Jim Eisenreich	.05
389	Kurt Abbott	.05
390	Kevin Appier	.05
391	Chris Bosio	.05
392	Randy Tomlin	.05
393	Bob Hamelin	.05
394	Kevin Gross	.05
395	Wil Cordero	.05
396	Joe Girardi	.05
397	Orestes Destrade	.05
398	Chris Haney	.05
399	Xavier Hernandez	.05
400	Mike Piazza	1.00
401	Alex Arias	.05
402	Tom Candiotti	.05
403	Kirk Gibson	.05
404	Chuck Carr	.05
405	Brady Anderson	.05
406	Greg Gagne	.05
407	Bruce Ruffin	.05
408	Scott Hemond	.05
409	Keith Miller	.05

410	John Wetteland	.05
411	Eric Anthony	.05
412	Andre Dawson	.15
413	Doug Henry	.05
414	John Franco	.05
415	Julio Franco	.05
416	Dave Hansen	.05
417	Mike Harkey	.05
418	Jack Armstrong	.05
419	Joe Orsulak	.05
420	John Smoltz	.10
421	Scott Livingstone	.05
422	Darren Holmes	.05
423	Ed Sprague	.05
424	Jay Buhner	.05
425	Kirby Puckett	.75
426	Phil Clark	.05
427	Anthony Young	.05
428	Reggie Jefferson	.05
429	Mariano Duncan	.05
430	Tom Glavine	.10
431	Dave Henderson	.05
432	Melido Perez	.05
433	Paul Wagner	.05
434	Tim Worrell	.05
435	Ozzie Guillen	.05
436	Mike Butcher	.05
437	Jim Deshaies	.05
438	Kevin Young	.05
439	Tom Browning	.05
440	Mike Greenwell	.05
441	Mike Stanton	.05
442	John Doherty	.05
443	John Dopson	.05
444	Carlos Baerga	.05
445	Jack McDowell	.05
446	Kent Mercker	.05
447	Ricky Jordan	.05
448	Jerry Browne	.05
449	Fernando Vina	.05
450	Jim Abbott	.05
451	Teddy Higuera	.05
452	Tim Naehring	.05
453	Jim Leyritz	.05
454	Frank Castillo	.05
455	Joe Carter	.05
456	Craig Biggio	.10
457	Geronimo Pena	.05
458	Alejandro Pena	.05
459	Mike Moore	.05
460	Randy Myers	.05
461	Greg Myers	.05
462	Greg Hibbard	.05
463	Jose Guzman	.05
464	Tom Pagnozzi	.05
465	Marquis Grissom	.05
466	Tim Wallach	.05
467	Joe Grahe	.05
468	Bob Tewksbury	.05
469	B.J. Surhoff	.05
470	Kevin Mitchell	.05
471	Bobby Witt	.05
472	Milt Thompson	.05
473	John Smiley	.05
474	Alan Trammell	.05
475	Mike Mussina	.30
476	Rick Aguilera	.05
477	Jose Valentin	.05
478	Harold Baines	.05
479	Bip Roberts	.05
480	Edgar Martinez	.05
481	Rheal Cormier	.05
482	Hal Morris	.05
483	Pat Kelly	.05
484	Roberto Kelly	.05
485	Chris Sabo	.05
486	Kent Hrbek	.05
487	Scott Kamieniecki	.05
488	Walt Weiss	.05
489	Karl Rhodes	.05
490	Derek Bell	.05
491	Chili Davis	.05
492	Brian Harper	.05
493	Felix Jose	.05
494	Trevor Hoffman	.05
495	Dennis Eckersley	.05
496	Pedro Astacio	.05
497	Jay Bell	.05
498	Randy Velarde	.05
499	David Wells	.05
500	Frank Thomas	1.25
501	Mark Lemke	.05
502	Mike Devereaux	.05
503	Chuck McElroy	.05
504	Luis Polonia	.05
505	Damion Easley	.05
506	Greg A. Harris	.05
507	Chris James	.05
508	Terry Mulholland	.05
509	Pete Smith	.05
510	Rickey Henderson	.30
511	Sid Fernandez	.05
512	Al Leiter	.05
513	Doug Jones	.05
514	Steve Farr	.05
515	Chuck Finley	.05
516	Bobby Thigpen	.05
517	Jim Edmonds	.05
518	Graeme Lloyd	.05
519	Dwight Gooden	.05
520	Pat Listach	.05
521	Kevin Bass	.05
522	Willie Banks	.05
523	Steve Finley	.05
524	Delino DeShields	.05
525	Mark McGwire	2.00
526	Greg Swindell	.05
527	Chris Nabholz	.05
528	Scott Sanders	.05
529	David Segui	.05
530	Howard Johnson	.05
531	Jaime Navarro	.05
532	Jose Vizcaino	.05
533	Mark Lewis	.05
534	Pete Harnisch	.05
535	Robby Thompson	.05
536	Marcus Moore	.05
537	Kevin Brown	.10
538	Mark Clark	.05
539	Sterling Hitchcock	.05
540	Will Clark	.10
541	Denis Boucher	.05
542	Jack Morris	.05
543	Pedro Munoz	.05
544	Bret Boone	.10
545	Ozzie Smith	.75
546	Dennis Martinez	.05
547	Dan Wilson	.05
548	Rick Sutcliffe	.05
549	Kevin McReynolds	.05
550	Roger Clemens	.75
551	Todd Benzinger	.05
552	Bill Haselman	.05
553	Bobby Munoz	.05
554	Ellis Burks	.05
555	Ryne Sandberg	.35
556	Lee Smith	.05
557	Danny Bautista	.05
558	Rey Sanchez	.05
559	Norm Charlton	.05
560	Jose Canseco	.35
561	Tim Belcher	.05
562	Denny Neagle	.05
563	Eric Davis	.05
564	Jody Reed	.05
565	Kenny Lofton	.05
566	Gary Gaetti	.05
567	Todd Worrell	.05
568	Mark Portugal	.05
569	Dick Schofield	.05
570	Andy Benes	.05
571	Zane Smith	.05
572	Bobby Ayala	.05
573	Chip Hale	.05
574	Bob Welch	.05
575	Deion Sanders	.10
576	Dave Nied	.05
577	Pat Mahomes	.05
578	Charles Nagy	.05
579	Otis Nixon	.05
580	Dean Palmer	.05
581	Roberto Petagine	.05
582	Dwight Smith	.05
583	Jeff Russell	.05
584	Mark Dewey	.05
585	Greg Vaughn	.05
586	Brian Hunter	.05
587	Willie McGee	.05
588	Pedro J. Martinez	.35
589	Roger Salkeld	.05
590	Jeff Bagwell	.60
591	Spike Owen	.05
592	Jeff Reardon	.05
593	Erik Pappas	.05
594	Brian Williams	.05
595	Eddie Murray	.35
596	Henry Rodriguez	.05
597	Erik Hanson	.05
598	Stan Javier	.05
599	Mitch Williams	.05
600	John Olerud	.05
601	Vince Coleman	.05
602	Damon Berryhill	.05
603	Tom Brunansky	.05
604	Robb Nen	.05
605	Rafael Palmeiro	.15
606	Cal Eldred	.05
607	Jeff Brantley	.05
608	Alan Mills	.05
609	Jeff Nelson	.05
610	Barry Bonds	.75
611	*Carlos Pulido*	.05
612	*Tim Hyers*	.05
613	Steve Howe	.05
614	*Brian Turang*	.05
615	Leo Gomez	.05
616	Jesse Orosco	.05
617	Dan Pasqua	.05
618	Marvin Freeman	.05
619	Tony Fernandez	.05
620	Albert Belle	.15
621	Eddie Taubensee	.05
622	Mike Jackson	.05
623	Jose Bautista	.05
624	Jim Thome	.05
625	Ivan Rodriguez	.30
626	Ben Rivera	.05
627	Dave Valle	.05
628	Tom Henke	.05
629	Omar Vizquel	.05
630	Juan Gonzalez	.60
631	Roberto Alomar (Up Close)	.10
632	Barry Bonds (Up Close)	.40
633	Juan Gonzalez (Up Close)	.25
634	Ken Griffey, Jr. (Up Close)	1.25
635	Michael Jordan (Up Close)	2.50
636	Dave Justice (Up Close)	.10
637	Mike Piazza (Up Close)	.50
638	Kirby Puckett (Up Close)	.25
639	Tim Salmon (Up Close)	.10
640	Frank Thomas (Up Close)	.35
641	*Alan Benes* (Future Foundation)	.25
642	Johnny Damon (Future Foundation)	.10
643	*Brad Fullmer* (Future Foundation)	1.00
644	Derek Jeter (Future Foundation)	1.00
645	*Derrek Lee* (Future Foundation)	.50
646	Alex Ochoa (Future Foundation)	.05
647	*Alex Rodriguez* (Future Foundation)	4.00
648	*Jose Silva* (Future Foundation)	.05
649	*Terrell Wade* (Future Foundation)	.05
650	Preston Wilson (Future Foundation)	.15
651	Shane Andrews (Rookie Class)	.05
652	James Baldwin (Rookie Class)	.05
653	*Ricky Bottalico* (Rookie Class)	.10
654	Tavo Alvarez (Rookie Class)	.05
655	Donnie Elliott (Rookie Class)	.05
656	Joey Eischen (Rookie Class)	.05
657	Jason Giambi (Rookie Class)	.35
658	Todd Hollandsworth (Rookie Class)	.05
659	Brian Hunter (Rookie Class)	.05
660	Charles Johnson (Rookie Class)	.05
661	*Michael Jordan* (Rookie Class)	5.00
662	Jeff Juden (Rookie Class)	.05
663	Mike Kelly (Rookie Class)	.05
664	James Mouton (Rookie Class)	.05
665	Ray Holbert (Rookie Class)	.05
666	Pokey Reese (Rookie Class)	.05
667	*Ruben Santana* (Rookie Class)	.05
668	Paul Spoljaric (Rookie Class)	.05
669	Luis Lopez (Rookie Class)	.05
670	Matt Walbeck (Rookie Class)	.05

1994 Collector's Choice Gold Signature

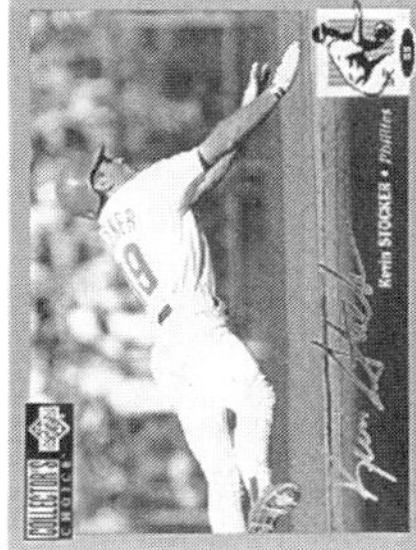

A super-scarce parallel set of the premiere-issue Collector's Choice in 1994 was the gold-signature version found on average of only once per 36 foil packs. In addition to a gold-foil facsimile signature on the card front, this edition features gold-colored borders on the regular player cards.

	MT
Common Player:	2.00
Stars:	20X

(See 1994 Collector's Choice for checklist and base card values.)

1994 Collector's Choice Silver Signature

Each of the cards in the debut edition of Upper Deck's Collector's Choice brand was also issued in a parallel edition bearing a facsimile silver-foil signature on front. The silver-signature cards were inserted at a one-per-pack rate in the set's foil packs, and proportionately in other types of packaging.

	MT
Common Player:	.15
Stars:	1.5X

(See 1994 Collector's Choice for checklist and base card values.)

1994 Collector's Choice Home Run All-Stars

Among the most attractive of the 1994 chase cards, the perceived high production (over a million sets according to stated odds of winning) of this set keeps it affordable. Sets were available by a mail-in offer to persons who found a winner card in Series 1 foil packs (about one per box). Cards feature a combination of brick-bordered hologram and color player photo on front, along with a gold-foil facsimile autograph. On back the brick border is repeated, as is the photo on the hologram, though this time in full color. There is a stadium photo in the background, over which is printed a description of the player's home run prowess. A numbering error resulted in two cards numbered HA4 and no card with the HA5 number.

	MT
Complete Set (8):	4.00
Common Player:	.25
1HA Juan Gonzalez	.75
2HA Ken Griffey, Jr.	2.50
3HA Barry Bonds	1.00
4HAaBobby Bonilla	.25
4HAbCecil Fielder	.25
6HA Albert Belle	.50
7HA David Justice	.40
8HA Mike Piazza	1.50

1995 Collector's Choice

Issued in a single series, Upper Deck's base-brand baseball series features a number of subsets within the main body of the issue, as well as several insert sets. Basic cards feature large photos on front and back, with the back having full major league stats. The set opens with a 27-card Rookie Class subset featuring front photos on which the background has been rendered in hot pink tones. Backs have a lime-green box with a scouting report on the player and a box featuring 1994 minor and major league stats. The next 18 cards are Future Foundation cards which have the prospects pictured with a posterized background on front, with backs similar to the Rookie Class cards. Career finale cards of five retired superstars follow, then a run of Best of the '90s cards honoring record-setting achievements, followed by cards depicting major award winners of the previous season. Each of the last three named subsets features borderless color photos on front, with backs similar to the regular cards. Immediately preceding the regular cards, which are arranged in team-set order, is a five-card What's the Call? subset featuring cartoon representations of the players. A set of five checklist cards marking career highlights ends the set.

		MT
Complete Set (530):		15.00
Unopened Factory Set (545):		20.00
Common Player:		.05
Pack (12):		1.00
Wax Box (36):		20.00
1	Charles Johnson (Rookie Class)	.05
2	Scott Ruffcorn (Rookie Class)	.05
3	Ray Durham (Rookie Class)	.05
4	Armando Benitez (Rookie Class)	.05
5	Alex Rodriguez (Rookie Class)	2.00
6	Julian Tavarez (Rookie Class)	.05
7	Chad Ogea (Rookie Class)	.05
8	Quilvio Veras (Rookie Class)	.05
9	Phil Nevin (Rookie Class)	.05
10	Michael Tucker (Rookie Class)	.05
11	Mark Thompson (Rookie Class)	.05
12	Rod Henderson (Rookie Class)	.05
13	Andrew Lorraine (Rookie Class)	.05
14	Joe Randa (Rookie Class)	.05
15	Derek Jeter (Rookie Class)	1.00
16	Tony Clark (Rookie Class)	.05
17	Juan Castillo (Rookie Class)	.05
18	Mark Acre (Rookie Class)	.05
19	Orlando Miller (Rookie Class)	.05
20	Paul Wilson (Rookie Class)	.05
21	John Mabry (Rookie Class)	.05
22	Garey Ingram (Rookie Class)	.05
23	*Garret Anderson* (Rookie Class)	.15
24	Dave Stevens (Rookie Class)	.05
25	Dustin Hermanson (Rookie Class)	.10
26	Paul Shuey (Rookie Class)	.05
27	J.R. Phillips (Rookie Class)	.05
28	Ruben Rivera (Future Foundation)	.05
29	Nomar Garciaparra (Future Foundation)	1.50
30	John Wasdin (Future Foundation)	.05
31	Jim Pittsley (Future Foundation)	.05
32	*Scott Elarton* (Future Foundation)	.20
33	*Raul Casanova* (Future Foundation)	.20
34	Todd Greene (Future Foundation)	.05
35	Bill Pulsipher (Future Foundation)	.05
36	Trey Beamon (Future Foundation)	.05
37	Curtis Goodwin (Future Foundation)	.05
38	Doug Million (Future Foundation)	.05
39	*Karim Garcia* (Future Foundation)	1.00
40	Ben Grieve (Future Foundation)	.30
41	Mark Farris (Future Foundation)	.10
42	*Juan Acevedo* (Future Foundation)	.05
43	C.J. Nitkowski (Future Foundation)	.05
44	*Travis Miller* (Future Foundation)	.15
45	Reid Ryan (Future Foundation)	.10
46	Nolan Ryan	2.00
47	Robin Yount	.50
48	Ryne Sandberg	.50
49	George Brett	.50
50	Mike Schmidt	.50
51	Cecil Fielder (Best of the 90's)	.05
52	Nolan Ryan (Best of the 90's)	.75
53	Rickey Henderson (Best of the 90's)	.10
54	George Brett, Robin Yount, Dave Winfield (Best of the 90's)	.25
55	Sid Bream (Best of the 90's)	.05
56	Carlos Baerga (Best of the 90's)	.05
57	Lee Smith (Best of the 90's)	.05
58	Mark Whiten (Best of the 90's)	.05
59	Joe Carter (Best of the 90's)	.05
60	Barry Bonds (Best of the 90's)	.45
61	Tony Gwynn (Best of the 90's)	.40
62	Ken Griffey Jr. (Best of the 90's)	.75
63	Greg Maddux (Best of the 90's)	.40
64	Frank Thomas (Best of the 90's)	.50
65	Dennis Martinez, Kenny Rogers (Best of the 90's)	.05
66	David Cone (Cy Young)	.05
67	Greg Maddux (Cy Young)	.50
68	Jimmy Key (Most Victories)	.05
69	Fred McGriff (All-Star MVP)	.05
70	Ken Griffey Jr. (HR Champ)	1.50
71	Matt Williams (HR Champ)	.10
72	Paul O'Neill (Batting Title)	.05
73	Tony Gwynn (Batting Title)	.40
74	Randy Johnson (Ks Leader)	.20
75	Frank Thomas (MVP)	.50
76	Jeff Bagwell (MVP)	.40
77	Kirby Puckett (RBI leader)	.50
78	Bob Hamelin (ROY)	.05
79	Raul Mondesi (ROY)	.15
80	Mike Piazza (All-Star)	1.00
81	Kenny Lofton (SB Leader)	.05
82	Barry Bonds (Gold Glove)	.50
83	Albert Belle (All-Star)	.20
84	Juan Gonzalez (HR Champ)	.40
85	Cal Ripken Jr. (2,000 Straight Games)	2.00
86	Barry Bonds (What's the Call?)	.50
87	Mike Piazza (What's the Call?)	.50
88	Ken Griffey Jr. (What's the Call?)	.50
89	Frank Thomas (What's the Call?)	.50
90	Juan Gonzalez (What's the Call?)	.15
91	Jorge Fabregas	.05
92	J.T. Snow	.05
93	Spike Owen	.05
94	Eduardo Perez	.05
95	Bo Jackson	.10
96	Damion Easley	.05
97	Gary DiSarcina	.05
98	Jim Edmonds	.05
99	Chad Curtis	.05
100	Tim Salmon	.10
101	Chili Davis	.05
102	Chuck Finley	.05
103	Mark Langston	.05
104	Brian Anderson	.05
105	Lee Smith	.05
106	Phil Leftwich	.05
107	Chris Donnels	.05
108	John Hudek	.05
109	Craig Biggio	.10
110	Luis Gonzalez	.25
111	Brian L. Hunter	.05
112	James Mouton	.05
113	Scott Servais	.05
114	Tony Eusebio	.05
115	Derek Bell	.05
116	Doug Drabek	.05
117	Shane Reynolds	.05
118	Darryl Kile	.05
119	Greg Swindell	.05
120	Phil Plantier	.05
121	Todd Jones	.05
122	Steve Ontiveros	.05
123	Bobby Witt	.05
124	Brent Gates	.05
125	Rickey Henderson	.35
126	Scott Brosius	.05
127	Mike Bordick	.05
128	Fausto Cruz	.05
129	Stan Javier	.05

No.	Player	Price
130	Mark McGwire	2.00
131	Geronimo Berroa	.05
132	Terry Steinbach	.05
133	Steve Karsay	.05
134	Dennis Eckersley	.05
135	Ruben Sierra	.05
136	Ron Darling	.05
137	Todd Van Poppel	.05
138	Alex Gonzalez	.10
139	John Olerud	.05
140	Roberto Alomar	.30
141	Darren Hall	.05
142	Ed Sprague	.05
143	Devon White	.05
144	Shawn Green	.10
145	Paul Molitor	.35
146	Pat Borders	.05
147	Carlos Delgado	.15
148	Juan Guzman	.05
149	Pat Hentgen	.05
150	Joe Carter	.05
151	Dave Stewart	.05
152	Todd Stottlemyre	.05
153	Dick Schofield	.05
154	Chipper Jones	1.00
155	Ryan Klesko	.05
156	Dave Justice	.25
157	Mike Kelly	.05
158	Roberto Kelly	.05
159	Tony Tarasco	.05
160	Javier Lopez	.05
161	Steve Avery	.05
162	Greg McMichael	.05
163	Kent Mercker	.05
164	Mark Lemke	.05
165	Tom Glavine	.10
166	Jose Oliva	.05
167	John Smoltz	.10
168	Jeff Blauser	.05
169	Troy O'Leary	.05
170	Greg Vaughn	.05
171	Jody Reed	.05
172	Kevin Seitzer	.05
173	Jeff Cirillo	.05
174	B.J. Surhoff	.05
175	Cal Eldred	.05
176	Jose Valentin	.05
177	Turner Ward	.05
178	Darryl Hamilton	.05
179	Pat Listach	.05
180	Matt Mieske	.05
181	Brian Harper	.05
182	Dave Nilsson	.05
183	Mike Fetters	.05
184	John Jaha	.05
185	Ricky Bones	.05
186	Geronimo Pena	.05
187	Bob Tewksbury	.05
188	Todd Zeile	.05
189	Danny Jackson	.05
190	Ray Lankford	.05
191	Bernard Gilkey	.05
192	Brian Jordan	.05
193	Tom Pagnozzi	.05
194	Rick Sutcliffe	.05
195	Mark Whiten	.05
196	Tom Henke	.05
197	Rene Arocha	.05
198	Allen Watson	.05
199	Mike Perez	.05
200	Ozzie Smith	.50
201	Anthony Young	.05
202	Rey Sanchez	.05
203	Steve Buechele	.05
204	Shawon Dunston	.05
205	Mark Grace	.15
206	Glenallen Hill	.05
207	Eddie Zambrano	.05
208	Rick Wilkins	.05
209	Derrick May	.05
210	Sammy Sosa	.75
211	Kevin Roberson	.05
212	Steve Trachsel	.05
213	Willie Banks	.05
214	Kevin Foster	.05
215	Randy Myers	.05
216	Mike Morgan	.05
217	Rafael Bournigal	.05
218	Delino DeShields	.05
219	Tim Wallach	.05
220	Eric Karros	.05
221	Jose Offerman	.05
222	Tom Candiotti	.05
223	Ismael Valdes	.05
224	Henry Rodriguez	.05
225	Billy Ashley	.05
226	Darren Dreifort	.05
227	Ramon Martinez	.05
228	Pedro Astacio	.05
229	Orel Hershiser	.05
230	Brett Butler	.05
231	Todd Hollandsworth	.05
232	Chan Ho Park	.20
233	Mike Lansing	.05
234	Sean Berry	.05
235	Rondell White	.15
236	Ken Hill	.05
237	Marquis Grissom	.05
238	Larry Walker	.20
239	John Wetteland	.05
240	Cliff Floyd	.05
241	Joey Eischen	.05
242	Lou Frazier	.05
243	Darrin Fletcher	.05
244	Pedro J. Martinez	.15
245	Wil Cordero	.05
246	Jeff Fassero	.05
247	Butch Henry	.05
248	Mel Rojas	.05
249	Kirk Rueter	.05
250	Moises Alou	.15
251	Rod Beck	.05
252	John Patterson	.05
253	Robby Thompson	.05
254	Royce Clayton	.05
255	William Van Landingham	.05
256	Darren Lewis	.05
257	Kirt Manwaring	.05
258	Mark Portugal	.05
259	Bill Swift	.05
260	Rikkert Faneyte	.05
261	Mike Jackson	.05
262	Todd Benzinger	.05
263	Bud Black	.05
264	Salomon Torres	.05
265	Eddie Murray	.35
266	Mark Clark	.05
267	Paul Sorrento	.05
268	Jim Thome	.05
269	Omar Vizquel	.05
270	Carlos Baerga	.05
271	Jeff Russell	.05
272	Herbert Perry	.05
273	Sandy Alomar Jr.	.05
274	Dennis Martinez	.05
275	Manny Ramirez	.40
276	Wayne Kirby	.05
277	Charles Nagy	.05
278	Albie Lopez	.05
279	Jeromy Burnitz	.05
280	Dave Winfield	.50
281	Tim Davis	.05
282	Marc Newfield	.05
283	Tino Martinez	.05
284	Mike Blowers	.05
285	Goose Gossage	.05
286	Luis Sojo	.05
287	Edgar Martinez	.05
288	Rich Amaral	.05
289	Felix Fermin	.05
290	Jay Buhner	.05
291	Dan Wilson	.05
292	Bobby Ayala	.05
293	Dave Fleming	.05
294	Greg Pirkl	.05
295	Reggie Jefferson	.05
296	Greg Hibbard	.05
297	Yorkis Perez	.05
298	Kurt Miller	.05
299	Chuck Carr	.05
300	Gary Sheffield	.15
301	Jerry Browne	.05
302	Dave Magadan	.05
303	Kurt Abbott	.05
304	Pat Rapp	.05
305	Jeff Conine	.05
306	Benito Santiago	.05
307	Dave Weathers	.05
308	Robb Nen	.05
309	Chris Hammond	.05
310	Bryan Harvey	.05
311	Charlie Hough	.05
312	Greg Colbrunn	.05
313	David Segui	.05
314	Rico Brogna	.05
315	Jeff Kent	.05
316	Jose Vizcaino	.05
317	Jim Lindeman	.05
318	Carl Everett	.10
319	Ryan Thompson	.05
320	Bobby Bonilla	.05
321	Joe Orsulak	.05
322	Pete Harnisch	.05
323	Doug Linton	.05
324	Todd Hundley	.05
325	Bret Saberhagen	.05
326	Kelly Stinnett	.05
327	Jason Jacome	.05
328	Bobby Jones	.05
329	John Franco	.05
330	Rafael Palmeiro	.10
331	Chris Hoiles	.05
332	Leo Gomez	.05
333	Chris Sabo	.05
334	Brady Anderson	.05
335	Jeffrey Hammonds	.05
336	Dwight Smith	.05
337	Jack Voigt	.05
338	Harold Baines	.05
339	Ben McDonald	.05
340	Mike Mussina	.30
341	Bret Barberie	.05
342	Jamie Moyer	.05
343	Mike Oquist	.05
344	Sid Fernandez	.05
345	Eddie Williams	.05
346	Joey Hamilton	.05
347	Brian Williams	.05
348	Luis Lopez	.05
349	Steve Finley	.05
350	Andy Benes	.05
351	Andujar Cedeno	.05
352	Bip Roberts	.05
353	Ray McDavid	.05
354	Ken Caminiti	.05
355	Trevor Hoffman	.05
356	Mel Nieves	.05
357	Brad Ausmus	.05
358	Andy Ashby	.05
359	Scott Sanders	.05
360	Gregg Jefferies	.05
361	Mariano Duncan	.05
362	Dave Hollins	.05
363	Kevin Stocker	.05
364	Fernando Valenzuela	.05
365	Lenny Dykstra	.05
366	Jim Eisenreich	.05
367	Ricky Bottalico	.05
368	Doug Jones	.05
369	Ricky Jordan	.05
370	Darren Daulton	.05
371	Mike Lieberthal	.05
372	Bobby Munoz	.05
373	John Kruk	.05
374	Curt Schilling	.15
375	Orlando Merced	.05
376	Carlos Garcia	.05
377	Lance Parrish	.05
378	Steve Cooke	.05
379	Jeff King	.05
380	Jay Bell	.05
381	Al Martin	.05
382	Paul Wagner	.05
383	Rick White	.05
384	Midre Cummings	.05
385	Jon Lieber	.05
386	Dave Clark	.05
387	Don Slaught	.05
388	Denny Neagle	.05
389	Zane Smith	.05
390	Andy Van Slyke	.05
391	Ivan Rodriguez	.30
392	David Hulse	.05
393	John Burkett	.05
394	Kevin Brown	.15
395	Dean Palmer	.05
396	Otis Nixon	.05
397	Rick Helling	.05
398	Kenny Rogers	.05
399	Darren Oliver	.05
400	Will Clark	.15
401	Jeff Frye	.05
402	Kevin Gross	.05
403	John Dettmer	.05
404	Manny Lee	.05
405	Rusty Greer	.05
406	Aaron Sele	.05
407	Carlos Rodriguez	.05
408	Scott Cooper	.05
409	John Valentin	.05
410	Roger Clemens	.50
411	Mike Greenwell	.05
412	Tim Vanegmond	.05
413	Tom Brunansky	.05
414	Steve Farr	.05
415	Jose Canseco	.20
416	Joe Hesketh	.05
417	Ken Ryan	.05
418	Tim Naehring	.05
419	Frank Viola	.05
420	Andre Dawson	.15
421	Mo Vaughn	.15
422	Jeff Brantley	.05
423	Pete Schourek	.05
424	Hal Morris	.05
425	Deion Sanders	.10
426	Brian L. Hunter	.05
427	Bret Boone	.10
428	Willie Greene	.05
429	Ron Gant	.05
430	Barry Larkin	.10
431	Reggie Sanders	.05
432	Eddie Taubensee	.05
433	Jack Morris	.05
434	Jose Rijo	.05
435	Johnny Ruffin	.05
436	John Smiley	.05
437	John Roper	.05
438	David Nied	.05
439	Roberto Mejia	.05
440	Andres Galarraga	.05
441	Mike Kingery	.05
442	Curt Leskanic	.05
443	Walt Weiss	.05
444	Marvin Freeman	.05
445	Charlie Hayes	.05
446	Eric Young	.05
447	Ellis Burks	.05
448	Joe Girardi	.05
449	Lance Painter	.05
450	Dante Bichette	.05
451	Bruce Ruffin	.05
452	Jeff Granger	.05
453	Wally Joyner	.05
454	Jose Lind	.05
455	Jeff Montgomery	.05
456	Gary Gaetti	.05
457	Greg Gagne	.05
458	Vince Coleman	.05
459	Mike Macfarlane	.05
460	Brian McRae	.05
461	Tom Gordon	.05
462	Kevin Appier	.05
463	Billy Brewer	.05
464	Mark Gubicza	.05
465	Travis Fryman	.05
466	Danny Bautista	.05
467	Sean Bergman	.05
468	Mike Henneman	.05
469	Mike Moore	.05
470	Cecil Fielder	.05
471	Alan Trammell	.05
472	Kirk Gibson	.05
473	Tony Phillips	.05
474	Mickey Tettleton	.05
475	Lou Whitaker	.05
476	Chris Gomez	.05
477	John Doherty	.05
478	Greg Gohr	.05
479	Bill Gullickson	.05
480	Rick Aguilera	.05
481	Matt Walbeck	.05
482	Kevin Tapani	.05
483	Scott Erickson	.05
484	Steve Dunn	.05
485	David McCarty	.05
486	Scott Leius	.05
487	Pat Meares	.05
488	Jeff Reboulet	.05
489	Pedro Munoz	.05
490	Chuck Knoblauch	.05
491	Rich Becker	.05
492	Alex Cole	.05
493	Pat Mahomes	.05
494	Ozzie Guillen	.05
495	Tim Raines	.05
496	Kirk McCaskill	.05
497	Olmedo Saenz	.05
498	Scott Sanderson	.05
499	Lance Johnson	.05
500	Michael Jordan	2.00
501	Warren Newson	.05
502	Ron Karkovice	.05
503	Wilson Alvarez	.05
504	Jason Bere	.05
505	Robin Ventura	.05
506	Alex Fernandez	.05
507	Roberto Hernandez	.05
508	Norberto Martin	.05
509	Bob Wickman	.05
510	Don Mattingly	.60
511	Melido Perez	.05
512	Pat Kelly	.05

513	Randy Velarde	.05
514	Tony Fernandez	.05
515	Jack McDowell	.05
516	Luis Polonia	.05
517	Bernie Williams	.20
518	Danny Tartabull	.05
519	Mike Stanley	.05
520	Wade Boggs	.40
521	Jim Leyritz	.05
522	Steve Howe	.05
523	Scott Kamieniecki	.05
524	Russ Davis	.05
525	Jim Abbott	.05
526	Checklist 1-106 (Eddie Murray)	.15
527	Checklist 107-212 (Alex Rodriguez)	.30
528	Checklist 213-318 (Jeff Bagwell)	.15
529	Checklist 319-424 (Joe Carter)	.05
530	Checklist 425-530 (Fred McGriff)	.05
---	National Packtime offer card	.05

1995 Collector's Choice Gold Signature

The top-of-the-line chase card in 1995 Collector's Choice is the Gold Signature parallel set. Each of the 530 cards in the set was created in a special gold version that was found on average only one per box of foil packs. Other than the addition of a gold-foil facsimile autograph on front, the cards are identical to regular-issue Collector's Choice.

	MT
Common Player:	1.00
Stars:	8X

(See 1995 Collector's Choice for checklist and base card values.)

1995 Collector's Choice Silver Signature

A silver-foil facsimile autograph added to the card front is the only difference between these chase cards and regular-issue Collector's Choice cards. The silver-signature inserts are found one per pack in regular foil packs, and two per pack in retail jumbo packs.

	MT
Common Player:	.10
Veteran Stars:	1.5X

(See 1995 Collector's Choice for checklist and base card values.)

1995 Collector's Choice Crash Winners

These 20-card sets were awarded to collectors who redeemed "You Crash the Game" winners cards. A silver-foil enhanced set was sent to winners with silver redemption cards, a gold version was sent to gold winners. A $3 redemption fee was required. Fronts are similar to the game cards, except for the foil printing down the left side in the place of the game date. Instead of redemption rules on the back of award cards there are career highlights at left and a panel at right with the names of the players in the set.

		MT
Complete Set, Silver (20):		12.50
Complete Set, Gold (20):		40.00
Common Player, Silver:		.40
Common Player, Gold:		1.50
	SILVER SET	
CR1	Jeff Bagwell	1.00
CR2	Albert Belle	.50
CR3	Barry Bonds	2.00
CR4	Jose Canseco	.75
CR5	Joe Carter	.40
CR6	Cecil Fielder	.40
CR7	Juan Gonzalez	1.00
CR8	Ken Griffey Jr.	3.00
CR9	Bob Hamelin	.40
CR10	Dave Justice	.40
CR11	Ryan Klesko	.40
CR12	Fred McGriff	.40
CR13	Mark McGwire	3.00
CR14	Raul Mondesi	.50
CR15	Mike Piazza	2.00
CR16	Manny Ramirez	.75
CR17	Alex Rodriguez	2.00
CR18	Gary Sheffield	.50
CR19	Frank Thomas	1.25
CR20	Matt Williams	.50
	GOLD SET	
CR1	Jeff Bagwell	3.00
CR2	Albert Belle	1.50
CR3	Barry Bonds	3.50
CR4	Jose Canseco	2.50
CR5	Joe Carter	1.50
CR6	Cecil Fielder	1.50
CR7	Juan Gonzalez	5.00
CR8	Ken Griffey Jr.	7.50
CR9	Bob Hamelin	1.50
CR10	Dave Justice	1.50
CR11	Ryan Klesko	1.50
CR12	Fred McGriff	1.50
CR13	Mark McGwire	8.00
CR14	Raul Mondesi	2.00
CR15	Mike Piazza	4.00
CR16	Manny Ramirez	2.50
CR17	Alex Rodriguez	4.00
CR18	Gary Sheffield	2.00
CR19	Frank Thomas	3.00
CR20	Matt Williams	1.50

1995 Collector's Choice Crash the Game

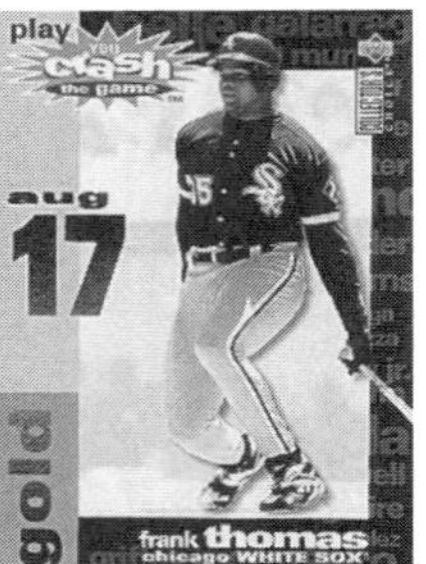

These insert cards gave collectors a reason to follow box scores around the major leagues between June 18-Oct. 1. Each of 20 noted home run hitters can be found with three different dates foil-stamped on the card front. If the player hit a home run on that day, the card could be redeemed for a set of 20 special prize cards. Stated odds of finding a You Crash the Game card were one in five packs. Most of the inserts are silver-foil enhanced, with about one in eight being found with gold foil. Winning cards are much scarcer than the others since they had to be mailed in for redemption.

		MT
Complete Set, Silver (20):		5.00
Common Player, Silver:		.15
Complete Set, Gold (20):		12.00
Common Player, Gold:		.35
	SILVER SET	
CG1	Jeff Bagwell (July 30)	.25
CG1	Jeff Bagwell (Aug. 13)	.25
CG1	Jeff Bagwell (Sept. 28)	.25
CG2	Albert Belle (June 18)	.15
CG2	Albert Belle (Aug. 26)	.15
CG2	Albert Belle (Sept. 20)	.15
CG3	Barry Bonds (June 28)	.50
CG3	Barry Bonds (July 9)	.50
CG3	Barry Bonds (Sept. 6)	.50
CG4	Jose Canseco (June 30) (winner)	1.00
CG4	Jose Canseco (July 30) (winner)	1.00
CG4	Jose Canseco (Sept. 3)	.35
CG5	Joe Carter (July 14)	.15
CG5	Joe Carter (Aug. 9)	.15
CG5	Joe Carter (Sept. 23)	.15
CG6	Cecil Fielder (July 4)	.15
CG6	Cecil Fielder (Aug. 2)	.15
CG6	Cecil Fielder (Oct. 1)	.15
CG7	Juan Gonzalez (June 29)	.40
CG7	Juan Gonzalez (Aug. 13)	.40
CG7	Juan Gonzalez (Sept. 3) (winner)	1.25
CG8	Ken Griffey Jr. (July 2)	.75
CG8	Ken Griffey Jr. (Aug. 24) (winner)	3.00
CG8	Ken Griffey Jr. (Sept. 15)	.75
CG9	Bob Hamelin (July 23)	.15
CG9	Bob Hamelin (Aug. 1)	.15
CG9	Bob Hamelin (Sept. 29)	.15
CG10	David Justice (June 24)	.15
CG10	David Justice (July 25)	.15
CG10	David Justice (Sept. 17)	.15
CG11	Ryan Klesko (July 13)	.15
CG11	Ryan Klesko (Aug. 20)	.15
CG11	Ryan Klesko (Sept. 10)	.15
CG12	Fred McGriff (Aug. 25)	.15
CG12	Fred McGriff (Sept. 8)	.15
CG12	Fred McGriff (Sept. 24)	.15
CG13	Mark McGwire (July 23)	.75
CG13	Mark McGwire (Aug. 3) (winner)	3.00
CG13	Mark McGwire (Sept. 27)	.75
CG14	Raul Mondesi (July 27) (winner)	1.00
CG14	Raul Mondesi (Aug. 13)	.15
CG14	Raul Mondesi (Sept. 15) (winner)	1.00
CG15	Mike Piazza (July 23) (winner)	2.00
CG15	Mike Piazza (Aug. 27) (winner)	2.00
CG15	Mike Piazza (Sept. 19)	.50
CG16	Manny Ramirez (June 21)	.25
CG16	Manny Ramirez (Aug. 13)	.25
CG16	Manny Ramirez (Sept. 26)	.25
CG17	Alex Rodriguez (Sept. 10)	.50
CG17	Alex Rodriguez (Sept. 18)	.50
CG17	Alex Rodriguez (Sept. 24)	.50
CG18	Gary Sheffield (July 5)	.15
CG18	Gary Sheffield (Aug. 13)	.15
CG18	Gary Sheffield (Sept. 4) (winner)	1.00
CG19	Frank Thomas (July 26)	.50
CG19	Frank Thomas (Aug. 17)	.50
CG19	Frank Thomas (Sept. 23)	.50
CG20	Matt Williams (July 29)	.15

CG20Matt Williams (Aug. 12)	.15
CG20Matt Williams (Sept. 19)	.15
GOLD SET	
CG1 Jeff Bagwell (July 30)	.75
CG1 Jeff Bagwell (Aug. 13)	.75
CG1 Jeff Bagwell (Sept. 28)	.75
CG2 Albert Belle (June 18)	.45
CG2 Albert Belle (Aug. 26)	.45
CG2 Albert Belle (Sept. 20)	.45
CG3 Barry Bonds (June 28)	1.00
CG3 Barry Bonds (July 9)	1.00
CG3 Barry Bonds (Sept. 6)	1.00
CG4 Jose Canseco (June 30) (winner)	2.00
CG4 Jose Canseco (July 30) (winner)	2.00
CG4 Jose Canseco (Sept. 3)	.75
CG5 Joe Carter (July 14)	.35
CG5 Joe Carter (Aug. 9)	.35
CG5 Joe Carter (Sept. 23)	.35
CG6 Cecil Fielder (July 4)	.35
CG6 Cecil Fielder (Aug. 2)	.35
CG6 Cecil Fielder (Oct. 1)	.35
CG7 Juan Gonzalez (June 29)	.75
CG7 Juan Gonzalez (Aug. 13)	.75
CG7 Juan Gonzalez (Sept. 3) (winner)	2.50
CG8 Ken Griffey Jr. (July 2)	2.00
CG8 Ken Griffey Jr. (Aug. 24) (winner)	4.00
CG8 Ken Griffey Jr. (Sept. 15)	2.00
CG9 Bob Hamelin (July 23)	.35
CG9 Bob Hamelin (Aug. 1)	.35
CG9 Bob Hamelin (Sept. 29)	.35
CG10David Justice (June 24)	.35
CG10David Justice (July 25)	.35
CG10David Justice (Sept. 17)	.35
CG11Ryan Klesko (July 13)	.35
CG11Ryan Klesko (Aug. 20)	.35
CG11Ryan Klesko (Sept. 10)	.35
CG12Fred McGriff (Aug. 25)	.35
CG12Fred McGriff (Sept. 8)	.35
CG12Fred McGriff (Sept. 24)	.35
CG13Mark McGwire (July 23)	2.00
CG13Mark McGwire (Aug. 3) (winner)	4.00
CG13Mark McGwire (Sept. 27)	2.00
CG14Raul Mondesi (July 27) (winner)	1.25
CG14Raul Mondesi (Aug. 13)	.45
CG14Raul Mondesi (Sept. 15) (winner)	1.25
CG15Mike Piazza (July 23) (winner)	3.00
CG15Mike Piazza (Aug. 27) (winner)	3.00
CG15Mike Piazza (Sept. 19)	1.00
CG16Manny Ramirez (June 21)	.50
CG16Manny Ramirez (Aug. 13)	.50
CG16Manny Ramirez (Sept. 26)	.50
CG17Alex Rodriguez (Sept. 10)	1.00
CG17Alex Rodriguez (Sept. 18)	1.00
CG17Alex Rodriguez (Sept. 24)	1.00
CG18Gary Sheffield (July 5)	.40
CG18Gary Sheffield (Aug. 13)	.40
CG18Gary Sheffield (Sept. 4) (winner)	1.50
CG19Frank Thomas (July 26)	.75
CG19Frank Thomas (Aug. 17)	.75
CG19Frank Thomas (Sept. 23)	.75
CG20Matt Williams (July 29)	.45
CG20Matt Williams (Aug. 12)	.45
CG20Matt Williams (Sept. 19)	.45

1995 Collector's Choice Redemption Cards

These update cards were available only via a mail-in offer involving trade cards found in foil packs. Each trade card was redeemable for a specific 11-card set of players shown in their new uniforms as a result of rookie call-ups, trades and free agent signings. The cards are in the same format as the regular 1995 Collector's Choice issue. The update redemption cards are numbered by team nickname from Angels through Yankees, the numbers running contiguously from the body of the CC set.

		MT
Complete Set (55):		4.00
Common Player:		.10
531	Tony Phillips	.10
532	Dave Magadan	.10
533	Mike Gallego	.10
534	Dave Stewart	.10
535	Todd Stottlemyre	.10
536	David Cone	.15
537	Marquis Grissom	.10
538	Derrick May	.10
539	Joe Oliver	.10
540	Scott Cooper	.10
541	Ken Hill	.10
542	Howard Johnson	.10
543	Brian McRae	.10
544	Jaime Navarro	.10
545	Ozzie Timmons	.10
546	Roberto Kelly	.10
547	Hideo Nomo	2.00
548	Shane Andrews	.25
549	Mark Grudzielanek	.15
550	Carlos Perez	.10
551	Henry Rodriguez	.10
552	Tony Tarasco	.10
553	Glenallen Hill	.10
554	Terry Mulholland	.10
555	Orel Hershiser	.15
556	Darren Bragg	.10
557	John Burkett	.10
558	Bobby Witt	.10
559	Terry Pendleton	.10
560	Andre Dawson	.50
561	Brett Butler	.10
562	Kevin Brown	.50
563	Doug Jones	.10
564	Andy Van Slyke	.10
565	Jody Reed	.10
566	Fernando Valenzuela	.10
567	Charlie Hayes	.10
568	Benji Gil	.10
569	Mark McLemore	.10
570	Mickey Tettleton	.10
571	Bob Tewksbury	.10
572	Rheal Cormier	.10
573	Vaughn Eshelman	.10
574	Mike Macfarlane	.10
575	Mark Whiten	.10
576	Benito Santiago	.10
577	Jason Bates	.10
578	Bill Swift	.10
579	Larry Walker	.25
580	Chad Curtis	.20
581	Bobby Higginson	.25
582	Marty Cordova	.25
583	Mike Devereaux	.10
584	John Kruk	.10
585	John Wetteland	.10

1995 Collector's Choice Trade Cards

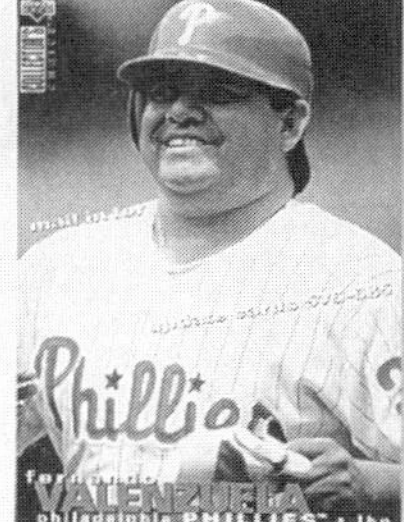

A series of five mail-in redemption cards was included as inserts into UD Collector's Choice, at the rate of approximately one per 11 packs. The cards could be sent in with $2 to receive 11 Collector's Choice Update cards, as specified on the front of the card. The trade offer expired on Feb. 1, 1996. Cards are numbered with the "TC" prefix.

		MT
Complete Set (5):		1.00
Common Player:		.25
1	Larry Walker (#531-541)	.50
2	David Cone (#542-552)	.25
3	Marquis Grissom (#553-563)	.25
4	Terry Pendleton (#564-574)	.25
5	Fernando Valenzuela (#575-585)	.25

1995 Collector's Choice/SE

The first Upper Deck baseball card issue for 1995 was this 265-card set which uses blue borders and a blue foil "Special Edition" trapezoidal logo to impart a premium look. The set opens with a Rookie Class subset of 25 cards on which the background has been rendered in orange hues. A series of six Record Pace cards, horizontal with blue and yellow backgrounds, immediately precedes the regular cards. Base cards in the set are arranged in team-alpha order. Front and back have large color photos, while backs offer complete major league stats. Interspersed within the teams are special cards with borderless front designs honoring players who won significant awards in the 1994 season. Another subset, Stat Leaders, pictures various players in a silver dollar-sized circle at the center of the card and lists the 1994 leaders in that category on the back. A dozen-card Fantasy Team subset near the end of the set lists on back the top-rated players at each position, picturing one of them on front, with a giant blue baseball. The set closes with five checklists honoring career highlights from the '94 season.

		MT
Complete Set (265):		15.00
Common Player:		.05
Pack (12):		1.25
Wax Box (36):		25.00
1	Alex Rodriguez	2.00
2	Derek Jeter	1.50
3	Dustin Hermanson	.05
4	Bill Pulsipher	.05
5	Terrell Wade	.05
6	Darren Dreifort	.05
7	LaTroy Hawkins	.05
8	Alex Ochoa	.05
9	Paul Wilson	.05
10	Ernie Young	.05
11	Alan Benes	.05
12	Garret Anderson	.05
13	Armando Benitez	.05
14	Robert Perez	.05
15	Herbert Perry	.05
16	Jose Silva	.05
17	Orlando Miller	.05
18	Russ Davis	.05
19	Jason Isringhausen	.05
20	Ray McDavid	.05
21	Duane Singleton	.05
22	Paul Shuey	.05
23	Steve Dunn	.05
24	Mike Lieberthal	.05
25	Chan Ho Park	.15

No.	Player	MT
26	Ken Griffey Jr. (Record Pace)	.75
27	Tony Gwynn (Record Pace)	.35
28	Chuck Knoblauch (Record Pace)	.05
29	Frank Thomas (Record Pace)	.50
30	Matt Williams (Record Pace)	.05
31	Chili Davis	.05
32	Chad Curtis	.05
33	Brian Anderson	.05
34	Chuck Finley	.05
35	Tim Salmon	.15
36	Bo Jackson	.10
37	Doug Drabek	.05
38	Craig Biggio	.10
39	Ken Caminiti	.05
40	Jeff Bagwell	.75
41	Darryl Kile	.05
42	John Hudek	.05
43	Brian L. Hunter	.05
44	Dennis Eckersley	.05
45	Mark McGwire	2.50
46	Brent Gates	.05
47	Steve Karsay	.05
48	Rickey Henderson	.45
49	Terry Steinbach	.05
50	Ruben Sierra	.05
51	Roberto Alomar	.50
52	Carlos Delgado	.15
53	Alex Gonzalez	.10
54	Joe Carter	.05
55	Paul Molitor	.50
56	Juan Guzman	.05
57	John Olerud	.05
58	Shawn Green	.15
59	Tom Glavine	.15
60	Greg Maddux	1.00
61	Roberto Kelly	.05
62	Ryan Klesko	.05
63	Javier Lopez	.05
64	Jose Oliva	.05
65	Fred McGriff	.05
66	Steve Avery	.05
67	Dave Justice	.25
68	Ricky Bones	.05
69	Cal Eldred	.05
70	Greg Vaughn	.05
71	Dave Nilsson	.05
72	Jose Valentin	.05
73	Matt Mieske	.05
74	Todd Zeile	.05
75	Ozzie Smith	1.00
76	Bernard Gilkey	.05
77	Ray Lankford	.05
78	Bob Tewksbury	.05
79	Mark Whiten	.05
80	Gregg Jefferies	.05
81	Randy Myers	.05
82	Shawon Dunston	.05
83	Mark Grace	.20
84	Derrick May	.05
85	Sammy Sosa	1.25
86	Steve Trachsel	.05
87	Brett Butler	.05
88	Delino DeShields	.05
89	Orel Hershiser	.05
90	Mike Piazza	1.50
91	Todd Hollandsworth	.05
92	Eric Karros	.05
93	Ramon Martinez	.05
94	Tim Wallach	.05
95	Raul Mondesi	.15
96	Larry Walker	.20
97	Wil Cordero	.05
98	Marquis Grissom	.05
99	Ken Hill	.05
100	Cliff Floyd	.05
101	Pedro J. Martinez	.25
102	John Wetteland	.05
103	Rondell White	.20
104	Moises Alou	.10
105	Barry Bonds	1.25
106	Darren Lewis	.05
107	Mark Portugal	.05
108	Matt Williams	.15
109	William VanLandingham	.05
110	Bill Swift	.05
111	Robby Thompson	.05
112	Rod Beck	.05
113	Darryl Strawberry	.05
114	Jim Thome	.05
115	Dave Winfield	.50
116	Eddie Murray	.35
117	Manny Ramirez	.75
118	Carlos Baerga	.05
119	Kenny Lofton	.05
120	Albert Belle	.20
121	Mark Clark	.05
122	Dennis Martinez	.05
123	Randy Johnson	.50
124	Jay Buhner	.05
125	Ken Griffey Jr.	2.00
125a	Ken Griffey Jr. (overprinted "For Promotional Use Only")	2.00
126	Rich Gossage	.05
127	Tino Martinez	.05
128	Reggie Jefferson	.05
129	Edgar Martinez	.05
130	Gary Sheffield	.15
131	Pat Rapp	.05
132	Bret Barberie	.05
133	Chuck Carr	.05
134	Jeff Conine	.05
135	Charles Johnson	.05
136	Benito Santiago	.05
137	Matt Williams (Stat Leaders)	.05
138	Jeff Bagwell (Stat Leaders)	.35
139	Kenny Lofton (Stat Leaders)	.05
140	Tony Gwynn (Stat Leaders)	.35
141	Jimmy Key (Stat Leaders)	.05
142	Greg Maddux (Stat Leaders)	.40
143	Randy Johnson (Stat Leaders)	.20
144	Lee Smith (Stat Leaders)	.05
145	Bobby Bonilla	.05
146	Jason Jacome	.05
147	Jeff Kent	.05
148	Ryan Thompson	.05
149	Bobby Jones	.05
150	Bret Saberhagen	.05
151	John Franco	.05
152	Lee Smith	.05
153	Rafael Palmeiro	.15
154	Brady Anderson	.05
155	Cal Ripken Jr.	2.50
156	Jeffrey Hammonds	.05
157	Mike Mussina	.45
158	Chris Hoiles	.05
159	Ben McDonald	.05
160	Tony Gwynn	1.00
161	Joey Hamilton	.05
162	Andy Benes	.05
163	Trevor Hoffman	.05
164	Phil Plantier	.05
165	Derek Bell	.05
166	Bip Roberts	.05
167	Eddie Williams	.05
168	Fernando Valenzuela	.05
169	Mariano Duncan	.05
170	Lenny Dykstra	.05
171	Darren Daulton	.05
172	Danny Jackson	.05
173	Bobby Munoz	.05
174	Doug Jones	.05
175	Jay Bell	.05
176	Zane Smith	.05
177	Jon Lieber	.05
178	Carlos Garcia	.05
179	Orlando Merced	.05
180	Andy Van Slyke	.05
181	Rick Helling	.05
182	Rusty Greer	.05
183	Kenny Rogers	.05
184	Will Clark	.15
185	Jose Canseco	.40
186	Juan Gonzalez	.75
187	Dean Palmer	.05
188	Ivan Rodriguez	.50
189	John Valentin	.05
190	Roger Clemens	1.00
191	Aaron Sele	.05
192	Scott Cooper	.05
193	Mike Greenwell	.05
194	Mo Vaughn	.20
195	Andre Dawson	.15
196	Ron Gant	.05
197	Jose Rijo	.05
198	Bret Boone	.10
199	Deion Sanders	.10
200	Barry Larkin	.10
201	Hal Morris	.05
202	Reggie Sanders	.05
203	Kevin Mitchell	.05
204	Marvin Freeman	.05
205	Andres Galarraga	.05
206	Walt Weiss	.05
207	Charlie Hayes	.05
208	David Nied	.05
209	Dante Bichette	.05
210	David Cone	.05
211	Jeff Montgomery	.05
212	Felix Jose	.05
213	Mike Macfarlane	.05
214	Wally Joyner	.05
215	Bob Hamelin	.05
216	Brian McRae	.05
217	Kirk Gibson	.05
218	Lou Whitaker	.05
219	Chris Gomez	.05
220	Cecil Fielder	.05
221	Mickey Tettleton	.05
222	Travis Fryman	.05
223	Tony Phillips	.05
224	Rick Aguilera	.05
225	Scott Erickson	.05
226	Chuck Knoblauch	.05
227	Kent Hrbek	.05
228	Shane Mack	.05
229	Kevin Tapani	.05
230	Kirby Puckett	1.00
231	Julio Franco	.05
232	Jack McDowell	.05
233	Jason Bere	.05
234	Alex Fernandez	.05
235	Frank Thomas	1.25
236	Ozzie Guillen	.05
237	Robin Ventura	.05
238	Michael Jordan	3.00
239	Wilson Alvarez	.05
240	Don Mattingly	1.00
241	Jim Abbott	.05
242	Jim Leyritz	.05
243	Paul O'Neill	.05
244	Melido Perez	.05
245	Wade Boggs	.50
246	Mike Stanley	.05
247	Danny Tartabull	.05
248	Jimmy Key	.05
249	Greg Maddux (Fantasy Team)	.40
250	Randy Johnson (Fantasy Team)	.20
251	Bret Saberhagen (Fantasy Team)	.05
252	John Wetteland (Fantasy Team)	.05
253	Mike Piazza (Fantasy Team)	.50
254	Jeff Bagwell (Fantasy Team)	.30
255	Craig Biggio (Fantasy Team)	.05
256	Matt Williams (Fantasy Team)	.05
257	Wil Cordero (Fantasy Team)	.05
258	Kenny Lofton (Fantasy Team)	.05
259	Barry Bonds (Fantasy Team)	.50
260	Dante Bichette (Fantasy Team)	.05
261	Checklist 1-53 (Ken Griffey Jr.)	.25
262	Checklist 54-106 (Goose Gossage)	.05
263	Checklist 107-159 (Cal Ripken Jr.)	.25
264	Checklist 160-212 (Kenny Rogers)	.05
265	Checklist 213-265 (John Valentin)	.05

1995 Collector's Choice/SE Gold

Each of the cards in the SE issue can be found in a premium chase card version which replaces the blue border and SE logo with gold, and adds a gold-foil facsimile autograph to the front of the card. The gold-version SE inserts are found on average of one per 36 packs.

	MT
Common Player:	1.00
Stars:	10X

(For checklist and base card values, see 1995 Collector's Choice SE.)

1995 Collector's Choice/SE Silver

The cards in this parallel edition feature the addition of a silver-foil facsimile autograph on the card front. Also, the blue SE logo and card borders have been replaced with silver on the chase cards, which are found on average of one per pack.

	MT
Common Player:	.15
Stars:	1.5X

(For checklist and base card values, see 1995 Collector's Choice SE.)

1996 Collector's Choice Promo

To introduce its base-brand set, Upper Deck issued a promotional sample card of Ken Griffey, Jr. Numbered 100 (he's #310 in the issued set), the back is overprinted "For Promotional Use Only".

		MT
100	Ken Griffey Jr.	5.00

1996 Collector's Choice

The third year for Collector's Choice includes 730 cards in two series with packs formatted in retail and hobby versions. The 280 regular player cards are joined by subsets of Rookie Class, International Flavor, Traditional Threads, Fantasy Team, Stat Leaders, Season Highlights, First Class, Arizona Fall League, Awards and Checklists. Packs feature a number of different insert sets including silver and gold signature parallel sets, interactive "You Make the Play" cards, four cards from the cross-brand Cal Ripken Collection and three postseason trade cards redeemable for 10-card sets recalling the League Championships and World Series. An additional 30 cards (#761-790) featuring traded players in their new uniforms was issued only in factory sets.

	MT
Complete Set: (760):	15.00
Complete Factory Set (790):	25.00
Traded Set (366T-395T):	6.00
Common Player:	.05
Series 1 Pack (12):	1.00
Series 1 Wax Box (36):	28.00
Series 2 Pack (14):	1.00
Series 2 Wax Box (40):	30.00

1 Cal Ripken Jr. 2.00
2 Edgar Martinez, Tony Gwynn (1995 Stat Leaders) .05
3 Albert Belle, Dante Bichette (1995 Stat Leaders) .05
4 Albert Belle, Mo Vaughn, Dante Bichette (1995 Stat Leaders) .05
5 Kenny Lofton, Quilvio Veras (1995 Stat Leaders) .05
6 Mike Mussina, Greg Maddux (1995 Stat Leaders) .40
7 Randy Johnson, Hideo Nomo (1995 Stat Leaders) .25
8 Randy Johnson, Greg Maddux (1995 Stat Leaders) .40
9 Jose Mesa, Randy Myers (1995 Stat Leaders) .05
10 Johnny Damon (Rookie Class) .15
11 Rick Krivda (Rookie Class) .05
12 Roger Cedeno (Rookie Class) .10
13 Angel Martinez (Rookie Class) .05
14 Ariel Prieto (Rookie Class) .05
15 John Wasdin (Rookie Class) .05
16 Edwin Hurtado (Rookie Class) .05
17 Lyle Mouton (Rookie Class) .05
18 Chris Snopek (Rookie Class) .05
19 Mariano Rivera (Rookie Class) .15
20 Ruben Rivera (Rookie Class) .05
21 *Juan Castro* (Rookie Class) .05
22 Jimmy Haynes (Rookie Class) .05
23 Bob Wolcott (Rookie Class) .05
24 Brian Barber (Rookie Class) .05
25 Frank Rodriguez (Rookie Class) .05
26 Jesus Tavarez (Rookie Class) .05
27 Glenn Dishman (Rookie Class) .05
28 Jose Herrera (Rookie Class) .05
29 Chan Ho Park (Rookie Class) .15
30 Jason Isringhausen (Rookie Class) .05
31 Doug Johns (Rookie Class) .05
32 Gene Schall (Rookie Class) .05
33 Kevin Jordan (Rookie Class) .05
34 *Matt Lawton* (Rookie Class) .10
35 Karim Garcia (Rookie Class) .10
36 George Williams (Rookie Class) .05
37 Orlando Palmeiro (Rookie Class) .05
38 Jamie Brewington (Rookie Class) .05
39 Robert Person (Rookie Class) .05
40 Greg Maddux .75
41 Marquis Grissom .05
42 Chipper Jones 1.25
43 David Justice .20
44 Mark Lemke .05
45 Fred McGriff .05
46 Javy Lopez .05
47 Mark Wohlers .05
48 Jason Schmidt .05
49 John Smoltz .10
50 Curtis Goodwin .05
51 Greg Zaun .05
52 Armando Benitez .05
53 Manny Alexander .05
54 Chris Hoiles .05
55 Harold Baines .05
56 Ben McDonald .05
57 Scott Erickson .05
58 Jeff Manto .05
59 Luis Alicea .05
60 Roger Clemens .75
61 Rheal Cormier .05
62 Vaughn Eshelman .05
63 Zane Smith .05
64 Mike Macfarlane .05
65 Erik Hanson .05
66 Tim Naehring .05
67 Lee Tinsley .05
68 Troy O'Leary .05
69 Garret Anderson .05
70 Chili Davis .05
71 Jim Edmonds .05
72 Troy Percival .05
73 Mark Langston .05
74 Spike Owen .05
75 Tim Salmon .10
76 Brian Anderson .05
77 Lee Smith .05
78 Jim Abbott .05
79 Jim Bullinger .05
80 Mark Grace .20
81 Todd Zeile .05
82 Kevin Foster .05
83 Howard Johnson .05
84 Brian McRae .05
85 Randy Myers .05
86 Jaime Navarro .05
87 Luis Gonzalez .05
88 Ozzie Timmons .05
89 Wilson Alvarez .05
90 Frank Thomas 1.00
91 James Baldwin .05
92 Ray Durham .05
93 Alex Fernandez .05
94 Ozzie Guillen .05
95 Tim Raines .05
96 Roberto Hernandez .05
97 Lance Johnson .05
98 John Kruk .05
99 Mark Portugal .05
100 Don Mattingly (Traditional Threads) .50
101 Jose Canseco (Traditional Threads) .20
102 Raul Mondesi (Traditional Threads) .05
103 Cecil Fielder (Traditional Threads) .05
104 Ozzie Smith (Traditional Threads) .40
105 Frank Thomas (Traditional Threads) .50
106 Sammy Sosa (Traditional Threads) .50
107 Fred McGriff (Traditional Threads) .05
108 Barry Bonds (Traditional Threads) .50
109 Thomas Howard .05
110 Ron Gant .05
111 Eddie Taubensee .05
112 Hal Morris .05
113 Jose Rijo .05
114 Pete Schourek .05
115 Reggie Sanders .05
116 Benito Santiago .05
117 Jeff Brantley .05
118 Julian Tavarez .05
119 Carlos Baerga .05
120 Jim Thome .05
121 Jose Mesa .05
122 Dennis Martinez .05
123 Dave Winfield .20
124 Eddie Murray .30
125 Manny Ramirez .60
126 Paul Sorrento .05
127 Kenny Lofton .05
128 Eric Young .05
129 Jason Bates .05
130 Bret Saberhagen .05
131 Andres Galarraga .05
132 Joe Girardi .05
133 John Vander Wal .05
134 David Nied .05
135 Dante Bichette .05
136 Vinny Castilla .05
137 Kevin Ritz .05
138 Felipe Lira .05
139 Joe Boever .05
140 Cecil Fielder .05
141 John Flaherty .05
142 Kirk Gibson .05
143 Brian Maxcy .05
144 Lou Whitaker .05
145 Alan Trammell .05
146 Bobby Higginson .10
147 Chad Curtis .05
148 Quilvio Veras .05
149 Jerry Browne .05
150 Andre Dawson .15
151 Robb Nen .05
152 Greg Colbrunn .05
153 Chris Hammond .05
154 Kurt Abbott .05
155 Charles Johnson .05
156 Terry Pendleton .05
157 Dave Weathers .05
158 Mike Hampton .05
159 Craig Biggio .10
160 Jeff Bagwell .60
161 Brian L. Hunter .05
162 Mike Henneman .05
163 Dave Magadan .05
164 Shane Reynolds .05
165 Derek Bell .05
166 Orlando Miller .05
167 James Mouton .05
168 Melvin Bunch .05
169 Tom Gordon .05
170 Kevin Appier .05
171 Tom Goodwin .05
172 Greg Gagne .05
173 Gary Gaetti .05
174 Jeff Montgomery .05
175 Jon Nunnally .05
176 Michael Tucker .05
177 Joe Vitiello .05
178 Billy Ashley .05
179 Tom Candiotti .05
180 Hideo Nomo .50
181 Chad Fonville .05
182 Todd Hollandsworth .05
183 Eric Karros .05
184 Roberto Kelly .05
185 Mike Piazza 1.25
186 Ramon Martinez .05
187 Tim Wallach .05
188 Jeff Cirillo .05
189 Sid Roberson .05
190 Kevin Seitzer .05
191 Mike Fetters .05
192 Steve Sparks .05
193 Matt Mieske .05
194 Joe Oliver .05
195 B.J. Surhoff .05
196 Alberto Reyes .05
197 Fernando Vina .05
198 LaTroy Hawkins .05
199 Marty Cordova .05
200 Kirby Puckett .75
201 Brad Radke .05
202 (Pedro Munoz) .05
203 Scott Klingenbeck .05
204 Pat Meares .05
205 Chuck Knoblauch .05
206 Scott Stahoviak .05
207 Dave Stevens .05
208 Shane Andrews .05
209 Moises Alou .10
210 David Segui .05
211 Cliff Floyd .05
212 Carlos Perez .05
213 Mark Grudzielanek .05
214 Butch Henry .05
215 Rondell White .15
216 Mel Rojas .05
217 Ugueth Urbina .05
218 Edgardo Alfonzo .05
219 Carl Everett .10
220 John Franco .05
221 Todd Hundley .05
222 Bobby Jones .05
223 Bill Pulsipher .05
224 Rico Brogna .05
225 Jeff Kent .05
226 Chris Jones .05
227 Butch Huskey .05
228 Robert Eenhoorn .05
229 Sterling Hitchcock .05
230 Wade Boggs .20
231 Derek Jeter 1.25
232 Tony Fernandez .05
233 Jack McDowell .05
234 Andy Pettitte .40
235 David Cone .05
236 Mike Stanley .05
237 Don Mattingly 1.00
238 Geronimo Berroa .05
239 Scott Brosius .05
240 Rickey Henderson .40
241 Terry Steinbach .05
242 Mike Gallego .05
243 Jason Giambi .25
244 Steve Ontiveros .05
245 Dennis Eckersley .05
246 Dave Stewart .05
247 Don Wengert .05
248 Paul Quantrill .05
249 Ricky Bottalico .05
250 Kevin Stocker .05
251 Lenny Dykstra .05
252 Tony Longmire .05
253 Tyler Green .05

254 Mike Mimbs .05
255 Charlie Hayes .05
256 Mickey Morandini .05
257 Heathcliff Slocumb .05
258 Jeff King .05
259 Midre Cummings .05
260 Mark Johnson .05
261 Freddy Garcia .05
262 Jon Lieber .05
263 Esteban Loaiza .05
264 Danny Miceli .05
265 Orlando Merced .05
266 Denny Neagle .05
267 Steve Parris .05
268 Fantasy Team '95 (Greg Maddux) .35
269 Fantasy Team '95 (Randy Johnson) .10
270 Fantasy Team '95 (Hideo Nomo) .25
271 Fantasy Team '95 (Jose Mesa) .05
272 Fantasy Team '95 (Mike Piazza) .50
273 Fantasy Team '95 (Mo Vaughn) .15
274 Fantasy Team '95 (Craig Biggio) .05
275 Fantasy Team '95 (Edgar Martinez) .05
276 Fantasy Team '95 (Barry Larkin) .05
277 Fantasy Team '95 (Sammy Sosa) .45
278 Fantasy Team '95 (Dante Bichette) .05
279 Fantasy Team '95 (Albert Belle) .10
280 Ozzie Smith .75
281 Mark Sweeney .05
282 Terry Bradshaw .05
283 Allen Battle .05
284 Danny Jackson .05
285 Tom Henke .05
286 Scott Cooper .05
287 Tripp Cromer .05
288 Bernard Gilkey .05
289 Brian Jordan .05
290 Tony Gwynn .75
291 Brad Ausmus .05
292 Bryce Florie .05
293 Andres Berumen .05
294 Ken Caminiti .05
295 Bip Roberts .05
296 Trevor Hoffman .05
297 Roberto Petagine .05
298 Jody Reed .05
299 Fernando Valenzuela .05
300 Barry Bonds 1.00
301 Mark Leiter .05
302 Mark Carreon .05
303 Royce Clayton .05
304 Kirt Manwaring .05
305 Glenallen Hill .05
306 Deion Sanders .10
307 Joe Rosselli .05
308 Robby Thompson .05
309 William VanLandingham .05
310 Ken Griffey Jr. 1.50
311 Bobby Ayala .05
312 Joey Cora .05
313 Mike Blowers .05
314 Darren Bragg .05
315 Randy Johnson .40
316 Alex Rodriguez 1.50
317 Andy Benes .05
318 Tino Martinez .05
319 Dan Wilson .05
320 Will Clark .15
321 Jeff Frye .05
322 Benji Gil .05
323 Rick Helling .05
324 Mark McLemore .05
325 Dave Nilsson (International Flavor) .05
326 Larry Walker (International Flavor) .20
327 Jose Canseco (International Flavor) .20
328 Raul Mondesi (International Flavor) .10
329 Manny Ramirez (International Flavor) .30
330 Robert Eenhoorn (International Flavor) .05
331 Chili Davis (International Flavor) .05
332 Hideo Nomo (International Flavor) .25
333 Benji Gil (International Flavor) .05
334 Fernando Valenzuela (International Flavor) .05
335 Dennis Martinez (International Flavor) .05
336 Roberto Kelly (International Flavor) .05
337 Carlos Baerga (International Flavor) .05
338 Juan Gonzalez (International Flavor) .30
339 Roberto Alomar (International Flavor) .15
340 Chan Ho Park (International Flavor) .10
341 Andres Galarraga (International Flavor) .05
342 Midre Cummings (International Flavor) .05
343 Otis Nixon .05
344 Jeff Russell .05
345 Ivan Rodriguez .40
346 Mickey Tettleton .05
347 Bob Tewksbury .05
348 Domingo Cedeno .05
349 Lance Parrish .05
350 Joe Carter .05
351 Devon White .05
352 Carlos Delgado .20
353 Alex Gonzalez .10
354 Darren Hall .05
355 Paul Molitor .40
356 Al Leiter .05
357 Randy Knorr .05
358 Checklist 1-46 (12-player Astros-Padres trade) .05
359 Checklist 47-92 (Hideo Nomo) .20
360 Checklist 93-138 (Ramon Martinez) .05
361 Checklist 139-184 (Robin Ventura) .05
362 Checklist 185-230 (Cal Ripken Jr.) .30
363 Checklist 231-275 (Ken Caminiti) .05
364 Checklist 276-320 (Eddie Murray) .15
365 Checklist 321-365 (Randy Johnson) .10
366 A.L. Divisional Series (Tony Pena) .10
367 A.L. Divisional Series (Jim Thome) .10
368 A.L. Divisional Series (Don Mattingly) .40
369 A.L. Divisional Series (Jim Leyritz) .10
370 A.L. Divisional Series (Ken Griffey Jr.) .75
371 A.L. Divisional Series (Edgar Martinez) .10
372 N.L. Divisional Series (Pete Schourek) .10
373 N.L. Divisional Series (Mark Lewis) .10
374 N.L. Divisonal Series (Chipper Jones) .75
375 N.L. Divisonal Series (Fred McGriff) .10
376 N.L. Championship Series (Javy Lopez) .10
377 N.L. Championship Series (Fred McGriff) .10
378 N.L. Championship Series (Charlie O'Brien) .10
379 N.L. Championship Series (Mike Devereaux) .10
380 N.L. Championship Series (Mark Wohlers) .10
381 A.L. Championship Series (Bob Wolcott) .10
382 A.L. Championship Series (Manny Ramirez) .20
383 A.L. Championship Series (Jay Buhner) .10
384 A.L. Championship Series (Orel Hershiser) .10
385 A.L. Championship Series (Kenny Lofton) .10
386 World Series (Greg Maddux) .50
387 World Series (Javy Lopez) .10
388 World Series (Kenny Lofton) .10
389 World Series (Eddie Murray) .10
390 World Series (Luis Polonia) .10
391 World Series (Pedro Borbon) .10
392 World Series (Jim Thome) .10
393 World Series (Orel Hershiser) .10
394 World Series (David Justice) .10
395 World Series (Tom Glavine) .10
396 Braves Team Checklist (Greg Maddux) .15
397 Mets Team Checklist (Brett Butler) .05
398 Phillies Team Checklist (Darren Daulton) .05
399 Marlins Team Checklist (Gary Sheffield) .05
400 Expos Team Checklist (Moises Alou) .05
401 Reds Team Checklist (Barry Larkin) .05
402 Astros Team Checklist (Jeff Bagwell) .15
403 Cubs Team Checklist (Sammy Sosa) .25
404 Cardinals Team Checklist (Ozzie Smith) .15
405 Pirates Team Checklist (Jeff King) .05
406 Dodgers Team Checklist (Mike Piazza) .25
407 Rockies Team Checklist (Dante Bichette) .05
408 Padres Team Checklist (Tony Gwynn) .15
409 Giants Team Checklist (Barry Bonds) .25
410 Indians Team Checklist (Kenny Lofton) .05
411 Royals Team Checklist (Jon Nunnally) .05
412 White Sox Team Checklist (Frank Thomas) .20
413 Brewers Team Checklist (Greg Vaughn) .05
414 Twins Team Checklist (Paul Molitor) .10
415 Mariners Team Checklist (Ken Griffey Jr.) .35
416 Angels Team Checklist (Jim Edmonds) .05
417 Rangers Team Checklist (Juan Gonzalez) .20
418 Athletics Team Checklist (Mark McGwire) .75
419 Red Sox Team Checklist (Roger Clemens) .15
420 Yankees Team Checklist (Wade Boggs) .20
421 Orioles Team Checklist (Cal Ripken Jr.) .40
422 Tigers Team Checklist (Cecil Fielder) .05
423 Blue Jays Team Checklist (Joe Carter) .05
424 *Osvaldo Fernandez* (Rookie Class) .15
425 Billy Wagner (Rookie Class) .05
426 George Arias (Rookie Class) .05
427 Mendy Lopez (Rookie Class) .05
428 Jeff Suppan (Rookie Class) .05
429 Rey Ordonez (Rookie Class) .10
430 Brooks Kieschnick (Rookie Class) .05
431 *Raul Ibanez* (Rookie Class) .05
432 *Livan Hernandez* (Rookie Class) .20
433 Shannon Stewart (Rookie Class) .10
434 Steve Cox (Rookie Class) .05
435 Trey Beamon (Rookie Class) .05
436 Sergio Nunez (Rookie Class) .05
437 Jermaine Dye (Rookie Class) .05
438 *Mike Sweeney* (Rookie Class) .30
439 Richard Hidalgo (Rookie Class) .10
440 Todd Greene (Rookie Class) .05
441 *Robert Smith* (Rookie Class) .10
442 Rafael Orellano (Rookie Class) .05
443 *Wilton Guerrero* (Rookie Class) .05
444 *David Doster* (Rookie Class) .05
445 Jason Kendall (Rookie Class) .05
446 Edgar Renteria (Rookie Class) .05
447 Scott Spiezio (Rookie Class) .05
448 Jay Canizaro (Rookie Class) .05
449 Enrique Wilson (Rookie Class) .05
450 Bob Abreu (Rookie Class) .10
451 Dwight Smith .05
452 Jeff Blauser .05
453 Steve Avery .05
454 Brad Clontz .05
455 Tom Glavine .10
456 Mike Mordecai .05
457 Rafael Belliard .05
458 Greg McMichael .05
459 Pedro Borbon .05
460 Ryan Klesko .05
461 Terrell Wade .05
462 Brady Anderson .05
463 Roberto Alomar .30
464 Bobby Bonilla .05
465 Mike Mussina .35
466 *Cesar Devarez* .05
467 Jeffrey Hammonds .05
468 Mike Devereaux .05
469 B.J. Surhoff .05
470 Rafael Palmeiro .15
471 John Valentin .05
472 Mike Greenwell .05
473 Dwayne Hosey .05
474 Tim Wakefield .05
475 Jose Canseco .35
476 Aaron Sele .05
477 Stan Belinda .05
478 Mike Stanley .05
479 Jamie Moyer .05
480 Mo Vaughn .20
481 Randy Velarde .05
482 Gary DiSarcina .05
483 Jorge Fabregas .05
484 Rex Hudler .05
485 Chuck Finley .05
486 Tim Wallach .05
487 Eduardo Perez .05
488 Scott Sanderson .05
489 J.T. Snow .05
490 Sammy Sosa 1.00
491 Terry Adams .05
492 Matt Franco .05
493 Scott Servais .05
494 Frank Castillo .05
495 Ryne Sandberg .45
496 Rey Sanchez .05
497 Steve Trachsel .05
498 Jose Hernandez .05
499 Dave Martinez .05
500 Babe Ruth (First Class) 1.00
501 Ty Cobb (First Class) .50
502 Walter Johnson (First Class) .10
503 Christy Mathewson (First Class) .10
504 Honus Wagner (First Class) .25
505 Robin Ventura .05
506 Jason Bere .05
507 *Mike Cameron* .25
508 Ron Karkovice .05

509 Matt Karchner .05
510 Harold Baines .05
511 Kirk McCaskill .05
512 Larry Thomas .05
513 Danny Tartabull .05
514 Steve Gibralter .05
515 Bret Boone .10
516 Jeff Branson .05
517 Kevin Jarvis .05
518 Xavier Hernandez .05
519 Eric Owens .05
520 Barry Larkin .10
521 Dave Burba .05
522 John Smiley .05
523 Paul Assenmacher .05
524 Chad Ogea .05
525 Orel Hershiser .05
526 Alan Embree .05
527 Tony Pena .05
528 Omar Vizquel .05
529 Mark Clark .05
530 Albert Belle .15
531 Charles Nagy .05
532 Herbert Perry .05
533 Darren Holmes .05
534 Ellis Burks .05
535 Bill Swift .05
536 Armando Reynoso .05
537 Curtis Leskanic .05
538 Quinton McCracken .05
539 Steve Reed .05
540 Larry Walker .15
541 Walt Weiss .05
542 Bryan Rekar .05
543 Tony Clark .05
544 Steve Rodriguez .05
545 C.J. Nitkowski .05
546 Todd Steverson .05
547 Jose Lima .05
548 Phil Nevin .05
549 Chris Gomez .05
550 Travis Fryman .05
551 Mark Lewis .05
552 Alex Arias .05
553 Marc Valdes .05
554 Kevin Brown .15
555 Jeff Conine .05
556 John Burkett .05
557 Devon White .05
558 Pat Rapp .05
559 Jay Powell .05
560 Gary Sheffield .20
561 Jim Dougherty .05
562 Todd Jones .05
563 Tony Eusebio .05
564 Darryl Kile .05
565 Doug Drabek .05
566 Mike Simms .05
567 Derrick May .05
568 *Donne Wall* .05
569 Greg Swindell .05
570 Jim Pittsley .05
571 Bob Hamelin .05
572 Mark Gubicza .05
573 Chris Haney .05
574 Keith Lockhart .05
575 Mike Macfarlane .05
576 Les Norman .05
577 Joe Randa .05
578 Chris Stynes .05
579 Greg Gagne .05
580 Raul Mondesi .10
581 Delino DeShields .05
582 Pedro Astacio .05
583 Antonio Osuna .05
584 Brett Butler .05
585 Todd Worrell .05
586 Mike Blowers .05
587 Felix Rodriguez .05
588 Ismael Valdes .05
589 Ricky Bones .05
590 Greg Vaughn .05
591 Mark Loretta .05
592 Cal Eldred .05
593 Chuck Carr .05
594 Dave Nilsson .05
595 John Jaha .05
596 Scott Karl .05
597 Pat Listach .05
598 *Jose Valentin* .05
599 Mike Trombley .05
600 Paul Molitor .40
601 Dave Hollins .05
602 Ron Coomer .05
603 Matt Walbeck .05
604 Roberto Kelly .05
605 Rick Aguilera .05
606 Pat Mahomes .05
607 Jeff Reboulet .05
608 Rich Becker .05
609 Tim Scott .05
610 Pedro J. Martinez .40
611 Kirk Rueter .05
612 Tavo Alvarez .05
613 Yamil Benitez .05
614 Darrin Fletcher .05
615 Mike Lansing .05
616 Henry Rodriguez .05
617 Tony Tarasco .05
618 Alex Ochoa .05
619 Tim Bogar .05
620 Bernard Gilkey .05
621 Dave Mlicki .05
622 Brent Mayne .05
623 Ryan Thompson .05
624 Pete Harnisch .05
625 Lance Johnson .05
626 Jose Vizcaino .05
627 Doug Henry .05
628 Scott Kamieniecki .05
629 Jim Leyritz .05
630 Ruben Sierra .05
631 Pat Kelly .05
632 Joe Girardi .05
633 John Wetteland .05
634 Melido Perez .05
635 Paul O'Neill .05
636 Jorge Posada .05
637 Bernie Williams .15
638 Mark Acre .05
639 Mike Bordick .05
640 Mark McGwire 2.00
641 Fausto Cruz .05
642 Ernie Young .05
643 Todd Van Poppel .05
644 Craig Paquette .05
645 Brent Gates .05
646 Pedro Munoz .05
647 Andrew Lorraine .05
648 Sid Fernandez .05
649 Jim Eisenreich .05
650 Johnny Damon (Arizona Fall League) .10
651 Dustin Hermanson (Arizona Fall League) .05
652 Joe Randa (Arizona Fall League) .05
653 Michael Tucker (Arizona Fall League) .05
654 Alan Benes (Arizona Fall League) .05
655 Chad Fonville (Arizona Fall League) .05
656 David Bell (Arizona Fall League) .05
657 Jon Nunnally (Arizona Fall League) .05
658 Chan Ho Park (Arizona Fall League) .15
659 LaTroy Hawkins (Arizona Fall League) .05
660 Jamie Brewington (Arizona Fall League) .05
661 Quinton McCracken (Arizona Fall League) .05
662 Tim Unroe (Arizona Fall League) .05
663 Jeff Ware (Arizona Fall League) .05
664 Todd Greene (Arizona Fall League) .05
665 Andrew Lorraine (Arizona Fall League) .05
666 Ernie Young (Arizona Fall League) .05
667 Toby Borland .05
668 Lenny Webster .05
669 Benito Santiago .05
670 Gregg Jefferies .05
671 Darren Daulton .05
672 Curt Schilling .20
673 Mark Whiten .05
674 Todd Zeile .05
675 Jay Bell .05
676 Paul Wagner .05
677 Dave Clark .05
678 Nelson Liriano .05
679 Ramon Morel .05
680 Charlie Hayes .05
681 Angelo Encaracion .05
682 Al Martin .05
683 Jacob Brumfield .05
684 Mike Kingery .05
685 Carlos Garcia .05
686 Tom Pagnozzi .05
687 David Bell .05
688 Todd Stottlemyre .05
689 Jose Oliva .05
690 Ray Lankford .05
691 Mike Morgan .05
692 John Frascatore .05
693 John Mabry .05
694 Mark Petkovsek .05
695 Alan Benes .05
696 Steve Finley .05
697 Marc Newfield .05
698 Andy Ashby .05
699 Marc Kroon .05
700 Wally Joyner .05
701 Joey Hamilton .05
702 Dustin Hermanson .05
703 Scott Sanders .05
704 Marty Cordova (Award Win.-ROY) .05
705 Hideo Nomo (Award Win.-ROY) .20
706 Mo Vaughn (Award Win.-MVP) .10
707 Barry Larkin (Award Win.-MVP) .05
708 Randy Johnson (Award Win.-CY) .15
709 Greg Maddux (Award Win.-CY) .35
710 Mark McGwire (Award-Comeback) .75
711 Ron Gant (Award-Comeback) .05
712 Andujar Cedeno .05
713 Brian Johnson .05
714 J.R. Phillips .05
715 Rod Beck .05
716 Sergio Valdez .05
717 *Marvin Benard* .25
718 Steve Scarsone .05
719 *Rich Aurilia* .10
720 Matt Williams .15
721 John Patterson .05
722 Shawn Estes .05
723 Russ Davis .05
724 Rich Amaral .05
725 Edgar Martinez .05
726 Norm Charlton .05
727 Paul Sorrento .05
728 Luis Sojo .05
729 Arquimedez Pozo .05
730 Jay Buhner .05
731 Chris Bosio .05
732 Chris Widger .05
733 Kevin Gross .05
734 Darren Oliver .05
735 Dean Palmer .05
736 Matt Whiteside .05
737 Luis Ortiz .05
738 Roger Pavlik .05
739 Damon Buford .05
740 Juan Gonzalez .60
741 Rusty Greer .05
742 Lou Frazier .05
743 Pat Hentgen .05
744 Tomas Perez .05
745 Juan Guzman .05
746 Otis Nixon .05
747 Robert Perez .05
748 Ed Sprague .05
749 Tony Castillo .05
750 John Olerud .05
751 Shawn Green .10
752 Jeff Ware .05
753 Checklist 396-441/ Blake St. Bombers (Dante Bichette, Larry Walker, Andres Galarraga, Vinny Castilla) .05
754 Checklist 442-487 (Greg Maddux) .25
755 Checklist 488-533 (Marty Cordova) .05
756 Checklist 534-579 (Ozzie Smith) .15
757 Checklist 580-625 (John Vander Wal) .05
758 Checklist 626-670 (Andres Galarraga) .05
759 Checklist 671-715 (Frank Thomas) .25
760 Checklist 716-760 (Tony Gwynn) .25
761 Randy Myers .10
762 Kent Mercker .10
763 David Wells .10
764 Tom Gordon .10
765 Wil Cordero .10
766 Dave Magadan .10
767 Doug Jones .10
768 Kevin Tapani .10
769 Curtis Goodwin .10
770 Julio Franco .10
771 Jack McDowell .10
772 Al Leiter .10
773 Sean Berry .10
774 Bip Roberts .10
775 Jose Offerman .10
776 Ben McDonald .10
777 Dan Serafini .10
778 Ryan McGuire .10
779 Tim Raines .10
780 Tino Martinez .10
781 Kenny Rogers .10
782 Bob Tewksbury .10
783 Rickey Henderson .60
784 Ron Gant .10
785 Gary Gaetti .10
786 Andy Benes .10
787 Royce Clayton .10
788 Darryl Hamilton .10
789 Ken Hill .10
790 Erik Hanson .10

1996 Collector's Choice Gold Signature

This insert set parallels each card in the regular Collector's Choice set. Found on average of one per 35 packs, the cards are nearly identical to the regular version except for the presence of a facsimile autograph in gold ink on the front and gold, instead of white, borders.

	MT
Common Player:	1.00
Veteran Stars:	10X

(See 1996 Collector's Choice for checklist and base card values.)

1996 Collector's Choice Silver Signature

A silver border instead of white, and a facsimile autograph in silver ink on the card front differentiate these parallel insert cards from the regular-issue Collector's Choice. The inserts are seeded at the rate of one per pack.

	MT
Complete Set (730):	50.00
Common Player:	.10
Stars:	1.5X

(See 1996 Collector's Choice for checklist and base card values.)

1996 Collector's Choice A Cut Above

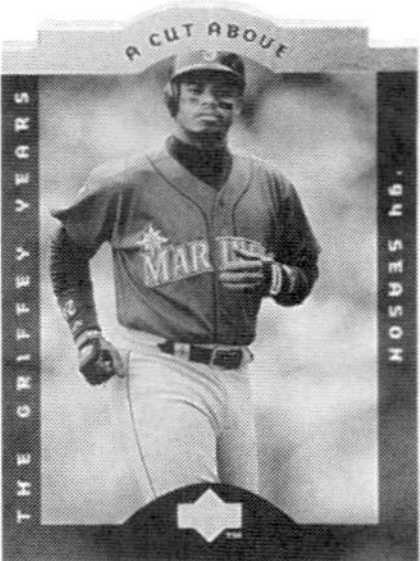

This 10-card set highlights the career of Ken Griffey Jr. The front has a color photo with "The Griffey Years" printed in the left border and a title in the right border. Die-cut gold-foil tops have "A CUT ABOVE". in black. Backs have a portrait photo on a marbled border and a narrative. This set was inserted one per six-card Wal-Mart exclusive pack.

		MT
Complete Set (10):		8.00
Common Card:		1.00
CA1	Ken Griffey Jr. (Teenage Rookie)	1.00
CA2	Ken Griffey Jr. (Great Defense)	1.00
CA3	Ken Griffey Jr. (Fun-Loving)	1.00
CA4	Ken Griffey Jr. (All-Star Games)	1.00
CA5	Ken Griffey Jr. ('93 Season)	1.00
CA6	Ken Griffey Jr. ('94 HR Records)	1.00
CA7	Ken Griffey Jr. ('94 Season)	1.00
CA8	Ken Griffey Jr. ('95 Season)	1.00
CA9	Ken Griffey Jr. ('95 Postseason)	1.00
CA10	Ken Griffey Jr. ('96: A Look Ahead)	1.00

1996 Collector's Choice Crash the Game

For a second season, UD continued its interactive chase card series, "You Crash the Game." At a ratio of about one per five packs for a silver version and one per 49 packs for a gold version, cards of the game's top sluggers can be found bearing one of three date ranges representing a three- or four-game series in which that player was scheduled to play during the 1996 season. If the player hit a home run during the series shown on the card, the card could be redeemed (for $1.75) by mail for a "Super Premium" wood-and-plastic card of the player. Both silver and gold Crash cards feature silver and red prismatic foil behind the player action photo. Silver versions have the Crash logo, series dates and player ID in silver foil on front; those details are in gold foil on the gold cards. Backs have contest rules printed on a gray (silver) or yellow (gold) background. Card numbers are preceded by a "CG" prefix. Cards were redeemable only until Nov. 25, 1996. Winning cards are indicated with an asterisk; they would be in shorter supply than those which could not be redeemed.

		MT
Complete Set (90):		90.00
Common Silver Player:		.50
Golds:		2X
1a	Chipper Jones (July 11-14*)	3.50
1b	Chipper Jones (Aug. 27-29*)	3.50
1c	Chipper Jones (Sept. 19-23)	2.00
2a	Fred McGriff (July 1-3)	.50
2b	Fred McGriff (Aug. 30-Sept. 1)	.50
2c	Fred McGriff (Sept. 10-12*)	1.00
3a	Rafael Palmeiro (July 4-7*)	1.00
3b	Rafael Palmeiro (Aug. 29-Sept. 1)	.60
3c	Rafael Palmeiro (Sept. 26-29)	.60
4a	Cal Ripken Jr. (June 27-30)	2.50
4b	Cal Ripken Jr. (July 25-28*)	4.50
4c	Cal Ripken Jr. (Sept. 2-4)	2.50
5a	Jose Canseco (June 27-30)	.75
5b	Jose Canseco (July 11-14*)	1.50
5c	Jose Canseco (Aug. 23-25)	.75
6a	Mo Vaughn (June 21-23*)	1.25
6b	Mo Vaughn (July 18-21*)	1.25
6c	Mo Vaughn (Sept. 20-22)	.60
7a	Jim Edmonds (July 18-21*)	1.00
7b	Jim Edmonds (Aug. 16-18*)	1.00
7c	Jim Edmonds (Sept. 20-22)	.50
8a	Tim Salmon (June 20-23)	.50
8b	Tim Salmon (July 30-Aug. 1)	.50
8c	Tim Salmon (Sept. 9-12)	.50
9a	Sammy Sosa (July 4-7*)	3.00
9b	Sammy Sosa (Aug. 1-4*)	3.00
9c	Sammy Sosa (Sept. 2-4)	1.50
10a	Frank Thomas (June 27-30)	1.50
10b	Frank Thomas (July 4-7)	1.50
10c	Frank Thomas (Sept. 2-4*)	3.00
11a	Albert Belle (June 25-26)	.60
11b	Albert Belle (Aug. 2-5*)	1.25
11c	Albert Belle (Sept. 6-8)	.60
12a	Manny Ramirez (July 18-21*)	2.00
12b	Manny Ramirez (Aug. 26-28)	1.00
12c	Manny Ramirez (Sept. 9-12*)	2.00
13a	Jim Thome (June 27-30)	.50
13b	Jim Thome (July 4-7*)	1.00
13c	Jim Thome (Sept. 23-25)	.50
14a	Dante Bichette (July 11-14*)	1.00
14b	Dante Bichette (Aug. 9-11)	.50
14c	Dante Bichette (Sept. 9-12)	.50
15a	Vinny Castilla (July 1-3)	.50
15b	Vinny Castilla (Aug. 23-25*)	1.00
15c	Vinny Castilla (Sept. 13-15*)	1.00
16a	Larry Walker (June 24-26)	.60
16b	Larry Walker (July 18-21)	.60
16c	Larry Walker (Sept. 27-29)	.60
17a	Cecil Fielder (June 27-30)	.50
17b	Cecil Fielder (July 30-Aug. 1*)	1.00
17c	Cecil Fielder (Sept. 17-19*)	1.00
18a	Gary Sheffield (July 4-7)	.60
18b	Gary Sheffield (Aug. 2-4)	.60
18c	Gary Sheffield (Sept. 5-8*)	1.25
19a	Jeff Bagwell (July 4-7*)	2.00
19b	Jeff Bagwell (Aug. 16-18)	1.00
19c	Jeff Bagwell (Sept. 13-15)	1.00
20a	Eric Karros (July 4-7*)	1.00
20b	Eric Karros (Aug. 13-15*)	1.00
20c	Eric Karros (Sept. 16-18)	.50
21a	Mike Piazza (June 27-30*)	3.50
21b	Mike Piazza (July 26-28)	2.00
21c	Mike Piazza (Sept. 12-15*)	3.50
22a	Ken Caminiti (July 11-14*)	1.00
22b	Ken Caminiti (Aug. 16-18*)	1.00
22c	Ken Caminiti (Sept. 19-22*)	1.00
23a	Barry Bonds (June 27-30*)	3.00
23b	Barry Bonds (July 22-24)	2.00
23c	Barry Bonds (Sept. 24-26)	2.00
24a	Matt Williams (July 11-14*)	1.00
24b	Matt Williams (Aug. 19-21)	.50
24c	Matt Williams (Sept. 27-29)	.50
25a	Jay Buhner (June 20-23)	.50
25b	Jay Buhner (July 25-28)	.50
25c	Jay Buhner (Aug. 29-Sept. 1*)	1.00
26a	Ken Griffey Jr. (July 18-21*)	4.00
26b	Ken Griffey Jr. (Aug. 16-18*)	4.00
26c	Ken Griffey Jr. (Sept. 20-22*)	4.00
27a	Ron Gant (June 24-27*)	1.00
27b	Ron Gant (July 11-14*)	1.00
27c	Ron Gant (Sept. 27-29*)	1.00
28a	Juan Gonzalez (June 28-30*)	2.00
28b	Juan Gonzalez (July 15-17*)	2.00
28c	Juan Gonzalez (Aug. 6-8)	1.00
29a	Mickey Tettleton (July 4-7*)	1.00
29b	Mickey Tettleton (Aug. 6-8)	.50
29c	Mickey Tettleton (Sept. 6-8*)	1.00
30a	Joe Carter (June 25-27)	.50
30b	Joe Carter (Aug. 5-8)	.50
30c	Joe Carter (Sept. 23-25)	.50

1996 Collector's Choice Crash Winners

Collectors who held "You Crash The Game" insert cards with date ranges on which the pictured player hit a home run could redeem them (for $1.75 per card) for a premium card of that player. The redemption cards have a layer of clear plastic bonded to a wood-laminate front. Within a starburst cutout at center is the player photo with a red background. Cards have a Crash/Game logo in the lower-right corner, in either silver or gold, depending on which winning card was submitted for exchange. Backs have 1995 and career stats along with licensing and copyright data. There were no winning cards of Tim Salmon, Larry Walker or Joe Carter.

	MT
Complete Set (27):	75.00
Common Player:	2.00
Golds:	2X
CR1 Chipper Jones	6.50
CR2 Fred McGriff	2.00
CR3 Rafael Palmeiro	2.50
CR4 Cal Ripken Jr.	8.00
CR5 Jose Canseco	4.00
CR6 Mo Vaughn	3.75
CR7 Jim Edmonds	2.00
CR9 Sammy Sosa	5.75
CR10Frank Thomas	5.75
CR11Albert Belle	3.50
CR12Manny Ramirez	4.75
CR13Jim Thome	2.00
CR14Dante Bichette	2.00
CR15Vinny Castilla	2.00
CR17Cecil Fielder	2.00
CR18Gary Sheffield	2.50
CR19Jeff Bagwell	4.75
CR20Eric Karros	2.00
CR21Mike Piazza	6.50
CR22Ken Caminiti	2.00
CR23Barry Bonds	5.75
CR24Matt Williams	2.50
CR25Jay Buhner	2.00
CR26Ken Griffey Jr.	7.50
CR27Ron Gant	2.00
CR28Juan Gonzalez	4.75
CR29Mickey Tettleton	2.00

1996 Collector's Choice Nomo Scrapbook

The five-card, regular-sized set was randomly inserted in 1996 Collector's Choice baseball. Fronts depict the Dodgers pitcher in action with his name in atypical lower-case type up the right border. Backs feature in-depth text below Nomo's name.

	MT
Complete Set (5):	10.00
Common Card:	2.00
1-5 Hideo Nomo	2.00

1996 Collector's Choice Ripken Collection

The 23-card, regular-sized Cal Ripken Collection was randomly inserted in various Upper Deck baseball releases in 1996. Cards #1-4 were found in Series 1 Collector's Choice; cards 5-8 were found in Upper Deck Series 1; cards 9-12 in Collector's Choice Series 2; cards 13-17 in Upper Deck Series 2; cards 18-22 in SP baseball and the header card in Collector's Choice.

	MT
Complete Set (1-4, 9-12)	30.00
Common Card:	3.00
Header Card:	3.00

(See also Upper Deck Series 1 and 2, and Upper Deck/SP)

1996 Collector's Choice "You Make the Play"

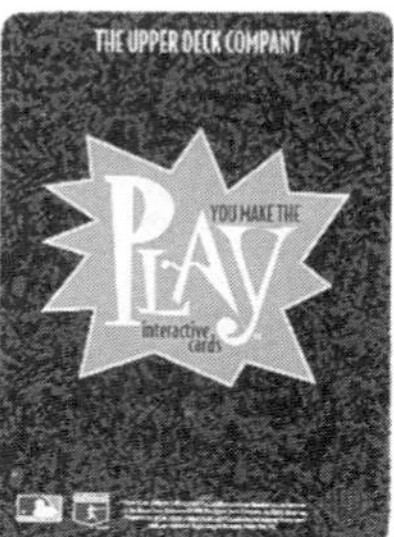

This insert series of interactive game cards was packaged with Series 1 Collector's Choice. Each player's card can be found with one of two play outcomes printed thereon, which are then used to play a baseball card game utilizing a playing field and scorecard found on box bottoms. Regular versions of the cards are seeded one per pack, while gold-signature versions are found one per 36 packs.

	MT
Complete Set (45):	80.00
Common Player:	.50
Golds:	8X
1a Kevin Appier (Strike out)	.50
1b Kevin Appier (Pick off)	.50
2a Carlos Baerga (Home run)	.50
2b Carlos Baerga (Ground out)	.50
3a Jeff Bagwell (Walk)	1.50
3b Jeff Bagwell (Strike out)	1.50
4a Jay Bell (Sacrifice)	.50
4b Jay Bell (Walk)	.50
5a Albert Belle (Fly out)	.60
5b Albert Belle (Home run)	.60
6a Craig Biggio (Single)	.50
6b Craig Biggio (Strike out)	.50
7a Wade Boggs (Single)	1.00
7b Wade Boggs (Ground out)	1.00
8a Barry Bonds (Strike out)	2.25
8b Barry Bonds (Reach on error)	2.25
9a Bobby Bonilla (Walk)	.50
9b Bobby Bonilla (Strike out)	.50
10a Jose Canseco (Strike out)	.75
10b Jose Canseco (Double)	.75
11a Joe Carter (Double)	.50
11b Joe Carter (Fly out)	.50
12a Darren Daulton (Ground out)	.50
12b Darren Daulton (Catcher's interference)	.50
13a Cecil Fielder (Stolen base)	.50
13b Cecil Fielder (Home run)	.50
14a Ron Gant (Home run)	.50
14b Ron Gant (Fly out)	.50
15a Juan Gonzalez (Double)	1.50
15b Juan Gonzalez (Fly out)	1.50
16a Ken Griffey Jr. (Home run)	3.00
16b Ken Griffey Jr. (Hit by pitch)	3.00
17a Tony Gwynn (Single)	2.00
17b Tony Gwynn (Ground out)	2.00
18a Randy Johnson (Strike out)	1.00
18b Randy Johnson (K - reach on wild pitch)	1.00
19a Chipper Jones (Walk)	2.50
19b Chipper Jones (Strike out)	2.50
20a Barry Larkin (Ground out)	.50
20b Barry Larkin (Stolen base)	.50
21a Kenny Lofton (Triple)	.50
21b Kenny Lofton (Stolen base)	.50
22a Greg Maddux (Single)	2.00
22b Greg Maddux (Strike out)	2.00
23a Don Mattingly (Fly out)	2.00
23b Don Mattingly (Double)	2.00
24a Fred McGriff (Double)	.50
24b Fred McGriff (Home run)	.50
25a Mark McGwire (Strike out)	3.25
25b Mark McGwire (Home run)	3.25
26a Paul Molitor (Ground out)	1.00
26b Paul Molitor (Single)	1.00
27a Raul Mondesi (Single)	.50
27b Raul Mondesi (Fly out)	.50
28a Eddie Murray (Sacrifice fly)	1.00
28b Eddie Murray (Ground out)	1.00
29a Hideo Nomo (Strike out)	1.00
29b Hideo Nomo (Balk)	1.00
30a Jon Nunnally (Single)	.50
30b Jon Nunnally (Error)	.50
31a Mike Piazza (Strike out)	2.50
31b Mike Piazza (Single)	2.50
32a Kirby Puckett (Walk)	2.00
32b Kirby Puckett (Ground out)	2.00
33a Cal Ripken Jr. (Home run)	3.25
33b Cal Ripken Jr. (Double)	3.25
34a Alex Rodriguez (Strike out)	3.00
34b Alex Rodriguez (Triple)	3.00
35a Tim Salmon (Sacrifice fly)	.50
35b Tim Salmon (Strike out)	.50
36a Gary Sheffield (Fly out)	.50
36b Gary Sheffield (Single)	.50
37a Lee Smith (Strike out)	.50
37b Lee Smith (Pick off of lead runner)	.50
38a Ozzie Smith (Ground out)	2.00
38b Ozzie Smith (Single)	2.00
39a Sammy Sosa (Stolen base)	2.25
39b Sammy Sosa (Single)	2.25
40a Frank Thomas (Walk)	2.50
40b Frank Thomas (Home run)	2.50
41a Greg Vaughn (Sacrifice fly)	.50
41b Greg Vaughn (Strike out)	.50
42a Mo Vaughn (Hit by Pitch)	.60
42b Mo Vaughn (Stolen base)	.60
43a Larry Walker (Strike out)	.60
43b Larry Walker (Walk)	.60
44a Rondell White (Triple)	.50
44b Rondell White (Fly out)	.50
45a Matt Williams (Home run)	.50
45b Matt Williams (Single)	.50

1997 Collector's Choice

The 506-card, standard-size set contains five subsets: Rookie Class (1-27), Leaders (56-63), Postseason (218-224), Ken Griffey Jr. Checklists (244-249) and Griffey Hot List (325-334). Insert sets are: All-Star Connection, Big Shots, Stick'Ums, Premier Power, Clearly Dominant, The Big Show. Toast of the Town and New Frontier. Basic card fronts feature a color action shot with the player's name appearing on the bottom edge. The team logo is located in the lower-left corner and each card features a white border. Backs contain another action shot on the upper half with biography, and career/season stats. The cards were issued in 12-card packs retailing for 99 cents.

	MT
Complete Set (506):	20.00
Common Player:	.05
Pack (12):	1.00
Wax Box (36):	25.00

1 Andruw Jones (Rookie Class) 1.00
2 Rocky Coppinger (Rookie Class) .05
3 Jeff D'Amico (Rookie Class) .05
4 Dmitri Young (Rookie Class) .05
5 Darin Erstad (Rookie Class) .75
6 Jermaine Allensworth (Rookie Class) .05
7 Damian Jackson (Rookie Class) .05
8 Bill Mueller (Rookie Class) .05
9 Jacob Cruz (Rookie Class) .05
10 Vladimir Guerrero (Rookie Class) 1.00
11 Marty Janzen (Rookie Class) .05
12 Kevin L. Brown (Rookie Class) .05
13 Willie Adams (Rookie Class) .05
14 Wendell Magee (Rookie Class) .05
15 Scott Rolen (Rookie Class) 1.00
16 Matt Beech (Rookie Class) .05
17 Neifi Perez (Rookie Class) .05
18 Jamey Wright (Rookie Class) .05
19 Jose Paniagua (Rookie Class) .05
20 Todd Walker (Rookie Class) .10
21 Justin Thompson (Rookie Class) .05
22 Robin Jennings (Rookie Class) .05
23 *Dario Veras* (Rookie Class) .05
24 Brian Lesher (Rookie Class) .05
25 Nomar Garciaparra (Rookie Class) 1.25
26 Luis Castillo (Rookie Class) .05
27 *Brian Giles* (Rookie Class) .75
28 Jermaine Dye .05
29 Terrell Wade .05
30 Fred McGriff .05
31 Marquis Grissom .05
32 Ryan Klesko .05
33 Javier Lopez .05
34 Mark Wohlers .05
35 Tom Glavine .10
36 Denny Neagle .05
37 Scott Erickson .05
38 Chris Hoiles .05
39 Roberto Alomar .40
40 Eddie Murray .30
41 Cal Ripken Jr. 2.00
42 Randy Myers .05
43 B.J. Surhoff .05
44 Rick Krivda .05
45 Jose Canseco .35
46 Heathcliff Slocumb .05
47 Jeff Suppan .05
48 Tom Gordon .05
49 Aaron Sele .05
50 Mo Vaughn .25
51 Darren Bragg .05
52 Wil Cordero .05
53 Scott Bullett .05
54 Terry Adams .05
55 Jackie Robinson .25
56 Tony Gwynn, Alex Rodriguez (Batting Leaders) .35
57 Andres Galarraga, Mark McGwire (Homer Leaders) .50
58 Andres Galarraga, Albert Belle (RBI Leaders) .05
59 Eric Young, Kenny Lofton (SB Leaders) .05
60 John Smoltz, Andy Pettitte (Victory Leaders) .05
61 John Smoltz, Roger Clemens (Strikout Leaders) .15
62 Kevin Brown, Juan Guzman (ERA Leaders) .05
63 John Wetteland, Todd Worrell, Jeff Brantley (Save Leaders) .05
64 Scott Servais .05
65 Sammy Sosa 1.00
66 Ryne Sandberg .60
67 Frank Castillo .05
68 Rey Sanchez .05
69 Steve Trachsel .05
70 Robin Ventura .05
71 Wilson Alvarez .05
72 Tony Phillips .05
73 Lyle Mouton .05
74 Mike Cameron .05
75 Harold Baines .05
76 Albert Belle .20
77 Chris Snopek .05
78 Reggie Sanders .05
79 Jeff Brantley .05
80 Barry Larkin .10
81 Kevin Jarvis .05
82 John Smiley .05
83 Pete Schourek .05
84 Thomas Howard .05
85 Lee Smith .05
86 Omar Vizquel .05
87 Julio Franco .05
88 Orel Hershiser .05
89 Charles Nagy .05
90 Matt Williams .15
91 Dennis Martinez .05
92 Jose Mesa .05
93 Sandy Alomar Jr. .05
94 Jim Thome .05
95 Vinny Castilla .05
96 Armando Reynoso .05
97 Kevin Ritz .05
98 Larry Walker .15
99 Eric Young .05
100 Dante Bichette .05
101 Quinton McCracken .05
102 John Vander Wal .05
103 Phil Nevin .05
104 Tony Clark .05
105 Alan Trammell .05
106 Felipe Lira .05
107 Curtis Pride .05
108 Bobby Higginson .10
109 Mark Lewis .05
110 Travis Fryman .05
111 Al Leiter .05
112 Devon White .05
113 Jeff Conine .05
114 Charles Johnson .05
115 Andre Dawson .15
116 Edgar Renteria .05
117 Robb Nen .05
118 Kevin Brown .15
119 Derek Bell .05
120 Bob Abreu .10
121 Mike Hampton .05
122 Todd Jones .05
123 Billy Wagner .05
124 Shane Reynolds .05
125 Jeff Bagwell .75
126 Brian L. Hunter .05
127 Jeff Montgomery .05
128 *Rod Myers* .05
129 Tim Belcher .05
130 Kevin Appier .05
131 Mike Sweeney .05
132 Craig Paquette .05
133 Joe Randa .05
134 Michael Tucker .05
135 Raul Mondesi .15
136 Tim Wallach .05
137 Brett Butler .05
138 Karim Garcia .10
139 Todd Hollandsworth .05
140 Eric Karros .05
141 Hideo Nomo .40
142 Ismael Valdes .05
143 Cal Eldred .05
144 Scott Karl .05
145 Matt Mieske .05
146 Mike Fetters .05
147 Mark Loretta .05
148 Fernando Vina .05
149 Jeff Cirillo .05
150 Dave Nilsson .05
151 Kirby Puckett 1.00
152 Rich Becker .05
153 Chuck Knoblauch .05
154 Marty Cordova .05
155 Paul Molitor .40
156 Rick Aguilera .05
157 Pat Meares .05
158 Frank Rodriguez .05
159 David Segui .05
160 Henry Rodriguez .05
161 Shane Andrews .05
162 Pedro J. Martinez .30
163 Mark Grudzielanek .05
164 Mike Lansing .05
165 Rondell White .15
166 Ugueth Urbina .05
167 Rey Ordonez .05
168 Robert Person .05
169 Carlos Baerga .05
170 Bernard Gilkey .05
171 John Franco .05
172 Pete Harnisch .05
173 Butch Huskey .05
174 Paul Wilson .05
175 Bernie Williams .20
176 Dwight Gooden .05
177 Wade Boggs .50
178 Ruben Rivera .05
179 Jim Leyritz .05
180 Derek Jeter 1.25
181 Tino Martinez .05
182 Tim Raines .05
183 Scott Brosius .05
184 Jason Giambi .25
185 Geronimo Berroa .05
186 Ariel Prieto .05
187 Scott Spiezio .05
188 John Wasdin .05
189 Ernie Young .05
190 Mark McGwire 2.00
191 Jim Eisenreich .05
192 Ricky Bottalico .05
193 Darren Daulton .05
194 David Doster .05
195 Gregg Jefferies .05
196 Lenny Dykstra .05
197 Curt Schilling .20
198 Todd Stottlemyre .05
199 Willie McGee .05
200 Ozzie Smith 1.00
201 Dennis Eckersley .05
202 Ray Lankford .05
203 John Mabry .05
204 Alan Benes .05
205 Ron Gant .05
206 Archi Cianfrocco .05
207 Fernando Valenzuela .05
208 Greg Vaughn .05
209 Steve Finley .05
210 Tony Gwynn 1.00
211 Rickey Henderson .40
212 Trevor Hoffman .05
213 Jason Thompson .05
214 Osvaldo Fernandez .05
215 Glenallen Hill .05
216 William VanLandingham .05
217 Marvin Benard .05
218 Juan Gonzalez (Postseason) .20
219 Roberto Alomar (Postseason) .05
220 Brian Jordan (Postseason) .05
221 John Smoltz (Postseason) .05
222 Javy Lopez (Postseason) .05
223 Bernie Williams (Postseason) .05
224 Jim Leyritz, John Wetteland (Postseason) .05
225 Barry Bonds 1.00
226 Rich Aurilia .05
227 Jay Canizaro .05
228 Dan Wilson .05
229 Bob Wolcott .05
230 Ken Griffey Jr. 1.50
231 Sterling Hitchcock .05
232 Edgar Martinez .05
233 Joey Cora .05
234 Norm Charlton .05
235 Alex Rodriguez 1.50
236 Bobby Witt .05
237 Darren Oliver .05
238 Kevin Elster .05
239 Rusty Greer .05
240 Juan Gonzalez .75
241 Will Clark .15
242 Dean Palmer .05
243 Ivan Rodriguez .30
244 Checklist (Ken Griffey Jr.) .25
245 Checklist (Ken Griffey Jr.) .25
246 Checklist (Ken Griffey Jr.) .25
247 Checklist (Ken Griffey Jr.) .25
248 Checklist (Ken Griffey Jr.) .25
249 Checklist (Ken Griffey Jr.) .25
250 Eddie Murray .30
251 Troy Percival .05
252 Garret Anderson .05
253 Allen Watson .05
254 Jason Dickson .05
255 Jim Edmonds .05
256 Chuck Finley .05
257 Randy Velarde .05
258 Shigetosi Hasegawa .05
259 Todd Greene .05
260 Tim Salmon .15
261 Mark Langston .05
262 Dave Hollins .05
263 Gary DiSarcina .05
264 Kenny Lofton .05
265 John Smoltz .10
266 Greg Maddux 1.00
267 Jeff Blauser .05
268 Alan Embree .05
269 Mark Lemke .05
270 Chipper Jones 1.25
271 Mike Mussina .40
272 Rafael Palmeiro .15
273 Jimmy Key .05
274 Mike Bordick .05
275 Brady Anderson .05
276 Eric Davis .05
277 Jeffrey Hammonds .05
278 Reggie Jefferson .05
279 Tim Naehring .05
280 John Valentin .05
281 Troy O'Leary .05
282 Shane Mack .05
283 Mike Stanley .05
284 Tim Wakefield .05

285	Brian McRae	.05
286	Brooks Kieschnick	.05
287	Shawon Dunston	.05
288	Kevin Foster	.05
289	Mel Rojas	.05
290	Mark Grace	.20
291	Brant Brown	.05
292	Amaury Telemaco	.05
293	Dave Martinez	.05
294	Jaime Navarro	.05
295	Ray Durham	.05
296	Ozzie Guillen	.05
297	Roberto Hernandez	.05
298	Ron Karkovice	.05
299	James Baldwin	.05
300	Frank Thomas	1.00
301	Eddie Taubensee	.05
302	Bret Boone	.10
303	Willie Greene	.05
304	Dave Burba	.05
305	Deion Sanders	.10
306	Reggie Sanders	.05
307	Hal Morris	.05
308	Pokey Reese	.05
309	Tony Fernandez	.05
310	Manny Ramirez	.75
311	Chad Ogea	.05
312	Jack McDowell	.05
313	Kevin Mitchell	.05
314	Chad Curtis	.05
315	Steve Kline	.05
316	Kevin Seitzer	.05
317	Kirt Manwaring	.05
318	Bill Swift	.05
319	Ellis Burks	.05
320	Andres Galarraga	.05
321	Bruce Ruffin	.05
322	Mark Thompson	.05
323	Walt Weiss	.05
324	Todd Jones	.05
325	Andruw Jones (Griffey Hot List)	.50
326	Chipper Jones (Griffey Hot List)	.65
327	Mo Vaughn (Griffey Hot List)	.15
328	Frank Thomas (Griffey Hot List)	.50
329	Albert Belle (Griffey Hot List)	.10
330	Mark McGwire (Griffey Hot List)	1.00
331	Derek Jeter (Griffey Hot List)	.65
332	Alex Rodriguez (Griffey Hot List)	1.00
333	Jay Buhner (Griffey Hot List)	.05
334	Ken Griffey Jr. (Griffey Hot List)	.75
335	Brian L. Hunter	.05
336	Brian Johnson	.05
337	Omar Olivares	.05
338	*Deivi Cruz*	.05
339	Damion Easley	.05
340	Melvin Nieves	.05
341	Moises Alou	.10
342	Jim Eisenreich	.05
343	Mark Hutton	.05
344	Alex Fernandez	.05
345	Gary Sheffield	.20
346	Pat Rapp	.05
347	Brad Ausmus	.05
348	Sean Berry	.05
349	Darryl Kile	.05
350	Craig Biggio	.10
351	Chris Holt	.05
352	Luis Gonzalez	.25
353	Pat Listach	.05
354	Jose Rosado	.05
355	Mike Macfarlane	.05
356	Tom Goodwin	.05
357	Chris Haney	.05
358	Chili Davis	.05
359	Jose Offerman	.05
360	Johnny Damon	.10
361	Bip Roberts	.05
362	Ramon Martinez	.05
363	Pedro Astacio	.05
364	Todd Zeile	.05
365	Mike Piazza	1.25
366	Greg Gagne	.05
367	Chan Ho Park	.15
368	Wilton Guerrero	.05
369	Todd Worrell	.05
370	John Jaha	.05
371	Steve Sparks	.05
372	Mike Matheny	.05
373	Marc Newfield	.05
374	Jeromy Burnitz	.05
375	Jose Valentin	.05
376	Ben McDonald	.05
377	Roberto Kelly	.05
378	Bob Tewksbury	.05
379	Ron Coomer	.05
380	Brad Radke	.05
381	Matt Lawton	.05
382	Dan Naulty	.05
383	Scott Stahoviak	.05
384	Matt Wagner	.05
385	Jim Bullinger	.05
386	Carlos Perez	.05
387	Darrin Fletcher	.05
388	Chris Widger	.05
389	F.P. Santangelo	.05
390	Lee Smith	.05
391	Bobby Jones	.05
392	John Olerud	.05
393	Mark Clark	.05
394	Jason Isringhausen	.05
395	Todd Hundley	.05
396	Lance Johnson	.05
397	Edgardo Alfonzo	.05
398	Alex Ochoa	.05
399	Darryl Strawberry	.05
400	David Cone	.05
401	Paul O'Neill	.05
402	Joe Girardi	.05
403	Charlie Hayes	.05
404	Andy Pettitte	.25
405	Mariano Rivera	.25
406	Mariano Duncan	.05
407	Kenny Rogers	.05
408	Cecil Fielder	.05
409	George Williams	.05
410	Jose Canseco	.35
411	Tony Batista	.05
412	Steve Karsay	.05
413	Dave Telgheder	.05
414	Billy Taylor	.05
415	Mickey Morandini	.05
416	Calvin Maduro	.05
417	Mark Leiter	.05
418	Kevin Stocker	.05
419	Mike Lieberthal	.05
420	Rico Brogna	.05
421	Mark Portugal	.05
422	Rex Hudler	.05
423	Mark Johnson	.05
424	Esteban Loiaza	.05
425	Lou Collier	.05
426	Kevin Elster	.05
427	Francisco Cordova	.05
428	Marc Wilkins	.05
429	Joe Randa	.05
430	Jason Kendall	.05
431	Jon Lieber	.05
432	Steve Cooke	.05
433	*Emil Brown*	.05
434	*Tony Womack*	.25
435	Al Martin	.05
436	Jason Schmidt	.05
437	Andy Benes	.05
438	Delino DeShields	.05
439	Royce Clayton	.05
440	Brian Jordan	.05
441	Donovan Osborne	.05
442	Gary Gaetti	.05
443	Tom Pagnozzi	.05
444	Joey Hamilton	.05
445	Wally Joyner	.05
446	John Flaherty	.05
447	Chris Gomez	.05
448	Sterling Hitchcock	.05
449	Andy Ashby	.05
450	Ken Caminiti	.05
451	Tim Worrell	.05
452	Jose Vizcaino	.05
453	Rod Beck	.05
454	Wilson Delgado	.05
455	Darryl Hamilton	.05
456	Mark Lewis	.05
457	Mark Gardner	.05
458	Rick Wilkins	.05
459	Scott Sanders	.05
460	Kevin Orie	.05
461	Glendon Rusch	.05
462	Juan Melo	.05
463	Richie Sexson	.05
464	Bartolo Colon	.05
465	Jose Guillen	.05
466	Heath Murray	.05
467	Aaron Boone	.05
468	*Bubba Trammell*	.40
469	Jeff Abbott	.05
470	Derrick Gibson	.05
471	Matt Morris	.05
472	Ryan Jones	.05
473	Pat Cline	.05
474	Adam Riggs	.05
475	Jay Payton	.05
476	Derrek Lee	.05
477	Elieser Marrero	.05
478	Lee Tinsley	.05
479	Jamie Moyer	.05
480	Jay Buhner	.05
481	Bob Wells	.05
482	Jeff Fassero	.05
483	Paul Sorrento	.05
484	Russ Davis	.05
485	Randy Johnson	.40
486	Roger Pavlik	.05
487	Damon Buford	.05
488	Julio Santana	.05
489	Mark McLemore	.05
490	Mickey Tettleton	.05
491	Ken Hill	.05
492	Benji Gil	.05
493	Ed Sprague	.05
494	Mike Timlin	.05
495	Pat Hentgen	.05
496	Orlando Merced	.05
497	Carlos Garcia	.05
498	Carlos Delgado	.15
499	Juan Guzman	.05
500	Roger Clemens	1.00
501	Erik Hanson	.05
502	Otis Nixon	.05
503	Shawn Green	.10
504	Charlie O'Brien	.05
505	Joe Carter	.05
506	Alex Gonzalez	.10

1997 Collector's Choice All-Star Connection

This 45-card insert from Series 2 highlights All-Star caliber players. Cards feature a large star-burst pattern on a metallic-foil background behind the player's photo. They were inserted one per pack.

		MT
Complete Set (45):		12.00
Common Player:		.10
1	Mark McGwire	1.50
2	Chuck Knoblauch	.10
3	Jim Thome	.10
4	Alex Rodriguez	1.25
5	Ken Griffey Jr.	1.25
6	Brady Anderson	.10
7	Albert Belle	.20
8	Ivan Rodriguez	.40
9	Pat Hentgen	.10
10	Frank Thomas	.65
11	Roberto Alomar	.35
12	Robin Ventura	.10
13	Cal Ripken Jr.	1.50
14	Juan Gonzalez	.50
15	Manny Ramirez	.50
16	Bernie Williams	.15
17	Terry Steinbach	.10
18	Andy Pettitte	.25
19	Jeff Bagwell	.50
20	Craig Biggio	.10
21	Ken Caminiti	.10
22	Barry Larkin	.10
23	Tony Gwynn	.55
24	Barry Bonds	.65
25	Kenny Lofton	.10
26	Mike Piazza	.75
27	John Smoltz	.10
28	Andres Galarraga	.10
29	Ryne Sandberg	.50
30	Chipper Jones	.75
31	Mark Grudzielanek	.10
32	Sammy Sosa	.65
33	Steve Finley	.10
34	Gary Sheffield	.15
35	Todd Hundley	.10
36	Greg Maddux	.55
37	Mo Vaughn	.20
38	Eric Young	.10
39	Vinny Castilla	.10
40	Derek Jeter	.75
41	Lance Johnson	.10
42	Ellis Burks	.10
43	Dante Bichette	.10
44	Javy Lopez	.10
45	Hideo Nomo	.50

1997 Collector's Choice Big Shots

This 20-card insert depicts the game's top stars in unique photos. Cards were inserted 1:12 packs. Gold Signature Editions, featuring a gold foil-stamped facsimile autograph, were inserted 1:144 packs. Fronts are highlighted in silver foil. Backs repeat a portion of the front photo, have a picture of the photographer and his comments about the picture.

		MT
Complete Set (19):		17.00
Common Player:		.20
Gold Signature Edition:		2X
1	Ken Griffey Jr.	2.25
2	Nomar Garciaparra	1.75
3	Brian Jordan	.20
4	Scott Rolen	.75
5	Alex Rodriguez	2.25
6	Larry Walker	.30
7	Mariano Rivera	.35
8	Cal Ripken Jr.	2.50
9	Deion Sanders	.20
10	Frank Thomas	1.75
11	Dean Palmer	.20
12	Ken Caminiti	.20
13	Derek Jeter	2.00
14	Barry Bonds	1.75
15	Chipper Jones	2.00
16	Mo Vaughn	.20
17	Jay Buhner	.20
18	Mike Piazza	2.00
19	Tony Gwynn	1.50

1997 Collector's Choice Clearly Dominant

The five-card, regular-sized set features Seattle outfielder Ken Griffey Jr. on each card and was inserted every 144 packs of 1997 Collector's Choice baseball.

		MT
Complete Set (5):		20.00
Common Card:		5.00
CD1	Ken Griffey Jr.	5.00
CD2	Ken Griffey Jr.	5.00
CD3	Ken Griffey Jr.	5.00
CD4	Ken Griffey Jr.	5.00
CD5	Ken Griffey Jr.	5.00

1997 Collector's Choice Clearly Dominant Jumbos

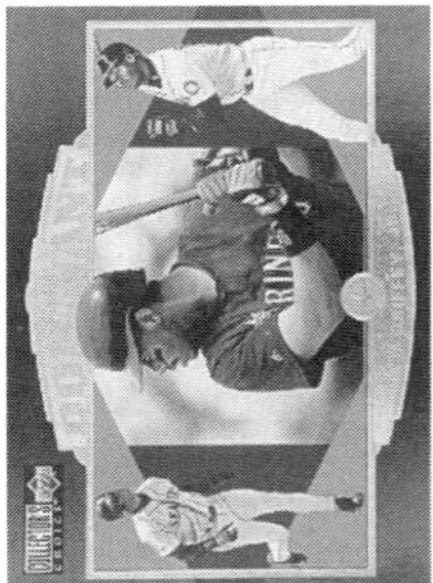

Each of the five Ken Griffey Jr. cards from the Collector's Choice insert set was also produced in a special retail-only 5" x 3-1/2" jumbo version. The supersize Clearly Dominant cards were packaged in a special collectors' kit which also included a Griffey stand-up figure and eight packs of CC cards, retailing for about $15. The cards could also be purchased as a complete set for $10. Cards are numbered with a "CD" prefix.

		MT
Complete Set (5):		10.00
Common Card:		2.00
1	Ken Griffey Jr.	2.00
2	Ken Griffey Jr.	2.00
3	Ken Griffey Jr.	2.00
4	Ken Griffey Jr.	2.00
5	Ken Griffey Jr.	2.00

1997 Collector's Choice Hot List Jumbos

These 5" x 7" versions of the "Ken Griffey Jr.'s Hot List" subset from Series 2 are an exclusive box-topper in certain retail packaging of Collector's Choice. Other than size, the jumbos are identical to the regular Hot List cards, including foil background printing on front.

		MT
Complete Set (10):		20.00
Common Player:		1.00
325	Andruw Jones	2.00
326	Chipper Jones	3.00
327	Mo Vaughn	1.50
328	Frank Thomas	2.50
329	Albert Belle	1.00
330	Mark McGwire	5.00
331	Derek Jeter	3.00
332	Alex Rodriguez	4.00
333	Jay Buhner	1.00
334	Ken Griffey Jr.	4.00

1997 Collector's Choice New Frontier

This is a 40-card Series 2 insert highlighting anticipated interleague matchups. Cards were designed with each player's action photo superimposed on a metallic-foil background depicting half of a ballfield. Pairs could then be displayed side-by-side. Cards were inserted 1:69 packs. They are numbered and carry a "NF" prefix.

		MT
Complete Set (40):		150.00
Common Player:		1.50
1	Alex Rodriguez	12.50
2	Tony Gwynn	6.50
3	Jose Canseco	3.00
4	Hideo Nomo	4.00
5	Mark McGwire	15.00
6	Barry Bonds	7.50
7	Juan Gonzalez	4.50
8	Ken Caminiti	1.50
9	Tim Salmon	2.00
10	Mike Piazza	10.00
11	Ken Griffey Jr.	12.50
12	Andres Galarraga	1.50
13	Jay Buhner	1.50
14	Dante Bichette	1.50
15	Frank Thomas	8.00
16	Ryne Sandberg	4.00
17	Roger Clemens	6.50
18	Andruw Jones	4.00
19	Jim Thome	1.50
20	Sammy Sosa	8.00
21	David Justice	2.00
22	Deion Sanders	1.50
23	Todd Walker	1.50
24	Kevin Orie	1.50
25	Albert Belle	2.00
26	Jeff Bagwell	4.50
27	Manny Ramirez	4.50
28	Brian Jordan	1.50
29	Derek Jeter	10.00
30	Chipper Jones	10.00
31	Mo Vaughn	2.50
32	Gary Sheffield	1.50
33	Carlos Delgado	2.00
34	Vladimir Guerrero	4.00
35	Cal Ripken Jr.	15.00
36	Greg Maddux	6.50
37	Cecil Fielder	1.50
38	Todd Hundley	1.50
39	Mike Mussina	3.50
40	Scott Rolen	3.50

1997 Collector's Choice Premier Power

The 20-card, regular-sized set was included one per 15 packs of Series 1. Fronts feature an action photo with the "Premier Power" logo in silver foil in the lower half and "spotlights" aiming out toward the sides. The bottom portion of the card is transparent red. Backs are bordered in red with the same card front shot appearing in black-and-white above a brief description and "Power Facts." The cards are numbered with a "PP" prefix. A parallel gold-foil version was available every 69 packs.

		MT
Complete Set (20):		25.00
Common Player:		.35
Gold:		2.5X
1	Mark McGwire	5.00
2	Brady Anderson	.35
3	Ken Griffey Jr.	4.00
4	Albert Belle	.75
5	Juan Gonzalez	1.75
6	Andres Galarraga	.35
7	Jay Buhner	.35
8	Mo Vaughn	1.00
9	Barry Bonds	2.00
10	Gary Sheffield	.35
11	Todd Hundley	.35
12	Frank Thomas	2.50
13	Sammy Sosa	2.50
14	Ken Caminiti	.35
15	Vinny Castilla	.35
16	Ellis Burks	.35
17	Rafael Palmeiro	.35
18	Alex Rodriguez	4.00
19	Mike Piazza	3.50
20	Eddie Murray	.75

1997 Collector's Choice Premier Power Jumbo

Each factory set of 1997 Collector's Choice included 10 super-size (3" x 5") versions of the Premier Power inserts. Besides the size, the jumbos differ from the insert version in the addition of a metallic facsimile autograph on front.

		MT
Complete Set (20):		20.00
Common Player:		.50
1	Mark McGwire	5.00
2	Brady Anderson	.50
3	Ken Griffey Jr.	5.00
4	Albert Belle	.65
5	Juan Gonzalez	1.50
6	Andres Galarraga	.50
7	Jay Buhner	.50
8	Mo Vaughn	1.00
9	Barry Bonds	2.00
10	Gary Sheffield	.50
11	Todd Hundley	.50
12	Frank Thomas	2.00
13	Sammy Sosa	2.00
14	Ken Caminiti	.50
15	Vinny Castilla	.50
16	Ellis Burks	.50
17	Rafael Palmeiro	.50
18	Alex Rodriguez	3.00
19	Mike Piazza	2.50
20	Eddie Murray	.75

1997 Collector's Choice Stick'Ums

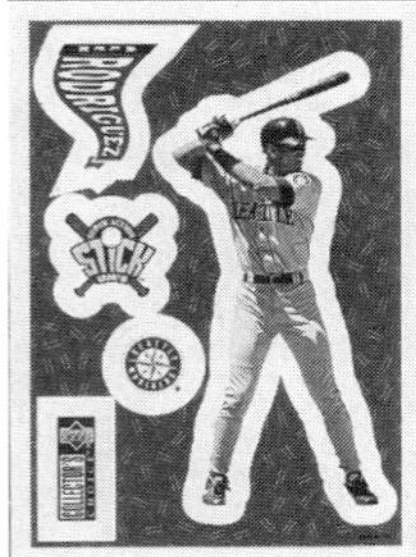

The 30-piece 2-1/2" x 3-1/2" sticker set was inserted one per three packs of Series 1 Collector's Choice. Fronts feature a bright background color and include five different peel-off stickers: An action shot of the player, a pennant in team colors featuring the player's name, a team logo, an Upper Deck Collector's Choice logo and a "Super Action Stick'Ums" decal. Backs feature the player checklist in black ink over a gray background. An unnumbered version of the stickers (without Smith and Puckett) was sold in a special retail-only package.

		MT
Complete Set (30):		17.00
Common Player:		.15
1	Ozzie Smith	.90
2	Andruw Jones	.75
3	Alex Rodriguez	1.75
4	Paul Molitor	.45
5	Jeff Bagwell	.75
6	Manny Ramirez	.75
7	Kenny Lofton	.15
8	Albert Belle	.25
9	Jay Buhner	.15
10	Chipper Jones	1.25
11	Barry Larkin	.15
12	Dante Bichette	.15
13	Mike Piazza	1.25
14	Andres Galarraga	.15
15	Barry Bonds	1.00
16	Brady Anderson	.15
17	Gary Sheffield	.15
18	Jim Thome	.15
19	Tony Gwynn	.90
20	Cal Ripken Jr.	2.00
21	Sammy Sosa	1.00
22	Juan Gonzalez	.75
23	Greg Maddux	.90
24	Ken Griffey Jr.	1.75
25	Mark McGwire	2.00
26	Kirby Puckett	.90
27	Mo Vaughn	.35
28	Vladimir Guerrero	.75
29	Ken Caminiti	.15
30	Frank Thomas	1.00

1997 Collector's Choice Team Sets

A special version of Collector's Choice cards for several popular major league teams was produced in two retail packages by Upper Deck. In one version, blister packs containing 13 player cards and a metallic-foil team logo/checklist card was sold for a suggested retail price of $1.99. The second version, exclusive to Wal-Mart, is a hard plastic blister pack containing two cello-wrapped packages. One holds a random assortment of 15 Series 1 Collector's Choice cards. The other has 13 player cards and a foil logo/checklist card for a specific team. The team-set cards are identical to the regular-issue cards, from either Series 1 or Series 2, except each of the team-set cards has a number on back which differs from the regular edition. Packaged with the Wal-Mart version is a 3-1/2" x 5" "Home Team Heroes" card, listed seperately.

		MT
Common Player:		.10
	Atlanta Braves team set:	4.00
AB	Team logo/checklist	.10
AB1	Andruw Jones	.65
AB2	Kenny Lofton	.10
AB3	Fred McGriff	.10
AB4	Michael Tucker	.10
AB5	Ryan Klesko	.10
AB6	Javy Lopez	.10
AB7	Mark Wohlers	.10
AB8	Tom Glavine	.15
AB9	Denny Neagle	.10
AB10	Chipper Jones	1.00
AB11	Jeff Blauser	.10
AB12	Greg Maddux	.75
AB13	John Smoltz	.15
	Baltimore Orioles team set:	2.00
BO	Team logo/checklist	.10
BO1	Rocky Coppinger	.10
BO2	Scott Erickson	.10
BO3	Chris Hoiles	.10
BO4	Roberto Alomar	.45
BO5	Cal Ripken Jr.	1.50
BO6	Randy Myers	.10
BO7	B.J. Surhoff	.10
BO8	Mike Mussina	.45
BO9	Rafael Palmeiro	.30
BO10	Jimmy Key	.10
BO11	Mike Bordick	.10
BO12	Brady Anderson	.10
BO13	Eric Davis	.10
	Chicago White Sox team set:	2.50
CW	Team logo/checklist	.10
CW1	Robin Ventura	.10
CW2	Wilson Alvarez	.10
CW3	Tony Phillips	.10
CW4	Lyle Mouton	.10
CW5	James Baldwin	.10
CW6	Harold Baines	.10
CW7	Albert Belle	.25
CW8	Chris Snopek	.10
CW9	Ray Durham	.10
CW10	Frank Thomas	.85
CW11	Ozzie Guillen	.10
CW12	Roberto Hernandez	.10
CW13	Jaime Navarro	.10
	Cleveland Indians team set:	1.50
CI	Team logo/checklist	.10
CI1	Brian Giles	.10
CI2	Omar Vizquel	.10
CI3	Julio Franco	.10
CI4	Orel Hershiser	.10
CI5	Charles Nagy	.10
CI6	Matt Williams	.15
CI7	Jose Mesa	.10
CI8	Sandy Alomar	.10
CI9	Jim Thome	.10
CI10	David Justice	.25
CI11	Marquis Grissom	.10
CI12	Chad Ogea	.10
CI13	Manny Ramirez	.65
	Colorado Rockies team set:	1.25
CR	Team logo/checklist	.10
CR1	Dante Bichette	.10
CR2	Vinny Castilla	.10
CR3	Kevin Ritz	.10
CR4	Larry Walker	.30
CR5	Eric Young	.10
CR6	Quinton McCracken	.10
CR7	John Vander Wal	.10
CR8	Jamey Wright	.10
CR9	Mark Thompson	.10
CR10	Andres Galarraga	.10
CR11	Ellis Burks	.10
CR12	Kirt Manwaring	.10
CR13	Walt Weiss	.10
	Florida Marlins team set:	2.00
FM	Team logo/checklist	.10
FM1	(Luis Castillo)	.10
FM2	(Al Leiter)	.10
FM3	(Devon White)	.10
FM4	(Jeff Conine)	.10
FM5	(Charles Johnson)	.10
FM6	(Edgar Renteria)	.10
FM7	(Robb Nen)	.10
FM8	(Kevin Brown)	.15
FM9	(Gary Sheffield)	.25
FM10	(Alex Fernandez)	.10
FM11	(Pat Rapp)	.10
FM12	(Moises Alou)	.15
FM13	(Bobby Bonilla)	.10
	L.A. Dodgers team set:	3.00
LA	Team logo/checklist	.10
LA1	(Raul Mondesi)	.15
LA2	(Brett Butler)	.10
LA3	(Todd Hollandsworth)	.10
LA4	(Eric Karros)	.10
LA5	(Hideo Nomo)	.50
LA6	(Ismael Valdes)	.10
LA7	(Wilton Guerrero)	.10
LA8	(Ramon Martinez)	.10
LA9	(Greg Gagne)	.10
LA10	(Mike Piazza)	1.00
LA11	(Chan Ho Park)	.35
LA12	(Todd Worrell)	.10
LA13	(Todd Zeile)	.10
	New York Yankees team set:	3.00
NY	Team logo/checklist	.10
NY1	Bernie Williams	.30
NY2	Dwight Gooden	.10
NY3	Wade Boggs	.50
NY4	Ruben Rivera	.10
NY5	Derek Jeter	1.00
NY6	Tino Martinez	.10
NY7	Tim Raines	.10
NY8	Joe Girardi	.10
NY9	Charlie Hayes	.10
NY10	Andy Pettitte	.30
NY11	Cecil Fielder	.10
NY12	Paul O'Neill	.10
NY13	David Cone	.10
	Seattle Mariners team set:	3.00
SM	Team logo/checklist	.10
SM1	Dan Wilson	.10
SM2	Ken Griffey Jr.	1.25
SM3	Edgar Martinez	.10
SM4	Joey Cora	.10
SM5	Norm Charlton	.10
SM6	Alex Rodriguez	1.25
SM7	Randy Johnson	.50
SM8	Paul Sorrento	.10
SM9	Jamie Moyer	.10
SM10	Jay Buhner	.10
SM11	Russ Davis	.10
SM12	Jeff Fassero	.10
SM13	Bob Wells	.10
	Texas Rangers team set:	3.00
TR	Team logo/checklist	.10
TR1	Bobby Witt	.10
TR2	Darren Oliver	.10
TR3	Rusty Greer	.10
TR4	Juan Gonzalez	.65
TR5	Will Clark	.15
TR6	Dean Palmer	.10
TR7	Ivan Rodriguez	.60
TR8	John Wetteland	.10
TR9	Mark McLemore	.10
TR10	John Burkett	.10
TR11	Benji Gil	.10
TR12	Ken Hill	.10
TR13	Mickey Tettleton	.10

1997 Collector's Choice Toast of the Town

This 30-card Series 2 insert features top stars on foil-enhanced cards. Odds of finding one are 1:35 packs. Cards are numbered with a "T" prefix.

		MT
Complete Set (30):		22.00
Common Player:		.25
1	Andruw Jones	.80
2	Chipper Jones	1.50
3	Greg Maddux	1.00
4	John Smoltz	.25
5	Kenny Lofton	.25
6	Brady Anderson	.25
7	Cal Ripken Jr.	2.75
8	Mo Vaughn	.35
9	Sammy Sosa	1.25
10	Albert Belle	.30
11	Frank Thomas	1.25
12	Barry Larkin	.25
13	Manny Ramirez	.80
14	Jeff Bagwell	.80
15	Mike Piazza	1.50
16	Paul Molitor	.45
17	Vladimir Guerrero	.80
18	Todd Hundley	.25
19	Derek Jeter	1.50
20	Andy Pettitte	.30
21	Bernie Williams	.30
22	Mark McGwire	2.75
23	Scott Rolen	.75
24	Ken Caminiti	.25
25	Tony Gwynn	1.00
26	Barry Bonds	1.25
27	Ken Griffey Jr.	2.25
28	Alex Rodriguez	2.25
29	Juan Gonzalez	.80
30	Roger Clemens	1.00

1997 Collector's Choice Update

This update set was offered via a mail-in redemption offer. Traded players in their new uniforms and 1997 rookies are the focus of the set. Fronts are color photos which are borderless at top and sides. Beneath each photo the player's name and team logo appear in a red (A.L.) or blue (N.L.) baseball design. Backs have another photo, major and minor league career stats and a trivia question. Cards are numbered with a "U" prefix.

		MT
Complete Set (30):		4.50
Common Player:		.15
1	Jim Leyritz	.15
2	Matt Perisho	.15
3	Michael Tucker	.15
4	Mike Johnson	.15
5	Jaime Navarro	.15
6	Doug Drabek	.15
7	Terry Mulholland	.15
8	Brett Tomko	.15
9	Marquis Grissom	.15
10	David Justice	.50
11	Brian Moehler	.15
12	Bobby Bonilla	.15
13	Todd Dunwoody	.40
14	Tony Saunders	.15
15	Jay Bell	.15
16	Jeff King	.15
17	Terry Steinbach	.15
18	Steve Bieser	.15
19	*Takashi Kashiwada*	.25
20	Hideki Irabu	.25
21	Damon Mashore	.15
22	Quilvio Veras	.15
23	Will Cunnane	.15
24	Jeff Kent	.40
25	J.T. Snow	.25
26	Dante Powell	.15
27	Jose Cruz Jr.	.50
28	John Burkett	.15
29	John Wetteland	.15
30	Benito Santiago	.15

1997 Collector's Choice You Crash the Game

A 30-player interactive set found in Series 2 packs features the game's top home run hitters. Cards were inserted 1:5 packs. Fronts feature a red-foil Crash logo and a range of game dates. Those holding cards of players who homered in that span could (for $2 per card handling fee) redeem them for high-tech versions. Instant winner cards (seeded 1:721) were redeemable for complete 30-card upgrade sets. Winning cards are marked with an asterisk; theoretically they would be scarcer than losing cards because many were redeemed. The contest cards expired on Sept. 8, 1997. Cards are numbered with a "CG" prefix.

		MT
Complete Set (90):		65.00
Common Player:		.25
1	Ryan Klesko	
	July 28-30	.25
	August 8-11	.25
	Sept. 19-21	.25
2	Chipper Jones	
	August 15-17	1.50
	August 29-31	1.50
	Sept. 12-14	1.50
3	Andruw Jones	
	August 22-24*	1.50
	Sept. 1-3	.75
	Sept. 19-22	.75
4	Brady Anderson	
	July 31-Aug. 3*	.50
	Sept. 4-7	.25
	Sept. 19-22	.25
5	Rafael Palmeiro	
	July 29-30	.25
	Aug. 29-31	.25
	Sept. 26-28	.25
6	Cal Ripken Jr.	
	August 8-10*	3.00
	Sept. 1-3*	3.00
	Sept. 11-14	1.50
7	Mo Vaughn	
	August 14-17	.40
	August 29-31*	.75
	Sept. 23-25*	.75
8	Sammy Sosa	
	August 1-3*	2.00
	August 29-31	1.00
	Sept. 19-21*	2.00
9	Albert Belle	
	August 7-10	.35
	Sept. 11-14	.35
	Sept. 19-21*	.75
10	Frank Thomas	
	August 29-31	1.00
	Sept. 1-3	1.00
	Sept. 23-25*	2.00
11	Manny Ramirez	
	August 12-14*	1.00
	August 29-31	.50
	Sept. 11-14*	1.00
12	Jim Thome	
	July 28-30	.25
	August 15-18*	.50
	Sept. 19-22	.25
13	Matt Williams	
	August 4-5	.25
	Sept. 1-3*	.50
	Sept. 23-25	.25
14	Dante Bichette	
	July 24-27*	.50
	August 28-29	.25
	Sept. 26-28*	.50
15	Vinny Castilla	
	August 12-13	.25
	Sept. 4-7*	.50
	Sept. 19-21	.25
16	Andres Galarraga	
	August 8-10*	.50
	August 30-31	.25
	Sept. 12-14	.25
17	Gary Sheffield	
	August 1-3*	.50
	Sept. 1-3*	.50
	Sept. 12-14*	.50
18	Jeff Bagwell	
	Sept. 9-10	.50
	Sept. 19-22*	1.00
	Sept. 23-25*	1.00
19	Eric Karros	
	August 1-3	.25
	August 15-17	.25
	Sept. 25-28*	.50
20	Mike Piazza	
	August 11-12	1.25
	Sept. 5-8*	2.50
	Sept. 19-21*	2.50
21	Vladimir Guerrero	
	August 22-24	.50
	August 29-31	.50
	Sept. 19-22	.50
22	Cecil Fielder	
	August 29-31	.25
	Sept. 4-7	.25
	Sept. 26-28*	.50
23	Jose Canseco	
	August 22-24	.35
	Sept. 12-14	.35
	Sept. 26-28	.35
24	Mark McGwire	
	July 31-Aug. 3	2.00
	August 30-31	2.00
	Sept. 19-22*	4.00
25	Ken Caminiti	
	August 8-10	.25
	Sept. 4-7	.25
	Sept. 17-18*	.50
26	Barry Bonds	
	August 5-7	.75
	Sept. 4-7*	1.50
	Sept. 23-24*	1.50
27	Jay Buhner	
	August 7-10	.25
	August 28-29	.25
	Sept. 1-3	.25
28	Ken Griffey Jr.	
	August 22-24*	3.00
	August 28-29	1.50
	Sept. 19-22*	3.00
29	Alex Rodriguez	
	July 29-31	1.50
	August 30-31	1.50
	Sept. 12-15	1.50
30	Juan Gonzalez	
	August 11-13*	1.00
	August 30-31	.50
	Sept. 19-21*	1.00

1997 Collector's Choice You Crash the Game Winners

These are the prize cards from CC's interactive "You Crash the Game" cards in Series 2. Persons who redeemed a Crash card with the correct date (s) on which the pictured player homered received (for a $2 handling fee) this high-end version of the Crash card. The redemption cards have the same basic design as the contest cards, but use different player photos with fronts printed on metallic-foil stock, and a team logo in place of the Crash foil logo. Where the contest cards have game rules on back, the redemption cards have another photo of the player and career highlights. Complete redemption sets were available upon redeeming an instant winner card, found on average of one per 721 packs. Because some cards were only available in complete redemption sets (marked with an "SP" here), and others might have been available for more than one date range, some cards will be scarcer than others.

		MT
Complete Set (30):		40.00
Common Player:		.50
CG1	Ryan Klesko (SP)	1.25
CG2	Chipper Jones (SP)	7.50
CG3	Andruw Jones	.75
CG4	Brady Anderson	.50
CG5	Rafael Palmeiro (SP)	1.50
CG6	Cal Ripken Jr.	3.00
CG7	Mo Vaughn	.60
CG8	Sammy Sosa	1.50
CG9	Albert Belle	.60
CG10	Frank Thomas	2.00
CG11	Manny Ramirez	.75
CG12	Jim Thome	.50
CG13	Matt Williams	.50
CG14	Dante Bichette	.50
CG15	Vinny Castilla	.50
CG16	Andres Galarraga	.50
CG17	Gary Sheffield	.50
CG18	Jeff Bagwell	.75
CG19	Eric Karros	.50
CG20	Mike Piazza	2.00
CG21	Vladimir Guerrero (SP)	3.00
CG22	Cecil Fielder (SP)	1.25
CG23	Jose Canseco (SP)	2.00
CG24	Mark McGwire	3.00
CG25	Ken Caminiti	.50
CG26	Barry Bonds	2.00
CG27	Jay Buhner (SP)	1.25
CG28	Ken Griffey Jr.	2.50
CG29	Alex Rodriguez (SP)	10.00
CG30	Juan Gonzalez	.75

1998 Collector's Choice

The 530-card Collectors Choice set was issued in two 265-card series. Series 1 features 197 regular cards, five checklists and four subsets: Cover Story features 18 of the leagues' top stars, Rookie Class has 27 young players, the nine-card Top of the Charts subset honors 1997's statistical leaders and Masked Marauders is a nine-card subset. Inserts in Series 1 are Super Action Stick-Ums, Evolution Revolution and StarQuest. Series 2 has 233 regular cards, five checklist cards, an 18-card Rookie Class subset and the nine-card Golden Jubilee subset. Inserts in Series 2 include Mini Bobbing Head Cards, You Crash the Game and StarQuest. Factory sets include a random assoirtment of 10 StarQuest cards.

		MT
Complete Set (530):		15.00
Unopened Factory Set (540):		20.00
Common Player:		.05
Pack (14):		1.00
Wax Box (36):		15.00
1	Nomar Garciaparra (Cover Glory)	.50

2 Roger Clemens (Cover Glory) .30
3 Larry Walker (Cover Glory) .05
4 Mike Piazza (Cover Glory) .60
5 Mark McGwire (Cover Glory) .75
6 Tony Gwynn (Cover Glory) .45
7 Jose Cruz Jr. (Cover Glory) .05
8 Frank Thomas (Cover Glory) .55
9 Tino Martinez (Cover Glory) .05
10 Ken Griffey Jr. (Cover Glory) .65
11 Barry Bonds (Cover Glory) .50
12 Scott Rolen (Cover Glory) .40
13 Randy Johnson (Cover Glory) .15
14 Ryne Sandberg (Cover Glory) .25
15 Eddie Murray (Cover Glory) .15
16 Kevin Brown (Cover Glory) .05
17 Greg Maddux (Cover Glory) .35
18 Sandy Alomar Jr. (Cover Glory) .05
19 Checklist (Ken Griffey Jr., Adam Riggs) .40
20 Checklist (Nomar Garciaparra, Charlie O'Brien) .10
21 Checklist (Ben Grieve, Ken Griffey Jr., Larry Walker, Mark McGwire) .50
22 Checklist (Mark McGwire, Cal Ripken Jr.) .50
23 Checklist (Tino Martinez) .05
24 Jason Dickson .05
25 Darin Erstad .60
26 Todd Greene .05
27 Chuck Finley .05
28 Garret Anderson .05
29 Dave Hollins .05
30 Rickey Henderson .40
31 John Smoltz .10
32 Michael Tucker .05
33 Jeff Blauser .05
34 Javier Lopez .05
35 Andruw Jones .65
36 Denny Neagle .05
37 Randall Simon .05
38 Mark Wohlers .05
39 Harold Baines .05
40 Cal Ripken Jr. 1.50
41 Mike Bordick .05
42 Jimmy Key .05
43 Armando Benitez .05
44 Scott Erickson .05
45 Eric Davis .05
46 Bret Saberhagen .05
47 Darren Bragg .05
48 Steve Avery .05
49 Jeff Frye .05
50 Aaron Sele .05
51 Scott Hatteberg .05
52 Tom Gordon .05
53 Kevin Orie .05
54 Kevin Foster .05
55 Ryne Sandberg .50
56 Doug Glanville .05
57 Tyler Houston .05
58 Steve Trachsel .05
59 Mark Grace .20
60 Frank Thomas .90
61 *Scott Eyre* .05
62 Jeff Abbott .05
63 Chris Clemons .05
64 Jorge Fabregas .05
65 Robin Ventura .05
66 Matt Karchner .05
67 Jon Nunnally .05
68 Aaron Boone .05
69 Pokey Reese .05
70 Deion Sanders .10
71 Jeff Shaw .05
72 Eduardo Perez .05
73 Brett Tomko .05
74 Bartolo Colon .05
75 Manny Ramirez .50
76 Jose Mesa .05
77 Brian Giles .05
78 Richie Sexson .05
79 Orel Hershiser .05
80 Matt Williams .20
81 Walt Weiss .05
82 Jerry DiPoto .05
83 Quinton McCracken .05
84 Neifi Perez .05
85 Vinny Castilla .05
86 Ellis Burks .05
87 John Thomson .05
88 Willie Blair .05
89 Bob Hamelin .05
90 Tony Clark .05
91 Todd Jones .05
92 Deivi Cruz .05
93 *Frank Catalanotto* .15
94 Justin Thompson .05
95 Gary Sheffield .25
96 Kevin Brown .15
97 Charles Johnson .05
98 Bobby Bonilla .05
99 Livan Hernandez .05
100 Paul Konerko (Rookie Class) .10
101 Craig Counsell (Rookie Class) .05
102 *Magglio Ordonez* (Rookie Class) 1.00
103 Garrett Stephenson (Rookie Class) .05
104 Ken Cloude (Rookie Class) .05
105 Miguel Tejada (Rookie Class) .30
106 Juan Encarnacion (Rookie Class) .10
107 Dennis Reyes (Rookie Class) .05
108 Orlando Cabrera (Rookie Class) .05
109 Kelvim Escobar (Rookie Class) .05
110 Ben Grieve (Rookie Class) .15
111 Brian Rose (Rookie Class) .05
112 Fernando Tatis (Rookie Class) .05
113 Tom Evans (Rookie Class) .05
114 Tom Fordham (Rookie Class) .05
115 Mark Kotsay (Rookie Class) .05
116 Mario Valdez (Rookie Class) .05
117 Jeremi Gonzalez (Rookie Class) .05
118 Todd Dunwoody (Rookie Class) .05
119 Javier Valentin (Rookie Class) .05
120 Todd Helton (Rookie Class) .50
121 Jason Varitek (Rookie Class) .05
122 Chris Carpenter (Rookie Class) .05
123 *Kevin Millwood* (Rookie Class) 1.00
124 Brad Fullmer (Rookie Class) .05
125 Jaret Wright (Rookie Class) .10
126 Brad Rigby (Rookie Class) .05
127 Edgar Renteria .05
128 Robb Nen .05
129 Tony Pena .05
130 Craig Biggio .10
131 Brad Ausmus .05
132 Shane Reynolds .05
133 Mike Hampton .05
134 Billy Wagner .05
135 Richard Hidalgo .10
136 Jose Rosado .05
137 Yamil Benitez .05
138 Felix Martinez .05
139 Jeff King .05
140 Jose Offerman .05
141 Joe Vitiello .05
142 Tim Belcher .05
143 Brett Butler .05
144 Greg Gagne .05
145 Mike Piazza 1.00
146 Ramon Martinez .05
147 Raul Mondesi .20
148 Adam Riggs .05
149 Eddie Murray .30
150 Jeff Cirillo .05
151 Scott Karl .05
152 Mike Fetters .05
153 Dave Nilsson .05
154 Antone Williamson .05
155 Jeff D'Amico .05
156 Jose Valentin .05
157 Brad Radke .05
158 Torii Hunter .05
159 Chuck Knoblauch .05
160 Paul Molitor .40
161 Travis Miller .05
162 Rich Robertson .05
163 Ron Coomer .05
164 Mark Grudzielanek .05
165 Lee Smith .05
166 Vladimir Guerrero .65
167 Dustin Hermanson .05
168 Ugueth Urbina .05
169 F.P. Santangelo .05
170 Rondell White .15
171 Bobby Jones .05
172 Edgardo Alfonzo .05
173 John Franco .05
174 Carlos Baerga .05
175 Butch Huskey .05
176 Rey Ordonez .05
177 Matt Franco .05
178 Dwight Gooden .05
179 Chad Curtis .05
180 Tino Martinez .05
181 Charlie O'Brien (Masked Marauders) .05
182 Sandy Alomar Jr. (Masked Marauders) .05
183 Raul Casanova (Masked Marauders) .05
184 Jim Leyritz (Masked Marauders) .05
185 Mike Piazza (Masked Marauders) .60
186 Ivan Rodriguez (Masked Marauders) .20
187 Charles Johnson (Masked Marauders) .05
188 Brad Ausmus (Masked Marauders) .05
189 Brian Johnson (Masked Marauders) .05
190 Wade Boggs .50
191 David Wells .05
192 Tim Raines .05
193 Ramiro Mendoza .05
194 Willie Adams .05
195 Matt Stairs .05
196 Jason McDonald .05
197 Dave Magadan .05
198 Mark Bellhorn .05
199 Ariel Prieto .05
200 Jose Canseco .35
201 Bobby Estalella .05
202 *Tony Barron* .05
203 Midre Cummings .05
204 Ricky Bottalico .05
205 Mike Grace .05
206 Rico Brogna .05
207 Mickey Morandini .05
208 Lou Collier .05
209 *Kevin Polcovich* .05
210 Kevin Young .05
211 Jose Guillen .05
212 Esteban Loaiza .05
213 Marc Wilkins .05
214 Jason Schmidt .05
215 Gary Gaetti .05
216 Fernando Valenzuela .05
217 Willie McGee .05
218 Alan Benes .05
219 Eli Marrero .05
220 Mark McGwire 1.50
221 Matt Morris .05
222 Trevor Hoffman .05
223 Will Cunnane .05
224 Joey Hamilton .05
225 Ken Caminiti .05
226 Derrek Lee .05
227 Mark Sweeney .05
228 Carlos Hernandez .05
229 Brian Johnson .05
230 Jeff Kent .05
231 Kirk Rueter .05
232 Bill Mueller .05
233 Dante Powell .05
234 J.T. Snow .05
235 Shawn Estes .05
236 Dennis Martinez .05
237 Jamie Moyer .05
238 Dan Wilson .05
239 Joey Cora .05
240 Ken Griffey Jr. 1.25
241 Paul Sorrento .05
242 Jay Buhner .05
243 *Hanley Frias* .05
244 John Burkett .05
245 Juan Gonzalez .50
246 Rick Helling .05
247 Darren Oliver .05
248 Mickey Tettleton .05
249 Ivan Rodriguez .40
250 Joe Carter .05
251 Pat Hentgen .05
252 Marty Janzen .05
253 Frank Thomas, Tony Gwynn (Top of the Charts) .25
254 Mark McGwire, Ken Griffey Jr., Larry Walker (Top of the Charts) .50
255 Ken Griffey Jr., Andres Galarraga (Top of the Charts) .40
256 Brian Hunter, Tony Womack (Top of the Charts) .05
257 Roger Clemens, Denny Neagle (Top of the Charts) .10
258 Roger Clemens, Curt Schilling (Top of the Charts) .30
259 Roger Clemens, Pedro J. Martinez (Top of the Charts) .25
260 Randy Myers, Jeff Shaw (Top of the Charts) .05
261 Nomar Garciaparra, Scott Rolen (Top of the Charts) .25
262 Charlie O'Brien .05
263 Shannon Stewart .10
264 Robert Person .05
265 Carlos Delgado .20
266 Checklist (Matt Williams, Travis Lee) .05
267 Checklist (Nomar Garciaparra, Cal Ripken Jr.) .50
268 Checklist (Mark McGwire, Mike Piazza) .50
269 Checklist (Tony Gwynn, Ken Griffey Jr.) .40
270 Checklist (Fred McGriff, Jose Cruz Jr.) .05
271 Andruw Jones (Golden Jubilee) .25
272 Alex Rodriguez (Golden Jubilee) .65
273 Juan Gonzalez (Golden Jubilee) .25
274 Nomar Garciaparra (Golden Jubilee) .50
275 Ken Griffey Jr. (Golden Jubilee) .65
276 Tino Martinez (Golden Jubilee) .05
277 Roger Clemens (Golden Jubilee) .40
278 Barry Bonds (Golden Jubilee) .50
279 Mike Piazza (Golden Jubilee) .60
280 Tim Salmon (Golden Jubilee) .05
281 Gary DiSarcina .05
282 Cecil Fielder .05
283 Ken Hill .05
284 Troy Percival .05
285 Jim Edmonds .05
286 Allen Watson .05
287 Brian Anderson .05
288 Jay Bell .05
289 Jorge Fabregas .05
290 Devon White .05
291 Yamil Benitez .05
292 Jeff Suppan .05

293	Tony Batista	.05
294	Brent Brede	.05
295	Andy Benes	.05
296	Felix Rodriguez	.05
297	Karim Garcia	.05
298	Omar Daal	.05
299	Andy Stankiewicz	.05
300	Matt Williams	.15
301	Willie Blair	.05
302	Ryan Klesko	.05
303	Tom Glavine	.10
304	Walt Weiss	.05
305	Greg Maddux	.75
306	Chipper Jones	1.00
307	Keith Lockhart	.05
308	Andres Galarraga	.05
309	Chris Hoiles	.05
310	Roberto Alomar	.40
311	Joe Carter	.05
312	Doug Drabek	.05
313	Jeffrey Hammonds	.05
314	Rafael Palmeiro	.15
315	Mike Mussina	.40
316	Brady Anderson	.05
317	B.J. Surhoff	.05
318	Dennis Eckersley	.05
319	Jim Leyritz	.05
320	Mo Vaughn	.20
321	Nomar Garciaparra	.90
322	Reggie Jefferson	.05
323	Tim Naehring	.05
324	Troy O'Leary	.05
325	Pedro J. Martinez	.30
326	John Valentin	.05
327	Mark Clark	.05
328	Rod Beck	.05
329	Mickey Morandini	.05
330	Sammy Sosa	.90
331	Jeff Blauser	.05
332	Lance Johnson	.05
333	Scott Servais	.05
334	Kevin Tapani	.05
335	Henry Rodriguez	.05
336	Jaime Navarro	.05
337	Benji Gil	.05
338	James Baldwin	.05
339	Mike Cameron	.05
340	Ray Durham	.05
341	Chris Snopek	.05
342	Eddie Taubensee	.05
343	Bret Boone	.10
344	Willie Greene	.05
345	Barry Larkin	.10
346	Chris Stynes	.05
347	Pete Harnisch	.05
348	Dave Burba	.05
349	Sandy Alomar Jr.	.05
350	Kenny Lofton	.05
351	Geronimo Berroa	.05
352	Omar Vizquel	.05
353	Travis Fryman	.05
354	Dwight Gooden	.05
355	Jim Thome	.05
356	David Justice	.20
357	Charles Nagy	.05
358	Chad Ogea	.05
359	Pedro Astacio	.05
360	Larry Walker	.15
361	Mike Lansing	.05
362	Kirt Manwaring	.05
363	Dante Bichette	.05
364	Jamey Wright	.05
365	Darryl Kile	.05
366	Luis Gonzalez	.25
367	Joe Randa	.05
368	Raul Casanova	.05
369	Damion Easley	.05
370	Brian L. Hunter	.05
371	Bobby Higginson	.10
372	Brian Moehler	.05
373	Scott Sanders	.05
374	Jim Eisenreich	.05
375	Derrek Lee	.05
376	Jay Powell	.05
377	Cliff Floyd	.05
378	Alex Fernandez	.05
379	Felix Heredia	.05
380	Jeff Bagwell	.60
381	Bill Spiers	.05
382	Chris Holt	.05
383	Carl Everett	.10
384	Derek Bell	.05
385	Moises Alou	.10
386	Ramon Garcia	.05
387	Mike Sweeney	.05
388	Glendon Rusch	.05
389	Kevin Appier	.05
390	Dean Palmer	.05
391	Jeff Conine	.05
392	Johnny Damon	.10
393	Jose Vizcaino	.05
394	Todd Hollandsworth	.05
395	Eric Karros	.05
396	Todd Zeile	.05
397	Chan Ho Park	.15
398	Ismael Valdes	.05
399	Eric Young	.05
400	Hideo Nomo	.40
401	Mark Loretta	.05
402	Doug Jones	.05
403	Jeromy Burnitz	.05
404	John Jaha	.05
405	Marquis Grissom	.05
406	Mike Matheny	.05
407	Todd Walker	.05
408	Marty Cordova	.05
409	Matt Lawton	.05
410	Terry Steinbach	.05
411	Pat Meares	.05
412	Rick Aguilera	.05
413	Otis Nixon	.05
414	Derrick May	.05
415	Carl Pavano (Rookie Class)	.05
416	A.J. Hinch (Rookie Class)	.10
417	*David Dellucci* (Rookie Class)	.20
418	Bruce Chen (Rookie Class)	.05
419	*Darron Ingram* (Rookie Class)	.05
420	Sean Casey (Rookie Class)	.30
421	Mark L. Johnson (Rookie Class)	.05
422	Gabe Alvarez (Rookie Class)	.05
423	Alex Gonzalez (Rookie Class)	.05
424	Daryle Ward (Rookie Class)	.05
425	Russell Branyan (Rookie Class)	.05
426	Mike Caruso (Rookie Class)	.05
427	*Mike Kinkade* (Rookie Class)	.25
428	Ramon Hernandez (Rookie Class)	.05
429	Matt Clement (Rookie Class)	.05
430	Travis Lee (Rookie Class)	.10
431	Shane Monahan (Rookie Class)	.05
432	*Rich Butler* (Rookie Class)	.05
433	Chris Widger	.05
434	Jose Vidro	.05
435	Carlos Perez	.05
436	Ryan McGuire	.05
437	Brian McRae	.05
438	Al Leiter	.05
439	Rich Becker	.05
440	Todd Hundley	.05
441	Dave Mlicki	.05
442	Bernard Gilkey	.05
443	John Olerud	.05
444	Paul O'Neill	.05
445	Andy Pettitte	.30
446	David Cone	.05
447	Chili Davis	.05
448	Bernie Williams	.30
449	Joe Girardi	.05
450	Derek Jeter	1.00
451	Mariano Rivera	.20
452	George Williams	.05
453	Kenny Rogers	.05
454	Tom Candiotti	.05
455	Rickey Henderson	.40
456	Jason Giambi	.30
457	Scott Spiezio	.05
458	Doug Glanville	.05
459	Desi Relaford	.05
460	Curt Schilling	.20
461	Bob Abreu	.10
462	Gregg Jefferies	.05
463	Scott Rolen	.60
464	Mike Lieberthal	.05
465	Tony Womack	.05
466	Jermaine Allensworth	.05
467	Francisco Cordova	.05
468	Jon Lieber	.05
469	Al Martin	.05
470	Jason Kendall	.05
471	Todd Stottlemyre	.05
472	Royce Clayton	.05
473	Brian Jordan	.05
474	John Mabry	.05
475	Ray Lankford	.05
476	Delino DeShields	.05
477	Ron Gant	.05
478	Mark Langston	.05
479	Steve Finley	.05
480	Tony Gwynn	.75
481	Andy Ashby	.05
482	Wally Joyner	.05
483	Greg Vaughn	.05
484	Sterling Hitchcock	.05
485	J. Kevin Brown	.05
486	Orel Hershiser	.05
487	Charlie Hayes	.05
488	Darryl Hamilton	.05
489	Mark Gardner	.05
490	Barry Bonds	.90
491	Robb Nen	.05
492	Kirk Rueter	.05
493	Randy Johnson	.40
494	Jeff Fassero	.05
495	Alex Rodriguez	1.25
496	David Segui	.05
497	Rich Amaral	.05
498	Russ Davis	.05
499	Bubba Trammell	.05
500	Wade Boggs	.50
501	Roberto Hernandez	.05
502	Dave Martinez	.05
503	Dennis Springer	.05
504	Paul Sorrento	.05
505	Wilson Alvarez	.05
506	Mike Kelly	.05
507	Albie Lopez	.05
508	Tony Saunders	.05
509	John Flaherty	.05
510	Fred McGriff	.05
511	Quinton McCracken	.05
512	Terrell Wade	.05
513	Kevin Stocker	.05
514	Kevin Elster	.05
515	Will Clark	.15
516	Bobby Witt	.05
517	Tom Goodwin	.05
518	Aaron Sele	.05
519	Lee Stevens	.05
520	Rusty Greer	.05
521	John Wetteland	.05
522	Darrin Fletcher	.05
523	Jose Canseco	.35
524	Randy Myers	.05
525	Jose Cruz Jr.	.15
526	Shawn Green	.10
527	Tony Fernandez	.05
528	Alex Gonzalez	.10
529	Ed Sprague	.05
530	Roger Clemens	.75

1998 Collector's Choice Cover Glory 5x7

		MT
Complete Set (10):		10.00
Common Player:		1.00
1	Nomar Garciaparra	1.50
2	Roger Clemens	1.00
3	Larry Walker	1.00
4	Mike Piazza	2.00
5	Mark McGwire	3.00
6	Tony Gwynn	1.25
7	Jose Cruz Jr.	1.00
8	Frank Thomas	1.50
9	Tino Martinez	1.00
10	Ken Griffey Jr.	2.50

1998 Collector's Choice Evolution Revolution

This 28-card insert features one player from each Major League team. The fronts picture the team jersey and open to reveal the player's top 1997 accomplishment. Evolution Revolution was inserted in Series 1 packs. Cards are numbered with an "ER" prefix.

		MT
Complete Set (28):		32.50
Common Player:		.40
Inserted 1:13		
1	Tim Salmon	.60
2	Greg Maddux	2.00
3	Cal Ripken Jr.	5.00
4	Mo Vaughn	.75
5	Sammy Sosa	2.50
6	Frank Thomas	2.50
7	Barry Larkin	.40
8	Jim Thome	.40
9	Larry Walker	.60
10	Travis Fryman	.40
11	Gary Sheffield	.60
12	Jeff Bagwell	1.50
13	Johnny Damon	.50
14	Mike Piazza	3.00
15	Jeff Cirillo	.40
16	Paul Molitor	1.00
17	Vladimir Guerrero	1.50
18	Todd Hundley	.40
19	Tino Martinez	.40
20	Jose Canseco	.75
21	Scott Rolen	1.25
22	Al Martin	.40
23	Mark McGwire	5.00
24	Tony Gwynn	2.00
25	Barry Bonds	2.50
26	Ken Griffey Jr.	4.00
27	Juan Gonzalez	1.50
28	Roger Clemens	2.00

Figure values of lower-grade cards from 1981-date as:
Near Mint (NM) 75%
Excellent (EX) 40%
of the listed Mint price

For cards through 1980, values should be figured as:
Excellent (EX) 50%
Very Good (VG) 30%
of the listed
Near Mint price

1998 Collector's Choice Mini Bobbing Heads

The cards in this 30-card insert series can be punched out and assembled into a stand-up figure with a removable bobbing head. They are a Series 2 insert.

		MT
Complete Set (30):		20.00
Common Player:		.25
Inserted 1:3		
1	Tim Salmon	.25
2	Travis Lee	.25
3	Matt Williams	.25
4	Chipper Jones	1.50
5	Greg Maddux	1.00
6	Cal Ripken Jr.	2.50
7	Nomar Garciaparra	1.25
8	Mo Vaughn	.40
9	Sammy Sosa	1.25
10	Frank Thomas	1.25
11	Kenny Lofton	.25
12	Jaret Wright	.25
13	Larry Walker	.35
14	Tony Clark	.25
15	Edgar Renteria	.25
16	Jeff Bagwell	.75
17	Mike Piazza	1.50
18	Vladimir Guerrero	.75
19	Derek Jeter	1.50
20	Ben Grieve	.50
21	Scott Rolen	.60
22	Mark McGwire	2.50
23	Tony Gwynn	1.00
24	Barry Bonds	1.25
25	Ken Griffey Jr.	2.00
26	Alex Rodriguez	2.00
27	Fred McGriff	.25
28	Juan Gonzalez	.75
29	Roger Clemens	1.00
30	Jose Cruz Jr.	.25

1998 Collector's Choice StarQuest Super Powers Jumbos

This enlarged (3-1/2" x 5") version of the StarQuest Super Powers cards from Series 1 were a retail-only variation found one per blister pack of specially marked Collector's Choice product.

	MT
Complete Set (10):	18.00
Common Player:	2.00
SQ67Andres Galarraga	2.00
SQ68Rafael Palmeiro	2.00
SQ69Manny Ramirez	3.00
SQ70Albert Belle	2.00
SQ71Jay Buhner	2.00
SQ72Mo Vaughn	2.00
SQ73Barry Bonds	3.00
SQ74Chipper Jones	4.00
SQ75Jeff Bagwell	2.50
SQ76Jim Thome	2.00

1998 Collector's Choice StarQuest - Series 1

The StarQuest insert in Series 1 consists of 90 cards within four tiers. The tiers are designated by the number of stars found on front, the more the better: Special Delivery (#1-45, one star), Students of the Game (two stars, #46-65), Super Powers (three stars, #66-80) and Super Star Domain (four stars, #81-90). All cards are numbered with a "SQ" prefix.

		MT
Complete Set (90):		200.00
Common Special Delivery (1-45):		.20
Inserted 1:1		
Common Student of the Game (46-65):		.75
Inserted 1:21		
Common Super Power (66-80):		2.00
Inserted 1:71		
Common Superstar Domain (81-90):		5.00
Inserted 1:145		
1	Nomar Garciaparra	2.00
2	Scott Rolen	1.50
3	Jason Dickson	.20
4	Jaret Wright	.75
5	Kevin Orie	.20
6	Jose Guillen	.50
7	Matt Morris	.20
8	Mike Cameron	.30
9	Kevin Polcovich	.20
10	Jose Cruz Jr.	.25
11	Miguel Tejada	.50
12	Fernando Tatis	.40
13	Todd Helton	.75
14	Ken Cloude	.20
15	Ben Grieve	.50
16	Dante Powell	.20
17	Bubba Trammell	.20
18	Juan Encarnacion	.40
19	Derrek Lee	.20
20	Paul Konerko	.50
21	Richard Hidalgo	.50
22	Denny Neagle	.20
23	David Justice	.30
24	Pedro J. Martinez	.40
25	Greg Maddux	1.00
26	Edgar Martinez	.20
27	Cal Ripken Jr.	2.50
28	Tim Salmon	.30
29	Shawn Estes	.20
30	Ken Griffey Jr.	2.50
31	Brad Radke	.35
32	Andy Pettitte	.50
33	Curt Schilling	.35
34	Raul Mondesi	.30
35	Alex Rodriguez	2.00
36	Jeff Kent	.20
37	Jeff Bagwell	1.00
38	Juan Gonzalez	1.00
39	Barry Bonds	1.50
40	Mark McGwire	3.00
41	Frank Thomas	1.50
42	Ray Lankford	.20
43	Tony Gwynn	1.50
44	Mike Piazza	2.00
45	Tino Martinez	.20
46	Nomar Garciaparra	5.00
47	Paul Molitor	1.50
48	Chuck Knoblauch	1.00
49	Rusty Greer	.75
50	Cal Ripken Jr.	6.00
51	Roberto Alomar	1.50
52	Scott Rolen	3.00
53	Derek Jeter	5.00
54	Mark Grace	1.00
55	Randy Johnson	1.00
56	Craig Biggio	.75
57	Kenny Lofton	.75
58	Eddie Murray	1.00
59	Ryne Sandberg	2.00
60	Rickey Henderson	1.00
61	Darin Erstad	2.00
62	Jim Edmonds	1.00
63	Ken Caminiti	1.00
64	Ivan Rodriguez	1.50
65	Tony Gwynn	2.00
66	Tony Clark	2.00
67	Andres Galarraga	2.00
68	Rafael Palmeiro	2.00
69	Manny Ramirez	4.00
70	Albert Belle	2.00
71	Jay Buhner	2.00
72	Mo Vaughn	2.00
73	Barry Bonds	7.50
74	Chipper Jones	12.50
75	Jeff Bagwell	6.00
76	Jim Thome	2.00
77	Sammy Sosa	6.00
78	Todd Hundley	2.00
79	Matt Williams	2.00
80	Vinny Castilla	2.00
81	Jose Cruz Jr.	5.00
82	Frank Thomas	9.00
83	Juan Gonzalez	7.50
84	Mike Piazza	15.00
85	Alex Rodriguez	20.00
86	Larry Walker	5.00
87	Tino Martinez	5.00
88	Greg Maddux	7.50
89	Mark McGwire	20.00
90	Ken Griffey Jr.	15.00

1998 Collector's Choice StarQuest - Series 2

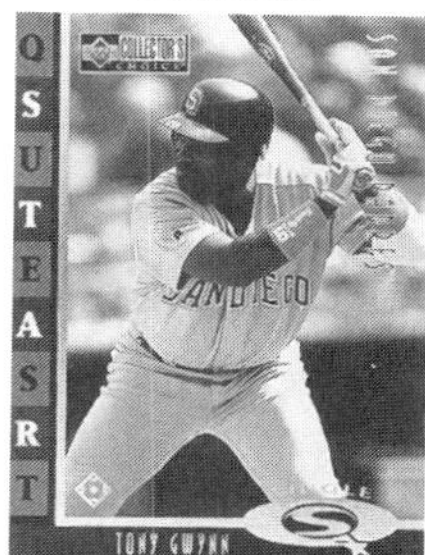

The 30-card StarQuest insert was included in Series 2 packs. The insert has four parallel tiers - Single, Double, Triple and Home Run - designated by the number of baseball diamond icons on the card front. Single cards were inserted 1:1, Doubles 1:21, Triples 1:71 and Home Runs are sequentially numbered to 100. The second series SQ cards feature a front design with the letters "QSUTEASRT" in color blocks vertically at left.

		MT
Complete Set (30):		17.00
Common Player:		.25
Singles 1:1		
Doubles 1:21		4X
Triples 1:71		10X
Home Runs		25X
1	Ken Griffey Jr.	1.50
2	Jose Cruz Jr.	.25
3	Cal Ripken Jr.	2.00
4	Roger Clemens	.75
5	Frank Thomas	1.00
6	Derek Jeter	1.25
7	Alex Rodriguez	1.50
8	Andruw Jones	.65
9	Vladimir Guerrero	.65
10	Mark McGwire	2.00
11	Kenny Lofton	.25
12	Pedro J. Martinez	.50
13	Greg Maddux	.75
14	Larry Walker	.25
15	Barry Bonds	1.00
16	Chipper Jones	1.25
17	Jeff Bagwell	.65
18	Juan Gonzalez	.65
19	Tony Gwynn	.75
20	Mike Piazza	1.25
21	Tino Martinez	.25
22	Mo Vaughn	.25
23	Ben Grieve	.40
24	Scott Rolen	.50
25	Nomar Garciaparra	1.00
26	Paul Konerko	.25
27	Jaret Wright	.25
28	Gary Sheffield	.25
29	Travis Lee	.25
30	Todd Helton	.50

1998 Collector's Choice Stickums

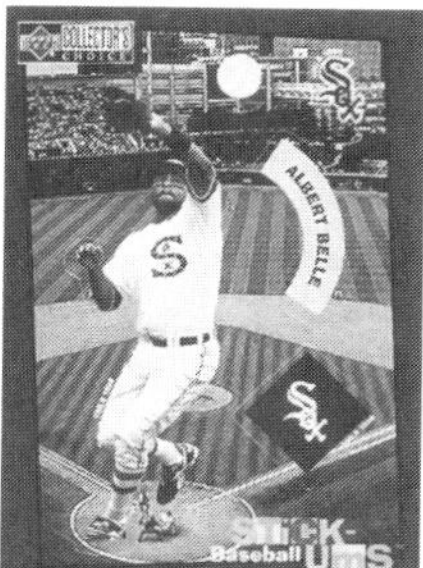

This 30-card insert was seeded 1:3 Series 1 packs. The stickers can be peeled off the card and reused.

		MT
Complete Set (30):		16.50
Common Player:		.25
Inserted 1:3		
1	Andruw Jones	.65
2	Chipper Jones	1.25
3	Cal Ripken Jr.	2.00
4	Nomar Garciaparra	1.00
5	Mo Vaughn	.35
6	Ryne Sandberg	.50
7	Sammy Sosa	1.00
8	Frank Thomas	1.00
9	Albert Belle	.35

10	Jim Thome	.25
11	Manny Ramirez	.65
12	Larry Walker	.25
13	Gary Sheffield	.25
14	Jeff Bagwell	.65
15	Mike Piazza	1.25
16	Paul Molitor	.40
17	Pedro J. Martinez	.50
18	Todd Hundley	.25
19	Derek Jeter	1.25
20	Tino Martinez	.25
21	Curt Schilling	.35
22	Mark McGwire	2.00
23	Tony Gwynn	.75
24	Barry Bonds	1.00
25	Ken Griffey Jr.	1.50
26	Alex Rodriguez	1.50
27	Juan Gonzalez	.65
28	Ivan Rodriguez	.40
29	Roger Clemens	.75
30	Jose Cruz Jr.	.25

1998 Collector's Choice Rookie Class: Prime Choice

This 18-card set is a parallel of the Rookie Class subset. Each card is foil-stamped with the words "Prime Choice Reserve." This hobby-only set is sequentially numbered to 500 and was inserted in Series 2 packs.

		MT
Complete Set (18):		32.50
Common Player:		2.00
415	Carl Pavano	2.00
416	A.J. Hinch	2.50
417	David Dellucci	2.00
418	Bruce Chen	2.00
419	Darron Ingram	2.00
420	Sean Casey	6.00
421	Mark L. Johnson	2.00
422	Gabe Alvarez	2.00
423	Alex Gonzalez	2.00
424	Daryle Ward	2.00
425	Russell Branyan	2.00
426	Mike Caruso	2.50
427	Mike Kinkade	2.00
428	Ramon Hernandez	2.00
429	Matt Clement	2.00
430	Travis Lee	4.50
431	Shane Monahan	2.00
432	Rich Butler	2.00

1998 Collector's Choice You Crash the Game

These 90 game cards were inserted one per five Series 2 packs. Each card features a player and a list of dates. If the pictured player hit a home run on one of those days, collectors with the card could mail it in for a graphically enhanced prize version. Instant Winner cards of each player were also inserted at the rate of 1:721 and could be exchanged for the complete 30-card prize set. Deadline for exchange of all winning cards was Dec. 1, 1998. Winning cards are designated here with an asterisk and can be expected to be somewhat scarcer than non-winning dates.

		MT
Complete Set (90):		90.00
Common Player:		.50
Instant Winner:		8X
Inserted 1:5		
CG1	Ken Griffey Jr. (June 26-28*)	3.50
CG1	Ken Griffey Jr. (July 7)	1.75
CG1	Ken Griffey Jr. (Sept. 21-24*)	3.50
CG2	Travis Lee (July 27-30)	.50
CG2	Travis Lee (Aug. 27-30)	.50
CG2	Travis Lee (Sept. 17-20)	.50
CG3	Larry Walker (July 17-19)	.50
CG3	Larry Walker (Aug. 27-30*)	1.00
CG3	Larry Walker (Sept. 25-27*)	1.00
CG4	Tony Clark (July 9-12*)	1.00
CG4	Tony Clark (June 30-July 2)	.50
CG4	Tony Clark (Sept. 4-6)	.50
CG5	Cal Ripken Jr. (June 22-25*)	4.00
CG5	Cal Ripken Jr. (July 7)	2.00
CG5	Cal Ripken Jr. (Sept. 4-6)	2.00
CG6	Tim Salmon (June 22-25)	.50
CG6	Tim Salmon (Aug. 28-30)	.50
CG6	Tim Salmon (Sept. 14-15)	.50
CG7	Vinny Castilla (June 30-July 2*)	1.00
CG7	Vinny Castilla (Aug. 27-30*)	1.00
CG7	Vinny Castilla (Sept. 7-10*)	1.00
CG8	Fred McGriff (June 22-25)	.50
CG8	Fred McGriff (July 3-5)	.50
CG8	Fred McGriff (Sept. 18-20*)	1.00
CG9	Matt Williams (July 17-29)	.50
CG9	Matt Williams (Sept. 14-16*)	1.00
CG9	Matt Williams (Sept. 18-20)	.50
CG10	Mark McGwire (July 7)	2.00
CG10	Mark McGwire (July 24-26*)	4.00
CG10	Mark McGwire (Aug. 18-19*)	4.00
CG11	Albert Belle (July 3-5)	.50
CG11	Albert Belle (Aug. 21-23*)	1.00
CG11	Albert Belle (Sept. 11-13)	.50
CG12	Jay Buhner (July 9-12*)	1.00
CG12	Jay Buhner (Aug. 6-9)	.50
CG12	Jay Buhner (Sept. 25-27)	.50
CG13	Vladimir Guerrero (June 22-25)	.75
CG13	Vladimir Guerrero (Aug. 10-12*)	1.50
CG13	Vladimir Guerrero (Sept. 14-16*)	1.50
CG14	Andruw Jones (July 16-19*)	1.50
CG14	Andruw Jones (Aug. 27-30*)	1.50
CG14	Andruw Jones (Sept. 17-20)	.75
CG15	Nomar Garciaparra (July 9-12)	1.25
CG15	Nomar Garciaparra (Aug. 13-16*)	2.50
CG15	Nomar Garciaparra (Sept. 24-27)	1.25
CG16	Ken Caminiti (June 26-28*)	1.00
CG16	Ken Caminiti (July 13-15*)	1.00
CG16	Ken Caminiti (Sept. 10-13)	.50
CG17	Sammy Sosa (July 9-12*)	2.50
CG17	Sammy Sosa (Aug. 27-30*)	2.50
CG17	Sammy Sosa (Sept. 18-20)	1.25
CG18	Ben Grieve (June 30-July 2*)	1.00
CG18	Ben Grieve (Aug. 14-16)	.50
CG18	Ben Grieve (Sept. 24-27)	.50
CG19	Mo Vaughn (July 7)	.50
CG19	Mo Vaughn (Sept. 7-9)	.50
CG19	Mo Vaughn (Sept. 24-27*)	1.00
CG20	Frank Thomas (July 7)	1.25
CG20	Frank Thomas (July 17-19*)	2.50
CG20	Frank Thomas (Sept. 4-6)	1.25
CG21	Manny Ramirez (July 9-12)	.75
CG21	Manny Ramirez (Aug. 13-16*)	1.50
CG21	Manny Ramirez (Sept. 18-20*)	1.50
CG22	Jeff Bagwell (July 7)	.75
CG22	Jeff Bagwell (Aug. 28-30*)	1.50
CG22	Jeff Bagwell (Sept. 4-6*)	1.50
CG23	Jose Cruz Jr. (July 9-12)	.50
CG23	Jose Cruz Jr. (Aug. 13-16)	.50
CG23	Jose Cruz Jr. (Sept. 18-20)	.50
CG24	Alex Rodriguez (July 7*)	3.50
CG24	Alex Rodriguez (Aug. 6-9*)	3.50
CG24	Alex Rodriguez (Sept. 21-23*)	3.50
CG25	Mike Piazza (June 22-25*)	3.00
CG25	Mike Piazza (July 7)	1.50
CG25	Mike Piazza (Sept. 10-13*)	3.00
CG26	Tino Martinez (June 26-28*)	1.00
CG26	Tino Martinez (July 9-12)	.50
CG26	Tino Martinez (Aug. 13-16)	.50
CG27	Chipper Jones (July 3-5)	1.00
CG27	Chipper Jones (Aug. 27-30)	1.00
CG27	Chipper Jones (Sept. 17-20)	1.00
CG28	Juan Gonzalez (July 7)	.75
CG28	Juan Gonzalez (Aug. 6-9*)	1.50
CG28	Juan Gonzalez (Sept. 11-13*)	.75
CG29	Jim Thome (June 22-23)	.50
CG29	Jim Thome (July 23-26*)	1.00
CG29	Jim Thome (Sept. 24-27)	.50
CG30	Barry Bonds (July 7*)	2.50
CG30	Barry Bonds (Sept. 4-6)	1.25
CG30	Barry Bonds (Sept. 18-20*)	2.50

1998 Collector's Choice You Crash the Game Winners

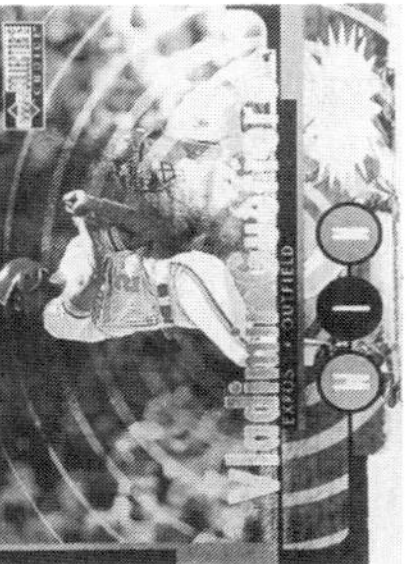

Collectors who redeemed winning "Crash" cards prior to the Dec. 1, 1998, deadline received an upgraded version of that player's card. Similar in format, the winners' cards have an action photo on front (different than the game card), with a metallic foil background. Instead of dates in the three circles at bottom are the letters "W I N". Backs have a career summary and stats, instead of the redemption instructions found on the game cards. The cards are numbered with a "CG" prefix. Cards of players who didn't homer during their designated dates were available only by redeeming a scarce (1:721 packs) Instant Win card. They are indicated here by "SP".

		MT
Complete Set (30):		70.00
Common Player:		1.00
CG1	Ken Griffey Jr.	5.00
CG2	Travis Lee (SP)	6.00
CG3	Larry Walker	1.00
CG4	Tony Clark	1.00
CG5	Cal Ripken Jr.	6.00
CG6	Tim Salmon (SP)	4.00
CG7	Vinny Castilla	1.00
CG8	Fred McGriff	1.00
CG9	Matt Williams	1.00

CG10 Mark McGwire 6.00
CG11 Albert Belle 1.00
CG12 Jay Buhner 1.00
CG13 Vladimir Guerrero 1.50
CG14 Andruw Jones 1.50
CG15 Nomar Garciaparra 4.00
CG16 Ken Caminiti 1.00
CG17 Sammy Sosa 3.50
CG18 Ben Grieve 1.00
CG19 Mo Vaughn 1.25
CG20 Frank Thomas 3.50
CG21 Manny Ramirez 1.50
CG22 Jeff Bagwell 3.00
CG23 Jose Cruz Jr. (SP) 4.00
CG24 Alex Rodriguez 5.00
CG25 Mike Piazza 5.00
CG26 Tino Martinez 1.00
CG27 Chipper Jones (SP) 15.00
CG28 Juan Gonzalez 3.00
CG29 Jim Thome 1.00
CG30 Barry Bonds 3.50

1998 Collector's Choice Jumbos (5x7)

These super-size (5" x 7") cards were one-per-box inserts in Series 2 retail packaging. Besides being four times the size of a normal card, the 5x7s are identical to the regular versions.

		MT
Complete Set (10):		15.00
Common Player:		1.00
306	Chipper Jones	3.00
321	Nomar Garciaparra	2.50
360	Larry Walker	1.00
450	Derek Jeter	3.00
463	Scott Rolen	1.50
480	Tony Gwynn	2.00
490	Barry Bonds	2.50
495	Alex Rodriguez	3.50
525	Jose Cruz Jr.	1.00
530	Roger Clemens	2.00

Values quoted in this guide reflect the retail price of a card — the price a collector can expect to pay when buying a card from a dealer.

The wholesale price — that which a collector can expect to receive from a dealer when selling cards — will be significantly lower, depending on desirability and condition.

1981 Donruss

TOM SEAVER PITCHER

The Donruss Co. of Memphis, Tenn., produced its premiere baseball card issue in 1981 with a set that consisted of 600 numbered cards and five unnumbered checklists. The cards, which measure 2-1/2" x 3-1/2", are printed on thin stock. The card fronts contain the Donruss logo plus the year of issue. The card backs are designed on a vertical format and have black print on red and white. The set, entitled "First Edition Collector Series," contains nearly 40 variations, those being first-printing errors that were corrected in a subsequent print run. The cards were sold in wax packs with bubblegum. The complete set price does not include the higher priced variations.

		MT
Complete Set (605):		25.00
Complete Set, Uncut Sheets (5):		50.00
Common Player:		.10
Pack (18):		1.75
Wax Box (36):		35.00
1	Ozzie Smith	2.00
2	Rollie Fingers	.75
3	Rick Wise	.10
4	Gene Richards	.10
5	Alan Trammell	.30
6	Tom Brookens	.10
7a	Duffy Dyer (1980 Avg. .185)	.50
7b	Duffy Dyer (1980 Avg. 185)	.10
8	Mark Fidrych	.15
9	Dave Rozema	.10
10	Ricky Peters	.10
11	Mike Schmidt	2.50
12	Willie Stargell	1.00
13	Tim Foli	.10
14	Manny Sanguillen	.10
15	Grant Jackson	.10
16	Eddie Solomon	.10
17	Omar Moreno	.10
18	Joe Morgan	.75
19	Rafael Landestoy	.10
20	Bruce Bochy	.10
21	Joe Sambito	.10
22	Manny Trillo	.10
23a	*Dave Smith* (incomplete box around stats)	.50
23b	*Dave Smith* (complete box around stats)	.30
24	Terry Puhl	.10
25	Bump Wills	.10
26a	John Ellis (Danny Walton photo - with bat)	.60
26b	John Ellis (John Ellis photo - with glove)	.10
27	Jim Kern	.10
28	Richie Zisk	.10
29	John Mayberry	.10
30	Bob Davis	.10
31	Jackson Todd	.10
32	Al Woods	.10
33	Steve Carlton	1.50
34	Lee Mazzilli	.10
35	John Stearns	.10
36	Roy Jackson	.10
37	Mike Scott	.10
38	Lamar Johnson	.10
39	Kevin Bell	.10
40	Ed Farmer	.10
41	Ross Baumgarten	.10
42	Leo Sutherland	.10
43	Dan Meyer	.10
44	Ron Reed	.10
45	Mario Mendoza	.10
46	Rick Honeycutt	.10
47	Glenn Abbott	.10
48	Leon Roberts	.10
49	Rod Carew	1.50
50	Bert Campaneris	.10
51a	Tom Donahue (incorrect spelling)	.50
51b	Tom Donohue (Donohue on front)	.10
52	Dave Frost	.10
53	Ed Halicki	.10
54	Dan Ford	.10
55	Garry Maddox	.10
56a	Steve Garvey (Surpassed 25 HR..)	1.25
56b	Steve Garvey (Surpassed 21 HR..)	.60
57	Bill Russell	.10
58	Don Sutton	.65
59	Reggie Smith	.10
60	Rick Monday	.10
61	Ray Knight	.10
62	Johnny Bench	1.25
63	Mario Soto	.10
64	Doug Bair	.10
65	George Foster	.10
66	Jeff Burroughs	.10
67	Keith Hernandez	.15
68	Tom Herr	.10
69	Bob Forsch	.10
70	John Fulgham	.10
71a	Bobby Bonds (lifetime HR 986)	.50
71b	Bobby Bonds (lifetime HR 326)	.15
72a	Rennie Stennett ("...breaking broke leg..." on back)	.50
72b	Rennie Stennett ("...breaking leg..." on back)	.10
73	Joe Strain	.10
74	Ed Whitson	.10
75	Tom Griffin	.10
76	Bill North	.10
77	Gene Garber	.10
78	Mike Hargrove	.10
79	Dave Rosello	.10
80	Ron Hassey	.10
81	Sid Monge	.10
82a	*Joe Charboneau* ("For some reason, Phillies..." on back)	1.00
82b	*Joe Charboneau* ("Phillies..." on back)	.25
83	Cecil Cooper	.10
84	Sal Bando	.10
85	Moose Haas	.10
86	Mike Caldwell	.10
87a	Larry Hisle ("...Twins with 28 RBI." on back)	.50
87b	Larry Hisle ("...Twins with 28 HR" on back)	.10
88	Luis Gomez	.10
89	Larry Parrish	.10
90	Gary Carter	.50
91	*Bill Gullickson*	.15
92	Fred Norman	.10
93	Tommy Hutton	.10
94	Carl Yastrzemski	1.25
95	Glenn Hoffman	.10
96	Dennis Eckersley	.50
97a	Tom Burgmeier (Throws: Right)	.50
97b	Tom Burgmeier (Throws: Left)	.10
98	Win Remmerswaal	.10
99	Bob Horner	.10
100	George Brett	3.00
101	Dave Chalk	.10
102	Dennis Leonard	.10
103	Renie Martin	.10
104	Amos Otis	.10
105	Graig Nettles	.15
106	Eric Soderholm	.10
107	Tommy John	.10
108	Tom Underwood	.10
109	Lou Piniella	.15
110	Mickey Klutts	.10
111	Bobby Murcer	.10
112	Eddie Murray	2.00
113	Rick Dempsey	.10
114	Scott McGregor	.10
115	Ken Singleton	.10
116	Gary Roenicke	.10
117	Dave Revering	.10
118	Mike Norris	.10
119	Rickey Henderson	2.00
120	Mike Heath	.10
121	Dave Cash	.10
122	Randy Jones	.10
123	Eric Rasmussen	.10
124	Jerry Mumphrey	.10
125	Richie Hebner	.10
126	Mark Wagner	.10
127	Jack Morris	.10
128	Dan Petry	.10
129	Bruce Robbins	.10
130	Champ Summers	.10
131a	Pete Rose ("see card 251" on back)	2.00
131b	Pete Rose ("see card 371" on back)	2.00
132	Willie Stargell	1.00
133	Ed Ott	.10
134	Jim Bibby	.10
135	Bert Blyleven	.10
136	Dave Parker	.25
137	Bill Robinson	.10
138	Enos Cabell	.10
139	Dave Bergman	.10
140	J.R. Richard	.10
141	Ken Forsch	.10
142	Larry Bowa	.15
143	Frank LaCorte (photo actually Randy Niemann)	.10
144	Dennis Walling	.10
145	Buddy Bell	.10
146	Fergie Jenkins	.75
147	Danny Darwin	.10
148	John Grubb	.10
149	Alfredo Griffin	.10
150	Jerry Garvin	.10
151	*Paul Mirabella*	.10
152	Rick Bosetti	.10
153	Dick Ruthven	.10
154	Frank Taveras	.10
155	Craig Swan	.10
156	*Jeff Reardon*	1.00
157	Steve Henderson	.10
158	Jim Morrison	.10
159	Glenn Borgmann	.10
160	*Lamarr Hoyt (LaMarr)*	.10
161	Rich Wortham	.10
162	Thad Bosley	.10
163	Julio Cruz	.10
164a	Del Unser (no 3B in stat heads)	.50
164b	Del Unser (3B in stat heads)	.10
165	Jim Anderson	.10
166	Jim Beattie	.10
167	Shane Rawley	.10
168	Joe Simpson	.10
169	Rod Carew	1.50
170	Fred Patek	.10
171	Frank Tanana	.10
172	Alfredo Martinez	.10
173	Chris Knapp	.10
174	Joe Rudi	.10
175	Greg Luzinski	.10
176	Steve Garvey	.65
177	Joe Ferguson	.10
178	Bob Welch	.10

No.	Player	Price
179	Dusty Baker	.15
180	Rudy Law	.10
181	Dave Concepcion	.10
182	Johnny Bench	1.25
183	Mike LaCoss	.10
184	Ken Griffey	.10
185	Dave Collins	.10
186	Brian Asselstine	.10
187	Garry Templeton	.10
188	Mike Phillips	.10
189	Pete Vukovich	.10
190	John Urrea	.10
191	Tony Scott	.10
192	Darrell Evans	.15
193	Milt May	.10
194	Bob Knepper	.10
195	Randy Moffitt	.10
196	Larry Herndon	.10
197	Rick Camp	.10
198	Andre Thornton	.10
199	Tom Veryzer	.10
200	Gary Alexander	.10
201	Rick Waits	.10
202	Rick Manning	.10
203	Paul Molitor	1.50
204	Jim Gantner	.10
205	Paul Mitchell	.10
206	Reggie Cleveland	.10
207	Sixto Lezcano	.10
208	Bruce Benedict	.10
209	Rodney Scott	.10
210	John Tamargo	.10
211	Bill Lee	.10
212	Andre Dawson	.50
213	Rowland Office	.10
214	Carl Yastrzemski	1.25
215	Jerry Remy	.10
216	Mike Torrez	.10
217	Skip Lockwood	.10
218	Fred Lynn	.10
219	Chris Chambliss	.10
220	Willie Aikens	.10
221	John Wathan	.10
222	Dan Quisenberry	.10
223	Willie Wilson	.10
224	Clint Hurdle	.10
225	Bob Watson	.10
226	Jim Spencer	.10
227	Ron Guidry	.25
228	Reggie Jackson	2.00
229	Oscar Gamble	.10
230	Jeff Cox	.10
231	Luis Tiant	.10
232	Rich Dauer	.10
233	Dan Graham	.10
234	Mike Flanagan	.10
235	John Lowenstein	.10
236	Benny Ayala	.10
237	Wayne Gross	.10
238	Rick Langford	.10
239	Tony Armas	.10
240a	Bob Lacy (incorrect spelling)	.50
240b	Bob Lacey (correct spelling)	.10
241	Gene Tenace	.10
242	Bob Shirley	.10
243	Gary Lucas	.10
244	Jerry Turner	.10
245	John Wockenfuss	.10
246	Stan Papi	.10
247	Milt Wilcox	.10
248	Dan Schatzeder	.10
249	Steve Kemp	.10
250	Jim Lentine	.10
251	Pete Rose	2.00
252	Bill Madlock	.10
253	Dale Berra	.10
254	Kent Tekulve	.10
255	Enrique Romo	.10
256	Mike Easler	.10
257	Chuck Tanner	.10
258	Art Howe	.10
259	Alan Ashby	.10
260	Nolan Ryan	6.00
261a	Vern Ruhle (Ken Forsch photo - head shot)	.50
261b	Vern Ruhle (Vern Ruhle photo - waist to head shot)	.10
262	Bob Boone	.10
263	Cesar Cedeno	.10
264	Jeff Leonard	.10
265	Pat Putnam	.10
266	Jon Matlack	.10
267	Dave Rajsich	.10
268	Billy Sample	.10
269	*Damaso Garcia*	.10
270	Tom Buskey	.10
271	Joey McLaughlin	.10
272	Barry Bonnell	.10
273	Tug McGraw	.10
274	Mike Jorgensen	.10
275	Pat Zachry	.10
276	Neil Allen	.10
277	Joel Youngblood	.10
278	Greg Pryor	.10
279	*Britt Burns*	.10
280	*Rich Dotson*	.25
281	Chet Lemon	.10
282	Rusty Kuntz	.10
283	Ted Cox	.10
284	Sparky Lyle	.10
285	Larry Cox	.10
286	Floyd Bannister	.10
287	Byron McLaughlin	.10
288	Rodney Craig	.10
289	Bobby Grich	.10
290	Dickie Thon	.10
291	Mark Clear	.10
292	Dave Lemanczyk	.10
293	Jason Thompson	.10
294	Rick Miller	.10
295	Lonnie Smith	.10
296	Ron Cey	.10
297	Steve Yeager	.10
298	Bobby Castillo	.10
299	Manny Mota	.10
300	Jay Johnstone	.10
301	Dan Driessen	.10
302	Joe Nolan	.10
303	Paul Householder	.10
304	Harry Spilman	.10
305	Cesar Geronimo	.10
306a	Gary Mathews (Mathews on front)	.65
306b	Gary Matthews (Matthews on front)	.10
307	Ken Reitz	.10
308	Ted Simmons	.10
309	John Littlefield	.10
310	George Frazier	.10
311	Dane Iorg	.10
312	Mike Ivie	.10
313	Dennis Littlejohn	.10
314	Gary LaVelle (Lavelle)	.10
315	Jack Clark	.10
316	Jim Wohlford	.10
317	Rick Matula	.10
318	Toby Harrah	.10
319a	Dwane Kuiper (Dwane on front)	.50
319b	Duane Kuiper (Duane on front)	.10
320	Len Barker	.10
321	Victor Cruz	.10
322	Dell Alston	.10
323	Robin Yount	2.00
324	Charlie Moore	.10
325	Lary Sorensen	.10
326a	Gorman Thomas ("...30-HR mark 4th..." on back)	.65
326b	Gorman Thomas ("...30-HR mark 3rd..." on back)	.10
327	Bob Rodgers	.10
328	Phil Niekro	.75
329	Chris Speier	.10
330a	Steve Rodgers (Rodgers on front)	.50
330b	Steve Rogers (Rogers on front)	.10
331	Woodie Fryman	.10
332	Warren Cromartie	.10
333	Jerry White	.10
334	Tony Perez	.50
335	Carlton Fisk	1.50
336	Dick Drago	.10
337	Steve Renko	.10
338	Jim Rice	.30
339	Jerry Royster	.10
340	Frank White	.10
341	Jamie Quirk	.10
342a	Paul Spittorff (Spittorff on front)	.50
342b	Paul Splittorff (Splittorff on front)	.10
343	Marty Pattin	.10
344	Pete LaCock	.10
345	Willie Randolph	.10
346	Rick Cerone	.10
347	Rich Gossage	.10
348	Reggie Jackson	2.00
349	Ruppert Jones	.10
350	Dave McKay	.10
351	Yogi Berra	.50
352	Doug Decinces (DeCinces)	.10
353	Jim Palmer	1.00
354	Tippy Martinez	.10
355	Al Bumbry	.10
356	Earl Weaver	.50
357a	Bob Picciolo (Bob on front)	.50
357b	Rob Picciolo (Rob on front)	.10
358	Matt Keough	.10
359	Dwayne Murphy	.10
360	Brian Kingman	.10
361	Bill Fahey	.10
362	Steve Mura	.10
363	Dennis Kinney	.10
364	Dave Winfield	2.00
365	Lou Whitaker	.10
366	Lance Parrish	.10
367	Tim Corcoran	.10
368	Pat Underwood	.10
369	Al Cowens	.10
370	Sparky Anderson	.30
371	Pete Rose	2.50
372	Phil Garner	.10
373	Steve Nicosia	.10
374	John Candelaria	.10
375	Don Robinson	.10
376	Lee Lacy	.10
377	John Milner	.10
378	Craig Reynolds	.10
379a	Luis Pujois (Pujois on front)	.50
379b	Luis Pujols (Pujols on front)	.10
380	Joe Niekro	.10
381	Joaquin Andujar	.10
382	*Keith Moreland*	.15
383	Jose Cruz	.10
384	Bill Virdon	.10
385	Jim Sundberg	.10
386	Doc Medich	.10
387	Al Oliver	.15
388	Jim Norris	.10
389	Bob Bailor	.10
390	Ernie Whitt	.10
391	Otto Velez	.10
392	Roy Howell	.10
393	*Bob Walk*	.10
394	Doug Flynn	.10
395	Pete Falcone	.10
396	Tom Hausman	.10
397	Elliott Maddox	.10
398	Mike Squires	.10
399	Marvis Foley	.10
400	Steve Trout	.10
401	Wayne Nordhagen	.10
402	Tony Larussa (LaRussa)	.10
403	Bruce Bochte	.10
404	Bake McBride	.10
405	Jerry Narron	.10
406	Rob Dressler	.10
407	Dave Heaverlo	.10
408	Tom Paciorek	.10
409	Carney Lansford	.10
410	Brian Downing	.10
411	Don Aase	.10
412	Jim Barr	.10
413	Don Baylor	.15
414	Jim Fregosi	.10
415	Dallas Green	.10
416	Dave Lopes	.10
417	Jerry Reuss	.10
418	Rick Sutcliffe	.10
419	Derrel Thomas	.10
420	Tommy LaSorda (Lasorda)	.50
421	*Charlie Leibrandt*	.50
422	Tom Seaver	2.00
423	Ron Oester	.10
424	Junior Kennedy	.10
425	Tom Seaver	2.00
426	Bobby Cox	.10
427	*Leon Durham*	.20
428	Terry Kennedy	.10
429	Silvio Martinez	.10
430	George Hendrick	.10
431	Red Schoendienst	.35
432	John LeMaster	.10
433	Vida Blue	.10
434	John Montefusco	.10
435	Terry Whitfield	.10
436	Dave Bristol	.10
437	Dale Murphy	.75
438	Jerry Dybzinski	.10
439	Jorge Orta	.10
440	Wayne Garland	.10
441	Miguel Dilone	.10
442	Dave Garcia	.10
443	Don Money	.10
444a	Buck Martinez (photo reversed)	.50
444b	Buck Martinez (photo correct)	.10
445	Jerry Augustine	.10
446	Ben Oglivie	.10
447	Jim Slaton	.10
448	Doyle Alexander	.10
449	Tony Bernazard	.10
450	Scott Sanderson	.10
451	Dave Palmer	.10
452	Stan Bahnsen	.10
453	Dick Williams	.10
454	Rick Burleson	.10
455	Gary Allenson	.10
456	Bob Stanley	.10
457a	*John Tudor* (lifetime W/L 9.7)	.75
457b	*John Tudor* (lifetime W/L 9-7)	.50
458	Dwight Evans	.15
459	Glenn Hubbard	.10
460	U L Washington	.10
461	Larry Gura	.10
462	Rich Gale	.10
463	Hal McRae	.10
464	Jim Frey	.10
465	Bucky Dent	.10
466	Dennis Werth	.10
467	Ron Davis	.10
468	Reggie Jackson	2.50
469	Bobby Brown	.10
470	*Mike Davis*	.10
471	Gaylord Perry	.75
472	Mark Belanger	.10
473	Jim Palmer	1.00
474	Sammy Stewart	.10
475	Tim Stoddard	.10
476	Steve Stone	.10
477	Jeff Newman	.10
478	Steve McCatty	.10
479	Billy Martin	.15
480	Mitchell Page	.10
481	Steve Carlton (CY)	.40
482	Bill Buckner	.10
483a	Ivan DeJesus (lifetime hits 702)	.50
483b	Ivan DeJesus (lifetime hits 642)	.10
484	Cliff Johnson	.10
485	Lenny Randle	.10
486	Larry Milbourne	.10
487	Roy Smalley	.10
488	John Castino	.10
489	Ron Jackson	.10
490a	Dave Roberts (1980 highlights begins "Showed pop...")	.50
490b	Dave Roberts (1980 highlights begins "Declared himself...")	.10
491	George Brett (MVP)	1.50
492	Mike Cubbage	.10
493	Rob Wilfong	.10
494	Danny Goodwin	.10
495	Jose Morales	.10
496	Mickey Rivers	.10
497	Mike Edwards	.10
498	Mike Sadek	.10
499	Lenn Sakata	.10
500	Gene Michael	.10
501	Dave Roberts	.10
502	Steve Dillard	.10
503	Jim Essian	.10
504	Rance Mulliniks	.10
505	Darrell Porter	.10
506	Joe Torre	.45
507	Terry Crowley	.10
508	Bill Travers	.10
509	Nelson Norman	.10
510	Bob McClure	.10
511	*Steve Howe*	.15
512	Dave Rader	.10
513	Mick Kelleher	.10
514	Kiko Garcia	.10

515 Larry Biittner .10
516a Willie Norwood (1980 highlights begins "Spent most...") .50
516b Willie Norwood (1980 highlights begins "Traded to...") .10
517 Bo Diaz .10
518 Juan Beniquez .10
519 Scot Thompson .10
520 Jim Tracy .10
521 Carlos Lezcano .10
522 Joe Amalfitano .10
523 Preston Hanna .10
524a Ray Burris (1980 highlights begins "Went on...") .50
524b Ray Burris (1980 highlights begins "Drafted by...") .10
525 Broderick Perkins .10
526 Mickey Hatcher .10
527 John Goryl .10
528 Dick Davis .10
529 Butch Wynegar .10
530 Sal Butera .10
531 Jerry Koosman .10
532a Jeff (Geoff) Zahn (1980 highlights begins "Was 2nd in...") .50
532b Jeff (Geoff) Zahn (1980 highlights begins "Signed a 3 year ...") .10
533 Dennis Martinez .10
534 Gary Thomasson .10
535 Steve Macko .10
536 Jim Kaat .15
537 Best Hitters (George Brett, Rod Carew) 1.50
538 *Tim Raines* 3.00
539 Keith Smith .10
540 Ken Macha .10
541 Burt Hooton .10
542 Butch Hobson .10
543 Bill Stein .10
544 Dave Stapleton .10
545 Bob Pate .10
546 Doug Corbett .10
547 Darrell Jackson .10
548 Pete Redfern .10
549 Roger Erickson .10
550 Al Hrabosky .10
551 Dick Tidrow .10
552 Dave Ford .10
553 Dave Kingman .15
554a Mike Vail (1980 highlights begins "After...") .50
554b Mike Vail (1980 highlights begins "Traded...") .10
555a Jerry Martin (1980 highlights begins "Overcame...") .50
555b Jerry Martin (1980 highlights begins "Traded...") .10
556a Jesus Figueroa (1980 highlights begins "Had...") .50
556b Jesus Figueroa (1980 highlights begins "Traded...") .10
557 Don Stanhouse .10
558 Barry Foote .10
559 Tim Blackwell .10
560 Bruce Sutter .10
561 Rick Reuschel .10
562 Lynn McGlothen .10
563a Bob Owchinko (1980 highlights begins "Traded...") .50
563b Bob Owchinko (1980 highlights begins "Involved...") .10
564 John Verhoeven .10
565 Ken Landreaux .10
566a Glen Adams (Glen on front) .50
566b Glenn Adams (Glenn on front) .10
567 Hosken Powell .10
568 Dick Noles .10
569 *Danny Ainge* 2.00
570 Bobby Mattick .10
571 Joe LeFebvre (Lefebvre) .10
572 Bobby Clark .10
573 Dennis Lamp .10
574 Randy Lerch .10
575 *Mookie Wilson* .30
576 Ron LeFlore .10
577 Jim Dwyer .10
578 Bill Castro .10
579 Greg Minton .10
580 Mark Littell .10
581 Andy Hassler .10
582 Dave Stieb .10
583 Ken Oberkfell .10
584 Larry Bradford .10
585 Fred Stanley .10
586 Bill Caudill .10
587 Doug Capilla .10
588 George Riley .10
589 Willie Hernandez .10
590 Mike Schmidt (MVP) 1.50
591 Steve Stone ((Cy Young 1980)) .10
592 Rick Sofield .10
593 Bombo Rivera .10
594 Gary Ward .10
595a Dave Edwards (1980 highlights begins "Sidelined...") .50
595b Dave Edwards (1980 highlights begins "Traded...") .10
596 Mike Proly .10
597 Tommy Boggs .10
598 Greg Gross .10
599 Elias Sosa .10
600 Pat Kelly .10
---- Checklist 1-120 (51 Tom Donohue) .25
---- Checklist 1-120 (51 Tom Donahue) .10
---- Checklist 121-240 .10
---- Checklist 241-360 (306 Gary Mathews) .25
---- Checklist 241-360 (306 Gary Matthews) .10
---- Checklist 361-480 (379 Luis Pujois) .25
---- Checklist 361-480 (379 Luis Pujols) .10
---- Checklist 481-600 (566 Glen Adams) .25
---- Checklist 481-600 (566 Glenn Adams) .10

1982 Donruss

Using card stock thicker than the previous year, Donruss issued a 660-card set which includes 653 numbered cards and seven unnumbered checklists. The cards were sold with puzzle pieces rather than gum as a result of a lawsuit by Topps. The puzzle pieces (three pieces on one card per pack) feature Babe Ruth. The first 26 cards of the set, entitled Diamond Kings, showcase the artwork of Dick Perez. Card fronts display the Donruss logo and the year of issue. Backs have black and blue ink on white stock and include the player's career highlights. The complete set price does not include the higher priced variations.

	MT
Complete Set (660):	50.00
Common Player:	.10
Babe Ruth Puzzle:	3.00
Pack (15):	3.50
Wax Box (36):	100.00

1 Pete Rose (Diamond King) 3.00
2 Gary Carter (DK) .50
3 Steve Garvey (DK) .30
4 Vida Blue (DK) .10
5a Alan Trammel (DK) (last name incorrect) 1.00
5b Alan Trammell (DK) (corrected) .30
6 Len Barker (DK) .10
7 Dwight Evans (DK) .15
8 Rod Carew (DK) .60
9 George Hendrick (DK) .10
10 Phil Niekro (DK) .50
11 Richie Zisk (DK) .10
12 Dave Parker (DK) .10
13 Nolan Ryan (DK) 4.00
14 Ivan DeJesus (DK) .10
15 George Brett (DK) 1.50
16 Tom Seaver (DK) .75
17 Dave Kingman (DK) .15
18 Dave Winfield (DK) 1.00
19 Mike Norris (DK) .10
20 Carlton Fisk (DK) .75
21 Ozzie Smith (DK) 1.50
22 Roy Smalley (DK) .10
23 Buddy Bell (DK) .10
24 Ken Singleton (DK) .10
25 John Mayberry (DK) .10
26 Gorman Thomas (DK) .10
27 Earl Weaver .45
28 Rollie Fingers .60
29 Sparky Anderson .25
30 Dennis Eckersley .25
31 Dave Winfield 1.50
32 Burt Hooton .10
33 Rick Waits .10
34 George Brett 2.00
35 Steve McCatty .10
36 Steve Rogers .10
37 Bill Stein .10
38 Steve Renko .10
39 Mike Squires .10
40 George Hendrick .10
41 Bob Knepper .10
42 Steve Carlton 1.00
43 Larry Biittner .10
44 Chris Welsh .10
45 Steve Nicosia .10
46 Jack Clark .10
47 Chris Chambliss .10
48 Ivan DeJesus .10
49 Lee Mazzilli .10
50 Julio Cruz .10
51 Pete Redfern .10
52 Dave Stieb .10
53 Doug Corbett .10
54 *George Bell* 1.00
55 Joe Simpson .10
56 Rusty Staub .15
57 Hector Cruz .10
58 Claudell Washington .10
59 Enrique Romo .10
60 Gary Lavelle .10
61 Tim Flannery .10
62 Joe Nolan .10
63 Larry Bowa .10
64 Sixto Lezcano .10
65 Joe Sambito .10
66 Bruce Kison .10
67 Wayne Nordhagen .10
68 Woodie Fryman .10
69 Billy Sample .10
70 Amos Otis .10
71 Matt Keough .10
72 Toby Harrah .10
73 *Dave Righetti* .30
74 Carl Yastrzemski 1.25
75 Bob Welch .10
76a Alan Trammel (last name misspelled) 1.00
76b Alan Trammell (corrected) .25
77 Rick Dempsey .10
78 Paul Molitor 1.50
79 Dennis Martinez .10
80 Jim Slaton .10
81 Champ Summers .10
82 Carney Lansford .10
83 Barry Foote .10
84 Steve Garvey .45
85 Rick Manning .10
86 John Wathan .10
87 Brian Kingman .10
88 Andre Dawson .50
89 Jim Kern .10
90 Bobby Grich .10
91 Bob Forsch .10
92 Art Howe .10
93 Marty Bystrom .10
94 Ozzie Smith 1.50
95 Dave Parker .20
96 Doyle Alexander .10
97 Al Hrabosky .10
98 Frank Taveras .10
99 Tim Blackwell .10
100 Floyd Bannister .10
101 Alfredo Griffin .10
102 Dave Engle .10
103 Mario Soto .10
104 Ross Baumgarten .10
105 Ken Singleton .10
106 Ted Simmons .10
107 Jack Morris .10
108 Bob Watson .10
109 Dwight Evans .10
110 Tom Lasorda .40
111 Bert Blyleven .10
112 Dan Quisenberry .10
113 Rickey Henderson 1.50
114 Gary Carter .50
115 Brian Downing .10
116 Al Oliver .10
117 LaMarr Hoyt .10
118 Cesar Cedeno .10
119 Keith Moreland .10
120 Bob Shirley .10
121 Terry Kennedy .10
122 Frank Pastore .10
123 Gene Garber .10
124 Tony Pena .10
125 Allen Ripley .10
126 Randy Martz .10
127 Richie Zisk .10
128 Mike Scott .10
129 Lloyd Moseby .10
130 Rob Wilfong .10
131 Tim Stoddard .10
132 Gorman Thomas .10
133 Dan Petry .10
134 Bob Stanley .10
135 Lou Piniella .15
136 Pedro Guerrero .10
137 Len Barker .10
138 Richard Gale .10
139 Wayne Gross .10
140 *Tim Wallach* 1.00
141 Gene Mauch .10
142 Doc Medich .10
143 Tony Bernazard .10
144 Bill Virdon .10
145 John Littlefield .10
146 Dave Bergman .10
147 Dick Davis .10
148 Tom Seaver 1.00
149 Matt Sinatro .10
150 Chuck Tanner .10
151 Leon Durham .10
152 Gene Tenace .10
153 Al Bumbry .10
154 Mark Brouhard .10
155 Rick Peters .10
156 Jerry Remy .10
157 Rick Reuschel .10
158 Steve Howe .10
159 Alan Bannister .10
160 U L Washington .10
161 Rick Langford .10
162 Bill Gullickson .10
163 Mark Wagner .10
164 Geoff Zahn .10
165 Ron LeFlore .10
166 Dane Iorg .10
167 Joe Niekro .10
168 Pete Rose 2.50
169 Dave Collins .10
170 Rick Wise .10

171 Jim Bibby .10
172 Larry Herndon .10
173 Bob Horner .10
174 Steve Dillard .10
175 Mookie Wilson .10
176 Dan Meyer .10
177 Fernando Arroyo .10
178 Jackson Todd .10
179 Darrell Jackson .10
180 Al Woods .10
181 Jim Anderson .10
182 Dave Kingman .15
183 Steve Henderson .10
184 Brian Asselstine .10
185 Rod Scurry .10
186 Fred Breining .10
187 Danny Boone .10
188 Junior Kennedy .10
189 Sparky Lyle .10
190 Whitey Herzog .10
191 Dave Smith .10
192 Ed Ott .10
193 Greg Luzinski .10
194 Bill Lee .10
195 Don Zimmer .10
196 Hal McRae .10
197 Mike Norris .10
198 Duane Kuiper .10
199 Rick Cerone .10
200 Jim Rice .25
201 Steve Yeager .10
202 Tom Brookens .10
203 Jose Morales .10
204 Roy Howell .10
205 Tippy Martinez .10
206 Moose Haas .10
207 Al Cowens .10
208 Dave Stapleton .10
209 Bucky Dent .10
210 Ron Cey .10
211 Jorge Orta .10
212 Jamie Quirk .10
213 Jeff Jones .10
214 Tim Raines .50
215 Jon Matlack .10
216 Rod Carew 1.00
217 Jim Kaat .15
218 Joe Pittman .10
219 Larry Christenson .10
220 Juan Bonilla .10
221 Mike Easler .10
222 Vida Blue .10
223 Rick Camp .10
224 Mike Jorgensen .10
225 *Jody Davis* .15
226 Mike Parrott .10
227 Jim Clancy .10
228 Hosken Powell .10
229 Tom Hume .10
230 Britt Burns .10
231 Jim Palmer 1.00
232 Bob Rodgers .10
233 Milt Wilcox .10
234 Dave Revering .10
235 Mike Torrez .10
236 Robert Castillo .10
237 *Von Hayes* .25
238 Renie Martin .10
239 Dwayne Murphy .10
240 Rodney Scott .10
241 Fred Patek .10
242 Mickey Rivers .10
243 Steve Trout .10
244 Jose Cruz .10
245 Manny Trillo .10
246 Lary Sorensen .10
247 Dave Edwards .10
248 Dan Driessen .10
249 Tommy Boggs .10
250 Dale Berra .10
251 Ed Whitson .10
252 *Lee Smith* 4.00
253 Tom Paciorek .10
254 Pat Zachry .10
255 Luis Leal .10
256 John Castino .10
257 Rich Dauer .10
258 Cecil Cooper .10
259 Dave Rozema .10
260 John Tudor .10
261 Jerry Mumphrey .10
262 Jay Johnstone .10
263 Bo Diaz .10
264 Dennis Leonard .10
265 Jim Spencer .10
266 John Milner .10
267 Don Aase .10
268 Jim Sundberg .10
269 Lamar Johnson .10
270 Frank LaCorte .10
271 Barry Evans .10
272 Enos Cabell .10
273 Del Unser .10
274 George Foster .10
275 *Brett Butler* 1.00
276 Lee Lacy .10
277 Ken Reitz .10
278 Keith Hernandez .15
279 Doug DeCinces .10
280 Charlie Moore .10
281 Lance Parrish .10
282 Ralph Houk .10
283 Rich Gossage .10
284 Jerry Reuss .10
285 Mike Stanton .10
286 Frank White .10
287 Bob Owchinko .10
288 Scott Sanderson .10
289 Bump Wills .10
290 Dave Frost .10
291 Chet Lemon .10
292 Tito Landrum .10
293 Vern Ruhle .10
294 Mike Schmidt 2.00
295 Sam Mejias .10
296 Gary Lucas .10
297 John Candelaria .10
298 Jerry Martin .10
299 Dale Murphy .50
300 Mike Lum .10
301 Tom Hausman .10
302 Glenn Abbott .10
303 Roger Erickson .10
304 Otto Velez .10
305 Danny Goodwin .10
306 John Mayberry .10
307 Lenny Randle .10
308 Bob Bailor .10
309 Jerry Morales .10
310 Rufino Linares .10
311 Kent Tekulve .10
312 Joe Morgan 1.00
313 John Urrea .10
314 Paul Householder .10
315 Garry Maddox .10
316 Mike Ramsey .10
317 Alan Ashby .10
318 Bob Clark .10
319 Tony LaRussa .15
320 Charlie Lea .10
321 Danny Darwin .10
322 Cesar Geronimo .10
323 Tom Underwood .10
324 Andre Thornton .10
325 Rudy May .10
326 Frank Tanana .10
327 Davey Lopes .10
328 Richie Hebner .10
329 Mike Flanagan .10
330 Mike Caldwell .10
331 Scott McGregor .10
332 Jerry Augustine .10
333 Stan Papi .10
334 Rick Miller .10
335 Graig Nettles .15
336 Dusty Baker .15
337 Dave Garcia .10
338 Larry Gura .10
339 Cliff Johnson .10
340 Warren Cromartie .10
341 Steve Comer .10
342 Rick Burleson .10
343 John Martin .10
344 Craig Reynolds .10
345 Mike Proly .10
346 Ruppert Jones .10
347 Omar Moreno .10
348 Greg Minton .10
349 *Rick Mahler* .10
350 Alex Trevino .10
351 Mike Krukow .10
352a Shane Rawley (Jim Anderson photo - shaking hands) .50
352b Shane Rawley (correct photo - kneeling) .15
353 Garth Iorg .10
354 Pete Mackanin .10
355 Paul Moskau .10
356 Richard Dotson .10
357 Steve Stone .10
358 Larry Hisle .10
359 Aurelio Lopez .10
360 Oscar Gamble .10
361 Tom Burgmeier .10
362 Terry Forster .10
363 Joe Charboneau .15
364 Ken Brett .10
365 Tony Armas .10
366 Chris Speier .10
367 Fred Lynn .10
368 Buddy Bell .10
369 Jim Essian .10
370 Terry Puhl .10
371 Greg Gross .10
372 Bruce Sutter .10
373 Joe Lefebvre .10
374 Ray Knight .10
375 Bruce Benedict .10
376 Tim Foli .10
377 Al Holland .10
378 Ken Kravec .10
379 Jeff Burroughs .10
380 Pete Falcone .10
381 Ernie Whitt .10
382 Brad Havens .10
383 Terry Crowley .10
384 Don Money .10
385 Dan Schatzeder .10
386 Gary Allenson .10
387 Yogi Berra .45
388 Ken Landreaux .10
389 Mike Hargrove .10
390 Darryl Motley .10
391 Dave McKay .10
392 Stan Bahnsen .10
393 Ken Forsch .10
394 Mario Mendoza .10
395 Jim Morrison .10
396 Mike Ivie .10
397 Broderick Perkins .10
398 Darrell Evans .15
399 Ron Reed .10
400 Johnny Bench 1.50
401 *Steve Bedrosian* .20
402 Bill Robinson .10
403 Bill Buckner .10
404 Ken Oberkfell .10
405 *Cal Ripken, Jr.* 40.00
406 Jim Gantner .10
407 Kirk Gibson .15
408 Tony Perez .75
409 Tommy John .10
410 *Dave Stewart* 2.50
411 Dan Spillner .10
412 Willie Aikens .10
413 Mike Heath .10
414 Ray Burris .10
415 Leon Roberts .10
416 *Mike Witt* .15
417 Bobby Molinaro .10
418 Steve Braun .10
419 Nolan Ryan 6.00
420 Tug McGraw .10
421 Dave Concepcion .10
422a Juan Eichelberger (Gary Lucas photo - white player) .50
422b Juan Eichelberger (correct photo - black player) .10
423 Rick Rhoden .10
424 Frank Robinson .50
425 Eddie Miller .10
426 Bill Caudill .10
427 Doug Flynn .10
428 Larry Anderson (Andersen) .10
429 Al Williams .10
430 Jerry Garvin .10
431 Glenn Adams .10
432 Barry Bonnell .10
433 Jerry Narron .10
434 John Stearns .10
435 Mike Tyson .10
436 Glenn Hubbard .10
437 Eddie Solomon .10
438 Jeff Leonard .10
439 Randy Bass .10
440 Mike LaCoss .10
441 Gary Matthews .10
442 Mark Littell .10
443 Don Sutton .60
444 John Harris .10
445 Vada Pinson .10
446 Elias Sosa .10
447 Charlie Hough .10
448 Willie Wilson .10
449 Fred Stanley .10
450 Tom Veryzer .10
451 Ron Davis .10
452 Mark Clear .10
453 Bill Russell .10
454 Lou Whitaker .10
455 Dan Graham .10
456 Reggie Cleveland .10
457 Sammy Stewart .10
458 Pete Vuckovich .10
459 John Wockenfuss .10
460 Glenn Hoffman .10
461 Willie Randolph .10
462 Fernando Valenzuela .10
463 Ron Hassey .10
464 Paul Splittorff .10
465 Rob Picciolo .10
466 Larry Parrish .10
467 Johnny Grubb .10
468 Dan Ford .10
469 Silvio Martinez .10
470 Kiko Garcia .10
471 Bob Boone .10
472 Luis Salazar .10
473 Randy Niemann .10
474 Tom Griffin .10
475 Phil Niekro .60
476 Hubie Brooks .10
477 Dick Tidrow .10
478 Jim Beattie .10
479 Damaso Garcia .10
480 Mickey Hatcher .10
481 Joe Price .10
482 Ed Farmer .10
483 Eddie Murray 1.50
484 Ben Oglivie .10
485 Kevin Saucier .10
486 Bobby Murcer .10
487 Bill Campbell .10
488 Reggie Smith .10
489 Wayne Garland .10
490 Jim Wright .10
491 Billy Martin .10
492 Jim Fanning .10
493 Don Baylor .15
494 Rick Honeycutt .10
495 Carlton Fisk 1.00
496 Denny Walling .10
497 Bake McBride .10
498 Darrell Porter .10
499 Gene Richards .10
500 Ron Oester .10
501 *Ken Dayley* .15
502 Jason Thompson .10
503 Milt May .10
504 Doug Bird .10
505 Bruce Bochte .10
506 Neil Allen .10
507 Joey McLaughlin .10
508 Butch Wynegar .10
509 Gary Roenicke .10
510 Robin Yount 1.00
511 Dave Tobik .10
512 *Rich Gedman* .15
513 *Gene Nelson* .10
514 Rick Monday .10
515 Miguel Dilone .10
516 Clint Hurdle .10
517 Jeff Newman .10
518 Grant Jackson .10
519 Andy Hassler .10
520 Pat Putnam .10
521 Greg Pryor .10
522 Tony Scott .10
523 Steve Mura .10
524 Johnnie LeMaster .10
525 Dick Ruthven .10
526 John McNamara .10
527 Larry McWilliams .10
528 *Johnny Ray* .15
529 *Pat Tabler* .15
530 Tom Herr .10
531a San Diego Chicken (w/ trademark symbol) .75
531b San Diego Chicken (no trademark symbol) .50
532 Sal Butera .10
533 Mike Griffin .10
534 Kelvin Moore .10
535 Reggie Jackson 2.00
536 Ed Romero .10
537 Derrel Thomas .10
538 Mike O'Berry .10
539 Jack O'Connor .10
540 *Bob Ojeda* .50

No.	Player	Price
541	Roy Lee Jackson	.10
542	Lynn Jones	.10
543	Gaylord Perry	.60
544a	Phil Garner (photo reversed)	.50
544b	Phil Garner (photo correct)	.10
545	Garry Templeton	.10
546	Rafael Ramirez	.10
547	Jeff Reardon	.10
548	Ron Guidry	.10
549	*Tim Laudner*	.15
550	John Henry Johnson	.10
551	Chris Bando	.10
552	Bobby Brown	.10
553	Larry Bradford	.10
554	*Scott Fletcher*	.20
555	Jerry Royster	.10
556	Shooty Babbitt	.10
557	*Kent Hrbek*	2.00
558	Yankee Winners (Ron Guidry, Tommy John)	.15
559	Mark Bomback	.10
560	Julio Valdez	.10
561	Buck Martinez	.10
562	*Mike Marshall*	.15
563	Rennie Stennett	.10
564	Steve Crawford	.10
565	Bob Babcock	.10
566	Johnny Podres	.10
567	Paul Serna	.10
568	Harold Baines	.50
569	Dave LaRoche	.10
570	Lee May	.10
571	Gary Ward	.10
572	John Denny	.10
573	Roy Smalley	.10
574	*Bob Brenly*	.20
575	Bronx Bombers (Reggie Jackson, Dave Winfield)	1.50
576	Luis Pujols	.10
577	Butch Hobson	.10
578	Harvey Kuenn	.10
579	Cal Ripken, Sr.	.10
580	Juan Berenguer	.10
581	Benny Ayala	.10
582	Vance Law	.10
583	*Rick Leach*	.15
584	George Frazier	.10
585	Phillies Finest (Pete Rose, Mike Schmidt)	1.00
586	Joe Rudi	.10
587	Juan Beniquez	.10
588	*Luis DeLeon*	.10
589	Craig Swan	.10
590	Dave Chalk	.10
591	Billy Gardner	.10
592	Sal Bando	.10
593	Bert Campaneris	.10
594	Steve Kemp	.10
595a	Randy Lerch (Braves)	.50
595b	Randy Lerch (Brewers)	.10
596	Bryan Clark	.10
597	Dave Ford	.10
598	Mike Scioscia	.10
599	John Lowenstein	.10
600	Rene Lachmann (Lachemann)	.10
601	Mick Kelleher	.10
602	Ron Jackson	.10
603	Jerry Koosman	.10
604	Dave Goltz	.10
605	Ellis Valentine	.10
606	Lonnie Smith	.10
607	Joaquin Andujar	.10
608	Garry Hancock	.10
609	Jerry Turner	.10
610	Bob Bonner	.10
611	Jim Dwyer	.10
612	Terry Bulling	.10
613	Joel Youngblood	.10
614	Larry Milbourne	.10
615	Phil Roof (photo actually Gene Roof)	.10
616	Keith Drumright	.10
617	Dave Rosello	.10
618	Rickey Keeton	.10
619	Dennis Lamp	.10
620	Sid Monge	.10
621	Jerry White	.10
622	*Luis Aguayo*	.10
623	Jamie Easterly	.10
624	*Steve Sax*	.75
625	Dave Roberts	.10
626	Rick Bosetti	.10
627	*Terry Francona*	.15
628	Pride of the Reds (Johnny Bench, Tom Seaver)	.75
629	Paul Mirabella	.10
630	Rance Mulliniks	.10
631	Kevin Hickey	.10
632	Reid Nichols	.10
633	Dave Geisel	.10
634	Ken Griffey	.10
635	Bob Lemon	.25
636	Orlando Sanchez	.10
637	Bill Almon	.10
638	Danny Ainge	1.00
639	Willie Stargell	1.00
640	Bob Sykes	.10
641	Ed Lynch	.10
642	John Ellis	.10
643	Fergie Jenkins	.60
644	Lenn Sakata	.10
645	Julio Gonzales	.10
646	Jesse Orosco	.10
647	Jerry Dybzinski	.10
648	Tommy Davis	.10
649	Ron Gardenhire	.10
650	Felipe Alou	.15
651	Harvey Haddix	.10
652	Willie Upshaw	.10
653	Bill Madlock	.10
----	Checklist 1-26 DK (5 Trammel)	.25
----	Checklist 1-26 DK (5 Trammell)	.10
----	Checklist 27-130	.10
----	Checklist 131-234	.10
----	Checklist 235-338	.10
----	Checklist 339-442	.10
----	Checklist 443-544	.10
----	Checklist 545-653	.10

1983 Donruss

The 1983 Donruss set consists of 653 numbered cards plus seven unnumbered checklists. The 2-1/2" x 3-1/2" cards were issued with puzzle pieces (three pieces on one card per pack) that feature Ty Cobb. The first 26 cards in the set were once again the Diamond Kings series. The card fronts display the Donruss logo and the year of issue. The card backs have black print on yellow and white and include statistics, career highlights, and the player's contract status. (DK) in the checklist below indicates cards which belong to the Diamond Kings series.

	MT
Factory Set (660):	45.00
Complete Set (660):	35.00
Common Player:	.10
Ty Cobb Puzzle:	3.00
Pack (15):	3.00
Wax Box (36):	60.00

No.	Player	Price
1	Fernando Valenzuela (DK)	.25
2	Rollie Fingers (DK)	.60
3	Reggie Jackson (DK)	1.00
4	Jim Palmer (DK)	.75
5	Jack Morris (DK)	.25
6	George Foster (DK)	.25
7	Jim Sundberg (DK)	.10
8	Willie Stargell (DK)	1.00
9	Dave Stieb (DK)	.15
10	Joe Niekro (DK)	.15
11	Rickey Henderson (DK)	2.00
12	Dale Murphy (DK)	.75
13	Toby Harrah (DK)	.10
14	Bill Buckner (DK)	.15
15	Willie Wilson (DK)	.20
16	Steve Carlton (DK)	1.00
17	Ron Guidry (DK)	.20
18	Steve Rogers (DK)	.10
19	Kent Hrbek (DK)	.20
20	Keith Hernandez (DK)	.20
21	Floyd Bannister (DK)	.10
22	Johnny Bench (DK)	1.00
23	Britt Burns (DK)	.10
24	Joe Morgan (DK)	1.00
25	Carl Yastrzemski (DK)	1.00
26	Terry Kennedy (DK)	.10
27	Gary Roenicke	.10
28	Dwight Bernard	.10
29	Pat Underwood	.10
30	Gary Allenson	.10
31	Ron Guidry	.10
32	Burt Hooton	.10
33	Chris Bando	.10
34	Vida Blue	.10
35	Rickey Henderson	1.50
36	Ray Burris	.10
37	John Butcher	.10
38	Don Aase	.10
39	Jerry Koosman	.10
40	Bruce Sutter	.10
41	Jose Cruz	.10
42	Pete Rose	3.00
43	Cesar Cedeno	.10
44	Floyd Chiffer	.10
45	Larry McWilliams	.10
46	Alan Fowlkes	.10
47	Dale Murphy	.75
48	Doug Bird	.10
49	Hubie Brooks	.10
50	Floyd Bannister	.10
51	Jack O'Connor	.10
52	Steve Senteney	.10
53	*Gary Gaetti*	.75
54	Damaso Garcia	.10
55	Gene Nelson	.10
56	Mookie Wilson	.10
57	Allen Ripley	.10
58	Bob Horner	.10
59	Tony Pena	.10
60	Gary Lavelle	.10
61	Tim Lollar	.10
62	Frank Pastore	.10
63	Garry Maddox	.10
64	Bob Forsch	.10
65	Harry Spilman	.10
66	Geoff Zahn	.10
67	Salome Barojas	.10
68	David Palmer	.10
69	Charlie Hough	.10
70	Dan Quisenberry	.10
71	Tony Armas	.10
72	Rick Sutcliffe	.10
73	Steve Balboni	.10
74	Jerry Remy	.10
75	Mike Scioscia	.10
76	John Wockenfuss	.10
77	Jim Palmer	.80
78	Rollie Fingers	.60
79	Joe Nolan	.10
80	Pete Vuckovich	.10
81	Rick Leach	.10
82	Rick Miller	.10
83	Graig Nettles	.15
84	Ron Cey	.10
85	Miguel Dilone	.10
86	John Wathan	.10
87	Kelvin Moore	.10
88a	Byrn Smith (first name incorrect)	.35
88b	Bryn Smith (first name correct)	.10
89	Dave Hostetler	.10
90	Rod Carew	1.00
91	Lonnie Smith	.10
92	Bob Knepper	.10
93	Marty Bystrom	.10
94	Chris Welsh	.10
95	Jason Thompson	.10
96	Tom O'Malley	.10
97	Phil Niekro	.60
98	Neil Allen	.10
99	Bill Buckner	.10
100	*Ed Vande Berg*	.10
101	Jim Clancy	.10
102	Robert Castillo	.10
103	Bruce Berenyi	.10
104	Carlton Fisk	1.00
105	Mike Flanagan	.10
106	Cecil Cooper	.10
107	Jack Morris	.10
108	Mike Morgan	.15
109	Luis Aponte	.10
110	Pedro Guerrero	.10
111	Len Barker	.10
112	Willie Wilson	.10
113	Dave Beard	.10
114	Mike Gates	.10
115	Reggie Jackson	1.50
116	George Wright	.10
117	Vance Law	.10
118	Nolan Ryan	6.00
119	Mike Krukow	.10
120	Ozzie Smith	1.50
121	Broderick Perkins	.10
122	Tom Seaver	1.50
123	Chris Chambliss	.10
124	Chuck Tanner	.10
125	Johnnie LeMaster	.10
126	*Mel Hall*	.15
127	Bruce Bochte	.10
128	*Charlie Puleo*	.10
129	Luis Leal	.10
130	John Pacella	.10
131	Glenn Gulliver	.10
132	Don Money	.10
133	Dave Rozema	.10
134	Bruce Hurst	.10
135	Rudy May	.10
136	Tom LaSorda (Lasorda)	.50
137	Dan Spillner (photo actually Ed Whitson)	.10
138	Jerry Martin	.10
139	Mike Norris	.10
140	Al Oliver	.10
141	Daryl Sconiers	.10
142	Lamar Johnson	.10
143	Harold Baines	.15
144	Alan Ashby	.10
145	Garry Templeton	.10
146	Al Holland	.10
147	Bo Diaz	.10
148	Dave Concepcion	.10
149	Rick Camp	.10
150	Jim Morrison	.10
151	Randy Martz	.10
152	Keith Hernandez	.15
153	John Lowenstein	.10
154	Mike Caldwell	.10
155	Milt Wilcox	.10
156	Rich Gedman	.10
157	Rich Gossage	.20
158	Jerry Reuss	.10
159	Ron Hassey	.10
160	Larry Gura	.10
161	Dwayne Murphy	.10
162	Woodie Fryman	.10
163	Steve Comer	.10
164	Ken Forsch	.10
165	Dennis Lamp	.10
166	David Green	.10
167	Terry Puhl	.10
168	Mike Schmidt	2.50
169	*Eddie Milner*	.10
170	John Curtis	.10
171	Don Robinson	.10
172	Richard Gale	.10
173	Steve Bedrosian	.10
174	Willie Hernandez	.10
175	Ron Gardenhire	.10
176	Jim Beattie	.10
177	Tim Laudner	.10
178	Buck Martinez	.10
179	Kent Hrbek	.10
180	Alfredo Griffin	.10

No.	Player	Value
181	Larry Andersen	.10
182	Pete Falcone	.10
183	Jody Davis	.10
184	Glenn Hubbard	.10
185	Dale Berra	.10
186	Greg Minton	.10
187	Gary Lucas	.10
188	Dave Van Gorder	.10
189	Bob Dernier	.10
190	*Willie McGee*	1.50
191	Dickie Thon	.10
192	Bob Boone	.10
193	Britt Burns	.10
194	Jeff Reardon	.10
195	Jon Matlack	.10
196	*Don Slaught*	.20
197	Fred Stanley	.10
198	Rick Manning	.10
199	Dave Righetti	.10
200	Dave Stapleton	.10
201	Steve Yeager	.10
202	Enos Cabell	.10
203	Sammy Stewart	.10
204	Moose Haas	.10
205	Lenn Sakata	.10
206	Charlie Moore	.10
207	Alan Trammell	.30
208	Jim Rice	.25
209	Roy Smalley	.10
210	Bill Russell	.10
211	Andre Thornton	.10
212	Willie Aikens	.10
213	Dave McKay	.10
214	Tim Blackwell	.10
215	Buddy Bell	.10
216	Doug DeCinces	.10
217	Tom Herr	.10
218	Frank LaCorte	.10
219	Steve Carlton	1.00
220	Terry Kennedy	.10
221	Mike Easler	.10
222	Jack Clark	.10
223	Gene Garber	.10
224	Scott Holman	.10
225	Mike Proly	.10
226	Terry Bulling	.10
227	Jerry Garvin	.10
228	Ron Davis	.10
229	Tom Hume	.10
230	Marc Hill	.10
231	Dennis Martinez	.10
232	Jim Gantner	.10
233	Larry Pashnick	.10
234	Dave Collins	.10
235	Tom Burgmeier	.10
236	Ken Landreaux	.10
237	John Denny	.10
238	Hal McRae	.10
239	Matt Keough	.10
240	Doug Flynn	.10
241	Fred Lynn	.10
242	Billy Sample	.10
243	Tom Paciorek	.10
244	Joe Sambito	.10
245	Sid Monge	.10
246	Ken Oberkfell	.10
247	Joe Pittman (photo actually Juan Eichelberger)	.10
248	Mario Soto	.10
249	Claudell Washington	.10
250	Rick Rhoden	.10
251	Darrell Evans	.10
252	Steve Henderson	.10
253	Manny Castillo	.10
254	Craig Swan	.10
255	Joey McLaughlin	.10
256	Pete Redfern	.10
257	Ken Singleton	.10
258	Robin Yount	1.50
259	Elias Sosa	.10
260	Bob Ojeda	.10
261	Bobby Murcer	.10
262	*Candy Maldonado*	.10
263	Rick Waits	.10
264	Greg Pryor	.10
265	Bob Owchinko	.10
266	Chris Speier	.10
267	Bruce Kison	.10
268	Mark Wagner	.10
269	Steve Kemp	.10
270	Phil Garner	.10
271	Gene Richards	.10
272	Renie Martin	.10
273	Dave Roberts	.10
274	Dan Driessen	.10
275	Rufino Linares	.10
276	Lee Lacy	.10
277	*Ryne Sandberg*	10.00
278	Darrell Porter	.10
279	Cal Ripken, Jr.	8.00
280	Jamie Easterly	.10
281	Bill Fahey	.10
282	Glenn Hoffman	.10
283	Willie Randolph	.10
284	Fernando Valenzuela	.10
285	Alan Bannister	.10
286	Paul Splittorff	.10
287	Joe Rudi	.10
288	Bill Gullickson	.10
289	Danny Darwin	.10
290	Andy Hassler	.10
291	Ernesto Escarrega	.10
292	Steve Mura	.10
293	Tony Scott	.10
294	Manny Trillo	.10
295	Greg Harris	.10
296	Luis DeLeon	.10
297	Kent Tekulve	.10
298	Atlee Hammaker	.10
299	Bruce Benedict	.10
300	Fergie Jenkins	.60
301	Dave Kingman	.15
302	Bill Caudill	.10
303	John Castino	.10
304	Ernie Whitt	.10
305	Randy S. Johnson	.10
306	Garth Iorg	.10
307	Gaylord Perry	.60
308	Ed Lynch	.10
309	Keith Moreland	.10
310	Rafael Ramirez	.10
311	Bill Madlock	.10
312	Milt May	.10
313	John Montefusco	.10
314	Wayne Krenchicki	.10
315	George Vukovich	.10
316	Joaquin Andujar	.10
317	Craig Reynolds	.10
318	Rick Burleson	.10
319	Richard Dotson	.10
320	Steve Rogers	.10
321	Dave Schmidt	.10
322	*Bud Black*	.15
323	Jeff Burroughs	.10
324	Von Hayes	.10
325	Butch Wynegar	.10
326	Carl Yastrzemski	1.00
327	Ron Roenicke	.10
328	*Howard Johnson*	1.00
329	Rick Dempsey	.10
330a	Jim Slaton (one yellow box on back)	.35
330b	Jim Slaton (two yellow boxes on back)	.10
331	Benny Ayala	.10
332	Ted Simmons	.10
333	Lou Whitaker	.10
334	Chuck Rainey	.10
335	Lou Piniella	.15
336	Steve Sax	.10
337	Toby Harrah	.10
338	George Brett	3.00
339	Davey Lopes	.10
340	Gary Carter	.50
341	John Grubb	.10
342	Tim Foli	.10
343	Jim Kaat	.15
344	Mike LaCoss	.10
345	Larry Christenson	.10
346	Juan Bonilla	.10
347	Omar Moreno	.10
348	Chili Davis	.10
349	Tommy Boggs	.10
350	Rusty Staub	.15
351	Bump Wills	.10
352	Rick Sweet	.10
353	*Jim Gott*	.15
354	Terry Felton	.10
355	Jim Kern	.10
356	Bill Almon	.10
357	Tippy Martinez	.10
358	Roy Howell	.10
359	Dan Petry	.10
360	Jerry Mumphrey	.10
361	Mark Clear	.10
362	Mike Marshall	.10
363	Lary Sorensen	.10
364	Amos Otis	.10
365	Rick Langford	.10
366	Brad Mills	.10
367	Brian Downing	.10
368	Mike Richardt	.10
369	Aurelio Rodriguez	.10
370	Dave Smith	.10
371	Tug McGraw	.10
372	Doug Bair	.10
373	Ruppert Jones	.10
374	Alex Trevino	.10
375	Ken Dayley	.10
376	Rod Scurry	.10
377	Bob Brenly	.10
378	Scot Thompson	.10
379	Julio Cruz	.10
380	John Stearns	.10
381	Dale Murray	.10
382	*Frank Viola*	1.50
383	Al Bumbry	.10
384	Ben Oglivie	.10
385	Dave Tobik	.10
386	Bob Stanley	.10
387	Andre Robertson	.10
388	Jorge Orta	.10
389	Ed Whitson	.10
390	Don Hood	.10
391	Tom Underwood	.10
392	Tim Wallach	.10
393	Steve Renko	.10
394	Mickey Rivers	.10
395	Greg Luzinski	.10
396	Art Howe	.10
397	Alan Wiggins	.10
398	Jim Barr	.10
399	Ivan DeJesus	.10
400	*Tom Lawless*	.10
401	Bob Walk	.10
402	Jimmy Smith	.10
403	Lee Smith	.20
404	George Hendrick	.10
405	Eddie Murray	1.50
406	Marshall Edwards	.10
407	Lance Parrish	.10
408	Carney Lansford	.10
409	Dave Winfield	1.50
410	Bob Welch	.10
411	Larry Milbourne	.10
412	Dennis Leonard	.10
413	Dan Meyer	.10
414	Charlie Lea	.10
415	Rick Honeycutt	.10
416	Mike Witt	.10
417	Steve Trout	.10
418	Glenn Brummer	.10
419	Denny Walling	.10
420	Gary Matthews	.10
421	Charlie Liebrandt (Leibrandt)	.10
422	Juan Eichelberger	.10
423	*Matt Guante (Cecilio)*	.10
424	Bill Laskey	.10
425	Jerry Royster	.10
426	Dickie Noles	.10
427	George Foster	.15
428	*Mike Moore*	.50
429	Gary Ward	.10
430	Barry Bonnell	.10
431	Ron Washington	.10
432	Rance Mulliniks	.10
433	Mike Stanton	.10
434	Jesse Orosco	.10
435	Larry Bowa	.10
436	Biff Pocoroba	.10
437	Johnny Ray	.10
438	Joe Morgan	.75
439	*Eric Show*	.15
440	Larry Biittner	.10
441	Greg Gross	.10
442	Gene Tenace	.10
443	Danny Heep	.10
444	Bobby Clark	.10
445	Kevin Hickey	.10
446	Scott Sanderson	.10
447	Frank Tanana	.10
448	Cesar Geronimo	.10
449	Jimmy Sexton	.10
450	Mike Hargrove	.10
451	Doyle Alexander	.10
452	Dwight Evans	.10
453	Terry Forster	.10
454	Tom Brookens	.10
455	Rich Dauer	.10
456	Rob Picciolo	.10
457	Terry Crowley	.10
458	Ned Yost	.10
459	Kirk Gibson	.10
460	Reid Nichols	.10
461	Oscar Gamble	.10
462	Dusty Baker	.15
463	Jack Perconte	.10
464	Frank White	.10
465	Mickey Klutts	.10
466	Warren Cromartie	.10
467	Larry Parrish	.10
468	Bobby Grich	.10
469	Dane Iorg	.10
470	Joe Niekro	.10
471	Ed Farmer	.10
472	Tim Flannery	.10
473	Dave Parker	.10
474	Jeff Leonard	.10
475	Al Hrabosky	.10
476	Ron Hodges	.10
477	Leon Durham	.10
478	Jim Essian	.10
479	Roy Lee Jackson	.10
480	Brad Havens	.10
481	Joe Price	.10
482	Tony Bernazard	.10
483	Scott McGregor	.10
484	Paul Molitor	1.50
485	Mike Ivie	.10
486	Ken Griffey	.10
487	Dennis Eckersley	.60
488	Steve Garvey	.60
489	Mike Fischlin	.10
490	U.L. Washington	.10
491	Steve McCatty	.10
492	Roy Johnson	.10
493	Don Baylor	.20
494	Bobby Johnson	.10
495	Mike Squires	.10
496	Bert Roberge	.10
497	Dick Ruthven	.10
498	Tito Landrum	.10
499	Sixto Lezcano	.10
500	Johnny Bench	1.50
501	Larry Whisenton	.10
502	Manny Sarmiento	.10
503	Fred Breining	.10
504	Bill Campbell	.10
505	Todd Cruz	.10
506	Bob Bailor	.10
507	Dave Stieb	.10
508	Al Williams	.10
509	Dan Ford	.10
510	Gorman Thomas	.10
511	Chet Lemon	.10
512	Mike Torrez	.10
513	Shane Rawley	.10
514	Mark Belanger	.10
515	Rodney Craig	.10
516	Onix Concepcion	.10
517	Mike Heath	.10
518	Andre Dawson	.75
519	Luis Sanchez	.10
520	Terry Bogener	.10
521	Rudy Law	.10
522	Ray Knight	.15
523	Joe Lefebvre	.10
524	Jim Wohlford	.10
525	*Julio Franco*	2.00
526	Ron Oester	.10
527	Rick Mahler	.10
528	Steve Nicosia	.10
529	Junior Kennedy	.10
530a	Whitey Herzog (one yellow box on back)	.35
530b	Whitey Herzog (two yellow boxes on back)	.15
531a	Don Sutton (blue frame)	.60
531b	Don Sutton (green frame)	.60
532	Mark Brouhard	.10
533a	Sparky Anderson (one yellow box on back)	.50
533b	Sparky Anderson (two yellow boxes on back)	.40
534	Roger LaFrancois	.10
535	George Frazier	.10
536	Tom Niedenfuer	.10
537	Ed Glynn	.10
538	Lee May	.10
539	Bob Kearney	.10
540	Tim Raines	.35
541	Paul Mirabella	.10
542	Luis Tiant	.10
543	Ron LeFlore	.10
544	*Dave LaPoint*	.15
545	Randy Moffitt	.10
546	Luis Aguayo	.10
547	Brad Lesley	.10

548 Luis Salazar .10
549 John Candelaria .10
550 Dave Bergman .10
551 Bob Watson .10
552 Pat Tabler .10
553 Brent Gaff .10
554 Al Cowens .10
555 Tom Brunansky .10
556 Lloyd Moseby .10
557a Pascual Perez (Twins) .45
557b Pascual Perez (Braves) .10
558 Willie Upshaw .10
559 Richie Zisk .10
560 Pat Zachry .10
561 Jay Johnstone .10
562 Carlos Diaz .10
563 John Tudor .10
564 Frank Robinson .50
565 Dave Edwards .10
566 Paul Householder .10
567 Ron Reed .10
568 Mike Ramsey .10
569 Kiko Garcia .10
570 Tommy John .10
571 Tony LaRussa .10
572 Joel Youngblood .10
573 *Wayne Tolleson* .10
574 Keith Creel .10
575 Billy Martin .20
576 Jerry Dybzinski .10
577 Rick Cerone .10
578 Tony Perez .60
579 *Greg Brock* .10
580 Glen Wilson (Glenn) .10
581 Tim Stoddard .10
582 Bob McClure .10
583 Jim Dwyer .10
584 Ed Romero .10
585 Larry Herndon .10
586 *Wade Boggs* 10.00
587 Jay Howell .10
588 Dave Stewart .25
589 Bert Blyleven .10
590 Dick Howser .10
591 Wayne Gross .10
592 Terry Francona .10
593 Don Werner .10
594 Bill Stein .10
595 Jesse Barfield .10
596 Bobby Molinaro .10
597 Mike Vail .10
598 *Tony Gwynn* 20.00
599 Gary Rajsich .10
600 Jerry Ujdur .10
601 Cliff Johnson .10
602 Jerry White .10
603 Bryan Clark .10
604 Joe Ferguson .10
605 Guy Sularz .10
606a Ozzie Virgil (green frame around photo) .45
606b Ozzie Virgil (orange frame around photo) .10
607 Terry Harper .10
608 Harvey Kuenn .10
609 Jim Sundberg .10
610 Willie Stargell 1.00
611 Reggie Smith .10
612 Rob Wilfong .10
613 Niekro Brothers (Joe Niekro, Phil Niekro) .25
614 Lee Elia .10
615 Mickey Hatcher .10
616 Jerry Hairston Sr. .10
617 John Martin .10
618 Wally Backman .10
619 *Storm Davis* .15
620 Alan Knicely .10
621 John Stuper .10
622 Matt Sinatro .10
623 *Gene Petralli* .10
624 Duane Walker .10
625 Dick Williams .10
626 Pat Corrales .10
627 Vern Ruhle .10
628 Joe Torre .10
629 Anthony Johnson .10
630 Steve Howe .10
631 Gary Woods .10
632 Lamarr Hoyt (LaMarr) .10
633 Steve Swisher .10
634 Terry Leach .10
635 Jeff Newman .10
636 Brett Butler .10
637 Gary Gray .10
638 Lee Mazzilli .10
639a Ron Jackson (A's) 3.00
639b Ron Jackson (Angels - green frame around photo) .45
639c Ron Jackson (Angels - red frame around photo) .15
640 Juan Beniquez .10
641 Dave Rucker .10
642 Luis Pujols .10
643 Rick Monday .10
644 Hosken Powell .10
645 San Diego Chicken .20
646 Dave Engle .10
647 Dick Davis .10
648 MVP's (Vida Blue, Joe Morgan, Frank Robinson) .15
649 Al Chambers .10
650 Jesus Vega .10
651 Jeff Jones .10
652 Marvis Foley .10
653 Ty Cobb (puzzle) .10
---- DK checklist (Dick Perez) (no word "Checklist" on back) .35
---- DK Checklist (Dick Perez) (word "Checklist" on back) .10
---- Checklist 27-130 .10
---- Checklist 131-234 .10
---- Checklist 235-338 .10
---- Checklist 339-442 .10
---- Checklist 443-546 .10
---- Checklist 547-653 .10

1983 Donruss Action All-Stars

The cards in this 60-card set are designed on a horizontal format and contain a large close-up photo of the player on the left and a smaller action photo on the right. The 5" x 3-1/2" cards have deep red borders and contain the Donruss logo and the year of issue. Backs are printed in black on red and white and contain statistical and biographical information. The cards were sold with puzzle pieces (three pieces on one card per pack) that feature Mickey Mantle.

MT
Complete Set (60): 6.00
Common Player: .05
Mickey Mantle puzzle: 12.50
1 Eddie Murray .30
2 Dwight Evans .05
3a Reggie Jackson (red covers part of statistics on back) .30
3b Reggie Jackson (red does not cover any statistics on back) .30
4 Greg Luzinski .05
5 Larry Herndon .05
6 Al Oliver .05
7 Bill Buckner .05
8 Jason Thompson .05
9 Andre Dawson .15
10 Greg Minton .05
11 Terry Kennedy .05
12 Phil Niekro .20
13 Willie Wilson .05
14 Johnny Bench .30
15 Ron Guidry .05
16 Hal McRae .05
17 Damaso Garcia .05
18 Gary Ward .05
19 Cecil Cooper .05
20 Keith Hernandez .05
21 Ron Cey .05
22 Rickey Henderson .30
23 Nolan Ryan 2.50
24 Steve Carlton .30
25 John Stearns .05
26 Jim Sundberg .05
27 Joaquin Andujar .05
28 Gaylord Perry .20
29 Jack Clark .05
30 Bill Madlock .05
31 Pete Rose 1.50
32 Mookie Wilson .05
33 Rollie Fingers .20
34 Lonnie Smith .05
35 Tony Pena .05
36 Dave Winfield .30
37 Tim Lollar .05
38 Rod Carew .30
39 Toby Harrah .05
40 Buddy Bell .05
41 Bruce Sutter .05
42 George Brett .75
43 Carlton Fisk .30
44 Carl Yastrzemski .50
45 Dale Murphy .20
46 Bob Horner .05
47 Dave Concepcion .05
48 Dave Stieb .05
49 Kent Hrbek .05
50 Lance Parrish .05
51 Joe Niekro .05
52 Cal Ripken, Jr. 2.50
53 Fernando Valenzuela .05
54 Rickie Zisk .05
55 Leon Durham .05
56 Robin Yount .30
57 Mike Schmidt .75
58 Gary Carter .15
59 Fred Lynn .05
60 Checklist .05

1983 Donruss Hall of Fame Heroes

The artwork of Dick Perez is featured in the 44-card Hall of Fame Heroes set issued in 1983. The 2-1/2" x 3-1/2" cards were available in wax packs that contained eight cards plus a Mickey Mantle puzzle piece card (three pieces on one card). Backs display red and blue print on white stock and contain a short biograpical sketch.

MT
Complete Set (44): 7.50
Common Player: .10
Mickey Mantle Puzzle: 12.50
1 Ty Cobb .75
2 Walter Johnson .15
3 Christy Mathewson .15
4 Josh Gibson .15
5 Honus Wagner .35
6 Jackie Robinson .75
7 Mickey Mantle 2.00
8 Luke Appling .10
9 Ted Williams .75
10 Johnny Mize .10
11 Satchel Paige .35
12 Lou Boudreau .10
13 Jimmie Foxx .10
14 Duke Snider .35
15 Monte Irvin .10
16 Hank Greenberg .25
17 Roberto Clemente 1.00
18 Al Kaline .25
19 Frank Robinson .25
20 Joe Cronin .10
21 Burleigh Grimes .10
22 The Waner Brothers (Lloyd Waner, Paul Waner) .10
23 Grover Alexander .10
24 Yogi Berra .35
25 James Bell .10
26 Bill Dickey .10
27 Cy Young .15
28 Charlie Gehringer .10
29 Dizzy Dean .15
30 Bob Lemon .10
31 Red Ruffing .10
32 Stan Musial .75
33 Carl Hubbell .10
34 Hank Aaron .75
35 John McGraw .10
36 Bob Feller .20
37 Casey Stengel .10
38 Ralph Kiner .10
39 Roy Campanella .35
40 Mel Ott .10
41 Robin Roberts .10
42 Early Wynn .10
43 Mickey Mantle Puzzle Card .25
--- Checklist .05

1984 Donruss

The 1984 Donruss set consists of 651 numbered cards, seven unnumbered checklists and two "Living Legends" cards (designated A and B). The A and B cards were issued only in wax packs and were not available to hobby dealers purchasing factory sets. The card fronts differ in style from the previous years, however the Donruss logo and year of issue are still included. Backs have black print on green and white and are identical in format to the preceding year. The 2-1/2" x 3-1/2" cards were issued in packs with three pieces of a 63-piece puzzle of Duke Snider. The complete set price in the checklist that follows does not include the higher priced variations. Cards marked with (DK) or (RR) in the checklist refer to the Diamond Kings and Rated Rookies subsets. Each of the Diamond Kings cards and the DK checklist can be found in two varieties. The more common has Frank Steele's name misspelled "Steel" in the credit line at the bottom-right corner on the back. The error was later corrected.

	MT
Factory Set (660):	125.00
Complete Set (660):	80.00
Common Player:	.15
Duke Snider Puzzle:	3.50
Pack (15):	9.00
Wax Box (36):	150.00

A Living Legends (Rollie Fingers, Gaylord Perry) 5.00
B Living Legends (Johnny Bench, Carl Yastrzemski) 6.00
1a Robin Yount (DK) (Steel) 1.00
1b Robin Yount (DK) (Steele) 2.00
2a Dave Concepcion (DK) (Steel) .25
2b Dave Concepcion (DK) (Steele) .50
3a Dwayne Murphy (DK) (Steel) .25
3b Dwayne Murphy (DK) (Steele) .50
4a John Castino (DK) (Steel) .25
4b John Castino (DK) (Steele) .50
5a Leon Durham (DK) (Steel) .25
5b Leon Durham (DK) (Steele) .50
6a Rusty Staub (DK) (Steel) .30
6b Rusty Staub (DK) (Steele) .60
7a Jack Clark (DK) (Steel) .25
7b Jack Clark (DK) (Steele) .50
8a Dave Dravecky (DK) (Steel) .25
8b Dave Dravecky (DK) (Steele) .50
9a Al Oliver (DK) (Steel) .35
9b Al Oliver (DK) (Steele) .70
10a Dave Righetti (DK) (Steel) .25
10b Dave Righetti (DK) (Steele) .50
11a Hal McRae (DK) (Steel) .25
11b Hal McRae (DK) (Steele) .50
12a Ray Knight (DK) (Steel) .25
12b Ray Knight (DK) (Steele) .50
13a Bruce Sutter (DK) (Steel) .25
13b Bruce Sutter (DK) (Steele) .50
14a Bob Horner (DK) (Steel) .25
14b Bob Horner (DK) (Steele) .50
15a Lance Parrish (DK) (Steel) .25
15b Lance Parrish (DK) (Steele) .50
16a Matt Young (DK) (Steel) .25
16b Matt Young (DK) (Steele) .50
17a Fred Lynn (DK) (Steel) .35
17b Fred Lynn (DK) (Steele) .70
18a Ron Kittle (DK) (Steel) .25
18b Ron Kittle (DK) (Steele) .50
19a Jim Clancy (DK) (Steel) .25
19b Jim Clancy (DK) (Steele) .50
20a Bill Madlock (DK) (Steel) .30
20b Bill Madlock (DK) (Steele) .60
21a Larry Parrish (DK) (Steel) .25
21b Larry Parrish (DK) (Steele) .50
22a Eddie Murray (DK) (Steel) 1.00
22b Eddie Murray (DK) (Steele) 2.00
23a Mike Schmidt (DK) (Steel) 2.50
23b Mike Schmidt (DK) (Steele) 5.00
24a Pedro Guerrero (DK) (Steel) .25
24b Pedro Guerrero (DK) (Steele) .50
25a Andre Thornton (DK) (Steel) .25
25b Andre Thornton (DK) (Steele) .50
26a Wade Boggs (DK) (Steel) 1.50
26b Wade Boggs (DK) (Steele) 3.00
27 *Joel Skinner* (RR) .20
28 Tom Dunbar (RR) .15
29a Mike Stenhouse (RR) (no number on back) .15
29b Mike Stenhouse (RR) (29 on back) 3.00
30a *Ron Darling* (RR) (no number on back) 2.00
30b *Ron Darling* (RR) (30 on back) 3.00
31 *Dion James* (RR) .15
32 *Tony Fernandez* (RR) 3.00
33 Angel Salazar (RR) .15
34 *Kevin McReynolds* (RR) 1.50
35 *Dick Schofield* (RR) .20
36 *Brad Komminsk* (RR) .15
37 *Tim Teufel* (RR) .30
38 Doug Frobel (RR) .15
39 *Greg Gagne* (RR) .75
40 Mike Fuentes (RR) .15
41 *Joe Carter* (RR) 8.00
42 Mike Brown (RR) .15
43 Mike Jeffcoat (RR) .15
44 *Sid Fernandez* (RR) 3.00
45 Brian Dayett (RR) .15
46 Chris Smith (RR) .15
47 Eddie Murray 4.00
48 Robin Yount 4.00
49 Lance Parrish .20
50 Jim Rice .50
51 Dave Winfield 4.00
52 Fernando Valenzuela .20
53 George Brett 8.00
54 Rickey Henderson 4.00
55 Gary Carter .65
56 Buddy Bell .20
57 Reggie Jackson 5.00
58 Harold Baines .20
59 Ozzie Smith 5.00
60 Nolan Ryan 15.00
61 Pete Rose 8.00
62 Ron Oester .15
63 Steve Garvey .75
64 Jason Thompson .15
65 Jack Clark .15
66 Dale Murphy 1.50
67 Leon Durham .15
68 Darryl Strawberry 2.00
69 Richie Zisk .15
70 Kent Hrbek .20
71 Dave Stieb .15
72 Ken Schrom .15
73 George Bell .20
74 John Moses .15
75 Ed Lynch .15
76 Chuck Rainey .15
77 Biff Pocoroba .15
78 Cecilio Guante .15
79 Jim Barr .15
80 Kurt Bevacqua .15
81 Tom Foley .15
82 Joe Lefebvre .15
83 *Andy Van Slyke* 2.00
84 Bob Lillis .15
85 Rick Adams .15
86 Jerry Hairston Sr. .15
87 Bob James .15
88 Joe Altobelli .15
89 Ed Romero .15
90 John Grubb .15
91 John Henry Johnson .15
92 Juan Espino .15
93 Candy Maldonado .15
94 Andre Thornton .15
95 Onix Concepcion .15
96 *Don Hill* .15
97 Andre Dawson 1.50
98 Frank Tanana .15
99 *Curt Wilkerson* .15
100 Larry Gura .15
101 Dwayne Murphy .15
102 Tom Brennan .15
103 Dave Righetti .15
104 Steve Sax .15
105 Dan Petry .15
106 Cal Ripken, Jr. 20.00
107 Paul Molitor 4.00
108 Fred Lynn .25
109 Neil Allen .15
110 Joe Niekro .15
111 Steve Carlton 3.00
112 Terry Kennedy .15
113 Bill Madlock .20
114 Chili Davis .15
115 Jim Gantner .15
116 Tom Seaver 4.00
117 Bill Buckner .20
118 Bill Caudill .15
119 Jim Clancy .15
120 John Castino .15
121 Dave Concepcion .15
122 Greg Luzinski .15
123 Mike Boddicker .15
124 Pete Ladd .15
125 Juan Berenguer .15
126 John Montefusco .15
127 Ed Jurak .15
128 Tom Niedenfuer .15
129 Bert Blyleven .20
130 Bud Black .15
131 Gorman Heimueller .15
132 Dan Schatzeder .15
133 Ron Jackson .15
134 *Tom Henke* 1.00
135 Kevin Hickey .15
136 Mike Scott .15
137 Bo Diaz .15
138 Glenn Brummer .15
139 Sid Monge .15
140 Rich Gale .15
141 Brett Butler .15
142 Brian Harper .15
143 John Rabb .15
144 Gary Woods .15
145 Pat Putnam .15
146 *Jim Acker* .15
147 Mickey Hatcher .15
148 Todd Cruz .15
149 Tom Tellmann .15
150 John Wockenfuss .15
151 Wade Boggs 10.00
152 Don Baylor .20
153 Bob Welch .15
154 Alan Bannister .15
155 Willie Aikens .15
156 Jeff Burroughs .15
157 Bryan Little .15
158 Bob Boone .20
159 Dave Hostetler .15
160 Jerry Dybzinski .15
161 Mike Madden .15
162 Luis DeLeon .15
163 Willie Hernandez .15
164 Frank Pastore .15
165 Rick Camp .15
166 Lee Mazzilli .15
167 Scot Thompson .15
168 Bob Forsch .15
169 Mike Flanagan .15
170 Rick Manning .15
171 Chet Lemon .15
172 Jerry Remy .15
173 Ron Guidry .20
174 Pedro Guerrero .15
175 Willie Wilson .15
176 Carney Lansford .15
177 Al Oliver .20
178 Jim Sundberg .15
179 Bobby Grich .20
180 Richard Dotson .15
181 Joaquin Andujar .15
182 Jose Cruz .15
183 Mike Schmidt 6.00
184 *Gary Redus* .25
185 Garry Templeton .15
186 Tony Pena .15
187 Greg Minton .15
188 Phil Niekro 1.00
189 Fergie Jenkins 1.00
190 Mookie Wilson .20
191 Jim Beattie .15
192 Gary Ward .15
193 Jesse Barfield .15
194 Pete Filson .15
195 Roy Lee Jackson .15
196 Rick Sweet .15
197 Jesse Orosco .15
198 *Steve Lake* .15
199 Ken Dayley .15
200 Manny Sarmiento .15
201 Mark Davis .15
202 Tim Flannery .15
203 Bill Scherrer .15
204 Al Holland .15
205 David Von Ohlen .15
206 Mike LaCoss .15
207 Juan Beniquez .15
208 *Juan Agosto* .15
209 Bobby Ramos .15
210 Al Bumbry .15
211 Mark Brouhard .15
212 Howard Bailey .15
213 Bruce Hurst .15
214 Bob Shirley .15
215 Pat Zachry .15
216 Julio Franco .15
217 Mike Armstrong .15
218 Dave Beard .15
219 Steve Rogers .15
220 John Butcher .15
221 *Mike Smithson* .15
222 Frank White .20
223 Mike Heath .15
224 Chris Bando .15
225 Roy Smalley .15
226 Dusty Baker .20
227 Lou Whitaker .20
228 John Lowenstein .15
229 Ben Oglivie .15
230 Doug DeCinces .15
231 Lonnie Smith .15
232 Ray Knight .15
233 Gary Matthews .15
234 Juan Bonilla .15
235 Rod Scurry .15
236 Atlee Hammaker .15
237 Mike Caldwell .15
238 Keith Hernandez .25
239 Larry Bowa .20
240 Tony Bernazard .15
241 Damaso Garcia .15
242 Tom Brunansky .15
243 Dan Driessen .15
244 Ron Kittle .15
245 Tim Stoddard .15
246 Bob L. Gibson .15
247 Marty Castillo .15
248 *Don Mattingly* 30.00
249 Jeff Newman .15
250 *Alejandro Pena* .25
251 Toby Harrah .15
252 Cesar Geronimo .15
253 Tom Underwood .15
254 Doug Flynn .15
255 Andy Hassler .15
256 Odell Jones .15
257 Rudy Law .15
258 Harry Spilman .15

No.	Player	Price
259	Marty Bystrom	.15
260	Dave Rucker	.15
261	Ruppert Jones	.15
262	Jeff Jones	.15
263	*Gerald Perry*	.25
264	Gene Tenace	.15
265	Brad Wellman	.15
266	Dickie Noles	.15
267	Jamie Allen	.15
268	Jim Gott	.15
269	Ron Davis	.15
270	Benny Ayala	.15
271	Ned Yost	.15
272	Dave Rozema	.15
273	Dave Stapleton	.15
274	Lou Piniella	.20
275	Jose Morales	.15
276	Brod Perkins	.15
277	Butch Davis	.15
278	Tony Phillips	.15
279	Jeff Reardon	.25
280	Ken Forsch	.15
281	*Pete O'Brien*	.50
282	Tom Paciorek	.15
283	Frank LaCorte	.15
284	Tim Lollar	.15
285	Greg Gross	.15
286	Alex Trevino	.15
287	Gene Garber	.15
288	Dave Parker	.25
289	Lee Smith	.75
290	Dave LaPoint	.15
291	*John Shelby*	.15
292	Charlie Moore	.15
293	Alan Trammell	1.00
294	Tony Armas	.15
295	Shane Rawley	.15
296	Greg Brock	.15
297	Hal McRae	.15
298	Mike Davis	.15
299	Tim Raines	.75
300	Bucky Dent	.15
301	Tommy John	.25
302	Carlton Fisk	4.00
303	Darrell Porter	.15
304	Dickie Thon	.15
305	Garry Maddox	.15
306	Cesar Cedeno	.15
307	Gary Lucas	.15
308	Johnny Ray	.15
309	Andy McGaffigan	.15
310	Claudell Washington	.15
311	Ryne Sandberg	10.00
312	George Foster	.25
313	*Spike Owen*	.50
314	Gary Gaetti	.20
315	Willie Upshaw	.15
316	Al Williams	.15
317	Jorge Orta	.15
318	Orlando Mercado	.15
319	*Junior Ortiz*	.15
320	Mike Proly	.15
321	Randy S. Johnson	.15
322	Jim Morrison	.15
323	Max Venable	.15
324	Tony Gwynn	15.00
325	Duane Walker	.15
326	Ozzie Virgil	.15
327	Jeff Lahti	.15
328	*Bill Dawley*	.15
329	Rob Wilfong	.15
330	Marc Hill	.15
331	Ray Burris	.15
332	Allan Ramirez	.15
333	Chuck Porter	.15
334	Wayne Krenchicki	.15
335	Gary Allenson	.15
336	*Bob Meacham*	.15
337	Joe Beckwith	.15
338	Rick Sutcliffe	.25
339	*Mark Huismann*	.15
340	*Tim Conroy*	.15
341	Scott Sanderson	.15
342	Larry Biittner	.15
343	Dave Stewart	.25
344	Darryl Motley	.15
345	*Chris Codiroli*	.15
346	Rick Behenna	.15
347	Andre Robertson	.15
348	Mike Marshall	.15
349	Larry Herndon	.15
350	Rich Dauer	.15
351	Cecil Cooper	.15
352	Rod Carew	3.00
353	Willie McGee	.20
354	Phil Garner	.15
355	Joe Morgan	1.50
356	Luis Salazar	.15
357	John Candelaria	.15
358	Bill Laskey	.15
359	Bob McClure	.15
360	Dave Kingman	.20
361	Ron Cey	.15
362	*Matt Young*	.15
363	Lloyd Moseby	.15
364	Frank Viola	.15
365	Eddie Milner	.15
366	Floyd Bannister	.15
367	Dan Ford	.15
368	Moose Haas	.15
369	Doug Bair	.15
370	*Ray Fontenot*	.15
371	Luis Aponte	.15
372	Jack Fimple	.15
373	*Neal Heaton*	.20
374	Greg Pryor	.15
375	Wayne Gross	.15
376	Charlie Lea	.15
377	Steve Lubratich	.15
378	Jon Matlack	.15
379	Julio Cruz	.15
380	John Mizerock	.15
381	*Kevin Gross*	.50
382	Mike Ramsey	.15
383	Doug Gwosdz	.15
384	Kelly Paris	.15
385	Pete Falcone	.15
386	Milt May	.15
387	Fred Breining	.15
388	*Craig Lefferts*	.25
389	Steve Henderson	.15
390	Randy Moffitt	.15
391	Ron Washington	.15
392	Gary Roenicke	.15
393	*Tom Candiotti*	.75
394	Larry Pashnick	.15
395	Dwight Evans	.25
396	Goose Gossage	.25
397	Derrel Thomas	.15
398	Juan Eichelberger	.15
399	Leon Roberts	.15
400	Davey Lopes	.15
401	Bill Gullickson	.15
402	Geoff Zahn	.15
403	Billy Sample	.15
404	Mike Squires	.15
405	Craig Reynolds	.15
406	Eric Show	.15
407	John Denny	.15
408	Dann Bilardello	.15
409	Bruce Benedict	.15
410	Kent Tekulve	.15
411	Mel Hall	.15
412	John Stuper	.15
413	Rick Dempsey	.15
414	Don Sutton	1.00
415	Jack Morris	.25
416	John Tudor	.15
417	Willie Randolph	.20
418	Jerry Reuss	.15
419	Don Slaught	.15
420	Steve McCatty	.15
421	Tim Wallach	.15
422	Larry Parrish	.15
423	Brian Downing	.15
424	Britt Burns	.15
425	David Green	.15
426	Jerry Mumphrey	.15
427	Ivan DeJesus	.15
428	Mario Soto	.15
429	Gene Richards	.15
430	Dale Berra	.15
431	Darrell Evans	.25
432	Glenn Hubbard	.15
433	Jody Davis	.15
434	Danny Heep	.15
435	*Ed Nunez*	.15
436	Bobby Castillo	.15
437	Ernie Whitt	.15
438	Scott Ullger	.15
439	Doyle Alexander	.15
440	Domingo Ramos	.15
441	Craig Swan	.15
442	Warren Brusstar	.15
443	Len Barker	.15
444	Mike Easler	.15
445	Renie Martin	.15
446	*Dennis Rasmussen*	.30
447	Ted Power	.15
448	*Charlie Hudson*	.15
449	*Danny Cox*	.50
450	Kevin Bass	.15
451	Daryl Sconiers	.15
452	Scott Fletcher	.15
453	Bryn Smith	.15
454	Jim Dwyer	.15
455	Rob Picciolo	.15
456	Enos Cabell	.15
457	*Dennis Boyd*	.20
458	Butch Wynegar	.15
459	Burt Hooton	.15
460	Ron Hassey	.15
461	*Danny Jackson*	.50
462	Bob Kearney	.15
463	Terry Francona	.15
464	Wayne Tolleson	.15
465	Mickey Rivers	.15
466	John Wathan	.15
467	Bill Almon	.15
468	George Vukovich	.15
469	Steve Kemp	.15
470	Ken Landreaux	.15
471	Milt Wilcox	.15
472	Tippy Martinez	.15
473	Ted Simmons	.15
474	Tim Foli	.15
475	George Hendrick	.15
476	Terry Puhl	.15
477	Von Hayes	.15
478	Bobby Brown	.15
479	Lee Lacy	.15
480	Joel Youngblood	.15
481	Jim Slaton	.15
482	*Mike Fitzgerald*	.15
483	Keith Moreland	.15
484	Ron Roenicke	.15
485	Luis Leal	.15
486	Bryan Oelkers	.15
487	Bruce Berenyi	.15
488	LaMarr Hoyt	.15
489	Joe Nolan	.15
490	Marshall Edwards	.15
491	*Mike Laga*	.15
492	Rick Cerone	.15
493	Mike Miller (Rick)	.15
494	Rick Honeycutt	.15
495	Mike Hargrove	.15
496	Joe Simpson	.15
497	*Keith Atherton*	.15
498	Chris Welsh	.15
499	Bruce Kison	.15
500	Bob Johnson	.15
501	Jerry Koosman	.15
502	Frank DiPino	.15
503	Tony Perez	1.00
504	Ken Oberkfell	.15
505	*Mark Thurmond*	.15
506	Joe Price	.15
507	Pascual Perez	.15
508	*Marvell Wynne*	.15
509	Mike Krukow	.15
510	Dick Ruthven	.15
511	Al Cowens	.15
512	Cliff Johnson	.15
513	*Randy Bush*	.15
514	Sammy Stewart	.15
515	*Bill Schroeder*	.15
516	Aurelio Lopez	.15
517	Mike Brown	.15
518	Graig Nettles	.35
519	Dave Sax	.15
520	Gerry Willard	.15
521	Paul Splittorff	.15
522	Tom Burgmeier	.15
523	Chris Speier	.15
524	Bobby Clark	.15
525	George Wright	.15
526	Dennis Lamp	.15
527	Tony Scott	.15
528	Ed Whitson	.15
529	Ron Reed	.15
530	Charlie Puleo	.15
531	Jerry Royster	.15
532	Don Robinson	.15
533	Steve Trout	.15
534	Bruce Sutter	.15
535	Bob Horner	.15
536	Pat Tabler	.15
537	Chris Chambliss	.15
538	Bob Ojeda	.15
539	Alan Ashby	.15
540	Jay Johnstone	.15
541	Bob Dernier	.15
542	*Brook Jacoby*	.25
543	U.L. Washington	.15
544	Danny Darwin	.15
545	Kiko Garcia	.15
546	Vance Law	.15
547	Tug McGraw	.20
548	Dave Smith	.15
549	Len Matuszek	.15
550	Tom Hume	.15
551	Dave Dravecky	.15
552	Rick Rhoden	.15
553	Duane Kuiper	.15
554	Rusty Staub	.20
555	Bill Campbell	.15
556	Mike Torrez	.15
557	Dave Henderson	.15
558	Len Whitehouse	.15
559	Barry Bonnell	.15
560	Rick Lysander	.15
561	Garth Iorg	.15
562	Bryan Clark	.15
563	Brian Giles	.15
564	Vern Ruhle	.15
565	Steve Bedrosian	.15
566	Larry McWilliams	.15
567	Jeff Leonard	.15
568	Alan Wiggins	.15
569	*Jeff Russell*	.50
570	Salome Barojas	.15
571	Dane Iorg	.15
572	Bob Knepper	.15
573	Gary Lavelle	.15
574	Gorman Thomas	.15
575	Manny Trillo	.15
576	Jim Palmer	3.00
577	Dale Murray	.15
578	Tom Brookens	.15
579	Rich Gedman	.15
580	*Bill Doran*	.50
581	Steve Yeager	.15
582	Dan Spillner	.15
583	Dan Quisenberry	.15
584	Rance Mulliniks	.15
585	Storm Davis	.15
586	Dave Schmidt	.15
587	Bill Russell	.15
588	*Pat Sheridan*	.15
589	Rafael Ramirez	.15
590	Bud Anderson	.15
591	George Frazier	.15
592	*Lee Tunnell*	.15
593	Kirk Gibson	.20
594	Scott McGregor	.15
595	Bob Bailor	.15
596	Tom Herr	.15
597	Luis Sanchez	.15
598	Dave Engle	.15
599	*Craig McMurtry*	.15
600	Carlos Diaz	.15
601	Tom O'Malley	.15
602	*Nick Esasky*	.15
603	Ron Hodges	.15
604	Ed Vande Berg	.15
605	Alfredo Griffin	.15
606	Glenn Hoffman	.15
607	Hubie Brooks	.15
608	Richard Barnes (photo actually Neal Heaton)	.15
609	*Greg Walker*	.20
610	Ken Singleton	.15
611	Mark Clear	.15
612	Buck Martinez	.15
613	Ken Griffey	.20
614	Reid Nichols	.15
615	*Doug Sisk*	.15
616	Bob Brenly	.15
617	Joey McLaughlin	.15
618	Glenn Wilson	.15
619	Bob Stoddard	.15
620	Len Sakata (Lenn)	.15
621	*Mike Young*	.15
622	John Stefero	.15
623	*Carmelo Martinez*	.15
624	Dave Bergman	.15
625	Runnin' Reds (David Green, Willie McGee, Lonnie Smith, Ozzie Smith)	.75
626	Rudy May	.15
627	Matt Keough	.15
628	*Jose DeLeon*	.15
629	Jim Essian	.15
630	*Darnell Coles*	.15
631	Mike Warren	.15
632	Del Crandall	.15
633	Dennis Martinez	.15
634	Mike Moore	.15
635	Lary Sorensen	.15
636	Ricky Nelson	.15

637	Omar Moreno	.15
638	Charlie Hough	.15
639	Dennis Eckersley	1.50
640	*Walt Terrell*	.20
641	Denny Walling	.15
642	*Dave Anderson*	.15
643	*Jose Oquendo*	.25
644	Bob Stanley	.15
645	Dave Geisel	.15
646	*Scott Garrelts*	.25
647	*Gary Pettis*	.25
648	Duke Snider Puzzle Card	.15
649	Johnnie LeMaster	.15
650	Dave Collins	.15
651	San Diego Chicken	.25
----	Checklist 1-26 DK (Perez-Steel on back)	.15
----	Checklist 1-26 DK (Perez-Steele on back)	.15
----	Checklist 27-130	.15
----	Checklist 131-234	.15
----	Checklist 235-338	.15
----	Checklist 339-442	.15
----	Checklist 443-546	.15
----	Checklist 547-651	.15

1984 Donruss Action All-Stars

Full-color photos on the card fronts and backs make the 1984 Donruss Action All-Stars set somewhat unusual. Fronts contain a large action photo plus the Donruss logo and year of issue inside a deep red border. The top half of the backs features a close-up photo with the bottom portion containing biographical and statistical information. The 3-1/2" x 5" cards were sold with Ted Williams puzzle pieces.

		MT
Complete Set (60):		3.75
Common Player:		.05
Ted Williams Puzzle:		5.00
1	Gary Lavelle	.05
2	Willie McGee	.05
3	Tony Pena	.05
4	Lou Whitaker	.05
5	Robin Yount	.30
6	Doug DeCinces	.05
7	John Castino	.05
8	Terry Kennedy	.05
9	Rickey Henderson	.30
10	Bob Horner	.05
11	Harold Baines	.05
12	Buddy Bell	.05
13	Fernando Valenzuela	.05
14	Nolan Ryan	1.50
15	Andre Thornton	.05
16	Gary Redus	.05
17	Pedro Guerrero	.05
18	Andre Dawson	.15
19	Dave Stieb	.05
20	Cal Ripken, Jr.	1.50
21	Ken Griffey	.05
22	Wade Boggs	.35
23	Keith Hernandez	.05
24	Steve Carlton	.25
25	Hal McRae	.05
26	John Lowenstein	.05
27	Fred Lynn	.05
28	Bill Buckner	.05
29	Chris Chambliss	.05
30	Richie Zisk	.05
31	Jack Clark	.05
32	George Hendrick	.05
33	Bill Madlock	.05
34	Lance Parrish	.05
35	Paul Molitor	.30
36	Reggie Jackson	.35
37	Kent Hrbek	.05
38	Steve Garvey	.15
39	Carney Lansford	.05
40	Dale Murphy	.15
41	Greg Luzinski	.05
42	Larry Parrish	.05
43	Ryne Sandberg	.35
44	Dickie Thon	.05
45	Bert Blyleven	.05
46	Ron Oester	.05
47	Dusty Baker	.05
48	Steve Rogers	.05
49	Jim Clancy	.05
50	Eddie Murray	.30
51	Ron Guidry	.05
52	Jim Rice	.10
53	Tom Seaver	.25
54	Pete Rose	1.00
55	George Brett	.40
56	Dan Quisenberry	.05
57	Mike Schmidt	.40
58	Ted Simmons	.05
59	Dave Righetti	.05
60	Checklist	.05

1984 Donruss Champions

The 60-card Donruss Champions set includes ten Hall of Famers, forty-nine current players and a numbered checklist. The Hall of Famers' cards (called Grand Champions) feature the artwork of Dick Perez, while cards of the current players (called Champions) are color photos. All cards measure 3-1/2" x 5". The Grand Champions represent hallmarks of excellence in various statistical categories, while the Champions are the leaders among then-active players in each category. The cards were issued with Duke Snider puzzle pieces.

		MT
Complete Set (60):		3.50
Common Player:		.05
Duke Snider Puzzle:		1.75
Pack (5):		2.00
Box (36):		15.00
1	Babe Ruth	.75
2	George Foster	.05
3	Dave Kingman	.05
4	Jim Rice	.10
5	Gorman Thomas	.05
6	Ben Oglivie	.05
7	Jeff Burroughs	.05
8	Hank Aaron	.50
9	Reggie Jackson	.20
10	Carl Yastrzemski	.20
11	Mike Schmidt	.25
12	Graig Nettles	.05
13	Greg Luzinski	.05
14	Ted Williams	.40
15	George Brett	.30
16	Wade Boggs	.20
17	Hal McRae	.05
18	Bill Buckner	.05
19	Eddie Murray	.15
20	Rogers Hornsby	.05
21	Rod Carew	.15
22	Bill Madlock	.05
23	Lonnie Smith	.05
24	Cecil Cooper	.05
25	Ken Griffey	.05
26	Ty Cobb	.30
27	Pete Rose	.30
28	Rusty Staub	.05
29	Tony Perez	.10
30	Al Oliver	.05
31	Cy Young	.10
32	Gaylord Perry	.10
33	Ferguson Jenkins	.10
34	Phil Niekro	.10
35	Jim Palmer	.10
36	Tommy John	.05
37	Walter Johnson	.10
38	Steve Carlton	.10
39	Nolan Ryan	.75
40	Tom Seaver	.20
41	Don Sutton	.10
42	Bert Blyleven	.05
43	Frank Robinson	.20
44	Joe Morgan	.15
45	Rollie Fingers	.10
46	Keith Hernandez	.05
47	Robin Yount	.15
48	Cal Ripken, Jr.	.75
49	Dale Murphy	.10
50	Mickey Mantle	1.00
51	Johnny Bench	.20
52	Carlton Fisk	.10
53	Tug McGraw	.05
54	Paul Molitor	.15
55	Carl Hubbell	.05
56	Steve Garvey	.10
57	Dave Parker	.05
58	Gary Carter	.10
59	Fred Lynn	.05
60	Checklist	.03

1985 Donruss

The black-bordered 1985 Donruss set includes 653 numbered cards and seven unnumbered checklists. Displaying the artwork of Dick Perez for the fourth consecutive year, cards #1-26 feature the Diamond Kings series. Donruss, reacting to the hobby craze over rookie cards, included a Rated Rookies subset (cards #27-46). The cards, in standard 2-1/2" x 3-1/2", were issued with a Lou Gehrig puzzle. Backs repeat the format of previous years with black print on yellow and white. The complete set price does not include the higher priced variations. (DK) and (RR) refer to the Diamond Kings and Rated Rookies subsets.

		MT
Unopened Factory Set (660):		100.00
Complete Set (660):		50.00
Common Player:		.10
Lou Gehrig Puzzle:		3.00
Pack (15):		5.00
Wax Box (36):		125.00
1	Ryne Sandberg (DK)	2.50
2	Doug DeCinces (DK)	.10
3	Rich Dotson (DK)	.10
4	Bert Blyleven (DK)	.15
5	Lou Whitaker (DK)	.15
6	Dan Quisenberry (DK)	.10
7	Don Mattingly (DK)	4.50
8	Carney Lansford (DK)	.10
9	Frank Tanana (DK)	.10
10	Willie Upshaw (DK)	.10
11	Claudell Washington (DK)	.10
12	Mike Marshall (DK)	.10
13	Joaquin Andujar (DK)	.10
14	Cal Ripken, Jr. (DK)	6.00
15	Jim Rice (DK)	.25
16	Don Sutton (DK)	.30
17	Frank Viola (DK)	.10
18	Alvin Davis (DK)	.10
19	Mario Soto (DK)	.10
20	Jose Cruz (DK)	.10
21	Charlie Lea (DK)	.10
22	Jesse Orosco (DK)	.10
23	Juan Samuel (DK)	.10
24	Tony Pena (DK)	.10
25	Tony Gwynn (DK)	3.00
26	Bob Brenly (DK)	.10
27	*Danny Tartabull* (RR)	1.50
28	*Mike Bielecki* (RR)	.15
29	*Steve Lyons* (RR)	.20
30	*Jeff Reed* (RR)	.15
31	Tony Brewer (RR)	.10
32	*John Morris* (RR)	.10
33	*Daryl Boston* (RR)	.15
34	Alfonso Pulido (RR)	.10
35	*Steve Kiefer* (RR)	.10
36	*Larry Sheets* (RR)	.10
37	*Scott Bradley* (RR)	.10
38	*Calvin Schiraldi* (RR)	.10
39	*Shawon Dunston* (RR)	1.50
40	Charlie Mitchell (RR)	.10
41	*Billy Hatcher* (RR)	.50
42	Russ Stephans (RR)	.10
43	Alejandro Sanchez (RR)	.10
44	*Steve Jeltz* (RR)	.10
45	*Jim Traber* (RR)	.10
46	Doug Loman (RR)	.10
47	Eddie Murray	2.50
48	Robin Yount	2.50
49	Lance Parrish	.15
50	Jim Rice	.25
51	Dave Winfield	1.25
52	Fernando Valenzuela	.15
53	George Brett	4.00
54	Dave Kingman	.15
55	Gary Carter	.40
56	Buddy Bell	.15
57	Reggie Jackson	2.00
58	Harold Baines	.15
59	Ozzie Smith	2.50
60	Nolan Ryan	8.00
61	Mike Schmidt	4.00
62	Dave Parker	.20
63	Tony Gwynn	7.50
64	Tony Pena	.10
65	Jack Clark	.10
66	Dale Murphy	.60

67 Ryne Sandberg 6.00
68 Keith Hernandez .20
69 Alvin Davis .25
70 Kent Hrbek .15
71 Willie Upshaw .10
72 Dave Engle .10
73 Alfredo Griffin .10
74a Jack Perconte (last line of highlights begins "Batted .346...") .10
74b Jack Perconte (last line of highlights begins "Led the ...") .25
75 Jesse Orosco .10
76 Jody Davis .10
77 Bob Horner .10
78 Larry McWilliams .10
79 Joel Youngblood .10
80 Alan Wiggins .10
81 Ron Oester .10
82 Ozzie Virgil .10
83 *Ricky Horton* .10
84 Bill Doran .10
85 Rod Carew 1.00
86 LaMarr Hoyt .10
87 Tim Wallach .10
88 Mike Flanagan .10
89 Jim Sundberg .10
90 Chet Lemon .10
91 Bob Stanley .10
92 Willie Randolph .15
93 Bill Russell .10
94 Julio Franco .10
95 Dan Quisenberry .10
96 Bill Caudill .10
97 Bill Gullickson .10
98 Danny Darwin .10
99 Curtis Wilkerson .10
100 Bud Black .10
101 Tony Phillips .10
102 Tony Bernazard .10
103 Jay Howell .10
104 Burt Hooton .10
105 Milt Wilcox .10
106 Rich Dauer .10
107 Don Sutton .75
108 Mike Witt .10
109 Bruce Sutter .15
110 Enos Cabell .10
111 John Denny .10
112 Dave Dravecky .10
113 Marvell Wynne .10
114 Johnnie LeMaster .10
115 Chuck Porter .10
116 John Gibbons .10
117 Keith Moreland .10
118 Darnell Coles .10
119 Dennis Lamp .10
120 Ron Davis .10
121 Nick Esasky .10
122 Vance Law .10
123 Gary Roenicke .10
124 Bill Schroeder .10
125 Dave Rozema .10
126 Bobby Meacham .10
127 Marty Barrett .10
128 *R.J. Reynolds* .15
129 Ernie Camacho .10
130 Jorge Orta .10
131 Lary Sorensen .10
132 Terry Francona .10
133 Fred Lynn .15
134 Bobby Jones .10
135 Jerry Hairston Sr. .10
136 Kevin Bass .10
137 Garry Maddox .10
138 Dave LaPoint .10
139 Kevin McReynolds .20
140 Wayne Krenchicki .10
141 Rafael Ramirez .10
142 Rod Scurry .10
143 Greg Minton .10
144 Tim Stoddard .10
145 Steve Henderson .10
146 George Bell .10
147 Dave Meier .10
148 Sammy Stewart .10
149 Mark Brouhard .10
150 Larry Herndon .10
151 Oil Can Boyd .10
152 Brian Dayett .10
153 Tom Niedenfuer .10
154 Brook Jacoby .10
155 Onix Concepcion .10
156 Tim Conroy .10
157 *Joe Hesketh* .15
158 Brian Downing .10
159 Tommy Dunbar .10
160 Marc Hill .10
161 Phil Garner .10
162 Jerry Davis .10
163 Bill Campbell .10
164 *John Franco* 1.00
165 Len Barker .10
166 *Benny Distefano* .10
167 George Frazier .10
168 Tito Landrum .10
169 Cal Ripken, Jr. 8.00
170 Cecil Cooper .10
171 Alan Trammell .35
172 Wade Boggs 3.00
173 Don Baylor .15
174 Pedro Guerrero .10
175 Frank White .15
176 Rickey Henderson 2.00
177 Charlie Lea .10
178 Pete O'Brien .10
179 Doug DeCinces .10
180 Ron Kittle .10
181 George Hendrick .10
182 Joe Niekro .10
183 Juan Samuel .10
184 Mario Soto .10
185 Goose Gossage .25
186 Johnny Ray .10
187 Bob Brenly .10
188 Craig McMurtry .10
189 Leon Durham .10
190 Dwight Gooden .50
191 Barry Bonnell .10
192 Tim Teufel .10
193 Dave Stieb .10
194 Mickey Hatcher .10
195 Jesse Barfield .10
196 Al Cowens .10
197 Hubie Brooks .10
198 Steve Trout .10
199 Glenn Hubbard .10
200 Bill Madlock .10
201 *Jeff Robinson* .10
202 Eric Show .10
203 Dave Concepcion .10
204 Ivan DeJesus .10
205 Neil Allen .10
206 Jerry Mumphrey .10
207 Mike Brown .10
208 Carlton Fisk 1.00
209 Bryn Smith .10
210 Tippy Martinez .10
211 Dion James .10
212 Willie Hernandez .10
213 Mike Easler .10
214 Ron Guidry .10
215 Rick Honeycutt .10
216 Brett Butler .10
217 Larry Gura .10
218 Ray Burris .10
219 Steve Rogers .10
220 Frank Tanana .10
221 Ned Yost .10
222 Bret Saberhagen .50
223 Mike Davis .10
224 Bert Blyleven .15
225 Steve Kemp .10
226 Jerry Reuss .10
227 Darrell Evans .15
228 Wayne Gross .10
229 Jim Gantner .10
230 Bob Boone .15
231 Lonnie Smith .10
232 Frank DiPino .10
233 Jerry Koosman .10
234 Graig Nettles .15
235 John Tudor .10
236 John Rabb .10
237 Rick Manning .10
238 Mike Fitzgerald .10
239 Gary Matthews .10
240 *Jim Presley* .10
241 Dave Collins .10
242 Gary Gaetti .15
243 Dann Bilardello .10
244 Rudy Law .10
245 John Lowenstein .10
246 Tom Tellmann .10
247 Howard Johnson .10
248 Ray Fontenot .10
249 Tony Armas .10
250 Candy Maldonado .10
251 *Mike Jeffcoat* .10
252 Dane Iorg .10
253 Bruce Bochte .10
254 Pete Rose 3.50
255 Don Aase .10
256 George Wright .10
257 Britt Burns .10
258 Mike Scott .15
259 Len Matuszek .10
260 Dave Rucker .10
261 Craig Lefferts .10
262 *Jay Tibbs* .10
263 Bruce Benedict .10
264 Don Robinson .10
265 Gary Lavelle .10
266 Scott Sanderson .10
267 Matt Young .10
268 Ernie Whitt .10
269 Houston Jimenez .10
270 *Ken Dixon* .10
271 Peter Ladd .10
272 Juan Berenguer .10
273 Roger Clemens 40.00
274 Rick Cerone .10
275 Dave Anderson .10
276 George Vukovich .10
277 Greg Pryor .10
278 Mike Warren .10
279 Bob James .10
280 Bobby Grich .15
281 *Mike Mason* .10
282 Ron Reed .10
283 Alan Ashby .10
284 Mark Thurmond .10
285 Joe Lefebvre .10
286 Ted Power .10
287 Chris Chambliss .10
288 Lee Tunnell .10
289 Rich Bordi .10
290 Glenn Brummer .10
291 Mike Boddicker .10
292 Rollie Fingers .50
293 Lou Whitaker .15
294 Dwight Evans .15
295 Don Mattingly 6.00
296 Mike Marshall .10
297 Willie Wilson .10
298 Mike Heath .10
299 Tim Raines .25
300 Larry Parrish .10
301 Geoff Zahn .10
302 Rich Dotson .10
303 David Green .10
304 Jose Cruz .10
305 Steve Carlton 1.25
306 Gary Redus .10
307 Steve Garvey .40
308 Jose DeLeon .10
309 Randy Lerch .10
310 Claudell Washington .10
311 Lee Smith .50
312 Darryl Strawberry .30
313 Jim Beattie .10
314 John Butcher .10
315 Damaso Garcia .10
316 Mike Smithson .10
317 Luis Leal .10
318 Ken Phelps .10
319 Wally Backman .10
320 Ron Cey .10
321 Brad Komminsk .10
322 Jason Thompson .10
323 *Frank Williams* .10
324 Tim Lollar .10
325 *Eric Davis* 1.50
326 Von Hayes .10
327 Andy Van Slyke .15
328 Craig Reynolds .10
329 Dick Schofield .10
330 Scott Fletcher .10
331 Jeff Reardon .10
332 Rick Dempsey .10
333 Ben Oglivie .10
334 Dan Petry .10
335 Jackie Gutierrez .10
336 Dave Righetti .10
337 Alejandro Pena .10
338 Mel Hall .10
339 Pat Sheridan .10
340 Keith Atherton .10
341 David Palmer .10
342 Gary Ward .10
343 Dave Stewart .15
344 *Mark Gubicza* .50
345 Carney Lansford .10
346 Jerry Willard .10
347 Ken Griffey .15
348 *Franklin Stubbs* .10
349 Aurelio Lopez .10
350 Al Bumbry .10
351 Charlie Moore .10
352 Luis Sanchez .10
353 Darrell Porter .10
354 Bill Dawley .10
355 Charlie Hudson .10
356 Garry Templeton .10
357 Cecilio Guante .10
358 Jeff Leonard .10
359 Paul Molitor 2.50
360 Ron Gardenhire .10
361 Larry Bowa .15
362 Bob Kearney .10
363 Garth Iorg .10
364 Tom Brunansky .10
365 Brad Gulden .10
366 Greg Walker .10
367 Mike Young .10
368 Rick Waits .10
369 Doug Bair .10
370 Bob Shirley .10
371 Bob Ojeda .10
372 Bob Welch .10
373 Neal Heaton .10
374 Danny Jackson (photo actually Steve Farr) .25
375 Donnie Hill .10
376 Mike Stenhouse .10
377 Bruce Kison .10
378 Wayne Tolleson .10
379 Floyd Bannister .10
380 Vern Ruhle .10
381 Tim Corcoran .10
382 Kurt Kepshire .10
383 Bobby Brown .10
384 Dave Van Gorder .10
385 Rick Mahler .10
386 Lee Mazzilli .10
387 Bill Laskey .10
388 Thad Bosley .10
389 Al Chambers .10
390 Tony Fernandez .10
391 Ron Washington .10
392 Bill Swaggerty .10
393 Bob L. Gibson .10
394 Marty Castillo .10
395 Steve Crawford .10
396 Clay Christiansen .10
397 Bob Bailor .10
398 Mike Hargrove .10
399 Charlie Leibrandt .10
400 Tom Burgmeier .10
401 Razor Shines .10
402 Rob Wilfong .10
403 Tom Henke .10
404 Al Jones .10
405 Mike LaCoss .10
406 Luis DeLeon .10
407 Greg Gross .10
408 Tom Hume .10
409 Rick Camp .10
410 Milt May .10
411 *Henry Cotto* .10
412 Dave Von Ohlen .10
413 Scott McGregor .10
414 Ted Simmons .10
415 Jack Morris .15
416 Bill Buckner .15
417 Butch Wynegar .10
418 Steve Sax .10
419 Steve Balboni .10
420 Dwayne Murphy .10
421 Andre Dawson .50
422 Charlie Hough .10
423 Tommy John .25
424a Tom Seaver (Floyd Bannister photo, left-hander) 2.00
424b Tom Seaver (correct photo) 30.00
425 Tom Herr .10
426 Terry Puhl .10
427 Al Holland .10
428 Eddie Milner .10
429 Terry Kennedy .10
430 John Candelaria .10
431 Manny Trillo .10
432 Ken Oberkfell .10
433 Rick Sutcliffe .15
434 Ron Darling .10
435 Spike Owen .10
436 Frank Viola .10
437 Lloyd Moseby .10
438 Kirby Puckett 20.00
439 Jim Clancy .10
440 Mike Moore .10

441	Doug Sisk	.10
442	Dennis Eckersley	.75
443	Gerald Perry	.10
444	Dale Berra	.10
445	Dusty Baker	.15
446	Ed Whitson	.10
447	Cesar Cedeno	.10
448	*Rick Schu*	.10
449	Joaquin Andujar	.10
450	*Mark Bailey*	.10
451	*Ron Romanick*	.10
452	Julio Cruz	.10
453	Miguel Dilone	.10
454	Storm Davis	.10
455	Jaime Cocanower	.10
456	Barbaro Garbey	.10
457	Rich Gedman	.10
458	Phil Niekro	.50
459	Mike Scioscia	.10
460	Pat Tabler	.10
461	Darryl Motley	.10
462	Chris Codoroli (Codiroli)	.10
463	Doug Flynn	.10
464	Billy Sample	.10
465	Mickey Rivers	.10
466	John Wathan	.10
467	Bill Krueger	.10
468	Andre Thornton	.10
469	Rex Hudler	.10
470	*Sid Bream*	.60
471	Kirk Gibson	.15
472	John Shelby	.10
473	Moose Haas	.10
474	Doug Corbett	.10
475	Willie McGee	.15
476	Bob Knepper	.10
477	Kevin Gross	.10
478	Carmelo Martinez	.10
479	Kent Tekulve	.10
480	Chili Davis	.10
481	Bobby Clark	.10
482	Mookie Wilson	.15
483	Dave Owen	.10
484	Ed Nunez	.10
485	Rance Mulliniks	.10
486	Ken Schrom	.10
487	Jeff Russell	.10
488	Tom Paciorek	.10
489	Dan Ford	.10
490	Mike Caldwell	.10
491	Scottie Earl	.10
492	Jose Rijo	.10
493	Bruce Hurst	.10
494	Ken Landreaux	.10
495	Mike Fischlin	.10
496	Don Slaught	.10
497	Steve McCatty	.10
498	Gary Lucas	.10
499	Gary Pettis	.10
500	Marvis Foley	.10
501	Mike Squires	.10
502	*Jim Pankovitz*	.10
503	Luis Aguayo	.10
504	Ralph Citarella	.10
505	Bruce Bochy	.10
506	Bob Owchinko	.10
507	Pascual Perez	.10
508	Lee Lacy	.10
509	Atlee Hammaker	.10
510	Bob Dernier	.10
511	Ed Vande Berg	.10
512	Cliff Johnson	.10
513	Len Whitehouse	.10
514	Dennis Martinez	.10
515	Ed Romero	.10
516	Rusty Kuntz	.10
517	Rick Miller	.10
518	Dennis Rasmussen	.10
519	Steve Yeager	.10
520	Chris Bando	.10
521	U.L. Washington	.10
522	*Curt Young*	.10
523	Angel Salazar	.10
524	Curt Kaufman	.10
525	Odell Jones	.10
526	Juan Agosto	.10
527	Denny Walling	.10
528	Andy Hawkins	.10
529	Sixto Lezcano	.10
530	Skeeter Barnes	.10
531	Randy S. Johnson	.10
532	Jim Morrison	.10
533	Warren Brusstar	.10
534a	*Jeff Pendleton* (error)	1.00
534b	*Terry Pendleton* (correct)	8.00
535	Vic Rodriguez	.10
536	Bob McClure	.10
537	Dave Bergman	.10
538	Mark Clear	.10
539	*Mike Pagliarulo*	.35
540	Terry Whitfield	.10
541	Joe Beckwith	.10
542	Jeff Burroughs	.10
543	Dan Schatzeder	.10
544	Donnie Scott	.10
545	Jim Slaton	.10
546	Greg Luzinski	.10
547	*Mark Salas*	.10
548	Dave Smith	.10
549	John Wockenfuss	.10
550	Frank Pastore	.10
551	Tim Flannery	.10
552	Rick Rhoden	.10
553	Mark Davis	.10
554	*Jeff Dedmon*	.15
555	Gary Woods	.10
556	Danny Heep	.10
557	Mark Langston	.50
558	Darrell Brown	.10
559	Jimmy Key	.10
560	Rick Lysander	.10
561	Doyle Alexander	.10
562	Mike Stanton	.10
563	Sid Fernandez	.10
564	Richie Hebner	.10
565	Alex Trevino	.10
566	Brian Harper	.10
567	*Dan Gladden*	.30
568	Luis Salazar	.10
569	Tom Foley	.10
570	Larry Andersen	.10
571	Danny Cox	.10
572	Joe Sambito	.10
573	Juan Beniquez	.10
574	Joel Skinner	.10
575	*Randy St. Claire*	.10
576	Floyd Rayford	.10
577	Roy Howell	.10
578	John Grubb	.10
579	Ed Jurak	.10
580	John Montefusco	.10
581	*Orel Hershiser*	3.00
582	*Tom Waddell*	.10
583	Mark Huismann	.10
584	Joe Morgan	.60
585	Jim Wohlford	.10
586	Dave Schmidt	.10
587	*Jeff Kunkel*	.10
588	Hal McRae	.10
589	Bill Almon	.10
590	Carmen Castillo	.10
591	Omar Moreno	.10
592	*Ken Howell*	.10
593	Tom Brookens	.10
594	Joe Nolan	.10
595	Willie Lozado	.10
596	*Tom Nieto*	.10
597	Walt Terrell	.10
598	Al Oliver	.15
599	Shane Rawley	.10
600	*Denny Gonzalez*	.10
601	*Mark Grant*	.10
602	Mike Armstrong	.10
603	George Foster	.15
604	Davey Lopes	.10
605	Salome Barojas	.10
606	Roy Lee Jackson	.10
607	Pete Filson	.10
608	Duane Walker	.10
609	Glenn Wilson	.10
610	*Rafael Santana*	.10
611	Roy Smith	.10
612	Ruppert Jones	.10
613	Joe Cowley	.10
614	*Al Nipper* (photo actually Mike Brown)	.15
615	Gene Nelson	.10
616	Joe Carter	.50
617	Ray Knight	.15
618	Chuck Rainey	.10
619	Dan Driessen	.10
620	Daryl Sconiers	.10
621	Bill Stein	.10
622	Roy Smalley	.10
623	Ed Lynch	.10
624	*Jeff Stone*	.10
625	Bruce Berenyi	.10
626	Kelvin Chapman	.10
627	Joe Price	.10
628	Steve Bedrosian	.10
629	Vic Mata	.10
630	Mike Krukow	.10
631	*Phil Bradley*	.15
632	Jim Gott	.10
633	Randy Bush	.10
634	*Tom Browning*	.60
635	Lou Gehrig Puzzle Card	.10
636	Reid Nichols	.10
637	*Dan Pasqua*	.60
638	German Rivera	.10
639	*Don Schulze*	.10
640a	Mike Jones (last line of highlights begins "Was 11- 7...")	.10
640b	Mike Jones (last line of highlights begins "Spent some ...")	.25
641	Pete Rose	3.00
642	*Wade Rowdon*	.10
643	Jerry Narron	.10
644	*Darrell Miller*	.10
645	*Tim Hulett*	.10
646	Andy McGaffigan	.10
647	Kurt Bevacqua	.10
648	*John Russell*	.10
649	*Ron Robinson*	.10
650	Donnie Moore	.10
651a	Two for the Title (Don Mattingly, Dave Winfield) (yellow letters)	3.00
651b	Two for the Title (Don Mattingly, Dave Winfield) (white letters)	6.00
652	Tim Laudner	.10
653	*Steve Farr*	.15
----	Checklist 1-26 DK	.10
----	Checklist 27-130	.10
----	Checklist 131-234	.10
----	Checklist 235-338	.10
----	Checklist 339-442	.10
----	Checklist 443-546	.10
----	Checklist 547-653	.10

1985 Donruss Action All-Stars

In 1985, Donruss issued an Action All-Stars set for the third consecutive year. Card fronts feature an action photo with an inset portrait of the player inside a black border with grey boxes through it. The card backs have black print on blue and white and include statistical and biographical information. The cards were issued with a Lou Gehrig puzzle.

		MT
Complete Set (60):		6.00
Common Player:		.10
Lou Gehrig Puzzle:		2.25
1	Tim Raines	.15
2	Jim Gantner	.10
3	Mario Soto	.10
4	Spike Owen	.10
5	Lloyd Moseby	.10
6	Damaso Garcia	.10
7	Cal Ripken, Jr.	2.50
8	Dan Quisenberry	.10
9	Eddie Murray	.60
10	Tony Pena	.10
11	Buddy Bell	.10
12	Dave Winfield	.45
13	Ron Kittle	.10
14	Rich Gossage	.10
15	Dwight Evans	.10
16	Al Davis	.10
17	Mike Schmidt	.75
18	Pascual Perez	.10
19	Tony Gwynn	1.50
20	Nolan Ryan	2.50
21	Robin Yount	.50
22	Mike Marshall	.10
23	Brett Butler	.10
24	Ryne Sandberg	.75
25	Dale Murphy	.25
26	George Brett	.75
27	Jim Rice	.15
28	Ozzie Smith	.60
29	Larry Parrish	.10
30	Jack Clark	.10
31	Manny Trillo	.10
32	Dave Kingman	.10
33	Geoff Zahn	.10
34	Pedro Guerrero	.10
35	Dave Parker	.10
36	Rollie Fingers	.20
37	Fernando Valenzuela	.15
38	Wade Boggs	.50
39	Reggie Jackson	.40
40	Kent Hrbek	.10
41	Keith Hernandez	.10
42	Lou Whitaker	.10
43	Tom Herr	.10
44	Alan Trammell	.15
45	Butch Wynegar	.10
46	Leon Durham	.10
47	Dwight Gooden	.25
48	Don Mattingly	.75
49	Phil Niekro	.20
50	Johnny Ray	.10
51	Doug DeCinces	.10
52	Willie Upshaw	.10
53	Lance Parrish	.10
54	Jody Davis	.10
55	Steve Carlton	.30
56	Juan Samuel	.10
57	Gary Carter	.20
58	Harold Baines	.10
59	Eric Show	.10
60	Checklist	.04

1985 Donruss Box Panels

In 1985, Donruss placed on the bottoms of its wax pack boxes a four-card panel which included three player cards and a Lou Gehrig puzzle card. The player cards, numbered PC1 through PC3, have backs identical to the regular 1985 Donruss issue. The card fronts are identical in design to the regular issue, but carry different photos.

	MT
Complete Panel:	3.00
Complete Singles Set (4):	3.50
Common Player:	.10

PC1	Dwight Gooden	.75
PC2	Ryne Sandberg	3.00
PC3	Ron Kittle	.10
---	Lou Gehrig (puzzle card)	.10

1985 Donruss Diamond Kings Supers

The 1985 Donruss Diamond Kings Supers are enlarged versions of the Diamond Kings cards in the regular 1985 Donruss set. The cards measure 4-15/16" x 6-3/4". The Diamond Kings series features the artwork of Dick Perez. Twenty-eight cards make up the Super set - 26 DK cards, an unnumbered checklist, and an unnumbered Dick Perez card. The back of the Perez card contains a brief history of Dick Perez and the Perez-Steele Galleries. The set could be obtained through a mail-in offer found on wax pack wrappers.

		MT
Complete Set (28):		12.00
Common Player:		.20
1	Ryne Sandberg	2.50
2	Doug DeCinces	.20
3	Richard Dotson	.20
4	Bert Blyleven	.20
5	Lou Whitaker	.20
6	Dan Quisenberry	.20
7	Don Mattingly	4.00
8	Carney Lansford	.20
9	Frank Tanana	.20
10	Willie Upshaw	.20
11	Claudell Washington	.20
12	Mike Marshall	.20
13	Joaquin Andujar	.20
14	Cal Ripken, Jr.	6.00
15	Jim Rice	.40
16	Don Sutton	.60
17	Frank Viola	.20
18	Alvin Davis	.20
19	Mario Soto	.20
20	Jose Cruz	.20
21	Charlie Lea	.20
22	Jesse Orosco	.20
23	Juan Samuel	.20
24	Tony Pena	.20
25	Tony Gwynn	4.00
26	Bob Brenly	.20
	Checklist	.05
	Dick Perez (DK artist)	.20

1985 Donruss Highlights

Designed in the style of the regular 1985 Donruss set, this issue features the Player of the Month in the major leagues plus highlight cards of special baseball events and milestones of the 1985 season. Fifty-six cards, including an unnumbered checklist, comprise the set which was available only through hobby dealers. The cards measure 2-1/2" x 3-1/2" and have glossy fronts. The last two cards in the set feature Donruss' picks for the A.L. and N.L. Rookies of the Year. The set was issued in a specially designed box.

		MT
Complete Set (56):		5.00
Common Player:		.05
1	Sets Opening Day Record (Tom Seaver)	.10
2	Establishes A.L. Save Mark (Rollie Fingers)	.10
3	A.L. Player of the Month - April (Mike Davis)	.05
4	A.L. Pitcher of the Month - April (Charlie Leibrandt)	.05
5	N.L. Player of the Month - April (Dale Murphy)	.10
6	N.L. Pitcher of the Month - April (Fernando Valenzuela)	.05
7	N.L. Shortstop Record (Larry Bowa)	.05
8	Joins Reds 2000 Hit Club (Dave Concepcion)	.05
9	Eldest Grand Slammer (Tony Perez)	.10
10	N.L. Career Run Leader (Pete Rose)	.30
11	A.L. Player of the Month - May (George Brett)	.25
12	A.L. Pitcher of the Month - May (Dave Stieb)	.05
13	N.L. Player of the Month - May (Dave Parker)	.05
14	N.L. Pitcher of the Month - May (Andy Hawkins)	.05
15	Records 11th Straight Win (Andy Hawkins)	.05
16	Two Homers In First Inning (Von Hayes)	.05
17	A.L. Player of the Month - June (Rickey Henderson)	.15
18	A.L. Pitcher of the Month - June (Jay Howell)	.05
19	N.L. Player of the Month - June (Pedro Guerrero)	.05
20	N.L. Pitcher of the Month - June (John Tudor)	.05
21	Marathon Game Iron Men (Gary Carter, Keith Hernandez)	.05
22	Records 4000th K (Nolan Ryan)	.50
23	All-Star Game MVP (LaMarr Hoyt)	.05
24	1st Ranger To Hit For Cycle (Oddibe McDowell)	.05
25	A.L. Player of the Month - July (George Brett)	.25
26	A.L. Pitcher of the Month - July (Bret Saberhagen)	.05
27	N.L. Player of the Month - July (Keith Hernandez)	.05
28	N.L. Pitcher of the Month - July (Fernando Valenzuela)	.05
29	Record Setting Base Stealers (Vince Coleman, Willie McGee)	.05
30	Notches 300th Career Win (Tom Seaver)	.10
31	Strokes 3000th Hit (Rod Carew)	.10
32	Establishes Met Record (Dwight Gooden)	.10
33	Achieves Strikeout Milestone (Dwight Gooden)	.10
34	Explodes For 9 RBI (Eddie Murray)	.10
35	A.L. Career Hbp Leader (Don Baylor)	.05
36	A.L. Player of the Month - August (Don Mattingly)	.40
37	A.L. Pitcher of the Month - August (Dave Righetti)	.05
38	N.L. Player of the Month (Willie McGee)	.05
39	N.L. Pitcher of the Month - August (Shane Rawley)	.05
40	Ty-Breaking Hit (Pete Rose)	.50
41	Hits 3 HRs, Drives In 8 Runs (Andre Dawson)	.05
42	Sets Yankee Theft Mark (Rickey Henderson)	.15
43	20 Wins In Rookie Season (Tom Browning)	.05
44	Yankee Milestone For Hits (Don Mattingly)	.40
45	A.L. Player of the Month - September (Don Mattingly)	.40
46	A.L. Pitcher of the Month - September (Charlie Leibrandt)	.05
47	N.L. Player of the Month - September (Gary Carter)	.05
48	N.L. Pitcher of the Month - September (Dwight Gooden)	.10
49	Major League Record Setter (Wade Boggs)	.25
50	Hurls Shutout For 300th Win (Phil Niekro)	.10
51	Venerable HR King (Darrell Evans)	.05
52	N.L. Switch-hitting Record (Willie McGee)	.05
53	Equals DiMaggio Feat (Dave Winfield)	.10
54	Donruss N.L. Rookie of the Year (Vince Coleman)	.10
55	Donruss A.L. Rookie of the Year (Ozzie Guillen)	.10
----	Checklist	.05

1985 Donruss Sluggers of The Hall of Fame

In much the same manner as the 1959-71 Bazooka cards were issued, this eight-player set consists of cards printed on the bottom panel of a box of bubble gum. When cut off the box, cards measure 3-1/2" x 6-1/2", with blank backs. Players are pictured on the cards in paintings done by Dick Perez.

		MT
Complete Set (8):		12.00
Common Player:		.60
1	Babe Ruth	2.50
2	Ted Williams	1.50
3	Lou Gehrig	2.00
4	Johnny Mize	.60
5	Stan Musial	1.50
6	Mickey Mantle	3.00
7	Hank Aaron	1.50
8	Frank Robinson	.90

1986 Donruss

In 1986, Donruss issued a 660-card set which included 653 numbered cards and seven unnumbered checklists. The 2-1/2" x 3-1/2" cards have fronts that feature blue borders and backs that have black print on blue and white. For the fifth year in a row, the first 26 cards in the set are Diamond Kings. The Rated Rookies subset (#27-46) appears once again. The cards were distributed with a Hank Aaron puzzle. The complete set price does not include the higher priced variations. In the checklist that follows, (DK) and (RR) refer to the Diamond Kings and Rated Rookies series.

	MT
Complete Set (660):	35.00
Complete Factory Set (660):	50.00
Common Player:	.08

Hank Aaron Puzzle: 5.00
Pack (15): 3.00
Wax Box (36): 60.00

1 Kirk Gibson (DK) .15
2 Goose Gossage (DK) .15
3 Willie McGee (DK) .15
4 George Bell (DK) .15
5 Tony Armas (DK) .15
6 Chili Davis (DK) .15
7 Cecil Cooper (DK) .08
8 Mike Boddicker (DK) .08
9 Davey Lopes (DK) .08
10 Bill Doran (DK) .08
11 Bret Saberhagen (DK) .25
12 Brett Butler (DK) .15
13 Harold Baines (DK) .25
14 Mike Davis (DK) .08
15 Tony Perez (DK) .40
16 Willie Randolph (DK) .15
17 Bob Boone (DK) .15
18 Orel Hershiser (DK) .20
19 Johnny Ray (DK) .08
20 Gary Ward (DK) .08
21 Rick Mahler (DK) .08
22 Phil Bradley (DK) .15
23 Jerry Koosman (DK) .15
24 Tom Brunansky (DK) .15
25 Andre Dawson (DK) .50
26 Dwight Gooden (DK) .20
27 *Kal Daniels* (RR) .15
28 *Fred McGriff* (RR) 5.00
29 *Cory Snyder* (RR) .20
30 *Jose Guzman* (RR) .15
31 *Ty Gainey* (RR) .08
32 *Johnny Abrego* (RR) .08
33a *Andres Galarraga* (RR) accent mark over e o Andres on back) 5.00
33b *Andres Galarraga* (RR) no accent mark) 5.00
34 *Dave Shipanoff* (RR) .08
35 *Mark McLemore* (RR) .50
36 *Marty Clary* (RR) .08
37 *Paul O'Neill* (RR) 5.00
38 Danny Tartabull (RR) .25
39 *Jose Canseco* (RR) 15.00
40 *Juan Nieves* (RR) .15
41 *Lance McCullers* (RR) .20
42 *Rick Surhoff* (RR) .08
43 *Todd Worrell* (RR) .40
44 Bob Kipper (RR) .08
45 *John Habyan* (RR) .15
46 *Mike Woodard* (RR) .08
47 Mike Boddicker .08
48 Robin Yount 1.50
49 Lou Whitaker .15
50 Dennis Boyd .08
51 Rickey Henderson 1.00
52 Mike Marshall .08
53 George Brett 2.00
54 Dave Kingman .15
55 Hubie Brooks .08
56 *Oddibe McDowell* .15
57 Doug DeCinces .08
58 Britt Burns .08
59 Ozzie Smith 1.50
q0 Jose Cruz .08
61 Mike Schmidt 2.00
62 Pete Rose 2.50
63 Steve Garvey .40
64 Tony Pena .08
65 Chili Davis .08
66 Dale Murphy .40
67 Ryne Sandberg 1.50
68 Gary Carter .40
69 Alvin Davis .08
70 Kent Hrbek .15
71 George Bell .15
72 Kirby Puckett 6.00
73 Lloyd Moseby .08
74 Bob Kearney .08
75 Dwight Gooden .25
76 Gary Matthews .08
77 Rick Mahler .08
78 Benny Distefano .08
79 Jeff Leonard .08
80 Kevin McReynolds .15
81 Ron Oester .08
82 John Russell .08
83 Tommy Herr .08
84 Jerry Mumphrey .08
85 Ron Romanick .08
86 Daryl Boston .08
87 Andre Dawson .75
88 Eddie Murray 1.50
89 Dion James .08
90 Chet Lemon .08
91 Bob Stanley .08
92 Willie Randolph .15
93 Mike Scioscia .08
94 Tom Waddell .08
95 Danny Jackson .08
96 Mike Davis .08
97 Mike Fitzgerald .08
98 Gary Ward .08
99 Pete O'Brien .08
100 Bret Saberhagen .15
101 Alfredo Griffin .08
102 Brett Butler .08
103 Ron Guidry .15
104 Jerry Reuss .08
105 Jack Morris .20
106 Rick Dempsey .08
107 Ray Burris .08
108 Brian Downing .08
109 Willie McGee .15
110 Bill Doran .08
111 Kent Tekulve .08
112 Tony Gwynn 4.00
113 Marvell Wynne .08
114 David Green .08
115 Jim Gantner .08
116 George Foster .15
117 Steve Trout .08
118 Mark Langston .15
119 Tony Fernandez .08
120 John Butcher .08
121 Ron Robinson .08
122 Dan Spillner .08
123 Mike Young .08
124 Paul Molitor 1.50
125 Kirk Gibson .15
126 Ken Griffey .15
127 Tony Armas .08
128 *Mariano Duncan* .15
129 Pat Tabler (Mr. Clutch) .08
130 Frank White .08
131 Carney Lansford .08
132 Vance Law .08
133 Dick Schofield .08
134 Wayne Tolleson .08
135 Greg Walker .08
136 Denny Walling .08
137 Ozzie Virgil .08
138 Ricky Horton .08
139 LaMarr Hoyt .08
140 Wayne Krenchicki .08
141 Glenn Hubbard .08
142 Cecilio Guante .08
143 Mike Krukow .08
144 Lee Smith .15
145 Edwin Nunez .08
146 Dave Stieb .15
147 Mike Smithson .08
148 Ken Dixon .08
149 Danny Darwin .08
150 Chris Pittaro .08
151 Bill Buckner .15
152 Mike Pagliarulo .08
153 Bill Russell .08
154 Brook Jacoby .08
155 Pat Sheridan .08
156 *Mike Gallego* .15
157 Jim Wohlford .08
158 Gary Pettis .08
159 Toby Harrah .08
160 Richard Dotson .08
161 Bob Knepper .08
162 Dave Dravecky .08
163 Greg Gross .08
164 Eric Davis .40
165 Gerald Perry .08
166 Rick Rhoden .08
167 Keith Moreland .08
168 Jack Clark .08
169 Storm Davis .08
170 Cecil Cooper .08
171 Alan Trammell .25
172 Roger Clemens 5.00
173 Don Mattingly 4.00
174 Pedro Guerrero .08
175 Willie Wilson .08
176 Dwayne Murphy .08
177 Tim Raines .30
178 Larry Parrish .08
179 Mike Witt .08
180 Harold Baines .15
181 *Vince Coleman* .35
182 *Jeff Heathcock* .08
183 Steve Carlton 1.00
184 Mario Soto .08
185 Goose Gossage .20
186 Johnny Ray .08
187 Dan Gladden .08
188 Bob Horner .08
189 Rick Sutcliffe .15
190 Keith Hernandez .15
191 Phil Bradley .08
192 Tom Brunansky .08
193 Jesse Barfield .08
194 Frank Viola .08
195 Willie Upshaw .08
196 Jim Beattie .08
197 Darryl Strawberry .15
198 Ron Cey .08
199 Steve Bedrosian .08
200 Steve Kemp .08
201 Manny Trillo .08
202 Garry Templeton .08
203 Dave Parker .15
204 John Denny .08
205 Terry Pendleton .08
206 Terry Puhl .08
207 Bobby Grich .08
208 *Ozzie Guillen* .75
209 Jeff Reardon .08
210 Cal Ripken, Jr. 6.00
211 Bill Schroeder .08
212 Dan Petry .08
213 Jim Rice .25
214 Dave Righetti .08
215 Fernando Valenzuela .15
216 Julio Franco .08
217 Darryl Motley .08
218 Dave Collins .08
219 Tim Wallach .08
220 George Wright .08
221 Tommy Dunbar .08
222 Steve Balboni .08
223 Jay Howell .08
224 Joe Carter .25
225 Ed Whitson .08
226 Orel Hershiser .25
227 Willie Hernandez .08
228 Lee Lacy .08
229 Rollie Fingers .45
230 Bob Boone .15
231 Joaquin Andujar .08
232 Craig Reynolds .08
233 Shane Rawley .08
234 Eric Show .08
235 Jose DeLeon .08
236 *Jose Uribe* .08
237 Moose Haas .08
238 Wally Backman .08
239 Dennis Eckersley .15
240 Mike Moore .08
241 Damaso Garcia .08
242 Tim Teufel .08
243 Dave Concepcion .08
244 Floyd Bannister .08
245 Fred Lynn .15
246 Charlie Moore .08
247 Walt Terrell .08
248 Dave Winfield 1.00
249 Dwight Evans .15
250 *Dennis Powell* .08
251 Andre Thornton .08
252 Onix Concepcion .08
253 Mike Heath .08
254a David Palmer (2B on front) .08
254b David Palmer (P on front) .25
255 Donnie Moore .08
256 Curtis Wilkerson .08
257 Julio Cruz .08
258 Nolan Ryan 6.00
259 Jeff Stone .08
260a John Tudor (1981 Games is .18) .08
260b John Tudor (1981 Games is 18) .25
261 Mark Thurmond .08
262 Jay Tibbs .08
263 Rafael Ramirez .08
264 Larry McWilliams .08
265 Mark Davis .08
266 Bob Dernier .08
267 Matt Young .08
268 Jim Clancy .08
269 Mickey Hatcher .08
270 Sammy Stewart .08
271 Bob L. Gibson .08
272 Nelson Simmons .08
273 Rich Gedman .08
274 Butch Wynegar .08
275 Ken Howell .08
276 Mel Hall .08
277 Jim Sundberg .08
278 Chris Codiroli .08
279 *Herman Winningham* .08
280 Rod Carew 1.00
281 Don Slaught .08
282 Scott Fletcher .08
283 Bill Dawley .08
284 Andy Hawkins .08
285 Glenn Wilson .08
286 Nick Esasky .08
287 Claudell Washington .08
288 Lee Mazzilli .08
289 Jody Davis .08
290 Darrell Porter .08
291 Scott McGregor .08
292 Ted Simmons .08
293 Aurelio Lopez .08
294 Marty Barrett .08
295 Dale Berra .08
296 Greg Brock .08
297 Charlie Leibrandt .08
298 Bill Krueger .08
299 Bryn Smith .08
300 Burt Hooton .08
301 *Stu Cliburn* .08
302 Luis Salazar .08
303 Ken Dayley .08
304 Frank DiPino .08
305 Von Hayes .08
306a Gary Redus (1983 2B is .20) .08
306b Gary Redus (1983 2B is 20) .25
307 Craig Lefferts .08
308 Sam Khalifa .08
309 Scott Garrelts .08
310 Rick Cerone .08
311 Shawon Dunston .08
312 Howard Johnson .08
313 Jim Presley .08
314 Gary Gaetti .15
315 Luis Leal .08
316 Mark Salas .08
317 Bill Caudill .08
318 Dave Henderson .08
319 Rafael Santana .08
320 Leon Durham .08
321 Bruce Sutter .08
322 Jason Thompson .08
323 Bob Brenly .08
324 Carmelo Martinez .08
325 Eddie Milner .08
326 Juan Samuel .08
327 Tom Nieto .08
328 Dave Smith .08
329 *Urbano Lugo* .08
330 Joel Skinner .08
331 Bill Gullickson .08
332 Floyd Rayford .08
333 Ben Oglivie .08
334 Lance Parrish .15
335 Jackie Gutierrez .08
336 Dennis Rasmussen .08
337 Terry Whitfield .08
338 Neal Heaton .08
339 Jorge Orta .08
340 Donnie Hill .08
341 Joe Hesketh .08
342 Charlie Hough .08
343 Dave Rozema .08
344 Greg Pryor .08
345 Mickey Tettleton .25
346 George Vukovich .08
347 Don Baylor .15
348 Carlos Diaz .08
349 Barbaro Garbey .08
350 Larry Sheets .08
351 *Ted Higuera* .15
352 Juan Beniquez .08
353 Bob Forsch .08
354 Mark Bailey .08
355 Larry Andersen .08
356 Terry Kennedy .08
357 Don Robinson .08
358 Jim Gott .08
359 *Earnest Riles* .08
360 *John Christensen* .08
361 Ray Fontenot .08
362 Spike Owen .08
363 Jim Acker .08
364a Ron Davis (last line in highlights ends with "... in May.") .08

No.	Player	Price
364b	Ron Davis (last line in highlights ends with "... relievers (9).")	.25
365	Tom Hume	.08
366	Carlton Fisk	1.00
367	Nate Snell	.08
368	Rick Manning	.08
369	Darrell Evans	.15
370	Ron Hassey	.08
371	Wade Boggs	1.50
372	Rick Honeycutt	.08
373	Chris Bando	.08
374	Bud Black	.08
375	Steve Henderson	.08
376	Charlie Lea	.08
377	Reggie Jackson	1.50
378	Dave Schmidt	.08
379	Bob James	.08
380	Glenn Davis	.08
381	Tim Corcoran	.08
382	Danny Cox	.08
383	Tim Flannery	.08
384	Tom Browning	.08
385	Rick Camp	.08
386	Jim Morrison	.08
387	Dave LaPoint	.08
388	Davey Lopes	.08
389	Al Cowens	.08
390	Doyle Alexander	.08
391	Tim Laudner	.08
392	Don Aase	.08
393	Jaime Cocanower	.08
394	Randy O'Neal	.08
395	Mike Easler	.08
396	Scott Bradley	.08
397	Tom Niedenfuer	.08
398	Jerry Willard	.08
399	Lonnie Smith	.08
400	Bruce Bochte	.08
401	Terry Francona	.08
402	Jim Slaton	.08
403	Bill Stein	.08
404	Tim Hulett	.08
405	Alan Ashby	.08
406	Tim Stoddard	.08
407	Garry Maddox	.08
408	Ted Power	.08
409	Len Barker	.08
410	Denny Gonzalez	.08
411	George Frazier	.08
412	Andy Van Slyke	.15
413	Jim Dwyer	.08
414	Paul Householder	.08
415	Alejandro Sanchez	.08
416	Steve Crawford	.08
417	Dan Pasqua	.08
418	Enos Cabell	.08
419	Mike Jones	.08
420	Steve Kiefer	.08
421	*Tim Burke*	.08
422	Mike Mason	.08
423	Ruppert Jones	.08
424	Jerry Hairston Sr.	.08
425	Tito Landrum	.08
426	Jeff Calhoun	.08
427	*Don Carman*	.08
428	Tony Perez	.50
429	Jerry Davis	.08
430	Bob Walk	.08
431	Brad Wellman	.08
432	Terry Forster	.08
433	Billy Hatcher	.08
434	Clint Hurdle	.08
435	*Ivan Calderon*	.15
436	Pete Filson	.08
437	Tom Henke	.08
438	Dave Engle	.08
439	Tom Filer	.08
440	Gorman Thomas	.08
441	*Rick Aguilera*	.50
442	Scott Sanderson	.08
443	Jeff Dedmon	.08
444	*Joe Orsulak*	.15
445	Atlee Hammaker	.08
446	Jerry Royster	.08
447	Buddy Bell	.15
448	Dave Rucker	.08
449	Ivan DeJesus	.08
450	Jim Pankovits	.08
451	Jerry Narron	.08
452	Bryan Little	.08
453	Gary Lucas	.08
454	Dennis Martinez	.08
455	Ed Romero	.08
456	*Bob Melvin*	.08
457	Glenn Hoffman	.08
458	Bob Shirley	.08
459	Bob Welch	.08
460	Carmen Castillo	.08
461	Dave Leeper	.08
462	*Tim Birtsas*	.08
463	Randy St. Claire	.08
464	Chris Welsh	.08
465	Greg Harris	.08
466	Lynn Jones	.08
467	Dusty Baker	.15
468	Roy Smith	.08
469	Andre Robertson	.08
470	Ken Landreaux	.08
471	Dave Bergman	.08
472	Gary Roenicke	.08
473	Pete Vuckovich	.08
474	*Kirk McCaskill*	.30
475	Jeff Lahti	.08
476	Mike Scott	.08
477	*Darren Daulton*	1.50
478	Graig Nettles	.15
479	Bill Almon	.08
480	Greg Minton	.08
481	Randy Ready	.08
482	*Len Dykstra*	1.50
483	Thad Bosley	.08
484	*Harold Reynolds*	.40
485	Al Oliver	.15
486	Roy Smalley	.08
487	John Franco	.15
488	Juan Agosto	.08
489	Al Pardo	.08
490	*Bill Wegman*	.15
491	Frank Tanana	.08
492	*Brian Fisher*	.08
493	Mark Clear	.08
494	Len Matuszek	.08
495	Ramon Romero	.08
496	John Wathan	.08
497	Rob Picciolo	.08
498	U.L. Washington	.08
499	John Candelaria	.08
500	Duane Walker	.08
501	Gene Nelson	.08
502	John Mizerock	.08
503	Luis Aguayo	.08
504	Kurt Kepshire	.08
505	Ed Wojna	.08
506	Joe Price	.08
507	*Milt Thompson*	.20
508	Junior Ortiz	.08
509	Vida Blue	.08
510	Steve Engel	.08
511	Karl Best	.08
512	*Cecil Fielder*	2.00
513	Frank Eufemia	.08
514	Tippy Martinez	.08
515	*Billy Robidoux*	.08
516	Bill Scherrer	.08
517	Bruce Hurst	.08
518	Rich Bordi	.08
519	Steve Yeager	.08
520	Tony Bernazard	.08
521	Hal McRae	.08
522	Jose Rijo	.08
523	*Mitch Webster*	.08
524	*Jack Howell*	.08
525	Alan Bannister	.08
526	Ron Kittle	.08
527	Phil Garner	.08
528	Kurt Bevacqua	.08
529	Kevin Gross	.08
530	Bo Diaz	.08
531	Ken Oberkfell	.08
532	Rick Reuschel	.08
533	Ron Meridith	.08
534	Steve Braun	.08
535	Wayne Gross	.08
536	Ray Searage	.08
537	Tom Brookens	.08
538	Al Nipper	.08
539	Billy Sample	.08
540	Steve Sax	.08
541	Dan Quisenberry	.08
542	Tony Phillips	.08
543	*Floyd Youmans*	.08
544	*Steve Buechele*	.35
545	Craig Gerber	.08
546	Joe DeSa	.08
547	Brian Harper	.08
548	Kevin Bass	.08
549	Tom Foley	.08
550	Dave Van Gorder	.08
551	Bruce Bochy	.08
552	R.J. Reynolds	.08
553	*Chris Brown*	.08
554	Bruce Benedict	.08
555	Warren Brusstar	.08
556	Danny Heep	.08
557	Darnell Coles	.08
558	Greg Gagne	.08
559	Ernie Whitt	.08
560	Ron Washington	.08
561	Jimmy Key	.08
562	Billy Swift	.08
563	Ron Darling	.08
564	Dick Ruthven	.08
565	Zane Smith	.08
566	Sid Bream	.08
567a	Joel Youngblood (P on front)	.08
567b	Joel Youngblood (IF on front)	.25
568	Mario Ramirez	.08
569	Tom Runnells	.08
570	Rick Schu	.08
571	Bill Campbell	.08
572	Dickie Thon	.08
573	Al Holland	.08
574	Reid Nichols	.08
575	Bert Roberge	.08
576	Mike Flanagan	.08
577	Tim Leary	.08
578	Mike Laga	.08
579	Steve Lyons	.15
580	Phil Niekro	.45
581	Gilberto Reyes	.08
582	Jamie Easterly	.08
583	Mark Gubicza	.08
584	*Stan Javier*	.15
585	Bill Laskey	.08
586	Jeff Russell	.08
587	Dickie Noles	.08
588	Steve Farr	.08
589	*Steve Ontiveros*	.15
590	Mike Hargrove	.15
591	Marty Bystrom	.08
592	Franklin Stubbs	.08
593	Larry Herndon	.08
594	Bill Swaggerty	.08
595	Carlos Ponce	.08
596	*Pat Perry*	.08
597	Ray Knight	.08
598	*Steve Lombardozzi*	.08
599	Brad Havens	.08
600	*Pat Clements*	.08
601	Joe Niekro	.08
602	Hank Aaron Puzzle Card	.08
603	*Dwayne Henry*	.08
604	Mookie Wilson	.15
605	Buddy Biancalana	.08
606	Rance Mulliniks	.08
607	Alan Wiggins	.08
608	Joe Cowley	.08
609a	Tom Seaver (green stripes around name)	1.00
609b	Tom Seaver (yellow stripes around name)	3.00
610	Neil Allen	.08
611	Don Sutton	.45
612	*Fred Toliver*	.08
613	Jay Baller	.08
614	Marc Sullivan	.08
615	John Grubb	.08
616	Bruce Kison	.08
617	Bill Madlock	.08
618	Chris Chambliss	.08
619	Dave Stewart	.15
620	Tim Lollar	.08
621	Gary Lavelle	.08
622	Charles Hudson	.08
623	*Joel Davis*	.08
624	*Joe Johnson*	.08
625	Sid Fernandez	.08
626	Dennis Lamp	.08
627	Terry Harper	.08
628	Jack Lazorko	.08
629	*Roger McDowell*	.25
630	Mark Funderburk	.08
631	Ed Lynch	.08
632	Rudy Law	.08
633	*Roger Mason*	.08
634	*Mike Felder*	.08
635	Ken Schrom	.08
636	Bob Ojeda	.08
637	Ed Vande Berg	.08
638	Bobby Meacham	.08
639	Cliff Johnson	.08
640	Garth Iorg	.08
641	Dan Driessen	.08
642	Mike Brown	.08
643	John Shelby	.08
644	Pete Rose (RB)	.50
645	Knuckle Brothers (Joe Niekro, Phil Niekro)	.25
646	Jesse Orosco	.08
647	*Billy Beane*	.08
648	Cesar Cedeno	.08
649	Bert Blyleven	.15
650	Max Venable	.08
651	Fleet Feet (Vince Coleman, Willie McGee)	.35
652	Calvin Schiraldi	.08
653	King of Kings (Pete Rose)	2.50
----	Checklist 1-26 DK	.08
----	Checklist 27-130 (45 is Beane)	.08
----	Checklist 27-130 (45 is Habyan)	.15
----	Checklist 131-234	.08
----	Checklist 235-338	.08
----	Checklist 339-442	.08
----	Checklist 443-546	.08
----	Checklist 547-653	.08

1986 Donruss All-Stars

Issued in conjunction with the 1986 Donruss Pop-Ups set, the All-Stars consist of 60 cards in 3-1/2" x 5" format. Fifty-nine players involved in the 1985 All-Star game plus an unnumbered checklist comprise the set. Card fronts have the same blue border found on the regular 1986 Donruss issue. Retail packs included one Pop-up card, three All-Star cards and one Hank Aaron puzzle-piece card.

		MT
Complete Set (60):		4.00
Common Player:		.05
Hank Aaron puzzle:		2.50
1	Tony Gwynn	.50
2	Tommy Herr	.05
3	Steve Garvey	.15
4	Dale Murphy	.15
5	Darryl Strawberry	.10
6	Graig Nettles	.05
7	Terry Kennedy	.05
8	Ozzie Smith	.40
9	LaMarr Hoyt	.05
10	Rickey Henderson	.25
11	Lou Whitaker	.05
12	George Brett	.40
13	Eddie Murray	.25
14	Cal Ripken, Jr.	1.25
15	Dave Winfield	.25
16	Jim Rice	.10
17	Carlton Fisk	.25
18	Jack Morris	.05
19	Jose Cruz	.05
20	Tim Raines	.10
21	Nolan Ryan	1.25

22	Tony Pena	.05
23	Jack Clark	.05
24	Dave Parker	.05
25	Tim Wallach	.05
26	Ozzie Virgil	.05
27	Fernando Valenzuela	.05
28	Dwight Gooden	.10
29	Glenn Wilson	.05
30	Garry Templeton	.05
31	Goose Gossage	.05
32	Ryne Sandberg	.30
33	Jeff Reardon	.05
34	Pete Rose	.75
35	Scott Garrelts	.05
36	Willie McGee	.05
37	Ron Darling	.05
38	Dick Williams	.05
39	Paul Molitor	.25
40	Damaso Garcia	.05
41	Phil Bradley	.05
42	Dan Petry	.05
43	Willie Hernandez	.05
44	Tom Brunansky	.05
45	Alan Trammell	.10
46	Donnie Moore	.05
47	Wade Boggs	.30
48	Ernie Whitt	.05
49	Harold Baines	.05
50	Don Mattingly	.50
51	Gary Ward	.05
52	Bert Blyleven	.05
53	Jimmy Key	.05
54	Cecil Cooper	.05
55	Dave Stieb	.05
56	Rich Gedman	.05
57	Jay Howell	.05
58	Sparky Anderson	.10
59	Minneapolis Metrodome	.05
---	Checklist	.03

1986 Donruss Box Panels

For the second year in a row, Donruss placed baseball cards on the bottom of its wax and cello pack boxes. The cards, printed four to a panel, are standard 2-1/2" x 3-1/2". With numbering that begins where Donruss left off in 1985, cards PC4 through PC6 were found on boxes of regular Donruss issue wax packs. Cards PC7 through PC9 were found on boxes of the 1986 All-Star/Pop-up packs. An unnumbered Hank Aaron puzzle card was included on each box.

		MT
Complete Panel Set (2):		3.00
Complete Singles Set (8):		3.00
Common Single Player:		.15
Panel		1.00
PC4	Kirk Gibson	.25
PC5	Willie Hernandez	.15
PC6	Doug DeCinces	.15
---	Aaron Puzzle Card	.05
Panel		2.00
PC7	Wade Boggs	.75
PC8	Lee Smith	.20
PC9	Cecil Cooper	.15
---	Aaron Puzzle Card	.05

1986 Donruss Diamond Kings Supers

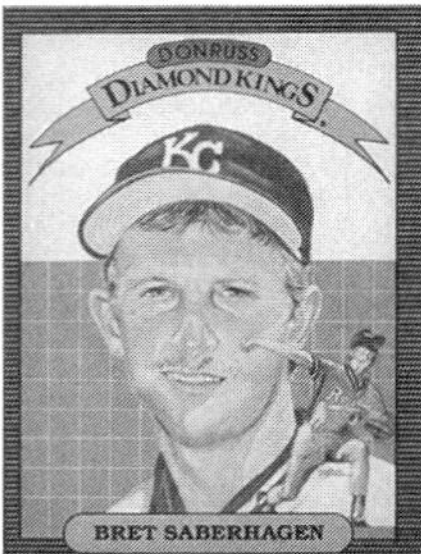

Donruss produced a set of large-format Diamond Kings in 1986 for the second year in a row. The 4-11/16" x 6-3/4" cards are enlarged versions of the 26 Diamond Kings cards found in the regular 1986 Donruss set, plus an unnumbered checklist and an unnumbered Pete Rose "King of Kings" card.

		MT
Complete Set (28):		10.00
Common Player:		.50
1	Kirk Gibson	.60
2	Goose Gossage	.60
3	Willie McGee	.60
4	George Bell	.50
5	Tony Armas	.50
6	Chili Davis	.50
7	Cecil Cooper	.50
8	Mike Boddicker	.50
9	Davey Lopes	.50
10	Bill Doran	.50
11	Bret Saberhagen	.60
12	Brett Butler	.50
13	Harold Baines	.50
14	Mike Davis	.50
15	Tony Perez	.75
16	Willie Randolph	.50
18	Orel Hershiser	.60
19	Johnny Ray	.50
20	Gary Ward	.50
21	Rick Mahler	.50
22	Phil Bradley	.50
23	Jerry Koosman	.50
24	Tom Brunansky	.50
25	Andre Dawson	.75
26	Dwight Gooden	.60
	Checklist	.05
	King of Kings (Pete Rose)	2.00

1986 Donruss Highlights

Donruss, for the second year in a row, issued a 56-card highlights set featuring cards of each league's Player of the Month plus significant events of the 1986 season. The cards, 2-1/2" x 3-1/2," are similar in design to the regular 1986 Donruss set but have a gold border instead of blue. A yellow "Highlights" logo appears in the lower-left corner of each card front. Backs are designed on a vertical format and feature black print on a yellow background. As in 1985, the set includes Donruss' picks for the Rookies of the Year. A new feature was three cards honoring the 1986 Hall of Fame inductees. The set, available only through hobby dealers, was issued in a specially designed box. Each card can also be found with the word "Highlights" in the logo in white, a much scarcer variation that sometimes attracts significant premiums from single-player specialist collectors.

		MT
Complete Set (56):		5.00
Common Player:		.05
White "Highlights":		20X
1	Homers In First At-Bat (Will Clark)	.30
2	Oakland Milestone For Strikeouts (Jose Rijo)	.05
3	Royals' All-Time Hit Man (George Brett)	.50
4	Phillies RBI Leader (Mike Schmidt)	.50
5	KKKKKKKKKKKKKKKKKKK (Roger Clemens)	1.00
6	A.L. Pitcher of the Month-April (Roger Clemens)	.50
7	A.L. Player of the Month-April (Kirby Puckett)	.50
8	N.L. Pitcher of the Month-April (Dwight Gooden)	.10
9	N.L. Player of the Month-April (Johnny Ray)	.05
10	Eclipses Mantle HR Record (Reggie Jackson)	.50
11	First Five Hit Game of Career (Wade Boggs)	.35
12	A.L. Pitcher of the Month-May (Don Aase)	.05
13	A.L. Player of the Month-May (Wade Boggs)	.35
14	N.L. Pitcher of the Month-May (Jeff Reardon)	.05
15	N.L. Player of the Month-May (Hubie Brooks)	.05
16	Notches 300th Career Win (Don Sutton)	.10
17	Starts Season 14-0 (Roger Clemens)	.50
18	A.L. Pitcher of the Month-June (Roger Clemens)	.50
19	A.L. Player of the Month-June (Kent Hrbek)	.05
20	N.L. Pitcher of the Month-June (Rick Rhoden)	.05
21	N.L. Player of the Month-June (Kevin Bass)	.05
22	Blasts 4 HRS in 1 Game (Bob Horner)	.10
23	Starting All Star Rookie (Wally Joyner)	.05
24	Starts 3rd Straight All Star Game (Darryl Strawberry)	.10
25	Ties All Star Game Record (Fernando Valenzuela)	.05
26	All Star Game MVP (Roger Clemens)	.50
27	A.L. Pitcher of the Month-July (Jack Morris)	.05
28	A.L. Player of the Month-July (Scott Fletcher)	.05
29	N.L. Pitcher of the Month-July (Todd Worrell)	.05
30	N.L. PLayer of the Month-July (Eric Davis)	.05
31	Records 3000th Strikeout (Bert Blyleven)	.05
32	1986 Hall of Fame Inductee (Bobby Doerr)	.05
33	1986 Hall of Fame Inductee (Ernie Lombardi)	.05
34	1986 Hall of Fame Inductee (Willie McCovey)	.20
35	Notches 4000th K (Steve Carlton)	.20
36	Surpasses DiMaggio Record (Mike Schmidt)	.50
37	Records 3rd "Quadruple Double" (Juan Samuel)	.05
38	A.L. Pitcher of the Month-August (Mike Witt)	.05
39	A.L. Player of the Month-August (Doug DeCinces)	.05
40	N.L. Pitcher of the Month-August (Bill Gullickson)	.05
41	N.L. Player of the Month-August (Dale Murphy)	.10
42	Sets Tribe Offensive Record (Joe Carter)	.05
43	Longest HR In Royals Stadium (Bo Jackson)	.25
44	Majors 1st No-Hitter In 2 Years (Joe Cowley)	.05
45	Sets M.L. Strikeout Record (Jim Deshaies)	.05
46	No Hitter Clinches Division (Mike Scott)	.05
47	A.L. Pitcher of the Month-September (Bruce Hurst)	.05
48	A.L. Player of the Month-September (Don Mattingly)	.50
49	N.L. Pitcher of the Month-September (Mike Krukow)	.05
50	N.L. Player of the Month-September (Steve Sax)	.05
51	A.L. Record For Steals By A Rookie (John Cangelosi)	.05
52	Shatters M.L. Save Mark (Dave Righetti)	.05
53	Yankee Record For Hits & Doubles (Don Mattingly)	.50
54	Donruss N.L. Rookie of the Year (Todd Worrell)	.05
55	Donruss A.L. Rookie of the Year (Jose Canseco)	.75
56	Highlight Checklist	.05

1986 Donruss Pop-Ups

Issued in conjunction with the 1986 Donruss All-Stars set, the Pop-Ups (18 unnumbered cards) feature the 1985 All-Star Game starting lineups. The cards, 2-1/2" x 5", are die-cut and fold out to form a three-dimensional stand-up card. The background for the cards is the Minneapolis Metrodome, site of the 1985 All-Star Game. Retail packs included one Pop-Up card, three All-Star cards and one Hank Aaron puzzle card.

		MT
Complete Set (18):		2.00
Common Player:		.05
Hank Aaron Puzzle:		3.25
(1)	George Brett	.45
(2)	Carlton Fisk	.20
(3)	Steve Garvey	.15
(4)	Tony Gwynn	.50
(5)	Rickey Henderson	.25
(6)	Tommy Herr	.05
(7)	LaMarr Hoyt	.05
(8)	Terry Kennedy	.05
(9)	Jack Morris	.05
(10)	Dale Murphy	.15
(11)	Eddie Murray	.25
(12)	Graig Nettles	.05
(13)	Jim Rice	.10
(14)	Cal Ripken, Jr.	.75
(15)	Ozzie Smith	.25
(16)	Darryl Strawberry	.10
(17)	Lou Whitaker	.05
(18)	Dave Winfield	.20

1986 Donruss Rookies

Entitled "The Rookies," this 56-card set includes the top 55 rookies of 1986 plus an unnumbered checklist. The cards are similar in format to the 1986 Donruss regular issue, except that the borders are green rather than blue. Several of the rookies who had cards in the regular 1986 Donruss set appear again in "The Rookies" set. The sets, which were only available through hobby dealers, came in a specially designed box.

		MT
Comp. Unopened Set (56):		30.00
Complete Opened Set (56):		20.00
Common Player:		.05
1	*Wally Joyner*	.75
2	Tracy Jones	.05
3	Allan Anderson	.05
4	Ed Correa	.05
5	Reggie Williams	.05
6	Charlie Kerfeld	.05
7	Andres Galarraga	2.00
8	Bob Tewksbury	.25
9	Al Newman	.05
10	Andres Thomas	.05
11	*Barry Bonds*	25.00
12	Juan Nieves	.05
13	Mark Eichhorn	.05
14	Dan Plesac	.05
15	Cory Snyder	.05
16	Kelly Gruber	.05
17	*Kevin Mitchell*	.15
18	Steve Lombardozzi	.05
19	Mitch Williams	.05
20	John Cerutti	.05
21	Todd Worrell	.05
22	Jose Canseco	4.00
23	*Pete Incaviglia*	.15
24	Jose Guzman	.05
25	Scott Bailes	.05
26	Greg Mathews	.05
27	Eric King	.05
28	Paul Assenmacher	.05
29	Jeff Sellers	.05
30	*Bobby Bonilla*	.50
31	*Doug Drabek*	.50
32	*Will Clark*	2.00
33	Bip Roberts	.05
34	Jim Deshaies	.05
35	Mike LaValliere	.05
36	Scott Bankhead	.05
37	Dale Sveum	.05
38	*Bo Jackson*	2.00
39	Rob Thompson	.05
40	Eric Plunk	.05
41	Bill Bathe	.05
42	*John Kruk*	.25
43	Andy Allanson	.05
44	Mark Portugal	.05
45	Danny Tartabull	.05
46	Bob Kipper	.05
47	Gene Walter	.05
48	Rey Quinonez	.05
49	Bobby Witt	.05
50	Bill Mooneyham	.05
51	John Cangelosi	.05
52	*Ruben Sierra*	.50
53	Rob Woodward	.05
54	Ed Hearn	.05
55	Joel McKeon	.05
56	Checklist 1-56	.05

1987 Donruss

The 1987 Donruss set consists of 660 numbered cards, each measuring 2-1/2" x 3-1/2". Color photos are surrounded by a bold black border separated by two narrow bands of yellow which enclose a brown area filled with baseballs. The player's name, team and team logo appear on the card fronts along with the words "Donruss '87". The card backs are designed on a horizontal format and contain black print on a yellow and white background. The backs are very similar to those in previous years' sets. Backs of cards issued in wax and rack packs face to the left when turned over, while those issued in factory sets face to the right. Cards were sold with Roberto Clemente puzzle pieces in each pack. Cards checklisted with a (DK) suffix are Diamond Kings; cards with an (RR) suffix are Rated Rookies.

		MT
Unopened Factory Set (660):		45.00
Complete Set (660):		35.00
Common Player:		.05
Roberto Clemente Puzzle:		6.00
Pack (15):		3.00
Wax Box (36):		50.00
1	Wally Joyner (DK)	.25
2	Roger Clemens (DK)	1.50
3	Dale Murphy (DK)	.15
4	Darryl Strawberry (DK)	.15
5	Ozzie Smith (DK)	.45
6	Jose Canseco (DK)	.65
7	Charlie Hough (DK)	.05
8	Brook Jacoby (DK)	.05
9	Fred Lynn (DK)	.15
10	Rick Rhoden (DK)	.05
11	Chris Brown (DK)	.05
12	Von Hayes (DK)	.05
13	Jack Morris (DK)	.10
14a	Kevin McReynolds (DK) (no yellow stripe on back)	.50
14b	Kevin McReynolds (DK) (yellow stripe on back)	.20
15	George Brett (DK)	.75
16	Ted Higuera (DK)	.05
17	Hubie Brooks (DK)	.05
18	Mike Scott (DK)	.05
19	Kirby Puckett (DK)	.75
20	Dave Winfield (DK)	.45
21	Lloyd Moseby (DK)	.05
22a	Eric Davis (DK) (no yellow stripe on back)	.50
22b	Eric Davis (DK) (yellow stripe on back)	.15
23	Jim Presley (DK)	.05
24	Keith Moreland (DK)	.05
25a	Greg Walker (DK) (no yellow stripe on back)	.50
25b	Greg Walker (DK) (yellow stripe on back)	.10
26	Steve Sax (DK)	.10
27	Checklist 1-27	.05
28	*B.J. Surhoff* (RR)	.30
29	*Randy Myers* (RR)	.65
30	*Ken Gerhart* (RR)	.05
31	Benito Santiago (RR)	.30
32	*Greg Swindell* (RR)	.15
33	*Mike Birkbeck* (RR)	.10
34	*Terry Steinbach* (RR)	.50
35	Bo Jackson (RR)	2.00
36	*Greg Maddux* (RR)	10.00
37	*Jim Lindeman* (RR)	.05
38	*Devon White* (RR)	.75
39	*Eric Bell* (RR)	.10
40	*Will Fraser* (RR)	.10
41	*Jerry Browne* (RR)	.15
42	*Chris James* (RR)	.10
43	*Rafael Palmeiro* (RR)	5.00
44	*Pat Dodson* (RR)	.05
45	*Duane Ward* (RR)	.25
46	Mark McGwire (RR)	15.00
47	*Bruce Fields* (RR) (Photo actually Darnell Coles)	.10
48	Eddie Murray	.60
49	Ted Higuera	.05
50	Kirk Gibson	.10
51	Oil Can Boyd	.05
52	Don Mattingly	1.00
53	Pedro Guerrero	.05
54	George Brett	1.00
55	Jose Rijo	.05
56	Tim Raines	.20
57	*Ed Correa*	.05
58	Mike Witt	.05
59	Greg Walker	.05
60	Ozzie Smith	.60
61	Glenn Davis	.05
62	Glenn Wilson	.05
63	Tom Browning	.05
64	Tony Gwynn	1.00
65	R.J. Reynolds	.05
66	Will Clark	.50
67	Ozzie Virgil	.05
68	Rick Sutcliffe	.10
69	Gary Carter	.15
70	Mike Moore	.05
71	Bert Blyleven	.10
72	Tony Fernandez	.05
73	Kent Hrbek	.10
74	Lloyd Moseby	.05
75	Alvin Davis	.05
76	Keith Hernandez	.10
77	Ryne Sandberg	.90
78	Dale Murphy	.30
79	Sid Bream	.05
80	Chris Brown	.05
81	Steve Garvey	.25
82	Mario Soto	.05
83	Shane Rawley	.05
84	Willie McGee	.10
85	Jose Cruz	.05
86	Brian Downing	.05
87	Ozzie Guillen	.05
88	Hubie Brooks	.05
89	Cal Ripken, Jr.	2.50
90	Juan Nieves	.05
91	Lance Parrish	.10
92	Jim Rice	.15
93	Ron Guidry	.15
94	Fernando Valenzuela	.10
95	*Andy Allanson*	.05
96	Willie Wilson	.05
97	Jose Canseco	.50
98	Jeff Reardon	.05
99	*Bobby Witt*	.20
100	Checklist 28-133	.05
101	Jose Guzman	.05
102	Steve Balboni	.05
103	Tony Phillips	.05
104	Brook Jacoby	.05
105	Dave Winfield	.40
106	Orel Hershiser	.10
107	Lou Whitaker	.05
108	Fred Lynn	.10
109	Bill Wegman	.05
110	Donnie Moore	.05
111	Jack Clark	.10
112	Bob Knepper	.05
113	Von Hayes	.05
114	*Bip Roberts*	.40
115	Tony Pena	.05
116	Scott Garrelts	.05
117	Paul Molitor	.75
118	Darryl Strawberry	.10
119	Shawon Dunston	.05
120	Jim Presley	.05
121	Jesse Barfield	.05
122	Gary Gaetti	.10
123	*Kurt Stillwell*	.10
124	Joel Davis	.05
125	Mike Boddicker	.05
126	Robin Yount	.75
127	Alan Trammell	.10

No.	Player	Price
128	Dave Righetti	.05
129	Dwight Evans	.10
130	Mike Scioscia	.05
131	Julio Franco	.05
132	Bret Saberhagen	.10
133	Mike Davis	.05
134	Joe Hesketh	.05
135	Wally Joyner	.05
136	Don Slaught	.05
137	Daryl Boston	.05
138	Nolan Ryan	2.50
139	Mike Schmidt	1.00
140	Tommy Herr	.05
141	Garry Templeton	.05
142	Kal Daniels	.05
143	Billy Sample	.05
144	Johnny Ray	.05
145	*Rob Thompson*	.25
146	Bob Dernier	.05
147	Danny Tartabull	.05
148	Ernie Whitt	.05
149	Kirby Puckett	1.00
150	Mike Young	.05
151	Ernest Riles	.05
152	Frank Tanana	.05
153	Rich Gedman	.05
154	Willie Randolph	.10
155a	Bill Madlock (name in brown band)	.10
155b	Bill Madlock (name in red band)	.50
156a	Joe Carter (name in brown band)	.10
156b	Joe Carter (name in red band)	.40
157	Danny Jackson	.05
158	Carney Lansford	.05
159	Bryn Smith	.05
160	Gary Pettis	.05
161	Oddibe McDowell	.05
162	*John Cangelosi*	.10
163	Mike Scott	.05
164	Eric Show	.05
165	Juan Samuel	.05
166	Nick Esasky	.05
167	Zane Smith	.05
168	Mike Brown	.05
169	Keith Moreland	.05
170	John Tudor	.05
171	Ken Dixon	.05
172	Jim Gantner	.05
173	Jack Morris	.15
174	Bruce Hurst	.05
175	Dennis Rasmussen	.05
176	Mike Marshall	.05
177	Dan Quisenberry	.05
178	Eric Plunk	.05
179	Tim Wallach	.05
180	Steve Buechele	.05
181	Don Sutton	.40
182	Dave Schmidt	.05
183	Terry Pendleton	.05
184	*Jim Deshaies*	.15
185	Steve Bedrosian	.05
186	Pete Rose	1.25
187	Dave Dravecky	.05
188	Rick Reuschel	.05
189	Dan Gladden	.05
190	Rick Mahler	.05
191	Thad Bosley	.05
192	Ron Darling	.05
193	Matt Young	.05
194	Tom Brunansky	.05
195	Dave Stieb	.05
196	Frank Viola	.05
197	Tom Henke	.05
198	Karl Best	.05
199	Dwight Gooden	.15
200	Checklist 134-239	.05
201	Steve Trout	.05
202	Rafael Ramirez	.05
203	Bob Walk	.05
204	Roger Mason	.05
205	Terry Kennedy	.05
206	Ron Oester	.05
207	John Russell	.05
208	*Greg Mathews*	.05
209	Charlie Kerfeld	.05
210	Reggie Jackson	.40
211	Floyd Bannister	.05
212	Vance Law	.05
213	Rich Bordi	.05
214	*Dan Plesac*	.10
215	Dave Collins	.05
216	Bob Stanley	.05
217	Joe Niekro	.10
218	Tom Niedenfuer	.05
219	Brett Butler	.05
220	Charlie Leibrandt	.05
221	Steve Ontiveros	.05
222	Tim Burke	.05
223	Curtis Wilkerson	.05
224	*Pete Incaviglia*	.25
225	Lonnie Smith	.05
226	Chris Codiroli	.05
227	*Scott Bailes*	.05
228	Rickey Henderson	.65
229	Ken Howell	.05
230	Darnell Coles	.05
231	Don Aase	.05
232	Tim Leary	.05
233	Bob Boone	.10
234	Ricky Horton	.05
235	Mark Bailey	.05
236	Kevin Gross	.05
237	Lance McCullers	.05
238	Cecilio Guante	.05
239	Bob Melvin	.05
240	Billy Jo Robidoux	.05
241	Roger McDowell	.05
242	Leon Durham	.05
243	Ed Nunez	.05
244	Jimmy Key	.05
245	Mike Smithson	.05
246	Bo Diaz	.05
247	Carlton Fisk	.40
248	Larry Sheets	.05
249	*Juan Castillo*	.05
250	*Eric King*	.05
251	Doug Drabek	.10
252	Wade Boggs	.90
253	Mariano Duncan	.05
254	Pat Tabler	.05
255	Frank White	.10
256	Alfredo Griffin	.05
257	Floyd Youmans	.05
258	Rob Wilfong	.05
259	Pete O'Brien	.05
260	Tim Hulett	.05
261	Dickie Thon	.05
262	Darren Daulton	.10
263	Vince Coleman	.10
264	Andy Hawkins	.05
265	Eric Davis	.20
266	*Andres Thomas*	.05
267	*Mike Diaz*	.05
268	Chili Davis	.05
269	Jody Davis	.05
270	Phil Bradley	.05
271	George Bell	.05
272	Keith Atherton	.05
273	Storm Davis	.05
274	Rob Deer	.05
275	Walt Terrell	.05
276	Roger Clemens	1.00
277	Mike Easler	.05
278	Steve Sax	.05
279	Andre Thornton	.05
280	Jim Sundberg	.05
281	Bill Bathe	.05
282	Jay Tibbs	.05
283	Dick Schofield	.05
284	Mike Mason	.05
285	Jerry Hairston Sr.	.05
286	Bill Doran	.05
287	Tim Flannery	.05
288	Gary Redus	.05
289	John Franco	.10
290	*Paul Assenmacher*	.15
291	Joe Orsulak	.05
292	Lee Smith	.15
293	Mike Laga	.05
294	Rick Dempsey	.05
295	Mike Felder	.05
296	Tom Brookens	.05
297	Al Nipper	.05
298	Mike Pagliarulo	.05
299	Franklin Stubbs	.05
300	Checklist 240-345	.05
301	Steve Farr	.05
302	*Bill Mooneyham*	.05
303	Andres Galarraga	.25
304	Scott Fletcher	.05
305	Jack Howell	.05
306	*Russ Morman*	.10
307	Todd Worrell	.05
308	Dave Smith	.05
309	Jeff Stone	.05
310	Ron Robinson	.05
311	Bruce Bochy	.05
312	Jim Winn	.05
313	Mark Davis	.05
314	Jeff Dedmon	.05
315	*Jamie Moyer*	.10
316	Wally Backman	.05
317	Ken Phelps	.05
318	Steve Lombardozzi	.05
319	Rance Mulliniks	.05
320	Tim Laudner	.05
321	*Mark Eichhorn*	.10
322	*Lee Guetterman*	.05
323	Sid Fernandez	.05
324	Jerry Mumphrey	.05
325	David Palmer	.05
326	Bill Almon	.05
327	Candy Maldonado	.05
328	John Kruk	.10
329	John Denny	.05
330	Milt Thompson	.05
331	*Mike LaValliere*	.15
332	Alan Ashby	.05
333	Doug Corbett	.05
334	*Ron Karkovice*	.10
335	Mitch Webster	.05
336	Lee Lacy	.05
337	*Glenn Braggs*	.15
338	Dwight Lowry	.05
339	Don Baylor	.15
340	Brian Fisher	.05
341	*Reggie Williams*	.05
342	Tom Candiotti	.05
343	Rudy Law	.05
344	Curt Young	.05
345	Mike Fitzgerald	.05
346	Ruben Sierra	.10
347	*Mitch Williams*	.25
348	Jorge Orta	.05
349	Mickey Tettleton	.10
350	Ernie Camacho	.05
351	Ron Kittle	.05
352	Ken Landreaux	.05
353	Chet Lemon	.05
354	John Shelby	.05
355	Mark Clear	.05
356	Doug DeCinces	.05
357	Ken Dayley	.05
358	Phil Garner	.05
359	Steve Jeltz	.05
360	Ed Whitson	.05
361	Barry Bonds	12.00
362	Vida Blue	.05
363	Cecil Cooper	.05
364	Bob Ojeda	.05
365	Dennis Eckersley	.25
366	Mike Morgan	.05
367	Willie Upshaw	.05
368	*Allan Anderson*	.05
369	Bill Gullickson	.05
370	*Bobby Thigpen*	.10
371	Juan Beniquez	.05
372	Charlie Moore	.05
373	Dan Petry	.05
374	Rod Scurry	.05
375	Tom Seaver	.50
376	Ed Vande Berg	.05
377	Tony Bernazard	.05
378	Greg Pryor	.05
379	Dwayne Murphy	.05
380	Andy McGaffigan	.05
381	Kirk McCaskill	.05
382	Greg Harris	.05
383	Rich Dotson	.05
384	Craig Reynolds	.05
385	Greg Gross	.05
386	Tito Landrum	.05
387	Craig Lefferts	.05
388	Dave Parker	.10
389	Bob Horner	.05
390	Pat Clements	.05
391	Jeff Leonard	.05
392	Chris Speier	.05
393	John Moses	.05
394	Garth Iorg	.05
395	Greg Gagne	.05
396	Nate Snell	.05
397	*Bryan Clutterbuck*	.05
398	Darrell Evans	.15
399	Steve Crawford	.05
400	Checklist 346-451	.05
401	*Phil Lombardi*	.05
402	Rick Honeycutt	.05
403	Ken Schrom	.05
404	Bud Black	.05
405	Donnie Hill	.05
406	Wayne Krenchicki	.05
407	*Chuck Finley*	.35
408	Toby Harrah	.05
409	Steve Lyons	.10
410	Kevin Bass	.05
411	Marvell Wynne	.05
412	Ron Roenicke	.05
413	*Tracy Jones*	.10
414	Gene Garber	.05
415	Mike Bielecki	.05
416	Frank DiPino	.05
417	Andy Van Slyke	.10
418	Jim Dwyer	.05
419	Ben Oglivie	.05
420	Dave Bergman	.05
421	Joe Sambito	.05
422	*Bob Tewksbury*	.30
423	Len Matuszek	.05
424	*Mike Kingery*	.05
425	Dave Kingman	.10
426	*Al Newman*	.05
427	Gary Ward	.05
428	Ruppert Jones	.05
429	Harold Baines	.10
430	Pat Perry	.05
431	Terry Puhl	.05
432	Don Carman	.05
433	Eddie Milner	.05
434	LaMarr Hoyt	.05
435	Rick Rhoden	.05
436	Jose Uribe	.05
437	Ken Oberkfell	.05
438	Ron Davis	.05
439	Jesse Orosco	.05
440	Scott Bradley	.05
441	Randy Bush	.05
442	*John Cerutti*	.10
443	Roy Smalley	.05
444	Kelly Gruber	.05
445	Bob Kearney	.05
446	*Ed Hearn*	.05
447	Scott Sanderson	.05
448	Bruce Benedict	.05
449	Junior Ortiz	.05
450	*Mike Aldrete*	.05
451	Kevin McReynolds	.05
452	*Rob Murphy*	.10
453	Kent Tekulve	.05
454	Curt Ford	.05
455	Davey Lopes	.05
456	Bobby Grich	.05
457	Jose DeLeon	.05
458	Andre Dawson	.30
459	Mike Flanagan	.05
460	*Joey Meyer*	.10
461	*Chuck Cary*	.05
462	Bill Buckner	.10
463	Bob Shirley	.05
464	*Jeff Hamilton*	.10
465	Phil Niekro	.30
466	Mark Gubicza	.05
467	Jerry Willard	.05
468	*Bob Sebra*	.05
469	Larry Parrish	.05
470	Charlie Hough	.05
471	Hal McRae	.05
472	*Dave Leiper*	.05
473	Mel Hall	.05
474	Dan Pasqua	.05
475	Bob Welch	.05
476	Johnny Grubb	.05
477	Jim Traber	.05
478	*Chris Bosio*	.25
479	Mark McLemore	.10
480	John Morris	.05
481	Billy Hatcher	.05
482	Dan Schatzeder	.05
483	Rich Gossage	.15
484	Jim Morrison	.05
485	Bob Brenly	.05
486	Bill Schroeder	.05
487	Mookie Wilson	.10
488	*Dave Martinez*	.15
489	Harold Reynolds	.10
490	Jeff Hearron	.05
491	Mickey Hatcher	.05
492	*Barry Larkin*	2.00
493	Bob James	.05
494	John Habyan	.05
495	*Jim Adduci*	.05
496	Mike Heath	.05
497	Tim Stoddard	.05
498	Tony Armas	.05
499	Dennis Powell	.05
500	Checklist 452-557	.05
501	Chris Bando	.05
502	*David Cone*	2.00
503	Jay Howell	.05
504	Tom Foley	.05
505	*Ray Chadwick*	.05

506 *Mike Loynd* .05
507 Neil Allen .05
508 Danny Darwin .05
509 Rick Schu .05
510 Jose Oquendo .05
511 Gene Walter .05
512 *Terry McGriff* .05
513 Ken Griffey .10
514 Benny Distefano .05
515 *Terry Mulholland* .40
516 Ed Lynch .05
517 Bill Swift .05
518 Manny Lee .05
519 Andre David .05
520 Scott McGregor .05
521 Rick Manning .05
522 Willie Hernandez .05
523 Marty Barrett .05
524 Wayne Tolleson .05
525 *Jose Gonzalez* .05
526 Cory Snyder .05
527 Buddy Biancalana .05
528 Moose Haas .05
529 *Wilfredo Tejada* .05
530 Stu Cliburn .05
531 *Dale Mohorcic* .05
532 Ron Hassey .05
533 Ty Gainey .05
534 Jerry Royster .05
535 *Mike Maddux* .05
536 Ted Power .05
537 Ted Simmons .05
538 *Rafael Belliard* .10
539 Chico Walker .05
540 Bob Forsch .05
541 John Stefero .05
542 *Dale Sveum* .10
543 Mark Thurmond .05
544 *Jeff Sellers* .05
545 Joel Skinner .05
546 Alex Trevino .05
547 *Randy Kutcher* .05
548 Joaquin Andujar .05
549 *Casey Candaele* .10
550 Jeff Russell .05
551 John Candelaria .05
552 Joe Cowley .05
553 Danny Cox .05
554 Denny Walling .05
555 *Bruce Ruffin* .20
556 Buddy Bell .10
557 *Jimmy Jones* .10
558 Bobby Bonilla .20
559 Jeff Robinson .05
560 Ed Olwine .05
561 *Glenallen Hill* .75
562 Lee Mazzilli .05
563 Mike Brown .05
564 George Frazier .05
565 *Mike Sharperson* .10
566 *Mark Portugal* .10
567 Rick Leach .05
568 Mark Langston .10
569 Rafael Santana .05
570 Manny Trillo .05
571 Cliff Speck .05
572 Bob Kipper .05
573 *Kelly Downs* .10
574 *Randy Asadoor* .05
575 *Dave Magadan* .25
576 *Marvin Freeman* .05
577 Jeff Lahti .05
578 Jeff Calhoun .05
579 Gus Polidor .05
580 Gene Nelson .05
581 Tim Teufel .05
582 Odell Jones .05
583 Mark Ryal .05
584 Randy O'Neal .05
585 *Mike Greenwell* .50
586 Ray Knight .05
587 *Ralph Bryant* .05
588 Carmen Castillo .05
589 Ed Wojna .05
590 Stan Javier .05
591 *Jeff Musselman* .10
592 *Mike Stanley* .20
593 Darrell Porter .05
594 *Drew Hall* .05
595 *Rob Nelson* .05
596 Bryan Oelkers .05
597 *Scott Nielsen* .05
598 *Brian Holton* .10
599 Kevin Mitchell .10
600 Checklist 558-660 .05
601 Jackie Gutierrez .05
602 *Barry Jones* .10
603 Jerry Narron .05
604 Steve Lake .05
605 Jim Pankovits .05
606 Ed Romero .05
607 Dave LaPoint .05
608 Don Robinson .05
609 Mike Krukow .05
610 *Dave Valle* .10
611 Len Dykstra .10
612 Roberto Clemente Puzzle Card .25
613 Mike Trujillo .05
614 Damaso Garcia .05
615 Neal Heaton .05
616 Juan Berenguer .05
617 Steve Carlton .40
618 Gary Lucas .05
619 Geno Petralli .05
620 Rick Aguilera .05
621 Fred McGriff .20
622 Dave Henderson .05
623 *Dave Clark* .05
624 Angel Salazar .05
625 Randy Hunt .05
626 John Gibbons .05
627 *Kevin Brown* 3.00
628 Bill Dawley .05
629 Aurelio Lopez .05
630 Charlie Hudson .05
631 Ray Soff .05
632 *Ray Hayward* .05
633 Spike Owen .05
634 Glenn Hubbard .05
635 *Kevin Elster* .10
636 Mike LaCoss .05
637 Dwayne Henry .05
638 *Rey Quinones* .05
639 Jim Clancy .05
640 Larry Andersen .05
641 Calvin Schiraldi .05
642 *Stan Jefferson* .05
643 Marc Sullivan .05
644 Mark Grant .05
645 Cliff Johnson .05
646 Howard Johnson .05
647 Dave Sax .05
648 Dave Stewart .10
649 Danny Heep .05
650 Joe Johnson .05
651 *Bob Brower* .05
652 Rob Woodward .05
653 John Mizerock .05
654 *Tim Pyznarski* .05
655 *Luis Aquino* .05
656 Mickey Brantley .10
657 Doyle Alexander .05
658 Sammy Stewart .05
659 Jim Acker .05
660 Pete Ladd .05

1987 Donruss All-Stars

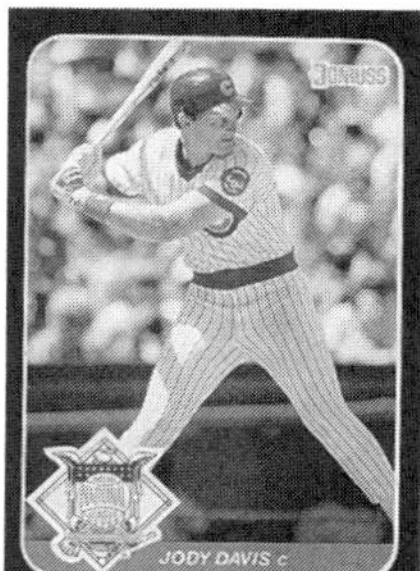

Issued in conjunction with the Donruss Pop-Ups set for the second consecutive year, the 1987 Donruss All-Stars consist of 59 players (plus a checklist) who were selected to the 1986 All-Star Game. Measuring 3-1/2" x 5" in size, the card fronts feature black borders and American or National League logos. Included on back are the player's career highlights and All-Star Game statistics. Retail packs included one Pop-Up card, three All-Star cards and one Roberto Clemente puzzle card.

	MT
Complete Set (60):	4.00
Common Player:	.10
Roberto Clemente Puzzle:	6.00

1 Wally Joyner .10
2 Dave Winfield .40
3 Lou Whitaker .10
4 Kirby Puckett .50
5 Cal Ripken, Jr. 1.00
6 Rickey Henderson .40
7 Wade Boggs .40
8 Roger Clemens .50
9 Lance Parrish .10
10 Dick Howser .10
11 Keith Hernandez .10
12 Darryl Strawberry .15
13 Ryne Sandberg .40
14 Dale Murphy .35
15 Ozzie Smith .40
16 Tony Gwynn .50
17 Mike Schmidt .50
18 Dwight Gooden .15
19 Gary Carter .20
20 Whitey Herzog .10
21 Jose Canseco .35
22 John Franco .10
23 Jesse Barfield .10
24 Rick Rhoden .10
25 Harold Baines .10
26 Sid Fernandez .10
27 George Brett .50
28 Steve Sax .10
29 Jim Presley .10
30 Dave Smith .10
31 Eddie Murray .35
32 Mike Scott .10
33 Don Mattingly .50
34 Dave Parker .10
35 Tony Fernandez .10
36 Tim Raines .10
37 Brook Jacoby .10
38 Chili Davis .10
39 Rich Gedman .10
40 Kevin Bass .10
41 Frank White .10
42 Glenn Davis .10
43 Willie Hernandez .10
44 Chris Brown .10
45 Jim Rice .20
46 Tony Pena .10
47 Don Aase .10
48 Hubie Brooks .10
49 Charlie Hough .10
50 Jody Davis .10
51 Mike Witt .10
52 Jeff Reardon .10
53 Ken Schrom .10
54 Fernando Valenzuela .10
55 Dave Righetti .10
56 Shane Rawley .10
57 Ted Higuera .10
58 Mike Krukow .10
59 Lloyd Moseby .10
60 Checklist .05

1987 Donruss Box Panels

Continuing with an idea they initiated in 1985, Donruss once again placed baseball cards on the bottoms of their retail boxes. The cards, which are 2-1/2" x 3-1/2" in size, come four to a panel with each panel containing an unnumbered Roberto Clemente puzzle card. With numbering that begins where Donruss left off in 1986, cards PC 10 through PC 12 were found on boxes of Donruss regular issue wax packs. Cards PC 13 through PC 15 were located on boxes of the 1987 All-Star/Pop-Up packs.

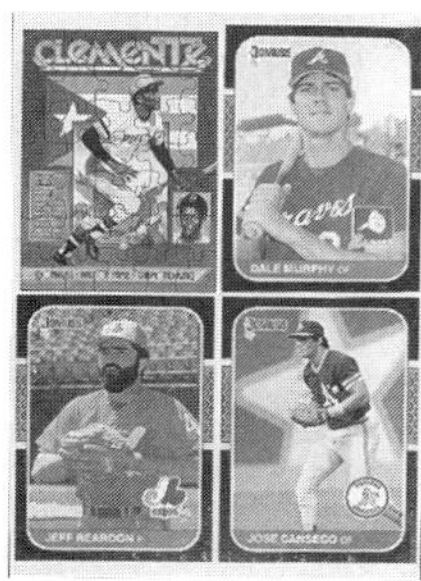

	MT
Complete Panel Set (2):	3.00
Complete Singles Set (8):	3.00
Common Single Player:	.15
Panel	2.00
10 Dale Murphy	.40
11 Jeff Reardon	.15
12 Jose Canseco	1.00
---- Roberto Clemente Puzzle Card	.15
Panel	2.00
13 Mike Scott	.15
14 Roger Clemens	1.50
15 Mike Krukow	.15
---- Roberto Clemente Puzzle Card	.15

1987 Donruss Diamond Kings Supers

For a third season, Donruss produced a set of enlarged Diamond Kings, measuring 4-11/16" x 6-3/4". The 28-cards feature the artwork of Dick Perez, and contain 26 player cards, a checklist and a Roberto Clemente puzzle card. The set was available through a mail-in offer for $9.50 plus three wrappers.

	MT
Complete Set (28):	5.00
Common Player:	.15
1 Wally Joyner	.15
2 Roger Clemens	1.50
3 Dale Murphy	.30
4 Darryl Strawberry	.20
5 Ozzie Smith	.50
6 Jose Canseco	.30
7 Charlie Hough	.15
8 Brook Jacoby	.15

9	Fred Lynn	.15
10	Rick Rhoden	.15
11	Chris Brown	.15
12	Von Hayes	.15
13	Jack Morris	.15
14	Kevin McReynolds	.15
15	George Brett	1.00
16	Ted Higuera	.15
17	Hubie Brooks	.15
18	Mike Scott	.15
19	Kirby Puckett	1.50
20	Dave Winfield	.50
21	Lloyd Moseby	.15
22	Eric Davis	.20
23	Jim Presley	.15
24	Keith Moreland	.15
25	Greg Walker	.15
26	Steve Sax	.15
27	Checklist	.05
---	Roberto Clemente Puzzle Card	.50

1987 Donruss Highlights

For a third consecutive year, Donruss produced a 56-card set which highlighted the special events of the 1987 baseball season. The 2-1/2" x 3-1/2" cards have a front design similar to the regular 1987 Donruss set. A blue border and the "Highlights" logo are the significant differences. The backs feature black print on a white background and include the date the event took place plus the particulars. As in the past, the set includes Donruss' picks for the A.L. and N.L. Rookies of the Year. The set was issued in a specially designed box and was available only through hobby dealers.

		MT
	Complete Unopened Set (56):	3.00
	Complete Set (56):	1.50
	Common Player:	.05
1	First No-Hitter For Brewers (Juan Nieves)	.05
2	Hits 500th Homer (Mike Schmidt)	.50
3	N.L. Player of the Month - April (Eric Davis)	.05
4	N.L. Pitcher of the Month - April (Sid Fernandez)	.05
5	A.L. Player of the Month - April (Brian Downing)	.05
6	A.L. Pitcher of the Month - April (Bret Saberhagen)	.05
7	Free Agent Holdout Returns (Tim Raines)	.05
8	N.L. Player of the Month - May (Eric Davis)	.05
9	N.L. Pitcher of the Month - May (Steve Bedrosian)	.05
10	A.L. Player of the Month - May (Larry Parrish)	.05
11	A.L. Pitcher of the Month - May (Jim Clancy)	.05
12	N.L. Player of the Month - June (Tony Gwynn)	.25
13	N.L. Pitcher of the Month - June (Orel Hershiser)	.05
14	A.L. Player of the Month - June (Wade Boggs)	.20
15	A.L. Pitcher of the Month - June (Steve Ontiveros)	.05
16	All Star Game Hero (Tim Raines)	.05
17	Consecutive Game Homer Streak (Don Mattingly)	.50
18	1987 Hall of Fame Inductee (Jim "Catfish" Hunter)	.15
19	1987 Hall of Fame Inductee (Ray Dandridge)	.15
20	1987 Hall of Fame Inductee (Billy Williams)	.15
21	N.L. Player of the Month - July (Bo Diaz)	.05
22	N.L. Pitcher of the Month - July (Floyd Youmans)	.05
23	A.L. Player of the Month - July (Don Mattingly)	.50
24	A.L. Pitcher of the Month - July (Frank Viola)	.05
25	Strikes Out 4 Batters In 1 Inning (Bobby Witt)	.05
26	Ties A.L. 9-Inning Game Hit Mark (Kevin Seitzer)	.05
27	Sets Rookie Home Run Record (Mark McGwire)	.75
28	Sets Cubs' 1st Year Homer Mark (Andre Dawson)	.05
29	Hits In 39 Straight Games (Paul Molitor)	.15
30	Record Weekend (Kirby Puckett)	.50
31	N.L. Player of the Month - August (Andre Dawson)	.05
32	N.L. Pitcher of the Month - August (Doug Drabek)	.05
33	A.L. Player of the Month - August (Dwight Evans)	.05
34	A.L. Pitcher of the Month - August (Mark Langston)	.05
35	100 RBI In 1st 2 Major League Seasons (Wally Joyner)	.05
36	100 SB In 1st 3 Major League Seasons (Vince Coleman)	.05
37	Orioles' All Time Homer King (Eddie Murray)	.20
38	Ends Consecutive Innings Streak (Cal Ripken)	.75
39	Blue Jays Hit Record 10 Homers In 1 Game (Rob Ducey, Fred McGriff, Ernie Whitt)	.05
40	Equal A's RBI Marks (Jose Canseco, Mark McGwire)	.60
41	Sets All-Time Catching Record (Bob Boone)	.05
42	Sets Mets' One-Season HR Mark (Darryl Strawberry)	.05
43	N.L.'s All-Time Switch Hit HR King (Howard Johnson)	.05
44	Five Straight 200-Hit Seasons (Wade Boggs)	.20
45	Eclipses Rookie Game Hitting Streak (Benito Santiago)	.05
46	Eclipses Jackson's A's HR Record (Mark McGwire)	.75
47	13th Rookie To Collect 200 Hits (Kevin Seitzer)	.05
48	Sets Slam Record (Don Mattingly)	.50
49	N.L. Player of the Month - September (Darryl Strawberry)	.05
50	N.L. Pitcher of the Month - September (Pascual Perez)	.05
51	A.L. Player of the Month - September (Alan Trammell)	.05
52	A.L. Pitcher of the Month - September (Doyle Alexander)	.05
53	Strikeout King - Again (Nolan Ryan)	.75
54	Donruss A.L. Rookie of the Year (Mark McGwire)	.75
55	Donruss N.L. Rookie of the Year (Benito Santiago)	.05
56	Highlight Checklist	.05

1987 Donruss Opening Day

The Donruss Opening Day set includes all players in major league baseball's starting lineups on the opening day of the 1987 baseball season. Cards in the 272-piece set measure 2-1/2" x 3-1/2" and have a glossy coating. The fronts are identical in design to the regular Donruss set, but new photos were utilized along with maroon borders as opposed to black. The backs carry black printing on white and yellow and offer a brief player biography plus the player's career statistics. The set was packaged in a sturdy 15" by 5" by 2" box with a clear acetate lid.

		MT
	Complete Set (272):	8.00
	Complete Set, Unopened (272):	40.00
	Common Player:	.10
1	Doug DeCinces	.10
2	Mike Witt	.10
3	George Hendrick	.10
4	Dick Schofield	.10
5	Devon White	.10
6	Butch Wynegar	.10
7	Wally Joyner	.10
8	Mark McLemore	.10
9	Brian Downing	.10
10	Gary Pettis	.10
11	Bill Doran	.10
12	Phil Garner	.10
13	Jose Cruz	.10
14	Kevin Bass	.10
15	Mike Scott	.10
16	Glenn Davis	.10
17	Alan Ashby	.10
18	Billy Hatcher	.10
19	Craig Reynolds	.10
20	Carney Lansford	.10
21	Mike Davis	.10
22	Reggie Jackson	.50
23	Mickey Tettleton	.10
24	Jose Canseco	.75
25	Rob Nelson	.10
26	Tony Phillips	.10
27	Dwayne Murphy	.10
28	Alfredo Griffin	.10
29	Curt Young	.10
30	Willie Upshaw	.10
31	Mike Sharperson	.10
32	Rance Mulliniks	.10
33	Ernie Whitt	.10
34	Jesse Barfield	.10
35	Tony Fernandez	.10
36	Lloyd Moseby	.10
37	Jimmy Key	.10
38	Fred McGriff	.10
39	George Bell	.10
40	Dale Murphy	.40
41	Rick Mahler	.10
42	Ken Griffey	.10
43	Andres Thomas	.10
44	Dion James	.10
45	Ozzie Virgil	.10
46	Ken Oberkfell	.10
47	Gary Roenicke	.10
48	Glenn Hubbard	.10
49	Bill Schroeder	.10
50	Greg Brock	.10
51	Billy Jo Robidoux	.10
52	Glenn Braggs	.10
53	Jim Gantner	.10
54	Paul Molitor	.40
55	Dale Sveum	.10
56	Ted Higuera	.10
57	Rob Deer	.10
58	Robin Yount	.50
59	Jim Lindeman	.10
60	Vince Coleman	.10
61	Tommy Herr	.10
62	Terry Pendleton	.10
63	John Tudor	.10
64	Tony Pena	.10
65	Ozzie Smith	.55
66	Tito Landrum	.10
67	Jack Clark	.10
68	Bob Dernier	.10
69	Rick Sutcliffe	.10
70	Andre Dawson	.25
71	Keith Moreland	.10
72	Jody Davis	.10
73	Brian Dayett	.10
74	Leon Durham	.10
75	Ryne Sandberg	.75
76	Shawon Dunston	.10
77	Mike Marshall	.10
78	Bill Madlock	.10
79	Orel Hershiser	.15
80	Mike Ramsey	.10
81	Ken Landreaux	.10
82	Mike Scioscia	.10
83	Franklin Stubbs	.10
84	Mariano Duncan	.10
85	Steve Sax	.10
86	Mitch Webster	.10
87	Reid Nichols	.10
88	Tim Wallach	.10
89	Floyd Youmans	.10
90	Andres Galarraga	.15
91	Hubie Brooks	.10
92	Jeff Reed	.10
93	Alonzo Powell	.10
94	Vance Law	.10
95	Bob Brenly	.10
96	Will Clark	.30
97	Chili Davis	.10
98	Mike Krukow	.10
99	Jose Uribe	.10
100	Chris Brown	.10
101	Rob Thompson	.10

102	Candy Maldonado	.10
103	Jeff Leonard	.10
104	Tom Candiotti	.10
105	Chris Bando	.10
106	Cory Snyder	.10
107	Pat Tabler	.10
108	Andre Thornton	.10
109	Joe Carter	.10
110	Tony Bernazard	.10
111	Julio Franco	.10
112	Brook Jacoby	.10
113	Brett Butler	.10
114	Donnell Nixon	.10
115	Alvin Davis	.10
116	Mark Langston	.10
117	Harold Reynolds	.10
118	Ken Phelps	.10
119	Mike Kingery	.10
120	Dave Valle	.10
121	Rey Quinones	.10
122	Phil Bradley	.10
123	Jim Presley	.10
124	Keith Hernandez	.10
125	Kevin McReynolds	.10
126	Rafael Santana	.10
127	Bob Ojeda	.10
128	Darryl Strawberry	.15
129	Mookie Wilson	.10
130	Gary Carter	.20
131	Tim Teufel	.10
132	Howard Johnson	.10
133	Cal Ripken, Jr.	2.50
134	Rick Burleson	.10
135	Fred Lynn	.10
136	Eddie Murray	.40
137	Ray Knight	.10
138	Alan Wiggins	.10
139	John Shelby	.10
140	Mike Boddicker	.10
141	Ken Gerhart	.10
142	Terry Kennedy	.10
143	Steve Garvey	.25
144	Marvell Wynne	.10
145	Kevin Mitchell	.10
146	Tony Gwynn	.75
147	Joey Cora	.10
148	Benito Santiago	.10
149	Eric Show	.10
150	Garry Templeton	.10
151	Carmelo Martinez	.10
152	Von Hayes	.10
153	Lance Parrish	.10
154	Milt Thompson	.10
155	Mike Easler	.10
156	Juan Samuel	.10
157	Steve Jeltz	.10
158	Glenn Wilson	.10
159	Shane Rawley	.10
160	Mike Schmidt	.75
161	Andy Van Slyke	.10
162	Johnny Ray	.10
163a	Barry Bonds (dark jersey, photo actually Johnny Ray)	375.00
163b	Barry Bonds (white jersey, correct photo)	5.00
164	Junior Ortiz	.10
165	Rafael Belliard	.10
166	Bob Patterson	.10
167	Bobby Bonilla	.15
168	Sid Bream	.10
169	Jim Morrison	.10
170	Jerry Browne	.10
171	Scott Fletcher	.10
172	Ruben Sierra	.10
173	Larry Parrish	.10
174	Pete O'Brien	.10
175	Pete Incaviglia	.10
176	Don Slaught	.10
177	Oddibe McDowell	.10
178	Charlie Hough	.10
179	Steve Buechele	.10
180	Bob Stanley	.10
181	Wade Boggs	.65
182	Jim Rice	.15
183	Bill Buckner	.10
184	Dwight Evans	.10
185	Spike Owen	.10
186	Don Baylor	.10
187	Marc Sullivan	.10
188	Marty Barrett	.10
189	Dave Henderson	.10
190	Bo Diaz	.10
191	Barry Larkin	.30
192	Kal Daniels	.10
193	Terry Francona	.10
194	Tom Browning	.10
195	Ron Oester	.10
196	Buddy Bell	.10
197	Eric Davis	.10
198	Dave Parker	.10
199	Steve Balboni	.10
200	Danny Tartabull	.10
201	Ed Hearn	.10
202	Buddy Biancalana	.10
203	Danny Jackson	.10
204	Frank White	.10
205	Bo Jackson	.30
206	George Brett	.75
207	Kevin Seitzer	.10
208	Willie Wilson	.10
209	Orlando Mercado	.10
210	Darrell Evans	.10
211	Larry Herndon	.10
212	Jack Morris	.10
213	Chet Lemon	.10
214	Mike Heath	.10
215	Darnell Coles	.10
216	Alan Trammell	.15
217	Terry Harper	.10
218	Lou Whitaker	.10
219	Gary Gaetti	.10
220	Tom Nieto	.10
221	Kirby Puckett	.75
222	Tom Brunansky	.10
223	Greg Gagne	.10
224	Dan Gladden	.10
225	Mark Davidson	.10
226	Bert Blyleven	.10
227	Steve Lombardozzi	.10
228	Kent Hrbek	.10
229	Gary Redus	.10
230	Ivan Calderon	.10
231	Tim Hulett	.10
232	Carlton Fisk	.25
233	Greg Walker	.10
234	Ron Karkovice	.10
235	Ozzie Guillen	.10
236	Harold Baines	.10
237	Donnie Hill	.10
238	Rich Dotson	.10
239	Mike Pagliarulo	.10
240	Joel Skinner	.10
241	Don Mattingly	1.50
242	Gary Ward	.10
243	Dave Winfield	.50
244	Dan Pasqua	.10
245	Wayne Tolleson	.10
246	Willie Randolph	.10
247	Dennis Rasmussen	.10
248	Rickey Henderson	.40
249	Angels Checklist	.05
250	Astros Checklist	.05
251	Athletics Checklist	.05
252	Blue Jays Checklist	.05
253	Braves Checklist	.05
254	Brewers Checklist	.05
255	Cardinals Checklist	.05
256	Dodgers Checklist	.05
257	Expos Checklist	.05
258	Giants Checklist	.05
259	Indians Checklist	.05
260	Mariners Checklist	.05
261	Orioles Checklist	.05
262	Padres Checklist	.05
263	Phillies Checklist	.05
264	Pirates Checklist	.05
265	Rangers Checklist	.05
266	Red Sox Checklist	.05
267	Reds Checklist	.05
268	Royals Checklist	.05
269	Tigers Checklist	.05
270	Twins Checklist	.05
271	White Sox/ Cubs Checklist	.05
272	Yankees/ Mets Checklist	.05

1987 Donruss Pop-Ups

For the second straight year, Donruss released in conjunction with its All-Stars issue a set of cards designed to fold out to form a three-dimensional stand-up card. Consisting of 20 cards, as opposed to the previous year's 18, the 1987 Donruss Pop-Ups set contains players selected to the 1986 All-Star Game. Background for the 2-1/2" x 5" cards is the Houston Astrodome, site of the 1986 mid-summer classic. Retail packs included one Pop-Up card, three All-Star cards and one Roberto Clemente puzzle card.

		MT
Complete Set (20):		3.00
Common Player:		.10
Roberto Clemente Puzzle:		6.00
(1)	Wade Boggs	.50
(2)	Gary Carter	.25
(3)	Roger Clemens	.75
(4)	Dwight Gooden	.25
(5)	Tony Gwynn	.75
(6)	Rickey Henderson	.40
(7)	Keith Hernandez	.15
(8)	Whitey Herzog	.10
(9)	Dick Howser	.10
(10)	Wally Joyner	.10
(11)	Dale Murphy	.30
(12)	Lance Parrish	.10
(13)	Kirby Puckett	.75
(14)	Cal Ripken, Jr.	1.00
(15)	Ryne Sandberg	.60
(16)	Mike Schmidt	.75
(17)	Ozzie Smith	.40
(18)	Darryl Strawberry	.25
(19)	Lou Whitaker	.10
(20)	Dave Winfield	.35

1987 Donruss Rookies

As they did in 1986, Donruss issued a 56-card set highlighting the major leagues' most promising rookies. The cards are standard 2-1/2" x 3-1/2" and are identical in design to the regular Donruss issue. The card fronts have green borders as opposed to the black found in the regular issue and carry the words "The Rookies" in the lower-left portion of the card. The set came housed in a specially designed box and was available only through hobby dealers.

		MT
Comp. Unopened Set (56):		20.00
Complete Set (56):		15.00
Common Player:		.05
1	Mark McGwire	10.00
2	Eric Bell	.05
3	Mark Williamson	.05
4	Mike Greenwell	.05
5	Ellis Burks	.10
6	DeWayne Buice	.05
7	Mark Mclemore (McLemore)	.10
8	Devon White	.10
9	Willie Fraser	.05
10	Lester Lancaster	.05
11	Ken Williams	.05
12	Matt Nokes	.05
13	Jeff Robinson	.05
14	Bo Jackson	.50
15	Kevin Seitzer	.05
16	Billy Ripken	.05
17	B.J. Surhoff	.10
18	Chuck Crim	.05
19	Mike Birbeck	.05
20	Chris Bosio	.05
21	Les Straker	.05
22	Mark Davidson	.05
23	Gene Larkin	.05
24	Ken Gerhart	.05
25	Luis Polonia	.05
26	Terry Steinbach	.05
27	Mickey Brantley	.05
28	Mike Stanley	.05
29	Jerry Browne	.05
30	Todd Benzinger	.05
31	Fred McGriff	.75
32	Mike Henneman	.05
33	Casey Candaele	.05
34	Dave Magadan	.05
35	David Cone	.75
36	Mike Jackson	.05
37	John Mitchell	.05
38	Mike Dunne	.05
39	John Smiley	.05
40	Joe Magrane	.05
41	Jim Lindeman	.05
42	Shane Mack	.05
43	Stan Jefferson	.05
44	Benito Santiago	.10
45	*Matt Williams*	2.00
46	Dave Meads	.05
47	Rafael Palmeiro	2.00
48	Bill Long	.05
49	Bob Brower	.05
50	James Steels	.05
51	Paul Noce	.05
52	Greg Maddux	6.00
53	Jeff Musselman	.05
54	Brian Holton	.05
55	Chuck Jackson	.05
56	Checklist 1-56	.03

1988 Donruss

The 1988 Donruss set consists of 660 cards, each measuring 2-1/2" x 3-1/2". Fronts feature a full-color photo surrounded by a colorful border - alternating stripes of black, red, black, blue, black, blue, black, red and black (in that order) - separated by soft-focus edges and airbrushed fades. The player's name and position appear in a red band at the bottom of the card. The Donruss logo is situated in the upper-left corner, while the team logo is located in the lower-right. For the seventh consecutive season, Donruss included a subset of "Diamond Kings" cards (#1-27) in the issue. And for the fifth straight year, Donruss incorporated the popular "Rated Rookies" (card #28-47) with the set. Twenty-six of the cards between #603-660 were short-printed to accommodate the printing of the 26 MVP insert cards.

	MT
Comp. Factory Set, Sealed (660):	10.00
Complete Set (660):	7.50
Common Player:	.05
Stan Musial Puzzle:	1.00
Pack (15):	.60
Wax Box (36):	10.00

1 Mark McGwire (DK) .75
2 Tim Raines (DK) .10
3 Benito Santiago (DK) .05
4 Alan Trammell (DK) .10
5 Danny Tartabull (DK) .05
6 Ron Darling (DK) .05
7 Paul Molitor (DK) .15
8 Devon White (DK) .10
9 Andre Dawson (DK) .15
10 Julio Franco (DK) .05
11 Scott Fletcher (DK) .05
12 Tony Fernandez (DK) .10
13 Shane Rawley (DK) .05
14 Kal Daniels (DK) .05
15 Jack Clark (DK) .10
16 Dwight Evans (DK) .10
17 Tommy John (DK) .10
18 Andy Van Slyke (DK) .10
19 Gary Gaetti (DK) .10
20 Mark Langston (DK) .10
21 Will Clark (DK) .20
22 Glenn Hubbard (DK) .05
23 Billy Hatcher (DK) .05
24 Bob Welch (DK) .05
25 Ivan Calderon (DK) .05
26 Cal Ripken, Jr. (DK) .50
27 Checklist 1-27 .05
28 *Mackey Sasser* (RR) .10
29 *Jeff Treadway* (RR) .05
30 *Mike Campbell* (RR) .05
31 *Lance Johnson* (RR) .15
32 *Nelson Liriano* (RR) .10
33 Shawn Abner (RR) .05
34 *Roberto Alomar* (RR) 1.50
35 *Shawn Hillegas* (RR) .05
36 Joey Meyer (RR) .05
37 Kevin Elster (RR) .05
38 *Jose Lind* (RR) .10
39 *Kirt Manwaring* (RR) .15
40 *Mark Grace* (RR) .50
41 *Jody Reed* (RR) .15
42 *John Farrell* (RR) .05
43 *Al Leiter* (RR) .25
44 *Gary Thurman* (RR) .10
45 *Vicente Palacios* (RR) .05
46 *Eddie Williams* (RR) .10
47 *Jack McDowell* (RR) .25
48 Ken Dixon .05
49 Mike Birkbeck .05
50 Eric King .05
51 Roger Clemens .40
52 Pat Clements .05
53 Fernando Valenzuela .10
54 Mark Gubicza .05
55 Jay Howell .05
56 Floyd Youmans .05
57 Ed Correa .05
58 *DeWayne Buice* .10
59 Jose DeLeon .05
60 Danny Cox .05
61 Nolan Ryan .60
62 Steve Bedrosian .05
63 Tom Browning .05
64 Mark Davis .05
65 R.J. Reynolds .05
66 Kevin Mitchell .05
67 Ken Oberkfell .05
68 Rick Sutcliffe .10
69 Dwight Gooden .10
70 Scott Bankhead .05
71 Bert Blyleven .10
72 Jimmy Key .05
73 *Les Straker* .05
74 Jim Clancy .05
75 Mike Moore .05
76 Ron Darling .05
77 Ed Lynch .05
78 Dale Murphy .15
79 Doug Drabek .05
80 Scott Garrelts .05
81 Ed Whitson .05
82 Rob Murphy .05
83 Shane Rawley .05
84 Greg Mathews .05
85 Jim Deshaies .05
86 Mike Witt .05
87 Donnie Hill .05
88 Jeff Reed .05
89 Mike Boddicker .05
90 Ted Higuera .05
91 Walt Terrell .05
92 Bob Stanley .05
93 Dave Righetti .05
94 Orel Hershiser .10
95 Chris Bando .05
96 Bret Saberhagen .05
97 Curt Young .05
98 Tim Burke .05
99 Charlie Hough .05
100a Checklist 28-137 .05
100b Checklist 28-133 .05
101 Bobby Witt .05
102 George Brett .40
103 Mickey Tettleton .05
104 Scott Bailes .05
105 Mike Pagliarulo .05
106 Mike Scioscia .05
107 Tom Brookens .05
108 Ray Knight .10
109 Dan Plesac .05
110 Wally Joyner .05
111 Bob Forsch .05
112 Mike Scott .05
113 Kevin Gross .05
114 Benito Santiago .05
115 Bob Kipper .05
116 Mike Krukow .05
117 Chris Bosio .05
118 Sid Fernandez .05
119 Jody Davis .05
120 Mike Morgan .05
121 Mark Eichhorn .05
122 Jeff Reardon .05
123 John Franco .10
124 Richard Dotson .05
125 Eric Bell .05
126 Juan Nieves .05
127 Jack Morris .10
128 Rick Rhoden .05
129 Rich Gedman .05
130 Ken Howell .05
131 Brook Jacoby .05
132 Danny Jackson .05
133 Gene Nelson .05
134 Neal Heaton .05
135 Willie Fraser .05
136 Jose Guzman .05
137 Ozzie Guillen .05
138 Bob Knepper .05
139 *Mike Jackson* .10
140 *Joe Magrane* .05
141 Jimmy Jones .05
142 Ted Power .05
143 Ozzie Virgil .05
144 *Felix Fermin* .10
145 Kelly Downs .05
146 Shawon Dunston .05
147 Scott Bradley .05
148 Dave Stieb .05
149 Frank Viola .05
150 Terry Kennedy .05
151 Bill Wegman .05
152 *Matt Nokes* .10
153 Wade Boggs .35
154 Wayne Tolleson .05
155 Mariano Duncan .05
156 Julio Franco .05
157 Charlie Leibrandt .05
158 Terry Steinbach .05
159 Mike Fitzgerald .05
160 Jack Lazorko .05
161 Mitch Williams .05
162 Greg Walker .05
163 Alan Ashby .05
164 Tony Gwynn .40
165 Bruce Ruffin .05
166 Ron Robinson .05
167 Zane Smith .05
168 Junior Ortiz .05
169 Jamie Moyer .05
170 Tony Pena .05
171 Cal Ripken, Jr. .60
172 B.J. Surhoff .10
173 Lou Whitaker .10
174 *Ellis Burks* .25
175 Ron Guidry .10
176 Steve Sax .05
177 Danny Tartabull .05
178 Carney Lansford .05
179 Casey Candaele .05
180 Scott Fletcher .05
181 Mark McLemore .05
182 Ivan Calderon .05
183 Jack Clark .10
184 Glenn Davis .05
185 Luis Aguayo .05
186 Bo Diaz .05
187 Stan Jefferson .05
188 Sid Bream .05
189 Bob Brenly .05
190 Dion James .05
191 Leon Durham .05
192 Jesse Orosco .05
193 Alvin Davis .05
194 Gary Gaetti .10
195 Fred McGriff .05
196 Steve Lombardozzi .05
197 Rance Mulliniks .05
198 Rey Quinones .05
199 Gary Carter .10
200a Checklist 138-247 .05
200b Checklist 134-239 .05
201 Keith Moreland .05
202 Ken Griffey .10
203 *Tommy Gregg* .05
204 Will Clark .15
205 John Kruk .10
206 Buddy Bell .10
207 Von Hayes .05
208 Tommy Herr .05
209 Craig Reynolds .05
210 Gary Pettis .05
211 Harold Baines .10
212 Vance Law .05
213 Ken Gerhart .05
214 Jim Gantner .05
215 Chet Lemon .05
216 Dwight Evans .10
217 Don Mattingly .35
218 Franklin Stubbs .05
219 Pat Tabler .05
220 Bo Jackson .20
221 Tony Phillips .05
222 Tim Wallach .05
223 Ruben Sierra .05
224 Steve Buechele .05
225 Frank White .05
226 Alfredo Griffin .05
227 Greg Swindell .05
228 Willie Randolph .10
229 Mike Marshall .05
230 Alan Trammell .15
231 Eddie Murray .30
232 Dale Sveum .05
233 Dick Schofield .05
234 Jose Oquendo .05
235 Bill Doran .05
236 Milt Thompson .05
237 Marvell Wynne .05
238 Bobby Bonilla .10
239 Chris Speier .05
240 Glenn Braggs .05
241 Wally Backman .05
242 Ryne Sandberg .35
243 Phil Bradley .05
244 Kelly Gruber .05
245 Tom Brunansky .05
246 Ron Oester .05
247 Bobby Thigpen .05
248 Fred Lynn .10
249 Paul Molitor .35
250 Darrell Evans .10
251 Gary Ward .05
252 Bruce Hurst .05
253 Bob Welch .05
254 Joe Carter .05
255 Willie Wilson .05
256 Mark McGwire 1.50
257 Mitch Webster .05
258 Brian Downing .05
259 Mike Stanley .05
260 Carlton Fisk .25
261 Billy Hatcher .05
262 Glenn Wilson .05
263 Ozzie Smith .35
264 Randy Ready .05
265 Kurt Stillwell .05
266 David Palmer .05
267 Mike Diaz .05
268 Rob Thompson .05
269 Andre Dawson .15
270 Lee Guetterman .05
271 Willie Upshaw .05
272 Randy Bush .05
273 Larry Sheets .05
274 Rob Deer .05
275 Kirk Gibson .10
276 Marty Barrett .05
277 Rickey Henderson .35
278 Pedro Guerrero .05
279 Brett Butler .05
280 Kevin Seitzer .05
281 Mike Davis .05
282 Andres Galarraga .10
283 Devon White .10
284 Pete O'Brien .05
285 Jerry Hairston Sr. .05
286 Kevin Bass .05
287 Carmelo Martinez .05
288 Juan Samuel .05
289 Kal Daniels .05
290 Albert Hall .05
291 Andy Van Slyke .10
292 Lee Smith .10
293 Vince Coleman .10
294 Tom Niedenfuer .05
295 Robin Yount .35
296 *Jeff Robinson* .05
297 *Todd Benzinger* .10
298 Dave Winfield .25
299 Mickey Hatcher .05
300a Checklist 248-357 .05
300b Checklist 240-345 .05
301 Bud Black .05
302 Jose Canseco .20
303 Tom Foley .05
304 Pete Incaviglia .05
305 Bob Boone .10
306 *Bill Long* .05
307 Willie McGee .10
308 *Ken Caminiti* .40
309 Darren Daulton .10
310 Tracy Jones .05
311 Greg Booker .05
312 Mike LaValliere .05
313 Chili Davis .05
314 Glenn Hubbard .05
315 *Paul Noce* .05
316 Keith Hernandez .10
317 Mark Langston .10
318 Keith Atherton .05
319 Tony Fernandez .05
320 Kent Hrbek .10
321 John Cerutti .05
322 Mike Kingery .05
323 Dave Magadan .10
324 Rafael Palmeiro .20
325 Jeff Dedmon .05
326 Barry Bonds .50
327 Jeffrey Leonard .05
328 Tim Flannery .05

No.	Player	Value
329	Dave Concepcion	.05
330	Mike Schmidt	.35
331	Bill Dawley	.05
332	Larry Andersen	.05
333	Jack Howell	.05
334	*Ken Williams*	.05
335	Bryn Smith	.05
336	*Billy Ripken*	.10
337	Greg Brock	.05
338	Mike Heath	.05
339	Mike Greenwell	.05
340	Claudell Washington	.05
341	Jose Gonzalez	.05
342	Mel Hall	.05
343	Jim Eisenreich	.05
344	Tony Bernazard	.05
345	Tim Raines	.10
346	Bob Brower	.05
347	Larry Parrish	.05
348	Thad Bosley	.05
349	Dennis Eckersley	.10
350	Cory Snyder	.05
351	Rick Cerone	.05
352	John Shelby	.05
353	Larry Herndon	.05
354	John Habyan	.05
355	*Chuck Crim*	.05
356	Gus Polidor	.05
357	Ken Dayley	.05
358	Danny Darwin	.05
359	Lance Parrish	.10
360	*James Steels*	.05
361	*Al Pedrique*	.05
362	Mike Aldrete	.05
363	Juan Castillo	.05
364	Len Dykstra	.10
365	Luis Quinones	.05
366	Jim Presley	.05
367	Lloyd Moseby	.05
368	Kirby Puckett	.50
369	Eric Davis	.10
370	Gary Redus	.05
371	Dave Schmidt	.05
372	Mark Clear	.05
373	Dave Bergman	.05
374	Charles Hudson	.05
375	Calvin Schiraldi	.05
376	Alex Trevino	.05
377	Tom Candiotti	.05
378	Steve Farr	.05
379	Mike Gallego	.05
380	Andy McGaffigan	.05
381	Kirk McCaskill	.05
382	Oddibe McDowell	.05
383	Floyd Bannister	.05
384	Denny Walling	.05
385	Don Carman	.05
386	Todd Worrell	.05
387	Eric Show	.05
388	Dave Parker	.10
389	Rick Mahler	.05
390	*Mike Dunne*	.10
391	Candy Maldonado	.05
392	Bob Dernier	.05
393	Dave Valle	.05
394	Ernie Whitt	.05
395	Juan Berenguer	.05
396	Mike Young	.05
397	Mike Felder	.05
398	Willie Hernandez	.05
399	Jim Rice	.15
400a	Checklist 358-467	.05
400b	Checklist 346-451	.05
401	Tommy John	.10
402	Brian Holton	.05
403	Carmen Castillo	.05
404	Jamie Quirk	.05
405	Dwayne Murphy	.05
406	*Jeff Parrett*	.05
407	Don Sutton	.20
408	Jerry Browne	.05
409	Jim Winn	.05
410	Dave Smith	.05
411	*Shane Mack*	.15
412	Greg Gross	.05
413	Nick Esasky	.05
414	Damaso Garcia	.05
415	Brian Fisher	.05
416	Brian Dayett	.05
417	Curt Ford	.05
418	*Mark Williamson*	.05
419	Bill Schroeder	.05
420	*Mike Henneman*	.15
421	*John Marzano*	.05
422	Ron Kittle	.05
423	Matt Young	.05
424	Steve Balboni	.05
425	*Luis Polonia*	.10
426	Randy St. Claire	.05
427	Greg Harris	.05
428	Johnny Ray	.05
429	Ray Searage	.05
430	Ricky Horton	.05
431	*Gerald Young*	.05
432	Rick Schu	.05
433	Paul O'Neill	.10
434	Rich Gossage	.10
435	John Cangelosi	.05
436	Mike LaCoss	.05
437	Gerald Perry	.05
438	Dave Martinez	.05
439	Darryl Strawberry	.10
440	John Moses	.05
441	Greg Gagne	.05
442	Jesse Barfield	.05
443	George Frazier	.05
444	Garth Iorg	.05
445	Ed Nunez	.05
446	Rick Aguilera	.05
447	Jerry Mumphrey	.05
448	Rafael Ramirez	.05
449	*John Smiley*	.10
450	Atlee Hammaker	.05
451	Lance McCullers	.05
452	Guy Hoffman	.05
453	Chris James	.05
454	Terry Pendleton	.05
455	*Dave Meads*	.05
456	Bill Buckner	.10
457	*John Pawlowski*	.05
458	Bob Sebra	.05
459	Jim Dwyer	.05
460	*Jay Aldrich*	.05
461	Frank Tanana	.05
462	Oil Can Boyd	.05
463	Dan Pasqua	.05
464	*Tim Crews*	.10
465	Andy Allanson	.05
466	*Bill Pecota*	.05
467	Steve Ontiveros	.05
468	Hubie Brooks	.05
469	*Paul Kilgus*	.05
470	Dale Mohorcic	.05
471	Dan Quisenberry	.05
472	Dave Stewart	.10
473	Dave Clark	.05
474	Joel Skinner	.05
475	Dave Anderson	.05
476	Dan Petry	.05
477	*Carl Nichols*	.05
478	Ernest Riles	.05
479	George Hendrick	.05
480	John Morris	.05
481	*Manny Hernandez*	.05
482	Jeff Stone	.05
483	Chris Brown	.05
484	Mike Bielecki	.05
485	Dave Dravecky	.05
486	Rick Manning	.05
487	Bill Almon	.05
488	Jim Sundberg	.05
489	Ken Phelps	.05
490	Tom Henke	.05
491	Dan Gladden	.05
492	Barry Larkin	.15
493	*Fred Manrique*	.05
494	Mike Griffin	.05
495	*Mark Knudson*	.05
496	Bill Madlock	.05
497	Tim Stoddard	.05
498	*Sam Horn*	.05
499	*Tracy Woodson*	.05
500a	Checklist 468-577	.05
500b	Checklist 452-557	.05
501	Ken Schrom	.05
502	Angel Salazar	.05
503	Eric Plunk	.05
504	Joe Hesketh	.05
505	Greg Minton	.05
506	Geno Petralli	.05
507	Bob James	.05
508	*Robbie Wine*	.05
509	Jeff Calhoun	.05
510	Steve Lake	.05
511	Mark Grant	.05
512	Frank Williams	.05
513	*Jeff Blauser*	.15
514	Bob Walk	.05
515	Craig Lefferts	.05
516	Manny Trillo	.05
517	Jerry Reed	.05
518	Rick Leach	.05
519	*Mark Davidson*	.05
520	*Jeff Ballard*	.05
521	*Dave Stapleton*	.05
522	Pat Sheridan	.05
523	Al Nipper	.05
524	Steve Trout	.05
525	Jeff Hamilton	.05
526	*Tommy Hinzo*	.05
527	Lonnie Smith	.05
528	*Greg Cadaret*	.05
529	Rob McClure (Bob)	.05
530	Chuck Finley	.05
531	Jeff Russell	.05
532	Steve Lyons	.05
533	Terry Puhl	.05
534	*Eric Nolte*	.05
535	Kent Tekulve	.05
536	*Pat Pacillo*	.05
537	Charlie Puleo	.05
538	*Tom Prince*	.05
539	Greg Maddux	.50
540	Jim Lindeman	.05
541	*Pete Stanicek*	.05
542	Steve Kiefer	.05
543	Jim Morrison	.05
544	Spike Owen	.05
545	*Jay Buhner*	.75
546	*Mike Devereaux*	.15
547	Jerry Don Gleaton	.05
548	Jose Rijo	.05
549	Dennis Martinez	.05
550	Mike Loynd	.05
551	Darrell Miller	.05
552	Dave LaPoint	.05
553	John Tudor	.05
554	*Rocky Childress*	.05
555	*Wally Ritchie*	.05
556	Terry McGriff	.05
557	Dave Leiper	.05
558	Jeff Robinson	.05
559	Jose Uribe	.05
560	Ted Simmons	.05
561	*Lester Lancaster*	.10
562	*Keith Miller*	.05
563	Harold Reynolds	.10
564	*Gene Larkin*	.05
565	Cecil Fielder	.05
566	Roy Smalley	.05
567	Duane Ward	.05
568	*Bill Wilkinson*	.05
569	Howard Johnson	.05
570	Frank DiPino	.05
571	*Pete Smith*	.05
572	Darnell Coles	.05
573	Don Robinson	.05
574	Rob Nelson	.05
575	Dennis Rasmussen	.05
576	Steve Jeltz (photo actually Juan Samuel)	.05
577	*Tom Pagnozzi*	.10
578	Ty Gainey	.05
579	Gary Lucas	.05
580	Ron Hassey	.05
581	Herm Winningham	.05
582	*Rene Gonzales*	.05
583	Brad Komminsk	.05
584	Doyle Alexander	.05
585	Jeff Sellers	.05
586	Bill Gullickson	.05
587	Tim Belcher	.05
588	*Doug Jones*	.10
589	*Melido Perez*	.10
590	Rick Honeycutt	.05
591	Pascual Perez	.05
592	Curt Wilkerson	.05
593	Steve Howe	.05
594	*John Davis*	.05
595	Storm Davis	.05
596	Sammy Stewart	.05
597	Neil Allen	.05
598	Alejandro Pena	.05
599	Mark Thurmond	.05
600a	Checklist 578-BC26	.05
600b	Checklist 558-660	.05
601	*Jose Mesa*	.15
602	*Don August*	.05
603	Terry Leach (SP)	.10
604	*Tom Newell*	.05
605	*Randall Byers* (SP)	.10
606	Jim Gott	.05
607	Harry Spilman	.05
608	John Candelaria	.05
609	*Mike Brumley*	.05
610	Mickey Brantley	.05
611	*Jose Nunez* (SP)	.10
612	Tom Nieto	.05
613	Rick Reuschel	.05
614	Lee Mazzilli (SP)	.10
615	*Scott Lusader*	.05
616	Bobby Meacham	.05
617	Kevin McReynolds (SP)	.15
618	Gene Garber	.05
619	*Barry Lyons* (SP)	.10
620	Randy Myers	.05
621	Donnie Moore	.05
622	Domingo Ramos	.05
623	Ed Romero	.05
624	*Greg Myers*	.10
625	Ripken Baseball Family (Billy Ripken, Cal Ripken, Jr., Cal Ripken, Sr.)	.30
626	Pat Perry	.05
627	Andres Thomas (SP)	.10
628	Matt Williams (SP)	.60
629	*Dave Hengel*	.05
630	Jeff Musselman (SP)	.10
631	Tim Laudner	.05
632	Bob Ojeda (SP)	.10
633	Rafael Santana	.05
634	*Wes Gardner*	.05
635	*Roberto Kelly* (SP)	.15
636	Mike Flanagan (SP)	.10
637	*Jay Bell*	.35
638	Bob Melvin	.05
639	*Damon Berryhill*	.10
640	*David Wells* (SP)	.40
641	Stan Musial Puzzle Card	.05
642	Doug Sisk	.05
643	*Keith Hughes*	.05
644	*Tom Glavine*	.50
645	Al Newman	.05
646	Scott Sanderson	.05
647	Scott Terry	.05
648	Tim Teufel (SP)	.10
649	Garry Templeton (SP)	.10
650	Manny Lee (SP)	.10
651	Roger McDowell (SP)	.15
652	Mookie Wilson (SP)	.15
653	David Cone (SP)	.15
654	*Ron Gant* (SP)	.25
655	Joe Price (SP)	.10
656	George Bell (SP)	.15
657	*Gregg Jefferies* (SP)	.25
658	*Todd Stottlemyre* (SP)	.25
659	*Geronimo Berroa* (SP)	.25
660	Jerry Royster (SP)	.10

1988 Donruss All-Stars

For the third consecutive year, this set of 64 cards was marketed in conjunction with Donruss Pop-Ups. The 1988 issue included a major change - the cards were reduced in size from 3-1/2" x 5" to a standard 2-1/2" x 3-1/2". The set features players from the 1987 All-Star Game starting lineup. Card fronts feature full-color photos, framed in blue, black and white, with a Donruss logo at upper-left.

Player name and position appear in a red banner below the photo, along with the appropriate National or American League logo. Backs include player stats and All-Star Game record. In 1988, All-Stars cards were distributed in individual packages containing three All-Stars, one Pop-Up and three Stan Musial puzzle pieces.

		MT
Complete Set (64):		2.50
Common Player:		.10
Stan Musial Puzzle:		1.00
1	Don Mattingly	.75
2	Dave Winfield	.50
3	Willie Randolph	.10
4	Rickey Henderson	.40
5	Cal Ripken, Jr.	1.25
6	George Bell	.10
7	Wade Boggs	.60
8	Bret Saberhagen	.10
9	Terry Kennedy	.10
10	John McNamara	.10
11	Jay Howell	.10
12	Harold Baines	.10
13	Harold Reynolds	.10
14	Bruce Hurst	.10
15	Kirby Puckett	.75
16	Matt Nokes	.10
17	Pat Tabler	.10
18	Dan Plesac	.10
19	Mark McGwire	1.25
20	Mike Witt	.10
21	Larry Parrish	.10
22	Alan Trammell	.10
23	Dwight Evans	.10
24	Jack Morris	.10
25	Tony Fernandez	.10
26	Mark Langston	.10
27	Kevin Seitzer	.10
28	Tom Henke	.10
29	Dave Righetti	.10
30	Oakland Coliseum	.10
31	Wade Boggs (Top Vote Getter)	.35
32	Checklist 1-32	.05
33	Jack Clark	.10
34	Darryl Strawberry	.10
35	Ryne Sandberg	.75
36	Andre Dawson	.10
37	Ozzie Smith	.40
38	Eric Davis	.10
39	Mike Schmidt	.75
40	Mike Scott	.10
41	Gary Carter	.15
42	Davey Johnson	.10
43	Rick Sutcliffe	.10
44	Willie McGee	.10
45	Hubie Brooks	.10
46	Dale Murphy	.30
47	Bo Diaz	.10
48	Pedro Guerrero	.10
49	Keith Hernandez	.10
50	Ozzie Virgil	.10
51	Tony Gwynn	.75
52	Rick Reuschel	.10
53	John Franco	.10
54	Jeffrey Leonard	.10
55	Juan Samuel	.10
56	Orel Hershiser	.10
57	Tim Raines	.10
58	Sid Fernandez	.10
59	Tim Wallach	.10
60	Lee Smith	.10
61	Steve Bedrosian	.10
62	(Tim Raines) (MVP)	.10
63	(Ozzie Smith) (Top Vote Getter)	.15
64	Checklist 33-64	.05

1988 Donruss Baseball's Best

The design of this 336-card set is similar to the regular 1988 Donruss issue with the exception of the borders which are orange, instead of blue. Player photos on the glossy front are framed by the Donruss logo upper-left, team logo lower-right and a bright red and white player name that spans the bottom margin. Backs are black and white, framed by a yellow border, and include personal information, year-by-year stats and major league totals. This set was packaged in a bright red cardboard box containing six individually shrink-wrapped packs of 56 cards. Donruss marketed the set via retail chain outlets with a suggested retail price of $21.95.

		MT
Complete Set (336):		9.00
Common Player:		.05
1	Don Mattingly	.75
2	Ron Gant	.05
3	Bob Boone	.05
4	Mark Grace	.30
5	Andy Allanson	.05
6	Kal Daniels	.05
7	Floyd Bannister	.05
8	Alan Ashby	.05
9	Marty Barrett	.05
10	Tim Belcher	.05
11	Harold Baines	.05
12	Hubie Brooks	.05
13	Doyle Alexander	.05
14	Gary Carter	.10
15	Glenn Braggs	.05
16	Steve Bedrosian	.05
17	Barry Bonds	.75
18	Bert Blyleven	.10
19	Tom Brunansky	.05
20	John Candelaria	.05
21	Shawn Abner	.05
22	Jose Canseco	.30
23	Brett Butler	.05
24	Scott Bradley	.05
25	Ivan Calderon	.05
26	Rich Gossage	.05
27	Brian Downing	.05
28	Jim Rice	.10
29	Dion James	.05
30	Terry Kennedy	.05
31	George Bell	.05
32	Scott Fletcher	.05
33	Bobby Bonilla	.05
34	Tim Burke	.05
35	Darrell Evans	.10
36	Mike Davis	.05
37	Shawon Dunston	.05
38	Kevin Bass	.05
39	George Brett	.60
40	David Cone	.05
41	Ron Darling	.05
42	Roberto Alomar	.30
43	Dennis Eckersley	.10
44	Vince Coleman	.05
45	Sid Bream	.05
46	Gary Gaetti	.05
47	Phil Bradley	.05
48	Jim Clancy	.05
49	Jack Clark	.05
50	Mike Krukow	.05
51	Henry Cotto	.05
52	Rich Dotson	.05
53	Jim Gantner	.05
54	John Franco	.05
55	Pete Incaviglia	.05
56	Joe Carter	.05
57	Roger Clemens	.75
58	Gerald Perry	.05
59	Jack Howell	.05
60	Vance Law	.05
61	Jay Bell	.05
62	Eric Davis	.05
63	Gene Garber	.05
64	Glenn Davis	.05
65	Wade Boggs	.45
66	Kirk Gibson	.05
67	Carlton Fisk	.30
68	Casey Candaele	.05
69	Mike Heath	.05
70	Kevin Elster	.05
71	Greg Brock	.05
72	Don Carman	.05
73	Doug Drabek	.05
74	Greg Gagne	.05
75	Danny Cox	.05
76	Rickey Henderson	.35
77	Chris Brown	.05
78	Terry Steinbach	.05
79	Will Clark	.15
80	Mickey Brantley	.05
81	Ozzie Guillen	.05
82	Greg Maddux	.50
83	Kirk McCaskill	.05
84	Dwight Evans	.10
85	Ozzie Virgil	.05
86	Mike Morgan	.05
87	Tony Fernandez	.05
88	Jose Guzman	.05
89	Mike Dunne	.05
90	Andres Galarraga	.10
91	Mike Henneman	.05
92	Alfredo Griffin	.05
93	Rafael Palmeiro	.10
94	Jim Deshaies	.05
95	Mark Gubicza	.05
96	Dwight Gooden	.05
97	Howard Johnson	.05
98	Mark Davis	.05
99	Dave Stewart	.05
100	Joe Magrane	.05
101	Brian Fisher	.05
102	Kent Hrbek	.05
103	Kevin Gross	.05
104	Tom Henke	.05
105	Mike Pagliarulo	.05
106	Kelly Downs	.05
107	Alvin Davis	.05
108	Willie Randolph	.05
109	Rob Deer	.05
110	Bo Diaz	.05
111	Paul Kilgus	.05
112	Tom Candiotti	.05
113	Dale Murphy	.15
114	Rick Mahler	.05
115	Wally Joyner	.05
116	Ryne Sandberg	.50
117	John Farrell	.05
118	Nick Esasky	.05
119	Bo Jackson	.25
120	Bill Doran	.05
121	Ellis Burks	.05
122	Pedro Guerrero	.05
123	Dave LaPoint	.05
124	Neal Heaton	.05
125	Willie Hernandez	.05
126	Roger McDowell	.05
127	Ted Higuera	.05
128	Von Hayes	.05
129	Mike LaValliere	.05
130	Dan Gladden	.05
131	Willie McGee	.05
132	Al Lieter	.05
133	Mark Grant	.05
134	Bob Welch	.05
135	Dave Dravecky	.05
136	Mark Langston	.05
137	Dan Pasqua	.05
138	Rick Sutcliffe	.05
139	Dan Petry	.05
140	Rich Gedman	.05
141	Ken Griffey	.05
142	Eddie Murray	.30
143	Jimmy Key	.05
144	Dale Mohorcic	.05
145	Jose Lind	.05
146	Dennis Martinez	.05
147	Chet Lemon	.05
148	Orel Hershiser	.05
149	Dave Martinez	.05
150	Billy Hatcher	.05
151	Charlie Leibrandt	.05
152	Keith Hernandez	.05
153	Kevin McReynolds	.05
154	Tony Gwynn	.75
155	Stan Javier	.05
156	Tony Pena	.05
157	Andy Van Slyke	.05
158	Gene Larkin	.05
159	Chris James	.05
160	Fred McGriff	.05
161	Rick Rhoden	.05
162	Scott Garrelts	.05
163	Mike Campbell	.05
164	Dave Righetti	.05
165	Paul Molitor	.20
166	Danny Jackson	.05
167	Pete O'Brien	.05
168	Julio Franco	.05
169	Mark McGwire	1.00
170	Zane Smith	.05
171	Johnny Ray	.05
172	Lester Lancaster	.05
173	Mel Hall	.05
174	Tracy Jones	.05
175	Kevin Seitzer	.05
176	Bob Knepper	.05
177	Mike Greenwell	.05
178	Mike Marshall	.05
179	Melido Perez	.05
180	Tim Raines	.05
181	Jack Morris	.05
182	Darryl Strawberry	.05
183	Robin Yount	.30
184	Lance Parrish	.05
185	Darnell Coles	.05
186	Kirby Puckett	.45
187	Terry Pendleton	.05
188	Don Slaught	.05
189	Jimmy Jones	.05
190	Dave Parker	.05
191	Mike Aldrete	.05
192	Mike Moore	.05
193	Greg Walker	.05
194	Calvin Schiraldi	.05
195	Dick Schofield	.05
196	Jody Reed	.05
197	Pete Smith	.05
198	Cal Ripken, Jr.	1.00
199	Lloyd Moseby	.05
200	Ruben Sierra	.05
201	R.J. Reynolds	.05
202	Bryn Smith	.05
203	Gary Pettis	.05
204	Steve Sax	.05
205	Frank DiPino	.05
206	Mike Scott	.05
207	Kurt Stillwell	.05
208	Mookie Wilson	.05
209	Lee Mazzilli	.05
210	Lance McCullers	.05
211	Rick Honeycutt	.05
212	John Tudor	.05
213	Jim Gott	.05
214	Frank Viola	.05
215	Juan Samuel	.05
216	Jesse Barfield	.05
217	Claudell Washington	.05
218	Rick Reuschel	.05
219	Jim Presley	.05
220	Tommy John	.05
221	Dan Plesac	.05
222	Barry Larkin	.10
223	Mike Stanley	.05
224	Cory Snyder	.05
225	Andre Dawson	.10
226	Ken Oberkfell	.05
227	Devon White	.10
228	Jamie Moyer	.05
229	Brook Jacoby	.05
230	Rob Murphy	.05
231	Bret Saberhagen	.10
232	Nolan Ryan	1.00
233	Bruce Hurst	.05
234	Jesse Orosco	.05
235	Bobby Thigpen	.05
236	Pascual Perez	.05
237	Matt Nokes	.05
238	Bob Ojeda	.05
239	Joey Meyer	.05

240	Shane Rawley	.05
241	Jeff Robinson	.05
242	Jeff Reardon	.05
243	Ozzie Smith	.30
244	Dave Winfield	.30
245	John Kruk	.05
246	Carney Lansford	.05
247	Candy Maldonado	.05
248	Ken Phelps	.05
249	Ken Williams	.05
250	Al Nipper	.05
251	Mark McLemore	.05
252	Lee Smith	.10
253	Albert Hall	.05
254	Billy Ripken	.05
255	Kelly Gruber	.05
256	Charlie Hough	.05
257	John Smiley	.05
258	Tim Wallach	.05
259	Frank Tanana	.05
260	Mike Scioscia	.05
261	Damon Berryhill	.05
262	Dave Smith	.05
263	Willie Wilson	.05
264	Len Dykstra	.05
265	Randy Myers	.05
266	Keith Moreland	.05
267	Eric Plunk	.05
268	Todd Worrell	.05
269	Bob Walk	.05
270	Keith Atherton	.05
271	Mike Schmidt	.60
272	Mike Flanagan	.05
273	Rafael Santana	.05
274	Rob Thompson	.05
275	Rey Quinones	.05
276	Cecilio Guante	.05
277	B.J. Surhoff	.10
278	Chris Sabo	.05
279	Mitch Williams	.05
280	Greg Swindell	.05
281	Alan Trammell	.10
282	Storm Davis	.05
283	Chuck Finley	.05
284	Dave Stieb	.05
285	Scott Bailes	.05
286	Larry Sheets	.05
287	Danny Tartabull	.05
288	Checklist	.05
289	Todd Benzinger	.05
290	John Shelby	.05
291	Steve Lyons	.05
292	Mitch Webster	.05
293	Walt Terrell	.05
294	Pete Stanicek	.05
295	Chris Bosio	.05
296	Milt Thompson	.05
297	Fred Lynn	.05
298	Juan Berenguer	.05
299	Ken Dayley	.05
300	Joel Skinner	.05
301	Benito Santiago	.05
302	Ron Hassey	.05
303	Jose Uribe	.05
304	Harold Reynolds	.05
305	Dale Sveum	.05
306	Glenn Wilson	.05
307	Mike Witt	.05
308	Ron Robinson	.05
309	Denny Walling	.05
310	Joe Orsulak	.05
311	David Wells	.05
312	Steve Buechele	.05
313	Jose Oquendo	.05
314	Floyd Youmans	.05
315	Lou Whitaker	.05
316	Fernando Valenzuela	.05
317	Mike Boddicker	.05
318	Gerald Young	.05
319	Frank White	.05
320	Bill Wegman	.05
321	Tom Niedenfuer	.05
322	Ed Whitson	.05
323	Curt Young	.05
324	Greg Mathews	.05
325	Doug Jones	.05
326	Tommy Herr	.05
327	Kent Tekulve	.05
328	Rance Mulliniks	.05
329	Checklist	.05
330	Craig Lefferts	.05
331	Franklin Stubbs	.05
332	Rick Cerone	.05
333	Dave Schmidt	.05
334	Larry Parrish	.05
335	Tom Browning	.05
336	Checklist	.05

1988 Donruss Diamond Kings Supers

This 28-card set (including the checklist) marks the fourth edition of Donruss' super-size (5" x 7") set. These cards are exact duplicates of the 1988 Diamond Kings that feature player portraits by Dick Perez. A 12-piece Stan Musial puzzle was also included with the purchase of the super-size set which was marketed via a mail-in offer printed on Donruss wrappers.

		MT
Complete Set (28):		5.00
Common Player:		.12
1	Mark McGwire	2.00
2	Tim Raines	.10
3	Benito Santiago	.10
4	Alan Trammell	.15
5	Danny Tartabull	.10
6	Ron Darling	.10
7	Paul Molitor	.25
8	Devon White	.10
9	Andre Dawson	.15
10	Julio Franco	.10
11	Scott Fletcher	.10
12	Tony Fernandez	.10
13	Shane Rawley	.10
14	Kal Daniels	.10
15	Jack Clark	.10
16	Dwight Evans	.10
17	Tommy John	.15
18	Andy Van Slyke	.10
19	Gary Gaetti	.10
20	Mark Langston	.10
21	Will Clark	.15
22	Glenn Hubbard	.10
23	Billy Hatcher	.10
24	Bob Welch	.10
25	Ivan Calderon	.10
26	Cal Ripken, Jr.	2.00
27	Checklist	.05
641	Stan Musial Puzzle Card	.10

1988 Donruss MVP

This 26-card set of standard-size player cards replaced the Donruss box-bottom cards in 1988. The bonus cards (numbered BC1 - BC26) were randomly inserted in Donruss wax or rack packs. Cards feature the company's choice of Most Valuable Player for each major league team and are titled "Donruss MVP." The MVP cards were not included in the factory-collated sets. Fronts carry the same basic red-blue-black border design as the 1988 Donruss basic issue. Backs are the same as the regular issue, except for the numbering system.

		MT
Complete Set (26):		4.00
Common Player:		.15
1	Cal Ripken, Jr.	1.00
2	Eric Davis	.15
3	Paul Molitor	.40
4	Mike Schmidt	.50
5	Ivan Calderon	.15
6	Tony Gwynn	.50
7	Wade Boggs	.40
8	Andy Van Slyke	.15
9	Joe Carter	.15
10	Andre Dawson	.20
11	Alan Trammell	.20
12	Mike Scott	.15
13	Wally Joyner	.15
14	Dale Murphy	.20
15	Kirby Puckett	.60
16	Pedro Guerrero	.15
17	Kevin Seitzer	.15
18	Tim Raines	.15
19	George Bell	.15
20	Darryl Strawberry	.25
21	Don Mattingly	.60
22	Ozzie Smith	.40
23	Mark McGwire	1.00
24	Will Clark	.25
25	Alvin Davis	.15
26	Ruben Sierra	.15

1988 Donruss Pop-Ups

Donruss' 1988 Pop-Up cards were reduced to the standard 2-1/2" x 3-1/2". The set includes 20 cards that fold out so that the upper portion of the player stands upright, giving a three-dimensional effect. Pop-Ups feature players from the All-Star Game starting lineup. Card fronts feature full-color photos, with the player's name, team and position printed in black on a yellow banner near the bottom. As in previous issues, the backs contain only the player's name, league and position. Pop-Ups were distributed in individual packages containing one Pop-Up, three Stan Musial puzzle pieces and three All-Star cards.

		MT
Complete Set (20):		2.00
Common Player:		.10
Stan Musial Puzzle:		1.00
(1)	George Bell	.10
(2)	Wade Boggs	.50
(3)	Gary Carter	.15
(4)	Jack Clark	.10
(5)	Eric Davis	.10
(6)	Andre Dawson	.15
(7)	Rickey Henderson	.35
(8)	Davey Johnson	.10
(9)	Don Mattingly	.75
(10)	Terry Kennedy	.10
(11)	John McNamara	.10
(12)	Willie Randolph	.10
(13)	Cal Ripken, Jr.	1.00
(14)	Bret Saberhagen	.10
(15)	Ryne Sandberg	.65
(16)	Mike Schmidt	.75
(17)	Mike Scott	.10
(18)	Ozzie Smith	.35
(19)	Darryl Strawberry	.10
(20)	Dave Winfield	.40

1988 Donruss Rookies

For the third consecutive year, Donruss issued a 56-card boxed set highlighting current rookies. The complete set includes a checklist and a 15-piece Stan Musial Diamond Kings puzzle. As in previous years, the set is similar to the company's basic issue, with the exception of the logo and border color. Card fronts feature red, green and black-striped borders, with a red-and-white player name printed in the lower-left corner beneath the photo. "The Rookies" logo is printed in red, white and black in the lower-right corner. Backs are printed in black on bright aqua and include personal data, recent performance stats and major league totals, as well as

1984-88 minor league stats. The cards are the standard 2-1/2" x 3-1/2".

		MT
Complete Set (56):		9.00
Common Player:		.10
1	Mark Grace	2.00
2	Mike Campbell	.10
3	Todd Frowirth	.10
4	Dave Stapleton	.10
5	Shawn Abner	.10
6	Jose Cecena	.10
7	Dave Gallagher	.10
8	Mark Parent	.10
9	Cecil Espy	.10
10	Pete Smith	.10
11	Jay Buhner	1.00
12	Pat Borders	.20
13	Doug Jennings	.10
14	*Brady Anderson*	1.00
15	Pete Stanicek	.10
16	Roberto Kelly	.15
17	Jeff Treadway	.10
18	Walt Weiss	.25
19	Paul Gibson	.10
20	Tim Crews	.10
21	Melido Perez	.10
22	Steve Peters	.10
23	Craig Worthington	.10
24	John Trautwein	.10
25	DeWayne Vaughn	.10
26	David Wells	1.50
27	Al Leiter	.15
28	Tim Belcher	.15
29	Johnny Paredes	.10
30	Chris Sabo	.20
31	Damon Berryhill	.10
32	Randy Milligan	.10
33	Gary Thurman	.10
34	Kevin Elster	.15
35	Roberto Alomar	5.00
36	*Edgar Martinez* (photo actually Edwin Nunez)	1.25
37	Todd Stottlemyre	.15
38	Joey Meyer	.10
39	Carl Nichols	.10
40	Jack McDowell	.20
41	Jose Bautista	.10
42	Sil Campusano	.10
43	John Dopson	.10
44	Jody Reed	.15
45	Darrin Jackson	.20
46	Mike Capel	.10
47	Ron Gant	.40
48	John Davis	.10
49	Kevin Coffman	.10
50	Cris Carpenter	.10
51	Mackey Sasser	.10
52	Luis Alicea	.10
53	Bryan Harvey	.10
54	Steve Ellsworth	.10
55	Mike Macfarlane	.10
56	Checklist 1-56	.05

1989 Donruss

This basic annual issue consists of 660 2-1/2" x 3-1/2" cards, including 26 Diamond Kings (DK) portrait cards and 20 Rated Rookies (RR) cards. Top and bottom borders of the cards are printed in a variety of colors that fade from dark to light. A white-lettered player name is printed across the top margin. The team logo appears upper-right and the Donruss logo lower-left. A black outer stripe varnish gives faintly visible film-strip texture to the border. Backs are in orange and black, similar to the 1988 design, with personal info, recent stats and major league totals. Team logo sticker cards (22 total) and Warren Spahn puzzle cards (63 total) are included in individual wax packs of cards. Each regular player card can be found with a back variation in the header line above the stats: i.e., "*Denotes" or "*Denotes*". Neither version carries a premium.

		MT
Unopened Factory Set (660):		30.00
Complete Set (660):		15.00
Common Player:		.05
Warren Spahn Puzzle:		1.00
Wax Pack (15):		1.25
Wax Box (36):		30.00
1	Mike Greenwell (DK)	.05
2	Bobby Bonilla (DK)	.10
3	Pete Incaviglia (DK)	.05
4	Chris Sabo (DK)	.10
5	Robin Yount (DK)	.20
6	Tony Gwynn (DK)	.35
7	Carlton Fisk (DK)	.20
8	Cory Snyder (DK)	.05
9	David Cone (DK)	.10
10	Kevin Seitzer (DK)	.05
11	Rick Reuschel (DK)	.05
12	Johnny Ray (DK)	.05
13	Dave Schmidt (DK)	.05
14	Andres Galarraga (DK)	.10
15	Kirk Gibson (DK)	.10
16	Fred McGriff (DK)	.05
17	Mark Grace (DK)	.25
18	Jeff Robinson (DK)	.05
19	Vince Coleman (DK)	.05
20	Dave Henderson (DK)	.05
21	Harold Reynolds (DK)	.10
22	Gerald Perry (DK)	.05
23	Frank Viola (DK)	.05
24	Steve Bedrosian (DK)	.05
25	Glenn Davis (DK)	.05
26	Don Mattingly (DK)	.30
27	Checklist 1-27	.05
28	*Sandy Alomar, Jr.* (RR)	.45
29	*Steve Searcy* (RR)	.10
30	*Cameron Drew* (RR)	.05
31	*Gary Sheffield* (RR)	.75
32	*Erik Hanson* (RR)	.25
33	*Ken Griffey, Jr.* (RR)	10.00
34	*Greg Harris* (RR)	.05
35	Gregg Jefferies (RR)	.10
36	*Luis Medina* (RR)	.05
37	*Carlos Quintana* (RR)	.05
38	*Felix Jose* (RR)	.15
39	*Cris Carpenter* (RR)	.05
40	*Ron Jones* (RR)	.05
41	*Dave West* (RR)	.10
42	*Randy Johnson* (RR)	3.00
43	*Mike Harkey* (RR)	.10
44	*Pete Harnisch* (RR)	.15
45	*Tom Gordon* (RR)	.25
46	*Gregg Olson* (RR)	.10
47	*Alex Sanchez* (RR)	.05
48	Ruben Sierra	.05
49	Rafael Palmeiro	.15
50	Ron Gant	.05
51	Cal Ripken, Jr.	.75
52	Wally Joyner	.05
53	Gary Carter	.10
54	Andy Van Slyke	.10
55	Robin Yount	.25
56	Pete Incaviglia	.05
57	Greg Brock	.05
58	Melido Perez	.05
59	Craig Lefferts	.05
60	Gary Pettis	.05
61	Danny Tartabull	.05
62	Guillermo Hernandez	.05
63	Ozzie Smith	.25
64	Gary Gaetti	.10
65	Mark Davis	.05
66	Lee Smith	.10
67	Dennis Eckersley	.10
68	Wade Boggs	.30
69	Mike Scott	.05
70	Fred McGriff	.05
71	Tom Browning	.05
72	Claudell Washington	.05
73	Mel Hall	.05
74	Don Mattingly	.50
75	Steve Bedrosian	.05
76	Juan Samuel	.05
77	Mike Scioscia	.05
78	Dave Righetti	.05
79	Alfredo Griffin	.05
80	Eric Davis	.10
81	Juan Berenguer	.05
82	Todd Worrell	.05
83	Joe Carter	.05
84	Steve Sax	.05
85	Frank White	.05
86	John Kruk	.10
87	Rance Mulliniks	.05
88	Alan Ashby	.05
89	Charlie Leibrandt	.05
90	Frank Tanana	.05
91	Jose Canseco	.35
92	Barry Bonds	.50
93	Harold Reynolds	.10
94	Mark McLemore	.05
95	Mark McGwire	.75
96	Eddie Murray	.25
97	Tim Raines	.10
98	Rob Thompson	.05
99	Kevin McReynolds	.05
100	Checklist 28-137	.05
101	Carlton Fisk	.20
102	Dave Martinez	.05
103	Glenn Braggs	.05
104	Dale Murphy	.15
105	Ryne Sandberg	.40
106	Dennis Martinez	.05
107	Pete O'Brien	.05
108	Dick Schofield	.05
109	Henry Cotto	.05
110	Mike Marshall	.05
111	Keith Moreland	.05
112	Tom Brunansky	.05
113	Kelly Gruber	.05
114	Brook Jacoby	.05
115	*Keith Brown*	.05
116	Matt Nokes	.05
117	Keith Hernandez	.05
118	Bob Forsch	.05
119	Bert Blyleven	.10
120	Willie Wilson	.05
121	Tommy Gregg	.05
122	Jim Rice	.10
123	Bob Knepper	.05
124	Danny Jackson	.05
125	Eric Plunk	.05
126	Brian Fisher	.05
127	Mike Pagliarulo	.05
128	Tony Gwynn	.45
129	Lance McCullers	.05
130	Andres Galarraga	.15
131	Jose Uribe	.05
132	Kirk Gibson	.10
133	David Palmer	.05
134	R.J. Reynolds	.05
135	Greg Walker	.05
136	Kirk McCaskill	.05
137	Shawon Dunston	.05
138	Andy Allanson	.05
139	Rob Murphy	.05
140	Mike Aldrete	.05
141	Terry Kennedy	.05
142	Scott Fletcher	.05
143	Steve Balboni	.05
144	Bret Saberhagen	.05
145	Ozzie Virgil	.05
146	Dale Sveum	.05
147	Darryl Strawberry	.10
148	Harold Baines	.10
149	George Bell	.05
150	Dave Parker	.10
151	Bobby Bonilla	.10
152	Mookie Wilson	.05
153	Ted Power	.05
154	Nolan Ryan	.75
155	Jeff Reardon	.05
156	Tim Wallach	.05
157	Jamie Moyer	.05
158	Rich Gossage	.10
159	Dave Winfield	.25
160	Von Hayes	.05
161	Willie McGee	.10
162	Rich Gedman	.05
163	Tony Pena	.05
164	Mike Morgan	.05
165	Charlie Hough	.05
166	Mike Stanley	.05
167	Andre Dawson	.15
168	Joe Boever	.05
169	Pete Stanicek	.05
170	Bob Boone	.10
171	Ron Darling	.05
172	Bob Walk	.05
173	Rob Deer	.05
174	Steve Buechele	.05
175	Ted Higuera	.05
176	Ozzie Guillen	.05
177	Candy Maldonado	.05
178	Doyle Alexander	.05
179	Mark Gubicza	.05
180	Alan Trammell	.10
181	Vince Coleman	.05
182	Kirby Puckett	.45
183	Chris Brown	.05
184	Marty Barrett	.05
185	Stan Javier	.05
186	Mike Greenwell	.05
187	Billy Hatcher	.05
188	Jimmy Key	.05
189	Nick Esasky	.05
190	Don Slaught	.05
191	Cory Snyder	.05
192	John Candelaria	.05
193	Mike Schmidt	.45
194	Kevin Gross	.05
195	John Tudor	.05
196	Neil Allen	.05
197	Orel Hershiser	.10
198	Kal Daniels	.05
199	Kent Hrbek	.10
200	Checklist 138-247	.05
201	Joe Magrane	.05
202	Scott Bailes	.05
203	Tim Belcher	.05
204	George Brett	.40
205	Benito Santiago	.05
206	Tony Fernandez	.05
207	Gerald Young	.05
208	Bo Jackson	.20
209	Chet Lemon	.05
210	Storm Davis	.05
211	Doug Drabek	.05
212	Mickey Brantley (photo actually Nelson Simmons)	.05
213	Devon White	.10
214	Dave Stewart	.05
215	Dave Schmidt	.05
216	Bryn Smith	.05
217	Brett Butler	.05
218	Bob Ojeda	.05
219	*Steve Rosenberg*	.05
220	Hubie Brooks	.05
221	B.J. Surhoff	.05
222	Rick Mahler	.05
223	Rick Sutcliffe	.05
224	Neal Heaton	.05
225	Mitch Williams	.05
226	Chuck Finley	.05
227	Mark Langston	.10
228	Jesse Orosco	.05
229	Ed Whitson	.05
230	Terry Pendleton	.05
231	Lloyd Moseby	.05
232	Greg Swindell	.05
233	John Franco	.05
234	Jack Morris	.10
235	Howard Johnson	.05
236	Glenn Davis	.05
237	Frank Viola	.05
238	Kevin Seitzer	.05
239	Gerald Perry	.05
240	Dwight Evans	.10
241	Jim Deshaies	.05
242	Bo Diaz	.05

243 Carney Lansford .05
244 Mike LaValliere .05
245 Rickey Henderson .30
246 Roberto Alomar .20
247 Jimmy Jones .05
248 Pascual Perez .05
249 Will Clark .15
250 Fernando Valenzuela .10
251 Shane Rawley .05
252 Sid Bream .05
253 Steve Lyons .05
254 Brian Downing .05
255 Mark Grace .20
256 Tom Candiotti .05
257 Barry Larkin .10
258 Mike Krukow .05
259 Billy Ripken .05
260 Cecilio Guante .05
261 Scott Bradley .05
262 Floyd Bannister .05
263 Pete Smith .05
264 Jim Gantner .05
265 Roger McDowell .05
266 Bobby Thigpen .05
267 Jim Clancy .05
268 Terry Steinbach .05
269 Mike Dunne .05
270 Dwight Gooden .10
271 Mike Heath .05
272 Dave Smith .05
273 Keith Atherton .05
274 Tim Burke .05
275 Damon Berryhill .05
276 Vance Law .05
277 Rich Dotson .05
278 Lance Parrish .05
279 Geronimo Berroa .05
280 Roger Clemens .45
281 Greg Mathews .05
282 Tom Niedenfuer .05
283 Paul Kilgus .05
284 Jose Guzman .05
285 Calvin Schiraldi .05
286 Charlie Puleo .05
287 Joe Orsulak .05
288 Jack Howell .05
289 Kevin Elster .05
290 Jose Lind .05
291 Paul Molitor .25
292 Cecil Espy .05
293 Bill Wegman .05
294 Dan Pasqua .05
295 Scott Garrelts .05
296 Walt Terrell .05
297 Ed Hearn .05
298 Lou Whitaker .05
299 Ken Dayley .05
300 Checklist 248-357 .05
301 Tommy Herr .05
302 Mike Brumley .05
303 Ellis Burks .10
304 Curt Young .05
305 Jody Reed .05
306 Bill Doran .05
307 David Wells .10
308 Ron Robinson .05
309 Rafael Santana .05
310 Julio Franco .05
311 Jack Clark .05
312 Chris James .05
313 Milt Thompson .05
314 John Shelby .05
315 Al Leiter .05
316 Mike Davis .05
317 *Chris Sabo* .15
318 Greg Gagne .05
319 Jose Oquendo .05
320 John Farrell .05
321 Franklin Stubbs .05
322 Kurt Stillwell .05
323 Shawn Abner .05
324 Mike Flanagan .05
325 Kevin Bass .05
326 Pat Tabler .05
327 Mike Henneman .05
328 Rick Honeycutt .05
329 John Smiley .05
330 Rey Quinones .05
331 Johnny Ray .05
332 Bob Welch .05
333 Larry Sheets .05
334 Jeff Parrett .05
335 Rick Reuschel .05
336 Randy Myers .05
337 Ken Williams .05
338 Andy McGaffigan .05
339 Joey Meyer .05
340 Dion James .05
341 Les Lancaster .05
342 Tom Foley .05
343 Geno Petralli .05
344 Dan Petry .05
345 Alvin Davis .05
346 Mickey Hatcher .05
347 Marvell Wynne .05
348 Danny Cox .05
349 Dave Stieb .05
350 Jay Bell .10
351 Jeff Treadway .05
352 Luis Salazar .05
353 Len Dykstra .10
354 Juan Agosto .05
355 Gene Larkin .05
356 Steve Farr .05
357 Paul Assenmacher .05
358 Todd Benzinger .05
359 Larry Andersen .05
360 Paul O'Neill .10
361 Ron Hassey .05
362 Jim Gott .05
363 Ken Phelps .05
364 Tim Flannery .05
365 Randy Ready .05
366 *Nelson Santovenia* .05
367 Kelly Downs .05
368 Danny Heep .05
369 Phil Bradley .05
370 Jeff Robinson .05
371 Ivan Calderon .05
372 Mike Witt .05
373 Greg Maddux .45
374 Carmen Castillo .05
375 Jose Rijo .05
376 Joe Price .05
377 R.C. Gonzalez .05
378 Oddibe McDowell .05
379 Jim Presley .05
380 Brad Wellman .05
381 Tom Glavine .25
382 Dan Plesac .05
383 Wally Backman .05
384 *Dave Gallagher* .05
385 Tom Henke .05
386 Luis Polonia .05
387 Junior Ortiz .05
388 David Cone .05
389 Dave Bergman .05
390 Danny Darwin .05
391 Dan Gladden .05
392 *John Dopson* .05
393 Frank DiPino .05
394 Al Nipper .05
395 Willie Randolph .05
396 Don Carman .05
397 Scott Terry .05
398 Rick Cerone .05
399 Tom Pagnozzi .05
400 Checklist 358-467 .05
401 Mickey Tettleton .05
402 Curtis Wilkerson .05
403 Jeff Russell .05
404 Pat Perry .05
405 *Jose Alvarez* .05
406 Rick Schu .05
407 *Sherman Corbett* .05
408 Dave Magadan .05
409 Bob Kipper .05
410 Don August .05
411 Bob Brower .05
412 Chris Bosio .05
413 Jerry Reuss .05
414 Atlee Hammaker .05
415 Jim Walewander .05
416 *Mike Macfarlane* .10
417 Pat Sheridan .05
418 Pedro Guerrero .05
419 Allan Anderson .05
420 *Mark Parent* .10
421 Bob Stanley .05
422 Mike Gallego .05
423 Bruce Hurst .05
424 Dave Meads .05
425 Jesse Barfield .05
426 *Rob Dibble* .15
427 Joel Skinner .05
428 Ron Kittle .05
429 Rick Rhoden .05
430 Bob Dernier .05
431 Steve Jeltz .05
432 Rick Dempsey .05
433 Roberto Kelly .05
434 Dave Anderson .05
435 Herm Winningham .05
436 Al Newman .05
437 Jose DeLeon .05
438 Doug Jones .05
439 Brian Holton .05
440 Jeff Montgomery .05
441 Dickie Thon .05
442 Cecil Fielder .05
443 *John Fishel* .05
444 Jerry Don Gleaton .05
445 *Paul Gibson* .05
446 Walt Weiss .05
447 Glenn Wilson .05
448 Mike Moore .05
449 Chili Davis .05
450 Dave Henderson .05
451 *Jose Bautista* .05
452 Rex Hudler .05
453 Bob Brenly .05
454 Mackey Sasser .05
455 Daryl Boston .05
456 Mike Fitzgerald .05
457 Jeffery Leonard .05
458 Bruce Sutter .05
459 Mitch Webster .05
460 Joe Hesketh .05
461 Bobby Witt .05
462 Stew Cliburn .05
463 Scott Bankhead .05
464 *Ramon Martinez* .40
465 Dave Leiper .05
466 *Luis Alicea* .10
467 John Cerutti .05
468 Ron Washington .05
469 Jeff Reed .05
470 Jeff Robinson .05
471 Sid Fernandez .05
472 Terry Puhl .05
473 Charlie Lea .05
474 *Israel Sanchez* .05
475 Bruce Benedict .05
476 Oil Can Boyd .05
477 Craig Reynolds .05
478 Frank Williams .05
479 Greg Cadaret .05
480 *Randy Kramer* .05
481 *Dave Eiland* .05
482 Eric Show .05
483 Garry Templeton .05
484 Wallace Johnson .05
485 Kevin Mitchell .05
486 Tim Crews .05
487 Mike Maddux .05
488 Dave LaPoint .05
489 Fred Manrique .05
490 Greg Minton .05
491 *Doug Dascenzo* .10
492 Willie Upshaw .05
493 *Jack Armstrong* .10
494 Kirt Manwaring .05
495 Jeff Ballard .05
496 Jeff Kunkel .05
497 Mike Campbell .05
498 Gary Thurman .05
499 Zane Smith .05
500 Checklist 468-577 .05
501 Mike Birkbeck .05
502 Terry Leach .05
503 Shawn Hillegas .05
504 Manny Lee .05
505 *Doug Jennings* .10
506 Ken Oberkfell .05
507 Tim Teufel .05
508 Tom Brookens .05
509 Rafael Ramirez .05
510 Fred Toliver .05
511 *Brian Holman* .05
512 Mike Bielecki .05
513 *Jeff Pico* .05
514 Charles Hudson .05
515 Bruce Ruffin .05
516 Larry McWilliams .05
517 Jeff Sellers .05
518 *John Costello* .05
519 Brady Anderson .10
520 Craig McMurtry .05
521 Ray Hayward .05
522 Drew Hall .05
523 *Mark Lemke* .05
524 *Oswald Peraza* .05
525 *Bryan Harvey* .10
526 Rick Aguilera .05
527 Tom Prince .05
528 Mark Clear .05
529 Jerry Browne .05
530 Juan Castillo .05
531 Jack McDowell .05
532 Chris Speier .05
533 Darrell Evans .10
534 Luis Aquino .05
535 Eric King .05
536 *Ken Hill* .25
537 Randy Bush .05
538 Shane Mack .05
539 Tom Bolton .05
540 Gene Nelson .05
541 Wes Gardner .05
542 Ken Caminiti .10
543 Duane Ward .05
544 *Norm Charlton* .10
545 *Hal Morris* .25
546 Rich Yett .05
547 *Hensley Meulens* .10
548 Greg Harris .05
549 Darren Daulton .10
550 Jeff Hamilton .05
551 Luis Aguayo .05
552 Tim Leary .05
553 Ron Oester .05
554 Steve Lombardozzi .05
555 *Tim Jones* .05
556 Bud Black .05
557 Alejandro Pena .05
558 *Jose DeJesus* .05
559 Dennis Rasmussen .05
560 *Pat Borders* 1.00
561 Craig Biggio .50
562 *Luis de los Santos* .05
563 Fred Lynn .10
564 *Todd Burns* .05
565 Felix Fermin .05
566 Darnell Coles .05
567 Willie Fraser .05
568 Glenn Hubbard .05
569 *Craig Worthington* .05
570 *Johnny Paredes* .05
571 Don Robinson .05
572 Barry Lyons .05
573 Bill Long .05
574 Tracy Jones .05
575 Juan Nieves .05
576 Andres Thomas .05
577 *Rolando Roomes* .05
578 Luis Rivera .05
579 *Chad Kreuter* .15
580 Tony Armas .05
581 Jay Buhner .15
582 Ricky Horton .05
583 Andy Hawkins .05
584 *Sil Campusano* .05
585 Dave Clark .05
586 *Van Snider* .05
587 Todd Frohwirth .05
588 Warren Spahn Puzzle Card .05
589 *William Brennan* .05
590 *German Gonzalez* .05
591 Ernie Whitt .05
592 Jeff Blauser .05
593 Spike Owen .05
594 Matt Williams .15
595 Lloyd McClendon .05
596 Steve Ontiveros .05
597 *Scott Medvin* .05
598 *Hipolito Pena* .05
599 *Jerald Clark* .05
600a Checklist 578-BC26 (#635 is Kurt Schilling) .10
600b Checklist 578-BC26 (#635 is Curt Schilling) .05
601 Carmelo Martinez .05
602 Mike LaCoss .05
603 Mike Devereaux .05
604 *Alex Madrid* .05
605 Gary Redus .05
606 Lance Johnson .05
607 *Terry Clark* .05
608 Manny Trillo .05
609 *Scott Jordan* .05
610 Jay Howell .05
611 *Francisco Melendez* .05
612 Mike Boddicker .05
613 Kevin Brown .10
614 Dave Valle .05
615 Tim Laudner .05
616 *Andy Nezelek* .05
617 Chuck Crim .05
618 Jack Savage .05
619 Adam Peterson .05
620 Todd Stottlemyre .05
621 *Lance Blankenship* .10

622	*Miguel Garcia*	.05
623	Keith Miller	.05
624	*Ricky Jordan*	.10
625	Ernest Riles	.05
626	John Moses	.05
627	Nelson Liriano	.05
628	Mike Smithson	.05
629	Scott Sanderson	.05
630	Dale Mohorcic	.05
631	Marvin Freeman	.05
632	Mike Young	.05
633	Dennis Lamp	.05
634	*Dante Bichette*	.40
635	*Curt Schilling*	3.00
636	*Scott May*	.05
637	*Mike Schooler*	.05
638	Rick Leach	.05
639	*Tom Lampkin*	.05
640	*Brian Meyer*	.05
641	Brian Harper	.05
642	John Smoltz	.15
643	Jose Canseco (40/40)	.15
644	Bill Schroeder	.05
645	Edgar Martinez	.10
646	*Dennis Cook*	.10
647	Barry Jones	.05
648	(Orel Hershiser) (59 and Counting)	.10
649	*Rod Nichols*	.05
650	Jody Davis	.05
651	*Bob Milacki*	.05
652	Mike Jackson	.05
653	*Derek Lilliquist*	.10
654	Paul Mirabella	.05
655	Mike Diaz	.05
656	Jeff Musselman	.05
657	Jerry Reed	.05
658	*Kevin Blankenship*	.10
659	Wayne Tolleson	.05
660	*Eric Hetzel*	.05

1989 Donruss All-Stars

For the fourth consecutive year Donruss featured a 64-card set with players from the 1988 All-Star Game. The card fronts include a red-to-gold fade or gold-to-red fade border and blue vertical side borders. The top border features the player's name and position along with the "Donruss 89" logo. Each full-color player photo is highlighted by a thin white line and includes a league logo in the lower right corner. Card backs reveal an orange-gold border and black and white printing. The player's ID and personal information is displayed with a gold star on both sides. The star in the left corner includes the card number. 1988 All-Star game statistics and run totals follow along with a career highlights feature surrounded by the team, All-Star Game MLB, MLBPA, and Leaf Inc. logos. The All-Stars were distributed in wax packages containing five All-Stars, one Pop-Up, and one three-piece Warren Spahn puzzle card.

		MT
Complete Set (64):		5.00
Common Player:		.10
Warren Spahn Puzzle:		1.00
1	Mark McGwire	1.50
2	Jose Canseco	.35
3	Paul Molitor	.40
4	Rickey Henderson	.35
5	Cal Ripken, Jr.	1.50
6	Dave Winfield	.40
7	Wade Boggs	.50
8	Frank Viola	.10
9	Terry Steinbach	.10
10	Tom Kelly	.10
11	George Brett	.75
12	Doyle Alexander	.10
13	Gary Gaetti	.10
14	Roger Clemens	.75
15	Mike Greenwell	.10
16	Dennis Eckersley	.10
17	Carney Lansford	.10
18	Mark Gubicza	.10
19	Tim Laudner	.10
20	Doug Jones	.10
21	Don Mattingly	.75
22	Dan Plesac	.10
23	Kirby Puckett	.75
24	Jeff Reardon	.10
25	Johnny Ray	.10
26	Jeff Russell	.10
27	Harold Reynolds	.10
28	Dave Stieb	.10
29	Kurt Stillwell	.10
30	Jose Canseco	.30
31	Terry Steinbach	.10
32	A.L. Checklist	.05
33	Will Clark	.25
34	Darryl Strawberry	.10
35	Ryne Sandberg	.65
36	Andre Dawson	.15
37	Ozzie Smith	.35
38	Vince Coleman	.10
39	Bobby Bonilla	.10
40	Dwight Gooden	.10
41	Gary Carter	.15
42	Whitey Herzog	.10
43	Shawon Dunston	.10
44	David Cone	.10
45	Andres Galarraga	.15
46	Mark Davis	.10
47	Barry Larkin	.15
48	Kevin Gross	.10
49	Vance Law	.10
50	Orel Hershiser	.10
51	Willie McGee	.10
52	Danny Jackson	.10
53	Rafael Palmeiro	.25
54	Bob Knepper	.10
55	Lance Parrish	.10
56	Greg Maddux	.60
57	Gerald Perry	.10
58	Bob Walk	.10
59	Chris Sabo	.10
60	Todd Worrell	.10
61	Andy Van Slyke	.10
62	Ozzie Smith	.35
63	Riverfront Stadium	.10
64	N.L. Checklist	.05

1989 Donruss Baseball's Best

For the second consecutive year, Donruss issued a "Baseball's Best" set in 1989 to highlight the game's top players. The special 336-card set was packaged in a special box and was sold at various retail chains nationwide following the conclusion of the 1989 baseball season. The cards are styled after the regular 1989 Donruss set with green borders and a glossy finish. The set included a Warren Spahn puzzle.

		MT
Complete Unopened Set (336):		150.00
Complete Set (336):		35.00
Common Player:		.05
1	Don Mattingly	1.00
2	Tom Glavine	.15
3	Bert Blyleven	.10
4	Andre Dawson	.10
5	Pete O'Brien	.05
6	Eric Davis	.05
7	George Brett	1.00
8	Glenn Davis	.05
9	Ellis Burks	.05
10	Kirk Gibson	.05
11	Carlton Fisk	.30
12	Andres Galarraga	.10
13	Alan Trammell	.10
14	Dwight Gooden	.05
15	Paul Molitor	.15
16	Roger McDowell	.05
17	Doug Drabek	.05
18	Kent Hrbek	.05
19	Vince Coleman	.05
20	Steve Sax	.05
21	Roberto Alomar	.20
22	Carney Lansford	.05
23	Will Clark	.15
24	Alvin Davis	.05
25	Bobby Thigpen	.05
26	Ryne Sandberg	.75
27	Devon White	.05
28	Mike Greenwell	.05
29	Dale Murphy	.20
30	Jeff Ballard	.05
31	Kelly Gruber	.05
32	Julio Franco	.05
33	Bobby Bonilla	.05
34	Tim Wallach	.05
35	Lou Whitaker	.05
36	Jay Howell	.05
37	Greg Maddux	.75
38	Bill Doran	.05
39	Danny Tartabull	.05
40	Darryl Strawberry	.05
41	Ron Darling	.05
42	Tony Gwynn	.75
43	Mark McGwire	1.50
44	Ozzie Smith	.30
45	Andy Van Slyke	.05
46	Juan Berenguer	.05
47	Von Hayes	.05
48	Tony Fernandez	.05
49	Eric Plunk	.05
50	Ernest Riles	.05
51	Harold Reynolds	.05
52	Andy Hawkins	.05
53	Robin Yount	.30
54	Danny Jackson	.05
55	Nolan Ryan	1.50
56	Joe Carter	.05
57	Jose Canseco	.45
58	Jody Davis	.05
59	Lance Parrish	.05
60	Mitch Williams	.05
61	Brook Jacoby	.05
62	Tom Browning	.05
63	Kurt Stillwell	.05
64	Rafael Ramirez	.05
65	Roger Clemens	.75
66	Mike Scioscia	.05
67	Dave Gallagher	.05
68	Mark Langston	.05
69	Chet Lemon	.05
70	Kevin McReynolds	.05
71	Rob Deer	.05
72	Tommy Herr	.05
73	Barry Bonds	1.00
74	Frank Viola	.05
75	Pedro Guerrero	.05
76	Dave Righetti	.05
77	Bruce Hurst	.05
78	Rickey Henderson	.30
79	Robby Thompson	.05
80	Randy Johnson	.35
81	Harold Baines	.05
82	Calvin Schiraldi	.05
83	Kirk McCaskill	.05
84	Lee Smith	.05
85	John Smoltz	.10
86	Mickey Tettleton	.05
87	Jimmy Key	.05
88	Rafael Palmeiro	.10
89	Sid Bream	.05
90	Dennis Martinez	.05
91	Frank Tanana	.05
92	Eddie Murray	.30
93	Shawon Dunston	.05
94	Mike Scott	.05
95	Bret Saberhagen	.05
96	David Cone	.05
97	Kevin Elster	.05
98	Jack Clark	.05
99	Dave Stewart	.05
100	Jose Oquendo	.05
101	Jose Lind	.05
102	Gary Gaetti	.05
103	Ricky Jordan	.05
104	Fred McGriff	.05
105	Don Slaught	.05
106	Jose Uribe	.05
107	Jeffrey Leonard	.05
108	Lee Guetterman	.05
109	Chris Bosio	.05
110	Barry Larkin	.10
111	Ruben Sierra	.05
112	Greg Swindell	.05
113	Gary Sheffield	.15
114	Lonnie Smith	.05
115	Chili Davis	.05
116	Damon Berryhill	.05
117	Tom Candiotti	.05
118	Kal Daniels	.05
119	Mark Gubicza	.05
120	Jim Deshaies	.05
121	Dwight Evans	.05
122	Mike Morgan	.05
123	Dan Pasqua	.05
124	Bryn Smith	.05
125	Doyle Alexander	.05
126	Howard Johnson	.05
127	Chuck Crim	.05
128	Darren Daulton	.05
129	Jeff Robinson	.05
130	Kirby Puckett	1.00
131	Joe Magrane	.05
132	Jesse Barfield	.05
133	Mark Davis (Photo actually Dave Leiper)	.05
134	Dennis Eckersley	.05
135	Mike Krukow	.05
136	Jay Buhner	.05
137	Ozzie Guillen	.05
138	Rick Sutcliffe	.05
139	Wally Joyner	.05
140	Wade Boggs	.60
141	Jeff Treadway	.05
142	Cal Ripken	1.50
143	Dave Steib	.05
144	Pete Incaviglia	.05
145	Bob Walk	.05
146	Nelson Santovenia	.05
147	Mike Heath	.05
148	Willie Randolph	.05
149	Paul Kilgus	.05
150	Billy Hatcher	.05
151	Steve Farr	.05
152	Gregg Jefferies	.05
153	Randy Myers	.05
154	Garry Templeton	.05
155	Walt Weiss	.05
156	Terry Pendleton	.05
157	John Smiley	.05
158	Greg Gagne	.05
159	Lenny Dykstra	.05

160	Nelson Liriano	.05
161	Alvaro Espinoza	.05
162	Rick Reuschel	.05
163	Omar Vizquel	.05
164	Clay Parker	.05
165	Dan Plesac	.05
166	John Franco	.05
167	Scott Fletcher	.05
168	Cory Snyder	.05
169	Bo Jackson	.20
170	Tommy Gregg	.05
171	Jim Abbott	.05
172	Jerome Walton	.05
173	Doug Jones	.05
174	Todd Benzinger	.05
175	Frank White	.05
176	Craig Biggio	.10
177	John Dopson	.05
178	Alfredo Griffin	.05
179	Melido Perez	.05
180	Tim Burke	.05
181	Matt Nokes	.05
182	Gary Carter	.10
183	Ted Higuera	.05
184	Ken Howell	.05
185	Rey Quinones	.05
186	Wally Backman	.05
187	Tom Brunansky	.05
188	Steve Balboni	.05
189	Marvell Wynne	.05
190	Dave Henderson	.05
191	Don Robinson	.05
192	Ken Griffey, Jr.	8.00
193	Ivan Calderon	.05
194	Mike Bielecki	.05
195	Johnny Ray	.05
196	Rob Murphy	.05
197	Andres Thomas	.05
198	Phil Bradley	.05
199	Junior Felix	.05
200	Jeff Russell	.05
201	Mike LaValliere	.05
202	Kevin Gross	.05
203	Keith Moreland	.05
204	Mike Marshall	.05
205	Dwight Smith	.05
206	Jim Clancy	.05
207	Kevin Seitzer	.05
208	Keith Hernandez	.05
209	Bob Ojeda	.05
210	Ed Whitson	.05
211	Tony Phillips	.05
212	Milt Thompson	.05
213	Randy Kramer	.05
214	Randy Bush	.05
215	Randy Ready	.05
216	Duane Ward	.05
217	Jimmy Jones	.05
218	Scott Garrelts	.05
219	Scott Bankhead	.05
220	Lance McCullers	.05
221	B.J. Surhoff	.05
222	Chris Sabo	.05
223	Steve Buechele	.05
224	Joel Skinner	.05
225	Orel Hershiser	.05
226	Derek Lilliquist	.05
227	Claudell Washington	.05
228	Lloyd McClendon	.05
229	Felix Fermin	.05
230	Paul O'Neill	.10
231	Charlie Leibrandt	.05
232	Dave Smith	.05
233	Bob Stanley	.05
234	Tim Belcher	.05
235	Eric King	.05
236	Spike Owen	.05
237	Mike Henneman	.05
238	Juan Samuel	.05
239	Greg Brock	.05
240	John Kruk	.05
241	Glenn Wilson	.05
242	Jeff Reardon	.05
243	Todd Worrell	.05
244	Dave LaPoint	.05
245	Walt Terrell	.05
246	Mike Moore	.05
247	Kelly Downs	.05
248	Dave Valle	.05
249	Ron Kittle	.05
250	Steve Wilson	.05
251	Dick Schofield	.05
252	Marty Barrett	.05
253	Dion James	.05
254	Bob Milacki	.05
255	Ernie Whitt	.05
256	Kevin Brown	.05
257	R.J. Reynolds	.05
258	Tim Raines	.05
259	Frank Williams	.05
260	Jose Gonzalez	.05
261	Mitch Webster	.05
262	Ken Caminiti	.10
263	Bob Boone	.05
264	Dave Magadan	.05
265	Rick Aguilera	.05
266	Chris James	.05
267	Bob Welch	.05
268	Ken Dayley	.05
269	Junior Ortiz	.05
270	Allan Anderson	.05
271	Steve Jeltz	.05
272	George Bell	.05
273	Roberto Kelly	.05
274	Brett Butler	.05
275	Mike Schooler	.05
276	Ken Phelps	.05
277	Glenn Braggs	.05
278	Jose Rijo	.05
279	Bobby Witt	.05
280	Jerry Browne	.05
281	Kevin Mitchell	.05
282	Craig Worthington	.05
283	Greg Minton	.05
284	Nick Esasky	.05
285	John Farrell	.05
286	Rick Mahler	.05
287	Tom Gordon	.05
288	Gerald Young	.05
289	Jody Reed	.05
290	Jeff Hamilton	.05
291	Gerald Perry	.05
292	Hubie Brooks	.05
293	Bo Diaz	.05
294	Terry Puhl	.05
295	Jim Gantner	.05
296	Jeff Parrett	.05
297	Mike Boddicker	.05
298	Dan Gladden	.05
299	Tony Pena	.05
300	Checklist	.05
301	Tom Henke	.05
302	Pascual Perez	.05
303	Steve Bedrosian	.05
304	Ken Hill	.05
305	Jerry Reuss	.05
306	Jim Eisenreich	.05
307	Jack Howell	.05
308	Rick Cerone	.05
309	Tim Leary	.05
310	Joe Orsulak	.05
311	Jim Dwyer	.05
312	Geno Petralli	.05
313	Rick Honeycutt	.05
314	Tom Foley	.05
315	Kenny Rogers	.05
316	Mike Flanagan	.05
317	Bryan Harvey	.05
318	Billy Ripken	.05
319	Jeff Montgomery	.05
320	Erik Hanson	.05
321	Brian Downing	.05
322	Gregg Olson	.05
323	Terry Steinbach	.05
324	Sammy Sosa	25.00
325	Gene Harris	.05
326	Mike Devereaux	.05
327	Dennis Cook	.05
328	David Wells	.10
329	Checklist	.05
330	Kirt Manwaring	.05
331	Jim Presley	.05
332	Checklist	.05
333	Chuck Finley	.05
334	Rob Dibble	.05
335	Cecil Espy	.05
336	Dave Parker	.05

1989 Donruss Diamond King Supers

Once again for 1989, collectors could acquire a 4-3/4" x 6-3/4" version of the Diamond King subset via a wrapper mail-in offer. Other than size, cards are identical to the DKs in the regular issue.

		MT
Complete Set (27):		10.00
Common Player:		.25
1	Mike Greenwell	.25
2	Bobby Bonilla	.25
3	Pete Incaviglia	.25
4	Chris Sabo	.25
5	Robin Yount	1.50
6	Tony Gwynn	3.00
7	Carlton Fisk	1.50
8	Cory Snyder	.25
9	David Cone	.50
10	Kevin Seitzer	.25
11	Rick Reuschel	.25
12	Johnny Ray	.25
13	Dave Schmidt	.25
14	Andres Galarraga	.50
15	Kirk Gibson	.25
16	Fred McGriff	.25
17	Mark Grace	1.50
18	Jeff Robinson	.25
19	Vince Coleman	.25
20	Dave Henderson	.25
21	Harold Reynolds	.25
22	Gerald Perry	.25
23	Frank Viola	.25
24	Steve Bedrosian	.25
25	Glenn Davis	.25
26	Don Mattingly	4.00
27	Checklist	.05

1989 Donruss Grand Slammers

One card from this 12-card set was included in each Donruss cello pack. The complete insert set was included in factory sets. The featured players all hit grand slams in 1988. The 2-1/2" x 3-1/2" cards feature full color action photos. Backs tell the story of the player's grand slam. Border color variations on the front of the card have been discovered, but the prices are consistent with all forms of the cards.

		MT
Complete Set (12):		2.50
Common Player:		.25
1	Jose Canseco	.30
2	Mike Marshall	.25
3	Walt Weiss	.25
4	Kevin McReynolds	.25
5	Mike Greenwell	.25
6	Dave Winfield	.40
7	Mark McGwire	1.00
8	Keith Hernandez	.25
9	Franklin Stubbs	.25
10	Danny Tartabull	.25
11	Jesse Barfield	.25
12	Ellis Burks	.25

1989 Donruss MVP

This set, numbered BC1-BC26, was randomly inserted in Donruss wax packs, but not included in factory sets or other card packs. Players highlighted were selected by Donruss, one player per team. MVP cards feature a variation of the design in the basic Donruss issue, with multi-color upper and lower borders and black side borders. The "MVP" designation in large, bright letters serves as a backdrop for the full-color player photo. The cards measure 2-1/2" x 3-1/2".

		MT
Complete Set (26):		3.00
Common Player:		.10
1	Kirby Puckett	.50
2	Mike Scott	.10
3	Joe Carter	.10
4	Orel Hershiser	.10
5	Jose Canseco	.40
6	Darryl Strawberry	.15
7	George Brett	.50
8	Andre Dawson	.20
9	Paul Molitor	.45
10	Andy Van Slyke	.10
11	Dave Winfield	.40
12	Kevin Gross	.10
13	Mike Greenwell	.10
14	Ozzie Smith	.40
15	Cal Ripken	1.00
16	Andres Galarraga	.15
17	Alan Trammell	.15
18	Kal Daniels	.10
19	Fred McGriff	.10
20	Tony Gwynn	.50
21	Wally Joyner	.10
22	Will Clark	.25
23	Ozzie Guillen	.10
24	Gerald Perry	.10
25	Alvin Davis	.10
26	Ruben Sierra	.10

1989 Donruss Pop-Ups

This set features the eighteen starters from the 1988 Major League All-Star game. The cards are designed with a perforated outline so each player can be popped up to stand upright. The flip side features a red, white, and blue "Cincinnati Reds All-Star Game" logo at the top, a league designation, and the player's name and position. The lower portion displays instructions for creating the base of the Pop-Up. The Pop-Ups were marketed in conjunction with All-Star and Warren Spahn Puzzle Cards.

		MT
Complete Set (20):		3.00
Common Player:		.20
Warren Spahn Puzzle:		1.00
(1)	Mark McGwire	1.00
(2)	Jose Canseco	.30
(3)	Paul Molitor	.35
(4)	Rickey Henderson	.35
(5)	Cal Ripken, Jr.	.75
(6)	Dave Winfield	.35
(7)	Wade Boggs	.50
(8)	Frank Viola	.20
(9)	Terry Steinbach	.20
(10)	Tom Kelly	.20
(11)	Will Clark	.25
(12)	Darryl Strawberry	.20
(13)	Ryne Sandberg	.50
(14)	Andre Dawson	.20
(15)	Ozzie Smith	.35
(16)	Vince Coleman	.20
(17)	Bobby Bonilla	.20
(18)	Dwight Gooden	.20
(19)	Gary Carter	.25
(20)	Whitey Herzog	.20

1989 Donruss Rookies

For the fourth straight year, Donruss issued a 56-card "Rookies" set in 1989. As in previous years, the set is similar in design to the regular Donruss set, except for a new "The Rookies" logo and a green and black border.

		MT
Complete Unopened Set (56):		20.00
Complete Set (56):		15.00
Common Player:		.10
1	Gary Sheffield	.50
2	Gregg Jefferies	.15
3	Ken Griffey, Jr.	15.00
4	Tom Gordon	.15
5	Billy Spiers	.10
6	*Deion Sanders*	.75
7	Donn Pall	.10
8	Steve Carter	.10
9	Francisco Oliveras	.10
10	Steve Wilson	.10
11	Bob Geren	.10
12	Tony Castillo	.10
13	Kenny Rogers	.10
14	Carlos Martinez	.10
15	Edgar Martinez	.10
16	Jim Abbott	.10
17	Torey Lovullo	.10
18	Mark Carreon	.10
19	Geronimo Berroa	.10
20	Luis Medina	.10
21	Sandy Alomar, Jr.	.30
22	Bob Milacki	.10
23	*Joe Girardi*	.15
24	German Gonzalez	.10
25	Craig Worthington	.10
26	Jerome Walton	.10
27	Gary Wayne	.10
28	Tim Jones	.10
29	Dante Bichette	.75
30	Alexis Infante	.10
31	Ken Hill	.10
32	Dwight Smith	.10
33	Luis de los Santos	.10
34	Eric Yelding	.10
35	Gregg Olson	.10
36	Phil Stephenson	.10
37	Ken Patterson	.10
38	Rick Wrona	.10
39	Mike Brumley	.10
40	Cris Carpenter	.10
41	Jeff Brantley	.10
42	Ron Jones	.10
43	Randy Johnson	6.00
44	Kevin Brown	.10
45	Ramon Martinez	.30
46	Greg Harris	.10
47	Steve Finley	.10
48	Randy Kramer	.10
49	Erik Hanson	.10
50	Matt Merullo	.10
51	Mike Devereaux	.10
52	Clay Parker	.10
53	Omar Vizquel	.15
54	Derek Lilliquist	.10
55	Junior Felix	.10
56	Checklist	.05

1989 Donruss Traded

Donruss issued its first "Traded" set in 1989, releasing a 56-card boxed set designed in the same style as the regular 1989 Donruss set. The set included a Stan Musial puzzle card and a checklist.

		MT
Complete Set (56):		3.00
Common Player:		.10
1	Jeffrey Leonard	.10
2	Jack Clark	.10
3	Kevin Gross	.10
4	Tommy Herr	.10
5	Bob Boone	.15
6	Rafael Palmeiro	.30
7	John Dopson	.10
8	Willie Randolph	.10
9	Chris Brown	.10
10	Wally Backman	.10
11	Steve Ontiveros	.10
12	Eddie Murray	.30
13	Lance McCullers	.10
14	Spike Owen	.10
15	Rob Murphy	.10
16	Pete O'Brien	.10
17	Ken Williams	.10
18	Nick Esasky	.10
19	Nolan Ryan	1.50
20	Brian Holton	.10
21	Mike Moore	.10
22	Joel Skinner	.10
23	Steve Sax	.10
24	Rick Mahler	.10
25	Mike Aldrete	.10
26	Jesse Orosco	.10
27	Dave LaPoint	.10
28	Walt Terrell	.10
29	Eddie Williams	.10
30	Mike Devereaux	.10
31	Julio Franco	.10
32	Jim Clancy	.10
33	Felix Fermin	.10
34	Curtis Wilkerson	.10
35	Bert Blyleven	.10
36	Mel Hall	.10
37	Eric King	.10
38	Mitch Williams	.10
39	Jamie Moyer	.10
40	Rick Rhoden	.10
41	Phil Bradley	.10
42	Paul Kilgus	.10
43	Milt Thompson	.10
44	Jerry Browne	.10
45	Bruce Hurst	.10
46	Claudell Washington	.10
47	Todd Benzinger	.10
48	Steve Balboni	.10
49	Oddibe McDowell	.10
50	Charles Hudson	.10
51	Ron Kittle	.10
52	Andy Hawkins	.10
53	Tom Brookens	.10
54	Tom Niedenfuer	.10
55	Jeff Parrett	.10
56	Checklist	.10

1990 Donruss Previews

To introduce its 1990 baseball issue, Donruss sent two preview cards from a set of 12 to each member of its dealers' network. Though the photos are different than those used on the issued versions, the front format was the same. Backs are printed in black on white and contain career highlights, but no stats. Issued at the dawn of the "promo card" craze, and succeeding the relatively valueless sample sheets used by most companies in earlier years, little value was attached to these preview cards initially. Today they are among the scarcest of the early-1990s promos.

		MT
Complete Set (12):		150.00
Common Player:		5.00
1	Todd Zeile	5.00
2	Ben McDonald	5.00
3	Bo Jackson	10.00
4	Will Clark	10.00
5	Dave Stewart	5.00
6	Kevin Mitchell	5.00
7	Nolan Ryan	100.00
8	Howard Johnson	5.00
9	Tony Gwynn	35.00
10	Jerome Walton	5.00
11	Wade Boggs	20.00
12	Kirby Puckett	35.00

1990 Donruss

Donruss marked its 10th anniversary in the baseball card hobby with a 715-card set in 1990, up from previous 660-card sets. The standard-size cards feature bright red borders with the player's name in script at the top. The set includes 26 "Diamond Kings" (DK) in the checklist, 20 "Rated Rookies" (RR) and a Carl Yastrzemski puzzle. Each All-Star card back has two variations. The more common has the stats box headed "All-Star Performance". Slightly scarcer versions say "Recent Major League Performance", and are worth about twice the value of the correct version.

	MT
Unopened Factory Set (716):	12.50
Complete Set (716):	10.00
Common Player:	.05
Carl Yastrzemski Puzzle:	1.00
Wax Pack (16):	.85
Wax Box (36):	17.50

No.	Player	Value
1	Bo Jackson (Diamond King)	.15
2	Steve Sax (DK)	.05
3a	Ruben Sierra (DK) (no vertical black line at top-right on back)	.25
3b	Ruben Sierra (DK) (vertical line at top-right on back)	.10
4	Ken Griffey, Jr. (DK)	.50
5	Mickey Tettleton (DK)	.05
6	Dave Stewart (DK)	.10
7	Jim Deshaies (DK)	.05
8	John Smoltz (DK)	.10
9	Mike Bielecki (DK)	.05
10a	Brian Downing (DK) (reversed negative)	.50
10b	Brian Downing (DK) (corrected)	.10
11	Kevin Mitchell (DK)	.05
12	Kelly Gruber (DK)	.05
13	Joe Magrane (DK)	.05
14	John Franco (DK)	.05
15	Ozzie Guillen (DK)	.05
16	Lou Whitaker (DK)	.05
17	John Smiley (DK)	.05
18	Howard Johnson (DK)	.05
19	Willie Randolph (DK)	.10
20	Chris Bosio (DK)	.05
21	Tommy Herr (DK)	.05
22	Dan Gladden (DK)	.05
23	Ellis Burks (DK)	.10
24	Pete O'Brien (DK)	.05
25	Bryn Smith (DK)	.05
26	Ed Whitson (DK)	.05
27	Checklist 1-27	.05
28	Robin Ventura (Rated Rookie)	.15
29	*Todd Zeile* (RR)	.15
30	Sandy Alomar, Jr. (RR)	.10
31	*Kent Mercker* (RR)	.20
32	*Ben McDonald* (RR)	.25
33a	*Juan Gonzalez (reversed negative)* (RR)	2.00
33b	*Juan Gonzalez* (RR) (corrected)	2.00
34	*Eric Anthony* (RR)	.15
35	*Mike Fetters* (RR)	.10
36	*Marquis Grissom* (RR)	.50
37	*Greg Vaughn* (RR)	.25
38	*Brian Dubois* (RR)	.05
39	*Steve Avery* (RR)	.20
40	*Mark Gardner* (RR)	.15
41	Andy Benes (RR)	.10
42	*Delino DeShields* (RR)	.15
43	*Scott Coolbaugh* (RR)	.05
44	*Pat Combs* (RR)	.10
45	*Alex Sanchez* (RR)	.05
46	*Kelly Mann* (RR)	.05
47	*Julio Machado* (RR)	.05
48	Pete Incaviglia	.05
49	Shawon Dunston	.05
50	Jeff Treadway	.05
51	Jeff Ballard	.05
52	Claudell Washington	.05
53	Juan Samuel	.05
54	John Smiley	.05
55	Rob Deer	.05
56	Geno Petralli	.05
57	Chris Bosio	.05
58	Carlton Fisk	.20
59	Kirt Manwaring	.05
60	Chet Lemon	.05
61	Bo Jackson	.20
62	Doyle Alexander	.05
63	Pedro Guerrero	.05
64	Allan Anderson	.05
65	Greg Harris	.05
66	Mike Greenwell	.05
67	Walt Weiss	.05
68	Wade Boggs	.25
69	Jim Clancy	.05
70	*Junior Felix*	.05
71	Barry Larkin	.10
72	Dave LaPoint	.05
73	Joel Skinner	.05
74	Jesse Barfield	.05
75	Tommy Herr	.05
76	Ricky Jordan	.05
77	Eddie Murray	.20
78	Steve Sax	.05
79	Tim Belcher	.05
80	Danny Jackson	.05
81	Kent Hrbek	.10
82	Milt Thompson	.05
83	Brook Jacoby	.05
84	Mike Marshall	.05
85	Kevin Seitzer	.05
86	Tony Gwynn	.35
87	Dave Steib	.05
88	Dave Smith	.05
89	Bret Saberhagen	.05
90	Alan Trammell	.10
91	Tony Phillips	.05
92	Doug Drabek	.05
93	Jeffrey Leonard	.05
94	Wally Joyner	.05
95	Carney Lansford	.05
96	Cal Ripken, Jr.	.75
97	Andres Galarraga	.10
98	Kevin Mitchell	.05
99	Howard Johnson	.05
100a	Checklist 28-129	.05
100b	Checklist 28-125	.05
101	Melido Perez	.05
102	Spike Owen	.05
103	Paul Molitor	.25
104	Geronimo Berroa	.05
105	Ryne Sandberg	.25
106	Bryn Smith	.05
107	Steve Buechele	.05
108	Jim Abbott	.05
109	Alvin Davis	.05
110	Lee Smith	.10
111	Roberto Alomar	.20
112	Rick Reuschel	.05
113a	Kelly Gruber (Born 2/22)	.05
113b	Kelly Gruber (Born 2/26)	.20
114	Joe Carter	.05
115	Jose Rijo	.05
116	Greg Minton	.05
117	Bob Ojeda	.05
118	Glenn Davis	.05
119	Jeff Reardon	.05
120	Kurt Stillwell	.05
121	John Smoltz	.10
122	Dwight Evans	.10
123	Eric Yelding	.05
124	John Franco	.05
125	Jose Canseco	.20
126	Barry Bonds	.50
127	Lee Guetterman	.05
128	Jack Clark	.05
129	Dave Valle	.05
130	Hubie Brooks	.05
131	Ernest Riles	.05
132	Mike Morgan	.05
133	Steve Jeltz	.05
134	Jeff Robinson	.05
135	Ozzie Guillen	.05
136	Chili Davis	.05
137	Mitch Webster	.05
138	Jerry Browne	.05
139	Bo Diaz	.05
140	Robby Thompson	.05
141	Craig Worthington	.05
142	Julio Franco	.05
143	Brian Holman	.05
144	George Brett	.25
145	Tom Glavine	.20
146	Robin Yount	.20
147	Gary Carter	.10
148	Ron Kittle	.05
149	Tony Fernandez	.05
150	Dave Stewart	.05
151	Gary Gaetti	.05
152	Kevin Elster	.05
153	Gerald Perry	.05
154	Jesse Orosco	.05
155	Wally Backman	.05
156	Dennis Martinez	.05
157	Rick Sutcliffe	.05
158	Greg Maddux	.60
159	Andy Hawkins	.05
160	John Kruk	.05
161	Jose Oquendo	.05
162	John Dopson	.05
163	Joe Magrane	.05
164	Billy Ripken	.05
165	Fred Manrique	.05
166	Nolan Ryan	.75
167	Damon Berryhill	.05
168	Dale Murphy	.10
169	Mickey Tettleton	.05
170a	Kirk McCaskill (Born 4/19)	.05
170b	Kirk McCaskill (Born 4/9)	.10
171	Dwight Gooden	.10
172	Jose Lind	.05
173	B.J. Surhoff	.05
174	Ruben Sierra	.05
175	Dan Plesac	.05
176	Dan Pasqua	.05
177	Kelly Downs	.05
178	Matt Nokes	.05
179	Luis Aquino	.05
180	Frank Tanana	.05
181	Tony Pena	.05
182	Dan Gladden	.05
183	Bruce Hurst	.05
184	Roger Clemens	.35
185	Mark McGwire	1.00
186	Rob Murphy	.05
187	Jim Deshaies	.05
188	Fred McGriff	.05
189	Rob Dibble	.05
190	Don Mattingly	.35
191	Felix Fermin	.05
192	Roberto Kelly	.05
193	Dennis Cook	.05
194	Darren Daulton	.05
195	Alfredo Griffin	.05
196	Eric Plunk	.05
197	Orel Hershiser	.10
198	Paul O'Neill	.10
199	Randy Bush	.05
200a	Checklist 130-231	.05
200b	Checklist 126-223	.05
201	Ozzie Smith	.20
202	Pete O'Brien	.05
203	Jay Howell	.05
204	Mark Gubicza	.05
205	Ed Whitson	.05
206	George Bell	.05
207	Mike Scott	.05
208	Charlie Leibrandt	.05
209	Mike Heath	.05
210	Dennis Eckersley	.10
211	Mike LaValliere	.05
212	Darnell Coles	.05
213	Lance Parrish	.05
214	Mike Moore	.05
215	*Steve Finley*	.20
216	Tim Raines	.10
217a	Scott Garrelts (Born 10/20)	.05
217b	Scott Garrelts (Born 10/30)	.20
218	Kevin McReynolds	.05
219	Dave Gallagher	.05
220	Tim Wallach	.05
221	Chuck Crim	.05
222	Lonnie Smith	.05
223	Andre Dawson	.10
224	Nelson Santovenia	.05
225	Rafael Palmeiro	.10
226	Devon White	.05
227	Harold Reynolds	.05
228	Ellis Burks	.05
229	Mark Parent	.05
230	Will Clark	.15
231	Jimmy Key	.05
232	John Farrell	.05
233	Eric Davis	.10
234	Johnny Ray	.05
235	Darryl Strawberry	.10
236	Bill Doran	.05
237	Greg Gagne	.05
238	Jim Eisenreich	.05
239	Tommy Gregg	.05
240	Marty Barrett	.05
241	Rafael Ramirez	.05
242	Chris Sabo	.05
243	Dave Henderson	.05
244	Andy Van Slyke	.05
245	Alvaro Espinoza	.05
246	Garry Templeton	.05
247	Gene Harris	.05
248	Kevin Gross	.05
249	Brett Butler	.05
250	Willie Randolph	.05
251	Roger McDowell	.05
252	Rafael Belliard	.05
253	Steve Rosenberg	.05
254	Jack Howell	.05
255	Marvell Wynne	.05
256	Tom Candiotti	.05
257	Todd Benzinger	.05
258	Don Robinson	.05
259	Phil Bradley	.05
260	Cecil Espy	.05
261	Scott Bankhead	.05
262	Frank White	.05
263	Andres Thomas	.05
264	Glenn Braggs	.05
265	David Cone	.05
266	Bobby Thigpen	.05
267	Nelson Liriano	.05
268	Terry Steinbach	.05
269	Kirby Puckett	.35
270	Gregg Jefferies	.10
271	Jeff Blauser	.05
272	Cory Snyder	.05
273	Roy Smith	.05
274	Tom Foley	.05
275	Mitch Williams	.05
276	Paul Kilgus	.05
277	Don Slaught	.05
278	Von Hayes	.05
279	Vince Coleman	.05
280	Mike Boddicker	.05
281	Ken Dayley	.05
282	Mike Devereaux	.05
283	*Kenny Rogers*	.05
284	Jeff Russell	.05
285	*Jerome Walton*	.10
286	Derek Lilliquist	.05
287	Joe Orsulak	.05
288	Dick Schofield	.05
289	Ron Darling	.05
290	Bobby Bonilla	.10
291	Jim Gantner	.05
292	Bobby Witt	.05
293	Greg Brock	.05
294	Ivan Calderon	.05
295	Steve Bedrosian	.05
296	Mike Henneman	.05
297	Tom Gordon	.05
298	Lou Whitaker	.05
299	Terry Pendleton	.05
300a	Checklist 232-333	.05
300b	Checklist 224-321	.05
301	Juan Berenguer	.05
302	Mark Davis	.05
303	Nick Esasky	.05
304	Rickey Henderson	.20
305	Rick Cerone	.05
306	Craig Biggio	.15
307	Duane Ward	.05
308	Tom Browning	.05
309	Walt Terrell	.05
310	Greg Swindell	.05
311	Dave Righetti	.05
312	Mike Maddux	.05
313	Len Dykstra	.10
314	Jose Gonzalez	.05
315	Steve Balboni	.05
316	Mike Scioscia	.05
317	Ron Oester	.05
318	*Gary Wayne*	.05
319	Todd Worrell	.05
320	Doug Jones	.05
321	Jeff Hamilton	.05
322	Danny Tartabull	.05
323	Chris James	.05
324	Mike Flanagan	.05
325	Gerald Young	.05
326	Bob Boone	.10
327	Frank Williams	.05
328	Dave Parker	.10
329	Sid Bream	.05
330	Mike Schooler	.05
331	Bert Blyleven	.10
332	Bob Welch	.05
333	Bob Milacki	.05
334	Tim Burke	.05
335	Jose Uribe	.05
336	Randy Myers	.05
337	Eric King	.05
338	Mark Langston	.05
339	Ted Higuera	.05
340	Oddibe McDowell	.05
341	Lloyd McClendon	.05
342	Pascual Perez	.05
343	Kevin Brown	.05
344	Chuck Finley	.05
345	Erik Hanson	.05
346	Rich Gedman	.05
347	Bip Roberts	.05
348	Matt Williams	.15
349	Tom Henke	.05
350	Brad Komminsk	.05
351	Jeff Reed	.05
352	Brian Downing	.05
353	Frank Viola	.05
354	Terry Puhl	.05
355	Brian Harper	.05
356	Steve Farr	.05
357	Joe Boever	.05

358 Danny Heep .05
359 Larry Andersen .05
360 Rolando Roomes .05
361 Mike Gallego .05
362 Bob Kipper .05
363 Clay Parker .05
364 Mike Pagliarulo .05
365 Ken Griffey, Jr. 1.50
366 Rex Hudler .05
367 Pat Sheridan .05
368 Kirk Gibson .10
369 Jeff Parrett .05
370 Bob Walk .05
371 Ken Patterson .05
372 Bryan Harvey .05
373 Mike Bielecki .05
374 *Tom Magrann* .05
375 Rick Mahler .05
376 Craig Lefferts .05
377 Gregg Olson .05
378 Jamie Moyer .05
379 Randy Johnson .25
380 Jeff Montgomery .05
381 Marty Clary .05
382 *Bill Spiers* .05
383 Dave Magadan .05
384 *Greg Hibbard* .05
385 Ernie Whitt .05
386 Rick Honeycutt .05
387 Dave West .05
388 Keith Hernandez .05
389 Jose Alvarez .05
390 Albert Belle .50
391 Rick Aguilera .05
392 Mike Fitzgerald .05
393 *Dwight Smith* .05
394 *Steve Wilson* .05
395 *Bob Geren* .05
396 Randy Ready .05
397 Ken Hill .05
398 Jody Reed .05
399 Tom Brunansky .05
400a Checklist 334-435 .05
400b Checklist 322-419 .05
401 Rene Gonzales .05
402 Harold Baines .10
403 Cecilio Guante .05
404 Joe Girardi .05
405a *Sergio Valdez* (black line crosses S in Sergio) .25
405b Sergio Valdez (corrected) .05
406 Mark Williamson .05
407 Glenn Hoffman .05
408 *Jeff Innis* .05
409 Randy Kramer .05
410 Charlie O'Brien .05
411 Charlie Hough .05
412 Gus Polidor .05
413 Ron Karkovice .05
414 Trevor Wilson .05
415 *Kevin Ritz* .10
416 Gary Thurman .05
417 Jeff Robinson .05
418 Scott Terry .05
419 Tim Laudner .05
420 Dennis Rasmussen .05
421 Luis Rivera .05
422 Jim Corsi .05
423 Dennis Lamp .05
424 Ken Caminiti .10
425 David Wells .10
426 Norm Charlton .05
427 Deion Sanders .15
428 Dion James .05
429 Chuck Cary .05
430 Ken Howell .05
431 Steve Lake .05
432 Kal Daniels .05
433 Lance McCullers .05
434 Lenny Harris .05
435 *Scott Scudder* .05
436 Gene Larkin .05
437 Dan Quisenberry .05
438 *Steve Olin* .05
439 Mickey Hatcher .05
440 Willie Wilson .05
441 Mark Grant .05
442 Mookie Wilson .05
443 Alex Trevino .05
444 Pat Tabler .05
445 Dave Bergman .05
446 Todd Burns .05
447 R.J. Reynolds .05
448 Jay Buhner .05
449 *Lee Stevens* .10
450 Ron Hassey .05
451 Bob Melvin .05
452 Dave Martinez .05
453 *Greg Litton* .05
454 Mark Carreon .05
455 Scott Fletcher .05
456 Otis Nixon .05
457 *Tony Fossas* .05
458 John Russell .05
459 Paul Assenmacher .05
460 Zane Smith .05
461 *Jack Daugherty* .05
462 *Rich Monteleone* .05
463 Greg Briley .05
464 Mike Smithson .05
465 Benito Santiago .05
466 *Jeff Brantley* .10
467 Jose Nunez .05
468 Scott Bailes .05
469 Ken Griffey .10
470 Bob McClure .05
471 Mackey Sasser .05
472 Glenn Wilson .05
473 *Kevin Tapani* .25
474 Bill Buckner .05
475 Ron Gant .05
476 Kevin Romine .05
477 Juan Agosto .05
478 Herm Winningham .05
479 Storm Davis .05
480 Jeff King .05
481 *Kevin Mmahat* .05
482 Carmelo Martinez .05
483 Omar Vizquel .10
484 Jim Dwyer .05
485 Bob Knepper .05
486 Dave Anderson .05
487 Ron Jones .05
488 Jay Bell .05
489 *Sammy Sosa* 5.00
490 *Kent Anderson* .05
491 Domingo Ramos .05
492 Dave Clark .05
493 Tim Birtsas .05
494 Ken Oberkfell .05
495 Larry Sheets .05
496 Jeff Kunkel .05
497 Jim Presley .05
498 Mike Macfarlane .05
499 Pete Smith .05
500a Checklist 436-537 .05
500b Checklist 420-517 .05
501 Gary Sheffield .15
502 *Terry Bross* .05
503 *Jerry Kutzler* .05
504 Lloyd Moseby .05
505 Curt Young .05
506 Al Newman .05
507 Keith Miller .05
508 *Mike Stanton* .15
509 Rich Yett .05
510 *Tim Drummond* .05
511 Joe Hesketh .05
512 *Rick Wrona* .10
513 Luis Salazar .05
514 Hal Morris .05
515 Terry Mullholland .10
516 John Morris .05
517 Carlos Quintana .05
518 Frank DiPino .05
519 Randy Milligan .05
520 Chad Kreuter .05
521 Mike Jeffcoat .05
522 Mike Harkey .05
523a Andy Nezelek (Born 1985) .05
523b Andy Nezelek (Born 1965) .15
524 Dave Schmidt .05
525 Tony Armas .05
526 Barry Lyons .05
527 *Rick Reed* .05
528 Jerry Reuss .05
529 *Dean Palmer* .15
530 *Jeff Peterek* .05
531 *Carlos Martinez* .10
532 Atlee Hammaker .05
533 Mike Brumley .05
534 Terry Leach .05
535 *Doug Strange* .05
536 Jose DeLeon .05
537 Shane Rawley .05
538 Joey Cora .05
539 Eric Hetzel .05
540 Gene Nelson .05
541 Wes Gardner .05
542 Mark Portugal .05
543 Al Leiter .05
544 Jack Armstrong .05
545 Greg Cadaret .05
546 Rod Nichols .05
547 Luis Polonia .05
548 Charlie Hayes .05
549 Dickie Thon .05
550 Tim Crews .05
551 Dave Winfield .20
552 Mike Davis .05
553 Ron Robinson .05
554 Carmen Castillo .05
555 John Costello .05
556 Bud Black .05
557 Rick Dempsey .05
558 Jim Acker .05
559 Eric Show .05
560 Pat Borders .05
561 Danny Darwin .05
562 *Rick Luecken* .05
563 Edwin Nunez .05
564 Felix Jose .05
565 John Cangelosi .05
566 Billy Swift .05
567 Bill Schroeder .05
568 Stan Javier .05
569 Jim Traber .05
570 Wallace Johnson .05
571 Donell Nixon .05
572 Sid Fernandez .05
573 Lance Johnson .05
574 Andy McGaffigan .05
575 Mark Knudson .05
576 *Tommy Greene* .20
577 Mark Grace .15
578 *Larry Walker* 1.50
579 Mike Stanley .05
580 Mike Witt .05
581 Scott Bradley .05
582 Greg Harris .05
583a Kevin Hickey (black stripe over top of "K" vertical stroke) .05
583b Kevin Hickey (black stripe under "K") .05
584 Lee Mazzilli .05
585 Jeff Pico .05
586 *Joe Oliver* .05
587 Willie Fraser .05
588 Puzzle card (Carl Yastrzemski) .05
589 Kevin Bass .05
590 John Moses .05
591 Tom Pagnozzi .05
592 *Tony Castillo* .05
593 Jerald Clark .05
594 Dan Schatzeder .05
595 Luis Quinones .05
596 Pete Harnisch .05
597 Gary Redus .05
598 Mel Hall .05
599 Rick Schu .05
600a Checklist 538-639 .05
600b Checklist 518-617 .05
601 Mike Kingery .05
602 Terry Kennedy .05
603 Mike Sharperson .05
604 Don Carman .05
605 Jim Gott .05
606 Donn Pall .05
607 Rance Mulliniks .05
608 Curt Wilkerson .05
609 Mike Felder .05
610 Guillermo Hernandez .05
611 Candy Maldonado .05
612 Mark Thurmond .05
613 Rick Leach .05
614 Jerry Reed .05
615 Franklin Stubbs .05
616 Billy Hatcher .05
617 Don August .05
618 Tim Teufel .05
619 Shawn Hillegas .05
620 Manny Lee .05
621 Gary Ward .05
622 *Mark Guthrie* .05
623 Jeff Musselman .05
624 Mark Lemke .05
625 Fernando Valenzuela .10
626 *Paul Sorrento* .10
627 Glenallen Hill .05
628 Les Lancaster .05
629 Vance Law .05
630 Randy Velarde .05
631 Todd Frohwirth .05
632 Willie McGee .05
633 Oil Can Boyd .05
634 Cris Carpenter .05
635 Brian Holton .05
636 Tracy Jones .05
637 Terry Steinbach (AS) .05
638 Brady Anderson .10
639a Jack Morris (black line crosses J of Jack) .25
639b Jack Morris (corrected) .10
640 *Jaime Navarro* .05
641 Darrin Jackson .05
642 *Mike Dyer* .05
643 Mike Schmidt .25
644 Henry Cotto .05
645 John Cerutti .05
646 *Francisco Cabrera* .05
647 Scott Sanderson .05
648 Brian Meyer .05
649 Ray Searage .05
650 Bo Jackson (AS) .15
651 Steve Lyons .05
652 Mike LaCoss .05
653 Ted Power .05
654 Howard Johnson (AS) .05
655 *Mauro Gozzo* .05
656 *Mike Blowers* .15
657 Paul Gibson .05
658 Neal Heaton .05
659a Nolan Ryan 5,000 K's (King of Kings (#665) back) 2.50
659b Nolan Ryan 5,000 K's (correct back) .50
660a Harold Baines (AS) (black line through star on front, Recent Major League Performance on back) .50
660b Harold Baines (AS) (black line through star on front, All-Star Game Performance on back) 1.00
660c Harold Baines (AS) (black line behind star on front, Recent Major League Performance on back) .50
660d Harold Baines (AS) (black line behind star on front, All-Star Game Performance on back) .10
661 Gary Pettis .05
662 *Clint Zavaras* .05
663 Rick Reuschel (AS) .05
664 Alejandro Pena .05
665a Nolan Ryan (King of Kings) 5,000 K's (#659) back) 2.50
665b Nolan Ryan (King of Kings) (correct back) .50
665c Nolan Ryan (King of Kings) (no number on back) 1.00
666 Ricky Horton .05
667 Curt Schilling .05
668 Bill Landrum .05
669 Todd Stottlemyre .05
670 Tim Leary .05
671 *John Wetteland* .25
672 Calvin Schiraldi .05
673 Ruben Sierra (AS) .05
674 Pedro Guerrero (AS) .05
675 Ken Phelps .05
676 Cal Ripken (AS) .30
677 Denny Walling .05
678 Goose Gossage .05
679 *Gary Mielke* .05
680 Bill Bathe .05
681 Tom Lawless .05
682 *Xavier Hernandez* .15
683 Kirby Puckett (AS) .20
684 Mariano Duncan .05
685 Ramon Martinez .10
686 Tim Jones .05
687 Tom Filer .05
688 Steve Lombardozzi .05
689 *Bernie Williams* 1.00
690 *Chip Hale* .05
691 *Beau Allred* .05
692 Ryne Sandberg (AS) .25
693 *Jeff Huson* .10
694 Curt Ford .05

695	Eric Davis (AS)	.05
696	Scott Lusader	.05
697	Mark McGwire (AS)	.50
698	*Steve Cummings*	.05
699	*George Canale*	.05
700a	Checklist 640-715/ BC1-BC26	.05
700b	Checklist 640-716/ BC1-BC26	.05
700c	Checklist 618-716	.05
701	Julio Franco (AS)	.05
702	*Dave Johnson*	.05
703	Dave Stewart (AS)	.05
704	*Dave Justice*	.50
705	Tony Gwynn (AS)	.15
706	Greg Myers	.05
707	Will Clark (AS)	.05
708	Benito Santiago (AS)	.05
709	Larry McWilliams	.05
710	Ozzie Smith (AS)	.10
711	*John Olerud*	.50
712	Wade Boggs (AS)	.10
713	*Gary Eave*	.05
714	Bob Tewksbury	.05
715	Kevin Mitchell (AS)	.05
716	A. Bartlett Giamatti	.25

1990 Donruss Best A.L.

This 144-card set features the top players of the American League. The 2-1/2" x 3-1/2" cards feature the same front design as the regular Donruss set, exception with blue borders instead of red. Backs feature a yellow frame with complete statistics and biographical information provided. This marks the first year that Donruss divided its baseball-best issue into two sets designated by league.

		MT
	Complete Set (144):	8.00
	Common Player:	.05
1	Ken Griffey, Jr.	2.00
2	Bob Milacki	.05
3	Mike Boddicker	.05
4	Bert Blyleven	.05
5	Carlton Fisk	.40
6	Greg Swindell	.05
7	Alan Trammell	.10
8	Mark Davis	.05
9	Chris Bosio	.05
10	Gary Gaetti	.05
11	Matt Nokes	.05
12	Dennis Eckersley	.05
13	Kevin Brown	.05
14	Tom Henke	.05
15	Mickey Tettleton	.05
16	Jody Reed	.05
17	Mark Langston	.05
18	Melido Perez	.05
19	John Farrell	.05
20	Tony Phillips	.05
21	Bret Saberhagen	.05
22	Robin Yount	.40
23	Kirby Puckett	.50
24	Steve Sax	.05
25	Dave Stewart	.05
26	Alvin Davis	.05
27	Geno Petralli	.05
28	Mookie Wilson	.05
29	Jeff Ballard	.05
30	Ellis Burks	.05
31	Wally Joyner	.05
32	Bobby Thigpen	.05
33	Keith Hernandez	.05
34	Jack Morris	.05
35	George Brett	.45
36	Dan Plesac	.05
37	Brian Harper	.05
38	Don Mattingly	.50
39	Dave Henderson	.05
40	Scott Bankhead	.05
41	Rafael Palmeiro	.10
42	Jimmy Key	.05
43	Gregg Olson	.05
44	Tony Pena	.05
45	Jack Howell	.05
46	Eric King	.05
47	Cory Snyder	.05
48	Frank Tanana	.05
49	Nolan Ryan	1.00
50	Bob Boone	.05
51	Dave Parker	.05
52	Allan Anderson	.05
53	Tim Leary	.05
54	Mark McGwire	2.00
55	Dave Valle	.05
56	Fred McGriff	.05
57	Cal Ripken	1.00
58	Roger Clemens	.50
59	Lance Parrish	.05
60	Robin Ventura	.10
61	Doug Jones	.05
62	Lloyd Moseby	.05
63	Bo Jackson	.15
64	Paul Molitor	.30
65	Kent Hrbek	.05
66	Mel Hall	.05
67	Bob Welch	.05
68	Erik Hanson	.05
69	Harold Baines	.05
70	Junior Felix	.05
71	Craig Worthington	.05
72	Jeff Reardon	.05
73	Johnny Ray	.05
74	Ozzie Guillen	.05
75	Brook Jacoby	.05
76	Chet Lemon	.05
77	Mark Gubicza	.05
78	B.J. Surhoff	.05
79	Rick Aguilera	.05
80	Pascual Perez	.05
81	Jose Canseco	.35
82	Mike Schooler	.05
83	Jeff Huson	.05
84	Kelly Gruber	.05
85	Randy Milligan	.05
86	Wade Boggs	.35
87	Dave Winfield	.40
88	Scott Fletcher	.05
89	Tom Candiotti	.05
90	Mike Heath	.05
91	Kevin Seitzer	.05
92	Ted Higuera	.05
93	Kevin Tapani	.05
94	Roberto Kelly	.05
95	Walt Weiss	.05
96	Checklist	.05
97	Sandy Alomar	.05
98	Pete O'Brien	.05
99	Jeff Russell	.05
100	John Olerud	.15
101	Pete Harnisch	.05
102	Dwight Evans	.05
103	Chuck Finley	.05
104	Sammy Sosa	2.00
105	Mike Henneman	.05
106	Kurt Stillwell	.05
107	Greg Vaughn	.10
108	Dan Gladden	.05
109	Jesse Barfield	.05
110	Willie Randolph	.05
111	Randy Johnson	.40
112	Julio Franco	.05
113	Tony Fernandez	.05
114	Ben McDonald	.05
115	Mike Greenwell	.05
116	Luis Polonia	.05
117	Carney Lansford	.05
118	Bud Black	.05
119	Lou Whitaker	.05
120	Jim Eisenreich	.05
121	Gary Sheffield	.10
122	Shane Mack	.05
123	Alvaro Espinoza	.05
124	Rickey Henderson	.35
125	Jeffrey Leonard	.05
126	Gary Pettis	.05
127	Dave Steib	.05
128	Danny Tartabull	.05
129	Joe Orsulak	.05
130	Tom Brunansky	.05
131	Dick Schofield	.05
132	Candy Maldonado	.05
133	Cecil Fielder	.05
134	Terry Shumpert	.05
135	Greg Gagne	.05
136	Dave Righetti	.05
137	Terry Steinbach	.05
138	Harold Reynolds	.05
139	George Bell	.05
140	Carlos Quintana	.05
141	Ivan Calderon	.05
142	Greg Brock	.05
143	Ruben Sierra	.05
144	Checklist	.05

1990 Donruss Best N.L.

This 144-card set features the top players in the National League for 1990. The 2-1/2" x 3-1/2" cards feature the same design as the regular 1990 Donruss cards, except they have blue, rather than red borders. Traded players are featured with their new teams. This set, along with the A.L. Best set, was available at select retail stores and within the hobby.

		MT
	Complete Set (144):	6.00
	Common Player:	.05
1	Eric Davis	.05
2	Tom Glavine	.20
3	Mike Bielecki	.05
4	Jim Deshaies	.05
5	Mike Scioscia	.05
6	Spike Owen	.05
7	Dwight Gooden	.05
8	Ricky Jordan	.05
9	Doug Drabek	.05
10	Bryn Smith	.05
11	Tony Gwynn	1.00
12	John Burkett	.05
13	Nick Esasky	.05
14	Greg Maddux	.75
15	Joe Oliver	.05
16	Mike Scott	.05
17	Tim Belcher	.05
18	Kevin Gross	.05
19	Howard Johnson	.05
20	Darren Daulton	.05
21	John Smiley	.05
22	Ken Dayley	.05
23	Craig Lefferts	.05
24	Will Clark	.15
25	Greg Olson	.05
26	Ryne Sandberg	.75
27	Tom Browning	.05
28	Eric Anthony	.05
29	Juan Samuel	.05
30	Dennis Martinez	.05
31	Kevin Elster	.05
32	Tom Herr	.05
33	Sid Bream	.05
34	Terry Pendleton	.05
35	Roberto Alomar	.20
36	Kevin Bass	.05
37	Jim Presley	.05
38	Les Lancaster	.05
39	Paul O'Neill	.10
40	Dave Smith	.05
41	Kirk Gibson	.05
42	Tim Burke	.05
43	David Cone	.05
44	Ken Howell	.05
45	Barry Bonds	1.00
46	Joe Magrane	.05
47	Andy Benes	.05
48	Gary Carter	.15
49	Pat Combs	.05
50	John Smoltz	.10
51	Mark Grace	.20
52	Barry Larkin	.15
53	Danny Darwin	.05
54	Orel Hershiser	.05
55	Tim Wallach	.05
56	Dave Magadan	.05
57	Roger McDowell	.05
58	Bill Landrum	.05
59	Jose DeLeon	.05
60	Bip Roberts	.05
61	Matt Williams	.10
62	Dale Murphy	.15
63	Dwight Smith	.05
64	Chris Sabo	.05
65	Glenn Davis	.05
66	Jay Howell	.05
67	Andres Galarraga	.10
68	Frank Viola	.05
69	John Kruk	.05
70	Bobby Bonilla	.05
71	Todd Zeile	.05
72	Joe Carter	.05
73	Robby Thompson	.05
74	Jeff Blauser	.05
75	Mitch Williams	.05
76	Rob Dibble	.05
77	Rafael Ramirez	.05
78	Eddie Murray	.20
79	Dave Martinez	.05
80	Darryl Strawberry	.05
81	Dickie Thon	.05
82	Jose Lind	.05
83	Ozzie Smith	.25
84	Bruce Hurst	.05
85	Kevin Mitchell	.05
86	Lonnie Smith	.05
87	Joe Girardi	.05
88	Randy Myers	.05
89	Craig Biggio	.10
90	Fernando Valenzuela	.05
91	Larry Walker	.20
92	John Franco	.05
93	Dennis Cook	.05
94	Bob Walk	.05
95	Pedro Guerrero	.05
96	Checklist	.05
97	Andre Dawson	.15
98	Ed Whitson	.05
99	Steve Bedrosian	.05
100	Oddibe McDowell	.05
101	Todd Benzinger	.05
102	Bill Doran	.05
103	Alfredo Griffin	.05
104	Tim Raines	.05
105	Sid Fernandez	.05
106	Charlie Hayes	.05
107	Mike LaValliere	.05
108	Jose Oquendo	.05
109	Jack Clark	.05
110	Scott Garrelts	.05
111	Ron Gant	.05
112	Shawon Dunston	.05
113	Mariano Duncan	.05
114	Eric Yelding	.05
115	Hubie Brooks	.05
116	Delino DeShields	.05
117	Gregg Jefferies	.05
118	Len Dykstra	.05
119	Andy Van Slyke	.05
120	Lee Smith	.05
121	Benito Santiago	.05
122	Jose Uribe	.05
123	Jeff Treadway	.05

124	Jerome Walton	.05
125	Billy Hatcher	.05
126	Ken Caminiti	.10
127	Kal Daniels	.05
128	Marquis Grissom	.05
129	Kevin McReynolds	.05
130	Wally Backman	.05
131	Willie McGee	.05
132	Terry Kennedy	.05
133	Garry Templeton	.05
134	Lloyd McClendon	.05
135	Daryl Boston	.05
136	Jay Bell	.05
137	Mike Pagliarulo	.05
138	Vince Coleman	.05
139	Brett Butler	.05
140	Von Hayes	.05
141	Ramon Martinez	.05
142	Jack Armstrong	.05
143	Franklin Stubbs	.05
144	Checklist	.05

1990 Donruss Diamond Kings Supers

Donruss made this set available through a mail-in offer. Three wrappers, $10 and $2 for postage were necessary to obtain this set. The cards are exactly the same design as the regular Donruss Diamond Kings except they measure approximately 5" x 6-3/4" in size. The artwork of Dick Perez is featured.

		MT
Complete Set (26):		4.00
Common Player:		.10
1	Bo Jackson	.50
2	Steve Sax	.10
3	Ruben Sierra	.10
4	Ken Griffey, Jr.	3.00
5	Mickey Tettleton	.10
6	Dave Stewart	.10
7	Jim Deshaies	.10
8	John Smoltz	.35
9	Mike Bielecki	.10
10	Brian Downing	.10
11	Kevin Mitchell	.10
12	Kelly Gruber	.10
13	Joe Magrane	.10
14	John Franco	.10
15	Ozzie Guillen	.10
16	Lou Whitaker	.10
17	John Smiley	.10
18	Howard Johnson	.10
19	Willie Randolph	.10
20	Chris Bosio	.10
21	Tommy Herr	.10
22	Dan Gladden	.10
23	Ellis Burks	.10
24	Pete O'Brien	.10
25	Bryn Smith	.10
26	Ed Whitson	.10

1990 Donruss Grand Slammers

For the second consecutive year Donruss produced a set in honor of players who hit grand slams in the previous season. The cards are styled after the 1990 Donruss regular issue. The cards were inserted into 1990 Donruss factory sets, and one card per cello pack. Some, perhaps all, of the cards can be found without the split black stripe near the right end on back.

		MT
Complete Set (12):		1.50
Common Player:		.10
1	Matt Williams	.25
2	Jeffrey Leonard	.10
3	Chris James	.10
4	Mark McGwire	1.00
5	Dwight Evans	.10
6	Will Clark	.20
7	Mike Scioscia	.10
8	Todd Benzinger	.10
9	Fred McGriff	.10
10	Kevin Bass	.10
11	Jack Clark	.10
12	Bo Jackson	.25

1990 Donruss Learning Series

Cards from this 55-card set were released as part of an educational package available to schools. The cards are styled like the regular-issue 1990 Donruss cards, but feature a special "learning series" logo on the front. The backs feature career highlights, statistics and card numbers. The cards were not released directly to the hobby.

		MT
Complete Set (55):		25.00
Common Player:		.25
1	George Brett (DK)	2.00
2	Kevin Mitchell	.25
3	Andy Van Slyke	.25
4	Benito Santiago	.25
5	Gary Carter	.40
6	Jose Canseco	.60
7	Rickey Henderson	.85
8	Ken Griffey, Jr.	6.00
9	Ozzie Smith	2.00
10	Dwight Gooden	.25
11	Ryne Sandberg (DK)	2.00
12	Don Mattingly	3.00
13	Ozzie Guillen	.25
14	Dave Righetti	.25
15	Rick Dempsey	.25
16	Tom Herr	.25
17	Julio Franco	.25
18	Von Hayes	.25
19	Cal Ripken	5.00
20	Alan Trammell	.35
21	Wade Boggs	1.50
22	Glenn Davis	.25
23	Will Clark	.50
24	Nolan Ryan	5.00
25	George Bell	.25
26	Cecil Fielder	.25
27	Gregg Olson	.25
28	Tim Wallach	.25
29	Ron Darling	.25
30	Kelly Gruber	.25
31	Shawn Boskie	.25
32	Mike Greenwell	.25
33	Dave Parker	.25
34	Joe Magrane	.25
35	Dave Stewart	.25
36	Kent Hrbek	.25
37	Robin Yount	1.00
38	Bo Jackson	.50
39	Fernando Valenzuela	.25
40	Sandy Alomar, Jr.	.25
41	Lance Parrish	.25
42	Candy Maldonado	.25
43	Mike LaValliere	.25
44	Jim Abbott	.25
45	Edgar Martinez	.25
46	Kirby Puckett	2.50
47	Delino DeShields	.25
48	Tony Gwynn	2.00
49	Carlton Fisk	.75
50	Mike Scott	.25
51	Barry Larkin	.30
52	Andre Dawson	.40
53	Tom Glavine	.35
54	Tom Browning	.25
55	Checklist	.05

1990 Donruss MVP

This special 26-card set includes one player from each Major League team. Numbered BC-1 (the "BC" stands for "Bonus Card") through BC-26, the cards from this set were randomly packed in 1990 Donruss wax packs and were not available in factory sets or other types of packaging. The red-bordered cards are similar in design to the regular 1990 Donruss set, except the player photos are set against a special background made up of the "MVP" logo.

		MT
Complete Set (26):		1.25
Common Player:		.10
1	Bo Jackson	.25
2	Howard Johnson	.10
3	Dave Stewart	.10
4	Tony Gwynn	.35
5	Orel Hershiser	.10
6	Pedro Guerrero	.10
7	Tim Raines	.10
8	Kirby Puckett	.35
9	Alvin Davis	.10
10	Ryne Sandberg	.40
11	Kevin Mitchell	.10
12a	John Smoltz (photo of Tom Glavine)	2.00
12b	John Smoltz (corrected)	.30
13	George Bell	.10
14	Julio Franco	.10
15	Paul Molitor	.25
16	Bobby Bonilla	.10
17	Mike Greenwell	.10
18	Cal Ripken	.75
19	Carlton Fisk	.25
20	Chili Davis	.10
21	Glenn Davis	.10
22	Steve Sax	.10
23	Eric Davis	.10
24	Greg Swindell	.10
25	Von Hayes	.10
26	Alan Trammell	.10

1990 Donruss Rookies

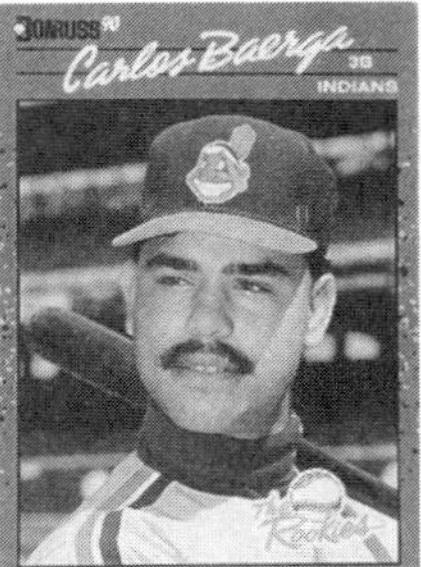

For the fifth straight year, Donruss issued a 56-card "Rookies" set in 1990. As in previous years, the set is similar in design to the regular Donruss set, except for a new "The Rookies" logo and green borders instead of red. The set is packaged in a special box and includes a Carl Yastrzemski puzzle card.

		MT
Complete Set (56):		2.00
Common Player:		.10
1	Sandy Alomar	.25
2	John Olerud	.40
3	Pat Combs	.10
4	Brian Dubois	.10
5	Felix Jose	.10
6	Delino DeShields	.10
7	Mike Stanton	.10
8	Mike Munoz	.10
9	Craig Grebeck	.10
10	Joe Kraemer	.10
11	Jeff Huson	.10
12	Bill Sampen	.10
13	Brian Bohanon	.10
14	Dave Justice	.50
15	Robin Ventura	.30
16	Greg Vaughn	.20
17	Wayne Edwards	.10
18	Shawn Boskie	.10
19	*Carlos Baerga*	.20
20	Mark Gardner	.10
21	Kevin Appier	.30
22	Mike Harkey	.10
23	Tim Layana	.10
24	Glenallen Hill	.10
25	Jerry Kutzler	.10
26	Mike Blowers	.10
27	Scott Ruskin	.10
28	Dana Kiecker	.10
29	Willie Blair	.10
30	Ben McDonald	.15
31	Todd Zeile	.15
32	Scott Coolbaugh	.10
33	Xavier Hernandez	.10
34	Mike Hartley	.10
35	Kevin Tapani	.10
36	Kevin Wickander	.10
37	Carlos Hernandez	.10
38	Brian Traxler	.10
39	Marty Brown	.10
40	Scott Radinsky	.10

41 Julio Machado .10
42 Steve Avery .10
43 Mark Lemke .10
44 Alan Mills .10
45 Marquis Grissom .25
46 Greg Olson .10
47 Dave Hollins .15
48 Jerald Clark .10
49 Eric Anthony .10
50 Tim Drummond .10
51 John Burkett .15
52 Brent Knackert .10
53 Jeff Shaw .10
54 John Orton .10
55 Terry Shumpert .10
56 Checklist .05

1991 Donruss Previews

Once again in late 1990 Donruss distributed individual cards from a 12-card preview issue to its dealer network as an introduction to its 1991 issue. Like the previous year's preview cards, the '91 samples utilized the format which would follow on the regular-issue cards, but the photos were different. This has helped create demand for these cards from superstar collectors. Backs are printed in black-and-white and have little more than a player name, card number and MLB logos.

		MT
Complete Set (12):		375.00
Common Player:		4.50
1	Dave Justice	20.00
2	Doug Drabek	4.50
3	Scott Chiamparino	4.50
4	Ken Griffey, Jr.	125.00
5	Bob Welch	4.50
6	Tino Martinez	8.00
7	Nolan Ryan	125.00
8	Dwight Gooden	6.00
9	Ryne Sandberg	40.00
10	Barry Bonds	50.00
11	Jose Canseco	20.00
12	Eddie Murray	20.00

1991 Donruss

Donruss used a two-series format in 1991. The first series was released in December, 1990, and the second in February, 1991. The 1991 design is somewhat reminiscent of the 1986 set, with blue borders on Series I cards; green on Series II. Limited edition cards including an autographed Ryne Sandberg card (5,000) were randomly inserted in wax packs. Other features of the set include 40 Rated Rookies, (RR) in the checklist, Legends and Elite insert series, and another Diamond King (DK) subset. Cards were distributed in packs with Willie Stargell puzzle pieces.

		MT
Factory Set w/Leaf or Studio Previews:		16.00
Complete Set (792):		8.00
Common Player:		.05
Willie Stargell Puzzle:		1.00
Series 1 or 2 Pack (15):		.40
Series 1 or 2 Wax Box (36):		15.00
1	Dave Steib (Diamond King)	.05
2	Craig Biggio (DK)	.10
3	Cecil Fielder (DK)	.05
4	Barry Bonds (DK)	.35
5	Barry Larkin (DK)	.10
6	Dave Parker (DK)	.05
7	Len Dykstra (DK)	.05
8	Bobby Thigpen (DK)	.05
9	Roger Clemens (DK)	.20
10	Ron Gant (DK)	.05
11	Delino DeShields (DK)	.05
12	Roberto Alomar (DK)	.20
13	Sandy Alomar (DK)	.10
14	Ryne Sandberg (DK)	.20
15	Ramon Martinez (DK)	.05
16	Edgar Martinez (DK)	.05
17	Dave Magadan (DK)	.05
18	Matt Williams (DK)	.10
19	Rafael Palmeiro (DK)	.10
20	Bob Welch (DK)	.05
21	Dave Righetti (DK)	.05
22	Brian Harper (DK)	.05
23	Gregg Olson (DK)	.05
24	Kurt Stillwell (DK)	.05
25	Pedro Guerrero (DK)	.05
26	Chuck Finley (DK)	.05
27	Diamond King checklist	.05
28	Tino Martinez (Rated Rookie)	.15
29	Mark Lewis (RR)	.10
30	*Bernard Gilkey* (RR)	.15
31	Hensley Meulens (RR)	.05
32	*Derek Bell* (RR)	.30
33	Jose Offerman (RR)	.05
34	Terry Bross (RR)	.05
35	*Leo Gomez* (RR)	.10
36	Derrick May (RR)	.05
37	*Kevin Morton* (RR)	.05
38	Moises Alou (RR)	.15
39	*Julio Valera* (RR)	.05
40	Milt Cuyler (RR)	.05
41	*Phil Plantier* (RR)	.10
42	*Scott Chiamparino* (RR)	.05
43	*Ray Lankford* (RR)	.20
44	*Mickey Morandini* (RR)	.10
45	Dave Hansen (RR)	.05
46	*Kevin Belcher* (RR)	.10
47	Darrin Fletcher (RR)	.05
48	Steve Sax (All Star)	.05
49	Ken Griffey, Jr. (AS)	.50
50a	Jose Canseco (AS) (A's in stat line on back)	.10
50b	Jose Canseco (AS) (AL in stat line on back)	.15
51	Sandy Alomar (AS)	.05
52	Cal Ripken, Jr. (AS)	.25
53	Rickey Henderson (AS)	.15
54	Bob Welch (AS)	.05
55	Wade Boggs (AS)	.10
56	Mark McGwire (AS)	.50
57	Jack McDowell	.05
58	Jose Lind	.05
59	Alex Fernandez	.10
60	Pat Combs	.05
61	*Mike Walker*	.05
62	Juan Samuel	.05
63	Mike Blowers	.05
64	Mark Guthrie	.05
65	Mark Salas	.05
66	Tim Jones	.05
67	Tim Leary	.05
68	Andres Galarraga	.10
69	Bob Milacki	.05
70	Tim Belcher	.05
71	Todd Zeile	.05
72	Jerome Walton	.05
73	Kevin Seitzer	.05
74	Jerald Clark	.05
75	John Smoltz	.10
76	Mike Henneman	.05
77	Ken Griffey, Jr.	1.00
78	Jim Abbott	.05
79	Gregg Jefferies	.10
80	Kevin Reimer	.05
81	Roger Clemens	.40
82	Mike Fitzgerald	.05
83	Bruce Hurst	.05
84	Eric Davis	.10
85	Paul Molitor	.25
86	Will Clark	.15
87	Mike Bielecki	.05
88	Bret Saberhagen	.05
89	Nolan Ryan	.75
90	Bobby Thigpen	.05
91	Dickie Thon	.05
92	Duane Ward	.05
93	Luis Polonia	.05
94	Terry Kennedy	.05
95	Kent Hrbek	.05
96	Danny Jackson	.05
97	Sid Fernandez	.05
98	Jimmy Key	.05
99	Franklin Stubbs	.05
100	Checklist 28-103	.05
101	R.J. Reynolds	.05
102	Dave Stewart	.05
103	Dan Pasqua	.05
104	Dan Plesac	.05
105	Mark McGwire	1.00
106	John Farrell	.05
107	Don Mattingly	.35
108	Carlton Fisk	.20
109	Ken Oberkfell	.05
110	Darrel Akerfelds	.05
111	Gregg Olson	.05
112	Mike Scioscia	.05
113	Bryn Smith	.05
114	Bob Geren	.05
115	Tom Candiotti	.05
116	Kevin Tapani	.05
117	Jeff Treadway	.05
118	Alan Trammell	.10
119	Pete O'Brien	.05
120	Joel Skinner	.05
121	Mike LaValliere	.05
122	Dwight Evans	.10
123	Jody Reed	.05
124	Lee Guetterman	.05
125	Tim Burke	.05
126	Dave Johnson	.05
127	Fernando Valenzuela	.10
128	Jose DeLeon	.05
129	Andre Dawson	.10
130	Gerald Perry	.05
131	Greg Harris	.05
132	Tom Glavine	.10
133	Lance McCullers	.05
134	Randy Johnson	.25
135	Lance Parrish	.05
136	Mackey Sasser	.05
137	Geno Petralli	.05
138	Dennis Lamp	.05
139	Dennis Martinez	.05
140	Mike Pagliarulo	.05
141	Hal Morris	.05
142	Dave Parker	.10
143	Brett Butler	.05
144	Paul Assenmacher	.05
145	Mark Gubicza	.05
146	Charlie Hough	.05
147	Sammy Sosa	.75
148	Randy Ready	.05
149	Kelly Gruber	.05
150	Devon White	.10
151	Gary Carter	.10
152	Gene Larkin	.05
153	Chris Sabo	.05
154	David Cone	.05
155	Todd Stottlemyre	.10
156	Glenn Wilson	.05
157	Bob Walk	.05
158	Mike Gallego	.05
159	Greg Hibbard	.05
160	Chris Bosio	.05
161	Mike Moore	.05
162	Jerry Browne	.05
163	Steve Sax	.05
164	Melido Perez	.05
165	Danny Darwin	.05
166	Roger McDowell	.05
167	Bill Ripken	.05
168	Mike Sharperson	.05
169	Lee Smith	.10
170	Matt Nokes	.05
171	Jesse Orosco	.05
172	Rick Aguilera	.05
173	Jim Presley	.05
174	Lou Whitaker	.05
175	Harold Reynolds	.10
176	Brook Jacoby	.05
177	Wally Backman	.05
178	Wade Boggs	.25
179	Chuck Cary	.05
180	Tom Foley	.05
181	Pete Harnisch	.05
182	Mike Morgan	.05
183	Bob Tewksbury	.05
184	Joe Girardi	.05
185	Storm Davis	.05
186	Ed Whitson	.05
187	Steve Avery	.05
188	Lloyd Moseby	.05
189	Scott Bankhead	.05
190	Mark Langston	.05
191	Kevin McReynolds	.05
192	Julio Franco	.05
193	John Dopson	.05
194	Oil Can Boyd	.05
195	Bip Roberts	.05
196	Billy Hatcher	.05
197	Edgar Diaz	.05
198	Greg Litton	.05
199	Mark Grace	.20
200	Checklist 104-179	.05
201	George Brett	.30
202	Jeff Russell	.05
203	Ivan Calderon	.05
204	Ken Howell	.05
205	Tom Henke	.05
206	Bryan Harvey	.05
207	Steve Bedrosian	.05
208	Al Newman	.05
209	Randy Myers	.05
210	Daryl Boston	.05
211	Manny Lee	.05
212	Dave Smith	.05
213	Don Slaught	.05
214	Walt Weiss	.05
215	Donn Pall	.05
216	Jamie Navarro	.05
217	Willie Randolph	.05
218	Rudy Seanez	.05
219	*Jim Leyritz*	.15
220	Ron Karkovice	.05
221	Ken Caminiti	.10
222a	Von Hayes (Traded players' first names included in How Acquired on back)	.05
222b	Von Hayes (No first names)	.05
223	Cal Ripken, Jr.	.75
224	Lenny Harris	.05
225	Milt Thompson	.05
226	Alvaro Espinoza	.05
227	Chris James	.05
228	Dan Gladden	.05

229 Jeff Blauser .05
230 Mike Heath .05
231 Omar Vizquel .05
232 Doug Jones .05
233 Jeff King .05
234 Luis Rivera .05
235 Ellis Burks .05
236 Greg Cadaret .05
237 Dave Martinez .05
238 Mark Williamson .05
239 Stan Javier .05
240 Ozzie Smith .25
241 *Shawn Boskie* .05
242 Tom Gordon .05
243 Tony Gwynn .35
244 Tommy Gregg .05
245 Jeff Robinson .05
246 Keith Comstock .05
247 Jack Howell .05
248 Keith Miller .05
249 Bobby Witt .05
250 Rob Murphy .05
251 Spike Owen .05
252 Garry Templeton .05
253 Glenn Braggs .05
254 Ron Robinson .05
255 Kevin Mitchell .05
256 Les Lancaster .05
257 *Mel Stottlemyre* .10
258 Kenny Rogers .05
259 Lance Johnson .05
260 John Kruk .05
261 Fred McGriff .05
262 Dick Schofield .05
263 Trevor Wilson .05
264 David West .05
265 Scott Scudder .05
266 Dwight Gooden .10
267 *Willie Blair* .10
268 Mark Portugal .05
269 Doug Drabek .05
270 Dennis Eckersley .10
271 Eric King .05
272 Robin Yount .25
273 Carney Lansford .05
274 Carlos Baerga .05
275 Dave Righetti .05
276 Scott Fletcher .05
277 Eric Yelding .05
278 Charlie Hayes .05
279 Jeff Ballard .05
280 Orel Hershiser .10
281 Jose Oquendo .05
282 Mike Witt .05
283 Mitch Webster .05
284 Greg Gagne .05
285 *Greg Olson* .05
286 Tony Phillips .05
287 Scott Bradley .05
288 Cory Snyder .05
289 Jay Bell .10
290 Kevin Romine .05
291 Jeff Robinson .05
292 Steve Frey .05
293 Craig Worthington .05
294 Tim Crews .05
295 Joe Magrane .05
296 *Hector Villanueva* .05
297 *Terry Shumpert* .05
298 Joe Carter .05
299 Kent Mercker .05
300 Checklist 180-255 .05
301 Chet Lemon .05
302 Mike Schooler .05
303 Dante Bichette .10
304 Kevin Elster .05
305 Jeff Huson .05
306 Greg Harris .05
307 Marquis Grissom .05
308 Calvin Schiraldi .05
309 Mariano Duncan .05
310 Bill Spiers .05
311 Scott Garrelts .05
312 Mitch Williams .05
313 Mike Macfarlane .05
314 Kevin Brown .05
315 Robin Ventura .10
316 Darren Daulton .05
317 Pat Borders .05
318 Mark Eichhorn .05
319 Jeff Brantley .05
320 Shane Mack .05
321 Rob Dibble .05
322 John Franco .05
323 Junior Felix .05
324 Casey Candaele .05
325 Bobby Bonilla .05
326 Dave Henderson .05
327 Wayne Edwards .05
328 Mark Knudson .05
329 Terry Steinbach .05
330 *Colby Ward* .05
331 *Oscar Azocar* .05
332 *Scott Radinsky* .10
333 Eric Anthony .05
334 Steve Lake .05
335 Bob Melvin .05
336 Kal Daniels .05
337 Tom Pagnozzi .05
338 *Alan Mills* .05
339 Steve Olin .05
340 Juan Berenguer .05
341 Francisco Cabrera .05
342 Dave Bergman .05
343 Henry Cotto .05
344 Sergio Valdez .05
345 Bob Patterson .05
346 John Marzano .05
347 *Dana Kiecker* .05
348 Dion James .05
349 Hubie Brooks .05
350 Bill Landrum .05
351 *Bill Sampen* .05
352 Greg Briley .05
353 Paul Gibson .05
354 Dave Eiland .05
355 Steve Finley .05
356 Bob Boone .05
357 Steve Buechele .05
358 Chris Hoiles .10
359 Larry Walker .15
360 Frank DiPino .05
361 Mark Grant .05
362 Dave Magadan .05
363 Robby Thompson .05
364 Lonnie Smith .05
365 Steve Farr .05
366 Dave Valle .05
367 *Tim Naehring* .05
368 Jim Acker .05
369 Jeff Reardon .05
370 Tim Teufel .05
371 Juan Gonzalez .60
372 Luis Salazar .05
373 Rick Honeycutt .05
374 Greg Maddux .60
375 Jose Uribe .05
376 Donnie Hill .05
377 Don Carman .05
378 *Craig Grebeck* .05
379 Willie Fraser .05
380 Glenallen Hill .05
381 Joe Oliver .05
382 Randy Bush .05
383 Alex Cole .05
384 Norm Charlton .05
385 Gene Nelson .05
386a Checklist 256-331 (blue borders) .05
386b Checklist 256-331 (green borders) .05
387 Rickey Henderson (MVP) .15
388 Lance Parrish (MVP) .05
389 Fred McGriff (MVP) .05
390 Dave Parker (MVP) .05
391 Candy Maldonado (MVP) .05
392 Ken Griffey, Jr. (MVP) .40
393 Gregg Olson (MVP) .05
394 Rafael Palmeiro (MVP) .10
395 Roger Clemens (MVP) .25
396 George Brett (MVP) .20
397 Cecil Fielder (MVP) .05
398 Brian Harper (MVP) .05
399 Bobby Thigpen (MVP) .05
400 Roberto Kelly (MVP) .05
401 Danny Darwin (MVP) .05
402 Dave Justice (MVP) .10
403 Lee Smith (MVP) .05
404 Ryne Sandberg (MVP) .15
405 Eddie Murray (MVP) .15
406 Tim Wallach (MVP) .05
407 Kevin Mitchell (MVP) .05
408 Darryl Strawberry (MVP) .10
409 Joe Carter (MVP) .05
410 Len Dykstra (MVP) .05
411 Doug Drabek (MVP) .05
412 Chris Sabo (MVP) .05
413 *Paul Marak* (RR) .05
414 Tim McIntosh (RR) .05
415 *Brian Barnes* (RR) .05
416 *Eric Gunderson* (RR) .05
417 *Mike Gardiner* (RR) .10
418 Steve Carter (RR) .05
419 *Gerald Alexander* (RR) .05
420 *Rich Garces* (RR) .05
421 *Chuck Knoblauch* (RR) .45
422 *Scott Aldred* (RR) .05
423 *Wes Chamberlain* (RR) .10
424 *Lance Dickson* (RR) .10
425 *Greg Colbrunn* (RR) .15
426 *Rich Delucia* (RR) .10
427 *Jeff Conine* (RR) .40
428 *Steve Decker* (RR) .10
429 *Turner Ward* (RR) .10
430 Mo Vaughn (RR) .50
431 *Steve Chitren* (RR) .10
432 Mike Benjamin (RR) .05
433 Ryne Sandberg (AS) .15
434 Len Dykstra (AS) .05
435 Andre Dawson (AS) .10
436 Mike Scioscia (AS) .05
437 Ozzie Smith (AS) .15
438 Kevin Mitchell (AS) .05
439 Jack Armstrong (AS) .05
440 Chris Sabo (AS) .05
441 Will Clark (AS) .10
442 Mel Hall .05
443 Mark Gardner .05
444 Mike Devereaux .05
445 Kirk Gibson .05
446 Terry Pendleton .05
447 Mike Harkey .05
448 Jim Eisenreich .05
449 Benito Santiago .05
450 Oddibe McDowell .05
451 Cecil Fielder .05
452 Ken Griffey, Sr. .10
453 Bert Blyleven .10
454 Howard Johnson .05
455 Monty Farris .05
456 Tony Pena .05
457 Tim Raines .10
458 Dennis Rasmussen .05
459 Luis Quinones .05
460 B.J. Surhoff .05
461 Ernest Riles .05
462 Rick Sutcliffe .05
463 Danny Tartabull .05
464 Pete Incaviglia .05
465 Carlos Martinez .05
466 Ricky Jordan .05
467 John Cerutti .05
468 Dave Winfield .25
469 Francisco Oliveras .05
470 Roy Smith .05
471 Barry Larkin .10
472 Ron Darling .05
473 David Wells .10
474 Glenn Davis .05
475 Neal Heaton .05
476 Ron Hassey .05
477 Frank Thomas .60
478 Greg Vaughn .05
479 Todd Burns .05
480 Candy Maldonado .05
481 Dave LaPoint .05
482 Alvin Davis .05
483 Mike Scott .05
484 Dale Murphy .15
485 Ben McDonald .05
486 Jay Howell .05
487 Vince Coleman .05
488 Alfredo Griffin .05
489 Sandy Alomar .10
490 Kirby Puckett .35
491 Andres Thomas .05
492 Jack Morris .10
493 Matt Young .05
494 Greg Myers .05
495 Barry Bonds .50
496 Scott Cooper .05
497 Dan Schatzeder .05
498 Jesse Barfield .05
499 Jerry Goff .05
500 Checklist 332-408 .05
501 *Anthony Telford* .10
502 Eddie Murray .20
503 *Omar Olivares* .10
504 Ryne Sandberg .25
505 Jeff Montgomery .05
506 Mark Parent .05
507 Ron Gant .05
508 Frank Tanana .05
509 Jay Buhner .10
510 Max Venable .05
511 Wally Whitehurst .05
512 Gary Pettis .05
513 Tom Brunansky .05
514 Tim Wallach .05
515 Craig Lefferts .05
516 *Tim Layana* .05
517 Darryl Hamilton .05
518 Rick Reuschel .05
519 Steve Wilson .05
520 Kurt Stillwell .05
521 Rafael Palmeiro .20
522 Ken Patterson .05
523 Len Dykstra .10
524 Tony Fernandez .05
525 Kent Anderson .05
526 *Mark Leonard* .10
527 Allan Anderson .05
528 Tom Browning .05
529 Frank Viola .05
530 John Olerud .10
531 Juan Agosto .05
532 Zane Smith .05
533 Scott Sanderson .05
534 Barry Jones .05
535 Mike Felder .05
536 Jose Canseco .25
537 Felix Fermin .05
538 Roberto Kelly .05
539 Brian Holman .05
540 Mark Davidson .05
541 Terry Mulholland .05
542 Randy Milligan .05
543 Jose Gonzalez .05
544 *Craig Wilson* .10
545 Mike Hartley .05
546 Greg Swindell .05
547 Gary Gaetti .05
548 Dave Justice .15
549 Steve Searcy .05
550 Erik Hanson .05
551 Dave Stieb .05
552 Andy Van Slyke .05
553 Mike Greenwell .05
554 Kevin Maas .05
555 Delino Deshields .05
556 Curt Schilling .10
557 Ramon Martinez .05
558 Pedro Guerrero .05
559 Dwight Smith .05
560 Mark Davis .05
561 Shawn Abner .05
562 Charlie Leibrandt .05
563 John Shelby .05
564 Bill Swift .05
565 Mike Fetters .05
566 Alejandro Pena .05
567 Ruben Sierra .05
568 Carlos Quintana .05
569 Kevin Gross .05
570 Derek Lilliquist .05
571 Jack Armstrong .05
572 Greg Brock .05
573 Mike Kingery .05
574 Greg Smith .05
575 *Brian McRae* .25
576 Jack Daugherty .05
577 Ozzie Guillen .05
578 Joe Boever .05
579 Luis Sojo .05
580 Chili Davis .05
581 Don Robinson .05
582 Brian Harper .05
583 Paul O'Neill .10
584 Bob Ojeda .05
585 Mookie Wilson .05
586 Rafael Ramirez .05
587 Gary Redus .05
588 Jamie Quirk .05
589 Shawn Hilligas .05
590 *Tom Edens* .05
591 Joe Klink .05
592 Charles Nagy .10
593 Eric Plunk .05
594 Tracy Jones .05
595 Craig Biggio .10
596 Jose DeJesus .05
597 Mickey Tettleton .05
598 Chris Gwynn .05
599 Rex Hudler .05
600 Checklist 409-506 .05
601 Jim Gott .05

602 Jeff Manto .05
603 Nelson Liriano .05
604 Mark Lemke .05
605 Clay Parker .05
606 Edgar Martinez .05
607 *Mark Whiten* .20
608 Ted Power .05
609 Tom Bolton .05
610 Tom Herr .05
611 Andy Hawkins .05
612 Scott Ruskin .05
613 Ron Kittle .05
614 John Wetteland .05
615 *Mike Perez* .05
616 Dave Clark .05
617 Brent Mayne .05
618 Jack Clark .05
619 Marvin Freeman .05
620 Edwin Nunez .05
621 Russ Swan .05
622 Johnny Ray .05
623 Charlie O'Brien .05
624 *Joe Bitker* .05
625 Mike Marshall .05
626 Otis Nixon .05
627 Andy Benes .05
628 Ron Oester .05
629 Ted Higuera .05
630 Kevin Bass .05
631 Damon Berryhill .05
632 Bo Jackson .10
633 Brad Arnsberg .05
634 Jerry Willard .05
635 Tommy Greene .05
636 *Bob MacDonald* .05
637 Kirk McCaskill .05
638 John Burkett .05
639 *Paul Abbott* .05
640 Todd Benzinger .05
641 Todd Hundley .05
642 George Bell .05
643 *Javier Ortiz* .05
644 Sid Bream .05
645 Bob Welch .05
646 Phil Bradley .05
647 Bill Krueger .05
648 Rickey Henderson .20
649 Kevin Wickander .05
650 Steve Balboni .05
651 Gene Harris .05
652 Jim Deshaies .05
653 Jason Grimsley .05
654 Joe Orsulak .05
655 *Jimmy Poole* .05
656 Felix Jose .05
657 Dennis Cook .05
658 Tom Brookens .05
659 Junior Ortiz .05
660 Jeff Parrett .05
661 Jerry Don Gleaton .05
662 Brent Knackert .05
663 Rance Mulliniks .05
664 John Smiley .05
665 Larry Andersen .05
666 Willie McGee .05
667 *Chris Nabholz* .05
668 Brady Anderson .10
669 *Darren Holmes* .10
670 Ken Hill .05
671 Gary Varsho .05
672 Bill Pecota .05
673 Fred Lynn .10
674 Kevin D. Brown .05
675 Dan Petry .05
676 Mike Jackson .05
677 Wally Joyner .05
678 Danny Jackson .05
679 *Bill Haselman* .05
680 Mike Boddicker .05
681 *Mel Rojas* .10
682 Roberto Alomar .20
683 Dave Justice (R.O.Y.) .10
684 Chuck Crim .05
685a Matt Williams (Last line of Career Highlights ends, "most DP's in") .20
685b Matt Williams (last line ends "8/24-27/87.") .25
686 Shawon Dunston .05
687 *Jeff Schulz* .05
688 *John Barfield* .05
689 Gerald Young .05
690 *Luis Gonzalez* .50
691 Frank Wills .05
692 Chuck Finley .05
693 Sandy Alomar (R.O.Y.) .10
694 Tim Drummond .05
695 Herm Winningham .05
696 Darryl Strawberry .10
697 Al Leiter .10
698 *Karl Rhodes* .10
699 Stan Belinda .05
700 Checklist 507-604 .05
701 Lance Blankenship .05
702 Willie Stargell (Puzzle Card) .05
703 Jim Gantner .05
704 *Reggie Harris* .05
705 Rob Ducey .05
706 Tim Hulett .05
707 Atlee Hammaker .05
708 Xavier Hernandez .05
709 Chuck McElroy .05
710 John Mitchell .05
711 Carlos Hernandez .05
712 Geronimo Pena .05
713 *Jim Neidlinger* .05
714 John Orton .05
715 Terry Leach .05
716 Mike Stanton .05
717 Walt Terrell .05
718 Luis Aquino .05
719 Bud Black .05
720 Bob Kipper .05
721 *Jeff Gray* .05
722 Jose Rijo .05
723 Curt Young .05
724 Jose Vizcaino .05
725 *Randy Tomlin* .05
726 Junior Noboa .05
727 Bob Welch (Award Winner) .05
728 Gary Ward .05
729 Rob Deer .05
730 *David Segui* .10
731 Mark Carreon .05
732 Vicente Palacios .05
733 Sam Horn .05
734 *Howard Farmer* .05
735 Ken Dayley .05
736 Kelly Mann .05
737 *Joe Grahe* .05
738 Kelly Downs .05
739 *Jimmy Kremers* .05
740 Kevin Appier .10
741 Jeff Reed .05
742 Jose Rijo (World Series) .05
743 *Dave Rohde* .05
744 Dr. Dirt/Mr. Clean (Len Dykstra, Dale Murphy) .10
745 Paul Sorrento .05
746 Thomas Howard .05
747 *Matt Stark* .05
748 Harold Baines .10
749 Doug Dascenzo .05
750 Doug Drabek (Award Winner) .05
751 Gary Sheffield .10
752 *Terry Lee* .05
753 *Jim Vatcher* .05
754 Lee Stevens .05
755 Randy Veres .05
756 Bill Doran .05
757 Gary Wayne .05
758 *Pedro Munoz* .10
759 Chris Hammond .05
760 Checklist 605-702 .05
761 Rickey Henderson (MVP) .15
762 Barry Bonds (MVP) .30
763 Billy Hatcher (World Series) .05
764 Julio Machado .05
765 Jose Mesa .05
766 Willie Randolph (World Series) .05
767 *Scott Erickson* .10
768 Travis Fryman .05
769 *Rich Rodriguez* .10
770 Checklist 703-770; BC1-BC22 .05

1991 Donruss Diamond Kings Supers

Donruss made this set available through a mail-in offer. Three wrappers, $12 and postage were necessary to obtain this set. The cards are exactly the same design as the regular Donruss Diamond Kings except they measure approximately 5" x 6-3/4" in size. The artwork of Dick Perez is featured.

		MT
Complete Set (26):		10.00
Common Player:		.25
1	Dave Steib	.25
2	Craig Biggio	.50
3	Cecil Fielder	.25
4	Barry Bonds	2.00
5	Barry Larkin	.35
6	Dave Parker	.25
7	Len Dykstra	.25
8	Bobby Thigpen	.25
9	Roger Clemens	2.00
10	Ron Gant	.25
11	Delino DeShields	.25
12	Roberto Alomar	1.00
13	Sandy Alomar	.50
14	Ryne Sandberg	1.50
15	Ramon Martinez	.25
16	Edgar Martinez	.25
17	Dave Magadan	.25
18	Matt Williams	.35
19	Rafael Palmeiro	.75
20	Bob Welch	.25
21	Dave Righetti	.25
22	Brian Harper	.25
23	Gregg Olson	.25
24	Kurt Stillwell	.25
25	Pedro Guerrero	.25
26	Chuck Finley	.25

1991 Donruss Elite

Donruss released a series of special inserts in 1991. Ten thousand of each Elite card was released, while 7,500 Legend cards and 5,000 Signature cards were issued. Cards were inserted in wax packs and feature marble borders. The Legend card features a Dick Perez drawing. Each card is designated with a serial number on the back.

		MT
Complete Set (10):		300.00
Common Player:		7.50
1	Barry Bonds	40.00
2	George Brett	65.00
3	Jose Canseco	30.00
4	Andre Dawson	10.00
5	Doug Drabek	7.50
6	Cecil Fielder	7.50
7	Rickey Henderson	30.00
8	Matt Williams	10.00
---	Nolan Ryan (Legend)	100.00
---	Ryne Sandberg (Signature)	175.00

1991 Donruss Grand Slammers

This set features players who hit grand slams in 1990. The cards are styled after the 1991 Donruss regular-issue cards. The featured player is showcased with a star in the background. The set was included in factory sets and randomly in jumbo packs.

		MT
Complete Set (14):		1.50
Common Player:		.10
1	Joe Carter	.10
2	Bobby Bonilla	.10
3	Kal Daniels	.10
4	Jose Canseco	.30
5	Barry Bonds	.50
6	Jay Buhner	.10
7	Cecil Fielder	.10
8	Matt Williams	.25
9	Andres Galarraga	.15
10	Luis Polonia	.10
11	Mark McGwire	.75
12	Ron Karkovice	.10
13	Darryl Strawberry	.10
14	Mike Greenwell	.10

1991 Donruss Highlights

This insert features highlights from the 1990 season. Cards have a "BC" prefix to the number and are styled after the 1991 regular-issue Donruss cards. Cards 1-10 feature blue borders due to their release with Series I cards. Cards 11-22 feature green borders and were released with Series II cards. A highlight logo appears on the front of the card. Each highlight is explained in depth on the card back.

		MT
Complete Set (22):		2.00
Common Player:		.10
1	Mark Langston, Mike Witt (No-Hit Mariners)	.10
2	Randy Johnson (No-Hits Tigers)	.25
3	Nolan Ryan (No-Hits A's)	.50
4	Dave Stewart (No-Hits Blue Jays)	.10
5	Cecil Fielder (50 Homer Club)	.10
6	Carlton Fisk (Record Home Run)	.20
7	Ryne Sandberg (Sets Fielding Records)	.25
8	Gary Carter (Breaks Catching Mark)	.10
9	Mark McGwire (Home Run Milestone)	.50
10	Bo Jackson (4 Consecutive HRs)	.25
11	Fernando Valenzuela (No-Hits Cardinals)	.10
12	Andy Hawkins (No-Hits White Sox)	.10
13	Melido Perez (No-Hits Yankees)	.10
14	Terry Mulholland (No-Hits Giants)	.10
15	Nolan Ryan (300th Win)	.50
16	Delino DeShields (4 Hits In Debut)	.10
17	Cal Ripken (Errorless Games)	.50
18	Eddie Murray (Switch Hit Homers)	.25
19	George Brett (3 Decade Champ)	.25
20	Bobby Thigpen (Shatters Save Mark)	.10
21	Dave Stieb (No-Hits Indians)	.10
22	Willie McGee (NL Batting Champ)	.10

1991 Donruss Rookies

Red borders highlight the 1991 Donruss Rookies cards. This set marks the sixth year that Donruss produced such an issue. As in past years, "The Rookies" logo appears on the card fronts. The set is packaged in a special box and includes a Willie Stargell puzzle card.

		MT
Complete Set (56):		6.00
Common Player:		.10
1	Pat Kelly	.10
2	Rich DeLucia	.10
3	Wes Chamberlain	.10
4	Scott Leius	.10
5	Darryl Kile	.10
6	Milt Cuyler	.10
7	Todd Van Poppel	.10
8	Ray Lankford	.25
9	Brian Hunter	.10
10	Tony Perezchica	.10
11	Ced Landrum	.10
12	Dave Burba	.10
13	Ramon Garcia	.10
14	Ed Sprague	.10
15	Warren Newson	.10
16	Paul Faries	.10
17	Luis Gonzalez	.35
18	Charles Nagy	.15
19	Chris Hammond	.10
20	Frank Castillo	.10
21	Pedro Munoz	.10
22	Orlando Merced	.10
23	Jose Melendez	.10
24	Kirk Dressendorfer	.10
25	Heathcliff Slocumb	.10
26	Doug Simons	.10
27	Mike Timlin	.10
28	Jeff Fassero	.10
29	Mark Leiter	.10
30	*Jeff Bagwell*	4.00
31	Brian McRae	.15
32	Mark Whiten	.10
33	*Ivan Rodriguez*	2.00
34	Wade Taylor	.10
35	Darren Lewis	.10
36	Mo Vaughn	.50
37	Mike Remlinger	.10
38	Rick Wilkins	.10
39	Chuck Knoblauch	.50
40	Kevin Morton	.10
41	Carlos Rodriguez	.10
42	Mark Lewis	.10
43	Brent Mayne	.10
44	Chris Haney	.10
45	Denis Boucher	.10
46	Mike Gardiner	.10
47	Jeff Johnson	.10
48	Dean Palmer	.15
49	Chuck McElroy	.10
50	Chris Jones	.10
51	Scott Kamieniecki	.10
52	Al Osuna	.10
53	Rusty Meacham	.10
54	Chito Martinez	.10
55	Reggie Jefferson	.10
56	Checklist	.05

1992 Donruss Previews

Four-card cello packs distributed to members of the Donruss dealers' network previewed the forthcoming 1992 baseball card issue. The preview cards have the same format, front and back photos as their counterparts in the regular set. Only the card number, the security underprinting, "Donruss Preview Card", and the stats, complete only through 1990, differ.

		MT
Complete Set (12):		150.00
Common Player:		2.50
1	Wade Boggs	12.50
2	Barry Bonds	20.00
3	Will Clark	6.00
4	Andre Dawson	4.50
5	Dennis Eckersley	3.00
6	Robin Ventura	7.50
7	Ken Griffey, Jr.	45.00
8	Kelly Gruber	2.50
9	Ryan Klesko (Rated Rookie)	12.50
10	Cal Ripken, Jr.	40.00
11	Nolan Ryan (Highlight)	35.00
12	Todd Van Poppel	2.50

1992 Donruss

For the second consecutive year, Donruss released its card set in two series. The 1992 cards feature improved stock, an anti-counterfeit feature and include both front and back photos. Once again Rated Rookies and All-Stars are included in the set. Special highlight cards also can be found in the 1992 Donruss set. Production was reduced in 1992 compared to 1988-1991.

		MT
Complete Factory Set, Retail (788):		11.00
Complete Factory Set, Hobby (784):		8.00
Complete Set (784):		6.00
Common Player:		.05
Rod Carew Puzzle:		1.00
Series 1 or 2 Pack (15):		.50
Series 1 or 2 Wax Box (36):		15.00
1	*Mark Wohlers* (Rated Rookie)	.20
2	Wil Cordero (Rated Rookie)	.05
3	Kyle Abbott (Rated Rookie)	.05
4	*Dave Nilsson* (Rated Rookie)	.10
5	Kenny Lofton (Rated Rookie)	.50
6	*Luis Mercedes* (Rated Rookie)	.10
7	*Roger Salkeld* (Rated Rookie)	.15
8	Eddie Zosky (Rated Rookie)	.05
9	*Todd Van Poppel* (Rated Rookie)	.10
10	*Frank Seminara* (Rated Rookie)	.05
11	*Andy Ashby* (Rated Rookie)	.20
12	Reggie Jefferson (Rated Rookie)	.10
13	Ryan Klesko (Rated Rookie)	.50
14	*Carlos Garcia* (Rated Rookie)	.15
15	*John Ramos* (Rated Rookie)	.05
16	Eric Karros (Rated Rookie)	.10
17	*Pat Lennon* (Rated Rookie)	.05
18	*Eddie Taubensee* (Rated Rookie)	.10
19	*Roberto Hernandez* (Rated Rookie)	.10
20	D.J. Dozier (Rated Rookie)	.05
21	Dave Henderson (All-Star)	.05
22	Cal Ripken, Jr. (All-Star)	.30
23	Wade Boggs (All-Star)	.10
24	Ken Griffey, Jr. (All-Star)	.50
25	Jack Morris (All-Star)	.05
26	Danny Tartabull (All-Star)	.05
27	Cecil Fielder (All-Star)	.05
28	Roberto Alomar (All-Star)	.10
29	Sandy Alomar (All-Star)	.05
30	Rickey Henderson (All-Star)	.15
31	Ken Hill	.05
32	John Habyan	.05
33	Otis Nixon (Highlight)	.05
34	Tim Wallach	.05
35	Cal Ripken, Jr.	.75
36	Gary Carter	.10
37	Juan Agosto	.05
38	Doug Dascenzo	.05
39	Kirk Gibson	.05
40	Benito Santiago	.05
41	Otis Nixon	.05
42	Andy Allanson	.05
43	Brian Holman	.05
44	Dick Schofield	.05
45	Dave Magadan	.05
46	Rafael Palmeiro	.20
47	Jody Reed	.05
48	Ivan Calderon	.05
49	Greg Harris	.05
50	Chris Sabo	.05
51	Paul Molitor	.25
52	Robby Thompson	.05
53	Dave Smith	.05
54	Mark Davis	.05
55	Kevin Brown	.05
56	Donn Pall	.05
57	Len Dykstra	.05
58	Roberto Alomar	.20
59	Jeff Robinson	.05
60	Willie McGee	.05
61	Jay Buhner	.10
62	Mike Pagliarulo	.05
63	Paul O'Neill	.10
64	Hubie Brooks	.05
65	Kelly Gruber	.05
66	Ken Caminiti	.10
67	Gary Redus	.05
68	Harold Baines	.05
69	Charlie Hough	.05
70	B.J. Surhoff	.05
71	Walt Weiss	.05
72	Shawn Hillegas	.05
73	Roberto Kelly	.05
74	Jeff Ballard	.05
75	Craig Biggio	.10
76	Pat Combs	.05
77	Jeff Robinson	.05
78	Tim Belcher	.05
79	Cris Carpenter	.05
80	Checklist 1-79	.05
81	Steve Avery	.05
82	Chris James	.05
83	Brian Harper	.05
84	Charlie Leibrandt	.05
85	Mickey Tettleton	.05
86	Pete O'Brien	.05
87	Danny Darwin	.05
88	Bob Walk	.05
89	Jeff Reardon	.05
90	Bobby Rose	.05
91	Danny Jackson	.05
92	John Morris	.05
93	Bud Black	.05
94	Tommy Greene (Highlight)	.05
95	Rick Aguilera	.05
96	Gary Gaetti	.05
97	David Cone	.05
98	John Olerud	.10
99	Joel Skinner	.05
100	Jay Bell	.10

No.	Player	Price
101	Bob Milacki	.05
102	Norm Charlton	.05
103	Chuck Crim	.05
104	Terry Steinbach	.05
105	Juan Samuel	.05
106	Steve Howe	.05
107	Rafael Belliard	.05
108	Joey Cora	.05
109	Tommy Greene	.05
110	Gregg Olson	.05
111	Frank Tanana	.05
112	Lee Smith	.10
113	Greg Harris	.05
114	Dwayne Henry	.05
115	Chili Davis	.05
116	Kent Mercker	.05
117	Brian Barnes	.05
118	Rich DeLucia	.05
119	Andre Dawson	.15
120	Carlos Baerga	.05
121	Mike LaValliere	.05
122	Jeff Gray	.05
123	Bruce Hurst	.05
124	Alvin Davis	.05
125	John Candelaria	.05
126	Matt Nokes	.05
127	George Bell	.05
128	Bret Saberhagen	.05
129	Jeff Russell	.05
130	Jim Abbott	.05
131	Bill Gullickson	.05
132	Todd Zeile	.05
133	Dave Winfield	.20
134	Wally Whitehurst	.05
135	Matt Williams	.15
136	Tom Browning	.05
137	Marquis Grissom	.10
138	Erik Hanson	.05
139	Rob Dibble	.05
140	Don August	.05
141	Tom Henke	.05
142	Dan Pasqua	.05
143	George Brett	.30
144	Jerald Clark	.05
145	Robin Ventura	.10
146	Dale Murphy	.15
147	Dennis Eckersley	.10
148	Eric Yelding	.05
149	Mario Diaz	.05
150	Casey Candaele	.05
151	Steve Olin	.05
152	Luis Salazar	.05
153	Kevin Maas	.05
154	Nolan Ryan (Highlight)	.40
155	Barry Jones	.05
156	Chris Hoiles	.05
157	Bobby Ojeda	.05
158	Pedro Guerrero	.05
159	Paul Assenmacher	.05
160	Checklist 80-157	.05
161	Mike Macfarlane	.05
162	Craig Lefferts	.05
163	*Brian Hunter*	.05
164	Alan Trammell	.10
165	Ken Griffey, Jr.	1.50
166	Lance Parrish	.05
167	Brian Downing	.05
168	John Barfield	.05
169	Jack Clark	.05
170	Chris Nabholz	.05
171	Tim Teufel	.05
172	Chris Hammond	.05
173	Robin Yount	.25
174	Dave Righetti	.05
175	Joe Girardi	.05
176	Mike Boddicker	.05
177	Dean Palmer	.05
178	Greg Hibbard	.05
179	Randy Ready	.05
180	Devon White	.10
181	Mark Eichhorn	.05
182	Mike Felder	.05
183	Joe Klink	.05
184	Steve Bedrosian	.05
185	Barry Larkin	.10
186	John Franco	.05
187	*Ed Sprague*	.10
188	Mark Portugal	.05
189	Jose Lind	.05
190	Bob Welch	.05
191	Alex Fernandez	.05
192	Gary Sheffield	.15
193	Rickey Henderson	.25
194	Rod Nichols	.05
195	*Scott Kamieniecki*	.10
196	Mike Flanagan	.05
197	Steve Finley	.10
198	Darren Daulton	.05
199	Leo Gomez	.05
200	Mike Morgan	.05
201	Bob Tewksbury	.05
202	Sid Bream	.05
203	Sandy Alomar	.10
204	Greg Gagne	.05
205	Juan Berenguer	.05
206	Cecil Fielder	.05
207	Randy Johnson	.25
208	Tony Pena	.05
209	Doug Drabek	.05
210	Wade Boggs	.25
211	Bryan Harvey	.05
212	Jose Vizcaino	.05
213	*Alonzo Powell*	.05
214	Will Clark	.15
215	Rickey Henderson (Highlight)	.10
216	Jack Morris	.10
217	Junior Felix	.05
218	Vince Coleman	.05
219	Jimmy Key	.05
220	Alex Cole	.05
221	Bill Landrum	.05
222	Randy Milligan	.05
223	Jose Rijo	.05
224	Greg Vaughn	.10
225	Dave Stewart	.05
226	Lenny Harris	.05
227	Scott Sanderson	.05
228	Jeff Blauser	.05
229	Ozzie Guillen	.05
230	John Kruk	.05
231	Bob Melvin	.05
232	Milt Cuyler	.05
233	Felix Jose	.05
234	Ellis Burks	.05
235	Pete Harnisch	.05
236	Kevin Tapani	.05
237	Terry Pendleton	.05
238	Mark Gardner	.05
239	Harold Reynolds	.05
240	Checklist 158-237	.05
241	Mike Harkey	.05
242	Felix Fermin	.05
243	Barry Bonds	.40
244	Roger Clemens	.35
245	Dennis Rasmussen	.05
246	Jose DeLeon	.05
247	Orel Hershiser	.10
248	Mel Hall	.05
249	*Rick Wilkins*	.15
250	Tom Gordon	.05
251	Kevin Reimer	.05
252	Luis Polonia	.05
253	Mike Henneman	.05
254	Tom Pagnozzi	.05
255	Chuck Finley	.05
256	Mackey Sasser	.05
257	John Burkett	.05
258	Hal Morris	.05
259	Larry Walker	.15
260	Billy Swift	.05
261	Joe Oliver	.05
262	Julio Machado	.05
263	Todd Stottlemyre	.05
264	Matt Merullo	.05
265	Brent Mayne	.05
266	Thomas Howard	.05
267	Lance Johnson	.05
268	Terry Mulholland	.05
269	Rick Honeycutt	.05
270	Luis Gonzalez	.15
271	Jose Guzman	.05
272	Jimmy Jones	.05
273	Mark Lewis	.05
274	Rene Gonzales	.05
275	*Jeff Johnson*	.05
276	Dennis Martinez (Highlight)	.05
277	Delino DeShields	.05
278	Sam Horn	.05
279	Kevin Gross	.05
280	Jose Oquendo	.05
281	Mark Grace	.20
282	Mark Gubicza	.05
283	Fred McGriff	.05
284	Ron Gant	.05
285	Lou Whitaker	.05
286	Edgar Martinez	.05
287	Ron Tingley	.05
288	Kevin McReynolds	.05
289	Ivan Rodriguez	.20
290	Mike Gardiner	.05
291	*Chris Haney*	.05
292	Darrin Jackson	.05
293	Bill Doran	.05
294	Ted Higuera	.05
295	Jeff Brantley	.05
296	Les Lancaster	.05
297	Jim Eisenreich	.05
298	Ruben Sierra	.05
299	Scott Radinsky	.05
300	Jose DeJesus	.05
301	*Mike Timlin*	.10
302	Luis Sojo	.05
303	Kelly Downs	.05
304	Scott Bankhead	.05
305	Pedro Munoz	.05
306	Scott Scudder	.05
307	Kevin Elster	.05
308	Duane Ward	.05
309	*Darryl Kile*	.15
310	Orlando Merced	.05
311	Dave Henderson	.05
312	Tim Raines	.10
313	Mark Lee	.05
314	Mike Gallego	.05
315	Charles Nagy	.05
316	Jesse Barfield	.05
317	Todd Frohwirth	.05
318	Al Osuna	.05
319	Darrin Fletcher	.05
320	Checklist 238-316	.05
321	David Segui	.05
322	Stan Javier	.05
323	Bryn Smith	.05
324	Jeff Treadway	.05
325	Mark Whiten	.05
326	Kent Hrbek	.05
327	Dave Justice	.15
328	Tony Phillips	.05
329	Rob Murphy	.05
330	Kevin Morton	.05
331	John Smiley	.05
332	Luis Rivera	.05
333	Wally Joyner	.05
334	*Heathcliff Slocumb*	.10
335	Rick Cerone	.05
336	*Mike Remlinger*	.05
337	Mike Moore	.05
338	Lloyd McClendon	.05
339	Al Newman	.05
340	Kirk McCaskill	.05
341	Howard Johnson	.05
342	Greg Myers	.05
343	Kal Daniels	.05
344	Bernie Williams	.15
345	Shane Mack	.05
346	Gary Thurman	.05
347	Dante Bichette	.05
348	Mark McGwire	1.50
349	Travis Fryman	.05
350	Ray Lankford	.05
351	Mike Jeffcoat	.05
352	Jack McDowell	.05
353	Mitch Williams	.05
354	Mike Devereaux	.05
355	Andres Galarraga	.10
356	Henry Cotto	.05
357	Scott Bailes	.05
358	Jeff Bagwell	.60
359	Scott Leius	.05
360	Zane Smith	.05
361	Bill Pecota	.05
362	Tony Fernandez	.05
363	Glenn Braggs	.05
364	Bill Spiers	.05
365	Vicente Palacios	.05
366	Tim Burke	.05
367	Randy Tomlin	.05
368	Kenny Rogers	.05
369	Brett Butler	.05
370	Pat Kelly	.05
371	Bip Roberts	.05
372	Gregg Jefferies	.05
373	Kevin Bass	.05
374	Ron Karkovice	.05
375	Paul Gibson	.05
376	Bernard Gilkey	.05
377	Dave Gallagher	.05
378	Bill Wegman	.05
379	Pat Borders	.05
380	Ed Whitson	.05
381	Gilberto Reyes	.05
382	Russ Swan	.05
383	Andy Van Slyke	.05
384	Wes Chamberlain	.05
385	Steve Chitren	.05
386	Greg Olson	.05
387	Brian McRae	.05
388	Rich Rodriguez	.05
389	Steve Decker	.05
390	Chuck Knoblauch	.10
391	Bobby Witt	.05
392	Eddie Murray	.25
393	Juan Gonzalez	.60
394	Scott Ruskin	.05
395	Jay Howell	.05
396	Checklist 317-396	.05
397	Royce Clayton (Rated Rookie)	.05
398	*John Jaha* (Rated Rookie)	.10
399	Dan Wilson (Rated Rookie)	.10
400	*Archie Corbin* (Rated Rookie)	.05
401	*Barry Manuel* (Rated Rookie)	.05
402	Kim Batiste (Rated Rookie)	.05
403	*Pat Mahomes* (Rated Rookie)	.10
404	Dave Fleming (Rated Rookie)	.05
405	Jeff Juden (Rated Rookie)	.05
406	Jim Thome (Rated Rookie)	.45
407	Sam Militello (Rated Rookie)	.05
408	*Jeff Nelson* (Rated Rookie)	.05
409	Anthony Young (Rated Rookie)	.10
410	Tino Martinez (Rated Rookie)	.10
411	*Jeff Mutis* (Rated Rookie)	.05
412	*Rey Sanchez* (Rated Rookie)	.10
413	*Chris Gardner* (Rated Rookie)	.05
414	*John Vander Wal* (Rated Rookie)	.10
415	Reggie Sanders (Rated Rookie)	.10
416	*Brian Williams* (Rated Rookie)	.10
417	Mo Sanford (Rated Rookie)	.05
418	*David Weathers* (Rated Rookie)	.05
419	*Hector Fajardo* (Rated Rookie)	.10
420	*Steve Foster* (Rated Rookie)	.05
421	Lance Dickson (Rated Rookie)	.05
422	Andre Dawson (All-Star)	.10
423	Ozzie Smith (All-Star)	.10
424	Chris Sabo (All-Star)	.05
425	Tony Gwynn (All-Star)	.10
426	Tom Glavine (All-Star)	.05
427	Bobby Bonilla (All-Star)	.05
428	Will Clark (All-Star)	.05
429	Ryne Sandberg (All-Star)	.15
430	Benito Santiago (All-Star)	.05
431	Ivan Calderon (All-Star)	.05
432	Ozzie Smith	.25
433	Tim Leary	.05
434	Bret Saberhagen (Highlight)	.05
435	Mel Rojas	.05
436	Ben McDonald	.05
437	Tim Crews	.05
438	Rex Hudler	.05
439	Chico Walker	.05
440	Kurt Stillwell	.05
441	Tony Gwynn	.35
442	John Smoltz	.10
443	Lloyd Moseby	.05
444	Mike Schooler	.05
445	Joe Grahe	.05
446	Dwight Gooden	.10
447	Oil Can Boyd	.05
448	John Marzano	.05

449	Bret Barberie	.05
450	Mike Maddux	.05
451	Jeff Reed	.05
452	Dale Sveum	.05
453	Jose Uribe	.05
454	Bob Scanlan	.05
455	Kevin Appier	.05
456	Jeff Huson	.05
457	Ken Patterson	.05
458	Ricky Jordan	.05
459	Tom Candiotti	.05
460	Lee Stevens	.05
461	*Rod Beck*	.15
462	Dave Valle	.05
463	Scott Erickson	.05
464	Chris Jones	.05
465	Mark Carreon	.05
466	Rob Ducey	.05
467	Jim Corsi	.05
468	Jeff King	.05
469	Curt Young	.05
470	Bo Jackson	.15
471	Chris Bosio	.05
472	Jamie Quirk	.05
473	Jesse Orosco	.05
474	Alvaro Espinoza	.05
475	Joe Orsulak	.05
476	Checklist 397-477	.05
477	Gerald Young	.05
478	Wally Backman	.05
479	Juan Bell	.05
480	Mike Scioscia	.05
481	Omar Olivares	.05
482	Francisco Cabrera	.05
483	Greg Swindell	.05
484	Terry Leach	.05
485	Tommy Gregg	.05
486	Scott Aldred	.05
487	Greg Briley	.05
488	Phil Plantier	.05
489	Curtis Wilkerson	.05
490	Tom Brunansky	.05
491	Mike Fetters	.05
492	Frank Castillo	.05
493	Joe Boever	.05
494	Kirt Manwaring	.05
495	Wilson Alvarez (Highlight)	.05
496	Gene Larkin	.05
497	Gary DiSarcina	.05
498	Frank Viola	.05
499	Manuel Lee	.05
500	Albert Belle	.25
501	Stan Belinda	.05
502	Dwight Evans	.05
503	Eric Davis	.10
504	Darren Holmes	.05
505	Mike Bordick	.05
506	Dave Hansen	.05
507	Lee Guetterman	.05
508	*Keith Mitchell*	.05
509	Melido Perez	.05
510	Dickie Thon	.05
511	Mark Williamson	.05
512	Mark Salas	.05
513	Milt Thompson	.05
514	Mo Vaughn	.15
515	Jim Deshaies	.05
516	Rich Garces	.05
517	Lonnie Smith	.05
518	Spike Owen	.05
519	Tracy Jones	.05
520	Greg Maddux	.60
521	Carlos Martinez	.05
522	Neal Heaton	.05
523	Mike Greenwell	.05
524	Andy Benes	.05
525	Jeff Schaefer	.05
526	Mike Sharperson	.05
527	Wade Taylor	.05
528	Jerome Walton	.05
529	Storm Davis	.05
530	*Jose Hernandez*	.05
531	Mark Langston	.05
532	Rob Deer	.05
533	Geronimo Pena	.05
534	*Juan Guzman*	.10
535	Pete Schourek	.05
536	Todd Benzinger	.05
537	Billy Hatcher	.05
538	Tom Foley	.05
539	Dave Cochrane	.05
540	Mariano Duncan	.05
541	Edwin Nunez	.05
542	Rance Mulliniks	.05
543	Carlton Fisk	.20
544	Luis Aquino	.05
545	Ricky Bones	.05
546	Craig Grebeck	.05
547	Charlie Hayes	.05
548	Jose Canseco	.25
549	Andujar Cedeno	.05
550	Geno Petralli	.05
551	Javier Ortiz	.05
552	Rudy Seanez	.05
553	Rich Gedman	.05
554	Eric Plunk	.05
555	Nolan Ryan, Rich Gossage (Highlight)	.20
556	Checklist 478-555	.05
557	Greg Colbrunn	.05
558	*Chito Martinez*	.05
559	Darryl Strawberry	.10
560	Luis Alicea	.05
561	Dwight Smith	.05
562	Terry Shumpert	.05
563	Jim Vatcher	.05
564	Deion Sanders	.10
565	Walt Terrell	.05
566	Dave Burba	.05
567	Dave Howard	.05
568	Todd Hundley	.05
569	Jack Daugherty	.05
570	Scott Cooper	.05
571	Bill Sampen	.05
572	Jose Melendez	.05
573	Freddie Benavides	.05
574	Jim Gantner	.05
575	Trevor Wilson	.05
576	Ryne Sandberg	.20
577	Kevin Seitzer	.05
578	Gerald Alexander	.05
579	Mike Huff	.05
580	Von Hayes	.05
581	Derek Bell	.10
582	Mike Stanley	.05
583	Kevin Mitchell	.05
584	Mike Jackson	.05
585	Dan Gladden	.05
586	Ted Power	.05
587	Jeff Innis	.05
588	Bob MacDonald	.05
589	*Jose Tolentino*	.05
590	Bob Patterson	.05
591	*Scott Brosius*	.10
592	Frank Thomas	.60
593	Darryl Hamilton	.05
594	Kirk Dressendorfer	.05
595	Jeff Shaw	.05
596	Don Mattingly	.35
597	Glenn Davis	.05
598	Andy Mota	.05
599	Jason Grimsley	.05
600	Jimmy Poole	.05
601	Jim Gott	.05
602	Stan Royer	.05
603	Marvin Freeman	.05
604	Denis Boucher	.05
605	Denny Neagle	.05
606	Mark Lemke	.05
607	Jerry Don Gleaton	.05
608	Brent Knackert	.05
609	Carlos Quintana	.05
610	Bobby Bonilla	.05
611	Joe Hesketh	.05
612	Daryl Boston	.05
613	Shawon Dunston	.05
614	Danny Cox	.05
615	Darren Lewis	.05
616	Alejandro Pena, Kent Mercker, Mark Wohlers (Highlight)	.05
617	Kirby Puckett	.35
618	Franklin Stubbs	.05
619	Chris Donnels	.05
620	David Wells	.10
621	Mike Aldrete	.05
622	Bob Kipper	.05
623	Anthony Telford	.05
624	Randy Myers	.05
625	Willie Randolph	.05
626	Joe Slusarski	.05
627	John Wetteland	.05
628	Greg Cadaret	.05
629	Tom Glavine	.10
630	Wilson Alvarez	.05
631	Wally Ritchie	.05
632	Mike Mussina	.30
633	Mark Leiter	.05
634	Gerald Perry	.05
635	Matt Young	.05
636	Checklist 556-635	.05
637	Scott Hemond	.05
638	David West	.05
639	Jim Clancy	.05
640	Doug Piatt	.05
641	Omar Vizquel	.05
642	Rick Sutcliffe	.05
643	Glenallen Hill	.05
644	Gary Varsho	.05
645	Tony Fossas	.05
646	Jack Howell	.05
647	*Jim Campanis*	.10
648	Chris Gwynn	.05
649	Jim Leyritz	.05
650	Chuck McElroy	.05
651	Sean Berry	.05
652	Donald Harris	.05
653	Don Slaught	.05
654	*Rusty Meacham*	.05
655	Scott Terry	.05
656	Ramon Martinez	.05
657	Keith Miller	.05
658	Ramon Garcia	.05
659	*Milt Hill*	.05
660	Steve Frey	.05
661	Bob McClure	.05
662	*Ced Landrum*	.05
663	*Doug Henry*	.05
664	Candy Maldonado	.05
665	Carl Willis	.05
666	Jeff Montgomery	.05
667	*Craig Shipley*	.05
668	*Warren Newson*	.05
669	Mickey Morandini	.05
670	Brook Jacoby	.05
671	*Ryan Bowen*	.10
672	Bill Krueger	.05
673	Rob Mallicoat	.05
674	Doug Jones	.05
675	Scott Livingstone	.05
676	Danny Tartabull	.05
677	Joe Carter (Highlight)	.05
678	Cecil Espy	.05
679	Randy Velarde	.05
680	Bruce Ruffin	.05
681	*Ted Wood*	.05
682	Dan Plesac	.05
683	Eric Bullock	.05
684	Junior Ortiz	.05
685	Dave Hollins	.05
686	Dennis Martinez	.05
687	Larry Andersen	.05
688	Doug Simons	.05
689	*Tim Spehr*	.05
690	*Calvin Jones*	.05
691	Mark Guthrie	.05
692	Alfredo Griffin	.05
693	Joe Carter	.05
694	*Terry Mathews*	.05
695	Pascual Perez	.05
696	Gene Nelson	.05
697	Gerald Williams	.05
698	*Chris Cron*	.05
699	Steve Buechele	.05
700	Paul McClellan	.05
701	Jim Lindeman	.05
702	Francisco Oliveras	.05
703	*Rob Maurer*	.05
704	*Pat Hentgen*	.25
705	Jaime Navarro	.05
706	*Mike Magnante*	.05
707	Nolan Ryan	.75
708	Bobby Thigpen	.05
709	John Cerutti	.05
710	Steve Wilson	.05
711	Hensley Meulens	.05
712	*Rheal Cormier*	.10
713	Scott Bradley	.05
714	Mitch Webster	.05
715	Roger Mason	.05
716	Checklist 636-716	.05
717	*Jeff Fassero*	.10
718	Cal Eldred	.05
719	Sid Fernandez	.05
720	*Bob Zupcic*	.05
721	Jose Offerman	.05
722	*Cliff Brantley*	.10
723	Ron Darling	.05
724	Dave Stieb	.05
725	Hector Villanueva	.05
726	Mike Hartley	.05
727	*Arthur Rhodes*	.15
728	Randy Bush	.05
729	Steve Sax	.05
730	Dave Otto	.05
731	*John Wehner*	.05
732	Dave Martinez	.05
733	*Ruben Amaro*	.05
734	Billy Ripken	.05
735	Steve Farr	.05
736	Shawn Abner	.05
737	*Gil Heredia*	.10
738	Ron Jones	.05
739	Tony Castillo	.05
740	Sammy Sosa	.75
741	Julio Franco	.05
742	Tim Naehring	.05
743	*Steve Wapnick*	.05
744	Craig Wilson	.05
745	*Darrin Chapin*	.05
746	*Chris George*	.05
747	Mike Simms	.05
748	Rosario Rodriguez	.05
749	Skeeter Barnes	.05
750	Roger McDowell	.05
751	Dann Howitt	.05
752	Paul Sorrento	.05
753	*Braulio Castillo*	.05
754	*Yorkis Perez*	.05
755	Willie Fraser	.05
756	*Jeremy Hernandez*	.05
757	Curt Schilling	.10
758	Steve Lyons	.05
759	Dave Anderson	.05
760	Willie Banks	.05
761	Mark Leonard	.05
762	Jack Armstrong	.05
763	Scott Servais	.05
764	Ray Stephens	.05
765	Junior Noboa	.05
766	*Jim Olander*	.05
767	Joe Magrane	.05
768	Lance Blankenship	.05
769	*Mike Humphreys*	.10
770	*Jarvis Brown*	.05
771	Damon Berryhill	.05
772	Alejandro Pena	.05
773	Jose Mesa	.05
774	*Gary Cooper*	.05
775	Carney Lansford	.05
776	Mike Bielecki	.05
777	Charlie O'Brien	.05
778	Carlos Hernandez	.05
779	Howard Farmer	.05
780	Mike Stanton	.05
781	Reggie Harris	.05
782	Xavier Hernandez	.05
783	*Bryan Hickerson*	.05
784	Checklist 717-BC8	.05

1992 Donruss Bonus Cards

The eight bonus cards were randomly inserted in 1992 foil packs and are numbered with a "BC" prefix. Both leagues' MVPs, Cy Young and Rookie of the Year award winners are featured, as are logo cards for the expansion Colorado Rockies and Florida Marlins. Cards are standard size in a format similar to the regular issue.

		MT
Complete Set (8):		4.00
Common Player:		.30
1	Cal Ripken, Jr. (MVP)	2.00
2	Terry Pendleton (MVP)	.30
3	Roger Clemens (Cy Young)	1.00

4	Tom Glavine (Cy Young)	.40
5	Chuck Knoblauch (Rookie of the Year)	.60
6	Jeff Bagwell (Rookie of the Year)	1.50
7	Colorado Rockies	.50
8	Florida Marlins	.50

1992 Donruss Diamond Kings

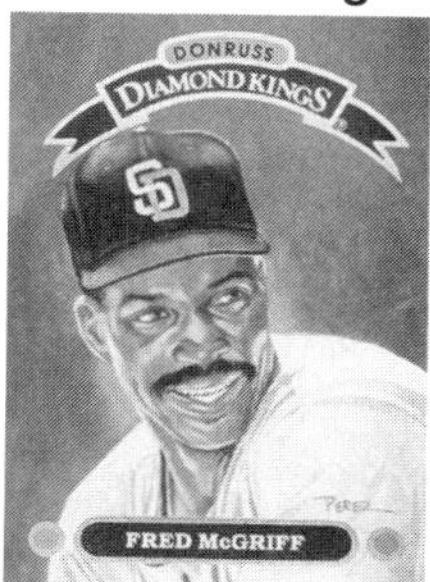

Donruss changed its Diamond Kings style and distribution in 1992. The cards still feature the art of Dick Perez, but quality was improved from past years. The cards were randomly inserted in foil packs. One player from each team is featured. Card numbers have a "DK" prefix.

		MT
Complete Set (27):		11.00
Common Player:		.20
1	Paul Molitor	1.00
2	Will Clark	.25
3	Joe Carter	.20
4	Julio Franco	.20
5	Cal Ripken, Jr.	4.00
6	Dave Justice	.25
7	George Bell	.20
8	Frank Thomas	2.00
9	Wade Boggs	.75
10	Scott Sanderson	.20
11	Jeff Bagwell	2.00
12	John Kruk	.20
13	Felix Jose	.20
14	Harold Baines	.20
15	Dwight Gooden	.20
16	Brian McRae	.20
17	Jay Bell	.25
18	Brett Butler	.20
19	Hal Morris	.20
20	Mark Langston	.20
21	Scott Erickson	.20
22	Randy Johnson	.75
23	Greg Swindell	.20
24	Dennis Martinez	.20
25	Tony Phillips	.20
26	Fred McGriff	.20
27	Checklist	.05

1992 Donruss Diamond Kings Supers

Produced in very limited numbers, possibly as a prototype for use in a sales presentation to a major retail chain, these 4-7/8" x 6-3/4" cards are identical in virtually everything but size to the regular 1992 DK inserts. Both front and back feature a high-gloss finish.

		MT
Complete Set (27):		1600.
Common Player:		25.00
1	Paul Molitor	150.00
2	Will Clark	35.00
3	Joe Carter	25.00
4	Julio Franco	25.00
5	Cal Ripken, Jr.	600.00
6	Dave Justice	60.00
7	George Bell	25.00
8	Frank Thomas	300.00
9	Wade Boggs	150.00
10	Scott Sanderson	25.00
11	Jeff Bagwell	200.00
12	John Kruk	25.00
13	Felix Jose	25.00
14	Harold Baines	25.00
15	Dwight Gooden	25.00
16	Brian McRae	25.00
17	Jay Bell	25.00
18	Brett Butler	25.00
19	Hal Morris	25.00
20	Mark Langston	25.00
21	Scott Erickson	25.00
22	Randy Johnson	75.00
23	Greg Swindell	25.00
24	Dennis Martinez	25.00
25	Tony Phillips	25.00
26	Fred McGriff	25.00
27	Checklist (Dick Perez)	10.00

1992 Donruss Elite

Donruss continued its Elite series in 1992 by inserting cards in foil packs. Each card was released in the same quantity as the 1991 inserts - 10,000 Elite, 7,500 Legend and 5,000 Signature. The Elite cards, now featuring a prismatic border, are numbered as a continuation of the 1991 issue.

		MT
Complete Set (12):		400.00
Common Player:		7.50
9	Wade Boggs	15.00
10	Joe Carter	7.50
11	Will Clark	10.00
12	Dwight Gooden	7.50
13	Ken Griffey, Jr.	50.00
14	Tony Gwynn	20.00
15	Howard Johnson	7.50
16	Terry Pendleton	7.50
17	Kirby Puckett	25.00
18	Frank Thomas	20.00
---	Rickey Henderson (Legend)	35.00
---	Cal Ripken, Jr. (Signature)	200.00

1992 Donruss Rookies

Donruss increased the size of its Rookies set in 1992 to include 132 cards. In the past the cards were released only in boxed set form, but the 1992 cards were available in packs. Special "Phenoms" cards were randomly inserted into Rookies packs. The Phenoms cards feature black borders, while the Rookies cards are styled after the regular 1992 Donruss issue. The cards are numbered alphabetically.

		MT
Complete Set (132):		10.00
Common Player:		.05
Pack (12):		2.00
Wax Box (36):		35.00
1	Kyle Abbott	.05
2	Troy Afenir	.05
3	Rich Amaral	.05
4	Ruben Amaro	.05
5	Billy Ashley	.05
6	Pedro Astacio	.10
7	Jim Austin	.05
8	Robert Ayrault	.05
9	Kevin Baez	.05
10	Estaban Beltre	.05
11	Brian Bohanon	.05
12	Kent Bottenfield	.05
13	Jeff Branson	.05
14	Brad Brink	.05
15	John Briscoe	.05
16	Doug Brocail	.05
17	Rico Brogna	.05
18	J.T. Bruett	.05
19	Jacob Brumfield	.05
20	Jim Bullinger	.05
21	Kevin Campbell	.05
22	Pedro Castellano	.05
23	Mike Christopher	.05
24	Archi Cianfrocco	.05
25	Mark Clark	.05
26	Craig Colbert	.05
27	Victor Cole	.05
28	Steve Cooke	.05
29	Tim Costo	.05
30	Chad Curtis	.25
31	Doug Davis	.05
32	Gary DiSarcina	.05
33	John Doherty	.05
34	Mike Draper	.05
35	Monty Fariss	.05
36	Bien Figueroa	.05
37	John Flaherty	.05
38	Tim Fortugno	.05
39	Eric Fox	.05
40	*Jeff Frye*	.05
41	Ramon Garcia	.05
42	Brent Gates	.05
43	Tom Goodwin	.05
44	Buddy Groom	.05
45	Jeff Grotewold	.05
46	Juan Guerrero	.05
47	Johnny Guzman	.05
48	Shawn Hare	.05
49	Ryan Hawblitzel	.05
50	Bert Heffernan	.05
51	Butch Henry	.05
52	Cesar Hernandez	.05
53	Vince Horsman	.05
54	Steve Hosey	.05
55	Pat Howell	.05
56	Peter Hoy	.05
57	Jon Hurst	.05
58	Mark Hutton	.05
59	Shawn Jeter	.05
60	Joel Johnston	.05
61	Jeff Kent	.40
62	Kurt Knudsen	.05
63	Kevin Koslofski	.05
64	Danny Leon	.05
65	Jesse Levis	.05
66	Tom Marsh	.05
67	Ed Martel	.05
68	Al Martin	.05
69	Pedro Martinez	2.00
70	Derrick May	.05
71	Matt Maysey	.05
72	Russ McGinnis	.05
73	Tim McIntosh	.05
74	Jim McNamara	.05
75	Jeff McNeely	.05
76	Rusty Meacham	.05
77	Tony Melendez	.05
78	Henry Mercedes	.05
79	Paul Miller	.05
80	Joe Millette	.05
81	Blas Minor	.05
82	Dennis Moeller	.05
83	Raul Mondesi	.75
84	Rob Natal	.05
85	Troy Neel	.05
86	David Nied	.05
87	Jerry Nielsen	.05
88	Donovan Osborne	.05
89	John Patterson	.05
90	Roger Pavlik	.05
91	Dan Peltier	.05
92	Jim Pena	.05
93	William Pennyfeather	.05
94	Mike Perez	.05
95	Hipolito Pichardo	.05
96	Greg Pirkl	.05
97	Harvey Pulliam	.05
98	*Manny Ramirez*	6.00
99	Pat Rapp	.05
100	Jeff Reboulet	.05
101	Darren Reed	.05
102	Shane Reynolds	.05
103	Bill Risley	.05
104	Ben Rivera	.05
105	Henry Rodriguez	.05
106	Rico Rossy	.05
107	Johnny Ruffin	.05
108	Steve Scarsone	.05
109	Tim Scott	.05
110	Steve Shifflett	.05
111	Dave Silvestri	.05
112	Matt Stairs	.10
113	William Suero	.05
114	Jeff Tackett	.05
115	Eddie Taubensee	.25
116	Rick Trlicek	.05
117	Scooter Tucker	.05
118	Shane Turner	.05
119	Julio Valera	.05
120	Paul Wagner	.05
121	Tim Wakefield	.05
122	Mike Walker	.05
123	Bruce Walton	.05
124	Lenny Webster	.05
125	Bob Wickman	.05
126	Mike Williams	.05
127	Kerry Woodson	.05
128	Eric Young	.25
129	Kevin Young	.10
130	Pete Young	.05
131	Checklist	.05
132	Checklist	.05

1992 Donruss Rookie Phenoms

The first 12 cards in this insert set were available in Donruss Rookies foil packs. Cards 13-20 were found randomly packed in jumbo packs. Predominantly black on both front and back, the borders are highlighted with gold. A gold-foil "Phenoms" appears at top front.

		MT
Complete Set (20):		30.00
Common Player:		.40
1	Moises Alou	3.00
2	Bret Boone	2.00
3	Jeff Conine	.75
4	Dave Fleming	.40
5	Tyler Green	.40
6	Eric Karros	1.00
7	Pat Listach	.40
8	Kenny Lofton	1.50
9	Mike Piazza	20.00
10	Tim Salmon	3.00
11	Andy Stankiewicz	.40
12	Dan Walters	.40
13	Ramon Caraballo	.40
14	Brian Jordan	2.00
15	Ryan Klesko	.50
16	Sam Militello	.40
17	Frank Seminara	.40
18	Salomon Torres	.40
19	John Valentin	1.00
20	Wil Cordero	.40

1992 Donruss Update

Each retail factory set of 1992 Donruss cards contained a cello-wrapped four-card selection from this 22-card Update set. The cards feature the same basic format as the regular '92 Donruss, except they carry a "U" prefix to the card number on back. The cards feature rookies, highlights and traded players from the 1992 season.

		MT
Complete Set (22):		25.00
Common Player:		.75
1	Pat Listach (Rated Rookie)	.75
2	Andy Stankiewicz (Rated Rookie)	.75
3	Brian Jordan (Rated Rookie)	1.50
4	Dan Walters (Rated Rookie)	.75
5	Chad Curtis (Rated Rookie)	1.00
6	Kenny Lofton (Rated Rookie)	4.00
7	Mark McGwire (Highlight)	10.00
8	Eddie Murray (Highlight)	1.00
9	Jeff Reardon (Highlight)	.75
10	Frank Viola	.75
11	Gary Sheffield	1.00
12	George Bell	.75
13	Rick Sutcliffe	.75
14	Wally Joyner	.75
15	Kevin Seitzer	.75
16	Bill Krueger	.75
17	Danny Tartabull	.75
18	Dave Winfield	2.50
19	Gary Carter	.75
20	Bobby Bonilla	.75
21	Cory Snyder	.75
22	Bill Swift	.75

1993 Donruss Previews

Twenty-two of the game's biggest stars were selected for inclusion in the preview version of Donruss' 1993 baseball card set. The previews follow the same basic format of the regular-issue 1993 except for the addition of the word "PREVIEW" above the card number in the home plate on back. Front photos are different between the preview and issued versions.

		MT
Complete Set (22):		70.00
Common Player:		2.00
1	Tom Glavine	2.50
2	Ryne Sandberg	6.00
3	Barry Larkin	2.50
4	Jeff Bagwell	5.00
5	Eric Karros	2.00
6	Larry Walker	3.00
7	Eddie Murray	4.00
8	Darren Daulton	2.00
9	Andy Van Slyke	2.00
10	Gary Sheffield	2.50
11	Will Clark	3.00
12	Cal Ripken Jr.	10.00
13	Roger Clemens	8.00
14	Frank Thomas	6.00
15	Cecil Fielder	2.00
16	George Brett	6.00
17	Robin Yount	4.00
18	Don Mattingly	8.00
19	Dennis Eckersley	2.00
20	Ken Griffey Jr.	10.00
21	Jose Canseco	3.00
22	Roberto Alomar	2.50

1993 Donruss

Rated Rookies and a randomly inserted Diamond Kings subset once again are featured in the 1993 Donruss set. Series I of the set includes 396 cards. Card fronts feature white borders surrounding a full-color player photo. The flip sides feature an additional photo, biographical information and career statistics. The cards are numbered on the back and the card's series is given with the number. The cards are UV coated. Series II contains a subset of players labeled with an "Expansion Draft" headline over their Marlins or Rockies team logo on front, even though the player photos are in the uniform of their previous team.

		MT
Complete Set (792):		12.00
Common Player:		.05
Series 1 or 2 Pack (14):		.75
Series 1 or 2 Wax Box (36):		15.00
1	Craig Lefferts	.05
2	Kent Mercker	.05
3	Phil Plantier	.05
4	*Alex Arias*	.15
5	Julio Valera	.05
6	Dan Wilson	.05
7	Frank Thomas	1.00
8	Eric Anthony	.05
9	Derek Lilliquist	.05
10	*Rafael Bournigal*	.10
11	*Manny Alexander* (Rated Rookie)	.10
12	Bret Barberie	.05
13	Mickey Tettleton	.05
14	Anthony Young	.05
15	Tim Spehr	.05
16	*Bob Ayrault*	.10
17	Bill Wegman	.05
18	Jay Bell	.10
19	Rick Aguilera	.05
20	Todd Zeile	.05
21	Steve Farr	.05
22	Andy Benes	.05
23	Lance Blankenship	.05
24	Ted Wood	.05
25	Omar Vizquel	.05
26	Steve Avery	.05
27	Brian Bohanon	.05
28	Rick Wilkins	.05
29	Devon White	.10
30	*Bobby Ayala*	.10
31	Leo Gomez	.05
32	Mike Simms	.05
33	Ellis Burks	.10
34	Steve Wilson	.05
35	Jim Abbott	.05
36	Tim Wallach	.05
37	Wilson Alvarez	.05
38	Daryl Boston	.05
39	Sandy Alomar, Jr.	.10
40	Mitch Williams	.05
41	Rico Brogna	.05
42	Gary Varsho	.05
43	Kevin Appier	.05
44	Eric Wedge (Rated Rookie)	.05
45	Dante Bichette	.05
46	Jose Oquendo	.05
47	*Mike Trombley*	.05
48	Dan Walters	.05
49	Gerald Williams	.05
50	Bud Black	.05
51	Bobby Witt	.05
52	Mark Davis	.05
53	*Shawn Barton*	.10
54	Paul Assenmacher	.05
55	Kevin Reimer	.05
56	*Billy Ashley* (Rated Rookie)	.15
57	Eddie Zosky	.05
58	Chris Sabo	.05
59	Billy Ripken	.05
60	*Scooter Tucker*	.10
61	*Tim Wakefield* (Rated Rookie)	.10
62	Mitch Webster	.05
63	Jack Clark	.05
64	Mark Gardner	.05
65	Lee Stevens	.05
66	Todd Hundley	.05
67	Bobby Thigpen	.05
68	Dave Hollins	.05
69	Jack Armstrong	.05
70	Alex Cole	.05
71	Mark Carreon	.05
72	Todd Worrell	.05
73	*Steve Shifflett*	.05
74	Jerald Clark	.05
75	Paul Molitor	.25
76	*Larry Carter*	.05
77	Rich Rowland	.05
78	Damon Berryhill	.05
79	Willie Banks	.05
80	Hector Villanueva	.05
81	Mike Gallego	.05
82	Tim Belcher	.05
83	Mike Bordick	.05
84	Craig Biggio	.10
85	Lance Parrish	.05
86	Brett Butler	.05
87	Mike Timlin	.05
88	Brian Barnes	.05
89	Brady Anderson	.05
90	D.J. Dozier	.05
91	Frank Viola	.05
92	Darren Daulton	.05
93	Chad Curtis	.05
94	Zane Smith	.05
95	George Bell	.05
96	Rex Hudler	.05
97	Mark Whiten	.05
98	Tim Teufel	.05
99	Kevin Ritz	.05
100	Jeff Brantley	.05
101	Jeff Conine	.05
102	Vinny Castilla	.10
103	Greg Vaughn	.10
104	Steve Buechele	.05
105	Darren Reed	.05
106	Bip Roberts	.05
107	John Habyan	.05
108	Scott Servais	.05
109	Walt Weiss	.05
110	*J.T. Snow* (Rated Rookie)	.75
111	Jay Buhner	.05
112	Darryl Strawberry	.10
113	*Roger Pavlik*	.10
114	Chris Nabholz	.05
115	Pat Borders	.05
116	*Pat Howell*	.10
117	Gregg Olson	.05
118	Curt Schilling	.10
119	Roger Clemens	.40

No.	Player	Price
120	*Victor Cole*	.05
121	Gary DiSarcina	.05
122	Checklist 1-80	.05
123	Steve Sax	.05
124	Chuck Carr	.05
125	Mark Lewis	.05
126	Tony Gwynn	.40
127	Travis Fryman	.05
128	Dave Burba	.05
129	Wally Joyner	.05
130	John Smoltz	.10
131	Cal Eldred	.05
132	Checklist 81-159	.05
133	Arthur Rhodes	.05
134	Jeff Blauser	.05
135	Scott Cooper	.05
136	Doug Strange	.05
137	Luis Sojo	.05
138	*Jeff Branson*	.10
139	Alex Fernandez	.05
140	Ken Caminiti	.10
141	Charles Nagy	.05
142	Tom Candiotti	.05
143	Willie Green (Rated Rookie)	.05
144	John Vander Wal	.05
145	*Kurt Knudsen*	.05
146	John Franco	.05
147	*Eddie Pierce*	.05
148	Kim Batiste	.05
149	Darren Holmes	.05
150	*Steve Cooke*	.15
151	Terry Jorgensen	.05
152	*Mark Clark*	.10
153	Randy Velarde	.05
154	Greg Harris	.05
155	*Kevin Campbell*	.05
156	John Burkett	.05
157	Kevin Mitchell	.05
158	Deion Sanders	.15
159	Jose Canseco	.20
160	*Jeff Hartsock*	.05
161	*Tom Quinlan*	.05
162	*Tim Pugh*	.10
163	Glenn Davis	.05
164	*Shane Reynolds*	.10
165	Jody Reed	.05
166	Mike Sharperson	.05
167	Scott Lewis	.05
168	Dennis Martinez	.05
169	Scott Radinsky	.05
170	Dave Gallagher	.05
171	Jim Thome	.10
172	Terry Mulholland	.05
173	Milt Cuyler	.05
174	Bob Patterson	.05
175	Jeff Montgomery	.05
176	Tim Salmon (Rated Rookie)	.20
177	Franklin Stubbs	.05
178	Donovan Osborne	.05
179	*Jeff Reboulet*	.05
180	*Jeremy Hernandez*	.10
181	Charlie Hayes	.05
182	Matt Williams	.15
183	Mike Raczka	.05
184	Francisco Cabrera	.05
185	Rich DeLucia	.05
186	Sammy Sosa	1.00
187	Ivan Rodriguez	.30
188	Bret Boone (Rated Rookie)	.15
189	Juan Guzman	.05
190	Tom Browning	.05
191	Randy Milligan	.05
192	Steve Finley	.10
193	John Patterson (Rated Rookie)	.05
194	Kip Gross	.05
195	Tony Fossas	.05
196	Ivan Calderon	.05
197	Junior Felix	.05
198	Pete Schourek	.05
199	Craig Grebeck	.05
200	Juan Bell	.05
201	Glenallen Hill	.05
202	Danny Jackson	.05
203	John Kiely	.05
204	Bob Tewksbury	.05
205	*Kevin Koslofski*	.05
206	Craig Shipley	.05
207	John Jaha	.05
208	Royce Clayton	.05
209	Mike Piazza (Rated Rookie)	1.50
210	Ron Gant	.05
211	Scott Erickson	.05
212	Doug Dascenzo	.05
213	Andy Stankiewicz	.05
214	Geronimo Berroa	.05
215	Dennis Eckersley	.10
216	Al Osuna	.05
217	Tino Martinez	.10
218	*Henry Rodriguez*	.10
219	Ed Sprague	.05
220	Ken Hill	.05
221	Chito Martinez	.05
222	Bret Saberhagen	.05
223	Mike Greenwell	.05
224	Mickey Morandini	.05
225	Chuck Finley	.05
226	Denny Neagle	.05
227	Kirk McCaskill	.05
228	Rheal Cormier	.05
229	Paul Sorrento	.05
230	Darrin Jackson	.05
231	Rob Deer	.05
232	Bill Swift	.05
233	Kevin McReynolds	.05
234	Terry Pendleton	.05
235	Dave Nilsson	.05
236	Chuck McElroy	.05
237	Derek Parks	.05
238	Norm Charlton	.05
239	Matt Nokes	.05
240	*Juan Guerrero*	.05
241	Jeff Parrett	.05
242	Ryan Thompson (Rated Rookie)	.10
243	Dave Fleming	.05
244	Dave Hansen	.05
245	Monty Fariss	.05
246	*Archi Cianfrocco*	.05
247	*Pat Hentgen*	.15
248	Bill Pecota	.05
249	Ben McDonald	.05
250	Cliff Brantley	.05
251	*John Valentin*	.15
252	Jeff King	.05
253	*Reggie Williams*	.10
254	Checklist 160-238	.05
255	Ozzie Guillen	.05
256	Mike Perez	.05
257	Thomas Howard	.05
258	Kurt Stillwell	.05
259	Mike Henneman	.05
260	Steve Decker	.05
261	Brent Mayne	.05
262	Otis Nixon	.05
263	*Mark Keifer*	.05
264	Checklist 239-317	.05
265	*Richie Lewis*	.05
266	*Pat Gomez*	.10
267	*Scott Taylor*	.10
268	Shawon Dunston	.05
269	Greg Myers	.05
270	Tim Costo	.05
271	Greg Hibbard	.05
272	Pete Harnisch	.05
273	*Dave Mlicki*	.05
274	Orel Hershiser	.10
275	Sean Berry (Rated Rookie)	.05
276	Doug Simons	.05
277	*John Doherty*	.10
278	Eddie Murray	.20
279	Chris Haney	.05
280	Stan Javier	.05
281	Jaime Navarro	.05
282	Orlando Merced	.05
283	Kent Hrbek	.05
284	Bernard Gilkey	.05
285	Russ Springer	.05
286	Mike Maddux	.05
287	*Eric Fox*	.10
288	Mark Leonard	.05
289	Tim Leary	.05
290	Brian Hunter	.05
291	Donald Harris	.05
292	Bob Scanlan	.05
293	Turner Ward	.05
294	Hal Morris	.05
295	Jimmy Poole	.05
296	Doug Jones	.05
297	Tony Pena	.05
298	Ramon Martinez	.05
299	*Tim Fortugno*	.10
300	Marquis Grissom	.10
301	Lance Johnson	.05
302	*Jeff Kent*	.15
303	Reggie Jefferson	.05
304	Wes Chamberlain	.05
305	*Shawn Hare*	.10
306	Mike LaValliere	.05
307	Gregg Jefferies	.05
308	*Troy Neel* (Rated Rookie)	.15
309	Pat Listach	.05
310	Geronimo Pena	.05
311	Pedro Munoz	.05
312	*Guillermo Velasquez*	.10
313	Roberto Kelly	.05
314	Mike Jackson	.05
315	Rickey Henderson	.25
316	Mark Lemke	.05
317	Erik Hanson	.05
318	Derrick May	.05
319	Geno Petralli	.05
320	Melvin Nieves (Rated Rookie)	.05
321	*Doug Linton*	.10
322	Rob Dibble	.05
323	Chris Hoiles	.05
324	Jimmy Jones	.05
325	Dave Staton (Rated Rookie)	.05
326	Pedro Martinez	.05
327	*Paul Quantrill*	.10
328	Greg Colbrunn	.05
329	*Hilly Hathaway*	.10
330	Jeff Innis	.05
331	Ron Karkovice	.05
332	*Keith Shepherd*	.10
333	*Alan Embree*	.10
334	*Paul Wagner*	.10
335	*Dave Haas*	.05
336	Ozzie Canseco	.05
337	Bill Sampen	.05
338	Rich Rodriguez	.05
339	Dean Palmer	.05
340	Greg Litton	.05
341	Jim Tatum (Rated Rookie)	.05
342	*Todd Haney*	.05
343	Larry Casian	.05
344	Ryne Sandberg	.35
345	*Sterling Hitchcock*	.15
346	Chris Hammond	.05
347	*Vince Horsman*	.05
348	*Butch Henry*	.10
349	Dann Howitt	.05
350	Roger McDowell	.05
351	Jack Morris	.05
352	Bill Krueger	.05
353	*Cris Colon*	.10
354	*Joe Vitko*	.10
355	Willie McGee	.05
356	Jay Baller	.05
357	Pat Mahomes	.05
358	Roger Mason	.05
359	*Jerry Nielsen*	.05
360	Tom Pagnozzi	.05
361	*Kevin Baez*	.05
362	*Tim Scott*	.05
363	*Domingo Martinez*	.10
364	Kirt Manwaring	.05
365	Rafael Palmeiro	.10
366	Ray Lankford	.05
367	Tim McIntosh	.05
368	*Jessie Hollins*	.05
369	Scott Leius	.05
370	Bill Doran	.05
371	*Sam Militello*	.10
372	Ryan Bowen	.05
373	Dave Henderson	.05
374	Dan Smith (Rated Rookie)	.05
375	*Steve Reed*	.10
376	Jose Offerman	.05
377	Kevin Brown	.05
378	Darrin Fletcher	.05
379	Duane Ward	.05
380	Wayne Kirby (Rated Rookie)	.05
381	*Steve Scarsone*	.10
382	Mariano Duncan	.05
383	*Ken Ryan*	.10
384	Lloyd McClendon	.05
385	Brian Holman	.05
386	Braulio Castillo	.05
387	*Danny Leon*	.05
388	Omar Olivares	.05
389	Kevin Wickander	.05
390	Fred McGriff	.05
391	Phil Clark	.05
392	Darren Lewis	.05
393	*Phil Hiatt*	.10
394	Mike Morgan	.05
395	Shane Mack	.05
396	Checklist 318-396	.05
397	David Segui	.05
398	Rafael Belliard	.05
399	Tim Naehring	.05
400	Frank Castillo	.05
401	Joe Grahe	.05
402	Reggie Sanders	.05
403	Roberto Hernandez	.05
404	Luis Gonzalez	.15
405	Carlos Baerga	.05
406	Carlos Hernandez	.05
407	Pedro Astacio (Rated Rookie)	.05
408	Mel Rojas	.05
409	Scott Livingstone	.05
410	Chico Walker	.05
411	Brian McRae	.05
412	Ben Rivera	.05
413	Ricky Bones	.05
414	Andy Van Slyke	.05
415	Chuck Knoblauch	.10
416	Luis Alicea	.05
417	Bob Wickman	.05
418	Doug Brocail	.05
419	Scott Brosius	.05
420	Rod Beck	.05
421	Edgar Martinez	.05
422	Ryan Klesko	.05
423	Nolan Ryan	1.00
424	Rey Sanchez	.05
425	Roberto Alomar	.15
426	Barry Larkin	.10
427	Mike Mussina	.25
428	Jeff Bagwell	.75
429	Mo Vaughn	.10
430	Eric Karros	.05
431	John Orton	.05
432	Wil Cordero	.05
433	Jack McDowell	.05
434	Howard Johnson	.05
435	Albert Belle	.25
436	John Kruk	.05
437	Skeeter Barnes	.05
438	Don Slaught	.05
439	Rusty Meacham	.05
440	Tim Laker (Rated Rookie)	.05
441	Robin Yount	.25
442	Brian Jordan	.10
443	Kevin Tapani	.05
444	Gary Sheffield	.15
445	Rich Monteleone	.05
446	Will Clark	.15
447	Jerry Browne	.05
448	Jeff Treadway	.05
449	Mike Schooler	.05
450	Mike Harkey	.05
451	Julio Franco	.05
452	Kevin Young (Rated Rookie)	.05
453	Kelly Gruber	.05
454	Jose Rijo	.05
455	Mike Devereaux	.05
456	Andujar Cedeno	.05
457	Damion Easley (Rated Rookie)	.10
458	Kevin Gross	.05
459	Matt Young	.05
460	Matt Stairs	.05
461	Luis Polonia	.05
462	Dwight Gooden	.05
463	Warren Newson	.05
464	Jose DeLeon	.05
465	Jose Mesa	.05
466	Danny Cox	.05
467	Dan Gladden	.05
468	Gerald Perry	.05
469	Mike Boddicker	.05
470	Jeff Gardner	.05
471	Doug Henry	.05
472	Mike Benajmin	.05
473	Dan Peltier (Rated Rookie)	.05
474	Mike Stanton	.05
475	John Smiley	.05
476	Dwight Smith	.05
477	Jim Leyritz	.05
478	Dwayne Henry	.05
479	Mark McGwire	2.00
480	Pete Incaviglia	.05
481	Dave Cochrane	.05
482	Eric Davis	.10
483	John Olerud	.15
484	Ken Bottenfield	.05
485	Mark McLemore	.05

486 Dave Magadan .05
487 John Marzano .05
488 Ruben Amaro .05
489 Rob Ducey .05
490 Stan Belinda .05
491 Dan Pasqua .05
492 Joe Magrane .05
493 Brook Jacoby .05
494 Gene Harris .05
495 Mark Leiter .05
496 Bryan Hickerson .05
497 Tom Gordon .05
498 Pete Smith .05
499 Chris Bosio .05
500 Shawn Boskie .05
501 Dave West .05
502 Milt Hill .05
503 Pat Kelly .05
504 Joe Boever .05
505 Terry Steinbach .05
506 Butch Huskey (Rated Rookie) .10
507 David Valle .05
508 Mike Scioscia .05
509 Kenny Rogers .05
510 Moises Alou .10
511 David Wells .10
512 Mackey Sasser .05
513 Todd Frohwirth .05
514 Ricky Jordan .05
515 Mike Gardiner .05
516 Gary Redus .05
517 Gary Gaetti .05
518 Checklist 397-476 .05
519 Carlton Fisk .15
520 Ozzie Smith .25
521 Rod Nichols .05
522 Benito Santiago .05
523 Bill Gullickson .05
524 Robby Thompson .05
525 Mike Macfarlane .05
526 Sid Bream .05
527 Darryl Hamilton .05
528 Checklist 477-555 .05
529 Jeff Tackett .05
530 Greg Olson .05
531 Bob Zupcic .05
532 Mark Grace .10
533 Steve Frey .05
534 Dave Martinez .05
535 Robin Ventura .10
536 Casey Candaele .05
537 Kenny Lofton .10
538 Jay Howell .05
539 Fernando Ramsey (Rated Rookie) .05
540 Larry Walker .10
541 Cecil Fielder .05
542 Lee Guetterman .05
543 Keith Miller .05
544 Len Dykstra .05
545 B.J. Surhoff .05
546 Bob Walk .05
547 Brian Harper .05
548 Lee Smith .05
549 Danny Tartabull .05
550 Frank Seminara .05
551 Henry Mercedes .05
552 Dave Righetti .05
553 Ken Griffey, Jr. 1.50
554 Tom Glavine .10
555 Juan Gonzalez .60
556 Jim Bullinger .05
557 Derek Bell .05
558 Cesar Hernandez .05
559 Cal Ripken, Jr. 2.00
560 Eddie Taubensee .05
561 John Flaherty .05
562 Todd Benzinger .05
563 Hubie Brooks .05
564 Delino DeShields .05
565 Tim Raines .10
566 Sid Fernandez .05
567 Steve Olin .05
568 Tommy Greene .05
569 Buddy Groom .05
570 Randy Tomlin .05
571 Hipolito Pichardo .05
572 Rene Arocha (Rated Rookie) .05
573 Mike Fetters .05
574 Felix Jose .05
575 Gene Larkin .05
576 Bruce Hurst .05
577 Bernie Williams .10
578 Trevor Wilson .05
579 Bob Welch .05
580 Dave Justice .10
581 Randy Johnson .25
582 Jose Vizcaino .05
583 Jeff Huson .05
584 Rob Maurer (Rated Rookie) .05
585 Todd Stottlemyre .05
586 Joe Oliver .05
587 Bob Milacki .05
588 Rob Murphy .05
589 Greg Pirkl (Rated Rookie) .05
590 Lenny Harris .05
591 Luis Rivera .05
592 John Wetteland .05
593 Mark Langston .05
594 Bobby Bonilla .05
595 Esteban Beltre .05
596 Mike Hartley .05
597 Felix Fermin .05
598 Carlos Garcia .05
599 Frank Tanana .05
600 Pedro Guerrero .05
601 Terry Shumpert .05
602 Wally Whitehurst .05
603 Kevin Seitzer .05
604 Chris James .05
605 Greg Gohr (Rated Rookie) .05
606 Mark Wohlers .05
607 Kirby Puckett .40
608 Greg Maddux .60
609 Don Mattingly .75
610 Greg Cadaret .05
611 Dave Stewart .05
612 Mark Portugal .05
613 Pete O'Brien .05
614 Bobby Ojeda .05
615 Joe Carter .05
616 Pete Young .05
617 Sam Horn .05
618 Vince Coleman .05
619 Wade Boggs .25
620 *Todd Pratt* .10
621 Ron Tingley .05
622 Doug Drabek .05
623 Scott Hemond .05
624 Tim Jones .05
625 Dennis Cook .05
626 Jose Melendez .05
627 Mike Munoz .05
628 Jim Pena .05
629 Gary Thurman .05
630 Charlie Leibrandt .05
631 Scott Fletcher .05
632 Andre Dawson .10
633 Greg Gagne .05
634 Greg Swindell .05
635 Kevin Maas .05
636 Xavier Hernandez .05
637 Ruben Sierra .05
638 Dimitri Young (Rated Rookie) .05
639 Harold Reynolds .05
640 Tom Goodwin .05
641 Todd Burns .05
642 Jeff Fassero .05
643 Dave Winfield .20
644 Willie Randolph .05
645 Luis Mercedes .05
646 Dale Murphy .10
647 Danny Darwin .05
648 Dennis Moeller .05
649 Chuck Crim .05
650 Checklist 556-634 .05
651 Shawn Abner .05
652 Tracy Woodson .05
653 Scott Scudder .05
654 Tom Lampkin .05
655 Alan Trammell .10
656 Cory Snyder .05
657 Chris Gwynn .05
658 Lonnie Smith .05
659 Jim Austin .05
660 Checklist 635-713 .05
661 (Tim Hulett) .05
662 Marvin Freeman .05
663 Greg Harris .05
664 Heathcliff Slocumb .05
665 Mike Butcher .05
666 Steve Foster .05
667 Donn Pall .05
668 Darryl Kile .05
669 Jesse Levis .05
670 Jim Gott .05
671 *Mark Hutton* .05
672 Brian Drahman .05
673 Chad Kreuter .05
674 Tony Fernandez .05
675 Jose Lind .05
676 Kyle Abbott .05
677 Dan Plesac .05
678 Barry Bonds .75
679 Chili Davis .05
680 Stan Royer .05
681 Scott Kamieniecki .05
682 Carlos Martinez .05
683 Mike Moore .05
684 Candy Maldanado .05
685 Jeff Nelson .05
686 Lou Whitaker .05
687 Jose Guzman .05
688 Manuel Lee .05
689 Bob MacDonald .05
690 Scott Bankhead .05
691 Alan Mills .05
692 Brian Williams .05
693 Tom Brunansky .05
694 Lenny Webster .05
695 Greg Briley .05
696 Paul O'Neill .10
697 Joey Cora .05
698 Charlie O'Brien .05
699 Junior Ortiz .05
700 Ron Darling .05
701 Tony Phillips .05
702 William Pennyfeather .05
703 Mark Gubicza .05
704 Steve Hosey (Rated Rookie) .05
705 Henry Cotto .05
706 *David Hulse* .15
707 Mike Pagliarulo .05
708 Dave Stieb .05
709 Melido Perez .05
710 Jimmy Key .05
711 Jeff Russell .05
712 David Cone .05
713 Russ Swan .05
714 Mark Guthrie .05
715 Checklist 714-792 .05
716 Al Martin (Rated Rookie) .05
717 Randy Knorr .05
718 Mike Stanley .05
719 Rick Sutcliffe .05
720 Terry Leach .05
721 Chipper Jones (Rated Rookie) 1.50
722 Jim Eisenreich .05
723 Tom Henke .05
724 Jeff Frye .05
725 Harold Baines .05
726 Scott Sanderson .05
727 Tom Foley .05
728 Bryan Harvey (Expansion Draft) .05
729 Tom Edens .05
730 Eric Young (Expansion Draft) .10
731 Dave Weathers (Expansion Draft) .05
732 Spike Owen .05
733 Scott Aldred (Expansion Draft) .05
734 Cris Carpenter (Expansion Draft) .05
735 Dion James .05
736 Joe Girardi (Expansion Draft) .05
737 Nigel Wilson (Expansion Draft) .05
738 Scott Chiamparino (Expansion Draft) .05
739 Jeff Reardon .05
740 Willie Blair (Expansion Draft) .05
741 Jim Corsi (Expansion Draft) .05
742 Ken Patterson .05
743 Andy Ashby (Expansion Draft) .05
744 Rob Natal (Expansion Draft) .05
745 Kevin Bass .05
746 Freddie Benavides (Expansion Draft) .05
747 Chris Donnels (Expansion Draft) .05
748 *Kerry Woodson* .10
749 Calvin Jones (Expansion Draft) .05
750 Gary Scott .05
751 Joe Orsulak .05
752 Armando Reynoso (Expansion Draft) .05
753 Monty Farriss (Expansion Draft) .05
754 Billy Hatcher .05
755 Denis Boucher (Expansion Draft) .05
756 Walt Weiss .05
757 Mike Fitzgerald .05
758 Rudy Seanez .05
759 Bret Barberie (Expansion Draft) .05
760 Mo Sanford (Expansion Draft) .05
761 *Pedro Castellano* (Expansion Draft) .10
762 Chuck Carr (Expansion Draft) .05
763 Steve Howe .05
764 Andres Galarraga .10
765 Jeff Conine (Expansion Draft) .10
766 Ted Power .05
767 Butch Henry (Expansion Draft) .05
768 Steve Decker (Expansion Draft) .05
769 Storm Davis .05
770 Vinny Castilla (Expansion Draft) .10
771 Junior Felix (Expansion Draft) .05
772 Walt Terrell .05
773 Brad Ausmus (Expansion Draft) .05
774 Jamie McAndrew (Expansion Draft) .05
775 Milt Thompson .05
776 Charlie Hayes (Expansion Draft) .05
777 Jack Armstrong (Expansion Draft) .05
778 Dennis Rasmussen .05
779 Darren Holmes (Expansion Draft) .05
780 *Alex Arias* .10
781 Randy Bush .05
782 Javier Lopez (Rated Rookie) .10
783 Dante Bichette .05
784 John Johnstone (Expansion Draft) .05
785 Rene Gonzales .05
786 Alex Cole (Expansion Draft) .05
787 Jeromy Burnitz (Rated Rookie) .15
788 Michael Huff .05
789 Anthony Telford .05
790 Jerald Clark (Expansion Draft) .05
791 Joel Johnston .05
792 David Nied (Rated Rookie) .05

1993 Donruss Diamond Kings

The traditional Donruss Diamond Kings cards were again used as an insert in Series I and Series

II foil packs in 1993. The first 15 cards were found in Series I packs, while cards 16-31 were available in the second series packs.

		MT
Complete Set (31):		12.00
Common Player:		.30
1	Ken Griffey, Jr.	3.00
2	Ryne Sandberg	1.50
3	Roger Clemens	1.50
4	Kirby Puckett	2.00
5	Bill Swift	.30
6	Larry Walker	.40
7	Juan Gonzalez	1.00
8	Wally Joyner	.30
9	Andy Van Slyke	.30
10	Robin Ventura	.40
11	Bip Roberts	.30
12	Roberto Kelly	.30
13	Carlos Baerga	.30
14	Orel Hershiser	.30
15	Cecil Fielder	.30
16	Robin Yount	.75
17	Darren Daulton	.30
18	Mark McGwire	3.00
19	Tom Glavine	.40
20	Roberto Alomar	.60
21	Gary Sheffield	.35
22	Bob Tewksbury	.30
23	Brady Anderson	.30
24	Craig Biggio	.40
25	Eddie Murray	.60
26	Luis Polonia	.30
27	Nigel Wilson	.30
28	David Nied	.30
29	Pat Listach	.30
30	Eric Karros	.30
31	Checklist	.05

1993 Donruss Elite

Continuing the card numbering from the 1992 Elite set, the Elite '93 inserts utilized a silver-foil prismatic front border with blue back printing. Each card is serial numbered as one of 10,000; this identified production number helping to make the Elites among the more valuable of insert cards.

		MT
Complete Set (20):		175.00
Common Player:		5.00
19	Fred McGriff	5.00
20	Ryne Sandberg	12.50
21	Eddie Murray	12.50
22	Paul Molitor	12.50
23	Barry Larkin	7.50
24	Don Mattingly	15.00
25	Dennis Eckersley	5.00
26	Roberto Alomar	10.00
27	Edgar Martinez	5.00
28	Gary Sheffield	7.50
29	Darren Daulton	5.00
30	Larry Walker	10.00
31	Barry Bonds	15.00
32	Andy Van Slyke	5.00
33	Mark McGwire	20.00
34	Cecil Fielder	5.00
35	Dave Winfield	10.00
36	Juan Gonzalez	12.50
---	Robin Yount (Legend)	12.50
---	Will Clark (Signature)	50.00

1993 Donruss Elite Supers

A Wal-Mart exclusive, Donruss produced 3-1/2" x 5" versions of its 1993 Elite inserts, added Nolan Ryan and Frank Thomas and a new card of Barry Bonds in his Giants uniform and packaged them one per shrink-wrapped box with Series I Donruss left-overs. Each super-size card features a color player photo and silver-foil prismatic borders on front. Backs are printed in blue and include a serial number identifying each of the cards from an edition of 5,000.

		MT
Complete Set (20):		300.00
Common Player:		6.00
1	Fred McGriff	6.00
2	Ryne Sandberg	30.00
3	Eddie Murray	20.00
4	Paul Molitor	20.00
5	Barry Larkin	10.00
6	Don Mattingly	40.00
7	Dennis Eckersley	6.00
8	Roberto Alomar	17.50
9	Edgar Martinez	6.00
10	Gary Sheffield	10.00
11	Darren Daulton	6.00
12	Larry Walker	12.50
13	Barry Bonds	35.00
14	Andy Van Slyke	6.00
15	Mark McGwire	50.00
16	Cecil Fielder	6.00
17	Dave Winfield	20.00
18	Juan Gonzalez	25.00
19	Frank Thomas	35.00
20	Nolan Ryan	75.00

1993 Donruss Elite Dominators

Created as a premium to move left-over boxes of its 1993 product on a home shopping network at $100 apiece, this special edition was produced in standard 2-1/2" x 3-1/2" size in a format similar to the 1991-93 Donruss Elite chase cards. Cards feature green prismatic borders, liberal use of foil stamping, etc. Only 5,000 of each card were produced, and each card is serially numbered on the back. Half of the cards of Nolan Ryan, Juan Gonzalez, Don Mattingly and Paul Molitor were personally autographed by the player.

		MT
Complete Set (20):		285.00
Common Player:		4.00
1	Ryne Sandberg	10.00
2	Fred McGriff	4.00
3	Greg Maddux	10.00
4	Ron Gant	4.00
5	Dave Justice	6.00
6	Don Mattingly	15.00
7	Tim Salmon	4.00
8	Mike Piazza	15.00
9	John Olerud	4.00
10	Nolan Ryan	25.00
11	Juan Gonzalez	7.50
12	Ken Griffey, Jr.	25.00
13	Frank Thomas	10.00
14	Tom Glavine	7.50
15	George Brett	12.50
16	Barry Bonds	12.50
17	Albert Belle	4.00
18	Paul Molitor	7.50
19	Cal Ripken, Jr.	25.00
20	Roberto Alomar	7.50
Autographed Cards:		
6	Don Mattingly	40.00
10	Nolan Ryan	55.00
11	Juan Gonzalez	30.00
18	Paul Molitor	30.00

1993 Donruss Long Ball Leaders

Carrying a prefix of "LL" before the card number, these inserts were released in Series I (LL1-9) and Series II (LL10-18) jumbo packs, detailing mammoth home runs of the previous season.

		MT
Complete Set (18):		11.00
Common Player:		.20
1	Rob Deer	.20
2	Fred McGriff	.20
3	Albert Belle	.30
4	Mark McGwire	3.50
5	Dave Justice	.25
6	Jose Canseco	.50
7	Kent Hrbek	.20
8	Roberto Alomar	.50
9	Ken Griffey, Jr.	3.00
10	Frank Thomas	1.50
11	Darryl Strawberry	.20
12	Felix Jose	.20
13	Cecil Fielder	.20
14	Juan Gonzalez	.50
15	Ryne Sandberg	.75
16	Gary Sheffield	.30
17	Jeff Bagwell	1.25
18	Larry Walker	.40

1993 Donruss Masters of the Game

Donruss issued a series of "Masters of the Game" art cards that were available only at Wal-Mart stores. The oversized cards (3-1/2" x 5") feature the artwork of Dick Perez, creator of the Diamond Kings cards for the same company. The cards came issued one to a pack, along with a foil pack of 1993 Donruss cards for a retail price of about $3.

		MT
Complete Set (16):		40.00
Common Player:		2.00
1	Frank Thomas	3.00
2	Nolan Ryan	6.00
3	Gary Sheffield	2.00
4	Fred McGriff	2.00
5	Ryne Sandberg	3.00
6	Cal Ripken, Jr.	6.00
7	Jose Canseco	2.50
8	Ken Griffey, Jr.	6.00
9	Will Clark	2.00
10	Roberto Alomar	2.00
11	Juan Gonzalez	3.00
12	David Justice	2.00
13	Kirby Puckett	4.00
14	Barry Bonds	4.00
15	Robin Yount	2.50
16	Deion Sanders	2.00

1993 Donruss MVPs

This set was inserted in jumbo packs of both Series I and Series II. Cards carry a MVP prefix to the card number.

		MT
Complete Set (26):		13.00
Common Player:		.20
1	Luis Polonia	.20
2	Frank Thomas	1.00
3	George Brett	1.00
4	Paul Molitor	.50
5	Don Mattingly	1.25
6	Roberto Alomar	.30
7	Terry Pendleton	.20
8	Eric Karros	.20
9	Larry Walker	.30
10	Eddie Murray	.40
11	Darren Daulton	.20
12	Ray Lankford	.20
13	Will Clark	.30
14	Cal Ripken, Jr.	2.00
15	Roger Clemens	1.00
16	Carlos Baerga	.20
17	Cecil Fielder	.20
18	Kirby Puckett	1.00
19	Mark McGwire	2.00
20	Ken Griffey, Jr.	1.50
21	Juan Gonzalez	.50
22	Ryne Sandberg	.75
23	Bip Roberts	.20
24	Jeff Bagwell	1.00
25	Barry Bonds	.75
26	Gary Sheffield	.30

1993 Donruss Spirit of the Game

Series I and Series II foil and jumbo packs could be found with these cards randomly inserted. Several multi-player cards are included in the set. Card numbers bear an SG prefix.

		MT
Complete Set (20):		10.00
Common Player:		.50
1	Turning Two (Dave Winfield, Mike Bordick)	.50
2	Play at the Plate (David Justice)	.50
3	In There (Roberto Alomar)	.75
4	Pumped (Dennis Eckersley)	.50
5	Dynamic Duo (Juan Gonzalez, Jose Canseco)	1.00
6	Gone (Frank Thomas, George Bell)	.75
7	Safe or Out? (Wade Boggs)	.75
8	The Thrill (Will Clark)	.50
9	Safe at Home (Damon Berryhill, Bip Roberts, Glenn Braggs)	.50
10	Thirty X 31 (Cecil Fielder, Mickey Tettleton, Rob Deer)	.50
11	Bag Bandit (Kenny Lofton)	.50
12	Back to Back (Fred McGriff, Gary Sheffield)	.50
13	Range Rovers (Greg Gagne, Barry Larkin)	.50
14	The Ball Stops Here (Ryne Sandberg)	1.00
15	Over the Top (Carlos Baerga, Gary Gaetti)	.50
16	At the Wall (Danny Tartabull)	.50
17	Head First (Brady Anderson)	.50
18	Big Hurt (Frank Thomas)	1.50
19	No-Hitter (Kevin Gross)	.50
20	3,000 (Robin Yount)	.75

1994 Donruss Promotional Samples

To introduce both its regular 1994 issue and the "Special Edition" gold cards, Donruss produced this 12-card promo set for distribution to its dealer network. The promos are virtually identical in format to the regular cards except for the large gray diagonal overprint "PROMOTIONAL SAMPLE" on both front and back. Card numbers also differ on the promos.

		MT
Complete Set (12):		20.00
Common Player:		.75
1	Barry Bonds	2.00
2	Darren Daulton	.75
3	John Olerud	1.00
4	Frank Thomas	2.00
5	Mike Piazza	2.50
6	Tim Salmon	1.00
7	Ken Griffey, Jr.	3.00
8	Fred McGriff	.75
9	Don Mattingly	2.50
10	Gary Sheffield	1.00
Special Edition Gold:		
1G	Barry Bonds (Special Edition Gold)	3.00
4G	Frank Thomas (Special Edition Gold)	3.00

1994 Donruss

Donruss released its 1994 set in two 330-card series. Each series also includes, 50 Special Edition gold cards and several insert sets. Regular cards have full-bleed photos and are UV coated and foil stamped. Special Edition cards are gold-foil stamped on both sides and are included in each pack. Insert sets titled Spirit of the Game and Decade Dominators were produced in regular and super (3-1/2" x 5") formats. Other inserts were MVPs and Long Ball Leaders in regular size and super-size Award Winners. An Elite series of cards, continuing from previous years with #37-48, was also issued as inserts. A 10th Anniversary insert set features 10 popular 1984 Donruss cards in gold-foil enhanced reprint versions.

		MT
Complete Set (660):		25.00
Common Player:		.05
Series 1 Pack (13):		1.50
Series 1 Wax Box (36):		25.00
Series 2 Pack (13):		1.25
Series 2 Wax Box (36):		20.00
1	Nolan Ryan (Career Salute 27 Years)	2.50
2	Mike Piazza	1.50
3	Moises Alou	.10
4	Ken Griffey, Jr.	2.50
5	Gary Sheffield	.15
6	Roberto Alomar	.50
7	John Kruk	.05
8	Gregg Olson	.05
9	Gregg Jefferies	.05
10	Tony Gwynn	1.00
11	Chad Curtis	.05
12	Craig Biggio	.10
13	John Burkett	.05
14	Carlos Baerga	.05
15	Robin Yount	.40
16	Dennis Eckersley	.10
17	Dwight Gooden	.05
18	Ryne Sandberg	.50
19	Rickey Henderson	.30
20	Jack McDowell	.05
21	Jay Bell	.10
22	Kevin Brown	.10
23	Robin Ventura	.10
24	Paul Molitor	.25
25	Dave Justice	.15
26	Rafael Palmeiro	.10
27	Cecil Fielder	.05
28	Chuck Knoblauch	.10
29	Dave Hollins	.05
30	Jimmy Key	.05
31	Mark Langston	.05
32	Darryl Kile	.05
33	Ruben Sierra	.05
34	Ron Gant	.05
35	Ozzie Smith	.40
36	Wade Boggs	.30
37	Marquis Grissom	.10
38	Will Clark	.15
39	Kenny Lofton	.10
40	Cal Ripken, Jr.	2.50
41	Steve Avery	.05
42	Mo Vaughn	.15
43	Brian McRae	.05
44	Mickey Tettleton	.05
45	Barry Larkin	.10
46	Charlie Hayes	.05
47	Kevin Appier	.05
48	Robby Thompson	.05
49	Juan Gonzalez	.75
50	Paul O'Neill	.10
51	Marcos Armas	.05
52	Mike Butcher	.05
53	Ken Caminiti	.15
54	Pat Borders	.05
55	Pedro Munoz	.05
56	Tim Belcher	.05
57	Paul Assenmacher	.05
58	Damon Berryhill	.05
59	Ricky Bones	.05
60	Rene Arocha	.05
61	Shawn Boskie	.05
62	Pedro Astacio	.05
63	Frank Bolick	.05
64	Bud Black	.05
65	Sandy Alomar, Jr.	.10
66	Rich Amaral	.05
67	Luis Aquino	.05
68	Kevin Baez	.05
69	Mike Devereaux	.05
70	Andy Ashby	.05
71	Larry Andersen	.05
72	Steve Cooke	.05
73	Mario Daiz	.05
74	Rob Deer	.05
75	Bobby Ayala	.05
76	Freddie Benavides	.05
77	Stan Belinda	.05
78	John Doherty	.05
79	Willie Banks	.05
80	Spike Owen	.05
81	Mike Bordick	.05
82	Chili Davis	.05
83	Luis Gonzalez	.15
84	Ed Sprague	.05
85	Jeff Reboulet	.05
86	Jason Bere	.10
87	Mark Hutton	.05
88	Jeff Blauser	.05
89	Cal Eldred	.05
90	Bernard Gilkey	.05
91	Frank Castillo	.05
92	Jim Gott	.05
93	Greg Colbrunn	.05
94	Jeff Brantley	.05
95	Jeremy Hernandez	.05
96	Norm Charlton	.05
97	Alex Arias	.05
98	John Franco	.05
99	Chris Hoiles	.05
100	Brad Ausmus	.05
101	Wes Chamberlain	.05
102	Mark Dewey	.05
103	Benji Gil (Rated Rookie)	.05
104	John Dopson	.05
105	John Smiley	.05
106	David Nied	.05
107	George Brett (Career Salute 21 Years)	1.00
108	Kirk Gibson	.05
109	Larry Casian	.05
110	Checklist (Ryne Sandberg 2,000 Hits)	.15
111	Brent Gates	.05
112	Damion Easley	.05
113	Pete Harnisch	.05
114	Danny Cox	.05
115	Kevin Tapani	.05
116	Roberto Hernandez	.05
117	Domingo Jean	.05
118	Sid Bream	.05
119	Doug Henry	.05
120	Omar Olivares	.05
121	Mike Harkey	.05
122	Carlos Hernandez	.05
123	Jeff Fassero	.05
124	Dave Burba	.05

125 Wayne Kirby .05
126 John Cummings .05
127 Bret Barberie .05
128 Todd Hundley .05
129 Tim Hulett .05
130 Phil Clark .05
131 Danny Jackson .05
132 Tom Foley .05
133 Donald Harris .05
134 Scott Fletcher .05
135 Johnny Ruffin (Rated Rookie) .05
136 Jerald Clark .05
137 Billy Brewer .05
138 Dan Gladden .05
139 Eddie Guardado .05
140 Checklist (Cal Ripken, Jr. 2,000 Hits) .25
141 Scott Hemond .05
142 Steve Frey .05
143 Xavier Hernandez .05
144 Mark Eichhorn .05
145 Ellis Burks .05
146 Jim Leyritz .05
147 Mark Lemke .05
148 Pat Listach .05
149 Donovan Osborne .05
150 Glenallen Hill .05
151 Orel Hershiser .05
152 Darrin Fletcher .05
153 Royce Clayton .05
154 Derek Lilliquist .05
155 Mike Felder .05
156 Jeff Conine .05
157 Ryan Thompson .05
158 Ben McDonald .05
159 Ricky Gutierrez .05
160 Terry Mulholland .05
161 Carlos Garcia .05
162 Tom Henke .05
163 Mike Greenwell .05
164 Thomas Howard .05
165 Joe Girardi .05
166 Hubie Brooks .05
167 Greg Gohr .05
168 Chip Hale .05
169 Rick Honeycutt .05
170 Hilly Hathaway .05
171 Todd Jones .05
172 Tony Fernandez .05
173 Bo Jackson .10
174 Bobby Munoz .05
175 Greg McMichael .05
176 Graeme Lloyd .05
177 Tom Pagnozzi .05
178 Derrick May .05
179 Pedro Martinez .50
180 Ken Hill .05
181 Bryan Hickerson .05
182 Jose Mesa .05
183 Dave Fleming .05
184 Henry Cotto .05
185 Jeff Kent .05
186 Mark McLemore .05
187 Trevor Hoffman .05
188 Todd Pratt .05
189 Blas Minor .05
190 Charlie Leibrandt .05
191 Tony Pena .05
192 *Larry Luebbers* .10
193 Greg Harris .05
194 David Cone .05
195 Bill Gullickson .05
196 Brian Harper .05
197 Steve Karsay (Rated Rookie) .05
198 Greg Myers .05
199 Mark Portugal .05
200 Pat Hentgen .05
201 Mike La Valliere .05
202 Mike Stanley .05
203 Kent Mercker .05
204 Dave Nilsson .05
205 Erik Pappas .05
206 Mike Morgan .05
207 Roger McDowell .05
208 Mike Lansing .10
209 Kirt Manwaring .05
210 Randy Milligan .05
211 Erik Hanson .05
212 Orestes Destrade .05
213 Mike Maddux .05
214 Alan Mills .05
215 Tim Mauser .05
216 Ben Rivera .05
217 Don Slaught .05
218 Bob Patterson .05
219 Carlos Quintana .05
220 Checklist (Tim Raines 2,000 Hits) .05
221 Hal Morris .05
222 Darren Holmes .05
223 Chris Gwynn .05
224 Chad Kreuter .05
225 Mike Hartley .05
226 Scott Lydy .05
227 Eduardo Perez .05
228 Greg Swindell .05
229 Al Leiter .10
230 Scott Radinsky .05
231 Bob Wickman .05
232 Otis Nixon .05
233 Kevin Reimer .05
234 Geronimo Pena .05
235 Kevin Roberson (Rated Rookie) .10
236 Jody Reed .05
237 Kirk Rueter (Rated Rookie) .10
238 Willie McGee .05
239 Charles Nagy .05
240 Tim Leary .05
241 Carl Everett .10
242 Charlie O'Brien .05
243 Mike Pagliarulo .05
244 Kerry Taylor .05
245 Kevin Stocker .05
246 Joel Johnston .05
247 Geno Petralli .05
248 Jeff Russell .05
249 Joe Oliver .05
250 Robert Mejia .05
251 Chris Haney .05
252 Bill Krueger .05
253 Shane Mack .05
254 Terry Steinbach .05
255 Luis Polonia .05
256 Eddie Taubensee .05
257 Dave Stewart .05
258 Tim Raines .10
259 Bernie Williams .25
260 John Smoltz .10
261 Kevin Seitzer .05
262 Bob Tewksbury .05
263 Bob Scanlan .05
264 Henry Rodriguez .05
265 Tim Scott .05
266 Scott Sanderson .05
267 Eric Plunk .05
268 Edgar Martinez .05
269 Charlie Hough .05
270 Joe Orsulak .05
271 Harold Reynolds .05
272 Tim Teufel .05
273 Bobby Thigpen .05
274 Randy Tomlin .05
275 Gary Redus .05
276 Ken Ryan .05
277 Tim Pugh .05
278 Jayhawk Owens .05
279 Phil Hiatt (Rated Rookie) .05
280 Alan Trammell .10
281 Dave McCarty (Rated Rookie) .05
282 Bob Welch .05
283 J.T. Snow .10
284 Brian Williams .05
285 Devon White .05
286 Steve Sax .05
287 Tony Tarasco .05
288 Bill Spiers .05
289 Allen Watson .05
290 Checklist (Rickey Henderson 2,000 Hits) .05
291 Joe Vizcaino .05
292 Darryl Strawberry .10
293 John Wetteland .05
294 Bill Swift .05
295 Jeff Treadway .05
296 Tino Martinez .10
297 Richie Lewis .05
298 Bret Saberhagen .05
299 Arthur Rhodes .05
300 Guillermo Velasquez .05
301 Milt Thompson .05
302 Doug Strange .05
303 Aaron Sele .10
304 Bip Roberts .05
305 Bruce Ruffin .05
306 Jose Lind .05
307 David Wells .10
308 Bobby Witt .05
309 Mark Wohlers .05
310 B.J. Surhoff .05
311 Mark Whiten .05
312 Turk Wendell .05
313 Raul Mondesi .10
314 *Brian Turang* .05
315 Chris Hammond .05
316 Tim Bogar .05
317 Brad Pennington .05
318 Tim Worrell .05
319 Mitch Williams .05
320 Rondell White (Rated Rookie) .20
321 Frank Viola .05
322 Manny Ramirez (Rated Rookie) 1.50
323 Gary Wayne .05
324 Mike Macfarlane .05
325 Russ Springer .05
326 Tim Wallach .05
327 Salomon Torres (Rated Rookie) .05
328 Omar Vizquel .05
329 *Andy Tomberlin* .10
330 Chris Sabo .05
331 Mike Mussina .40
332 Andy Benes .05
333 Darren Daulton .05
334 Orlando Merced .05
335 Mark McGwire 2.50
336 Dave Winfield .25
337 Sammy Sosa 1.00
338 Eric Karros .05
339 Greg Vaughn .10
340 Don Mattingly 1.00
341 Frank Thomas 1.00
342 Fred McGriff .05
343 Kirby Puckett 1.00
344 Roberto Kelly .05
345 Wally Joyner .05
346 Andres Galarraga .10
347 Bobby Bonilla .05
348 Benito Santiago .05
349 Barry Bonds 1.00
350 Delino DeShields .05
351 Albert Belle .25
352 Randy Johnson .50
353 Tim Salmon .10
354 John Olerud .10
355 Dean Palmer .05
356 Roger Clemens 1.00
357 Jim Abbott .05
358 Mark Grace .15
359 Ozzie Guillen .05
360 Lou Whitaker .05
361 Jose Rijo .05
362 Jeff Montgomery .05
363 Chuck Finley .05
364 Tom Glavine .10
365 Jeff Bagwell .75
366 Joe Carter .05
367 Ray Lankford .05
368 Ramon Martinez .05
369 Jay Buhner .10
370 Matt Williams .10
371 Larry Walker .10
372 Jose Canseco .30
373 Len Dykstra .05
374 Bryan Harvey .05
375 Andy Van Slyke .05
376 Ivan Rodriguez .35
377 Kevin Mitchell .05
378 Travis Fryman .05
379 Duane Ward .05
380 Greg Maddux .60
381 Scott Servais .05
382 Greg Olson .05
383 Rey Sanchez .05
384 Tom Kramer .05
385 David Valle .05
386 Eddie Murray .20
387 Kevin Higgins .05
388 Dan Wilson .05
389 Todd Frohwirth .05
390 Gerald Williams .05
391 Hipolito Pichardo .05
392 Pat Meares .05
393 Luis Lopez .05
394 Ricky Jordan .05
395 Bob Walk .05
396 Sid Fernandez .05
397 Todd Worrell .05
398 Darryl Hamilton .05
399 Randy Myers .05
400 Rod Brewer .05
401 Lance Blankenship .05
402 Steve Finley .05
403 *Phil Leftwich* .05
404 Juan Guzman .05
405 Anthony Young .05
406 Jeff Gardner .05
407 Ryan Bowen .05
408 Fernando Valenzuela .05
409 David West .05
410 Kenny Rogers .05
411 Bob Zupcic .05
412 Eric Young .10
413 Bret Boone .10
414 Danny Tartabull .05
415 Bob MacDonald .05
416 Ron Karkovice .05
417 Scott Cooper .05
418 Dante Bichette .05
419 Tripp Cromer .05
420 Billy Ashley .05
421 Roger Smithberg .05
422 Dennis Martinez .05
423 Mike Blowers .05
424 Darren Lewis .05
425 Junior Ortiz .05
426 Butch Huskey .05
427 Jimmy Poole .05
428 Walt Weiss .05
429 Scott Bankhead .05
430 Deion Sanders .10
431 Scott Bullett .05
432 Jeff Huson .05
433 Tyler Green .05
434 Billy Hatcher .05
435 Bob Hamelin .05
436 Reggie Sanders .05
437 Scott Erickson .05
438 Steve Reed .05
439 Randy Velarde .05
440 Checklist (Tony Gwynn 2,000 Hits) .15
441 Terry Leach .05
442 Danny Bautista .05
443 Kent Hrbek .05
444 Rick Wilkins .05
445 Tony Phillips .05
446 Dion James .05
447 Joey Cora .05
448 Andre Dawson .10
449 Pedro Castellano .05
450 Tom Gordon .05
451 Rob Dibble .05
452 Ron Darling .05
453 Chipper Jones .75
454 Joe Grahe .05
455 Domingo Cedeno .05
456 Tom Edens .05
457 Mitch Webster .05
458 Jose Bautista .05
459 Troy O'Leary .05
460 Todd Zeile .05
461 Sean Berry .05
462 *Brad Holman* .05
463 Dave Martinez .05
464 Mark Lewis .05
465 Paul Carey .05
466 Jack Armstrong .05
467 David Telgheder .05
468 Gene Harris .05
469 Danny Darwin .05
470 Kim Batiste .05
471 Tim Wakefield .05
472 Craig Lefferts .05
473 Jacob Brumfield .05
474 Lance Painter .05
475 Milt Cuyler .05
476 Melido Perez .05
477 Derek Parks .05
478 Gary DiSarcina .05
479 Steve Bedrosian .05
480 Eric Anthony .05
481 Julio Franco .05
482 Tommy Greene .05
483 Pat Kelly .05
484 Nate Minchey (Rated Rookie) .05
485 William Pennyfeather .05
486 Harold Baines .05
487 Howard Johnson .05
488 Angel Miranda .05
489 Scott Sanders .05
490 Shawon Dunston .05
491 Mel Rojas .05
492 Jeff Nelson .05
493 Archi Cianfrocco .05

494	Al Martin	.05
495	Mike Gallego	.05
496	Mike Henneman	.05
497	Armando Reynoso	.05
498	Mickey Morandini	.05
499	Rick Renteria	.05
500	Rick Sutcliffe	.05
501	Bobby Jones (Rated Rookie)	.05
502	Gary Gaetti	.05
503	Rick Aguilera	.05
504	Todd Stottlemyre	.05
505	Mike Mohler	.05
506	Mike Stanton	.05
507	Jose Guzman	.05
508	Kevin Rogers	.05
509	Chuck Carr	.05
510	Chris Jones	.05
511	Brent Mayne	.05
512	Greg Harris	.05
513	Dave Henderson	.05
514	Eric Hillman	.05
515	Dan Peltier	.05
516	Craig Shipley	.05
517	John Valentin	.05
518	Wilson Alvarez	.05
519	Andujar Cedeno	.05
520	Troy Neel	.05
521	Tom Candiotti	.05
522	Matt Mieske	.05
523	Jim Thome	.10
524	Lou Frazier	.05
525	Mike Jackson	.05
526	Pedro Martinez	.05
527	Roger Pavlik	.05
528	Kent Bottenfield	.05
529	Felix Jose	.05
530	Mark Guthrie	.05
531	Steve Farr	.05
532	Craig Paquette	.05
533	Doug Jones	.05
534	Luis Alicea	.05
535	Cory Snyder	.05
536	Paul Sorrento	.05
537	Nigel Wilson	.05
538	Jeff King	.05
539	Willie Green	.05
540	Kirk McCaskill	.05
541	Al Osuna	.05
542	Greg Hibbard	.05
543	Brett Butler	.05
544	Jose Valentin	.05
545	Wil Cordero	.05
546	Chris Bosio	.05
547	Jamie Moyer	.05
548	Jim Eisenreich	.05
549	Vinny Castilla	.05
550	Checklist (Dave Winfield 3,000 Hits)	.05
551	John Roper	.05
552	Lance Johnson	.05
553	Scott Kamieniecki	.05
554	Mike Moore	.05
555	Steve Buechele	.05
556	Terry Pendleton	.05
557	Todd Van Poppel	.05
558	Rob Butler	.05
559	Zane Smith	.05
560	David Hulse	.05
561	Tim Costo	.05
562	John Habyan	.05
563	Terry Jorgensen	.05
564	Matt Nokes	.05
565	Kevin McReynolds	.05
566	Phil Plantier	.05
567	Chris Turner	.05
568	Carlos Delgado	.25
569	John Jaha	.05
570	Dwight Smith	.05
571	John Vander Wal	.05
572	Trevor Wilson	.05
573	Felix Fermin	.05
574	Marc Newfield (Rated Rookie)	.05
575	Jeromy Burnitz	.10
576	Leo Gomez	.05
577	Curt Schilling	.10
578	Kevin Young	.05
579	*Jerry Spradlin*	.05
580	Curt Leskanic	.05
581	Carl Willis	.05
582	Alex Fernandez	.05
583	Mark Holzemer	.05
584	Domingo Martinez	.05
585	Pete Smith	.05
586	Brian Jordan	.05
587	Kevin Gross	.05
588	J.R. Phillips (Rated Rookie)	.05
589	Chris Nabholz	.05
590	Bill Wertz	.05
591	Derek Bell	.05
592	Brady Anderson	.05
593	Matt Turner	.05
594	Pete Incaviglia	.05
595	Greg Gagne	.05
596	John Flaherty	.05
597	Scott Livingstone	.05
598	Rod Bolton	.05
599	Mike Perez	.05
600	Checklist (Roger Clemens 2,000 Strikeouts)	.10
601	Tony Castillo	.05
602	Henry Mercedes	.05
603	Mike Fetters	.05
604	Rod Beck	.05
605	Damon Buford	.05
606	Matt Whiteside	.05
607	Shawn Green	.35
608	Midre Cummings (Rated Rookie)	.10
609	Jeff McNeeley	.05
610	Danny Sheaffer	.05
611	Paul Wagner	.05
612	Torey Lovullo	.05
613	Javier Lopez	.05
614	Mariano Duncan	.05
615	Doug Brocail	.05
616	Dave Hansen	.05
617	Ryan Klesko	.05
618	Eric Davis	.10
619	Scott Ruffcorn (Rated Rookie)	.05
620	Mike Trombley	.05
621	Jaime Navarro	.05
622	Rheal Cormier	.05
623	Jose Offerman	.05
624	David Segui	.05
625	Robb Nen (Rated Rookie)	.05
626	Dave Gallagher	.05
627	*Julian Tavarez*	.10
628	Chris Gomez	.05
629	Jeffrey Hammonds (Rated Rookie)	.10
630	Scott Brosius	.05
631	Willie Blair	.05
632	Doug Drabek	.05
633	Bill Wegman	.05
634	Jeff McKnight	.05
635	Rich Rodriguez	.05
636	Steve Trachsel	.05
637	Buddy Groom	.05
638	Sterling Hitchcock	.05
639	Chuck McElroy	.05
640	Rene Gonzales	.05
641	Dan Plesac	.05
642	Jeff Branson	.05
643	Darrell Whitmore	.05
644	Paul Quantrill	.05
645	Rich Rowland	.05
646	*Curtis Pride*	.10
647	Erik Plantenberg	.05
648	Albie Lopez	.05
649	*Rich Batchelor*	.05
650	Lee Smith	.10
651	Cliff Floyd	.10
652	Pete Schourek	.05
653	Reggie Jefferson	.05
654	Bill Haselman	.05
655	Steve Hosey	.05
656	Mark Clark	.05
657	Mark Davis	.05
658	Dave Magadan	.05
659	Candy Maldonado	.05
660	Checklist (Mark Langston 2,0000 Strikeouts)	.05

1994 Donruss Special Edition - Gold

In 1994 Donruss added a Special Edition subset of 100 of the game's top players. Fifty cards each were included one or two per pack in all types of Donruss' Series 1 and 2 packaging. The cards use the same photos and format as the regular-issue version, but have special gold-foil stamping on front in the area of the team logo and player name, and on back in a "Special Edition" number box in the upper-left corner.

		MT
Complete Set (100):		15.00
Common Player:		.10
1	Nolan Ryan	2.00
2	Mike Piazza	1.50
3	Moises Alou	.10
4	Ken Griffey, Jr.	2.00
5	Gary Sheffield	.25
6	Roberto Alomar	.50
7	John Kruk	.10
8	Gregg Olson	.10
9	Gregg Jefferies	.10
10	Tony Gwynn	1.00
11	Chad Curtis	.10
12	Craig Biggio	.20
13	John Burkett	.10
14	Carlos Baerga	.10
15	Robin Yount	.40
16	Dennis Eckersley	.10
17	Dwight Gooden	.10
18	Ryne Sandberg	.50
19	Rickey Henderson	.25
20	Jack McDowell	.10
21	Jay Bell	.10
22	Kevin Brown	.20
23	Robin Ventura	.20
24	Paul Molitor	.50
25	David Justice	.20
26	Rafael Palmeiro	.20
27	Cecil Fielder	.10
28	Chuck Knoblauch	.15
29	Dave Hollins	.10
30	Jimmy Key	.10
31	Mark Langston	.10
32	Darryl Kile	.10
33	Ruben Sierra	.10
34	Ron Gant	.10
35	Ozzie Smith	.50
36	Wade Boggs	.30
37	Marquis Grissom	.15
38	Will Clark	.20
39	Kenny Lofton	.15
40	Cal Ripken, Jr.	2.00
41	Steve Avery	.10
42	Mo Vaughn	.20
43	Brian McRae	.10
44	Mickey Tettleton	.10
45	Barry Larkin	.20
46	Charlie Hayes	.10
47	Kevin Appier	.10
48	Robby Thompson	.10
49	Juan Gonzalez	.60
50	Paul O'Neill	.15
51	Mike Mussina	.40
52	Andy Benes	.10
53	Darren Daulton	.10
54	Orlando Merced	.10
55	Mark McGwire	2.00
56	Dave Winfield	.25
57	Sammy Sosa	1.25
58	Eric Karros	.10
59	Greg Vaughn	.10
60	Don Mattingly	1.00
61	Frank Thomas	1.00
62	Fred McGriff	.10
63	Kirby Puckett	.75
64	Roberto Kelly	.10
65	Wally Joyner	.10
66	Andres Galarraga	.15
67	Bobby Bonilla	.10
68	Benito Santiago	.10
69	Barry Bonds	1.00
70	Delino DeShields	.10
71	Albert Belle	.25
72	Randy Johnson	.60
73	Tim Salmon	.15
74	John Olerud	.15
75	Dean Palmer	.10
76	Roger Clemens	1.00
77	Jim Abbott	.10
78	Mark Grace	.20
79	Ozzie Guillen	.10
80	Lou Whitaker	.10
81	Jose Rijo	.10
82	Jeff Montgomery	.10
83	Chuck Finley	.10
84	Tom Glavine	.20
85	Jeff Bagwell	.60
86	Joe Carter	.10
87	Ray Lankford	.10
88	Ramon Martinez	.10
89	Jay Buhner	.10
90	Matt Williams	.15
91	Larry Walker	.20
92	Jose Canseco	.30
93	Len Dykstra	.10
94	Bryan Harvey	.10
95	Andy Van Slyke	.10
96	Ivan Rodriguez	.30
97	Kevin Mitchell	.10
98	Travis Fryman	.10
99	Duane Ward	.10
100	Greg Maddux	.75

1994 Donruss Anniversary-1984

This set commemorates and features 10 of the most popular cards from Donruss' 1984 set. The cards, inserted in Series I hobby foil packs only, are "holographically enhanced" with foil stamping and UV coating.

		MT
Complete Set (10):		24.00
Common Player:		1.00
1	Joe Carter	1.00
2	Robin Yount	1.50
3	George Brett	2.50
4	Rickey Henderson	1.50
5	Nolan Ryan	7.50
6	Cal Ripken, Jr.	7.50
7	Wade Boggs	1.50
8	Don Mattingly	4.00
9	Ryne Sandberg	2.00
10	Tony Gwynn	3.00

1994 Donruss Award Winners Supers

Major award winners of the 1993 season are honored in in this super-size (3-1/2" x 5") insert set. One card was packaged in each box of U.S. jumbo packs and in each Canadian foil-pack box. On a gold-tone background, the card backs have another player photo, a description of his award winning performance and a white strip with a serial number identifying the card's place in an edition of 10,000.

		MT
Complete Set (10):		18.00
Common Player:		1.50
1	Barry Bonds (N.L. MVP)	3.00
2	Greg Maddux (N.L. Cy Young)	2.00
3	Mike Piazza (N.L. ROY)	3.00
4	Barry Bonds (N.L. HR Champ)	3.00
5	Kirby Puckett (All-Star MVP)	2.50
6	Frank Thomas (A.L. MVP)	2.50
7	Jack McDowell (A.L. Cy Young)	1.50
8	Tim Salmon (A.L. ROY)	2.00
9	Juan Gonzalez (A.L. HR Champ)	2.00
10	Paul Molitor (World Series MVP)	2.00

1994 Donruss Decade Dominators

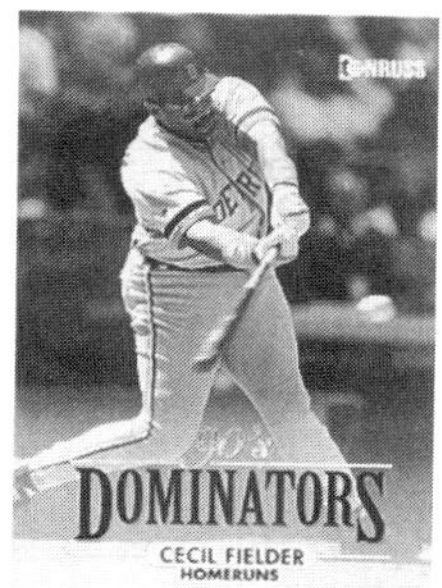

Donruss selected 10 top home run hitters (Series I) and 10 RBI leaders of the 1990s for this insert set. Cards were issued in all types of Series I and II packs. Full-bleed UV-coated cards were gold-foil enhanced on the front. Backs featured another full-color player photo and charted information on his 1990s home run or RBI output and ranking.

		MT
Complete Set (20):		22.50
Common Player:		.50
Series 1		
1	Cecil Fielder	.50
2	Barry Bonds	1.50
3	Fred McGriff	.50
4	Matt Williams	.50
5	Joe Carter	.50
6	Juan Gonzalez	1.00
7	Jose Canseco	.75
8	Ron Gant	.50
9	Ken Griffey, Jr.	3.50
10	Mark McGwire	4.00
Series 2		
1	Tony Gwynn	2.00
2	Frank Thomas	2.00
3	Paul Molitor	1.75
4	Edgar Martinez	.50
5	Kirby Puckett	2.00
6	Ken Griffey, Jr.	3.50
7	Barry Bonds	2.00
8	Willie McGee	.50
9	Len Dykstra	.50
10	John Kruk	.50

1994 Donruss Decade Dominators Supers

Super-size (3-1/2" x 5") versions of the 1994 Donruss Decade Dominators insert cards were produced as a premium, one card being packaged in a paper checklist envelope in each hobby box of Donruss foil packs. The supers are identical in format to the regular-size cards with the exception of a white serial number strip on the back, identifying each card's position in an edition of 10,000.

		MT
Complete Set (20):		45.00
Common Player:		2.00
Series 1		
1	Cecil Fielder	2.00
2	Barry Bonds	3.00
3	Fred McGriff	2.00
4	Matt Williams	2.00
5	Joe Carter	2.00
6	Juan Gonzalez	2.50
7	Jose Canseco	2.50
8	Ron Gant	2.00
9	Ken Griffey, Jr.	4.00
10	Mark McGwire	6.00
Series 2		
1	Tony Gwynn	3.00
2	Frank Thomas	3.00
3	Paul Molitor	2.50
4	Edgar Martinez	2.00
5	Kirby Puckett	3.00
6	Ken Griffey, Jr.	5.00
7	Barry Bonds	4.00
8	Willie McGee	2.00
9	Lenny Dykstra	2.00
10	John Kruk	2.00

1994 Donruss Diamond Kings

The artwork of Dick Perez is again featured on this insert set included in foil packs. Player art is set against garish color backgrounds with a red-and-silver "Diamond Kings" foil logo above, and the player's name in script at bottom. Backs are printed in red on pale yellow and feature a 1993 season summary. Cards have a DK preface to the number. Cards #1-14 and #29, Dave Winfield, were included in Series I packs; cards #15-28 were found in Series II, along with the checklist card (#30), featuring a Dick Perez self-portrait.

		MT
Complete Set (30):		20.00
Common Player:		.30
1	Barry Bonds	1.75
2	Mo Vaughn	.50
3	Steve Avery	.30
4	Tim Salmon	.30
5	Rick Wilkins	.30
6	Brian Harper	.30
7	Andres Galarraga	.40
8	Albert Belle	.50
9	John Kruk	.30
10	Ivan Rodriguez	1.00
11	Tony Gwynn	2.00
12	Brian McRae	.30
13	Bobby Bonilla	.30
14	Ken Griffey, Jr.	3.00
15	Mike Piazza	2.50
16	Don Mattingly	1.75
17	Barry Larkin	.35
18	Ruben Sierra	.30
19	Orlando Merced	.30
20	Greg Vaughn	.30
21	Gregg Jefferies	.30
22	Cecil Fielder	.30
23	Moises Alou	.30
24	John Olerud	.30
25	Gary Sheffield	.30
26	Mike Mussina	.75
27	Jeff Bagwell	1.25
28	Frank Thomas	1.50
29	Dave Winfield (King of Kings)	1.50
30	Dick Perez (Checklist)	.30

1994 Donruss Diamond Kings Supers

Each retail box of 1994 Donruss foil packs contains one super-size (4-7/8" x 6-13/16") version of the Diamond Kings inserts. Series 1 boxes offer cards #1-14, while #15-28 are found in Series 2 boxes. A 29th card, honoring Dave Winfield, was also produced. Super DKs are identical in format to the regular-size inserts, with the exception of a white serial number strip on the back which identifies the card within an edition of 10,000.

		MT
Complete Set (29):		65.00
Common Player:		2.00
1	Barry Bonds	5.00
2	Mo Vaughn	3.00
3	Steve Avery	2.00
4	Tim Salmon	2.00
5	Rick Wilkins	2.00
6	Brian Harper	2.00
7	Andres Galarraga	2.50
8	Albert Belle	3.00
9	John Kruk	2.00
10	Ivan Rodriguez	3.00
11	Tony Gwynn	4.00
12	Brian McRae	2.00
13	Bobby Bonilla	2.00
14	Ken Griffey, Jr.	6.00
15	Mike Piazza	5.00
16	Don Mattingly	4.00
17	Barry Larkin	2.50
18	Ruben Sierra	2.00
19	Orlando Merced	2.00
20	Greg Vaughn	2.00
21	Gregg Jefferies	2.00
22	Cecil Fielder	2.00
23	Moises Alou	2.00
24	John Olerud	2.00
25	Gary Sheffield	2.00
26	Mike Mussina	3.00
27	Jeff Bagwell	3.00
28	Frank Thomas	4.00
29	Dave Winfield (King of Kings)	4.00

1994 Donruss Elite

Donruss continued its popular Elite Series with 12 more players in 1994. The cards, numbered #37-48, were inserted in foil packs only. The cards feature the player in a diamond on the front; the back offers an opinion of why the player is considered an elite and is serially numbered to 10,000.

		MT
Complete Set (12):		65.00
Common Player:		5.00
37	Frank Thomas	7.50
38	Tony Gwynn	8.00
39	Tim Salmon	5.00
40	Albert Belle	5.00
41	John Kruk	5.00
42	Juan Gonzalez	6.00
43	John Olerud	5.00
44	Barry Bonds	7.50
45	Ken Griffey, Jr.	15.00
46	Mike Piazza	10.00
47	Jack McDowell	5.00
48	Andres Galarraga	5.00

1994 Donruss Long Ball Leaders

The "Tale of the Tape" for the 1993 season is chronicled in this Series II hobby-only foil-pack insert. Silver prismatic foil highlights the typography on the front of the card which includes the "Long Ball Leaders" logos (complete with embossed baseball), the player's last name and the distance of his blast. Cards backs have another player photo superimposed on the venue in which the home run was hit. The distance is repeated in silver over the ballpark photo. In a wide silver box at bottom are data about the home run.

		MT
Complete Set (10):		8.00
Common Player:		.25
1	Cecil Fielder	.25
2	Dean Palmer	.25
3	Andres Galarraga	.25
4	Bo Jackson	.40
5	Ken Griffey, Jr.	2.50
6	Dave Justice	.35
7	Mike Piazza	2.00
8	Frank Thomas	1.50
9	Barry Bonds	2.00
10	Juan Gonzalez	.75

1994 Donruss MVPs

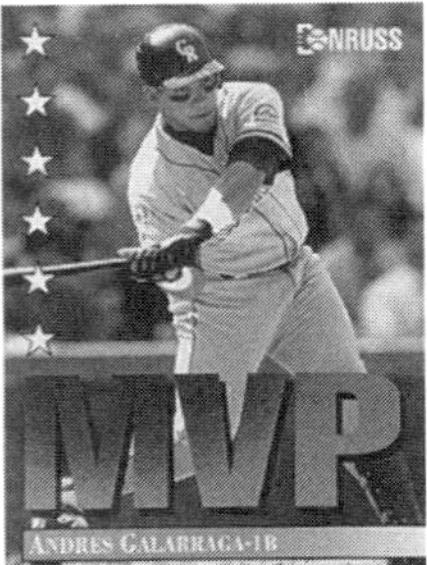

These inserts were included in 1994 jumbo packs only. The fronts have a large metallic blue MVP logo, beneath which is a red stripe with the player's name and position in white. Backs have a portrait photo, stats for 1993 and a summary of why the player was selected as team MVP.

		MT
Complete Set (28):		30.00
Common Player:		.25
1	Dave Justice	.50
2	Mark Grace	.50
3	Jose Rijo	.25
4	Andres Galarraga	.50
5	Bryan Harvey	.25
6	Jeff Bagwell	1.50
7	Mike Piazza	3.50
8	Moises Alou	.25
9	Bobby Bonilla	.25
10	Len Dykstra	.25
11	Jeff King	.25
12	Gregg Jefferies	.25
13	Tony Gwynn	3.00
14	Barry Bonds	3.00
15	Cal Ripken, Jr.	5.00
16	Mo Vaughn	.50
17	Tim Salmon	.50
18	Frank Thomas	3.00
19	Albert Belle	.75
20	Cecil Fielder	.25
21	Wally Joyner	.25
22	Greg Vaughn	.25
23	Kirby Puckett	2.50
24	Don Mattingly	2.50
25	Ruben Sierra	.25
26	Ken Griffey, Jr.	5.00
27	Juan Gonzalez	2.00
28	John Olerud	.25

1994 Donruss Spirit of the Game

Ten players are featured in this insert set, packaged exclusively in retail boxes. Horizontal in format, fronts feature a color player action photo set against a gold-tone background which has the appearance of a multiple-exposure photo. On back a player portrait photo is set against a backdrop of red, white and blue bunting. There is a short previous-season write-up at right. Cards #1-5 were included with Series I, cards 6-10 were in Series II packs.

		MT
Complete Set (10):		10.00
Common Player:		.70
1	John Olerud	.50
2	Barry Bonds	2.00
3	Ken Griffey, Jr.	3.00
4	Mike Piazza	2.00
5	Juan Gonzalez	1.00
6	Frank Thomas	1.50
7	Tim Salmon	.50
8	Dave Justice	.50
9	Don Mattingly	1.50
10	Len Dykstra	.50

1994 Donruss Spirit of the Game Supers

Virtually identical in format to the regular-size "Spirit of the Game" cards, these 3-1/2" x 5" versions have gold-foil, rather than holographic printing on the front, and have a serial number on back identifying it from an edition of 10,000. One super card was inserted in each specially designated retail box.

		MT
Complete Set (10):		18.00
Common Player:		1.50
1	John Olerud	1.50
2	Barry Bonds	3.00
3	Ken Griffey, Jr.	4.00
4	Mike Piazza	3.50
5	Juan Gonzalez	2.00
6	Frank Thomas	2.50
7	Tim Salmon	1.50
8	Dave Justice	1.50
9	Don Mattingly	3.00
10	Len Dykstra	1.50

1995 Donruss Samples

The cards in this preview release of Donruss' 1995 baseball issue are virtually identical to the issued versions of the same players' cards except for the overprinted notation of sample status on each side.

		MT
Complete Set (7):		27.50
Common Player:		3.75
5	Mike Piazza	6.00
8	Barry Bonds	5.00
20	Jeff Bagwell	4.00
42	Juan Gonzalez	4.00
55	Don Mattingly	7.50
275	Frank Thomas	4.00
331	Greg Maddux	4.00

1995 Donruss

A pair of player photos on the front of each card and silver-foil highlights are featured on the 1995 Donruss set. Besides the main action photo on front, each card has a second photo in a home plate frame at lower-left. A silver-foil ribbon beneath has the player's team and name embossed. Above the small photo is the player's position, with a half-circle of stars over all; both elements in silver foil. Completing the silver-foil highlights is the Donruss logo at upper-left. Full-bleed backs have yet another action photo at center, with a large team logo at left and five years' worth of stats plus career numbers at bottom. Donruss was issued in retail and hobby 12-card packs, magazine distributor packs of 16 and jumbo packs of 20 cards. New to Donruss in 1995 were Super Packs. These were packs that contained complete insert sets and were seeded every 90 packs.

	MT
Complete Set (550):	35.00
Complete Series 1:	20.00
Complete Series 2:	15.00
Common Player:	.05
Press Proofs:	10X
Series 1 or 2 Pack (12):	1.00
Series 1 or 2 Wax Box (36):	25.00

1 Dave Justice .10
2 Rene Arocha .05
3 Sandy Alomar Jr. .10
4 Luis Lopez .05
5 Mike Piazza 1.50
6 Bobby Jones .05
7 Damion Easley .05
8 Barry Bonds 1.50
9 Mike Mussina .35
10 Kevin Seitzer .05
11 John Smiley .05
12 W. VanLandingham .05
13 Ron Darling .05
14 Walt Weiss .05
15 Mike Lansing .05
16 Allen Watson .05
17 Aaron Sele .05
18 Randy Johnson .50
19 Dean Palmer .05
20 Jeff Bagwell .75
21 Curt Schilling .15
22 Darrell Whitmore .05
23 Steve Trachsel .05
24 Dan Wilson .05
25 Steve Finley .05
26 Bret Boone .10
27 Charles Johnson .10
28 Mike Stanton .05
29 Ismael Valdes .05
30 Salomon Torres .05
31 Eric Anthony .05
32 Spike Owen .05
33 Joey Cora .05
34 Robert Eenhoorn .05
35 Rick White .05
36 Omar Vizquel .10
37 Carlos Delgado .25
38 Eddie Williams .05
39 Shawon Dunston .05
40 Darrin Fletcher .05
41 Leo Gomez .05
42 Juan Gonzalez 1.00
43 Luis Alicea .05
44 Ken Ryan .05
45 Lou Whitaker .05
46 Mike Blowers .05
47 Willie Blair .05
48 Todd Van Poppel .05
49 Roberto Alomar .35
50 Ozzie Smith .75
51 Sterling Hitchcock .05
52 Mo Vaughn .25
53 Rick Aguilera .05
54 Kent Mercker .05
55 Don Mattingly 1.00
56 Bob Scanlan .05
57 Wilson Alvarez .05
58 Jose Mesa .05
59 Scott Kamieniecki .05
60 Todd Jones .05
61 John Kruk .05
62 Mike Stanley .05
63 Tino Martinez .05
64 Eddie Zambrano .05
65 Todd Hundley .10
66 Jamie Moyer .05
67 Rich Amaral .05
68 Jose Valentin .05
69 Alex Gonzalez .05
70 Kurt Abbott .05
71 Delino DeShields .05
72 Brian Anderson .05
73 John Vander Wal .05
74 Turner Ward .05
75 Tim Raines .10
76 Mark Acre .05
77 Jose Offerman .05
78 Jimmy Key .05
79 Mark Whiten .05
80 Mark Gubicza .05
81 Darren Hall .05
82 Travis Fryman .10
83 Cal Ripken, Jr. 3.00
84 Geronimo Berroa .05
85 Bret Barberie .05
86 Andy Ashby .05
87 Steve Avery .05
88 Rich Becker .05
89 John Valentin .05
90 Glenallen Hill .05
91 Carlos Garcia .10
92 Dennis Martinez .05
93 Pat Kelly .05
94 Orlando Miller .10
95 Felix Jose .05
96 Mike Kingery .05
97 Jeff Kent .05
98 Pete Incaviglia .05
99 Chad Curtis .05
100 Thomas Howard .05
101 Hector Carrasco .05
102 Tom Pagnozzi .05
103 Danny Tartabull .05
104 Donnie Elliott .05
105 Danny Jackson .05
106 Steve Dunn .05
107 Roger Salkeld .05
108 Jeff King .05
109 Cecil Fielder .10
110 Checklist .05
111 Denny Neagle .05
112 Troy Neel .05
113 Rod Beck .05
114 Alex Rodriguez 3.00
115 Joey Eischen .05
116 Tom Candiotti .05
117 Ray McDavid .05
118 Vince Coleman .05
119 Pete Harnisch .05
120 David Nied .05
121 Pat Rapp .10
122 Sammy Sosa 1.50
123 Steve Reed .05
124 Jose Oliva .05
125 Rick Bottalico .10
126 Jose DeLeon .05
127 Pat Hentgen .05
128 Will Clark .15
129 Mark Dewey .05
130 Greg Vaughn .10
131 Darren Dreifort .05
132 Ed Sprague .05
133 Lee Smith .10
134 Charles Nagy .10
135 Phil Plantier .05
136 Jason Jacome .05
137 Jose Lima .05
138 J.R. Phillips .05
139 J.T. Snow .10
140 Mike Huff .05
141 Billy Brewer .05
142 Jeromy Burnitz .10
143 Ricky Bones .05
144 Carlos Rodriguez .05
145 Luis Gonzalez .20
146 Mark Lemke .05
147 Al Martin .05
148 Mike Bordick .05
149 Robb Nen .05
150 Wil Cordero .05
151 Edgar Martinez .05
152 Gerald Williams .05
153 Esteban Beltre .05
154 Mike Moore .05
155 Mark Langston .05
156 Mark Clark .05
157 Bobby Ayala .05
158 Rick Wilkins .05
159 Bobby Munoz .05
160 Checklist .05
161 Scott Erickson .05
162 Paul Molitor .35
163 Jon Lieber .10
164 Jason Grimsley .05
165 Norberto Martin .05
166 Javier Lopez .05
167 Brian McRae .05
168 Gary Sheffield .20
169 Marcus Moore .05
170 John Hudek .05
171 Kelly Stinett .05
172 Chris Gomez .05
173 Rey Sanchez .05
174 Juan Guzman .05
175 Chan Ho Park .15
176 Terry Shumpert .05
177 Steve Ontiveros .05
178 Brad Ausmus .05
179 Tim Davis .05
180 Billy Ashley .05
181 Vinny Castilla .10
182 Bill Spiers .05
183 Randy Knorr .05
184 Brian Hunter .05
185 Pat Meares .05
186 Steve Buechele .05
187 Kirt Manwaring .05
188 Tim Naehring .05
189 Matt Mieske .05
190 Josias Manzanillo .05
191 Greg McMichael .05
192 Chuck Carr .05
193 Midre Cummings .05
194 Darryl Strawberry .10
195 Greg Gagne .05
196 Steve Cooke .05
197 Woody Williams .05
198 Ron Karkovice .05
199 Phil Leftwich .05
200 Jim Thome .15
201 Brady Anderson .10
202 Pedro Martinez .15
203 Steve Karsay .05
204 Reggie Sanders .10
205 Bill Risley .05
206 Jay Bell .05
207 Kevin Brown .15
208 Tim Scott .05
209 Len Dykstra .05
210 Willie Greene .05
211 Jim Eisenreich .05
212 Cliff Floyd .10
213 Otis Nixon .05
214 Eduardo Perez .05
215 Manuel Lee .05
216 *Armando Benitez* .15
217 Dave McCarty .05
218 Scott Livingstone .05
219 Chad Kreuter .05
220 Checklist .05
221 Brian Jordan .05
222 Matt Whiteside .05
223 Jim Edmonds .15
224 Tony Gwynn .75
225 Jose Lind .05
226 Marvin Freeman .05
227 Ken Hill .05
228 David Hulse .05
229 Joe Hesketh .05
230 Roberto Petagine .05
231 Jeffrey Hammonds .05
232 John Jaha .05
233 John Burkett .05
234 Hal Morris .05
235 Tony Castillo .05
236 Ryan Bowen .05
237 Wayne Kirby .05
238 Brent Mayne .05
239 Jim Bullinger .05
240 Mike Lieberthal .10
241 Barry Larkin .15
242 David Segui .05
243 Jose Bautista .05
244 Hector Fajardo .05
245 Orel Hershiser .10
246 James Mouton .05
247 Scott Leius .05
248 Tom Glavine .15
249 Danny Bautista .05
250 Jose Mercedes .05
251 Marquis Grissom .05
252 Charlie Hayes .05
253 Ryan Klesko .05
254 Vicente Palacios .05
255 Matias Carillo .05
256 Gary DiSarcina .05
257 Kirk Gibson .05
258 Garey Ingram .05
259 Alex Fernandez .05
260 John Mabry .05
261 Chris Howard .05
262 Miguel Jimenez .05
263 Heath Slocumb .05
264 Albert Belle .25
265 Dave Clark .05
266 Joe Orsulak .05
267 Joey Hamilton .05
268 Mark Portugal .05
269 Kevin Tapani .05
270 Sid Fernandez .05
271 Steve Dreyer .05
272 Denny Hocking .05
273 Troy O'Leary .05
274 Milt Cuyler .05
275 Frank Thomas 1.00
276 Jorge Fabregas .05
277 Mike Gallego .05
278 Mickey Morandini .05
279 Roberto Hernandez .05
280 Henry Rodriguez .05
281 Garret Anderson .05
282 Bob Wickman .05
283 Gar Finnvold .05
284 Paul O'Neill .05
285 Royce Clayton .05
286 Chuck Knoblauch .05
287 Johnny Ruffin .05
288 Dave Nilsson .05
289 David Cone .10
290 Chuck McElroy .05
291 Kevin Stocker .05
292 Jose Rijo .05
293 Sean Berry .05
294 Ozzie Guillen .05
295 Chris Hoiles .05
296 Kevin Foster .05
297 Jeff Frye .05
298 Lance Johnson .05
299 Mike Kelly .05
300 Ellis Burks .05
301 Roberto Kelly .05
302 Dante Bichette .05
303 Alvaro Espinoza .05
304 Alex Cole .05
305 Rickey Henderson .30
306 Dave Weathers .05
307 Shane Reynolds .05
308 Bobby Bonilla .05
309 Junior Felix .05
310 Jeff Fassero .05
311 Darren Lewis .05
312 John Doherty .05
313 Scott Servais .05
314 Rick Helling .05
315 Pedro Martinez .15
316 Wes Chamberlain .05
317 Bryan Eversgerd .05
318 Trevor Hoffman .05
319 John Patterson .05
320 Matt Walbeck .05
321 Jeff Montgomery .05
322 Mel Rojas .05
323 Eddie Taubensee .05
324 Ray Lankford .05
325 Jose Vizcaino .05
326 Carlos Baerga .05
327 Jack Voigt .05
328 Julio Franco .05
329 Brent Gates .05
330 Checklist .05
331 Greg Maddux 1.00
332 Jason Bere .05
333 Bill Wegman .05
334 Tuffy Rhodes .05
335 Kevin Young .10
336 Andy Benes .05
337 Pedro Astacio .05
338 Reggie Jefferson .05
339 Tim Belcher .05
340 Ken Griffey Jr. 2.50
341 Mariano Duncan .05
342 Andres Galarraga .05
343 Rondell White .10
344 Cory Bailey .05
345 Bryan Harvey .05
346 John Franco .05
347 Greg Swindell .05
348 David West .05
349 Fred McGriff .05
350 Jose Canseco .25
351 Orlando Merced .05
352 Rheal Cormier .05
353 Carlos Pulido .05
354 Terry Steinbach .05
355 Wade Boggs .25
356 B.J. Surhoff .05
357 Rafael Palmeiro .15
358 Anthony Young .05
359 Tom Brunansky .05
360 Todd Stottlemyre .10
361 Chris Turner .05
362 Joe Boever .05
363 Jeff Blauser .05
364 Derek Bell .05
365 Matt Williams .15
366 Jeremy Hernandez .05
367 Joe Girardi .05
368 Mike Devereaux .05
369 Jim Abbott .05
370 Manny Ramirez 1.00
371 Kenny Lofton .10

#	Player	MT
372	Mark Smith	.05
373	Dave Fleming	.05
374	Dave Stewart	.10
375	Roger Pavlik	.05
376	Hipolito Pichardo	.05
377	Bill Taylor	.05
378	Robin Ventura	.10
379	Bernard Gilkey	.05
380	Kirby Puckett	1.00
381	Steve Howe	.05
382	Devon White	.10
383	Roberto Mejia	.05
384	Darrin Jackson	.05
385	Mike Morgan	.05
386	Rusty Meacham	.05
387	Bill Swift	.05
388	Lou Frazier	.05
389	Andy Van Slyke	.05
390	Brett Butler	.05
391	Bobby Witt	.05
392	Jeff Conine	.10
393	Tim Hyers	.05
394	Terry Pendleton	.05
395	Ricky Jordan	.05
396	Eric Plunk	.05
397	Melido Perez	.05
398	Darryl Kile	.10
399	Mark McLemore	.05
400	Greg Harris	.05
401	Jim Leyritz	.05
402	Doug Strange	.05
403	Tim Salmon	.15
404	Terry Mulholland	.05
405	Robby Thompson	.05
406	Ruben Sierra	.05
407	Tony Phillips	.05
408	Moises Alou	.10
409	Felix Fermin	.05
410	Pat Listach	.05
411	Kevin Bass	.05
412	Ben McDonald	.05
413	Scott Cooper	.05
414	Jody Reed	.05
415	Deion Sanders	.10
416	Ricky Gutierrez	.05
417	Gregg Jefferies	.05
418	Jack McDowell	.05
419	Al Leiter	.10
420	Tony Longmire	.05
421	Paul Wagner	.05
422	Geronimo Pena	.05
423	Ivan Rodriguez	.50
424	Kevin Gross	.05
425	Kirk McCaskill	.05
426	Greg Myers	.05
427	Roger Clemens	1.00
428	Chris Hammond	.05
429	Randy Myers	.05
430	Roger Mason	.05
431	Bret Saberhagen	.10
432	Jeff Reboulet	.05
433	John Olerud	.10
434	Bill Gullickson	.05
435	Eddie Murray	.60
436	Pedro Munoz	.05
437	Charlie O'Brien	.05
438	Jeff Nelson	.05
439	Mike Macfarlane	.05
440	Checklist	.05
441	Derrick May	.05
442	John Roper	.05
443	Darryl Hamilton	.05
444	Dan Miceli	.05
445	Tony Eusebio	.05
446	Jerry Browne	.05
447	Wally Joyner	.05
448	Brian Harper	.05
449	Scott Fletcher	.05
450	Bip Roberts	.05
451	Pete Smith	.05
452	Chili Davis	.05
453	Dave Hollins	.05
454	Tony Pena	.05
455	Butch Henry	.05
456	Craig Biggio	.15
457	Zane Smith	.05
458	Ryan Thompson	.05
459	Mike Jackson	.05
460	Mark McGwire	2.50
461	John Smoltz	.10
462	Steve Scarsone	.05
463	Greg Colbrunn	.05
464	Shawn Green	.25
465	David Wells	.10
466	Jose Hernandez	.05
467	Chip Hale	.05
468	Tony Tarasco	.05
469	Kevin Mitchell	.05
470	Billy Hatcher	.05
471	Jay Buhner	.05
472	Ken Caminiti	.10
473	Tom Henke	.05
474	Todd Worrell	.05
475	Mark Eichhorn	.05
476	Bruce Ruffin	.05
477	Chuck Finley	.05
478	Marc Newfield	.05
479	Paul Shuey	.05
480	Bob Tewksbury	.05
481	Ramon Martinez	.05
482	Melvin Nieves	.05
483	Todd Zeile	.05
484	Benito Santiago	.05
485	Stan Javier	.05
486	Kirk Rueter	.05
487	Andre Dawson	.15
488	Eric Karros	.05
489	Dave Magadan	.05
490	Checklist	.05
491	Randy Velarde	.05
492	Larry Walker	.20
493	Cris Carpenter	.05
494	Tom Gordon	.05
495	Dave Burba	.05
496	Darren Bragg	.05
497	Darren Daulton	.05
498	Don Slaught	.05
499	Pat Borders	.05
500	Lenny Harris	.05
501	Joe Ausanio	.05
502	Alan Trammell	.10
503	Mike Fetters	.05
504	Scott Ruffcorn	.05
505	Rich Rowland	.05
506	Juan Samuel	.05
507	Bo Jackson	.10
508	Jeff Branson	.05
509	Bernie Williams	.25
510	Paul Sorrento	.05
511	Dennis Eckersley	.10
512	Pat Mahomes	.05
513	Rusty Greer	.05
514	Luis Polonia	.05
515	Willie Banks	.05
516	John Wetteland	.05
517	Mike LaVaillere	.05
518	Tommy Greene	.05
519	Mark Grace	.20
520	Bob Hamelin	.05
521	Scott Sanderson	.05
522	Joe Carter	.05
523	Jeff Brantley	.05
524	Andrew Lorraine	.05
525	Rico Brogna	.05
526	Shane Mack	.05
527	Mark Wohlers	.05
528	Scott Sanders	.05
529	Chris Bosio	.05
530	Andujar Cedeno	.05
531	Kenny Rogers	.05
532	Doug Drabek	.05
533	Curt Leskanic	.05
534	Craig Shipley	.05
535	Craig Grebeck	.05
536	Cal Eldred	.05
537	Mickey Tettleton	.05
538	Harold Baines	.10
539	Tim Wallach	.05
540	Damon Buford	.05
541	Lenny Webster	.05
542	Kevin Appier	.05
543	Raul Mondesi	.10
544	Eric Young	.10
545	Russ Davis	.05
546	Mike Benjamin	.05
547	Mike Greenwell	.05
548	Scott Brosius	.05
549	Brian Dorsett	.05
550	Checklist	.05

1995 Donruss Press Proofs

Designated as Press Proofs, the first 2,000 cards of each player in the '95 Donruss set were enhanced with gold, rather than silver, foil and inserted into packs at an average rate of one per 20 packs.

	MT
Complete Set (550):	400.00
Complete Series 1 (330):	250.00
Complete Series 2 (220):	200.00
Common Player:	1.00
Stars:	10X

(See 1995 Donruss for checklist and base card values.)

1995 Donruss All-Stars

Exclusive to Wal-Mart jumbo packs were Donruss All-Stars. Nine cards featuring American Leaguers were inserted into Series 1, while nine National League All-Stars were inserted into Series 2 jumbos.

		MT
Complete Set (18):		35.00
Common Player:		.50
AL1	Jimmy Key	.50
AL2	Ivan Rodriguez	2.00
AL3	Frank Thomas	4.00
AL4	Roberto Alomar	1.50
AL5	Wade Boggs	1.50
AL6	Cal Ripken, Jr.	6.00
AL7	Joe Carter	.50
AL8	Ken Griffey, Jr.	6.00
AL9	Kirby Puckett	4.00
NL1	Greg Maddux	4.00
NL2	Mike Piazza	5.00
NL3	Gregg Jefferies	.50
NL4	Mariano Duncan	.50
NL5	Matt Williams	.60
NL6	Ozzie Smith	1.50
NL7	Barry Bonds	3.00
NL8	Tony Gwynn	4.00
NL9	Dave Justice	.75

1995 Donruss Bomb Squad

Bomb Squad features the top six home run hitters in each league on double-sided cards. These cards were only inserted into Series I retail and magazine distributor packs at a rate of one per 24 retail packs and one per 16 magazine distributor packs.

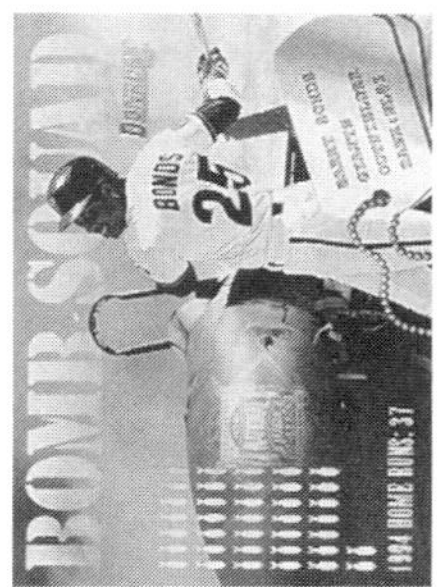

		MT
Complete Set (6):		6.00
Common Player:		.50
1	Ken Griffey, Jr., Matt Williams	2.00
2	Frank Thomas, Jeff Bagwell	1.00
3	Albert Belle, Barry Bonds	1.00
4	Jose Canseco, Fred McGriff	.75
5	Cecil Fielder, Andres Galarraga	.50
6	Joe Carter, Kevin Mitchell	.50

1995 Donruss Diamond Kings

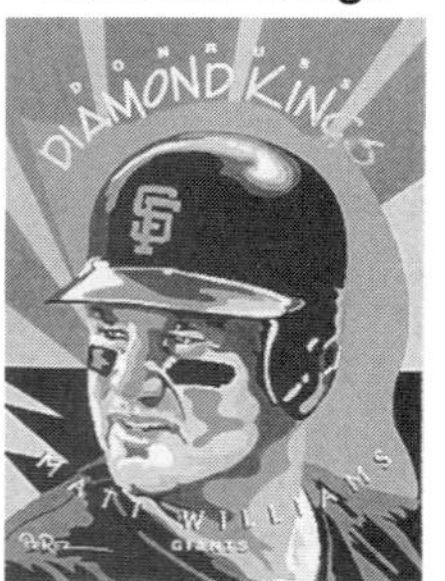

Continuing a tradition begun in 1982, artist Dick Perez painted a series of 28 water colors to produce insert cards of the game's best; 14 in each series. A portrait of the player appears on a party-colored background, with Diamond Kings in gold across the top. DKs were inserted in Series 1 and 2 packs at a rate of one per 10.

		MT
Complete Set (29):		22.00
Common Player:		.50
1	Frank Thomas	2.50
2	Jeff Bagwell	2.50
3	Chili Davis	.50
4	Dante Bichette	.50
5	Ruben Sierra	.50
6	Jeff Conine	.50
7	Paul O'Neill	.50
8	Bobby Bonilla	.50
9	Joe Carter	.50
10	Moises Alou	.50

11	Kenny Lofton	.50
12	Matt Williams	.50
13	Kevin Seitzer	.50
14	Sammy Sosa	2.50
15	Scott Cooper	.50
16	Raul Mondesi	.50
17	Will Clark	.60
18	Lenny Dykstra	.50
19	Kirby Puckett	3.00
20	Hal Morris	.50
21	Travis Fryman	.50
22	Greg Maddux	3.00
23	Rafael Palmeiro	.60
24	Tony Gwynn	2.50
25	David Cone	.50
26	Al Martin	.50
27	Ken Griffey Jr.	3.00
28	Gregg Jefferies	.50
29	Checklist	.10

1995 Donruss Elite

Another Donruss insert tradition continues with the fifth annual presentation of the Elite series. Each of the 12 cards (six each Series 1 and 2) is produced in a numbered edition of 10,000 and inserted into all types of packaging at the rate of one per 210 packs.

		MT
Complete Set (12):		150.00
Common Player:		4.00
49	Jeff Bagwell	15.00
50	Paul O'Neill	4.00
51	Greg Maddux	15.00
52	Mike Piazza	20.00
53	Matt Williams	4.50
54	Ken Griffey, Jr.	30.00
55	Frank Thomas	15.00
56	Barry Bonds	15.00
57	Kirby Puckett	20.00
58	Fred McGriff	4.00
59	Jose Canseco	5.00
60	Albert Belle	7.50

1995 Donruss Long Ball Leaders

Exclusive to Series 1 hobby packs, these cards feature the top long-distance home runs of 1994 in an eye-popping holographic foil presentation. Stated odds of picking one from a hobby pack are one in 24.

		MT
Complete Set (8):		24.00
Common Player:		1.00
1	Frank Thomas	2.50
2	Fred McGriff	1.00
3	Ken Griffey, Jr.	4.00
4	Matt Williams	1.00
5	Mike Piazza	3.00
6	Jose Canseco	1.50
7	Barry Bonds	2.50
8	Jeff Bagwell	2.00

1995 Donruss Mound Marvels

Mound Marvels is an eight-card insert set containing some of the best pitchers in baseball. Cards were inserted into one per 18 retail and magazine packs of Donruss Series II. Each card features a two-way mirror that allows collectors to see the players' face through the mirror.

		MT
Complete Set (8):		15.00
Common Player:		1.00
1	Greg Maddux	6.00
2	David Cone	1.00
3	Mike Mussina	2.50
4	Bret Saberhagen	1.00
5	Jimmy Key	1.00
6	Doug Drabek	1.00
7	Randy Johnson	3.00
8	Jason Bere	1.00

1995 Donruss Dominators

Dominators is a nine-card chase set inserted into hobby packs of Series II Donruss baseball at a rate of one per 24 packs. These acetate cards feature three of the top players at each position on a horizontal format.

		MT
Complete Set (9):		15.00
Common Player:		.50
1	David Cone, Mike Mussina, Greg Maddux	1.50
2	Ivan Rodriguez, Mike Piazza, Darren Daulton	3.00
3	Fred McGriff, Frank Thomas, Jeff Bagwell	2.00
4	Roberto Alomar, Carlos Baerga, Craig Biggio	1.00
5	Robin Ventura, Travis Fryman, Matt Williams	1.00
6	Cal Ripken Jr., Barry Larkin, Wil Cordero	3.50
7	Albert Belle, Barry Bonds, Moises Alou	2.50
8	Ken Griffey Jr., Kenny Lofton, Marquis Grissom	3.50
9	Kirby Puckett, Paul O'Neill, Tony Gwynn	3.00

1995 Donruss/ Top of the Order Card Game

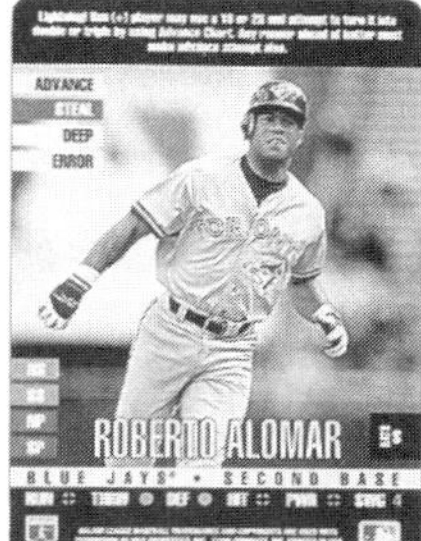

In one of the earliest efforts to wed the play factor and collectibility that had made various fantasy card games so successful in 1994-95, Donruss created the interactive Top of the Order baseball card game. Printed on playing card stock with rounded corners and semi-gloss surface, the player cards feature color action photos and all manners of game-action indicators. Backs of each card are printed primarily in green with Donruss logos. Cards were sold in several types of packaging, including 80- and 160-card boxed sets, and 12-card foil "booster" packs. Stars' cards were printed in lesser quantities than those of journeyman players, resulting in values higher than would be the case based on player popularity alone if all cards were printed in equal quantities. The unnumbered cards are checklisted here in alphabetical order within team and league.

		MT
Complete Set (360):		175.00
Common Player:		.10
(1)	Brady Anderson	.10
(2)	Harold Baines	.10
(3)	Bret Barberie	.10
(4)	Armando Benitez	.10
(5)	Bobby Bonilla	.10
(6)	Scott Erickson	.15
(7)	Leo Gomez	.10
(8)	Curtis Goodwin	.10
(9)	Jeffrey Hammonds	.10
(10)	Chris Hoiles	.10
(11)	Doug Jones	.10
(12)	Ben McDonald	.10
(13)	Mike Mussina	3.00
(14)	Rafael Palmeiro	1.50
(15)	Cal Ripken Jr.	25.00
(16)	Rick Aguilera	.10
(17)	Luis Alicea	.10
(18)	Jose Canseco	2.00
(19)	Roger Clemens	12.50
(20)	Mike Greenwell	.10
(21)	Erik Hanson	.10
(22)	Mike Macfarlane	.10
(23)	Tim Naehring	.10
(24)	Troy O'Leary	.10
(25)	Ken Ryan	.10
(26)	Aaron Sele	.10
(27)	Lee Tinsley	.10
(28)	John Valentin	.10
(29)	Mo Vaughn	1.00
(30)	Jim Abbott	.10
(31)	Mike Butcher	.10
(32)	Chili Davis	.10
(33)	Gary DiSarcina	.10
(34)	Damion Easley	.10
(35)	Jim Edmonds	3.00
(36)	Chuck Finley	.10
(37)	Mark Langston	.10
(38)	Greg Myers	.10
(39)	Spike Owen	.10
(40)	Troy Percival	.10
(41)	Tony Phillips	.10
(42)	Tim Salmon	1.00
(43)	Lee Smith	.25
(44)	J.T. Snow	.10
(45)	Jason Bere	.10
(46)	Mike Devereaux	.10
(47)	Ray Durham	.10
(48)	Alex Fernandez	.10
(49)	Ozzie Guillen	.10
(50)	Roberto Hernandez	.10
(51)	Lance Johnson	.10
(52)	Ron Karkovice	.10
(53)	Tim Raines	.10
(54)	Frank Thomas	12.50
(55)	Robin Ventura	1.00
(56)	Sandy Alomar Jr.	.10
(57)	Carlos Baerga	.10
(58)	Albert Belle	1.00
(59)	Kenny Lofton	1.00
(60)	Dennis Martinez	.10
(61)	Jose Mesa	.10
(62)	Eddie Murray	5.00
(63)	Charles Nagy	.10
(64)	Tony Pena	.10
(65)	Eric Plunk	.10
(66)	Manny Ramirez	10.00
(67)	Paul Sorrento	.10
(68)	Jim Thome	1.00
(69)	Omar Vizquel	.10
(70)	Danny Bautista	.10
(71)	Joe Boever	.10
(72)	Chad Curtis	.10
(73)	Cecil Fielder	.10
(74)	John Flaherty	.10
(75)	Travis Fryman	.40
(76)	Kirk Gibson	.10
(77)	Chris Gomez	.10
(78)	Mike Henneman	.10
(79)	Bob Higginson	.10
(80)	Alan Trammell	.25
(81)	Lou Whitaker	.10
(82)	Kevin Appier	.10
(83)	Billy Brewer	.10
(84)	Vince Coleman	.10
(85)	Gary Gaetti	.10
(86)	Greg Gagne	.10

(87) Tom Goodwin .10
(88) Tom Gordon .10
(89) Mark Gubicza .10
(90) Bob Hamelin .10
(91) Phil Hiatt .10
(92) Wally Joyner .10
(93) Brent Mayne .10
(94) Jeff Montgomery .10
(95) Ricky Bones .10
(96) Mike Fetters .10
(97) Darryl Hamilton .10
(98) Pat Listach .10
(99) Matt Mieske .10
(100) Dave Nilsson .10
(101) Joe Oliver .10
(102) Kevin Seitzer .10
(103) B.J. Surhoff .10
(104) Jose Valentin .10
(105) Greg Vaughn .15
(106) Bill Wegman .10
(107) Alex Cole .10
(108) Marty Cordova .10
(109) Chuck Knoblauch .65
(110) Scott Leius .10
(111) Pat Meares .10
(112) Pedro Munoz .10
(113) Kirby Puckett 17.50
(114) Scott Stahoviak .10
(115) Mike Trombley .10
(116) Matt Walbeck .10
(117) Wade Boggs 9.00
(118) David Cone .15
(119) Tony Fernandez .10
(120) Don Mattingly 15.00
(121) Jack McDowell .10
(122) Paul O'Neill .15
(123) Melido Perez .10
(124) Luis Polonia .10
(125) Ruben Sierra .10
(126) Mike Stanley .10
(127) Randy Velarde .10
(128) John Wetteland .10
(129) Bob Wickman .10
(130) Bernie Williams .35
(131) Gerald Williams .10
(132) Geronimo Berroa .10
(133) Mike Bordick .10
(134) Scott Brosius .10
(135) Dennis Eckersley .10
(136) Brent Gates .10
(137) Rickey Henderson 5.00
(138) Stan Javier .10
(139) Mark McGwire 25.00
(140) Steve Ontiveros .10
(141) Terry Steinbach .10
(142) Todd Stottlemyre .10
(143) Danny Tartabull .10
(144) Bobby Ayala .10
(145) Andy Benes .10
(146) Mike Blowers .10
(147) Jay Buhner .10
(148) Joey Cora .10
(149) Alex Diaz .10
(150) Ken Griffey Jr. 25.00
(151) Randy Johnson 6.00
(152) Edgar Martinez .10
(153) Tino Martinez .15
(154) Bill Risley .10
(155) Alex Rodriguez 20.00
(156) Dan Wilson .10
(157) Will Clark 1.00
(158) Jeff Frye .10
(159) Benji Gil .10
(160) Juan Gonzalez 3.00
(161) Rusty Greer .10
(162) Mark McLemore .10
(163) Otis Nixon .10
(164) Dean Palmer .10
(165) Ivan Rodriguez 5.00
(166) Kenny Rogers .10
(167) Jeff Russell .10
(168) Mickey Tettleton .10
(169) Bob Tewksbury .10
(170) Bobby Witt .10
(171) Roberto Alomar 9.00
(172) Joe Carter .10
(173) Alex Gonzalez .10
(174) Candy Maldonado .10
(175) Paul Molitor 3.00
(176) John Olerud .20
(177) Lance Parrish .10
(178) Ed Sprague .10
(179) Devon White .10
(180) Woody Williams .10
(181) Steve Avery .10
(182) Jeff Blauser .10
(183) Tom Glavine 1.50
(184) Marquis Grissom .10
(185) Chipper Jones 15.00
(186) Dave Justice 1.00
(187) Ryan Klesko .10
(188) Mark Lemke .10
(189) Javier Lopez .10
(190) Greg Maddux 15.00
(191) Fred McGriff .10
(192) Greg McMichael .10
(193) John Smoltz 2.00
(194) Mark Wohlers .10
(195) Jim Bullinger .10
(196) Shawon Dunston .10
(197) Kevin Foster .10
(198) Luis Gonzalez .10
(199) Mark Grace 3.00
(200) Brian McRae .10
(201) Randy Myers .10
(202) Jaime Navarro .10
(203) Rey Sanchez .10
(204) Scott Servais .10
(205) Sammy Sosa 9.00
(206) Steve Trachsel .10
(207) Todd Zeile .10
(208) Bret Boone .50
(209) Jeff Branson .10
(210) Jeff Brantley .10
(211) Hector Carrasco .10
(212) Ron Gant .20
(213) Lenny Harris .10
(214) Barry Larkin 1.00
(215) Darren Lewis .10
(216) Hal Morris .10
(217) Mark Portugal .10
(218) Jose Rijo .10
(219) Reggie Sanders .15
(220) Pete Schourek .10
(221) John Smiley .10
(222) Eddie Taubensee .10
(223) Dave Wells .15
(224) Jason Bates .10
(225) Dante Bichette .75
(226) Vinny Castilla .20
(227) Andres Galarraga .15
(228) Joe Girardi .10
(229) Mike Kingery .10
(230) Steve Reed .10
(231) Bruce Ruffin .10
(232) Bret Saberhagen .15
(233) Bill Swift .10
(234) Larry Walker 2.50
(235) Walt Weiss .10
(236) Eric Young .10
(237) Kurt Abbott .10
(238) John Burkett .10
(239) Chuck Carr .10
(240) Greg Colbrunn .10
(241) Jeff Conine .10
(242) Andre Dawson .25
(243) Chris Hammond .10
(244) Charles Johnson .10
(245) Robb Nen .10
(246) Terry Pendleton .10
(247) Gary Sheffield 1.00
(248) Quilvio Veras .10
(249) Jeff Bagwell 6.00
(250) Derek Bell .10
(251) Craig Biggio .25
(252) Doug Drabek .10
(253) Tony Eusebio .10
(254) John Hudek .10
(255) Brian Hunter .10
(256) Todd Jones .10
(257) Dave Magadan .10
(258) Orlando Miller .10
(259) James Mouton .10
(260) Shane Reynolds .10
(261) Greg Swindell .10
(262) Billy Ashley .10
(263) Tom Candiotti .10
(264) Delino DeShields .10
(265) Eric Karros .15
(266) Roberto Kelly .10
(267) Ramon Martinez .10
(268) Raul Mondesi .50
(269) Hideo Nomo 9.00
(270) Jose Offerman .10
(271) Mike Piazza 20.00
(272) Kevin Tapani .10
(273) Ismael Valdes .10
(274) Tim Wallach .10
(275) Todd Worrell .10
(276) Moises Alou 1.00
(277) Sean Berry .10
(278) Wil Cordero .10
(279) Jeff Fassero .10
(280) Darrin Fletcher .10
(281) Mike Lansing .10
(282) Pedro J. Martinez 5.00
(283) Carlos Perez .10
(284) Mel Rojas .10
(285) Tim Scott .10
(286) David Segui .10
(287) Tony Tarasco .10
(288) Rondell White .20
(289) Rico Brogna .10
(290) Brett Butler .10
(291) John Franco .10
(292) Pete Harnisch .10
(293) Todd Hundley .15
(294) Bobby Jones .10
(295) Jeff Kent .10
(296) Joe Orsulak .10
(297) Ryan Thompson .10
(298) Jose Vizcaino .10
(299) Ricky Bottalico .10
(300) Darren Daulton .10
(301) Mariano Duncan .10
(302) Lenny Dykstra .10
(303) Jim Eisenreich .10
(304) Tyler Green .10
(305) Charlie Hayes .10
(306) Dave Hollins .10
(307) Gregg Jefferies .10
(308) Mickey Morandini .10
(309) Curt Schilling .20
(310) Heathcliff Slocumb .10
(311) Kevin Stocker .10
(312) Jay Bell .10
(313) Jacob Brumfield .10
(314) Dave Clark .10
(315) Carlos Garcia .10
(316) Mark Johnson .10
(317) Jeff King .10
(318) Nelson Liriano .10
(319) Al Martin .10
(320) Orlando Merced .10
(321) Dan Miceli .10
(322) Denny Neagle .10
(323) Mark Parent .10
(324) Dan Plesac .10
(325) Scott Cooper .10
(326) Bernard Gilkey .10
(327) Tom Henke .10
(328) Ken Hill .10
(329) Danny Jackson .10
(330) Brian Jordan .15
(331) Ray Lankford .10
(332) John Mabry .10
(333) Jose Oquendo .10
(334) Tom Pagnozzi .10
(335) Ozzie Smith 3.00
(336) Andy Ashby .10
(337) Brad Ausmus .10
(338) Ken Caminiti .20
(339) Andujar Cedeno .10
(340) Steve Finley .10
(341) Tony Gwynn 15.00
(342) Joey Hamilton .10
(343) Trevor Hoffman .10
(344) Jody Reed .10
(345) Bip Roberts .10
(346) Eddie Williams .10
(347) Rod Beck .10
(348) Mike Benjamin .10
(349) Barry Bonds 15.00
(350) Royce Clayton .10
(351) Glenallen Hill .10
(352) Kirt Manwaring .10
(353) Terry Mulholland .10
(354) John Patterson .10
(355) J.R. Phillips .10
(356) Deion Sanders 2.00
(357) Steve Scarsone .10
(358) Robby Thompson .10
(359) William VanLandingham .10
(360) Matt Williams 1.50

1996 Donruss Samples

To introduce its 1996 series to dealers and the hobby press, Donruss issued an eight-card sample set. Identical in format to the issued version, the samples are numbered differently from the same players' cards in the regular issue (except #1, Frank Thomas). The samples also differ in that they lack 1995 stats on back, may have slightly different wording in the career highlights, and have printed on front and back a diagonal gray "PROMOTIONAL SAMPLE".

		MT
Complete Set (8):		15.00
Common Player:		2.00
1	Frank Thomas	2.00
2	Barry Bonds	2.00
3	Hideo Nomo	2.00
4	Ken Griffey Jr.	3.00
5	Cal Ripken Jr.	3.00
6	Manny Ramirez	2.00
7	Mike Piazza	2.50
8	Greg Maddux	2.00

1996 Donruss

A clean, borderless look marks the 1996 Donruss regular-issue cards. Besides the player name in white inside a fading team-color stripe at top-right, the only graphic enhancement on front is a 7/8" square foil box at bottom-center with the company and team name, team logo, player position and uniform number. The foil box is enhanced with team colors, which are carried over to the horizontal backs. Backs also feature a color action photo, a large gray team logo, stats and career highlights. Basic packaging was 12-card foil packs with a suggested retail price of $1.79. Several types of insert cards were offered, each at a virtually unprecedented rate of scarcity. The set was issued in two series; Series 1 with 330 cards, Series 2 with 220 cards.

	MT
Complete Set (550):	40.00
Complete Series 1 (330):	22.50
Complete Series 2 (220):	17.50
Common Player:	.05
Press Proofs:	10X
Series 1 Pack (12):	1.50
Series 1 Wax Box (36):	30.00
Series 2 Pack (12):	2.00
Series 2 Wax Box (18):	25.00

1 Frank Thomas 1.50
2 Jason Bates .05
3 Steve Sparks .05
4 Scott Servais .05
5 Angelo Encarnacion .05
6 Scott Sanders .05
7 Billy Ashley .05
8 Alex Rodriguez 3.00
9 Sean Bergman .05
10 Brad Radke .10
11 Andy Van Slyke .05
12 Joe Girardi .05
13 Mark Grudzielanek .10
14 Rick Aguilera .05
15 Randy Veres .05
16 Tim Bogar .05
17 Dave Veres .05
18 Kevin Stocker .05
19 Marquis Grissom .10
20 Will Clark .15
21 Jay Bell .05
22 Allen Battle .05
23 Frank Rodriguez .05
24 Terry Steinbach .05
25 Gerald Williams .05
26 Sid Roberson .05
27 Greg Zaun .05
28 Ozzie Timmons .05
29 Vaughn Eshelman .05
30 Ed Sprague .05
31 Gary DiSarcina .05
32 Joe Boever .05
33 Steve Avery .05
34 Brad Ausmus .05
35 Kirt Manwaring .05
36 Gary Sheffield .20
37 Jason Bere .05
38 Jeff Manto .05
39 David Cone .10
40 Manny Ramirez 1.00
41 Sandy Alomar .10
42 Curtis Goodwin (Rated Rookie) .05
43 Tino Martinez .10
44 Woody Williams .05
45 Dean Palmer .05
46 Hipolito Pichardo .05
47 Jason Giambi .25
48 Lance Johnson .05
49 Bernard Gilkey .05
50 Kirby Puckett 1.50
51 Tony Fernandez .05
52 Alex Gonzalez .05
53 Bret Saberhagen .10
54 Lyle Mouton (Rated Rookie) .05
55 Brian McRae .05
56 Mark Gubicza .05
57 Sergio Valdez .05
58 Darrin Fletcher .05
59 Steve Parris .05
60 Johnny Damon (Rated Rookie) .20
61 Rickey Henderson .20
62 Darrell Whitmore .05
63 Roberto Petagine .05
64 Trenidad Hubbard .05
65 Heathcliff Slocumb .05
66 Steve Finley .05
67 Mariano Rivera .35
68 Brian Hunter .05
69 Jamie Moyer .05
70 Ellis Burks .05
71 Pat Kelly .05
72 Mickey Tettleton .05
73 Garret Anderson .10
74 Andy Pettitte (Rated Rookie) 1.00
75 Glenallen Hill .05
76 Brent Gates .05
77 Lou Whitaker .05
78 David Segui .05
79 Dan Wilson .05
80 Pat Listach .05
81 Jeff Bagwell 1.00
82 Ben McDonald .05
83 John Valentin .10
84 John Jaha .05
85 Pete Schourek .05
86 Bryce Florie .05
87 Brian Jordan .10
88 Ron Karkovice .05
89 Al Leiter .10
90 Tony Longmire .05
91 Nelson Liriano .05
92 David Bell .05
93 Kevin Gross .05
94 Tom Candiotti .05
95 Dave Martinez .05
96 Greg Myers .05
97 Rheal Cormier .05
98 Chris Hammond .05
99 Randy Myers .05
100 Bill Pulsipher (Rated Rookie) .15
101 Jason Isringhausen (Rated Rookie) .20
102 Dave Stevens .05
103 Roberto Alomar .60
104 Bob Higginson (Rated Rookie) .25
105 Eddie Murray .35
106 Matt Walbeck .05
107 Mark Wohlers .05
108 Jeff Nelson .05
109 Tom Goodwin .05
110 Checklist 1-83 (Cal Ripken Jr.) (2,131 Consecutive Games) 1.50
111 Rey Sanchez .05
112 Hector Carrasco .05
113 B.J. Surhoff .05
114 Dan Miceli .05
115 Dean Hartgraves .05
116 John Burkett .05
117 Gary Gaetti .05
118 Ricky Bones .05
119 Mike Macfarlane .05
120 Bip Roberts .05
121 Dave Mlicki .05
122 Chili Davis .05
123 Mark Whiten .05
124 Herbert Perry .05
125 Butch Henry .05
126 Derek Bell .05
127 Al Martin .05
128 John Franco .05
129 William VanLandingham .05
130 Mike Bordick .05
131 Mike Mordecai .05
132 Robby Thompson .05
133 Greg Colbrunn .05
134 Domingo Cedeno .05
135 Chad Curtis .05
136 Jose Hernandez .05
137 Scott Klingenbeck .05
138 Ryan Klesko .05
139 John Smiley .05
140 Charlie Hayes .05
141 Jay Buhner .10
142 Doug Drabek .05
143 Roger Pavlik .05
144 Todd Worrell .05
145 Cal Ripken Jr. 2.50
146 Steve Reed .05
147 Chuck Finley .05
148 Mike Blowers .05
149 Orel Hershiser .05
150 Allen Watson .05
151 Ramon Martinez .05
152 Melvin Nieves .05
153 Tripp Cromer .05
154 Yorkis Perez .05
155 Stan Javier .05
156 Mel Rojas .05
157 Aaron Sele .05
158 Eric Karros .10
159 Robb Nen .05
160 Raul Mondesi .15
161 John Wetteland .05
162 Tim Scott .05
163 Kenny Rogers .05
164 Melvin Bunch .05
165 Rod Beck .05
166 Andy Benes .05
167 Lenny Dykstra .05
168 Orlando Merced .05
169 Tomas Perez .05
170 Xavier Hernandez .05
171 Ruben Sierra .05
172 Alan Trammell .10
173 Mike Fetters .05
174 Wilson Alvarez .05
175 Erik Hanson .05
176 Travis Fryman .10
177 Jim Abbott .05
178 Bret Boone .10
179 Sterling Hitchcock .05
180 Pat Mahomes .05
181 Mark Acre .05
182 Charles Nagy .10
183 Rusty Greer .05
184 Mike Stanley .05
185 Jim Bullinger .05
186 Shane Andrews .05
187 Brian Keyser .05
188 Tyler Green .05
189 Mark Grace .20
190 Bob Hamelin .05
191 Luis Ortiz .05
192 Joe Carter .05
193 Eddie Taubensee .05
194 Brian Anderson .05
195 Edgardo Alfonzo .10
196 Pedro Munoz .05
197 David Justice .15
198 Trevor Hoffman .05
199 Bobby Ayala .05
200 Tony Eusebio .05
201 Jeff Russell .05
202 Mike Hampton .05
203 Walt Weiss .05
204 Joey Hamilton .05
205 Roberto Hernandez .05
206 Greg Vaughn .10
207 Felipe Lira .05
208 Harold Baines .05
209 Tim Wallach .05
210 Manny Alexander .05
211 Tim Laker .05
212 Chris Haney .05
213 Brian Maxcy .05
214 Eric Young .10
215 Darryl Strawberry .10
216 Barry Bonds 1.50
217 Tim Naehring .05
218 Scott Brosius .05
219 Reggie Sanders .05
220 Checklist 84-166 (Eddie Murray) (3,000 Career Hits) .20
221 Luis Alicea .05
222 Albert Belle .25
223 Benji Gil .05
224 Dante Bichette .10
225 Bobby Bonilla .05
226 Todd Stottlemyre .05
227 Jim Edmonds .10
228 Todd Jones .05
229 Shawn Green .15
230 Javy Lopez .05
231 Ariel Prieto .05
232 Tony Phillips .05
233 James Mouton .05
234 Jose Oquendo .05
235 Royce Clayton .05
236 Chuck Carr .05
237 Doug Jones .05
238 Mark Mclemore (McLemore) .05
239 Bill Swift .05
240 Scott Leius .05
241 Russ Davis .05
242 Ray Durham (Rated Rookie) .10
243 Matt Mieske .05
244 Brent Mayne .05
245 Thomas Howard .05
246 Troy O'Leary .05
247 Jacob Brumfield .05
248 Mickey Morandini .05
249 Todd Hundley .10
250 Chris Bosio .05
251 Omar Vizquel .10
252 Mike Lansing .05
253 John Mabry .05
254 Mike Perez .05
255 Delino DeShields .05
256 Wil Cordero .05
257 Mike James .05
258 Todd Van Poppel .05
259 Joey Cora .05
260 Andre Dawson .20
261 Jerry DiPoto .05
262 Rick Krivda .05
263 Glenn Dishman .05
264 Mike Mimbs .05
265 John Ericks .05
266 Jose Canseco .25
267 Jeff Branson .05
268 Curt Leskanic .05
269 Jon Nunnally .05
270 Scott Stahoviak .05
271 Jeff Montgomery .05
272 Hal Morris .05
273 Esteban Loaiza .05
274 Rico Brogna .05
275 Dave Winfield .25
276 J.R. Phillips .05
277 Todd Zeile .05
278 Tom Pagnozzi .05
279 Mark Lemke .05
280 Dave Magadan .05
281 Greg McMichael .05
282 Mike Morgan .05
283 Moises Alou .15
284 Dennis Martinez .05
285 Jeff Kent .05
286 Mark Johnson .05
287 Darren Lewis .05
288 Brad Clontz .05
289 Chad Fonville (Rated Rookie) .15
290 Paul Sorrento .05
291 Lee Smith .10
292 Tom Glavine .15
293 Antonio Osuna .05
294 Kevin Foster .05
295 *Sandy Martinez* .05
296 Mark Leiter .05
297 Julian Tavarez .05
298 Mike Kelly .05
299 Joe Oliver .05
300 John Flaherty .05
301 Don Mattingly 1.00
302 Pat Meares .05
303 John Doherty .05
304 Joe Vitiello .05
305 Vinny Castilla .10
306 Jeff Brantley .05
307 Mike Greenwell .05
308 Midre Cummings .05
309 Curt Schilling .10
310 Ken Caminiti .10
311 Scott Erickson .05
312 Carl Everett .10
313 Charles Johnson .10
314 Alex Diaz .05
315 Jose Mesa .05
316 Mark Carreon .05
317 Carlos Perez (Rated Rookie) .15
318 Ismael Valdes .05
319 Frank Castillo .05
320 Tom Henke .05
321 Spike Owen .05
322 Joe Orsulak .05
323 Paul Menhart .05
324 Pedro Borbon .05
325 Checklist 167-249 (Paul Molitor) (1,000 Career RBI) .25
326 Jeff Cirillo .05
327 Edwin Hurtado .05
328 Orlando Miller .05
329 Steve Ontiveros .05
330 Checklist 250-330 (Kirby Puckett) (1,000 Career RBI) .50
331 Scott Bullett .05
332 Andres Galarraga .05
333 Cal Eldred .05
334 Sammy Sosa 1.50
335 Don Slaught .05
336 Jody Reed .05
337 Roger Cedeno .05
338 Ken Griffey Jr. 2.50
339 Todd Hollandsworth .05
340 Mike Trombley .05
341 Gregg Jefferies .05
342 Larry Walker .15
343 Pedro Martinez .05
344 Dwayne Hosey .05
345 Terry Pendleton .05
346 Pete Harnisch .05

No.	Player	MT
347	Tony Castillo	.05
348	Paul Quantrill	.05
349	Fred McGriff	.05
350	Ivan Rodriguez	.50
351	Butch Huskey	.05
352	Ozzie Smith	.50
353	Marty Cordova	.10
354	John Wasdin	.05
355	Wade Boggs	.25
356	Dave Nilsson	.05
357	Rafael Palmeiro	.15
358	Luis Gonzalez	.20
359	Reggie Jefferson	.05
360	Carlos Delgado	.20
361	Orlando Palmeiro	.05
362	Chris Gomez	.05
363	John Smoltz	.10
364	Marc Newfield	.05
365	Matt Williams	.20
366	Jesus Tavarez	.05
367	Bruce Ruffin	.05
368	Sean Berry	.05
369	Randy Velarde	.05
370	Tony Pena	.05
371	Jim Thome	.10
372	Jeffrey Hammonds	.05
373	Bob Wolcott	.05
374	Juan Guzman	.05
375	Juan Gonzalez	1.00
376	Michael Tucker	.05
377	Doug Johns	.05
378	*Mike Cameron*	1.00
379	Ray Lankford	.05
380	Jose Parra	.05
381	Jimmy Key	.05
382	John Olerud	.15
383	Kevin Ritz	.05
384	Tim Raines	.10
385	Rich Amaral	.05
386	Keith Lockhart	.05
387	Steve Scarsone	.05
388	Cliff Floyd	.10
389	Rich Aude	.05
390	Hideo Nomo	.60
391	Geronimo Berroa	.05
392	Pat Rapp	.05
393	Dustin Hermanson	.05
394	Greg Maddux	2.00
395	Darren Daulton	.05
396	Kenny Lofton	.60
397	Ruben Rivera	.10
398	Billy Wagner	.10
399	Kevin Brown	.15
400	Mike Kingery	.05
401	Bernie Williams	.20
402	Otis Nixon	.05
403	Damion Easley	.05
404	Paul O'Neill	.10
405	Deion Sanders	.10
406	Dennis Eckersley	.10
407	Tony Clark	.10
408	Rondell White	.15
409	Luis Sojo	.05
410	David Hulse	.05
411	Shane Reynolds	.05
412	Chris Hoiles	.05
413	Lee Tinsley	.05
414	Scott Karl	.05
415	Ron Gant	.10
416	Brian Johnson	.05
417	Jose Oliva	.05
418	Jack McDowell	.05
419	Paul Molitor	.35
420	Ricky Bottalico	.05
421	Paul Wagner	.05
422	Terry Bradshaw	.05
423	Bob Tewksbury	.05
424	Mike Piazza	2.00
425	*Luis Andujar*	.05
426	Mark Langston	.05
427	Stan Belinda	.05
428	Kurt Abbott	.05
429	Shawon Dunston	.05
430	Bobby Jones	.05
431	Jose Vizcaino	.05
432	*Matt Lawton*	.05
433	Pat Hentgen	.05
434	Cecil Fielder	.05
435	Carlos Baerga	.05
436	Rich Becker	.05
437	Chipper Jones	2.00
438	Bill Risley	.05
439	Kevin Appier	.05
440	Checklist	.05
441	Jaime Navarro	.05
442	Barry Larkin	.15
443	*Jose Valentin*	.10
444	Bryan Rekar	.05
445	Rick Wilkins	.05
446	Quilvio Veras	.05
447	Greg Gagne	.05
448	Mark Kiefer	.05
449	Bobby Witt	.05
450	Andy Ashby	.05
451	Alex Ochoa	.05
452	Jorge Fabregas	.05
453	Gene Schall	.05
454	Ken Hill	.05
455	Tony Tarasco	.05
456	Donnie Wall	.05
457	Carlos Garcia	.05
458	Ryan Thompson	.05
459	*Marvin Benard*	.10
460	Jose Herrera	.05
461	Jeff Blauser	.05
462	Chris Hook	.05
463	Jeff Conine	.10
464	Devon White	.05
465	Danny Bautista	.05
466	Steve Trachsel	.05
467	C.J. Nitkowski	.05
468	Mike Devereaux	.05
469	David Wells	.10
470	Jim Eisenreich	.05
471	Edgar Martinez	.05
472	Craig Biggio	.10
473	Jeff Frye	.05
474	Karim Garcia	.10
475	Jimmy Haynes	.05
476	Darren Holmes	.05
477	Tim Salmon	.15
478	Randy Johnson	.35
479	Eric Plunk	.05
480	Scott Cooper	.05
481	Chan Ho Park	.10
482	Ray McDavid	.05
483	Mark Petkovsek	.05
484	Greg Swindell	.05
485	George Williams	.05
486	Yamil Benitez	.05
487	Tim Wakefield	.05
488	Kevin Tapani	.05
489	Derrick May	.05
490	Checklist (Ken Griffey Jr.)	1.00
491	Derek Jeter	2.00
492	Jeff Fassero	.05
493	Benito Santiago	.05
494	Tom Gordon	.05
495	Jamie Brewington	.05
496	Vince Coleman	.05
497	Kevin Jordan	.05
498	Jeff King	.05
499	Mike Simms	.05
500	Jose Rijo	.05
501	Denny Neagle	.05
502	Jose Lima	.05
503	Kevin Seitzer	.05
504	Alex Fernandez	.05
505	Mo Vaughn	.35
506	Phil Nevin	.10
507	J.T. Snow	.10
508	Andujar Cedeno	.05
509	Ozzie Guillen	.05
510	Mark Clark	.05
511	Mark McGwire	2.50
512	Jeff Reboulet	.05
513	Armando Benitez	.05
514	LaTroy Hawkins	.05
515	Brett Butler	.05
516	Tavo Alvarez	.05
517	Chris Snopek	.05
518	Mike Mussina	.30
519	Darryl Kile	.10
520	Wally Joyner	.05
521	Willie McGee	.10
522	Kent Mercker	.05
523	Mike Jackson	.05
524	Troy Percival	.05
525	Tony Gwynn	1.50
526	Ron Coomer	.05
527	Darryl Hamilton	.05
528	Phil Plantier	.05
529	Norm Charlton	.05
530	Craig Paquette	.05
531	Dave Burba	.05
532	Mike Henneman	.05
533	Terrell Wade	.05
534	Eddie Williams	.05
535	Robin Ventura	.10
536	Chuck Knoblauch	.10
537	Les Norman	.05
538	Brady Anderson	.10
539	Roger Clemens	1.50
540	Mark Portugal	.05
541	Mike Matheny	.05
542	Jeff Parrett	.05
543	Roberto Kelly	.05
544	Damon Buford	.05
545	Chad Ogea	.05
546	Jose Offerman	.05
547	Brian Barber	.05
548	Danny Tartabull	.05
549	Duane Singleton	.05
550	Checklist (Tony Gwynn)	.50

1996 Donruss Press Proofs

The first 2,000 of each regular card issued in the 1996 Donruss set are distinguished by the addition of a gold-foil "PRESS PROOF" stamped along the right side. As opposed to regular-issue cards which have silver-and-black card numbers and personal data strip at bottom, the Press Proof cards have those elements printed in black-on-gold. Stated odds of finding a Press Proof are one per 12 packs in Series 1, one per 10 packs in Series 2, on average.

	MT
Complete Set (550):	600.00
Complete Series 1 (330):	325.00
Complete Series 2 (220):	300.00
Common Player:	1.00

(Star cards valued 10X corresponding regular-issue cards.)

1996 Donruss Diamond Kings

The most "common" of the '96 Donruss inserts are the popular Diamond Kings, featuring the portraits of Dick Perez on a black background within a mottled gold-foil frame. Once again, the DKs feature one player from each team, with 14 issued in each of Series 1 and 2. Like all '96 Donruss inserts, the DKs are numbered on back, within an edition of 10,000. Also on back are color action photos and career highlights. Diamond Kings are inserted at the rate of one per 60 foil packs (Series 1), and one per 30 packs (Series 2), on average.

		MT
Complete Set (31):		190.00
Complete Series 1 (1-14):		110.00
Complete Series 2 (15-31):		80.00
Common Player Series 1:		3.00
Common Player Series 2:		3.00
1	Frank Thomas	12.50
2	Mo Vaughn	5.00
3	Manny Ramirez	8.00
4	Mark McGwire	20.00
5	Juan Gonzalez	8.00
6	Roberto Alomar	6.00
7	Tim Salmon	3.00
8	Barry Bonds	12.50
9	Tony Gwynn	15.00
10	Reggie Sanders	3.00
11	Larry Walker	3.00
12	Pedro Martinez	8.00
13	Jeff King	3.00
14	Mark Grace	5.00
15	Greg Maddux	15.00
16	Don Mattingly	12.50
17	Gregg Jefferies	3.00
18	Chad Curtis	3.00
19	Jason Isringhausen	3.00
20	B.J. Surhoff	3.00
21	Jeff Conine	3.00
22	Kirby Puckett	12.50
23	Derek Bell	3.00
24	Wally Joyner	3.00
25	Brian Jordan	3.00
26	Edgar Martinez	3.00
27	Hideo Nomo	5.00
28	Mike Mussina	5.00
29	Eddie Murray	5.00
30	Cal Ripken Jr.	20.00
31	Checklist	.50

1996 Donruss Elite

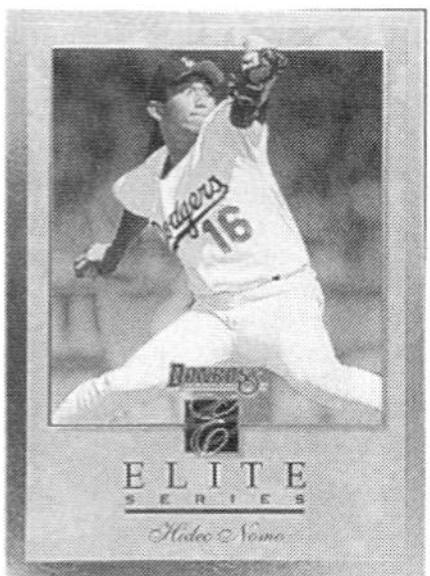

The Elite series continued as a Donruss insert in 1996, and they are the elite of the chase cards, being found on average only once per 140 packs (Series 1) or once per 75 packs (Series 2). The '96 Elite cards have a classic look bespeaking value. Player action photos at top center are framed in mottled silver foil and bordered in bright silver. Backs have another action photo, a few words about the player and a serial number from within an edition of 10,000 cards each. As usual, card numbering continues from the previous year.

		MT
Complete Set (12):		90.00
Complete Series 1 (61-66):		40.00
Complete Series 2 (67-72):		55.00
Common Player Series 1:		4.00
Common Player Series 2:		3.00
61	Cal Ripken Jr.	15.00
62	Hideo Nomo	7.50
63	Reggie Sanders	4.00
64	Mo Vaughn	4.00
65	Tim Salmon	4.00
66	Chipper Jones	12.00
67	Manny Ramirez	6.00
68	Greg Maddux	10.00
69	Frank Thomas	10.00
70	Ken Griffey Jr.	15.00
71	Dante Bichette	3.00
72	Tony Gwynn	10.00

1996 Donruss Freeze Frame

One of two insert sets exclusive to Series 2 Donruss is the Freeze Frame issue. Printed on heavy, round-cornered cardboard stock, the inserts feature multiple photos of the player on both front and back. Fronts combine matte and glossy finish plus a gold-foil Donruss logo. Backs are conventionally printed, include 1995 season highlights and a serial number from within the edition of 5,000. Stated odds of pulling a Freeze Frame insert are one per 60 packs.

		MT
Complete Set (8):		35.00
Common Player:		2.00
1	Frank Thomas	5.00
2	Ken Griffey Jr.	7.50
3	Cal Ripken Jr.	7.50
4	Hideo Nomo	3.00
5	Greg Maddux	5.00
6	Albert Belle	2.00
7	Chipper Jones	6.00
8	Mike Piazza	6.00

1996 Donruss Hit List

Printed on metallic foil with gold-foil graphic highlights, players who hit for high average with power or who collected milestone hits are featured in this insert set. Eight inserts were included in each of Series 1 and 2. Backs have a color action photo, a description of the player's batting prowess and a serial number from an edition of 10,000 cards each. Hit List inserts are found at an average rate of once per 106 foil packs in Series 1 and once per 60 packs in Series 2.

		MT
Complete Set (16):		60.00
Common Player:		1.00
1	Tony Gwynn	7.50
2	Ken Griffey Jr.	12.00
3	Will Clark	1.50
4	Mike Piazza	10.00
5	Carlos Baerga	1.00
6	Mo Vaughn	2.50
7	Mark Grace	1.50
8	Kirby Puckett	5.00
9	Frank Thomas	6.00
10	Barry Bonds	6.00
11	Jeff Bagwell	4.00
12	Edgar Martinez	1.00
13	Tim Salmon	2.00
14	Wade Boggs	2.50
15	Don Mattingly	5.00
16	Eddie Murray	2.50

1996 Donruss Long Ball Leaders

Once again the previous season's longest home runs are recalled in this retail-only insert set, found at an average rate of once per 96 packs in Series 1 only. Fronts are bordered and trimmed in bright silver foil and feature the player in his home run stroke against a black background. The date, location and distance of his tape-measure shot are in an arc across the card front. Backs feature another batting action photo, further details of the home run and a serial number within an edition of 5,000.

		MT
Complete Set (8):		75.00
Common Player:		3.00
1	Barry Bonds	12.00
2	Ryan Klesko	3.00
3	Mark McGwire	30.00
4	Raul Mondesi	3.00
5	Cecil Fielder	3.00
6	Ken Griffey Jr.	30.00
7	Larry Walker	5.00
8	Frank Thomas	12.00

1996 Donruss Power Alley

Among the most visually dazzling of 1996's inserts is this hobby-only chase set featuring baseball's top sluggers. Action batting photos are found within several layers of prismatic foil in geometric patterns on front. Backs are horizontally formatted, feature portrait photos at left and power stats at right and bottom. In the lower-left corner is an individual serial number from within an edition of 5,000 cards each. The first 500 of each player's cards are specially die-cut at left- and right-center. Found only in Series 1 hobby foil packs, Power Alley inserts are a one per 92 pack pick.

		MT
Complete Set (10):		35.00
Common Player		2.00
Die-cuts		2-3X
1	Frank Thomas	5.00
2	Barry Bonds	6.00
3	Reggie Sanders	2.00
4	Albert Belle	3.00
5	Tim Salmon	2.00
6	Dante Bichette	2.00
7	Mo Vaughn	3.50
8	Jim Edmonds	3.00
9	Manny Ramirez	5.00
10	Ken Griffey Jr.	12.50

1996 Donruss Pure Power

These cards were random inserts found only in Series 2 retail packs. Fronts are printed on foil backgrounds and at bottom have a die-cut hole giving the impression a baseball has been batted through the card. On back the inserts are individually serial numbered within an edition of 5,000.

		MT
Complete Set (8):		20.00
Common Player:		1.50
1	Raul Mondesi	1.50
2	Barry Bonds	4.50
3	Albert Belle	2.00
4	Frank Thomas	3.00
5	Mike Piazza	7.50
6	Dante Bichette	1.50
7	Manny Ramirez	3.00
8	Mo Vaughn	2.50

1996 Donruss Round Trippers

An embossed white home plate design bearing the player's 1995 dinger output is featured on this Series 2 insert set. The entire background has been rendered in gold-flecked sepia tones. Typography on front is in bronze foil. Backs repeat the sepia background photo and include a month-by-month bar graph of the player's 1995 and career homers. Within the white home plate frame is the card's unique serial number from within an edition of 5,000. Odds of finding a Round Trippers card are stated at one per 55 packs, in hobby packs only.

		MT
Complete Set (10):		75.00
Common Player:		3.00
1	Albert Belle	4.00
2	Barry Bonds	6.00

3	Jeff Bagwell	5.00
4	Tim Salmon	3.00
5	Mo Vaughn	4.00
6	Ken Griffey Jr.	15.00
7	Mike Piazza	12.50
8	Cal Ripken Jr.	15.00
9	Frank Thomas	7.50
9p	Frank Thomas (Promo)	3.00
10	Dante Bichette	3.00

1996 Donruss Showdown

Baseball's top hitters and pitchers are matched on a silver and black foil background in this insert set. Gold-foil graphic highlights complete the horizontal front design. Backs are printed on a black and gold background with color action photos and write-ups about each player. At top is a serial number from within an edition of 10,000 cards each. Showdown inserts are found at an average rate of one per Series 1 foil packs.

		MT
Complete Set (8):		30.00
Common Player:		1.00
1	Frank Thomas, Hideo Nomo	4.00
2	Barry Bonds, Randy Johnson	4.00
3	Greg Maddux, Ken Griffey Jr.	7.50
4	Roger Clemens, Tony Gwynn	6.00
5	Mike Piazza, Mike Mussina	5.00
6	Cal Ripken Jr., Pedro Martinez	7.50
7	Tim Wakefield, Matt Williams	1.00
8	Manny Ramirez, Carlos Perez	2.00

1997 Donruss

Donruss' 1997 Series 1 features 270 base cards with a full-bleed color action photo on the front. Horizontal backs have a photo, career statistics, a brief player profile and biographical tidbits. A Press Proofs parallel was made of the base cards in an edition of 2,000 each. Other Series 1 inserts include the annual Diamond Kings, Elites, Armed and Dangerous cards, Longball Leaders and Rocket Launchers. A 180-card Update set was released later as a follow-up to the regular. '97 Donruss series. The Updates are numbered contiguously, #271-450, from the first series. Press Proofs and Gold Press Proof parallel inserts were available; other Update inserts include Dominators, Franchise Futures, Power Alley, Rookie Diamond Kings and a special Cal Ripken Jr. set.

		MT
Complete Set (450):		30.00
Series 1 Set (270):		15.00
Update Set (180):		15.00
Common Player:		.10
Pack (10):		2.00
Hobby Wax Box (18):		32.00
Retail Wax Box (36):		60.00
Update Pack (10):		2.00
Update Wax Box (24):		45.00
1	Juan Gonzalez	.75
2	Jim Edmonds	.15
3	Tony Gwynn	1.50
4	Andres Galarraga	.10
5	Joe Carter	.10
6	Raul Mondesi	.15
7	Greg Maddux	1.50
8	Travis Fryman	.10
9	Brian Jordan	.10
10	Henry Rodriguez	.10
11	Manny Ramirez	1.00
12	Mark McGwire	2.00
13	Marc Newfield	.10
14	Craig Biggio	.10
15	Sammy Sosa	1.50
16	Brady Anderson	.10
17	Wade Boggs	.25
18	Charles Johnson	.10
19	Matt Williams	.20
20	Denny Neagle	.10
21	Ken Griffey Jr.	2.00
22	Robin Ventura	.10
23	Barry Larkin	.15
24	Todd Zeile	.10
25	Chuck Knoblauch	.10
26	Todd Hundley	.10
27	Roger Clemens	.75
28	Michael Tucker	.10
29	Rondell White	.10
30	Osvaldo Fernandez	.10
31	Ivan Rodriguez	.50
32	Alex Fernandez	.10
33	Jason Isringhausen	.10
34	Chipper Jones	1.50
35	Paul O'Neill	.10
36	Hideo Nomo	.50
37	Roberto Alomar	.50
38	Derek Bell	.10
39	Paul Molitor	.40
40	Andy Benes	.10
41	Steve Trachsel	.10
42	J.T. Snow	.10
43	Jason Kendall	.10
44	Alex Rodriguez	2.50
45	Joey Hamilton	.10
46	Carlos Delgado	.30
47	Jason Giambi	.25
48	Larry Walker	.30
49	Derek Jeter	1.50
50	Kenny Lofton	.15
51	Devon White	.10
52	Matt Mieske	.10
53	Melvin Nieves	.10
54	Jose Canseco	.25
55	Tino Martinez	.15
56	Rafael Palmeiro	.15
57	Edgardo Alfonzo	.15
58	Jay Buhner	.15
59	Shane Reynolds	.10
60	Steve Finley	.10
61	Bobby Higginson	.10
62	Dean Palmer	.10
63	Terry Pendleton	.10
64	Marquis Grissom	.10
65	Mike Stanley	.10
66	Moises Alou	.15
67	Ray Lankford	.10
68	Marty Cordova	.10
69	John Olerud	.10
70	David Cone	.10
71	Benito Santiago	.10
72	Ryne Sandberg	.60
73	Rickey Henderson	.30
74	Roger Cedeno	.10
75	Wilson Alvarez	.10
76	Tim Salmon	.15
77	Orlando Merced	.10
78	Vinny Castilla	.10
79	Ismael Valdes	.10
80	Dante Bichette	.15
81	Kevin Brown	.15
82	Andy Pettitte	.50
83	Scott Stahoviak	.10
84	Mickey Tettleton	.10
85	Jack McDowell	.10
86	Tom Glavine	.15
87	Gregg Jefferies	.10
88	Chili Davis	.10
89	Randy Johnson	.35
90	John Mabry	.10
91	Billy Wagner	.10
92	Jeff Cirillo	.10
93	Trevor Hoffman	.10
94	Juan Guzman	.10
95	Geronimo Berroa	.10
96	Bernard Gilkey	.10
97	Danny Tartabull	.10
98	Johnny Damon	.20
99	Charlie Hayes	.10
100	Reggie Sanders	.10
101	Robby Thompson	.10
102	Bobby Bonilla	.10
103	Reggie Jefferson	.10
104	John Smoltz	.10
105	Jim Thome	.20
106	Ruben Rivera	.15
107	Darren Oliver	.10
108	Mo Vaughn	.30
109	Roger Pavlik	.10
110	Terry Steinbach	.10
111	Jermaine Dye	.10
112	Mark Grudzielanek	.10
113	Rick Aguilera	.10
114	Jamey Wright	.10
115	Eddie Murray	.35
116	Brian Hunter	.10
117	Hal Morris	.10
118	Tom Pagnozzi	.10
119	Mike Mussina	.35
120	Mark Grace	.25
121	Cal Ripken Jr.	2.00
122	Tom Goodwin	.10
123	Paul Sorrento	.10
124	Jay Bell	.10
125	Todd Hollandsworth	.10
126	Edgar Martinez	.10
127	George Arias	.10
128	Greg Vaughn	.10
129	Roberto Hernandez	.10
130	Delino DeShields	.10
131	Bill Pulsipher	.10
132	Joey Cora	.10
133	Mariano Rivera	.25
134	Mike Piazza	1.50
135	Carlos Baerga	.10
136	Jose Mesa	.10
137	Will Clark	.25
138	Frank Thomas	1.25
139	John Wetteland	.10
140	Shawn Estes	.10
141	Garret Anderson	.10
142	Andre Dawson	.15
143	Eddie Taubensee	.10
144	Ryan Klesko	.10
145	Rocky Coppinger	.10
146	Jeff Bagwell	1.00
147	Donovan Osborne	.10
148	Greg Myers	.10
149	Brant Brown	.10
150	Kevin Elster	.10
151	Bob Wells	.10
152	Wally Joyner	.10
153	Rico Brogna	.10
154	Dwight Gooden	.10
155	Jermaine Allensworth	.10
156	Ray Durham	.10
157	Cecil Fielder	.10
158	Ryan Hancock	.10
159	Gary Sheffield	.20
160	Albert Belle	.25
161	Tomas Perez	.10
162	David Doster	.10
163	John Valentin	.10
164	Danny Graves	.10
165	Jose Paniagua	.10
166	*Brian Giles*	1.00
167	Barry Bonds	1.25
168	Sterling Hitchcock	.10
169	Bernie Williams	.30
170	Fred McGriff	.10
171	George Williams	.10
172	Amaury Telemaco	.10
173	Ken Caminiti	.10
174	Ron Gant	.10
175	David Justice	.15
176	James Baldwin	.10
177	Pat Hentgen	.10
178	Ben McDonald	.10
179	Tim Naehring	.10
180	Jim Eisenreich	.10
181	Ken Hill	.10
182	Paul Wilson	.10
183	Marvin Benard	.10
184	Alan Benes	.10
185	Ellis Burks	.10
186	Scott Servais	.10
187	David Segui	.10
188	Scott Brosius	.10
189	Jose Offerman	.10
190	Eric Davis	.10
191	Brett Butler	.10
192	Curtis Pride	.10
193	Yamil Benitez	.10
194	Chan Ho Park	.15
195	Bret Boone	.15
196	Omar Vizquel	.10
197	Orlando Miller	.10
198	Ramon Martinez	.10
199	Harold Baines	.10
200	Eric Young	.10
201	Fernando Vina	.10
202	Alex Gonzalez	.10
203	Fernando Valenzuela	.10
204	Steve Avery	.10
205	Ernie Young	.10
206	Kevin Appier	.10
207	Randy Myers	.10
208	Jeff Suppan	.10
209	James Mouton	.10
210	Russ Davis	.10
211	Al Martin	.10
212	Troy Percival	.10
213	Al Leiter	.10
214	Dennis Eckersley	.10
215	Mark Johnson	.10
216	Eric Karros	.10
217	Royce Clayton	.10
218	Tony Phillips	.10
219	Tim Wakefield	.10
220	Alan Trammell	.10
221	Eduardo Perez	.10
222	Butch Huskey	.10
223	Tim Belcher	.10
224	Jamie Moyer	.10
225	F.P. Santangelo	.10
226	Rusty Greer	.10
227	Jeff Brantley	.10
228	Mark Langston	.10
229	Ray Montgomery	.10
230	Rich Becker	.10
231	Ozzie Smith	.75
232	Rey Ordonez	.15
233	Ricky Otero	.10
234	Mike Cameron	.10
235	Mike Sweeney	.10
236	Mark Lewis	.10
237	Luis Gonzalez	.10
238	Marcus Jensen	.10
239	Ed Sprague	.10
240	Jose Valentin	.10
241	Jeff Frye	.10

242	Charles Nagy	.10
243	Carlos Garcia	.10
244	Mike Hampton	.10
245	B.J. Surhoff	.10
246	Wilton Guerrero	.10
247	Frank Rodriguez	.10
248	Gary Gaetti	.10
249	Lance Johnson	.10
250	Darren Bragg	.10
251	Darryl Hamilton	.10
252	John Jaha	.10
253	Craig Paquette	.10
254	Jaime Navarro	.10
255	Shawon Dunston	.10
256	Ron Wright	.15
257	Tim Belk	.10
258	Jeff Darwin	.10
259	Ruben Sierra	.10
260	Chuck Finley	.10
261	Darryl Strawberry	.10
262	Shannon Stewart	.10
263	Pedro Martinez	.10
264	Neifi Perez	.10
265	Jeff Conine	.10
266	Orel Hershiser	.10
267	Checklist 1-90 (Eddie Murray) (500 Career HR)	.10
268	Checklist 91-180 (Paul Molitor) (3,000 Career Hits)	.10
269	Checklist 181-270 (Barry Bonds) (300 Career HR)	.60
270	Checklist - inserts (Mark McGwire) (300 Career HR)	.75
271	Matt Williams	.20
272	Todd Zeile	.10
273	Roger Clemens	.75
274	Michael Tucker	.10
275	J.T. Snow	.10
276	Kenny Lofton	.15
277	Jose Canseco	.25
278	Marquis Grissom	.10
279	Moises Alou	.15
280	Benito Santiago	.10
281	Willie McGee	.10
282	Chili Davis	.10
283	Ron Coomer	.10
284	Orlando Merced	.10
285	Delino DeShields	.10
286	John Wetteland	.10
287	Darren Daulton	.10
288	Lee Stevens	.10
289	Albert Belle	.25
290	Sterling Hitchcock	.10
291	David Justice	.15
292	Eric Davis	.10
293	Brian Hunter	.10
294	Darryl Hamilton	.10
295	Steve Avery	.10
296	Joe Vitiello	.10
297	Jaime Navarro	.10
298	Eddie Murray	.30
299	Randy Myers	.10
300	Francisco Cordova	.10
301	Javier Lopez	.10
302	Geronimo Berroa	.10
303	Jeffrey Hammonds	.10
304	Deion Sanders	.15
305	Jeff Fassero	.10
306	Curt Schilling	.15
307	Robb Nen	.10
308	Mark McLemore	.10
309	Jimmy Key	.10
310	Quilvio Veras	.10
311	Bip Roberts	.10
312	Esteban Loaiza	.10
313	Andy Ashby	.10
314	Sandy Alomar Jr.	.10
315	Shawn Green	.15
316	Luis Castillo	.10
317	Benji Gil	.10
318	Otis Nixon	.10
319	Aaron Sele	.10
320	Brad Ausmus	.10
321	Troy O'Leary	.10
322	Terrell Wade	.10
323	Jeff King	.10
324	Kevin Seitzer	.10
325	Mark Wohlers	.10
326	Edgar Renteria	.10
327	Dan Wilson	.10
328	Brian McRae	.10
329	Rod Beck	.10
330	Julio Franco	.10
331	Dave Nilsson	.10
332	Glenallen Hill	.10
333	Kevin Elster	.10
334	Joe Girardi	.10
335	David Wells	.10
336	Jeff Blauser	.10
337	Darryl Kile	.10
338	Jeff Kent	.10
339	Jim Leyritz	.10
340	Todd Stottlemyre	.10
341	Tony Clark	.10
342	Chris Hoiles	.10
343	Mike Lieberthal	.10
344	Matt Lawton	.10
345	Alex Ochoa	.10
346	Chris Snopek	.10
347	Rudy Pemberton	.10
348	Eric Owens	.10
349	Joe Randa	.10
350	John Olerud	.10
351	Steve Karsay	.10
352	Mark Whiten	.10
353	Bob Abreu	.10
354	Bartolo Colon	.10
355	Vladimir Guerrero	1.25
356	Darin Erstad	.50
357	Scott Rolen	.50
358	Andruw Jones	1.25
359	Scott Spiezio	.10
360	Karim Garcia	.10
361	*Hideki Irabu*	.40
362	Nomar Garciaparra	1.25
363	Dmitri Young	.10
364	*Bubba Trammell*	1.00
365	Kevin Orie	.10
366	Jose Rosado	.10
367	Jose Guillen	.50
368	Brooks Kieschnick	.10
369	Pokey Reese	.10
370	Glendon Rusch	.10
371	Jason Dickson	.15
372	Todd Walker	.15
373	Justin Thompson	.10
374	Todd Greene	.10
375	Jeff Suppan	.10
376	Trey Beamon	.10
377	Damon Mashore	.10
378	Wendell Magee	.10
379	Shigetosi Hasegawa	.10
380	Bill Mueller	.10
381	Chris Widger	.10
382	Tony Grafannino	.10
383	Derrek Lee	.10
384	Brian Moehler	.10
385	Quinton McCracken	.10
386	Matt Morris	.10
387	Marvin Benard	.10
388	*Deivi Cruz*	.50
389	*Javier Valentin*	.15
390	Todd Dunwoody	.15
391	Derrick Gibson	.10
392	Raul Casanova	.10
393	George Arias	.10
394	*Tony Womack*	.25
395	Antone Williamson	.10
396	*Jose Cruz Jr.*	.75
397	Desi Relaford	.10
398	Frank Thomas (Hit List)	.75
399	Ken Griffey Jr. (Hit List)	1.00
400	Cal Ripken Jr. (Hit List)	1.00
401	Chipper Jones (Hit List)	.75
402	Mike Piazza (Hit List)	.75
403	Gary Sheffield (Hit List)	.15
404	Alex Rodriguez (Hit List)	1.00
405	Wade Boggs (Hit List)	.15
406	Juan Gonzalez (Hit List)	.40
407	Tony Gwynn (Hit List)	.65
408	Edgar Martinez (Hit List)	.10
409	Jeff Bagwell (Hit List)	.60
410	Larry Walker (Hit List)	.15
411	Kenny Lofton (Hit List)	.10
412	Manny Ramirez (Hit List)	.50
413	Mark McGwire (Hit List)	1.00
414	Roberto Alomar (Hit List)	.25
415	Derek Jeter (Hit List)	.75
416	Brady Anderson (Hit List)	.10
417	Paul Molitor (Hit List)	.20
418	Dante Bichette (Hit List)	.15
419	Jim Edmonds (Hit List)	.10
420	Mo Vaughn (Hit List)	.15
421	Barry Bonds (Hit List)	.50
422	Rusty Greer (Hit List)	.10
423	Greg Maddux (King of the Hill)	.75
424	Andy Pettitte (King of the Hill)	.15
425	John Smoltz (King of the Hill)	.10
426	Randy Johnson (King of the Hill)	.25
427	Hideo Nomo (King of the Hill)	.25
428	Roger Clemens (King of the Hill)	.35
429	Tom Glavine (King of the Hill)	.15
430	Pat Hentgen (King of the Hill)	.10
431	Kevin Brown (King of the Hill)	.10
432	Mike Mussina (King of the Hill)	.25
433	Alex Fernandez (King of the Hill)	.10
434	Kevin Appier (King of the Hill)	.10
435	David Cone (King of the Hill)	.10
436	Jeff Fassero (King of the Hill)	.10
437	John Wetteland (King of the Hill)	.10
438	Barry Bonds, Ivan Rodriguez (Interleague Showdown)	.35
439	Ken Griffey Jr., Andres Galarraga (Interleague Showdown)	.75
440	Fred McGriff, Rafael Palmeiro (Interleague Showdown)	.10
441	Barry Larkin, Jim Thome (Interleague Showdown)	.10
442	Sammy Sosa, Albert Belle (Interleague Showdown)	1.50
443	Bernie Williams, Todd Hundley (Interleague Showdown)	.10
444	Chuck Knoblauch, Brian Jordan (Interleague Showdown)	.10
445	Mo Vaughn, Jeff Conine (Interleague Showdown)	.15
446	Ken Caminiti, Jason Giambi (Interleague Showdown)	.50
447	Raul Mondesi, Tim Salmon (Interleague Showdown)	.15
448	Checklist (Cal Ripken Jr.)	.75
449	Checklist (Greg Maddux)	.60
450	Checklist (Ken Griffey Jr.)	.75

1997 Donruss Press Proofs

Each of the 450 cards in the Donruss base set was also produced in a Press Proof parallel edition of 2,000 cards. Virtually identical in design to the regular cards, the Press Proofs are printed on a metallic background with silver-foil highlights. Most Press Proof backs carry the notation "1 of 2000". Stated odds of finding a press proof are one per eight packs. A special "gold" press proof chase set features cards with gold-foil highlights, die-cut at top and bottom and the note "1 of 500" on back. Gold press proofs are found on average of once per 32 packs.

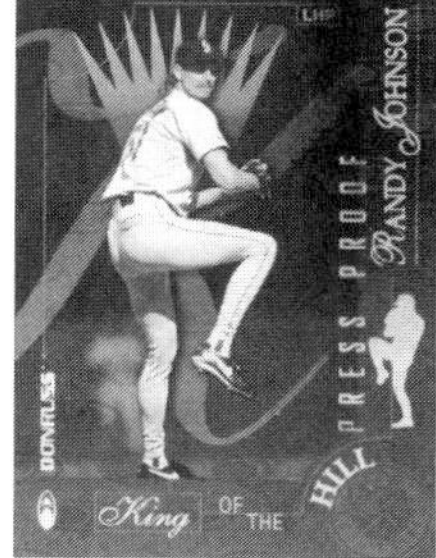

	MT
Complete Set (270):	350.00
Common Player:	1.00
Stars/Rookies:	6-10X
Complete Gold Set (270):	1100.
Common Gold Player:	4.00
Gold Stars/Rookies:	15-25X

(See 1997 Donruss for checklist and base card values.)

1997 Donruss Armed and Dangerous

These 15 cards are numbered up to 5,000. They were inserted in 1997 Donruss Series 1 retail packs only.

		MT
Complete Set (15):		65.00
Common Player:		1.50
1	Ken Griffey Jr.	12.00
2	Raul Mondesi	1.50
3	Chipper Jones	10.00
4	Ivan Rodriguez	3.00
5	Randy Johnson	3.00
6	Alex Rodriguez	12.00
7	Larry Walker	2.00
8	Cal Ripken Jr.	12.00
9	Kenny Lofton	1.50
10	Barry Bonds	5.00
11	Derek Jeter	10.00
12	Charles Johnson	1.50
13	Greg Maddux	9.00
14	Roberto Alomar	2.50
15	Barry Larkin	1.50

1997 Donruss Diamond Kings

Diamond Kings for 1997 are sequentially numbered from 1 to 10,000. To celebrate 15 years of this popular insert set, Donruss offered collectors a one-of-a-kind piece of artwork if they find one of the 10 cards with the serial number 1,982 (1982 was the first year of the Diamond Kings). Those who find these cards can redeem them for an original artwork provided by artist Dan Gardiner. In addition, Donruss printed the first 500 of each card on canvas stock.

		MT
Complete Set (10):		55.00
Common Player:		2.50
Canvas (1st 500):		2-4X
1	Ken Griffey Jr.	12.00
2	Cal Ripken Jr.	12.00
3	Mo Vaughn	3.50
4	Chuck Knoblauch	2.50
5	Jeff Bagwell	6.00
6	Henry Rodriguez	2.50
7	Mike Piazza	10.00
8	Ivan Rodriguez	3.50
9	Frank Thomas	7.50
10	Chipper Jones	9.00

1997 Donruss Elite Inserts

There were 2,500 sets of these insert cards made. The cards were randomly included in 1997 Donruss Series I packs. Fronts have a white marbled border and are graphically enhanced with silver foil, including a large script "E". On back is another photo, a career summary and a serial number from within the edition limit of 2,500.

		MT
Complete Set (12):		175.00
Common Player:		7.50
1	Frank Thomas	17.50
2	Paul Molitor	7.50
3	Sammy Sosa	17.50
4	Barry Bonds	15.00
5	Chipper Jones	20.00
6	Alex Rodriguez	30.00
7	Ken Griffey Jr.	30.00
8	Jeff Bagwell	9.00
9	Cal Ripken Jr.	30.00
10	Mo Vaughn	7.50
11	Mike Piazza	25.00
12	Juan Gonzalez	7.50

1997 Donruss Frank Thomas The Big Heart

In one of several specialty card charitable endeavors, Thomas and Donruss teamed up to issue this set as a fund raiser for "The Big Hurt's" charitable foundation. Each of the cards was available in an edition limited to 2,500 for a $20 donation. Cards are standard 2-1/2" x 3-1/2" with posed photos on front and "THE BIG HEART", a play on his nickname. Backs have information on the foundation.

		MT
Complete Set (4):		75.00
Common Card:		20.00
(1)	Frank Thomas (black jersey)	20.00
(2)	Frank Thomas (gray jersey)	20.00
(3)	Frank Thomas	20.00
(4)	Frank Thomas, Rod Carew	20.00

1997 Donruss Jackie Robinson Rookie Reprint

In conjunction with its program of special issues and giveaways honoring the 50th anniversary of Robinson's major league debut, Donruss issued this "Commemorative Rookie Card". Printed in the same size as the 1949 Leaf Robinson, and on heavier, coarser stock than modern cards, the card carries a reprint notice and is serially numbered on back in gold foil from within an edition of 1,948.

		MT
79	Jackie Robinson	12.00

1997 Donruss Longball Leaders

These 1997 Donruss Series 1 inserts have an action photo printed on a metallic foil background. Printed on the gold-foil border is a gauge with the player's 1996 home run total indicated. Horizontal backs have a player photo and record of career HRs by season. Each card is serially numbered within an edition of 5,000. The set was seeded in retail packs only.

		MT
Complete Set (15):		45.00
Common Player:		1.00
1	Frank Thomas	5.00
2	Albert Belle	2.00
3	Mo Vaughn	2.00
4	Brady Anderson	1.00
5	Greg Vaughn	1.00
6	Ken Griffey Jr.	10.00
7	Jay Buhner	1.00
8	Juan Gonzalez	3.00
9	Mike Piazza	7.50
10	Jeff Bagwell	4.00
11	Sammy Sosa	6.00
12	Mark McGwire	10.00
13	Cecil Fielder	1.00
14	Ryan Klesko	1.00
15	Jose Canseco	2.00

1997 Donruss Rocket Launchers

These 1997 Donruss Series 1 inserts are limited to 5,000 each. They were only included in magazine packs.

		MT
Complete Set (15):		35.00
Common Player:		1.00
1	Frank Thomas	4.50
2	Albert Belle	1.50
3	Chipper Jones	6.00
4	Mike Piazza	6.00
5	Mo Vaughn	2.00
6	Juan Gonzalez	3.00
7	Fred McGriff	1.00
8	Jeff Bagwell	2.50
9	Matt Williams	1.00
10	Gary Sheffield	1.00
11	Barry Bonds	3.00
12	Manny Ramirez	2.50
13	Henry Rodriguez	1.00
14	Jason Giambi	2.00
15	Cal Ripken Jr.	7.50

1997 Donruss Rated Rookies

Although numbered more like an insert set, Rated Rookies qre part of the regular-issue set. Cards are numbered 1-30, with no ratio given on packs. The cards are differentiated by a large silver-foil strip on the top right side with the words Rated Rookie.

		MT
Complete Set (30):		22.50
Common Player:		.50
1	Jason Thompson	.50
2	LaTroy Hawkins	.50
3	Scott Rolen	3.00
4	Trey Beamon	.50
5	Kimera Bartee	.50
6	Nerio Rodriguez	.50
7	Jeff D'Amico	.50
8	Quinton McCracken	.50
9	John Wasdin	.50
10	Robin Jennings	.50
11	Steve Gibralter	.50
12	Tyler Houston	.50
13	Tony Clark	1.00
14	Ugueth Urbina	.50
15	Billy McMillon	.50
16	Raul Casanova	.50
17	Brooks Kieschnick	.50
18	Luis Castillo	.50
19	Edgar Renteria	1.00
20	Andruw Jones	3.00
21	Chad Mottola	.50
22	Makoto Suzuki	.50
23	Justin Thompson	.50
24	Darin Erstad	3.00
25	Todd Walker	1.50
26	Todd Greene	.50
27	Vladimir Guerrero	3.00
28	Darren Dreifort	.50
29	John Burke	.50
30	Damon Mashore	.50

1997 Donruss Update Press Proofs

This 180-card parallel set is printed on an all-foil stock with bright foil accents. Each card is numbered "1 of 2,000". Special die-cut gold versions are numbered as "1 of 500".

	MT
Complete Set (180):	450.00
Common Player:	2.00
Stars:	15-25X
Complete Set, Gold (180):	1800.
Common Player, Gold:	6.00
Gold Stars:	45-60X

(See 1997 Donruss (#271-450) for checklist, base card values.)

1997 Donruss Update Cal Ripken

This 10-card set salutes Cal Ripken Jr. and is printed on an all-foil stock with foil highlights. Photos and text are taken from Ripken's autobiography, "The Only Way I Know." The first nine cards of the set were randomly inserted into packs. The 10th card was only available inside the book. Each card found within packs was numbered to 5,000.

		MT
Complete Set (10):		80.00
Common Card:		10.00
1-9	Cal Ripken Jr.	10.00
10	Cal Ripken Jr. (book insert)	15.00

1997 Donruss Update Dominators

This 20-card insert highlights players known for being able to "take over a game." Each card features silver-foil highlights on front and stats on back.

		MT
Complete Set (20):		25.00
Common Player:		.50
1	Frank Thomas	2.00
2	Ken Griffey Jr.	3.00
3	Greg Maddux	2.00
4	Cal Ripken Jr.	3.00
5	Alex Rodriguez	3.00
6	Albert Belle	.75
7	Mark McGwire	3.00
8	Juan Gonzalez	1.00
9	Chipper Jones	2.50
10	Hideo Nomo	1.00
11	Roger Clemens	1.50
12	John Smoltz	.50
13	Mike Piazza	2.50
14	Sammy Sosa	2.00
15	Matt Williams	.50
16	Kenny Lofton	.50
17	Barry Larkin	.50
18	Rafael Palmeiro	.50
19	Ken Caminiti	.50
20	Gary Sheffield	.50

1997 Donruss Update Franchise Features

This hobby-exclusive insert consists of 15 cards designed with a movie poster theme. The double-front design highlights a top veteran player on one side with an up-and-coming rookie on the other. The side featuring the veteran has the designation "Now Playing," while the rookie side carries the banner "Coming Attraction." Each card is printed on an all-foil stock and numbered to 3,000.

		MT
Complete Set (15):		85.00
Common Player:		2.50
1	Ken Griffey Jr., Andruw Jones	10.00
2	Frank Thomas, Darin Erstad	5.00
3	Alex Rodriguez, Nomar Garciaparra	10.00
4	Chuck Knoblauch, Wilton Guerrero	2.50
5	Juan Gonzalez, Bubba Trammell	6.50
6	Chipper Jones, Todd Walker	7.50
7	Barry Bonds, Vladimir Guerrero	5.00
8	Mark McGwire, Dmitri Young	10.00
9	Mike Piazza, Mike Sweeney	7.50
10	Mo Vaughn, Tony Clark	3.00
11	Gary Sheffield, Jose Guillen	2.50
12	Kenny Lofton, Shannon Stewart	2.50
13	Cal Ripken Jr., Scott Rolen	10.00
14	Derek Jeter, Pokey Reese	7.50
15	Tony Gwynn, Bob Abreu	6.50

1997 Donruss Update Power Alley

This 24-card insert is fractured into three different styles: Gold, Blue and Green. Each card is micro-etched and printed on holographic foil board. All cards are sequentially numbered, with the first 250 cards in each level being die-cut. Twelve players' cards feature a green finish and are numbered to 4,000. Eight players are printed on blue cards that are numbered to 2,000. Four players are found on gold cards numbered to 1,000.

		MT
Complete Set (24):		275.00
Common Gold:		17.50
Common Blue:		7.50
Common Green:		4.00
Die-Cuts:		2X
1	Frank Thomas (G)	17.50
2	Ken Griffey Jr. (G)	35.00
3	Cal Ripken Jr. (G)	35.00
4	Jeff Bagwell (B)	15.00
5	Mike Piazza (B)	22.50
6	Andruw Jones (GR)	9.00
7	Alex Rodriguez (G)	32.50
8	Albert Belle (GR)	6.00
9	Mo Vaughn (GR)	6.00
10	Chipper Jones (B)	22.50
11	Juan Gonzalez (B)	11.00
12	Ken Caminiti (GR)	4.00
13	Manny Ramirez (GR)	9.00
14	Mark McGwire (GR)	20.00
15	Kenny Lofton (B)	7.50
16	Barry Bonds (GR)	9.00
17	Gary Sheffield (GR)	4.00
18	Tony Gwynn (GR)	12.50
19	Vladimir Guerrero (B)	12.50
20	Ivan Rodriguez (B)	9.00
21	Paul Molitor (B)	11.00
22	Sammy Sosa (GR)	12.50
23	Matt Williams (GR)	4.00
24	Derek Jeter (GR)	15.00

1997 Donruss Update Rookie Diamond Kings

This popular Donruss Update insert set features a new twist - all 10 cards feature promising rookies. Each card is sequentially numbered to 10,000, with the first 500 cards of each player printed on actual canvas.

		MT
Complete Set (10):		60.00
Common Player:		3.00
Canvas:		3X
1	Andruw Jones	12.00
2	Vladimir Guerrero	11.00
3	Scott Rolen	10.00
4	Todd Walker	4.50
5	Bartolo Colon	3.50
6	Jose Guillen	6.00
7	Nomar Garciaparra	15.00
8	Darin Erstad	9.00
9	Dmitri Young	3.00
10	Wilton Guerrero	3.00

1997 Donruss Team Sets

A total of 163 cards were part of the Donruss Team Set issue. Packs consisted solely of players from one of 11 different teams. In addition, a full 163-card parallel set called Pennant Edition was available, featuring red and gold foil and a special "Pennant Edition" logo. Cards were sold in five-card packs for $1.99 each. The Angels and Indians set were sold only at their teams' souvenir outlets. Cards #131 Bernie Williams and #144 Russ Davis were never issued. The Team Set cards utilize team-color foil highlights and the numbers on back differ from the regular-issue version.

		MT
Comp. Angels Set (1-15):		2.50
Comp. Braves Set (16-30):		6.00
Comp. Orioles Set (31-45):		5.00
Comp. Red Sox Set (46-60):		3.00
Comp. White Sox Set (61-75):		4.00
Comp. Indians Set (76-90):		3.00
Comp. Rockies Set (91-105):		3.00
Comp. Dodgers Set (106-120):		4.50
Comp. Yankees Set (121-135):		9.00
Comp. Mariners Set (136-150):		9.00
Comp. Cardinals Set (151-165)		4.00
Common Player:		.10
Pennant Edition Stars:		8-12X
1	Jim Edmonds	.15
2	Tim Salmon	.20
3	Tony Phillips	.10
4	Garret Anderson	.10
5	Troy Percival	.10
6	Mark Langston	.10
7	Chuck Finley	.10
8	Eddie Murray	.50
9	Jim Leyritz	.10
10	Darin Erstad	.75
11	Jason Dickson	.10
12	Allen Watson	.10
13	Shigetosi Hasegawa	.10
14	Dave Hollins	.10
15	Gary DiSarcina	.10
16	Greg Maddux	2.00
17	Denny Neagle	.10
18	Chipper Jones	2.50
19	Tom Glavine	.15
20	John Smoltz	.15
21	Ryan Klesko	.10
22	Fred McGriff	.10
23	Michael Tucker	.10
24	Kenny Lofton	.10
25	Javier Lopez	.10
26	Mark Wohlers	.10
27	Jeff Blauser	.10
28	Andruw Jones	1.50
29	Tony Graffanino	.10
30	Terrell Wade	.10
31	Brady Anderson	.10
32	Roberto Alomar	.60
33	Rafael Palmeiro	.20
34	Mike Mussina	.60
35	Cal Ripken Jr.	3.50
36	Rocky Coppinger	.10
37	Randy Myers	.10
38	B.J. Surhoff	.10
39	Eric Davis	.10
40	Armando Benitez	.10
41	Jeffrey Hammonds	.10
42	Jimmy Key	.10
43	Chris Hoiles	.10
44	Mike Bordick	.10
45	Pete Incaviglia	.10
46	Mike Stanley	.10
47	Reggie Jefferson	.10
48	Mo Vaughn	.50
49	John Valentin	.10
50	Tim Naehring	.10
51	Jeff Suppan	.10
52	Tim Wakefield	.10
53	Jeff Frye	.10
54	Darren Bragg	.10
55	Steve Avery	.10
56	Shane Mack	.10
57	Aaron Sele	.10
58	Troy O'Leary	.10
59	Rudy Pemberton	.10
60	Nomar Garciaparra	2.00
61	Robin Ventura	.10
62	Wilson Alvarez	.10
63	Roberto Hernandez	.10
64	Frank Thomas	2.00
65	Ray Durham	.10
66	James Baldwin	.10
67	Harold Baines	.10
68	Doug Drabek	.10
69	Mike Cameron	.10
70	Albert Belle	.40
71	Jaime Navarro	.10
72	Chris Snopek	.10
73	Lyle Mouton	.10
74	Dave Martinez	.10
75	Ozzie Guillen	.10
76	Manny Ramirez	1.00
77	Jack McDowell	.10
78	Jim Thome	.10
79	Jose Mesa	.10
80	Brian Giles	.10
81	Omar Vizquel	.10
82	Charles Nagy	.10
83	Orel Hershiser	.10
84	Matt Williams	.15
85	Marquis Grissom	.10
86	David Justice	.15
87	Sandy Alomar	.10
88	Kevin Seitzer	.10
89	Julio Franco	.10
90	Bartolo Colon	.10
91	Andres Galarraga	.10
92	Larry Walker	.20
93	Vinny Castilla	.10
94	Dante Bichette	.10
95	Jamey Wright	.10
96	Ellis Burks	.10
97	Eric Young	.10
98	Neifi Perez	.10
99	Quinton McCracken	.10
100	Bruce Ruffin	.10
101	Walt Weiss	.10
102	Roger Bailey	.10
103	Jeff Reed	.10
104	Bill Swift	.10
105	Kirt Manwaring	.10
106	Raul Mondesi	.10
107	Hideo Nomo	.50
108	Roger Cedeno	.10
109	Ismael Valdes	.10
110	Todd Hollandsworth	.10
111	Mike Piazza	2.50
112	Brett Butler	.10
113	Chan Ho Park	.10
114	Ramon Martinez	.10
115	Eric Karros	.10
116	Wilton Guerrero	.10
117	Todd Zeile	.10
118	Karim Garcia	.10
119	Greg Gagne	.10
120	Darren Dreifort	.10
121	Wade Boggs	.75
122	Paul O'Neill	.10
123	Derek Jeter	2.50
124	Tino Martinez	.10
125	David Cone	.10
126	Andy Pettitte	.50
127	Charlie Hayes	.10
128	Mariano Rivera	.30
129	Dwight Gooden	.10
130	Cecil Fielder	.10
131	Not Issued	
132	Darryl Strawberry	.10
133	Joe Girardi	.10
134	David Wells	.10
135	Hideki Irabu	.10
136	Ken Griffey Jr.	3.50
137	Alex Rodriguez	3.50
138	Jay Buhner	.10
139	Randy Johnson	.65
140	Paul Sorrento	.10
141	Edgar Martinez	.10
142	Joey Cora	.10
143	Bob Wells	.10
144	Not Issued	
145	Jamie Moyer	.10
146	Jeff Fassero	.10
147	Dan Wilson	.10
148	Jose Cruz, Jr.	.50
149	Scott Sanders	.10
150	Rich Amaral	.10
151	Brian Jordan	.10
152	Andy Benes	.10
153	Ray Lankford	.10
154	John Mabry	.10
155	Tom Pagnozzi	.10
156	Ron Gant	.10
157	Alan Benes	.10
158	Dennis Eckersley	.15
159	Royce Clayton	.10
160	Todd Stottlemyre	.10
161	Gary Gaetti	.10
162	Willie McGee	.10
163	Delino DeShields	.10
164	Dmitri Young	.10
165	Matt Morris	.10

1997 Donruss Team Sets MVP

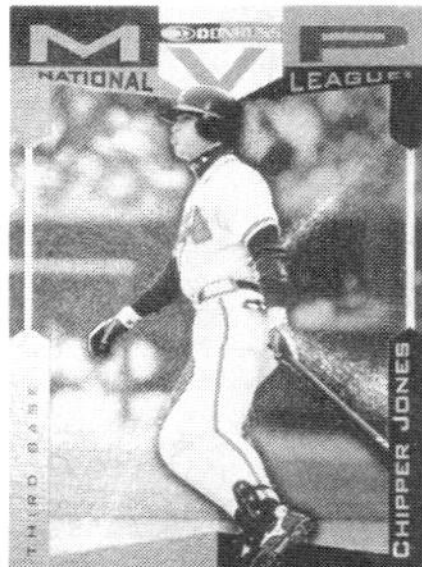

The top players at each position were available in this 18-card insert set. Each card is sequentially numbered to 1,000. Fronts are printed with a textured foil background and holographic foil highlights. Backs have a portrait photo.

		MT
Complete Set (18):		95.00
Common Player:		1.00
1	Ivan Rodriguez	3.50
2	Mike Piazza	12.50
3	Frank Thomas	10.00
4	Jeff Bagwell	6.00
5	Chuck Knoblauch	1.00
6	Eric Young	1.00
7	Alex Rodriguez	15.00
8	Barry Larkin	1.00
9	Cal Ripken Jr.	15.00
10	Chipper Jones	12.50
11	Albert Belle	2.00
12	Barry Bonds	7.50
13	Ken Griffey Jr.	15.00
14	Kenny Lofton	1.00
15	Juan Gonzalez	4.00
16	Larry Walker	1.50
17	Roger Clemens	8.00
18	Greg Maddux	10.00

1997 Donruss Elite Promos

Each of the 12 cards in Series 1 Donruss Elite inserts can be found in a sample card version. The promos differ from the issued version in the diagonal black overprint "SAMPLE CARD" on front and back, and the "PROMO/2500" at back bottom in place of the issued version's serial number.

		MT
Complete Set (12):		90.00
Common Player:		4.00
1	Frank Thomas	7.50
2	Paul Molitor	6.00
3	Sammy Sosa	7.50
4	Barry Bonds	9.00
5	Chipper Jones	10.00
6	Alex Rodriguez	15.00
7	Ken Griffey Jr.	15.00
8	Jeff Bagwell	6.00
9	Cal Ripken Jr.	15.00
10	Mo Vaughn	4.00
11	Mike Piazza	12.00
12	Juan Gonzalez	6.00

1997 Donruss Elite

Donruss Elite Baseball is a 150-card, single-series set distributed as a hobby-only product. The regular-issue cards feature a silver border around the entire card, with a marblized frame around a color player photo at center. Backs feature a color player photo and minimal statistics and personal data. Elite was accompanied by an Elite Stars parallel set and three inserts: Leather and Lumber, Passing the Torch and Turn of the Century.

		MT
Complete Set (150):		10.00
Common Player:		.10
Pack (6):		2.50
Wax Box (18):		35.00
1	Juan Gonzalez	.75
2	Alex Rodriguez	2.00
3	Frank Thomas	1.00
4	Greg Maddux	1.00
5	Ken Griffey Jr.	2.00
6	Cal Ripken Jr.	2.00
7	Mike Piazza	1.25
8	Chipper Jones	1.25
9	Albert Belle	.40
10	Andruw Jones	.65
11	Vladimir Guerrero	.65
12	Mo Vaughn	.50
13	Ivan Rodriguez	.65
14	Andy Pettitte	.50
15	Tony Gwynn	1.00
16	Barry Bonds	1.00
17	Jeff Bagwell	.65
18	Manny Ramirez	.75
19	Kenny Lofton	.10
20	Roberto Alomar	.65
21	Mark McGwire	2.00

22	Ryan Klesko	.10
23	Tim Salmon	.15
24	Derek Jeter	1.00
25	Eddie Murray	.50
26	Jermaine Dye	.10
27	Ruben Rivera	.10
28	Jim Edmonds	.10
29	Mike Mussina	.50
30	Randy Johnson	.50
31	Sammy Sosa	1.00
32	Hideo Nomo	.25
33	Chuck Knoblauch	.10
34	Paul Molitor	.50
35	Rafael Palmeiro	.15
36	Brady Anderson	.10
37	Will Clark	.15
38	Craig Biggio	.10
39	Jason Giambi	.25
40	Roger Clemens	.75
41	Jay Buhner	.10
42	Edgar Martinez	.10
43	Gary Sheffield	.15
44	Fred McGriff	.10
45	Bobby Bonilla	.10
46	Tom Glavine	.20
47	Wade Boggs	.25
48	Jeff Conine	.10
49	John Smoltz	.10
50	Jim Thome	.10
51	Billy Wagner	.10
52	Jose Canseco	.20
53	Javy Lopez	.10
54	Cecil Fielder	.10
55	Garret Anderson	.10
56	Alex Ochoa	.10
57	Scott Rolen	.50
58	Darin Erstad	.50
59	Rey Ordonez	.15
60	Dante Bichette	.10
61	Joe Carter	.10
62	Moises Alou	.15
63	Jason Isringhausen	.10
64	Karim Garcia	.15
65	Brian Jordan	.10
66	Ruben Sierra	.10
67	Todd Hollandsworth	.10
68	Paul Wilson	.10
69	Ernie Young	.10
70	Ryne Sandberg	.75
71	Raul Mondesi	.20
72	George Arias	.10
73	Ray Durham	.10
74	Dean Palmer	.10
75	Shawn Green	.25
76	Eric Young	.10
77	Jason Kendall	.10
78	Greg Vaughn	.10
79	Terrell Wade	.10
80	Bill Pulsipher	.10
81	Bobby Higginson	.10
82	Mark Grudzielanek	.10
83	Ken Caminiti	.15
84	Todd Greene	.10
85	Carlos Delgado	.25
86	Mark Grace	.25
87	Rondell White	.15
88	Barry Larkin	.15
89	J.T. Snow	.10
90	Alex Gonzalez	.10
91	Raul Casanova	.10
92	Marc Newfield	.10
93	Jermaine Allensworth	.10
94	John Mabry	.10
95	Kirby Puckett	1.00
96	Travis Fryman	.10
97	Kevin Brown	.15
98	Andres Galarraga	.10
99	Marty Cordova	.10
100	Henry Rodriguez	.10
101	Sterling Hitchcock	.10
102	Trey Beamon	.10
103	Brett Butler	.10
104	Rickey Henderson	.25
105	Tino Martinez	.10
106	Kevin Appier	.10
107	Brian Hunter	.10
108	Eric Karros	.10
109	Andre Dawson	.10
110	Darryl Strawberry	.10
111	James Baldwin	.10
112	Chad Mottola	.10
113	Dave Nilsson	.10
114	Carlos Baerga	.10
115	Chan Ho Park	.15
116	John Jaha	.10
117	Alan Benes	.10
118	Mariano Rivera	.25
119	Ellis Burks	.10
120	Tony Clark	.10
121	Todd Walker	.20
122	Dwight Gooden	.10
123	Ugueth Urbina	.10
124	David Cone	.10
125	Ozzie Smith	1.00
126	Kimera Bartee	.10
127	Rusty Greer	.10
128	Pat Hentgen	.10
129	Charles Johnson	.10
130	Quinton McCracken	.10
131	Troy Percival	.10
132	Shane Reynolds	.10
133	Charles Nagy	.10
134	Tom Goodwin	.10
135	Ron Gant	.10
136	Dan Wilson	.10
137	Matt Williams	.15
138	LaTroy Hawkins	.10
139	Kevin Seitzer	.10
140	Michael Tucker	.10
141	Todd Hundley	.10
142	Alex Fernandez	.10
143	Marquis Grissom	.10
144	Steve Finley	.10
145	Curtis Pride	.10
146	Derek Bell	.10
147	Butch Huskey	.10
148	Dwight Gooden	.10
149	Al Leiter	.10
150	Hideo Nomo	.25

1997 Donruss Elite Stars

Gold, rather than silver, foil differentiates the parallel set of Elite Stars from the regular-issue versions of each of the base cards in the Elite set. The parallels also have a small "Elite Stars" printed at top, flanking the position. Stated odds of finding a Stars insert are about one per five packs.

		MT
Complete Set (150):		150.00
Common Player:		1.00

(Star players in the Elite Star parallel issue valued at 5-8X regular Elites.)

1997 Donruss Elite Leather & Lumber

Leather and Lumber is a 10-card insert set filled with veterans. Genuine leather is featured on one side of the card, while wood card stock is on the other. There were 500 sequentially numbered sets produced.

		MT
Complete Set (10):		160.00
Common Player:		6.00
1	Ken Griffey Jr.	30.00
2	Alex Rodriguez	30.00
3	Frank Thomas	15.00
4	Chipper Jones	22.50
5	Ivan Rodriguez	10.00
6	Cal Ripken Jr.	35.00
7	Barry Bonds	15.00
8	Chuck Knoblauch	6.00
9	Manny Ramirez	12.50
10	Mark McGwire	30.00

1997 Donruss Elite Passing the Torch

Passing the Torch is a 12-card insert limited to 1,500 individually numbered sets. It features eight different stars, each with their own cards and then featured on a double-sided card with another player from the set.

		MT
Complete Set (12):		210.00
Common Player:		10.00
1	Cal Ripken Jr.	45.00
2	Alex Rodriguez	45.00
3	Cal Ripken Jr., Alex Rodriguez	35.00
4	Kirby Puckett	20.00
5	Andruw Jones	15.00
6	Kirby Puckett, Andruw Jones	15.00
7	Cecil Fielder	10.00
8	Frank Thomas	15.00
9	Cecil Fielder, Frank Thomas	15.00
10	Ozzie Smith	20.00
11	Derek Jeter	25.00
12	Ozzie Smith, Derek Jeter	15.00

1997 Donruss Elite Turn of the Century

Turn of the Century includes 20 potential year 2000 superstars on an insert set numbered to 3,500. The first 500 of these sets feature an external die-cut design. Cards feature the player over a framed background image on silver foil board, with black strips down each side. Backs have a color photo, a few words about the player and the serial number.

		MT
Complete Set (20):		60.00
Common Player:		1.50
Complete Die-Cut Set (20):		180.00
Die-Cuts:		3X
1	Alex Rodriguez	15.00
2	Andruw Jones	9.00
3	Chipper Jones	12.50
4	Todd Walker	1.50
5	Scott Rolen	7.50
6	Trey Beamon	1.50
7	Derek Jeter	12.50
7s	Derek Jeter ("SAMPLE" overprint)	5.00
8	Darin Erstad	6.50
9	Tony Clark	1.50
10	Todd Greene	1.50
11	Jason Giambi	6.00
12	Justin Thompson	1.50
13	Ernie Young	1.50
14	Jason Kendall	2.00
15	Alex Ochoa	1.50
15s	Alex Ochoa ("SAMPLE" overprint)	1.50
16	Brooks Kieschnick	1.50
17	Bobby Higginson	1.50
17s	Bobby Higginson ("SAMPLE" overprint)	1.50
18	Ruben Rivera	1.50
18s	Ruben Rivera ("SAMPLE" overprint)	1.50
19	Chan Ho Park	2.00
20	Chad Mottola	1.50

1997 Donruss Elite Passing the Torch Autographs

The first 150 individually numbered sets of the Passing the Torch insert were autographed. This means that cards 3, 6, 9 and 12 are dual-autographed on their double-sided format.

		MT
Complete Set (12):		1300.
Common Card:		35.00
1	Cal Ripken Jr.	150.00
2	Alex Rodriguez	100.00
3	Cal Ripken Jr., Alex Rodriguez	600.00
4	Kirby Puckett	125.00
5	Andruw Jones	75.00
6	Kirby Puckett, Andruw Jones	100.00
7	Cecil Fielder	35.00
8	Frank Thomas	75.00
9	Cecil Fielder, Frank Thomas	75.00
10	Ozzie Smith	100.00
11	Derek Jeter	100.00
12	Ozzie Smith, Derek Jeter	200.00

1997 Donruss Limited

Each of the 200 base cards in this set features a double-front design showcasing an action photo on each side. The set is divided into four subsets. Counterparts (100 cards) highlights two different players from the same position; Double Team (40 cards) features some of the majors' top teammate duos; Star Factor (40 cards) consists of two photos of some of the hobby's favorite players; and Unlimited Potential/Talent (20 cards) combines a top veteran with a top prospect. The issue also includes a Limited Exposure parallel set and a multi-tiered insert called Fabric of the Game. Odds of finding any insert card were 1:5 packs. Less than 1,100 base sets were available. Cards were sold in five-card packs for $4.99.

		MT
Complete Set (200):		750.00
Common Counterpart:		.25
Common Double Team:		1.00
Common Star Factor:		2.50
Common Unlimited:		2.00
Pack (5):		2.50
Wax Box (24):		55.00
1	Ken Griffey Jr., Rondell White (Counterparts)	2.00
2	Greg Maddux, David Cone (Counterparts)	1.00
3	Gary Sheffield, Moises Alou (Double Team)	1.50
4	Frank Thomas (Star Factor)	12.50
5	Cal Ripken Jr., Kevin Orie (Counterparts)	2.00
6	Vladimir Guerrero, Barry Bonds (Unlimited Potential/Talent)	15.00
7	Eddie Murray, Reggie Jefferson (Counterparts)	.30
8	Manny Ramirez, Marquis Grissom (Double Team)	3.00
9	Mike Piazza (Star Factor)	25.00
10	Barry Larkin, Rey Ordonez (Counterparts)	.30
11	Jeff Bagwell, Eric Karros (Counterparts)	1.00
12	Chuck Knoblauch, Ray Durham (Counterparts)	.25
13	Alex Rodriguez, Edgar Renteria (Counterparts)	2.00
14	Matt Williams, Vinny Castilla (Counterparts)	.30
15	Todd Hollandsworth, Bob Abreu (Counterparts)	.25
16	John Smoltz, Pedro Martinez (Counterparts)	.40
17	Jose Canseco, Chili Davis (Counterparts)	.30
18	Jose Cruz, Jr., Ken Griffey Jr. (Unlimited Potential/Talent)	20.00
19	Ken Griffey Jr. (Star Factor)	30.00
20	Paul Molitor, John Olerud (Counterparts)	.75
21	Roberto Alomar, Luis Castillo (Counterparts)	.50
22	Derek Jeter, Lou Collier (Counterparts)	1.50
23	Chipper Jones, Robin Ventura (Counterparts)	1.50
24	Gary Sheffield, Ron Gant (Counterparts)	.30
25	Ramon Martinez, Bobby Jones (Counterparts)	.25
26	Mike Piazza, Raul Mondesi (Double Team)	12.50
27	Darin Erstad, Jeff Bagwell (Unlimited Potential/Talent)	4.00
28	Ivan Rodriguez (Star Factor)	10.00
29	J.T. Snow, Kevin Young (Counterparts)	.25
30	Ryne Sandberg, Julio Franco (Counterparts)	.65
31	Travis Fryman, Chris Snopek (Counterparts)	.25
32	Wade Boggs, Russ Davis (Counterparts)	.40
33	Brooks Kieschnick, Marty Cordova (Counterparts)	.25
34	Andy Pettitte, Denny Neagle (Counterparts)	.65
35	Paul Molitor, Matt Lawton (Double Team)	1.25
36	Scott Rolen, Cal Ripken Jr. (Unlimited Potential/Talent)	30.00
37	Cal Ripken Jr. (Star Factor)	30.00
38	Jim Thome, Dave Nilsson (Counterparts)	.30
39	*Tony Womack*, Carlos Baerga (Counterparts)	.25
40	Nomar Garciaparra, Mark Grudzielanek (Counterparts)	1.25
41	Todd Greene, Chris Widger (Counterparts)	.25
42	Deion Sanders, Bernard Gilkey (Counterparts)	.30
43	Hideo Nomo, Charles Nagy (Counterparts)	.40
44	Ivan Rodriguez, Rusty Greer (Double Team)	3.00
45	Todd Walker, Chipper Jones (Unlimited Potential/Talent)	10.00
46	Greg Maddux (Star Factor)	10.00
47	Mo Vaughn, Cecil Fielder (Counterparts)	.40
48	Craig Biggio, Scott Spiezio (Counterparts)	.25
49	Pokey Reese, Jeff Blauser (Counterparts)	.25
50	Ken Caminiti, Joe Randa (Counterparts)	.25
51	Albert Belle, Shawn Green (Counterparts)	.60
52	Randy Johnson, Jason Dickson (Counterparts)	.60
53	Hideo Nomo, Chan Ho Park (Double Team)	2.50
54	Scott Spiezio, Chuck Knoblauch (Unlimited Potential/Talent)	2.00
55	Chipper Jone s (Star Factor)	25.00
56	Tino Martinez, Ryan McGuire (Counterparts)	.25
57	Eric Young, Wilton Guerrero (Counterparts)	.25
58	Ron Coomer, Dave Hollins (Counterparts)	.25
59	Sammy Sosa, Angel Echevarria (Counterparts)	1.25
60	*Dennis Reyes*, Jimmy Key (Counterparts)	.25
61	Barry Larkin, Deion Sanders (Double Team)	1.00
62	Wilton Guerrero, Roberto Alomar (Unlimited Potential/Talent)	2.00
63	Albert Belle (Star Factor)	4.00
64	Mark McGwire, Andres Galarraga (Counterparts)	2.00
65	Edgar Martinez, Todd Walker (Counterparts)	.25
66	Steve Finley, Rich Becker (Counterparts)	.25
67	Tom Glavine, Andy Ashby (Counterparts)	.35
68	Sammy Sosa, Ryne Sandberg (Double Team)	10.00
69	Nomar Garciaparra, Alex Rodriguez (Unlimited Potential/Talent)	30.00
70	Jeff Bagwell (Star Factor)	12.50
71	Darin Erstad, Mark Grace (Counterparts)	.75
72	Scott Rolen, Edgardo Alfonzo (Counterparts)	.75
73	Kenny Lofton, Lance Johnson (Counterparts)	.25
74	Joey Hamilton, Brett Tomko (Counterparts)	.25
75	Eddie Murray, Tim Salmon (Double Team)	1.50
76	Dmitri Young, Mo Vaughn (Unlimited Potential/Talent)	2.00
77	Juan Gonzalez (Star Factor)	7.50
78	Frank Thomas, Tony Clark (Counterparts)	.75
79	Shannon Stewart, Bip Roberts (Counterparts)	.25
80	Shawn Estes, Alex Fernandez (Counterparts)	.25
81	John Smoltz, Javier Lopez (Double Team)	.50
82	Todd Greene, Mike Piazza (Unlimited Potential/Talent)	20.00
83	Derek Jeter (Star Factor)	25.00
84	Dmitri Young, Antone Williamson (Counterparts)	.25
85	Rickey Henderson, Darryl Hamilton (Counterparts)	.35
86	Billy Wagner, Dennis Eckersley (Counterparts)	.50
87	Larry Walker, Eric Young (Double Team)	1.50
88	Mark Kotsay, Juan Gonzalez (Unlimited Potential/Talent)	4.00
89	Barry Bonds (Star Factor)	10.00
90	Will Clark, Jeff Conine (Counterparts)	.35
91	Tony Gwynn, Brett Butler (Counterparts)	1.25
92	John Wetteland, Rod Beck (Counterparts)	.25
93	Bernie Williams, Tino Martinez (Double Team)	1.25
94	Andruw Jones, Kenny Lofton (Unlimited Potential/Talent)	4.00
95	Mo Vaughn (Star Factor)	4.00
96	Joe Carter, Derrek Lee (Counterparts)	.25
97	John Mabry, F.P. Santangelo (Counterparts)	.25
98	Esteban Loaiza, Wilson Alvarez (Counterparts)	.25
99	Matt Williams, David Justice (Double Team)	1.25
100	Derrek Lee, Frank Thomas (Unlimited Potential/Talent)	3.00
101	Mark McGwire (Star Factor)	30.00
102	Fred McGriff, Paul Sorrento (Counterparts)	.25
103	Jermaine Allensworth, Bernie Williams (Counterparts)	.25
104	Ismael Valdes, Chris Holt (Counterparts)	.25
105	Fred McGriff, Ryan Klesko (Double Team)	1.00
106	Tony Clark, Mark McGwire (Unlimited Potential/Talent)	30.00
107	Tony Gwynn (Star Factor)	20.00
108	Jeffrey Hammonds, Ellis Burks (Counterparts)	.25
109	Shane Reynolds, Andy Benes (Counterparts)	.25
110	Roger Clemens, Carlos Delgado (Double Team)	3.00
111	Karim Garcia, Albert Belle (Unlimited Potential/Talent)	2.50
112	Paul Molitor (Star Factor)	7.50

113 Trey Beamon, Eric Owens (Counterparts) .25
114 Curt Schilling, Darryl Kile (Counterparts) .35
115 Tom Glavine, Michael Tucker (Double Team) 1.00
116 Pokey Reese, Derek Jeter (Unlimited Potential/Talent) 17.50
117 Manny Ramirez (Star Factor) 9.00
118 Juan Gonzalez, Brant Brown (Counterparts) 1.00
119 Juan Guzman, Francisco Cordova (Counterparts) .25
120 Randy Johnson, Edgar Martinez (Double Team) 1.50
121 Hideki Irabu, Greg Maddux (Unlimited Potential/Talent) 5.50
122 Alex Rodriguez (Star Factor) 30.00
123 Barry Bonds, Quinton McCracken (Counterparts) 1.25
124 Roger Clemens, Alan Benes (Counterparts) .60
125 Wade Boggs, Paul O'Neill (Double Team) 1.25
126 Mike Cameron, Larry Walker (Unlimited Potential/Talent) 2.00
127 Gary Sheffield (Star Factor) 2.50
128 Andruw Jones, Raul Mondesi (Counterparts) 1.00
129 Brian Anderson, Terrell Wade (Counterparts) .25
130 Brady Anderson, Rafael Palmeiro (Double Team) 2.50
131 Neifi Perez, Barry Larkin (Unlimited Potential/ Talent) 2.00
132 Ken Caminiti (Star Factor) 2.50
133 Larry Walker, Rusty Greer (Counterparts) .35
134 Mariano Rivera, Mark Wohlers (Counterparts) .35
135 Hideki Irabu, Andy Pettitte (Double Team) 1.50
136 Jose Guillen, Tony Gwynn (Unlimited Potential/ Talent) 6.00
137 Hideo Nomo (Star Factor) 4.00
138 Vladimir Guerrero, Jim Edmonds (Counterparts) .75
139 Justin Thompson, Dwight Gooden (Counterparts) .25
140 Andres Galarraga, Dante Bichette (Double Team) 1.00
141 Kenny Lofton (Star Factor) 2.50
142 Tim Salmon, Manny Ramirez (Counterparts) 1.00
143 Kevin Brown, Matt Morris (Counterparts) .25
144 Craig Biggio, Bob Abreu (Double Team) 1.00
145 Roberto Alomar (Star Factor) 5.00
146 Jose Guillen, Brian Jordan (Counterparts) .25
147 Bartolo Colon, Kevin Appier (Counterparts) .25
148 Ray Lankford, Brian Jordan (Double Team) 1.00
149 Chuck Knoblauch (Star Factor) 2.50
150 Henry Rodriguez, Ray Lankford (Counterparts) .25
151 *Jaret Wright*, Ben McDonald (Counterparts) .65
152 Bobby Bonilla, Kevin Brown (Double Team) 1.00
153 Barry Larkin (Star Factor) 2.50
154 David Justice, Reggie Sanders (Counterparts) .40
155 Mike Mussina, Ken Hill (Counterparts) .50
156 Mark Grace, Brooks Kieschnick (Double Team) 1.25
157 Jim Thome (Star Factor) 2.50
158 Michael Tucker, Curtis Goodwin (Counterparts) .25
159 Jeff Suppan, Jeff Fassero (Counterparts) .25
160 Mike Mussina, Jeffrey Hammonds (Double Team) 1.25
161 John Smoltz (Star Factor) 2.50
162 Moises Alou, Eric Davis (Counterparts) .25
163 Sandy Alomar Jr., Dan Wilson (Counterparts) .25
164 Rondell White, Henry Rodriguez (Double Team) 1.00
165 Roger Clemens (Star Factor) 10.00
166 Brady Anderson, Al Martin (Counterparts) .25
167 Jason Kendall, Charles Johnson (Counterparts) .25
168 Jason Giambi, Jose Canseco (Double Team) 6.50
169 Larry Walker (Star Factor) 2.50
170 Jay Buhner, Geronimo Berroa (Counterparts) .25
171 Ivan Rodriguez, Mike Sweeney (Counterparts) .60
172 Kevin Appier, Jose Rosado (Double Team) 1.00
173 Bernie Williams (Star Factor) 2.50
174 Todd Dunwoody, *Brian Giles* (Counterparts) .60
175 Javier Lopez, Scott Hatteberg (Counterparts) .25
176 John Jaha, Jeff Cirillo (Double Team) 1.00
177 Andy Pettitte (Star Factor) 2.50
178 Dante Bichette, Butch Huskey (Counterparts) .25
179 Raul Casanova, Todd Hundley (Counterparts) .25
180 Jim Edmonds, Garret Anderson (Double Team) 1.25
181 Deion Sanders (Star Factor) 2.50
182 Ryan Klesko, Paul O'Neill (Counterparts) .25
183 Joe Carter, Pat Hentgen (Double Team) 1.00
184 Brady Anderson (Star Factor) 2.50
185 Carlos Delgado, Wally Joyner (Counterparts) .30
186 Jermaine Dye, Johnny Damon (Double Team) 1.00
187 Randy Johnson (Star Factor) 4.00
188 Todd Hundley, Carlos Baerga (Double Team) 1.00
189 Tom Glavine (Star Factor) 2.50
190 Damon Mashore, Jason McDonald (Double Team) 1.25
191 Wade Boggs (Star Factor) 4.00
192 Al Martin, Jason Kendall (Double Team) 1.00
193 Matt Williams (Star Factor) 2.50
194 Will Clark, Dean Palmer (Double Team) 1.25
195 Sammy Sosa (Star Factor) 17.50
196 Jose Cruz, Jr., Jay Buhner (Double Team) 1.00
197 Eddie Murray (Star Factor) 3.50
198 Darin Erstad, Jason Dickson (Double Team) 1.25
199 Fred McGriff (Star Factor) 2.50
200 Bubba Trammell, Bobby Higginson (Double Team) 1.00

1997 Donruss Limited Exposure

A complete 200-card parallel set printed with Holographic Poly-Chromium technology on both sides and featuring a special "Limited Exposure" stamp. Less than 40 sets of the Star Factor Limited Exposures are thought to exist.

	MT
Complete Set (200):	4500.
Common Counterparts:	2.00
Counterparts Stars:	6X
Common Double Team:	6.00
Double Team Stars:	6X
Common Star Factor:	10.00
Star Factor Stars:	4X
Common Unlimited:	8.00
Unlimited Stars:	4X

(See 1997 Donruss Limited for checklist and base card values.)

1997 Donruss Limited Exposure Non-Glossy

In error, half (100 cards) of the Limited Exposure parallels were produced in regular technology (non-chrome) on regular (non-glossy) cardboard stock. These cards do carry the Limited Exposure identification in the card-number box on back, but do not carry the correct cards' higher values. No checklist of which 100 cards were involved in the error is available.

	MT
Common Non-Glossy:	1.00
Stars: 15-25%	

(See 1997 Donruss Limited and Limited Exposure to calculate base card values.)

1997 Donruss Limited Fabric of the Game

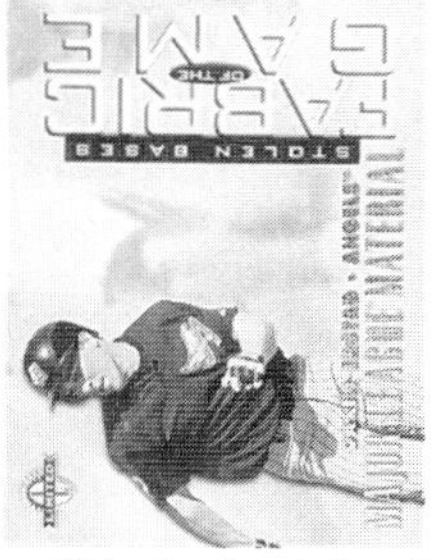

This fractured insert set consists of 69 different cards highlighting three different technologies representing three statistical categories: Canvas (stolen bases), Leather (doubles) and Wood (home runs). Each of the 23 cards in each category are found in varying levels of scarcity: Legendary Material (one card per theme; numbered to 100), Hall of Fame Material (four cards numbered to 250), Superstar Material (five cards numbered to 500), Star Material (six cards numbered to 750), and Major League Material (seven cards numbered to 1,000).

	MT
Complete Set: (69):	550.00
Common Player:	2.50
Complete Canvas Set (23):	160.00
Rickey Henderson (100)	22.50
Barry Bonds (250)	17.50
Kenny Lofton (250)	4.00
Roberto Alomar (250)	12.50
Ryne Sandberg (250)	15.00
Tony Gwynn (500)	15.00
Barry Larkin (500)	4.00
Brady Anderson (500)	5.00
Chuck Knoblauch (500)	4.00
Craig Biggio (500)	4.00
Sammy Sosa (750)	15.00
Gary Sheffield (750)	4.00
Eric Young (750)	3.50
Larry Walker (750)	6.00
Ken Griffey Jr. (750)	30.00

Deion Sanders (750)	5.00
Raul Mondesi (1,000)	3.00
Rondell White (1,000)	3.50
Derek Jeter (1,000)	12.50
Nomar Garciaparra (1,000)	10.00
Wilton Guerrero (1,000)	2.50
Pokey Reese (1,000)	2.50
Darin Erstad (1,000)	4.00
Complete Leather Set (23):	185.00
Paul Molitor (100)	30.00
Wade Boggs (250)	12.50
Cal Ripken Jr. (250)	40.00
Tony Gwynn (250)	25.00
Joe Carter (250)	6.00
Rafael Palmeiro (500)	6.00
Mark Grace (500)	8.00
Bobby Bonilla (500)	3.00
Andres Galarraga (500)	3.00
Edgar Martinez (500)	3.00
Ken Caminiti (750)	5.00
Ivan Rodriguez (750)	8.00
Frank Thomas (750)	15.00
Jeff Bagwell (750)	10.00
Albert Belle (750)	6.00
Bernie Williams (750)	6.00
Chipper Jones (1,000)	12.50
Rusty Greer (1,000)	3.00
Todd Walker (1,000)	5.00
Scott Rolen (1,000)	6.00
Bob Abreu (1,000)	3.00
Jose Guillen (1,000)	3.00
Jose Cruz, Jr. (1,000)	3.00
Complete Wood Set (23);	195.00
Eddie Murray (100)	25.00
Cal Ripken Jr. (250)	35.00
Barry Bonds (250)	25.00
Mark McGwire (250)	35.00
Fred McGriff (250)	3.00
Ken Griffey Jr. (500)	30.00
Albert Belle (500)	4.00
Frank Thomas (500)	15.00
Juan Gonzalez (500)	10.00
Matt Williams (500)	4.00
Mike Piazza (750)	15.00
Jeff Bagwell (750)	10.00
Mo Vaughn (750)	6.50
Gary Sheffield (750)	3.00
Tim Salmon (750)	3.00
David Justice (750)	4.00
Manny Ramirez (1,000)	7.50
Jim Thome (1,000)	3.00
Tino Martinez (1,000)	3.00
Andruw Jones (1,000)	5.00
Vladimir Guerrero (1,000)	6.50
Tony Clark (1,000)	3.00
Dmitri Young (1,000)	3.00

1997 Donruss Preferred

Each of the 200 base cards is printed on all-foil microetched stock. Conventional backs have a color player photo and a few stats. The set is fractured into four increasingly scarce levels: 100 Bronze cards, 70 Silver, 20 Gold and 10 Platinum. Instead of traditional packs, cards were sold in five-card collectible tins. Four different inserts were included with the product: Staremaster, X-Ponential Power, Cut To The Chase (a die-cut parallel) and Precious Metals. Odds of finding any insert were 1:4 packs.

		MT
Complete Set (200):		350.00
Common Bronze:		.10
Common Silver:		.75
Common Gold:		2.00
Common Platinum:		5.00
Cut to the Chase Bronze:		4X
Cut to the Chase Silver:		3X
Cut to the Chase Gold:		2X
Cut to the Chase Platinum:		2X
Wax Box (24):		120.00
1	Frank Thomas P	12.50
2	Ken Griffey Jr. P	20.00
3	Cecil Fielder B	.10
4	Chuck Knoblauch G	2.00
5	Garret Anderson B	.10
6	Greg Maddux P	10.00
7	Matt Williams S	1.00
8	Marquis Grissom S	.75
9	Jason Isringhausen B	.10
10	Larry Walker S	1.25
11	Charles Nagy B	.10
12	Dan Wilson B	.10
13	Albert Belle G	3.00
14	Javier Lopez B	.10
15	David Cone B	.10
16	Bernard Gilkey B	.10
17	Andres Galarraga S	.75
18	Bill Pulsipher B	.10
19	Alex Fernandez B	.10
20	Andy Pettitte S	2.00
21	Mark Grudzielanek B	.10
22	Juan Gonzalez P	9.00
23	Reggie Sanders B	.10
24	Kenny Lofton G	2.00
25	Andy Ashby B	.10
26	John Wetteland B	.10
27	Bobby Bonilla B	.10
28	Hideo Nomo G	4.00
29	Joe Carter B	.10
30	Jose Canseco B	.25
31	Ellis Burks B	.10
32	Edgar Martinez S	.75
33	Chan Ho Park B	.15
34	David Justice B	.20
35	Carlos Delgado B	.25
36	Jeff Cirillo S	.75
37	Charles Johnson B	.10
38	Manny Ramirez G	6.00
39	Greg Vaughn B	.10
40	Henry Rodriguez B	.10
41	Darryl Strawberry B	.10
42	Jim Thome G	2.00
43	Ryan Klesko S	.75
44	Jermaine Allensworth B	.10
45	Brian Jordan G	2.00
46	Tony Gwynn P	15.00
47	Rafael Palmeiro G	2.50
48	Dante Bichette S	.75
49	Ivan Rodriguez G	6.00
50	Mark McGwire G	20.00
51	Tim Salmon S	1.00
52	Roger Clemens B	.50
53	Matt Lawton B	.10
54	Wade Boggs S	1.50
55	Travis Fryman B	.10
56	Bobby Higginson S	.75
57	John Jaha S	.75
58	Rondell White S	.75
59	Tom Glavine S	1.00
60	Eddie Murray S	2.50
61	Vinny Castilla B	.10
62	Todd Hundley B	.10
63	Jay Buhner S	.75
64	Paul O'Neill B	.10
65	Steve Finley B	.10
66	Kevin Appier B	.10
67	Ray Durham B	.10
68	Dave Nilsson B	.10
69	Jeff Bagwell G	5.00
70	Al Martin S	.75
71	Paul Molitor G	5.00
72	Kevin Brown S	1.00
73	Ron Gant B	.10
74	Dwight Gooden B	.10
75	Quinton McCracken B	.10
76	Rusty Greer S	.75
77	Juan Guzman B	.10
78	Fred McGriff S	.75
79	Tino Martinez B	.10
80	Ray Lankford B	.10
81	Ken Caminiti G	2.00
82	James Baldwin B	.10
83	Jermaine Dye G	2.00
84	Mark Grace S	1.25
85	Pat Hentgen S	.75
86	Jason Giambi S	1.50
87	Brian Hunter B	.10
88	Andy Benes B	.10
89	Jose Rosado B	.10
90	Shawn Green B	.20
91	Jason Kendall B	.10
92	Alex Rodriguez P	20.00
93	Chipper Jones P	15.00
94	Barry Bonds G	7.50
95	Brady Anderson G	2.00
96	Ryne Sandberg S	2.50
97	Lance Johnson B	.10
98	Cal Ripken Jr. P	20.00
99	Craig Biggio S	.75
100	Dean Palmer B	.10
101	Gary Sheffield G	2.50
102	Johnny Damon B	.15
103	Mo Vaughn G	3.50
104	Randy Johnson S	1.50
105	Raul Mondesi S	.75
106	Roberto Alomar G	4.00
107	Mike Piazza P	15.00
108	Rey Ordonez B	.10
109	Barry Larkin G	2.00
110	Tony Clark S	.75
111	Bernie Williams S	2.00
112	John Smoltz G	2.50
113	Moises Alou B	.15
114	Will Clark B	.15
115	Sammy Sosa G	12.50
116	Jim Edmonds S	1.00
117	Jeff Conine B	.10
118	Joey Hamilton B	.10
119	Todd Hollandsworth B	.10
120	Troy Percival B	.10
121	Paul Wilson B	.10
122	Ken Hill B	.10
123	Mariano Rivera S	1.00
124	Eric Karros B	.10
125	Derek Jeter G	12.50
126	Eric Young S	.75
127	John Mabry B	.10
128	Gregg Jefferies B	.10
129	Ismael Valdes S	.75
130	Marty Cordova B	.10
131	Omar Vizquel B	.10
132	Mike Mussina S	2.00
133	Darin Erstad B	.25
134	Edgar Renteria S	.75
135	Billy Wagner B	.10
136	Alex Ochoa B	.10
137	Luis Castillo B	.10
138	Rocky Coppinger B	.10
139	Mike Sweeney B	.10
140	Michael Tucker B	.10
141	Chris Snopek B	.10
142	Dmitri Young S	.75
143	Andruw Jones P	12.00
144	Mike Cameron S	.75
145	Brant Brown B	.10
146	Todd Walker G	2.00
147	Nomar Garciaparra G	12.00
148	Glendon Rusch B	.10
149	Karim Garcia S	.75
150	*Bubba Trammell S*	1.50
151	Todd Greene B	.10
152	Wilton Guerrero G	2.00
153	Scott Spiezio B	.10
154	Brooks Kieschnick B	.10
155	Vladimir Guerrero G	12.00
156	*Brian Giles S*	5.00
157	Pokey Reese B	.10
158	Jason Dickson G	2.00
159	Kevin Orie S	.75
160	Scott Rolen G	5.00
161	Bartolo Colon S	.75
162	Shannon Stewart G	2.00
163	Wendell Magee B	.10
164	Jose Guillen S	1.75
165	Bob Abreu S	.75
166	*Deivi Cruz B*	.25
167	Alex Rodriguez B (National Treasures)	3.00
168	Frank Thomas B (National Treasures)	1.00
169	Cal Ripken Jr. B (National Treasures)	3.00
170	Chipper Jones B (National Treasures)	2.00
171	Mike Piazza B (National Treasures)	2.00
172	Tony Gwynn S (National Treasures)	3.50
173	Juan Gonzalez B (National Treasures)	.25
174	Kenny Lofton S (National Treasures)	.75
175	Ken Griffey Jr. B (National Treasures)	5.00
176	Mark McGwire B (National Treasures)	4.00
177	Jeff Bagwell B (National Treasures)	.25
178	Paul Molitor S (National Treasures)	1.50
179	Andruw Jones B (National Treasures)	1.00
180	Manny Ramirez S (National Treasures)	2.00
181	Ken Caminiti S (National Treasures)	.75
182	Barry Bonds B (National Treasures)	.50
183	Mo Vaughn B (National Treasures)	.30
184	Derek Jeter B (National Treasures)	2.00
185	Barry Larkin S (National Treasures)	.75
186	Ivan Rodriguez B (National Treasures)	.25
187	Albert Belle S (National Treasures)	.75
188	John Smoltz S (National Treasures)	.75
189	Chuck Knoblauch S (National Treasures)	.75
190	Brian Jordan S (National Treasures)	.75
191	Gary Sheffield S (National Treasures)	.75
192	Jim Thome S (National Treasures)	2.00
193	Brady Anderson S (National Treasures)	.75
194	Hideo Nomo S (National Treasures)	1.50
195	Sammy Sosa S (National Treasures)	6.00
196	Greg Maddux B (National Treasures)	.60
197	Checklist (Vladimir Guerrero B)	.25
198	Checklist (Scott Rolen B)	.20

199	Checklist (Todd Walker B)	.10
200	Checklist m(Nomar Garciaparra B)	.50

1997 Donruss Preferred Tin Boxes

Twenty-five different players are featured on the lithographed steel boxes in which the "packs" of Donruss Preferred baseball were sold. Boxes measure about 5-1/4" x 9-1/4" x 5-3/8". Inside the removable lid is a serial number from within an edition of 1,200 (blue) or 299 (gold). The gold versions were a later, hobby-only release.

		MT
Complete Set, Blue (25):		100.00
Common Box:		3.00
Gold:		4X
1	Frank Thomas	6.00
2	Ken Griffey Jr.	10.00
3	Andruw Jones	4.50
4	Cal Ripken Jr.	10.00
5	Mike Piazza	7.50
6	Chipper Jones	7.50
7	Alex Rodriguez	7.50
8	Derek Jeter	7.50
9	Juan Gonzalez	4.00
10	Albert Belle	3.50
11	Tony Gwynn	4.50
12	Greg Maddux	4.00
13	Jeff Bagwell	3.50
14	Roger Clemens	4.50
15	Mark McGwire	10.00
16	Gary Sheffield	3.00
17	Manny Ramirez	3.50
18	Hideo Nomo	3.50
19	Kenny Lofton	3.00
20	Mo Vaughn	3.50
21	Ryne Sandberg	3.50
22	Barry Bonds	5.00
23	Sammy Sosa	4.50
24	John Smoltz	3.00
25	Ivan Rodriguez	3.50

1997 Donruss Preferred Tins

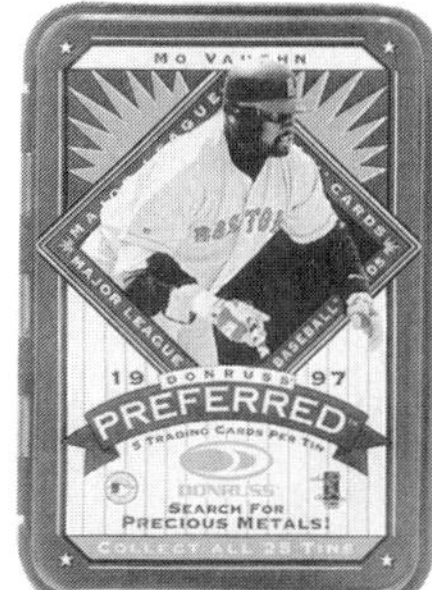

Twenty-five different players are featured on the lithographed steel tins which were the "packs" of Donruss Preferred baseball. The 3" x 4-1/2" x 5/8" tins are hinged along the left side and were produced in two versions. Predominantly blue tins are the standard package. A premium parallel version is gold-colored and serially numbered within an edition of 1,200. Gold tins were packed one per 24-pack box of Preferred. Values shown are for opened tins. Shrink-wrapped unopened tins are valued about 1.5-3X the figures shown.

		MT
Complete Set, Blue (25):		15.00
Common Tin:		.50
Gold: 6X		
1	Frank Thomas	1.00
2	Ken Griffey Jr.	1.50
3	Andruw Jones	1.00
4	Cal Ripken Jr.	1.50
5	Mike Piazza	1.25
6	Chipper Jones	1.25
7	Alex Rodriguez	1.50
8	Derek Jeter	1.25
9	Juan Gonzalez	.75
10	Albert Belle	.60
11	Tony Gwynn	1.00
12	Greg Maddux	.75
13	Jeff Bagwell	.60
14	Roger Clemens	.75
15	Mark McGwire	1.50
16	Gary Sheffield	.50
17	Manny Ramirez	.60
18	Hideo Nomo	.60
19	Kenny Lofton	.50
20	Mo Vaughn	.60
21	Ryne Sandberg	.60
22	Barry Bonds	.75
23	Sammy Sosa	1.00
24	John Smoltz	.50
25	Ivan Rodriguez	.60

1997 Donruss Preferred Cut To The Chase

Each of the cards in the Donruss Preferred series can also be found in this parallel set with die-cut borders, in the same bronze, silver, gold and platinum finishes. Multiplier values of the die-cuts are inverse to that usually found, with platinum cards the lowest, followed by gold, silver and bronze. Besides die-cutting, the chase cards feature a "CUT TO THE CHASE" designation at bottom.

	MT
Complete Set (200):	2000.
Common Bronze:	.50
Bronze Stars:	4X
Common Silver:	1.50
Silver Stars:	3X
Common Gold:	4.00
Gold Stars:	2X
Common Platinum:	10.00
Platinum Stars:	2X

(See 1997 Donruss Preferred for checklist and base card values.)

1997 Donruss Preferred Precious Metals

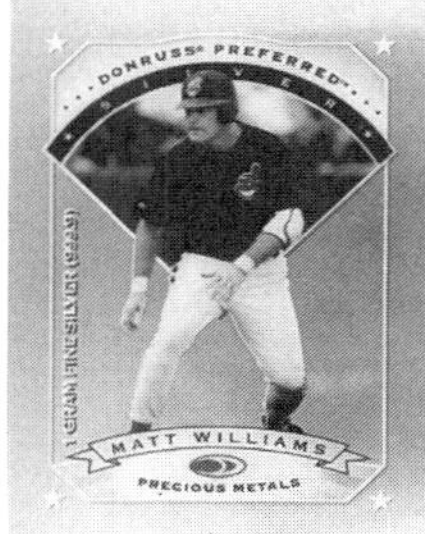

This 25-card partial parallel set features cards printed on actual silver, gold and platinum stock. Only 100 of each card were produced.

		MT
Complete Set (25):		850.00
Common Player:		12.50
1	Frank Thomas (P)	60.00
2	Ken Griffey Jr. (P)	100.00
3	Greg Maddux (P)	60.00
4	Albert Belle (G)	15.00
5	Juan Gonzalez (P)	30.00
6	Kenny Lofton (G)	12.50
7	Tony Gwynn (P)	65.00
8	Ivan Rodriguez (G)	20.00
9	Mark McGwire (G)	100.00
10	Matt Williams (S)	12.50
11	Wade Boggs (S)	25.00
12	Eddie Murray (S)	25.00
13	Jeff Bagwell (G)	20.00
14	Ken Caminiti (G)	12.50
15	Alex Rodriguez (P)	100.00
16	Chipper Jones (P)	75.00
17	Barry Bonds (G)	40.00
18	Cal Ripken Jr. (P)	100.00
19	Mo Vaughn (G)	17.50
20	Mike Piazza (P)	75.00
21	Derek Jeter (G)	75.00
22	Bernie Williams (S)	15.00
23	Andruw Jones (P)	30.00
24	Vladimir Guerrero (G)	20.00
25	Jose Guillen (S)	12.50

1997 Donruss Preferred Staremasters

A 20-card insert printed on foil stock and accented with holographic foil, Staremasters is designed to show up-close "game-face" photography. Each card is sequentially numbered to 1,500. Each of the Staremasters inserts can also be found in a version overprinted with a large diagonal black "SAMPLE" on front and back. These were distributed to dealers and the media. The sample cards have a "PROMO/1500" on back in place of a serial number.

		MT
Complete Set (20):		135.00
Common Player:		3.00
Samples: 25%		
1	Alex Rodriguez	12.50
2	Frank Thomas	10.00
3	Chipper Jones	12.50
4	Cal Ripken Jr.	15.00
5	Mike Piazza	12.50
6	Juan Gonzalez	5.00
7	Derek Jeter	12.50
8	Jeff Bagwell	7.50
9	Ken Griffey Jr.	15.00
10	Tony Gwynn	10.00
11	Barry Bonds	7.50
12	Albert Belle	3.00
13	Greg Maddux	10.00
14	Mark McGwire	15.00
15	Ken Caminiti	3.00
16	Hideo Nomo	5.00
17	Gary Sheffield	3.00
18	Andruw Jones	7.50
19	Mo Vaughn	3.50
20	Ivan Rodriguez	4.50

1997 Donruss Preferred X-Ponential Power

This 20-card die-cut insert contains two top hitters from 10 different teams. Placing the cards of teammates together forms an "X" shape. Cards are printed on thick plastic stock and gold holographic foil stamping and are sequentially numbered to 3,000.

		MT
Complete Set (20):		110.00
Common Player:		2.00
1A	Manny Ramirez	5.50
1B	Jim Thome	2.00
2A	Paul Molitor	4.00
2B	Chuck Knoblauch	2.00

3A	Ivan Rodriguez	3.50
3B	Juan Gonzalez	6.00
4A	Albert Belle	3.00
4B	Frank Thomas	9.00
5A	Roberto Alomar	4.00
5B	Cal Ripken Jr.	18.00
6A	Tim Salmon	2.00
6B	Jim Edmonds	2.00
7A	Ken Griffey Jr.	18.00
7B	Alex Rodriguez	15.00
8A	Chipper Jones	12.00
8B	Andruw Jones	7.00
9A	Mike Piazza	12.00
9B	Raul Mondesi	2.00
10A	Tony Gwynn	8.00
10B	Ken Caminiti	2.00

1997 Donruss Signature

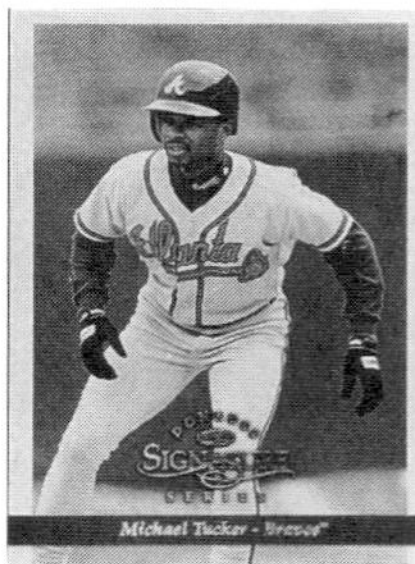

Donruss ventured in the autograph-per-pack market with this series featuring 100 base cards (unsigned) and various types and versions of authentically autographed cards. The suggested retail price for each five-card pack was $14.99. Base cards have textured silver-foil borders and highlights on front. Backs have a second photo and lengthy stats. A parallel insert edition of each base card was also issued. labeled "Platinum Press Proof", the parallels have blue metallic foil on front and are designated "1 of 150" on the back.

		MT
Complete Set (100):		30.00
Common Player:		.20
Pack (5):		15.00
Wax Box (12):		160.00
1	Mark McGwire	3.00
2	Kenny Lofton	.20
3	Tony Gwynn	2.00
4	Tony Clark	.20
5	Tim Salmon	.25
6	Ken Griffey Jr.	3.00
7	Mike Piazza	2.50
8	Greg Maddux	2.00
9	Roberto Alomar	.75
10	Andres Galarraga	.20
11	Roger Clemens	1.50
12	Bernie Williams	.50
13	Rondell White	.30
14	Kevin Appler	.20
15	Ray Lankford	.20
16	Frank Thomas	2.00
17	Will Clark	.35
18	Chipper Jones	2.50
19	Jeff Bagwell	1.00
20	Manny Ramirez	1.00
21	Ryne Sandberg	1.00
22	Paul Molitor	.80
23	Gary Sheffield	.20
24	Jim Edmonds	.20
25	Barry Larkin	.30
26	Rafael Palmeiro	.30
27	Alan Benes	.20
28	David Justice	.30
29	Randy Johnson	.60
30	Barry Bonds	1.50
31	Mo Vaughn	.50
32	Michael Tucker	.20
33	Larry Walker	.25
34	Tino Martinez	.20
35	Jose Guillen	.60
36	Carlos Delgado	.40
37	Jason Dickson	.20
38	Tom Glavine	.30
39	Raul Mondesi	.30
40	*Jose Cruz Jr.*	.75
41	Johnny Damon	.20
42	Mark Grace	.30
43	Juan Gonzalez	1.00
44	Vladimir Guerrero	1.50
45	Kevin Brown	.20
46	Justin Thompson	.20
47	Eric Young	.20
48	Ron Coomer	.20
49	Mark Kotsay	.20
50	Scott Rolen	.60
51	Derek Jeter	2.50
52	Jim Thome	.20
53	Fred McGriff	.20
54	Albert Belle	.40
55	Garret Anderson	.20
56	Wilton Guerrero	.20
57	Jose Canseco	.30
58	Cal Ripken Jr.	3.00
59	Sammy Sosa	2.00
60	Dmitri Young	.20
61	Alex Rodriguez	3.00
62	Javier Lopez	.20
63	Sandy Alomar Jr.	.20
64	Joe Carter	.20
65	Dante Bichette	.20
66	Al Martin	.20
67	Darin Erstad	.60
68	Pokey Reese	.20
69	Brady Anderson	.20
70	Andruw Jones	1.50
71	Ivan Rodriguez	.75
72	Nomar Garciaparra	1.50
73	Moises Alou	.25
74	Andy Pettitte	.50
75	Jay Buhner	.20
76	Craig Biggio	.20
77	Wade Boggs	.50
78	Shawn Estes	.20
79	Neifi Perez	.20
80	Rusty Greer	.20
81	Pedro Martinez	.40
82	Mike Mussina	.60
83	Jason Giambi	.40
84	Hideo Nomo	.50
85	Todd Hundley	.20
86	Deion Sanders	.25
87	Mike Cameron	.20
88	Bobby Bonilla	.20
89	Todd Greene	.20
90	Kevin Orie	.20
91	Ken Caminiti	.20
92	Chuck Knoblauch	.20
93	Matt Morris	.20
94	Matt Williams	.35
95	Pat Hentgen	.20
96	John Smoltz	.20
97	Edgar Martinez	.20
98	Jason Kendall	.20
99	Ken Griffey Jr.	1.50
100	Frank Thomas	.90

1997 Donruss Signature Platinum Press Proofs

This parallel insert set features metallic blue borders and graphics on front and has a "1 of 150" notation on back.

	MT
Complete Set (100):	650.00
Common Player:	3.00
Stars:	15-25X

(See 1997 Donruss Signature for checklist and base card prices.)

1997 Donruss Signature Autographs (Red)

The basic level of authentically autographed cards found one per ($15) pack in Donruss Signature is the unnumbered "red" version. Cards have the background of the front photo printed only in red. For most players, 3,900 cards of the red version were autographed for insertion. Some players, however, signed fewer reds. Exchange cards had to be issued for Raul Mondesi and Edgar Renteria, whose signed cards were not ready when the set was first issued. It has been reported that Mondesi never signed any of the red version autograph cards. Cards are checklisted here in alphabetical order, in concordance with the larger Millenium checklist. The reported number of red cards signed appears in parentheses. This list differs significantly from the original list announced by Donruss in Nov. 1997 due to last minute additions and deletions. Players signed in black and/or blue ink. Some players also added personal touches to some or all of their signatures, such as Bible verse citations, uniform numbers, etc.

		MT
Complete Set (116):		700.00
Common Player:		3.00
(1)	Jeff Abbott (3900)	3.00
(2)	Bob Abreu (3900)	4.50
(3)	Edgardo Alfonzo (3900)	6.00
(4)	Roberto Alomar (150)	55.00
(5)	Sandy Alomar Jr. (1400)	7.50
(6)	Moises Alou (900)	8.00
(7)	Garret Anderson (3900)	4.00
(8)	Andy Ashby (3900)	3.50
(10)	Trey Beamon (3900)	3.00
(12)	Alan Benes (3900)	3.00
(13)	Geronimo Berroa (3900)	3.00
(14)	Wade Boggs (150)	60.00
(18)	Kevin L. Brown (3900)	3.00
(20)	Brett Butler (1400)	9.00
(21)	Mike Cameron (3900)	3.00
(22)	Giovanni Carrara (2900)	3.00
(23)	Luis Castillo (3900)	3.00
(24)	Tony Clark (3900)	4.00
(25)	Will Clark (1400)	12.00
(27)	Lou Collier (3900)	3.00
(28)	Bartolo Colon (3900)	4.50
(29)	Ron Coomer (3900)	3.00
(30)	Marty Cordova (3900)	3.00
(31)	Jacob Cruz (3900)	3.50
(32)	Jose Cruz Jr. (900)	9.00
(33)	Russ Davis (3900)	3.00
(34)	Jason Dickson (3900)	3.50
(35)	Todd Dunwoody (3900)	3.00
(36)	Jermaine Dye (3900)	4.50
(37)	Jim Edmonds (3900)	9.00
(38)	Darin Erstad (900)	15.00
(39)	Bobby Estalella (3900)	4.50
(40)	Shawn Estes (3900)	3.00
(41)	Jeff Fassero (3900)	3.00
(42)	Andres Galarraga (900)	6.00
(43)	Karim Garcia (3900)	3.00
(45)	Derrick Gibson (3900)	3.00
(46)	Brian Giles (3900)	3.00
(47)	Tom Glavine (150)	30.00
(49)	Rick Gorecki (900)	4.50
(50)	Shawn Green (1900)	15.00
(51)	Todd Greene (3900)	3.50
(52)	Rusty Greer (3900)	3.00
(53)	Ben Grieve (3900)	3.00
(54)	Mark Grudzielanek (3900)	3.00
(55)	Vladimir Guerrero (1900)	25.00
(56)	Wilton Guerrero (2150)	3.00
(57)	Jose Guillen (2900)	4.50
(59)	Jeffrey Hammonds (2150)	3.50
(60)	Todd Helton (1400)	20.00
(61)	Todd Hollandsworth (2900)	4.00
(62)	Trenidad Hubbard (900)	3.50
(63)	Todd Hundley (1400)	6.00
(66)	Bobby Jones (3900)	3.00
(68)	Brian Jordan (1400)	6.00
(69)	David Justice (900)	9.00
(70)	Eric Karros (650)	9.00

(71) Jason Kendall (3900) 8.00
(72) Jimmy Key (3900) 4.50
(73) Brooks Kieschnick (3900) 3.00
(74) Ryan Klesko (225) 12.00
(76) Paul Konerko (3900) 4.00
(77) Mark Kotsay (2400) 4.50
(78) Ray Lankford (3900) 4.50
(79) Barry Larkin (150) 30.00
(80) Derrek Lee (3900) 4.00
(81) Esteban Loaiza (3900) 3.00
(82) Javier Lopez (1400) 6.00
(84) Edgar Martinez (150) 20.00
(85) Pedro Martinez (900) 35.00
(87) Rafael Medina (3900) 3.00
(88) Raul Mondesi (may not exist)
(88) Raul Mondesi (Exchange card) 3.00
(89) Matt Morris (3900) 9.00
(92) Paul O'Neill (900) 10.00
(93) Kevin Orie (3900) 3.00
(94) David Ortiz (3900) 3.00
(95) Rafael Palmeiro (900) 15.00
(96) Jay Payton (3900) 4.50
(97) Neifi Perez (3900) 3.00
(99) Manny Ramirez (900) 22.50
(100) Joe Randa (3900) 3.00
(101) Calvin Reese (3900) 3.00
(102) Edgar Renteria (?) 15.00
(102) Edgar Renteria (Exchange card) 3.00
(103) Dennis Reyes (3900) 3.00
(106) Henry Rodriguez (3900) 3.00
(108) Scott Rolen (1900) 10.00
(109) Kirk Rueter (2900) 3.00
(110) Ryne Sandberg (400) 60.00
(112) Dwight Smith (2900) 3.00
(113) J.T. Snow (900) 5.00
(114) Scott Spiezio (3900) 3.00
(115) Shannon Stewart (2900) 4.50
(116) Jeff Suppan (1900) 4.00
(117) Mike Sweeney (3900) 3.00
(118) Miguel Tejada (3900) 10.00
(121) Justin Thompson (2400) 3.50
(122) Brett Tomko (3900) 3.00
(123) Bubba Trammell (3900) 3.00
(124) Michael Tucker (3900) 3.00
(125) Javier Valentin (3900) 3.00
(126) Mo Vaughn (150) 20.00
(127) Robin Ventura (1400) 9.00
(128) Terrell Wade (3900) 3.00
(129) Billy Wagner (3900) 4.00
(130) Larry Walker (900) 8.00
(131) Todd Walker (2400) 5.00
(132) Rondell White (3900) 4.50
(133) Kevin Wickander (900) 4.50
(134) Chris Widger (3900) 3.00
(136) Matt Williams (150) 20.00
(137) Antone Williamson (3900) 3.00
(138) Dan Wilson (3900) 3.00
(139) Tony Womack (3900) 4.50
(140) Jaret Wright (3900) 4.50
(141) Dmitri Young (3900) 3.00
(142) Eric Young (3900) 3.00
(143) Kevin Young (3900) 3.00

1997 Donruss Signature Century Marks (Blue)

Only the top-name stars and rookies from the Signature series autograph line-up are included in the top level of scarcity. Virtually identical to the more common red and green (Millenium) versions, the Century Marks are identifiable at first glance by the use of blue ink in the background of the front photo and the "Century Marks" designation at top. On back, the cards are numbered from 0001 through 0100 in metallic foil at center. Several players initially had to be represented in the set by exchange cards. The unnumbered cards are checklisted here alphabetically, with the assigned card numbered keyed to the full 143-card issue in green.

	MT
Common Player:	20.00
(4) Roberto Alomar	50.00
(9) Jeff Bagwell	75.00
(11) Albert Belle	25.00
(14) Wade Boggs	50.00
(15) Barry Bonds	120.00
(19) Jay Buhner	20.00
(24) Tony Clark	20.00
(25) Will Clark	30.00
(26) Roger Clemens	150.00
(32) Jose Cruz Jr.	20.00
(37) Jim Edmonds	25.00
(38) Darin Erstad	25.00
(42) Andres Galarraga	20.00
(44) Nomar Garciaparra (SP)	200.00
(48) Juan Gonzalez	40.00
(53) Ben Grieve	25.00
(55) Vladimir Guerrero	75.00
(57) Jose Guillen	25.00
(58) Tony Gwynn	120.00
(60) Todd Helton	60.00
(64) Derek Jeter	150.00
(65) Andruw Jones	40.00
(67) Chipper Jones	120.00
(69) David Justice	20.00
(74) Ryan Klesko	20.00
(75) Chuck Knoblauch	20.00
(76) Paul Konerko	20.00
(77) Mark Kotsay	20.00
(79) Barry Larkin	30.00
(83) Greg Maddux	150.00
(84) Edgar Martinez	20.00
(85) Pedro Martinez	100.00
(86) Tino Martinez	20.00
(88) Raul Mondesi	30.00
(88) Raul Mondesi (Exchange card)	5.00
(90) Eddie Murray	40.00
(90) Eddie Murray (Exchange card)	5.00
(91) Mike Mussina	35.00
(95) Rafael Palmeiro	30.00
(98) Andy Pettitte	25.00
(99) Manny Ramirez	60.00
(104) Cal Ripken Jr.	200.00
(105) Alex Rodriguez	175.00
(107) Ivan Rodriguez	75.00
(108) Scott Rolen	30.00
(110) Ryne Sandberg	75.00
(111) Gary Sheffield	30.00
(118) Miguel Tejada	30.00
(119) Frank Thomas	75.00
(120) Jim Thome	25.00
(120) Jim Thome (Exchange card)	5.00
(126) Mo Vaughn	30.00
(130) Larry Walker	30.00
(135) Bernie Williams	30.00
(136) Matt Williams	30.00
(140) Jaret Wright	20.00

1997 Donruss Signature Millennium Marks (Green)

One thousand cards of most of the players who signed Signature Autographs are found in an edition marked on front as "Millenium Marks". These cards are also distinguished by the use of green ink in the background of the front photo. On back, the cards have a silver-foil serial number between (generally) 0101-1,000. Some cards as noted in the alphabetical checklist here were produced in lower numbers. The MM autographs were a random insert among the one-per-pack autographed cards found in $15 packs of Donruss Signature. Packs carried exchange cards redeemable for autographed cards of Raul Mondesi, Edgar Renteria and Jim Thome. This checklist differs significantly from that released in Nov., 1997, by Donruss due to the last-minute addition, deletion and substitution of players. It is possible that cards exist of players not shown here.

	MT
Complete Set (143):	1450.
Common Player:	3.00
(1) Jeff Abbott	3.00
(2) Bob Abreu	4.50
(3) Edgardo Alfonzo	12.00
(4) Roberto Alomar	15.00
(5) Sandy Alomar Jr.	10.00
(6) Moises Alou	8.00
(7) Garret Anderson	4.50
(8) Andy Ashby	7.50
(9) Jeff Bagwell (400)	50.00
(10) Trey Beamon	3.00
(11) Albert Belle (400)	35.00
(12) Alan Benes	3.00
(13) Geronimo Berroa	3.00
(14) Wade Boggs	30.00
(15) Barry Bonds (400)	80.00
(16) Bobby Bonilla (900)	7.50
(17) Kevin Brown (900)	3.00
(18) Kevin L. Brown	10.00
(19) Jay Buhner (900)	6.00
(20) Brett Butler	7.50
(21) Mike Cameron	3.00
(22) Giovanni Carrara	3.00
(23) Luis Castillo	3.00
(24) Tony Clark	4.50
(25) Will Clark	15.00
(26) Roger Clemens (400)	75.00
(27) Lou Collier	3.00
(28) Bartolo Colon	10.00
(29) Ron Coomer	3.00
(30) Marty Cordova	3.00
(31) Jacob Cruz	3.00
(32) Jose Cruz Jr.	7.50
(33) Russ Davis	3.00
(34) Jason Dickson	7.50
(35) Todd Dunwoody	7.50
(36) Jermaine Dye	3.00
(37) Jim Edmonds	7.50
(38) Darin Erstad	15.00
(39) Bobby Estalella	3.00
(40) Shawn Estes	3.00
(41) Jeff Fassero	3.00
(42) Andres Galarraga	8.00
(43) Karim Garcia	4.50
(44) Nomar Garciaparra (650)	75.00
(45) Derrick Gibson	4.50
(46) Brian Giles	7.50
(47) Tom Glavine	15.00
(48) Juan Gonzalez (900)	25.00
(49) Rick Gorecki	3.00
(50) Shawn Green	20.00
(51) Todd Greene	7.50
(52) Rusty Greer	3.00
(53) Ben Grieve	15.00
(54) Mark Grudzielanek	3.00
(55) Vladimir Guerrero	20.00
(56) Wilton Guerrero	3.00
(57) Jose Guillen	10.00
(58) Tony Gwynn (900)	35.00
(59) Jeffrey Hammonds	3.00
(60) Todd Helton	10.00
(61) Todd Hollandsworth	3.00
(62) Trenidad Hubbard	3.00
(63) Todd Hundley	6.00
(64) Derek Jeter (400)	100.00
(65) Andruw Jones (900)	15.00
(66) Bobby Jones	3.00
(67) Chipper Jones	45.00
(68) Brian Jordan	7.50
(69) David Justice	9.00
(70) Eric Karros	6.00
(71) Jason Kendall	7.50
(72) Jimmy Key	3.00
(73) Brooks Kieschnick	3.00
(74) Ryan Klesko	3.00
(75) Chuck Knoblauch (900)	10.00
(76) Paul Konerko	4.50
(77) Mark Kotsay	6.00
(78) Ray Lankford	3.00
(79) Barry Larkin	9.00
(80) Derrek Lee	4.50
(81) Esteban Loaiza	3.00
(82) Javy Lopez	8.00
(83) Greg Maddux (400)	75.00
(84) Edgar Martinez	6.00
(85) Pedro Martinez	25.00
(86) Tino Martinez (900)	9.00
(87) Rafael Medina	3.00
(88) Raul Mondesi	10.00
(88) Raul Mondesi (Exchange card)	3.00

(89)	Matt Morris	3.00
(90)	Eddie Murray (900)	25.00
(91)	Mike Mussina (900)	12.00
(92)	Paul O'Neill	10.00
(93)	Kevin Orie	3.00
(94)	David Ortiz	3.00
(95)	Rafael Palmeiro	12.00
(96)	Jay Payton	4.50
(97)	Neifi Perez	3.00
(98)	Andy Petitte (900)	9.00
(99)	Manny Ramirez	15.00
(100)	Joe Randa	3.00
(101)	Calvin Reese	3.00
(102)	Edgar Renteria	10.00
(102)	Edgar Renteria (Exchange card)	3.00
(103)	Dennis Reyes	3.00
(104)	Cal Ripken Jr. (400)	150.00
(105)	Alex Rodriguez (400)	100.00
(106)	Henry Rodriguez	4.50
(107)	Ivan Rodriguez (900)	20.00
(108)	Scott Rolen	25.00
(109)	Kirk Rueter	3.00
(110)	Ryne Sandberg	35.00
(111)	Gary Sheffield (400)	25.00
(112)	Dwight Smith	3.00
(113)	J.T. Snow	7.50
(114)	Scott Spiezio	3.00
(115)	Shannon Stewart	3.00
(116)	Jeff Suppan	3.00
(117)	Mike Sweeney	3.00
(118)	Miguel Tejada	15.00
(119)	Frank Thomas (400)	75.00
(120)	Jim Thome (900)	10.00
(120)	Jim Thome (Exchange card)	3.00
(121)	Justin Thompson	3.00
(122)	Brett Tomko	3.00
(123)	Bubba Trammell	4.50
(124)	Michael Tucker	3.00
(125)	Javier Valentin	3.00
(126)	Mo Vaughn	15.00
(127)	Robin Ventura	10.00
(128)	Terrell Wade	3.00
(129)	Billy Wagner	8.00
(130)	Larry Walker	12.00
(131)	Todd Walker	6.00
(132)	Rondell White	7.50
(133)	Kevin Wickander	3.00
(134)	Chris Widger	3.00
(135)	Bernie Williams (400)	25.00
(136)	Matt Williams	12.00
(137)	Antone Williamson	3.00
(138)	Dan Wilson	3.00
(139)	Tony Womack	3.00
(140)	Jaret Wright	6.00
(141)	Dmitri Young	3.00
(142)	Eric Young	6.00
(143)	Kevin Young	3.00

1997 Donruss Signature Notable Nicknames

Current and former players whose nicknames are instantly recognized are featured in this Signature Series insert. The autographs are generally enhanced by the appearance of those nicknames, though Roger Clemens omitted "The Rocket" from many of his cards. Backs have a serial number from within an edition of 200 of each card.

		MT
Complete Set (13):		950.00
Common Player:		50.00
(1)	Ernie Banks (Mr. Cub)	100.00
(2)	Tony Clark (The Tiger)	50.00
(3)	Roger Clemens (The Rocket)	150.00
(4)	Reggie Jackson (Mr. October)	125.00
(5)	Randy Johnson (Big Unit)	100.00
(6)	Stan Musial (The Man)	150.00
(7)	Ivan Rodriguez (Pudge)	100.00
(8)	Frank Thomas (The Big Hurt)	125.00
(9)	Mo Vaughn (Hit Dog)	100.00
(10)	Billy Wagner (The Kid)	50.00

1997 Donruss Signature Significant Signatures

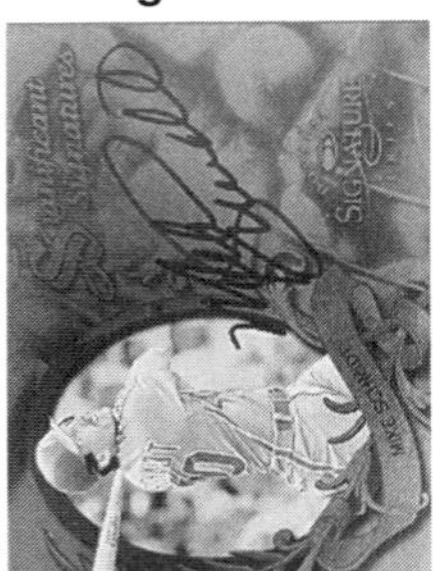

Retired superstars from the early 1960s through the mid 1990s are featured in this insert series. Cards are horizontal in format with color photos on front and back. Generally autographed on front, each card is serially numbered on back from within an edition of 2,000. The unnumbered cards are listed here in alphabetical order.

		MT
Complete Set (22):		750.00
Common Player:		25.00
(1)	Ernie Banks	45.00
(2)	Johnny Bench	55.00
(3)	Yogi Berra	45.00
(4)	George Brett	65.00
(5)	Lou Brock	25.00
(6)	Rod Carew	25.00
(7)	Steve Carlton	25.00
(8)	Larry Doby	25.00
(9)	Carlton Fisk	30.00
(10)	Bob Gibson	25.00
(11)	Reggie Jackson	50.00
(12)	Al Kaline	25.00
(13)	Harmon Killebrew	25.00
(14)	Don Mattingly	65.00
(15)	Stan Musial	65.00
(16)	Jim Palmer	25.00
(17)	Brooks Robinson	35.00
(18)	Frank Robinson	25.00
(19)	Mike Schmidt	65.00
(20)	Tom Seaver	35.00
(21)	Duke Snider	25.00
(22)	Carl Yastrzemski	45.00

1997 Donruss VXP 1.0 CDs

One of the earliest attempts to bring baseball cards into the computer age was Donruss "VXP 1.0 CD ROM" trading cards. Retailed, with 10 special-series player cards for about $10, the 4" x 2-3/4" "card" is a CD with player portrait and action photos on front. The CD was sold in a cardboard folder with the player's picture on front and instructions for use inside. CDs feature player stats, action footage and other interactive elements.

		MT
Complete Set (6):		16.00
Common Player:		3.00
(1)	Ken Griffey Jr.	4.00
(2)	Greg Maddux	3.00
(3)	Mike Piazza	3.00
(4)	Cal Ripken Jr.	4.00
(5)	Alex Rodriguez	4.00
(6)	Frank Thomas	3.00

1997 Donruss VXP 1.0

This set was issued to accompany the hobby's first major effort to bring baseball cards into the computer age. The standard-format cards have motion-variable portrait and action photos on front and another photo on back. Cards were sold in packs of 10 with one of six CD ROMs for about $10.

		MT
Complete Set (50):		17.50
Common Player:		.25
1	Darin Erstad	.60
2	Jim Thome	.25
3	Alex Rodriguez	1.75
4	Greg Maddux	1.00
5	Scott Rolen	.60
6	Roberto Alomar	.25
7	Tony Clark	.25
8	Randy Johnson	.50
9	Sammy Sosa	1.00
10	Jose Guillen	.25
11	Cal Ripken Jr.	2.00
12	Paul Molitor	.75
13	Jose Cruz Jr.	.25
14	Barry Larkin	.25
15	Ken Caminiti	.25
16	Rafael Palmeiro	.35
17	Chuck Knoblauch	.25
18	Juan Gonzalez	.75
19	Larry Walker	.35
20	Tony Gwynn	1.00
21	Brady Anderson	.25
22	Derek Jeter	1.25
23	Rusty Greer	.25
24	Gary Sheffield	.25
25	Barry Bonds	1.25
26	Mo Vaughn	.40
27	Tino Martinez	.25
28	Ivan Rodriguez	.40
29	Jeff Bagwell	.40
30	Tim Salmon	.25
31	Nomar Garciaparra	1.00
32	Bernie Williams	.25
33	Kenny Lofton	.25
34	Mike Piazza	1.50
35	Jim Edmonds	.25
36	Frank Thomas	1.25
37	Andy Pettitte	.25
38	Andruw Jones	.60
39	Raul Mondesi	.30
40	John Smoltz	.25
41	Albert Belle	.30
42	Mark McGwire	2.00
43	Chipper Jones	1.50
44	Hideo Nomo	.45
45	David Justice	.25
46	Manny Ramirez	.40
47	Ken Griffey Jr.	2.00
48	Roger Clemens	.75
49	Vladimir Guerrero	.60
50	Ryne Sandberg	.50

1998 Donruss

This 170-card set includes 155 regular player cards, the 10-card Fan Club subset and five checklists. The cards have color photos and the player's name listed at the bottom. The backs have a horizontal layout with stats and a biography on the left and another photo on the right. The base set is paralleled twice. Silver Press Proofs is a silver foil and die-cut parallel numbered "1 of 1,500." Gold Press Proofs is die-cut, has gold foil and is numbered "1 of 500." The inserts are Crusade, Diamond Kings, Longball Leaders, Production Line and Rated Rookies.

	MT
Complete Set (420):	45.00
Complete Series 1 (170):	20.00
Complete Update 2 (250):	25.00
Common Player:	.10
Pack (10):	1.75
Wax Box (24):	35.00

No.	Player	MT
1	Paul Molitor	.50
2	Juan Gonzalez	.75
3	Darryl Kile	.15
4	Randy Johnson	.40
5	Tom Glavine	.15
6	Pat Hentgen	.10
7	David Justice	.20
8	Kevin Brown	.15
9	Mike Mussina	.60
10	Ken Caminiti	.10
11	Todd Hundley	.10
12	Frank Thomas	1.50
13	Ray Lankford	.10
14	Justin Thompson	.10
15	Jason Dickson	.10
16	Kenny Lofton	.10
17	Ivan Rodriguez	.60
18	Pedro Martinez	.40
19	Brady Anderson	.10
20	Barry Larkin	.15
21	Chipper Jones	2.00
22	Tony Gwynn	1.50
23	Roger Clemens	1.00
24	Sandy Alomar Jr.	.10
25	Tino Martinez	.10
26	Jeff Bagwell	.90
27	Shawn Estes	.10
28	Ken Griffey Jr.	2.50
29	Javier Lopez	.10
30	Denny Neagle	.10
31	Mike Piazza	2.00
32	Andres Galarraga	.10
33	Larry Walker	.20
34	Alex Rodriguez	2.50
35	Greg Maddux	1.50
36	Albert Belle	.25
37	Barry Bonds	1.25
38	Mo Vaughn	.25
39	Kevin Appier	.10
40	Wade Boggs	.35
41	Garret Anderson	.10
42	Jeffrey Hammonds	.10
43	Marquis Grissom	.10
44	Jim Edmonds	.15
45	Brian Jordan	.10
46	Raul Mondesi	.15
47	John Valentin	.10
48	Brad Radke	.15
49	Ismael Valdes	.10
50	Matt Stairs	.10
51	Matt Williams	.15
52	Reggie Jefferson	.10
53	Alan Benes	.10
54	Charles Johnson	.10
55	Chuck Knoblauch	.10
56	Edgar Martinez	.10
57	Nomar Garciaparra	1.25
58	Craig Biggio	.10
59	Bernie Williams	.30
60	David Cone	.10
61	Cal Ripken Jr.	2.50
62	Mark McGwire	2.50
63	Roberto Alomar	.45
64	Fred McGriff	.10
65	Eric Karros	.10
66	Robin Ventura	.15
67	Darin Erstad	.35
68	Michael Tucker	.10
69	Jim Thome	.10
70	Mark Grace	.25
71	Lou Collier	.10
72	Karim Garcia	.10
73	Alex Fernandez	.10
74	J.T. Snow	.10
75	Reggie Sanders	.10
76	John Smoltz	.10
77	Tim Salmon	.15
78	Paul O'Neill	.10
79	Vinny Castilla	.10
80	Rafael Palmeiro	.15
81	Jaret Wright	.25
82	Jay Buhner	.10
83	Brett Butler	.10
84	Todd Greene	.10
85	Scott Rolen	.90
86	Sammy Sosa	2.00
87	Jason Giambi	.25
88	Carlos Delgado	.20
89	Deion Sanders	.15
90	Wilton Guerrero	.10
91	Andy Pettitte	.30
92	Brian Giles	.10
93	Dmitri Young	.10
94	Ron Coomer	.10
95	Mike Cameron	.10
96	Edgardo Alfonzo	.20
97	Jimmy Key	.10
98	Ryan Klesko	.10
99	Andy Benes	.10
100	Derek Jeter	2.00
101	Jeff Fassero	.10
102	Neifi Perez	.10
103	Hideo Nomo	.35
104	Andruw Jones	.90
105	Todd Helton	.30
106	Livan Hernandez	.15
107	Brett Tomko	.10
108	Shannon Stewart	.10
109	Bartolo Colon	.15
110	Matt Morris	.15
111	Miguel Tejada	.30
112	Pokey Reese	.10
113	Fernando Tatis	.15
114	Todd Dunwoody	.10
115	Jose Cruz Jr.	.25
116	Chan Ho Park	.15
117	Kevin Young	.10
118	Rickey Henderson	.35
119	Hideki Irabu	.15
120	Francisco Cordova	.10
121	Al Martin	.10
122	Tony Clark	.15
123	Curt Schilling	.15
124	Rusty Greer	.10
125	Jose Canseco	.25
126	Edgar Renteria	.10
127	Todd Walker	.15
128	Wally Joyner	.10
129	Bill Mueller	.10
130	Jose Guillen	.30
131	Manny Ramirez	.75
132	Bobby Higginson	.10
133	Kevin Orie	.10
134	Will Clark	.20
135	Dave Nilsson	.10
136	Jason Kendall	.10
137	Ivan Cruz	.10
138	Gary Sheffield	.15
139	Bubba Trammell	.15
140	Vladimir Guerrero	.90
141	Dennis Reyes	.10
142	Bobby Bonilla	.10
143	Ruben Rivera	.10
144	Ben Grieve	.30
145	Moises Alou	.20
146	Tony Womack	.10
147	Eric Young	.10
148	Paul Konerko	.15
149	Dante Bichette	.10
150	Joe Carter	.10
151	Rondell White	.15
152	Chris Holt	.10
153	Shawn Green	.25
154	Mark Grudzielanek	.10
155	Jermaine Dye	.10
156	Ken Griffey Jr. (Fan Club)	1.00
157	Frank Thomas (Fan Club)	.60
158	Chipper Jones (Fan Club)	.75
159	Mike Piazza (Fan Club)	.75
160	Cal Ripken Jr. (Fan Club)	1.00
161	Greg Maddux (Fan Club)	.60
162	Juan Gonzalez (Fan Club)	.35
163	Alex Rodriguez (Fan Club)	1.00
164	Mark McGwire (Fan Club)	1.00
165	Derek Jeter (Fan Club)	.75
166	Larry Walker CL	.10
167	Tony Gwynn CL	.75
168	Tino Martinez CL	.10
169	Scott Rolen CL	.25
170	Nomar Garciaparra CL	.45
171	Mike Sweeney	.10
172	Dustin Hermanson	.10
173	Darren Dreifort	.10
174	Ron Gant	.10
175	Todd Hollandsworth	.10
176	John Jaha	.10
177	Kerry Wood	.35
178	Chris Stynes	.10
179	Kevin Elster	.10
180	Derek Bell	.10
181	Darryl Strawberry	.10
182	Damion Easley	.10
183	Jeff Cirillo	.10
184	John Thomson	.10
185	Dan Wilson	.10
186	Jay Bell	.10
187	Bernard Gilkey	.10
188	Marc Valdes	.10
189	Ramon Martinez	.10
190	Charles Nagy	.10
191	Derek Lowe	.10
192	Andy Benes	.10
193	Delino DeShields	.10
194	*Ryan Jackson*	.30
195	Kenny Lofton	.10
196	Chuck Knoblauch	.10
197	Andres Galarraga	.10
198	Jose Canseco	.25
199	John Olerud	.15
200	Lance Johnson	.10
201	Darryl Kile	.15
202	Luis Castillo	.10
203	Joe Carter	.10
204	Dennis Eckersley	.15
205	Steve Finley	.10
206	Esteban Loaiza	.10
207	*Ryan Christenson*	.25
208	Deivi Cruz	.10
209	Mariano Rivera	.15
210	*Mike Judd*	.25
211	Billy Wagner	.10
212	Scott Spiezio	.10
213	Russ Davis	.10
214	Jeff Suppan	.10
215	Doug Glanville	.10
216	Dmitri Young	.10
217	Rey Ordonez	.10
218	Cecil Fielder	.10
219	*Masato Yoshii*	.50
220	Raul Casanova	.10
221	*Rolando Arrojo*	.30
222	Ellis Burks	.10
223	Butch Huskey	.10
224	Brian Hunter	.10
225	Marquis Grissom	.10
226	Kevin Brown	.15
227	Joe Randa	.10
228	Henry Rodriguez	.10
229	Omar Vizquel	.10
230	Fred McGriff	.10
231	Matt Williams	.15
232	Moises Alou	.20
233	Travis Fryman	.10
234	Wade Boggs	.35
235	Pedro Martinez	.50
236	Rickey Henderson	.35
237	Bubba Trammell	.10
238	Mike Caruso	.10
239	Wilson Alvarez	.10
240	Geronimo Berroa	.10
241	Eric Milton	.10
242	Scott Erickson	.10
243	*Todd Erdos*	.15
244	Bobby Hughes	.10
245	Dave Hollins	.10
246	Dean Palmer	.10
247	Carlos Baerga	.10
248	Jose Silva	.10
249	*Jose Cabrera*	.25
250	Tom Evans	.10
251	Marty Cordova	.10
252	*Hanley Frias*	.10
253	Javier Valentin	.10
254	Mario Valdez	.10
255	Joey Cora	.10
256	Mike Lansing	.10
257	Jeff Kent	.10
258	*David Dellucci*	.25
259	*Curtis King*	.10
260	David Segui	.10
261	Royce Clayton	.10
262	Jeff Blauser	.10
263	*Manny Aybar*	.25
264	*Mike Cather*	.15
265	Todd Zeile	.10
266	Richard Hidalgo	.10
267	Dante Powell	.10
268	*Mike DeJean*	.10
269	Ken Cloude	.10
270	Danny Klassen	.15
271	Sean Casey	.25
272	A.J. Hinch	.25
273	*Rich Butler*	.20
274	*Ben Ford*	.10
275	Billy McMillon	.10
276	Wilson Delgado	.10
277	Orlando Cabrera	.10
278	Geoff Jenkins	.10
279	Enrique Wilson	.10
280	Derrek Lee	.10
281	*Marc Pisciotta*	.10
282	Abraham Nunez	.20
283	Aaron Boone	.10
284	Brad Fullmer	.15
285	*Rob Stanifer*	.15
286	Preston Wilson	.10
287	Greg Norton	.10
288	Bobby Smith	.10
289	Josh Booty	.10
290	Russell Branyan	.10
291	Jeremi Gonzalez	.10
292	Michael Coleman	.10
293	Cliff Politte	.10
294	Eric Ludwick	.10
295	Rafael Medina	.10
296	Jason Varitek	.10
297	Ron Wright	.10
298	Mark Kotsay	.15
299	David Ortiz	.10
300	*Frank Catalanotto*	.20
301	Robinson Checo	.10
302	*Kevin Millwood*	2.00
303	Jacob Cruz	.10
304	Javier Vazquez	.10
305	*Magglio Ordonez*	1.50
306	Kevin Witt	.10
307	Derrick Gibson	.10
308	Shane Monahan	.10
309	Brian Rose	.10
310	Bobby Estalella	.10
311	Felix Heredia	.10
312	Desi Relaford	.10
313	*Esteban Yan*	.20
314	Ricky Ledee	.10
315	*Steve Woodard*	.25
316	Pat Watkins	.10
317	Damian Moss	.10
318	Bob Abreu	.10
319	Jeff Abbott	.10
320	Miguel Cairo	.10
321	*Rigo Beltran*	.10
322	Tony Saunders	.10
323	Randall Simon	.10
324	Hiram Bocachica	.10
325	Richie Sexson	.10
326	Karim Garcia	.10
327	*Mike Lowell*	.50
328	Pat Cline	.10
329	Matt Clement	.10
330	Scott Elarton	.10
331	*Manuel Barrios*	.10
332	Bruce Chen	.10
333	Juan Encarnacion	.10
334	Travis Lee	.15
335	Wes Helms	.10
336	*Chad Fox*	.10
337	Donnie Sadler	.10
338	*Carlos Mendoza*	.30
339	Damian Jackson	.10
340	*Julio Ramirez*	.40
341	*John Halama*	.30
342	Edwin Diaz	.10
343	Felix Martinez	.10
344	Eli Marrero	.10
345	Carl Pavano	.10
346	Vladimir Guerrero (Hit List)	.30
347	Barry Bonds (Hit List)	.75
348	Darin Erstad (Hit List)	.25
349	Albert Belle (Hit List)	.15
350	Kenny Lofton (Hit List)	.10

351	Mo Vaughn (Hit List)	.15
352	Jose Cruz Jr. (Hit List)	.25
353	Tony Clark (Hit List)	.10
354	Roberto Alomar (Hit List)	.15
355	Manny Ramirez (Hit List)	.50
356	Paul Molitor (Hit List)	.20
357	Jim Thome (Hit List)	.10
358	Tino Martinez (Hit List)	.10
359	Tim Salmon (Hit List)	.10
360	David Justice (Hit List)	.10
361	Raul Mondesi (Hit List)	.10
362	Mark Grace (Hit List)	.10
363	Craig Biggio (Hit List)	.10
364	Larry Walker (Hit List)	.10
365	Mark McGwire (Hit List)	1.00
366	Juan Gonzalez (Hit List)	.25
367	Derek Jeter (Hit List)	.75
368	Chipper Jones (Hit List)	.75
369	Frank Thomas (Hit List)	.50
370	Alex Rodriguez (Hit List)	1.00
371	Mike Piazza (Hit List)	.75
372	Tony Gwynn (Hit List)	.75
373	Jeff Bagwell (Hit List)	.50
374	Nomar Garciaparra (Hit List)	.75
375	Ken Griffey Jr. (Hit List)	1.00
376	Livan Hernandez (Untouchables)	.10
377	Chan Ho Park (Untouchables)	.10
378	Mike Mussina (Untouchables)	.25
379	Andy Pettitte (Untouchables)	.10
380	Greg Maddux (Untouchables)	.60
381	Hideo Nomo (Untouchables)	.25
382	Roger Clemens (Untouchables)	.60
383	Randy Johnson (Untouchables)	.25
384	Pedro Martinez (Untouchables)	.25
385	Jaret Wright (Untouchables)	.10
386	Ken Griffey Jr. (Spirit of the Game)	1.00
387	Todd Helton (Spirit of the Game)	.10
388	Paul Konerko (Spirit of the Game)	.10
389	Cal Ripken Jr. (Spirit of the Game)	1.00
390	Larry Walker (Spirit of the Game)	.10
391	Ken Caminiti (Spirit of the Game)	.10
392	Jose Guillen (Spirit of the Game)	.10
393	Jim Edmonds (Spirit of the Game)	.10
394	Barry Larkin (Spirit of the Game)	.10
395	Bernie Williams (Spirit of the Game)	.15
396	Tony Clark (Spirit of the Game)	.10
397	Jose Cruz Jr. (Spirit of the Game)	.15
398	Ivan Rodriguez (Spirit of the Game)	.15
399	Darin Erstad (Spirit of the Game)	.15
400	Scott Rolen (Spirit of the Game)	.40
401	Mark McGwire (Spirit of the Game)	1.00
402	Andruw Jones (Spirit of the Game)	.40
403	Juan Gonzalez (Spirit of the Game)	.40
404	Derek Jeter (Spirit of the Game)	.75
405	Chipper Jones (Spirit of the Game)	.75
406	Greg Maddux (Spirit of the Game)	.75
407	Frank Thomas (Spirit of the Game)	.50
408	Alex Rodriguez (Spirit of the Game)	1.00
409	Mike Piazza (Spirit of the Game)	.75
410	Tony Gwynn (Spirit of the Game)	.75
411	Jeff Bagwell (Spirit of the Game)	.40
412	Nomar Garciaparra (Spirit of the Game)	.75
413	Hideo Nomo (Spirit of the Game)	.25
414	Barry Bonds (Spirit of the Game)	.65
415	Ben Grieve (Spirit of the Game)	.15
416	Checklist (Barry Bonds)	.40
417	Checklist (Mark McGwire)	1.00
418	Checklist (Roger Clemens)	.40
419	Checklist (Livan Hernandez)	.10
420	Checklist (Ken Griffey Jr.)	.75

1998 Donruss Silver Press Proofs

Silver Press Proofs paralleled all 420 cards in the Donruss and Donruss Update Baseball. Cards featured silver foil stamping and a die-cut top right corner. Backs had a silver tint and were numbered "1 of 1500" in the bottom left corner.

	MT
Complete Set (420):	300.00
Common Player:	1.00
Stars/RCs:	4X
Production 1,500 sets	

(See 1998 Donruss for checklist and base card values.)

1998 Donruss Gold Press Proofs

All 420 cards in Donruss and Donruss Update were also issued in Gold Press Proofs. These cards were die-cut on the top right corner and contained gold foil stamping. Backs featured a gold tint and "1 of 500" was printed in black in the bottome left corner.

	MT
Complete Set (420):	500.00
Common Player:	2.00
Stars/RCs:	8X
Production 500 sets	

(See 1998 Donruss for checklist and base card values.)

1998 Donruss Crusade

This 100-card insert was included in 1998 Donruss (40 cards), Leaf (30) and Donruss Update (30). The cards use refractive technology and the background features heraldic-style lions. The cards are sequentially numbered to 250. Crusade Purple (numbered to 100) and Red (25) parallels were also inserted in the three products.

		MT
Complete Set, Green (40):		475.00
Common Player:		5.00
Production: 250 sets		
Purples (100 sets):		1.5X
Reds (25 sets):		6X
5	Jason Dickson	5.00
6	Todd Greene	7.50
7	Roberto Alomar	15.00
8	Cal Ripken Jr.	75.00
12	Mo Vaughn	20.00
13	Nomar Garciaparra	40.00
16	Mike Cameron	7.50
20	Sandy Alomar Jr.	7.50
21	David Justice	10.00
25	Justin Thompson	5.00
27	Kevin Appier	5.00
33	Tino Martinez	5.00
36	Hideki Irabu	7.50
37	Jose Canseco	12.50
39	Ken Griffey Jr.	75.00
42	Edgar Martinez	5.00
45	Will Clark	7.50
47	Rusty Greer	5.00
50	Shawn Green	17.50
51	Jose Cruz Jr.	7.50
52	Kenny Lofton	7.50
53	Chipper Jones	45.00
62	Kevin Orie	5.00
65	Deion Sanders	7.50
67	Larry Walker	7.50
68	Dante Bichette	7.50
71	Todd Helton	20.00
74	Bobby Bonilla	5.00
75	Kevin Brown	7.50
78	Craig Biggio	7.50
82	Wilton Guerrero	5.00
85	Pedro Martinez	20.00
86	Edgardo Alfonzo	7.50
88	Scott Rolen	17.50
89	Francisco Cordova	5.00
90	Jose Guillen	10.00
92	Ray Lankford	5.00
93	Mark McGwire	75.00
94	Matt Morris	9.00
100	Shawn Estes	5.00

1998 Donruss Diamond Kings

Diamond Kings is a 20-card insert featuring a painted portrait by Dan Gardiner. Backs have a ghosted image of the portrait with a player biography and the card's number overprinted. A total of 10,000 sets were produced with the first 500 of each card printed on canvas. A Frank Thomas sample card was also created.

		MT
Complete Set (20):		100.00
Common Player:		2.50
Production 9,500 sets		
Canvas (1st 500 sets):		3X
1	Cal Ripken Jr.	12.50
2	Greg Maddux	8.00
3	Ivan Rodriguez	5.00
4	Tony Gwynn	6.50
5	Paul Molitor	4.00
6	Kenny Lofton	2.50
7	Andy Pettitte	2.50
8	Darin Erstad	5.00
9	Randy Johnson	4.00
10	Derek Jeter	10.00
11	Hideo Nomo	4.00
12	David Justice	2.50
13	Bernie Williams	2.50
14	Roger Clemens	6.50
15	Barry Larkin	2.50
16	Andruw Jones	5.00
17	Mike Piazza	10.00
18	Frank Thomas	8.00
18s	Frank Thomas (sample)	4.00
19	Alex Rodriguez	12.50
20	Ken Griffey Jr.	12.50

1998 Donruss Longball Leaders

Longball Leaders features 24 top home run hitters. The right border features a home run meter with zero at the bottom, 61 at the top and the player's 1997

home run total marked. Each card is sequentially numbered to 5,000.

		MT
Complete Set (24):		90.00
Common Player:		1.00
Production 5,000 sets		
1	Ken Griffey Jr.	15.00
2	Mark McGwire	15.00
3	Tino Martinez	1.00
4	Barry Bonds	5.00
5	Frank Thomas	7.50
6	Albert Belle	2.00
7	Mike Piazza	10.00
8	Chipper Jones	10.00
9	Vladimir Guerrero	5.00
10	Matt Williams	1.50
11	Sammy Sosa	9.00
12	Tim Salmon	1.00
13	Raul Mondesi	1.00
14	Jeff Bagwell	5.00
15	Mo Vaughn	2.00
16	Manny Ramirez	4.00
17	Jim Thome	1.00
18	Jim Edmonds	1.00
19	Tony Clark	1.00
20	Nomar Garciaparra	7.50
21	Juan Gonzalez	5.00
22	Scott Rolen	2.00
23	Larry Walker	2.00
24	Andres Galarraga	1.00

1998 Donruss Production Line-ob

This 20-card insert is printed on holographic foil board. Inserted in magazine packs, this insert features player's with a high on-base percentage in 1997. Each player's card is sequentially numbered to his on-base percentage from that season. The card back has a player photo and a list of the 20 players with their stat.

		MT
Complete Set (20):		225.00
Common Player:		3.50
1	Frank Thomas (456)	17.50
2	Edgar Martinez (456)	3.50
3	Barry Bonds (446)	20.00
4	Barry Larkin (440)	3.50
5	Mike Piazza (431)	25.00
6	Jeff Bagwell (425)	15.00
7	Gary Sheffield (424)	3.50
8	Mo Vaughn (420)	7.50
9	Craig Biggio (415)	3.50
10	Kenny Lofton (409)	3.50
11	Tony Gwynn (409)	25.00
12	Bernie Williams (408)	5.00
13	Rusty Greer (405)	3.50
14	Brady Anderson (393)	3.50
15	Mark McGwire (393)	40.00
16	Chuck Knoblauch (390)	3.50
17	Roberto Alomar (390)	7.50
18	Ken Griffey Jr. (382)	40.00
19	Chipper Jones (371)	30.00
20	Derek Jeter (370)	30.00

1998 Donruss Production Line-pi

This 20-card insert was printed on holographic board. The set features players with a high power index from 1997. Each card is sequentially numbered to that player's power index from that season.

		MT
Complete Set (20):		130.00
Common Player:		2.50
1	Larry Walker (1,172)	3.00
2	Mike Piazza (1,070)	15.00
3	Frank Thomas (1,067)	10.00
4	Mark McGwire (1,039)	20.00
5	Barry Bonds (1,031)	10.00
6	Ken Griffey Jr. (1,028)	20.00
7	Jeff Bagwell (1,017)	7.50
8	David Justice (1,013)	2.50
9	Jim Thome (1,001)	3.00
10	Mo Vaughn (980)	4.00
11	Tony Gwynn (957)	12.50
12	Manny Ramirez (953)	7.50
13	Bernie Williams (952)	3.00
14	Tino Martinez (948)	2.50
15	Brady Anderson (863)	2.50
16	Chipper Jones (850)	15.00
17	Scott Rolen (846)	4.00
18	Alex Rodriguez (846)	20.00
19	Vladimir Guerrero (833)	5.00
20	Albert Belle (823)	4.00

1998 Donruss Production Line-sg

This 20-card insert was printed on holographic board. It featured players with high slugging percentages in 1997. Each card is sequentially numbered to the player's slugging percentage from that season.

		MT
Complete Set (20):		285.00
Common Player:		5.00
1	Larry Walker (720)	5.00
2	Ken Griffey Jr. (646)	45.00
3	Mark McGwire (646)	45.00
4	Mike Piazza (638)	30.00
5	Frank Thomas (611)	25.00
6	Jeff Bagwell (592)	15.00
7	Juan Gonzalez (589)	15.00
8	Andres Galarraga (585)	5.00
9	Barry Bonds (585)	20.00
10	Jim Thome (579)	5.00
11	Tino Martinez (577)	5.00
12	Mo Vaughn (560)	7.50
13	Raul Mondesi (541)	5.00
14	Manny Ramirez (538)	15.00
15	Nomar Garciaparra (534)	30.00
16	Tim Salmon (517)	5.00
17	Tony Clark (500)	5.00
18	Jose Cruz Jr. (499)	6.00
19	Alex Rodriguez (496)	45.00
20	Cal Ripken Jr. (402)	45.00

1998 Donruss Rated Rookies

This 30-card insert features top young players. The fronts have a color player photo in front of a stars and stripes background, with "Rated Rookies" and the player's name printed on the right. The backs have another photo, basic player information and career highlights. A rare (250 each) Medalist version is micro-etched on gold holographic foil.

		MT
Complete Set (30):		35.00
Common Player:		1.00
Medalists (250 sets):		5X
1	Mark Kotsay	2.00
2	Neifi Perez	1.00
3	Paul Konerko	1.50
4	Jose Cruz Jr.	1.50
5	Hideki Irabu	1.25
6	Mike Cameron	1.00
7	Jeff Suppan	1.00
8	Kevin Orie	1.00
9	Pokey Reese	1.00
10	Todd Dunwoody	1.00
11	Miguel Tejada	2.50
12	Jose Guillen	1.50
13	Bartolo Colon	1.50
14	Derrek Lee	1.00
15	Antone Williamson	1.00
16	Wilton Guerrero	1.00
17	Jaret Wright	2.00
18	Todd Helton	2.50
19	Shannon Stewart	1.00
20	Nomar Garciaparra	7.50
21	Brett Tomko	1.00
22	Fernando Tatis	1.25
23	Raul Ibanez	1.00
24	Dennis Reyes	1.00
25	Bobby Estalella	1.00
26	Lou Collier	1.00
27	Bubba Trammell	1.00
28	Ben Grieve	2.50
29	Ivan Cruz	1.00
30	Karim Garcia	1.00

1998 Donruss Update Crusade

This 30-card insert is continued from 1998 Donruss and Leaf baseball sets. Each card features a color action photo in front of a Medieval background. The player's name and background are green and each card is serial numbered to 250. Purple (numbered to 100) and Red (25) parallel versions were also created. Crusade is a 130-card cross-brand insert with 40 cards included in 1998 Donruss and 30 each in 1998 Leaf and Leaf Rookies & Stars.

		MT
Complete Set, Green (30):		375.00
Common Player:		5.00
Production 250 sets		
Purples (100 sets):		1.5X
Reds (25 sets):		4X
1	Tim Salmon	7.50
2	Garret Anderson	5.00
9	Rafael Palmeiro	15.00
10	Brady Anderson	5.00
14	Frank Thomas	40.00
17	Robin Ventura	7.50
22	Matt Williams	7.50
23	Tony Clark	5.00
29	Chuck Knoblauch	5.00
31	Bernie Williams	15.00
32	Derek Jeter	60.00
38	Jason Giambi	20.00
43	Jay Buhner	5.00
44	Juan Gonzalez	25.00
49	Carlos Delgado	20.00
55	Greg Maddux	45.00
57	Tom Glavine	7.50
60	Mark Grace	15.00
61	Sammy Sosa	45.00
63	Barry Larkin	7.50
69	Neifi Perez	5.00
72	Gary Sheffield	6.50
77	Jeff Bagwell	25.00
80	Raul Mondesi	5.00
81	Hideo Nomo	9.00
83	Rondell White	6.50
84	Vladimir Guerrero	25.00
87	Todd Hundley	5.00
96	Brian Jordan	5.00
99	Barry Bonds	35.00

1998 Donruss Update Dominators

This 30-card insert features color player photos and holographic foil.

		MT
Complete Set (30):		100.00
Common Player:		1.50
Approx: 1:12		
1	Roger Clemens	5.00
2	Tony Clark	1.50
3	Darin Erstad	3.00
4	Jeff Bagwell	4.00
5	Ken Griffey Jr.	10.00
6	Andruw Jones	3.00
7	Juan Gonzalez	3.00
8	Ivan Rodriguez	3.00
9	Randy Johnson	2.50
10	Tino Martinez	1.50
11	Mark McGwire	10.00
12	Chuck Knoblauch	1.50
13	Jim Thome	1.50
14	Alex Rodriguez	10.00
15	Hideo Nomo	2.00
16	Jose Cruz Jr.	2.00
17	Chipper Jones	7.50
18	Tony Gwynn	6.00
19	Barry Bonds	4.00
20	Mo Vaughn	2.00
21	Cal Ripken Jr.	10.00
22	Greg Maddux	6.00
23	Manny Ramirez	2.50
24	Andres Galarraga	1.50
25	Vladimir Guerrero	3.00
26	Albert Belle	2.00
27	Nomar Garciaparra	5.00
28	Kenny Lofton	1.50
29	Mike Piazza	7.50
30	Frank Thomas	5.00

1998 Donruss Update Elite

This 20-card insert features color player photos in a diamond-shaped border at the top with the Elite Series logo and player's name at the bottom. The fronts have a cream-colored border.

		MT
Complete Set (20):		90.00
Common Player:		3.00
Production 2,500 sets		
1	Jeff Bagwell	3.00
2	Andruw Jones	3.00
3	Ken Griffey Jr.	10.00
4	Derek Jeter	7.50
5	Juan Gonzalez	4.00
6	Mark McGwire	10.00
7	Ivan Rodriguez	3.00
8	Paul Molitor	3.00
9	Hideo Nomo	4.00
10	Mo Vaughn	3.00
11	Chipper Jones	7.50
12	Nomar Garciaparra	6.00
13	Mike Piazza	7.50
14	Frank Thomas	5.00
15	Greg Maddux	6.00
16	Cal Ripken Jr.	10.00
17	Alex Rodriguez	10.00
18	Scott Rolen	3.00
19	Barry Bonds	5.00
20	Tony Gwynn	6.00

1998 Donruss Update FANtasy Team

This 20-card set features the top vote getters from the Donruss online Fan Club ballot box. The top ten make up the 1st Team FANtasy Team and are sequentially numbered to 2,000. The other players are included in the 2nd Team FANtasy Team and are numbered to 4,000. The first 250 cards of each player are die-cut. The front of the cards feature a color photo inside a stars and stripes border.

		MT
Complete Set (20):		90.00
Common Player (1-10) (1,750 sets):		4.00
Common Player (11-20) (3,750 sets):		2.00
Die-Cuts (250 each):		3X
1	Frank Thomas	7.50
2	Ken Griffey Jr.	15.00
3	Cal Ripken Jr.	15.00
4	Jose Cruz Jr.	4.00
5	Travis Lee	3.00
6	Greg Maddux	10.00
7	Alex Rodriguez	15.00
8	Mark McGwire	15.00
9	Chipper Jones	12.50
10	Andruw Jones	5.00
11	Mike Piazza	9.00
12	Tony Gwynn	6.00
13	Larry Walker	2.00
14	Nomar Garciaparra	6.00
15	Jaret Wright	3.00
16	Livan Hernandez	2.00
17	Roger Clemens	6.50
18	Derek Jeter	9.00
19	Scott Rolen	4.00
20	Jeff Bagwell	5.00

1998 Donruss Update Rookie Diamond Kings

The Rookie Diamond Kings insert features color portraits by artist Dan Gardiner of young players inside a golden border. Player identification and Rookie Diamond Kings logo are at the bottom. Each card is sequentially numbered to 10,000 with the first 500 printed on canvas.

		MT
Complete Set (12):		35.00
Common Player:		2.00
Production 9,500 sets		
Canvas (500 sets):		3X
1	Travis Lee	3.00
2	Fernando Tatis	2.00
3	Livan Hernandez	2.00
4	Todd Helton	5.00
5	Derrek Lee	2.00
6	Jaret Wright	5.00
7	Ben Grieve	5.00
8	Paul Konerko	2.00
9	Jose Cruz Jr.	3.00
10	Mark Kotsay	3.00
11	Todd Greene	2.00
12	Brad Fullmer	3.00

1998 Donruss Update Sony MLB 99

This 20-card set promotes the MLB '99 game for Sony PlayStation systems. The card front has a color player photo with a red border on two sides. The Donruss, PlayStation and MLB '99 logos appear on the front as well. The backs have a MLB '99 Tip and instructions on entering the PlayStation MLB '99 Sweepstakes.

		MT
Complete Set (20):		4.00
Common Player:		.10
1	Cal Ripken Jr.	.75
2	Nomar Garciaparra	.40
3	Barry Bonds	.50
4	Mike Mussina	.20
5	Pedro Martinez	.20
6	Derek Jeter	.50
7	Andruw Jones	.25
8	Kenny Lofton	.10
9	Gary Sheffield	.10
10	Raul Mondesi	.10
11	Jeff Bagwell	.25
12	Tim Salmon	.10
13	Tom Glavine	.10
14	Ben Grieve	.15
15	Matt Williams	.10
16	Juan Gonzalez	.25
17	Mark McGwire	.75
18	Bernie Williams	.10
19	Andres Galarraga	.10
20	Jose Cruz Jr.	.15

1998 Donruss Elite

Donruss Elite consists of a 150-card base set with two parallels and five inserts. The base cards feature a foil background with player photo on front. Another photo is on the back with stats and basic player information. The Aspirations parallel is numbered to 750 and the Status parallel is numbered to 100. The base set also includes the 30-card Generations subset and three checklists. The inserts are Back to the Future, Back to the Future Autographs, Craftsmen, Prime Numbers and Prime Numbers Die-Cuts.

		MT
Complete Set (150):		20.00
Common Player:		.15
Pack (5):		4.00
Wax Box (18):		60.00
1	Ken Griffey Jr.	3.00
2	Frank Thomas	2.00
3	Alex Rodriguez	3.00
4	Mike Piazza	2.50
5	Greg Maddux	2.00
6	Cal Ripken Jr.	3.00
7	Chipper Jones	2.50
8	Derek Jeter	2.50
9	Tony Gwynn	2.00
10	Andruw Jones	.75
11	Juan Gonzalez	.75
12	Jeff Bagwell	.60
13	Mark McGwire	3.00
14	Roger Clemens	1.50
15	Albert Belle	.25
16	Barry Bonds	1.50
17	Kenny Lofton	.15
18	Ivan Rodriguez	.50
19	Manny Ramirez	.75
20	Jim Thome	.20
21	Chuck Knoblauch	.15
22	Paul Molitor	.60
23	Barry Larkin	.25
24	Andy Pettitte	.40
25	John Smoltz	.15
26	Randy Johnson	.50
27	Bernie Williams	.40
28	Larry Walker	.25
29	Mo Vaughn	.40
30	Bobby Higginson	.15
31	Edgardo Alfonzo	.20
32	Justin Thompson	.15
33	Jeff Suppan	.15
34	Roberto Alomar	.40
35	Hideo Nomo	.50
36	Rusty Greer	.15
37	Tim Salmon	.25
38	Jim Edmonds	.15
39	Gary Sheffield	.25
40	Ken Caminiti	.15
41	Sammy Sosa	2.00
42	Tony Womack	.15
43	Matt Williams	.25
44	Andres Galarraga	.15
45	Garret Anderson	.15
46	Rafael Palmeiro	.25

47	Mike Mussina	.50
48	Craig Biggio	.15
49	Wade Boggs	.35
50	Tom Glavine	.25
51	Jason Giambi	.35
52	Will Clark	.25
53	David Justice	.25
54	Sandy Alomar Jr.	.15
55	Edgar Martinez	.15
56	Brady Anderson	.15
57	Eric Young	.15
58	Ray Lankford	.15
59	Kevin Brown	.25
60	Raul Mondesi	.25
61	Bobby Bonilla	.15
62	Javier Lopez	.15
63	Fred McGriff	.15
64	Rondell White	.25
65	Todd Hundley	.15
66	Mark Grace	.35
67	Alan Benes	.15
68	Jeff Abbott	.15
69	Bob Abreu	.15
70	Deion Sanders	.20
71	Tino Martinez	.15
72	Shannon Stewart	.15
73	Homer Bush	.15
74	Carlos Delgado	.50
75	Raul Ibanez	.15
76	Hideki Irabu	.15
77	Jose Cruz Jr.	.50
78	Tony Clark	.15
79	Wilton Guerrero	.15
80	Vladimir Guerrero	.75
81	Scott Rolen	.75
82	Nomar Garciaparra	2.00
83	Darin Erstad	.50
84	Chan Ho Park	.25
85	Mike Cameron	.15
86	Todd Walker	.25
87	Todd Dunwoody	.15
88	Neifi Perez	.15
89	Brett Tomko	.15
90	Jose Guillen	.40
91	Matt Morris	.20
92	Bartolo Colon	.20
93	Jaret Wright	.30
94	Shawn Estes	.15
95	Livan Hernandez	.15
96	Bobby Estalella	.15
97	Ben Grieve	.30
98	Paul Konerko	.25
99	David Ortiz	.25
100	Todd Helton	.50
101	Juan Encarnacion	.30
102	Bubba Trammell	.15
103	Miguel Tejada	.75
104	Jacob Cruz	.15
105	Todd Greene	.15
106	Kevin Orie	.15
107	Mark Kotsay	.25
108	Fernando Tatis	.25
109	Jay Payton	.20
110	Pokey Reese	.15
111	Derrek Lee	.15
112	Richard Hidalgo	.20
113	Ricky Ledee	.25
114	Lou Collier	.15
115	Ruben Rivera	.15
116	Shawn Green	.25
117	Moises Alou	.25
118	Ken Griffey Jr. (Generations)	1.50
119	Frank Thomas (Generations)	1.00
120	Alex Rodriguez (Generations)	1.50
121	Mike Piazza (Generations)	1.25
122	Greg Maddux (Generations)	1.00
123	Cal Ripken Jr. (Generations)	1.50
124	Chipper Jones (Generations)	1.25
125	Derek Jeter (Generations)	1.25
126	Tony Gwynn (Generations)	1.00
127	Andruw Jones (Generations)	.75
128	Juan Gonzalez (Generations)	.50
129	Jeff Bagwell (Generations)	.75
130	Mark McGwire (Generations)	1.50
131	Roger Clemens (Generations)	.75
132	Albert Belle (Generations)	.25
133	Barry Bonds (Generations)	.75
134	Kenny Lofton (Generations)	.15
135	Ivan Rodriguez (Generations)	.35
136	Manny Ramirez (Generations)	.40
137	Jim Thome (Generations)	.15
138	Chuck Knoblauch (Generations)	.15
139	Paul Molitor (Generations)	.35
140	Barry Larkin (Generations)	.15
141	Mo Vaughn (Generations)	.25
142	Hideki Irabu (Generations)	.15
143	Jose Cruz Jr. (Generations)	.25
144	Tony Clark (Generations)	.15
145	Vladimir Guerrero (Generations)	.75
146	Scott Rolen (Generations)	.75
147	Nomar Garciaparra (Generations)	1.00
148	Checklist (Nomar Garciaparra) (Hit Streaks)	.50
149	Checklist (Larry Walker) (Long HR-Coors)	.15
150	Checklist (Tino Martinez) (3 HR in game)	.15

1998 Donruss Elite Aspirations

A parallel edition of 750 of each player are found in this die-cut set. Cards have a scalloped treatment cut into the top and sides and red, rather than silver metallic borders. The word "ASPIRATIONS" in printed on front at bottom-right. Backs have the notation "1 of 750".

	MT
Complete Set (150):	100.00
Common Player:	.75
Stars and rookies:	4X

(See 1998 Donruss Elite for checklist and base card values.)

1998 Donruss Elite Status

Just 100 serially numbered cards of each player are found in this die-cut parallel set. Cards have a scalloped treatment cut into the top and sides and red, rather than silver metallic borders.

	MT
Complete Set (150):	600.00
Common Player:	3.00
Stars and rookies:	20X

(See 1998 Donruss Elite for checklist and base card values.)

1998 Donruss Elite Back to the Future

These double-front cards feature a veteran or retired star on one side and a young player on the other. Each player's name, team and "Back to the Future" are printed in the border. The cards are numbered to 1,500, with the first 100 of each card signed by both players. Exceptions are cards #1 and #6. Ripken and Konerko did not sign the same cards and Frank Thomas did not sign his Back to the Future card. Thomas instead signed 100 copies of his Elite base set card which was specially marked.

		MT
Complete Set (8):		110.00
Common Player:		7.50
Production 1,400 sets		
1	Cal Ripken Jr., Paul Konerko	22.50
2	Jeff Bagwell, Todd Helton	10.00
3	Eddie Mathews, Chipper Jones	20.00
4	Juan Gonzalez, Ben Grieve	10.00
5	Hank Aaron, Jose Cruz Jr.	15.00
6	Frank Thomas, David Ortiz	7.50
7	Nolan Ryan, Greg Maddux	25.00
8	Alex Rodriguez, Nomar Garciaparra	25.00

1998 Donruss Elite Back to the Future Autographs

The first 100 of each card in the Back to the Future insert was autographed by both players. Exceptions are cards #1 and #6. Ripken and Konerko did not sign the same cards and Frank Thomas did not sign his Back to the Future card. Thomas instead signed 100 specially marked copies of his Elite base-set card.

		MT
Production 100 sets		
1a	Paul Konerko	25.00
1b	Cal Ripken Jr.	200.00
2	Jeff Bagwell, Todd Helton	175.00
3	Eddie Mathews, Chipper Jones	200.00
4	Juan Gonzalez, Ben Grieve	175.00
5	Hank Aaron, Jose Cruz Jr.	200.00
6	NOT ISSUED IN AUTOGRAPHED FORM	
7	Nolan Ryan, Greg Maddux	500.00
8	Alex Rodriguez, Nomar Garciaparra	300.00
2	Frank Thomas (Specially autographed Elite)	75.00

1998 Donruss Elite Craftsmen

This 30-card insert has color player photos on the front and back. The set is sequentially numbered to 3,500. The Master Craftsmen parallel is numbered to 100.

		MT
Complete Set (30):		70.00
Common Player:		1.00
Production 3,500 sets		
Master Craftsman (100 sets):		3X
1	Ken Griffey Jr.	6.00
2	Frank Thomas	4.00
3	Alex Rodriguez	6.00
4	Cal Ripken Jr.	6.00
5	Greg Maddux	4.00
6	Mike Piazza	4.50
7	Chipper Jones	4.50
8	Derek Jeter	4.50
9	Tony Gwynn	4.00
10	Nomar Garciaparra	4.00
11	Scott Rolen	2.50
12	Jose Cruz Jr.	1.25

13 Tony Clark 1.00
14 Vladimir Guerrero 2.50
15 Todd Helton 1.50
16 Ben Grieve 2.00
17 Andruw Jones 2.50
18 Jeff Bagwell 2.50
19 Mark McGwire 6.00
20 Juan Gonzalez 2.00
21 Roger Clemens 4.00
22 Albert Belle 1.00
23 Barry Bonds 2.50
24 Kenny Lofton 1.00
25 Ivan Rodriguez 1.50
26 Paul Molitor 1.50
27 Barry Larkin (incorrect "CARDINALS" on front) 1.00
28 Mo Vaughn 1.50
29 Larry Walker 1.50
30 Tino Martinez 1.00

1998 Donruss Elite Prime Numbers

This 36-card insert includes three cards for each of 12 players. Each card has a single number in the background. The three numbers for each player represent a key statistic for the player (ex. Mark McGwire's cards are 3-8-7; his career home run total at the time was 387). Each card in the set is sequentially numbered. The total is dependent upon the player's statistic.

MT
Common Player: 7.50
1A Ken Griffey Jr. 2 (94) 60.00
1B Ken Griffey Jr. 9 (204) 30.00
1C Ken Griffey Jr. 4 (290) 25.00
2A Frank Thomas 4 (56) 40.00
2B Frank Thomas 5 (406) 10.00
2C Frank Thomas 6 (450) 10.00
3A Mark McGwire 3 (87) 60.00
3B Mark McGwire 8 (307) 30.00
3C Mark McGwire 7 (380) 30.00
4A Cal Ripken Jr. 5 (17) 200.00
4B Cal Ripken Jr. 1 (507) 20.00
4C Cal Ripken Jr. 7 (510) 20.00
5A Mike Piazza 5 (76) 45.00
5B Mike Piazza 7 (506) 15.00
5C Mike Piazza 6 (570) 15.00
6A Chipper Jones 4 (89) 35.00
6B Chipper Jones 8 (409) 10.00
6C Chipper Jones 9 (480) 10.00
7A Tony Gwynn 3 (72) 40.00
7B Tony Gwynn 7 (302) 15.00
7C Tony Gwynn 2 (370) 15.00
8A Barry Bonds 3 (74) 30.00
8B Barry Bonds 7 (304) 12.50
8C Barry Bonds 4 (370) 12.50
9A Jeff Bagwell 4 (25) 60.00
9B Jeff Bagwell 2 (405) 10.00
9C Jeff Bagwell 5 (420) 10.00
10A Juan Gonzalez 5 (89) 30.00
10B Juan Gonzalez 8 (509) 7.50
10C Juan Gonzalez 9 (580) 7.50
11A Alex Rodriguez 5 (34) 75.00
11B Alex Rodriguez 3 (504) 15.00
11C Alex Rodriguez 4 (530) 15.00
12A Kenny Lofton 3 (54) 20.00
12B Kenny Lofton 5 (304) 7.50
12C Kenny Lofton 4 (350) 7.50

1998 Donruss Elite Prime Numbers Die-Cuts

This set is a die-cut parallel of the Prime Numbers insert. Each card is sequentially numbered. The production run for each player is the number featured on his first card times 100, his second card times 10 and his third card is sequentially numbered to the number featured on the card.

MT
Common Player: 7.50
1A Ken Griffey Jr. 2 (200) 40.00
1B Ken Griffey Jr. 9 (90) 70.00
1C Ken Griffey Jr. 4 (4) 250.00
2A Frank Thomas 4 (400) 12.50
2B Frank Thomas 5 (50) 40.00
2C Frank Thomas 6 (6) 125.00
3A Mark McGwire 3 (300) 35.00
3B Mark McGwire 8 (80) 100.00
3C Mark McGwire 7 (7) 225.00
4A Cal Ripken Jr. 5 (500) 25.00
4B Cal Ripken Jr. 1 (10) 175.00
4C Cal Ripken Jr. 7 (7) 200.00
5A Mike Piazza 5 (500) 20.00
5B Mike Piazza 7 (70) 50.00
5C Mike Piazza 6 (6) 125.00
6A Chipper Jones 4 (400) 12.50
6B Chipper Jones 8 (80) 50.00
6C Chipper Jones 9 (9) 100.00
7A Tony Gwynn 3 (300) 17.50
7B Tony Gwynn 7 (70) 45.00
7C Tony Gwynn 2 (2) 300.00
8A Barry Bonds 3 (300) 17.50
8B Barry Bonds 7 (70) 40.00
8C Barry Bonds 4 (4) 175.00
9A Jeff Bagwell 4 (400) 7.50
9B Jeff Bagwell 2 (20) 50.00
9C Jeff Bagwell 5 (5) 100.00
10A Juan Gonzalez 5 (500) 7.50
10B Juan Gonzalez 8 (80) 30.00
10C Juan Gonzalez 9 (9) 100.00
11A Alex Rodriguez 5 (500) 15.00
11B Alex Rodriguez 3 (30) 110.00
11C Alex Rodriguez 4 (4) 300.00
12A Kenny Lofton 3 (300) 7.50
12B Kenny Lofton 5 (50) 20.00
12C Kenny Lofton 4 (4) 60.00

1998 Donruss Preferred

The Donruss Preferred 200-card base set is broken down into five subsets: 100 Grand Stand cards (5:1), 40 Mezzanine (1:6), 30 Club Level (1:12), 20 Field Box (1:23) and 10 Executive Suite (1:65). The base set is paralleled in the Preferred Seating set. Each subset has a different die-cut in the parallel. Inserts in this product include Great X-Pectations, Precious Metals and Title Waves.

MT
Complete Set (200): 450.00
Common Grand Stand (5:1): .10
Common Mezzanine (1:6): .75
Common Club Level (1:12): 1.00
Common Field Box: (1:23) 1.50
Common Executive Suite (1:65): 15.00
Pack (5): 4.00
Wax Box (24): 80.00
1 Ken Griffey Jr. EX 30.00
2 Frank Thomas EX 20.00
3 Cal Ripken Jr. EX 30.00
4 Alex Rodriguez EX 30.00
5 Greg Maddux EX 20.00
6 Mike Piazza EX 25.00
7 Chipper Jones EX 25.00
8 Tony Gwynn FB 15.00
9 Derek Jeter FB 15.00
10 Jeff Bagwell EX 10.00
11 Juan Gonzalez EX 12.50
12 Nomar Garciaparra EX 20.00
13 Andruw Jones FB 6.00
14 Hideo Nomo FB 5.00
15 Roger Clemens FB 10.00
16 Mark McGwire FB 30.00
17 Scott Rolen FB 6.00
18 Vladimir Guerrero FB 6.00
19 Barry Bonds FB 10.00
20 Darin Erstad FB 6.00
21 Albert Belle FB 4.50
22 Kenny Lofton FB 3.00
23 Mo Vaughn FB 5.00
24 Tony Clark FB 3.00
25 Ivan Rodriguez FB 6.00
26 Larry Walker CL 2.00
27 Eddie Murray CL 2.00
28 Andy Pettitte CL 4.00
29 Roberto Alomar CL 4.00
30 Randy Johnson CL 4.00
31 Manny Ramirez CL 5.00
32 Paul Molitor FB 6.00
33 Mike Mussina CL 4.00
34 Jim Thome FB 3.00
35 Tino Martinez CL 1.50
36 Gary Sheffield CL 2.50
37 Chuck Knoblauch CL 1.50
38 Bernie Williams CL 3.00
39 Tim Salmon CL 3.00
40 Sammy Sosa CL 6.00
41 Wade Boggs MZ 1.50
42 Will Clark GS .25
43 Andres Galarraga CL 1.50
44 Raul Mondesi CL 2.00
45 Rickey Henderson GS .25
46 Jose Canseco GS .25
47 Pedro Martinez GS .40
48 Jay Buhner GS .10
49 Ryan Klesko GS .10
50 Barry Larkin CL 2.00
51 Charles Johnson GS .10
52 Tom Glavine GS .20
53 Edgar Martinez CL 1.50
54 Fred McGriff GS .10
55 Moises Alou MZ .75
56 Dante Bichette GS .10
57 Jim Edmonds CL 1.50
58 Mark Grace MZ 1.50
59 Chan Ho Park MZ 1.25
60 Justin Thompson MZ .75
61 John Smoltz MZ 1.25
62 Craig Biggio CL 1.50
63 Ken Caminiti MZ 1.00
64 Deion Sanders MZ 1.00
65 Carlos Delgado GS .50
66 David Justice CL 2.00
67 J.T. Snow GS .10
68 Jason Giambi CL 3.00
69 Garret Anderson MZ .10
70 Rondell White MZ .75
71 Matt Williams MZ .85
72 Brady Anderson MZ .75
73 Eric Karros GS .10
74 Javier Lopez GS .10
75 Pat Hentgen GS .10
76 Todd Hundley GS .10
77 Ray Lankford GS .10
78 Denny Neagle GS .10
79 Henry Rodriguez GS .10
80 Sandy Alomar Jr. MZ .75
81 Rafael Palmeiro MZ 1.25
82 Robin Ventura GS .15
83 John Olerud GS .15
84 Omar Vizquel GS .10
85 Joe Randa GS .10
86 Lance Johnson GS .10
87 Kevin Brown GS .20
88 Curt Schilling GS .25
89 Ismael Valdes GS .10
90 Francisco Cordova GS .10
91 David Cone GS .10
92 Paul O'Neill GS .10
93 Jimmy Key GS .10

94	Brad Radke GS	.15
95	Kevin Appier GS	.10
96	Al Martin GS	.10
97	Rusty Greer MZ	.75
98	Reggie Jefferson GS	.10
99	Ron Coomer GS	.10
100	Vinny Castilla GS	.10
101	Bobby Bonilla MZ	.75
102	Eric Young GS	.10
103	Tony Womack GS	.10
104	Jason Kendall GS	.10
105	Jeff Suppan GS	.10
106	Shawn Estes MZ	.75
107	Shawn Green GS	.25
108	Edgardo Alfonzo MZ	.75
109	Alan Benes MZ	.75
110	Bobby Higginson GS	.10
111	Mark Grudzielanek GS	.10
112	Wilton Guerrero GS	.10
113	Todd Greene MZ	.75
114	Pokey Reese GS	.10
115	Jose Guillen CL	1.50
116	Neifi Perez MZ	.75
117	Luis Castillo GS	.10
118	Edgar Renteria GS	.10
119	Karim Garcia GS	.10
120	Butch Huskey GS	.10
121	Michael Tucker GS	.10
122	Jason Dickson GS	.10
123	Todd Walker MZ	1.25
124	Brian Jordan GS	.10
125	Joe Carter GS	.10
126	Matt Morris MZ	.85
127	Brett Tomko MZ	.75
128	Mike Cameron CL	1.50
129	Russ Davis GS	.10
130	Shannon Stewart MZ	.80
131	Kevin Orie GS	.10
132	Scott Spiezio GS	.10
133	Brian Giles GS	.10
134	Raul Casanova GS	.10
135	Jose Cruz Jr. CL	3.00
136	Hideki Irabu GS	.10
137	Bubba Trammell GS	.10
138	Richard Hidalgo CL	2.00
139	Paul Konerko CL	2.00
140	Todd Helton FB	4.00
141	Miguel Tejada CL	2.50
142	Fernando Tatis MZ	.75
143	Ben Grieve FB	4.00
144	Travis Lee FB	4.50
145	Mark Kotsay CL	2.00
146	Eli Marrero MZ	.75
147	David Ortiz CL	2.00
148	Juan Encarnacion MZ	.75
149	Jaret Wright MZ	2.50
150	Livan Hernandez CL	1.50
151	Ruben Rivera GS	.10
152	Brad Fullmer MZ	1.00
153	Dennis Reyes GS	.10
154	Enrique Wilson MZ	.75
155	Todd Dunwoody MZ	.75
156	Derrick Gibson MZ	.75
157	Aaron Boone MZ	.75
158	Ron Wright MZ	.75
159	Preston Wilson MZ	.85
160	Abraham Nunez GS	.15
161	Shane Monahan GS	.10
162	Carl Pavano GS	.25
163	Derrek Lee GS	.25
164	Jeff Abbott GS	.10
165	Wes Helms MZ	.10
166	Brian Rose GS	.10
167	Bobby Estalella GS	.10
168	Ken Griffey Jr. GS	2.00
169	Frank Thomas GS	1.00
170	Cal Ripken Jr. GS	2.00
171	Alex Rodriguez GS	2.00
172	Greg Maddux GS	1.00
173	Mike Piazza GS	1.50
174	Chipper Jones GS	1.50
175	Tony Gwynn GS	1.00
176	Derek Jeter GS	1.50
177	Jeff Bagwell GS	.50
178	Juan Gonzalez GS	.50
179	Nomar Garciaparra GS	1.00
180	Andruw Jones GS	.40
181	Hideo Nomo GS	.25
182	Roger Clemens GS	1.00
183	Mark McGwire GS	2.00
184	Scott Rolen GS	.40
185	Barry Bonds GS	.65
186	Darin Erstad GS	.40
187	Mo Vaughn GS	.30
188	Ivan Rodriguez GS	.45
189	Larry Walker MZ	2.00
190	Andy Pettitte GS	.25
191	Randy Johnson MZ	2.00
192	Paul Molitor GS	.30
193	Jim Thome GS	.10
194	Tino Martinez MZ	.75
195	Gary Sheffield GS	.20
196	Albert Belle GS	.30
197	Jose Cruz Jr. GS	.25
198	Todd Helton GS	.45
199	Ben Grieve GS	.30
200	Paul Konerko GS	.20

1998 Donruss Preferred Seating

Preferred Seating is a die-cut parallel of the base set. Each section of the base set has a different die-cut.

	MT
Common Grand Stand:	.50
Stars and Rookies:	5X
Common Mezzanine:	2.50
Stars and Rookies:	2X
Common Club Level:	4.00
Stars and Rookies:	2X
Common Field Box:	7.50
Stars and Rookies:	2X
Common Executive Suite:	20.00
Stars and Rookies:	2X

(See 1998 Donruss Preferred for checklist and base card values.)

1998 Donruss Preferred Tins

Donruss Preferred was packaged in collectible tins. Each tin contained five cards and featured one of 24 players on the top. Silver (numbered to 999) and gold (199) parallel tins were also produced and included in hobby-only boxes. The values shown are for empty tins.

		MT
Complete Set (24):		18.00
Common Player:		.25
Gold Tins (199):		5X
Silver Tins (999):		2X
1	Todd Helton	.50
2	Ben Grieve	.35
3	Cal Ripken Jr.	2.00
4	Alex Rodriguez	2.00
5	Greg Maddux	1.00
6	Mike Piazza	1.50
7	Chipper Jones	1.50
8	Travis Lee	.35
9	Derek Jeter	1.50
10	Jeff Bagwell	1.00
11	Juan Gonzalez	.75
12	Mark McGwire	2.00
13	Hideo Nomo	.75
14	Roger Clemens	1.00
15	Andruw Jones	.75
16	Paul Molitor	.75
17	Vladimir Guerrero	.75
18	Jose Cruz Jr.	.25
19	Nomar Garciaparra	1.00
20	Scott Rolen	.75
21	Ken Griffey Jr.	2.00
22	Larry Walker	.25
23	Frank Thomas	1.00
24	Tony Gwynn	1.00

1998 Donruss Preferred Tin Boxes

The boxes for 1998 Donruss Preferred consisted of a lithographed steel lidded box which contained 24 tin packs. The basic tin box was green in color and individually serial numbered to 999. A parallel gold box issue was randomly inserted in Preferred cases and had boxes numbered to 199. Values shown are for empty boxes.

		MT
Complete Set (24):		100.00
Common Player:		2.00
Gold:		2X
1	Todd Helton	3.50
2	Ben Grieve	3.00
3	Cal Ripken Jr.	10.00
4	Alex Rodriguez	10.00
5	Greg Maddux	6.00
6	Mike Piazza	7.50
7	Chipper Jones	7.50
8	Travis Lee	2.00
9	Derek Jeter	7.50
10	Jeff Bagwell	5.00
11	Juan Gonzalez	5.00
12	Mark McGwire	10.00
13	Hideo Nomo	4.00
14	Roger Clemens	5.00
15	Andruw Jones	4.00
16	Paul Molitor	3.50
17	Vladimir Guerrero	4.00
18	Jose Cruz Jr.	2.50
19	Nomar Garciaparra	6.00
20	Scott Rolen	4.00
21	Ken Griffey Jr.	10.00
22	Larry Walker	2.00
23	Frank Thomas	5.00
24	Tony Gwynn	6.00

1998 Donruss Preferred Double-Wide Tins

Double-wide flip-top tins of Donruss Preferred cards were a reail exclusive with a price tag of about $6. The double-wide retail tins use the same player checklist and photo as the green hobby-version single tins, but have predominantly blue color. Values shown are for opened tins.

		MT
Complete Set (12):		15.00
Common Tin:		.75
1	Todd Helton, Ben Grieve	.75
2	Cal Ripken Jr., Alex Rodriguez	2.50
3	Greg Maddux, Mike Piazza	2.00
4	Chipper Jones, Travis Lee	2.00
5	Derek Jeter, Jeff Bagwell	2.00
6	Juan Gonzalez, Mark McGwire	2.50
7	Hideo Nomo, Roger Clemens	1.50
8	Andruw Jones, Paul Molitor	.75
9	Vladimir Guerrero, Jose Cruz Jr.	.75
10	Nomar Garciaparra, Scott Rolen	1.00
11	Ken Griffey Jr., Larry Walker	2.50
12	Tony Gwynn, Frank Thomas	1.50

1998 Donruss Preferred Great X-pectations

This 26-card insert features a veteran player on one side and a young player on the other. A large "GX" appears in the background on each side. The cards are sequentially numbered to 2,700, with the first 300 of each die-cut around the "GX".

		MT
Complete Set (26):		125.00
Common Player:		2.00
Die-Cuts:		2X
1	Jeff Bagwell, Travis Lee	6.00
2	Jose Cruz Jr., Ken Griffey Jr.	12.50
3	Larry Walker, Ben Grieve	4.00
4	Frank Thomas, Todd Helton	7.50
5	Jim Thome, Paul Konerko	2.00
6	Alex Rodriguez, Miguel Tejada	12.50
7	Greg Maddux, Livan Hernandez	8.00
8	Roger Clemens, Jaret Wright	7.50

9	Albert Belle, Juan Encarnacion	3.00
10	Mo Vaughn, David Ortiz	3.50
11	Manny Ramirez, Mark Kotsay	3.50
12	Tim Salmon, Brad Fullmer	2.00
13	Cal Ripken Jr., Fernando Tatis	12.50
14	Hideo Nomo, Hideki Irabu	3.50
15	Mike Piazza, Todd Greene	10.00
16	Gary Sheffield, Richard Hidalgo	2.50
17	Paul Molitor, Darin Erstad	3.50
18	Ivan Rodriguez, Eli Marrero	3.50
19	Ken Caminiti, Todd Walker	2.00
20	Tony Gwynn, Jose Guillen	8.00
21	Derek Jeter, Nomar Garciaparra	10.00
22	Chipper Jones, Scott Rolen	10.00
23	Juan Gonzalez, Andruw Jones	6.50
24	Barry Bonds, Vladimir Guerrero	6.00
25	Mark McGwire, Tony Clark	12.50
26	Bernie Williams, Mike Cameron	3.00

1998 Donruss Preferred Precious Metals

Precious Metals is a 30-card partial parallel of the Preferred base set. Each card was printed on stock using real silver, gold or platinum. Fifty complete sets were produced.

		MT
Complete Set (30):		1200.
Common Player:		15.00
1	Ken Griffey Jr.	100.00
2	Frank Thomas	65.00
3	Cal Ripken Jr.	100.00
4	Alex Rodriguez	100.00
5	Greg Maddux	75.00
6	Mike Piazza	90.00
7	Chipper Jones	90.00
8	Tony Gwynn	75.00
9	Derek Jeter	90.00
10	Jeff Bagwell	45.00
11	Juan Gonzalez	45.00
12	Nomar Garciaparra	75.00
13	Andruw Jones	40.00
14	Hideo Nomo	25.00
15	Roger Clemens	65.00
16	Mark McGwire	100.00
17	Scott Rolen	35.00
18	Barry Bonds	65.00
19	Darin Erstad	25.00
20	Kenny Lofton	15.00
21	Mo Vaughn	25.00
22	Ivan Rodriguez	35.00
23	Randy Johnson	35.00
24	Paul Molitor	35.00
25	Jose Cruz Jr.	20.00
26	Paul Konerko	15.00
27	Todd Helton	40.00
28	Ben Grieve	20.00
29	Travis Lee	15.00
30	Mark Kotsay	15.00

1998 Donruss Preferred Title Waves

This 30-card set features players who won awards or titles between 1993-1997. Printed on plastic stock, each card is sequentially numbered to the year the player won the award. The card fronts feature the Title Waves logo, a color player photo in front of a background of fans and the name of the award the player won.

		MT
Complete Set (30):		150.00
Common Player:		2.00
1	Nomar Garciaparra	9.00
2	Scott Rolen	5.00
3	Roger Clemens	7.50
4	Gary Sheffield	2.00
5	Jeff Bagwell	6.50
6	Cal Ripken Jr.	15.00
7	Frank Thomas	7.50
8	Ken Griffey Jr.	15.00
9	Larry Walker	2.50
10	Derek Jeter	10.00
11	Juan Gonzalez	5.00
12	Bernie Williams	2.50
13	Andruw Jones	5.00
14	Andy Pettitte	2.50
15	Ivan Rodriguez	5.00
16	Alex Rodriguez	15.00
17	Mark McGwire	15.00
18	Andres Galarraga	2.00
19	Hideo Nomo	2.50
20	Mo Vaughn	3.00
21	Randy Johnson	3.00
22	Chipper Jones	10.00
23	Greg Maddux	9.00
24	Manny Ramirez	3.50
25	Tony Gwynn	9.00
26	Albert Belle	2.50
27	Kenny Lofton	2.00
28	Mike Piazza	10.00
29	Paul Molitor	3.50
30	Barry Bonds	7.50

1998 Donruss Signature Series

The 140-card base set has a white border encasing the player photo with the logo stamped with silver foil. Card backs have a small photo and complete year-by-year statistics. Signature Proofs are a parallel to the base set utilizing holo-foil treatment and "Signature Proof" written down the left edge of the card front. Each card is numbered "1 of 150" on the card back.

		MT
Complete Set (140):		60.00
Common Player:		.15
Signature Proofs:		10X
Pack (5):		20.00
Wax Box (12):		225.00
1	David Justice	.30
2	Derek Jeter	2.50
3	Nomar Garciaparra	2.00
4	Ryan Klesko	.15
5	Jeff Bagwell	1.00
6	Dante Bichette	.15
7	Ivan Rodriguez	.60
8	Albert Belle	.35
9	Cal Ripken Jr.	4.00
10	Craig Biggio	.15
11	Barry Larkin	.25
12	Jose Guillen	.25
13	Will Clark	.30
14	J.T. Snow	.15
15	Chuck Knoblauch	.15
16	Todd Walker	.20
17	Scott Rolen	.60
18	Rickey Henderson	.40
19	Juan Gonzalez	.75
20	Justin Thompson	.15
21	Roger Clemens	1.50
22	Ray Lankford	.15
23	Jose Cruz Jr.	.25
24	Ken Griffey Jr.	4.00
25	Andruw Jones	.60
26	Darin Erstad	.60
27	Jim Thome	.15
28	Wade Boggs	.40
29	Ken Caminiti	.15
30	Todd Hundley	.15
31	Mike Piazza	2.50
32	Sammy Sosa	2.00
33	Larry Walker	.35
34	Matt Williams	.30
35	Frank Thomas	1.50
36	Gary Sheffield	.25
37	Alex Rodriguez	4.00
38	Hideo Nomo	.25
39	Kenny Lofton	.15
40	John Smoltz	.15
41	Mo Vaughn	.30
42	Edgar Martinez	.15
43	Paul Molitor	.50
44	Rafael Palmeiro	.30
45	Barry Bonds	1.50
46	Vladimir Guerrero	1.00
47	Carlos Delgado	.40
48	Bobby Higginson	.15
49	Greg Maddux	2.00
50	Jim Edmonds	.15
51	Randy Johnson	.75
52	Mark McGwire	4.00
53	Rondell White	.20
54	Raul Mondesi	.20
55	Manny Ramirez	1.00
56	Pedro Martinez	.75
57	Tim Salmon	.25
58	Moises Alou	.20
59	Fred McGriff	.15
60	Garret Anderson	.15
61	Sandy Alomar Jr.	.15
62	Chan Ho Park	.20
63	Mark Kotsay	.20
64	Mike Mussina	.50
65	Tom Glavine	.20
66	Tony Clark	.15
67	Mark Grace	.25
68	Tony Gwynn	2.00
69	Tino Martinez	.15
70	Kevin Brown	.25
71	Todd Greene	.15
72	Andy Pettitte	.30
73	Livan Hernandez	.15
74	Curt Schilling	.25
75	Andres Galarraga	.15
76	Rusty Greer	.15
77	Jay Buhner	.15
78	Bobby Bonilla	.15
79	Chipper Jones	2.50
80	Eric Young	.15
81	Jason Giambi	.25
82	Javy Lopez	.15
83	Roberto Alomar	.40
84	Bernie Williams	.40
85	A.J. Hinch	.15
86	Kerry Wood	.75
87	Juan Encarnacion	.25
88	Brad Fullmer	.15
89	Ben Grieve	.40
90	*Maggio Ordonez*	7.50
91	Todd Helton	.40
92	Richard Hidalgo	.20
93	Paul Konerko	.20
94	Aramis Ramirez	.25
95	Ricky Ledee	.15
96	Derrek Lee	.15
97	Travis Lee	.35
98	*Matt Anderson*	1.00
99	Jaret Wright	.35
100	David Ortiz	.20
101	Carl Pavano	.20
102	*Orlando Hernandez*	2.50
103	Fernando Tatis	.20
104	Miguel Tejada	.20
105	*Rolando Arrojo*	2.00
106	*Kevin Millwood*	3.00
107	Ken Griffey Jr. (Checklist)	1.00
108	Frank Thomas (Checklist)	.75
109	Cal Ripken Jr. (Checklist)	1.00
110	Greg Maddux (Checklist)	.75
111	John Olerud	.20
112	David Cone	.15
113	Vinny Castilla	.15
114	Jason Kendall	.20
115	Brian Jordan	.15
116	Hideki Irabu	.15
117	Bartolo Colon	.20
118	Greg Vaughn	.15
119	David Segui	.15
120	Bruce Chen	.15
121	*Julio Ramirez*	.50
122	*Troy Glaus*	10.00
123	*Jeremy Giambi*	2.00
124	*Ryan Minor*	.50
125	Richie Sexson	.15
126	Dermal Brown	.25
127	Adrian Beltre	.35
128	Eric Chavez	.50
129	*J.D. Drew*	7.50
130	*Gabe Kapler*	2.50
131	*Masato Yoshii*	.50
132	*Mike Lowell*	2.00
133	*Jim Parque*	.50
134	Roy Halladay	.20
135	*Carlos Lee*	2.00
136	*Jin Ho Cho*	.40
137	Michael Barrett	.25
138	*Fernando Seguignol*	1.50
139	*Odalis Perez*	.50
140	Mark McGwire (Checklist)	1.50

1998 Donruss Signature Series Proofs

This parallel set differs from the regular issue Signature Series base cards in the presence at left-front of a vertical stack of gold refractive foil strips on which SIGNATURE PROOF is spelled out. Also, backs of the proofs have a gold, rather than white, background.

	MT
Complete Set (140):	750.00
Common Player:	2.00
Stars/Rookies:	10X

(See 1998 Donruss Signature Series for checklist and base card values.)

1998 Donruss Signature Series Autographs (Red)

Autographs were inserted one per pack and feature the player photo over a silver and red foil background. The featured player's autograph appears on the bottom portion on front with the Donruss logo stamped in gold foil. Autographs are unnumbered. The first 100 cards signed by each player are blue, sequentially numbered and designated as "Century Marks". The next 1,000 signed are green, sequentially numbered and designated as "Millennium Marks." Greg Maddux signed only 12 regular Donruss Signature Autographs.

	MT
Common Player:	2.50
Roberto Alomar (150)	35.00
Sandy Alomar Jr. (700)	12.50
Moises Alou (900)	12.50
Gabe Alvarez (2,900)	2.50
Wilson Alvarez (1,600)	4.00
Jay Bell (1,500)	4.00
Adrian Beltre (1,900)	10.00
Andy Benes (2,600)	5.00
Aaron Boone (3,400)	2.50
Russell Branyan (1,650)	4.00
Orlando Cabrera (3,100)	2.50
Mike Cameron (1,150)	7.50
Joe Carter (400)	12.00
Sean Casey (2,275)	15.00
Bruce Chen (150)	20.00
Tony Clark (2,275)	7.50
Will Clark (1,400)	15.00
Matt Clement (1,400)	7.50
Pat Cline (400)	10.00
Ken Cloude (3,400)	4.00
Michael Coleman (2,800)	2.50
David Cone (25)	75.00
Jeff Conine (1,400)	5.00
Jacob Cruz (3,200)	2.50
Russ Davis (3,500)	2.50
Jason Dickson (1,400)	4.00
Todd Dunwoody (3,500)	2.50
Juan Encarnacion (3,400)	7.50
Darin Erstad (700)	25.00
Bobby Estalella (3,400)	2.50
Jeff Fassero (3,400)	2.50
John Franco (1,800)	2.50
Brad Fullmer (3,100)	5.00
Jason Giambi (3,100)	5.00
Derrick Gibson (1,200)	5.00
Todd Greene (1,400)	5.00
Ben Grieve (1,400)	20.00
Mark Grudzielanek (3,200)	4.00
Vladimir Guerrero (2,100)	30.00
Wilton Guerrero (1,900)	4.00
Jose Guillen (2,400)	6.00
Todd Helton (1,300)	20.00
Richard Hidalgo (3,400)	4.00
A.J. Hinch (2,900)	4.00
Butch Huskey (1,900)	4.00
Raul Ibanez (3,300)	2.50
Damian Jackson (900)	2.50
Geoff Jenkins (3,100)	4.00
Eric Karros (650)	9.00
Ryan Klesko (400)	12.00
Mark Kotsay (3,600)	5.00
Ricky Ledee (2,200)	10.00
Derrek Lee (3,400)	4.00
Travis Lee (150)	35.00
Travis Lee (facsimile autograph, "SAMPLE" on back)	3.00
Javier Lopez (650)	10.00
Mike Lowell (3,500)	10.00
Greg Maddux (12)	250.00
Eli Marrero (3,400)	2.50
Al Martin (1,300)	4.00
Rafael Medina (1,400)	2.50
Scott Morgan (900)	7.50
Abraham Nunez (3,500)	2.50
Paul O'Neill (1,000)	10.00
Luis Ordaz (2,700)	4.00
Magglio Ordonez (3,200)	6.00
Kevin Orie (1,350)	5.00
David Ortiz (3,400)	5.00
Rafael Palmeiro (1,000)	15.00
Carl Pavano (2,600)	4.00
Neifi Perez (3,300)	2.50
Dante Powell (3,050)	2.50
Aramis Ramirez (2,800)	7.50
Mariano Rivera (900)	10.00
Felix Rodriguez (1,400)	5.00
Henry Rodriguez (3,400)	4.00
Scott Rolen (1,900)	30.00
Brian Rose (1,400)	5.00
Curt Schilling (900)	20.00
Richie Sexson (3,500)	7.50
Randall Simon (3,500)	5.00
J.T. Snow (400)	10.00
Jeff Suppan (1,400)	5.00
Fernando Tatis (3,900)	5.00
Miguel Tejada (3,800)	10.00
Brett Tomko (3,400)	2.50
Bubba Trammell (3,900)	2.50
Ismael Valdez (1,900)	5.00
Robin Ventura (1,400)	10.00
Billy Wagner (3,900)	4.00
Todd Walker (1,900)	7.50
Daryle Ward (400)	7.50
Rondell White (3,400)	7.50
Antone Williamson (3,350)	2.50
Dan Wilson (2,400)	2.50
Enrique Wilson (3,400)	2.50
Preston Wilson (2,100)	5.00
Tony Womack (3,500)	2.50
Kerry Wood (3,400)	10.00

1998 Donruss Signature Series Century Marks (Blue)

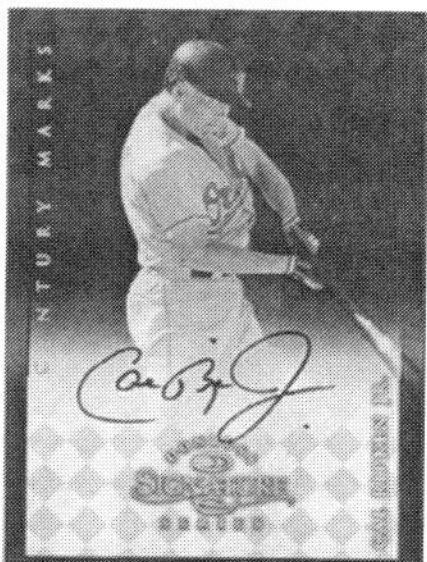

This 121-card set is a serially numbered, blue-foil parallel of the Autographs insert set and limited to 100 cards signed by each featured player (unless otherwise shown in the checklist).

	MT
Common Player:	7.50
Roberto Alomar	30.00
Sandy Alomar Jr.	10.00
Moises Alou	10.00
Gabe Alvarez	7.50
Wilson Alvarez	7.50
Brady Anderson	7.50
Jay Bell	7.50
Albert Belle	20.00
Adrian Beltre	25.00
Andy Benes	7.50
Wade Boggs	32.50
Barry Bonds	65.00
Aaron Boone	7.50
Russell Branyan	7.50
Jay Buhner	7.50
Ellis Burks	7.50
Orlando Cabrera	7.50
Mike Cameron	7.50
Ken Caminiti	7.50
Joe Carter	7.50
Sean Casey	10.00
Bruce Chen	7.50
Tony Clark	7.50
Will Clark	17.50
Roger Clemens	65.00
Matt Clement	7.50
Pat Cline	7.50
Ken Cloude	7.50
Michael Coleman	7.50
David Cone	10.00
Jeff Conine	7.50
Jacob Cruz	7.50
Jose Cruz Jr.	10.00
Russ Davis	7.50
Jason Dickson	7.50
Todd Dunwoody	7.50
Scott Elarton	7.50
Darin Erstad	17.50
Bobby Estalella	7.50
Jeff Fassero	7.50
John Franco	7.50
Brad Fullmer	7.50
Andres Galarraga	17.50
Nomar Garciaparra	75.00
Jason Giambi	30.00
Derrick Gibson	7.50
Tom Glavine	12.50
Juan Gonzalez	50.00
Todd Greene	7.50
Ben Grieve	20.00
Mark Grudzielanek	7.50
Vladimir Guerrero	35.00
Wilton Guerrero	7.50
Jose Guillen	10.00
Tony Gwynn	75.00
Todd Helton	20.00
Richard Hidalgo	10.00
A.J. Hinch	10.00
Butch Huskey	7.50
Raul Ibanez	7.50
Damian Jackson	7.50
Geoff Jenkins	10.00
Derek Jeter	75.00
Randy Johnson	30.00
Chipper Jones	75.00
Eric Karros (50)	12.50
Ryan Klesko	7.50
Chuck Knoblauch	20.00
Mark Kotsay	10.00
Ricky Ledee	7.50
Derrek Lee	7.50
Travis Lee	17.50
Javier Lopez	7.50
Mike Lowell	12.00
Greg Maddux	75.00
Eli Marrero	7.50
Al Martin	7.50
Rafael Medina	7.50
Paul Molitor	32.50
Scott Morgan	7.50
Mike Mussina	30.00
Abraham Nunez	10.00
Paul O'Neill	10.00
Luis Ordaz	7.50
Magglio Ordonez	10.00
Kevin Orie	7.50
David Ortiz	10.00
Rafael Palmeiro	20.00
Carl Pavano	10.00
Neifi Perez	7.50
Andy Pettitte	20.00
Aramis Ramirez	10.00
Cal Ripken Jr.	200.00
Mariano Rivera	17.50
Alex Rodriguez	150.00
Felix Rodriguez	7.50
Henry Rodriguez	7.50
Scott Rolen	35.00
Brian Rose	7.50
Curt Schilling	20.00
Richie Sexson	20.00
Randall Simon	7.50
J.T. Snow	7.50
Darryl Strawberry	15.00
Jeff Suppan	10.00
Fernando Tatis	10.00
Brett Tomko	7.50
Bubba Trammell	7.50
Ismael Valdez	10.00
Robin Ventura	15.00
Billy Wagner	10.00
Todd Walker	10.00
Daryle Ward	10.00
Rondell White	12.50
Matt Williams (80)	25.00

Antone Williamson	7.50
Dan Wilson	7.50
Enrique Wilson	7.50
Preston Wilson	10.00
Tony Womack	7.50
Kerry Wood	17.50

1998 Donruss Signature Series Millennium Marks (Green)

This is a green-foil parallel version of the Autographs insert set and features 1,000 cards signed by the featured player (unless otherwise shown in the checklist. Cards are not numbered.

	MT
Complete Set (125):	
Common Player:	3.00
Roberto Alomar	12.50
Sandy Alomar Jr.	5.00
Moises Alou	6.00
Gabe Alvarez	3.00
Wilson Alvarez	3.00
Brady Anderson (800)	5.00
Jay Bell	3.00
Albert Belle (400)	20.00
Adrian Beltre	10.00
Andy Benes	3.00
Wade Boggs (900)	15.00
Barry Bonds (400)	50.00
Aaron Boone	3.00
Russell Branyan	4.00
Jay Buhner (400)	12.50
Ellis Burks (900)	3.50
Orlando Cabrera	3.00
Mike Cameron	3.00
Ken Caminiti (900)	4.50
Joe Carter	4.00
Sean Casey	10.00
Bruce Chen	3.00
Tony Clark	4.50
Will Clark	10.00
Roger Clemens (400)	50.00
Matt Clement (900)	3.00
Pat Cline	3.00
Ken Cloude	3.00
Michael Coleman	3.00
David Cone	5.00
Jeff Conine	3.00
Jacob Cruz	3.00
Jose Cruz Jr. (850)	5.00
Russ Davis (950)	3.00
Jason Dickson (950)	3.00
Todd Dunwoody	3.00
Scott Elarton (900)	3.00
Juan Encarnacion	5.00
Darin Erstad	10.00
Bobby Estalella	3.00
Jeff Fassero	3.00
John Franco (950)	3.00
Brad Fullmer	5.00
Andres Galarraga (900)	4.50
Nomar Garciaparra (400)	50.00
Jason Giambi	15.00
Derrick Gibson	3.00
Tom Glavine (700)	10.00
Juan Gonzalez	25.00
Todd Greene	3.00
Ben Grieve	10.00
Mark Grudzielanek	3.00
Vladimir Guerrero	20.00
Wilton Guerrero	3.00
Jose Guillen	4.00
Tony Gwynn (900)	30.00
Todd Helton	12.50
Richard Hidalgo	4.00
A.J. Hinch	3.00
Butch Huskey	3.00
Raul Ibanez	3.00
Damian Jackson	3.00
Geoff Jenkins	3.50
Derek Jeter (400)	50.00
Randy Johnson (800)	15.00
Chipper Jones (900)	35.00
Eric Karros	3.50
Ryan Klesko	3.50
Chuck Knoblauch (900)	10.00
Mark Kotsay	5.00
Ricky Ledee	3.00
Derrek Lee	3.50
Travis Lee	10.00
Javier Lopez (800)	5.00
Mike Lowell	8.00
Greg Maddux (400)	60.00
Eli Marrero	3.00
Al Martin (950)	3.00
Rafael Medina (850)	3.00
Paul Molitor (900)	15.00
Scott Morgan	3.50
Mike Mussina (900)	7.50
Abraham Nunez	3.00
Paul O'Neill (900)	4.50
Luis Ordaz	3.00
Magglio Ordonez	5.00
Kevin Orie	3.00
David Ortiz	5.00
Rafael Palmeiro (900)	10.00
Carl Pavano	3.50
Neifi Perez	3.00
Andy Pettitte (900)	7.50
Dante Powell (950)	3.00
Aramis Ramirez	6.00
Cal Ripken Jr. (375)	75.00
Mariano Rivera	7.50
Alex Rodriguez (350)	75.00
Felix Rodriguez	3.00
Henry Rodriguez	3.00
Scott Rolen	20.00
Brian Rose	3.50
Curt Schilling	7.50
Richie Sexson	10.00
Randall Simon	3.00
J.T. Snow	3.00
Darryl Strawberry (900)	7.50
Jeff Suppan	3.50
Fernando Tatis	6.00
Miguel Tejada	10.00
Brett Tomko	3.00
Bubba Trammell	3.00
Ismael Valdes	3.50
Robin Ventura	6.00
Billy Wagner (900)	3.50
Todd Walker	6.00
Daryle Ward	3.00
Rondell White	6.00
Matt Williams (820)	10.00
Antone Williamson	3.00
Dan Wilson	3.00
Enrique Wilson	3.00
Preston Wilson (400)	7.50
Tony Womack	3.00
Kerry Wood	12.50

1998 Donruss Signature Series Preview Autographs

This insert was a surprise addition to Donruss Update. The set features autographs from top rookies and stars. The number of cards produced varies for each player. The card fronts have a color player photo in front of a gold checkered border with the signature in a white area near the bottom. Cards of a number of players (Alou, Casey, Jenkins, Wilson, etc.) were never officially released, having been returned too late by the players; specimens, have, however made their way into the hobby market in unknown numbers.

	MT
Common Player:	15.00
Sandy Alomar Jr. (96)	45.00
Moises Alou	75.00
Andy Benes (135)	25.00
Russell Branyan (188)	25.00
Sean Casey	125.00
Tony Clark (188)	25.00
Juan Encarnacion (193)	25.00
Brad Fullmer (396)	25.00
Juan Gonzalez (108)	175.00
Ben Grieve (100)	75.00
Todd Helton (101)	75.00
Richard Hidalgo (380)	25.00
A.J. Hinch (400)	15.00
Damian Jackson (15)	100.00
Geoff Jenkins	275.00
Chipper Jones (112)	300.00
Chuck Knoblauch (98)	75.00
Travis Lee (101)	30.00
Mike Lowell (450)	25.00
Greg Maddux (92)	250.00
Kevin Millwood (395)	60.00
Magglio Ordonez (420)	60.00
David Ortiz (393)	15.00
Rafael Palmeiro (107)	75.00
Cal Ripken Jr. (22)	1000.
Alex Rodriguez (23)	1000.
Curt Schilling (100)	75.00
Randall Simon (380)	15.00
Fernando Tatis (400)	25.00
Miguel Tejada (375)	20.00
Robin Ventura (95)	45.00
Dan Wilson	125.00
Kerry Wood (373)	40.00

1998 Donruss Signature Series Redemption Baseballs

Redemption cards authentically autographed baseballs were randomly inserted in Donruss Signature Series packs. Baseballs are laser burned with a Donruss seal to ensure authenticity. Every ball, except Ben Grieve's, is serial numbered within the edition limit shown. Redemption cards, no longer valid, are valued about 10% of the corresponding ball.

	MT
Common Autographed Ball:	15.00
Signing Bonus Redemption Card: 10%	
Roberto Alomar 60)	45.00
Sandy Alomar Jr. (60)	20.00
Ernie Banks (12)	85.00
Ken Caminiti (60)	25.00
Tony Clark (60)	20.00
Jacob Cruz (12)	50.00
Russ Davis (60)	15.00
Juan Encarnacion (60)	25.00
Bobby Estalella (60)	15.00
Jeff Fassero (60)	15.00
Mark Grudzielanek (60)	15.00
Ben Grieve (30)	25.00
Jose Guillen (120)	25.00
Tony Gwynn (60)	100.00
Al Kaline (12)	80.00
Paul Konerko (100)	15.00
Travis Lee (100)	25.00
Mike Lowell (60)	15.00
Eli Marrero (60)	15.00
Eddie Mathews (12)	80.00
Paul Molitor (60)	50.00
Stan Musial (12)	125.00
Abraham Nunez (12)	50.00
Luis Ordaz (12)	35.00
Magglio Ordonez (12)	35.00
Scott Rolen (60)	45.00
Bubba Trammell (24)	25.00
Robin Ventura (60)	25.00
Billy Wagner (60)	20.00
Rondell White (60)	20.00
Antone Williamson (12)	15.00
Tony Womack (60)	15.00

1998 Donruss Signature Series Significant Signatures

This 18-card autographed set features some of baseball's all-time great players. Each card is sequentially numbered to 2,000. The Sandy Koufax autographs weren't received in time prior to release and was redeemable by sending in the Billy Williams autograph, the collector would then receive both the Williams and Koufax back. Exchange cards were also initially released for Nolan Ryan and Ozzie Smith.

	MT
Complete Set (18):	800.00
Common Player:	12.50
Ernie Banks	25.00
Yogi Berra	30.00
George Brett	40.00
Catfish Hunter	12.50
Al Kaline	20.00
Harmon Killebrew	20.00
Ralph Kiner	15.00
Sandy Koufax	125.00
Eddie Mathews	25.00
Don Mattingly	40.00
Willie McCovey	12.50
Stan Musial	35.00
Phil Rizzuto (edition of 1,000)	25.00
Nolan Ryan	75.00
Nolan Ryan (Exchange card)	5.00
Ozzie Smith	30.00
Ozzie Smith (Exchange card)	5.00
Duke Snider	25.00
Don Sutton	12.50
Billy Williams	25.00

2001 Donruss

	MT
Complete Set (220):	600.00
Common Player:	.15
Common Rated Rookie (151-200):	5.00
Production 2001	
Hobby Pack (5):	3.50
Hobby Box (24):	75.00
The Rookies Coupon:	20.00
Inserted 1:72	
Baseball's Best Coupon:	100.00
Inserted 1:720	

Exchange Deadline 11/01/01

1	Alex Rodriguez	2.00
2	Barry Bonds	1.00
3	Cal Ripken Jr.	2.50
4	Chipper Jones	1.50
5	Derek Jeter	2.50
6	Troy Glaus	.75
7	Frank Thomas	1.00
8	Greg Maddux	1.50
9	Ivan Rodriguez	.75
10	Jeff Bagwell	.75
11	Jose Canseco	.40
12	Todd Helton	.75
13	Ken Griffey Jr.	2.00
14	Manny Ramirez	.75
15	Mark McGwire	2.50
16	Mike Piazza	2.00
17	Nomar Garciaparra	2.00
18	Pedro Martinez	1.00
19	Randy Johnson	.75
20	Rick Ankiel	.40
21	Ricky Henderson	.25
22	Roger Clemens	1.00
23	Sammy Sosa	1.50
24	Tony Gwynn	1.00
25	Vladimir Guerrero	1.00
26	Eric Davis	.15
27	Roberto Alomar	.50
28	Mark Mulder	.15
29	Pat Burrell	.50
30	Harold Baines	.15
31	Carlos Delgado	.60
32	J.D. Drew	.25
33	Jim Edmonds	.25
34	Darin Erstad	.25
35	Jason Giambi	.30
36	Tom Glavine	.30
37	Juan Gonzalez	.75
38	Mark Grace	.25
39	Shawn Green	.25
40	Tim Hudson	.25
41	Andruw Jones	.60
42	David Justice	.40
43	Jeff Kent	.15
44	Barry Larkin	.25
45	Pokey Reese	.15
46	Mike Mussina	.50
47	Hideo Nomo	.25
48	Rafael Palmeiro	.40
49	Adam Piatt	.15
50	Scott Rolen	.40
51	Gary Sheffield	.25
52	Bernie Williams	.50
53	Bob Abreu	.15
54	Edgardo Alfonzo	.15
55	*Jermaine Clark*	.15
56	Albert Belle	.15
57	Craig Biggio	.25
58	Andres Galarraga	.25
59	Edgar Martinez	.15
60	Fred McGriff	.25
61	Magglio Ordonez	.25
62	Jim Thome	.25
63	Matt Williams	.25
64	Kerry Wood	.25
65	Moises Alou	.15
66	Brady Anderson	.20
67	Garret Anderson	.15
68	Tony Armas Jr.	.15
69	Tony Batista	.15
70	Jose Cruz Jr.	.15
71	Carlos Beltran	.15
72	Adrian Beltre	.25
73	Kris Benson	.15
74	Lance Berkman	.15
75	Kevin Brown	.25
76	Jay Buhner	.15
77	Jeromy Burnitz	.15
78	Ken Caminiti	.15
79	Sean Casey	.25
80	Luis Castillo	.15
81	Eric Chavez	.25
82	Jeff Cirillo	.15
83	Bartolo Colon	.15
84	David Cone	.15
85	Freddy Garcia	.15
86	Johnny Damon	.15
87	Ray Durham	.15
88	Jermaine Dye	.15
89	Juan Encarnacion	.15
90	Terrence Long	.15
91	Carl Everett	.15
92	Steve Finley	.15
93	Cliff Floyd	.15
94	Brad Fullmer	.15
95	Brian Giles	.25
96	Luis Gonzalez	.25
97	Rusty Greer	.15
98	Jeffrey Hammonds	.15
99	Mike Hampton	.25
100	Orlando Hernandez	.25
101	Richard Hidalgo	.25
102	Geoff Jenkins	.25
103	Jacque Jones	.15
104	Brian Jordan	.15
105	Gabe Kapler	.25
106	Eric Karros	.15
107	Jason Kendall	.15
108	Adam Kennedy	.15
109	Byung-Hyun Kim	.15
110	Ryan Klesko	.15
111	Chuck Knoblauch	.25
112	Paul Konerko	.15
113	Carlos Lee	.15
114	Kenny Lofton	.25
115	Javy Lopez	.25
116	Tino Martinez	.15
117	Ruben Mateo	.15
118	Kevin Millwood	.15
119	Ben Molina	.15
120	Raul Mondesi	.25
121	Trot Nixon	.15
122	John Olerud	.25
123	Paul O'Neill	.25
124	Chan Ho Park	.15
125	Andy Pettite	.25
126	Jorge Posada	.25
127	Mark Quinn	.15
128	Aramis Ramirez	.15
129	Mariano Rivera	.25
130	Tim Salmon	.25
131	Curt Schilling	.25
132	Richie Sexson	.15
133	John Smoltz	.15
134	J.T. Snow	.15
135	Jay Payton	.15
136	Shannon Stewart	.15
137	B.J. Surhoff	.15
138	Mike Sweeney	.15
139	Fernando Tatis	.15
140	Miguel Tejada	.25
141	Jason Varitek	.15
142	Greg Vaughn	.15
143	Mo Vaughn	.25
144	Robin Ventura	.25
145	Jose Vidro	.15
146	Omar Vizquel	.25
147	Larry Walker	.25
148	David Wells	.15
149	Rondell White	.25
150	Preston Wilson	.15
151	Brent Abernathy	5.00
152	*Cory Aldridge*	15.00
153	*Gene Altman*	8.00
154	Josh Beckett	6.00
155	*Wilson Betemit*	20.00
156	*Albert Pujols/500*	140.00
157	Joe Crede	6.00
158	Jack Cust	6.00
159	J.J. Davis	5.00
160	Alex Escobar	5.00
161	*Adrian Hernandez*	15.00
162	Pedro Feliz	5.00
163	*Nate Frese*	8.00
164	*Carlos Garcia*	6.00
165	Marcus Giles	5.00
166	*Alexis Gomez*	8.00
167	Jason Hart	8.00
168	*Eric Hinske*	15.00
169	Cesar Izturis	5.00
170	Nick Johnson	8.00
171	Mike Young	5.00
172	*Brian Lawrence*	10.00
173	Steve Lomasney	5.00
174	*Nick Maness*	10.00
175	*Jose Mieses*	6.00
176	*Greg Miller*	8.00
177	Eric Munson	6.00
178	Xavier Nady	12.00
179	*Blaine Neal*	6.00
180	Abraham Nunez	5.00
181	Jose Ortiz	5.00
182	*Jeremy Owens*	10.00
183	Pablo Ozuna	5.00
184	Corey Patterson	8.00
185	Carlos Pena	5.00
186	Wily Mo Pena	5.00
187	Timo Perez	5.00
188	*Adam Pettyjohn*	8.00
189	Luis Rivas	5.00
190	*Jackson Melian*	25.00
191	*Wilken Ruan*	6.00
192	*Duaner Sanchez*	8.00
193	Alfonso Soriano	10.00
194	*Rafael Soriano*	8.00
195	*Ichiro Suzuki*	90.00
196	*Billy Sylvester*	8.00
197	*Juan Uribe*	6.00
198	Eric Valent	5.00
199	*Carlos Valderrama*	8.00
200	*Matt White*	15.00
201	Alex Rodriguez	1.00
202	Barry Bonds	.50
203	Cal Ripken Jr.	1.25
204	Chipper Jones	.75
205	Derek Jeter	1.25
206	Troy Glaus	.40
207	Frank Thomas	.50
208	Greg Maddux	.75
209	Ivan Rodriguez	.40
210	Jeff Bagwell	.40
211	Todd Helton	.40
212	Ken Griffey Jr.	1.00
213	Manny Ramirez	.40
214	Mark McGwire	1.25
215	Mike Piazza	1.00
216	Pedro Martinez	.50
217	Sammy Sosa	.75
218	Tony Gwynn	.50
219	Vladimir Guerrero	.50
220	Nomar Garciaparra	1.00

2001 Donruss All-Time Diamond Kings

		MT
Complete Set (10):		200.00
Common Player:		10.00
Production 2,500 sets		
Studio Series:		2-3X
Production 250		
#9 undetermined redemp.		
1a	Frank Robinson	10.00
1b	Willie Mays (should have been ATDK-9)	35.00
2	Harmon Killebrew	20.00
3	Mike Schmidt	25.00
4	Reggie Jackson	25.00
5	Nolan Ryan	50.00
6	George Brett	25.00
7	Tom Seaver	10.00
8	Hank Aaron	35.00
9	Redemption, Willie Mays (See #1b)	
10	Stan Musial	25.00

2001 Donruss All-Time Diamond Kings Autograph

		MT
Common Autograph:		40.00
Production 50 sets		
1	Frank Robinson	100.00
2	Harmon Killebrew	
3	Mike Schmidt	250.00
4	Reggie Jackson	
5	Nolan Ryan	400.00
6	George Brett	
7	Tom Seaver	180.00
8	Hank Aaron	
9	TBD Exchange	
10	Stan Musial	250.00

2001 Donruss Bat Kings

		MT
Common Card:		40.00
Production 250 sets		
1	Ivan Rodriguez	50.00
2	Tony Gwynn	60.00
3	Barry Bonds	70.00
4	Todd Helton	50.00
5	Troy Glaus	60.00
6	Mike Schmidt	90.00
7	Reggie Jackson	90.00
8	Harmon Killebrew	90.00
9	Frank Robinson	50.00
10	Hank Aaron	120.00

2001 Donruss Bat Kings Autograph

		MT
Common Autograph:		125.00
Production 50 sets		
1	Ivan Rodriguez	125.00
2	Tony Gwynn	160.00
3	TBD Redemption	
4	Todd Helton	125.00
5	Troy Glaus	125.00
6	Mike Schmidt	300.00
7	Reggie Jackson	180.00
8	Harmon Killebrew	150.00
9	Frank Robinson	125.00
10	Hank Aaron	

2001 Donruss Diamond Kings Reprints

		MT
Complete Set (20):		
Common Player:		6.00
#'d to yr. produced		
1	Rod Carew	6.00
2	Nolan Ryan	30.00
3	Tom Seaver	10.00
4	Carlton Fisk	8.00
5	Reggie Jackson	10.00
6	Steve Carlton	8.00
7	Johnny Bench	10.00
8	Joe Morgan	6.00
9	Mike Schmidt	15.00
10	Wade Boggs	10.00
11	Cal Ripken Jr.	25.00
12	Tony Gwynn	10.00
13	Andre Dawson	8.00
14	Ozzie Smith	15.00
15	George Brett	15.00
16	Dave Winfield	6.00
17	Paul Molitor	8.00
18	Will Clark	
19	Robin Yount	10.00
20	Barry Bonds	

2001 Donruss Elite Series

		MT
Complete Set (20):		250.00
Common Player:		5.00
Production 2,500 sets		
Dominators:		5-8X
Production 25 sets		
1	Vladimir Guerrero	10.00
2	Cal Ripken Jr.	25.00
3	Greg Maddux	15.00
4	Alex Rodriguez	20.00
5	Barry Bonds	10.00
6	Chipper Jones	15.00
7	Derek Jeter	25.00
8	Ivan Rodriguez	8.00
9	Ken Griffey Jr.	25.00
10	Mark McGwire	25.00
11	Mike Piazza	20.00
12	Nomar Garciaparra	20.00
13	Pedro Martinez	10.00
14	Randy Johnson	8.00
15	Roger Clemens	10.00
16	Sammy Sosa	15.00
17	Tony Gwynn	10.00
18	Darin Erstad	5.00
19	Andruw Jones	6.00
20	Bernie Williams	6.00

2001 Donruss Jersey Kings

		MT
Common Card:		40.00
Production 250 sets		
1	Vladimir Guerrero	40.00
2	Cal Ripken Jr.	150.00
3	Greg Maddux	75.00
4	Chipper Jones	
5	Roger Clemens	75.00
6	George Brett	100.00
7	Tom Seaver	75.00
8	Nolan Ryan	150.00
9	Stan Musial	100.00
10	Willie Mays	

2001 Donruss Jersey Kings Autographs

		MT
Common Autograph:		120.00
Production 50 sets		
1	Vladimir Guerrero	120.00
2	Cal Ripken Jr.	350.00
3	Greg Maddux	250.00
4	TBD Redemption	
5	Roger Clemens	150.00
6	George Brett	250.00
7	Tom Seaver	200.00
8	Nolan Ryan	500.00
9	Stan Musial	250.00
10	TBD Redemption	

2001 Donruss Longball Leaders

		MT
Complete Set (20):		200.00
Common Player:		5.00
Production 1,000 sets		
Die-Cut Parallel:		3-5X
#'d to '00 HR Total		
1	Vladimir Guerrero	12.00
2	Alex Rodriguez	30.00
3	Barry Bonds	10.00
4	Troy Glaus	10.00
5	Frank Thomas	12.00
6	Jeff Bagwell	10.00
7	Todd Helton	10.00
8	Ken Griffey Jr.	35.00
9	Manny Ramirez	10.00
10	Mike Piazza	30.00
11	Sammy Sosa	20.00
12	Carlos Delgado	8.00
13	Jim Edmonds	5.00
14	Jason Giambi	6.00
15	David Justice	6.00
16	Rafael Palmeiro	6.00
17	Gary Sheffield	5.00
18	Jim Thome	5.00
19	Tony Batista	5.00
20	Richard Hidalgo	6.00

2001 Donruss Production Line

		MT
Complete Set (60):		450.00
Common Player:		2.50
Die-Cut OBP (1-20):		1-2X
Die-Cut SLG (21-40):		1-2.5X
Die-Cut PI (41-60):		1.5-3X
Production 100 sets		
1	Jason Giambi/476	6.00
2	Carlos Delgado/470	8.00
3	Todd Helton/463	10.00
4	Manny Ramirez/457	12.00
5	Barry Bonds/440	12.00
6	Gary Sheffield/438	5.00
7	Frank Thomas/436	12.00
8	Nomar Garciaparra/434	25.00
9	Brian Giles/432	4.00
10	Edgardo Alfonzo/425	3.00
11	Jeff Kent/424	4.00
12	Jeff Bagwell/424	10.00
13	Edgar Martinez/423	5.00
14	Alex Rodriguez/420	25.00
15	Luis Castillo/418	3.00
16	Will Clark/418	6.00
17	Jorge Posada/417	4.00
18	Derek Jeter/416	30.00
19	Bob Abreu/416	4.00
20	Moises Alou/416	4.00
21	Todd Helton/698	8.00
22	Manny Ramirez/697	10.00
23	Barry Bonds/688	10.00
24	Carlos Delgado/664	6.00
25	Vladimir Guerrero/664	10.00
26	Jason Giambi/647	6.00
27	Gary Sheffield/643	5.00
28	Richard Hidalgo/636	4.00
29	Sammy Sosa/634	12.00
30	Frank Thomas/625	10.00
31	Moises Alou/623	3.00
32	Jeff Bagwell/615	10.00
33	Mike Piazza/614	20.00
34	Alex Rodriguez/606	20.00
35	Troy Glaus/604	8.00
36	Nomar Garciaparra/599	20.00
37	Jeff Kent/596	4.00
38	Brian Giles/594	3.00
39	Geoff Jenkins/588	4.00
40	Carl Everett/587	2.50
41	Todd Helton/1161	6.00
42	Manny Ramirez/1154	8.00
43	Carlos Delgado/1134	5.00
44	Barry Bonds/1128	8.00
45	Jason Giambi/1123	5.00
46	Gary Sheffield/1081	4.00
47	Vladimir Guerrero/1074	8.00
48	Frank Thomas/1061	8.00
49	Sammy Sosa/1040	10.00
50	Moises Alou/1039	2.50
51	Jeff Bagwell/1039	6.00
52	Nomar Garciaparra/1033	15.00
53	Richard Hidalgo/1027	3.00
54	Alex Rodriguez/1026	15.00
55	Brian Giles/1026	3.00
56	Jeff Kent/1020	3.00
57	Mike Piazza/1012	15.00
58	Troy Glaus/1008	6.00
59	Edgar Martinez/1002	3.00
60	Jim Edmonds/994	4.00

2001 Donruss Rookie Reprints

		MT
Complete Set (40):		300.00
Common Player:		3.00
#'d to Original Yr. issued		
1	Cal Ripken Jr.	25.00
2	Wade Boggs	8.00
3	Tony Gwynn	15.00
4	Ryne Sandberg	20.00
5	Don Mattingly	25.00
6	Joe Carter	3.00
7	Roger Clemens	15.00
8	Kirby Puckett	25.00
9	Orel Hershiser	3.00
10	Andres Galarraga	5.00
11	Jose Canseco	8.00
12	Fred McGriff	5.00
13	Paul O'Neill	5.00
14	Mark McGwire	20.00
15	Barry Bonds	10.00
16	Kevin Brown	4.00
17	David Cone	3.00
18	Rafael Palmeiro	6.00
19	Barry Larkin	5.00
20	Bo Jackson	4.00
21	Greg Maddux	15.00
22	Roberto Alomar	6.00
23	Mark Grace	5.00
24	David Wells	3.00
25	Tom Glavine	6.00
26	Matt Williams	4.00
27	Ken Griffey Jr.	25.00
28	Randy Johnson	8.00
29	Gary Sheffield	4.00
30	Craig Biggio	4.00
31	Curt Schilling	3.00
32	Larry Walker	4.00
33	Bernie Williams	6.00
34	Sammy Sosa	15.00
35	Juan Gonzalez	8.00
36	David Justice	5.00
37	Ivan Rodriguez	8.00
38	Jeff Bagwell	8.00
39	Jeff Kent	4.00
40	Manny Ramirez	8.00

2001 Donruss Rookie Reprints Autographs

		MT
Common Player:		
#'d to last 2 digits of yr. issued		
1	Cal Ripken/82	220.00
2	Wade Boggs/83	70.00
3	Tony Gwynn/83	100.00
4	Ryne Sandberg/83	125.00
5	Don Mattingly/84	300.00
6	Joe Carter/84	30.00
7	Roger Clemens/85	100.00
8	Kirby Puckett/85	150.00
9	Orel Hershiser/85	30.00
10	Andres Galarraga/86	40.00
15	Barry Bonds/87	200.00

16	Kevin Brown/87	30.00
17	David Cone/87	40.00
18	Rafael Palmeiro/ 87	50.00
20	Bo Jackson/87	75.00
21	Greg Maddux/87	150.00
22	Roberto Alomar/ 88	40.00
24	David Wells/88	30.00
25	Tom Glavine/88	40.00
28	Randy Johnson/ 89	75.00
29	Gary Sheffield/89	30.00
31	Curt Schilling/89	30.00
35	Juan Gonzalez/90	100.00
36	David Justice/90	50.00
37	Ivan Rodriguez/91	70.00
39	Manny Ramirez/92	75.00

2001 Donruss Stat Line Career

	MT
Cards #1-150 print run 251-400:	4-8X
1-150 p/r 201-250:	5-10X
1-150 p/r 151-200:	6-12X
1-150 p/r 101-150:	8-15X
1-150 p/r 61-100:	15-25X
1-150 p/r 41-60:	20-40X
1-150 p/r 21-40:	25-50X
1-150 p/r 15-20:	30-70X
Common (151-200) p/r 251-400:	2.00
Common (151-200) p/r 151-250:	4.00
Common (151-200) p/r 101-150:	6.00
Common (151-200) p/r 76-100:	8.00
Common (151-200) p/r 31-75	10.00
Common (151-200) p/r 20-30	12.00
cards 201-220 p/r 201-400:	1-2X
201-220 p/r 101-200:	2-4X
201-220 p/r 75-100:	3-5X
201-220 p/r 40-74:	4-8X
156 Albert Pujols/154	250.00
190 Jackson Melian/ 26	50.00
195 Ichiro Suzuki/106	250.00

2001 Donruss Stat Line Season

	MT
Cards #1-150 print run 151-200:	6-12X
1-150 p/r 101-150:	8-15X
1-150 p/r 76-100:	10-20X
1-150 p/r 51-75:	15-25X
1-150 p/r 36-50:	20-35X
1-150 p/r 21-35:	25-50X
Common (151-200) p/r 151-200:	3.00
Common (151-200) p/r 101-150:	4.00
Common (151-200) p/r 101-150:	6.00
Common (151-200) p/r 76-100:	8.00
Common (151-200) p/r 31-75	10.00
Common (151-200) p/r 20-30	12.00
cards 201-220 p/r 151-200:	1-3X
201-220 p/r 101-150:	2-4X
201-220 p/r 75-100:	3-5X
201-220 p/r 40-74:	4-8X
156 Albert Pujols/17	500.00
190 Jackson Melian/73	40.00
195 Ichiro Suzuki/153	200.00

A player's name in *italic* type indicates a rookie card.

2001 Donruss 1999 Diamond Kings

		MT
Complete Set (5):		70.00
Common Player:		10.00
Production 2,500 sets		
1	Scott Rolen	8.00
2	Sammy Sosa	15.00
3	Juan Gonzalez	10.00
4	Ken Griffey Jr.	25.00
5	Derek Jeter	25.00

2001 Donruss 2000 Diamond Kings

		MT
Complete Set (5):		40.00
Common Player:		8.00
Production 2,500 sets		
Studio:		1-2X
Production 250 sets		
1	Frank Thomas	8.00
2	Greg Maddux	12.00
3	Alex Rodriguez	15.00
4	Jeff Bagwell	8.00
5	Manny Ramirez	8.00

2001 Donruss 2001 Diamond Kings

		MT
Complete Set (20):		240.00
Common Player:		5.00
Production 2,500 sets		
Studio Canvas Parallel:		1-2X
Production 250		
1	Alex Rodriguez	20.00
2	Cal Ripken Jr.	25.00
3	Mark McGwire	25.00
4	Ken Griffey Jr.	25.00
5	Derek Jeter	25.00
6	Nomar Garciaparra	20.00
7	Mike Piazza	20.00
8	Roger Clemens	10.00
9	Greg Maddux	15.00
10	Chipper Jones	15.00
11	Tony Gwynn	10.00
12	Barry Bonds	8.00
13	Sammy Sosa	15.00
14	Vladimir Guerrero	10.00
15	Frank Thomas	10.00
16	Troy Glaus	8.00
17	Todd Helton	8.00
18	Ivan Rodriguez	8.00
19	Pedro Martinez	10.00
20	Carlos Delgado	6.00

2001 Donruss 1999 Retro

		MT
Complete Set (100):		200.00
Common Player:		.25
Inserted 1:hobby pack		
Common (81-100):		5.00
Production 1,999		
1	Ken Griffey Jr.	4.00
2	Nomar Garciaparra	3.00
3	Alex Rodriguez	3.00
4	Mark McGwire	4.00
5	Sammy Sosa	2.50
6	Chipper Jones	2.50
7	Mike Piazza	3.00
8	Barry Larkin	.40
9	Andruw Jones	1.00
10	Albert Belle	.25
11	Jeff Bagwell	1.25
12	Tony Gwynn	1.50
13	Manny Ramirez	1.25
14	Mo Vaughn	.40
15	Barry Bonds	2.00
16	Frank Thomas	1.50
17	Vladimir Guerrero	1.50
18	Derek Jeter	4.00
19	Randy Johnson	1.25
20	Greg Maddux	2.50
21	Pedro Martinez	1.50
22	Cal Ripken Jr.	4.00
23	Ivan Rodriguez	1.25
24	Matt Williams	.40
25	Javy Lopez	.25
26	Tim Salmon	.25
27	Raul Mondesi	.25
28	Todd Helton	1.25
29	Magglio Ordonez	.35
30	Sean Casey	.35
31	Jeromy Burnitz	.25
32	Jeff Kent	.35
33	Jim Edmonds	.35
34	Jim Thome	.35
35	Dante Bichette	.25
36	Larry Walker	.40
37	Will Clark	.50
38	Omar Vizquel	.25
39	Mike Mussina	.75
40	Eric Karros	.25
41	Kenny Lofton	.25
42	David Justice	.50
43	Craig Biggio	.25
44	J.D. Drew	.25
45	Rickey Henderson	.40
46	Bernie Williams	1.00
47	Brian Giles	.25
48	Paul O'Neill	.40
49	Orlando Hernandez	.40
50	Jason Giambi	.50
51	Curt Schilling	.25
52	Scott Rolen	.50
53	Mark Grace	.50
54	Moises Alou	.25
55	Jason Kendall	.25
56	Ray Lankford	.25
57	Kerry Wood	.40
58	Gary Sheffield	.40
59	Ruben Mateo	.25
60	Darin Erstad	.40
61	Troy Glaus	1.25
62	Jose Canseco	.75
63	Wade Boggs	.50
64	Tom Glavine	.50
65	Gabe Kapler	.25
66	Juan Gonzalez	1.25
67	Rafael Palmeiro	.75
68	Richie Sexson	.25
69	Carl Everett	.25
70	David Wells	.25
71	Carlos Delgado	1.00
72	Eric Davis	.25
73	Shawn Green	.40
74	Andres Galarraga	.40
75	Edgar Martinez	.25
76	Roberto Alomar	1.00
77	John Olerud	.40
78	Luis Gonzalez	.25
79	Kevin Brown	.25
80	Roger Clemens	1.50
81	Josh Beckett	10.00
82	Alfonso Soriano	10.00
83	Alex Escobar	8.00
84	Pat Burrell	15.00
85	Eric Chavez	8.00
86	Erubiel Durazo	5.00
87	Abraham Nunez	5.00
88	Carlos Pena	6.00
89	Nick Johnson	10.00
90	Eric Munson	8.00
91	Corey Patterson	8.00
92	Wily Mo Pena	8.00
93	Rafael Furcal	15.00
94	Eric Valent	8.00
95	Mark Mulder	12.00
96	Chad Hutchinson	5.00
97	Freddy Garcia	8.00
98	Tim Hudson	10.00
99	Rick Ankiel	6.00
100	Kip Wells	5.00

2001 Donruss 1999 Retro Stat Line Career

		MT
Cards #1-80 print run 251-400:		2-4X
(1-80) p/r 151-250:		3-6X
(1-80) p/r 101-150:		4-8X
(1-80) p/r 76-100:		5-10X
(1-80) p/r 51-75:		6-12X
(1-80) p/r 30-50:		8-20X
1	Ken Griffey Jr./350	20.00
2	Nomar Garciaparra/ 309	20.00
3	Alex Rodriguez/ 313	20.00
4	Mark McGwire/219	25.00
5	Sammy Sosa/273	12.00
6	Chipper Jones/297	15.00
7	Mike Piazza/333	20.00
8	Barry Larkin/305	5.00
9	Andruw Jones/273	6.00
10	Albert Belle/321	2.50
11	Jeff Bagwell/304	8.00
12	Tony Gwynn/339	12.00
13	Manny Ramirez/ 154	15.00
14	Mo Vaughn/304	2.50
15	Barry Bonds/290	12.00
16	Frank Thomas/286	10.00
17	Vladimir Guerrero/ 305	10.00
18	Derek Jeter/308	25.00
19	Randy Johnson/ 336	8.00
20	Greg Maddux/202	20.00
21	Pedro Martinez/ 298	10.00
22	Cal Ripken Jr./276	25.00
23	Ivan Rodriguez/232	8.00
24	Matt Williams/299	4.00
25	Javy Lopez/333	2.50
26	Tim Salmon/179	4.00
27	Raul Mondesi/295	2.50
28	Todd Helton/310	8.00
29	Magglio Ordonez/ 173	4.00
30	Sean Casey/269	2.50
31	Jeromy Burnitz/294	2.50
32	Jeff Kent/193	5.00
33	Jim Edmonds/294	5.00
34	Jim Thome/163	4.00

35 Dante Bichette/300 2.50
36 Larry Walker/225 8.00
37 Will Clark/302 6.00
38 Omar Vizquel/196 4.00
39 Mike Mussina/118 10.00
40 Eric Karros/177 4.00
41 Kenny Lofton/311 2.50
42 David Justice/214 5.00
43 Craig Biggio/318 2.50
44 J.D. Drew/35 25.00
45 Rickey Henderson/283 6.00
46 Bernie Williams/213 6.00
47 Brian Giles/157 4.00
48 Paul O'Neill/223 5.00
49 Orlando Hernandez/313 2.50
50 Jason Giambi/73 15.00
51 Curt Schilling/336 2.50
52 Scott Rolen/220 5.00
53 Mark Grace/310 6.00
54 Moises Alou/201 3.00
55 Jason Kendall/308 2.50
56 Ray Lankford/225 3.00
57 Kerry Wood/233 3.00
58 Gary Sheffield/202 5.00
59 Ruben Mateo/384 2.50
60 Darin Erstad/179 8.00
61 Troy Glaus/218 10.00
62 Jose Canseco/296 6.00
63 Wade Boggs/329 8.00
64 Tom Glavine/331 5.00
65 Gabe Kapler/5
66 Juan Gonzalez/301 8.00
67 Rafael Palmeiro/314 5.00
68 Richie Sexson/308 2.50
69 Carl Everett/209 3.00
70 David Wells/124 5.00
71 Carlos Delgado/333 6.00
72 Eric Davis/342 2.50
73 Shawn Green/77 15.00
74 Andres Galarraga/364 4.00
75 Edgar Martinez/318 4.00
76 Roberto Alomar/302 6.00
77 John Olerud/301 2.50
78 Luis Gonzalez/237 3.00
79 Kevin Brown/330 2.50
80 Roger Clemens/295 12.00
81 Josh Beckett/13
82 Alfonso Soriano/113 20.00
83 Alex Escobar/181 10.00
84 Pat Burrell/303 12.00
85 Eric Chavez/314 2.50
86 Erubiel Durazo/147 5.00
87 Abraham Nunez/106 15.00
88 Carlos Pena/46 25.00
89 Nick Johnson/259 6.00
90 Eric Munson/392 6.00
91 Corey Patterson/117 15.00
92 Wily Mo Pena/247 8.00
93 Rafael Furcal/137 20.00
94 Eric Valent/53 10.00
95 Mark Mulder/340 4.00
96 Chad Hutchinson/2
97 Freddy Garcia/397 6.00
98 Tim Hudson/17 50.00
99 Rick Ankiel/222 10.00
100 Kip Wells/371 2.50

2001 Donruss 1999 Retro Stat Line Season

MT

Cards #1-80 print run 251-400: 2-4X
(1-80) p/r 151-250: 3-6X
(1-80) p/r 101-150: 4-8X
(1-80) p/r 76-100: 5-10X
(1-80) p/r 51-75: 6-12X
(1-80) p/r 30-50: 8-20X
1 Ken Griffey Jr./56 70.00
2 Nomar Garciaparra/35 100.00
3 Alex Rodriguez/42 100.00
4 Mark McGwire/70 80.00
5 Sammy Sosa/66 40.00
6 Chipper Jones/123 30.00
7 Mike Piazza/111 50.00
8 Barry Larkin/166 8.00
9 Andruw Jones/31 30.00
10 Albert Belle/49 8.00
11 Jeff Bagwell/164 12.00
12 Tony Gwynn/148 25.00
13 Manny Ramirez/145 20.00
14 Mo Vaughn/40 10.00
15 Barry Bonds/120 25.00
16 Frank Thomas/155 15.00
17 Vladimir Guerrero/38 40.00
18 Derek Jeter/127 60.00
19 Randy Johnson/19 75.00
20 Greg Maddux/5
21 Pedro Martinez/19 80.00
22 Cal Ripken Jr./163 40.00
23 Ivan Rodriguez/186 12.00
24 Matt Williams/136 8.00
25 Javy Lopez/106 6.00
26 Tim Salmon/139 5.00
27 Raul Mondesi/162 4.00
28 Todd Helton/25 60.00
29 Magglio Ordonez/151 4.00
30 Sean Casey/82 8.00
31 Jeromy Burnitz/125 5.00
32 Jeff Kent/128 8.00
33 Jim Edmonds/115 12.00
34 Jim Thome/129 6.00
35 Dante Bichette/122 5.00
36 Larry Walker/113 15.00
37 Will Clark/169 10.00
38 Omar Vizquel/166 4.00
39 Mike Mussina/175 10.00
40 Eric Karros/150 5.00
41 Kenny Lofton/54 10.00
42 David Justice/151 6.00
43 Craig Biggio/51 10.00
44 J.D. Drew/5
45 Rickey Henderson/66 25.00
46 Bernie Williams/26 30.00
47 Brian Giles/94 6.00
48 Paul O'Neill/116 10.00
49 Orlando Hernandez/12 35.00
50 Jason Giambi/166 10.00
51 Curt Schilling/15 40.00
52 Scott Rolen/31 30.00
53 Mark Grace/92 15.00
54 Moises Alou/124 5.00
55 Jason Kendall/175 4.00
56 Ray Lankford/156 4.00
57 Kerry Wood/13 50.00
58 Gary Sheffield/132 10.00
59 Ruben Mateo/134 5.00
60 Darin Erstad/159 10.00
61 Troy Glaus/1
62 Jose Canseco/46 30.00
63 Wade Boggs/122 15.00
64 Tom Glavine/20 50.00
65 Gabe Kapler/25 20.00
66 Juan Gonzalez/50 30.00
67 Rafael Palmeiro/121 10.00
68 Richie Sexson/11
69 Carl Everett/138 5.00
70 David Wells/163 4.00
71 Carlos Delgado/155 10.00
72 Eric Davis/148 5.00
73 Shawn Green/100 12.00
74 Andres Galarraga/44 20.00
75 Edgar Martinez/102 10.00
76 Roberto Alomar/166 15.00
77 John Olerud/22 20.00
78 Luis Gonzalez/146 5.00
79 Kevin Brown/18 25.00
80 Roger Clemens/20 120.00
81 Josh Beckett/178 10.00
82 Alfonso Soriano/7
83 Alex Escobar/27 40.00
84 Pat Burrell/7
85 Eric Chavez/33 15.00
86 Erubiel Durazo/19 20.00
87 Abraham Nunez/95 10.00
88 Carlos Pena/319 6.00
89 Nick Johnson/17 50.00
90 Eric Munson/16 40.00
91 Corey Patterson/22 40.00
92 Wily Mo Pena/7
93 Rafael Furcal/88 20.00
94 Eric Valent/13
95 Mark Mulder/113 6.00
96 Chad Hutchinson/51 6.00
97 Freddy Garcia/10
98 Tim Hudson/152 15.00
99 Rick Ankiel/12 40.00
100 Kip Wells/135 2.50

2001 Donruss 2000 Retro

MT

Complete Set (100): 200.00
Common Player: .25
Common (81-100): 5.00
Production 2,000
1 Vladimir Guerrero 1.50
2 Alex Rodriguez 3.00
3 Ken Griffey Jr. 3.00
4 Nomar Garciaparra 3.00
5 Mike Piazza 3.00
6 Mark McGwire 4.00
7 Sammy Sosa 2.50
8 Chipper Jones 2.50
9 Jim Edmonds .35
10 Tony Gwynn 1.50
11 Andruw Jones 1.00
12 Albert Belle .25
13 Jeff Bagwell 1.25
14 Manny Ramirez 1.50
15 Mo Vaughn .30
16 Barry Bonds 2.00
17 Frank Thomas 1.50
18 Ivan Rodriguez 1.25
19 Derek Jeter 4.00
20 Randy Johnson 1.25
21 Greg Maddux 2.50
22 Pedro Martinez 1.50
23 Cal Ripken Jr. 4.00
24 Mark Grace .60
25 Javy Lopez .25
26 Ray Durham .25
27 Todd Helton 1.25
28 Magglio Ordonez .40
29 Sean Casey .40
30 Darin Erstad .50
31 Barry Larkin .50
32 Will Clark .50
33 Jim Thome .40
34 Dante Bichette .25
35 Larry Walker .60
36 Ken Caminiti .25
37 Omar Vizquel .35
38 Miguel Tejada .40
39 Eric Karros .25
40 Gary Sheffield .50
41 Jeff Cirillo .25
42 Rondell White .25
43 Rickey Henderson .50
44 Bernie Williams 1.00
45 Brian Giles .40
46 Paul O'Neill .40
47 Orlando Hernandez .40
48 Ben Grieve .40
49 Jason Giambi .60
50 Curt Schilling .35
51 Scott Rolen .50
52 Bobby Abreu .25
53 Jason Kendall .25
54 Fernando Tatis .25
55 Jeff Kent .40
56 Mike Mussina .75
57 Troy Glaus 1.25
58 Jose Canseco .75
59 Wade Boggs .50
60 Fred McGriff .40
61 Juan Gonzalez 1.25
62 Rafael Palmeiro .75
63 Rusty Greer .25
64 Carl Everett .25
65 David Wells .25
66 Carlos Delgado 1.00
67 Shawn Green .40
68 David Justice .50
69 Edgar Martinez .25
70 Andres Galarraga .40
71 Roberto Alomar 1.00
72 Jermaine Dye .25
73 John Olerud .40
74 Luis Gonzalez .50
75 Craig Biggio .40
76 Kevin Millwood .25
77 Kevin Brown .40
78 John Smoltz .25
79 Roger Clemens 1.50
80 Mike Hampton .25
81 Tomas De La Rosa 5.00
82 C.C. Sabathia 15.00
83 Ryan Christenson 5.00
84 Pedro Feliz 6.00
85 Jose Ortiz 8.00
86 Xavier Nady 10.00
87 Julio Zuleta 6.00
88 Jason Hart 10.00
89 Keith Ginter 6.00
90 Brent Abernathy 5.00
91 Timo Perez 5.00
92 Juan Pierre 6.00
93 Tike Redman 5.00
94 Mike Lamb 5.00
95 Ben Sheets 15.00
96 Kazuhiro Sasaki 15.00
97 Barry Zito 15.00
98 Adam Bernero 5.00
99 Chad Durbin 5.00
100 Matt Ginter 5.00

2001 Donruss 2000 Retro Stat Line Career

MT

Cards #1-80 print run 251-400: 2-4X
1-80 p/r 151-250: 3-6X
1-80 p/r 101-150: 4-8X
1-80 p/r 76-100: 5-10X
1-80 p/r 51-75: 8-15X
1-80 p/r 31-50: 10-20X
1-80 p/r 21-30: 15-30X
Common (81-100) p/r 251-400: 1.50
Common (81-100) p/r 151-250: 2.50
Common (81-100) p/r 101-150: 4.00
Common (81-100) p/r 76-100: 5.00
Common (81-100) p/r 31-75 6.00
88 Jason Hart/19 30.00
95 Ben Sheets/159 25.00
96 Kazuhiro Sasaki/229 35.00

2001 Donruss 2000 Retro Stat Line Season

MT

Cards #1-80 print run 251-400: 2-4X
1-80 p/r 151-250: 3-6X
1-80 p/r 101-150: 4-8X
1-80 p/r 76-100: 5-10X

1-80 p/r 51-75: 8-15X
1-80 p/r 31-50: 10-20X
1-80 p/r 21-30: 15-30X
Common (81-100) p/r 151-200: 2.50
Common (81-100) p/r 81-150: 5.00
Common (81-100) p/r 51-80: 6.00
86 Xavier Nady/23 40.00
96 Kazuhiro Sasaki/34 80.00
97 Barry Zito/97 25.00

2001 Donruss 2001 Diamond Kings Studio Series Autograph

MT
Common Autograph: 100.00
Production 50 sets
1 Alex Rodriguez 200.00
2 Cal Ripken Jr. 300.00
8 Roger Clemens 150.00
9 Greg Maddux 200.00
10 TBD Redemption
11 Tony Gwynn 125.00
12 TBD Redemption
14 Vladimir Guerrero 100.00
16 Troy Glaus 100.00
17 Todd Helton 100.00
18 Ivan Rodriguez 100.00

2001 Donruss Classics

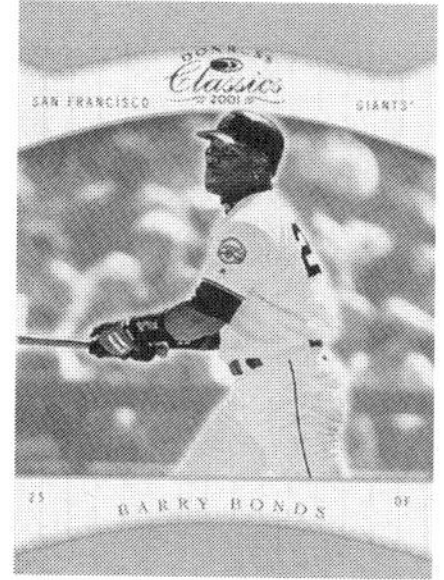

MT
Common Player: .50
Common SP (101-150): 10.00
Production 585
Common SP (151-200): 4.00
Production 1,755
Pack (6): 9.00
Box (18): 150.00
1 Alex Rodriguez 5.00
2 Barry Bonds 4.00
3 Cal Ripken Jr. 6.00
4 Chipper Jones 4.00
5 Derek Jeter 6.00
6 Troy Glaus 2.00
7 Frank Thomas 2.00
8 Greg Maddux 4.00
9 Ivan Rodriguez 2.00
10 Jeff Bagwell 2.00
11 Cliff Floyd .50
12 Todd Helton 2.00
13 Ken Griffey Jr. 5.00
14 Manny Ramirez 2.00
15 Mark McGwire 6.00
16 Mike Piazza 5.00
17 Nomar Garciaparra 5.00
18 Pedro Martinez 2.50
19 Randy Johnson 2.00
20 Rick Ankiel .75
21 Rickey Henderson .75
22 Roger Clemens 3.00
23 Sammy Sosa 4.00
24 Tony Gwynn 2.50
25 Vladimir Guerrero 2.00
26 Kazuhiro Sasaki .75
27 Roberto Alomar 1.50
28 Barry Zito .75
29 Pat Burrell 1.00
30 Harold Baines .50
31 Carlos Delgado 1.50
32 J.D. Drew 1.00
33 Jim Edmonds .75
34 Darin Erstad 1.00
35 Jason Giambi 1.50
36 Tom Glavine 1.00
37 Juan Gonzalez 2.00
38 Mark Grace 1.00
39 Shawn Green .75
40 Tim Hudson 1.00
41 Andruw Jones 1.50
42 Jeff Kent .75
43 Barry Larkin 1.00
44 Rafael Furcal .75
45 Mike Mussina 1.00
46 Hideo Nomo 1.00
47 Rafael Palmeiro 1.00
48 Scott Rolen 1.00
49 Gary Sheffield .75
50 Bernie Williams 1.50
51 Bob Abreu .50
52 Edgardo Alfonzo .50
53 Edgar Martinez .50
54 Magglio Ordonez .75
55 Kerry Wood .75
56 Adrian Beltre .75
57 Lance Berkman .75
58 Kevin Brown .75
59 Sean Casey .75
60 Eric Chavez .50
61 Bartolo Colon .50
62 Johnny Damon .50
63 Jermaine Dye .50
64 Juan Encarnacion .50
65 Carl Everett .50
66 Brian Giles .50
67 Mike Hampton .75
68 Richard Hidalgo .50
69 Geoff Jenkins .75
70 Jacque Jones .50
71 Jason Kendall .50
72 Ryan Klesko .50
73 Chan Ho Park .75
74 Richie Sexson .50
75 Mike Sweeney .50
76 Fernando Tatis .50
77 Miguel Tejada .75
78 Jose Vidro .50
79 Larry Walker 1.00
80 Preston Wilson .50
81 Craig Biggio .75
82 Fred McGriff .75
83 Jim Thome 1.00
84 Garret Anderson .50
85 Russell Branyan .50
86 Tony Batista .50
87 Terrence Long .50
88 Brad Fullmer .50
89 Rusty Greer .50
90 Orlando Hernandez .50
91 Gabe Kapler .50
92 Paul Konerko .50
93 Carlos Lee .50
94 Kenny Lofton .75
95 Raul Mondesi .50
96 Jorge Posada .75
97 Tim Salmon .75
98 Greg Vaughn .50
99 Mo Vaughn .50
100 Omar Vizquel .50
101 Aubrey Huff 12.00
102 Jimmy Rollins 12.00
103 *Cory Aldridge* 15.00
104 *Wilmy Caceres* 15.00
105 Josh Beckett 15.00
106 *Wilson Betemit* 25.00
107 Timo Perez 12.00
108 *Albert Pujols* 60.00
109 *Bud Smith* 15.00
110 *Jack Wilson* 15.00
111 Alex Escobar 12.00
112 *Johnny Estrada* 15.00
113 Pedro Feliz 12.00
114 *Nate Frese* 15.00
115 *Carlos Garcia* 15.00
116 *Brandon Larson* 15.00
117 *Alexis Gomez* 15.00
118 Jason Hart 15.00
119 Adam Dunn 25.00
120 Marcus Giles 12.00
121 *Christian Parker* 15.00
122 *Jackson Melian* 12.00
123 Eric Chavez 12.00
124 *Adrian Hernandez* 15.00
125 *Joe Kennedy* 15.00
126 *Jose Mieses* 15.00
127 C.C. Sabathia 15.00
128 Eric Munson 12.00
129 Xavier Nady 12.00
130 *Horacio Ramirez* 15.00
131 Abraham Nunez 12.00
132 Jose Ortiz 12.00
133 *Jeremy Owens* 15.00
134 *Claudio Vargas* 15.00
135 Corey Patterson 15.00
136 Audres Torres 12.00
137 Ben Sheets 15.00
138 Joe Crede 12.00
139 *Adam Pettyjohn* 15.00
140 *Elpidio Guzman* 15.00
141 *Jay Gibbons* 20.00
142 *Wilkin Ruan* 12.00
143 *Tsuyoshi Shinjo* 25.00
144 Alfonso Soriano 15.00
145 Nick Johnson 12.00
146 *Ichiro Suzuki* 80.00
147 *Juan Uribe* 15.00
148 Jack Cust 12.00
149 *Carlos Valderrama* 15.00
150 *Matt White* 15.00
151 Hank Aaron 15.00
152 Ernie Banks 6.00
153 Johnny Bench 8.00
154 George Brett 10.00
155 Lou Brock 6.00
156 Rod Carew 6.00
157 Steve Carlton 6.00
158 Bob Feller 4.00
159 Bob Gibson 6.00
160 Reggie Jackson 8.00
161 Al Kaline 8.00
162 Sandy Koufax
163 Don Mattingly 15.00
164 Willie Mays 15.00
165 Willie McCovey 6.00
166 Joe Morgan 6.00
167 Stan Musial 10.00
168 Jim Palmer 6.00
169 Brooks Robinson 8.00
170 Frank Robinson 6.00
171 Nolan Ryan 20.00
172 Mike Schmidt 10.00
173 Tom Seaver 8.00
174 Warren Spahn 8.00
175 Robin Yount 8.00
176 Wade Boggs 6.00
177 Ty Cobb 10.00
178 Lou Gehrig 12.00
179 Luis Aparicio 4.00
180 Babe Ruth 20.00
181 Ryne Sandberg 12.00
182 Yogi Berra 8.00
183 Roberto Clemente 15.00
184 Eddie Murray 6.00
185 Robin Roberts 4.00
186 Duke Snider 6.00
187 Orlando Cepeda 4.00
188 Billy Williams 4.00
189 Juan Marichal 4.00
190 Harmon Killebrew 6.00
191 Kirby Puckett 15.00
192 Carlton Fisk 6.00
193 Dave Winfield 6.00
194 Whitey Ford 6.00
195 Paul Molitor 6.00
196 Tony Perez 4.00
197 Ozzie Smith 8.00
198 Ralph Kiner 4.00
199 Fergie Jenkins 4.00
200 Phil Rizzuto 6.00

Figure values of lower-grade cards from 1981-date as:
Near Mint (NM) 75%
Excellent (EX) 40%
of the listed Mint price

For cards through 1980, values should be figured as:
Excellent (EX) 50%
Very Good (VG) 30%
of the listed Near Mint price

2001 Donruss Classics Benchmarks

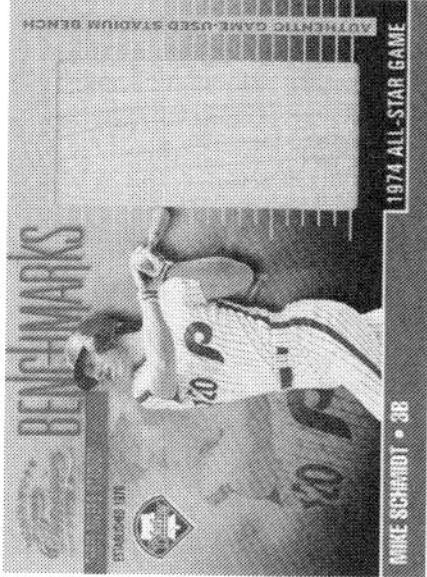

MT
Common Player: 10.00
Inserted 1:18
1 Todd Helton 15.00
2 Roberto Clemente 60.00
3 Mark McGwire 40.00
4 Barry Bonds 30.00
5 Bob Gibson 20.00
6 Ken Griffey Jr. 30.00
7 Frank Robinson 15.00
8 Greg Maddux 20.00
9 Reggie Jackson 20.00
10 Sammy Sosa 25.00
11 Willie Stargell 20.00
12 Vladimir Guerrero 15.00
13 Johnny Bench 20.00
14 Tony Gwynn 20.00
15 Mike Schmidt 20.00
16 Ivan Rodriguez 15.00
17 Jeff Bagwell 20.00
18 Cal Ripken Jr. 40.00
20 Kirby Puckett 40.00
21 Frank Thomas 15.00
22 Joe Morgan 10.00
23 Mike Piazza 25.00
24 Hank Aaron
25 Andruw Jones 10.00

2001 Donruss Classics Benchmarks Autographs

MT
Common Autograph:
5 Bob Gibson 60.00
7 Frank Robinson 50.00
9 Reggie Jackson 100.00
12 Vladimir Guerrero
13 Johnny Bench
15 Mike Schmidt 100.00
20 Kirby Puckett
22 Joe Morgan 50.00
25 Andruw Jones 60.00

2001 Donruss Classics Classic Combos

MT
Common Card: 30.00
1 Roberto Clemente 250.00
2 Willie Stargell
3 Babe Ruth 800.00
4 Lou Gehrig 600.00
5 Hank Aaron
6 Eddie Mathews 125.00
7 Johnny Bench 100.00
8 Joe Morgan 50.00
9 Robin Yount 120.00
10 Paul Molitor 75.00
11 Steve Carlton 75.00
12 Mike Schmidt 125.00
13 Stan Musial 125.00
14 Lou Brock
15 Yogi Berra 125.00
16 Phil Rizzuto 80.00
17 Ernie Banks

18 Billy Williams 50.00
21 Jackie Robinson
22 Duke Snider 75.00
23 Frank Robinson 50.00
24 Brooks Robinson 75.00
26 Willie McCovey 50.00
29 Harmon Killebrew 100.00
30 Rod Carew 90.00
31 Roberto Clemente
32 Babe Ruth, Lou Gehrig 1400.
33 Hank Aaron, Eddie Mathews
34 Johnny Bench, Joe Morgan 125.00
35 Robin Yount, Paul Molitor 150.00
36 Steve Carlton, Mike Schmidt
37 Stan Musial, Lou Brock 200.00
38 Phil Rizzuto, Yogi Berra 250.00
39 Ernie Banks, Billy Williams
41 Jackie Robinson, Duke Snider
42 Brooks Robinson, Frank Robinson
43 Willie McCovey, Orlando Cepeda 90.00
45 Harmon Killebrew, Rod Carew 200.00

2001 Donruss Classics Legendary Lumberjacks

MT
Common Player: 15.00
Inserted 1:18
1 TBD
2 Chipper Jones 25.00
3 TBD
4 Nellie Fox
5 Ivan Rodriguez 20.00
6 Jimmie Foxx
7 Hank Aaron
8 Yogi Berra 30.00
9 Ernie Banks 40.00
10 George Brett 40.00
11 Ty Cobb 180.00
12 Roberto Clemente 150.00
13 Carlton Fisk 25.00
14 Reggie Jackson 25.00
15 Al Kaline 40.00
16 Harmon Killebrew 40.00
17 Ralph Kiner 20.00
18 Roger Maris
19 Eddie Mathews 40.00
20 Ted Williams
21 Willie McCovey 20.00
22 Eddie Murray 20.00
23 Joe Morgan 15.00
24 Frank Robinson 20.00
25 Tony Perez 15.00
26 Mike Schmidt 40.00
27 Ryne Sandberg 40.00
28 Duke Snider 25.00
29 Willie Stargell
30 Billy Williams 20.00
31 Dave Winfield 20.00
32 Robin Yount 30.00
33 Barry Bonds 40.00
34 Stan Musial 50.00
35 Johnny Bench 40.00
36 Orlando Cepeda 20.00
37 Jeff Bagwell 20.00
38 Frank Thomas 20.00
39 Juan Gonzalez 20.00
40 Cal Ripken Jr. 40.00
41 Rafael Palmeiro 20.00
42 Troy Glaus 20.00
43 Manny Ramirez 20.00
44 Paul Molitor 30.00
45 Tony Gwynn 25.00
46 Rod Carew 20.00
47 Lou Brock 20.00
48 Wade Boggs 15.00
49 Babe Ruth 300.00
50 Lou Gehrig 250.00

2001 Donruss Classics Significant Signatures

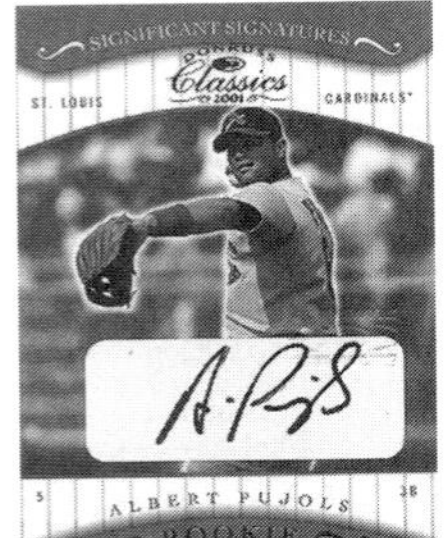

MT
Common Autograph: 12.00
Inserted 1:18
101 Aubrey Huff 12.00
103 Cory Aldridge 15.00
105 Josh Beckett 30.00
106 Wilson Betemit 30.00
107 Timo Perez 15.00
108 Albert Pujols 150.00
110 Jack Wilson 12.00
111 Alex Escobar 15.00
112 Johnny Estrada 25.00
113 Pedro Feliz 12.00
114 Nate Frese 12.00
115 Carlos Garcia 12.00
116 Brandon Larson 12.00
118 Jason Hart 15.00
119 Adam Dunn 75.00
120 Marcus Giles 15.00
121 Christian Parker 12.00
126 Jose Mieses 12.00
127 C.C. Sabathia 30.00
129 Xavier Nady 15.00
130 Horacio Ramirez 15.00
131 Abraham Nunez 12.00
132 Jose Ortiz 20.00
133 Jeremy Owens 12.00
134 Claudio Vargas 12.00
135 Corey Patterson 25.00
136 Andres Torres 12.00
137 Ben Sheets 30.00
138 Joe Crede 15.00
139 Adam Pettyjohn 12.00
140 Elpidio Guzman 12.00
141 Jay Gibbons 25.00
142 Wilkin Ruan 12.00
144 Alfonso Soriano 40.00
145 Nick Johnson 30.00
147 Juan Uribe 15.00
149 Carlos Valderrama 12.00
151 Hank Aaron
152 Ernie Banks 50.00
153 Johnny Bench 100.00
154 George Brett 120.00
155 Lou Brock 35.00
156 Rod Carew 30.00
157 Steve Carlton 30.00
158 Bob Feller
159 Bob Gibson 35.00
160 Reggie Jackson
161 Al Kaline 40.00
162 Sandy Koufax 300.00
163 Don Mattingly 100.00
164 Willie Mays 150.00
165 Willie McCovey 40.00
166 Joe Morgan 25.00
167 Stan Musial 100.00
168 Jim Palmer 25.00
169 Brooks Robinson 35.00
170 Frank Robinson 25.00
171 Nolan Ryan 175.00
172 Mike Schmidt 75.00
173 Tom Seaver 50.00
174 Warren Spahn 30.00
175 Robin Yount 120.00
176 Wade Boggs 75.00
179 Luis Aparicio 25.00
181 Ryne Sandberg 75.00
182 Yogi Berra 30.00
184 Eddie Murray 40.00
185 Robin Roberts 20.00
186 Duke Snider 40.00
187 Orlando Cepeda 20.00
188 Billy Williams 25.00
189 Juan Marichal 20.00
190 Harmon Killebrew 30.00
191 Kirby Puckett 220.00
192 Carlton Fisk 40.00
193 Dave Winfield 50.00
194 Whitey Ford 50.00
195 Paul Molitor 75.00
196 Tony Perez 20.00
197 Ozzie Smith 75.00
198 Ralph Kiner 25.00
199 Fergie Jenkins 25.00
200 Phil Rizzuto 40.00

2001 Donruss Classics Stadium Stars

MT
Common Player: 8.00
Inserted 1:18
1 Babe Ruth 50.00
2 Cal Ripken Jr. 25.00
3 Brooks Robinson 10.00
4 Tony Gwynn 10.00
5 Ty Cobb 25.00
6 Vladimir Guerrero 10.00
7 Lou Gehrig 40.00
8 Nomar Garciaparra 20.00
9 Sammy Sosa 15.00
10 Reggie Jackson 10.00
11 Alex Rodriguez 20.00
12 Derek Jeter 25.00
13 Willie McCovey 8.00
14 Mark McGwire 20.00
15 Chipper Jones 15.00
16 Honus Wagner 20.00
17 Ken Griffey Jr. 15.00
18 Frank Robinson 10.00
19 Barry Bonds 20.00
20 Yogi Berra 15.00
21 Mike Piazza 15.00
22 Roger Clemens 15.00
23 Duke Snider 15.00
24 Frank Thomas 10.00
25 Andruw Jones 8.00

2001 Donruss Classics Timeless Treasures

MT
Common Player: 75.00
Inserted 1:420
1 Mark McGwire ball 400.00
2 Babe Ruth seat 100.00
3 Harmon Killebrew bat 75.00
4 Derek Jeter base 75.00
5 Barry Bonds ball 150.00

2001 Donruss Classics Timeless Tributes

MT
Stars (1-100): 4-8X
SP's (101-150): 1-1.5X
SP's (151-200): 1-2.5X
Production 100 sets
(See 2001 Donruss Classics for checklist and base cards values.)

2001 Donruss The Rookies

MT
Complete Set (105): 40.00
Complete Factory Set (106): 50.00
Common Player: .25
1 Adam Dunn 2.50
2 *Ryan Drese* .40
3 *Bud Smith* 3.00
4 *Tsuyoshi Shinjo* 2.00
5 Roy Oswalt .75
6 *Wilmy Caceres* .25
7 *Willie Harris* .25
8 *Andres Torres* .25
9 *Brandon Knight* .25
10 *Horacio Ramirez* .25
11 *Benito Baez* .25
12 *Jeremy Affeldt* .25
13 *Ryan Jensen* .25
14 *Casey Fossum* .75
15 *Ramon Vazquez* 1.00
16 *Dustan Mohr* .25
17 *Saul Rivera* .25
18 *Zach Day* .25
19 *Erik Hiljus* .25
20 *Cesar Crespo* .25
21 *Wilson Guzman* .25
22 *Travis Hafner* 1.00
23 *Grant Balfour* .25
24 *Johnny Estrada* .75
25 *Morgan Ensberg* 1.50
26 *Jack Wilson* .25
27 Aubrey Huff .25
28 *Endy Chavez* .50
29 *Delvin James* .25
30 Michael Cuddyer .25
31 *Jason Michaels* .25
32 *Martin Vargas* .25
33 *Donaldo Mendez* .25
34 *Jorge Julio* .25
35 *Tim Spooneybarger* .25
36 Kurt Ainsworth .25
37 *Josh Fogg* 1.00
38 *Brian Reith* .25
39 *Rick Baurer* .25
40 Tim Redding .25
41 *Erick Almonte* .50
42 Juan Pena .50
43 Ken Harvey .25
44 *David Brous* .25
45 *Kevin Olsen* .25
46 *Henry Mateo* .25
47 Nick Neugebauer .50
48 *Mike Penney* .25
49 *Jay Gibbons* 2.00
50 *Tim Christman* .25
51 *Brandon Duckworth* 2.00
52 *Brett Jodie* .25
53 *Christian Parker* .25
54 *Carlos Hernandez* .25
55 *Brandon Larson* .25
56 *Nick Punto* .25
57 *Elpidio Guzman* .25
58 *Joe Beimel* .25
59 *Junior Spivey* .50
60 *Will Ohman* .25
61 *Brandon Lyon* .25
62 *Stubby Clapp* .25
63 *Justin Duchscherer* .25
64 Jimmy Rollins .25

65	*David Williams*	.75
66	*Craig Monroe*	1.00
67	*Jose Acevedo*	.25
68	Jason Jennings	.25
69	Josh Phelps	.25
70	*Brian Roberts*	.25
71	*Claudio Vargas*	.25
72	Adam Johnson	.25
73	*Bart Miadich*	.25
74	Juan Rivera	.25
75	*Brad Voyles*	.25
76	Nate Cornejo	.25
77	*Juan Moreno*	.25
78	*Brian Rogers*	.25
79	*Ricardo Rodriguez*	1.00
80	*Geronimo Gil*	.25
81	*Joe Kennedy*	2.00
82	*Kevin Joseph*	.25
83	*Josue Perez*	.25
84	*Victor Zambrano*	.25
85	*Josh Towers*	1.00
86	*Mike Rivera*	.25
87	*Mark Prior*	10.00
88	*Juan Cruz*	2.00
89	*Dewon Brazelton*	2.00
90	*Angel Berroa*	1.00
91	*Mark Teixeira*	6.00
92	*Cody Ransom*	.25
93	*Angel Santos*	.25
94	*Corky Miller*	1.50
95	*Brandon Berger*	1.00
96	Corey Patterson	.25
97	*Albert Pujols*	10.00
98	Josh Beckett	.75
99	C.C. Sabathia	.25
100	Alfonso Soriano	.50
101	Ben Sheets	.40
102	*Rafael Soriano*	.75
103	*Wilson Betemit*	3.00
104	*Ichiro Suzuki*	8.00
105	Jose Ortiz	.50

2001 Donruss The Rookies Rookie Diamond Kings

		MT
Complete Set (5):		8.00
Inserted 1:Rookies Set		
106	C.C. Sabathia	8.00
107	Tsuyoshi Shinjo	10.00
108	Albert Pujols	25.00
109	Roy Oswalt	8.00
110	Ichiro Suzuki	30.00

2001 Donruss Class of 2001

		MT
Complete Set (300):		NA
Common Player:		.20
Common (101-200):		3.00
Production 1,875		
Common (201-300):		8.00
Production 625		
Pack (3):		3.50
Box (24 + bobble head):		75.00
1	Alex Rodriguez	2.00
2	Barry Bonds	1.50
3	Vladimir Guerrero	.75
4	Jim Edmonds	.40
5	Derek Jeter	3.00
6	Jose Canseco	.40
7	Rafael Furcal	.20
8	Cal Ripken Jr.	3.00
9	Brad Radke	.20
10	Miguel Tejada	.30
11	Pat Burrell	.40
12	Ken Griffey Jr.	2.50
13	Cliff Floyd	.20
14	Luis Gonzalez	.50
15	Frank Thomas	.75
16	Mike Sweeney	.20
17	Paul LoDuca	.20
18	Lance Berkman	.30
19	Tony Gwynn	.75
20	Chipper Jones	1.50
21	Eric Chavez	.30
22	Kerry Wood	.40
23	Jorge Posada	.40
24	J.D. Drew	.40
25	Garret Anderson	.20
26	Mike Piazza	2.00
27	Kenny Lofton	.30
28	Mike Mussina	.60
29	Paul Konerko	.20
30	Bernie Williams	.50
31	Eric Milton	.20
32	Shawn Green	.40
33	Paul O'Neill	.40
34	Juan Gonzalez	.75
35	Andres Galarraga	.30
36	Gary Sheffield	.30
37	Ben Grieve	.20
38	Scott Rolen	.40
39	Mark Grace	.50
40	Hideo Nomo	.50
41	Barry Zito	.30
42	Edgar Martinez	.20
43	Jarrod Washburn	.20
44	Greg Maddux	1.50
45	Mark Buehrle	.20
46	Larry Walker	.40
47	Trot Nixon	.20
48	Nomar Garciaparra	2.00
49	Robert Fick	.20
50	Sean Casey	.40
51	Joe Mays	.20
52	Roger Clemens	1.00
53	Chan Ho Park	.40
54	Carlos Delgado	.50
55	Phil Nevin	.20
56	Jason Giambi	.60
57	Raul Mondesi	.20
58	Roberto Alomar	.60
59	Ryan Klesko	.20
60	Andruw Jones	.50
61	Gabe Kapler	.30
62	Darin Erstad	.30
63	Cristian Guzman	.20
64	Kazuhiro Sasaki	.20
65	Doug Mientkiewicz	.20
66	Sammy Sosa	1.50
67	Mike Hampton	.30
68	Rickey Henderson	.40
69	Mark Mulder	.40
70	Mark McGwire	2.50
71	Freddy Garcia	.20
72	Ivan Rodriguez	.75
73	Terrence Long	.20
74	Jeff Bagwell	.75
75	Moises Alou	.30
76	Todd Helton	.75
77	Preston Wilson	.20
78	Pedro Martinez	.75
79	Bobby Abreu	.20
80	Manny Ramirez	.75
81	Jose Vidro	.20
82	Randy Johnson	.75
83	Richie Sexson	.20
84	Troy Glaus	.50
85	Kevin Brown	.40
86	Carlos Lee	.20
87	Adrian Beltre	.30
88	Brian Giles	.30
89	Jermaine Dye	.20
90	Craig Biggio	.30
91	Richard Hidalgo	.20
92	Magglio Ordonez	.20
93	Aramis Ramirez	.20
94	Jeff Kent	.30
95	Curt Schilling	.40
96	Tim Hudson	.40
97	Fred McGriff	.30
98	Barry Larkin	.40
99	Jim Thome	.40
100	Tom Glavine	.40
101	*Sean Douglass*	4.00
102	*Rob Mackowiak*	3.00
103	*Jeremy Fikac*	4.00
104	*Henry Mateo*	4.00
105	*Geronimo Gil*	4.00
106	*Ramon Vazquez*	8.00
107	*Pedro Santana*	6.00
108	*Ryan Jensen*	4.00
109	*Paul Phillips*	4.00
110	*Saul Rivera*	5.00
111	Larry Bigbie	3.00
112	Josh Phelps	3.00
113	*Justin Kaye*	4.00
114	*Kris Keller*	5.00
115	Adam Bernero	3.00
116	*Victor Zambrano*	4.00
117	Felipe Lopez	3.00
118	*Brian Roberts*	4.00
119	Kurt Ainsworth	3.00
120	*George Perez*	5.00
121	*Wilson Guzman*	6.00
122	*Derrick Lewis*	3.00
123	*Nate Teut*	8.00
124	*Martin Vargas*	4.00
125	Brandon Inge	3.00
126	*Travis Phelps*	4.00
127	*Les Walrond*	4.00
128	*Justin Atchley*	4.00
129	*Stubby Clapp*	4.00
130	*Bret Prinz*	3.00
131	*Bert Snow*	3.00
132	Joe Crede	3.00
133	*Nick Punto*	5.00
134	*Carlos Hernandez*	4.00
135	*Ken Vining*	4.00
136	*Luis Pineda*	4.00
137	*Winston Abreu*	4.00
138	Matt Ginter	3.00
139	*Jason Smith*	4.00
140	*Gene Altman*	4.00
141	*Brian Rogers*	4.00
142	Michael Cuddyer	3.00
143	*Mike Penney*	3.00
144	*Scott Podsednik*	3.00
145	*Esix Snead*	4.00
146	*Steve Watkins*	4.00
147	*Orlando Woodards*	4.00
148	Mike Young	3.00
149	Chris George	3.00
150	*Blaine Neal*	4.00
151	Ben Sheets	4.00
152	*Scott Stewart*	3.00
153	*Mike Koplove*	5.00
154	*Kyle Lohse*	8.00
155	Dee Brown	3.00
156	Aubrey Huff	3.00
157	Pablo Ozuna	3.00
158	Bill Ortega	3.00
159	Toby Hall	3.00
160	*Kevin Olsen*	4.00
161	*Will Ohman*	4.00
162	Nate Cornejo	3.00
163	Jack Cust	3.00
164	Juan Rivera	3.00
165	*Jerrod Riggan*	4.00
166	*Dustan Mohr*	4.00
167	*Doug Nickle*	6.00
168	*Craig Monroe*	5.00
169	Jason Jennings	3.00
170	*Bart Miadich*	5.00
171	Luis Rivas	3.00
172	*Tim Christman*	6.00
173	*Luke Hudson*	4.00
174	*Brett Jodie*	5.00
175	*Jorge Julio*	4.00
176	David Espinosa	3.00
177	*Mike Maroth*	4.00
178	Keith Ginter	3.00
179	*Juan Moreno*	4.00
180	*Brandon Knight*	5.00
181	Steve Lomasney	3.00
182	*John Grabow*	4.00
183	*Steve Green*	4.00
184	*Jason Karnuth*	5.00
185	*Bob File*	4.00
186	Brent Abernathy	3.00
187	*Morgan Ensberg*	5.00
188	Wily Mo Pena	3.00
189	Ken Harvey	3.00
190	*Josh Pearce*	3.00
191	Cesar Izturis	3.00
192	*Eric Hinske*	10.00
193	*Joe Beimel*	6.00
194	Timo Perez	3.00
195	*Troy Mattes*	5.00
196	Eric Valent	3.00
197	*Ed Rogers*	3.00
198	*Grant Balfour*	4.00
199	*Benito Baez*	4.00
200	Vernon Wells	3.00
201	*Joe Kennedy*	10.00
202	*Wilson Betemit*	20.00
203	*Christian Parker*	8.00
204	*Jay Gibbons*	20.00
205	*Carlos Garcia*	8.00
206	*Jack Wilson*	8.00
207	*Johnny Estrada*	10.00
208	*Wilkin Ruan*	8.00
209	*Brandon Duckworth*	15.00
210	*Willie Harris*	8.00
211	*Marlon Byrd*	25.00
212	C.C. Sabathia	8.00
213	*Dennis Tankersley*	12.00
214	*Brandon Larson*	8.00
215	*Alexis Gomez*	12.00
216	*Bill Hall*	8.00
217	*Antonio Perez*	10.00
218	*Jeremy Affeldt*	8.00
219	*Junior Spivey*	10.00
220	*Casey Fossum*	10.00
221	*Brandon Lyon*	8.00
222	*Angel Santos*	8.00
223	*Lance Davis*	15.00
224	*Zach Day*	8.00
225	*David Williams*	8.00
226	*Cesar Crespo*	8.00
227	*Jose Acevedo*	8.00
228	*Travis Hafner*	8.00
229	*Orlando Hudson*	15.00
230	*Jose Mieses*	8.00
231	*Ricardo Rodriguez*	10.00
232	Alfonso Soriano	8.00
233	Jason Hart	8.00
234	*Endy Chavez*	8.00
235	*Delvin James*	12.00
236	*Ryan Drese*	8.00
237	*Jeremy Owens*	10.00
238	*Brad Voyles*	8.00
239	Nate Frese	8.00
240	Josh Beckett	10.00
241	Roy Oswalt	10.00
242	*Juan Uribe*	8.00
243	*Cory Aldridge*	8.00
244	Adam Dunn	20.00
245	*Bud Smith*	25.00
246	*Adrian Hernandez*	8.00
247	*Matt Guerrier*	10.00
248	Jimmy Rollins	8.00
249	*Wilmy Caceres*	8.00
250	*Jason Michaels*	8.00
251	*Ichiro Suzuki*	60.00
252	*John Buck*	10.00
253	*Andres Torres*	8.00
254	*Alfredo Amezaga*	8.00
255	*Corky Miller*	10.00
256	*Rafael Soriano*	8.00
257	*Donaldo Mendez*	15.00
258	*Victor Martinez*	10.00
259	Corey Patterson	8.00
260	*Horacio Ramirez*	8.00
261	*Elpidio Guzman*	8.00
262	*Juan Diaz*	10.00
263	*Mike Rivera*	8.00
264	*Brian Lawrence*	8.00
265	*Josue Perez*	8.00
266	Jose Nunez	8.00
267	*Erik Bedard*	8.00
268	*Albert Pujols*	40.00
269	*Duaner Sanchez*	8.00
270	*Cody Ransom*	8.00
271	*Greg Miller*	8.00
272	*Adam Pettyjohn*	8.00
273	*Tsuyoshi Shinjo*	15.00
274	*Claudio Vargas*	8.00
275	*Justin Duchscherer*	8.00
276	*Tim Spooneybarger*	8.00
277	*Rick Bauer*	8.00
278	*Josh Fogg*	15.00
279	*Brian Reith*	8.00
280	*Scott MacRae*	8.00
281	*Ryan Ludwick*	10.00
282	*Erick Almonte*	8.00
283	*Josh Towers*	10.00
284	Juan Pena	8.00
285	*David Brous*	8.00
286	*Erik Hiljus*	10.00
287	Nick Neugebauer	8.00
288	*Jackson Melian*	8.00
289	*Billy Sylvester*	8.00
290	*Carlos Valderrama*	8.00
291	*Jose Cueto*	8.00
292	*Matt White*	8.00
293	*Nick Maness*	8.00
294	*Jason Lane*	20.00

295	*Brandon Berger*	8.00
296	*Angel Berroa*	8.00
297	*Juan Cruz*	15.00
298	*Dewon Brazelton*	12.00
299	*Mark Prior*	50.00
300	*Mark Teixeira*	30.00

2001 Donruss Class of 2001 First Class

	MT
Stars (1-100):	8-15X
Production 100	
SP's (101-300):	1-3X
Production 50	

2001 Donruss Class of 2001 Aces

		MT
Complete Set (20):		70.00
Common Player:		3.00
Inserted 1:30		
1	Roger Clemens	10.00
2	Randy Johnson	5.00
3	Freddy Garcia	3.00
4	Greg Maddux	10.00
5	Tim Hudson	5.00
6	Curt Schilling	5.00
7	Mark Buehrle	3.00
8	Matt Morris	3.00
9	Joe Mays	3.00
10	Javier Vazquez	3.00
11	Mark Mulder	4.00
12	Wade Miller	3.00
13	Barry Zito	3.00
14	Pedro Martinez	8.00
15	Al Leiter	4.00
16	Chan Ho Park	3.00
17	John Burkett	3.00
18	C.C. Sabathia	3.00
19	Jamie Moyer	3.00
20	Mike Mussina	5.00

2001 Donruss Class of 2001 Bobblehead

		MT
Common Bobblehead:		15.00
One per box		
1	Ichiro Suzuki	50.00
2	Cal Ripken Jr.	50.00
3	Derek Jeter	50.00
4	Mark McGwire	50.00
5	Albert Pujols	40.00
6	Ken Griffey Jr.	40.00
7	Nomar Garciaparra	25.00
8	Mike Piazza	30.00
9	Alex Rodriguez	25.00
10	Manny Ramirez	20.00
11	Tsuyoshi Shinjo	25.00
12	Hideo Nomo	25.00
13	Chipper Jones	20.00
14	Sammy Sosa	25.00
15	Roger Clemens	25.00
16	Tony Gwynn	20.00
17	Barry Bonds	25.00
18	Kazuhiro Sasaki	15.00
19	Pedro Martinez	20.00
20	Jeff Bagwell	20.00
21	Ichiro Suzuki ROY	70.00
22	Albert Pujols ROY	50.00

2001 Donruss Class of 2001 Bobblehead Cards

		MT
Common Player:		4.00
1-20 2,000 produced		
21-22 1,000 produced		
1	Ichiro Suzuki	15.00
2	Cal Ripken Jr.	12.00
3	Derek Jeter	12.00
4	Mark McGwire	10.00
5	Albert Pujols	10.00
6	Ken Griffey Jr.	10.00
7	Nomar Garciaparra	8.00
8	Mike Piazza	8.00
9	Alex Rodriguez	8.00
10	Manny Ramirez	5.00
11	Tsuyoshi Shinjo	4.00
12	Hideo Nomo	4.00
13	Chipper Jones	6.00
14	Sammy Sosa	6.00
15	Roger Clemens	6.00
16	Tony Gwynn	5.00
17	Barry Bonds	6.00
18	Kazuhiro Sasaki	4.00
19	Pedro Martinez	5.00
20	Jeff Bagwell	5.00
21	Ichiro Suzuki	20.00
22	Albert Pujols	15.00

2001 Donruss Class of 2001 Crusade

		MT
Complete Set (25):		140.00
Common Player:		4.00
Production 300		
1	Roger Clemens	15.00
2	Luis Gonzalez	8.00
3	Troy Glaus	8.00
4	Freddy Garcia	4.00
5	Sean Casey	5.00
6	Bobby Abreu	4.00
7	Matt Morris	4.00
8	Cal Ripken Jr.	25.00
9	Miguel Tejada	5.00
10	Vladimir Guerrero	8.00
11	Mark Buehrle	4.00
12	Mike Sweeney	4.00
13	Ivan Rodriguez	8.00
14	Jeff Bagwell	10.00
15	Joe Mays	4.00
16	Cliff Floyd	4.00
17	Lance Berkman	6.00
18	Aramis Ramirez	4.00
19	Tony Gwynn	10.00
20	Shannon Stewart	4.00
21	Todd Helton	10.00
22	Chipper Jones	12.00
23	Javier Vazquez	4.00
24	Shawn Green	5.00
25	Barry Bonds	12.00

2001 Donruss Class of 2001 Rookie Crusade

		MT
Complete Set (25):		150.00
Common Player:		3.00
Production 300		
26	Albert Pujols	30.00
27	Wilson Betemit	12.00
28	C.C. Sabathia	3.00
29	Roy Oswalt	6.00
30	Johnny Estrada	6.00
31	Nick Johnson	3.00
32	Aubrey Huff	3.00
33	Corey Patterson	3.00
34	Jay Gibbons	5.00
35	Marcus Giles	3.00
36	Juan Cruz	15.00
37	Tsuyoshi Shinjo	10.00
38	Ben Sheets	5.00
39	Bud Smith	12.00
40	Alex Escobar	3.00
41	Joe Kennedy	3.00
42	Alexis Gomez	3.00
43	Jimmy Rollins	3.00
44	Josh Towers	5.00
45	Joe Crede	3.00
46	Brandon Duckworth	8.00
47	Ichiro Suzuki	50.00
48	Jose Ortiz	3.00
49	Casey Fossum	5.00
50	Adam Dunn	10.00

2001 Donruss Class of 2001 Diamond Aces

		MT
Common Player:		10.00
Varying quantities produced		
1	Roger Clemens/200	50.00
2	Randy Johnson/750	20.00
3	Freddy Garcia/350	10.00
4	Greg Maddux/750	30.00
5	Tim Hudson/550	15.00
6	Curt Schilling/525	15.00
7	Mark Buehrle/750	10.00
9	Joe Mays/750	10.00
10	Javier Vazquez/500	10.00
11	Mark Mulder/300	10.00
12	Wade Miller/525	10.00
13	Barry Zito/550	10.00
14	Pedro Martinez/550	25.00
15	Al Leiter/525	15.00
16	Chan Ho Park/400	10.00
17	John Burkett/700	10.00
18	C.C. Sabathia/550	10.00
19	Jamie Moyer/700	10.00
20	Mike Mussina/75	

2001 Donruss Class of 2001 Diamond Dominators

		MT
Common Player:		8.00
Varying quantities produced		
1	Manny Ramirez/725	10.00
2	Lance Berkman/725	8.00
3	Juan Gonzalez/500	10.00
4	Albert Pujols/125	65.00
5	Jason Giambi/250	25.00
6	Mike Sweeney/325	8.00
7	Rafael Palmeiro/550	10.00
8	Luis Gonzalez/725	15.00
9	Ichiro Suzuki/50	
10	Cliff Floyd/725	8.00
11	Roberto Alomar/200	15.00
12	Paul LoDuca/600	8.00
13	Shannon Stewart/725	8.00
14	Barry Bonds/250	40.00
15	Larry Walker/725	10.00
16	Shawn Green/500	10.00
17	Moises Alou/550	8.00
18	Cal Ripken/250	80.00
19	Brian Giles/725	8.00
20	Magglio Ordonez/725	8.00
21	Jose Vidro/725	8.00
22	Edgar Martinez/200	15.00
23	Aramis Ramirez/200	10.00
24	Tony Gwynn/500	20.00
25	Richie Sexson/725	8.00
26	Todd Helton/725	12.00
27	Garret Anderson/725	8.00
28	Chipper Jones/725	20.00
29	Troy Glaus/200	15.00
30	Jeff Bagwell/325	20.00

2001 Donruss Class of 2001 Dominators

		MT
Complete Set (30):		120.00
Common Player:		3.00
Inserted 1:20		
1	Manny Ramirez	4.00
2	Lance Berkman	3.00
3	Juan Gonzalez	4.00
4	Albert Pujols	15.00
5	Jason Giambi	4.00
6	Mike Sweeney	3.00
7	Rafael Palmeiro	4.00
8	Luis Gonzalez	4.00
9	Ichiro Suzuki	20.00
10	Cliff Floyd	3.00
11	Roberto Alomar	4.00
12	Paul LoDuca	3.00
13	Shannon Stewart	3.00
14	Barry Bonds	8.00
15	Larry Walker	3.00
16	Shawn Green	4.00
17	Moises Alou	3.00
18	Cal Ripken Jr.	15.00
19	Brian Giles	3.00
20	Magglio Ordonez	3.00
21	Jose Vidro	3.00
22	Edgar Martinez	3.00
23	Aramis Ramirez	3.00
24	Tony Gwynn	5.00
25	Richie Sexson	3.00
26	Todd Helton	5.00
27	Garret Anderson	3.00
28	Chipper Jones	6.00
29	Troy Glaus	4.00
30	Jeff Bagwell	5.00

2001 Donruss Class of 2001 Final Rewards

		MT
Common Player:		8.00
Varying quantities produced		
1	Jason Giambi/250	20.00
2	Ichiro Suzuki/50	200.00
3	Roger Clemens/200	50.00
4	Freddy Garcia/250	10.00
5	Ichiro Suzuki/50	200.00
6	Albert Pujols/125	60.00
7	Barry Bonds/200	45.00
8	Albert Pujols/125	60.00
9	Randy Johnson/250	25.00

2001 Donruss Class of 2001 First Class Autographs

MT

Common Player:
1 Alex Rodriguez/25
3 Vladimir Guerrero/25
10 Miguel Tejada/75
14 Luis Gonzalez/25
15 Frank Thomas/25
17 Paul LoDuca/100
18 Lance Berkman/25
20 Chipper Jones/25
21 Eric Chavez/100
22 Kerry Wood/25
24 J.D. Drew/25
27 Kenny Lofton/25
28 Mike Mussina/25
30 Bernie Williams/25
32 Shawn Green/15
34 Juan Gonzalez/25
35 Andres Galarraga/25
36 Gary Sheffield/25
38 Scott Rolen/25
41 Barry Zito/100
44 Greg Maddux/25
45 Mark Buehrle/100
48 Nomar Garciaparra/15
49 Robert Fick/100
50 Sean Casey/100
51 Joe Mays/100
52 Roger Clemens/25
53 Chan Ho Park/15
58 Roberto Alomar/15
59 Ryan Klesko/50
62 Darin Erstad/25
69 Mark Mulder/100
72 Ivan Rodriguez/25
73 Terrence Long/100
74 Jeff Bagwell/15
75 Moises Alou/25
76 Todd Helton/25
78 Pedro Martinez/15
80 Manny Ramirez/15
81 Jose Vidro/100
82 Randy Johnson/15
83 Richie Sexson/100
84 Troy Glaus/100
85 Kevin Brown/25
88 Brian Giles/25
89 Jermaine Dye/100
90 Craig Biggio/15
91 Richard Hidalgo/100
93 Aramis Ramirez/100
95 Curt Schilling/25
96 Tim Hudson/100
98 Barry Larkin/15
100 Tom Glavine/25

2001 Donruss Class of 2001 Rewards

		MT
Complete Set (10):		200.00
Common Player:		8.00
Inserted 1:212		
1	Jason Giambi	10.00
2	Ichiro Suzuki	50.00
3	Roger Clemens	25.00
4	Freddy Garcia	8.00
5	Ichiro Suzuki	50.00
6	Albert Pujols	30.00
7	Barry Bonds	25.00
8	Albert Pujols	30.00
9	Randy Johnson	12.00
10	Matt Morris	8.00

2001 Donruss Class of 2001 Rookie Team

		MT
Complete Set (15):		100.00
Common Player:		5.00
Inserted 1:83		
1	Jay Gibbons	5.00
2	Alfonso Soriano	5.00
3	Jimmy Rollins	5.00
4	Wilson Betemit	8.00
5	Albert Pujols	20.00
6	Johnny Estrada	5.00
7	Ichiro Suzuki	30.00
8	Tsuyoshi Shinjo	8.00
9	Adam Dunn	8.00
10	C.C. Sabathia	5.00
11	Ben Sheets	5.00
12	Roy Oswalt	5.00
13	Bud Smith	8.00
14	Josh Towers	5.00
15	Juan Cruz	8.00

2001 Donruss Class of 2001 Rookie Team Materials

		MT
Common Player:		5.00
Varying quantities produced		
1	Jay Gibbons/100	10.00
2	Alfonso Soriano/100	20.00
3	Jimmy Rollins/200	10.00
4	Wilson Betemit/100	
5	Albert Pujols/100	65.00
6	Johnny Estrada/100	10.00
7	Ichiro Suzuki/50	200.00
8	Tsuyoshi Shinjo/200	30.00
9	Adam Dunn/200	35.00
10	C.C. Sabathia/200	10.00
11	Ben Sheets/200	12.00
12	Roy Oswalt/50	
13	Bud Smith/250	25.00
14	Josh Towers/200	15.00
15	Juan Cruz/200	30.00

2001 Donruss Class of 2001 Rookie Autographs

		MT
Common Autograph:		8.00
109	Paul Phillips/250	8.00
114	Kris Keller/250	10.00
115	Adam Bernero/250	8.00
120	George Perez/250	8.00
123	Nate Teut/250	10.00
124	Martin Vargas/250	10.00
127	Les Walrond/250	8.00
132	Joe Crede/250	10.00
137	Winston Abreu/250	8.00
138	Matt Ginter/250	10.00
140	Gene Altman/250	8.00
142	Michael Cuddyer/250	8.00
143	Mike Penney/250	8.00
145	Esix Snead/250	8.00
147	Orlando Woodards/250	8.00
148	Jeff Deardorff/100	8.00
150	Blaine Neal/250	8.00
156	Aubrey Huff/250	8.00
157	Pablo Ozuna/250	10.00
158	Bill Ortega/250	8.00
160	Kevin Olsen/250	8.00
161	Will Ohman/250	8.00
163	Jack Cust/250	8.00
168	Craig Monroe/250	8.00
169	Jason Jennings/250	8.00
171	Luis Rivas/250	8.00
173	Luke Hudson/250	12.00
176	David Espinosa/250	8.00
177	Mike Maroth/250	8.00
178	Keith Ginter/250	8.00
181	Steve Lomasney/250	8.00
182	John Grabow/250	8.00
184	Jason Karnuth/250	8.00
186	Brent Abernathy/250	10.00
188	Wily Mo Pena/250	8.00
191	Cesar Izturis/250	8.00
192	Eric Hinske/250	20.00
194	Timo Perez/100	8.00
196	Eric Valent/250	10.00
201	Joe Kennedy/100	25.00
202	Wilson Betemit/100	50.00
203	Christian Parker/100	12.00
204	Jay Gibbons/100	40.00
205	Carlos Garcia/200	8.00
206	Jack Wilson/100	12.00
207	Johnny Estrada/200	10.00
208	Wilkin Ruan/200	8.00
209	Brandon Duckworth/100	40.00
211	Marlon Byrd/100	60.00
212	C.C. Sabathia/25	
213	Dennis Tankersley/100	40.00
214	Brandon Larson/200	8.00
215	Alexis Gomez/200	10.00
216	Bill Hall/100	15.00
217	Antonio Perez/100	25.00
218	Jeremy Affeldt/200	8.00
220	Casey Fossum/200	10.00
224	Zach Day/200	8.00
225	David Williams/200	8.00
227	Jose Acevedo/200	8.00
229	Orlando Hudson/100	20.00
230	Jose Mieses/200	8.00
231	Ric Rodriguez/200	8.00
232	Alfonso Soriano/100	30.00
233	Jason Hart/100	12.00
234	Endy Chavez/200	8.00
235	Delvin James/100	10.00
237	Jeremy Owens/200	8.00
238	Brad Voyles/200	8.00
239	Nate Frese/200	8.00
240	Josh Beckett/25	20.00
241	Roy Oswalt/100	25.00
242	Juan Uribe/150	10.00
243	Cory Aldridge/200	8.00
244	Adam Dunn/100	50.00
245	Bud Smith/100	50.00
246	Adrian Hernandez/100	10.00
249	Wilmy Caceres/200	8.00
250	Jason Michaels/200	8.00
252	John Buck/100	15.00
253	Andres Torres/100	10.00
255	Corky Miller/100	20.00
256	Rafael Soriano/200	10.00
257	Donaldo Mendez/200	8.00
259	Corey Patterson/100	15.00
260	Horacio Ramirez/200	8.00
261	Elpidio Guzman/200	8.00
262	Juan Diaz/200	8.00
264	Brian Lawrence/200	10.00
265	Josue Perez/200	8.00
266	Jose Nunez/200	8.00
268	Albert Pujols/100	150.00
269	Duaner Sanchez/200	8.00
271	Greg Miller/200	8.00
272	Adam Pettyjohn/200	8.00
274	Claudio Vargas/200	8.00
279	Brian Reith/200	8.00
283	Josh Towers/100	15.00
285	David Brous/200	8.00
287	Nick Neugebauer/100	12.00
289	Billy Sylvester/200	8.00
290	Carlos Valderrama/200	8.00
292	Matt White/200	10.00
293	Nick Maness/200	8.00
296	Angel Berroa/100	20.00
297	Juan Cruz/100	50.00
298	Dewon Brazelton/100	25.00
299	Mark Prior/100	150.00
300	Mark Teixeira /100	100.00

2001 Donruss Class of 2001 Yearbook

		MT
Complete Set (25):		90.00
Common Player:		2.50
Inserted 1:24		
1	Barry Bonds	8.00
2	Mark Mulder	3.00
3	Luis Gonzalez	3.00
4	Lance Berkman	2.50
5	Matt Morris	2.50
6	Roy Oswalt	3.00
7	Todd Helton	4.00
8	Tsuyoshi Shinjo	4.00
9	C.C. Sabathia	2.50
10	Curt Schilling	4.00
11	Rickey Henderson	3.00
12	Jamie Moyer	2.50
13	Shawn Green	3.00
14	Randy Johnson	4.00
15	Jim Thome	3.00
16	Larry Walker	3.00
17	Jimmy Rollins	2.50
18	Kazuhiro Sasaki	2.50
19	Hideo Nomo	3.00
20	Roger Clemens	8.00
21	Bud Smith	5.00
22	Ichiro Suzuki	20.00
23	Albert Pujols	15.00
24	Cal Ripken Jr.	15.00
25	Tony Gwynn	5.00

2001 Donruss Class of 2001 Yearbook Scrapbook

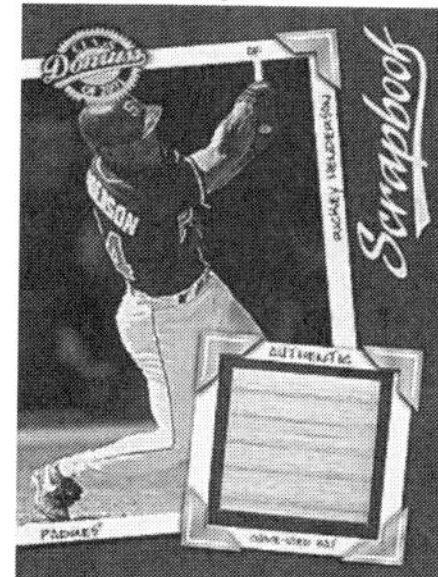

		MT
Common Player:		10.00
Varying quantities produced		
1	Barry Bonds/525	30.00
2	Mark Mulder/500	10.00
3	Luis Gonzalez/500	20.00
4	Lance Berkman/525	10.00
6	Roy Oswalt/150	20.00
7	Todd Helton/525	15.00
8	Tsuyoshi Shinjo/75	50.00
9	C.C. Sabathia/500	10.00
10	Curt Schilling/525	15.00
11	Rickey Henderson/200	40.00

12	Jamie Moyer/500	10.00
13	Shawn Green/525	12.00
14	Randy Johnson/ 500	20.00
15	Jim Thome/400	15.00
16	Larry Walker/500	10.00
17	Jimmy Rollins/25	
18	Kazuhiro Sasaki/ 500	15.00
19	Hideo Nomo/150	75.00
20	Roger Clemens/ 475	30.00
21	Bud Smith/525	25.00
22	Ichiro Suzuki/75	150.00
23	Albert Pujols/150	60.00
24	Cal Ripken/525	70.00
25	Tony Gwynn/500	15.00

2001 Donruss Elite

	MT
Complete Set (200):	NA
Common Player:	.25
Common (151-200):	8.00
Production 900	
Common Coupon (201-250):	4.00
Pack (5):	8.00
Box (18):	150.00
Cards 201-250 available through redempt.	
Common 201-250:	5.00

1	Alex Rodriguez	2.50
2	Barry Bonds	1.50
3	Cal Ripken Jr.	3.00
4	Chipper Jones	2.00
5	Derek Jeter	3.00
6	Troy Glaus	1.00
7	Frank Thomas	1.25
8	Greg Maddux	2.00
9	Ivan Rodriguez	1.00
10	Jeff Bagwell	1.00
11	Jose Canseco	.50
12	Todd Helton	1.00
13	Ken Griffey Jr.	2.50
14	Manny Ramirez	1.00
15	Mark McGwire	3.00
16	Mike Piazza	2.50
17	Nomar Garciaparra	2.50
18	Pedro Martinez	1.25
19	Randy Johnson	1.00
20	Rick Ankiel	.40
21	Ricky Henderson	.40
22	Roger Clemens	1.50
23	Sammy Sosa	2.00
24	Tony Gwynn	1.25
25	Vladimir Guerrero	1.25
26	Eric Davis	.25
27	Roberto Alomar	.75
28	Mark Mulder	.25
29	Pat Burrell	.75
30	Harold Baines	.25
31	Carlos Delgado	.75
32	J.D. Drew	.40
33	Jim Edmonds	.40
34	Darin Erstad	.50
35	Jason Giambi	.50
36	Tom Glavine	.50
37	Juan Gonzalez	1.00
38	Mark Grace	.50
39	Shawn Green	.40
40	Tim Hudson	.40
41	Andruw Jones	.75
42	David Justice	.50
43	Jeff Kent	.40
44	Barry Larkin	.50
45	Pokey Reese	.25
46	Mike Mussina	.50
47	Hideo Nomo	.40
48	Rafael Palmeiro	.50
49	Adam Piatt	.25
50	Scott Rolen	.50
51	Gary Sheffield	.40
52	Bernie Williams	.75
53	Bob Abreu	.25
54	Edgardo Alfonzo	.25
55	*Jermaine Clark*	.25
56	Albert Belle	.25
57	Craig Biggio	.40
58	Andres Galarraga	.40
59	Edgar Martinez	.25
60	Fred McGriff	.25
61	Maggio Ordonez	.40
62	Jim Thome	.40
63	Matt Williams	.40
64	Kerry Wood	.40
65	Moises Alou	.25
66	Brady Anderson	.25
67	Garret Anderson	.25
68	Tony Armas Jr.	.25
69	Tony Batista	.25
70	Jose Cruz Jr.	.25
71	Carlos Beltran	.25
72	Adrian Beltre	.40
73	Kris Benson	.25
74	Lance Berkman	.25
75	Kevin Brown	.40
76	Jay Buhner	.25
77	Jeromy Burnitz	.25
78	Ken Caminiti	.25
79	Sean Casey	.40
80	Luis Castillo	.25
81	Eric Chavez	.40
82	Jeff Cirillo	.25
83	Bartolo Colon	.25
84	David Cone	.25
85	Freddy Garcia	.25
86	Johnny Damon	.25
87	Ray Durham	.25
88	Jermaine Dye	.25
89	Juan Encarnacion	.25
90	Terrence Long	.25
91	Carl Everett	.25
92	Steve Finley	.25
93	Cliff Floyd	.25
94	Brad Fulmer	.25
95	Brian Giles	.40
96	Luis Gonzalez	.40
97	Rusty Greer	.25
98	Jeffrey Hammonds	.25
99	Mike Hampton	.40
100	Orlando Hernandez	.40
101	Richard Hidalgo	.40
102	Geoff Jenkins	.40
103	Jacque Jones	.25
104	Brian Jordan	.25
105	Gabe Kapler	.40
106	Eric Karros	.25
107	Jason Kendall	.25
108	Adam Kennedy	.25
109	Byung-Hyun Kim	.25
110	Ryan Klesko	.25
111	Chuck Knoblauch	.25
112	Paul Konerko	.25
113	Carlos Lee	.25
114	Kenny Lofton	.40
115	Javy Lopez	.25
116	Tino Martinez	.25
117	Ruben Mateo	.25
118	Kevin Millwood	.25
119	Ben Molina	.25
120	Raul Mondesi	.40
121	Trot Nixon	.25
122	John Olerud	.40
123	Paul O'Neill	.25
124	Chan Ho Park	.40
125	Andy Pettite	.40
126	Jorge Posada	.40
127	Mark Quinn	.25
128	Aramis Ramirez	.25
129	Mariano Rivera	.40
130	Tim Salmon	.25
131	Curt Schilling	.40
132	Richie Sexson	.25
133	John Smoltz	.25
134	J.T. Snow	.25
135	Jay Payton	.25
136	Shannon Stewart	.25
137	B.J. Surhoff	.25
138	Mike Sweeney	.25
139	Fernando Tatis	.25
140	Miguel Tejada	.40
141	Jason Varitek	.25
142	Greg Vaughn	.25
143	Mo Vaughn	.25
144	Robin Ventura	.25
145	Jose Vidro	.25
146	Omar Vizquel	.40
147	Larry Walker	.50
148	David Wells	.25
149	Rondell White	.25
150	Preston Wilson	.25
151	Brent Abernathy	8.00
152	*Cory Aldridge*	10.00
153	*Gene Altman*	10.00
154	Josh Beckett	10.00
155	*Wilson Betemit*	20.00
156	*Albert Pujols*	100.00
157	Joe Crede	8.00
158	Jack Cust	8.00
159	Ben Sheets	15.00
160	Alex Escobar	8.00
161	*Adrian Hernandez*	10.00
162	Pedro Feliz	8.00
163	*Nate Frese*	10.00
164	*Carlos Garcia*	10.00
165	Marcus Giles	8.00
166	*Alexis Gomez*	10.00
167	Jason Hart	10.00
168	Aubrey Huff	8.00
169	Cesar Izturis	8.00
170	Nick Johnson	10.00
171	*Jack Wilson*	10.00
172	*Brian Lawrence*	12.00
173	*Christian Parker*	10.00
174	*Nick Maness*	10.00
175	*Jose Mieses*	10.00
176	*Greg Miller*	10.00
177	Eric Munson	8.00
178	Xavier Nady	15.00
179	*Blaine Neal*	10.00
180	Abraham Nunez	8.00
181	Jose Ortiz	12.00
182	*Jeremy Owens*	10.00
183	*Jay Gibbons*	20.00
184	Corey Patterson	10.00
185	Carlos Pena	8.00
186	C.C. Sabathia	8.00
187	Timo Perez	8.00
188	*Adam Pettyjohn*	10.00
189	*Donaldo Mendez*	10.00
190	*Jackson Melian*	15.00
191	*Wilken Ruan*	10.00
192	*Duaner Sanchez*	10.00
193	Alfonso Soriano	10.00
194	*Rafael Soriano*	10.00
195	*Ichiro Suzuki*	120.00
196	*Billy Sylvester*	10.00
197	*Juan Uribe*	10.00
198	*Tsuyoshi Shinjo*	20.00
199	*Carlos Valderrama*	10.00
200	*Matt White*	10.00
201	Adam Dunn	20.00
202	Joe Kennedy	8.00
203	Mike Rivera	5.00
204	Erick Almonte	5.00
205	Brandon Duckworth	15.00
206	*Victor Martinez*	15.00
207	Rick Bauer	5.00
208	Jeff Deardorff	5.00
209	Antonio Perez	15.00
210	Bill Hall	15.00
211	Dennis Tankersley	25.00
212	Jeremy Affeldt	5.00
213	Junior Spivey	15.00
214	Casey Fossum	6.00
215	Brandon Lyon	5.00
216	Angel Santos	5.00
217	Cody Ransom	5.00
218	Jason Lane	30.00
219	David Williams	15.00
220	Alex Herrera	5.00
221	Ryan Drese	5.00
222	Travis Hafner	8.00
223	Bud Smith	15.00
224	Johnny Estrada	6.00
225	Ricardo Rodriguez	6.00
226	Brandon Berger	15.00
227	Claudio Vargas	5.00
228	Luis Garcia	5.00
229	Marlon Byrd	40.00
230	Hee Seop Choi	30.00
231	Corky Miller	15.00
232	Justin Duchscherer	5.00
233	Tim Spooneybarger	5.00
234	Roy Oswalt	8.00
235	Willie Harris	5.00
236	Josh Towers	6.00
237	Juan Pena	5.00
238	Alfredo Amezaga	10.00
239	Geronimo Gil	5.00
240	Juan Cruz	15.00
241	Ed Rogers	5.00
242	Joe Thurston	5.00
243	*Orlando Hudson*	15.00
244	*John Buck*	15.00
245	Martin Vargas	5.00
246	David Brous	5.00
247	Dewon Brazelton	15.00
248	Mark Prior	140.00
249	Angel Berroa	15.00
250	Mark Teixeira	40.00

2001 Donruss Elite Back 2 Back Jacks

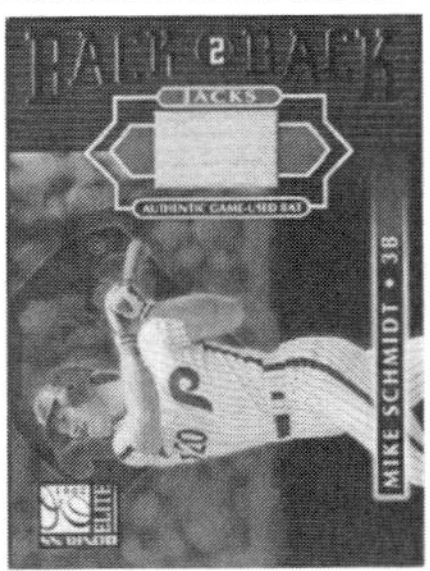

	MT
Common Player:	40.00
Singles production 100	
Doubles production 50	
SP print runs listed	

1	Ernie Banks/75	50.00
2	Ryne Sandberg/ 75	100.00
3	Babe Ruth	275.00
4	Lou Gehrig	240.00
5	Eddie Matthews	50.00
6	Troy Glaus	50.00
7	Don Mattingly/50	200.00
8	Todd Helton	50.00
9	Wade Boggs	50.00
10	Tony Gwynn	60.00
11	Robin Yount	50.00
12	Paul Molitor/50	60.00
13	Mike Schmidt/50	125.00
14	Scott Rolen/75	40.00
15	Reggie Jackson	60.00
16	Dave Winfield	40.00
17	Johnny Bench/50	70.00
18	Joe Morgan	40.00
19	Brooks Robinson/ 50	60.00
20	Cal Ripken Jr.	90.00
21	Ty Cobb	180.00
22	Al Kaline/50	80.00
23	Frank Robinson/ 50	40.00
24	Frank Thomas	40.00
25	Roberto Clemente	200.00
26	Vladimir Guerrero/ 50	40.00
27	Harmon Killebrew/ 50	80.00
28	Kirby Puckett	120.00
29	Yogi Berra/75	50.00
30	Phil Rizzuto/75	50.00
31	Ernie Banks, Ryne Sandberg	150.00
32	Babe Ruth, Lou Gehrig	1000.
33	Troy Glaus, Eddie Matthews	60.00
34	Don Mattingly, Todd Helton	200.00
35	Tony Gwynn, Wade Boggs	125.00
36	Paul Molitor, Robin Yount	120.00
37	Mike Schmidt, Scott Rolen	125.00
38	Dave Winfield, Reggie Jackson	80.00

39 Joe Morgan, Johnny Bench 90.00
40 Brooks Robinson, Cal Ripken Jr. 250.00
41 Al Kaline, Ty Cobb 200.00
42 Frank Robinson, Frank Thomas 60.00
43 Roberto Clemente, Vladimir Guerrero 175.00
44 Harmon Killebrew, Kirby Puckett 175.00
45 Phil Rizzuto, Yogi Berra/25 150.00

2001 Donruss Elite Back 2 Back Jacks Autograph

MT
Common Autograph: 125.00
Print runs listed
1 Ernie Banks/25 300.00
2 Ryne Sandberg/25 275.00
6 Troy Glaus/50 125.00
7 Don Mattingly/50 500.00
12 Paul Molitor/50 150.00
13 Mike Schmidt/50 225.00
14 Scott Rolen/25 175.00
17 Johnny Bench/50 200.00
19 Brooks Robinson/50 150.00
22 Al Kaline/50 180.00
23 Frank Robinson/50 125.00
26 Vladimir Guerrero/50 150.00
27 Harmon Killebrew/50 150.00
29 Yogi Berra/25 200.00
30 Phil Rizzuto/25 150.00
45 Phil Rizzuto, Yogi Berra/25 350.00

2001 Donruss Elite Passing the Torch

MT
Complete Set (24): 400.00
Common Player: 6.00
Singles production 1,000
Doubles production 500
1 Stan Musial 15.00
2 Tony Gwynn 12.00
3 Willie Mays 20.00
4 Barry Bonds 12.00
5 Mike Schmidt 12.00
6 Scott Rolen 6.00
7 Cal Ripken Jr. 25.00
8 Alex Rodriguez 20.00
9 Hank Aaron 20.00
10 Andruw Jones 8.00
11 Nolan Ryan 30.00
12 Pedro Martinez 12.00
13 Wade Boggs 6.00
14 Nomar Garciaparra 20.00
15 Don Mattingly 20.00
16 Todd Helton 10.00
17 Stan Musial, Tony Gwynn 20.00
18 Barry Bonds, Willie Mays 35.00
19 Mike Schmidt, Scott Rolen 20.00
20 Alex Rodriguez, Cal Ripken Jr. 40.00
21 Andruw Jones, Hank Aaron 25.00
22 Nolan Ryan, Pedro Martinez 50.00
23 Nomar Garciaparra, Wade Boggs 25.00
24 Don Mattingly, Todd Helton 35.00

2001 Donruss Elite Passing the Torch Autographs

MT
Common Player: 40.00
Singles production 100
Doubles production 50
1 Stan Musial 120.00
2 Tony Gwynn 75.00
3 Willie Mays 200.00
4 Barry Bonds 120.00
5 Mike Schmidt 100.00
6 Scott Rolen 40.00
7 Cal Ripken Jr. 200.00
8 Alex Rodriguez 125.00
9 Hank Aaron 150.00
10 Andruw Jones 50.00
11 Nolan Ryan 275.00
12 Pedro Martinez 125.00
13 Wade Boggs 60.00
14 Exchange TBD
15 Don Mattingly 200.00
16 Todd Helton 60.00
17 Stan Musial, Tony Gwynn 275.00
18 Barry Bonds, Willie Mays 525.00
19 Mike Schmidt, Scott Rolen 225.00
20 Alex Rodriguez, Cal Ripken Jr. 650.00
21 Andruw Jones, Hank Aaron 300.00
22 Nolan Ryan, Pedro Martinez 700.00
22 Nolan Ryan, Roger Clemens FB redemp.
23 Wade Boggs FB Redemp. 25.00
24 Don Mattingly, Todd Helton 500.00

2001 Donruss Elite Primary Colors Red

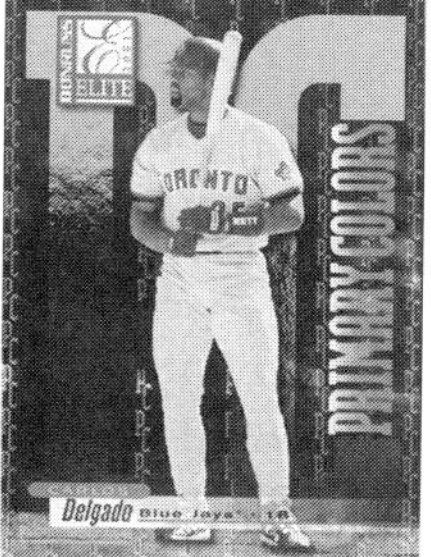

MT
Complete Set (40): 325.00
Common Player: 4.00
Production 975 sets
Red Die-Cut: 3-5X
Production 25
Blues: 1-1.5X
Production 200
Blue Die-Cut: 1.5-3X
Production 50
Yellows: 3-5X
Production 25
Yellow Die-Cut: 1.5-2X
Production 75
1 Alex Rodriguez 20.00
2 Barry Bonds 10.00
3 Cal Ripken Jr. 25.00
4 Chipper Jones 15.00
5 Derek Jeter 25.00
6 Troy Glaus 8.00
7 Frank Thomas 10.00
8 Greg Maddux 15.00
9 Ivan Rodriguez 10.00
10 Jeff Bagwell 10.00
11 Todd Helton 10.00
12 Ken Griffey Jr. 20.00
13 Manny Ramirez 10.00
14 Mark McGwire 25.00
15 Mike Piazza 20.00
16 Nomar Garciaparra 20.00
17 Pedro Martinez 10.00
18 Randy Johnson 8.00
19 Rick Ankiel 4.00
20 Roger Clemens 10.00
21 Sammy Sosa 15.00
22 Tony Gwynn 10.00
23 Vladimir Guerrero 10.00
24 Carlos Delgado 6.00
25 Jason Giambi 6.00
26 Andruw Jones 6.00
27 Bernie Williams 6.00
28 Roberto Alomar 6.00
29 Shawn Green 4.00
30 Barry Larkin 4.00
31 Scott Rolen 4.00
32 Gary Sheffield 4.00
33 Rafael Palmeiro 5.00
34 Albert Belle 4.00
35 Magglio Ordonez 4.00
36 Jim Thome 4.00
37 Jim Edmonds 4.00
38 Darin Erstad 4.00
39 Kris Benson 4.00
40 Sean Casey 4.00

2001 Donruss Elite Prime Numbers

MT
Common Player: 10.00
Print runs listed
1a Alex Rodriguez/300 25.00
1b Alex Rodriguez/308 25.00
1c Alex Rodriguez/350 25.00
2a Ken Griffey Jr./400 25.00
2b Ken Griffey Jr./408 25.00
2c Ken Griffey Jr./430 25.00
3a Mark McGwire/500 30.00
3b Mark McGwire/504 30.00
3c Mark McGwire/550 30.00
4a Cal Ripken Jr./400 30.00
4b Cal Ripken Jr./407 30.00
4c Cal Ripken Jr./410 30.00
5a Derek Jeter/300 30.00
5b Derek Jeter/302 30.00
5c Derek Jeter/320 30.00
6a Mike Piazza/300 25.00
6b Mike Piazza/302 25.00
6c Mike Piazza/360 25.00
7a Nomar Garciaparra/300 25.00
7b Nomar Garciaparra/302 25.00
7c Nomar Garciaparra/370 25.00
8a Sammy Sosa/300 20.00
8b Sammy Sosa/306 20.00
8c Sammy Sosa/380 20.00
9a Vladimir Guerrero/300 10.00
9b Vladimir Guerrero/305 10.00
9c Vladimir Guerrero/340 10.00
10a Tony Gwynn/300 15.00
10b Tony Gwynn/304 15.00
10c Tony Gwynn/390 15.00

2001 Donruss Elite Prime Numbers Die-Cut

MT
Common Player: 10.00
Print runs listed
1a Alex Rodriguez/58 60.00
1b Alex Rodriguez/50 60.00
1c Alex Rodriguez/8
2a Ken Griffey Jr./38 80.00
2b Ken Griffey Jr./30 90.00
2c Ken Griffey Jr./8
3a Mark McGwire/54 100.00
3b Mark McGwire/50 100.00
3c Mark McGwire/4
4a Cal Ripken Jr./17 200.00
4b Cal Ripken Jr./10
4c Cal Ripken Jr./7
5a Derek Jeter/22 200.00
5b Derek Jeter/20 200.00
5c Derek Jeter/2
6a Mike Piazza/62 50.00
6b Mike Piazza/60 50.00
6c Mike Piazza/2
7a Nomar Garciaparra/72 50.00
7b Nomar Garciaparra/70 50.00
7c Nomar Garciaparra/2
8a Sammy Sosa/86 25.00
8b Sammy Sosa/80 25.00
8c Sammy Sosa/6
9a Vladimir Guerrero/45 35.00
9b Vladimir Guerrero/40 35.00
9c Vladimir Guerrero/5
10a Tony Gwynn/94 25.00
10b Tony Gwynn/90 25.00
10c Tony Gwynn/4

2001 Donruss Elite Throwback Threads

MT
Common Player: 30.00
Singles production 100
Doubles production 50
SP production listed
1 Stan Musial/75 100.00
2 Tony Gwynn/75 60.00
3 Willie McCovey 40.00
4 Barry Bonds 80.00
5 Babe Ruth 575.00
6 Lou Gehrig 500.00
7 Mike Schmidt/75 90.00
8 Scott Rolen 30.00
9 Harmon Killebrew/75 75.00
10 Kirby Puckett 180.00

11	Al Kaline/75	75.00
12	Eddie Matthews	75.00
13	Hank Aaron/75	140.00
14	Andruw Jones/50	50.00
15	Lou Brock	30.00
16	Ozzie Smith	60.00
17	Ernie Banks/75	100.00
18	Ryne Sandberg	80.00
19	Roberto Clemente	200.00
20	Vladimir Guerrero/ 50	50.00
21	Frank Robinson/ 50	40.00
22	Frank Thomas	50.00
23	Brooks Robinson/ 50	75.00
24	Cal Ripken Jr.	125.00
25	Roger Clemens	60.00
26	Pedro Martinez	75.00
27	Reggie Jackson	60.00
28	Dave Winfield	40.00
29	Don Mattingly/50	200.00
30	Todd Helton	50.00
31	Stan Musial, Tony Gwynn/25	225.00
32	Barry Bonds, Willie McCovey	200.00
33	Babe Ruth, Lou Gehrig	1250.
34	Mike Schmidt, Scott Rolen/25	250.00
35	Harmon Killebrew, Kirby Puckett	375.00
36	Al Kaline, Eddie Matthews	125.00
37	Andruw Jones, Hank Aaron	180.00
38	Lou Brock, Ozzie Smith	180.00
39	Ernie Banks, Ryne Sandberg/25	250.00
40	Roberto Clemente, Vladimir Guerrero	325.00
41	Frank Robinson, Frank Thomas	90.00
42	Brooks Robinson, Cal Ripken Jr.	250.00
43	Pedro Martinez, Roger Clemens	200.00
44	Dave Winfield, Reggie Jackson	100.00
45	Don Mattingly, Todd Helton	250.00

2001 Donruss Elite Throwback Threads Autograph

MT

Common Autograph: 30.00
Production listed
Football Exchange for 21 & 22 will be redeemed for #'s listed for 21 & 22

1	Stan Musial/25	275.00
2	Tony Gwynn/25	180.00
7	Mike Schmidt/25	350.00
9	Harmon Killebrew/ 25	200.00
11	Al Kaline/25	200.00
13	Hank Aaron/25	400.00
14	Andruw Jones/50	100.00
17	Ernie Banks/25	300.00
20	Vladimir Guerrero/ 50	125.00
21	Frank Robinson/ 50 FB Redemp	40.00
22	Frank Thomas/ 50 FB redemp	50.00
23	Brooks Robinson/ 50	150.00
29	Don Mattingly/50	500.00
31	Stan Musial, Tony Gwynn/25	425.00
34	Mike Schmidt, Scott Rolen/25	450.00
39	Ernie Banks, Ryne Sandberg/25	500.00

2001 Donruss Elite Title Waves

MT

Common Player: 2.50
numbered to title year
Holofoil: 2-3X
Production 100 sets

1	Tony Gwynn/1994	6.00
2	Todd Helton/2000	5.00
3	Nomar Garciaparra/ 2000	12.00
4	Frank Thomas/ 1997	6.00
5	Alex Rodriguez/ 1996	12.00
6	Jeff Bagwell/1994	5.00
7	Mark McGwire/ 1998	15.00
8	Sammy Sosa/ 2000	10.00
9	Ken Griffey Jr./ 1997	12.00
10	Albert Belle/1995	2.50
11	Barry Bonds/1993	8.00
12	Jose Canseco/ 1991	3.00
13	Manny Ramirez/ 1999	6.00
14	Sammy Sosa/1998	10.00
15	Andres Galarraga/ 1996	2.50
16	Todd Helton/2000	5.00
17	Ken Griffey Jr./ 1997	12.00
18	Jeff Bagwell/1994	5.00
19	Mike Piazza/1995	12.00
20	Alex Rodriguez/ 1995	12.00
21	Jason Giambi/2000	3.00
22	Ivan Rodriguez/ 1999	5.00
23	Greg Maddux/ 1997	10.00
24	Pedro Martinez/ 1994	6.00
25	Derek Jeter/2000	15.00
26	Bernie Williams/ 1998	4.00
27	Roger Clemens/ 1999	6.00
28	Chipper Jones/ 1995	10.00
29	Mark McGwire/ 1990	15.00
30	Cal Ripken Jr./ 1983	15.00

2001 Donruss Elite Turn of the Century Autographs

MT

Common Autograph: 10.00
Production 100 sets
Redemp. deadline 5/01/03

151	Brent Abernathy	10.00
152	Cory Aldridge	20.00
153	Gene Altman	10.00
154	Josh Beckett	25.00
155	Wilson Betemit	60.00
156	Albert Pujols	300.00
157	Joe Crede	15.00
158	Jack Cust	15.00
159	Ben Sheets	50.00
160	Alex Escobar	20.00
161	Adrian Hernandez	20.00
162	Pedro Feliz	20.00
163	Nate Frese	15.00
164	Carlos Garcia	15.00
165	Marcus Giles	20.00
166	Alexis Gomez	20.00
167	Jason Hart	35.00
168	Aubrey Huff	15.00
169	Cesar Izturis	10.00
170	Nick Johnson	20.00
171	Jack Wilson	15.00
172	Brian Lawrence	15.00
173	Christian Parker	10.00
174	Nick Maness	10.00
175	Jose Mieses	15.00
176	Greg Miller	10.00
177	Eric Munson	20.00
178	Xavier Nady	30.00
179	Blaine Neal	15.00
180	Abraham Nunez	15.00
181	Jose Ortiz	30.00
182	Jeremy Owens	10.00
183	Jay Gibbons	40.00
184	Corey Patterson	40.00
185	Carlos Pena	20.00
186	C.C. Sabathia	20.00
187	Timoniel Perez	20.00
188	Adam Pettyjohn	10.00
189	Donaldo Mendez	20.00
190	Jackson Melian	35.00
191	Wilken Ruan	15.00
192	Duaner Sanchez	10.00
193	Alfonso Soriano	45.00
194	Rafael Soriano	15.00
196	Billy Sylvester	10.00
197	Juan Uribe	20.00
199	Carlos Valderrama	15.00
200	Matt White	20.00

2001 Donruss Signature Series

MT

Complete Set (311):
Common Player: .50
Common (111-165): 10.00
Auto. print run 330
Common (166-311): 6.00
Production 800
Box: 50.00

1	Alex Rodriguez	4.00
2	Barry Bonds	3.00
3	Cal Ripken Jr.	6.00
4	Chipper Jones	3.00
5	Derek Jeter	6.00
6	Troy Glaus	1.00
7	Frank Thomas	1.50
8	Greg Maddux	3.00
9	Ivan Rodriguez	1.50
10	Jeff Bagwell	1.50
11	John Olerud	.75
12	Todd Helton	1.50
13	Ken Griffey Jr.	4.00
14	Manny Ramirez	1.50
15	Mark McGwire	5.00
16	Mike Piazza	4.00
17	Nomar Garciaparra	4.00
18	Moises Alou	.50
19	Aramis Ramirez	.50
20	Curt Schilling	.75
21	Pat Burrell	1.00
22	Doug Mientkiewicz	.50
23	Carlos Delgado	1.00
24	J.D. Drew	1.00
25	Cliff Floyd	.50
26	Freddy Garcia	.50
27	Roberto Alomar	1.25
28	Barry Zito	.50
29	Juan Encarnacion	.50
30	Paul Konerko	.50
31	Mark Mulder	.75
32	Andy Pettitte	1.00
33	Jim Edmonds	.75
34	Darin Erstad	.75
35	Jason Giambi	1.25
36	Tom Glavine	1.00
37	Juan Gonzalez	1.50
38	Fred McGriff	.75
39	Shawn Green	.75
40	Tim Hudson	.75
41	Andruw Jones	1.00
42	Jeff Kent	.50
43	Barry Larkin	1.00
44	Brad Radke	.50
45	Mike Mussina	1.25
46	Hideo Nomo	1.00
47	Rafael Palmeiro	1.00
48	Scott Rolen	.75
49	Gary Sheffield	.75
50	Bernie Williams	1.25
51	Bobby Abreu	.50
52	Edgardo Alfonzo	.50
53	Edgar Martinez	.50
54	Magglio Ordonez	.50
55	Kerry Wood	.75
56	Adrian Beltre	.50
57	Lance Berkman	.75
58	Kevin Brown	.75
59	Sean Casey	.75
60	Eric Chavez	.75
61	Bartolo Colon	.50
62	Sammy Sosa	3.00
63	Jermaine Dye	.50
64	Tony Gwynn	1.50
65	Carl Everett	.50
66	Brian Giles	.75
67	Mike Hampton	.50
68	Richard Hidalgo	.50
69	Geoff Jenkins	.75
70	Tony Clark	.50
71	Roger Clemens	2.00
72	Ryan Klesko	.50
73	Chan Ho Park	.50
74	Richie Sexson	.50
75	Mike Sweeney	.50
76	Kazuhiro Sasaki	.50
77	Miguel Tejada	.75
78	Jose Vidro	.50
79	Larry Walker	1.00
80	Preston Wilson	.50
81	Craig Biggio	.75
82	Andres Galarraga	.75
83	Jim Thome	1.00
84	Vladimir Guerrero	1.50
85	Rafael Furcal	.75
86	Cristian Guzman	.50
87	Terrence Long	.50
88	Bret Boone	.50
89	Wade Miller	.50
90	Eric Milton	.50
91	Gabe Kapler	.75
92	Johnny Damon	.50
93	Carlos Lee	.50
94	Kenny Lofton	.75
95	Raul Mondesi	.50
96	Jorge Posada	.75
97	Mark Grace	1.00
98	Robert Fick	.50
99	Joe Mays	.50
100	Aaron Sele	.50

101 Ben Grieve .50
102 Luis Gonzalez 1.00
103 Ray Durham .50
104 Mark Quinn .50
105 Jose Canseco 1.00
106 David Justice 1.00
107 Pedro Martinez 1.50
108 Randy Johnson 1.50
109 Phil Nevin .50
110 Ricky Henderson 1.00
111 Alex Escobar Auto 10.00
112 *Johnny Estrada Auto* 25.00
113 Pedro Feliz Auto 12.00
114 Nate Frese Auto 10.00
115 *Ricardo Rodriguez Auto* 20.00
116 *Brandon Larson Auto* 10.00
117 *Alexis Gomez Auto* 15.00
118 Jason Hart Auto 15.00
119 C.C. Sabathia Auto 25.00
120 *Endy Chavez Auto* 15.00
121 *Christian Parker Auto* 10.00
122 *Jackson Melian* 10.00
123 *Joe Kennedy Auto* 20.00
124 *Adrian Hernandez Auto* 10.00
125 Cesar Izturis Auto 12.00
126 *Jose Mieses Auto* 10.00
127 Roy Oswalt Auto 40.00
128 Eric Munson Auto 15.00
129 Xavier Nady Auto 15.00
130 *Horacio Ramirez Auto* 10.00
131 Abraham Nunez Auto 10.00
132 Jose Ortiz Auto 15.00
133 *Jeremy Owens Auto* 10.00
134 *Claudio Vargas Auto* 10.00
135 Corey Patterson Auto 20.00
136 Carlos Pena 10.00
137 *Bud Smith Auto* 25.00
138 Adam Dunn Auto 40.00
139 Adam Pettyjohn Auto 10.00
140 *Elpidio Guzman Auto* 10.00
141 *Jay Gibbons Auto* 30.00
142 *Wilken Ruan Auto* 10.00
143 *Tsuyoshi Shinjo* 35.00
144 Alfonso Soriano Auto 40.00
145 Marcus Giles Auto 15.00
146 *Ichiro Suzuki* 90.00
147 Juan Uribe Auto 25.00
148 *David Williams Auto* 20.00
149 *Carlos Valderrama Auto* 10.00
150 *Matt White Auto* 10.00
151 *Albert Pujols Auto* 120.00
152 *Donaldo Mendez Auto* 10.00
153 *Cory Aldridge Auto* 10.00
154 *Brandon Duckworth Auto* 30.00
155 Josh Beckett Auto 30.00
156 *Wilson Betemit Auto* 40.00
157 Ben Sheets Auto 20.00
158 *Andres Torres Auto* 10.00
159 Aubrey Huff Auto 10.00
160 *Jack Wilson Auto* 10.00
161 *Rafael Soriano Auto* 15.00
162 Nick Johnson Auto 20.00
163 *Carlos Garcia Auto* 10.00
164 *Josh Towers Auto* 25.00
165 *Jason Michaels Auto* 10.00
166 *Ryan Drese* 6.00
167 *Dewon Brazelton* 12.00
168 *Kevin Olsen* 6.00
169 *Benito Baez* 6.00
170 *Mark Prior* 60.00
171 *Wilmy Caceres* 6.00
172 *Mark Teixeira* 40.00
173 *Willie Harris* 6.00
174 *Mike Koplove* 6.00
175 *Brandon Knight* 6.00
176 *John Grabow* 6.00
177 *Jeremy Affeldt* 8.00
178 Brandon Inge 6.00
179 *Casey Fossum* 10.00
180 *Scott Stewart* 6.00
181 *Luke Hudson* 6.00
182 *Ken Vining* 6.00
183 Toby Hall 6.00
184 *Eric Knott* 6.00
185 *Kris Foster* 6.00
186 *David Brous* 6.00
187 *Roy Smith* 6.00
188 *Grant Balfour* 8.00
189 *Jeremy Fikac* 6.00
190 *Morgan Ensberg* 10.00
191 *Ryan Freel* 8.00
192 *Ryan Jensen* 6.00
193 *Lance Davis* 6.00
194 *Delvin James* 8.00
195 Timo Perez 6.00
196 Michael Cuddyer 6.00
197 *Bob File* 6.00
198 *Martin Vargas* 6.00
199 *Kris Keller* 6.00
200 *Tim Spooneybarger* 6.00
201 Adam Everett 6.00
202 *Josh Fogg* 10.00
203 Kip Wells 8.00
204 *Rick Bauer* 6.00
205 Brent Abernathy 8.00
206 *Erick Almonte* 8.00
207 *Pedro Santana* 6.00
208 Ken Harvey 6.00
209 *Jerrod Riggan* 6.00
210 *Nick Punto* 6.00
211 *Steve Green* 6.00
212 Nick Neugebauer 12.00
213 Chris George 6.00
214 Mike Penny 6.00
215 *Bret Prinz* 6.00
216 *Tim Christman* 6.00
217 *Sean Douglass* 6.00
218 *Brett Jodie* 6.00
219 *Juan Diaz* 6.00
220 *Carlos Hernandez* 6.00
221 Alex Cintron 6.00
222 *Juan Cruz* 15.00
223 Larry Bigbie 6.00
224 *Junior Spivey* 6.00
225 Luis Rivas 6.00
226 *Brandon Lyon* 6.00
227 *Tony Cogan* 6.00
228 *Justin Duchscherer* 6.00
229 Tike Redman 6.00
230 Jimmy Rollins 6.00
231 *Scott Podsednik* 8.00
232 *Jose Acevedo* 8.00
233 *Luis Pineda* 6.00
234 Josh Phelps 6.00
235 *Paul Phillips* 6.00
236 *Brian Roberts* 6.00
237 Orlando Woodwards 6.00
238 *Bart Miadich* 6.00
239 *Les Walrond* 8.00
240 *Brad Voyles* 6.00
241 Joe Crede 6.00
242 *Juan Moreno* 6.00
243 Matt Ginter 6.00
244 *Brian Rogers* 8.00
245 Pablo Ozuna 6.00
246 *Geronimo Gil* 6.00
247 *Mike Maroth* 6.00
248 *Josue Perez* 6.00
249 Dee Brown 6.00
250 *Victor Zambrano* 6.00
251 *Nick Maness* 6.00
252 *Kyle Lohse* 12.00
253 *Greg Miller* 6.00
254 *Henry Mateo* 6.00
255 *Duaner Sanchez* 6.00
256 *Rob Mackowiak* 6.00
257 Steve Lomasney 6.00
258 *Angel Santos* 6.00
259 *Winston Abreu* 6.00
260 *Brandon Berger* 6.00
261 Tomas De La Rosa 6.00
262 *Ramon Vazquez* 8.00
263 Mickey Callaway 6.00
264 *Corky Miller* 6.00
265 Keith Ginter 6.00
266 *Cody Ransom* 6.00
267 *Doug Nickle* 6.00
268 *Derrick Lewis* 6.00
269 *Eric Hinske* 15.00
270 *Travis Phelps* 6.00
271 Eric Valent 6.00
272 *Michael Rivera* 6.00
273 *Esix Snead* 6.00
274 *Troy Mattes* 6.00
275 Jermaine Clark 6.00
276 Nate Cornejo 6.00
277 *George Perez* 6.00
278 Juan Rivera 6.00
279 *Justin Atchley* 6.00
280 Adam Johnson 6.00
281 *Gene Altman* 6.00
282 Jason Jennings 6.00
283 *Scott MacRae* 6.00
284 *Craig Monroe* 6.00
285 *Bert Snow* 6.00
286 *Stubby Clapp* 6.00
287 Jack Cust 6.00
288 *Will Ohman* 6.00
289 Wily Mo Pena 6.00
290 *Joe Beimel* 8.00
291 *Jason Karnuth* 6.00
292 Bill Ortega 6.00
293 *Nate Teut* 8.00
294 *Erik Hiljus* 6.00
295 *Jason Smith* 6.00
296 Juan Pena 6.00
297 David Espinosa 8.00
298 Tim Redding 10.00
299 *Brian Lawrence* 8.00
300 *Brian Reith* 8.00
301 Chad Durbin 6.00
302 Kurt Ainsworth 6.00
303 *Blaine Neal* 6.00
304 *Jorge Julio* 6.00
305 Adam Bernero 8.00
306 *Travis Hafner* 10.00
307 *Dustan Mohr* 6.00
308 *Cesar Crespo* 6.00
309 *Billy Sylvester* 6.00
310 *Zach Day* 6.00
311 *Angel Berroa* 6.00

2001 Donruss Signature Series Signature Proofs

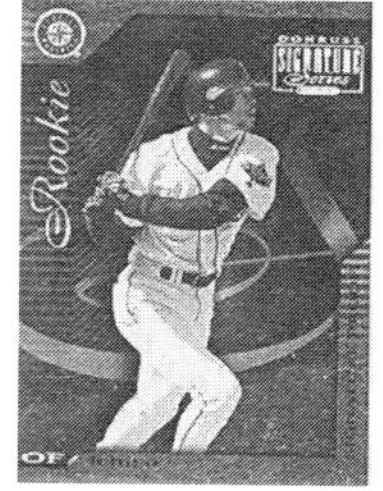

MT
Stars (1-110): 2-4X
Production 175
Cards (111-311) production 25

2001 Donruss Signature Series Award Winning Signatures

MT
Common Player: 20.00
Jeff Bagwell/94 75.00
Carlos Beltran/99 20.00
Johnny Bench/68 80.00
Yogi Berra/55 80.00
Craig Biggio/97 40.00
Barry Bonds/93 125.00
Rod Carew/77 50.00
Orlando Cepeda/67 25.00
Andre Dawson/77 30.00
Dennis Eckersley/92 40.00
Dennis Eckersley/92 40.00
Whitey Ford/61 75.00
Jason Giambi/100 40.00
Bob Gibson/68 40.00
Juan Gonzalez/96 60.00
Orel Hershiser/88 35.00
Al Kaline/67 60.00
Fred Lynn/75 20.00
Fred Lynn/75 20.00
Jim Palmer/76 40.00
Cal Ripken/83 200.00
Phil Rizzuto/50 40.00
Brooks Robinson/64 60.00
Scott Rolen/97 30.00
Ryne Sandberg/84 90.00
Warren Spahn/57 50.00
Frank Thomas/94 50.00
Billy Williams/61 35.00
Kerry Wood/98 25.00
Robin Yount/89 75.00

2001 Donruss Signature Series Century Marks

MT
Complete Set (48):
Common Autograph: 8.00
Brent Abernathy/184 8.00
Roberto Alomar/102 50.00
Rick Ankiel/119 25.00
Lance Berkman/121 20.00
Mark Buerhle/224 15.00
Wilmy Caceres/194 8.00
Eric Chavez/170 15.00
Joe Crede/154 10.00
Jack Cust/178 8.00
Brandon Duckworth/183 15.00
David Espinosa/199 8.00
Johnny Estrada/198 20.00
Pedro Feliz/180 8.00
Robert Fick/232 8.00
Cliff Floyd/146 12.00
Casey Fossum/100 20.00
Jay Gibbons/175 15.00
Keith Ginter/163 8.00
Troy Glaus/144 30.00
Luis Gonzalez/101 40.00
Vladimir Guerrero/187 30.00
Richard Hidalgo/173 10.00
Tim Hudson/145 25.00
Adam Johnson/130 8.00
Gabe Kapler/150 12.00
Joe Kennedy/219 8.00
Ryan Klesko/176 10.00
Carlos Lee/179 10.00
Terrence Long/180 8.00
Edgar Martinez/110 20.00

Joe Mays/209	10.00
Greg Miller/194	8.00
Wade Miller/180	8.00
Mark Mulder/203	20.00
Xavier Nady/180	8.00
Magglio Ordonez/104	15.00
Jose Ortiz/187	10.00
Roy Oswalt/192	25.00
Wily Mo Pena/203	8.00
Brad Penny/198	8.00
Aramis Ramirez/241	15.00
Luis Rivas/163	8.00
Alex Rodriguez/110	75.00
Scott Rolen/106	30.00
Mike Sweeney/99	15.00
Eric Valent/163	8.00
Kip Wells/223	8.00
Kerry Wood/109	25.00

2001 Donruss Signature Series Milestone Marks

	MT
Common Player:	15.00
Ernie Banks/285	40.00
Yogi Berra/120	60.00
Wade Boggs/98	75.00
Barry Bonds/55	150.00
George Brett/27	200.00
George Brett/23	200.00
Lou Brock/83	30.00
Rod Carew/110	35.00
Steve Carlton/75	40.00
Gary Carter/213	30.00
Bobby Doerr/192	20.00
Bob Feller/202	20.00
Whitey Ford/186	40.00
Steve Garvey/175	20.00
Tony Gwynn/99	60.00
Fergie Jenkins/149	20.00
Al Kaline/149	50.00
Harmon Killebrew/127	50.00
Ralph Kiner/105	25.00
Willie McCovey/20	90.00
Paul Molitor/96	50.00
Eddie Murray/46	80.00
Eddie Murray/17	
Stan Musial/109	75.00
Phil Niekro/300	15.00
Tony Perez/146	20.00
Cal Ripken/25	300.00
Frank Robinson/136	25.00
Mike Schmidt/40	180.00
Mike Schmidt/23	225.00
Enos Slaughter/117	20.00
Warren Spahn/300	25.00
Alan Trammell/154	35.00
Hoyt Wilhelm/227	15.00
Dave Winfield/31	60.00
Dave Winfield/15	90.00

2001 Donruss Signature Series Notable Nicknames

	MT
Common Player:	40.00
Production 100	
Ernie Banks	75.00
Orlando Cepeda	40.00
Will Clark	90.00
Roger Clemens/50	200.00
Andre Dawson	50.00
Bob Feller	60.00
Carlton Fisk	90.00
Andres Galarraga	40.00
Luis Gonzalez	60.00
Reggie Jackson	100.00
Harmon Killebrew	75.00
Stan Musial	150.00
Brooks Robinson	75.00
Nolan Ryan	250.00
Ryne Sandberg	150.00
Enos Slaughter	40.00
Duke Snider	80.00
Frank Thomas	60.00

2001 Donruss Signature Series Signature Stats

MT

Complete Set (52):
Common Player:
Roberto Alomar
Moises Alou
Luis Aparicio
Lance Berkman
Wade Boggs
Lou Brock
Gary Carter
Joe Carter
Sean Casey
Darin Erstad
Bob Feller
Cliff Floyd
Whitey Ford
Andres Galarraga
Bob Gibson
Brian Giles
Troy Glaus
Luis Gonzalez
Vladimir Guerrero
Tony Gwynn
Richard Hidalgo
Bo Jackson
Fergie Jenkins
Randy Johnson
Al Kaline
Gabe Kapler
Ralph Kiner
Ryan Klesko
Carlos Lee
Kenny Lofton
Edgar Martinez
Joe Mays
Paul Molitor
Mark Mulder
Phil Niekro
Magglio Ordonez
Jim Palmer
Rafael Palmeiro
Chan Ho Park
Kirby Puckett
Manny Ramirez
Alex Rodriguez
Ivan Rodriguez
Curt Schilling
Tom Seaver
Shannon Stewart
Mike Sweeney
Miguel Tejada
Joe Torre
Javier Vazquez
Jose Vidro
Hoyt Wilhelm

2001 Donruss Studio

		MT
Complete Set (200):		NA
Common Player:		.25
Common SP (151-200):		10.00
Production 700		
Pack (6):		7.50
Box (18) + 5x7 Auto.		125.00
1	Alex Rodriguez	3.00
2	Barry Bonds	2.50
3	Cal Ripken Jr.	4.00
4	Chipper Jones	2.50
5	Derek Jeter	4.00
6	Troy Glaus	1.25
7	Frank Thomas	1.50
8	Greg Maddux	2.50
9	Ivan Rodriguez	1.25
10	Jeff Bagwell	1.25
11	Mark Quinn	.25
12	Todd Helton	1.25
13	Ken Griffey Jr.	3.00
14	Manny Ramirez	1.25
15	Mark McGwire	3.00
16	Mike Piazza	3.00
17	Nomar Garciaparra	3.00
18	Robin Ventura	.40
19	Aramis Ramirez	.25
20	J.T. Snow	.25
21	Pat Burrell	.75
22	Curt Schilling	.50
23	Carlos Delgado	.75
24	J.D. Drew	.50
25	Cliff Floyd	.25
26	Brian Jordan	.25
27	Roberto Alomar	1.00
28	Barry Zito	.50
29	Harold Baines	.25
30	Brad Penny	.25
31	Jose Cruz	.25
32	Andy Pettitte	.50
33	Jim Edmonds	.40
34	Darin Erstad	.75
35	Jason Giambi	1.00
36	Tom Glavine	.75
37	Juan Gonzalez	1.25
38	Mark Grace	.75
39	Shawn Green	.50
40	Tim Hudson	.50
41	Andruw Jones	.75
42	Jeff Kent	.40
43	Barry Larkin	.75
44	Rafael Furcal	.50
45	Mike Mussina	1.00
46	Hideo Nomo	.75
47	Rafael Palmeiro	.75
48	Scott Rolen	.75
49	Gary Sheffield	.50
50	Bernie Williams	1.00
51	Bobby Abreu	.25
52	Edgardo Alfonzo	.25
53	Edgar Martinez	.25
54	Magglio Ordonez	.40
55	Kerry Wood	.75
56	Matt Morris	.25
57	Lance Berkman	.50
58	Kevin Brown	.25
59	Sean Casey	.40
60	Eric Chavez	.40
61	Bartolo Colon	.25
62	Johnny Damon	.25
63	Jermaine Dye	.25
64	Juan Encarnacion	.25
65	Carl Everett	.25
66	Brian Giles	.50
67	Mike Hampton	.40
68	Richard Hidalgo	.25
69	Geoff Jenkins	.25
70	Jacque Jones	.25
71	Jason Kendall	.25
72	Ryan Klesko	.25
73	Chan Ho Park	.25
74	Richie Sexson	.25
75	Mike Sweeney	.25
76	Fernando Tatis	.25
77	Miguel Tejada	.50
78	Jose Vidro	.25
79	Larry Walker	.75
80	Preston Wilson	.25
81	Craig Biggio	.50
82	Fred McGriff	.50
83	Jim Thome	.50
84	Garret Anderson	.25
85	Mark Mulder	.25
86	Tony Batista	.25
87	Terrence Long	.25
88	Brad Fullmer	.25
89	Rusty Greer	.25
90	Orlando Hernandez	.25
91	Gabe Kapler	.25
92	Paul Konerko	.25
93	Carlos Lee	.25
94	Kenny Lofton	.40
95	Raul Mondesi	.25
96	Jorge Posada	.50
97	Tim Salmon	.40
98	Greg Vaughn	.25
99	Mo Vaughn	.40
100	Omar Vizquel	.40
101	Ben Grieve	.25
102	Luis Gonzalez	.75
103	Ray Durham	.25
104	Ryan Dempster	.25
105	Eric Karros	.25
106	David Justice	.50
107	Pedro Martinez	1.50
108	Randy Johnson	1.50
109	Rick Ankiel	.50
110	Rickey Henderson	.50
111	Roger Clemens	2.00
112	Sammy Sosa	2.50
113	Tony Gwynn	1.50
114	Vladimir Guerrero	1.00
115	Kazuhiro Sasaki	.25
116	Phil Nevin	.25
117	Ruben Mateo	.25
118	Shannon Stewart	.25
119	Matt Williams	.50
120	Tino Martinez	.50
121	Ken Caminiti	.25
122	Edgar Renteria	.25
123	Charles Johnson	.25
124	Aaron Sele	.25
125	Javy Lopez	.25
126	Mariano Rivera	.50
127	Shea Hillenbrand	.25
128	Jeff D'Amico	.25
129	Brady Anderson	.25
130	Kevin Millwood	.25
131	Trot Nixon	.25
132	Mike Lieberthal	.25
133	Juan Pierre	.25
134	Russ Ortiz	.25
135	Jose Macias	.25
136	John Smoltz	.25
137	Jason Varitek	.25
138	Dean Palmer	.25
139	Jeff Cirillo	.25
140	Paul O'Neill	.50
141	Andres Galarraga	.40
142	David Wells	.25
143	Brad Radke	.25
144	Wade Miller	.25
145	John Olerud	.75
146	Moises Alou	.40
147	Carlos Beltran	.25
148	Jeromy Burnitz	.25

149	Steve Finley	.25
150	Joe Mays	.25
151	Alex Escobar	10.00
152	*Johnny Estrada*	15.00
153	Pedro Feliz	10.00
154	*Nate Frese*	10.00
155	Dee Brown	10.00
156	*Brandon Larson*	10.00
157	*Alexis Gomez*	10.00
158	Jason Hart	15.00
159	C.C. Sabathia	15.00
160	*Josh Towers*	15.00
161	*Christian Parker*	10.00
162	*Jackson Melian*	10.00
163	*Joe Kennedy*	10.00
164	*Adrian Hernandez*	10.00
165	Jimmy Rollins	15.00
166	*Jose Mieses*	15.00
167	Roy Oswalt	15.00
168	Eric Munson	10.00
169	Xavier Nady	10.00
170	*Horacio Ramirez*	10.00
171	Abraham Nunez	10.00
172	Jose Ortiz	10.00
173	*Jeremy Owens*	15.00
174	*Claudio Vargas*	10.00
175	Corey Patterson	15.00
176	Carlos Pena	15.00
177	*Bud Smith*	15.00
178	Adam Dunn	25.00
179	*Adam Pettyjohn*	10.00
180	*Elpidio Guzman*	10.00
181	*Jay Gibbons*	20.00
182	*Wilkin Ruan*	10.00
183	*Tsuyoshi Shinjo*	25.00
184	Alfonso Soriano	15.00
185	Marcus Giles	15.00
186	*Ichiro Suzuki*	90.00
187	*Juan Uribe*	10.00
188	*David Williams*	10.00
189	*Carlos Valderrama*	10.00
190	*Matt White*	10.00
191	*Albert Pujols*	60.00
192	*Donaldo Mendez*	10.00
193	*Cory Aldridge*	10.00
194	*Endy Chavez*	10.00
195	Josh Beckett	15.00
196	*Wilson Betemit*	25.00
197	Ben Sheets	15.00
198	*Andres Torres*	10.00
199	Aubrey Huff	10.00
200	*Jack Wilson*	10.00

2001 Donruss Studio Diamond Collection

		MT
Common Player:		10.00
1	Vladimir Guerrero	20.00
2	Barry Bonds	35.00
3	Cal Ripken Jr.	50.00
4	Nomar Garciaparra	50.00
5	Greg Maddux	25.00
6	Frank Thomas	25.00
7	Roger Clemens	30.00
8	Luis Gonzalez SP	40.00
9	Tony Gwynn	25.00
10	Carlos Lee SP	10.00
11	Troy Glaus	15.00
12	Randy Johnson	25.00
13	Manny Ramirez SP	25.00
14	Pedro Martinez	25.00
15	Todd Helton	20.00
16	Jeff Bagwell	25.00
17	Rickey Henderson	35.00
18	Kazuhiro Sasaki	35.00
19	Albert Pujols SP	
20	Ivan Rodriguez	20.00
21	Darin Erstad	15.00
22	Andruw Jones	15.00
23	Roberto Alomar	25.00
25	Juan Gonzalez	20.00
26	Shawn Green	10.00
27	Lance Berkman	25.00
28	Scott Rolen	15.00
29	Rafael Palmeiro	15.00
30	J.D. Drew	20.00
31	Kerry Wood	30.00
32	Jim Edmonds	15.00
33	Tom Glavine SP	25.00
34	Hideo Nomo SP	80.00
36	Tim Hudson	20.00
37	Miguel Tejada	15.00
38	Chipper Jones	30.00
39	Edgar Martinez SP	20.00
40	Chan Ho Park	20.00
41	Magglio Ordonez	10.00
42	Sean Casey	20.00
43	Larry Walker	15.00
45	Cliff Floyd	10.00
46	Mike Sweeney	10.00
47	Kevin Brown	10.00
48	Richie Sexson	10.00
49	Jermaine Dye	10.00
50	Craig Biggio	20.00

2001 Donruss Studio Leather & Lumber

		MT
Common Player:		10.00
1	Barry Bonds	30.00
2	Cal Ripken Jr.	40.00
3	Miguel Tejada	15.00
5	Frank Thomas	20.00
6	Greg Maddux	25.00
7	Ivan Rodriguez	20.00
8	Jeff Bagwell SP	25.00
9	Sean Casey SP	15.00
10	Todd Helton	20.00
11	Cliff Floyd	10.00
12	Hideo Nomo	60.00
13	Chipper Jones	20.00
14	Rickey Henderson	30.00
15	Richard Hidalgo	10.00
16	Mike Piazza	30.00
17	Larry Walker	15.00
18	Tony Gwynn	20.00
19	Vladimir Guerrero	20.00
20	Rafael Furcal	15.00
21	Roberto Alomar SP	25.00
23	Albert Pujols	60.00
24	Raul Mondesi	10.00
25	J.D. Drew	15.00
26	Jim Edmonds	10.00
27	Darin Erstad SP	15.00
28	Craig Biggio	15.00
29	Kenny Lofton	10.00
30	Juan Gonzalez	20.00
31	John Olerud	10.00
32	Shawn Green	15.00
33	Andruw Jones SP	15.00
34	Moises Alou	10.00
35	Jeff Kent	10.00
36	Ryan Klesko	10.00
37	Luis Gonzalez	20.00
38	Rafael Palmeiro	15.00
40	Scott Rolen	15.00
41	Carlos Lee	10.00
42	Bobby Abreu	10.00
43	Edgardo Alfonzo	15.00
44	Bernie Williams	20.00
45	Brian Giles	15.00
46	Jermaine Dye	10.00
47	Lance Berkman	20.00
48	Edgar Martinez	15.00
49	Richie Sexson	10.00
50	Magglio Ordonez	10.00

2001 Donruss Studio Masterstokes

		MT
Common Player:		15.00
Production 200 sets		
1	Tony Gwynn	60.00
2	Ivan Rodriguez	30.00
3	J.D. Drew	40.00
4	Cal Ripken Jr.	100.00
5	Hideo Nomo	150.00
6	Darin Erstad	25.00
7	Frank Thomas	40.00
8	Andruw Jones	25.00
9	Roberto Alomar	40.00
10	Larry Walker	25.00
11	Vladimir Guerrero	40.00
12	Barry Bonds	60.00
14	Luis Gonzalez	40.00
16	Juan Gonzalez	40.00
17	Todd Helton	40.00
18	Jeff Bagwell	40.00
19	Albert Pujols	125.00
20	Shawn Green	20.00
21	Magglio Ordonez	20.00
22	Scott Rolen	30.00
23	Rafael Palmeiro	30.00
24	Sean Casey	25.00
25	Jim Edmonds	25.00
26	Chipper Jones	40.00
27	Cliff Floyd	20.00
28	Carlos Lee	20.00
29	Edgar Martinez	25.00
30	Lance Berkman	

2001 Donruss Studio Round Trip Tickets

		MT
Complete Set (20):		
Common Player:		
1	Mark McGwire	
2	Frank Robinson	
3	Joe Morgan	
4	Mike Piazza	
5	Barry Bonds	
6	Johnny Bench	
7	Vladimir Guerrero	
8	Mike Schmidt	
9	Andruw Jones	
10	Todd Helton	
11	Sammy Sosa	
12	Reggie Jackson	
13	Cal Ripken Jr.	
15	Willie Stargell	
16	Jeff Bagwell	
18	Tony Gwynn	
19	Ivan Rodriguez	
20	Roberto Clemente	

2001 Donruss Studio Private Signings

		MT
Common Player:		15.00
Inserted 1:hobby box		
1	Alex Rodriguez	80.00
2	Miguel Tejada	15.00
3	Ben Sheets	20.00
4	Tony Gwynn SP/190	60.00
5	Wilson Betemit	20.00
6	Rick Ankiel	30.00
7	Ivan Rodriguez SP/150	40.00
8	Ryan Klesko	15.00
9	Jason Giambi SP/250	40.00
10	Brad Penny	15.00
11	Gabe Kapler	15.00
12	Vladimir Guerrero	35.00
13	Alex Escobar	15.00
14	Edgar Martinez	30.00
15	Cal Ripken SP/50	200.00
16	Brian Giles	20.00
17	Todd Helton SP/125	40.00
18	Mike Sweeney	20.00
19	Cliff Floyd	15.00
20	Corey Patterson	20.00
21	Alfonso Soriano	40.00
22	Bobby Abreu	20.00
23	Shawn Green SP/190	25.00
24	C.C. Sabathia	40.00
25	Luis Gonzalez	40.00
26	Barry Bonds SP/95	90.00
27	Rafael Palmeiro SP/250	30.00
28	Mike Mussina SP/144	50.00
29	Roger Clemens SP/200	90.00
30	Greg Maddux SP/200	75.00
31	Troy Glaus	20.00
32	Kerry Wood	40.00
33	Roberto Alomar SP/200	40.00
34	Tom Glavine	35.00
35	Frank Thomas	40.00
36	Carlos Lee	15.00
37	Scott Rolen	25.00
38	Andruw Jones SP/250	30.00

39	Manny Ramirez SP/ 115	60.00
40	Magglio Ordonez	20.00
41	Lance Berkman	20.00
42	Josh Beckett	25.00
43	Adam Dunn	50.00
44	Albert Pujols SP/ 50	150.00
45	Darin Erstad	40.00
46	Curt Schilling	40.00
47	Barry Zito	20.00
48	Sean Casey	15.00

2001 Donruss Studio Warning Track

		MT
Common Player:		10.00
1	Andruw Jones	10.00
2	Rafael Palmeiro	15.00
3	Gary Sheffield	10.00
4	Larry Walker	15.00
5	Shawn Green	30.00
6	Mike Piazza	35.00
7	Barry Bonds	30.00
8	J.D. Drew	20.00
9	Magglio Ordonez	15.00
10	Todd Helton	15.00
11	Juan Gonzalez	20.00
12	Pat Burrell	15.00
13	Mark McGwire	40.00
14	Frank Robinson	15.00
15	Manny Ramirez	20.00
16	Lance Berkman	15.00
18	Johnny Bench	30.00
19	Chipper Jones	15.00
20	Mike Schmidt	30.00
21	Vladimir Guerrero	15.00
22	Sammy Sosa	20.00
23	Cal Ripken Jr.	30.00
24	Roberto Alomar	20.00
25	Willie Stargell	15.00
27	Scott Rolen	10.00
28	Roberto Clemente	75.00
29	Tony Gwynn	20.00
30	Ivan Rodriguez	15.00
31	Sean Casey	15.00
32	Frank Thomas	20.00
33	Jeff Bagwell	25.00
34	Jeff Kent	10.00
35	Reggie Jackson	20.00

2002 Donruss

		MT
Complete Set (220):		100.00
Common Player:		.15
Common (151-200):		1.00
Inserted 1:4		
Common (201-220):		1.00
Inserted 1:12		
Pack (5):		2.50
Box (24):		50.00
1	Alex Rodriguez	1.50
2	Barry Bonds	1.50
3	Derek Jeter	2.50
4	Robert Fick	.15
5	Juan Pierre	.15
6	Torii Hunter	.15
7	Todd Helton	.60
8	Cal Ripken Jr.	2.50
9	Manny Ramirez	.60
10	Johnny Damon	.15
11	Mike Piazza	1.50
12	Nomar Garciaparra	1.50
13	Pedro Martinez	.60
14	Brian Giles	.25
15	Albert Pujols	1.50
16	Roger Clemens	1.00
17	Sammy Sosa	1.25
18	Vladimir Guerrero	.60
19	Tony Gwynn	.60
20	Pat Burrell	.25
21	Carlos Delgado	.50
22	Tino Martinez	.25
23	Jim Edmonds	.25
24	Jason Giambi	.50
25	Tom Glavine	.30
26	Mark Grace	.40
27	Tony Armas Jr.	.15
28	Andruw Jones	.40
29	Ben Sheets	.25
30	Jeff Kent	.15
31	Barry Larkin	.25
32	Joe Mays	.15
33	Mike Mussina	.50
34	Hideo Nomo	.40
35	Rafael Palmeiro	.40
36	Scott Brosius	.15
37	Scott Rolen	.30
38	Gary Sheffield	.25
39	Bernie Williams	.50
40	Bobby Abreu	.15
41	Edgardo Alfonzo	.15
42	C.C. Sabathia	.15
43	Jeremy Giambi	.15
44	Craig Biggio	.25
45	Andres Galarraga	.25
46	Edgar Martinez	.20
47	Fred McGriff	.25
48	Magglio Ordonez	.20
49	Jim Thome	.30
50	Matt Williams	.25
51	Kerry Wood	.30
52	Moises Alou	.20
53	Brady Anderson	.15
54	Garret Anderson	.15
55	Juan Gonzalez	.60
56	Bret Boone	.15
57	Jose Cruz Jr.	.15
58	Carlos Beltran	.15
59	Adrian Beltre	.25
60	Joe Kennedy	.15
61	Lance Berkman	.30
62	Kevin Brown	.25
63	Tim Hudson	.40
64	Jeromy Burnitz	.15
65	Jarrod Washburn	.15
66	Sean Casey	.30
67	Eric Chavez	.25
68	Bartolo Colon	.15
69	Freddy Garcia	.15
70	Jermaine Dye	.15
71	Terrence Long	.15
72	Cliff Floyd	.15
73	Luis Gonzalez	.50
74	Ichiro Suzuki	3.00
75	Mike Hampton	.20
76	Richard Hidalgo	.15
77	Geoff Jenkins	.25
78	Gabe Kapler	.20
79	Ken Griffey Jr.	2.00
80	Jason Kendall	.15
81	Josh Towers	.15
82	Ryan Klesko	.15
83	Paul Konerko	.15
84	Carlos Lee	.15
85	Kenny Lofton	.20
86	Josh Beckett	.25
87	Raul Mondesi	.15
88	Trot Nixon	.15
89	John Olerud	.25
90	Paul O'Neill	.20
91	Chan Ho Park	.20
92	Andy Pettitte	.25
93	Jorge Posada	.25
94	Mark Quinn	.15
95	Aramis Ramirez	.15
96	Curt Schilling	.25
97	Richie Sexson	.15
98	John Smoltz	.15
99	Wilson Betemit	.25
100	Shannon Stewart	.15
101	Alfonso Soriano	.25
102	Mike Sweeney	.15
103	Miguel Tejada	.25
104	Greg Vaughn	.15
105	Robin Ventura	.25
106	Jose Vidro	.15
107	Larry Walker	.25
108	Preston Wilson	.15
109	Corey Patterson	.20
110	Mark Mulder	.25
111	Tony Clark	.15
112	Roy Oswalt	.25
113	Jimmy Rollins	.15
114	Kazuhiro Sasaki	.15
115	Barry Zito	.15
116	Javier Vazquez	.15
117	Mike Cameron	.15
118	Phil Nevin	.20
119	Bud Smith	.20
120	Cristian Guzman	.15
121	Al Leiter	.20
122	Brad Radke	.15
123	Bobby Higginson	.15
124	Robert Person	.15
125	Adam Dunn	.75
126	Ben Grieve	.15
127	Rafael Furcal	.15
128	Jay Gibbons	.15
129	Paul LoDuca	.15
130	Wade Miller	.15
131	Tsuyoshi Shinjo	.25
132	Eric Milton	.15
133	Rickey Henderson	.40
134	Roberto Alomar	.50
135	Darin Erstad	.25
136	J.D. Drew	.30
137	Shawn Green	.25
138	Randy Johnson	.60
139	Mark McGwire	2.00
139		.15
140	Jose Canseco	.40
141	Jeff Bagwell	.60
142	Greg Maddux	1.25
143	Mark Buehrle	.15
144	Ivan Rodriguez	.60
145	Frank Thomas	.60
146	Rich Aurilia	.15
147	Troy Glaus	.60
148	Ryan Dempster	.15
149	Chipper Jones	1.25
150	Matt Morris	.15
151	Marlon Byrd	3.00
152	*Ben Howard*	8.00
153	*Brandon Backe*	2.00
154	*Jorge De La Rosa*	2.00
155	Corky Miller	1.00
156	Dennis Tankersley	2.00
157	*Kyle Kane*	5.00
158	Justin Duchscherer	1.00
159	*Brian Mallette*	5.00
160	*Chris Baker*	3.00
161	Jason Lane	1.00
162	Hee Seop Choi	2.00
163	Juan Cruz	1.50
164	*Rodrigo Rosario*	2.00
165	Matt Guerrier	1.00
166	*Anderson Machado*	3.00
167	Geronimo Gil	1.00
168	Dewon Brazelton	1.00
169	Mark Prior	4.00
170	Bill Hall	1.00
171	*Jorge Padilla*	5.00
172	Jose Cueto	1.00
173	*Allan Simpson*	3.00
174	*Doug Devore*	3.00
175	Josh Pearce	1.00
176	Angel Berroa	1.00
177	*Steve Bechler*	4.00
178	Antonio Perez	1.00
179	Mark Teixeira	5.00
180	Erick Almonte	1.00
181	Orlando Hudson	1.00
182	Mike Rivera	1.00
183	*Raul Chavez*	2.00
184	Juan Pena	1.00
185	*Travis Hughes*	2.00
186	Ryan Ludwick	1.00
187	Ed Rogers	1.00
188	*Andy Pratt*	3.00
189	Nick Neugebauer	1.00
190	*Tom Shearn*	3.00
191	*Eric Cyr*	3.00
192	Victor Martinez	1.00
193	Brandon Berger	1.00
194	Erik Bedard	1.00
195	Fernando Rodney	1.00
196	Joe Thurston	1.00
197	John Buck	1.00
198	*Jeff Deardorff*	4.00
199	*Ryan Jamison*	3.00
200	Alfredo Amezaga	1.00
201	Luis Gonzalez	2.00
202	Roger Clemens	4.00
203	Barry Zito	1.00
204	Bud Smith	1.50
205	Magglio Ordonez	1.00
206	Kerry Wood	1.50
207	Freddy Garcia	1.00
208	Adam Dunn	2.00
209	Curt Schilling	2.00
210	Lance Berkman	1.50
211	Rafael Palmeiro	2.00
212	Ichiro Suzuki	8.00
213	Bobby Abreu	1.00
214	Mark Mulder	1.00
215	Roy Oswalt	1.50
216	Mike Sweeney	1.00
217	Paul LoDuca	1.00
218	Aramis Ramirez	1.00
219	Randy Johnson	2.00
220	Albert Pujols	5.00

2002 Donruss Stat Line Career

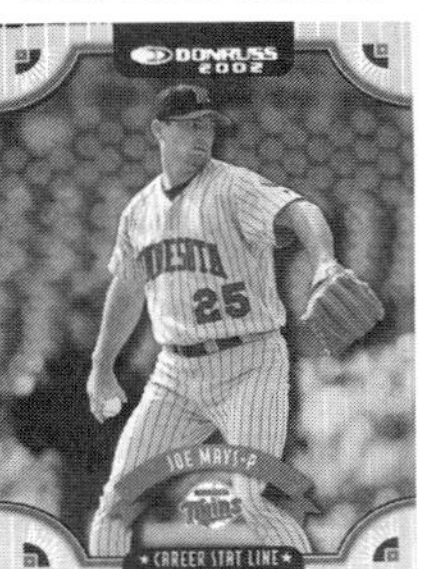

	MT
cards 1-150 print run 251-400:	4-8X
1-150 p/r 151-250:	5-10X
1-150 p/r 101-150:	6-12X
1-150 p/r 61-100:	12-25X
1-150 p/r 31-60:	15-30X
1-150 p/r 15-30:	25-40X
Comm. 151-200 p/r 251-400:	2.00
Comm. 151-200 p/r 151-250:	3.00
Comm. 151-200 p/r 76-150:	5.00
Comm. 151-200 p/r 30-75:	8.00

2002 Donruss Stat Line Season

	MT
cards 1-150 print run 151-200:	5-10X
1-150 p/r 101-150:	6-12X
1-150 p/r 76-100:	8-15X
1-150 p/r 51-75:	10-20X
1-150 p/r 31-50:	15-30X
1-150 p/r 15-30:	20-40X
Comm. 151-200 p/r 151-200:	3.00
Comm. 151-200 p/r 101-150:	4.00
Comm. 151-200 p/r 76-100:	6.00
Comm. 151-200 p/r 30-75:	10.00

2002 Donruss All-Time Diamond Kings

		MT
Complete Set (10):		160.00
Common Player:		10.00
Production 2,500 sets		
Studio Series:		2-3X
Production 250 sets		
1	Ted Williams	25.00
2	Cal Ripken Jr.	25.00
3	Lou Gehrig	20.00
4	Babe Ruth	25.00
5	Roberto Clemente	20.00

6 Don Mattingly 25.00
7 Kirby Puckett 15.00
8 Stan Musial 15.00
9 Yogi Berra 15.00
10 Ernie Banks 15.00

2002 Donruss Bat Kings

MT
Quantities produced listed
Studio Series: 1.5-3X
Production 25 or 50
1 Jason Giambi/250 25.00
2 Alex Rodriguez/250 30.00
3 Mike Piazza/250 45.00
4 Roberto Clemente/125 100.00
5 Babe Ruth/125 260.00

2002 Donruss Diamond Kings

MT
Complete Set (20): 220.00
Common Player: 8.00
Production 2,500 sets
Studio Series: 2-3X
Production 250 sets
1 Nomar Garciaparra 20.00
2 Shawn Green 8.00
3 Randy Johnson 12.00
4 Derek Jeter 25.00
5 Carlos Delgado 10.00
6 Roger Clemens 15.00
7 Jeff Bagwell 12.00
8 Vladimir Guerrero 10.00
9 Luis Gonzalez 8.00
10 Mike Piazza 20.00
11 Ichiro Suzuki 25.00
12 Pedro Martinez 12.00
13 Todd Helton 12.00
14 Sammy Sosa 15.00
15 Ivan Rodriguez 12.00
16 Barry Bonds 15.00
17 Albert Pujols 15.00
18 Jim Thome 12.00
19 Alex Rodriguez 15.00
20 Jason Giambi 15.00

2002 Donruss Elite Series

MT
Complete Set (15): 95.00
Common Player: 4.00
Production 2,500 sets
1 Barry Bonds 15.00
2 Lance Berkman 8.00
3 Jason Giambi 10.00
4 Nomar Garciaparra 15.00
5 Curt Schilling 8.00
6 Vladimir Guerrero 8.00
7 Shawn Green 5.00
8 Troy Glaus 8.00
9 Jeff Bagwell 10.00
10 Manny Ramirez 10.00
11 Eric Chavez 4.00
12 Carlos Delgado 6.00
13 Mike Sweeney 4.00
14 Todd Helton 10.00
15 Luis Gonzalez 8.00

2002 Donruss Elite Series Legends

MT
Complete Set (5): 40.00
Common Player: 8.00
Production 2,500
16 Enos Slaughter 8.00
17 Frank Robinson 10.00
18 Bob Gibson 10.00
19 Warren Spahn 8.00
20 Whitey Ford 10.00

2002 Donruss Elite Series Legends Autographs

MT
Production 250 sets
16 Enos Slaughter 40.00
17 Frank Robinson 40.00
18 Bob Gibson 40.00
19 Warren Spahn 50.00
20 Whitey Ford 50.00

2002 Donruss Jersey Kings

MT
Quantity Produced Listed
1 Alex Rodriguez/250 40.00
2 Jason Giambi/250 35.00
3 Carlos Delgado/250 25.00
4 Barry Bonds/250 50.00
5 Randy Johnson/250 40.00
6 Jim Thome/250 40.00
7 Shawn Green/250 20.00
8 Pedro Martinez/250 35.00
9 Jeff Bagwell/250 30.00
10 Vladimir Guerrero/250 30.00
11 Ivan Rodriguez/250 25.00
12 Nomar Garciaparra/250 50.00
13 Don Mattingly/125 110.00
14 Ted Williams/125 200.00
15 Lou Gehrig/125 250.00

2002 Donruss Longball Leaders

MT
Complete Set (20): 100.00
Common Player: 4.00
Production 1,000 sets
Parallel: 2-4X
Parallel #'d to 2001 HR Total
1 Barry Bonds 12.00
2 Sammy Sosa 12.00
3 Luis Gonzalez 6.00
4 Alex Rodriguez 10.00
5 Shawn Green 5.00
6 Todd Helton 8.00
7 Jim Thome 6.00
8 Rafael Palmeiro 6.00
9 Richie Sexson 4.00
10 Troy Glaus 8.00
11 Manny Ramirez 8.00
12 Phil Nevin 4.00
13 Jeff Bagwell 8.00
14 Carlos Delgado 6.00
15 Jason Giambi 6.00
16 Chipper Jones 10.00
17 Larry Walker 5.00
18 Albert Pujols 12.00
19 Brian Giles 4.00
20 Bret Boone 4.00

2002 Donruss Production Line

MT
Common Card: 2.00
Numbered to category stat
1 Barry Bonds/515 10.00
2 Jason Giambi/477 6.00
3 Larry Walker/449 3.00
4 Sammy Sosa/437 10.00
5 Todd Helton/432 5.00
6 Lance Berkman/430 3.00
7 Luis Gonzalez/429 3.00
8 Chipper Jones/427 10.00
9 Edgar Martinez/423 2.00
10 Gary Sheffield/417 2.00
11 Jim Thome/416 3.00
12 Roberto Alomar/415 4.00
13 J.D. Drew/414 3.00
14 Jim Edmonds/410 2.00
15 Carlos Delgado/408 4.00
16 Manny Ramirez/405 5.00
17 Brian Giles/404 2.00
18 Albert Pujols/403 10.00
19 John Olerud/401 3.00
20 Alex Rodriguez/399 12.00
21 Barry Bonds/863 8.00
22 Sammy Sosa/737 8.00
23 Luis Gonzalez/688 3.00
24 Todd Helton/685 4.00
25 Larry Walker/662 2.00
26 Jason Giambi/660 3.00
27 Jim Thome/624 3.00
28 Alex Rodriguez/620 10.00
29 Lance Berkman/620 2.00
30 J.D. Drew/613 3.00
31 Albert Pujols/610 8.00
32 Manny Ramirez/609 4.00
33 Chipper Jones/605 8.00
34 Shawn Green/598 2.00
35 Brian Giles/590 2.00
36 Juan Gonzalez/590 4.00
37 Phil Nevin/588 2.00
38 Gary Sheffield/583 2.00
39 Bret Boone/578 2.00
40 Cliff Floyd/578 2.00
41 Barry Bonds/1,378 6.00
42 Sammy Sosa/1,174 6.00
43 Jason Giambi/1,137 3.00
44 Todd Helton/1,117 3.00
45 Luis Gonzalez/1,117 2.50
46 Larry Walker/1,111 2.50
47 Lance Berkman/1,050 2.00
48 Jim Thome/1,040 2.50
49 Chipper Jones/1,032 6.00
50 J.D. Drew/1,027 2.50
51 Alex Rodriguez/1,021 8.00
52 Manny Ramirez/1,014 3.00
53 Albert Pujols/1,013 6.00
54 Gary Sheffield/1,000 2.00
55 Brian Giles/994 2.00
56 Phil Nevin/976 2.00
57 Jim Edmonds/974 2.00
58 Shawn Green/970 2.50
59 Cliff Floyd/968 2.00
60 Edgar Martinez/966 2.00

2002 Donruss Rookie Year Materials - Bats

MT
Production 250 sets
1 Barry Bonds 60.00
2 Cal Ripken Jr. 90.00
3 Kirby Puckett 80.00
4 Johnny Bench 50.00

2002 Donruss Rookie Year Materials - Jerseys

MT
Quantity produced listed
Parallel #'d to 25 or 50
1 Nomar Garciaparra/250 80.00
2 Randy Johnson/250 70.00
3 Ivan Rodriguez/250 40.00
4 Vladimir Guerrero/250 30.00
5 Stan Musial/50 160.00
6 Yogi Berra/50 100.00

2002 Donruss Rookie Year Materials - Bats Autograph

MT
Numbered to debut year
1 Barry Bonds/86
2 Cal Ripken Jr/81 140.00
3 Kirby Puckett/84 120.00
4 Johnny Bench/68

2002 Donruss Classics

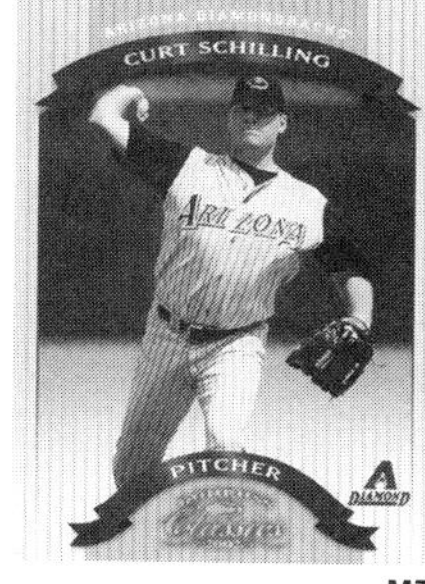

MT
Complete Set (200): NA
Common Player: .50
Common (101-150): 5.00
Common (151-200): 4.00
Production 1,500
Pack (6): 7.00
Box (18): 100.00
1 Alex Rodriguez 4.00
2 Barry Bonds 3.00
3 C.C. Sabathia .50
4 Chipper Jones 2.50
5 Derek Jeter 5.00
6 Troy Glaus 1.00
7 Frank Thomas 1.25
8 Greg Maddux 2.50
9 Ivan Rodriguez 1.00
10 Jeff Bagwell 1.25
11 Mark Buehrle .50
12 Todd Helton 1.25
13 Ken Griffey Jr. 3.00
14 Manny Ramirez 1.25
15 Brad Penny .50
16 Mike Piazza 3.00
17 Nomar Garciaparra 3.00
18 Pedro J. Martinez 1.50
19 Randy Johnson 1.50
20 Bud Smith .50

21	Rickey Henderson	1.00
22	Roger Clemens	2.00
23	Sammy Sosa	2.50
24	Brandon Duckworth	.50
25	Vladimir Guerrero	1.50
26	Kazuhiro Sasaki	.50
27	Roberto Alomar	1.00
28	Barry Zito	.50
29	Rich Aurilia	.50
30	Ben Sheets	.75
31	Carlos Delgado	1.00
32	J.D. Drew	.75
33	Jermaine Dye	.50
34	Darin Erstad	.75
35	Jason Giambi	1.50
36	Tom Glavine	.75
37	Juan Gonzalez	1.00
38	Luis Gonzalez	1.00
39	Shawn Green	.75
40	Tim Hudson	.75
41	Andruw Jones	1.00
42	Shannon Stewart	.50
43	Barry Larkin	.75
44	Wade Miller	.50
45	Mike Mussina	1.00
46	Hideo Nomo	1.00
47	Rafael Palmeiro	.75
48	Scott Rolen	.75
49	Gary Sheffield	.75
50	Bernie Williams	1.00
51	Bobby Abreu	.50
52	Javier Vazquez	.50
53	Edgar Martinez	.50
54	Magglio Ordonez	.75
55	Kerry Wood	1.00
56	Adrian Beltre	.50
57	Lance Berkman	1.00
58	Kevin Brown	.50
59	Sean Casey	.50
60	Eric Chavez	.75
61	Robert Person	.50
62	Jeremy Giambi	.50
63	Freddy Garcia	.50
64	Alfonso Soriano	3.00
65	Doug Davis	.50
66	Brian Giles	.75
67	Moises Alou	.50
68	Richard Hidalgo	.50
69	Paul LoDuca	.50
70	Aramis Ramirez	.50
71	Andres Galarraga	.50
72	Ryan Klesko	.50
73	Chan Ho Park	.50
74	Richie Sexson	.75
75	Mike Sweeney	.50
76	Aubrey Huff	.50
77	Miguel Tejada	.75
78	Jose Vidro	.50
79	Larry Walker	.75
80	Roy Oswalt	.75
81	Craig Biggio	.75
82	Juan Pierre	.50
83	Jim Thome	1.00
84	Josh Towers	.50
85	Alex Escobar	.50
86	Cliff Floyd	.50
87	Terrence Long	.50
88	Curt Schilling	1.00
89	Carlos Beltran	.50
90	Albert Pujols	2.50
91	Gabe Kapler	.50
92	Mark Mulder	.50
93	Carlos Lee	.50
94	Robert Fick	.50
95	Raul Mondesi	.50
96	Ichiro Suzuki	4.00
97	Adam Dunn	1.25
98	Corey Patterson	.75
99	Tsuyoshi Shinjo	.75
100	Joe Mays	.50
101	Juan Cruz	5.00
102	Marlon Byrd	8.00
103	Luis Garcia	5.00
104	*Jorge Padilla*	10.00
105	Dennis Tankersley	5.00
106	Josh Pearce	5.00
107	Ramon Vazquez	5.00
108	*Chris Baker*	6.00
109	*Eric Cyr*	5.00
110	*Reed Johnson*	5.00
111	*Ryan Jamison*	5.00
112	Antonio Perez	5.00
113	*Satoru Komiyama*	8.00
114	Austin Kearns	10.00
115	Juan Pena	5.00
116	Orlando Hudson	5.00
117	*Kazuhisa Ishii*	15.00
118	Eric Bedard	5.00
119	*Luis Ugueto*	8.00
120	*Ben Howard*	8.00
121	Morgan Ensberg	5.00
122	*Doug Devore*	10.00
123	Josh Phelps	10.00
124	Angel Berroa	5.00
125	Ed Rogers	5.00
126	*Takahito Nomura*	5.00
127	*John Ennis*	5.00
128	Bill Hall	5.00
129	Dewon Brazelton	5.00
130	Hank Blalock	8.00
131	*So Taguchi*	10.00
132	*Jorge De La Rosa*	5.00
133	Matt Thornton	5.00
134	*Brandon Backe*	5.00
135	*Jeff Deardorff*	5.00
136	Steve Smyth	5.00
137	*Anderson Machado*	5.00
138	John Buck	5.00
139	Mark Prior	20.00
140	Sean Burroughs	5.00
141	Alex Herrera	5.00
142	*Francis Beltran*	5.00
143	Jason Romano	5.00
144	Michael Cuddyer	5.00
145	*Steve Bechler*	5.00
146	Alfredo Amezaga	5.00
147	Ryan Ludwick	5.00
148	Martin Vargas	5.00
149	*Allan Simpson*	5.00
150	Mark Teixeira	8.00
151	TBD	
152	Ernie Banks	8.00
153	Johnny Bench	8.00
154	George Brett	12.00
155	Lou Brock	6.00
156	Rod Carew	5.00
157	Steve Carlton	5.00
158	Joe Torre	4.00
159	Dennis Eckersley	4.00
160	Reggie Jackson	6.00
161	Al Kaline	8.00
162	Dave Parker	4.00
163	Don Mattingly	15.00
164	Tony Gwynn	8.00
165	Willie McCovey	4.00
166	Joe Morgan	4.00
167	Stan Musial	8.00
168	Jim Palmer	4.00
169	Brooks Robinson	6.00
170	Bo Jackson	8.00
171	Nolan Ryan	20.00
172	Mike Schmidt	8.00
173	Tom Seaver	6.00
174	Cal Ripken Jr.	15.00
175	Robin Yount	8.00
176	Wade Boggs	5.00
177	Gary Carter	4.00
178	Ron Santo	4.00
179	Luis Aparicio	4.00
180	Bobby Doerr	4.00
181	Ryne Sandberg	40.00
182	Yogi Berra	6.00
183	Will Clark	6.00
184	Eddie Murray	5.00
185	Andre Dawson	5.00
186	Duke Snider	6.00
187	Orlando Cepeda	4.00
188	Billy Williams	4.00
189	Juan Marichal	4.00
190	Harmon Killebrew	8.00
191	Kirby Puckett	8.00
192	Carlton Fisk	5.00
193	Dave Winfield	5.00
194	Alan Trammell	4.00
195	Paul Molitor	6.00
196	Tony Perez	4.00
197	Ozzie Smith	8.00
198	Ralph Kiner	4.00
199	Fergie Jenkins	4.00
200	Phil Rizzuto	5.00

2002 Donruss Classics Classic Combos

		MT
Common Player:		
Too scarce to price		
1	Eddie Murray, Cal Ripken Jr.	
2	George Brett, Bo Jackson	
3	Ted Williams, Jimmie Foxx	
4	Nolan Ryan, Steve Carlton	
5	Mel Ott, Babe Ruth	
6	Nolan Ryan, George Brett	
7	Babe Ruth, Ty Cobb	
8	Jackie Robinson, Duke Snider	
9	Nolan Ryan, George Brett, Robin Yount, Orlando Cepeda	
10	Rickey Henderson, Ty Cobb	
11	Ted Williams, Tony Gwynn	
12	Tony Gwynn, Rickey Henderson	
13	Ty Cobb, Tony Gwynn	
14	Dave Parker, Willie Stargell	
15	Ted Williams, Ty Cobb	
16	Jimmie Foxx, Lou Gehrig	
17	Jim "Catfish" Hunter, Reggie Jackson	
18	Ted Williams, Ty Cobb, Jimmie Foxx, Lou Gehrig	
19	Bobby Doerr, Ted Williams	
20	Mike Schmidt, George Brett	

2002 Donruss Classics Classic Singles

		MT
Common Player:		15.00
Some too scarce to price		
1	Cal Ripken Jr/jsy/50	50.00
2	Eddie Murray/jsy/100	20.00
3	George Brett/jsy/100	40.00
4	Bo Jackson/jsy/100	25.00
5	Ted Williams/bat/50	200.00
6	Jimmie Foxx/bat/50	70.00
7	Reggie Jackson/jsy/100	25.00
8	Steve Carlton/jsy/50	40.00
9	Mel Ott/jsy/50	90.00
10	"Catfish" Hunter/jsy/100	40.00
11	Nolan Ryan/jsy/100	80.00
12	Rickey Henderson/jsy/100	40.00
13	Robin Yount/jsy/100	40.00
14	Orlando Cepeda/jsy/100	15.00
15	Ty Cobb	
16	Babe Ruth/bat/50	275.00
17	Dave Parker/jsy/100	15.00
18	Willie Stargell/jsy/100	20.00
19	Ernie Banks/bat/100	45.00
20	Mike Schmidt/jsy/100	70.00
21	Duke Snider/jsy/50	35.00
22	Jackie Robinson/jsy/50	75.00
23	Rickey Henderson/bat/100	40.00
24	TBD	
25	Lou Gehrig/bat/50	175.00
26	Jimmie Foxx/50	
27	Reggie Jackson	
28	Tony Gwynn/bat/100	30.00
29	Bobby Doerr/jsy/100	25.00
30	Joe Torre/jsy/100	15.00

2002 Donruss Classics Legendary Hats

		MT
50 sets produced		
1	Don Mattingly/50	210.00
2	George Brett	190.00
3	Wade Boggs	50.00
4	Reggie Jackson	
5	Ryne Sandberg	120.00

2002 Donruss Classics Legendary Spikes

		MT
50 sets produced		
1	Don Mattingly	
2	Eddie Murray	90.00
3	Paul Molitor	80.00
4	Harmon Killebrew	65.00
5	Mike Schmidt	150.00

2002 Donruss Classics Legendary Leather

		MT
50 sets produced		
1	Don Mattingly	160.00
2	Wade Boggs	50.00
3	Tony Gwynn	
4	Kirby Puckett	165.00
5	Mike Schmidt	120.00

2002 Donruss Classics Legendary Lumberjacks

		MT
Varying quantities produced		
1	Don Mattingly/500	30.00
2	George Brett/400	25.00
3	Stan Musial/100	45.00
4	Lou Gehrig/50	175.00
5	Mike Piazza/500	20.00
6	Mel Ott/50	75.00
7	Ted Williams/50	200.00
8	Bo Jackson/500	15.00
9	Kirby Puckett/500	20.00
10	Rafael Palmeiro/500	10.00
11	Andre Dawson/500	12.00
12	Ozzie Smith/500	20.00
13	Paul Molitor/500	12.00
14	Babe Ruth/50	220.00
15	Carlton Fisk/500	15.00
16	Rickey Henderson/500	20.00
17	Gary Carter/500	10.00
18	Cal Ripken Jr/100	50.00
19	Eddie Matthews/100	40.00
20	Luis Aparicio/500	15.00
21	Al Kaline/100	40.00
22	Eddie Murray/500	15.00
23	Yogi Berra/100	40.00
24	Alex Rodriguez/500	15.00

25 Tony Gwynn/500 15.00
26 Roberto Clemente/100 80.00
27 Mike Schmidt/400 30.00
28 Reggie Jackson/500 15.00
29 Ryne Sandberg/500 30.00
30 Joe Morgan/400 15.00
31 Joe Torre/500 10.00
32 Gary Sheffield/500 8.00
33 Nomar Garciaparra/500 20.00
34 Jeff Bagwell/500 10.00
35 Manny Ramirez/500 10.00

2002 Donruss Classics New Millennium Classics

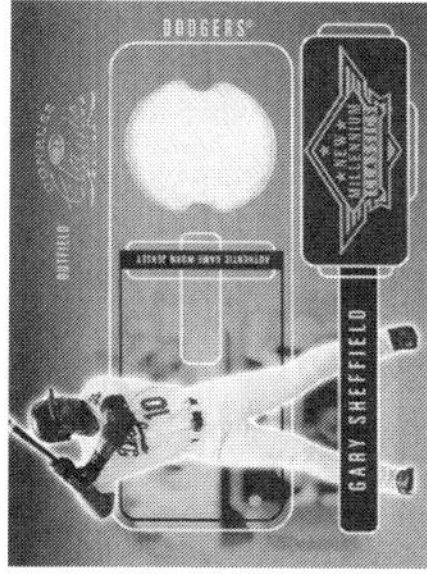

MT
Common Player: 8.00
Varying quantities produced
All jerseys unless noted
1 Curt Schilling/500 12.00
2 Vladimir Guerrero/100 25.00
3 Jim Thome/500 12.00
4 Troy Glaus/400 10.00
5 Ivan Rodriguez/200 12.00
6 Todd Helton/400 10.00
7 Sean Casey/500 8.00
8 Scott Rolen/475 8.00
9 Ken Griffey Jr/150/base 20.00
10 Hideo Nomo/100 65.00
11 Tom Glavine/350 10.00
12 Pedro Martinez/100 30.00
13 Cliff Floyd/500 8.00
14 Shawn Green/125 20.00
15 Rafael Palmeiro/250 12.00
16 Luis Gonzalez/100 20.00
17 Lance Berkman/100 25.00
18 Frank Thomas/500 10.00
19 Randy Johnson/400 15.00
20 Moises Alou/500 8.00
21 Chipper Jones/500 15.00
22 Larry Walker/300 8.00
23 Mike Sweeney/500 8.00
24 Juan Gonzalez/300 10.00
25 Roger Clemens/100 25.00
26 Albert Pujols/300/base 15.00
27 Magglio Ordonez/500 8.00
28 Alex Rodriguez/400 15.00
29 Jeff Bagwell/125 20.00
30 Kazuhiro Sasaki/500 8.00
31 Barry Larkin/300 8.00
32 Andruw Jones/350 8.00
33 Kerry Wood/200 20.00
34 Rickey Henderson/100 40.00
35 Greg Maddux/100 30.00
36 Brian Giles/400 8.00
37 Craig Biggio/100 15.00
38 Roberto Alomar/400 8.00
39 Mike Piazza/400 20.00
40 Bernie Williams/100 20.00
41 Ichiro Suzuki/150/ball 60.00
42 Kenny Lofton/450 8.00
43 Mark Mulder/500 8.00
44 Kazuhisa Ishii/100
45 Darin Erstad/500 8.00
46 Jose Vidro/500 8.00
47 Miguel Tejada/475 10.00
48 Roy Oswalt/500 10.00
49 So Taguchi/100
50 Barry Zito/500 8.00
51 Manny Ramirez/400 12.00
52 Nomar Garciaparra/400 30.00
53 C.C. Sabathia/500 8.00
54 Carlos Delgado/500 8.00
55 Gary Sheffield/500 8.00
56 J.D. Drew/500 10.00
57 Barry Bonds/150/ball 30.00
58 Derek Jeter/150/ball 40.00
59 Edgar Martinez/400 8.00
60 Sammy Sosa/150/ball 20.00

2002 Donruss Classics Significant Signatures

MT
Common Prospect Autograph: 10.00
Varying quantities produced, many not priced due to scarcity
1 Alex Rodriguez
2 Barry Bonds
3 C.C. Sabathia
4 Chipper Jones/15
5 Derek Jeter
6 Troy Glaus
7 Frank Thomas
8 Greg Maddux
9 Ivan Rodriguez
10 Jeff Bagwell
11 Mark Buehrle
12 Todd Helton
13 Ken Griffey Jr.
14 Manny Ramirez
15 Brad Penny
16 Mike Piazza
17 Nomar Garciaparra
18 Pedro J. Martinez
19 Randy Johnson
20 Bud Smith
21 Rickey Henderson
22 Roger Clemens
23 Sammy Sosa
24 Brandon Duckworth
25 Vladimir Guerrero
26 Kazuhiro Sasaki
27 Roberto Alomar
28 Barry Zito
29 Rich Aurilia
30 Ben Sheets
31 Carlos Delgado
32 J.D. Drew
33 Jermaine Dye
34 Darin Erstad
35 Jason Giambi
36 Tom Glavine
37 Juan Gonzalez
38 Luis Gonzalez
39 Shawn Green
40 Tim Hudson
41 Andruw Jones
42 Shannon Stewart
43 Barry Larkin
44 Wade Miller
45 Mike Mussina
46 Hideo Nomo
47 Rafael Palmeiro
48 Scott Rolen
49 Gary Sheffield
50 Bernie Williams
51 Bobby Abreu
52 Javier Vazquez
53 Edgar Martinez
54 Magglio Ordonez
55 Kerry Wood
56 Adrian Beltre
57 Lance Berkman
58 Kevin Brown
59 Sean Casey
60 Eric Chavez
61 Robert Person
62 Jeremy Giambi
63 Freddy Garcia
64 Alfonso Soriano
65 Doug Davis
66 Brian Giles
67 Moises Alou
68 Richard Hidalgo
69 Paul LoDuca
70 Aramis Ramirez
71 Andres Galarraga
72 Ryan Klesko
73 Chan Ho Park
74 Richie Sexson
75 Mike Sweeney
76 Aubrey Huff
77 Miguel Tejada
78 Jose Vidro
79 Larry Walker
80 Roy Oswalt
81 Craig Biggio
82 Juan Pierre
83 Jim Thome
84 Josh Towers
85 Alex Escobar
86 Cliff Floyd
87 Terrence Long
88 Curt Schilling
89 Carlos Beltran
90 Albert Pujols
91 Gabe Kapler
92 Mark Mulder
93 Carlos Lee
94 Robert Fick
95 Raul Mondesi
96 Ichiro Suzuki
97 Adam Dunn
98 Corey Patterson
99 Tsuyoshi Shinjo
100 Joe Mays
101 Juan Cruz/400 15.00
102 Marlon Byrd/500 20.00
103 Luis Garcia/500 10.00
104 *Jorge Padilla/500* 15.00
105 Dennis Tankersley/250 10.00
106 Josh Pearce/500 10.00
107 Ramon Vazquez/500 15.00
108 *Chris Baker/500* 10.00
109 Eric Cyr/500 10.00
110 Reed Johnson/500 10.00
111 Ryan Jamison/500 10.00
112 Antonio Perez/500 10.00
113 Satoru Komiyama/50 125.00
114 Austin Kearns/500 40.00
115 Juan Pena/500 10.00
116 Orlando Hudson/400 15.00
117 Kazuhisa Ishii/50 180.00
118 Eric Bedard/500 10.00
119 Luis Ugueto/250 20.00
120 Ben Howard/500 15.00
121 Morgan Ensberg/500 10.00
122 Doug Devore/500 15.00
123 Josh Phelps/500 25.00
124 Angel Berroa/500 10.00
125 Ed Rogers/500 10.00
126 Takahito Nomura/25
127 John Ennis/500 10.00
128 Bill Hall/400 12.00
129 Dewon Brazelton/400 12.00
130 Hank Blalock/100 40.00
131 So Taguchi/150 40.00
132 Jorge De La Rosa/500 10.00
133 Matt Thornton/500 10.00
134 Brandon Backe/500 15.00
135 Jeff Deardorff/500 10.00
136 Steve Smyth/400 12.00
137 Anderson Machado/500 10.00
138 John Buck/500 12.00
139 Mark Prior/250 85.00
140 Sean Burroughs/50 50.00
141 Alex Herrera/500 10.00
142 Francis Beltran/500 10.00
143 Jason Romano/500 15.00
144 Michael Cuddyer/400 20.00
145 Steve Bechler/500 10.00
146 Alfredo Amezaga/500 10.00
147 Ryan Ludwick/500 10.00
148 Martin Vargas/500 15.00
149 Allan Simpson/500 10.00
150 Mark Teixeira/200 25.00
151 TBD
152 Ernie Banks/25 100.00
153 Johnny Bench/25 125.00
154 George Brett/25 260.00
155 Lou Brock/100 40.00
156 Rod Carew/25
157 Steve Carlton/125 35.00
158 Joe Torre/25
159 Dennis Eckersley/500 20.00
160 Reggie Jackson/25
161 Al Kaline/125 35.00
162 Dave Parker/500 15.00
163 Don Mattingly/50
164 Tony Gwynn/25
165 Willie McCovey/25
166 Joe Morgan/25
167 Stan Musial/25
168 Jim Palmer/125 25.00
169 Brooks Robinson/125 40.00
170 Bo Jackson/25
171 Nolan Ryan/25
172 Mike Schmidt/25
173 Tom Seaver/25
174 Cal Ripken Jr/25
175 Robin Yount/25
176 Wade Boggs/25
177 Gary Carter/150 30.00
178 Ron Santo/500 20.00
179 Luis Aparicio/400 15.00
180 Bobby Doerr/500 15.00
181 Ryne Sandberg
182 Yogi Berra/25 125.00
183 Will Clark/50
184 Eddie Murray/25 75.00
185 Andre Dawson/200 30.00
186 Duke Snider/25 70.00
187 Orlando Cepeda/125 25.00
188 Billy Williams/200 15.00
189 Juan Marichal/500 15.00
190 Harmon Killebrew/100 90.00
191 Kirby Puckett
192 Carlton Fisk/25
193 Dave Winfield
194 Alan Trammell/200 25.00
195 Paul Molitor/25
196 Tony Perez
197 Ozzie Smith/25
198 Ralph Kiner/125 25.00
199 Fergie Jenkins/200 15.00
200 Phil Rizzuto/125 40.00

2002 Donruss Classics Timeless Tributes

	MT
Stars (1-100):	5-10X
SP's (101-150):	1-2X
SP's (151-200):	2-3X
Production 100 sets	

2002 Donruss Diamond Kings

		MT
Complete Set (150):		200.00
Common Player:		.40
Common SP (101-150):		2.50
Inserted 1:3		
Pack (4):		4.50
Box (24):		95.00
1	Vladimir Guerrero	.75
2	Adam Dunn	.75
3	Tsuyoshi Shinjo	.50
4	Adrian Beltre	.40
5	Troy Glaus	.50
6	Albert Pujols	1.50
7	Trot Nixon	.40
8	Alex Rodriguez	2.50
9	Tom Glavine	.50
10	Alfonso Soriano	1.00
11	Todd Helton	.75
12	Joe Torre	.40
13	Tim Hudson	.50
14	Andruw Jones	.50
15	Shawn Green	.50
16	Aramis Ramirez	.40
17	Shannon Stewart	.40
18	Barry Bonds	1.50
19	Sean Casey	.40
20	Barry Larkin	.50
21	Scott Rolen	.50
22	Barry Zito	.40
23	Sammy Sosa	1.50
24	Bartolo Colon	.40
25	Ryan Klesko	.40
26	Ben Grieve	.40
27	Roy Oswalt	.50
28	Kazuhiro Sasaki	.40
29	Roger Clemens	1.00
30	Bernie Williams	.50
31	Roberto Alomar	.50
32	Bobby Abreu	.40
33	Robert Fick	.40
34	Bret Boone	.40
35	Rickey Henderson	.50
36	Brian Giles	.50
37	Richie Sexson	.50
38	Bud Smith	.40
39	Richard Hidalgo	.40
40	C.C. Sabathia	.40
41	Rich Aurilia	.40
42	Carlos Beltran	.40
43	Raul Mondesi	.40
44	Carlos Delgado	.50
45	Randy Johnson	.75
46	Chan Ho Park	.40
47	Rafael Palmeiro	.50
48	Chipper Jones	1.50
49	Phil Nevin	.40
50	Cliff Floyd	.40
51	Pedro Martinez	.75
52	Craig Biggio	.50
53	Paul LoDuca	.40
54	Cristian Guzman	.40
55	Pat Burrell	.50
56	Curt Schilling	.50
57	Orlando Cabrera	.40
58	Darin Erstad	.50
59	Omar Vizquel	.50
60	Derek Jeter	3.00
61	Nomar Garciaparra	2.00
62	Edgar Martinez	.40
63	Moises Alou	.40
64	Eric Chavez	.50
65	Mike Sweeney	.40
66	Frank Thomas	.75
67	Mike Piazza	2.50
68	Gary Sheffield	.50
69	Mike Mussina	.50
70	Greg Maddux	1.50
71	Juan Gonzalez	.75
72	Hideo Nomo	.50
73	Miguel Tejada	.50
74	Ichiro Suzuki	2.50
75	Matt Morris	.40
76	Ivan Rodriguez	.50
77	Mark Mulder	.40
78	J.D. Drew	.40
79	Mark Grace	.50
80	Jason Giambi	.75
81	Mark Buehrle	.40
82	Jose Vidro	.40
83	Manny Ramirez	.75
84	Jeff Bagwell	.75
85	Magglio Ordonez	.50
86	Ken Griffey Jr.	2.00
87	Luis Gonzalez	.50
88	Jim Edmonds	.50
89	Larry Walker	.50
90	Jim Thome	.50
91	Lance Berkman	.50
92	Jorge Posada	.50
93	Kevin Brown	.40
94	Joe Mays	.40
95	Kerry Wood	.60
96	Mark Ellis	.40
97	Austin Kearns	.75
98	*Jorge De La Rosa*	.50
99	Brandon Berger	.40
100	Ryan Ludwick	.40
101	Marlon Byrd	2.50
102	*Brandon Backe*	2.50
103	Juan Cruz	2.50
104	*Anderson Machado*	2.50
105	*So Taguchi*	4.00
106	Dewon Brazelton	2.50
107	Josh Beckett	4.00
108	John Buck	2.50
109	*Jorge Padilla*	3.00
110	Hee Seop Choi	3.00
111	Angel Berroa	2.50
112	Mark Teixeira	3.00
113	Victor Martinez	2.50
114	*Kazuhisa Ishii*	12.00
115	Dennis Tankersley	2.50
116	*Wilson Valdez*	2.50
117	Antonio Perez	2.50
118	Ed Rogers	2.50
119	Wilson Betemit	2.50
120	Mike Rivera	2.50
121	Mark Prior	6.00
122	Roberto Clemente	6.00
123	Roberto Clemente	6.00
124	Roberto Clemente	6.00
125	Roberto Clemente	6.00
126	Roberto Clemente	6.00
127	Babe Ruth	10.00
128	Ted Williams	8.00
129	Andre Dawson	2.50
130	Eddie Murray	4.00
131	Juan Marichal	3.00
132	Kirby Puckett	6.00
133	Alan Trammell	2.50
134	Bobby Doerr	2.50
135	Carlton Fisk	3.00
136	Eddie Mathews	4.00
137	Mike Schmidt	6.00
138	Jim "Catfish" Hunter	2.50
139	Nolan Ryan	10.00
140	George Brett	6.00
141	Gary Carter	2.50
142	Paul Molitor	4.00
143	Lou Gehrig	8.00
144	Ryne Sandberg	6.00
145	Tony Gwynn	5.00
146	Ron Santo	2.50
147	Cal Ripken Jr.	10.00
148	Al Kaline	4.00
149	Bo Jackson	3.00
150	Don Mattingly	8.00

2002 Donruss Diamond Kings Bronze Foil

	MT
Cards 1-100:	1-2.5X
Cards 101-150:	.5X
Inserted 1:6	
Gold Foil (1-100):	5-10X
Gold Foil (101-150):	2-4X
Production 100 sets	
Silver Foil (1-100):	3-5X
Silver Foil (101-150):	1-2X
Production 400 sets	

2002 Donruss Diamond Kings Diamond Cut

		MT
Common Card:		10.00
1	Vladimir Guerrero/400	35.00
2	Mark Prior/400	80.00
3	Victor Martinez/500	10.00
4	Marlon Byrd/500	20.00
5	Bud Smith/400	15.00
6	Joe Mays/500	15.00
7	Troy Glaus/500	25.00
8	Ron Santo/500	20.00
9	Roy Oswalt/500	25.00
10	Angel Berroa/500	10.00
11	Mark Buehrle/500	15.00
12	John Buck/500	15.00
13	Barry Larkin/250	40.00
14	Gary Carter/300	30.00
15	Mark Teixeira/300	40.00
16	Alan Trammell/500	20.00
17	Kazuhisa Ishii/100	125.00
18	Rafael Palmeiro/125	50.00
19	Austin Kearns/500	40.00
20	Joe Torre/125	60.00
21	J.D. Drew/400	40.00
22	So Taguchi/400	35.00
23	Juan Marichal/500	20.00
24	Bobby Doerr/500	20.00
25	Carlos Beltran/500	15.00
26	Robert Fick/500	10.00
27	Albert Pujols/200	70.00
28	Shannon Stewart/500	15.00
29	Antonio Perez/500	10.00
30	Wilson Betemit/500	20.00
Signatures (1-30):		
1	Vladimir Guerrero	
2	Mark Prior	
3	Victor Martinez	
4	Marlon Byrd	
5	Bud Smith	
6	Joe Mays	
7	Troy Glaus	
8	Ron Santo	
9	Roy Oswalt	
10	Angel Berroa	
11	Mark Buehrle	
12	John Buck	
13	Barry Larkin	
14	Gary Carter	
15	Mark Teixeira	
16	Alan Trammell	
17	Kazuhisa Ishii	
18	Rafael Palmeiro	
19	Austin Kearns	
20	Joe Torre	
21	J.D. Drew	
22	So Taguchi	
23	Juan Marichal	
24	Bobby Doerr	
25	Carlos Beltran	
26	Robert Fick	
27	Albert Pujols	
28	Shannon Stewart	
29	Antonio Perez	
30	Wilson Betemit	
Jerseys (31-80):		
31	Alex Rodriguez/500	20.00
32	Curt Schilling/500	15.00
33	George Brett/300	40.00
34	Hideo Nomo/100	75.00
35	Ivan Rodriguez/500	15.00
36	Don Mattingly/200	50.00
37	Joe Mays/500	10.00
38	Lance Berkman/400	20.00
39	Tony Gwynn/500	20.00
40	Darin Erstad/400	10.00
41	Adrian Beltre/400	15.00
42	Frank Thomas/500	15.00
43	Cal Ripken Jr./300	30.00
44	Jose Vidro/500	10.00
45	Randy Johnson/300	15.00
46	Carlos Delgado/500	10.00
47	Roger Clemens/400	25.00
48	Luis Gonzalez/500	15.00
49	Marlon Byrd/500	15.00
50	Carlton Fisk/500	15.00
51	Manny Ramirez/500	15.00
52	Vladimir Guerrero/500	15.00
53	Barry Larkin/500	12.00
54	Aramis Ramirez/500	10.00
55	Todd Helton/300	20.00
56	Carlos Beltran/250	12.00
57	Jeff Bagwell/250	15.00
58	Larry Walker/500	10.00
59	Al Kaline/200	45.00
60	Chipper Jones/500	20.00
61	Bernie Williams/500	10.00
62	Bud Smith/500	10.00
63	Edgar Martinez/500	12.00
64	Pedro Martinez/500	15.00
65	Andre Dawson/200	20.00
66	Mike Piazza/100	75.00
67	Barry Zito/500	15.00
68	Bo Jackson/300	25.00
69	Nolan Ryan/400	75.00
70	Troy Glaus/500	15.00
71	Jorge Posada/500	15.00
72	Ted Williams/100	240.00
73	Nomar Garciaparra/500	30.00
74	"Catfish" Hunter/100	30.00
75	Gary Carter/500	15.00
76	Craig Biggio/500	10.00
77	Andruw Jones/500	15.00
78	Rickey Henderson/250	40.00
79	Greg Maddux/400	25.00
80	Kerry Wood/500	15.00
Bats (81-100):		
81	Alex Rodriguez/500	20.00
82	Don Mattingly/425	40.00
83	Craig Biggio/500	10.00
84	Kazuhisa Ishii/375	60.00
85	Eddie Murray/500	15.00
86	Carlton Fisk/500	15.00
87	Tsuyoshi Shinjo/500	15.00
88	Bo Jackson/500	20.00

89	Eddie Mathews/ 100	40.00
90	Chipper Jones/ 500	20.00
91	Adam Dunn/375	25.00
92	Tony Gwynn/200	25.00
93	Kirby Puckett/500	20.00
94	Andre Dawson/ 500	15.00
95	Bernie Williams/ 500	10.00
96	Roberto Clemente/ 300	70.00
97	Babe Ruth/100	250.00
98	Roberto Alomar/ 500	15.00
99	Frank Thomas/ 500	15.00
100	So Taguchi/500	15.00

2002 Donruss Diamond Kings DK Originals

		MT
Complete Set (15):		90.00
Common Player:		4.00
Production 1,000 sets		
1	Alex Rodriguez	12.00
2	Kazuhisa Ishii	15.00
3	Pedro Martinez	5.00
4	Nomar Garciaparra	10.00
5	Albert Pujols	8.00
6	Chipper Jones	8.00
7	So Taguchi	4.00
8	Jeff Bagwell	4.00
9	Vladimir Guerrero	4.00
10	Derek Jeter	15.00
11	Sammy Sosa	8.00
12	Ichiro Suzuki	12.00
13	Barry Bonds	8.00
14	Jason Giambi	5.00
15	Mike Piazza	10.00

2002 Donruss Diamond Kings Heritage Collection

		MT
Complete Set (25):		150.00
Common Player:		2.50
Inserted 1:23		
1	Lou Gehrig	10.00
2	Nolan Ryan	15.00
3	Ryne Sandberg	8.00
4	Ted Williams	12.00
5	Roberto Clemente	10.00
6	Mike Schmidt	8.00
7	Roger Clemens	6.00
8	Kirby Puckett	6.00
9	Andre Dawson	2.50
10	Carlton Fisk	2.50
11	Don Mattingly	12.00
12	Juan Marichal	2.50
13	George Brett	10.00
14	Bo Jackson	4.00
15	Eddie Mathews	5.00
16	Randy Johnson	4.00
17	Alan Trammell	2.50
18	Tony Gwynn	6.00
19	Paul Molitor	5.00
20	Barry Bonds	8.00
21	Eddie Murray	3.00
22	Jim "Catfish" Hunter	2.50
23	Rickey Henderson	4.00
24	Cal Ripken Jr.	15.00
25	Babe Ruth	15.00

2002 Donruss Diamond Kings Original Paintings

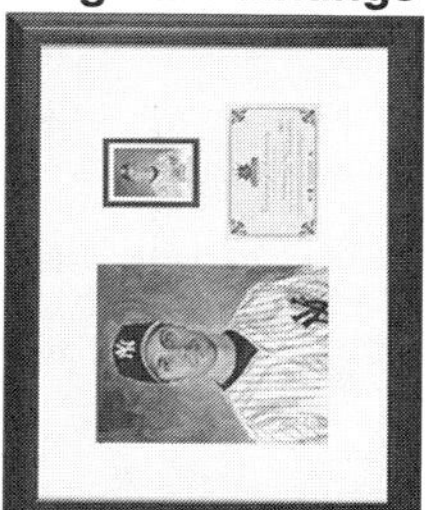

The original 8" x 10" oil paintings which were commissioned to create the player cards in 2002 Donruss Diamond Kings were offered to collectors in a series of Internet auctions during June-July, 2002. Of the 150 cards in the set, 131 paintings were offered. Each original came framed (about 24" x 18") with an example of the issued card and a certificate of authenticity from Donruss. Most of the pieces sold in the $300-500 range, with 25 of the more popular players bringing 1,000 or more and a handful selling at or slightly above $2,000. Because of the unique nature of the items and wildly varying demand, attribution of a current "catalog" value is impossible.

		MT
-	(See 2002 Donruss Diamond Kings for checklist.)	

2002 Donruss Diamond Kings Ramly T204

		MT
Complete Set (25):		150.00
Common Player:		3.00
Production 1,000 sets		
1	Vladimir Guerrero	4.00
2	Jeff Bagwell	4.00
3	Barry Bonds	10.00
4	Rickey Henderson	5.00
5	Mike Piazza	10.00
6	Derek Jeter	15.00
7	Kazuhisa Ishii	15.00
8	Ichiro Suzuki	10.00
9	Chipper Jones	8.00
10	Sammy Sosa	8.00
11	Don Mattingly	10.00
12	Shawn Green	3.00
13	Nomar Garciaparra	10.00
14	Luis Gonzalez	4.00
15	Albert Pujols	8.00
16	Cal Ripken Jr.	15.00
17	Todd Helton	4.00
18	Hideo Nomo	3.00
19	Alex Rodriguez	10.00
20	So Taguchi	3.00
21	Lance Berkman	3.00
22	Tony Gwynn	6.00
23	Roger Clemens	6.00
24	Jason Giambi	5.00
25	Ken Griffey Jr.	10.00

2002 Donruss Diamond Kings Recollection Collection

		MT
1	Roberto Alomar 91 DK/39	
2	Johnny Bench 83 DK/4	
3	Craig Biggio 91 DK/5	
4	Wade Boggs 84 DK/6	
5	Wade Boggs 92 DK/2	
6	George Brett 83 DK/11	
7	George Brett 87 DK/6	
8	Rod Carew 82 DK/21	
9	Steve Carlton 83 DK/10	
10	Gary Carter 82 DK/4	
11	Will Clark 88 DK/24	
12	Carlton Fisk 82 DK/18	
13	Carlton Fisk 89 DK/5	
14	Andres Galarraga 89 DK/10	
15	Nomar Garciaparra 01 DK/3	
16	Tony Gwynn 85 DK/12	
17	Tony Gwynn 89 DK/11	
18	Orel Hershiser 86 DK/12	
19	Bo Jackson 90 DK/5	
20	Reggie Jackson 83 DK/2	
21	Fred Lynn 84 DK/14	
22	Fred Lynn 87 DK/28	
23	Greg Maddux 01 Retro 00 DK/1	
24	Edgar Martinez 91 DK/30	
25	Don Mattingly 85 DK/12	
26	Don Mattingly 89 DK/13	
27	Paul Molitor 88 DK/18	
28	Joe Morgan 83 DK/10	
29	Eddie Murray 84 DK/8	
30	Roy Oswalt 01 RDK Black/48	
31	Roy Oswalt 01 RDK Blue/2	
32	Jim Palmer 83 DK/14	
33	Dave Parker 82 DK/11	
34	Dave Parker 91 DK/2	
35	Kirby Puckett 87 DK/23	
36	Nolan Ryan 90 DK COR/2	
37	Nolan Ryan 90 DK ERR/3	
38	C.C. Sabathia 01 RDK/23	
39	Ryne Sandberg 85 DK/6	
40	Ryne Sandberg 91 DK/15	
41	Tom Seaver 82 DK/9	
42	Ozzie Smith 82 DK/14	
43	Ozzie Smith 87 DK/15	
44	Frank Thomas 92 DK/3	
45	Alan Trammell 83 DK COR/14	
46	Alan Trammell 82 DK ERR/8	
47	Alan Trammell 88 DK/110	
48	Dave Winfield 82 DK/7	
49	Dave Winfield 87 DK/15	

2002 Donruss Diamond Kings Timeline

		MT
Complete Set (10):		75.00
Common Card:		6.00
Inserted 1:60		
1	Lou Gehrig, Don Mattingly	15.00
2	Hideo Nomo, Ichiro Suzuki	12.00
3	Cal Ripken Jr., Alex Rodriguez	15.00
4	Mike Schmidt, Scott Rolen	8.00
5	Ichiro Suzuki, Albert Pujols	12.00
6	Curt Schilling, Randy Johnson	6.00
7	Chipper Jones, Eddie Mathews	8.00
8	Lou Gehrig, Cal Ripken Jr.	15.00
9	Derek Jeter, Roger Clemens	15.00
10	Kazuhiko Ishimine, So Taguchi	6.00

2002 Donruss Elite

		MT
Complete Set (200):		NA
Common Player:		.25
Common (101-150):		2.00
Inserted 1:10		
Common (151-200):		5.00
Production 1,500		
Pack (5):		4.50
Box (20):		85.00
1	Vladimir Guerrero	.75
2	Bernie Williams	.50
3	Ichiro Suzuki	3.00
4	Roger Clemens	1.00
5	Greg Maddux	1.50
6	Fred McGriff	.25
7	Jermaine Dye	.25
8	Ken Griffey Jr.	2.00
9	Todd Helton	.75
10	Torii Hunter	.25
11	Pat Burrell	.40
12	Chipper Jones	1.50
13	Ivan Rodriguez	.50
14	Roy Oswalt	.40
15	Shannon Stewart	.25
16	Magglio Ordonez	.40
17	Lance Berkman	.50
18	Mark Mulder	.25
19	Al Leiter	.25
20	Sammy Sosa	1.50
21	Scott Rolen	.40
22	Aramis Ramirez	.25
23	Alfonso Soriano	.75
24	Phil Nevin	.25
25	Barry Bonds	1.50
26	Joe Mays	.25
27	Jeff Kent	.25
28	Mark Quinn	.25
29	Adrian Beltre	.25
30	Freddy Garcia	.25
31	Pedro J. Martinez	.75
32	Darryl Kile	.25
33	Mike Cameron	.25
34	Frank Catalanotto	.25
35	Jose Vidro	.25
36	Jim Thome	.40
37	Javy Lopez	.25
38	Paul Konerko	.25
39	Jeff Bagwell	.75
40	Curt Schilling	.50
41	Miguel Tejada	.40
42	Jim Edmonds	.40
43	Ellis Burks	.25

44 Mark Grace .50
45 Robb Nen .25
46 Jeff Conine .25
47 Derek Jeter 3.00
48 Mike Lowell .25
49 Javier Vazquez .25
50 Manny Ramirez .75
51 Bartolo Colon .25
52 Carlos Beltran .25
53 Tim Hudson .40
54 Rafael Palmeiro .40
55 Jimmy Rollins .25
56 Andruw Jones .50
57 Orlando Cabrera .25
58 Dean Palmer .25
59 Bret Boone .25
60 Carlos Febles .25
61 Ben Grieve .25
62 Richie Sexson .40
63 Alex Rodriguez 2.50
64 Juan Pierre .25
65 Bobby Higginson .25
66 Barry Zito .40
67 Raul Mondesi .25
68 Albert Pujols 1.50
69 Omar Vizquel .25
70 Bobby Abreu .25
71 Corey Koskie .25
72 Tom Glavine .40
73 Paul LoDuca .25
74 Terrence Long .25
75 Matt Morris .25
76 Andy Pettitte .40
77 Rich Aurilia .25
78 Todd Walker .25
79 John Olerud .50
80 Mike Sweeney .25
81 Ray Durham .25
82 Fernando Vina .25
83 Nomar Garciaparra 2.00
84 Mariano Rivera .40
85 Mike Piazza 2.00
86 Mark Buehrle .25
87 Adam Dunn .75
88 Luis Gonzalez .50
89 Richard Hidalgo .25
90 Brad Radke .25
91 Russ Ortiz .25
92 Brian Giles .40
93 Billy Wagner .25
94 Cliff Floyd .25
95 Eric Milton .25
96 Bud Smith .25
97 Wade Miller .25
98 Jon Lieber .25
99 Derrek Lee .25
100 Jose Cruz Jr. .25
101 Dmitri Young 2.00
102 Mo Vaughn 2.50
103 Tino Martinez 2.00
104 Larry Walker 2.50
105 Chuck Knoblauch 2.00
106 Troy Glaus 4.00
107 Jason Giambi 10.00
108 Travis Fryman 2.00
109 Josh Beckett 3.00
110 Edgar Martinez 2.00
111 Tim Salmon 2.00
112 C.C. Sabathia 2.00
113 Randy Johnson 8.00
114 Juan Gonzalez 6.00
115 Carlos Delgado 4.00
116 Hideo Nomo 4.00
117 Kerry Wood 4.00
118 Brian Jordan 2.00
119 Carlos Pena 2.00
120 Roger Cedeno 2.00
121 Chan Ho Park 2.00
122 Rafael Furcal 2.00
123 Frank Thomas 6.00
124 Mike Mussina 4.00
125 Rickey Henderson 5.00
126 Sean Casey 3.00
127 Barry Larkin 4.00
128 Kazuhiro Sasaki 2.00
129 Moises Alou 2.00
130 Jeff Cirillo 2.00
131 Jason Kendall 2.00
132 Gary Sheffield 3.00
133 Ryan Klesko 2.00
134 Kevin Brown 2.00
135 Darin Erstad 3.00
136 Roberto Alomar 4.00
137 Brad Fullmer 2.00
138 Eric Chavez 2.50
139 Ben Sheets 2.50
140 Trot Nixon 2.00
141 Garret Anderson 2.00
142 Shawn Green 2.50
143 Troy Percival 2.00
144 Craig Biggio 2.50
145 Jorge Posada 2.00
146 J.D. Drew 3.00
147 Johnny Damon 2.00
148 Jeromy Burnitz 2.00
149 Robin Ventura 2.00
150 Aaron Sele 2.00
151 *Cam Esslinger* 6.00
152 *Ben Howard* 10.00
153 *Brandon Backe* 5.00
154 *Jorge De La Rosa* 5.00
155 Austin Kearns 8.00
156 Carlos Zambrano 5.00
157 *Kyle Kane* 5.00
158 *So Taguchi* 10.00
159 *Brian Mallette* 5.00
160 Brett Jodie 5.00
161 *Elio Serrano* 5.00
162 Joe Thurston 5.00
163 Kevin Olsen 5.00
164 *Rodrigo Rosario* 8.00
165 Matt Guerrier 5.00
166 *Anderson Machado* 5.00
167 Bert Snow 5.00
168 *Franklyn German* 5.00
169 Brandon Claussen 5.00
170 Jason Romano 5.00
171 *Jorge Padilla* 8.00
172 Jose Cueto 5.00
173 *Allan Simpson* 5.00
174 *Doug Devore* 5.00
175 Justin Duchscherer 5.00
176 Josh Pearce 5.00
177 *Steve Bechler* 5.00
178 Josh Phelps 5.00
179 Juan Diaz 5.00
180 *Victor Alvarez* 5.00
181 Ramon Vazquez 5.00
182 Mike Rivera 5.00
183 *Kazuhisa Ishii* 30.00
184 Henry Mateo 5.00
185 *Travis Hughes* 5.00
186 Zach Day 5.00
187 Brad Voyles 5.00
188 Sean Douglass 5.00
189 Nick Neugebauer 5.00
190 *Tom Shearn* 5.00
191 *Eric Cyr* 5.00
192 Adam Johnson 5.00
193 Michael Cuddyer 5.00
194 Erik Bedard 5.00
195 Mark Ellis 5.00
196 Carlos Hernandez 5.00
197 Deivi Santos 5.00
198 Morgan Ensberg 5.00
199 *Ryan Jamison* 5.00
200 Cody Ransom 5.00

2002 Donruss Elite Aspirations

MT
1-100 print run 26-50: 15-30X
1-100 p/r 51-80: 8-15X
101-150 p/r 26-50: 1.5-3X
101-150 p/r 51-99: 1-2X

2002 Donruss Elite Status

MT
1-100 print run 36-70: 10-20X
1-100 p/r 71-100: 5-10X
101-150 p/r 36-70: 1-2X
101-150 p/r 71-100: 1X

2002 Donruss Elite All-Star Salutes

MT
Common Player: 2.00
Century: 1-2X
Production 100
1 Ichiro Suzuki 12.00
2 Tony Gwynn 6.00
3 Magglio Ordonez 2.00
4 Cal Ripken Jr. 15.00
5 Tony Gwynn 6.00
6 Kazuhiro Sasaki 2.00
7 Freddy Garcia 2.00
8 Luis Gonzalez 2.00
9 Lance Berkman 2.00
10 Derek Jeter 15.00
11 Chipper Jones 6.00
12 Randy Johnson 6.00
13 Andruw Jones 2.00
14 Pedro J. Martinez 4.00
15 Jim Thome 4.00
16 Rafael Palmeiro 2.00
17 Barry Larkin 3.00
18 Ivan Rodriguez 3.00
19 Omar Vizquel 2.00
20 Edgar Martinez 2.00
21 Larry Walker 2.00
22 Javy Lopez 2.00
23 Mariano Rivera 2.00
24 Frank Thomas 4.00
25 Greg Maddux 8.00

2002 Donruss Elite Back to the Future

MT
Complete Set (24): 75.00
Common Player: 2.00
Duals 500 produced, Singles 1,000
1 Scott Rolen, Marlon Byrd 5.00
2 Joe Crede, Frank Thomas 6.00
3 Lance Berkman, Jeff Bagwell 6.00
4 Marcus Giles, Chipper Jones 10.00
5 Shawn Green, Paul LoDuca 4.00
7 Kerry Wood, Juan Cruz 4.00
8 Vladimir Guerrero, Orlando Cabrera 6.00
9 Scott Rolen 3.00
10 Marlon Byrd 3.00
11 Frank Thomas 4.00
12 Joe Crede 2.00
13 Jeff Bagwell 4.00
14 Lance Berkman 3.00
15 Chipper Jones 6.00
16 Marcus Giles 2.00
17 Shawn Green 2.50
18 Paul LoDuca 2.00
19 Jim Edmonds 2.00
21 Kerry Wood 3.00
22 Juan Cruz 2.00
23 Vladimir Guerrero 4.00
24 Orlando Cabrera 2.00

2002 Donruss Elite Back to the Future Threads

MT
Common Card: 10.00
Duals 50 produced, Singles 100
1 Scott Rolen, Marlon Byrd 30.00
2 Joe Crede, Frank Thomas 40.00
3 Lance Berkman, Jeff Bagwell 40.00
4 Marcus Giles, Chipper Jones 50.00
5 Shawn Green, Paul LoDuca 30.00
7 Kerry Wood, Juan Cruz 35.00
8 Vladimir Guerrero, Orlando Cabrera 40.00
9 Scott Rolen 15.00
10 Marlon Byrd 20.00
11 Frank Thomas 25.00
12 Joe Crede 10.00
13 Jeff Bagwell 25.00
14 Lance Berkman 15.00
15 Chipper Jones 25.00
16 Marcus Giles 10.00
17 Shawn Green 15.00
18 Paul LoDuca 10.00
19 Jim Edmonds 10.00
20 So Taguchi 50.00
21 Kerry Wood 15.00
22 Juan Cruz 10.00
23 Vladimir Guerrero 25.00
24 Orlando Cabrera 10.00

2002 Donruss Elite Back 2 Back Jacks

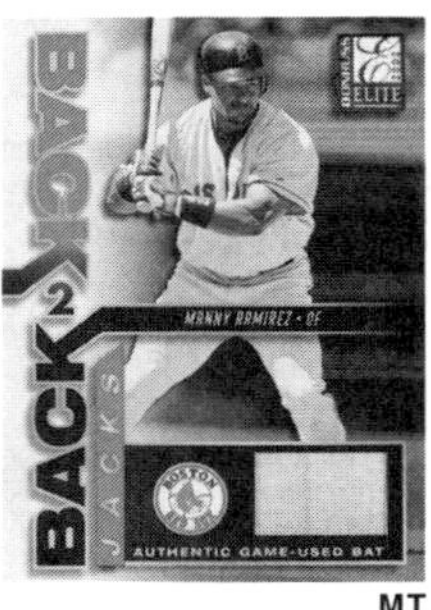

MT
Common Card: 10.00
Dual production 75
Single production 150
1 Ivan Rodriguez, Alex Rodriguez 40.00
2 Kirby Puckett, Dave Winfield 75.00
3 Ted Williams, Nomar Garciaparra 280.00
4 Jeff Bagwell, Craig Biggio 35.00
5 Eddie Murray, Cal Ripken Jr. 200.00
6 Andruw Jones, Chipper Jones 45.00
7 Roberto Clemente, Willie Stargell 120.00
8 Lou Gehrig, Don Mattingly 275.00
9 Larry Walker, Todd Helton 30.00
10 Manny Ramirez, Trot Nixon 30.00
11 Alex Rodriguez 30.00
12 Ivan Rodriguez 15.00
13 Kirby Puckett 50.00
14 Dave Winfield 15.00
15 Ted Williams 190.00
16 Nomar Garciaparra 40.00
17 Jeff Bagwell 20.00
18 Craig Biggio 10.00
19 Eddie Murray 25.00
20 Cal Ripken Jr. 60.00
21 Andruw Jones 10.00
22 Chipper Jones 20.00
23 Roberto Clemente 90.00
25 Lou Gehrig 190.00
26 Don Mattingly 75.00
27 Larry Walker 10.00
28 Todd Helton 15.00
29 Manny Ramirez 20.00
30 Trot Nixon 10.00

A player's name in *italic* type indicates a rookie card.

2002 Donruss Elite Career Bests

MT
Common Player: 2.00
1 Albert Pujols/1,013 6.00
2 Alex Rodriguez/52 20.00
3 Alex Rodriguez/135 15.00
4 Andruw Jones/104 6.00
5 Barry Bonds/73 25.00
6 Barry Bonds/1379 8.00
7 Barry Bonds/177 15.00
8 C.C. Sabathia/171 4.00
9 Carlos Beltran/876 2.00
10 Chipper Jones/330 6.00
11 Derek Jeter/900 15.00
12 Eric Chavez/114 4.00
13 Frank Catalanotto/330 2.00
14 Ichiro Suzuki/838 10.00
15 Ichiro Suzuki/127 25.00
16 Ichiro Suzuki/8
17 J.D. Drew/27 20.00
18 J.D. Drew/1027 2.00
19 Jason Giambi/660 8.00
20 Jim Thome/49 25.00
21 Jim Thome/624 4.00
22 Jorge Posada/95 8.00
23 Jose Cruz Jr/856 2.00
24 Kazuhiro Sasaki/45 15.00
25 Kerry Wood/336 4.00
26 Lance Berkman/1050 3.00
27 Magglio Ordonez/382 3.00
28 Mark Mulder/345 2.00
29 Pat Burrell/27 20.00
30 Pat Burrell/469 3.00
31 Randy Johnson/372 6.00
32 Randy Johnson/21
33 Richie Sexson/547 2.00
34 Roberto Alomar/956 4.00
35 Sammy Sosa/160 12.00
36 Sammy Sosa/1174 6.00
37 Shawn Green/125 4.00
38 Tsuyoshi Shinjo/10
39 Trot Nixon/150 3.00
40 Troy Glaus/108 5.00

2002 Donruss Elite Passing the Torch

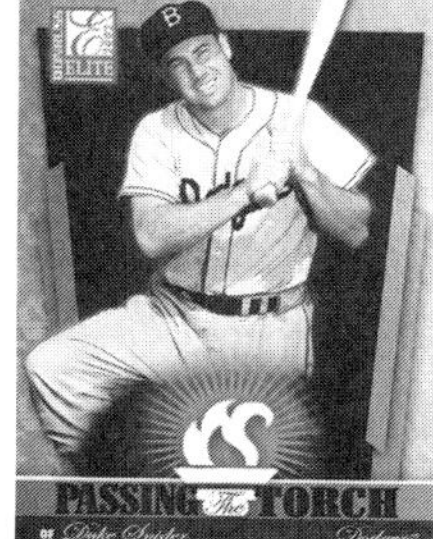

MT
Common Card: 4.00
Dual 500, Single 1,000 produced
1 Fergie Jenkins, Mark Prior 10.00
2 Nolan Ryan, Roy Oswalt 25.00
3 Ozzie Smith, J.D. Drew 8.00
4 George Brett, Carlos Beltran 15.00
5 Kirby Puckett, Michael Cuddyer 10.00
6 Johnny Bench, Adam Dunn 8.00
7 Duke Snider, Paul LoDuca 6.00
8 Tony Gwynn, Xavier Nady 15.00
9 Fergie Jenkins 4.00
10 Mark Prior 8.00
11 Nolan Ryan 15.00
12 Roy Oswalt 4.00
13 Ozzie Smith 6.00
14 J.D. Drew 4.00
15 George Brett 10.00
16 Carlos Beltran 4.00
17 Kirby Puckett 8.00
18 Michael Cuddyer 4.00
19 Johnny Bench 6.00
20 Adam Dunn 6.00
21 Duke Snider 6.00
22 Paul LoDuca 4.00
23 Tony Gwynn 8.00
24 Xavier Nady 4.00

2002 Donruss Elite Passing the Torch Autographs

MT
Common Autograph: 15.00
1 Ferguson Jenkins, Mark Prior/50 125.00
2 Nolan Ryan, Roy Oswalt/50 300.00
3 Ozzie Smith, J.D. Drew/50 125.00
4 George Brett, Carlos Beltran/25 300.00
5 Kirby Puckett, Michael Cuddyer/50 175.00
6 Johnny Bench, Adam Dunn/50 150.00
7 Duke Snider, Paul LoDuca/50 80.00
8 Tony Gwynn, Xavier Nady/50 120.00
9 Fergie Jenkins/50 40.00
10 Mark Prior/100 75.00
11 Nolan Ryan/100 180.00
12 Roy Oswalt/100 25.00
13 Ozzie Smith/25 160.00
14 J.D. Drew/100 35.00
15 George Brett/25 300.00
16 Carlos Beltran/100 15.00
17 Kirby Puckett/25 200.00
18 Michael Cuddyer/100 15.00
19 Johnny Bench/100 75.00
20 Adam Dunn/50 75.00
21 Duke Snider/100 40.00
22 Paul LoDuca/100 15.00
23 Tony Gwynn/100 60.00
24 Xavier Nady/100 15.00

2002 Donruss Elite Throwback Threads

MT
Common Card: 15.00
Dual 50, Single 100 produced
1 Manny Ramirez, Ted Williams 275.00
2 Mike Piazza, Carlton Fisk 90.00
3 George Brett, Bo Jackson 150.00
4 Randy Johnson, Curt Schilling 65.00
5 Don Mattingly, Lou Gehrig 450.00
6 Bernie Williams, Dave Winfield 40.00
7 Rickey Henderson 100.00
8 Paul Molitor, Robin Yount 100.00
9 J.D. Drew, Stan Musial 125.00
10 Andre Dawson, Ryne Sandberg 125.00
11 Babe Ruth, Reggie Jackson 500.00
12 Brooks Robinson, Cal Ripken Jr. 140.00
13 Ted Williams, Nomar Garciaparra 350.00
14 Shawn Green, Jackie Robinson 125.00
15 Tony Gwynn, Cal Ripken Jr. 140.00
16 Ted Williams 180.00
17 Manny Ramirez 25.00
18 Carlton Fisk 40.00
19 Mike Piazza 40.00
20 Bo Jackson 30.00
21 George Brett 60.00
22 Curt Schilling 25.00
23 Randy Johnson 25.00
24 Don Mattingly 85.00
25 Lou Gehrig 250.00
26 Bernie Williams 15.00
27 Dave Winfield 20.00
29 Rickey Henderson 50.00
30 Robin Yount 50.00
31 Paul Molitor 40.00
32 Stan Musial 65.00
33 J.D. Drew 15.00
34 Andre Dawson 20.00
35 Ryne Sandberg 85.00
36 Babe Ruth 300.00
37 Reggie Jackson 40.00
38 Brooks Robinson 25.00
39 Cal Ripken Jr. 75.00
40 Nomar Garciaparra 40.00
41 Jackie Robinson 80.00
42 Shawn Green 15.00
43 Pedro J. Martinez 20.00
44 Nolan Ryan 90.00
45 Kazuhiro Sasaki 15.00
46 Tony Gwynn 25.00
47 Carlton Fisk 30.00
48 Cal Ripken Jr. 75.00
49 Rod Carew 20.00
50 Nolan Ryan 90.00
51 Alex Rodriguez 25.00
52 Greg Maddux 35.00
53 Pedro J. Martinez 25.00
54 Rickey Henderson 50.00
55 Rod Carew 40.00
56 Roberto Clemente 100.00
57 Hideo Nomo 60.00
58 Rickey Henderson 50.00
59 Dave Parker 20.00
60 Eddie Mathews 40.00
61 Eddie Murray 30.00
62 Nolan Ryan 90.00
63 Tom Seaver 40.00
64 Roger Clemens 40.00
65 Rickey Henderson 50.00

2002 Donruss Elite Throwback Threads Autographs

MT
Complete Set (29):
Common Player:
17 Manny Ramirez/10
18 Carlton Fisk Red Sox/15
20 Bo Jackson/10
21 George Brett/5
22 Curt Schilling/10
24 Don Mattingly/20
26 Bernie Williams/5
27 Dave Winfield/10
28 Rickey Henderson/100 EXCH
30 Robin Yount/10
31 Paul Molitor/15
32 Stan Musial/10
33 J.D. Drew/25
34 Andre Dawson/15
35 Ryne Sandberg/20
37 Reggie Jackson/10
43 Pedro J. Martinez/10
44 Nolan Ryan Astros/10
46 Tony Gwynn/10
47 Carlton Fisk White Sox/10
49 Rod Carew Angels/10
50 Nolan Ryan Rangers/10
51 Alex Rodriguez/10
52 Greg Maddux/10
56 Rod Carew Twins/10
59 Dave Parker/25
61 Eddie Murray/10
62 Nolan Ryan Angels/10
63 Tom Seaver/15

2002 Donruss Elite Turn of the Century

MT
Common Player: 8.00
154 Jorge De La Rosa/50 8.00
156 Carlos Zambrano/50 8.00
157 Kyle Kane/50 8.00
158 So Taguchi/25 15.00
159 Brian Mallette/50 8.00
160 Brett Jodie/50 8.00
165 Matt Guerrier/50 8.00
168 Franklyn German/50 8.00
169 Brandon Claussen/50 15.00
171 Jorge Padilla/50 15.00
172 Jose Cueto/50 8.00
176 Josh Pearce/50 8.00
177 Steve Bechler/50 8.00
178 Josh Phelps/50 8.00
180 Victor Alvarez/50 8.00
182 Michael Rivera/50 8.00
183 Kazuhisa Ishii/125 100.00
184 Henry Mateo/50 8.00
186 Zach Day/50 8.00
189 Nick Neugebauer/100 8.00
192 Adam Johnson/125 8.00
193 Michael Cuddyer/50 8.00
195 Mark Ellis/25 12.00
196 Carlos Hernandez/150 8.00
198 Morgan Ensberg/50 8.00
200 Cody Ransom/150 8.00

2002 Donruss Elite Turn of the Century Autographs

MT
Common Autograph: 10.00
151 Cam Esslinger/150 12.00
152 Ben Howard/150 20.00
153 Brandon Backe/150 10.00
154 Jorge De La Rosa/100 10.00
155 Austin Kearns/150 45.00
15 Carlos Zambrano/100 12.00
157 Kyle Kane/100 10.00
158 So Taguchi/125 50.00
159 Brian Mallette/100 10.00
160 Brett Jodie/100 10.00
161 Elio Serrano/150 12.00
162 Joe Thurston/150 10.00
163 Kevin Olsen/150 10.00
164 Rodrigo Rosario/150 15.00
165 Matt Guerrier/100 10.00
166 Anderson Machado/150 12.00
167 Bert Snow/150 10.00
168 Franklyn German/100 10.00
169 Brandon Claussen/100 20.00
170 Jason Romano/150 10.00
171 Jorge Padilla/100 15.00

172	Jose Cueto/100	10.00
173	Allan Simpson/150	10.00
174	Doug Devore/150	15.00
175	Justin Duchscherer/150	10.00
176	Josh Pearce/100	10.00
177	Steve Bechler/100	10.00
178	Josh Phelps/100	20.00
179	Juan Diaz/150	10.00
180	Victor Alvarez/100	15.00
181	Ramon Vazquez/150	15.00
182	Michael Rivera/100	10.00
183	Kazuhisa Ishii/25	360.00
184	Henry Mateo/100	10.00
185	Travis Hughes/150	10.00
186	Zach Day/100	10.00
187	Brad Voyles/150	10.00
188	Sean Douglass/150	10.00
189	Nick Neugebauer/50	20.00
190	Tom Shearn/150	10.00
191	Eric Cyr/150	10.00
192	Adam Johnson/25	18.00
193	Michael Cuddyer/100	10.00
194	Erik Bedard/150	10.00
195	Mark Ellis/125	10.00
197	Deivis Santos/150	10.00
198	Morgan Ensberg/100	10.00
199	Ryan Jamison/150	10.00

2002 Donruss Fan Club

	MT
Complete Set (300):	NA
Common Player:	.25
Common (201-260):	6.00
Production 1,350	
Common (261-300):	2.00
Production 2,025	
Pack (5):	5.00
Box (20):	80.00

1	Alex Rodriguez	2.50
2	Pedro Martinez	1.00
3	Vladimir Guerrero	1.00
4	Jim Edmonds	.40
5	Derek Jeter	4.00
6	Johnny Damon	.25
7	Rafael Furcal	.25
8	Cal Ripken Jr.	4.00
9	Brad Radke	.25
10	Bret Boone	.25
11	Pat Burrell	.50
12	Roy Oswalt	.50
13	Cliff Floyd	.25
14	Robin Ventura	.40
15	Frank Thomas	1.00
16	Mariano Rivera	.50
17	Paul LoDuca	.25
18	Geoff Jenkins	.40
19	Tony Gwynn	1.00
20	Chipper Jones	2.00
21	Eric Chavez	.50
22	Kerry Wood	.50
23	Jorge Posada	.50
24	J.D. Drew	.50
25	Garret Anderson	.25
26	Javier Vazquez	.25
27	Kenny Lofton	.40
28	Mike Mussina	.75
29	Paul Konerko	.25
30	Bernie Williams	.75
31	Eric Milton	.25
32	Craig Wilson	.25
33	Paul O'Neill	.50
34	Dmitri Young	.25
35	Andres Galarraga	.50
36	Gary Sheffield	.50
37	Ben Grieve	.25
38	Scott Rolen	.50
39	Mark Grace	.50
40	Albert Pujols	2.00
41	Barry Zito	.40
42	Edgar Martinez	.40
43	Jarrod Washburn	.25
44	Juan Pierre	.25
45	Mark Buehrle	.25
46	Larry Walker	.50
47	Trot Nixon	.25
48	Wade Miller	.25
49	Robert Fick	.25
50	Sean Casey	.40
51	Joe Mays	.25
52	Brad Fullmer	.25
53	Chan Ho Park	.50
54	Carlos Delgado	.75
55	Phil Nevin	.25
56	Mike Cameron	.25
57	Raul Mondesi	.25
58	Roberto Alomar	.75
59	Ryan Klesko	.25
60	Andruw Jones	.50
61	Gabe Kapler	.25
62	Darin Erstad	.40
63	Cristian Guzman	.25
64	Kazuhiro Sasaki	.25
65	Doug Mientkiewicz	.25
66	Sammy Sosa	2.00
67	Mike Hampton	.25
68	Rickey Henderson	.50
69	Mark Mulder	.40
70	Jeff Conine	.25
71	Freddy Garcia	.25
72	Ivan Rodriguez	1.00
73	Terrence Long	.25
74	Adam Dunn	1.00
75	Moises Alou	.40
76	Todd Helton	1.00
77	Preston Wilson	.25
78	Roger Cedeno	.25
79	Tony Armas Jr.	.25
80	Manny Ramirez	1.00
81	Jose Vidro	.25
82	Randy Johnson	1.00
83	Richie Sexson	.25
84	Troy Glaus	.75
85	Kevin Brown	.40
86	Woody Williams	.25
87	Adrian Beltre	.40
88	Brian Giles	.40
89	Jermaine Dye	.40
90	Craig Biggio	.50
91	Richard Hidalgo	.40
92	Magglio Ordonez	.40
93	Al Leiter	.40
94	Jeff Kent	.40
95	Curt Schilling	.50
96	Tim Hudson	.50
97	Fred McGriff	.50
98	Barry Larkin	.50
99	Jim Thome	.50
100	Tom Glavine	.50
101	Alfonso Soriano	.50
102	Jamie Moyer	.25
103	Vinny Castilla	.25
104	Rich Aurilia	.25
105	Matt Morris	.25
106	Rafael Palmeiro	.75
107	Joe Crede	.25
108	Barry Bonds	2.00
109	Robert Person	.25
110	Nomar Garciaparra	2.50
111	Brandon Duckworth	.25
112	Russ Ortiz	.25
113	Jeff Weaver	.25
114	Carlos Beltran	.25
115	Ellis Burks	.25
116	Jeremy Giambi	.25
117	Carlos Lee	.25
118	Ken Griffey Jr.	3.00
119	Torii Hunter	.25
120	Andy Petitte	.50
121	Jose Canseco	.50
122	Charles Johnson	.25
123	Nick Johnson	.25
124	Luis Gonzalez	.75
125	Rondell White	.25
126	Miguel Tejada	.25
127	Jose Cruz Jr.	.25
128	Brent Abernathy	.25
129	Scott Brosius	.25
130	Jon Lieber	.25
131	John Smoltz	.25
132	Mike Sweeney	.25
133	Shannon Stewart	.25
134	Derrek Lee	.25
135	Brian Jordan	.25
136	Rusty Greer	.25
137	Mike Piazza	3.00
138	Billy Wagner	.25
139	Shawn Green	.50
140	Orlando Cabrera	.25
141	Jeff Bagwell	1.00
142	Aaron Sele	.25
143	Hideo Nomo	.75
144	Marlon Anderson	.25
145	Todd Walker	.25
146	Bobby Higginson	.25
147	Ichiro Suzuki	4.00
148	Juan Uribe	.25
149	Jason Kendall	.25
150	Mark Quinn	.25
151	Ben Sheets	.40
152	Paul Abbott	.25
153	Aubrey Huff	.25
154	Greg Maddux	2.00
155	Darryl Kile	.25
156	John Burkett	.25
157	Juan Gonzalez	1.00
158	Javy Lopez	.40
159	Aramis Ramirez	.40
160	Lance Berkman	.40
161	David Cone	.25
162	Edgar Renteria	.25
163	Roger Clemens	1.50
164	Frank Catalanotto	.25
165	Bartolo Colon	.25
166	Mark McGwire	3.00
167	Jay Gibbons	.25
168	Tony Clark	.25
169	Tsuyoshi Shinjo	.50
170	Brad Penny	.25
171	Marcus Giles	.25
172	Matt Williams	.50
173	Bud Smith	.75
174	Tino Martinez	.40
175	Ryan Dempster	.25
176	Jimmy Rollins	.25
177	Edgardo Alfonzo	.25
178	Jason Giambi	.75
179	Aaron Boone	.25
180	Matt Dunigan	.25
181	Mike Lowell	.25
182	Jose Ortiz	.25
183	Johnny Estrada	.25
184	Shane Reynolds	.25
185	Joe Kennedy	.25
186	Corey Patterson	.25
187	Jeromy Burnitz	.25
188	C.C. Sabathia	.25
189	Doug Davis	.25
190	Omar Vizquel	.25
191	John Olerud	.50
192	Dee Brown	.25
193	Kip Wells	.25
194	A.J. Burnett	.25
195	Josh Towers	.25
196	Jason Varitek	.25
197	Jason Isringhausen	.25
198	Fernando Vina	.25
199	Ramon Ortiz	.25
200	Bobby Abreu	.25
201	Willie Harris	6.00
202	Angel Santos	6.00
203	Corky Miller	6.00
204	Mike Rivera	6.00
205	Justin Duchscherer	6.00
206	Rick Bauer	6.00
207	Angel Berroa	6.00
208	Juan Cruz	6.00
209	Dewon Brazelton	6.00
210	Mark Prior	15.00
211	Mark Teixeira	20.00
212	Geronimo Gil	6.00
213	Casey Fossum	6.00
214	Ken Harvey	6.00
215	Michael Cuddyer	6.00
216	Wilson Betemit	8.00
217	David Brous	6.00
218	Juan Pena	6.00
219	Travis Hafner	6.00
220	Erick Almonte	6.00
221	Morgan Ensberg	6.00
222	Martin Vargas	6.00
223	Brandon Berger	6.00
224	Zach Day	6.00
225	Brad Voyles	6.00
226	Jeremy Affeldt	6.00
227	Nick Neugebauer	6.00
228	Tim Redding	6.00
229	Adam Johnson	6.00
230	*Doug DeVore*	8.00
231	Cody Ransom	6.00
232	Marlon Byrd	6.00
233	Delvin James	6.00
234	Eric Munson	6.00
235	Dennis Tankersley	6.00
236	Josh Beckett	8.00
237	Bill Hall	6.00
238	Kevin Olsen	6.00
239	*Francis Beltran*	6.00
240	Antonio Perez	6.00
241	Orlando Hudson	6.00
242	*Anderson Machado*	6.00
243	*Tom Shearn*	6.00
244	*Brian Mallette*	8.00
245	*Raul Chavez*	6.00
246	*Andy Pratt*	8.00
247	*Jorge De La Rosa*	6.00
248	*Jeff Deardorff*	6.00
249	*Ben Howard*	8.00
250	*Brandon Backe*	6.00
251	Ed Rogers	.25
252	*Travis Hughes*	8.00
253	*Rodrigo Rosario*	6.00
254	Alfredo Amezaga	6.00
255	*Jorge Padilla*	6.00
256	Victor Martinez	6.00
257	*Steve Bechler*	6.00
258	*Chris Baker*	6.00
259	Ryan Freel	6.00
260	*Allan Simpson*	6.00
261	Alex Rodriguez	8.00
262	Vladimir Guerrero	3.00
263	Bud Smith	3.00
264	Miguel Tejada	2.00
265	Craig Biggio	2.00
266	Luis Gonzalez	3.00
267	Ivan Rodriguez	3.00
268	C.C. Sabathia	2.00
269	Jeff Bagwell	3.00
270	Aramis Ramirez	2.00
271	Bobby Abreu	2.00
272	Rich Aurilia	2.00
273	Jason Giambi	3.00
274	Rickey Henderson	3.00
275	Wade Miller	2.00
276	Andruw Jones	3.00
277	Troy Glaus	3.00
278	Roy Oswalt	3.00
279	Tony Gwynn	3.00
280	Adam Dunn	4.00
281	Larry Walker	3.00
282	Jose Canseco	3.00
283	Todd Helton	3.00
284	Lance Berkman	3.00
285	Cal Ripken Jr.	12.00
286	Albert Pujols	8.00
287	Alfonso Soriano	3.00
288	Mark Mulder	2.00
289	Mike Hampton	2.00
290	Andres Galarraga	2.00
291	Barry Bonds	6.00
292	Ben Sheets	2.00
293	Ichiro Suzuki	12.00
294	J.D. Drew	3.00
295	Jose Ortiz	2.00
296	Kerry Wood	3.00
297	Mark McGwire	10.00
298	Mike Sweeney	2.00
299	Pat Burrell	3.00
300	Tim Hudson	3.00

2002 Donruss Fan Club Autographs

		MT
Common Player:		8.00
Varying quantities produced		
201	Willie Harris/500	8.00
203	Corky Miller/500	8.00
205	Justin Duchscherer/500	8.00

207 Angel Berroa/100 15.00
208 Juan Cruz/175 30.00
209 Dewon Brazelton/52 20.00
210 Mark Prior/425 40.00
211 Mark Teixeira/425 50.00
213 Casey Fossum/100 12.00
215 Michael Cuddyer/52 15.00
216 Wilson Betemit/500 15.00
217 David Brous/500 8.00
218 Juan A. Pena/188 12.00
219 Travis Hafner/375 8.00
221 Morgan Ensberg/52 8.00
222 Martin Vargas/500 8.00
223 Brandon Berger/500 8.00
224 Zach Day/500 8.00
225 Brad Voyles/500 8.00
226 Jeremy Affeldt/250 8.00
227 Nick Neugebauer/225 12.00
228 Tim Redding/500 8.00
229 Adam Johnson/425 8.00
230 Doug DeVore/300 8.00
231 Cody Ransom/500 8.00
232 Marlon Byrd/475 20.00
233 Delvin James/375 8.00
234 Eric Munson/325 10.00
235 Dennis Tankersley/500 8.00
236 Josh Beckett/25
238 Kevin Olsen/325 8.00
240 Antonio Perez/525 8.00
241 Orlando Hudson/525 8.00
248 Jeff Deardorff/475 8.00
251 Ed Rogers/400 8.00
255 Jorge Padilla/450 8.00
260 Allan Simpson/475 8.00
261 Alex Rodriguez/25
263 Bud Smith/23
265 Craig Biggio/15
266 Luis Gonzalez/15
268 C.C. Sabathia/25
269 Jeff Bagwell/15
275 Wade Miller/23
278 Roy Oswalt/75 35.00
280 Adam Dunn/25
284 Lance Berkman/15
285 Cal Ripken Jr./15
286 Albert Pujols/25
287 Alfonso Soriano/25
290 Andres Galarraga/25
292 Ben Sheets/15
294 J.D. Drew/25
296 Kerry Wood/15
300 Tim Hudson/25

2002 Donruss Fan Club Artist

MT
Complete Set (14): 70.00
Common Player: 3.00
Production 300 sets
1 Pedro Martinez 8.00
2 Curt Schilling 6.00
3 Kevin Brown 4.00
4 Tim Hudson 6.00
5 Kerry Wood 6.00
6 Barry Zito 4.00
7 Hideo Nomo 6.00
8 Randy Johnson 8.00
9 Greg Maddux 15.00
10 Roger Clemens 15.00
11 Kazuhiro Sasaki 3.00
12 Joe Mays 3.00
13 Mark Mulder 4.00
14 Javier Vazquez 3.00

2002 Donruss Fan Club Artist Autographs

MT
Common Player:
Varying quantities produced
1 Pedro Martinez/15
2 Curt Schilling/15
3 Kevin Brown/25
4 Tim Hudson/25
5 Kerry Wood/15
6 Barry Zito/100
8 Randy Johnson/15
9 Greg Maddux/15
10 Roger Clemens/15

2002 Donruss Fan Club Craftsmen

MT
Complete Set (18): 125.00
Common Player: 3.00
Production 300 sets
1 Ichiro Suzuki 25.00
2 Todd Helton 8.00
3 Manny Ramirez 8.00
4 Luis Gonzalez 6.00
5 Roberto Alomar 6.00
6 Moises Alou 3.00
7 Darin Erstad 3.00
8 Mike Piazza 20.00
9 Edgar Martinez 3.00
10 Vladimir Guerrero 8.00
11 Juan Gonzalez 8.00
12 Nomar Garciaparra 15.00
13 Tony Gwynn 8.00
14 Jeff Bagwell 8.00
15 Albert Pujols 15.00
16 Larry Walker 5.00
17 Paul LoDuca 3.00
18 Lance Berkman 4.00

2002 Donruss Fan Club Craftsmen Autographs

MT
Common Player:
Production 300 sets
2 Todd Helton/15
3 Manny Ramirez/15
4 Luis Gonzalez/15
5 Roberto Alomar/15
6 Moises Alou/25
7 Darin Erstad/25
9 Edgar Martinez/15
10 Vladimir Guerrero/25
11 Juan Gonzalez/15
12 Nomar Garciaparra/15
13 Tony Gwynn/15
14 Jeff Bagwell/15
15 Albert Pujols/25
17 Paul LoDuca/100 20.00

2002 Donruss Fan Club Double Features

MT
Complete Set (10): 140.00
Common Card: 10.00
Production 125 sets
1 Larry Walker, Todd Helton 15.00
2 Jose Vidro, Vladimir Guerrero 15.00
3 Jason Giambi, Jeremy Giambi 10.00
4 Nomar Garciaparra, Manny Ramirez 30.00
5 Troy Glaus, Darin Erstad 12.00
6 Shawn Green, Paul LoDuca 10.00
7 Jeff Bagwell, Craig Biggio 15.00
8 Pedro Martinez, Hideo Nomo 25.00
9 Curt Schilling, Randy Johnson 15.00
10 Andruw Jones, Chipper Jones 20.00

2002 Donruss Fan Club Double Features Game-Used

MT
Common Card: 30.00
Production 50 sets
1 Larry Walker, Todd Helton 40.00
2 Jose Vidro, Vladimir Guerrero 40.00
3 Jason Giambi, Jeremy Giambi 40.00
4 Nomar Garciaparra, Manny Ramirez 100.00
5 Troy Glaus, Darin Erstad 40.00
6 Shawn Green, Paul LoDuca 30.00
7 Jeff Bagwell, Craig Biggio 60.00
8 Pedro Martinez, Hideo Nomo 120.00
9 Curt Schilling, Randy Johnson 70.00
10 Andruw Jones, Chipper Jones 65.00

2002 Donruss Fan Club Franchise Features

MT
Complete Set (40): 200.00
Common Player: 3.00
Production 300 sets
1 Cliff Floyd 3.00
2 Mike Piazza 15.00
3 Cal Ripken Jr. 25.00
4 Mike Sweeney 3.00
5 Curt Schilling 5.00
6 Aramis Ramirez 3.00
7 Vladimir Guerrero 6.00
8 Andruw Jones 4.00
9 Tim Hudson 4.00
10 Bernie Williams 5.00
11 Pedro Martinez 6.00
12 Roberto Alomar 5.00
13 Joe Mays 3.00
14 Jason Giambi 5.00
15 Kazuhiro Sasaki 3.00
16 Magglio Ordonez 3.00
17 Nomar Garciaparra 15.00
18 Juan Gonzalez 6.00
19 Carlos Beltran 3.00
20 Javier Vazquez 3.00
21 Miguel Tejada 3.00
22 Luis Gonzalez 5.00
23 Greg Maddux 12.00
24 Rafael Palmeiro 5.00
25 Freddy Garcia 3.00
26 Barry Zito 4.00
27 Paul LoDuca 3.00
28 Robert Fick 3.00
29 Roger Clemens 10.00
30 Eric Chavez 3.00
31 Ivan Rodriguez 6.00
32 Chipper Jones 12.00
33 Kerry Wood 4.00
34 Randy Johnson 6.00
35 Alex Rodriguez 15.00
36 Manny Ramirez 6.00
37 Mark Buehrle 3.00
38 Mark Mulder 4.00
39 Ichiro Suzuki 25.00
40 Troy Glaus 6.00

2002 Donruss Fan Club Franchise Features Game-Used

MT
Common Player: 8.00
Production 150 sets
All Jerseys unless noted
1 Cliff Floyd 10.00
2 Mike Piazza 40.00
3 Cal Ripken Jr. 75.00
4 Mike Sweeney 8.00
5 Curt Schilling 15.00
6 Aramis Ramirez 10.00
7 Vladimir Guerrero 20.00
8 Andruw Jones 15.00
9 Tim Hudson 15.00
10 Bernie Williams 15.00
11 Pedro Martinez 20.00
12 Roberto Alomar 20.00
13 Joe Mays 10.00
14 Jason Giambi 20.00
15 Kazuhiro Sasaki 15.00
16 Magglio Ordonez 10.00
17 Nomar Garciaparra 40.00
18 Juan Gonzalez 15.00
19 Carlos Beltran 10.00
20 Javier Vazquez 8.00
21 Miguel Tejada 12.00
22 Luis Gonzalez 20.00
23 Greg Maddux 30.00
24 Rafael Palmeiro 15.00
25 Freddy Garcia 15.00
26 Barry Zito 12.00
27 Paul LoDuca 8.00
28 Robert Fick 8.00
29 Roger Clemens 40.00
30 Eric Chavez/bat 10.00
31 Ivan Rodriguez 15.00
32 Chipper Jones 30.00
33 Kerry Wood 20.00
34 Randy Johnson 20.00
35 Alex Rodriguez 35.00
36 Manny Ramirez 15.00
37 Mark Buehrle 8.00
38 Mark Mulder 15.00
39 Ichiro Suzuki/ball 160.00
40 Troy Glaus 15.00

2002 Donruss Fan Club Franchise Features Autographs

MT
Common Player: 3.00
Varying quantities produced
3 Cal Ripken/25
5 Curt Schilling/25
6 Aramis Ramirez/100 25.00
7 Vladimir Guerrero/25
9 Tim Hudson/50
10 Bernie Williams/25
11 Pedro Martinez/15
12 Roberto Alomar/15
13 Joe Mays/75 10.00
17 Nomar Garciaparra/15
18 Juan Gonzalez/25

19	Carlos Beltran/100	20.00
20	Javier Vazquez/25	
22	Luis Gonzalez/15	
23	Greg Maddux/15	
24	Rafael Palmeiro/25	
25	Freddy Garcia/100	20.00
26	Barry Zito/100	20.00
27	Paul LoDuca/100	15.00
28	Robert Fick/100	15.00
29	Roger Clemens/15	
30	Eric Chavez/50	20.00
31	Ivan Rodriguez/15	
33	Kerry Wood/15	
34	Randy Johnson/15	
35	Alex Rodriguez/15	
36	Manny Ramirez/25	
37	Mark Buehrle/100	15.00
40	Troy Glaus/25	

2002 Donruss Fan Club League Leaders

		MT
Complete Set (44):		260.00
Common Player:		3.00
Production 300 sets		
1	Roger Clemens	12.00
2	Curt Schilling	5.00
3	Matt Morris	3.00
4	Randy Johnson	6.00
5	Mark Mulder	4.00
6	Curt Schilling	5.00
7	Mike Mussina	5.00
8	Joe Mays	3.00
9	Matt Morris	3.00
10	Tim Hudson	5.00
11	Mark Buehrle	3.00
12	Greg Maddux	15.00
13	Freddy Garcia	4.00
14	Randy Johnson	6.00
15	Curt Schilling	5.00
16	Chan Ho Park	3.00
17	Roger Clemens	12.00
18	Mike Mussina	5.00
19	Javier Vazquez	3.00
20	Kerry Wood	5.00
21	Randy Johnson	6.00
22	Barry Zito	4.00
23	Hideo Nomo	6.00
24	Ichiro Suzuki	25.00
25	Todd Helton	6.00
26	Albert Pujols	20.00
27	Alex Rodriguez	18.00
28	Shannon Stewart	3.00
29	Luis Gonzalez	5.00
30	Alex Rodriguez	18.00
31	Barry Bonds	12.00
32	Sammy Sosa	15.00
33	Luis Gonzalez	5.00
34	Todd Helton	6.00
35	Jim Thome	4.00
36	Shawn Green	4.00
37	Jeff Bagwell	6.00
38	Todd Helton	6.00
39	Luis Gonzalez	5.00
40	Lance Berkman	3.00
41	Juan Gonzalez	6.00
42	Larry Walker	4.00
43	Ichiro Suzuki	25.00
44	Lance Berkman	4.00
45	Todd Helton	6.00

2002 Donruss Fan Club League Leaders Game-Used

		MT
Common Player:		10.00
Production 150 or 175		
1	Roger Clemens	40.00
2	Curt Schilling	15.00
4	Randy Johnson	20.00
5	Mark Mulder	10.00
6	Curt Schilling	15.00
7	Mike Mussina/Shoe/ 50	50.00
8	Joe Mays	10.00
10	Tim Hudson	15.00
11	Mark Buehrle	10.00
12	Greg Maddux	35.00
13	Freddy Garcia	15.00
14	Randy Johnson	20.00
15	Curt Schilling	15.00
16	Chan Ho Park	10.00
17	Roger Clemens	40.00
18	Mike Mussina/Shoe/ 50	50.00
19	Javier Vazquez	10.00
20	Kerry Wood	20.00
21	Randy Johnson	20.00
22	Barry Zito	10.00
23	Hideo Nomo	75.00
24	Ichiro Suzuki/Ball/ 51	160.00
25	Todd Helton	20.00
26	Albert Pujols	35.00
27	Alex Rodriguez	30.00
28	Shannon Stewart	10.00
29	Luis Gonzalez	20.00
30	Alex Rodriguez	30.00
31	Barry Bonds	40.00
32	Sammy Sosa	35.00
33	Luis Gonzalez	20.00
34	Todd Helton	20.00
35	Jim Thome	20.00
36	Shawn Green	15.00
37	Jeff Bagwell	20.00
38	Todd Helton	20.00
39	Luis Gonzalez	20.00
40	Lance Berkman	10.00
41	Juan Gonzalez	15.00
42	Larry Walker	10.00
43	Ichiro Suzuki/Ball/ 51	160.00
44	Lance Berkman	15.00
45	Todd Helton	20.00

2002 Donruss Fan Club League Leaders Autographs

		MT
Common Player:		
Varying quantities produced		
1	Roger Clemens/25	
2	Curt Schilling/25	
4	Randy Johnson/15	
5	Mark Mulder/100	20.00
6	Curt Schilling/25	
7	Mike Mussina/25	
8	Joe Mays/25	
10	Tim Hudson/50	
11	Mark Buehrle/100	15.00
12	Greg Maddux/25	
13	Freddy Garcia/100	20.00
14	Randy Johnson/25	
15	Curt Schilling/25	
16	Chan Ho Park/15	
17	Roger Clemens/15	
18	Mike Mussina/15	
19	Javier Vazquez/ 100	15.00
20	Kerry Wood/30	
21	Randy Johnson/15	
22	Barry Zito/100	
25	Todd Helton/25	
26	Albert Pujols/100	75.00
27	Alex Rodriguez/15	
28	Shannon Stewart/ 100	18.00
29	Luis Gonzalez/15	
30	Alex Rodriguez/15	
33	Luis Gonzalez/15	
34	Todd Helton/25	
36	Shawn Green/15	
37	Jeff Bagwell/15	
38	Todd Helton/15	
39	Luis Gonzalez/15	
41	Juan Gonzalez/25	
44	Lance Berkman/15	

2002 Donruss Fan Club Master Artists

		MT
Common Player:		10.00
Production 150 sets		
1	Pedro Martinez	25.00
2	Curt Schilling	20.00
3	Kevin Brown	12.00
4	Tim Hudson	15.00
5	Kerry Wood	15.00
6	Barry Zito	12.00
7	Hideo Nomo	75.00
8	Randy Johnson	25.00
9	Greg Maddux	35.00
10	Roger Clemens	40.00
11	Kazuhiro Sasaki	15.00
12	Joe Mays	10.00
13	Mark Mulder	12.00
14	Javier Vazquez	10.00

2002 Donruss Fan Club Master Craftsmen

		MT
Common Player:		8.00
Production 150 sets/H		
1	Ichiro Suzuki/ball/ 51	150.00
2	Todd Helton	20.00
3	Manny Ramirez	20.00
4	Luis Gonzalez	20.00
5	Roberto Alomar	20.00
6	Moises Alou	10.00
7	Darin Erstad	15.00
8	Mike Piazza	40.00
9	Edgar Martinez	15.00
10	Vladimir Guerrero	20.00
11	Juan Gonzalez	15.00
12	Nomar Garciaparra	40.00
13	Tony Gwynn/175	30.00
14	Jeff Bagwell	20.00
15	Albert Pujols/175	40.00
16	Larry Walker/175	10.00
17	Paul LoDuca/175	8.00
18	Lance Berkman	12.00

2002 Donruss Fan Club Pure Power

		MT
Complete Set (18):		100.00
Common Player:		3.00
Production 300 sets		
1	Sammy Sosa	12.00
2	Lance Berkman	3.00
3	Chipper Jones	12.00
4	Troy Glaus	6.00
5	Barry Bonds	12.00
6	Todd Helton	6.00
7	Manny Ramirez	6.00
8	Jason Giambi	6.00
9	Juan Gonzalez	6.00
10	Albert Pujols	20.00
11	Jim Thome	5.00
12	Mike Piazza	15.00
13	Frank Thomas	6.00
14	Richie Sexson	3.00
15	Jeff Bagwell	6.00
16	Rafael Palmeiro	5.00
17	Luis Gonzalez	5.00
18	Shawn Green	4.00

2002 Donruss Fan Club Pure Power Masters

		MT
Common Player:		10.00
Production 150		
1	Sammy Sosa	35.00
2	Lance Berkman	10.00
3	Chipper Jones	30.00
4	Troy Glaus	15.00
5	Barry Bonds	40.00
6	Todd Helton	20.00
7	Manny Ramirez	20.00
8	Jason Giambi	18.00
9	Juan Gonzalez	15.00
10	Albert Pujols	40.00
11	Jim Thome	15.00
12	Mike Piazza	40.00
13	Frank Thomas	20.00
14	Richie Sexson	10.00
15	Jeff Bagwell	20.00
16	Rafael Palmeiro	15.00
17	Luis Gonzalez	20.00
18	Shawn Green	15.00

2002 Donruss Fan Club Pure Power Autographs

		MT
Varying quantities produced		
4	Troy Glaus/25	
6	Todd Helton/25	
7	Manny Ramirez/15	
9	Juan Gonzalez/15	
10	Albert Pujols/25	
13	Frank Thomas/25	
14	Richie Sexson/100	20.00
15	Jeff Bagwell/15	
16	Rafael Palmeiro/25	
17	Luis Gonzalez/15	

2002 Donruss Fan Club Records

		MT
Complete Set (5):		50.00
Common Player:		8.00
Production 300		
1	Barry Bonds	15.00
2	Barry Bonds	15.00
3	Barry Bonds	15.00
4	Rickey Henderson	8.00
5	Rickey Henderson	8.00

2002 Donruss Fan Club Records Autographs

		MT
1	Barry Bonds	
2	Barry Bonds	
3	Barry Bonds	
4	Rickey Henderson	
5	Rickey Henderson	

2002 Donruss Fan Club Records Game-Used

		MT
Common Card:		35.00
Production 150		
1	Barry Bonds	40.00
2	Barry Bonds	40.00
3	Barry Bonds	40.00
4	Rickey Henderson	35.00
5	Rickey Henderson	35.00

2002 Donruss Originals

		MT
Complete Set (400):		75.00
Common Player:		.10
Common Rated Rookie:		.50
Pack (5):		2.75
Hobby Box (24):		55.00
1	*So Taguchi* (Rated Rookie)	1.50
2	*Allan Simpson* (Rated Rookie)	.50
3	*Brian Mallette* (Rated Rookie)	.50
4	*Ben Howard*	

(Rated Rookie) .50
5 *Kazuhisa Ishii* (Rated Rookie) 2.50
6 *Francis Beltran* (Rated Rookie) .50
7 *Jorge Padilla* (Rated Rookie) .75
8 *Brandon Puffer* (Rated Rookie) .50
9 *Oliver Perez* (Rated Rookie) 4.00
10 Kirk Saarloos (Rated Rookie) 2.50
11 *Travis Driskill* (Rated Rookie) 2.00
12 *Jeremy Lambert* (Rated Rookie) .50
13 *John Foster* (Rated Rookie) 1.00
14 *Steve Kent* (Rated Rookie) .50
15 *Shawn Sedlacek* (Rated Rookie) .50
16 Alex Rodriguez 1.25
17 Lance Berkman .40
18 Kevin Brown .10
19 Garret Anderson .20
20 Bobby Abreu .20
21 Richard Hidalgo .10
22 Matt Morris .20
23 Manny Ramirez .40
24 Derek Jeter 1.50
25 Kerry Wood .25
26 Mark Grace .25
27 Edgar Martinez .10
28 Nomar Garciaparra 1.00
29 Roberto Alomar .30
30 Jason Giambi .75
31 Juan Gonzalez .40
32 Albert Pujols .75
33 Juan Cruz .10
34 Troy Glaus .30
35 Greg Maddux .75
36 Adam Dunn .40
37 J.D. Drew .25
38 Tsuyoshi Shinjo .25
39 Vladimir Guerrero .50
40 Barry Bonds 1.00
41 Carlos Delgado .20
42 Ken Griffey Jr. 1.00
43 Carlos Pena .10
44 Jeff Kent .20
45 Roger Clemens .75
46 Frank Thomas .40
47 Larry Walker .20
48 Pedro J. Martinez .40
49 Moises Alou .10
50 Andruw Jones .30
51 Luis Gonzalez .30
52 Adrian Beltre .10
53 Bobby Hill .10
54 Roy Oswalt .20
55 Tim Hudson .20
56 Trot Nixon .10
57 Jeff Bagwell .40
58 Bernie Williams .30
59 Magglio Ordonez .20
60 Bartolo Colon .15
61 Shawn Green .20
62 Mark Buerhle .10
63 Sean Casey .10
64 Rickey Henderson .25
65 Aramis Ramirez .10
66 Ichiro Suzuki 1.00
67 Cliff Floyd .10
68 Darin Erstad .20
69 Paul LoDuca .10
70 Ivan Rodriguez .25
71 Mo Vaughn .10
72 Todd Helton .25
73 Raul Mondesi .10
74 Sammy Sosa .75
75 Cristian Guzman .10
76 Jimmy Rollins .10
77 Hideo Nomo .25
78 C.C. Sabathia .10
79 Wade Miller .10
80 Drew Henson .20
81 Chipper Jones .75
82 Miguel Tejada .40
83 Freddy Garcia .10
84 Richie Sexson .20
85 Robin Ventura .20
86 Jose Vidro .10
87 Rich Aurilia .10
88 Scott Rolen .25
89 Carlos Beltran .10
90 Austin Kearns .25
91 Kazuhiro Sasaki .10
92 Carlos Hernandez .10
93 Randy Johnson .40
94 Jim Thome .40
95 Curt Schilling .40
96 Alfonso Soriano 1.00
97 Barry Larkin .20
98 Rafael Palmeiro .25
99 Tom Glavine .25
100 Barry Zito .25
101 Craig Biggio .20
102 Mike Piazza 1.00
103 Ben Sheets .10
104 Mark Mulder .20
105 Mike Mussina .25
106 Jim Edmonds .20
107 Paul Konerko .10
108 Pat Burrell .25
109 Chan Ho Park .10
110 Mike Sweeney .10
111 Phil Nevin .10
112 Brian Giles .20
113 Eric Chavez .20
114 Corey Patterson .10
115 Gary Sheffield .20
116 Kazuhisa Ishii (Rated Rookie) 2.50
117 *Kyle Kane* (Rated Rookie) .50
118 *Eric Junge* (Rated Rookie) .50
119 *Luis Ugueto* (Rated Rookie) .50
120 *Cam Esslinger* (Rated Rookie) .50
121 *Earl Snyder* (Rated Rookie) .50
122 Oliver Perez (Rated Rookie) 4.00
123 *Victor Alvarez* (Rated Rookie) .50
124 *Tom Shearn* (Rated Rookie) .50
125 *Corey Thurman* (Rated Rookie) .50
126 *Satoru Komiyama* (Rated Rookie) .50
127 *Hansel Izquierdo* (Rated Rookie) .50
128 *Elio Serrano* (Rated Rookie) .50
129 *Michael Crudale* (Rated Rookie) .50
130 *Chris Snelling* (Rated Rookie) 2.00
131 Nomar Garciaparra 1.00
132 Roger Clemens .75
133 Hank Blalock .10
134 Eric Chavez .20
135 Corey Patterson .10
136 Richie Sexson .20
137 Freddy Garcia .10
138 Miguel Tejada .40
139 Alex Rodriguez 1.00
140 Adrian Beltre .10
141 Bobby Abreu .20
142 Bret Boone .10
143 Tim Hudson .20
144 Roy Oswalt .20
145 Derek Jeter 1.50
146 Rich Aurilia .10
147 Mark Grace .25
148 Kerry Wood .25
149 Geronimo Gil .10
150 Mark Buehrle .10
151 Jim Edmonds .15
152 Ichiro Suzuki 1.00
153 Juan Gonzalez .40
154 Darin Erstad .20
155 Barry Bonds 1.00
156 Greg Maddux .75
157 Adam Dunn .40
158 Todd Helton .25
159 Roberto Alomar .30
160 Sammy Sosa .75
161 Sean Burroughs .10
162 Albert Pujols .75
163 Carlos Delgado .20
164 Frank Thomas .40
165 Ken Griffey Jr. 1.00
166 Jason Giambi .75
167 Chipper Jones .75
168 Ivan Rodriguez .30
169 Pedro J. Martinez .50
170 Gary Sheffield .20
171 Andruw Jones .25
172 Luis Gonzalez .25
173 Raul Mondesi .10
174 Jose Vidro .10
175 Garret Anderson .15
176 Scott Rolen .25
177 Kazuhiro Sasaki .10
178 Jeff Bagwell .40
179 Manny Ramirez .40
180 Jim Thome .40
181 Ben Sheets .10
182 Randy Johnson .40
183 Lance Berkman .40
184 Shawn Green .20
185 Rickey Henderson .25
186 Edgar Martinez .10
187 Barry Larkin .20
188 Bernie Williams .30
189 Luis Aparicio .10
190 Troy Glaus .25
191 Mike Mussina .30
192 Pee Wee Reese .20
193 Craig Biggio .20
194 Vladimir Guerrero .50
195 J.D. Drew .20
196 Jeff Kent .20
197 Dewon Brazelton .10
198 Tsuyoshi Shinjo .20
199 Sean Casey .10
200 Hideo Nomo .25
201 C.C. Sabathia .10
202 Larry Walker .20
203 Mark Teixeira .20
204 Mike Sweeney .10
205 Moises Alou .10
206 Mark Prior .25
207 Javier Vazquez .10
208 Phil Nevin .10
209 Harmon Killebrew .50
210 Brian Giles .20
211 Carlos Beltran .10
212 Don Drysdale .40
213 Matt Morris .20
214 Trot Nixon .10
215 Magglio Ordonez .20
216 Curt Schilling .40
217 Mark Mulder .20
218 Alfonso Soriano 1.00
219 Rafael Palmeiro .25
220 Tom Glavine .25
221 Barry Zito .25
222 Mike Piazza 1.00
223 Bartolo Colon .15
224 Cliff Floyd .10
225 Paul LoDuca .10
226 Cristian Guzman .10
227 Mo Vaughn .10
228 Aramis Ramirez .10
229 Pat Burrell .25
230 Chan Ho Park .10
231 Satoru Komiyama (Rated Rookie) .75
232 *Brandon Backe* (Rated Rookie) .50
233 *Anderson Machado* (Rated Rookie) .50
234 *Doug Devore* (Rated Rookie) .50
235 *Steve Bechler* (Rated Rookie) .50
236 *John Ennis* (Rated Rookie) .50
237 *Rodrigo Rosario* (Rated Rookie) .50
238 *Jorge Sosa* (Rated Rookie) .50
239 *Ken Huckaby* (Rated Rookie) .50
240 *Mike Moriarty* (Rated Rookie) .50
241 Kirk Saarloos (Rated Rookie) 2.50
242 *Kevin Frederick* (Rated Rookie) .50
243 *Aaron Guiel* (Rated Rookie) 3.00
244 Jose Rodriguez (Rated Rookie) .50
245 So Taguchi (Rated Rookie) 1.50
246 Albert Pujols .75
247 Derek Jeter 1.50
248 Brian Giles .20
249 Mike Cameron .10
250 Josh Beckett .10
251 Ken Griffey Jr. 1.00
252 Aramis Ramirez .10
253 Miguel Tejada .30
254 Carlos Delgado .20
255 Pedro J. Martinez .50
256 Raul Mondesi .10
257 Roger Clemens .75
258 Gary Sheffield .20
259 Jose Vidro .10
260 Alex Rodriguez 1.25
261 Larry Walker .20
262 Mark Mulder .20
263 Scott Rolen .25
264 Tim Hudson .20
265 Manny Ramirez .40
266 Rich Aurilia .10
267 Roy Oswalt .20
268 Mark Grace .25
269 Lance Berkman .40
270 Nomar Garciaparra 1.00
271 Barry Bonds 1.00
272 Ryan Klesko .10
273 Ichiro Suzuki 1.00
274 Shawn Green .20
275 Darin Erstad .20
276 Bernie Williams .30
277 Greg Maddux .75
278 Eric Hinske .10
279 Randy Johnson .40
280 Todd Helton .25
281 Sammy Sosa .75
282 Nick Johnson .20
283 Jose Cruz Jr. .10
284 Frank Thomas .40
285 Tsuyoshi Shinjo .20
286 Troy Glaus .30
287 Jason Giambi .75
288 Chipper Jones .75
289 Roberto Alomar .30
290 Bobby Hill .10
291 Garret Anderson .20
292 Andruw Jones .25
293 Luis Gonzalez .25
294 Mike Mussina .30
295 Ivan Rodriguez .30
296 Barry Larkin .20
297 Kazuhiro Sasaki .10
298 Alfonso Soriano 1.00
299 Jeff Bagwell .40
300 Bobby Abreu .20
301 Ben Sheets .10
302 Curt Schilling .30
303 Jim Thome .30
304 Kerry Wood .25
305 Mark Buehrle .10
306 Rickey Henderson .25
307 Rafael Palmeiro .25
308 Jim Edmonds .20
309 Mike Piazza 1.00
310 Edgar Martinez .10
311 Tom Glavine .25
312 Adrian Beltre .10
313 Adam Dunn .40
314 Craig Biggio .20
315 Vladimir Guerrero .50
316 Bret Boone .10
317 Hideo Nomo .25
318 Jeff Kent .20
319 Juan Gonzalez .40
320 Sean Casey .10
321 C.C. Sabathia .10
322 J.D. Drew .20
323 Torii Hunter .10
324 Chan Ho Park .10
325 Mike Sweeney .10
326 Javier Vazquez .10
327 Jorge Posada .20
328 Barry Zito .25
329 Willie McCovey .10
330 Kevin Brown .10
331 Mo Vaughn .10
332 Carlos Beltran .10
333 Bobby Doerr .10
334 Matt Morris .20
335 Trot Nixon .10
336 Magglio Ordonez .10
337 Paul LoDuca .10
338 Phil Nevin .10
339 Eric Chavez .20
340 Corey Patterson .10
341 Richie Sexson .10
342 Pat Burrell .25
343 Freddy Garcia .10
344 Bartolo Colon .10
345 Cliff Floyd .10
346 Deivis Santos (Rated Rookie) .50

347	*Felix Escalona* (Rated Rookie)	.50
348	*Miguel Asencio* (Rated Rookie)	.50
349	*Takahito Nomura* (Rated Rookie)	.50
350	Jorge Padilla (Rated Rookie)	.50
351	Vladimir Guerrero	.50
352	Ichiro Suzuki	1.00
353	Jay Gibbons	.10
354	Alfonso Soriano	1.00
355	Mark Buehrle	.10
356	Shawn Green	.20
357	Barry Larkin	.20
358	Josh Fogg	.10
359	Shannon Stewart	.10
360	Andruw Jones	.25
361	Juan Gonzalez	.40
362	Ken Griffey Jr.	1.00
363	Tim Hudson	.20
364	Roy Oswalt	.20
365	Carlos Delgado	.20
366	Albert Pujols	.75
367	Willie Stargell	.25
368	Roger Clemens	.75
369	Luis Gonzalez	.25
370	Barry Zito	.25
371	Alex Rodriguez	1.25
372	Troy Glaus	.30
373	Vladimir Guerrero	.50
374	Jeff Bagwell	.40
375	Randy Johnson	.40
376	Manny Ramirez	.40
377	Derek Jeter	1.00
378	C.C. Sabathia	.10
379	Rickey Henderson	.25
380	J.D. Drew	.20
381	Nomar Garciaparra	1.00
382	Darin Erstad	.20
383	Ben Sheets	.10
384	Frank Thomas	.40
385	Barry Bonds	1.00
386	Pedro J. Martinez	.50
387	Mark Mulder	.20
388	Greg Maddux	.75
389	Todd Helton	.25
390	Lance Berkman	.40
391	Sammy Sosa	.75
392	Mike Piazza	1.00
393	Chipper Jones	.75
394	Adam Dunn	.40
395	Jason Giambi	.75
396	Eric Chavez	.20
397	Bobby Abreu	.20
398	Aramis Ramirez	.10
399	Paul LoDuca	.10
400	Miguel Tejada	.30

2002 Donruss Originals Aqueous Glossy

	MT
Stars (1-400):	8-15X
Average of 1:box	

2002 Donruss Originals All-Stars

		MT
Complete Set (25):		90.00
Common Player:		2.00
Inserted 1:30		
1	George Brett	8.00
2	Rickey Henderson	4.00
3	Mike Schmidt	6.00
4	Vladimir Guerrero	3.00
5	Tony Gwynn	3.00
6	Curt Schilling	2.00
7	Don Mattingly	8.00
8	Roberto Alomar	2.00
9	Cal Ripken Jr.	8.00
10	Carlton Fisk	2.00
11	Roger Clemens	5.00
12	Jeff Bagwell	3.00
13	Kirby Puckett	8.00
14	Nolan Ryan	10.00
15	Ryne Sandberg	5.00
16	Ivan Rodriguez	2.00
17	Sammy Sosa	5.00
18	Greg Maddux	5.00
19	Alex Rodriguez	8.00
20	Todd Helton	2.00
21	Randy Johnson	3.00
22	Troy Glaus	2.00
23	Ichiro Suzuki	6.00
24	Barry Bonds	8.00
25	Derek Jeter	10.00

2002 Donruss Originals Champions

		MT
Complete Set (25):		75.00
Common Player:		2.00
Production 800 sets		
1	Nolan Ryan	10.00
2	George Brett	8.00
3	Edgar Martinez	2.00
4	Mike Schmidt	6.00
5	Randy Johnson	3.00
6	Tony Gwynn	3.00
7	John Smoltz	2.00
8	Roger Clemens	5.00
9	Mel Ott	2.00
10	Todd Helton	2.00
11	Bernie Williams	2.00
12	Troy Glaus	2.00
13	Steve Carlton	2.00
14	Ryne Sandberg	5.00
15	Ted Williams	8.00
16	Alex Rodriguez	8.00
17	Lou Boudreau	2.00
18	Luis Gonzalez	2.00
19	Rickey Henderson	2.00
20	Jose Canseco	2.00
21	Stan Musial	5.00
22	Randy Johnson	3.00
23	Don Mattingly	8.00
24	Nomar Garciaparra	6.00
25	Wade Boggs	2.00

2002 Donruss Originals Champions Materials

		MT
Varying quantities produced		
1	Nolan Ryan/78	95.00
2	George Brett	
3	Edgar Martinez/92	12.00
4	Mike Schmidt	
5	Randy Johnson/94	20.00
6	Tony Gwynn/84	35.00
7	John Smoltz/96	12.00
8	Roger Clemens/88	20.00
9	Mel Ott	
10	Todd Helton/100	15.00
11	Bernie Williams/98	12.00
12	Troy Glaus/100	12.00
13	Steve Carlton/80	20.00
14	Ryne Sandberg/90	55.00
15	Ted Williams/42	200.00
16	Alex Rodriguez/96	25.00
17	Lou Boudreau	
18	Luis Gonzalez/99	10.00
19	Rickey Henderson/ 82	40.00
20	Jose Canseco	
21	Stan Musial/50	60.00
22	Randy Johnson	
23	Don Mattingly/84	75.00
24	Nomar Garciaparra/ 100	30.00
25	Wade Boggs	

2002 Donruss Originals Gamers

		MT
Common Player:		5.00
Varying quantities produced		
1	Alfonso Soriano/ 400	40.00
2	Shawn Green/500	8.00
3	Curt Schilling/250	15.00
4	Hideo Nomo/100	60.00
5	Toby Hall	
6	Andruw Jones/500	10.00
7	Cliff Floyd/500	5.00
8	Mark Ellis	
9	Gabe Kapler/500	5.00
10	Andres Galarraga/ 500	5.00
11	Freddy Garcia/500	5.00
12	Tsuyoshi Shinjo/ 200	25.00
13	Robin Ventura	
14	Paul LoDuca/500	5.00
15	Manny Ramirez/ 500	10.00
16	Garret Anderson/ 250	8.00
17	Joe Kennedy	
18	Roger Clemens/ 500	20.00
19	Gary Sheffield/500	5.00
20	Vernon Wells/500	5.00
21	Matt Guerrier	
22	Hideo Nomo/100	60.00
23	Tim Hudson/500	10.00
24	Larry Bigbie	
25	Larry Walker/500	5.00
26	Ryan Ludwick	
27	John Olerud/500	5.00
28	Chipper Jones/500	20.00
29	Tony Gwynn/500	15.00
30	Juan Gonzalez/500	8.00
31	Jacque Jones/500	15.00
32	Frank Thomas/500	10.00
33	Luis Gonzalez/500	8.00
34	Geoff Jenkins	
35	J.D. Drew/500	15.00
36	Edgardo Alfonzo	
37	Todd Helton/500	8.00
38	Brad Penny	
39	Robert Fick/500	5.00
40	Will Clark/500	25.00
41	Tony Armas Jr.	
42	Nick Johnson/400	8.00
43	Ben Grieve/500	5.00
44	Vladimir Guerrero/ 500	12.00
45	Jason Jennings/ 500	8.00
46	Carlos Lee/500	5.00
47	Carlos Delgado/ 500	5.00
48	Chan Ho Park	
49	Juan Diaz	
50	Alex Rodriguez/ 400	20.00

2002 Donruss Originals Hit List

		MT
Complete Set (20):		40.00
Common Player:		1.00
Production 1,500 sets		
1	Ichiro Suzuki	5.00
2	Shawn Green	1.00
3	Alex Rodriguez	5.00
4	Nomar Garciaparra	4.00
5	Derek Jeter	6.00
6	Barry Bonds	5.00
7	Mike Piazza	4.00
8	Albert Pujols	3.00
9	Chipper Jones	3.00
10	Sammy Sosa	3.00
11	Rickey Henderson	1.50
12	Frank Thomas	1.50
13	Jeff Bagwell	1.50
14	Vladimir Guerrero	2.00
15	Todd Helton	1.00
16	Adam Dunn	1.00
17	Rafael Palmeiro	1.00
18	Manny Ramirez	1.50
19	Lance Berkman	1.00
20	Jason Giambi	2.50

2002 Donruss Originals Hit List Total Bases

		MT
Numbered to career high total bases		
1	Ichiro Suzuki/base/ 316	20.00
2	Shawn Green/bat/ 370	5.00
3	Alex Rodriguez/bat/ 393	15.00
4	Nomar Garciaparra/ bat/365	20.00
5	Derek Jeter/346/ base	25.00
6	Barry Bonds/base/ 411	12.00
7	Mike Piazza	
8	Albert Pujols/base/ 360	10.00
9	Chipper Jones/bat/ 359	12.00
10	Sammy Sosa/base/ 425	10.00
11	Rickey Henderson	
12	Frank Thomas/bat/ 364	10.00
13	Jeff Bagwell/bat/ 363	10.00
14	Vladimir Guerrero	
15	Todd Helton/bat/ 405	8.00
16	Adam Dunn/bat/ 141	10.00
17	Rafael Palmeiro/bat/ 356	10.00
18	Manny Ramirez/bat/ 346	10.00
19	Lance Berkman/bat/ 358	10.00
20	Jason Giambi/base/ 343	8.00

2002 Donruss Originals Making History

		MT
Complete Set (10):		30.00
Common Player:		2.00
Production 800 sets		
1	Rafael Palmeiro	2.00
2	Roger Clemens	5.00
3	Greg Maddux	5.00
4	Randy Johnson	3.00
5	Barry Bonds	8.00
6	Mike Piazza	8.00
7	Roberto Alomar	2.00
8	Rickey Henderson	2.00
9	Sammy Sosa	5.00
10	Tom Glavine	2.00

2002 Donruss Originals Making History Materials

		MT
Production 100 sets		
1	Rafael Palmeiro	15.00
2	Roger Clemens	20.00
3	Greg Maddux	35.00
4	Randy Johnson	20.00
5	Barry Bonds	
6	Mike Piazza	25.00
7	Roberto Alomar	
8	Rickey Henderson	35.00
9	Sammy Sosa	
10	Tom Glavine	

2002 Donruss Originals Mound Marvels

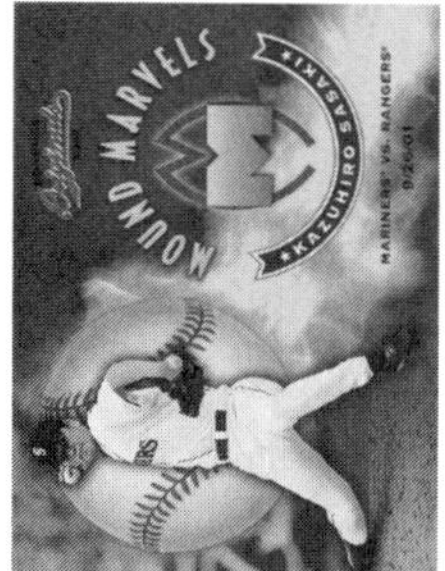

		MT
Complete Set (15):		30.00
Common Player:		1.00
Inserted 1:40		
1	Roger Clemens	6.00
2	Matt Morris	1.00
3	Pedro J. Martinez	5.00
4	Randy Johnson	5.00
5	Wade Miller	1.00
6	Tim Hudson	1.50
7	Mike Mussina	3.00
8	C.C. Sabathia	1.00
9	Kazuhiro Sasaki	1.00
10	Curt Schilling	4.00
11	Hideo Nomo	1.50
12	Roger Clemens	6.00
13	Mark Buehrle	1.00
14	Barry Zito	2.00
15	Roy Oswalt	1.50

2002 Donruss Originals Mound Marvels High Heat

		MT
Production 100 sets		
1	Roger Clemens	25.00
2	Matt Morris	15.00
3	Pedro J. Martinez	25.00
4	Randy Johnson	25.00
5	Wade Miller	
6	Tim Hudson	20.00
7	Mike Mussina	20.00
8	C.C. Sabathia	15.00
9	Kazuhiro Sasaki	15.00
10	Curt Schilling	25.00
11	Hideo Nomo	40.00
12	Roger Clemens	25.00
13	Mark Buehrle	10.00
14	Barry Zito	20.00
15	Roy Oswalt	

2002 Donruss Originals Nifty Fifty

		MT
Complete Set (50):		
Common Player:		
1	Alex Rodriguez	
2	Kerry Wood	
3	Ivan Rodriguez	
4	Geronimo Gil	
5	Vladimir Guerrero	
6	Corky Miller	
7	Todd Helton	
8	Rickey Henderson	
9	Andruw Jones	
10	Barry Bonds	
11	Tom Glavine	
12	Mark Teixeira	
13	Mike Piazza	
14	Austin Kearns	
15	Rickey Henderson	
16	Derek Jeter	
17	Barry Larkin	
18	Jeff Bagwell	
19	Bernie Williams	
20	Frank Thomas	
21	Magglio Ordonez	
22	Marlon Byrd	
23	Randy Johnson	
24	Ichiro Suzuki	
25	Darin Erstad	
26	Jason Lane	
27	Roberto Alomar	
28	Ken Griffey Jr.	
29	Tsuyoshi Shinjo	
30	Miguel Tejada	
31	Rickey Henderson	
32	Albert Pujols	
33	Nomar Garciaparra	
34	Troy Glaus	
35	Chipper Jones	
36	Adam Dunn	
37	Jason Giambi	
38	Greg Maddux	
39	Mike Piazza	
40	So Taguchi	
41	Manny Ramirez	
42	Scott Rolen	
43	Sammy Sosa	
44	Shawn Green	
45	Rickey Henderson	
46	Alex Rodriguez	
47	Hideo Nomo	
48	Kazuhisa Ishii	
49	Luis Gonzalez	
50	Jim Thome	

2002 Donruss Originals On The Record

		MT
Complete Set (15):		60.00
Common Player:		3.00
Production 800 sets		
1	Ty Cobb	6.00
2	Jimmie Foxx	4.00
3	Lou Gehrig	8.00
4	Dale Murphy	3.00
5	Steve Carlton	3.00
6	Randy Johnson	4.00
7	Greg Maddux	6.00
8	Roger Clemens	6.00
9	Yogi Berra	5.00
10	Don Mattingly	8.00
11	Rickey Henderson	4.00
12	Stan Musial	6.00
13	Jackie Robinson	6.00
14	Roberto Clemente	6.00
15	Mike Schmidt	6.00

2002 Donruss Originals On the Record Materials

		MT
Varying quantities produced		
1	Ty Cobb	
2	Jimmie Foxx	
3	Lou Gehrig/34	220.00
4	Dale Murphy	
5	Steve Carlton	
6	Randy Johnson	
7	Greg Maddux/93	35.00
8	Roger Clemens/87	20.00
9	Yogi Berra/51	30.00
10	Don Mattingly/85	85.00
11	Rickey Henderson/ 90	35.00
12	Stan Musial	
13	Jackie Robinson/ 49	50.00
14	Roberto Clemente/ 66	150.00
15	Mike Schmidt/80	50.00

2002 Donruss Originals Power Alley

		MT
Complete Set (15):		35.00
Common Player:		1.00
Production 1,500 sets		
Die-Cut Parallel:		2-5X
Production 100 sets		
1	Barry Bonds	5.00
2	Sammy Sosa	3.00
3	Lance Berkman	1.50
4	Luis Gonzalez	1.00
5	Alex Rodriguez	5.00
6	Troy Glaus	1.50
7	Vladimir Guerrero	2.00
8	Jason Giambi	3.00
9	Mike Piazza	4.00
10	Todd Helton	1.00
11	Mike Schmidt	4.00
12	Don Mattingly	6.00
13	Andre Dawson	1.50
14	Reggie Jackson	2.00
15	Dale Murphy	1.00

2002 Donruss Originals Signature Marks

		MT
Common Autograph:		8.00
Varying quantities produced		
Many not priced, lack of market info		
1	Kazuhisa Ishii	
2	Eric Hinske/200	15.00
3	Cesar Izturis	
4	Roy Oswalt/100	20.00
5	Jack Cust/200	10.00
6	Nick Johnson/200	20.00
7	Jason Hart/200	12.00
8	Mark Prior	
9	Luis Garcia/200	10.00
10	Jay Gibbons	
11	Corky Miller	
12	Antonio Perez/100	10.00
13	Andres Torres	
14	Brandon Claussen	
15	Ed Rogers/200	8.00
16	Jorge Padilla/200	15.00
17	Francis Beltran/200	8.00
18	Kip Wells	
19	Ryan Ludwick/200	10.00
20	Juan Cruz	
21	Juan Diaz	
22	Marcus Giles/200	15.00
23	Joe Kennedy/200	10.00
24	Wade Miller	
25	Corey Patterson/ 100	15.00
26	Angel Berroa	
27	Ricardo Rodriguez/ 200	10.00
28	Toby Hall/200	10.00
29	Carlos Pena/50	30.00
30	Jason Jennings/ 200	15.00
31	Rafael Soriano/ 200	10.00
32	Marlon Byrd	
33	Rodrigo Rosario/ 200	8.00
34	Rick Ankiel	
35	Brent Abernathy	
36	Bill Hall/200	8.00
37	Fernando Rodney	
38	Josh Pearce/200	10.00
39	Brian Lawrence	
40	Tim Redding/200	10.00
41	Matt Guerrier	
42	Jeremy Giambi	
43	Victor Martinez/ 200	30.00
44	Hank Blalock	
45	Larry Bigbie	
46	Geronimo Gil/200	8.00
47	So Taguchi/50	30.00
48	Austin Kearns/200	35.00
49	Alfonso Soriano	
50	Jose Ortiz	

2002 Donruss Originals What If - Rookies

		MT
Complete Set (23):		100.00
Common Player:		1.50
Inserted 1:12		
1	Wade Boggs	3.00
2	Ryne Sandberg	8.00
3	Cal Ripken Jr.	15.00
4	Tony Gwynn	4.00
5	Don Mattingly	12.00
6	Wade Boggs	3.00
7	Roger Clemens	8.00
8	Kirby Puckett	10.00
9	Eric Davis	1.50
10	Dwight Gooden	1.50
11	Eric Davis	1.50
12	Roger Clemens	8.00
13	Kirby Puckett	10.00
14	Dwight Gooden	1.50
15	Barry Larkin	1.50
16	Will Clark	3.00
17	Barry Bonds	10.00
18	Greg Maddux	8.00
19	Rafael Palmeiro	3.00
20	Craig Biggio	1.50
21	Gary Sheffield	1.50
22	Randy Johnson	4.00
23	Curt Schilling	4.00

2002 Donruss Originals What If - '78

		MT
Complete Set (27):		75.00
Common Player:		1.50
Inserted 1:12		
1	Paul Molitor	4.00
2	Alan Trammell	1.50
3	Ozzie Smith	6.00
4	George Brett	10.00
5	Johnny Bench	8.00
6	Rod Carew	2.00
7	Carlton Fisk	1.50
8	Reggie Jackson	5.00

9	Dale Murphy	1.50
10	Joe Morgan	1.50
11	Eddie Murray	2.00
12	Jim Palmer	2.00
13	Tom Seaver	4.00
14	Willie Stargell	2.00
15	Dave Winfield	2.00
16	Dave Parker	1.50
17	Mike Schmidt	8.00
18	Eddie Mathews	4.00
19	Lou Brock	1.50
20	Willie McCovey	1.50
21	Andre Dawson	1.50
22	Dennis Eckersley	1.50
23	Robin Yount	4.00
24	Nolan Ryan	15.00
25	Steve Carlton	1.50
26	Paul Molitor	4.00
27	Ozzie Smith	6.00

2002 Donruss Originals What If - '80

	MT
Complete Set (25):	75.00
Common Player:	1.50
Inserted 1:12	

1	Rickey Henderson	3.00
2	Johnny Bench	8.00
3	George Brett	10.00
4	Steve Carlton	2.50
5	Rod Carew	2.00
6	Gary Carter	1.50
7	Carlton Fisk	1.50
8	Reggie Jackson	4.00
9	Dave Parker	1.50
10	Dale Murphy	1.50
11	Paul Molitor	4.00
12	Mike Schmidt	8.00
13	Alan Trammell	1.50
14	Dave Winfield	1.50
15	Robin Yount	4.00
16	Joe Morgan	1.50
17	Jim Palmer	1.50
18	Nolan Ryan	15.00
19	Tom Seaver	4.00
20	Ozzie Smith	6.00
21	Willie McCovey	1.50
22	Andre Dawson	1.50
23	Eddie Murray	2.00
24	Al Kaline	5.00
25	Duke Snider	4.00

2002 Donruss Studio

	MT
Complete Set (250):	275.00
Common Player:	.25
Common (201-250):	5.00
Production 1,500	
Pack (5):	4.00
Box (18):	70.00

1	Vladimir Guerrero	.75
2	Chipper Jones	1.50
3	Bobby Abreu	.25
4	Barry Zito	.40
5	Larry Walker	.40
6	Miguel Tejada	.40
7	Mike Sweeney	.25
8	Shannon Stewart	.25
9	Sammy Sosa	1.50
10	Bud Smith	.25
11	Wilson Betemit	.35
12	Kevin Brown	.25
13	Ellis Burks	.25
14	Pat Burrell	.40
15	Cliff Floyd	.25
16	Marcus Giles	.25
17	Troy Glaus	.50
18	Barry Larkin	.40
19	Carlos Lee	.25
20	Brian Lawrence	.25
21	Paul LoDuca	.25
22	Ben Grieve	.25
23	Shawn Green	.40
24	Mike Cameron	.25
25	Roger Clemens	1.00
26	Joe Crede	.25
27	Jose Cruz	.25
28	Jeremy Affeldt	.25
29	Adrian Beltre	.25
30	Josh Beckett	.25
31	Roberto Alomar	.50
32	Toby Hall	.25
33	Mike Hampton	.25
34	Eric Milton	.25
35	Eric Munson	.25
36	Trot Nixon	.25
37	Roy Oswalt	.40
38	Chan Ho Park	.25
39	Charles Johnson	.25
40	Nick Johnson	.40
41	Tim Hudson	.40
42	Cristian Guzman	.25
43	Drew Henson	.40
44	Mark Grace	.50
45	Luis Gonzalez	.50
46	Pedro J. Martinez	1.00
47	Joe Mays	.25
48	Jorge Posada	.50
49	Aramis Ramirez	.25
50	Kip Wells	.25
51	Moises Alou	.25
52	Omar Vizquel	.40
53	Ichiro Suzuki	2.50
54	Jimmy Rollins	.25
55	Freddy Garcia	.25
56	Steve Green	.25
57	Brian Jordan	.25
58	Paul Konerko	.40
59	Jack Cust	.25
60	Sean Casey	.25
61	Bret Boone	.25
62	Hideo Nomo	.50
63	Magglio Ordonez	.40
64	Frank Thomas	.75
65	Josh Towers	.25
66	Javier Vazquez	.25
67	Robin Ventura	.25
68	Aubrey Huff	.25
69	Richard Hidalgo	.25
70	Brandon Claussen	.25
71	Bartolo Colon	.25
72	John Buck	.25
73	Dee Brown	.25
74	Barry Bonds	2.00
75	Jason Giambi	1.00
76	Erick Almonte	.25
77	Ryan Dempster	.25
78	Jim Edmonds	.40
79	Jay Gibbons	.25
80	Shigetoshi Hasegawa	.25
81	Todd Helton	.75
82	Erik Bedard	.25
83	Carlos Beltran	.25
84	Rafael Soriano	.25
85	Gary Sheffield	.40
86	Richie Sexson	.40
87	Mike Rivera	.25
88	Jose Ortiz	.25
89	Abraham Nunez	.25
90	Dave Williams	.25
91	Preston Wilson	.25
92	Jason Jennings	.25
93	Juan Diaz	.25
94	Steve Smyth	.25
95	Phil Nevin	.25
96	John Olerud	.40
97	Brad Penny	.25
98	Andy Pettitte	.50
99	Juan Pierre	.25
100	Manny Ramirez	.75
101	Edgardo Alfonzo	.25
102	Michael Cuddyer	.25
103	Johnny Damon	.25
104	Carlos Zambrano	.25
105	Jose Vidro	.25
106	Tsuyoshi Shinjo	.25
107	Ed Rogers	.25
108	Scott Rolen	.50
109	Mariano Rivera	.50
110	Tim Redding	.25
111	Josh Phelps	.25
112	Gabe Kapler	.25
113	Edgar Martinez	.25
114	Fred McGriff	.25
115	Raul Mondesi	.40
116	Wade Miller	.25
117	Mike Mussina	.50
118	Rafael Palmeiro	.50
119	Adam Johnson	.25
120	Rickey Henderson	.50
121	Bill Hall	.25
122	Ken Griffey Jr.	2.00
123	Geronimo Gil	.25
124	Robert Fick	.25
125	Darin Erstad	.40
126	Brandon Duckworth	.25
127	Garret Anderson	.25
128	Pedro Feliz	.25
129	Jeff Cirillo	.25
130	Brian Giles	.40
131	Craig Biggio	.40
132	Willie Harris	.25
133	Doug Davis	.25
134	Jeff Kent	.25
135	Terrence Long	.25
136	Carlos Delgado	.50
137	Tino Martinez	.40
138	Donaldo Mendez	.25
139	Sean Douglass	.25
140	Eric Chavez	.40
141	Rick Ankiel	.25
142	Jeremy Giambi	.25
143	Juan Pena	.25
144	Bernie Williams	.50
145	Craig Wilson	.25
146	Ricardo Rodriguez	.25
147	Albert Pujols	1.50
148	Antonio Perez	.25
149	Russ Ortiz	.25
150	Corky Miller	.25
151	Rich Aurilia	.25
152	Kerry Wood	.50
153	Joe Thurston	.25
154	Jeff Deardorff	.25
155	Jermaine Dye	.25
156	Andruw Jones	.50
157	Victor Martinez	.25
158	Nick Neugebauer	.25
159	Matt Morris	.25
160	Casey Fossum	.25
161	J.D. Drew	.50
162	*Matt Childers*	.50
163	Mark Buehrle	.25
164	Jeff Bagwell	.75
165	Kazuhiro Sasaki	.25
166	Ben Sheets	.25
167	Alex Rodriguez	2.50
168	Adam Pettyjohn	.25
169	*Chris Snelling*	.25
170	Robert Person	.25
171	Juan Uribe	.25
172	Mo Vaughn	.50
173	Alfredo Amezaga	.25
174	Ryan Drese	.25
175	*Corey Thurman*	.25
176	Jim Thome	.50
177	Orlando Cabrera	.25
178	*Eric Cyr*	.50
179	Greg Maddux	1.50
180	*Earl Snyder*	.25
181	C.C. Sabathia	.25
182	Mark Mulder	.40
183	Jose Mieses	.25
184	Joe Kennedy	.25
185	Randy Johnson	.75
186	Tom Glavine	.50
187	*Eric Junge*	.25
188	Mike Piazza	2.00
189	Corey Patterson	.25
190	Carlos Pena	.25
191	Curt Schilling	.75
192	Nomar Garciaparra	2.00
193	Lance Berkman	.75
194	Ryan Klesko	.25
195	Ivan Rodriguez	.50
196	Alfonso Soriano	1.50
197	Derek Jeter	3.00
198	David Justice	.50
199	Juan Gonzalez	.75
200	Adam Dunn	.50
201	*Victor Alvarez*	8.00
202	*Miguel Asencio*	6.00
203	*Brandon Backe*	8.00
204	*Chris Baker*	5.00
205	*Steve Bechler*	15.00
206	*Francis Beltran*	5.00
207	Angel Berroa	5.00
208	Hank Blalock	5.00
209	Dewon Brazelton	5.00
210	Sean Burroughs	5.00
211	Marlon Byrd	8.00
212	*Raul Chavez*	5.00
213	Juan Cruz	5.00
214	*Jorge De La Rosa*	5.00
215	*Doug Devore*	5.00
216	*John Ennis*	8.00
217	*Felix Escalona*	5.00
218	Morgan Ensberg	5.00
219	*Cam Esslinger*	5.00
220	*Kevin Frederick*	5.00
221	*Franklyn German*	5.00
222	Eric Hinske	10.00
223	*Ben Howard*	8.00
224	Orlando Hudson	5.00
225	*Travis Hughes*	5.00
226	*Kazuhisa Ishii*	10.00
227	*Ryan Jamison*	5.00
228	*Reed Johnson*	8.00
229	*Kyle Kane*	5.00
230	Austin Kearns	10.00
231	*Satoru Komiyama*	8.00
232	Jason Lane	5.00
233	*Jeremy Lambert*	5.00
234	*Anderson Machado*	8.00
235	*Brian Mallette*	10.00
236	*Takahito Nomura*	8.00
237	*Jorge Padilla*	8.00
238	*Luis Ugueto*	8.00
239	Mark Prior	15.00
240	*Rene Reyes*	5.00
241	Deivis Santos	5.00
242	*Elio Serrano*	5.00
243	*Tom Shearn*	6.00
244	*Allan Simpson*	5.00
245	*So Taguchi*	8.00
246	Dennis Tankersley	5.00
247	Mark Teixeira	8.00
248	Matt Thornton	5.00
249	Bobby Hill	8.00
250	Ramon Vazquez	5.00

2002 Donruss Studio Classic Studio

	MT
Complete Set (25):	120.00
Common Player:	3.00
Production 1,000 sets	

1	Kirby Puckett	8.00
2	George Brett	10.00
3	Nolan Ryan	12.00
4	Mike Schmidt	10.00
5	Steve Carlton	4.00
6	Reggie Jackson	5.00
7	Tom Seaver	5.00
8	Joe Morgan	3.00
9	Jim Palmer	3.00
10	Johnny Bench	6.00
11	Willie McCovey	3.00
12	Brooks Robinson	5.00
13	Al Kaline	6.00
14	Stan Musial	8.00
15	Ozzie Smith	8.00
16	Dave Winfield	4.00
17	Robin Yount	6.00

18	Rod Carew	4.00
19	Willie Stargell	3.00
20	Lou Brock	3.00
21	Ernie Banks	5.00
22	Ted Williams	10.00
23	Jackie Robinson	8.00
24	Roberto Clemente	10.00
25	Lou Gehrig	10.00

2002 Donruss Studio Diamond Collection

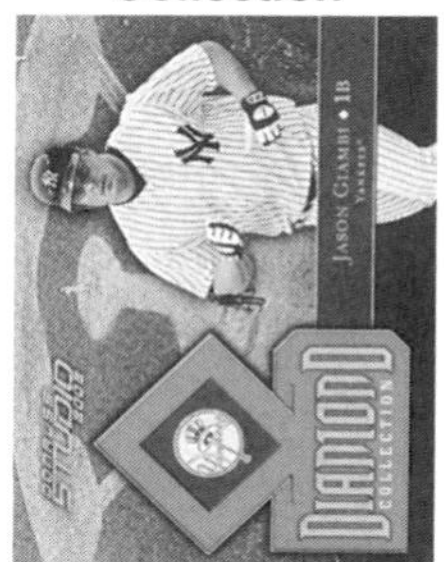

		MT
Complete Set (25):		80.00
Common Player:		2.00
Inserted 1:17		
1	Todd Helton	2.50
2	Chipper Jones	6.00
3	Lance Berkman	3.00
4	Derek Jeter	10.00
5	Hideo Nomo	2.00
6	Kazuhisa Ishii	6.00
7	Barry Bonds	8.00
8	Alex Rodriguez	8.00
9	Ichiro Suzuki	8.00
10	Mike Piazza	6.00
11	Jim Thome	2.00
12	Greg Maddux	5.00
13	Jeff Bagwell	2.50
14	Vladimir Guerrero	3.00
15	Ken Griffey Jr.	6.00
16	Jason Giambi	4.00
17	Nomar Garciaparra	6.00
18	Albert Pujols	5.00
19	Manny Ramirez	2.50
20	Pedro J. Martinez	2.50
21	Roger Clemens	3.00
22	Randy Johnson	3.00
23	Mark Prior	3.00
24	So Taguchi	2.00
25	Sammy Sosa	5.00

2002 Donruss Studio Diamond Collection Artist's Proof

		MT
Common Jersey card:		8.00
Varying quantities produced		
1	Todd Helton/200	8.00
2	Chipper Jones/150	30.00
3	Lance Berkman/200	20.00
4	Derek Jeter/200/base	40.00
5	Hideo Nomo/150	100.00
6	Kazuhisa Ishii/150	45.00
7	Barry Bonds/200/base	25.00
8	Alex Rodriguez/150	30.00
9	Ichiro Suzuki/200/base	30.00
10	Mike Piazza/150	30.00
11	Jim Thome/150	20.00
12	Greg Maddux/150	40.00
13	Jeff Bagwell/150	20.00
14	Vladimir Guerrero/200	25.00
15	Ken Griffey Jr/200/base	20.00
16	Jason Giambi/200/base	15.00
17	Nomar Garciaparra/150	40.00
18	Albert Pujols/base/200	15.00
19	Manny Ramirez/150	15.00
20	Pedro Martinez/150	15.00
21	Roger Clemens/150	30.00
22	Randy Johnson/150	25.00
23	Mark Prior	
24	So Taguchi/200	15.00
25	Sammy Sosa/200/base	20.00

2002 Donruss Studio Hats Off

		MT
Common Player:		
Production 100		
1	Alex Rodriguez	
2	Curt Schilling	
3	Hideo Nomo	
5	Mike Sweeney	
6	Mike Piazza	
7	Roger Clemens	
8	Shawn Green	
9	Vladimir Guerrero	
10	Carlos Lee	10.00
11	Edgar Martinez	
12	Albert Pujols	
13	Mark Prior	
14	Mark Buehrle	20.00
15	Chipper Jones	
16	Paul LoDuca	10.00
17	Frank Thomas	
18	Randy Johnson	
19	Cliff Floyd	
20	Todd Helton	
21	Luis Gonzalez	
22	Brandon Duckworth	20.00
23	Jason Giambi	
24	Juan Uribe	
25	Dewon Brazelton	
26	J.D. Drew	30.00
27	Troy Glaus	
28	Wade Miller	20.00
29	Darin Erstad	
30	Brian Giles	25.00
31	Lance Berkman	30.00
32	Shannon Stewart	
33	Kazuhisa Ishii/50	
34	Corey Patterson	
35	Rafael Palmeiro	20.00
36	Roy Oswalt	20.00
37	Jason Lane	10.00
38	Andruw Jones	30.00
39	Brad Penny	10.00
40	Bud Smith	20.00
41	Carlos Beltran	10.00
42	Magglio Ordonez	20.00
43	Craig Biggio	20.00
44	Hank Blalock	
45	Jeff Bagwell	25.00
46	Josh Beckett	
47	Juan Cruz	10.00
48	Kerry Wood	20.00
49	Brandon Berger	10.00
50	Juan Pierre	10.00

2002 Donruss Studio Leather & Lumber

		MT
Common Player:		10.00
Production 200 unless noted		
Parallel:		2-3X
Production 50		
1	Nomar Garciaparra	40.00
2	Jeff Bagwell/150	20.00
3	Alex Rodriguez	25.00
4	Vladimir Guerrero/100	20.00
5	Luis Gonzalez	12.00
6	Chipper Jones	20.00
7	Shawn Green	10.00
8	Kirby Puckett/100	60.00
9	Juan Gonzalez	12.00
10	Troy Glaus	10.00
11	Don Mattingly/100	60.00
12	Todd Helton	10.00
13	Jim Thome	15.00
14	Rickey Henderson	35.00
15	Mike Schmidt/100	60.00
16	Adam Dunn/100	35.00
17	Ivan Rodriguez	10.00
18	Manny Ramirez/150	15.00
19	Tsuyoshi Shinjo	20.00
20	Andruw Jones/150	15.00
21	Roberto Alomar	15.00
22	Lance Berkman	20.00
23	Derek Jeter/50/ball	50.00
24	Ichiro Suzuki/50/ball	75.00
25	Mike Piazza	25.00

2002 Donruss Studio Masterstrokes

		MT
Complete Set (25):		70.00
Common Player:		2.00
Inserted 1:17		
1	Vladimir Guerrero	3.00
2	Frank Thomas	2.50
3	Alex Rodriguez	8.00
4	Manny Ramirez	2.50
5	Jeff Bagwell	2.50
6	Jim Thome	2.00
7	Ichiro Suzuki	8.00
8	Andruw Jones	2.00
9	Troy Glaus	2.00
10	Chipper Jones	5.00
11	Juan Gonzalez	2.50
12	Lance Berkman	3.00
13	Mike Piazza	6.00
14	Darin Erstad	2.00
15	Albert Pujols	5.00
16	Kazuhisa Ishii	6.00
17	Shawn Green	2.00
18	Rafael Palmeiro	2.00
19	Todd Helton	2.00
20	Carlos Delgado	2.00
21	Ivan Rodriguez	2.00
22	Luis Gonzalez	2.00
23	Derek Jeter	10.00
24	Nomar Garciaparra	6.00
15	J.D. Drew	2.00

2002 Donruss Studio Masterstrokes Artist's Proof

		MT
All Jersey/bat unless noted		
Varying quantities produced		
1	Vladimir Guerrero/200	25.00
2	Frank Thomas/200	20.00
3	Alex Rodriguez/100	50.00
4	Manny Ramirez/200	20.00
5	Jeff Bagwell/150	45.00
6	Jim Thome/200	25.00
7	Ichiro Suzuki/100/ball/base	80.00
8	Andruw Jones/200	20.00
9	Troy Glaus/200	15.00
10	Chipper Jones/200	40.00
11	Juan Gonzalez/200	25.00
12	Lance Berkman/200	25.00
13	Mike Piazza/200	40.00
14	Darin Erstad/200	20.00
15	Albert Pujols/100/ball/base	30.00
16	Kazuhisa Ishii/150	110.00
17	Shawn Green/200	20.00
18	Rafael Palmeiro/200	20.00
19	Todd Helton/200	20.00
20	Carlos Delgado/200	15.00
21	Ivan Rodriguez/200	15.00
22	Luis Gonzalez/200	20.00
23	Derek Jeter/100/ball/base	45.00
24	Nomar Garciaparra/150	45.00
25	J.D. Drew/150	25.00

2002 Donruss Studio Private Signings

		MT
Common Autograph:		10.00
Varying quantities produced		
1	Vladimir Guerrero/25	100.00
2	Chipper Jones/15	170.00
3	Bobby Abreu/30	30.00
4	Barry Zito/25	50.00
5	Larry Walker	
6	Miguel Tejada/50	65.00
7	Mike Sweeney/50	20.00
8	Shannon Stewart/100	10.00
9	Sammy Sosa	
10	Bud Smith/100	20.00
11	Wilson Betemit/250	15.00
12	Kevin Brown/25	45.00
13	Ellis Burks	
14	Pat Burrell	
15	Cliff Floyd/50	20.00
16	Marcus Giles/250	10.00
17	Troy Glaus/50	40.00
18	Barry Larkin	
19	Carlos Lee/25	20.00
20	Brian Lawrence/250	10.00
21	Paul LoDuca/50	25.00
22	Ben Grieve	
23	Shawn Green	
24	Mike Cameron	
25	Roger Clemens/15	175.00
26	Joe Crede/250	10.00
27	Jose Cruz	
28	Jeremy Affeldt/250	10.00
29	Adrian Beltre/25	25.00
30	Josh Beckett	40.00
31	Roberto Alomar	90.00
32	Toby Hall	10.00
33	Mike Hampton	
34	Eric Milton	
35	Eric Munson	
36	Trot Nixon	
37	Roy Oswalt/50	50.00
38	Chan Ho Park	
39	Charles Johnson	
40	Nick Johnson/250	25.00
41	Tim Hudson	
42	Cristian Guzman	
43	Drew Henson/150	40.00
44	Mark Grace	
45	Luis Gonzalez/15	65.00
46	Pedro Martinez/15	160.00

47 Joe Mays/100 15.00
48 Jorge Posada
49 Aramis Ramirez/50 20.00
50 Kip Wells/250
51 Moises Alou/15 30.00
52 Omar Vizquel
53 Ichiro Suzuki
54 Jimmy Rollins
55 Freddy Garcia
56 Steve Green/250 10.00
57 Brian Jordan
58 Paul Konerko
59 Jack Cust/250 15.00
60 Sean Casey
61 Bret Boone
62 Hideo Nomo
63 Magglio Ordonez/15 90.00
64 Frank Thomas/15 100.00
65 Josh Towers
66 Javier Vazquez/100
67 Robin Ventura
68 Aubrey Huff
69 Richard Hidalgo/25 20.00
70 Brandon Claussen/250 10.00
71 Bartolo Colon
72 John Buck/250 10.00
73 Dee Brown
74 Barry Bonds
75 Jason Giambi
76 Erick Almonte/250 10.00
77 Ryan Dempster
78 Jim Edmonds
79 Jay Gibbons/250 25.00
80 Shigetoshi Hasegawa
81 Todd Helton/15 85.00
82 Erik Bedard/250 15.00
83 Carlos Beltran
84 Rafael Soriano
85 Gary Sheffield/15 60.00
86 Richie Sexson/50 35.00
87 Mike Rivera/250 10.00
88 Jose Ortiz/250 10.00
89 Abraham Nunez/250 10.00
90 Dave Williams/250 10.00
91 Preston Wilson
92 Jason Jennings/250 10.00
93 Juan Diaz/250 10.00
94 Steve Smyth/250 10.00
95 Phil Nevin
96 John Olerud
97 Brad Penny/80 10.00
98 Andy Pettitte
99 Juan Pierre/100 10.00
100 Manny Ramirez/15 75.00
101 Edgardo Alfonzo
102 Michael Cuddyer/250 15.00
103 Johnny Damon
104 Carlos Zambrano/250 12.00
105 Jose Vidro/100 15.00
106 Tsuyoshi Shinjo
107 Ed Rogers/250 10.00
108 Scott Rolen
109 Mariano Rivera
110 Tim Redding
111 Josh Phelps/250 15.00
112 Gabe Kapler/100 15.00
113 Edgar Martinez/50 40.00
114 Fred McGriff
115 Raul Mondesi
116 Wade Miller/250 15.00
117 Mike Mussina/15 170.00
118 Rafael Palmeiro/25 75.00
119 Adam Johnson
120 Rickey Henderson/15
121 Bill Hall/250 10.00
122 Ken Griffey Jr.
123 Geronimo Gil/250 10.00
124 Robert Fick/150 15.00
125 Darin Erstad
126 Brandon Duckworth/250 15.00
127 Garret Anderson
128 Pedro Feliz
129 Jeff Cirillo
130 Brian Giles/15 50.00
131 Craig Biggio/15 70.00
132 Willie Harris
133 Doug Davis
134 Jeff Kent
135 Terrence Long/150 10.00
136 Carlos Delgado
137 Tino Martinez
138 Donaldo Mendez/250 10.00
139 Sean Douglass/250 10.00
140 Eric Chavez/15 75.00
141 Rick Ankiel/250 20.00
142 Jeremy Giambi/100 10.00
143 Juan Pena/250 10.00
144 Bernie Williams/15 75.00
145 Craig Wilson/250 10.00
146 Ricardo Rodriguez/250 10.00
147 Albert Pujols/25 120.00
148 Antonio Perez/250 10.00
149 Russ Ortiz
150 Corky Miller/250 15.00
151 Rich Aurilia/25 25.00
152 Kerry Wood/25 70.00
153 Joe Thurston/250 10.00
154 Jeff Deardorff/250 15.00
155 Jermaine Dye/15 35.00
156 Andruw Jones/15 140.00
157 Victor Martinez/250 15.00
158 Nick Neugebauer
159 Matt Morris
160 Casey Fossum/250 15.00
161 J.D. Drew/25 60.00
162 Matt Childers/250 15.00
163 Mark Buehrle/150 20.00
164 Jeff Bagwell
165 Kazuhiro Sasaki
166 Ben Sheets/100 15.00
167 Alex Rodriguez/15 165.00
168 Adam Pettyjohn
169 Chris Snelling/250 25.00
170 Robert Person/250 10.00
171 Juan Uribe/250 10.00
172 Mo Vaughn
173 Alfredo Amezaga/250 10.00
174 Ryan Drese
175 Corey Thurman/250 10.00
176 Jim Thome/15 95.00
177 Orlando Cabrera
178 Eric Cyr
179 Greg Maddux/15 200.00
180 Earl Snyder/250 15.00
181 C.C. Sabathia/50 20.00
182 Mark Mulder/50 50.00
183 Jose Mieses
184 Joe Kennedy
185 Randy Johnson
186 Tom Glavine
187 Eric Junge/250 10.00
188 Mike Piazza
189 Corey Patterson/205 20.00
190 Carlos Pena/250 10.00
191 Curt Schilling/15 80.00
192 Nomar Garciaparra/15 220.00
193 Lance Berkman/15 60.00
194 Ryan Klesko
195 Ivan Rodriguez/15 100.00
196 Alfonso Soriano/50 90.00
197 Derek Jeter
198 David Justice/15 65.00
199 Juan Gonzalez/15 100.00
200 Adam Dunn/25
201 Victor Alvarez/250 10.00
202 Miguel Asencio
203 Brandon Backe/250 10.00
204 Chris Baker/250 10.00
205 Steve Bechler/250 20.00
206 Francis Beltran/250 10.00
207 Angel Berroa/250 10.00
208 Hank Blalock/100 35.00
209 Dewon Brazelton/200 10.00
210 Sean Burroughs/50 40.00
211 Marlon Byrd/200 25.00
212 Raul Chavez/250 15.00
213 Juan Cruz/50 20.00
214 Jorge De La Rosa
215 Doug Devore/250 10.00
216 John Ennis/250 25.00
217 Felix Escalona/250 15.00
218 Morgan Ensberg/250 10.00
219 Cam Esslinger/250 10.00
220 Kevin Frederick
221 Franklyn German/250 10.00
222 Eric Hinske/250 35.00
223 Ben Howard/250 15.00
224 Orlando Hudson/250 15.00
225 Travis Hughes/250 10.00
226 Kazuhisa Ishii/50 175.00
227 Ryan Jamison/250 10.00
228 Reed Johnson/250 10.00
229 Kyle Kane/250 10.00
230 Austin Kearns/250 35.00
231 Satoru Komiyama/50 130.00
232 Jason Lane
233 Jeremy Lambert/250 15.00
234 Anderson Machado/200 15.00
235 Brian Mallette/250 10.00
236 Takahito Nomura/100 50.00
237 Jorge Padilla/200 20.00
238 Luis Ugueto/250 20.00
239 Mark Prior/100 60.00
240 Rene Reyes/250 10.00
241 Deivis Santos 10.00
242 Elio Serrano
243 Tom Shearn/250 10.00
244 Allan Simpson/250 10.00
245 So Taguchi/100 40.00
246 Dennis Tankersley/100 10.00
247 Mark Teixeira/50 35.00
248 Matt Thornton/250 10.00
249 Bobby Hill/100 35.00
250 Ramon Vazquez/250 10.00

2002 Donruss Studio Spirit of the Game

		MT
Complete Set (50):		80.00
Common Player:		1.50
Inserted 1:9		
1	Alex Rodriguez	8.00
2	Curt Schilling	2.50
3	Hideo Nomo	2.00
4	Derek Jeter	10.00
5	Mike Sweeney	1.50
6	Mike Piazza	6.00
7	Roger Clemens	3.00
8	Shawn Green	1.50
9	Vladimir Guerrero	3.00
10	Carlos Lee	1.50
11	Edgar Martinez	1.50
12	Albert Pujols	5.00
13	Mark Prior	4.00
14	Mark Buehrle	1.50
15	Chipper Jones	5.00
16	Paul LoDuca	1.50
17	Frank Thomas	2.50
18	Randy Johnson	2.50
19	Cliff Floyd	1.50
20	Todd Helton	2.00
21	Luis Gonzalez	2.00
22	Brandon Duckworth	1.50
23	Jason Giambi	4.00
24	Juan Uribe	1.50
25	Dewon Brazelton	1.50
26	J.D. Drew	1.50
27	Troy Glaus	1.50
28	Wade Miller	1.50
29	Darin Erstad	1.50
30	Brian Giles	2.00
31	Lance Berkman	3.00
32	Shannon Stewart	1.50
33	Kazuhisa Ishii	5.00
34	Corey Patterson	1.50
35	Rafael Palmeiro	2.50
36	Roy Oswalt	2.00
37	Jason Lane	1.50
38	Andruw Jones	2.00
39	Brad Penny	1.50
40	Bud Smith	1.50
41	Carlos Beltran	1.50
42	Magglio Ordonez	1.50
43	Craig Biggio	1.50
44	Hank Blalock	1.50
45	Jeff Bagwell	2.50
46	Josh Beckett	1.50
47	Juan Cruz	1.50
48	Kerry Wood	2.00
49	Brandon Berger	1.50
50	Juan Pierre	1.50

2002 Donruss Studio Studio Stars

		MT
Complete Set (50):		110.00
Common Player:		1.50
Production 700 sets		
Golds:		1.5-2.5X
Production 250 sets		
Platinums:		3-5X
Production 50 sets		
1	Mike Piazza	6.00
2	Ivan Rodriguez	2.00
3	Albert Pujols	5.00
4	Scott Rolen	2.00
5	Alex Rodriguez	8.00
6	Curt Schilling	2.50
7	Vladimir Guerrero	3.00
8	Jim Thome	2.00
9	Derek Jeter	10.00
10	C.C. Sabathia	1.50
11	Sammy Sosa	5.00
12	Adam Dunn	2.50
13	Bernie Williams	2.00
14	Ichiro Suzuki	8.00
15	Barry Bonds	8.00
16	Rickey Henderson	2.00
17	Ken Griffey Jr.	6.00
18	Kazuhisa Ishii	6.00
19	Kerry Wood	2.00
20	Todd Helton	2.00
21	Hideo Nomo	2.00
22	Frank Thomas	2.50

23	Manny Ramirez	2.50
24	Luis Gonzalez	2.00
25	Rafael Palmeiro	2.00
26	Mike Mussina	2.00
27	Roy Oswalt	2.00
28	Darin Erstad	1.50
29	Barry Larkin	1.50
30	Randy Johnson	2.50
31	Tom Glavine	1.50
32	Lance Berkman	3.00
33	Juan Gonzalez	2.50
34	Shawn Green	2.00
35	Nomar Garciaparra	6.00
36	Troy Glaus	2.00
37	Tim Hudson	2.00
38	Carlos Delgado	2.00
39	Jason Giambi	4.00
40	Andruw Jones	2.00
41	Roberto Alomar	2.00
42	Greg Maddux	5.00
43	Pedro J. Martinez	3.00
44	Tony Gwynn	4.00
45	Alfonso Soriano	5.00
46	Chipper Jones	5.00
47	J.D. Drew	1.50
48	Roger Clemens	4.00
49	Barry Zito	1.50
50	Jeff Bagwell	2.50

E

2000 E-X

Released as a 90-card set the card fronts have a holo-foil card front, with the E-X logo and player name stamped in silver foil. Card backs have a player image, 1999 stats and the featured player's career totals.

		MT
Complete Set (90):		300.00
Common Player:		.25
Common Prospect (61-90):		5.00
Production 3,499 sets		
Pack:		4.00
Wax Box:		80.00
1	Alex Rodriguez	5.00
2	Jeff Bagwell	1.50
3	Mike Piazza	4.00
4	Tony Gwynn	2.50
5	Ken Griffey Jr.	5.00
6	Juan Gonzalez	1.50
7	Vladimir Guerrero	3.00
8	Cal Ripken Jr.	5.00
9	Mo Vaughn	1.00
10	Chipper Jones	3.00
11	Derek Jeter	4.00
12	Nomar Garciaparra	4.00
13	Mark McGwire	6.00
14	Sammy Sosa	4.00
15	Pedro Martinez	1.50
16	Greg Maddux	3.00
17	Frank Thomas	2.00
18	Shawn Green	1.00
19	Carlos Beltran	.40
20	Roger Clemens	2.00
21	Randy Johnson	1.50
22	Bernie Williams	1.00
23	Carlos Delgado	1.00
24	Manny Ramirez	1.50
25	Freddy Garcia	.25
26	Barry Bonds	2.00
27	Tim Hudson	.50
28	Larry Walker	.75
29	Raul Mondesi	.50
30	Ivan Rodriguez	1.50
31	Magglio Ordonez	.50
32	Scott Rolen	1.50
33	Mike Mussina	.75
34	J.D. Drew	.40
35	Tom Glavine	.40
36	Barry Larkin	.50
37	Jim Thome	.75
38	Erubiel Durazo	.25
39	Curt Schilling	.40
40	Orlando Hernandez	.40
41	Rafael Palmeiro	1.00
42	Gabe Kapler	.25
43	Mark Grace	.50
44	Jeff Cirillo	.25
45	Jeromy Burnitz	.25
46	Sean Casey	.25
47	Kevin Millwood	.25
48	Vinny Castilla	.25
49	Jose Canseco	1.00
50	Roberto Alomar	1.00
51	Craig Biggio	.50
52	Preston Wilson	.25
53	Jeff Weaver	.25
54	Robin Ventura	.40
55	Ben Grieve	.50
56	Troy Glaus	1.50
57	Jacque Jones	.25
58	Brian Giles	.25
59	Kevin Brown	.40
60	Todd Helton	1.50
61	Ben Petrick (Prospects)	5.00
62	Chad Hermansen (Prospects)	5.00
63	Kevin Barker (Prospects)	5.00
64	Matt LeCroy (Prospects)	5.00
65	Brad Penny (Prospects)	5.00
66	D.T. Cromer (Prospects)	5.00
67	Steve Lomasney (Prospects)	5.00
68	Cole Liniak (Prospects)	5.00
69	B.J. Ryan (Prospects)	5.00
70	Wilton Veras (Prospects)	10.00
71	*Aaron McNeal* (Prospects)	12.00
72	Nick Johnson (Prospects)	15.00
73	Adam Piatt (Prospects)	10.00
74	Adam Kennedy (Prospects)	6.00
75	Cesar King (Prospects)	5.00
76	Peter Bergeron (Prospects)	6.00
77	Rob Bell (Prospects)	5.00
78	Wily Pena (Prospects)	20.00
79	Ruben Mateo (Prospects)	5.00
80	Kip Wells (Prospects)	6.00
81	Alex Escobar (Prospects)	5.00
82	*Danys Baez* (Prospects)	10.00
83	Travis Dawkins (Prospects)	5.00
84	Mark Quinn (Prospects)	6.00
85	Jimmy Anderson (Prospects)	5.00
86	Rick Ankiel (Prospects)	8.00
87	Alfonso Soriano (Prospects)	8.00
88	Pat Burrell (Prospects)	15.00
89	Eric Munson (Prospects)	15.00
90	Josh Beckett (Prospects)	18.00

2000 E-X Essential Credentials Now

Like Future, this is a parallel of the base set, with the production of cards 1-60 limited to that player's card number. Production for cards 61-90 can be determined by subtracting 60 from the card number. Quantity issued is listed in parantheses.

		MT
Common Player:		15.00
1	Alex Rodriguez (1)	
2	Jeff Bagwell (2)	
3	Mike Piazza (3)	
4	Tony Gwynn (4)	
5	Ken Griffey Jr. (5)	
6	Juan Gonzalez (6)	
7	Vladimir Guerrero (7)	
8	Cal Ripken Jr. (8)	
9	Mo Vaughn (9)	
10	Chipper Jones (10)	
11	Derek Jeter (11)	
12	Nomar Garciaparra (12)	
13	Mark McGwire (13)	
14	Sammy Sosa (14)	
15	Pedro Martinez (15)	
16	Greg Maddux (16)	
17	Frank Thomas (17)	
18	Shawn Green (18)	
19	Carlos Beltran (19)	
20	Roger Clemens (20)	200.00
21	Randy Johnson (21)	125.00
22	Bernie Williams (22)	125.00
23	Carlos Delgado (23)	90.00
24	Manny Ramirez (24)	100.00
25	Freddy Garcia (25)	30.00
26	Barry Bonds (26)	125.00
27	Tim Hudson (27)	40.00
28	Larry Walker (28)	75.00
29	Raul Mondesi (29)	50.00
30	Ivan Rodriguez (30)	125.00
31	Magglio Ordonez (31)	50.00
32	Scott Rolen (32)	100.00
33	Mike Mussina (33)	75.00
34	J.D. Drew (34)	35.00
35	Tom Glavine (35)	35.00
36	Barry Larkin (36)	40.00
37	Jim Thome (37)	40.00
38	Erubiel Durazo (38)	20.00
39	Curt Schilling (39)	25.00
40	Orlando Hernandez (40)	25.00
41	Rafael Palmeiro (41)	40.00
42	Gabe Kapler (42)	20.00
43	Mark Grace (43)	25.00
44	Jeff Cirillo (44)	20.00
45	Jeromy Burnitz (45)	15.00
46	Sean Casey (46)	15.00
47	Kevin Millwood (47)	15.00
48	Vinny Castilla (48)	15.00
49	Jose Canseco (49)	40.00
50	Roberto Alomar (50)	40.00
51	Craig Biggio (51)	25.00
52	Preston Wilson (52)	10.00
53	Jeff Weaver (53)	10.00
54	Robin Ventura (54)	15.00
55	Ben Grieve (55)	20.00
56	Troy Glaus (56)	20.00
57	Jacque Jones (57)	10.00
58	Brian Giles (58)	10.00
59	Kevin Brown (59)	15.00
60	Todd Helton (60)	40.00
61	Ben Petrick (1) (Prospects)	
62	Chad Hermansen (2) (Prospects)	
63	Kevin Barker (3) (Prospects)	
64	Matt LeCroy (4) (Prospects)	
65	Brad Penny (5) (Prospects)	
66	D.T. Cromer (6) (Prospects)	
67	Steve Lomasney (7) (Prospects)	
68	Cole Liniak (8) (Prospects)	
69	B.J. Ryan (9) (Prospects)	
70	Wilton Veras (10) (Prospects)	
71	Aaron McNeal (11) (Prospects)	
72	Nick Johnson (12) (Prospects)	
73	Adam Piatt (13) (Prospects)	
74	Adam Kennedy (14) (Prospects)	65.00
75	Cesar King (15) (Prospects)	15.00
76	Peter Bergeron (16) (Prospects)	65.00
77	Rob Bell (17) (Prospects)	25.00
78	Wily Pena (18) (Prospects)	100.00
79	Ruben Mateo (19) (Prospects)	20.00
80	Kip Wells (20) (Prospects)	20.00
81	Alex Escobar (21) (Prospects)	20.00
82	Danys Baez (22) (Prospects)	50.00
83	Travis Dawkins (23) (Prospects)	20.00
84	Mark Quinn (24) (Prospects)	15.00
85	Jimmy Anderson (25) (Prospects)	15.00
86	Rick Ankiel (26) (Prospects)	100.00
87	Alfonso Soriano (27) (Prospects)	65.00
88	Pat Burrell (28) (Prospects)	100.00
89	Eric Munson (29) (Prospects)	75.00
90	Josh Beckett (30) (Prospects)	75.00

2000 E-X Essential Credentials Future

Production varied for these parallel inserts depending on the card number, with the exact production number for cards 1-60 determined by subtracting the card number from 61. Cards 61-90 are determined by subtracting the card number from 91. Quantity issued is listed in parantheses.

		MT
Common Player:		15.00
1	Alex Rodriguez (60)	160.00
2	Jeff Bagwell (59)	60.00
3	Mike Piazza (58)	150.00
4	Tony Gwynn (57)	100.00
5	Ken Griffey Jr. (56)	200.00
6	Juan Gonzalez (55)	60.00
7	Vladimir Guerrero (54)	75.00
8	Cal Ripken Jr. (53)	180.00
9	Mo Vaughn (52)	50.00

10 Chipper Jones (51) 125.00
11 Derek Jeter (50) 160.00
12 Nomar Garciaparra (49) 150.00
13 Mark McGwire (48) 275.00
14 Sammy Sosa (47) 150.00
15 Pedro Martinez (46) 70.00
16 Greg Maddux (45) 125.00
17 Frank Thomas (44) 80.00
18 Shawn Green (43) 50.00
19 Carlos Beltran (42) 25.00
20 Roger Clemens (41) 80.00
21 Randy Johnson (40) 60.00
22 Bernie Williams (39) 50.00
23 Carlos Delgado (38) 50.00
24 Manny Ramirez (37) 60.00
25 Freddy Garcia (36) 25.00
26 Barry Bonds (35) 70.00
27 Tim Hudson (34) 30.00
28 Larry Walker (33) 50.00
29 Raul Mondesi (32) 30.00
30 Ivan Rodriguez (31) 80.00
31 Magglio Ordonez (30) 25.00
32 Scott Rolen (29) 60.00
33 Mike Mussina (28) 40.00
34 J.D. Drew (27) 30.00
35 Tom Glavine (26) 40.00
36 Barry Larkin (25) 40.00
37 Jim Thome (24) 40.00
38 Erubiel Durazo (23) 25.00
39 Curt Schilling (22) 25.00
40 Orlando Hernandez (21) 20.00
41 Rafael Palmeiro (20) 60.00
42 Gabe Kapler (19) 25.00
43 Mark Grace (18) 30.00
44 Jeff Cirillo (17) 20.00
45 Jeromy Burnitz (16) 20.00
46 Sean Casey (15) 20.00
47 Kevin Millwood (14) 20.00
48 Vinny Castilla (13) 25.00
49 Jose Canseco (12) 80.00
50 Roberto Alomar (11) 80.00
51 Craig Biggio (10) 50.00
52 Preston Wilson (9)
53 Jeff Weaver (8)
54 Robin Ventura (7)
55 Ben Grieve (6)
56 Troy Glaus (5)
57 Jacque Jones (4)
58 Brian Giles (3)
59 Kevin Brown (2)
60 Todd Helton (1)
61 Ben Petrick (30) (Prospects) 15.00
62 Chad Hermansen (29) (Prospects) 15.00
63 Kevin Barker (28) (Prospects) 15.00
64 Matt LeCroy (27) (Prospects) 15.00
65 Brad Penny (26) (Prospects) 15.00
66 D.T. Cromer (25) (Prospects) 15.00
67 Steve Lomasney (24) (Prospects) 15.00
68 Cole Liniak (23) (Prospects) 15.00
69 B.J. Ryan (22) (Prospects) 20.00
70 Wilton Veras (21) (Prospects) 75.00
71 Aaron McNeal (20) (Prospects) 90.00
72 Nick Johnson (19) (Prospects) 125.00
73 Adam Piatt (18) (Prospects) 100.00
74 Adam Kennedy (17) (Prospects) 35.00
75 Cesar King (16) (Prospects) 25.00
76 Peter Bergeron (15) (Prospects) 35.00
77 Rob Bell (14) (Prospects) 25.00
78 Wily Pena (13) (Prospects) 150.00
79 Ruben Mateo (12) (Prospects) 25.00
80 Kip Wells (11) (Prospects) 25.00
81 Alex Escobar (10) (Prospects) 35.00
82 Danys Baez (9) (Prospects)
83 Travis Dawkins (8) (Prospects)
84 Mark Quinn (7) (Prospects)
85 Jimmy Anderson (6) (Prospects)
86 Rick Ankiel (5) (Prospects)
87 Alfonso Soriano (4) (Prospects)
88 Pat Burrell (3) (Prospects)
89 Eric Munson (2) (Prospects)
90 Josh Beckett (1) (Prospects)

2000 E-X Autographics

	MT
Common Player:	10.00
Inserted 1:24	
Bob Abreu	15.00
Moises Alou	15.00
Rick Ankiel	25.00
Michael Barrett	10.00
Josh Beckett	25.00
Rob Bell	10.00
Adrian Beltre	15.00
Carlos Beltran	12.00
Wade Boggs	60.00
Barry Bonds	80.00
Kent Bottenfield	10.00
Milton Bradley	10.00
Pat Burrell	25.00
Chris Carpenter	10.00
Sean Casey	15.00
Eric Chavez	15.00
Will Clark	35.00
Johnny Damon	15.00
Mike Darr	10.00
Ben Davis	10.00
Russ Davis	10.00
Carlos Delgado	35.00
Jason Dewey	10.00
Octavio Dotel	10.00
J.D. Drew	30.00
Ray Durham	15.00
Damion Easley	10.00
Kelvim Escobar	10.00
Carlos Febles	10.00
Freddy Garcia	10.00
Jeremy Giambi	10.00
Todd Greene	10.00
Jason Grilli	10.00
Vladimir Guerrero	40.00
Tony Gwynn	50.00
Jerry Hairston Jr.	10.00
Mike Hampton	15.00
Todd Helton	40.00
Trevor Hoffman	10.00
Tim Hudson	25.00
John Jaha	10.00
Derek Jeter	100.00
D'Angelo Jimenez	10.00
Randy Johnson	60.00
Jason Kendall	15.00
Adam Kennedy	10.00
Cesar King	10.00
Paul Konerko	15.00
Mark Kotsay	10.00
Ray Lankford	15.00
Jason LaRue	10.00
Matt Lawton	10.00
Carlos Lee	10.00
Mike Lieberthal	10.00
Cole Liniak	10.00
Steve Lomasney	10.00
Jose Macias	10.00
Greg Maddux	60.00
Edgar Martinez	20.00
Pedro Martinez	75.00
Ruben Mateo	10.00
Gary Matthews Jr.	10.00
Aaron McNeal	10.00
Raul Mondesi	15.00
Orber Moreno	10.00
Warren Morris	10.00
Eric Munson	15.00
Heath Murray	10.00
Mike Mussina	30.00
Joe Nathan	10.00
Rafael Palmeiro	30.00
Jim Parque	10.00
Angel Pena	10.00
Wily Pena	12.00
Pokey Reese	15.00
Matt Riley	10.00
Cal Ripken Jr.	100.00
Alex Rodriguez	75.00
Scott Rolen	25.00
Jimmy Rollins	10.00
B.J. Ryan	10.00
Randall Simon	10.00
Chris Singleton	10.00
Alfonso Soriano	20.00
Shannon Stewart	15.00
Mike Sweeney	15.00
Miguel Tejada	15.00
Wilton Veras	12.00
Frank Thomas	50.00
Billy Wagner	15.00
Jeff Weaver	10.00
Rondell White	15.00
Scott Williamson	10.00
Randy Wolf	10.00
Jaret Wright	10.00
Ed Yarnall	10.00
Kevin Young	10.00

2000 E-X Generation E-X

This 15-card set spotlights the top young players in the game and were seeded 1:8 packs. Card fronts have silver foil stamping over a background resembling a sky. These were seeded 1:8 packs. Card backs are numbered with a "GX" suffix.

		MT
Complete Set (15):		50.00
Common Player:		1.50
Inserted 1:8		
1	Rick Ankiel	3.00
2	Josh Beckett	4.00
3	Carlos Beltran	1.50
4	Pat Burrell	5.00
5	Freddy Garcia	1.50
6	Alex Rodriguez	12.00
7	Derek Jeter	10.00
8	Tim Hudson	2.00
9	Shawn Green	3.00
10	Eric Munson	3.00
11	Adam Piatt	2.50
12	Adam Kennedy	1.50
13	Nick Johnson	3.00
14	Alfonso Soriano	4.00
15	Nomar Garciaparra	10.00

2000 E-X E-Xplosive

These inserts have a traditional format, with a holographic star like image in the background and "explosive" running down the top left side. Card backs are numbered with an "XP" suffix and are serial numbered on the bottom portion in an edition of 2,499 sets.

		MT
Complete Set (20):		150.00
Common Player:		4.00
Production 2,499 sets		
1	Tony Gwynn	8.00
2	Alex Rodriguez	15.00
3	Pedro Martinez	5.00
4	Sammy Sosa	12.00
5	Cal Ripken Jr.	15.00
6	Adam Piatt	4.00
7	Pat Burrell	6.00
8	J.D. Drew	4.00
9	Mike Piazza	12.00
10	Shawn Green	4.00
11	Troy Glaus	5.00
12	Randy Johnson	5.00
13	Juan Gonzalez	5.00
14	Chipper Jones	10.00
15	Ivan Rodriguez	5.00
16	Nomar Garciaparra	12.00
17	Ken Griffey Jr.	15.00
18	Nick Johnson	5.00
19	Mark McGwire	20.00
20	Frank Thomas	8.00

2000 E-X E-Xceptional Red

Die-cut in a shape similar to an oval, these inserts have a cloth like feel with silver foil stamping with a red background. Card backs are numbered consecutively "1 0f 15XC" and so on. These are seeded 1:14 packs. Two parallels are also inserted: Blues are seeded 1:288 packs and Greens are limited to 999 serial numbered sets.

		MT
Complete Set (15):		190.00
Common Player:		6.00
Inserted 1:14		
Blue:		2-3X
Inserted 1:288		
Green:		1-1.5X
Production 999 sets		
1	Ken Griffey Jr.	25.00
2	Derek Jeter	20.00
3	Nomar Garciaparra	20.00
4	Mark McGwire	30.00
5	Sammy Sosa	20.00
6	Mike Piazza	20.00
7	Alex Rodriguez	25.00
8	Cal Ripken Jr.	25.00
9	Chipper Jones	15.00
10	Pedro Martinez	8.00
11	Jeff Bagwell	8.00
12	Greg Maddux	15.00
13	Roger Clemens	10.00
14	Tony Gwynn	12.00
15	Frank Thomas	10.00

2000 E-X E-Xciting

Die-cut in the shape of a jersey card fronts have a holograpic appearance with silver foil stamping. These were seeded 1:24 packs. Card backs are numbered with an "XT" suffix.

		MT
Complete Set (10):		75.00
Common Player:		4.00
Inserted 1:24		
1	Mark McGwire	20.00
2	Ken Griffey Jr.	15.00
3	Randy Johnson	5.00
4	Sammy Sosa	12.00
5	Manny Ramirez	5.00
6	Jose Canseco	4.00
7	Derek Jeter	12.00
8	Scott Rolen	5.00
9	Juan Gonzalez	5.00
10	Barry Bonds	6.00

2000 E-X Genuine Coverage

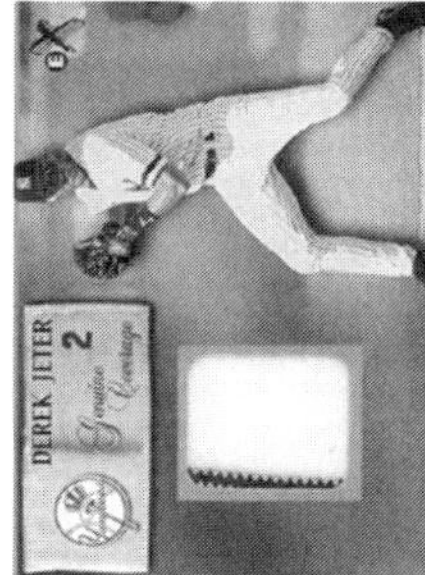

	MT
Common Player:	15.00
Inserted 1:144	

1	Alex Rodriguez	50.00
2	Tom Glavine	25.00
3	Cal Ripken Jr.	60.00
4	Edgar Martinez	25.00
5	Raul Mondesi	20.00
6	Carlos Beltran	20.00
7	Chipper Jones	35.00
8	Barry Bonds	60.00
9	Heath Murray	15.00
10	Tim Hudson	25.00
11	Mike Mussina	35.00
12	Derek Jeter	75.00

2001 E-X

		MT
Complete Set (130):		400.00
Common Player:		.25
Common SP (101-130):		8.00
Production listed		
Pack (5):		5.00
Box (24):		100.00
1	Jason Kendall	.25
2	Derek Jeter	4.00
3	Greg Vaughn	.25
4	Eric Chavez	.40
5	Nomar Garciaparra	3.00
6	Roberto Alomar	1.00
7	Barry Larkin	.50
8	Matt Lawton	.25
9	Larry Walker	.50
10	Chipper Jones	2.50
11	Scott Rolen	.75
12	Carlos Lee	.25
13	Adrian Beltre	.25
14	Ben Grieve	.25
15	Mike Sweeney	.25
16	John Olerud	.40
17	Gabe Kapler	.40
18	Brian Giles	.40
19	Luis Gonzalez	.50
20	Sammy Sosa	2.50
21	Roger Clemens	1.50
22	Vladimir Guerrero	1.50
23	Ken Griffey Jr.	3.00
24	Mark McGwire	4.00
25	Orlando Hernandez	.50
26	Shannon Stewart	.25
27	Fred McGriff	.25
28	Lance Berkman	.25
29	Carlos Delgado	1.00
30	Mike Piazza	3.00
31	Juan Encarnacion	.25
32	David Justice	.50
33	Greg Maddux	2.50
34	Frank Thomas	1.50
35	Jason Giambi	.75
36	Ruben Mateo	.25
37	Todd Helton	1.25
38	Jim Edmonds	.40
39	Steve Finley	.25
40	Tom Glavine	.50
41	Mo Vaughn	.25
42	Phil Nevin	.25
43	Richie Sexson	.25
44	Craig Biggio	.40
45	Kerry Wood	.40
46	Pat Burrell	.75
47	Edgar Martinez	.25
48	Jim Thome	.40
49	Jeff Bagwell	1.25
50	Bernie Williams	1.00
51	Andruw Jones	1.00
52	Gary Sheffield	.40
53	Johnny Damon	.25
54	Rondell White	.25
55	J.D. Drew	.50
56	Tony Batista	.25
57	Paul Konerko	.25
58	Rafael Palmeiro	.75
59	Cal Ripken Jr.	4.00
60	Darin Erstad	.50
61	Ivan Rodriguez	1.25
62	Barry Bonds	2.00
63	Edgardo Alfonzo	.25
64	Ellis Burks	.25
65	Mike Lieberthal	.25
66	Robin Ventura	.25
67	Richard Hidalgo	.50
68	Magglio Ordonez	.25
69	Kazuhiro Sasaki	.25
70	Miguel Tejada	.50
71	David Wells	.25
72	Troy Glaus	1.25
73	Jose Vidro	.25
74	Shawn Green	.25
75	Barry Zito	.25
76	Jermaine Dye	.25
77	Geoff Jenkins	.25
78	Jeff Kent	.25
79	Al Leiter	.40
80	Deivi Cruz	.25
81	Eric Karros	.25
82	Albert Belle	.25
83	Pedro Martinez	1.50
84	Raul Mondesi	.25
85	Preston Wilson	.25
86	Rafael Furcal	.40
87	Rick Ankiel	.25
88	Randy Johnson	1.25
89	Kevin Brown	.25
90	Sean Casey	.25
91	Mike Mussina	.75
92	Alex Rodriguez	3.00
93	Andres Galarraga	.50
94	Juan Gonzalez	1.25
95	Manny Ramirez	1.50
96	Mark Grace	.50
97	Carl Everett	.25
98	Tony Gwynn	1.50
99	Mike Hampton	.40
100	Ken Caminiti	.25
101	Jason Hart/1749	12.00
102	Corey Patterson/ 1199	10.00
103	Timo Perez/1999	8.00
104	Marcus Giles/1999	8.00
105	*Ichiro Suzuki/1999*	110.00
106	Aubrey Huff/1499	8.00
107	Joe Crede/1999	8.00
108	Larry Barnes/1499	8.00
109	*Esix Snead/1499*	8.00
110	Kenny Kelly/2249	8.00
111	Justin Miller/2249	8.00
112	Jack Cust/1999	10.00
113	Xavier Nady/999	15.00
114	Eric Munson/1499	10.00
115	*Elpidio Guzman/ 1749*	12.00
116	Juan Pierre/2189	8.00
117	*Winston Abreu/1749*	8.00
118	Keith Ginter/1999	8.00
119	Jace Brewer/2699	8.00
120	Paxton Crawford/ 2249	8.00
121	Jason Tyner/2249	8.00
122	Tike Redman/1999	8.00
123	John Riedling/2499	8.00
124	Jose Ortiz/1499	12.00
125	Oswaldo Mairena/ 2499	10.00
126	Eric Byrnes/2249	8.00
127	Brian Cole/999	8.00
128	Adam Piatt/2249	8.00
129	Nate Rolison/2499	8.00
130	Keith McDonald/ 2249	8.00

A card number in parentheses ( ) indicates the set is unnumbered.

2001 E-X Essential Credentials

	MT
Stars (1-100):	5-10X
Production 299	
Common (101-130):	15.00
Minor Stars (101-130):	25.00
Production 29	

(See 2001 E-X for checklist and base card values.)

2001 E-X Behind the Numbers

		MT
Common Player:		20.00
Inserted 1:33		
1BN	Johnny Bench	50.00
2BN	Wade Boggs	40.00
3BN	George Brett	60.00
4BN	Lou Brock	30.00
5BN	Rollie Fingers	20.00
6BN	Carlton Fisk	40.00
7BN	Reggie Jackson	35.00
8BN	Al Kaline	75.00
9BN	Willie Mays	
10BN	Willie McCovey	30.00
11BN	Paul Molitor	40.00
12BN	Eddie Murray	50.00
13BN	Jim Palmer	25.00
14BN	Ozzie Smith	60.00
15BN	Nolan Ryan	100.00
16BN	Mike Schmidt	75.00
17BN	Tom Seaver	50.00
18BN	Dave Winfield	40.00
19BN	Ted Williams	275.00
20BN	Robin Yount	60.00
21BN	Brady Anderson	20.00
22BN	Rick Ankiel	20.00
23BN	Albert Belle	20.00
24BN	Adrian Beltre	20.00
25BN	Barry Bonds	60.00
26BN	Eric Chavez	20.00
27BN	J.D. Drew	25.00
28BN	Darin Erstad	25.00
29BN	Troy Glaus	35.00
30BN	Mark Grace	30.00
31BN	Ben Grieve	20.00
32BN	Tony Gwynn	40.00
33BN	Todd Helton	40.00
34BN	Derek Jeter	75.00

35BNJeff Kent 20.00
36BNJason Kendall 20.00
37BNGreg Maddux 40.00
38BNJohn Olerud 20.00
39BNCal Ripken Jr. 75.00
40BNChipper Jones 40.00
41BNJohn Smoltz 20.00
42BNFrank Thomas 30.00
43BNRobin Ventura 20.00
44BNBernie Williams 25.00

2001 E-X Behind the Numbers Autograph

	MT
Common Player:	50.00
1BN Johnny Bench/5	
2BN Wade Boggs/26	300.00
3BN George Brett/5	
4BN Lou Brock/20	175.00
5BN Rollie Fingers/34	75.00
6BN Carlton Fisk/27	200.00
7BN Reggie Jackson/44	200.00
8BN Al Kaline/6	
10BNWillie McCovey/44	120.00
11BNPaul Molitor/4	
12BNEddie Murray/33	325.00
13BNJim Palmer/22	150.00
14BNOzzie Smith/1	
15BNNolan Ryan/34	750.00
16BNMike Schmidt/20	500.00
17BNTom Seaver/41	225.00
18BNDave Winfield/31	150.00
20BNRobin Yount/19	350.00
21BNBrady Anderson/9	
22BNRick Ankiel/66	50.00
23BNAlbert Belle/88	50.00
24BNAdrian Beltre/29	50.00
25BNBarry Bonds/25	375.00
26BNEric Chavez/3	
27BNJ.D. Drew/7	
28BNDarin Erstad/17	200.00
29BNTroy Glaus/25	200.00
30BNMark Grace/17	250.00
31BNBen Grieve/14	
32BNTony Gwynn/19	350.00
33BNTodd Helton/17	350.00
34BNDerek Jeter/2	
35BNJeff Kent/21	90.00
36BNJason Kendall/18	75.00
37BNGreg Maddux/31	400.00
38BNJohn Olerud/5	
39BNCal Ripken Jr./8	
40BNChipper Jones/10	
41BNJohn Smoltz/29	75.00
42BNFrank Thomas/35	250.00
43BNRobin Ventura/4	
44BNBernie Williams/51	100.00

A player's name in *italic* type indicates a rookie card.

2001 E-X Base Inks

	MT
Random Inserts	
Derek Jeter/1996	20.00
Derek Jeter AU/500	180.00
Derek Jeter AU/96	200.00

2001 E-X E-Xtra Innings

	MT
Complete Set (10):	80.00
Common Player:	4.00
Inserted 1:20 R	
1XI Mark McGwire	12.00
2XI Sammy Sosa	8.00
3XI Chipper Jones	8.00
4XI Mike Piazza	10.00
5XI Cal Ripken Jr.	12.00
6XI Ken Griffey Jr.	10.00
7XI Alex Rodriguez	10.00
8XI Vladimir Guerrero	5.00
9XI Nomar Garciaparra	10.00
10XI Derek Jeter	12.00

2001 E-X Prospects Autograph

	MT
Common Autograph:	15.00
Prod. #'s listed	
101 Jason Hart/250	25.00
102 Corey Patterson/800	25.00
103 Timoniel Perez/1000	15.00
104 Marcus Giles/500	20.00
106 Aubrey Huff/500	20.00
107 Joe Crede/500	25.00
108 Larry Barnes/500	15.00
109 Esix Snead/500	15.00
110 Kenny Kelly/250	15.00
111 Justin Miller/250	15.00
112 Jack Cust/1000	20.00
113 Xavier Nady/1000	25.00
114 Eric Munson/1500	20.00
115 Elpidio Guzman/250	20.00
116 Juan Pierre/810	20.00
117 Winston Abreu/250	20.00
118 Keith Ginter/500	15.00
119 Jace Brewer/300	15.00
120 Paxton Crawford/250	15.00
121 Jason Tyner/250	15.00
122 Tike Redman/250	15.00
123 John Riedling/500	15.00
124 Jose Ortiz/500	25.00
125 Oswaldo Mairena/500	20.00
126 Eric Byrnes/250	15.00
127 Brian Cole/2000	15.00
128 Adam Piatt/250	20.00
129 Nate Rolison/500	15.00
130 Keith McDonald/250	15.00

2001 E-X Wall of Fame

	MT
Common Player:	10.00
Inserted 1:24	
1WF Robin Yount	25.00
2WF Paul Molitor	20.00
3WF Geoff Jenkins	10.00
4WF Mark McGwire	60.00
5WF Sammy Sosa	25.00
6WF Greg Maddux	25.00
7WF Mike Piazza	40.00
8WF Cal Ripken Jr.	60.00
9WF Todd Helton	20.00
10WFKen Griffey Jr.	40.00
11WFAlex Rodriguez	30.00
12WFVladimir Guerrero	20.00
13WFJeff Bagwell	20.00
14WFIvan Rodriguez	15.00
15WFJuan Gonzalez	20.00
16WFBarry Bonds	30.00
17WFDerek Jeter	50.00
18WFChipper Jones	25.00
19WFFrank Thomas	15.00
20WFTony Gwynn	15.00
21WFNomar Garciaparra	40.00
22WFManny Ramirez	20.00
23WFAndruw Jones	15.00
24WFScott Rolen	10.00
25WFJason Kendall	10.00
26WFRoger Clemens	25.00
27WFTroy Glaus	15.00
28WFPedro Martinez	25.00
29WFJason Giambi	15.00
30WFPat Burrell	15.00

F

1993 Finest Promos

Debuting at the 1993 National Convention in Chicago, this three-card set introduced the hobby to the Topps Finest baseball issue. While the promos are identical in high-tech format to the regular Finest cards issued later, including the same card numbers, there are differences in the promos; some subtle, some glaring. For instance, the Ryan and Alomar cards were issued in promo form in the "gray" style of the basic set. In the regularly issued set, those cards were in the green All-Star format. Each of the promos is overprinted in red on the back, "Promotional Sample 1 of 5000". Of considerably greater rarity are refractor versions of these promo cards, with production numbers unknown.

	MT
Complete Set (3):	25.00
Complete Set, Refractors (3):	2500.
88 Roberto Alomar	7.50
88r Roberto Alomar (refractor)	750.00
98 Don Mattingly	12.50
98r Don Mattingly (refractor)	1000.
107 Nolan Ryan	15.00
107r Nolan Ryan (refractor)	1500.

1993 Finest

This 199-card set uses a process of multi-color metallization; this chromium technology adds depth and dimension to the card. The set has a 33-card subset of All-Stars; a parallel version of these cards (Refractors) were also created with refracting foil using the metallization enhancement process. There is one refracting foil card in every nine packs. Packs have five cards. Each 18-count box contains a 5" x 7" version of one of the 33 All-Star players in the set.

	MT
Complete Set (199):	175.00
Common Player:	1.00
Pack (6):	24.00
Wax Box (18):	300.00
1 Dave Justice	2.00
2 Lou Whitaker	1.00
3 Bryan Harvey	1.00
4 Carlos Garcia	1.00
5 Sid Fernandez	1.00
6 Brett Butler	1.00
7 Scott Cooper	1.00
8 B.J. Surhoff	1.00

9 Steve Finley 1.50
10 Curt Schilling 2.00
11 Jeff Bagwell 7.50
12 Alex Cole 1.00
13 John Olerud 1.50
14 John Smiley 1.00
15 Bip Roberts 1.00
16 Albert Belle 3.00
17 Duane Ward 1.00
18 Alan Trammell 1.00
19 Andy Benes 1.00
20 Reggie Sanders 1.00
21 Todd Zeile 1.00
22 Rick Aguilera 1.00
23 Dave Hollins 1.00
24 Jose Rijo 1.00
25 Matt Williams 2.00
26 Sandy Alomar 1.00
27 Alex Fernandez 1.00
28 Ozzie Smith 10.00
29 Ramon Martinez 1.00
30 Bernie Williams 4.00
31 Gary Sheffield 2.00
32 Eric Karros 1.00
33 Frank Viola 1.00
34 Kevin Young 1.00
35 Ken Hill 1.00
36 Tony Fernandez 1.00
37 Tim Wakefield 1.00
38 John Kruk 1.00
39 Chris Sabo 1.00
40 Marquis Grissom 1.00
41 Glenn Davis 1.00
42 Jeff Montgomery 1.00
43 Kenny Lofton 1.00
44 John Burkett 1.00
45 Darryl Hamilton 1.00
46 Jim Abbott 1.00
47 Ivan Rodriguez 6.00
48 Eric Young 1.00
49 Mitch Williams 1.00
50 Harold Reynolds 1.00
51 Brian Harper 1.00
52 Rafael Palmeiro 2.50
53 Bret Saberhagen 1.00
54 Jeff Conine 1.00
55 Ivan Calderon 1.00
56 Juan Guzman 1.00
57 Carlos Baerga 1.00
58 Charles Nagy 1.00
59 Wally Joyner 1.00
60 Charlie Hayes 1.00
61 Shane Mack 1.00
62 Pete Harnisch 1.00
63 George Brett 10.00
64 Lance Johnson 1.00
65 Ben McDonald 1.00
66 Bobby Bonilla 1.00
67 Terry Steinbach 1.00
68 Ron Gant 1.00
69 Doug Jones 1.00
70 Paul Molitor 5.00
71 Brady Anderson 1.00
72 Chuck Finley 1.00
73 Mark Grace 2.50
74 Mike Devereaux 1.00
75 Tony Phillips 1.00
76 Chuck Knoblauch 1.00
77 Tony Gwynn 12.50
78 Kevin Appier 1.00
79 Sammy Sosa 12.50
80 Mickey Tettleton 1.00
81 Felix Jose 1.00
82 Mark Langston 1.00
83 Gregg Jefferies 1.00
84 Andre Dawson (AS) 1.50
85 Greg Maddux (AS) 12.50
86 Rickey Henderson (AS) 4.00
87 Tom Glavine (AS) 2.50
88 Roberto Alomar (AS) 5.00
89 Darryl Strawberry (AS) 1.00
90 Wade Boggs (AS) 4.00
91 Bo Jackson (AS) 2.00
92 Mark McGwire (AS) 15.00
93 Robin Ventura (AS) 1.00
94 Joe Carter (AS) 1.00
95 Lee Smith (AS) 1.00
96 Cal Ripken, Jr. (AS) 15.00
97 Larry Walker (AS) 4.00
98 Don Mattingly (AS) 12.50
99 Jose Canseco (AS) 2.50
100 Dennis Eckersley (AS) 1.00
101 Terry Pendleton (AS) 1.00
102 Frank Thomas (AS) 12.50
103 Barry Bonds (AS) 9.00
104 Roger Clemens 10.00
105 Ryne Sandberg (AS) 6.00
106 Fred McGriff (AS) 1.00
107 Nolan Ryan (AS) 15.00
108 Will Clark (AS) 3.00
109 Pat Listach (AS) 1.00
110 Ken Griffey, Jr. (AS) 15.00
111 Cecil Fielder (AS) 1.00
112 Kirby Puckett (AS) 10.00
113 Dwight Gooden (AS) 1.25
114 Barry Larkin (AS) 3.00
115 David Cone (AS) 1.00
116 Juan Gonzalez (AS) 7.50
117 Kent Hrbek 1.00
118 Tim Wallach 1.00
119 Craig Biggio 1.00
120 Bobby Kelly 1.00
121 Greg Olson 1.00
122 Eddie Murray 5.00
123 Wil Cordero 1.00
124 Jay Buhner 1.00
125 Carlton Fisk 4.00
126 Eric Davis 1.00
127 Doug Drabek 1.00
128 Ozzie Guillen 1.00
129 John Wetteland 1.00
130 Andres Galarraga 1.00
131 Ken Caminiti 1.00
132 Tom Candiotti 1.00
133 Pat Borders 1.00
134 Kevin Brown 1.50
135 Travis Fryman 1.00
136 Kevin Mitchell 1.00
137 Greg Swindell 1.00
138 Benny Santiago 1.00
139 Reggie Jefferson 1.00
140 Chris Bosio 1.00
141 Deion Sanders 2.00
142 Scott Erickson 1.00
143 Howard Johnson 1.00
144 Orestes Destrade 1.00
145 Jose Guzman 1.00
146 Chad Curtis 1.00
147 Cal Eldred 1.00
148 Willie Greene 1.00
149 Tommy Greene 1.00
150 Erik Hanson 1.00
151 Bob Welch 1.00
152 John Jaha 1.00
153 Harold Baines 1.00
154 Randy Johnson 5.00
155 Al Martin 1.00
156 *J.T. Snow* 3.00
157 Mike Mussina 5.00
158 Ruben Sierra 1.00
159 Dean Palmer 1.00
160 Steve Avery 1.00
161 Julio Franco 1.00
162 Dave Winfield 4.00
163 Tim Salmon 3.00
164 Tom Henke 1.00
165 Mo Vaughn 4.00
166 John Smoltz 1.50
167 Danny Tartabull 1.00
168 Delino DeShields 1.00
169 Charlie Hough 1.00
170 Paul O'Neill 1.00
171 Darren Daulton 1.00
172 Jack McDowell 1.00
173 Junior Felix 1.00
174 Jimmy Key 1.00
175 George Bell 1.00
176 Mike Stanton 1.00
177 Len Dykstra 1.00
178 Norm Charlton 1.00
179 Eric Anthony 1.00
180 Bob Dibble 1.00
181 Otis Nixon 1.00
182 Randy Myers 1.00
183 Tim Raines 1.00
184 Orel Hershiser 1.25
185 Andy Van Slyke 1.00
186 *Mike Lansing* 2.00
187 Ray Lankford 1.00
188 Mike Morgan 1.00
189 Moises Alou 2.00
190 Edgar Martinez 1.00
191 John Franco 1.00
192 Robin Yount 7.50
193 Bob Tewksbury 1.00
194 Jay Bell 1.00
195 Luis Gonzalez 1.00
196 Dave Fleming 1.00
197 Mike Greenwell 1.00
198 David Nied 1.00
199 Mike Piazza 25.00

1993 Finest Refractors

This parallel insert set comprises each of the 199 cards from the regular Topps Finest set recreated with refracting foil using the metallization enhancement process. One refracting foil card was inserted in every nine packs, on average. Estimated production is about 250 of each card.

MT

Complete Set (199): 8000.
Common Player: 20.00
1 Dave Justice 45.00
2 Lou Whitaker 20.00
3 Bryan Harvey 20.00
4 Carlos Garcia 20.00
5 Sid Fernandez 20.00
6 Brett Butler 20.00
7 Scott Cooper 20.00
8 B.J. Surhoff 20.00
9 Steve Finley 20.00
10 Curt Schilling 40.00
11 Jeff Bagwell 150.00
12 Alex Cole 20.00
13 John Olerud 30.00
14 John Smiley 20.00
15 Bip Roberts 20.00
16 Albert Belle 40.00
17 Duane Ward 20.00
18 Alan Trammell 25.00
19 Andy Benes 20.00
20 Reggie Sanders 20.00
21 Todd Zeile 20.00
22 Rick Aguilera 20.00
23 Dave Hollins 20.00
24 Jose Rijo 20.00
25 Matt Williams 40.00
26 Sandy Alomar 20.00
27 Alex Fernandez 20.00
28 Ozzie Smith 200.00
29 Ramon Martinez 20.00
30 Bernie Williams 40.00
31 Gary Sheffield 40.00
32 Eric Karros 20.00
33 Frank Viola 20.00
34 Kevin Young 20.00
35 Ken Hill 20.00
36 Tony Fernandez 20.00
37 Tim Wakefield 20.00
38 John Kruk 20.00
39 Chris Sabo 20.00
40 Marquis Grissom 20.00
41 Glenn Davis 20.00
42 Jeff Montgomery 20.00
43 Kenny Lofton 20.00
44 John Burkett 20.00
45 Darryl Hamilton 20.00
46 Jim Abbott 20.00
47 Ivan Rodriguez 150.00
48 Eric Young 20.00
49 Mitch Williams 20.00
50 Harold Reynolds 20.00
51 Brian Harper 20.00
52 Rafael Palmeiro 60.00
53 Bret Saberhagen 20.00
54 Jeff Conine 20.00
55 Ivan Calderon 20.00
56 Juan Guzman 20.00
57 Carlos Baerga 20.00
58 Charles Nagy 20.00
59 Wally Joyner 20.00
60 Charlie Hayes 20.00
61 Shane Mack 20.00
62 Pete Harnisch 20.00
63 George Brett 200.00
64 Lance Johnson 20.00
65 Ben McDonald 20.00
66 Bobby Bonilla 20.00
67 Terry Steinbach 20.00
68 Ron Gant 20.00
69 Doug Jones 20.00
70 Paul Molitor 150.00
71 Brady Anderson 20.00
72 Chuck Finley 20.00
73 Mark Grace 60.00
74 Mike Devereaux 20.00
75 Tony Phillips 20.00
76 Chuck Knoblauch 20.00
77 Tony Gwynn 200.00
78 Kevin Appier 20.00
79 Sammy Sosa 250.00
80 Mickey Tettleton 20.00
81 Felix Jose 20.00
82 Mark Langston 20.00
83 Gregg Jefferies 20.00
84 Andre Dawson (AS) 30.00
85 Greg Maddux (AS) 250.00
86 Rickey Henderson (AS) 75.00
87 Tom Glavine (AS) 30.00
88 Roberto Alomar (AS) 60.00
89 Darryl Strawberry (AS) 20.00
90 Wade Boggs (AS) 45.00
91 Bo Jackson (AS) 35.00
92 Mark McGwire (AS) 600.00
93 Robin Ventura (AS) 20.00
94 Joe Carter (AS) 20.00
95 Lee Smith (AS) 20.00
96 Cal Ripken, Jr. (AS) 600.00
97 Larry Walker (AS) 30.00
98 Don Mattingly (AS) 200.00
99 Jose Canseco (AS) 60.00
100 Dennis Eckersley (AS) 20.00
101 Terry Pendleton (AS) 20.00
102 Frank Thomas (AS) 250.00
103 Barry Bonds (AS) 200.00
104 Roger Clemens 200.00
105 Ryne Sandberg (AS) 150.00
106 Fred McGriff (AS) 20.00
107 Nolan Ryan (AS) 600.00
108 Will Clark (AS) 30.00
109 Pat Listach (AS) 20.00
110 Ken Griffey, Jr. (AS) 600.00
111 Cecil Fielder (AS) 20.00
112 Kirby Puckett (AS) 200.00
113 Dwight Gooden (AS) 20.00
114 Barry Larkin (AS) 30.00
115 David Cone (AS) 25.00
116 Juan Gonzalez (AS) 150.00
117 Kent Hrbek 20.00
118 Tim Wallach 20.00
119 Craig Biggio 20.00
120 Bobby Kelly 20.00
121 Greg Olson 20.00
122 Eddie Murray 100.00
123 Wil Cordero 20.00
124 Jay Buhner 20.00
125 Carlton Fisk 150.00
126 Eric Davis 20.00
127 Doug Drabek 20.00
128 Ozzie Guillen 20.00
129 John Wetteland 20.00
130 Andres Galarraga 20.00
131 Ken Caminiti 20.00
132 Tom Candiotti 20.00
133 Pat Borders 20.00
134 Kevin Brown 25.00
135 Travis Fryman 20.00
136 Kevin Mitchell 20.00
137 Greg Swindell 20.00
138 Benny Santiago 20.00
139 Reggie Jefferson 20.00
140 Chris Bosio 20.00
141 Deion Sanders 25.00
142 Scott Erickson 20.00
143 Howard Johnson 20.00

144 Orestes Destrade 20.00
145 Jose Guzman 20.00
146 Chad Curtis 20.00
147 Cal Eldred 20.00
148 Willie Greene 20.00
149 Tommy Greene 20.00
150 Erik Hanson 20.00
151 Bob Welch 20.00
152 John Jaha 20.00
153 Harold Baines 20.00
154 Randy Johnson 75.00
155 Al Martin 20.00
156 J.T. Snow 25.00
157 Mike Mussina 60.00
158 Ruben Sierra 20.00
159 Dean Palmer 20.00
160 Steve Avery 20.00
161 Julio Franco 20.00
162 Dave Winfield 150.00
163 Tim Salmon 30.00
164 Tom Henke 20.00
165 Mo Vaughn 50.00
166 John Smoltz 25.00
167 Danny Tartabull 20.00
168 Delino DeShields 20.00
169 Charlie Hough 20.00
170 Paul O'Neill 20.00
171 Darren Daulton 20.00
172 Jack McDowell 20.00
173 Junior Felix 20.00
174 Jimmy Key 20.00
175 George Bell 20.00
176 Mike Stanton 20.00
177 Len Dykstra 20.00
178 Norm Charlton 20.00
179 Eric Anthony 20.00
180 Bob Dibble 20.00
181 Otis Nixon 20.00
182 Randy Myers 20.00
183 Tim Raines 20.00
184 Orel Hershiser 20.00
185 Andy Van Slyke 20.00
186 Mike Lansing 25.00
187 Ray Lankford 20.00
188 Mike Morgan 20.00
189 Moises Alou 25.00
190 Edgar Martinez 20.00
191 John Franco 20.00
192 Robin Yount 200.00
193 Bob Tewksbury 20.00
194 Jay Bell 20.00
195 Luis Gonzalez 20.00
196 Dave Fleming 20.00
197 Mike Greenwell 20.00
198 David Nied 20.00
199 Mike Piazza 300.00

1993 Finest Jumbo All-Stars

These 4-1/2" x 6" cards were produced using the chromium metallization process. Each 18-pack Finest box contains one of the All-Star jumbo cards. Based on '93 Finest production, it is estimated fewer than 1,500 of each were issued.

MT
Complete Set (33): 100.00
Common Player: 1.00
84 Andre Dawson 1.25
85 Greg Maddux 7.50
86 Rickey Henderson 3.00
87 Tom Glavine 1.50
88 Roberto Alomar 2.50
89 Darryl Strawberry 1.00
90 Wade Boggs 2.50
91 Bo Jackson 1.00
92 Mark McGwire 12.50
93 Robin Ventura 1.00
94 Joe Carter 1.00
95 Lee Smith 1.00
96 Cal Ripken, Jr. 12.50
97 Larry Walker 2.00
98 Don Mattingly 7.50
99 Jose Canseco 2.00
100 Dennis Eckersley 1.00
101 Terry Pendleton 1.00
102 Frank Thomas 7.50
103 Barry Bonds 5.00
104 Roger Clemens 5.00
105 Ryne Sandberg 4.00
106 Fred McGriff 1.00
107 Nolan Ryan 12.50
108 Will Clark 2.00
109 Pat Listach 1.00
110 Ken Griffey, Jr. 12.50
111 Cecil Fielder 1.00
112 Kirby Puckett 5.00
113 Dwight Gooden 1.00
114 Barry Larkin 1.25
115 David Cone 1.00
116 Juan Gonzalez 4.00

1994 Finest Pre-Production

Forty cards premiering the upcoming 1994 Topps Finest set were issued as a random insert in packs of Topps Series 2 regular-issue cards. The promos are in the same format as the regular-issue Finest cards and share the same card numbers. On back there is a red "Pre-Production" notice printed diagonally over the statistics.

MT
Complete Set (40): 60.00
Common Player: 1.50
22 Deion Sanders 2.50
23 Jose Offerman 1.50
26 Alex Fernandez 1.50
31 Steve Finley 1.50
35 Andres Galarraga 1.50
43 Reggie Sanders 1.50
47 Dave Hollins 1.50
52 David Cone 1.50
59 Dante Bichette 1.50
61 Orlando Merced 1.50
62 Brian McRae 1.50
66 Mike Mussina 2.50
76 Mike Stanley 1.50
78 Mark McGwire 10.00
79 Pat Listach 1.50
82 Dwight Gooden 1.75
84 Phil Plantier 1.50
90 Jeff Russell 1.50
92 Gregg Jefferies 1.50
93 Jose Guzman 1.50
100 John Smoltz 1.75
102 Jim Thome 1.50
121 Moises Alou 2.00
125 Devon White 1.50
126 Ivan Rodriguez 3.50
130 Dave Magadan 1.50
136 Ozzie Smith 7.50
141 Chris Hoiles 1.50
149 Jim Abbott 1.50
151 Bill Swift 1.50
154 Edgar Martinez 1.50
157 J.T. Snow 1.75
159 Alan Trammell 1.75
163 Roberto Kelly 1.50
166 Scott Erickson 1.50
168 Scott Cooper 1.50
169 Rod Beck 1.50
177 Dean Palmer 1.50
182 Todd Van Poppel 1.50
185 Paul Sorrento 1.50

1994 Finest

The 1994 Finest set comprises two series of 220 cards each; subsets of 20 superstars and 20 top rookies are featured in each series. Each card has a metallic look to it, using Topps Finest technology. Backs picture the player on the top half and statistics on the bottom. Baseball's Finest was limited to 4,000 cases and available to dealers through an allocation process, based on their sales the previous year. Along with the regular-issue set, there was a parallel set, called Refractors, of 440 cards and a 4 x 6-inch version of the 80 subset cards.

MT
Complete Set (440): 100.00
Common Player: .50
Refractors: 3X
Series 1 or 2 Pack (7): 2.50
Series 1 or 2 Wax Box (24): 50.00
1 Mike Piazza 8.00
2 Kevin Stocker .50
3 Greg McMichael .50
4 Jeff Conine .50
5 Rene Arocha .50
6 Aaron Sele .50
7 Brent Gates .50
8 Chuck Carr .50
9 Kirk Rueter .50
10 Mike Lansing .50
11 Al Martin .50
12 Jason Bere .50
13 Troy Neel .50
14 Armando Reynoso .50
15 Jeromy Burnitz .50
16 Rich Amaral .50
17 David McCarty .50
18 Tim Salmon 1.00
19 Steve Cooke .50
20 Wil Cordero .50
21 Kevin Tapani .50
22 Deion Sanders .75
23 Jose Offerman .50
24 Mark Langston .50
25 Ken Hill .50
26 Alex Fernandez .50
27 Jeff Blauser .50
28 Royce Clayton .50
29 Brad Ausmus .50
30 Ryan Bowen .50
31 Steve Finley .50
32 Charlie Hayes .50
33 Jeff Kent .50
34 Mike Henneman .50
35 Andres Galarraga .50
36 Wayne Kirby .50
37 Joe Oliver .50
38 Terry Steinbach .50
39 Ryan Thompson .50
40 Luis Alicea .50
41 Randy Velarde .50
42 Bob Tewksbury .50
43 Reggie Sanders .50
44 Brian Williams .50
45 Joe Orsulak .50
46 Jose Lind .50
47 Dave Hollins .50
48 Graeme Lloyd .50
49 Jim Gott .50
50 Andre Dawson 1.00
51 Steve Buechele .50
52 David Cone .50
53 Ricky Gutierrez .50
54 Lance Johnson .50
55 Tino Martinez .50
56 Phil Hiatt .50
57 Carlos Garcia .50
58 Danny Darwin .50
59 Dante Bichette .50
60 Scott Kamieniecki .50
61 Orlando Merced .50
62 Brian McRae .50
63 Pat Kelly .50
64 Tom Henke .50
65 Jeff King .50
66 Mike Mussina 2.00
67 Tim Pugh .50
68 Robby Thompson .50
69 Paul O'Neill .50
70 Hal Morris .50
71 Ron Karkovice .50
72 Joe Girardi .50
73 Eduardo Perez .50
74 Raul Mondesi 1.00
75 Mike Gallego .50
76 Mike Stanley .50
77 Kevin Roberson .50
78 Mark McGwire 10.00
79 Pat Listach .50
80 Eric Davis .50
81 Mike Bordick .50
82 Dwight Gooden .50
83 Mike Moore .50
84 Phil Plantier .50
85 Darren Lewis .50
86 Rick Wilkins .50
87 Darryl Strawberry .50
88 Rob Dibble .50
89 Greg Vaughn .50
90 Jeff Russell .50
91 Mark Lewis .50
92 Gregg Jefferies .50
93 Jose Guzman .50
94 Kenny Rogers .50
95 Mark Lemke .50
96 Mike Morgan .50
97 Andujar Cedeno .50
98 Orel Hershiser .50
99 Greg Swindell .50
100 John Smoltz .65
101 Pedro Martinez .50
102 Jim Thome .50
103 David Segui .50
104 Charles Nagy .50
105 Shane Mack .50
106 John Jaha .50
107 Tom Candiotti .50
108 David Wells .75
109 Bobby Jones .50
110 Bob Hamelin .50
111 Bernard Gilkey .50
112 Chili Davis .50
113 Todd Stottlemyre .50
114 Derek Bell .50
115 Mark McLemore .50

#	Player	MT
116	Mark Whiten	.50
117	Mike Devereaux	.50
118	Terry Pendleton	.50
119	Pat Meares	.50
120	Pete Harnisch	.50
121	Moises Alou	.75
122	Jay Buhner	.50
123	Wes Chamberlain	.50
124	Mike Perez	.50
125	Devon White	.50
126	Ivan Rodriguez	2.50
127	Don Slaught	.50
128	John Valentin	.50
129	Jaime Navarro	.50
130	Dave Magadan	.50
131	Brady Anderson	.50
132	Juan Guzman	.50
133	John Wetteland	.50
134	Dave Stewart	.50
135	Scott Servais	.50
136	Ozzie Smith	5.00
137	Darrin Fletcher	.50
138	Jose Mesa	.50
139	Wilson Alvarez	.50
140	Pete Incaviglia	.50
141	Chris Hoiles	.50
142	Darryl Hamilton	.50
143	Chuck Finley	.50
144	Archi Cianfrocco	.50
145	Bill Wegman	.50
146	Joey Cora	.50
147	Darrell Whitmore	.50
148	David Hulse	.50
149	Jim Abbott	.50
150	Curt Schilling	.75
151	Bill Swift	.50
152	Tommy Greene	.50
153	Roberto Mejia	.50
154	Edgar Martinez	.50
155	Roger Pavlik	.50
156	Randy Tomlin	.50
157	J.T. Snow	.50
158	Bob Welch	.50
159	Alan Trammell	.50
160	Ed Sprague	.50
161	Ben McDonald	.50
162	Derrick May	.50
163	Roberto Kelly	.50
164	Bryan Harvey	.50
165	Ron Gant	.50
166	Scott Erickson	.50
167	Anthony Young	.50
168	Scott Cooper	.50
169	Rod Beck	.50
170	John Franco	.50
171	Gary DiSarcina	.50
172	Dave Fleming	.50
173	Wade Boggs	1.50
174	Kevin Appier	.50
175	Jose Bautista	.50
176	Wally Joyner	.50
177	Dean Palmer	.50
178	Tony Phillips	.50
179	John Smiley	.50
180	Charlie Hough	.50
181	Scott Fletcher	.50
182	Todd Van Poppel	.50
183	Mike Blowers	.50
184	Willie McGee	.50
185	Paul Sorrento	.50
186	Eric Young	.50
187	Bret Barberie	.50
188	Manuel Lee	.50
189	Jeff Branson	.50
190	Jim Deshaies	.50
191	Ken Caminiti	.50
192	Tim Raines	.50
193	Joe Grahe	.50
194	Hipolito Pichardo	.50
195	Denny Neagle	.50
196	Jeff Gardner	.50
197	Mike Benjamin	.50
198	Milt Thompson	.50
199	Bruce Ruffin	.50
200	Chris Hammond	.50
201	Tony Gwynn	6.00
202	Robin Ventura	.50
203	Frank Thomas	6.00
204	Kirby Puckett	5.00
205	Roberto Alomar	2.50
206	Dennis Eckersley	.50
207	Joe Carter	.50
208	Albert Belle	1.50
209	Greg Maddux	7.00
210	Ryne Sandberg	3.00
211	Juan Gonzalez	3.00
212	Jeff Bagwell	2.50
213	Randy Johnson	3.00
214	Matt Williams	1.00
215	Dave Winfield	3.00
216	Larry Walker	1.00
217	Roger Clemens	5.00
218	Kenny Lofton	.50
219	Cecil Fielder	.50
220	Darren Daulton	.50
221	John Olerud	.75
222	Jose Canseco	2.00
223	Rickey Henderson	3.00
224	Fred McGriff	.50
225	Gary Sheffield	1.50
226	Jack McDowell	.50
227	Rafael Palmeiro	1.50
228	Travis Fryman	.50
229	Marquis Grissom	.50
230	Barry Bonds	5.00
231	Carlos Baerga	.50
232	Ken Griffey, Jr.	10.00
233	Dave Justice	.75
234	Bobby Bonilla	.50
235	Cal Ripken	10.00
236	Sammy Sosa	6.00
237	Len Dykstra	.50
238	Will Clark	1.00
239	Paul Molitor	3.50
240	Barry Larkin	1.00
241	Bo Jackson	.75
242	Mitch Williams	.50
243	Ron Darling	.50
244	Darryl Kile	.50
245	Geronimo Berroa	.50
246	Gregg Olson	.50
247	Brian Harper	.50
248	Rheal Cormier	.50
249	Rey Sanchez	.50
250	Jeff Fassero	.50
251	Sandy Alomar	.50
252	Chris Bosio	.50
253	Andy Stankiewicz	.50
254	Harold Baines	.50
255	Andy Ashby	.50
256	Tyler Green	.50
257	Kevin Brown	.75
258	Mo Vaughn	2.50
259	Mike Harkey	.50
260	Dave Henderson	.50
261	Kent Hrbek	.50
262	Darrin Jackson	.50
263	Bob Wickman	.50
264	Spike Owen	.50
265	Todd Jones	.50
266	Pat Borders	.50
267	Tom Glavine	1.25
268	Dave Nilsson	.50
269	Rich Batchelor	.50
270	Delino DeShields	.50
271	Felix Fermin	.50
272	Orestes Destrade	.50
273	Mickey Morandini	.50
274	Otis Nixon	.50
275	Ellis Burks	.50
276	Greg Gagne	.50
277	John Doherty	.50
278	Julio Franco	.50
279	Bernie Williams	2.00
280	Rick Aguilera	.50
281	Mickey Tettleton	.50
282	David Nied	.50
283	Johnny Ruffin	.50
284	Dan Wilson	.50
285	Omar Vizquel	.50
286	Willie Banks	.50
287	Erik Pappas	.50
288	Cal Eldred	.50
289	Bobby Witt	.50
290	Luis Gonzalez	.75
291	Greg Pirkl	.50
292	Alex Cole	.50
293	Ricky Bones	.50
294	Denis Boucher	.50
295	John Burkett	.50
296	Steve Trachsel	.50
297	Ricky Jordan	.50
298	Mark Dewey	.50
299	Jimmy Key	.50
300	Mike MacFarlane	.50
301	Tim Belcher	.50
302	Carlos Reyes	.50
303	Greg Harris	.50
304	*Brian Anderson*	1.00
305	Terry Mulholland	.50
306	Felix Jose	.50
307	Darren Holmes	.50
308	Jose Rijo	.50
309	Paul Wagner	.50
310	Bob Scanlan	.50
311	Mike Jackson	.50
312	Jose Vizcaino	.50
313	Rob Butler	.50
314	Kevin Seitzer	.50
315	Geronimo Pena	.50
316	Hector Carrasco	.50
317	Eddie Murray	3.00
318	Roger Salkeld	.50
319	Todd Hundley	.50
320	Danny Jackson	.50
321	Kevin Young	.50
322	Mike Greenwell	.50
323	Kevin Mitchell	.50
324	Chuck Knoblauch	.50
325	Danny Tartabull	.50
326	Vince Coleman	.50
327	Marvin Freeman	.50
328	Andy Benes	.50
329	Mike Kelly	.50
330	Karl Rhodes	.50
331	Allen Watson	.50
332	Damion Easley	.50
333	Reggie Jefferson	.50
334	Kevin McReynolds	.50
335	Arthur Rhodes	.50
336	Brian Hunter	.50
337	Tom Browning	.50
338	Pedro Munoz	.50
339	Billy Ripken	.50
340	Gene Harris	.50
341	Fernando Vina	.50
342	Sean Berry	.50
343	Pedro Astacio	.50
344	B.J. Surhoff	.50
345	Doug Drabek	.50
346	Jody Reed	.50
347	Ray Lankford	.50
348	Steve Farr	.50
349	Eric Anthony	.50
350	Pete Smith	.50
351	Lee Smith	.50
352	Mariano Duncan	.50
353	Doug Strange	.50
354	Tim Bogar	.50
355	Dave Weathers	.50
356	Eric Karros	.50
357	Randy Myers	.50
358	Chad Curtis	.50
359	Steve Avery	.50
360	Brian Jordan	.50
361	Tim Wallach	.50
362	Pedro Martinez	3.00
363	Bip Roberts	.50
364	Lou Whitaker	.50
365	Luis Polonia	.50
366	Benny Santiago	.50
367	Brett Butler	.50
368	Shawon Dunston	.50
369	Kelly Stinnett	.50
370	Chris Turner	.50
371	Ruben Sierra	.50
372	Greg Harris	.50
373	Xavier Hernandez	.50
374	Howard Johnson	.50
375	Duane Ward	.50
376	Roberto Hernandez	.50
377	Scott Leius	.50
378	Dave Valle	.50
379	Sid Fernandez	.50
380	Doug Jones	.50
381	Zane Smith	.50
382	Craig Biggio	.50
383	Rick White	.50
384	Tom Pagnozzi	.50
385	Chris James	.50
386	Bret Boone	.60
387	Jeff Montgomery	.50
388	Chad Kreuter	.50
389	Greg Hibbard	.50
390	Mark Grace	2.00
391	Phil Leftwich	.50
392	Don Mattingly	6.00
393	Ozzie Guillen	.50
394	Gary Gaetti	.50
395	Erik Hanson	.50
396	Scott Brosius	.50
397	Tom Gordon	.50
398	Bill Gullickson	.50
399	Matt Mieske	.50
400	Pat Hentgen	.50
401	Walt Weiss	.50
402	Greg Blosser	.50
403	Stan Javier	.50
404	Doug Henry	.50
405	Ramon Martinez	.50
406	Frank Viola	.50
407	Mike Hampton	.50
408	Andy Van Slyke	.50
409	Bobby Ayala	.50
410	Todd Zeile	.50
411	Jay Bell	.50
412	Denny Martinez	.50
413	Mark Portugal	.50
414	Bobby Munoz	.50
415	Kirt Manwaring	.50
416	John Kruk	.50
417	Trevor Hoffman	.50
418	Chris Sabo	.50
419	Bret Saberhagen	.50
420	Chris Nabholz	.50
421	James Mouton	.50
422	Tony Tarasco	.50
423	Carlos Delgado	2.50
424	Rondell White	1.00
425	Javier Lopez	.50
426	*Chan Ho Park*	1.50
427	Cliff Floyd	.50
428	Dave Staton	.50
429	J.R. Phillips	.50
430	Manny Ramirez	3.00
431	Kurt Abbott	.50
432	Melvin Nieves	.50
433	Alex Gonzalez	.50
434	Rick Helling	.50
435	Danny Bautista	.50
436	Matt Walbeck	.50
437	Ryan Klesko	.50
438	Steve Karsay	.50
439	Salomon Torres	.50
440	Scott Ruffcorn	.50

1994 Finest Refractors

It takes an experienced eye and good light to detect a Refractor parallel card from a regular-issue Topps Finest. The Refractor utilizes a variation of the Finest metallic printing process to produce rainbow-effect highlights on the card front. The Refractors share the checklist with the regular-issue Finest and were inserted at a rate of about one per 10 packs.

	MT
Complete Set (440):	600.00
Common Player:	1.50
Stars/Rookies:	3X

(See 1994 Finest for checklist and base card prices.)

1994 Finest Bronze

This three-card set was included as part of the purchase of a 1994 Topps Stadium Club Members

Only set, but was also made available on a limited basis via newspaper ads. The cards feature a version of Topps' Finest technology with the multi-colored front design laminated to a bronze base by a heavy lucite overlay. Backs are engraved in black on bronze and contain complete major and minor league stats and a few personal data. The Finest bronze cards are slightly larger than current standard suze, measuring 2-3/4" x 3-3/4".

		MT
Complete Set (3):		75.00
Common Player:		25.00
1	Barry Bonds	30.00
2	Ken Griffey, Jr.	35.00
3	Frank Thomas	20.00

1994 Finest Superstar Jumbos

Identical in format to the Superstars subset in the Finest issue, these cards measure about 4" x 5-1/2" and were distributed one per box in Finest foil packs. Backs carry a card number under the banner with the player's name and position. Since there were 20 rookies and 20 superstars from both Series 1 and Series 2, this is an 80-card set.

		MT
Complete Set (80):		250.00
Common Player:		1.00
1	Mike Piazza	20.00
2	Kevin Stocker	1.00
3	Greg McMichael	1.00
4	Jeff Conine	1.00
5	Rene Arocha	1.00
6	Aaron Sele	1.00
7	Brent Gates	1.00
8	Chuck Carr	1.00
9	Kirk Rueter	1.00
10	Mike Lansing	1.00
11	Al Martin	1.00
12	Jason Bere	1.00
13	Troy Neel	1.00
14	Armando Reynoso	1.00
15	Jeromy Burnitz	1.00
16	Rich Amaral	1.00
17	David McCarty	1.00
18	Tim Salmon	2.00
19	Steve Cooke	1.00
20	Wil Cordero	1.00
201	Tony Gwynn	15.00
202	Robin Ventura	1.00
203	Frank Thomas	17.50
204	Kirby Puckett	17.50
205	Roberto Alomar	6.00
206	Dennis Eckersley	1.00
207	Joe Carter	1.00
208	Albert Belle	3.00
209	Greg Maddux	17.50
210	Ryne Sandberg	7.50
211	Juan Gonzalez	7.50
212	Jeff Bagwell	6.00
213	Randy Johnson	5.00
214	Matt Williams	2.00
215	Dave Winfield	5.00
216	Larry Walker	2.50
217	Roger Clemens	7.50
218	Kenny Lofton	1.00
219	Cecil Fielder	1.00
220	Darren Daulton	1.00
221	John Olerud	1.00
222	Jose Canseco	4.00
223	Rickey Henderson	4.00
224	Fred McGriff	1.00
225	Gary Sheffield	2.00
226	Jack McDowell	1.00
227	Rafael Palmeiro	2.50
228	Travis Fryman	1.00
229	Marquis Grissom	1.00
230	Barry Bonds	12.50
231	Carlos Baerga	1.00
232	Ken Griffey Jr.	25.00
233	Dave Justice	3.00
234	Bobby Bonilla	1.00
235	Cal Ripken	25.00
236	Sammy Sosa	15.00
237	Len Dykstra	1.00
238	Will Clark	2.50
239	Paul Molitor	5.00
240	Barry Larkin	2.00
421	James Mouton	1.00
422	Tony Tarasco	1.00
423	Carlos Delgado	1.50
424	Rondell White	1.50
425	Javier Lopez	1.00
426	Chan Ho Park	2.00
427	Cliff Floyd	1.50
428	Dave Staton	1.00
429	J.R. Phillips	1.00
430	Manny Ramirez	10.00
431	Kurt Abbott	1.00
432	Melvin Nieves	1.00
433	Alex Gonzalez	1.00
434	Rick Helling	1.00
435	Danny Bautista	1.00
436	Matt Walbeck	1.00
437	Ryan Klesko	1.00
438	Steve Karsay	1.00
439	Salomon Torres	1.00
440	Scott Ruffcorn	1.00

1994 Finest Superstar Sampler

This special version of 45 of the biggest-name stars from the 1994 Topps Finest set was issued in a three-card cello pack with the same player's '94 Bowman and Stadium Club cards. The packs were available only in 1994 Topps retail factory sets. Cards are identical to the regular-issue Finest cards except for a round, red "Topps Superstar Sampler" logo printed at bottom center on back.

		MT
Complete Set (45):		275.00
Common Player:		3.00
1	Mike Piazza	22.50
18	Tim Salmon	4.50
35	Andres Galarraga	3.00
74	Raul Mondesi	4.50
92	Gregg Jefferies	3.00
201	Tony Gwynn	12.50
203	Frank Thomas	20.00
204	Kirby Puckett	12.50
205	Roberto Alomar	5.00
207	Joe Carter	3.00
208	Albert Belle	4.50
209	Greg Maddux	20.00
210	Ryne Sandberg	12.50
211	Juan Gonzalez	10.00
212	Jeff Bagwell	10.00
213	Randy Johnson	5.00
214	Matt Williams	4.50
216	Larry Walker	4.50
217	Roger Clemens	7.50
219	Cecil Fielder	3.00
220	Darren Daulton	3.00
221	John Olerud	3.00
222	Jose Canseco	4.50
224	Fred McGriff	3.00
225	Gary Sheffield	4.50
226	Jack McDowell	3.00
227	Rafael Palmeiro	4.50
229	Marquis Grissom	3.00
230	Barry Bonds	15.00
231	Carlos Baerga	3.00
232	Ken Griffey Jr.	30.00
233	Dave Justice	4.50
234	Bobby Bonilla	3.00
235	Cal Ripken Jr.	30.00
237	Len Dykstra	3.00
238	Will Clark	4.50
239	Paul Molitor	6.00
240	Barry Larkin	3.00
258	Mo Vaughn	5.00
267	Tom Glavine	4.50
390	Mark Grace	5.00
392	Don Mattingly	20.00
408	Andy Van Slyke	3.00
427	Cliff Floyd	3.00
430	Manny Ramirez	6.00

1995 Finest

In its third year Finest baseball was reduced to a 220-card base set. All cards feature the chrome-printing technology associated with the Finest logo and include a peel-off plastic protector on the card front. Backgrounds are green with gold pinstripes. Behind the action photo at center is a large diamond with each corner intersected by a silver semi-circle. On the Finest Rookies subset which makes up the first 30 cards of the issue, the diamond has a graduated pink to orange center, with flecks of red throughout. Veterans cards have a graduated blue to purple center of the diamond. On the rookies cards there is a teal brand name at top, while the vets show a gold "FINEST". Backs repeat the front background motif in shades of green. There is a player photo at right, with biographical data, 1994 and career stats, and a "Finest Moment" career highlight at left. Finest was sold in seven-card packs with a suggested retail price of $4.99.

		MT
Complete Set (220):		75.00
Common Player:		.25
Refractors:		4X
Series 1 Pack (7):		2.00
Series 1 Wax Box (24):		45.00
Series 2 Pack (7):		2.00
Series 2 Wax Box (24):		35.00
1	Raul Mondesi (Rookie Theme)	.75
2	Kurt Abbott (Rookie Theme)	.25
3	Chris Gomez (Rookie Theme)	.25
4	Manny Ramirez (Rookie Theme)	2.50
5	Rondell White (Rookie Theme)	.50
6	William Van Landingham (Rookie Theme)	.25
7	Jon Lieber (Rookie Theme)	.25
8	Ryan Klesko (Rookie Theme)	.25
9	John Hudek (Rookie Theme)	.25
10	Joey Hamilton (Rookie Theme)	.25
11	Bob Hamelin (Rookie Theme)	.25
12	Brian Anderson (Rookie Theme)	.25
13	Mike Lieberthal (Rookie Theme)	.35
14	Rico Brogna (Rookie Theme)	.25
15	Rusty Greer (Rookie Theme)	.25
16	Carlos Delgado (Rookie Theme)	.75
17	Jim Edmonds (Rookie Theme)	.75
18	Steve Trachsel (Rookie Theme)	.25
19	Matt Walbeck (Rookie Theme)	.25
20	Armando Benitez (Rookie Theme)	.25
21	Steve Karsay (Rookie Theme)	.25
22	Jose Oliva (Rookie Theme)	.25
23	Cliff Floyd (Rookie Theme)	.30

24 Kevin Foster (Rookie Theme) .25
25 Javier Lopez (Rookie Theme) .25
26 Jose Valentin (Rookie Theme) .25
27 James Mouton (Rookie Theme) .25
28 Hector Carrasco (Rookie Theme) .25
29 Orlando Miller (Rookie Theme) .25
30 Garret Anderson (Rookie Theme) .25
31 Marvin Freeman .25
32 Brett Butler .25
33 Roberto Kelly .25
34 Rod Beck .25
35 Jose Rijo .25
36 Edgar Martinez .25
37 Jim Thome .25
38 Rick Wilkins .25
39 Wally Joyner .25
40 Wil Cordero .25
41 Tommy Greene .25
42 Travis Fryman .25
43 Don Slaught .25
44 Brady Anderson .25
45 Matt Williams .75
46 Rene Arocha .25
47 Rickey Henderson 1.00
48 Mike Mussina 1.00
49 Greg McMichael .25
50 Jody Reed .25
51 Tino Martinez .25
52 Dave Clark .25
53 John Valentin .25
54 Bret Boone .25
55 Walt Weiss .25
56 Kenny Lofton .25
57 Scott Leius .25
58 Eric Karros .25
59 John Olerud .25
60 Chris Hoiles .25
61 Sandy Alomar .25
62 Tim Wallach .25
63 Cal Eldred .25
64 Tom Glavine .35
65 Mark Grace .75
66 Rey Sanchez .25
67 Bobby Ayala .25
68 Dante Bichette .25
69 Andres Galarraga .25
70 Chuck Carr .25
71 Bobby Witt .25
72 Steve Avery .25
73 Bobby Jones .25
74 Delino DeShields .25
75 Kevin Tapani .25
76 Randy Johnson 2.00
77 David Nied .25
78 Pat Hentgen .25
79 Tim Salmon .75
80 Todd Zeile .25
81 John Wetteland .25
82 Albert Belle 1.00
83 Ben McDonald .25
84 Bobby Munoz .25
85 Bip Roberts .25
86 Mo Vaughn 1.50
87 Chuck Finley .25
88 Chuck Knoblauch .25
89 Frank Thomas 4.00
90 Danny Tartabull .25
91 Dean Palmer .25
92 Len Dykstra .25
93 J.R. Phillips .25
94 Tom Candiotti .25
95 Marquis Grissom .25
96 Barry Larkin .50
97 Bryan Harvey .25
98 Dave Justice .50
99 David Cone .25
100 Wade Boggs 1.00
101 Jason Bere .25
102 Hal Morris .25
103 Fred McGriff .25
104 Bobby Bonilla .25
105 Jay Buhner .25
106 Allen Watson .25
107 Mickey Tettleton .25
108 Kevin Appier .25
109 Ivan Rodriguez 2.00
110 Carlos Garcia .25
111 Andy Benes .25
112 Eddie Murray 2.00
113 Mike Piazza 6.50
114 Greg Vaughn .25
115 Paul Molitor 2.00
116 Terry Steinbach .25
117 Jeff Bagwell 2.00
118 Ken Griffey Jr. 8.00
119 Gary Sheffield .50
120 Cal Ripken Jr. 8.00
121 Jeff Kent .25
122 Jay Bell .25
123 Will Clark .75
124 Cecil Fielder .25
125 Alex Fernandez .25
126 Don Mattingly 5.00
127 Reggie Sanders .25
128 Moises Alou .30
129 Craig Biggio .25
130 Eddie Williams .25
131 John Franco .25
132 John Kruk .25
133 Jeff King .25
134 Royce Clayton .25
135 Doug Drabek .25
136 Ray Lankford .25
137 Roberto Alomar 1.50
138 Todd Hundley .25
139 Alex Cole .25
140 Shawon Dunston .25
141 John Roper .25
142 Mark Langston .25
143 Tom Pagnozzi .25
144 Wilson Alvarez .25
145 Scott Cooper .25
146 Kevin Mitchell .25
147 Mark Whiten .25
148 Jeff Conine .25
149 Chili Davis .25
150 Luis Gonzalez .35
151 Juan Guzman .25
152 Mike Greenwell .25
153 Mike Henneman .25
154 Rick Aguilera .25
155 Dennis Eckersley .25
156 Darrin Fletcher .25
157 Darren Lewis .25
158 Juan Gonzalez 2.50
159 Dave Hollins .25
160 Jimmy Key .25
161 Roberto Hernandez .25
162 Randy Myers .25
163 Joe Carter .25
164 Darren Daulton .25
165 Mike MacFarlane .25
166 Bret Saberhagen .25
167 Kirby Puckett 4.00
168 Lance Johnson .25
169 Mark McGwire 8.00
170 Jose Canseco .75
171 Mike Stanley .25
172 Lee Smith .25
173 Robin Ventura .25
174 Greg Gagne .25
175 Brian McRae .25
176 Mike Bordick .25
177 Rafael Palmeiro .50
178 Kenny Rogers .25
179 Chad Curtis .25
180 Devon White .30
181 Paul O'Neill .25
182 Ken Caminiti .25
183 Dave Nilsson .25
184 Tim Naehring .25
185 Roger Clemens 3.00
186 Otis Nixon .25
187 Tim Raines .25
188 Dennis Martinez .25
189 Pedro Martinez .40
190 Jim Abbott .25
191 Ryan Thompson .25
192 Barry Bonds 3.00
193 Joe Girardi .25
194 Steve Finley .25
195 John Jaha .25
196 Tony Gwynn 4.00
197 Sammy Sosa 4.00
198 John Burkett .25
199 Carlos Baerga .25
200 Ramon Martinez .25
201 Aaron Sele .25
202 Eduardo Perez .25
203 Alan Trammell .25
204 Orlando Merced .25
205 Deion Sanders .30
206 Robb Nen .25
207 Jack McDowell .25
208 Ruben Sierra .25
209 Bernie Williams .50
210 Kevin Seitzer .25
211 Charles Nagy .25
212 Tony Phillips .25
213 Greg Maddux 5.00
214 Jeff Montgomery .25
215 Larry Walker .75
216 Andy Van Slyke .25
217 Ozzie Smith 4.00
218 Geronimo Pena .25
219 Gregg Jefferies .25
220 Lou Whitaker .25

1995 Finest Refractors

A parallel set with a counterpart to each of the 220 cards in the regular Finest emission, the Refractors are printed in a version of the Finest chrome technology that produces a rainbow effect when viewed at the proper angle. The relatively open spaces of the 1995 Finest design make the Refractors easier to spot than the previous years' versions, but just to assist the identification process, Topps placed a small black "REFRACTOR" in the dark green background on the cards' backs, as well. Advertised rate of insertion for the Refractors was about one per 12 packs.

	MT
Complete Set (220):	1100.
Common Player:	2.00
Stars:	4X

(See 1995 Finest for checklist and base card values.)

1995 Finest Bronze League Leaders

Available only by mail directly from Topps, this set features N.L. and A.L. leaders in various batting categories for the 1994 season. Fronts employ Topps' Finest technology with a stained-glass effect in the background, overlaid with a heavy layer of resin. Backs are bronze and feature 1994 stats and highlights embossed in blue. The cards are oversized, measuring 2-3/4" x 3-3/4".

		MT
Complete Set (6):		90.00
Common Player:		10.00
1	Matt Williams	10.00
2	Tony Gwynn	25.00
3	Jeff Bagwell	20.00
4	Ken Griffey Jr.	35.00
5	Paul O'Neill	10.00
6	Frank Thomas	20.00

1995 Finest Flame Throwers

The scarcest of the Finest inserts is the nine-card set of baseball hardest throwing pitchers. Flame Throwers cards are found at an average rate of one per 48 packs. Fronts have a central photo of a pitcher bringing his best heat. Behind the photo is the Flame Throwers typographic logo in tones of red, yellow and orange. Backs have another photo and a bar graph rating the pitcher's skill levels.

		MT
Complete Set (9):		18.00
Common Player:		1.50
1	Jason Bere	1.50
2	Roger Clemens	7.50
3	Juan Guzman	1.50
4	John Hudek	1.50
5	Randy Johnson	4.00
6	Pedro Martinez	3.50
7	Jose Rijo	1.50
8	Bret Saberhagen	1.50
9	John Wetteland	1.50

1995 Finest Power Kings

The emphasis in on youth in this chase set of baseball's top distance threats. Found at a rate of one per 24 packs, on average, the Power Kings inserts have a central photo of the player in batting action. The background, in shades of blue, features lightning strokes. Backs feature another pair of player photos and a bar graph charting the hitter's power skills.

		MT
Complete Set (18):		35.00
Common Player:		.75
1	Bob Hamelin	.75
2	Raul Mondesi	.75
3	Ryan Klesko	.75
4	Carlos Delgado	1.50
5	Manny Ramirez	3.50
6	Mike Piazza	6.00
7	Jeff Bagwell	3.00
8	Mo Vaughn	3.00
9	Frank Thomas	4.00
10	Ken Griffey Jr.	8.00
11	Albert Belle	2.00
12	Sammy Sosa	4.00
13	Dante Bichette	.75
14	Gary Sheffield	.75
15	Matt Williams	.75
16	Fred McGriff	.75
17	Barry Bonds	4.00
18	Cecil Fielder	.75

1995 Finest Update

Players who changed teams through trades or free agent signings and more of the season's rookie player crop are included in the Finest Update series of 110 cards. The cards are numbered contiguously with the base Finest set and share the same design. Once again, Refractor cards were found on an average of once per 12 packs. Finest Update was sold in seven-card packs with a suggested retail price of $4.99.

		MT
Complete Set (110):		25.00
Common Player:		.25
Refractors:		4X
Pack (7):		3.00
Box (24):		50.00
221	Chipper Jones	8.00
222	Benji Gil	.25
223	Tony Phillips	.25
224	Trevor Wilson	.25
225	Tony Tarasco	.25
226	Roberto Petagine	.25
227	Mike MacFarlane	.25
228	*Hideo Nomo*	8.00
229	Mark McLemore	.25
230	Ron Gant	.25
231	Andujar Cedeno	.25
232	*Mike Mimbs*	.25
233	Jim Abbott	.25
234	Ricky Bones	.25
235	Marty Cordova	.50
236	Mark Johnson	.25
237	Marquis Grissom	.25
238	Tom Henke	.25
239	Terry Pendleton	.25
240	John Wetteland	.25
241	Lee Smith	.25
242	Jaime Navarro	.25
243	Luis Alicea	.25
244	Scott Cooper	.25
245	Gary Gaetti	.25
246	Edgardo Alfonzo	.50
247	Brad Clontz	.25
248	Dave Mlicki	.25
249	Dave Winfield	2.00
250	*Mark Grudzielanek*	2.00
251	Alex Gonzalez	.25
252	Kevin Brown	.50
253	Esteban Loaiza	.25
254	Vaughn Eshelman	.25
255	Bill Swift	.25
256	Brian McRae	.25
257	*Bobby Higginson*	3.00
258	Jack McDowell	.25
259	Scott Stahoviak	.25
260	Jon Nunnally	.25
261	Charlie Hayes	.25
262	Jacob Brumfield	.25
263	Chad Curtis	.25
264	Heathcliff Slocumb	.25
265	Mark Whiten	.25
266	Mickey Tettleton	.25
267	Jose Mesa	.25
268	Doug Jones	.25
269	Trevor Hoffman	.25
270	Paul Sorrento	.25
271	Shane Andrews	.25
272	Brett Butler	.25
273	Curtis Goodwin	.25
274	Larry Walker	.75
275	Phil Plantier	.25
276	Ken Hill	.25
277	Vinny Castilla	.25
278	Billy Ashley	.25
279	Derek Jeter	8.00
280	Bob Tewksbury	.25
281	Jose Offerman	.25
282	Glenallen Hill	.25
283	Tony Fernandez	.25
284	Mike Devereaux	.25
285	John Burkett	.25
286	Geronimo Berroa	.25
287	Quilvio Veras	.25
288	Jason Bates	.25
289	Lee Tinsley	.25
290	Derek Bell	.25
291	Jeff Fassero	.25
292	Ray Durham	.25
293	Chad Ogea	.25
294	Bill Pulsipher	.25
295	Phil Nevin	.25
296	*Carlos Perez*	1.00
297	Roberto Kelly	.25
298	Tim Wakefield	.25
299	Jeff Manto	.25
300	Brian Hunter	.25
301	C.J. Nitkowski	.25
302	Dustin Hermanson	.25
303	John Mabry	.25
304	Orel Hershiser	.25
305	Ron Villone	.25
306	Sean Bergman	.25
307	Tom Goodwin	.25
308	Al Reyes	.25
309	Todd Stottlemyre	.25
310	Rich Becker	.25
311	Joey Cora	.25
312	Ed Sprague	.25
313	John Smoltz	.50
314	Frank Castillo	.25
315	Chris Hammond	.25
316	Ismael Valdes	.25
317	Pete Harnisch	.25
318	Bernard Gilkey	.25
319	John Kruk	.25
320	Marc Newfield	.25
321	Brian Johnson	.25
322	Mark Portugal	.25
323	David Hulse	.25
324	Luis Ortiz	.25
325	Mike Benjamin	.25
326	Brian Jordan	.25
327	Shawn Green	1.00
328	Joe Oliver	.25
329	Felipe Lira	.25
330	Andre Dawson	.75

1995 Finest Update Refractors

The special version of Topps' chromium printing process which creates a rainbow effect was applied to a limited number of each card in the Finest Update set to create a parallel Refractor edition. To assist in identification, a small black "REFRACTOR" is printed on the cards' backs, as well. Refractors are found on average once every 12 packs of Finest Update.

	MT
Complete Set (110):	225.00
Common Player:	2.00
Stars:	4X

(See 1995 Finest Update for checklist and base card values.)

1996 Finest

Utilizing three levels of base-card scarcity, the 359-card Finest set comprises 220 Commons (Bronze), 91 Uncommons (Silver) and 49 Rares (Gold). Cards were somewhat randomly assigned a status. Uncommon cards are found one in four packs; Rare cards are seeded one per 24 packs. The set has eight themes. Series 1 themes are Phenoms, Intimidators, Gamers and Sterling, the latter of which consists of star players already included within the first three themes. Series 2 themes are Franchise, Additions, Prodigies and Sterling. Regular-issue cards are not only numbered from 1-359 in the set as a whole, but also numbered within each subset. Finest Refractor parallel cards were also made. Rare Refractor cards are found one every 288 packs (fewer than 150 of each produced), while Uncommon Refractors are found one per 48 packs. Common Refractors are seeded 1:12.

		MT
Complete Set (359):		375.00
Bronze Set (220):		20.00
Common Bronze:		.15
Silver Set (91):		100.00
Typical Silver:		.50
Gold Set (47):		300.00
Typical Gold:		2.50
Series 1 Pack (6):		2.50
Series 1 Wax Box (24):		45.00
Series 2 Pack (6):		2.00
Series 2 Wax Box (24):		30.00
1	Greg Maddux S (Intimidators)	4.50
2	Bernie Williams S (Gamers)	1.25
3	Ivan Rodriguez S (Intimidators)	1.50
4	Marty Cordova G (Phenoms)	2.50
5	Roberto Hernandez (Intimidators)	.15
6	Tony Gwynn G (Gamers)	7.50
7	Barry Larkin S (Sterling)	.75
8	Terry Pendleton (Gamers)	.15
9	Albert Belle G (Sterling)	3.00
10	Ray Lankford S (Gamers)	.50
11	Mike Piazza S (Sterling)	5.00
12	Ken Caminiti (Gamers)	.15
13	Larry Walker S (Intimidators)	1.00
14	Matt Williams S (Intimidators)	.75
15	Dan Miceli (Phenoms)	.15
16	Chipper Jones (Sterling)	2.50
17	John Wetteland (Intimidators)	.15
18	Kirby Puckett G (Sterling)	7.50
19	Tim Naehring (Gamers)	.15
20	Karim Garcia G (Phenoms)	2.50
21	Eddie Murray (Gamers)	.35
22	Tim Salmon S (Intimidators)	.75
23	Kevin Appier (Intimidators)	.15
24	Ken Griffey Jr. (Sterling)	4.00
25	Cal Ripken Jr. G (Gamers)	15.00
26	Brian McRae (Gamers)	.15
27	Pedro Martinez (Intimidators)	.35
28	Brian Jordan (Gamers)	.15
29	Mike Fetters (Intimidators)	.15
30	Carlos Delgado (Phenoms)	.25
31	Shane Reynolds (Intimidators)	.15
32	Terry Steinbach (Gamers)	.15
33	Hideo Nomo G (Sterling)	4.00
34	Mark Leiter (Gamers)	.15
35	Edgar Martinez S (Intimidators)	.50

36 David Segui (Gamers) .15
37 Gregg Jefferies S (Gamers) .50
38 Bill Pulsipher S (Phenoms) .50
39 Ryne Sandberg G (Gamers) 5.00
40 Fred McGriff (Intimidators) .15
41 Shawn Green S (Phenoms) 1.25
42 Jeff Bagwell G (Sterling) 4.00
43 Jim Abbott S (Gamers) .50
44 Glenallen Hill (Intimidators) .15
45 Brady Anderson (Gamers) .15
46 Roger Clemens S (Intimidators) 2.00
47 Jim Thome (Gamers) .15
48 Frank Thomas (Sterling) 1.00
49 Chuck Knoblauch (Gamers) .15
50 Lenny Dykstra (Gamers) .15
51 Jason Isringhausen G (Phenoms) 2.50
52 Rondell White S (Phenoms) .50
53 Tom Pagnozzi (Gamers) .15
54 Dennis Eckersley S (Intimidators) .50
55 Ricky Bones (Gamers) .15
56 David Justice (Intimidators) .25
57 Steve Avery (Gamers) .15
58 Robby Thompson (Gamers) .15
59 Hideo Nomo S (Phenoms) 1.50
60 Gary Sheffield S (Intimidators) .75
61 Tony Gwynn (Sterling) 1.00
62 Will Clark S (Gamers) .75
63 Denny Neagle (Gamers) .15
64 Mo Vaughn G (Intimidators) 3.50
65 Bret Boone S (Gamers) .50
66 Dante Bichette G (Sterling) 2.50
67 Robin Ventura (Gamers) .15
68 Rafael Palmeiro S (Intimidators) .75
69 Carlos Baerga S (Gamers) .50
70 Kevin Seitzer (Gamers) .15
71 Ramon Martinez (Intimidators) .15
72 Tom Glavine S (Gamers) .75
73 Garret Anderson S (Phenoms) .50
74 Mark McGwire G (Intimidators) 15.00
75 Brian Hunter (Phenoms) .15
76 Alan Benes (Phenoms) .15
77 Randy Johnson S (Intimidators) 2.00
78 Jeff King S (Gamers) .50
79 Kirby Puckett S (Intimidators) 3.00
80 Ozzie Guillen (Gamers) .15
81 Kenny Lofton G (Intimidators) 2.50
82 Benji Gil (Phenoms) .15
83 Jim Edmonds G (Gamers) 2.50
84 Cecil Fielder S (Intimidators) .50
85 Todd Hundley (Gamers) .15
86 Reggie Sanders S (Intimidators) .50
87 Pat Hentgen (Gamers) .15
88 Ryan Klesko S (Intimidators) .50
89 Chuck Finley (Gamers) .15
90 Mike Mussina G (Intimidators) 4.00
91 John Valentin S (Intimidators) .50
92 Derek Jeter (Phenoms) 3.00
93 Paul O'Neill (Intimidators) .15
94 Darrin Fletcher (Gamers) .15
95 Manny Ramirez S (Phenoms) 3.00
96 Delino DeShields (Gamers) .15
97 Tim Salmon (Sterling) .25
98 John Olerud (Gamers) .15
99 Vinny Castilla S (Intimidators) .50
100 Jeff Conine G (Gamers) 2.50
101 Tim Wakefield (Gamers) .15
102 Johnny Damon G (Phenoms) 2.50
103 Dave Stevens (Gamers) .15
104 Orlando Merced (Gamers) .15
105 Barry Bonds G (Sterling) 7.50
106 Jay Bell (Gamers) .15
107 John Burkett (Gamers) .15
108 Chris Hoiles (Gamers) .15
109 Carlos Perez S (Phenoms) .50
110 Dave Nilsson (Gamers) .15
111 Rod Beck (Intimidators) .15
112 Craig Biggio S (Gamers) .50
113 Mike Piazza (Intimidators) 3.00
114 Mark Langston (Gamers) .15
115 Juan Gonzalez S (Intimidators) 2.00
116 Rico Brogna (Gamers) .15
117 Jose Canseco G (Intimidators) 3.00
118 Tom Goodwin (Gamers) .15
119 Bryan Rekar (Phenoms) .15
120 David Cone (Intimidators) .15
121 Ray Durham S (Phenoms) .50
122 Andy Pettitte (Phenoms) .35
123 Chili Davis (Intimidators) .15
124 John Smoltz (Gamers) .20
125 Heathcliff Slocumb (Intimidators) .15
126 Dante Bichette (Intimidators) .15
127 C.J. Nitkowski S (Phenoms) .50
128 Alex Gonzalez (Phenoms) .15
129 Jeff Montgomery (Intimidators) .15
130 Raul Mondesi S (Intimidators) .75
131 Denny Martinez (Gamers) .15
132 Mel Rojas (Intimidators) .15
133 Derek Bell (Gamers) .15
134 Trevor Hoffman (Intimidators) .15
135 Ken Griffey Jr. G (Intimidators) 15.00
136 Darren Daulton (Gamers) .15
137 Pete Schourek (Gamers) .15
138 Phil Nevin (Phenoms) .15
139 Andres Galarraga (Intimidators) .15
140 Chad Fonville (Phenoms) .15
141 Chipper Jones G (Phenoms) 12.00
142 Lee Smith S (Intimidators) .50
143 Joe Carter S (Gamers) .50
144 J.T. Snow (Gamers) .15
145 Greg Maddux G (Sterling) 10.00
146 Barry Bonds (Intimidators) .75
147 Orel Hershiser (Gamers) .15
148 Quilvio Veras (Phenoms) .15
149 Will Clark (Sterling) .25
150 Jose Rijo (Gamers) .15
151 Mo Vaughn S (Sterling) 2.00
152 Travis Fryman (Gamers) .15
153 Frank Rodriguez S (Phenoms) .50
154 Alex Fernandez (Gamers) .15
155 Wade Boggs (Gamers) .35
156 Troy Percival (Phenoms) .15
157 Moises Alou (Gamers) .25
158 Javy Lopez (Gamers) .15
159 Jason Giambi (Phenoms) .50
160 Steve Finley S (Gamers) .50
161 Jeff Bagwell S (Intimidators) 3.00
162 Mark McGwire (Sterling) 4.00
163 Eric Karros (Gamers) .15
164 Jay Buhner G (Intimidators) 2.50
165 Cal Ripken Jr. S (Sterling) 6.00
166 Mickey Tettleton (Intimidators) .15
167 Barry Larkin (Intimidators) .20
168 Lyle Mouton S (Phenoms) .50
169 Ruben Sierra (Intimidators) .15
170 Bill Swift (Gamers) .15
171 Sammy Sosa S (Intimidators) 4.50
172 Chad Curtis (Gamers) .15
173 Dean Palmer (Gamers) .15
174 John Franco S (Gamers) .50
175 Bobby Bonilla (Intimidators) .15
176 Greg Colbrunn (Gamers) .15
177 Jose Mesa (Intimidators) .15
178 Mike Greenwell (Gamers) .15
179 Greg Vaughn S (Intimidators) .50
180 Mark Wohlers S (Intimidators) .50
181 Doug Drabek (Gamers) .15
182 Paul O'Neill S (Sterling) .50
183 Wilson Alvarez (Gamers) .15
184 Marty Cordova (Sterling) .15
185 Hal Morris (Gamers) .15
186 Frank Thomas G (Intimidators) 7.50
187 Carlos Garcia (Gamers) .15
188 Albert Belle S (Intimidators) 1.50
189 Mark Grace S (Gamers) 1.25
190 Marquis Grissom (Gamers) .15
191 Checklist .15
192 Chipper Jones G 12.00
193 Will Clark .20
194 Paul Molitor .50
195 Kenny Rogers .15
196 Reggie Sanders .15
197 Roberto Alomar G 4.00
198 Dennis Eckersley G 2.50
199 Raul Mondesi .20
200 Lance Johnson .15
201 Alvin Mormon .15
202 George Arias G 2.50
203 Jack McDowell .15
204 Randy Myers .15
205 Harold Baines .15
206 Marty Cordova .15
207 *Rich Hunter* .15
208 Al Leiter .15
209 Greg Gagne .15
210 Ben McDonald .15
211 Ernie Young S .50
212 Terry Adams .15
213 Paul Sorrento .15
214 Albert Belle .30
215 Mike Blowers .15
216 Jim Edmonds .20
217 Felipe Crespo .15
218 Fred McGriff S .50
219 Shawon Dunston .15
220 Jimmy Haynes .15
221 Jose Canseco .35
222 Eric Davis .15
223 Kimera Bartee S .50
224 Tim Raines .15
225 Tony Phillips .15
226 Charlie Hayes .15
227 Eric Owens .15
228 Roberto Alomar .30
229 Rickey Henderson S 2.00
230 Sterling Hitchcock S .50
231 Bernard Gilkey S .50
232 Hideo Nomo G 4.00
233 Kenny Lofton .15
234 Ryne Sandberg S 1.50
235 Greg Maddux S 4.50
236 Mark McGwire 4.00
237 Jay Buhner .15
238 Craig Biggio .15
239 Todd Stottlemyre S .50
240 Barry Bonds .75
241 Jason Kendall S .50
242 Paul O'Neill S .50
243 Chris Snopek G 2.50
244 Ron Gant .15
245 Paul Wilson .15
246 Todd Hollandsworth .15
247 Todd Zeile .15
248 David Justice .25
249 Tim Salmon G 2.50
250 Moises Alou .20
251 Bob Wolcott .15
252 David Wells .15
253 Juan Gonzalez .60
254 Andres Galarraga .15
255 Dave Hollins .15
256 Devon White S .50
257 Sammy Sosa 1.50
258 Ivan Rodriguez .50
259 Bip Roberts .15
260 Tino Martinez .15
261 Chuck Knoblauch S .50
262 Mike Stanley .15
263 Wally Joyner S .50
264 Butch Huskey .15
265 Jeff Conine .15
266 Matt Williams G 2.50
267 Mark Grace .25
268 Jason Schmidt .15
269 Otis Nixon .15
270 Randy Johnson G 4.00
271 Kirby Puckett 1.00
272 *Andy Fox S* .50
273 Andy Benes .15
274 Sean Berry S .50
275 Mike Piazza 3.00
276 Rey Ordonez .20
277 Benito Santiago S .50

278	Gary Gaetti	.15
279	Paul Molitor G	3.50
280	Robin Ventura	.15
281	Cal Ripken Jr.	4.00
282	Carlos Baerga	.15
283	Roger Cedeno	.15
284	Chad Mottola S	.50
285	Terrell Wade	.15
286	Kevin Brown	.20
287	Rafael Palmeiro	.20
288	Mo Vaughn	.35
289	Dante Bichette S	.50
290	Cecil Fielder G	2.50
291	Doc Gooden S	.50
292	Bob Tewksbury	.15
293	Kevin Mitchell S	.50
294	*Livan Hernandez G*	3.50
295	Russ Davis S	.50
296	Chan Ho Park S	1.00
297	T.J. Mathews	.15
298	Manny Ramirez	.60
299	Jeff Bagwell	.60
300	*Marty Janzen G*	2.50
301	Wade Boggs	.35
302	Larry Walker S	1.00
303	Steve Gibralter	.15
304	B.J. Surhoff	.15
305	Ken Griffey Jr. S	6.00
306	Royce Clayton	.15
307	Sal Fasano	.15
308	Ron Gant G	2.50
309	Gary Sheffield	.20
310	Ken Hill	.15
311	Joe Girardi	.15
312	*Matt Lawton*	.15
313	Billy Wagner S	.50
314	Julio Franco	.15
315	Joe Carter	.15
316	Brooks Kieschnick	.15
317	*Mike Grace S*	.50
318	Heathcliff Slocumb	.15
319	Barry Larkin	.20
320	Tony Gwynn	1.00
321	Ryan Klesko G	2.50
322	Frank Thomas	1.00
323	Edgar Martinez	.15
324	Jermaine Dye G	2.50
325	Henry Rodriguez	.15
326	*Marvin Benard*	.50
327	Kenny Lofton S	.50
328	Derek Bell S	.50
329	Ugueth Urbina	.15
330	Jason Giambi G	2.50
331	Roger Salkeld	.15
332	Edgar Renteria	.15
333	Ryan Klesko	.15
334	Ray Lankford	.15
335	Edgar Martinez G	2.50
336	Justin Thompson	.15
337	Gary Sheffield S	.75
338	Rey Ordonez G	2.50
339	Mark Clark	.15
340	Ruben Rivera	.15
341	Mark Grace S	.75
342	Matt Williams	.25
343	*Francisco Cordova*	.25
344	Cecil Fielder	.15
345	Andres Galarraga S	.50
346	Brady Anderson S	.50
347	Sammy Sosa G	9.00
348	Mark Grudzielanek	.15
349	Ron Coomer	.15
350	Derek Jeter S	4.50
351	Rich Aurilla	.15
352	Jose Herrera	.15
353	Jay Buhner S	.50
354	Juan Gonzalez G	5.00
355	Craig Biggio G	2.50
356	Tony Clark	.15
357	Tino Martinez S	.50
358	*Dan Naulty*	.15
359	Checklist	.15

1996 Finest Refractors

Finest Refractor cards were created as a parallel set to Topps' 1996 Finest set. Rare Refractor cards are found about one per 288 packs (less than 150 of these sets were produced), while Uncommon Refractors are found one every 48 packs. Common Refractors are seeded one every 12 packs.

	MT
Complete Set (359):	1200.
Bronze Set (220):	300.00
Common Bronze:	1.00
Bronze Stars:	6X
Silver Set (91):	300.00
Typical Silver:	2.00
Silver Stars:	3X
Gold Set (48):	600.00
Typical Gold:	6.00
Gold Stars:	2.5X

(See 1996 Finest for checklist and base card values.)

1997 Finest Samples

Many of the subsets included in the 1997 Finest issue were previewed with a cello-wrapped pack of five cards distributed to hobby dealers. Cards are virtually identical to the issued versions and are designated a Refractor on back. Overprinted on back is a red notice, "PROMOTIONAL SAMPLE / NOT FOR RESALE".

		MT
Complete Set (5):		15.00
Common Player:		2.00
1	Barry Bonds	3.00
15	Derek Jeter	3.50
30	Mark McGwire	4.00
143	Hideo Nomo	2.50
159	Jeff Bagwell	2.50

1997 Finest

Finest returned for 1997 in its three-tiered format from 1996, but added several new twists. Issued in two series of 175 cards each, cards numbered 1-100 and 176-275 are bronze; 101-150 and 276-325 are silver and 151-175 and 326-350 are gold. All cards are designated among one of five different subsets per series. In Series 1 they are: Warriors, Blue Chips, Power, Hurlers and Masters. Series 2 subsets are: Power, Masters, Blue Chips, Competitors and Acquisitions. The bronze cards are the "common" card, while silvers are found every four packs and golds every 24 packs. Each card has a parallel Refractor version: bronze (1:12), silver (1:48) and gold (1:288). In addition, silver and gold cards have an additional parallel set. Silvers are found in an embossed version (1:16) and embossed Refractor version (1:192), while golds are found in a die-cut embossed version (1:96) and a die-cut embossed Refractor (1:1152).

		MT
Complete Set (350):		300.00
Bronze Set (200):		17.50
Common Bronze:		.07
Silver Set (100):		100.00
Typical Silver:		.50
Embossed Silvers:		3X
Complete Gold Set (50):		200.00
Typical Gold:		2.00
Embossed Die-Cut Golds:		2X
Series 1 or 2 Pack (6):		2.50
Series 1 or 2 Wax Box (24):		45.00
1	Barry Bonds B	.60
2	Ryne Sandberg B	.40
3	Brian Jordan B	.15
4	Rocky Coppinger B	.15
5	Dante Bichette B	.15
6	Al Martin B	.15
7	Charles Nagy B	.15
8	Otis Nixon B	.15
9	Mark Johnson B	.15
10	Jeff Bagwell B	.60
11	Ken Hill B	.15
12	Willie Adams B	.15
13	Raul Mondesi B	.15
14	Reggie Sanders B	.15
15	Derek Jeter B	1.50
16	Jermaine Dye B	.15
17	Edgar Renteria B	.15
18	Travis Fryman B	.15
19	Roberto Hernandez B	.15
20	Sammy Sosa B	1.00
21	Garret Anderson B	.15
22	Rey Ordonez B	.15
23	Glenallen Hill B	.15
24	Dave Nilsson B	.15
25	Kevin Brown B	.15
26	Brian McRae B	.15
27	Joey Hamilton B	.15
28	Jamey Wright B	.15
29	Frank Thomas B	1.00
30	Mark McGwire B	3.00
31	Ramon Martinez B	.15
32	Jaime Bluma B	.15
33	Frank Rodriguez B	.15
34	Andy Benes B	.15
35	Jay Buhner B	.10
36	Justin Thompson B	.15
37	Darin Erstad B	.40
38	Gregg Jefferies B	.15
39	Jeff D'Amico B	.15
40	Pedro Martinez B	.50
41	Nomar Garciaparra B	.60
42	Jose Valentin B	.15
43	Pat Hentgen B	.15
44	Will Clark B	.20
45	Bernie Williams B	.25
46	Luis Castillo B	.15
47	B.J. Surhoff B	.15
48	Greg Gagne B	.15
49	Pete Schourek B	.15
50	Mike Piazza B	1.50
51	Dwight Gooden B	.15
52	Javy Lopez B	.15
53	Chuck Finley B	.15
54	James Baldwin B	.15
55	Jack McDowell B	.15
56	Royce Clayton B	.15
57	Carlos Delgado B	.25
58	Neifi Perez B	.15
59	Eddie Taubensee B	.15
60	Rafael Palmeiro B	.20
61	Marty Cordova B	.15
62	Wade Boggs B	.35
63	Rickey Henderson B	.50
64	Mike Hampton B	.15
65	Troy Percival B	.15
66	Barry Larkin B	.20
67	Jermaine Allensworth B	.15
68	Mark Clark B	.15
69	Mike Lansing B	.15
70	Mark Grudzielanek B	.15
71	Todd Stottlemyre B	.15
72	Juan Guzman B	.15
73	John Burkett B	.15
74	Wilson Alvarez B	.15
75	Ellis Burks B	.15
76	Bobby Higginson B	.15
77	Ricky Bottalico B	.15
78	Omar Vizquel B	.15
79	Paul Sorrento B	.15
80	Denny Neagle B	.15
81	Roger Pavlik B	.15
82	Mike Lieberthal B	.15
83	Devon White B	.15
84	John Olerud B	.15
85	Kevin Appier B	.15
86	Joe Girardi B	.15
87	Paul O'Neill B	.15
88	Mike Sweeney B	.15
89	John Smiley B	.15
90	Ivan Rodriguez B	.40
91	Randy Myers B	.15
92	Bip Roberts B	.15
93	Jose Mesa B	.15
94	Paul Wilson B	.15
95	Mike Mussina B	.35
96	Ben McDonald B	.15
97	John Mabry B	.15
98	Tom Goodwin B	.15
99	Edgar Martinez B	.15
100	Andruw Jones B	1.50
101	Jose Canseco S	.75
102	Billy Wagner S	.50
103	Dante Bichette S	.50
104	Curt Schilling S	.75
105	Dean Palmer S	.50
106	Larry Walker S	1.00

No.	Player	MT
107	Bernie Williams S	1.00
108	Chipper Jones S	4.00
109	Gary Sheffield S	1.00
110	Randy Johnson S	1.50
111	Roberto Alomar S	1.50
112	Todd Walker S	1.25
113	Sandy Alomar S	.50
114	John Jaha S	.50
115	Ken Caminiti S	.50
116	Ryan Klesko S	.50
117	Mariano Rivera S	1.00
118	Jason Giambi S	1.50
119	Lance Johnson S	.50
120	Robin Ventura S	.50
121	Todd Hollandsworth S	.50
122	Johnny Damon S	.75
123	William VanLandingham S	.50
124	Jason Kendall S	.50
125	Vinny Castilla S	.50
126	Harold Baines S	.50
127	Joe Carter S	.50
128	Craig Biggio S	.50
129	Tony Clark S	.75
130	Ron Gant S	.50
131	David Segui S	.50
132	Steve Trachsel S	.50
133	Scott Rolen S	1.50
134	Mike Stanley S	.50
135	Cal Ripken Jr. S	5.00
136	John Smoltz S	.65
137	Bobby Jones S	.50
138	Manny Ramirez S	2.50
139	Ken Griffey Jr. S	6.00
140	Chuck Knoblauch S	.50
141	Mark Grace S	.75
142	Chris Snopek S	.50
143	Hideo Nomo S	1.50
144	Tim Salmon S	.75
145	David Cone S	.50
146	Eric Young S	.50
147	Jeff Brantley S	.50
148	Jim Thome S	.50
149	Trevor Hoffman S	.50
150	Juan Gonzalez S	2.00
151	Mike Piazza G	10.00
152	Ivan Rodriguez G	4.50
153	Mo Vaughn G	3.00
154	Brady Anderson G	2.00
155	Mark McGwire G	15.00
156	Rafael Palmeiro G	3.00
157	Barry Larkin G	2.00
158	Greg Maddux G	8.00
159	Jeff Bagwell G	6.00
160	Frank Thomas G	7.50
161	Ken Caminiti G	2.00
162	Andruw Jones G	5.00
163	Dennis Eckersley G	2.00
164	Jeff Conine G	2.00
165	Jim Edmonds G	2.00
166	Derek Jeter G	10.00
167	Vladimir Guerrero G	5.00
168	Sammy Sosa G	10.00
169	Tony Gwynn G	7.50
170	Andres Galarraga G	2.00
171	Todd Hundley G	2.00
172	Jay Buhner G	2.00
173	Paul Molitor G	4.00
174	Kenny Lofton G	2.00
175	Barry Bonds G	7.50
176	Gary Sheffield B	.20
177	Dmitri Young B	.15
178	Jay Bell B	.15
179	David Wells B	.15
180	Walt Weiss B	.15
181	Paul Molitor B	.50
182	Jose Guillen B	.40
183	Al Leiter B	.15
184	Mike Fetters B	.15
185	Mark Langston B	.15
186	Fred McGriff B	.15
187	Darrin Fletcher B	.15
188	Brant Brown B	.15
189	Geronimo Berroa B	.15
190	Jim Thome B	.15
191	Jose Vizcaino B	.15
192	Andy Ashby B	.15
193	Rusty Greer B	.15
194	Brian Hunter B	.15
195	Chris Hoiles B	.15
196	Orlando Merced B	.15
197	Brett Butler B	.15
198	Derek Bell B	.15
199	Bobby Bonilla B	.15
200	Alex Ochoa B	.15
201	Wally Joyner B	.15
202	Mo Vaughn B	.45
203	Doug Drabek B	.15
204	Tino Martinez B	.15
205	Roberto Alomar B	.50
206	*Brian Giles B*	2.00
207	Todd Worrell B	.15
208	Alan Benes B	.15
209	Jim Leyritz B	.15
210	Darryl Hamilton B	.15
211	Jimmy Key B	.15
212	Juan Gonzalez B	.60
213	Vinny Castilla B	.15
214	Chuck Knoblauch B	.15
215	Tony Phillips B	.15
216	Jeff Cirillo B	.15
217	Carlos Garcia B	.15
218	Brooks Kieschnick B	.15
219	Marquis Grissom B	.15
220	Dan Wilson B	.15
221	Greg Vaughn B	.15
222	John Wetteland B	.15
223	Andres Galarraga B	.15
224	Ozzie Guillen B	.15
225	Kevin Elster B	.15
226	Bernard Gilkey B	.15
227	Mike MacFarlane B	.15
228	Heathcliff Slocumb B	.15
229	Wendell Magee Jr. B	.15
230	Carlos Baerga B	.15
231	Kevin Seitzer B	.15
232	Henry Rodriguez B	.15
233	Roger Clemens B	.50
234	Mark Wohlers B	.15
235	Eddie Murray B	.40
236	Todd Zeile B	.15
237	J.T. Snow B	.15
238	Ken Griffey Jr. B	2.00
239	Sterling Hitchcock B	.15
240	Albert Belle B	.30
241	Terry Steinbach B	.15
242	Robb Nen B	.15
243	Mark McLemore B	.15
244	Jeff King B	.15
245	Tony Clark B	.15
246	Tim Salmon B	.20
247	Benito Santiago B	.15
248	Robin Ventura B	.15
249	*Bubba Trammell B*	.40
250	Chili Davis B	.15
251	John Valentin B	.15
252	Cal Ripken Jr. B	2.00
253	Matt Williams B	.20
254	Jeff Kent B	.15
255	Eric Karros B	.15
256	Ray Lankford B	.15
257	Ed Sprague B	.15
258	Shane Reynolds B	.15
259	Jaime Navarro B	.15
260	Eric Davis B	.15
261	Orel Hershiser B	.15
262	Mark Grace B	.25
263	Rod Beck B	.15
264	Ismael Valdes B	.15
265	Manny Ramirez B	.40
266	Ken Caminiti B	.15
267	Tim Naehring B	.15
268	Jose Rosado B	.15
269	Greg Colbrunn B	.15
270	Dean Palmer B	.15
271	David Justice B	.25
272	Scott Spiezio B	.15
273	Chipper Jones B	1.50
274	Mel Rojas B	.15
275	Bartolo Colon B	.15
276	Darin Erstad S	2.00
277	Sammy Sosa S	3.50
278	Rafael Palmeiro S	.75
279	Frank Thomas S	3.50
280	Ruben Rivera S	.50
281	Hal Morris S	.50
282	Jay Buhner S	.50
283	Kenny Lofton S	.50
284	Jose Canseco S	.75
285	Alex Fernandez S	.50
286	Todd Helton S	2.00
287	Andy Pettitte S	1.50
288	John Franco S	.50
289	Ivan Rodriguez S	2.50
290	Ellis Burks S	.50
291	Julio Franco S	.50
292	Mike Piazza S	4.50
293	Brian Jordan S	.50
294	Greg Maddux S	3.75
295	Bob Abreu S	.60
296	Rondell White S	.60
297	Moises Alou S	.60
298	Tony Gwynn S	2.75
299	Deion Sanders S	.60
300	Jeff Montgomery S	.50
301	Ray Durham S	.50
302	John Wasdin S	.50
303	Ryne Sandberg S	2.00
304	Delino DeShields S	.50
305	Mark McGwire S	6.00
306	Andruw Jones S	1.50
307	Kevin Orie S	.50
308	Matt Williams S	.60
309	Karim Garcia S	.50
310	Derek Jeter S	5.00
311	Mo Vaughn S	1.50
312	Brady Anderson S	.50
313	Barry Bonds S	3.00
314	Steve Finley S	.50
315	Vladimir Guerrero S	1.50
316	Matt Morris S	.50
317	Tom Glavine S	.75
318	Jeff Bagwell S	2.00
319	Albert Belle S	1.50
320	*Hideki Irabu S*	1.00
321	Andres Galarraga S	.50
322	Cecil Fielder S	.50
323	Barry Larkin S	.65
324	Todd Hundley S	.50
325	Fred McGriff S	.50
326	Gary Sheffield G	3.00
327	Craig Biggio G	2.00
328	Raul Mondesi G	2.50
329	Edgar Martinez G	2.00
330	Chipper Jones G	10.00
331	Bernie Williams G	4.00
332	Juan Gonzalez G	5.00
333	Ron Gant G	2.00
334	Cal Ripken Jr. G	12.50
335	Larry Walker G	3.00
336	Matt Williams G	3.00
337	Jose Cruz Jr. G	3.00
338	Joe Carter G	2.00
339	Wilton Guerrero G	2.00
340	Cecil Fielder G	2.00
341	Todd Walker G	2.00
342	Ken Griffey Jr. G	12.50
343	Ryan Klesko G	2.00
344	Roger Clemens G	5.00
345	Hideo Nomo G	4.00
346	Dante Bichette G	2.00
347	Albert Belle G	1.50
348	Randy Johnson G	3.50
349	Manny Ramirez G	5.00
350	John Smoltz G	2.00

1997 Finest Refractors

Every card in '97 Finest - both regular and embossed parallel - has a Refractor version. The Uncommon parallel set of Refractors features a mosaic pattern in the background while the Rare embossed die-cut parallel set of Refractors are produced with a hyper-plaid foil design. The number of cards and the insertion ratios for each level of Refractors is as follows: Common (200 cards, 1:12 packs), Uncommon (100, 1:48), Rare (50, 1:288), Embossed Uncommon (100, 1:192), Embossed Die-cut Rare (50, 1:1152).

	MT
Common Bronze:	2.00
Bronze Stars:	6X
Typical Silver:	3.00
Silver Stars:	3X
Typical Gold:	8.00
Gold Stars:	2X
Typical Embossed Silver:	7.50
Embossed Silver Stars:	8X
Typical Embossed Gold:	20.00
Embossed Gold Stars:	2X

(See 1997 Finest for cheklist and base card values.)

1997 Finest Embossed

Each Uncommon (silver) and Rare (gold) card in both Series 1 and 2 Finest was also issued in a parallel Embossed version. The Embossed Silver were a 1:16 find, while the die-cut Embossed Gold were found on average of just one per 96 packs.

	MT
Common Embossed Silver:	1.00
Embossed Silver Stars:	3X
Common Embossed Gold:	5.00
Embossed/Die-Cut Gold Stars:	2X

(See 1997 Finest for checklist and base card values.)

1998 Fines Pre-Production

Five-card cello packs of '98 Finest were distributed in the hobby market to preview the always-popular issue. The cards are virtually identical to the issued versions except for the card number, which bears a "PP" prefix.

		MT
Complete Set (5):		10.00
Common Player:		1.50
1	Nomar Garciaparra	3.00
2	Mark McGwire	4.00
3	Ivan Rodriguez	3.00
4	Ken Griffey Jr.	4.50
5	Roger Clemens	3.00

1998 Finest

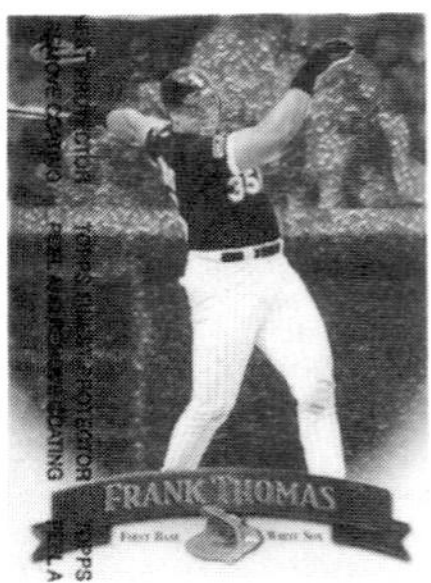

Finest dropped its three-tiered format in 1998 and produced a 275-card set on a thicker 26-point stock, with 150 cards in Series 1 and 125 in Series 2. The catch in 1998 was that each card arrived in Protector, No-Protector, Protector Refractor and No-Protector Refractor versions. Six-card packs sold for a suggested retail price of $5. Finest also included insert sets for the first time since 1995. Included in Series 1 packs were Centurions, Mystery Finest and Power Zone inserts. Series 2 had Mystery Finest, Stadium Stars and The Man. Throughout both series, Finest Protector cards are considered base cards, while No-Protector are inserted one per two packs (HTA odds 1:1), No-Protector Refractors are seeded 1:24 packs (HTA odds 1:10) and Finest Refractors are seeded 1:12 packs (HTA odds 1:5).

		MT
Complete Set (275):		35.00
Complete Series 1 Set (150):		20.00
Complete Series 2 Set (125):		15.00
Common Player:		.07
No-Protector:		2.5X
Refractors:		4X
No-Protector Refractor:		8X
Pack (6):		2.00
Wax Box (24):		45.00
1	Larry Walker	.25
2	Andruw Jones	.40
3	Ramon Martinez	.15
4	Geronimo Berroa	.15
5	David Justice	.25
6	Rusty Greer	.15
7	Chad Ogea	.15
8	Tom Goodwin	.15
9	Tino Martinez	.15
10	Jose Guillen	.20
11	Jeffrey Hammonds	.15
12	Brian McRae	.15
13	Jeremi Gonzalez	.15
14	Craig Counsell	.15
15	Mike Piazza	1.25
16	Greg Maddux	1.00
17	Todd Greene	.15
18	Rondell White	.15
19	Kirk Rueter	.15
20	Tony Clark	.15
21	Brad Radke	.15
22	Jaret Wright	.15
23	Carlos Delgado	.40
24	Dustin Hermanson	.15
25	Gary Sheffield	.20
26	Jose Canseco	.20
27	Kevin Young	.15
28	David Wells	.15
29	Mariano Rivera	.25
30	Reggie Sanders	.15
31	Mike Cameron	.15
32	Bobby Witt	.15
33	Kevin Orie	.15
34	Royce Clayton	.15
35	Edgar Martinez	.15
36	Neifi Perez	.15
37	Kevin Appier	.15
38	Darryl Hamilton	.15
39	Michael Tucker	.15
40	Roger Clemens	.75
41	Carl Everett	.15
42	Mike Sweeney	.15
43	Pat Meares	.15
44	Brian Giles	.15
45	Matt Morris	.15
46	Jason Dickson	.15
47	Rich Loiselle	.15
48	Joe Girardi	.15
49	Steve Trachsel	.15
50	Ben Grieve	.25
51	Jose Vizcaino	.15
52	Hideki Irabu	.20
53	J.T. Snow	.15
54	Mike Hampton	.15
55	Dave Nilsson	.15
56	Alex Fernandez	.15
57	Brett Tomko	.15
58	Wally Joyner	.15
59	Kelvim Escobar	.15
60	Roberto Alomar	.30
61	Todd Jones	.15
62	Paul O'Neill	.15
63	Jamie Moyer	.15
64	Mark Wohlers	.15
65	Jose Cruz Jr.	.20
66	Troy Percival	.15
67	Rick Reed	.15
68	Will Clark	.20
69	Jamey Wright	.15
70	Mike Mussina	.30
71	David Cone	.15
72	Ryan Klesko	.15
73	Scott Hatteberg	.15
74	James Baldwin	.15
75	Tony Womack	.15
76	Carlos Perez	.15
77	Charles Nagy	.15
78	Jeromy Burnitz	.15
79	Shane Reynolds	.15
80	Cliff Floyd	.15
81	Jason Kendall	.15
82	Chad Curtis	.15
83	Matt Karchner	.15
84	Ricky Bottalico	.15
85	Sammy Sosa	1.00
86	Javy Lopez	.15
87	Jeff Kent	.15
88	Shawn Green	.20
89	Devon White	.15
90	Tony Gwynn	.75
91	Bob Tewksbury	.15
92	Derek Jeter	1.25
93	Eric Davis	.15
94	Jeff Fassero	.15
95	Denny Neagle	.15
96	Ismael Valdes	.15
97	Tim Salmon	.20
98	Mark Grudzielanek	.15
99	Curt Schilling	.20
100	Ken Griffey Jr.	2.00
101	Edgardo Alfonzo	.20
102	Vinny Castilla	.15
103	Jose Rosado	.15
104	Scott Erickson	.15
105	Alan Benes	.15
106	Shannon Stewart	.15
107	Delino DeShields	.15
108	Mark Loretta	.15
109	Todd Hundley	.15
110	Chuck Knoblauch	.15
111	Quinton McCracken	.15
112	F.P. Santangelo	.15
113	Gerald Williams	.15
114	Omar Vizquel	.15
115	John Valentin	.15
116	Damion Easley	.15
117	Matt Lawton	.15
118	Jim Thome	.15
119	Sandy Alomar	.15
120	Albert Belle	.35
121	Chris Stynes	.15
122	Butch Huskey	.15
123	Shawn Estes	.15
124	Terry Adams	.15
125	Ivan Rodriguez	.40
126	Ron Gant	.15
127	John Mabry	.15
128	Jeff Shaw	.15
129	Jeff Montgomery	.15
130	Justin Thompson	.15
131	Livan Hernandez	.15
132	Ugueth Urbina	.15
133	Doug Glanville	.15
134	Troy O'Leary	.15
135	Cal Ripken Jr.	2.00
136	Quilvio Veras	.15
137	Pedro Astacio	.15
138	Willie Greene	.15
139	Lance Johnson	.15
140	Nomar Garciaparra	1.00
141	Jose Offerman	.15
142	Scott Rolen	.40
143	Derek Bell	.15
144	Johnny Damon	.20
145	Mark McGwire	2.00
146	Chan Ho Park	.20
147	Edgar Renteria	.15
148	Eric Young	.15
149	Craig Biggio	.15
150	Checklist 1-150	.15
151	Frank Thomas	1.00
152	John Wetteland	.15
153	Mike Lansing	.15
154	Pedro Martinez	.50
155	Rico Brogna	.15
156	Kevin Brown	.15
157	Alex Rodriguez	2.00
158	Wade Boggs	.30
159	Richard Hidalgo	.20
160	Mark Grace	.15
161	Jose Mesa	.15
162	John Olerud	.15
163	Tim Belcher	.15
164	Chuck Finley	.15
165	Brian Hunter	.15
166	Joe Carter	.15
167	Stan Javier	.15
168	Jay Bell	.15
169	Ray Lankford	.15
170	John Smoltz	.15
171	Ed Sprague	.15
172	Jason Giambi	.30
173	Todd Walker	.15
174	Paul Konerko	.15
175	Rey Ordonez	.15
176	Dante Bichette	.15
177	Bernie Williams	.25
178	Jon Nunnally	.15
179	Rafael Palmeiro	.25
180	Jay Buhner	.15
181	Devon White	.15
182	Jeff D'Amico	.15
183	Walt Weiss	.15
184	Scott Spiezio	.15
185	Moises Alou	.20
186	Carlos Baerga	.15
187	Todd Zeile	.15
188	Gregg Jefferies	.15
189	Mo Vaughn	.40
190	Terry Steinbach	.15
191	Ray Durham	.15
192	Robin Ventura	.15
193	Jeff Reed	.15
194	Ken Caminiti	.15
195	Eric Karros	.15
196	Wilson Alvarez	.15
197	Gary Gaetti	.15
198	Andres Galarraga	.15
199	Alex Gonzalez	.15
200	Garret Anderson	.15
201	Andy Benes	.15
202	Harold Baines	.15
203	Ron Coomer	.15
204	Dean Palmer	.15
205	Reggie Jefferson	.15
206	John Burkett	.15
207	Jermaine Allensworth	.15
208	Bernard Gilkey	.15
209	Jeff Bagwell	.50
210	Kenny Lofton	.15
211	Bobby Jones	.15
212	Bartolo Colon	.20
213	Jim Edmonds	.20
214	Pat Hentgen	.15
215	Matt Williams	.20
216	Bob Abreu	.15
217	Jorge Posada	.15
218	Marty Cordova	.15
219	Ken Hill	.15
220	Steve Finley	.15
221	Jeff King	.15
222	Quinton McCracken	.15
223	Matt Stairs	.15
224	Darin Erstad	.40
225	Fred McGriff	.15
226	Marquis Grissom	.15
227	Doug Glanville	.15
228	Tom Glavine	.20
229	John Franco	.15
230	Darren Bragg	.15
231	Barry Larkin	.20
232	Trevor Hoffman	.15
233	Brady Anderson	.15
234	Al Martin	.15
235	B.J. Surhoff	.15
236	Ellis Burks	.15
237	Randy Johnson	.50
238	Mark Clark	.15
239	Tony Saunders	.15
240	Hideo Nomo	.25
241	Brad Fullmer	.15
242	Chipper Jones	1.25
243	Jose Valentin	.15
244	Manny Ramirez	.50
245	Derrek Lee	.15
246	Jimmy Key	.15
247	Tim Naehring	.15
248	Bobby Higginson	.15
249	Charles Johnson	.15
250	Chili Davis	.15
251	Tom Gordon	.15
252	Mike Lieberthal	.15
253	Billy Wagner	.15
254	Juan Guzman	.15
255	Todd Stottlemyre	.15
256	Brian Jordan	.15
257	Barry Bonds	1.00
258	Dan Wilson	.15
259	Paul Molitor	.30
260	Juan Gonzalez	.50
261	Francisco Cordova	.15
262	Cecil Fielder	.15
263	Travis Lee	.15
264	Kevin Tapani	.15
265	Raul Mondesi	.20
266	Travis Fryman	.15
267	Armando Benitez	.15
268	Pokey Reese	.15
269	Rick Aguilera	.15
270	Andy Pettitte	.25
271	Jose Vizcaino	.15
272	Kerry Wood	.25
273	Vladimir Guerrero	.40
274	John Smiley	.15
275	Checklist 151-275	.15

1998 Finest Refractors

All 275 cards from Finest Series 1 and 2 are available in a Refractor version. seeded one per 12 packs. Besides the refractive quality of the printing of front, Refractors are designated with an "R" suffix to the card number on back.

	MT
Complete Set (275):	250.00
Common Player:	1.00
Stars/Rookies:	4X

(See 1998 Finest for checklist and base card values.)

1998 Finest No-Protector

This parallel to the 275-card base set foregoes the peel-off front protector and adds Finest technology to the back of the card. Stated insertion rates were one per two packs or one per pack in Home Team Advantage (HTA) boxes.

	MT
Complete Set (275):	150.00
Common Player:	.50
Stars/Rookies:	2.5X

(See 1998 Finest for checklist and base card values.)

1998 Finest No-Protector Refractor

A Refractor parallel to the 275 No-Protector parallel cards was a 1:24 pack insert. In Series 1, only the refractive quality of the front and back printing reveals this insert. Series 2 No-Protector Refractors have an "R" suffix to the card number on back.

	MT
Complete Set (275):	400.00
Common Player:	2.00
Stars/Rookies:	8X

(See 1998 Finest for checklist and base card values.)

1998 Finest Centurions

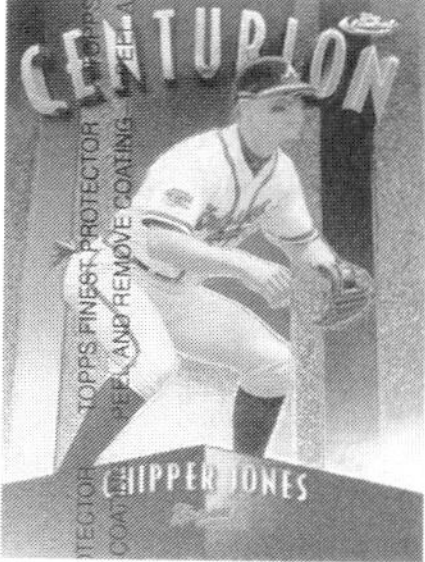

Centurions is a 20-card insert found only Series 1 hobby (1:153) and Home Team Advantage packs (1:71). The theme of the insert to top players who will lead the game into the next century. Each card is sequentially numbered on the back to 500, while Refractor versions are numbered to 75.

		MT
Complete Set (20):		50.00
Common Player:		1.00
Production 500 sets		
Refractors (75 sets):		4X
C1	Andruw Jones	2.00
C2	Vladimir Guerrero	4.00
C3	Nomar Garciaparra	5.00
C4	Scott Rolen	2.00
C5	Ken Griffey Jr.	6.00
C6	Jose Cruz Jr.	1.50
C7	Barry Bonds	5.00
C8	Mark McGwire	8.00
C9	Juan Gonzalez	2.50
C10	Jeff Bagwell	2.50
C11	Frank Thomas	4.00
C12	Paul Konerko	1.00
C13	Alex Rodriguez	8.00
C14	Mike Piazza	6.00
C15	Travis Lee	1.00
C16	Chipper Jones	6.00
C17	Larry Walker	1.50
C18	Mo Vaughn	2.00
C19	Livan Hernandez	1.00
C20	Jaret Wright	1.00

1998 Finest Jumbo

Eight oversized cards were inserted into both Series 1 and Series 2 boxes as box toppers. The cards measure 3" x 5" and are inserted one per three boxes, with Refractor versions every six boxes. The oversized cards are similar to the regular-issed cards except for the numbering which designates each "X of 8".

		MT
Complete Set (16):		55.00
Common Player:		1.50
Refractors:		1.5X
	FIRST SERIES	
1	Mark McGwire	7.50
2	Cal Ripken Jr.	7.50
3	Nomar Garciaparra	5.00
4	Mike Piazza	6.00
5	Greg Maddux	4.50
6	Jose Cruz Jr.	1.50
7	Roger Clemens	3.50
8	Ken Griffey Jr.	7.00
	SECOND SERIES	
1	Frank Thomas	5.00
2	Bernie Williams	1.50
3	Randy Johnson	1.50
4	Chipper Jones	6.00
5	Manny Ramirez	2.50
6	Barry Bonds	4.00
7	Juan Gonzalez	4.00
8	Jeff Bagwell	3.00

1998 Finest Power Zone

This Series 1 insert features Topps' new "Flop Inks" technology which changes the color of the card depending at what angle it is viewed. They are inserted one per 72 hobby packs (HTA odds 1:32). Cards are numbered with a "P" prefix.

		MT
Complete Set (20):		95.00
Common Player:		1.50
1	Ken Griffey Jr.	17.50
2	Jeff Bagwell	5.00
3	Jose Cruz Jr.	2.50
4	Barry Bonds	7.50
5	Mark McGwire	20.00
6	Jim Thome	1.50
7	Mo Vaughn	3.00
8	Gary Sheffield	2.00
9	Andres Galarraga	3.00
10	Nomar Garciaparra	10.00
11	Rafael Palmeiro	3.00
12	Sammy Sosa	10.00
13	Jay Buhner	1.50
14	Tony Clark	1.50
15	Mike Piazza	12.50
16	Larry Walker	2.00
17	Albert Belle	3.00
18	Tino Martinez	1.50
19	Juan Gonzalez	5.00
20	Frank Thomas	9.00

1998 Finest Mystery Finest

This 50-card insert was seeded one per 36 Series 1 packs and one per 15 HTA packs. The set includes 20 top players, each matched on a double-sided card with three other players and once with himself. Each side of the card is printed on a chromium finish and arrives with a black opaque protector. Mystery Finest inserts are numbered with an "M" prefix. Refractor versions were seeded one per 64 packs (HTA odds 1:15).

		MT
Complete Set (50):		265.00
Common Player:		2.50
Refractors:		2X
M1	Frank Thomas, Ken Griffey Jr.	10.00
M2	Frank Thomas, Mike Piazza	9.00
M3	Frank Thomas, Mark McGwire	12.50
M4	Frank Thomas, Frank Thomas	7.50
M5	Ken Griffey Jr., Mike Piazza	10.00
M6	Ken Griffey Jr., Mark McGwire	12.50
M7	Ken Griffey Jr., Ken Griffey Jr.	12.50
M8	Mike Piazza, Mark McGwire	13.50
M9	Mike Piazza, Mike Piazza	12.50
M10	Mark McGwire, Mark McGwire	15.00
M11	Nomar Garciaparra, Jose Cruz Jr.	4.50
M12	Nomar Garciaparra, Derek Jeter	9.00
M13	Nomar Garciaparra, Andruw Jones	4.50
M14	Nomar Garciaparra, Nomar Garciaparra	9.00
M15	Jose Cruz Jr., Derek Jeter	6.00
M16	Jose Cruz Jr., Andruw Jones	2.50
M17	Jose Cruz Jr., Jose Cruz Jr.	2.50
M18	Derek Jeter, Andruw Jones	7.50
M19	Derek Jeter, Derek Jeter	12.50
M20	Andruw Jones, Andruw Jones	5.00
M21	Cal Ripken Jr., Tony Gwynn	10.00
M22	Cal Ripken Jr., Barry Bonds	12.50
M23	Cal Ripken Jr., Greg Maddux	10.00
M24	Cal Ripken Jr., Cal Ripken Jr.	15.00
M25	Tony Gwynn, Barry Bonds	6.00
M26	Tony Gwynn, Greg Maddux	5.00
M27	Tony Gwynn, Tony Gwynn	7.50
M28	Barry Bonds, Greg Maddux	5.50

M29	Barry Bonds, Barry Bonds	6.00
M30	Greg Maddux, Greg Maddux	7.50
M31	Juan Gonzalez, Larry Walker	2.50
M32	Juan Gonzalez, Andres Galarraga	2.50
M33	Juan Gonzalez, Chipper Jones	7.50
M34	Juan Gonzalez, Juan Gonzalez	4.00
M35	Larry Walker, Andres Galarraga	2.50
M36	Larry Walker, Chipper Jones	5.00
M37	Larry Walker, Larry Walker	2.50
M38	Andres Galarraga, Chipper Jones	5.00
M39	Andres Galarraga, Andres Galarraga	2.50
M40	Chipper Jones, Chipper Jones	10.00
M41	Gary Sheffield, Sammy Sosa	3.50
M42	Gary Sheffield, Jeff Bagwell	2.50
M43	Gary Sheffield, Tino Martinez	2.50
M44	Gary Sheffield, Gary Sheffield	2.50
M45	Sammy Sosa, Jeff Bagwell	4.50
M46	Sammy Sosa, Tino Martinez	3.00
M47	Sammy Sosa, Sammy Sosa	9.00
M48	Jeff Bagwell, Tino Martinez	2.50
M49	Jeff Bagwell, Jeff Bagwell	4.00
M50	Tino Martinez, Tino Martinez	2.50

1998 Finest Mystery Finest 2

Forty more Mystery Finest inserts were seeded in Series 2 packs at a rate of one per 36 packs (HTA odds 1:15), with Refrators every 1:144 packs (HTA odds 1:64). As with Series 1, 20 players are in the checklist; some players are found with another player on the back or by himself on each side. Each side is printed in Finest technology with an opaque black protector.

		MT
Complete Set (40):		225.00
Common Player:		2.50
Refractors:		2X
M1	Nomar Garciaparra, Frank Thomas	10.00
M2	Nomar Garciaparra, Albert Belle	7.50
M3	Nomar Garciaparra, Scott Rolen	7.50
M4	Frank Thomas, Albert Belle	7.50
M5	Frank Thomas, Scott Rolen	7.50
M6	Albert Belle, Scott Rolen	2.50
M7	Ken Griffey Jr., Jose Cruz	10.00
M8	Ken Griffey Jr., Alex Rodriguez	15.00
M9	Ken Griffey Jr., Roger Clemens	12.50
M10	Jose Cruz, Alex Rodriguez	10.00
M11	Jose Cruz, Roger Clemens	5.00
M12	Alex Rodriguez, Roger Clemens	15.00
M13	Mike Piazza, Barry Bonds	12.50
M14	Mike Piazza, Derek Jeter	12.50
M15	Mike Piazza, Bernie Williams	10.00
M16	Barry Bonds, Derek Jeter	12.50
M17	Barry Bonds, Bernie Williams	5.00
M18	Derek Jeter, Bernie Williams	10.00
M19	Mark McGwire, Jeff Bagwell	15.00
M20	Mark McGwire, Mo Vaughn	12.50
M21	Mark McGwire, Jim Thome	11.00
M22	Jeff Bagwell, Mo Vaughn	4.00
M23	Jeff Bagwell, Jim Thome	3.50
M24	Mo Vaughn, Jim Thome	2.50
M25	Juan Gonzalez, Travis Lee	4.00
M26	Juan Gonzalez, Ben Grieve	5.00
M27	Juan Gonzalez, Fred McGriff	4.00
M28	Travis Lee, Ben Grieve	2.50
M29	Travis Lee, Fred McGriff	2.50
M30	Ben Grieve, Fred McGriff	2.50
M31	Albert Belle, Albert Belle	3.00
M32	Scott Rolen, Scott Rolen	4.00
M33	Alex Rodriguez, Alex Rodriguez	12.50
M34	Roger Clemens, Roger Clemens	6.00
M35	Bernie Williams, Bernie Williams	3.00
M36	Mo Vaughn, Mo Vaughn	3.00
M37	Jim Thome, Jim Thome	2.50
M38	Travis Lee, Travis Lee	2.50
M39	Fred McGriff, Fred McGriff	2.50
M40	Ben Grieve, Ben Grieve	3.00

1998 Finest Mystery Finest Jumbo

Series 2 Home Team Advantage (HTA) boxes were the exclusive venue for these large-format (3" x 5") versions of Mystery Finest. Regular cards were found one per six boxes of HTA, while Refractor versions were a 1:12 seed.

		MT
Complete Set (3):		12.50
Common Card:		2.50
Refractor:		1.5X
1	Ken Griffey Jr., Alex Rodriguez	5.00
2	Derek Jeter, Bernie Williams	2.50
3	Mark McGwire, Jeff Bagwell	5.00

1998 Finest Stadium Stars

Stadium Stars is a 24-card insert that features Topps' new lenticular holographic chromium technology. These are exclusive to Series 2 packs and carried an insertion rate of one per 72 packs (HTA odds 1:32).

		MT
Complete Set (24):		250.00
Common Player:		3.00
SS1	Ken Griffey Jr.	25.00
SS2	Alex Rodriguez	30.00
SS3	Mo Vaughn	4.00
SS4	Nomar Garciaparra	20.00
SS5	Frank Thomas	15.00
SS6	Albert Belle	4.00
SS7	Derek Jeter	25.00
SS8	Chipper Jones	20.00
SS9	Cal Ripken Jr.	30.00
SS10	Jim Thome	3.00
SS11	Mike Piazza	25.00
SS12	Juan Gonzalez	11.00
SS13	Jeff Bagwell	11.00
SS14	Sammy Sosa	17.50
SS15	Jose Cruz Jr.	3.50
SS16	Gary Sheffield	4.50
SS17	Larry Walker	5.00
SS18	Tony Gwynn	15.00
SS19	Mark McGwire	30.00
SS20	Barry Bonds	15.00
SS21	Tino Martinez	3.00
SS22	Manny Ramirez	11.00
SS23	Ken Caminiti	3.00
SS24	Andres Galarraga	3.00

1998 Finest The Man

This 20-card insert features the top players in baseball and was exclusively found in Series 2 packs. Regular versions are sequentially numbered to 500 and inserted one per 119 packs, while Refractor versions are numbered to 75 and inserted one per 793 packs.

		MT
Complete Set (20):		225.00
Common Player:		2.50
Refractors:		2X
TM1	Ken Griffey Jr.	25.00
TM2	Barry Bonds	10.00
TM3	Frank Thomas	10.00
TM4	Chipper Jones	20.00
TM5	Cal Ripken Jr.	30.00
TM6	Nomar Garciaparra	20.00
TM7	Mark McGwire	30.00
TM8	Mike Piazza	20.00
TM9	Derek Jeter	25.00
TM10	Alex Rodriguez	25.00
TM11	Jose Cruz Jr.	3.00
TM12	Larry Walker	4.00
TM13	Jeff Bagwell	7.50
TM14	Tony Gwynn	10.00
TM15	Travis Lee	2.50
TM16	Juan Gonzalez	7.50
TM17	Scott Rolen	4.00
TM18	Randy Johnson	6.00
TM19	Roger Clemens	9.00
TM20	Greg Maddux	15.00

1999 Finest

Released in two series, with each consisting of 100 regular and 50 subset cards divided into three categories: Gems, Sensations and Rookies in Series 1, and Sterling, Gamers and Rookies in the second series. The subset cards are short-printed, seeded one per pack. Cards are printed on 27 pt. stock utilizing chromium technology. There are two parallels: Refractors and die-cut Gold Refractors. Refractors are seeded 1:12 packs, while Gold Refractors are numbered to 100 sets. Six-cards packs carried an SRP of $4.99.

		MT
Complete Set (300):		160.00
Complete Series 1 (150):		80.00
Complete Series 2 (150):		80.00
Common Player:		.15
Common SP (101-150, 251-300):		.50
Star Refractors:		6X
SP Refractors:		3X
Star Gold Refractors:		15X
SP Gold Refractors:		10X
Pack (6):		3.00
Wax Box (24):		65.00
1	Darin Erstad	.50
2	Javy Lopez	.15

3 Vinny Castilla .15
4 Jim Thome .15
5 Tino Martinez .15
6 Mark Grace .25
7 Shawn Green .40
8 Dustin Hermanson .15
9 Kevin Young .15
10 Tony Clark .15
11 Scott Brosius .15
12 Craig Biggio .15
13 Brian McRae .15
14 Chan Ho Park .25
15 Manny Ramirez 1.00
16 Chipper Jones 2.00
17 Rico Brogna .15
18 Quinton McCracken .15
19 J.T. Snow Jr. .15
20 Tony Gwynn 1.50
21 Juan Guzman .15
22 John Valentin .15
23 Rick Helling .15
24 Sandy Alomar .15
25 Frank Thomas 1.50
26 Jorge Posada .15
27 Dmitri Young .15
28 Rick Reed .15
29 Kevin Tapani .15
30 Troy Glaus 1.50
31 Kenny Rogers .15
32 Jeromy Burnitz .15
33 Mark Grudzielanek .15
34 Mike Mussina .75
35 Scott Rolen .75
36 Neifi Perez .15
37 Brad Radke .25
38 Darryl Strawberry .15
39 Robb Nen .15
40 Moises Alou .25
41 Eric Young .15
42 Livan Hernandez .15
43 John Wetteland .15
44 Matt Lawton .15
45 Ben Grieve .25
46 Fernando Tatis .25
47 Travis Fryman .15
48 David Segui .15
49 Bob Abreu .15
50 Nomar Garciaparra 2.00
51 Paul O'Neill .15
52 Jeff King .15
53 Francisco Cordova .15
54 John Olerud .25
55 Vladimir Guerrero 1.00
56 Fernando Vina .15
57 Shane Reynolds .15
58 Chuck Finley .15
59 Rondell White .20
60 Greg Vaughn .15
61 Ryan Minor .15
62 Tom Gordon .15
63 Damion Easley .15
64 Ray Durham .15
65 Orlando Hernandez .40
66 Bartolo Colon .20
67 Jaret Wright .15
68 Royce Clayton .15
69 Tim Salmon .20
70 Mark McGwire 3.00
71 Alex Gonzalez .15
72 Tom Glavine .25
73 David Justice .40
74 Omar Vizquel .15
75 Juan Gonzalez 1.00
76 Bobby Higginson .15
77 Todd Walker .15
78 Dante Bichette .15
79 Kevin Millwood .15
80 Roger Clemens 1.50
81 Kerry Wood .40
82 Cal Ripken Jr. 3.00
83 Jay Bell .15
84 Barry Bonds 1.50
85 Alex Rodriguez 3.00
86 Doug Glanville .15
87 Jason Kendall .20
88 Sean Casey .25
89 Aaron Sele .15
90 Derek Jeter 2.50
91 Andy Ashby .15
92 Rusty Greer .15
93 Rod Beck .15
94 Matt Williams .25
95 Mike Piazza 2.50
96 Wally Joyner .15
97 Barry Larkin .25
98 Eric Milton .15
99 Gary Sheffield .30
100 Greg Maddux 1.50
101 Ken Griffey Jr. (Gem) 4.00
102 Frank Thomas (Gem) 2.00
103 Nomar Garciaparra (Gem) 3.00
104 Mark McGwire (Gem) 5.00
105 Alex Rodriguez (Gem) 5.00
106 Tony Gwynn (Gem) 2.50
107 Juan Gonzalez (Gem) 1.50
108 Jeff Bagwell (Gem) 1.50
109 Sammy Sosa (Gem) 4.00
110 Vladimir Guerrero (Gem) 1.50
111 Roger Clemens (Gem) 2.00
112 Barry Bonds (Gem) 4.00
113 Darin Erstad (Gem) 1.00
114 Mike Piazza (Gem) 4.00
115 Derek Jeter (Gem) 4.00
116 Chipper Jones (Gem) 4.00
117 Larry Walker (Gem) .75
118 Scott Rolen (Gem) 1.50
119 Cal Ripken Jr. (Gem) 5.00
120 Greg Maddux (Gem) 3.00
121 Troy Glaus (Sensations) 2.50
122 Ben Grieve (Sensations) .50
123 Ryan Minor (Sensations) .50
124 Kerry Wood (Sensations) .75
125 Travis Lee (Sensations) .50
126 Adrian Beltre (Sensations) .50
127 Brad Fullmer (Sensations) .50
128 Aramis Ramirez (Sensations) .50
129 Eric Chavez (Sensations) .60
130 Todd Helton (Sensations) 1.00
131 *Pat Burrell* (Finest Rookies) 6.00
132 *Ryan Mills* (Finest Rookies) 1.00
133 *Austin Kearns* (Finest Rookies) 6.00
134 *Josh McKinley* (Finest Rookies) 1.00
135 *Adam Everett* (Finest Rookies) 1.00
136 Marlon Anderson .50
137 Bruce Chen .50
138 Matt Clement .50
139 Alex Gonzalez .50
140 Roy Halladay .50
141 Calvin Pickering .50
142 Randy Wolf .50
143 Ryan Anderson .75
144 Ruben Mateo .75
145 *Alex Escobar* 4.00
146 Jeremy Giambi .50
147 Lance Berkman .50
148 Michael Barrett .50
149 Preston Wilson .50
150 Gabe Kapler .50
151 Roger Clemens 1.50
152 Jay Buhner .15
153 Brad Fullmer .15
154 Ray Lankford .15
155 Jim Edmonds .25
156 Jason Giambi .40
157 Bret Boone .20
158 Jeff Cirillo .15
159 Rickey Henderson .40
160 Edgar Martinez .15
161 Ron Gant .15
162 Mark Kotsay .15
163 Trevor Hoffman .15
164 Jason Schmidt .15
165 Brett Tomko .15
166 David Ortiz .15
167 Dean Palmer .15
168 Hideki Irabu .20
169 Mike Cameron .15
170 Pedro Martinez .75
171 Tom Goodwin .15
172 Brian Hunter .15
173 Al Leiter .15
174 Charles Johnson .15
175 Curt Schilling .25
176 Robin Ventura .15
177 Travis Lee .15
178 Jeff Shaw .15
179 Ugueth Urbina .15
180 Roberto Alomar .60
181 Cliff Floyd .15
182 Adrian Beltre .30
183 Tony Womack .15
184 Brian Jordan .15
185 Randy Johnson .75
186 Mickey Morandini .15
187 Todd Hundley .15
188 Jose Valentin .15
189 Eric Davis .15
190 Ken Caminiti .15
191 David Wells .15
192 Ryan Klesko .15
193 Garret Anderson .15
194 Eric Karros .15
195 Ivan Rodriguez 1.00
196 Aramis Ramirez .15
197 Mike Lieberthal .15
198 Will Clark .25
199 Rey Ordonez .15
200 Ken Griffey Jr. 2.00
201 Jose Guillen .20
202 Scott Erickson .15
203 Paul Konerko .15
204 Johnny Damon .20
205 Larry Walker .30
206 Denny Neagle .15
207 Jose Offerman .15
208 Andy Pettitte .25
209 Bobby Jones .15
210 Kevin Brown .25
211 John Smoltz .15
212 Henry Rodriguez .15
213 Tim Belcher .15
214 Carlos Delgado .50
215 Andruw Jones 1.00
216 Andy Benes .15
217 Fred McGriff .15
218 Edgar Renteria .15
219 Miguel Tejada .30
220 Bernie Williams .50
221 Justin Thompson .15
222 Marty Cordova .15
223 Delino DeShields .15
224 Ellis Burks .15
225 Kenny Lofton .15
226 Steve Finley .15
227 Eric Chavez .25
228 Jose Cruz Jr. .25
229 Marquis Grissom .15
230 Jeff Bagwell 1.00
231 Jose Canseco .50
232 Edgardo Alfonzo .25
233 Richie Sexson .25
234 Jeff Kent .25
235 Rafael Palmeiro .35
236 David Cone .25
237 Gregg Jefferies .15
238 Mike Lansing .15
239 Mariano Rivera .35
240 Albert Belle .45
241 Chuck Knoblauch .15
242 Derek Bell .15
243 Pat Hentgen .15
244 Andres Galarraga .15
245 Mo Vaughn .50
246 Wade Boggs .50
247 Devon White .15
248 Todd Helton .50
249 Raul Mondesi .30
250 Sammy Sosa 2.00
251 Nomar Garciaparra (Sterling) 4.00
252 Mark McGwire (Sterling) 6.00
253 Alex Rodriguez (Sterling) 5.00
254 Juan Gonzalez (Sterling) 1.50
255 Vladimir Guerrero (Sterling) 1.50
256 Ken Griffey Jr. (Sterling) 4.00
257 Mike Piazza (Sterling) 4.00
258 Derek Jeter (Sterling) 4.00
259 Albert Belle (Sterling) 1.00
260 Greg Vaughn (Sterling) .50
261 Sammy Sosa (Sterling) 4.00
262 Greg Maddux (Sterling) 3.50
263 Frank Thomas (Sterling) 3.00
264 Mark Grace (Sterling) 1.00
265 Ivan Rodriguez (Sterling) 1.00
266 Roger Clemens (Gamers) 2.00
267 Mo Vaughn (Gamers) 1.00
268 Jim Thome (Gamers) .50
269 Darin Erstad (Gamers) 1.00
270 Chipper Jones (Gamers) 3.00
271 Larry Walker (Gamers) 1.00
272 Cal Ripken Jr. (Gamers) 5.00
273 Scott Rolen (Gamers) 1.00
274 Randy Johnson (Gamers) 1.50
275 Tony Gwynn (Gamers) 3.00
276 Barry Bonds (Gamers) 3.00
277 *Sean Burroughs* 6.00
278 *J.M. Gold* 1.00
279 Carlos Lee .50
280 George Lombard .50
281 Carlos Beltran .50
282 Fernando Seguignol .50
283 Eric Chavez .50
284 *Carlos Pena* 6.00
285 *Corey Patterson* 6.00
286 *Alfonso Soriano* 8.00
287 *Nick Johnson* 8.00
288 *Jorge Toca* 1.00
289 *A.J. Burnett* 2.00
290 *Andy Brown* 1.50
291 *Doug Mientkiewicz* 1.00
292 *Bobby Seay* 1.00
293 *Chip Ambres* 1.00
294 *C.C. Sabathia* 5.00
295 *Choo Freeman* 1.50
296 *Eric Valent* 2.00
297 *Matt Belisle* 2.00
298 *Jason Tyner* 1.50
299 *Masao Kida* 1.50
300 Hank Aaron, Mark McGwire (Homerun Kings) 3.00

1999 Finest Refractors

Inserted at the rate of one card per 12 packs, Refractors use special technology to impart a more colorful sheen to the card fronts. To eliminate doubt, the backs have the word

"REFRACTOR" printed to the right of the card number at top.

	MT
Complete Set (300):	1000.
Common Player:	2.00
Stars:	6X
SPs:	3X

(See 1999 Finest for checklist and base card values.)

1999 Finest Gold Refractors

At the top of Finest's chase-card line-up for 1999 are the Gold Refractors. Fronts have an overall gold tone in the background. Backs are individually serial numbered in gold foil with an edition of 100 each, and have the words "GOLD REFRACTOR" printed at top, to the right of the card number. The Gold Refractors are die-cut along the edges to create a deckled effect. Stated pack insertion rates were between 1:26 and 1:82 depending on series and type.

	MT
Common Player:	6.00
Stars:	15X
SPs:	10X

(See 1999 Finest for checklist and base card values.)

1999 Finest Complements

This Series 2 insert set pairs two players on a "split-screen" card front. There are three different versions for each card, Non-Refractor/Refractor (1:56), Refractor/Non-Refractor (1:56) and Refractor/Refractor (1:168). Each card is numbered with a "C" prefix. Values shown are for cards with either the left- or right-side player as Refractor; dual-refractor cards valued at 2X.

		MT
Complete Set (7):		35.00
Common Player:		2.50
Inserted 1:56		
Dual-Refractors:		2X
Inserted 1:168		
1	Mike Piazza, Ivan Rodriguez	6.00
2	Tony Gwynn, Wade Boggs	5.00
3	Kerry Wood, Roger Clemens	3.00
4	Juan Gonzalez, Sammy Sosa	5.00
5	Derek Jeter, Nomar Garciaparra	6.00
6	Mark McGwire, Frank Thomas	7.50
7	Vladimir Guerrero, Andruw Jones	3.00

1999 Finest Double Feature

Similar to Finest Complements, this Series 2 set utilizes split-screen fronts to accomodate two players on a horizontal format. Each card has three versions: Non- Refractor/Refractor (1:56), Refractor/Non-Refractor (1:56) and Refractor/Refractor (1:168). Card numbers have a "DF" prefix. Values shown are for cards with either left- or right-side Refractor; Dual-Refractor cards are valued at 2X.

		MT
Complete Set (7):		30.00
Common Player:		2.00
Dual-Refractors:		2X
1	Ken Griffey Jr., Alex Rodriguez	10.00
2	Chipper Jones, Andruw Jones	6.00
3	Darin Erstad, Mo Vaughn	2.50
4	Craig Biggio, Jeff Bagwell	3.00
5	Ben Grieve, Eric Chavez	3.00
6	Albert Belle, Cal Ripken Jr.	7.50
7	Scott Rolen, Pat Burrell	4.00

1999 Finest Franchise Records

This Series 2 insert set focuses on players who led their teams in various statistical categories. They are randomly seeded in 1:129 packs, while a parallel Refractor version is inserted 1:378. Card numbers have a "FR" prefix.

		MT
Complete Set (10):		65.00
Common Player:		3.50
Refractors:		1.5X
1	Frank Thomas	4.00
2	Ken Griffey Jr.	10.00
3	Mark McGwire	13.50
4	Juan Gonzalez	3.50
5	Nomar Garciaparra	9.00
6	Mike Piazza	10.00
7	Cal Ripken Jr.	13.50
8	Sammy Sosa	6.00
9	Barry Bonds	7.50
10	Tony Gwynn	5.00

1999 Finest Future's Finest

This Series 2 insert focuses on up-and-coming players who are primed to emerge as superstars. These are seeded 1:171 packs and limited to 500 numbered sets. Card numbers have a "FF" prefix.

		MT
Complete Set (10):		35.00
Common Player:		2.00
1	Pat Burrell	10.00
2	Troy Glaus	12.50
3	Eric Chavez	5.00
4	Ryan Anderson	3.00
5	Ruben Mateo	3.00
6	Gabe Kapler	5.00
7	Alex Gonzalez	2.00
8	Michael Barrett	2.00
9	Lance Berkman	2.00
10	Fernando Seguignol	2.00

1999 Finest Hank Aaron Award Contenders

This insert set focuses on nine players who had the best chance to win baseball's newest award. Production varies from card to card, with nine times as many of card #9 as of card #1, and so on. Insertion odds thus vary greatly, from 1:12 to 1:216. Refractor versions are found at odds which vary from 1:96 to 1:1728. Card numbers have an "HA" prefix.

		MT
Complete Set (9):		27.50
Common Player:		2.50
Refractors:		3X
1	Juan Gonzalez	4.00
2	Vladimir Guerrero	4.00
3	Nomar Garciaparra	8.00
4	Albert Belle	2.50
5	Frank Thomas	2.50
6	Sammy Sosa	3.00
7	Alex Rodriguez	3.50
8	Ken Griffey Jr.	3.50
9	Mark McGwire	4.00

1999 Finest Leading Indicators

Utilizing a heat-sensitive, thermal ink technology, these cards highlight the 1998 home run totals of 10 players. Touching the left, right or center field portion of the card behind each player's image reveals his 1998 season home run total in that specific direction. These are seeded in Series 1 packs.

		MT
Complete Set (10):		22.00
Common Player:		.50
Inserted 1:24		
L1	Mark McGwire	6.00
L2	Sammy Sosa	4.00
L3	Ken Griffey Jr.	5.00
L4	Greg Vaughn	.50
L5	Albert Belle	1.00
L6	Juan Gonzalez	1.50
L7	Andres Galarraga	.50

L8	Alex Rodriguez	5.00
L9	Barry Bonds	2.00
L10	Jeff Bagwell	1.50

1999 Finest Milestones

This Series 2 insert set is fractured into four subsets, each focusing on a statistical category: Hits, Home Runs, RBIs and Doubles. The Hits category is limited to 3,000 numbered sets. Home Runs are limited to 500 numbered sets. RBIs are limited to 1,400 numbered sets and Doubles is limited to 500 numbered sets. Each card number carries an "M" prefix.

		MT
	Complete Set (40):	200.00
	Common Hits (1-10):	1.50
	Common Homeruns (11-20):	3.75
	Common RBI (21-30):	1.50
	Common Doubles (31-40):	3.00
1	Tony Gwynn (Hits)	4.00
2	Cal Ripken Jr. (Hits)	6.00
3	Wade Boggs (Hits)	1.50
4	Ken Griffey Jr. (Hits)	5.00
5	Frank Thomas (Hits)	3.00
6	Barry Bonds (Hits)	4.00
7	Travis Lee (Hits)	1.50
8	Alex Rodriguez (Hits)	6.00
9	Derek Jeter (Hits)	5.00
10	Vladimir Guerrero (Hits)	3.00
11	Mark McGwire (Home Runs)	18.50
12	Ken Griffey Jr. (Home Runs)	15.00
13	Vladimir Guerrero (Home Runs)	6.00
14	Alex Rodriguez (Home Runs)	15.00
15	Barry Bonds (Home Runs)	7.50
16	Sammy Sosa (Home Runs)	9.00
17	Albert Belle (Home Runs)	2.50
18	Frank Thomas (Home Runs)	4.00
19	Jose Canseco (Home Runs)	3.00
20	Mike Piazza (Home Runs)	15.00
21	Jeff Bagwell (RBI)	3.50
22	Barry Bonds (RBI)	4.00
23	Ken Griffey Jr. (RBI)	9.00
24	Albert Belle (RBI)	3.00
25	Juan Gonzalez (RBI)	3.50
26	Vinny Castilla (RBI)	1.50
27	Mark McGwire (RBI)	9.00
28	Alex Rodriguez (RBI)	9.00
29	Nomar Garciaparra (RBI)	6.00
30	Frank Thomas (RBI)	5.00
31	Barry Bonds (Doubles)	6.00
32	Albert Belle (Doubles)	3.00
33	Ben Grieve (Doubles)	3.00
34	Craig Biggio (Doubles)	3.00
35	Vladimir Guerrero (Doubles)	6.00
36	Nomar Garciaparra (Doubles)	12.00
37	Alex Rodriguez (Doubles)	15.00
38	Derek Jeter (Doubles)	15.00
39	Ken Griffey Jr. (Doubles)	15.00
40	Brad Fullmer (Doubles)	3.00

1999 Finest Peel & Reveal

This Series 1 insert offers 20 players produced in varying levels of scarcity designated by background design: Sparkle is common, Hyperplaid is uncommon and Stadium Stars is rare. Each card has a peel-off opaque protective coating on both front and back. Stated insertion odds are: Sparkle 1:30; Hyperplaid 1:60, and Stadium Stars 1:120. Home Team Advantage (HTA) boxes have odds which are twice as good.

		MT
	Complete Set (20):	55.00
	Common Player:	1.25
	Hyperplaid:	1.5X
	Stadium Stars:	2.5X
1	Kerry Wood	2.00
2	Mark McGwire	7.50
3	Sammy Sosa	5.00
4	Ken Griffey Jr.	6.50
5	Nomar Garciaparra	4.00
6	Greg Maddux	4.00
7	Derek Jeter	5.00
8	Andres Galarraga	1.25
9	Alex Rodriguez	6.50
10	Frank Thomas	3.00
11	Roger Clemens	2.50
12	Juan Gonzalez	2.00
13	Ben Grieve	1.50
14	Jeff Bagwell	2.00
15	Todd Helton	1.50
16	Chipper Jones	4.00
17	Barry Bonds	2.50
18	Travis Lee	1.25
19	Vladimir Guerrero	3.00
20	Pat Burrell	3.00

1999 Finest Prominent Figures

Fifty cards on Refractor technology highlight superstars chasing the all-time records in five different statistical categories: Home Runs, Slugging Percentage, Batting Average, RBIs and Total Bases. Ten players are featured in each category, each sequentially numbered to the all-time single season record statistic for that category. Home Run category is numbered to 70, Slugging Percentage to 847, Batting Average to 424, RBIs to 190 and Total Bases to 457.

		MT
	Complete Set (50):	500.00
	Common Home Runs (1-10); #d to 70:	6.00
	Common Slugging % (11-20); #d to 847:	2.00
	Common Batting Ave. (21-30); #d to 424:	3.50
	Common RBIs (31-40); #d to 190:	3.50
	Common Total Bases (41-50); #d to 457:	3.50
1	Mark McGwire (HR)	75.00
2	Sammy Sosa (HR)	35.00
3	Ken Griffey Jr. (HR)	50.00
4	Mike Piazza (HR)	40.00
5	Juan Gonzalez (HR)	15.00
6	Greg Vaughn (HR)	6.00
7	Alex Rodriguez (HR)	40.00
8	Manny Ramirez (HR)	15.00
9	Jeff Bagwell (HR)	15.00
10	Andres Galarraga (HR)	6.00
11	Mark McGwire (S%)	15.00
12	Sammy Sosa (S%)	10.00
13	Juan Gonzalez (S%)	4.00
14	Ken Griffey Jr. (S%)	12.50
15	Barry Bonds (S%)	6.00
16	Greg Vaughn (S%)	2.00
17	Larry Walker (S%)	2.50
18	Andres Galarraga (S%)	2.00
19	Jeff Bagwell (S%)	4.00
20	Albert Belle (S%)	3.00
21	Tony Gwynn (BA)	10.00
22	Mike Piazza (BA)	12.50
23	Larry Walker (BA)	3.50
24	Alex Rodriguez (BA)	15.00
25	John Olerud (BA)	3.50
26	Frank Thomas (BA)	7.50
27	Bernie Williams (BA)	3.50
28	Chipper Jones (BA)	10.00
29	Jim Thome (BA)	3.50
30	Barry Bonds (BA)	7.50
31	Juan Gonzalez (RBI)	10.00
32	Sammy Sosa (RBI)	20.00
33	Mark McGwire (RBI)	40.00
34	Albert Belle (RBI)	5.00
35	Ken Griffey Jr. (RBI)	30.00
36	Jeff Bagwell (RBI)	9.00
37	Chipper Jones (RBI)	17.50
38	Vinny Castilla (RBI)	3.50
39	Alex Rodriguez (RBI)	30.00
40	Andres Galarraga (RBI)	3.50
41	Sammy Sosa (TB)	10.00
42	Mark McGwire (TB)	20.00
43	Albert Belle (TB)	3.50
44	Ken Griffey Jr. (TB)	15.00
45	Jeff Bagwell (TB)	5.00
46	Juan Gonzalez (TB)	5.00
47	Barry Bonds (TB)	7.50
48	Vladimir Guerrero (TB)	5.00
49	Larry Walker (TB)	3.50
50	Alex Rodriguez (TB)	15.00

1999 Finest Split Screen

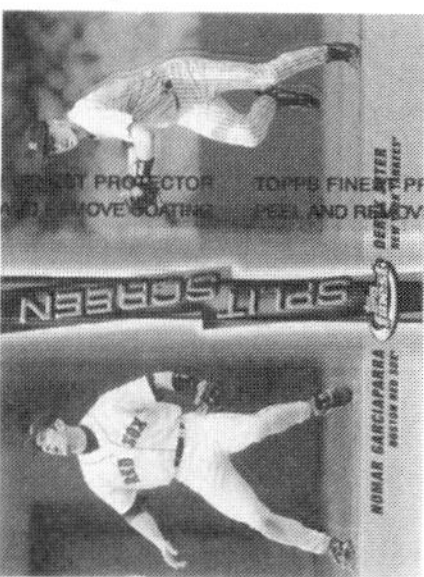

Players who share a common bond are highlighted in this Series 1 insert set which includes 14 paired players. Each card is available in three variations: Non-Refractor/Refractor (1:28), Refractor/Non-Refractor (1:28) and Refractor/Refractor (1:84). Values shown are for a card with either left- or right-side Refractor; dual-Refractor cards are worth 2X.

		MT
	Complete Set (14):	40.00
	Common Card:	1.50
	Dual-Refractor:	2X
1	Mark McGwire, Sammy Sosa	7.50
2	Ken Griffey Jr., Alex Rodriguez	6.00
3	Nomar Garciaparra, Derek Jeter	4.00
4	Barry Bonds, Albert Belle	2.00
5	Cal Ripken Jr., Tony Gwynn	5.00
6	Manny Ramirez, Juan Gonzalez	2.00
7	Frank Thomas, Andres Galarraga	3.00
8	Scott Rolen, Chipper Jones	2.50
9	Ivan Rodriguez, Mike Piazza	4.00
10	Kerry Wood, Roger Clemens	3.00
11	Greg Maddux, Tom Glavine	3.00
12	Troy Glaus, Eric Chavez	2.00
13	Ben Grieve, Todd Helton	1.50
14	Travis Lee, Pat Burrell	4.00

1999 Finest Team Finest

The first 10 cards are showcased in Series 1 while the last 10 cards showcased in Series 2. Team Finest are available in three colors: Blue, Red and Gold (Red and Gold are only available in Home Team Advantage packs). All Team Finest are serially numbered as follows: Blue, numbered to 1,500; Blue Refractors to 150; Red to 500; Red Refractors to 50; Gold to 250 and Gold Refractors to 25. Cards have a TF prefix to the card number.

		MT
Complete Set (20):		100.00
Common Blue:		2.00
Production 1,500 sets		
Blue Refractors:		3X
Production 150 sets		
Reds:		1.5X
Production 500 sets		
Red Refractors:		7X
Production 50 sets		
Golds:		2X
Production 250 sets		
Gold Refractors:		10X
Production 25 sets		
1	Greg Maddux	7.50
2	Mark McGwire	12.50
3	Sammy Sosa	7.50
4	Juan Gonzalez	3.50
5	Alex Rodriguez	9.00
6	Travis Lee	2.00
7	Roger Clemens	6.00
8	Darin Erstad	2.50
9	Todd Helton	3.00
10	Mike Piazza	9.00
11	Kerry Wood	3.00
12	Ken Griffey Jr.	10.00
13	Frank Thomas	5.00
14	Jeff Bagwell	3.50
15	Nomar Garciaparra	7.50
16	Derek Jeter	9.00
17	Chipper Jones	9.00
18	Barry Bonds	5.00
19	Tony Gwynn	4.50
20	Ben Grieve	2.25

2000 Finest

The 286-card base set has the traditional chromium finish with the Topps Finest logo in the upper left portion on the front. Also in the upper left portion is a partial image of a baseball with seams in the background of the player photo. Card backs have a small photo with '99 stats and career totals. The rookies from Series 1 are serial numbered to 2,000 and in Series 2 to 3,000.

		MT
Complete Set (286):		750.00
Complete Series 1 (147)		450.00
Complete Series 2 (140):		300.00
Common Player:		.25
Common Rookie (101-120):		8.00
Production 2,000		
Common Rookie (247-266)		6.00
Production 3,000		
Common Counterpart (267-276)		1.00
Inserted 1:8		
Common Gem (136-145):		
Inserted 1:24		
Pack (6):		4.00
Series 1 & 2 Box:		95.00
1	Nomar Garciaparra	2.50
2	Chipper Jones	2.00
3	Erubiel Durazo	.50
4	Robin Ventura	.50
5	Garret Anderson	.25
6	Dean Palmer	.40
7	Mariano Rivera	.50
8	Rusty Greer	.25
9	Jim Thome	.75
10	Jeff Bagwell	1.00
11	Jason Giambi	.25
12	Jeromy Burnitz	.40
13	Mark Grace	.50
14	Russ Ortiz	.25
15	Kevin Brown	.50
16	Kevin Millwood	.40
17	Scott Williamson	.25
18	Orlando Hernandez	.50
19	Todd Walker	.25
20	Carlos Beltran	.40
21	Ruben Rivera	.25
22	Curt Schilling	.40
23	Brian Giles	.25
24	Eric Karros	.40
25	Preston Wilson	.25
26	Al Leiter	.40
27	Juan Encarnacion	.25
28	Tim Salmon	.40
29	B.J. Surhoff	.25
30	Bernie Williams	.75
31	Lee Stevens	.25
32	Pokey Reese	.25
33	Mike Sweeney	.25
34	Corey Koskie	.25
35	Roberto Alomar	.75
36	Tim Hudson	.25
37	Tom Glavine	.50
38	Jeff Kent	.25
39	Mike Lieberthal	.25
40	Barry Larkin	.60
41	Paul O'Neill	.40
42	Rico Brogna	.25
43	Brian Daubach	.25
44	Rich Aurilia	.25
45	Vladimir Guerrero	1.50
46	Luis Castillo	.25
47	Bartolo Colon	.25
48	Kevin Appier	.25
49	Mo Vaughn	.75
50	Alex Rodriguez	3.00
51	Randy Johnson	.75
52	Kris Benson	.25
53	Tony Clark	.50
54	Chad Allen	.25
55	Larry Walker	.75
56	Freddy Garcia	.25
57	Paul Konerko	.40
58	Edgardo Alfonzo	.40
59	Brady Anderson	.40
60	Derek Jeter	2.50
61	Mike Hampton	.25
62	Jeff Cirillo	.40
63	Shannon Stewart	.25
64	Greg Maddux	2.00
65	Mark McGwire	4.00
66	Gary Sheffield	.50
67	Kevin Young	.25
68	Tony Gwynn	2.00
69	Rey Ordonez	.25
70	Cal Ripken Jr.	3.00
71	Todd Helton	1.00
72	Brian Jordan	.25
73	Jose Canseco	.50
74	Luis Gonzalez	.25
75	Barry Bonds	1.50
76	Jermaine Dye	.25
77	Jose Offerman	.25
78	Magglio Ordonez	.25
79	Fred McGriff	.50
80	Ivan Rodriguez	1.00
81	Josh Hamilton (Prospects)	2.00
82	Vernon Wells (Prospects)	.25
83	Mark Mulder (Prospects)	.25
84	John Patterson (Prospects)	.25
85	Nick Johnson (Prospects)	1.00
86	Pablo Ozuna (Prospects)	.25
87	A.J. Burnett (Prospects)	.25
88	Jack Cust (Prospects)	.25
89	Adam Piatt (Prospects)	1.00
90	Rob Ryan (Prospects)	.25
91	Sean Burroughs (Prospects)	1.50
92	D'Angelo Jimenez (Prospects)	.25
93	Chad Hermansen (Prospects)	.25
94	Rob Fick (Prospects)	.25
95	Ruben Mateo (Prospects)	.25
96	Alex Escobar (Prospects)	.25
97	Willi Mo Pena (Prospects)	1.00
98	Corey Patterson (Prospects)	.50
99	Eric Munson (Prospects)	.40
100	Pat Burrell (Prospects)	1.50
101	*Michael Tejera*	8.00
102	*Bobby Bradley*	15.00
103	*Larry Bigbie*	10.00
104	*B.J. Garbe*	12.00
105	*Josh Kalinowski*	8.00
106	*Brett Myers*	20.00
107	*Chris Mears*	8.00
108	*Aaron Rowand*	12.00
109	*Corey Myers*	10.00
110	*John Sneed*	8.00
111	*Ryan Christensen*	15.00
112	*Kyle Snyder*	8.00
113	*Mike Paradis*	8.00
114	*Chance Caple*	10.00
115	*Ben Christiansen*	8.00
116	*Brad Baker*	10.00
117	*Rob Purvis*	8.00
118	*Rick Asadoorian*	12.00
119	*Ruben Salazar*	12.00
120	*Julio Zuleta*	10.00
121	Ken Griffey Jr., Alex Rodriguez (Features)	6.00
122	Nomar Garciaparra, Derek Jeter (Features)	5.00
123	Mark McGwire, Sammy Sosa (Features)	8.00
124	Randy Johnson, Pedro Martinez (Features)	2.00
125	Mike Piazza, Ivan Rodriguez (Features)	5.00
126	Manny Ramirez, Roberto Alomar (Features)	2.00
127	Chipper Jones, Andruw Jones (Features)	4.00
128	Cal Ripken Jr., Tony Gwynn (Features)	6.00
129	Jeff Bagwell, Craig Biggio (Features)	2.00
130	Vladimir Guerrero, Barry Bonds (Features)	3.00
131	Alfonso Soriano, Nick Johnson (Features)	2.00
132	Josh Hamilton, Pat Burrell (Features)	3.00
133	Corey Patterson, Ruben Mateo (Features)	1.00
134	Larry Walker, Todd Helton (Features)	1.50
135	Edgardo Alfonzo, Rey Ordonez (Features)	1.00
136	Derek Jeter (Gems)	12.00
137	Alex Rodriguez (Gems)	15.00
138	Chipper Jones (Gems)	10.00
139	Mike Piazza (Gems)	12.00
140	Mark McGwire (Gems)	20.00
141	Ivan Rodriguez (Gems)	5.00
142	Cal Ripken Jr. (Gems)	15.00
143	Vladimir Guerrero (Gems)	8.00
144	Randy Johnson (Gems)	4.00
145	Jeff Bagwell (Gems)	5.00
146	Ken Griffey Jr. field	4.00
146a	Ken Griffey Jr. press	4.00
147	Andruw Jones	.50
148	Kerry Wood	.40
149	Jim Edmonds	.40
150	Pedro Martinez	1.00
151	Warren Morris	.25
152	Trevor Hoffman	.25
153	Eric Young	.25
154	Andy Pettitte	.25
155	Frank Thomas	1.50
156	Damion Easley	.25
157	Cliff Floyd	.25
158	Ben Davis	.25
159	John Valentin	.25
160	Rafael Palmeiro	.75
161	Andy Ashby	.25
162	J.D. Drew	.40
163	Jay Bell	.25
164	Adam Kennedy	.25
165	Manny Ramirez	1.00
166	John Halama	.25
167	Octavio Dotel	.25
168	Darin Erstad	.50
169	Jose Lima	.25
170	Andres Galarraga	.75
171	Scott Rolen	.75
172	Delino DeShields	.25
173	J.T. Snow Jr.	.25
174	Tony Womack	.25
175	John Olerud	.40
176	Jason Kendall	.40
177	Carlos Lee	.25
178	Eric Milton	.25
179	Jeff Cirillo	.25
180	Gabe Kapler	.50
181	Greg Vaughn	.40
182	Denny Neagle	.25
183	Tino Martinez	.40
184	Doug Mientkiewicz	.25
185	Juan Gonzalez	1.00
186	Ellis Burks	.25
187	Mike Hampton	.25
188	Royce Clayton	.25
189	Mike Mussina	.50
190	Carlos Delgado	.75
191	Ben Grieve	.50

192	Fernando Tatis	.25
193	Matt Williams	.50
194	Rondell White	.40
195	Shawn Green	.75
196	Justin Thompson	.25
197	Troy Glaus	1.00
198	Roger Cedeno	.25
199	Ray Lankford	.25
200	Sammy Sosa	2.50
201	Kenny Lofton	.50
202	Edgar Martinez	.40
203	Mark Kotsay	.25
204	David Wells	.25
205	Craig Biggio	.50
206	Ray Durham	.25
207	Troy O'Leary	.25
208	Rickey Henderson	.50
209	Bob Abreu	.25
210	Neifi Perez	.25
211	Carlos Febles	.25
212	Chuck Knoblauch	.25
213	Moises Alou	.25
214	Omar Vizquel	.25
215	Vinny Castilla	.25
216	Javy Lopez	.25
217	Johnny Damon	.40
218	Roger Clemens	1.25
219	Miguel Tejada	.25
220	Deion Sanders	.40
221	Matt Lawton	.25
222	Albert Belle	.75
223	Adrian Beltre	.40
224	Dante Bichette	.40
225	Raul Mondesi	.40
226	Mike Piazza	2.50
227	Brad Penny (Prospects)	.25
228	Kip Wells (Prospects)	.25
229	Adam Everett (Prospects)	.25
230	Eddie Yarnall (Prospects)	.25
231	Matt LeCroy (Prospects)	.25
232	Ryan Anderson (Prospects)	.50
233	Rick Ankiel (Prospects)	.75
234	Daryle Ward (Prospects)	.25
235	Rafael Furcal (Prospects)	.75
236	Dee Brown (Prospects)	.25
237	Travis Dawkins (Prospects)	.25
238	Eric Valent (Prospects)	.25
239	Peter Bergeron (Prospects)	.25
240	Alfonso Soriano (Prospects)	.50
241	John Patterson (Prospects)	.25
242	Jorge Toca (Prospects)	.25
243	Ryan Anderson (Prospects)	.50
244	Jason Dallaero (Prospects)	.25
245	Jason Grilli (Prospects)	.25
246	Chad Hermansen (Prospects)	.25
247	*Scott Downs*	6.00
248	*Keith Reed*	10.00
249	*Edgar Cruz*	6.00
250	*Wes Anderson*	8.00
251	*Lyle Overbay*	10.00
252	*Mike Lamb*	8.00
253	*Vince Faison*	10.00
254	*Chad Alexander*	6.00
255	Chris Wakeland	6.00
256	*Aaron McNeal*	8.00
257	*Tomokazu Ohka*	10.00
258	*Ty Howington*	10.00
259	*Javier Colina*	6.00
260	Jason Jennings	6.00
261	*Ramon Santiago*	8.00
262	*Johan Santana*	6.00
263	*Quincey Foster*	6.00
264	*Junior Brignac*	6.00
265	*Rico Washington*	6.00
266	*Scott Sobkowiak*	6.00
267	Pedro Martinez, Rick Ankiel (Counterparts)	3.00
268	Manny Ramirez, Vladimir Guerrero (Counterparts)	3.00
269	A.J. Burnett, Mark Mulder (Counterparts)	1.00
270	Mike Piazza, Eric Munson (Counterparts)	6.00
271	Josh Hamilton, Corey Patterson (Counterparts)	1.50
272	Ken Griffey Jr., Sammy Sosa (Counterparts)	6.00
273	Derek Jeter, Alfonso Soriano (Counterparts)	6.00
274	Mark McGwire, Pat Burrell (Counterparts)	8.00
275	Chipper Jones, Cal Ripken Jr. (Counterparts)	8.00
276	Nomar Garciaparra, Alex Rodriguez (Counterparts)	8.00
277	Pedro Martinez (Gems)	4.00
278	Tony Gwynn (Gems)	5.00
279	Barry Bonds (Gems)	5.00
280	Juan Gonzalez (Gems)	4.00
281	Larry Walker (Gems)	3.00
282	Nomar Garciaparra (Gems)	10.00
283	Ken Griffey Jr. (Gems)	10.00
284	Manny Ramirez (Gems)	4.00
285	Shawn Green (Gems)	2.50
286	Sammy Sosa (Gems)	8.00

2000 Finest Refractor

These are a parallel to the base set and have a mirror like sheen. Card backs have "refractor" written underneath the card number.

	MT
Stars (1-100):	6-10X
Inserted 1:24	
Rookies (101-120, 247-266):	1X
Production 500 sets	
Features (121-135):	2-3X
Inserted 1:96	
Counterparts (267-276):	2-3X
Inserted 1:96	
Gems (136-145, 277-286):	2-3X
Inserted 1:288	

2000 Finest Gold Refractor

A parallel to the base set, these have the usual mirror like appearance with a deckle edged border. Regular cards are seeded 1:240 packs, Rookies are limited to 100 serial numbered sets, Features and Counterparts subsets (1:960) and Gems (1:2,880).

	MT
Stars (1-100):	20-40X
Inserted 1:240	
Rookies (101-120, 247-266):	1-2X
Production 100 sets	
Features:	4-8X
Inserted 1:960	
Counterparts:	4-8X
Inserted 1:960	
Gems:	4-8X
Inserted 1:2,880	

2000 Finest Ballpark Bounties

Seeded across both Series 1 and 2 these inserts use Serigraph Fresnal technology and have a metallic looking image of a baseball in the background of the player photo. Card backs are numbered with a "BB" prefix.

		MT
Complete Set (30):		170.00
Complete Series 1 (15):		80.00
Complete Series 2 (15):		90.00
Common Player:		3.00
Inserted 1:24		
1	Chipper Jones	10.00
2	Mike Piazza	12.00
3	Vladimir Guerrero	8.00
4	Sammy Sosa	12.00
5	Nomar Garciaparra	12.00
6	Manny Ramirez	5.00
7	Jeff Bagwell	5.00
8	Scott Rolen	5.00
9	Carlos Beltran	3.00
10	Pedro Martinez	5.00
11	Greg Maddux	10.00
12	Josh Hamilton	6.00
13	Adam Piatt	3.00
14	Pat Burrell	5.00
15	Alfonso Soriano	4.00
16	Alex Rodriguez	15.00
17	Derek Jeter	12.00
18	Cal Ripken Jr.	15.00
19	Larry Walker	3.00
20	Barry Bonds	5.00
21	Ken Griffey Jr.	15.00
22	Mark McGwire	20.00
23	Ivan Rodriguez	5.00
24	Andruw Jones	4.00
25	Todd Helton	5.00
26	Randy Johnson	5.00
27	Ruben Mateo	3.00
28	Corey Patterson	3.00
29	Sean Burroughs	4.00
30	Eric Munson	3.00

2000 Finest Dream Cast

These inserts are found exclusively in Series 2 packs and utilize Duflex technology. The card fronts try to portray a "dream sequence" with sky and clouds in the background. They are numbered with a "DC" prefix on the card back.

		MT
Complete Set (10):		80.00
Common Player:		4.00
Inserted 1:36		
1	Mark McGwire	20.00
2	Roberto Alomar	4.00
3	Chipper Jones	10.00
4	Derek Jeter	12.00
5	Barry Bonds	5.00
6	Ken Griffey Jr.	15.00
7	Sammy Sosa	12.00
8	Mike Piazza	12.00
9	Pedro Martinez	5.00
10	Randy Johnson	5.00

2000 Finest Finest Moments

This four-card set pays tribute to milestone achievements accomplished during the 1999 season. They are numbered with a "FM" prefix. A Refractor parallel version is seeded 1:20 packs.

		MT
Complete Set (4):		
Common Player:		1.00
Inserted 1:9		
Refractor:		1-2X
Inserted 1:20		
1	Chipper Jones	3.00
2	Ivan Rodriguez	1.50
3	Tony Gwynn	2.50
4	Wade Boggs	1.00

2000 Finest For The Record

Printed on Finest Clear Card technology, each of

the 10 players featured has three cards. Each card sequentially numbered to the distance of the outfield wall in their home ballpark (left, center and right). Combining all three cards forms a panaromic view of the stadium.

		MT
Complete Set (30):		700.00
Common Player:		10.00
1A	Derek Jeter (318)	35.00
1B	Derek Jeter (408)	30.00
1C	Derek Jeter (314)	35.00
2A	Mark McGwire (330)	55.00
2B	Mark McGwire (402)	50.00
2C	Mark McGwire (330)	55.00
3A	Ken Griffey Jr. (331)	50.00
3B	Ken Griffey Jr. (405)	40.00
3C	Ken Griffey Jr. (327)	50.00
4A	Alex Rodriguez (331)	40.00
4B	Alex Rodriguez (405)	35.00
4C	Alex Rodriguez (327)	40.00
5A	Nomar Garciaparra (310)	35.00
5B	Nomar Garciaparra (390)	30.00
5C	Nomar Garciaparra (302)	35.00
6A	Cal Ripken Jr. (333)	40.00
6B	Cal Ripken Jr. (410)	35.00
6C	Cal Ripken Jr. (318)	40.00
7A	Sammy Sosa (355)	30.00
7B	Sammy Sosa (400)	30.00
7C	Sammy Sosa (353)	30.00
8A	Manny Ramirez (325)	15.00
8B	Manny Ramirez (410)	12.00
8C	Manny Ramirez (325)	15.00
9A	Mike Piazza (338)	35.00
9B	Mike Piazza (410)	30.00
9C	Mike Piazza (338)	35.00
10A	Chipper Jones (335)	30.00
10B	Chipper Jones (401)	25.00
10C	Chipper Jones (330)	30.00

2000 Finest Gems Oversized

Each of the 10 Gems subset cards in series 1 and 2 were also done on an oversized format. The oversized cards were added as a box topper to each box. Home Team Advantage stores received Refractor versions of the Gems Oversized cards as a box topper.

		MT
Complete Set (20):		90.00
Complete Series 1 (10):		50.00
Complete Series 2 (10):		40.00
Common Player:		2.00
Inserted 1:box		
1	Derek Jeter	8.00
2	Alex Rodriguez	10.00
3	Chipper Jones	6.00
4	Mike Piazza	8.00
5	Mark McGwire	12.00
6	Ivan Rodriguez	3.00
7	Cal Ripken Jr.	10.00
8	Vladimir Guerrero	5.00
9	Randy Johnson	3.00
10	Jeff Bagwell	3.00
11	Nomar Garciaparra	8.00
12	Ken Griffey Jr.	10.00
13	Manny Ramirez	3.00
14	Shawn Green	2.00
15	Sammy Sosa	8.00
16	Pedro Martinez	3.00
17	Tony Gwynn	5.00
18	Barry Bonds	4.00
19	Juan Gonzalez	3.00
20	Larry Walker	2.00

2000 Finest Going the Distance

This 12-card set highlights the top hitters in baseball, utilizing Photopolymer hologram technology. Card backs are numbered with a "GTD" prefix.

		MT
Complete Set (12):		90.00
Common Player:		3.00
Inserted 1:24		
1	Tony Gwynn	8.00
2	Alex Rodriguez	12.00
3	Derek Jeter	10.00
4	Chipper Jones	8.00
5	Nomar Garciaparra	10.00
6	Sammy Sosa	10.00
7	Ken Griffey Jr.	12.00
8	Vladimir Guerrero	6.00
9	Mark McGwire	15.00
10	Mike Piazza	10.00
11	Manny Ramirez	4.00
12	Cal Ripken Jr.	12.00

2000 Finest Moments Autographs

An autographed version of the four-card set, these were seeded 1:425 packs.

		MT
Complete Set (4):		325.00
Common Player:		80.00
Inserted 1:425		
1	Chipper Jones	100.00
2	Ivan Rodriguez	80.00
3	Tony Gwynn	100.00
4	Wade Boggs	80.00

2001 Finest

		MT
Complete Set (140):		400.00
Common Player:		.25
Common Standout Veteran (10):		8.00
Production 1999		
Common Rookie (111-140):		8.00
Production 999		
Pack (6):		4.75
Box (20):		85.00
1	Mike Piazza SV	20.00
2	Andruw Jones	.75
3	Jason Giambi	.75
4	Fred McGriff	.25
5	Vladimir Guerrero SV	10.00
6	Adrian Gonzalez	.25
7	Pedro Martinez	1.25
8	Mike Lieberthal	.25
9	Warren Morris	.25
10	Juan Gonzalez	1.00
11	Jose Canseco	.50
12	Jose Valentin	.25
13	Jeff Cirillo	.25
14	Pokey Reese	.25
15	Scott Rolen	.50
16	Greg Maddux	2.00
17	Carlos Delgado	.75
18	Rick Ankiel	.25
19	Steve Finley	.25
20	Shawn Green	.40
21	Orlando Cabrerra	.25
22	Roberto Alomar	.75
23	John Olerud	.35
24	Albert Belle	.25
25	Edgardo Alfonzo	.25
26	Rafael Palmeiro	.50
27	Mike Sweeney	.25
28	Bernie Williams	.75
29	Larry Walker	.50
30	Barry Bonds SV	10.00
31	Orlando Hernandez	.40
32	Randy Johnson	1.00
33	Shannon Stewart	.25
34	Mark Grace	.40
35	Alex Rodriguez SV	18.00
36	Tino Martinez	.25
37	Carlos Febles	.25
38	Al Leiter	.35
39	Omar Vizquel	.35
40	Chuck Knoblauch	.25
41	Tim Salmon	.25
42	Brian Jordan	.25
43	Edgar Renteria	.25
44	Preston Wilson	.25
45	Mariano Rivera	.35
46	Gabe Kapler	.35
47	Jason Kendall	.25
48	Rickey Henderson	.40
49	Luis Gonzalez	.40
50	Tom Glavine	.50
51	Jeromy Burnitz	.25
52	Garret Anderson	.25
53	Craig Biggio	.35
54	Vinny Castilla	.25
55	Jeff Kent	.35
56	Gary Sheffield	.40
57	Jorge Posada	.40
58	Sean Casey	.40
59	Johnny Damon	.25
60	Dean Palmer	.25
61	Todd Helton	1.00
62	Barry Larkin	.40
63	Robin Ventura	.25
64	Kenny Lofton	.35
65	Sammy Sosa SV	15.00
66	Rafael Furcal	.25
67	Jay Bell	.25
68	J.T. Snow Jr.	.25
69	Jose Vidro	.25
70	Ivan Rodriguez	1.00
71	Jermaine Dye	.25
72	Chipper Jones SV	15.00
73	Fernando Vina	.25
74	Ben Grieve	.25
75	Mark McGwire SV	25.00
76	Matt Williams	.40
77	Mark Grudzielanek	.25
78	Mike Hampton	.25
79	Brian Giles	.35
80	Tony Gwynn	1.25
81	Carlos Beltran	.25
82	Ray Durham	.25
83	Brad Radke	.25
84	David Justice	.50
85	Frank Thomas	1.25
86	Todd Zeile	.25
87	Pat Burrell	.50
88	Jim Thome	.35
89	Greg Vaughn	.25
90	Ken Griffey Jr. SV	20.00
91	Mike Mussina	.50
92	Maggiio Ordonez	.35
93	Bobby Abreu	.25
94	Alex Gonzalez	.25
95	Kevin Brown	.35
96	Jay Buhner	.25
97	Roger Clemens	1.50
98	Nomar Garciaparra SV	18.00
99	Derek Lee	.25
100	Derek Jeter SV	25.00
101	Adrian Beltre	.25
102	Geoff Jenkins	.40
103	Javy Lopez	.25
104	Raul Mondesi	.25
105	Troy Glaus	1.00
106	Jeff Bagwell	1.00
107	Eric Karros	.25
108	Mo Vaughn	.25
109	Cal Ripken Jr.	3.00
110	Manny Ramirez	1.25
111	Scott Heard	8.00
112	*Luis Montanez*	25.00
113	Ben Diggins	8.00
114	*Shaun Boyd*	15.00
115	Sean Burnett	8.00
116	*Carmen Cali*	12.00
117	Derek Thompson	8.00
118	*David Parrish*	20.00
119	*Dominic Rich*	15.00
120	*Chad Petty*	12.00
121	*Steve Smyth*	15.00
122	John Lackey	8.00
123	*Matt Galante*	12.00
124	*Danny Borrell*	10.00
125	*Bob Keppel*	12.00
126	*Justin Wayne*	20.00
127	J.R. House	15.00
128	*Brian Sellier*	15.00
129	*Dan Moylan*	15.00
130	*Scott Pratt*	15.00
131	*Victor Hall*	20.00

132	Joel Pineiro	8.00
133	*Josh Axelson*	15.00
134	*Jose Reyes*	20.00
135	*Greg Runser*	10.00
136	*Bryan Hebson*	10.00
137	*Sammy Serrano*	15.00
138	*Kevin Joseph*	20.00
139	*Juan Richardson*	20.00
140	*Mark Fischer*	15.00

2001 Finest Refractors

	MT
Stars (1-110):	4-8X
Production 499	
SP's:	.5-1.5X
Production 399	
Cards (111-140):	1-2X
Production 241	

2001 Finest Autographed

		MT
Common Player:		10.00
Inserted 1:22		
MB	Milton Bradley	15.00
SB	Sean Burnett	10.00
BKC	Brian Cole	10.00
JC	Joe Crede	15.00
BC	Brad Creese	10.00
BD	Ben Diggins	10.00
CD	Chad Durham	10.00
TF	Troy Farnsworth	10.00
RF	Rafael Furcal	25.00
KG	Keith Ginter	10.00
AG	Adrian Gonzalez	20.00
JHH	Josh Hamilton	35.00
JH	Jason Hart	20.00
JRH	J.R. House	25.00
AH	Adam Hyzdu	10.00
DKC	David Kelton	10.00
AK	Adam Kennedy	10.00
DK	David Krynzel	15.00
ML	Mike Lamb	10.00
TL	Terrence Long	10.00
KM	Kevin Mench	15.00
BM	Ben Molina	10.00
JM	Justin Morneau	25.00
CM	Chad Mottola	10.00
JO	Jose Ortiz	20.00
DP	David Parrish	10.00
DCP	Corey Patterson	25.00
JP	Jay Payton	15.00
CP	Carlos Pena	15.00
AP	Albert Pujols	200.00
MQ	Mark Quinn	15.00
MR	Mark Redman	10.00
BS	Ben Sheets	30.00
JS	Juan Silvestre	10.00
JNS	Jamal Strong	10.00
BZ	Barry Zito	25.00

A card number in parentheses ( ) indicates the set is unnumbered.

2001 Finest All-Stars

		MT
Complete Set (10):		60.00
Common Player:		3.00
Inserted 1:10		
Refractors:		1.5-2X
Inserted 1:40		
1	Mark McGwire	10.00
2	Derek Jeter	10.00
3	Alex Rodriguez	8.00
4	Chipper Jones	6.00
5	Nomar Garciaparra	8.00
6	Sammy Sosa	6.00
7	Mike Piazza	8.00
8	Barry Bonds	4.00
9	Vladimir Guerrero	4.00
10	Ken Griffey Jr.	8.00

2001 Finest Moments Autographs

		MT
Common Autograph:		30.00
Inserted 1:250		
BB	Barry Bonds	100.00
GB	George Brett	100.00
JG	Jason Giambi	30.00
TG	Troy Glaus	40.00
TH	Todd Helton	50.00
PM	Paul Molitor	60.00
EM	Eddie Murray	75.00
CR	Cal Ripken Jr.	150.00
DW	Dave Winfield	50.00
RY	Robin Yount	70.00

2001 Finest Moments

		MT
Complete Set (25):		100.00
Common Player:		1.50
Inserted 1:12		
Refractors:		1.5-2X
Inserted 1:40		
1	Pat Burrell	5.00
2	Adam Kennedy	1.50
3	Mike Lamb	1.50
4	Rafael Furcal	2.00
5	Terrence Long	1.50
6	Jay Payton	1.50
7	Mark Quinn	1.50
8	Ben Molina	1.50
9	Kazuhiro Sasaki	1.50
10	Mark Redman	1.50
11	Barry Bonds	8.00
12	Alex Rodriguez	15.00
13	Roger Clemens	8.00
14	Jim Edmonds	2.50
15	Jason Giambi	4.00
16	Todd Helton	6.00
17	Troy Glaus	6.00
18	Carlos Delgado	5.00
19	Darin Erstad	4.00
20	Cal Ripken Jr.	20.00
21	Paul Molitor	6.00
22	Robin Yount	6.00
23	George Brett	10.00
24	Dave Winfield	3.00
25	Wade Boggs	4.00

2001 Finest Origins

		MT
Complete Set (15):		40.00
Common Player:		1.50
Inserted 1:7		
Refractors:		1.5-2X
Inserted 1:40		
1	Derek Jeter	12.00
2	Jason Kendall	1.50
3	Jose Vidro	1.50
4	Preston Wilson	1.50
5	Jim Edmonds	2.50
6	Vladimir Guerrero	5.00
7	Andruw Jones	4.00
8	Scott Rolen	4.00
9	Edgardo Alfonzo	1.50
10	Mike Sweeney	1.50
11	Alex Rodriguez	10.00
12	Jermaine Dye	1.50
13	Charles Johnson	1.50
14	Darren Dreifort	1.50
15	Neifi Perez	1.50

2002 Finest

		MT
Complete Set (110):		175.00
Common Player:		.25
Common SP Auto. (101-110):		10.00
Pack (5):		6.00
Box (18):		95.00
1	Mike Mussina	.75
2	Steve Sparks	.25
3	Randy Johnson	1.00
4	Orlando Cabrera	.25
5	Jeff Kent	.40
6	Carlos Delgado	.50
7	Ivan Rodriguez	.75
8	Jose Cruz	.25
9	Jason Giambi	1.00
10	Brad Penny	.25
11	Moises Alou	.40
12	Mike Piazza	2.50
13	Ben Grieve	.40
14	Derek Jeter	4.00
15	Roy Oswalt	.50
16	Pat Burrell	.50
17	Preston Wilson	.25
18	Kevin Brown	.25
19	Barry Bonds	2.00
20	Phil Nevin	.25
21	Juan Gonzalez	1.00
22	Carlos Beltran	.25
23	Chipper Jones	2.00
24	Curt Schilling	.75
25	Jorge Posada	.50
26	Alfonso Soriano	1.00
27	Cliff Floyd	.40
28	Rafael Palmeiro	.50
29	Terrence Long	.25
30	Ken Griffey Jr.	3.00
31	Jason Kendall	.25
32	Jose Vidro	.25
33	Jermaine Dye	.25
34	Bobby Higginson	.25
35	Albert Pujols	2.00
36	Miguel Tejada	.50
37	Jim Edmonds	.40
38	Barry Zito	.40
39	Jimmy Rollins	.25
40	Rafael Furcal	.25
41	Omar Vizquel	.25
42	Kazuhiro Sasaki	.25
43	Brian Giles	.50
44	Darin Erstad	.50
45	Mariano Rivera	.50
46	Troy Percival	.25
47	Mike Sweeney	.25
48	Vladimir Guerrero	1.00
49	Troy Glaus	.75
50	Hideo Nomo	.50
51	Edgardo Alfonzo	.25
52	Roger Clemens	1.50
53	Eric Chavez	.50
54	Alex Rodriguez	2.50
55	Cristian Guzman	.25
56	Jeff Bagwell	1.00
57	Bernie Williams	.75
58	Kerry Wood	.50
59	Ryan Klesko	.40
60	Ichiro Suzuki	4.00
61	Larry Walker	.50
62	Nomar Garciaparra	2.50
63	Craig Biggio	.40
64	J.D. Drew	.50
65	Juan Pierre	.25
66	Roberto Alomar	.75
67	Luis Gonzalez	.75
68	Bud Smith	.25
69	Magglio Ordonez	.50
70	Scott Rolen	.50
71	Tsuyoshi Shinjo	.50
72	Reggie Sanders	.25
73	Garret Anderson	.25
74	Tim Hudson	.50
75	Adam Dunn	1.00
76	Gary Sheffield	.50
77	Johnny Damon	.25
78	Todd Helton	1.00
79	Geoff Jenkins	.50
80	Shawn Green	.50
81	C.C. Sabathia	.25
82	*Kazuhisa Ishii*	6.00
83	Rich Aurilia	.25
84	Mike Hampton	.25
85	Ben Sheets	.50
86	Andruw Jones	.75
87	Richie Sexson	.50
88	Jim Thome	.50
89	Sammy Sosa	2.00
90	Greg Maddux	2.00
91	Pedro Martinez	1.00
92	Jeromy Burnitz	.25
93	Raul Mondesi	.25
94	Bret Boone	.25
95	Jerry Hairston Jr.	.25
96	Carlos Pena	.50
97	Juan Cruz	.25
98	Morgan Ensberg	.25
99	Nathan Haynes	.25
100	Xavier Nady	.25
101	*Nic Jackson Auto.*	25.00
102	*Mauricio Lara Auto.*	15.00
103	*Freddy Sanchez Auto.*	20.00
104	*Clint Nageotte Auto.*	25.00
105	*Beltran Perez Auto.*	25.00
106	*Garrett Gentry Auto.*	15.00
107	*Chad Qualls Auto.*	20.00
108	*Jason Bay Auto.*	20.00
109	*Michael Hill Auto.*	15.00
110	Brian Tallet Auto.	20.00

2002 Finest Refractors

	MT
Star Refractors:	2-5X
Numbered to 499	
X-Fractors:	3-6X

Numbered to 299
X-Fractor Protector: 5-10X
Numbered to 99

2002 Finest Finest Moments Autographs

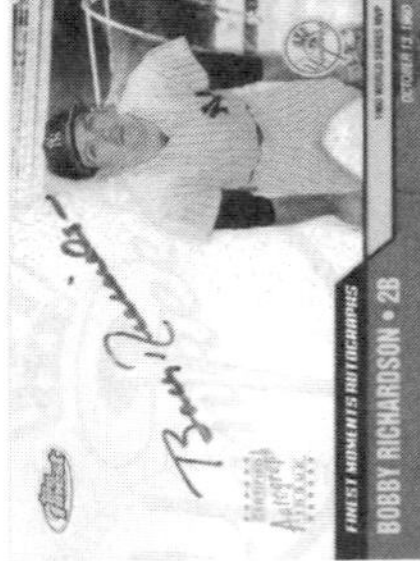

		MT
Common Autograph:		15.00
Inserted 1:18		
LA	Luis Aparicio	20.00
YB	Yogi Berra	45.00
WB	Wade Boggs	
JB	Jim Bunning	25.00
CF	Carlton Fisk	
BG	Bob Gibson	35.00
GG	Rich "Goose" Gossage	15.00
FJ	Fergie Jenkins	18.00
DL	Don Larsen	25.00
DM	Don Mattingly	75.00
JM	Joe Morgan	
GP	Gaylord Perry	20.00
BR	Bobby Richardson	20.00
BRO	Brooks Robinson	35.00
JS	Johnny Sain	20.00
MS	Mike Schmidt	50.00
RS	Red Schoendienst	15.00
BT	Bobby Thomson	15.00
BW	Billy Williams	
RY	Robin Yount	

2002 Finest Finest Uniform Relics

		MT
Common Player:		10.00
Inserted 1:24		
RA	Roberto Alomar	15.00
JB	Jeff Bagwell	15.00
BB	Barry Bonds	30.00
BBO	Bret Boone	10.00
CD	Carlos Delgado	10.00
LG	Luis Gonzalez	10.00
MG	Mark Grace	15.00
SG	Shawn Green	10.00
TG	Tony Gwynn	20.00
TH	Todd Helton	15.00
RH	Rickey Henderson	25.00
AJ	Andruw Jones	
CJ	Chipper Jones	25.00
GM	Greg Maddux	25.00
PM	Pedro Martinez	20.00
HN	Hideo Nomo	45.00
RP	Rafael Palmeiro	20.00
MP	Mike Piazza	25.00
AR	Alex Rodriguez	20.00
IR	Ivan Rodriguez	15.00
CS	Curt Schilling	12.00
TS	Tsuyoshi Shinjo	25.00
FT	Frank Thomas	15.00
LW	Larry Walker	10.00

2002 Finest Finest Bat Relics

		MT
Common Player:		12.00
Inserted 1:72		
BB	Barry Bonds	40.00
BBO	Bret Boone	12.00
NG	Nomar Garciaparra	35.00
LG	Luis Gonzalez	12.00
TG	Tony Gwynn	20.00
TH	Todd Helton	15.00
AJ	Andruw Jones	20.00
CJ	Chipper Jones	30.00
MP	Mike Piazza	30.00
AP	Albert Pujols	25.00
AR	Alex Rodriguez	25.00
IR	Ivan Rodriguez	12.00
TS	Tsuyoshi Shinjo	20.00
AS	Alfonso Soriano	25.00
BW	Bernie Williams	20.00

2002 Finest Team Topps Legends

MT

Common Autograph
Paul Blair
Ralph Branca
Vern Law
Willie Mays
Graig Nettles
Bobby Richardson
Robin Roberts
Bill "Moose" Skowron
Bobby Thomson
Carl Yastrzemski

1993 Flair Promos

Among the scarcest modern baseball promo cards are those produced to introduce Fleer's new premium product for 1993, Flair. Basically similar to the issued versions, the promo cards have "000" in place of the card number on back. The promos are checklisted here in alphabetical order.

		MT
Complete Set (8):		400.00
Common Player:		25.00
(1)	Will Clark	50.00
(2)	Darren Daulton	25.00
(3)	Andres Galarraga	25.00
(4)	Bryan Harvey	25.00
(5)	David Justice	50.00
(6)	Jody Reed	25.00
(7)	Nolan Ryan	200.00
(8)	Sammy Sosa	125.00

1993 Flair

Designed as Fleer's super-premium card brand, this 300-card set contains extra-thick cards which feature gold-foil highlights and UV coating front and back. Portrait and action photos are combined in a high-tech front picture and there is a muted photo on the back, as well.

		MT
Complete Set (300):		20.00
Common Player:		.15
Pack (10):		2.00
Wax Box (24):		25.00
1	Steve Avery	.15
2	Jeff Blauser	.15
3	Ron Gant	.15
4	Tom Glavine	.20
5	Dave Justice	.25
6	Mark Lemke	.15
7	Greg Maddux	1.25
8	Fred McGriff	.15
9	Terry Pendleton	.15
10	Deion Sanders	.20
11	John Smoltz	.20
12	Mike Stanton	.15
13	Steve Buechele	.15
14	Mark Grace	.25
15	Greg Hibbard	.15
16	Derrick May	.15
17	Chuck McElroy	.15
18	Mike Morgan	.15
19	Randy Myers	.15
20	Ryne Sandberg	.75
21	Dwight Smith	.15
22	Sammy Sosa	1.50
23	Jose Vizcaino	.15
24	Tim Belcher	.15
25	Rob Dibble	.15
26	Roberto Kelly	.15
27	Barry Larkin	.25
28	Kevin Mitchell	.15
29	Hal Morris	.15
30	Joe Oliver	.15
31	Jose Rijo	.15
32	Bip Roberts	.15
33	Chris Sabo	.15
34	Reggie Sanders	.15
35	Dante Bichette	.15
36	Willie Blair	.15
37	Jerald Clark	.15
38	Alex Cole	.15
39	Andres Galarraga	.15
40	Joe Girardi	.15
41	Charlie Hayes	.15
42	Chris Jones	.15
43	David Nied	.15
44	Eric Young	.15
45	Alex Arias	.15
46	Jack Armstrong	.15
47	Bret Barberie	.15
48	Chuck Carr	.15
49	Jeff Conine	.15
50	Orestes Destrade	.15
51	Chris Hammond	.15
52	Bryan Harvey	.15
53	Benito Santiago	.15
54	Gary Sheffield	.25
55	Walt Weiss	.15
56	Eric Anthony	.15
57	Jeff Bagwell	.50
58	Craig Biggio	.15
59	Ken Caminiti	.15
60	Andujar Cedeno	.15
61	Doug Drabek	.15
62	Steve Finley	.15
63	Luis Gonzalez	.25
64	Pete Harnisch	.15
65	Doug Jones	.15
66	Darryl Kile	.20
67	Greg Swindell	.15
68	Brett Butler	.15
69	Jim Gott	.15
70	Orel Hershiser	.15
71	Eric Karros	.15
72	Pedro Martinez	.75
73	Ramon Martinez	.15
74	Roger McDowell	.15
75	Mike Piazza	1.50
76	Jody Reed	.15
77	Tim Wallach	.15
78	Moises Alou	.20
79	Greg Colbrunn	.15
80	Wil Cordero	.15
81	Delino DeShields	.15
82	Jeff Fassero	.15
83	Marquis Grissom	.15
84	Ken Hill	.15
85	*Mike Lansing*	.30
86	Dennis Martinez	.15
87	Larry Walker	.30
88	John Wetteland	.15
89	Bobby Bonilla	.15
90	Vince Coleman	.15
91	Dwight Gooden	.15
92	Todd Hundley	.15
93	Howard Johnson	.15
94	Eddie Murray	.25
95	Joe Orsulak	.15
96	Bret Saberhagen	.15
97	Darren Daulton	.15
98	Mariano Duncan	.15
99	Len Dykstra	.15
100	Jim Eisenreich	.15
101	Tommy Greene	.15
102	Dave Hollins	.15
103	Pete Incaviglia	.15
104	Danny Jackson	.15
105	John Kruk	.15
106	Terry Mulholland	.15
107	Curt Schilling	.25
108	Mitch Williams	.15
109	Stan Belinda	.15
110	Jay Bell	.15
111	Steve Cooke	.15
112	Carlos Garcia	.15
113	Jeff King	.15
114	Al Martin	.15
115	Orlando Merced	.15
116	Don Slaught	.15
117	Andy Van Slyke	.15
118	Tim Wakefield	.15
119	*Rene Arocha*	.20
120	Bernard Gilkey	.15
121	Gregg Jefferies	.15
122	Ray Lankford	.15
123	Donovan Osborne	.15
124	Tom Pagnozzi	.15
125	Erik Pappas	.15
126	Geronimo Pena	.15
127	Lee Smith	.15
128	Ozzie Smith	1.00
129	Bob Tewksbury	.15
130	Mark Whiten	.15
131	Derek Bell	.15
132	Andy Benes	.15
133	Tony Gwynn	1.00
134	Gene Harris	.15
135	Trevor Hoffman	.15
136	Phil Plantier	.15
137	Rod Beck	.15
138	Barry Bonds	1.00
139	John Burkett	.15
140	Will Clark	.25
141	Royce Clayton	.15
142	Mike Jackson	.15
143	Darren Lewis	.15
144	Kirt Manwaring	.15
145	Willie McGee	.15
146	Bill Swift	.15
147	Robby Thompson	.15
148	Matt Williams	.25

149	Brady Anderson	.15
150	Mike Devereaux	.15
151	Chris Hoiles	.15
152	Ben McDonald	.15
153	Mark McLemore	.15
154	Mike Mussina	.50
155	Gregg Olson	.15
156	Harold Reynolds	.15
157	Cal Ripken, Jr.	2.00
158	Rick Sutcliffe	.15
159	Fernando Valenzuela	.15
160	Roger Clemens	1.00
161	Scott Cooper	.15
162	Andre Dawson	.20
163	Scott Fletcher	.15
164	Mike Greenwell	.15
165	Greg Harris	.15
166	Billy Hatcher	.15
167	Jeff Russell	.15
168	Mo Vaughn	.30
169	Frank Viola	.15
170	Chad Curtis	.15
171	Chili Davis	.15
172	Gary DiSarcina	.15
173	Damion Easley	.15
174	Chuck Finley	.15
175	Mark Langston	.15
176	Luis Polonia	.15
177	Tim Salmon	.25
178	Scott Sanderson	.15
179	*J.T. Snow*	.75
180	Wilson Alvarez	.15
181	Ellis Burks	.15
182	Joey Cora	.15
183	Alex Fernandez	.15
184	Ozzie Guillen	.15
185	Roberto Hernandez	.15
186	Bo Jackson	.20
187	Lance Johnson	.15
188	Jack McDowell	.15
189	Frank Thomas	1.00
190	Robin Ventura	.15
191	Carlos Baerga	.15
192	Albert Belle	.25
193	Wayne Kirby	.15
194	Derek Lilliquist	.15
195	Kenny Lofton	.15
196	Carlos Martinez	.15
197	Jose Mesa	.15
198	Eric Plunk	.15
199	Paul Sorrento	.15
200	John Doherty	.15
201	Cecil Fielder	.15
202	Travis Fryman	.15
203	Kirk Gibson	.15
204	Mike Henneman	.15
205	Chad Kreuter	.15
206	Scott Livingstone	.15
207	Tony Phillips	.15
208	Mickey Tettleton	.15
209	Alan Trammell	.20
210	David Wells	.20
211	Lou Whitaker	.15
212	Kevin Appier	.15
213	George Brett	1.00
214	David Cone	.15
215	Tom Gordon	.15
216	Phil Hiatt	.15
217	Felix Jose	.15
218	Wally Joyner	.15
219	Jose Lind	.15
220	Mike Macfarlane	.15
221	Brian McRae	.15
222	Jeff Montgomery	.15
223	Cal Eldred	.15
224	Darryl Hamilton	.15
225	John Jaha	.15
226	Pat Listach	.15
227	*Graeme Lloyd*	.20
228	Kevin Reimer	.15
229	Bill Spiers	.15
230	B.J. Surhoff	.15
231	Greg Vaughn	.15
232	Robin Yount	.75
233	Rick Aguilera	.15
234	Jim Deshaies	.15
235	Brian Harper	.15
236	Kent Hrbek	.15
237	Chuck Knoblauch	.15
238	Shane Mack	.15
239	David McCarty	.15
240	Pedro Munoz	.15
241	Mike Pagliarulo	.15
242	Kirby Puckett	1.00
243	Dave Winfield	.75
244	Jim Abbott	.15
245	Wade Boggs	.50
246	Pat Kelly	.15
247	Jimmy Key	.15
248	Jim Leyritz	.15
249	Don Mattingly	1.00
250	Matt Nokes	.15
251	Paul O'Neill	.15
252	Mike Stanley	.15
253	Danny Tartabull	.15
254	Bob Wickman	.15
255	Bernie Williams	.30
256	Mike Bordick	.15
257	Dennis Eckersley	.15
258	Brent Gates	.15
259	Goose Gossage	.15
260	Rickey Henderson	.30
261	Mark McGwire	2.50
262	Ruben Sierra	.15
263	Terry Steinbach	.15
264	Bob Welch	.15
265	Bobby Witt	.15
266	Rich Amaral	.15
267	Chris Bosio	.15
268	Jay Buhner	.15
269	Norm Charlton	.15
270	Ken Griffey, Jr.	1.50
271	Erik Hanson	.15
272	Randy Johnson	.60
273	Edgar Martinez	.15
274	Tino Martinez	.15
275	Dave Valle	.15
276	Omar Vizquel	.15
277	Kevin Brown	.20
278	Jose Canseco	.40
279	Julio Franco	.15
280	Juan Gonzalez	.60
281	Tom Henke	.15
282	David Hulse	.15
283	Rafael Palmeiro	.30
284	Dean Palmer	.15
285	Ivan Rodriguez	.45
286	Nolan Ryan	2.50
287	Roberto Alomar	.40
288	Pat Borders	.15
289	Joe Carter	.15
290	Juan Guzman	.15
291	Pat Hentgen	.15
292	Paul Molitor	.60
293	John Olerud	.20
294	Ed Sprague	.15
295	Dave Stewart	.15
296	Duane Ward	.15
297	Devon White	.15
298	Checklist	.05
299	Checklist	.05
300	Checklist	.05

1993 Flair Wave of the Future

The game's top prospects are featured in this insert issue randomly packaged in Flair packs. Cards #19-20, Darrell Whitmore and Nigel Wilson, were printed with each other's back; no corrected version was made.

		MT
Complete Set (20):		7.50
Common Player:		.15
1	Jason Bere	.15
2	Jeremy Burnitz	.50
3	Russ Davis	.15
4	Jim Edmonds	.75
5	Cliff Floyd	.25
6	Jeffrey Hammonds	.15
7	Trevor Hoffman	.25
8	Domingo Jean	.15
9	David McCarty	.15
10	Bobby Munoz	.15
11	Brad Pennington	.15
12	Mike Piazza	3.00
13	Manny Ramirez	1.25
14	John Roper	.15
15	Tim Salmon	.75
16	Aaron Sele	.25
17	Allen Watson	.15
18	Rondell White	.50
19	Darell Whitmore	.15
20	Nigel Wilson	.15

1994 Flair

One of the success stories of 1993 returned with the release of Fleer Flair for 1994. At $4 per pack this was pricey stuff, but collectors apparently liked the look that includes an extremely thick card stock, full-bleed photos and gold-foil graphics on both sides with a protective polyester laminate described as "far beyond mere UV coating." In addition to the 250 regular-issue cards, there are three 10-card, insert sets; Wave of the Future, Outfield Power and Hot Numbers in Series 1, the last with players' images printed on 100% etched foil. Series 2 has 200 base cards and Hot Glove, Infield Power and 10 more Wave of the Future insert cards.

		MT
Complete Set (450):		60.00
Common Player:		.15
Series 1 Pack (10):		2.00
Series 1 Wax Box (24):		35.00
Series 2 Pack (10):		4.00
Series 2 Wax Box (24):		90.00
1	Harold Baines	.15
2	Jeffrey Hammonds	.15
3	Chris Hoiles	.15
4	Ben McDonald	.15
5	Mark McLemore	.15
6	Jamie Moyer	.15
7	Jim Poole	.15
8	Cal Ripken, Jr.	4.00
9	Chris Sabo	.15
10	Scott Bankhead	.15
11	Scott Cooper	.15
12	Danny Darwin	.15
13	Andre Dawson	.35
14	Billy Hatcher	.15
15	Aaron Sele	.25
15a	Aaron Sele (overprinted "PROMOTIONAL SAMPLE")	2.00
16	John Valentin	.15
17	Dave Valle	.15
18	Mo Vaughn	.50
19	*Brian Anderson*	.75
20	Gary DiSarcina	.15
21	Jim Edmonds	.35
22	Chuck Finley	.15
23	Bo Jackson	.35
24	Mark Leiter	.15
25	Greg Myers	.15
26	Eduardo Perez	.15
27	Tim Salmon	.50
28	Wilson Alvarez	.15
29	Jason Bere	.15
30	Alex Fernandez	.15
31	Ozzie Guillen	.15
32	Joe Hall	.15
33	Darrin Jackson	.15
34	Kirk McCaskill	.15
35	Tim Raines	.15
36	Frank Thomas	2.00
37	Carlos Baerga	.15
38	Albert Belle	.45
39	Mark Clark	.15
40	Wayne Kirby	.15
41	Dennis Martinez	.15
42	Charles Nagy	.15
43	Manny Ramirez	1.25
44	Paul Sorrento	.15
45	Jim Thome	.15
46	Eric Davis	.15
47	John Doherty	.15
48	Junior Felix	.15
49	Cecil Fielder	.15
50	Kirk Gibson	.15
51	Mike Moore	.15
52	Tony Phillips	.15
53	Alan Trammell	.15
54	Kevin Appier	.15
55	Stan Belinda	.15
56	Vince Coleman	.15
57	Greg Gagne	.15
58	Bob Hamelin	.15
59	Dave Henderson	.15
60	Wally Joyner	.15
61	Mike Macfarlane	.15
62	Jeff Montgomery	.15
63	Ricky Bones	.15
64	Jeff Bronkey	.15
65	Alex Diaz	.15
66	Cal Eldred	.15
67	Darryl Hamilton	.15
68	John Jaha	.15
69	Mark Kiefer	.15
70	Kevin Seitzer	.15
71	Turner Ward	.15
72	Rich Becker	.15
73	Scott Erickson	.15
74	Keith Garagozzo	.15
75	Kent Hrbek	.15
76	Scott Leius	.15
77	Kirby Puckett	1.50
78	Matt Walbeck	.15
79	Dave Winfield	.75
80	Mike Gallego	.15
81	Xavier Hernandez	.15
82	Jimmy Key	.15
83	Jim Leyritz	.15
84	Don Mattingly	2.00
85	Matt Nokes	.15
86	Paul O'Neill	.15
87	Melido Perez	.15
88	Danny Tartabull	.15
89	Mike Bordick	.15
90	Ron Darling	.15
91	Dennis Eckersley	.20
92	Stan Javier	.15
93	Steve Karsay	.15
94	Mark McGwire	4.00
95	Troy Neel	.15
96	Terry Steinbach	.15
97	Bill Taylor	.15
98	Eric Anthony	.15
99	Chris Bosio	.15
100	Tim Davis	.15
101	Felix Fermin	.15
102	Dave Fleming	.15
103	Ken Griffey, Jr.	3.00
104	Greg Hibbard	.15
105	Reggie Jefferson	.15
106	Tino Martinez	.15
107	Jack Armstrong	.15
108	Will Clark	.45
109	Juan Gonzalez	1.25
110	Rick Helling	.15
111	Tom Henke	.15

No.	Player	MT
112	David Hulse	.15
113	Manuel Lee	.15
114	Doug Strange	.15
115	Roberto Alomar	.75
116	Joe Carter	.15
117	Carlos Delgado	.75
118	Pat Hentgen	.15
119	Paul Molitor	1.00
120	John Olerud	.15
121	Dave Stewart	.15
122	Todd Stottlemyre	.15
123	Mike Timlin	.15
124	Jeff Blauser	.15
125	Tom Glavine	.30
126	Dave Justice	.30
127	Mike Kelly	.15
128	Ryan Klesko	.15
129	Javier Lopez	.15
130	Greg Maddux	2.00
131	Fred McGriff	.15
132	Kent Mercker	.15
133	Mark Wohlers	.15
134	Willie Banks	.15
135	Steve Buechele	.15
136	Shawon Dunston	.15
137	Jose Guzman	.15
138	Glenallen Hill	.15
139	Randy Myers	.15
140	Karl Rhodes	.15
141	Ryne Sandberg	1.25
142	Steve Trachsel	.15
143	Bret Boone	.20
144	Tom Browning	.15
145	Hector Carrasco	.15
146	Barry Larkin	.25
147	Hal Morris	.15
148	Jose Rijo	.15
149	Reggie Sanders	.15
150	John Smiley	.15
151	Dante Bichette	.15
152	Ellis Burks	.15
153	Joe Girardi	.15
154	Mike Harkey	.15
155	Roberto Mejia	.15
156	Marcus Moore	.15
157	Armando Reynoso	.15
158	Bruce Ruffin	.15
159	Eric Young	.15
160	*Kurt Abbott*	.40
161	Jeff Conine	.15
162	Orestes Destrade	.15
163	Chris Hammond	.15
164	Bryan Harvey	.15
165	Dave Magadan	.15
166	Gary Sheffield	.35
167	David Weathers	.15
168	Andujar Cedeno	.15
169	Tom Edens	.15
170	Luis Gonzalez	.25
171	Pete Harnisch	.15
172	Todd Jones	.15
173	Darryl Kile	.20
174	James Mouton	.15
175	Scott Servais	.15
176	Mitch Williams	.15
177	Pedro Astacio	.15
178	Orel Hershiser	.15
179	Raul Mondesi	.30
180	Jose Offerman	.15
181	*Chan Ho Park*	1.50
182	Mike Piazza	3.00
183	Cory Snyder	.15
184	Tim Wallach	.15
185	Todd Worrell	.15
186	Sean Berry	.15
187	Wil Cordero	.15
188	Darrin Fletcher	.15
189	Cliff Floyd	.20
190	Marquis Grissom	.15
191	Rod Henderson	.15
192	Ken Hill	.15
193	Pedro Martinez	1.50
194	Kirk Rueter	.15
195	Jeromy Burnitz	.15
196	John Franco	.15
197	Dwight Gooden	.15
198	Todd Hundley	.15
199	Bobby Jones	.15
200	Jeff Kent	.15
201	Mike Maddux	.15
202	Ryan Thompson	.15
203	Jose Vizcaino	.15
204	Darren Daulton	.15
205	Len Dykstra	.15
206	Jim Eisenreich	.15
207	Dave Hollins	.15
208	Danny Jackson	.15
209	Doug Jones	.15
210	Jeff Juden	.15
211	Ben Rivera	.15
212	Kevin Stocker	.15
213	Milt Thompson	.15
214	Jay Bell	.15
215	Steve Cooke	.15
216	Mark Dewey	.15
217	Al Martin	.15
218	Orlando Merced	.15
219	Don Slaught	.15
220	Zane Smith	.15
221	Rick White	.15
222	Kevin Young	.15
223	Rene Arocha	.15
224	Rheal Cormier	.15
225	Brian Jordan	.15
226	Ray Lankford	.15
227	Mike Perez	.15
228	Ozzie Smith	1.25
229	Mark Whiten	.15
230	Todd Zeile	.15
231	Derek Bell	.15
232	Archi Cianfrocco	.15
233	Ricky Gutierrez	.15
234	Trevor Hoffman	.15
235	Phil Plantier	.15
236	Dave Staton	.15
237	Wally Whitehurst	.15
238	Todd Benzinger	.15
239	Barry Bonds	2.00
240	John Burkett	.15
241	Royce Clayton	.15
242	Bryan Hickerson	.15
243	Mike Jackson	.15
244	Darren Lewis	.15
245	Kirt Manwaring	.15
246	Mark Portugal	.15
247	Salomon Torres	.15
248	Checklist	.15
249	Checklist	.15
250	Checklist	.15
251	Brady Anderson	.15
252	Mike Devereaux	.15
253	Sid Fernandez	.15
254	Leo Gomez	.15
255	Mike Mussina	1.00
256	Mike Oquist	.15
257	Rafael Palmeiro	.60
258	Lee Smith	.20
259	Damon Berryhill	.15
260	Wes Chamberlain	.15
261	Roger Clemens	2.00
262	Gar Finnvold	.15
263	Mike Greenwell	.15
264	Tim Naehring	.15
265	Otis Nixon	.15
266	Ken Ryan	.15
267	Chad Curtis	.15
268	Chili Davis	.15
269	Damion Easley	.15
270	Jorge Fabregas	.15
271	Mark Langston	.15
272	Phil Leftwich	.15
273	Harold Reynolds	.15
274	J.T. Snow	.25
275	Joey Cora	.15
276	Julio Franco	.15
277	Roberto Hernandez	.15
278	Lance Johnson	.15
279	Ron Karkovice	.15
280	Jack McDowell	.15
281	Robin Ventura	.20
282	Sandy Alomar Jr.	.15
283	Kenny Lofton	.15
284	Jose Mesa	.15
285	Jack Morris	.15
286	Eddie Murray	.35
287	Chad Ogea	.15
288	Eric Plunk	.15
289	Paul Shuey	.15
290	Omar Vizquel	.15
291	Danny Bautista	.15
292	Travis Fryman	.15
293	Greg Gohr	.15
294	Chris Gomez	.15
295	Mickey Tettleton	.15
296	Lou Whitaker	.15
297	David Cone	.15
298	Gary Gaetti	.15
299	Tom Gordon	.15
300	Felix Jose	.15
301	Jose Lind	.15
302	Brian McRae	.15
303	Mike Fetters	.15
304	Brian Harper	.15
305	Pat Listach	.15
306	Matt Mieske	.15
307	Dave Nilsson	.15
308	Jody Reed	.15
309	Greg Vaughn	.15
310	Bill Wegman	.15
311	Rick Aguilera	.15
312	Alex Cole	.15
313	Denny Hocking	.15
314	Chuck Knoblauch	.15
315	Shane Mack	.15
316	Pat Meares	.15
317	Kevin Tapani	.15
318	Jim Abbott	.15
319	Wade Boggs	.65
320	Sterling Hitchcock	.15
321	Pat Kelly	.15
322	Terry Mulholland	.15
323	Luis Polonia	.15
324	Mike Stanley	.15
325	Bob Wickman	.15
326	Bernie Williams	.50
327	Mark Acre	.15
328	Geronimo Berroa	.15
329	Scott Brosius	.15
330	Brent Gates	.15
331	Rickey Henderson	.75
332	Carlos Reyes	.15
333	Ruben Sierra	.15
334	Bobby Witt	.15
335	Bobby Ayala	.15
336	Jay Buhner	.15
337	Randy Johnson	1.00
338	Edgar Martinez	.15
339	Bill Risley	.15
340	*Alex Rodriguez*	25.00
341	Roger Salkeld	.15
342	Dan Wilson	.15
343	Kevin Brown	.25
344	Jose Canseco	.60
345	Dean Palmer	.15
346	Ivan Rodriguez	1.00
347	Kenny Rogers	.15
348	Pat Borders	.15
349	Juan Guzman	.15
350	Ed Sprague	.15
351	Devon White	.15
352	Steve Avery	.15
353	Roberto Kelly	.15
354	Mark Lemke	.15
355	Greg McMichael	.15
356	Terry Pendleton	.15
357	John Smoltz	.20
358	Mike Stanton	.15
359	Tony Tarasco	.15
360	Mark Grace	.30
361	Derrick May	.15
362	Rey Sanchez	.15
363	Sammy Sosa	2.50
364	Rick Wilkins	.15
365	Jeff Brantley	.15
366	Tony Fernandez	.15
367	Chuck McElroy	.15
368	Kevin Mitchell	.15
369	John Roper	.15
370	Johnny Ruffin	.15
371	Deion Sanders	.25
372	Marvin Freeman	.15
373	Andres Galarraga	.15
374	Charlie Hayes	.15
375	Nelson Liriano	.15
376	David Nied	.15
377	Walt Weiss	.15
378	Bret Barberie	.15
379	Jerry Browne	.15
380	Chuck Carr	.15
381	Greg Colbrunn	.15
382	Charlie Hough	.15
383	Kurt Miller	.15
384	Benito Santiago	.15
385	Jeff Bagwell	1.00
386	Craig Biggio	.15
387	Ken Caminiti	.15
388	Doug Drabek	.15
389	Steve Finley	.15
390	John Hudek	.15
391	Orlando Miller	.15
392	Shane Reynolds	.15
393	Brett Butler	.15
394	Tom Candiotti	.15
395	Delino DeShields	.15
396	Kevin Gross	.15
397	Eric Karros	.15
398	Ramon Martinez	.15
399	Henry Rodriguez	.15
400	Moises Alou	.25
401	Jeff Fassero	.15
402	Mike Lansing	.15
403	Mel Rojas	.15
404	Larry Walker	.60
405	John Wetteland	.15
406	Gabe White	.20
407	Bobby Bonilla	.15
408	Josias Manzanillo	.15
409	Bret Saberhagen	.15
410	David Segui	.15
411	Mariano Duncan	.15
412	Tommy Greene	.15
413	Billy Hatcher	.15
414	Ricky Jordan	.15
415	John Kruk	.15
416	Bobby Munoz	.15
417	Curt Schilling	.25
418	Fernando Valenzuela	.15
419	David West	.15
420	Carlos Garcia	.15
421	Brian Hunter	.15
422	Jeff King	.15
423	Jon Lieber	.20
424	Ravelo Manzanillo	.15
425	Denny Neagle	.15
426	Andy Van Slyke	.15
427	Bryan Eversgerd	.15
428	Bernard Gilkey	.15
429	Gregg Jefferies	.15
430	Tom Pagnozzi	.15
431	Bob Tewksbury	.15
432	Allen Watson	.15
433	Andy Ashby	.15
434	Andy Benes	.15
435	Donnie Elliott	.15
436	Tony Gwynn	1.50
437	Joey Hamilton	.15
438	Tim Hyers	.15
439	Luis Lopez	.15
440	Bip Roberts	.15
441	Scott Sanders	.15
442	Rod Beck	.15
443	Dave Burba	.15
444	Darryl Strawberry	.15
445	Bill Swift	.15
446	Robby Thompson	.15
447	*William VanLandingham*	.45
448	Matt Williams	.45
449	Checklist	.15
450	Checklist	.15

1994 Flair Hot Gloves

Hot Glove is a 10-card Series 2 insert set. It focuses on players with outstanding defensive ability. Cards feature a die-cut design, with the player photo in front of a baseball glove. Player identification and a "Hot Glove" logo are in gold foil in the lower-left corner.

		MT
Complete Set (10):		60.00
Common Player:		3.00
1	Barry Bonds	7.00
2	Will Clark	3.00
3	Ken Griffey, Jr.	15.00

		MT
4	Kenny Lofton	3.00
5	Greg Maddux	10.00
6	Don Mattingly	7.00
7	Kirby Puckett	7.00
8	Cal Ripken, Jr.	15.00
9	Tim Salmon	3.00
10	Matt Williams	3.00

1994 Flair Hot Numbers

Hot Numbers is an insert set found in Series 1 packs at an average rate of 1:24. Each card is printed on 100% etched foil and displays the player in the forefront with a background made up of floating numbers. The player's name is in gold foil across the bottom-right side and a large foil "Hot Numbers" and that player's uniform number are in a square at bottom-left.

		MT
Complete Set (10):		45.00
Common Player:		1.00
1	Roberto Alomar	4.00
2	Carlos Baerga	1.00
3	Will Clark	1.50
4	Fred McGriff	1.00
5	Paul Molitor	5.00
6	John Olerud	1.00
7	Mike Piazza	12.00
8	Cal Ripken, Jr.	15.00
9	Ryne Sandberg	6.00
10	Frank Thomas	6.00

1994 Flair Infield Power

Infield Power is a horizontally formatted insert set. Cards show the player batting on one half and in the field on the other half of the card, divided by a black, diagonal strip that reads "Infield Power" and the player's name. The set spotlights infielders that often hit the longball. Infield Power was inserted into Series 2 packs at an average rate of 1:5.

		MT
Complete Set (10):		12.00
Common Player:		.50
1	Jeff Bagwell	1.50
2	Will Clark	.60
3	Darren Daulton	.50
4	Don Mattingly	2.00
5	Fred McGriff	.50
6	Rafael Palmeiro	.75
7	Mike Piazza	4.00
8	Cal Ripken, Jr.	5.00
9	Frank Thomas	2.00
10	Matt Williams	.60

1994 Flair Outfield Power

Flair's Outfield Power was randomly inserted in Series 1 packs at a 1:5 rate. This vertically formatted card shows the player in the field on top, while the bottom half shows the player at the plate. The photos divided by a black strip with "Outfield Power" and the player's name on it.

		MT
Complete Set (10):		7.50
Common Player:		.40
1	Albert Belle	.60
2	Barry Bonds	1.00
3	Joe Carter	.40
4	Len Dykstra	.40
5	Juan Gonzalez	1.00
6	Ken Griffey, Jr.	3.00
7	Dave Justice	.60
8	Kirby Puckett	1.25
9	Tim Salmon	.50
10	Dave Winfield	.75

1994 Flair Wave of the Future 1

Series 1 Wave of the Future is horizontally formatted and depicts 10 outstanding 1994 rookies who have the potential to become superstars. Each player is featured on a colorful wavelike background. A Wave of the Future gold-foil stamp is placed in the bottom-right corner with the player name in gold foil starting in the opposite bottom corner and running across the bottom. Advertised insertion rate was 1:5.

		MT
Complete Set (10):		10.00
Common Player:		.50
1	Kurt Abbott	.50
2	Carlos Delgado	6.00
3	Steve Karsay	.50
4	Ryan Klesko	.50
5	Javier Lopez	.50
6	Raul Mondesi	2.00
7	James Mouton	.50
8	Chan Ho Park	2.00
9	Dave Staton	.50
10	Rick White	.50

1994 Flair Wave of the Future 2

Series 2 Flair also has a Wave of the Future insert set. Unlike the earlier series, this 10-card set is vertically formated. The Wave of the Future logo appears in the bottom-left with the player's name stretching across the rest of the bottom. The background has a swirling water effect, on which the player is superimposed. Insertion rate is one per five packs.

		MT
Complete Set (10):		27.50
Common Player:		.75
1	Mark Acre	.75
2	Chris Gomez	.75
3	Joey Hamilton	.75
4	John Hudek	.75
5	Jon Lieber	1.50
6	Matt Mieske	.75
7	Orlando Miller	1.00
8	Alex Rodriguez	25.00
9	Tony Tarasco	.75
10	Bill VanLandingham	.75

1995 Flair

There's no mistaking that 1995 Flair is Fleer's super-premium brand. Cards are printed on double-thick cardboard with a background of etched metallic foil: Gold for National Leaguers, silver for American. A portrait and an action photo are featured on the horizontal front design. Backs are vertically formatted with a borderless action photo, several years worth of stats and foil trim. The basic set was issued in two series of 216 basic cards each, along with several insert sets exclusive to each series. Cards were sold in a hard pack of nine with a suggested retail price of $5.

		MT
Complete Set (432):		40.00
Common Player:		.20
Series 1 or 2 Pack (9):		2.50
Series 1 or 2 Wax Box (24):		45.00
1	Brady Anderson	.20
2	Harold Baines	.20
3	Leo Gomez	.20
4	Alan Mills	.20
5	Jamie Moyer	.20
6	Mike Mussina	.75
7	Mike Oquist	.20
8	Arthur Rhodes	.20
9	Cal Ripken Jr.	4.00
10	Roger Clemens	1.50
11	Scott Cooper	.20
12	Mike Greenwell	.20
13	Aaron Sele	.20
14	John Valentin	.20
15	Mo Vaughn	.75
16	Chad Curtis	.20
17	Gary DiSarcina	.20
18	Chuck Finley	.20
19	Andrew Lorraine	.20
20	Spike Owen	.20
21	Tim Salmon	.40
22	J.T. Snow	.25
23	Wilson Alvarez	.20
24	Jason Bere	.20
25	Ozzie Guillen	.20
26	Mike LaValliere	.20
27	Frank Thomas	1.50
28	Robin Ventura	.20
29	Carlos Baerga	.20
30	Albert Belle	.50
31	Jason Grimsley	.20
32	Dennis Martinez	.20
33	Eddie Murray	.50
34	Charles Nagy	.25
35	Manny Ramirez	1.25
36	Paul Sorrento	.20
37	John Doherty	.20
38	Cecil Fielder	.20
39	Travis Fryman	.20
40	Chris Gomez	.20
41	Tony Phillips	.20
42	Lou Whitaker	.20
43	David Cone	.20
44	Gary Gaetti	.20
45	Mark Gubicza	.20
46	Bob Hamelin	.20
47	Wally Joyner	.20
48	Rusty Meacham	.20
49	Jeff Montgomery	.20
50	Ricky Bones	.20

No.	Player	Price
51	Cal Eldred	.20
52	Pat Listach	.20
53	Matt Mieske	.20
54	Dave Nilsson	.20
55	Greg Vaughn	.20
56	Bill Wegman	.20
57	Chuck Knoblauch	.20
58	Scott Leius	.20
59	Pat Mahomes	.20
60	Pat Meares	.20
61	Pedro Munoz	.20
62	Kirby Puckett	2.00
63	Wade Boggs	.50
64	Jimmy Key	.20
65	Jim Leyritz	.20
66	Don Mattingly	2.00
67	Paul O'Neill	.20
68	Melido Perez	.20
69	Danny Tartabull	.20
70	John Briscoe	.20
71	Scott Brosius	.20
72	Ron Darling	.20
73	Brent Gates	.20
74	Rickey Henderson	.60
75	Stan Javier	.20
76	Mark McGwire	4.00
77	Todd Van Poppel	.20
78	Bobby Ayala	.20
79	Mike Blowers	.20
80	Jay Buhner	.20
81	Ken Griffey Jr.	3.00
82	Randy Johnson	1.25
83	Tino Martinez	.20
84	Jeff Nelson	.20
85	Alex Rodriguez	4.00
86	Will Clark	.50
87	Jeff Frye	.20
88	Juan Gonzalez	1.25
89	Rusty Greer	.20
90	Darren Oliver	.20
91	Dean Palmer	.20
92	Ivan Rodriguez	1.00
93	Matt Whiteside	.20
94	Roberto Alomar	.75
95	Joe Carter	.20
96	Tony Castillo	.20
97	Juan Guzman	.20
98	Pat Hentgen	.20
99	Mike Huff	.20
100	John Olerud	.20
101	Woody Williams	.20
102	Roberto Kelly	.20
103	Ryan Klesko	.20
104	Javier Lopez	.20
105	Greg Maddux	2.50
106	Fred McGriff	.20
107	Jose Oliva	.20
108	John Smoltz	.25
109	Tony Tarasco	.20
110	Mark Wohlers	.20
111	Jim Bullinger	.20
112	Shawon Dunston	.20
113	Derrick May	.20
114	Randy Myers	.20
115	Karl Rhodes	.20
116	Rey Sanchez	.20
117	Steve Trachsel	.20
118	Eddie Zambrano	.20
119	Bret Boone	.25
120	Brian Dorsett	.20
121	Hal Morris	.20
122	Jose Rijo	.20
123	John Roper	.20
124	Reggie Sanders	.20
125	Pete Schourek	.20
126	John Smiley	.20
127	Ellis Burks	.20
128	Vinny Castilla	.20
129	Marvin Freeman	.20
130	Andres Galarraga	.20
131	Mike Munoz	.20
132	David Nied	.20
133	Bruce Ruffin	.20
134	Walt Weiss	.20
135	Eric Young	.20
136	Greg Colbrunn	.20
137	Jeff Conine	.20
138	Jeremy Hernandez	.20
139	Charles Johnson	.20
140	Robb Nen	.20
141	Gary Sheffield	.45
142	Dave Weathers	.20
143	Jeff Bagwell	1.00
144	Craig Biggio	.20
145	Tony Eusebio	.20
146	Luis Gonzalez	.30
147	John Hudek	.20
148	Darryl Kile	.25
149	Dave Veres	.20
150	Billy Ashley	.20
151	Pedro Astacio	.20
152	Rafael Bournigal	.20
153	Delino DeShields	.20
154	Raul Mondesi	.40
155	Mike Piazza	3.00
156	Rudy Seanez	.20
157	Ismael Valdes	.20
158	Tim Wallach	.20
159	Todd Worrell	.20
160	Moises Alou	.25
161	Cliff Floyd	.20
162	Gil Heredia	.20
163	Mike Lansing	.20
164	Pedro Martinez	1.00
165	Kirk Rueter	.20
166	Tim Scott	.20
167	Jeff Shaw	.20
168	Rondell White	.20
169	Bobby Bonilla	.20
170	Rico Brogna	.20
171	Todd Hundley	.20
172	Jeff Kent	.20
173	Jim Lindeman	.20
174	Joe Orsulak	.20
175	Bret Saberhagen	.20
176	Toby Borland	.20
177	Darren Daulton	.20
178	Lenny Dykstra	.20
179	Jim Eisenreich	.20
180	Tommy Greene	.20
181	Tony Longmire	.20
182	Bobby Munoz	.20
183	Kevin Stocker	.20
184	Jay Bell	.20
185	Steve Cooke	.20
186	Ravelo Manzanillo	.20
187	Al Martin	.20
188	Denny Neagle	.20
189	Don Slaught	.20
190	Paul Wagner	.20
191	Rene Arocha	.20
192	Bernard Gilkey	.20
193	Jose Oquendo	.20
194	Tom Pagnozzi	.20
195	Ozzie Smith	1.50
196	Allen Watson	.20
197	Mark Whiten	.20
198	Andy Ashby	.20
199	Donnie Elliott	.20
200	Bryce Florie	.20
201	Tony Gwynn	1.50
202	Trevor Hoffman	.25
203	Brian Johnson	.20
204	Tim Mauser	.20
205	Bip Roberts	.20
206	Rod Beck	.20
207	Barry Bonds	1.50
208	Royce Clayton	.20
209	Darren Lewis	.20
210	Mark Portugal	.20
211	Kevin Rogers	.20
212	William Van Landingham	.20
213	Matt Williams	.50
214	Checklist	.20
215	Checklist	.20
216	Checklist	.20
217	Bret Barberie	.20
218	Armando Benitez	.20
219	Kevin Brown	.25
220	Sid Fernandez	.20
221	Chris Hoiles	.20
222	Doug Jones	.20
223	Ben McDonald	.20
224	Rafael Palmeiro	.60
225	Andy Van Slyke	.20
226	Jose Canseco	.50
227	Vaughn Eshelman	.20
228	Mike Macfarlane	.20
229	Tim Naehring	.20
230	Frank Rodriguez	.20
231	Lee Tinsley	.20
232	Mark Whiten	.20
233	Garret Anderson	.20
234	Chili Davis	.20
235	Jim Edmonds	.35
236	Mark Langston	.20
237	Troy Percival	.20
238	Tony Phillips	.20
239	Lee Smith	.20
240	Jim Abbott	.20
241	James Baldwin	.20
242	Mike Devereaux	.20
243	Ray Durham	.20
244	Alex Fernandez	.20
245	Roberto Hernandez	.20
246	Lance Johnson	.20
247	Ron Karkovice	.20
248	Tim Raines	.20
249	Sandy Alomar Jr.	.20
250	Orel Hershiser	.20
251	Julian Tavarez	.20
252	Jim Thome	.20
253	Omar Vizquel	.20
254	Dave Winfield	.75
255	Chad Curtis	.20
256	Kirk Gibson	.20
257	Mike Henneman	.20
258	*Bob Higginson*	1.50
259	Felipe Lira	.20
260	Rudy Pemberton	.20
261	Alan Trammell	.20
262	Kevin Appier	.20
263	Pat Borders	.20
264	Tom Gordon	.20
265	Jose Lind	.20
266	Jon Nunnally	.20
267	Dilson Torres	.20
268	Michael Tucker	.20
269	Jeff Cirillo	.20
270	Darryl Hamilton	.20
271	David Hulse	.20
272	Mark Kiefer	.20
273	Graeme Lloyd	.20
274	Joe Oliver	.20
275	Al Reyes	.20
276	Kevin Seitzer	.20
277	Rick Aguilera	.20
278	Marty Cordova	.20
279	Scott Erickson	.20
280	LaTroy Hawkins	.20
281	Brad Radke	.30
282	Kevin Tapani	.20
283	Tony Fernandez	.20
284	Sterling Hitchcock	.20
285	Pat Kelly	.20
286	Jack McDowell	.20
287	Andy Pettitte	.60
288	Mike Stanley	.20
289	John Wetteland	.20
290	Bernie Williams	.60
291	Mark Acre	.20
292	Geronimo Berroa	.20
293	Dennis Eckersley	.25
294	Steve Ontiveros	.20
295	Ruben Sierra	.20
296	Terry Steinbach	.20
297	Dave Stewart	.20
298	Todd Stottlemyre	.20
299	Darren Bragg	.20
300	Joey Cora	.20
301	Edgar Martinez	.20
302	Bill Risley	.20
303	Ron Villone	.20
304	Dan Wilson	.20
305	Benji Gil	.20
306	Wilson Heredia	.20
307	Mark McLemore	.20
308	Otis Nixon	.20
309	Kenny Rogers	.20
310	Jeff Russell	.20
311	Mickey Tettleton	.20
312	Bob Tewksbury	.20
313	David Cone	.20
314	Carlos Delgado	.75
315	Alex Gonzalez	.20
316	Shawn Green	.65
317	Paul Molitor	.60
318	Ed Sprague	.20
319	Devon White	.25
320	Steve Avery	.20
321	Jeff Blauser	.20
322	Brad Clontz	.20
323	Tom Glavine	.35
324	Marquis Grissom	.20
325	Chipper Jones	2.50
326	Dave Justice	.40
327	Mark Lemke	.20
328	Kent Mercker	.20
329	Jason Schmidt	.20
330	Steve Buechele	.20
331	Kevin Foster	.20
332	Mark Grace	.40
333	Brian McRae	.20
334	Sammy Sosa	2.00
335	Ozzie Timmons	.20
336	Rick Wilkins	.20
337	Hector Carrasco	.20
338	Ron Gant	.20
339	Barry Larkin	.35
340	Deion Sanders	.30
341	Benito Santiago	.20
342	Roger Bailey	.20
343	Jason Bates	.20
344	Dante Bichette	.20
345	Joe Girardi	.20
346	Bill Swift	.20
347	Mark Thompson	.20
348	Larry Walker	.35
349	Kurt Abbott	.20
350	John Burkett	.20
351	Chuck Carr	.20
352	Andre Dawson	.25
353	Chris Hammond	.20
354	Charles Johnson	.25
355	Terry Pendleton	.20
356	Quilvio Veras	.20
357	Derek Bell	.20
358	Jim Dougherty	.20
359	Doug Drabek	.20
360	Todd Jones	.20
361	Orlando Miller	.20
362	James Mouton	.20
363	Phil Plantier	.20
364	Shane Reynolds	.20
365	Todd Hollandsworth	.20
366	Eric Karros	.20
367	Ramon Martinez	.20
368	*Hideo Nomo*	3.00
369	Jose Offerman	.20
370	Antonio Osuna	.20
371	Todd Williams	.20
372	Shane Andrews	.20
373	Wil Cordero	.20
374	Jeff Fassero	.20
375	Darrin Fletcher	.20
376	*Mark Grudzielanek*	.60
377	*Carlos Perez*	.25
378	Mel Rojas	.20
379	Tony Tarasco	.20
380	Edgardo Alfonzo	.35
381	Brett Butler	.20
382	Carl Everett	.25
383	John Franco	.20
384	Pete Harnisch	.20
385	Bobby Jones	.20
386	Dave Mlicki	.20
387	Jose Vizcaino	.20
388	Ricky Bottalico	.20
389	Tyler Green	.20
390	Charlie Hayes	.20
391	Dave Hollins	.20
392	Gregg Jefferies	.20
393	*Michael Mimbs*	.20
394	Mickey Morandini	.20
395	Curt Schilling	.30
396	Heathcliff Slocumb	.20
397	Jason Christiansen	.20
398	Midre Cummings	.20
399	Carlos Garcia	.20
400	Mark Johnson	.20
401	Jeff King	.20
402	Jon Lieber	.25
403	Esteban Loaiza	.20
404	Orlando Merced	.20
405	*Gary Wilson*	.20
406	Scott Cooper	.20
407	Tom Henke	.20
408	Ken Hill	.20
409	Danny Jackson	.20
410	Brian Jordan	.20
411	Ray Lankford	.20
412	John Mabry	.20
413	Todd Zeile	.20
414	Andy Benes	.20
415	Andres Berumen	.20
416	Ken Caminiti	.20
417	Andujar Cedeno	.20
418	Steve Finley	.20
419	Joey Hamilton	.20
420	Dustin Hermanson	.25
421	Melvin Nieves	.20
422	Roberto Petagine	.20
423	Eddie Williams	.20
424	Glenallen Hill	.20
425	Kirt Manwaring	.20
426	Terry Mulholland	.20
427	J.R. Phillips	.20
428	Joe Rosselli	.20
429	Robby Thompson	.20
430	Checklist	.20
431	Checklist	.20
432	Checklist	.20

1995 Flair Cal Ripken, Jr. Enduring Flair

The career of Cal Ripken, Jr., is traced in this insert set found in Series 2 Flair at the average rate of once per dozen packs. Each card has a vintage photo on front, with a large silver-foil "ENDURING" logo toward bottom. Backs have another color photo, a quote and other information about the milestone. The series was extended by a special mail-in offer for five additional cards which chronicled Ripken's record- breaking 1995 season.

		MT
Complete Set (15):		50.00
Common Card:		3.50
1	Rookie Of The Year	3.50
2	1st MVP Season	3.50
3	World Series Highlight	3.50
4	Family Tradition	3.50
5	8,243 Consecutive Innings	3.50
6	95 Consecutive Errorless Games	3.50
7	All-Star MVP	3.50
8	1,000th RBI	3.50
9	287th Home Run	3.50
10	2,000th Consecutive Game	3.50
11	Record-tying Game	4.00
12	Record-breaking Game	4.00
13	Defensive Prowess	4.00
14	Literacy Work	4.00
15	2,153 and Counting	4.00

1995 Flair Hot Gloves

The cream of the crop among Series 2 Flair inserts is this set featuring fine fielders. Cards have a background of an embossed gold-foil glove, with a color player photo centered in front. Silver foil comprises the card title and player name at bottom and the Flair logo at top. Backs have a white background, a photo of a glove with a career summary overprinted and a player portrait photo in a lower corner. These inserts are found at the average rate of once per 25 packs.

		MT
Complete Set (12):		25.00
Common Player:		1.00
1	Roberto Alomar	2.00
2	Barry Bonds	3.00
3	Ken Griffey Jr.	6.50
4	Marquis Grissom	1.00
5	Barry Larkin	1.25
6	Darren Lewis	1.00
7	Kenny Lofton	1.00
8	Don Mattingly	3.50
9	Cal Ripken Jr.	6.50
10	Ivan Rodriguez	2.00
11	Devon White	1.00
12	Matt Williams	1.25

1995 Flair Hot Numbers

These Series 1 inserts are a 1:9 find. Gold metallic-foil background with 1994 seasonal stat numbers are the background for a color action photo on front. Horizontal backs have a ghosted portrait photo at right and career highlights at left.

		MT
Complete Set (10):		20.00
Common Player:		1.25
1	Jeff Bagwell	2.00
2	Albert Belle	1.50
3	Barry Bonds	2.50
4	Ken Griffey Jr.	4.50
5	Kenny Lofton	1.25
6	Greg Maddux	2.50
7	Mike Piazza	4.00
8	Cal Ripken Jr.	4.50
9	Frank Thomas	2.50
10	Matt Williams	1.25

1995 Flair Infield Power

Power rays and waves eminating from the player's bat in an action photo are the front design of this Series 2 chase set. The card title, name and team at bottom, and the Flair logo at top are in silver foil. Backs repeat the wave theme with a player photo on one end and a career summary at the other. These inserts are seeded at the average rate of one per five packs.

		MT
Complete Set (10):		4.00
Common Player:		.25
1	Jeff Bagwell	.75
2	Darren Daulton	.25
3	Cecil Fielder	.25
4	Andres Galarraga	.25
5	Fred McGriff	.25
6	Rafael Palmeiro	.40
7	Mike Piazza	1.00
8	Frank Thomas	1.00
9	Mo Vaughn	.50
10	Matt Williams	.25

1995 Flair Outfield Power

Laser-like colored rays are the background to the action photo on front and portrait on back of this series. The card title, player identification and Flair logo on front are in silver foil. Backs are horizontal, silver-foil enhanced and include a career summary. This chase set is seeded at the average rate of one card per six packs of Series 1 Flair.

		MT
Complete Set (10):		9.00
Common Player:		.50
1	Albert Belle	1.00
2	Dante Bichette	.50
3	Barry Bonds	1.50
4	Jose Canseco	1.00
5	Joe Carter	.50
6	Juan Gonzalez	1.00
7	Ken Griffey Jr.	3.50
8	Kirby Puckett	1.50
9	Gary Sheffield	.60
10	Ruben Sierra	.50

1995 Flair Today's Spotlight

The premier insert set in Flair Series I, found once every 30 packs or so, this die-cut issue has the player action photo spotlighted in a 2-3/8" bright spot, with the rest of the photo muted in gray and dark gray. The card title, Flair logo, player name and team are in silver foil. The horizontal backs have a portrait photo in the spotlight and career summary on the side.

		MT
Complete Set (12):		30.00
Common Player:		1.50
1	Jeff Bagwell	3.00
2	Jason Bere	1.50
3	Cliff Floyd	1.50
4	Chuck Knoblauch	1.50
5	Kenny Lofton	1.50
6	Javier Lopez	1.50
7	Raul Mondesi	2.50
8	Mike Mussina	3.00
9	Mike Piazza	10.00
10	Manny Ramirez	4.00
11	Tim Salmon	2.00
12	Frank Thomas	7.50

1995 Flair Wave Of The Future

The cream of baseball's rookie crop is featured in this Series 2 insert set, found once per eight packs on average. Fronts have a graduated color background with a baseball/wave morph, which is repeated at the bottom in silver foil, along with the player name. A color action photo is at center. The player's name, team and

"Wave of the Future" are repeated in horizontal rows behind the photo. Horizontal backs repeat the wave logo, have another player photo and a career summary.

		MT
Complete Set (10):		13.50
Common Player:		.50
1	Jason Bates	.50
2	Armando Benitez	.50
3	Marty Cordova	.50
4	Ray Durham	.50
5	Vaughn Eshelman	.50
6	Carl Everett	.75
7	Shawn Green	3.00
8	Dustin Hermanson	.75
9	Chipper Jones	6.00
10	Hideo Nomo	5.00

1996 Flair Promotional Sheet

Three samples of Flair's 1996 issue and an information card are included on this 5" x 7" promotional sheet.

	MT
Complete Sheet:	7.50
Manny Ramirez, Cal Ripken Jr., Matt Williams, Information card	

1996 Flair

Fleer's 1996 Flair baseball set has 400 cards, a parallel set and four insert types. Regular card fronts have two photos of the featured player; backs have a photo and career statistics. All cards have a silver-foil version and a gold-foil version, with each version appearing in equal numbers. Seven-card packs carried an issue price of $4.99.

		MT
Complete Set (400):		100.00
Common Player:		.25
Pack (9):		3.00
Wax Box (18):		50.00
1	Roberto Alomar	1.00
2	Brady Anderson	.25
3	Bobby Bonilla	.25
4	Scott Erickson	.25
5	Jeffrey Hammonds	.25
6	Jimmy Haynes	.25
7	Chris Hoiles	.25
8	Kent Mercker	.25
9	Mike Mussina	1.50
10	Randy Myers	.25
11	Rafael Palmeiro	.75
12	Cal Ripken Jr.	6.00
(12p)	Cal Ripken Jr. (no card #, overprinted "PROMOTIONAL SAMPLE")	3.50
13	B.J. Surhoff	.25
14	David Wells	.30
15	Jose Canseco	.75
16	Roger Clemens	3.00
17	Wil Cordero	.25
18	Tom Gordon	.25
19	Mike Greenwell	.25
20	Dwayne Hosey	.25
21	Jose Malave	.25
22	Tim Naehring	.25
23	Troy O'Leary	.25
24	Aaron Sele	.25
25	Heathcliff Slocumb	.25
26	Mike Stanley	.25
27	Jeff Suppan	.25
28	John Valentin	.25
29	Mo Vaughn	1.00
30	Tim Wakefield	.25
31	Jim Abbott	.25
32	Garret Anderson	.25
33	George Arias	.25
34	Chili Davis	.25
35	Gary DiSarcina	.25
36	Jim Edmonds	.50
37	Chuck Finley	.25
38	Todd Greene	.25
39	Mark Langston	.25
40	Troy Percival	.25
41	Tim Salmon	.45
42	Lee Smith	.25
43	J.T. Snow	.30
44	Randy Velarde	.25
45	Tim Wallach	.25
46	Wilson Alvarez	.25
47	Harold Baines	.25
48	Jason Bere	.25
49	Ray Durham	.25
50	Alex Fernandez	.25
51	Ozzie Guillen	.25
52	Roberto Hernandez	.25
53	Ron Karkovice	.25
54	Darren Lewis	.25
55	Lyle Mouton	.25
56	Tony Phillips	.25
57	Chris Snopek	.25
58	Kevin Tapani	.25
59	Danny Tartabull	.25
30	Frank Thomas	3.00
61	Robin Ventura	.25
62	Sandy Alomar	.25
63	Carlos Baerga	.25
64	Albert Belle	1.00
65	Julio Franco	.25
66	Orel Hershiser	.25
67	Kenny Lofton	.25
68	Dennis Martinez	.25
69	Jack McDowell	.25
70	Jose Mesa	.25
71	Eddie Murray	1.00
72	Charles Nagy	.25
73	Tony Pena	.25
74	Manny Ramirez	2.50
75	Julian Tavarez	.25
76	Jim Thome	.25
77	Omar Vizquel	.25
78	Chad Curtis	.25
79	Cecil Fielder	.25
80	Travis Fryman	.25
81	Chris Gomez	.25
82	Bob Higginson	.25
83	Mark Lewis	.25
84	Felipe Lira	.25
85	Alan Trammell	.25
86	Kevin Appier	.25
87	Johnny Damon	.40
88	Tom Goodwin	.25
89	Mark Gubicza	.25
90	Bob Hamelin	.25
91	Keith Lockhart	.25
92	Jeff Montgomery	.25
93	Jon Nunnally	.25
94	Bip Roberts	.25
95	Michael Tucker	.25
96	Joe Vitiello	.25
97	Ricky Bones	.25
98	Chuck Carr	.25
99	Jeff Cirillo	.25
100	Mike Fetters	.25
101	John Jaha	.25
102	Mike Matheny	.25
103	Ben McDonald	.25
104	Matt Mieske	.25
105	Dave Nilsson	.25
106	Kevin Seitzer	.25
107	Steve Sparks	.25
108	Jose Valentin	.25
109	Greg Vaughn	.25
110	Rick Aguilera	.25
111	Rich Becker	.25
112	Marty Cordova	.25
113	LaTroy Hawkins	.25
114	Dave Hollins	.25
115	Roberto Kelly	.25
116	Chuck Knoblauch	.25
117	*Matt Lawton*	1.50
118	Pat Meares	.25
119	Paul Molitor	1.50
120	Kirby Puckett	2.50
121	Brad Radke	.35
122	Frank Rodriguez	.25
123	Scott Stahoviak	.25
124	Matt Walbeck	.25
125	Wade Boggs	.75
126	David Cone	.25
127	Joe Girardi	.25
128	Dwight Gooden	.25
129	Derek Jeter	4.50
130	Jimmy Key	.25
131	Jim Leyritz	.25
132	Tino Martinez	.25
133	Paul O'Neill	.25
134	Andy Pettitte	.75
135	Tim Raines	.25
136	Ruben Rivera	.25
137	Kenny Rogers	.25
138	Ruben Sierra	.25
139	John Wetteland	.25
140	Bernie Williams	.75
141	*Tony Batista*	3.50
142	Allen Battle	.25
143	Geronimo Berroa	.25
144	Mike Bordick	.25
145	Scott Brosius	.25
146	Steve Cox	.25
147	Brent Gates	.25
148	Jason Giambi	.75
149	Doug Johns	.25
150	Mark McGwire	6.00
151	Pedro Munoz	.25
152	Ariel Prieto	.25
153	Terry Steinbach	.25
154	Todd Van Poppel	.25
155	Bobby Ayala	.25
156	Chris Bosio	.25
157	Jay Buhner	.25
158	Joey Cora	.25
159	Russ Davis	.25
160	Ken Griffey Jr.	6.00
161	Sterling Hitchcock	.25
162	Randy Johnson	2.00
163	Edgar Martinez	.25
164	Alex Rodriguez	6.00
165	Paul Sorrento	.25
166	Dan Wilson	.25
167	Will Clark	.50
168	Benji Gil	.25
169	Juan Gonzalez	2.50
170	Rusty Greer	.25
171	Kevin Gross	.25
172	Darryl Hamilton	.25
173	Mike Henneman	.25
174	Ken Hill	.25
175	Mark McLemore	.25
176	Dean Palmer	.25
177	Roger Pavlik	.25
178	Ivan Rodriguez	1.50
179	Mickey Tettleton	.25
180	Bobby Witt	.25
181	Joe Carter	.25
182	Felipe Crespo	.25
183	Alex Gonzalez	.25
184	Shawn Green	.75
185	Juan Guzman	.25
186	Erik Hanson	.25
187	Pat Hentgen	.25
188	*Sandy Martinez*	.25
189	Otis Nixon	.25
190	John Olerud	.25
191	Paul Quantrill	.25
192	Bill Risley	.25
193	Ed Sprague	.25
194	Steve Avery	.25
195	Jeff Blauser	.25
196	Brad Clontz	.25
197	Jermaine Dye	.25
198	Tom Glavine	.40
199	Marquis Grissom	.25
200	Chipper Jones	4.50
201	David Justice	.50
202	Ryan Klesko	.25
203	Mark Lemke	.25
204	Javier Lopez	.25
205	Greg Maddux	4.00
206	Fred McGriff	.25
207	Greg McMichael	.25
208	Wonderful Monds	.25
209	Jason Schmidt	.25
210	John Smoltz	.25
211	Mark Wohlers	.25
212	Jim Bullinger	.25
213	Frank Castillo	.25
214	Kevin Foster	.25
215	Luis Gonzalez	.35
216	Mark Grace	.45
217	*Robin Jennings*	.25
218	Doug Jones	.25
219	Dave Magadan	.25
220	Brian McRae	.25
221	Jaime Navarro	.25
222	Rey Sanchez	.25
223	Ryne Sandberg	2.00
224	Scott Servais	.25
225	Sammy Sosa	4.00
226	Ozzie Timmons	.25
227	Bret Boone	.30
228	Jeff Branson	.25
229	Jeff Brantley	.25
230	Dave Burba	.25
231	Vince Coleman	.25
232	Steve Gibralter	.25
233	Mike Kelly	.25
234	Barry Larkin	.50
235	Hal Morris	.25
236	Mark Portugal	.25
237	Jose Rijo	.25
238	Reggie Sanders	.25
239	Pete Schourek	.25
240	John Smiley	.25
241	Eddie Taubensee	.25
242	Jason Bates	.25
243	Dante Bichette	.25
244	Ellis Burks	.25
245	Vinny Castilla	.25
246	Andres Galarraga	.25
247	Darren Holmes	.25
248	Curt Leskanic	.25
249	Steve Reed	.25
250	Kevin Ritz	.25
251	Bret Saberhagen	.25
252	Bill Swift	.25
253	Larry Walker	.50
254	Walt Weiss	.25
255	Eric Young	.25
256	Kurt Abbott	.25
257	Kevin Brown	.25
258	John Burkett	.25
259	Greg Colbrunn	.25
260	Jeff Conine	.25
261	Andre Dawson	.40
262	Chris Hammond	.25
263	Charles Johnson	.25
264	Al Leiter	.25
265	Robb Nen	.25
266	Terry Pendleton	.25
267	Pat Rapp	.25
268	Gary Sheffield	.75
269	Quilvio Veras	.25
270	Devon White	.25
271	Bob Abreu	.50
272	Jeff Bagwell	2.00
273	Derek Bell	.25
274	Sean Berry	.25
275	Craig Biggio	.25
276	Doug Drabek	.25
277	Tony Eusebio	.25
278	Richard Hidalgo	.50
279	Brian Hunter	.25
280	Todd Jones	.25
281	Derrick May	.25
282	Orlando Miller	.25
283	James Mouton	.25

284 Shane Reynolds .25
285 Greg Swindell .25
286 Mike Blowers .25
287 Brett Butler .25
288 Tom Candiotti .25
289 Roger Cedeno .25
290 Delino DeShields .25
291 Greg Gagne .25
292 Karim Garcia .25
293 Todd Hollandsworth .25
294 Eric Karros .25
295 Ramon Martinez .25
296 Raul Mondesi .50
297 Hideo Nomo 1.00
298 Mike Piazza 4.50
299 Ismael Valdes .25
300 Todd Worrell .25
301 Moises Alou .25
302 Shane Andrews .25
303 Yamil Benitez .25
304 Jeff Fassero .25
305 Darrin Fletcher .25
306 Cliff Floyd .25
307 Mark Grudzielanek .25
308 Mike Lansing .25
309 Pedro Martinez 1.50
310 Ryan McGuire .25
311 Carlos Perez .25
312 Mel Rojas .25
313 David Segui .25
314 Rondell White .25
315 Edgardo Alfonzo .35
316 Rico Brogna .25
317 Carl Everett .25
318 John Franco .25
319 Bernard Gilkey .25
320 Todd Hundley .25
321 Jason Isringhausen .25
322 Lance Johnson .25
323 Bobby Jones .25
324 Jeff Kent .25
325 Rey Ordonez .25
326 Bill Pulsipher .25
327 Jose Vizcaino .25
328 Paul Wilson .25
329 Ricky Bottalico .25
330 Darren Daulton .25
331 *David Doster* .25
332 Lenny Dykstra .25
333 Jim Eisenreich .25
334 Sid Fernandez .25
335 Gregg Jefferies .25
336 Mickey Morandini .25
337 Benito Santiago .25
338 Curt Schilling .30
339 Kevin Stocker .25
340 David West .25
341 Mark Whiten .25
342 Todd Zeile .25
343 Jay Bell .25
344 John Ericks .25
345 Carlos Garcia .25
346 Charlie Hayes .25
347 Jason Kendall .25
348 Jeff King .25
349 Mike Kingery .25
350 Al Martin .25
351 Orlando Merced .25
352 Dan Miceli .25
353 Denny Neagle .25
354 Alan Benes .25
355 Andy Benes .25
356 Royce Clayton .25
357 Dennis Eckersley .25
358 Gary Gaetti .25
359 Ron Gant .25
360 Brian Jordan .25
361 Ray Lankford .25
362 John Mabry .25
363 T.J. Mathews .25
364 Mike Morgan .25
365 Donovan Osborne .25
366 Tom Pagnozzi .25
367 Ozzie Smith 2.00
368 Todd Stottlemyre .25
369 Andy Ashby .25
370 Brad Ausmus .25
371 Ken Caminiti .25
372 Andujar Cedeno .25
373 Steve Finley .25
374 Tony Gwynn 3.00
375 Joey Hamilton .25
376 Rickey Henderson .75
377 Trevor Hoffman .25
378 Wally Joyner .25
379 Marc Newfield .25
380 Jody Reed .25
381 Bob Tewksbury .25
382 Fernando Valenzuela .25
383 Rod Beck .25
384 Barry Bonds 3.00
385 Mark Carreon .25
386 Shawon Dunston .25
387 *Osvaldo Fernandez* .40
388 Glenallen Hill .25
389 Stan Javier .25
390 Mark Leiter .25
391 Kirt Manwaring .25
392 Robby Thompson .25
393 William VanLandingham .25
394 Allen Watson .25
395 Matt Williams .50
396 Checklist .25
397 Checklist .25
398 Checklist .25
399 Checklist .25
400 Checklist .25

1996 Flair Diamond Cuts

Ten of the game's top stars are showcased on these 1996 Flair inserts. They are seeded one per 20 packs. Fronts have a textured background rainbow metallic foil and silver glitter.

		MT
Complete Set (12):		30.00
Common Player:		1.25
1	Jeff Bagwell	3.50
2	Albert Belle	1.25
3	Barry Bonds	3.50
4	Juan Gonzalez	2.50
5	Ken Griffey Jr.	7.50
6	Greg Maddux	5.00
7	Eddie Murray	2.00
8	Mike Piazza	6.00
9	Cal Ripken Jr.	7.50
10	Frank Thomas	5.00
11	Mo Vaughn	2.00
12	Matt Williams	1.25

1996 Flair Hot Gloves

Ten top defensive players are highlighted on these die-cut insert cards, a design first made popular in 1994. Hot Gloves can only be found in hobby packs, at a rate of one per every 90 packs.

		MT
Complete Set (10):		100.00
Common Player:		5.00
1	Roberto Alomar	8.00
2	Barry Bonds	12.50
3	Will Clark	5.00
4	Ken Griffey Jr.	25.00
5	Kenny Lofton	5.00
6	Greg Maddux	15.00
7	Mike Piazza	20.00
8	Cal Ripken Jr.	25.00
9	Ivan Rodriguez	10.00
10	Matt Williams	5.00

1996 Flair Powerline

Ten of baseball's top sluggers are featured on these Flair inserts. They are the easiest of the Flair inserts to obtain; seeded one per six packs. Fronts combine yellow-green artwork with the player photo. Backs have a vertical color photo and career information.

		MT
Complete Set (10):		10.00
Common Player:		.50
1	Albert Belle	.50
2	Barry Bonds	1.00
3	Juan Gonzalez	1.00
4	Ken Griffey Jr.	3.00
5	Mark McGwire	3.00
6	Mike Piazza	2.00
7	Manny Ramirez	1.00
8	Sammy Sosa	1.75
9	Frank Thomas	1.75
10	Matt Williams	.50

1996 Flair Wave of the Future

These inserts feature up-and-coming young talent in baseball. Twenty 1996 rookies and prospects are printed on lenticular cards. They are seeded one per every 72 packs.

		MT
Complete Set (20):		65.00
Common Player:		3.00
1	Bob Abreu	7.50
2	George Arias	3.00
3	Tony Batista	7.50
4	Alan Benes	3.00
5	Yamil Benitez	3.00
6	Steve Cox	3.00
7	David Doster	3.00
8	Jermaine Dye	5.00
9	Osvaldo Fernandez	3.00
10	Karim Garcia	3.00
11	Steve Gibralter	3.00
12	Todd Greene	3.00
13	Richard Hidalgo	12.50
14	Robin Jennings	3.00
15	Jason Kendall	7.50
16	Jose Malave	3.00
17	Wonderful Monds	3.00
18	Rey Ordonez	4.50
19	Ruben Rivera	3.00
20	Paul Wilson	4.50

1997 Flair Showcase Row 2 (Style)

The 1997 Flair issue is actually three different versions of a 180-player set printed on a super-glossy thick stock. The most common version, Style, is designated Row 2 on back. Fronts have a color action photo with a black-and-white portrait image in the background, all printed on silver foil. Cards #1-60 are designated "Showtime" on back; #61-120 are "Showpiece" and #121-180 are labeled "Showstopper" and were inserted in varying ratios: Showtime - 1.5:1; Showpiece 1:1.5 and Showstopper 1:1. Cards were sold exclusively at hobby shops in five-card packs for $4.99.

		MT
Complete Set (180):		30.00
Common Style/Showtime (1-60):		.20
Common Style/Showpiece (61-120):		.35
Common Style/Showstopper (121-180):		.25
A-Rod Glove Exchange:		250.00
Pack (5):		2.50
Wax Box (24):		45.00
1	Andruw Jones	1.50
2	Derek Jeter	3.00

#	Player	MT
3	Alex Rodriguez	4.00
4	Paul Molitor	1.50
5	Jeff Bagwell	1.50
6	Scott Rolen	1.50
7	Kenny Lofton	.20
8	Cal Ripken Jr.	4.00
9	Brady Anderson	.20
10	Chipper Jones	3.00
11	Todd Greene	.20
12	Todd Walker	.50
13	Billy Wagner	.30
14	Craig Biggio	.20
15	Kevin Orie	.20
16	Hideo Nomo	.75
17	Kevin Appier	.20
18	*Bubba Trammell*	.50
19	Juan Gonzalez	1.50
20	Randy Johnson	1.00
21	Roger Clemens	1.50
22	Johnny Damon	.30
23	Ryne Sandberg	1.50
24	Ken Griffey Jr.	4.00
25	Barry Bonds	1.50
26	Nomar Garciaparra	2.50
27	Vladimir Guerrero	1.50
28	Ron Gant	.20
29	Joe Carter	.20
30	Tim Salmon	.75
31	Mike Piazza	3.00
32	Barry Larkin	.75
33	Manny Ramirez	1.50
34	Sammy Sosa	2.50
35	Frank Thomas	1.50
36	Melvin Nieves	.20
37	Tony Gwynn	2.50
38	Gary Sheffield	.40
39	Darin Erstad	1.50
40	Ken Caminiti	.20
41	Jermaine Dye	.20
42	Mo Vaughn	1.00
43	Raul Mondesi	.40
44	Greg Maddux	2.50
45	Chuck Knoblauch	.20
46	Andy Pettitte	.50
47	Deion Sanders	.40
48	Albert Belle	.75
49	Jamey Wright	.20
50	Rey Ordonez	.35
51	Bernie Williams	.75
52	Mark McGwire	4.00
53	Mike Mussina	1.00
54	Bob Abreu	.25
55	Reggie Sanders	.20
56	Brian Jordan	.20
57	Ivan Rodriguez	1.25
58	Roberto Alomar	.75
59	Tim Naehring	.20
60	Edgar Renteria	.25
61	Dean Palmer	.35
62	Benito Santiago	.35
63	David Cone	.35
64	Carlos Delgado	1.00
65	*Brian Giles*	3.00
66	Alex Ochoa	.35
67	Rondell White	.35
68	Robin Ventura	.35
69	Eric Karros	.35
70	Jose Valentin	.35
71	Rafael Palmeiro	.75
72	Chris Snopek	.35
73	David Justice	.75
74	Tom Glavine	.45
75	Rudy Pemberton	.35
76	Larry Walker	1.00
77	Jim Thome	.35
78	Charles Johnson	.35
79	Dante Powell	.35
80	Derrek Lee	.35
81	Jason Kendall	.35
82	Todd Hollandsworth	.35
83	Bernard Gilkey	.35
84	Mel Rojas	.35
85	Dmitri Young	.35
86	Bret Boone	.35
87	Pat Hentgen	.35
88	Bobby Bonilla	.35
89	John Wetteland	.35
90	Todd Hundley	.35
91	Wilton Guerrero	.35
92	Geronimo Berroa	.35
93	Al Martin	.35
94	Danny Tartabull	.35
95	Brian McRae	.35
96	Steve Finley	.35
97	Todd Stottlemyre	.35
98	John Smoltz	.40
99	Matt Williams	1.00
100	Eddie Murray	1.50
101	Henry Rodriguez	.35
102	Marty Cordova	.35
103	Juan Guzman	.35
104	Chili Davis	.35
105	Eric Young	.35
106	Jeff Abbott	.35
107	Shannon Stewart	.35
108	Rocky Coppinger	.35
109	Jose Canseco	1.50
110	Dante Bichette	.35
111	Dwight Gooden	.35
112	Scott Brosius	.35
113	Steve Avery	.35
114	Andres Galarraga	.35
115	Sandy Alomar Jr.	.35
116	Ray Lankford	.35
117	Jorge Posada	.35
118	Ryan Klesko	.35
119	Jay Buhner	.35
120	Jose Guillen	.40
121	Paul O'Neill	.25
122	Jimmy Key	.25
123	Hal Morris	.25
124	Travis Fryman	.25
125	Jim Edmonds	.30
126	Jeff Cirillo	.25
127	Fred McGriff	.25
128	Alan Benes	.25
129	Derek Bell	.25
130	Tony Graffanino	.25
131	Shawn Green	.75
132	Denny Neagle	.25
133	Alex Fernandez	.25
134	Mickey Morandini	.25
135	Royce Clayton	.25
136	Jose Mesa	.25
137	Edgar Martinez	.25
138	Curt Schilling	.35
139	Lance Johnson	.25
140	Andy Benes	.25
141	Charles Nagy	.25
142	Mariano Rivera	.75
143	Mark Wohlers	.25
144	Ken Hill	.25
145	Jay Bell	.25
146	Bob Higginson	.40
147	Mark Grudzielanek	.25
148	Ray Durham	.25
149	John Olerud	.25
150	Joey Hamilton	.25
151	Trevor Hoffman	.30
152	Dan Wilson	.25
153	J.T. Snow	.25
154	Marquis Grissom	.25
155	Yamil Benitez	.25
156	Rusty Greer	.25
157	Darryl Kile	.25
158	Ismael Valdes	.25
159	Jeff Conine	.25
160	Darren Daulton	.25
161	Chan Ho Park	.35
162	Troy Percival	.25
163	Wade Boggs	.75
164	Dave Nilsson	.25
165	Vinny Castilla	.25
166	Kevin Brown	.35
167	Dennis Eckersley	.25
168	Wendell Magee Jr.	.25
169	John Jaha	.25
170	Garret Anderson	.25
171	Jason Giambi	.50
172	Mark Grace	.60
173	Tony Clark	.50
174	Moises Alou	.35
175	Brett Butler	.25
176	Cecil Fielder	.25
177	Chris Widger	.25
178	Doug Drabek	.25
179	Ellis Burks	.25
180	Shigetosi Hasegawa	.25

1997 Flair Showcase Row 1 (Grace)

The second level of '97 Flair scarcity is represented by the Row 1/Grace cards (so designated on back). These are visually differentiated on front by the use of a full background to the action photo, and the addition of a color portrait. Row 1/Grace cards are further broken down by their designation on back as: "Showstopper" (#1-60; seeded 1:2.5 packs), "Showtime" (#61-120; 1:2) and "Showpiece" (#121-180; 1:3) with varying insertion rates as shown.

	MT
Complete Set (180):	150.00
Common Showstopper (1-60):	.50
Stars:	2X
Common Showtime (#61-120):	.35
Stars:	1X
Common Showpiece (#121-180):	.75
Stars:	2X

(See 1997 Flair Showcase Row 2 for checklist and base card values.)

1997 Flair Showcase Row 0 (Showcase)

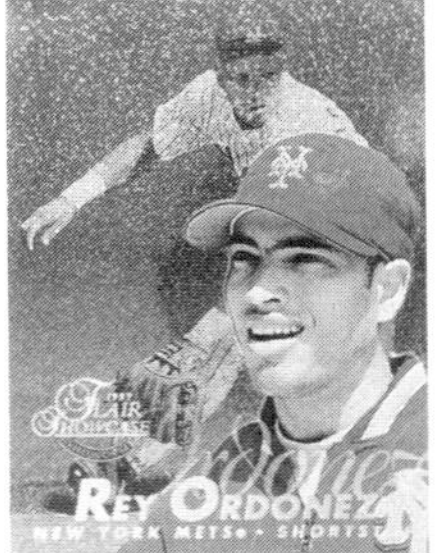

The scarcest level of '97 Flair is the Row 0/Showcase cards (so designated on front and back). These are identifiable on front by the use of a color portrait in the foreground, with a large action photo behind, printed on a gold-flecked metallic background. Row 0/ Showcase cards are further broken down by their designation on back as: "Showpiece" (#1-60; seeded 1:24 packs), "Showstopper" (#61-120; 1:12) and "Showtime" (#121-180; 1:5) with varying insertion rates as shown.

	MT
Complete Set (180):	950.00
Common Showpiece (1-60):	3.00
Stars:	10X
Common Showstopper (61-120):	1.50
Stars:	4X
Common Showtime (121-180):	.50
Stars:	3X

(See 1997 Flair Showcase Row 2 for checklist and base card values.)

1997 Flair Showcase Legacy Collection

This 540-card parallel set is printed on matte-finish stock rather than the high-gloss of the regular cards. Front graphic highlights are in blue foil, as is the serial number on back from within each card's edition of just 100. Stated odds of insertion are one per 30 packs. Because all Legacies are printed in identical numbers, there is no premium for cards of different rows.

	MT
Common Player:	10.00
Stars:	25-50X

(See 1997 Flair Showcase Row 2 for checkist and base card values.)

1997 Flair Showcase Legacy Masterpiece

The insert card chase reached its inevitable zenith with the creation of this series of one-of-a-kind inserts. Each of the 180 players' three cards (Row 2/Style, Row 1/Grace, Row 0/Showcase) in the '97 Flair Legacy Collection was also produced in an edition of one card and inserted at a rate of about one per 3,000 packs. Instead of the blue metallic foil highlights on front and back of the regular Legacy cards, the one-of-a-kind Masterpieces are highlighted in purple and carry a notation on back, "The Only 1 of 1 Masterpiece". Because of the unique nature of each card, value depends solely on demand, thus presentation of meaningful "catalog" values is not possible.

	MT
Common Player:	100.00

(Values undertermined)

1997 Flair Showcase Diamond Cuts

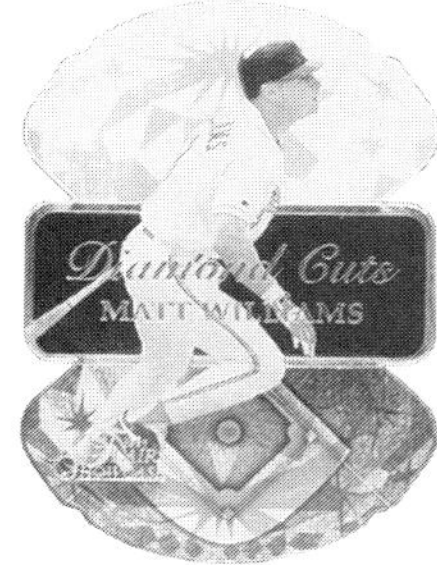

This 20-card insert, found 1:20 packs, features a die-cut design with an action photo of the player appearing above a baseball diamond in the lower background.

		MT
Complete Set (20):		55.00
Common Player:		1.50
1	Jeff Bagwell	3.50
2	Albert Belle	1.50
3	Ken Caminiti	1.50
4	Juan Gonzalez	2.50
5	Ken Griffey Jr.	6.00
6	Tony Gwynn	4.00
7	Todd Hundley	1.50
8	Andruw Jones	2.50
9	Chipper Jones	5.00
10	Greg Maddux	4.00
11	Mark McGwire	6.50
12	Mike Piazza	5.00
13	Derek Jeter	5.00
14	Manny Ramirez	2.50
15	Cal Ripken Jr.	6.50
16	Alex Rodriguez	6.00
17	Frank Thomas	4.00
18	Mo Vaughn	2.00
19	Bernie Williams	1.50
20	Matt Williams	1.50

1997 Flair Showcase Hot Gloves

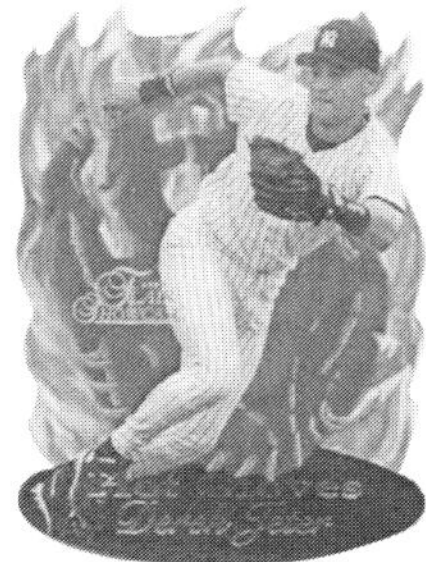

Inserted 1:90 packs, Hot Gloves features 15 cards with a die-cut "flaming glove" design printed in thermally active inks and saluting some of baseball's best defensive players.

		MT
Complete Set (15):		185.00
Common Player:		3.50
1	Roberto Alomar	7.50
2	Barry Bonds	15.00
3	Juan Gonzalez	12.50
4	Ken Griffey Jr.	30.00
5	Marquis Grissom	3.50
6	Derek Jeter	22.50
7	Chipper Jones	22.50
8	Barry Larkin	3.50
9	Kenny Lofton	3.50
10	Greg Maddux	17.50
11	Mike Piazza	22.50
12	Cal Ripken Jr.	30.00
13	Alex Rodriguez	30.00
14	Ivan Rodriguez	7.50
15	Frank Thomas	17.50

1997 Flair Showcase Wave of the Future

This insert focuses on some of the up-and-coming young stars in the game. Cards were seeded 1:4 packs. A large ocean wave makes up the background of each card front.

		MT
Complete Set (27):		20.00
Common Player:		.50
1	Todd Greene	.60
2	Andruw Jones	2.50
3	Randall Simon	.50
4	Wady Almonte	.50
5	Pat Cline	.75
6	Jeff Abbott	.50
7	Justin Towle	.50
8	Richie Sexson	.75
9	Bubba Trammell	1.00
10	Bob Abreu	.75
11	David Arias (last name actually Ortiz)	.75
12	Todd Walker	1.50
13	Orlando Cabrera	.65
14	Vladimir Guerrero	2.50
15	Ricky Ledee	.50
16	Jorge Posada	.75
17	Ruben Rivera	.50
18	Scott Spiezio	.50
19	Scott Rolen	2.50
20	Emil Brown	.50
21	Jose Guillen	1.25
22	T.J. Staton	.50
23	Elieser Marrero	.50
24	Fernando Tatis	1.25
25	Ryan Jones	.50
WF1	Hideki Irabu	.50
WF2	Jose Cruz Jr.	1.50

1998 Flair Showcase Row 3

Row 3, or Flair, cards are considered the base cards of '98 Showcase. They feature a close-up black-and-white portrait photo in the background and an action shot in front, overprinted on a silver-foil background. Flair/Showtime (#1-30) cards are inserted 1:.9 packs, Flair/Showstopper (#31-60) are found 1:1.1 packs, Flair/Showdown (#61-90) cards are inserted 1:1.5 packs and Flair/Showdown (#91-120) cards are inserted 1:2 packs.

		MT
Complete Set (120):		20.00
Common Player (1-30):		.25
Common Player (31-60):		.25
Common Player (61-90):		.35
Common Player (91-120):		.45
Pack (5):		3.00
Wax Box (24):		65.00
1	Ken Griffey Jr.	5.00
2	Travis Lee	1.00
3	Frank Thomas	3.00
4	Ben Grieve	1.00
5	Nomar Garciaparra	4.00
6	Jose Cruz Jr.	.40
7	Alex Rodriguez	4.00
8	Cal Ripken Jr.	5.00
9	Mark McGwire	5.00
10	Chipper Jones	3.50
11	Paul Konerko	.35
12	Todd Helton	1.50
13	Greg Maddux	4.00
14	Derek Jeter	4.00
15	Jaret Wright	.50
16	Livan Hernandez	.25
17	Mike Piazza	4.00
18	Juan Encarnacion	.25
19	Tony Gwynn	3.00
20	Scott Rolen	2.00
21	Roger Clemens	3.00
22	Tony Clark	.35
23	Albert Belle	1.00
24	Mo Vaughn	1.25
25	Andruw Jones	1.50
26	Jason Dickson	.25
27	Fernando Tatis	.35
28	Ivan Rodriguez	1.25
29	Ricky Ledee	.25
30	Darin Erstad	1.50
31	Brian Rose	.25
32	*Magglio Ordonez*	4.00
33	Larry Walker	.75
34	Bobby Higginson	.25
35	Chili Davis	.25
36	Barry Bonds	3.00
37	Vladimir Guerrero	2.00
38	Jeff Bagwell	1.50
39	Kenny Lofton	.25
40	Ryan Klesko	.25
41	Mike Cameron	.25
42	Charles Johnson	.25
43	Andy Pettitte	1.00
44	Juan Gonzalez	1.50
45	Tim Salmon	.75
46	Hideki Irabu	.25
47	Paul Molitor	1.50
48	Edgar Renteria	.25
49	Manny Ramirez	2.00
50	Jim Edmonds	.40
51	Bernie Williams	.75
52	Roberto Alomar	.75
53	David Justice	.50
54	Rey Ordonez	.25
55	Ken Caminiti	.25
56	Jose Guillen	.50
57	Randy Johnson	1.00
58	Brady Anderson	.25
59	Hideo Nomo	.50
60	Tino Martinez	.25
61	John Smoltz	.35
62	Joe Carter	.35
63	Matt Williams	.50
64	Robin Ventura	.35
65	Barry Larkin	.45
66	Dante Bichette	.35
67	Travis Fryman	.35
68	Gary Sheffield	.65
69	Eric Karros	.35
70	Matt Stairs	.35
71	Al Martin	.35
72	Jay Buhner	.35
73	Ray Lankford	.35
74	Carlos Delgado	.50
75	Edgardo Alfonzo	.40
76	Rondell White	.35
77	Chuck Knoblauch	.35
78	Raul Mondesi	.45
79	Johnny Damon	.45
80	Matt Morris	.35
81	Tom Glavine	.45
82	Kevin Brown	.45
83	Garret Anderson	.35
84	Mike Mussina	1.00
85	Pedro Martinez	.75
86	Craig Biggio	.35
87	Darryl Kile	.40
88	Rafael Palmeiro	.50
89	Jim Thome	.35
90	Andres Galarraga	.35
91	Sammy Sosa	3.50
92	Willie Greene	.45
93	Vinny Castilla	.45
94	Justin Thompson	.45
95	Jeff King	.45
96	Jeff Cirillo	.45
97	Mark Grudzielanek	.45
98	Brad Radke	.50
99	John Olerud	.45
100	Curt Schilling	.60
101	Steve Finley	.45
102	J.T. Snow	.45
103	Edgar Martinez	.45
104	Wilson Alvarez	.45
105	Rusty Greer	.45
106	Pat Hentgen	.45
107	David Cone	.45
108	Fred McGriff	.45
109	Jason Giambi	1.00
110	Tony Womack	.45
111	Bernard Gilkey	.45
112	Alan Benes	.45
113	Mark Grace	.75
114	Reggie Sanders	.45
115	Moises Alou	.50
116	John Jaha	.45
117	Henry Rodriguez	.45
118	Dean Palmer	.45
119	Mike Lieberthal	.50
120	Shawn Estes	.45

1998 Flair Showcase Row 2

Row 2, or Style (as they are designated on front) cards in Flair Showcase are the second easiest type of card to pull from packs. Fronts are similar to Row 3 base cards, but include the entire background of the action photo and have a color portrait photo. Cards #1-30 are inserted one per three packs, #31-60 are found

1:2.5 packs, #61-90 cards are 1:4 and #91-120 are inserted one per three packs.

	MT
Complete Set (120):	50.00
Common Player (1-30):	.50
Stars:	2X
Common Player (31-60):	.50
Stars:	1.5X
Common Player (61-90):	.75
Stars:	2X
Common Player (91-120):	.75
Stars:	1.5X

(See 1998 Flair Showcase Row 3 for checklist and base card values.)

1998 Flair Showcase Row 1

Row 1, also referred to as Grace, was the second most difficult type of card to pull from Flair Showcase. The front design has an action photo overprinted on a large portrait which is printed on a rainbow metallic-foil background. Cards #1-30 are seeded one per 16 packs, #31-60 are 1:24, #61-90 are 1:6 and #91-120 are 1:10.

	MT
Complete Set (1-120):	200.00
Commons (1-30):	2.00
Stars:	4X
Commons (31-60):	2.50
Stars:	6X
Commons (61-90):	.75
Stars:	2X
Commons (91-120):	1.50
Stars:	3X

(See 1998 Flair Showcase Row 3 for checklist and base cards values.)

1998 Flair Showcase Row 0

Row 0 is the most difficult of the four tiers to obtain from packs. Two action photos are combined on a horizontal format with one in a prismatic foil background. The first 30 cards are serially numbered to 250, cards #30-60 are numbered to 500, #61-90 are numbered to 1,000 and #91-120 are numbered within an edition of 2,000.

	MT
Complete Set (120):	750.00
Common Player (1-30):	5.00
Stars:	20X
Common Player (31-60):	3.00
Stars:	15X
Common Player (61-90):	2.00
Stars:	9X
Common Player (91-120):	1.00
Stars:	5X

(See 1998 Flair Showcase Row 3 for checklist and base card values.)

1998 Flair Showcase Legacy Collection

Legacy Collection parallels all 480 cards in the Flair Showcase set. Each Legacy Collection card displays the player's name in black plate laminated on the back, with the card's sequential numbering to 100 in gold foil.

	MT
Common Player:	4.00
Stars:	15-25X

(See 1998 Flair Showcase Row 3 for checklist and base card values.)

1998 Flair Showcase Legacy Masterpiece

Each of the 120 players' four cards (Rows 3, 2, 1 and 0) in the '98 Flair Legacy Collection was also produced in an edition of one card and inserted at a rate of about one per 3,000 packs. The one-of-a-kind cards carry a notation on back: "The Only 1 of 1 Masterpiece". With supply a fixed quantity, value depends on demand at any particular time, thus it is not possible to present meaningful "catalog" values.

	MT
Common Player:	100.00

(Values undetermined)

1998 Flair Showcase Perfect 10

Perfect 10 features the game's most popular players on a silk-screen technology design. The cards were serial numbered to 10 on the back and were inserted into packs of Flair Showcase.

		MT
	Complete Set (10):	3750.
	Common Player:	100.00
1	Ken Griffey Jr.	750.00
2	Cal Ripken Jr.	750.00
3	Frank Thomas	375.00
4	Mike Piazza	550.00
5	Greg Maddux	450.00
6	Nomar Garciaparra	500.00
7	Mark McGwire	750.00
8	Scott Rolen	100.00
9	Alex Rodriguez	750.00
10	Roger Clemens	325.00

1998 Flair Showcase Wave of the Future

Twelve up-and-coming players with hot minor league stats and Major League potential are displayed in Wave of the Future. The cards contain a clear acetate card inside a plastic covering that is filled with vegetable oil and glitter. These were inserted one per 20 packs and are numbered with a "WF" prefix.

		MT
	Complete Set (12):	20.00
	Common Player:	.70
WF1	Travis Lee	1.50
WF2	Todd Helton	7.50
WF3	Ben Grieve	4.00
WF4	Juan Encarnacion	1.50
WF5	Brad Fullmer	1.50
WF6	Ruben Rivera	.75
WF7	Paul Konerko	1.50
WF8	Derrek Lee	.75
WF9	Mike Lowell	1.25
WF10	Magglio Ordonez	2.50
WF11	Rich Butler	.75
WF12	Eli Marrero	1.25

1999 Flair Showcase Row 3 (Power)

Power is one of three tiers in 1999 Showcase. The front on this base-level version is rainbow holofoil including the large portrait photo in the background. In the foreground is a color action photo. Matte textured silver spot embossing is printed over the player's name and team at lower-right. All three Rows of Showcase can be found with three different back designs. Showtime presents traditional annual and career stats. Horizontally formatted Showpiece cards have a black-and-white player photo as a "Classic Matchup" of the player's stats to those of a past star. Showdown backs have a color action photo on a brightly-colored wave-pattern background. A stat box at center offers career numbers in four unique categories like day-night, grass-turf, etc. Each of these three back-design levels of scarcity has a different advertised insertion rate. Within Row 3/Power, these vary only between one card in .9 packs, and one card in 1.2

packs, thus there is no practical value differential. Five-card packs of Flair Showcase had a $4.99 SRP.

		MT
Complete Set (144):		30.00
Common Player:		.25
Pack (5):		3.00
Wax Box (24):		75.00
1	Mark McGwire	4.00
2	Sammy Sosa	2.00
3	Ken Griffey Jr.	4.00
4	Chipper Jones	3.00
5	Ben Grieve	.50
6	J.D. Drew	.50
7	Jeff Bagwell	1.25
8	Cal Ripken Jr.	4.00
9	Tony Gwynn	2.50
10	Nomar Garciaparra	3.00
11	Travis Lee	.40
12	Troy Glaus	2.00
13	Mike Piazza	3.00
14	Alex Rodriguez	4.00
15	Kevin Brown	.50
16	Darin Erstad	1.00
17	Scott Rolen	1.50
18	*Micah Bowie*	.75
19	Juan Gonzalez	1.50
20	Kerry Wood	1.00
21	Roger Clemens	2.00
22	Derek Jeter	3.00
23	*Pat Burrell*	5.00
24	Tim Salmon	.60
25	Barry Bonds	2.00
26	*Roosevelt Brown*	1.00
27	Vladimir Guerrero	1.50
28	Randy Johnson	1.00
29	Mo Vaughn	1.00
30	Fernando Seguignol	.25
31	Greg Maddux	2.50
32	Tony Clark	.35
33	Eric Chavez	.50
34	Kris Benson	.25
35	Frank Thomas	2.00
36	Mario Encarnacion	.25
37	Gabe Kapler	.50
38	Jeremy Giambi	.75
39	*Peter Tucci*	.50
40	Manny Ramirez	2.00
41	Albert Belle	.75
42	Warren Morris	.25
43	Michael Barrett	.40
44	Andruw Jones	1.25
45	Carlos Delgado	.75
46	Jaret Wright	.50
47	Juan Encarnacion	.40
48	Scott Hunter	.25
49	Tino Martinez	.25
50	Craig Biggio	.25
51	Jim Thome	.25
52	Vinny Castilla	.25
53	Tom Glavine	.35
54	Bob Higginson	.25
55	Moises Alou	.40
56	Robin Ventura	.25
57	Bernie Williams	.75
58	Pedro J. Martinez	1.00
59	Greg Vaughn	.25
60	Ray Lankford	.25
61	Jose Canseco	1.00
62	Ivan Rodriguez	1.00
63	Shawn Green	.75
64	Rafael Palmeiro	.60
65	Ellis Burks	.25
66	Jason Kendall	.35
67	David Wells	.25
68	Rondell White	.30
69	Gary Sheffield	.40
70	Ken Caminiti	.25
71	Cliff Floyd	.25
72	Larry Walker	1.00
73	Bartolo Colon	.25
74	Barry Larkin	.45
75	Calvin Pickering	.25
76	Jim Edmonds	.25
77	Henry Rodriguez	.25
78	Roberto Alomar	1.00
79	Andres Galarraga	.25
80	Richie Sexson	.35
81	Todd Helton	1.50
82	Damion Easley	.25
83	Livan Hernandez	.25
84	Carlos Beltran	.40
85	Todd Hundley	.25
86	Todd Walker	.25
87	Scott Brosius	.25
88	Bob Abreu	.25
89	Corey Koskie	.25
90	Ruben Rivera	.25
91	Edgar Renteria	.25
92	Quinton McCracken	.25
93	Bernard Gilkey	.25
94	Shannon Stewart	.25
95	Dustin Hermanson	.25
96	Mike Caruso	.25
97	Alex Gonzalez	.25
98	Raul Mondesi	.35
99	David Cone	.25
100	Curt Schilling	.45
101	Brian Giles	.25
102	Edgar Martinez	.25
103	Rolando Arrojo	.25
104	Derek Bell	.25
105	Denny Neagle	.25
106	Marquis Grissom	.25
107	Bret Boone	.25
108	Mike Mussina	1.00
109	John Smoltz	.25
110	Brett Tomko	.25
111	David Justice	.50
112	Andy Pettitte	.40
113	Eric Karros	.25
114	Dante Bichette	.25
115	Jeromy Burnitz	.25
116	Paul Konerko	.25
117	Steve Finley	.25
118	Ricky Ledee	.25
119	Edgardo Alfonzo	.25
120	Dean Palmer	.25
121	Rusty Greer	.25
122	Luis Gonzalez	.35
123	Randy Winn	.25
124	Jeff Kent	.25
125	Doug Glanville	.25
126	Justin Thompson	.25
127	Bret Saberhagen	.25
128	Wade Boggs	.75
129	Al Leiter	.25
130	Paul O'Neill	.25
131	Chan Ho Park	.50
132	Johnny Damon	.35
133	Darryl Kile	.30
134	Reggie Sanders	.25
135	Kevin Millwood	.50
136	Charles Johnson	.25
137	Ray Durham	.25
138	Rico Brogna	.25
139	Matt Williams	.75
140	Sandy Alomar	.25
141	Jeff Cirillo	.25
142	Devon White	.25
143	Andy Benes	.25
144	Mike Stanley	.25
	Checklist card	.05

1999 Flair Showcase Row 2 (Passion)

The metallic-foil background in the second level of Flair Showcase - Row 2/Passion - has an action photo printed in front of large textured numerals representing the player's uniform number. In the foreground is another action shot. Backs have the same three designs as Row 3, but only vary in insertion rate from one card per 1.3 packs to one card per three packs.

	MT
Complete Set (144):	75.00
Common Player:	.25
Showdown (1-48):	2X
Showpiece (49-96):	1X
Showtime (97-144):	1X

(See 1999 Flair Showcase Row 3 for checklist and base card values.)

1999 Flair Showcase Row 1 (Showcase)

Showcase level - Row 1 - presents two portraits and an action photo and the player's uniform number on a platic laminate in a horizontal format. A gold-foil serial number is stamped into the upper-left corner in one of three levels of scarcity: Showpiece (#1-48) is limited to 1,500 numbered sets, Showtime (#49-96) is limited to 3,000 sets and Showdown (#97-144) is numbered to 6,000 sets.

	MT
Complete Set (144):	550.00
Common Showpiece (1-48):	2.00
Showpiece Stars:	7X
Common Showtime (49-96):	1.00
Showtime Stars:	5X
Common Showdown (97-144):	.75
Showdown Stars:	2X

(See 1999 Flair Showcase Row 1 for checklist and base card values.)

1999 Flair Showcase Legacy / Masterpiece

Each of the 432 total cards in Flair Showcase was also produced in a pair of extremely limited parallels. The blue-foil enhanced Legacy Collection cards are serially numbered within an edition of just 99. The presence of purple foil on front signifies a Legacy Masterpiece card, which is identified on back by the notation, "The Only 1 of 1 Masterpiece". Because of their unique nature, determination of a "book value" for Masterpiece cards is not possible.

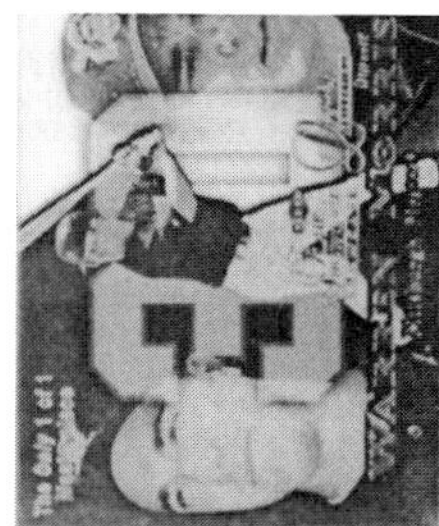

	MT
Common Legacy:	4.00
Legacy Stars:	15x to 20x
Common Masterpiece:	75.00

(See 1999 Flair Showcase for checklist.)

1999 Flair Showcase Measure of Greatness

This 15-card set captures baseball's top superstars who were closing in on milestones during the 1999 season. Each card is sequentially numbered to 500.

		MT
Complete Set (15):		200.00
Common Player:		7.50
Production 500 sets		
1	Roger Clemens	12.50
2	Nomar Garciaparra	15.00
3	Juan Gonzalez	7.50
4	Ken Griffey Jr.	30.00
5	Vladimir Guerrero	7.50
6	Tony Gwynn	12.50
7	Derek Jeter	20.00
8	Chipper Jones	20.00
9	Mark McGwire	30.00
10	Mike Piazza	20.00
11	Manny Ramirez	7.50
12	Cal Ripken Jr.	30.00
13	Alex Rodriguez	30.00
14	Sammy Sosa	15.00
15	Frank Thomas	7.50

A card number in parentheses ( ) indicates the set is unnumbered.

1999 Flair Showcase Wave of the Future

This insert set spotlights young stars on the rise and is limited to 1,000 serial numbered sets.

		MT
Complete Set (15):		45.00
Common Player:		2.00
Production 1,000 sets		
1	Kerry Wood	3.50
2	Ben Grieve	3.00
3	J.D. Drew	4.00
4	Juan Encarnacion	2.50
5	Travis Lee	2.50
6	Todd Helton	6.50
7	Troy Glaus	8.00
8	Ricky Ledee	2.00
9	Eric Chavez	5.00
10	Ben Davis	2.00
11	George Lombard	2.00
12	Jeremy Giambi	2.00
13	Roosevelt Brown	2.00
14	Pat Burrell	12.50
15	Preston Wilson	2.50

1981 Fleer

For the first time in 18 years, Fleer issued a baseball card set featuring current players. The 660-card effort included numerous errors in the first print run which were subsequently corrected. The 2-1/2" x 3-1/2" cards are numbered by team in order of the previous season's finish. Card fronts feature a full-color photo inside a border which is color-coded by team. Backs are printed in black, grey and yellow on white stock and carry full player statistical information. The player's batting average or earned run average is located in a circle in the upper-right corner of the back. The complete set price in the checklist that follows does not include the higher priced variations.

		MT
Complete Set (660):		25.00
Common Player:		.08
Pack (17 - 2nd print):		1.50
Wax Box (38 - 2nd print)_:		35.00
1	Pete Rose	3.00
2	Larry Bowa	.10
3	Manny Trillo	.08
4	Bob Boone	.10
5a	Mike Schmidt (portrait)	2.50
5b	Mike Schmidt (batting)	2.00
6a	Steve Carlton ("Lefty" on front)	1.00
6b	Steve Carlton (Pitcher of the Year on front, date 1066 on back)	2.00
6c	Steve Carlton (Pitcher of the Year on front, date 1966 on back)	2.50
7a	Tug McGraw (Game Saver on front)	.50
7b	Tug McGraw (Pitcher on front)	.08
8	Larry Christenson	.08
9	Bake McBride	.08
10	Greg Luzinski	.08
11	Ron Reed	.08
12	Dickie Noles	.08
13	*Keith Moreland*	.15
14	*Bob Walk*	.08
15	Lonnie Smith	.08
16	Dick Ruthven	.08
17	Sparky Lyle	.08
18	Greg Gross	.08
19	Garry Maddox	.08
20	Nino Espinosa	.08
21	George Vukovich	.08
22	John Vukovich	.08
23	Ramon Aviles	.08
24a	Kevin Saucier (Ken Saucier on back)	.10
24b	Kevin Saucier (Kevin Saucier on back)	.50
25	Randy Lerch	.08
26	Del Unser	.08
27	Tim McCarver	.15
28a	George Brett (batting)	3.00
28b	George Brett (portrait)	1.00
29a	Willie Wilson (portrait)	.50
29b	Willie Wilson (batting)	.15
30	Paul Splittorff	.08
31	Dan Quisenberry	.08
32a	Amos Otis (batting)	.50
32b	Amos Otis (portrait)	.10
33	Steve Busby	.08
34	U.L. Washington	.08
35	Dave Chalk	.08
36	Darrell Porter	.08
37	Marty Pattin	.08
38	Larry Gura	.08
39	Renie Martin	.08
40	Rich Gale	.08
41a	Hal McRae (dark blue "Royals" on front)	.40
41b	Hal McRae (light blue "Royals" on front)	.10
42	Dennis Leonard	.08
43	Willie Aikens	.08
44	Frank White	.08
45	Clint Hurdle	.08
46	John Wathan	.08
47	Pete LaCock	.08
48	Rance Mulliniks	.08
49	Jeff Twitty	.08
50	Jamie Quirk	.08
51	Art Howe	.08
52	Ken Forsch	.08
53	Vern Ruhle	.08
54	Joe Niekro	.10
55	Frank LaCorte	.08
56	J.R. Richard	.10
57	Nolan Ryan	4.00
58	Enos Cabell	.08
59	Cesar Cedeno	.10
60	Jose Cruz	.10
61	Bill Virdon	.08
62	Terry Puhl	.08
63	Joaquin Andujar	.08
64	Alan Ashby	.08
65	Joe Sambito	.08
66	Denny Walling	.08
67	Jeff Leonard	.08
68	Luis Pujols	.08
69	Bruce Bochy	.08
70	Rafael Landestoy	.08
71	*Dave Smith*	.08
72	*Danny Heep*	.08
73	Julio Gonzalez	.08
74	Craig Reynolds	.08
75	Gary Woods	.08
76	Dave Bergman	.08
77	Randy Niemann	.08
78	Joe Morgan	.75
79a	Reggie Jackson (portrait)	2.50
79b	Reggie Jackson (batting)	2.00
80	Bucky Dent	.10
81	Tommy John	.20
82	Luis Tiant	.10
83	Rick Cerone	.08
84	Dick Howser	.08
85	Lou Piniella	.15
86	Ron Davis	.08
87a	Graig Nettles (Craig on back)	8.00
87b	Graig Nettles (Graig on back)	.15
88	Ron Guidry	.15
89	Rich Gossage	.10
90	Rudy May	.08
91	Gaylord Perry	.75
92	Eric Soderholm	.08
93	Bob Watson	.08
94	Bobby Murcer	.10
95	Bobby Brown	.08
96	Jim Spencer	.08
97	Tom Underwood	.08
98	Oscar Gamble	.08
99	Johnny Oates	.08
100	Fred Stanley	.08
101	Ruppert Jones	.08
102	Dennis Werth	.08
103	Joe Lefebvre	.08
104	Brian Doyle	.08
105	Aurelio Rodriguez	.08
106	Doug Bird	.08
107	Mike Griffin	.08
108	Tim Lollar	.08
109	Willie Randolph	.08
110	Steve Garvey	.40
111	Reggie Smith	.08
112	Don Sutton	.75
113	Burt Hooton	.08
114a	Davy Lopes (Davey) (no finger on back)	.08
114b	Davy Lopes (Davey) (small finger on back)	.50
115	Dusty Baker	.15
116	Tom Lasorda	.45
117	Bill Russell	.08
118	Jerry Reuss	.08
119	Terry Forster	.08
120a	Bob Welch (Bob on back)	.10
120b	Bob Welch (Robert)	.50
121	Don Stanhouse	.08
122	Rick Monday	.08
123	Derrel Thomas	.08
124	Joe Ferguson	.08
125	Rick Sutcliffe	.10
126a	Ron Cey (no finger on back)	.08
126b	Ron Cey (small finger on back)	.50
127	Dave Goltz	.08
128	Jay Johnstone	.08
129	Steve Yeager	.08
130	Gary Weiss	.08
131	*Mike Scioscia*	.25
132	Vic Davalillo	.08
133	Doug Rau	.08
134	Pepe Frias	.08
135	Mickey Hatcher	.08
136	*Steve Howe*	.10
137	Robert Castillo	.08
138	Gary Thomasson	.08
139	Rudy Law	.08
140	*Fernando Valenzuela*	1.50
141	Manny Mota	.08
142	Gary Carter	.65
143	Steve Rogers	.08
144	Warren Cromartie	.08
145	Andre Dawson	1.00
146	Larry Parrish	.08
147	Rowland Office	.08
148	Ellis Valentine	.08
149	Dick Williams	.08
150	*Bill Gullickson*	.15
151	Elias Sosa	.08
152	John Tamargo	.08
153	Chris Speier	.08
154	Ron LeFlore	.08
155	Rodney Scott	.08
156	Stan Bahnsen	.08
157	Bill Lee	.08
158	Fred Norman	.08
159	Woodie Fryman	.08
160	Dave Palmer	.08
161	Jerry White	.08
162	Roberto Ramos	.08
163	John D'Acquisto	.08
164	Tommy Hutton	.08
165	*Charlie Lea*	.15
166	Scott Sanderson	.08
167	Ken Macha	.08
168	Tony Bernazard	.08
169	Jim Palmer	1.00
170	Steve Stone	.10
171	Mike Flanagan	.08
172	Al Bumbry	.08
173	Doug DeCinces	.08
174	Scott McGregor	.08
175	Mark Belanger	.08
176	Tim Stoddard	.08
177a	Rick Dempsey (no finger on front)	.08
177b	Rick Dempsey (small finger on front)	.50
178	Earl Weaver	.45
179	Tippy Martinez	.08
180	Dennis Martinez	.08
181	Sammy Stewart	.08
182	Rich Dauer	.08
183	Lee May	.08
184	Eddie Murray	1.50
185	Benny Ayala	.08
186	John Lowenstein	.08
187	Gary Roenicke	.08
188	Ken Singleton	.08
189	Dan Graham	.08
190	Terry Crowley	.08
191	Kiko Garcia	.08
192	Dave Ford	.08
193	Mark Corey	.08
194	Lenn Sakata	.08
195	Doug DeCinces	.08
196	Johnny Bench	1.50
197	Dave Concepcion	.15
198	Ray Knight	.10
199	Ken Griffey	.10
200	Tom Seaver	1.50
201	Dave Collins	.08
202	George Foster	.10
203	Junior Kennedy	.08
204	Frank Pastore	.08
205	Dan Driessen	.08
206	Hector Cruz	.08
207	Paul Moskau	.08
208	*Charlie Leibrandt*	.25
209	Harry Spilman	.08
210	*Joe Price*	.08
211	Tom Hume	.08
212	Joe Nolan	.08
213	Doug Bair	.08
214	Mario Soto	.08
215a	Bill Bonham (no finger on back)	.08
215b	Bill Bonham (small finger on back)	.50
216a	George Foster (Slugger on front)	.25
216b	George Foster (Outfield on front)	.15
217	Paul Householder	.08
218	Ron Oester	.08
219	Sam Mejias	.08
220	Sheldon Burnside	.08
221	Carl Yastrzemski	1.50
222	Jim Rice	.50
223	Fred Lynn	.15
224	Carlton Fisk	1.50
225	Rick Burleson	.08
226	Dennis Eckersley	.65
227	Butch Hobson	.08
228	Tom Burgmeier	.08
229	Garry Hancock	.08
230	Don Zimmer	.08
231	Steve Renko	.08
232	Dwight Evans	.15
233	Mike Torrez	.08
234	Bob Stanley	.08
235	Jim Dwyer	.08
236	Dave Stapleton	.08
237	Glenn Hoffman	.08
238	Jerry Remy	.08
239	Dick Drago	.08
240	Bill Campbell	.08
241	Tony Perez	.75
242	Phil Niekro	.75
243	Dale Murphy	.75
244	Bob Horner	.10
245	Jeff Burroughs	.08
246	Rick Camp	.08
247	Bob Cox	.15
248	Bruce Benedict	.08

No.	Player	Price
249	Gene Garber	.08
250	Jerry Royster	.08
251a	Gary Matthews (no finger on back)	.08
251b	Gary Matthews (small finger on back)	.50
252	Chris Chambliss	.08
253	Luis Gomez	.08
254	Bill Nahorodny	.08
255	Doyle Alexander	.08
256	Brian Asselstine	.08
257	Biff Pocoroba	.08
258	Mike Lum	.08
259	Charlie Spikes	.08
260	Glenn Hubbard	.08
261	Tommy Boggs	.08
262	Al Hrabosky	.08
263	Rick Matula	.08
264	Preston Hanna	.08
265	Larry Bradford	.08
266	*Rafael Ramirez*	.08
267	Larry McWilliams	.08
268	Rod Carew	1.50
269	Bobby Grich	.10
270	Carney Lansford	.08
271	Don Baylor	.15
272	Joe Rudi	.08
273	Dan Ford	.08
274	Jim Fregosi	.08
275	Dave Frost	.08
276	Frank Tanana	.08
277	Dickie Thon	.08
278	Jason Thompson	.08
279	Rick Miller	.08
280	Bert Campaneris	.08
281	Tom Donohue	.08
282	Brian Downing	.08
283	Fred Patek	.08
284	Bruce Kison	.08
285	Dave LaRoche	.08
286	Don Aase	.08
287	Jim Barr	.08
288	Alfredo Martinez	.08
289	Larry Harlow	.08
290	Andy Hassler	.08
291	Dave Kingman	.10
292	Bill Buckner	.15
293	Rick Reuschel	.08
294	Bruce Sutter	.08
295	Jerry Martin	.08
296	Scot Thompson	.08
297	Ivan DeJesus	.08
298	Steve Dillard	.08
299	Dick Tidrow	.08
300	Randy Martz	.08
301	Lenny Randle	.08
302	Lynn McGlothen	.08
303	Cliff Johnson	.08
304	Tim Blackwell	.08
305	Dennis Lamp	.08
306	Bill Caudill	.08
307	Carlos Lezcano	.08
308	Jim Tracy	.08
309	Doug Capilla	.08
310	Willie Hernandez	.08
311	Mike Vail	.08
312	Mike Krukow	.08
313	Barry Foote	.08
314	Larry Biittner	.08
315	Mike Tyson	.08
316	Lee Mazzilli	.08
317	John Stearns	.08
318	Alex Trevino	.08
319	Craig Swan	.08
320	Frank Taveras	.08
321	Steve Henderson	.08
322	Neil Allen	.08
323	Mark Bomback	.08
324	Mike Jorgensen	.08
325	Joe Torre	.25
326	Elliott Maddox	.08
327	Pete Falcone	.08
328	Ray Burris	.08
329	Claudell Washington	.08
330	Doug Flynn	.08
331	Joel Youngblood	.08
332	Bill Almon	.08
333	Tom Hausman	.08
334	Pat Zachry	.08
335	*Jeff Reardon*	2.00
336	*Wally Backman*	.15
337	Dan Norman	.08
338	Jerry Morales	.08
339	Ed Farmer	.08
340	Bob Molinaro	.08
341	Todd Cruz	.08
342a	*Britt Burns* (no finger on front)	.10
342b	*Britt Burns* (small finger on front)	.50
343	Kevin Bell	.08
344	Tony LaRussa	.15
345	Steve Trout	.08
346	*Harold Baines*	4.00
347	Richard Wortham	.08
348	Wayne Nordhagen	.08
349	Mike Squires	.08
350	Lamar Johnson	.08
351	Rickey Henderson	3.00
352	Francisco Barrios	.08
353	Thad Bosley	.08
354	Chet Lemon	.08
355	Bruce Kimm	.08
356	*Richard Dotson*	.08
357	Jim Morrison	.08
358	Mike Proly	.08
359	Greg Pryor	.08
360	Dave Parker	.15
361	Omar Moreno	.08
362a	Kent Tekulve (1071 Waterbury on back)	.15
362b	Kent Tekulve (1971 Waterbury on back)	.50
363	Willie Stargell	.75
364	Phil Garner	.08
365	Ed Ott	.08
366	Don Robinson	.08
367	Chuck Tanner	.08
368	Jim Rooker	.08
369	Dale Berra	.08
370	Jim Bibby	.08
371	Steve Nicosia	.08
372	Mike Easler	.08
373	Bill Robinson	.08
374	Lee Lacy	.08
375	John Candelaria	.08
376	Manny Sanguillen	.08
377	Rick Rhoden	.08
378	Grant Jackson	.08
379	Tim Foli	.08
380	*Rod Scurry*	.08
381	Bill Madlock	.10
382a	Kurt Bevacqua (photo reversed, backwards "P" on cap)	.15
382b	Kurt Bevacqua (correct photo)	.50
383	Bert Blyleven	.10
384	Eddie Solomon	.08
385	Enrique Romo	.08
386	John Milner	.08
387	Mike Hargrove	.08
388	Jorge Orta	.08
389	Toby Harrah	.08
390	Tom Veryzer	.08
391	Miguel Dilone	.08
392	Dan Spillner	.08
393	Jack Brohamer	.08
394	Wayne Garland	.08
395	Sid Monge	.08
396	Rick Waits	.08
397	*Joe Charboneau*	.35
398	Gary Alexander	.08
399	Jerry Dybzinski	.08
400	Mike Stanton	.08
401	Mike Paxton	.08
402	Gary Gray	.08
403	Rick Manning	.08
404	Bo Diaz	.08
405	Ron Hassey	.08
406	Ross Grimsley	.08
407	Victor Cruz	.08
408	Len Barker	.08
409	Bob Bailor	.08
410	Otto Velez	.08
411	Ernie Whitt	.08
412	Jim Clancy	.08
413	Barry Bonnell	.08
414	Dave Stieb	.20
415	*Damaso Garcia*	.10
416	John Mayberry	.08
417	Roy Howell	.08
418	*Dan Ainge*	4.00
419a	Jesse Jefferson (Pirates on back)	.10
419b	Jesse Jefferson (Blue Jays on back)	.50
420	Joey McLaughlin	.08
421	*Lloyd Moseby*	.10
422	Al Woods	.08
423	Garth Iorg	.08
424	Doug Ault	.08
425	*Ken Schrom*	.08
426	Mike Willis	.08
427	Steve Braun	.08
428	Bob Davis	.08
429	Jerry Garvin	.08
430	Alfredo Griffin	.08
431	Bob Mattick	.08
432	Vida Blue	.10
433	Jack Clark	.10
434	Willie McCovey	1.00
435	Mike Ivie	.08
436a	Darrel Evans (Darrel on front)	.15
436b	Darrell Evans (Darrell on front)	.50
437	Terry Whitfield	.08
438	Rennie Stennett	.08
439	John Montefusco	.08
440	Jim Wohlford	.08
441	Bill North	.08
442	Milt May	.08
443	Max Venable	.08
444	Ed Whitson	.08
445	*Al Holland*	.08
446	Randy Moffitt	.08
447	Bob Knepper	.08
448	Gary Lavelle	.08
449	Greg Minton	.08
450	Johnnie LeMaster	.08
451	Larry Herndon	.08
452	Rich Murray	.08
453	Joe Pettini	.08
454	Allen Ripley	.08
455	Dennis Littlejohn	.08
456	Tom Griffin	.08
457	Alan Hargesheimer	.08
458	Joe Strain	.08
459	Steve Kemp	.08
460	Sparky Anderson	.40
461	Alan Trammell	.50
462	Mark Fidrych	.20
463	Lou Whitaker	.20
464	Dave Rozema	.08
465	Milt Wilcox	.08
466	Champ Summers	.08
467	Lance Parrish	.10
468	Dan Petry	.08
469	Pat Underwood	.08
470	Rick Peters	.08
471	Al Cowens	.08
472	John Wockenfuss	.08
473	Tom Brookens	.08
474	Richie Hebner	.08
475	Jack Morris	.10
476	Jim Lentine	.08
477	Bruce Robbins	.08
478	Mark Wagner	.08
479	Tim Corcoran	.08
480a	Stan Papi (Pitcher on front)	.15
480b	Stan Papi (Shortstop on front)	.50
481	*Kirk Gibson*	3.00
482	Dan Schatzeder	.08
483	Amos Otis	.10
484	Dave Winfield	1.50
485	Rollie Fingers	.75
486	Gene Richards	.08
487	Randy Jones	.08
488	Ozzie Smith	2.00
489	Gene Tenace	.08
490	Bill Fahey	.08
491	John Curtis	.08
492	Dave Cash	.08
493a	Tim Flannery (photo reversed, batting righty)	.15
493b	Tim Flannery (photo correct, batting lefty)	.50
494	Jerry Mumphrey	.08
495	Bob Shirley	.08
496	Steve Mura	.08
497	Eric Rasmussen	.08
498	Broderick Perkins	.08
499	Barry Evans	.08
500	Chuck Baker	.08
501	*Luis Salazar*	.08
502	Gary Lucas	.08
503	Mike Armstrong	.08
504	Jerry Turner	.08
505	Dennis Kinney	.08
506	Willy Montanez (Willie)	.08
507	Gorman Thomas	.08
508	Ben Oglivie	.08
509	Larry Hisle	.08
510	Sal Bando	.08
511	Robin Yount	1.50
512	Mike Caldwell	.08
513	Sixto Lezcano	.08
514a	Jerry Augustine (Billy Travers photo)	.15
514b	Billy Travers (correct name with photo)	.50
515	Paul Molitor	1.50
516	Moose Haas	.08
517	Bill Castro	.08
518	Jim Slaton	.08
519	Lary Sorensen	.08
520	Bob McClure	.08
521	Charlie Moore	.08
522	Jim Gantner	.08
523	Reggie Cleveland	.08
524	Don Money	.08
525	Billy Travers	.08
526	Buck Martinez	.08
527	Dick Davis	.08
528	Ted Simmons	.08
529	Garry Templeton	.08
530	Ken Reitz	.08
531	Tony Scott	.08
532	Ken Oberkfell	.08
533	Bob Sykes	.08
534	Keith Smith	.08
535	John Littlefield	.08
536	Jim Kaat	.20
537	Bob Forsch	.08
538	Mike Phillips	.08
539	*Terry Landrum*	.08
540	*Leon Durham*	.10
541	Terry Kennedy	.08
542	George Hendrick	.08
543	Dane Iorg	.08
544	Mark Littell (photo actually Jeff Little)	.08
545	Keith Hernandez	.15
546	Silvio Martinez	.08
547a	Pete Vuckovich (photo actually Don Hood)	.15
547b	Don Hood (correct name with photo)	.50
548	Bobby Bonds	.10
549	Mike Ramsey	.08
550	Tom Herr	.08
551	Roy Smalley	.08
552	Jerry Koosman	.08
553	Ken Landreaux	.08
554	John Castino	.08
555	Doug Corbett	.08
556	Bombo Rivera	.08
557	Ron Jackson	.08
558	Butch Wynegar	.08
559	Hosken Powell	.08
560	Pete Redfern	.08
561	Roger Erickson	.08
562	Glenn Adams	.08
563	Rick Sofield	.08
564	Geoff Zahn	.08
565	Pete Mackanin	.08
566	Mike Cubbage	.08
567	Darrell Jackson	.08
568	Dave Edwards	.08
569	Rob Wilfong	.08
570	Sal Butera	.08
571	Jose Morales	.08
572	Rick Langford	.08
573	Mike Norris	.08
574	Rickey Henderson	3.50
575	Tony Armas	.08
576	Dave Revering	.08
577	Jeff Newman	.08
578	Bob Lacey	.08
579	Brian Kingman (photo actually Alan Wirth)	.08
580	Mitchell Page	.08
581	Billy Martin	.20
582	Rob Picciolo	.08
583	Mike Heath	.08
584	Mickey Klutts	.08
585	Orlando Gonzalez	.08
586	*Mike Davis*	.08
587	Wayne Gross	.08
588	Matt Keough	.08
589	Steve McCatty	.08
590	Dwayne Murphy	.08
591	Mario Guerrero	.08
592	Dave McKay	.08
593	Jim Essian	.08
594	Dave Heaverlo	.08
595	Maury Wills	.10
596	Juan Beniquez	.08
597	Rodney Craig	.08
598	Jim Anderson	.08

599	Floyd Bannister	.08
600	Bruce Bochte	.08
601	Julio Cruz	.08
602	Ted Cox	.08
603	Dan Meyer	.08
604	Larry Cox	.08
605	Bill Stein	.08
606	Steve Garvey	.45
607	Dave Roberts	.08
608	Leon Roberts	.08
609	Reggie Walton	.08
610	Dave Edler	.08
611	Larry Milbourne	.08
612	Kim Allen	.08
613	Mario Mendoza	.08
614	Tom Paciorek	.08
615	Glenn Abbott	.08
616	Joe Simpson	.08
617	Mickey Rivers	.08
618	Jim Kern	.08
619	Jim Sundberg	.08
620	Richie Zisk	.08
621	Jon Matlack	.08
622	Fergie Jenkins	.75
623	Pat Corrales	.08
624	Ed Figueroa	.08
625	Buddy Bell	.10
626	Al Oliver	.15
627	Doc Medich	.08
628	Bump Wills	.08
629	Rusty Staub	.10
630	Pat Putnam	.08
631	John Grubb	.08
632	Danny Darwin	.08
633	Ken Clay	.08
634	Jim Norris	.08
635	John Butcher	.08
636	Dave Roberts	.08
637	Billy Sample	.08
638	Carl Yastrzemski	1.50
639	Cecil Cooper	.08
640	Mike Schmidt	2.00
641a	Checklist 1-50 (41 Hal McRae)	.10
641b	Checklist 1-50 (41 Hal McRae Double Threat)	.15
642	Checklist 51-109	.08
643	Checklist 110-168	.08
644a	Checklist 169-220 (202 George Foster)	.10
644b	Checklist 169-220 (202 George Foster "Slugger")	.15
(645a)	Triple Threat (Larry Bowa, Pete Rose, Mike Schmidt) (no number on back)	2.00
645b	Triple Threat (Pete Rose, Larry Bowa, Mike Schmidt) (number on back)	2.00
646	Checklist 221-267	.08
647	Checklist 268-315	.08
648	Checklist 316-359	.08
649	Checklist 360-408	.08
650	Reggie Jackson	2.50
651	Checklist 409-458	.08
652a	Checklist 459-509 (483 Aurelio Lopez)	.10
652b	Checklist 459-506 (no 483)	.15
653	Willie Wilson	.25
654a	Checklist 507-550 (514 Jerry Augustine)	.10
654b	Checklist 507-550 (514 Billy Travers)	.15
655	George Brett	4.00
656	Checklist 551-593	.08
657	Tug McGraw	.15
658	Checklist 594-637	.08
659a	Checklist 640-660 (last number on front is 551)	.10
659b	Checklist 640-660 (last number on front is 483)	.15
660a	Steve Carlton (date 1066 on back)	1.00
660b	Steve Carlton (date 1966 on back)	2.00

1981 Fleer Star Stickers

The 128-card 1981 Fleer Star Sticker set was designed to allow the card fronts to be peeled away from the cardboard backs. Fronts feature color photos with blue and yellow trim. Backs are identical in design to the regular 1981 Fleer set except for color and numbering. The set contains three unnumbered checklist cards whose fronts depict Reggie Jackson, George Brett and Mike Schmidt. The sticker-cards, which are the standard 2-1/2" x 3-1/2", were issued in gum wax packs.

		MT
Complete Set (128):		35.00
Common Player:		.15
Wax Pack (5):		1.50
Wax Box (36):		30.00
1	Steve Garvey	.50
2	Ron LeFlore	.15
3	Ron Cey	.15
4	Dave Revering	.15
5	Tony Armas	.15
6	Mike Norris	.15
7	Steve Kemp	.15
8	Bruce Bochte	.15
9	Mike Schmidt	3.00
10	Scott McGregor	.15
11	Buddy Bell	.15
12	Carney Lansford	.15
13	Carl Yastrzemski	2.00
14	Ben Oglivie	.15
15	Willie Stargell	1.00
16	Cecil Cooper	.15
17	Gene Richards	.15
18	Jim Kern	.15
19	Jerry Koosman	.15
20	Larry Bowa	.15
21	Kent Tekulve	.15
22	Dan Driessen	.15
23	Phil Niekro	.75
24	Dan Quisenberry	.15
25	Dave Winfield	1.00
26	Dave Parker	.25
27	Rick Langford	.15
28	Amos Otis	.15
29	Bill Buckner	.15
30	Al Bumbry	.15
31	Bake McBride	.15
32	Mickey Rivers	.15
33	Rick Burleson	.15
34	Dennis Eckersley	.50
35	Cesar Cedeno	.15
36	Enos Cabell	.15
37	Johnny Bench	2.00
38	Robin Yount	1.00
39	Mark Belanger	.15
40	Rod Carew	1.00
41	George Foster	.15
42	Lee Mazzilli	.15
43	Triple Threat (Larry Bowa, Pete Rose, Mike Schmidt)	3.00
44	J.R. Richard	.15
45	Lou Piniella	.15
46	Ken Landreaux	.15
47	Rollie Fingers	.75
48	Joaquin Andujar	.15
49	Tom Seaver	1.50
50	Bobby Grich	.15
51	Jon Matlack	.15
52	Jack Clark	.15
53	Jim Rice	.15
54	Rickey Henderson	4.00
55	Roy Smalley	.15
56	Mike Flanagan	.15
57	Steve Rogers	.15
58	Carlton Fisk	.75
59	Don Sutton	.75
60	Ken Griffey	.20
61	Burt Hooton	.15
62	Dusty Baker	.20
63	Vida Blue	.15
64	Al Oliver	.20
65	Jim Bibby	.15
66	Tony Perez	.75
67	Davy Lopes (Davey)	.15
68	Bill Russell	.15
69	Larry Parrish	.15
70	Garry Maddox	.15
71	Phil Garner	.15
72	Graig Nettles	.20
73	Gary Carter	.60
74	Pete Rose	4.00
75	Greg Luzinski	.15
76	Ron Guidry	.15
77	Gorman Thomas	.15
78	Jose Cruz	.15
79	Bob Boone	.20
80	Bruce Sutter	.15
81	Chris Chambliss	.15
82	Paul Molitor	1.00
83	Tug McGraw	.15
84	Ferguson Jenkins	.75
85	Steve Carlton	1.00
86	Miguel Dilone	.15
87	Reggie Smith	.15
88	Rick Cerone	.15
89	Alan Trammell	.25
90	Doug DeCinces	.15
91	Sparky Lyle	.15
92	Warren Cromartie	.15
93	Rick Reuschel	.15
94	Larry Hisle	.15
95	Paul Splittorff	.15
96	Manny Trillo	.15
97	Frank White	.15
98	Fred Lynn	.20
99	Bob Horner	.15
100	Omar Moreno	.15
101	Dave Concepcion	.15
102	Larry Gura	.15
103	Ken Singleton	.15
104	Steve Stone	.20
105	Richie Zisk	.15
106	Willie Wilson	.15
107	Willie Randolph	.15
108	Nolan Ryan	5.00
109	Joe Morgan	1.00
110	Bucky Dent	.20
111	Dave Kingman	.20
112	John Castino	.15
113	Joe Rudi	.15
114	Ed Farmer	.15
115	Reggie Jackson	2.50
116	George Brett	2.50
117	Eddie Murray	1.00
118	Rich Gossage	.20
119	Dale Murphy	.60
120	Ted Simmons	.15
121	Tommy John	.25
122	Don Baylor	.25
123	Andre Dawson	.50
124	Jim Palmer	1.00
125	Garry Templeton	.15
----	Checklist 1-42 (Reggie Jackson)	1.00
----	Checklist 43-83 (George Brett)	1.00
----	Checklist 84-125 (Mike Schmidt)	1.00

1982 Fleer

Fleer's 1982 set did not match the quality of the previous year's effort. Many of the card photos are blurred and have muddied backgrounds. The 2-1/2" x 3-1/2" cards feature color photos bordered by a frame which is color-coded by team. Backs are blue, white, and yellow and contain the player's team logo plus the logos of Major League Baseball and the Major League Baseball Players Association. Due to a lawsuit by Topps, Fleer was forced to issue the set with team logo stickers rather than gum. The complete set price does not include the higher priced variations.

		MT
Complete Set (660):		45.00
Common Player:		.08
Pack (15):		3.00
Wax Box (36):		75.00
1	Dusty Baker	.10
2	Robert Castillo	.08
3	Ron Cey	.08
4	Terry Forster	.08
5	Steve Garvey	.20
6	Dave Goltz	.08
7	Pedro Guerrero	.08
8	Burt Hooton	.08
9	Steve Howe	.08
10	Jay Johnstone	.08
11	Ken Landreaux	.08
12	Davey Lopes	.08
13	*Mike Marshall*	.15
14	Bobby Mitchell	.08
15	Rick Monday	.08
16	*Tom Niedenfuer*	.08
17	*Ted Power*	.08
18	Jerry Reuss	.08
19	Ron Roenicke	.08
20	Bill Russell	.08
21	*Steve Sax*	.45
22	Mike Scioscia	.08
23	Reggie Smith	.08
24	*Dave Stewart*	2.00
25	Rick Sutcliffe	.08
26	Derrel Thomas	.08
27	Fernando Valenzuela	.15
28	Bob Welch	.08
29	Steve Yeager	.08
30	Bobby Brown	.08
31	Rick Cerone	.08
32	Ron Davis	.08
33	Bucky Dent	.10
34	Barry Foote	.08
35	George Frazier	.08
36	Oscar Gamble	.08
37	Rich Gossage	.10
38	Ron Guidry	.15
39	Reggie Jackson	1.50
40	Tommy John	.15
41	Rudy May	.08
42	Larry Milbourne	.08
43	Jerry Mumphrey	.08
44	Bobby Murcer	.10
45	*Gene Nelson*	.08
46	Graig Nettles	.10
47	Johnny Oates	.08
48	Lou Piniella	.15
49	Willie Randolph	.08
50	Rick Reuschel	.08
51	Dave Revering	.08
52	*Dave Righetti*	.45
53	Aurelio Rodriguez	.08

54 Bob Watson .08
55 Dennis Werth .08
56 Dave Winfield 1.00
57 Johnny Bench 1.00
58 Bruce Berenyi .08
59 Larry Biittner .08
60 Scott Brown .08
61 Dave Collins .08
62 Geoff Combe .08
63 Dave Concepcion .08
64 Dan Driessen .08
65 Joe Edelen .08
66 George Foster .10
67 Ken Griffey .10
68 Paul Householder .08
69 Tom Hume .08
70 Junior Kennedy .08
71 Ray Knight .10
72 Mike LaCoss .08
73 Rafael Landestoy .08
74 Charlie Leibrandt .08
75 Sam Mejias .08
76 Paul Moskau .08
77 Joe Nolan .08
78 Mike O'Berry .08
79 Ron Oester .08
80 Frank Pastore .08
81 Joe Price .08
82 Tom Seaver 1.00
83 Mario Soto .08
84 Mike Vail .08
85 Tony Armas .08
86 Shooty Babitt .08
87 Dave Beard .08
88 Rick Bosetti .08
89 Keith Drumright .08
90 Wayne Gross .08
91 Mike Heath .08
92 Rickey Henderson 1.00
93 Cliff Johnson .08
94 Jeff Jones .08
95 Matt Keough .08
96 Brian Kingman .08
97 Mickey Klutts .08
98 Rick Langford .08
99 Steve McCatty .08
100 Dave McKay .08
101 Dwayne Murphy .08
102 Jeff Newman .08
103 Mike Norris .08
104 Bob Owchinko .08
105 Mitchell Page .08
106 Rob Picciolo .08
107 Jim Spencer .08
108 Fred Stanley .08
109 Tom Underwood .08
110 Joaquin Andujar .08
111 Steve Braun .08
112 Bob Forsch .08
113 George Hendrick .08
114 Keith Hernandez .15
115 Tom Herr .08
116 Dane Iorg .08
117 Jim Kaat .10
118 Tito Landrum .08
119 Sixto Lezcano .08
120 Mark Littell .08
121 John Martin .08
122 Silvio Martinez .08
123 Ken Oberkfell .08
124 Darrell Porter .08
125 Mike Ramsey .08
126 Orlando Sanchez .08
127 Bob Shirley .08
128 Lary Sorensen .08
129 Bruce Sutter .08
130 Bob Sykes .08
131 Garry Templeton .08
132 Gene Tenace .08
133 Jerry Augustine .08
134 Sal Bando .08
135 Mark Brouhard .08
136 Mike Caldwell .08
137 Reggie Cleveland .08
138 Cecil Cooper .08
139 Jamie Easterly .08
140 Marshall Edwards .08
141 Rollie Fingers .65
142 Jim Gantner .08
143 Moose Haas .08
144 Larry Hisle .08
145 Roy Howell .08
146 Rickey Keeton .08
147 Randy Lerch .08
148 Paul Molitor 1.00
149 Don Money .08
150 Charlie Moore .08
151 Ben Oglivie .08
152 Ted Simmons .08
153 Jim Slaton .08
154 Gorman Thomas .08
155 Robin Yount 1.00
156 Pete Vukovich .08
157 Benny Ayala .08
158 Mark Belanger .08
159 Al Bumbry .08
160 Terry Crowley .08
161 Rich Dauer .08
162 Doug DeCinces .08
163 Rick Dempsey .08
164 Jim Dwyer .08
165 Mike Flanagan .08
166 Dave Ford .08
167 Dan Graham .08
168 Wayne Krenchicki .08
169 John Lowenstein .08
170 Dennis Martinez .08
171 Tippy Martinez .08
172 Scott McGregor .08
173 Jose Morales .08
174 Eddie Murray 1.00
175 Jim Palmer .75
176 *Cal Ripken, Jr.* 35.00
177 Gary Roenicke .08
178 Lenn Sakata .08
179 Ken Singleton .08
180 Sammy Stewart .08
181 Tim Stoddard .08
182 Steve Stone .08
183 Stan Bahnsen .08
184 Ray Burris .08
185 Gary Carter .75
186 Warren Cromartie .08
187 Andre Dawson .25
188 *Terry Francona* .08
189 Woodie Fryman .08
190 Bill Gullickson .08
191 Grant Jackson .08
192 Wallace Johnson .08
193 Charlie Lea .08
194 Bill Lee .08
195 Jerry Manuel .08
196 Brad Mills .08
197 John Milner .08
198 Rowland Office .08
199 David Palmer .08
200 Larry Parrish .08
201 Mike Phillips .08
202 Tim Raines .50
203 Bobby Ramos .08
204 Jeff Reardon .08
205 Steve Rogers .08
206 Scott Sanderson .08
207 Rodney Scott (photo actually Tim Raines) .10
208 Elias Sosa .08
209 Chris Speier .08
210 *Tim Wallach* 1.00
211 Jerry White .08
212 Alan Ashby .08
213 Cesar Cedeno .08
214 Jose Cruz .08
215 Kiko Garcia .08
216 Phil Garner .08
217 Danny Heep .08
218 Art Howe .08
219 Bob Knepper .08
220 Frank LaCorte .08
221 Joe Niekro .10
222 Joe Pittman .08
223 Terry Puhl .08
224 Luis Pujols .08
225 Craig Reynolds .08
226 J.R. Richard .10
227 Dave Roberts .08
228 Vern Ruhle .08
229 Nolan Ryan 5.00
230 Joe Sambito .08
231 Tony Scott .08
232 Dave Smith .08
233 Harry Spilman .08
234 Don Sutton .65
235 Dickie Thon .08
236 Denny Walling .08
237 Gary Woods .08
238 *Luis Aguayo* .08
239 Ramon Aviles .08
240 Bob Boone .10
241 Larry Bowa .08
242 Warren Brusstar .08
243 Steve Carlton 1.00
244 Larry Christenson .08
245 Dick Davis .08
246 Greg Gross .08
247 Sparky Lyle .08
248 Garry Maddox .08
249 Gary Matthews .08
250 Bake McBride .08
251 Tug McGraw .10
252 Keith Moreland .08
253 Dickie Noles .08
254 Mike Proly .08
255 Ron Reed .08
256 Pete Rose 2.50
257 Dick Ruthven .08
258 Mike Schmidt 2.00
259 Lonnie Smith .08
260 Manny Trillo .08
261 Del Unser .08
262 George Vukovich .08
263 Tom Brookens .08
264 George Cappuzzello .08
265 Marty Castillo .08
266 Al Cowens .08
267 Kirk Gibson .10
268 Richie Hebner .08
269 Ron Jackson .08
270 Lynn Jones .08
271 Steve Kemp .08
272 *Rick Leach* .25
273 Aurelio Lopez .08
274 Jack Morris .10
275 Kevin Saucier .08
276 Lance Parrish .10
277 Rick Peters .08
278 Dan Petry .08
279 David Rozema .08
280 Stan Papi .08
281 Dan Schatzeder .08
282 Champ Summers .08
283 Alan Trammell .30
284 Lou Whitaker .10
285 Milt Wilcox .08
286 John Wockenfuss .08
287 Gary Allenson .08
288 Tom Burgmeier .08
289 Bill Campbell .08
290 Mark Clear .08
291 Steve Crawford .08
292 Dennis Eckersley .50
293 Dwight Evans .15
294 *Rich Gedman* .20
295 Garry Hancock .08
296 Glenn Hoffman .08
297 Bruce Hurst .08
298 Carney Lansford .08
299 Rick Miller .08
300 Reid Nichols .08
301 *Bob Ojeda* .25
302 Tony Perez .65
303 Chuck Rainey .08
304 Jerry Remy .08
305 Jim Rice .25
306 Joe Rudi .08
307 Bob Stanley .08
308 Dave Stapleton .08
309 Frank Tanana .08
310 Mike Torrez .08
311 John Tudor .08
312 Carl Yastrzemski 1.25
313 Buddy Bell .10
314 Steve Comer .08
315 Danny Darwin .08
316 John Ellis .08
317 John Grubb .08
318 Rick Honeycutt .08
319 Charlie Hough .08
320 Fergie Jenkins .65
321 John Henry Johnson .08
322 Jim Kern .08
323 Jon Matlack .08
324 Doc Medich .08
325 Mario Mendoza .08
326 Al Oliver .10
327 Pat Putnam .08
328 Mickey Rivers .08
329 Leon Roberts .08
330 Billy Sample .08
331 Bill Stein .08
332 Jim Sundberg .08
333 Mark Wagner .08
334 Bump Wills .08
335 Bill Almon .08
336 Harold Baines .15
337 Ross Baumgarten .08
338 Tony Bernazard .08
339 Britt Burns .08
340 Richard Dotson .08
341 Jim Essian .08
342 Ed Farmer .08
343 Carlton Fisk .75
344 Kevin Hickey .08
345 Lamarr Hoyt (LaMarr) .08
346 Lamar Johnson .08
347 Jerry Koosman .08
348 Rusty Kuntz .08
349 Dennis Lamp .08
350 Ron LeFlore .08
351 Chet Lemon .08
352 Greg Luzinski .08
353 Bob Molinaro .08
354 Jim Morrison .08
355 Wayne Nordhagen .08
356 Greg Pryor .08
357 Mike Squires .08
358 Steve Trout .08
359 Alan Bannister .08
360 Len Barker .08
361 Bert Blyleven .10
362 Joe Charboneau .10
363 John Denny .08
364 Bo Diaz .08
365 Miguel Dilone .08
366 Jerry Dybzinski .08
367 Wayne Garland .08
368 Mike Hargrove .08
369 Toby Harrah .08
370 Ron Hassey .08
371 *Von Hayes* .25
372 Pat Kelly .08
373 Duane Kuiper .08
374 Rick Manning .08
375 Sid Monge .08
376 Jorge Orta .08
377 Dave Rosello .08
378 Dan Spillner .08
379 Mike Stanton .08
380 Andre Thornton .08
381 Tom Veryzer .08
382 Rick Waits .08
383 Doyle Alexander .08
384 Vida Blue .10
385 Fred Breining .08
386 Enos Cabell .08
387 Jack Clark .08
388 Darrell Evans .15
389 Tom Griffin .08
390 Larry Herndon .08
391 Al Holland .08
392 Gary Lavelle .08
393 Johnnie LeMaster .08
394 Jerry Martin .08
395 Milt May .08
396 Greg Minton .08
397 Joe Morgan .75
398 Joe Pettini .08
399 Alan Ripley .08
400 Billy Smith .08
401 Rennie Stennett .08
402 Ed Whitson .08
403 Jim Wohlford .08
404 Willie Aikens .08
405 George Brett 2.00
406 Ken Brett .08
407 Dave Chalk .08
408 Rich Gale .08
409 Cesar Geronimo .08
410 Larry Gura .08
411 Clint Hurdle .08
412 Mike Jones .08
413 Dennis Leonard .08
414 Renie Martin .08
415 Lee May .08
416 Hal McRae .10
417 Darryl Motley .08
418 Rance Mulliniks .08
419 Amos Otis .08
420 *Ken Phelps* .10
421 Jamie Quirk .08
422 Dan Quisenberry .08
423 Paul Splittorff .08
424 U.L. Washington .08
425 John Wathan .08
426 Frank White .08
427 Willie Wilson .10
428 Brian Asselstine .08
429 Bruce Benedict .08
430 Tom Boggs .08
431 Larry Bradford .08
432 Rick Camp .08
433 Chris Chambliss .08
434 Gene Garber .08
435 Preston Hanna .08

436 Bob Horner .08
437 Glenn Hubbard .08
438a Al Hrabosky (All Hrabosky, 5'1" on back) 12.00
438b Al Hrabosky (Al Hrabosky, 5'1" on back) 1.00
438c Al Hrabosky (Al Hrabosky, 5'10" on back) .25
439 Rufino Linares .08
440 *Rick Mahler* .10
441 Ed Miller .08
442 John Montefusco .08
443 Dale Murphy .60
444 Phil Niekro .65
445 Gaylord Perry .65
446 Biff Pocoroba .08
447 Rafael Ramirez .08
448 Jerry Royster .08
449 Claudell Washington .08
450 Don Aase .08
451 Don Baylor .15
452 Juan Beniquez .08
453 Rick Burleson .08
454 Bert Campaneris .08
455 Rod Carew 1.00
456 Bob Clark .08
457 Brian Downing .08
458 Dan Ford .08
459 Ken Forsch .08
460 Dave Frost .08
461 Bobby Grich .08
462 Larry Harlow .08
463 John Harris .08
464 Andy Hassler .08
465 Butch Hobson .08
466 Jesse Jefferson .08
467 Bruce Kison .08
468 Fred Lynn .10
469 Angel Moreno .08
470 Ed Ott .08
471 Fred Patek .08
472 Steve Renko .08
473 *Mike Witt* .20
474 Geoff Zahn .08
475 Gary Alexander .08
476 Dale Berra .08
477 Kurt Bevacqua .08
478 Jim Bibby .08
479 John Candelaria .08
480 Victor Cruz .08
481 Mike Easler .08
482 Tim Foli .08
483 Lee Lacy .08
484 Vance Law .08
485 Bill Madlock .10
486 Willie Montanez .08
487 Omar Moreno .08
488 Steve Nicosia .08
489 Dave Parker .15
490 Tony Pena .08
491 Pascual Perez .08
492 *Johnny Ray* .08
493 Rick Rhoden .08
494 Bill Robinson .08
495 Don Robinson .08
496 Enrique Romo .08
497 Rod Scurry .08
498 Eddie Solomon .08
499 Willie Stargell 1.00
500 Kent Tekulve .08
501 Jason Thompson .08
502 Glenn Abbott .08
503 Jim Anderson .08
504 Floyd Bannister .08
505 Bruce Bochte .08
506 Jeff Burroughs .08
507 Bryan Clark .08
508 Ken Clay .08
509 Julio Cruz .08
510 Dick Drago .08
511 Gary Gray .08
512 Dan Meyer .08
513 Jerry Narron .08
514 Tom Paciorek .08
515 Casey Parsons .08
516 Lenny Randle .08
517 Shane Rawley .08
518 Joe Simpson .08
519 Richie Zisk .08
520 Neil Allen .08
521 Bob Bailor .08
522 Hubie Brooks .08
523 Mike Cubbage .08
524 Pete Falcone .08
525 Doug Flynn .08
526 Tom Hausman .08
527 Ron Hodges .08
528 Randy Jones .08
529 Mike Jorgensen .08
530 Dave Kingman .10
531 Ed Lynch .08
532 Mike Marshall .08
533 Lee Mazzilli .08
534 Dyar Miller .08
535 Mike Scott .08
536 Rusty Staub .10
537 John Stearns .08
538 Craig Swan .08
539 Frank Taveras .08
540 Alex Trevino .08
541 Ellis Valentine .08
542 Mookie Wilson .15
543 Joel Youngblood .08
544 Pat Zachry .08
545 Glenn Adams .08
546 Fernando Arroyo .08
547 John Verhoeven .08
548 Sal Butera .08
549 John Castino .08
550 Don Cooper .08
551 Doug Corbett .08
552 Dave Engle .08
553 Roger Erickson .08
554 Danny Goodwin .08
555a Darrell Jackson (black cap) .65
555b Darrell Jackson (red cap with emblem) .10
555c Darrell Jackson (red cap, no emblem) .20
556 Pete Mackanin .08
557 Jack O'Connor .08
558 Hosken Powell .08
559 Pete Redfern .08
560 Roy Smalley .08
561 Chuck Baker .08
562 Gary Ward .08
563 Rob Wilfong .08
564 Al Williams .08
565 Butch Wynegar .08
566 Randy Bass .08
567 Juan Bonilla .08
568 Danny Boone .08
569 John Curtis .08
570 Juan Eichelberger .08
571 Barry Evans .08
572 Tim Flannery .08
573 Ruppert Jones .08
574 Terry Kennedy .08
575 Joe Lefebvre .08
576a John Littlefield (pitching lefty) 150.00
576b John Littlefield (pitching righty) .08
577 Gary Lucas .08
578 Steve Mura .08
579 Broderick Perkins .08
580 Gene Richards .08
581 Luis Salazar .08
582 Ozzie Smith 1.00
583 John Urrea .08
584 Chris Welsh .08
585 Rick Wise .08
586 Doug Bird .08
587 Tim Blackwell .08
588 Bobby Bonds .10
589 Bill Buckner .10
590 Bill Caudill .08
591 Hector Cruz .08
592 *Jody Davis* .10
593 Ivan DeJesus .08
594 Steve Dillard .08
595 Leon Durham .08
596 Rawly Eastwick .08
597 Steve Henderson .08
598 Mike Krukow .08
599 Mike Lum .08
600 Randy Martz .08
601 Jerry Morales .08
602 Ken Reitz .08
603a *Lee Smith* (Cubs logo reversed on back) 4.00
603b *Lee Smith* (corrected) 4.00
604 Dick Tidrow .08
605 Jim Tracy .08
606 Mike Tyson .08
607 Ty Waller .08
608 Danny Ainge 1.00
609 *Jorge Bell* 1.00
610 Mark Bomback .08
611 Barry Bonnell .08
612 Jim Clancy .08
613 Damaso Garcia .08
614 Jerry Garvin .08
615 Alfredo Griffin .08
616 Garth Iorg .08
617 Luis Leal .08
618 Ken Macha .08
619 John Mayberry .08
620 Joey McLaughlin .08
621 Lloyd Moseby .08
622 Dave Stieb .08
623 Jackson Todd .08
624 Willie Upshaw .08
625 Otto Velez .08
626 Ernie Whitt .08
627 Al Woods .08
628 1981 All-Star Game .08
629 All-Star Infielders (Bucky Dent, Frank White) .08
630 Big Red Machine (Dave Concepcion, Dan Driessen, George Foster) .10
631 Top N.L. Relief Pitcher (Bruce Sutter) .08
632 Steve & Carlton (Steve Carlton, Carlton Fisk) .25
633 3000th Game, May 25, 1981 (Carl Yastrzemski) .35
634 Dynamic Duo (Johnny Bench, Tom Seaver) .30
635 West Meets East (Gary Carter, Fernando Valenzuela) .20
636a N.L. Strikeout King (Fernando Valenzuela) ("...led the National League...") .50
636b N.L. Strikeout King (Fernando Valenzuela) ("... led the National League) .25
637 Home Run King (Mike Schmidt) .50
638 N.L. All-Stars (Gary Carter, Dave Parker) .15
639 Perfect Game! (Len Barker, Bo Diaz) .08
640 Pete Rose, Pete Rose, Jr. (Re-Pete) 2.00
641 Phillies' Finest (Steve Carlton, Mike Schmidt, Lonnie Smith) .50
642 Red Sox Reunion (Dwight Evans, Fred Lynn) .15
643 Most Hits and Runs (Rickey Henderson) 1.00
644 Most Saves 1981 A.L. (Rollie Fingers) .15
645 Most 1981 Wins (Tom Seaver) .25
646a Yankee Powerhouse (Reggie Jackson, Dave Winfield) (comma after "outfielder" on back) 2.00
646b Yankee Powerhouse (Reggie Jackson, Dave Winfield) (no comma) 2.00
647 Checklist 1-56 .08
648 Checklist 57-109 .08
649 Checklist 110-156 .08
650 Checklist 157-211 .08
651 Checklist 212-262 .08
652 Checklist 263-312 .08
653 Checklist 313-358 .08
654 Checklist 359-403 .08
655 Checklist 404-449 .08
656 Checklist 450-501 .08
657 Checklist 502-544 .08
658 Checklist 545-585 .08
659 Checklist 586-627 .08
660 Checklist 628-646 .08

1982 Fleer Stamps

Issued by Fleer in 1982, this set consists of 242 player stamps, each measuring 1-13/16" x 2-1/2". Originally issued in perforated strips of 10, the full-color stamps are numbered in the lower-left corner and were designed to be placed in an album. Six stamps feature two players each.

	MT
Complete Set (242):	12.00
Common Player:	.05
Stamp Album:	1.50
Wax Pack (10):	.25
Wax Box (60):	15.00

1 Fernando Valenzuela .05
2 Rick Monday .05
3 Ron Cey .05
4 Dusty Baker .10
5 Burt Hooton .05
6 Pedro Guerrero .05
7 Jerry Reuss .05
8 Bill Russell .05
9 Steve Garvey .20
10 Davey Lopes .05
11 Tom Seaver .25
12 George Foster .05
13 Frank Pastore .05
14 Dave Collins .05
15 Dave Concepcion .05
16 Ken Griffey .10
17 Johnny Bench .25
18 Ray Knight .05
19 Mario Soto .05
20 Ron Oester .05
21 Ken Oberkfell .05
22 Bob Forsch .05
23 Keith Hernandez .10
24 Dane Iorg .05
25 George Hendrick .05
26 Gene Tenace .05
27 Garry Templeton .05
28 Bruce Sutter .05
29 Darrell Porter .05
30 Tom Herr .05
31 Tim Raines .05
32 Chris Speier .05
33 Warren Cromartie .05
34 Larry Parrish .05
35 Andre Dawson .15
36 Steve Rogers .05
37 Jeff Reardon .05
38 Rodney Scott .05
39 Gary Carter .15
40 Scott Sanderson .05
41 Cesar Cedeno .05
42 Nolan Ryan 1.00
43 Don Sutton .20
44 Terry Puhl .05
45 Joe Niekro .05
46 Tony Scott .05
47 Joe Sambito .05
48 Art Howe .05
49 Bob Knepper .05
50 Jose Cruz .05
51 Pete Rose .50
52 Dick Ruthven .05
53 Mike Schmidt .40
54 Steve Carlton .25
55 Tug McGraw .05
56 Larry Bowa .05
57 Garry Maddox .05
58 Gary Matthews .05

59	Manny Trillo	.05
60	Lonnie Smith	.05
61	Vida Blue	.05
62	Milt May	.05
63	Joe Morgan	.25
64	Enos Cabell	.05
65	Jack Clark	.05
66	Claudell Washington	.05
67	Gaylord Perry	.20
68	Phil Niekro	.20
69	Bob Horner	.05
70	Chris Chambliss	.05
71	Dave Parker	.05
72	Tony Pena	.05
73	Kent Tekulve	.05
74	Mike Easler	.05
75	Tim Foli	.05
76	Willie Stargell	.25
77	Bill Madlock	.05
78	Jim Bibby	.05
79	Omar Moreno	.05
80	Lee Lacy	.05
81	Hubie Brooks	.05
82	Rusty Staub	.10
83	Ellis Valentine	.05
84	Neil Allen	.05
85	Dave Kingman	.05
86	Mookie Wilson	.05
87	Doug Flynn	.05
88	Pat Zachry	.05
89	John Stearns	.05
90	Lee Mazzilli	.05
91	Ken Reitz	.05
92	Mike Krukow	.05
93	Jerry Morales	.05
94	Leon Durham	.05
95	Ivan DeJesus	.05
96	Bill Buckner	.05
97	Jim Tracy	.05
98	Steve Henderson	.05
99	Dick Tidrow	.05
100	Mike Tyson	.05
101	Ozzie Smith	.25
102	Ruppert Jones	.05
103	Broderick Perkins	.05
104	Gene Richrds	.05
105	Terry Kennedy	.05
106	Jim Bibby, Willie Stargell	.10
107	Larry Bowa, Pete Rose	.20
108	Warren Spahn, Fernando Valenzuela	.15
109	Dave Concepcion, Pete Rose	.25
110	Reggie Jackson, Dave Winfield	.25
111	Tom Lasorda, Fernando Valenzuela	.20
112	Reggie Jackson	.25
113	Dave Winfield	.25
114	Lou Piniella	.10
115	Tommy John	.10
116	Rich Gossage	.10
117	Ron Davis	.05
118	Rick Cerone	.05
119	Graig Nettles	.05
120	Ron Guidry	.05
121	Willie Randolph	.05
122	Dwayne Murphy	.05
123	Rickey Henderson	.25
124	Wayne Gross	.05
125	Mike Norris	.05
126	Rick Langford	.05
127	Jim Spencer	.05
128	Tony Armas	.05
129	Matt Keough	.05
130	Jeff Jones	.05
131	Steve McCatty	.05
132	Rollie Fingers	.20
133	Jim Gantner	.05
134	Gorman Thomas	.05
135	Robin Yount	.25
136	Paul Molitor	.25
137	Ted Simmons	.05
138	Ben Oglivie	.05
139	Moose Haas	.05
140	Cecil Cooper	.05
141	Pete Vuckovich	.05
142	Doug DeCinces	.05
143	Jim Palmer	.25
144	Steve Stone	.05
145	Mike Flanagan	.05
146	Rick Dempsey	.05
147	Al Bumbry	.05
148	Mark Belanger	.05
149	Scott McGregor	.05
150	Ken Singleton	.05
151	Eddie Murray	.25
152	Lance Parrish	.10
153	David Rozema	.05
154	Champ Summers	.05
155	Alan Trammell	.10
156	Lou Whitaker	.05
157	Milt Wilcox	.05
158	Kevin Saucier	.05
159	Jack Morris	.05
160	Steve Kemp	.05
161	Kirk Gibson	.05
162	Carl Yastrzemski	.25
163	Jim Rice	.10
164	Carney Lansford	.05
165	Dennis Eckersley	.10
166	Mike Torrez	.05
167	Dwight Evans	.05
168	Glenn Hoffman	.05
169	Bob Stanley	.05
170	Tony Perez	.25
171	Jerry Remy	.05
172	Buddy Bell	.05
173	Ferguson Jenkins	.20
174	Mickey Rivers	.05
175	Bump Wills	.05
176	Jon Matlack	.05
177	Steve Comer	.05
178	Al Oliver	.05
179	Bill Stein	.05
180	Pat Putnam	.05
181	Jim Sundberg	.05
182	Ron LeFlore	.05
183	Carlton Fisk	.15
184	Harold Baines	.05
185	Bill Almon	.05
186	Richard Dotson	.05
187	Greg Luzinski	.05
188	Mike Squires	.05
189	Britt Burns	.05
190	Lamarr Hoyt	.05
191	Chet Lemon	.05
192	Joe Charboneau	.10
193	Toby Harrah	.05
194	John Denny	.05
195	Rick Manning	.05
196	Miguel Dilone	.05
197	Bo Diaz	.05
198	Mike Hargrove	.05
199	Bert Blyleven	.05
200	Len Barker	.05
201	Andre Thornton	.05
202	George Brett	.25
203	U.L. Washington	.05
204	Dan Quisenberry	.05
205	Larry Gura	.05
206	Willie Aikens	.05
207	Willie Wilson	.05
208	Dennis Leonard	.05
209	Frank White	.05
210	Hal McRae	.05
211	Amos Otis	.05
212	Don Aase	.05
213	Butch Hobson	.05
214	Fred Lynn	.05
215	Brian Downing	.05
216	Dan Ford	.05
217	Rod Carew	.25
218	Bobby Grich	.05
219	Rick Burleson	.05
220	Don Baylor	.10
221	Ken Forsch	.05
222	Bruce Bochte	.05
223	Richie Zisk	.05
224	Tom Paciorek	.05
225	Julio Cruz	.05
226	Jeff Burroughs	.05
227	Doug Corbett	.05
228	Roy Smalley	.05
229	Gary Ward	.05
230	John Castino	.05
231	Rob Wilfong	.05
232	Dave Stieb	.05
233	Otto Velez	.05
234	Damaso Garcia	.05
235	John Mayberry	.05
236	Alfredo Griffin	.05
237	Ted Williams, Carl Yastrzemski	.50
238	Rick Cerone, Graig Nettles	.10
239	Buddy Bell, George Brett	.15
240	Steve Carlton, Jim Kaat	.10
241	Steve Carlton, Dave Parker	.10
242	Ron Davis, Nolan Ryan	.40

1983 Fleer

The 1983 Fleer set features color photos set inside a light brown border. The cards are standard 2-1/2" x 3-1/2". A team logo is located at the card bottom and the word "Fleer" is found at the top. The card backs are designed on a vertical format and include a small black and white photo of the player along with biographical and statistical information. The reverses are done in two shades of brown on white stock. The set was issued with team logo stickers.

		MT
Complete Set (660):		50.00
Common Player:		.08
Pack (15):		4.00
Wax Box (38):		90.00
1	Joaquin Andujar	.08
2	Doug Bair	.08
3	Steve Braun	.08
4	Glenn Brummer	.08
5	Bob Forsch	.08
6	David Green	.08
7	George Hendrick	.08
8	Keith Hernandez	.10
9	Tom Herr	.08
10	Dane Iorg	.08
11	Jim Kaat	.10
12	Jeff Lahti	.08
13	Tito Landrum	.08
14	*Dave LaPoint*	.08
15	*Willie McGee*	1.50
16	Steve Mura	.08
17	Ken Oberkfell	.08
18	Darrell Porter	.08
19	Mike Ramsey	.08
20	Gene Roof	.08
21	Lonnie Smith	.08
22	Ozzie Smith	2.50
23	John Stuper	.08
24	Bruce Sutter	.08
25	Gene Tenace	.08
26	Jerry Augustine	.08
27	Dwight Bernard	.08
28	Mark Brouhard	.08
29	Mike Caldwell	.08
30	Cecil Cooper	.08
31	Jamie Easterly	.08
32	Marshall Edwards	.08
33	Rollie Fingers	.60
34	Jim Gantner	.08
35	Moose Haas	.08
36	Roy Howell	.08
37	Peter Ladd	.08
38	Bob McClure	.08
39	Doc Medich	.08
40	Paul Molitor	2.00
41	Don Money	.08
42	Charlie Moore	.08
43	Ben Oglivie	.08
44	Ed Romero	.08
45	Ted Simmons	.08
46	Jim Slaton	.08
47	Don Sutton	.60
48	Gorman Thomas	.08
49	Pete Vuckovich	.08
50	Ned Yost	.08
51	Robin Yount	2.00
52	Benny Ayala	.08
53	Bob Bonner	.08
54	Al Bumbry	.08
55	Terry Crowley	.08
56	*Storm Davis*	.10
57	Rich Dauer	.08
58	Rick Dempsey	.08
59	Jim Dwyer	.08
60	Mike Flanagan	.08
61	Dan Ford	.08
62	Glenn Gulliver	.08
63	John Lowenstein	.08
64	Dennis Martinez	.08
65	Tippy Martinez	.08
66	Scott McGregor	.08
67	Eddie Murray	1.50
68	Joe Nolan	.08
69	Jim Palmer	1.00
70	Cal Ripken, Jr.	7.50
71	Gary Roenicke	.08
72	Lenn Sakata	.08
73	Ken Singleton	.08
74	Sammy Stewart	.08
75	Tim Stoddard	.08
76	Don Aase	.08
77	Don Baylor	.10
78	Juan Beniquez	.08
79	Bob Boone	.10
80	Rick Burleson	.08
81	Rod Carew	1.00
82	Bobby Clark	.08
83	Doug Corbett	.08
84	John Curtis	.08
85	Doug DeCinces	.08
86	Brian Downing	.08
87	Joe Ferguson	.08
88	Tim Foli	.08
89	Ken Forsch	.08
90	Dave Goltz	.08
91	Bobby Grich	.08
92	Andy Hassler	.08
93	Reggie Jackson	1.00
94	Ron Jackson	.08
95	Tommy John	.10
96	Bruce Kison	.08
97	Fred Lynn	.08
98	Ed Ott	.08
99	Steve Renko	.08
100	Luis Sanchez	.08
101	Rob Wilfong	.08
102	Mike Witt	.08
103	Geoff Zahn	.08
104	Willie Aikens	.08
105	Mike Armstrong	.08
106	Vida Blue	.08
107	*Bud Black*	.50
108	George Brett	2.50
109	Bill Castro	.08
110	Onix Concepcion	.08
111	Dave Frost	.08
112	Cesar Geronimo	.08
113	Larry Gura	.08
114	Steve Hammond	.08
115	Don Hood	.08
116	Dennis Leonard	.08
117	Jerry Martin	.08
118	Lee May	.08
119	Hal McRae	.08
120	Amos Otis	.08
121	Greg Pryor	.08
122	Dan Quisenberry	.08
123	*Don Slaught*	.20
124	Paul Splittorff	.08
125	U.L. Washington	.08
126	John Wathan	.08
127	Frank White	.08
128	Willie Wilson	.08
129	Steve Bedrosian	.08
130	Bruce Benedict	.08
131	Tommy Boggs	.08
132	Brett Butler	.08
133	Rick Camp	.08
134	Chris Chambliss	.08
135	Ken Dayley	.08
136	Gene Garber	.08
137	Terry Harper	.08
138	Bob Horner	.08

139 Glenn Hubbard .08
140 Rufino Linares .08
141 Rick Mahler .08
142 Dale Murphy .50
143 Phil Niekro .60
144 Pascual Perez .08
145 Biff Pocoroba .08
146 Rafael Ramirez .08
147 Jerry Royster .08
148 Ken Smith .08
149 Bob Walk .08
150 Claudell Washington .08
151 Bob Watson .08
152 Larry Whisenton .08
153 Porfirio Altamirano .08
154 Marty Bystrom .08
155 Steve Carlton 1.00
156 Larry Christenson .08
157 Ivan DeJesus .08
158 John Denny .08
159 Bob Dernier .08
160 Bo Diaz .08
161 Ed Farmer .08
162 Greg Gross .08
163 Mike Krukow .08
164 Garry Maddox .08
165 Gary Matthews .08
166 Tug McGraw .08
167 Bob Molinaro .08
168 Sid Monge .08
169 Ron Reed .08
170 Bill Robinson .08
171 Pete Rose 2.50
172 Dick Ruthven .08
173 Mike Schmidt 2.00
174 Manny Trillo .08
175 Ozzie Virgil .08
176 George Vukovich .08
177 Gary Allenson .08
178 Luis Aponte .08
179 *Wade Boggs* 9.00
180 Tom Burgmeier .08
181 Mark Clear .08
182 Dennis Eckersley .25
183 Dwight Evans .10
184 Rich Gedman .08
185 Glenn Hoffman .08
186 Bruce Hurst .08
187 Carney Lansford .08
188 Rick Miller .08
189 Reid Nichols .08
190 Bob Ojeda .08
191 Tony Perez .60
192 Chuck Rainey .08
193 Jerry Remy .08
194 Jim Rice .20
195 Bob Stanley .08
196 Dave Stapleton .08
197 Mike Torrez .08
198 John Tudor .08
199 Julio Valdez .08
200 Carl Yastrzemski 1.00
201 Dusty Baker .08
202 Joe Beckwith .08
203 *Greg Brock* .08
204 Ron Cey .08
205 Terry Forster .08
206 Steve Garvey .30
207 Pedro Guerrero .08
208 Burt Hooton .08
209 Steve Howe .08
210 Ken Landreaux .08
211 Mike Marshall .08
212 *Candy Maldonado* .10
213 Rick Monday .08
214 Tom Niedenfuer .08
215 Jorge Orta .08
216 Jerry Reuss .08
217 Ron Roenicke .08
218 Vicente Romo .08
219 Bill Russell .08
220 Steve Sax .08
221 Mike Scioscia .08
222 Dave Stewart .20
223 Derrel Thomas .08
224 Fernando Valenzuela .10
225 Bob Welch .08
226 Ricky Wright .08
227 Steve Yeager .08
228 Bill Almon .08
229 Harold Baines .10
230 Salome Barojas .08
231 Tony Bernazard .08
232 Britt Burns .08
233 Richard Dotson .08
234 Ernesto Escarrega .08
235 Carlton Fisk .65
236 Jerry Hairston Sr. .08
237 Kevin Hickey .08
238 LaMarr Hoyt .08
239 Steve Kemp .08
240 Jim Kern .08
241 *Ron Kittle* .15
242 Jerry Koosman .08
243 Dennis Lamp .08
244 Rudy Law .08
245 Vance Law .08
246 Ron LeFlore .08
247 Greg Luzinski .08
248 Tom Paciorek .08
249 Aurelio Rodriguez .08
250 Mike Squires .08
251 Steve Trout .08
252 Jim Barr .08
253 Dave Bergman .08
254 Fred Breining .08
255 Bob Brenly .08
256 Jack Clark .08
257 Chili Davis .10
258 Darrell Evans .15
259 Alan Fowlkes .08
260 Rich Gale .08
261 Atlee Hammaker .08
262 Al Holland .08
263 Duane Kuiper .08
264 Bill Laskey .08
265 Gary Lavelle .08
266 Johnnie LeMaster .08
267 Renie Martin .08
268 Milt May .08
269 Greg Minton .08
270 Joe Morgan .75
271 Tom O'Malley .08
272 Reggie Smith .08
273 Guy Sularz .08
274 Champ Summers .08
275 Max Venable .08
276 Jim Wohlford .08
277 Ray Burris .08
278 Gary Carter .45
279 Warren Cromartie .08
280 Andre Dawson .40
281 Terry Francona .08
282 Doug Flynn .08
283 Woody Fryman .08
284 Bill Gullickson .08
285 Wallace Johnson .08
286 Charlie Lea .08
287 Randy Lerch .08
288 Brad Mills .08
289 Dan Norman .08
290 Al Oliver .08
291 David Palmer .08
292 Tim Raines .15
293 Jeff Reardon .08
294 Steve Rogers .08
295 Scott Sanderson .08
296 Dan Schatzeder .08
297 Bryn Smith .08
298 Chris Speier .08
299 Tim Wallach .08
300 Jerry White .08
301 Joel Youngblood .08
302 Ross Baumgarten .08
303 Dale Berra .08
304 John Candelaria .08
305 Dick Davis .08
306 Mike Easler .08
307 Richie Hebner .08
308 Lee Lacy .08
309 Bill Madlock .08
310 Larry McWilliams .08
311 John Milner .08
312 Omar Moreno .08
313 Jim Morrison .08
314 Steve Nicosia .08
315 Dave Parker .10
316 Tony Pena .08
317 Johnny Ray .08
318 Rick Rhoden .08
319 Don Robinson .08
320 Enrique Romo .08
321 Manny Sarmiento .08
322 Rod Scurry .08
323 Jim Smith .08
324 Willie Stargell .75
325 Jason Thompson .08
326 Kent Tekulve .08
327a Tom Brookens (narrow (1/4") brown box at bottom on back) .45
327b Tom Brookens (wide (1-1/4") brown box at bottom on back) .08
328 Enos Cabell .08
329 Kirk Gibson .08
330 Larry Herndon .08
331 Mike Ivie .08
332 *Howard Johnson* 1.00
333 Lynn Jones .08
334 Rick Leach .08
335 Chet Lemon .08
336 Jack Morris .10
337 Lance Parrish .10
338 Larry Pashnick .08
339 Dan Petry .08
340 Dave Rozema .08
341 Dave Rucker .08
342 Elias Sosa .08
343 Dave Tobik .08
344 Alan Trammell .25
345 Jerry Turner .08
346 Jerry Ujdur .08
347 Pat Underwood .08
348 Lou Whitaker .08
349 Milt Wilcox .08
350 *Glenn Wilson* .08
351 John Wockenfuss .08
352 Kurt Bevacqua .08
353 Juan Bonilla .08
354 Floyd Chiffer .08
355 Luis DeLeon .08
356 *Dave Dravecky* .30
357 Dave Edwards .08
358 Juan Eichelberger .08
359 Tim Flannery .08
360 *Tony Gwynn* 15.00
361 Ruppert Jones .08
362 Terry Kennedy .08
363 Joe Lefebvre .08
364 Sixto Lezcano .08
365 Tim Lollar .08
366 Gary Lucas .08
367 John Montefusco .08
368 Broderick Perkins .08
369 Joe Pittman .08
370 Gene Richards .08
371 Luis Salazar .08
372 *Eric Show* .08
373 Garry Templeton .08
374 Chris Welsh .08
375 Alan Wiggins .08
376 Rick Cerone .08
377 Dave Collins .08
378 Roger Erickson .08
379 George Frazier .08
380 Oscar Gamble .08
381 Goose Gossage .10
382 Ken Griffey .10
383 Ron Guidry .10
384 Dave LaRoche .08
385 Rudy May .08
386 John Mayberry .08
387 Lee Mazzilli .08
388 Mike Morgan .08
389 Jerry Mumphrey .08
390 Bobby Murcer .10
391 Graig Nettles .10
392 Lou Piniella .15
393 Willie Randolph .08
394 Shane Rawley .08
395 Dave Righetti .08
396 Andre Robertson .08
397 Roy Smalley .08
398 Dave Winfield 1.00
399 Butch Wynegar .08
400 Chris Bando .08
401 Alan Bannister .08
402 Len Barker .08
403 Tom Brennan .08
404 *Carmelo Castillo* .08
405 Miguel Dilone .08
406 Jerry Dybzinski .08
407 Mike Fischlin .08
408 Ed Glynn (photo actually Bud Anderson) .08
409 Mike Hargrove .08
410 Toby Harrah .08
411 Ron Hassey .08
412 Von Hayes .08
413 Rick Manning .08
414 Bake McBride .08
415 Larry Milbourne .08
416 Bill Nahorodny .08
417 Jack Perconte .08
418 Larry Sorensen .08
419 Dan Spillner .08
420 Rick Sutcliffe .08
421 Andre Thornton .08
422 Rick Waits .08
423 Eddie Whitson .08
424 Jesse Barfield .08
425 Barry Bonnell .08
426 Jim Clancy .08
427 Damaso Garcia .08
428 Jerry Garvin .08
429 Alfredo Griffin .08
430 Garth Iorg .08
431 Roy Lee Jackson .08
432 Luis Leal .08
433 Buck Martinez .08
434 Joey McLaughlin .08
435 Lloyd Moseby .08
436 Rance Mulliniks .08
437 Dale Murray .08
438 Wayne Nordhagen .08
439 *Gene Petralli* .08
440 Hosken Powell .08
441 Dave Stieb .08
442 Willie Upshaw .08
443 Ernie Whitt .08
444 Al Woods .08
445 Alan Ashby .08
446 Jose Cruz .08
447 Kiko Garcia .08
448 Phil Garner .08
449 Danny Heep .08
450 Art Howe .08
451 Bob Knepper .08
452 Alan Knicely .08
453 Ray Knight .08
454 Frank LaCorte .08
455 Mike LaCoss .08
456 Randy Moffitt .08
457 Joe Niekro .08
458 Terry Puhl .08
459 Luis Pujols .08
460 Craig Reynolds .08
461 Bert Roberge .08
462 Vern Ruhle .08
463 Nolan Ryan 4.00
464 Joe Sambito .08
465 Tony Scott .08
466 Dave Smith .08
467 Harry Spilman .08
468 Dickie Thon .08
469 Denny Walling .08
470 Larry Andersen .08
471 Floyd Bannister .08
472 Jim Beattie .08
473 Bruce Bochte .08
474 Manny Castillo .08
475 Bill Caudill .08
476 Bryan Clark .08
477 Al Cowens .08
478 Julio Cruz .08
479 Todd Cruz .08
480 Gary Gray .08
481 Dave Henderson .08
482 *Mike Moore* .20
483 Gaylord Perry .65
484 Dave Revering .08
485 Joe Simpson .08
486 Mike Stanton .08
487 Rick Sweet .08
488 *Ed Vande Berg* .08
489 Richie Zisk .08
490 Doug Bird .08
491 Larry Bowa .08
492 Bill Buckner .10
493 Bill Campbell .08
494 Jody Davis .08
495 Leon Durham .08
496 Steve Henderson .08
497 Willie Hernandez .08
498 Fergie Jenkins .65
499 Jay Johnstone .08
500 Junior Kennedy .08
501 Randy Martz .08
502 Jerry Morales .08
503 Keith Moreland .08
504 Dickie Noles .08
505 Mike Proly .08
506 Allen Ripley .08
507 *Ryne Sandberg* 10.00
508 Lee Smith .50
509 Pat Tabler .08
510 Dick Tidrow .08
511 Bump Wills .08
512 Gary Woods .08
513 Tony Armas .08
514 Dave Beard .08
515 Jeff Burroughs .08

516 John D'Acquisto .08
517 Wayne Gross .08
518 Mike Heath .08
519 Rickey Henderson 1.00
520 Cliff Johnson .08
521 Matt Keough .08
522 Brian Kingman .08
523 Rick Langford .08
524 Davey Lopes .08
525 Steve McCatty .08
526 Dave McKay .08
527 Dan Meyer .08
528 Dwayne Murphy .08
529 Jeff Newman .08
530 Mike Norris .08
531 Bob Owchinko .08
532 Joe Rudi .08
533 Jimmy Sexton .08
534 Fred Stanley .08
535 Tom Underwood .08
536 Neil Allen .08
537 Wally Backman .08
538 Bob Bailor .08
539 Hubie Brooks .08
540 Carlos Diaz .08
541 Pete Falcone .08
542 George Foster .08
543 Ron Gardenhire .08
544 Brian Giles .08
545 Ron Hodges .08
546 Randy Jones .08
547 Mike Jorgensen .08
548 Dave Kingman .10
549 Ed Lynch .08
550 Jesse Orosco .08
551 Rick Ownbey .08
552 *Charlie Puleo* .08
553 Gary Rajsich .08
554 Mike Scott .08
555 Rusty Staub .10
556 John Stearns .08
557 Craig Swan .08
558 Ellis Valentine .08
559 Tom Veryzer .08
560 Mookie Wilson .08
561 Pat Zachry .08
562 Buddy Bell .08
563 John Butcher .08
564 Steve Comer .08
565 Danny Darwin .08
566 Bucky Dent .08
567 John Grubb .08
568 Rick Honeycutt .08
569 Dave Hostetler .08
570 Charlie Hough .08
571 Lamar Johnson .08
572 Jon Matlack .08
573 Paul Mirabella .08
574 Larry Parrish .08
575 Mike Richardt .08
576 Mickey Rivers .08
577 Billy Sample .08
578 *Dave Schmidt* .08
579 Bill Stein .08
580 Jim Sundberg .08
581 Frank Tanana .08
582 Mark Wagner .08
583 George Wright .08
584 Johnny Bench 1.00
585 Bruce Berenyi .08
586 Larry Biittner .08
587 Cesar Cedeno .08
588 Dave Concepcion .08
589 Dan Driessen .08
590 Greg Harris .08
591 Ben Hayes .08
592 Paul Householder .08
593 Tom Hume .08
594 Wayne Krenchicki .08
595 Rafael Landestoy .08
596 Charlie Leibrandt .08
597 *Eddie Milner* .08
598 Ron Oester .08
599 Frank Pastore .08
600 Joe Price .08
601 Tom Seaver 1.00
602 Bob Shirley .08
603 Mario Soto .08
604 Alex Trevino .08
605 Mike Vail .08
606 Duane Walker .08
607 Tom Brunansky .08
608 Bobby Castillo .08
609 John Castino .08
610 Ron Davis .08
611 Lenny Faedo .08
612 Terry Felton .08
613 *Gary Gaetti* .35
614 Mickey Hatcher .08
615 Brad Havens .08
616 Kent Hrbek .15
617 Randy S. Johnson .08
618 Tim Laudner .08
619 Jeff Little .08
620 Bob Mitchell .08
621 Jack O'Connor .08
622 John Pacella .08
623 Pete Redfern .08
624 Jesus Vega .08
625 *Frank Viola* .90
626 Ron Washington .08
627 Gary Ward .08
628 Al Williams .08
629 Red Sox All-Stars (Mark Clear, Dennis Eckersley, Carl Yastrzemski) .25
630 300 Career Wins (Terry Bulling, Gaylord Perry) .10
631 Pride of Venezuela (Dave Concepcion, Manny Trillo) .10
632 All-Star Infielders (Buddy Bell, Robin Yount) .20
633 Mr. Vet & Mr. Rookie (Kent Hrbek, Dave Winfield) .25
634 Fountain of Youth (Pete Rose, Willie Stargell) .40
635 Big Chiefs (Toby Harrah, Andre Thornton) .08
636 "Smith Bros." (Lonnie Smith, Ozzie Smith) .15
637 Base Stealers' Threat (Gary Carter, Bo Diaz) .10
638 All-Star Catchers (Gary Carter, Carlton Fisk) .15
639 Rickey Henderson (In Action) .50
640 Home Run Threats (Reggie Jackson, Ben Oglivie) .25
641 Two Teams - Same Day (Joel Youngblood) .08
642 Last Perfect Game (Len Barker, Ron Hassey) .08
643 Blue (Vida Blue) .08
644 Black & (Bud Black) .08
645 Power (Reggie Jackson) .30
646 Speed & (Rickey Henderson) .30
647 Checklist 1-51 .08
648 Checklist 52-103 .08
649 Checklist 104-152 .08
650 Checklist 153-200 .08
651 Checklist 201-251 .08
652 Checklist 252-301 .08
653 Checklist 302-351 .08
654 Checklist 352-399 .08
655 Checklist 400-444 .08
656 Checklist 445-489 .08
657 Checklist 490-535 .08
658 Checklist 536-583 .08
659 Checklist 584-628 .08
660 Checklist 629-646 .08

1983 Fleer Star Stamps

The 1983 Fleer Stamp set consists of 288 stamps, including 224 player stamps and 64 team logo stamps. They were originally issued on four different sheets of 72 stamps each (checklisted below) and in "Vend-A-Stamp" dispensers of 18 stamps each. Sixteen different dispenser strips were needed to complete the set (strips 1-4 comprise Sheet 1; strips 5-8 comprise Sheet 2; strips 9-12 comprise Sheet 3; and strips 13-16 comprise Sheet 4.) Stamps measure 1-1/4" x 1-13/16".

		MT
Complete Sheet Set (4):		7.50
Complete Vend-A-Stamp Set (288):		7.50
Common Sheet:		3.50
Common Stamp Dispenser:		.50
Common Single Stamp:		.02
1	Sheet 1 (A's Logo, Angels Logo, Astros Logo, Cardinals Logo, Cubs Logo, Dodgers Logo, Expos Logo, Giants Logo, Indians Logo, Mets Logo, Orioles Logo, Phillies Logo, Pirates Logo, Red Sox Logo, Twins Logo, White Sox L	
2	Sheet 2 (Angels Logo, Astros Logo, Braves Logo, Cardinals logo, Dodgers Logo, Expos Logo, Indians Logo, Mariners Logo, Mets Logo, Phillies Logo, Pirates Logo, Rangers Logo, Reds Logo, Royals Logo, Tigers Logo, Yank	
3	Sheet 3 (A's Logo, Angels Logo, Blue Jays Logo, Braves Logo, Brewers Logo, Dodgers Logo, Giants Logo, Indians Logo, Mariners Logo, Orioles Logo, Padres Logo, Reds Logo, Royals Logo, Tigers Logo, Twins Logo, White Sox	
4	Sheet 4 (Blue Jays Logo, Braves logo, Brewers Logo, Cubs Logo, Expos Logo, Giants Logo, Padres Logo, Phillies Logo, Pirates Logo, Rangers Logo, Red Sox Logo, Reds Logo, Royals Logo, Twins Logo, White Sox Logo, Yank	

1983 Fleer Stickers

This 270-sticker set consists of both player stickers and team logo stickers, all measuring 1-13/16" x 2-1/2". The player stickers are numbered on the back. The front features a full-color photo surrounded by a blue border with two stars at the top. The stickers were issued in strips of ten player stickers plus two team logo stickers. The 26 logo stickers have been assigned numbers 271 through 296.

		MT
Complete Set (296):		13.00
Common Player:		.05
Wax Pack (12):		.50
Wax Box (48):		15.00
1	Bruce Sutter	.05
2	Willie McGee	.10
3	Darrell Porter	.05
4	Lonnie Smith	.05
5	Dane Iorg	.05
6	Keith Hernandez	.05
7	Joaquin Andujar	.05
8	Ken Oberkfell	.05
9	John Stuper	.05
10	Ozzie Smith	.25
11	Bob Forsch	.05
12	Jim Gantner	.05
13	Rollie Fingers	.15
14	Pete Vuckovich	.05
15	Ben Oglivie	.05
16	Don Sutton	.15
17	Bob McClure	.05
18	Robin Yount	.20
19	Paul Molitor	.20
20	Gorman Thomas	.05
21	Mike Caldwell	.05
22	Ted Simmons	.05
23	Cecil Cooper	.05
24	Steve Renko	.05
25	Tommy John	.10
26	Rod Carew	.25
27	Bruce Kison	.05
28	Ken Forsch	.05
29	Geoff Zahn	.05
30	Doug DiCinces	.05
31	Fred Lynn	.05
32	Reggie Jackson	.25
33	Don Baylor	.10
34	Bob Boone	.05
35	Brian Downing	.05
36	Goose Gossage	.05
37	Roy Smalley	.05
38	Graig Nettles	.05
39	Dave Winfield	.20
40	Lee Mazzilli	.05
41	Jerry Mumphrey	.05
42	Dave Collins	.05
43	Rick Cerone	.05
44	Willie Randolph	.05
45	Lou Piniella	.10
46	Ken Griffey	.05
47	Ron Guidry	.05
48	Jack Clark	.05
49	Reggie Smith	.05
50	Atlee Hammaker	.05
51	Fred Breining	.05
52	Gary Lavelle	.05
53	Chili Davis	.05
54	Greg Minton	.05
55	Joe Morgan	.15

56 Al Holland .05
57 Bill Laskey .05
58 Duane Kuiper .05
59 Tom Burgmeier .05
60 Carl Yastrzemski .25
61 Mark Clear .05
62 Mike Torrez .05
63 Dennis Eckersley .10
64 Wade Boggs .40
65 Bob Stanley .05
66 Jim Rice .10
67 Carney Lansford .05
68 Jerry Remy .05
69 Dwight Evans .10
70 John Candelaria .05
71 Bill Madlock .05
72 Dave Parker .05
73 Kent Tekulve .05
74 Tony Pena .05
75 Manny Sarmiento .05
76 Johnny Ray .05
77 Dale Berra .05
78 Lee Lacy .05
79 Jason Thompson .05
80 Mike Easler .05
81 Willie Stargell .20
82 Rick Camp .05
83 Bob Watson .05
84 Bob Horner .05
85 Rafael Ramirez .05
86 Chris Chambliss .05
87 Gene Garber .05
88 Claudell Washington .05
89 Steve Bedrosian .05
90 Dale Murphy .15
91 Phil Niekro .15
92 Jerry Royster .05
93 Bob Walk .05
94 Frank White .05
95 Dennis Leonard .05
96 Vida Blue .05
97 U.L. Washington .05
98 George Brett .45
99 Amos Otis .05
100 Dan Quisenberry .05
101 Willie Aikens .05
102 Hal McRae .05
103 Larry Gura .05
104 Willie Wilson .05
105 Damaso Garcia .05
106 Hosken Powell .05
107 Joey McLaughlin .05
108 Jim Clancy .05
109 Barry Bonnell .05
110 Garth Lorg .05
111 Dave Stieb .05
112 Fernando Valenzuela .05
113 Steve Garvey .10
114 Rick Monday .05
115 Burt Hooton .05
116 Bill Russell .05
117 Pedro Guerrero .05
118 Steve Sax .05
119 Steve Howe .05
120 Ken Landreaux .05
121 Dusty Baker .10
122 Ron Cey .05
123 Jerry Reuss .05
124 Bump Wills .05
125 Keith Moreland .05
126 Dick Tidrow .05
127 Bill Campbell .05
128 Larry Bowa .05
129 Randy Martz .05
130 Ferguson Jenkins .15
131 Leon Durham .05
132 Bill Buckner .05
133 Ron Davis .05
134 Jack O'Connor .05
135 Kent Hrbek .05
136 Gary Ward .05
137 Al Williams .05
138 Tom Brunansky .05
139 Bobby Castillo .05
140 Dusty Baker, Dale Murphy .10
141 Nolan Ryan .50
142 Lee Lacey (Lacy), Omar Moreno .05
143 Al Oliver, Pete Rose .25
144 Rickey Henderson .20
145 Ray Knight, Pete Rose, Mike Schmidt .30
146 Hal McRae, Ben Oglivie .05
147 Tom Hume, Ray Knight .05
148 Buddy Bell, Carlton Fisk .05
149 Steve Kemp .05
150 Rudy Law .05
151 Ron LeFlore .05
152 Jerry Koosman .05
153 Carlton Fisk .15
154 Salome Barojas .05
155 Harold Baines .05
156 Britt Burns .05
157 Tom Paciorek .05
158 Greg Luzinski .05
159 LaMarr Hoyt .05
160 George Wright .05
161 Danny Darwin .05
162 Lamar Johnson .05
163 Charlie Hough .05
164 Buddy Bell .05
165 John Matlack (Jon) .05
166 Billy Sample .05
167 John Grubb .05
168 Larry Parrish .05
169 Ivan DeJesus .05
170 Mike Schmidt .40
171 Tug McGraw .05
172 Ron Reed .05
173 Garry Maddox .05
174 Pete Rose .50
175 Manny Trillo .05
176 Steve Carlton .20
177 Bo Diaz .05
178 Gary Matthews .05
179 Bill Caudill .05
180 Ed Vande Berg .05
181 Gaylord Perry .15
182 Floyd Bannister .05
183 Richie Zisk .05
184 Al Cowens .05
185 Bruce Bochte .05
186 Jeff Burroughs .05
187 Dave Beard .05
188 Davey Lopes .05
189 Dwayne Murphy .05
190 Rick Langford .05
191 Tom Underwood .05
192 Rickey Henderson .20
193 Mike Flanagan .05
194 Scott McGregor .05
195 Ken Singleton .05
196 Rich Dauer .05
197 John Lowenstein .05
198 Cal Ripken, Jr. 1.00
199 Dennis Martinez .05
200 Jim Palmer .20
201 Tippy Martinez .05
202 Eddie Murray .15
203 Al Bumbry .05
204 Dickie Thon .05
205 Phil Garner .05
206 Jose Cruz .05
207 Nolan Ryan .50
208 Ray Knight .05
209 Terry Puhl .05
210 Joe Niekro .05
211 Art Howe .05
212 Alan Ashby .05
213 Tom Hume .05
214 Johnny Bench .25
215 Larry Biittner .05
216 Mario Soto .05
217 Dan Driessen .05
218 Tom Seaver .25
219 Dave Concepcion .05
220 Wayne Krenchicki .05
221 Cesar Cedeno .05
222 Ruppert Jones .05
223 Terry Kennedy .05
224 Luis DeLeon .05
225 Eric Show .05
226 Tim Flannery .05
227 Garry Templeton .05
228 Tim Lollar .05
229 Sixto Lezcano .05
230 Bob Bailor .05
231 Craig Swan .05
232 Dave Kingman .05
233 Mookie Wilson .05
234 John Stearns .05
235 Ellis Valentine .05
236 Neil Allen .05
237 Pat Zachry .05
238 Rusty Staub .05
239 George Foster .05
240 Rick Sutcliffe .05
241 Andre Thornton .05
242 Mike Hargrove .05
243 Dan Spillner .05
244 Lary Sorensen .05
245 Len Barker .05
246 Rick Manning .05
247 Toby Harrah .05
248 Milt Wilcox .05
249 Lou Whitaker .05
250 Tom Brookens .05
251 Chet Lemon .05
252 Jack Morris .05
253 Alan Trammell .05
254 John Wockenfuss .05
255 Lance Parrish .05
256 Larry Herndon .05
257 Chris Speier .05
258 Woody Fryman .05
259 Scott Sanderson .05
260 Steve Rogers .05
261 Warren Cromartie .05
262 Gary Carter .15
263 Bill Gullickson .05
264 Andre Dawson .10
265 Tim Raines .05
266 Charlie Lea .05
267 Jeff Reardon .05
268 Al Oliver .05
269 George Hendrick .05
270 John Montefusco .05
(271) A's Logo .05
(272) Angels Logo .05
(273) Astros Logo .05
(274) Blue Jays Logo .05
(275) Braves Logo .05
(276) Brewers Logo .05
(277) Cardinals Logo .05
(278) Cubs Logo .05
(279) Dodgers Logo .05
(280) Expos Logo .05
(281) Giants Logo .05
(282) Indians Logo .05
(283) Mariners Logo .05
(284) Mets Logo .05
(285) Orioles Logo .05
(286) Padres Logo .05
(287) Phillies Logo .05
(288) Pirates Logo .05
(289) Rangers Logo .05
(290) Red Sox Logo .05
(291) Reds Logo .05
(292) Royals Logo .05
(293) Tigers Logo .05
(294) Twins Logo .05
(295) Yankees Logo .05
(296) White Sox Logo .05

1984 Fleer

The 1984 Fleer set contained 660 cards for the fourth consecutive year. The 2-1/2" x 3-1/2" cards feature a color photo surrounded by white borders and horizontal dark blue stripes. The top stripe contains the word "Fleer" with the lower carrying the player's name. Backs have a small black-and-white player photo and are done in blue ink on white stock. The set was issued with team logo stickers.

		MT
Complete Set (660):		35.00
Common Player:		.08
Pack (15):		3.00
Wax Box (36):		85.00
1	Mike Boddicker	.08
2	Al Bumbry	.08
3	Todd Cruz	.08
4	Rich Dauer	.08
5	Storm Davis	.08
6	Rick Dempsey	.08
7	Jim Dwyer	.08
8	Mike Flanagan	.08
9	Dan Ford	.08
10	John Lowenstein	.08
11	Dennis Martinez	.08
12	Tippy Martinez	.08
13	Scott McGregor	.08
14	Eddie Murray	1.00
15	Joe Nolan	.08
16	Jim Palmer	1.00
17	Cal Ripken, Jr.	6.00
18	Gary Roenicke	.08
19	Lenn Sakata	.08
20	*John Shelby*	.08
21	Ken Singleton	.08
22	Sammy Stewart	.08
23	Tim Stoddard	.08
24	Marty Bystrom	.08
25	Steve Carlton	1.50
26	Ivan DeJesus	.08
27	John Denny	.08
28	Bob Dernier	.08
29	Bo Diaz	.08
30	Kiko Garcia	.08
31	Greg Gross	.08
32	*Kevin Gross*	.08
33	Von Hayes	.08
34	Willie Hernandez	.08
35	Al Holland	.08
36	*Charles Hudson*	.08
37	Joe Lefebvre	.08
38	Sixto Lezcano	.08
39	Garry Maddox	.08
40	Gary Matthews	.08
41	Len Matuszek	.08
42	Tug McGraw	.08
43	Joe Morgan	1.00
44	Tony Perez	1.00
45	Ron Reed	.08
46	Pete Rose	3.50
47	*Juan Samuel*	.40
48	Mike Schmidt	3.00
49	Ozzie Virgil	.08
50	*Juan Agosto*	.08
51	Harold Baines	.08
52	Floyd Bannister	.08
53	Salome Barojas	.08
54	Britt Burns	.08
55	Julio Cruz	.08
56	Richard Dotson	.08
57	Jerry Dybzinski	.08
58	Carlton Fisk	1.00
59	Scott Fletcher	.08
60	Jerry Hairston Sr.	.08
61	Kevin Hickey	.08
62	Marc Hill	.08
63	LaMarr Hoyt	.08
64	Ron Kittle	.08
65	Jerry Koosman	.08
66	Dennis Lamp	.08
67	Rudy Law	.08
68	Vance Law	.08
69	Greg Luzinski	.08
70	Tom Paciorek	.08
71	Mike Squires	.08
72	Dick Tidrow	.08
73	*Greg Walker*	.08
74	Glenn Abbott	.08
75	Howard Bailey	.08
76	Doug Bair	.08
77	Juan Berenguer	.08
78	Tom Brookens	.08
79	Enos Cabell	.08
80	Kirk Gibson	.08
81	John Grubb	.08
82	Larry Herndon	.08
83	Wayne Krenchicki	.08
84	Rick Leach	.08
85	Chet Lemon	.08
86	Aurelio Lopez	.08
87	Jack Morris	.08

No.	Player	Price
88	Lance Parrish	.10
89	Dan Petry	.08
90	Dave Rozema	.08
91	Alan Trammell	.15
92	Lou Whitaker	.08
93	Milt Wilcox	.08
94	Glenn Wilson	.08
95	John Wockenfuss	.08
96	Dusty Baker	.10
97	Joe Beckwith	.08
98	Greg Brock	.08
99	Jack Fimple	.08
100	Pedro Guerrero	.08
101	Rick Honeycutt	.08
102	Burt Hooton	.08
103	Steve Howe	.08
104	Ken Landreaux	.08
105	Mike Marshall	.08
106	Rick Monday	.08
107	Jose Morales	.08
108	Tom Niedenfuer	.08
109	*Alejandro Pena*	.08
110	Jerry Reuss	.08
111	Bill Russell	.08
112	Steve Sax	.08
113	Mike Scioscia	.08
114	Derrel Thomas	.08
115	Fernando Valenzuela	.08
116	Bob Welch	.08
117	Steve Yeager	.08
118	Pat Zachry	.08
119	Don Baylor	.15
120	Bert Campaneris	.08
121	Rick Cerone	.08
122	*Ray Fontenot*	.08
123	George Frazier	.08
124	Oscar Gamble	.08
125	Goose Gossage	.10
126	Ken Griffey	.08
127	Ron Guidry	.10
128	Jay Howell	.08
129	Steve Kemp	.08
130	Matt Keough	.08
131	*Don Mattingly*	12.00
132	John Montefusco	.08
133	Omar Moreno	.08
134	Dale Murray	.08
135	Graig Nettles	.10
136	Lou Piniella	.10
137	Willie Randolph	.08
138	Shane Rawley	.08
139	Dave Righetti	.08
140	Andre Robertson	.08
141	Bob Shirley	.08
142	Roy Smalley	.08
143	Dave Winfield	1.00
144	Butch Wynegar	.08
145	*Jim Acker*	.08
146	Doyle Alexander	.08
147	Jesse Barfield	.08
148	George Bell	.08
149	Barry Bonnell	.08
150	Jim Clancy	.08
151	Dave Collins	.08
152	*Tony Fernandez*	.50
153	Damaso Garcia	.08
154	Dave Geisel	.08
155	Jim Gott	.08
156	Alfredo Griffin	.08
157	Garth Iorg	.08
158	Roy Lee Jackson	.08
159	Cliff Johnson	.08
160	Luis Leal	.08
161	Buck Martinez	.08
162	Joey McLaughlin	.08
163	Randy Moffitt	.08
164	Lloyd Moseby	.08
165	Rance Mulliniks	.08
166	Jorge Orta	.08
167	Dave Stieb	.08
168	Willie Upshaw	.08
169	Ernie Whitt	.08
170	Len Barker	.08
171	Steve Bedrosian	.08
172	Bruce Benedict	.08
173	Brett Butler	.08
174	Rick Camp	.08
175	Chris Chambliss	.08
176	Ken Dayley	.08
177	Pete Falcone	.08
178	Terry Forster	.08
179	Gene Garber	.08
180	Terry Harper	.08
181	Bob Horner	.08
182	Glenn Hubbard	.08
183	Randy Johnson	.08
184	*Craig McMurtry*	.08
185	Donnie Moore	.08
186	Dale Murphy	.60
187	Phil Niekro	.75
188	Pascual Perez	.08
189	Biff Pocoroba	.08
190	Rafael Ramirez	.08
191	Jerry Royster	.08
192	Claudell Washington	.08
193	Bob Watson	.08
194	Jerry Augustine	.08
195	Mark Brouhard	.08
196	Mike Caldwell	.08
197	*Tom Candiotti*	.30
198	Cecil Cooper	.08
199	Rollie Fingers	.75
200	Jim Gantner	.08
201	Bob L. Gibson	.08
202	Moose Haas	.08
203	Roy Howell	.08
204	Pete Ladd	.08
205	Rick Manning	.08
206	Bob McClure	.08
207	Paul Molitor	1.00
208	Don Money	.08
209	Charlie Moore	.08
210	Ben Oglivie	.08
211	Chuck Porter	.08
212	Ed Romero	.08
213	Ted Simmons	.08
214	Jim Slaton	.08
215	Don Sutton	.75
216	Tom Tellmann	.08
217	Pete Vuckovich	.08
218	Ned Yost	.08
219	Robin Yount	1.00
220	Alan Ashby	.08
221	Kevin Bass	.08
222	Jose Cruz	.08
223	*Bill Dawley*	.08
224	Frank DiPino	.08
225	*Bill Doran*	.08
226	Phil Garner	.08
227	Art Howe	.08
228	Bob Knepper	.08
229	Ray Knight	.08
230	Frank LaCorte	.08
231	Mike LaCoss	.08
232	Mike Madden	.08
233	Jerry Mumphrey	.08
235	Terry Puhl	.08
236	Luis Pujols	.08
237	Craig Reynolds	.08
238	Vern Ruhle	.08
239	Nolan Ryan	4.00
240	Mike Scott	.08
241	Tony Scott	.08
242	Dave Smith	.08
243	Dickie Thon	.08
244	Denny Walling	.08
245	Dale Berra	.08
246	Jim Bibby	.08
247	John Candelaria	.08
248	*Jose DeLeon*	.08
249	Mike Easler	.08
250	Cecilio Guante	.08
251	Richie Hebner	.08
252	Lee Lacy	.08
253	Bill Madlock	.08
254	Milt May	.08
255	Lee Mazzilli	.08
256	Larry McWilliams	.08
257	Jim Morrison	.08
258	Dave Parker	.10
259	Tony Pena	.08
260	Johnny Ray	.08
261	Rick Rhoden	.08
262	Don Robinson	.08
263	Manny Sarmiento	.08
264	Rod Scurry	.08
265	Kent Tekulve	.08
266	Gene Tenace	.08
267	Jason Thompson	.08
268	*Lee Tunnell*	.08
269	*Marvell Wynne*	.08
270	Ray Burris	.08
271	Gary Carter	.60
272	Warren Cromartie	.08
273	Andre Dawson	.50
274	Doug Flynn	.08
275	Terry Francona	.08
276	Bill Gullickson	.08
277	Bob James	.08
278	Charlie Lea	.08
279	Bryan Little	.08
280	Al Oliver	.10
281	Tim Raines	.08
282	Bobby Ramos	.08
283	Jeff Reardon	.08
284	Steve Rogers	.08
285	Scott Sanderson	.08
286	Dan Schatzeder	.08
287	Bryn Smith	.08
288	Chris Speier	.08
289	Manny Trillo	.08
290	Mike Vail	.08
291	Tim Wallach	.08
292	Chris Welsh	.08
293	Jim Wohlford	.08
294	Kurt Bevacqua	.08
295	Juan Bonilla	.08
296	Bobby Brown	.08
297	Luis DeLeon	.08
298	Dave Dravecky	.08
299	Tim Flannery	.08
300	Steve Garvey	.25
301	Tony Gwynn	2.00
302	*Andy Hawkins*	.10
303	Ruppert Jones	.08
304	Terry Kennedy	.08
305	Tim Lollar	.08
306	Gary Lucas	.08
307	*Kevin McReynolds*	.30
308	Sid Monge	.08
309	Mario Ramirez	.08
310	Gene Richards	.08
311	Luis Salazar	.08
312	Eric Show	.08
313	Elias Sosa	.08
314	Garry Templeton	.08
315	*Mark Thurmond*	.08
316	Ed Whitson	.08
317	Alan Wiggins	.08
318	Neil Allen	.08
319	Joaquin Andujar	.08
320	Steve Braun	.08
321	Glenn Brummer	.08
322	Bob Forsch	.08
323	David Green	.08
324	George Hendrick	.08
325	Tom Herr	.08
326	Dane Iorg	.08
327	Jeff Lahti	.08
328	Dave LaPoint	.08
329	Willie McGee	.10
330	Ken Oberkfell	.08
331	Darrell Porter	.08
332	Jamie Quirk	.08
333	Mike Ramsey	.08
334	Floyd Rayford	.08
335	Lonnie Smith	.08
336	Ozzie Smith	1.50
337	John Stuper	.08
338	Bruce Sutter	.08
339	*Andy Van Slyke*	1.00
340	Dave Von Ohlen	.08
341	Willie Aikens	.08
342	Mike Armstrong	.08
343	Bud Black	.08
344	George Brett	3.00
345	Onix Concepcion	.08
346	Keith Creel	.08
347	Larry Gura	.08
348	Don Hood	.08
349	Dennis Leonard	.08
350	Hal McRae	.08
351	Amos Otis	.08
352	Gaylord Perry	.75
353	Greg Pryor	.08
354	Dan Quisenberry	.08
355	Steve Renko	.08
356	Leon Roberts	.08
357	*Pat Sheridan*	.08
358	Joe Simpson	.08
359	Don Slaught	.08
360	Paul Splittorff	.08
361	U.L. Washington	.08
362	John Wathan	.08
363	Frank White	.08
364	Willie Wilson	.08
365	Jim Barr	.08
366	Dave Bergman	.08
367	Fred Breining	.08
368	Bob Brenly	.08
369	Jack Clark	.08
370	Chili Davis	.08
371	Mark Davis	.08
372	Darrell Evans	.08
373	Atlee Hammaker	.08
374	Mike Krukow	.08
375	Duane Kuiper	.08
376	Bill Laskey	.08
377	Gary Lavelle	.08
378	Johnnie LeMaster	.08
379	Jeff Leonard	.08
380	Randy Lerch	.08
381	Renie Martin	.08
382	Andy McGaffigan	.08
383	Greg Minton	.08
384	Tom O'Malley	.08
385	Max Venable	.08
386	Brad Wellman	.08
387	Joel Youngblood	.08
388	Gary Allenson	.08
389	Luis Aponte	.08
390	Tony Armas	.08
391	Doug Bird	.08
392	Wade Boggs	1.50
393	*Dennis Boyd*	.08
394	Mike Brown	.08
395	Mark Clear	.08
396	Dennis Eckersley	.10
397	Dwight Evans	.10
398	Rich Gedman	.08
399	Glenn Hoffman	.08
400	Bruce Hurst	.08
401	John Henry Johnson	.08
402	Ed Jurak	.08
403	Rick Miller	.08
404	Jeff Newman	.08
405	Reid Nichols	.08
406	Bob Ojeda	.08
407	Jerry Remy	.08
408	Jim Rice	.08
409	Bob Stanley	.08
410	Dave Stapleton	.08
411	John Tudor	.08
412	Carl Yastrzemski	1.00
413	Buddy Bell	.08
414	Larry Biittner	.08
415	John Butcher	.08
416	Danny Darwin	.08
417	Bucky Dent	.08
418	Dave Hostetler	.08
419	Charlie Hough	.08
420	Bobby Johnson	.08
421	Odell Jones	.08
422	Jon Matlack	.08
423	*Pete O'Brien*	.15
424	Larry Parrish	.08
425	Mickey Rivers	.08
426	Billy Sample	.08
427	Dave Schmidt	.08
428	*Mike Smithson*	.08
429	Bill Stein	.08
430	Dave Stewart	.08
431	Jim Sundberg	.08
432	Frank Tanana	.08
433	Dave Tobik	.08
434	Wayne Tolleson	.08
435	George Wright	.08
436	Bill Almon	.08
437	*Keith Atherton*	.08
438	Dave Beard	.08
439	Tom Burgmeier	.08
440	Jeff Burroughs	.08
441	*Chris Codiroli*	.08
442	*Tim Conroy*	.08
443	Mike Davis	.08
444	Wayne Gross	.08
445	Garry Hancock	.08
446	Mike Heath	.08
447	Rickey Henderson	1.00
448	*Don Hill*	.08
449	Bob Kearney	.08
450	Bill Krueger	.08
451	Rick Langford	.08
452	Carney Lansford	.08
453	Davey Lopes	.08
454	Steve McCatty	.08
455	Dan Meyer	.08
456	Dwayne Murphy	.08
457	Mike Norris	.08
458	Ricky Peters	.08
459	Tony Phillips	.08
460	Tom Underwood	.08
461	Mike Warren	.08
462	Johnny Bench	1.00
463	Bruce Berenyi	.08
464	Dann Bilardello	.08
465	Cesar Cedeno	.08
466	Dave Concepcion	.08
467	Dan Driessen	.08
468	*Nick Esasky*	.08
469	Rich Gale	.08
470	Ben Hayes	.08
471	Paul Householder	.08

472 Tom Hume .08
473 Alan Knicely .08
474 Eddie Milner .08
475 Ron Oester .08
476 Kelly Paris .08
477 Frank Pastore .08
478 Ted Power .08
479 Joe Price .08
480 Charlie Puleo .08
481 *Gary Redus* .15
482 Bill Scherrer .08
483 Mario Soto .08
484 Alex Trevino .08
485 Duane Walker .08
486 Larry Bowa .08
487 Warren Brusstar .08
488 Bill Buckner .08
489 Bill Campbell .08
490 Ron Cey .08
491 Jody Davis .08
492 Leon Durham .08
493 Mel Hall .08
494 Fergie Jenkins .75
495 Jay Johnstone .08
496 *Craig Lefferts* .10
497 *Carmelo Martinez* .08
498 Jerry Morales .08
499 Keith Moreland .08
500 Dickie Noles .08
501 Mike Proly .08
502 Chuck Rainey .08
503 Dick Ruthven .08
504 Ryne Sandberg 2.00
505 Lee Smith .08
506 Steve Trout .08
507 Gary Woods .08
508 Juan Beniquez .08
509 Bob Boone .10
510 Rick Burleson .08
511 Rod Carew 1.00
512 Bobby Clark .08
513 John Curtis .08
514 Doug DeCinces .08
515 Brian Downing .08
516 Tim Foli .08
517 Ken Forsch .08
518 Bobby Grich .08
519 Andy Hassler .08
520 Reggie Jackson 1.50
521 Ron Jackson .08
522 Tommy John .10
523 Bruce Kison .08
524 Steve Lubratich .08
525 Fred Lynn .08
526 *Gary Pettis* .08
527 Luis Sanchez .08
528 Daryl Sconiers .08
529 Ellis Valentine .08
530 Rob Wilfong .08
531 Mike Witt .08
532 Geoff Zahn .08
533 Bud Anderson .08
534 Chris Bando .08
535 Alan Bannister .08
536 Bert Blyleven .10
537 Tom Brennan .08
538 Jamie Easterly .08
539 Juan Eichelberger .08
540 Jim Essian .08
541 Mike Fischlin .08
542 Julio Franco .08
543 Mike Hargrove .08
544 Toby Harrah .08
545 Ron Hassey .08
546 *Neal Heaton* .08
547 Bake McBride .08
548 Broderick Perkins .08
549 Lary Sorensen .08
550 Dan Spillner .08
551 Rick Sutcliffe .08
552 Pat Tabler .08
553 Gorman Thomas .08
554 Andre Thornton .08
555 George Vukovich .08
556 Darrell Brown .08
557 Tom Brunansky .08
558 *Randy Bush* .08
559 Bobby Castillo .08
560 John Castino .08
561 Ron Davis .08
562 Dave Engle .08
563 Lenny Faedo .08
564 Pete Filson .08
565 Gary Gaetti .08
566 Mickey Hatcher .08
567 Kent Hrbek .10
568 Rusty Kuntz .08
569 Tim Laudner .08
570 Rick Lysander .08
571 Bobby Mitchell .08
572 Ken Schrom .08
573 Ray Smith .08
574 *Tim Teufel* .15
575 Frank Viola .08
576 Gary Ward .08
577 Ron Washington .08
578 Len Whitehouse .08
579 Al Williams .08
580 Bob Bailor .08
581 Mark Bradley .08
582 Hubie Brooks .08
583 Carlos Diaz .08
584 George Foster .08
585 Brian Giles .08
586 Danny Heep .08
587 Keith Hernandez .08
588 Ron Hodges .08
589 Scott Holman .08
590 Dave Kingman .10
591 Ed Lynch .08
592 *Jose Oquendo* .08
593 Jesse Orosco .08
594 *Junior Ortiz* .08
595 Tom Seaver 1.00
596 *Doug Sisk* .08
597 Rusty Staub .10
598 John Stearns .08
599 Darryl Strawberry 2.00
600 Craig Swan .08
601 *Walt Terrell* .08
602 Mike Torrez .08
603 Mookie Wilson .08
604 Jamie Allen .08
605 Jim Beattie .08
606 Tony Bernazard .08
607 Manny Castillo .08
608 Bill Caudill .08
609 Bryan Clark .08
610 Al Cowens .08
611 Dave Henderson .08
612 Steve Henderson .08
613 Orlando Mercado .08
614 Mike Moore .08
615 Ricky Nelson .08
616 *Spike Owen* .10
617 Pat Putnam .08
618 Ron Roenicke .08
619 Mike Stanton .08
620 Bob Stoddard .08
621 Rick Sweet .08
622 Roy Thomas .08
623 Ed Vande Berg .08
624 *Matt Young* .08
625 Richie Zisk .08
626 '83 All-Star Game Record Breaker (Fred Lynn) .08
627 '83 All-Star Game Record Breaker (Manny Trillo) .08
628 N.L. Iron Man (Steve Garvey) .10
629 A.L. Batting Runner-Up (Rod Carew) .15
630 A.L. Batting Champion (Wade Boggs) .50
631 Letting Go Of The Raines (Tim Raines) .10
632 Double Trouble (Al Oliver) .08
633 All-Star Second Base (Steve Sax) .08
634 All-Star Shortstop (Dickie Thon) .08
635 Ace Firemen (Tippy Martinez, Dan Quisenberry) .08
636 Reds Reunited (Joe Morgan, Tony Perez, Pete Rose) .75
637 Backstop Stars (Bob Boone, Lance Parrish) .08
638 The Pine Tar Incident, 7/24/83 (George Brett, Gaylord Perry) .25
639 1983 No-Hitters (Bob Forsch, Dave Righetti, Mike Warren) .08
640 Retiring Superstars (Johnny Bench, Carl Yastrzemski) .50
641 Going Out In Style (Gaylord Perry) .08
642 300 Club & Strikeout Record (Steve Carlton) .10
643 The Managers (Joe Altobelli, Paul Owens) .08
644 The MVP (Rick Dempsey) .08
645 The Rookie Winner (Mike Boddicker) .08
646 The Clincher (Scott McGregor) .08
647 Checklist: Orioles/Royals (Joe Altobelli) .08
648 Checklist: Phillies/ Giants (Paul Owens) .08
649 Checklist: White Sox/Red Sox (Tony LaRussa) .08
650 Checklist: Tigers/ Rangers (Sparky Anderson) .10
651 Checklist: Dodgers/A's (Tommy Lasorda) .10
652 Checklist: Yankees/ Reds (Billy Martin) .08
653 Checklist: Blue Jays/Cubs (Bobby Cox) .10
654 Checklist: Braves/ Angels (Joe Torre) .10
655 Checklist: Brewers/ Indians (Rene Lacheman) .08
656 Checklist: Astros/ Twins (Bob Lillis) .08
657 Checklist: Pirates/Mets (Chuck Tanner) .08
658 Checklist: Expos/Mariners (Bill Virdon) .08
659 Checklist: Padres/Specials (Dick Williams) .08
660 Checklist: Cardinals/ Specials (Whitey Herzog) .08

1984 Fleer Stickers

This set was designed to be housed in a special collector's album that was organized according to various league leader categories, resulting in some players being pictured on more than one sticker. Each full-color sticker measures 1-15/16" x 2-1/2" and is framed with a beige border. The stickers, which were sold in packs of six, are numbered on the back.

	MT
Complete Set (126):	10.00
Common Player:	.05
Sticker Album:	1.00

1 Dickie Thon .05
2 Ken Landreaux .05
3 Darrell Evans .05
4 Harold Baines .05
5 Dave Winfield .25
6 Bill Madlock .05
7 Lonnie Smith .05
8 Jose Cruz .05
9 George Hendrick .05
10 Ray Knight .05
11 Wade Boggs .30
12 Rod Carew .25
13 Lou Whitaker .05
14 Alan Trammell .05
15 Cal Ripken, Jr. .50
16 Mike Schmidt .40
17 Dale Murphy .20
18 Andre Dawson .15
19 Pedro Guerrero .05
20 Jim Rice .10
21 Tony Armas .05
22 Ron Kittle .05
23 Eddie Murray .25
24 Jose Cruz .05
25 Andre Dawson .15
26 Rafael Ramirez .05
27 Al Oliver .05
28 Wade Boggs .30
29 Cal Ripken, Jr. .50
30 Lou Whitaker .05
31 Cecil Cooper .05
32 Dale Murphy .20
33 Andre Dawson .15
34 Pedro Guerrero .05
35 Mike Schmidt .40
36 George Brett .40
37 Jim Rice .10
38 Eddie Murray .25
39 Carlton Fisk .25
40 Rusty Staub .05
41 Duane Walker .05
42 Steve Braun .05
43 Kurt Bevacqua .05
44 Hal McRae .05
45 Don Baylor .10
46 Ken Singleton .05
47 Greg Luzinski .05
48 Mike Schmidt .40
49 Keith Hernandez .05
50 Dale Murphy .20
51 Tim Raines .05
52 Wade Boggs .30
53 Rickey Henderson .25
54 Rod Carew .25
55 Ken Singleton .05
56 John Denny .05
57 John Candelaria .05
58 Larry McWilliams .05
59 Pascual Perez .05
60 Jesse Orosco .05
61 Moose Haas .05
62 Richard Dotson .05
63 Mike Flanagan .05
64 Scott McGregor .05
65 Atlee Hammaker .05
66 Rick Honeycutt .05
67 Lee Smith .05
68 Al Holland .05
69 Greg Minton .05
70 Bruce Sutter .05
71 Jeff Reardon .05
72 Frank DiPino .05
73 Dan Quisenberry .05
74 Bob Stanley .05
75 Ron Davis .05
76 Bill Caudill .05
77 Peter Ladd .05
78 Steve Carlton .25
79 Mario Soto .05
80 Larry McWilliams .05
81 Fernando Valenzuela .05
82 Nolan Ryan .75
83 Jack Morris .05
84 Floyd Bannister .05
85 Dave Stieb .05
86 Dave Righetti .05
87 Rick Sutcliffe .05
88 Tim Raines .05
89 Alan Wiggins .05
90 Steve Sax .05
91 Mookie Wilson .05
92 Rickey Henderson .25
93 Rudy Law .05
94 Willie Wilson .05
95 Julio Cruz .05
96 Johnny Bench .30
97 Carl Yastrzemski .25
98 Gaylord Perry .15
99 Pete Rose .45
100 Joe Morgan .25
101 Steve Carlton .25

102	Jim Palmer	.25
103	Rod Carew	.25
104	Darryl Strawberry	.20
105	Craig McMurtry	.05
106	Mel Hall	.05
107	Lee Tunnell	.05
108	Bill Dawley	.05
109	Ron Kittle	.05
110	Mike Boddicker	.05
111	Julio Franco	.05
112	Daryl Sconiers	.05
113	Neal Heaton	.05
114	John Shelby	.05
115	Rick Dempsey	.05
116	John Lowenstein	.05
117	Jim Dwyer	.05
118	Bo Diaz	.05
119	Pete Rose	.45
120	Joe Morgan	.25
121	Gary Matthews	.05
122	Garry Maddox	.05
123	Paul Owens	.05
124	Tom Lasorda	.10
125	Joe Altobelli	.05
126	Tony LaRussa	.05

1984 Fleer Update

Following the lead of Topps, Fleer issued near the end of the baseball season a 132-card set to update player trades and include rookies not depicted in the regular issue. The cards are identical in design to the regular issue but are numbered U-1 through U-132. Available only as a boxed set through hobby dealers, the set was printed in limited quantities.

		MT
Complete Set (132):		300.00
Common Player:		.25
1	Willie Aikens	.25
2	Luis Aponte	.25
3	Mark Bailey	.25
4	Bob Bailor	.25
5	Dusty Baker	.50
6	Steve Balboni	.25
7	Alan Bannister	.25
8	Marty Barrett	.25
9	Dave Beard	.25
10	Joe Beckwith	.25
11	Dave Bergman	.25
12	Tony Bernazard	.25
13	Bruce Bochte	.25
14	Barry Bonnell	.25
15	Phil Bradley	.25
16	Fred Breining	.25
17	Mike Brown	.25
18	Bill Buckner	.35
19	Ray Burris	.25
20	John Butcher	.25
21	Brett Butler	.25
22	Enos Cabell	.25
23	Bill Campbell	.25
24	Bill Caudill	.25
25	Bobby Clark	.25
26	Bryan Clark	.25
27	*Roger Clemens*	200.00
28	Jaime Cocanower	.25
29	*Ron Darling*	2.50
30	*Alvin Davis*	.25
31	Bob Dernier	.25
32	Carlos Diaz	.25
33	Mike Easler	.25
34	Dennis Eckersley	6.00
35	Jim Essian	.25
36	Darrell Evans	.35
37	Mike Fitzgerald	.25
38	Tim Foli	.25
39	*John Franco*	4.00
40	George Frazier	.25
41	Rich Gale	.25
42	Barbaro Garbey	.25
43	*Dwight Gooden*	7.50
44	Goose Gossage	.40
45	Wayne Gross	.25
46	Mark Gubicza	2.00
47	Jackie Gutierrez	.25
48	Toby Harrah	.25
49	Ron Hassey	.25
50	Richie Hebner	.25
51	Willie Hernandez	.25
52	Ed Hodge	.25
53	Ricky Horton	.25
54	Art Howe	.25
55	Dane Iorg	.25
56	Brook Jacoby	.25
57	Dion James	.25
58	Mike Jeffcoat	.25
59	Ruppert Jones	.25
60	Bob Kearney	.25
61	*Jimmy Key*	2.00
62	Dave Kingman	.35
63	Brad Komminsk	.25
64	Jerry Koosman	.25
65	Wayne Krenchicki	.25
66	Rusty Kuntz	.25
67	Frank LaCorte	.25
68	Dennis Lamp	.25
69	Tito Landrum	.25
70	*Mark Langston*	7.50
71	Rick Leach	.25
72	Craig Lefferts	.25
73	Gary Lucas	.25
74	Jerry Martin	.25
75	Carmelo Martinez	.25
76	Mike Mason	.25
77	Gary Matthews	.25
78	Andy McGaffigan	.25
79	Joey McLaughlin	.25
80	Joe Morgan	5.00
81	Darryl Motley	.25
82	Graig Nettles	.50
83	Phil Niekro	3.00
84	Ken Oberkfell	.25
85	Al Oliver	.35
86	Jorge Orta	.25
87	Amos Otis	.25
88	Bob Owchinko	.25
89	Dave Parker	1.00
90	Jack Perconte	.25
91	Tony Perez	3.00
92	Gerald Perry	.25
93	*Kirby Puckett*	80.00
94	Shane Rawley	.25
95	Floyd Rayford	.25
96	Ron Reed	.25
97	R.J. Reynolds	.25
98	Gene Richards	.25
99	*Jose Rijo*	2.00
100	Jeff Robinson	.25
101	Ron Romanick	.25
102	Pete Rose	10.00
103	*Bret Saberhagen*	7.50
104	Scott Sanderson	.25
105	Dick Schofield	.25
106	Tom Seaver	7.50
107	Jim Slaton	.25
108	Mike Smithson	.25
109	Lary Sorensen	.25
110	Tim Stoddard	.25
111	Jeff Stone	.25
112	Champ Summers	.25
113	Jim Sundberg	.25
114	Rick Sutcliffe	.35
115	Craig Swan	.25
116	Derrel Thomas	.25
117	Gorman Thomas	.25
118	Alex Trevino	.25
119	Manny Trillo	.25
120	John Tudor	.25
121	Tom Underwood	.25
122	Mike Vail	.25
123	Tom Waddell	.25
124	Gary Ward	.25
125	Terry Whitfield	.25
126	Curtis Wilkerson	.25
127	Frank Williams	.25
128	Glenn Wilson	.25
129	John Wockenfuss	.25
130	Ned Yost	.25
131	Mike Young	.25
132	Checklist 1-132	.10

1985 Fleer

The 1985 Fleer set consists of 660 cards, each measuring 2-1/2" x 3-1/2". Card fronts feature a color photo plus the player's team logo and the word "Fleer." The photos have a color-coded frame which corresponds to the player's team. A grey border surrounds the frame. Backs are similar in design to previous years, but have two shades of red and black ink on white stock. For the fourth consecutive year, Fleer included special cards and team checklists in the set. Also incorporated in a set for the first time were ten "Major League Prospect" cards, each featuring two rookie hopefuls. The set was issued with team logo stickers.

		MT
Complete Set (660):		45.00
Unopened Factory Set (660):		65.00
Common Player:		.06
Pack (15):		4.00
Wax Box (36):		115.00
1	Doug Bair	.06
2	Juan Berenguer	.06
3	Dave Bergman	.06
4	Tom Brookens	.06
5	Marty Castillo	.06
6	Darrell Evans	.10
7	Barbaro Garbey	.06
8	Kirk Gibson	.06
9	John Grubb	.06
10	Willie Hernandez	.06
11	Larry Herndon	.06
12	Howard Johnson	.06
13	Ruppert Jones	.06
14	Rusty Kuntz	.06
15	Chet Lemon	.06
16	Aurelio Lopez	.06
17	Sid Monge	.06
18	Jack Morris	.10
19	Lance Parrish	.10
20	Dan Petry	.06
21	Dave Rozema	.06
22	Bill Scherrer	.06
23	Alan Trammell	.20
24	Lou Whitaker	.06
25	Milt Wilcox	.06
26	Kurt Bevacqua	.06
27	*Greg Booker*	.06
28	Bobby Brown	.06
29	Luis DeLeon	.06
30	Dave Dravecky	.06
31	Tim Flannery	.06
32	Steve Garvey	.35
33	Goose Gossage	.10
34	Tony Gwynn	2.00
35	Greg Harris	.06
36	Andy Hawkins	.06
37	Terry Kennedy	.06
38	Craig Lefferts	.06
39	Tim Lollar	.06
40	Carmelo Martinez	.06
41	Kevin McReynolds	.06
42	Graig Nettles	.10
43	Luis Salazar	.06
44	Eric Show	.06
45	Garry Templeton	.06
46	Mark Thurmond	.06
47	Ed Whitson	.06
48	Alan Wiggins	.06
49	Rich Bordi	.06
50	Larry Bowa	.06
51	Warren Brusstar	.06
52	Ron Cey	.06
53	*Henry Cotto*	.06
54	Jody Davis	.06
55	Bob Dernier	.06
56	Leon Durham	.06
57	Dennis Eckersley	.30
58	George Frazier	.06
59	Richie Hebner	.06
60	Dave Lopes	.06
61	Gary Matthews	.06
62	Keith Moreland	.06
63	Rick Reuschel	.06
64	Dick Ruthven	.06
65	Ryne Sandberg	1.50
66	Scott Sanderson	.06
67	Lee Smith	.10
68	Tim Stoddard	.06
69	Rick Sutcliffe	.06
70	Steve Trout	.06
71	Gary Woods	.06
72	Wally Backman	.06
73	Bruce Berenyi	.06
74	Hubie Brooks	.06
75	Kelvin Chapman	.06
76	Ron Darling	.06
77	Sid Fernandez	.06
78	Mike Fitzgerald	.06
79	George Foster	.06
80	Brent Gaff	.06
81	Ron Gardenhire	.06
82	Dwight Gooden	.25
83	Tom Gorman	.06
84	Danny Heep	.06
85	Keith Hernandez	.10
86	Ray Knight	.06
87	Ed Lynch	.06
88	Jose Oquendo	.06
89	Jesse Orosco	.06
90	*Rafael Santana*	.06
91	Doug Sisk	.06
92	Rusty Staub	.10
93	Darryl Strawberry	.50
94	Walt Terrell	.06
95	Mookie Wilson	.06
96	Jim Acker	.06
97	Willie Aikens	.06
98	Doyle Alexander	.06
99	Jesse Barfield	.06
100	George Bell	.06
101	Jim Clancy	.06
102	Dave Collins	.06
103	Tony Fernandez	.06
104	Damaso Garcia	.06
105	Jim Gott	.06
106	Alfredo Griffin	.06
107	Garth Iorg	.06
108	Roy Lee Jackson	.06
109	Cliff Johnson	.06
110	Jimmy Key	.50
111	Dennis Lamp	.06
112	Rick Leach	.06
113	Luis Leal	.06
114	Buck Martinez	.06
115	Lloyd Moseby	.06
116	Rance Mulliniks	.06
117	Dave Stieb	.06
118	Willie Upshaw	.06
119	Ernie Whitt	.06
120	Mike Armstrong	.06
121	Don Baylor	.15
122	Marty Bystrom	.06
123	Rick Cerone	.06
124	Joe Cowley	.06
125	Brian Dayett	.06
126	Tim Foli	.06

127 Ray Fontenot .06
128 Ken Griffey .06
129 Ron Guidry .10
130 Toby Harrah .06
131 Jay Howell .06
132 Steve Kemp .06
133 Don Mattingly 4.00
134 Bobby Meacham .06
135 John Montefusco .06
136 Omar Moreno .06
137 Dale Murray .06
138 Phil Niekro .65
139 *Mike Pagliarulo* .20
140 Willie Randolph .06
141 Dennis Rasmussen .06
142 Dave Righetti .06
143 Jose Rijo .06
144 Andre Robertson .06
145 Bob Shirley .06
146 Dave Winfield 1.00
147 Butch Wynegar .06
148 Gary Allenson .06
149 Tony Armas .06
150 Marty Barrett .06
151 Wade Boggs 1.00
152 Dennis Boyd .06
153 Bill Buckner .06
154 Mark Clear .06
155 Roger Clemens 25.00
156 Steve Crawford .06
157 Mike Easler .06
158 Dwight Evans .06
159 Rich Gedman .06
160 Jackie Gutierrez .06
161 Bruce Hurst .06
162 John Henry Johnson .06
163 Rick Miller .06
164 Reid Nichols .06
165 *Al Nipper* .06
166 Bob Ojeda .06
167 Jerry Remy .06
168 Jim Rice .10
169 Bob Stanley .06
170 Mike Boddicker .06
171 Al Bumbry .06
172 Todd Cruz .06
173 Rich Dauer .06
174 Storm Davis .06
175 Rick Dempsey .06
176 Jim Dwyer .06
177 Mike Flanagan .06
178 Dan Ford .06
179 Wayne Gross .06
180 John Lowenstein .06
181 Dennis Martinez .06
182 Tippy Martinez .06
183 Scott McGregor .06
184 Eddie Murray 1.00
185 Joe Nolan .06
186 Floyd Rayford .06
187 Cal Ripken, Jr. 5.00
188 Gary Roenicke .06
189 Lenn Sakata .06
190 John Shelby .06
191 Ken Singleton .06
192 Sammy Stewart .06
193 Bill Swaggerty .06
194 Tom Underwood .06
195 Mike Young .06
196 Steve Balboni .06
197 Joe Beckwith .06
198 Bud Black .06
199 George Brett 2.50
200 Onix Concepcion .06
201 *Mark Gubicza* .75
202 Larry Gura .06
203 Mark Huismann .06
204 Dane Iorg .06
205 Danny Jackson .06
206 Charlie Leibrandt .06
207 Hal McRae .06
208 Darryl Motley .06
209 Jorge Orta .06
210 Greg Pryor .06
211 Dan Quisenberry .06
212 Bret Saberhagen 1.00
213 Pat Sheridan .06
214 Don Slaught .06
215 U.L. Washington .06
216 John Wathan .06
217 Frank White .06
218 Willie Wilson .06
219 Neil Allen .06
220 Joaquin Andujar .06
221 Steve Braun .06
222 Danny Cox .06
223 Bob Forsch .06
224 David Green .06
225 George Hendrick .06
226 Tom Herr .06
227 *Ricky Horton* .06
228 Art Howe .06
229 Mike Jorgensen .06
230 Kurt Kepshire .06
231 Jeff Lahti .06
232 Tito Landrum .06
233 Dave LaPoint .06
234 Willie McGee .06
235 *Tom Nieto* .06
236 *Terry Pendleton* 1.50
237 Darrell Porter .06
238 Dave Rucker .06
239 Lonnie Smith .06
240 Ozzie Smith 1.50
241 Bruce Sutter .06
242 Andy Van Slyke .10
243 Dave Von Ohlen .06
244 Larry Andersen .06
245 Bill Campbell .06
246 Steve Carlton 1.00
247 Tim Corcoran .06
248 Ivan DeJesus .06
249 John Denny .06
250 Bo Diaz .06
251 Greg Gross .06
252 Kevin Gross .06
253 Von Hayes .06
254 Al Holland .06
255 Charles Hudson .06
256 Jerry Koosman .06
257 Joe Lefebvre .06
258 Sixto Lezcano .06
259 Garry Maddox .06
260 Len Matuszek .06
261 Tug McGraw .06
262 Al Oliver .10
263 Shane Rawley .06
264 Juan Samuel .06
265 Mike Schmidt 2.50
266 *Jeff Stone* .06
267 Ozzie Virgil .06
268 Glenn Wilson .06
269 John Wockenfuss .06
270 Darrell Brown .06
271 Tom Brunansky .06
272 Randy Bush .06
273 John Butcher .06
274 Bobby Castillo .06
275 Ron Davis .06
276 Dave Engle .06
277 Pete Filson .06
278 Gary Gaetti .06
279 Mickey Hatcher .06
280 Ed Hodge .06
281 Kent Hrbek .10
282 Houston Jimenez .06
283 Tim Laudner .06
284 Rick Lysander .06
285 Dave Meier .06
286 Kirby Puckett 15.00
287 Pat Putnam .06
288 Ken Schrom .06
289 Mike Smithson .06
290 Tim Teufel .06
291 Frank Viola .06
292 Ron Washington .06
293 Don Aase .06
294 Juan Beniquez .06
295 Bob Boone .10
296 Mike Brown .06
297 Rod Carew 1.00
298 Doug Corbett .06
299 Doug DeCinces .06
300 Brian Downing .06
301 Ken Forsch .06
302 Bobby Grich .06
303 Reggie Jackson 1.50
304 Tommy John .10
305 Curt Kaufman .06
306 Bruce Kison .06
307 Fred Lynn .10
308 Gary Pettis .06
309 *Ron Romanick* .06
310 Luis Sanchez .06
311 Dick Schofield .06
312 Daryl Sconiers .06
313 Jim Slaton .06
314 Derrel Thomas .06
315 Rob Wilfong .06
316 Mike Witt .06
317 Geoff Zahn .06
318 Len Barker .06
319 Steve Bedrosian .06
320 Bruce Benedict .06
321 Rick Camp .06
322 Chris Chambliss .06
323 *Jeff Dedmon* .06
324 Terry Forster .06
325 Gene Garber .06
326 *Albert Hall* .06
327 Terry Harper .06
328 Bob Horner .06
329 Glenn Hubbard .06
330 Randy Johnson .06
331 Brad Komminsk .06
332 Rick Mahler .06
333 Craig McMurtry .06
334 Donnie Moore .06
335 Dale Murphy .50
336 Ken Oberkfell .06
337 Pascual Perez .06
338 Gerald Perry .06
339 Rafael Ramirez .06
340 Jerry Royster .06
341 Alex Trevino .06
342 Claudell Washington .06
343 Alan Ashby .06
344 *Mark Bailey* .06
345 Kevin Bass .06
346 Enos Cabell .06
347 Jose Cruz .06
348 Bill Dawley .06
349 Frank DiPino .06
350 Bill Doran .06
351 Phil Garner .06
352 Bob Knepper .06
353 Mike LaCoss .06
354 Jerry Mumphrey .06
355 Joe Niekro .06
356 Terry Puhl .06
357 Craig Reynolds .06
358 Vern Ruhle .06
359 Nolan Ryan 5.00
360 Joe Sambito .06
361 Mike Scott .06
362 Dave Smith .06
363 *Julio Solano* .06
364 Dickie Thon .06
365 Denny Walling .06
366 Dave Anderson .06
367 Bob Bailor .06
368 Greg Brock .06
369 Carlos Diaz .06
370 Pedro Guerrero .06
371 *Orel Hershiser* 3.50
372 Rick Honeycutt .06
373 Burt Hooton .06
374 *Ken Howell* .15
375 Ken Landreaux .06
376 Candy Maldonado .06
377 Mike Marshall .06
378 Tom Niedenfuer .06
379 Alejandro Pena .06
380 Jerry Reuss .06
381 *R.J. Reynolds* .06
382 German Rivera .06
383 Bill Russell .06
384 Steve Sax .06
385 Mike Scioscia .06
386 *Franklin Stubbs* .06
387 Fernando Valenzuela .06
388 Bob Welch .06
389 Terry Whitfield .06
390 Steve Yeager .06
391 Pat Zachry .06
392 Fred Breining .06
393 Gary Carter .40
394 Andre Dawson .35
395 Miguel Dilone .06
396 Dan Driessen .06
397 Doug Flynn .06
398 Terry Francona .06
399 Bill Gullickson .06
400 Bob James .06
401 Charlie Lea .06
402 Bryan Little .06
403 Gary Lucas .06
404 David Palmer .06
405 Tim Raines .06
406 Mike Ramsey .06
407 Jeff Reardon .06
408 Steve Rogers .06
409 Dan Schatzeder .06
410 Bryn Smith .06
411 Mike Stenhouse .06
412 Tim Wallach .06
413 Jim Wohlford .06
414 Bill Almon .06
415 Keith Atherton .06
416 Bruce Bochte .06
417 Tom Burgmeier .06
418 Ray Burris .06
419 Bill Caudill .06
420 Chris Codiroli .06
421 Tim Conroy .06
422 Mike Davis .06
423 Jim Essian .06
424 Mike Heath .06
425 Rickey Henderson 1.00
426 Donnie Hill .06
427 Dave Kingman .10
428 Bill Krueger .06
429 Carney Lansford .06
430 Steve McCatty .06
431 Joe Morgan 1.00
432 Dwayne Murphy .06
433 Tony Phillips .06
434 Lary Sorensen .06
435 Mike Warren .06
436 *Curt Young* .06
437 Luis Aponte .06
438 Chris Bando .06
439 Tony Bernazard .06
440 Bert Blyleven .10
441 Brett Butler .06
442 Ernie Camacho .06
443 Joe Carter 1.00
444 Carmelo Castillo .06
445 Jamie Easterly .06
446 *Steve Farr* .06
447 Mike Fischlin .06
448 Julio Franco .06
449 Mel Hall .06
450 Mike Hargrove .06
451 Neal Heaton .06
452 Brook Jacoby .06
453 *Mike Jeffcoat* .06
454 *Don Schulze* .06
455 Roy Smith .06
456 Pat Tabler .06
457 Andre Thornton .06
458 George Vukovich .06
459 Tom Waddell .06
460 Jerry Willard .06
461 Dale Berra .06
462 John Candelaria .06
463 Jose DeLeon .06
464 Doug Frobel .06
465 Cecilio Guante .06
466 Brian Harper .06
467 Lee Lacy .06
468 Bill Madlock .06
469 Lee Mazzilli .06
470 Larry McWilliams .06
471 Jim Morrison .06
472 Tony Pena .06
473 Johnny Ray .06
474 Rick Rhoden .06
475 Don Robinson .06
476 Rod Scurry .06
477 Kent Tekulve .06
478 Jason Thompson .06
479 John Tudor .06
480 Lee Tunnell .06
481 Marvell Wynne .06
482 Salome Barojas .06
483 Dave Beard .06
484 Jim Beattie .06
485 Barry Bonnell .06
486 *Phil Bradley* .06
487 Al Cowens .06
488 Alvin Davis .06
489 Dave Henderson .06
490 Steve Henderson .06
491 Bob Kearney .06
492 Mark Langston .50
493 Larry Milbourne .06
494 Paul Mirabella .06
495 Mike Moore .06
496 Edwin Nunez .06
497 Spike Owen .06
498 Jack Perconte .06
499 Ken Phelps .06
500 *Jim Presley* .06
501 Mike Stanton .06
502 Bob Stoddard .06
503 Gorman Thomas .06
504 Ed Vande Berg .06
505 Matt Young .06
506 Juan Agosto .06
507 Harold Baines .10
508 Floyd Bannister .06
509 Britt Burns .06

510 Julio Cruz .06
511 Richard Dotson .06
512 Jerry Dybzinski .06
513 Carlton Fisk .75
514 Scott Fletcher .06
515 Jerry Hairston Sr. .06
516 Marc Hill .06
517 LaMarr Hoyt .06
518 Ron Kittle .06
519 Rudy Law .06
520 Vance Law .06
521 Greg Luzinski .06
522 Gene Nelson .06
523 Tom Paciorek .06
524 Ron Reed .06
525 Bert Roberge .06
526 Tom Seaver 1.00
527 Roy Smalley .06
528 Dan Spillner .06
529 Mike Squires .06
530 Greg Walker .06
531 Cesar Cedeno .06
532 Dave Concepcion .06
533 *Eric Davis* 2.50
534 Nick Esasky .06
535 Tom Foley .06
536 John Franco .10
537 Brad Gulden .06
538 Tom Hume .06
539 Wayne Krenchicki .06
540 Andy McGaffigan .06
541 Eddie Milner .06
542 Ron Oester .06
543 Bob Owchinko .06
544 Dave Parker .15
545 Frank Pastore .06
546 Tony Perez .75
547 Ted Power .06
548 Joe Price .06
549 Gary Redus .06
550 Pete Rose 3.00
551 Jeff Russell .06
552 Mario Soto .06
553 *Jay Tibbs* .06
554 Duane Walker .06
555 Alan Bannister .06
556 Buddy Bell .06
557 Danny Darwin .06
558 Charlie Hough .06
559 Bobby Jones .06
560 Odell Jones .06
561 *Jeff Kunkel* .06
562 *Mike Mason* .06
563 Pete O'Brien .06
564 Larry Parrish .06
565 Mickey Rivers .06
566 Billy Sample .06
567 Dave Schmidt .06
568 Donnie Scott .06
569 Dave Stewart .10
570 Frank Tanana .06
571 Wayne Tolleson .06
572 Gary Ward .06
573 Curtis Wilkerson .06
574 George Wright .06
575 Ned Yost .06
576 Mark Brouhard .06
577 Mike Caldwell .06
578 Bobby Clark .06
579 Jaime Cocanower .06
580 Cecil Cooper .06
581 Rollie Fingers .75
582 Jim Gantner .06
583 Moose Haas .06
584 Dion James .06
585 Pete Ladd .06
586 Rick Manning .06
587 Bob McClure .06
588 Paul Molitor 1.00
589 Charlie Moore .06
590 Ben Oglivie .06
591 Chuck Porter .06
592 *Randy Ready* .06
593 Ed Romero .06
594 Bill Schroeder .06
595 Ray Searage .06
596 Ted Simmons .06
597 Jim Sundberg .06
598 Don Sutton .65
599 Tom Tellmann .06
600 Rick Waits .06
601 Robin Yount 1.00
602 Dusty Baker .15
603 Bob Brenly .06
604 Jack Clark .06
605 Chili Davis .06
606 Mark Davis .06
607 *Dan Gladden* .25
608 Atlee Hammaker .06
609 Mike Krukow .06
610 Duane Kuiper .06
611 Bob Lacey .06
612 Bill Laskey .06
613 Gary Lavelle .06
614 Johnnie LeMaster .06
615 Jeff Leonard .06
616 Randy Lerch .06
617 Greg Minton .06
618 Steve Nicosia .06
619 Gene Richards .06
620 *Jeff Robinson* .06
621 Scot Thompson .06
622 Manny Trillo .06
623 Brad Wellman .06
624 *Frank Williams* .06
625 Joel Youngblood .06
626 Cal Ripken, Jr. (In Action) 1.00
627 Mike Schmidt (In Action) 1.00
628 Giving the Signs (Sparky Anderson) .10
629 A.L. Pitcher's Nightmare (Rickey Henderson, Dave Winfield) .50
630 N.L. Pitcher's Nightmare (Ryne Sandberg, Mike Schmidt) 1.00
631 N.L. All-Stars (Gary Carter, Steve Garvey, Ozzie Smith, Darryl Strawberry) .25
632 All-Star Game Winning Battery (Gary Carter, Charlie Lea) .10
633 N.L. Pennant Clinchers (Steve Garvey, Goose Gossage) .10
634 N.L. Rookie Phenoms (Dwight Gooden, Juan Samuel) .15
635 Toronto's Big Guns (Willie Upshaw) .06
636 Toronto's Big Guns (Lloyd Moseby) .06
637 Holland (Al Holland) .06
638 Tunnell (Lee Tunnell) .06
639 Reggie Jackson (In Action) .50
640 Pete Rose (In Action) .75
641 Father & Son (Cal Ripken, Jr., Cal Ripken, Sr.) 1.00
642 Cubs team .10
643 1984's Two Perfect Games & One No-Hitter (Jack Morris, David Palmer, Mike Witt) .06
644 Major League Prospect (Willie Lozado, Vic Mata) .06
645 Major League Prospect (*Kelly Gruber*), (*Randy O'Neal*) .15
646 Major League Prospect (*Jose Roman*), (*Joel Skinner*) .06
647 Major League Prospect (*Steve Kiefer*), (*Danny Tartabull*) .75
648 Major League Prospect (*Rob Deer*), (*Alejandro Sanchez*) .25
649 Major League Prospect (*Shawon Dunston*), (*Bill Hatcher*) 1.00
650 Major League Prospect (*Mike Bielecki*), (*Ron Robinson*) .10
651 Major League Prospect (*Zane Smith*), (*Paul Zuvella*) .15
652 Major League Prospect (*Glenn Davis*), (*Joe Hesketh*) .20
653 Major League Prospect (*Steve Jeltz*), (*John Russell*) .10
654 Checklist 1-95 .06
655 Checklist 96-195 .06
656 Checklist 196-292 .06
657 Checklist 293-391 .06
658 Checklist 392-481 .06
659 Checklist 482-575 .06
660 Checklist 576-660 .06

1985 Fleer Star Stickers

The 1985 Fleer sticker set consists of 126 player stickers, each measuring 1-15/16" x 2-1/2". Numbered on the back, the stickers were designed to be put in a special album. Distributed in packs of six, the 1985 stickers are the scarcest of all Fleer baseball sticker issues.

		MT
Complete Set (126):		25.00
Common Player:		.10
Sticker Album:		1.25
1	Pete Rose	1.00
2	Pete Rose	1.00
3	Pete Rose	1.00
4	Don Mattingly	1.50
5	Dave Winfield	.50
6	Wade Boggs	1.00
7	Buddy Bell	.10
8	Tony Gwynn	1.00
9	Lee Lacy	.10
10	Chili Davis	.10
11	Ryne Sandberg	1.00
12	Tony Armas	.10
13	Jim Rice	.15
14	Dave Kingman	.10
15	Alvin Davis	.10
16	Gary Carter	.15
17	Mike Schmidt	1.50
18	Dale Murphy	.20
19	Ron Cey	.10
20	Eddie Murray	.40
21	Harold Baines	.10
22	Kirk Gibson	.10
23	Jim Rice	.15
24	Gary Matthews	.10
25	Keith Hernandez	.10
26	Gary Carter	.15
27	George Hendrick	.10
28	Tony Armas	.10
29	Dave Kingman	.10
30	Dwayne Murphy	.10
31	Lance Parrish	.10
32	Andre Thornton	.10
33	Dale Murphy	.20
34	Mike Schmidt	1.50
35	Gary Carter	.15
36	Darryl Strawberry	.10
37	Don Mattingly	1.50
38	Larry Parrish	.10
39	George Bell	.10
40	Dwight Evans	.10
41	Cal Ripken, Jr.	2.50
42	Tim Raines	.10
43	Johnny Ray	.10
44	Juan Samuel	.10
45	Ryne Sandberg	1.00
46	Mike Easler	.10
47	Andre Thornton	.10
48	Dave Kingman	.10
49	Don Baylor	.15
50	Rusty Staub	.10
51	Steve Braun	.10
52	Kevin Bass	.10
53	Greg Gross	.10
54	Rickey Henderson	.40
55	Dave Collins	.10
56	Brett Butler	.10
57	Gary Pettis	.10
58	Tim Raines	.10
59	Juan Samuel	.10
60	Alan Wiggins	.10
61	Lonnie Smith	.10
62	Eddie Murray	.10
63	Eddie Murray	.10
64	Eddie Murray	.10
65	Eddie Murray	.10
66	Eddie Murray	.10
67	Eddie Murray	.10
68	Tom Seaver	.10
69	Tom Seaver	.10
70	Tom Seaver	.10
71	Tom Seaver	.10
72	Tom Seaver	.10
73	Tom Seaver	.10
74	Mike Schmidt	.25
75	Mike Schmidt	.25
76	Mike Schmidt	.25
77	Mike Schmidt	.25
78	Mike Schmidt	.25
79	Mike Schmidt	.25
80	Mike Boddicker	.10
81	Bert Blyleven	.10
82	Jack Morris	.10
83	Dan Petry	.10
84	Frank Viola	.10
85	Joaquin Andujar	.10
86	Mario Soto	.10
87	Dwight Gooden	.10
88	Joe Niekro	.10
89	Rick Sutcliffe	.10
90	Mike Boddicker	.10
91	Dave Stieb	.10
92	Bert Blyleven	.10
93	Phil Niekro	.25
94	Alejandro Pena	.10
95	Dwight Gooden	.10
96	Orel Hershiser	.15
97	Rick Rhoden	.10
98	John Candelaria	.10
99	Dan Quisenberry	.10
100	Bill Caudill	.10
101	Willie Hernandez	.10
102	Dave Righetti	.10
103	Ron Davis	.10
104	Bruce Sutter	.10
105	Lee Smith	.10
106	Jesse Orosco	.10
107	Al Holland	.10
108	Goose Gossage	.10
109	Mark Langston	.10
110	Dave Stieb	.10
111	Mike Witt	.10
112	Bert Blyleven	.10
113	Dwight Gooden	.10
114	Fernando Valenzuela	.10
115	Nolan Ryan	2.50
116	Mario Soto	.10
117	Ron Darling	.10
118	Dan Gladden	.10
119	Jeff Stone	.10
120	John Franco	.10
121	Barbaro Garbey	.10
122	Kirby Puckett	2.50
123	Roger Clemens	2.50
124	Bret Saberhagen	.10
125	Sparky Anderson	.10
126	Dick Williams	.10

1985 Fleer Update

For the second straight year, Fleer issued a 132-card update set. Cards portray traded players on their new teams and also include rookies not depicted in the regular issue. The cards are identical in design to the 1985 Fleer set but are numbered U-1 through U-132. The set was issued with team logo stickers in a specially designed box and was available only through hobby dealers.

		MT
Complete Set (132):		8.00
Common Player:		.10
1	Don Aase	.10
2	Bill Almon	.10
3	Dusty Baker	.20
4	Dale Berra	.10
5	Karl Best	.10
6	Tim Birtsas	.10
7	Vida Blue	.10
8	Rich Bordi	.10
9	Daryl Boston	.10
10	Hubie Brooks	.10
11	Chris Brown	.10
12	Tom Browning	.15
13	Al Bumbry	.10
14	Tim Burke	.10
15	Ray Burris	.10
16	Jeff Burroughs	.10
17	Ivan Calderon	.10
18	Jeff Calhoun	.10
19	Bill Campbell	.10
20	Don Carman	.10
21	Gary Carter	.75
22	Bobby Castillo	.10
23	Bill Caudill	.10
24	Rick Cerone	.10
25	Jack Clark	.10
26	Pat Clements	.10
27	Stewart Cliburn	.10
28	Vince Coleman	.75
29	Dave Collins	.10
30	Fritz Connally	.10
31	Henry Cotto	.10
32	Danny Darwin	.10
33	*Darren Daulton*	2.00
34	Jerry Davis	.10
35	Brian Dayett	.10
36	Ken Dixon	.10
37	Tommy Dunbar	.10
38	Mariano Duncan	.20
39	Bob Fallon	.10
40	Brian Fisher	.10
41	Mike Fitzgerald	.10
42	Ray Fontenot	.10
43	Greg Gagne	.25
44	Oscar Gamble	.10
45	Jim Gott	.10
46	David Green	.10
47	Alfredo Griffin	.10
48	*Ozzie Guillen*	1.00
49	Toby Harrah	.10
50	Ron Hassey	.10
51	Rickey Henderson	3.00
52	Steve Henderson	.10
53	George Hendrick	.10
54	Teddy Higuera	.10
55	Al Holland	.10
56	Burt Hooton	.10
57	Jay Howell	.10
58	LaMarr Hoyt	.10
59	Tim Hulett	.10
60	Bob James	.10
61	Cliff Johnson	.10
62	Howard Johnson	.15
63	Ruppert Jones	.10
64	Steve Kemp	.10
65	Bruce Kison	.10
66	Mike LaCoss	.10
67	Lee Lacy	.10
68	Dave LaPoint	.10
69	Gary Lavelle	.10
70	Vance Law	.10
71	Manny Lee	.10
72	Sixto Lezcano	.10
73	Tim Lollar	.10
74	Urbano Lugo	.10
75	Fred Lynn	.25
76	Steve Lyons	.15
77	Mickey Mahler	.10
78	Ron Mathis	.10
79	Len Matuszek	.10
80	Oddibe McDowell	.10
81	Roger McDowell	.20
82	Donnie Moore	.10
83	Ron Musselman	.10
84	Al Oliver	.15
85	Joe Orsulak	.10
86	Dan Pasqua	.20
87	Chris Pittaro	.10
88	Rick Reuschel	.10
89	Earnie Riles	.10
90	Jerry Royster	.10
91	Dave Rozema	.10
92	Dave Rucker	.10
93	Vern Ruhle	.10
94	Mark Salas	.10
95	Luis Salazar	.10
96	Joe Sambito	.10
97	Billy Sample	.10
98	Alex Sanchez	.10
99	Calvin Schiraldi	.10
100	Rick Schu	.10
101	Larry Sheets	.10
102	Ron Shepherd	.10
103	Nelson Simmons	.10
104	Don Slaught	.10
105	Roy Smalley	.10
106	Lonnie Smith	.10
107	Nate Snell	.10
108	Lary Sorensen	.10
109	Chris Speier	.10
110	Mike Stenhouse	.10
111	Tim Stoddard	.10
112	John Stuper	.10
113	Jim Sundberg	.10
114	Bruce Sutter	.10
115	Don Sutton	.75
116	Bruce Tanner	.10
117	Kent Tekulve	.10
118	Walt Terrell	.10
119	*Mickey Tettleton*	2.00
120	Rich Thompson	.10
121	Louis Thornton	.10
122	Alex Trevino	.10
123	John Tudor	.10
124	Jose Uribe	.10
125	Dave Valle	.10
126	Dave Von Ohlen	.10
127	Curt Wardle	.10
128	U.L. Washington	.10
129	Ed Whitson	.10
130	Herm Winningham	.10
131	Rich Yett	.10
132	Checklist	.10

1986 Fleer

The 1986 Fleer set contains 660 color cards measuring 2-1/2" x 3-1/2". The card fronts feature a player photo enclosed by a dark blue border. The card backs are minus the black-and-white photo that was included in past Fleer efforts. Player biographical and statistical information appear in black and yellow on white stock. As in 1985, Fleer devoted ten cards, entitled "Major League Prospects," to twenty promising rookie players. The 1986 set, as in the previous four years was issued with team logo stickers.

		MT
Complete Set (660):		25.00
Unopened Factory Set (660):		35.00
Common Player:		.08
Wax Pack:		1.50
Wax Box (36):		50.00
1	Steve Balboni	.08
2	Joe Beckwith	.08
3	Buddy Biancalana	.08
4	Bud Black	.08
5	George Brett	2.00
6	Onix Concepcion	.08
7	Steve Farr	.08
8	Mark Gubicza	.08
9	Dane Iorg	.08
10	Danny Jackson	.08
11	Lynn Jones	.08
12	Mike Jones	.08
13	Charlie Leibrandt	.08
14	Hal McRae	.08
15	Omar Moreno	.08
16	Darryl Motley	.08
17	Jorge Orta	.08
18	Dan Quisenberry	.08
19	Bret Saberhagen	.15
20	Pat Sheridan	.08
21	Lonnie Smith	.08
22	Jim Sundberg	.08
23	John Wathan	.08
24	Frank White	.08
25	Willie Wilson	.08
26	Joaquin Andujar	.08
27	Steve Braun	.08
28	Bill Campbell	.08
29	Cesar Cedeno	.08
30	Jack Clark	.08
31	Vince Coleman	.10
32	Danny Cox	.08
33	Ken Dayley	.08
34	Ivan DeJesus	.08
35	Bob Forsch	.08
36	Brian Harper	.08
37	Tom Herr	.08
38	Ricky Horton	.08
39	Kurt Kepshire	.08
40	Jeff Lahti	.08
41	Tito Landrum	.08
42	Willie McGee	.08
43	Tom Nieto	.08
44	Terry Pendleton	.08
45	Darrell Porter	.08
46	Ozzie Smith	1.00
47	John Tudor	.08
48	Andy Van Slyke	.08
49	*Todd Worrell*	.35
50	Jim Acker	.08
51	Doyle Alexander	.08
52	Jesse Barfield	.08
53	George Bell	.08
54	Jeff Burroughs	.08
55	Bill Caudill	.08
56	Jim Clancy	.08
57	Tony Fernandez	.08
58	Tom Filer	.08
59	Damaso Garcia	.08
60	Tom Henke	.08
61	Garth Iorg	.08
62	Cliff Johnson	.08
63	Jimmy Key	.08
64	Dennis Lamp	.08
65	Gary Lavelle	.08
66	Buck Martinez	.08
67	Lloyd Moseby	.08
68	Rance Mulliniks	.08
69	Al Oliver	.08
70	Dave Stieb	.08
71	Louis Thornton	.08
72	Willie Upshaw	.08
73	Ernie Whitt	.08
74	*Rick Aguilera*	1.00
75	Wally Backman	.08
76	Gary Carter	.50
77	Ron Darling	.08
78	*Len Dykstra*	2.00
79	Sid Fernandez	.08
80	George Foster	.08
81	Dwight Gooden	.15
82	Tom Gorman	.08
83	Danny Heep	.08
84	Keith Hernandez	.08
85	Howard Johnson	.08
86	Ray Knight	.08
87	Terry Leach	.08
88	Ed Lynch	.08
89	Roger McDowell	.10
90	Jesse Orosco	.08
91	Tom Paciorek	.08
92	Ronn Reynolds	.08
93	Rafael Santana	.08
94	Doug Sisk	.08
95	Rusty Staub	.10
96	Darryl Strawberry	.15
97	Mookie Wilson	.08
98	Neil Allen	.08
99	Don Baylor	.15
100	Dale Berra	.08
101	Rich Bordi	.08
102	Marty Bystrom	.08
103	Joe Cowley	.08
104	*Brian Fisher*	.08
105	Ken Griffey	.08
106	Ron Guidry	.10
107	Ron Hassey	.08
108	Rickey Henderson	1.00
109	Don Mattingly	1.50
110	Bobby Meacham	.08
111	John Montefusco	.08
112	Phil Niekro	.75
113	Mike Pagliarulo	.08
114	Dan Pasqua	.08
115	Willie Randolph	.08
116	Dave Righetti	.08
117	Andre Robertson	.08
118	Billy Sample	.08
119	Bob Shirley	.08
120	Ed Whitson	.08
121	Dave Winfield	1.00
122	Butch Wynegar	.08
123	Dave Anderson	.08
124	Bob Bailor	.08
125	Greg Brock	.08
126	Enos Cabell	.08
127	Bobby Castillo	.08
128	Carlos Diaz	.08
129	Mariano Duncan	.10
130	Pedro Guerrero	.08
131	Orel Hershiser	.15
132	Rick Honeycutt	.08
133	Ken Howell	.08
134	Ken Landreaux	.08
135	Bill Madlock	.08
136	Candy Maldonado	.08
137	Mike Marshall	.08
138	Len Matuszek	.08
139	Tom Niedenfuer	.08
140	Alejandro Pena	.08
141	Jerry Reuss	.08
142	Bill Russell	.08
143	Steve Sax	.08
144	Mike Scioscia	.08
145	Fernando Valenzuela	.08
146	Bob Welch	.08
147	Terry Whitfield	.08
148	Juan Beniquez	.08
149	Bob Boone	.10
150	John Candelaria	.08
151	Rod Carew	1.00
152	*Stewart Cliburn*	.08
153	Doug DeCinces	.08
154	Brian Downing	.08
155	Ken Forsch	.08
156	Craig Gerber	.08
157	Bobby Grich	.08
158	George Hendrick	.08
159	Al Holland	.08
160	Reggie Jackson	1.00
161	Ruppert Jones	.08
162	*Urbano Lugo*	.08
163	*Kirk McCaskill*	.25
164	Donnie Moore	.08
165	Gary Pettis	.08
166	Ron Romanick	.08
167	Dick Schofield	.08
168	Daryl Sconiers	.08
169	Jim Slaton	.08
170	Don Sutton	.75

171	Mike Witt	.08
172	Buddy Bell	.08
173	Tom Browning	.08
174	Dave Concepcion	.08
175	Eric Davis	.25
176	Bo Diaz	.08
177	Nick Esasky	.08
178	John Franco	.08
179	Tom Hume	.08
180	Wayne Krenchicki	.08
181	Andy McGaffigan	.08
182	Eddie Milner	.08
183	Ron Oester	.08
184	Dave Parker	.10
185	Frank Pastore	.08
186	Tony Perez	1.00
187	Ted Power	.08
188	Joe Price	.08
189	Gary Redus	.08
190	Ron Robinson	.08
191	Pete Rose	2.00
192	Mario Soto	.08
193	John Stuper	.08
194	Jay Tibbs	.08
195	Dave Van Gorder	.08
196	Max Venable	.08
197	Juan Agosto	.08
198	Harold Baines	.10
199	Floyd Bannister	.08
200	Britt Burns	.08
201	Julio Cruz	.08
202	*Joel Davis*	.08
203	Richard Dotson	.08
204	Carlton Fisk	1.00
205	Scott Fletcher	.08
206	Ozzie Guillen	.15
207	Jerry Hairston Sr.	.08
208	Tim Hulett	.08
209	Bob James	.08
210	Ron Kittle	.08
211	Rudy Law	.08
212	Bryan Little	.08
213	Gene Nelson	.08
214	Reid Nichols	.08
215	Luis Salazar	.08
216	Tom Seaver	1.00
217	Dan Spillner	.08
218	Bruce Tanner	.08
219	Greg Walker	.08
220	Dave Wehrmeister	.08
221	Juan Berenguer	.08
222	Dave Bergman	.08
223	Tom Brookens	.08
224	Darrell Evans	.10
225	Barbaro Garbey	.08
226	Kirk Gibson	.08
227	John Grubb	.08
228	Willie Hernandez	.08
229	Larry Herndon	.08
230	Chet Lemon	.08
231	Aurelio Lopez	.08
232	Jack Morris	.08
233	Randy O'Neal	.08
234	Lance Parrish	.08
235	Dan Petry	.08
236	Alex Sanchez	.08
237	Bill Scherrer	.08
238	Nelson Simmons	.08
239	Frank Tanana	.08
240	Walt Terrell	.08
241	Alan Trammell	.15
242	Lou Whitaker	.08
243	Milt Wilcox	.08
244	Hubie Brooks	.08
245	*Tim Burke*	.10
246	Andre Dawson	.30
247	Mike Fitzgerald	.08
248	Terry Francona	.08
249	Bill Gullickson	.08
250	Joe Hesketh	.08
251	Bill Laskey	.08
252	Vance Law	.08
253	Charlie Lea	.08
254	Gary Lucas	.08
255	David Palmer	.08
256	Tim Raines	.08
257	Jeff Reardon	.08
258	Bert Roberge	.08
259	Dan Schatzeder	.08
260	Bryn Smith	.08
261	Randy St. Claire	.08
262	Scot Thompson	.08
263	Tim Wallach	.08
264	U.L. Washington	.08
265	*Mitch Webster*	.08
266	*Herm Winningham*	.08
267	*Floyd Youmans*	.08
268	Don Aase	.08
269	Mike Boddicker	.08
270	Rich Dauer	.08
271	Storm Davis	.08
272	Rick Dempsey	.08
273	Ken Dixon	.08
274	Jim Dwyer	.08
275	Mike Flanagan	.08
276	Wayne Gross	.08
277	Lee Lacy	.08
278	Fred Lynn	.10
279	Tippy Martinez	.08
280	Dennis Martinez	.08
281	Scott McGregor	.08
282	Eddie Murray	1.00
283	Floyd Rayford	.08
284	Cal Ripken, Jr.	4.00
285	Gary Roenicke	.08
286	Larry Sheets	.08
287	John Shelby	.08
288	Nate Snell	.08
289	Sammy Stewart	.08
290	Alan Wiggins	.08
291	Mike Young	.08
292	Alan Ashby	.08
293	Mark Bailey	.08
294	Kevin Bass	.08
295	Jeff Calhoun	.08
296	Jose Cruz	.08
297	Glenn Davis	.08
298	Bill Dawley	.08
299	Frank DiPino	.08
300	Bill Doran	.08
301	Phil Garner	.08
302	*Jeff Heathcock*	.08
303	*Charlie Kerfeld*	.08
304	Bob Knepper	.08
305	Ron Mathis	.08
306	Jerry Mumphrey	.08
307	Jim Pankovits	.08
308	Terry Puhl	.08
309	Craig Reynolds	.08
310	Nolan Ryan	4.00
311	Mike Scott	.08
312	Dave Smith	.08
313	Dickie Thon	.08
314	Denny Walling	.08
315	Kurt Bevacqua	.08
316	Al Bumbry	.08
317	Jerry Davis	.08
318	Luis DeLeon	.08
319	Dave Dravecky	.08
320	Tim Flannery	.08
321	Steve Garvey	.30
322	Goose Gossage	.08
323	Tony Gwynn	1.50
324	Andy Hawkins	.08
325	LaMarr Hoyt	.08
326	Roy Lee Jackson	.08
327	Terry Kennedy	.08
328	Craig Lefferts	.08
329	Carmelo Martinez	.08
330	*Lance McCullers*	.08
331	Kevin McReynolds	.08
332	Graig Nettles	.08
333	Jerry Royster	.08
334	Eric Show	.08
335	Tim Stoddard	.08
336	Garry Templeton	.08
337	Mark Thurmond	.08
338	Ed Wojna	.08
339	Tony Armas	.08
340	Marty Barrett	.08
341	Wade Boggs	1.00
342	Dennis Boyd	.08
343	Bill Buckner	.10
344	Mark Clear	.08
345	Roger Clemens	3.00
346	Steve Crawford	.08
347	Mike Easler	.08
348	Dwight Evans	.10
349	Rich Gedman	.08
350	Jackie Gutierrez	.08
351	Glenn Hoffman	.08
352	Bruce Hurst	.08
353	Bruce Kison	.08
354	Tim Lollar	.08
355	Steve Lyons	.08
356	Al Nipper	.08
357	Bob Ojeda	.08
358	Jim Rice	.20
359	Bob Stanley	.08
360	Mike Trujillo	.08
361	Thad Bosley	.08
362	Warren Brusstar	.08
363	Ron Cey	.08
364	Jody Davis	.08
365	Bob Dernier	.08
366	Shawon Dunston	.08
367	Leon Durham	.08
368	Dennis Eckersley	.15
369	Ray Fontenot	.08
370	George Frazier	.08
371	Bill Hatcher	.08
372	Dave Lopes	.08
373	Gary Matthews	.08
374	Ron Meredith	.08
375	Keith Moreland	.08
376	Reggie Patterson	.08
377	Dick Ruthven	.08
378	Ryne Sandberg	1.50
379	Scott Sanderson	.08
380	Lee Smith	.10
381	Lary Sorensen	.08
382	Chris Speier	.08
383	Rick Sutcliffe	.08
384	Steve Trout	.08
385	Gary Woods	.08
386	Bert Blyleven	.10
387	Tom Brunansky	.08
388	Randy Bush	.08
389	John Butcher	.08
390	Ron Davis	.08
391	Dave Engle	.08
392	Frank Eufemia	.08
393	Pete Filson	.08
394	Gary Gaetti	.08
395	Greg Gagne	.08
396	Mickey Hatcher	.08
397	Kent Hrbek	.10
398	Tim Laudner	.08
399	Rick Lysander	.08
400	Dave Meier	.08
401	Kirby Puckett	3.00
402	Mark Salas	.08
403	Ken Schrom	.08
404	Roy Smalley	.08
405	Mike Smithson	.08
406	Mike Stenhouse	.08
407	Tim Teufel	.08
408	Frank Viola	.08
409	Ron Washington	.08
410	Keith Atherton	.08
411	Dusty Baker	.10
412	*Tim Birtsas*	.08
413	Bruce Bochte	.08
414	Chris Codiroli	.08
415	Dave Collins	.08
416	Mike Davis	.08
417	Alfredo Griffin	.08
418	Mike Heath	.08
419	Steve Henderson	.08
420	Donnie Hill	.08
421	Jay Howell	.08
422	Tommy John	.10
423	Dave Kingman	.10
424	Bill Krueger	.08
425	Rick Langford	.08
426	Carney Lansford	.08
427	Steve McCatty	.08
428	Dwayne Murphy	.08
429	*Steve Ontiveros*	.08
430	Tony Phillips	.08
431	Jose Rijo	.08
432	Mickey Tettleton	.25
433	Luis Aguayo	.08
434	Larry Andersen	.08
435	Steve Carlton	1.00
436	*Don Carman*	.08
437	Tim Corcoran	.08
438	Darren Daulton	1.00
439	John Denny	.08
440	Tom Foley	.08
441	Greg Gross	.08
442	Kevin Gross	.08
443	Von Hayes	.08
444	Charles Hudson	.08
445	Garry Maddox	.08
446	Shane Rawley	.08
447	Dave Rucker	.08
448	John Russell	.08
449	Juan Samuel	.08
450	Mike Schmidt	2.00
451	Rick Schu	.08
452	Dave Shipanoff	.08
453	Dave Stewart	.10
454	Jeff Stone	.08
455	Kent Tekulve	.08
456	Ozzie Virgil	.08
457	Glenn Wilson	.08
458	Jim Beattie	.08
459	Karl Best	.08
460	Barry Bonnell	.08
461	Phil Bradley	.08
462	*Ivan Calderon*	.08
463	Al Cowens	.08
464	Alvin Davis	.08
465	Dave Henderson	.08
466	Bob Kearney	.08
467	Mark Langston	.10
468	Bob Long	.08
469	Mike Moore	.08
470	Edwin Nunez	.08
471	Spike Owen	.08
472	Jack Perconte	.08
473	Jim Presley	.08
474	Donnie Scott	.08
475	Bill Swift	.08
476	Danny Tartabull	.08
477	Gorman Thomas	.08
478	Roy Thomas	.08
479	Ed Vande Berg	.08
480	Frank Wills	.08
481	Matt Young	.08
482	Ray Burris	.08
483	Jaime Cocanower	.08
484	Cecil Cooper	.08
485	Danny Darwin	.08
486	Rollie Fingers	.75
487	Jim Gantner	.08
488	Bob Gibson	.08
489	Moose Haas	.08
490	*Teddy Higuera*	.08
491	Paul Householder	.08
492	Pete Ladd	.08
493	Rick Manning	.08
494	Bob McClure	.08
495	Paul Molitor	1.00
496	Charlie Moore	.08
497	Ben Oglivie	.08
498	Randy Ready	.08
499	*Earnie Riles*	.08
500	Ed Romero	.08
501	Bill Schroeder	.08
502	Ray Searage	.08
503	Ted Simmons	.08
504	Pete Vuckovich	.08
505	Rick Waits	.08
506	Robin Yount	1.00
507	Len Barker	.08
508	Steve Bedrosian	.08
509	Bruce Benedict	.08
510	Rick Camp	.08
511	Rick Cerone	.08
512	Chris Chambliss	.08
513	Jeff Dedmon	.08
514	Terry Forster	.08
515	Gene Garber	.08
516	Terry Harper	.08
517	Bob Horner	.08
518	Glenn Hubbard	.08
519	*Joe Johnson*	.08
520	Brad Komminsk	.08
521	Rick Mahler	.08
522	Dale Murphy	.35
523	Ken Oberkfell	.08
524	Pascual Perez	.08
525	Gerald Perry	.08
526	Rafael Ramirez	.08
527	*Steve Shields*	.08
528	Zane Smith	.08
529	Bruce Sutter	.08
530	*Milt Thompson*	.10
531	Claudell Washington	.08
532	Paul Zuvella	.08
533	Vida Blue	.08
534	Bob Brenly	.08
535	*Chris Brown*	.08
536	Chili Davis	.08
537	Mark Davis	.08
538	Rob Deer	.08
539	Dan Driessen	.08
540	Scott Garrelts	.08
541	Dan Gladden	.08
542	Jim Gott	.08
543	David Green	.08
544	Atlee Hammaker	.08
545	Mike Jeffcoat	.08
546	Mike Krukow	.08
547	Dave LaPoint	.08
548	Jeff Leonard	.08
549	Greg Minton	.08
550	Alex Trevino	.08
551	Manny Trillo	.08
552	*Jose Uribe*	.08
553	Brad Wellman	.08
554	Frank Williams	.08

555	Joel Youngblood	.08
556	Alan Bannister	.08
557	Glenn Brummer	.08
558	*Steve Buechele*	.10
559	*Jose Guzman*	.08
560	Toby Harrah	.08
561	Greg Harris	.08
562	*Dwayne Henry*	.08
563	Burt Hooton	.08
564	Charlie Hough	.08
565	Mike Mason	.08
566	*Oddibe McDowell*	.08
567	Dickie Noles	.08
568	Pete O'Brien	.08
569	Larry Parrish	.08
570	Dave Rozema	.08
571	Dave Schmidt	.08
572	Don Slaught	.08
573	Wayne Tolleson	.08
574	Duane Walker	.08
575	Gary Ward	.08
576	Chris Welsh	.08
577	Curtis Wilkerson	.08
578	George Wright	.08
579	Chris Bando	.08
580	Tony Bernazard	.08
581	Brett Butler	.08
582	Ernie Camacho	.08
583	Joe Carter	.15
584	Carmello Castillo (Carmelo)	.08
585	Jamie Easterly	.08
586	Julio Franco	.08
587	Mel Hall	.08
588	Mike Hargrove	.08
589	Neal Heaton	.08
590	Brook Jacoby	.08
591	*Otis Nixon*	.25
592	Jerry Reed	.08
593	Vern Ruhle	.08
594	Pat Tabler	.08
595	Rich Thompson	.08
596	Andre Thornton	.08
597	Dave Von Ohlen	.08
598	George Vukovich	.08
599	Tom Waddell	.08
600	Curt Wardle	.08
601	Jerry Willard	.08
602	Bill Almon	.08
603	Mike Bielecki	.08
604	Sid Bream	.08
605	Mike Brown	.08
606	*Pat Clements*	.08
607	Jose DeLeon	.08
608	Denny Gonzalez	.08
609	Cecilio Guante	.08
610	Steve Kemp	.08
611	Sam Khalifa	.08
612	Lee Mazzilli	.08
613	Larry McWilliams	.08
614	Jim Morrison	.08
615	*Joe Orsulak*	.25
616	Tony Pena	.08
617	Johnny Ray	.08
618	Rick Reuschel	.08
619	R.J. Reynolds	.08
620	Rick Rhoden	.08
621	Don Robinson	.08
622	Jason Thompson	.08
623	Lee Tunnell	.08
624	Jim Winn	.08
625	Marvell Wynne	.08
626	Dwight Gooden (In Action)	.10
627	Don Mattingly (In Action)	1.00
628	Pete Rose (4,192 hits)	1.00
629	Rod Carew (3,000 Hits)	.25
630	Phil Niekro, Tom Seaver (300 Wins)	.25
631	Ouch! (Don Baylor)	.10
632	Instant Offense (Tim Raines, Darryl Strawberry)	.10
633	Shortstops Supreme (Cal Ripken, Jr., Alan Trammell)	1.00
634	Boggs & "Hero" (Wade Boggs, George Brett)	1.00
635	Braves Dynamic Duo (Bob Horner, Dale Murphy)	.25
636	Cardinal Ignitors (Vince Coleman, Willie McGee)	.25
637	Terror on the Basepaths (Vince Coleman)	.10
638	Charlie Hustle & Dr. K (Dwight Gooden, Pete Rose)	.50
639	1984 and 1985 A.L. Batting Champs (Wade Boggs, Don Mattingly)	1.00
640	N.L. West Sluggers (Steve Garvey, Dale Murphy, Dave Parker)	.25
641	Staff Aces (Dwight Gooden, Fernando Valenzuela)	.10
642	Blue Jay Stoppers (Jimmy Key, Dave Stieb)	.08
643	A.L. All-Star Backstops (Carlton Fisk, Rich Gedman)	.10
644	Major League Prospect (*Benito Santiago*), (*Gene Walter*)	.75
645	Major League Prospect (*Colin Ward*), (*Mike Woodard*)	.10
646	Major League Prospect (*Kal Daniels*), (*Paul O'Neill*)	2.00
647	Major League Prospect (*Andres Galarraga*), (*Fred Toliver*)	3.00
648	Major League Prospect (*Curt Ford*), (*Bob Kipper*)	.10
649	Major League Prospect (*Jose Canseco*), (*Eric Plunk*)	5.00
650	Major League Prospect (*Mark McLemore*), (*Gus Polidor*)	.75
651	Major League Prospect (*Mickey Brantley*), (*Rob Woodward*)	.10
652	Major League Prospect (*Mark Funderburk*), (*Billy Joe Robidoux*)	.10
653	Major League Prospect (*Cecil Fielder*), (*Cory Snyder*)	1.50
654	Checklist 1-97	.08
655	Checklist 98-196	.08
656	Checklist 197-291	.08
657	Checklist 292-385	.08
658	Checklist 386-482	.08
659	Checklist 483-578	.08
660	Checklist 579-660	.08

1986 Fleer All Stars

Fleer's choices for a major league All-Star team make up this 12-card set. The cards were randomly inserted in 35Û wax packs and 59Û cello packs. The card fronts have a color photo set against a bright red background for A.L. players or a bright blue background for N.L. players. Backs feature the player's career highlights on a red and blue background.

		MT
Complete Set (12):		6.00
Common Player:		.10
1	Don Mattingly	1.50
2	Tom Herr	.10
3	George Brett	1.25
4	Gary Carter	.50
5	Cal Ripken, Jr.	4.00
6	Dave Parker	.10
7	Rickey Henderson	1.00
8	Pedro Guerrero	.10
9	Dan Quisenberry	.10
10	Dwight Gooden	.15
11	Gorman Thomas	.10
12	John Tudor	.10

1986 Fleer Box Panels

Picking up on a Donruss idea, Fleer issued eight cards in panels of four on the bottoms of the wax and cello pack boxes. The cards are numbered C-1 through C-8 and are 2-1/2" x 3-1/2", with a complete panel measuring 5" x 7-1/8". Included in the eight cards are six players and two team logo/checklist cards.

		MT
Complete Panel Set (2):		3.00
Complete Singles Set (8):		3.50
Common Single Player:		.20
Panel		2.50
1	Royals logo/ checklist	.05
2	George Brett	1.00
3	Ozzie Guillen	.20
4	Dale Murphy	.40
Panel		1.50
5	Cardinals Logo/ Checklist	.05
6	Tom Browning	.20
7	Gary Carter	.50
8	Carlton Fisk	.75

1986 Fleer Future Hall Of Famers

The 1986 Future Hall of Famers set is comprised of six players Fleer felt would gain eventual entrance into the Baseball Hall of Fame. The cards are the standard 2-1/2" x 3-1/2" and were randomly inserted in three-pack rack packs. Card fronts feature a player photo set against a blue background with horizontal light blue stripes. Backs are printed in black on blue and feature career highlights in narrative form.

		MT
Complete Set (6):		5.00
Common Player:		.75
1	Pete Rose	2.00
2	Steve Carlton	.75
3	Tom Seaver	.75
4	Rod Carew	.75
5	Nolan Ryan	3.00
6	Reggie Jackson	1.00

1986 Fleer Mini

Fleer's 1986 "Classic Miniatures" set contains 120 cards that measure 1-13/16" x 2-9/16". The design of the high-gloss cards is identical to the regular 1986 Fleer set but the player photos are entirely different. The set, which was issued in a specially designed box along with 18 team logo stickers, was available only through hobby dealers.

		MT
Complete Set (120):		3.00
Common Player:		.05
1	George Brett	.75
2	Dan Quisenberry	.05
3	Bret Saberhagen	.05
4	Lonnie Smith	.05
5	Willie Wilson	.05
6	Jack Clark	.05
7	Vince Coleman	.05
8	Tom Herr	.05
9	Willie McGee	.05
10	Ozzie Smith	.50
11	John Tudor	.05
12	Jesse Barfield	.05
13	George Bell	.05
14	Tony Fernandez	.05
15	Damaso Garcia	.05
16	Dave Stieb	.05
17	Gary Carter	.15
18	Ron Darling	.05
19	Dwight Gooden	.05
20	Keith Hernandez	.05
21	Darryl Strawberry	.05

#	Player	MT
22	Ron Guidry	.05
23	Rickey Henderson	.40
24	Don Mattingly	.75
25	Dave Righetti	.05
26	Dave Winfield	.40
27	Mariano Duncan	.05
28	Pedro Guerrero	.05
29	Bill Madlock	.05
30	Mike Marshall	.05
31	Fernando Valenzuela	.05
32	Reggie Jackson	.40
33	Gary Pettis	.05
34	Ron Romanick	.05
35	Don Sutton	.25
36	Mike Witt	.05
37	Buddy Bell	.05
38	Tom Browning	.05
39	Dave Parker	.05
40	Pete Rose	1.00
41	Mario Soto	.05
42	Harold Baines	.05
43	Carlton Fisk	.25
44	Ozzie Guillen	.05
45	Ron Kittle	.05
46	Tom Seaver	.40
47	Kirk Gibson	.05
48	Jack Morris	.05
49	Lance Parrish	.05
50	Alan Trammell	.05
51	Lou Whitaker	.05
52	Hubie Brooks	.05
53	Andre Dawson	.10
54	Tim Raines	.05
55	Bryn Smith	.05
56	Tim Wallach	.05
57	Mike Boddicker	.05
58	Eddie Murray	.35
59	Cal Ripken, Jr.	1.00
60	John Shelby	.05
61	Mike Young	.05
62	Jose Cruz	.05
63	Glenn Davis	.05
64	Phil Garner	.05
65	Nolan Ryan	1.00
66	Mike Scott	.05
67	Steve Garvey	.15
68	Goose Gossage	.05
69	Tony Gwynn	.60
70	Andy Hawkins	.05
71	Garry Templeton	.05
72	Wade Boggs	.35
73	Roger Clemens	.60
74	Dwight Evans	.05
75	Rich Gedman	.05
76	Jim Rice	.10
77	Shawon Dunston	.05
78	Leon Durham	.05
79	Keith Moreland	.05
80	Ryne Sandberg	.60
81	Rick Sutcliffe	.05
82	Bert Blyleven	.05
83	Tom Brunansky	.05
84	Kent Hrbek	.05
85	Kirby Puckett	.75
86	Bruce Bochte	.05
87	Jose Canseco	.40
88	Mike Davis	.05
89	Jay Howell	.05
90	Dwayne Murphy	.05
91	Steve Carlton	.40
92	Von Hayes	.05
93	Juan Samuel	.05
94	Mike Schmidt	.60
95	Glenn Wilson	.05
96	Phil Bradley	.05
97	Alvin Davis	.05
98	Jim Presley	.05
99	Danny Tartabull	.05
100	Cecil Cooper	.05
101	Paul Molitor	.40
102	Earnie Riles	.05
103	Robin Yount	.40
104	Bob Horner	.05
105	Dale Murphy	.20
106	Bruce Sutter	.05
107	Claudell Washington	.05
108	Chris Brown	.05
109	Chili Davis	.05
110	Scott Garrelts	.05
111	Oddibe McDowell	.05
112	Pete O'Brien	.05
113	Gary Ward	.05
114	Brett Butler	.05
115	Julio Franco	.05
116	Brook Jacoby	.05
117	Mike Brown	.05
118	Joe Orsulak	.05
119	Tony Pena	.05
120	R.J. Reynolds	.05

1986 Fleer Star Stickers

Fleer's 1986 sticker-card set again measures 2-1/2" x 3-1/2" and features color photos inside dark maroon borders. Backs are identical to the 1986 baseball card issue except for the 1-132 numbering system and blue ink instead of yellow. Card #132 is a multi-player card featuring Dwight Gooden and Dale Murphy on the front and a complete checklist for the set on the reverse. The cards were sold in wax packs with team logo stickers.

		MT
Complete Set (132):		20.00
Common Player:		.10
1	Harold Baines	.10
2	Jesse Barfield	.10
3	Don Baylor	.15
4	Juan Beniquez	.10
5	Tim Birtsas	.10
6	Bert Blyleven	.10
7	Bruce Bochte	.10
8	Wade Boggs	.75
9	Dennis Boyd	.10
10	Phil Bradley	.10
11	George Brett	2.00
12	Hubie Brooks	.10
13	Chris Brown	.10
14	Tom Browning	.10
15	Tom Brunansky	.10
16	Bill Buckner	.10
17	Britt Burns	.10
18	Brett Butler	.10
19	Jose Canseco	.75
20	Rod Carew	.75
21	Steve Carlton	.75
22	Don Carman	.10
23	Gary Carter	.35
24	Jack Clark	.10
25	Vince Coleman	.10
26	Cecil Cooper	.10
27	Jose Cruz	.10
28	Ron Darling	.10
29	Alvin Davis	.10
30	Jody Davis	.10
31	Mike Davis	.10
32	Andre Dawson	.30
33	Mariano Duncan	.10
34	Shawon Dunston	.10
35	Leon Durham	.10
36	Darrell Evans	.10
37	Tony Fernandez	.10
38	Carlton Fisk	.60
39	John Franco	.10
40	Julio Franco	.10
41	Damaso Garcia	.10
42	Scott Garrelts	.10
43	Steve Garvey	.30
44	Rich Gedman	.10
45	Kirk Gibson	.10
46	Dwight Gooden	.10
47	Pedro Guerrero	.10
48	Ron Guidry	.10
49	Ozzie Guillen	.10
50	Tony Gwynn	1.00
51	Andy Hawkins	.10
52	Von Hayes	.10
53	Rickey Henderson	.75
54	Tom Henke	.10
55	Keith Hernandez	.10
56	Willie Hernandez	.10
57	Tom Herr	.10
58	Orel Hershiser	.10
59	Teddy Higuera	.10
60	Bob Horner	.10
61	Charlie Hough	.10
62	Jay Howell	.10
63	LaMarr Hoyt	.10
64	Kent Hrbek	.10
65	Reggie Jackson	1.00
66	Bob James	.10
67	Dave Kingman	.10
68	Ron Kittle	.10
69	Charlie Leibrandt	.10
70	Fred Lynn	.10
71	Mike Marshall	.10
72	Don Mattingly	1.50
73	Oddibe McDowell	.10
74	Willie McGee	.10
75	Scott McGregor	.10
76	Paul Molitor	.75
77	Donnie Moore	.10
78	Keith Moreland	.10
79	Jack Morris	.10
80	Dale Murphy	.30
81	Eddie Murray	.75
82	Phil Niekro	.50
83	Joe Orsulak	.10
84	Dave Parker	.10
85	Lance Parrish	.10
86	Larry Parrish	.10
87	Tony Pena	.10
88	Gary Pettis	.10
89	Jim Presley	.10
90	Kirby Puckett	1.50
91	Dan Quisenberry	.10
92	Tim Raines	.10
93	Johnny Ray	.10
94	Jeff Reardon	.10
95	Rick Reuschel	.10
96	Jim Rice	.15
97	Dave Righetti	.10
98	Earnie Riles	.10
99	Cal Ripken, Jr.	3.00
100	Ron Romanick	.10
101	Pete Rose	2.00
102	Nolan Ryan	3.00
103	Bret Saberhagen	.10
104	Mark Salas	.10
105	Juan Samuel	.10
106	Ryne Sandberg	.75
107	Mike Schmidt	2.00
108	Mike Scott	.10
109	Tom Seaver	.75
110	Bryn Smith	.10
111	Dave Smith	.10
112	Lee Smith	.10
113	Ozzie Smith	.75
114	Mario Soto	.10
115	Dave Stieb	.10
116	Darryl Strawberry	.10
117	Bruce Sutter	.10
118	Garry Templeton	.10
119	Gorman Thomas	.10
120	Andre Thornton	.10
121	Alan Trammell	.15
122	John Tudor	.10
123	Fernando Valenzuela	.10
124	Frank Viola	.10
125	Gary Ward	.10
126	Lou Whitaker	.10
127	Frank White	.10
128	Glenn Wilson	.10
129	Willie Wilson	.10
130	Dave Winfield	.75
131	Robin Yount	.60
132	Dwight Gooden, Dale Murphy	.20

1986 Fleer Update

Issued near the end of the baseball season, the 1986 Fleer Update set consists of cards numbered U-1 through U-132. The 2-1/2" x 3-1/2" cards are identical in design to the regular 1986 Fleer set. The purpose of the set is to update player trades and include rookies not depicted in the regular issue. The set was issued with team logo stickers in a specially designed box and was available only through hobby dealers.

		MT
Complete Set (132):		30.00
Common Player:		.08
1	Mike Aldrete	.08
2	Andy Allanson	.08
3	Neil Allen	.08
4	Joaquin Andujar	.08
5	Paul Assenmacher	.08
6	Scott Bailes	.08
7	Jay Baller	.08
8	Scott Bankhead	.08
9	Bill Bathe	.08
10	Don Baylor	.25
11	Billy Beane	.08
12	Steve Bedrosian	.08
13	Juan Beniquez	.08
14	*Barry Bonds*	25.00
15	*Bobby Bonilla*	1.00
16	Rich Bordi	.08
17	Bill Campbell	.08
18	Tom Candiotti	.08
19	John Cangelosi	.08
20	Jose Canseco	4.00
21	Chuck Cary	.08
22	Juan Castillo	.08
23	Rick Cerone	.08
24	John Cerutti	.10
25	*Will Clark*	3.00
26	Mark Clear	.08
27	Darnell Coles	.08
28	Dave Collins	.08
29	Tim Conroy	.08
30	Ed Correa	.08
31	Joe Cowley	.08
32	Bill Dawley	.08
33	Rob Deer	.08
34	John Denny	.08
35	Jim DeShaies	.08
36	*Doug Drabek*	1.00
37	Mike Easler	.08
38	Mark Eichhorn	.08
39	Dave Engle	.08
40	Mike Fischlin	.08
41	Scott Fletcher	.08
42	Terry Forster	.08
43	Terry Francona	.08
44	Andres Galarraga	3.00
45	Lee Guetterman	.08
46	Bill Gullickson	.08
47	Jackie Gutierrez	.08
48	Moose Haas	.08
49	Billy Hatcher	.08
50	Mike Heath	.08
51	Guy Hoffman	.08
52	Tom Hume	.08
53	*Pete Incaviglia*	.40
54	Dane Iorg	.08
55	Chris James	.08
56	Stan Javier	.08
57	Tommy John	.15

58	Tracy Jones	.08
59	*Wally Joyner*	1.00
60	Wayne Krenchicki	.08
61	*John Kruk*	1.00
62	Mike LaCoss	.08
63	Pete Ladd	.08
64	Dave LaPoint	.08
65	Mike LaValliere	.20
66	Rudy Law	.08
67	Dennis Leonard	.08
68	Steve Lombardozzi	.08
69	Aurelio Lopez	.08
70	Mickey Mahler	.08
71	Candy Maldonado	.08
72	Roger Mason	.08
73	Greg Mathews	.08
74	Andy McGaffigan	.08
75	Joel McKeon	.08
76	*Kevin Mitchell*	.50
77	Bill Mooneyham	.08
78	Omar Moreno	.08
79	Jerry Mumphrey	.08
80	Al Newman	.08
81	Phil Niekro	.50
82	Randy Niemann	.08
83	Juan Nieves	.08
84	Bob Ojeda	.08
85	Rick Ownbey	.08
86	Tom Paciorek	.08
87	David Palmer	.08
88	Jeff Parrett	.08
89	Pat Perry	.08
90	Dan Plesac	.08
91	Darrell Porter	.08
92	Luis Quinones	.08
93	Rey Quinonez	.08
94	Gary Redus	.08
95	Jeff Reed	.08
96	Bip Roberts	.25
97	Billy Joe Robidoux	.08
98	Gary Roenicke	.08
99	Ron Roenicke	.08
100	Angel Salazar	.08
101	Joe Sambito	.08
102	Billy Sample	.08
103	Dave Schmidt	.08
104	Ken Schrom	.08
105	*Ruben Sierra*	.75
106	Ted Simmons	.08
107	Sammy Stewart	.08
108	Kurt Stillwell	.08
109	Dale Sveum	.08
110	Tim Teufel	.08
111	Bob Tewksbury	.25
112	Andres Thomas	.08
113	Jason Thompson	.08
114	Milt Thompson	.08
115	Rob Thompson	.15
116	Jay Tibbs	.08
117	Fred Toliver	.08
118	Wayne Tolleson	.08
119	Alex Trevino	.08
120	Manny Trillo	.08
121	Ed Vande Berg	.08
122	Ozzie Virgil	.08
123	Tony Walker	.08
124	Gene Walter	.08
125	Duane Ward	.15
126	Jerry Willard	.08
127	Mitch Williams	.15
128	Reggie Williams	.08
129	Bobby Witt	.20
130	Marvell Wynne	.08
131	Steve Yeager	.08
132	Checklist	.05

1987 Fleer

The 1987 Fleer set consists of 660 cards. Fronts feature a graduated blue-to-white border design. The player's name and position appear in the upper-left corner of the card; his team logo is located in the lower-right. Backs are done in blue, red and white and contain an innovative "Pro Scouts Report" feature which rates the player's batting or pitching skills. For the third year in a row, Fleer included its "Major League Prospects" subset. Fleer produced a glossy-finish Collectors Edition set which came housed in a specially-designed tin box. After experiencing a dramatic hike in price during 1987, the glossy set now sells for only a few dollars more than the regular issue.

	MT
Complete Set (660):	35.00
Unopened Factory Set (672):	45.00
Common Player:	.06
Wax Pack (15 - Red Test)	4.00
Wax Box (36 - Red Test):	80.00
Wax Pack (17 - Blue Wr.)	4.25
Wax Box (36 - Blue Wr.)	90.00

1	Rick Aguilera	.06
2	Richard Anderson	.06
3	Wally Backman	.06
4	Gary Carter	.35
5	Ron Darling	.06
6	Len Dykstra	.10
7	*Kevin Elster*	.15
8	Sid Fernandez	.06
9	Dwight Gooden	.10
10	*Ed Hearn*	.06
11	Danny Heep	.06
12	Keith Hernandez	.10
13	Howard Johnson	.06
14	Ray Knight	.06
15	Lee Mazzilli	.06
16	Roger McDowell	.06
17	Kevin Mitchell	.06
18	Randy Niemann	.06
19	Bob Ojeda	.06
20	Jesse Orosco	.06
21	Rafael Santana	.06
22	Doug Sisk	.06
23	Darryl Strawberry	.06
24	Tim Teufel	.06
25	Mookie Wilson	.06
26	Tony Armas	.06
27	Marty Barrett	.06
28	Don Baylor	.15
29	Wade Boggs	1.00
30	Oil Can Boyd	.06
31	Bill Buckner	.10
32	Roger Clemens	1.50
33	Steve Crawford	.06
34	Dwight Evans	.10
35	Rich Gedman	.06
36	Dave Henderson	.06
37	Bruce Hurst	.06
38	Tim Lollar	.06
39	Al Nipper	.06
40	Spike Owen	.06
41	Jim Rice	.20
42	Ed Romero	.06
43	Joe Sambito	.06
44	Calvin Schiraldi	.06
45	Tom Seaver	.75
46	*Jeff Sellers*	.06
47	Bob Stanley	.06
48	Sammy Stewart	.06
49	Larry Andersen	.06
50	Alan Ashby	.06
51	Kevin Bass	.06
52	Jeff Calhoun	.06
53	Jose Cruz	.06
54	Danny Darwin	.06
55	Glenn Davis	.06
56	*Jim Deshaies*	.15
57	Bill Doran	.06
58	Phil Garner	.06
59	Billy Hatcher	.06
60	Charlie Kerfeld	.06
61	Bob Knepper	.06
62	Dave Lopes	.06
63	Aurelio Lopez	.06
64	Jim Pankovits	.06
65	Terry Puhl	.06
66	Craig Reynolds	.06
67	Nolan Ryan	3.00
68	Mike Scott	.06
69	Dave Smith	.06
70	Dickie Thon	.06
71	Tony Walker	.06
72	Denny Walling	.06
73	Bob Boone	.06
74	Rick Burleson	.06
75	John Candelaria	.06
76	Doug Corbett	.06
77	Doug DeCinces	.06
78	Brian Downing	.06
79	*Chuck Finley*	1.00
80	Terry Forster	.06
81	Bobby Grich	.06
82	George Hendrick	.06
83	Jack Howell	.06
84	Reggie Jackson	1.00
85	Ruppert Jones	.06
86	Wally Joyner	.25
87	Gary Lucas	.06
88	Kirk McCaskill	.06
89	Donnie Moore	.06
90	Gary Pettis	.06
91	Vern Ruhle	.06
92	Dick Schofield	.06
93	Don Sutton	.50
94	Rob Wilfong	.06
95	Mike Witt	.06
96	Doug Drabek	.06
97	Mike Easler	.06
98	Mike Fischlin	.06
99	Brian Fisher	.06
100	Ron Guidry	.10
101	Rickey Henderson	.75
102	Tommy John	.10
103	Ron Kittle	.06
104	Don Mattingly	1.50
105	Bobby Meacham	.06
106	Joe Niekro	.06
107	Mike Pagliarulo	.06
108	Dan Pasqua	.06
109	Willie Randolph	.06
110	Dennis Rasmussen	.06
111	Dave Righetti	.06
112	Gary Roenicke	.06
113	Rod Scurry	.06
114	Bob Shirley	.06
115	Joel Skinner	.06
116	Tim Stoddard	.06
117	*Bob Tewksbury*	.50
118	Wayne Tolleson	.06
119	Claudell Washington	.06
120	Dave Winfield	.75
121	Steve Buechele	.06
122	*Ed Correa*	.06
123	Scott Fletcher	.06
124	Jose Guzman	.06
125	Toby Harrah	.06
126	Greg Harris	.06
127	Charlie Hough	.06
128	Pete Incaviglia	.10
129	Mike Mason	.06
130	Oddibe McDowell	.06
131	*Dale Mohorcic*	.06
132	Pete O'Brien	.06
133	Tom Paciorek	.06
134	Larry Parrish	.06
135	Geno Petralli	.06
136	Darrell Porter	.06
137	Jeff Russell	.06
138	Ruben Sierra	.10
139	Don Slaught	.06
140	Gary Ward	.06
141	Curtis Wilkerson	.06
142	*Mitch Williams*	.10
143	*Bobby Witt*	.10
144	Dave Bergman	.06
145	Tom Brookens	.06
146	Bill Campbell	.06
147	*Chuck Cary*	.06
148	Darnell Coles	.06
149	Dave Collins	.06
150	Darrell Evans	.10
151	Kirk Gibson	.06
152	John Grubb	.06
153	Willie Hernandez	.06
154	Larry Herndon	.06
155	*Eric King*	.06
156	Chet Lemon	.06
157	Dwight Lowry	.06
158	Jack Morris	.06
159	Randy O'Neal	.06
160	Lance Parrish	.10
161	Dan Petry	.06
162	Pat Sheridan	.06
163	Jim Slaton	.06
164	Frank Tanana	.06
165	Walt Terrell	.06
166	Mark Thurmond	.06
167	Alan Trammell	.06
168	Lou Whitaker	.06
169	Luis Aguayo	.06
170	Steve Bedrosian	.06
171	Don Carman	.06
172	Darren Daulton	.06
173	Greg Gross	.06
174	Kevin Gross	.06
175	Von Hayes	.06
176	Charles Hudson	.06
177	Tom Hume	.06
178	Steve Jeltz	.06
179	*Mike Maddux*	.06
180	Shane Rawley	.06
181	Gary Redus	.06
182	Ron Roenicke	.06
183	*Bruce Ruffin*	.10
184	John Russell	.06
185	Juan Samuel	.06
186	Dan Schatzeder	.06
187	Mike Schmidt	1.25
188	Rick Schu	.06
189	Jeff Stone	.06
190	Kent Tekulve	.06
191	Milt Thompson	.06
192	Glenn Wilson	.06
193	Buddy Bell	.06
194	Tom Browning	.06
195	Sal Butera	.06
196	Dave Concepcion	.06
197	Kal Daniels	.06
198	Eric Davis	.10
199	John Denny	.06
200	Bo Diaz	.06
201	Nick Esasky	.06
202	John Franco	.06
203	Bill Gullickson	.06
204	*Barry Larkin*	3.00
205	Eddie Milner	.06
206	*Rob Murphy*	.06
207	Ron Oester	.06
208	Dave Parker	.10
209	Tony Perez	.75
210	Ted Power	.06
211	Joe Price	.06
212	Ron Robinson	.06
213	Pete Rose	2.00
214	Mario Soto	.06
215	*Kurt Stillwell*	.06
216	Max Venable	.06
217	Chris Welsh	.06
218	*Carl Willis*	.06
219	Jesse Barfield	.06
220	George Bell	.06
221	Bill Caudill	.06
222	*John Cerutti*	.06
223	Jim Clancy	.06
224	*Mark Eichhorn*	.10
225	Tony Fernandez	.06
226	Damaso Garcia	.06
227	Kelly Gruber	.06
228	Tom Henke	.06
229	Garth Iorg	.06
230	Cliff Johnson	.06
231	Joe Johnson	.06
232	Jimmy Key	.06
233	Dennis Lamp	.06
234	Rick Leach	.06
235	Buck Martinez	.06
236	Lloyd Moseby	.06
237	Rance Mulliniks	.06
238	Dave Stieb	.06
239	Willie Upshaw	.06
240	Ernie Whitt	.06
241	*Andy Allanson*	.06
242	*Scott Bailes*	.06
243	Chris Bando	.06
244	Tony Bernazard	.06

No.	Player	Price
245	John Butcher	.06
246	Brett Butler	.06
247	Ernie Camacho	.06
248	Tom Candiotti	.06
249	Joe Carter	.06
250	Carmen Castillo	.06
251	Julio Franco	.06
252	Mel Hall	.06
253	Brook Jacoby	.06
254	Phil Niekro	.50
255	Otis Nixon	.06
256	Dickie Noles	.06
257	Bryan Oelkers	.06
258	Ken Schrom	.06
259	Don Schulze	.06
260	Cory Snyder	.06
261	Pat Tabler	.06
262	Andre Thornton	.06
263	*Rich Yett*	.06
264	*Mike Aldrete*	.06
265	Juan Berenguer	.06
266	Vida Blue	.06
267	Bob Brenly	.06
268	Chris Brown	.06
269	Will Clark	1.00
270	Chili Davis	.06
271	Mark Davis	.06
272	*Kelly Downs*	.06
273	Scott Garrelts	.06
274	Dan Gladden	.06
275	Mike Krukow	.06
276	*Randy Kutcher*	.06
277	Mike LaCoss	.06
278	Jeff Leonard	.06
279	Candy Maldonado	.06
280	Roger Mason	.06
281	Bob Melvin	.06
282	Greg Minton	.06
283	Jeff Robinson	.06
284	Harry Spilman	.06
285	*Rob Thompson*	.06
286	Jose Uribe	.06
287	Frank Williams	.06
288	Joel Youngblood	.06
289	Jack Clark	.06
290	Vince Coleman	.06
291	Tim Conroy	.06
292	Danny Cox	.06
293	Ken Dayley	.06
294	Curt Ford	.06
295	Bob Forsch	.06
296	Tom Herr	.06
297	Ricky Horton	.06
298	Clint Hurdle	.06
299	Jeff Lahti	.06
300	Steve Lake	.06
301	Tito Landrum	.06
302	*Mike LaValliere*	.06
303	*Greg Mathews*	.06
304	Willie McGee	.06
305	Jose Oquendo	.06
306	Terry Pendleton	.06
307	Pat Perry	.06
308	Ozzie Smith	1.25
309	Ray Soff	.06
310	John Tudor	.06
311	Andy Van Slyke	.06
312	Todd Worrell	.06
313	Dann Bilardello	.06
314	Hubie Brooks	.06
315	Tim Burke	.06
316	Andre Dawson	.25
317	Mike Fitzgerald	.06
318	Tom Foley	.06
319	Andres Galarraga	.15
320	Joe Hesketh	.06
321	Wallace Johnson	.06
322	Wayne Krenchicki	.06
323	Vance Law	.06
324	Dennis Martinez	.06
325	Bob McClure	.06
326	Andy McGaffigan	.06
327	*Al Newman*	.06
328	Tim Raines	.06
329	Jeff Reardon	.06
330	*Luis Rivera*	.06
331	*Bob Sebra*	.06
332	Bryn Smith	.06
333	Jay Tibbs	.06
334	Tim Wallach	.06
335	Mitch Webster	.06
336	Jim Wohlford	.06
337	Floyd Youmans	.06
338	*Chris Bosio*	.25
339	*Glenn Braggs*	.06
340	Rick Cerone	.06
341	Mark Clear	.06
342	*Bryan Clutterbuck*	.06
343	Cecil Cooper	.06
344	Rob Deer	.06
345	Jim Gantner	.06
346	Ted Higuera	.06
347	John Henry Johnson	.06
348	Tim Leary	.06
349	Rick Manning	.06
350	Paul Molitor	.75
351	Charlie Moore	.06
352	Juan Nieves	.06
353	Ben Oglivie	.06
354	*Dan Plesac*	.10
355	Ernest Riles	.06
356	Billy Joe Robidoux	.06
357	Bill Schroeder	.06
358	*Dale Sveum*	.06
359	Gorman Thomas	.06
360	Bill Wegman	.10
361	Robin Yount	.75
362	Steve Balboni	.06
363	*Scott Bankhead*	.06
364	Buddy Biancalana	.06
365	Bud Black	.06
366	George Brett	1.50
367	Steve Farr	.06
368	Mark Gubicza	.06
369	Bo Jackson	.75
370	Danny Jackson	.06
371	*Mike Kingery*	.06
372	Rudy Law	.06
373	Charlie Leibrandt	.06
374	Dennis Leonard	.06
375	Hal McRae	.06
376	Jorge Orta	.06
377	Jamie Quirk	.06
378	Dan Quisenberry	.06
379	Bret Saberhagen	.06
380	Angel Salazar	.06
381	Lonnie Smith	.06
382	Jim Sundberg	.06
383	Frank White	.06
384	Willie Wilson	.06
385	Joaquin Andujar	.06
386	Doug Bair	.06
387	Dusty Baker	.10
388	Bruce Bochte	.06
389	Jose Canseco	.75
390	Chris Codiroli	.06
391	Mike Davis	.06
392	Alfredo Griffin	.06
393	Moose Haas	.06
394	Donnie Hill	.06
395	Jay Howell	.06
396	Dave Kingman	.10
397	Carney Lansford	.06
398	*David Leiper*	.06
399	*Bill Mooneyham*	.06
400	Dwayne Murphy	.06
401	Steve Ontiveros	.06
402	Tony Phillips	.06
403	Eric Plunk	.06
404	Jose Rijo	.06
405	*Terry Steinbach*	.50
406	Dave Stewart	.10
407	Mickey Tettleton	.06
408	Dave Von Ohlen	.06
409	Jerry Willard	.06
410	Curt Young	.06
411	Bruce Bochy	.06
412	Dave Dravecky	.06
413	Tim Flannery	.06
414	Steve Garvey	.35
415	Goose Gossage	.10
416	Tony Gwynn	1.50
417	Andy Hawkins	.06
418	LaMarr Hoyt	.06
419	Terry Kennedy	.06
420	John Kruk	.10
421	Dave LaPoint	.06
422	Craig Lefferts	.06
423	Carmelo Martinez	.06
424	Lance McCullers	.06
425	Kevin McReynolds	.06
426	Graig Nettles	.06
427	Bip Roberts	.15
428	Jerry Royster	.06
429	Benito Santiago	.06
430	Eric Show	.06
431	Bob Stoddard	.06
432	Garry Templeton	.06
433	Gene Walter	.06
434	Ed Whitson	.06
435	Marvell Wynne	.06
436	Dave Anderson	.06
437	Greg Brock	.06
438	Enos Cabell	.06
439	Mariano Duncan	.06
440	Pedro Guerrero	.06
441	Orel Hershiser	.10
442	Rick Honeycutt	.06
443	Ken Howell	.06
444	Ken Landreaux	.06
445	Bill Madlock	.06
446	Mike Marshall	.06
447	Len Matuszek	.06
448	Tom Niedenfuer	.06
449	Alejandro Pena	.06
450	Dennis Powell	.06
451	Jerry Reuss	.06
452	Bill Russell	.06
453	Steve Sax	.06
454	Mike Scioscia	.06
455	Franklin Stubbs	.06
456	Alex Trevino	.06
457	Fernando Valenzuela	.06
458	Ed Vande Berg	.06
459	Bob Welch	.06
460	*Reggie Williams*	.06
461	Don Aase	.06
462	Juan Beniquez	.06
463	Mike Boddicker	.06
464	Juan Bonilla	.06
465	Rich Bordi	.06
466	Storm Davis	.06
467	Rick Dempsey	.06
468	Ken Dixon	.06
469	Jim Dwyer	.06
470	Mike Flanagan	.06
471	Jackie Gutierrez	.06
472	Brad Havens	.06
473	Lee Lacy	.06
474	Fred Lynn	.10
475	Scott McGregor	.06
476	Eddie Murray	.75
477	Tom O'Malley	.06
478	Cal Ripken, Jr.	3.00
479	Larry Sheets	.06
480	John Shelby	.06
481	Nate Snell	.06
482	Jim Traber	.06
483	Mike Young	.06
484	Neil Allen	.06
485	Harold Baines	.06
486	Floyd Bannister	.06
487	Daryl Boston	.06
488	Ivan Calderon	.06
489	*John Cangelosi*	.06
490	Steve Carlton	.75
491	Joe Cowley	.06
492	Julio Cruz	.06
493	Bill Dawley	.06
494	Jose DeLeon	.06
495	Richard Dotson	.06
496	Carlton Fisk	.75
497	Ozzie Guillen	.06
498	Jerry Hairston Sr.	.06
499	Ron Hassey	.06
500	Tim Hulett	.06
501	Bob James	.06
502	Steve Lyons	.06
503	*Joel McKeon*	.06
504	Gene Nelson	.06
505	Dave Schmidt	.06
506	Ray Searage	.06
507	*Bobby Thigpen*	.15
508	Greg Walker	.06
509	Jim Acker	.06
510	Doyle Alexander	.06
511	*Paul Assenmacher*	.06
512	Bruce Benedict	.06
513	Chris Chambliss	.06
514	Jeff Dedmon	.06
515	Gene Garber	.06
516	Ken Griffey	.06
517	Terry Harper	.06
518	Bob Horner	.06
519	Glenn Hubbard	.06
520	Rick Mahler	.06
521	Omar Moreno	.06
522	Dale Murphy	.35
523	Ken Oberkfell	.06
524	Ed Olwine	.06
525	David Palmer	.06
526	Rafael Ramirez	.06
527	Billy Sample	.06
528	Ted Simmons	.06
529	Zane Smith	.06
530	Bruce Sutter	.06
531	*Andres Thomas*	.06
532	Ozzie Virgil	.06
533	*Allan Anderson*	.06
534	Keith Atherton	.06
535	Billy Beane	.06
536	Bert Blyleven	.10
537	Tom Brunansky	.06
538	Randy Bush	.06
539	George Frazier	.06
540	Gary Gaetti	.06
541	Greg Gagne	.06
542	Mickey Hatcher	.06
543	Neal Heaton	.06
544	Kent Hrbek	.06
545	Roy Lee Jackson	.06
546	Tim Laudner	.06
547	Steve Lombardozzi	.06
548	*Mark Portugal*	.20
549	Kirby Puckett	1.50
550	Jeff Reed	.06
551	Mark Salas	.06
552	Roy Smalley	.06
553	Mike Smithson	.06
554	Frank Viola	.06
555	Thad Bosley	.06
556	Ron Cey	.06
557	Jody Davis	.06
558	Ron Davis	.06
559	Bob Dernier	.06
560	Frank DiPino	.06
561	Shawon Dunston	.06
562	Leon Durham	.06
563	Dennis Eckersley	.15
564	Terry Francona	.06
565	Dave Gumpert	.06
566	Guy Hoffman	.06
567	Ed Lynch	.06
568	Gary Matthews	.06
569	Keith Moreland	.06
570	*Jamie Moyer*	.06
571	Jerry Mumphrey	.06
572	Ryne Sandberg	1.00
573	Scott Sanderson	.06
574	Lee Smith	.10
575	Chris Speier	.06
576	Rick Sutcliffe	.06
577	Manny Trillo	.06
578	Steve Trout	.06
579	Karl Best	.06
580	Scott Bradley	.06
581	Phil Bradley	.06
582	Mickey Brantley	.06
583	Mike Brown	.06
584	Alvin Davis	.06
585	*Lee Guetterman*	.06
586	Mark Huismann	.06
587	Bob Kearney	.06
588	Pete Ladd	.06
589	Mark Langston	.06
590	Mike Moore	.06
591	Mike Morgan	.06
592	John Moses	.06
593	Ken Phelps	.06
594	Jim Presley	.06
595	*Rey Quinonez (Quinones)*	.06
596	Harold Reynolds	.06
597	Billy Swift	.06
598	Danny Tartabull	.05
599	Steve Yeager	.06
600	Matt Young	.06
601	Bill Almon	.06
602	*Rafael Belliard*	.06
603	Mike Bielecki	.06
604	Barry Bonds	45.00
605	Bobby Bonilla	.25
606	Sid Bream	.06
607	Mike Brown	.06
608	Pat Clements	.06
609	*Mike Diaz*	.06
610	Cecillo Guante	.06
611	*Barry Jones*	.06
612	Bob Kipper	.06
613	Larry McWilliams	.06
614	Jim Morrison	.06
615	Joe Orsulak	.06
616	Junior Ortiz	.06
617	Tony Pena	.06
618	Johnny Ray	.06
619	Rick Reuschel	.06
620	R.J. Reynolds	.06
621	Rick Rhoden	.06
622	Don Robinson	.06
623	Bob Walk	.06
624	Jim Winn	.06
625	Youthful Power (Jose Canseco, Pete Incaviglia)	.15

626 300 Game Winners (Phil Niekro, Don Sutton) .25
627 A.L. Firemen (Don Aase, Dave Righetti) .06
628 Rookie All-Stars (Jose Canseco, Wally Joyner) .15
629 Magic Mets (Gary Carter, Dwight Gooden, Keith Hernandez, Darryl Strawberry) .15
630 N.L. Best Righties (Mike Krukow, Mike Scott) .06
631 Sensational Southpaws (John Franco, Fernando Valenzuela) .06
632 Count 'Em (Bob Horner) .06
633 A.L. Pitcher's Nightmare (Jose Canseco, Kirby Puckett, Jim Rice) .25
634 All Star Battery (Gary Carter, Roger Clemens) .25
635 4,000 Strikeouts (Steve Carlton) .15
636 Big Bats At First Sack (Glenn Davis, Eddie Murray) .15
637 On Base (Wade Boggs, Keith Hernandez) .15
638 Sluggers From Left Side (Don Mattingly, Darryl Strawberry) .35
639 Former MVP's (Dave Parker, Ryne Sandberg) .10
640 Dr. K. & Super K (Roger Clemens, Dwight Gooden) .50
641 A.L. West Stoppers (Charlie Hough, Mike Witt) .06
642 Doubles & Triples (Tim Raines, Juan Samuel) .06
643 Outfielders With Punch (Harold Baines, Jesse Barfield) .06
644 Major League Prospects *(Dave Clark)*, *(Greg Swindell)* .35
645 Major League Prospects *(Ron Karkovice)*, *(Russ Morman)* .25
646 Major League Prospects *(Willie Fraser)*, *(Devon White)* 1.00
647 Major League Prospects *(Jerry Browne)*, *(Mike Stanley)* .25
648 Major League Prospects *(Phil Lombardi)*, *(Dave Magadan)* .20
649 Major League Prospects *(Ralph Bryant)*, *(Jose Gonzalez)* .10
650 Major League Prospects *(Randy Asadoor)*, *(Jimmy Jones)* .10
651 Major League Prospects *(Marvin Freeman)*, *(Tracy Jones)* .10
652 Major League Prospects *(Kevin Seitzer*, John Stefero) .25
653 Major League Prospects *(Steve Fireovid)*, *(Rob Nelson)* .10
654 Checklist 1-95 .06
655 Checklist 96-192 .06
656 Checklist 193-288 .06
657 Checklist 289-384 .06
658 Checklist 385-483 .06
659 Checklist 484-578 .06
660 Checklist 579-660 .06

1987 Fleer Glossy Tin

The three-year run of limited edition, glossy collectors' issues by Fleer from 1987-89 has become known to the hobby as "tins" for the colorful lithographed metal boxes in which complete sets were sold. In their debut year a reported 100,000 sets were made, each serial numbered on a sticker attached to the shrink-wrapped tin box. While the glossy version of the 1987 Fleer set once enjoyed a significant premium over regular cards, today that premium has evaporated and, indeed, it can be harder to find a buyer for the glossy version.

	MT
Complete Set (672):	60.00
Common Player:	.10

(Single star cards valued at .75-1X regular-issue 1987 Fleer.)

1987 Fleer All Stars

As in 1986, Fleer All Star Team cards were randomly inserted in wax and cello packs. Twelve cards, measuring the standard 2-1/2" x 3-1/2", comprise the set. Fronts feature a full-color player photo set against a gray background for American League players and a black background for National Leaguers. Backs are printed in black, red and white and feature a lengthy player biography. Fleer's choices for a major league All-Star team is once again the theme for the set.

		MT
Complete Set (12):		7.50
Common Player:		.15
1	Don Mattingly	2.00
2	Gary Carter	.60
3	Tony Fernandez	.15
4	Steve Sax	.15
5	Kirby Puckett	1.50
6	Mike Schmidt	1.50
7	Mike Easler	.15
8	Todd Worrell	.15
9	George Bell	.15
10	Fernando Valenzuela	.15
11	Roger Clemens	1.50
12	Tim Raines	.15

1987 Fleer Headliners

A continuation of the 1986 Future Hall of Famers idea, Fleer encountered legal problems with using the Hall of Fame name and abated them by entitling the set "Headliners." The cards were randomly inserted in three-pack rack packs. Fronts feature a player photo set against a beige background with bright red stripes. Backs are printed in black, red and gray and offer a brief biography with an emphasis on the player's performance during the 1986 season.

		MT
Complete Set (6):		5.00
Common Player:		.50
1	Wade Boggs	1.50
2	Jose Canseco	1.50
3	Dwight Gooden	.50
4	Rickey Henderson	1.50
5	Keith Hernandez	.50
6	Jim Rice	.75

1987 Fleer '86 World Series

Fleer issued a set of 12 cards highlighting the 1986 World Series between the Boston Red Sox and New York Mets. The sets were available only with Fleer factory sets, both regular and glossy. The cards, 2-1/2" x 3-1/2", have either horizontal or vertical formats. The fronts are bordered in red, white and blue stars and stripes with a thin gold frame around the photo. Backs are printed in red and blue on white stock and include information regarding the photo on the card fronts.

		MT
Complete Set, Regular (12):		2.00
Complete Set, Glossy (12):		2.00
Common Card:		.25
1	Left-Hand Finesse Beats Mets (Bruce Hurst)	.25
2	Wade Boggs, Keith Hernandez	.50
3	Roger Clemens	.75
4	Gary Carter	.35
5	Ron Darling	.25
6	.433 Series Batting Average (Marty Barrett)	.25
7	Dwight Gooden	.35
8	Strategy At Work	.25
9	Dewey! (Dwight Evans)	.25
10	One Strike From Boston Victory (Dave Henderson, Spike Owen)	.25
11	Ray Knight, Darryl Strawberry	.25
12	Series M.V.P. (Ray Knight)	.25

1987 Fleer Box Panels

For the second straight year, Fleer produced a special set of cards designed to stimulate sales of their wax and cello pack boxes. In 1987, Fleer issued 16 cards in panels of four on the bottoms of retail boxes. The cards are numbered C-1 through C-16 and are 2-1/2" x 3-1/2" in size. The cards have the same design as the regular issue set with the player photos and card numbers being different.

		MT
Complete Panel Set (4):		6.00
Complete Singles Set (16):		6.00
Common Panel:		2.00
Common Single Player:		.15
Panel		2.50
1	Mets Logo	.05
6	Keith Hernandez	.25
8	Dale Murphy	.45
14	Ryne Sandberg	.75
Panel		2.25
2	Jesse Barfield	.15
3	George Brett	1.00
5	Red Sox Logo	.05
11	Kirby Puckett	1.00
Panel		2.75
4	Dwight Gooden	.20
9	Astros Logo	.05
10	Dave Parker	.15
15	Mike Schmidt	1.00
Panel		2.50
7	Wally Joyner	.25
12	Dave Righetti	.15
13	Angels Logo	.05
16	Robin Yount	.75

1987 Fleer Mini

Continuing with an idea originated the previous

year, the Fleer "Classic Miniatures" set consists of 120 cards that measure 1-13/16" x 2-9/16". The cards are identical in design to the regular-issue set, but use completely different photos. The set was issued in a specially prepared collectors box along with 18 team logo stickers. The mini set was available only through hobby dealers.

		MT
Complete Set (120):		5.00
Common Player:		.05
1	Don Aase	.05
2	Joaquin Andujar	.05
3	Harold Baines	.10
4	Jesse Barfield	.05
5	Kevin Bass	.05
6	Don Baylor	.10
7	George Bell	.05
8	Tony Bernazard	.05
9	Bert Blyleven	.05
10	Wade Boggs	.75
11	Phil Bradley	.05
12	Sid Bream	.05
13	George Brett	1.00
14	Hubie Brooks	.05
15	Chris Brown	.05
16	Tom Candiotti	.05
17	Jose Canseco	.60
18	Gary Carter	.25
19	Joe Carter	.05
20	Roger Clemens	1.00
21	Vince Coleman	.05
22	Cecil Cooper	.05
23	Ron Darling	.05
24	Alvin Davis	.05
25	Chili Davis	.05
26	Eric Davis	.10
27	Glenn Davis	.05
28	Mike Davis	.05
29	Doug DeCinces	.05
30	Rob Deer	.05
31	Jim Deshaies	.05
32	Bo Diaz	.05
33	Richard Dotson	.05
34	Brian Downing	.05
35	Shawon Dunston	.05
36	Mark Eichhorn	.05
37	Dwight Evans	.05
38	Tony Fernandez	.05
39	Julio Franco	.05
40	Gary Gaetti	.05
41	Andres Galarraga	.05
42	Scott Garrelts	.05
43	Steve Garvey	.15
44	Kirk Gibson	.05
45	Dwight Gooden	.10
46	Ken Griffey	.05
47	Mark Gubicza	.05
48	Ozzie Guillen	.05
49	Bill Gullickson	.05
50	Tony Gwynn	1.00
51	Von Hayes	.05
52	Rickey Henderson	.60
53	Keith Hernandez	.05
54	Willie Hernandez	.05
55	Ted Higuera	.05
56	Charlie Hough	.05
57	Kent Hrbek	.05
58	Pete Incaviglia	.05
59	Wally Joyner	.05
60	Bob Knepper	.05
61	Mike Krukow	.05
62	Mark Langston	.05
63	Carney Lansford	.05
64	Jim Lindeman	.05
65	Bill Madlock	.05
66	Don Mattingly	1.00
67	Kirk McCaskill	.05
68	Lance McCullers	.05
69	Keith Moreland	.05
70	Jack Morris	.05
71	Jim Morrison	.05
72	Lloyd Moseby	.05
73	Jerry Mumphrey	.05
74	Dale Murphy	.15
75	Eddie Murray	.50
76	Pete O'Brien	.05
77	Bob Ojeda	.05
78	Jesse Orosco	.05
79	Dan Pasqua	.05
80	Dave Parker	.05
81	Larry Parrish	.05
82	Jim Presley	.05
83	Kirby Puckett	1.00
84	Dan Quisenberry	.05
85	Tim Raines	.10
86	Dennis Rasmussen	.05
87	Johnny Ray	.05
88	Jeff Reardon	.05
89	Jim Rice	.10
90	Dave Righetti	.05
91	Earnest Riles	.05
92	Cal Ripken, Jr.	2.00
93	Ron Robinson	.05
94	Juan Samuel	.05
95	Ryne Sandberg	.75
96	Steve Sax	.05
97	Mike Schmidt	1.00
98	Ken Schrom	.05
99	Mike Scott	.05
100	Ruben Sierra	.05
101	Lee Smith	.05
102	Ozzie Smith	.75
103	Cory Snyder	.05
104	Kent Tekulve	.05
105	Andres Thomas	.05
106	Rob Thompson	.05
107	Alan Trammell	.10
108	John Tudor	.05
109	Fernando Valenzuela	.05
110	Greg Walker	.05
111	Mitch Webster	.05
112	Lou Whitaker	.05
113	Frank White	.05
114	Reggie Williams	.05
115	Glenn Wilson	.05
116	Willie Wilson	.05
117	Dave Winfield	.40
118	Mike Witt	.05
119	Todd Worrell	.05
120	Floyd Youmans	.05

1987 Fleer Star Stickers

The 1987 Fleer Star Stickers set contains 132 cards which become stickers if the back is bent and peeled off. As in the previous year, the card backs are identical, save the numbering system, to the regular-issue cards. The cards measure 2-1/2" x 3-1/2" and were sold in wax packs with team logo stickers. The fronts have a green border with a red and white banner wrapped across the upper left corner and the sides. The backs are printed in green and yellow.

		MT
Complete Set (132):		12.00
Common Player:		.05
1	Don Aase	.05
2	Harold Baines	.05
3	Floyd Bannister	.05
4	Jesse Barfield	.05
5	Marty Barrett	.05
6	Kevin Bass	.05
7	Don Baylor	.05
8	Steve Bedrosian	.05
9	George Bell	.05
10	Bert Blyleven	.05
11	Mike Boddicker	.05
12	Wade Boggs	.50
13	Phil Bradley	.05
14	Sid Bream	.05
15	George Brett	.75
16	Hubie Brooks	.05
17	Tom Brunansky	.05
18	Tom Candiotti	.05
19	Jose Canseco	.50
20	Gary Carter	.25
21	Joe Carter	.05
22	Will Clark	.15
23	Mark Clear	.05
24	Roger Clemens	.75
25	Vince Coleman	.05
26	Jose Cruz	.05
27	Ron Darling	.05
28	Alvin Davis	.05
29	Chili Davis	.05
30	Eric Davis	.05
31	Glenn Davis	.05
32	Mike Davis	.05
33	Andre Dawson	.20
34	Doug DeCinces	.05
35	Brian Downing	.05
36	Shawon Dunston	.05
37	Mark Eichhorn	.05
38	Dwight Evans	.05
39	Tony Fernandez	.05
40	Bob Forsch	.05
41	John Franco	.05
42	Julio Franco	.05
43	Gary Gaetti	.05
44	Gene Garber	.05
45	Scott Garrelts	.05
46	Steve Garvey	.20
47	Kirk Gibson	.05
48	Dwight Gooden	.05
49	Ken Griffey	.05
50	Ozzie Guillen	.05
51	Bill Gullickson	.05
52	Tony Gwynn	.65
53	Mel Hall	.05
54	Greg Harris	.05
55	Von Hayes	.05
56	Rickey Henderson	.50
57	Tom Henke	.05
58	Keith Hernandez	.05
59	Willie Hernandez	.05
60	Ted Higuera	.05
61	Bob Horner	.05
62	Charlie Hough	.05
63	Jay Howell	.05
64	Kent Hrbek	.05
65	Bruce Hurst	.05
66	Pete Incaviglia	.05
67	Bob James	.05
68	Wally Joyner	.05
69	Mike Krukow	.05
70	Mark Langston	.05
71	Carney Lansford	.05
72	Fred Lynn	.05
73	Bill Madlock	.05
74	Don Mattingly	.75
75	Kirk McCaskill	.05
76	Lance McCullers	.05
77	Oddibe McDowell	.05
78	Paul Molitor	.50
79	Keith Moreland	.05
80	Jack Morris	.05
81	Jim Morrison	.05
82	Jerry Mumphrey	.05
83	Dale Murphy	.20
84	Eddie Murray	.50
85	Ben Oglivie	.05
86	Bob Ojeda	.05
87	Jesse Orosco	.05
88	Dave Parker	.05
89	Larry Parrish	.05
90	Tony Pena	.05
91	Jim Presley	.05
92	Kirby Puckett	.75
93	Dan Quisenberry	.05
94	Tim Raines	.05
95	Dennis Rasmussen	.05
96	Shane Rawley	.05
97	Johnny Ray	.05
98	Jeff Reardon	.05
99	Jim Rice	.15
100	Dave Righetti	.05
101	Cal Ripken, Jr.	2.00
102	Pete Rose	1.00
103	Nolan Ryan	2.00
104	Juan Samuel	.05
105	Ryne Sandberg	.60
106	Steve Sax	.05
107	Mike Schmidt	.75
108	Mike Scott	.05
109	Dave Smith	.05
110	Lee Smith	.05
111	Lonnie Smith	.05
112	Ozzie Smith	.65
113	Cory Snyder	.05
114	Darryl Strawberry	.05
115	Don Sutton	.35
116	Kent Tekulve	.05
117	Gorman Thomas	.05
118	Alan Trammell	.05
119	John Tudor	.05
120	Fernando Valenzuela	.05
121	Bob Welch	.05
122	Lou Whitaker	.05
123	Frank White	.05
124	Reggie Williams	.05
125	Willie Wilson	.05
126	Dave Winfield	.50
127	Mike Witt	.05
128	Todd Worrell	.05
129	Curt Young	.05
130	Robin Yount	.50
131	Checklist (Jose Canseco, Don Mattingly)	.25
132	Checklist (Bo Jackson, Eric Davis)	.10

1987 Fleer Star Stickers Box Panels

Fleer issued on the bottoms of its Fleer Star Stickers wax pack boxes six player cards plus two team logo/checklist cards. The cards, which measure 2-1/2" x 3-1/2", are numbered S-1 through S-8, and are identical in design to the Star Stickers.

	MT
Complete Panel Set (2):	2.50
Complete Singles Set (8):	2.50

Common Single Player:		.10
Panel		3.50
2	Wade Boggs	.50
3	Bert Blyleven	.10
6	Phillies Logo	.05
8	Don Mattingly	1.50
Panel		1.00
1	Tigers Logo	.05
4	Jose Cruz	.10
5	Glenn Davis	.10
7	Bob Horner	.10

1987 Fleer Update

The 1987 update edition brings the regular Fleer set up to date by including traded players and hot rookies. The cards measure 2-1/2" x 3-1/2" and are housed in a specially designed box with 25 team logo stickers. A glossy-coated Fleer Collectors Edition set was also produced.

		MT
Complete Set (132):		15.00
Common Player:		.08
1	Scott Bankhead	.08
2	Eric Bell	.08
3	Juan Beniquez	.08
4	Juan Berenguer	.08
5	Mike Birkbeck	.08
6	Randy Bockus	.08
7	Rod Booker	.08
8	Thad Bosley	.08
9	Greg Brock	.08
10	Bob Brower	.08
11	Chris Brown	.08
12	Jerry Browne	.08
13	Ralph Bryant	.08
14	DeWayne Buice	.08
15	Ellis Burks	.25
16	Casey Candaele	.08
17	Steve Carlton	.50
18	Juan Castillo	.08
19	Chuck Crim	.08
20	Mark Davidson	.08
21	Mark Davis	.08
22	Storm Davis	.08
23	Bill Dawley	.08
24	Andre Dawson	.30
25	Brian Dayett	.08
26	Rick Dempsey	.08
27	Ken Dowell	.08
28	Dave Dravecky	.08
29	Mike Dunne	.08
30	Dennis Eckersley	.25
31	Cecil Fielder	.15
32	Brian Fisher	.08
33	Willie Fraser	.08
34	Ken Gerhart	.08
35	Jim Gott	.08
36	Dan Gladden	.08
37	Mike Greenwell	.10
38	Cecilio Guante	.08
39	Albert Hall	.08
40	Atlee Hammaker	.08
41	Mickey Hatcher	.08
42	Mike Heath	.08
43	Neal Heaton	.08
44	Mike Henneman	.15
45	Guy Hoffman	.08
46	Charles Hudson	.08
47	Chuck Jackson	.08
48	Mike Jackson	.08
49	Reggie Jackson	.60
50	Chris James	.08
51	Dion James	.08
52	Stan Javier	.08
53	Stan Jefferson	.08
54	Jimmy Jones	.08
55	Tracy Jones	.08
56	Terry Kennedy	.08
57	Mike Kingery	.08
58	Ray Knight	.10
59	Gene Larkin	.08
60	Mike LaValliere	.08
61	Jack Lazorko	.08
62	Terry Leach	.08
63	Rick Leach	.08
64	Craig Lefferts	.08
65	Jim Lindeman	.08
66	Bill Long	.08
67	Mike Loynd	.08
68	*Greg Maddux*	5.00
69	Bill Madlock	.08
70	Dave Magadan	.08
71	Joe Magrane	.10
72	Fred Manrique	.08
73	Mike Mason	.08
74	Lloyd McClendon	.08
75	Fred McGriff	1.00
76	Mark McGwire	10.00
77	Mark McLemore	.08
78	Kevin McReynolds	.08
79	Dave Meads	.08
80	Greg Minton	.08
81	John Mitchell	.08
82	Kevin Mitchell	.08
83	John Morris	.08
84	Jeff Musselman	.10
85	Randy Myers	.35
86	Gene Nelson	.08
87	Joe Niekro	.08
88	Tom Nieto	.08
89	Reid Nichols	.08
90	Matt Nokes	.08
91	Dickie Noles	.08
92	Edwin Nunez	.08
93	Jose Nunez	.08
94	Paul O'Neill	.25
95	Jim Paciorek	.08
96	Lance Parrish	.08
97	Bill Pecota	.08
98	Tony Pena	.08
99	Luis Polonia	.10
100	Randy Ready	.08
101	Jeff Reardon	.08
102	Gary Redus	.08
103	Rick Rhoden	.08
104	Wally Ritchie	.08
105	Jeff Robinson	.08
106	Mark Salas	.08
107	Dave Schmidt	.08
108	Kevin Seitzer	.08
109	John Shelby	.08
110	John Smiley	.10
111	Lary Sorenson	.08
112	Chris Speier	.08
113	Randy St. Claire	.08
114	Jim Sundberg	.08
115	B.J. Surhoff	.15
116	Greg Swindell	.08
117	Danny Tartabull	.08
118	Dorn Taylor	.08
119	Lee Tunnell	.08
120	Ed Vande Berg	.08
121	Andy Van Slyke	.08
122	Gary Ward	.08
123	Devon White	.15
124	Alan Wiggins	.08
125	Bill Wilkinson	.08
126	Jim Winn	.08
127	Frank Williams	.08
128	Ken Williams	.08
129	*Matt Williams*	1.50
130	Herm Winningham	.08
131	Matt Young	.08
132	Checklist 1-132	.08

1987 Fleer Update Glossy Tin

The 1987 Fleer glossy tin update set is identical to the regular-issue updates, except for the high-gloss coating on the cards' fronts and the lithographed metal box in which the sets were sold. Production was estimated at 100,000. Because of perceived overproduction, the glossy tin update set and singles currently carry little, if any, premium over the regular-issue updates.

	MT
Complete Set (132):	20.00
Common Player:	.10

(Star cards valued at .75-1X regular version 1987 Fleer updates.)

1988 Fleer

A clean, uncluttered look was featured in the 1988 Fleer set. Cards in the standard 2-1/2" x 3-1/2" format feature blue and red diagonal lines on a white background. Player identification and team logo appears at top. Backs include personal information and career statistics, plus a new feature called "At Their Best." This feature graphically shows a player's pitching or hitting statistics for home and road games and how he fared during day games as opposed to night contests. The set includes 19 special cards (#622-640) and 12 "Major League Prospects" cards.

		MT
Complete Set (660):		8.00
Unopened Factory Set (672):		15.00
Common Player:		.06
Pack (15):		1.00
Wax Box (36):		15.00
1	Keith Atherton	.06
2	Don Baylor	.10
3	Juan Berenguer	.06
4	Bert Blyleven	.10
5	Tom Brunansky	.06
6	Randy Bush	.06
7	Steve Carlton	.50
8	*Mark Davidson*	.06
9	George Frazier	.06
10	Gary Gaetti	.06
11	Greg Gagne	.06
12	Dan Gladden	.06
13	Kent Hrbek	.06
14	*Gene Larkin*	.06
15	Tim Laudner	.06
16	Steve Lombardozzi	.06
17	Al Newman	.06
18	Joe Niekro	.06
19	Kirby Puckett	.75
20	Jeff Reardon	.06
21a	Dan Schatzader (incorrect spelling)	.20
21b	Dan Schatzeder (correct spelling)	.06
22	Roy Smalley	.06
23	Mike Smithson	.06
24	*Les Straker*	.06
25	Frank Viola	.06
26	Jack Clark	.06
27	Vince Coleman	.06
28	Danny Cox	.06
29	Bill Dawley	.06
30	Ken Dayley	.06
31	Doug DeCinces	.06
32	Curt Ford	.06
33	Bob Forsch	.06
34	David Green	.06
35	Tom Herr	.06
36	Ricky Horton	.06
37	*Lance Johnson*	.40
38	Steve Lake	.06
39	Jim Lindeman	.06
40	*Joe Magrane*	.10
41	Greg Mathews	.06
42	Willie McGee	.06
43	John Morris	.06
44	Jose Oquendo	.06
45	Tony Pena	.06
46	Terry Pendleton	.06
47	Ozzie Smith	.65
48	John Tudor	.06
49	Lee Tunnell	.06
50	Todd Worrell	.06
51	Doyle Alexander	.06
52	Dave Bergman	.06
53	Tom Brookens	.06
54	Darrell Evans	.10
55	Kirk Gibson	.06
56	Mike Heath	.06
57	Mike Henneman	.10
58	Willie Hernandez	.06
59	Larry Herndon	.06
60	Eric King	.06
61	Chet Lemon	.06
62	*Scott Lusader*	.06
63	Bill Madlock	.06
64	Jack Morris	.06
65	Jim Morrison	.06
66	Matt Nokes	.10
67	Dan Petry	.06
68a	*Jeff Robinson* (Born 12-13-60 on back)	.25
68b	*Jeff Robinson* (Born 12/14/61 on back)	.10
69	Pat Sheridan	.06
70	Nate Snell	.06
71	Frank Tanana	.06
72	Walt Terrell	.06
73	Mark Thurmond	.06
74	Alan Trammell	.10
75	Lou Whitaker	.06
76	Mike Aldrete	.06
77	Bob Brenly	.06
78	Will Clark	.20
79	Chili Davis	.06
80	Kelly Downs	.06
81	Dave Dravecky	.06
82	Scott Garrelts	.06
83	Atlee Hammaker	.06
84	Dave Henderson	.06
85	Mike Krukow	.06
86	Mike LaCoss	.06
87	Craig Lefferts	.06
88	Jeff Leonard	.06
89	Candy Maldonado	.06
90	Ed Milner	.06
91	Bob Melvin	.06
92	Kevin Mitchell	.06
93	*Jon Perlman*	.06
94	Rick Reuschel	.06
95	Don Robinson	.06
96	Chris Speier	.06
97	Harry Spilman	.06
98	Robbie Thompson	.06
99	Jose Uribe	.06
100	*Mark Wasinger*	.06
101	Matt Williams	.40
102	Jesse Barfield	.06
103	George Bell	.06
104	Juan Beniquez	.06
105	John Cerutti	.06
106	Jim Clancy	.06
107	*Rob Ducey*	.06
108	Mark Eichhorn	.06
109	Tony Fernandez	.06

No.	Player	Price
110	Cecil Fielder	.06
111	Kelly Gruber	.06
112	Tom Henke	.06
113	Garth Iorq (Iorg)	.06
114	Jimmy Key	.06
115	Rick Leach	.06
116	Manny Lee	.06
117	*Nelson Liriano*	.06
118	Fred McGriff	.06
119	Lloyd Moseby	.06
120	Rance Mulliniks	.06
121	Jeff Musselman	.06
122	*Jose Nunez*	.06
123	Dave Stieb	.06
124	Willie Upshaw	.06
125	Duane Ward	.06
126	Ernie Whitt	.06
127	Rick Aguilera	.06
128	Wally Backman	.06
129	*Mark Carreon*	.10
130	Gary Carter	.25
131	David Cone	.25
132	Ron Darling	.06
133	Len Dykstra	.08
134	Sid Fernandez	.06
135	Dwight Gooden	.06
136	Keith Hernandez	.06
137	*Gregg Jefferies*	.75
138	Howard Johnson	.06
139	Terry Leach	.06
140	*Barry Lyons*	.06
141	Dave Magadan	.06
142	Roger McDowell	.06
143	Kevin McReynolds	.06
144	*Keith Miller*	.06
145	*John Mitchell*	.06
146	Randy Myers	.06
147	Bob Ojeda	.06
148	Jesse Orosco	.06
149	Rafael Santana	.06
150	Doug Sisk	.06
151	Darryl Strawberry	.06
152	Tim Teufel	.06
153	Gene Walter	.06
154	Mookie Wilson	.06
155	*Jay Aldrich*	.06
156	Chris Bosio	.06
157	Glenn Braggs	.06
158	Greg Brock	.06
159	Juan Castillo	.06
160	Mark Clear	.06
161	Cecil Cooper	.06
162	*Chuck Crim*	.06
163	Rob Deer	.06
164	Mike Felder	.06
165	Jim Gantner	.06
166	Ted Higuera	.06
167	Steve Kiefer	.06
168	Rick Manning	.06
169	Paul Molitor	.50
170	Juan Nieves	.06
171	Dan Plesac	.06
172	Earnest Riles	.06
173	Bill Schroeder	.06
174	*Steve Stanicek*	.06
175	B.J. Surhoff	.06
176	Dale Sveum	.06
177	Bill Wegman	.06
178	Robin Yount	.50
179	Hubie Brooks	.06
180	Tim Burke	.06
181	Casey Candaele	.06
182	Mike Fitzgerald	.06
183	Tom Foley	.06
184	Andres Galarraga	.06
185	Neal Heaton	.06
186	Wallace Johnson	.06
187	Vance Law	.06
188	Dennis Martinez	.06
189	Bob McClure	.06
190	Andy McGaffigan	.06
191	Reid Nichols	.06
192	Pascual Perez	.06
193	Tim Raines	.06
194	Jeff Reed	.06
195	Bob Sebra	.06
196	Bryn Smith	.06
197	Randy St. Claire	.06
198	Tim Wallach	.06
199	Mitch Webster	.06
200	Herm Winningham	.06
201	Floyd Youmans	.06
202	*Brad Arnsberg*	.06
203	Rick Cerone	.06
204	Pat Clements	.06
205	Henry Cotto	.06
206	Mike Easler	.06
207	Ron Guidry	.10
208	Bill Gullickson	.06
209	Rickey Henderson	.50
210	Charles Hudson	.06
211	Tommy John	.10
212	*Roberto Kelly*	.40
213	Ron Kittle	.06
214	Don Mattingly	.75
215	Bobby Meacham	.06
216	Mike Pagliarulo	.06
217	Dan Pasqua	.06
218	Willie Randolph	.06
219	Rick Rhoden	.06
220	Dave Righetti	.06
221	Jerry Royster	.06
222	Tim Stoddard	.06
223	Wayne Tolleson	.06
224	Gary Ward	.06
225	Claudell Washington	.06
226	Dave Winfield	.50
227	Buddy Bell	.06
228	Tom Browning	.06
229	Dave Concepcion	.06
230	Kal Daniels	.06
231	Eric Davis	.06
232	Bo Diaz	.06
233	Nick Esasky	.06
234	John Franco	.06
235	Guy Hoffman	.06
236	Tom Hume	.06
237	Tracy Jones	.06
238	*Bill Landrum*	.06
239	Barry Larkin	.20
240	Terry McGriff	.06
241	Rob Murphy	.06
242	Ron Oester	.06
243	Dave Parker	.10
244	Pat Perry	.06
245	Ted Power	.06
246	Dennis Rasmussen	.06
247	Ron Robinson	.06
248	Kurt Stillwell	.06
249	*Jeff Treadway*	.06
250	Frank Williams	.06
251	Steve Balboni	.06
252	Bud Black	.06
253	Thad Bosley	.06
254	George Brett	.75
255	*John Davis*	.06
256	Steve Farr	.06
257	Gene Garber	.06
258	Jerry Gleaton	.06
259	Mark Gubicza	.06
260	Bo Jackson	.25
261	Danny Jackson	.06
262	*Ross Jones*	.06
263	Charlie Leibrandt	.06
264	*Bill Pecota*	.06
265	*Melido Perez*	.15
266	Jamie Quirk	.06
267	Dan Quisenberry	.06
268	Bret Saberhagen	.10
269	Angel Salazar	.06
270	Kevin Seitzer	.06
271	Danny Tartabull	.06
272	*Gary Thurman*	.06
273	Frank White	.06
274	Willie Wilson	.06
275	Tony Bernazard	.06
276	Jose Canseco	.40
277	Mike Davis	.06
278	Storm Davis	.06
279	Dennis Eckersley	.10
280	Alfredo Griffin	.06
281	Rick Honeycutt	.06
282	Jay Howell	.06
283	Reggie Jackson	.50
284	Dennis Lamp	.06
285	Carney Lansford	.06
286	Mark McGwire	2.00
287	Dwayne Murphy	.06
288	Gene Nelson	.06
289	Steve Ontiveros	.06
290	Tony Phillips	.06
291	Eric Plunk	.06
292	*Luis Polonia*	.15
293	*Rick Rodriguez*	.06
294	Terry Steinbach	.06
295	Dave Stewart	.10
296	Curt Young	.06
297	Luis Aguayo	.06
298	Steve Bedrosian	.06
299	Jeff Calhoun	.06
300	Don Carman	.06
301	*Todd Frohwirth*	.06
302	Greg Gross	.06
303	Kevin Gross	.06
304	Von Hayes	.06
305	*Keith Hughes*	.06
306	*Mike Jackson*	.06
307	Chris James	.06
308	Steve Jeltz	.06
309	Mike Maddux	.06
310	Lance Parrish	.10
311	Shane Rawley	.06
312	*Wally Ritchie*	.06
313	Bruce Ruffin	.06
314	Juan Samuel	.06
315	Mike Schmidt	.75
316	Rick Schu	.06
317	Jeff Stone	.06
318	Kent Tekulve	.06
319	Milt Thompson	.06
320	Glenn Wilson	.06
321	Rafael Belliard	.06
322	Barry Bonds	1.00
323	Bobby Bonilla	.06
324	Sid Bream	.06
325	John Cangelosi	.06
326	Mike Diaz	.06
327	Doug Drabek	.06
328	*Mike Dunne*	.06
329	Brian Fisher	.06
330	*Brett Gideon*	.06
331	Terry Harper	.06
332	Bob Kipper	.06
333	Mike LaValliere	.06
334	*Jose Lind*	.15
335	Junior Ortiz	.06
336	*Vicente Palacios*	.06
337	*Bob Patterson*	.10
338	*Al Pedrique*	.06
339	R.J. Reynolds	.06
340	John Smiley	.06
341	Andy Van Slyke	.06
342	Bob Walk	.06
343	Marty Barrett	.06
344	*Todd Benzinger*	.06
345	Wade Boggs	.40
346	*Tom Bolton*	.06
347	Oil Can Boyd	.06
348	Ellis Burks	.25
349	Roger Clemens	1.00
350	Steve Crawford	.06
351	Dwight Evans	.10
352	*Wes Gardner*	.06
353	Rich Gedman	.06
354	Mike Greenwell	.06
355	*Sam Horn*	.06
356	Bruce Hurst	.06
357	*John Marzano*	.06
358	Al Nipper	.06
359	Spike Owen	.06
360	*Jody Reed*	.20
361	Jim Rice	.08
362	Ed Romero	.06
363	Kevin Romine	.06
364	Joe Sambito	.06
365	Calvin Schiraldi	.06
366	Jeff Sellers	.06
367	Bob Stanley	.06
368	Scott Bankhead	.06
369	Phil Bradley	.06
370	Scott Bradley	.06
371	Mickey Brantley	.06
372	*Mike Campbell*	.06
373	Alvin Davis	.06
374	Lee Guetterman	.06
375	*Dave Hengel*	.06
376	Mike Kingery	.06
377	Mark Langston	.06
378	*Edgar Martinez*	1.00
379	Mike Moore	.06
380	Mike Morgan	.06
381	John Moses	.06
382	*Donnell Nixon*	.06
383	Edwin Nunez	.06
384	Ken Phelps	.06
385	Jim Presley	.06
386	Rey Quinones	.06
387	Jerry Reed	.06
388	Harold Reynolds	.06
389	Dave Valle	.06
390	*Bill Wilkinson*	.06
391	Harold Baines	.06
392	Floyd Bannister	.06
393	Daryl Boston	.06
394	Ivan Calderon	.06
395	Jose DeLeon	.06
396	Richard Dotson	.06
397	Carlton Fisk	.50
398	Ozzie Guillen	.06
399	Ron Hassey	.06
400	Donnie Hill	.06
401	Bob James	.06
402	Dave LaPoint	.06
403	*Bill Lindsey*	.06
404	*Bill Long*	.06
405	Steve Lyons	.06
406	*Fred Manrique*	.06
407	*Jack McDowell*	.50
408	Gary Redus	.06
409	Ray Searage	.06
410	Bobby Thigpen	.06
411	Greg Walker	.06
412	*Kenny Williams*	.06
413	Jim Winn	.06
414	Jody Davis	.06
415	Andre Dawson	.20
416	Brian Dayett	.06
417	Bob Dernier	.06
418	Frank DiPino	.06
419	Shawon Dunston	.06
420	Leon Durham	.06
421	*Les Lancaster*	.10
422	Ed Lynch	.06
423	Greg Maddux	1.50
424	Dave Martinez	.06
425a	Keith Moreland (bunting, photo actually Jody Davis)	2.00
425b	Keith Moreland (standing upright, correct photo)	.06
426	Jamie Moyer	.06
427	Jerry Mumphrey	.06
428	*Paul Noce*	.06
429	Rafael Palmeiro	.40
430	Wade Rowdon	.06
431	Ryne Sandberg	.50
432	Scott Sanderson	.06
433	Lee Smith	.10
434	Jim Sundberg	.06
435	Rick Sutcliffe	.06
436	Manny Trillo	.06
437	Juan Agosto	.06
438	Larry Andersen	.06
439	Alan Ashby	.06
440	Kevin Bass	.06
441	*Ken Caminiti*	.75
442	*Rocky Childress*	.06
443	Jose Cruz	.06
444	Danny Darwin	.06
445	Glenn Davis	.06
446	Jim Deshaies	.06
447	Bill Doran	.06
448	Ty Gainey	.06
449	Billy Hatcher	.06
450	Jeff Heathcock	.06
451	Bob Knepper	.06
452	*Rob Mallicoat*	.06
453	*Dave Meads*	.06
454	Craig Reynolds	.06
455	Nolan Ryan	2.00
456	Mike Scott	.06
457	Dave Smith	.06
458	Denny Walling	.06
459	*Robbie Wine*	.06
460	*Gerald Young*	.06
461	Bob Brower	.06
462a	Jerry Browne (white player, photo actually Bob Brower)	2.00
462b	Jerry Browne (black player, correct photo)	.06
463	Steve Buechele	.06
464	Edwin Correa	.06
465	*Cecil Espy*	.06
466	Scott Fletcher	.06
467	Jose Guzman	.06
468	Greg Harris	.06
469	Charlie Hough	.06
470	Pete Incaviglia	.06
471	*Paul Kilgus*	.06
472	Mike Loynd	.06
473	Oddibe McDowell	.06
474	Dale Mohorcic	.06
475	Pete O'Brien	.06
476	Larry Parrish	.06
477	Geno Petralli	.06
478	Jeff Russell	.06
479	Ruben Sierra	.06
480	Mike Stanley	.06
481	Curtis Wilkerson	.06
482	Mitch Williams	.06
483	Bobby Witt	.06
484	Tony Armas	.06

No.	Player	Value
485	Bob Boone	.10
486	Bill Buckner	.06
487	*DeWayne Buice*	.06
488	Brian Downing	.06
489	Chuck Finley	.06
490	Willie Fraser	.06
491	Jack Howell	.06
492	Ruppert Jones	.06
493	Wally Joyner	.06
494	Jack Lazorko	.06
495	Gary Lucas	.06
496	Kirk McCaskill	.06
497	Mark McLemore	.06
498	Darrell Miller	.06
499	Greg Minton	.06
500	Donnie Moore	.06
501	Gus Polidor	.06
502	Johnny Ray	.06
503	Mark Ryal	.06
504	Dick Schofield	.06
505	Don Sutton	.45
506	Devon White	.10
507	Mike Witt	.06
508	Dave Anderson	.06
509	Tim Belcher	.06
510	Ralph Bryant	.06
511	*Tim Crews*	.15
512	*Mike Devereaux*	.10
513	Mariano Duncan	.06
514	Pedro Guerrero	.06
515	Jeff Hamilton	.06
516	Mickey Hatcher	.06
517	Brad Havens	.06
518	Orel Hershiser	.10
519	*Shawn Hillegas*	.06
520	Ken Howell	.06
521	Tim Leary	.06
522	Mike Marshall	.06
523	Steve Sax	.06
524	Mike Scioscia	.06
525	Mike Sharperson	.06
526	John Shelby	.06
527	Franklin Stubbs	.06
528	Fernando Valenzuela	.06
529	Bob Welch	.06
530	Matt Young	.06
531	Jim Acker	.06
532	Paul Assenmacher	.06
533	*Jeff Blauser*	.25
534	*Joe Boever*	.06
535	Martin Clary	.06
536	*Kevin Coffman*	.06
537	Jeff Dedmon	.06
538	*Ron Gant*	2.00
539	*Tom Glavine*	3.00
540	Ken Griffey	.06
541	Al Hall	.06
542	Glenn Hubbard	.06
543	Dion James	.06
544	Dale Murphy	.20
545	Ken Oberkfell	.06
546	David Palmer	.06
547	Gerald Perry	.06
548	Charlie Puleo	.06
549	Ted Simmons	.06
550	Zane Smith	.06
551	Andres Thomas	.06
552	Ozzie Virgil	.06
553	Don Aase	.06
554	*Jeff Ballard*	.06
555	Eric Bell	.06
556	Mike Boddicker	.06
557	Ken Dixon	.06
558	Jim Dwyer	.06
559	Ken Gerhart	.06
560	*Rene Gonzales*	.06
561	Mike Griffin	.06
562	John Hayban (Habyan)	.06
563	Terry Kennedy	.06
564	Ray Knight	.06
565	Lee Lacy	.06
566	Fred Lynn	.06
567	Eddie Murray	.50
568	Tom Niedenfuer	.06
569	*Bill Ripken*	.06
570	Cal Ripken, Jr.	2.00
571	Dave Schmidt	.06
572	Larry Sheets	.06
573	*Pete Stanicek*	.06
574	*Mark Williamson*	.06
575	Mike Young	.06
576	Shawn Abner	.06
577	Greg Booker	.06
578	Chris Brown	.06
579	*Keith Comstock*	.06
580	*Joey Cora*	.06
581	Mark Davis	.06
582	Tim Flannery	.06
583	Goose Gossage	.10
584	Mark Grant	.06
585	Tony Gwynn	.60
586	Andy Hawkins	.06
587	Stan Jefferson	.06
588	Jimmy Jones	.06
589	John Kruk	.06
590	*Shane Mack*	.25
591	Carmelo Martinez	.06
592	Lance McCullers	.06
593	*Eric Nolte*	.06
594	Randy Ready	.06
595	Luis Salazar	.06
596	Benito Santiago	.06
597	Eric Show	.06
598	Garry Templeton	.06
599	Ed Whitson	.06
600	Scott Bailes	.06
601	Chris Bando	.06
602	*Jay Bell*	.75
603	Brett Butler	.06
604	Tom Candiotti	.06
605	Joe Carter	.06
606	Carmen Castillo	.06
607	*Brian Dorsett*	.06
608	*John Farrell*	.06
609	Julio Franco	.06
610	Mel Hall	.06
611	*Tommy Hinzo*	.06
612	Brook Jacoby	.06
613	*Doug Jones*	.30
614	Ken Schrom	.06
615	Cory Snyder	.06
616	Sammy Stewart	.06
617	Greg Swindell	.06
618	Pat Tabler	.06
619	Ed Vande Berg	.06
620	*Eddie Williams*	.06
621	Rich Yett	.06
622	Slugging Sophomores (Wally Joyner, Cory Snyder)	.15
623	Dominican Dynamite (George Bell, Pedro Guerrero)	.06
624	Oakland's Power Team (Jose Canseco, Mark McGwire)	1.00
625	Classic Relief (Dan Plesac, Dave Righetti)	.06
626	All Star Righties (Jack Morris, Bret Saberhagen, Mike Witt)	.06
627	Game Closers (Steve Bedrosian, John Franco)	.06
628	Masters of the Double Play (Ryne Sandberg, Ozzie Smith)	.35
629	Rookie Record Setter (Mark McGwire)	1.00
630	Changing the Guard in Boston (Todd Benzinger, Ellis Burks, Mike Greenwell)	.25
631	N.L. Batting Champs (Tony Gwynn, Tim Raines)	.20
632	Pitching Magic (Orel Hershiser, Mike Scott)	.06
633	Big Bats At First (Mark McGwire, Pat Tabler)	1.00
634	Hitting King and the Thief (Tony Gwynn, Vince Coleman)	.15
635	A.L. Slugging Shortstops (Tony Fernandez, Cal Ripken, Jr., Alan Trammell)	.30
636	Tried and True Sluggers (Gary Carter, Mike Schmidt)	.25
637	Crunch Time (Eric Davis)	.06
638	A.L. All Stars (Matt Nokes, Kirby Puckett)	.25
639	N.L. All Stars (Keith Hernandez, Dale Murphy)	.10
640	The "O's" Brothers (Bill Ripken, Cal Ripken, Jr.)	.50
641	Major League Prospects (*Mark Grace*), (*Darrin Jackson*)	3.00
642	Major League Prospects (*Damon Berryhill*), (*Jeff Montgomery*)	.20
643	Major League Prospects (*Felix Fermin*), (*Jessie Reid*)	.10
644	Major League Prospects (*Greg Myers*), (*Greg Tabor*)	.10
645	Major League Prospects (*Jim Eppard*, Joey Meyer)	.06
646	Major League Prospects (*Adam Peterson*), (*Randy Velarde*)	.15
647	Major League Prospects (*Chris Gwynn*), (*Peter Smith*)	.15
648	Major League Prospects (*Greg Jelks*), (*Tom Newell*)	.06
649	Major League Prospects (*Mario Diaz*), (*Clay Parker*)	.06
650	Major League Prospects (*Jack Savage*), (*Todd Simmons*)	.06
651	Major League Prospects (*John Burkett*), (*Kirt Manwaring*)	.40
652	Major League Prospects (*Dave Otto*), (*Walt Weiss*)	.30
653	Major League Prospects (*Randell Byers (Randall)*), (*Jeff King*)	.75
654a	Checklist 1-101 (21 is Schatzader)	.08
654b	Checklist 1-101 (21 is Schatzeder)	.06
655	Checklist 102-201	.06
656	Checklist 202-296	.06
657	Checklist 297-390	.06
658	Checklist 391-483	.06
659	Checklist 484-575	.06
660	Checklist 576-660	.06

1988 Fleer Glossy Tin

In its second year of production, Fleer radically reduced production numbers on its glossy version of the 1988 baseball card set. With production estimates in the 60,000 set range, values of the '88 tin glossies are about double those of the regular issue cards. Once again the issue was sold only as complete sets in colorful lithographed metal boxes.

	MT
Complete Set (672):	30.00
Common Player:	.15
(Star cards valued 1-1.5X regular-issue 1988 Fleer.)	

1988 Fleer All Stars

For the third consecutive year, Fleer randomly inserted All Star Team cards in its wax and cello packs. Twelve cards make up the set, with players chosen for the set being Fleer's idea of a major league All-Star team.

		MT
Complete Set (12):		4.00
Common Player:		.10
1	Matt Nokes	.10
2	Tom Henke	.10
3	Ted Higuera	.10
4	Roger Clemens	2.00
5	George Bell	.10
6	Andre Dawson	.25
7	Eric Davis	.10
8	Wade Boggs	.75
9	Alan Trammell	.10
10	Juan Samuel	.10
11	Jack Clark	.10
12	Paul Molitor	.75

1988 Fleer Headliners

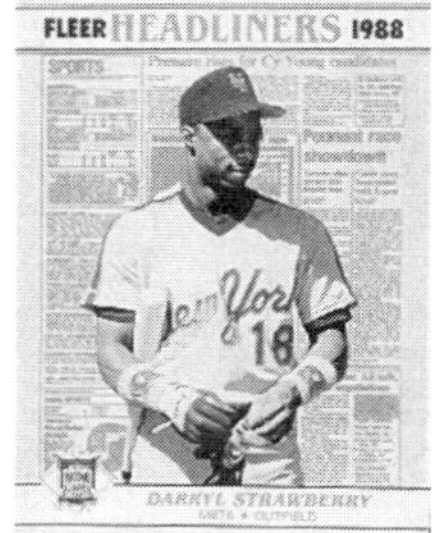

This six-card set was inserted in Fleer three-packs, sold by retail outlets and hobby dealers nationwide. The card fronts feature crisp full-color player cut-outs printed on a grey and white facsimile sports page. "Fleer Headliners 1988" is printed in black and red on a white banner across the top of the card, both front and back. A similar white banner across the card bottom bears the black and white National or American League logo and a red player/team name. Card backs are black on grey with red accents and include the card number and a narrative career summary.

		MT
Complete Set (6):		4.00
Common Player:		.25
1	Don Mattingly	1.50
2	Mark McGwire	2.50
3	Jack Morris	.25
4	Darryl Strawberry	.25
5	Dwight Gooden	.25
6	Tim Raines	.25

1988 Fleer Box Panels

Fleer's third annual box-bottom issue once again included 16 full-color trading cards printed on the bottoms of four different wax and cello pack retail display boxes. Each box contains three player cards and one team logo card. Player cards follow the same design as the basic 1988 Fleer issue. Standard size, the cards are numbered C-1 through C-16.

		MT
Complete Panel Set (4):		4.00
Complete Singles Set (16):		4.00
Common Panel:		1.50
Common Single Player:		.15
Panel		2.00
1	Cardinals Logo	.05
11	Mike Schmidt	1.00
14	Dave Stewart	.15
15	Tim Wallach	.15
Panel		2.75
2	Dwight Evans	.15
8	Shane Rawley	.15
10	Ryne Sandberg	.75
13	Tigers Logo	.05
Panel		2.00
3	Andres Galarraga	.15
6	Dale Murphy	.45
9	Giants Logo	.05
12	Kevin Seitzer	.15
Panel		2.75
4	Wally Joyner	.15
5	Twins Logo	.05
7	Kirby Puckett	1.00
16	Todd Worrell	.15

1988 Fleer Mini

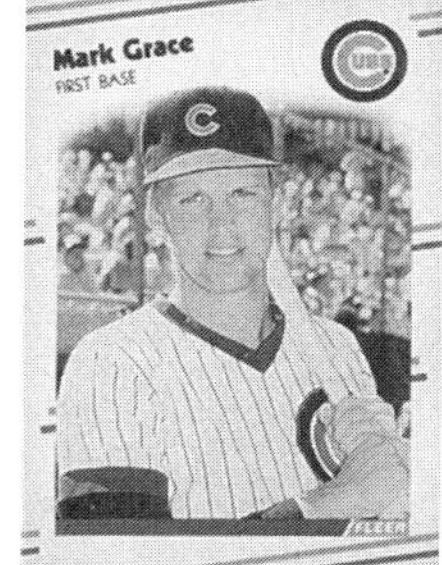

This third annual issue of miniatures (1-7/8" x 2-5/8") includes 120 high-gloss cards featuring new photos, not copies from the regular issue, although the card designs are identical. Card backs are red, white and blue and include personal data, yearly career stats and a stats breakdown of batting average, slugging percentage and on-base average, listed for day, night, home and road games. Card backs are numbered in alphabetical order by teams which are also listed alphabetically. The set includes 18 team logo stickers with black-and-white aerial stadium photos on the flip sides.

		MT
Complete Set (120):		7.00
Common Player:		.05
1	Eddie Murray	.50
2	Dave Schmidt	.05
3	Larry Sheets	.05
4	Wade Boggs	.50
5	Roger Clemens	.75
6	Dwight Evans	.05
7	Mike Greenwell	.05
8	Sam Horn	.05
9	Lee Smith	.05
10	Brian Downing	.05
11	Wally Joyner	.05
12	Devon White	.05
13	Mike Witt	.05
14	Ivan Calderon	.05
15	Ozzie Guillen	.05
16	Jack McDowell	.05
17	Kenny Williams	.05
18	Joe Carter	.05
19	Julio Franco	.05
20	Pat Tabler	.05
21	Doyle Alexander	.05
22	Jack Morris	.05
23	Matt Nokes	.05
24	Walt Terrell	.05
25	Alan Trammell	.05
26	Bret Saberhagen	.05
27	Kevin Seitzer	.05
28	Danny Tartabull	.05
29	Gary Thurman	.05
30	Ted Higuera	.05
31	Paul Molitor	.50
32	Dan Plesac	.05
33	Robin Yount	.50
34	Gary Gaetti	.05
35	Kent Hrbek	.05
36	Kirby Puckett	.75
37	Jeff Reardon	.05
38	Frank Viola	.05
39	Jack Clark	.05
40	Rickey Henderson	.50
41	Don Mattingly	.75
42	Willie Randolph	.05
43	Dave Righetti	.05
44	Dave Winfield	.50
45	Jose Canseco	.50
46	Mark McGwire	2.00
47	Dave Parker	.05
48	Dave Stewart	.05
49	Walt Weiss	.05
50	Bob Welch	.05
51	Mickey Brantley	.05
52	Mark Langston	.05
53	Harold Reynolds	.05
54	Scott Fletcher	.05
55	Charlie Hough	.05
56	Pete Incaviglia	.05
57	Larry Parrish	.05
58	Ruben Sierra	.05
59	George Bell	.05
60	Mark Eichhorn	.05
61	Tony Fernandez	.05
62	Tom Henke	.05
63	Jimmy Key	.05
64	Dion James	.05
65	Dale Murphy	.15
66	Zane Smith	.05
67	Andre Dawson	.15
68	Mark Grace	.75
69	Jerry Mumphrey	.05
70	Ryne Sandberg	.60
71	Rick Sutcliffe	.05
72	Kal Daniels	.05
73	Eric Davis	.05
74	John Franco	.05
75	Ron Robinson	.05
76	Jeff Treadway	.05
77	Kevin Bass	.05
78	Glenn Davis	.05
79	Nolan Ryan	1.00
80	Mike Scott	.05
81	Dave Smith	.05
82	Kirk Gibson	.05
83	Pedro Guerrero	.05
84	Orel Hershiser	.05
85	Steve Sax	.05
86	Fernando Valenzuela	.05
87	Tim Burke	.05
88	Andres Galarraga	.05
89	Neal Heaton	.05
90	Tim Raines	.05
91	Tim Wallach	.05
92	Dwight Gooden	.05
93	Keith Hernandez	.05
94	Gregg Jefferies	.25
95	Howard Johnson	.05
96	Roger McDowell	.05
97	Darryl Strawberry	.05
98	Steve Bedrosian	.05
99	Von Hayes	.05
100	Shane Rawley	.05
101	Juan Samuel	.05
102	Mike Schmidt	.75
103	Bobby Bonilla	.05
104	Mike Dunne	.05
105	Andy Van Slyke	.05
106	Vince Coleman	.05
107	Bob Horner	.05
108	Willie McGee	.05
109	Ozzie Smith	.75
110	John Tudor	.05
111	Todd Worrell	.05
112	Tony Gwynn	.60
113	John Kruk	.05
114	Lance McCullers	.05
115	Benito Santiago	.05
116	Will Clark	.25
117	Jeff Leonard	.05
118	Candy Maldonado	.05
119	Kirt Manwaring	.05
120	Don Robinson	.05

1988 Fleer Star Stickers

This set of 132 standard-size sticker cards (including a checklist card) features exclusive player photos, different from those in the Fleer regular issue. Card fronts have light gray borders sprinkled with multi-colored stars. Card backs are printed in red, gray and black on white and include personal data and a breakdown of pitching and batting stats into day, night, home and road categories. Cards were marketed in two different display boxes that feature six players and two team logos on the bottoms.

		MT
Complete Set (132):		10.00
Common Player:		.05
Wax Pack (5):		.50
Wax Box (36):		12.00
1	Mike Boddicker	.05
2	Eddie Murray	.50
3	Cal Ripken, Jr.	2.00
4	Larry Sheets	.05
5	Wade Boggs	.50
6	Ellis Burks	.05
7	Roger Clemens	.75
8	Dwight Evans	.05
9	Mike Greenwell	.05
10	Bruce Hurst	.05
11	Brian Downing	.05
12	Wally Joyner	.05
13	Mike Witt	.05
14	Ivan Calderon	.05
15	Jose DeLeon	.05
16	Ozzie Guillen	.05
17	Bobby Thigpen	.05
18	Joe Carter	.05
19	Julio Franco	.05
20	Brook Jacoby	.05
21	Cory Snyder	.05
22	Pat Tabler	.05
23	Doyle Alexander	.05
24	Kirk Gibson	.05
25	Mike Henneman	.05
26	Jack Morris	.05
27	Matt Nokes	.05
28	Walt Terrell	.05
29	Alan Trammell	.05
30	George Brett	.75
31	Charlie Leibrandt	.05
32	Bret Saberhagen	.05
33	Kevin Seitzer	.05
34	Danny Tartabull	.05
35	Frank White	.05
36	Rob Deer	.05
37	Ted Higuera	.05
38	Paul Molitor	.50
39	Dan Plesac	.05
40	Robin Yount	.50
41	Bert Blyleven	.05
42	Tom Brunansky	.05
43	Gary Gaetti	.05
44	Kent Hrbek	.05
45	Kirby Puckett	.75
46	Jeff Reardon	.05
47	Frank Viola	.05
48	Don Mattingly	.75
49	Mike Pagliarulo	.05
50	Willie Randolph	.05
51	Rick Rhoden	.05
52	Dave Righetti	.05
53	Dave Winfield	.60
54	Jose Canseco	.40
55	Carney Lansford	.05
56	Mark McGwire	2.00
57	Dave Stewart	.05
58	Curt Young	.05
59	Alvin Davis	.05
60	Mark Langston	.05
61	Ken Phelps	.05
62	Harold Reynolds	.05
63	Scott Fletcher	.05
64	Charlie Hough	.05
65	Pete Incaviglia	.05
66	Oddibe McDowell	.05
67	Pete O'Brien	.05
68	Larry Parrish	.05
69	Ruben Sierra	.05
70	Jesse Barfield	.05
71	George Bell	.05
72	Tony Fernandez	.05
73	Tom Henke	.05
74	Jimmy Key	.05
75	Lloyd Moseby	.05
76	Dion James	.05
77	Dale Murphy	.15
78	Zane Smith	.05
79	Andre Dawson	.15
80	Ryne Sandberg	.65
81	Rick Sutcliffe	.05
82	Kal Daniels	.05
83	Eric Davis	.05
84	John Franco	.05
85	Kevin Bass	.05
86	Glenn Davis	.05
87	Bill Doran	.05
88	Nolan Ryan	2.00
89	Mike Scott	.05
90	Dave Smith	.05
91	Pedro Guerrero	.05

92	Orel Hershiser	.05
93	Steve Sax	.05
94	Fernando Valenzuela	.05
95	Tim Burke	.05
96	Andres Galarraga	.05
97	Tim Raines	.05
98	Tim Wallach	.05
99	Mitch Webster	.05
100	Ron Darling	.05
101	Sid Fernandez	.05
102	Dwight Gooden	.05
103	Keith Hernandez	.05
104	Howard Johnson	.05
105	Roger McDowell	.05
106	Darryl Strawberry	.05
107	Steve Bedrosian	.05
108	Von Hayes	.05
109	Shane Rawley	.05
110	Juan Samuel	.05
111	Mike Schmidt	.75
112	Milt Thompson	.05
113	Sid Bream	.05
114	Bobby Bonilla	.05
115	Mike Dunne	.05
116	Andy Van Slyke	.05
117	Vince Coleman	.05
118	Willie McGee	.05
119	Terry Pendleton	.05
120	Ozzie Smith	.75
121	John Tudor	.05
122	Todd Worrell	.05
123	Tony Gwynn	.65
124	John Kruk	.05
125	Benito Santiago	.05
126	Will Clark	.15
127	Dave Dravecky	.05
128	Jeff Leonard	.05
129	Candy Maldonado	.05
130	Rick Rueschel	.05
131	Don Robinson	.05
132	Checklist	.05

1988 Fleer Star Stickers Box Panels

This set of eight box-bottom cards was printed on two different retail display boxes. Six players and two team logo sticker cards are included in the set, three player photos and one team photo per box. The full-color player photos are exclusive to the Fleer Star Sticker set. The cards, which measure 2-1/2" x 3-1/2", have a light gray border sprinkled with multi-color stars. The backs are printed in navy blue and red.

		MT
Complete Panel Set (2):		1.50
Complete Singles Set (8):		1.50
Common Singles Player:		.15
Panel		1.00
1	Eric Davis	.10
3	Kevin Mitchell	.10
5	Rickey Henderson	.75
7	Tigers Logo	.05
Panel		1.00
2	Gary Carter	.25
4	Ron Guidry	.10
6	Don Baylor	.10
8	Giants Logo	.05

1988 Fleer Update

This update set (numbered U-1 through U-132 are 2-1/2" x 3-1/2") features traded veterans and rookies in a mixture of full-color action shots and close-ups, framed by white borders with red and blue stripes. The backs are red, white and blue-grey and include personal info, along with yearly and "At Their Best" (day, night, home, road) stats charts. The set was packaged in white cardboard boxes with red and blue stripes. A glossy-coated edition of the update set was issued in its own box and is valued at two times the regular issue.

		MT
Complete Set (132):		6.00
Common Player:		.06
1	Jose Bautista	.06
2	Joe Orsulak	.06
3	Doug Sisk	.06
4	Craig Worthington	.06
5	Mike Boddicker	.06
6	Rick Cerone	.06
7	Larry Parrish	.06
8	Lee Smith	.10
9	Mike Smithson	.06
10	John Trautwein	.06
11	Sherman Corbett	.06
12	Chili Davis	.06
13	Jim Eppard	.06
14	Bryan Harvey	.10
15	John Davis	.06
16	Dave Gallagher	.06
17	Ricky Horton	.06
18	Dan Pasqua	.06
19	Melido Perez	.06
20	Jose Segura	.06
21	Andy Allanson	.06
22	Jon Perlman	.06
23	Domingo Ramos	.06
24	Rick Rodriguez	.06
25	Willie Upshaw	.06
26	Paul Gibson	.06
27	Don Heinkel	.06
28	Ray Knight	.06
29	Gary Pettis	.06
30	Luis Salazar	.06
31	Mike MacFarlane	.06
32	Jeff Montgomery	.06
33	Ted Power	.06
34	Israel Sanchez	.06
35	Kurt Stillwell	.06
36	Pat Tabler	.06
37	Don August	.06
38	Darryl Hamilton	.25
39	Jeff Leonard	.06
40	Joey Meyer	.06
41	Allan Anderson	.06
42	Brian Harper	.06
43	Tom Herr	.06
44	Charlie Lea	.06
45	John Moses	.06
46	John Candelaria	.06
47	Jack Clark	.06
48	Richard Dotson	.06
49	Al Leiter	.10
50	Rafael Santana	.06
51	Don Slaught	.06
52	Todd Burns	.06
53	Dave Henderson	.06
54	Doug Jennings	.06
55	Dave Parker	.10
56	Walt Weiss	.06
57	Bob Welch	.06
58	Henry Cotto	.06
59	Marion Diaz (Mario)	.06
60	Mike Jackson	.06
61	Bill Swift	.06
62	Jose Cecena	.06
63	Ray Hayward	.06
64	Jim Steels	.06
65	Pat Borders	.06
66	Sil Campusano	.06
67	Mike Flanagan	.06
68	Todd Stottlemyre	.25
69	David Wells	1.50
70	Jose Alvarez	.06
71	Paul Runge	.06
72	Cesar Jimenez (German)	.06
73	Pete Smith	.06
74	*John Smoltz*	1.50
75	Damon Berryhill	.06
76	Goose Gossage	.10
77	Mark Grace	1.00
78	Darrin Jackson	.06
79	Vance Law	.06
80	Jeff Pico	.06
81	Gary Varsho	.06
82	Tim Birtsas	.06
83	Rob Dibble	.10
84	Danny Jackson	.06
85	Paul O'Neill	.15
86	Jose Rijo	.06
87	*Chris Sabo*	.15
88	John Fishel	.06
89	*Craig Biggio*	1.50
90	Terry Puhl	.06
91	Rafael Ramirez	.06
92	Louie Meadows	.06
93	Kirk Gibson	.06
94	Alfredo Griffin	.06
95	Jay Howell	.06
96	Jesse Orosco	.06
97	Alejandro Pena	.06
98	Tracy Woodson	.06
99	John Dopson	.06
100	Brian Holman	.06
101	Rex Hudler	.06
102	Jeff Parrett	.06
103	Nelson Santovenia	.06
104	Kevin Elster	.06
105	Jeff Innis	.06
106	Mackey Sasser	.06
107	Phil Bradley	.06
108	Danny Clay	.06
109	Greg Harris	.06
110	Ricky Jordan	.06
111	David Palmer	.06
112	Jim Gott	.06
113	Tommy Gregg (photo actually Randy Milligan)	.06
114	Barry Jones	.06
115	Randy Milligan	.06
116	Luis Alicea	.10
117	Tom Brunansky	.06
118	John Costello	.06
119	Jose DeLeon	.06
120	Bob Horner	.06
121	Scott Terry	.06
122	*Roberto Alomar*	4.00
123	Dave Leiper	.06
124	Keith Moreland	.06
125	Mark Parent	.06
126	Dennis Rasmussen	.06
127	Randy Bockus	.06
128	Brett Butler	.06
129	Donell Nixon	.06
130	Earnest Riles	.06
131	Roger Samuels	.06
132	Checklist	.06

1988 Fleer Update Glossy Tin

The glossy version of the 1988 Fleer Update set differs from the regular-issue Update set only in the high-gloss finish applied to the cards' fronts and the lithographed metal box in which sets were sold.

	MT
Complete Set (132):	15.00
Common Player:	.15

(Star cards valued about 2X regular-issue 1988 Fleer Updates.)

1989 Fleer

This set includes 660 standard-size cards and was issued with 45 team logo stickers. Individual card fronts feature a grey and white striped background with full-color player photos framed by a bright line of color that slants upward to the right. The set also includes two subsets: 15 Major League Prospects and 12 SuperStar Specials. A special bonus set of 12 All-Star Team cards was randomly inserted in individual wax packs of 15 cards. The last seven cards in the set are checklists, with players listed alphabetically by teams.

		MT
Unopened Factory Set, Hobby (660):		20.00
Unopened Factory Set, Retail (672):		20.00
Complete Set (660):		12.50
Common Player:		.05
Wax Pack (15):		1.25
Wax Box (36):		30.00
1	Don Baylor	.15
2	*Lance Blankenship*	.10
3	*Todd Burns*	.05
4	Greg Cadaret	.05
5	Jose Canseco	.35
6	Storm Davis	.05
7	Dennis Eckersley	.10
8	Mike Gallego	.05
9	Ron Hassey	.05
10	Dave Henderson	.05
11	Rick Honeycutt	.05
12	Glenn Hubbard	.05
13	Stan Javier	.05
14	*Doug Jennings*	.05
15	*Felix Jose*	.05
16	Carney Lansford	.05
17	Mark McGwire	1.00
18	Gene Nelson	.05
19	Dave Parker	.10
20	Eric Plunk	.05

21 Luis Polonia .05
22 Terry Steinbach .05
23 Dave Stewart .05
24 Walt Weiss .05
25 Bob Welch .05
26 Curt Young .05
27 Rick Aguilera .05
28 Wally Backman .05
29 Mark Carreon .05
30 Gary Carter .25
31 David Cone .10
32 Ron Darling .05
33 Len Dykstra .05
34 Kevin Elster .05
35 Sid Fernandez .05
36 Dwight Gooden .05
37 Keith Hernandez .05
38 Gregg Jefferies .10
39 Howard Johnson .05
40 Terry Leach .05
41 Dave Magadan .05
42 Bob McClure .05
43 Roger McDowell .05
44 Kevin McReynolds .05
45 Keith Miller .05
46 Randy Myers .05
47 Bob Ojeda .05
48 Mackey Sasser .05
49 Darryl Strawberry .05
50 Tim Teufel .05
51 *Dave West* .10
52 Mookie Wilson .05
53 Dave Anderson .05
54 Tim Belcher .05
55 Mike Davis .05
56 Mike Devereaux .05
57 Kirk Gibson .05
58 Alfredo Griffin .05
59 Chris Gwynn .05
60 Jeff Hamilton .05
61a Danny Heep (Home: San Antonio, TX) .25
61b Danny Heep (Home: Lake Hills, TX) .05
62 Orel Hershiser .05
63 Brian Holton .05
64 Jay Howell .05
65 Tim Leary .05
66 Mike Marshall .05
67 *Ramon Martinez* .40
68 Jesse Orosco .05
69 Alejandro Pena .05
70 Steve Sax .05
71 Mike Scioscia .05
72 Mike Sharperson .05
73 John Shelby .05
74 Franklin Stubbs .05
75 John Tudor .05
76 Fernando Valenzuela .05
77 Tracy Woodson .05
78 Marty Barrett .05
79 Todd Benzinger .05
80 Mike Boddicker .05
81 Wade Boggs .25
82 "Oil Can" Boyd .05
83 Ellis Burks .05
84 Rick Cerone .05
85 Roger Clemens .50
86 *Steve Curry* .05
87 Dwight Evans .10
88 Wes Gardner .05
89 Rich Gedman .05
90 Mike Greenwell .05
91 Bruce Hurst .05
92 Dennis Lamp .05
93 Spike Owen .05
94 Larry Parrish .05
95 *Carlos Quintana* .05
96 Jody Reed .05
97 Jim Rice .15
98a Kevin Romine (batting follow-thru, photo actually Randy Kutcher) .25
98b Kevin Romine (arms crossed on chest, correct photo) .25
99 Lee Smith .10
100 Mike Smithson .05
101 Bob Stanley .05
102 Allan Anderson .05
103 Keith Atherton .05
104 Juan Berenguer .05
105 Bert Blyleven .10
106 *Eric Bullock* .05
107 Randy Bush .05
108 John Christensen .05
109 Mark Davidson .05
110 Gary Gaetti .05
111 Greg Gagne .05
112 Dan Gladden .05
113 *German Gonzalez* .05
114 Brian Harper .05
115 Tom Herr .05
116 Kent Hrbek .05
117 Gene Larkin .05
118 Tim Laudner .05
119 Charlie Lea .05
120 Steve Lombardozzi .05
121a John Moses (Home: Phoenix, AZ) .25
121b John Moses (Home: Tempe, AZ) .05
122 Al Newman .05
123 Mark Portugal .05
124 Kirby Puckett .50
125 Jeff Reardon .05
126 Fred Toliver .05
127 Frank Viola .05
128 Doyle Alexander .05
129 Dave Bergman .05
130a Tom Brookens (Mike Heath stats on back) .50
130b Tom Brookens (correct stats on back) .10
131 *Paul Gibson* .05
132a Mike Heath (Tom Brookens stats on back) .50
132b Mike Heath (correct stats on back) .10
133 *Don Heinkel* .05
134 Mike Henneman .05
135 Guillermo Hernandez .05
136 Eric King .05
137 Chet Lemon .05
138 Fred Lynn .05
139 Jack Morris .05
140 Matt Nokes .05
141 Gary Pettis .05
142 Ted Power .05
143 Jeff Robinson .05
144 Luis Salazar .05
145 *Steve Searcy* .10
146 Pat Sheridan .05
147 Frank Tanana .05
148 Alan Trammell .05
149 Walt Terrell .05
150 Jim Walewander .05
151 Lou Whitaker .05
152 Tim Birtsas .05
153 Tom Browning .05
154 *Keith Brown* .05
155 *Norm Charlton* .15
156 Dave Concepcion .05
157 Kal Daniels .05
158 Eric Davis .05
159 Bo Diaz .05
160 Rob Dibble .05
161 Nick Esasky .05
162 John Franco .05
163 Danny Jackson .05
164 Barry Larkin .15
165 Rob Murphy .05
166 Paul O'Neill .05
167 Jeff Reed .05
168 Jose Rijo .05
169 Ron Robinson .05
170 Chris Sabo .10
171 *Candy Sierra* .05
172 *Van Snider* .05
173a Jeff Treadway (blue "target" above head) 15.00
173b Jeff Treadway (no "target") .05
174 Frank Williams .05
175 Herm Winningham .05
176 Jim Adduci .05
177 Don August .05
178 Mike Birkbeck .05
179 Chris Bosio .05
180 Glenn Braggs .05
181 Greg Brock .05
182 Mark Clear .05
183 Chuck Crim .05
184 Rob Deer .05
185 Tom Filer .05
186 Jim Gantner .05
187 Darryl Hamilton .05
188 Ted Higuera .05
189 Odell Jones .05
190 Jeffrey Leonard .05
191 Joey Meyer .05
192 Paul Mirabella .05
193 Paul Molitor .30
194 Charlie O'Brien .05
195 Dan Plesac .05
196 *Gary Sheffield* .75
197 B.J. Surhoff .05
198 Dale Sveum .05
199 Bill Wegman .05
200 Robin Yount .30
201 Rafael Belliard .05
202 Barry Bonds .75
203 Bobby Bonilla .05
204 Sid Bream .05
205 Benny Distefano .05
206 Doug Drabek .05
207 Mike Dunne .05
208 Felix Fermin .05
209 Brian Fisher .05
210 Jim Gott .05
211 Bob Kipper .05
212 Dave LaPoint .05
213 Mike LaValliere .05
214 Jose Lind .05
215 Junior Ortiz .05
216 Vicente Palacios .05
217 Tom Prince .05
218 Gary Redus .05
219 R.J. Reynolds .05
220 Jeff Robinson .05
221 John Smiley .05
222 Andy Van Slyke .05
223 Bob Walk .05
224 Glenn Wilson .05
225 Jesse Barfield .05
226 George Bell .05
227 Pat Borders .05
228 John Cerutti .05
229 Jim Clancy .05
230 Mark Eichhorn .05
231 Tony Fernandez .05
232 Cecil Fielder .05
233 Mike Flanagan .05
234 Kelly Gruber .05
235 Tom Henke .05
236 Jimmy Key .05
237 Rick Leach .05
238 Manny Lee .05
239 Nelson Liriano .05
240 Fred McGriff .05
241 Lloyd Moseby .05
242 Rance Mulliniks .05
243 Jeff Musselman .05
244 Dave Stieb .05
245 Todd Stottlemyre .05
246 Duane Ward .05
247 David Wells .10
248 Ernie Whitt .05
249 Luis Aguayo .05
250a Neil Allen (Home: Sarasota, FL) .25
250b Neil Allen (Home: Syosset, NY) .05
251 John Candelaria .05
252 Jack Clark .05
253 Richard Dotson .05
254 Rickey Henderson .30
255 Tommy John .10
256 Roberto Kelly .05
257 Al Leiter .05
258 Don Mattingly .50
259 Dale Mohorcic .05
260 *Hal Morris* .25
261 Scott Nielsen .05
262 Mike Pagliarulo .05
263 *Hipolito Pena* .05
264 Ken Phelps .05
265 Willie Randolph .05
266 Rick Rhoden .05
267 Dave Righetti .05
268 Rafael Santana .05
269 Steve Shields .05
270 Joel Skinner .05
271 Don Slaught .05
272 Claudell Washington .05
273 Gary Ward .05
274 Dave Winfield .40
275 Luis Aquino .05
276 Floyd Bannister .05
277 George Brett .50
278 Bill Buckner .05
279 *Nick Capra* .05
280 *Jose DeJesus* .05
281 Steve Farr .05
282 Jerry Gleaton .05
283 Mark Gubicza .05
284 *Tom Gordon* .25
285 Bo Jackson .15
286 Charlie Leibrandt .05
287 *Mike Macfarlane* .15
288 Jeff Montgomery .05
289 Bill Pecota .05
290 Jamie Quirk .05
291 Bret Saberhagen .05
292 Kevin Seitzer .05
293 Kurt Stillwell .05
294 Pat Tabler .05
295 Danny Tartabull .05
296 Gary Thurman .05
297 Frank White .05
298 Willie Wilson .05
299 Roberto Alomar .40
300 *Sandy Alomar, Jr.* .40
301 Chris Brown .05
302 Mike Brumley .05
303 Mark Davis .05
304 Mark Grant .05
305 Tony Gwynn .40
306 *Greg Harris* .05
307 Andy Hawkins .05
308 Jimmy Jones .05
309 John Kruk .05
310 Dave Leiper .05
311 Carmelo Martinez .05
312 Lance McCullers .05
313 Keith Moreland .05
314 Dennis Rasmussen .05
315 Randy Ready .05
316 Benito Santiago .05
317 Eric Show .05
318 Todd Simmons .05
319 Garry Templeton .05
320 Dickie Thon .05
321 Ed Whitson .05
322 Marvell Wynne .05
323 Mike Aldrete .05
324 Brett Butler .05
325 Will Clark .15
326 Kelly Downs .05
327 Dave Dravecky .05
328 Scott Garrelts .05
329 Atlee Hammaker .05
330 *Charlie Hayes* .25
331 Mike Krukow .05
332 Craig Lefferts .05
333 Candy Maldonado .05
334 Kirt Manwaring .05
335 Bob Melvin .05
336 Kevin Mitchell .05
337 Donell Nixon .05
338 *Tony Perezchica* .05
339 Joe Price .05
340 Rick Reuschel .05
341 Earnest Riles .05
342 Don Robinson .05
343 Chris Speier .05
344 Robby Thompson .05
345 Jose Uribe .05
346 Matt Williams .20
347 *Trevor Wilson* .15
348 Juan Agosto .05
349 Larry Andersen .05
350a Alan Ashby ("Throws Rig") .25
350b Alan Ashby ("Throws Right") .05
351 Kevin Bass .05
352 Buddy Bell .05
353 Craig Biggio .15
354 Danny Darwin .05
355 Glenn Davis .05
356 Jim Deshaies .05
357 Bill Doran .05
358 *John Fishel* .05
359 Billy Hatcher .05
360 Bob Knepper .05
361 *Louie Meadows* .05
362 Dave Meads .05
363 Jim Pankovits .05
364 Terry Puhl .05
365 Rafael Ramirez .05
366 Craig Reynolds .05
367 Mike Scott .05
368 Nolan Ryan .75
369 Dave Smith .05
370 Gerald Young .05
371 Hubie Brooks .05
372 Tim Burke .05
373 *John Dopson* .10
374 Mike Fitzgerald .05
375 Tom Foley .05
376 Andres Galarraga .05

377 Neal Heaton .05
378 Joe Hesketh .05
379 *Brian Holman* .10
380 Rex Hudler .05
381 *Randy Johnson* 2.50
382 Wallace Johnson .05
383 Tracy Jones .05
384 Dave Martinez .05
385 Dennis Martinez .05
386 Andy McGaffigan .05
387 Otis Nixon .05
388 *Johnny Paredes* .05
389 Jeff Parrett .05
390 Pascual Perez .05
391 Tim Raines .05
392 Luis Rivera .05
393 *Nelson Santovenia* .05
394 Bryn Smith .05
395 Tim Wallach .05
396 Andy Allanson .05
397 *Rod Allen* .05
398 Scott Bailes .05
399 Tom Candiotti .05
400 Joe Carter .05
401 Carmen Castillo .05
402 Dave Clark .05
403 John Farrell .05
404 Julio Franco .05
405 Don Gordon .05
406 Mel Hall .05
407 Brad Havens .05
408 Brook Jacoby .05
409 Doug Jones .05
410 *Jeff Kaiser* .05
411 *Luis Medina* .05
412 Cory Snyder .05
413 Greg Swindell .05
414 *Ron Tingley* .05
415 Willie Upshaw .05
416 Ron Washington .05
417 Rich Yett .05
418 Damon Berryhill .05
419 Mike Bielecki .05
420 *Doug Dascenzo* .05
421 Jody Davis .05
422 Andre Dawson .15
423 Frank DiPino .05
424 Shawon Dunston .05
425 "Goose" Gossage .10
426 Mark Grace .30
427 *Mike Harkey* .05
428 Darrin Jackson .05
429 Les Lancaster .05
430 Vance Law .05
431 Greg Maddux .65
432 Jamie Moyer .05
433 Al Nipper .05
434 Rafael Palmeiro .20
435 Pat Perry .05
436 *Jeff Pico* .05
437 Ryne Sandberg .40
438 Calvin Schiraldi .05
439 Rick Sutcliffe .05
440a Manny Trillo ("Throws Rig") .35
440b Manny Trillo ("Throws Right") .05
441 *Gary Varsho* .05
442 Mitch Webster .05
443 Luis Alicea .05
444 Tom Brunansky .05
445 Vince Coleman .05
446 *John Costello* .05
447 Danny Cox .05
448 Ken Dayley .05
449 Jose DeLeon .05
450 Curt Ford .05
451 Pedro Guerrero .05
452 Bob Horner .05
453 *Tim Jones* .05
454 Steve Lake .05
455 Joe Magrane .05
456 Greg Mathews .05
457 Willie McGee .08
458 Larry McWilliams .05
459 Jose Oquendo .05
460 Tony Pena .05
461 Terry Pendleton .05
462 *Steve Peters* .05
463 Ozzie Smith .45
464 Scott Terry .05
465 Denny Walling .05
466 Todd Worrell .05
467 Tony Armas .05
468 *Dante Bichette* .50
469 Bob Boone .10
470 *Terry Clark* .05
471 Stew Cliburn .05
472 *Mike Cook* .05
473 *Sherman Corbett* .05
474 Chili Davis .05
475 Brian Downing .05
476 Jim Eppard .05
477 Chuck Finley .05
478 Willie Fraser .05
479 Bryan Harvey .05
480 Jack Howell .05
481 Wally Joyner .05
482 Jack Lazorko .05
483 Kirk McCaskill .05
484 Mark McLemore .05
485 Greg Minton .05
486 Dan Petry .05
487 Johnny Ray .05
488 Dick Schofield .05
489 Devon White .10
490 Mike Witt .05
491 Harold Baines .05
492 Daryl Boston .05
493 Ivan Calderon .05
494 Mike Diaz .05
495 Carlton Fisk .35
496 *Dave Gallagher* .05
497 Ozzie Guillen .05
498 Shawn Hillegas .05
499 Lance Johnson .05
500 Barry Jones .05
501 Bill Long .05
502 Steve Lyons .05
503 Fred Manrique .05
504 Jack McDowell .05
505 *Donn Pall* .10
506 Kelly Paris .05
507 Dan Pasqua .05
508 *Ken Patterson* .05
509 Melido Perez .05
510 Jerry Reuss .05
511 Mark Salas .05
512 Bobby Thigpen .05
513 Mike Woodard .05
514 Bob Brower .05
515 Steve Buechele .05
516 *Jose Cecena* .05
517 Cecil Espy .05
518 Scott Fletcher .05
519 Cecilio Guante .05
520 Jose Guzman .05
521 Ray Hayward .05
522 Charlie Hough .05
523 Pete Incaviglia .05
524 Mike Jeffcoat .05
525 Paul Kilgus .05
526 *Chad Kreuter* .15
527 Jeff Kunkel .05
528 Oddibe McDowell .05
529 Pete O'Brien .05
530 Geno Petralli .05
531 Jeff Russell .05
532 Ruben Sierra .05
533 Mike Stanley .05
534 Ed Vande Berg .05
535 Curtis Wilkerson .05
536 Mitch Williams .05
537 Bobby Witt .05
538 Steve Balboni .05
539 Scott Bankhead .05
540 Scott Bradley .05
541 Mickey Brantley .05
542 Jay Buhner .10
543 Mike Campbell .05
544 Darnell Coles .05
545 Henry Cotto .05
546 Alvin Davis .05
547 Mario Diaz .05
548 *Ken Griffey, Jr.* 10.00
549 *Erik Hanson* .15
550 Mike Jackson .05
551 Mark Langston .05
552 Edgar Martinez .10
553 *Bill McGuire* .05
554 Mike Moore .05
555 Jim Presley .05
556 Rey Quinones .05
557 Jerry Reed .05
558 Harold Reynolds .05
559 *Mike Schooler* .05
560 Bill Swift .05
561 Dave Valle .05
562 Steve Bedrosian .05
563 Phil Bradley .05
564 Don Carman .05
565 Bob Dernier .05
566 Marvin Freeman .05
567 Todd Frohwirth .05
568 Greg Gross .05
569 Kevin Gross .05
570 Greg Harris .05
571 Von Hayes .05
572 Chris James .05
573 Steve Jeltz .05
574 *Ron Jones* .05
575 *Ricky Jordan* .05
576 Mike Maddux .05
577 David Palmer .05
578 Lance Parrish .05
579 Shane Rawley .05
580 Bruce Ruffin .05
581 Juan Samuel .05
582 Mike Schmidt .45
583 Kent Tekulve .05
584 Milt Thompson .05
585 *Jose Alvarez* .05
586 Paul Assenmacher .05
587 Bruce Benedict .05
588 Jeff Blauser .05
589 *Terry Blocker* .05
590 Ron Gant .10
591 Tom Glavine .20
592 Tommy Gregg .05
593 Albert Hall .05
594 Dion James .05
595 Rick Mahler .05
596 Dale Murphy .20
597 Gerald Perry .05
598 Charlie Puleo .05
599 Ted Simmons .05
600 Pete Smith .05
601 Zane Smith .05
602 John Smoltz .15
603 Bruce Sutter .05
604 Andres Thomas .05
605 Ozzie Virgil .05
606 Brady Anderson .10
607 Jeff Ballard .05
608 *Jose Bautista* .05
609 Ken Gerhart .05
610 Terry Kennedy .05
611 Eddie Murray .30
612 Carl Nichols .05
613 Tom Niedenfuer .05
614 Joe Orsulak .05
615 *Oswaldo Peraza* ((Oswald)) .05
616a Bill Ripken (vulgarity on bat knob) 7.50
616b Bill Ripken (scribble over vulgarity) 7.50
616c Bill Ripken (black box over vulgarity) .10
616d Bill Ripken (vulgarity whited out) 20.00
616e Billy Ripken (strip cut out of bottom of card) .10
617 Cal Ripken, Jr. .75
618 Dave Schmidt .05
619 Rick Schu .05
620 Larry Sheets .05
621 Doug Sisk .05
622 Pete Stanicek .05
623 Mickey Tettleton .05
624 Jay Tibbs .05
625 Jim Traber .05
626 Mark Williamson .05
627 *Craig Worthington* .10
628 Speed and Power (Jose Canseco) .20
629 Pitcher Perfect (Tom Browning) .05
630 Like Father Like Sons (Roberto Alomar, Sandy Alomar, Jr.) .20
631 N.L. All-Stars (Will Clark, Rafael Palmeiro) .10
632 Homeruns Coast to Coast (Will Clark, Darryl Strawberry) .10
633 Hot Corner's Hot Hitters (Wade Boggs, Carney Lansford) .10
634 Triple A's (Jose Canseco, Mark McGwire, Terry Steinbach) .45
635 Dual Heat (Mark Davis, Dwight Gooden) .10
636 N.L. Pitching Power (David Cone, Danny Jackson) .05
637 Cannon Arms (Bobby Bonilla, Chris Sabo) .05
638 Double Trouble (Andres Galarraga, Gerald Perry) .05
639 Power Center (Eric Davis) .05
640 Major League Prospects (*Cameron Drew*), (*Steve Wilson*) .05
641 Major League Prospects (Kevin Brown), (*Kevin Reimer*) .30
642 Major League Prospects (*Jerald Clark*), (*Brad Pounders*) .05
643 Major League Prospects (*Mike Capel*), (*Drew Hall*) .05
644 Major League Prospects (*Joe Girardi*), (*Rolando Roomes*) .20
645 Major League Prospects (*Marty Brown*), (*Lenny Harris*) .15
646 Major League Prospects (*Luis de los Santos*), (*Jim Campbell*) .05
647 Major League Prospects (*Miguel Garcia*), (*Randy Kramer*) .05
648 Major League Prospects (*Torey Lovullo*), (*Robert Palacios*) .05
649 Major League Prospects (*Jim Corsi*), (*Bob Milacki*) .10
650 Major League Prospects (*Grady Hall*), (*Mike Rochford*) .05
651 Major League Prospects (*Vance Lovelace*), (*Terry Taylor*) .05
652 Major League Prospects (*Dennis Cook*), (*Ken Hill*) .20
653 Major League Prospects (*Scott Service*), (*Shane Turner*) .05
654 Checklist 1-101 .05
655 Checklist 102-200 .05
656 Checklist 201-298 .05
657 Checklist 299-395 .05
658 Checklist 396-490 .05
659 Checklist 491-584 .05
660 Checklist 585-660 .05

1989 Fleer Glossy Tin

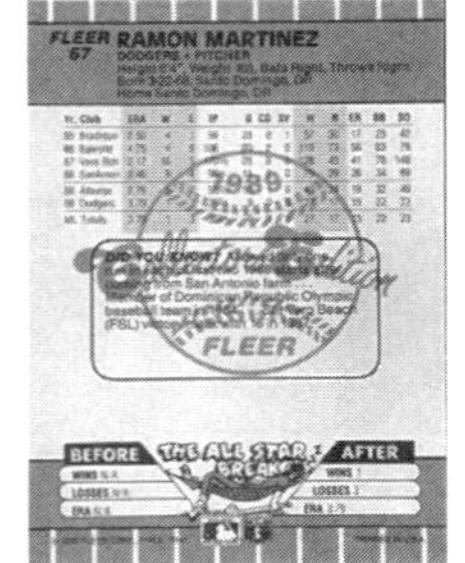

The last of the limited-edition, collector-version glossy tin sets is estimated to have been produced in an edition of 30,000-60,000, creating a significant premium over their counterparts in the regualr Fleer set. The issue was sold only in complete-set form in a lithographed metal box. The 1989 glossies differ from the regular cards on back in the use of blue, rather than yellow ink, and the appearance at center of a large baseball logo with 1989 / Collector's Edition / Fleer at center. No glossy version of the '89 Update set was made. Fleer glossy sets were originally wholesaled at $40 each.

	MT
Complete Set, Unopened (672):	150.00
Complete Set (672):	80.00
Common Player:	.25

(Star cards valued at 3-4X regular 1989 Fleer cards.)

1989 Fleer All Star Team

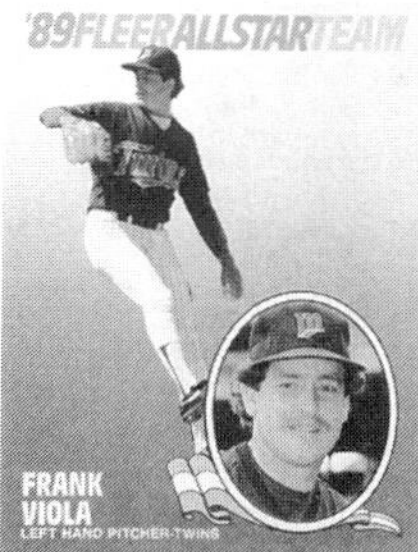

This special 12-card set represents Fleer's choices for its 1989 Major League All-Star Team. For the fourth consecutive year, Fleer inserted the special cards randomly in wax and cello packs. The cards feature two player photos set against a green background with the "'89 Fleer All Star Team" logo bannered across the top, and the player's name, position and team in the lower left corner. The backs contain a narrative player profile.

		MT
Complete Set (12):		3.50
Common Player:		.25
1	Bobby Bonilla	.25
2	Jose Canseco	1.00
3	Will Clark	.40
4	Dennis Eckersley	.25
5	Julio Franco	.25
6	Mike Greenwell	.25
7	Orel Hershiser	.25
8	Paul Molitor	1.00
9	Mike Scioscia	.25
10	Darryl Strawberry	.25
11	Alan Trammell	.25
12	Frank Viola	.25

1989 Fleer For The Record

Fleer's "For the Record" set features six players and their achievements from 1988. Fronts of the standard 2-1/2" x 3-1/2" cards feature a photo of the player set against a red scoreboard background. Card backs are grey and describe individual accomplishments. The cards were distributed randomly in rack packs.

		MT
Complete Set (6):		4.00
Common Player:		.25
1	Wade Boggs	.75
2	Roger Clemens	1.00
3	Andres Galarraga	.25
4	Kirk Gibson	.25
5	Greg Maddux	1.00
6	Don Mattingly	1.50

1989 Fleer World Series

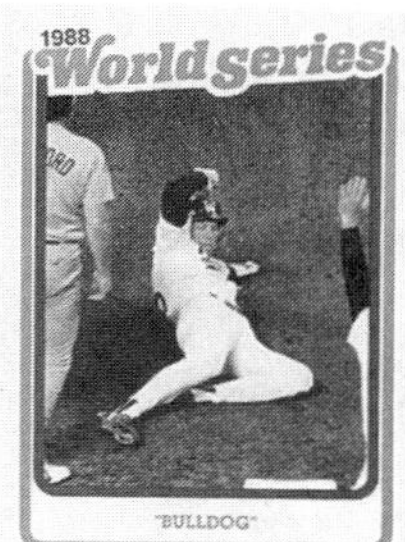

This 12-card set, which depicts highlights of the 1988 World Series, was included as a special sub-set with the regular and glossy factory-collated Fleer set. It was not available as individual cards in wax packs, cello packs or any other form.

		MT
Complete Set, Regular (12):		1.50
Complete Set, Glossy (12):		1.00
Common Card:		.10
1	Dodgers Secret Weapon (Mickey Hatcher)	.10
2	Rookie Starts Series (Tim Belcher)	.10
3	Jose Canseco	.25
4	Dramatic Comeback (Mike Scioscia)	.10
5	Kirk Gibson	.25
6	Orel Hershiser	.15
7	One Swings, Three RBIs (Mike Marshall)	.10
8	Mark McGwire	1.00
9	Sax's Speed Wins Game 4 (Steve Sax)	.10
10	Series Caps Award Winning Year (Walt Weiss)	.10
11	Orel Hershiser	.15
12	Dodger Blue, World Champs	.25

1989 Fleer Box Panels

For the fourth consecutive year, Fleer issued a series of cards on the bottom panels of its regular 1989 wax pack boxes. The 28-card set includes 20 players and eight team logo cards, all designed in the identical style of the regular 1989 Fleer set. The box-bottom cards were randomly printed, four cards (three player cards and one team logo) on each bottom panel. The cards are numbered from C-1 to C-28.

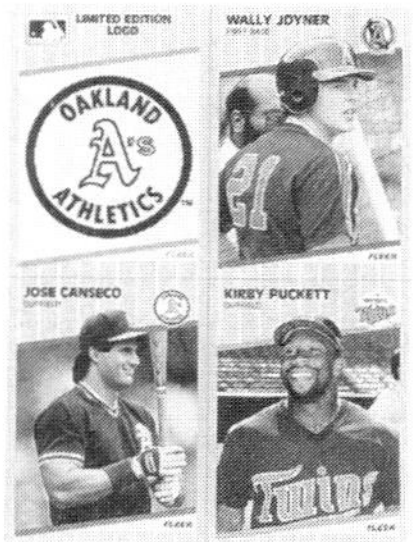

		MT
Complete Panel Set (7):		6.00
Complete Singles Set (28):		3.00
Common Single Player:		.15
1	Mets Logo	.05
2	Wade Boggs	.50
3	George Brett	.75
4	Jose Canseco	.50
5	A's Logo	.05
6	Will Clark	.25
7	David Cone	.10
8	Andres Galarraga	.20
9	Dodgers Logo	.05
10	Kirk Gibson	.10
11	Mike Greenwell	.10
12	Tony Gwynn	.75
13	Tigers Logo	.05
14	Orel Hershiser	.10
15	Danny Jackson	.10
16	Wally Joyner	.10
17	Red Sox Logo	.05
18	Yankees Logo	.05
19	Fred McGriff	.10
20	Kirby Puckett	.75
21	Chris Sabo	.10
22	Kevin Seitzer	.10
23	Pirates logo	.05
24	Astros logo	.05
25	Darryl Strawberry	.10
26	Alan Trammell	.20
27	Andy Van Slyke	.10
28	Frank Viola	.10

1989 Fleer Update

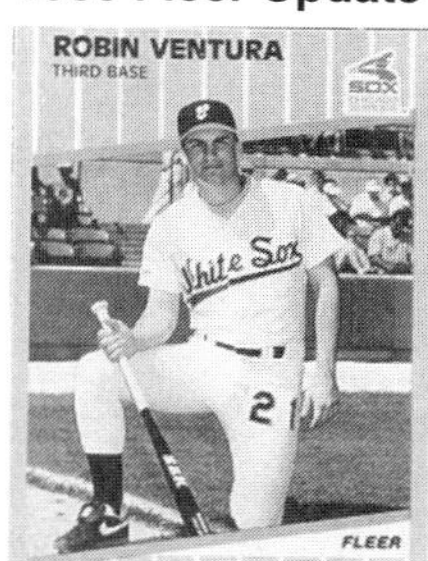

Fleer produced its sixth consecutive "Update" set in 1989 to supplement the company's regular set. As in the past, the set consisted of 132 cards (numbered U-1 through U-132) that were sold by hobby dealers in special collector's boxes.

		MT
Complete Set (132):		4.00
Common Player:		.06
1	Phil Bradley	.06
2	Mike Devereaux	.06
3	Steve Finley	.15
4	Kevin Hickey	.06
5	Brian Holton	.06
6	Bob Milacki	.06
7	Randy Milligan	.06
8	John Dopson	.06
9	Nick Esasky	.06
10	Rob Murphy	.06
11	Jim Abbott	.20
12	Bert Blyleven	.10
13	Jeff Manto	.06
14	Bob McClure	.06
15	Lance Parrish	.06
16	Lee Stevens	.06
17	Claudell Washington	.06
18	Mark Davis	.06
19	Eric King	.06
20	Ron Kittle	.06
21	Matt Merullo	.06
22	Steve Rosenberg	.06
23	Robin Ventura	.40
24	Keith Atherton	.06
25	*Joey (Albert) Belle*	1.00
26	Jerry Browne	.06
27	Felix Fermin	.06
28	Brad Komminsk	.06
29	Pete O'Brien	.06
30	Mike Brumley	.06
31	Tracy Jones	.06
32	Mike Schwabe	.06
33	Gary Ward	.06
34	Frank Williams	.06
35	*Kevin Appier*	.25
36	Bob Boone	.06
37	Luis de los Santos	.06
38	Jim Eisenreich	.06
39	*Jaime Navarro*	.06
40	Bill Spiers	.06
41	*Greg Vaughn*	1.00
42	Randy Veres	.06
43	Wally Backman	.06
44	Shane Rawley	.06
45	Steve Balboni	.06
46	Jesse Barfield	.06
47	Alvaro Espinoza	.06
48	Bob Geren	.06
49	Mel Hall	.06
50	Andy Hawkins	.06
51	Hensley Meulens	.06
52	Steve Sax	.06
53	*Deion Sanders*	.60
54	Rickey Henderson	.40
55	Mike Moore	.06
56	Tony Phillips	.06
57	Greg Briley	.06
58	Gene Harris	.06
59	Randy Johnson	1.50
60	Jeffrey Leonard	.06
61	Dennis Powell	.06
62	Omar Vizquel	.06
63	Kevin Brown	.10
64	Julio Franco	.06
65	Jamie Moyer	.06
66	Rafael Palmeiro	.15
67	Nolan Ryan	1.00
68	Francisco Cabrera	.06
69	Junior Felix	.06
70	Al Leiter	.06
71	Alex Sanchez	.06
72	Geronimo Berroa	.06
73	Derek Lilliquist	.06
74	Lonnie Smith	.06
75	Jeff Treadway	.06
76	Paul Kilgus	.06
77	Lloyd McClendon	.06
78	Scott Sanderson	.06
79	Dwight Smith	.06
80	Jerome Walton	.06
81	Mitch Williams	.06
82	Steve Wilson	.06
83	Todd Benzinger	.06
84	Ken Griffey	.06
85	Rick Mahler	.06
86	Rolando Roomes	.06

87	Scott Scudder	.06
88	Jim Clancy	.06
89	Rick Rhoden	.06
90	Dan Schatzeder	.06
91	Mike Morgan	.06
92	Eddie Murray	.35
93	Willie Randolph	.06
94	Ray Searage	.06
95	Mike Aldrete	.06
96	Kevin Gross	.06
97	Mark Langston	.06
98	Spike Owen	.06
99	Zane Smith	.06
100	Don Aase	.06
101	Barry Lyons	.06
102	Juan Samuel	.06
103	Wally Whitehurst	.06
104	Dennis Cook	.06
105	Len Dykstra	.06
106	Charlie Hayes	.06
107	Tommy Herr	.06
108	Ken Howell	.06
109	John Kruk	.06
110	Roger McDowell	.06
111	Terry Mulholland	.06
112	Jeff Parrett	.06
113	Neal Heaton	.06
114	Jeff King	.10
115	Randy Kramer	.06
116	Bill Landrum	.06
117	Cris Carpenter	.06
118	Frank DiPino	.06
119	Ken Hill	.06
120	Dan Quisenberry	.06
121	Milt Thompson	.06
122	*Todd Zeile*	.25
123	Jack Clark	.06
124	Bruce Hurst	.06
125	Mark Parent	.06
126	Bip Roberts	.06
127	Jeff Brantley	.06
128	Terry Kennedy	.06
129	Mike LaCoss	.06
130	Greg Litton	.06
131	Mike Schmidt	.50
132	Checklist	.06

1990 Fleer

Fleer's 1990 set, its 10th annual baseball card offering, again consisted of 660 cards numbered by team. The front of the cards feature mostly action photos surrounded by one of several different color bands and a white border. The set includes various special cards, including a series of "Major League Prospects," Players of the Decade, team checklist cards and a series of multi-player cards. The backs include complete career stats, player data, and a special "Vital Signs" section showing on-base percentage, slugging percentage, etc. for batters; and strikeout and walk ratios, opposing batting averages, etc. for pitchers.

	MT
Complete Set (660):	10.00
Unopened Factory Set (672):	12.50
Common Player:	.05
Wax Pack (15):	.75
Wax Box (36):	15.00

1	Lance Blankenship	.05
2	Todd Burns	.05
3	Jose Canseco	.25
4	Jim Corsi	.05
5	Storm Davis	.05
6	Dennis Eckersley	.10
7	Mike Gallego	.05
8	Ron Hassey	.05
9	Dave Henderson	.05
10	Rickey Henderson	.30
11	Rick Honeycutt	.05
12	Stan Javier	.05
13	Felix Jose	.05
14	Carney Lansford	.05
15	Mark McGwire	1.00
16	Mike Moore	.05
17	Gene Nelson	.05
18	Dave Parker	.10
19	Tony Phillips	.05
20	Terry Steinbach	.05
21	Dave Stewart	.05
22	Walt Weiss	.05
23	Bob Welch	.05
24	Curt Young	.05
25	Paul Assenmacher	.05
26	Damon Berryhill	.05
27	Mike Bielecki	.05
28	Kevin Blankenship	.05
29	Andre Dawson	.15
30	Shawon Dunston	.05
31	Joe Girardi	.10
32	Mark Grace	.25
33	Mike Harkey	.05
34	Paul Kilgus	.05
35	Les Lancaster	.05
36	Vance Law	.05
37	Greg Maddux	.60
38	Lloyd McClendon	.05
39	Jeff Pico	.05
40	Ryne Sandberg	.30
41	Scott Sanderson	.05
42	Dwight Smith	.05
43	Rick Sutcliffe	.05
44	*Jerome Walton*	.05
45	Mitch Webster	.05
46	Curt Wilkerson	.05
47	*Dean Wilkins*	.05
48	Mitch Williams	.05
49	Steve Wilson	.05
50	Steve Bedrosian	.05
51	*Mike Benjamin*	.05
52	*Jeff Brantley*	.10
53	Brett Butler	.05
54	Will Clark	.15
55	Kelly Downs	.05
56	Scott Garrelts	.05
57	Atlee Hammaker	.05
58	Terry Kennedy	.05
59	Mike LaCoss	.05
60	Craig Lefferts	.05
61	*Greg Litton*	.05
62	Candy Maldonado	.05
63	Kirt Manwaring	.05
64	*Randy McCament*	.05
65	Kevin Mitchell	.05
66	Donell Nixon	.05
67	Ken Oberkfell	.05
68	Rick Reuschel	.05
69	Ernest Riles	.05
70	Don Robinson	.05
71	Pat Sheridan	.05
72	Chris Speier	.05
73	Robby Thompson	.05
74	Jose Uribe	.05
75	Matt Williams	.20
76	George Bell	.05
77	Pat Borders	.05
78	John Cerutti	.05
79	*Junior Felix*	.05
80	Tony Fernandez	.05
81	Mike Flanagan	.05
82	*Mauro Gozzo*	.05
83	Kelly Gruber	.05
84	Tom Henke	.05
85	Jimmy Key	.05
86	Manny Lee	.05
87	Nelson Liriano	.05
88	Lee Mazzilli	.05
89	Fred McGriff	.05
90	Lloyd Moseby	.05
91	Rance Mulliniks	.05
92	Alex Sanchez	.05
93	Dave Steib	.05
94	Todd Stottlemyre	.05
95	Duane Ward	.05
96	David Wells	.10
97	Ernie Whitt	.05
98	Frank Wills	.05
99	Mookie Wilson	.05
100	Kevin Appier	.10
101	Luis Aquino	.05
102	Bob Boone	.10
103	George Brett	.50
104	Jose DeJesus	.05
105	Luis de los Santos	.05
106	Jim Eisenreich	.05
107	Steve Farr	.05
108	Tom Gordon	.05
109	Mark Gubicza	.05
110	Bo Jackson	.15
111	Terry Leach	.05
112	Charlie Leibrandt	.05
113	*Rick Luecken*	.05
114	Mike Macfarlane	.05
115	Jeff Montgomery	.05
116	Bret Saberhagen	.05
117	Kevin Seitzer	.05
118	Kurt Stillwell	.05
119	Pat Tabler	.05
120	Danny Tartabull	.05
121	Gary Thurman	.05
122	Frank White	.05
123	Willie Wilson	.05
124	*Matt Winters*	.05
125	Jim Abbott	.05
126	Tony Armas	.05
127	Dante Bichette	.10
128	Bert Blyleven	.10
129	Chili Davis	.05
130	Brian Downing	.05
131	*Mike Fetters*	.05
132	Chuck Finley	.05
133	Willie Fraser	.05
134	Bryan Harvey	.05
135	Jack Howell	.05
136	Wally Joyner	.05
137	*Jeff Manto*	.05
138	Kirk McCaskill	.05
139	Bob McClure	.05
140	Greg Minton	.05
141	Lance Parrish	.05
142	Dan Petry	.05
143	Johnny Ray	.05
144	Dick Schofield	.05
145	*Lee Stevens*	.05
146	Claudell Washington	.05
147	Devon White	.08
148	Mike Witt	.05
149	Roberto Alomar	.25
150	Sandy Alomar, Jr.	.10
151	Andy Benes	.10
152	Jack Clark	.05
153	Pat Clements	.05
154	Joey Cora	.05
155	Mark Davis	.05
156	Mark Grant	.05
157	Tony Gwynn	.40
158	Greg Harris	.05
159	Bruce Hurst	.05
160	Darrin Jackson	.05
161	Chris James	.05
162	Carmelo Martinez	.05
163	Mike Pagliarulo	.05
164	Mark Parent	.05
165	Dennis Rasmussen	.05
166	Bip Roberts	.05
167	Benito Santiago	.05
168	Calvin Schiraldi	.05
169	Eric Show	.05
170	Garry Templeton	.05
171	Ed Whitson	.05
172	Brady Anderson	.05
173	Jeff Ballard	.05
174	Phil Bradley	.05
175	Mike Devereaux	.05
176	Steve Finley	.10
177	Pete Harnisch	.05
178	Kevin Hickey	.05
179	Brian Holton	.05
180	*Ben McDonald*	.15
181	Bob Melvin	.05
182	Bob Milacki	.05
183	Randy Milligan	.05
184	Gregg Olson	.05
185	Joe Orsulak	.05
186	Bill Ripken	.05
187	Cal Ripken, Jr.	.75
188	Dave Schmidt	.05
189	Larry Sheets	.05
190	Mickey Tettleton	.05
191	Mark Thurmond	.05
192	Jay Tibbs	.05
193	Jim Traber	.05
194	Mark Williamson	.05
195	Craig Worthington	.05
196	Don Aase	.05
197	*Blaine Beatty*	.05
198	Mark Carreon	.05
199	Gary Carter	.20
200	David Cone	.05
201	Ron Darling	.05
202	Kevin Elster	.05
203	Sid Fernandez	.05
204	Dwight Gooden	.05
205	Keith Hernandez	.05
206	*Jeff Innis*	.05
207	Gregg Jefferies	.05
208	Howard Johnson	.05
209	Barry Lyons	.05
210	Dave Magadan	.05
211	Kevin McReynolds	.05
212	Jeff Musselman	.05
213	Randy Myers	.05
214	Bob Ojeda	.05
215	Juan Samuel	.05
216	Mackey Sasser	.05
217	Darryl Strawberry	.05
218	Tim Teufel	.05
219	Frank Viola	.05
220	Juan Agosto	.05
221	Larry Anderson	.05
222	*Eric Anthony*	.10
223	Kevin Bass	.05
224	Craig Biggio	.10
225	Ken Caminiti	.05
226	Jim Clancy	.05
227	Danny Darwin	.05
228	Glenn Davis	.05
229	Jim Deshaies	.05
230	Bill Doran	.05
231	Bob Forsch	.05
232	Brian Meyer	.05
233	Terry Puhl	.05
234	Rafael Ramirez	.05
235	Rick Rhoden	.05
236	Dan Schatzeder	.05
237	Mike Scott	.05
238	Dave Smith	.05
239	Alex Trevino	.05
240	Glenn Wilson	.05
241	Gerald Young	.05
242	Tom Brunansky	.05
243	Cris Carpenter	.05
244	*Alex Cole*	.05
245	Vince Coleman	.05
246	John Costello	.05
247	Ken Dayley	.05
248	Jose DeLeon	.05
249	Frank DiPino	.05
250	Pedro Guerrero	.05
251	Ken Hill	.05
252	Joe Magrane	.05
253	Willie McGee	.05
254	John Morris	.05
255	Jose Oquendo	.05
256	Tony Pena	.05
257	Terry Pendleton	.05
258	Ted Power	.05
259	Dan Quisenberry	.05
260	Ozzie Smith	.40
261	Scott Terry	.05
262	Milt Thompson	.05
263	Denny Walling	.05
264	Todd Worrell	.05
265	Todd Zeile	.10
266	Marty Barrett	.05
267	Mike Boddicker	.05
268	Wade Boggs	.35
269	Ellis Burks	.05
270	Rick Cerone	.05
271	Roger Clemens	.50
272	John Dopson	.05
273	Nick Esasky	.05
274	Dwight Evans	.10
275	Wes Gardner	.05
276	Rich Gedman	.05
277	Mike Greenwell	.05

No.	Player	Price
278	Danny Heep	.05
279	Eric Hetzel	.05
280	Dennis Lamp	.05
281	Rob Murphy	.05
282	Joe Price	.05
283	Carlos Quintana	.05
284	Jody Reed	.05
285	Luis Rivera	.05
286	Kevin Romine	.05
287	Lee Smith	.05
288	Mike Smithson	.05
289	Bob Stanley	.05
290	Harold Baines	.05
291	Kevin Brown	.10
292	Steve Buechele	.05
293	*Scott Coolbaugh*	.05
294	*Jack Daugherty*	.05
295	Cecil Espy	.05
296	Julio Franco	.05
297	*Juan Gonzalez*	3.00
298	Cecilio Guante	.05
299	Drew Hall	.05
300	Charlie Hough	.05
301	Pete Incaviglia	.05
302	Mike Jeffcoat	.05
303	Chad Kreuter	.05
304	Jeff Kunkel	.05
305	Rick Leach	.05
306	Fred Manrique	.05
307	Jamie Moyer	.05
308	Rafael Palmeiro	.15
309	Geno Petralli	.05
310	Kevin Reimer	.05
311	*Kenny Rogers*	.15
312	Jeff Russell	.05
313	Nolan Ryan	.75
314	Ruben Sierra	.05
315	Bobby Witt	.05
316	Chris Bosio	.05
317	Glenn Braggs	.05
318	Greg Brock	.05
319	Chuck Crim	.05
320	Rob Deer	.05
321	Mike Felder	.05
322	Tom Filer	.05
323	*Tony Fossas*	.05
324	Jim Gantner	.05
325	Darryl Hamilton	.05
326	Ted Higuera	.05
327	Mark Knudson	.05
328	Bill Krueger	.05
329	*Tim McIntosh*	.05
330	Paul Molitor	.30
331	Jaime Navarro	.05
332	Charlie O'Brien	.05
333	*Jeff Peterek*	.05
334	Dan Plesac	.05
335	Jerry Reuss	.05
336	Gary Sheffield	.25
337	*Bill Spiers*	.05
338	B.J. Surhoff	.05
339	Greg Vaughn	.10
340	Robin Yount	.30
341	Hubie Brooks	.05
342	Tim Burke	.05
343	Mike Fitzgerald	.05
344	Tom Foley	.05
345	Andres Galarraga	.05
346	Damaso Garcia	.05
347	*Marquis Grissom*	.50
348	Kevin Gross	.05
349	Joe Hesketh	.05
350	*Jeff Huson*	.10
351	Wallace Johnson	.05
352	Mark Langston	.05
353	Dave Martinez	.05
354	Dennis Martinez	.05
355	Andy McGaffigan	.05
356	Otis Nixon	.05
357	Spike Owen	.05
358	Pascual Perez	.05
359	Tim Raines	.05
360	Nelson Santovenia	.05
361	Bryn Smith	.05
362	Zane Smith	.05
363	*Larry Walker*	1.25
364	Tim Wallach	.05
365	Rick Aguilera	.05
366	Allan Anderson	.05
367	Wally Backman	.05
368	Doug Baker	.05
369	Juan Berenguer	.05
370	Randy Bush	.05
371	Carmen Castillo	.05
372	*Mike Dyer*	.05
373	Gary Gaetti	.05
374	Greg Gagne	.05
375	Dan Gladden	.05
376	German Gonzalez	.05
377	Brian Harper	.05
378	Kent Hrbek	.05
379	Gene Larkin	.05
380	Tim Laudner	.05
381	John Moses	.05
382	Al Newman	.05
383	Kirby Puckett	.50
384	Shane Rawley	.05
385	Jeff Reardon	.05
386	Roy Smith	.05
387	*Gary Wayne*	.05
388	Dave West	.05
389	Tim Belcher	.05
390	Tim Crews	.05
391	Mike Davis	.05
392	Rick Dempsey	.05
393	Kirk Gibson	.05
394	Jose Gonzalez	.05
395	Alfredo Griffin	.05
396	Jeff Hamilton	.05
397	Lenny Harris	.05
398	Mickey Hatcher	.05
399	Orel Hershiser	.05
400	Jay Howell	.05
401	Mike Marshall	.05
402	Ramon Martinez	.05
403	Mike Morgan	.05
404	Eddie Murray	.25
405	Alejandro Pena	.05
406	Willie Randolph	.05
407	Mike Scioscia	.05
408	Ray Searage	.05
409	Fernando Valenzuela	.05
410	*Jose Vizcaino*	.20
411	*John Wetteland*	.20
412	Jack Armstrong	.05
413	Todd Benzinger	.05
414	Tim Birtsas	.05
415	Tom Browning	.05
416	Norm Charlton	.05
417	Eric Davis	.05
418	Rob Dibble	.05
419	John Franco	.05
420	Ken Griffey, Sr.	.05
421	*Chris Hammond*	.15
422	Danny Jackson	.05
423	Barry Larkin	.15
424	Tim Leary	.05
425	Rick Mahler	.05
426	*Joe Oliver*	.05
427	Paul O'Neill	.05
428	Luis Quinones	.05
429	Jeff Reed	.05
430	Jose Rijo	.05
431	Ron Robinson	.05
432	Rolando Roomes	.05
433	Chris Sabo	.05
434	*Scott Scudder*	.10
435	Herm Winningham	.05
436	Steve Balboni	.05
437	Jesse Barfield	.05
438	*Mike Blowers*	.05
439	Tom Brookens	.05
440	Greg Cadaret	.05
441	Alvaro Espinoza	.05
442	*Bob Geren*	.05
443	Lee Guetterman	.05
444	Mel Hall	.05
445	Andy Hawkins	.05
446	Roberto Kelly	.05
447	Don Mattingly	.50
448	Lance McCullers	.05
449	Hensley Meulens	.05
450	Dale Mohorcic	.05
451	Clay Parker	.05
452	Eric Plunk	.05
453	Dave Righetti	.05
454	Deion Sanders	.15
455	Steve Sax	.05
456	Don Slaught	.05
457	Walt Terrell	.05
458	Dave Winfield	.35
459	Jay Bell	.10
460	Rafael Belliard	.05
461	Barry Bonds	.60
462	Bobby Bonilla	.05
463	Sid Bream	.05
464	Benny Distefano	.05
465	Doug Drabek	.05
466	Jim Gott	.05
467	Billy Hatcher	.05
468	Neal Heaton	.05
469	Jeff King	.05
470	Bob Kipper	.05
471	Randy Kramer	.05
472	Bill Landrum	.05
473	Mike LaValliere	.05
474	Jose Lind	.05
475	Junior Ortiz	.05
476	Gary Redus	.05
477	*Rick Reed*	.05
478	R.J. Reynolds	.05
479	Jeff Robinson	.05
480	John Smiley	.05
481	Andy Van Slyke	.05
482	Bob Walk	.05
483	Andy Allanson	.05
484	Scott Bailes	.05
485	Albert Belle	.20
486	Bud Black	.05
487	Jerry Browne	.05
488	Tom Candiotti	.05
489	Joe Carter	.05
490	David Clark	.05
491	John Farrell	.05
492	Felix Fermin	.05
493	Brook Jacoby	.05
494	Dion James	.05
495	Doug Jones	.05
496	Brad Komminsk	.05
497	Rod Nichols	.05
498	Pete O'Brien	.05
499	*Steve Olin*	.10
500	Jesse Orosco	.05
501	Joel Skinner	.05
502	Cory Snyder	.05
503	Greg Swindell	.05
504	Rich Yett	.05
505	Scott Bankhead	.05
506	Scott Bradley	.05
507	Greg Briley	.05
508	Jay Buhner	.05
509	Darnell Coles	.05
510	Keith Comstock	.05
511	Henry Cotto	.05
512	Alvin Davis	.05
513	Ken Griffey, Jr.	1.00
514	Erik Hanson	.05
515	Gene Harris	.05
516	Brian Holman	.05
517	Mike Jackson	.05
518	Randy Johnson	.35
519	Jeffrey Leonard	.05
520	Edgar Martinez	.05
521	Dennis Powell	.05
522	Jim Presley	.05
523	Jerry Reed	.05
524	Harold Reynolds	.05
525	Mike Schooler	.05
526	Bill Swift	.05
527	David Valle	.05
528	Omar Vizquel	.10
529	Ivan Calderon	.05
530	Carlton Fisk	.25
531	Scott Fletcher	.05
532	Dave Gallagher	.05
533	Ozzie Guillen	.05
534	*Greg Hibbard*	.05
535	Shawn Hillegas	.05
536	Lance Johnson	.05
537	Eric King	.05
538	Ron Kittle	.05
539	Steve Lyons	.05
540	Carlos Martinez	.05
541	*Tom McCarthy*	.05
542	*Matt Merullo*	.05
543	Donn Pall	.05
544	Dan Pasqua	.05
545	Ken Patterson	.05
546	Melido Perez	.05
547	Steve Rosenberg	.05
548	*Sammy Sosa*	5.00
549	Bobby Thigpen	.05
550	Robin Ventura	.10
551	Greg Walker	.05
552	Don Carman	.05
553	*Pat Combs*	.05
554	Dennis Cook	.05
555	Darren Daulton	.05
556	Len Dykstra	.05
557	Curt Ford	.05
558	Charlie Hayes	.05
559	Von Hayes	.05
560	Tom Herr	.05
561	Ken Howell	.05
562	Steve Jeltz	.05
563	Ron Jones	.05
564	Ricky Jordan	.05
565	John Kruk	.05
566	Steve Lake	.05
567	Roger McDowell	.05
568	Terry Mulholland	.05
569	Dwayne Murphy	.05
570	Jeff Parrett	.05
571	Randy Ready	.05
572	Bruce Ruffin	.05
573	Dickie Thon	.05
574	Jose Alvarez	.05
575	Geronimo Berroa	.05
576	Jeff Blauser	.05
577	Joe Boever	.05
578	Marty Clary	.05
579	Jody Davis	.05
580	Mark Eichhorn	.05
581	Darrell Evans	.10
582	Ron Gant	.05
583	Tom Glavine	.10
584	*Tommy Greene*	.05
585	Tommy Gregg	.05
586	*Dave Justice*	.40
587	Mark Lemke	.05
588	Derek Lilliquist	.05
589	Oddibe McDowell	.05
590	*Kent Mercker*	.05
591	Dale Murphy	.20
592	Gerald Perry	.05
593	Lonnie Smith	.05
594	Pete Smith	.05
595	John Smoltz	.10
596	*Mike Stanton*	.10
597	Andres Thomas	.05
598	Jeff Treadway	.05
599	Doyle Alexander	.05
600	Dave Bergman	.05
601	*Brian Dubois*	.05
602	Paul Gibson	.05
603	Mike Heath	.05
604	Mike Henneman	.05
605	Guillermo Hernandez	.05
606	*Shawn Holman*	.05
607	Tracy Jones	.05
608	Chet Lemon	.05
609	Fred Lynn	.05
610	Jack Morris	.05
611	Matt Nokes	.05
612	Gary Pettis	.05
613	*Kevin Ritz*	.10
614	Jeff Robinson	.05
615	Steve Searcy	.05
616	Frank Tanana	.05
617	Alan Trammell	.05
618	Gary Ward	.05
619	Lou Whitaker	.05
620	Frank Williams	.05
621a	Players of the Decade - 1980 (George Brett) (... .390 hitting ...)	1.00
621b	Players of the Decade - 1980 (George Brett)	.20
622	Players of the Decade - 1981 (Fernando Valenzuela)	.05
623	Players of the Decade - 1982 (Dale Murphy)	.05
624a	Players of the Decade - 1983 (Cal Ripkin, Jr.) (Ripken)	1.50
624b	Players of the Decade - 1983 (Cal Ripken, Jr.)	.25
625	Players of the Decade - 1984 (Ryne Sandberg)	.15
626	Players of the Decade - 1985 (Don Mattingly)	.25
627	Players of the Decade - 1986 (Roger Clemens)	.25
628	Players of the Decade - 1987 (George Bell)	.05
629	Players of the Decade - 1988 (Jose Canseco)	.10
630a	Players of the Decade - 1989 (Will Clark) (total bases 32)	.50
630b	Players of the Decade - 1989 (Will Clark) (total bases 321)	.10
631	Game Savers (Mark Davis, Mitch Williams)	.05
632	Boston Igniters (Wade Boggs, Mike Greenwell)	.10

633 Starter & Stopper (Mark Gubicza, Jeff Russell) .05
634 League's Best Shortstops (Tony Fernandez, Cal Ripken Jr.) .15
635 Human Dynamos (Kirby Puckett, Bo Jackson) .15
636 300 Strikeout Club (Mike Scott, Nolan Ryan) .20
637 The Dymanic Duo (Will Clark, Kevin Mitchell) .10
638 A.L. All-Stars (Don Mattingly, Mark McGwire) .50
639 N.L. East Rivals (Howard Johnson, Ryne Sandberg) .10
640 Major League Prospects *(Rudy Seanez), (Colin Charland)* .10
641 Major League Prospects *(George Canale), (Kevin Maas)* .15
642 Major League Prospects *(Kelly Mann), (Dave Hansen)* .15
643 Major League Prospects *(Greg Smith), (Stu Tate)* .10
644 Major League Prospects *(Tom Drees), (Dan Howitt)* .05
645 Major League Prospects *(Mike Roesler), (Derrick May)* .05
646 Major League Prospects *(Scott Hemond), (Mark Gardner)* .10
647 Major League Prospects *(John Orton), (Scott Leius)* .10
648 Major League Prospects *(Rich Monteleone), (Dana Williams)* .05
649 Major League Prospects *(Mike Huff), (Steve Frey)* .10
650 Major League Prospects *(Chuck McElroy), (Moises Alou)* .65
651 Major League Prospects *(Bobby Rose), (Mike Hartley)* .10
652 Major League Prospects *(Matt Kinzer), (Wayne Edwards)* .05
653 Major League Prospects *(Delino DeShields), (Jason Grimsley)* .15
654 Athletics, Cubs, Giants & Blue Jays (Checklist) .05
655 Royals, Angels, Padres & Orioles (Checklist) .05
656 Mets, Astros, Cardinals & Red Sox (Checklist) .05
657 Rangers, Brewers, Expos & Twins (Checklist) .05
658 Dodgers, Reds, Yankees & Pirates (Checklist) .05
659 Indians, Mariners, White Sox & Phillies (Checklist) .05
660 Braves, Tigers & Special Cards (Checklist) .05

1990 Fleer All-Stars

The top players at each position, as selected by Fleer, are featured in this 12-card set inserted in cello packs and some wax packs. The cards measure 2-1/2" x 3-1/2" and feature a unique two-photo format on the card fronts.

		MT
Complete Set (12):		4.00
Common Player:		.20
1	Harold Baines	.20
2	Will Clark	.40
3	Mark Davis	.20
4	Howard Johnson	.20
5	Joe Magrane	.20
6	Kevin Mitchell	.20
7	Kirby Puckett	1.00
8	Cal Ripken	2.00
9	Ryne Sandberg	.75
10	Mike Scott	.20
11	Ruben Sierra	.20
12	Mickey Tettleton	.20

1990 Fleer Box Panels

For the fifth consecutive year, Fleer issued a series of cards on the bottom panels of its wax pack boxes. This 28-card set features both players and team logo cards. The cards were numbered C-1 to C-28.

		MT
Complete Set, Panels (7):		5.00
Complete Set, Singles (28):		5.00
Common Player:		.05
1	Giants Logo	.05
2	Tim Belcher	.05
3	Roger Clemens	.75
4	Eric Davis	.10
5	Glenn Davis	.05
6	Cubs Logo	.05
7	John Franco	.05
8	Mike Greenwell	.05
9	Athletics logo	.05
10	Ken Griffey, Jr.	1.00
11	Pedro Guerrero	.05
12	Tony Gwynn	.60
13	Blue Jays Logo	.05
14	Orel Hershiser	.10
15	Bo Jackson	.20
16	Howard Johnson	.05
17	Mets Logo	.05
18	Cardinals Logo	.05
19	Don Mattingly	.75
20	Mark McGwire	1.00
21	Kevin Mitchell	.05
22	Kirby Puckett	.75
23	Royals Logo	.05
24	Orioles Logo	.05
25	Ruben Sierra	.05
26	Dave Stewart	.10
27	Jerome Walton	.05
28	Robin Yount	.35

1990 Fleer League Standouts

Fleer's "League Standouts" are six of baseball's top players distributed randomly in Fleer rack packs. Fronts feature full color photos with a six-dimensional effect. A black and gold frame borders the photo. Backs are yellow and describe the player's accomplishments. The cards measure 2-1/2" x 3-1/2".

		MT
Complete Set (6):		3.00
Common Player:		.50
1	Barry Larkin	.50
2	Don Mattingly	1.50
3	Darryl Strawberry	.50
4	Jose Canseco	.60
5	Wade Boggs	.75
6	Mark Grace	.60

1990 Fleer Soaring Stars

Cards from this 12-card set could be found in 1990 Fleer jumbo cello packs. The cards are styled with a cartoon flavor, featuring astronomical graphics surrounding the player. Backs feature information about the promising young player.

		MT
Complete Set (12):		11.00
Common Player:		.20
1	Todd Zeile	.25
2	Mike Stanton	.20
3	Larry Walker	2.00
4	Robin Ventura	2.00
5	Scott Coolbaugh	.20
6	Ken Griffey, Jr.	7.50
7	Tom Gordon	.25
8	Jerome Walton	.20
9	Junior Felix	.20
10	Jim Abbott	.25
11	Ricky Jordan	.20
12	Dwight Smith	.20

1990 Fleer World Series

This 12-card set depicts highlights of the 1989 World Series and was included in the factory-collated Fleer set. Single World Series cards were discovered in cello and rack packs, but this was not intended to happen. Fronts of the 2-1/2" x 3-1/2" cards feature action photos set against a white background with a red and blue "'89 World Series" banner. Backs are pink and white and describe the events of the 1989 Fall Classic.

		MT
Complete Set (12):		1.50
Common Player:		.10
1	The Final Piece To The Puzzle (Mike Moore)	.10
2	Kevin Mitchell	.15
3	Game Two's Crushing Blow	.20
4	Will Clark	.50
5	Jose Canseco	.75
6	Great Leather in the Field	.10
7	Game One And A's Break Out On Top	.10
8	Dave Stewart	.25
9	Parker's Bat Produces Power (Dave Parker)	.25
10	World Series Record Book Game 3	.10
11	Rickey Henderson	.75
12	Oakland A's - Baseball's Best In '89	.25

1990 Fleer Update

Fleer produced its seventh consecutive "Update"

set in 1990. As in the past, the set consists of 132 cards (numbered U-1 through U-132) that were sold by hobby dealers in special collectors boxes. The cards are designed in the same style as the regular issue. A special Nolan Ryan commemorative card is included in the set.

		MT
Complete Set (132):		4.00
Common Player:		.05
1	Steve Avery	.05
2	Francisco Cabrera	.05
3	Nick Esasky	.05
4	Jim Kremers	.05
5	Greg Olson	.05
6	Jim Presley	.05
7	Shawn Boskie	.05
8	Joe Kraemer	.05
9	Luis Salazar	.05
10	Hector Villanueva	.05
11	Glenn Braggs	.05
12	Mariano Duncan	.05
13	Billy Hatcher	.05
14	Tim Layana	.05
15	Hal Morris	.05
16	Javier Ortiz	.05
17	Dave Rohde	.05
18	Eric Yelding	.05
19	Hubie Brooks	.05
20	Kal Daniels	.05
21	Dave Hansen	.05
22	Mike Hartley	.05
23	Stan Javier	.05
24	Jose Offerman	.05
25	Juan Samuel	.05
26	Dennis Boyd	.05
27	Delino DeShields	.05
28	Steve Frey	.05
29	Mark Gardner	.05
30	Chris Nabholz	.05
31	Bill Sampen	.05
32	Dave Schmidt	.05
33	Daryl Boston	.05
34	Chuck Carr	.05
35	John Franco	.05
36	*Todd Hundley*	.75
37	Julio Machado	.05
38	Alejandro Pena	.05
39	Darren Reed	.05
40	Kelvin Torve	.05
41	Darrel Akerfelds	.05
42	Jose DeJesus	.05
43	Dave Hollins	.05
44	Carmelo Martinez	.05
45	Brad Moore	.05
46	Dale Murphy	.15
47	Wally Backman	.05
48	Stan Belinda	.05
49	Bob Patterson	.05
50	Ted Power	.05
51	Don Slaught	.05
52	Geronimo Pena	.05
53	Lee Smith	.05
54	John Tudor	.05
55	Joe Carter	.05
56	Tom Howard	.05
57	Craig Lefferts	.05
58	Rafael Valdez	.05
59	Dave Anderson	.05
60	Kevin Bass	.05
61	John Burkett	.05
62	Gary Carter	.15
63	Rick Parker	.05
64	Trevor Wilson	.05
65	Chris Hoiles	.05
66	Tim Hulett	.05
67	Dave Johnson	.05
68	Curt Schilling	.35
69	David Segui	.05
70	Tom Brunansky	.05
71	Greg Harris	.05
72	Dana Kiecker	.05
73	Tim Naehring	.05
74	Tony Pena	.05
75	Jeff Reardon	.05
76	Jerry Reed	.05
77	Mark Eichhorn	.05
78	Mark Langston	.05
79	John Orton	.05
80	Luis Polonia	.05
81	Dave Winfield	.45
82	Cliff Young	.05
83	Wayne Edwards	.05
84	Alex Fernandez	.05
85	Craig Grebeck	.05
86	Scott Radinsky	.05
87	Frank Thomas	3.00
88	Beau Allred	.05
89	Sandy Alomar, Jr.	.05
90	*Carlos Baerga*	.10
91	Kevin Bearse	.05
92	Chris James	.05
93	Candy Maldonado	.05
94	Jeff Manto	.05
95	Cecil Fielder	.05
96	*Travis Fryman*	.25
97	Lloyd Moseby	.05
98	Edwin Nunez	.05
99	Tony Phillips	.05
100	Larry Sheets	.05
101	Mark Davis	.05
102	Storm Davis	.05
103	Gerald Perry	.05
104	Terry Shumpert	.05
105	Edgar Diaz	.05
106	Dave Parker	.05
107	Tim Drummond	.05
108	Junior Ortiz	.05
109	Park Pittman	.05
110	Kevin Tapani	.05
111	Oscar Azocar	.05
112	Jim Leyritz	.15
113	Kevin Maas	.05
114	Alan Mills	.05
115	Matt Nokes	.05
116	Pascual Perez	.05
117	Ozzie Canseco	.10
118	Scott Sanderson	.05
119	Tino Martinez	.10
120	Jeff Schaefer	.05
121	Matt Young	.05
122	Brian Bohanon	.05
123	Jeff Huson	.05
124	Ramon Manon	.05
125	Gary Mielke	.05
126	Willie Blair	.05
127	Glenallen Hill	.05
128	*John Olerud*	.35
129	Luis Sojo	.05
130	Mark Whiten	.05
131	Three Decades of No Hitters (Nolan Ryan)	.75
132	Checklist	.05

1990 Fleer "Printed in Canada"

Whether these cards were printed for distribution in Canada or simply the work of a Canadian printer engaged by Fleer to meet U.S. demand is unknown. Each of the 660 cards in the 1990 Fleer issue can be found with a "1990 FLEER LTD./LTEE PTD. IN CANADA" copyright notice on back in the bottom border. Except for various superstar cards, little demand attaches to this variation.

	MT
Complete Set (660):	25.00
Common Player:	.25

(See 1990 Fleer for checklist and base values; stars bring 2-4X base price.)

1991 Fleer

Fleer expanded its 1991 set to include 720 cards. The cards feature yellow borders surrounding full-color action photos. Backs feature a circular portrait photo, biographical information, complete statistics, and career highlights. Once again the cards are numbered alphabetically within team. Because Fleer used more than one printer, many minor variations in photo cropping and typography can be found. The most notable are included in the checklist here.

		MT
Unopened Factory Set (732):		10.00
Complete Set (720):		8.00
Common Player:		.05
Pack (15):		.30
Wax Box (36):		8.00
1	*Troy Afenir*	.05
2	Harold Baines	.05
3	Lance Blankenship	.05
4	Todd Burns	.05
5	Jose Canseco	.30
6	Dennis Eckersley	.10
7	Mike Gallego	.05
8	Ron Hassey	.05
9	Dave Henderson	.05
10	Rickey Henderson	.30
11	Rick Honeycutt	.05
12	Doug Jennings	.05
13	*Joe Klink*	.05
14	Carney Lansford	.05
15	*Darren Lewis*	.10
16	Willie McGee	.05
17a	Mark McGwire (six-line career summary)	1.50
17b	Mark McGwire (seven-line career summary)	1.50
18	Mike Moore	.05
19	Gene Nelson	.05
20	Dave Otto	.05
21	Jamie Quirk	.05
22	Willie Randolph	.05
23	Scott Sanderson	.05
24	Terry Steinbach	.05
25	Dave Stewart	.05
26	Walt Weiss	.05
27	Bob Welch	.05
28	Curt Young	.05
29	Wally Backman	.05
30	*Stan Belinda*	.05
31	Jay Bell	.05
32	Rafael Belliard	.05
33	Barry Bonds	.50
34	Bobby Bonilla	.05
35	Sid Bream	.05
36	Doug Drabek	.05
37	*Carlos Garcia*	.15
38	Neal Heaton	.05
39	Jeff King	.05
40	Bob Kipper	.05
41	Bill Landrum	.05
42	Mike LaValliere	.05
43	Jose Lind	.05
44	Carmelo Martinez	.05
45	Bob Patterson	.05
46	Ted Power	.05
47	Gary Redus	.05
48	R.J. Reynolds	.05
49	Don Slaught	.05
50	John Smiley	.05
51	Zane Smith	.05
52	*Randy Tomlin*	.10
53	Andy Van Slyke	.05
54	Bob Walk	.05
55	Jack Armstrong	.05
56	Todd Benzinger	.05
57	Glenn Braggs	.05
58	Keith Brown	.05
59	Tom Browning	.05
60	Norm Charlton	.05
61	Eric Davis	.05
62	Rob Dibble	.05
63	Bill Doran	.05
64	Mariano Duncan	.05
65	Chris Hammond	.05
66	Billy Hatcher	.05
67	Danny Jackson	.05
68	Barry Larkin	.10
69	*Tim Layana*	.05
70	*Terry Lee*	.05
71	Rick Mahler	.05
72	Hal Morris	.05
73	Randy Myers	.05
74	Ron Oester	.05
75	Joe Oliver	.05
76	Paul O'Neill	.05
77	Luis Quinones	.05
78	Jeff Reed	.05
79	Jose Rijo	.05
80	Chris Sabo	.05
81	Scott Scudder	.05
82	Herm Winningham	.05
83	Larry Andersen	.05
84	Marty Barrett	.05
85	Mike Boddicker	.05
86	Wade Boggs	.30
87	Tom Bolton	.05
88	Tom Brunansky	.05
89	Ellis Burks	.05
90	Roger Clemens	.50
91	Scott Cooper	.05
92	John Dopson	.05
93	Dwight Evans	.05
94	Wes Gardner	.05
95	*Jeff Gray*	.05
96	Mike Greenwell	.05
97	Greg Harris	.05
98	*Daryl Irvine*	.05
99	*Dana Kiecker*	.05
100	Randy Kutcher	.05
101	Dennis Lamp	.05
102	Mike Marshall	.05
103	John Marzano	.05
104	Rob Murphy	.05
105a	*Tim Naehring* (seven-line career summary)	.05
105b	*Tim Naehring* (nine-line career summary)	.05
106	Tony Pena	.05
107	*Phil Plantier*	.05
108	Carlos Quintana	.05
109	Jeff Reardon	.05
110	Jerry Reed	.05
111	Jody Reed	.05
112	Luis Rivera	.05
113a	Kevin Romine (one-line career summary)	.05
113b	Kevin Romine (two-line career summary)	.05
114	Phil Bradley	.05
115	Ivan Calderon	.05
116	Wayne Edwards	.05
117	Alex Fernandez	.05

118 Carlton Fisk .35
119 Scott Fletcher .05
120 *Craig Grebeck* .10
121 Ozzie Guillen .05
122 Greg Hibbard .05
123 Lance Johnson .05
124 Barry Jones .05
125a Ron Karkovice (two-line career summary) .05
125b Ron Karkovice (one-line career summary) .05
126 Eric King .05
127 Steve Lyons .05
128 Carlos Martinez .05
129 Jack McDowell .05
130 Donn Pall .05
131 Dan Pasqua .05
132 Ken Patterson .05
133 Melido Perez .05
134 Adam Peterson .05
135 *Scott Radinsky* .10
136 Sammy Sosa .75
137 Bobby Thigpen .05
138 Frank Thomas 1.00
139 Robin Ventura .05
140 Daryl Boston .05
141 *Chuck Carr* .10
142 Mark Carreon .05
143 David Cone .05
144 Ron Darling .05
145 Kevin Elster .05
146 Sid Fernandez .05
147 John Franco .05
148 Dwight Gooden .05
149 Tom Herr .05
150 Todd Hundley .05
151 Gregg Jefferies .05
152 Howard Johnson .05
153 Dave Magadan .05
154 Kevin McReynolds .05
155 Keith Miller .05
156 Bob Ojeda .05
157 Tom O'Malley .05
158 Alejandro Pena .05
159 *Darren Reed* .10
160 Mackey Sasser .05
161 Darryl Strawberry .05
162 Tim Teufel .05
163 Kelvin Torve .05
164 Julio Valera .05
165 Frank Viola .05
166 Wally Whitehurst .05
167 Jim Acker .05
168 *Derek Bell* .15
169 George Bell .05
170 *Willie Blair* .05
171 Pat Borders .05
172 John Cerutti .05
173 Junior Felix .05
174 Tony Fernandez .05
175 Kelly Gruber .05
176 Tom Henke .05
177 Glenallen Hill .05
178 Jimmy Key .05
179 Manny Lee .05
180 Fred McGriff .05
181 Rance Mulliniks .05
182 Greg Myers .05
183 John Olerud .10
184 Luis Sojo .05
185 Dave Steib .05
186 Todd Stottlemyre .05
187 Duane Ward .05
188 David Wells .10
189 *Mark Whiten* .10
190 Ken Williams .05
191 Frank Wills .05
192 Mookie Wilson .05
193 Don Aase .05
194 Tim Belcher .05
195 Hubie Brooks .05
196 Dennis Cook .05
197 Tim Crews .05
198 Kal Daniels .05
199 Kirk Gibson .05
200 Jim Gott .05
201 Alfredo Griffin .05
202 Chris Gwynn .05
203 Dave Hansen .05
204 Lenny Harris .05
205 Mike Hartley .05
206 Mickey Hatcher .05
207 *Carlos Hernandez* .10
208 Orel Hershiser .05
209 Jay Howell .05
210 Mike Huff .05
211 Stan Javier .05
212 Ramon Martinez .05
213 Mike Morgan .05
214 Eddie Murray .25
215 *Jim Neidlinger* .05
216 Jose Offerman .05
217 *Jim Poole* .05
218 Juan Samuel .05
219 Mike Scioscia .05
220 Ray Searage .05
221 Mike Sharperson .05
222 Fernando Valenzuela .05
223 Jose Vizcaino .05
224 Mike Aldrete .05
225 *Scott Anderson* .05
226 Dennis Boyd .05
227 Tim Burke .05
228 Delino DeShields .05
229 Mike Fitzgerald .05
230 Tom Foley .05
231 Steve Frey .05
232 Andres Galarraga .05
233 Mark Gardner .05
234 Marquis Grissom .05
235 Kevin Gross .05
236 Drew Hall .05
237 Dave Martinez .05
238 Dennis Martinez .05
239 Dale Mohorcic .05
240 *Chris Nabholz* .05
241 Otis Nixon .05
242 Junior Noboa .05
243 Spike Owen .05
244 Tim Raines .05
245 *Mel Rojas* .10
246 *Scott Ruskin* .05
247 *Bill Sampen* .05
248 Nelson Santovenia .05
249 Dave Schmidt .05
250 Larry Walker .25
251 Tim Wallach .05
252 Dave Anderson .05
253 Kevin Bass .05
254 Steve Bedrosian .05
255 Jeff Brantley .05
256 John Burkett .05
257 Brett Butler .05
258 Gary Carter .15
259 Will Clark .15
260 *Steve Decker* .05
261 Kelly Downs .05
262 Scott Garrelts .05
263 Terry Kennedy .05
264 Mike LaCoss (photo on back actually Ken Oberkfell) .05
265 *Mark Leonard* .05
266 Greg Litton .05
267 Kevin Mitchell .05
268 Randy O'Neal .05
269 *Rick Parker* .05
270 Rick Reuschel .05
271 Ernest Riles .05
272 Don Robinson .05
273 Robby Thompson .05
274 Mark Thurmond .05
275 Jose Uribe .05
276 Matt Williams .20
277 Trevor Wilson .05
278 *Gerald Alexander* .05
279 Brad Arnsberg .05
280 *Kevin Belcher* .05
281 *Joe Bitker* .05
282 Kevin Brown .10
283 Steve Buechele .05
284 Jack Daugherty .05
285 Julio Franco .05
286 Juan Gonzalez .35
287 *Bill Haselman* .15
288 Charlie Hough .05
289 Jeff Huson .05
290 Pete Incaviglia .05
291 Mike Jeffcoat .05
292 Jeff Kunkel .05
293 Gary Mielke .05
294 Jamie Moyer .05
295 Rafael Palmeiro .10
296 Geno Petralli .05
297 Gary Pettis .05
298 Kevin Reimer .05
299 Kenny Rogers .05
300 Jeff Russell .05
301 John Russell .05
302 Nolan Ryan .65
303 Ruben Sierra .05
304 Bobby Witt .05
305 Jim Abbott .05
306 Kent Anderson .05
307 Dante Bichette .05
308 Bert Blyleven .05
309 Chili Davis .05
310 Brian Downing .05
311 Mark Eichhorn .05
312 Mike Fetters .05
313 Chuck Finley .05
314 Willie Fraser .05
315 Bryan Harvey .05
316 Donnie Hill .05
317 Wally Joyner .05
318 Mark Langston .05
319 Kirk McCaskill .05
320 John Orton .05
321 Lance Parrish .05
322 Luis Polonia .05
323 Johnny Ray .05
324 Bobby Rose .05
325 Dick Schofield .05
326 Rick Schu .05
327a Lee Stevens (six-line career summary) .05
327b Lee Stevens (seven-line career summary) .05
328 Devon White .05
329 Dave Winfield .35
330 *Cliff Young* .05
331 Dave Bergman .05
332 *Phil Clark* .10
333 Darnell Coles .05
334 Milt Cuyler .05
335 Cecil Fielder .05
336 Travis Fryman .05
337 Paul Gibson .05
338 Jerry Don Gleaton .05
339 Mike Heath .05
340 Mike Henneman .05
341 Chet Lemon .05
342 Lance McCullers .05
343 Jack Morris .05
344 Lloyd Moseby .05
345 Edwin Nunez .05
346 Clay Parker .05
347 Dan Petry .05
348 Tony Phillips .05
349 Jeff Robinson .05
350 Mark Salas .05
351 *Mike Schwabe* .05
352 Larry Sheets .05
353 John Shelby .05
354 Frank Tanana .05
355 Alan Trammell .05
356 Gary Ward .05
357 Lou Whitaker .05
358 Beau Allred .05
359 Sandy Alomar,Jr. .05
360 Carlos Baerga .05
361 *Kevin Bearse* .05
362 Tom Brookens .05
363 Jerry Browne .05
364 Tom Candiotti .05
365 Alex Cole .05
366 John Farrell .05
367 Felix Fermin .05
368 Keith Hernandez .05
369 Brook Jacoby .05
370 Chris James .05
371 Dion James .05
372 Doug Jones .05
373 Candy Maldonado .05
374 Steve Olin .05
375 Jesse Orosco .05
376 Rudy Seanez .05
377 Joel Skinner .05
378 Cory Snyder .05
379 Greg Swindell .05
380 Sergio Valdez .05
381 *Mike Walker* .05
382 *Colby Ward* .05
383 *Turner Ward* .05
384 Mitch Webster .05
385 Kevin Wickander .05
386 Darrel Akerfelds .05
387 Joe Boever .05
388a Rod Booker (no 1981 stats) .05
388b Rod Booker (1981 stats included) .05
389 Sil Campusano .05
390 Don Carman .05
391 *Wes Chamberlain* .05
392 Pat Combs .05
393 Darren Daulton .05
394 Jose DeJesus .05
395 Len Dykstra .05
396 Jason Grimsley .05
397 Charlie Hayes .05
398 Von Hayes .05
399 *Dave Hollins* .20
400 Ken Howell .05
401 Ricky Jordan .05
402 John Kruk .05
403 Steve Lake .05
404 *Chuck Malone* .05
405 Roger McDowell .05
406 Chuck McElroy .05
407 *Mickey Morandini* .10
408 Terry Mulholland .05
409 Dale Murphy .15
410 Randy Ready .05
411 Bruce Ruffin .05
412 Dickie Thon .05
413 Paul Assenmacher .05
414 Damon Berryhill .05
415 Mike Bielecki .05
416 *Shawn Boskie* .10
417 Dave Clark .05
418 Doug Dascenzo .05
419a Andre Dawson (no 1976 stats) .15
419b Andre Dawson (1976 stats included) .15
420 Shawon Dunston .05
421 Joe Girardi .05
422 Mark Grace .25
423 Mike Harkey .05
424 Les Lancaster .05
425 Bill Long .05
426 Greg Maddux .50
427 Derrick May .05
428 Jeff Pico .05
429 Domingo Ramos .05
430 Luis Salazar .05
431 Ryne Sandberg .30
432 Dwight Smith .05
433 Greg Smith .05
434 Rick Sutcliffe .05
435 Gary Varsho .05
436 *Hector Villanueva* .05
437 Jerome Walton .05
438 Curtis Wilkerson .05
439 Mitch Williams .05
440 Steve Wilson .05
441 Marvell Wynne .05
442 Scott Bankhead .05
443 Scott Bradley .05
444 Greg Briley .05
445 Mike Brumley .05
446 Jay Buhner .05
447 *Dave Burba* .10
448 Henry Cotto .05
449 Alvin Davis .05
450 Ken Griffey, Jr. 1.00
451 Erik Hanson .05
452 Gene Harris .05
453 Brian Holman .05
454 Mike Jackson .05
455 Randy Johnson .25
456 Jeffrey Leonard .05
457 Edgar Martinez .05
458 Tino Martinez .05
459 Pete O'Brien .05
460 Harold Reynolds .05
461 Mike Schooler .05
462 Bill Swift .05
463 David Valle .05
464 Omar Vizquel .05
465 Matt Young .05
466 Brady Anderson .05
467 Jeff Ballard .05
468 Juan Bell .05
469a Mike Devereaux ("six" last word in career summary top line) .05
469b Mike Devereaux ("runs" last word in career summary top line) .05
470 Steve Finley .05
471 Dave Gallagher .05
472 *Leo Gomez* .10
473 Rene Gonzales .05
474 Pete Harnisch .05
475 Kevin Hickey .05
476 *Chris Hoiles* .10
477 Sam Horn .05
478 Tim Hulett .05
479 Dave Johnson .05
480 Ron Kittle .05
481 Ben McDonald .05

482 Bob Melvin .05
483 Bob Milacki .05
484 Randy Milligan .05
485 *John Mitchell* .05
486 Gregg Olson .05
487 Joe Orsulak .05
488 Joe Price .05
489 Bill Ripken .05
490 Cal Ripken, Jr. .75
491 Curt Schilling .10
492 *David Segui* .10
493 *Anthony Telford* .05
494 Mickey Tettleton .05
495 Mark Williamson .05
496 Craig Worthington .05
497 Juan Agosto .05
498 Eric Anthony .05
499 Craig Biggio .10
500 Ken Caminiti .05
501 Casey Candaele .05
502 *Andujar Cedeno* .05
503 Danny Darwin .05
504 Mark Davidson .05
505 Glenn Davis .05
506 Jim Deshaies .05
507 *Luis Gonzalez* .50
508 Bill Gullickson .05
509 Xavier Hernandez .05
510 Brian Meyer .05
511 Ken Oberkfell .05
512 Mark Portugal .05
513 Rafael Ramirez .05
514 *Karl Rhodes* .10
515 Mike Scott .05
516 *Mike Simms* .05
517 Dave Smith .05
518 Franklin Stubbs .05
519 Glenn Wilson .05
520 Eric Yelding .05
521 Gerald Young .05
522 Shawn Abner .05
523 Roberto Alomar .25
524 Andy Benes .05
525 Joe Carter .05
526 Jack Clark .05
527 Joey Cora .05
528 *Paul Faries* .05
529 Tony Gwynn .40
530 Atlee Hammaker .05
531 Greg Harris .05
532 *Thomas Howard* .05
533 Bruce Hurst .05
534 Craig Lefferts .05
535 Derek Lilliquist .05
536 Fred Lynn .05
537 Mike Pagliarulo .05
538 Mark Parent .05
539 Dennis Rasmussen .05
540 Bip Roberts .05
541 *Richard Rodriguez* .05
542 Benito Santiago .05
543 Calvin Schiraldi .05
544 Eric Show .05
545 Phil Stephenson .05
546 Garry Templeton .05
547 Ed Whitson .05
548 Eddie Williams .05
549 Kevin Appier .05
550 Luis Aquino .05
551 Bob Boone .05
552 George Brett .35
553 *Jeff Conine* .30
554 Steve Crawford .05
555 Mark Davis .05
556 Storm Davis .05
557 Jim Eisenreich .05
558 Steve Farr .05
559 Tom Gordon .05
560 Mark Gubicza .05
561 Bo Jackson .15
562 Mike Macfarlane .05
563 *Brian McRae* .20
564 Jeff Montgomery .05
565 Bill Pecota .05
566 Gerald Perry .05
567 Bret Saberhagen .05
568 *Jeff Schulz* .05
569 Kevin Seitzer .05
570 *Terry Shumpert* .05
571 Kurt Stillwell .05
572 Danny Tartabull .05
573 Gary Thurman .05
574 Frank White .05
575 Willie Wilson .05
576 Chris Bosio .05
577 Greg Brock .05
578 George Canale .05
579 Chuck Crim .05
580 Rob Deer .05
581 *Edgar Diaz* .05
582 *Tom Edens* .05
583 Mike Felder .05
584 Jim Gantner .05
585 Darryl Hamilton .05
586 Ted Higuera .05
587 Mark Knudson .05
588 Bill Krueger .05
589 Tim McIntosh .05
590 Paul Mirabella .05
591 Paul Molitor .30
592 Jaime Navarro .05
593 Dave Parker .05
594 Dan Plesac .05
595 Ron Robinson .05
596 Gary Sheffield .20
597 Bill Spiers .05
598 B.J. Surhoff .05
599 Greg Vaughn .05
600 Randy Veres .05
601 Robin Yount .35
602a Rick Aguilera (five-line career summary) .05
602b Rick Aguilera (four-line career summary) .05
603 Allan Anderson .05
604 Juan Berenguer .05
605 Randy Bush .05
606 Carmen Castillo .05
607 Tim Drummond .05
608 *Scott Erickson* .10
609 Gary Gaetti .05
610 Greg Gagne .05
611 Dan Gladden .05
612 Mark Guthrie .05
613 Brian Harper .05
614 Kent Hrbek .05
615 Gene Larkin .05
616 Terry Leach .05
617 Nelson Liriano .05
618 Shane Mack .05
619 John Moses .05
620 *Pedro Munoz* .05
621 Al Newman .05
622 Junior Ortiz .05
623 Kirby Puckett .40
624 Roy Smith .05
625 Kevin Tapani .05
626 Gary Wayne .05
627 David West .05
628 Cris Carpenter .05
629 Vince Coleman .05
630 Ken Dayley .05
631 Jose DeLeon .05
632 Frank DiPino .05
633 *Bernard Gilkey* .25
634 Pedro Guerrero .05
635 Ken Hill .05
636 Felix Jose .05
637 *Ray Lankford* .25
638 Joe Magrane .05
639 Tom Niedenfuer .05
640 Jose Oquendo .05
641 Tom Pagnozzi .05
642 Terry Pendleton .05
643 *Mike Perez* .05
644 Bryn Smith .05
645 Lee Smith .05
646 Ozzie Smith .35
647 Scott Terry .05
648 Bob Tewksbury .05
649 Milt Thompson .05
650 John Tudor .05
651 Denny Walling .05
652 *Craig Wilson* .05
653 Todd Worrell .05
654 Todd Zeile .05
655 *Oscar Azocar* .05
656 Steve Balboni .05
657 Jesse Barfield .05
658 Greg Cadaret .05
659 Chuck Cary .05
660 Rick Cerone .05
661 Dave Eiland .05
662a Alvaro Espinoza (no 1979-80 stats) .05
662b Alvaro Espinoza (1979-80 stats included) .05
663 Bob Geren .05
664 Lee Guetterman .05
665 Mel Hall .05
666a Andy Hawkins (no 1978 stats) .05
666b Andy Hawkins (1978 stats included) .05
667 Jimmy Jones .05
668 Roberto Kelly .05
669 Dave LaPoint .05
670 Tim Leary .05
671 *Jim Leyritz* .20
672 Kevin Maas .05
673 Don Mattingly .40
674 Matt Nokes .05
675 Pascual Perez .05
676 Eric Plunk .05
677 Dave Righetti .05
678 Jeff Robinson .05
679 Steve Sax .05
680 Mike Witt .05
681 Steve Avery .05
682 Mike Bell .05
683 Jeff Blauser .05
684 Francisco Cabrera .05
685 Tony Castillo .05
686 Marty Clary .05
687 Nick Esasky .05
688 Ron Gant .05
689 Tom Glavine .10
690 Mark Grant .05
691 Tommy Gregg .05
692 Dwayne Henry .05
693 Dave Justice .25
694 *Jimmy Kremers* .05
695 Charlie Leibrandt .05
696 Mark Lemke .05
697 Oddibe McDowell .05
698 *Greg Olson* .05
699 Jeff Parrett .05
700 Jim Presley .05
701 *Victor Rosario* .05
702 Lonnie Smith .05
703 Pete Smith .05
704 John Smoltz .10
705 Mike Stanton .05
706 Andres Thomas .05
707 Jeff Treadway .05
708 *Jim Vatcher* .05
709 Home Run Kings (Ryne Sandberg, Cecil Fielder) .10
710 Second Generation Superstars (Barry Bonds, Ken Griffey, Jr.) .40
711 NLCS Team Leaders (Bobby Bonilla, Barry Larkin) .05
712 Top Game Savers (Bobby Thigpen, John Franco) .05
713 Chicago's 100 Club (Andre Dawson, Ryne Sandberg) .10
714 Checklists (Athletics, Pirates, Reds, Red Sox) .05
715 Checklists - White Sox, Mets, Blue Jays, Dodgers .05
716 Checklists (Expos, Giants, Rangers, Angels) .05
717 Checklists (Tigers, Indians, Phillies, Cubs) .05
718 Checklists (Mariners, Orioles, Astros, Padres) .05
719 Checklists (Royals, Brewers, Twins, Cardinals) .05
720 Checklists (Yankees, Braves, Super Stars) .05

1991 Fleer All Stars

Three player photos are featured on each card in this special insert set. An action shot and portrait close-up are featured on the front, while a full-figure pose is showcased on the back. The cards were inserted into 1991 Fleer cello packs.

		MT
Complete Set (10):		8.00
Common Player:		.50
1	Ryne Sandberg	1.00
2	Barry Larkin	.50
3	Matt Williams	.50
4	Cecil Fielder	.50
5	Barry Bonds	2.00
6	Rickey Henderson	.60
7	Ken Griffey, Jr.	3.00
8	Jose Canseco	.50
9	Benito Santiago	.50
10	Roger Clemens	1.50

1991 Fleer Box Panels

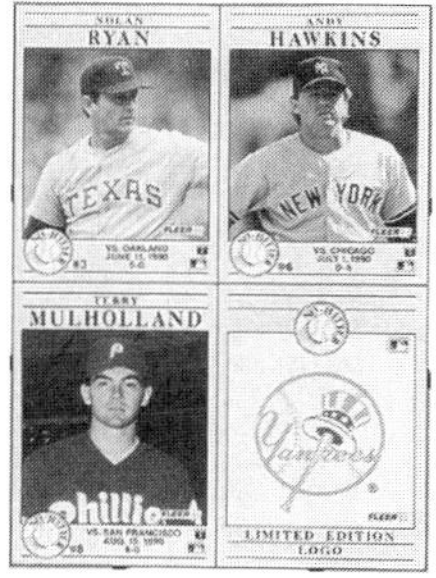

Unlike past box panel sets, the 1991 Fleer box panels feature a theme; 1990 no-hitters are celebrated on the three different boxes. The cards feature blank backs and are numbered in order of no-hitter on the front. A team logo was included on each box. The card fronts are styled after the 1991 Fleer cards. A special no-hitter logo appears in the lower left corner.

		MT
Complete Set, Singles (10):		3.00
Complete Set, Panels (3):		3.00
Common Player:		.10
1	Mark Langston, Mike Witt	.10
2	Randy Johnson	.50
3	Nolan Ryan	2.50
4	Dave Stewart	.10
5	Fernando Valenzuela	.10
6	Andy Hawkins	.10
7	Melido Perez	.10
8	Terry Mulholland	.10
9	Dave Steib	.10
----	Team Logos	.05

1991 Fleer ProVisions

The illustrations of artist Terry Smith are showcased in this special set. Twelve fantasy portraits were produced for cards inserted into rack packs. Four other ProVision cards were inserted into factory sets. The rack pack cards feature black borders, while the factory set cards have white borders. Information on the card backs explains the manner in which Smith painted each player. Factory insert ProVisions are indicated by an "F" suffix in the checklist here.

		MT
Complete Set (12):		5.00
Common Player:		.15
Complete Factory Set (4):		5.00
Common Player:		.40
1	Kirby Puckett	1.00
2	Will Clark	.30
3	Ruben Sierra	.15
4	Mark McGwire	1.50
5	Bo Jackson	.25
6	Jose Canseco	.50
7	Dwight Gooden	.15
8	Mike Greenwell	.15
9	Roger Clemens	1.00
10	Eric Davis	.15
11	Don Mattingly	1.00
12	Darryl Strawberry	.15
1F	Barry Bonds	3.50
2F	Rickey Henderson	.50
3F	Ryne Sandberg	1.00
4F	Dave Stewart	.40

1991 Fleer World Series

Once again Fleer released a set in honor of the World Series from the previous season. The 1991 issue features only eight cards compared to twelve in 1990. The cards feature white borders surrounding full-color action shots from the 1990 Fall Classic. The card backs feature an overview of the World Series action.

		MT
Complete Set (8):		1.50
Common Player:		.20
1	Eric Davis	.25
2	Billy Hatcher	.20
3	Jose Canseco	.35
4	Rickey Henderson	.35
5	Chris Sabo, Carney Lansford	.20
6	Dave Stewart	.25
7	Jose Rijo	.20
8	Reds Celebrate	.20

1991 Fleer Update

Fleer produced its eighth consecutive "Update" set in 1991 to supplement the company's regular set. As in the past, the set consists of 132 cards that were sold by hobby dealers in special collectors boxes. The cards are designed in the same style as the regular Fleer issue.

		MT
Complete Set (132):		5.00
Common Player:		.06
1	Glenn Davis	.06
2	Dwight Evans	.06
3	Jose Mesa	.15
4	Jack Clark	.06
5	Danny Darwin	.06
6	Steve Lyons	.06
7	Mo Vaughn	.50
8	Floyd Bannister	.06
9	Gary Gaetti	.06
10	Dave Parker	.06
11	Joey Cora	.06
12	Charlie Hough	.06
13	Matt Merullo	.06
14	Warren Newson	.10
15	Tim Raines	.06
16	Albert Belle	.20
17	Glenallen Hill	.06
18	Shawn Hillegas	.06
19	Mark Lewis	.06
20	Charles Nagy	.25
21	Mark Whiten	.06
22	John Cerutti	.06
23	Rob Deer	.06
24	Mickey Tettleton	.06
25	Warren Cromartie	.06
26	Kirk Gibson	.06
27	David Howard	.06
28	Brent Mayne	.10
29	Dante Bichette	.10
30	Mark Lee	.06
31	Julio Machado	.06
32	Edwin Nunez	.06
33	Willie Randolph	.06
34	Franklin Stubbs	.06
35	Bill Wegman	.06
36	Chili Davis	.06
37	Chuck Knoblauch	.25
38	Scott Leius	.06
39	Jack Morris	.06
40	Mike Pagliarulo	.06
41	Lenny Webster	.06
42	John Habyan	.06
43	Steve Howe	.06
44	Jeff Johnson	.06
45	Scott Kamieniecki	.10
46	Pat Kelly	.06
47	Hensley Meulens	.06
48	Wade Taylor	.06
49	Bernie Williams	.30
50	Kirk Dressendorfer	.10
51	Ernest Riles	.06
52	Rich DeLucia	.06
53	Tracy Jones	.06
54	Bill Krueger	.06
55	Alonzo Powell	.06
56	Jeff Schaefer	.06
57	Russ Swan	.06
58	John Barfield	.06
59	Rich Gossage	.10
60	Jose Guzman	.06
61	Dean Palmer	.06
62	*Ivan Rodriguez*	2.00
63	Roberto Alomar	.30
64	Tom Candiotti	.06
65	Joe Carter	.06
66	Ed Sprague	.06
67	Pat Tabler	.06
68	Mike Timlin	.15
69	Devon White	.10
70	Rafael Belliard	.06
71	Juan Berenguer	.06
72	Sid Bream	.06
73	Marvin Freeman	.06
74	Kent Mercker	.06
75	Otis Nixon	.06
76	Terry Pendleton	.06
77	George Bell	.06
78	Danny Jackson	.06
79	Chuck McElroy	.06
80	Gary Scott	.06
81	Heathcliff Slocumb	.06
82	Dave Smith	.06
83	Rick Wilkins	.10
84	Freddie Benavides	.06
85	Ted Power	.06
86	Mo Sanford	.06
87	*Jeff Bagwell*	2.00
88	Steve Finley	.10
89	Pete Harnisch	.06
90	Darryl Kile	.15
91	Brett Butler	.06
92	John Candelaria	.06
93	Gary Carter	.20
94	Kevin Gross	.06
95	Bob Ojeda	.06
96	Darryl Strawberry	.06
97	Ivan Calderon	.06
98	Ron Hassey	.06
99	Gilberto Reyes	.06
100	Hubie Brooks	.06
101	Rick Cerone	.06
102	Vince Coleman	.06
103	Jeff Innis	.06
104	Pete Schourek	.06
105	Andy Ashby	.10
106	Wally Backman	.06
107	Darrin Fletcher	.10
108	Tommy Greene	.06
109	John Morris	.06
110	Mitch Williams	.06
111	Lloyd McClendon	.06
112	Orlando Merced	.25
113	Vicente Palacios	.06
114	Gary Varsho	.06
115	John Wehner	.06
116	Rex Hudler	.06
117	Tim Jones	.06
118	Geronimo Pena	.10
119	Gerald Perry	.06
120	Larry Andersen	.06
121	Jerald Clark	.06
122	Scott Coolbaugh	.06
123	Tony Fernandez	.06
124	Darrin Jackson	.06
125	Fred McGriff	.06
126	Jose Mota	.06
127	Tim Teufel	.06
128	Bud Black	.06
129	Mike Felder	.06
130	Willie McGee	.06
131	Dave Righetti	.06
132	Checklist	.06

1992 Fleer

For the second consecutive year, Fleer produced a 720-card set. The standard card fronts feature full-color action photos bordered in green with the player's name, position and team logo on the right border. The backs feature another full-color action photo, biographical information and statistics. A special 12-card Roger Clemens subset is also included in the 1992 Fleer set. Three more Clemens cards were available through a mail-in offer, and 2,000 Roger Clemens autographed cards were inserted in 1992 packs. Once again the cards are numbered according to team. Subsets in the issue included Major League Propects (#652-680), Record Setters (#681-687), League Leaders (#688-697), Superstar Specials (#698-707) and ProVisions (#708-713), which for the first time were part of the regular numbered set rather than limited edition insert cards.

		MT
Unopened Factory Set (732):		15.00
Complete Set (720):		12.50
Common Player:		.05
Pack (15):		.50
Wax Box (36):		15.00
1	Brady Anderson	.05
2	Jose Bautista	.05
3	Juan Bell	.05
4	Glenn Davis	.05
5	Mike Devereaux	.05
6	Dwight Evans	.05
7	Mike Flanagan	.05
8	Leo Gomez	.05
9	Chris Hoiles	.05
10	Sam Horn	.05
11	Tim Hulett	.05
12	Dave Johnson	.05
13	*Chito Martinez*	.05
14	Ben McDonald	.05
15	Bob Melvin	.05
16	*Luis Mercedes*	.10
17	Jose Mesa	.05
18	Bob Milacki	.05
19	Randy Milligan	.05
20	Mike Mussina	.25
21	Gregg Olson	.05
22	Joe Orsulak	.05
23	Jim Poole	.05
24	*Arthur Rhodes*	.10
25	Billy Ripken	.05
26	Cal Ripken, Jr.	1.00
27	David Segui	.05
28	Roy Smith	.05
29	Anthony Telford	.05
30	Mark Williamson	.05
31	Craig Worthington	.05
32	Wade Boggs	.20
33	Tom Bolton	.05
34	Tom Brunansky	.05

No.	Player	Price
35	Ellis Burks	.05
36	Jack Clark	.05
37	Roger Clemens	.40
38	Danny Darwin	.05
39	Mike Greenwell	.05
40	Joe Hesketh	.05
41	Daryl Irvine	.05
42	Dennis Lamp	.05
43	Tony Pena	.05
44	Phil Plantier	.05
45	Carlos Quintana	.05
46	Jeff Reardon	.05
47	Jody Reed	.05
48	Luis Rivera	.05
49	Mo Vaughn	.25
50	Jim Abbott	.05
51	Kyle Abbott	.05
52	*Ruben Amaro, Jr.*	.05
53	Scott Bailes	.05
54	*Chris Beasley*	.05
55	Mark Eichhorn	.05
56	Mike Fetters	.05
57	Chuck Finley	.05
58	Gary Gaetti	.05
59	Dave Gallagher	.05
60	Donnie Hill	.05
61	Bryan Harvey	.05
62	Wally Joyner	.05
63	Mark Langston	.05
64	Kirk McCaskill	.05
65	John Orton	.05
66	Lance Parrish	.05
67	Luis Polonia	.05
68	Bobby Rose	.05
69	Dick Schofield	.05
70	Luis Sojo	.05
71	Lee Stevens	.05
72	Dave Winfield	.30
73	Cliff Young	.05
74	Wilson Alvarez	.05
75	*Esteban Beltre*	.10
76	Joey Cora	.05
77	*Brian Drahman*	.05
78	Alex Fernandez	.05
79	Carlton Fisk	.30
80	Scott Fletcher	.05
81	Craig Grebeck	.05
82	Ozzie Guillen	.05
83	Greg Hibbard	.05
84	Charlie Hough	.05
85	Mike Huff	.05
86	Bo Jackson	.15
87	Lance Johnson	.05
88	Ron Karkovice	.05
89	Jack McDowell	.05
90	Matt Merullo	.05
91	*Warren Newson*	.10
92	Donn Pall	.05
93	Dan Pasqua	.05
94	Ken Patterson	.05
95	Melido Perez	.05
96	Scott Radinsky	.05
97	Tim Raines	.05
98	Sammy Sosa	.50
99	Bobby Thigpen	.05
100	Frank Thomas	.50
101	Robin Ventura	.05
102	Mike Aldrete	.05
103	Sandy Alomar, Jr.	.05
104	Carlos Baerga	.05
105	Albert Belle	.20
106	Willie Blair	.05
107	Jerry Browne	.05
108	Alex Cole	.05
109	Felix Fermin	.05
110	Glenallen Hill	.05
111	Shawn Hillegas	.05
112	Chris James	.05
113	Reggie Jefferson	.05
114	Doug Jones	.05
115	Eric King	.05
116	Mark Lewis	.05
117	Carlos Martinez	.05
118	Charles Nagy	.10
119	Rod Nichols	.05
120	Steve Olin	.05
121	Jesse Orosco	.05
122	Rudy Seanez	.05
123	Joel Skinner	.05
124	Greg Swindell	.05
125	Jim Thome	.20
126	Mark Whiten	.05
127	Scott Aldred	.05
128	Andy Allanson	.05
129	John Cerutti	.05
130	Milt Cuyler	.05
131	*Mike Dalton*	.05
132	Rob Deer	.05
133	Cecil Fielder	.05
134	Travis Fryman	.05
135	*Dan Gakeler*	.05
136	Paul Gibson	.05
137	Bill Gullickson	.05
138	Mike Henneman	.05
139	Pete Incaviglia	.05
140	*Mark Leiter*	.05
141	*Scott Livingstone*	.15
142	Lloyd Moseby	.05
143	Tony Phillips	.05
144	Mark Salas	.05
145	Frank Tanana	.05
146	Walt Terrell	.05
147	Mickey Tettleton	.05
148	Alan Trammell	.05
149	Lou Whitaker	.05
150	Kevin Appier	.05
151	Luis Aquino	.05
152	Todd Benzinger	.05
153	Mike Boddicker	.05
154	George Brett	.45
155	Storm Davis	.05
156	Jim Eisenreich	.05
157	Kirk Gibson	.05
158	Tom Gordon	.05
159	Mark Gubicza	.05
160	*David Howard*	.05
161	Mike Macfarlane	.05
162	Brent Mayne	.05
163	Brian McRae	.05
164	Jeff Montgomery	.05
165	Bill Pecota	.05
166	*Harvey Pulliam*	.05
167	Bret Saberhagen	.05
168	Kevin Seitzer	.05
169	Terry Shumpert	.05
170	Kurt Stillwell	.05
171	Danny Tartabull	.05
172	Gary Thurman	.05
173	Dante Bichette	.05
174	Kevin Brown	.05
175	Chuck Crim	.05
176	Jim Gantner	.05
177	Darryl Hamilton	.05
178	Ted Higuera	.05
179	Darren Holmes	.05
180	Mark Lee	.05
181	Julio Machado	.05
182	Paul Molitor	.25
183	Jaime Navarro	.05
184	Edwin Nunez	.05
185	Dan Plesac	.05
186	Willie Randolph	.05
187	Ron Robinson	.05
188	Gary Sheffield	.15
189	Bill Spiers	.05
190	B.J. Surhoff	.05
191	Dale Sveum	.05
192	Greg Vaughn	.05
193	Bill Wegman	.05
194	Robin Yount	.35
195	Rick Aguilera	.05
196	Allan Anderson	.05
197	Steve Bedrosian	.05
198	Randy Bush	.05
199	Larry Casian	.05
200	Chili Davis	.05
201	Scott Erickson	.05
202	Greg Gagne	.05
203	Dan Gladden	.05
204	Brian Harper	.05
205	Kent Hrbek	.05
206	Chuck Knoblauch	.05
207	Gene Larkin	.05
208	Terry Leach	.05
209	Scott Leius	.05
210	Shane Mack	.05
211	Jack Morris	.05
212	Pedro Munoz	.05
213	*Denny Neagle*	.10
214	Al Newman	.05
215	Junior Ortiz	.05
216	Mike Pagliarulo	.05
217	Kirby Puckett	.60
218	Paul Sorrento	.05
219	Kevin Tapani	.05
220	Lenny Webster	.05
221	Jesse Barfield	.05
222	Greg Cadaret	.05
223	Dave Eiland	.05
224	Alvaro Espinoza	.05
225	Steve Farr	.05
226	Bob Geren	.05
227	Lee Guetterman	.05
228	John Habyan	.05
229	Mel Hall	.05
230	Steve Howe	.05
231	*Mike Humphreys*	.05
232	*Scott Kamieniecki*	.10
233	Pat Kelly	.05
234	Roberto Kelly	.05
235	Tim Leary	.05
236	Kevin Maas	.05
237	Don Mattingly	.75
238	Hensley Meulens	.05
239	Matt Nokes	.05
240	Pascual Perez	.05
241	Eric Plunk	.05
242	*John Ramos*	.05
243	Scott Sanderson	.05
244	Steve Sax	.05
245	*Wade Taylor*	.05
246	Randy Velarde	.05
247	Bernie Williams	.20
248	Troy Afenir	.05
249	Harold Baines	.05
250	Lance Blankenship	.05
251	*Mike Bordick*	.10
252	Jose Canseco	.20
253	Steve Chitren	.05
254	Ron Darling	.05
255	Dennis Eckersley	.10
256	Mike Gallego	.05
257	Dave Henderson	.05
258	Rickey Henderson	.25
259	Rick Honeycutt	.05
260	Brook Jacoby	.05
261	Carney Lansford	.05
262	Mark McGwire	1.00
263	Mike Moore	.05
264	Gene Nelson	.05
265	Jamie Quirk	.05
266	*Joe Slusarski*	.10
267	Terry Steinbach	.05
268	Dave Stewart	.05
269	Todd Van Poppel	.05
270	Walt Weiss	.05
271	Bob Welch	.05
272	Curt Young	.05
273	Scott Bradley	.05
274	Greg Briley	.05
275	Jay Buhner	.05
276	Henry Cotto	.05
277	Alvin Davis	.05
278	Rich DeLucia	.05
279	Ken Griffey, Jr.	1.00
280	Erik Hanson	.05
281	Brian Holman	.05
282	Mike Jackson	.05
283	Randy Johnson	.25
284	Tracy Jones	.05
285	Bill Krueger	.05
286	Edgar Martinez	.05
287	Tino Martinez	.05
288	Rob Murphy	.05
289	Pete O'Brien	.05
290	Alonzo Powell	.05
291	Harold Reynolds	.05
292	Mike Schooler	.05
293	Russ Swan	.05
294	Bill Swift	.05
295	Dave Valle	.05
296	Omar Vizquel	.05
297	Gerald Alexander	.05
298	Brad Arnsberg	.05
299	Kevin Brown	.10
300	Jack Daugherty	.05
301	Mario Diaz	.05
302	Brian Downing	.05
303	Julio Franco	.05
304	Juan Gonzalez	.45
305	Rich Gossage	.10
306	Jose Guzman	.05
307	*Jose Hernandez*	.05
308	Jeff Huson	.05
309	Mike Jeffcoat	.05
310	*Terry Mathews*	.05
311	Rafael Palmeiro	.10
312	Dean Palmer	.05
313	Geno Petralli	.05
314	Gary Pettis	.05
315	Kevin Reimer	.05
316	Ivan Rodriguez	.20
317	Kenny Rogers	.05
318	*Wayne Rosenthal*	.05
319	Jeff Russell	.05
320	Nolan Ryan	.75
321	Ruben Sierra	.05
322	Jim Acker	.05
323	Roberto Alomar	.25
324	Derek Bell	.05
325	Pat Borders	.05
326	Tom Candiotti	.05
327	Joe Carter	.05
328	Rob Ducey	.05
329	Kelly Gruber	.05
330	*Juan Guzman*	.25
331	Tom Henke	.05
332	Jimmy Key	.05
333	Manny Lee	.05
334	Al Leiter	.10
335	*Bob MacDonald*	.05
336	Candy Maldonado	.05
337	Rance Mulliniks	.05
338	Greg Myers	.05
339	John Olerud	.05
340	*Ed Sprague*	.10
341	Dave Stieb	.05
342	Todd Stottlemyre	.05
343	*Mike Timlin*	.15
344	Duane Ward	.05
345	David Wells	.10
346	Devon White	.10
347	Mookie Wilson	.05
348	Eddie Zosky	.05
349	Steve Avery	.05
350	Mike Bell	.05
351	Rafael Belliard	.05
352	Juan Berenguer	.05
353	Jeff Blauser	.05
354	Sid Bream	.05
355	Francisco Cabrera	.05
356	Marvin Freeman	.05
357	Ron Gant	.05
358	Tom Glavine	.10
359	*Brian Hunter*	.05
360	Dave Justice	.15
361	Charlie Leibrandt	.05
362	Mark Lemke	.05
363	Kent Mercker	.05
364	*Keith Mitchell*	.05
365	Greg Olson	.05
366	Terry Pendleton	.05
367	*Armando Reynoso*	.05
368	Deion Sanders	.15
369	Lonnie Smith	.05
370	Pete Smith	.05
371	John Smoltz	.10
372	Mike Stanton	.05
373	Jeff Treadway	.05
374	*Mark Wohlers*	.10
375	Paul Assenmacher	.05
376	George Bell	.05
377	Shawn Boskie	.05
378	*Frank Castillo*	.05
379	Andre Dawson	.10
380	Shawon Dunston	.05
381	Mark Grace	.20
382	Mike Harkey	.05
383	Danny Jackson	.05
384	Les Lancaster	.05
385	*Cedric Landrum*	.05
386	Greg Maddux	.60
387	Derrick May	.05
388	Chuck McElroy	.05
389	Ryne Sandberg	.35
390	*Heathcliff Slocumb*	.10
391	Dave Smith	.05
392	Dwight Smith	.05
393	Rick Sutcliffe	.05
394	Hector Villanueva	.05
395	*Chico Walker*	.05
396	Jerome Walton	.05
397	*Rick Wilkins*	.15
398	Jack Armstrong	.05
399	*Freddie Benavides*	.10
400	Glenn Braggs	.05
401	Tom Browning	.05
402	Norm Charlton	.05
403	Eric Davis	.05
404	Rob Dibble	.05
405	Bill Doran	.05
406	Mariano Duncan	.05
407	*Kip Gross*	.05
408	Chris Hammond	.05
409	Billy Hatcher	.05
410	*Chris Jones*	.10
411	Barry Larkin	.10
412	Hal Morris	.05
413	Randy Myers	.05
414	Joe Oliver	.05
415	Paul O'Neill	.05
416	Ted Power	.05
417	Luis Quinones	.05
418	Jeff Reed	.05

419 Jose Rijo .05
420 Chris Sabo .05
421 Reggie Sanders .10
422 Scott Scudder .05
423 Glenn Sutko .05
424 Eric Anthony .05
425 Jeff Bagwell .75
426 Craig Biggio .10
427 Ken Caminiti .05
428 Casey Candaele .05
429 Mike Capel .05
430 Andujar Cedeno .05
431 Jim Corsi .05
432 Mark Davidson .05
433 Steve Finley .05
434 Luis Gonzalez .15
435 Pete Harnisch .05
436 Dwayne Henry .05
437 Xavier Hernandez .05
438 Jimmy Jones .05
439 *Darryl Kile* .10
440 *Rob Mallicoat* .05
441 *Andy Mota* .05
442 Al Osuna .05
443 Mark Portugal .05
444 *Scott Servais* .10
445 Mike Simms .05
446 Gerald Young .05
447 Tim Belcher .05
448 Brett Butler .05
449 John Candelaria .05
450 Gary Carter .15
451 Dennis Cook .05
452 Tim Crews .05
453 Kal Daniels .05
454 Jim Gott .05
455 Alfredo Griffin .05
456 Kevin Gross .05
457 Chris Gwynn .05
458 Lenny Harris .05
459 Orel Hershiser .05
460 Jay Howell .05
461 Stan Javier .05
462 Eric Karros .05
463 Ramon Martinez .05
464 Roger McDowell .05
465 Mike Morgan .05
466 Eddie Murray .25
467 Jose Offerman .05
468 Bob Ojeda .05
469 Juan Samuel .05
470 Mike Scioscia .05
471 Darryl Strawberry .05
472 *Bret Barberie* .10
473 Brian Barnes .05
474 Eric Bullock .05
475 Ivan Calderon .05
476 Delino DeShields .05
477 *Jeff Fassero* .10
478 Mike Fitzgerald .05
479 Steve Frey .05
480 Andres Galarraga .05
481 Mark Gardner .05
482 Marquis Grissom .05
483 *Chris Haney* .05
484 Barry Jones .05
485 Dave Martinez .05
486 Dennis Martinez .05
487 Chris Nabholz .05
488 Spike Owen .05
489 Gilberto Reyes .05
490 Mel Rojas .05
491 Scott Ruskin .05
492 Bill Sampen .05
493 Larry Walker .10
494 Tim Wallach .05
495 Daryl Boston .05
496 Hubie Brooks .05
497 Tim Burke .05
498 Mark Carreon .05
499 Tony Castillo .05
500 Vince Coleman .05
501 David Cone .05
502 Kevin Elster .05
503 Sid Fernandez .05
504 John Franco .05
505 Dwight Gooden .05
506 Todd Hundley .05
507 Jeff Innis .05
508 Gregg Jefferies .05
509 Howard Johnson .05
510 Dave Magadan .05
511 *Terry McDaniel* .05
512 Kevin McReynolds .05
513 Keith Miller .05
514 Charlie O'Brien .05
515 Mackey Sasser .05
516 *Pete Schourek* .10
517 Julio Valera .05
518 Frank Viola .05
519 Wally Whitehurst .05
520 *Anthony Young* .10
521 *Andy Ashby* .10
522 *Kim Batiste* .05
523 Joe Boever .05
524 Wes Chamberlain .05
525 Pat Combs .05
526 Danny Cox .05
527 Darren Daulton .05
528 Jose DeJesus .05
529 Len Dykstra .05
530 Darrin Fletcher .05
531 Tommy Greene .05
532 Jason Grimsley .05
533 Charlie Hayes .05
534 Von Hayes .05
535 Dave Hollins .05
536 Ricky Jordan .05
537 John Kruk .05
538 Jim Lindeman .05
539 Mickey Morandini .05
540 Terry Mulholland .05
541 Dale Murphy .15
542 Randy Ready .05
543 Wally Ritchie .05
544 Bruce Ruffin .05
545 Steve Searcy .05
546 Dickie Thon .05
547 Mitch Williams .05
548 Stan Belinda .05
549 Jay Bell .05
550 Barry Bonds .40
551 Bobby Bonilla .05
552 Steve Buechele .05
553 Doug Drabek .05
554 Neal Heaton .05
555 Jeff King .05
556 Bob Kipper .05
557 Bill Landrum .05
558 Mike LaValliere .05
559 Jose Lind .05
560 Lloyd McClendon .05
561 Orlando Merced .05
562 Bob Patterson .05
563 *Joe Redfield* .05
564 Gary Redus .05
565 Rosario Rodriguez .05
566 Don Slaught .05
567 John Smiley .05
568 Zane Smith .05
569 Randy Tomlin .05
570 Andy Van Slyke .05
571 Gary Varsho .05
572 Bob Walk .05
573 *John Wehner* .10
574 Juan Agosto .05
575 Cris Carpenter .05
576 Jose DeLeon .05
577 Rich Gedman .05
578 Bernard Gilkey .05
579 Pedro Guerrero .05
580 Ken Hill .05
581 Rex Hudler .05
582 Felix Jose .05
583 Ray Lankford .05
584 Omar Olivares .05
585 Jose Oquendo .05
586 Tom Pagnozzi .05
587 Geronimo Pena .05
588 Mike Perez .05
589 Gerald Perry .05
590 Bryn Smith .05
591 Lee Smith .05
592 Ozzie Smith .35
593 Scott Terry .05
594 Bob Tewksbury .05
595 Milt Thompson .05
596 Todd Zeile .10
597 Larry Andersen .05
598 Oscar Azocar .05
599 Andy Benes .05
600 *Ricky Bones* .05
601 Jerald Clark .05
602 Pat Clements .05
603 Paul Faries .05
604 Tony Fernandez .05
605 Tony Gwynn .35
606 Greg Harris .05
607 Thomas Howard .05
608 Bruce Hurst .05
609 Darrin Jackson .05
610 Tom Lampkin .05
611 Craig Lefferts .05
612 *Jim Lewis* .05
613 Mike Maddux .05
614 Fred McGriff .05
615 *Jose Melendez* .05
616 *Jose Mota* .10
617 Dennis Rasmussen .05
618 Bip Roberts .05
619 Rich Rodriguez .05
620 Benito Santiago .05
621 *Craig Shipley* .05
622 Tim Teufel .05
623 *Kevin Ward* .05
624 Ed Whitson .05
625 Dave Anderson .05
626 Kevin Bass .05
627 *Rod Beck* .10
628 Bud Black .05
629 Jeff Brantley .05
630 John Burkett .05
631 Will Clark .15
632 Royce Clayton .05
633 Steve Decker .05
634 Kelly Downs .05
635 Mike Felder .05
636 Scott Garrelts .05
637 Eric Gunderson .05
638 *Bryan Hickerson* .10
639 Darren Lewis .05
640 Greg Litton .05
641 Kirt Manwaring .05
642 *Paul McClellan* .05
643 Willie McGee .05
644 Kevin Mitchell .05
645 Francisco Olivares .05
646 *Mike Remlinger* .10
647 Dave Righetti .05
648 Robby Thompson .05
649 Jose Uribe .05
650 Matt Williams .15
651 Trevor Wilson .05
652 Tom Goodwin (Prospects) .25
653 Terry Bross (Prospects) .05
654 *Mike Christopher* (Prospects) .10
655 Kenny Lofton (Prospects) .25
656 *Chris Cron* (Prospects) .05
657 Willie Banks (Prospects) .05
658 *Pat Rice* (Prospects) .05
659a *Rob Mauer* (Prospects) (last name misspelled) .75
659b *Rob Maurer* (Prospects) (corrected) .10
660 Don Harris (Prospects) .05
661 Henry Rodriguez (Prospects) .25
662 *Cliff Brantley* (Prospects) .10
663 *Mike Linskey* (Prospects) .05
664 Gary Disarcina (Prospects) .10
665 *Gil Heredia* (Prospects) .10
666 *Vinny Castilla* (Prospects) 1.00
667 Paul Abbott (Prospects) .10
668 Monty Fariss (Prospects) .05
669 *Jarvis Brown* (Prospects) .05
670 *Wayne Kirby* (Prospects) .15
671 *Scott Brosius* (Prospects) .15
672 Bob Hamelin (Prospects) .05
673 *Joel Johnston* (Prospects) .05
674 *Tim Spehr* (Prospects) .10
675 *Jeff Gardner* (Prospects) .10
676 *Rico Rossy* (Prospects) .10
677 *Roberto Hernandez* (Prospects) .20
678 *Ted Wood* (Prospects) .05
679 Cal Eldred (Prospects) .10
680 Sean Berry (Prospects) .10
681 Rickey Henderson (Stolen Base Record) .15
682 Nolan Ryan (Record 7th No-hitter) .25
683 Dennis Martinez (Perfect Game) .05
684 Wilson Alvarez (Rookie No-hitter) .05
685 Joe Carter (3 100 RBI Seasons) .05
686 Dave Winfield (400 Home Runs) .10
687 David Cone (Ties NL Record Strikeouts) .05
688 Jose Canseco (League Leaders) .15
689 Howard Johnson (League Leaders) .05
690 Julio Franco (League Leaders) .05
691 Terry Pendleton (League Leaders) .05
692 Cecil Fielder (League Leaders) .05
693 Scott Erickson (League Leaders) .05
694 Tom Glavine (League Leaders) .05
695 Dennis Martinez (League Leaders) .05
696 Bryan Harvey (League Leaders) .05
697 Lee Smith (League Leaders) .05
698 Super Siblings (Roberto & Sandy Alomar, Roberto & Sandy Alomar) .10
699 The Indispensables (Bobby Bonilla, Will Clark) .05
700 Teamwork (Mark Wohlers, Kent Mercker, Alejandro Pena) .05
701 Tiger Tandems (Chris Jones, Bo Jackson, Gregg Olson, Frank Thomas) .30
702 The Ignitors (Brett Butler, Paul Molitor) .10
703 The Indispensables II (Cal Ripken Jr., Joe Carter) .15
704 Power Packs (Barry Larkin, Kirby Puckett) .15
705 Today and Tomorrow (Mo Vaughn, Cecil Fielder) .10
706 Teenage Sensations (Ramon Martinez, Ozzie Guillen) .05
707 Designated Hitters (Harold Baines, Wade Boggs) .10
708 Robin Yount (ProVision) .25
709 Ken Griffey, Jr. (ProVision) .75
710 Nolan Ryan (ProVision) .75
711 Cal Ripken, Jr. (ProVision) .75
712 Frank Thomas (ProVision) .75
713 Dave Justice (ProVision) .20
714 Checklist 1-101 .05
715 Checklist 102-194 .05
716 Checklist 195-296 .05
717 Checklist 297-397 .05
718 Checklist 398-494 .05
719 Checklist 495-596 .05
720a Checklist 597-720 (659 Rob Mauer) .05
720b Checklist 597-720 (659 Rob Maurer) .05

1992 Fleer All-Stars

Black borders with gold highlights are featured on these special wax pack insert cards. The fronts feature glossy action photos with a portrait photo inset. Backs feature career highlights.

		MT
Complete Set (24):		5.00
Common Player:		.05
1	Felix Jose	.05
2	Tony Gwynn	.50
3	Barry Bonds	.75
4	Bobby Bonilla	.05
5	Mike LaValliere	.05
6	Tom Glavine	.10
7	Ramon Martinez	.05
8	Lee Smith	.05
9	Mickey Tettleton	.05
10	Scott Erickson	.05
11	Frank Thomas	.75
12	Danny Tartabull	.05
13	Will Clark	.15
14	Ryne Sandberg	.50
15	Terry Pendleton	.05
16	Barry Larkin	.05
17	Rafael Palmeiro	.15
18	Julio Franco	.05
19	Robin Ventura	.05
20	Cal Ripken, Jr.	1.00
21	Joe Carter	.05
22	Kirby Puckett	.50
23	Ken Griffey, Jr.	1.00
24	Jose Canseco	.35

1992 Fleer Lumber Co.

Baseball's top power hitters at each position are featured in this nine-card set. Fronts feature full-color action photos bordered in black. Backs feature posed player photos and career highlights. The set was included only in factory sets released to the hobby trade.

		MT
Complete Set (9):		4.00
Common Player:		.25
1	Cecil Fielder	.25
2	Mickey Tettleton	.25
3	Darryl Strawberry	.25
4	Ryne Sandberg	.65
5	Jose Canseco	.40
6	Matt Williams	.25
7	Cal Ripken, Jr.	1.50
8	Barry Bonds	1.00
9	Ron Gant	.25

1992 Fleer Roger Clemens

This set chronicles the career highlights of Roger Clemens. The initial 12 cards from the set were inserted in 1992 Fleer wax packs. A limited number of autographed cards were inserted as well. The additional three cards from the set were available through a mail-in offer. The card fronts feature black borders with metallic gold type. The flip side is yellow with black borders.

		MT
Complete Set (15):		7.00
Common Card:		.50
Autographed Card:		40.00
1	Quiet Storm	.50
2	Courted by the Mets and Twins	.50
3	The Show	.50
4	A Rocket Launched	.50
5	Time of Trial	.50
6	Break Through	.50
7	Play it Again Roger	.50
8	Business as Usual	.50
9	Heee's Back	.50
10	Blood, Sweat and Tears	.50
11	Prime of Life	.50
12	Man for Every Season	.50
13	Cooperstown Bound	1.00
14	The Heat of the Moment	1.00
15	Final Words	1.00

1992 Fleer Rookie Sensations

This 20-card set features the top rookies of 1991 and rookie prospects from 1992. The card fronts feature blue borders with "Rookie Sensations" in gold along the top border. The flip sides feature background information on the player. The cards were randomly inserted in 1992 Fleer cello packs. This issue saw very high prices when initially released then suffered long-term declines as the hobby became inundated with more and more insert sets.

		MT
Complete Set (20):		12.00
Common Player:		.25
1	Frank Thomas	3.50
2	Todd Van Poppel	.25
3	Orlando Merced	.25
4	Jeff Bagwell	3.00
5	Jeff Fassero	.25
6	Darren Lewis	.25
7	Milt Cuyler	.25
8	Mike Timlin	.25
9	Brian McRae	.25
10	Chuck Knoblauch	.75
11	Rich DeLucia	.25
12	Ivan Rodriguez	2.50
13	Juan Guzman	.40
14	Steve Chitren	.25
15	Mark Wohlers	.25
16	Wes Chamberlain	.25
17	Ray Lankford	.50
18	Chito Martinez	.25
19	Phil Plantier	.25
20	Scott Leius	.25

1992 Fleer Smoke 'N Heat

This 12-card set of top pitchers was included in factory sets designated for sale within the general retail trade. Card numbers have an "S" prefix.

		MT
Complete Set (12):		5.00
Common Player:		.25
1	Lee Smith	.25
2	Jack McDowell	.25
3	David Cone	.50
4	Roger Clemens	1.00
5	Nolan Ryan	2.00
6	Scott Erickson	.25
7	Tom Glavine	.40
8	Dwight Gooden	.25
9	Andy Benes	.25
10	Steve Avery	.25
11	Randy Johnson	.75
12	Jim Abbott	.25

1992 Fleer Team Leaders

White and green borders highlight this insert set from Fleer. The card fronts also feature a special gold-foil "team leaders" logo beneath the full-color player photo. The card backs feature player information. The cards were randomly inserted in 1992 Fleer rack packs.

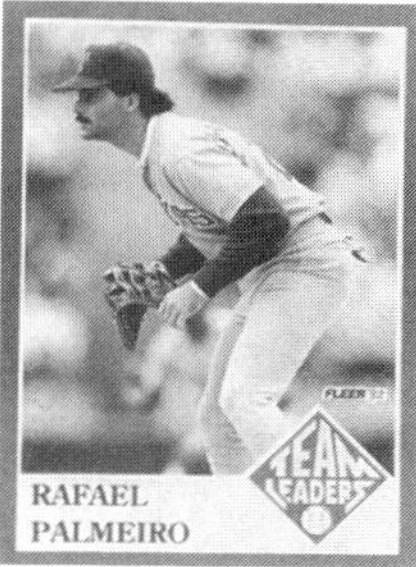

		MT
Complete Set (20):		10.00
Common Player:		.10
1	Don Mattingly	2.00
2	Howard Johnson	.10
3	Chris Sabo	.10
4	Carlton Fisk	1.00
5	Kirby Puckett	1.50
6	Cecil Fielder	.10
7	Tony Gwynn	1.50
8	Will Clark	.30
9	Bobby Bonilla	.10
10	Len Dykstra	.10
11	Tom Glavine	.30
12	Rafael Palmeiro	.40
13	Wade Boggs	.60
14	Joe Carter	.10
15	Ken Griffey, Jr.	2.50
16	Darryl Strawberry	.10
17	Cal Ripken, Jr.	2.50
18	Danny Tartabull	.10
19	Jose Canseco	.50
20	Andre Dawson	.15

1992 Fleer Update

This 132-card set was released in boxed set form and features traded players, free agents and top rookies from 1992. The cards are styled after the regular 1992 Fleer and are numbered alphabetically according to team. This set marks the ninth year that Fleer has released an update set. The set includes four black-bordered "Headliner" cards.

		MT
Complete Set (136):		125.00
Common Player:		.20
H1	1992 All-Star Game MVP (Ken Griffey, Jr.)	10.00
H2	3000 Career Hits (Robin Yount)	1.50

H3	Major League Career Saves Record (Jeff Reardon)	.25
H4	Record RBI Performance (Cecil Fielder)	.50
1	Todd Frohwirth	.20
2	Alan Mills	.20
3	Rick Sutcliffe	.20
4	*John Valentin*	2.00
5	Frank Viola	.20
6	Bob Zupcic	.20
7	Mike Butcher	.20
8	*Chad Curtis*	.75
9	*Damion Easley*	1.50
10	Tim Salmon	2.00
11	Julio Valera	.20
12	George Bell	.20
13	Roberto Hernandez	.35
14	Shawn Jeter	.20
15	Thomas Howard	.20
16	Jesse Levis	.20
17	Kenny Lofton	2.00
18	Paul Sorrento	.20
19	Rico Brogna	.35
20	John Doherty	.20
21	Dan Gladden	.20
22	Buddy Groom	.20
23	Shawn Hare	.20
24	John Kiely	.20
25	Kurt Knudsen	.20
26	Gregg Jefferies	.20
27	Wally Joyner	.20
28	Kevin Koslofski	.20
29	Kevin McReynolds	.20
30	Rusty Meacham	.20
31	Keith Miller	.20
32	Hipolito Pichardo	.20
33	James Austin	.20
34	Scott Fletcher	.20
35	*John Jaha*	.50
36	Pat Listach	.50
37	Dave Nilsson	.50
38	Kevin Seitzer	.20
39	Tom Edens	.20
40	Pat Mahomes	.50
41	John Smiley	.20
42	Charlie Hayes	.20
43	Sam Militello	.20
44	Andy Stankiewicz	.35
45	Danny Tartabull	.20
46	Bob Wickman	.20
47	Jerry Browne	.20
48	Kevin Campbell	.20
49	Vince Horsman	.20
50	Troy Neel	.50
51	Ruben Sierra	.20
52	Bruce Walton	.20
53	Willie Wilson	.20
54	Bret Boone	.75
55	Dave Fleming	.50
56	Kevin Mitchell	.20
57	*Jeff Nelson*	.20
58	Shane Turner	.20
59	Jose Canseco	2.00
60	*Jeff Frye*	.30
61	Damilo Leon	.20
62	Roger Pavlik	.30
63	David Cone	.20
64	Pat Hentgen	.50
65	Randy Knorr	.20
66	Jack Morris	.20
67	Dave Winfield	1.50
68	*David Nied*	.20
69	Otis Nixon	.20
70	Alejandro Pena	.20
71	Jeff Reardon	.20
72	Alex Arias	.25
73	Jim Bullinger	.20
74	Mike Morgan	.20
75	Rey Sanchez	.20
76	Bob Scanlan	.20
77	Sammy Sosa	4.00
78	Scott Bankhead	.20
79	Tim Belcher	.20
80	Steve Foster	.20
81	Willie Greene	.50
82	Bip Roberts	.20
83	Scott Ruskin	.20
84	Greg Swindell	.20
85	Juan Guerrero	.20
86	Butch Henry	.20
87	Doug Jones	.20
88	Brian Williams	.30
89	Tom Candiotti	.20
90	Eric Davis	.20
91	Carlos Hernandez	.20
92	*Mike Piazza*	65.00
93	Mike Sharperson	.20
94	Eric Young	.75
95	Moises Alou	1.50
96	Greg Colbrunn	.20
97	Wil Cordero	.50
98	Ken Hill	.20
99	John Vander Wal	.25
100	John Wetteland	.20
101	Bobby Bonilla	.20
102	Eric Hilman	.20
103	Pat Howell	.20
104	*Jeff Kent*	6.00
105	Dick Schofield	.20
106	*Ryan Thompson*	.25
107	Chico Walker	.20
108	Juan Bell	.20
109	Mariano Duncan	.20
110	Jeff Grotewold	.25
111	Ben Rivera	.20
112	Curt Schilling	1.50
113	Victor Cole	.20
114	Al Martin	1.00
115	Roger Mason	.20
116	Blas Minor	.20
117	Tim Wakefield	.50
118	*Mark Clark*	.50
119	Rheal Cormier	.35
120	Donovan Osborne	.20
121	Todd Worrell	.20
122	Jeremy Hernandez	.25
123	Randy Myers	.20
124	Frank Seminara	.20
125	Gary Sheffield	1.50
126	Dan Walters	.20
127	Steve Hosey	.20
128	Mike Jackson	.20
129	Jim Pena	.20
130	Cory Snyder	.20
131	Bill Swift	.20
132	Checklist	.05

1993 Fleer

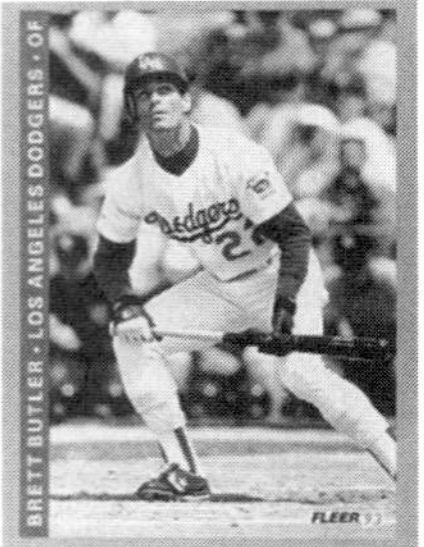

The card fronts feature silver borders with the player's name, team and position in a banner along the left side of the card. The backs feature an action photo of the player with his name in bold behind him. A box featuring biographical information, statistics and player information is located to the right of the action photo. The cards are numbered alphabetically by team. The basic Fleer issue for 1993 was issued in two series of 360 cards each. The 720-card set included a number of subsets and could be found in many different types of packaging with an unprecedented number of inserts sets to spice up each offering.

		MT
Complete Set (720):		25.00
Common Player:		.05
Series 1 or 2 Pack (15):		.50
Series 1 or 2 Wax Box (36):		16.00
1	Steve Avery	.05
2	Sid Bream	.05
3	Ron Gant	.05
4	Tom Glavine	.10
5	Brian Hunter	.05
6	Ryan Klesko	.05
7	Charlie Leibrandt	.05
8	Kent Mercker	.05
9	David Nied	.05
10	Otis Nixon	.05
11	Greg Olson	.05
12	Terry Pendleton	.05
13	Deion Sanders	.10
14	John Smoltz	.10
15	Mike Stanton	.05
16	Mark Wohlers	.05
17	Paul Assenmacher	.05
18	Steve Buechele	.05
19	Shawon Dunston	.05
20	Mark Grace	.20
21	Derrick May	.05
22	Chuck McElroy	.05
23	Mike Morgan	.05
24	Rey Sanchez	.05
25	Ryne Sandberg	.30
26	Bob Scanlan	.05
27	Sammy Sosa	.75
28	Rick Wilkins	.05
29	*Bobby Ayala*	.05
30	Tim Belcher	.05
31	*Jeff Branson*	.10
32	Norm Charlton	.05
33	*Steve Foster*	.05
34	Willie Greene	.05
35	Chris Hammond	.05
36	Milt Hill	.05
37	Hal Morris	.05
38	Joe Oliver	.05
39	Paul O'Neill	.05
40	*Tim Pugh*	.10
41	Jose Rijo	.05
42	Bip Roberts	.05
43	Chris Sabo	.05
44	Reggie Sanders	.05
45	Eric Anthony	.05
46	Jeff Bagwell	.50
47	Craig Biggio	.05
48	Joe Boever	.05
49	Casey Candaele	.05
50	Steve Finley	.05
51	Luis Gonzalez	.15
52	Pete Harnisch	.05
53	Xavier Hernandez	.05
54	Doug Jones	.05
55	Eddie Taubensee	.05
56	Brian Williams	.05
57	*Pedro Astacio*	.10
58	Todd Benzinger	.05
59	Brett Butler	.05
60	Tom Candiotti	.05
61	Lenny Harris	.05
62	Carlos Hernandez	.05
63	Orel Hershiser	.05
64	Eric Karros	.05
65	Ramon Martinez	.05
66	Jose Offerman	.05
67	Mike Scioscia	.05
68	Mike Sharperson	.05
69	*Eric Young*	.10
70	Moises Alou	.10
71	Ivan Calderon	.05
72	*Archi Cianfrocco*	.05
73	Wil Cordero	.05
74	Delino DeShields	.05
75	Mark Gardner	.05
76	Ken Hill	.05
77	*Tim Laker*	.05
78	Chris Nabholz	.05
79	Mel Rojas	.05
80	*John Vander Wal*	.10
81	Larry Walker	.15
82	Tim Wallach	.05
83	John Wetteland	.05
84	Bobby Bonilla	.05
85	Daryl Boston	.05
86	Sid Fernandez	.05
87	*Eric Hillman*	.10
88	Todd Hundley	.05
89	Howard Johnson	.05
90	Jeff Kent	.10
91	Eddie Murray	.30
92	Bill Pecota	.05
93	Bret Saberhagen	.05
94	Dick Schofield	.05
95	Pete Schourek	.05
96	Anthony Young	.05
97	Ruben Amaro Jr.	.05
98	Juan Bell	.05
99	Wes Chamberlain	.05
100	Darren Daulton	.05
101	Mariano Duncan	.05
102	Mike Hartley	.05
103	Ricky Jordan	.05
104	John Kruk	.05
105	Mickey Morandini	.05
106	Terry Mulholland	.05
107	*Ben Rivera*	.05
108	Curt Schilling	.10
109	*Keith Shepherd*	.05
110	Stan Belinda	.05
111	Jay Bell	.05
112	Barry Bonds	.75
113	Jeff King	.05
114	Mike LaValliere	.05
115	Jose Lind	.05
116	Roger Mason	.05
117	Orlando Merced	.05
118	Bob Patterson	.05
119	Don Slaught	.05
120	Zane Smith	.05
121	Randy Tomlin	.05
122	Andy Van Slyke	.05
123	*Tim Wakefield*	.10
124	Rheal Cormier	.05
125	Bernard Gilkey	.05
126	Felix Jose	.05
127	Ray Lankford	.05
128	Bob McClure	.05
129	Donovan Osborne	.05
130	Tom Pagnozzi	.05
131	Geronimo Pena	.05
132	Mike Perez	.05
133	Lee Smith	.05
134	Bob Tewksbury	.05
135	Todd Worrell	.05
136	Todd Zeile	.05
137	Jerald Clark	.05
138	Tony Gwynn	.40
139	Greg Harris	.05
140	Jeremy Hernandez	.05
141	Darrin Jackson	.05
142	Mike Maddux	.05
143	Fred McGriff	.05
144	Jose Melendez	.05
145	Rich Rodriguez	.05
146	Frank Seminara	.05
147	Gary Sheffield	.20
148	Kurt Stillwell	.05
149	*Dan Walters*	.10
150	Rod Beck	.05
151	Bud Black	.05
152	Jeff Brantley	.05
153	John Burkett	.05
154	Will Clark	.15
155	Royce Clayton	.05
156	Mike Jackson	.05
157	Darren Lewis	.05
158	Kirt Manwaring	.05
159	Willie McGee	.05
160	Cory Snyder	.05
161	Bill Swift	.05
162	Trevor Wilson	.05
163	Brady Anderson	.05
164	Glenn Davis	.05
165	Mike Devereaux	.05
166	Todd Frohwirth	.05
167	Leo Gomez	.05
168	Chris Hoiles	.05
169	Ben McDonald	.05
170	Randy Milligan	.05
171	Alan Mills	.05
172	Mike Mussina	.30
173	Gregg Olson	.05
174	Arthur Rhodes	.05
175	David Segui	.05
176	Ellis Burks	.05
177	Roger Clemens	.75
178	Scott Cooper	.05
179	Danny Darwin	.05
180	Tony Fossas	.05
181	*Paul Quantrill*	.10
182	Jody Reed	.05
183	*John Valentin*	.15
184	Mo Vaughn	.25
185	Frank Viola	.05
186	Bob Zupcic	.05
187	Jim Abbott	.05
188	Gary DiSarcina	.05
189	*Damion Easley*	.10

190	Junior Felix	.05
191	Chuck Finley	.05
192	Joe Grahe	.05
193	Bryan Harvey	.05
194	Mark Langston	.05
195	John Orton	.05
196	Luis Polonia	.05
197	Tim Salmon	.40
198	Luis Sojo	.05
199	Wilson Alvarez	.05
200	George Bell	.05
201	Alex Fernandez	.05
202	Craig Grebeck	.05
203	Ozzie Guillen	.05
204	Lance Johnson	.05
205	Ron Karkovice	.05
206	Kirk McCaskill	.05
207	Jack McDowell	.05
208	Scott Radinsky	.05
209	Tim Raines	.05
210	Frank Thomas	1.00
211	Robin Ventura	.05
212	Sandy Alomar Jr.	.05
213	Carlos Baerga	.05
214	Dennis Cook	.05
215	Thomas Howard	.05
216	Mark Lewis	.05
217	Derek Lilliquist	.05
218	Kenny Lofton	.25
219	Charles Nagy	.05
220	Steve Olin	.05
221	Paul Sorrento	.05
222	Jim Thome	.05
223	Mark Whiten	.05
224	Milt Cuyler	.05
225	Rob Deer	.05
226	*John Doherty*	.10
227	Cecil Fielder	.05
228	Travis Fryman	.05
229	Mike Henneman	.05
230	*John Kiely*	.05
231	*Kurt Knudsen*	.05
232	Scott Livingstone	.05
233	Tony Phillips	.05
234	Mickey Tettleton	.05
235	Kevin Appier	.05
236	George Brett	.40
237	Tom Gordon	.05
238	Gregg Jefferies	.10
239	Wally Joyner	.05
240	*Kevin Koslofski*	.10
241	Mike Macfarlane	.05
242	Brian McRae	.05
243	Rusty Meacham	.05
244	Keith Miller	.05
245	Jeff Montgomery	.05
246	*Hipolito Pichardo*	.05
247	Ricky Bones	.05
248	Cal Eldred	.05
249	Mike Fetters	.05
250	Darryl Hamilton	.05
251	Doug Henry	.05
252	John Jaha	.05
253	Pat Listach	.05
254	Paul Molitor	.30
255	Jaime Navarro	.05
256	Kevin Seitzer	.05
257	B.J. Surhoff	.05
258	Greg Vaughn	.05
259	Bill Wegman	.05
260	Robin Yount	.30
261	Rick Aguilera	.05
262	Chili Davis	.05
263	Scott Erickson	.05
264	Greg Gagne	.05
265	Mark Guthrie	.05
266	Brian Harper	.05
267	Kent Hrbek	.05
268	Terry Jorgensen	.05
269	Gene Larkin	.05
270	Scott Leius	.05
271	Pat Mahomes	.05
272	Pedro Munoz	.05
273	Kirby Puckett	.75
274	Kevin Tapani	.05
275	Carl Willis	.05
276	Steve Farr	.05
277	John Habyan	.05
278	Mel Hall	.05
279	Charlie Hayes	.05
280	Pat Kelly	.05
281	Don Mattingly	.40
282	Sam Militello	.05
283	Matt Nokes	.05
284	Melido Perez	.05
285	Andy Stankiewicz	.05
286	Danny Tartabull	.05
287	Randy Velarde	.05
288	Bob Wickman	.05
289	Bernie Williams	.30
290	Lance Blankenship	.05
291	Mike Bordick	.05
292	Jerry Browne	.05
293	Dennis Eckersley	.10
294	Rickey Henderson	.25
295	*Vince Horsman*	.10
296	Mark McGwire	1.50
297	Jeff Parrett	.05
298	Ruben Sierra	.05
299	Terry Steinbach	.05
300	Walt Weiss	.05
301	Bob Welch	.05
302	Willie Wilson	.05
303	Bobby Witt	.05
304	Bret Boone	.10
305	Jay Buhner	.05
306	Dave Fleming	.05
307	Ken Griffey, Jr.	1.50
308	Erik Hanson	.05
309	Edgar Martinez	.05
310	Tino Martinez	.05
311	Jeff Nelson	.05
312	Dennis Powell	.05
313	Mike Schooler	.05
314	Russ Swan	.05
315	Dave Valle	.05
316	Omar Vizquel	.05
317	Kevin Brown	.05
318	Todd Burns	.05
319	Jose Canseco	.30
320	Julio Franco	.05
321	Jeff Frye	.05
322	Juan Gonzalez	.50
323	Jose Guzman	.05
324	Jeff Huson	.05
325	Dean Palmer	.05
326	Kevin Reimer	.05
327	Ivan Rodriguez	.30
328	Kenny Rogers	.05
329	Dan Smith	.05
330	Roberto Alomar	.25
331	Derek Bell	.05
332	Pat Borders	.05
333	Joe Carter	.05
334	Kelly Gruber	.05
335	Tom Henke	.05
336	Jimmy Key	.05
337	Manuel Lee	.05
338	Candy Maldonado	.05
339	John Olerud	.05
340	Todd Stottlemyre	.05
341	Duane Ward	.05
342	Devon White	.05
343	Dave Winfield	.25
344	Edgar Martinez (League Leaders)	.05
345	Cecil Fielder (League Leaders)	.05
346	Kenny Lofton (League Leaders)	.05
347	Jack Morris (League Leaders)	.05
348	Roger Clemens (League Leaders)	.25
349	Fred McGriff (Round Trippers)	.05
350	Barry Bonds (Round Trippers)	.25
351	Gary Sheffield (Round Trippers)	.05
352	Darren Daulton (Round Trippers)	.05
353	Dave Hollins (Round Trippers)	.05
354	Brothers In Blue (Pedro Martinez, Ramon Martinez)	.50
355	Power Packs (Ivan Rodriguez, Kirby Puckett)	.25
356	Triple Threats (Ryne Sandberg, Gary Sheffield)	.10
357	Infield Trifecta (Roberto Alomar, Chuck Knoblauch, Carlos Baerga)	.05
358	Checklist	.05
359	Checklist	.05
360	Checklist	.05
361	Rafael Belliard	.05
362	Damon Berryhill	.05
363	Mike Bielecki	.05
364	Jeff Blauser	.05
365	Francisco Cabrera	.05
366	Marvin Freeman	.05
367	Dave Justice	.15
368	Mark Lemke	.05
369	Alejandro Pena	.05
370	Jeff Reardon	.05
371	Lonnie Smith	.05
372	Pete Smith	.05
373	Shawn Boskie	.05
374	Jim Bullinger	.05
375	Frank Castillo	.05
376	Doug Dascenzo	.05
377	Andre Dawson	.10
378	Mike Harkey	.05
379	Greg Hibbard	.05
380	Greg Maddux	.75
381	Ken Patterson	.05
382	Jeff Robinson	.05
383	Luis Salazar	.05
384	Dwight Smith	.05
385	Jose Vizcaino	.05
386	Scott Bankhead	.05
387	Tom Browning	.05
388	Darnell Coles	.05
389	Rob Dibble	.05
390	Bill Doran	.05
391	Dwayne Henry	.05
392	Cesar Hernandez	.05
393	Roberto Kelly	.05
394	Barry Larkin	.10
395	Dave Martinez	.05
396	Kevin Mitchell	.05
397	Jeff Reed	.05
398	Scott Ruskin	.05
399	Greg Swindell	.05
400	Dan Wilson	.05
401	Andy Ashby	.05
402	Freddie Benavides	.05
403	Dante Bichette	.05
404	Willie Blair	.05
405	Denis Boucher	.05
406	Vinny Castilla	.05
407	Braulio Castillo	.05
408	Alex Cole	.05
409	Andres Galarraga	.05
410	Joe Girardi	.05
411	Butch Henry	.05
412	Darren Holmes	.05
413	Calvin Jones	.05
414	*Steve Reed*	.10
415	Kevin Ritz	.05
416	*Jim Tatum*	.05
417	Jack Armstrong	.05
418	Bret Barberie	.05
419	Ryan Bowen	.05
420	Cris Carpenter	.05
421	Chuck Carr	.05
422	Scott Chiamparino	.05
423	Jeff Conine	.05
424	Jim Corsi	.05
425	Steve Decker	.05
426	Chris Donnels	.05
427	Monty Fariss	.05
428	Bob Natal	.05
429	*Pat Rapp*	.10
430	Dave Weathers	.05
431	*Nigel Wilson*	.10
432	Ken Caminiti	.05
433	Andujar Cedeno	.05
434	Tom Edens	.05
435	Juan Guerrero	.05
436	Pete Incaviglia	.05
437	Jimmy Jones	.05
438	Darryl Kile	.10
439	Rob Murphy	.05
440	Al Osuna	.05
441	Mark Portugal	.05
442	Scott Servais	.05
443	John Candelaria	.05
444	Tim Crews	.05
445	Eric Davis	.05
446	Tom Goodwin	.05
447	Jim Gott	.05
448	Kevin Gross	.05
449	Dave Hansen	.05
450	Jay Howell	.05
451	Roger McDowell	.05
452	Bob Ojeda	.05
453	Henry Rodriguez	.05
454	Darryl Strawberry	.05
455	Mitch Webster	.05
456	Steve Wilson	.05
457	Brian Barnes	.05
458	Sean Berry	.05
459	Jeff Fassero	.05
460	Darrin Fletcher	.05
461	Marquis Grissom	.05
462	Dennis Martinez	.05
463	Spike Owen	.05
464	Matt Stairs	.05
465	Sergio Valdez	.05
466	Kevin Bass	.05
467	Vince Coleman	.05
468	Mark Dewey	.05
469	Kevin Elster	.05
470	Tony Fernandez	.05
471	John Franco	.05
472	Dave Gallagher	.05
473	Paul Gibson	.05
474	Dwight Gooden	.05
475	Lee Guetterman	.05
476	Jeff Innis	.05
477	Dave Magadan	.05
478	Charlie O'Brien	.05
479	Willie Randolph	.05
480	Mackey Sasser	.05
481	Ryan Thompson	.05
482	Chico Walker	.05
483	Kyle Abbott	.05
484	Bob Ayrault	.05
485	Kim Batiste	.05
486	Cliff Brantley	.05
487	Jose DeLeon	.05
488	Len Dykstra	.05
489	Tommy Greene	.05
490	Jeff Grotewold	.05
491	Dave Hollins	.05
492	Danny Jackson	.05
493	Stan Javier	.05
494	Tom Marsh	.05
495	Greg Matthews	.05
496	Dale Murphy	.15
497	*Todd Pratt*	.10
498	Mitch Williams	.05
499	Danny Cox	.05
500	Doug Drabek	.05
501	Carlos Garcia	.05
502	Lloyd McClendon	.05
503	Denny Neagle	.05
504	Gary Redus	.05
505	Bob Walk	.05
506	John Wehner	.05
507	Luis Alicea	.05
508	Mark Clark	.05
509	Pedro Guerrero	.05
510	Rex Hudler	.05
511	Brian Jordan	.10
512	Omar Olivares	.05
513	Jose Oquendo	.05
514	Gerald Perry	.05
515	Bryn Smith	.05
516	Craig Wilson	.05
517	Tracy Woodson	.05
518	Larry Anderson	.05
519	Andy Benes	.05
520	Jim Deshaies	.05
521	Bruce Hurst	.05
522	Randy Myers	.05
523	Benito Santiago	.05
524	Tim Scott	.05
525	Tim Teufel	.05
526	Mike Benjamin	.05
527	Dave Burba	.05
528	Craig Colbert	.05
529	Mike Felder	.05
530	Bryan Hickerson	.05
531	Chris James	.05
532	Mark Leonard	.05
533	Greg Litton	.05
534	Francisco Oliveras	.05
535	John Patterson	.05
536	Jim Pena	.05
537	Dave Righetti	.05
538	Robby Thompson	.05
539	Jose Uribe	.05
540	Matt Williams	.15
541	Storm Davis	.05
542	Sam Horn	.05
543	Tim Hulett	.05
544	Craig Lefferts	.05
545	Chito Martinez	.05
546	Mark McLemore	.05
547	Luis Mercedes	.05
548	Bob Milacki	.05
549	Joe Orsulak	.05
550	Billy Ripken	.05
551	Cal Ripken, Jr.	1.25
552	Rick Sutcliffe	.05
553	Jeff Tackett	.05
554	Wade Boggs	.30

555	Tom Brunansky	.05
556	Jack Clark	.05
557	John Dopson	.05
558	Mike Gardiner	.05
559	Mike Greenwell	.05
560	Greg Harris	.05
561	Billy Hatcher	.05
562	Joe Hesketh	.05
563	Tony Pena	.05
564	Phil Plantier	.05
565	Luis Rivera	.05
566	Herm Winningham	.05
567	Matt Young	.05
568	Bert Blyleven	.05
569	Mike Butcher	.05
570	Chuck Crim	.05
571	*Chad Curtis*	.15
572	Tim Fortugno	.05
573	Steve Frey	.05
574	Gary Gaetti	.05
575	Scott Lewis	.05
576	Lee Stevens	.05
577	Ron Tingley	.05
578	Julio Valera	.05
579	Shawn Abner	.05
580	Joey Cora	.05
581	Chris Cron	.05
582	Carlton Fisk	.25
583	Roberto Hernandez	.05
584	Charlie Hough	.05
585	Terry Leach	.05
586	Donn Pall	.05
587	Dan Pasqua	.05
588	Steve Sax	.05
589	Bobby Thigpen	.05
590	Albert Belle	.20
591	Felix Fermin	.05
592	Glenallen Hill	.05
593	Brook Jacoby	.05
594	Reggie Jefferson	.05
595	Carlos Martinez	.05
596	Jose Mesa	.05
597	Rod Nichols	.05
598	Junior Ortiz	.05
599	Eric Plunk	.05
600	Ted Power	.05
601	Scott Scudder	.05
602	Kevin Wickander	.05
603	Skeeter Barnes	.05
604	Mark Carreon	.05
605	Dan Gladden	.05
606	Bill Gullickson	.05
607	Chad Kreuter	.05
608	Mark Leiter	.05
609	Mike Munoz	.05
610	Rich Rowland	.05
611	Frank Tanana	.05
612	Walt Terrell	.05
613	Alan Trammell	.05
614	Lou Whitaker	.05
615	Luis Aquino	.05
616	Mike Boddicker	.05
617	Jim Eisenreich	.05
618	Mark Gubicza	.05
619	David Howard	.05
620	Mike Magnante	.05
621	Brent Mayne	.05
622	Kevin McReynolds	.05
623	*Eddie Pierce*	.05
624	Bill Sampen	.05
625	Steve Shifflett	.05
626	Gary Thurman	.05
627	Curtis Wilkerson	.05
628	Chris Bosio	.05
629	Scott Fletcher	.05
630	Jim Gantner	.05
631	Dave Nilsson	.05
632	Jesse Orosco	.05
633	Dan Plesac	.05
634	Ron Robinson	.05
635	Bill Spiers	.05
636	Franklin Stubbs	.05
637	Willie Banks	.05
638	Randy Bush	.05
639	Chuck Knoblauch	.05
640	Shane Mack	.05
641	Mike Pagliarulo	.05
642	Jeff Reboulet	.05
643	John Smiley	.05
644	*Mike Trombley*	.10
645	Gary Wayne	.05
646	Lenny Webster	.05
647	Tim Burke	.05
648	Mike Gallego	.05
649	Dion James	.05
650	Jeff Johnson	.05
651	Scott Kamieniecki	.05
652	Kevin Maas	.05
653	Rich Monteleone	.05
654	Jerry Nielsen	.05
655	Scott Sanderson	.05
656	Mike Stanley	.05
657	Gerald Williams	.05
658	Curt Young	.05
659	Harold Baines	.05
660	Kevin Campbell	.05
661	Ron Darling	.05
662	Kelly Downs	.05
663	Eric Fox	.05
664	Dave Henderson	.05
665	Rick Honeycutt	.05
666	Mike Moore	.05
667	Jamie Quirk	.05
668	Jeff Russell	.05
669	Dave Stewart	.05
670	Greg Briley	.05
671	Dave Cochrane	.05
672	Henry Cotto	.05
673	Rich DeLucia	.05
674	Brian Fisher	.05
675	Mark Grant	.05
676	Randy Johnson	.35
677	Tim Leary	.05
678	Pete O'Brien	.05
679	Lance Parrish	.05
680	Harold Reynolds	.05
681	Shane Turner	.05
682	Jack Daugherty	.05
683	*David Hulse*	.10
684	Terry Mathews	.05
685	Al Newman	.05
686	Edwin Nunez	.05
687	Rafael Palmeiro	.15
688	Roger Pavlik	.05
689	Geno Petralli	.05
690	Nolan Ryan	1.00
691	David Cone	.05
692	Alfredo Griffin	.05
693	Juan Guzman	.05
694	Pat Hentgen	.05
695	Randy Knorr	.05
696	Bob MacDonald	.05
697	Jack Morris	.05
698	Ed Sprague	.05
699	Dave Stieb	.05
700	Pat Tabler	.05
701	Mike Timlin	.05
702	David Wells	.10
703	Eddie Zosky	.05
704	Gary Sheffield (League Leaders)	.05
705	Darren Daulton (League Leaders)	.05
706	Marquis Grissom (League Leaders)	.05
707	Greg Maddux (League Leaders)	.10
708	Bill Swift (League Leaders)	.05
709	Juan Gonzalez (Round Trippers)	.25
710	Mark McGwire (Round Trippers)	.50
711	Cecil Fielder (Round Trippers)	.05
712	Albert Belle (Round Trippers)	.05
713	Joe Carter (Round Trippers)	.05
714	Power Brokers (Frank Thomas, Cecil Fielder)	.10
715	Unsung Heroes (Larry Walker, Darren Daulton)	.05
716	Hot Corner Hammers (Edgar Martinez, Robin Ventura)	.05
717	Start to Finish (Roger Clemens, Dennis Eckersley)	.10
718	Checklist	.05
719	Checklist	.05
720	Checklist	.05

1993 Fleer All-Stars

Horizontal-format All-Star cards comprised one of the many 1993 Fleer insert issues. Twelve cards of National League All-Stars were included in Series I wax packs, while a dozen American League All-Stars were found in Series II packs. They are among the more popular and valuable of the '93 Fleer inserts.

		MT
Complete Set A.L. (12):		6.00
Complete Set N.L. (12):		3.75
Common Player:		.15
AMERICAN LEAGUE		
1	Frank Thomas	1.50
2	Roberto Alomar	.50
3	Edgar Martinez	.15
4	Pat Listach	.15
5	Cecil Fielder	.15
6	Juan Gonzalez	.75
7	Ken Griffey, Jr.	2.25
8	Joe Carter	.15
9	Kirby Puckett	1.25
10	Brian Harper	.15
11	Dave Fleming	.15
12	Jack McDowell	.15
NATIONAL LEAGUE		
1	Fred McGriff	.15
2	Delino DeShields	.15
3	Gary Sheffield	.40
4	Barry Larkin	.15
5	Felix Jose	.15
6	Larry Walker	.40
7	Barry Bonds	1.25
8	Andy Van Slyke	.15
9	Darren Daulton	.15
10	Greg Maddux	1.50
11	Tom Glavine	.25
12	Lee Smith	.15

1993 Fleer Golden Moments

Three cards of this insert set were available in both series of wax packs. Fronts feature black borders with gold-foil baseballs in the corners. The player's name appears in a "Golden Moments" banner at the bottom of the photo. Backs have a portrait photo of the player at top-center and a information on the highlight. The cards are unnumbered and are checklisted here alphabetically within series.

		MT
Complete Set (6):		4.00
Common Player:		.25
	SERIES 1	2.00
(1)	George Brett	1.50
(2)	Mickey Morandini	.25
(3)	Dave Winfield	.60
	SERIES 2	2.00
(1)	Dennis Eckersley	.40
(2)	Bip Roberts	.25
(3)	Frank Thomas, Juan Gonzalez	2.00

1993 Fleer Major League Prospects

Yet another way to package currently hot rookies and future prospects to increase sales of the base product, there were 18 insert cards found in each series' wax packs. Fronts are bordered in black and have gold-foil highlights. Most of the depicted players were a few seasons away from everyday play in the major leagues.

		MT
Complete Set (36):		10.00
Common Player:		.20
	SERIES 1	7.50
1	Melvin Nieves	.20
2	Sterling Hitchcock	.20
3	Tim Costo	.20
4	Manny Alexander	.20
5	Alan Embree	.20
6	Kevin Young	.20
7	J.T. Snow	.50
8	Russ Springer	.20
9	Billy Ashley	.20
10	Kevin Rogers	.20
11	Steve Hosey	.20
12	Eric Wedge	.20
13	Mike Piazza	4.50
14	Jesse Levis	.20
15	Rico Brogna	.20
16	Alex Arias	.20
17	Rod Brewer	.20
18	Troy Neel	.20
	SERIES 2	3.50
1	Scooter Tucker	.20
2	Kerry Woodson	.20
3	Greg Colbrunn	.20
4	Pedro Martinez	1.50
5	Dave Silvestri	.20
6	Kent Bottenfield	.20
7	Rafael Bournigal	.20
8	J.T. Bruett	.20
9	Dave Mlicki	.20

10	Paul Wagner	.20
11	Mike Williams	.20
12	Henry Mercedes	.20
13	Scott Taylor	.20
14	Dennis Moeller	.20
15	Javier Lopez	.50
16	Steve Cooke	.20
17	Pete Young	.20
18	Ken Ryan	.20

1993 Fleer ProVisions

This three-card insert set in Series I wax packs features the baseball art of Wayne Still. Black-bordered fronts feature a player-fantasy painting at center, with the player's name gold-foil stamped beneath. Backs are also bordered in black and have a white box with a career summary.

		MT
Complete Set (6):		3.00
Common Player:		.40
	SERIES 1	2.00
1	Roberto Alomar	1.00
2	Dennis Eckersley	.40
3	Gary Sheffield	1.00
	SERIES 2	1.00
1	Andy Van Slyke	.40
2	Tom Glavine	.75
3	Cecil Fielder	.40

1993 Fleer Rookie Sensations

Ten rookie sensations - some of whom had not been true rookies for several seasons - were featured in this insert issue packaged exclusively in Series 1 and Series 2 cello packs. Card fronts have a player photo set against a silver background and surrounded by a blue border. The player's name and other front printing are in gold foil. Backs are also printed in silver with a blue border. There is a player portrait photo and career summary.

		MT
Complete Set (20):		12.50
Common Player:		.50
	SERIES 1	7.50
1	Kenny Lofton	2.50
2	Cal Eldred	.50
3	Pat Listach	.50
4	Roberto Hernandez	.50
5	Dave Fleming	.50
6	Eric Karros	1.00
7	Reggie Sanders	1.00
8	Derrick May	.50
9	Mike Perez	.50
10	Donovan Osborne	.50
	SERIES 2	5.00
1	Moises Alou	1.50
2	Pedro Astacio	.50
3	Jim Austin	.50
4	Chad Curtis	.50
5	Gary DiSarcina	.50
6	Scott Livingstone	.50
7	Sam Militello	.50
8	Arthur Rhodes	.50
9	Tim Wakefield	.50
10	Bob Zupcic	.50

1993 Fleer Team Leaders

This 20-card insert issue was exclusive to Series 1 and 2 rack packs. Fronts have a portrait photo, with a small action photo superimposed. At the side is a colored bar with the player's name and "Team Leaders" printed vertically. On back is a career summary. Card borders are a light metallic green and both sides of the card are UV coated.

		MT
Complete Set (20):		11.00
Common Player:		.15
	SERIES 1	9.00
1	Kirby Puckett	1.25
2	Mark McGwire	2.50
3	Pat Listach	.15
4	Roger Clemens	.75
5	Frank Thomas	1.00
6	Carlos Baerga	.15
7	Brady Anderson	.15
8	Juan Gonzalez	.75
9	Roberto Alomar	.30
10	Ken Griffey, Jr.	2.50
	SERIES 2	3.00
1	Will Clark	.35
2	Terry Pendleton	.15
3	Ray Lankford	.15
4	Eric Karros	.20
5	Gary Sheffield	.30
6	Ryne Sandberg	.60
7	Marquis Grissom	.15
8	John Kruk	.15
9	Jeff Bagwell	1.25
10	Andy Van Slyke	.15

1993 Fleer Tom Glavine Career Highlights

This 15-card insert set spotlighted career highlights of Fleer's 1993 spokesman, Tom Glavine. Twelve cards were available in Series 1 and Series 2 packs; cards #13-15 could be obtained only via a special mail offer. A limited number of certified autograph cards were also inserted into packs. Cards #1-4 and 7-10 can each be found with two variations of the write-ups on the back. The versions found in Series 2 packaging are the "correct" backs. Neither version carries a premium value.

		MT
Complete Set (15):		5.00
Common Card:		.50
Autographed Card:		35.00
1	Tom Glavine	.50
2	Tom Glavine	.50
3	Tom Glavine	.50
4	Tom Glavine	.50
5	Tom Glavine	.50
6	Tom Glavine	.50
7	Tom Glavine	.50
8	Tom Glavine	.50
9	Tom Glavine	.50
10	Tom Glavine	.50
11	Tom Glavine	.50
12	Tom Glavine	.50
13	Tom Glavine	.50
14	Tom Glavine	.50
15	Tom Glavine	.50

1993 Fleer Final Edition

This 310-card set was sold as a complete set in its own box. Card numbers have the prefix "F". The set also includes 10 Diamond Tribute cards, which are numbered DT1-DT10.

		MT
Complete Set (310):		7.00
Common Player:		.05
1	Steve Bedrosian	.05
2	Jay Howell	.05
3	Greg Maddux	1.00
4	*Greg McMichael*	.05
5	*Tony Tarasco*	.05
6	Jose Bautista	.05
7	Jose Guzman	.05
8	Greg Hibbard	.05
9	Candy Maldonado	.05
10	Randy Myers	.05
11	*Matt Walbeck*	.10
12	Turk Wendell	.05
13	Willie Nelson	.05
14	Greg Cadaret	.05
15	Roberto Kelly	.05
16	Randy Milligan	.05
17	Kevin Mitchell	.05
18	Jeff Reardon	.05
19	John Roper	.05
20	John Smiley	.05
21	Andy Ashby	.05
22	Dante Bichette	.10
23	Willie Blair	.05
24	Pedro Castellano	.05
25	Vinny Castilla	.05
26	Jerald Clark	.05
27	Alex Cole	.05
28	*Scott Fredrickson*	.05
29	*Jay Gainer*	.05
30	Andres Galarraga	.05
31	Joe Girardi	.05
32	Ryan Hawblitzel	.05
33	Charlie Hayes	.05
34	Darren Holmes	.05
35	Chris Jones	.05
36	David Nied	.05
37	*J. Owens*	.10
38	*Lance Painter*	.05
39	Jeff Parrett	.05
40	*Steve Reed*	.05
41	Armando Reynoso	.05
42	Bruce Ruffin	.05
43	*Danny Sheaffer*	.10
44	Keith Shepherd	.05
45	Jim Tatum	.05
46	Gary Wayne	.05
47	Eric Young	.10
48	Luis Aquino	.05
49	Alex Arias	.05
50	Jack Armstrong	.05
51	Bret Barberie	.05
52	Geronimo Berroa	.05
53	Ryan Bowen	.05
54	Greg Briley	.05
55	Chris Carpenter	.05
56	Chuck Carr	.05
57	Jeff Conine	.05
58	Jim Corsi	.05
59	Orestes Destrade	.05
60	Junior Felix	.05
61	Chris Hammond	.05
62	Bryan Harvey	.05
63	Charlie Hough	.05
64	Joe Klink	.05
65	*Richie Lewis*	.10
66	*Mitch Lyden*	.05
67	Bob Natal	.05
68	*Scott Pose*	.05
69	Rich Renteria	.05
70	Benito Santiago	.05
71	Gary Sheffield	.25
72	*Matt Turner*	.10
73	Walt Weiss	.05
74	*Darrell Whitmore*	.10
75	Nigel Wilson	.05
76	Kevin Bass	.05
77	Doug Drabek	.05
78	Tom Edens	.05
79	Chris James	.05
80	Greg Swindell	.05
81	*Omar Daal*	.10
82	Raul Mondesi	.25
83	Jody Reed	.05
84	Cory Snyder	.05
85	Rick Trlicek	.05
86	Tim Wallach	.05

87	Todd Worrell	.05
88	Tavo Alvarez	.05
89	Frank Bolick	.05
90	Kent Bottenfield	.05
91	Greg Colbrunn	.05
92	Cliff Floyd	.15
93	*Lou Frazier*	.10
94	Mike Gardiner	.05
95	*Mike Lansing*	.30
96	Bill Risley	.05
97	Jeff Shaw	.05
98	Kevin Baez	.05
99	*Tim Bogar*	.10
100	Jeromy Burnitz	.15
101	Mike Draper	.05
102	Darrin Jackson	.05
103	Mike Maddux	.05
104	Joe Orsulak	.05
105	Doug Saunders	.05
106	Frank Tanana	.05
107	Dave Telgheder	.05
108	Larry Anderson	.05
109	Jim Eisenreich	.05
110	Pete Incaviglia	.05
111	Danny Jackson	.05
112	David West	.05
113	Al Martin	.05
114	Blas Minor	.05
115	Dennis Moeller	.05
116	Will Pennyfeather	.05
117	Rich Robertson	.05
118	Ben Shelton	.05
119	Lonnie Smith	.05
120	Freddie Toliver	.05
121	Paul Wagner	.05
122	Kevin Young	.05
123	*Rene Arocha*	.10
124	Gregg Jefferies	.05
125	Paul Kilgus	.05
126	Les Lancaster	.05
127	Joe Magrane	.05
128	Rob Murphy	.05
129	Erik Pappas	.05
130	Stan Royer	.05
131	Ozzie Smith	.75
132	Tom Urbani	.05
133	Mark Whiten	.05
134	Derek Bell	.05
135	Doug Brocall	.05
136	Phil Clark	.05
137	*Mark Ettles*	.05
138	Jeff Gardner	.05
139	*Pat Gomez*	.10
140	Ricky Gutierrez	.05
141	Gene Harris	.05
142	*Kevin Higgins*	.05
143	Trevor Hoffman	.05
144	Phil Plantier	.05
145	*Kerry Taylor*	.05
146	Guillermo Velasquez	.05
147	Wally Whitehurst	.05
148	*Tim Worrell*	.05
149	Todd Benzinger	.05
150	Barry Bonds	1.00
151	Greg Brummett	.05
152	Mark Carreon	.05
153	Dave Martinez	.05
154	Jeff Reed	.05
155	Kevin Rogers	.05
156	Harold Baines	.05
157	Damon Buford	.05
158	*Paul Carey*	.05
159	Jeffrey Hammonds	.05
160	Jaime Moyer	.05
161	*Sherman Obando*	.10
162	*John O'Donoghue*	.10
163	Brad Pennington	.05
164	Jim Poole	.05
165	Harold Reynolds	.05
166	Fernando Valenzuela	.05
167	*Jack Voight*	.05
168	Mark Williamson	.05
169	Scott Bankhead	.05
170	Greg Blosser	.05
171	*Jim Byrd*	.05
172	Ivan Calderon	.05
173	Andre Dawson	.15
174	Scott Fletcher	.05
175	Jose Melendez	.05
176	Carlos Quintana	.05
177	Jeff Russell	.05
178	Aaron Sele	.10
179	*Rod Correia*	.05
180	Chili Davis	.05
181	*Jim Edmonds*	3.00
182	Rene Gonzales	.05
183	*Hilly Hathaway*	.05
184	Torey Lovullo	.05
185	Greg Myers	.05
186	Gene Nelson	.05
187	Troy Percival	.05
188	Scott Sanderson	.05
189	*Darryl Scott*	.05
190	*J.T. Snow*	.50
191	Russ Springer	.05
192	Jason Bere	.10
193	Rodney Bolton	.05
194	Ellis Burks	.05
195	Bo Jackson	.10
196	Mike LaValliere	.05
197	Scott Ruffcorn	.05
198	*Jeff Schwartz*	.05
199	Jerry DiPoto	.05
200	Alvaro Espinoza	.05
201	Wayne Kirby	.05
202	*Tom Kramer*	.05
203	Jesse Levis	.05
204	Manny Ramirez	1.50
205	Jeff Treadway	.05
206	*Bill Wertz*	.05
207	Cliff Young	.05
208	Matt Young	.05
209	Kirk Gibson	.05
210	Greg Gohr	.05
211	Bill Krueger	.05
212	Bob MacDonald	.05
213	Mike Moore	.05
214	David Wells	.10
215	*Billy Brewer*	.05
216	David Cone	.10
217	Greg Gagne	.05
218	Mark Gardner	.05
219	Chis Haney	.05
220	Phil Hiatt	.05
221	Jose Lind	.05
222	Juan Bell	.05
223	Tom Brunansky	.05
224	Mike Ignasiak	.05
225	Joe Kmak	.05
226	Tom Lampkin	.05
227	*Graeme Lloyd*	.10
228	Carlos Maldonado	.05
229	Matt Mieske	.05
230	Angel Miranda	.05
231	*Troy O'Leary*	.10
232	Kevin Reimer	.05
233	Larry Casian	.05
234	Jim Deshaies	.05
235	*Eddie Guardado*	.10
236	Chip Hale	.05
237	*Mike Maksudian*	.05
238	David McCarty	.05
239	*Pat Meares*	.10
240	*George Tsamis*	.05
241	Dave Winfield	.25
242	Jim Abbott	.05
243	Wade Boggs	.50
244	*Andy Cook*	.05
245	*Russ Davis*	.15
246	Mike Humphreys	.05
247	Jimmy Key	.05
248	Jim Leyritz	.10
249	Bobby Munoz	.05
250	Paul O'Neill	.05
251	Spike Owen	.05
252	Dave Silvestri	.05
253	*Marcos Armas*	.05
254	Brent Gates	.05
255	Goose Gossage	.05
256	*Scott Lydy*	.05
257	Henry Mercedes	.05
258	*Mike Mohler*	.05
259	Troy Neel	.05
260	Edwin Nunez	.05
261	Craig Paquette	.05
262	Kevin Seitzer	.05
263	Rich Amaral	.05
264	Mike Blowers	.05
265	Chris Bosio	.05
266	Norm Charlton	.05
267	*Jim Converse*	.05
268	*John Cummings*	.10
269	Mike Felder	.05
270	Mike Hampton	.05
271	Bill Haselman	.05
272	Dwayne Henry	.05
273	Greg Litton	.05
274	Mackey Sasser	.05
275	Lee Tinsley	.05
276	David Wainhouse	.05
277	*Jeff Bronkey*	.05
278	Benji Gil	.05
279	Tom Henke	.05
280	Charlie Leibrandt	.05
281	Robb Nen	.05
282	Bill Ripken	.05
283	*Jon Shave*	.05
284	Doug Strange	.05
285	*Matt Whiteside*	.10
286	*Scott Brow*	.05
287	*Willie Canate*	.05
288	Tony Castillo	.05
289	*Domingo Cedeno*	.10
290	Darnell Coles	.05
291	Danny Cox	.05
292	Mark Eichhorn	.05
293	Tony Fernandez	.05
294	Al Leiter	.05
295	Paul Molitor	.75
296	Dave Stewart	.05
297	*Woody Williams*	.05
298	Checklist	.05
299	Checklist	.05
300	Checklist	.05
	DIAMOND TRIBUTE	
1DT	Wade Boggs	.60
2DT	George Brett	1.00
3DT	Andre Dawson	.25
4DT	Carlton Fisk	.25
5DT	Paul Molitor	.50
6DT	Nolan Ryan	2.00
7DT	Lee Smith	.10
8DT	Ozzie Smith	.75
9DT	Dave Winfield	.50
10DT	Robin Yount	.50

1994 Fleer

Fleer's 720-card 1994 set, released in one series, includes another 204 insert cards to be pursued by collectors. Every pack includes one of the cards, randomly inserted from among the 12 insert sets. Regular cards have action photos on front, with a team logo in one of the lower corners. The player's name and position is stamped in gold foil around the logo. On back, another color player photo is overprinted with color boxes, data and stats, leaving a clear image of the player's face, 1-1/2" x 1-3/4" in size. Cards are UV coated on both sides.

		MT
Complete Set (720):		30.00
Common Player:		.05
Pack (15):		1.00
Wax Box (36):		30.00
1	Brady Anderson	.05
2	Harold Baines	.05
3	Mike Devereaux	.05
4	Todd Frohwirth	.05
5	Jeffrey Hammonds	.05
6	Chris Hoiles	.05
7	Tim Hulett	.05
8	Ben McDonald	.05
9	Mark McLemore	.05
10	Alan Mills	.05
11	Jamie Moyer	.05
12	Mike Mussina	.50
13	Gregg Olson	.05
14	Mike Pagliarulo	.05
15	Brad Pennington	.05
16	Jim Poole	.05
17	Harold Reynolds	.05
18	Arthur Rhodes	.05
19	Cal Ripken, Jr.	2.50
20	David Segui	.05
21	Rick Sutcliffe	.05
22	Fernando Valenzuela	.05
23	Jack Voigt	.05
24	Mark Williamson	.05
25	Scott Bankhead	.05
26	Roger Clemens	1.50
27	Scott Cooper	.05
28	Danny Darwin	.05
29	Andre Dawson	.10
30	Rob Deer	.05
31	John Dopson	.05
32	Scott Fletcher	.05
33	Mike Greenwell	.05
34	Greg Harris	.05
35	Billy Hatcher	.05
36	Bob Melvin	.05
37	Tony Pena	.05
38	Paul Quantrill	.05
39	Carlos Quintana	.05
40	Ernest Riles	.05
41	Jeff Russell	.05
42	Ken Ryan	.05
43	Aaron Sele	.05
44	John Valentin	.10
45	Mo Vaughn	.35
46	Frank Viola	.05
47	Bob Zupcic	.05
48	Mike Butcher	.05
49	Rod Correia	.05
50	Chad Curtis	.05
51	Chili Davis	.05
52	Gary DiSarcina	.05
53	Damion Easley	.05
54	Jim Edmonds	.25
55	Chuck Finley	.05
56	Steve Frey	.05
57	Rene Gonzales	.05
58	Joe Grahe	.05
59	Hilly Hathaway	.05
60	Stan Javier	.05
61	Mark Langston	.05
62	Phil Leftwich	.05
63	Torey Lovullo	.05
64	Joe Magrane	.05
65	Greg Myers	.05
66	Ken Patterson	.05
67	Eduardo Perez	.05
68	Luis Polonia	.05
69	Tim Salmon	.25
69a	Tim Salmon (overprinted PROMOTIONAL SAMPLE)	3.00
70	J.T. Snow	.15
71	Ron Tingley	.05
72	Julio Valera	.05
73	Wilson Alvarez	.05
74	Tim Belcher	.05
75	George Bell	.05
76	Jason Bere	.05
77	Rod Bolton	.05
78	Ellis Burks	.05
79	Joey Cora	.05
80	Alex Fernandez	.05
81	Craig Grebeck	.05
82	Ozzie Guillen	.05
83	Roberto Hernandez	.05
84	Bo Jackson	.15
85	Lance Johnson	.05
86	Ron Karkovice	.05
87	Mike LaValliere	.05
88	Kirk McCaskill	.05
89	Jack McDowell	.05
90	Warren Newson	.05
91	Dan Pasqua	.05
92	Scott Radinsky	.05
93	Tim Raines	.05
94	Steve Sax	.05
95	Jeff Schwarz	.05
96	Frank Thomas	1.50
97	Robin Ventura	.05
98	Sandy Alomar, Jr.	.05
99	Carlos Baerga	.05
100	Albert Belle	.25
101	Mark Clark	.05

102 Jerry DiPoto .05
103 Alvaro Espinoza .05
104 Felix Fermin .05
105 Jeremy Hernandez .05
106 Reggie Jefferson .05
107 Wayne Kirby .05
108 Tom Kramer .05
109 Mark Lewis .05
110 Derek Lilliquist .05
111 Kenny Lofton .05
112 Candy Maldonado .05
113 Jose Mesa .05
114 Jeff Mutis .05
115 Charles Nagy .05
116 Bob Ojeda .05
117 Junior Ortiz .05
118 Eric Plunk .05
119 Manny Ramirez 1.00
120 Paul Sorrento .05
121 Jim Thome .05
122 Jeff Treadway .05
123 Bill Wertz .05
124 Skeeter Barnes .05
125 Milt Cuyler .05
126 Eric Davis .05
127 John Doherty .05
128 Cecil Fielder .05
129 Travis Fryman .05
130 Kirk Gibson .05
131 Dan Gladden .05
132 Greg Gohr .05
133 Chris Gomez .05
134 Bill Gullickson .05
135 Mike Henneman .05
136 Kurt Knudsen .05
137 Chad Kreuter .05
138 Bill Krueger .05
139 Scott Livingstone .05
140 Bob MacDonald .05
141 Mike Moore .05
142 Tony Phillips .05
143 Mickey Tettleton .05
144 Alan Trammell .05
145 David Wells .10
146 Lou Whitaker .05
147 Kevin Appier .05
148 Stan Belinda .05
149 George Brett .60
150 Billy Brewer .05
151 Hubie Brooks .05
152 David Cone .05
153 Gary Gaetti .05
154 Greg Gagne .05
155 Tom Gordon .05
156 Mark Gubicza .05
157 Chris Gwynn .05
158 John Habyan .05
159 Chris Haney .05
160 Phil Hiatt .05
161 Felix Jose .05
162 Wally Joyner .05
163 Jose Lind .05
164 Mike Macfarlane .05
165 Mike Magnante .05
166 Brent Mayne .05
167 Brian McRae .05
168 Kevin McReynolds .05
169 Keith Miller .05
170 Jeff Montgomery .05
171 Hipolito Pichardo .05
172 Rico Rossy .05
173 Juan Bell .05
174 Ricky Bones .05
175 Cal Eldred .05
176 Mike Fetters .05
177 Darryl Hamilton .05
178 Doug Henry .05
179 Mike Ignasiak .05
180 John Jaha .05
181 Pat Listach .05
182 Graeme Lloyd .05
183 Matt Mieske .05
184 Angel Miranda .05
185 Jaime Navarro .05
186 Dave Nilsson .05
187 Troy O'Leary .05
188 Jesse Orosco .05
189 Kevin Reimer .05
190 Kevin Seitzer .05
191 Bill Spiers .05
192 B.J. Surhoff .05
193 Dickie Thon .05
194 Jose Valentin .05
195 Greg Vaughn .05
196 Bill Wegman .05
197 Robin Yount .35
198 Rick Aguilera .05
199 Willie Banks .05
200 Bernardo Brito .05
201 Larry Casian .05
202 Scott Erickson .05
203 Eddie Guardado .05
204 Mark Guthrie .05
205 Chip Hale .05
206 Brian Harper .05
207 Mike Hartley .05
208 Kent Hrbek .05
209 Terry Jorgensen .05
210 Chuck Knoblauch .05
211 Gene Larkin .05
212 Shane Mack .05
213 David McCarty .05
214 Pat Meares .05
215 Pedro Munoz .05
216 Derek Parks .05
217 Kirby Puckett 1.50
218 Jeff Reboulet .05
219 Kevin Tapani .05
220 Mike Trombley .05
221 George Tsamis .05
222 Carl Willis .05
223 Dave Winfield .35
224 Jim Abbott .05
225 Paul Assenmacher .05
226 Wade Boggs .40
227 Russ Davis .05
228 Steve Farr .05
229 Mike Gallego .05
230 Paul Gibson .05
231 Steve Howe .05
232 Dion James .05
233 Domingo Jean .05
234 Scott Kamieniecki .05
235 Pat Kelly .05
236 Jimmy Key .05
237 Jim Leyritz .05
238 Kevin Maas .05
239 Don Mattingly 1.50
240 Rich Monteleone .05
241 Bobby Munoz .05
242 Matt Nokes .05
243 Paul O'Neill .05
244 Spike Owen .05
245 Melido Perez .05
246 Lee Smith .05
247 Mike Stanley .05
248 Danny Tartabull .05
249 Randy Velarde .05
250 Bob Wickman .05
251 Bernie Williams .40
252 Mike Aldrete .05
253 Marcos Armas .05
254 Lance Blankenship .05
255 Mike Bordick .05
256 Scott Brosius .05
257 Jerry Browne .05
258 Ron Darling .05
259 Kelly Downs .05
260 Dennis Eckersley .05
261 Brent Gates .05
262 Goose Gossage .05
263 Scott Hemond .05
264 Dave Henderson .05
265 Rick Honeycutt .05
266 Vince Horsman .05
267 Scott Lydy .05
268 Mark McGwire 2.50
269 Mike Mohler .05
270 Troy Neel .05
271 Edwin Nunez .05
272 Craig Paquette .05
273 Ruben Sierra .05
274 Terry Steinbach .05
275 Todd Van Poppel .05
276 Bob Welch .05
277 Bobby Witt .05
278 Rich Amaral .05
279 Mike Blowers .05
280 Bret Boone .10
281 Chris Bosio .05
282 Jay Buhner .05
283 Norm Charlton .05
284 Mike Felder .05
285 Dave Fleming .05
286 Ken Griffey, Jr. 2.50
287 Erik Hanson .05
288 Bill Haselman .05
289 *Brad Holman* .10
290 Randy Johnson .75
291 Tim Leary .05
292 Greg Litton .05
293 Dave Magadan .05
294 Edgar Martinez .05
295 Tino Martinez .05
296 Jeff Nelson .05
297 *Erik Plantenberg* .05
298 Mackey Sasser .05
299 *Brian Turang* .05
300 Dave Valle .05
301 Omar Vizquel .05
302 Brian Bohanon .05
303 Kevin Brown .05
304 Jose Canseco .40
305 Mario Diaz .05
306 Julio Franco .05
307 Juan Gonzalez .75
308 Tom Henke .05
309 David Hulse .05
310 Manuel Lee .05
311 Craig Lefferts .05
312 Charlie Leibrandt .05
313 Rafael Palmeiro .25
314 Dean Palmer .05
315 Roger Pavlik .05
316 Dan Peltier .05
317 Geno Petralli .05
318 Gary Redus .05
319 Ivan Rodriguez .60
320 Kenny Rogers .05
321 Nolan Ryan 2.50
322 Doug Strange .05
323 Matt Whiteside .05
324 Roberto Alomar .60
325 Pat Borders .05
326 Joe Carter .05
327 Tony Castillo .05
328 Darnell Coles .05
329 Danny Cox .05
330 Mark Eichhorn .05
331 Tony Fernandez .05
332 Alfredo Griffin .05
333 Juan Guzman .05
334 Rickey Henderson .25
335 Pat Hentgen .05
336 Randy Knorr .05
337 Al Leiter .05
338 Paul Molitor .40
339 Jack Morris .05
340 John Olerud .05
341 Dick Schofield .05
342 Ed Sprague .05
343 Dave Stewart .05
344 Todd Stottlemyre .05
345 Mike Timlin .05
346 Duane Ward .05
347 Turner Ward .05
348 Devon White .10
349 Woody Williams .05
350 Steve Avery .05
351 Steve Bedrosian .05
352 Rafael Belliard .05
353 Damon Berryhill .05
354 Jeff Blauser .05
355 Sid Bream .05
356 Francisco Cabrera .05
357 Marvin Freeman .05
358 Ron Gant .05
359 Tom Glavine .10
360 Jay Howell .05
361 Dave Justice .10
362 Ryan Klesko .05
363 Mark Lemke .05
364 Javier Lopez .05
365 Greg Maddux 2.00
366 Fred McGriff .05
367 Greg McMichael .05
368 Kent Mercker .05
369 Otis Nixon .05
370 Greg Olson .05
371 Bill Pecota .05
372 Terry Pendleton .05
373 Deion Sanders .10
374 Pete Smith .05
375 John Smoltz .10
376 Mike Stanton .05
377 Tony Tarasco .05
378 Mark Wohlers .05
379 Jose Bautista .05
380 Shawn Boskie .05
381 Steve Buechele .05
382 Frank Castillo .05
383 Mark Grace .20
384 Jose Guzman .05
385 Mike Harkey .05
386 Greg Hibbard .05
387 Glenallen Hill .05
388 Steve Lake .05
389 Derrick May .05
390 Chuck McElroy .05
391 Mike Morgan .05
392 Randy Myers .05
393 Dan Plesac .05
394 Kevin Roberson .05
395 Rey Sanchez .05
396 Ryne Sandberg .50
397 Bob Scanlan .05
398 Dwight Smith .05
399 Sammy Sosa 1.50
400 Jose Vizcaino .05
401 Rick Wilkins .05
402 Willie Wilson .05
403 Eric Yelding .05
404 Bobby Ayala .05
405 Jeff Branson .05
406 Tom Browning .05
407 Jacob Brumfield .05
408 Tim Costo .05
409 Rob Dibble .05
410 Willie Greene .05
411 Thomas Howard .05
412 Roberto Kelly .05
413 Bill Landrum .05
414 Barry Larkin .10
415 *Larry Luebbers* .05
416 Kevin Mitchell .05
417 Hal Morris .05
418 Joe Oliver .05
419 Tim Pugh .05
420 Jeff Reardon .05
421 Jose Rijo .05
422 Bip Roberts .05
423 John Roper .05
424 Johnny Ruffin .05
425 Chris Sabo .05
426 Juan Samuel .05
427 Reggie Sanders .05
428 Scott Service .05
429 John Smiley .05
430 *Jerry Spradlin* .05
431 Kevin Wickander .05
432 Freddie Benavides .05
433 Dante Bichette .05
434 Willie Blair .05
435 Daryl Boston .05
436 Kent Bottenfield .05
437 Vinny Castilla .05
438 Jerald Clark .05
439 Alex Cole .05
440 Andres Galarraga .05
441 Joe Girardi .05
442 Greg Harris .05
443 Charlie Hayes .05
444 Darren Holmes .05
445 Chris Jones .05
446 Roberto Mejia .05
447 David Nied .05
448 J. Owens .05
449 Jeff Parrett .05
450 Steve Reed .05
451 Armando Reynoso .05
452 Bruce Ruffin .05
453 Mo Sanford .05
454 Danny Sheaffer .05
455 Jim Tatum .05
456 Gary Wayne .05
457 Eric Young .05
458 Luis Aquino .05
459 Alex Arias .05
460 Jack Armstrong .05
461 Bret Barberie .05
462 Ryan Bowen .05
463 Chuck Carr .05
464 Jeff Conine .05
465 Henry Cotto .05
466 Orestes Destrade .05
467 Chris Hammond .05
468 Bryan Harvey .05
469 Charlie Hough .05
470 Joe Klink .05
471 Richie Lewis .05
472 *Bob Natal* .10
473 *Pat Rapp* .15
474 *Rich Renteria* .10
475 Rich Rodriguez .05
476 Benito Santiago .05
477 Gary Sheffield .20
478 Matt Turner .05
479 David Weathers .05
480 Walt Weiss .05
481 Darrell Whitmore .05
482 Eric Anthony .05
483 Jeff Bagwell .75
484 Kevin Bass .05
485 Craig Biggio .10

486 Ken Caminiti .05
487 Andujar Cedeno .05
488 Chris Donnels .05
489 Doug Drabek .05
490 Steve Finley .05
491 Luis Gonzalez .15
492 Pete Harnisch .05
493 Xavier Hernandez .05
494 Doug Jones .05
495 Todd Jones .05
496 Darryl Kile .05
497 Al Osuna .05
498 Mark Portugal .05
499 Scott Servais .05
500 Greg Swindell .05
501 Eddie Taubensee .05
502 Jose Uribe .05
503 Brian Williams .05
504 Billy Ashley .05
505 Pedro Astacio .05
506 Brett Butler .05
507 Tom Candiotti .05
508 Omar Daal .05
509 Jim Gott .05
510 Kevin Gross .05
511 Dave Hansen .05
512 Carlos Hernandez .05
513 Orel Hershiser .05
514 Eric Karros .05
515 Pedro Martinez .75
516 Ramon Martinez .05
517 Roger McDowell .05
518 Raul Mondesi .25
519 Jose Offerman .05
520 Mike Piazza 2.00
521 Jody Reed .05
522 Henry Rodriguez .05
523 Mike Sharperson .05
524 Cory Snyder .05
525 Darryl Strawberry .05
526 Rick Trlicek .05
527 Tim Wallach .05
528 Mitch Webster .05
529 Steve Wilson .05
530 Todd Worrell .05
531 Moises Alou .10
532 Brian Barnes .05
533 Sean Berry .05
534 Greg Colbrunn .05
535 Delino DeShields .05
536 Jeff Fassero .05
537 Darrin Fletcher .05
538 Cliff Floyd .10
539 Lou Frazier .05
540 Marquis Grissom .05
541 Butch Henry .05
542 Ken Hill .05
543 Mike Lansing .05
544 *Brian Looney* .05
545 Dennis Martinez .05
546 Chris Nabholz .05
547 Randy Ready .05
548 Mel Rojas .05
549 Kirk Rueter .05
550 Tim Scott .05
551 Jeff Shaw .05
552 Tim Spehr .05
553 John VanderWal .05
554 Larry Walker .15
555 John Wetteland .05
556 Rondell White .10
557 Tim Bogar .05
558 Bobby Bonilla .05
559 Jeremy Burnitz .10
560 Sid Fernandez .05
561 John Franco .05
562 Dave Gallagher .05
563 Dwight Gooden .05
564 Eric Hillman .05
565 Todd Hundley .05
566 Jeff Innis .05
567 Darrin Jackson .05
568 Howard Johnson .05
569 Bobby Jones .05
570 Jeff Kent .05
571 Mike Maddux .05
572 Jeff McKnight .05
573 Eddie Murray .20
574 Charlie O'Brien .05
575 Joe Orsulak .05
576 Bret Saberhagen .05
577 Pete Schourek .05
578 Dave Telgheder .05
579 Ryan Thompson .05
580 Anthony Young .05
581 Ruben Amaro .05
582 Larry Andersen .05
583 Kim Batiste .05
584 Wes Chamberlain .05
585 Darren Daulton .05
586 Mariano Duncan .05
587 Len Dykstra .05
588 Jim Eisenreich .05
589 Tommy Greene .05
590 Dave Hollins .05
591 Pete Incaviglia .05
592 Danny Jackson .05
593 Ricky Jordan .05
594 John Kruk .05
595 Roger Mason .05
596 Mickey Morandini .05
597 Terry Mulholland .05
598 Todd Pratt .05
599 Ben Rivera .05
600 Curt Schilling .10
601 Kevin Stocker .05
602 Milt Thompson .05
603 David West .05
604 Mitch Williams .05
605 Jay Bell .05
606 Dave Clark .05
607 Steve Cooke .05
608 Tom Foley .05
609 Carlos Garcia .05
610 Joel Johnston .05
611 Jeff King .05
612 Al Martin .05
613 Lloyd McClendon .05
614 Orlando Merced .05
615 Blas Minor .05
616 Denny Neagle .05
617 *Mark Petkovsek* .10
618 Tom Prince .05
619 Don Slaught .05
620 Zane Smith .05
621 Randy Tomlin .05
622 Andy Van Slyke .05
623 Paul Wagner .05
624 Tim Wakefield .05
625 Bob Walk .05
626 Kevin Young .05
627 Luis Alicea .05
628 Rene Arocha .05
629 Rod Brewer .05
630 Rheal Cormier .05
631 Bernard Gilkey .05
632 Lee Guetterman .05
633 Gregg Jefferies .05
634 Brian Jordan .05
635 Les Lancaster .05
636 Ray Lankford .05
637 Rob Murphy .05
638 Omar Olivares .05
639 Jose Oquendo .05
640 Donovan Osborne .05
641 Tom Pagnozzi .05
642 Erik Pappas .05
643 Geronimo Pena .05
644 Mike Perez .05
645 Gerald Perry .05
646 Ozzie Smith .60
647 Bob Tewksbury .05
648 Allen Watson .05
649 Mark Whiten .05
650 Tracy Woodson .05
651 Todd Zeile .05
652 Andy Ashby .05
653 Brad Ausmus .05
654 Billy Bean .05
655 Derek Bell .05
656 Andy Benes .05
657 Doug Brocail .05
658 Jarvis Brown .05
659 Archi Cianfrocco .05
660 Phil Clark .05
661 Mark Davis .05
662 Jeff Gardner .05
663 Pat Gomez .05
664 Ricky Gutierrez .05
665 Tony Gwynn 1.25
666 Gene Harris .05
667 Kevin Higgins .05
668 Trevor Hoffman .05
669 *Pedro A. Martinez* .05
670 Tim Mauser .05
671 Melvin Nieves .05
672 Phil Plantier .05
673 Frank Seminara .05
674 Craig Shipley .05
675 Kerry Taylor .05
676 Tim Teufel .05
677 Guillermo Velasquez .05
678 Wally Whitehurst .05
679 Tim Worrell .05
680 Rod Beck .05
681 Mike Benjamin .05
682 Todd Benzinger .05
683 Bud Black .05
684 Barry Bonds 1.00
685 Jeff Brantley .05
686 Dave Burba .05
687 John Burkett .05
688 Mark Carreon .05
689 Will Clark .15
690 Royce Clayton .05
691 Bryan Hickerson .05
692 Mike Jackson .05
693 Darren Lewis .05
694 Kirt Manwaring .05
695 Dave Martinez .05
696 Willie McGee .05
697 John Patterson .05
698 Jeff Reed .05
699 Kevin Rogers .05
700 Scott Sanderson .05
701 Steve Scarsone .05
702 Billy Swift .05
703 Robby Thompson .05
704 Matt Williams .15
705 Trevor Wilson .05
706 "Brave New World" (Fred McGriff, Ron Gant, Dave Justice) .10
707 "1-2 Punch" (Paul Molitor, John Olerud) .10
708 "American Heat" (Mike Mussina, Jack McDowell) .10
709 "Together Again" (Lou Whitaker, Alan Trammell) .10
710 "Lone Star Lumber" (Rafael Palmeiro, Juan Gonzalez) .20
711 "Batmen" (Brett Butler, Tony Gwynn) .10
712 "Twin Peaks" (Kirby Puckett, Chuck Knoblauch) .20
713 "Back to Back" (Mike Piazza, Eric Karros) .20
714 Checklist .05
715 Checklist .05
716 Checklist .05
717 Checklist .05
718 Checklist .05
719 Checklist .05
720 Checklist .05

1994 Fleer All-Stars

Each league's 25 representatives for the 1993 All-Star Game are featured in this insert set. Fronts have a player action photo with a rippling American flag in the top half of the background. The '93 All-Star logo is featured at the bottom, along with a gold-foil impression of the player's name. The flag motif is repeated at top of the card back, along with a player portrait photo set against a red (American League) or blue (National League) background. Odds of finding one of the 50 All-Star inserts are one in every two 15-card foil packs.

		MT
Complete Set (50):		20.00
Common Player:		.25
1	Roberto Alomar	.60
2	Carlos Baerga	.25
3	Albert Belle	.75
4	Wade Boggs	.75
5	Joe Carter	.25
6	Scott Cooper	.25
7	Cecil Fielder	.25
8	Travis Fryman	.25
9	Juan Gonzalez	1.00
10	Ken Griffey, Jr.	3.00
11	Pat Hentgen	.25
12	Randy Johnson	.75
13	Jimmy Key	.25
14	Mark Langston	.25
15	Jack McDowell	.25
16	Paul Molitor	.75
17	Jeff Montgomery	.25
18	Mike Mussina	.75
19	John Olerud	.25
20	Kirby Puckett	1.00
21	Cal Ripken, Jr.	3.00
22	Ivan Rodriguez	.60
23	Frank Thomas	2.00
24	Greg Vaughn	.25
25	Duane Ward	.25
26	Steve Avery	.25
27	Rod Beck	.25
28	Jay Bell	.25
29	Andy Benes	.25
30	Jeff Blauser	.25
31	Barry Bonds	1.50
32	Bobby Bonilla	.25
33	John Burkett	.25
34	Darren Daulton	.25
35	Andres Galarraga	.25
36	Tom Glavine	.35
37	Mark Grace	.50
38	Marquis Grissom	.25
39	Tony Gwynn	1.50
40	Bryan Harvey	.25
41	Dave Hollins	.25
42	Dave Justice	.35
43	Darryl Kile	.25
44	John Kruk	.25
45	Barry Larkin	.35
46	Terry Mulholland	.25
47	Mike Piazza	2.50
48	Ryne Sandberg	.75
49	Gary Sheffield	.50
50	John Smoltz	.35

1994 Fleer Award Winners

The 1993 MVP, Cy Young and Rookie of the Year award winners from each league are featured in this insert set. Cards are UV coated on both sides. Three different croppings of the same player action photo are featured on the front, with the player's name and other printing in gold foil. Backs have a player portrait and short summary of his previous season's performance. According to the company, odds of finding one of these horizontal-format inserts were one in 37 packs.

		MT
Complete Set (6):		4.50
Common Player:		.25
1	Frank Thomas	1.50
2	Barry Bonds	1.00
3	Jack McDowell	.25
4	Greg Maddux	1.50
5	Tim Salmon	.50
6	Mike Piazza	2.00

1994 Fleer Golden Moments

Ten highlights from the 1993 Major League baseball season are commemorated in this insert set. Each of the cards has a title which summarizes the historical moment. These inserts were available exclusively in Fleer cards packaged for large retail outlets.

		MT
Complete Set (10):		10.00
Common Player:		.25
1	"Four in One" (Mark Whiten)	.25
2	"Left and Right" (Carlos Baerga)	.25
3	"3,000 Hit Club" (Dave Winfield)	.75
4	"Eight Straight" (Ken Griffey, Jr.)	4.00
5	"Triumphant Return" (Bo Jackson)	.75
6	"Farewell to Baseball" (George Brett)	1.50
7	"Farewell to Baseball" (Nolan Ryan)	4.00
8	"Thirty Times Six" (Fred McGriff)	.25
9	"Enters 5th Dimension" (Frank Thomas)	2.00
10	"The No-Hit Parade" (Chris Bosio, Jim Abbott, Darryl Kile)	.25

1994 Fleer Golden Moments Super

Super-size (3-1/2" x 5") versions of the Golden Moments insert set were included in hobby cases at the rate of one set, in a specially-printed folder, per 20-box case. Each card carries a serial number designating its position in an edition of 10,000.

		MT
Complete Set (10):		20.00
Common Player:		1.00
1	"Four in One" (Mark Whiten)	1.00
2	"Left and Right" (Carlos Baerga)	1.00
3	"3,000 Hit Club" (Dave Winfield)	2.00
4	"Eight Straight" (Ken Griffey, Jr.)	5.00
5	"Triumphant Return" (Bo Jackson)	2.00
6	"Farewell to Baseball" (George Brett)	3.00
7	"Farewell to Baseball" (Nolan Ryan)	5.00
8	"Thirty Times Six" (Fred McGriff)	1.00
9	"Enters 5th Dimension" (Frank Thomas)	3.00
10	"The No-Hit Parade" (Chris Bosio, Jim Abbott, Darryl Kile)	1.00

1994 Fleer League Leaders

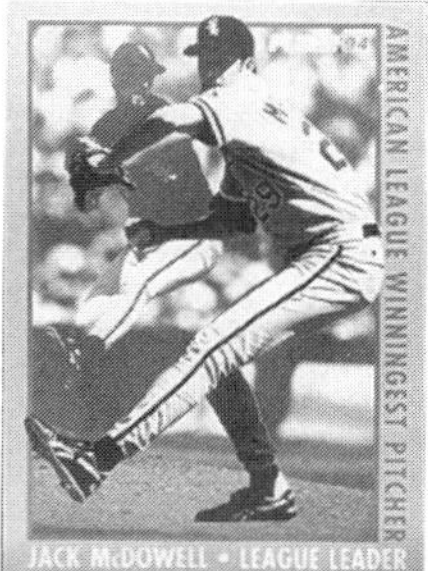

Twelve players who led the major leagues in various statistical categories in 1993 are featured in this insert set. Cards are UV coated and have gold-foil stamping on both sides. Within a light metallic green border, card fronts feature a color action photo superimposed over a similar photo in black-and-white. The category in which the player led his league is printed down the right border. Other printing is gold-foil. On back is a color photo and details of the league-leading performance. Stated odds of finding a League Leaders card were one per 17 packs.

		MT
Complete Set (12):		3.00
Common Player:		.10
1	John Olerud	.10
2	Albert Belle	.30
3	Rafael Palmeiro	.25
4	Kenny Lofton	.10
5	Jack McDowell	.10
6	Kevin Appier	.10
7	Andres Galarraga	.10
8	Barry Bonds	1.00
9	Len Dykstra	.10
10	Chuck Carr	.10
11	Tom Glavine	.20
12	Greg Maddux	1.00

1994 Fleer Lumber Co.

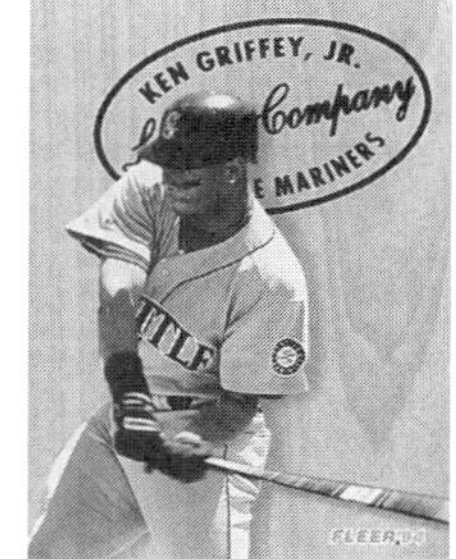

This insert set features the major leagues' top home run hitters. Inserted only in 21-card jumbo packs, odds of finding one were given as one per five packs. Card fronts feature player action photos against a background resembling the label area of a baseball bat. On back is a background photo of a row of bats on the dirt. A player write-up and close-up photo complete the design.

		MT
Complete Set (10):		10.00
Common Player:		.50
1	Albert Belle	1.00
2	Barry Bonds	2.00
3	Ron Gant	.50
4	Juan Gonzalez	1.50
5	Ken Griffey, Jr.	4.00
6	Dave Justice	.75
7	Fred McGriff	.50
8	Rafael Palmeiro	1.00
9	Frank Thomas	1.50
10	Matt Williams	.75

1994 Fleer Major League Prospects

Thirty-five of the game's promising young stars are featured in this insert set. A light green metallic border frames a player photo, with his team logo lightly printed over the background. Most of the printing is gold-foil stamped. Backs have a player photo against a pin-striped background. A light blue box contains career details. Given odds of finding a "Major League Prospects" card are one in six packs.

		MT
Complete Set (35):		7.00
Common Player:		.20
1	Kurt Abbott	.30
2	Brian Anderson	.20
3	Rich Aude	.20
4	Cory Bailey	.20
5	Danny Bautista	.20
6	Marty Cordova	.50
7	Tripp Cromer	.20
8	Midre Cummings	.20
9	Carlos Delgado	1.00
10	Steve Dreyer	.20
11	Steve Dunn	.20
12	Jeff Granger	.20
13	Tyrone Hill	.20
14	Denny Hocking	.20
15	John Hope	.20
16	Butch Huskey	.40
17	Miguel Jimenez	.20
18	Chipper Jones	3.00
19	Steve Karsay	.20
20	Mike Kelly	.20
21	Mike Lieberthal	.50
22	Albie Lopez	.20
23	Jeff McNeely	.20
24	Dan Miceli	.20
25	Nate Minchey	.20
26	Marc Newfield	.20
27	Darren Oliver	.20
28	Luis Ortiz	.20
29	Curtis Pride	.20
30	Roger Salkeld	.20
31	Scott Sanders	.20
32	Dave Staton	.20
33	Salomon Torres	.20
34	Steve Trachsel	.20
35	Chris Turner	.20

1994 Fleer ProVisions

Nine players are featured in this insert set. Cards feature the fantasy artwork of Wayne Still in a format that produces one large image when all nine cards are properly arranged. Besides the art, card fronts feature the player's name in gold-foil. Backs have a background in several shades of red, with the player's name and team at the top in white. A short career summary is printed in black. Odds of finding this particular insert in a pack are one in 12.

		MT
Complete Set (9):		3.00
Common Player:		.20
1	Darren Daulton	.20
2	John Olerud	.25
3	Matt Williams	.25
4	Carlos Baerga	.20
5	Ozzie Smith	1.00
6	Juan Gonzalez	1.00
7	Jack McDowell	.20
8	Mike Piazza	2.00
9	Tony Gwynn	1.00

1994 Fleer Rookie Sensations

This insert set features the top rookies from 1993. These inserts were available only in 21-card jumbo packs, with stated odds of one in four packs. Full-bleed fronts have a pair of player photos - one highlighted by a neon outline - superimposed on a graduated background approximating the team colors. Team uniform logo details appear vertically at the right or left side. The player's name is gold-foil stamped in a banner at bottom. The Rookie Sensations and Fleer logos are also gold-imprinted. On back, the team uniform logo is repeated on a white background, along with another player photo and a short write-up.

		MT
Complete Set (20):		10.00
Common Player:		.40
1	Rene Arocha	.40
2	Jason Bere	.50
3	Jeromy Burnitz	.75
4	Chuck Carr	.40
5	Jeff Conine	.50
6	Steve Cooke	.40
7	Cliff Floyd	.60
8	Jeffrey Hammonds	.40
9	Wayne Kirby	.40
10	Mike Lansing	.50
11	Al Martin	.40
12	Greg McMichael	.40
13	Troy Neel	.40
14	Mike Piazza	4.00
15	Armando Reynoso	.40
16	Kirk Rueter	.40
17	Tim Salmon	1.50
18	Aaron Sele	.60
19	J.T. Snow	.75
20	Kevin Stocker	.40

1994 Fleer Smoke N' Heat

Among the scarcest of the '94 Fleer inserts, available at a stated rate of one per 30 packs, these feature 10 of the top strikeout pitchers in the major leagues. "Metallized" card fronts have a player photo set against an infernal background with large letters, "Smoke 'N Heat". The player's name is in gold foil at bottom. Backs have a similar chaotic hot-red background, a player photo and career summary.

		MT
Complete Set (12):		20.00
Common Player:		.25
1	Roger Clemens	5.00
2	David Cone	.50
3	Juan Guzman	.25
4	Pete Harnisch	.25
5	Randy Johnson	2.50
6	Mark Langston	.25
7	Greg Maddux	5.00
8	Mike Mussina	2.00
9	Jose Rijo	.25
10	Nolan Ryan	9.00
11	Curt Schilling	1.00
12	John Smoltz	1.00

1994 Fleer Tim Salmon A.L. Rookie of the Year

The popular Angels Rookie of the Year is featured in a 15-card set produced in what Fleer terms "metallized" format. The first 12 cards in the set were inserted into foil packs at the rate of about one card per box. Three additional cards could be obtained by sending $1.50 and 10 '94 Fleer wrappers to a mail-in offer. On both front and back, the cards have a color player photo set against a metallic-image background.

		MT
Complete Set (15):		12.50
Common Card:		1.00
Autograph/2,000:		25.00
1	Tim Salmon	1.00
2	Tim Salmon	1.00
3	Tim Salmon	1.00
4	Tim Salmon	1.00
5	Tim Salmon	1.00
6	Tim Salmon	1.00
7	Tim Salmon	1.00
8	Tim Salmon	1.00
9	Tim Salmon	1.00
10	Tim Salmon	1.00
11	Tim Salmon	1.00
12	Tim Salmon	1.00
13	Tim Salmon	1.50
14	Tim Salmon	1.50
15	Tim Salmon	1.50

1994 Fleer Team Leaders

A player from each major league team has been chosen for this 28-card insert set. Fronts feature a team logo against a backgound of graduated team colors. Player portrait and action photos are superimposed. At bottom is the player name, team and position, all in gold foil. Backs have a team logo and player photo set against a white background, with a short write-up justifying the player's selection as a "Team Leader." Odds of finding one of these inserts were given as one in eight packs.

		MT
Complete Set (28):		20.00
Common Player:		.15
1	Cal Ripken, Jr.	3.00
2	Mo Vaughn	.45
3	Tim Salmon	.30
4	Frank Thomas	1.25
5	Carlos Baerga	.15
6	Cecil Fielder	.15
7	Brian McRae	.15
8	Greg Vaughn	.15
9	Kirby Puckett	1.50
10	Don Mattingly	1.50
11	Mark McGwire	3.50
12	Ken Griffey, Jr.	3.00
13	Juan Gonzalez	1.00
14	Paul Molitor	.50
15	Dave Justice	.25
16	Ryne Sandberg	.75
17	Barry Larkin	.25
18	Andres Galarraga	.15
19	Gary Sheffield	.45
20	Jeff Bagwell	.75
21	Mike Piazza	2.50
22	Marquis Grissom	.15
23	Bobby Bonilla	.15
24	Len Dykstra	.15
25	Jay Bell	.15
26	Gregg Jefferies	.15
27	Tony Gwynn	1.50
28	Will Clark	.30

1994 Fleer Update

Rookies, traded players and free agents who changed teams are included in the annual update issue. Cards are in the same format as the regular-issue '94 Fleer set. Cards are numbered alphabetically within team.

		MT
Complete Set (200):		50.00
Common Player:		.10
1	Mark Eichhorn	.10
2	Sid Fernandez	.10
3	Leo Gomez	.10
4	Mike Oquist	.10
5	Rafael Palmeiro	.40
6	Chris Sabo	.10
7	Dwight Smith	.10
8	Lee Smith	.10
9	Damon Berryhill	.10
10	Wes Chamberlain	.10
11	Gar Finnvold	.10
12	Chris Howard	.10
13	Tim Naehring	.10
14	Otis Nixon	.10
15	Brian Anderson	.10
16	Jorge Fabregas	.10
17	Rex Hudler	.10
18	Bo Jackson	.20
19	Mark Leiter	.10
20	Spike Owen	.10
21	Harold Reynolds	.10
22	Chris Turner	.10
23	Dennis Cook	.10
24	Jose DeLeon	.10
25	Julio Franco	.10
26	Joe Hall	.10
27	Darrin Jackson	.10
28	Dane Johnson	.10
29	Norberto Martin	.10
30	Scott Sanderson	.10
31	Jason Grimsley	.10
32	Dennis Martinez	.10
33	Jack Morris	.10
34	Eddie Murray	.35
35	Chad Ogea	.10
36	Tony Pena	.10
37	Paul Shuey	.10
38	Omar Vizquel	.10
39	Danny Bautista	.10
40	Tim Belcher	.10
41	Joe Boever	.10
42	Storm Davis	.10
43	Junior Felix	.10

44	Mike Gardiner	.10
45	Buddy Groom	.10
46	Juan Samuel	.10
47	Vince Coleman	.10
48	Bob Hamelin	.10
49	Dave Henderson	.10
50	Rusty Meacham	.10
51	Terry Shumpert	.10
52	Jeff Bronkey	.10
53	Alex Diaz	.10
54	Brian Harper	.10
55	Jose Mercedes	.10
56	Jody Reed	.10
57	Bob Scanlan	.10
58	Turner Ward	.10
59	Rich Becker	.10
60	Alex Cole	.10
61	Denny Hocking	.10
63	Pat Mahomes	.10
64	Carlos Pulido	.10
65	Dave Stevens	.10
66	Matt Walbeck	.10
67	Xavier Hernandez	.10
68	Sterling Hitchcock	.10
69	Terry Mulholland	.10
70	Luis Polonia	.10
71	Gerald Williams	.10
72	Mark Acre	.10
73	Geronimo Berroa	.10
74	Rickey Henderson	.50
75	Stan Javier	.10
76	Steve Karsay	.10
77	Carlos Reyes	.10
78	Bill Taylor	.10
79	Eric Anthony	.10
80	Bobby Ayala	.10
81	Tim Davis	.10
82	Felix Fermin	.10
83	Reggie Jefferson	.10
84	Keith Mitchell	.10
85	Bill Risley	.10
86	*Alex Rodriguez*	30.00
87	Roger Salkeld	.10
88	Dan Wilson	.10
89	Cris Carpenter	.10
90	Will Clark	.30
91	Jeff Frye	.10
92	Rick Helling	.10
93	Chris James	.10
94	Oddibe McDowell	.10
95	Billy Ripken	.10
96	Carlos Delgado	1.50
97	Alex Gonzalez	.30
98	Shawn Green	1.00
100	Mike Huff	.10
101	Mike Kelly	.10
102	Roberto Kelly	.10
103	Charlie O'Brien	.10
104	Jose Oliva	.10
105	Gregg Olson	.10
106	Willie Banks	.10
107	Jim Bullinger	.10
108	Chuck Crim	.10
109	Shawon Dunston	.10
110	Karl Rhodes	.10
111	Steve Trachsel	.10
112	Anthony Young	.10
113	Eddie Zambrano	.10
114	Bret Boone	.15
115	Jeff Brantley	.10
116	Hector Carrasco	.10
117	Tony Fernandez	.10
118	Tim Fortugno	.10
119	Erik Hanson	.10
120	Chuck McElroy	.10
121	Deion Sanders	.25
122	Ellis Burks	.10
123	Marvin Freeman	.10
124	Mike Harkey	.10
125	Howard Johnson	.10
126	Mike Kingery	.10
127	Nelson Liriano	.10
128	Marcus Moore	.10
129	Mike Munoz	.10
130	Kevin Ritz	.10
131	Walt Weiss	.10
132	Kurt Abbott	.10
133	Jerry Browne	.10
134	Greg Colbrunn	.10
135	Jeremy Hernandez	.10
136	Dave Magadan	.10
137	Kurt Miller	.10
138	Robb Nen	.10
139	Jesus Taverez	.10
140	Sid Bream	.10
141	Tom Edens	.10
142	Tony Eusebio	.10
143	John Hudek	.10
144	Brian Hunter	.10
145	Orlando Miller	.15
146	James Mouton	.10
147	Shane Reynolds	.10
148	Rafael Bournigal	.10
149	Delino DeShields	.10
150	Garey Ingram	.10
151	Chan Ho Park	2.00
152	Wil Cordero	.10
153	Pedro Martinez	1.50
154	Randy Milligan	.10
155	Lenny Webster	.10
156	Rico Brogna	.10
157	Josias Manzanillo	.10
158	Kevin McReynolds	.10
159	Mike Remlinger	.10
160	David Segui	.10
161	Pete Smith	.10
162	Kelly Stinnett	.10
163	Jose Vizcaino	.10
164	Billy Hatcher	.10
165	Doug Jones	.10
166	Mike Lieberthal	.20
167	Tony Longmire	.10
168	Bobby Munoz	.10
169	Paul Quantrill	.10
170	Heathcliff Slocumb	.10
171	Fernando Valenzuela	.10
172	Mark Dewey	.10
173	Brian Hunter	.10
174	Jon Lieber	.10
175	Ravelo Manzanillo	.10
176	Dan Miceli	.10
177	Rick White	.10
178	Bryan Eversgerd	.10
179	John Habyan	.10
180	Terry McGriff	.10
181	Vicente Palacios	.10
182	Rich Rodriguez	.10
183	Rick Sutcliffe	.10
184	Donnie Elliott	.10
185	Joey Hamilton	.15
186	Tim Hyers	.10
187	Luis Lopez	.10
188	Ray McDavid	.10
189	Bip Roberts	.10
190	Scott Sanders	.10
191	Eddie Williams	.10
192	Steve Frey	.10
193	Pat Gomez	.10
194	Rich Monteleone	.10
195	Mark Portugal	.10
196	Darryl Strawberry	.10
197	Salomon Torres	.10
198	W. Van Landingham	.10
199	Checklist	.05
200	Checklist	.05

1994 Fleer Update Diamond Tribute

These special cards included in the 1994 Fleer Update set feature 10 of baseball's proven superstars. The card front has a color action shot of the player, against a skyline with a baseball pattern among the clouds. The card back is numbered 1 of 8, etc., and includes another photo against a background similar to that used for the card front. A "Diamond Tribute" logo and career summary are also included on the back.

		MT
Complete Set (10):		7.00
Common Player:		.50
1	Barry Bonds	1.00
2	Joe Carter	.50
3	Will Clark	.50
4	Roger Clemens	1.00
5	Tony Gwynn	1.00
6	Don Mattingly	1.00
7	Fred McGriff	.50
8	Eddie Murray	.75
9	Kirby Puckett	1.00
10	Cal Ripken Jr.	3.00

1994 Fleer/ Extra Bases

Extra Bases was a 400-card, oversized set, plus 80 insert cards in four different subsets. The cards, 4-11/16" by 2-1/2", have a full-bleed photo on the front and back, as well as UV coating and color coding by team. As was the case in other Fleer products, Extra Bases contained an insert card in every pack. All 80 insert cards feature gold or silver foil stamping.

		MT
Complete Set (400):		20.00
Common Player:		.10
Wax Pack:		.50
Wax Box (36):		15.00
1	Brady Anderson	.10
2	Harold Baines	.10
3	Mike Devereaux	.10
4	Sid Fernandez	.10
5	Jeffrey Hammonds	.10
6	Chris Hoiles	.10
7	Ben McDonald	.10
8	Mark McLemore	.10
9	Mike Mussina	.50
10	Mike Oquist	.10
11	Rafael Palmeiro	.25
12	Cal Ripken, Jr.	2.50
13	Chris Sabo	.10
14	Lee Smith	.10
15	Wes Chamberlain	.10
16	Roger Clemens	.75
17	Scott Cooper	.10
18	Danny Darwin	.10
19	Andre Dawson	.20
20	Mike Greenwell	.10
21	Tim Naehring	.10
22	Otis Nixon	.10
23	Jeff Russell	.10
24	Ken Ryan	.10
25	Aaron Sele	.15
26	John Valentin	.15
27	Mo Vaughn	.35
28	Frank Viola	.10
29	*Brian Anderson*	.15
30	Chad Curtis	.10
31	Chili Davis	.10
32	Gary DiSarcina	.10
33	Damion Easley	.10
34	Jim Edmonds	.25
35	Chuck Finley	.10
36	Bo Jackson	.15
37	Mark Langston	.10
38	Harold Reynolds	.10
39	Tim Salmon	.30
40	Wilson Alvarez	.10
41	James Baldwin	.10
42	Jason Bere	.10
43	Joey Cora	.10
44	*Ray Durham*	.60
45	Alex Fernandez	.10
46	Julio Franco	.10
47	Ozzie Guillen	.10
48	Darrin Jackson	.10
49	Lance Johnson	.10
50	Ron Karkovice	.10
51	Jack McDowell	.10
52	Tim Raines	.10
53	Frank Thomas	1.50
54	Robin Ventura	.10
55	Sandy Alomar Jr.	.10
56	Carlos Baerga	.10
57	Albert Belle	.35
58	Mark Clark	.10
59	Wayne Kirby	.10
60	Kenny Lofton	.10
61	Dennis Martinez	.10
62	Jose Mesa	.10
63	Jack Morris	.10
64	Eddie Murray	.30
65	Charles Nagy	.10
66	Manny Ramirez	.75
67	Paul Shuey	.10
68	Paul Sorrento	.10
69	Jim Thome	.10
70	Omar Vizquel	.10
71	Eric Davis	.10
72	John Doherty	.10
73	Cecil Fielder	.10
74	Travis Fryman	.10
75	Kirk Gibson	.10
76	Gene Harris	.10
77	Mike Henneman	.10
78	Mike Moore	.10
79	Tony Phillips	.10
80	Mickey Tettleton	.10
81	Alan Trammell	.10
82	Lou Whitaker	.10
83	Kevin Appier	.10
84	Vince Coleman	.10
85	David Cone	.10
86	Gary Gaetti	.10
87	Greg Gagne	.10
88	Tom Gordon	.10
89	Jeff Granger	.10
90	Bob Hamelin	.10
91	Dave Henderson	.10
92	Felix Jose	.10
93	Wally Joyner	.10
94	Jose Lind	.10
95	Mike Macfarlane	.10
96	Brian McRae	.10
97	Jeff Montgomery	.10
98	Ricky Bones	.10
99	Jeff Bronkey	.10
100	Alex Diaz	.10
101	Cal Eldred	.10
102	Darryl Hamilton	.10
103	Brian Harper	.10
104	John Jaha	.10
105	Pat Listach	.10
106	Dave Nilsson	.10
107	Jody Reed	.10
108	Kevin Seitzer	.10
109	Greg Vaughn	.10
110	Turner Ward	.10
111	Wes Weger	.10
112	Bill Wegman	.10
113	Rick Aguilera	.10
114	Rich Becker	.10
115	Alex Cole	.10
116	Scott Erickson	.10
117	Kent Hrbek	.10

118 Chuck Knoblauch .10
119 Scott Leius .10
120 Shane Mack .10
121 Pat Mahomes .10
122 Pat Meares .10
123 Kirby Puckett 1.00
124 Kevin Tapani .10
125 Matt Walbeck .10
126 Dave Winfield .45
127 Jim Abbott .10
128 Wade Boggs .45
129 Mike Gallego .10
130 Xavier Hernandez .10
131 Pat Kelly .10
132 Jimmy Key .10
133 Don Mattingly 1.00
134 Terry Mulholland .10
135 Matt Nokes .10
136 Paul O'Neill .10
137 Melido Perez .10
138 Luis Polonia .10
139 Mike Stanley .10
140 Danny Tartabull .10
141 Randy Velarde .10
142 Bernie Williams .35
143 Mark Acre .10
144 Geronimo Berroa .10
145 Mike Bordick .10
146 Scott Brosius .10
147 Ron Darling .10
148 Dennis Eckersley .10
149 Brent Gates .10
150 Rickey Henderson .40
151 Stan Javier .10
152 Steve Karsay .10
153 Mark McGwire 2.50
154 Troy Neel .10
155 Ruben Sierra .10
156 Terry Steinbach .10
157 Bill Taylor .10
158 Rich Amaral .10
159 Eric Anthony .10
160 Bobby Ayala .10
161 Chris Bosio .10
162 Jay Buhner .10
163 Tim Davis .10
164 Felix Fermin .10
165 Dave Fleming .10
166 Ken Griffey, Jr. 2.50
167 Reggie Jefferson .10
168 Randy Johnson .60
169 Edgar Martinez .10
170 Tino Martinez .10
171 Bill Risley .10
172 Roger Salkeld .10
173 *Mac Suzuki* .20
174 Dan Wilson .10
175 Kevin Brown .20
176 Jose Canseco .40
177 Will Clark .30
178 Juan Gonzalez .75
179 Rick Helling .10
180 Tom Henke .10
181 Chris James .10
182 Manuel Lee .10
183 Dean Palmer .10
184 Ivan Rodriguez .40
185 Kenny Rogers .10
186 Roberto Alomar .60
187 Pat Borders .10
188 Joe Carter .10
189 Carlos Delgado .50
190 Juan Guzman .10
191 Pat Hentgen .10
192 Paul Molitor .50
192a Paul Molitor (promotional sample) 3.00
193 John Olerud .10
194 Ed Sprague .10
195 Dave Stewart .10
196 Todd Stottlemyre .10
197 Duane Ward .10
198 Devon White .15
199 Steve Avery .10
200 Jeff Blauser .10
201 Tom Glavine .20
202 Dave Justice .30
203 Mike Kelly .10
204 Roberto Kelly .10
205 Ryan Klesko .10
206 Mark Lemke .10
207 Javier Lopez .10
208 Greg Maddux 1.50
209 Fred McGriff .10
210 Greg McMichael .10
211 Kent Mercker .10
212 Terry Pendleton .10
213 John Smoltz .15
214 Tony Tarasco .10
215 Willie Banks .10
216 Steve Buechele .10
217 Shawon Dunston .10
218 Mark Grace .30
219 *Brooks Kieschnick* .10
220 Derrick May .10
221 Randy Myers .10
222 Karl Rhodes .10
223 Rey Sanchez .10
224 Sammy Sosa 1.50
225 Steve Traschel .10
226 Rick Wilkins .10
227 Bret Boone .15
228 Jeff Brantley .10
229 Tom Browning .10
230 Hector Carrasco .10
231 Rob Dibble .10
232 Erik Hanson .10
233 Barry Larkin .15
234 Kevin Mitchell .10
235 Hal Morris .10
236 Joe Oliver .10
237 Jose Rijo .10
238 Johnny Ruffin .10
239 Deion Sanders .25
240 Reggie Sanders .10
241 John Smiley .10
242 Dante Bichette .30
243 Ellis Burks .10
244 Andres Galarraga .10
245 Joe Girardi .10
246 Greg Harris .10
247 Charlie Hayes .10
248 Howard Johnson .10
249 Roberto Mejia .10
250 Marcus Moore .10
251 David Nied .10
252 Armando Reynoso .10
253 Bruce Ruffin .10
254 Mark Thompson .10
255 Walt Weiss .10
256 *Kurt Abbott* .20
257 Bret Barberie .10
258 Chuck Carr .10
259 Jeff Conine .10
260 Chris Hammond .10
261 Bryan Harvey .10
262 Jeremy Hernandez .10
263 Charlie Hough .10
264 Dave Magadan .10
265 Benito Santiago .10
266 Gary Sheffield .25
267 David Weathers .10
268 Jeff Bagwell .75
269 Craig Biggio .15
270 Ken Caminiti .10
271 Andujar Cedeno .10
272 Doug Drabek .10
273 Steve Finley .10
274 Luis Gonzalez .20
275 Pete Harnisch .10
276 John Hudek .10
277 Darryl Kile .10
278 Orlando Miller .10
279 James Mouton .10
280 Shane Reynolds .10
281 Scott Servais .10
282 Greg Swindell .10
283 Pedro Astacio .10
284 Brett Butler .10
285 Tom Candiotti .10
286 Delino DeShields .10
287 Kevin Gross .10
288 Orel Hershiser .10
289 Eric Karros .10
290 Ramon Martinez .10
291 Raul Mondesi .25
292 Jose Offerman .10
293 *Chan Ho Park* 2.00
294 Mike Piazza 2.00
295 Henry Rodriguez .10
296 Cory Snyder .10
297 Tim Wallach .10
298 Todd Worrell .10
299 Moises Alou .15
300 Sean Berry .10
301 Wil Cordero .10
302 Joey Eischen .10
303 Jeff Fassero .10
304 Darrin Fletcher .10
305 Cliff Floyd .20
306 Marquis Grissom .10
307 Ken Hill .10
308 Mike Lansing .10
309 Pedro Martinez .50
310 Mel Rojas .10
311 Kirk Rueter .10
312 Larry Walker .30
313 John Wetteland .10
314 Rondell White .20
315 Bobby Bonilla .10
316 John Franco .10
317 Dwight Gooden .10
318 Todd Hundley .10
319 Bobby Jones .10
320 Jeff Kent .10
321 Kevin McReynolds .10
322 Bill Pulsipher .10
323 Bret Saberhagen .10
324 David Segui .10
325 Pete Smith .10
326 Kelly Stinnett .10
327 Ryan Thompson .10
328 Jose Vizcaino .10
329 Ricky Bottalico .10
330 Darren Daulton .10
331 Mariano Duncan .10
332 Len Dykstra .10
333 Tommy Greene .10
334 Billy Hatcher .10
335 Dave Hollins .10
336 Pete Incaviglia .10
337 Danny Jackson .10
338 Doug Jones .10
339 Ricky Jordan .10
340 John Kruk .10
341 Curt Schilling .20
342 Kevin Stocker .10
343 Jay Bell .10
344 Steve Cooke .10
345 Carlos Garcia .10
346 Brian Hunter .10
347 Jeff King .10
348 Al Martin .10
349 Orlando Merced .10
350 Denny Neagle .10
351 Don Slaught .10
352 Andy Van Slyke .10
353 Paul Wagner .10
354 Rick White .10
355 Luis Alicea .10
356 Rene Arocha .10
357 Rheal Cormier .10
358 Bernard Gilkey .10
359 Gregg Jefferies .10
360 Ray Lankford .10
361 Tom Pagnozzi .10
362 Mike Perez .10
363 Ozzie Smith .75
364 Bob Tewksbury .10
365 Mark Whiten .10
366 Todd Zeile .10
367 Andy Ashby .10
368 Brad Ausmus .10
369 Derek Bell .10
370 Andy Benes .10
371 Archi Cianfrocco .10
372 Tony Gwynn 1.00
373 Trevor Hoffman .10
374 Tim Hyers .10
375 Pedro Martinez .10
376 Phil Plantier .10
377 Bip Roberts .10
378 Scott Sanders .10
379 Dave Staton .10
380 Wally Whitehurst .10
381 Rod Beck .10
382 Todd Benzinger .10
383 Barry Bonds .75
384 John Burkett .10
385 Royce Clayton .10
386 Bryan Hickerson .10
387 Mike Jackson .10
388 Darren Lewis .10
389 Kirt Manwaring .10
390 Willie McGee .10
391 Mark Portugal .10
392 Bill Swift .10
393 Robby Thompson .10
394 Salomon Torres .10
395 Matt Williams .30
396 Checklist .10
397 Checklist .10
398 Checklist .10
399 Checklist .10
400 Checklist .10

1994 Fleer/ Extra Bases Game Breakers

Game Breakers featured 30 big-name stars from both leagues who have exhibited offensive firepower. This insert set was done in a horizontal format picturing the player in two different shots, one close-up and one slightly further away. The words "Game Breakers" is written across the bottom, with the player name and team in much smaller letters, printed under it.

		MT
Complete Set (30):		15.00
Common Player:		.25
1	Jeff Bagwell	1.00
2	Rod Beck	.25
3	Albert Belle	.75
4	Barry Bonds	1.50
5	Jose Canseco	.75
6	Joe Carter	.25
7	Roger Clemens	1.00
8	Darren Daulton	.25
9	Len Dykstra	.25
10	Cecil Fielder	.25
11	Tom Glavine	.45
12	Juan Gonzalez	1.00
13	Mark Grace	.50
14	Ken Griffey, Jr.	3.00
15	Dave Justice	.50
16	Greg Maddux	2.00
17	Don Mattingly	2.00
18	Ben McDonald	.25
19	Fred McGriff	.25
20	Paul Molitor	.75
21	John Olerud	.25
22	Mike Piazza	2.50
23	Kirby Puckett	1.50
24	Cal Ripken, Jr.	3.00
25	Tim Salmon	.75
26	Gary Sheffield	.50
27	Frank Thomas	2.00
28	Mo Vaughn	.75
29	Matt Williams	.50
30	Dave Winfield	.75

1994 Fleer/ Extra Bases Major League Hopefuls

Minor league standouts with impressive credentials were showcased in Major League Hopefuls. Each card in this insert set shows the player over a computer enhanced background, with three smaller photos running down the top half, on the left side of the card. The insert set title runs across the bottom and the player's name is just under it on a black strip.

		MT
Complete Set (10):		3.00
Common Player:		.25
1	James Baldwin	.50
2	Ricky Bottalico	.50
3	Ray Durham	1.00
4	Joey Eischen	.35
5	Brooks Kieschnick	.25
6	Orlando Miller	.50
7	Bill Pulsipher	.25
8	Mac Suzuki	.25
9	Mark Thompson	.25
10	Wes Weger	.25

1994 Fleer/ Extra Bases Rookie Standouts

Rookie Standouts highlights 20 of the best and brightest first-year players of the 1994 season. Cards picture the player on a baseball background, with a black, jagged-edged "aura" around the player. Names and teams were placed in the bottom-left corner, running up the side. The Rookie Standouts logo, which is a gold glove with a baseball in it and "Rookie Standouts" printed under it, was placed in the bottom-right corner and the Extra Bases logo appears in the upper-left.

		MT
Complete Set (20):		10.00
Common Player:		.25
1	Kurt Abbott	.50
2	Brian Anderson	.35
3	Hector Carrasco	.25
4	Tim Davis	.25
5	Carlos Delgado	2.00
6	Cliff Floyd	.60
7	Bob Hamelin	.25
8	Jeffrey Hammonds	.25
9	Rick Helling	.35
10	Steve Karsay	.25
11	Ryan Klesko	.50
12	Javier Lopez	.50
13	Raul Mondesi	1.00
14	James Mouton	.25
15	Chan Ho Park	1.50
16	Manny Ramirez	2.00
17	Tony Tarasco	.25
18	Steve Trachsel	.25
19	Rick White	.25
20	Rondell White	1.00

1994 Fleer/ Extra Bases Second Year Stars

Second-Year Stars contains 1993 rookies who were expected to have an even bigger impact in the 1994 season. Each card features five photos of the player. Four are in a filmstrip down the left side; the remaining two-thirds of the card contain a larger photo. "Second-Year Stars" is printed across the bottom, along with the player name and team. Backs repeat the film-strip motif.

		MT
Complete Set (20):		9.00
Common Player:		.25
1	Bobby Ayala	.25
2	Jason Bere	.50
3	Chuck Carr	.25
4	Jeff Conine	.40
5	Steve Cooke	.25
6	Wil Cordero	.25
7	Carlos Garcia	.25
8	Brent Gates	.25
9	Trevor Hoffman	.50
10	Wayne Kirby	.25
11	Al Martin	.25
12	Pedro Martinez	1.50
13	Greg McMichael	.25
14	Troy Neel	.25
15	David Nied	.25
16	Mike Piazza	3.50
17	Kirk Rueter	.25
18	Tim Salmon	1.00
19	Aaron Sele	.35
20	Kevin Stocker	.25

1994 Fleer/ Extra Bases Pitcher's Duel

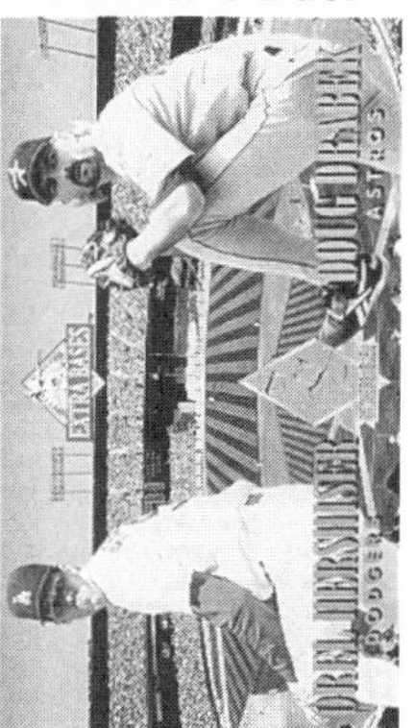

Pitcher's Duel was available to collectors who mailed in 10 Extra Bases wrappers. The set features 20 of the top pitchers is baseball. Contained in the set were five American League and five National League cards, with two pitchers from the same league on each card. The front background pictures a wide-angle photo of a major league stadium, viewed from above the diamond, behind home plate. Backs have two more action photos set against a sepia-toned background photo of an Old West street to enhance the shootout theme of the set. Cards are numbered with an "M" prefix.

		MT
Complete Set (10):		7.50
Common Player:		.50
1	Roger Clemens, Jack McDowell	2.00
2	Ben McDonald, Randy Johnson	1.25
3	Jimmy Key, David Cone	.50
4	Mike Mussina, Aaron Sele	1.00
5	Chuck Finley, Wilson Alvarez	.50
6	Steve Avery, Curt Schilling	.75
7	Greg Maddux, Jose Rijo	2.00
8	Bret Saberhagen, Bob Tewksbury	.50
9	Tom Glavine, Bill Swift	.75
10	Doug Drabek, Orel Hershiser	.50

1995 Fleer Promos

This eight-player (plus a header card), cello-wrapped promo set was included in a special "Fleer" national newsstand magazine in early 1995. At first glance the cards seem identical to the regularly issued cards of the same players, but there are subtle differences on the back of each card.

		MT
Complete Set (9):		5.00
Common Player:		1.00
26	Roger Clemens (1988 291 SO and 1992 2.41 ERA boxed)	2.50
78	Paul O'Neill (1991 boxed)	1.00
155	David Cone (1990 233 SO boxed, white shadow on team names)	1.00
235	Tim Salmon (No box on 1992 101 R)	1.00
285	Juan Gonzalez (Black stats, 1993 boxed)	1.50
351	Marquis Grissom (No box on 1988 291 AB)	1.00
509	Ozzie Smith (Black stats, no box on 1986 Cardinals)	2.00
514	Dante Bichette (Black stats)	1.00
--	Header card "Different by Design"	.10

1995 Fleer

Fleer baseball arrived in 1995 with six different designs, one for each division. The basic set contains 600 cards and was sold in 12-card and 18-card packs. National League West cards feature many smaller pictures in the background that are identical to the picture in the forefront, while AL West cards contain an action photo over top of a close-up on the right side and a water colored look on the left side. AL Central cards exhibit numbers pertinant to each player througout the front design, with the player in the middle. NL East players appear in action on the left half of the card with a colorful, encripted look on the rest. National League Central and American League East feature more standard designs with the player in the forefront, with vital numbers and a color background.

		MT
Complete Set (600):		35.00
Common Player:		.05
Pack (12):		.75
Wax Box (36):		25.00
1	Brady Anderson	.05
2	Harold Baines	.05
3	Damon Buford	.05
4	Mike Devereaux	.05
5	Mark Eichhorn	.05
6	Sid Fernandez	.05
7	Leo Gomez	.05
8	Jeffrey Hammonds	.05
9	Chris Hoiles	.05
10	Rick Krivda	.05
11	Ben McDonald	.05
12	Mark McLemore	.05
13	Alan Mills	.05
14	Jamie Moyer	.05
15	Mike Mussina	.40
16	Mike Oquist	.05
17	Rafael Palmeiro	.30
18	Arthur Rhodes	.05
19	Cal Ripken, Jr.	2.50
20	Chris Sabo	.05
21	Lee Smith	.05
22	Jack Voight	.05
23	Damon Berryhill	.05
24	Tom Brunansky	.05
25	Wes Chamberlain	.05
26	Roger Clemens	1.00
27	Scott Cooper	.05
28	Andre Dawson	.15
29	Gar Finnvold	.05
30	Tony Fossas	.05
31	Mike Greenwell	.05
32	Joe Hesketh	.05
33	Chris Howard	.05
34	Chris Nabholz	.05
35	Tim Naehring	.05
36	Otis Nixon	.05
37	Carlos Rodriguez	.05
38	Rich Rowland	.05
39	Ken Ryan	.05
40	Aaron Sele	.10
41	John Valentin	.10
42	Mo Vaughn	.25
43	Frank Viola	.05
44	Danny Bautista	.05
45	Joe Boeven	.05
46	Milt Cuyler	.05
47	Storm Davis	.05
48	John Doherty	.05
49	Junior Felix	.05
50	Cecil Fielder	.05
51	Travis Fryman	.05
52	Mike Gardiner	.05
53	Kirk Gibson	.05
54	Chris Gomez	.05
55	Buddy Groom	.05
56	Mike Henneman	.05
57	Chad Kreuter	.05
58	Mike Moore	.05
59	Tony Phillips	.05
60	Juan Samuel	.05
61	Mickey Tettleton	.05
62	Alan Trammell	.05
63	David Wells	.10
64	Lou Whitaker	.05
65	Jim Abbott	.05
66	Joe Ausanio	.05
67	Wade Boggs	.30
68	Mike Gallego	.05
69	Xavier Hernandez	.05
70	Sterling Hitchcock	.05
71	Steve Howe	.05
72	Scott Kamieniecki	.05
73	Pat Kelly	.05
74	Jimmy Key	.05
75	Jim Leyritz	.05
76	Don Mattingly	1.00
77	Terry Mulholland	.05
78	Paul O'Neill	.05
79	Melido Perez	.05
80	Luis Polonia	.05
81	Mike Stanley	.05
82	Danny Tartabull	.05
83	Randy Velarde	.05
84	Bob Wickman	.05
85	Bernie Williams	.30
86	Gerald Williams	.05
87	Roberto Alomar	.40
88	Pat Borders	.05
89	Joe Carter	.05
90	Tony Castillo	.05
91	Brad Cornett	.05
92	Carlos Delgado	.50
93	Alex Gonzalez	.10
94	Shawn Green	.50
95	Juan Guzman	.05
96	Darren Hall	.05
97	Pat Hentgen	.05
98	Mike Huff	.05
99	Randy Knorr	.05
100	Al Leiter	.05
101	Paul Molitor	.45
102	John Olerud	.05
103	Dick Schofield	.05
104	Ed Sprague	.05
105	Dave Stewart	.05
106	Todd Stottlemyre	.05
107	Devon White	.05
108	Woody Williams	.05
109	Wilson Alvarez	.05
110	Paul Assenmacher	.05
111	Jason Bere	.05
112	Dennis Cook	.05
113	Joey Cora	.05
114	Jose DeLeon	.05
115	Alex Fernandez	.05
116	Julio Franco	.05
117	Craig Graboeck	.05
118	Ozzie Guillen	.05
119	Roberto Hernandez	.05
120	Darrin Jackson	.05
121	Lance Johnson	.05
122	Ron Karkovice	.05
123	Mike LaValliere	.05
124	Norberto Martin	.05
125	Kirk McCaskill	.05
126	Jack McDowell	.05
127	Tim Raines	.05
128	Frank Thomas	1.00
129	Robin Ventura	.05
130	Sandy Alomar Jr.	.05
131	Carlos Baerga	.05
132	Albert Belle	.25
133	Mark Clark	.05
134	Alvaro Espinoza	.05
135	Jason Grimsley	.05
136	Wayne Kirby	.05
137	Kenny Lofton	.05
138	Albie Lopez	.05
139	Dennis Martinez	.05
140	Jose Mesa	.05
141	Eddie Murray	.25
142	Charles Nagy	.05
143	Tony Pena	.05
144	Eric Plunk	.05
145	Manny Ramirez	.75
146	Jeff Russell	.05
147	Paul Shuey	.05
148	Paul Sorrento	.05
149	Jim Thome	.05
150	Omar Vizquel	.05
151	Dave Winfield	.50
152	Kevin Appier	.05
153	Billy Brewer	.05
154	Vince Coleman	.05
155	David Cone	.05
156	Gary Gaetti	.05
157	Greg Gagne	.05
158	Tom Gordon	.05
159	Mark Gubicza	.05
160	Bob Hamelin	.05
161	Dave Henderson	.05
162	Felix Jose	.05
163	Wally Joyner	.05
164	Jose Lind	.05
165	Mike Macfarlane	.05
166	Mike Magnante	.05
167	Brent Mayne	.05
168	Brian McRae	.05
169	Rusty Meacham	.05
170	Jeff Montgomery	.05
171	Hipolito Pichardo	.05
172	Terry Shumpert	.05
173	Michael Tucker	.05
174	Ricky Bones	.05
175	*Jeff Cirillo*	.40
176	Alex Diaz	.05
177	Cal Eldred	.05
178	Mike Fetters	.05
179	Darryl Hamilton	.05
180	Brian Harper	.05
181	John Jaha	.05
182	Pat Listach	.05
183	Graeme Lloyd	.05
184	Jose Mercedes	.05
185	Matt Mieske	.05
186	Dave Nilsson	.05
187	Jody Reed	.05
188	Bob Scanlan	.05
189	Kevin Seitzer	.05
190	Bill Spiers	.05
191	B.J. Surhoff	.05
192	Jose Valentin	.05
193	Greg Vaughn	.05
194	Turner Ward	.05
195	Bill Wegman	.05
196	Rick Aguilera	.05
197	Rich Becker	.05
198	Alex Cole	.05
199	Marty Cordova	.10
200	Steve Dunn	.05
201	Scott Erickson	.05
202	Mark Guthrie	.05
203	Chip Hale	.05
204	LaTroy Hawkins	.05
205	Denny Hocking	.05
206	Chuck Knoblauch	.05
207	Scott Leius	.05
208	Shane Mack	.05
209	Pat Mahomes	.05
210	Pat Meares	.05
211	Pedro Munoz	.05
212	Kirby Puckett	1.00
213	Jeff Reboulet	.05
214	Dave Stevens	.05
215	Kevin Tapani	.05
216	Matt Walbeck	.05
217	Carl Willis	.05
218	Brian Anderson	.05
219	Chad Curtis	.05
220	Chili Davis	.05
221	Gary DiSarcina	.05
222	Damion Easley	.05
223	Jim Edmonds	.10
224	Chuck Finley	.05
225	Joe Grahe	.05
226	Rex Hudler	.05
227	Bo Jackson	.10
228	Mark Langston	.05
229	Phil Leftwich	.05
230	Mark Leiter	.05
231	Spike Owen	.05
232	Bob Patterson	.05
233	Troy Percival	.05
234	Eduardo Perez	.05
235	Tim Salmon	.10
236	J.T. Snow	.10
237	Chris Turner	.05
238	Mark Acre	.05
239	Geronimo Berroa	.05
240	Mike Bordick	.05
241	John Briscoe	.05
242	Scott Brosius	.05
243	Ron Darling	.05
244	Dennis Eckersley	.05
245	Brent Gates	.05
246	Rickey Henderson	.35
247	Stan Javier	.05
248	Steve Karsay	.05
249	Mark McGwire	2.50
250	Troy Neel	.05
251	Steve Ontiveros	.05
252	Carlos Reyes	.05
253	Ruben Sierra	.05
254	Terry Steinbach	.05
255	Bill Taylor	.05
256	Todd Van Poppel	.05
257	Bobby Witt	.05
258	Rich Amaral	.05
259	Eric Anthony	.05
260	Bobby Ayala	.05
261	Mike Blowers	.05
262	Chris Bosio	.05
263	Jay Buhner	.05
264	John Cummings	.05
265	Tim Davis	.05
266	Felix Fermin	.05
267	Dave Fleming	.05
268	Goose Gossage	.05
269	Ken Griffey, Jr.	2.50
270	Reggie Jefferson	.05
271	Randy Johnson	.75
272	Edgar Martinez	.05
273	Tino Martinez	.05
274	Greg Pirkl	.05
275	Bill Risley	.05
276	Roger Salkeld	.05
277	Luis Sojo	.05
278	Mac Suzuki	.05
279	Dan Wilson	.05
280	Kevin Brown	.10
281	Jose Canseco	.35
282	Cris Carpenter	.05
283	Will Clark	.15
284	Jeff Frye	.05
285	Juan Gonzalez	.75
286	Rick Helling	.05
287	Tom Henke	.05
288	David Hulse	.05
289	Chris James	.05
290	Manuel Lee	.05
291	Oddibe McDowell	.05
292	Dean Palmer	.05
293	Roger Pavlik	.05
294	Bill Ripken	.05
295	Ivan Rodriguez	.60
296	Kenny Rogers	.05
297	Doug Strange	.05
298	Matt Whiteside	.05
299	Steve Avery	.05
300	Steve Bedrosian	.05
301	Rafael Belliard	.05
302	Jeff Blauser	.05
303	Dave Gallagher	.05
304	Tom Glavine	.10
305	Dave Justice	.15
306	Mike Kelly	.05
307	Roberto Kelly	.05
308	Ryan Klesko	.05
309	Mark Lemke	.05
310	Javier Lopez	.05
311	Greg Maddux	1.00
312	Fred McGriff	.05
313	Greg McMichael	.05
314	Kent Mercker	.05
315	Charlie O'Brien	.05
316	Jose Oliva	.05
317	Terry Pendleton	.05
318	John Smoltz	.10
319	Mike Stanton	.05
320	Tony Tarasco	.05
321	Terrell Wade	.05
322	Mark Wohlers	.05
323	Kurt Abbott	.05
324	Luis Aquino	.05
325	Bret Barberie	.05
326	Ryan Bowen	.05
327	Jerry Browne	.05
328	Chuck Carr	.05
329	Matias Carrillo	.05
330	Greg Colbrunn	.05
331	Jeff Conine	.05
332	Mark Gardner	.05
333	Chris Hammond	.05
334	Bryan Harvey	.05
335	Richie Lewis	.05
336	Dave Magadan	.05
337	Terry Mathews	.05
338	Robb Nen	.05
339	Yorkis Perez	.05
340	Pat Rapp	.05
341	Benito Santiago	.05
342	Gary Sheffield	.35
343	Dave Weathers	.05
344	Moises Alou	.10
345	Sean Berry	.05
346	Wil Cordero	.05
347	Joe Eischen	.05
348	Jeff Fassero	.05
349	Darrin Fletcher	.05
350	Cliff Floyd	.10
351	Marquis Grissom	.05
352	Butch Henry	.05
353	Gil Heredia	.05
354	Ken Hill	.05
355	Mike Lansing	.05
356	Pedro Martinez	.75
357	Mel Rojas	.05
358	Kirk Rueter	.05
359	Tim Scott	.05
360	Jeff Shaw	.05
361	Larry Walker	.20
362	Lenny Webster	.05
363	John Wetteland	.05

364	Rondell White	.10
365	Bobby Bonilla	.05
366	Rico Brogna	.05
367	Jeromy Burnitz	.10
368	John Franco	.05
369	Dwight Gooden	.05
370	Todd Hundley	.05
371	Jason Jacome	.05
372	Bobby Jones	.05
373	Jeff Kent	.05
374	Jim Lindeman	.05
375	Josias Manzanillo	.05
376	Roger Mason	.05
377	Kevin McReynolds	.05
378	Joe Orsulak	.05
379	Bill Pulsipher	.05
380	Bret Saberhagen	.05
381	David Segui	.05
382	Pete Smith	.05
383	Kelly Stinnett	.05
384	Ryan Thompson	.05
385	Jose Vizcaino	.05
386	Toby Borland	.05
387	Ricky Bettalico	.05
388	Darren Daulton	.05
389	Mariano Duncan	.05
390	Len Dykstra	.05
391	Jim Eisenreich	.05
392	Tommy Greene	.05
393	Dave Hollins	.05
394	Pete Incaviglia	.05
395	Danny Jackson	.05
396	Doug Jones	.05
397	Ricky Jordan	.05
398	John Kruk	.05
399	Mike Lieberthal	.10
400	Tony Longmire	.05
401	Mickey Morandini	.05
402	Bobby Munoz	.05
403	Curt Schilling	.10
404	Heathcliff Slocumb	.05
405	Kevin Stocker	.05
406	Fernando Valenzuela	.05
407	David West	.05
408	Willie Banks	.05
409	Jose Bautista	.05
410	Steve Buechele	.05
411	Jim Bullinger	.05
412	Chuck Crim	.05
413	Shawon Dunston	.05
414	Kevin Foster	.05
415	Mark Grace	.20
416	Jose Hernandez	.05
417	Glenallen Hill	.05
418	Brooks Kieschnick	.05
419	Derrick May	.05
420	Randy Myers	.05
421	Dan Plesac	.05
422	Karl Rhodes	.05
423	Rey Sanchez	.05
424	Sammy Sosa	1.50
425	Steve Trachsel	.05
426	Rick Wilkins	.05
427	Anthony Young	.05
428	Eddie Zambrano	.05
429	Bret Boone	.05
430	Jeff Branson	.05
431	Jeff Brantley	.05
432	Hector Carrasco	.05
433	Brian Dorsett	.05
434	Tony Fernandez	.05
435	Tim Fortugno	.05
436	Erik Hanson	.05
437	Thomas Howard	.05
438	Kevin Jarvis	.05
439	Barry Larkin	.10
440	Chuck McElroy	.05
441	Kevin Mitchell	.05
442	Hal Morris	.05
443	Jose Rijo	.05
444	John Roper	.05
445	Johnny Ruffin	.05
446	Deion Sanders	.10
447	Reggie Sanders	.05
448	Pete Schourek	.05
449	John Smiley	.05
450	Eddie Taubensee	.05
451	Jeff Bagwell	.60
452	Kevin Bass	.05
453	Craig Biggio	.10
454	Ken Caminiti	.05
455	Andujar Cedeno	.05
456	Doug Drabek	.05
457	Tony Eusebio	.05
458	Mike Felder	.05
459	Steve Finley	.05
460	Luis Gonzalez	.15
461	Mike Hampton	.05
462	Pete Harnisch	.05
463	John Hudek	.05
464	Todd Jones	.05
465	Darryl Kile	.05
466	James Mouton	.05
467	Shane Reynolds	.05
468	Scott Servais	.05
469	Greg Swindell	.05
470	Dave Veres	.05
471	Brian Williams	.05
472	Jay Bell	.05
473	Jacob Brumfield	.05
474	Dave Clark	.05
475	Steve Cooke	.05
476	Midre Cummings	.05
477	Mark Dewey	.05
478	Tom Foley	.05
479	Carlos Garcia	.05
480	Jeff King	.05
481	Jon Lieber	.10
482	Ravelo Manzanillo	.05
483	Al Martin	.05
484	Orlando Merced	.05
485	Danny Miceli	.05
486	Denny Neagle	.05
487	Lance Parrish	.05
488	Don Slaught	.05
489	Zane Smith	.05
490	Andy Van Slyke	.05
491	Paul Wagner	.05
492	Rick White	.05
493	Luis Alicea	.05
494	Rene Arocha	.05
495	Rheal Cormier	.05
496	Bryan Eversgerd	.05
497	Bernard Gilkey	.05
498	John Habyan	.05
499	Gregg Jefferies	.05
500	Brian Jordan	.05
501	Ray Lankford	.05
502	John Mabry	.05
503	Terry McGriff	.05
504	Tom Pagnozzi	.05
505	Vicente Palacios	.05
506	Geronimo Pena	.05
507	Gerald Perry	.05
508	Rich Rodriguez	.05
509	Ozzie Smith	.65
510	Bob Tewksbury	.05
511	Allen Watson	.05
512	Mark Whiten	.05
513	Todd Zeile	.05
514	Dante Bichette	.05
515	Willie Blair	.05
516	Ellis Burks	.05
517	Marvin Freeman	.05
518	Andres Galarraga	.05
519	Joe Girardi	.05
520	Greg Harris	.05
521	Charlie Hayes	.05
522	Mike Kingery	.05
523	Nelson Liriano	.05
524	Mike Munoz	.05
525	David Nied	.05
526	Steve Reed	.05
527	Kevin Ritz	.05
528	Bruce Ruffin	.05
529	John Vander Wal	.05
530	Walt Weiss	.05
531	Eric Young	.05
532	Billy Ashley	.05
533	Pedro Astacio	.05
534	Rafael Bournigal	.05
535	Brett Butler	.05
536	Tom Candiotti	.05
537	Omar Daal	.05
538	Delino DeShields	.05
539	Darren Dreifort	.05
540	Kevin Gross	.05
541	Orel Hershiser	.05
542	Garey Ingram	.05
543	Eric Karros	.05
544	Ramon Martinez	.05
545	Raul Mondesi	.20
546	Chan Ho Park	.15
547	Mike Piazza	2.00
548	Henry Rodriguez	.05
549	Rudy Seanez	.05
550	Ismael Valdes	.05
551	Tim Wallach	.05
552	Todd Worrell	.05
553	Andy Ashby	.05
554	Brad Ausmus	.05
555	Derek Bell	.05
556	Andy Benes	.05
557	Phil Clark	.05
558	Donnie Elliott	.05
559	Ricky Gutierrez	.05
560	Tony Gwynn	.75
561	Joey Hamilton	.05
562	Trevor Hoffman	.05
563	Luis Lopez	.05
564	Pedro Martinez	.05
565	Tim Mauser	.05
566	Phil Plantier	.05
567	Bip Roberts	.05
568	Scott Sanders	.05
569	Craig Shipley	.05
570	Jeff Tabaka	.05
571	Eddie Williams	.05
572	Rod Beck	.05
573	Mike Benjamin	.05
574	Barry Bonds	1.00
575	Dave Burba	.05
576	John Burkett	.05
577	Mark Carreon	.05
578	Royce Clayton	.05
579	Steve Frey	.05
580	Bryan Hickerson	.05
581	Mike Jackson	.05
582	Darren Lewis	.05
583	Kirt Manwaring	.05
584	Rich Monteleone	.05
585	John Patterson	.05
586	J.R. Phillips	.05
587	Mark Portugal	.05
588	Joe Rosselli	.05
589	Darryl Strawberry	.05
590	Bill Swift	.05
591	Robby Thompson	.05
592	William Van Landingham	.05
593	Matt Williams	.15
594	Checklist	.05
595	Checklist	.05
596	Checklist	.05
597	Checklist	.05
598	Checklist	.05
599	Checklist	.05
600	Checklist	.05

1995 Fleer Award Winners

Fleer Award Winners contain Fleer's choices of baseball's most outstanding players. This six-card set was only inserted at a rate of one per 24 packs. Each card has an embossed gold foil design, with the gold strip running up the left side and containing the words "Fleer Award Winner" and the player name.

		MT
Complete Set (6):		5.00
Common Player:		.25
1	Frank Thomas	2.00
2	Jeff Bagwell	1.50
3	David Cone	.25
4	Greg Maddux	2.00
5	Bob Hamelin	.25
6	Raul Mondesi	.50

1995 Fleer All-Fleer 9

Available only by mailing in 10 Fleer wrappers and $3, this set presents an all-star lineup in a unique design. Colored scribbles down one side of the card front offer a background for gold-foil printing of the card title, player name, position and team. Backs repeat the colored scribbles across virtually the entire surface, making it extremely difficult to read the career summary printed in white over it.

		MT
Complete Set (9):		4.50
Common Player:		.25
1	Mike Piazza	.75
2	Frank Thomas	.65
3	Roberto Alomar	.40
4	Cal Ripken Jr.	1.00
5	Matt Williams	.25
6	Barry Bonds	.60
7	Ken Griffey Jr.	1.00
8	Tony Gwynn	.50
9	Greg Maddux	.50

1995 Fleer All-Stars

All-Stars are a horizontal, two-sided insert set consisting of 25 cards. A National League All-Star is on one side, while an American League All-Star is on the other, by position. All-Stars are the most common insert in Fleer 1995 baseball, with an insertion ratio of one per three packs.

		MT
Complete Set (25):		5.00
Common Player:		.10
1	Ivan Rodriguez, Mike Piazza	.75
2	Frank Thomas, Gregg Jefferies	.75

3	Roberto Alomar, Mariano Duncan	.25
4	Wade Boggs, Matt Williams	.25
5	Cal Ripken, Jr., Ozzie Smith	1.00
6	Joe Carter, Barry Bonds	.45
7	Ken Griffey, Jr., Tony Gwynn	1.00
8	Kirby Puckett, Dave Justice	.50
9	Jimmy Key, Greg Maddux	.50
10	Chuck Knoblauch, Wil Cordero	.10
11	Scott Cooper, Ken Caminiti	.10
12	Will Clark, Carlos Garcia	.15
13	Paul Molitor, Jeff Bagwell	.20
14	Travis Fryman, Craig Biggio	.10
15	Mickey Tettleton, Fred McGriff	.10
16	Kenny Lofton, Moises Alou	.10
17	Albert Belle, Marquis Grissom	.15
18	Paul O'Neill, Dante Bichette	.10
19	David Cone, Ken Hill	.10
20	Mike Mussina, Doug Drabek	.10
21	Randy Johnson, John Hudek	.25
22	Pat Hentgen, Danny Jackson	.10
23	Wilson Alvarez, Rod Beck	.10
24	Lee Smith, Randy Myers	.10
25	Jason Bere, Doug Jones	.10

1995 Fleer All-Rookies

This mail-in set was available by redeeming a randomly inserted trade card found in packs. The cards feature action player photos on a muted background, with the player ID in gold-foil beneath a huge rookie banner. Horizontal backs have a player photo at left and professional highlights at right. Cards have an "M" prefix to the card number.

		MT
Complete Set (9):		4.00
Common Player:		.50
Trade card (expired Sept. 30, 1995):		.25
1	Edgardo Alfonzo	2.00
2	Jason Bates	.50
3	Brian Boehringer	.50
4	Darren Bragg	.50
5	Brad Clontz	.50
6	Jim Dougherty	.50
7	Todd Hollandsworth	.50
8	Rudy Pemberton	.50
9	Frank Rodriguez	.50

1995 Fleer League Leaders

League Leaders feature players on a horizontal format from 10 statistical categories from both leagues. "League Leader" is placed in a blue strip down the left-side of the card, with their respective league and their name in it. These were inserted at a rate of one per 12 packs.

		MT
Complete Set (10):		4.00
Common Player:		.20
1	Paul O'Neill	.20
2	Ken Griffey, Jr.	1.50
3	Kirby Puckett	.75
4	Jimmy Key	.20
5	Randy Johnson	.50
6	Tony Gwynn	.75
7	Matt Williams	.25
8	Jeff Bagwell	.60
9	Greg Maddux, Ken Hill	.50
10	Andy Benes	.20

1995 Fleer Lumber Company

Ten of the top longball hitters were featured in Lumber Company, which were inserted into every 24 12-card retailer packs. They show the power hitter in action, with a wood-grain Lumber Co. logo across the bottom, contain the player's name and team.

		MT
Complete Set (10):		12.50
Common Player:		.40
1	Jeff Bagwell	1.50
2	Albert Belle	1.00
3	Barry Bonds	3.00
4	Jose Canseco	1.00
5	Joe Carter	.40
6	Ken Griffey, Jr.	5.00
7	Fred McGriff	.40
8	Kevin Mitchell	.40
9	Frank Thomas	2.00
10	Matt Williams	.50

1995 Fleer Major League Prospects

Major League Prospects showcases 10 of 1995's most promising young players. The set title is repeatedly printed across the background, with the player's name and team in a grey strip across the bottom. These cards were inserted into one every six packs.

		MT
Complete Set (10):		7.00
Common Player:		.25
1	Garret Anderson	.50
2	James Baldwin	.25
3	Alan Benes	.35
4	Armando Benitez	.25
5	Ray Durham	.50
6	Brian Hunter	.25
7a	Derek Jeter (no licensor logos on back)	4.00
7b	Derek Jeter (licensor logos on back)	4.00
8	Charles Johnson	.40
9	Orlando Miller	.50
10	Alex Rodriguez	5.00

1995 Fleer Pro-Visions

Pro-Visions contain six interlocking cards that form one giant picture. These original art cards exhibit the player in a fantasy art background and are inserted into every nine packs.

		MT
Complete Set (6):		2.00
Common Player:		.25
1	Mike Mussina	.25
2	Raul Mondesi	.25
3	Jeff Bagwell	.75
4	Greg Maddux	1.00
5	Tim Salmon	.25
6	Manny Ramirez	.75

1995 Fleer Rookie Sensations

A perenial favorite within Fleer products, Rookie Sensations cards were inserted in 18-card packs only, at a rate of one per 16 packs. This 20-card set featured the top rookies from the 1994 season. The player's name and team run up the right side of the card, while the words "Rookie Sensations" appear in the bottom-left corner, separated by a colorful, zig-zagged image of a player.

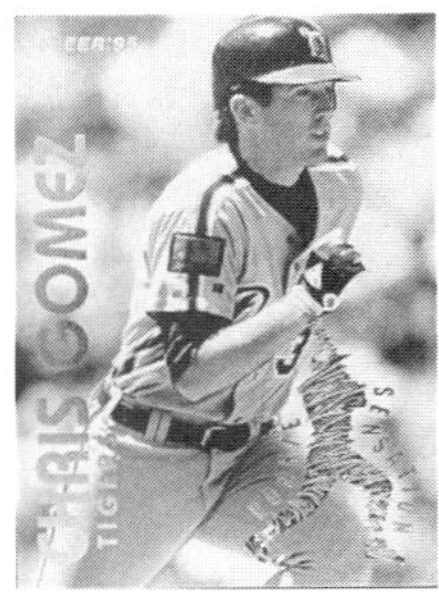

		MT
Complete Set (20):		12.00
Common Player:		.50
1	Kurt Abbott	.50
2	Rico Brogna	.50
3	Hector Carrasco	.50
4	Kevin Foster	.50
5	Chris Gomez	.50
6	Darren Hall	.50
7	Bob Hamelin	.50
8	Joey Hamilton	.50
9	John Hudek	.50
10	Ryan Klesko	.75
11	Javier Lopez	.75
12	Matt Mieske	.50
13	Raul Mondesi	1.00
14	Manny Ramirez	5.00
15	Shane Reynolds	.50
16	Bill Risley	.50
17	Johnny Ruffin	.50
18	Steve Trachsel	.50
19	William Van Landingham	.50
20	Rondell White	1.00

1995 Fleer Team Leaders

Team Leaders are two-player cards featuring the leading hitter and pitcher from each major league team, one on each side. Inserted at a rate of one per 24 packs, these are only found in 12-card hobby packs. Team Leaders consisted of 28 cards and included a Team Leader logo in the bottom-left corner.

		MT
Complete Set (28):		60.00
Common Player:		.50
1	Cal Ripken, Jr., Mike Mussina	10.00
2	Mo Vaughn, Roger Clemens	6.00
3	Tim Salmon, Chuck Finley	1.00
4	Frank Thomas, Jack McDowell	5.00
5	Albert Belle, Dennis Martinez	2.50
6	Cecil Fielder, Mike Moore	.50
7	Bob Hamelin, David Cone	.50
8	Greg Vaughn, Ricky Bones	.50
9	Kirby Puckett, Rick Aguilera	5.00
10	Don Mattingly, Jimmy Key	5.00
11	Ruben Sierra, Dennis Eckersley	.50
12	Ken Griffey, Jr., Randy Johnson	10.00
13	Jose Canseco, Kenny Rogers	2.50
14	Joe Carter, Pat Hentgen	.50
15	Dave Justice, Greg Maddux	7.50
16	Sammy Sosa, Steve Trachsel	7.50
17	Kevin Mitchell, Jose Rijo	.50
18	Dante Bichette, Bruce Ruffin	.50
19	Jeff Conine, Robb Nen	.50
20	Jeff Bagwell, Doug Drabek	4.00
21	Mike Piazza, Ramon Martinez	7.50
22	Moises Alou, Ken Hill	.75
23	Bobby Bonilla, Bret Saberhagen	.50
24	Darren Daulton, Danny Jackson	.50
25	Jay Bell, Zane Smith	.50
26	Gregg Jefferies, Bob Tewksbury	.50
27	Tony Gwynn, Andy Benes	5.00
28	Matt Williams, Rod Beck	.75

1995 Fleer Update

Fleer carried its "different by design" concept of six formats (one for each division in each league) from the regular set into its 1995 Update issue. The issue consists of 200 cards of 1995's traded, rookie and free agent players, plus five different insert sets. One insert card was found in each regular (12-card, $1.49) and jumbo (18-card, $2.29) pack. Cards are numbered with a "U" prefix.

		MT
Complete Set (200):		12.00
Common Player:		.10
Pack (12):		1.00
Wax Box (36):		30.00
1	Manny Alexander	.10
2	Bret Barberie	.10
3	Armando Benitez	.10
4	Kevin Brown	.10
5	Doug Jones	.10
6	Sherman Obando	.10
7	Andy Van Slyke	.10
8	Stan Belinda	.10
9	Jose Canseco	.30
10	Vaughn Eshelman	.10
11	Mike Macfarlane	.10
12	Troy O'Leary	.10
13	Steve Rodriguez	.10
14	Lee Tinsley	.10
15	Tim Vanegmond	.10
16	Mark Whiten	.10
17	Sean Bergman	.10
18	Chad Curtis	.10
19	John Flaherty	.10
20	*Bob Higginson*	.25
21	Felipe Lira	.10
22	Shannon Penn	.10
23	Todd Steverson	.10
24	Sean Whiteside	.10
25	Tony Fernandez	.10
26	Jack McDowell	.10
27	Andy Petitte	.15
28	John Wetteland	.10
29	David Cone	.10
30	Mike Timlin	.10
31	Duane Ward	.10
32	Jim Abbott	.10
33	James Baldwin	.10
34	Mike Devereaux	.10
35	Ray Durham	.15
36	Tim Fortugno	.10
37	Scott Ruffcorn	.10
38	Chris Sabo	.10
39	Paul Assenmacher	.10
40	Bud Black	.10
41	Orel Hershiser	.10
42	Julian Tavarez	.10
43	Dave Winfield	.30
44	Pat Borders	.10
45	*Melvin Bunch*	.10
46	Tom Goodwin	.10
47	Jon Nunnally	.10
48	Joe Randa	.10
49	*Dilson Torres*	.10
50	Joe Vitiello	.10
51	David Hulse	.10
52	Scott Karl	.10
53	Mark Kiefer	.10
54	Derrick May	.10
55	Joe Oliver	.10
56	Al Reyes	.10
57	*Steve Sparks*	.10
58	Jerald Clark	.10
59	Eddie Guardado	.10
60	Kevin Maas	.10
61	David McCarty	.10
62	*Brad Radke*	.75
63	Scott Stahoviak	.10
64	Garret Anderson	.15
65	Shawn Boskie	.10
66	Mike James	.10
67	Tony Phillips	.10
68	Lee Smith	.10
69	Mitch Williams	.10
70	Jim Corsi	.10
71	Mark Harkey	.10
72	Dave Stewart	.10
73	Todd Stottlemyre	.10
74	Joey Cora	.10
75	Chad Kreuter	.10
76	Jeff Nelson	.10
77	Alex Rodriguez	2.00
78	Ron Villone	.10
79	*Bob Wells*	.15
80	*Jose Alberro*	.10
81	Terry Burrows	.10
82	Kevin Gross	.10
83	Wilson Heredia	.10
84	Mark McLemore	.10
85	Otis Nixon	.10
86	Jeff Russell	.10
87	Mickey Tettleton	.10
88	Bob Tewksbury	.10
89	Pedro Borbon	.10
90	Marquis Grissom	.10
91	Chipper Jones	.75
92	Mike Mordecai	.10
93	*Jason Schmidt*	.25
94	John Burkett	.10
95	Andre Dawson	.25
96	*Matt Dunbar*	.15
97	Charles Johnson	.15
98	Terry Pendleton	.10
99	Rich Scheid	.10
100	Quilvio Veras	.10
101	Bobby Witt	.10
102	Eddie Zosky	.10
103	Shane Andrews	.10
104	Reid Cornelius	.10
105	*Chad Fonville*	.20
106	*Mark Grudzielanek*	.30
107	Roberto Kelly	.10
108	*Carlos Perez*	.15
109	Tony Tarasco	.10
110	Brett Butler	.10
111	Carl Everett	.15
112	Pete Harnisch	.10
113	Doug Henry	.10
114	Kevin Lomon	.10
115	Blas Minor	.10
116	Dave Mlicki	.10
117	*Ricky Otero*	.15
118	Norm Charlton	.10
119	Tyler Green	.10
120	Gene Harris	.10
121	Charlie Hayes	.10
122	Gregg Jefferies	.10
123	*Michael Mimbs*	.20
124	Paul Quantrill	.10
125	Frank Castillo	.10
126	Brian McRae	.10
127	Jaime Navarro	.10
128	Mike Perez	.10
129	Tanyon Sturtze	.10
130	Ozzie Timmons	.10
131	John Courtright	.10
132	Ron Gant	.10
133	Xavier Hernandez	.10
134	Brian Hunter	.10
135	Benito Santiago	.10
136	Pete Smith	.10
137	Scott Sullivan	.10
138	Derek Bell	.10
139	Doug Brocail	.10
140	Ricky Gutierrez	.10
141	Pedro Martinez	.10
142	Orlando Miller	.10
143	Phil Plantier	.10
144	Craig Shipley	.10
145	Rich Aude	.10
146	*Jason Christiansen*	.15
147	*Freddy Garcia*	.25
148	Jim Gott	.10
149	*Mark Johnson*	.20
150	Esteban Loaiza	.10
151	Dan Plesac	.10
152	*Gary Wilson*	.10
153	Allen Battle	.10
154	Terry Bradshaw	.10
155	Scott Cooper	.10
156	Tripp Cromer	.10
157	John Frascatore	.10
158	John Habyan	.10
159	Tom Henke	.10
160	Ken Hill	.10
161	Danny Jackson	.10
162	Donovan Osborne	.10
163	Tom Urbani	.10
164	Roger Bailey	.10
165	*Jorge Brito*	.10
166	Vinny Castilla	.10
167	Darren Holmes	.10
168	Roberto Mejia	.10
169	Bill Swift	.10
170	Mark Thompson	.10
171	Larry Walker	.30
172	Greg Hansell	.10
173	Dave Hansen	.10
174	Carlos Hernandez	.10
175	*Hideo Nomo*	2.00
176	Jose Offerman	.10
177	Antonio Osuna	.10
178	Reggie Williams	.10
179	Todd Williams	.10
180	Andres Berumen	.10
181	Ken Caminiti	.10
182	Andujar Cedeno	.10
183	Steve Finley	.10
184	Bryce Florie	.10
185	Dustin Hermanson	.15
186	Ray Holbert	.10
187	Melvin Nieves	.10
188	Roberto Petagine	.10
189	Jody Reed	.10
190	Fernando Valenzuela	.10
191	Brian Williams	.10
192	Mark Dewey	.10
193	Glenallen Hill	.10
194	*Chris Hook*	.15
195	Terry Mulholland	.10
196	Steve Scarsone	.10
197	Trevor Wilson	.10
198	Checklist	.10
199	Checklist	.10
200	Checklist	.10

1995 Fleer Update Diamond Tribute

Borderless action photos and gold-foil graphics are front features of this chase set honoring perhaps the 10 top names among baseball's veteran players. Backs have another photo and a few sentences describing what makes the player worthy of inclusion in such a set. The Diamond Tribute cards are found on the average of one per five packs.

		MT
Complete Set (10):		3.50
Common Player:		.15
1	Jeff Bagwell	.50
2	Albert Belle	.40
3	Barry Bonds	.65
4	David Cone	.15
5	Dennis Eckersley	.15
6	Ken Griffey Jr.	1.00
7	Rickey Henderson	.50
8	Greg Maddux	.75
9	Frank Thomas	.75
10	Matt Williams	.20

1995 Fleer Update Headliners

The most common of the Fleer Update inserts are

the Headliners cards found on average of one per three packs. Fronts have an action photo set against a collage of newspaper clippings. The graphics are gold-foil. Backs have another color photo and a "Fleer Times" newspaper background with career summary and/or quotes about the featured player.

		MT
Complete Set (20):		6.50
Common Player:		.15
1	Jeff Bagwell	.60
2	Albert Belle	.25
3	Barry Bonds	1.00
4	Jose Canseco	.35
5	Joe Carter	.15
6	Will Clark	.25
7	Roger Clemens	.75
8	Lenny Dykstra	.15
9	Cecil Fielder	.15
10	Juan Gonzalez	.75
11	Ken Griffey Jr.	2.00
12	Kenny Lofton	.15
13	Greg Maddux	1.25
14	Fred McGriff	.15
15	Mike Piazza	1.50
16	Kirby Puckett	.75
17	Tim Salmon	.25
18	Frank Thomas	1.25
19	Mo Vaughn	.40
20	Matt Williams	.25

1995 Fleer Update Rookie Update

Ten of 1995's top rookies are featured in this horizontally formatted insert set. Fronts have an action photo with a large gold-foil "ROOKIE UPDATE" headline at top. Backs have another photo and career summary. Rookie Update chase cards are found on the average of one per four packs.

		MT
Complete Set (10):		4.50
Common Player:		.15
1	Shane Andrews	.15
2	Ray Durham	.40
3	Shawn Green	1.00
4	Charles Johnson	.40
5	Chipper Jones	1.50
6	Esteban Loaiza	.15
7	Hideo Nomo	1.00
8	Jon Nunnally	.15
9	Alex Rodriguez	2.00
10	Julian Tavarez	.15

1995 Fleer Update Smooth Leather

These inserts featuring top fielders were found only in pre-priced (magazine) foil packs, at an average rate of one card per 12 packs. Fronts are highlighted with gold-foil graphics. Backs have a glove in the background and explain the player's defensive abilities.

		MT
Complete Set (10):		10.00
Common Player:		.25
1	Roberto Alomar	.60
2	Barry Bonds	1.50
3	Ken Griffey Jr.	4.00
4	Marquis Grissom	.25
5	Darren Lewis	.25
6	Kenny Lofton	.25
7	Don Mattingly	2.00
8	Cal Ripken Jr.	4.00
9	Ivan Rodriguez	.55
10	Matt Williams	.45

1995 Fleer Update Soaring Stars

A metallic foil-etched background behind the color player action photo identifies this chase set as the toughest among those in the 1995 Fleer Update issue. The Soaring Star cards are found at the average rate of one per box. Backs are conventionally printed and featured a colorful posterized version of the front background, along with another color photo and a career summary.

		MT
Complete Set (9):		12.00
Common Player:		.50
1	Moises Alou	1.50
2	Jason Bere	.75
3	Jeff Conine	.75
4	Cliff Floyd	1.00
5	Pat Hentgen	.75
6	Kenny Lofton	1.00
7	Raul Mondesi	1.50
8	Mike Piazza	6.00
9	Tim Salmon	1.00

1995 Fleer/Panini Stickers

Following Fleer's purchase of the well-known Italian sticker company, Panini, it was no surprise to see the companies produce a 1995 baseball issue. Titled "Major League Baseball All-Stars," the set consists of 156 player and team logo stickers. A 36-page color album to house the stickers was sold for $1.19. Sold in six-sticker packs for about .50, the individual stickers measure 1-15/16" x 3". Borders are team color-coded and have the player name and team logo at bottom, with the position abbreviation in a diamond at top-right. Backs are printed in black-and-white and include a sticker number, copyright notice and large logos of the licensors and Fleer/Panini. Each sticker can be found with backs that do, or do not, include a promotional message beginning, "Collect all 156 . . ."

		MT
Complete Set (156):		18.00
Common Player:		.10
Album:		1.25
1	Tom Glavine	.15
2	Doug Drabek	.10
3	Rod Beck	.10
4	Pedro J. Martinez	.35
5	Danny Jackson	.10
6	Greg Maddux	.30
7	Bret Saberhagen	.10
8	Ken Hill	.10
9	Marvin Freeman	.10
10	Andy Benes	.10
11	Wilson Alvarez	.10
12	Jimmy Key	.10
13	Mike Mussina	.15
14	Roger Clemens	.25
15	Pat Hentgen	.10
16	Randy Johnson	.20
17	Lee Smith	.10
18	David Cone	.10
19	Jason Bere	.10
20	Dennis Martinez	.10
21	Darren Daulton	.10
22	Darrin Fletcher	.10
23	Tom Pagnozzi	.10
24	Mike Piazza	.45
25	Benito Santiago	.10
26	Sandy Alomar Jr.	.10
27	Chris Hoiles	.10
28	Ivan Rodriguez	.25
29	Mike Stanley	.10
30	Dave Nilsson	.10
31	Jeff Bagwell	.30
32	Mark Grace	.20
33	Gregg Jefferies	.10
34	Andres Galarraga	.10
35	Fred McGriff	.10
36	Will Clark	.15
37	Mo Vaughn	.15
38	Don Mattingly	.40
39	Frank Thomas	.35
40	Cecil Fielder	.10
41	Robby Thompson	.10
42	Delino DeShields	.10
43	Carlos Garcia	.10
44	Bret Boone	.10
45	Craig Biggio	.10
46	Roberto Alomar	.20
47	Chuck Knoblauch	.10
48	Jose Lind	.10
49	Carlos Baerga	.10
50	Lou Whitaker	.10
51	Bobby Bonilla	.10
52	Tim Wallach	.10
53	Todd Zeile	.10
54	Matt Williams	.15
55	Ken Caminiti	.10
56	Robin Ventura	.10
57	Wade Boggs	.20
58	Scott Cooper	.10
59	Travis Fryman	.10
60	Dean Palmer	.10
61	Jay Bell	.10
62	Barry Larkin	.15
63	Ozzie Smith	.30
64	Wil Cordero	.10
65	Royce Clayton	.10
66	Chris Gomez	.10
67	Ozzie Guillen	.10
68	Cal Ripken Jr.	.50
69	Omar Vizquel	.10
70	Gary DiSarcina	.10
71	Dante Bichette	.10
72	Lenny Dykstra	.10
73	Barry Bonds	.40
74	Gary Sheffield	.15
75	Larry Walker	.15
76	Raul Mondesi	.10
77	Dave Justice	.15
78	Moises Alou	.15
79	Tony Gwynn	.30
80	Deion Sanders	.15
81	Kenny Lofton	.10
82	Kirby Puckett	.40
83	Juan Gonzalez	.25
84	Jay Buhner	.10
85	Joe Carter	.10
86	Ken Griffey Jr.	.50
87	Ruben Sierra	.10
88	Tim Salmon	.10
89	Paul O'Neill	.10
90	Albert Belle	.15
91	Danny Tartabull	.10
92	Jose Canseco	.20
93	Harold Baines	.10
94	Kirk Gibson	.10
95	Chili Davis	.10
96	Eddie Murray	.20
97	Bob Hamelin	.10
98	Paul Molitor	.25
99	Raul Mondesi	.15
100	Ryan Klesko	.10
101	Cliff Floyd	.10
102	William VanLandingham	.10
103	Joey Hamilton	.10
104	John Hudek	.10
105	Manny Ramirez	.25
106	Bob Hamelin	.10
107	Rusty Greer	.10
108	Chris Gomez	.10
	Award Winners	
109	Greg Maddux	.15
110	Jeff Bagwell	.15
111	Raul Mondesi	.10
112	David Cone	.10
113	Frank Thomas	.35
114	Bob Hamelin	.10
	League Leaders	
115	Tony Gwynn	.15
116	Matt Williams	.10
117	Jeff Bagwell	.15
118	Craig Biggio	.10
119	Andy Benes	.10
120	Greg Maddux	.20
121	John Franco	.10
122	Paul O'Neill	.10

123 Ken Griffey Jr. .35
124 Kirby Puckett .20
125 Kenny Lofton .10
126 Randy Johnson .10
127 Jimmy Key .10
128 Lee Smith .10
129 San Francisco Giants logo .10
130 Montreal Expos logo .10
131 Cincinnati Reds logo .10
132 Los Angeles Dodgers logo .10
133 New York Mets logo .10
134 San Diego Padres logo .10
135 Colorado Rockies logo .10
136 Pittsburgh Pirates logo .10
137 Florida Marlins logo .10
138 Philadelphia Phillies logo .10
139 Atlanta Braves logo .10
140 Houston Astros logo .10
141 St. Louis Cardinals logo .10
142 Chicago Cubs logo .10
143 Cleveland Indians logo .10
144 New York Yankees logo .10
145 Kansas City Royals logo .10
146 Chicago White Sox logo .10
147 Baltimore Orioles logo .10
148 Seattle Mariners logo .10
149 Boston Red Sox logo .10
150 California Angels logo .10
151 Toronto Blue Jays logo .10
152 Detroit Tigers logo .10
153 Texas Rangers logo .10
154 Oakland A's logo .10
155 Milwaukee Brewers logo .10
156 Minnesota Twins logo .10

1996 Fleer

In a radical departure from the UV-coated standard for even base-brand baseball cards, Fleer's 1996 issue is printed on a matte surface. Fronts feature borderless game-action photos with minimal (player ID, Fleer logo) graphic enhancement in gold foil. Backs have a white background, a portrait photo, full pro stats and a few career highlights. The single-series set was sold in basic 11-card packs with one of nearly a dozen insert-set cards in each $1.49 pack. The set is arranged alphabetically by player within team and league. A glossy-surface Tiffany Collection parallel was included in each pack.

	MT
Complete Set (600):	45.00
Common Player:	.05
Complete Tiffany Set (600):	150.00
Tiffanies:	3X
Pack (11):	1.50
Wax Box (36):	45.00

1 Manny Alexander .05
2 Brady Anderson .05
3 Harold Baines .05
4 Armando Benitez .05
5 Bobby Bonilla .05
6 Kevin Brown .05
7 Scott Erickson .05
8 Curtis Goodwin .05
9 Jeffrey Hammonds .05
10 Jimmy Haynes .05
11 Chris Hoiles .05
12 Doug Jones .05
13 Rick Krivda .05
14 Jeff Manto .05
15 Ben McDonald .05
16 Jamie Moyer .05
17 Mike Mussina .50
18 Jesse Orosco .05
19 Rafael Palmeiro .25
20 Cal Ripken Jr. 2.50
20 (p) Cal Ripken Jr. (overprinted "PROMOTIONAL SAMPLE") 4.00
21 Rick Aguilera .05
22 Luis Alicea .05
23 Stan Belinda .05
24 Jose Canseco .35
25 Roger Clemens 1.00
26 Vaughn Eshelman .05
27 Mike Greenwell .05
28 Erik Hanson .05
29 Dwayne Hosey .05
30 Mike Macfarlane .05
31 Tim Naehring .05
32 Troy O'Leary .05
33 Aaron Sele .05
34 Zane Smith .05
35 Jeff Suppan .05
36 Lee Tinsley .05
37 John Valentin .10
38 Mo Vaughn .25
39 Tim Wakefield .05
40 Jim Abbott .05
41 Brian Anderson .05
42 Garret Anderson .10
43 Chili Davis .05
44 Gary DiSarcina .05
45 Damion Easley .05
46 Jim Edmonds .15
47 Chuck Finley .05
48 Todd Greene .05
49 Mike Harkey .05
50 Mike James .05
51 Mark Langston .05
52 Greg Myers .05
53 Orlando Palmeiro .05
54 Bob Patterson .05
55 Troy Percival .05
56 Tony Phillips .05
57 Tim Salmon .10
58 Lee Smith .05
59 J.T. Snow .10
60 Randy Velarde .05
61 Wilson Alvarez .05
62 *Luis Andujar* .05
63 Jason Bere .05
64 Ray Durham .05
65 Alex Fernandez .05
66 Ozzie Guillen .05
67 Roberto Hernandez .05
68 Lance Johnson .05
69 Matt Karchner .05
70 Ron Karkovice .05
71 Norberto Martin .05
72 Dave Martinez .05
73 Kirk McCaskill .05
74 Lyle Mouton .05
75 Tim Raines .05
76 *Mike Sirotka* .25
77 Frank Thomas 1.00
78 Larry Thomas .05
79 Robin Ventura .05
80 Sandy Alomar Jr. .05
81 Paul Assenmacher .05
82 Carlos Baerga .05
83 Albert Belle .15
84 Mark Clark .05
85 Alan Embree .05
86 Alvaro Espinoza .05
87 Orel Hershiser .05
88 Ken Hill .05
89 Kenny Lofton .05
90 Dennis Martinez .05
91 Jose Mesa .05
92 Eddie Murray .35
93 Charles Nagy .05
94 Chad Ogea .05
95 Tony Pena .05
96 Herb Perry .05
97 Eric Plunk .05
98 Jim Poole .05
99 Manny Ramirez .75
100 Paul Sorrento .05
101 Julian Travarez .05
102 Jim Thome .05
103 Omar Vizquel .05
104 Dave Winfield .30
105 Danny Bautista .05
106 Joe Boever .05
107 Chad Curtis .05
108 John Doherty .05
109 Cecil Fielder .05
110 John Flaherty .05
111 Travis Fryman .05
112 Chris Gomez .05
113 Bob Higginson .05
114 Mark Lewis .05
115 Jose Lima .05
116 Felipe Lira .05
117 Brian Maxcy .05
118 C.J. Nitkowski .05
119 Phil Plantier .05
120 Clint Sodowsky .05
121 Alan Trammell .05
122 Lou Whitaker .05
123 Kevin Appier .05
124 Johnny Damon .20
125 Gary Gaetti .05
126 Tom Goodwin .05
127 Tom Gordon .05
128 Mark Gubicza .05
129 Bob Hamelin .05
130 David Howard .05
131 Jason Jacome .05
132 Wally Joyner .05
133 Keith Lockhart .05
134 Brent Mayne .05
135 Jeff Montgomery .05
136 Jon Nunnally .05
137 Juan Samuel .05
138 *Mike Sweeney* 1.00
139 Michael Tucker .05
140 Joe Vitiello .05
141 Ricky Bones .05
142 Chuck Carr .05
143 Jeff Cirillo .05
144 Mike Fetters .05
145 Darryl Hamilton .05
146 David Hulse .05
147 John Jaha .05
148 Scott Karl .05
149 Mark Kiefer .05
150 Pat Listach .05
151 Mark Loretta .05
152 Mike Matheny .05
153 Matt Mieske .05
154 Dave Nilsson .05
155 Joe Oliver .05
156 Al Reyes .05
157 Kevin Seitzer .05
158 Steve Sparks .05
159 B.J. Surhoff .05
160 Jose Valentin .05
161 Greg Vaughn .05
162 Fernando Vina .05
163 Rich Becker .05
164 Ron Coomer .05
165 Marty Cordova .10
166 Chuck Knoblauch .05
167 *Matt Lawton* .50
168 Pat Meares .05
169 Paul Molitor .40
170 Pedro Munoz .05
171 Jose Parra .05
172 Kirby Puckett 1.00
173 Brad Radke .10
174 Jeff Reboulet .05
175 Rich Robertson .05
176 Frank Rodriguez .05
177 Scott Stahoviak .05
178 Dave Stevens .05
179 Matt Walbeck .05
180 Wade Boggs .30
181 David Cone .05
182 Tony Fernandez .05
183 Joe Girardi .05
184 Derek Jeter 2.00
185 Scott Kamieniecki .05
186 Pat Kelly .05
187 Jim Leyritz .05
188 Tino Martinez .05
189 Don Mattingly 1.00
190 Jack McDowell .05
191 Jeff Nelson .05
192 Paul O'Neill .05
193 Melido Perez .05
194 Andy Pettitte .40
195 Mariano Rivera .15
196 Ruben Sierra .05
197 Mike Stanley .05
198 Darryl Strawberry .05
199 John Wetteland .05
200 Bob Wickman .05
201 Bernie Williams .30
202 Mark Acre .05
203 Geronimo Berroa .05
204 Mike Bordick .05
205 Scott Brosius .05
206 Dennis Eckersley .05
207 Brent Gates .05
208 Jason Giambi .40
209 Rickey Henderson .35
210 Jose Herrera .05
211 Stan Javier .05
212 Doug Johns .05
213 Mark McGwire 2.50
214 Steve Ontiveros .05
215 Craig Paquette .05
216 Ariel Prieto .05
217 Carlos Reyes .05
218 Terry Steinbach .05
219 Todd Stottlemyre .05
220 Danny Tartabull .05
221 Todd Van Poppel .05
222 John Wasdin .05
223 George Williams .05
224 Steve Wojciechowski .05
225 Rich Amaral .05
226 Bobby Ayala .05
227 Tim Belcher .05
228 Andy Benes .05
229 Chris Bosio .05
230 Darren Bragg .05
231 Jay Buhner .05
232 Norm Charlton .05
233 Vince Coleman .05
234 Joey Cora .05
235 Russ Davis .05
236 Alex Diaz .05
237 Felix Fermin .05
238 Ken Griffey Jr. 2.50
239 Sterling Hitchcock .05
240 Randy Johnson .60
241 Edgar Martinez .05
242 Bill Risley .05
243 Alex Rodriquez 2.50
244 Luis Sojo .05
245 Dan Wilson .05
246 Bob Wolcott .05
247 Will Clark .15
248 Jeff Frye .05
249 Benji Gil .05
250 Juan Gonzalez .75
251 Rusty Greer .05
252 Kevin Gross .05
253 Roger McDowell .05
254 Mark McLemore .05
255 Otis Nixon .05
256 Luis Ortiz .05
257 Mike Pagliarulo .05
258 Dean Palmer .05
259 Roger Pavlik .05
260 Ivan Rodriguez .60
261 Kenny Rogers .05
262 Jeff Russell .05
263 Mickey Tettleton .05
264 Bob Tewksbury .05
265 Dave Valle .05
266 Matt Whiteside .05
267 Roberto Alomar .45
268 Joe Carter .05
269 Tony Castillo .05
270 Domingo Cedeno .05
271 Timothy Crabtree .05

No.	Player	Value
272	Carlos Delgado	.50
273	Alex Gonzalez	.10
274	Shawn Green	.20
275	Juan Guzman	.05
276	Pat Hentgen	.05
277	Al Leiter	.05
278	*Sandy Martinez*	.05
279	Paul Menhart	.05
280	John Olerud	.05
281	Paul Quantrill	.05
282	Ken Robinson	.05
283	Ed Sprague	.05
284	Mike Timlin	.05
285	Steve Avery	.05
286	Rafael Belliard	.05
287	Jeff Blauser	.05
288	Pedro Borbon	.05
289	Brad Clontz	.05
290	Mike Devereaux	.05
291	Tom Glavine	.10
292	Marquis Grissom	.05
293	Chipper Jones	1.50
294	David Justice	.10
295	Mike Kelly	.05
296	Ryan Klesko	.05
297	Mark Lemke	.05
298	Javier Lopez	.05
299	Greg Maddux	1.50
300	Fred McGriff	.05
301	Greg McMichael	.05
302	Kent Mercker	.05
303	Mike Mordecai	.05
304	Charlie O'Brien	.05
305	Eduardo Perez	.05
306	Luis Polonia	.05
307	Jason Schmidt	.05
308	John Smoltz	.10
309	Terrell Wade	.05
310	Mark Wohlers	.05
311	Scott Bullett	.05
312	Jim Bullinger	.05
313	Larry Casian	.05
314	Frank Castillo	.05
315	Shawon Dunston	.05
316	Kevin Foster	.05
317	Matt Franco	.05
318	Luis Gonzalez	.15
319	Mark Grace	.25
320	Jose Hernandez	.05
321	Mike Hubbard	.05
322	Brian McRae	.05
323	Randy Myers	.05
324	Jaime Navarro	.05
325	Mark Parent	.05
326	Mike Perez	.05
327	Rey Sanchez	.05
328	Ryne Sandberg	.75
329	Scott Servais	.05
330	Sammy Sosa	1.50
331	Ozzie Timmons	.05
332	Steve Trachsel	.05
333	Todd Zeile	.05
334	Bret Boone	.10
335	Jeff Branson	.05
336	Jeff Brantley	.05
337	Dave Burba	.05
338	Hector Carrasco	.05
339	Mariano Duncan	.05
340	Ron Gant	.05
341	Lenny Harris	.05
342	Xavier Hernandez	.05
343	Thomas Howard	.05
344	Mike Jackson	.05
345	Barry Larkin	.10
346	Darren Lewis	.05
347	Hal Morris	.05
348	Eric Owens	.05
349	Mark Portugal	.05
350	Jose Rijo	.05
351	Reggie Sanders	.05
352	Benito Santiago	.05
353	Pete Schourek	.05
354	John Smiley	.05
355	Eddie Taubensee	.05
356	Jerome Walton	.05
357	David Wells	.10
358	Roger Bailey	.05
359	Jason Bates	.05
360	Dante Bichette	.05
361	Ellis Burks	.05
362	Vinny Castilla	.05
363	Andres Galarraga	.05
364	Darren Holmes	.05
365	Mike Kingery	.05
366	Curt Leskanic	.05
367	Quinton McCracken	.05
368	Mike Munoz	.05
369	David Nied	.05
370	Steve Reed	.05
371	Bryan Rekar	.05
372	Kevin Ritz	.05
373	Bruce Ruffin	.05
374	Bret Saberhagen	.05
375	Bill Swift	.05
376	John Vander Wal	.05
377	Larry Walker	.15
378	Walt Weiss	.05
379	Eric Young	.05
380	Kurt Abbott	.05
381	Alex Arias	.05
382	Jerry Browne	.05
383	John Burkett	.05
384	Greg Colbrunn	.05
385	Jeff Conine	.05
386	Andre Dawson	.15
387	Chris Hammond	.05
388	Charles Johnson	.05
389	Terry Mathews	.05
390	Robb Nen	.05
391	Joe Orsulak	.05
392	Terry Pendleton	.05
393	Pat Rapp	.05
394	Gary Sheffield	.25
395	Jesus Tavarez	.05
396	Marc Valdes	.05
397	Quilvio Veras	.05
398	Randy Veres	.05
399	Devon White	.05
400	Jeff Bagwell	.60
401	Derek Bell	.05
402	Craig Biggio	.10
403	John Cangelosi	.05
404	Jim Dougherty	.05
405	Doug Drabek	.05
406	Tony Eusebio	.05
407	Ricky Gutierrez	.05
408	Mike Hampton	.10
409	Dean Hartgraves	.05
410	John Hudek	.05
411	Brian Hunter	.05
412	Todd Jones	.05
413	Darryl Kile	.05
414	Dave Magadan	.05
415	Derrick May	.05
416	Orlando Miller	.05
417	James Mouton	.05
418	Shane Reynolds	.05
419	Greg Swindell	.05
420	Jeff Tabaka	.05
421	Dave Veres	.05
422	Billy Wagner	.05
423	*Donne Wall*	.05
424	Rick Wilkins	.05
425	Billy Ashley	.05
426	Mike Blowers	.05
427	Brett Butler	.05
428	Tom Candiotti	.05
429	Juan Castro	.05
430	John Cummings	.05
431	Delino DeShields	.05
432	Joey Eischen	.05
433	Chad Fonville	.05
434	Greg Gagne	.05
435	Dave Hansen	.05
436	Carlos Hernandez	.05
437	Todd Hollandsworth	.05
438	Eric Karros	.05
439	Roberto Kelly	.05
440	Ramon Martinez	.05
441	Raul Mondesi	.15
442	Hideo Nomo	.60
443	Antonio Osuna	.05
444	Chan Ho Park	.15
445	Mike Piazza	2.00
446	Felix Rodriguez	.05
447	Kevin Tapani	.05
448	Ismael Valdes	.05
449	Todd Worrell	.05
450	Moises Alou	.10
451	Shane Andrews	.05
452	Yamil Benitez	.05
453	Sean Berry	.05
454	Wil Cordero	.05
455	Jeff Fassero	.05
456	Darrin Fletcher	.05
457	Cliff Floyd	.05
458	Mark Grudzielanek	.10
459	Gil Heredia	.05
460	Tim Laker	.05
461	Mike Lansing	.05
462	Pedro Martinez	.75
463	Carlos Perez	.05
464	Curtis Pride	.05
465	Mel Rojas	.05
466	Kirk Rueter	.05
467	*F.P. Santangelo*	.10
468	Tim Scott	.05
469	David Segui	.05
470	Tony Tarasco	.05
471	Rondell White	.10
472	Edgardo Alfonzo	.10
473	Tim Bogar	.05
474	Rico Brogna	.05
475	Damon Buford	.05
476	Paul Byrd	.05
477	Carl Everett	.10
478	John Franco	.05
479	Todd Hundley	.05
480	Butch Huskey	.05
481	Jason Isringhausen	.10
482	Bobby Jones	.05
483	Chris Jones	.05
484	Jeff Kent	.10
485	Dave Mlicki	.05
486	Robert Person	.05
487	Bill Pulsipher	.05
488	Kelly Stinnett	.05
489	Ryan Thompson	.05
490	Jose Vizcaino	.05
491	Howard Battle	.05
492	Toby Borland	.05
493	Ricky Bottalico	.05
494	Darren Daulton	.05
495	Lenny Dykstra	.05
496	Jim Eisenreich	.05
497	Sid Fernandez	.05
498	Tyler Green	.05
499	Charlie Hayes	.05
500	Gregg Jefferies	.05
501	Kevin Jordan	.05
502	Tony Longmire	.05
503	Tom Marsh	.05
504	Michael Mimbs	.05
505	Mickey Morandini	.05
506	Gene Schall	.05
507	Curt Schilling	.10
508	Heathcliff Slocumb	.05
509	Kevin Stocker	.05
510	Andy Van Slyke	.05
511	Lenny Webster	.05
512	Mark Whiten	.05
513	Mike Williams	.05
514	Jay Bell	.05
515	Jacob Brumfield	.05
516	Jason Christiansen	.05
517	Dave Clark	.05
518	Midre Cummings	.05
519	Angelo Encarnacion	.05
520	John Ericks	.05
521	Carlos Garcia	.05
522	Mark Johnson	.10
523	Jeff King	.05
524	Nelson Liriano	.05
525	Esteban Loaiza	.05
526	Al Martin	.05
527	Orlando Merced	.05
528	Dan Miceli	.05
529	Ramon Morel	.05
530	Denny Neagle	.05
531	Steve Parris	.05
532	Dan Plesac	.05
533	Don Slaught	.05
534	Paul Wagner	.05
535	John Wehner	.05
536	Kevin Young	.05
537	Allen Battle	.05
538	David Bell	.05
539	Alan Benes	.05
540	Scott Cooper	.05
541	Tripp Cromer	.05
542	Tony Fossas	.05
543	Bernard Gilkey	.05
544	Tom Henke	.05
545	Brian Jordan	.05
546	Ray Lankford	.05
547	John Mabry	.05
548	T.J. Mathews	.05
549	Mike Morgan	.05
550	Jose Oliva	.05
551	Jose Oquendo	.05
552	Donovan Osborne	.05
553	Tom Pagnozzi	.05
554	Mark Petkovsek	.05
555	Danny Sheaffer	.05
556	Ozzie Smith	.50
557	Mark Sweeney	.05
558	Allen Watson	.05
559	Andy Ashby	.05
560	Brad Ausmus	.05
561	Willie Blair	.05
562	Ken Caminiti	.05
563	Andujar Cedeno	.05
564	Glenn Dishman	.05
565	Steve Finley	.05
566	Bryce Florie	.05
567	Tony Gwynn	.75
568	Joey Hamilton	.05
569	Dustin Hermanson	.05
570	Trevor Hoffman	.05
571	Brian Johnson	.05
572	Marc Kroon	.05
573	Scott Livingstone	.05
574	Marc Newfield	.05
575	Melvin Nieves	.05
576	Jody Reed	.05
577	Bip Roberts	.05
578	Scott Sanders	.05
579	Fernando Valenzuela	.05
580	Eddie Williams	.05
581	Rod Beck	.05
582	*Marvin Benard*	.10
583	Barry Bonds	1.00
584	Jamie Brewington	.05
585	Mark Carreon	.05
586	Royce Clayton	.05
587	Shawn Estes	.05
588	Glenallen Hill	.05
589	Mark Leiter	.05
590	Kirt Manwaring	.05
591	David McCarty	.05
592	Terry Mulholland	.05
593	John Patterson	.05
594	J.R. Phillips	.05
595	Deion Sanders	.10
596	Steve Scarsone	.05
597	Robby Thompson	.05
598	Sergio Valdez	.05
599	William VanLandingham	.05
600	Matt Williams	.15

1996 Fleer Tiffany

While Fleer's basic card set for 1996 feature matte-surface cards, a glossy version of each regular card was also issued as a parallel insert set. Other than the UV coating on front and back and the use of silver- rather than gold-foil typography on front, the cards are identical to the regular '96 Fleer player cards. One glossy version card is found in each pack.

	MT
Complete Set (600):	150.00
Common Player:	.15
Stars:	3X

(See 1996 Fleer for checklist and base card values.)

1996 Fleer Checklists

Checklist cards are treated as an insert set in

1996 Fleer, appearing on average once every six packs. Like all other Fleer hobby inserts in the baseball set, the checklists are UV-coated front and back, in contrast to the matte-finish regular issue cards. Checklists have borderless game-action photos on front, with gold-foil typography. Backs have a large Fleer logo and checklist data on a white background.

		MT
Complete Set (10):		3.00
Common Player:		.25
1	Barry Bonds	.50
2	Ken Griffey Jr.	1.00
3	Chipper Jones	.75
4	Greg Maddux	.65
5	Mike Piazza	.75
6	Manny Ramirez	.50
7	Cal Ripken Jr.	1.00
8	Frank Thomas	.50
9	Mo Vaughn	.35
10	Matt Williams	.25

1996 Fleer Golden Memories

Some of the 1995 season's greatest moments are captured in this insert set, a one per 10 pack pick. Fronts have two photos of the player, one in full color in the foreground and one in monochrome as a backdrop. Typography is in prismatic foil vertically down one side. Backs have another color player photo, along with details of the milestone. Two of the cards feature multiple players.

		MT
Complete Set (10):		6.00
Common Player:		.10
1	Albert Belle	.40
2	Barry Bonds, Sammy Sosa	1.00
3	Greg Maddux	1.00
4	Edgar Martinez	.10
5	Ramon Martinez	.10
6	Mark McGwire	2.00
7	Eddie Murray	.25
8	Cal Ripken Jr.	2.00
9	Frank Thomas	.75
10	Alan Trammell, Lou Whitaker	.15

1996 Fleer Lumber Company

Once again for 1996, a Fleer "Lumber Company" chase set honors the game's top sluggers. The '96 version has a horizontal format with a rather small player action photo on a background resembling the trademark area of a bat. The "trademark" is actually the player and team name along with the "Lumber Company" ID, printed in textured glossy black ink. Backs repeat the trademark motif and also include a close-up player photo and a few words about his power-hitting numbers. Lumber Company cards are a one per nine pack pick, on average, found only in retail packs.

		MT
Complete Set (12):		16.00
Common Player:		.50
1	Albert Belle	.75
2	Dante Bichette	.50
3	Barry Bonds	2.00
4	Ken Griffey Jr.	4.00
5	Mark McGwire	4.00
6	Mike Piazza	3.00
7	Manny Ramirez	1.50
8	Tim Salmon	.50
9	Sammy Sosa	2.50
10	Frank Thomas	2.00
11	Mo Vaughn	.50
12	Matt Williams	.50

1996 Fleer Post-Season Glory

Highlights of the 1995 postseason are featured in this small chase card set. Against a stadium background are multiple photos of the featured player, arranged horizontally. The vertical backs have another player photo down one side, and a description of his play-off performance on the other. Stated odds of picking one of these cards are one per five packs.

		MT
Complete Set (5):		2.00
Common Player:		.15
1	Tom Glavine	.20
2	Ken Griffey Jr.	1.50
3	Orel Hershiser	.15
4	Randy Johnson	.30
5	Jim Thome	.15

1996 Fleer Prospects

Minor leaguers who are expected to make it big in the big time are featured in this insert issue. Fronts feature large portrait photos against pastel backgrounds with player and set ID in prismatic foil. Backs have an action photo and repeat the front background color in a box which details the player's potential and career to date. Average odds of finding a Prospects card are one per six packs.

		MT
Complete Set (10):		1.50
Common Player:		.15
1	Yamil Benitez	.15
2	Roger Cedeno	.25
3	Tony Clark	.50
4	Micah Franklin	.15
5	Karim Garcia	.30
6	Todd Greene	.15
7	Alex Ochoa	.15
8	Ruben Rivera	.20
9	Chris Snopek	.15
10	Shannon Stewart	.15

1996 Fleer Road Warriors

A black-and-white country highway photo is the background for the color player action photo on this insert set. Front typography is in silver foil. The players featured are those whose performance on the road is considered outstanding. Backs have a white background, portrait photo and stats bearing out the away-game superiority. These inserts are found at an average pace of one per 13 packs.

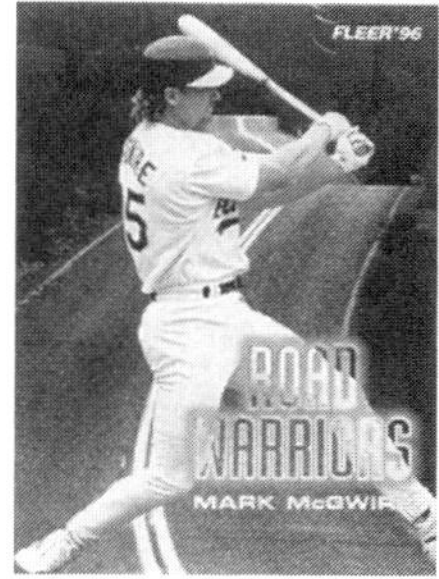

		MT
Complete Set (10):		9.00
Common Player:		.35
1	Derek Bell	.40
2	Tony Gwynn	1.25
3	Greg Maddux	1.25
4	Mark McGwire	3.00
5	Mike Piazza	2.00
6	Manny Ramirez	1.00
7	Tim Salmon	.50
8	Frank Thomas	1.25
9	Mo Vaughn	.75
10	Matt Williams	.40

1996 Fleer Rookie Sensations

Top rookies of the 1995 season are featured on this chase card set. Horizontally formatted, the cards have an action photo on one side and a large prismatic-foil end strip which displays the player name, team logo and card company identifiers. Backs have a portrait photo on as white background with a few sentences about the player's rookie season. Stated odds of finding one of these inserts is one per 11 packs, on average.

		MT
Complete Set (15):		7.50
Common Player:		.25
1	Garret Anderson	.40
2	Marty Cordova	.40

3	Johnny Damon	.40
4	Ray Durham	.25
5	Carl Everett	.40
6	Shawn Green	.75
7	Brian Hunter	.25
8	Jason Isringhausen	.35
9	Charles Johnson	.25
10	Chipper Jones	3.00
11	John Mabry	.25
12	Hideo Nomo	1.50
13	Troy Percival	.25
14	Andy Pettitte	1.50
15	Quilvio Veras	.25

1996 Fleer Smoke 'N Heat

Once more using the "Smoke 'N Heat" identifier for a chase set of the game's hardest throwers, Fleer presents these select pitchers in action photos against a black-and-flame background. Front typography is in gold foil. Backs have a large portrait photo, repeat the flame motif as background and have a description of the pitcher's prowess in a black box. The cards are found, on average, once per nine packs.

		MT
Complete Set (10):		4.00
Common Player:		.15
1	Kevin Appier	.15
2	Roger Clemens	1.25
3	David Cone	.15
4	Chuck Finley	.15
5	Randy Johnson	.50
6	Greg Maddux	1.50
7	Pedro Martinez	.50
8	Hideo Nomo	1.00
9	John Smoltz	.25
10	Todd Stottlemyre	.15

1996 Fleer Team Leaders

One player from each club has been selected for inclusion in the "Team Leaders" chase set. Fronts have action player photos on a background of metallic foil littered with multiple representations of the team logo. Gold-foil lettering identifies the player, team and chase set. Backs have a white background, portrait photo and description of the player's leadership role. Stated rate of insertion for this set is one card per nine packs, on average, found only in hobby packs.

		MT
Complete Set (28):		15.00
Common Player:		.15
1	Cal Ripken Jr.	2.50
2	Mo Vaughn	.45
3	Jim Edmonds	.25
4	Frank Thomas	1.25
5	Kenny Lofton	.15
6	Travis Fryman	.15
7	Gary Gaetti	.15
8	B.J. Surhoff	.15
9	Kirby Puckett	1.25
10	Don Mattingly	1.25
11	Mark McGwire	3.00
12	Ken Griffey Jr.	2.50
13	Juan Gonzalez	1.00
14	Joe Carter	.15
15	Greg Maddux	1.50
16	Sammy Sosa	1.50
17	Barry Larkin	.15
18	Dante Bichette	.15
19	Jeff Conine	.20
20	Jeff Bagwell	1.00
21	Mike Piazza	2.00
22	Rondell White	.20
23	Rico Brogna	.15
24	Darren Daulton	.15
25	Jeff King	.15
26	Ray Lankford	.15
27	Tony Gwynn	1.25
28	Barry Bonds	1.00

1996 Fleer Tomorrow's Legends

In this insert set the projected stars of tomorrow are featured in action poses on a busy multi-colored, quartered background of baseball symbols and the globe. Typography is in silver foil. Backs have a portrait photo and large team logo along with an early-career summary. Odds of finding a "Tomorrow's Legends" card are posted at one per 13 packs, on average.

		MT
Complete Set (10):		6.50
Common Player:		.25
1	Garret Anderson	.25
2	Jim Edmonds	.35
3	Brian Hunter	.25
4	Jason Isringhausen	.25
5	Charles Johnson	.25
6	Chipper Jones	3.00
7	Ryan Klesko	.25
8	Hideo Nomo	1.50
9	Manny Ramirez	1.50
10	Rondell White	.25

1996 Fleer Zone

The toughest pull (one in 90 packs, average) among the '96 Fleer chase cards is this set evoking the "zone" that the game's great players seek in which their performance is at its peak. The cards have action photos with a background of prismatic foil. Backs are conventionally printed but simulate the foil background and include a player portrait photo plus quotes about the player.

		MT
Complete Set (12):		30.00
Common Player:		1.00
1	Albert Belle	1.50
2	Barry Bonds	3.00
3	Ken Griffey Jr.	7.50
4	Tony Gwynn	4.00
5	Randy Johnson	2.50
6	Kenny Lofton	1.00
7	Greg Maddux	6.00
8	Edgar Martinez	1.00
9	Mike Piazza	7.00
10	Frank Thomas	4.00
11	Mo Vaughn	1.50
12	Matt Williams	1.50

1996 Fleer Update

Fleer Update Baseball has 250 cards, including more than 55 rookies, plus traded players and free agents in their new uniforms, 35 Encore subset cards and five checklists. Each card in the regular-issue set also has a parallel "Tiffany Collection" version, which has UV coating and holographic foil stamping in contrast to the matte finish and gold foil of the regular cards. Insert cards include Diamond Tribute, New Horizons, Smooth Leather and Soaring Stars. Each pack also contains a Fleer "Thanks a Million" scratch-off game card, redeemable for prizes. Cards are numbered with a "U" prefix.

		MT
Complete Set (250):		20.00
Common Player:		.05
Complete Tiffany Set (250):		75.00
Tiffany Stars:		3X
Pack (11):		1.25
Wax Box (24):		30.00
1	Roberto Alomar	.60
2	Mike Devereaux	.05
3	*Scott McClain*	.05
4	Roger McDowell	.05
5	Kent Mercker	.05
6	Jimmy Myers	.05
7	Randy Myers	.05
8	B.J. Surhoff	.05
9	Tony Tarasco	.05
10	David Wells	.10
11	Wil Cordero	.05
12	Tom Gordon	.05
13	Reggie Jefferson	.05
14	Jose Malave	.05
15	Kevin Mitchell	.05
16	Jamie Moyer	.05
17	Heathcliff Slocumb	.05
18	Mike Stanley	.05
19	George Arias	.05
20	Jorge Fabregas	.05
21	Don Slaught	.05
22	Randy Velarde	.05
23	Harold Baines	.05
24	*Mike Cameron*	1.00
25	Darren Lewis	.05
26	Tony Phillips	.05
27	Bill Simas	.05
28	Chris Snopek	.05
29	Kevin Tapani	.05
30	Danny Tartabull	.05
31	Julio Franco	.05
32	Jack McDowell	.05
33	Kimera Bartee	.05
34	Mark Lewis	.05
35	Melvin Nieves	.05
36	Mark Parent	.05
37	Eddie Williams	.05
38	Tim Belcher	.05
39	Sal Fasano	.05
40	Chris Haney	.05
41	Mike Macfarlane	.05
42	Jose Offerman	.05
43	Joe Randa	.05
44	Bip Roberts	.05
45	Chuck Carr	.05
46	Bobby Hughes	.05
47	Graeme Lloyd	.05
48	Ben McDonald	.05
49	Kevin Wickander	.05
50	Rick Aguilera	.05
51	Mike Durant	.05
52	Chip Hale	.05
53	LaTroy Hawkins	.05
54	Dave Hollins	.05
55	Roberto Kelly	.05
56	Paul Molitor	.35
57	*Dan Naulty*	.05
58	Mariano Duncan	.05
59	*Andy Fox*	.05
60	Joe Girardi	.05
61	Dwight Gooden	.05
62	Jimmy Key	.05
63	*Matt Luke*	.10
64	Tino Martinez	.05
65	Jeff Nelson	.05
66	Tim Raines	.05

67	Ruben Rivera	.05
68	Kenny Rogers	.05
69	Gerald Williams	.05
70	*Tony Batista*	1.50
71	Allen Battle	.05
72	Jim Corsi	.05
73	Steve Cox	.05
74	Pedro Munoz	.05
75	Phil Plantier	.05
76	Scott Spiezio	.05
77	Ernie Young	.05
78	Russ Davis	.05
79	Sterling Hitchcock	.05
80	Edwin Hurtado	.05
81	*Raul Ibanez*	.05
82	Mike Jackson	.05
83	Ricky Jordan	.05
84	Paul Sorrento	.05
85	Doug Strange	.05
86	Mark Brandenburg	.05
87	Damon Buford	.05
88	Kevin Elster	.05
89	Darryl Hamilton	.05
90	Ken Hill	.05
91	Ed Vosberg	.05
92	Craig Worthington	.05
93	Tilson Brito	.05
94	Giovanni Carrara	.05
95	Felipe Crespo	.05
96	Erik Hanson	.05
97	*Marty Janzen*	.05
98	Otis Nixon	.05
99	Charlie O'Brien	.05
100	Robert Perez	.05
101	Paul Quantrill	.05
102	Bill Risley	.05
103	Juan Samuel	.05
104	Jermaine Dye	.25
105	Wonderful Monds	.05
106	Dwight Smith	.05
107	Jerome Walton	.05
108	Terry Adams	.05
109	Leo Gomez	.05
110	*Robin Jennings*	.05
111	Doug Jones	.05
112	Brooks Kieschnick	.05
113	Dave Magadan	.05
114	*Jason Maxwell*	.05
115	Rodney Myers	.05
116	Eric Anthony	.05
117	Vince Coleman	.05
118	Eric Davis	.05
119	Steve Gibralter	.05
120	Curtis Goodwin	.05
121	Willie Greene	.05
122	Mike Kelly	.05
123	Marcus Moore	.05
124	Chad Mottola	.05
125	Chris Sabo	.05
126	Roger Salkeld	.05
127	Pedro Castellano	.05
128	Trenidad Hubbard	.05
129	Jayhawk Owens	.05
130	Jeff Reed	.05
131	Kevin Brown	.10
132	Al Leiter	.05
133	*Matt Mantei*	.75
134	Dave Weathers	.05
135	Devon White	.05
136	Bob Abreu	.15
137	Sean Berry	.05
138	Doug Brocail	.05
139	Richard Hidalgo	.10
140	Alvin Morman	.05
141	Mike Blowers	.05
142	Roger Cedeno	.10
143	Greg Gagne	.05
144	Karim Garcia	.25
145	*Wilton Guerrero*	.25
146	*Israel Alcantara*	.05
147	Omar Daal	.05
148	Ryan McGuire	.10
149	Sherman Obando	.05
150	Jose Paniagua	.05
151	Henry Rodriguez	.05
152	Andy Stankiewicz	.05
153	Dave Veres	.05
154	Juan Acevedo	.05
155	Mark Clark	.05
156	Bernard Gilkey	.05
157	Pete Harnisch	.05
158	Lance Johnson	.05
159	Brent Mayne	.05
160	Rey Ordonez	.25
161	Kevin Roberson	.05
162	Paul Wilson	.10
163	*David Doster*	.05
164	*Mike Grace*	.10
165	*Rich Hunter*	.05
166	Pete Incaviglia	.05
167	Mike Lieberthal	.10
168	Terry Mulholland	.05
169	Ken Ryan	.05
170	Benito Santiago	.05
171	*Kevin Sefcik*	.05
172	Lee Tinsley	.05
173	Todd Zeile	.05
174	*Francisco Cordova*	.10
175	Danny Darwin	.05
176	Charlie Hayes	.05
177	Jason Kendall	.10
178	Mike Kingery	.05
179	Jon Lieber	.10
180	Zane Smith	.05
181	Luis Alicea	.05
182	Cory Bailey	.05
183	Andy Benes	.05
184	Pat Borders	.05
185	*Mike Busby*	.05
186	Royce Clayton	.05
187	Dennis Eckersley	.05
188	Gary Gaetti	.05
189	Ron Gant	.05
190	Aaron Holbert	.05
191	Willie McGee	.05
192	*Miguel Mejia*	.05
193	Jeff Parrett	.05
194	Todd Stottlemyre	.05
195	Sean Bergman	.05
196	Archi Cianfrocco	.05
197	Rickey Henderson	.25
198	Wally Joyner	.05
199	Craig Shipley	.05
200	Bob Tewksbury	.05
201	Tim Worrell	.05
202	*Rich Aurilia*	.10
203	Doug Creek	.05
204	Shawon Dunston	.05
205	*Osvaldo Fernandez*	.10
206	Mark Gardner	.05
207	Stan Javier	.05
208	Marcus Jensen	.05
209	*Chris Singleton*	2.00
210	Allen Watson	.05
211	Jeff Bagwell (Encore)	.60
212	Derek Bell (Encore)	.05
213	Albert Belle (Encore)	.15
214	Wade Boggs (Encore)	.15
215	Barry Bonds (Encore)	.75
216	Jose Canseco (Encore)	.15
217	Marty Cordova (Encore)	.05
218	Jim Edmonds (Encore)	.10
219	Cecil Fielder (Encore)	.05
220	Andres Galarraga (Encore)	.05
221	Juan Gonzalez (Encore)	.50
222	Mark Grace (Encore)	.10
223	Ken Griffey Jr. (Encore)	1.25
224	Tony Gwynn (Encore)	.60
225	Jason Isringhausen (Encore)	.10
226	Derek Jeter (Encore)	1.50
227	Randy Johnson (Encore)	.35
228	Chipper Jones (Encore)	1.00
229	Ryan Klesko (Encore)	.05
230	Barry Larkin (Encore)	.05
231	Kenny Lofton (Encore)	.05
232	Greg Maddux (Encore)	1.00
233	Raul Mondesi (Encore)	.10
234	Hideo Nomo (Encore)	.75
235	Mike Piazza (Encore)	1.00
236	Manny Ramirez (Encore)	.75
237	Cal Ripken Jr. (Encore)	1.25
238	Tim Salmon (Encore)	.10
239	Ryne Sandberg (Encore)	.40
240	Reggie Sanders (Encore)	.05
241	Gary Sheffield (Encore)	.20
242	Sammy Sosa (Encore)	1.00
243	Frank Thomas (Encore)	1.00
244	Mo Vaughn (Encore)	.15
245	Matt Williams (Encore)	.10
246	Checklist	.05
247	Checklist	.05
248	Checklist	.05
249	Checklist	.05
250	Checklist	.05

1996 Fleer Update Tiffany

	MT
Complete Set (250):	100.00
Common Player:	.15
Glossy Stars:	3X

(See 1996 Fleer Update for checklist and base card values.)

1996 Fleer Update Diamond Tribute

These insert cards are the most difficult to pull from 1996 Fleer Update packs; they are seeded one per every 100 packs. The 10-card set features cards of future Hall of Famers on stock utilizing two different holographic foils and a diamond design, similar to the "Zone" insert cards in Fleer Baseball.

		MT
Complete Set (10):		70.00
Common Player:		3.00
1	Wade Boggs	3.00
2	Barry Bonds	7.50
3	Ken Griffey Jr.	15.00
4	Tony Gwynn	10.00
5	Rickey Henderson	3.00
6	Greg Maddux	12.50
7	Eddie Murray	3.00
8	Cal Ripken Jr.	15.00
9	Ozzie Smith	6.00
10	Frank Thomas	10.00

1996 Fleer Update Headliners

These 20 cards feature newsmakers from 1996. The cards were random inserts in 1996 Fleer Update packs, one per every five retail packs.

		MT
Complete Set (20):		20.00
Common Player:		.25
1	Roberto Alomar	.75
2	Jeff Bagwell	1.25
3	Albert Belle	.50
4	Barry Bonds	1.00
5	Cecil Fielder	.25
6	Juan Gonzalez	1.00
7	Ken Griffey Jr.	3.50
8	Tony Gwynn	1.25
9	Randy Johnson	.75
10	Chipper Jones	2.50
11	Ryan Klesko	.25
12	Kenny Lofton	.25
13	Greg Maddux	2.25
14	Hideo Nomo	1.00
15	Mike Piazza	2.50
16	Manny Ramirez	1.00
17	Cal Ripken Jr.	3.50
18	Tim Salmon	.25
19	Frank Thomas	1.25
20	Matt Williams	.25

1996 Fleer Update New Horizons

These 1996 Fleer Update inserts feature 20 promising youngsters with bright futures in the majors. The cards were seeded one per every five hobby packs.

		MT
Complete Set (20):		8.00
Common Player:		.30
1	Bob Abreu	1.50
2	George Arias	.30
3	Tony Batista	.30
4	Steve Cox	.30
5	David Doster	.30
6	Jermaine Dye	1.00
7	Andy Fox	.30
8	Mike Grace	.30
9	Todd Greene	.30
10	Wilton Guerrero	.30
11	Richard Hidalgo	.75
12	Raul Ibanez	.30
13	Robin Jennings	.30
14	Marcus Jensen	.30
15	Jason Kendall	1.00
16	Brooks Kieschnick	.30
17	Ryan McGuire	.30
18	Miguel Mejia	.30
19	Rey Ordonez	2.00
20	Paul Wilson	.50

1996 Fleer Update Smooth Leather

Ten of the game's top fielders are showcased on these 1996 Fleer Update insert cards. The cards were seeded one per every five packs.

		MT
Complete Set (10):		7.50
Common Player:		.40
1	Roberto Alomar	.60
2	Barry Bonds	1.00
3	Will Clark	.40
4	Ken Griffey Jr.	2.50
5	Kenny Lofton	.40
6	Greg Maddux	1.50
7	Raul Mondesi	.50
8	Rey Ordonez	.50
9	Cal Ripken Jr.	2.50
10	Matt Williams	.40

1996 Fleer Update Soaring Stars

Ten of the game's top players are spotlighted on these 1996 Fleer Update inserts. The cards were seeded one per every 11 packs.

		MT
Complete Set (10):		8.00
Common Player:		.25
1	Jeff Bagwell	.60
2	Barry Bonds	.75
3	Juan Gonzalez	.75
4	Ken Griffey Jr.	2.00
5	Chipper Jones	1.50
6	Greg Maddux	1.00
7	Mike Piazza	1.50
8	Manny Ramirez	.75
9	Frank Thomas	1.00
10	Matt Williams	.25

1996 Fleer/Panini Stickers

For the second year of distribution by Fleer/SkyBox, the annual baseball sticker set once again used Panini as the dominant brand identification. Printed in Italy, the stickers were sold in packs of six for 49 cents in the U.S., 69 cents in Canada. At 2-1/8" x 3", the basic player stickers have a green border around the color action photo; a second, ghosted, version of the photo appear in the background. Team logo and player ID are in a bat at bottom. Backs are printed in blue with the sticker number, Panini and licensor logos, along with copyright information. Team logo and special rookie stickers were printed on silver foil. A 60-page album was issued to house the set.

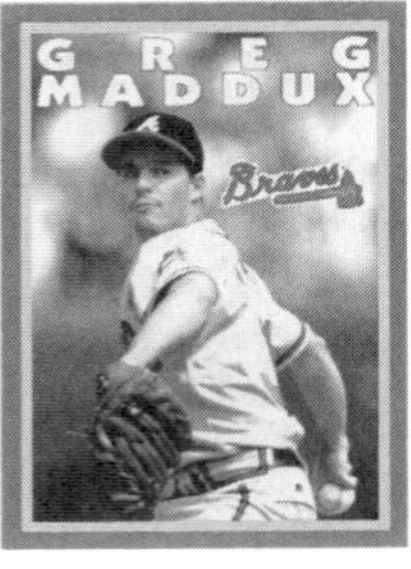

		MT
Complete Set (246):		5.00
Common Player:		.05
Album:		.70
1	David Justice	.10
2	Tom Glavine	.10
3	Javier Lopez	.05
4	Greg Maddux	.45
5	Marquis Grissom	.05
6	Braves logo	.05
7	Ryan Klesko	.05
8	Chipper Jones	.50
9	Quilvio Veras	.05
10	Chris Hammond	.05
11	Charles Johnson	.05
12	John Burkett	.05
13	Marlins logo	.05
14	Jeff Conine	.05
15	Gary Sheffield	.10
16	Greg Colbrunn	.05
17	Moises Alou	.10
18	Pedro J. Martinez	.25
19	Rondell White	.05
20	Tony Tarasco	.05
21	Expos logo	.05
22	Carlos Perez	.05
23	David Segui	.05
24	Wil Cordero	.05
25	Jason Isringhausen	.10
26	Rico Brogna	.05
27	Edgardo Alfonzo	.10
28	Todd Hundley	.05
29	Mets logo	.05
30	Bill Pulsipher	.05
31	Carl Everett	.10
32	Jose Vizcaino	.05
33	Lenny Dykstra	.05
34	Charlie Hayes	.05
35	Heathcliff Slocumb	.05
36	Darren Daulton	.05
37	Phillies logo	.05
38	Mickey Morandini	.05
39	Gregg Jefferies	.05
40	Jim Eisenreich	.05
41	Brian McRae	.05
42	Luis Gonzalez	.15
43	Randy Myers	.05
44	Shawon Dunston	.05
45	Cubs logo	.05
46	Jaime Navarro	.05
47	Mark Grace	.15
48	Sammy Sosa	.45
49	Barry Larkin	.10
50	Pete Schourek	.05
51	John Smiley	.05
52	Reggie Sanders	.05
53	Reds logo	.05
54	Hal Morris	.05
55	Ron Gant	.05
56	Bret Boone	.10
57	Craig Biggio	.10
58	Brian L. Hunter	.05
59	Jeff Bagwell	.25
60	Shane Reynolds	.05
61	Astros logo	.05
62	Derek Bell	.05
63	Doug Drabek	.05
64	Orlando Miller	.05
65	Jay Bell	.05
66	Dan Miceli	.05
67	Orlando Merced	.05
68	Jeff King	.05
69	Carlos Garcia	.05
70	Pirates logo	.05
71	Al Martin	.05
72	Denny Neagle	.05
73	Ray Lankford	.05
74	Ozzie Smith	.35
75	Bernard Gilkey	.05
76	John Mabry	.05
77	Cardinals logo	.05
78	Brian Jordan	.05
79	Scott Cooper	.05
80	Allen Watson	.05
81	Dante Bichette	.05
82	Bret Saberhagen	.05
83	Walt Weiss	.05
84	Andres Galarraga	.05
85	Rockies logo	.05
86	Larry Walker	.10
87	Bill Swift	.05
88	Vinny Castilla	.05
89	Raul Mondesi	.10
90	Roger Cedeno	.10
91	Chad Fonville	.05
92	Hideo Nomo	.25
93	Dodgers logo	.05
94	Ramon Martinez	.05
95	Mike Piazza	.50
96	Eric Karros	.05
97	Tony Gwynn	.35
98	Brad Ausmus	.05
99	Trevor Hoffman	.05
100	Ken Caminiti	.05
101	Padres logo	.05
102	Andy Ashby	.05
103	Steve Finley	.05
104	Joey Hamilton	.05
105	Matt Williams	.10
106	Rod Beck	.05
107	Barry Bonds	.35
108	William VanLandingham	.05
109	Giants logo	.05
110	Deion Sanders	.10
111	Royce Clayton	.05
112	Glenallen Hill	.05
113	Tony Gwynn (League Leader - BA)	.10
114	Dante Bichette (League Leader - HR)	.05
115	Dante Bichette (League Leader - RBI)	.05
116	Quilvio Veras (League Leader - SB)	.05
117	Hideo Nomo (League Leader - K)	.15
118	Greg Maddux (League Leader - W)	.15
119	Randy Myers (League Leader - Saves)	.05
120	Edgar Martinez (League Leader - BA)	.05
121	Albert Belle (League Leader - HR)	.10
122	Mo Vaughn (League Leader - RBI)	.05
123	Kenny Lofton (League Leader - SB)	.05
124	Randy Johnson (League Leader - K)	.10
125	Mike Mussina (League Leader - W)	.05
126	Jose Mesa (League Leader - Saves)	.05
127	Mike Mussina	.15
128	Cal Ripken Jr.	.75
129	Rafael Palmeiro	.10
130	Ben McDonald	.05
131	Orioles logo	.05
132	Chris Hoiles	.05
133	Bobby Bonilla	.05
134	Brady Anderson	.05
135	Jose Canseco	.15
136	Roger Clemens	.30
137	Mo Vaughn	.15
138	Mike Greenwell	.05
139	Red Sox logo	.05
140	Tim Wakefield	.05
141	John Valentin	.05
142	Tim Naehring	.05
143	Travis Fryman	.05
144	Chad Curtis	.05
145	Felipe Lira	.05
146	Cecil Fielder	.05
147	Tigers logo	.05
148	John Flaherty	.05
149	Chris Gomez	.05
150	Sean Bergman	.05
151	Don Mattingly	.45
152	Andy Pettitte	.10
153	Wade Boggs	.15
154	Paul O'Neill	.05
155	Yankees logo	.05
156	Bernie Williams	.15
157	Jack McDowell	.05
158	David Cone	.05
159	Roberto Alomar	.20
160	Paul Molitor	.25
161	Shawn Green	.10
162	Joe Carter	.05
163	Blue Jays logo	.05
164	Alex Gonzalez	.05
165	Al Leiter	.05
166	John Olerud	.05
167	Alex Fernandez	.05
168	Ray Durham	.05
169	Lance Johnson	.05
170	Ozzie Guillen	.05
171	White Sox logo	.05
172	Robin Ventura	.05
173	Frank Thomas	.35
174	Tim Raines	.05
175	Albert Belle	.15
176	Manny Ramirez	.30
177	Eddie Murray	.15
178	Orel Hershiser	.05
179	Indians logo	.05
180	Kenny Lofton	.05
181	Carlos Baerga	.05
182	Jose Mesa	.05
183	Gary Gaetti	.05
184	Tom Goodwin	.05
185	Kevin Appier	.05
186	Jon Nunnally	.05
187	Royals logo	.05
188	Wally Joyner	.05
189	Jeff Montgomery	.05
190	Johnny Damon	.10
191	B.J. Surhoff	.05
192	Ricky Bones	.05
193	John Jaha	.05
194	Dave Nilsson	.05
195	Brewers logo	.05
196	Greg Vaughn	.05
197	Kevin Seitzer	.05
198	Joe Oliver	.05
199	Chuck Knoblauch	.05
200	Kirby Puckett	.45
201	Marty Cordova	.05
202	Pat Meares	.05
203	Twins logo	.05
204	Scott Stahoviak	.05
205	Matt Walbeck	.05
206	Pedro Munoz	.05
207	Garret Anderson	.10
208	Chili Davis	.05
209	Tim Salmon	.10
210	J.T. Snow	.10
211	Angels logo	.05
212	Jim Edmonds	.10
213	Chuck Finley	.05
214	Mark Langston	.05
215	Dennis Eckersley	.05
216	Todd Stottlemyre	.05
217	Geronimo Berroa	.05
218	Mark McGwire	.75
219	A's logo	.05
220	Brent Gates	.05
221	Terry Steinbach	.05
222	Rickey Henderson	.15

223	Ken Griffey Jr.	.75
224	Alex Rodriguez	.75
225	Tino Martinez	.05
226	Randy Johnson	.15
227	Mariners logo	.05
228	Jay Buhner	.05
229	Vince Coleman	.05
230	Edgar Martinez	.05
231	Will Clark	.10
232	Juan Gonzalez	.25
233	Kenny Rogers	.05
234	Ivan Rodriguez	.15
235	Rangers logo	.05
236	Mickey Tettleton	.05
237	Dean Palmer	.05
238	Otis Nixon	.05
239	Hideo Nomo (Rookie)	.75
240	Quilvio Veras (Rookie)	.05
241	Jason Isringhausen (Rookie)	.10
242	Andy Pettitte (Rookie)	.05
243	Chipper Jones (Rookie)	.50
244	Garret Anderson (Rookie)	.10
245	Charles Johnson (Rookie)	.10
246	Marty Cordova (Rookie)	.10

1997 Fleer

Fleer maintained its matte-finish coating for 1997 after it debuted in the 1996 product. The regular-issue Series 1 has 500 cards equipped with icons designating All-Stars, League Leaders and World Series cards. There were also 10 checklist cards in the regular-issue set, featuring stars on the front. Fleer arrived in 10-card packs and had a Tiffany Collection parallel set and six different insert sets, including Rookie Sensations, Golden Memories, Team Leaders, Night and Day, Zone and Lumber Company. Series 2 comprises 261 cards plus inserts Decade of Excellence, Bleacher Bashers, Diamond Tributes, Goudey Greats, Headliners, New Horizons and Soaring Stars.

	MT
Complete Set (761):	75.00
Complete Series 1 Set (500):	45.00
Complete Series 2 Set (261):	35.00
Common Player:	.05
Complete Tiffany Set (1-761):	1500.
Tiffany Stars/RCs:	20X
A. Jones Circa AU/200:	35.00
Series 1 or 2 Pack (10):	1.50
Series 1 or 2 Wax Box (36):	50.00

1	Roberto Alomar	.50
2	Brady Anderson	.05
3	Bobby Bonilla	.05
4	Rocky Coppinger	.05
5	Cesar Devarez	.05
6	Scott Erickson	.05
7	Jeffrey Hammonds	.05
8	Chris Hoiles	.05
9	Eddie Murray	.40
10	Mike Mussina	.50
11	Randy Myers	.05
12	Rafael Palmeiro	.20
13	Cal Ripken Jr.	2.50
14	B.J. Surhoff	.05
15	David Wells	.10
16	Todd Zeile	.05
17	Darren Bragg	.05
18	Jose Canseco	.25
19	Roger Clemens	.75
20	Wil Cordero	.05
21	Jeff Frye	.05
22	Nomar Garciaparra	2.00
23	Tom Gordon	.05
24	Mike Greenwell	.05
25	Reggie Jefferson	.05
26	Jose Malave	.05
27	Tim Naehring	.05
28	Troy O'Leary	.05
29	Heathcliff Slocumb	.05
30	Mike Stanley	.05
31	John Valentin	.05
32	Mo Vaughn	.45
33	Tim Wakefield	.05
34	Garret Anderson	.05
35	George Arias	.05
36	Shawn Boskie	.05
37	Chili Davis	.05
38	Jason Dickson	.15
39	Gary DiSarcina	.05
40	Jim Edmonds	.10
41	Darin Erstad	1.00
42	Jorge Fabregas	.05
43	Chuck Finley	.05
44	Todd Greene	.05
45	*Mike Holtz*	.10
46	Rex Hudler	.05
47	Mike James	.05
48	Mark Langston	.05
49	Troy Percival	.05
50	Tim Salmon	.20
51	Jeff Schmidt	.05
52	J.T. Snow	.10
53	Randy Velarde	.05
54	Wilson Alvarez	.05
55	Harold Baines	.05
56	James Baldwin	.05
57	Jason Bere	.05
58	Mike Cameron	.05
59	Ray Durham	.05
60	Alex Fernandez	.05
61	Ozzie Guillen	.05
62	Roberto Hernandez	.05
63	Ron Karkovice	.05
64	Darren Lewis	.05
65	Dave Martinez	.05
66	Lyle Mouton	.05
67	Greg Norton	.05
68	Tony Phillips	.05
69	Chris Snopek	.05
70	Kevin Tapani	.05
71	Danny Tartabull	.05
72	Frank Thomas	1.50
73	Robin Ventura	.05
74	Sandy Alomar Jr.	.05
75	Albert Belle	.20
76	Mark Carreon	.05
77	Julio Franco	.05
78	*Brian Giles*	1.50
79	Orel Hershiser	.05
80	Kenny Lofton	.05
81	Dennis Martinez	.05
82	Jack McDowell	.05
83	Jose Mesa	.05
84	Charles Nagy	.05
85	Chad Ogea	.05
86	Eric Plunk	.05
87	Manny Ramirez	1.00
88	Kevin Seitzer	.05
89	Julian Tavarez	.05
90	Jim Thome	.05
91	Jose Vizcaino	.05
92	Omar Vizquel	.05
93	Brad Ausmus	.05
94	Kimera Bartee	.05
95	Raul Casanova	.05
96	Tony Clark	.25
97	John Cummings	.05
98	Travis Fryman	.05
99	Bob Higginson	.10
100	Mark Lewis	.05
101	Felipe Lira	.05
102	Phil Nevin	.05
103	Melvin Nieves	.05
104	Curtis Pride	.05
105	A.J. Sager	.05
106	Ruben Sierra	.05
107	Justin Thompson	.05
108	Alan Trammell	.05
109	Kevin Appier	.05
110	Tim Belcher	.05
111	Jaime Bluma	.05
112	Johnny Damon	.15
113	Tom Goodwin	.05
114	Chris Haney	.05
115	Keith Lockhart	.05
116	Mike Macfarlane	.05
117	Jeff Montgomery	.05
118	Jose Offerman	.05
119	Craig Paquette	.05
120	Joe Randa	.05
121	Bip Roberts	.05
122	Jose Rosado	.05
123	Mike Sweeney	.05
124	Michael Tucker	.05
125	Jeromy Burnitz	.05
126	Jeff Cirillo	.05
127	Jeff D'Amico	.05
128	Mike Fetters	.05
129	John Jaha	.05
130	Scott Karl	.05
131	Jesse Levis	.05
132	Mark Loretta	.05
133	Mike Matheny	.05
134	Ben McDonald	.05
135	Matt Mieske	.05
136	Marc Newfield	.05
137	Dave Nilsson	.05
138	Jose Valentin	.05
139	Fernando Vina	.05
140	Bob Wickman	.05
141	Gerald Williams	.05
142	Rick Aguilera	.05
143	Rich Becker	.05
144	Ron Coomer	.05
145	Marty Cordova	.10
146	Roberto Kelly	.05
147	Chuck Knoblauch	.05
148	Matt Lawton	.05
149	Pat Meares	.05
150	Travis Miller	.05
151	Paul Molitor	.40
152	Greg Myers	.05
153	Dan Naulty	.05
154	Kirby Puckett	1.00
155	Brad Radke	.10
156	Frank Rodriguez	.05
157	Scott Stahoviak	.05
158	Dave Stevens	.05
159	Matt Walbeck	.05
160	Todd Walker	.40
161	Wade Boggs	.25
162	David Cone	.05
163	Mariano Duncan	.05
164	Cecil Fielder	.05
165	Joe Girardi	.05
166	Dwight Gooden	.05
167	Charlie Hayes	.05
168	Derek Jeter	2.00
169	Jimmy Key	.05
170	Jim Leyritz	.05
171	Tino Martinez	.05
172	*Ramiro Mendoza*	.25
173	Jeff Nelson	.05
174	Paul O'Neill	.05
175	Andy Pettitte	.25
176	Mariano Rivera	.15
177	Ruben Rivera	.10
178	Kenny Rogers	.05
179	Darryl Strawberry	.05
180	John Wetteland	.05
181	Bernie Williams	.35
182	Willie Adams	.05
183	Tony Batista	.05
184	Geronimo Berroa	.05
185	Mike Bordick	.05
186	Scott Brosius	.05
187	Bobby Chouinard	.05
188	Jim Corsi	.05
189	Brent Gates	.05
190	Jason Giambi	.15
191	Jose Herrera	.05
192	*Damon Mashore*	.05
193	Mark McGwire	3.00
194	Mike Mohler	.05
195	Scott Spiezio	.05
196	Terry Steinbach	.05
197	Bill Taylor	.05
198	John Wasdin	.05
199	Steve Wojciechowski	.05
200	Ernie Young	.05
201	Rich Amaral	.05
202	Jay Buhner	.05
203	Norm Charlton	.05
204	Joey Cora	.05
205	Russ Davis	.05
206	Ken Griffey Jr.	2.50
207	Sterling Hitchcock	.05
208	Brian Hunter	.05
209	Raul Ibanez	.05
210	Randy Johnson	.30
211	Edgar Martinez	.05
212	Jamie Moyer	.05
213	Alex Rodriguez	2.50
214	Paul Sorrento	.05
215	Matt Wagner	.05
216	Bob Wells	.05
217	Dan Wilson	.05
218	Damon Buford	.05
219	Will Clark	.20
220	Kevin Elster	.05
221	Juan Gonzalez	.75
222	Rusty Greer	.05
223	Kevin Gross	.05
224	Darryl Hamilton	.05
225	Mike Henneman	.05
226	Ken Hill	.05
227	Mark McLemore	.05
228	Darren Oliver	.05
229	Dean Palmer	.05
230	Roger Pavlik	.05
231	Ivan Rodriguez	.40
232	Mickey Tettleton	.05
233	Bobby Witt	.05
234	Jacob Brumfield	.05
235	Joe Carter	.05
236	Tim Crabtree	.05
237	Carlos Delgado	.40
238	Huck Flener	.05
239	Alex Gonzalez	.05
240	Shawn Green	.10
241	Juan Guzman	.05
242	Pat Hentgen	.05
243	Marty Janzen	.05
244	Sandy Martinez	.05
245	Otis Nixon	.05
246	Charlie O'Brien	.05
247	John Olerud	.05
248	Robert Perez	.05
249	Ed Sprague	.05
250	Mike Timlin	.05
251	Steve Avery	.05
252	Jeff Blauser	.05
253	Brad Clontz	.05
254	Jermaine Dye	.10
255	Tom Glavine	.10
256	Marquis Grissom	.05
257	Andruw Jones	1.50
258	Chipper Jones	2.00
259	David Justice	.15
260	Ryan Klesko	.05
261	Mark Lemke	.05
262	Javier Lopez	.05
263	Greg Maddux	2.00
264	Fred McGriff	.05
265	Greg McMichael	.05
266	Denny Neagle	.05
267	Terry Pendleton	.05
268	Eddie Perez	.05
269	John Smoltz	.10
270	Terrell Wade	.05
271	Mark Wohlers	.05
272	Terry Adams	.05
273	Brant Brown	.05
274	Leo Gomez	.05
275	Luis Gonzalez	.15
276	Mark Grace	.15
277	Tyler Houston	.05
278	Robin Jennings	.05
279	Brooks Kieschnick	.05
280	Brian McRae	.05
281	Jaime Navarro	.05
282	Ryne Sandberg	.75
283	Scott Servais	.05
284	Sammy Sosa	1.50

No.	Player	Value
285	*Dave Swartzbaugh*	.05
286	Amaury Telemaco	.05
287	Steve Trachsel	.05
288	*Pedro Valdes*	.05
289	Turk Wendell	.05
290	Bret Boone	.10
291	Jeff Branson	.05
292	Jeff Brantley	.05
293	Eric Davis	.05
294	Willie Greene	.05
295	Thomas Howard	.05
296	Barry Larkin	.10
297	Kevin Mitchell	.05
298	Hal Morris	.05
299	Chad Mottola	.05
300	Joe Oliver	.05
301	Mark Portugal	.05
302	Roger Salkeld	.05
303	Reggie Sanders	.05
304	Pete Schourek	.05
305	John Smiley	.05
306	Eddie Taubensee	.05
307	Dante Bichette	.05
308	Ellis Burks	.05
309	Vinny Castilla	.05
310	Andres Galarraga	.05
311	Curt Leskanic	.05
312	Quinton McCracken	.05
313	Neifi Perez	.05
314	Jeff Reed	.05
315	Steve Reed	.05
316	Armando Reynoso	.05
317	Kevin Ritz	.05
318	Bruce Ruffin	.05
319	Larry Walker	.20
320	Walt Weiss	.05
321	Jamey Wright	.05
322	Eric Young	.05
323	Kurt Abbott	.05
324	Alex Arias	.05
325	Kevin Brown	.10
326	Luis Castillo	.05
327	Greg Colbrunn	.05
328	Jeff Conine	.05
329	Andre Dawson	.10
330	Charles Johnson	.05
331	Al Leiter	.05
332	Ralph Milliard	.05
333	Robb Nen	.05
334	Pat Rapp	.05
335	Edgar Renteria	.10
336	Gary Sheffield	.25
337	Devon White	.05
338	Bob Abreu	.10
339	Jeff Bagwell	.75
340	Derek Bell	.05
341	Sean Berry	.05
342	Craig Biggio	.10
343	Doug Drabek	.05
344	Tony Eusebio	.05
345	Ricky Gutierrez	.05
346	Mike Hampton	.05
347	Brian Hunter	.05
348	Todd Jones	.05
349	Darryl Kile	.05
350	Derrick May	.05
351	Orlando Miller	.05
352	James Mouton	.05
353	Shane Reynolds	.05
354	Billy Wagner	.05
355	Donne Wall	.05
356	Mike Blowers	.05
357	Brett Butler	.05
358	Roger Cedeno	.10
259	Chad Curtis	.05
360	Delino DeShields	.05
361	Greg Gagne	.05
362	Karim Garcia	.10
363	Wilton Guerrero	.05
364	Todd Hollandsworth	.05
365	Eric Karros	.05
366	Ramon Martinez	.05
367	Raul Mondesi	.20
368	Hideo Nomo	.75
369	Antonio Osuna	.05
370	Chan Ho Park	.15
371	Mike Piazza	2.00
372	Ismael Valdes	.05
373	Todd Worrell	.05
374	Moises Alou	.10
375	Shane Andrews	.05
376	Yamil Benitez	.05
377	Jeff Fassero	.05
378	Darrin Fletcher	.05
379	Cliff Floyd	.05
380	Mark Grudzielanek	.05
381	Mike Lansing	.05
382	Barry Manuel	.05
383	Pedro Martinez	.50
384	Henry Rodriguez	.05
385	Mel Rojas	.05
386	F.P. Santangelo	.05
387	David Segui	.05
388	Ugueth Urbina	.05
389	Rondell White	.10
390	Edgardo Alfonzo	.10
391	Carlos Baerga	.05
392	Mark Clark	.05
393	Alvaro Espinoza	.05
394	John Franco	.05
395	Bernard Gilkey	.05
396	Pete Harnisch	.05
397	Todd Hundley	.05
398	Butch Huskey	.05
399	Jason Isringhausen	.10
400	Lance Johnson	.05
401	Bobby Jones	.05
402	Alex Ochoa	.05
403	Rey Ordonez	.20
404	Robert Person	.05
405	Paul Wilson	.10
406	Matt Beech	.05
407	Ron Blazier	.05
408	Ricky Bottalico	.05
409	Lenny Dykstra	.05
410	Jim Eisenreich	.05
411	Bobby Estalella	.05
412	Mike Grace	.05
413	Gregg Jefferies	.05
414	Mike Lieberthal	.10
415	Wendell Magee Jr.	.05
416	Mickey Morandini	.05
417	Ricky Otero	.05
418	Scott Rolen	1.50
419	Ken Ryan	.05
420	Benito Santiago	.05
421	Curt Schilling	.10
422	Kevin Sefcik	.05
423	Jermaine Allensworth	.05
424	Trey Beamon	.05
425	Jay Bell	.05
426	Francisco Cordova	.05
427	Carlos Garcia	.05
428	Mark Johnson	.05
429	Jason Kendall	.10
430	Jeff King	.05
431	Jon Lieber	.05
432	Al Martin	.05
433	Orlando Merced	.05
434	Ramon Morel	.05
435	Matt Ruebel	.05
436	Jason Schmidt	.05
437	*Marc Wilkins*	.05
438	Alan Benes	.05
439	Andy Benes	.05
440	Royce Clayton	.05
441	Dennis Eckersley	.05
442	Gary Gaetti	.05
443	Ron Gant	.05
444	Aaron Holbert	.05
445	Brian Jordan	.05
446	Ray Lankford	.05
447	John Mabry	.05
448	T.J. Mathews	.05
449	Willie McGee	.05
450	Donovan Osborne	.05
451	Tom Pagnozzi	.05
452	Ozzie Smith	.60
453	Todd Stottlemyre	.05
454	Mark Sweeney	.05
455	Dmitri Young	.05
456	Andy Ashby	.05
457	Ken Caminiti	.05
458	Archi Cianfrocco	.05
459	Steve Finley	.05
460	John Flaherty	.05
461	Chris Gomez	.05
462	Tony Gwynn	.75
463	Joey Hamilton	.05
464	Rickey Henderson	.25
465	Trevor Hoffman	.05
466	Brian Johnson	.05
467	Wally Joyner	.05
468	Jody Reed	.05
469	Scott Sanders	.05
470	Bob Tewksbury	.05
471	Fernando Valenzuela	.05
472	Greg Vaughn	.05
473	Tim Worrell	.05
474	Rich Aurilla	.05
475	Rod Beck	.05
476	Marvin Benard	.05
477	Barry Bonds	1.00
478	Jay Canizaro	.05
479	Shawon Dunston	.05
480	Shawn Estes	.05
481	Mark Gardner	.05
482	Glenallen Hill	.05
483	Stan Javier	.05
484	Marcus Jensen	.05
485	*Bill Mueller*	.25
486	William VanLandingham	.05
487	Allen Watson	.05
488	Rick Wilkins	.05
489	Matt Williams	.20
489p	Matt Williams ("PROMOTIONAL SAMPLE")	6.00
490	Desi Wilson	.05
491	Checklist (Albert Belle)	.10
492	Checklist (Ken Griffey Jr.)	.75
493	Checklist (Andruw Jones)	.50
494	Checklist (Chipper Jones)	.60
495	Checklist (Mark McGwire)	1.00
496	Checklist (Paul Molitor)	.15
497	Checklist (Mike Piazza)	.60
498	Checklist (Cal Ripken Jr.)	.75
499	Checklist (Alex Rodriguez)	.75
500	Checklist (Frank Thomas)	.50
501	Kenny Lofton	.05
502	Carlos Perez	.05
503	Tim Raines	.05
504	*Danny Patterson*	.10
505	Derrick May	.05
506	Dave Hollins	.05
507	Felipe Crespo	.05
508	Brian Banks	.05
509	Jeff Kent	.05
510	*Bubba Trammell*	.60
511	Robert Person	.05
512	*David Arias* (last name actually Ortiz)	.50
513	Ryan Jones	.05
514	David Justice	.15
515	Will Cunnane	.05
516	Russ Johnson	.05
517	John Burkett	.05
518	*Robinson Checo*	.25
519	*Ricardo Rincon*	.10
520	Woody Williams	.05
521	Rick Helling	.05
522	Jorge Posada	.05
523	Kevin Orie	.05
524	*Fernando Tatis*	.50
525	Jermaine Dye	.10
526	Brian Hunter	.05
527	Greg McMichael	.05
528	Matt Wagner	.05
529	Richie Sexson	.05
530	Scott Ruffcorn	.05
531	Luis Gonzalez	.15
532	Mike Johnson	.05
533	Mark Petkovsek	.05
534	Doug Drabek	.05
535	Jose Canseco	.25
536	Bobby Bonilla	.05
537	J.T. Snow	.10
538	Shawon Dunston	.05
539	John Ericks	.05
540	Terry Steinbach	.05
541	Jay Bell	.05
542	Joe Borowski	.05
543	David Wells	.10
544	*Justin Towle*	.25
545	Mike Blowers	.05
546	Shannon Stewart	.05
547	Rudy Pemberton	.05
548	Bill Swift	.05
549	Osvaldo Fernandez	.05
550	Eddie Murray	.40
551	Don Wengert	.05
552	Brad Ausmus	.05
553	Carlos Garcia	.05
554	Jose Guillen	.25
555	Rheal Cormier	.05
556	Doug Brocail	.05
557	Rex Hudler	.05
558	Armando Benitez	.05
559	Elieser Marrero	.05
560	*Ricky Ledee*	.75
561	Bartolo Colon	.05
562	Quilvio Veras	.05
563	Alex Fernandez	.05
564	Darren Dreifort	.05
565	Benji Gil	.05
566	Kent Mercker	.05
567	Glendon Rusch	.05
568	*Ramon Tatis*	.05
569	Roger Clemens	1.00
570	Mark Lewis	.05
571	*Emil Brown*	.10
572	Jaime Navarro	.05
573	Sherman Obando	.05
574	John Wasdin	.05
575	Calvin Maduro	.05
576	Todd Jones	.05
577	Orlando Merced	.05
578	Cal Eldred	.05
579	Mark Gubicza	.05
580	Michael Tucker	.05
581	*Tony Saunders*	.45
582	Garvin Alston	.05
583	Joe Roa	.05
584	*Brady Raggio*	.05
585	Jimmy Key	.05
586	*Marc Sagmoen*	.05
587	Jim Bullinger	.05
588	Yorkis Perez	.05
589	*Jose Cruz Jr.*	.75
590	Mike Stanton	.05
591	*Deivi Cruz*	.50
592	Steve Karsay	.05
593	Mike Trombley	.05
594	Doug Glanville	.05
595	Scott Sanders	.05
596	Thomas Howard	.05
597	T.J. Staton	.05
598	Garrett Stephenson	.05
599	Rico Brogna	.05
600	Albert Belle	.20
601	Jose Vizcaino	.05
602	Chili Davis	.05
603	Shane Mack	.05
604	Jim Eisenreich	.05
605	Todd Zeile	.05
606	Brian Boehringer	.05
607	Paul Shuey	.05
608	Kevin Tapani	.05
609	John Wetteland	.05
610	Jim Leyritz	.05
611	Ray Montgomery	.05
612	Doug Bochtler	.05
613	Wady Almonte	.05
614	Danny Tartabull	.05
615	Orlando Miller	.05
616	Bobby Ayala	.05
617	Tony Graffanino	.05
618	Marc Valdes	.05
619	Ron Villone	.05
620	Derrek Lee	.05
621	Greg Colbrunn	.05
622	*Felix Heredia*	.25
623	Carl Everett	.10
624	Mark Thompson	.05
625	Jeff Granger	.05
626	Damian Jackson	.05
627	Mark Leiter	.05
628	Chris Holt	.05
629	*Dario Veras*	.10
630	Dave Burba	.05
631	Darryl Hamilton	.05
632	Mark Acre	.05
633	Fernando Hernandez	.05
634	Terry Mulholland	.05
635	Dustin Hermanson	.05
636	Delino DeShields	.05
637	Steve Avery	.05
638	*Tony Womack*	.25
639	Mark Whiten	.05
640	Marquis Grissom	.05
641	Xavier Hernandez	.05
642	Eric Davis	.05
643	Bob Tewksbury	.05
644	Dante Powell	.05
645	Carlos Castillo	.05
646	Chris Widger	.05
647	Moises Alou	.10
648	Pat Listach	.05
649	Edgar Ramos	.05
650	Deion Sanders	.15
651	John Olerud	.05

652	Todd Dunwoody	.10
653	*Randall Simon*	.10
654	Dan Carlson	.05
655	Matt Williams	.20
656	Jeff King	.05
657	Luis Alicea	.05
658	Brian Moehler	.05
659	Ariel Prieto	.05
660	Kevin Elster	.05
661	Mark Hutton	.05
662	Aaron Sele	.05
663	Graeme Lloyd	.05
664	John Burke	.05
665	Mel Rojas	.05
666	Sid Fernandez	.05
667	Pedro Astacio	.05
668	Jeff Abbott	.05
669	Darren Daulton	.05
670	Mike Bordick	.05
671	Sterling Hitchcock	.05
672	Damion Easley	.05
673	Armando Reynoso	.05
674	Pat Cline	.05
675	*Orlando Cabrera*	.30
676	Alan Embree	.05
677	Brian Bevil	.05
678	David Weathers	.05
679	Cliff Floyd	.05
680	Joe Randa	.05
681	Bill Haselman	.05
682	Jeff Fassero	.05
683	Matt Morris	.05
684	Mark Portugal	.05
685	Lee Smith	.05
686	Pokey Reese	.05
687	Benito Santiago	.05
688	Brian Johnson	.05
689	*Brent Brede*	.05
690	Shigetosi Hasegawa	.05
691	Julio Santana	.05
692	Steve Kline	.05
693	Julian Tavarez	.05
694	John Hudek	.05
695	Manny Alexander	.05
696	Roberto Alomar (Encore)	.25
697	Jeff Bagwell (Encore)	.45
698	Barry Bonds (Encore)	.75
699	Ken Caminiti (Encore)	.05
700	Juan Gonzalez (Encore)	.40
701	Ken Griffey Jr. (Encore)	1.25
702	Tony Gwynn (Encore)	.45
703	Derek Jeter (Encore)	1.00
704	Andruw Jones (Encore)	.40
705	Chipper Jones (Encore)	1.00
706	Barry Larkin (Encore)	.05
707	Greg Maddux (Encore)	1.00
708	Mark McGwire (Encore)	1.50
709	Paul Molitor (Encore)	.15
710	Hideo Nomo (Encore)	.50
711	Andy Pettitte (Encore)	.25
712	Mike Piazza (Encore)	1.00
713	Manny Ramirez (Encore)	.50
714	Cal Ripken Jr. (Encore)	1.25
715	Alex Rodriguez (Encore)	1.25
716	Ryne Sandberg (Encore)	.40
717	John Smoltz (Encore)	.05
718	Frank Thomas (Encore)	.75
719	Mo Vaughn (Encore)	.20
720	Bernie Williams (Encore)	.25
721	Checklist (Tim Salmon)	.05
722	Checklist (Greg Maddux)	.50
723	Checklist (Cal Ripken Jr.)	.75
724	Checklist (Mo Vaughn)	.20
725	Checklist (Ryne Sandberg)	.25
726	Checklist (Frank Thomas)	.50
727	Checklist (Barry Larkin)	.05
728	Checklist (Manny Ramirez)	.30
729	Checklist (Andres Galarraga)	.05
730	Checklist (Tony Clark)	.05
731	Checklist (Gary Sheffield)	.10
732	Checklist (Jeff Bagwell)	.40
733	Checklist (Kevin Appier)	.05
734	Checklist (Mike Piazza)	.50
735	Checklist (Jeff Cirillo)	.05
736	Checklist (Paul Molitor)	.15
737	Checklist (Henry Rodriguez)	.05
738	Checklist (Todd Hundley)	.05
739	Checklist (Derek Jeter)	.60
740	Checklist (Mark McGwire)	.75
741	Checklist (Curt Schilling)	.05
742	Checklist (Jason Kendall)	.05
743	Checklist (Tony Gwynn)	.40
744	Checklist (Barry Bonds)	.50
745	Checklist (Ken Griffey Jr.)	.75
746	Checklist (Brian Jordan)	.05
747	Checklist (Juan Gonzalez)	.40
748	Checklist (Joe Carter)	.05
749	Arizona Diamondbacks	.05
750	Tampa Bay Devil Rays	.05
751	*Hideki Irabu*	.30
752	*Jeremi Gonzalez*	.50
753	*Mario Valdez*	.25
754	Aaron Boone	.05
755	Brett Tomko	.05
756	*Jaret Wright*	2.00
757	Ryan McGuire	.05
758	Jason McDonald	.05
759	*Adrian Brown*	.15
760	*Keith Foulke*	.25
761	Checklist	.05

1997 Fleer Tiffany

Insertion odds were considerably lengthened for the UV-coated Tiffany Collection parallels in 1997 Fleer - to one card per 20 packs.

	MT
Complete Set (761):	1500.
Common Player:	2.00
Stars/Rcs:	20X

(See 1997 Fleer for checklist and base card values.)

1997 Fleer Bleacher Blasters

This 10-card insert features some of the game's top power hitters and was found in retail packs only. Cards featured a die-cut "burst" pattern on an etched foil background. Backs have a portrait photo and career highlights. Cards were inserted 1:36 packs.

		MT
Complete Set (10):		20.00
Common Player:		.75
1	Albert Belle	.75
2	Barry Bonds	2.00
3	Juan Gonzalez	1.25
4	Ken Griffey Jr.	4.00
5	Mark McGwire	5.00
6	Mike Piazza	3.00
7	Alex Rodriguez	5.00
8	Frank Thomas	2.00
9	Mo Vaughn	1.00
10	Matt Williams	.75

1997 Fleer Decade of Excellence

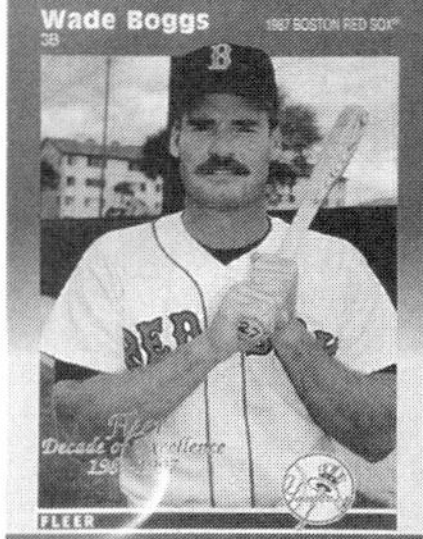

A 12-card insert found 1:36 in hobby shop packs, cards are in a format similar to the 1987 Fleer set and feature vintage photos of players who started their careers no later than the '87 season. Ten percent of the press run (1:360 packs) received a special foil treatment and designation as "Rare Traditions."

		MT
Complete Set (12):		70.00
Common Player:		3.00
Rare Tradition:		15X
1	Wade Boggs	5.00
2	Barry Bonds	10.00
3	Roger Clemens	10.00
4	Tony Gwynn	10.00
5	Rickey Henderson	4.00
6	Greg Maddux	10.00
7	Mark McGwire	15.00
8	Paul Molitor	5.00
9	Eddie Murray	4.00
10	Cal Ripken Jr.	15.00
11	Ryne Sandberg	6.00
12	Matt Williams	3.00

1997 Fleer Diamond Tribute

Twelve of the game's top stars are highlighted in this set. Fronts feature an embossed rainbow prismatic foil background and gold lettering. Backs have an action photo and a few sentences about the player. They were inserted 1:288 packs.

		MT
Complete Set (12):		160.00
Common Player:		4.00
1	Albert Belle	4.00
2	Barry Bonds	10.00
3	Juan Gonzalez	7.50
4	Ken Griffey Jr.	30.00
5	Tony Gwynn	17.50
6	Greg Maddux	20.00
7	Mark McGwire	30.00
8	Eddie Murray	4.00
9	Mike Piazza	22.50
10	Cal Ripken Jr.	25.00
11	Alex Rodriguez	25.00
12	Frank Thomas	15.00

1997 Fleer Golden Memories

Golden Memories captures 10 different highlights from the 1996 season, and is inserted one per 16 packs. Moments like Dwight Gooden's no hitter, Paul Molitor's 3000th hit and Eddie Murray's 500th home run are highlighted on a horizontal format.

		MT
Complete Set (10):		10.00
Common Player:		.40
1	Barry Bonds	1.50
2	Dwight Gooden	.40
3	Todd Hundley	.50
4	Mark McGwire	3.00
5	Paul Molitor	1.00
6	Eddie Murray	.75

7	Hideo Nomo	1.00
8	Mike Piazza	2.00
9	Cal Ripken Jr.	2.50
10	Ozzie Smith	1.50

1997 Fleer Goudey Greats

Using a 2-3/8" x 2-7/8" format reminiscent of 1933 Goudey cards, this 15-card insert offers today's top players in classic old-time design. Cards were inserted 1:8 packs. A limited number (1% of press run) of cards received a special gold-foil treatment and were found only in hobby packs.

		MT
Complete Set (15):		25.00
Common Player:		.50
Foils:		20X
1	Barry Bonds	1.00
2	Ken Griffey Jr.	3.00
3	Tony Gwynn	1.50
4	Derek Jeter	3.00
5	Chipper Jones	2.50
6	Kenny Lofton	.50
7	Greg Maddux	2.00
8	Mark McGwire	4.00
9	Eddie Murray	.50
10	Mike Piazza	3.00
11	Cal Ripken Jr.	4.00
12	Alex Rodriguez	4.00
13	Ryne Sandberg	1.00
14	Frank Thomas	1.50
15	Mo Vaughn	.75

1997 Fleer Headliners

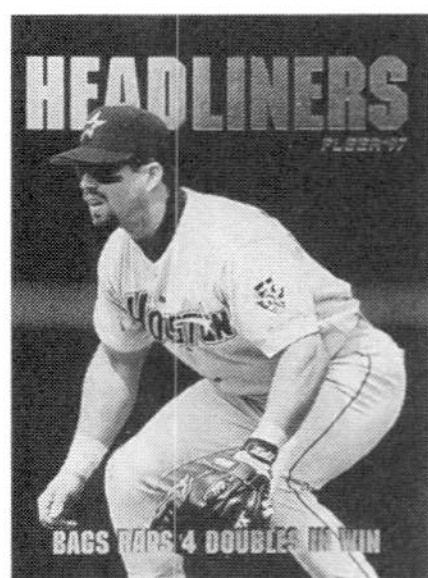

This 20-card insert highlights the personal achievements of each of the players depicted. Cards were inserted 1:2 packs and feature multi-color foil stamping on the fronts and a newspaper-style account of the player's achievement on the back.

		MT
Complete Set (20):		6.00
Common Player:		.10
1	Jeff Bagwell	.25
2	Albert Belle	.15
3	Barry Bonds	.50
4	Ken Caminiti	.10
5	Juan Gonzalez	.25
6	Ken Griffey Jr.	.75
7	Tony Gwynn	.40
8	Derek Jeter	.75
9	Andruw Jones	.25
10	Chipper Jones	.60
11	Greg Maddux	.50
12	Mark McGwire	1.00
13	Paul Molitor	.20
14	Eddie Murray	.15
15	Mike Piazza	.60
16	Cal Ripken Jr.	1.00
17	Alex Rodriguez	1.00
18	Ryne Sandberg	.25
19	John Smoltz	.10
20	Frank Thomas	.40

1997 Fleer Lumber Company

Lumber Company inserts were found every 48 retail packs. The cards were printed on a die-cut, spherical wood-like pattern, with the player imposed on the left side. Eighteen of the top power hitters in baseball are highlighted.

		MT
Complete Set (18):		50.00
Common Player:		1.00
1	Brady Anderson	1.00
2	Jeff Bagwell	3.50
3	Albert Belle	2.00
4	Barry Bonds	5.00
5	Jay Buhner	1.00
6	Ellis Burks	1.00
7	Andres Galarraga	1.00
8	Juan Gonzalez	3.00
9	Ken Griffey Jr.	8.50
10	Todd Hundley	1.00
11	Ryan Klesko	1.00
12	Mark McGwire	10.00
13	Mike Piazza	6.50
14	Alex Rodriguez	8.50
15	Gary Sheffield	1.25
16	Sammy Sosa	6.50
17	Frank Thomas	3.50
18	Mo Vaughn	2.00

1997 Fleer New Horizons

Rookies and prospects expected to make an impact during the 1996 season were featured in this 15-card insert set. Card fronts feature a rainbow foil background with the words "New Horizon" featured prominently on the bottom under the player's name. Cards were inserted 1:4 packs.

		MT
Complete Set (15):		3.00
Common Player:		.05
1	Bob Abreu	.10
2	Jose Cruz Jr.	.25
3	Darin Erstad	.30
4	Nomar Garciaparra	.50
5	Vladimir Guerrero	.50
6	Wilton Guerrero	.05
7	Jose Guillen	.25
8	Hideki Irabu	.25
9	Andruw Jones	.50
10	Kevin Orie	.05
11	Scott Rolen	.40
12	Scott Spiezio	.05
13	Bubba Trammell	.15
14	Todd Walker	.05
15	Dmitri Young	.05

1997 Fleer Night & Day

Night and Day spotlighted 10 stars with unusual prowess during night or day games. These lenticular cards carried the toughest insert ratios in Fleer Baseball at one per 288 packs.

		MT
Complete Set (10):		75.00
Common Player:		2.50
1	Barry Bonds	7.50
2	Ellis Burks	2.50
3	Juan Gonzalez	5.00
4	Ken Griffey Jr.	15.00
5	Mark McGwire	15.00
6	Mike Piazza	12.50
7	Manny Ramirez	5.00
8	Alex Rodriguez	15.00
9	John Smoltz	2.50
10	Frank Thomas	7.50

1997 Fleer Rookie Sensations

Rookies Sensations showcased 20 of the top up-and-coming stars in baseball. Appearing every six packs, these inserts have the feaured player in the foreground, with the background look of painted brush strokes.

		MT
Complete Set (20):		13.50
Common Player:		.30
1	Jermaine Allensworth	.30
2	James Baldwin	.30
3	Alan Benes	.30
4	Jermaine Dye	.40
5	Darin Erstad	1.50
6	Todd Hollandsworth	.30
7	Derek Jeter	3.00
8	Jason Kendall	.50
9	Alex Ochoa	.30
10	Rey Ordonez	.75
11	Edgar Renteria	.45
12	Bob Abreu	1.25
13	Nomar Garciaparra	2.50
14	Wilton Guerrero	.30
15	Andruw Jones	2.50
16	Wendell Magee	.30
17	Neifi Perez	.30
18	Scott Rolen	2.00
19	Scott Spiezio	.30
20	Todd Walker	.45

1997 Fleer Soaring Stars

A 12-card insert found 1:12 packs designed to profile players with outstanding statistical performances early in their careers. Fronts have player action photos set against a background of rainbow holographic stars which appear, disappear and twinkle as the viewing angle is changed. Conventionally printed backs have another player photo and a few sentences about his career. A parallel version on which the background stars glow was issued at a greatly reduced rate.

		MT
Complete Set (12):		13.00
Common Player:		.30
Glowing:		15X
1	Albert Belle	.30
2	Barry Bonds	1.25
3	Juan Gonzalez	.60
4	Ken Griffey Jr.	2.00
5	Derek Jeter	2.00
6	Andruw Jones	.75
7	Chipper Jones	1.50
8	Greg Maddux	1.25
9	Mark McGwire	2.50
10	Mike Piazza	1.50
11	Alex Rodriguez	2.50
12	Frank Thomas	1.00

1997 Fleer Team Leaders

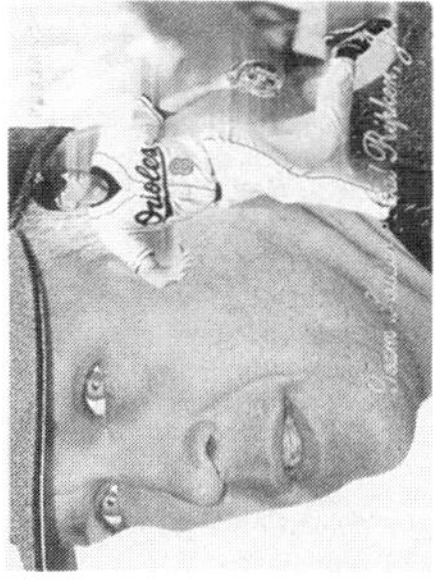

Team Leaders captured the statistical and/or inspirational leaders from all 28 teams. Inserted every 20 packs, these inserts were printed on a horizontal format, with the player's face die-cut in the perimeter of the card.

		MT
Complete Set (28):		18.00
Common Player:		.30
1	Cal Ripken Jr.	2.50
2	Mo Vaughn	.40
3	Jim Edmonds	.35
4	Frank Thomas	1.50
5	Albert Belle	.40
6	Bob Higginson	.30
7	Kevin Appier	.30
8	John Jaha	.30
9	Paul Molitor	.50
10	Andy Pettitte	.40
11	Mark McGwire	3.50
12	Ken Griffey Jr.	2.50
13	Juan Gonzalez	.75
14	Pat Hentgen	.30
15	Chipper Jones	1.75
16	Mark Grace	.50
17	Barry Larkin	.30
18	Ellis Burks	.30
19	Gary Sheffield	.45
20	Jeff Bagwell	1.25
21	Mike Piazza	1.75
22	Henry Rodriguez	.30
23	Todd Hundley	.30
24	Curt Schilling	.35
25	Jeff King	.30
26	Brian Jordan	.30
27	Tony Gwynn	1.50
28	Barry Bonds	1.00

1997 Fleer Zone

Twenty of the top hitters in baseball are featured on these holographic cards with the words Zone printed across the front. Zone inserts were found only in hobby packs at a rate of one per 80.

		MT
Complete Set (20):		70.00
Common Player:		1.50
1	Jeff Bagwell	4.50
2	Albert Belle	2.00
3	Barry Bonds	5.00
4	Ken Caminiti	1.50
5	Andres Galarraga	1.50
6	Juan Gonzalez	4.00
7	Ken Griffey Jr.	12.00
8	Tony Gwynn	5.00
9	Chipper Jones	7.50
10	Greg Maddux	6.50
11	Mark McGwire	12.50
12	Dean Palmer	1.50
13	Andy Petitte	2.00
14	Mike Piazza	7.50
15	Alex Rodriguez	12.00
16	Gary Sheffield	2.00
17	John Smoltz	1.50
18	Frank Thomas	5.00
19	Jim Thome	1.50
20	Matt Williams	1.75

1998 Fleer

Fleer was issued in two series in 1998, with 350 cards in Series 1 and 250 in Series 2. Each card features a borderless color action shot, with backs containing player information. Subsets in Series 1 included Smoke 'N Heat (301-310), Golden Memories (311-320) and Tale of the Tape (321-340). Golden Memories (1:6 packs) and Tale of the Tape (1:4) were shortprinted. Series 2 subsets included 25 shortprinted (1:4) Unforgetable Moments (571-595). Inserts in Series 1 were Vintage '63, Vintage '63 Classic, Decade of Excellence, Decade of Excellence Rare Traditions, Diamond Ink, Diamond Standouts, Lumber Company, Power Game, Rookie Sensations and Zone. Series 2 inserts include: Vintage '63, Vintage '63 Classic, Promising Forecast, In the Clutch, Mickey Mantle: Monumental Moments, Mickey Mantle: Monumental Moments Gold Edition, Diamond Tribute and Diamond Ink.

		MT
Complete Set (600):		100.00
Complete Series 1 (350):		60.00
Complete Series 2 (250):		40.00
Common Player:		.10
Series 1 or 2 Pack (10):		1.50
Series 1 or 2 Wax Box (36):		45.00
1	Ken Griffey Jr.	2.50
2	Derek Jeter	2.00
3	Gerald Williams	.10
4	Carlos Delgado	.75
5	Nomar Garciaparra	1.50
6	Gary Sheffield	.25
7	Jeff King	.10
8	Cal Ripken Jr.	2.50
9	Matt Williams	.25
10	Chipper Jones	1.50
11	Chuck Knoblauch	.10
12	Mark Grudzielanek	.10
13	Edgardo Alfonzo	.15
14	Andres Galarraga	.10
15	Tim Salmon	.15
16	Reggie Sanders	.10
17	Tony Clark	.10
18	Jason Kendall	.15
19	Juan Gonzalez	.75
20	Ben Grieve	.25
21	Roger Clemens	1.00
22	Raul Mondesi	.20
23	Robin Ventura	.10
24	Derrek Lee	.10
25	Mark McGwire	3.00
26	Luis Gonzalez	.20
27	Kevin Brown	.20
28	Kirk Rueter	.10
29	Bobby Estalella	.10
30	Shawn Green	.20
31	Greg Maddux	1.50
32	Jorge Velandia	.10
33	Larry Walker	.25
34	Joey Cora	.10
35	Frank Thomas	1.00
36	*Curtis King*	.10
37	Aaron Boone	.10
38	Curt Schilling	.15
39	Bruce Aven	.10
40	Ben McDonald	.10
41	Andy Ashby	.10
42	Jason McDonald	.10
43	Eric Davis	.10
44	Mark Grace	.25
45	Pedro Martinez	.75
46	Lou Collier	.10
47	Chan Ho Park	.20
48	Shane Halter	.10
49	Brian Hunter	.10
50	Jeff Bagwell	.75
51	Bernie Williams	.50
52	J.T. Snow	.15
53	Todd Greene	.10
54	Shannon Stewart	.10
55	Darren Bragg	.10
56	Fernando Tatis	.20
57	Darryl Kile	.10
58	Chris Stynes	.10
59	Javier Valentin	.10
60	Brian McRae	.10
61	Tom Evans	.10
62	Randall Simon	.10
63	Darrin Fletcher	.10
64	Jaret Wright	.20
65	Luis Ordaz	.10
66	Jose Canseco	.30
67	Edgar Renteria	.10
68	Jay Buhner	.10
69	Paul Konerko	.20
70	Adrian Brown	.10
71	Chris Carpenter	.10
72	Mike Lieberthal	.15
73	Dean Palmer	.10
74	Jorge Fabregas	.10
75	Stan Javier	.10
76	Damion Easley	.10
77	David Cone	.10
78	Aaron Sele	.10
79	Antonio Alfonseca	.10
80	Bobby Jones	.10
81	David Justice	.25
82	Jeffrey Hammonds	.10
83	Doug Glanville	.10
84	Jason Dickson	.10
85	Brad Radke	.15
86	David Segui	.10
87	Greg Vaughn	.10
88	*Mike Cather*	.20
89	Alex Fernandez	.10
90	Billy Taylor	.10
91	Jason Schmidt	.10
92	*Mike DeJean*	.10
93	Domingo Cedeno	.10
94	Jeff Cirillo	.10
95	*Manny Aybar*	.25
96	Jaime Navarro	.10
97	Dennis Reyes	.10
98	Barry Larkin	.20
99	Troy O'Leary	.10
100	Alex Rodriguez	2.50
100p	Alex Rodriguez (pver-printed PROMOTIONAL SAMPLE)	3.00
101	Pat Hentgen	.10
102	Bubba Trammell	.20
103	Glendon Rusch	.10
104	Kenny Lofton	.10
105	Craig Biggio	.15
106	Kelvim Escobar	.10
107	Mark Kotsay	.20
108	Rondell White	.20
109	Darren Oliver	.10
110	Jim Thome	.10
111	Rich Becker	.10
112	Chad Curtis	.10
113	Dave Hollins	.10
114	Bill Mueller	.10
115	Antone Williamson	.10
116	Tony Womack	.10
117	Randy Myers	.10
118	Rico Brogna	.10
119	Pat Watkins	.10
120	Eli Marrero	.10
121	Jay Bell	.10
122	Kevin Tapani	.10
123	*Todd Erdos*	.20
124	Neifi Perez	.10
125	Todd Hundley	.10
126	Jeff Abbott	.10
127	Todd Zeile	.10
128	Travis Fryman	.10
129	Sandy Alomar	.10
130	Fred McGriff	.10
131	Richard Hidalgo	.15
132	Scott Spiezio	.10
133	John Valentin	.10
134	Quilvio Veras	.10
135	Mike Lansing	.10
136	Paul Molitor	.50
137	Randy Johnson	.75
138	Harold Baines	.10
139	Doug Jones	.10
140	Abraham Nunez	.25
141	Alan Benes	.10
142	Matt Perisho	.10
143	Chris Clemons	.10
144	Andy Pettitte	.40
145	Jason Giambi	.25
146	Moises Alou	.20
147	*Chad Fox*	.25
148	Felix Martinez	.10
149	*Carlos Mendoza*	.25
150	Scott Rolen	.60
151	*Jose Cabrera*	.20
152	Justin Thompson	.10
153	Ellis Burks	.10
154	Pokey Reese	.10
155	Bartolo Colon	.10
156	Ray Durham	.10
157	Ugueth Urbina	.10
158	Tom Goodwin	.10
159	*David Dellucci*	.40
160	Rod Beck	.10
161	Ramon Martinez	.10
162	Joe Carter	.10
163	Kevin Orie	.10
164	Trevor Hoffman	.10
165	Emil Brown	.10
166	Robb Nen	.10
167	Paul O'Neill	.10
168	Ryan Long	.10

No.	Player	Price
169	Ray Lankford	.10
170	Ivan Rodriguez	.60
171	Rick Aguilera	.10
172	Deivi Cruz	.10
173	Ricky Bottalico	.10
174	Garret Anderson	.10
175	Jose Vizcaino	.10
176	Omar Vizquel	.10
177	Jeff Blauser	.10
178	Orlando Cabrera	.10
179	Russ Johnson	.10
180	Matt Stairs	.10
181	Will Cunnane	.10
182	Adam Riggs	.10
183	Matt Morris	.10
184	Mario Valdez	.10
185	Larry Sutton	.10
186	*Marc Pisciotta*	.10
187	Dan Wilson	.10
188	John Franco	.10
189	Darren Daulton	.10
190	Todd Helton	.60
191	Brady Anderson	.10
192	Ricardo Rincon	.10
193	Kevin Stocker	.10
194	Jose Valentin	.10
195	Ed Sprague	.10
196	Ryan McGuire	.10
197	*Scott Eyre*	.25
198	Steve Finley	.10
199	T.J. Mathews	.10
200	Mike Piazza	2.00
201	Mark Wohlers	.10
202	Brian Giles	.10
203	Eduardo Perez	.10
204	Shigetosi Hasegawa	.10
205	Mariano Rivera	.25
206	Jose Rosado	.10
207	Michael Coleman	.10
208	James Baldwin	.10
209	Russ Davis	.10
210	Billy Wagner	.10
211	Sammy Sosa	1.50
212	*Frank Catalanotto*	.25
213	Delino DeShields	.10
214	John Olerud	.10
215	Heath Murray	.10
216	Jose Vidro	.10
217	Jim Edmonds	.25
218	Shawon Dunston	.10
219	Homer Bush	.10
220	Midre Cummings	.10
221	Tony Saunders	.10
222	Jeromy Burnitz	.10
223	Enrique Wilson	.10
224	Chili Davis	.10
225	Jerry DiPoto	.10
226	Dante Powell	.10
227	Javier Lopez	.10
228	*Kevin Polcovich*	.20
229	Deion Sanders	.15
230	Jimmy Key	.10
231	Rusty Greer	.10
232	Reggie Jefferson	.10
233	Ron Coomer	.10
234	Bobby Higginson	.20
235	*Magglio Ordonez*	2.00
236	Miguel Tejada	.40
237	Rick Gorecki	.10
238	Charles Johnson	.10
239	Lance Johnson	.10
240	Derek Bell	.10
241	Will Clark	.30
242	Brady Raggio	.10
243	Orel Hershiser	.10
244	Vladimir Guerrero	.60
245	John LeRoy	.10
246	Shawn Estes	.10
247	Brett Tomko	.10
248	Dave Nilsson	.10
249	Edgar Martinez	.10
250	Tony Gwynn	1.00
251	Mark Bellhorn	.10
252	Jed Hansen	.10
253	Butch Huskey	.10
254	Eric Young	.10
255	Vinny Castilla	.10
256	Hideki Irabu	.15
257	Mike Cameron	.10
258	Juan Encarnacion	.25
259	Brian Rose	.25
260	Brad Ausmus	.10
261	Dan Serafini	.10
262	Willie Greene	.10
263	Troy Percival	.10
264	*Jeff Wallace*	.20
265	Richie Sexson	.10
266	Rafael Palmeiro	.35
267	Brad Fullmer	.10
268	Jeremi Gonzalez	.10
269	*Rob Stanifer*	.25
270	Mickey Morandini	.10
271	Andruw Jones	.60
272	Royce Clayton	.10
273	Takashi Kashiwada	.25
274	*Steve Woodard*	.25
275	Jose Cruz Jr.	.35
276	Keith Foulke	.10
277	Brad Rigby	.10
278	Tino Martinez	.10
279	Todd Jones	.10
280	John Wetteland	.10
281	Alex Gonzalez	.15
282	Ken Cloude	.10
283	Jose Guillen	.25
284	Danny Clyburn	.10
285	David Ortiz	.10
286	John Thomson	.10
287	Kevin Appier	.10
288	Ismael Valdes	.10
289	Gary DiSarcina	.10
290	Todd Dunwoody	.10
291	Wally Joyner	.10
292	Charles Nagy	.10
293	Jeff Shaw	.10
294	*Kevin Millwood*	2.50
295	*Rigo Beltran*	.20
296	Jeff Frye	.10
297	Oscar Henriquez	.10
298	Mike Thurman	.10
299	Garrett Stephenson	.10
300	Barry Bonds	1.00
301	Roger Clemens (Smoke 'N Heat)	.50
302	David Cone (Smoke 'N Heat)	.15
303	Hideki Irabu (Smoke 'N Heat)	.15
304	Randy Johnson (Smoke 'N Heat)	.20
305	Greg Maddux (Smoke 'N Heat)	1.00
306	Pedro Martinez (Smoke 'N Heat)	.35
307	Mike Mussina (Smoke 'N Heat)	.30
308	Andy Pettitte (Smoke 'N Heat)	.25
309	Curt Schilling (Smoke 'N Heat)	.15
310	John Smoltz (Smoke 'N Heat)	.15
311	Roger Clemens (Golden Memories)	.60
312	Jose Cruz Jr. (Golden Memories)	.25
313	Nomar Garciaparra (Golden Memories)	1.00
314	Ken Griffey Jr. (Golden Memories)	1.50
315	Tony Gwynn (Golden Memories)	.60
316	Hideki Irabu (Golden Memories)	.25
317	Randy Johnson (Golden Memories)	.75
318	Mark McGwire (Golden Memories)	2.50
319	Curt Schilling (Golden Memories)	.25
320	Larry Walker (Golden Memories)	.25
321	Jeff Bagwell (Tale of the Tape)	.60
322	Albert Belle (Tale of the Tape)	.25
323	Barry Bonds (Tale of the Tape)	.75
324	Jay Buhner (Tale of the Tape)	.15
325	Tony Clark (Tale of the Tape)	.20
326	Jose Cruz Jr. (Tale of the Tape)	.30
327	Andres Galarraga (Tale of the Tape)	.15
328	Juan Gonzalez (Tale of the Tape)	.50
329	Ken Griffey Jr. (Tale of the Tape)	1.50
330	Andruw Jones (Tale of the Tape)	.60
331	Tino Martinez (Tale of the Tape)	.15
332	Mark McGwire (Tale of the Tape)	2.00
333	Rafael Palmeiro (Tale of the Tape)	.25
334	Mike Piazza (Tale of the Tape)	1.25
335	Manny Ramirez (Tale of the Tape)	.50
336	Alex Rodriguez (Tale of the Tape)	1.50
337	Frank Thomas (Tale of the Tape)	.75
338	Jim Thome (Tale of the Tape)	.15
339	Mo Vaughn (Tale of the Tape)	.40
340	Larry Walker (Tale of the Tape)	.15
341	Checklist (Jose Cruz Jr.)	.25
342	Checklist (Ken Griffey Jr.)	1.00
343	Checklist (Derek Jeter)	1.00
344	Checklist (Andruw Jones)	.45
345	Checklist (Chipper Jones)	.60
346	Checklist (Greg Maddux)	.50
347	Checklist (Mike Piazza)	.60
348	Checklist (Cal Ripken Jr.)	1.00
349	Checklist (Alex Rodriguez)	1.00
350	Checklist (Frank Thomas)	.50
351	Mo Vaughn	.30
352	Andres Galarraga	.10
353	Roberto Alomar	.40
354	Darin Erstad	.75
355	Albert Belle	.25
356	Matt Williams	.25
357	Darryl Kile	.10
358	Kenny Lofton	.10
359	Orel Hershiser	.10
360	Bob Abreu	.10
361	Chris Widger	.10
362	Glenallen Hill	.10
363	Chili Davis	.10
364	Kevin Brown	.15
365	Marquis Grissom	.10
366	Livan Hernandez	.10
367	Moises Alou	.20
368	Matt Lawton	.10
369	Rey Ordonez	.10
370	Kenny Rogers	.10
371	Lee Stevens	.10
372	Wade Boggs	.25
373	Luis Gonzalez	.10
374	Jeff Conine	.10
375	Esteban Loaiza	.10
376	Jose Canseco	.25
377	Henry Rodriguez	.10
378	Dave Burba	.10
379	Todd Hollandsworth	.10
380	Ron Gant	.10
381	Pedro Martinez	.75
382	Ryan Klesko	.10
383	Derrek Lee	.10
384	Doug Glanville	.10
385	David Wells	.10
386	Ken Caminiti	.10
387	Damon Hollins	.10
388	Manny Ramirez	.75
389	Mike Mussina	.60
390	Jay Bell	.10
391	Mike Piazza	2.00
392	Mike Lansing	.10
393	Mike Hampton	.10
394	Geoff Jenkins	.10
395	Jimmy Haynes	.10
396	Scott Servais	.10
397	Kent Mercker	.10
398	Jeff Kent	.10
399	Kevin Elster	.10
400	*Masato Yoshii*	.75
401	Jose Vizcaino	.10
402	Javier Martinez	.10
403	David Segui	.10
404	Tony Saunders	.10
405	Karim Garcia	.10
406	Armando Benitez	.10
407	Joe Randa	.10
408	Vic Darensbourg	.10
409	Sean Casey	.20
410	Eric Milton	.20
411	Trey Moore	.10
412	Mike Stanley	.10
413	Tom Gordon	.10
414	Hal Morris	.10
415	Braden Looper	.10
416	Mike Kelly	.10
417	John Smoltz	.15
418	Roger Cedeno	.10
419	Al Leiter	.10
420	Chuck Knoblauch	.10
421	Felix Rodriguez	.10
422	Bip Roberts	.10
423	Ken Hill	.10
424	Jermaine Allensworth	.10
425	Esteban Yan	.10
426	Scott Karl	.10
427	Sean Berry	.10
428	Rafael Medina	.10
429	Javier Vazquez	.10
430	Rickey Henderson	.45
431	*Adam Butler*	.10
432	Todd Stottlemyre	.10
433	Yamil Benitez	.10
434	Sterling Hitchcock	.10
435	Paul Sorrento	.10
436	Bobby Ayala	.10
437	Tim Raines	.10
438	Chris Hoiles	.10
439	Rod Beck	.10
440	Donnie Sadler	.10
441	Charles Johnson	.10
442	Russ Ortiz	.10
443	Pedro Astacio	.10
444	Wilson Alvarez	.10
445	Mike Blowers	.10
446	Todd Zeile	.10
447	Mel Rojas	.10
448	F.P. Santangelo	.10
449	Dmitri Young	.10
450	Brian Anderson	.10
451	Cecil Fielder	.10
452	Roberto Hernandez	.10
453	Todd Walker	.20
454	Tyler Green	.10
455	Jorge Posada	.10
456	Geronimo Berroa	.10
457	Jose Silva	.10
458	Bobby Bonilla	.10
459	Walt Weiss	.10
460	Darren Dreifort	.10
461	B.J. Surhoff	.10
462	Quinton McCracken	.10
463	Derek Lowe	.10
464	Jorge Fabregas	.10
465	Joey Hamilton	.10
466	Brian Jordan	.10
467	Allen Watson	.10
468	John Jaha	.10
469	Heathcliff Slocumb	.10
470	Gregg Jefferies	.10
471	Scott Brosius	.10
472	Chad Ogea	.10
473	A.J. Hinch	.15
474	Bobby Smith	.10
475	Brian Moehler	.10
476	DaRond Stovall	.10
477	Kevin Young	.10
478	Jeff Suppan	.10
479	Marty Cordova	.10
480	*John Halama*	.25
481	Bubba Trammell	.10
482	Mike Caruso	.10
483	Eric Karros	.10
484	Jamey Wright	.10
485	Mike Sweeney	.10
486	Aaron Sele	.10
487	Cliff Floyd	.10
488	Jeff Brantley	.10
489	Jim Leyritz	.10
490	Denny Neagle	.10
491	Travis Fryman	.10
492	Carlos Baerga	.10
493	Eddie Taubensee	.10
494	Darryl Strawberry	.10
495	Brian Johnson	.10
496	Randy Myers	.10
497	Jeff Blauser	.10
498	Jason Wood	.10
499	*Rolando Arrojo*	.65
500	Johnny Damon	.10
501	Jose Mercedes	.10

502 Tony Batista .10
503 Mike Piazza 2.00
504 Hideo Nomo .60
505 Chris Gomez .10
506 *Jesus Sanchez* .10
507 Al Martin .10
508 Brian Edmondson .10
509 Joe Girardi .10
510 Shayne Bennett .10
511 Joe Carter .10
512 Dave Mlicki .10
513 *Rich Butler* .25
514 Dennis Eckersley .10
515 Travis Lee .25
516 John Mabry .10
517 Jose Mesa .10
518 Phil Nevin .10
519 Raul Casanova .10
520 Mike Fetters .10
521 Gary Sheffield .25
522 Terry Steinbach .10
523 Steve Trachsel .10
524 Josh Booty .10
525 Darryl Hamilton .10
526 Mark McLemore .10
527 Kevin Stocker .10
528 Bret Boone .15
529 Shane Andrews .10
530 Robb Nen .10
531 Carl Everett .15
532 LaTroy Hawkins .10
533 Fernando Vina .10
534 Michael Tucker .10
535 Mark Langston .10
536 Mickey Mantle 3.00
537 Bernard Gilkey .10
538 Francisco Cordova .10
539 Mike Bordick .10
540 Fred McGriff .10
541 Cliff Politte .10
542 Jason Varitek .10
543 Shawon Dunston .10
544 Brian Meadows .10
545 Pat Meares .10
546 Carlos Perez .10
547 Desi Relaford .10
548 Antonio Osuna .10
549 Devon White .10
550 Sean Runyan .10
551 Mickey Morandini .10
552 Dave Martinez .10
553 Jeff Fassero .10
554 *Ryan Jackson* .25
555 Stan Javier .10
556 Jaime Navarro .10
557 Jose Offerman .10
558 *Mike Lowell* .75
559 Darrin Fletcher .10
560 Mark Lewis .10
561 Dante Bichette .10
562 Chuck Finley .10
563 Kerry Wood .40
564 Andy Benes .10
565 Freddy Garcia .10
566 Tom Glavine .20
567 Jon Nunnally .05
568 Miguel Cairo .10
569 Shane Reynolds .10
570 Roberto Kelly .10
571 Checklist (Jose Cruz Jr.) .25
572 Checklist (Ken Griffey Jr.) 1.00
573 Checklist (Mark McGwire) 1.00
574 Checklist (Cal Ripken Jr.) 1.00
575 Checklist (Frank Thomas) .50
576 Jeff Bagwell (Unforgettable Moments) 1.50
577 Barry Bonds (Unforgettable Moments) 1.50
578 Tony Clark (Unforgettable Moments) .25
579 Roger Clemens (Unforgettable Moments) 1.50
580 Jose Cruz Jr. (Unforgettable Moments) .65
581 Nomar Garciaparra (Unforgettable Moments) 1.50
582 Juan Gonzalez (Unforgettable Moments) 1.50
583 Ben Grieve (Unforgettable Moments) .75
584 Ken Griffey Jr. (Unforgettable Moments) 2.50
585 Tony Gwynn (Unforgettable Moments) 2.00
586 Derek Jeter (Unforgettable Moments) 2.00
587 Randy Johnson (Unforgettable Moments) .75
588 Chipper Jones (Unforgettable Moments) 2.00
589 Greg Maddux (Unforgettable Moments) 1.75
590 Mark McGwire (Unforgettable Moments) 3.00
591 Andy Pettitte (Unforgettable Moments) .60
592 Paul Molitor (Unforgettable Moments) .50
593 Cal Ripken Jr. (Unforgettable Moments) 2.00
594 Alex Rodriguez (Unforgettable Moments) 2.00
595 Scott Rolen (Unforgettable Moments) 1.00
596 Curt Schilling (Unforgettable Moments) .50
597 Frank Thomas (Unforgettable Moments) 1.25
598 Jim Thome (Unforgettable Moments) .25
599 Larry Walker (Unforgettable Moments) .50
600 Bernie Williams (Unforgettable Moments) .35

1998 Fleer Decade of Excellence

Decade of Excellence inserts were found in one per 72 Series 1 hobby packs of Fleer Tradition. The 12-card set features 1988 season photos in Fleer's 1988 card design. The set includes only those current players who have been in baseball for ten years or more. The use of blue and red metallic foil stripes in the background differentiates a scarcer (1:720 hobby packs) "Rare Traditions" parallel to the insert.

		MT
Complete Set (12):		60.00
Common Player:		2.00
Inserted 1:72		
Rare Traditions:		3X
Inserted 1:720		
1	Roberto Alomar	3.00
2	Barry Bonds	7.50
3	Roger Clemens	6.00
4	David Cone	2.00
5	Andres Galarraga	2.00
6	Mark Grace	2.50
7	Tony Gwynn	7.50
8	Randy Johnson	3.00
9	Greg Maddux	12.00
10	Mark McGwire	20.00
11	Paul O'Neill	2.00
12	Cal Ripken Jr.	15.00

1998 Fleer Diamond Standouts

Diamond Standouts were inserted into Series I packs at a rate of one per 12. The 20-card insert set features players over a diamond design silver foil background.

		MT
Complete Set (20):		45.00
Common Player:		1.00
1	Jeff Bagwell	2.50
2	Barry Bonds	3.00
3	Roger Clemens	2.50
4	Jose Cruz Jr.	1.00
5	Andres Galarraga	1.00
6	Nomar Garciaparra	4.00
7	Juan Gonzalez	2.00
8	Ken Griffey Jr.	5.00
9	Derek Jeter	5.00
10	Randy Johnson	2.00
11	Chipper Jones	4.00
12	Kenny Lofton	1.00
13	Greg Maddux	3.50
14	Pedro Martinez	2.00
15	Mark McGwire	6.00
16	Mike Piazza	4.50
17	Alex Rodriguez	6.00
18	Curt Schilling	1.25
19	Frank Thomas	2.50
20	Larry Walker	1.25

1998 Fleer Diamond Tribute

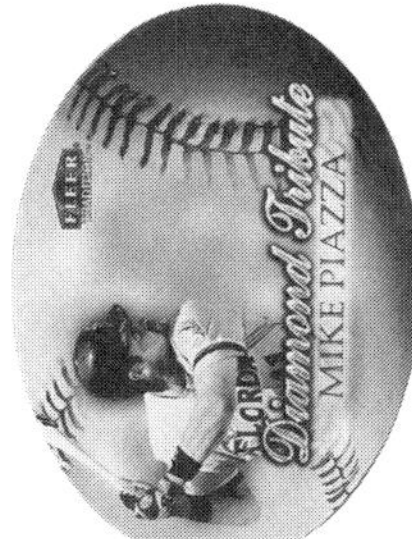

This 10-card insert was exclusive to Series II packs and seeded one per 300 packs. Cards were printed on a leather- like laminated stock and had silver holofoil stamping.

		MT
Complete Set (10):		65.00
Common Player:		3.50
DT1	Jeff Bagwell	3.50
DT2	Roger Clemens	6.00
DT3	Nomar Garciaparra	9.00
DT4	Juan Gonzalez	3.50
DT5	Ken Griffey Jr.	12.50
DT6	Mark McGwire	15.00
DT7	Mike Piazza	10.00
DT8	Cal Ripken Jr.	12.50
DT9	Alex Rodriguez	12.50
DT10	Frank Thomas	5.00

1998 Fleer Diamond Ink

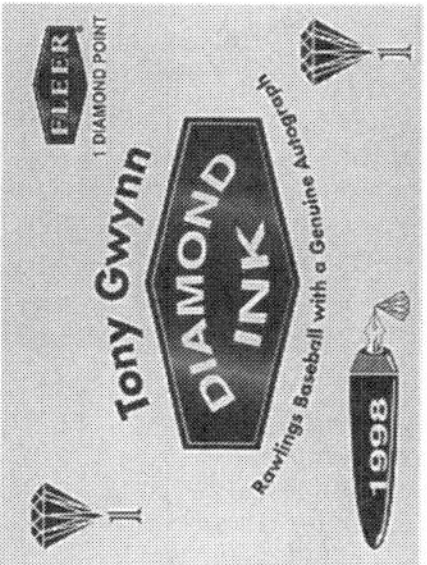

These one-per-pack inserts offer collectors a chance to acquire genuine autographed baseballs. Issued in denominations of 1, 5 and 10 points, the cards had to be accumulated to a total of 500 points of the same player to be redeemed for an autographed ball of that player. Cards are the standard 3-1/2" x 2-1/2" and are printed in black and purple on front and black and yellow on back. The point value of each card is embossed at center to prevent counterfeiting. The rules of the exchange program are printed on back. The deadline for redemption was Dec. 31, 1998. Values shown are for 1-pt. cards. The unnumbered players in the series are listed alphabetically.

		MT
Complete Set, 1 pt. (11):		1.25
Common Player, 1 pt.:		.05
5-pt. Cards:		5X
10-pt. Cards:		10X
(1)	Jay Buhner	.05
(2)	Roger Clemens	.10
(3)	Jose Cruz Jr.	.10
(4)	Nomar Garciaparra	.10
(5)	Tony Gwynn	.10
(6)	Roberto Hernandez	.05
(7)	Greg Maddux	.10
(8)	Cal Ripken Jr.	.25
(9)	Alex Rodriguez	.20
(10)	Scott Rolen	.10
(11)	Tony Womack	.05

1998 Fleer In the Clutch

This Series 2 insert features stars who can stand up to pressure of big league ball. Fronts have embossed action photos on a prismatic metallic foil background. Backs have a portrait photo and a few words about the player.

Stated insertion rate for the inserts was one per 20 packs on average.

		MT
Complete Set (15):		40.00
Common Player:		1.00
IC1	Jeff Bagwell	2.50
IC2	Barry Bonds	3.00
IC3	Roger Clemens	2.50
IC4	Jose Cruz Jr.	1.00
IC5	Nomar Garciaparra	4.00
IC6	Juan Gonzalez	2.00
IC7	Ken Griffey Jr.	6.00
IC8	Tony Gwynn	3.00
IC9	Derek Jeter	6.00
IC10	Chipper Jones	4.00
IC11	Greg Maddux	3.00
IC12	Mark McGwire	6.50
IC13	Mike Piazza	4.00
IC14	Frank Thomas	2.50
IC15	Larry Walker	1.00

1998 Fleer Lumber Company

This 15-card set was exclusive to Series I retail packs and inserted one per 36 packs. It included power hitters and featured the insert name in large letters across the top.

		MT
Complete Set (15):		65.00
Common Player:		1.00
Inserted 1:36 R		
1	Jeff Bagwell	3.25
2	Barry Bonds	5.00
3	Jose Cruz Jr.	1.00
4	Nomar Garciaparra	6.50
5	Juan Gonzalez	2.75
6	Ken Griffey Jr.	10.00
7	Tony Gwynn	4.00
8	Chipper Jones	6.50
9	Tino Martinez	1.00
10	Mark McGwire	12.00
11	Mike Piazza	8.00
12	Cal Ripken Jr.	10.00
13	Alex Rodriguez	10.00
14	Frank Thomas	4.00
15	Larry Walker	1.00

1998 Fleer Mark McGwire 62nd HR 23K Gold Commemorative

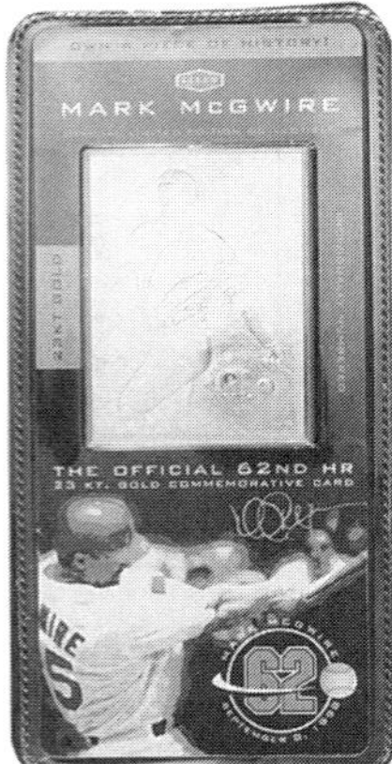

Marketed as a retail-exclusive "Official 62nd HR 23 Kt. Gold Commemorative Card," this 2-1/2" x 3-1/2" card was sold in a colorful blister pack. Embossed in 23-karat gold foil is an image of McGwire in action. Also on front are a 62-HR logo and a facsimile autograph, along with the legend "Smashing the Record". On back is a small picture of McGwire with the large 9-8-98 date and the details of the record blast. There are appropriate licensing logos and a serial number from within an edition of 200,000.

	MT
Mark McGwire	7.50

1998 Fleer Mickey Mantle promo postcard

This 4-1/4" x 5-1/2" color postcard was sent to Fleer dealers to announce a Mickey Mantle commemorative series in its Series 2 product. The address side has the Fleer Tradition logo in black, blue and red. The picture side has a color photo of one of the Mantle cards to be issued in the format of the 1963 Fleer issue. Cards are individually serial numbered within an edition of 3,500.

	MT
Mickey Mantle	5.00

1998 Fleer Mickey Mantle Monumental Moments

This 10-card insert honors Hall of Famer Mickey Mantle's legendary career and was seeded one per 68 packs of Series 2. Fleer/SkyBox worked closely with Mantle's family with each photo in the set personally selected by them. A gold-enhanced version was issued with each card serially numbered to 51.

		MT
Complete Set (10):		75.00
Common Card:		10.00
Inserted 1:68		
Golds (51 sets):		10X
1	Armed and Dangerous	10.00
2	Getting Ready in Spring Training	10.00
3	Mantle and Rizzuto Celebrate	10.00
4	Posed for Action	10.00
5	Signed, Sealed and Ready to Deliver	10.00
6	Triple Crown 1956 Season	10.00
7	Number 7 . . .	10.00
8	Mantle's Powerful Swing . . .	10.00
9	Old-Timers Day Introduction	10.00
10	Portrait of Determination	10.00

1998 Fleer Promising Forecast

Potential future stars are showcased in this Series 2 insert. Both front and back have a background of a colorful weather map. Fronts have a glossy player action photo on a matte-finish background. Backs are all-glossy and have a second photo and a few words about the player's potential. Average odds of pulling a Promising Forecast card were stated as one per 12 packs.

		MT
Complete Set (20):		11.00
Common Player:		.25
Inserted 1:12		
PF1	Rolando Arrojo	.60
PF2	Sean Casey	1.50
PF3	Brad Fullmer	.75
PF4	Karim Garcia	.25
PF5	Ben Grieve	1.00
PF6	Todd Helton	1.50
PF7	Richard Hidalgo	.35
PF8	A.J. Hinch	.25
PF9	Paul Konerko	.50
PF10	Mark Kotsay	.50
PF11	Derrek Lee	.25
PF12	Travis Lee	1.50
PF13	Eric Milton	.25
PF14	Magglio Ordonez	.75
PF15	David Ortiz	.25
PF16	Brian Rose	.25
PF17	Miguel Tejada	.75
PF18	Jason Varitek	.25
PF19	Enrique Wilson	.25
PF20	Kerry Wood	2.00

1998 Fleer Rookie Sensations

Rookie Sensations included 20 gray-bordered cards of the 1997 most promising players who were eligible for the Rookie of the Year award. Each card contained a multi-colored background and was inserted one per 18 packs.

		MT
Complete Set (20):		30.00
Common Player:		1.00
Inserted 1:18		
1	Mike Cameron	1.00
2	Jose Cruz Jr.	1.50
3	Jason Dickson	1.00
4	Kelvim Escobar	1.00
5	Nomar Garciaparra	6.00
6	Ben Grieve	1.50
7	Vladimir Guerrero	4.00
8	Wilton Guerrero	1.00
9	Jose Guillen	1.50

10 Todd Helton 2.00
11 Livan Hernandez 1.00
12 Hideki Irabu 1.00
13 Andruw Jones 4.00
14 Matt Morris 1.50
15 Magglio Ordonez 1.50
16 Neifi Perez 1.00
17 Scott Rolen 4.00
18 Fernando Tatis 1.25
19 Brett Tomko 1.00
20 Jaret Wright 2.00

1998 Fleer The Power Game

Pitchers and hitters are pictured over a purple metallic background with UV coating in this 20-card insert. Power Game inserts were exclusive to Series I and seeded one per 36 packs.

		MT
Complete Set (20):		32.50
Common Player:		.50
Inserted 1:36		
1	Jeff Bagwell	1.75
2	Albert Belle	.75
3	Barry Bonds	2.50
4	Tony Clark	.50
5	Roger Clemens	2.50
6	Jose Cruz Jr.	.75
7	Andres Galarraga	.50
8	Nomar Garciaparra	3.00
9	Juan Gonzalez	1.75
10	Ken Griffey Jr.	5.00
11	Randy Johnson	1.75
12	Greg Maddux	3.00
13	Pedro Martinez	1.75
14	Tino Martinez	.50
15	Mark McGwire	6.00
16	Mike Piazza	4.00
17	Curt Schilling	.75
18	Frank Thomas	2.50
19	Jim Thome	.50
20	Larry Walker	.75

1998 Fleer Vintage '63

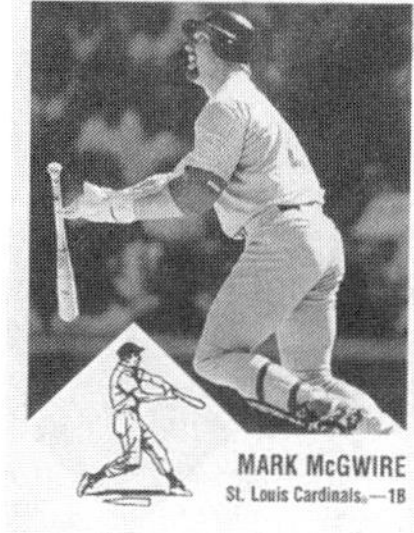

Vintage featured 126 different players, with 63 in Series I and 63 in Series II, on the design of 1963 Fleer cards. The insert commemorated the 35th anniversary of Fleer and was seeded one per hobby pack. In addition, Series II featured Mickey Mantle on card No. 67, which completed the original 1963 Fleer set that ended at card No. 66 and wasn't able to include Mantle for licensing reasons. The Mantle card was printed in vintage looking stock and was purposely made to look and feel like the originals. Fleer also printed a Classic parallel version to this insert that contained gold foil on the front and was sequentially numbered to 63 with a "C" prefix on the back.

		MT
Complete Set (126):		30.00
Complete Series 1 (63):		15.00
Complete Series 2 (63):		15.00
Common Player:		.25
Classics (63 sets):		25X
1	Jason Dickson	.25
2	Tim Salmon	.40
3	Andruw Jones	.75
4	Chipper Jones	2.00
5	Kenny Lofton	.25
6	Greg Maddux	1.50
7	Rafael Palmeiro	.40
8	Cal Ripken Jr.	3.00
9	Nomar Garciaparra	2.00
10	Mark Grace	.40
11	Sammy Sosa	1.50
12	Frank Thomas	1.00
13	Deion Sanders	.30
14	Sandy Alomar	.25
15	David Justice	.35
16	Jim Thome	.25
17	Matt Williams	.35
18	Jaret Wright	.25
19	Vinny Castilla	.25
20	Andres Galarraga	.25
21	Todd Helton	.75
22	Larry Walker	.40
23	Tony Clark	.25
24	Moises Alou	.25
25	Kevin Brown	.25
26	Charles Johnson	.25
27	Edgar Renteria	.25
28	Gary Sheffield	.40
29	Jeff Bagwell	.75
30	Craig Biggio	.25
31	Raul Mondesi	.25
32	Mike Piazza	2.00
33	Chuck Knoblauch	.25
34	Paul Molitor	.50
35	Vladimir Guerrero	.75
36	Pedro Martinez	.75
37	Todd Hundley	.25
38	Derek Jeter	2.50
39	Tino Martinez	.25
40	Paul O'Neill	.25
41	Andy Pettitte	.35
42	Mariano Rivera	.40
43	Bernie Williams	.40
44	Ben Grieve	.40
45	Scott Rolen	.75
46	Curt Schilling	.35
47	Jason Kendall	.25
48	Tony Womack	.25
49	Ray Lankford	.25
50	Mark McGwire	3.00
51	Matt Morris	.25
52	Tony Gwynn	1.00
53	Barry Bonds	1.50
54	Jay Buhner	.25
55	Ken Griffey Jr.	2.50
56	Randy Johnson	.75
57	Edgar Martinez	.25
58	Alex Rodriguez	2.50
59	Juan Gonzalez	.75
60	Rusty Greer	.25
61	Ivan Rodriguez	.60
62	Roger Clemens	1.25
63	Jose Cruz Jr.	.35
	Checklist #1-63	.25
64	Darin Erstad	.75
65	Jay Bell	.25
66	Andy Benes	.25
67	Mickey Mantle	5.00
68	Karim Garcia	.25
69	Travis Lee	.25
70	Matt Williams	.40
71	Andres Galarraga	.25
72	Tom Glavine	.35
73	Ryan Klesko	.25
74	Denny Neagle	.25
75	John Smoltz	.25
76	Roberto Alomar	.50
77	Joe Carter	.25
78	Mike Mussina	.50
79	B.J. Surhoff	.25
80	Dennis Eckersley	.25
81	Pedro Martinez	.75
82	Mo Vaughn	.40
83	Jeff Blauser	.25
84	Henry Rodriguez	.25
85	Albert Belle	.40
86	Sean Casey	.50
87	Travis Fryman	.25
88	Kenny Lofton	.25
89	Darryl Kile	.25
90	Mike Lansing	.25
91	Bobby Bonilla	.25
92	Cliff Floyd	.25
93	Livan Hernandez	.25
94	Derrek Lee	.25
95	Moises Alou	.25
96	Shane Reynolds	.25
97	Jeff Conine	.25
98	Johnny Damon	.25
99	Eric Karros	.25
100	Hideo Nomo	.40
101	Marquis Grissom	.25
102	Matt Lawton	.25
103	Todd Walker	.25
104	Gary Sheffield	.40
105	Bernard Gilkey	.25
106	Rey Ordonez	.25
107	Chili Davis	.25
108	Chuck Knoblauch	.25
109	Charles Johnson	.25
110	Rickey Henderson	.40
111	Bob Abreu	.25
112	Doug Glanville	.25
113	Gregg Jefferies	.25
114	Al Martin	.25
115	Kevin Young	.25
116	Ron Gant	.25
117	Kevin Brown	.25
118	Ken Caminiti	.25
119	Joey Hamilton	.25
120	Jeff Kent	.25
121	Wade Boggs	.40
122	Quinton McCracken	.25
123	Fred McGriff	.25
124	Paul Sorrento	.25
125	Jose Canseco	.40
126	Randy Myers	.25
	Checklist #64-126	.25

1998 Fleer Vintage '63 Classic

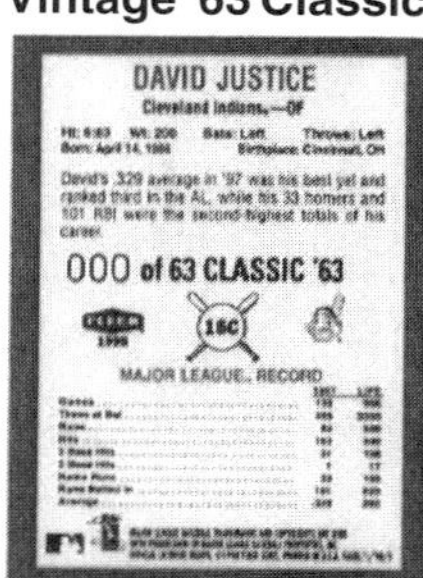

Vintage '63 Classic paralleled all 126 Vintage '63 inserts throughout Series 1 and 2, plus the checklists. These cards feature gold-foil stamping on front, specifically around the diamond in the lower-left corner, and are sequentailly numbered to 63 sets. Cards have a "C" suffix to the card number.

	MT
Complete Set (128):	900.00
Common Player:	7.50
Stars/RCs:	25X

(See 1998 Fleer Vintage '63 for checklist and base card values.)

1998 Fleer Zone

Inserted in one per 288 packs of Series I Fleer Tradition, Zone featured 15 top players printed on rainbow foil and etching.

		MT
Complete Set (15):		80.00
Common Player:		2.00
Inserted 1:288		
1	Jeff Bagwell	4.00
2	Barry Bonds	6.00
3	Roger Clemens	6.00
4	Jose Cruz Jr.	2.50
5	Nomar Garciaparra	9.00
6	Juan Gonzalez	4.00
7	Ken Griffey Jr.	12.50
8	Tony Gwynn	6.00
9	Chipper Jones	9.00
10	Greg Maddux	7.50
11	Mark McGwire	15.00
12	Mike Piazza	9.00
13	Alex Rodriguez	12.50
14	Frank Thomas	6.00
15	Larry Walker	2.00

1998 Fleer Update

Fleer produced its first Update set since 1994 with this 100-card boxed set. It arrived soon after the conclusion of the 1998 World Series and focused on rookies like J.D. Drew, Rich Croushore, Ryan Bradley, John Rocker, Mike Frank and Benj Sampson, who made their major league debut in September and have not yet had a rookie card yet. The set had 70 rookies, including 15 making their major league debut, 20 traded players and free agents. There was one subset called Season's Highlights that focused on feats like Mark McGwire's 70th home run, Sammy Sosa's single-month home run record and Kerry Wood's 20 strikeout performance.

		MT
Complete Set (100):		20.00
Common Player:		.10
U1	Mark McGwire (Season Highlights)	1.50
U2	Sammy Sosa (Season Highlights)	1.00
U3	Roger Clemens (Season Highlights)	.65
U4	Barry Bonds (Season Highlights)	.65
U5	Kerry Wood (Season Highlights)	.25
U6	Paul Molitor (Season Highlights)	.25
U7	Ken Griffey Jr. (Season Highlights)	1.00
U8	Cal Ripken Jr. (Season Highlights)	1.50
U9	David Wells (Season Highlights)	.10
U10	Alex Rodriguez (Season Highlights)	1.00
U11	*Angel Pena*	.25
U12	Bruce Chen	.10
U13	Craig Wilson	.10
U14	*Orlando Hernandez*	1.50
U15	Aramis Ramirez	.15
U16	Aaron Boone	.10
U17	Bob Henley	.10
U18	Juan Guzman	.10
U19	Darryl Hamilton	.10
U20	Jay Payton	.10
U21	*Jeremy Powell*	.15
U22	Ben Davis	.10
U23	Preston Wilson	.20
U24	*Jim Parque*	.25
U25	*Odalis Perez*	.75
U26	Ron Belliard	.10
U27	Royce Clayton	.10
U28	George Lombard	.15
U29	Tony Phillips	.10
U30	*Fernando Seguignol*	.40
U31	*Armando Rios*	.15
U32	*Jerry Hairston Jr.*	.50
U33	*Justin Baughman*	.10
U34	Seth Greisinger	.10
U35	Alex Gonzalez	.10
U36	Michael Barrett	.15
U37	Carlos Beltran	.20
U38	Ellis Burks	.10
U39	Jose Jimenez	.20
U40	Carlos Guillen	.10
U41	Marlon Anderson	.10
U42	Scott Elarton	.10
U43	Glenallen Hill	.10
U44	Shane Monahan	.10
U45	Dennis Martinez	.10
U46	*Carlos Febles*	.30
U47	Carlos Perez	.10
U48	Wilton Guerrero	.10
U49	Randy Johnson	.45
U50	*Brian Simmons*	.10
U51	Carlton Loewer	.10
U52	*Mark DeRosa*	1.00
U53	*Tim Young*	.10
U54	Gary Gaetti	.10
U55	Eric Chavez	.25
U56	Carl Pavano	.10
U57	Mike Stanley	.10
U58	Todd Stottlemyre	.10
U59	*Gabe Kapler*	1.50
U60	*Mike Jerzembeck*	.10
U61	*Mitch Meluskey*	.25
U62	Bill Pulsipher	.10
U63	Derrick Gibson	.10
U64	*John Rocker*	1.00
U65	Calvin Pickering	.10
U66	Blake Stein	.10
U67	Fernando Tatis	.15
U68	Gabe Alvarez	.10
U69	Jeffrey Hammonds	.10
U70	Adrian Beltre	.25
U71	*Ryan Bradley*	.25
U72	*Edgar Clemente*	.15
U73	*Rick Croushore*	.20
U74	Matt Clement	.15
U75	Dermal Brown	.10
U76	Paul Bako	.10
U77	*Placido Polanco*	.75
U78	Jay Tessmer	.10
U79	Jarrod Washburn	.10
U80	Kevin Witt	.10
U81	Mike Metcalfe	.10
U82	Daryle Ward	.10
U83	*Benj Sampson*	.15
U84	*Mike Kinkade*	.25
U85	Randy Winn	.10
U86	Jeff Shaw	.10
U87	*Troy Glaus*	2.00
U88	Hideo Nomo	.40
U89	Mark Grudzielanek	.10
U90	*Mike Frank*	.20
U91	*Bobby Howry*	.25
U92	*Ryan Minor*	.25
U93	*Corey Koskie*	1.00
U94	*Matt Anderson*	.35
U95	Joe Carter	.10
U96	Paul Konerko	.15
U97	Sidney Ponson	.10
U98	*Jeremy Giambi*	1.00
U99	*Jeff Kubenka*	.10
U100	*J.D. Drew*	4.00

1999 Fleer

Released as a single series in 10-card packs with a suggested retail price of $1.59, the base set consists of 600 cards, including 10 checklists and a 15-card Franchise Futures subset. Cards are UV coated, with borderless photos and gold-foil graphics. Backs have personal bio-information along with year-by-year career stats and a small photo. There are two parallels, Starting Nine, which are hobby-exclusive, numbered to nine sets with blue foil stamping and Warning Track. Found exclusively in retail packs, Warning Tracks can be identified by red foil stamping and a Warning Track logo.

		MT
Complete Set (600):		45.00
Common Player:		.10
Pack (10):		1.25
Wax Box (36):		40.00
1	Mark McGwire	3.00
2	Sammy Sosa	1.50
3	Ken Griffey Jr.	2.50
4	Kerry Wood	.75
5	Derek Jeter	2.50
6	Stan Musial	3.00
7	J.D. Drew	.75
7p	J.D. Drew (overprinted PROMOTIONAL SAMPLE)	1.50
8	Cal Ripken Jr.	2.50
9	Alex Rodriguez	2.50
10	Travis Lee	.50
11	Andres Galarraga	.10
12	Nomar Garciaparra	2.00
13	Albert Belle	.30
14	Barry Larkin	.15
15	Dante Bichette	.10
16	Tony Clark	.25
17	Moises Alou	.20
18	Rafael Palmeiro	.25
19	Raul Mondesi	.25
20	Vladimir Guerrero	.75
21	John Olerud	.10
22	Bernie Williams	.40
23	Ben Grieve	.75
24	Scott Rolen	.75
25	Jeromy Burnitz	.10
26	Ken Caminiti	.10
27	Barry Bonds	1.25
28	Todd Helton	.75
29	Juan Gonzalez	1.00
30	Roger Clemens	1.25
31	Andruw Jones	.75
32	Mo Vaughn	.40
33	Larry Walker	.35
34	Frank Thomas	1.00
35	Manny Ramirez	1.00
36	Randy Johnson	.50
37	Vinny Castilla	.10
38	Juan Encarnacion	.10
39	Jeff Bagwell	.75
40	Gary Sheffield	.25
41	Mike Piazza	2.50
42	Richie Sexson	.10
43	Tony Gwynn	1.50
44	Chipper Jones	2.00
45	Jim Thome	.10
46	Craig Biggio	.15
47	Carlos Delgado	.40
48	Greg Vaughn	.10
49	Greg Maddux	2.00
50	Troy Glaus	.75
51	Roberto Alomar	.40
52	Dennis Eckersley	.10
53	Mike Caruso	.10
54	Bruce Chen	.10
55	Aaron Boone	.10
56	Bartolo Colon	.10
57	Derrick Gibson	.10
58	Brian Anderson	.10
59	Gabe Alvarez	.10
60	Todd Dunwoody	.10
61	Rod Beck	.10
62	Derek Bell	.10
63	Francisco Cordova	.10
64	Johnny Damon	.15
65	Adrian Beltre	.10
66	Garret Anderson	.10
67	Armando Benitez	.10
68	Edgardo Alfonzo	.10
69	Ryan Bradley	.10
70	Eric Chavez	.50
71	Bobby Abreu	.10
72	Andy Ashby	.10
73	Ellis Burks	.10
74	Jeff Cirillo	.10
75	Jay Buhner	.10
76	Ron Gant	.10
77	Rolando Arrojo	.25
78	Will Clark	.30
79	Chris Carpenter	.10
80	Jim Edmonds	.15
81	Tony Batista	.10
82	Shane Andrews	.10
83	Mark DeRosa	.10
84	Brady Anderson	.10
85	Tony Gordon	.10
86	Brant Brown	.10
87	Ray Durham	.10
88	Ron Coomer	.10
89	Bret Boone	.15
90	Travis Fryman	.10
91	Darryl Kile	.10
92	Paul Bako	.10
93	Cliff Floyd	.10
94	Scott Elarton	.10
95	Jeremy Giambi	.10
96	Darren Dreifort	.10
97	Marquis Grissom	.10
98	Marty Cordova	.10
99	Fernando Seguignol	.15
100	Orlando Hernandez	.50
101	Jose Cruz Jr.	.50
102	Jason Giambi	.40
103	Damion Easley	.10
104	Freddy Garcia	.20
105	Marlon Anderson	.10
106	Kevin Brown	.20
107	Joe Carter	.10
108	Russ Davis	.10
109	Brian Jordan	.10
110	Wade Boggs	.40
111	Tom Goodwin	.10
112	Scott Brosius	.10
113	Darin Erstad	.75
114	Jay Bell	.10
115	Tom Glavine	.15
116	Pedro Martinez	.50
117	Mark Grace	.25
118	Russ Ortiz	.10
119	Magglio Ordonez	.20
120	Sean Casey	.25
121	*Rafael Roque*	.15
122	Brian Giles	.10
123	Mike Lansing	.10
124	David Cone	.10
125	Alex Gonzalez	.15
126	Carl Everett	.10
127	Jeff King	.10
128	Charles Johnson	.10
129	Geoff Jenkins	.10
130	Corey Koskie	.10
131	Brad Fullmer	.15
132	Al Leiter	.10
133	Rickey Henderson	.35
134	Rico Brogna	.10
135	Jose Guillen	.25
136	Matt Clement	.10
137	Carlos Guillen	.10
138	Orel Hershiser	.10
139	Ray Lankford	.10
140	Miguel Cairo	.10
141	Chuck Finley	.10
142	Rusty Greer	.10
143	Kelvim Escobar	.10
144	Ryan Klesko	.10
145	Andy Benes	.10
146	Eric Davis	.10
147	David Wells	.10
148	Trot Nixon	.25
149	Jose Hernandez	.10
150	Mark Johnson	.10
151	Mike Frank	.10
152	Joey Hamilton	.10
153	David Justice	.25
154	Mike Mussina	.50
155	Neifi Perez	.10
156	Luis Gonzalez	.20
157	Livan Hernandez	.10
158	Dermal Brown	.10
159	Jose Lima	.10
160	Eric Karros	.10
161	Ronnie Belliard	.10
162	Matt Lawton	.10
163	Dustin Hermanson	.10
164	Brian McRae	.10
165	Mike Kinkade	.10
166	A.J. Hinch	.10
167	Doug Glanville	.10
168	Hideo Nomo	.40
169	Jason Kendall	.10
170	Steve Finley	.10
171	Jeff Kent	.10
172	Ben Davis	.10
173	Edgar Martinez	.10
174	Eli Marrero	.10
175	Quinton McCracken	.10
176	Rick Helling	.10
177	Tom Evans	.10
178	Carl Pavano	.10
179	Todd Greene	.10
180	Omar Daal	.10
181	George Lombard	.10
182	Ryan Minor	.20
183	Troy O'Leary	.10
184	Robb Nen	.10
185	Mickey Morandini	.10
186	Robin Ventura	.10
187	Pete Harnisch	.10
188	Kenny Lofton	.10
189	Eric Milton	.10
190	Bobby Higginson	.10
191	Jamie Moyer	.10
192	Mark Kotsay	.15
193	Shane Reynolds	.10
194	Carlos Febles	.10
195	Jeff Kubenka	.10
196	Chuck Knoblauch	.10
197	Kenny Rogers	.10
198	Bill Mueller	.10
199	Shane Monahan	.10
200	Matt Morris	.10
201	Fred McGriff	.10
202	Ivan Rodriguez	.60
203	Kevin Witt	.10
204	Troy Percival	.10
205	David Dellucci	.10
206	Kevin Millwood	.50
207	Jerry Hairston Jr.	.15
208	Mike Stanley	.10
209	Henry Rodriguez	.10
210	Trevor Hoffman	.10

211 Craig Wilson .10
212 Reggie Sanders .10
213 Carlton Loewer .10
214 Omar Vizquel .10
215 Gabe Kapler .50
216 Derrek Lee .10
217 Billy Wagner .10
218 Dean Palmer .10
219 Chan Ho Park .50
220 Fernando Vina .10
221 Roy Halladay .15
222 Paul Molitor .50
223 Ugueth Urbina .10
224 Rey Ordonez .10
225 Ricky Ledee .15
226 Scott Spiezio .10
227 Wendell Magee Jr. .10
228 Aramis Ramirez .10
229 Brian Simmons .10
230 Fernando Tatis .10
231 Bobby Smith .10
232 Aaron Sele .10
233 Shawn Green .20
234 Mariano Rivera .25
235 Tim Salmon .30
236 Andy Fox .10
237 Denny Neagle .10
238 John Valentin .10
239 Kevin Tapani .10
240 Paul Konerko .15
241 Robert Fick .10
242 Edgar Renteria .10
243 Brett Tomko .10
244 Daryle Ward .10
245 Carlos Beltran .10
246 Angel Pena .10
247 Steve Woodard .10
248 David Ortiz .10
249 Justin Thompson .10
250 Rondell White .15
251 Jaret Wright .25
252 Ed Sprague .10
253 Jay Payton .10
254 Mike Lowell .15
255 Orlando Cabrera .10
256 Jason Schmidt .10
257 David Segui .10
258 Paul Sorrento .10
259 John Wetteland .10
260 Devon White .10
261 Odalis Perez .25
262 Calvin Pickering .10
263 Alex Ramirez .10
264 Preston Wilson .10
265 Brad Radke .10
266 Walt Weiss .10
267 Tim Young .10
268 Tino Martinez .10
269 Matt Stairs .10
270 Curt Schilling .20
271 Tony Womack .10
272 Ismael Valdes .10
273 Wally Joyner .10
274 Armando Rios .10
275 Andy Pettitte .40
276 Bubba Trammell .10
277 Todd Zeile .10
278 Shannon Stewart .10
279 Matt Williams .30
280 John Rocker .10
281 B.J. Surhoff .10
282 Eric Young .10
283 Dmitri Young .10
284 John Smoltz .15
285 Todd Walker .25
286 Paul O'Neill .10
287 Blake Stein .10
288 Kevin Young .10
289 Quilvio Veras .10
290 Kirk Rueter .10
291 Randy Winn .10
292 Miguel Tejada .10
293 J.T. Snow .10
294 Michael Tucker .10
295 Jay Tessmer .10
296 Scott Erickson .10
297 Tim Wakefield .10
298 Jeff Abbott .10
299 Eddie Taubensee .10
300 Darryl Hamilton .10
301 Kevin Orie .10
302 Jose Offerman .10
303 Scott Karl .10
304 Chris Widger .10
305 Todd Hundley .10
306 Desi Relaford .10
307 Sterling Hitchcock .10
308 Delino DeShields .10
309 Alex Gonzalez .10
310 Justin Baughman .10
311 Jamey Wright .10
312 Wes Helms .10
313 Dante Powell .10
314 Jim Abbott .10
315 Manny Alexander .10
316 Harold Baines .10
317 Danny Graves .10
318 Sandy Alomar .10
319 Pedro Astacio .10
320 Jermaine Allensworth .10
321 Matt Anderson .10
322 Chad Curtis .10
323 Antonio Osuna .10
324 Brad Ausmus .10
325 Steve Trachsel .10
326 Mike Blowers .10
327 Brian Bohanon .10
328 Chris Gomez .10
329 Valerio de los Santos .10
330 Rich Aurilia .10
331 Michael Barrett .45
332 Rick Aguilera .10
333 Adrian Brown .10
334 Bill Spiers .10
335 Matt Beech .10
336 David Bell .10
337 Juan Acevedo .10
338 Jose Canseco .40
339 Wilson Alvarez .10
340 Luis Alicea .10
341 Jason Dickson .10
342 Mike Bordick .10
343 Ben Ford .10
344 Keith Lockhart .10
345 Jason Christiansen .10
346 Darren Bragg .10
347 Doug Brocail .10
348 Jeff Blauser .10
349 James Baldwin .10
350 Jeffrey Hammonds .10
351 Ricky Bottalico .10
352 Russ Branyon .10
353 Mark Brownson .10
354 Dave Berg .10
355 Sean Bergman .10
356 Jeff Conine .10
357 Shayne Bennett .10
358 Bobby Bonilla .10
359 Bob Wickman .10
360 Carlos Baerga .10
361 Chris Fussell .10
362 Chili Davis .10
363 Jerry Spradlin .10
364 Carlos Hernandez .10
365 Roberto Hernandez .10
366 Marvin Benard .10
367 Ken Cloude .10
368 Tony Fernandez .10
369 John Burkett .10
370 Gary DiSarcina .10
371 Alan Benes .10
372 Karim Garcia .10
373 Carlos Perez .10
374 Damon Buford .10
375 Mark Clark .10
376 *Edgard Clemente* .10
377 Chad Bradford .10
378 Frank Catalanotto .10
379 Vic Darensbourg .10
380 Sean Berry .10
381 Dave Burba .10
382 Sal Fasano .10
383 Steve Parris .10
384 Roger Cedeno .10
385 Chad Fox .10
386 Wilton Guerrero .10
387 Dennis Cook .10
388 Joe Girardi .10
389 LaTroy Hawkins .10
390 Ryan Christenson .10
391 Paul Byrd .10
392 Lou Collier .10
393 Jeff Fassero .10
394 Jim Leyritz .10
395 Shawn Estes .10
396 Mike Kelly .10
397 Rich Croushore .10
398 Royce Clayton .10
399 Rudy Seanez .10
400 Darrin Fletcher .10
401 Shigetosi Hasegawa .10
402 Bernard Gilkey .10
403 Juan Guzman .10
404 Jeff Frye .10
405 Marino Santana .10
406 Alex Fernandez .10
407 Gary Gaetti .10
408 Dan Miceli .10
409 Mike Cameron .10
410 Mike Remlinger .10
411 Joey Cora .10
412 Mark Gardner .10
413 Aaron Ledesma .10
414 Jerry Dipoto .10
415 Ricky Gutierrez .10
416 John Franco .10
417 Mendy Lopez .10
418 Hideki Irabu .15
419 Mark Grudzielanek .10
420 Bobby Hughes .10
421 Pat Meares .10
422 Jimmy Haynes .10
423 Bob Henley .10
424 Bobby Estalella .10
425 Jon Lieber .10
426 *Giomar Guevara* .25
427 Jose Jimenez .10
428 Deivi Cruz .10
429 Jonathan Johnson .10
430 Ken Hill .10
431 Craig Grebeck .10
432 Jose Rosado .10
433 Danny Klassen .10
434 Bobby Howry .10
435 Gerald Williams .10
436 Omar Olivares .10
437 Chris Hoiles .10
438 Seth Greisinger .10
439 Scott Hatteberg .10
440 Jeremi Gonzalez .10
441 Wil Cordero .10
442 Jeff Montgomery .10
443 Chris Stynes .10
444 Tony Saunders .10
445 Einar Diaz .10
446 Laril Gonzalez .10
447 Ryan Jackson .10
448 Mike Hampton .10
449 Todd Hollandsworth .10
450 Gabe White .10
451 John Jaha .10
452 Bret Saberhagen .10
453 Otis Nixon .10
454 Steve Kline .10
455 Butch Huskey .10
456 Mike Jerzembeck .10
457 Wayne Gomes .10
458 Mike Macfarlane .10
459 Jesus Sanchez .10
460 Al Martin .10
461 Dwight Gooden .10
462 Ruben Rivera .10
463 Pat Hentgen .10
464 Jose Valentin .10
465 Vladimir Nunez .10
466 Charlie Hayes .10
467 Jay Powell .10
468 Raul Ibanez .10
469 Kent Mercker .10
470 John Mabry .10
471 Woody Williams .10
472 Roberto Kelly .10
473 Jim Mecir .10
474 Dave Hollins .10
475 Rafael Medina .10
476 Darren Lewis .10
477 Felix Heredia .10
478 Brian Hunter .10
479 Matt Mantei .10
480 Richard Hidalgo .10
481 Bobby Jones .10
482 Hal Morris .10
483 Ramiro Mendoza .10
484 Matt Luke .10
485 Esteban Loaiza .10
486 Mark Loretta .10
487 A.J. Pierzynski .10
488 Charles Nagy .10
489 Kevin Sefcik .10
490 Jason McDonald .10
491 Jeremy Powell .10
492 Scott Servais .10
493 Abraham Nunez .10
494 Stan Spencer .10
495 Stan Javier .10
496 Jose Paniagua .10
497 Gregg Jefferies .10
498 Gregg Olson .10
499 Derek Lowe .10
500 Willis Otanez .10
501 Brian Moehler .10
502 Glenallen Hill .10
503 Bobby Jones .10
504 Greg Norton .10
505 Mike Jackson .10
506 Kirt Manwaring .10
507 Eric Weaver .10
508 Mitch Meluskey .15
509 Todd Jones .10
510 Mike Matheny .10
511 Benj Sampson .10
512 Tony Phillips .10
513 Mike Thurman .10
514 Jorge Posada .10
515 Bill Taylor .10
516 Mike Sweeney .10
517 Jose Silva .10
518 Mark Lewis .10
519 Chris Peters .10
520 Brian Johnson .10
521 Mike Timlin .10
522 Mark McLemore .10
523 Dan Plesac .10
524 Kelly Stinnett .10
525 Sidney Ponson .10
526 Jim Parque .10
527 Tyler Houston .10
528 John Thomson .10
529 Mike Metcalfe .10
530 Robert Person .10
531 Marc Newfield .10
532 Javier Vazquez .10
533 Terry Steinbach .10
534 Turk Wendell .10
535 Tim Raines .10
536 Brian Meadows .10
537 Mike Lieberthal .10
538 Ricardo Rincon .10
539 Dan Wilson .10
540 John Johnstone .10
541 Todd Stottlemyre .10
542 Kevin Stocker .10
543 Ramon Martinez .10
544 Mike Simms .10
545 Paul Quantrill .10
546 Matt Walbeck .10
547 Turner Ward .10
548 Bill Pulsipher .10
549 Donnie Sadler .10
550 Lance Johnson .10
551 Bill Simas .10
552 Jeff Reed .10
553 Jeff Shaw .10
554 Joe Randa .10
555 Paul Shuey .10
556 Mike Redmond .50
557 Sean Runyan .10
558 Enrique Wilson .10
559 Scott Radinsky .10
560 Larry Sutton .10
561 Masato Yoshii .10
562 David Nilsson .10
563 Mike Trombley .10
564 Darryl Strawberry .10
565 Dave Mlicki .10
566 Placido Polanco .10
567 Yorkis Perez .10
568 Esteban Yan .10
569 Lee Stevens .10
570 Steve Sinclair .10
571 Jarrod Washburn .10
572 Lenny Webster .10
573 Mike Sirotka .10
574 Jason Varitek .10
575 Terry Mulholland .10
576 Adrian Beltre (Franchise Futures) .25
577 Eric Chavez (Franchise Futures) .50
578 J.D. Drew (Franchise Futures) .50
579 Juan Encarnacion (Franchise Futures) .25
580 Nomar Garciaparra (Franchise Futures) 1.00
581 Troy Glaus (Franchise Futures) .50
582 Ben Grieve (Franchise Futures) .40
583 Vladimir Guerrero (Franchise Futures) .50
584 Todd Helton (Franchise Futures) .40

585	Derek Jeter (Franchise Futures)	1.25
586	Travis Lee (Franchise Futures)	.40
587	Alex Rodriguez (Franchise Futures)	1.25
588	Scott Rolen (Franchise Futures)	.40
589	Richie Sexson (Franchise Futures)	.25
590	Kerry Wood (Franchise Futures)	.40
591	Ken Griffey Jr. (Checklist)	1.00
592	Chipper Jones (Checklist)	.50
593	Alex Rodriguez (Checklist)	1.00
594	Sammy Sosa (Checklist)	.75
595	Mark McGwire (Checklist)	1.50
596	Cal Ripken Jr. (Checklist)	1.00
597	Nomar Garciaparra (Checklist)	.75
598	Derek Jeter (Checklist)	1.00
599	Kerry Wood (Checklist)	.40
600	J.D. Drew (Checklist)	.40

1999 Fleer Starting Nine

This ultra-scarce, hobby-only parallel insert, found at the rate of about two cards per case, includes just nine cards of each player. Sharing the basic design of the Fleer Traditional set, the cards have blue metallic foil printing on front, including a "STARTING 9 NINElogo at lower-right. At bottom right, the card's individual serial number from within the edition of nine is printed. Backs have an "S" suffix to the card number.

	MT
Common Player:	20.00

(Star and rookie cards valued at 200-250X base versions.)

1999 Fleer Warning Track Collection

Each of the cards in '99 Fleer Tradition was paralleled in this retail-only issue found one per pack. Warning Track cards are distinguished by the use of red metallic foil on front for the player's name, team, position that are in gold-foil on the regular version. There is also a special "Warning Track Collection" logo in red foil at bottom-right. On back, WTC cards have a "W" suffix to the card number.

	MT
Complete Set (600):	150.00
Common Player:	.20
Stars:	3X

(See 1999 Fleer for checklist and base card values.)

1999 Fleer Date With Destiny

This 10-card set takes a look at what Hall of Fame plaques might look like for some of today's great players. These are serially numbered to 100 sets.

		MT
Complete Set (10):		325.00
Common Player:		20.00
Production 100 sets		
1	Barry Bonds	25.00
2	Roger Clemens	25.00
3	Ken Griffey Jr.	50.00
4	Tony Gwynn	20.00
5	Greg Maddux	35.00
6	Mark McGwire	75.00
7	Mike Piazza	45.00
8	Cal Ripken Jr.	60.00
9	Alex Rodriguez	60.00
10	Frank Thomas	20.00

1999 Fleer Diamond Magic

A multi-layer card, where collectors turn a "wheel" for a kaleidoscope effect behind the player image. These are seeded 1:96 packs.

		MT
Complete Set (15):		55.00
Common Player:		1.50
Inserted 1:96		
1	Barry Bonds	5.00
2	Roger Clemens	4.00
3	Nomar Garciaparra	6.00
4	Ken Griffey Jr.	7.50
5	Tony Gwynn	3.50
6	Orlando Hernandez	1.50
7	Derek Jeter	7.50
8	Randy Johnson	2.50
9	Chipper Jones	6.00
10	Greg Maddux	5.00
11	Mark McGwire	10.00
12	Alex Rodriguez	7.50
13	Sammy Sosa	5.00
14	Bernie Williams	1.50
15	Kerry Wood	1.50

1999 Fleer Going Yard

This 15-card set features the top home run hitters from the '98 season. These 1:18 pack inserts unfold to be twice as wide as regular cards and takes an unorthodox look at how far the longest home runs went.

		MT
Complete Set (15):		11.00
Common Player:		.20
Inserted 1:18		
1	Moises Alou	.25
2	Albert Belle	.45
3	Jose Canseco	.45
4	Vinny Castilla	.20
5	Andres Galarraga	.20
6	Juan Gonzalez	.60
7	Ken Griffey Jr.	2.00
8	Chipper Jones	1.50
9	Mark McGwire	3.00
10	Rafael Palmeiro	.25
11	Mike Piazza	1.50
12	Alex Rodriguez	2.00
13	Sammy Sosa	1.25
14	Greg Vaughn	.20
15	Mo Vaughn	.50

1999 Fleer Golden Memories

This 15-card set pays tribute to the great moments from the 1998 season including David Wells perfect game and McGwire's record breaking season. These are seeded 1:54 packs on an embossed frame design.

		MT
Complete Set (15):		35.00
Common Player:		.75
Inserted 1:54		
1	Albert Belle	1.00
2	Barry Bonds	2.50
3	Roger Clemens	2.50
4	Nomar Garciaparra	3.00
5	Juan Gonzalez	1.50
6	Ken Griffey Jr.	4.00
7	Randy Johnson	1.00
8	Greg Maddux	3.00
9	Mark McGwire	6.00
10	Mike Piazza	3.50
11	Cal Ripken Jr.	5.00
12	Alex Rodriguez	5.00
13	Sammy Sosa	3.00
14	David Wells	.75
15	Kerry Wood	1.00

1999 Fleer Rookie Flashback

This 15-card set features the impact rookies from the 1998 season. These are seeded 1:6 packs and feature sculpture embossing.

		MT
Complete Set (15):		9.00
Common Player:		.20
Inserted 1:6		
1	Matt Anderson	.20
2	Rolando Arrojo	.30
3	Adrian Beltre	.60
4	Mike Caruso	.20
5	Eric Chavez	1.00
6	J.D. Drew	1.50
7	Juan Encarnacion	.60
8	Brad Fullmer	.30
9	Troy Glaus	1.50
10	Ben Grieve	1.00
11	Todd Helton	.75
12	Orlando Hernandez	1.50
13	Travis Lee	1.25
14	Richie Sexson	.40
15	Kerry Wood	.75

1999 Fleer Stan Musial Monumental Moments

Great moments and insight from and about the St. Louis Cardinals great. This 10-card tribute set chronicles Musial's legendary career. These are seeded 1:36 packs with 500 autographed cards randomly seeded.

		MT
Complete Set (10):		15.00
Common Musial:		2.00
Autographed Card:		75.00
1	Life in Donora	2.00
2	Values	2.00
3	In the Beginning	2.00
4	In the Navy	2.00
5	The 1948 Season (w/ Red Schoendienst)	2.00
6	Success Stories (w/ Pres. Kennedy)	2.00
7	Mr. Cardinal	2.00
8	Most Valuable Player	2.00
9	... baseball's perfect knight	2.00
10	Hall of Fame	2.00

1999 Fleer Vintage '61

This 50-card set takes the first 50 cards from the base set and showcases them in the 1961 Fleer "Baseball Greats" card design. These are seeded one per hobby pack.

		MT
Complete Set (50):		30.00
Common Player:		.20
Inserted 1:1		
1	Mark McGwire	3.00
2	Sammy Sosa	1.50
3	Ken Griffey Jr.	2.50
4	Kerry Wood	.45
5	Derek Jeter	2.50
6	Stan Musial	3.00
7	J.D. Drew	.45
8	Cal Ripken Jr.	2.50
9	Alex Rodriguez	2.50
10	Travis Lee	.25
11	Andres Galarraga	.20
12	Nomar Garciaparra	1.50
13	Albert Belle	.40
14	Barry Larkin	.25
15	Dante Bichette	.20
16	Tony Clark	.20
17	Moises Alou	.25
18	Rafael Palmeiro	.45
19	Raul Mondesi	.25
20	Vladimir Guerrero	.75
21	John Olerud	.20
22	Bernie Williams	.45
23	Ben Grieve	.40
24	Scott Rolen	.75
25	Jeromy Burnitz	.20
26	Ken Caminiti	.20
27	Barry Bonds	1.00
28	Todd Helton	.75
29	Juan Gonzalez	.75
30	Roger Clemens	1.00
31	Andruw Jones	.75
32	Mo Vaughn	.40
33	Larry Walker	.35
34	Frank Thomas	1.00
35	Manny Ramirez	.75
36	Randy Johnson	.75
37	Vinny Castilla	.20
38	Juan Encarnacion	.20
39	Jeff Bagwell	.75
40	Gary Sheffield	.40
41	Mike Piazza	2.00
42	Richie Sexson	.20
43	Tony Gwynn	.75
44	Chipper Jones	2.00
45	Jim Thome	.20
46	Craig Biggio	.20
47	Carlos Delgado	.50
48	Greg Vaughn	.20
49	Greg Maddux	1.50
50	Troy Glaus	.75

1999 Fleer Update

Distributed as a 150-card boxed set, the main focus for this release is the inclusion of rookie cards of players called up late in the '99 season, including Rick Ankiel. Besides rookies, the set also features 10 traded players/ free agents and a 10-card Season Highlights subset.

		MT
Complete Set (150):		20.00
Common Player:		.10
1	*Rick Ankiel*	4.00
2	*Peter Bergeron*	.50
3	*Pat Burrell*	3.00
4	*Eric Munson*	1.00
5	*Alfonso Soriano*	5.00
6	*Tim Hudson*	2.50
7	*Erubiel Durazo*	1.00
8	Chad Hermansen	.10
9	Jeff Zimmerman	.15
10	*Jesus Pena*	.25
11	Ramon Hernandez	.10
12	*Trent Durrington*	.25
13	Tony Armas Jr.	.25
14	*Mike Fyhrie*	.20
15	*Danny Kolb*	.20
16	*Mike Porzio*	.20
17	*Will Brunson*	.20
18	*Mike Duvall*	.20
19	*Doug Mientkiewicz*	1.00
20	*Gabe Molina*	.25
21	*Luis Vizcaino*	.20
22	*Robinson Cancel*	.15
23	*Brett Laxton*	.20
24	*Joe McEwing*	.25
25	*Justin Speier*	.30
26	*Kip Wells*	.40
27	*Armando Almanza*	.25
28	*Joe Davenport*	.20
29	*Yamid Haad*	.20
30	John Halama	.10
31	Adam Kennedy	.10
32	*Vicente Padilla*	1.00
33	*Travis Dawkins*	.40
34	*Ryan Rupe*	.40
35	*B.J. Ryan*	.25
36	*Chance Sanford*	.20
37	*Anthony Shumaker*	.20
38	*Ryan Glynn*	.30
39	*Matt Herges*	.20
40	Ben Molina	.20
41	Scott Williamson	.10
42	*Eric Gagne*	.40
43	*John McDonald*	.25
44	*Scott Sauerbeck*	.20
45	*Mike Venafro*	.15
46	*Edwards Guzman*	.40
47	*Richard Barker*	.20
48	Braden Looper	.10
49	*Chad Meyers*	.20
50	*Scott Strickland*	.20
51	Billy Koch	.10
52	*Dave Newhan*	.20
53	*David Riske*	.15
54	Jose Santiago	.10
55	*Miguel Del Toro*	.15
56	*Orber Moreno*	.15
57	Dave Roberts	.10
58	*Tim Byrdak*	.20
59	*David Lee*	.15
60	*Guillermo Mota*	.20
61	*Wilton Veras*	.50
62	*Joe Mays*	.75
63	*Jose Fernandez*	.15
64	*Ray King*	.25
65	*Chris Petersen*	.20
66	Vernon Wells	.15
67	Ruben Mateo	.20
68	Ben Petrick	.10
69	*Chris Tremie*	.20
70	Lance Berkman	.25
71	Dan Smith	.10
72	*Carlos Hernandez*	.10
73	*Chad Harville*	.25
74	Damaso Marte	.10
75	*Aaron Myette*	.50
76	*Willis Roberts*	.15
77	*Erik Sabel*	.15
78	*Hector Almonte*	.25
79	Kris Benson	.10
80	*Pat Daneker*	.25
81	*Freddy Garcia*	2.50
82	*Byung-Hyun Kim*	.50
83	*Wily Pena*	1.50
84	*Dan Wheeler*	.25
85	*Tim Harikkala*	.25
86	*Derrin Ebert*	.25
87	*Horacio Estrada*	.15
88	*Liu Rodriguez*	.15
89	*Jordan Zimmerman*	.15
90	*A.J. Burnett*	.75
91	*Doug Davis*	.15
92	*Robert Ramsey*	.15
93	*Ryan Franklin*	.10
94	*Charlie Greene*	.15
95	*Bo Porter*	.15
96	*Jorge Toca*	.30
97	*Casey Blake*	.25
98	*Amaury Garcia*	.15
99	*Jose Molina*	.15
100	*Melvin Mora*	.30
101	*Joe Nathan*	.20
102	*Juan Pena*	.25
103	*Dave Borkowski*	.20
104	*Eddie Gaillard*	.10
105	Rob Radlosky	.10
106	*Brett Hinchliffe*	.10
107	Carlos Lee	.10
108	*Rob Ryan*	.10
109	*Jeff Weaver*	.50
110	Ed Yarnall	.10
111	*Nelson Cruz*	.10
112	*Cleatus Davidson*	.25
113	*Tim Kubinski*	.10
114	*Sean Spencer*	.10
115	*Joe Winkelsas*	.10
116	*Chris Clapinski*	.25
117	*Tom Davey*	.10
118	Warren Morris	.10
119	*Dan Murray*	.10
120	*Jose Nieves*	.10
121	*Mark Quinn*	.50
122	*Josh Beckett*	8.00
123	*Chad Allen*	.10
124	Mike Figga	.10
125	*Beiker Graterol*	.10
126	*Aaron Scheffer*	.10
127	*Wiki Gonzalez*	.20
128	Ramon E. Martinez	.10
129	*Matt Riley*	.40
130	*Chris Woodward*	.20
131	Albert Belle	.15
132	Roger Cedeno	.10
133	Roger Clemens	.50
134	Brian Giles	.10
135	Rickey Henderson	.25
136	Randy Johnson	.25
137	Brian Jordan	.10
138	Paul Konerko	.10
139	Hideo Nomo	.40
140	Kenny Rogers	.10
141	Wade Boggs	.25
142	Jose Canseco	.40
143	Roger Clemens	.75
144	David Cone	.10
145	Tony Gwynn	.75
146	Mark McGwire	1.50
147	Cal Ripken Jr.	1.50
148	Alex Rodriguez	1.00
149	Fernando Tatis	.10
150	Robin Ventura	.10

1999 Fleer Brilliants

This 175-card set features an action photo on a complete silver-foiled background swirl pattern. The featured player's name, team and postion are stamped in gold foil. Card backs have a small photo, vital information, 1998 statistics and a brief overview of the player's '98 season. Cards numbered 126-175 are part of a short-printed Rookies subset and are seeded 1:2 packs.

		MT
Complete Set (175):		90.00
Common Player:		.40
Common SP (126-175):		.75
Pack (5):		3.00
Wax Box (24):		60.00
1	Mark McGwire	4.00
2	Derek Jeter	3.00
3	Nomar Garciaparra	2.00
4	Travis Lee	.40
5	Jeff Bagwell	1.25
6	Andres Galarraga	.40
7	Pedro Martinez	1.25
8	Cal Ripken Jr.	4.00
9	Vladimir Guerrero	1.00
10	Chipper Jones	2.50
11	Rusty Greer	.40
12	Omar Vizquel	.40
13	Quinton McCracken	.40
14	Jaret Wright	.60
15	Mike Mussina	.75
16	Jason Giambi	.75
17	Tony Clark	.40
18	Troy O'Leary	.40

19	Troy Percival	.40
20	Kerry Wood	.75
21	Vinny Castilla	.40
22	Chris Carpenter	.40
23	Richie Sexson	.40
24	Ken Griffey Jr.	3.00
25	Barry Bonds	1.50
26	Carlos Delgado	1.25
27	Frank Thomas	1.50
28	Manny Ramirez	1.25
29	Shawn Green	.75
30	Mike Piazza	2.50
31	Tino Martinez	.40
32	Dante Bichette	.40
33	Scott Rolen	1.00
34	Gabe Alvarez	.40
35	Raul Mondesi	.60
36	Damion Easley	.40
37	Jeff Kent	.40
38	Al Leiter	.40
39	Alex Rodriguez	3.00
40	Jeff King	.40
41	Mark Grace	.60
42	Larry Walker	.60
43	Moises Alou	.60
44	Juan Gonzalez	1.25
45	Rolando Arrojo	.40
46	Tom Glavine	.60
47	Johnny Damon	.40
48	Livan Hernandez	.40
49	Craig Biggio	.50
50	Dmitri Young	.40
51	Chan Ho Park	.60
52	Todd Walker	.40
53	Derrek Lee	.40
54	Todd Helton	1.00
55	Ray Lankford	.40
56	Jim Thome	.40
57	Matt Lawton	.40
58	Matt Anderson	.40
59	Jose Offerman	.40
60	Eric Karros	.40
61	Orlando Hernandez	.60
62	Ben Grieve	.60
63	Bobby Abreu	.40
64	Kevin Young	.40
65	John Olerud	.40
66	Sammy Sosa	2.00
67	Andy Ashby	.40
68	Juan Encarnacion	.40
69	Shane Reynolds	.40
70	Bernie Williams	.60
71	Mike Cameron	.40
72	Troy Glaus	2.00
73	Gary Sheffield	.60
74	Jeromy Burnitz	.40
75	Mike Caruso	.40
76	Chuck Knoblauch	.40
77	Kenny Rogers	.40
78	David Cone	.40
79	Tony Gwynn	1.50
80	Aramis Ramirez	.40
81	Paul O'Neill	.40
82	Charles Nagy	.40
83	Javy Lopez	.40
84	Scott Erickson	.40
85	Trevor Hoffman	.40
86	Andruw Jones	1.00
87	Ray Durham	.40
88	Jorge Posada	.40
89	Edgar Martinez	.40
90	Tim Salmon	.75
91	Bobby Higginson	.40
92	Adrian Beltre	.75
93	Jason Kendall	.40
94	Henry Rodriguez	.40
95	Greg Maddux	2.50
96	David Justice	.75
97	Ivan Rodriguez	1.00
98	Curt Schilling	.60
99	Matt Williams	.75
100	Darin Erstad	1.00
101	Rafael Palmeiro	.75
102	David Wells	.40
103	Barry Larkin	.75
104	Robin Ventura	.40
105	Edgar Renteria	.40
106	Andy Pettitte	.60
107	Albert Belle	.75
108	Steve Finley	.40
109	Fernando Vina	.40
110	Rondell White	.40
111	Kevin Brown	.40
112	Jose Canseco	.75
113	Roger Clemens	1.50
114	Todd Hundley	.40
115	Will Clark	.75
116	Jim Edmonds	.40
117	Randy Johnson	1.25
118	Denny Neagle	.40
119	Brian Jordan	.40
120	Dean Palmer	.40
121	Roberto Alomar	.75
122	Ken Caminiti	.40
123	Brian Giles	.40
124	Todd Stottlemyre	.40
125	Mo Vaughn	.60
126	J.D. Drew	1.50
127	Ryan Minor	.75
128	Gabe Kapler	1.00
129	Jeremy Giambi	.75
130	Eric Chavez	1.50
131	Ben Davis	1.00
132	Rob Fick	.75
133	George Lombard	.75
134	Calvin Pickering	.75
135	Preston Wilson	1.00
136	Corey Koskie	1.00
137	Russell Branyan	1.00
138	Bruce Chen	.75
139	Matt Clement	.75
140	*Pat Burrell*	6.00
141	*Freddy Garcia*	3.00
142	Brian Simmons	.75
143	Carlos Febles	.75
144	Carlos Guillen	.75
145	Fernando Seguignol	1.00
146	Carlos Beltran	.75
147	Edgard Clemente	.75
148	Mitch Meluskey	.75
149	Ryan Bradley	.75
150	Marlon Anderson	.75
151	*A.J. Burnett*	1.50
152	*Scott Hunter*	.75
153	Mark Johnson	.75
154	Angel Pena	.75
155	Roy Halladay	.75
156	*Chad Allen*	1.00
157	Trot Nixon	.75
158	Ricky Ledee	.75
159	*Gary Bennett*	1.00
160	*Micah Bowie*	1.00
161	Doug Mientkiewicz	.75
162	Danny Klassen	.75
163	Willis Otanez	.75
164	Jin Ho Cho	.75
165	Mike Lowell	1.00
166	Armando Rios	.75
167	Tom Evans	.75
168	Michael Barrett	.75
169	Alex Gonzalez	.75
170	*Masao Kida*	1.00
171	*Peter Tucci*	1.00
172	Luis Saturria	.75
173	Kris Benson	1.00
174	*Mario Encarnacion*	1.00
175	*Roosevelt Brown*	1.00

1999 Fleer Brilliants Blue/Golds

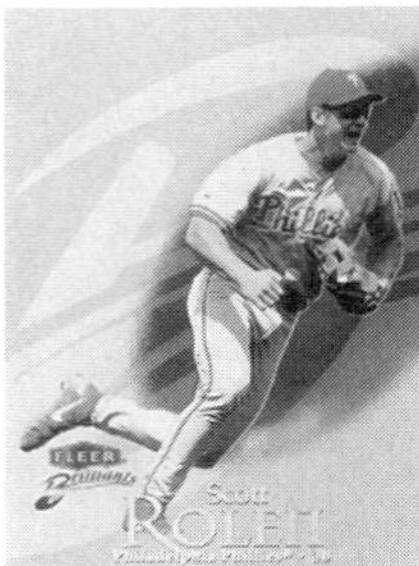

The 175 Fleer Brilliants base cards are paralleled in three insert sets of differing degrees of scarcity. Brilliant Blue parallels have a mirrored blue foil background on front and a "B" suffix to the card number on back. They are seeded one per three packs (125 veterans) and one per six packs (50 rookies). Gold parallels are printed with gold foil background and a "G" suffix. Each card is serially numbered on back within an edition of 99. The 24-karat Gold parallels have gold rainbow holographic foil backgrounds, a 24-karat gold logo and are serially numbered to just 24 of each card; numbers have a TG sugffix.

	MT
Brilliants Blue Common:	.50
Brilliants Blue Stars:	2X
Brilliants Blue Rookies:	1.5X
Brilliants Gold Common:	4.00
Brilliants Gold Stars:	15X
Brilliants Gold Rookies:	5X
Brilliants 24K Gold Common:	15.00
Brilliants 24K Gold Stars:	50X
Brilliants 24K Gold Rookies:	15X

(See 1999 Fleer Brilliants for checklist and base card values.)

1999 Fleer Brilliants Illuminators

This 15-card set highlights baseball's top young prospects on a team color-coded fully foiled front. Card backs are numbered with an "I" suffix and are inserted 1:10 packs.

		MT
Complete Set (15):		25.00
Common Player:		1.50
Inserted 1:10		
1	Kerry Wood	2.50
2	Ben Grieve	1.50
3	J.D. Drew	2.50
4	Juan Encarnacion	1.50
5	Travis Lee	1.50
6	Todd Helton	4.00
7	Troy Glaus	6.00
8	Ricky Ledee	1.50
9	Eric Chavez	3.00
10	Ben Davis	1.50
11	George Lombard	1.50
12	Jeremy Giambi	1.50
13	Richie Sexson	1.50
14	Corey Koskie	1.50
15	Russell Branyan	1.50

1999 Fleer Brilliants Shining Stars

Shining Stars is a 15-card set printed on styrene with two-sided mirrored foil. Card backs are numbered with a "S" suffix and are seeded 1:20 packs. Pulsars are a parallel set that are printed on two-sided rainbow holographic foil and styrene with an embossed star pattern in the background. Pulsars are seeded 1:400 packs.

		MT
Complete Set (15):		30.00
Common Player:		1.50
Inserted 1:20		
Pulsars:		6X
Inserted 1:400		
1	Ken Griffey Jr.	3.50
2	Mark McGwire	4.00
3	Sammy Sosa	2.50
4	Derek Jeter	3.50
5	Nomar Garciaparra	3.00
6	Alex Rodriguez	3.50
7	Mike Piazza	3.00
8	Juan Gonzalez	1.50
9	Chipper Jones	3.00
10	Cal Ripken Jr.	3.50
11	Frank Thomas	1.50
12	Greg Maddux	2.50
13	Roger Clemens	1.50
14	Vladimir Guerrero	1.50
15	Manny Ramirez	1.50

1999 Fleer Mystique

The "Mystique" of this issue lay partly in the fact that each four-card $4.99 pack included a card which was covered with a peel-off coating, either a short-printed star card from the #1-100 base set, one of the short-printed Rookie (#101-150) or Stars (#151-160) cards or one of the inserts. The Rookie cards are serial numbered to 2,999 apiece, while the red-foil highlighted Stars cards are in an edition of 2,500 each. Fronts have metallic foil backgrounds, backs have a player portrait photo, biographical and career notes and stats.

		MT
Complete Set (160):		250.00
Common Player:		.20
Common SP (1-100):		.75
Common (101-150):		2.50
Production 2,999 sets		
Common (151-160):		2.00
Production 2,500 sets		
Pack (4):		4.00
Wax Box (24):		80.00
1	Ken Griffey Jr. (SP)	5.00
2	Livan Hernandez	.20
3	Jeff Kent	.20
4	Brian Jordan	.20
5	Kevin Young	.20
6	Vinny Castilla	.20
7	Orlando Hernandez (SP)	.50
8	Bobby Abreu	.20
9	Vladimir Guerrero (SP)	1.00
10	Chuck Knoblauch	.20
11	Nomar Garciaparra (SP)	3.00
12	Jeff Bagwell	1.50
13	Todd Walker	.20
14	Johnny Damon	.20
15	Mike Caruso	.20
16	Cliff Floyd	.20
17	Andy Pettitte	.40
18	Cal Ripken Jr. (SP)	4.00
19	Brian Giles	.20
20	Robin Ventura	.20
21	Alex Gonzalez	.20
22	Randy Johnson	.75
23	Raul Mondesi	.30
24	Ken Caminiti	.20
25	Tom Glavine	.30
26	Derek Jeter (SP)	4.00
27	Carlos Delgado	.75
28	Adrian Beltre	.50
29	Tino Martinez	.20
30	Todd Helton	1.00
31	Juan Gonzalez (SP)	1.50
32	Henry Rodriguez	.20
33	Jim Thome	.20
34	Paul O'Neill	.20
35	Scott Rolen (SP)	1.50
36	Rafael Palmeiro	.60
37	Will Clark	.40
38	Todd Hundley	.20
39	Andruw Jones (SP)	1.00
40	Luis Rolando Arrojo	.20
41	Barry Larkin	.30
42	Tim Salmon	.30
43	Rondell White	.20
44	Curt Schilling	.40
45	Chipper Jones (SP)	3.00
46	Jeromy Burnitz	.20
47	Mo Vaughn	.50
48	Tony Clark	.30
49	Fernando Tatis	.20
50	Dmitri Young	.20
51	Wade Boggs	.50
52	Rickey Henderson	.50
53	Manny Ramirez (SP)	1.50
54	Edgar Martinez	.20
55	Jason Giambi	.50
56	Jason Kendall	.20
57	Eric Karros	.20
58	Jose Canseco (SP)	1.00
59	Shawn Green	.50
60	Ellis Burks	.20
61	Derek Bell	.20
62	Shannon Stewart	.20
63	Roger Clemens (SP)	2.00
64	Sean Casey (SP)	.75
65	Jose Offerman	.20
66	Sammy Sosa (SP)	3.00
67	Frank Thomas (SP)	1.50
68	Tony Gwynn (SP)	1.50
69	Roberto Alomar	.65
70	Mark McGwire (SP)	4.00
71	Troy Glaus	1.00
72	Ray Durham	.20
73	Jeff Cirillo	.20
74	Alex Rodriguez (SP)	4.00
75	Jose Cruz Jr.	.40
76	Juan Encarnacion	.20
77	Mark Grace	.40
78	Barry Bonds (SP)	2.00
79	Ivan Rodriguez (SP)	1.00
80	Greg Vaughn	.20
81	Greg Maddux (SP)	2.00
82	Albert Belle	.50
83	John Olerud	.20
84	Kenny Lofton	.20
85	Bernie Williams	.50
86	Matt Williams	.50
87	Ray Lankford	.20
88	Darin Erstad	.75
89	Ben Grieve	.40
90	Craig Biggio	.30
91	Dean Palmer	.20
92	Reggie Sanders	.20
93	Dante Bichette	.30
94	Pedro Martinez (SP)	1.50
95	Larry Walker	.50
96	David Wells	.20
97	Travis Lee (SP)	.50
98	Mike Piazza (SP)	3.00
99	Mike Mussina	.75
100	Kevin Brown	.30
101	Ruben Mateo (Rookie)	4.00
102	Roberto Ramirez (Rookie)	2.50
103	*Glen Barker* (Rookie)	2.50
104	*Clay Bellinger* (Rookie)	2.50
105	Carlos Guillen (Rookie)	3.00
106	Scott Schoeneweis (Rookie)	2.50
107	Creighton Gubanich (Rookie)	2.50
108	Scott Williamson (Rookie)	3.00
109	*Edwards Guzman* (Rookie)	3.00
110	*A.J. Burnett* (Rookie)	4.00
111	Jeremy Giambi (Rookie)	2.50
112	Trot Nixon (Rookie)	2.50
113	J.D. Drew (Rookie)	7.50
114	Roy Halladay (Rookie)	3.00
115	*Jose Macias* (Rookie)	3.00
116	Corey Koskie (Rookie)	2.50
117	*Ryan Rupe* (Rookie)	3.00
118	Scott Hunter (Rookie)	2.50
119	Rob Fick (Rookie)	2.50
120	McKay Christensen (Rookie)	2.50
121	Carlos Febles (Rookie)	3.00
122	Gabe Kapler (Rookie)	4.00
123	Jeff Liefer (Rookie)	2.50
124	Warren Morris (Rookie)	2.50
125	Chris Pritchett (Rookie)	2.50
126	Torii Hunter (Rookie)	2.50
127	Armando Rios (Rookie)	2.50
128	Ricky Ledee (Rookie)	2.50
129	*Kelly Dransfeldt* (Rookie)	3.00
130	Jeff Zimmerman (Rookie)	5.00
131	Eric Chavez (Rookie)	3.00
132	Freddy Garcia (Rookie)	10.00
133	Jose Jimenez (Rookie)	2.50
134	*Pat Burrell* (Rookie)	60.00
135	*Joe McEwing* (Rookie)	3.00
136	Kris Benson (Rookie)	2.50
137	*Joe Mays* (Rookie)	4.00
138	Rafael Roque (Rookie)	2.50
139	Cristian Guzman (Rookie)	2.50
140	Michael Barrett (Rookie)	2.50
141	Doug Mientkiewicz (Rookie)	3.00
142	*Jeff Weaver* (Rookie)	8.00
143	Mike Lowell (Rookie)	2.50
144	*Jason Phillips* (Rookie)	2.50
145	Marlon Anderson (Rookie)	2.50
146	*Brett Hinchliffe* (Rookie)	2.50
147	Matt Clement (Rookie)	2.50
148	Terrence Long (Rookie)	3.00
149	Carlos Beltran (Rookie)	3.00
150	Preston Wilson (Rookie)	3.50
151	Ken Griffey Jr. (Stars)	4.00
152	Mark McGwire (Stars)	5.00
153	Sammy Sosa (Stars)	4.00
154	Mike Piazza (Stars)	4.00
155	Alex Rodriguez (Stars)	4.00
156	Nomar Garciaparra (Stars)	3.00
157	Cal Ripken Jr. (Stars)	5.00
158	Greg Maddux (Stars)	3.00
159	Derek Jeter (Stars)	5.00
160	Juan Gonzalez (Stars)	2.00
	Checklist card	.10

1999 Fleer Mystique Gold

The first 100 cards of the base set are paralleled in this insert which features gold-foil highlights on front. Gold versions are found in one of eight packs, on average.

	MT
Common Player:	1.50
Stars (1-100):	4X
Inserted 1:8	

(See 1999 Fleer Mystique for checklist and base card values.)

1999 Fleer Mystique Masterpiece

Each of the cards in Fleer Mystique was also produced in a unique Masterpiece version. The super-rarities are labeled on front "The Only 1 of 1 / Masterpiece".

	MT
Common Player:	50.00

(Because of their unique nature Masterpiece values cannot be determined.)

1999 Fleer Mystique Destiny

A silver holofoil background on front and a serial number within an edition of 999 each marks this insert set. Backs have another photo along with career highlights.

		MT
Complete Set (10):		45.00
Common Player:		4.00
Production 999 sets		
1	Tony Gwynn	7.50
2	Juan Gonzalez	5.00
3	Scott Rolen	4.00
4	Nomar Garciaparra	15.00
5	Orlando Hernandez	4.00
6	Andruw Jones	5.00
7	Vladimir Guerrero	5.00
8	Darin Erstad	4.00
9	Manny Ramirez	5.00
10	Roger Clemens	7.50

1999 Fleer Mystique Established

A plastic stock, red holofoil background and silver foil highlights complement the action photo of a top star in this insert set. Backs have another photo, some career highlights and a serial number from within an edition of 100 each.

		MT
Complete Set (10):		500.00
Common Player:		40.00
Production 100 sets		
1	Ken Griffey Jr.	75.00
2	Derek Jeter	75.00
3	Chipper Jones	60.00
4	Greg Maddux	55.00
5	Mark McGwire	90.00
6	Mike Piazza	60.00
7	Cal Ripken Jr.	75.00
8	Alex Rodriguez	75.00

9	Sammy Sosa	55.00
10	Frank Thomas	40.00

1999 Fleer Mystique Fresh Ink

These inserts, found about one per 48 packs, have a white oval at bottom front containing an autograph of the player pictured. At bottom is a white panel with a hand-printed serial number from within each card's edition, which ranged from 140 to 1,000. Backs have a Fleer seal and statement of authenticity pertinent to the autograph. The unnumbered cards are listed here in alphabetical order.

	MT
Complete Set (26):	400.00
Common Player:	5.00
Inserted 1:48	
Roberto Alomar (500)	25.00
Michael Barrett (1,000)	5.00
Kris Benson (500)	10.00
Micah Bowie (1,000)	5.00
A.J. Burnett (500)	15.00
Pat Burrell (250)	30.00
Ken Caminiti (250)	15.00
Jose Canseco (250)	40.00
Sean Casey (1,000)	15.00
Edgard Clemente (1,000)	5.00
Bartolo Colon (500)	10.00
J.D. Drew (400)	20.00
Juan Encarnacion (1,000)	5.00
Troy Glaus (400)	25.00
Juan Gonzalez (250)	40.00
Shawn Green (250)	30.00
Tony Gwynn (250)	40.00
Chipper Jones (500)	40.00
Gabe Kapler (750)	12.50
Barry Larkin (250)	25.00
Doug Mientkiewicz (500)	10.00
Alex Rodriguez (200)	100.00
Scott Rolen (140)	40.00
Fernando Tatis (750)	10.00
Robin Ventura (500)	10.00
Todd Walker (1,000)	5.00

1999 Fleer Mystique Feel the Game

Swatches of various game-used equipment are featured in this insert series. Each card is hand-numbered from editions which range between 345 and 450.

	MT
Common Player:	15.00
Adrian Beltre (shoe, 430)	20.00
J.D. Drew (jersey, 450)	25.00
Juan Gonzalez (bat glove, 415)	40.00
Tony Gwynn (jersey, 435)	30.00
Kevin Millwood (jersey, 435)	15.00
Alex Rodriguez (bat glove, 345)	70.00
Frank Thomas (jersey, 450)	40.00

1999 Fleer Mystique Prophetic

Blue holofoil with silver highlights is the graphic treatment found on this insert set of young stars. Each card is numbered on front from within an edition of 1,999. Backs have a portrait photo and a few words about the player.

		MT
Complete Set (10):		18.00
Common Player:		1.25
Production 1,999 sets		
1	Eric Chavez	1.50
2	J.D. Drew	1.50
3	A.J. Burnett	1.25
4	Ben Grieve	1.50
5	Gabe Kapler	1.25
6	Todd Helton	2.50
7	Troy Glaus	3.50
8	Travis Lee	1.25
9	Pat Burrell	7.50
10	Kerry Wood	1.50

2000 Fleer Focus

The 250-card base set has two versions for the Prospects subset card numbers 226-250. The portrait versions are serial numbered from 1-999, while the remaining serial numbered from 1,000 to 3,999 capture an action shot. The base set design has a white border with gold foil stamping. Card backs have complete year-by-year statistics along with a career note and small photo.

		MT
Complete Set (250):		200.00
Common Player:		.15
Common Prospect (226-250):		4.00
Production 2,999 sets		
Common Portrait (226-250):		8.00
Portraits:		2X
Production 999 sets		
Pack:		2.50
Wax Box (24):		50.00
1	Nomar Garciaparra	2.00
2	Adrian Beltre	.25
3	Miguel Tejada	.15
4	Joe Randa	.15
5	Larry Walker	.50
6	Jeff Weaver	.15
7	Jay Bell	.15
8	Ivan Rodriguez	.75
9	Edgar Martinez	.15
10	Desi Relaford	.15
11	Derek Jeter	3.00
12	Delino DeShields	.15
13	Craig Biggio	.50
14	Chuck Knoblauch	.25
15	Chuck Finley	.15
16	Brett Tomko	.15
17	Bobby Higginson	.15
18	Pedro Martinez	.75
19	Troy O'Leary	.15
20	Rickey Henderson	.30
21	Robb Nen	.15
22	Rolando Arrojo	.15
23	Rondell White	.25
24	Royce Clayton	.15
25	Rusty Greer	.15
26	Stan Spencer	.15
27	Steve Finley	.25
28	Tom Goodwin	.15
29	Troy Percival	.15
30	Wilton Guerrero	.15
31	Roberto Alomar	.50
32	Mike Hampton	.15
33	Michael Barrett	.15
34	Curt Schilling	.25
35	Bill Mueller	.15
36	Bernie Williams	.50
37	John Smoltz	.15
38	B.J. Surhoff	.25
39	Pete Harnisch	.15
40	Juan Encarnacion	.25
41	Derrek Lee	.15
42	Jeff Shaw	.15
43	David Cone	.25
44	Jason Christiansen	.15
45	Jeff Kent	.25
46	Randy Johnson	.60
47	Todd Walker	.15
48	Jose Lima	.15
49	Jason Giambi	.25
50	Ken Griffey Jr.	2.50
51	Bartolo Colon	.15
52	Mike Lieberthal	.15
53	Shane Reynolds	.25
54	Travis Lee	.25
55	Travis Fryman	.25
56	John Valentin	.15
57	Joey Hamilton	.15
58	Jay Buhner	.25
59	Brad Radke	.15
60	A.J. Burnett	.15
61	Roy Halladay	.15
62	Raul Mondesi	.25
63	Matt Mantei	.15
64	Mark Grace	.30
65	David Justice	.30
66	Billy Wagner	.15
67	Eric Milton	.15
68	Eric Chavez	.25
69	Doug Glanville	.15
70	Ray Durham	.15
71	Mike Sirotka	.15
72	Greg Vaughn	.25
73	Brian Jordan	.25
74	Alex Gonzalez	.15
75	Alex Rodriguez	2.50
76	David Nilsson	.15
77	Robin Ventura	.25
78	Kevin Young	.25
79	Wilson Alvarez	.15
80	Matt Williams	.40
81	Ismael Valdes	.15
82	Kenny Lofton	.50
83	Carlos Beltran	.20
84	Doug Mientkiewicz	.15
85	Wally Joyner	.15
86	J.D. Drew	.25
87	Carlos Delgado	.50
88	Tony Womack	.15
89	Eric Young	.15
90	Manny Ramirez	.75
91	Johnny Damon	.15
92	Torii Hunter	.15
93	Kenny Rogers	.15
94	Trevor Hoffman	.15
95	John Wetteland	.15
96	Ray Lankford	.15
97	Tom Glavine	.25
98	Carlos Lee	.15
99	Richie Sexson	.25
100	Carlos Febles	.15
101	Chad Allen	.15
102	Sterling Hitchcock	.15
103	Joe McEwing	.15
104	Justin Thompson	.15
105	Jim Edmonds	.25
106	Kerry Wood	.40
107	Jim Thome	.40
108	Jeremy Giambi	.15
109	Mike Piazza	2.00
110	Darryl Kile	.15
111	Darin Erstad	.25
112	Kyle Farnsworth	.15
113	Omar Vizquel	.25
114	Orber Moreno	.15
115	Al Leiter	.25
116	John Olerud	.30
117	Aaron Sele	.15
118	Chipper Jones	1.50
119	Paul Konerko	.25
120	Chris Singleton	.15
121	Fernando Vina	.15
122	Andy Ashby	.15
123	Eli Marrero	.15
124	Edgar Renteria	.15
125	Roberto Hernandez	.15
126	Andruw Jones	.50
127	Maggio Ordonez	.30
128	Bob Wickman	.15
129	Tony Gwynn	1.50
130	Mark McGwire	3.00
131	Albert Belle	.50
132	Pokey Reese	.15
133	Tony Clark	.25
134	Jeff Bagwell	.75
135	Mark Grudzielanek	.15
136	Dustin Hermanson	.15

137	Reggie Sanders	.15
138	Ryan Rupe	.15
139	Kevin Millwood	.30
140	Bret Saberhagen	.15
141	Juan Guzman	.15
142	Alex Gonzalez	.15
143	Gary Sheffield	.30
144	Roger Clemens	1.00
145	Ben Grieve	.30
146	Bobby Abreu	.30
147	Brian Giles	.15
148	Quinton McCracken	.15
149	Freddy Garcia	.25
150	Erubiel Durazo	.25
151	Sidney Ponson	.15
152	Scott Williamson	.15
153	Ken Caminiti	.25
154	Vladimir Guerrero	1.50
155	Andy Pettitte	.30
156	Edwards Guzman	.15
157	Shannon Stewart	.15
158	Greg Maddux	1.50
159	Mike Stanley	.15
160	Sean Casey	.30
161	Cliff Floyd	.15
162	Devon White	.15
163	Scott Brosius	.15
164	Marlon Anderson	.15
165	Jason Kendall	.25
166	Ryan Klesko	.15
167	Sammy Sosa	2.00
168	Frank Thomas	1.00
169	Geoff Jenkins	.25
170	Jason Schmidt	.15
171	Dan Wilson	.15
172	Jose Canseco	.75
173	Troy Glaus	.50
174	Mariano Rivera	.25
175	Scott Rolen	.75
176	J.T. Snow	.15
177	Rafael Palmeiro	.40
178	A.J. Hinch	.15
179	Jose Offerman	.15
180	Jeff Cirillo	.15
181	Dean Palmer	.25
182	Jose Rosado	.15
183	Armando Benitez	.15
184	Brady Anderson	.25
185	Cal Ripken Jr.	2.50
186	Barry Larkin	.40
187	Damion Easley	.15
188	Moises Alou	.25
189	Todd Hundley	.25
190	Tim Hudson	.25
191	Livan Hernandez	.15
192	Fred McGriff	.30
193	Orlando Hernandez	.30
194	Tim Salmon	.25
195	Mike Mussina	.50
196	Todd Helton	.75
197	Juan Gonzalez	.75
198	Kevin Brown	.25
199	Ugueth Urbina	.15
200	Matt Stairs	.15
201	Shawn Estes	.15
202	Gabe Kapler	.25
203	Javy Lopez	.25
204	Henry Rodriguez	.15
205	Dante Bichette	.25
206	Jeromy Burnitz	.25
207	Todd Zeile	.15
208	Rico Brogna	.15
209	Warren Morris	.15
210	David Segui	.15
211	Vinny Castilla	.25
212	Mo Vaughn	.50
213	Charles Johnson	.15
214	Neifi Perez	.15
215	Shawn Green	.50
216	Carl Pavano	.15
217	Tino Martinez	.30
218	Barry Bonds	1.00
219	David Wells	.15
220	Paul O'Neill	.30
221	Masato Yoshii	.15
222	Kris Benson	.15
223	Fernando Tatis	.30
224	Lee Stevens	.15
225	Jose Cruz Jr.	.15
226	Rick Ankiel (Prospect)	8.00
227	Matt Riley (Prospect)	6.00
228	Norm Hutchins (Prospect)	4.00
229	Ruben Mateo (Prospect)	4.00
229		8.00
230	Ben Petrick (Prospect)	4.00
231	Mario Encarnacion (Prospect)	4.00
232	Nick Johnson (Prospect)	10.00
233	Adam Piatt (Prospect)	10.00
234	Mike Darr (Prospect)	4.00
235	Chad Hermansen (Prospect)	4.00
236	Wily Pena (Prospect)	12.00
237	Octavio Dotel (Prospect)	4.00
238	Vernon Wells (Prospect)	6.00
239	Daryle Ward (Prospect)	5.00
240	Adam Kennedy (Prospect)	6.00
241	Angel Pena (Prospect)	4.00
242	Lance Berkman (Prospect)	5.00
243	Gabe Molina (Prospect)	4.00
244	Steve Lomasney (Prospect)	4.00
245	Jacob Cruz (Prospect)	4.00
246	Mark Quinn (Prospect)	5.00
247	Eric Munson (Prospect)	12.00
248	Alfonso Soriano (Prospect)	8.00
249	Kip Wells (Prospect)	4.00
250	Josh Beckett (Prospect)	12.00
	Checklist #171	.05
	Checklist #172-25, inserts	.05
	Checklist inserts	.05

2000 Fleer Focus Masterpiece

Each of the cards in Fleer Focus was issued in a parallel edition of just one piece each. Fronts of Masterpiece 1/1s have purple metallic ink, instead of gold, for the player identification. On back, there is a notation "The Only 1 of 1 Masterpiece" along with an "M" suffix to the card number. An error version has all the attributes of the true Masterpiece, but lacks the "Only 1 . . . " notation on back (see 2000 Fleer Focus Masterpiece Errors).

	MT
Common Player:	100.00

(Values undetermined due to rarity and fluctuating demand. See 2000 Fleer Focus for checklist.)

2000 Fleer Focus Masterpiece Mania

Green, rather than gold, ink is used on front for the player name, team and position to distinguish this parallel insert set. On back, each card is numbered from within an edition of 300 each.

	MT
Common Player:	3.00
Stars:	8-15X
Yng Stars & RCs (226-250):	1-2X
Production 300 sets	

(See 2000 Fleer Focus for checklist and base card values.)

2000 Fleer Focus Masterpiece Errors

Thousands of collectors' hopes were crushed when it was determined that an unknown number of uncompleted Masterpiece 1-of-1 cards were erroneously inserted in Focus foil packs. Like the true Masterpiece cards, the fronts of the error cards have the player name, team and position at bottom front in purple, rather than gold foil. On back, the cards even have the "M" suffix to the card number at lower-right. Unfortunately, these do not have the foil-stamped "The Only 1 of 1 Masterpiece" notation on back; greatly reducing the value.

		MT
	Complete Set (25):	250.00
	Common Player:	4.00
50M	Ken Griffey Jr.	100.00
202M	Gabe Kapler	8.00
203M	Javy Lopez	6.00
204M	Henry Rodriguez	4.00
205M	Dante Bichette	5.00
206M	Jeromy Burnitz	5.00
207M	Todd Zeile	4.00
208M	Rico Brogna	4.00
209M	Warren Morris	4.00
210M	David Segui	4.00
211M	Vinny Castilla	5.00
212M	Mo Vaughn	6.00
213M	Charles Johnson	5.00
214M	Neifi Perez	5.00
215M	Shawn Green	20.00
216M	Carl Pavano	4.00
217M	Tino Martinez	5.00
218M	Barry Bonds	30.00
219M	David Wells	8.00
220M	Paul O'Neill	6.00
221M	Masato Yoshii	5.00
222M	Kris Benson	8.00
223M	Fernando Tatis	6.00
224M	Lee Stevens	4.00
225M	Jose Cruz Jr.	6.00

2000 Fleer Focus Club 3000

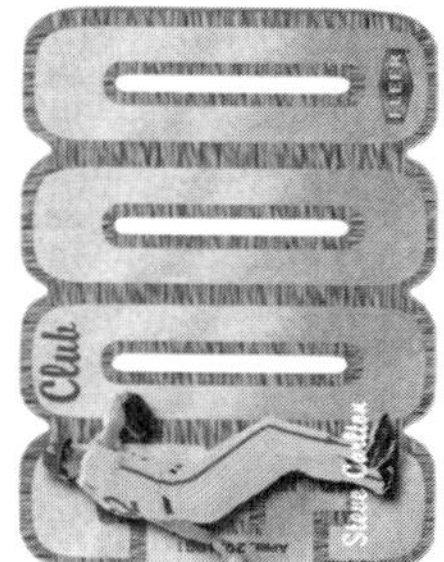

These inserts are die-cut around the numbers 3,000 and features three players who either have 3,000 hits or strikeouts, this set spotlights Stan Musial, Steve Carlton and Paul Molitor. These are seeded 1:36 packs.

		MT
	Complete Set (3):	4.00
	Common Player:	1.50
(1)	Steve Carlton	1.50
(2)	Paul Molitor	1.50
(3)	Stan Musial	1.50

2000 Fleer Focus Club 3000 Memorabilia

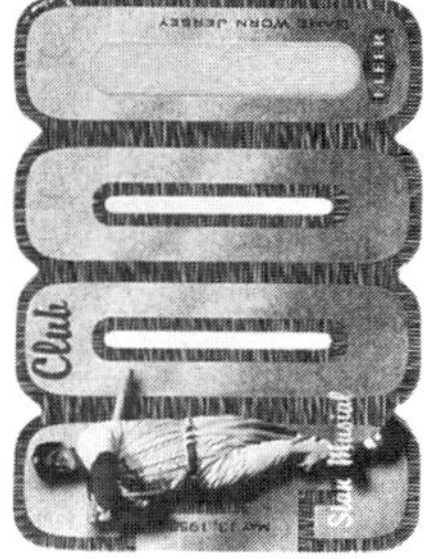

Five tiers featuring memorabilia from game-used bats, caps etc... make up this hand numbered set. Besides a bat and cap insert others include jersey, bat and jersey combo and a bat, jersey and cap combo.

	MT
Steve Carlton - bat/325	50.00
Steve Carlton - hat/65	125.00
Steve Carlton - jersey/750	40.00

Steve Carlton - bat, hat, jersey/25	400.00
Paul Molitor - bat/355	50.00
Paul Molitor - hat/65	120.00
Paul Molitor - jersey/975	40.00
Paul Molitor - bat, jersey/100	75.00
Stan Musial - bat/325	50.00
Stan Musial - hat/65	125.00
Stan Musial - jersey/975	45.00
Stan Musial - bat, jersey/100	150.00

2000 Fleer Focus Feel the Game

This 10-card set offers pieces of player-worn jersey from some of baseball's biggest stars embedded into the card front. These were seeded 1:288 packs.

	MT
Common Player:	15.00
Inserted 1:288	
Adrian Beltre	20.00
Tom Glavine	20.00
Vladimir Guerrero	25.00
Randy Johnson	25.00
Javy Lopez	15.00
Alex Rodriguez	40.00
Scott Rolen	20.00
Cal Ripken Jr.	50.00
Tim Salmon	20.00
Miguel Tejada	15.00

2000 Fleer Focus Focal Points

This 15-card set has silver foil etching around the border and silver foil stamping. These were seeded 1:6 packs and are numbered with an "F" suffix on the card back.

		MT
Complete Set (15):		35.00
Common Player:		1.00
Inserted 1:6		
1	Mark McGwire	5.00
2	Tony Gwynn	2.50
3	Nomar Garciaparra	3.00
4	Juan Gonzalez	1.25
5	Jeff Bagwell	1.25
6	Chipper Jones	2.50
7	Cal Ripken Jr.	4.00
8	Alex Rodriguez	4.00
9	Scott Rolen	1.00
10	Vladimir Guerrero	2.50
11	Mike Piazza	3.00
12	Frank Thomas	2.00
13	Ken Griffey Jr.	4.00
14	Sammy Sosa	3.00
15	Derek Jeter	4.00

2000 Fleer Focus Focus Pocus

This 10-card set has a silver prismatic, holofoil background with silver foil stamping. These were seeded 1:14 packs and are numbered with an "FP" suffix.

		MT
Complete Set (10):		40.00
Common Player:		1.50
Inserted 1:14		
1	Cal Ripken Jr.	6.00
2	Tony Gwynn	4.00
3	Nomar Garciaparra	5.00
4	Juan Gonzalez	2.00
5	Mike Piazza	5.00
6	Mark McGwire	8.00
7	Chipper Jones	4.00
8	Ken Griffey Jr.	6.00
9	Derek Jeter	6.00
10	Alex Rodriguez	6.00

2000 Fleer Focus Fresh Ink

These autographed inserts are seeded 1:96 packs.

	MT
Common Player:	10.00
Inserted 1:96	
Chad Allen	10.00
Michael Barrett	10.00
Josh Beckett	20.00
Rob Bell	10.00
Adrian Beltre	15.00
Milton Bradley	10.00
Rico Brogna	10.00
Mike Cameron	10.00
Eric Chavez	15.00
Bruce Chen	10.00
Johnny Damon	10.00
Ben Davis	10.00
J.D. Drew	30.00
Erubiel Durazo	15.00
Jeremy Giambi	10.00
Jason Giambi	25.00
Doug Glanville	10.00
Troy Glaus	30.00
Shawn Green	25.00
Mike Hampton	15.00
Tim Hudson	20.00
John Jaha	10.00
Derek Jeter	175.00
D'Angelo Jimenez	10.00
Nick Johnson	10.00
Andruw Jones	20.00
Jason Kendall	12.00
Adam Kennedy	10.00
Mike Lieberthal	10.00
Edgar Martinez	15.00
Aaron McNeal	10.00
Kevin Millwood	10.00
Mike Mussina	40.00
Magglio Ordonez	20.00
Eric Owens	10.00
Rafael Palmeiro	35.00
Wily Pena	15.00
Adam Piatt	15.00
Cal Ripken Jr.	125.00
Alex Rodriguez	75.00
Scott Rolen	20.00
Tim Salmon	20.00
Chris Singleton	10.00
Mike Sweeney	10.00
Jose Vidro	10.00
Rondell White	15.00
Jaret Wright	10.00

2000 Fleer Focus Future Vision

This 15-card set highlights the top prospects over a holo- foiled background with red foil etching and stamping. These were seeded 1:9 packs and are numbered with an "FV" suffix.

		MT
Complete Set (15):		25.00
Common Player:		1.00
Inserted 1:9		
1	Rick Ankiel	2.00
2	Matt Riley	1.50
3	Ruben Mateo	1.50
4	Ben Petrick	1.00
5	Mario Encarnacion	1.00
6	Octavio Dotel	1.00
7	Vernon Wells	1.50
8	Adam Kennedy	2.00
9	Lance Berkman	1.00
10	Chad Hermansen	1.00
11	Mark Quinn	1.00
12	Eric Munson	2.50
13	Alfonso Soriano	3.00
14	Kip Wells	1.00
15	Josh Beckett	3.00

2000 Fleer Gamers

The 120-card base set has silver foil etching down the left portion of the card with vertical stripes running down the right portion of the card front. The card back has career statistical totals as well as a small photo. Two short-printed subsets also make up the 120-card set. Next Gamers (91-110) are seeded 1:3 packs and Fame Game (111-120) are seeded 1:8 packs.

		MT
Complete Set (120):		125.00
Common Player (1-90):		.15
Common (91-110):		1.00
Inserted 1:3		
Common (111-120):		4.00
Inserted 1:8		
Pack:		3.50
Wax Box:		75.00
1	Cal Ripken Jr.	2.50
2	Derek Jeter	3.00
3	Alex Rodriguez	2.50
4	Alex Gonzalez	.15
5	Nomar Garciaparra	2.00
6	Brian Giles	.25
7	Chris Singleton	.15
8	Kevin Brown	.25
9	J.D. Drew	.40
10	Raul Mondesi	.40
11	Sammy Sosa	2.00
12	Carlos Beltran	.20
13	Eric Chavez	.15
14	Gabe Kapler	.25
15	Tim Salmon	.25
16	Manny Ramirez	.75
17	Orlando Hernandez	.40
18	Jeff Kent	.15
19	Juan Gonzalez	.75
20	Moises Alou	.25
21	Jason Giambi	.25
22	Ivan Rodriguez	.75
23	Geoff Jenkins	.25
24	Ken Griffey Jr.	2.50
25	Mark McGwire	3.00
26	Jose Canseco	.75
27	Roberto Alomar	.50
28	Craig Biggio	.40
29	Scott Rolen	.75
30	Vinny Castilla	.25
31	Greg Maddux	1.50
32	Pedro J. Martinez	.75
33	Mike Piazza	2.00
34	Albert Belle	.50
35	Frank Thomas	1.00
36	Bobby Abreu	.25
37	Edgar Martinez	.25
38	Pokey Reese	.15
39	Preston Wilson	.15
40	Mike Lieberthal	.15
41	Andruw Jones	.50
42	Damion Easley	.15
43	Mike Cameron	.15
44	Todd Walker	.15
45	Jason Kendall	.25
46	Sean Casey	.30
47	Corey Koskie	.15
48	Warren Morris	.15
49	Andres Galarraga	.50
50	Dean Palmer	.15
51	Jose Vidro	.15
52	Brian Jordan	.15
53	Tony Clark	.25
54	Vladimir Guerrero	1.50
55	Mo Vaughn	.50
56	Richie Sexson	.15
57	Tino Martinez	.40
58	Eric Owens	.15
59	Matt Williams	.40
60	Omar Vizquel	.25
61	Rickey Henderson	.40
62	J.T. Snow	.15
63	Mark Grace	.30

64	Carlos Febles	.15
65	Paul O'Neill	.40
66	Randy Johnson	.75
67	Kenny Lofton	.50
68	Roger Cedeno	.15
69	Shawn Green	.50
70	Chipper Jones	1.50
71	Jeff Cirillo	.25
72	Robin Ventura	.25
73	Paul Konerko	.25
74	Jeromy Burnitz	.25
75	Ben Grieve	.40
76	Troy Glaus	.50
77	Jim Thome	.40
78	Bernie Williams	.50
79	Barry Bonds	1.00
80	Ray Durham	.15
81	Adrian Beltre	.25
82	Ray Lankford	.15
83	Carlos Delgado	.50
84	Erubiel Durazo	.15
85	Larry Walker	.50
86	Edgardo Alfonzo	.25
87	Rafael Palmeiro	.50
88	Magglio Ordonez	.25
89	Jeff Bagwell	.75
90	Tony Gwynn	1.50
91	Norm Hutchins (Next Gamers)	1.00
92	*Derrick Turnbow* (Next Gamers)	3.00
93	Matt Riley (Next Gamers)	2.50
94	David Eckstein (Next Gamers)	1.00
95	Dernell Stenson (Next Gamers)	2.00
96	Joe Crede (Next Gamers)	1.00
97	Ben Petrick (Next Gamers)	1.00
98	Eric Munson (Next Gamers)	4.00
99	Pablo Ozuna (Next Gamers)	1.50
100	Josh Beckett (Next Gamers)	5.00
101	*Aaron McNeal* (Next Gamers)	4.00
102	Milton Bradley (Next Gamers)	2.00
103	Alex Escobar (Next Gamers)	2.00
104	Alfonso Soriano (Next Gamers)	2.50
105	Wily Pena (Next Gamers)	5.00
106	Nick Johnson (Next Gamers)	4.00
107	Adam Piatt (Next Gamers)	3.00
108	Pat Burrell (Next Gamers)	5.00
109	Rick Ankiel (Next Gamers)	1.50
110	(Vernon Wells) (Next Gamers)	2.00
111	Alex Rodriguez (Fame Game)	6.00
112	Cal Ripken Jr. (Fame Game)	6.00
113	Mark McGwire (Fame Game)	8.00
114	Ken Griffey Jr. (Fame Game)	6.00
115	Mike Piazza (Fame Game)	5.00
116	Nomar Garciaparra (Fame Game)	5.00
117	Derek Jeter (Fame Game)	8.00
118	Chipper Jones (Fame Game)	4.00
119	Sammy Sosa (Fame Game)	5.00
120	Tony Gwynn (Fame Game)	4.00

2000 Fleer Gamers Extra

A parallel to the 120-card base set, the gold foiled card front and "Extra" written down the right portion of the card can be used to differentiate these from regular cards. "Extra" is also written underneath the card number on the back as well. Extras 1-90 are seeded 1:24 packs and numbers 91-120 are seeded 1:36 packs.

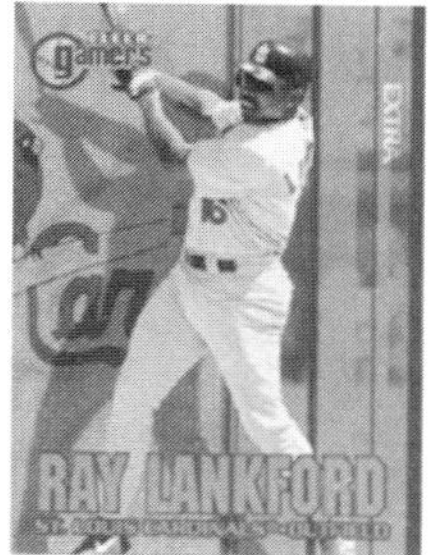

	MT
Stars (1-90):	6-12X
Inserted 1:24	
Next Gamers (91-110):	2X
Inserted 1:36	
Fame Game (110-120):	2X
Inserted 1:36	

(See Fleer Gamers for checklist and base card values.)

2000 Fleer Gamers Cal to Greatness

This 15-card tribute insert set to baseball's "Iron Man" is broken into three tiers. Cards 1-5 are seeded 1:9 packs, cards 6-10 are found 1:25 packs and cards 11-15 are inserted 1:144 packs. Card backs are numbered with a "C" suffix.

		MT
Complete Set (15):		
Common Ripken (1-5):		5.00
Inserted 1:9		
Common Ripken (6-10):		10.00
Inserted 1:25		
Common Ripken (11-15):		40.00
Inserted 1:144		
1	Cal Ripken Jr.	5.00
2	Cal Ripken Jr.	5.00
3	Cal Ripken Jr.	5.00
4	Cal Ripken Jr.	5.00
5	Cal Ripken Jr.	5.00
6	Cal Ripken Jr.	10.00
7	Cal Ripken Jr.	10.00
8	Cal Ripken Jr.	10.00
9	Cal Ripken Jr.	10.00
10	Cal Ripken Jr.	10.00
11	Cal Ripken Jr.	40.00
12	Cal Ripken Jr.	40.00
13	Cal Ripken Jr.	40.00
14	Cal Ripken Jr.	40.00
15	Cal Ripken Jr.	40.00

2000 Fleer Gamers Change the Game

This 15-card set has a holofoiled front with Change the Game printed behind the player image. Seeded 1:24 packs, card backs are numbered with a "CG" suffix.

		MT
Complete Set (15):		125.00
Common Player:		3.00
Inserted 1:24		
1	Alex Rodriguez	15.00
2	Cal Ripken Jr.	15.00
3	Chipper Jones	10.00
4	Derek Jeter	15.00
5	Ken Griffey Jr.	15.00
6	Mark McGwire	20.00
7	Mike Piazza	12.00
8	Nomar Garciaparra	12.00
9	Sammy Sosa	12.00
10	Tony Gwynn	10.00
11	Ivan Rodriguez	6.00
12	Pedro Martinez	6.00
13	Juan Gonzalez	6.00
14	Vladimir Guerrero	10.00
15	Manny Ramirez	6.00

2000 Fleer Gamers Determined

This 15-card set has a holo-foiled front with two player images on the card front. The second player photo is smaller than the primary image and is a close-up shot. Card backs are numbered with a "D" suffix and are seeded 1:12 packs.

		MT
Complete Set (15):		70.00
Common Player:		1.50
Inserted 1:12		
1	Nomar Garciaparra	6.00
2	Chipper Jones	5.00
3	Derek Jeter	8.00
4	Mike Piazza	6.00
5	Jeff Bagwell	2.50
6	Mark McGwire	10.00
7	Greg Maddux	5.00
8	Sammy Sosa	6.00
9	Ken Griffey Jr.	8.00
10	Alex Rodriguez	8.00
11	Tony Gwynn	5.00
12	Cal Ripken Jr.	8.00
13	Barry Bonds	3.00
14	Juan Gonzalez	2.50
15	Sean Casey	1.50

2000 Fleer Gamers Lumber

Seeded 1:36 packs, these inserts have a piece of game-used bat embedded into the card front and are numbered with an "GL" suffix

		MT
Common Player:		10.00
Inserted 1:36		
1	Alex Rodriguez	40.00
2	Carlos Delgado	20.00
3	Jose Vidro	10.00
4	Carlos Febles	10.00
5	J.D. Drew	20.00
6	Mike Cameron	10.00
7	Derek Jeter	75.00
8	Eric Chavez	15.00
9	Cal Ripken Jr.	65.00
10	Gabe Kapler	10.00
11	Damion Easley	10.00
12	Frank Thomas	35.00
13	Chris Singleton	10.00
14	Norm Hutchins	10.00
15	Pokey Reese	10.00
16	Rafael Palmeiro	20.00
17	Ray Durham	10.00
18	Ray Lankford	10.00
19	Roger Cedeno	10.00
20	Shawn Green	20.00
21	Wade Boggs	20.00
22	Roberto Alomar	25.00
23	Moises Alou	15.00
24	Adrian Beltre	15.00
25	Barry Bonds	50.00
26	Jason Giambi	20.00
27	Jason Kendall	12.00
28	Paul Konerko	10.00
29	Mike Lieberthal	10.00
30	Edgar Martinez	20.00
31	Raul Mondesi	10.00
32	Scott Rolen	15.00
33	Alfonso Soriano	15.00
34	Ivan Rodriguez	25.00
35	Magglio Ordonez	20.00
36	Chipper Jones	35.00
37	Sean Casey	10.00
38	Edgardo Alfonzo	10.00
39	Robin Ventura	12.00
40	Bernie Williams	20.00
41	Vladimir Guerrero	35.00
42	Tony Clark	10.00
43	Carlos Beltran	15.00
44	Warren Morris	10.00
45	Jim Thome	20.00
46	Jeromy Burnitz	10.00
47	Matt Williams	15.00
48	Erubiel Durazo	12.00

2000 Fleer Gamers Lumber Autograph

Twelve players also signed a limited number of their Lumber inserts. The number signed by each player is listed after the player name. These were seeded 1:287 packs.

		MT
Common Player:		25.00
Inserted 1:287		
1	Derek Jeter	220.00
2	Eric Chavez	40.00
3	Rafael Palmeiro	50.00
4	Shawn Green	50.00
5	Roberto Alomar	65.00
6	Paul Konerko	25.00
7	Sean Casey	30.00
8	Alex Rodriguez	120.00
9	Robin Ventura	45.00
10	Erubiel Durazo	25.00
11	Tony Clark	25.00
12	Alfonso Soriano	40.00

2000 Fleer Greats of the Game

The base set consists of 107-cards of retired stars. Card fronts have a brown border with "Fleer Greats of the Game" stamped in silver foil. Backs have a small photo along with complete career statistics and a brief career highlight.

		MT
Complete Set (108):		90.00
Common Player:		.50
Pack (6):		12.00
Wax Box:		250.00
1	Mickey Mantle	15.00
2	Gil Hodges	1.50
3	Monte Irvin	.50
4	Satchel Paige	2.50
5	Roy Campanella	2.00
6	Richie Ashburn	1.00
7	Roger Maris	2.00
8	Ozzie Smith	2.00
9	Reggie Jackson	2.50
10	Eddie Mathews	2.50
11	Dave Righetti	.50
12	Dave Winfield	1.00
13	Lou Whitaker	.50
14	Phil Garner	.50
15	Ron Cey	.50
16	Brooks Robinson	2.50
17	Bruce Sutter	.50
18	Dave Parker	.50
19	Johnny Bench	2.50
20	Fernando Valenzuela	.50
21	George Brett	3.00
22	Paul Molitor	2.00
23	Hoyt Wilhelm	.50
24	Luis Aparicio	.50
25	Frank White	.50
26	Herb Score	.50
27	Kirk Gibson	.50
28	Mike Schmidt	3.00
29	Don Baylor	.50
30	Joe Pepitone	.50
31	Hal McRae	.50
32	Lee Smith	.50
33	Nolan Ryan	7.00
33	Nolan Ryan (overprinted "PROMOTIONAL SAMPLE")	5.00
34	Bill Mazeroski	.75
35	Bobby Doerr	.50
36	Duke Snider	1.00
37	Dick Groat	.50
38	Larry Doby	.50
39	Kirby Puckett	2.00
40	Steve Carlton	1.00
41	Dennis Eckersley	.50
42	Jim Bunning	.50
43	Ron Guidry	.50
44	Alan Trammell	1.00
45	Bob Feller	1.50
46	Dave Concepcion	.50
47	Dwight Evans	.50
48	Enos Slaughter	.50
49	Tom Seaver	2.50
50	Tony Oliva	1.00
51	Mel Stottlemyre	.50
52	Tommy John	.50
53	Willie McCovey	1.00
54	Red Schoendienst	.50
55	Gorman Thomas	.50
56	Ralph Kiner	1.00
57	Robin Yount	2.00
58	Andre Dawson	1.00
59	Al Kaline	2.00
60	Dom DiMaggio	.50
61	Juan Marichal	1.00
62	Jack Morris	.50
63	Warren Spahn	2.00
64	Preacher Roe	.50
65	Darrell Evans	.50
66	Jim Bouton	.50
67	Rocky Colavito	1.00
68	Bob Gibson	2.00
69	Whitey Ford	1.50
70	Moose Skowron	.50
71	Boog Powell	1.00
72	Al Lopez	.50
73	Lou Brock	1.50
74	Mickey Lolich	.50
75	Rod Carew	2.50
76	Bob Lemon	.50
77	Frank Howard	.50
78	Phil Rizzuto	1.50
79	Carl Yastrzemski	2.00
80	Rico Carty	.50
81	Jim Kaat	.50
82	Bert Blyleven	.50
83	George Kell	.50
84	Jim Palmer	2.00
85	Maury Wills	1.00
86	Jim Rice	.50
87	Joe Carter	.50
88	Clete Boyer	.50
89	Yogi Berra	3.00
90	Cecil Cooper	.50
91	Davey Johnson	.50
92	Lou Boudreau	.50
93	Orlando Cepeda	1.00
94	Tommy Henrich	.50
95	Hank Bauer	.50
96	Don Larsen	1.50
97	Vida Blue	1.00
98	Ben Oglivie	.50
99	Don Mattingly	3.00
100	Dale Murphy	1.00
101	Ferguson Jenkins	1.00
102	Bobby Bonds	1.00
103	Dick Allen	.50
104	Stan Musial	3.00
105	Gaylord Perry	.50
106	Willie Randolph	.50
107	Willie Stargell	1.50
108	Checklist	.50

2000 Fleer Greats of the Game Autographs

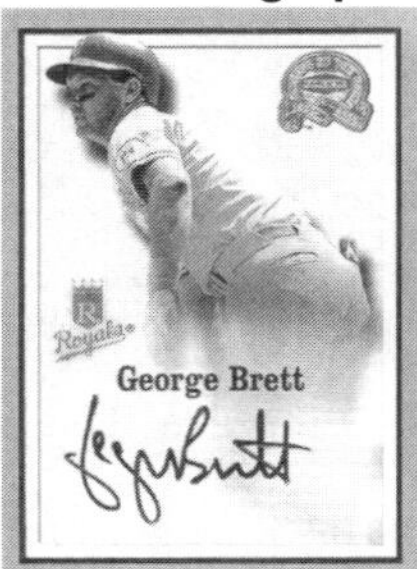

Seeded in every six packs, Autographs feature the signature on the bottom half of the card front in black sharpie. The autographed set features 89 retired players. Some cards were issued in condierably lower quantities than others, as noted in the checklist.

		MT
Common Player:		10.00
Inserted 1:6		
	Luis Aparicio	20.00
	Hank Bauer	10.00
	Don Baylor	20.00
	Johnny Bench	200.00
	Yogi Berra	125.00
	Vida Blue	20.00
	Bert Blyleven	10.00
	Bobby Bonds	30.00
	Lou Boudreau	40.00
	Jim Bouton	20.00
	Clete Boyer	25.00
	George Brett (275 or less)	200.00
	Lou Brock	35.00
	Jim Bunning	30.00
	Rod Carew	40.00
	Steve Carlton	35.00
	Joe Carter	75.00
	Orlando Cepeda	25.00
	Ron Cey	15.00
	Rocky Colavito	30.00
	Dave Concepcion (black autograph)	20.00
	Dave Concepcion (red autograph)	20.00
	Cecil Cooper	10.00
	Andre Dawson	30.00
	Dom DiMaggio	75.00
	Bobby Doerr	20.00
	Darrell Evans	20.00
	Bob Feller	20.00
	Whitey Ford (300 or less)	100.00
	Phil Garner	10.00
	Bob Gibson	35.00
	Kirk Gibson	30.00
	Dick Groat	10.00
	Ron Guidry	25.00
	Tommy Henrich (300 or less)	125.00
	Frank Howard	20.00
	Reggie Jackson (250 or less)	125.00
	Ferguson Jenkins	25.00
	Tommy John	10.00
	Davey Johnson	10.00
	Jim Kaat	15.00
	Al Kaline	50.00
	George Kell	20.00
	Ralph Kiner	35.00
	Don Larsen	40.00
	Mickey Lolich	10.00
	Juan Marichal	50.00
	Eddie Mathews	80.00
	Don Mattingly (300 or less)	250.00
	Bill Mazeroski	25.00
	Willie McCovey	50.00
	Hal McRae	10.00
	Paul Molitor	50.00
	Jack Morris	10.00
	Dale Murphy	50.00
	Stan Musial	125.00
	Ben Oglivie	10.00
	Tony Oliva	30.00
	Jim Palmer	80.00
	Dave Parker	20.00
	Joe Pepitone	20.00
	Gaylord Perry	25.00
	Boog Powell	20.00
	Kirby Puckett (200 or less)	200.00
	Willie Randolph	20.00
	Jim Rice	20.00
	Dave Righetti	15.00
	Phil Rizzuto (200 or less)	200.00
	Brooks Robinson	50.00
	Preacher Roe	30.00
	Nolan Ryan	150.00
	Mike Schmidt (175 or less)	300.00
	Red Schoendienst	20.00
	Herb Score	25.00
	Tom Seaver	75.00
	Moose Skowron	20.00
	Enos Slaughter	25.00
	Lee Smith	10.00
	Ozzie Smith	200.00
	Duke Snider	90.00
	Warren Spahn	200.00
	Bruce Sutter	10.00
	Gorman Thomas	10.00
	Alan Trammell	20.00
	Frank White	10.00
	Hoyt Wilhelm	20.00
	Maury Wills	20.00
	Dave Winfield	150.00
	Carl Yastrzemski	80.00
	Robin Yount	100.00

2000 Fleer Greats of the Game Memorable Moments Auto.

		MT
Common Player:		125.00
1	Ron Guidry /78	125.00
2	Nolan Ryan /99	350.00
3	Herb Score /55	125.00
4	Tom Seaver /69	250.00

2000 Fleer Greats of the Game Retrospection

The 15-card Retrospection insert set highlights some of the all-time greats with a design borrowed from 1960 Fleer. Former greats including Stan Musial and Al Kaline are featured. They were seeded 1:6 packs.

		MT
Complete Set (15):		120.00
Common Player:		4.00
Inserted 1:6		
1	Rod Carew	8.00
2	Stan Musial	12.00
3	Nolan Ryan	20.00
4	Tom Seaver	12.00
5	Brooks Robinson	8.00
6	Al Kaline	6.00
7	Mike Schmidt	10.00
8	Thurman Munson	8.00
9	Steve Carlton	6.00
10	Roger Maris	10.00
11	Duke Snider	8.00
12	Yogi Berra	12.00
13	Carl Yastrzemski	8.00
14	Reggie Jackson	12.00
15	Johnny Bench	12.00

2000 Fleer Greats of the Game Yankees Clippings

This 15-card memorabilia insert features an actual piece of New York Yankee uniform worn by former Yankee greats. The jersey swatch is formed in the shape of the interlocking "NY" logo and are seeded 1:48 packs. Players featured include Mickey Mantle and Don Mattingly.

		MT
Common Player:		40.00
Inserted 1:48		
1	Mickey Mantle	375.00
2	Ron Guidry	50.00
3	Don Larsen	60.00
4	Elston Howard	60.00
5	Mel Stottlemyre	50.00
6	Don Mattingly	200.00
7	Reggie Jackson	75.00
8	Tommy John	50.00
9	Dave Winfield	50.00
10	Willie Randolph	50.00
11	Tommy Henrich	50.00
12	Billy Martin	150.00
13	Dave Righetti	60.00
14	Joe Pepitone	60.00
15	Thurman Munson	100.00

2000 Fleer Impact

The base set consists of 200 cards with 25 of those being Prospect subset cards. The featured player's team logo appears beside the player name on the bottom portion with the Impact logo on the top left portion. Card backs have a maximum of 10 years of statistics along with a small photo and vital information. Impact was sold in 10-card packs with an SRP of $.99 per pack.

		MT
Complete Set (200):		15.00
Common Player:		.10
Pack (10):		1.00
Box (36):		32.00
1	Cal Ripken Jr.	1.50
2	Jose Canseco	.30
3	Manny Ramirez	.50
4	Bernie Williams	.40
5	Troy Glaus	.25
6	Jeff Bagwell	.50
7	Corey Koskie	.10
8	Barry Larkin	.25
9	Mark Quinn	.10
10	Russ Ortiz	.10
11	Tim Salmon	.15
12	Preston Wilson	.10
13	Mo Vaughn	.30
14	Ray Lankford	.10
15	Sterling Hitchcock	.10
16	Al Leiter	.10
17	Jim Morris	.10
18	Freddy Garcia	.10
19	Adrian Beltre	.10
20	Eric Chavez	.20
21	Robinson Cancel	.10
22	Edgar Renteria	.10
23	John Jaha	.10
24	Chuck Finley	.10
25	Andres Galarraga	.25
26	Paul Byrd	.10
27	John Halama	.10
28	Eric Karros	.15
29	Mike Piazza	1.25
30	Ryan Rupe	.10
31	Frank Thomas	.75
32	Randy Velarde	.10
33	Bobby Abreu	.10
34	Randy Johnson	.50
35	Matt Williams	.20
36	Tony Gwynn	.75
37	Dean Palmer	.10
38	Aaron Sele	.10
39	Rondell White	.15
40	Erubiel Durazo	.10
41	Curt Schilling	.10
42	Kip Wells	.10
43	Craig Biggio	.20
44	Tom Glavine	.20
45	Trevor Hoffman	.10
46	Greg Vaughn	.10
47	Edgar Martinez	.10
48	Magglio Ordonez	.10
49	Mark Mulder	.10
50	John Rocker	.10
51	Kenny Rogers	.10
52	Gary Sheffield	.20
53	Brian Simmons	.10
54	Tony Womack	.10
55	Ken Caminiti	.10
56	Jeff Cirillo	.10
57	Ray Durham	.10
58	Mike Lieberthal	.10
59	Ruben Mateo	.10
60	Mike Cameron	.10
61	Rusty Greer	.10
62	Alex Rodriguez	1.50
63	Robin Ventura	.10
64	Pokey Reese	.10
65	Jose Lima	.10
66	Neifi Perez	.10
67	Rafael Palmeiro	.25
68	Scott Rolen	.40
69	Mike Hampton	.10
70	Sammy Sosa	1.25
71	Mike Stanley	.10
72	Dan Wilson	.10
73	Kerry Wood	.25
74	Mike Mussina	.30
75	Masato Yoshii	.10
76	Peter Bergeron	.10
77	Carlos Delgado	.50
78	Juan Encarnacion	.10
79	Nomar Garciaparra	1.25
80	Jason Kendall	.10
81	Pedro Martinez	.50
82	Darin Erstad	.20
83	Larry Walker	.20
84	Rick Ankiel	.25
85	Scott Erickson	.10
86	Roger Clemens	.75
87	Matt Lawton	.10
88	Jon Lieber	.10
89	Shane Reynolds	.10
90	Ivan Rodriguez	.50
91	Pat Burrell	.30
92	Kent Bottenfield	.10
93	David Cone	.15
94	Mark Grace	.15
95	Paul Konerko	.10
96	Eric Milton	.10
97	Lee Stevens	.10
98	B.J. Surhoff	.10
99	Billy Wagner	.10
100	Ken Griffey Jr.	1.50
101	Randy Wolf	.10
102	Henry Rodriguez	.10
103	Carlos Beltran	.10
104	Rich Aurilia	.10
105	Chipper Jones	1.00
106	Homer Bush	.10
107	Johnny Damon	.10
108	J.D. Drew	.20
109	Orlando Hernandez	.10
110	Brad Radke	.10
111	Wilton Veras	.10
112	Dmitri Young	.10
113	Jermaine Dye	.10
114	Kris Benson	.10
115	Derek Jeter	1.50
116	Cole Liniak	.10
117	Jim Thome	.25
118	Pedro Astacio	.10
119	Carlos Febles	.10
120	Darryl Kile	.10
121	Alfonso Soriano	.25
122	Michael Barrett	.10
123	Ellis Burks	.10
124	Chad Hermansen	.10
125	Trot Nixon	.10
126	Bobby Higginson	.10
127	Rick Helling	.10
128	Chris Carpenter	.10
129	Vinny Castilla	.10
130	Brian Giles	.10
131	Todd Helton	.50
132	Jason Varitek	.10
133	Rob Ducey	.10
134	Octavio Dotel	.10
135	Adam Kennedy	.10
136	Jeff Kent	.10
137	Aaron Boone	.10
138	Todd Walker	.10
139	Jeromy Burnitz	.10
140	Roberto Hernandez	.10
141	Matt LeCroy	.10
142	Ugueth Urbina	.10
143	David Wells	.10
144	Luis Gonzalez	.10
145	Andruw Jones	.25
146	Juan Gonzalez	.50
147	Moises Alou	.10
148	Michael Tejera	.10
149	Brian Jordan	.10
150	Mark McGwire	2.00
151	Shawn Green	.30
152	Jay Bell	.10
153	Fred McGriff	.20
154	Rey Ordonez	.10
155	Matt Stairs	.10
156	A.J. Burnett	.10
157	Omar Vizquel	.10
158	Damion Easley	.10
159	Dante Bichette	.10
160	Javy Lopez	.10
161	Fernando Seguignol	.10
162	Richie Sexson	.10
163	Vladimir Guerrero	.75
164	Kevin Young	.10
165	Josh Beckett	.10
166	Albert Belle	.30
167	Cliff Floyd	.10
168	Gabe Kapler	.20
169	Nick Johnson	.10
170	Raul Mondesi	.15
171	Warren Morris	.10
172	Kenny Lofton	.20
173	Reggie Sanders	.10
174	Mike Sweeney	.10
175	Robert Fick	.10
176	Barry Bonds	.75
177	Luis Castillo	.10
178	Roger Cedeno	.10
179	Jim Edmonds	.15
180	Geoff Jenkins	.15
181	Adam Piatt	.10
182	Phil Nevin	.10
183	Roberto Alomar	.40
184	Kevin Brown	.15
185	D.T. Cromer	.10
186	Jason Giambi	.20
187	Fernando Tatis	.20
188	Brady Anderson	.15
189	Tony Clark	.10
190	Alex Fernandez	.10
191	Matt Blank	.10
192	Greg Maddux	1.00
193	Kevin Millwood	.10
194	Jason Schmidt	.10
195	Shannon Stewart	.10
196	Rolando Arrojo	.10
197	Darren Dreifort	.10
198	Ben Grieve	.20
199	Bartolo Colon	.10
200	Sean Casey	.20

2000 Fleer Impact Autographics

This autographed set has the player signature on the bottom portion of the card. These were seeded 1:216 packs.

		MT
Common Player:		10.00
Inserted 1:216		
1	Bobby Abreu	20.00
2	Marlon Anderson	10.00
3	Rick Ankiel	25.00
4	Rob Bell	10.00
5	Carlos Beltran	10.00
6	Wade Boggs	60.00
7	Barry Bonds	75.00
8	Milton Bradley	10.00
9	Pat Burrell	25.00
10	Orlando Cabrera	10.00
11	Chris Carpenter	10.00
12	Sean Casey	15.00
13	Carlos Delgado	35.00
14	J.D. Drew	30.00
15	Ray Durham	15.00
16	Kelvim Escobar	10.00

17	Vladimir Guerrero	40.00
18	Tony Gwynn	50.00
19	Jerry Hairston Jr.	10.00
20	Todd Helton	40.00
21	Nick Johnson	10.00
22	Jason Kendall	10.00
23	Mark Kotsay	10.00
24	Cole Liniak	10.00
25	Jose Macias	10.00
26	Greg Maddux	60.00
27	Ruben Mateo	10.00
28	Ober Moreno	10.00
29	Eric Munson	10.00
30	Joe Nathan	10.00
31	Angel Pena	10.00
32	Adam Piatt	10.00
33	Matt Riley	10.00
34	Cal Ripken Jr.	100.00
35	Alex Rodriguez	75.00
36	Scott Rolen	25.00
37	Jimmy Rollins	10.00
38	B.J. Ryan	10.00
39	Alfonso Soriano	30.00
40	Frank Thomas	50.00
41	Wilton Veras	10.00
42	Billy Wagner	10.00
43	Jeff Weaver	10.00
44	Scott Williamson	10.00

2000 Fleer Impact Genuine Coverage

This memorabilia insert set has pieces of game-used batting gloves embedded into the card front. They were seeded 1:720 packs.

		MT
Common Player:		10.00
Inserted 1:720		
1	Alex Rodriguez	100.00
2	Cole Liniak	10.00
3	Barry Bonds	75.00
4	Ben Davis	15.00
5	Bobby Abreu	35.00
6	Mike Sweeney	25.00
7	Rafael Palmeiro	40.00
8	Carlos Lee	25.00
9	Glen Barker	10.00
10	Jason Giambi	50.00
11	Jacque Jones	20.00
12	Joe Nathan	10.00
13	Jason LaRue	10.00
14	Magglio Ordonez	35.00
15	Shannon Stewart	25.00
16	Matt Lawton	20.00
18	Trevor Hoffman	30.00

2000 Fleer Impact Mighty Fine in '99

This 40-card set honors the 1999 World Series Champion New York Yankees as well as other various award winners from the '99 season. These were seeded one per pack.

		MT
Complete Set (40):		15.00
Common Player:		.15
Inserted 1:1		
1	Clay Bellinger	.15
2	Scott Brosius	.15
3	Roger Clemens	1.00
4	David Cone	.25
5	Chad Curtis	.15
6	Chili Davis	.15
7	Joe Girardi	.15
8	Jason Grimsley	.15
9	Orlando Hernandez	.25
10	Hideki Irabu	.15
11	Derek Jeter	2.00
12	Chuck Knoblauch	.25
13	Ricky Ledee	.15
14	Jim Leyritz	.15
15	Tino Martinez	.25
16	Ramiro Mendoza	.15
17	Jeff Nelson	.15
18	Paul O'Neill	.25
19	Andy Pettitte	.25
20	Jorge Posada	.25
21	Mariano Rivera	.25
22	Luis Sojo	.15
23	Mike Stanton	.15
24	Allen Watson	.15
25	Bernie Williams	.50
26	Chipper Jones	1.25
27	Ivan Rodriguez	.60
28	Randy Johnson	.60
29	Pedro Martinez	.60
30	Scott Williamson	.15
31	Carlos Beltran	.15
32	Mark McGwire	2.50
33	Ken Griffey Jr.	2.00
34	Robin Ventura	.15
35	Tony Gwynn	1.00
36	Wade Boggs	.40
37	Cal Ripken Jr.	2.00
38	Jose Canseco	.40
39	Alex Rodriguez	2.00
40	Fernando Tatis	.15

2000 Fleer Impact Point of Impact

Point of Impact honors some of the game's top sluggers on a die-cut design. Card fronts have silver foil stamping and cross hairs where the featured player finds his sweet spot. These were seeded 1:30 packs and are numbered with an "PI" suffix on the card back.

		MT
Complete Set (10):		50.00
Common Player:		2.00
Inserted 1:30		
1	Ken Griffey Jr.	8.00
2	Mark McGwire	10.00
3	Sammy Sosa	6.00
4	Jeff Bagwell	2.50
5	Derek Jeter	8.00
6	Chipper Jones	5.00
7	Nomar Garciaparra	6.00
8	Cal Ripken Jr.	8.00
9	Barry Bonds	2.50
10	Alex Rodriguez	8.00

2000 Fleer Mystique

The base set consists of 175-cards including a 50-card Prospects subset that each card is serially numbered to 2,000 and covered. The card fronts have a full bleed design with gold foil stamping. Card backs have complete year-by-year statistics and a small photo.

		MT
Complete Set (175):		500.00
Common Player:		.20
Common 126-175		8.00
Production 2,000 sets		
Pack (5):		4.00
Box (20):		70.00
1	Derek Jeter	4.00
2	David Justice	.40
3	Kevin Brown	.40
4	Jason Giambi	.40
5	Jose Canseco	.60
6	Mark Grace	.40
7	Hideo Nomo	.20
8	Edgardo Alfonzo	.40
9	Barry Bonds	1.50
10	Pedro Martinez	1.00
11	Juan Gonzalez	1.00
12	Vladimir Guerrero	1.50
13	Chuck Finley	.20
14	Brian Jordan	.20
15	Richie Sexson	.20
16	Chan Ho Park	.20
17	Tim Hudson	.40
18	Fred McGriff	.40
19	Darin Erstad	.40
20	Chris Singleton	.20
21	Jeff Bagwell	1.00
22	David Cone	.40
23	Edgar Martinez	.20
24	Greg Maddux	2.00
25	Jim Thome	.50
26	Eric Karros	.30
27	Bobby Abreu	.30
28	Greg Vaughn	.30
29	Kevin Millwood	.30
30	Omar Vizquel	.20
31	Marquis Grissom	.20
32	Mike Lieberthal	.20
33	Gabe Kapler	.40
34	Brady Anderson	.30
35	Jeff Cirillo	.20
36	Geoff Jenkins	.40
37	Scott Rolen	.75
38	Rafael Palmeiro	.60
39	Randy Johnson	1.00
40	Barry Larkin	.50
41	Johnny Damon	.20
42	Andy Pettitte	.40
43	Mark McGwire	4.00
44	Albert Belle	.60
45	Derrick Gibson	.20
46	Corey Koskie	.20
47	Curt Schilling	.30
48	Ivan Rodriguez	1.00
49	Mike Mussina	.60
50	Todd Helton	1.00
51	Matt Lawton	.20
52	Jason Kendall	.20
53	Kenny Rogers	.20
54	Cal Ripken Jr.	3.00
55	Larry Walker	.50
56	Eric Milton	.20
57	Warren Morris	.20
58	Carlos Delgado	1.00
59	Kerry Wood	.40
60	Cliff Floyd	.20
61	Mike Piazza	2.50
62	Jeff Kent	.20
63	Sammy Sosa	2.50
64	Alex Fernandez	.20
65	Mike Hampton	.20
66	Livan Hernandez	.20
67	Matt Williams	.40
68	Roberto Alomar	.75
69	Jermaine Dye	.20
70	Bernie Williams	.75
71	Edgar Renteria	.20
72	Tom Glavine	.40
73	Bartolo Colon	.20
74	Jason Varitek	.20
75	Eric Chavez	.40
76	Fernando Tatis	.20
77	Adrian Beltre	.40
78	Paul Konerko	.20
79	Mike Lowell	.20
80	Robin Ventura	.20
81	Russ Ortiz	.20
82	Troy Glaus	.75
83	Frank Thomas	1.50
84	Craig Biggio	.40
85	Orlando Hernandez	.20
86	John Olerud	.40
87	Chipper Jones	2.00
88	Manny Ramirez	1.00
89	Shawn Green	.40
90	Ben Grieve	.40
91	Vinny Castilla	.20
92	Tim Salmon	.40
93	Dante Bichette	.30
94	Ken Caminiti	.20
95	Andruw Jones	.50
96	Alex Rodriguez	3.00
97	Erubiel Durazo	.20
98	Sean Casey	.30
99	Carlos Beltran	.20
100	Paul O'Neill	.30
101	Ray Lankford	.20
102	Troy O'Leary	.20
103	Bobby Higginson	.20
104	Rondell White	.20
105	Tony Gwynn	1.50
106	Jim Edmonds	.30
107	Magglio Ordonez	.40
108	Preston Wilson	.20
109	Roger Clemens	1.50
110	Ken Griffey Jr.	3.00
111	Nomar Garciaparra	2.50
112	Juan Encarnacion	.20
113	Michael Barrett	.20
114	Matt Clement	.20
115	David Wells	.20
116	Mo Vaughn	.50
117	Mike Cameron	.20
118	Jose Lima	.20
119	Tino Martinez	.40
120	J.D. Drew	.40
121	Carl Everett	.20
122	Tony Clark	.20
123	Brad Radke	.20
124	Kevin Young	.20
125	Raul Mondesi	.40
126	Cole Liniak (Prospects)	8.00
127	Alfonso Soriano (Prospects)	10.00
128	Lance Berkman (Prospects)	10.00

129	Danny Young (Prospects)	8.00
130	Francisco Cordero (Prospects)	8.00
131	Rob Fick (Prospects)	10.00
132	Matt LeCroy (Prospects)	8.00
133	Adam Piatt (Prospects)	15.00
134	*Derrick Turnbow* (Prospects)	8.00
135	Mark Quinn (Prospects)	12.00
136	Kip Wells (Prospects)	10.00
137	Rob Bell (Prospects)	8.00
138	Brad Penny (Prospects)	8.00
139	Pat Burrell (Prospects)	25.00
140	*Danys Baez* (Prospects)	12.00
141	Chad Hermansen (Prospects)	8.00
142	Steve Lomasney (Prospects)	8.00
143	Peter Bergeron (Prospects)	12.00
144	Jimmy Anderson (Prospects)	8.00
145	Mike Darr (Prospects)	8.00
146	Jacob Cruz (Prospects)	8.00
147	*Kazuhiro Sasaki* (Prospects)	20.00
148	Ben Petrick (Prospects)	10.00
149	Rick Ankiel (Prospects)	10.00
150	*Aaron McNeal* (Prospects)	15.00
152	Octavio Dotel (Prospects)	8.00
152	Juan Pena (Prospects)	8.00
153	Nick Johnson (Prospects)	15.00
154	Wilton Veras (Prospects)	8.00
155	Wily Pena (Prospects)	15.00
156	Mark Mulder (Prospects)	8.00
157	Daryle Ward (Prospects)	10.00
158	*Chad Durbin* (Prospects)	8.00
159	Angel Pena (Prospects)	10.00
160	Dewayne Wise (Prospects)	8.00
161	Tarrik Brock (Prospects)	8.00
162	Marcus Jensen (Prospects)	8.00
163	Kevin Barker (Prospects)	10.00
164	B.J. Ryan (Prospects)	8.00
165	Cesar King (Prospects)	8.00
166	Geoff Blum (Prospects)	8.00
167	Ruben Mateo (Prospects)	10.00
168	Ramon Ortiz (Prospects)	8.00
169	Eric Munson (Prospects)	15.00
170	Josh Beckett (Prospects)	15.00
171	Rafael Furcal (Prospects)	10.00
172	Matt Riley (Prospects)	12.00
173	*Johan Santana* (Prospects)	8.00
174	Mark Johnson (Prospects)	8.00
175	Adam Kennedy (Prospects)	12.00

2000 Fleer Mystique Gold

These parallel inserts to the 175-card base set are identical to the base cards besides gold highlights throughout the background of the player photo. The word "Gold" also appears underneath the card number on the back. These were seeded 1:20 packs.

	MT
Stars (1-125):	5-10X
SPs (126-175):	1X
Inserted 1:20	

(See 2000 Fleer Mystique for checklist and base card values.)

2000 Fleer Mystique Club 3000

This three-card set is die-cut around the 3,000 numerals with a date on the left side when the featured player reached the 3,000 milestone. The player name is stamped in silver holo-foil. Card backs are not numbered and have a brief career note. These were seeded 1:20 packs.

		MT
Complete Set (3):		8.00
Common Player:		2.00
Inserted 1:20		
1	Cal Ripken Jr.	6.00
2	Bob Gibson	2.00
3	Dave Winfield	2.00

2000 Fleer Mystique Club 3000 Memorabilia

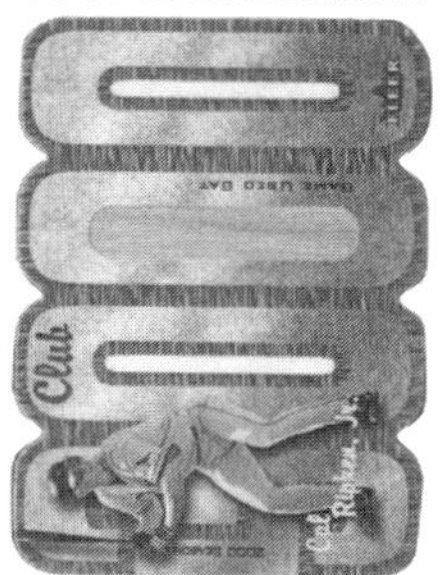

Five different memorabilia versions of each player exist, using pieces of game-used bat, jersey and cap which are embedded into each card. The amount of each card produced is listed after the player name.

	MT
Cal Ripken Jr. - jersey/825	75.00
Cal Ripken Jr. - bat/265	100.00
Cal Ripken Jr. - hat/55	275.00
Cal Ripken Jr. - bat, jersey/100	275.00
Cal Ripken - bat, hat, jersey/25	
Bob Gibson - jersey/825	35.00
Bob Gibson - bat/265	50.00
Bob Gibson - bat, jersey/100	60.00
Bob Gibson - hat, jersey/100	100.00
Bob Gibson - hat/55	125.00
Bob Gibson - bat, hat, jersey/25	
Dave Winfield - jersey/825	25.00
Dave Winfield - bat/270	40.00
Dave Winfield - bat, jersey/100	90.00
Dave Winfield - hat/55	100.00
Dave Winfield - bat, hat, jersey/25	

2000 Fleer Mystique Dave Winfield Auto. Memorabilia

This two-card set consists of 40 game-used helmet Winfield cards and 20 game-used ball cards.

		MT
1	Dave Winfield bat/20	175.00
2	Dave Winfield helmet/40	125.00

2000 Fleer Mystique Diamond Dominators

This 10-card set spotlights baseball's most dominating performers. Card fronts have a holofoil appearance. These were seeded 1:5 packs and are numbered with an "DD" suffix.

		MT
Complete Set (10):		15.00
Common Player:		.75
Inserted 1:5		
1	Manny Ramirez	1.00
2	Pedro Martinez	1.00
3	Sean Casey	.75
4	Vladimir Guerrero	1.50
5	Sammy Sosa	2.50
6	Nomar Garciaparra	2.50
7	Mark McGwire	4.00
8	Ken Griffey Jr.	3.00
9	Derek Jeter	4.00
10	Alex Rodriguez	3.00

2000 Fleer Mystique Feel the Game

This game-used memorabilia set features either game-used jerseys or bats from today's top stars. These were seeded 1:120 packs.

		MT
Common Player:		10.00
Inserted 1:120		
1	Tony Gwynn jersey	35.00
2	Alex Rodriguez jersey	50.00
3	Chipper Jones jersey	35.00
4	Cal Ripken Jr. jersey	60.00
5	Derek Jeter pants	70.00
7	Frank Thomas bat	35.00
8	Barry Bonds bat	60.00
9	Carlos Beltran bat	10.00
10	Shawn Green bat	20.00
11	Michael Barrett bat	10.00
12	Rafael Palmeiro bat	25.00
13	Vladimir Guerrero bat	25.00
14	Pat Burrell bat	25.00

2000 Fleer Mystique Fresh Ink

This autographed set features signatures from

many of the game's top players and are seeded 1:40 packs.

		MT
Common Player:		10.00
Inserted 1:40		
1	Chad Allen	10.00
2	Glen Barker	10.00
3	Michael Barrett	10.00
4	Josh Beckett	25.00
5	Rob Bell	10.00
6	Lance Berkman	10.00
7	Kent Bottenfield	10.00
8	Milton Bradley	10.00
9	Orlando Cabrera	10.00
10	Sean Casey	15.00
11	Roger Cedeno	10.00
12	Will Clark	25.00
13	Russ Davis	10.00
14	Carlos Delgado	30.00
15	Einar Diaz	10.00
16	J.D. Drew	30.00
17	Erubiel Durazo	15.00
18	Damion Easley	10.00
19	Carlos Febles	10.00
20	Doug Glanville	10.00
21	Alex Gonzalez	10.00
22	Tony Gwynn	50.00
23	Mike Hampton	15.00
24	Bobby Howry	10.00
25	John Jaha	10.00
26	Nick Johnson	15.00
27	Andruw Jones	30.00
28	Adam Kennedy	10.00
29	Mike Lieberthal	10.00
30	Jose Macias	10.00
31	Ruben Mateo	10.00
32	Raul Mondesi	15.00
33	Heath Murray	10.00
34	Mike Mussina	30.00
35	Hideo Nomo	200.00
36	Magglio Ordonez	20.00
37	Eric Owens	10.00
38	Adam Piatt	15.00
39	Cal Ripken Jr.	100.00
40	Tim Salmon	15.00
41	Chris Singleton	10.00
42	J.T. Snow	10.00
43	Mike Sweeney	15.00
44	Wilton Veras	10.00
45	Jose Vidro	10.00
46	Rondell White	15.00
47	Jaret Wright	10.00

2000 Fleer Mystique High Praise

This 10-card set has a holo-foiled card front with a "sky" background. These were inserted 1:20 packs and are numbered on the card back with an "HP" suffix.

		MT
Complete Set (10):		55.00
Common Player:		2.00
Inserted 1:20		
1	Mark McGwire	10.00
2	Ken Griffey Jr.	8.00
3	Alex Rodriguez	8.00
4	Derek Jeter	10.00
5	Sammy Sosa	6.00
6	Mike Piazza	6.00
7	Nomar Garciaparra	6.00
8	Cal Ripken Jr.	8.00
9	Tony Gwynn	4.00
10	Shawn Green	2.00

2000 Fleer Mystique Rookie I.P.O.

This 10-card set highlights the top young rookies on a holofoil design. Card backs are numbered with an "RI" suffix and are seeded 1:10 packs.

		MT
Complete Set (10):		15.00
Common Player:		1.00
Inserted 1:10		
1	Josh Beckett	2.00
2	Eric Munson	2.00
3	Pat Burrell	4.00
4	Alfonso Soriano	2.00
5	Rick Ankiel	1.50
6	Ruben Mateo	1.50
7	Mark Quinn	1.00
8	Kip Wells	1.00
9	Ben Petrick	1.00
10	Nick Johnson	2.00

2000 Fleer Mystique Seismic Activity

This 10-card set spotlights the top power hitters in the game. The player image is in the foreground of a warp like setting with golden highlights. Card backs are numbered with an "SA" suffix and are seeded 1:40 packs. A serial numbered parallel called Richter 100 is randomly seeded and is limited to 100 serial numbered sets.

		MT
Complete Set (10):		80.00
Common Player:		3.00
Inserted 1:40		
Richter parallel:		3-5X
Production 100 sets		
1	Ken Griffey Jr.	12.00
2	Sammy Sosa	10.00
3	Derek Jeter	18.00
4	Mark McGwire	18.00
5	Manny Ramirez	5.00
6	Mike Piazza	10.00
7	Vladimir Guerrero	6.00
8	Chipper Jones	8.00
9	Alex Rodriguez	12.00
10	Jeff Bagwell	5.00

2000 Fleer Mystique Supernaturals

This 10-card set has a warp like image of the player on the front with silver holo-foil highlights around the player image and gold foil stamping. Card backs are numbered with an "S" suffix. These were seeded 1:10 packs.

		MT
Complete Set (10):		30.00
Common Player:		1.50
Inserted 1:10		
1	Alex Rodriguez	5.00
2	Chipper Jones	3.00
3	Derek Jeter	5.00
4	Ivan Rodriguez	1.50
5	Ken Griffey Jr.	5.00
6	Mark McGwire	6.00
7	Mike Piazza	4.00
8	Nomar Garciaparra	4.00
9	Sammy Sosa	4.00
10	Vladimir Guerrero	2.00

2000 Fleer Showcase

The base set consists of 140 cards, including 40 Prospect Showcase subset cards. Cards 101-115 are serially numbered to 1,000 and cards 116-140 are serially numbered to 2,000. The card fronts are holo-foiled, with the player name and team stamped in gold foil. Card backs have year-by-year statistics and a small close-up photo. Five-card packs carried an SRP of $4.99.

		MT
Complete Set (140):		450.00
Common Player (1-100):		.25
Common (101-115):		8.00
Production 1,000 sets		
Common (116-140):		6.00
Production 2,000 sets		
Pack (5):		4.00
Box (24):		90.00
1	Alex Rodriguez	3.00
2	Derek Jeter	4.00
3	Jeromy Burnitz	.25
4	John Olerud	.25
5	Paul Konerko	.25
6	Johnny Damon	.25
7	Curt Schilling	.25
8	Barry Larkin	.50
9	Adrian Beltre	.25
10	Scott Rolen	1.00
11	Carlos Delgado	1.00
12	Pedro J. Martinez	1.00
13	Todd Helton	1.00
14	Jacque Jones	.25
15	Jeff Kent	.40
16	Darin Erstad	.50
17	Juan Encarnacion	.25
18	Roger Clemens	1.50
19	Tony Gwynn	1.50
20	Nomar Garciaparra	2.50
21	Roberto Alomar	.75
22	Matt Lawton	.25
23	Rich Aurilia	.25
24	Charles Johnson	.25
25	Jim Thome	.40
26	Eric Milton	.25
27	Barry Bonds	1.50
28	Albert Belle	.50
29	Travis Fryman	.25
30	Ken Griffey Jr.	2.50
31	Phil Nevin	.25
32	Chipper Jones	2.00
33	Craig Biggio	.40
34	Mike Hampton	.25
35	Fred McGriff	.40
36	Cal Ripken Jr.	3.00
37	Manny Ramirez	1.00
38	Jose Vidro	.25
39	Trevor Hoffman	.25
40	Tom Glavine	.50
41	Frank Thomas	1.50
42	Chris Widger	.25
43	J.D. Drew	.25
44	Andres Galarraga	.40
45	Pokey Reese	.25
46	Mike Piazza	2.50
47	Kevin Young	.25
48	Sean Casey	.25
49	Carlos Beltran	.25
50	Jason Kendall	.25
51	Vladimir Guerrero	1.50
52	Jermaine Dye	.25
53	Brian Giles	.25
54	Andruw Jones	.75
55	Richard Hidalgo	.40
56	Robin Ventura	.25
57	Ivan Rodriguez	1.00
58	Greg Maddux	2.00
59	Billy Wagner	.25
60	Ruben Mateo	.25
61	Troy Glaus	1.00
62	Dean Palmer	.25
63	Eric Chavez	.25
64	Edgar Martinez	.25
65	Randy Johnson	1.00
66	Preston Wilson	.25
67	Orlando Hernandez	.40
68	Jim Edmonds	.40
69	Carl Everett	.25
70	Larry Walker	.40
71	Ron Belliard	.25
72	Sammy Sosa	2.50
73	Matt Williams	.40
74	Cliff Floyd	.25
75	Bernie Williams	.75
76	Fernando Tatis	.25
77	Steve Finley	.25
78	Jeff Bagwell	1.00

79	Edgardo Alfonzo	.40
80	Jose Canseco	.50
81	Magglio Ordonez	.25
82	Shawn Green	.40
83	Bobby Abreu	.25
84	Tony Batista	.25
85	Mo Vaughn	.50
86	Juan Gonzalez	1.00
87	Paul O'Neill	.40
88	Mark McGwire	4.00
89	Mark Grace	.40
90	Kevin Brown	.40
91	Ben Grieve	.40
92	Shannon Stewart	.25
93	Erubiel Durazo	.25
94	Antonio Alfonseca	.25
95	Jeff Cirillo	.25
96	Greg Vaughn	.25
97	Kerry Wood	.40
98	Geoff Jenkins	.25
99	Jason Giambi	.40
100	Rafael Palmeiro	.50
101	Rafael Furcal	8.00
102	Pablo Ozuna	8.00
103	Brad Penny	8.00
104	Mark Mulder	10.00
105	Adam Piatt	10.00
106	*Mike Lamb*	15.00
107	*Kazuhiro Sasaki*	25.00
108	*Aaron McNeal*	15.00
109	Pat Burrell	18.00
110	Rick Ankiel	10.00
111	Eric Munson	12.00
112	Josh Beckett	20.00
113	Adam Kennedy	10.00
114	Alex Escobar	10.00
115	Chad Hermansen	8.00
116	Kip Wells	6.00
117	Matt LeCroy	6.00
118	Julio Ramirez	6.00
119	Ben Petrick	6.00
120	Nick Johnson	10.00
121	Gookie Dawkins	8.00
122	*Julio Zuleta*	10.00
123	Alfonso Soriano	10.00
124	*Keith McDonald*	8.00
125	Kory DeHaan	10.00
126	Vernon Wells	6.00
127	Dernell Stenson	8.00
128	David Eckstein	10.00
129	Robert Fick	8.00
130	Cole Liniak	8.00
131	Mark Quinn	10.00
132	Eric Gagne	8.00
133	Wily Pena	10.00
134	*Andy Thompson*	10.00
135	*Steve Sisco*	10.00
136	*Paul Rigdon*	15.00
137	Rob Bell	8.00
138	Carlos Guillen	6.00
139	Jimmy Rollins	6.00
140	Jason Conti	8.00

2000 Fleer Showcase Legacy

A parallel to the 140-card base set these feature a matte and holo-foil design and are serially numbered to 20.

	MT
Stars (1-100):	50-75X
Prospects (101-140):	4-8X
Production 20 sets	

(See 2000 Fleer Showcase for checklist and base card values.)

2000 Fleer Showcase Masterpiece

Each card in 2000 Showcase was issued in a unique Masterpiece edition. The front is enhanced with gold ink while on back is printed the notice "The Only 1 Of 1 / Masterpiece".

MT

(Because of each card's unique nature, catalog values cannot be presented.)

2000 Fleer Showcase Club 3000

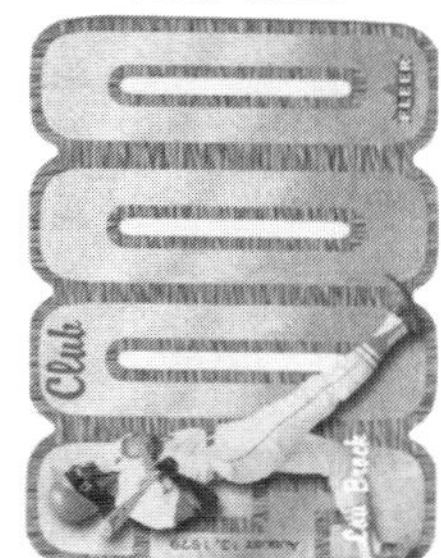

This two-card set pays tribute to Lou Brock and Nolan Ryan. Each card is die-cut around the numerals 3,000 with a date displaying the day Brock or Ryan reached their 3,000 milestone. The player name is stamped in silver holo-foil. These were inserted 1:24 packs.

		MT
Complete Set (2):		10.00
Common Player:		3.00
Inserted 1:24		
1	Lou Brock	3.00
2	Nolan Ryan	10.00

2000 Fleer Showcase Club 3000 Memorabilia

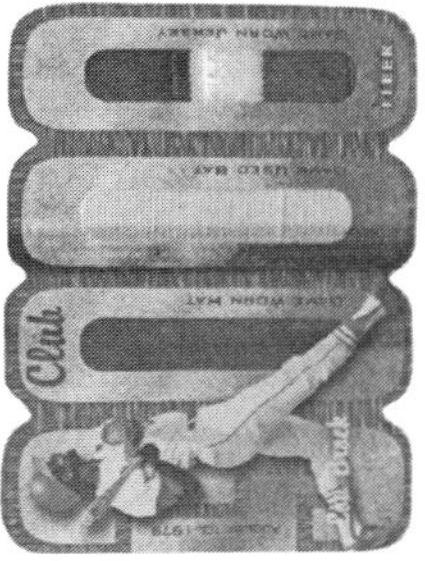

These inserts feature actual game-used pieces of memorabilia from Nolan Ryan and Lou Brock and are serial numbered. The number produced is listed after the player name.

	MT
Lou Brock - jersey/680	40.00
Lou Brock - bat/270	50.00
Lou Brock - hat, bat, jersey/25	300.00
Nolan Ryan - jersey/780	75.00
Nolan Ryan - hat/65	250.00
Nolan Ryan - bat/265	150.00
Nolan Ryan - bat, jersey/100	200.00

2000 Fleer Showcase Consummate Prose

This 15-card set has an image of a worn scroll of paper with consummate prose written on it in the background of the player image. The Showcase logo, player name and Consummate Prose are stamped in gold foil. Card backs are numbered with an "CP" suffix and are inserted 1:6 packs.

		MT
Complete Set (15):		40.00
Common Player:		1.00
Inserted 1:6		
1	Jeff Bagwell	1.50
2	Alex Rodriguez	5.00
3	Chipper Jones	3.00
4	Derek Jeter	6.00
5	Manny Ramirez	1.50
6	Tony Gwynn	2.00
7	Sammy Sosa	4.00
8	Ivan Rodriguez	1.50
9	Greg Maddux	3.00
10	Ken Griffey Jr.	4.00
11	Rick Ankiel	.75
12	Cal Ripken Jr.	5.00
13	Pedro Martinez	1.50
14	Mike Piazza	4.00
15	Mark McGwire	6.00

2000 Fleer Showcase Final Answer

These foiled inserts have a green border with the player inside a frame with question marks in the background. The card backs have trivia questions about the featured player. Card backs are numbered with a "FA" suffix. These were seeded 1:10 packs.

		MT
Complete Set (10):		30.00
Common Player:		1.50
Inserted 1:10		
1	Alex Rodriguez	5.00
2	Vladimir Guerrero	2.00
3	Cal Ripken Jr.	5.00
4	Sammy Sosa	4.00
5	Barry Bonds	2.00
6	Derek Jeter	6.00
7	Ken Griffey Jr.	4.00
8	Mike Piazza	4.00
9	Nomar Garciaparra	4.00
10	Mark McGwire	6.00

2000 Fleer Showcase Feel the Game

This 20-card set has swatches of game worn jersey embedded into the card front. These were seeded 1:72 packs.

		MT
Common Player:		10.00
Inserted 1:72		
1	Barry Bonds	50.00
2	Gookie Dawkins	10.00
3	Darin Erstad	25.00
4	Troy Glaus	25.00
5	Scott Rolen	25.00
6	Alex Rodriguez	50.00
7	Andruw Jones	25.00
8	Robin Ventura	20.00
9	Sean Casey	15.00
10	Cal Ripken Jr.	70.00

2000 Fleer Showcase Fresh Ink

These autographed inserts are inserted 1:24 packs.

	MT
Common Player:	10.00
Inserted 1:24	

1 Rick Ankiel 20.00
2 Josh Beckett 25.00
3 Barry Bonds 80.00
4 A.J. Burnett 10.00
5 Pat Burrell 20.00
6 Ken Caminiti 15.00
7 Sean Casey 15.00
8 Jose Cruz Jr. 10.00
9 Gookie Dawkins 10.00
10 Erubiel Durazo 15.00
11 Juan Encarnacion 10.00
12 Darin Erstad 20.00
13 Rafael Furcal 15.00
14 Nomar Garciaparra 100.00
15 Jason Giambi 30.00
16 Jeremy Giambi 10.00
17 Brian Giles 15.00
18 Troy Glaus 25.00
19 Mark Grace
20 Vladimir Guerrero 35.00
21 Chad Hermansen 10.00
22 Orlando Hernandez
23 Trevor Hoffman 10.00
24 Randy Johnson 60.00
25 Andruw Jones 25.00
26 Jason Kendall 10.00
27 Paul Konerko 15.00
28 Mike Lowell 10.00
29 Aaron McNeal 10.00
30 Warren Morris 10.00
31 Paul O'Neill 20.00
32 Magglio Ordonez 20.00
33 Pablo Ozuna 10.00
34 Brad Penny 10.00
35 Ben Petrick 10.00
36 Pokey Reese 10.00
37 Cal Ripken Jr. 125.00
38 Alex Rodriguez 80.00
39 Scott Rolen 25.00
40 Jose Vidro 10.00
41 Kip Wells 10.00

2000 Fleer Showcase License to Skill

License to Skill have a rounded, die-cut top with a background similar to that of a bullseye on a target. Silver and gold foil etching and foil stamping are used as well. Card backs are numbered with an "LS" suffix and are inserted 1:20 packs.

	MT
Complete Set (10):	40.00
Common Player:	2.50
Inserted 1:20	
1 Vladimir Guerrero	3.00
2 Pedro J. Martinez	2.50
3 Nomar Garciaparra	6.00
4 Ivan Rodriguez	2.50
5 Mark McGwire	10.00
6 Derek Jeter	10.00
7 Ken Griffey Jr.	6.00
8 Randy Johnson	2.50
9 Sammy Sosa	6.00
10 Alex Rodriguez	8.00

2000 Fleer Showcase Long Gone

These inserts are die-cut around the card top to mimic the outfield dimensions of the featured players' stadium. Gold foil stamping is also used. Card backs are numbered with an "LG" suffix and have an insertion ratio of 1:20 packs.

	MT
Complete Set (10):	45.00
Common Player:	2.50
Inserted 1:20	
1 Sammy Sosa	6.00
2 Derek Jeter	10.00
3 Nomar Garciaparra	6.00
4 Juan Gonzalez	2.50
5 Vladimir Guerrero	3.00
6 Barry Bonds	3.00
7 Jeff Bagwell	2.50
8 Alex Rodriguez	8.00
9 Ken Griffey Jr.	6.00
10 Mark McGwire	10.00

2000 Fleer Showcase Noise of Summer

This 10-card set has a kaleidoscope background with the insert name stamped in red foil and the logo, player name and team name stamped in gold foil. Card backs are numbered with an "NS" suffix. These were seeded 1:10 packs.

	MT
Complete Set (10):	25.00
Common Player:	1.50
Inserted 1:10	
1 Chipper Jones	3.00
2 Jeff Bagwell	1.50
3 Manny Ramirez	1.50
4 Mark McGwire	6.00
5 Ken Griffey Jr.	4.00
6 Mike Piazza	4.00
7 Pedro J. Martinez	1.50
8 Alex Rodriguez	5.00
9 Derek Jeter	6.00
10 Randy Johnson	1.50

2000 Fleer Showcase Prospect Showcase First

A parallel of the 40-card Prospects subset. These differ from the base cards in that they have a horizontal format and are serially numbered to 500.

	MT
Prospects (101-140):	1-2X
Production 500 sets	

(See Prospects subset in 2000 Fleer Showcase for checklist and base values.)

2000 Fleer Showcase Sweet Sigs

These autographed inserts have the featured players' autograph on an actual "sweet spot" from an authentic Major League baseball. These have an insertion ratio of 1:250 packs.

	MT
Common Player:	20.00
Inserted 1:250	
1 Nomar Garciaparra/53	200.00
2 Alex Rodriguez/67	200.00
3 Tony Gwynn	80.00
4 Roger Clemens/79	125.00
5 Scott Rolen	50.00
6 Greg Maddux	90.00
7 Jose Cruz Jr.	20.00
8 Tony Womack	20.00
9 Jay Buhner	30.00
10 Nolan Ryan	150.00

2000 Fleer Tradition

The Fleer Tradition base set consists of 450 cards including a 30-card rookies/prospects subset, 30 team cards, 10 league leaders, 6 award winners, 10 postseason recaps and 6 checklists. The card fronts have a close-up photo of the featured player as well as a small action photo surrounded by a white border. Like the fronts the card backs have a "throwback" look, which includes complete year-by-year statistics, a brief career note and vital information. 10-card packs had a SRP of $1.49.

	MT
Complete Set (450):	75.00
Common Player:	.10
Complete Glossy Factory Set (500):	800.00
Complete Glossy Factory Set (455):	100.00
Glossy (1-450):	1-2X
Common Glossy (451-500):	10.00
Five Glossy (451-500) per factory set 1,000 produced (451-500)	
Pack (10):	2.00
Wax Box:	65.00
1 AL HRs	.75
2 NL HRs	.75
3 AL RBIs	.75
4 NL RBIs	.75
5 AL Avg.	.50
6 NL Avg.	.15
7 AL Wins	.20
8 NL Wins	.40
9 AL ERA	.20
10 NL ERA	.25
11 Matt Mantei	.10
12 John Rocker	.10
13 Kyle Farnsworth	.10
14 Juan Guzman	.10
15 Manny Ramirez	1.00
16 Matt Riley-P, Calvin Pickering-1B	.10
17 Tony Clark	.40
18 Brian Meadows	.10
19 Orber Moreno	.10
20 Eric Karros	.20
21 Steve Woodard	.10
22 Scott Brosius	.10
23 Gary Bennett	.10
24 Jason Wood-3B, Dave Borkowski-P	.10
25 Joe McEwing	.10
26 Juan Gonzalez	1.00
27 Roy Halladay	.10
28 Trevor Hoffman	.10
29 Arizona Diamondbacks	.10
30 *Domingo Guzman-P*, Wiki Gonzalez-C	.50
31 Bret Boone	.10

32 Nomar Garciaparra 2.50
33 Bo Porter .10
34 Eddie Taubensee .10
35 Pedro Astacio .10
36 Derek Bell .10
37 Jacque Jones .10
38 Ricky Ledee .20
39 Jeff Kent .10
40 Matt Williams .50
41 Alfonso Soriano-SS, D'Angelo Jimenez-3B .50
42 B.J. Surhoff .10
43 Denny Neagle .10
44 Omar Vizquel .10
45 Jeff Bagwell 1.00
46 Mark Grudzielanek .10
47 LaTroy Hawkins .10
48 Orlando Hernandez .40
49 Ken Griffey Jr. 3.00
50 Fernando Tatis .20
51 Quilvio Veras .10
52 Wayne Gomes .10
53 Rick Helling .10
54 Shannon Stewart .10
55 Dermal Brown-OF, Mark Quinn-OF .25
56 Randy Johnson .75
57 Greg Maddux 2.00
58 Mike Cameron .10
59 Matt Anderson .10
60 Milwaukee Brewers .10
61 Derrek Lee .10
62 Mike Sweeney .10
63 Fernando Vina .10
64 Orlando Cabrera .10
65 Doug Glanville .10
66 Stan Spencer .10
67 Ray Lankford .10
68 Kelly Dransfeldt .10
69 Alex Gonzalez .10
70 Russell Branyan-3B, Danny Peoples-OF .10
71 Jim Edmonds .10
72 Brady Anderson .20
73 Mike Stanley .10
74 Travis Fryman .20
75 Carlos Febles .10
76 Bobby Higginson .10
77 Carlos Perez .10
78 Steve Cox-1B, Alex Sanchez-OF .10
79 Dustin Hermanson .10
80 Kenny Rogers .10
81 Miguel Tejada .10
82 Ben Davis .10
83 Reggie Sanders .10
84 Eric Davis .20
85 J.D. Drew .40
86 Ryan Rupe .10
87 Bobby Smith .10
88 Jose Cruz Jr. .10
89 Carlos Delgado .75
90 Toronto Blue Jays .10
91 *Denny Stark-P*, Gil Meche-P .25
92 Randy Velarde .10
93 Aaron Boone .10
94 Javy Lopez .10
95 Johnny Damon .10
96 Jon Lieber .10
97 Montreal Expos .10
98 Mark Kotsay .10
99 Luis Gonzalez .10
100 Larry Walker .75
101 Adrian Beltre .25
102 Alex Ochoa .10
103 Michael Barrett .10
104 Tampa Bay Devil Rays .10
105 Rey Ordonez .10
106 Derek Jeter 3.00
107 Mike Lieberthal .10
108 Ellis Burks .10
109 Steve Finley .10
110 Ryan Klesko .20
111 Steve Avery .10
112 Dave Veres .10
113 Cliff Floyd .10
114 Shane Reynolds .10
115 Kevin Brown .20
116 David Nilsson .10
117 Mike Trombley .10
118 Todd Walker .10
119 John Olerud .25
120 Chuck Knoblauch .40
121 Nomar Garciaparra 2.00
122 Trot Nixon .10
123 Erubiel Durazo .25
124 Edwards Guzman .10
125 Curt Schilling .20
126 Brian Jordan .10
127 Cleveland Indians .10
128 Benito Santiago .10
129 Frank Thomas 1.00
130 Neifi Perez .10
131 Alex Fernandez .10
132 Jose Lima .10
133 Jorge Toca-1B, Melvin Mora-OF .10
134 Scott Karl .10
135 Brad Radke .10
136 Paul O'Neill .25
137 Kris Benson .10
138 Colorado Rockies .10
139 Jason Phillips .10
140 Robb Nen .10
141 Ken Hill .10
142 Charles Johnson .10
143 Paul Konerko .10
144 Dmitri Young .10
145 Justin Thompson .10
146 Mark Loretta .10
147 Edgardo Alfonzo .25
148 Armando Benitez .10
149 Octavio Dotel .10
150 Wade Boggs .50
151 Ramon Hernandez .10
152 Freddy Garcia .25
153 Edgar Martinez .20
154 Ivan Rodriguez 1.00
155 Kansas City Royals .10
156 Cleatus Davidson-2B, Cristian Guzman-SS .10
157 Andy Benes .10
158 Todd Dunwoody .10
159 Pedro Martinez 1.00
160 Mike Caruso .10
161 Mike Sirotka .10
162 Houston Astros .10
163 Darryl Kile .10
164 Chipper Jones 2.00
165 Carl Everett .10
166 Geoff Jenkins .10
167 Dan Perkins .10
168 Andy Pettitte .25
169 Francisco Cordova .10
170 Jay Buhner .20
171 Jay Bell .10
172 Andruw Jones .75
173 Bobby Howry .10
174 Chris Singleton .10
175 Todd Helton .75
176 A.J. Burnett .25
177 Marquis Grissom .10
178 Eric Milton .10
179 Los Angeles Dodgers .10
180 Kevin Appier .10
181 Brian Giles .10
182 Tom Davey .10
183 Mo Vaughn .75
184 Jose Hernandez .10
185 Jim Parque .10
186 Derrick Gibson .10
187 Bruce Aven .10
188 Jeff Cirillo .10
189 Doug Mientkiewicz .10
190 Eric Chavez .10
191 Al Martin .10
192 Tom Glavine .25
193 Butch Huskey .10
194 Ray Durham .10
195 Greg Vaughn .25
196 Vinny Castilla .10
197 Ken Caminiti .20
198 Joe Mays .10
199 Chicago White Sox .10
200 Mariano Rivera .25
201 Mark McGwire 4.00
202 Pat Meares .10
203 Andres Galarraga .50
204 Tom Gordon .10
205 Henry Rodriguez .10
206 Brett Tomko .10
207 Dante Bichette .25
208 Craig Biggio .50
209 Matt Lawton .10
210 Tino Martinez .40
211 Aaron Myette-P, Josh Paul-C .10
212 Warren Morris .10
213 San Diego Padres .10
214 Ramon E. Martinez .10
215 Troy Percival .10
216 Jason Johnson .10
217 Carlos Lee .10
218 Scott Williamson .10
219 Jeff Weaver .10
220 Ronnie Belliard .10
221 Jason Giambi .10
222 Ken Griffey Jr. 3.00
223 John Halama .10
224 Brett Hinchliffe .10
225 Wilson Alvarez .10
226 Rolando Arrojo .10
227 Ruben Mateo .40
228 Rafael Palmeiro .75
229 David Wells .10
230 Eric Gagne-P, Jeff Williams-P .10
231 Tim Salmon .40
232 Mike Mussina .75
233 Magglio Ordonez .25
234 Ron Villone .10
235 Antonio Alfonseca .10
236 Jeromy Burnitz .10
237 Ben Grieve .40
238 Giomar Guevara .10
239 Garret Anderson .10
240 John Smoltz .20
241 Mark Grace .25
242 Cole Liniak-3B, Jose Molina-C .10
243 Damion Easley .10
244 Jeff Montgomery .10
245 Kenny Lofton .60
246 Masato Yoshii .10
247 Philadelphia Phillies .10
248 Raul Mondesi .25
249 Marlon Anderson .10
250 Shawn Green .75
251 Sterling Hitchcock .10
252 Randy Wolf-P, Anthony Shumaker-P .10
253 Jeff Fassero .10
254 Eli Marrero .10
255 Cincinnati Reds .10
256 Rick Ankiel-P, Adam Kennedy-2B .50
257 Darin Erstad .25
258 Albert Belle .75
259 Bartolo Colon .10
260 Bret Saberhagen .10
261 Carlos Beltran .25
262 Glenallen Hill .10
263 Gregg Jefferies .10
264 Matt Clement .10
265 Miguel Del Toro .10
266 Robinson Cancel-C, Kevin Barker-1B .10
267 San Francisco Giants .10
268 Kent Bottenfield .10
269 Fred McGriff .25
270 Chris Carpenter .10
271 Atlanta Braves .10
272 Wilton Veras-3B, *Tomokazu Ohka-P* .50
273 Will Clark .50
274 Troy O'Leary .10
275 Sammy Sosa 2.50
276 Travis Lee .25
277 Sean Casey .50
278 Ron Gant .25
279 Roger Clemens 1.50
280 Phil Nevin .10
281 Mike Piazza 2.50
282 Mike Lowell .10
283 Kevin Millwood .25
284 Joe Randa .10
285 Jeff Shaw .10
286 Jason Varitek .10
287 Harold Baines .10
288 Gabe Kapler .25
289 Chuck Finley .10
290 Carl Pavano .10
291 Brad Ausmus .10
292 Brad Fullmer .10
293 Boston Red Sox .10
294 Bob Wickman .10
295 Billy Wagner .10
296 Shawn Estes .10
297 Gary Sheffield .25
298 Fernando Seguignol .10
299 Omar Olivares .10
300 Baltimore Orioles .10
301 Matt Stairs .10
302 Andy Ashby .10
303 Todd Greene .10
304 Jesse Garcia .10
305 Kerry Wood .40
306 Roberto Alomar .75
307 New York Mets .10
308 Dean Palmer .10
309 Mike Hampton .10
310 Devon White .10
311 Chad Hermansen-OF, Mike Garcia-P .10
312 Tim Hudson .40
313 John Franco .10
314 Jason Schmidt .10
315 J.T. Snow .10
316 Ed Sprague .10
317 Chris Widger .10
318 Ben Petrick-C, *Luther Hackman-P* .50
319 Jose Mesa .10
320 Jose Canseco 1.00
321 John Wetteland .10
322 Minnesota Twins .10
323 *Jeff DaVanon-OF*, Brian Cooper-P .50
324 Tony Womack .10
325 Rod Beck .10
326 Mickey Morandini .10
327 Pokey Reese .10
328 Jaret Wright .10
329 Glen Barker .10
330 Darren Dreifort .10
331 Torii Hunter .10
332 Tony Armas Jr.-P, Peter Bergeron-OF .10
333 Hideki Irabu .20
334 Desi Relaford .10
335 Barry Bonds 1.25
336 Gary DiSarcina .10
337 Gerald Williams .10
338 John Valentin .10
339 David Justice .25
340 Juan Encarnacion .10
341 Jeremy Giambi .10
342 Chan Ho Park .10
343 Vladimir Guerrero 2.00
344 Robin Ventura .25
345 Bobby Abreu .10
346 Tony Gwynn 2.00
347 Jose Jimenez .10
348 Royce Clayton .10
349 Kelvim Escobar .10
350 Chicago Cubs .10
351 Travis Dawkins-SS, Jason LaRue-C .10
352 Barry Larkin .50
353 Cal Ripken Jr. 2.50
353s Cal Ripken Jr. (overprinted "PROMOTIONAL SAMPLE") 4.00
354 Alex Rodriguez 3.00
355 Todd Stottlemyre .20
356 Terry Adams .10
357 Pittsburgh Pirates .10
358 Jim Thome .50
359 Corey Lee-P, Doug Davis-P .10
360 Moises Alou .20
361 Todd Hollandsworth .10
362 Marty Cordova .10
363 David Cone .20
364 Joe Nathan-P, Wilson Delgado-SS .10
365 Paul Byrd .10
366 Edgar Renteria .10
367 Rusty Greer .10
368 David Segui .10
369 New York Yankees .50
370 Daryle Ward-OF/1B, Carlos Hernandez-2B .10
371 Troy Glaus .50
372 Delino DeShields .10
373 Jose Offerman .10
374 Sammy Sosa 2.50
375 Sandy Alomar Jr. .20
376 Masao Kida .10
377 Richard Hidalgo .10
378 Ismael Valdes .10
379 Ugueth Urbina .10
380 Darryl Hamilton .10
381 John Jaha .10
382 St. Louis Cardinals .10
383 Scott Sauerbeck .10
384 Russ Ortiz .10
385 Jamie Moyer .10

386 Dave Martinez .10
387 Todd Zeile .10
388 Anaheim Angels .10
389 Rob Ryan-OF, Nick Bierbrodt-P .10
390 Rickey Henderson .40
391 Alex Rodriguez 3.00
392 Texas Rangers .10
393 Roberto Hernandez .10
394 Tony Batista .10
395 Oakland Athletics .10
396 Randall Simon-1B, *David Cortes-P* .40
397 Gregg Olson .10
398 Sidney Ponson .10
399 Micah Bowie .10
400 Mark McGwire 4.00
401 Florida Marlins .10
402 Chad Allen .10
403 Casey Blake-3B, Vernon Wells-OF .10
404 Pete Harnisch .10
405 Preston Wilson .10
406 Richie Sexson .10
407 Rico Brogna .10
408 Todd Hundley .10
409 Wally Joyner .10
410 Tom Goodwin .10
411 Joey Hamilton .10
412 Detroit Tigers .10
413 *Michael Tejera-P*, Ramon Castro-C .25
414 Alex Gonzalez .10
415 Jermaine Dye .10
416 Jose Rosado .10
417 Wilton Guerrero .10
418 Rondell White .20
419 Al Leiter .20
420 Bernie Williams .75
421 A.J. Hinch .10
422 Pat Burrell 2.50
423 Scott Rolen 1.00
424 Jason Kendall .25
425 Kevin Young .10
426 Eric Owens .10
427 Derek Jeter 3.00
428 Livan Hernandez .10
429 Russ Davis .10
430 Dan Wilson .10
431 Quinton McCracken .10
432 Homer Bush .10
433 Seattle Mariners .10
434 Chad Harville-P, Luis Vizcaino-P .10
435 Carlos Beltran .15
436 Scott Williamson .10
437 Pedro Martinez .50
438 Randy Johnson .40
439 Ivan Rodriguez .50
440 Chipper Jones 1.00
441 AL Division (Bernie Williams) .40
442 AL Division (Pedro Martinez) .50
443 AL Champ (Derek Jeter) 1.50
444 NL Division (Brian Jordan) .10
445 NL Division (Todd Pratt) .10
446 NL Champ (Kevin Millwood) .10
447 World Series (Orlando Hernandez) .20
448 World Series (Derek Jeter) 1.50
449 World Series (Chad Curtis) .10
450 World Series (Roger Clemens) .75
451 *Carlos Casimiro* 10.00
452 *Adam Melhuse* 10.00
453 *Adam Bernero* 10.00
454 *Dusty Allen* 10.00
455 *Chan Perry* 10.00
456 *Damian Rolls* 10.00
457 *Josh Phelps* 40.00
458 *Barry Zito* 45.00
459 *Hector Ortiz* 10.00
460 *Juan Pierre* 15.00
461 *Jose Ortiz* 60.00
462 *Chad Zerbe* 10.00
463 *Julio Zuleta* 10.00
464 *Eric Byrnes* 10.00
465 *Wilfredo Rodriguez* 15.00
466 *Wascar Serrano* 10.00
467 *Aaron McNeal* 15.00
468 *Paul Rigdon* 15.00
469 *John Snyder* 10.00
470 *J.C. Romero* 10.00
471 *Talmadge Nunnari* 10.00
472 *Mike Lamb* 15.00
473 *Ryan Kohlmeier* 10.00
474 *Rodney Lindsey* 10.00
475 *Elvis Pena* 10.00
476 *Alex Cabrera* 10.00
477 *Chris Richard* 15.00
478 *Pedro Feliz* 25.00
479 *Ross Gload* 10.00
480 *Timoniel Perez* 20.00
481 *Jason Woolf* 10.00
482 *Kenny Kelly* 15.00
483 *Sang-Hoon Lee* 10.00
484 *John Riedling* 15.00
485 Chris Wakeland 10.00
486 *Britt Reames* 15.00
487 *Greg LaRocca* 10.00
488 *Randy Keisler* 15.00
489 *Xavier Nady* 40.00
490 *Keith Ginter* 20.00
491 *Joey Nation* 10.00
492 *Kazuhiro Sasaki* 25.00
493 *Lesli Brea* 10.00
494 *Jace Brewer* 10.00
495 *Yohanny Valera* 10.00
496 Adam Piatt 15.00
497 Nate Rolison 10.00
498 Aubrey Huff 10.00
499 Jason Tyner 10.00
500 Corey Patterson 20.00

2000 Fleer Tradition Club 3000

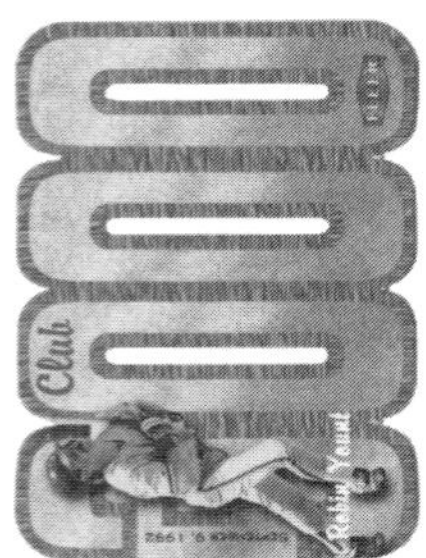

The Club 3000 inserts are die-cut around the number 3,000, commemmorating their reaching the 3,000 hit achievement. These are seeded 1:36 packs and features George Brett, Rod Carew and Robin Yount.

	MT
Complete Set (3):	10.00
Common Player:	3.00
Inserted 1:36	
(1) George Brett	5.00
(2) Rod Carew	3.00
(3) Robin Yount	3.00

2000 Fleer Tradition Club 3000 Memorabilia

These are a parallel to the base version and has five different memorabilia based tiers. Level 2 (cap), Level 3 (bat), Level 4 (jersey), Level 5 (bat and jersey) and Level 6 (bat, jersey and cap). Each card is hand-numbered.

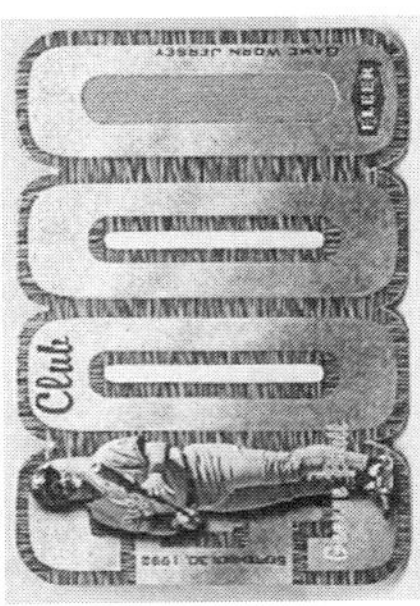

	MT
George Brett - bat/250	90.00
George Brett - hat/100	125.00
George Brett - jersey/445	75.00
George Brett - bat, jersey/100	175.00
George Brett - bat, hat, jersey/25	
Rod Carew - bat/225	65.00
Rod Carew - hat/100	100.00
Rod Carew - jersey/440	50.00
Rod Carew - bat, jersey/100	125.00
Rod Carew - bat, hat, jersey/25	
Robin Yount - bat/250	75.00
Robin Yount - hat/100	100.00
Robin Yount - jersey/440	60.00
Robin Yount - bat, jersey/100	125.00
Robin Yount - bat, hat, jersey/25	

2000 Fleer Tradition Dividends

This insert set consists of 15 cards and spotlights the top players on a horizontal format. Card fronts have silver foil stamping, a red border and are seeded 1:6 packs. They are numbered on the back with a "D" suffix.

	MT
Complete Set (15):	30.00
Common Player:	.75
Inserted 1:6	
1 Alex Rodriguez	5.00
2 Ben Grieve	1.00
3 Cal Ripken Jr.	4.00
4 Chipper Jones	3.00
5 Derek Jeter	4.00
6 Frank Thomas	1.50
7 Jeff Bagwell	1.50
8 Sammy Sosa	4.00
9 Tony Gwynn	3.00
10 Scott Rolen	1.50
11 Nomar Garciaparra	4.00
12 Mike Piazza	4.00
13 Mark McGwire	6.00
14 Ken Griffey Jr.	5.00
15 Juan Gonzalez	1.50

2000 Fleer Tradition Glossy Lumberjacks

	MT
Common Player:	15.00
One per Factory set	
Production listed	
1 Edgardo Alfonzo/145	25.00
2 Roberto Alomar/627	40.00
3 Moises Alou/529	15.00
4 Carlos Beltran/489	15.00
5 Adrian Beltre/127	20.00
6 Wade Boggs/30	
7 Barry Bonds/305	50.00
8 Jeromy Burnitz/34	
9 Pat Burrell/45	50.00
10 Sean Casey/50	30.00
11 Eric Chavez/259	15.00
12 Tony Clark/70	25.00
13 Carlos Delgado/70	75.00
14 J.D. Drew/135	40.00
15 Erubiel Durazo/70	25.00
16 Ray Durham/35	
17 Carlos Febles/120	20.00
18 Jason Giambi/220	40.00
19 Shawn Green/429	25.00
20 Vladimir Guerrero/809	40.00
21 Derek Jeter/180	125.00
22 Chipper Jones/725	40.00
23 Gabe Kapler/160	20.00
24 Jason Kendall/34	
25 Paul Konerko/70	25.00
26 Ray Lankford/35	
27 Mike Lieberthal/45	25.00
28 Edgar Martinez/211	25.00
29 Raul Mondesi/458	15.00
30 Warren Morris/35	20.00
31 Magglio Ordonez/190	20.00
32 Rafael Palmeiro/49	70.00
33 Pokey Reese/110	15.00
34 Cal Ripken/235	125.00
35 Alex Rodriguez/292	90.00
36 Ivan Rodriguez/602	35.00
37 Scott Rolen/502	25.00
38 Chris Singleton/68	25.00
39 Alfonso Soriano/285	20.00
40 Frank Thomas/489	50.00
41 Jim Thome/479	20.00
42 Robin Ventura/114	20.00

43	Jose Vidro/60	25.00
44	Bernie Williams/ 215	40.00
45	Matt Williams/152	35.00

2000 Fleer Tradition Grasskickers

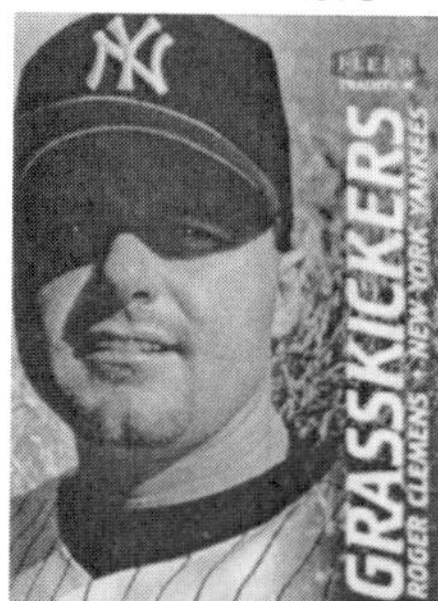

This 15-card set has a close-up photo of the featured player with holographic silver foil stamping. These are seeded 1:30 packs and are numbered on the back with a "GK" suffix.

		MT
Complete Set (15):		125.00
Common Player:		3.00
Inserted 1:30		
1	Tony Gwynn	10.00
2	Scott Rolen	5.00
3	Nomar Garciaparra	12.00
4	Mike Piazza	12.00
5	Mark McGwire	20.00
6	Frank Thomas	5.00
7	Cal Ripken Jr.	12.00
8	Chipper Jones	10.00
9	Greg Maddux	10.00
10	Ken Griffey Jr.	15.00
11	Juan Gonzalez	5.00
12	Derek Jeter	15.00
13	Sammy Sosa	12.00
14	Roger Clemens	8.00
15	Alex Rodriguez	15.00

2000 Fleer Tradition Hall's Well

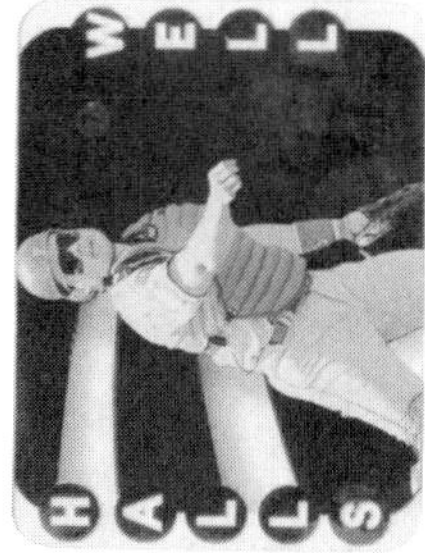

This 15-card set spotlights superstars destined for Cooperstown, featured on a transparent plastic stock with overlays of silver foil stamping. These were seeded 1:30 packs and are numbered with a "HW" suffix.

		MT
Complete Set (15):		125.00
Common Player:		3.00
Inserted 1:30		
1	Mark McGwire	20.00
2	Alex Rodriguez	15.00
3	Cal Ripken Jr.	12.00
4	Chipper Jones	10.00
5	Derek Jeter	15.00
6	Frank Thomas	5.00
7	Greg Maddux	10.00
8	Juan Gonzalez	5.00
9	Ken Griffey Jr.	15.00
10	Mike Piazza	12.00
11	Nomar Garciaparra	12.00
12	Sammy Sosa	12.00
13	Roger Clemens	8.00
14	Ivan Rodriguez	5.00
15	Tony Gwynn	10.00

2000 Fleer Tradition Fresh Ink

This autographed insert set consists of 38 cards on a vertical format with the autograph on the bottom third of the card below the player image. These were inserted 1:144 packs.

	MT
Common Player:	10.00
Inserted 1:144	
Rick Ankiel	20.00
Carlos Beltran	15.00
Pat Burrell	20.00
Miguel Cairo	10.00
Sean Casey	15.00
Will Clark	30.00
Mike Darr	20.00
J.D. Drew	40.00
Erubiel Durazo	15.00
Carlos Febles	10.00
Freddy Garcia	20.00
Greg Maddux	100.00
Jason Grilli	10.00
Vladimir Guerrero	50.00
Tony Gwynn	50.00
Jerry Hairston Jr.	10.00
Tim Hudson	25.00
John Jaha	10.00
D'Angelo Jimenez	10.00
Andruw Jones	25.00
Gabe Kapler	15.00
Cesar King	10.00
Jason LaRue	10.00
Mike Lieberthal	10.00
Pedro Martinez	75.00
Gary Matthews Jr.	10.00
Orber Moreno	10.00
Eric Munson	15.00
Rafael Palmeiro	35.00
Jim Parque	10.00
Willi Mo Pena	10.00
Cal Ripken Jr.	120.00
Alex Rodriguez	80.00
Tim Salmon	15.00
Chris Singleton	10.00
Alfonso Soriano	30.00
Ed Yarnall	10.00

2000 Fleer Tradition Ripken Collection

This 10-card set is devoted to Cal Ripken Jr. and features 10 different Fleer retro designs. These were seeded 1:30 packs.

	MT
Complete Set (10):	70.00
Common Card:	8.00
Inserted 1:30	

(Inserted at the rate of 1:30 packs.)

2000 Fleer Tradition Ten-4

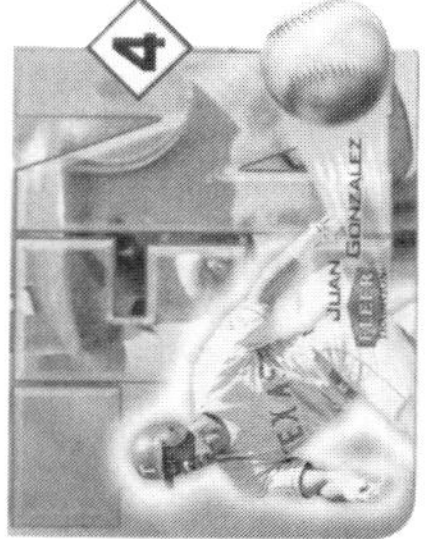

This 10-card insert set focuses on baseball's home run kings on a die-cut design enhanced with silver foil stamping. These were seeded 1:18 packs and are numbered on the card back with a "TF" suffix.

		MT
Complete Set (10):		60.00
Common Player:		2.00
Inserted 1:18		
1	Sammy Sosa	6.00
2	Nomar Garciaparra	6.00
3	Mike Piazza	6.00
4	Mark McGwire	10.00
5	Ken Griffey Jr.	8.00
6	Juan Gonzalez	3.00
7	Derek Jeter	8.00
8	Chipper Jones	5.00
9	Cal Ripken Jr.	6.00
10	Alex Rodriguez	8.00

2000 Fleer Tradition Who To Watch

Top prospects for the 2000 season are highlighted in this 15-card set, including Rick Ankiel. They have a die-cut design with gold foil stamping. These were inserted 1:3 packs and numbered on the back with a "WW" suffix.

		MT
Complete Set (15):		12.00
Common Player:		.50
Inserted 1:3		
1	Rick Ankiel	2.50
2	Matt Riley	.50
3	Wilton Veras	.50
4	Ben Petrick	.50
5	Chad Hermansen	.50
6	Peter Bergeron	1.00
7	Mark Quinn	1.00
8	Russell Branyan	.50
9	Alfonso Soriano	1.00
10	Randy Wolf	.50
11	Ben Davis	.50
12	Jeff DaVanon	.50
13	D'Angelo Jimenez	.50
14	Vernon Wells	1.00
15	Adam Kennedy	.50

2000 Fleer Tradition Update

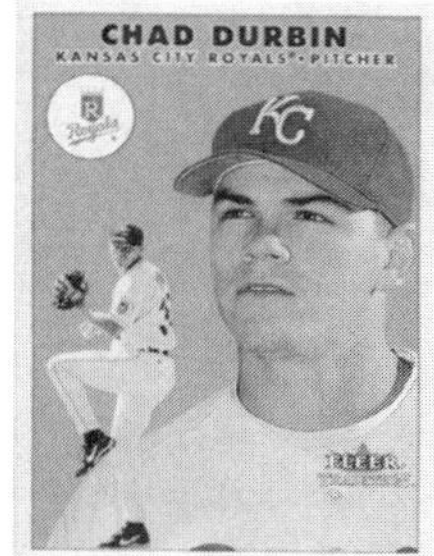

Card #50 was supposed to be Indians prospect C.C. Sabathia but it was never issued because he was not called up during the 2000 season.

		MT
Complete Set (149):		20.00
Common Player:		.15
1	Ken Griffey Jr. (Season Highlights)	.75
2	Cal Ripken Jr. (Season Highlights)	1.00
3	Randy Velarde (Season Highlights)	.15
4	Fred McGriff (Season Highlights)	.15
5	Derek Jeter (Season Highlights)	1.50
6	Tom Glavine (Season Highlights)	.25
7	Brent Mayne (Season Highlights)	.15
8	Alex Ochoa (Season Highlights)	.15
9	Scott Sheldon (Season Highlights)	.15
10	Randy Johnson (Season Highlights)	.25
11	*Daniel Garibay*	.25
12	Brad Fullmer	.15
13	*Kazuhiro Sasaki*	2.00
14	Andy Tracy	.15
15	Bret Boone	.15
16	*Chad Durbin*	.25
17	*Mark Buehrle*	.15
18	*Julio Zuleta*	.15
19	Jeremy Giambi	.15
20	*Gene Stechschulte*	.15
21	Lou Pote	.15
22	Darrell Einertson	.15
23	Ken Griffey Jr.	2.00
24	*Jeff Sparks*	.25
25	*Aaron Fultz*	.15
26	Derek Bell	.15
27	Rob Bell	.15
28	Rob Fick	.15
29	Darryl Kile	.15
30	Clayton Andrews	.15
31	Dave Veres	.15
32	*Hector Mercado*	.15

33 Willie Morales .15
34 Kelly Wunsch .15
35 Hideki Irabu .15
36 Sean DePaula .15
37 Dewayne Wise .15
38 Curt Schilling .15
39 Mark Johnson .15
40 Mike Cameron .15
41 Scott Sheldon .15
42 Brett Tomko .15
43 *Johan Santana* .15
44 Andy Benes .15
45 Matt LeCroy .15
46 Ryan Klesko .15
47 Andy Ashby .15
48 Octavio Dotel .15
49 *Eric Byrnes* .15
50 Not Issued
51 Kenny Rogers .15
52 Ben Weber .15
53 Matt Blank .15
54 Tom Goodwin .15
55 Jim Edmonds .50
56 *Derrick Turnbow* .25
57 Mark Mulder .15
58 Tarrik Brock .15
59 Danny Young .15
60 Fernando Vina .15
61 *Justin Brunette* .15
62 Jimmy Anderson .15
63 Reggie Sanders .15
64 Adam Kennedy .15
65 Jesse Garcia .15
66 Al Martin .15
67 Kevin Walker .15
68 Brad Penny .15
69 B.J. Surhoff .15
70 Geoff Blum .15
71 Jose Jimenez .15
72 Chuck Finley .15
73 Valerio DeLosSantos .15
74 Terry Adams .15
75 Rafael Furcal .25
76 Mike Darr .15
77 Quilvio Veras .15
78 Armando Almanza .15
79 Greg Vaughn .15
80 *Keith McDonald* .15
81 Eric Cammack .15
82 Horacio Estrada .15
83 Kory DeHaan .15
84 Kevin Hodges .15
85 *Mike Lamb* .50
86 Shawn Green .40
87 Dan Reichert .15
88 Adam Piatt .25
89 Mike Garcia .15
90 *Rodrigo Lopez* .15
91 John Olerud .25
92 Barry Zito 3.00
93 Jimmy Rollins .15
94 Denny Neagle .15
95 Rickey Henderson .40
96 Adam Eaton .15
97 Brian O'Connor .15
98 Andy Thompson .15
99 Jason Boyd .15
100 Carlos Guillen .15
101 Raul Gonzalez .15
102 *Brandon Kolb* .25
103 Jason Maxwell .15
104 *Luis Matos* .50
105 *Morgan Burkhart* .25
106 Ismael Villegas .15
107 David Justice .50
108 Pablo Ozuna .15
109 Jose Canseco .50
110 Alex Cora .15
111 Will Clark .50
112 Keith Luuloa .15
113 Bruce Chen .15
114 Adam Hyzdu .15
115 Scott Forster .15
116 Allen McDill .15
117 Kevin Nicholson .15
118 Israel Alcantara .15
119 Juan Alvarez .15
120 Julio Lugo .15
121 B.J. Waszgis .15
122 Jeff D'Amico .15
123 Ricky Ledee .15
124 Mark DeRosa .15
125 *Alex Cabrera* .50
126 Gary Matthews .15
127 Richie Sexson .15
128 Santiago Perez .15
129 Rondell White .15
130 *Craig House* .15
131 Kevin Beirne .15
132 Wayne Franklin .15
133 Henry Rodriguez .15
134 Jay Payton .15
135 Ron Gant .15
136 *Paxton Crawford* .25
137 Kent Bottenfield .15
138 *Rocky Biddle* .15
139 Travis Lee .15
140 Ryan Vogelsong .15
141 Jason Conti .15
142 Tim Drew .15
143 *John Parrish* .15
144 *Javier Cardona* .15
145 *Tike Redman* .15
146 Brian Schneider .15
147 *Pasqual Coco* .15
148 *Lorenzo Barcelo* .15
149 *Jace Brewer* .25
150 Milton Bradley .15

2000 Fleer Tradition Update Mantle Pieces

MT
Inserted 1:80 sets
1 Mickey Mantle 200.00

2001 Fleer Authority

MT
Complete Set (150): NA
Common Player: .25
Common (101-150): 4.00
Production 2,001
Pack (5): 4.00
Box (22 + 2 graded packs): 90.00
1 Mark Grace .50
2 Paul Konerko .25
3 Sean Casey .25
4 Jim Thome .50
5 Todd Helton .75
6 Tony Clark .40
7 Jeff Bagwell .75
8 Mike Sweeney .25
9 Eric Karros .25
10 Richie Sexson .25
11 Doug Mientkiewicz .25
12 Ryan Klesko .25
13 John Olerud .50
14 Mark McGwire 2.50
15 Fred McGriff .40
16 Rafael Palmeiro .40
17 Carlos Delgado .50
18 Roberto Alomar .60
19 Craig Biggio .40
20 Jose Vidro .25
21 Edgardo Alfonzo .25
22 Jeff Kent .25
23 Bret Boone .25
24 Rafael Furcal .25
25 Nomar Garciaparra 2.00
26 Barry Larkin .50
27 Cristian Guzman .25
28 Derek Jeter 3.00
29 Miguel Tejada .40
30 Jimmy Rollins .25
31 Rich Aurilia .25
32 Alex Rodriguez 2.00
33 Cal Ripken Jr. 3.00
34 Troy Glaus .60
35 Matt Williams .40
36 Chipper Jones 1.50
37 Jeff Cirillo .25
38 Robin Ventura .25
39 Eric Chavez .40
40 Scott Rolen .40
41 Phil Nevin .25
42 Mike Piazza 2.00
43 Jorge Posada .40
44 Jason Kendall .25
45 Ivan Rodriguez .75
46 Frank Thomas .75
47 Edgar Martinez .25
48 Darin Erstad .25
49 Tim Salmon .40
50 Luis Gonzalez .50
51 Andruw Jones .50
52 Carl Everett .25
53 Manny Ramirez .75
54 Sammy Sosa 1.50
55 Rondell White .25
56 Magglio Ordonez .25
57 Ken Griffey Jr. 2.50
58 Juan Gonzalez .75
59 Larry Walker .40
60 Bobby Higginson .25
61 Cliff Floyd .25
62 Preston Wilson .25
63 Moises Alou .40
64 Lance Berkman .40
65 Richard Hidalgo .25
66 Jermaine Dye .40
67 Mark Quinn .25
68 Shawn Green .40
69 Gary Sheffield .40
70 Jeromy Burnitz .25
71 Geoff Jenkins .40
72 Vladimir Guerrero .75
73 Bernie Williams .50
74 Johnny Damon .25
75 Jason Giambi .50
76 Bobby Abreu .25
77 Pat Burrell .40
78 Brian Giles .40
79 Tony Gwynn .75
80 Barry Bonds 1.50
81 J.D. Drew .40
82 Jim Edmonds .40
83 Greg Vaughn .25
84 Raul Mondesi .25
85 Shannon Stewart .25
86 Randy Johnson .75
87 Curt Schilling .40
88 Tom Glavine .40
89 Greg Maddux 1.50
90 Pedro Martinez .75
91 Kerry Wood .40
92 David Wells .25
93 Bartolo Colon .25
94 Mike Hampton .25
95 Kevin Brown .40
96 Al Leiter .40
97 Roger Clemens 1.00
98 Mike Mussina .60
99 Tim Hudson .50
100 Kazuhiro Sasaki .25
101 *Ichiro Suzuki* 45.00
102 *Albert Pujols* 40.00
103 *Drew Henson* 20.00
104 Adam Pettyjohn 4.00
105 *Adrian Hernandez* 4.00
106 Andy Morales 4.00
107 *Tsuyoshi Shinjo* 10.00
108 Juan Uribe 4.00
109 *Jack Wilson* 4.00
110 *Jason Smith* 4.00
111 *Junior Spivey* 4.00
112 *Wilson Betemit* 10.00
113 *Elpidio Guzman* 4.00
114 *Esix Snead* 4.00
115 *Winston Abreu* 4.00
116 *Jeremy Owens* 4.00
117 *Jay Gibbons* 8.00
118 Luis Lopez 4.00
119 *Ryan Freel* 4.00
120 *Rafael Soriano* 4.00
121 *Johnny Estrada* 4.00
122 *Bud Smith* 10.00
123 *Jackson Melian* 4.00
124 *Matt White* 4.00
125 *Travis Hafner* 4.00
126 *Morgan Ensberg* 4.00
127 *Endy Chavez* 4.00
128 *Bret Prinz* 4.00
129 *Juan Diaz* 4.00
130 *Erick Almonte* 4.00
131 *Rob Mackowiak* 4.00
132 *Carlos Valderrama* 4.00
133 *Wilkin Ruan* 4.00
134 *Angel Berroa* 4.00
135 *Henry Mateo* 4.00
136 Bill Ortega 4.00
137 *Billy Sylvester* 4.00
138 *Andres Torres* 4.00
139 Nate Frese 4.00
140 *Casey Fossum* 4.00
141 *Ricardo Rodriguez* 4.00
142 *Brian Roberts* 4.00
143 *Carlos Garcia* 4.00
144 *Brian Lawrence* 5.00
145 *Cory Aldridge* 4.00
146 *Mark Teixeira* 20.00
147 *Juan Cruz* 10.00
148 *Brandon Duckworth* 8.00
149 *Dewon Brazelton* 8.00
150 *Mark Prior* 35.00

2001 Fleer Authority Prominence

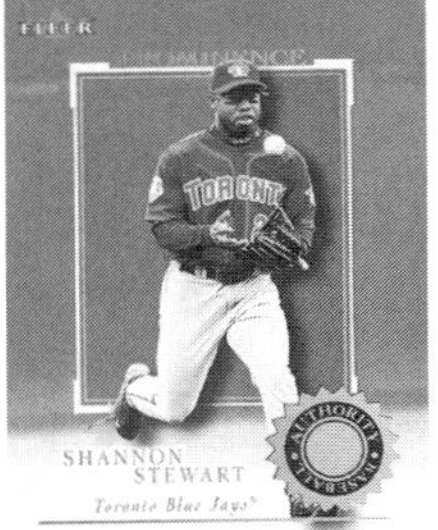

MT
Stars (1-100): 5-10X
Production 125
SP's (101-150): 3-5X
Production 75
(See 2001 Fleer Authority for checklist and base card values.)

2001 Fleer Authority Graded

MT
Mint: 1-1.5X
NrMt+: .8-1X
NrMt: .4-.6X
No Multipliers for Gem Mint
(See 2001 Fleer Authority for checklist and base card values.)

2001 Fleer Authority Authority Figures

MT
Complete Set (20):
Common Player: 2.00
1AF Mark McGwire, Albert Pujols 15.00

2AF Kazuhiro Sasaki, Ichiro Suzuki 20.00
3AF Derek Jeter, Drew Henson 15.00
4AF Ken Griffey Jr., Jackson Melian 12.00
5AF Wilson Betemit, Chipper Jones 8.00
6AF Jeff Bagwell, Morgan Ensberg 4.00
7AF Cal Ripken Jr., Jay Gibbons 15.00
8AF Mike Piazza, Tsuyoshi Shinjo 12.00
9AF Luis Gonzalez, Junior Spivey 3.00
10AF Barry Bonds, Carlos Valderrama 8.00
11AF Todd Helton, Juan Uribe 4.00
12AF Roger Clemens, Adrian Hernandez 5.00
13AF Alex Rodriguez, Travis Hafner 12.00
14AF Scott Rolen, Johnny Estrada 2.00
15AF Brian Giles, Rob Mackowiak 2.00
16AF Randy Johnson, Bret Prinz 4.00
17AF Carlos Delgado, Luis Lopez 3.00
18AF Manny Ramirez, Juan Diaz 4.00
19AF Mike Sweeney, Endy Chavez 3.00
20AF Sammy Sosa, Jaisen Randolph 8.00

2001 Fleer Authority Derek Jeter Reprint Autographs

MT

1DJRA Derek Jeter/500 160.00

2001 Fleer Authority Derek Jeter Monumental Moments

MT

1DJMM Derek Jeter/2000 10.00

2001 Fleer Authority Diamond Cuts

MT

Complete Set (63): 75.00
Common Player:
Rick Ankiel/Shoe 20.00
Jeff Bagwell/Jersey 20.00
Adrian Beltre/Hat 12.00
Craig Biggio/Bat 10.00
Barry Bonds/Hat 50.00
Barry Bonds/Jersey 25.00
Barry Bonds/Pants 25.00
Barry Bonds/Shoe 50.00
Barry Bonds/Wristband/100 60.00
Kevin Brown/Hat 15.00
Kevin Brown/Pants 10.00
Eric Byrnes/Bat 8.00
Sean Casey/Jersey 15.00
Eric Chavez/Hat 12.00
Chipper Jones/Jersey 15.00
Chipper Jones/Bat 15.00
Bartolo Colon/Hat 15.00
Erubiel Durazo/Bat 10.00
Ray Durham/Bat 8.00
Jim Edmonds/Hat 20.00
Jim Edmonds/Shoe 20.00
Darin Erstad/Hat 15.00
Carlos Febles/Bat
Carlos Febles/Shoe
Rafael Furcal/Hat 15.00
Juan Gonzalez/Bat Glove 25.00
Juan Gonzalez/Hat 25.00
Luis Gonzalez 20.00
Shawn Green/Bat Glove 25.00
Shawn Green/Bat 10.00
Vladimir Guerrero/Bat 12.00
Tony Gwynn/Bat 12.00
Mike Hampton/Hat 10.00
Mike Hampton/Shoe 10.00
Jerry Hairston Jr./Hat 12.00
Jason Hart/Bat 10.00
Todd Helton/Jersey 15.00
Todd Helton/Pants 15.00
Orlando Hernandez/Bat 10.00
Richard Hidalgo/Bat 10.00
Richard Hidalgo/Bat Glove 15.00
Derek Jeter/Bat 50.00
Derek Jeter/Bat Glove 80.00
Derek Jeter/Jersey 50.00
Derek Jeter/Pants 50.00
Derek Jeter/Shoe 60.00
Randy Johnson/Hat 30.00
Andruw Jones/Bat 12.00
Andruw Jones/Hat 20.00
Jason Kendall/Hat 12.00
Barry Larkin/Jersey 10.00
Matt Lawton/Hat 10.00
Mike Lieberthal/at Glove 15.00
Mike Lieberthal/Wristband
Kenny Lofton/Bat 10.00
Edgar Martinez/Bat Glove 20.00
Pedro Martinez/Shoe 20.00
Raul Mondesi/Bat 8.00
Raul Mondesi/Bat Glove 15.00
Hideo Nomo/Bat 25.00
Hideo Nomo/Hat 75.00
Magglio Ordonez/Bat Glove 15.00
Magglio Ordonez/Hat 10.00
David Ortiz/Bat 8.00
Rafael Palmeiro/Bat 15.00
Rafael Palmeiro/Hat 30.00
Chan Ho Park/Hat 25.00
Mike Piazza/Bat 25.00
Mike Piazza/Jersey 25.00
Mike Piazza/Shoe 50.00
Albert Pujols/Pants 30.00
Manny Ramirez/Bat 15.00
Manny Ramirez/Bat Glove 30.00
Manny Ramirez/Hat 30.00
Cal Ripken Jr./Bat Glove 100.00
Cal Ripken Jr./Pants 50.00
Ivan Rodriguez/Bat Glove 25.00
Ivan Rodriguez/Hat 25.00
Ivan Rodriguez/Pants 12.00
Ivan Rodriguez/Shoe 20.00
Scott Rolen/Hat 15.00
Jared Sandberg/Bat 8.00
Deion Sanders/Jersey 10.00
Tsuyoshi Shinjo/Wristband 75.00
Tsuyoshi Shinjo/Bat 25.00
J.T. Snow
Alfonso Soriano/Hat 25.00
Ichiro Suzuki/Bat 80.00
Ichiro Suzuki/Hat 100.00
Mike Sweeney/Hat 10.00
Miguel Tejada/Hat 15.00
Frank Thomas/Bat 15.00
Frank Thomas/Hat 30.00
Jim Thome/Bat 15.00
Larry Walker/Bat 10.00
Larry Walker/Jersey 10.00
Bernie Williams/Bat 12.00
Brian Giles/Pants

2001 Fleer Authority Seal of Approval

MT

Complete Set (15): 75.00
Common Player: 3.00
1SA Derek Jeter 12.00
2SA Alex Rodriguez 8.00
3SA Nomar Garciaparra 8.00
4SA Cal Ripken Jr. 12.00
5SA Mike Piazza 10.00
6SA Mark McGwire 10.00
7SA Tony Gwynn 3.00
8SA Barry Bonds 6.00
9SA Greg Maddux 6.00
10SA Chipper Jones 6.00
11SA Roger Clemens 4.00
12SA Ken Griffey Jr. 10.00
13SA Vladimir Guerrero 3.00
14SA Sammy Sosa 6.00
15SA Todd Helton 3.00

2001 Fleer Boston Red Sox 100th Anniversary

MT

Complete Set (100): 40.00
Common Player: .25
Field the Game/7150: 40.00
Pack (5): 4.00
Box (24): 90.00
1 Carl Yastrzemski 2.50
2 Mel Parnell .25
3 Birdie Tebbetts .25
4 Tex Hughson .25
5 Nomar Garciaparra 4.00
6 Fred Lynn .50
7 John Valentin .25
8 Rico Petrocelli .25
9 Ted Williams 5.00
10 Roger Clemens 3.00
11 Luis Aparicio .40
12 Cy Young 1.50
13 Carlton Fisk 1.00
14 Pedro Martinez 2.00
15 Joe Dobson .25
16 Babe Ruth 6.00
17 Doc Cramer .25
18 Pete Runnels .25
19 Tony Conigliaro .25
20 Bill Monbouquette .25
21 Boo Ferriss .25
22 Harry Hooper .25
23 Tony Armas .25
24 Joe Cronin 1.00
25 Rick Ferrell .25
26 Wade Boggs 1.50
27 Don Baylor .25
28 Jeff Reardon .25
29 Smokey Joe Wood .25
30 Mo Vaughn .40
31 Walt Dropo .25
32 Vern Stephens .25
33 Bernie Carbo .25
34 George Scott .25
35 Lefty Grove 1.00
36 Dom DiMaggio 1.00
37 Dennis Eckersley .25
38 Johnny Pesky .25
39 Jim Lonborg .25
40 Jimmy Piersall .25
41 Tris Speaker 1.50
42 Frank Malzone .25
43 Bobby Doerr .75
44 Jimmie Foxx 2.00
45 Tony Pena .25
46 Billy Goodman .25
47 Jim Rice .25
48 Reggie Smith .25
49 Bill Buckner .25
50 Earl Wilson .25
51 Rick Burleson .25
52 George Kell .25
53 Dick Radatz .25
54 Dwight Evans .25
55 Luis Tiant .25
56 Elijah "Pumpsie" Green .25
57 Gene Conley .25
58 Jackie Jensen .25
59 Mike Fornieles .25
60 Dutch Leonard .25
61 Jake Stahl .25
62 Don Schwall .25
63 Jimmy Collins .25
64 Herb Pennock .25
65 .25
66 Carney Lansford .25

67	Dick Stuart	.25
68	Dave Morehead	.25
69	Harry Agganis	.25
70	Lou Boudreau	.25
71	Joe Morgan	.75
72	Don Zimmer	.75
73	Tom Yawkey	.25
74	Jean Yawkey	.25
75	Origin of the Red Sox	.25
76	First Season	.25
77	World Series History	.25
78	Carl Yastrzemski (Beantown's Best)	1.00
79	Carlton Fisk (Beantown's Best)	.50
80	Dom DiMaggio (Beantown's Best)	.50
81	Wade Boggs (Beantown's Best)	.75
82	Nomar Garciaparra (Beantown's Best)	2.00
83	Pedro Martinez (Beantown's Best)	1.00
84	Ted Williams (Beantown's Best)	2.50
85	Jim Rice (Beantown's Best)	.25
86	Fred Lynn (Beantown's Best)	.25
87	Mo Vaughn (Beantown's Best)	.25
88	Bobby Doerr (Beantown's Best)	.40
89	Bernie Carbo (Beantown's Best)	.25
90	Dennis Eckersley (Beantown's Best)	.25
91	Jimmy Piersall (Beantown's Best)	.25
92	Luis Tiant (Beantown's Best)	.25
93	Jimmy Fund signage (Fenway Through the Years)	.25
94	Green Monster w/ Ads (Fenway Through the Years)	.25
95	Green Monster w/ All-Star logo (Fenway Through the Years)	.25
96	Ladder shot on Green Monster (Fenway Through the Years)	.25
97	Manual Scoreboard (Fenway Through the Years)	.25
98	Panoramic of Fenway (Fenway Through the Years)	.25
99	Lansdowne St. (Fenway Through the Years)	.25
100	1999 All-Star Game (Fenway Through the Years)	.25

2001 Fleer Boston Red Sox 100th Anniversary BoSox Sigs

	MT
Common Autograph:	20.00
Inserted 1:96	
Wade Boggs	80.00
Bill Buckner	20.00
Bernie Carbo	20.00
Roger Clemens/100	
Dom DiMaggio	60.00
Bobby Doerr	40.00
Dwight Evans	35.00
Carlton Fisk	80.00
Nomar Garciaparra	
Jim Lonborg	20.00
Fred Lynn	40.00
Rico Petrocelli	40.00
Jim Rice	40.00
Luis Tiant	40.00
Carl Yastrzemski	250.00

2001 Fleer Boston Red Sox 100th Anniversary Threads

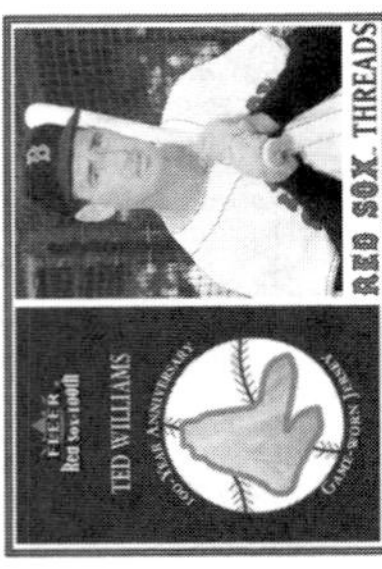

	MT
Common Player:	25.00
Inserted 1:96	
Wade Boggs	40.00
Roger Clemens	50.00
Dwight Evans	30.00
Carlton Fisk/100	100.00
Pedro Martinez/100	65.00
Jim Rice	40.00
Ted Williams/100	400.00
Carl Yastrzemski	100.00
Don Zimmer	25.00

2001 Fleer Boston Red Sox 100th Anniv. Yawkey's Heroes

		MT
Complete Set (20):		18.00
Common Player:		.50
Inserted 1:4		
1YH	Bobby Doerr	.75
2YH	Dom DiMaggio	1.00
3YH	Jim Rice	.50
4YH	Wade Boggs	1.50
5YH	Carlton Fisk	1.00
6YH	Nomar Garciaparra	4.00
7YH	Dennis Eckersley	.50
8YH	Carl Yastrzemski	2.50
9YH	Ted Williams	5.00
10YH	Tony Conigliaro	.75
11YH	Tony Armas	.50
12YH	Joe Cronin	1.00
13YH	Mo Vaughn	.50
14YH	Johnny Pesky	.50
15YH	Jim Lonborg	.50
16YH	Luis Tiant	.50
17YH	Tony Pena	.50
18YH	Dwight Evans	.50
19YH	Fred Lynn	.75
20YH	Jimmy Piersall	.50

Values quoted in this guide reflect the retail price of a card — the price a collector can expect to pay when buying a card from a dealer.

The wholesale price — that which a collector can expect to receive from a dealer when selling cards — will be significantly lower, depending on desirability and condition.

2001 Fleer Boston Red Sox 100th Ann. Splendid Splinters

		MT
Complete Set (15):		35.00
Common Player:		1.00
Inserted 1:10		
SS1	Babe Ruth	8.00
SS2	Dom DiMaggio	2.00
SS3	Carlton Fisk	2.00
SS4	Carl Yastrzemski	3.00
SS5	Nomar Garciaparra	6.00
SS6	Wade Boggs	2.50
SS7	Ted Williams	6.00
SS8	Jim Rice	1.00
SS9	Mo Vaughn	1.00
SS10	Tris Speaker	2.00
SS11	Dwight Evans	1.00
SS12	Jimmie Foxx	2.50
SS13	Bobby Doerr	1.50
SS14	Fred Lynn	1.00
SS15	Johnny Pesky	1.00

2001 Fleer Boston Red Sox Splendid Splinters Game Bat

	MT
Common Player:	25.00
Inserted 1:96	
Babe Ruth SP/100	500.00
Carl Yastrzemski	75.00
Nomar Garciaparra	75.00
Wade Boggs	40.00
Ted Williams SP/100	300.00
Jim Rice	25.00
Dwight Evans	25.00
Jimmie Foxx SP/100	180.00

A player's name in *italic* type indicates a rookie card.

2001 Fleer Focus

		MT
Complete Set (240):		250.00
Common Player:		.15
Common Prospect (201-224):		6.00
Common Prospect (225-250):		4.00
Pack (10):		3.00
Box (24):		65.00
1	Derek Jeter	2.50
2	Manny Ramirez	.75
3	Ken Griffey Jr.	2.00
4	Ken Caminiti	.15
5	Joe Randa	.15
6	Jason Kendall	.15
7	Ron Coomer	.15
8	Rondell White	.15
9	Tino Martinez	.25
10	Nomar Garciaparra	2.00
11	Tony Batista	.15
12	Todd Stottlemyre	.15
13	Ryan Klesko	.15
14	Darin Erstad	.40
15	Todd Walker	.15
16	Al Leiter	.25
17	Carl Everett	.15
18	Bobby Abreu	.15
19	Raul Mondesi	.25
20	Vladimir Guerrero	1.00
21	Mike Bordick	.15
22	Aaron Sele	.15
23	Ray Lankford	.15
24	Roger Clemens	1.00
25	Kevin Young	.15
26	Brad Radke	.15
27	Todd Hundley	.15
28	Ellis Burks	.15
29	Lee Stevens	.15
30	Eric Karros	.15
31	Darren Dreifort	.15
32	Ivan Rodriguez	.75
33	Pedro Martinez	1.00
34	Travis Fryman	.25
35	Garret Anderson	.15
36	Rafael Palmeiro	.50
37	Jason Giambi	.40
38	Jeromy Burnitz	.15
39	Robin Ventura	.25
40	Derek Bell	.15
41	Carlos Guillen	.15
42	Albert Belle	.30
43	Henry Rodriguez	.15
44	Brian Jordan	.15
45	Mike Sweeney	.15
46	Ruben Rivera	.15
47	Greg Maddux	1.50
48	Corey Koskie	.15
49	Sandy Alomar Jr.	.15
50	Mike Mussina	.50
51	Tom Glavine	.30
52	Aaron Boone	.15
53	Frank Thomas	1.00
54	Kenny Lofton	.30
55	Danny Graves	.15
56	Jose Valentin	.15
57	Travis Lee	.15
58	Jim Edmonds	.30
59	Jim Thome	.30
60	Steve Finley	.15
61	Shawn Green	.25
62	Lance Berkman	.15
63	Mark Quinn	.15
64	Randy Johnson	.75
65	Dmitri Young	.15
66	Andy Pettitte	.25
67	Paul O'Neill	.25

68 Gil Heredia .15
69 Russell Branyan .15
70 Alex Rodriguez 2.00
71 Geoff Jenkins .15
72 Eric Chavez .25
73 Cal Ripken Jr. 2.50
74 Mark Kotsay .15
75 Jeff D'Amico .15
76 Tony Womack .15
77 Eric Milton .15
78 Joe Girardi .15
79 Peter Bergeron .15
80 Miguel Tejada .15
81 Luis Gonzalez .25
82 Doug Glanville .15
83 Gerald Williams .15
84 Troy O'Leary .15
85 Brian Giles .25
86 Miguel Cairo .15
87 Magglio Ordonez .25
88 Rick Helling .15
89 Bruce Chen .15
90 Jason Varitek .15
91 Mike Lieberthal .15
92 Shawn Estes .15
93 Rick Ankiel .25
94 Tim Salmon .25
95 Jacque Jones .15
96 Johnny Damon .15
97 Larry Walker .30
98 Ruben Mateo .15
99 Brad Fullmer .15
100 Edgardo Alfonzo .25
101 Mark Mulder .15
102 Tony Gwynn 1.50
103 Mike Cameron .15
104 Richie Sexson .15
105 Barry Larkin .40
106 Mike Piazza 2.00
107 Eric Young .15
108 Edgar Renteria .15
109 Todd Zeile .15
110 Luis Castillo .15
111 Sammy Sosa 1.50
112 David Justice .50
113 Delino DeShields .15
114 Mariano Rivera .25
115 Edgar Martinez .15
116 Ray Durham .15
117 Brady Anderson .25
118 Eric Owens .15
119 Alex Gonzalez .15
120 Jay Buhner .15
121 Greg Vaughn .15
122 Mike Lowell .15
123 Marquis Grissom .15
124 Matt Williams .30
125 Dean Palmer .15
126 Troy Glaus .75
127 Bret Boone .15
128 David Ortiz .15
129 Glenallen Hill .15
130 Chipper Jones 1.50
131 Tony Clark .15
132 Terrence Long .15
133 Chuck Finley .15
134 Jeff Bagwell .75
135 J.T. Snow .15
136 Andruw Jones .75
137 Carlos Delgado .60
138 Mo Vaughn .30
139 Derrek Lee .15
140 Bobby Estalella .15
141 Kerry Wood .25
142 Jose Vidro .15
143 Ben Grieve .25
144 Barry Bonds 1.00
145 Javy Lopez .15
146 Adam Kennedy .15
147 Jeff Cirillo .15
148 Cliff Floyd .15
149 Carl Pavano .15
150 Bobby Higginson .15
151 Kevin Brown .25
152 Fernando Tatis .15
153 Matt Lawton .15
154 Damion Easley .15
155 Curt Schilling .25
156 Mark McGwire 2.50
157 Mark Grace .25
158 Adrian Beltre .25
159 Jorge Posada .25
160 Richard Hidalgo .25
161 Vinny Castilla .15
162 Bernie Williams .60
163 John Olerud .25
164 Todd Helton .75
165 Craig Biggio .25
166 David Wells .15
167 Phil Nevin .15
168 Andres Galarraga .30
169 Moises Alou .25
170 Denny Neagle .15
171 Jeffrey Hammonds .15
172 Sean Casey .25
173 Gary Sheffield .40
174 Carlos Lee .15
175 Juan Encarnacion .15
176 Roberto Alomar .60
177 Kenny Rogers .15
178 Charles Johnson .15
179 Shannon Stewart .15
180 B.J. Surhoff .15
181 Paul Konerko .15
182 Jermaine Dye .15
183 Scott Rolen .50
184 Fred McGriff .25
185 Juan Gonzalez .75
186 Carlos Beltran .15
187 Jay Payton .15
188 Chad Hermansen .15
189 Pat Burrell .50
190 Omar Vizquel .25
191 Trot Nixon .15
192 Mike Hampton .25
193 Kris Benson .15
194 Gabe Kapler .25
195 Rickey Henderson .30
196 J.D. Drew .25
197 Pokey Reese .15
198 Jeff Kent .25
199 Jose Cruz Jr. .15
200 Preston Wilson .15
201 Eric Munson 2,499 (Prospects) 10.00
202 Alex Cabrera 2,499 (Prospects) 6.00
203 Nate Rolison 2,499 (Prospects) 6.00
204 Julio Zuleta 2,499 (Prospects) 6.00
205 Chris Richard 2,499 (Prospects) 6.00
206 Dernell Stenson 2,499 (Prospects) 6.00
207 Aaron McNeal 2,499 (Prospects) 6.00
208 Aubrey Huff 2,999 (Prospects) 6.00
209 Mike Lamb 2,999 (Prospects) 6.00
210 Xavier Nady 2,999 (Prospects) 15.00
211 Joe Crede 2,999 (Prospects) 10.00
212 Ben Petrick 3,499 (Prospects) 6.00
213 Morgan Burkhart 3,499 (Prospects) 6.00
214 Jason Tyner 1,999 (Prospects) 8.00
215 Juan Pierre 1,999 (Prospects) 8.00
216 Adam Dunn 1,999 (Prospects) 8.00
117 Adam Piatt 1,999 (Prospects) 8.00
218 Eric Byrnes 1,999 (Prospects) 8.00
219 Corey Patterson 1,999 (Prospects) 8.00
220 Kenny Kelly 1,999 (Prospects) 6.00
221 Tike Redman 1,999 (Prospects) 6.00
222 Luis Matos 1,999 (Prospects) 8.00
223 Timoniel Perez 1,999 (Prospects) 8.00
224 Vernon Wells 1,999 (Prospects) 6.00
225 Barry Zito 4,999 (Prospects) 15.00
226 Adam Bernero 4,999 (Prospects) 4.00
227 Kazuhiro Sasaki 4,999 (Prospects) 8.00
228 Oswaldo Mairena 4,999 (Prospects) 4.00
229 Mark Buehrle 4,999 (Prospects) 4.00
230 Ryan Dempster 4,999 (Prospects) 4.00
231 Tim Hudson 4,999 (Prospects) 8.00
232 Scott Downs 4,999 (Prospects) 4.00
233 A.J. Burnett 4,999 (Prospects) 6.00
234 Adam Eaton 4,999 (Prospects) 4.00
235 Paxton Crawford 4,999 (Prospects) 4.00
236 Jace Brewer 3,999 (Prospects) 4.00
237 Jose Ortiz 3,999 (Prospects) 8.00
238 Rafael Furcal 3,999 (Prospects) 5.00
239 Julio Lugo 3,999 (Prospects) 4.00
240 Tomas de la Rosa 3,999 (Prospects) 4.00

2001 Fleer Focus Green

MT

Complete Set (240):
Common Player: 2.00
Random inserts in packs
Stated print runs listed below

1 Derek Jeter/339 30.00
2 Manny Ramirez/351 10.00
3 Ken Griffey Jr./271 25.00
4 Ken Caminiti/303 3.00
5 Joe Randa/304 2.00
6 Jason Kendall/270 3.00
7 Ron Coomer/270 2.00
8 Rondell White/258 3.00
9 Tino Martinez/258 4.00
10 Nomar Garciaparra/372 25.00
11 Tony Batista/263 3.00
12 Todd Stottlemyre/491 1.50
13 Ryan Klesko/283 3.00
14 Darin Erstad/355 8.00
15 Todd Walker/290 2.00
16 Al Leiter/320 3.00
17 Carl Everett/300 4.00
18 Bobby Abreu/316 4.00
19 Raul Mondesi/271 4.00
20 Vladimir Guerrero/345 12.00
21 Mike Bordick/285 3.00
22 Aaron Sele/451 2.50
23 Ray Lankford/253 3.00
24 Roger Clemens/370 15.00
25 Kevin Young/258 2.00
26 Brad Radke/445 2.50
27 Todd Hundley/284 2.00
28 Ellis Burks/344 3.00
29 Lee Stevens/265 2.00
30 Eric Karros/250 4.00
31 Darren Dreifort/416 2.50
32 Ivan Rodriguez/347 10.00
33 Pedro Martinez/174 20.00
34 Travis Fryman/321 3.00
35 Garret Anderson/286 3.00
36 Rafael Palmeiro/288 6.00
37 Jason Giambi/333 8.00
38 Jeromy Burnitz/232 4.00
39 Robin Ventura/232 5.00
40 Derek Bell/266 3.00
41 Carlos Guillen/257 2.00
42 Albert Belle/281 5.00
43 Henry Rodriguez/256 2.00
44 Brian Jordan/264 3.00
45 Mike Sweeney/333 4.00
46 Ruben Rivera/208 2.50
47 Greg Maddux/300 20.00
48 Corey Koskie/300 2.00
49 Sandy Alomar Jr./289 3.00
50 Mike Mussina/379 8.00
51 Tom Glavine/340 6.00
52 Aaron Boone/285 2.00
53 Frank Thomas/328 15.00
54 Kenny Lofton/278 4.00
55 Danny Graves/256 2.00
56 Jose Valentin/273 2.00
57 Travis Lee/235 4.00
58 Jim Edmonds/295 8.00
59 Jim Thome/269 4.00
60 Steve Finley/280 3.00
61 Shawn Green/269 6.00
62 Lance Berkman/297 3.00
63 Mark Quinn/294 3.00
64 Randy Johnson/264 10.00
65 Dmitri Young/303 3.00
66 Andy Pettitte/435 3.00
67 Paul O'Neill/283 4.00
68 Gil Heredia/412 1.50
69 Russell Branyan/238 4.00
70 Alex Rodriguez/316 25.00
71 Geoff Jenkins/303 3.00
72 Eric Chavez/277 4.00
73 Cal Ripken Jr./256 35.00
74 Mark Kotsay/298 3.00
75 Jeff D'Amico/266 3.00
76 Tony Womack/271 3.00
77 Eric Milton/486 2.50
78 Joe Girardi/278 2.00
79 Peter Bergeron/245 2.50
80 Miguel Tejada/275 5.00
81 Luis Gonzalez/311 3.00
82 Doug Glanville/275 2.00
83 Gerald Williams/274 2.00
84 Troy O'Leary/261 2.00
85 Brian Giles/315 4.00
86 Miguel Cairo/261 2.00
87 Magglio Ordonez/315 4.00
88 Rick Helling/448 2.50
89 Bruce Chen/329 3.00
90 Jason Varitek/248 4.00
91 Mike Lieberthal/278 3.00
92 Shawn Estes/426 2.50
93 Rick Ankiel/350 4.00
94 Tim Salmon/290 4.00
95 Jacque Jones/285 3.00
96 Johnny Damon/327 4.00
97 Larry Walker/309 4.00
98 Ruben Mateo/291 4.00
99 Brad Fullmer/295 3.00
100 Edgardo Alfonzo/324 4.00
101 Mark Mulder/544 2.50
102 Tony Gwynn/323 15.00
103 Mike Cameron/267 3.00
104 Richie Sexson/272 3.00
105 Barry Larkin/313 6.00
106 Mike Piazza/324 25.00
107 Eric Young/297 2.00
108 Edgar Renteria/278 3.00
109 Todd Zeile/268 3.00
110 Luis Castillo/334 3.00
111 Sammy Sosa/320 15.00
112 David Justice/286 5.00
113 Delino DeShields/296 2.00
114 Mariano Rivera/285 4.00
115 Edgar Martinez/324 5.00
116 Ray Durham/280 3.00
117 Brady Anderson/257 3.00
118 Eric Owens/293 2.00
119 Alex Gonzalez/252 2.00
120 Jay Buhner/253 3.00
121 Greg Vaughn/254 3.00
122 Mike Lowell/270 3.00
123 Marquis Grissom/244 2.50
124 Matt Williams/275 5.00
125 Dean Palmer/256 3.00
126 Troy Glaus/284 10.00
127 Bret Boone/251 2.00
128 David Ortiz/282 2.00
129 Glenallen Hill/293 2.00
130 Chipper Jones/311 20.00
131 Tony Clark/274 2.00
132 Terrence Long/288 3.00
133 Chuck Finley/417 2.50
134 Jeff Bagwell/310 10.00
135 J.T. Snow/284 3.00
136 Andruw Jones/303 8.00
137 Carlos Delgado/

	344	8.00
138	Mo Vaughn/272	4.00
139	Derek Lee/281	3.00
140	Bobby Estalella/234	2.50
141	Kerry Wood/480	3.00
142	Jose Vidro/330	3.00
143	Ben Grieve/279	4.00
144	Barry Bonds/306	12.00
145	Javy Lopez/287	3.00
146	Adam Kennedy/266	3.00
147	Jeff Cirillo/326	3.00
148	Cliff Floyd/300	3.00
149	Carl Pavano/306	3.00
150	Bobby Higginson/300	3.00
151	Kevin Brown/258	4.00
152	Fernando Tatis/253	3.00
153	Matt Lawton/305	3.00
154	Damion Easley/259	2.00
155	Curt Schilling/381	3.00
156	Mark McGwire/305	30.00
157	Mark Grace/280	8.00
158	Adrian Beltre/290	4.00
159	Jorge Posada/287	3.00
160	Richard Hidalgo/314	4.00
161	Vinny Castilla/221	4.00
162	Bernie Williams/307	6.00
163	John Olerud/285	3.00
164	Todd Helton/372	10.00
165	Craig Biggio/268	5.00
166	David Wells/411	2.50
167	Phil Nevin/303	3.00
168	Andres Galarraga/302	5.00
169	Moises Alou/355	3.00
170	Denny Neagle/452	1.50
171	Jeffrey Hammonds/335	3.00
172	Sean Casey/315	4.00
173	Gary Sheffield/325	6.00
174	Carlos Lee/301	3.00
175	Juan Encarnacion/289	3.00
176	Roberto Alomar/310	8.00
177	Kenny Rogers/455	1.50
178	Charles Johnson/304	3.00
179	Shannon Stewart/319	3.00
180	B.J. Surhoff/291	3.00
181	Paul Konerko/298	3.00
182	Jermaine Dye/321	4.00
183	Scott Rolen/298	6.00
184	Fred McGriff/277	5.00
185	Juan Gonzalez/289	6.00
186	Carlos Beltran/247	4.00
187	Jay Payton/291	3.00
188	Chad Hermansen/185	3.00
189	Pat Burrell/260	8.00
190	Omar Vizquel/287	4.00
191	Trot Nixon/276	3.00
192	Mike Hampton/314	4.00
193	Kris Benson/385	4.00
194	Gabe Kapler/302	4.00
195	Rickey Henderson/233	12.00
196	J.D. Drew/295	6.00
197	Pokey Reese/255	3.00
198	Jeff Kent/334	5.00
199	Jose Cruz Jr./242	4.00
200	Preston Wilson/264	3.00
201	Eric Munson/252	4.00
202	Alex Cabrera/263	3.00
203	Nate Rolison/77	6.00
204	Julio Zuleta/294	3.00
205	Chris Richard/265	3.00
206	Dernell Stenson/268	3.00
207	Aaron McNeal/310	3.00
208	Aubrey Huff/287	3.00
209	Mike Lamb/278	2.00
210	Xavier Nady/1	
211	Joe Crede/357	4.00
212	Ben Petrick/322	2.00
213	Morgan Burkhart/288	2.00
214	Jason Tyner/226	2.50
215	Juan Pierre/310	3.00
216	Adam Dunn/281	3.00
217	Adam Piatt/299	4.00
218	Eric Byrnes/300	3.00
219	Corey Patterson/167	6.00
220	Kenny Kelly/252	3.00
221	Tike Redman/333	2.00
222	Luis Matos/225	4.00
223	Timo Perez/286	3.00
224	Vernon Wells/243	4.00
225	Barry Zito/272	15.00
226	Adam Bernero/419	1.50
227	Kazuhiro Sasaki/316	10.00
228	Oswaldo Mairena/18	20.00
229	Mark Buehrle/421	1.50
230	Ryan Dempster/366	3.00
231	Tim Hudson/414	5.00
232	Scott Downs/529	1.50
233	A.J. Burnett/479	1.50
234	Adam Eaton/413	2.50
235	Paxton Crawford/341	2.00
236	Jace Brewer/1	
237	Jose Ortiz/182	15.00
238	Rafael Furcal/295	6.00
239	Julio Lugo/283	2.00
240	Tomas De La Rosa/288	2.00

2001 Fleer Focus Autographics

	MT
Common Player:	10.00
Inserted 1:72	
Silvers:	1-2X
Production 250 sets	
Roberto Alomar	50.00
Rick Ankiel	20.00
Albert Belle	
Adrian Beltre	15.00
Lance Berkman	10.00
Barry Bonds	65.00
Jeromy Burnitz	
Pat Burrell	25.00
Sean Casey	15.00
Eric Chavez	15.00
Carlos Delgado	30.00
J.D. Drew	20.00
Jermaine Dye	
Jim Edmonds	30.00
Troy Glaus	40.00
Ben Grieve	
Tony Gwynn	50.00
Randy Johnson	50.00
Chipper Jones	60.00
Mike Lamb	10.00
Mike Lieberthal	
Terrence Long	15.00
Greg Maddux	
Edgar Martinez	20.00
Kevin Millwood	25.00
Mike Mussina	30.00
Corey Patterson	25.00
Jay Payton	15.00
Juan Pierre	10.00
Brad Radke	15.00
Scott Rolen	
Gary Sheffield	30.00
Fernando Tatis	15.00
Robin Ventura	
Kerry Wood	20.00

2001 Fleer Focus Bat Company

		MT
Complete Set (10):		60.00
Common Player:		2.00
Inserted 1:24		
1	Barry Bonds	5.00
2	Mark McGwire	10.00
3	Sammy Sosa	6.00
4	Ken Griffey Jr.	8.00
5	Mike Piazza	8.00
6	Derek Jeter	10.00
7	Gary Sheffield	2.00
8	Frank Thomas	4.00
9	Chipper Jones	6.00
10	Alex Rodriguez	8.00

2001 Fleer Focus Big Innings

		MT
Complete Set (25):		40.00
Common Player:		.75
Inserted 1:6		
VIP:		15-25X
Production 50 sets		
1	Rick Ankiel	1.00
2	Andruw Jones	2.00
3	Brian Giles	1.00
4	Derek Jeter	6.00
5	Rafael Furcal	1.00
6	Richie Sexson	.75
7	Jay Payton	.75
8	Carlos Delgado	1.50
9	Jermaine Dye	1.00
10	Darin Erstad	1.00
11	Pat Burrell	1.50
12	Richard Hidalgo	1.00
13	Adrian Beltre	1.00
14	Todd Helton	2.00
15	Vladimir Guerrero	2.50
16	Nomar Garciaparra	5.00
17	Gabe Kapler	1.00
18	Carlos Lee	.75
19	J.D. Drew	.75
20	Troy Glaus	2.00
21	Scott Rolen	1.50
22	Alex Rodriguez	5.00
23	Magglio Ordonez	1.00
24	Miguel Tejada	1.00
25	Ruben Mateo	.75

2001 Fleer Focus Diamond Vision

		MT
Complete Set (15):		65.00
Common Player:		2.00
Inserted 1:12		
1	Derek Jeter	8.00
2	Nomar Garciaparra	6.00
3	Cal Ripken Jr.	8.00
4	Jeff Bagwell	2.50
5	Mark McGwire	8.00
6	Ken Griffey Jr.	6.00
7	Pedro Martinez	3.00
8	Carlos Delgado	2.00
9	Chipper Jones	5.00
10	Barry Bonds	4.00
11	Mike Piazza	6.00
12	Sammy Sosa	5.00
13	Alex Rodriguez	6.00
14	Frank Thomas	3.00
15	Randy Johnson	2.50

2001 Fleer Focus Feel the Game

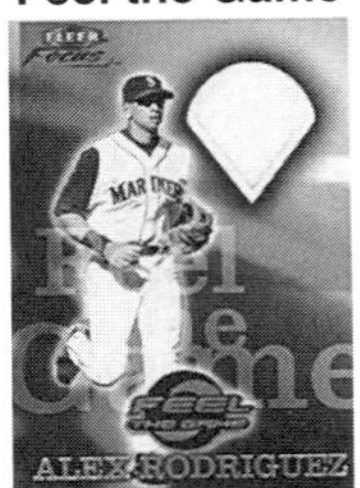

	MT
Common Player:	15.00
Inserted 1:72	
Moises Alou	20.00
Brady Anderson	20.00
Dante Bichette	25.00
Jermaine Dye	20.00
Brian Giles	25.00
Juan Gonzalez	30.00
Rickey Henderson	50.00
Javy Lopez	25.00
Tino Martinez	25.00
Phil Nevin	20.00
Matt Stairs	15.00
Shannon Stewart	20.00
Jose Vidro	20.00

2001 Fleer Focus ROY Collection

		MT
Complete Set (25):		140.00
Common Player:		3.00
Inserted 1:24		
1	Luis Aparicio	4.00
2	Johnny Bench	10.00
3	Joe Black	3.00
4	Rod Carew	6.00
5	Orlando Cepeda	3.00
6	Carlton Fisk	6.00
7	Ben Grieve	4.00
8	Frank Howard	3.00
9	Derek Jeter	20.00
10	Fred Lynn	3.00
11	Willie Mays	15.00
12	Willie McCovey	3.00
13	Mark McGwire	20.00
14	Raul Mondesi	3.00
15	Thurman Munson	10.00
16	Eddie Murray	5.00
17	Mike Piazza	15.00
18	Cal Ripken Jr.	20.00
19	Frank Robinson	6.00
20	Jackie Robinson	15.00
21	Scott Rolen	5.00
22	Tom Seaver	8.00
23	Fernando Valenzuela	3.00
24	David Justice	5.00
25	Billy Williams	3.00

2001 Fleer Focus ROY Collection Memorabilia

		MT
Common Player:		30.00
Inserted 1:288		
1	Luis Aparicio bat	35.00
2	Johnny Bench jersey	100.00
3	Orlando Cepeda bat	30.00
4	Carlton Fisk jersey	50.00
5	Ben Grieve jersey	40.00
6	Frank Howard bat	40.00
7	Derek Jeter jersey	200.00
8	Fred Lynn bat	35.00
9	Willie Mays jersey	150.00
10	Willie McCovey bat	50.00
11	Mark McGwire ball	200.00
12	Raul Mondesi bat	30.00
13	Thurman Munson bat	100.00
14	Eddie Murray jersey	100.00
15	Mike Piazza base	50.00
16	Cal Ripken jersey	150.00
17	Frank Robinson bat	50.00
18	Jackie Robinson jersey	200.00
19	Scott Rolen bat	40.00
20	Tom Seaver jersey	100.00
21	Fernando Valenzuela	
22	David Justice jersey	40.00

2001 Fleer Focus ROY Collection Signed Memorabilia

		MT
Common Player:		50.00
1	Luis Aparicio jsy/56	150.00
2	Johnny Bench/68	220.00
3	Orlando Cepeda/58	120.00
4	Carlton Fisk/72	150.00
5	Ben Grieve/98	100.00
6	Frank Howard/60	80.00
7	Derek Jeter/96	400.00
8	Fred Lynn/75	100.00
9	Willie Mays jsy/51	375.00
10	Willie McCovey bat/59	140.00
11	Raul Mondesi/94	70.00
12	Eddie Murray/77	225.00
13	Cal Ripken/82	375.00
14	Frank Robinson bat/225	225.00
15	Scott Rolen/97	75.00
16	Tom Seaver/67	300.00
18	David Justice/90	75.00

2001 Fleer Futures

		MT
Complete Set (220):		30.00
Common Player:		.15
Pack (8):		1.75
Box (28):		40.00
1	Darin Erstad	.30
2	Manny Ramirez	.75
3	Darryl Kile	.15
4	Troy O'Leary	.15
5	Mark Quinn	.15
6	Brian Giles	.15
7	Randy Johnson	.75
8	Todd Walker	.15
9	Mike Piazza	2.00
10	Fred McGriff	.25
11	Sammy Sosa	1.50
12	Chan Ho Park	.25
13	John Rocker	.15
14	Luis Castillo	.15
15	Eric Chavez	.25
16	Carlos Delgado	.60
17	Sean Casey	.25
18	Corey Koskie	.15
19	John Olerud	.25
20	Nomar Garciaparra	2.00
21	Craig Biggio	.25
22	Pat Burrell	.50
23	Bengie Molina	.15
24	Jim Thome	.30
25	Rey Ordonez	.15
26	Fernando Tatis	.15
27	Eric Young	.15
28	Eric Karros	.25
29	Adam Eaton	.15
30	Brian Jordan	.15
31	Jorge Posada	.25
32	Gabe Kapler	.25
33	Keith Foulke	.15
34	Ron Coomer	.15
35	Chipper Jones	1.50
36	Miguel Tejada	.25
37	David Wells	.15
38	Carlos Lee	.15
39	Barry Bonds	1.00
40	Derrek Lee	.15
41	Tim Hudson	.25
42	Billy Koch	.15
43	Dmitri Young	.15
44	Vladimir Guerrero	1.00
45	Rickey Henderson	.25
46	Jeff Bagwell	.75
47	Robert Person	.15
48	Brady Anderson	.15
49	Lance Berkman	.15
50	Mike Lieberthal	.15
51	Adam Kennedy	.15
52	Russ Branyan	.15
53	Robin Ventura	.25
54	Mark McGwire	2.50
55	Tony Gwynn	1.00
56	Matt Williams	.25
57	Jeff Cirillo	.15
58	Roger Clemens	1.00
59	Ivan Rodriguez	.75
60	Brad Radke	.15
61	Kazuhiro Sasaki	.15
62	Cal Ripken Jr.	2.50
63	Ken Caminiti	.15
64	Bobby Abreu	.15
65	Troy Glaus	.75
66	Sandy Alomar Jr.	.15
67	Jose Vidro	.15
68	Pedro Martinez	1.00
69	Kevin Young	.15
70	Jay Bell	.15
71	Larry Walker	.25
72	Derek Jeter	2.50
73	Miguel Cairo	.15
74	Magglio Ordonez	.25
75	Jeromy Burnitz	.15
76	J.T. Snow	.15
77	Andres Galarraga	.30
78	Ryan Dempster	.15
79	Ken Griffey Jr.	1.50
80	Aaron Sele	.15
81	Tom Glavine	.30
82	Hideo Nomo	.30
83	Orlando Hernandez	.25
84	Tony Batista	.15
85	Aaron Boone	.15
86	Jacque Jones	.15
87	Delino DeShields	.15
88	Garret Anderson	.15
89	Fernando Seguignol	.15
90	Jim Edmonds	.25
91	Frank Thomas	1.00
92	Adrian Beltre	.25
93	Ellis Burks	.15
94	Andruw Jones	.60
95	Tony Clark	.15
96	Danny Graves	.15
97	Alex Rodriguez	2.00
98	Mike Mussina	.50
99	Scott Elarton	.15
100	Jason Giambi	.25
101	Jay Payton	.15
102	Gerald Williams	.15
103	Kerry Wood	.25
104	Shawn Green	.25
105	Greg Maddux	1.50
106	Juan Encarnacion	.15
107	Bernie Williams	.60
108	Mike Lamb	.15
109	Charles Johnson	.15
110	Richie Sexson	.15
111	Jeff Kent	.25
112	Albert Belle	.15
113	Cliff Floyd	.15
114	Ben Grieve	.25
115	Tim Salmon	.25
116	Carl Pavano	.15
117	Rick Ankiel	.25
118	Dante Bichette	.15
119	Johnny Damon	.25
120	Brian Anderson	.15
121	Roberto Alomar	.60
122	Mike Hampton	.25
123	Greg Vaughn	.15
124	Carl Everett	.15
125	Moises Alou	.15
126	Jason Kendall	.15
127	Omar Vizquel	.25
128	Mark Grace	.25
129	Kevin Brown	.25
130	Phil Nevin	.15
131	Kevin Millwood	.15
132	Bobby Higginson	.15
133	Ruben Mateo	.25
134	Luis Gonzalez	.25
135	Dean Palmer	.15
136	Mariano Rivera	.25
137	Rick Helling	.15
138	Paul Konerko	.15
139	Marquis Grissom	.15
140	Robb Nen	.15
141	Javy Lopez	.15
142	Preston Wilson	.15
143	Terrence Long	.15
144	Shannon Stewart	.15
145	Barry Larkin	.30
146	Cristian Guzman	.15
147	Jay Buhner	.15
148	Jermaine Dye	.15
149	Kris Benson	.15
150	Curt Schilling	.25
151	Todd Helton	.75
152	Paul O'Neill	.25
153	Rafael Palmeiro	.40
154	Ray Durham	.15
155	Geoff Jenkins	.25
156	Livan Hernandez	.15
157	Rafael Furcal	.25
158	Juan Gonzalez	.75
159	Tino Martinez	.25
160	Raul Mondesi	.25
161	Matt Lawton	.15
162	Edgar Martinez	.15
163	Richard Hidalgo	.25
164	Scott Rolen	.50
165	Chuck Finley	.15
166	Edgardo Alfonzo	.25
167	J.D. Drew	.25
168	Trot Nixon	.15
169	Carlos Beltran	.25
170	Ryan Klesko	.15
171	Mo Vaughn	.15
172	Kenny Lofton	.25
173	Al Leiter	.25
174	Rondell White	.25
175	Mike Sweeney	.15
176	Trevor Hoffman	.15
177	Steve Finley	.15
178	Jeffrey Hammonds	.15
179	David Justice	.40
180	Gary Sheffield	.30
181	Eric Munson (Bright Futures)	.40
182	Luis Matos (Bright Futures)	.15
183	Alex Cabrera (Bright Futures)	.15
184	Randy Keisler (Bright Futures)	.15
185	Nate Rolison (Bright Futures)	.15
186	Jason Hart (Bright Futures)	.15
187	Timo Perez (Bright Futures)	.15
188	Adam Bernero (Bright Futures)	.15
189	Barry Zito (Bright Futures)	1.00
190	Ryan Kohlmeier (Bright Futures)	.15
191	Joey Nation (Bright Futures)	.15
192	Oswaldo Mairena (Bright Futures)	.15
193	Aubrey Huff (Bright Futures)	.15
194	Mark Buehrle (Bright Futures)	.15
195	Jace Brewer (Bright Futures)	.15
196	Julio Zuleta (Bright Futures)	.15
197	Xavier Nady (Bright Futures)	.75
198	Vernon Wells (Bright Futures)	.15
199	Joe Crede (Bright Futures)	.15
200	Scott Downs (Bright Futures)	.15
201	Ben Petrick (Bright Futures)	.15
202	A.J. Burnett (Bright Futures)	.15
203	Esix Snead (Bright Futures)	.50
204	Dernell Stenson (Bright Futures)	.15
205	Jose Ortiz (Bright Futures)	.50
206	Paxton Crawford (Bright Futures)	.15
207	Jason Tyner (Bright Futures)	.15
208	Jimmy Rollins (Bright Futures)	.15
209	Juan Pierre (Bright Futures)	.15
210	Keith Ginter (Bright Futures)	.15
211	Adam Dunn (Bright Futures)	.15
212	Larry Barnes (Bright Futures)	.15
213	Adam Piatt (Bright Futures)	.15
214	Rodney Lindsey (Bright Futures)	.15
215	Eric Byrnes (Bright Futures)	.15
216	Julio Lugo (Bright Futures)	.15
217	Corey Patterson (Bright Futures)	.25
218	Reggie Taylor (Bright Futures)	.15
219	Kenny Kelly (Bright Futures)	.15
220	Tike Redman (Bright Futures)	.15

2001 Fleer Futures Black Gold

	MT
Production 499 sets:	4-8X

(See 2001 Fleer Futures for checklist and base card values.)

2001 Fleer Futures Bases Loaded

		MT
Common Player:		10.00
Inserted 1:134		
BL1	Ken Griffey Jr.	40.00
BL2	Mark McGwire	50.00
BL3	Carlos Delgado	15.00
BL4	Chipper Jones	30.00
BL5	Nomar Garciaparra	40.00
BL6	Cal Ripken Jr.	50.00
BL7	Sammy Sosa	30.00
BL8	Jeff Bagwell	15.00
BL9	Vladimir Guerrero	20.00
BL10	Tony Gwynn	20.00
BL11	Frank Thomas	20.00
BL12	Mike Piazza	40.00
BL13	Jason Giambi	15.00
BL14	Troy Glaus	15.00
BL15	Pat Burrell	15.00

2001 Fleer Futures Bats to the Future

		MT
Complete Set (25):		140.00
Common Player:		3.00
Inserted 1:28		
1BF	Mike Schmidt	12.00
2BF	Carlton Fisk	6.00
3BF	Paul Molitor	6.00
4BF	Vladimir Guerrero	6.00
5BF	Dave Parker	3.00
6BF	Chipper Jones	10.00
7BF	Chris Delgado	4.00
8BF	Tony Gwynn	6.00
9BF	Reggie Jackson	8.00
10BF	Eddie Murray	6.00
11BF	Robin Yount	8.00
12BF	Alan Trammell	3.00
13BF	Frank Thomas	6.00
14BF	Cal Ripken Jr.	15.00
15BF	Don Mattingly	15.00
16BF	Jim Rice	3.00
17BF	Juan Gonzalez	4.00
18BF	Todd Helton	5.00
19BF	George Brett	12.00
20BF	Barry Bonds	4.00
21BF	Kirk Gibson	3.00
22BF	Matt Williams	3.00
23BF	Dave Winfield	6.00
24BF	Ryne Sandberg	8.00
25BF	Ivan Rodriguez	4.00

2001 Fleer Futures Bats to the Future Game Bat

		MT
Common Player:		20.00
Inserted 1:114		
1BF	Mike Schmidt	50.00
2BF	Carlton Fisk	35.00
3BF	Paul Molitor	40.00
4BF	Vladimir Guerrero	30.00
5BF	Dave Parker	20.00
6BF	Chipper Jones	40.00
7BF	Chris Delgado	25.00
8BF	Tony Gwynn	35.00
9BF	Reggie Jackson	40.00
10BF	Eddie Murray	40.00
11BF	Robin Yount	50.00
12BF	Alan Trammell	25.00
13BF	Frank Thomas	35.00
14BF	Cal Ripken Jr.	80.00
15BF	Don Mattingly	75.00
16BF	Jim Rice	20.00
17BF	Juan Gonzalez	25.00
18BF	Todd Helton	30.00
19BF	George Brett	60.00
20BF	Barry Bonds	35.00
21BF	Kirk Gibson	20.00
22BF	Matt Williams	20.00
23BF	Dave Winfield	25.00
24BF	Ryne Sandberg	60.00
25BF	Ivan Rodriguez	25.00

2001 Fleer Futures Bats to the Future Game Bat Auto.

		MT
Common Autograph:		80.00
Production 50 sets		
1BF	Mike Schmidt	375.00
2BF	Carlton Fisk	180.00
3BF	Paul Molitor	180.00
4BF	Vladimir Guerrero	200.00
5BF	Dave Parker	80.00
6BF	Chipper Jones	200.00
7BF	Chris Delgado	125.00
8BF	Tony Gwynn	200.00
9BF	Reggie Jackson	200.00
10BF	Eddie Murray	240.00
11BF	Robin Yount	240.00
12BF	Alan Trammell	100.00
13BF	Frank Thomas	175.00
14BF	Cal Ripken Jr.	400.00
15BF	Don Mattingly	450.00
16BF	Jim Rice	80.00
17BF	Juan Gonzalez	250.00
18BF	Todd Helton	150.00
19BF	George Brett	275.00
20BF	Barry Bonds	175.00
21BF	Kirk Gibson	80.00
22BF	Matt Williams	80.00
23BF	Dave Winfield	125.00
24BF	Ryne Sandberg	325.00
25BF	Ivan Rodriguez	125.00

2001 Fleer Futures Characteristics

		MT
Complete Set (15):		45.00
Common Player:		1.00
Inserted 1:9		
1C	Derek Jeter	6.00
2C	Mark McGwire	6.00
3C	Nomar Garciaparra	5.00
4C	Sammy Sosa	4.00
5C	Pedro Martinez	3.00
6C	Chipper Jones	4.00
7C	Cal Ripken Jr.	6.00
8C	Todd Helton	2.00
9C	Jim Edmonds	1.00
10C	Ken Griffey Jr.	4.00
11C	Alex Rodriguez	5.00
12C	Mike Piazza	5.00
13C	Vladimir Guerrero	2.50
14C	Frank Thomas	2.50
15C	Carlos Delgado	1.50

2001 Fleer Futures Hot Commodities

		MT
Complete Set (10):		40.00
Common Player:		1.00
Inserted 1:14		
1HC	Mark McGwire	6.00
2HC	Ken Griffey Jr.	4.00
3HC	Derek Jeter	6.00
4HC	Cal Ripken Jr.	6.00
5HC	Chipper Jones	4.00
6HC	Barry Bonds	2.00
7HC	Mike Piazza	5.00
8HC	Sammy Sosa	4.00
9HC	Alex Rodriguez	5.00
10HC	Frank Thomas	2.50

2001 Fleer Futures September Call-Ups Memorabilia

		MT
Common Card:		10.00
Production 200 sets		
184	Randy Keisler Cap/Cleat	20.00
185	Nate Rolison/Bat	10.00
187	Timoniel Perez/ Bat	20.00
191	Joey Nation/Glove	10.00
192	Oswaldo Mairena/ Glove	10.00
195	Jace Brewer/Bat	10.00
197	Xavier Nady/ Glove	35.00
199	Joe Crede/Bat	20.00
205	Jose Ortiz/Bat	40.00
208	Jimmy Rollins/ Glove	20.00
210	Keith Ginter/Bat	15.00
214	Rodney Lindsey/ Bat	15.00
217	Corey Patterson/ Bat	25.00
218	Reggie Taylor/Bat	10.00
219	Kenny Kelly/Bat	15.00

2001 Fleer Game Time

		MT
Complete Set (121):		NA
Common Player:		4.00
Common (91-121):		4.00
Production 2,000		
Pack (5):		3.00
Box (24):		65.00
1	Derek Jeter	3.00
2	Nomar Garciaparra	2.50
3	Alex Rodriguez	2.50
4	Jason Kendall	.25
5	Barry Bonds	1.50
6	David Wells	.25
7	Craig Biggio	.30
8	Adrian Beltre	.25
9	Pat Burrell	.50
10	Rafael Palmeiro	.75
11	Jim Thome	.40
12	Mike Lowell	.25
13	Trevor Hoffman	.25
14	Pokey Reese	.25
15	Juan Encarnacion	.25
16	Shawn Green	.30
17	Kerry Wood	.40
18	Richard Hidalgo	.40
19	Scott Rolen	.40
20	Jeff Kent	.40
21	Alex Gonzalez	.25
22	Matt Williams	.40
23	Mike Sweeney	.25
24	Edgar Martinez	.25
25	Sammy Sosa	2.00
26	Bobby Higginson	.25
27	Kevin Brown	.40
28	Mike Lieberthal	.25
29	Pedro J. Martinez	1.25
30	Jeff Weaver	.25
31	Greg Maddux	2.00
32	Mike Hampton	.25
33	Vladimir Guerrero	1.25
34	Greg Vaughn	.25
35	Manny Ramirez	1.25
36	Carlos Beltran	.25
37	Eric Chavez	.25
38	Troy Glaus	1.00
39	Todd Helton	1.00
40	Gary Sheffield	.40
41	Brady Anderson	.25
42	Juan Gonzalez	1.00
43	Tim Hudson	.40
44	Kenny Lofton	.30
45	Al Leiter	.25
46	Eric Owens	.25
47	Roberto Alomar	.75
48	Preston Wilson	.25
49	Tony Gwynn	1.50
50	Cal Ripken Jr.	3.00
51	Ben Petrick	.25
52	Jason Giambi	.50
53	Ben Grieve	.25
54	Albert Belle	.25
55	Jose Vidro	.25
56	Barry Zito	.40
57	Ivan Rodriguez	1.00
58	Jeff Bagwell	1.00
59	Geoff Jenkins	.40
60	Roger Clemens	1.50
61	John Olerud	.40
62	Randy Johnson	1.00
63	Matt Lawton	.25
64	Mark McGwire	3.00
65	Brad Radke	.25
66	Frank Thomas	1.25
67	Edgardo Alfonzo	.25
68	Brian Giles	.40
69	J.T. Snow	.25
70	Carlos Delgado	.75
71	Chipper Jones	2.00
72	Mark Quinn	.25
73	Mike Mussina	.50
74	Rick Ankiel	.40
75	Rafael Furcal	.25
76	Jim Edmonds	.25
77	Vinny Castilla	.25
78	Sean Casey	.40
79	Derrek Lee	.25
80	Mike Piazza	2.50
81	Warren Morris	.25
82	Tim Salmon	.25
83	Jeromy Burnitz	.25
84	Freddy Garcia	.25
85	Ken Griffey Jr.	2.50
86	Andruw Jones	.75
87	Darryl Kile	.25
88	Magglio Ordonez	.25
89	Bernie Williams	.75
90	Timo Perez	.25
91	*Ichiro Suzuki* (Next Game)	60.00
92	Larry Barnes, Darin Erstad (Next Game)	4.00
93	*Jaisen Randolph* (Next Game)	4.00
94	*Paul Phillips* (Next Game)	4.00
95	*Esix Snead* (Next Game)	4.00
96	*Matt White* (Next Game)	4.00
97	*Ryan Freel* (Next Game)	4.00
98	*Winston Abreu* (Next Game)	4.00
99	*Junior Spivey* (Next Game)	4.00
100	Randy Keisler, Roger Clemens (Next Game)	6.00
101	Brian Cole, Mike Piazza (Next Game)	10.00
102	Aubrey Huff, Chipper Jones (Next Game)	8.00
103	Corey Patterson, Sammy Sosa (Next Game)	6.00
104	Sun-Woo Kim, Pedro Martinez (Next Game)	5.00
105	*Drew Henson* (Next Game)	25.00
106	*Claudio Vargas* (Next Game)	4.00

107 Cesar Izturis, Rafael Furcal (Next Game) 4.00
108 Paxton Crawford, Pedro Martinez (Next Game) 5.00
109 *Adrian Hernandez* (Next Game) 6.00
110 Jace Brewer, Derek Jeter (Next Game) 12.00
111 *Andy Morales* (Next Game) 4.00
112 *Wilson Betemit* (Next Game) 12.00
113 *Juan Diaz* (Next Game) 4.00
114 *Erick Almonte* (Next Game) 5.00
115 *Nick Punto* (Next Game) 4.00
116 *Tsuyoshi Shinjo* (Next Game) 8.00
117 *Jay Gibbons* (Next Game) 12.00
118 *Andres Torres* (Next Game) 4.00
119 *Alexis Gomez* (Next Game) 4.00
120 *Wilken Ruan* (Next Game) 4.00
121 *Albert Pujols* (Next Game) 50.00

2001 Fleer Game Time Next Game Extra

MT
Cards (91-121): 2-3X
Production 200 sets
(See 2001 Fleer Game Time #91-121 for checklist and base card values.)

2001 Fleer Game Time Derek Jeter's Monumental Moments

MT
Complete Set (1):
1JM Derek Jeter/1996 15.00
1JMS Derek Jeter Auto/96 250.00

2001 Fleer Game Time Famers Lumber

MT
Common Player: 20.00
Production 100 sets
1FL Luis Aparicio 40.00
2FL Hank Bauer 25.00
3FL Paul Blair 20.00
4FL Bobby Bonds 25.00
5FL Orlando Cepeda 25.00
6FL Roberto Clemente 250.00
7FL Rocky Colavito 50.00
8FL Bucky Dent 20.00
9FL Bill Dickey 50.00
10FL Larry Doby 30.00
11FL Carlton Fisk 90.00
12FL Hank Greenberg 75.00
13FL Elston Howard 30.00
14FL Frank Howard 25.00
15FL Reggie Jackson 70.00
16FL Harmon Killebrew 60.00
17FL Tony Lazzeri 25.00
18FL Roger Maris 125.00
19FL Johnny Mize 30.00
20FL Thurman Munson 125.00
21FL Tony Perez 35.00
22FL Jim Rice 35.00
23FL Phil Rizzuto 50.00
24FL Bill Skowron 20.00
25FL Enos Slaughter 30.00
26FL Duke Snider 50.00
27FL Willie Stargell 40.00
28FL Bill Terry 40.00
29FL Ted Williams 400.00

2001 Fleer Game Time Famers Lumber Autograph

MT
Common Player: 75.00
Production 25 sets
1FLS Hank Bauer 75.00
2FLS Barry Bonds 80.00
3FLS Orlando Cepeda 75.00
4FLS Rocky Colavito 200.00
5FLS Bucky Dent 75.00
6FLS Larry Doby 75.00
7FLS Carlton Fisk 200.00
8FLS Frank Howard 75.00
9FLS Reggie Jackson 200.00
10FLS Harmon Killebrew 225.00
11FLS Tony Perez 100.00
12FLS Jim Rice 90.00
13FLS Phil Rizzuto 150.00
14FLS Bill Skowron 75.00
15FLS Enos Slaughter 100.00
16FLS Duke Snider 180.00

2001 Fleer Game Time Let's Play Two!

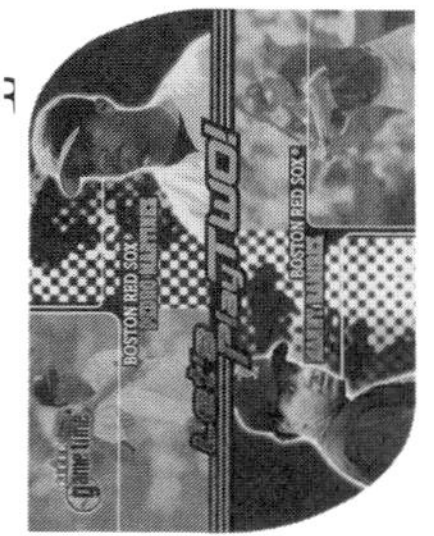

MT
Complete Set (15): 100.00
Common Player: 2.00
Inserted 1:24
1LT Derek Jeter, Nomar Garciaparra 12.00
2LT Mark McGwire, Sammy Sosa 12.00
3LT Pedro J. Martinez, Randy Johnson 5.00
4LT Vladimir Guerrero, Carlos Delgado 5.00
5LT Mike Piazza, Roger Clemens 10.00
6LT Alex Rodriguez, Miguel Tejada 10.00
7LT Troy Glaus, Chipper Jones 8.00
8LT Derek Jeter, Alex Rodriguez 12.00
9LT Cal Ripken Jr., Derek Jeter 12.00
10LT Jason Giambi, Mark McGwire 12.00
11LT Jeff Bagwell, Craig Biggio 4.00
12LT Tom Glavine, Greg Maddux 8.00
13LT Ken Griffey Jr., Barry Bonds 10.00
14LT Manny Ramirez, Pedro J. Martinez 5.00
15LT Alex Rodriguez, Ivan Rodriguez 10.00

2001 Fleer Game Time Lumber

MT
Common Player: 10.00
Inserted 1:40
1GL Roberto Alomar 25.00
2GL Rick Ankiel 15.00
3GL Adrian Beltre 15.00
4GL Barry Bonds 40.00
5GL Kevin Brown 15.00
7GL Ken Caminiti 15.00
8GL Eric Chavez 15.00
9GL Carlos Delgado 20.00
10GL J.D. Drew 20.00
11GL Erubiel Durazo 15.00
12GL Carl Everett 15.00
13GL Rafael Furcal 10.00
14GL Brian Giles 15.00
15GL Juan Gonzalez 25.00
16GL Todd Helton 25.00
18GL Randy Johnson 25.00
19GL Chipper Jones 30.00
20GL Pedro J. Martinez 30.00
21GL Tino Martinez 20.00
23GL Cal Ripken SP/275 90.00
24GL Ivan Rodriguez 25.00
25GL Frank Thomas 25.00
26GL Jim Thome 20.00
27GL Bernie Williams 25.00
28GL Nomar Garciaparra 50.00

2001 Fleer Game Time New Order

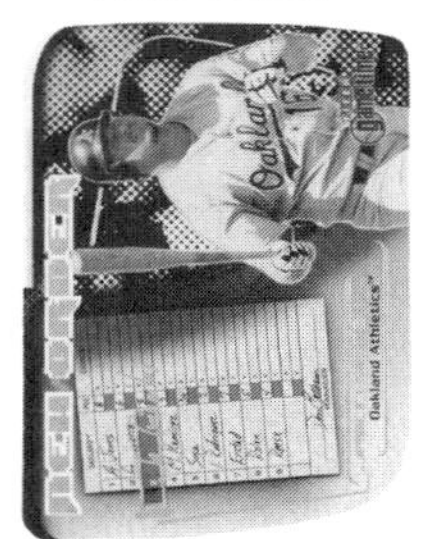

MT
Complete Set (20): 50.00
Common Player: 1.50
Inserted 1:12
1NO Derek Jeter 8.00
2NO Nomar Garciaparra 6.00
3NO Alex Rodriguez 6.00
4NO Mark McGwire 8.00
5NO Sammy Sosa 5.00
6NO Carlos Delgado 2.00
7NO Troy Glaus 2.50
8NO Jason Giambi 1.50
9NO Mike Piazza 6.00
10NO Todd Helton 2.50
11NO Vladimir Guerrero 3.00
12NO Manny Ramirez 3.00
13NO Frank Thomas 3.00
14NO Ken Griffey Jr. 6.00
15NO Chipper Jones 5.00

2001 Fleer Game Time Sticktoitness

MT
Complete Set (20): 40.00
Common Player: 1.00
Inserted 1:8
1S Derek Jeter 6.00
2S Nomar Garciaparra 5.00
3S Alex Rodriguez 5.00
4S Jeff Bagwell 2.00
5S Bernie Williams 1.50
6S Eric Chavez 1.00
7S Richard Hidalgo 1.50
8S Ichiro Suzuki 15.00
9S Troy Glaus 2.00
10S Magglio Ordonez 1.00
11S Corey Patterson 1.00
12S Todd Helton 2.00
13S Jim Edmonds 1.00
14S Rafael Furcal 1.00
15S Mo Vaughn 1.00
16S Pat Burrell 1.50
17S Adrian Beltre 1.00
18S Andruw Jones 1.50
19S Manny Ramirez 2.50
20S Sean Casey 1.00

2001 Fleer Game Time Uniformity

MT
Common Player: 10.00
Inserted 1:25
1GU Andres Galarraga 15.00
2GU Barry Bonds 40.00
3GU Ben Petrick 10.00
4GU Brad Radke 15.00
5GU Brian Jordan 10.00
6GU Carlos Guillen 10.00
7GU Fernando Seguignol 10.00
8GU Fred McGriff 15.00
9GU Gary Sheffield 15.00
10GU Greg Maddux 35.00
11GU Ivan Rodriguez 25.00
12GU Jay Buhner 15.00
13GU Jeromy Burnitz 10.00
14GU John Olerud 15.00
15GU Kevin Brown 15.00
16GU Larry Walker 15.00
17GU Magglio Ordonez 15.00
18GU Matt Williams 20.00
19GU Robin Ventura 15.00
20GU Rondell White 10.00
21GU Tony Gwynn 35.00
22GU Troy Glaus 20.00
23GU Vladimir Guerrero 25.00

2001 Fleer Genuine

MT
Complete Set (130): 500.00
Common Player: .25
Common (101-130): 5.00
Production 1,500

Pack (5): 4.50
Box (24): 90.00
1 Derek Jeter 3.00
2 Nomar Garciaparra 2.50
3 Alex Rodriguez 2.50
4 Frank Thomas 1.25
5 Travis Fryman .25
6 Gary Sheffield .50
7 Jason Giambi .75
8 Trevor Hoffman .25
9 Todd Helton 1.00
10 Ivan Rodriguez 1.00
11 Roberto Alomar .75
12 Barry Zito .50
13 Kevin Brown .40
14 Shawn Green .40
15 Kenny Lofton .40
16 Jeff Weaver .25
17 Geoff Jenkins .40
18 Carlos Delgado .75
19 Mark Grace .50
20 Ken Griffey Jr. 2.50
21 David Justice .50
22 Brian Giles .40
23 Scott Williamson .25
24 Richie Sexson .25
25 John Olerud .50
26 Sammy Sosa 2.00
27 Bobby Higginson .25
28 Matt Lawton .25
29 Vinny Castilla .25
30 Alex S. Gonzalez .25
31 Manny Ramirez 1.25
32 Brad Radke .25
33 Cal Ripken Jr. 3.00
34 Richard Hidalgo .40
35 Al Leiter .40
36 Freddy Garcia .25
37 Juan Encarnacion .25
38 Corey Koskie .25
39 Greg Vaughn .25
40 Rafael Palmeiro .75
41 Vladimir Guerrero 1.25
42 Troy Glaus 1.00
43 Mike Hampton .40
44 Jose Vidro .25
45 Ryan Rupe .25
46 Troy O'Leary .25
47 Ben Petrick .25
48 Mike Lieberthal .25
49 Mike Sweeney .25
50 Scott Rolen .50
51 Albert Belle .25
52 Mark Quinn .25
53 Mike Piazza 2.50
54 Mark McGwire 3.00
55 Brady Anderson .25
56 Carlos Beltran .25
57 Michael Barrett .25
58 Jason Kendall .25
59 Jim Edmonds .40
60 Matt Williams .50
61 Pokey Reese .25
62 Bernie Williams .75
63 Barry Bonds 1.50
64 David Wells .25
65 Chipper Jones 2.00
66 Jim Parque .25
67 Derrek Lee .25
68 Darin Erstad .50
69 Edgar Martinez .25
70 Kerry Wood .50
71 Omar Vizquel .40
72 Jeromy Burnitz .25
73 Warren Morris .25
74 Rick Ankiel .40
75 Andruw Jones .75
76 Paul Konerko .25
77 Mike Lowell .25
78 Roger Clemens 1.50
79 Tim Hudson .40
80 Rafael Furcal .40
81 Craig Biggio .40
82 Edgardo Alfonzo .25
83 Pat Burrell .75
84 Adrian Beltre .40
85 Tony Gwynn 1.25
86 J.T. Snow .25
87 Randy Johnson 1.00
88 Sean Casey .40
89 Preston Wilson .25
90 Mike Mussina .50
91 Eric Chavez .40
92 Tim Salmon .25
93 Pedro Martinez 1.25
94 Darryl Kile .25
95 Greg Maddux 2.00
96 Magglio Ordonez .40
97 Jeff Bagwell 1.00
98 Timo Perez .25
99 Jeff Kent .40
100 Eric Owens .25
101 *Ichiro Suzuki* (Genuine Upside) 75.00
102 *Elpidio Guzman* (Genuine Upside) 10.00
103 *Tsuyoshi Shinjo* (Genuine Upside) 18.00
104 *Travis Hafner* (Genuine Upside) 5.00
105 Larry Barnes (Genuine Upside) 5.00
106 *Jaisen Randolph* (Genuine Upside) 5.00
107 *Paul Phillips* (Genuine Upside) 6.00
108 *Erick Almonte* (Genuine Upside) 5.00
109 *Nick Punto* (Genuine Upside) 5.00
110 *Jack Wilson* (Genuine Upside) 5.00
111 *Jeremy Owens* (Genuine Upside) 8.00
112 *Esix Snead* (Genuine Upside) 12.00
113 *Jay Gibbons* (Genuine Upside) 15.00
114 *Adrian Hernandez* (Genuine Upside) 10.00
115 *Matt White* (Genuine Upside) 8.00
116 *Ryan Freel* (Genuine Upside) 5.00
117 *Martin Vargas* (Genuine Upside) 5.00
118 *Winston Abreu* (Genuine Upside) 5.00
119 *Junior Spivey* (Genuine Upside) 8.00
120 Paxton Crawford (Genuine Upside) 5.00
121 Randy Keisler (Genuine Upside) 5.00
122 *Juan Diaz* (Genuine Upside) 10.00
123 Aaron Rowand (Genuine Upside) 5.00
124 Toby Hall (Genuine Upside) 5.00
125 Brian Cole (Genuine Upside) 5.00
126 Aubrey Huff (Genuine Upside) 5.00
127 Corey Patterson (Genuine Upside) 10.00
128 Sun-Woo Kim (Genuine Upside) 5.00
129 Jace Brewer (Genuine Upside) 5.00
130 Cesar Izturis (Genuine Upside) 8.00

2001 Fleer Genuine Final Cut

Final Cut cards of Ron Guidry, Don Larsen and Reggie Jackson were prepared, but not intended for release. At least a few of each have made their way into hobby channels. Because of limited numbers extant, their values cannot be determined. Some, perhaps all, of Edgar Martinez' Final Cut cards have jersey patches rather than the described glove piece.

MT
Common Player: 15.00
Inserted 1:30
Miguel Tejada SP/170 25.00
Barry Bonds SP/330 60.00
Robin Ventura 15.00
Greg Maddux 30.00
Andruw Jones SP/135 35.00
J.D. Drew SP/75 40.00
Chipper Jones 30.00
Tim Salmon 15.00
Edgar Martinez SP/130 30.00
Troy Glaus 25.00
Frank Thomas 30.00
Pokey Reese 15.00
Larry Walker 20.00
Ivan Rodriguez SP/120 60.00
Scott Rolen 20.00
Cal Ripken Jr. 50.00
Tony Gwynn 30.00
Wade Boggs 25.00
George Brett 50.00
Sean Casey 15.00
Bob Gibson 40.00
Matt Williams 20.00
Robin Yount 40.00
Ron Guidry (not officially released)
Reggie Jackson (not officially released)
Don Larsen (not officially released)

2001 Fleer Genuine Genuine Coverage PLUS

MT
Common Player: 25.00
Production 150 sets
Troy Glaus 30.00
Randy Johnson 40.00
Andruw Jones 30.00
Frank Thomas 35.00
Darin Erstad 25.00
Chipper Jones 50.00
Derek Jeter 125.00
Tony Gwynn 50.00
Barry Bonds 65.00
Cal Ripken Jr. 125.00

2001 Fleer Genuine High Interest

MT
Complete Set (15): 90.00
Common Player: 2.50
Inserted 1:23
1HI Derek Jeter 15.00
2HI Nomar Garciaparra 12.00
3HI Greg Maddux 10.00
4HI Todd Helton 5.00
5HI Sammy Sosa 10.00
6HI Jeff Bagwell 5.00
7HI Jason Giambi 3.00
8HI Frank Thomas 6.00
9HI Andruw Jones 4.00
10HI Jim Edmonds 2.50
11HI Bernie Williams 4.00
12HI Randy Johnson 5.00
13HI Ken Griffey Jr. 12.00
14HI Pedro Martinez 6.00
15HI Mark McGwire 15.00

2001 Fleer Genuine Material Issue

MT
Common Player: 15.00
Inserted 1:30
Randy Johnson 20.00
Scott Rolen 15.00
Robin Ventura 15.00
Tony Gwynn 25.00
Troy Glaus 20.00
Kevin Millwood 15.00
Chipper Jones 25.00
Tom Glavine 15.00
Pedro Martinez SP/60 75.00
Greg Maddux 35.00
Frank Thomas 25.00
Curt Schilling SP/120 20.00
Edgar Martinez 20.00
Darin Erstad 15.00
J.D. Drew 20.00
Cal Ripken Jr. 40.00
Nolan Ryan 75.00
Steve Carlton 50.00

2001 Fleer Genuine Pennant Aggression

MT
Complete Set (10): 70.00
Common Player: 3.00
Inserted 1:23
1PA Derek Jeter 12.00
2PA Alex Rodriguez 10.00
3PA Nomar Garciaparra 10.00
4PA Mark McGwire 12.00
5PA Ken Griffey Jr. 10.00
6PA Mike Piazza 10.00
7PA Sammy Sosa 8.00
8PA Barry Bonds 5.00
9PA Chipper Jones 8.00
10PA Pedro Martinez 5.00

2001 Fleer Genuine Names of the Game - game used

MT
Common Player: 30.00
Production 50 sets
1NG Yogi Berra bat 90.00
2NG Orlando Cepeda bat 35.00
3NG Rocky Colavito bat 80.00
4NG Andre Dawson jsy 45.00
5NG Bucky Dent bat 30.00
6NG Rollie Fingers jsy 40.00
7NG Carlton Fisk bat 75.00
8NG Whitey Ford jsy 90.00
9NG Jimmie Foxx bat 225.00

10NGLou Gehrig
11NGHank Greenberg bat 200.00
12NG"Catfish" Hunter jsy 60.00
13NGReggie Jackson jsy 100.00
14NGRandy Johnson jsy 60.00
15NGChipper Jones bat 90.00
16NGHarmon Killebrew bat 125.00
17NGTony Lazzeri bat 50.00
18NGDon Mattingly bat 250.00
20NGWillie McCovey bat 50.00
21NGJohnny Mize bat 50.00
22NGPee Wee Reese jsy 100.00
23NGCal Ripken Jr. bat 225.00
24NGPhil Rizzuto bat 75.00
25NGIvan Rodriguez bat 50.00
26NGPreacher Roe jsy 50.00
27NGBabe Ruth bat 750.00
28NGNolan Ryan jsy 300.00
29NGTom Seaver jsy 75.00
30NGBill Skowron bat 40.00
31NGEnos Slaughter bat 50.00
32NGDuke Snider bat 75.00
33NGWillie Stargell bat 60.00
34NGBill Terry bat 75.00
35NGTed Williams bat 600.00
36NGHack Wilson bat 100.00

2001 Fleer Genuine Names of the Game - autograph

MT
Common Player: 40.00
1NGAYogi Berra 125.00
2NGAOrlando Cepeda 60.00
3NGARocky Colavito 110.00
4NGAAndre Dawson 75.00
5NGABucky Dent 40.00
6NGARollie Fingers 50.00
7NGACarlton Fisk 100.00
8NGAWhitey Ford 125.00
9NGAReggie Jackson 100.00
10NGARandy Johnson 100.00
11NGAChipper Jones 125.00
12NGAHarmon Killebrew 150.00
13NGADon Mattingly 300.00
15NGAWillie McCovey 80.00
16NGACal Ripken Jr. 275.00
18NGAIvan Rodriguez 80.00
19NGAPreacher Roe 50.00
20NGANolan Ryan 350.00
21NGATom Seaver 125.00
22NGABill Skowron 50.00
23NGAEnos Slaughter 75.00
24NGADuke Snider 125.00

2001 Fleer Genuine Tip of the Cap

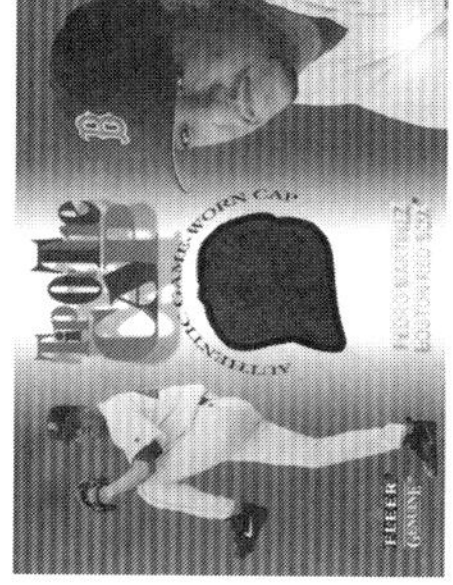

MT
Common Player: 25.00
Production 150 sets

Barry Bonds 100.00
Eric Chavez 25.00
Shawn Green 30.00
Vladimir Guerrero 40.00
Randy Johnson 50.00
Andruw Jones 40.00
Javy Lopez 25.00
Rafael Palmeiro 40.00
Ivan Rodriguez 40.00
Miguel Tejada 30.00
Roberto Alomar 50.00
Pedro Martinez 125.00

2001 Fleer Genuine LG

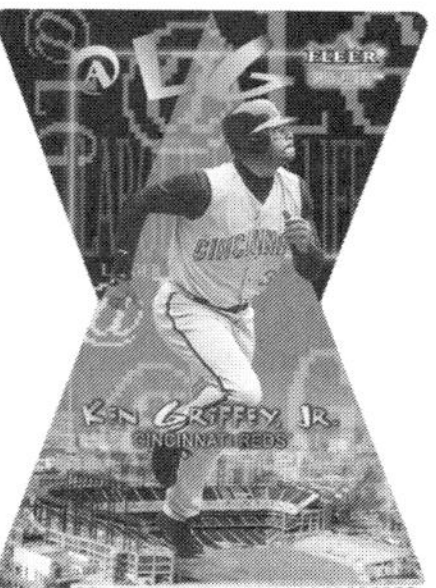

MT
Complete Set (15): 100.00
Common Player: 2.50
Inserted 1:23
1AL Derek Jeter 15.00
2AL Nomar Garciaparra 12.00
3AL Mark McGwire 15.00
4AL Pedro Martinez 6.00
5AL Tony Gwynn 6.00
6AL Roger Clemens 6.00
7AL Ivan Rodriguez 5.00
8AL Sammy Sosa 10.00
9AL Magglio Ordonez 2.50
10AL Jason Giambi 3.00
11AL Carlos Delgado 4.00
12AL Chipper Jones 10.00
13AL Mike Piazza 12.00
14AL Cal Ripken Jr. 15.00
15AL Ken Griffey Jr. 12.00

2001 Fleer Greats of the Game

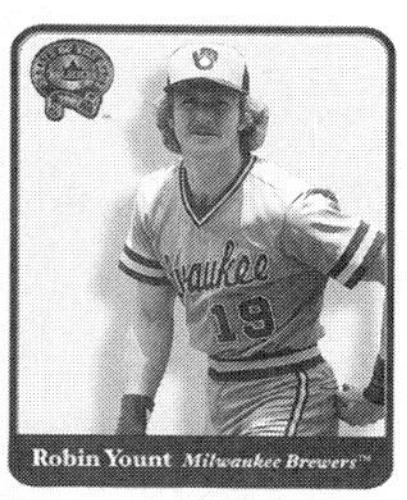

MT
Complete Set (137): 70.00
Common Player: .50
Hobby Pack (5): 8.00
Hobby Box (24): 175.00
1 Roberto Clemente 6.00
2 George "Sparky" Anderson .50
3 Babe Ruth 8.00
4 Paul Molitor 2.00
5 Don Larsen .50
6 Cy Young 1.50
7 Billy Martin .50
8 Lou Brock 1.00
9 Fred Lynn .50
10 Johnny Vander Meer .50
11 Harmon Killebrew .50
12 Dave Winfield 1.00
13 Orlando Cepeda .50
14 Johnny Mize 1.00
15 Walter Johnson 2.00
16 Roy Campanella 2.50
17 Monte Irvin .50
18 Mookie Wilson .50
19 Elston Howard .50
20 Walter Alston .50
21 Rollie Fingers .50
22 Brooks Robinson 2.00
23 Hank Greenberg 1.50
24 Maury Wills .50
25 Rich Gossage .50
26 Leon Day .50
27 Jimmie Foxx 2.50
28 Alan Trammell .50
29 Dennis Martinez .50
30 Don Drysdale 1.50
31 Bob Feller 1.00
32 Jackie Robinson 6.00
33 Whitey Ford 2.50
34 Enos Slaughter .50
35 Rod Carew 1.50
36 Eddie Mathews 2.50
37 Ron Cey .50
38 Thurman Munson 2.00
39 Henry Kimbro .50
40 Ty Cobb 4.00
41 Rocky Colavito .50
42 Satchel Paige 2.50
43 Andre Dawson .50
44 Phil Rizzuto 1.50
45 Roger Maris 3.00
46 Bobby Bonds .50
47 Joe Carter .50
48 Christy Mathewson .50
49 Tony Lazzeri .50
50 Gil Hodges .50
51 Ray Dandridge .50
52 Gaylord Perry .50
53 Ernie Banks 3.00
54 Lou Gehrig 8.00
55 George Kell .50
56 Wes Parker .50
57 Sam Jethroe .50
58 Joe Morgan 1.50
59 Steve Garvey .50
60 Joe Torre 1.00
61 Roger Craig .50
62 Warren Spahn 2.50
63 Willie McCovey .50
64 Cool Papa Bell 1.00
65 Frank Robinson 1.50
66 Richie Allen .50
67 Bucky Dent .50
68 George Foster .50
69 Hoyt Wilhelm .50
70 Phil Niekro .50
71 Buck Leonard .50
72 Preacher Roe .50
73 Yogi Berra 4.00
74 Joe Black .50
75 Nolan Ryan 8.00
76 Pop Lloyd .50
77 Lester Lockett .50
78 Paul Blair .50
79 Ryne Sandberg 1.50
80 Bill Perkins .50
81 Frank Howard .50
82 Hack Wilson 1.50
83 Robin Yount 1.50
84 Harry Heilmann .50
85 Mike Schmidt 3.00
86 Vida Blue .50
87 George Brett 3.00
88 Juan Marichal .50
89 Tom Seaver 2.50
90 Bill Skowron .50
91 Don Mattingly 4.00
92 Jim Bunning .50
93 Eddie Murray 1.50
94 Tommy Lasorda 1.00
95 Pee Wee Reese 1.50
96 Bill Dickey .50
97 Ozzie Smith 2.00
98 Dale Murphy .50
99 Artie Wilson .50
100 Bill Terry .50
101 Jim "Catfish" Hunter .50
102 Don Sutton .50
103 Luis Aparicio .50
104 Reggie Jackson 3.00
105 Ted Radcliffe .50
106 Carl Erskine .50
107 Johnny Bench 2.50
108 Carl Furillo .50
109 Stan Musial 3.00
110 Carlton Fisk .50
111 Rube Foster .50
112 Tony Oliva .50
113 Hank Bauer .50
114 Jim Rice .50
115 Willie Mays 4.00
116 Ralph Kiner 1.00
117 Al Kaline 1.00
118 Billy Williams .50
119 Buck O'Neil .50
120 Tony Perez .50
121 Dave Parker .50
122 Kirk Gibson .50
123 Lou Piniella .50
124 Ted Williams 8.00
125 Steve Carlton 1.00
126 Dizzy Dean .50
127 Willie Stargell .50
128 Joe Niekro .50
129 Lloyd Waner .50
130 Wade Boggs 1.00
131 Wilmer Fields .50
132 Bill Mazeroski .75
133 Duke Snider 2.00
134 Smoky Joe Williams .50
135 Bob Gibson 2.00
136 Jim Palmer 1.00
137 Oscar Charleston .50

2001 Fleer Greats of the Game Autographs

MT
Common Player: 15.00
Inserted 1:8
1 Richie Allen 20.00
2 George "Sparky" Anderson 40.00
3 Luis Aparicio 20.00
4 Ernie Banks SP/250 160.00
5 Hank Bauer 20.00
6 Johnny Bench SP/400 150.00
7 Yogi Berra SP/500 100.00
8 Joe Black 20.00
9 Paul Blair 15.00
9a Paul Blair double signed 15.00
10 Vida Blue 20.00
11 Wade Boggs 60.00
12 Barry Bonds 20.00
13 George Brett SP/247 160.00
14 Lou Brock SP/500 50.00
15 Jim Bunning 20.00
16 Rod Carew 40.00
17 Steve Carlton 30.00
18 Joe Carter 25.00
19 Orlando Cepeda 20.00
20 Ron Cey 15.00
21 Rocky Colavito 40.00
22 Roger Craig 15.00
23 Andre Dawson 20.00
24 Bucky Dent 15.00
25 Carl Erskine 25.00
26 Bob Feller 25.00
27 Wilmer Fields 20.00

28	Rollie Fingers	15.00
29	Carlton Fisk	50.00
30	Whitey Ford	75.00
31	George Foster	15.00
32	Steve Garvey SP/400	70.00
33	Bob Gibson	30.00
34	Kirk Gibson	20.00
35	Rich Gossage	20.00
36	Frank Howard	15.00
37	Monte Irvin	20.00
38	Reggie Jackson SP/400	120.00
39	Sam Jethroe	15.00
40	Al Kaline	30.00
41	George Kell	15.00
42	Harmon Killebrew	40.00
43	Ralph Kiner	20.00
44	Don Larsen	25.00
45	Tommy Lasorda SP/400	65.00
46	Lester Lockett	15.00
47	Fred Lynn	20.00
48	Juan Marichal	25.00
49	Dennis Martinez	15.00
50	Don Mattingly	150.00
51	Willie Mays SP/100	650.00
52	Bill Mazeroski	25.00
53	Willie McCovey	50.00
54	Paul Molitor	60.00
55	Joe Morgan	40.00
56	Dale Murphy	40.00
57	Eddie Murray SP/140	250.00
58	Stan Musial SP/525	125.00
59	Joe Niekro	15.00
60	Phil Niekro	20.00
61	Tony Oliva	15.00
62	Buck O'Neil	25.00
63	Jim Palmer SP/600	50.00
64	Dave Parker	15.00
65	Tony Perez	25.00
66	Gaylord Perry	15.00
67	Lou Piniella	25.00
68	Ted Radcliffe	20.00
69	Jim Rice	20.00
70	Phil Rizzuto SP/425	125.00
71	Brooks Robinson	30.00
72	Frank Robinson	40.00
73	Preacher Roe	20.00
74	Nolan Ryan SP/650	150.00
75	Ryne Sandberg	50.00
76	Mike Schmidt SP/213	225.00
77	Tom Seaver	60.00
78	Bill Skowron	15.00
79	Enos Slaughter	20.00
80	Ozzie Smith	75.00
81	Duke Snider SP/600	75.00
82	Warren Spahn	60.00
83	Willie Stargell	35.00
84	Don Sutton	20.00
85	Joe Torre SP/500	80.00
86	Alan Trammell	20.00
87	Hoyt Wilhelm	15.00
88	Billy Williams	25.00
89	Maury Wills	15.00
90	Artie Wilson	20.00
91	Mookie Wilson	15.00
92	Dave Winfield SP/370	125.00
93	Robin Yount SP/400	125.00

A card number in parentheses ( ) indicates the set is unnumbered.

2001 Fleer Greats of the Game Dodger Blues

		MT
Complete Set (13):		1000.
Common Player:		25.00
Inserted 1:36		
1	Walter Alston	30.00
2	Roy Campanella SP	280.00
3	Carl Furillo	40.00
4	Gil Hodges	50.00
5	Pee Wee Reese	75.00
6	Jackie Robinson SP	400.00
7	Preacher Roe	40.00
8	Duke Snider SP	180.00
9	Roger Craig	40.00
10	Don Drysdale	60.00
11	Wes Parker	25.00
12	Don Sutton	40.00
13	Steve Garvey	40.00

2001 Fleer Greats of the Game Feel the Game Classics

		MT
Common Player:		20.00
Inserted 1:72		
1	Luis Aparicio bat	50.00
2	George Brett jersey	90.00
3	Lou Brock jersey	40.00
4	Orlando Cepeda bat	25.00
5	Whitey Ford jersey	50.00
6	Hank Greenberg bat	80.00
7	Elston Howard bat	30.00
8	"Catfish" Hunter jersey	30.00
9	Harmon Killebrew bat	60.00
10	Roger Maris bat	100.00
11	Eddie Mathews bat	50.00
12	W. McCovey bat SP/200	50.00
13	Johnny Mize bat	40.00
14	Paul Molitor jersey	50.00
15	Jim Palmer jersey	40.00
16	Tony Perez bat	25.00
17	Brooks Robinson bat/144	125.00
18	Babe Ruth bat/250	400.00
19	Mike Schmidt jersey	60.00
20	Tom Seaver jersey	50.00
21	Enos Slaughter	40.00
22	Willie Stargell	40.00
23	Hack Wilson	50.00
24	Harry Heilmann	40.00

2001 Fleer Greats of the Game Retrospection Collection

		MT
Complete Set (10):		50.00
Common Player:		4.00
Inserted 1:6		
1	Babe Ruth	15.00
2	Stan Musial	6.00
3	Jimmie Foxx	6.00
4	Roberto Clemente	8.00
5	Ted Williams	10.00
6	Mike Schmidt	8.00
7	Cy Young	6.00
8	Satchel Paige	6.00
9	Hank Greenberg	4.00
10	Jim Bunning	4.00

2001 Fleer Legacy

		MT
Complete Set (105):		
Common Player:		.50
Common (91-105):		15.00
Production 799 sets		
Pack (5):		10.00
Box (15):		160.00
1	Pedro J. Martinez	2.50
2	Andruw Jones	1.50
3	Mike Hampton	.50
4	Gary Sheffield	.75
5	Barry Zito	.75
6	J.D. Drew	1.00
7	Charles Johnson	.50
8	David Wells	.50
9	Kazuhiro Sasaki	.50
10	Vladimir Guerrero	2.50
11	Pat Burrell	1.00
12	Ruben Mateo	.50
13	Greg Maddux	4.00
14	Sean Casey	1.00
15	Craig Biggio	.75
16	Bernie Williams	1.50
17	Jeff Kent	.75
18	Nomar Garciaparra	5.00
19	Cal Ripken Jr.	6.00
20	Larry Walker	1.00
21	Adrian Beltre	.75
22	Johnny Damon	.50
23	Rick Ankiel	.75
24	Matt Williams	.75
25	Magglio Ordonez	.75
26	Richard Hidalgo	.75
27	Robin Ventura	.50
28	Jason Kendall	.50
29	Tony Batista	.50
30	Chipper Jones	4.00
31	Jim Thome	1.00
32	Kevin Brown	.50
33	Mike Mussina	1.00
34	Mark McGwire	6.00
35	Darin Erstad	.75
36	Manny Ramirez	2.00
37	Bobby Higginson	.50
38	Richie Sexson	.50
39	Jason Giambi	1.00
40	Alex Rodriguez	5.00
41	Mark Grace	1.00
42	Ken Griffey Jr.	5.00
43	Moises Alou	.75
44	Edgardo Alfonzo	.50
45	Phil Nevin	.50
46	Rafael Palmeiro	1.00
47	Javy Lopez	.50
48	Juan Gonzalez	2.00
49	Jermaine Dye	.50
50	Roger Clemens	2.50
51	Barry Bonds	3.50
52	Carl Everett	.50
53	Ben Sheets	1.00
54	Juan Encarnacion	.50
55	Jeromy Burnitz	.50
56	Miguel Tejada	.75
57	Ben Grieve	.50
58	Randy Johnson	2.00
59	Frank Thomas	2.00
60	Preston Wilson	.50
61	Mike Piazza	5.00
62	Brian Giles	.75
63	Carlos Delgado	1.50
64	Tom Glavine	1.00
65	Roberto Alomar	1.50
66	Mike Sweeney	.50
67	Orlando Hernandez	.50
68	Edgar Martinez	.50
69	Tim Salmon	.50
70	Kerry Wood	.75
71	*Jack Wilson*	2.00
72	Matt Lawton	.50
73	Scott Rolen	.75
74	Ivan Rodriguez	2.00
75	Steve Finley	.50
76	Barry Larkin	.75
77	Jeff Bagwell	2.00
78	Derek Jeter	6.00
79	Tony Gwynn	2.50
80	Raul Mondesi	.50
81	Rafael Furcal	.50
82	Todd Helton	2.00
83	Shawn Green	.75
84	Tim Hudson	.75
85	Jim Edmonds	.75
86	Troy Glaus	2.00
87	Sammy Sosa	4.00
88	Cliff Floyd	.50
89	Jose Vidro	.50
90	Bobby Abreu	.50
91	*Drew Henson Auto*	100.00
92	*Andy Morales Auto*	25.00
93	*Wilson Betemit Auto*	40.00
94	*Elpidio Guzman*	20.00
95	*Esix Snead*	20.00
96	*Winston Abreu*	20.00
97	*Jeremy Owens*	20.00
99	*Junior Spivey*	20.00
100	*Jaisen Randolph*	20.00
101	*Ichiro Suzuki*	75.00
102	*Albert Pujols/549*	100.00
102	*Albert Pujols Auto/250*	200.00
103	*Tsuyoshi Shinjo*	25.00
104	*Jay Gibbons*	25.00
105	*Juan Uribe*	15.00

2001 Fleer Legacy Ultimate Legacy

	MT
Stars (1-90):	3-5X
Rookies (91-100):	.3-.75X
Rookies (101-105):	.75-1.5X
Production 250 sets	

(See 2001 Fleer Legacy for checklist and base card values.)

2001 Fleer Legacy Autographed MLB Fitted Cap

	MT
Common Player:	30.00
Inserted 1:15	
Edgardo Alfonzo	40.00
Roberto Alomar	80.00
Ernie Banks/100	
Adrian Beltre	40.00
Johnny Bench/100	
Lance Berkman	60.00
Yogi Berra/200	150.00
Craig Biggio	40.00
Barry Bonds	225.00
Jeromy Burnitz	30.00
Pat Burrell	40.00
Steve Carlton	75.00
Sean Casey	40.00
Orlando Cepeda	50.00
Eric Chavez	30.00
Tony Clark	30.00
Roger Clemens/100	
Johnny Damon	30.00
Dom DiMaggio /200	100.00
J.D. Drew	60.00
Jermaine Dye	30.00
Darin Erstad	50.00
Carlton Fisk/150	
Rafael Furcal	40.00
Nomar Garciaparra/150	
Jason Giambi	75.00
Troy Glaus	75.00
Tom Glavine	50.00
Juan Gonzalez	75.00
Luis Gonzalez	60.00
Tony Gwynn	100.00
Drew Henson	100.00
Derek Jeter	300.00
Andruw Jones	75.00
David Justice	40.00
Paul Konerko	30.00
Don Mattingly	200.00
Willie McCovey	50.00
Paul Molitor	75.00
Stan Musial/200	
Mike Mussina	75.00
Jim Palmer	50.00
Corey Patterson	50.00
Kirby Puckett/ 200	200.00
Cal Ripken/200	
Brooks Robinson	75.00
Ivan Rodriguez	60.00
Scott Rolen	50.00
Nolan Ryan/150	
Mike Schmidt/ 150	125.00
Tom Seaver/100	
Ben Sheets	75.00
Ozzie Smith	100.00
Duke Snider	75.00
Miguel Tejada	50.00
Jim Thome	60.00
Matt Williams	40.00
Dave Winfield/150	75.00
Carl Yastrzemski/150	
Robin Yount	75.00
Barry Zito	40.00

2001 Fleer Legacy Hit Kings

		MT
Common Player:		10.00
Inserted 1:13		
1HK	Stan Musial	50.00
2HK	Barry Bonds	40.00
3HK	Corey Patterson	10.00
4HK	Shawn Green	15.00
5HK	Ralph Kiner	20.00
6HK	Troy O'Leary	10.00
7HK	Ivan Rodriguez	15.00
8HK	Jose Vidro	10.00
9HK	Carlos Beltran	10.00
10HK	Jose Canseco	25.00
11HK	Juan Encarnacion	10.00
12HK	Reggie Jackson	40.00
13HK	Ruben Mateo	10.00
14HK	Juan Pierre	10.00
15HK	Tim Salmon	10.00
16HK	Adrian Beltre	10.00
17HK	Roger Cedeno	10.00
18HK	Troy Glaus	25.00
19HK	Jason Kendall	15.00
20HK	Rick Ankiel	15.00
21HK	Andruw Jones	20.00
22HK	Jim Thome	25.00
23HK	Tony Batista	10.00
24HK	George Brett	40.00
26HK	Vladimir Guerrero	25.00
27HK	Billy Martin	40.00
28HK	Magglio Ordonez	15.00
29HK	Johnny Damon	10.00

2001 Fleer Legacy Hit Kings Short Prints

		MT
Common Player:		30.00
Production 100 sets		
1HKSP	Robin Yount	75.00
2HKSP	Scott Rolen	30.00
3HKSP	Johnny Bench	180.00
4HKSP	Steve Garvey	50.00
5HKSP	Joe Morgan	
6HKSP	Frank Thomas	50.00
7HKSP	Eddie Mathews	125.00
8HKSP	Tony Gwynn	75.00
9HKSP	Roger Clemens	100.00
10HKSP	Wade Boggs	75.00

2001 Fleer Legacy Hot Gloves

		MT
Common Player:		35.00
Inserted 1:180		
1HG	Andruw Jones	40.00
2HG	Mike Mussina	75.00
3HG	Roberto Alomar	60.00
4HG	Tony Gwynn	75.00
5HG	Bernie Williams	50.00
6HG	Ivan Rodriguez	60.00
7HG	Ken Griffey Jr.	125.00
8HG	Robin Ventura	35.00
9HG	Cal Ripken Jr.	180.00
10HG	Jeff Bagwell	75.00
11HG	Mark McGwire	250.00
12HG	Rafael Palmeiro	60.00
13HG	Scott Rolen	50.00
14HG	Barry Bonds	100.00
15HG	Greg Maddux	100.00

2001 Fleer Legacy MLB Game Issue - Base

		MT
Common Player:		15.00
Inserted 1:52		
1GI	Mark McGwire	70.00
2GI	Ken Griffey Jr.	40.00
3GI	Sammy Sosa	30.00
4GI	Mike Piazza	30.00
5GI	Alex Rodriguez	25.00
6GI	Derek Jeter	50.00
7GI	Cal Ripken Jr.	50.00
8GI	Todd Helton	20.00
9GI	Tony Gwynn	20.00
10GI	Chipper Jones	25.00
11GI	Frank Thomas	20.00
12GI	Barry Bonds	30.00
13GI	Troy Glaus	20.00
14GI	Pat Burrell	15.00
15GI	Scott Rolen	15.00

2001 Fleer Legacy MLB Game Issue - Base/Ball

		MT
Common Player:		40.00
Production 100 sets		
1GIBB	Mark McGwire	160.00
2GIBB	Ken Griffey Jr.	100.00
3GIBB	Sammy Sosa	75.00
4GIBB	Mike Piazza	90.00
5GIBB	Alex Rodriguez	75.00
6GIBB	Derek Jeter	140.00
7GIBB	Cal Ripken Jr.	140.00
8GIBB	Todd Helton	50.00
9GIBB	Tony Gwynn	65.00
10GIBB	Chipper Jones	65.00
11GIBB	Frank Thomas	50.00
12GIBB	Barry Bonds	90.00
13GIBB	Troy Glaus	50.00
14GIBB	Pat Burrell	40.00
15GIBB	Scott Rolen	40.00

2001 Fleer Legacy MLB Game Issue - Base/Ball/Jersey

		MT
Common Player:		80.00
Production 50 sets		
1GIBBJ	Derek Jeter	250.00
2GIBBJ	Cal Ripken Jr.	250.00
3GIBBJ	Todd Helton	80.00
4GIBBJ	Tony Gwynn	120.00
5GIBBJ	Chipper Jones	120.00
6GIBBJ	Frank Thomas	90.00
7GIBBJ	Barry Bonds	180.00
8GIBBJ	Troy Glaus	90.00
9GIBBJ	Pat Burrell	80.00
10GIBBJ	Scott Rolen	80.00

2001 Fleer Legacy Tailor Made

		MT
Common Player:		10.00
Inserted 1:15		
2TM	Cal Ripken Jr.	60.00
3TM	Orlando Cepeda	15.00
4TM	Willie McCovey	15.00
5TM	Dave Winfield	15.00
6TM	Don Mattingly	75.00
7TM	Nolan Ryan	100.00
8TM	Manny Ramirez	25.00
9TM	Edgardo Alfonzo	10.00
10TM	Rondell White	10.00
11TM	Lou Piniella	10.00
12TM	Ivan Rodriguez	15.00
13TM	J.D. Drew	20.00
14TM	Barry Bonds	40.00
15TM	Greg Maddux	30.00
16TM	Rick Ankiel	15.00
17TM	Carlos Delgado	20.00
18TM	Kevin Brown	10.00
20TM	Reggie Jackson	30.00
21TM	Shawn Green	15.00
22TM	Jason Kendall	10.00
23TM	Rafael Palmeiro	20.00
24TM	Todd Helton	20.00
25	Curt Schilling	15.00

2001 Fleer Platinum

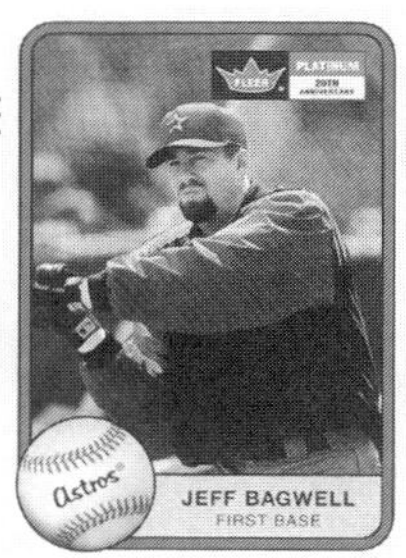

		MT
Complete Set (301):		275.00
Common Player:		.15
Common SP (251-300):		3.00
Inserted 1:6		
Card #301 production 1,500		
Pack (10):		3.50
Box (24):		75.00
1	Bobby Abreu	.25
2	Brad Radke	.15
3	Bill Mueller	.15
4	Adam Eaton	.15
5	Antonio Alfonseca	.15
6	Manny Ramirez	1.00
7	Adam Kennedy	.15
8	Jose Valentin	.15
9	Jaret Wright	.15
10	Aramis Ramirez	.15
11	Jeff Kent	.25
12	Juan Encarnacion	.15
13	Sandy Alomar Jr.	.15
14	Joe Randa	.15
15	Darryl Kile	.15
16	Darren Dreifort	.15
17	Matt Kinney	.15
18	Pokey Reese	.15
19	Ryan Klesko	.15
20	Shawn Estes	.15
21	Moises Alou	.25
22	Edgar Renteria	.15
23	Chuck Knoblauch	.25
24	Carl Everett	.15
25	Garret Anderson	.15
26	Shane Reynolds	.15
27	Billy Koch	.15
28	Carlos Febles	.15
29	Brian Anderson	.15
30	Armando Rios	.15
31	Ryan Kohlmeier	.15
32	Steve Finley	.15
33	Brady Anderson	.15
34	Cal Ripken Jr.	2.50
35	Paul Konerko	.15
36	Chuck Finley	.15
37	Rick Ankiel	.15
38	Mariano Rivera	.25
39	Corey Koskie	.15
40	Cliff Floyd	.25
41	Kevin Appier	.15
42	Henry Rodriguez	.15
43	Mark Kotsay	.15
44	Brook Fordyce	.15
45	Brad Ausmus	.15
46	Alfonso Soriano	.30
47	Ray Lankford	.15
48	Keith Foulke	.15
49	Rich Aurilia	.15
50	Alex Rodriguez	2.00
51	Eric Byrnes	.15
52	Travis Fryman	.15
53	Jeff Bagwell	.75
54	Scott Rolen	.40
55	Matt Lawton	.15
56	Brad Fullmer	.15
57	Tony Batista	.15
58	Nate Rolison	.15
59	Carlos Lee	.15
60	Rafael Furcal	.25
61	Jay Bell	.15
62	Jimmy Rollins	.15
63	Derrek Lee	.15
64	Andres Galarraga	.25
65	Derek Bell	.15
66	Tim Salmon	.15
67	Travis Lee	.15
68	Kevin Millwood	.15
69	Albert Belle	.15
70	Kazuhiro Sasaki	.15
71	Al Leiter	.25
72	Britt Reames	.15
73	Carlos Beltran	.15
74	Curt Schilling	.25
75	Curtis Leskanic	.15
76	Jeremy Giambi	.15
77	Adrian Beltre	.25
78	David Segui	.15
79	Mike Lieberthal	.15
80	Brian Giles	.25
81	Marvin Benard	.15
82	Aaron Sele	.15
83	Kenny Lofton	.25
84	Doug Glanville	.15
85	Kris Benson	.15
86	Richie Sexson	.15
87	Javy Lopez	.25
88	Doug Mientkiewicz	.15
89	Peter Bergeron	.15
90	Gary Sheffield	.30
91	Derek Lowe	.15
92	Tom Glavine	.30
93	Lance Berkman	.15
94	Chris Singleton	.15
95	Mike Lowell	.15
96	Luis Gonzalez	.30
97	Dante Bichette	.20
98	Mike Sirotka	.15
99	Julio Lugo	.15

100 Juan Gonzalez .75
101 Craig Biggio .25
102 Armando Benitez .15
103 Greg Maddux 1.50
104 Mark Grace .30
105 John Smoltz .15
106 J.T. Snow .15
107 Al Martin .15
108 Danny Graves .15
109 Barry Bonds 1.25
110 Lee Stevens .15
111 Pedro Martinez 1.00
112 Shawn Green .25
113 Bret Boone .15
114 Matt Stairs .15
115 Tino Martinez .15
116 Rusty Greer .15
117 Mike Bordick .15
118 Garrett Stephenson .15
119 Edgar Martinez .15
120 Ben Grieve .15
121 Milton Bradley .15
122 Aaron Boone .15
123 Ruben Mateo .15
124 Ken Griffey Jr. 2.00
125 Russell Branyan .15
126 Shannon Stewart .15
127 Fred McGriff .15
128 Ben Petrick .15
129 Kevin Brown .25
130 B.J. Surhoff .15
131 Mark McGwire 2.50
132 Carlos Guillen .15
133 Adrian Brown .15
134 Mike Sweeney .15
135 Eric Milton .15
136 Cristian Guzman .15
137 Ellis Burks .15
138 Fernando Tatis .15
139 Ben Molina .15
140 Tony Gwynn 1.00
141 Jeromy Burnitz .15
142 Miguel Tejada .25
143 Raul Mondesi .25
144 Jeffrey Hammonds .15
145 Pat Burrell .40
146 Frank Thomas 1.00
147 Eric Munson .15
148 Mike Hampton .25
149 Mike Cameron .15
150 Jim Thome .25
151 Mike Mussina .40
152 Rick Helling .15
153 Ken Caminiti .15
154 John Vander Wal .15
155 Denny Neagle .15
156 Robb Nen .15
157 Jose Canseco .50
158 Mo Vaughn .25
159 Phil Nevin .15
160 Pat Hentgen .15
161 Sean Casey .25
162 Greg Vaughn .15
163 Trot Nixon .15
164 Roberto Hernandez .15
165 Vinny Castilla .15
166 Robin Ventura .15
167 Alex Ochoa .15
168 Orlando Hernandez .15
169 Luis Castillo .15
170 Quilvio Veras .15
171 Troy O'Leary .15
172 Livan Hernandez .15
173 Roger Cedeno .15
174 Jose Vidro .15
175 John Olerud .25
176 Richard Hidalgo .25
177 Eric Chavez .25
178 Fernando Vina .15
179 Chris Stynes .15
180 Bobby Higginson .15
181 Bruce Chen .15
182 Omar Vizquel .25
183 Rey Ordonez .15
184 Trevor Hoffman .15
185 Jeff Cirillo .15
186 Billy Wagner .15
187 David Ortiz .15
188 Tim Hudson .25
189 Tony Clark .15
190 Larry Walker .30
191 Eric Owens .15
192 Aubrey Huff .15
193 Royce Clayton .15
194 Todd Walker .15
195 Rafael Palmeiro .40
196 Todd Hundley .15
197 Roger Clemens 1.00
198 Jeff Weaver .15
199 Dean Palmer .15
200 Geoff Jenkins .25
201 Matt Clement .15
202 David Wells .15
203 Chan Ho Park .15
204 Hideo Nomo .40
205 Bartolo Colon .15
206 John Wetteland .15
207 Corey Patterson .25
208 Freddy Garcia .15
209 David Cone .15
210 Rondell White .15
211 Carl Pavano .15
212 Charles Johnson .15
213 Ron Coomer .15
214 Matt Williams .25
215 Jay Payton .15
216 Nick Johnson .15
217 Deivi Cruz .15
218 Scott Elarton .15
219 Neifi Perez .15
220 Jason Isringhausen .15
221 Jose Cruz .15
222 Gerald Williams .15
223 Timo Perez .15
224 Damion Easley .15
225 Jeff D'Amico (photo actually Jamey Wright) .15
226 Preston Wilson .15
227 Robert Person .15
228 Jacque Jones .15
229 Johnny Damon .15
230 Tony Womack .15
231 Adam Piatt .15
232 Brian Jordan .15
233 Ben Davis .15
234 Kerry Wood .25
235 Mike Piazza 2.00
236 David Justice .40
237 Dave Veres .15
238 Eric Young .15
239 Juan Pierre .15
240 Gabe Kapler .25
241 Ryan Dempster .15
242 Dmitri Young .15
243 Jorge Posada .25
244 Eric Karros .25
245 J.D. Drew .25
246 Todd Zeile .15
247 Mark Quinn .15
248 Kenny Kelly .15
249 Jermaine Dye .15
250 Barry Zito .25
251 Jason Hart, Larry Barnes 6.00
252 *Ichiro Suzuki, Elpidio Guzman* 35.00
253 *Tsuyoshi Shinjo*, Brian Cole 6.00
254 John Barnes, *Adrian Hernandez* 5.00
255 Jason Tyner, Jace Brewer 3.00
256 Brian Buchanan, Luis Rivas 3.00
257 Brent Abernathy, Jose Ortiz 3.00
258 Marcus Giles, Keith Ginter 3.00
259 Tike Redman *Jaisen Randolph* 3.00
260 Dane Sardinha, David Espinosa 3.00
261 Josh Beckett, Craig House 3.00
262 Jack Cust, Hiram Bocachica 3.00
263 Alex Escobar, *Esix Snead* 3.00
264 Chris Richard, Vernon Wells 3.00
265 Pedro Feliz, Xavier Nady 4.00
266 Brandon Inge, Joe Crede 3.00
267 Ben Sheets, Roy Oswalt 6.00
268 *Drew Henson, Andy Morales* 12.00
269 C.C. Sabathia, Justin Miller 3.00
270 David Eckstein, Jason Gabrowski 3.00
271 Dee Brown, Chris Wakeland 3.00
272 *Junior Spivey*, Alex Cintron 3.00
273 Elvis Pena, *Juan Uribe* 4.00
274 Carlos Pena, Jason Romano 3.00
275 *Winston Abreu, Wilson Betemit* 4.00
276 *Jose Mieses*, Nick Neugebauer 4.00
277 Shea Hillenbrand, Dernell Stenson 3.00
278 Jared Sandberg, Toby Hall 3.00
279 *Jay Gibbons*, Ivanon Coffie 5.00
280 Pablo Ozuna, Santiago Perez 3.00
281 Nomar Garciaparra (All-Stars) 10.00
282 Derek Jeter (All-Stars) 12.00
283 Jason Giambi (All-Stars) 3.00
284 Magglio Ordonez (All-Stars) 3.00
285 Ivan Rodriguez (All-Stars) 4.00
286 Troy Glaus (All-Stars) 4.00
287 Carlos Delgado (All-Stars) 3.00
288 Darin Erstad (All-Stars) 3.00
289 Bernie Williams (All-Stars) 3.00
290 Roberto Alomar (All-Stars) 3.00
291 Barry Larkin (All-Stars) 3.00
292 Chipper Jones (All-Stars) 8.00
293 Vladimir Guerrero (All-Stars) 5.00
294 Sammy Sosa (All-Stars) 8.00
295 Todd Helton (All-Stars) 4.00
296 Randy Johnson (All-Stars) 4.00
297 Jason Kendall (All-Stars) 3.00
298 Jim Edmonds (All-Stars) 3.00
299 Andruw Jones (All-Stars) 3.00
300 Edgardo Alfonzo (All-Stars) 3.00
301 *Albert Pujols, Donaldo Mendez* 75.00

2001 Fleer Platinum Platinum

MT
Cards (1-250): 5-10X
Production 201 sets
SP's (251-280): 8-20X
SP's (281-300): 5-10X
SP Production 21 sets
(See 2001 Fleer Platinum for checklist and base card values.)

2001 Fleer Platinum Classic Combinations

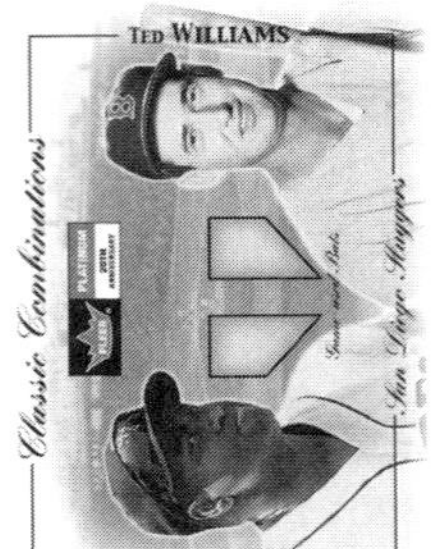

MT
Common Card: 6.00
#1-10 numbered to 250
11-20 numbered to 500
21-30 numbered to 1,000
31-40 numbered to 2,000
1CC Derek Jeter, Alex Rodriguez 40.00
2CC Willie Mays, Willie McCovey 30.00
3CC Lou Gehrig, Babe Ruth 40.00
4CC Mark McGwire, Ken Griffey Jr. 40.00
5CC Johnny Bench, Roy Campanella 20.00
6CC Ted Williams, Nomar Garciaparra 40.00
7CC Yogi Berra, Mike Piazza 30.00
8CC Ernie Banks, Sammy Sosa 25.00
9CC Nolan Ryan, Randy Johnson 50.00
10CC Roberto Clemente, Vladimir Guerrero 30.00
11CC Lou Gehrig, Stan Musial 25.00
12CC Bill Mazeroski, Roberto Clemente 20.00
13CC Ernie Banks, Alex Rodriguez 20.00
14CC Phil Rizzuto, Derek Jeter 25.00
15CC Mike Piazza, Johnny Bench 20.00
16CC Mark McGwire, Sammy Sosa 25.00
17CC Ted Williams, Tony Gwynn 25.00
18CC Eddie Mathews, Mike Schmidt 20.00
19CC Barry Bonds, Willie Mays 20.00
20CC Nolan Ryan, Pedro Martinez 30.00
21CC Barry Bonds, Ken Griffey Jr. 15.00
22CC Willie McCovey, Reggie Jackson 10.00
23CC Roberto Clemente, Sammy Sosa 15.00
24CC Willie Mays, Ernie Banks 15.00
25CC Eddie Mathews, Chipper Jones 12.00
26CC Mike Schmidt, Brooks Robinson 10.00
27CC Stan Musial, Mark McGwire 15.00
28CC Ted Williams, Roger Maris 15.00
29CC Yogi Berra, Roy Campanella 10.00
30CC Johnny Bench, Tony Perez 10.00
31CC Bill Mazeroski, Joe Carter 6.00
32CC Mike Piazza, Roy Campanella 12.00
33CC Ernie Banks, Craig Biggio 8.00
34CC Frank Robinson, Brooks Robinson 8.00
35CC Mike Schmidt, Scott Rolen 8.00
36CC Roger Maris, Mark McGwire 25.00
37CC Stan Musial, Tony Gwynn 8.00
38CC Ted Williams, Bill Terry 12.00
39CC Derek Jeter, Reggie Jackson 15.00
40CC Yogi Berra, Bill Dickey 10.00

A player's name in *italic* type indicates a rookie card.

2001 Fleer Platinum Classic Combinations Memorabilia

		MT
Common Card:		125.00
Production 25 sets		
1	Yogi Berra, Bill Dickey	125.00
2	Yogi Berra, Roy Campanella	175.00
3	Roberto Clemente, Vladimir Guerrero	300.00
4	Eddie Mathews, Chipper Jones	125.00
5	Willie McCovey, Reggie Jackson	150.00
6	Phil Rizzuto, Derek Jeter	300.00
7	Brooks Robinson, Frank Robinson	180.00
8	Brooks Robinson, Mike Schmidt	250.00
9	Mike Schmidt, Scott Rolen	225.00
10	Ted Williams, Bill Terry	600.00
11	Ted Williams, Tony Gwynn	800.00

2001 Fleer Platinum Grandstand Greats

		MT
Complete Set (20):		120.00
Common Player:		2.00
Inserted 1:12		
1GG	Chipper Jones	8.00
2GG	Alex Rodriguez	10.00
3GG	Jeff Bagwell	4.00
4GG	Troy Glaus	4.00
5GG	Manny Ramirez	5.00
6GG	Derek Jeter	12.00
7GG	Tony Gwynn	5.00
8GG	Greg Maddux	8.00
9GG	Nomar Garciaparra	10.00
10GG	Sammy Sosa	8.00
11GG	Mike Piazza	10.00
12GG	Barry Bonds	5.00
13GG	Mark McGwire	12.00
14GG	Vladimir Guerrero	5.00
15GG	Ivan Rodriguez	4.00
16GG	Ken Griffey Jr.	10.00
17GG	Todd Helton	4.00
18GG	Cal Ripken Jr.	12.00
19GG	Pedro Martinez	5.00
20GG	Frank Thomas	5.00

2001 Fleer Platinum Nameplates

	MT
Common Player:	20.00
Inserted 1:12	
Cal Ripken /19	300.00
Cal Ripken /21	300.00
Cal Ripken /23	300.00
Cal Ripken /110	125.00
Randy Johnson/99	60.00
Nolan Ryan/40	275.00
Javy Lopez/49	25.00
Frank Thomas/35	75.00
Frank Thomas/75	50.00
Frank Thomas/80	50.00
Jeffrey Hammonds/135	20.00
Larry Walker/79	35.00
Larry Walker/85	35.00
Dave Winfield/80	50.00
Vladimir Guerrero/80	60.00
Vladimir Guerrero/90	60.00
Kevin Millwood/130	20.00
Mike Mussina/91	60.00
Edgar Martinez/87	90.00
Edgar Martinez/120	70.00
Scott Rolen/65	60.00
Ivan Rodriguez/177	40.00
Manny Ramirez/75	90.00
Manny Ramirez/105	80.00
J.D. Drew/170	50.00
Greg Maddux/180	70.00
Chipper Jones/95	80.00
Carlos Beltran/90	30.00
Adrian Beltre	30.00
Matt Williams/175	30.00
Curt Schilling	30.00
Pedro Martinez/120	100.00
Robin Ventura/99	30.00
Tom Glavine/125	40.00
Tony Gwynn/35	125.00
Tony Gwynn/65	75.00
Tony Gwynn/70	75.00
Troy Glaus/85	70.00
Sean Casey/21	60.00
Darin Erstad/39	60.00
Stan Musial/30	275.00

2001 Fleer Platinum National Patch Time

	MT
Common Player:	8.00
Inserted 1:24 H	
Tony Gwynn	15.00
Manny Ramirez	15.00
Freddy Garcia	8.00
Rondell White	8.00
Ivan Rodriguez	15.00
Brady Anderson	8.00
Adam Piatt	8.00
Carl Everett	8.00
Magglio Ordonez	8.00
Edgardo Alfonzo	8.00
Jason Kendall	8.00
Greg Maddux	20.00
Cal Ripken Jr.	40.00
Fred McGriff	8.00
Pedro Martinez	20.00
Roger Clemens	25.00
Wade Boggs	15.00
George Brett	25.00
Ozzie Smith	20.00
Dave Winfield	15.00
Tom Seaver	20.00
Rollie Fingers	8.00
Mike Schmidt	25.00
Eddie Murray	15.00
Nolan Ryan	50.00
Jeff Cirillo	8.00
Mike Mussina	10.00

2001 Fleer Platinum Rack Pack Autographs

	MT
Common Player:	
Hank Aaron 1997/90	160.00
Lou Brock 1998/15	
Roger Clemens 1998/125	100.00
Jose Cruz Jr. 1997	5.00
J.D. Drew 1999/10	
Steve Garvey 1997/15	
Bob Gibson 1998/300	40.00
Ben Grieve 100	15.00
Tony Gwynn 1998/125	100.00
Wes Helms 1997	5.00
Harmon Killebrew 1998/300	40.00
Paul Konerko 135	5.00
Willie Mays 1997/115	180.00
Willie Mays 1998/120	180.00
Kirby Puckett 1997/105	150.00
Cal Ripken Jr. /5	
Brooks Robinson 1998/40	125.00
Frank Robinson 1998/115	40.00
Scott Rolen 1998/150	40.00
Alex Rodriguez 1997/94	180.00
Alex Rodriguez 1998/150	90.00

2001 Fleer Platinum Tickets

		MT
Complete Set (44):		
Common Player:		
1	George Brett 9/30/92	
2	Rod Carew 8/4/85	
3	Steve Carlton 9/23/83	
4	Chicago White Sox 7/29/66	
5	David Cone 7/18/99	
6	Tony Gwynn 8/5/99	
7	Reggie Jackson 9/17/84	
8	Mark McGwire 9/15/98	
9	Mark McGwire 9/18/98	
10	Mark McGwire 9/20/98	
11	Mark McGwire 9/25/98	
12	Mark McGwire 9/26/98	
13	Mark McGwire 4/5/99	
14	Mark McGwire 9/26/99	
15	Eddie Murray 6/30/95	
16	Eddie Murray 9/6/96	
17	Stan Musial 9/29/63	
18	Cal Ripken Jr. 8/1/94	
19	Cal Ripken Jr.	
20	Cal Ripken Jr. 9/5/96	
21	Cal Ripken Jr. 6/14/96	
22	Cal Ripken Jr. 7/96	
23	Cal Ripken Jr. 6/13/99	
24	Cal Ripken Jr. 4/25/98	
25	Cal Ripken Jr. 9/2/99	
26	Cal Ripken Jr. 4/18/00	
27	Babe Ruth 1926	
28	Nolan Ryan 7/31/90	
29	Nolan Ryan 5/1/91	
30	Tom Seaver 8/4/85	
31	Ozzie Smith	
32	Sammy Sosa 8/21/98	
33	Sammy Sosa 9/2/98	
34	Sammy Sosa 9/13/98	
35	Sammy Sosa 9/23/98	
36	Sammy Sosa 6/3/99	
37	Sammy Sosa 6/26/99	
38	Sammy Sosa 8/4/99	
39	Sammy Sosa 8/9/99	
40	Sammy Sosa 8/26/99	
41	Sammy Sosa 9/6/99	
42	Sammy Sosa 9/9/99	
43	Kerry Wood 5/24/99	
44	World Series 1964	

2001 Fleer Platinum Tickets Autographs

		MT
Complete Set (9):		
Common Player:		
1	George Brett 9/30/92	
2	Rod Carew 8/4/85	
3	Steve Carlton 9/23/83	
4	Bob Gibson 1968	
5	Stan Musial 9/29/63	
6	Cal Ripken Jr. 1991	
7	Cal Ripken Jr. 9/2/99	
8	Mike Schmidt 4/18/87	
9	Mike Schmidt	

2001 Fleer Platinum 20th Anniversary Reprints

		MT
Complete Set (18):		75.00
Common Player:		2.00
Inserted 1:8		
1AR	Cal Ripken Jr.	12.00
2AR	Wade Boggs	3.00
3AR	Ryne Sandberg	4.00
4AR	Tony Gwynn	5.00
5AR	Don Mattingly	10.00

6AR	Roger Clemens	5.00
7AR	Kirby Puckett	5.00
8AR	Jose Canseco	3.00
9AR	Barry Bonds	5.00
10AR	Ken Griffey Jr.	10.00
11AR	Sammy Sosa	8.00
12AR	Ivan Rodriguez	4.00
13AR	Jeff Bagwell	4.00
14AR	J.D. Drew	3.00
15AR	Troy Glaus	4.00
16AR	Rick Ankiel	2.00
17AR	Xavier Nady	2.00
18AR	Jose Ortiz	2.00

2001 Fleer Platinum RC

		MT
Complete Set (300):		
Common Player:		.15
Common (502-601):		1.50
Inserted 1:3 hobby		
Pack (10):		2.50
Box (24):		55.00
302	Shawn Wooten	.15
303	Todd Walker	.15
304	Brian Buchanan	.15
305	Jim Edmonds	.25
306	Jarrod Washburn	.15
307	Jose Rijo	.15
308	Tim Raines	.15
309	Matt Morris	.15
310	Troy Glaus	.50
311	Barry Larkin	.40
312	Javier Vazquez	.15
313	Placido Polanco	.15
314	Darin Erstad	.25
315	Marty Cordova	.15
316	Vladimir Guerrero	.75
317	Kerry Robinson	.15
318	Byung-Hyun Kim	.15
319	C.C. Sabathia	.15
320	Edgardo Alfonzo	.15
321	Jason Tyner	.15
322	Reggie Sanders	.15
323	Roberto Alomar	.60
324	Matt Lawton	.15
325	Brent Abernathy	.15
326	Randy Johnson	.75
327	Todd Helton	.75
328	Andy Pettitte	.40
329	Josh Beckett	.40
330	Mark DeRosa	.15
331	Jose Ortiz	.15
332	Derek Jeter	2.50
333	Toby Hall	.15
334	Wes Helms	.15
335	Jose Macias	.15
336	Bernie Williams	.60
337	Ivan Rodriguez	.75
338	Chipper Jones	1.25
339	Brandon Inge	.15
340	Jason Giambi	.60
341	Frank Catalanotto	.15
342	Andruw Jones	.50
343	*Carlos Hernandez*	.25
344	Jermaine Dye	.15
345	Mike Lamb	.15
346	Ken Caminiti	.15
347	A.J. Burnett	.15
348	Terrence Long	.15
349	Ruben Sierra	.15
350	Marcus Giles	.15
351	Wade Miller	.15
352	Mark Mulder	.15
353	Carlos Delgado	.50
354	Chris Richard	.15
355	Daryle Ward	.15
356	Brad Penny	.15
357	Vernon Wells	.15
358	Jason Johnson	.15
359	Tim Redding	.15
360	Marlon Anderson	.15
361	Carlos Pena	.15
362	Nomar Garciaparra	2.00
363	Roy Oswalt	.40
364	Todd Ritchie	.15
365	Jose Mesa	.15
366	Shea Hillenbrand	.15
367	Dee Brown	.15
368	Jason Kendall	.15
369	Vinny Castilla	.15
370	Fred McGriff	.25
371	Neifi Perez	.15
372	Xavier Nady	.15
373	Abraham Nunez	.15
374	Jon Lieber	.15
375	Paul LoDuca	.15
376	Bubba Trammell	.15
377	Brady Clark	.15
378	Joel Pineiro	.15
379	Mark Grudzielanek	.15
380	D'Angelo Jimenez	.15
381	Junior Herndon	.15
382	Magglio Ordonez	.15
383	Ben Sheets	.25
384	John Vander Wal	.15
385	Pedro Astacio	.15
386	Jose Canseco	.40
387	Jose Hernandez	.15
388	Eric Davis	.15
389	Sammy Sosa	1.25
390	Mark Buerhle	.15
391	Mark Loretta	.15
392	Andres Galarraga	.25
393	Scott Spiezio	.15
394	Joe Crede	.15
395	Luis Rivas	.15
396	David Bell	.15
397	Einar Diaz	.15
398	Adam Dunn	.75
399	A.J. Pierzynski	.15
400	Jamie Moyer	.15
401	Nick Johnson	.15
402	Freddy Garcia	4.00
403	Hideo Nomo	.50
404	Mark Mudler	.15
405	Steve Sparks	.15
406	Mariano Rivera	.25
407	Mark Buerhle, Mike Mussina	.25
408	Randy Johnson	.40
409	Randy Johnson	.40
410	Curt Schilling, Matt Morris	.20
411	Greg Maddux	.60
412	Robb Nen	.15
413	Randy Johnson	.40
414	Barry Bonds	.75
415	Jason Giambi	.30
416	Ichiro Suzuki	3.00
417	Ichiro Suzuki	3.00
418	Alex Rodriguez	1.00
419	Bret Boone	.15
420	Ichiro Suzuki	3.00
421	Alex Rodriguez	1.00
422	Jason Giambi	.30
423	Alex Rodriguez	1.00
424	Larry Walker	.20
425	Rich Aurilia	.15
426	Barry Bonds	.75
427	Sammy Sosa	.75
428	Jimmy Rollins, Juan Pierre	.15
429	Sammy Sosa	.75
430	Lance Berkman	.15
431	Sammy Sosa	.75
432	Carlos Delgado	.25
433	Alex Rodriguez	1.00
434	Greg Vaughn	.15
435	Albert Pujols	2.00
436	Ichiro Suzuki	3.00
437	Barry Bonds	.75
438	Phil Nevin	.15
439	Brian Giles	.15
440	Bobby Abreu	.15
441	Jason Giambi	.30
442	Derek Jeter	1.25
443	Mike Piazza	1.00
444	Vladimir Guerrero	.40
445	Corey Koskie	.15
446	Richie Sexson	.15
447	Shawn Green	.20
448	Mike Sweeney	.15
449	Jeff Bagwell	.40
450	Cliff Floyd	.15
451	Roger Cedeno	.15
452	Todd Helton	.40
453	Juan Gonzalez	.30
454	Sean Casey	.15
455	Magglio Ordonez	.15
456	Sammy Sosa	.75
457	Manny Ramirez	.40
458	Jeff Conine	.15
459	Chipper Jones	.60
460	Luis Gonzalez	.25
461	Troy Glaus	.25
462	Ivan Rodriguez	.40
463	Luis Gonzalez, Jack Cust	.25
464	Jim Thome, C.C. Sabathia	.20
465	Jason Hart, Jason Giambi	.20
466	Jeff Bagwell, Roy Oswalt	.30
467	Sammy Sosa, Corey Patterson	.50
468	Mike Piazza, Alex Escobar	.75
469	Ken Griffey Jr., Adam Dunn	.75
470	Roger Clemens, Nick Johnson	.50
471	Cliff Floyd, Josh Beckett	.15
472	Cal Ripken Jr., Jerry Hairston Jr.	.75
473	Phil Nevin, Xavier Nady	.15
474	Scott Rolen, Jimmy Rollins	.20
475	Barry Larkin, David Espinosa	.20
476	Larry Walker, Jose Ortiz	.15
477	Chipper Jones, Marcus Giles	.40
478	Craig Biggio, Keith Ginter	.15
479	Magglio Ordonez, Aaron Rowand	.15
480	Alex Rodriguez, Carlos Pena	.75
481	Derek Jeter, Alfonso Soriano	.75
482	Curt Schilling (Post Season Glory)	.20
483	(Post Season Glory)	.25
484	(Post Season Glory)	.25
485	(Post Season Glory)	.25
486	(Post Season Glory)	.25
487	(Post Season Glory)	.25
488	(Post Season Glory)	.25
489	Rudolph Giuliani (Post Season Glory)	.50
490	George Bush (Post Season Glory)	.75
491	(Post Season Glory)	.25
492	(Post Season Glory)	.25
493	(Post Season Glory)	.25
494	Derek Jeter (Post Season Glory)	.75
495	(Post Season Glory)	.25
496	(Post Season Glory)	.25
497	(Post Season Glory)	.25
498	(Post Season Glory)	.25
499	(Post Season Glory)	.25
500	(Post Season Glory)	.25
501	(Post Season Glory)	.25
502	*Josh Fogg*	1.50
503	Elpidio Guzman	1.50
504	*Corky Miller*	2.00
505	*Cesar Crespo*	1.50
506	*Carlos Garcia*	2.00
507	*Carlos Valderrama*	1.50
508	*Joe Kennedy*	2.00
509	*Henry Mateo*	1.50
510	*Brandon Duckworth*	3.00
511	Ichiro Suzuki	12.00
512	*Zach Day*	1.50
513	*Ryan Freel*	1.50
514	*Brian Lawrence*	1.50
515	*Alexis Gomez*	1.50
516	*Will Ohman*	1.50
517	*Juan Diaz*	1.50
518	*Juan Moreno*	1.50
519	*Rob Mackowiak*	1.50
520	*Horacio Ramirez*	1.50
521	Albert Pujols	10.00
522	Tsuyoshi Shinjo	5.00
523	*Ryan Drese*	1.50
524	*Angel Berroa*	1.50
525	*Josh Towers*	2.00
526	Junior Spivey	1.50
527	*Greg Miller*	1.50
528	*Esix Snead*	1.50
529	*Mark Prior*	6.00
530	Drew Henson	6.00
531	*Brian Reith*	1.50
532	*Andres Torres*	1.50
533	*Casey Fossum*	1.50
534	*Wilmy Caceres*	1.50
535	*Matt White*	1.50
536	*Wilkin Ruan*	1.50
537	*Rick Bauer*	1.50
538	*Morgan Ensberg*	1.50
539	*Geronimo Gil*	1.50
540	*Dewon Brazelton*	3.00
541	*Johnny Estrada*	1.50
542	*Claudio Vargas*	1.50
543	*Donaldo Mendez*	1.50
544	*Kyle Lohse*	2.00
545	*Nate Frese*	1.50
546	*Christian Parker*	1.50
547	*Blaine Neal*	1.50
548	*Travis Hafner*	1.50
549	*Billy Sylvester*	1.50
550	Adam Pettyjohn	1.50
551	Bill Ortega	1.50
552	*Jose Acevedo*	1.50
553	*Steve Green*	1.50
554	*Jay Gibbons*	2.00
555	*Bert Snow*	1.50
556	*Erick Almonte*	1.50
557	*Jeremy Owens*	1.50
558	*Sean Douglass*	1.50
559	*Jason Smith*	1.50
560	*Ricardo Rodriguez*	1.50
561	*Mark Teixeira*	7.00
562	*Tyler Walker*	1.50
563	*Juan Uribe*	1.50
564	*Bud Smith*	5.00
565	*Angel Santos*	1.50
566	*Brandon Lyon*	2.00
567	*Eric Hinske*	2.50
568	*Nick Punto*	1.50
569	*Winston Abreu*	1.50
570	*Jason Phillips*	1.50
571	*Rafael Soriano*	1.50
572	Wilson Betemit	3.00
573	*Endy Chavez*	1.50
574	*Juan Cruz*	4.00
575	*Cory Aldridge*	1.50
576	Adrian Hernandez	1.50
577	*Brandon Larson*	1.50
578	*Bret Prinz*	1.50
579	*Jackson Melian*	1.50
580	*Dave Maurer*	1.50
581	*Jason Michaels*	1.50
582	*Travis Phelps*	1.50
583	*Cody Ransom*	1.50
584	*Benito Baez*	1.50
585	*Brian Roberts*	1.50
586	*Nate Teut*	2.00
587	*Jack Wilson*	2.00
588	*Willie Harris*	1.50
589	*Martin Vargas*	1.50
590	*Steve Torrealba*	1.50
591	*Stubby Clapp*	1.50
592	*Danny Wright*	1.50
593	*Mike Rivera*	1.50
594	*Luis Pineda*	1.50
595	*Lance Davis*	1.50
596	*Ramon Vazquez*	2.50
597	*Dustan Mohr*	1.50
598	*Troy Mattes*	1.50
599	*Grant Balfour*	1.50
600	*Jared Fernandez*	1.50
601	*Jorge Julio*	2.00
E-X		
131	Albert Pujols/499	75.00
132	Bud Smith/499	40.00
133	Tsuyoshi Shinjo/499	25.00
134	Wilson Betemit/499	25.00
135	Adrian Hernandez/499	10.00
136	Jackson Melian/499	10.00
137	Jay Gibbons/499	15.00
138	Johnny Estrada/499	10.00
139	Morgan Ensberg/499	10.00
140	Drew Henson/499	45.00
Focus		
241	Tsuyoshi Shinjo/999	12.00
242	Wilson Betemit/999	15.00
243	Jeremy Owens/999	8.00

244 Drew Henson/999 20.00
245 Albert Pujols/999 30.00
246 Travis Hafner/999 8.00
247 Ichiro Suzuki/999 50.00
248 Elpidio Guzman/ 999 8.00
249 Matt White/999 8.00
250 Junior Spivey/ 999 8.00

Futures
221 Drew Henson/ 2499 10.00
222 Johnny Estrada/ 2499 3.00
223 Elpidio Guzman/ 2499 3.00
224 Albert Pujols/2499 15.00
225 Wilson Betemit/ 2499 8.00
226 Mark Teixeira/ 2499 12.00
227 Tsuyoshi Shinjo/ 2499 6.00
228 Matt White/2499 3.00
229 Adrian Hernandez/ 2499 3.00
230 Ichiro Suzuki/2499 20.00

Triple Crown
301 Elpidio Guzman/ 2999 4.00
302 Drew Henson/ 2999 10.00
303 Bud Smith/2999 8.00
304 Carlos Valderrama/ 2999 4.00
305 Tsuyoshi Shinjo/ 2999 8.00
306 Ichiro Suzuki/2999 20.00
307 Jackson Melian/ 2999 4.00
308 Morgan Ensberg/ 2999 4.00
309 Albert Pujols/2999 15.00
310 Johnny Estrada/ 2999 4.00

Ultra
276 Junior Spivey, Juan Uribe 6.00
277 Albert Pujols, Bud Smith 30.00
278 Ichiro Suzuki, Tsuyoshi Shinjo 30.00
279 Drew Henson, Jackson Melian 15.00
280 Matt White, Adrian Hernandez 6.00

2001 Fleer Platinum RC Platinum

MT
Cards (302-501): 5-10X
Production 201
SPs (502-601):
Production 21 not priced
(See 2001 Fleer Platinum RC for checklist and base card values.)

2001 Fleer Platinum RC Lumberjacks

MT
Common Player: 6.00
Inserted 1:1 Rack pack
Barry Bonds 20.00
Cal Ripken Jr.
Derek Jeter 40.00
Luis Gonzalez 12.00
Mike Sweeney 6.00
Albert Pujols 30.00
Tony Gwynn 15.00
Adam Dunn 20.00
J.D. Drew
Brian Giles 6.00
Adrian Beltre 6.00
Bret Boone 6.00
Chipper Jones 15.00
Cliff Floyd 6.00
Darin Erstad 8.00
Gary Sheffield 6.00
Manny Ramirez 12.00
Mike Piazza 20.00
Todd Helton 12.00
Ivan Rodriguez 12.00
Lance Berkman 6.00
Vladimir Guerrero 10.00
Drew Henson 25.00
Cristian Guzman 6.00
Roberto Alomar 10.00
Moises Alou 6.00
Larry Walker 6.00

2001 Fleer Platinum RC National Patch Time

MT
Common Player: 8.00
Inserted 1:24 H
Edgardo Alfonzo 8.00
Brady Anderson 8.00
Adrian Beltre 8.00
Barry Bonds 25.00
Jeromy Burnitz 8.00
Eric Chavez 8.00
Roger Clemens 25.00
J.D. Drew 15.00
Darin Erstad 10.00
Carl Everett 8.00
Freddy Garcia 8.00
Jason Giambi 20.00
Juan Gonzalez 15.00
Mark Grace 15.00
Shawn Green 8.00
Ben Grieve 8.00
Vladimir Guerrero 12.00
Tony Gwynn 15.00
Randy Johnson 15.00
Chipper Jones 20.00
David Justice 8.00
Jeff Kent 8.00
Greg Maddux 20.00
Fred McGriff 8.00
John Olerud 10.00
Magglio Ordonez 8.00
Jorge Posada 10.00
Cal Ripken Jr. 50.00
Mariano Rivera 12.00
Ivan Rodriguez 12.00
Scott Rolen 10.00
Kazuhiro Sasaki 15.00
Aaron Sele 8.00
Gary Sheffield 8.00
John Smoltz 8.00
Frank Thomas 15.00
Mo Vaughn 8.00
Robin Ventura 8.00
Bernie Williams 12.00
Carlos Delgado 10.00
Chan Ho Park 10.00
Todd Helton 15.00
Craig Biggio 8.00
Jeff Bagwell 15.00
Paul LoDuca 8.00

2001 Fleer Platinum RC Prime Numbers

MT
Common Player: 20.00
Inserted 1:12 Jumbo pack
1PN Jeff Bagwell 40.00
2PN Cal Ripken Jr. 120.00
3PN Barry Bonds 60.00
4PN Todd Helton 25.00
5PN Derek Jeter 80.00
6PN Tony Gwynn 50.00
7PN Kazuhiro Sasaki 40.00
8PN Chan Ho Park 40.00
9PN Sean Casey 40.00
10PNChipper Jones 40.00
11PNPedro Martinez 35.00
12PNMike Piazza 65.00
13PNCarlos Delgado 25.00
14PNCraig Biggio 20.00
15PNRoger Clemens 50.00

2001 Fleer Platinum RC Winning Combinations

MT
Common Card: 5.00
Varying quantities produced
1WC Derek Jeter, Ozzie Smith/2000 15.00
2WC Barry Bonds,Mark McGwire/500 25.00
3WC Ichiro Suzuki, Albert Pujols/250 50.00
4WC Ted Williams, Manny Ramirez/1000 15.00
5WC Tony Gwynn, Cal Ripken/250 35.00
6WC Mike Piazza, Derek Jeter/500 25.00
7WC Dave Winfield, Tony Gwynn/2000 5.00
8WC Hideo Nomo, Ichiro Suzuki/2000 15.00
9WC Cal Ripken, Ozzie Smith/1000 20.00
10WCMark McGwire, Albert Pujols/2000 15.00
11WCJeff Bagwell, Craig Biggio/1000 5.00
12WCBobby Bonds, Barry Bonds/250 15.00
13WCTed Williams, Stan Musial/250 25.00
14WCBabe Ruth, Reggie Jackson/500 25.00
15WCKazuhiro Sasaki, Ichiro Suzuki/500 25.00
16WCNolan Ryan, Roger Clemens/500 20.00
17WCRoger Clemens, Derek Jeter/250 30.00
18WCIvan Rodriguez, Mike Piazza/1000 8.00
19WCVladimir Guerrero, Sammy Sosa/2000 8.00
20WCBarry Bonds, Sammy Sosa/250 20.00
21WCRoger Clemens, Greg Maddux/1000 10.00
22WCJuan Gonzalez, Manny Ramirez/2000 5.00
23WCTodd Helton, Jason Giambi/2000 5.00
24WCJeff Bagwell, Lance Berkman/2000 5.00
25WCMike Sweeney, George Brett/1000 8.00
26WCLuis Gonzalez, Babe Ruth/2000 15.00
27WCBill Skowron, Don Mattingly/250 25.00
28WCYogi Berra, Cal Ripken/2000 10.00
29WCPedro Martinez, Nomar Garciaparra/500 12.00
30WCTed Kluszewski, Frank Robinson/1000 5.00
31WCCurt Schilling, Randy Johnson/1000 6.00
32WCKen Griffey Jr., Cal Ripken/500 10.00
33WCMike Piazza, Johnny Bench/1000 10.00
34WCStan Musial, Albert Pujols/500 20.00
35WCJackie Robinson, Nellie Fox/500 15.00
36WCLefty Grove, Steve Carlton/250 10.00
37WCTy Cobb, Tony Gwynn/250 15.00
38WCAlbert Pujols, Frank Robinson/1000 15.00
39WCRyne Sandberg, Sammy Sosa/500 15.00
40WCCal Ripken Jr., Lou Gehrig/250 50.00

2001 Fleer Premium

MT
Complete Set (235): NA
Common Player: .20
Common SP (201-230): 8.00
Production 1,999
Cards 231-235 are redemptions
Hobby Pack (8): 4.00
Hobby Box (24): 90.00
1 Cal Ripken Jr. 3.00
2 Derek Jeter 3.00
3 Edgardo Alfonzo .30
4 Luis Castillo .20
5 Mike Lieberthal .20
6 Kazuhiro Sasaki .20
7 Jeff Kent .30
8 Eric Karros .20
9 Tom Glavine .40
10 Jeremy Burnitz .20
11 Travis Fryman .30
12 Ron Coomer .20
13 Jeff D'Amico .20
14 Carlos Febles .20
15 Kevin Brown .30
16 Deivi Cruz .20
17 Tino Martinez .30
18 Bobby Abreu .20
19 Roger Clemens 1.50
20 Jeffrey Hammonds .20

21 Peter Bergeron .20
22 Ray Lankford .20
23 Scott Rolen .50
24 Jermaine Dye .20
25 Rusty Greer .20
26 Frank Thomas 1.25
27 Jeff Bagwell 1.00
28 Cliff Floyd .20
29 Chris Singleton .20
30 Steve Finley .20
31 Orlando Hernandez .30
32 Tom Goodwin .20
33 Larry Walker .30
34 Mike Sweeney .20
35 Tim Hudson .40
36 Kerry Wood .40
37 Mike Lowell .20
38 Andruw Jones .75
39 Alex S. Gonzalez .20
40 Juan Gonzalez 1.00
41 J.D. Drew .40
42 Mark McLemore .20
43 Royce Clayton .20
44 Paul O'Neill .40
45 Carlos Beltran .30
46 Phil Nevin .20
47 Rondell White .30
48 Gerald Williams .20
49 Geoff Jenkins .40
50 Marvin Benard .20
51 Alex Rodriguez 2.50
52 Moises Alou .20
53 Mike Lansing .20
54 Omar Vizquel .30
55 Eric Chavez .40
56 Mark Quinn .20
57 Mike Lamb .20
58 Rick Ankiel .25
59 Lance Berkman .20
60 Jeff Conine .20
61 B.J. Surhoff .20
62 Todd Helton 1.00
63 J.T. Snow .20
64 John Vander Wal .20
65 Johnny Damon .20
66 Bobby Higginson .20
67 Carlos Delgado .75
68 Shawn Green .30
69 Mike Redmond .20
70 Mike Piazza 2.50
71 Adrian Beltre .30
72 Juan Encarnacion .20
73 Chipper Jones 2.00
74 Garret Anderson .20
75 Paul Konerko .20
76 Barry Larkin .40
77 Tony Gwynn 1.25
78 Rafael Palmeiro .75
79 Randy Johnson 1.00
80 Mark Grace .40
81 Javy Lopez .20
82 Gabe Kapler .30
83 Henry Rodriguez .20
84 Raul Mondesi .30
85 Adam Piatt .20
86 Marquis Grissom .20
87 Charles Johnson .20
88 Sean Casey .30
89 Manny Ramirez 1.00
90 Curt Schilling .30
91 Fernando Tatis .20
92 Derek Bell .20
93 Tony Clark .20
94 Homer Bush .20
95 Nomar Garciaparra 2.50
96 Vinny Castilla .20
97 Ben Davis .20
98 Carl Everett .20
99 Damion Easley .20
100 Craig Biggio .30
101 Todd Hollandsworth .20
102 Jay Payton .20
103 Gary Sheffield .40
104 Sandy Alomar Jr. .20
105 Doug Glanville .20
106 Barry Bonds 1.25
107 Tim Salmon .30
108 Terrence Long .20
109 Jorge Posada .30
110 Jose Offerman .20
111 Edgar Martinez .20
112 Jeremy Giambi .20
113 Dean Palmer .20
114 Roberto Alomar .75
115 Aaron Boone .20
116 Adam Kennedy .20
117 Joe Randa .20
118 Jose Vidro .20
119 Tony Batista .20
120 Kevin Young .20
121 Preston Wilson .20
122 Jason Kendall .20
123 Mark Kotsay .20
124 Timoniel Perez .20
125 Eric Young .20
126 Greg Maddux 2.00
127 Richard Hidalgo .40
128 Brian Giles .30
129 Fred McGriff .30
130 Troy Glaus 1.00
131 Todd Walker .20
132 Brady Anderson .20
133 Jim Edmonds .30
134 Ben Grieve .40
135 Greg Vaughn .20
136 Robin Ventura .30
137 Sammy Sosa 2.00
138 Rich Aurilla .20
139 Jose Valentin .20
140 Trot Nixon .20
141 Troy Percival .20
142 Bernie Williams .75
143 Warren Morris .20
144 Jacque Jones .20
145 Danny Bautista .20
146 A.J. Pierzynski .20
147 Mark McGwire 3.00
148 Rafael Furcal .25
149 Ray Durham .20
150 Mike Mussina .60
151 Jay Bell .20
152 David Wells .20
153 Ken Caminiti .20
154 Jim Thome .40
155 Ivan Rodriguez 1.00
156 Milton Bradley .20
157 Ken Griffey Jr. 2.50
158 Al Leiter .30
159 Corey Koskie .20
160 Shannon Stewart .20
161 Mo Vaughn .20
162 Pedro Martinez 1.25
163 Todd Hundley .20
164 Darin Erstad .30
165 Ruben Rivera .20
166 Richie Sexson .20
167 Andres Galarraga .40
168 Darryl Kile .20
169 Jose Cruz Jr. .20
170 David Justice .40
171 Vladimir Guerrero 1.25
172 Jeff Cirillo .20
173 John Olerud .30
174 Devon White .20
175 Ron Belliard .20
176 Pokey Reese .20
177 Mike Hampton .30
178 David Ortiz .20
179 Magglio Ordonez .30
180 Ruben Mateo .20
181 Carlos Lee .20
182 Matt Williams .40
183 Miguel Tejada .30
184 Scott Elarton .20
185 Bret Boone .20
186 Pat Burrell .50
187 Brad Radke .20
188 Brian Jordan .20
189 Matt Lawton .20
190 Al Martin .20
191 Albert Belle .20
192 Tony Womack .20
193 Roger Cedeno .20
194 Travis Lee .20
195 Dmitri Young .20
196 Jay Buhner .20
197 Jason Giambi .50
198 Jason Tyner .20
199 Ben Petrick .20
200 Jose Canseco .50
201 Nick Johnson 10.00
202 Jace Brewer 8.00
203 *Ryan Freel* 10.00
204 *Jaisen Randolph* 8.00
205 Marcus Giles 8.00
206 *Claudio Vargas* 8.00
207 Brian Cole 8.00
208 Scott Hodges 8.00
209 *Winston Abreu* 8.00
210 Shea Hillenbrand 10.00
211 Larry Barnes 8.00
212 *Paul Phillips* 8.00
213 *Pedro Santana* 8.00
214 Ivanon Coffie 8.00
215 *Junior Spivey* 10.00
216 Donzell McDonald 8.00
217 Vernon Wells 8.00
218 Corey Patterson 10.00
219 Sang-Hoon Lee 8.00
220 Jack Cust 8.00
221 Jason Romano 8.00
222 *Jack Wilson* 10.00
223 Adam Everett 8.00
224 *Esix Snead* 10.00
225 Jason Hart 8.00
226 Joe Lawrence 8.00
227 Brandon Inge 8.00
228 Alex Escobar 8.00
229 Abraham Nunez 8.00
230 Jared Sandberg 8.00
231 *Ichiro Suzuki* 90.00
232 *Tsuyoshi Shinjo* 20.00
233 *Albert Pujols* 60.00
234 *Wilson Betemit* 20.00
235 *Drew Henson* 35.00

2001 Fleer Premium Star Ruby

MT
Stars (1-200): 8-15X
SPs (201-230): . 4-.8X
Production 125 sets
(See 2001 Fleer Premium for checklist and base card values.)

2001 Fleer Premium A Time for Heroes

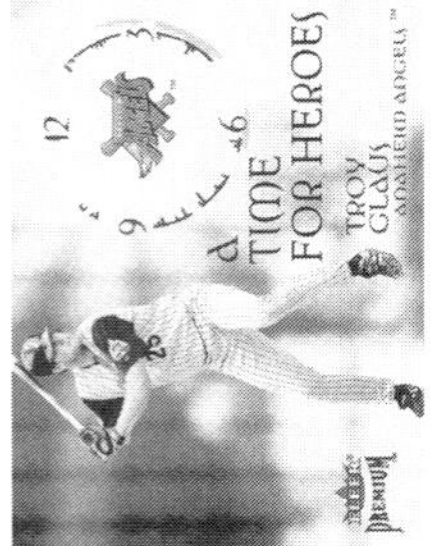

MT
Complete Set (20): 75.00
Common Player: 1.50
Inserted 1:20
1ATFHDarin Erstad 1.50
2ATFHAlex Rodriguez 10.00
3ATFHShawn Green 2.00
4ATFHJeff Bagwell 4.00
5ATFHSammy Sosa 8.00
6ATFHDerek Jeter 12.00
7ATFHNomar Garciaparra 10.00
8ATFHCarlos Delgado 3.00
9ATFHPat Burrell 2.50
10ATFHTony Gwynn 5.00
11ATFHChipper Jones 8.00
12ATFHJason Giambi 2.00
13ATFHMaggio Ordonez 1.50
14ATFHTroy Glaus 4.00
15ATFHIvan Rodriguez 4.00
16ATFHAndruw Jones 3.00
17ATFHVladimir Guerrero 5.00
18ATFHKen Griffey Jr. 10.00
19ATFHJ.D. Drew 1.50
20ATFHTodd Helton 4.00

2001 Fleer Premium A Time for Heroes Memorabilia

MT
Common Player: 25.00
Inserted 1:82
Shawn Green 25.00
Derek Jeter 125.00
Pat Burrell 30.00
Chipper Jones 50.00
Jason Giambi 30.00
Troy Glaus 40.00
Ivan Rodriguez 40.00
Andruw Jones 35.00
J.D. Drew 30.00
Todd Helton 40.00

2001 Fleer Premium Brother Wood

MT
Complete Set (9): 175.00
Common Player: 15.00
Inserted 1:108
1BW Vladimir Guerrero 30.00
2BW Andruw Jones 25.00
3BW Corey Patterson 20.00
4BW Magglio Ordonez 20.00
5BW Jason Giambi 25.00
6BW Rafael Palmeiro 25.00
7BW Eric Chavez 20.00
8BW Pat Burrell 25.00
9BW Adrian Beltre 15.00

2001 Fleer Premium Decades of Excellence

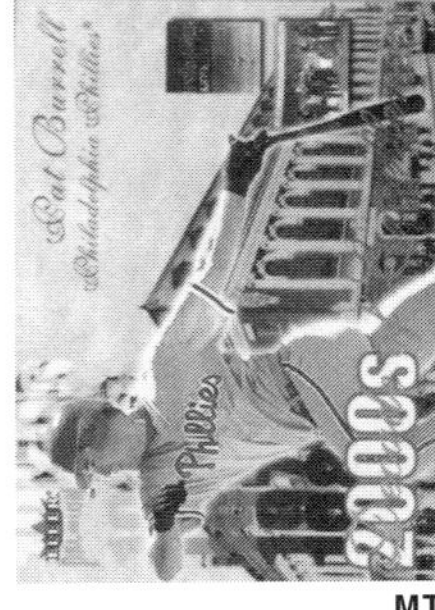

MT
Complete Set (50): 250.00
Common Player: 3.00
Inserted 1:12
Card #17 does not exist
1DOEBabe Ruth, Lou Gehrig 20.00
2DOELloyd Waner 3.00
3DOEJimmie Foxx 5.00
4DOEHank Greenberg 4.00
5DOETed Williams 15.00
6DOEJohnny Mize 4.00

7DOEEnos Slaughter 3.00
8DOEJackie Robinson 12.00
9DOEStan Musial 8.00
10DOEDuke Snider 6.00
11DOEEddie Mathews 6.00
12DOERoy Campanella 5.00
13DOEYogi Berra 8.00
14DOEPee Wee Reese 4.00
15DOEPhil Rizzuto 4.00
16DOEAl Kaline 5.00
18DOEFrank Howard 3.00
19DOERoberto Clemente 15.00
20DOEBob Gibson 5.00
21DOERoger Maris 8.00
22DOEDon Drysdale 5.00
23DOEMaury Wills 3.00
24DOETom Seaver 5.00
25DOEReggie Jackson 8.00
26DOEJohnny Bench 8.00
27DOECarlton Fisk 5.00
28DOERod Carew 4.00
29DOESteve Carlton 3.00
30DOEMike Schmidt 8.00
31DOENolan Ryan 20.00
32DOERickey Henderson 4.00
33DOERoger Clemens 8.00
34DOEDon Mattingly 10.00
35DOEGeorge Brett 10.00
36DOEGreg Maddux 10.00
37DOECal Ripken Jr. 15.00
38DOEChipper Jones 10.00
39DOEBarry Bonds 6.00
40DOEIvan Rodriguez 5.00
41DOESammy Sosa, Mark McGwire 20.00
42DOEKen Griffey Jr. 12.00
43DOETony Gwynn 6.00
44DOEVladimir Guerrero 6.00
45DOEShawn Green 3.00
46DOEAlex Rodriguez, Derek Jeter, Nomar Garciaparra 15.00
47DOEPat Burrell 4.00
48DOERick Ankiel 3.00
49DOEEric Chavez 3.00
50DOETroy Glaus 5.00

2001 Fleer Premium Decades of Excellence Autograph

MT
Common Autograph: 40.00
Production #'s listed
1 Rick Ankiel/99 40.00
2 Johnny Bench/67 160.00
3 Barry Bonds/86 125.00
4 George Brett/73 200.00
5 Rod Carew/67 100.00
6 Steve Carlton/65 100.00
7 Eric Chavez/98 40.00
8 Carlton Fisk/69 125.00
9 Bob Gibson/59 100.00
10 Tony Gwynn/82 100.00
11 Reggie Jackson/67 125.00
12 Chipper Jones/93 100.00
13 Al Kaline/53 175.00
14 Don Mattingly/82 350.00
15 Cal Ripken Jr./82 350.00
16 Nolan Ryan/66 500.00
17 Mike Schmidt/72 325.00
18 Tom Seaver/67 150.00
19 Enos Slaughter/38 75.00
20 Maury Wills/59 40.00

2001 Fleer Premium Decades of Excellence Memorabilia

MT
Common Player: 20.00
Inserted 1:217 H
1 Rick Ankiel/Jrsy 25.00
2 Barry Bonds/Jrsy
3 Pat Burrell/jrsy 30.00
4 Roy Campanella/bat/50 100.00
5 Eric Chavez/bat 20.00
6 Roberto Clemente/bat/50 200.00
7 Carlton Fisk/uni. 50.00
8 Jimmie Foxx/bat/50 200.00
9 Shawn Green/bat 20.00
10 Tony Gwynn/jrsy 60.00
11 Reggie Jackson/jrsy 75.00
12 Greg Maddux/jrsy 75.00
13 Roger Maris/uni.
14 Pee Wee Reese/jrsy
15 Cal Ripken /jrsy/50
16 Ivan Rodriguez/bat
17 Nolan Ryan/jrsy
18 Mike Schmidt/jrsy
19 Tom Seaver/jrsy
20 Duke Snider/bat 75.00
21 Ted Williams/jrsy/50 650.00

2001 Fleer Premium Derek Jeter Monumental Moments

MT
Numbered to 1,995
Autograph numbered to 95
DJMMDerek Jeter 20.00
DJMMDerek Jeter Auto./95 300.00

2001 Fleer Premium Diamond Dominators

MT
Common Player: 20.00
Inserted 1:51
1DD Troy Glaus 40.00
2DD Darin Erstad 25.00
3DD J.D. Drew 30.00
4DD Barry Bonds 60.00
5DD Roger Clemens 50.00
6DD Vladimir Guerrero 40.00
7DD Tony Gwynn 40.00
8DD Greg Maddux 50.00
9DD Cal Ripken Jr. 75.00
10DDIvan Rodriguez 30.00
11DDFrank Thomas 40.00
12DDBernie Williams 25.00
13DDJeremy Burnitz 20.00
14DDJuan Gonzalez 35.00

2001 Fleer Premium Diamond Dominators Patches

MT
Common Player: 20.00
Production 100 sets
1DD Troy Glaus 120.00
2DD Darin Erstad 80.00
3DD J.D. Drew 100.00
4DD Barry Bonds 150.00
5DD Roger Clemens 150.00
6DD Vladimir Guerrero 125.00
7DD Tony Gwynn 125.00
8DD Greg Maddux 150.00
9DD Cal Ripken Jr. 200.00
10DDIvan Rodriguez 125.00
11DDFrank Thomas 150.00
12DDBernie Williams 125.00
13DDJeremy Burnitz 50.00
14DDJuan Gonzalez 150.00

2001 Fleer Premium Grip It and Rip It

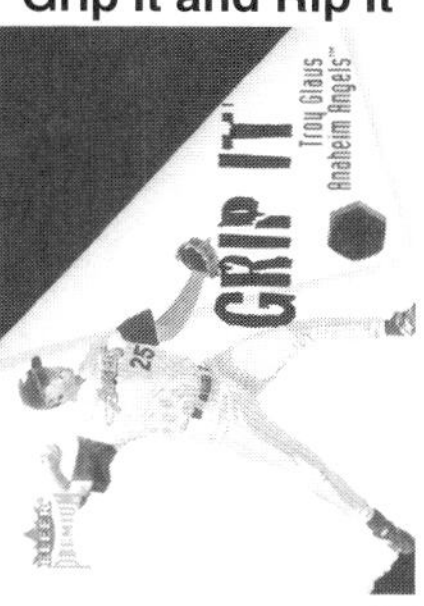

MT
Complete Set (15): 20.00
Common Player: .50
Inserted 1:6
1GRPRoger Clemens, Derek Jeter 4.00
2GRPScott Rolen, Pat Burrell .75
3GRPGreg Maddux, Andruw Jones 2.50
4GRPShannon Stewart, Carlos Delgado 1.00
5GRPShawn Estes, Barry Bonds 1.50
6GRPCal Eldred, Frank Thomas 1.50
7GRPMark McGwire, Jim Edmonds 4.00
8GRPJose Vidro, Vladimir Guerrero 1.50
9GRPPedro Martinez, Nomar Garciaparra 3.00
10GRPTom Glavine, Chipper Jones 2.50
11GRPKen Griffey Jr., Sean Casey 3.00
12GRPJeff Bagwell, Moises Alou 1.25
13GRPTroy Glaus, Darin Erstad 1.25
14GRPMike Piazza, Robin Ventura 3.00
15GRPEric Chavez, Jason Giambi .50

2001 Fleer Premium Grip It and Rip It Plus

MT
Common Card: .50
200 Base/Bat Produced
100 Ball/Bat Produced
1GRPRoger Clemens, Derek Jeter/100 180.00
2GRPScott Rolen, Pat Burrell/200 40.00
3GRPGreg Maddux, Andruw Jones/100 125.00
4GRPShannon Stewart, Carlos Delgado/200 40.00
5GRPShawn Estes, Barry Bonds/100 80.00
6GRPCal Eldred, Frank Thomas/200 40.00
7GRPMark McGwire, Jim Edmonds/100 180.00
8GRPJose Vidro, Vladimir Guerrero/200 40.00
9GRPPedro Martinez, Nomar Garciaparra/100 150.00
10GRPTom Glavine, Chipper Jones/200 50.00
11GRPKen Griffey Jr., Sean Casey/200 90.00
12GRPJeff Bagwell, Moises Alou/200 50.00
13GRPTroy Glaus, Darin Erstad/200 50.00
14GRPMike Piazza, Robin Ventura/100 120.00
15GRPEric Chavez, Jason Giambi/200 35.00

2001 Fleer Premium Home Field Advantage

MT
Complete Set (15): 150.00
Common Player: 3.00
Inserted 1:72
1HFAMike Piazza 15.00
2HFADerek Jeter 20.00
3HFAKen Griffey Jr. 15.00
4HFACarlos Delgado 5.00
5HFAChipper Jones 12.00
6HFAAlex Rodriguez 15.00
7HFASammy Sosa 12.00
8HFAScott Rolen 4.00
9HFANomar Garciaparra 15.00
10HFATodd Helton 6.00
11HFAVladimir Guerrero 8.00
12HFAJeff Bagwell 6.00
13HFABarry Bonds 8.00
14HFACal Ripken Jr. 20.00
15HFAMark McGwire 20.00

2001 Fleer Premium Home Field Advantage Game Wall

MT
Common Player: 20.00
Production 100 sets
1HFAMike Piazza 60.00
2HFADerek Jeter 120.00
3HFAKen Griffey Jr. 80.00
4HFACarlos Delgado 20.00
5HFAChipper Jones 40.00
6HFAAlex Rodriguez 60.00
7HFASammy Sosa 40.00
8HFAScott Rolen 20.00
9HFANomar Garciaparra 60.00
10HFATodd Helton 40.00
11HFAVladimir Guerrero 40.00
12HFAJeff Bagwell 40.00
13HFABarry Bonds 40.00
14HFACal Ripken Jr. 150.00
15HFAMark McGwire 150.00

A card number in parentheses ( ) indicates the set is unnumbered.

2001 Fleer Premium Solid Performers

MT
Complete Set (15): 75.00
Common Player: 2.00
Inserted 1:20
1SP Mark McGwire 10.00
2SP Alex Rodriguez 8.00
3SP Nomar Garciaparra 8.00
4SP Derek Jeter 10.00
5SP Vladimir Guerrero 4.00
6SP Todd Helton 3.00
7SP Chipper Jones 6.00
8SP Mike Piazza 8.00
9SP Ivan Rodriguez 3.00
10SP Tony Gwynn 4.00
11SP Cal Ripken Jr. 10.00
12SP Barry Bonds 4.00
13SP Jeff Bagwell 3.00
14SP Ken Griffey Jr. 8.00
15SP Sammy Sosa 6.00

2001 Fleer Premium Solid Performers Game Base

MT
Common Player: 2.00
Production 150 sets
1SP Mark McGwire 100.00
2SP Alex Rodriguez 70.00
3SP Nomar Garciaparra 70.00
4SP Derek Jeter 90.00
5SP Vladimir Guerrero 40.00
6SP Todd Helton 40.00
7SP Chipper Jones 50.00
8SP Mike Piazza 70.00
9SP Ivan Rodriguez 30.00
10SP Tony Gwynn 40.00
11SP Cal Ripken Jr. 100.00
12SP Barry Bonds 40.00
13SP Jeff Bagwell 40.00
14SP Ken Griffey Jr. 75.00
15SP Sammy Sosa 50.00

2001 Fleer Showcase

MT
Complete Set (160): NA
Common Player: .25
Common SP (116-125): 15.00
Production 500
Common SP (126-145): 6.00
Production 1,500
Common SP (146-160): 6.00
Production 2,000
Pack (5): 4.75
Box (24): 100.00
1 Tony Gwynn 1.50
2 Barry Larkin .50
3 Chan Ho Park .25
4 Darin Erstad .50
5 Rafael Furcal .40
6 Roger Cedeno .25
7 Timo Perez .25
8 Rick Ankiel .40
9 Pokey Reese .25
10 Jeromy Burnitz .25
11 Phil Nevin .25
12 Matt Williams .40
13 Mike Hampton .25
14 Fernando Tatis .25
15 Kazuhiro Sasaki .40
16 Jim Thome .50
17 Geoff Jenkins .40
18 Jeff Kent .25
19 Tom Glavine .40
20 Dean Palmer .25
21 Todd Zeile .25
22 Edgar Renteria .25
23 Andruw Jones .75
24 Juan Encarnacion .25
25 Robin Ventura .25
26 J.D. Drew .50
27 Ray Durham .25
28 Richard Hidalgo .25
29 Eric Chavez .40
30 Rafael Palmeiro .75
31 Steve Finley .25
32 Jeff Weaver .25
33 Al Leiter .40
34 Jim Edmonds .40
35 Garret Anderson .25
36 Larry Walker .50
37 Jose Vidro .25
38 Mike Cameron .25
39 Brady Anderson .25
40 Mike Lowell .25
41 Bernie Williams .75
42 Gary Sheffield .40
43 John Smoltz .25
44 Mike Mussina .50
45 Greg Vaughn .25
46 Juan Gonzalez 1.00
47 Matt Lawton .25
48 Robb Nen .25
49 Brad Radke .25
50 Edgar Martinez .25
51 Mike Bordick .25
52 Shawn Green .25
53 Carl Everett .25
54 Adrian Beltre .40
55 Kerry Wood .40
56 Kevin Brown .25
57 Brian Giles .40
58 Greg Maddux 2.00
59 Preston Wilson .25
60 Orlando Hernandez .40
61 Ben Grieve .25
62 Jermaine Dye .25
63 Travis Lee .25
64 Jose Cruz Jr. .25
65 Rondell White .25
66 Carlos Beltran .25
67 Scott Rolen .50
68 Brad Fullmer .25
69 David Wells .25
70 Mike Sweeney .25
71 Barry Zito .40
72 Tony Batista .25
73 Curt Schilling .40
74 Jeff Cirillo .25
75 Edgardo Alfonzo .25
76 John Olerud .40
77 Carlos Lee .25
78 Moises Alou .40
79 Tim Hudson .40
80 Andres Galarraga .40
81 Roberto Alomar .75
82 Richie Sexson .25
83 Trevor Hoffman .25
84 Omar Vizquel .40
85 Jacque Jones .25
86 J.T. Snow .25
87 Sean Casey .40
88 Craig Biggio .40
89 Mariano Rivera .40
90 Rusty Greer .25
91 Barry Bonds 2.00
92 Pedro Martinez 1.00
93 Cal Ripken Jr. 3.00
94 Pat Burrell .50
95 Chipper Jones 2.00
96 Magglio Ordonez .25
97 Jeff Bagwell 1.00
98 Randy Johnson 1.00
99 Frank Thomas 1.00
100 Jason Kendall .25
101 Nomar Garciaparra (Avant Card) 2.00
102 Mark McGwire (Avant Card) 2.50
103 Troy Glaus (Avant Card) .75
104 Ivan Rodriguez (Avant Card) .75
105 Manny Ramirez (Avant Card) .75
106 Derek Jeter (Avant Card) 2.50
107 Alex Rodriguez (Avant Card) 2.00
108 Ken Griffey Jr. (Avant Card) 2.00
109 Todd Helton (Avant Card) .75
110 Sammy Sosa (Avant Card) 1.50
111 Vladimir Guerrero (Avant Card) .75
112 Mike Piazza (Avant Card) 2.00
113 Roger Clemens (Avant Card) 1.00
114 Jason Giambi (Avant Card) .50
115 Carlos Delgado (Avant Card) .50
116 *Ichiro Suzuki* (Rookie Avant) 150.00
117 *Morgan Ensberg* (Rookie Avant) 25.00
118 *Carlos Valderrama* (Rookie Avant) 15.00
119 *Erick Almonte* (Rookie Avant) 15.00
120 *Tsuyoshi Shinjo* (Rookie Avant) 35.00
121 *Albert Pujols* (Rookie Avant) 100.00
122 *Wilson Betemit* (Rookie Avant) 40.00
123 *Adrian Hernandez* (Rookie Avant) 20.00
124 *Jackson Melian* (Rookie Avant) 15.00
125 *Drew Henson* (Rookie Avant) 50.00
126 *Paul Phillips* 6.00
127 *Esix Snead* 12.00
128 *Ryan Freel* 6.00
129 *Junior Spivey* 8.00
130 *Elpidio Guzman* 6.00
131 *Juan Diaz* 6.00
132 *Andres Torres* 6.00
133 *Jay Gibbons* 15.00
134 Bill Ortega 6.00
135 *Alexis Gomez* 6.00
136 *Wilken Ruan* 6.00
137 *Henry Mateo* 6.00
138 *Juan Uribe* 15.00
139 *Johnny Estrada* 8.00
140 *Jaisen Randolph* 6.00
141 *Eric Hinske* 18.00
142 *Jack Wilson* 8.00
143 *Cody Ransom* 6.00
144 *Nate Frese* 6.00
145 *John Grabow* 6.00
146 *Christian Parker* 6.00
147 *Brian Lawrence* 15.00
148 *Brandon Duckworth* 15.00
149 *Winston Abreu* 6.00
150 *Horacio Ramirez* 8.00
151 *Nick Maness* 6.00
152 *Blaine Neal* 6.00
153 *Billy Sylvester* 6.00
154 *David Elder* 6.00
155 *Bert Snow* 6.00
156 *Claudio Vargas* 6.00
157 *Martin Vargas* 6.00
158 *Grant Balfour* 6.00
159 Randy Keisler 6.00
160 *Zach Day* 6.00

2001 Fleer Showcase Autographics

MT
Complete Set (63):
Common Player:
Roberto Alomar
Rick Ankiel
Albert Belle
Carlos Beltran
Adrian Beltre
Milton Bradley
Dee Brown
Jeromy Burnitz
Pat Burrell
Sean Casey
Joseph Crede
Jose Cruz Jr.
Ryan Dempster
J.D. Drew
Adam Dunn
Erubiel Durazo
Jermaine Dye
David Eckstein
Alex Escobar
Seth Etherton
Adam Everett
Carlos Febles
Troy Glaus
Ben Grieve
Toby Hall
Todd Helton
Shea Hillenbrand
Aubrey Huff
D'Angelo Jimenez
Paul Konerko
Mike Lamb
Matt Lawton
Derrek Lee
Mike Lieberthal
Mike Lowell
Julio Lugo
Jason Marquis
Edgar Martinez
Kevin Millwood
Eric Milton
Bengie Molina
Mike Mussina
Russ Ortiz
Corey Patterson
Jay Payton
Adam Piatt
Juan Pierre
Brad Radke
John Rocker
Alex Rodriguez
Scott Rolen
Richie Sexson
Gary Sheffield
Shannon Stewart
Miguel Tejada
Robin Ventura
Jose Vidro
Billy Wagner
Kip Wells
Rondell White
Preston Wilson
Kerry Wood
Julio Zuleta

2001 Fleer Showcase Awards Showcase Memorabilia

MT
Common Player: 20.00
Production 100 sets
Johnny Bench 40.00
Yogi Berra 50.00
George Brett 80.00
Lou Brock 40.00
Roy Campanella 70.00
Steve Carlton 40.00
Roger Clemens 60.00
Andre Dawson 30.00
Whitey Ford 40.00
Jimmie Foxx 65.00
Kirk Gibson 30.00
Tom Glavine 35.00
Juan Gonzalez 40.00
Elston Howard 35.00
Jim "Catfish" Hunter 30.00
Reggie Jackson 40.00

Randy Johnson 40.00
Chipper Jones 50.00
Harmon Killebrew 75.00
Fred Lynn
Greg Maddux 50.00
Don Mattingly 180.00
Willie McCovey 30.00
Jim Palmer 30.00
Jim Rice 25.00
Brooks Robinson 50.00
Frank Robinson 40.00
Jackie Robinson 150.00
Ivan Rodriguez 40.00
Mike Schmidt 80.00
Tom Seaver 50.00
Willie Stargell 40.00
Ted Williams 325.00
Robin Yount 50.00

2001 Fleer Showcase Awards Showcase Autograph

MT
Common Player: 50.00
Production 25 sets
Johnny Bench 200.00
Yogi Berra 175.00
George Brett 350.00
Steve Carlton 125.00
Roger Clemens 300.00
Andre Dawson 75.00
Whitey Ford 150.00
Kirk Gibson
Tom Glavine 100.00
Juan Gonzalez 100.00
Reggie Jackson 200.00
Randy Johnson 150.00
Chipper Jones 175.00
Harmon Killebrew 150.00
Fred Lynn 50.00
Greg Maddux 300.00
Don Mattingly 400.00
Willie McCoyey 100.00
Jim Palmer 100.00
Jim Rice 50.00
Brooks Robinson 120.00
Frank Robinson 100.00
Ivan Rodriguez 100.00
Mike Schmidt 250.00
Tom Seaver 200.00
Robin Yount

2001 Fleer Showcase Derek Jeter's Monumental Moments

MT
Production 2,000:
Derek Jeter 15.00
Derek Jeter/ Auto/100 200.00

2001 Fleer Showcase Showcase Sticks

MT
Common Player: 10.00
Inserted 1:24
Roberto Alomar 20.00
Adrian Beltre 15.00
Pat Burrell 15.00
J.D. Drew 15.00
Juan Gonzalez 20.00
Andruw Jones 15.00
Chipper Jones 20.00
Magglio Ordonez 10.00
Ivan Rodriguez 15.00
Scott Rolen 15.00
Frank Thomas 15.00
Roger Cedeno 10.00
Shawn Green 10.00
Richard Hidalgo 10.00
Tony Clark 10.00
Preston Wilson 10.00
Barry Bonds 30.00
Rafael Furcal 15.00
Randy Johnson 15.00
Vladimir Guerrero 15.00
Al Kaline 40.00
George Kell 15.00
Jason Kendall 15.00
Carlos Delgado 15.00
Adam Piatt 10.00
Alex Gonzalez 10.00
Jorge Posada 10.00
Jose Vidro 10.00
Roger Clemens 30.00
Steve Finley 10.00
Reggie Jackson 20.00
Shannon Stewart 10.00
Rick Ankiel 15.00
Jim Thome 20.00
Tsuyoshi Shinjo 25.00
Ichiro Suzuki 125.00

2001 Fleer Showcase Sweet Sigs

MT
Common Player: 15.00
Inserted 1:24
Prices for Lumber Wall: .75-1.25X
Leather: 1-2X
Bobby Abreu 30.00
Wilson Betemit 50.00
Russell Branyan 20.00
Pat Burrell 40.00
Eric Chavez 20.00
Rafael Furcal 20.00
Nomar Garciaparra 200.00
Juan Gonzalez 60.00
Elpidio Guzman 15.00
Drew Henson 80.00
Brandon Inge 15.00
Derek Jeter 175.00
Andruw Jones 35.00
Willie Mays 200.00
Jackson Melian 15.00
Xavier Nady 20.00
Jose Ortiz 15.00
Ben Sheets 30.00
Mike Sweeney 15.00
Miguel Tejada 20.00
Albert Pujols 125.00

2001 Fleer Tradition

MT
Complete Set (450): 50.00
Common Player: .15
Comp. Factory Set (485): 65.00
Pack (10): 1.75
Box (36): 55.00
1 Andres Galarraga .30
2 Armando Rios .15
3 Julio Lugo .15
4 Darryl Hamilton .15
5 Dave Veres .15
6 Edgardo Alfonzo .25
7 Brook Fordyce .15
8 Eric Karros .20
9 Neifi Perez .15
10 Jim Edmonds .30
11 Barry Larkin .40
12 Trot Nixon .15
13 Andy Pettitte .30
14 Jose Guillen .15
15 David Wells .15
16 Magglio Ordonez .25
17 David Segui .15
18 Juan Encarnacion .15
19 Robert Person .15
20 Quilvio Veras .15
21 Mo Vaughn .30
22 B.J. Surhoff .15
23 Ken Caminiti .15
24 Frank Catalanotto .15
25 Luis Gonzalez .25
26 Pete Harnisch .15
27 Alex Gonzalez .15
28 Mark Quinn .15
29 Luis Castillo .15
30 Rick Helling .15
31 Barry Bonds 1.00
32 Warren Morris .15
33 Aaron Boone .15
34 Ricky Gutierrez .15
35 Preston Wilson .15
36 Erubiel Durazo .15
37 Jermaine Dye .15
38 John Rocker .15
39 Mark Grudzielanek .15
40 Pedro Martinez 1.00
41 Phil Nevin .15
42 Luis Matos .15
43 Orlando Hernandez .25
44 Steve Cox .15
45 James Baldwin .15
46 Rafael Furcal .25
47 Todd Zeile .15
48 Elmer Dessens .15
49 Russell Branyan .15
50 Juan Gonzalez .75
51 Mac Suzuki .15
52 Adam Kennedy .15
53 Randy Velarde .15
54 David Bell .15
55 Royce Clayton .15
56 Greg Colbrunn .15
57 Rey Ordonez .15
58 Kevin Millwood .15
59 Fernando Vina .15
60 Eddie Taubensee .15
61 Enrique Wilson .15
62 Jay Bell .15
63 Brian Moehler .15
64 Brad Fullmer .15
65 Ben Petrick .15
66 Orlando Cabrera .15
67 Shane Reynolds .15
68 Mitch Meluskey .15
69 Jeff Shaw .15
70 Chipper Jones 1.50
71 Tomo Ohka .15
72 Ruben Rivera .15
73 Mike Sirotka .15
74 Scott Rolen .50
75 Glendon Rusch .15
76 Miguel Tejada .15
77 Brady Anderson .25
78 Bartolo Colon .15
79 Ron Coomer .15
80 Gary DiSarcina .15
81 Geoff Jenkins .25
82 Billy Koch .15
83 Mike Lamb .15
84 Alex Rodriguez 2.00
85 Denny Neagle .15
86 Michael Tucker .15
87 Edgar Renteria .15
88 Brian Anderson .15
89 Glenallen Hill .15
90 Aramis Ramirez .15
91 Rondell White .20
92 Tony Womack .15
93 Jeffrey Hammonds .15
94 Freddy Garcia .15
95 Bill Mueller .15
96 Mike Lieberthal .15
97 Michael Barrett .15
98 Derrek Lee .15
99 Bill Spiers .15
100 Derek Lowe .15
101 Javy Lopez .15
102 Adrian Beltre .25
103 Jim Parque .15
104 Marquis Grissom .15
105 Eric Chavez .25
106 Todd Jones .15
107 Eric Owens .15
108 Roger Clemens 1.00
109 Denny Hocking .15
110 Roberto Hernandez .15
111 Albert Belle .30
112 Troy Glaus .75
113 Ivan Rodriguez .75
114 Carlos Guillen .15
115 Chuck Finley .15
116 Dmitri Young .15
117 Paul Konerko .15
118 Damon Buford .15
119 Fernando Tatis .15
120 Larry Walker .30
121 Jason Kendall .20
122 Matt Williams .30
123 Henry Rodriguez .15
124 Placido Polanco .15
125 Bobby Estalella .15
126 Pat Burrell .50
127 Mark Loretta .15
128 Moises Alou .20
129 Tino Martinez .25
130 Milton Bradley .15
131 Todd Hundley .15
132 Keith Foulke .15
133 Robert Fick .15
134 Cristian Guzman .15
135 Rusty Greer .15
136 John Olerud .25
137 Mariano Rivera .25
138 Jeromy Burnitz .15
139 Dave Burba .15
140 Ken Griffey Jr. 2.00
141 Tony Gwynn 1.00
142 Carlos Delgado .60
143 Edgar Martinez .25
144 Ramon Hernandez .15
145 Pedro Astacio .15
146 Ray Lankford .15
147 Mike Mussina .50
148 Ray Durham .15
149 Lee Stevens .15
150 Jay Canizaro .15
151 Adrian Brown .15
152 Mike Piazza 2.00
153 Cliff Floyd .15
154 Jose Vidro .15
155 Jason Giambi .40
156 Andruw Jones .60
157 Robin Ventura .25
158 Gary Sheffield .40
159 Jeff D'Amico .15
160 Chuck Knoblauch .25
161 Roger Cedeno .15
162 Jim Thome .40
163 Peter Bergeron .15
164 Kerry Wood .25
165 Gabe Kapler .25
166 Corey Koskie .15
167 Doug Glanville .15
168 Brent Mayne .15
169 Scott Spiezio .15
170 Steve Karsay .15
171 Al Martin .15

172 Fred McGriff .30
173 Gabe White .15
174 Alex Gonzalez .15
175 Mike Darr .15
176 Bengie Molina .15
177 Ben Grieve .25
178 Marlon Anderson .15
179 Brian Giles .25
180 Jose Valentin .15
181 Brian Jordan .15
182 Randy Johnson .75
183 Ricky Ledee .15
184 Russ Ortiz .15
185 Mike Lowell .15
186 Curtis Leskanic .15
187 Bobby Abreu .15
188 Derek Jeter 2.50
189 Lance Berkman .15
190 Roberto Alomar .60
191 Darin Erstad .40
192 Richie Sexson .15
193 Alex Ochoa .15
194 Carlos Febles .15
195 David Ortiz .15
196 Shawn Green .30
197 Mike Sweeney .15
198 Vladimir Guerrero 1.00
199 Jose Jimenez .15
200 Travis Lee .15
201 Rickey Henderson .25
202 Bob Wickman .15
203 Miguel Cairo .15
204 Steve Finley .15
205 Tony Batista .15
206 Jamey Wright .15
207 Terrence Long .15
208 Trevor Hoffman .15
209 John Vander Wal .15
210 Greg Maddux 1.50
211 Tim Salmon .25
212 Herbert Perry .15
213 Marvin Benard .15
214 Jose Offerman .15
215 Jay Payton .15
216 Jon Lieber .15
217 Mark Kotsay .15
218 Scott Brosius .15
219 Scott Williamson .15
220 Omar Vizquel .25
221 Mike Hampton .25
222 Richard Hidalgo .25
223 Rey Sanchez .15
224 Matt Lawton .15
225 Bruce Chen .15
226 Ryan Klesko .15
227 Garret Anderson .15
228 Kevin Brown .25
229 Mike Cameron .15
230 Tony Clark .15
231 Curt Schilling .20
232 Vinny Castilla .15
233 Carl Pavano .15
234 Eric Davis .20
235 Darrin Fletcher .15
236 Matt Stairs .15
237 Octavio Dotel .15
238 Mark Grace .30
239 John Smoltz .15
240 Matt Clement .15
241 Ellis Burks .15
242 Charles Johnson .15
243 Jeff Bagwell .75
244 Derek Bell .15
245 Nomar Garciaparra 2.00
246 Jorge Posada .25
247 Ryan Dempster .15
248 J.T. Snow .15
249 Eric Young .15
250 Daryle Ward .15
251 Joe Randa .15
252 Travis Fryman .25
253 Mike Williams .15
254 Jacque Jones .15
255 Scott Elarton .15
256 Mark McGwire 2.50
257 Jay Buhner .15
258 Randy Wolf .15
259 Sammy Sosa 1.50
260 Chan Ho Park .15
261 Damion Easley .15
262 Rick Ankiel .25
263 Frank Thomas 1.00
264 Kris Benson .15
265 Luis Alicea .15
266 Jeremy Giambi .15
267 Geoff Blum .15
268 Joe Girardi .15
269 Livan Hernandez .15
270 Jeff Conine .15
271 Danny Graves .15
272 Craig Biggio .25
273 Jose Canseco .50
274 Tom Glavine .30
275 Ruben Mateo .15
276 Jeff Kent .25
277 Kevin Young .15
278 A.J. Burnett .15
279 Dante Bichette .20
280 Sandy Alomar Jr. .15
281 John Wetteland .15
282 Torii Hunter .15
283 Jarrod Washburn .15
284 Rich Aurilia .15
285 Jeff Cirillo .15
286 Fernando Seguignol .15
287 Darren Dreifort .15
288 Deivi Cruz .15
289 Pokey Reese .15
290 Garrett Stephenson .15
291 Pat Boone .15
292 Tim Hudson .25
293 John Flaherty .15
294 Shannon Stewart .15
295 Shawn Estes .15
296 Wilton Guerrero .15
297 Delino DeShields .15
298 David Justice .40
299 Harold Baines .15
300 Al Leiter .25
301 Wil Cordero .15
302 Antonio Alfonseca .15
303 Sean Casey .25
304 Carlos Beltran .15
305 Brad Radke .15
306 Jason Varitek .15
307 Shigetosi Hasegawa .15
308 Todd Stottlemyre .15
309 Raul Mondesi .25
310 Mike Bordick .15
311 Darryl Kile .15
312 Dean Palmer .15
313 Johnny Damon .15
314 Todd Helton .75
315 Chad Hermansen .15
316 Kevin Appier .15
317 Greg Vaughn .15
318 Robb Nen .15
319 Jose Cruz Jr. .15
320 Ron Belliard .15
321 Bernie Williams .60
322 Melvin Mora .15
323 Kenny Lofton .30
324 Armando Benitez .15
325 Carlos Lee .15
326 Damian Jackson .15
327 Eric Milton .15
328 J.D. Drew .25
329 Byung-Hyun Kim .15
330 Chris Stynes .15
331 Kazuhiro Sasaki .50
332 Troy O'Leary .15
333 Pat Hentgen .15
334 Brad Ausmus .15
335 Todd Walker .15
336 Jason Isringhausen .15
337 Gerald Williams .15
338 Aaron Sele .15
339 Paul O'Neill .25
340 Cal Ripken Jr. 2.50
341 Manny Ramirez .75
342 Will Clark .40
343 Mark Redman .15
344 Bubba Trammell .15
345 Troy Percival .15
346 Chris Singleton .15
347 Rafael Palmeiro .50
348 Carl Everett .15
349 Andy Benes .15
350 Bobby Higginson .15
351 Alex Cabrera (Prospects) .15
352 Barry Zito (Prospects) 1.00
353 Jace Brewer (Prospects) .15
354 Paxton Crawford (Prospects) .15
355 Oswaldo Mairena (Prospects) .15
356 Joe Crede (Prospects) .15
357 A.J. Pierzynski (Prospects) .15
358 Daniel Garibay (Prospects) .15
359 Jason Tyner (Prospects) .15
360 Nate Rolison (Prospects) .15
361 Scott Downs (Prospects) .15
362 Keith Ginter (Prospects) .15
363 Juan Pierre (Prospects) .15
364 Adam Bernero (Prospects) .15
365 Chris Richard (Prospects) .15
366 Joey Nation (Prospects) .15
367 Aubrey Huff (Prospects) .15
368 Adam Eaton (Prospects) .15
369 Jose Ortiz (Prospects) .15
370 Eric Munson (Prospects) .15
371 Matt Kinney (Prospects) .15
372 Eric Byrnes (Prospects) .15
373 Keith McDonald (Prospects) .15
374 Matt Wise (Prospects) .15
375 Timo Perez (Prospects) .15
376 Julio Zuleta (Prospects) .15
377 Jimmy Rollins (Prospects) .15
378 Xavier Nady (Prospects) 1.50
379 Ryan Kohlmeier (Prospects) .15
380 Corey Patterson (Prospects) .25
381 Todd Helton (League Leaders) .40
382 Moises Alou (League Leaders) .15
383 Vladimir Guerrero (League Leaders) .50
384 Luis Castillo (League Leaders) .15
385 Jeffrey Hammonds (League Leaders) .15
386 Nomar Garciaparra (League Leaders) 1.00
387 Carlos Delgado (League Leaders) .30
388 Darin Erstad (League Leaders) .20
389 Manny Ramirez (League Leaders) .40
390 Mike Sweeney (League Leaders) .15
391 Sammy Sosa (League Leaders) .75
392 Barry Bonds (League Leaders) .50
393 Jeff Bagwell (League Leaders) .40
394 Richard Hidalgo (League Leaders) .20
395 Vladimir Guerrero (League Leaders) .50
396 Troy Glaus (League Leaders) .40
397 Frank Thomas (League Leaders) .50
398 Carlos Delgado (League Leaders) .30
399 David Justice (League Leaders) .20
400 Jason Giambi (League Leaders) .20
401 Randy Johnson (League Leaders) .40
402 Kevin Brown (League Leaders) .15
403 Greg Maddux (League Leaders) .75
404 Al Leiter (League Leaders) .15
405 Mike Hampton (League Leaders) .15
406 Pedro Martinez (League Leaders) .40
407 Roger Clemens (League Leaders) .50
408 Mike Sirotka (League Leaders) .15
409 Mike Mussina (League Leaders) .25
410 Bartolo Colon (League Leaders) .15
411 World Series Update .15
412 World Series Update .15
413 World Series Update .15
414 World Series Update .15
415 World Series Update .15
416 World Series Update .15
417 World Series Update .15
418 World Series Update .15
419 World Series Update .15
420 World Series Update .15
421 Atlanta Braves (Team Checklists) .15
422 New York Mets (Team Checklists) .15
423 Florida Marlins (Team Checklists) .15
424 Philadelphia Phillies (Team Checklists) .15
425 Montreal Expos (Team Checklists) .15
426 St. Louis Cardinals (Team Checklists) .15
427 Cincinnati Reds (Team Checklists) .15
428 Chicago Cubs (Team Checklists) .15
429 Milwaukee Brewers (Team Checklists) .15
430 Houston Astros (Team Checklists) .15
431 Pittsburgh Pirates (Team Checklists) .15
432 San Francisco Giants (Team Checklists) .15
433 Arizona Diamondbacks (Team Checklists) .15
434 Los Angeles Dodgers (Team Checklists) .15
435 Colorado Rockies (Team Checklists) .15
436 San Diego Padres (Team Checklists) .15
437 New York Yankees (Team Checklists) .15
438 Boston Red Sox (Team Checklists) .15
439 Baltimore Orioles (Team Checklists) .15
440 Toronto Blue Jays (Team Checklists) .15
441 Tampa Bay Devil Rays (Team Checklists) .15
442 Chicago White Sox (Team Checklists) .15
443 Cleveland Indians (Team Checklists) .15
444 Detroit Tigers (Team Checklists) .15
445 Kansas City Royals (Team Checklists) .15
446 Minnesota Twins (Team Checklists) .15
447 Seattle Mariners (Team Checklists) .15
448 Oakland Athletics (Team Checklists) .15
449 Anaheim Angels (Team Checklists) .15
450 Texas Rangers (Team Checklists) .15
451 *Albert Pujols* 8.00
452 *Ichiro Suzuki* 12.00
453 *Tsuyoshi Shinjo* 2.00
454 *Johnny Estrada* .75
455 *Elpidio Guzman* .40
456 *Adrian Hernandez* .30
457 *Rafael Soriano* .75
458 *Drew Henson* 3.00
459 *Juan Uribe* .75
460 *Matt White* .40
461 *Endy Chavez* .30
462 *Bud Smith* 2.00
463 *Morgan Ensberg* .75
464 *Jay Gibbons* 2.00
465 *Jackson Melian* .30
466 *Junior Spivey* .30
467 *Juan Cruz* 2.00
468 *Wilson Betemit* 2.00
469 *Alexis Gomez* .30
470 *Mark Teixeira* 10.00
471 *Erick Almonte* .30
472 *Travis Hafner* .60
473 *Carlos Valderrama* .30
474 *Brandon Duckworth* 1.00
475 *Ryan Freel* .30
476 *Wilkin Ruan* .30
477 *Andres Torres* .30
478 *Josh Towers* .50
479 *Kyle Lohse* .75
480 *Jason Michaels* .30
481 Alfonso Soriano .40
482 C.C. Sabathia .25
483 Roy Oswalt .25
484 Ben Sheets .15
485 Adam Dunn 2.00

2001 Fleer Tradition Warning Track

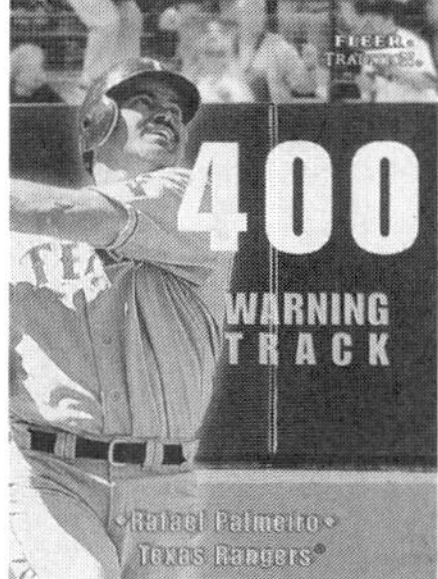

		MT
Complete Set (23):		200.00
Common Player:		3.00
Inserted 1:72		
1	Josh Gibson	6.00
2	Willie Mays	20.00
3	Mark McGwire	20.00
4	Barry Bonds	12.00
5	Jose Canseco	5.00
6	Ken Griffey Jr.	20.00
7	Cal Ripken Jr.	25.00
8	Rafael Palmeiro	5.00
9	Sammy Sosa	12.00
10	Juan Gonzalez	6.00
11	Frank Thomas	6.00
12	Jeff Bagwell	6.00
13	Gary Sheffield	4.00
14	Larry Walker	3.00
15	Mike Piazza	15.00
16	Larry Doby	5.00
17	Roy Campanella	8.00
18	Manny Ramirez	6.00
19	Chipper Jones	12.00
20	Alex Rodriguez	15.00
21	Ivan Rodriguez	6.00
22	Vladimir Guerrero	6.00
23	Nomar Garciaparra	15.00
24	Andres Galarraga	4.00
25	Jim Thome	4.00

2001 Fleer Tradition Diamond Tributes

		MT
Complete Set (30):		50.00
Common Player:		.75
Inserted 1:7		
1	Jackie Robinson	5.00
2	Mike Piazza	3.00
3	Alex Rodriguez	3.00
4	Barry Bonds	2.50
5	Nomar Garciaparra	3.00
6	Roger Clemens	2.00
7	Ivan Rodriguez	1.25
8	Cal Ripken Jr.	5.00
9	Manny Ramirez	1.25
10	Chipper Jones	2.50
11	Barry Larkin	.75
12	Carlos Delgado	.75
13	J.D. Drew	.75
14	Carl Everett	.75
15	Todd Helton	1.25
16	Greg Maddux	2.50
17	Scott Rolen	.75
18	Troy Glaus	1.00
19	Brian Giles	.75
20	Jeff Bagwell	1.25
21	Sammy Sosa	2.50
22	Randy Johnson	1.25
23	Andruw Jones	1.00
24	Ken Griffey Jr.	4.00
25	Mark McGwire	4.00
26	Derek Jeter	5.00
27	Vladimir Guerrero	1.25
28	Frank Thomas	1.25
29	Pedro Martinez	1.25
30	Bernie Williams	1.00

2001 Fleer Tradition Grass Roots

		MT
Complete Set (15):		70.00
Common Player:		2.00
Inserted 1:18		
1	Derek Jeter	8.00
2	Greg Maddux	5.00
3	Sammy Sosa	5.00
4	Alex Rodriguez	6.00
5	Vladimir Guerrero	3.00
6	Scott Rolen	2.00
7	Frank Thomas	2.50
8	Nomar Garciaparra	6.00
9	Cal Ripken Jr.	8.00
10	Mike Piazza	6.00
11	Ivan Rodriguez	2.50
12	Chipper Jones	5.00
13	Tony Gwynn	3.00
14	Ken Griffey Jr.	6.00
15	Mark McGwire	8.00

2001 Fleer Tradition Lumber Company

		MT
Complete Set (20):		30.00
Common Player:		1.00
Inserted 1:12		
1	Vladimir Guerrero	1.25
2	Mo Vaughn	.75
3	Ken Griffey Jr.	4.00
4	Juan Gonzalez	1.25
5	Tony Gwynn	1.50
6	Jim Edmonds	.75
7	Jason Giambi	1.00
8	Alex Rodriguez	3.00
9	Derek Jeter	5.00
10	Darin Erstad	.75
11	Andruw Jones	1.00
12	Cal Ripken Jr.	5.00
13	Magglio Ordonez	.75
14	Nomar Garciaparra	3.00
15	Chipper Jones	2.50
16	Sean Casey	.75
17	Shawn Green	.75
18	Mike Piazza	3.00
19	Sammy Sosa	2.50
20	Barry Bonds	2.50

2001 Fleer Tradition Stitches in Time

		MT
Complete Set (25):		60.00
Common Player:		1.50
Inserted 1:18		
1	Henry Kimbro	1.50
2	Ernie Banks	8.00
3	James "Cool Papa" Bell	3.00
4	Joe Black	1.50
5	Roy Campanella	5.00
6	Ray Dandridge	1.50
7	Leon Day	1.50
8	Larry Doby	3.00
9	Josh Gibson	5.00
10	Elston Howard	3.00
11	Monte Irvin	3.00
12	Buck Leonard	3.00
13	Max Manning	1.50
14	Willie Mays	10.00
15	Buck O'Neil	3.00
16	Satchel Paige	6.00
17	Ted Radcliffe	2.00
18	Jackie Robinson	10.00
19	Bill Perkins	1.50
20	Andrew "Rube" Foster	2.00
21	William "Judy" Johnson	1.50
22	Oscar Charleston	1.50
23	John Henry "Pop" Lloyd	1.50
24	Artie Wilson	1.50
25	Sam Jethroe	1.50

2001 Fleer Tradition Stitches in Time Game-Used

		MT
Common Card:		40.00
5	Roy Campanella	80.00
8	Larry Doby bat	50.00
10	Elston Howard bat	60.00
14	Willie Mays jersey	200.00
18	Jackie Robinson jersey	325.00

2001 Fleer Tradition Stitches in Time Autographs

		MT
Common Autograph:		25.00
2	Ernie Banks	75.00
4	Joe Black	25.00
11	Monte Irvin	40.00
14	Willie Mays	200.00
15	Buck O'Neil	30.00
17	Ted Radcliffe	25.00
24	Artie Wilson	25.00

2001 Fleer Tradition Turn Back the Clock

		MT
Common Card:		10.00
Inserted 1:352		
1	Tom Glavine	25.00
2	Greg Maddux	50.00
3	Sean Casey	15.00
4	Pokey Reese	10.00
5	Jason Giambi	25.00
6	Tim Hudson	25.00
7	Larry Walker	10.00
8	Jeffrey Hammonds	10.00
9	Scott Rolen	25.00
10	Pat Burrell	15.00
11	Chipper Jones	40.00
13	Troy Glaus	25.00
14	Tony Gwynn	40.00
15	Cal Ripken Jr.	80.00
16	Tom Glavine, Greg Maddux	90.00
17	Sean Casey, Pokey Reese	40.00
18	Chipper Jones, Greg Maddux	150.00
19	Larry Walker, Jeffrey Hammonds	40.00
20	Scott Rolen, Pat Burrell	80.00
21	Jason Giambi, Tim Hudson	50.00

2001 Fleer Triple Crown

		MT
Complete Set (300):		40.00
Common Player:		.15
Pack (10):		2.00
Box (24):		40.00
1	Derek Jeter	3.00
2	Vladimir Guerrero	1.00
3	Henry Rodriguez	.15
4	Jason Giambi	.50
5	Nomar Garciaparra	2.00
6	Jeff Kent	.25
7	Garret Anderson	.15
8	Todd Helton	.75
9	Barry Bonds	1.00
10	Preston Wilson	.15
11	Troy Glaus	.75
12	Geoff Jenkins	.25
13	Jim Edmonds	.25
14	Bobby Higginson	.15

15	Mark Quinn	.15
16	Barry Larkin	.40
17	Richie Sexson	.15
18	Fernando Tatis	.15
19	John Vander Wal	.15
20	Darin Erstad	.40
21	Shawn Green	.40
22	Scott Rolen	.50
23	Tony Batista	.25
24	Phil Nevin	.15
25	Tim Salmon	.25
26	Gary Sheffield	.40
27	Ben Grieve	.25
28	Jermaine Dye	.15
29	Andres Galarraga	.30
30	Adrian Beltre	.25
31	Rafael Palmeiro	.40
32	J.T. Snow	.15
33	Edgardo Alfonzo	.25
34	Paul Konerko	.15
35	Jim Thome	.40
36	Andruw Jones	.50
37	Mike Sweeney	.15
38	Jose Cruz Jr.	.15
39	David Ortiz	.15
40	Pat Burrell	.40
41	Chipper Jones	1.50
42	Jeff Bagwell	.75
43	Raul Mondesi	.25
44	Rondell White	.15
45	Edgar Martinez	.15
46	Cal Ripken Jr.	3.00
47	Moises Alou	.15
48	Shannon Stewart	.15
49	Tino Martinez	.25
50	Jason Kendall	.15
51	Richard Hidalgo	.25
52	Albert Belle	.30
53	Jay Payton	.15
54	Cliff Floyd	.15
55	Rusty Greer	.15
56	Matt Williams	.30
57	Sammy Sosa	1.50
58	Carl Everett	.15
59	Carlos Delgado	.50
60	Jeremy Giambi	.15
61	Jose Canseco	.50
62	David Segui	.15
63	Jose Vidro	.15
64	Matt Stairs	.15
65	Travis Fryman	.25
66	Ken Griffey Jr.	2.50
67	Mike Piazza	2.00
68	Mark McGwire	3.00
69	Craig Biggio	.25
70	Eric Chavez	.25
71	Mo Vaughn	.25
72	Matt Lawton	.15
73	Miguel Tejada	.25
74	Brian Giles	.25
75	Sean Casey	.25
76	Robin Ventura	.25
77	Ivan Rodriguez	.75
78	Dean Palmer	.15
79	Frank Thomas	1.00
80	Bernie Williams	.50
81	Juan Encarnacion	.15
82	John Olerud	.25
83	Rich Aurilla	.15
84	Juan Gonzalez	.75
85	Ray Durham	.15
86	Steve Finley	.15
87	Ken Caminiti	.15
88	Roberto Alomar	.60
89	Jeromy Burnitz	.15
90	J.D. Drew	.25
91	Lance Berkman	.15
92	Gabe Kapler	.25
93	Larry Walker	.30
94	Alex Rodriguez	2.50
95	Jeffrey Hammonds	.15
96	Magglio Ordonez	.25
97	David Justice	.40
98	Eric Karros	.15
99	Manny Ramirez	.75
100	Paul O'Neill	.25
101	Ron Gant	.15
102	Erubiel Durazo	.15
103	Jason Varitek	.15
104	Chan Ho Park	.15
105	Corey Koskie	.15
106	Jeff Conine	.15
107	Kevin Tapani	.15
108	Mike Lowell	.15
109	Tim Hudson	.25
110	Bobby Abreu	.15
111	Bret Boone	.15
112	David Wells	.15
113	Brian Jordan	.15
114	Mitch Meluskey	.15
115	Terrence Long	.15
116	Matt Clement	.15
117	Fernando Vina	.15
118	Luis Alicea	.15
119	Jay Bell	.15
120	Mark Grace	.25
121	Carlos Febles	.15
122	Mark Redman	.15
123	Kevin Jordan	.15
124	Pat Meares	.15
125	Mark McLemore	.15
126	Chris Singleton	.15
127	Trot Nixon	.15
128	Carlos Beltran	.15
129	Lee Stevens	.15
130	Kris Benson	.15
131	Jay Buhner	.15
132	Greg Vaughn	.15
133	Eric Young	.15
134	Tony Womack	.15
135	Roger Cedeno	.15
136	Travis Lee	.15
137	Marvin Benard	.15
138	Aaron Sele	.15
139	Rick Ankiel	.25
140	Ruben Mateo	.15
141	Randy Johnson	.75
142	Jason Tyner	.15
143	Mike Redmond	.15
144	Ron Coomer	.15
145	Scott Elarton	.15
146	Javy Lopez	.15
147	Carlos Lee	.15
148	Tony Clark	.15
149	Roger Clemens	1.00
150	Mike Lieberthal	.15
151	Shawn Estes	.15
152	Vinny Castilla	.15
153	Alex Gonzalez	.15
154	Troy Percival	.15
155	Pokey Reese	.15
156	Todd Hollandsworth	.15
157	Marquis Grissom	.15
158	Greg Maddux	1.50
159	Dante Bichette	.25
160	Hideo Nomo	.40
161	Jacque Jones	.15
162	Kevin Young	.15
163	B.J. Surhoff	.15
164	Eddie Taubensee	.15
165	Neifi Perez	.15
166	Orlando Hernandez	.25
167	Francisco Cordova	.15
168	Miguel Cairo	.15
169	Rafael Furcal	.25
170	Sandy Alomar Jr.	.15
171	Jeff Cirillo	.15
172	A.J. Pierzynski	.15
173	Fred McGriff	.30
174	Mike Mussina	.50
175	Aaron Boone	.15
176	Nick Johnson	.15
177	Kent Bottenfield	.15
178	Felipe Crespo	.15
179	Ryan Minor	.15
180	Charles Johnson	.15
181	Damion Easley	.15
182	Michael Barrett	.15
183	Doug Glanville	.15
184	Ben Davis	.15
185	Rickey Henderson	.30
186	Edgard Clemente	.15
187	Dmitri Young	.15
188	Tom Goodwin	.15
189	Mike Hampton	.25
190	Gerald Williams	.15
191	Omar Vizquel	.25
192	Ben Petrick	.15
193	Brad Radke	.15
194	Russ Davis	.15
195	Milton Bradley	.15
196	John Parrish	.15
197	Todd Hundley	.15
198	Carl Pavano	.15
199	Bruce Chen	.15
200	Royce Clayton	.15
201	Homer Bush	.15
202	Mark Grudzielanek	.15
203	Mike Lansing	.15
204	Daryle Ward	.15
205	Jeff D'Amico	.15
206	Ray Lankford	.15
207	Curt Schilling	.15
208	Pedro Martinez	.75
209	Johnny Damon	.15
210	Al Leiter	.25
211	Ruben Rivera	.15
212	Kazuhiro Sasaki	.15
213	Will Clark	.40
214	Rick Helling	.15
215	Adam Piatt	.15
216	Joe Girardi	.15
217	A.J. Burnett	.15
218	Mike Bordick	.15
219	Mike Cameron	.15
220	Tony Gwynn	1.50
221	Deivi Cruz	.15
222	Bubba Trammell	.15
223	Scott Erickson	.15
224	Kerry Wood	.25
225	Derrek Lee	.15
226	Peter Bergeron	.15
227	Chris Gomez	.15
228	Al Martin	.15
229	Brady Anderson	.25
230	Ramon Martinez	.15
231	Darryl Kile	.15
232	Devon White	.15
233	Charlie Hayes	.15
234	Aramis Ramirez	.15
235	Mike Lamb	.15
236	Tom Glavine	.30
237	Troy O'Leary	.15
238	Joe Randa	.15
239	Dustin Hermanson	.15
240	Adam Kennedy	.15
241	Jose Valentin	.15
242	Derek Bell	.15
243	Mark Kotsay	.15
244	Ron Belliard	.15
245	Warren Morris	.15
246	Ozzie Guillen	.15
247	Andy Ashby	.15
248	Jose Offerman	.15
249	Kevin Brown	.15
250	Jorge Posada	.25
251	Alex Cabrera (Prospects)	.15
252	Chan Perry (Prospects)	.15
253	Augie Ojeda (Prospects)	.15
254	Santiago Perez (Prospects)	.15
255	Grant Roberts (Prospects)	.15
256	Dusty Allen (Prospects)	.15
257	Elvis Pena (Prospects)	.15
258	Matt Kinney (Prospects)	.15
259	Timoniel Perez (Prospects)	.40
260	Adam Eaton (Prospects)	.15
261	Geraldo Guzman (Prospects)	.15
262	Damian Rolls (Prospects)	.15
263	Alfonso Soriano (Prospects)	.40
264	Corey Patterson (Prospects)	.25
265	Juan Alvarez (Prospects)	.15
266	Shawn Gilbert (Prospects)	.15
267	Adam Bernero (Prospects)	.15
268	Ben Weber (Prospects)	.15
269	Tike Redman (Prospects)	.15
270	Willie Morales (Prospects)	.15
271	Tomas De La Rosa (Prospects)	.15
272	Rodney Lindsey (Prospects)	.15
273	Carlos Casimiro (Prospects)	.15
274	Jim Mann (Prospects)	.15
275	Pasqual Coco (Prospects)	.15
276	Julio Zuleta (Prospects)	.15
277	Damon Minor (Prospects)	.15
278	Jose Ortiz (Prospects)	1.00
279	Eric Munson (Prospects)	.25
280	Andy Thompson (Prospects)	.15
281	Aubrey Huff (Prospects)	.15
282	Chris Richard (Prospects)	.15
283	Ross Gload (Prospects)	.15
284	Travis Dawkins (Prospects)	.15
285	Tim Drew (Prospects)	.15
286	Barry Zito (Prospects)	1.50
287	Andy Tracy (Prospects)	.15
288	Julio Lugo (Prospects)	.15
289	Matt DeWitt (Prospects)	.15
290	Keith McDonald (Prospects)	.15
291	J.C. Romero (Prospects)	.15
292	Adam Melhuse (Prospects)	.15
293	Ryan Kohlmeier (Prospects)	.15
294	John Bale (Prospects)	.15
295	Eric Cammack (Prospects)	.15
296	Morgan Burkhart (Prospects)	.15
297	Kory DeHaan (Prospects)	.15
298	Raul Gonzalez (Prospects)	.15
299	Hector Ortiz (Prospects)	.15
300	Talmadge Nunnari (Prospects)	.15

2001 Fleer Triple Crown Blue

		MT
Common Player:		15.00
Produced to # of 2000 HR's		
1	Derek Jeter (15)	275.00
2	Vladimir Guerrero (44)	60.00
3	Henry Rodriguez (20)	15.00
4	Jason Giambi (43)	40.00
5	Nomar Garciaparra (21)	180.00
6	Jeff Kent (33)	25.00
7	Garret Anderson (35)	15.00
8	Todd Helton (42)	50.00
9	Barry Bonds (49)	60.00
10	Preston Wilson (31)	15.00
11	Troy Glaus (47)	60.00
12	Geoff Jenkins (34)	20.00
13	Jim Edmonds (42)	30.00
14	Bobby Higginson (30)	15.00
15	Mark Quinn (20)	25.00
16	Barry Larkin (11)	75.00
17	Richie Sexson (30)	20.00
18	Fernando Tatis (18)	25.00
19	John Vander Wal (24)	15.00
20	Darin Erstad (25)	50.00
21	Shawn Green (24)	50.00
22	Scott Rolen (26)	40.00
23	Tony Batista (41)	15.00
24	Phil Nevin (31)	15.00
25	Tim Salmon (34)	25.00
26	Gary Sheffield (43)	30.00
27	Ben Grieve (27)	25.00
28	Jermaine Dye (33)	20.00
29	Andres Galarraga (28)	30.00

30 Adrian Beltre (20) 30.00
31 Rafael Palmeiro (39) 30.00
32 J.T. Snow (19) 20.00
33 Edgardo Alfonzo (25) 25.00
34 Paul Konerko (21) 25.00
35 Jim Thome (37) 25.00
36 Andruw Jones (36) 40.00
37 Mike Sweeney (29) 15.00
38 Jose Cruz Jr. (31) 15.00
39 David Ortiz (10) 40.00
40 Pat Burrell (18) 75.00
41 Chipper Jones (36) 80.00
42 Jeff Bagwell (47) 50.00
43 Raul Mondesi (24) 25.00
44 Rondell White (13) 40.00
45 Edgar Martinez (37) 25.00
46 Cal Ripken Jr. (15) 300.00
47 Moises Alou (30) 20.00
48 Shannon Stewart (21) 25.00
49 Tino Martinez (16) 35.00
50 Jason Kendall (14) 40.00
51 Richard Hidalgo (44) 20.00
52 Albert Belle (23) 40.00
53 Jay Payton (17) 30.00
54 Cliff Floyd (22) 20.00
55 Rusty Greer (8) 40.00
56 Matt Williams (12) 60.00
57 Sammy Sosa (50) 75.00
58 Carl Everett (34) 25.00
59 Carlos Delgado (41) 40.00
60 Jeremy Giambi (10) 60.00
61 Jose Canseco (15) 60.00
62 David Segui (19) 20.00
63 Jose Vidro (24) 20.00
64 Matt Stairs (21) 15.00
65 Travis Fryman (22) 25.00
66 Ken Griffey Jr. (40) 100.00
67 Mike Piazza (38) 100.00
68 Mark McGwire (32) 180.00
69 Craig Biggio (8) 50.00
70 Eric Chavez (26) 20.00
71 Mo Vaughn (36) 20.00
72 Matt Lawton (13) 30.00
73 Miguel Tejada (30) 30.00
74 Brian Giles (35) 25.00
75 Sean Casey (20) 30.00
76 Robin Ventura (24) 25.00
77 Ivan Rodriguez (27) 60.00
78 Dean Palmer (29) 20.00
79 Frank Thomas (43) 75.00
80 Bernie Williams (30) 40.00
81 Juan Encarnacion (14) 30.00
82 John Olerud (14) 35.00
83 Rich Aurilia (20) 20.00
84 Juan Gonzalez (22) 50.00
85 Ray Durham (17) 25.00
86 Steve Finley (35) 10.00
87 Ken Caminiti (15) 30.00
88 Roberto Alomar (19) 75.00
89 Jeromy Burnitz (31) 20.00
90 J.D. Drew (18) 50.00
91 Lance Berkman (21) 30.00
92 Gabe Kapler (14) 35.00
93 Larry Walker (9) 50.00
94 Alex Rodriguez (41) 100.00
95 Jeffrey Hammonds (20) 25.00
96 Magglio Ordonez (32) 25.00
97 David Justice (41) 25.00
98 Eric Karros (31) 20.00
99 Manny Ramirez (38) 50.00
100 Paul O'Neill (18) 35.00

2001 Fleer Triple Crown Green

MT
Common Player: 4.00
Produced to # of 2000 RBI's
1 Derek Jeter (73) 100.00
2 Vladimir Guerrero (123) 25.00
3 Henry Rodriguez (61) 6.00
4 Jason Giambi (137) 15.00
5 Nomar Garciaparra (96) 60.00
6 Jeff Kent (125) 10.00
7 Garret Anderson (117) 6.00
8 Todd Helton (147) 20.00
9 Barry Bonds (106) 30.00
10 Preston Wilson (121) 4.00
11 Troy Glaus (102) 30.00
12 Geoff Jenkins (94) 8.00
13 Jim Edmonds (108) 15.00
14 Bobby Higginson (102) 6.00
15 Mark Quinn (78) 8.00
16 Barry Larkin (41) 30.00
17 Richie Sexson (91) 8.00
18 Fernando Tatis (64) 8.00
19 John Vander Wal (94) 4.00
20 Darin Erstad (100) 15.00
21 Shawn Green (99) 15.00
22 Scott Rolen (89) 20.00
23 Tony Batista (114) 6.00
24 Phil Nevin (107) 4.00
25 Tim Salmon (97) 10.00
26 Gary Sheffield (109) 15.00
27 Ben Grieve (104) 8.00
28 Jermaine Dye (118) 6.00
29 Andres Galarraga (100) 15.00
30 Adrian Beltre (85) 10.00
31 Rafael Palmeiro (120) 20.00
32 J.T. Snow (96) 4.00
33 Edgardo Alfonzo (94) 10.00
34 Paul Konerko (97) 6.00
35 Jim Thome (106) 10.00
36 Andruw Jones (104) 20.00
37 Mike Sweeney (144) 4.00
38 Jose Cruz Jr. (76) 8.00
39 David Ortiz (63) 5.00
40 Pat Burrell (79) 25.00
41 Chipper Jones (111) 50.00
42 Jeff Bagwell (132) 20.00
43 Raul Mondesi (67) 10.00
44 Rondell White (61) 8.00
45 Edgar Martinez (145) 8.00
46 Cal Ripken Jr. (56) 125.00
47 Moises Alou (114) 5.00
'8 Shannon Stewart (69) 6.00
49 Tino Martinez (91) 10.00
50 Jason Kendall (58) 8.00
51 Richard Hidalgo (122) 8.00
52 Albert Belle (103) 12.00
53 Jay Payton (62) 10.00
54 Cliff Floyd (91) 8.00
55 Rusty Greer (65) 6.00
56 Matt Williams (47) 25.00
57 Sammy Sosa (138) 30.00
58 Carl Everett (108) 10.00
59 Carlos Delgado (137) 20.00
60 Jeremy Giambi (50) 6.00
61 Jose Canseco (49) 40.00
62 David Segui (103) 4.00
63 Jose Vidro (97) 6.00
64 Matt Stairs (81) 4.00
65 Travis Fryman (106) 8.00
66 Ken Griffey Jr. (118) 60.00
67 Mike Piazza (113) 60.00
68 Mark McGwire (73) 100.00
69 Craig Biggio (35) 25.00
70 Eric Chavez (86) 8.00
71 Mo Vaughn (117) 8.00
72 Matt Lawton (88) 5.00
73 Miguel Tejada (115) 12.00
74 Brian Giles (123) 8.00
75 Sean Casey (85) 8.00
76 Robin Ventura (84) 8.00
77 Ivan Rodriguez (83) 25.00
78 Dean Palmer (102) 6.00
79 Frank Thomas (143) 30.00
80 Bernie Williams (121) 15.00
81 Juan Encarnacion (72) 8.00
82 John Olerud (103) 8.00
83 Rich Aurilia (79) 4.00
84 Juan Gonzalez (67) 25.00
85 Ray Durham (75) 6.00
86 Steve Finley (96) 8.00
87 Ken Caminiti (45) 10.00
88 Roberto Alomar (89) 20.00
89 Jeromy Burnitz (98) 6.00
90 J.D. Drew (57) 20.00
91 Lance Berkman (67) 10.00
92 Gabe Kapler (66) 10.00
93 Larry Walker (51) 15.00
94 Alex Rodriguez (132) 60.00
95 Jeffrey Hammonds (106) 4.00
96 Magglio Ordonez (126) 8.00
97 David Justice (118) 15.00
98 Eric Karros (106) 6.00
99 Manny Ramirez (122) 25.00
100 Paul O'Neill (100) 8.00

2001 Fleer Triple Crown Red

MT
Common Player (1-100):
Stars: 5-10X
Produced to 2000 Bat Avg.
(See 2001 Fleer Triple Crown #1-100 for checklist and base card values.)

2001 Fleer Triple Crown Autographics

MT
Common Autograph: 10.00
Inserted 1:72
Silvers: 1-2X
Production 250 sets
1 Roberto Alomar 50.00
2 Jimmy Anderson 10.00
3 Ryan Anderson 20.00
4 Rick Ankiel 20.00
5 Adrian Beltre 15.00
6 Peter Bergeron 15.00
7 Lance Berkman 10.00
8 Barry Bonds 60.00
9 Milton Bradley 10.00
10 Dee Brown 10.00
11 Roosevelt Brown 10.00
12 Pat Burrell 25.00
13 Sean Casey 15.00
14 Eric Chavez 15.00
15 Giuseppe Chiaramonte 20.00
16 Joe Crede 15.00
17 Jose Cruz Jr. 10.00
18 Carlos Delgado 30.00
19 Ryan Dempster 10.00
20 Adam Dunn 15.00
21 David Eckstein 10.00
22 Jim Edmonds 30.00
23 Troy Glaus 40.00
24 Chad Green 10.00
25 Tony Gwynn 50.00
26 Todd Helton 40.00
27 Chad Hermansen 15.00
28 Shea Hillenbrand 15.00
29 Aubrey Huff 10.00
30 Randy Johnson 50.00
31 Chipper Jones 60.00
32 Mike Lamb 10.00
33 Corey Lee 10.00
34 Steve Lomasney 10.00
35 Terrence Long 15.00
36 Julio Lugo 15.00
37 Jason Marquis 15.00
38 Bengie Molina 15.00
39 Mike Mussina 30.00
40 Pablo Ozuna 10.00
41 Corey Patterson 25.00
42 Jay Payton 15.00
43 Wily Pena 15.00
44 Josh Phelps 15.00
45 Adam Piatt 20.00
46 Matt Riley 10.00
47 Alex Rodriguez 125.00
48 Alex Sanchez 10.00
49 Gary Sheffield 30.00
50 Alfonso Soriano 25.00
51 Shannon Stewart 15.00
52 Fernando Tatis 15.00
53 Jose Vidro 15.00
54 Preston Wilson 15.00
55 Kerry Wood 20.00
56 Julio Zuleta 10.00

2001 Fleer Triple Crown Crowns of Gold

MT
Common Player: 30.00
Random inserts in Hobby packs
Rick Ankiel jersey 40.00
Steve Carlton Jersey 75.00
Roger Clemens jersey 100.00
Carlos Delgado bat 40.00
Darin Erstad bat 40.00
Jimmie Foxx bat 200.00
Todd Helton bat 40.00
Randy Johnson jersey 75.00
Frank Robinson bat 60.00
Gary Sheffield jersey 30.00
Frank Thomas bat 50.00
Ted Williams bat 450.00

2001 Fleer Triple Crown Crowns of Gold Autograph

MT
Random inserts in Hobby packs
Steve Carlton jersey/72 150.00
Roger Clemens jersey/98 200.00
Frank Robinson bat/66 150.00
Ted Williams bat/9

2001 Fleer Triple Crown Crowning Achievements

		MT
Complete Set (15):		40.00
Common Player:		1.00
Inserted 1:9		
1	Troy Glaus	2.00
2	Mark McGwire	6.00
3	Barry Larkin, Craig Biggio	1.00
4	Ken Griffey Jr.	5.00
5	Rafael Palmeiro	1.50
6	Alex Rodriguez	5.00
7	Roger Clemens	3.00
8	Mike Piazza	5.00
9	Cal Ripken Jr.	6.00
10	Randy Johnson	2.00
11	Jeff Bagwell	2.00
12	Sammy Sosa	4.00
13	Greg Maddux	4.00
14	Barry Bonds	2.00
15	Fred McGriff	1.00

2001 Fleer Triple Crown Feel the Game

		MT
Common Player:		15.00
Inserted 1:72		
Golds:		1.5-2X
Production 50 sets		
	Adrian Beltre	25.00
	Dante Bichette	25.00
	Roger Cedeno	15.00
	Ben Davis	15.00
	Carlos Delgado	40.00
	J.D. Drew	25.00
	Jason Giambi	40.00
	Brian Giles	25.00
	Juan Gonzalez	30.00
	Richard Hidalgo	25.00
	Chipper Jones	60.00
	Eric Karros	25.00
	Javy Lopez	25.00
	Tino Martinez	25.00
	Raul Mondesi	20.00
	Phil Nevin	20.00
	Chan Ho Park	25.00
	Ivan Rodriguez	40.00
	Shannon Stewart	20.00
	Frank Thomas	50.00
	Jose Vidro	20.00
	Matt Williams	30.00
	Preston Wilson	20.00

2001 Fleer Triple Crown Future Threats

		MT
Complete Set (15):		30.00
Common Player:		1.00
Inserted 1:7		
1	Derek Jeter	5.00
2	Alex Rodriguez	5.00
3	Magglio Ordonez, Shawn Green	1.00
4	Larry Walker	1.00
5	Vladimir Guerrero	2.00
6	Nomar Garciaparra	4.00
7	Ken Griffey Jr.	4.00
8	Barry Bonds	1.50
9	Chipper Jones	3.00
10	Todd Helton	1.50
11	Ivan Rodriguez	1.50
12	Jeff Bagwell	1.50
13	Frank Thomas	2.00
14	Carlos Delgado	1.00
15	Mike Piazza	4.00

2001 Fleer Triple Crown Glamour Boys

		MT
Complete Set (15):		90.00
Common Player:		4.00
Inserted 1:24		
1	Derek Jeter	12.00
2	Vladimir Guerrero	5.00
3	Scott Rolen, Jeff Bagwell	4.00
4	Sammy Sosa	8.00
5	Ken Griffey Jr.	10.00
6	Mark McGwire	12.00
7	Ivan Rodriguez	4.00
8	Mike Piazza	10.00
9	Nomar Garciaparra	10.00
10	Cal Ripken Jr.	12.00
11	Tony Gwynn	8.00
12	Barry Bonds	4.00
13	Randy Johnson	4.00
14	Alex Rodriguez	10.00
15	Pedro Martinez	4.00

2002 Fleer

		MT
Complete Set (540):		75.00
Common Player:		.15
Pack (10):		2.50
Box (24):		40.00
31	Miguel Tejada	.25
32	Todd Hollandsworth	.15
33	Marlon Anderson	.15
34	Kerry Robinson	.15
35	Chris Richard	.15
36	Jamey Wright	.15
37	Ray Lankford	.15
38	Mike Bordick	.15
39	Danny Graves	.15
40	A.J. Pierzynski	.15
41	Shannon Stewart	.15
42	Tony Armas Jr.	.15
43	Brad Ausmus	.15
44	Alfonso Soriano	1.00
45	Junior Spivey	.15
46	Brent Mayne	.15
47	Jim Thome	.50
48	Dan Wilson	.15
49	Geoff Jenkins	.25
50	Kris Benson	.15
51	Rafael Furcal	.15
52	Wiki Gonzalez	.15
53	Jeff Kent	.25
54	Curt Schilling	.50
55	Ken Harvey	.15
56	Roosevelt Brown	.15
57	David Segui	.15
58	Mario Valdez	.15
59	Adam Dunn	.75
60	Bob Howry	.15
61	Michael Barrett	.15
62	Garret Anderson	.15
63	Kelvim Escobar	.15
64	Ben Grieve	.15
65	Randy Johnson	.75
66	Jose Offerman	.15
67	Jason Kendall	.15
68	Joel Pineiro	.15
69	Alex Escobar	.15
70	Chris George	.15
71	Bobby Higginson	.15
72	Nomar Garciaparra	2.00
73	Pat Burrell	.40
74	Lee Stevens	.15
75	Felipe Lopez	.15
76	Al Leiter	.25
77	Jim Edmonds	.25
78	Al Levine	.15
79	Raul Mondesi	.25
80	Jose Valentin	.15
81	Matt Clement	.15
82	Richard Hidalgo	.15
83	Jamie Moyer	.15
84	Brian Schneider	.15
85	John Franco	.15
86	Brian Buchanan	.15
87	Roy Oswalt	.40
88	Johnny Estrada	.15
89	Marcus Giles	.15
90	Carlos Valderrama	.15
91	Mark Mulder	.25
92	Mark Grace	.40
93	Andy Ashby	.15
94	Woody Williams	.15
95	Ben Petrick	.15
96	Roy Halladay	.15
97	Fred McGriff	.40
98	Shawn Green	.40
99	Todd Hundley	.15
100	Carlos Febles	.15
101	Jason Marquis	.15
102	Mike Redmond	.15
103	Shane Halter	.15
104	Trot Nixon	.15
105	Jeremy Giambi	.15
106	Carlos Delgado	.50
107	Richie Sexson	.40
108	Russ Ortiz	.15
109	David Ortiz	.15
110	Curtis Leskanic	.15
111	Jay Payton	.15
112	Travis Phelps	.15
113	J.T. Snow	.15
114	Edgar Renteria	.15
115	Freddy Garcia	.15
116	Cliff Floyd	.15
117	Charles Nagy	.15
118	Tony Batista	.15
119	Rafael Palmeiro	.50
120	Darren Dreifort	.15
121	Warren Morris	.15
122	Augie Ojeda	.15
123	Rusty Greer	.15
124	Esteban Yan	.15
125	Corey Patterson	.25
126	Matt Ginter	.15
127	Matt Lawton	.15
128	Miguel Batista	.15
129	Randy Winn	.15
130	Eric Milton	.15
131	Jack Wilson	.15
132	Sean Casey	.25
133	Mike Sweeney	.15
134	Jason Tyner	.15
135	Carlos Hernandez	.15
136	Shea Hillenbrand	.15
137	Shawn Wooten	.15
138	Peter Bergeron	.15
139	Travis Lee	.15
140	Craig Wilson	.15
141	Carlos Guillen	.15
142	Chipper Jones	1.50
143	Gabe Kapler	.15
144	Raul Ibanez	.15
145	Eric Chavez	.25
146	D'Angelo Jiminez	.15
147	Chad Hermansen	.15
148	Joe Kennedy	.15
149	Mariano Rivera	.25
150	Jeff Bagwell	.75
151	Joe McEwing	.15
152	Ronnie Belliard	.15
153	Desi Relaford	.15
154	Vinny Castilla	.15
155	Tim Hudson	.25
156	Wilton Guerrero	.15
157	Raul Casanova	.15
158	Edgardo Alfonzo	.15
159	Derrek Lee	.15
160	Phil Nevin	.15
161	Roger Clemens	1.00
162	Jason LaRue	.15
163	Brian Lawrence	.15
164	Adrian Beltre	.25
165	Troy Glaus	.50
166	Jeff Weaver	.15
167	B.J. Surhoff	.15
168	Eric Byrnes	.15
169	Mike Sirotka	.15
170	Bill Haselman	.15
171	Javier Vazquez	.15
172	Sidney Ponson	.15
173	Adam Everett	.15
174	Bubba Trammell	.15
175	Robb Nen	.15
176	Barry Larkin	.40
177	Tony Graffanino	.15
178	Rich Garces	.15
179	Juan Uribe	.15
180	Tom Glavine	.40
181	Eric Karros	.15
182	Michael Cuddyer	.15
183	Wade Miller	.15
184	Matt Williams	.25
185	Matt Morris	.15
186	Rickey Henderson	.40
187	Trevor Hoffman	.15
188	Wilson Betemit	.25
189	Steve Karsay	.15
190	Frank Catalanotto	.15
191	Jason Schmidt	.15
192	Roger Cedeno	.15
193	Magglio Ordonez	.40
194	Pat Hentgen	.15
195	Mike Lieberthal	.15
196	Andy Pettitte	.40
197	Jay Gibbons	.15
198	Rolando Arrojo	.15
199	Joe Mays	.15
200	Aubrey Huff	.15
201	Nelson Figueroa	.15
202	Paul Konerko	.40
203	Ken Griffey Jr.	2.00
204	Brandon Duckworth	.15
205	Sammy Sosa	1.50
206	Carl Everett	.15
207	Scott Rolen	.40
208	Orlando Hernandez	.25
209	Todd Helton	.75
210	Preston Wilson	.15
211	Gil Meche	.15
212	Bill Mueller	.15
213	Craig Biggio	.25
214	Dean Palmer	.15
215	Randy Wolf	.15
216	Jeff Suppan	.15
217	Jimmy Rollins	.25
218	Alexis Gomez	.15
219	Ellis Burks	.15
220	Ramon E. Martinez	.15
221	Ramiro Mendoza	.15
222	Einar Diaz	.15
223	Brent Abernathy	.15
224	Darin Erstad	.25
225	Reggie Taylor	.15
226	Jason Jennings	.15
227	Ray Durham	.15
228	John Parrish	.15
229	Kevin Young	.15
230	Xavier Nady	.15
231	Juan Cruz	.15
232	Greg Norton	.15
233	Barry Bonds	1.50
234	Kip Wells	.15
235	Paul LoDuca	.15
236	Javy Lopez	.15
237	Luis Castillo	.15

238 Tom Gordon .15
239 Mike Mordecai .15
240 Damian Rolls .15
241 Julio Lugo .15
242 Ichiro Suzuki 2.50
243 Tony Womack .15
244 Matt Anderson .15
245 Carlos Lee .15
246 Alex Rodriguez 2.50
247 Bernie Williams .50
248 Scott Sullivan .15
249 Mike Hampton .15
250 Orlando Cabrera .15
251 Benito Santiago .15
252 Steve Finley .15
253 Dave Williams .15
254 Adam Kennedy .15
255 Omar Vizquel .25
256 Garrett Stephenson .15
257 Fernando Tatis .15
258 Mike Piazza 2.00
259 Scott Spiezio .15
260 Jacque Jones .15
261 Russell Branyan .15
262 Mark McLemore .15
263 Mitch Meluskey .15
264 Marlon Byrd .15
265 Kyle Farnsworth .15
266 Billy Sylvester .15
267 C.C. Sabathia .15
268 Mark Buehrle .15
269 Geoff Blum .15
270 Bret Prinz .15
271 Placido Polanco .15
272 John Olerud .40
273 Pedro J. Martinez 1.00
274 Doug Mientkiewicz .15
275 Jason Bere .15
276 Bud Smith .15
277 Terrence Long .15
278 Troy Percival .15
279 Derek Jeter 3.00
280 Eric Owens .15
281 Jay Bell .15
282 Mike Cameron .15
283 Joe Randa .15
284 Brian Roberts .15
285 Ryan Klesko .15
286 Ryan Dempster .15
287 Cristian Guzman .15
288 Tim Salmon .25
289 Mark Johnson .15
290 Brian Giles .40
291 Jon Lieber .15
292 Fernando Vina .15
293 Mike Mussina .40
294 Juan Pierre .15
295 Carlos Beltran .15
296 Vladimir Guerrero .75
297 Orlando Merced .15
298 Jose Hernandez .15
299 Mike Lamb .15
300 David Eckstein .15
301 Mark Loretta .15
302 Greg Vaughn .15
303 Jose Vidro .15
304 Jose Ortiz .15
305 Mark Grudzielanek .15
306 Rob Bell .15
307 Elmer Dessens .15
308 Tomas Perez .15
309 Jerry Hairston Jr. .15
310 Mike Stanton .15
311 Todd Walker .15
312 Jason Varitek .15
313 Masato Yoshii .15
314 Ben Sheets .25
315 Roberto Hernandez .15
316 Eli Marrero .15
317 Josh Beckett .25
318 Robert Fick .15
319 Aramis Ramirez .15
320 Bartolo Colon .15
321 Kenny Kelly .15
322 Luis Gonzalez .50
323 John Smoltz .15
324 Homer Bush .15
325 Kevin Millwood .15
326 Manny Ramirez .75
327 Armando Benitez .15
328 Luis Alicea .15
329 Mark Kotsay .15
330 Felix Rodriguez .15
331 Eddie Taubensee .15
332 John Burkett .15
333 Ramon Ortiz .15
334 Daryle Ward .15
335 Jarrod Washburn .15
336 Benji Gil .15
337 Mike Lowell .15
338 Larry Walker .40
339 Andruw Jones .50
340 Scott Elarton .15
341 Tony McKnight .15
342 Frank Thomas .75
343 Kevin Brown .15
344 Jermaine Dye .15
345 Luis Rivas .15
346 Jeff Conine .15
347 Bobby Kielty .15
348 Jeffrey Hammonds .15
349 Keith Foulke .15
350 Dave Martinez .15
351 Adam Eaton .15
352 Brandon Inge .15
353 Tyler Houston .15
354 Bobby Abreu .15
355 Ivan Rodriguez .60
356 Doug Glanville .15
357 Jorge Julio .15
358 Kerry Wood .50
359 Eric Munson .15
360 Joe Crede .15
361 Denny Neagle .15
362 Vance Wilson .15
363 Neifi Perez .15
364 Darryl Kile .15
365 Jose Macias .15
366 Michael Coleman .15
367 Erubiel Durazo .15
368 Darrin Fletcher .15
369 Matt White .15
370 Marvin Benard .15
371 Brad Penny .15
372 Chuck Finley .15
373 Delino DeShields .15
374 Adrian Brown .15
375 Corey Koskie .15
376 Kazuhiro Sasaki .15
377 Brent Butler .15
378 Paul Wilson .15
379 Scott Williamson .15
380 Mike Young .15
381 Toby Hall .15
382 Shane Reynolds .15
383 Tom Goodwin .15
384 Seth Etherton .15
385 Billy Wagner .15
386 Josh Phelps .15
387 Kyle Lohse .15
388 Jeremy Fikac .15
389 Jorge Posada .40
390 Bret Boone .15
391 Angel Berroa .15
392 Matt Mantei .15
393 Alex Gonzalez .15
394 Scott Strickland .15
395 Charles Johnson .15
396 Ramon Hernandez .15
397 Damian Jackson .15
398 Albert Pujols 1.50
399 Gary Bennett .15
400 Edgar Martinez .15
401 Carl Pavano .15
402 Chris Gomez .15
403 Jaret Wright .15
404 Lance Berkman .50
405 Robert Person .15
406 Brook Fordyce .15
407 Adam Pettyjohn .15
408 Chris Carpenter .15
409 Rey Ordonez .15
410 Eric Gagne .15
411 Damion Easley .15
412 A.J. Burnett .15
413 Aaron Boone .15
414 J.D. Drew .25
415 Kelly Stinnett .15
416 Mark Quinn .15
417 Brad Radke .15
418 Jose Cruz Jr. .15
419 Greg Maddux 1.50
420 Steve Cox .15
421 Torii Hunter .15
422 Sandy Alomar .15
423 Barry Zito .25
424 Bill Hall .15
425 Marquis Grissom .15
426 Rich Aurilia .15
427 Royce Clayton .15
428 Travis Fryman .15
429 Pablo Ozuna .15
430 David Dellucci .15
431 Vernon Wells .15
432 Gregg Zaun .15
433 Alex Gonzalez .15
434 Hideo Nomo .40
435 Jeromy Burnitz .15
436 Gary Sheffield .25
437 Tino Martinez .25
438 Tsuyoshi Shinjo .40
439 Chan Ho Park .15
440 Tony Clark .15
441 Brad Fullmer .15
442 Jason Giambi 1.00
443 Billy Koch .15
444 Mo Vaughn .40
445 Alex Ochoa .15
446 Darren Lewis .15
447 John Rocker .15
448 Scott Hatteberg .15
449 Brady Anderson .15
450 Chuck Knoblauch .15
451 Pokey Reese .15
452 Brian Jordan .15
453 Albie Lopez .15
454 David Bell .15
455 Juan Gonzalez .75
456 Terry Adams .15
457 Kenny Lofton .25
458 Shawn Estes .15
459 Josh Fogg .15
460 Dmitri Young .15
461 Johnny Damon .15
462 Chris Singleton .15
463 Ricky Ledee .15
464 Dustin Hermanson .15
465 Aaron Sele .15
466 Chris Stynes .15
467 Matt Stairs .15
468 Kevin Appier .15
469 Omar Daal .15
470 Moises Alou .15
471 Juan Encarnacion .15
472 Robin Ventura .25
473 Eric Hinske .25
474 Rondell White .15
475 Carlos Pena .15
476 Craig Paquette .15
477 Marty Cordova .15
478 Brett Tomko .15
479 Reggie Sanders .15
480 Roberto Alomar .15
481 Jeff Cirillo .15
482 Todd Zeile .15
483 John Vander Wal .15
484 Rick Helling .15
485 Jeff D'Amico .15
486 David Justice .40
487 Jason Isringhausen .15
488 Shigetoshi Hasegawa .15
489 Eric Young .15
490 David Wells .15
491 Ruben Sierra .15
492 *Aaron Cook* .75
493 *Takahito Nomura* .50
494 Austin Kearns 1.00
495 *Kazuhisa Ishii* 4.00
496 Mark Teixeira .50
497 *Rene Reyes* .50
498 Tim Spooneybarger .15
499 Ben Broussard .15
500 *Eric Cyr* .25
501 *Anastacio Martinez* 1.00
502 Morgan Ensberg .15
503 *Steve Kent* .40
504 *Franklin Nunez* .15
505 *Adam Walker* .40
506 *Anderson Machado* .75
507 Ryan Drese .15
508 *Luis Ugueto* .15
509 *Jorge Nunez* .15
510 Colby Lewis .15
511 *Ron Calloway* .40
512 *Hansel Izquierdo* .50
513 Jason Lane .15
514 Rafael Soriano .15
515 Jackson Melian .15
516 *Edwin Almonte* .50
517 *Satoru Komiyama* .50
518 *Corey Thurman* .15
519 *Jorge De La Rosa* .75
520 Victor Martinez .15
521 Dewan Brazleton .15
522 Marlon Byrd .50
523 Jae Weong Seo .15
524 Orlando Hudson .15
525 Sean Burroughs .40
526 Ryan Langerhans .15
527 David Kelton .15
528 *So Taguchi* 1.00
529 Tyler Walker .15
530 Hank Blalock .50
531 Mark Prior 4.00
532 Yankee Stadium .50
533 Fenway Park .50
534 Wrigley Field .50
535 Dodger Stadium .15
536 Camden Yards .15
537 PacBell Park .15
538 Jacobs Field .15
539 SAFECO Field .15
540 Miller Field .15

2002 Fleer Tiffany

	MT
Stars (1-540):	4-8X
Production 200 sets	

2002 Fleer Barry Bonds Career Highlights

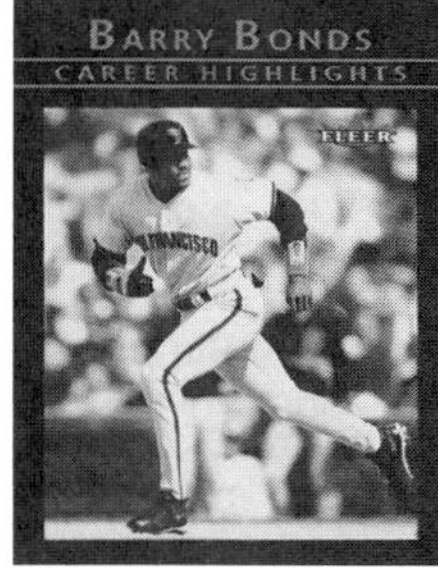

	MT
Complete Set (10):	40.00
Common Bonds 1-3:	3.00
Common 4-6 inserted 1:125 H	4.00
7-9 1:250 H	6.00
#10 1:383	6.00
1CH Barry Bonds	3.00
2CH Barry Bonds	3.00
3CH Barry Bonds	3.00
4CH Barry Bonds	4.00
5CH Barry Bonds	4.00
6CH Barry Bonds	4.00
7CH Barry Bonds	6.00
8CH Barry Bonds	6.00
9CH Barry Bonds	6.00
10CHBarry Bonds	6.00

2002 Fleer Barry Bonds Career Highlights Autographs

MT

Common Bonds Auto.
25 sets produced
1CHABarry Bonds
2CHABarry Bonds
3CHABarry Bonds
4CHABarry Bonds
5CHABarry Bonds
6CHABarry Bonds
7CHABarry Bonds
8CHABarry Bonds
9CHABarry Bonds
10CHABarry Bonds

2002 Fleer Barry Bonds 600 HR Supers

To commemorate his career 600th home run, Fleer produced a pair of jumbo-format (3-1/2" x 5") cards for sale on a tv home shopping show. Oen version of the card bears a facsimile autograph. A premium version, limited to 600 numbered cards, has a game-used bat chip and an authentic Bonds signature.

	MT
Barry Bonds (facsimile signature)	55.00
Barry Bonds (autograph w/bat chip)	250.00

2002 Fleer Classic Cuts Autographs

	MT
Inserted 1:432	
LA-A Luis Aparicio	15.00
RC-A Ron Cey	8.00
RF-A Rollie Fingers SP/35	
HK-A Harmon Killebrew	30.00
TL-A Tommy Lasorda SP/35	
JM-A Juan Marichal	15.00
GP-A Gaylord Perry SP/225	15.00
PR-A Phil Rizzuto SP/125	50.00
BR-A Brooks Robinson SP/200	40.00

2002 Fleer Classic Cuts Game Used

	MT
Common Player:	6.00
Inserted 1:24	
SA-P Sparky Anderson Pants	6.00
HB-B Hank Bauer Bat	8.00
JB-B Johnny Bench Bat/100	
JB-J Johnny Bench Jsy	20.00
YBB Yogi Berra Bat/72	
PB-B Paul Blair Bat	6.00
WB-B Wade Boggs Bat/99	30.00
WB-J Wade Boggs Jsy	15.00
WB-P Wade Boggs Patch/50	
BB-B Bobby Bonds Bat	8.00
BB-J Bobby Bonds Jsy	8.00
GB-B George Brett Bat/250	40.00
GB-J George Brett Jsy/250	40.00
RC-B Roy Campanella Bat/7	
SC-H Steve Carlton Hat/25	6.00
SC-P Steve Carlton Pants	6.00
OC-B Orlando Cepeda Bat/45	
OC-P Orlando Cepeda Pants	8.00
AD-J Andre Dawson Jsy	15.00
BD-B Bill Dickey Bat/200	20.00
LD-B Larry Doby Bat/250	15.00
DE-B Dwight Evans Bat/250	12.00
DE-J Dwight Evans Jsy	8.00
RF-J Rollie Fingers Jsy	6.00
CF-B Carlton Fisk Bat	15.00
CF-J Carlton Fisk Jsy/150	25.00
NF-B Nellie Fox Bat/200	25.00
SG-B Steve Garvey Bat	6.00
KG-B Kirk Gibson Bat	10.00
HG-B Hank Greenberg Bat/13	
GH-B Gil Hodges Bat/200	25.00
CH-J Jim Hunter Jsy	15.00
BJ-J Bo Jackson Jsy	15.00
RJ-B Reggie Jackson Bat/50	
RJ-P Reggie Jackson Pants	15.00
TJ-J Tommy John Jsy/55	
TJ-P Tommy John Patch/15	
GK-B George Kell Bat/150	20.00
RK-B Ralph Kiner Bat/47	
TK-B Ted Kluszewski Bat/200	20.00
TK-P Ted Kluszewski Pants	15.00
TL-B Tony Lazzeri Bat/25	
FL-B Fred Lynn Bat/25	
RM-P Roger Maris Pants/200	70.00
BM-B Billy Martin Bat/65	
EM-B Eddie Mathews Bat/200	30.00
DM-B Don Mattingly Bat/200	50.00
DM-J Don Mattingly Jsy	40.00
DM-P Don Mattingly Patch/50	
WM-J Willie McCovey Jsy/300	15.00
PM-B Paul Molitor Bat/250	30.00
PM-P Paul Molitor Patch/110	
JM-B Joe Morgan Bat/250	15.00
TM-P Thurman Munson Pants/10	
EM-B Eddie Murray Bat	15.00
EM-J Eddie Murray Jsy	15.00
EM-P Eddie Murray Patch/45	
JP-J Jim Palmer Jsy/273	15.00
DP-B Dave Parker Bat	8.00
TP-B Tony Perez Bat/250	20.00
TP-J Tony Perez Jsy	10.00
LP-P Lou Piniella Pants	6.00
KP-B Kirby Puckett Bat/25	
KP-J Kirby Puckett Jsy	30.00
WR-P Willie Randolph Patch/18	
PWR-J Pee Wee Reese Jsy/20	
JR-B Jim Rice Bat/225	15.00
JR-J Jim Rice Jsy/90	
CR-BG Cal Ripken Jr. Big Glv/100	75.00
CR-FG Cal Ripken Jr. Fld Glv/50	125.00
CR-J Cal Ripken Jr. Jsy	35.00
CR-P Cal Ripken Jr. Pants/200	40.00
BR-B Brooks Robinson Bat/250	20.00
PR-J Preacher Roe Jsy/19	
NR-J Nolan Ryan Jsy	65.00
NR-P Nolan Ryan Pants/200	6.00
RS-B Ryne Sandberg Bat	30.00
OS-J Ozzie Smith Jsy/250	30.00
WS-B Willie Stargell Bat/250	15.00
BT-B Bill Terry Bat/85	
JT-J Joe Torre Jsy/125	25.00
AT-B Alan Trammell Bat	10.00
EW-J Earl Weaver Jsy	6.00
HW-P Hoyt Wilhelm Pants/150	15.00
TW-B Ted Williams Bat	120.00
TW-P Ted Williams Pants	120.00
HW-B Hack Wilson Bat/8	
DW-B Dave Winfield Bat	10.00
DW-J Dave Winfield Jsy/231	15.00
DW-P Dave Winfield Pants	10.00
DW-P Dave Winfield Patch/25	
RY-B Robin Yount Bat	25.00
DZ-J Don Zimmer Jsy/90	

2002 Fleer Classic Cuts Game Used Autographs

	MT
Complete Set (3):	
Common Player:	
LA-B Luis Aparicio Bat/45	
RF-J Rollie Fingers Jsy/35	
BR-B Brooks Robinson Bat/45	

2002 Fleer Diamond Standouts

	MT
Complete Set (10):	50.00
Common Player:	3.00
Production 1,200 sets	
1DS Mike Piazza	6.00
2DS Derek Jeter	10.00
3DS Ken Griffey Jr.	6.00
4DS Barry Bonds	5.00
5DS Sammy Sosa	5.00
6DS Alex Rodriguez	8.00
7DS Ichiro Suzuki	8.00
8DS Greg Maddux	5.00
9DS Jason Giambi	4.00
10DS Nomar Garciaparra	6.00

2002 Fleer Golden Memories

	MT
Complete Set (15):	30.00
Common Player:	1.00
Inserted 1:24	
1GM Frank Thomas	1.50
2GM Derek Jeter	6.00
3GM Albert Pujols	3.00
4GM Barry Bonds	3.00
5GM Alex Rodriguez	5.00
6GM Randy Johnson	1.50
7GM Jeff Bagwell	1.50
8GM Greg Maddux	3.00
9GM Ivan Rodriguez	1.00
10GM Ichiro Suzuki	5.00
11GM Mike Piazza	4.00
12GM Pat Burrell	1.00
13GM Rickey Henderson	1.50
14GM Vladimir Guerrero	1.50
15GM Sammy Sosa	3.00

2002 Fleer Headliners

	MT
Complete Set (20):	18.00
Common Player:	.50
Inserted 1:8	
1HL Randy Johnson	.75
2HL Alex Rodriguez	2.50
3HL Todd Helton	.75
4HL Pedro J. Martinez	.75
5HL Ichiro Suzuki	2.50
6HL Vladimir Guerrero	.75
7HL Derek Jeter	3.00
8HL Adam Dunn	.75
9HL Luis Gonzalez	.50
10HL Kazuhiro Sasaki	.50
11HL Sammy Sosa	1.50
12HL Jason Giambi	1.00
13HL Ken Griffey Jr.	2.00
14HL Roger Clemens	1.00
15HL Brandon Duckworth	.50
16HL Nomar Garciaparra	2.00
17HL Bud Smith	.50
18HL Juan Gonzalez	.75
19HL Chipper Jones	1.50
20HL Barry Bonds	1.50

2002 Fleer Rookie Flashback

	MT
Complete Set (20):	12.00
Common Player:	.50
Inserted 1:3 Retail	
1RF Bret Prinz	.50
2RF Albert Pujols	2.00
3RF C.C. Sabathia	.50
4RF Ichiro Suzuki	3.00
5RF Juan Cruz	.50
6RF Jay Gibbons	.50
7RF Bud Smith	.75
8RF Johnny Estrada	.50
9RF Roy Oswalt	1.00
10RF Tsuyoshi Shinjo	1.00
11RF Brandon Duckworth	.50
12RF Jackson Melian	.50
13RF Josh Beckett	1.00
14RF Morgan Ensberg	.50
15RF Brian Lawrence	.50
16RF Eric Hinske	1.50
17RF Juan Uribe	.50
18RF Matt White	.50
19RF Junior Spivey	.50
20RF Wilson Betemit	.75

2002 Fleer Rookie Sensations

	MT
Complete Set (20):	50.00
Common Player:	2.00
Production 1,500 sets	
1RS Bret Prinz	2.00
2RS Albert Pujols	10.00
3RS C.C. Sabathia	2.00
4RS Ichiro Suzuki	15.00
5RS Juan Cruz	2.00
6RS Jay Gibbons	3.00
7RS Bud Smith	2.00
8RS Johnny Estrada	2.00
9RS Roy Oswalt	4.00
10RS Tsuyoshi Shinjo	4.00
11RS Brandon Duckworth	2.00
12RS Jackson Melian	2.00
13RS Josh Beckett	3.00
14RS Morgan Ensberg	2.00
15RS Brian Lawrence	2.00
16RS Eric Hinske	4.00
17RS Juan Uribe	2.00
18RS Matt White	2.00
19RS Junior Spivey	3.00
20RS Wilson Betemit	3.00

2002 Fleer Then and Now

		MT
Common Card:		15.00
Production 275 sets		
1TN	Eddie Mathews, Chipper Jones	20.00
2TN	Willie McCovey, Barry Bonds	20.00
3TN	Johnny Bench, Mike Piazza	25.00
4TN	Ernie Banks, Alex Rodriguez	25.00
5TN	Rickey Henderson, Ichiro Suzuki	35.00
6TN	Tom Seaver, Roger Clemens	15.00
7TN	Juan Marichal, Pedro J. Martinez	15.00
8TN	Reggie Jackson, Derek Jeter	35.00
9TN	Nolan Ryan, Kerry Wood	40.00
10TN	Joe Morgan, Ken Griffey Jr.	25.00

2002 Fleer Authentix

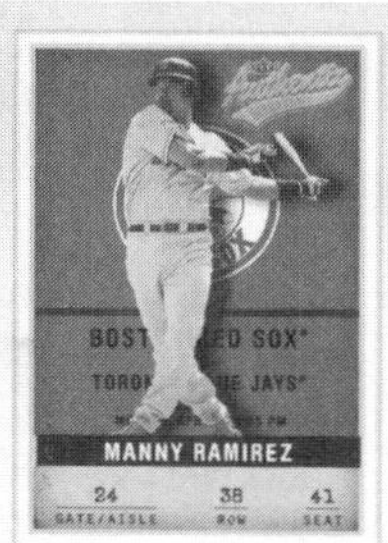

		MT
Complete Set (170):		125.00
Common Player:		.25
Common SP (151-170):		5.00
Production 1,850		
Front Row:		5-10X
Front Row SP:		1-3X
Production 150		
Second Row:		3-6X
Second Row SP:		.75-2X
Production 250		
Pack (5):		4.00
Box (24):		80.00
1	Derek Jeter	3.00
2	Tim Hudson	.40
3	Robert Fick	.25
4	Javy Lopez	.25
5	Alfonso Soriano	.75
6	Ken Griffey Jr.	2.50
7	Rafael Palmeiro	.50
8	Bernie Williams	.60
9	Adam Dunn	.75
10	Ivan Rodriguez	.50
11	Vladimir Guerrero	.75
12	Pedro J. Martinez	.75
13	Bret Boone	.25
14	Paul LoDuca	.25
15	Tony Batista	.25
16	Barry Bonds	1.50
17	Craig Biggio	.25
18	Garret Anderson	.25
19	Mark Mulder	.25
20	Frank Thomas	.75
21	Alex Rodriguez	2.00
22	Cristian Guzman	.25
23	Sammy Sosa	1.50
24	Ichiro Suzuki	3.00
25	Carlos Beltran	.25
26	Edgardo Alfonzo	.25
27	Josh Beckett	.25
28	Eric Chavez	.40
29	Roberto Alomar	.60
30	Raul Mondesi	.25
31	Mike Piazza	2.00
32	Barry Larkin	.40
33	Ruben Sierra	.25
34	Tsuyoshi Shinjo	.25
35	Magglio Ordonez	.40
36	Ben Grieve	.25
37	Richie Sexson	.25
38	Manny Ramirez	.75
39	Jeff Kent	.25
40	Shawn Green	.35
41	Andruw Jones	.50
42	Aramis Ramirez	.25
43	Cliff Floyd	.25
44	Juan Pierre	.25
45	Jose Vidro	.25
46	Paul Konerko	.25
47	Greg Vaughn	.25
48	Geoff Jenkins	.40
49	Greg Maddux	1.50
50	Ryan Klesko	.25
51	Corey Koskie	.25
52	Nomar Garciaparra	2.00
53	Edgar Martinez	.25
54	Gary Sheffield	.40
55	Randy Johnson	.75
56	Bobby Abreu	.25
57	Mike Sweeney	.25
58	Chipper Jones	1.50
59	Brian Giles	.40
60	Charles Johnson	.25
61	Ben Sheets	.25
62	Jason Giambi	.60
63	Todd Helton	.75
64	David Eckstein	.25
65	Troy Glaus	.60
66	Sean Casey	.40
67	Gabe Kapler	.25
68	Doug Mientkiewicz	.25
69	Curt Schilling	.50
70	Pat Burrell	.40
71	Albert Pujols	1.50
72	Jermaine Dye	.25
73	Miguel Tejada	.40
74	Jim Thome	.40
75	Carlos Delgado	.40
76	Fred McGriff	.40
77	Mike Cameron	.25
78	Jeromy Burnitz	.25
79	Jay Gibbons	.25
80	Rich Aurilia	.25
81	Lance Berkman	.50
82	Brian Jordan	.25
83	Phil Nevin	.25
84	Moises Alou	.30
85	Reggie Sanders	.25
86	Scott Rolen	.40
87	Larry Walker	.40
88	Matt Williams	.40
89	Roger Clemens	1.00
90	Juan Gonzalez	.75
91	Jose Cruz Jr.	.25
92	Tino Martinez	.25
93	Kerry Wood	.50
94	Freddy Garcia	.25
95	Jeff Bagwell	.75
96	Luis Gonzalez	.50
97	Jimmy Rollins	.25
98	Bobby Higginson	.25
99	Rondell White	.25
100	Jorge Posada	.40
101	Trot Nixon	.25
102	Jason Kendall	.25
103	Preston Wilson	.25
104	Corey Patterson	.40
105	Jose Valentin	.25
106	Carlos Lee	.25
107	Chris Richard	.25
108	Todd Walker	.25
109	Ellis Burks	.25
110	Brady Anderson	.25
111	Kazuhiro Sasaki	.25
112	Roy Oswalt	.40
113	Kevin Brown	.25
114	Jeff Weaver	.25
115	Todd Hollandsworth	.25
116	Joe Crede	.25
117	Tom Glavine	.40
118	Mike Lieberthal	.25
119	Tim Salmon	.40
120	Johnny Damon	.25
121	Brad Fullmer	.25
122	Mo Vaughn	.40
123	Torii Hunter	.25
124	Jamie Moyer	.25
125	Terrence Long	.25
126	Travis Lee	.25
127	Jacque Jones	.25
128	Lee Stevens	.25
129	Russ Ortiz	.25
130	Jeremy Giambi	.25
131	Mike Mussina	.50
132	Orlando Cabrera	.25
133	Barry Zito	.40
134	Robert Person	.25
135	Andy Pettitte	.40
136	Drew Henson	.50
137	Mark Teixeira	.50
138	David Espinosa	.25
139	Orlando Hudson	.25
140	Colby Lewis	.25
141	Bill Hall	.25
142	Michael Restovich	.25
143	Angel Berroa	.25
144	Dewon Brazelton	.25
145	Joe Thurston	.25
146	Mark Prior	.75
147	Dane Sardinha	.25
148	Marlon Byrd	.25
149	*Jeff Deardorff*	.25
150	Austin Kearns	.25
151	*Anderson Machado*	5.00
152	*Kazuhisa Ishii*	15.00
153	*Eric Junge*	5.00
154	*Mark Corey*	5.00
155	*So Taguchi*	8.00
156	*Jorge Padilla*	5.00
157	*Steve Kent*	5.00
158	*Jaime Cerda*	5.00
159	*Hansel Izquierdo*	5.00
160	*Rene Reyes*	5.00
161	*Jorge Nunez*	5.00
162	*Corey Thurman*	5.00
163	*Jorge Sosa*	8.00
164	*Franklin Nunez*	8.00
165	*Adam Walker*	5.00
166	*Ryan Baerlocher*	5.00
167	*Ron Calloway*	5.00
168	*Miguel Asencio*	5.00
169	*Luis Ugueto*	8.00
170	*Felix Escalona*	5.00

2002 Fleer Authentix Autographed AuthenTIX

		MT
Common Player:		10.00
Inserted 1:780		
Unripped no pricing		
Numbered to 25		
1AA	Derek Jeter	240.00
2AA	Marlon Byrd	
3AA	Drew Henson	
4AA	Mark Teixeira	35.00
5AA	Barry Bonds	
6AA	Brooks Robinson	50.00
7AA	Ben Sheets	35.00
8AA	Mark Prior	80.00
9AA	Kazuhisa Ishii	100.00
10AA	So Taguchi	45.00
11AA	Dane Sardinha	10.00
12AA	David Espinosa	10.00

2002 Fleer Authentix Autographed Jersey AuthenTIX

		MT
Inserted 1:1,387		
1AJA	Barry Bonds	
2AJA	Chipper Jones	
3AJA	Greg Maddux	
4AJA	Derek Jeter	250.00
5AJA	Jeff Bagwell	80.00

A card number in parentheses ( ) indicates the set is unnumbered.

2002 Fleer Authentix Ballpark Classics

		MT
Complete Set (15):		65.00
Common Player:		2.00
Inserted 1:22		
1BC	Reggie Jackson	4.00
2BC	Don Mattingly	10.00
3BC	Duke Snider	3.00
4BC	Carlton Fisk	3.00
5BC	Cal Ripken Jr.	10.00
6BC	Willie McCovey	2.00
7BC	Robin Yount	4.00
8BC	Paul Molitor	3.00
9BC	George Brett	8.00
10BC	Ryne Sandberg	5.00
11BC	Nolan Ryan	10.00
12BC	Thurman Munson	5.00
13BC	Joe Morgan	3.00
14BC	Jim Rice	2.00
15BC	Babe Ruth	10.00

2002 Fleer Authentix Ballpark Classics Memorabilia

		MT
Common Player:		15.00
Inserted 1:83		
Golds:		2-3X
Production 100		
RJ	Reggie Jackson	30.00
DM	Don Mattingly	40.00
DS	Duke Snider	25.00
CF	Carlton Fisk	20.00
CR	Cal Ripken Jr.	50.00
WC	Willie McCovey	15.00
RY	Robin Yount	40.00
PM	Paul Molitor	15.00
GB	George Brett	35.00
RS	Ryne Sandberg	100.00
NR	Nolan Ryan	40.00
TM	Thurman Munson	50.00
JM	Joe Morgan	15.00
JR	Jim Rice	15.00
BR	Babe Ruth	150.00

2002 Fleer Authentix Bat AuthenTIX

		MT
Common Player:		8.00
Inserted 1:68		
Unripped:		2-3X
Production 50		
1BA	Pat Burrell	15.00
2BA	Ray Durham	8.00
3BA	Juan Gonzalez	12.00
4BA	Drew Henson	18.00
5BA	Orlando Hernandez	10.00
6BA	Hideo Nomo	30.00
7BA	Jimmy Rollins	15.00
8BA	Manny Ramirez	12.00
9BA	Bernie Williams	12.00
10BA	Derek Jeter	40.00
11BA	Andruw Jones	10.00
12BA	Chipper Jones	20.00

13BA Barry Bonds 20.00
14BA Nomar Garciaparra 25.00

2002 Fleer Authentix Jersey AuthenTIX

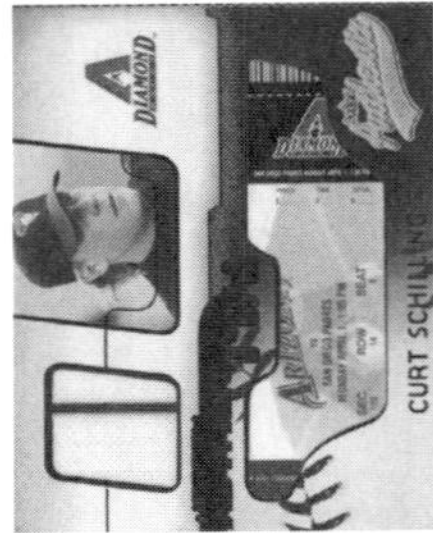

MT
Common Player: 8.00
Inserted 1:12
Unripped: 2-3X
Production 50
1JA Barry Bonds 20.00
2JA Chipper Jones 18.00
3JA Scott Rolen 12.00
4JA Greg Maddux 15.00
5JA Curt Schilling 10.00
6JA Mike Piazza 20.00
7JA Nomar Garciaparra 25.00
8JA Derek Jeter 35.00
9JA Luis Gonzalez 10.00
10JA Jeff Bagwell 12.00
11JA Frank Thomas 12.00
12JA Manny Ramirez 12.00
13JA Shawn Green 8.00
14JA Todd Helton 10.00
15JA Jim Edmonds 10.00
16JA Paul LoDuca 8.00
17JA Alex Rodriguez 15.00
18JA Roberto Alomar 12.00
19JA Andruw Jones 10.00
20JA Barry Zito 10.00
21JA J.D. Drew 12.00
22JA Magglio Ordonez 8.00
23JA Eric Chavez 8.00
24JA Darren Erstad 8.00
25JA Freddy Garcia 10.00
26JA Jim Thome 12.00
27JA Pedro J. Martinez 15.00
28JA Ivan Rodriguez 12.00
29JA Bernie Williams 12.00
30JA Randy Johnson 15.00

2002 Fleer Authentix Power Alley

MT
Complete Set (15): 35.00
Common Player: 1.00
Inserted 1:11
1PA Sammy Sosa 4.00
2PA Ken Griffey Jr. 6.00
3PA Luis Gonzalez 1.50
4PA Alex Rodriguez 5.00
5PA Shawn Green 1.00
6PA Barry Bonds 4.00
7PA Todd Helton 2.00
8PA Jim Thome 1.50
9PA Troy Glaus 1.50
10PA Manny Ramirez 2.00
11PA Jeff Bagwell 2.00
12PA Jason Giambi 2.00
13PA Chipper Jones 4.00
14PA Mike Piazza 5.00
15PA Albert Pujols 4.00

2002 Fleer Box Score

MT
Complete Set (310): NA
Common Player: .25
Common (126-150): 5.00
Production 2,499
Complete Rising Star set (40): 30.00
Common (151-190): 1.00
Complete Intl. Set (40): 18.00
Common (191-230): 1.00
Complete All-Star set (40): 20.00
Common (231-270): 1.00
Comp. Cooperstown set (40): 30.00
Common Cooperstown (271-310): 1.50
Print run for all subsets is 2,950
Pack (7): 4.00
Box (18 packs + supp. box): 90.00
1 Derek Jeter 3.00
2 Kevin Brown .25
3 Nomar Garciaparra 2.00
4 Mark Buehrle .25
5 Mike Piazza 2.00
6 David Justice .40
7 Tino Martinez .25
8 Paul Konerko .40
9 Larry Walker .40
10 Ben Sheets .40
11 Mike Cameron .25
12 David Wells .25
13 Barry Zito .40
14 Pat Burrell .50
15 Mike Mussina .50
16 Bud Smith .25
17 Brian Jordan .25
18 Chris Singleton .25
19 Daryle Ward .25
20 Russ Ortiz .25
21 Jason Kendall .25
22 Kerry Wood .50
23 Jeff Weaver .25
24 Tony Armas .25
25 Toby Hall .25
26 Brian Giles .40
27 Juan Pierre .25
28 Ken Griffey Jr. 2.00
29 Mike Sweeney .25
30 John Smoltz .25
31 Sean Casey .25
32 Jeremy Giambi .25
33 Mike Lieberthal .25
34 Rich Aurilia .25
35 Matt Lawton .25
36 Dmitri Young .25
37 Wade Miller .25
38 Jason Giambi 1.25
39 Jeff Cirillo .25
40 Mark Grace .40
41 Frank Thomas .75
42 Preston Wilson .25
43 Brad Radke .25
44 Greg Maddux 1.50
45 Adam Dunn .75
46 Roy Oswalt .40
47 Troy Glaus .50
48 Edgar Martinez .40
49 Billy Koch .25
50 Chipper Jones 1.50
51 Lance Berkman .75
52 Shannon Stewart .25
53 Eddie Guardado .25
54 C.C. Sabathia .25
55 Craig Biggio .40
56 Roger Clemens 1.50
57 Jimmy Rollins .25
58 Carlos Delgado .50
59 Tony Clark .25
60 Mike Hampton .25
61 Jeromy Burnitz .25
62 Jorge Posada .50
63 Todd Helton .75
64 Richie Sexson .40
65 Ryan Klesko .25
66 Cliff Floyd .25
67 Eric Milton .25
68 Scott Rolen .40
69 Steve Finley .25
70 Ray Durham .25
71 Jeff Bagwell .75
72 Geoff Jenkins .40
73 Jamie Moyer .25
74 David Eckstein .25
75 Johnny Damon .25
76 Pokey Reese .25
77 Mo Vaughn .40
78 Trevor Hoffman .25
79 Albert Pujols 1.50
80 Ben Grieve .25
81 Matt Morris .40
82 Aubrey Huff .25
83 Darin Erstad .40
84 Garret Anderson .25
85 Jacque Jones .25
86 Matt Anderson .25
87 Jose Vidro .25
88 Carlos Lee .25
89 Jeff Suppan .25
90 Al Leiter .40
91 Jeff Kent .40
92 Randy Johnson .75
93 Moises Alou .25
94 Bobby Higginson .25
95 Phil Nevin .25
96 Alex Rodriguez 2.50
97 Luis Gonzalez .50
98 A.J. Burnett .25
99 Torii Hunter .25
100 Ivan Rodriguez .50
101 Pedro J. Martinez 1.00
102 Brady Anderson .25
103 Paul LoDuca .25
104 Eric Chavez .40
105 Tim Salmon .40
106 Javier Vazquez .25
107 Bret Boone .25
108 Greg Vaughn .25
109 J.D. Drew .40
110 Jay Gibbons .25
111 Jim Thome .75
112 Shawn Green .50
113 Tim Hudson .40
114 John Olerud .50
115 Raul Mondesi .40
116 Curt Schilling .75
117 Corey Patterson .25
118 Robert Fick .25
119 Corey Koskie .25
120 Juan Gonzalez .75
121 Jerry Hairston Jr. .25
122 Gary Sheffield .50
123 Mark Mulder .40
124 Barry Bonds 2.00
125 Jim Edmonds .40
126 *Franklyn German* 5.00
127 *Rodrigo Rosario* 8.00
128 Ryan Ludwick 5.00
129 Jorge de la Rosa 5.00
130 Jason Lane 5.00
131 *Brian Mallette* 5.00
132 *Chris Baker* 5.00
133 *Kyle Kane* 5.00
134 *Doug Devore* 6.00
135 *Raul Chavez* 5.00
136 *Miguel Asencio* 5.00
137 Luis Garcia 5.00
138 Nick Johnson 6.00
139 *Michael Crudale* 5.00
140 *P.J. Bevis* 5.00
141 *Josh Hancock* 5.00
142 *Jeremy Lambert* 5.00
143 Ben Broussard 5.00
144 *John Ennis* 6.00
145 *Wilson Valdez* 5.00
146 *Eric Good* 5.00
147 *Elio Serrano* 5.00
148 *Jamie Cerda* 5.00
149 Hank Blalock 6.00
150 Brandon Duckworth 5.00
151 Drew Henson 3.00
152 *Kazuhisa Ishii* 8.00
153 *Earl Snyder* 2.00
154 J.M. Gold 1.00
155 *Satoru Komiyama* 1.00
156 Marlon Byrd 1.50
157 *So Taguchi* 3.00
158 Eric Hinske 2.00
159 Mark Prior 8.00
160 *Jorge Padilla* 2.50
161 *Rene Reyes* 1.00
162 *Jorge Nunez* 1.00
163 *Nelson Castro* 1.50
164 *Anderson Machado* 1.50
165 Mark Teixeira 2.00
166 Orlando Hudson 1.00
167 *Edwin Almonte* 1.50
168 *Luis Ugueto* 1.00
169 *Felix Escalona* 1.50
170 *Ron Calloway* 1.50
171 Kevin Mench 1.00
172 *Takahito Nomura* 1.00
173 Sean Burroughs 1.50
174 *Steve Kent* 1.00
175 *Jorge Sosa* 1.00
176 *Mike Moriarty* 1.00
177 Carlos Pena 1.00
178 *Anastacio Martinez* 1.50
179 *Reed Johnson* 1.50
180 *Juan Brito* 1.00
181 Wilson Betemit 1.50
182 Mike Rivera 1.00
183 David Espinosa 1.00
184 *Todd Donovan* 1.00
185 Morgan Ensberg 1.00
186 Dewon Brazelton 1.00
187 *Ben Howard* 2.50
188 Austin Kearns 2.50
189 Josh Beckett 2.00
190 *Brandon Backe* 2.00
191 Ichiro Suzuki 6.00
192 Tsuyoshi Shinjo 1.50
193 Hideo Nomo 2.00
194 Kazuhiro Sasaki 2.00
195 Edgardo Alfonzo 1.00
196 Chan Ho Park 1.00
197 Carlos Hernandez 1.00
198 Byung Kim 1.00
199 Omar Vizquel 1.50
200 Freddy Garcia 1.00
201 Richard Hidalgo 1.00
202 Magglio Ordonez 1.50
203 Bobby Abreu 1.50
204 Roger Cedeno 1.00
205 Andruw Jones 2.00
206 Mariano Rivera 1.50
207 Jose Macias 1.00
208 Orlando Hernandez 1.50
209 Rafael Palmeiro 2.00
210 Danys Baez 1.00
211 Bernie Williams 2.00
212 Carlos Beltran 1.00
213 Roberto Alomar 2.00
214 Jose Cruz Jr. 1.00
215 Ryan Dempster 1.00
216 Erubiel Durazo 1.00
217 Carlos Pena 1.00
218 Sammy Sosa 4.00
219 Adrian Beltre 1.50
220 Aramis Ramirez 1.00
221 Alfonso Soriano 4.00
222 Vladimir Guerrero 2.50
223 Juan Uribe 1.00
224 Cristian Guzman 1.00
225 Manny Ramirez 2.50
226 Juan Cruz 1.00
227 Ramon Ortiz 1.00
228 Juan Encarnacion 1.00
229 Bartolo Colon 1.00
230 Miguel Tejada 2.00
231 Cal Ripken Jr. 8.00
232 Derek Jeter 8.00
233 Pedro J. Martinez 3.00
234 Roberto Alomar 1.50

235 Sandy Alomar 1.00
236 Mike Piazza 5.00
237 Jeff Conine 1.00
238 Fred McGriff 1.00
239 Kirby Puckett 5.00
240 Ken Griffey Jr. 5.00
241 Roger Clemens 4.00
242 Joe Morgan 1.50
243 Willie McCovey 1.50
244 Brooks Robinson 2.50
245 Juan Marichal 1.00
246 Todd Helton 2.00
247 Alex Rodriguez 6.00
248 Barry Bonds 6.00
249 Nomar Garciaparra 5.00
250 Jeff Bagwell 2.50
251 Kenny Lofton 1.00
252 Barry Larkin 1.50
253 Tom Glavine 1.50
254 Magglio Ordonez 1.50
255 Randy Johnson 2.00
256 Chipper Jones 4.00
257 Kevin Brown 1.00
258 Rickey Henderson 2.00
259 Greg Maddux 4.00
260 Jim Thome 2.00
261 Rafael Palmeiro 2.00
262 Frank Thomas 2.00
263 Manny Ramirez 2.00
264 Travis Fryman 1.00
265 Gary Sheffield 1.50
266 Bernie Williams 1.50
267 Matt Williams 1.00
268 Ivan Rodriguez 1.50
269 Mike Mussina 1.50
270 Larry Walker 1.00
271 Jim Palmer 1.00
272 Cal Ripken Jr. 8.00
273 Brooks Robinson 2.50
274 Bobby Doerr 1.00
275 Ernie Banks 3.00
276 Fergie Jenkins 1.00
277 Luis Aparicio 1.00
278 Hoyt Wilhelm 1.00
279 Tom Seaver 3.00
280 Joe Morgan 1.50
281 Lou Boudreau 1.00
282 Larry Doby 1.00
283 Jim Bunning 1.00
284 George Kell 1.00
285 Pee Wee Reese 1.00
286 Eddie Mathews 3.00
287 Robin Yount 3.00
288 Rod Carew 2.50
289 Monte Irvin 2.00
290 Yogi Berra 4.00
291 Whitey Ford 2.00
292 Reggie Jackson 4.00
293 Rollie Fingers 1.00
294 Jim "Catfish" Hunter 1.00
295 Richie Ashburn 1.00
296 Willie Stargell 2.00
297 Ralph Kiner 1.00
298 Orlando Cepeda 1.00
299 Juan Marichal 1.00
300 Gaylord Perry 1.00
301 Willie McCovey 1.50
302 Red Schoendienst 1.00
303 Nolan Ryan 10.00
304 Bob Gibson 3.00
305 Al Kaline 3.00
306 Harmon Killebrew 3.00
307 Stan Musial 4.00
308 Phil Rizzuto 2.00
309 Mike Schmidt 5.00
310 Enos Slaughter 1.00

2002 Fleer Box Score First Edition

MT
Cards (1-125): 5-10X
Cards (126-150): .5-1X
Cards (151-310): 1-2.5X
Production 100 sets

2002 Fleer Box Score Classic Miniatures

MT
Complete Set (40): 30.00
Stars: 1.5-3X base card
Production 2,950 sets
One set per classic mini box
First Editions: 5-10X
Production 100 sets

2002 Fleer Box Score All-Star Lineup

MT
Common Card: 15.00
1:All-Stars Box
Derek Jeter, Nomar Garciaparra, Alex Rodriguez 50.00
Joe Morgan, Willie McCovey, Brooks Robinson 15.00
Alex Rodriguez, Ivan Rodriguez, Rafael Palmeiro 20.00
Derek Jeter, Mike Mussina, Bernie Williams 35.00
Barry Bonds, Cal Ripken Jr., Frank Thomas 40.00
Cal Ripken Jr., Derek Jeter, Roberto Alomar, Pedro J. Martinez 60.00
Mike Piazza, Barry Bonds, Ken Griffey Jr., Jeff Bagwell 40.00
Roger Clemens, Greg Maddux, Randy Johnson, Pedro J. Martinez 60.00
Todd Helton, Roberto Alomar, Alex Rodriguez, Chipper Jones 25.00
Ken Griffey Jr., Barry Bonds, Larry Walker, Manny Ramirez 35.00

2002 Fleer Box Score Amazing Greats

MT
Complete Set (20): 25.00
Common Player: 1.00
Inserted 1:5
1AG Derek Jeter 5.00
2AG Barry Bonds 4.00
3AG Mike Piazza 3.00
4AG Ivan Rodriguez 1.00
5AG Todd Helton 1.00
6AG Nomar Garciaparra 3.00
7AG Jim Thome 1.00
8AG Bernie Williams 1.00
9AG Kazuhiro Sasaki 1.00
10AG Torii Hunter 1.00
11AG Bret Boone 1.00
12AG Tim Hudson 1.00
13AG Randy Johnson 1.50
14AG Rafael Palmeiro 1.50
15AG Scott Rolen 1.00
16AG Carlos Delgado 1.00
17AG Chipper Jones 2.50
18AG Lance Berkman 1.50
19AG Frank Thomas 1.50
20AG Greg Maddux 2.50

2002 Fleer Box Score Amazing Greats Single Swatch

MT
Common Player: 6.00
Inserted 1:13
Dual Swatches: 1-2X
Inserted 1:90
Derek Jeter 25.00
Barry Bonds 20.00
Mike Piazza 15.00
Ivan Rodriguez 6.00
Nomar Garciaparra 20.00
Jim Thome/bat 12.00
Bernie Williams 10.00
Kazuhiro Sasaki 8.00
Torii Hunter 10.00
Bret Boone 6.00
Rafael Palmeiro 8.00
Scott Rolen 6.00
Carlos Delgado 6.00
Lance Berkman 15.00
Frank Thomas 10.00
Greg Maddux 15.00

2002 Fleer Box Score Amazing Greats Patch

MT
Common Player: 15.00
Production 150 sets
Derek Jeter 60.00
Barry Bonds 50.00
Mike Piazza 35.00
Ivan Rodriguez 25.00
Nomar Garciaparra 60.00
Bernie Williams 25.00
Kazuhiro Sasaki 25.00
Torii Hunter 30.00
Bret Boone 15.00
Rafael Palmeiro 25.00
Scott Rolen 25.00
Carlos Delgado 25.00
Lance Berkman 30.00
Frank Thomas 25.00
Greg Maddux 35.00

2002 Fleer Box Score Bat Rack

MT
Common Card: 20.00
Production 300 sets
1BR Derek Jeter, Alfonso Soriano, Bernie Williams 60.00
2BR Mike Piazza, Roberto Alomar, Mo Vaughn 35.00
3BR Jeff Bagwell, Lance Berkman, Craig Biggio 40.00
4BR Eric Chavez, Miguel Tejada, Carlos Pena 20.00
5BR Alex Rodriguez, Ivan Rodriguez, Rafael Palmeiro 30.00
6BR Chipper Jones, Gary Sheffield, Andruw Jones 25.00
7BR Carlos Delgado, Jim Thome, Frank Thomas 25.00
8BR Derek Jeter, Nomar Garciaparra, Alex Rodriguez 60.00
9BR Barry Bonds, Adam Dunn, Chipper Jones 35.00
10BR Magglio Ordonez, Juan Gonzalez, Manny Ramirez 20.00

2002 Fleer Box Score Bat Rack Quad

MT
Common Card 25.00
Production 150 sets
Torii Hunter, Cristian Guzman, Frank Thomas, Magglio Ordonez 25.00
Alex Rodriguez, Ivan Rodriguez, Eric Chavez, Miguel Tejada 40.00
Mike Piazza, Roberto Alomar, Alfonso Soriano, Derek Jeter 90.00
Barry Bonds, Lance Berkman, Alex Rodriguez, Nomar Garciaparra 75.00
Barry Bonds, Chipper Jones, Mike Piazza, Ivan Rodriguez 85.00
Derek Jeter, Miguel Tejada, Nomar Garciaparra, Alex Rodriguez 125.00
Roberto Alomar, Mo Vaughn, Jeff Bagwell, Craig Biggio 25.00
Jim Palmer, Carlos Delgado, Jim Thome, Frank Thomas 25.00
Magglio Ordonez, Bernie Williams, Juan Gonzalez, Manny Ramirez 25.00
Chipper Jones, Adam Dunn, Jeff Bagwell, Mo Vaughn 40.00
Alex Rodriguez, Jim Palmer, Bernie Williams, Alfonso Soriano 40.00
Carlos Pena, Eric Chavez, Carlos Delgado, Juan Gonzalez 25.00
Adam Dunn, Lance Berkman, Jim Thome, Manny Ramirez 50.00

2002 Fleer Box Score Box Score Debuts

MT
Complete Set (15): 70.00
Common Player: 2.50
Production 2,002 sets
1BSD Hank Blalock 6.00
2BSD Eric Hinske 5.00
3BSD Kazuhisa Ishii 12.00
4BSD Sean Burroughs 4.00
5BSD Andres Torres 2.50
6BSD Satoru Komiyama 2.50
7BSD Mark Prior 15.00
8BSD Kevin Mench 2.50
9BSD Austin Kearns 6.00
10BSD Earl Snyder 2.50
11BSD Jon Rauch 2.50
12BSD Jason Lane 3.00
13BSD Ben Howard 5.00
14BSD Bobby Hill 4.00
15BSD Dennis Tankersley 2.50

2002 Fleer Box Score Hall of Fame Material

MT
Common Player: 8.00
1:Cooperstown box
1HFM Jim Palmer/jsy 10.00
2HFM Cal Ripken Jr/jsy 25.00
3HFM Brooks Robinson/bat 10.00
4HFM Joe Morgan/bat 8.00
5HFM Eddie Mathews/bat 20.00
6HFM Robin Yount/jsy 15.00
7HFM Reggie Jackson/jsy 10.00
8HFM "Catfish" Hunter/jsy 10.00
9HFM Willie McCovey/jsy 10.00
10HFM Nolan Ryan/jsy 30.00

2002 Fleer Box Score Press Clippings

MT
Complete Set (20): 125.00
Common Player: 4.00
Inserted 1:90
1PC Mark Mudler 4.00
2PC Curt Schilling 6.00
3PC Alfonso Soriano 10.00
4PC Jeff Bagwell 6.00
5PC J.D. Drew 4.00
6PC Pedro J. Martinez 6.00
7PC Bobby Abreu 4.00
8PC Alex Rodriguez 12.00

9PC	Mike Sweeney	4.00
10PC	Carlos Pena	4.00
11PC	Josh Beckett	4.00
12PC	Roger Clemens	8.00
13PC	Manny Ramirez	6.00
14PC	Adam Dunn	6.00
15PC	Kazuhisa Ishii	15.00
16PC	Ken Griffey Jr.	12.00
17PC	Sammy Sosa	10.00
18PC	Ichiro Suzuki	15.00
19PC	Albert Pujols	8.00
20PC	Troy Glaus	4.00

2002 Fleer Box Score Press Clippings Game-Used

		MT
Common Player:		4.00
1PC	Mark Mudler/jsy	8.00
2PC	Curt Schilling/jsy	10.00
3PC	Alfonso Soriano/ bat	25.00
4PC	Jeff Bagwell/jsy	8.00
5PC	J.D. Drew/jsy	10.00
6PC	Pedro Martinez/ jsy	10.00
7PC	Bobby Abreu/jsy	6.00
8PC	Alex Rodriguez /jsy	10.00
9PC	Mike Sweeney/jsy	6.00
10PC	Carlos Pena/jsy	6.00
11PC	Josh Beckett/jsy	8.00
13PC	Manny Ramirez/ jsy	10.00
14PC	Adam Dunn/jsy	25.00
15PC	Kazuhisa Ishii/jsy	30.00
16PC	Ken Griffey Jr/ base	15.00
17PC	Sammy Sosa/ base	15.00
18PC	Ichiro Suzuki/base	15.00
19PC	Albert Pujols/base	10.00
20PC	Troy Glaus/base	8.00

2002 Fleer Box Score Wave of the Future

		MT
Common Player:		
1: Rising Stars box		
1WF	Drew Henson/bat	10.00
2WF	Kazuhisa Ishii/bat	15.00
3WF	Marlon Byrd/jsy	8.00
4WF	So Taguchi/bat	8.00
5WF	Jorge Padilla/ pants	12.00
6WF	Rene Reyes/jsy	6.00
7WF	Mark Teixeira/100	10.00
8WF	Carlos Pena/bat	6.00
9WF	Austin Kearns/ pants	20.00
10WF	Josh Beckett/jsy	25.00

2002 Fleer Box Score World Piece

		MT
Common Player:		8.00
1:International box		
1WP	Ichiro Suzuki/base	20.00
2WP	Tsuyoshi Shinjo/bat	8.00
3WP	Hideo Nomo/jsy	20.00
4WP	Kazuhiro Sasaki/jsy	8.00
5WP	Chan Ho Park/jsy	8.00
6WP	Magglio Ordonez/ jsy	10.00
7WP	Andruw Jones/jsy	10.00
8WP	Rafael Palmeiro/ jsy	12.00
9WP	Bernie Williams/ jsy	10.00
10WP	Roberto Alomar/ bat	8.00

2002 Fleer E-X

		MT
Complete Set (140):		NA
Common Player:		.25
Common SP (101-125):		5.00
Common (126-140):		5.00
Inserted 1:24		
Pack (4):		3.50
Box (24):		65.00
1	Alex Rodriguez	3.00
2	Albert Pujols	2.00
3	Ken Griffey Jr.	3.00
4	Vladimir Guerrero	1.00
5	Sammy Sosa	2.00
6	Ichiro Suzuki	3.00
7	Jorge Posada	.75
8	Matt Williams	.50
9	Adrian Beltre	.50
10	Pat Burrell	.50
11	Roger Cedeno	.25
12	Tony Clark	.25
13	Steve Finley	.25
14	Rafael Furcal	.25
15	Rickey Henderson	.75
16	Richard Hidalgo	.25
17	Jason Kendall	.25
18	Tino Martinez	.50
19	Scott Rolen	.75
20	Shannon Stewart	.25
21	Jose Vidro	.25
22	Preston Wilson	.25
23	Raul Mondesi	.25
24	Lance Berkman	.75
25	Rick Ankiel	.25
26	Kevin Brown	.50
27	Jeromy Burnitz	.25
28	Jeff Cirillo	.25
29	Carl Everett	.25
30	Eric Chavez	.25
31	Freddy Garcia	.25
32	Mark Grace	.50
33	David Justice	.50
34	Fred McGriff	.50
35	Mike Mussina	.75
36	John Olerud	.50
37	Magglio Ordonez	.50
38	Curt Schilling	.75
39	Aaron Sele	.25
40	Robin Ventura	.50
41	Adam Dunn	1.00
42	Jeff Bagwell	1.00
43	Barry Bonds	2.00
44	Roger Clemens	1.50
45	Cliff Floyd	.50
46	Jason Giambi	1.50
47	Juan Gonzalez	1.00
48	Luis Gonzalez	.75
49	Cristian Guzman	.25
50	Todd Helton	1.00
51	Derek Jeter	4.00
52	Rafael Palmeiro	.75
53	Mike Sweeney	.25
54	Ben Grieve	.25
55	Phil Nevin	.25
56	Mike Piazza	3.00
57	Moises Alou	.25
58	Ivan Rodriguez	.75
59	Manny Ramirez	1.00
60	Brian Giles	.50
61	Jim Thome	.75
62	Larry Walker	.50
63	Bobby Abreu	.25
64	Troy Glaus	1.00
65	Garret Anderson	.25
66	Roberto Alomar	.75
67	Bret Boone	.25
68	Marty Cardova	.25
69	Craig Biggio	.50
70	Omar Vizquel	.50
71	Jermaine Dye	.25
72	Darin Erstad	.50
73	Carlos Delgado	.75
74	Nomar Garciaparra	2.50
75	Greg Maddux	2.00
76	Tom Glavine	.50
77	Frank Thomas	1.00
78	Shawn Green	.50
79	Bobby Higginson	.25
80	Jeff Kent	.50
81	Chuck Knoblauch	.25
82	Paul Konerko	.50
83	Carlos Lee	.25
84	Jon Lieber	.25
85	Paul LoDuca	.25
86	Mike Lowell	.25
87	Edgar Martinez	.25
88	Doug Mientkiewicz	.25
89	Pedro J. Martinez	1.00
90	Randy Johnson	1.00
91	Aramis Ramirez	.25
92	J.D. Drew	.50
93	Chris Richard	.25
94	Jimmy Rollins	.50
95	Ryan Klesko	.25
96	Gary Sheffield	.50
97	Chipper Jones	2.00
98	Greg Vaughn	.25
99	Mo Vaughn	.50
100	Bernie Williams	.75
101	*John Foster/2,999*	5.00
102	*Jorge De La Rosa/ 2,999*	5.00
103	*Edwin Almonte/ 2,999*	5.00
104	*Chris Booker/2,999*	5.00
105	*Victor Alvarez/2,999*	5.00
106	*Clifford Bartosh2,999*	5.00
107	*Felix Escalona/2,999*	5.00
108	*Corey Thurman/ 2,999*	5.00
109	*Kazuhisa Ishii/ 2,999*	15.00
110	*Miguel Ascencio/ 2,999*	5.00
111	*P.J. Bevis/2,499*	5.00
112	*Gustavo Chacin/ 2,499*	5.00
113	*Steve Kent/2,499*	5.00
114	*Takahito Nomura/ 2,499*	5.00
115	*Adam Walker/2,499*	5.00
116	*So Taguchi/2,499*	8.00
117	*Reed Johnson/2,499*	5.00
118	*Rodrigo Rosario/ 2,499*	5.00
119	*Luis Martinez/2,499*	5.00
120	*Satoru Komiyama/ 2,499*	5.00
121	Sean Burroughs/ 1,999	8.00
122	Hank Blalock/1,999	8.00
123	Marlon Byrd/1,999	8.00
124	Nick Johnson/1,999	6.00
125	Mark Teixeira/ 1,999	6.00
126	David Espinosa	5.00
127	*Adrian Burnside*	5.00
128	*Mark Corey*	5.00
129	Matt Thornton	5.00
130	Dane Sardinha	5.00
131	Juan Rivera	5.00
132	Austin Kearns	8.00
133	Drew Henson	6.00
134	Ben Broussard	5.00
135	Orlando Hudson	5.00
136	Carlos Pena	5.00
137	Kenny Kelly	5.00
138	Bill Hall	5.00
139	Ron Chiavacci	5.00
140	Mark Prior	12.00

2002 Fleer E-X Barry Bonds 4X MVP

		MT
Complete Set (4):		20.00
Common Bonds:		6.00
1BB4X	Barry Bonds/1990	6.00
2BB4X	Barry Bonds/ 1,992	6.00
3BB4X	Barry Bonds/ 1,993	6.00
4BB4X	Barry Bonds/ 2,001	6.00

2002 Fleer E-X Behind the Numbers

		MT
Complete Set (35):		75.00
Common Player:		1.00
Inserted 1:8		
1BTN	Ichiro Suzuki	6.00
2BTN	Jason Giambi	3.00
3BTN	Mike Piazza	6.00
4BTN	Brian Giles	1.50
5BTN	Barry Bonds	5.00
6BTN	Pedro J. Martinez	3.00
7BTN	Nomar Garciaparra	5.00
8BTN	Randy Johnson	2.00
9BTN	Craig Biggio	1.00
10BTN	Manny Ramirez	2.00
11BTN	Mike Mussina	1.50
12BTN	Kerry Wood	1.50
13BTN	Jim Edmonds	1.00
14BTN	Ivan Rodriguez	1.50
15BTN	Jeff Bagwell	2.00
16BTN	Roger Clemens	3.00
17BTN	Chipper Jones	4.00
18BTN	Shawn Green	1.50
19BTN	Albert Pujols	4.00
20BTN	Andruw Jones	1.50
21BTN	Luis Gonzalez	1.50
22BTN	Todd Helton	2.00
23BTN	Jorge Posada	1.50
24BTN	Scott Rolen	1.50
25BTN	Ben Sheets	1.00
26BTN	Alfonso Soriano	3.00
27BTN	Greg Maddux	4.00
28BTN	Gary Sheffield	1.00
29BTN	Barry Zito	1.00
30BTN	Alex Rodriguez	6.00
31BTN	Larry Walker	1.00
32BTN	Derek Jeter	8.00
33BTN	Ken Griffey Jr.	5.00
34BTN	Vladimir Guerrero	2.00
35BTN	Sammy Sosa	4.00

2002 Fleer E-X Behind the Numbers Game Jersey

		MT
Common Player:		5.00
Inserted 1:24		
1	Jeff Bagwell	10.00
2	Craig Biggio Pants	10.00
3	Barry Bonds SP/50	
4	Roger Clemens	20.00
5	Jim Edmonds	5.00
6	Brian Giles	8.00
7	Luis Gonzalez	8.00
8	Shawn Green	5.00
9	Todd Helton	8.00
10	Derek Jeter SP	40.00
11	Randy Johnson SP	15.00
12	Andruw Jones	10.00
13	Chipper Jones	15.00
14	Greg Maddux	15.00
15	Pedro J. Martinez	10.00
16	Mike Mussina	10.00
17	Mike Piazza Pants	20.00
18	Jorge Posada	10.00
19	Manny Ramirez	12.00
20	Alex Rodriguez	15.00
21	Ivan Rodriguez	8.00
22	Scott Rolen	8.00
23	Alfonso Soriano SP	25.00
24	Barry Zito	5.00

2002 Fleer E-X Behind the Numbers Game Jersey Dual

		MT
Common Card:		
Production 25 sets		
1	Craig Biggio, Ivan Rodriguez	
2	Barry Bonds, Andruw Jones	
3	Jim Edmonds, Shawn Green	
4	Brian Giles, Manny Ramirez	
5	Greg Maddux, Mike Piazza	
6	Scott Rolen, Todd Helton	
7	Alfonso Soriano, Larry Walker	

2002 Fleer E-X Derek Jeter 4X Champ

	MT
Complete Set (4):	30.00
Common Jeter:	10.00
1DJFXDerek Jeter/ 1,996	10.00
2DJFXDerek Jeter/ 1,998	10.00
3DJFXDerek Jeter/ 1,999	10.00
4DJFXDerek Jeter/ 2,000	10.00

Figure values of lower-grade cards from 1981-date as: Near Mint (NM) 75% Excellent (EX) 40% of the listed Mint price

For cards through 1980, values should be figured as: Excellent (EX) 50% Very Good (VG) 30% of the listed Near Mint price

2002 Fleer E-X Game Essentials

	MT
Common Player:	6.00
1GE Carlos Beltran	6.00
2GE Barry Bonds	
3GE Kevin Brown	6.00
4GE Jeromy Burnitz	8.00
5GE Carlos Delgado	10.00
6GE Jason Hart/SP	8.00
7GE Rickey Henderson	25.00
8GE Drew Henson	20.00
9GE Derek Jeter/shoe	50.00
10GEJason Kendall	8.00
11GEJeff Kent	10.00
12GEBarry Larkin	25.00
13GEJavy Lopez	8.00
14GERaul Mondesi	10.00
15GERafael Palmeiro	10.00
16GEAdam Piatt	6.00
17GEBrad Radke	6.00
18GECal Ripken Jr.	35.00
19GEMariano Rivera	10.00
20GEAlex Rodriguez	20.00
21GEIvan Rodriguez	15.00
22GEKazuhiro Sasaki	10.00
23GEJ.T. Snow	10.00
24GEMo Vaughn	10.00
25GERobin Ventura	10.00
26GEJose Vidro	6.00
27GEMatt Williams	8.00

2002 Fleer E-X HardWear

	MT
Complete Set (10):	
Common Player:	
1HW Ivan Rodriguez	
2HW Mike Piazza	
3HW Derek Jeter	
4HW Barry Bonds	
5HW Todd Helton	
6HW Roberto Alomar	
7HW Albert Pujols	
8HW Ichiro Suzuki	
9HW Ken Griffey Jr.	
10HWJason Giambi	

2002 Fleer E-X Hit and Run

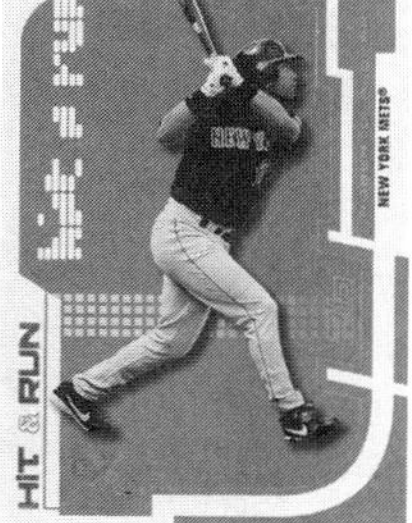

	MT
Complete Set (30):	60.00
Common Player:	1.00
Inserted 1:12	
1HNRAdam Dunn	2.00
2HNRDerek Jeter	8.00
3HNRFrank Thomas	2.00
4HNRAlbert Pujols	4.00
5HNRJ.D. Drew	1.00
6HNRRichard Hidalgo	1.00
7HNRJohn Olerud	1.50
8HNRRoberto Alomar	1.50
9HNRPat Burrell	1.50
10HNRDarin Erstad	1.50
11HNRMark Grace	1.50
12HNRChipper Jones	4.00
13HNRJose Vidro	1.00
14HNRCliff Floyd	1.00
15HNRMo Vaughn	1.00
16HNRNomar Garciaparra	5.00
17HNRIvan Rodriguez	1.50
18HNRLuis Gonzalez	1.50
19HNRJason Giambi	3.00
20HNRBernie Williams	1.50
21HNRMike Piazza	5.00
22HNRBarry Bonds	5.00
23HNRJose Ortiz	1.00
24HNRMagglio Ordonez	1.00
25HNRTroy Glaus	1.50
26HNRAlex Rodriguez	6.00
27HNRIchiro Suzuki	6.00
28HNRSammy Sosa	4.00
29HNRKen Griffey Jr.	5.00
30HNRVladimir Guerrero	2.00

2002 Fleer E-X Hit and Run Game Base

		MT
Inserted 1:240		
1	J.D. Drew	8.00
2	Adam Dunn	15.00
3	Jason Giambi	15.00
4	Troy Glaus	10.00
5	Ken Griffey Jr.	20.00
6	Vladimir Guerrero	10.00
7	Albert Pujols	15.00
8	Sammy Sosa	15.00
9	Ichiro Suzuki	30.00
10	Bernie Williams	8.00

2002 Fleer E-X Hit and Run Game Bat

		MT
Common Player:		5.00
Inserted 1:24		
1	Roberto Alomar	8.00
2	J.D. Drew	8.00
3	Darin Erstad	8.00
4	Cliff Floyd	5.00
5	Nomar Garciaparra	20.00
6	Luis Gonzalez	10.00
7	Richard Hidalgo	5.00
8	Derek Jeter	35.00
9	Chipper Jones	12.00
10	John Olerud	5.00
11	Magglio Ordonez	8.00
12	Jose Ortiz	5.00
13	Mike Piazza	15.00
14	Alex Rodriguez	15.00
15	Ivan Rodriguez	8.00
16	Frank Thomas	12.00
17	Mo Vaughn	8.00
18	Jose Vidro	5.00
19	Bernie Williams	8.00

2002 Fleer E-X Hit and Run Game Bat and Base

		MT
Common Player:		
Inserted 1:240		
1	Roberto Alomar	15.00
2	Barry Bonds SP	50.00
3	Nomar Garciaparra	35.00
4	Derek Jeter	40.00
5	Chipper Jones	20.00
6	Mike Piazza	35.00
7	Alex Rodriguez	25.00
8	Mo Vaughn	10.00

2002 Fleer Fall Classic

		MT
Complete Set (100):		30.00
Common Player:		.25
Common SP:		3.00
Inserted 1:18 hobby		
Golds:		4-10X
Production 50 set		
Pack (5):		6.00
Box (24):		125.00
1	Rabbit Maranville	.25
2	Tris Speaker	.75
3	Harmon Killebrew	1.50
4	Lou Gehrig	3.00
5	Lou Boudreau	.25
6	Al Kaline	1.50
7	Paul Molitor	1.00
7	Paul Molitor/ Brewers	4.00
8	Cal Ripken Jr.	4.00
9	Yogi Berra	2.00
10	Phil Rizzuto	1.00
11	Luis Aparicio	.25
11	Luis Aparicio/ Orioles	4.00
12	Stan Musial	2.00
13	Mel Ott	.50
14	Larry Doby	.25
15	Ozzie Smith	1.00
16	Babe Ruth	4.00
16	Babe Ruth/ Red Sox	12.00
17	Red Schoendienst	.25
17	Red Schoendienst/ Cards	3.00
18	Rollie Fingers	.25
19	Thurman Munson	1.50
20	Lou Brock	.50
21	Paul O'Neill	.25
21	Paul O'Neill/Reds	3.00
22	Jim Palmer	.50
23	Kirby Puckett	2.00
24	Tony Perez	.25
24	Tony Perez/Phila.	3.00
25	Don Larsen	.75
26	Steve Garvey	.25
26	Steve Garvey/ Padres	3.00
27	Jim "Catfish" Hunter	.25

27 "Catfish" Hunter/Yanks 4.00
28 Juan Marichal .50
29 Pee Wee Reese .25
30 Orlando Cepeda .25
31 Rich "Goose" Gossage .25
32 Ray Knight .25
33 Eddie Murray .75
34 Nolan Ryan 4.00
35 Alan Trammell .25
36 Grover Alexander .25
37 Joe Carter .25
38 Rogers Hornsby 1.00
39 Jimmie Foxx 1.00
40 Mike Schmidt 1.50
41 Eddie Mathews 1.50
42 Jackie Robinson 2.00
43 Eddie Collins .25
43 Eddie Collins/White Sox 3.00
44 Willie McCovey .25
45 Bob Gibson 1.50
46 Keith Hernandez .25
46 Keith Hernandez/Cards 3.00
47 Brooks Robinson 1.00
48 Mordecai Brown .25
49 Gary Carter .25
50 Kirk Gibson .25
50 Kirk Gibson/Tigers 3.00
51 Johnny Mize .25
52 Johnny Podres .25
53 Darrell Porter .25
54 Willie Stargell .75
55 Lenny Dykstra .25
55 Lenny Dykstra/Phila. 3.00
56 Christy Mathewson .25
57 Walter Johnson 1.00
58 Whitey Ford .75
59 Lefty Grove .25
60 Duke Snider 1.00
61 Cy Young 1.00
62 Dave Winfield .75
62 Dave Winfield/Yanks 5.00
63 Robin Yount 1.00
64 Fred Lynn .25
65 Ty Cobb 2.50
66 Joe Morgan .25
67 Bill Mazeroski .25
68 Frank Baker .25
69 Chief Bender .25
70 Carlton Fisk .25
71 Jerry Coleman .25
72 Frankie Frisch .25
73 Wade Boggs .75
73 Wade Boggs/Yanks 4.00
74 Johnny Bench 1.50
75 Roger Maris 2.00
75 Roger Maris/Cards 8.00
76 Dom DiMaggio .25
77 George Brett 3.00
78 Dave Parker .25
78 Dave Parker/A's 3.00
79 Hank Greenberg .25
80 Pepper Martin .25
81 Graig Nettles .25
81 Graig Nettles/Padres 3.00
82 Dennis Eckersley .25
83 Donn Clendenon .25
84 Tom Seaver 1.50
85 Honus Wagner 1.50
86 Reggie Jackson 1.50
86 Reggie Jackson/A's 5.00
87 Goose Goslin .25
87 Goose Goslin/Tigers 3.00
88 Tony Kubek .25
90 Roy Campanella 1.00
91 Steve Carlton/Cards 4.00
91 Steve Carlton .75
92 Lou Gehrig, Mel Ott 2.00
93 Eddie Collins, Joe Morgan .25
94 George Brett, Mike Schmidt 2.00
95 Cal Ripken Jr., Ozzie Smith 3.00
96 Thurman Munson, Johnny Bench 1.50
97 Willie Stargell, Stan Musial, Pepper Martin 1.00
98 Babe Ruth, Kirby Puckett, Reggie Jackson 3.00
99 Cy Young, Bob Gibson 1.00
100 Paul Molitor, Lou Brock .50

2002 Fleer Fall Classic HOF Plaque

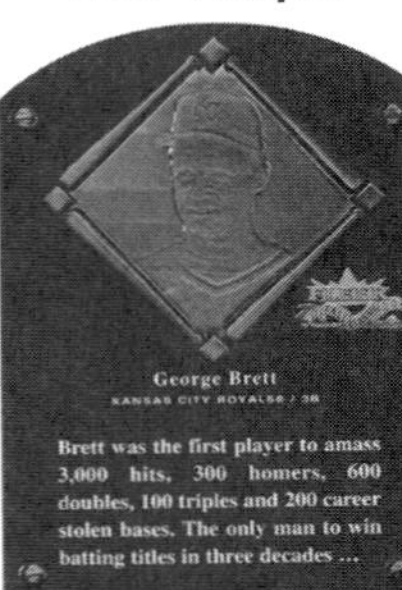

George Brett
KANSAS CITY ROYALS / 38
Brett was the first player to amass 3,000 hits, 300 homers, 600 doubles, 100 triples and 200 career stolen bases. The only man to win batting titles in three decades ...

MT
Complete Set (30): 90.00
Common Player: 3.00
#'d to HOF induction year
1HOF Babe Ruth 8.00
2HOF Christy Mathewson 3.00
3HOF Honus Wagner 4.00
4HOF Ty Cobb 5.00
5HOF Walter Johnson 4.00
6HOF Cy Young 4.00
7HOF Tris Speaker 3.00
8HOF Eddie Collins 3.00
9HOF Lou Gehrig 6.00
10HOF Jimmie Foxx 4.00
11HOF Jackie Robinson 6.00
12HOF Stan Musial 5.00
13HOF Yogi Berra 4.00
14HOF Duke Snider 4.00
15HOF Juan Marichal 3.00
16HOF Luis Aparicio 3.00
17HOF Pee Wee Reese 3.00
18HOF Willie McCovey 3.00
19HOF Willie Stargell 3.00
20HOF Johnny Bench 5.00
21HOF Joe Morgan 3.00
22HOF Jim Palmer 3.00
23HOF Tom Seaver 5.00
24HOF Reggie Jackson 4.00
25HOF Steve Carlton 3.00
26HOF George Brett 6.00
27HOF Nolan Ryan 8.00
28HOF Robin Yount 4.00
29HOF Kirby Puckett 5.00
30HOF Ozzie Smith 4.00

2002 Fleer Fall Classic MVP Collection Game-Used

MT
Common Player: 8.00
Inserted 1:100
Golds: .75-2X
Production 100 sets
JB Johnny Bench/200 20.00
DC Donn Clendenon 8.00
RF Rollie Fingers/200 8.00
RJOK Reggie Jackson/50 30.00
RJNY Reggie Jackson 15.00
RK Ray Knight 8.00
PM Paul Molitor/250 15.00
DP Darrell Porter/250 10.00
BR Brooks Robinson/250 20.00
WS Willie Stargell/200 10.00
AT Alan Trammell 10.00

2002 Fleer Fall Classic MVP Collection Patch

MT
Numbered to MVP Year
JB Johnny Bench/76 45.00
RF Rollie Fingers/74 20.00
RJNY Reggie Jackson/77 40.00
BR Brooks Robinson/70
AT Alan Trammell/84 35.00

2002 Fleer Fall Classic October Legends

MT
Common Player: 8.00
Inserted 1:48
Golds: .75-1.5X
Production 100 sets
Joe Morgan 8.00
Wade Boggs/60 10.00
Keith Hernandez/100 30.00
Robin Yount 12.00
Eddie Murray 10.00
Lenny Dykstra/200 10.00
Paul O'Neill 10.00
Red Schoendienst/210 8.00
Pepper Martin/50 15.00
Keith Hernandez/150 20.00
Willie Stargell/225 12.00
Cal Ripken Jr/50
George Brett 20.00
Dave Parker/50
Tony Perez 8.00
Rollie Fingers 8.00
Gary Carter/200 10.00
Dennis Eckersley 8.00
Juan Marichal 10.00
Pee Wee Reese/200 15.00
Roger Maris 60.00
Frankie Frisch/25
Duke Snider/200 25.00
Darrell Porter/150
Willie McCovey/150 15.00
Paul Molitor/150

2002 Fleer Fall Classic October Legends Dual

MT
Common Card
SP's noted
RFDE Rollie Fingers, Dennis Eckersley 10.00
KHRS Keith Hernandez, Red Schoendienst 12.00
JMWS Joe Morgan, Tony Perez 15.00
WBKH Wade Boggs, Keith Hernandez 12.00
LDGC Lenny Dykstra, Gary Carter 12.00
RYPM Robin Yount, Paul Molitor/150 45.00
RMPO Roger Maris, Paul O'Neill/200 50.00
DSPWR Duke Snider, Pee Wee Reese/200 35.00
JMWM Juan Marichal, Willie McCovey 15.00
GBDP George Brett, Darrell Porter/150 40.00
WSDP Willie Stargell, Dave Parker 15.00
GCKH Gary Carter, Keith Hernandez 12.00
CREM Cal Ripken Jr., Eddie Murray/200 40.00
CREM Cal Ripken Jr., Eddie Murray/100 50.00
PMFF Pepper Martin, Frankie Frisch 20.00

2002 Fleer Fall Classic Pennant Chase

MT
Common Player: 10.00
Inserted 1:48 hobby
2PC Yogi Berra/pants/150 20.00
3PC Carlton Fisk/bat 15.00
4PC Reggie Jackson/jsy 15.00
5PC Fred Lynn/bat 10.00
6PC Thurman Munson/bat 30.00
7PC Wade Boggs/jsy 10.00
8PC Dave Winfield/bat 10.00

2002 Fleer Fall Classic Pennant Chase Dual

MT
Production 50 sets
CFRJ Carlton Fisk/bat, Reggie Jackson/jsy 45.00
FLTM Fred Lynn/bat, Thurman Munson/bat 60.00
WBDW Wade Boggs/jsy, Dave Winfield/bat 40.00

2002 Fleer Fall Classic Rival Factions

MT
Common Card: 2.00
1-24 #'d to 1,000
25-36 #'d to 500
37-43 #'d to 50 not priced
1RF Carlton Fisk, Thurman Munson 3.00
2RF Frank Baker, Babe Ruth 8.00
3RF Jimmie Foxx, Lou Gehrig 6.00
4RF Steve Carlton, Nolan Ryan 8.00
5RF Mordecai Brown, Honus Wagner 3.00
6RF Frankie Frisch, Duke Snider 3.00
7RF Ozzie Smith, Alan Trammell 3.00
8RF Larry Doby, Jackie Robinson 5.00
9RF Steve Garvey, Tony Perez 2.00
10RF Johnny Bench, Willie Stargell 4.00
11RF Ty Cobb, Eddie Collins 5.00
12RF Reggie Jackson, Brooks Robinson 4.00
13RF Yogi Berra, Roy Campanella 4.00
14RF Orlando Cepeda, Willie McCovey 2.00
15RF Al Kaline, Jim Palmer 4.00
16RF George Brett, Kirby Puckett 6.00
17RF Bob Gibson, Tom Seaver 4.00
18RF Cal Ripken Jr., Robin Yount 8.00
19RF Johnny Mize, Mel Ott 3.00
20RF Stan Musial, Pee Wee Reese 4.00
21RF Phil Rizzuto, Ted Williams 8.00
22RF Hank Greenberg, Lefty Grove 2.00
23RF Dave Parker, Mike Schmidt 4.00
24RF Bill Mazeroski, Joe Morgan 2.00

25RFJohnny Bench, Carlton Fisk 5.00
26RFGeorge Brett, Mike Schmidt 6.00
27RFPee Wee Reese, Phil Rizzuto 4.00
28RFStan Musial, Ted Williams 10.00
29RFCal Ripken Jr., Alan Trammell 10.00
30RFJim "Catfish" Hunter, Tom Seaver 4.00
31RFTy Cobb, Honus Wagner 5.00
32RFSteve Carlton, Lefty Grove 2.00
33RFOzzie Smith, Robin Yount 4.00
34RFFrankie Frisch, Joe Morgan 2.00
35RFHank Greenberg, Jackie Robinson 6.00
36RFJimmie Foxx, Pepper Martin 4.00
37RFLou Gehrig, Cal Ripken Jr.
38RFOzzie Smith, Honus Wagner
39RFReggie Jackson, Dave Winfield
40RFTy Cobb, Rogers Hornsby
41RFBabe Ruth, Roger Maris
42RFYogi Berra, Thurman Munson
43RFNolan Ryan, Tom Seaver
44RFJoe Morgan, Jackie Robinson
45RFJimmie Foxx, Mel Ott

2002 Fleer Fall Classic Rival Factions Game-used Single

	MT
Common Card:	8.00
Inserted 1:32	
Carlton Fisk, Thurman Munson	25.00
Frank Baker, Babe Ruth	25.00
Jimmie Foxx, Lou Gehrig	35.00
Steve Carlton, Nolan Ryan	25.00
Frankie Frisch, Duke Snider	20.00
Ozzie Smith, Alan Trammell	15.00
Larry Doby, Jackie Robinson	15.00
Steve Garvey, Tony Perez	10.00
Johnny Bench, Willie Stargell	10.00
Reggie Jackson, Brooks Robinson	12.00
Orlando Cepeda, Willie McCovey	10.00
Al Kaline, Jim Palmer	10.00
George Brett, Kirby Puckett	25.00
Bob Gibson, Tom Seaver	20.00
Cal Ripken Jr., Robin Yount	30.00
Stan Musial, Pee Wee Reese	25.00
Hank Greenberg, Lefty Grove	20.00
Bill Mazeroski, Joe Morgan	8.00
Johnny Bench, Carlton Fisk	10.00
George Brett, Mike Schmidt	25.00
Pee Wee Reese, Phil Rizzuto	15.00
Cal Ripken Jr., Alan Trammell	35.00
Steve Carlton, Lefty Grove	15.00
Ozzie Smith, Robin Yount	15.00
Frankie Frisch, Joe Morgan	25.00
Hank Greenberg, Jackie Robinson	20.00
Jimmie Foxx, Pepper Martin	30.00
Lou Gehrig, Cal Ripken Jr.	40.00
Reggie Jackson, Dave Winfield	10.00
Babe Ruth, Roger Maris	60.00
Nolan Ryan, Tom Seaver	35.00

2002 Fleer Fall Classic Rival Factions Game-Used Dual

	MT
Common Card:	12.00
CFTMCarlton Fisk, Thurman Munson	30.00
FBBRFrank Baker, Babe Ruth/25	
SCNRSteve Carlton, Nolan Ryan	30.00
FFDSFrankie Frisch, Duke Snider	15.00
OSATOzzie Smith, Alan Trammell	25.00
LDJRLarry Doby, Jackie Robinson/75	60.00
SGTPSteve Garvey, Tony Perez	12.00
JBWSJohnny Bench, Willie Stargell	25.00
RJBRReggie Jackson, Brooks Robinson	25.00
OCWMOrlando Cepeda, Willie McCovey/200	15.00
GBKPGeorge Brett, Kirby Puckett	40.00
CRRYCal Ripken Jr., Robin Yount	30.00
JBCFJohnny Bench, Carlton Fisk	20.00
CRATCal Ripken Jr., Alan Trammell	30.00
CHTSJim "Catfish" Hunter, Tom Seaver	18.00
OSRYOzzie Smith, Robin Yount	25.00
FFJMFrankie Frisch, Joe Morgan	15.00
HGJRHank Greenberg, Jackie Robinson/50	100.00
JFPMJimmie Foxx, Pepper Martin/200	40.00
RJDWReggie Jackson, Dave Winfield/150	20.00
BRRMBabe Ruth, Roger Maris/25	
YBTMYogi Berra, Thurman Munson	40.00
NRTSNolan Ryan, Tom Seaver	45.00
JMJRJoe Morgan, Jackie Robinson/50	

2002 Fleer Fall Classic Rival Factions Dual Patch

	MT
Production 50 sets	12.00
CFTMCarlton Fisk, Thurman Munson	60.00
SCNRSteve Carlton, Nolan Ryan	200.00
OSATOzzie Smith, Alan Trammell	70.00
SGTPSteve Garvey, Tony Perez	60.00
JBWSJohnny Bench, Willie Stargell	65.00
CRRYCal Ripken Jr., Robin Yount	125.00
JBCFJohnny Bench, Carlton Fisk	70.00
CRATCal Ripken Jr., Alan Trammell	125.00
OSRYOzzie Smith, Robin Yount	90.00
RJDWReggie Jackson, Dave Winfield	

2002 Fleer Fall Classic Series of Champions

	MT
Complete Set (20):	25.00
Common Player:	1.00
Inserted 1:6	
1SOCYogi Berra	2.00
2SOCWade Boggs	1.50
3SOCDave Parker	1.00
4SOCJoe Carter	1.00
5SOCKirk Gibson	1.00
6SOCReggie Jackson	2.00
7SOCTony Kubek	1.00
8SOCDon Larsen	1.00
9SOCBill Mazeroski	1.00
10SOCEddie Murray	1.50
11SOCGraig Nettles	1.00
12SOCTony Perez	1.00
13SOCPhil Rizzuto	1.50
14SOCMike Schmidt	2.50
15SOCRed Schoendienst	1.00
16SOCDuke Snider	2.00
17SOCTy Cobb	2.50
18SOCLou Gehrig	3.00
19SOCBabe Ruth	4.00

2002 Fleer Fall Classic Series of Champions Game-Used

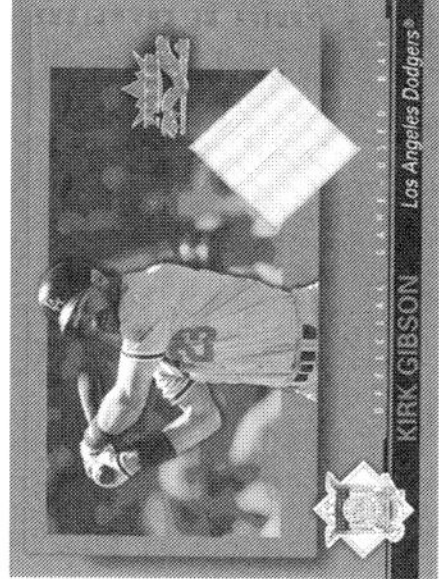

	MT
Common Player:	6.00
Inserted 1:36	
Golds:	.75-1.5X
Production 100 sets	
Bat Knob numbered to 10 not priced	
Yogi Berra/bat	20.00
Wade Boggs/jsy	10.00
Dave Parker/bat	6.00
Joe Carter/bat	8.00
Kirk Gibson/bat	8.00
Reggie Jackson bat	10.00
Tony Kubek/bat	10.00
Eddie Murray/bat	10.00
Graig Nettles/bat	10.00
Tony Perez/bat	10.00
Red Schoendienst/jsy	8.00
Duke Snider/bat	12.00
Babe Ruth/bat/25	180.00

2002 Fleer Flair

		MT
Complete Set (138):		NA
Common Player:		.25
Common (101-138):		5.00
Production 1,750		
Pack (5):		6.00
Hobby Box (20):		110.00
1	Scott Rolen	.40
2	Derek Jeter	3.00
3	Sean Casey	.40
4	Hideo Nomo	.50
5	Craig Biggio	.40
6	Randy Johnson	.75
7	J.D. Drew	.50
8	Greg Maddux	1.50
9	Paul LoDuca	.25
10	John Olerud	.50
11	Barry Larkin	.40
12	Mark Grace	.50
13	Jimmy Rollins	.25
14	Todd Helton	.75
15	Jim Edmonds	.40
16	Roy Oswalt	.40

17	Phil Nevin	.25
18	Tim Salmon	.25
19	Magglio Ordonez	.40
20	Roger Clemens	1.25
21	Raul Mondesi	.25
22	Edgar Martinez	.25
23	Pedro J. Martinez	.75
24	Edgardo Alfonzo	.25
25	Bernie Williams	.50
26	Gary Sheffield	.40
27	D'Angelo Jimenez	.25
28	Toby Hall	.25
29	Joe Mays	.25
30	Alfonso Soriano	.75
31	Mike Piazza	2.00
32	Lance Berkman	.50
33	Jim Thome	.50
34	Ben Sheets	.40
35	Brandon Inge	.25
36	Luis Gonzalez	.50
37	Jeff Kent	.25
38	Ben Grieve	.25
39	Carlos Delgado	.50
40	Pat Burrell	.50
41	Mark Buehrle	.25
42	Cristian Guzman	.25
43	Shawn Green	.40
44	Nomar Garciaparra	2.00
45	Carlos Beltran	.25
46	Troy Glaus	.50
47	Paul Konerko	.25
48	Moises Alou	.25
49	Kerry Wood	.50
50	Jose Vidro	.25
51	Juan Encarnacion	.25
52	Bobby Abreu	.25
53	C.C. Sabathia	.25
54	Alex Rodriguez	2.50
55	Albert Pujols	1.50
56	Bret Boone	.25
57	Orlando Hernandez	.40
58	Jason Kendall	.25
59	Tim Hudson	.40
60	Darin Erstad	.40
61	Mike Mussina	.60
62	Ken Griffey Jr.	2.00
63	Adrian Beltre	.25
64	Jeff Bagwell	.75
65	Vladimir Guerrero	.75
66	Mike Sweeney	.25
67	Sammy Sosa	1.50
68	Andruw Jones	.50
69	Richie Sexson	.40
70	Matt Morris	.25
71	Ivan Rodriguez	.50
72	Shannon Stewart	.25
73	Barry Bonds	1.50
74	Matt Williams	.40
75	Jason Giambi	.75
76	Brian Giles	.40
77	Cliff Floyd	.25
78	Tino Martinez	.25
79	Juan Gonzalez	.75
80	Frank Thomas	.75
81	Ichiro Suzuki	3.00
82	Barry Zito	.40
83	Chipper Jones	1.50
84	Adam Dunn	.75
85	Kazuhiro Sasaki	.25
86	Mark Quinn	.25
87	Rafael Palmeiro	.40
88	Jeromy Burnitz	.25
89	Curt Schilling	.40
90	Chris Richards	.25
91	Jon Leiber	.25
92	Doug Mientkiewicz	.25
93	Roberto Alomar	.50
94	Rich Aurilia	.25
95	Eric Chavez	.40
96	Larry Walker	.40
97	Manny Ramirez	.75
98	Tony Clark	.25
99	Tsuyoshi Shinjo	.25
100	Josh Beckett	.25
101	Dewon Brazelton	8.00
102	*Jeremy Lambert*	6.00
103	Andres Torres	5.00
104	*Matt Childers*	5.00
105	Wilson Betemit	6.00
106	Willie Harris	5.00
107	Drew Henson	10.00
108	Rafael Soriano	8.00
109	Carlos Valderrama	5.00
110	Victor Martinez	10.00
111	Juan Rivera	8.00
112	Felipe Lopez	6.00
113	Brandon Duckworth	5.00
114	Jeremy Owens	8.00
115	*Aaron Cook*	8.00
116	Derrick Lewis	5.00
117	Mark Teixeira	6.00
118	Ken Harvey	5.00
119	Tim Spooneybarger	10.00
120	Bill Hall	8.00
121	Adam Pettyjohn	5.00
122	Ramon Castro	6.00
123	Marlon Byrd	8.00
124	Matt White	8.00
125	*Eric Cyr*	5.00
126	Morgan Ensberg	5.00
127	Horacio Ramirez	5.00
128	*Ron Calloway*	6.00
129	Nick Punto	6.00
130	Joe Kennedy	6.00
131	*So Taguchi*	12.00
132	Austin Kearns	8.00
133	Mark Prior	15.00
134	*Kazuhisa Ishii*	35.00
135	Steve Torrealba	5.00
136	*Adam Walker*	8.00
137	Travis Hafner	5.00
138	Zach Day	5.00

2002 Fleer Flair Collection

	MT
Collection (1-100):	4-8X
Production 175	
Collection (101-138):	1-2X
Production 50	

2002 Fleer Flair Hot Numbers

	MT
Common Player:	15.00
Production 100 sets	
Manny Ramirez	35.00
Randy Johnson	40.00
Curt Schilling	35.00
Pedro J. Martinez	40.00
Nomar Garciaparra	75.00
Barry Larkin	35.00
Todd Helton	35.00
Larry Walker	25.00
Sean Casey	25.00
Jeff Bagwell	40.00
Craig Biggio	25.00
Shawn Green	25.00
Edgardo Alfonzo	15.00
Mike Piazza	60.00
Derek Jeter	90.00
Roger Clemens	
Chipper Jones	50.00
Jim Edmonds	15.00
J.D. Drew	30.00
Ivan Rodriguez	35.00
Rafael Palmeiro	30.00
Alex Rodriguez	65.00
Greg Maddux	60.00
Carlos Delgado	25.00

2002 Fleer Flair Jersey Heights

		MT
Common Player:		8.00
Inserted 1:18		
1JH	Edgardo Alfonzo	8.00
2JH	Jeff Bagwell	12.00
3JH	Craig Biggio	8.00
4JH	Barry Bonds	20.00
5JH	Sean Casey	8.00
6JH	Roger Clemens	20.00
7JH	Carlos Delgado	8.00
8JH	J.D. Drew	10.00
9JH	Jim Edmonds	8.00
10JH	Nomar Garciaparra	20.00
11JH	Shawn Green	8.00
12JH	Todd Helton	10.00
13JH	Derek Jeter	30.00
14JH	Randy Johnson	12.00
15JH	Chipper Jones	15.00
16JH	Barry Larkin	10.00
17JH	Greg Maddux	15.00
18JH	Pedro J. Martinez	12.00
19JH	Rafael Palmeiro	10.00
20JH	Mike Piazza	15.00
21JH	Manny Ramirez	10.00
22JH	Alex Rodriguez	15.00
23JH	Ivan Rodriguez	8.00
24JH	Curt Schilling	10.00
25JH	Larry Walker	8.00

2002 Fleer Flair Jersey Heights (Dual)

	MT
Common Card:	15.00
Production 100 sets	
Randy Johnson, Curt Schilling	35.00
Pedro J. Martinez, Nomar Garciaparra	50.00
Edgardo Alfonzo, Mike Piazza	35.00
Derek Jeter, Roger Clemens	75.00
Greg Maddux, Chipper Jones	50.00
Jim Edmonds, Jeff Bagwell	20.00
Jeff Bagwell, Craig Biggio	25.00
Rafael Palmeiro, Ivan Rodriguez	25.00
Carlos Delgado, Shawn Green	15.00
Todd Helton, Larry Walker	20.00
Sean Casey, Barry Larkin	30.00
Alex Rodriguez, Manny Ramirez	40.00

2002 Fleer Flair Power Tools

		MT
Common Player:		8.00
Inserted 1:19		
Golds:		1-2.5X
Production 100		
1PT	Roberto Alomar	10.00
2PT	Jeff Bagwell/150	15.00
3PT	Craig Biggio	10.00
4PT	Barry Bonds	20.00
5PT	Bret Boone	8.00
6PT	Pat Burrell/225	12.00
8PT	Eric Chavez	8.00
9PT	J.D. Drew/150	15.00
10PT	Jim Edmonds	8.00
11PT	Juan Gonzalez	10.00
12PT	Luis Gonzalez	8.00
13PT	Shawn Green	8.00
15PT	Derek Jeter	25.00
16PT	Doug Mientkiewicz	8.00
17PT	Magglio Ordonez	8.00
18PT	Rafael Palmeiro/100	15.00
19PT	Mike Piazza	15.00
20PT	Alex Rodriguez	15.00
21PT	Ivan Rodriguez	8.00
22PT	Scott Rolen/42	15.00
23PT	Reggie Sanders/120	12.00
24PT	Gary Sheffield	8.00
25PT	Tsuyoshi Shinjo	12.00
26PT	Miguel Tejada	8.00
27PT	Frank Thomas	12.00
28PT	Jim Thome/225	15.00
29PT	Larry Walker	8.00
30PT	Bernie Williams	10.00

2002 Fleer Flair Power Tools Dual

		MT
Common Card:		10.00
Inserted 1:40		
Golds:		1-2.5X
Production 50 sets		
1	Eric Chavez, Miguel Tejada	10.00
2	Barry Bonds, Tsuyoshi Shinjo	25.00
3	Jim Edmonds, J.D. Drew	15.00
4	Jeff Bagwell, Craig Biggio	15.00
5	Bernie Williams, Derek Jeter	35.00
6	Roberto Alomar, Mike Piazza	20.00
7	Sean Casey, Jim Thome/40	30.00
8	Pat Burrell, Scott Rolen	15.00
9	Gary Sheffield, Shawn Green	10.00
10	Ivan Rodriguez, Alex Rodriguez	15.00
11	Juan Gonzalez, Rafael Palmeiro	15.00
12	Magglio Ordonez, Frank Thomas	15.00
13	Larry Walker, Todd Helton/225	20.00
14	Luis Gonzalez, Reggie Sanders	10.00
15	Doug Mientkiewicz, Bret Boone	10.00

2002 Fleer Flair Sweet Swatch Patch

	MT
Common Player:	25.00
Random Box Topper	
Jeff Bagwell/45	75.00
Josh Beckett/60	50.00
Darin Erstad/50	40.00
Freddy Garcia/50	40.00
Juan Gonzalez/55	75.00
Mark Grace/75	60.00
Derek Jeter/20	
Jason Kendall/120	25.00
Paul LoDuca/50	35.00
Greg Maddux/50	90.00
Magglio Ordonez/55	40.00
Rafael Palmeiro/60	40.00
Mike Piazza/95	100.00
Alex Rodriguez/50	90.00
Ivan Rodriguez/50	60.00
Tim Salmon/40	40.00
Kazuhiro Sasaki/80	50.00
Alfonso Soriano/35	65.00
Larry Walker/60	40.00
Ted Williams/15	

2002 Fleer Flair Sweet Swatch Autographs

	MT
Common Player:	15.00
Quantity produced listed	
Derek Jeter/405	175.00

Barry Bonds/35	225.00
Drew Henson/785	40.00
Mark Teixeira/185	40.00
Dewon Brazelton/ 185	15.00
Mark Prior/285	90.00
Marlon Byrd/185	40.00
Ozzie Smith/185	65.00
Ron Cey/285	20.00
Paul Molitor/85	70.00
Maury Wills/285	25.00
Dale Murphy/285	60.00
David Espinosa/ 485	15.00
Dane Sardinha/ 485	15.00
Ben Sheets/85	50.00
Tony Perez/115	40.00
Brooks Robinson/ 185	50.00
So Taguchi/335	30.00
Al Kaline/285	60.00
Kazuhisa Ishii/ 335	120.00
Albert Pujols/50	80.00
Don Mattingly/85	150.00

2002 Fleer Flair Sweet Swatch Game-Used

	MT
Common Player:	10.00
1:hobby box	
Jeff Bagwell/490	20.00
Josh Beckett/500	20.00
Darin Erstad/525	15.00
Freddy Garcia/ 620	20.00
Brian Giles/445	15.00
Juan Gonzalez/ 505	15.00
Mark Grace/795	20.00
Derek Jeter/525	50.00
Jason Kendall/990	15.00
Paul LoDuca/440	15.00
Greg Maddux/475	25.00
Magglio Ordonez/ 495	12.00
Rafael Palmeiro/535	15.00
Mike Piazza/1,000	25.00
Alex Rodriguez/ 550	25.00
Ivan Rodriguez/ 475	15.00
Tim Salmon/465	10.00
Kazuhiro Sasaki/ 770	10.00
Alfonso Soriano/ 775	40.00
Larry Walker/430	12.00
Ted Williams/250	125.00

2002 Fleer Focus Jersey Edition

	MT
Complete Set (260):	65.00
Common Player:	.15
Common (226-260):	1.00
Inserted 1:4	
Pack (10):	2.50
Box (24):	50.00

1	Mike Piazza	2.00
2	Jason Giambi	.75
3	Jim Thome	.50
4	John Olerud	.40
5	J.D. Drew	.25
6	Richard Hidalgo	.15
7	Rusty Greer	.15
8	Tony Batista	.15
9	Omar Vizquel	.25
10	Randy Johnson	.75
11	Cristian Guzman	.15
12	Mark Grace	.40
13	Jeff Cirillo	.15
14	Mike Cameron	.15
15	Jeromy Burnitz	.15
16	Pokey Reese	.15
17	Richie Sexson	.25
18	Joe Randa	.15
19	Aramis Ramirez	.15
20	Pedro J. Martinez	1.00
21	Todd Hollandsworth	.15
22	Rondell White	.15
23	Tsuyoshi Shinjo	.40
24	Melvin Mora	.15
25	Tim Hudson	.40
26	Darrin Fletcher	.15
27	Bill Mueller	.15
28	Jeff Weaver	.15
29	Tony Clark	.15
30	Tom Glavine	.40
31	Jarrod Washburn	.25
32	Greg Vaughn	.15
33	Lee Stevens	.15
34	Charles Johnson	.15
35	Lance Berkman	.75
36	Bud Smith	.15
37	Keith Foulke	.15
38	Ben Davis	.15
39	Daryle Ward	.15
40	Bernie Williams	.50
41	Dean Palmer	.15
42	Mark Mulder	.25
43	Jason LaRue	.15
44	Jay Gibbons	.15
45	Brandon Duckworth	.15
46	Carlos Delgado	.40
47	Barry Zito	.25
48	Matt Morris	.15
49	J.T. Snow	.15
50	Albert Pujols	1.50
51	Brad Fullmer	.15
52	Damion Easley	.15
53	Pat Burrell	.50
54	Kevin Brown	.15
55	Todd Walker	.15
56	Rich Garces	.15
57	Carlos Pena	.15
58	Paul LoDuca	.15
59	Mike Lieberthal	.15
60	Barry Larkin	.40
61	Jon Lieber	.15
62	Jose Cruz	.15
63	Mo Vaughn	.40
64	Ivan Rodriguez	.50
65	Jorge Posada	.50
66	Magglio Ordonez	.40
67	Juan Encarnacion	.15
68	Shawn Estes	.15
69	Kevin Appier	.15
70	Jeff Bagwell	.75
71	Tim Wakefield	.15
72	Shannon Stewart	.15
73	Scott Rolen	.40
74	Bobby Higginson	.15
75	Jim Edmonds	.40
76	Adam Dunn	.75
77	Eric Chavez	.40
78	Adrian Beltre	.25
79	Jason Varitek	.15
80	Barry Bonds	2.00
81	Edgar Renteria	.15
82	Raul Mondesi	.25
83	Eric Karros	.15
84	Ken Griffey Jr.	1.50
85	Jermaine Dye	.15
86	Carlos Beltran	.15
87	Mark Quinn	.15
88	Terrence Long	.15
89	Shawn Green	.40
90	Nomar Garciaparra	1.50
91	Sean Casey	.25
92	Homer Bush	.15
93	Bobby Abreu	.25
94	Jamey Wright	.15
95	Tony Womack	.15
96	Larry Walker	.40
97	Doug Mientkiewicz	.15
98	Jimmy Rollins	.15
99	Brady Anderson	.15
100	Derek Jeter	2.50
101	Kevin Young	.15
102	Juan Pierre	.15
103	Edgar Martinez	.15
104	Corey Koskie	.15
105	Jeffrey Hammonds	.15
106	Luis Gonzalez	.40
107	Travis Fryman	.15
108	Kerry Wood	.40
109	Rafael Palmeiro	.40
110	Ichiro Suzuki	2.00
111	Russ Ortiz	.15
112	Jeff Kent	.25
113	Scott Erickson	.15
114	Bruce Chen	.15
115	Craig Biggio	.25
116	Robin Ventura	.25
117	Alex Rodriguez	2.00
118	Roy Oswalt	.40
119	Fred McGriff	.40
120	Juan Gonzalez	.75
121	David Justice	.40
122	Pat Hentgen	.15
123	Hideo Nomo	.40
124	Ramon Ortiz	.15
125	David Ortiz	.15
126	Phil Nevin	.15
127	Ryan Dempster	.15
128	Toby Hall	.15
129	Vladimir Guerrero	.75
130	Chipper Jones	1.50
131	Russell Branyan	.15
132	Jose Vidro	.15
133	Bubba Trammell	.15
134	Tino Martinez	.25
135	Greg Maddux	1.50
136	Derrek Lee	.15
137	Troy Glaus	.50
138	Joe Crede	.15
139	Steve Cox	.15
140	Sammy Sosa	1.50
141	Corey Patterson	.15
142	Vernon Wells	.15
143	Matt Lawton	.15
144	Gabe Kapler	.15
145	Johnny Damon	.15
146	Marty Cordova	.15
147	Moises Alou	.15
148	Fernando Tatis	.15
149	Tanyon Sturtze	.15
150	Roger Clemens	1.25
151	Paul Konerko	.40
152	Chan Ho Park	.15
153	Marcus Giles	.15
154	David Eckstein	.15
155	Mike Lowell	.15
156	Preston Wilson	.15
157	John Vander Wal	.15
158	Tim Salmon	.25
159	Andy Pettitte	.40
160	Mike Mussina	.50
161	Doug Davis	.15
162	Peter Bergeron	.15
163	Rich Aurilia	.15
164	Eric Milton	.15
165	Geoff Jenkins	.15
166	Todd Helton	.75
167	Bret Boone	.15
168	Kris Benson	.15
169	Brian Anderson	.15
170	Roberto Alomar	.50
171	Javier Vazquez	.15
172	Scott Schoeneweis	.15
173	Ryan Klesko	.15
174	Jacque Jones	.15
175	Andruw Jones	.50
176	Aubrey Huff	.15
177	Mark Buehrle	.15
178	Josh Beckett	.40
179	Ben Sheets	.25
180	Curt Schilling	.75
181	C.C. Sabathia	.15
182	Denny Neagle	.15
183	Jamie Moyer	.15
184	Jason Kendall	.15
185	Dee Brown	.15
186	Frank Thomas	.75
187	Damian Rolls	.15
188	Carlos Lee	.15
189	Kevin Jarvis	.15
190	Manny Ramirez	.75
191	Cliff Floyd	.25
192	Freddy Garcia	.25
193	Orlando Cabrera	.15
194	Mike Sweeney	.15
195	Gary Sheffield	.40
196	Rafael Furcal	.25
197	Esteban Loaiza	.15
198	Mike Hampton	.15
199	Brian Giles	.40
200	Darin Erstad	.40
201	David Wells	.15
202	Kenny Lofton	.25
203	Aaron Sele	.15
204	Jason Schmidt	.15
205	Javy Lopez	.15
206	Dmitri Young	.15
207	Darryl Kile	.15
208	Matt Williams	.25
209	Joe Kennedy	.15
210	Chuck Knoblauch	.15
211	Brian Jordan	.15
212	Roberto Person	.15
213	Alex Ochoa	.15
214	Steve Finley	.15
215	Ben Petrick	.15
216	Al Leiter	.25
217	Mark Kotsay	.15
218	Miguel Tejada	.40
219	David Segui	.15
220	A.J. Burnett	.15
221	Marlon Anderson	.15
222	Wiki Gonzalez	.15
223	Jeff Suppan	.15
224	Dave Roberts	.15
225	Jose Hernandez	.15
226	Angel Berroa	1.00
227	Sean Burroughs	1.50
228	*Luis Martinez*	1.00
229	*Adrian Burnside*	1.50
230	*John Ennis*	1.50
231	*Anastacio Martinez*	1.00
232	Hank Blalock	2.50
233	Eric Hinske	2.50
234	*Chris Booker*	1.00
235	*Colin Young*	1.00
236	*Mark Corey*	1.00
237	*Satoru Komiyama*	1.00
238	*So Taguchi*	3.00
239	*Elio Serrano*	1.00
240	*Reed Johnson*	1.00
241	*Jeremy Lambert*	1.00
242	*Chris Baker*	1.00
243	Orlando Hudson	1.00
244	*Travis Hughes*	1.00
245	*Kevin Frederick*	1.00
246	*Rodrigo Rosario*	2.00
247	*Jeremy Ward*	1.00
248	*Kazuhisa Ishii*	5.00
249	Austin Kearns	2.00
250	*Kyle Kane*	1.00
251	*Cam Esslinger*	1.00
252	*Jeff Austin*	1.00
253	*Brian Mallette*	1.00
254	Mark Prior	8.00
255	Mark Teixeira	2.00
256	Carlos Valderrama	1.00
257	Jason Hart	1.00
258	*Takahito Nomura*	1.00
259	Matt Thornton	1.00
260	Marlon Byrd	1.50

2002 Fleer Focus Jersey Edition Century

	MT
Cards (1-225):	6-10X
Cards (226-260):	.75-1.5X
Production 101-199	

A card number in parentheses ( ) indicates the set is unnumbered.

2002 Fleer Focus Jersey Edition Blue Chips

	MT
Complete Set (15):	12.00
Common Player:	.50
Inserted 1:6	
1BC Albert Pujols	2.50
2BC Sean Burroughs	.75
3BC Vernon Wells	.50
4BC Adam Dunn	2.00
5BC Pat Burrell	1.00
6BC Juan Pierre	.50
7BC Russell Branyan	.50
8BC Carlos Pena	.75
9BC Toby Hall	.50
10BCHank Blalock	1.00
11BCAlfonso Soriano	3.00
12BCJimmy Rollins	.75
13BCJose Ortiz	.50
14BCEric Hinske	1.00
15BCNick Johnson	1.00

2002 Fleer Focus Jersey Edition Blue Chips Game-Used

	MT
Inserted 1:96 Hobby	
Russell Branyan/jsy	8.00
Nick Johnson/jsy	10.00
Nick Johnson/patch/ 100	20.00

2002 Fleer Focus Jersey Ed. International Diamond Co.

	MT
Complete Set (25):	25.00
Common Player:	1.00
Inserted 1:8	
1IDC Bobby Abreu	1.00
2IDC Adrian Beltre	1.00
3IDC Jorge Posada	1.50
4IDC Vladimir Guerrero	2.00
5IDC Rafael Palmeiro	1.50
6IDC Sammy Sosa	4.00
7IDC Larry Walker	1.00
8IDC Manny Ramirez	2.00
9IDC Ichiro Suzuki	6.00
10IDCJose Cruz	1.00
11IDCJuan Gonzalez	2.00
12IDCBernie Williams	1.50
13IDCIvan Rodriguez	1.50
14IDCMoises Alou	1.00
15IDCCristian Guzman	1.00
16IDCAndruw Jones	1.50
17IDCAramis Ramirez	1.00
18IDCRaul Mondesi	1.00
19IDCEdgar Martinez	1.00
20IDCMagglio Ordonez	1.00
21IDCRoberto Alomar	1.50
22IDCChan Ho Park	1.00
23IDCKazuhiro Sasaki	1.00
24IDCTsuyoshi Shinjo	1.00
25IDCHideo Nomo	1.50

2002 Fleer Focus Jersey Ed. Int. Diam. Co. Game-Used

	MT
Common Player:	5.00
Inserted 1:144	
3IDC Jorge Posada/jsy	15.00
5IDC Rafael Palmeiro/jsy	8.00
8IDC Manny Ramirez/ jsy	10.00
13IDCIvan Rodriguez/jsy	6.00
16IDCAndruw Jones/jsy	6.00
17IDCAramis Ramirez/ jsy	5.00
18IDCRaul Mondesi/jsy	5.00
19IDCEdgar Martinez/jsy	6.00
22IDCChan Ho Park/jsy	6.00
23IDCKazuhiro Sasaki/ jsy	10.00
25IDCHideo Nomo/jsy	20.00

2002 Fleer Focus Jersey Ed. Int. Diam. Co. Patch

	MT
Common Player:	15.00
Production 100	
8IDC Manny Ramirez	30.00
13IDCIvan Rodriguez	20.00
18IDCRaul Mondesi	15.00
19IDCEdgar Martinez	20.00
22IDCChan Ho Park	20.00
25IDCHideo Nomo	90.00

2002 Fleer Focus Jersey Edition Jersey Number Parallel

	MT
(1-225) print run 26-50:	15-35X
(1-225) p/r 51-75:	10-20X
(1-225) p/r 76-99:	5-10X
Produced to player's jsy #	

Values quoted in this guide reflect the retail price of a card — the price a collector can expect to pay when buying a card from a dealer.

The wholesale price — that which a collector can expect to receive from a dealer when selling cards — will be significantly lower, depending on desirability and condition.

2002 Fleer Focus Jersey Edition K Corps

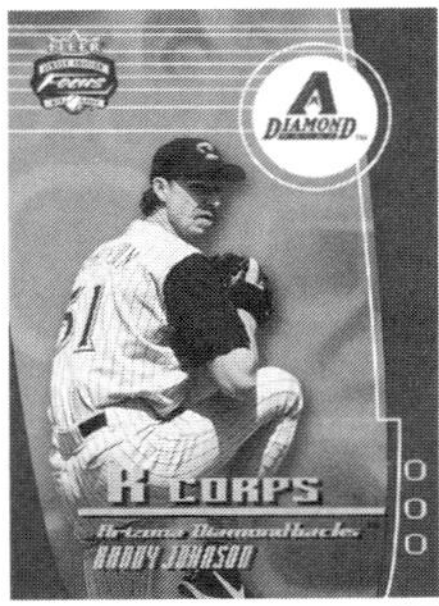

	MT
Complete Set (15):	20.00
Common Player:	1.00
Inserted 1:12	
1KC Roger Clemens	5.00
2KC Randy Johnson	3.00
3KC Tom Glavine	1.50
4KC Josh Beckett	1.50
5KC Matt Morris	1.00
6KC Curt Schilling	1.50
7KC Greg Maddux	5.00
8KC Tim Hudson	1.50
9KC Roy Oswalt	1.00
10KCKerry Wood	1.50
11KCBarry Zito	1.00
12KCKevin Brown	1.00
13KCRyan Dempster	1.00
14KCBen Sheets	1.00
15KCPedro J. Martinez	3.00

2002 Fleer Focus Jersey Edition K Corps Game-Used

	MT
Common Player:	5.00
Inserted 1:96	
2KC Randy Johnson/jsy	15.00
6KC Curt Schilling/jsy	12.00
7KC Greg Maddux/jsy	15.00
11KCBarry Zito/jsy	10.00
12KCKevin Brown/jsy	5.00
15KCPedro Martinez/jsy	12.00

2002 Fleer Focus Jersey Edition K Corps Patch

	MT
Production 100	
6KC Curt Schilling	20.00
12KCKevin Brown	30.00
15KCPedro Martinez	30.00

2002 Fleer Focus Jersey Edition Kings of Swing

	MT
Complete Set (20):	80.00
Common Player:	2.00
Inserted 1:48	
1KS Barry Bonds	10.00
2KS Mike Piazza	8.00
3KS Albert Pujols	6.00
4KS Todd Helton	3.00
5KS Ken Griffey Jr.	8.00
6KS Alex Rodriguez	10.00
7KS Sammy Sosa	6.00
8KS Troy Glaus	2.00
9KS Derek Jeter	12.00
10KSIchiro Suzuki	10.00
11KSManny Ramirez	3.00
12KSRoberto Alomar	2.50
13KSJuan Gonzalez	3.00
14KSShawn Green	2.00
15KSVladimir Guerrero	3.00
16KSNomar Garciaparra	8.00
17KSAdam Dunn	3.00
18KSJason Giambi	5.00
19KSEdgar Martinez	2.00
20KSChipper Jones	6.00

2002 Fleer Focus Jersey Ed. Kings of Swing Game-Used

	MT
Common Player:	5.00
Inserted 1:108	
Mike Piazza	15.00
Todd Helton	8.00
Alex Rodriguez	15.00
Derek Jeter	30.00
Manny Ramirez	8.00
Shawn Green	5.00
Edgar Martinez	6.00
Chipper Jones	15.00

2002 Fleer Focus Jersey Ed. Kings of Swing Patch

	MT
Production 100	
Todd Helton	25.00
Manny Ramirez	30.00
Shawn Green	20.00
Edgar Martinez	25.00
Mike Piazza	75.00

2002 Fleer Focus Jersey Edition Larger Than Life

	MT
Common Player:	4.00
Inserted 1:240	
1LL Jason Giambi	10.00
2LL Carlos Delgado	4.00
3LL Alex Rodriguez	20.00
4LL Preston Wilson	4.00
5LL Frank Thomas	6.00
6LL Nomar Garciaparra	15.00
7LL Jim Edmonds	4.00
8LL Jim Thome	5.00
9LL Barry Bonds	15.00
10LL Mo Vaughn	4.00
11LL Ichiro Suzuki	20.00
12LL Ivan Rodriguez	5.00
13LL Gary Sheffield	4.00
14LL Derek Jeter	25.00
15LL Jeff Bagwell	6.00
16LL Mike Piazza	15.00
17LL J.D. Drew	4.00
18LL Sammy Sosa	12.00
19LL Albert Pujols	12.00
20LL Luis Gonzalez	5.00

2002 Fleer Focus Jersey Ed. Larger Than Life Game-Used

	MT
Common Player:	6.00
Inserted 1:144	
Alex Rodriguez/jsy	20.00
Preston Wilson/jsy	6.00
Frank Thomas/jsy	10.00
Jim Edmonds/jsy	6.00
Mo Vaughn/jsy	6.00
Ivan Rodriguez/jsy	8.00
Derek Jeter/jsy	40.00
Jeff Bagwell/jsy	15.00
Mike Piazza/jsy	20.00
Luis Gonzalez/jsy	6.00

2002 Fleer Focus Jersey Ed. Larger Than Life Patch

	MT
Common Player:	15.00
Production 100	
Preston Wilson	15.00
Frank Thomas	25.00
Jim Edmonds	15.00
Ivan Rodriguez	20.00
Mike Piazza	65.00
Luis Gonzalez	15.00

2002 Fleer Focus Jersey Edition Lettermen

	MT
Complete Set (18):	
Common Player:	
1LTTRJ.D. Drew	
2LTTRBarry Bonds	
3LTTRTom Glavine	
4LTTRLarry Walker	
5LTTRChan Ho Park	
6LTTREdgar Martinez	
7LTTRIvan Rodriguez	
8LTTRLuis Gonzalez	
9LTTRManny Ramirez	
10LTTRHideo Nomo	
11LTTRMike Piazza	
12LTTRAlex Rodriguez	
13LTTRFrank Thomas	
14LTTRCurt Schilling	
15LTTRTodd Helton	
16LTTRJeff Bagwell	
17LTTRCarlos Delgado	
18LTTRPedro J. Martinez	

A card number in parentheses ( ) indicates the set is unnumbered.

2002 Fleer Focus Jersey Edition Materialistic Away

	MT
Complete Set (15):	90.00
Common Player:	4.00
Inserted 1:24	
Home:	2-5X
Production 50 sets	
Away Oversized:	.75-1.5X
One per hobby box	
Home Oversized:	2-5X
Production 50 sets	
1MA Derek Jeter	12.00
2MA Alex Rodriguez	10.00
3MA Mike Piazza	8.00
4MA Ivan Rodriguez	4.00
5MA Chipper Jones	6.00
6MA Todd Helton	4.00
7MA Nomar Garciaparra	8.00
8MA Barry Bonds	10.00
9MA Ichiro Suzuki	12.00
10MAKen Griffey Jr.	8.00
11MAJason Giambi	8.00
12MASammy Sosa	8.00
13MAAlbert Pujols	8.00
14MAPedro J. Martinez	6.00
15MAVladimir Guerrero	6.00

2002 Fleer Genuine

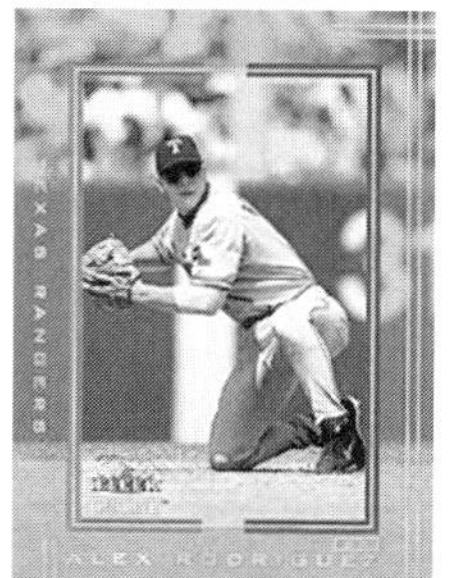

		MT
Complete Set (140):		NA
Common Player:		.15
Common (101-140):		5.00
Production 2,002		
Pack (5):		5.50
Box (20):		90.00
1	Alex Rodriguez	2.00
2	Manny Ramirez	.75
3	Jim Thome	.40
4	Eric Milton	.15
5	Todd Helton	.60
6	Mike Mussina	.50
7	Ichiro Suzuki	3.00
8	Randy Johnson	.75
9	Mark Mulder	.15
10	Johnny Damon	.15
11	Sean Casey	.25
12	Albert Pujols	1.50
13	Mark Grace	.40
14	Moises Alou, Mark Mulder	.15
15	Raul Mondesi, Roberto Alomar	.25
16	Cliff Floyd, Scott Rolen	.15
17	Vladimir Guerrero, Tom Glavine	.40
18	Pat Burrell, Bobby Abreu	.25
19	Ryan Klesko, Nomar Garciaparra	.50
20	Mike Hampton, Darin Erstad	.15
21	Shawn Green Cliff Floyd	.15
22	Rich Aurilia, Tim Hudson	.15
23	Matt Morris, Jim Thome	.20
24	Curt Schilling, Nolan Ryan	.75
25	Kevin Brown, Reggie Jackson	.40
26	Adrian Beltre, Rafael Palmeiro	.40
27	Joe Mays, Ken Griffey Jr.	.75
28	Luis Gonzalez, Sammy Sosa	.75
29	Barry Larkin, Vladimir Guerrero	.40
30	A.J. Burnett, Ichiro Suzuki	1.00
31	Eric Munson	.15
32	Juan Gonzalez	.75
33	Lance Berkman	.40
34	Fred McGriff	.25
35	Paul Konerko	.15
36	Pedro J. Martinez	.75
37	Adam Dunn	.75
38	Jeromy Burnitz	.15
39	Mike Sweeney	.15
40	Bret Boone	.15
41	Ken Griffey Jr.	2.00
42	Eric Chavez	.25
43	Mark Quinn	.15
44	Roberto Alomar	.50
45	Bobby Abreu	.15
46	Bartolo Colon	.25
47	Jimmy Rollins	.15
48	Chipper Jones	1.50
49	Ben Sheets	.15
50	Freddy Garcia	.15
51	Sammy Sosa	1.50
52	Rafael Palmeiro	.50
53	Preston Wilson	.15
54	Troy Glaus	.50
55	Josh Beckett	.15
56	C.C. Sabathia	.15
57	Magglio Ordonez	.40
58	Brian Giles	.40
59	Darin Erstad	.25
60	Gary Sheffield	.30
61	Paul LoDuca	.15
62	Derek Jeter	3.00
63	Greg Maddux	1.50
64	Kerry Wood	.50
65	Toby Hall	.15
66	Barry Bonds	1.50
67	Jeff Bagwell	.75
68	Jason Kendall	.15
69	Richard Hidalgo	.15
70	J.D. Drew	.40
71	Tom Glavine	.25
72	Javier Vazquez	.15
73	Doug Mientkiewicz	.15
74	Jason Giambi	.75
75	Carlos Delgado	.40
76	Aramis Ramirez	.15
77	Torii Hunter	.15
78	Ivan Rodriguez	.50
79	Charles Johnson	.15
80	Jeff Kent	.25
81	Jacque Jones	.15
82	Larry Walker	.40
83	Cristian Guzman	.15
84	Jermaine Dye	.15
85	Roger Clemens	1.00
86	Mike Piazza	2.00
87	Craig Biggio	.25
88	Phil Nevin	.25
89	Jeff Cirillo	.15
90	Barry Zito	.25
91	Ryan Dempster	.15
92	Mark Buehrle	.15
93	Nomar Garciaparra	2.00
94	Frank Thomas	.75
95	Jim Edmonds	.25
96	Geoff Jenkins	.25
97	Scott Rolen	.30
98	Tim Hudson	.25
99	Shannon Stewart	.15
100	Richie Sexson	.25
101	Orlando Hudson	5.00
102	*Doug Devore*	5.00
103	*Rene Reyes*	5.00
104	*Steve Bechler*	8.00
105	*Jorge Nunez*	5.00
106	*Mitch Wylie*	5.00
107	*Jaime Cerda*	5.00
108	*Brandon Puffer*	10.00
109	*Tyler Yates*	6.00
110	Bill Hall	5.00
111	*Peter Zamora*	6.00
112	*Jeff Deardorff*	5.00
113	*J.J. Putz*	5.00
114	*Scotty Layfield*	6.00
115	*Brandon Backe*	5.00
116	*Andy Pratt*	5.00
117	Mark Prior	15.00
118	*Franklyn German*	5.00
119	*Todd Donovan*	6.00
120	*Franklin Nunez*	5.00
121	*Adam Walker*	5.00
122	*Ron Calloway*	5.00
123	*Tim Kalita*	5.00
124	*Kazuhisa Ishii*	15.00
125	Mark Teixeira	6.00
126	*Nate Field*	5.00
127	*Nelson Castro*	5.00
128	*So Taguchi*	8.00
129	Marlon Byrd	6.00
130	Drew Henson	8.00
131	Kenny Kelly	5.00
132	*John Ennis*	8.00
133	*Anastacio Martinez*	5.00
134	Matt Guerrier	5.00
135	*Tom Wilson*	6.00
136	*Ben Howard*	8.00
137	*Chris Baker*	5.00
138	*Kevin Frederick*	5.00
159	*Wilson Valdez*	5.00
140	Austin Kearns	8.00

2002 Fleer Genuine Bat's Incredible

		MT
Complete Set (25):		70.00
Common Player:		1.50
Inserted 1:10		
1BI	Todd Helton	2.50
2BI	Chipper Jones	5.00
3BI	Luis Gonzalez	2.00
4BI	Barry Bonds	5.00
5BI	Jason Giambi	2.50
6BI	Alex Rodriguez	8.00
7BI	Manny Ramirez	2.50
8BI	Jeff Bagwell	2.50
9BI	Shawn Green	1.50
10BI	Albert Pujols	4.00
11BI	Paul LoDuca	1.50
12BI	Mike Piazza	6.00
13BI	Derek Jeter	10.00
14BI	Edgar Martinez	1.50
15BI	Juan Gonzalez	2.50
16BI	Magglio Ordonez	1.50
17BI	Jermaine Dye	1.50
18BI	Larry Walker	1.50
19BI	Phil Nevin	1.50
20BI	Ivan Rodriguez	2.00
21BI	Ichiro Suzuki	10.00
22BI	J.D. Drew	1.50
23BI	Vladimir Guerrero	2.50
24BI	Sammy Sosa	5.00
25BI	Ken Griffey Jr.	6.00

2002 Fleer Genuine Bat's Incredible Game-used

		MT
Common Player:		8.00
Inserted 1:20		
1BIGU	Todd Helton	10.00
2BIGU	Chipper Jones	15.00
4BIGU	J.D. Drew	15.00
5BIGU	Alex Rodriguez	15.00
6BIGU	Manny Ramirez	12.00
7BIGU	Shawn Green	8.00
8BIGU	Derek Jeter	30.00
9BIGU	Edgar Martinez	8.00
10BIGU	Juan Gonzalez	10.00
11BIGU	Jermaine Dye	8.00
12BIGU	Phil Nevin	8.00
13BIGU	Ivan Rodriguez	10.00

2002 Fleer Genuine Genuine Ink

		MT
Common Autograph		15.00
Production varies		
1GI	Barry Bonds/150	140.00
2GI	Ron Cey/175	15.00
3GI	Derek Jeter/150	160.00
4GI	Al Kaline/300	60.00
5GI	Don Mattingly/50	220.00
6GI	Paul Molitor	50.00
7GI	Dale Murphy/700	40.00
8GI	Phil Rizzuto/700	50.00
9GI	Brooks Robinson/140	60.00
10GI	Maury Willis/975	15.00

2002 Fleer Genuine Leaders

		MT
Complete Set (15):		25.00
Common Player:		1.00
Inserted 1:6		
1GL	Sammy Sosa	3.00
2GL	Todd Helton	1.50
3GL	Alex Rodriguez	4.00
4GL	Roger Clemens	2.00
5GL	Barry Bonds	3.00
6GL	Randy Johnson	1.50
7GL	Albert Pujols	2.50
8GL	Curt Schilling	1.00
9GL	Bernie Williams	1.00
10GL	Ken Griffey Jr.	4.00
11GL	Pedro J. Martinez	1.50
12GL	Juan Gonzalez	1.50
13GL	Hideo Nomo	1.00
14GL	Bret Boone	1.00
15GL	Ichiro Suzuki	6.00

2002 Fleer Genuine Leaders Game-Used

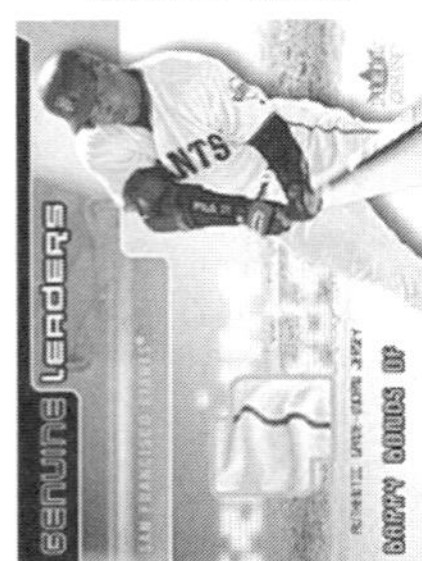

		MT
Common Player:		10.00
Inserted 1:16		
2GL	Todd Helton	10.00
3GL	Alex Rodriguez	15.00
4GL	Roger Clemens	15.00
5GL	Barry Bonds	20.00
6GL	Randy Johnson	12.00
8GL	Curt Schilling	10.00
9GL	Bernie Williams	10.00
11GL	Pedro J. Martinez	10.00
13GL	Hideo Nomo	15.00

2002 Fleer Genuine Names of the Game

		MT
Complete Set (30):		75.00
Common Player:		1.50
Inserted 1:10 H, 1:20 R		
1	Mike Piazza	6.00
2	Chipper Jones	5.00
3	Jim Edmonds	1.50
4	Barry Larkin	1.50
5	Frank Thomas	2.50
6	Manny Ramirez	2.50
7	Carlos Delgado	2.00
8	Brian Giles	1.50
9	Kerry Wood	2.00
10	Derek Jeter	10.00
11	Adam Dunn	2.50
12	Gary Sheffield	1.50
13	Luis Gonzalez	2.00
14	Mark Mulder	1.50
15	Roberto Alomar	2.00
16	Scott Rolen	1.50
17	Tom Glavine	1.50
18	Bobby Abreu	1.50
19	Nomar Garciaparra	6.00
20	Darin Erstad	1.50
21	Cliff Floyd	1.50
22	Tim Hudson	1.50
23	Jim Thome	1.50
24	Nolan Ryan	10.00
25	Reggie Jackson	3.00
26	Rafael Palmeiro	1.50
27	Ken Griffey Jr.	6.00
28	Sammy Sosa	5.00
29	Vladimir Guerrero	2.50
30	Ichiro Suzuki	10.00

2002 Fleer Genuine Names of the Game Memorabilia

		MT
Common Player:		8.00
1:24 H, 1:100 R		
1	Roberto Alomar	10.00
2	Carlos Delgado	10.00
3	Jim Edmonds	8.00
4	Darin Erstad	8.00
5	Cliff Floyd	8.00
6	Nomar Garciaparra SP/90	60.00
7	Brian Giles	8.00
8	Luis Gonzalez	10.00
9	Tim Hudson	8.00
10	Derek Jeter	30.00
11	Chipper Jones	15.00
12	Barry Larkin	10.00
13	Mark Mulder	8.00
14	Rafael Palmeiro	10.00
15	Mike Piazza	20.00
16	Manny Ramirez	12.00
17	Scott Rolen	10.00
18	Nolan Ryan	40.00
19	Jim Thome	12.00

2002 Fleer Genuine Tip of the Cap

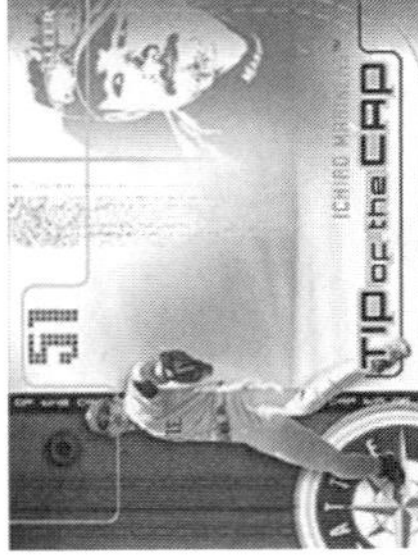

		MT
Complete Set (25):		45.00
Common Player:		.75
Inserted 1:6		
1TC	Alex Rodriguez	6.00
2TC	Derek Jeter	8.00
3TC	Kazuhiro Sasaki	.75
4TC	Barry Bonds	4.00
5TC	J.D. Drew	1.00
6TC	Tsuyoshi Shinjo	.75
7TC	Alfonso Soriano	2.00
8TC	Albert Pujols	3.00
9TC	Tom Seaver	2.50
10TC	Drew Henson	1.00
11TC	Dave Winfield	1.00
12TC	Carlos Delgado	1.00
13TC	Lou Boudreau	.75
14TC	Shawn Green	.75
15TC	Roger Clemens	3.00
16TC	Randy Johnson	2.00
17TC	Sammy Sosa	4.00
18TC	Rafael Palmeiro	1.50
19TC	Ken Griffey Jr.	6.00
20TC	Ichiro Suzuki	8.00
21TC	Eric Chavez	.75
22TC	Andruw Jones	.75
23TC	Miguel Tejada	.75
24TC	Pedro J. Martinez	2.00
25TC	Tim Salmon	.75

2002 Fleer Genuine Tip of the Cap Game-Used

		MT
Common Player:		
1TC	Alex Rodriguez/670	20.00
2TC	Derek Jeter	
4TC	Barry Bonds/32	75.00
5TC	J.D. Drew/8	
7TC	Alfonso Soriano/4	
9TC	Tom Seaver/224	25.00
10TC	Drew Henson/361	20.00
11TC	Dave Winfield/363	20.00
12TC	Carlos Delgado/219	25.00
13TC	Lou Boudreau/303	20.00
16TC	Randy Johnson/74	40.00
18TC	Rafael Palmeiro/300	20.00
21TC	Eric Chavez/14	
22TC	Andruw Jones/19	65.00
23TC	Miguel Tejada/225	15.00
24TC	Pedro Martinez/2	
25TC	Tim Salmon/6	

2002 Fleer Genuine Touch 'Em All

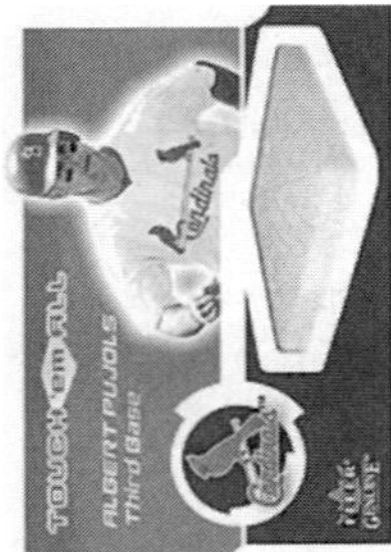

		MT
Complete Set (25):		70.00
Common Player:		1.50
Inserted 1:10		
1TEA	Derek Jeter	10.00
2TEA	Sammy Sosa	5.00
3TEA	Albert Pujols	4.00
4TEA	Vladimir Guerrero	2.50
5TEA	Ken Griffey Jr.	6.00
6TEA	Nomar Garciaparra	6.00
7TEA	Luis Gonzalez	1.50
8TEA	Barry Bonds	5.00
9TEA	Manny Ramirez	2.50
10TEA	Jason Giambi	2.50
11TEA	Chipper Jones	5.00
12TEA	Ichiro Suzuki	10.00

13TEAAlex Rodriguez 8.00
14TEAJuan Gonzalez 2.50
15TEATodd Helton 2.00
16TEARoberto Alomar 2.00
17TEAJeff Bagwell 2.50
18TEAMike Piazza 6.00
19TEAGary Sheffield 1.50
20TEAIvan Rodriguez 2.00
21TEAFrank Thomas 2.50
22TEABobby Abreu 1.50
23TEAJ.D. Drew 1.50
24TEAScott Rolen 1.50
25TEADarin Erstad 1.50

2002 Fleer Genuine Touch 'Em All Base

MT
Common Player: 6.00
Production 350 sets
1TEADerek Jeter 20.00
2TEASammy Sosa 15.00
3TEAAlbert Pujols 15.00
4TEAVladimir Guerrero 15.00
5TEAKen Griffey Jr. 20.00
6TEANomar Garciaparra 15.00
7TEALuis Gonzalez 10.00
8TEABarry Bonds 15.00
9TEAManny Ramirez 10.00
10TEAJason Giambi 10.00
11TEAChipper Jones 15.00
12TEAIchiro Suzuki 35.00
13TEAAlex Rodriguez 15.00
14TEAJuan Gonzalez 12.00
15TEATodd Helton 12.00
16TEARoberto Alomar 15.00
17TEAJeff Bagwell 12.00
18TEAMike Piazza 15.00
19TEAGary Sheffield 6.00
20TEAIvan Rodriguez 8.00
21TEAFrank Thomas 10.00
22TEABobby Abreu 6.00
23TEAJ.D. Drew 8.00
24TEAScott Rolen 8.00
25TEADarin Erstad 6.00

2002 Fleer Greats of the Game

MT
Complete Set (100): 45.00
Common Player: .40
Pack (5): 5.00
Box (24): 100.00
1 Cal Ripken Jr. 6.00
2 Paul Molitor 1.50
3 Roberto Clemente 4.00
4 Cy Young 1.50
5 Tris Speaker .75
6 Lou Brock .40
7 Fred Lynn .40
8 Harmon Killebrew 1.50
9 Ted Williams 6.00
10 Dave Winfield 1.00
11 Orlando Cepeda .40
12 Johnny Mize .40
13 Walter Johnson 2.00
14 Roy Campanella 1.50
15 George Sisler .40
16 Bo Jackson .40
17 Rollie Fingers .40
18 Brooks Robinson 1.50
19 Billy Williams .40
20 Maury Wills .40
21 Jimmie Foxx 1.50
22 Alan Trammell .40
23 Rogers Hornsby 1.50
24 Don Drysdale 1.00
25 Bob Feller .75
26 Jackie Robinson 5.00
27 Whitey Ford 1.50
28 Enos Slaughter .40
29 Rod Carew 1.00
30 Eddie Mathews 1.50
31 Ron Cey .40
32 Thurman Munson 2.00
33 Ty Cobb 3.00
34 Rocky Colavito .75
35 Satchel Paige 1.50
36 Andre Dawson .75
37 Phil Rizzuto .75
38 Roger Maris 3.00
39 Earl Weaver .40
40 Joe Carter .40
41 Christy Mathewson 1.50
42 Tony Lazzeri .40
43 Gil Hodges .75
44 Gaylord Perry .40
45 Steve Carlton 1.00
46 George Kell .40
47 Mickey Cochrane 1.00
48 Joe Morgan .60
49 Steve Garvey .40
50 Bob Gibson 1.50
51 Lefty Grove .40
52 Warren Spahn 1.00
53 Willie McCovey .40
54 Frank Robinson 1.50
55 Rich "Goose" Gossage .40
56 Hank Bauer .40
57 Hoyt Wilhelm .40
58 Mel Ott .75
59 Preacher Roe .75
60 Yogi Berra 2.00
61 Nolan Ryan 6.00
62 Dizzy Dean .75
63 Ryne Sandberg 2.00
64 Frank Howard .40
65 Hack Wilson .40
66 Robin Yount 1.50
67 Al Kaline 1.50
68 Mike Schmidt 2.00
69 Vida Blue .40
70 George Brett 2.00
71 Sparky Anderson .40
72 Tom Seaver 1.50
73 Bill "Moose" Skowron .40
74 Don Mattingly 2.00
75 Carl Yastrzemski 1.50
76 Eddie Murray 1.00
77 Jim Palmer 1.00
78 Bill Dickey .75
79 Ozzie Smith 1.50
80 Dale Murphy .75
81 Nap Lajoie 1.00
82 Jim "Catfish" Hunter 1.00
83 Duke Snider 1.00
84 Luis Aparicio .40
85 Reggie Jackson 1.50
86 Honus Wagner 1.50
87 Johnny Bench 2.00
88 Stan Musial 3.00
89 Carlton Fisk .75
90 Tony Oliva .75
91 Wade Boggs .75
92 Jim Rice .40
93 Bill Mazeroski .40
94 Ralph Kiner .40
95 Tony Perez .40
96 Kirby Puckett 2.50
97 Bobby Bonds .75
98 Bill Terry .40
99 Juan Marichal .75
100 Hank Greenberg 1.00

2002 Fleer Greats of the Game Autographs

MT
Common Player: 10.00
Inserted 1:24
SA Sparky Anderson 15.00
LA Luis Aparicio 15.00
HB Hank Bauer 10.00
JB Johnny Bench 65.00
YB Yogi Berra 45.00
PB Paul Blair 12.00
VB Vida Blue 15.00
WB Wade Boggs 35.00
BB Bobby Bonds 15.00
GB George Brett/150 140.00
LB Lou Brock/250 25.00
RC Rod Carew/250 40.00
SC Steve Carlton 25.00
JC Joe Carter 15.00
OC Orlando Cepeda 20.00
CE Ron Cey 12.00
CO Rocky Colavito 45.00
AD Andre Dawson 20.00
BF Bob Feller 35.00
RF Rollie Fingers 15.00
CF Carlton Fisk/100 65.00
WF Whitey Ford 40.00
SG Steve Garvey 15.00
BG Bob Gibson/200 40.00
RG Rich "Goose" Gossage 12.00
FH Frank Howard 15.00
RJ Reggie Jackson/150 70.00
AK Al Kaline 40.00
GK George Kell 12.00
HK Harmon Killebrew 35.00
RK Ralph Kiner/250 35.00
FL Fred Lynn 15.00
JM Juan Marichal 20.00
DM Don Mattingly/300 100.00
BM Bill Mazeroski/200 20.00
WM Willie McCovey 30.00
PM Paul Molitor 30.00
JM Joe Morgan 35.00
MU Dale Murphy 40.00
EM Eddie Murray/250 70.00
SM Stan Musial/200 75.00
TO Tony Oliva 20.00
JP Jim Palmer 20.00
DP Dave Parker 15.00
TP Tony Perez 20.00
GP Gaylord Perry 15.00
KP Kirby Puckett/250 100.00
JR Jim Rice 20.00
CR Cal Ripken Jr./100 260.00
PR Phil Rizzuto/300 80.00
BR Brooks Robinson 30.00
FR Frank Robinson/250 40.00
PR Preacher Roe 20.00
NR Nolan Ryan/150 175.00
RS Ryne Sandberg/200 75.00
MS Mike Schmidt/150 100.00
TS Tom Seaver/150 70.00
BS Bill "Moose" Skowron 10.00
ES Enos Slaughter 15.00
OS Ozzie Smith/300 65.00
DS Duke Snider 35.00
WS Warren Spahn 40.00
AT Alan Trammell 30.00
HW Hoyt Wilhelm 15.00
BW Billy Williams 25.00
MW Maury Wills 15.00
DW Dave Winfield/250 25.00
CY Carl Yastrzemski/200 100.00
RY Robin Yount 70.00

2002 Fleer Greats of the Game Dueling Duos

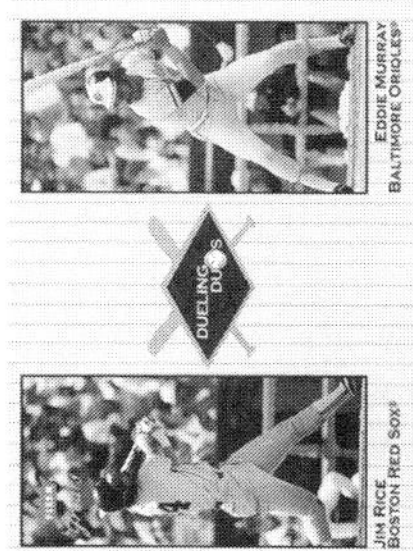

MT
Complete Set (29): 90.00
Common Player: 2.00
Inserted 1:6
1DD Johnny Bench, Carlton Fisk 4.00
2DD Roy Campanella, Yogi Berra 5.00
3DD Stan Musial, Ted Williams 8.00
4DD Carl Yastrzemski, Reggie Jackson 3.00
5DD Babe Ruth, Jimmie Foxx 8.00
6DD Steve Carlton, Nolan Ryan 8.00
7DD Wade Boggs, Don Mattingly 6.00
8DD Brooks Robinson, Roger Maris 5.00
9DD Paul Molitor, Don Mattingly 6.00
10DDSparky Anderson, Earl Weaver 2.00
11DDBob Gibson, Duke Snider 3.00
12DDYogi Berra, Gil Hodges 4.00
13DDJoe Morgan, Ryne Sandberg 3.00
14DDTony Perez, Carl Yastrzemski 3.00
15DDJimmie Foxx, Bill Dickey 3.00
16DDRalph Kiner, Duke Snider 2.00
17DDNellie Fox, Rocky Colavito 2.00
18DDWillie McCovey, Johnny Bench 3.00
19DDDuke Snider, Eddie Mathews 4.00
20DDReggie Jackson, Jim Rice 3.00
21DDEddie Murray, Jim Rice 2.00
22DDPaul Molitor, Dave Winfield 3.00
23DDRobin Yount, Dave Winfield 3.00
24DDEnos Slaughter, Ted Kluszewski 2.00
25DDWade Boggs, George Brett 4.00
26DDGeorge Brett, Eddie Murray 4.00
27DDGeorge Brett, Cal Ripken Jr. 8.00
28DDKirby Puckett, Don Mattingly 8.00

29DDGeorge Brett, Mike Schmidt 5.00

2002 Fleer Greats of Game Dueling Duos Game Used Dual

MT

Common Player:
Production 25 sets
1DDDJohnny Bench, Carlton Fisk
2DDDRoy Campanella, Yogi Berra
3DDDCarl Yastrzemski, Reggie Jackson
4DDDBabe Ruth, Jimmie Foxx
5DDDKirby Puckett, Don Mattingly
6DDDSteve Carlton, Nolan Ryan
7DDDWade Boggs, Don Mattingly
8DDDBrooks Robinson, Roger Maris
9DDDPaul Molitor, Don Mattingly
10DDDSparky Anderson, Earl Weaver
11DDDBob Gibson, Duke Snider
12DDDYogi Berra, Gil Hodges
13DDDJoe Morgan, Ryne Sandberg
14DDDTony Perez, Carl Yastrzemski
15DDDJimmie Foxx, Bill Dickey
16DDDRalph Kiner, Duke Snider
17DDDNellie Fox, Rocky Colavito
18DDDWillie McCovey, Johnny Bench
19DDDDuke Snider, Eddie Mathews
20DDDReggie Jackson, Jim Rice
21DDDEddie Murray, Jim Rice
22DDDPaul Molitor, Dave Winfield
23DDDRobin Yount, Dave Winfield
24DDDEnos Slaughter, Ted Kluszewski
25DDDWade Boggs, George Brett
26DDDGeorge Brett, Eddie Murray
27DDDGeorge Brett, Cal Ripken Jr.

2002 Fleer Greats of the Game Dueling Duos G-U Single

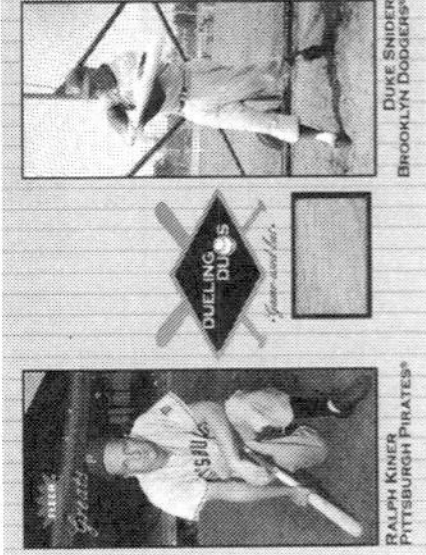

MT

Common Card: 15.00
Inserted 1:24
Johnny Bench, Carlton Fisk 20.00
Roy Campanella, Yogi Berra 25.00
Carl Yastrzemski, Reggie Jackson 30.00
Babe Ruth, Jimmie Foxx/75 80.00
Kirby Puckett, Don Mattingly 40.00
Steve Carlton, Nolan Ryan 80.00
Wade Boggs, Don Mattingly 35.00
Brooks Robinson, Roger Maris 40.00
Paul Molitor, Don Mattingly 30.00
Sparky Anderson, Earl Weaver 15.00
Bob Gibson, Duke Snider/200 25.00
Yogi Berra, Gil Hodges 25.00
Joe Morgan, Ryne Sandberg 30.00
Tony Perez, Carl Yastrzemski 25.00
Jimmie Foxx, Bill Dickey 30.00
Ralph Kiner, Duke Snider 25.00
Nellie Fox, Rocky Colavito 20.00
Willie McCovey, Johnny Bench 25.00
Duke Snider, Eddie Mathews 20.00
Reggie Jackson, Jim Rice 20.00
Eddie Murray, Jim Rice 15.00
Paul Molitor, Dave Winfield 20.00
Robin Yount, Dave Winfield 20.00
Enos Slaughter, Ted Kluszewski 15.00
Wade Boggs, George Brett 25.00
George Brett, Eddie Murray 20.00
George Brett, Cal Ripken Jr. 40.00

2002 Fleer Greats of the Game Through the Years Level 1

MT

Common Player: 10.00
Inserted 1:24
George Brett 25.00
Reggie Jackson A's 25.00
Reggie Jackson Angels 20.00
Ted Williams/350 125.00
Robin Yount 20.00
Willie McCovey 10.00
Paul Molitor Brewers 20.00
Paul Molitor Blue Jays 15.00
Jim Palmer 10.00
Brooks Robinson 15.00
Carl Yastrzemski 30.00
Don Mattingly 35.00
Carlton Fisk hitting 15.00
Carlton Fisk fielding 15.00
Nolan Ryan 60.00
Eddie Murray 10.00
Wade Boggs 15.00
Tony Perez 10.00
Ted Kluszewski 20.00
Bo Jackson Royals 15.00
Bo Jackson White Sox 15.00
Johnny Bench 25.00
Jackie Robinson 65.00
Hoyt Wilhelm 10.00
Vida Blue 10.00
Dave Winfield 10.00
Frank Robinson 15.00
Jim Rice 10.00
Jim Rice 10.00
Cal Ripken Hitting 50.00
Cal Ripken Fielding 50.00

2002 Fleer Greats of the Game Through the Years Level 2

MT

Common Player: 25.00
Production 100 sets
George Brett 80.00
Reggie Jackson 50.00
Ted Williams 250.00
Robin Yount 50.00
Willie McCovey 30.00
Paul Molitor 50.00
Jim Palmer 25.00
Carl Yastrzemski 75.00
Don Mattingly 125.00
Carlton Fisk 50.00
Nolan Ryan 150.00
Eddie Murray 25.00
Wade Boggs 40.00
Ted Kluszewski 50.00
Bo Jackson Royals 40.00
Bo Jackson White Sox 40.00
Johnny Bench 70.00
Dave Winfield 35.00
Jim Rice 25.00
Jim Rice 25.00
Cal Ripken Jr. 100.00
Cal Ripken Jr. 100.00

2002 Fleer Greats of the Game Through the Years Level 3

MT

Complete Set (19):
Common Player:
1TYCGeorge Brett
2TYCReggie Jackson
3TYCTed Williams
4TYCRobin Yount
5TYCWillie McCovey
6TYCPaul Molitor
7TYCCarl Yastrzemski
8TYCDon Mattingly
9TYCCarlton Fisk
10TYCNolan Ryan
11TYCEddie Murray
12TYCWade Boggs
13TYCTed Kluszewski
14TYCJohnny Bench
15TYCDave Winfield
16TYCJim Rice
17TYCJim Rice
18TYCCal Ripken Jr.
19TYCCal Ripken Jr.

2002 Fleer Greats the Game Through Years Patch Edition

MT

Common Player: 25.00
Production 100 sets
George Brett 80.00
Reggie Jackson A's 50.00
Reggie Jackson Angels 50.00
Ted Williams 250.00
Robin Yount 50.00
Willie McCovey 30.00
Paul Molitor Brewers 50.00
Paul Molitor Blue Jays 40.00
Jim Palmer 25.00
Carl Yastrzemski 75.00
Don Mattingly 125.00
Carlton Fisk 50.00
Carlton Fisk 50.00
Nolan Ryan 150.00
Eddie Murray 25.00
Wade Boggs 40.00
Tony Perez 25.00
Ted Kluszewski 50.00
Bo Jackson Royals 40.00
Bo Jackson White Sox 40.00
Johnny Bench 70.00
Dave Winfield 35.00
Frank Robinson 50.00
Jim Rice 25.00
Jim Rice 25.00
Cal Ripken Jr. 100.00
Cal Ripken Jr. 100.00

2002 Fleer Hot Prospects

MT

Complete Set (125):
Common Player: .25
Common (81-105): 8.00
Production 1,000
Common (106-125): 5.00
Production 1,500
Pack (5): 6.00
Box (18): 100.00
1 Derek Jeter 3.00
2 Garret Anderson .25
3 Scott Rolen .40
4 Bret Boone .25
5 Lance Berkman .75
6 Andruw Jones .50
7 Ivan Rodriguez .50
8 Bernie Williams .50
9 Cristian Guzman .25
10 Mo Vaughn .25
11 Troy Glaus .50
12 Tim Salmon .40
13 Jason Giambi 1.50
14 Cliff Floyd .25
15 Tim Hudson .50
16 Curt Schilling .75
17 Sammy Sosa 1.50
18 Alex Rodriguez 2.50
19 Chuck Knoblauch .25
20 Jason Kendall .25
21 Ben Sheets .25
22 Nomar Garciaparra 2.00
23 Ryan Klesko .25
24 Greg Vaughn .25
25 Rafael Palmeiro .50
26 Miguel Tejada .75
27 Shea Hillenbrand .25
28 Jim Thome .75
29 Randy Johnson .75
30 Barry Larkin .50
31 Paul LoDuca .25
32 Pedro J. Martinez 1.00
33 Luis Gonzalez .50
34 Carlos Delgado .40
35 Richie Sexson .40
36 Albert Pujols 1.00
37 Bobby Abreu .25
38 Gary Sheffield .40
39 Magglio Ordonez .40
40 Eric Chavez .50
41 Jeff Bagwell .75
42 Doug Mientkiewicz .25
43 Moises Alou .25

44	Todd Helton	.60
45	Ichiro Suzuki	2.00
46	Jose Cruz Jr.	.25
47	Freddy Garcia	.25
48	Tino Martinez	.40
49	Roger Clemens	1.50
50	Greg Maddux	1.50
51	Mike Piazza	2.00
52	Roberto Alomar	.50
53	Adam Dunn	.50
54	Kerry Wood	.50
55	Edgar Martinez	.25
56	Ken Griffey Jr.	1.50
57	Juan Gonzalez	.50
58	Pat Burrell	.50
59	Corey Koskie	.25
60	Jose Vidro	.25
61	Ben Grieve	.25
62	Barry Bonds	2.50
63	Raul Mondesi	.25
64	Jimmy Rollins	.25
65	Mike Sweeney	.25
66	Josh Beckett	.25
67	Chipper Jones	1.50
68	Jeff Kent	.40
69	Tony Batista	.25
70	Phil Nevin	.25
71	Brian Jordan	.25
72	Rich Aurilia	.25
73	Brian Giles	.50
74	Frank Thomas	.60
75	Larry Walker	.40
76	Shawn Green	.40
77	Manny Ramirez	.75
78	Craig Biggio	.40
79	Vladimir Guerrero	1.00
80	Jeromy Burnitz	.25
81	Mark Teixeira	15.00
82	*Corey Thurman*	10.00
83	Mark Prior	25.00
84	Marlon Byrd	10.00
85	Austin Kearns	15.00
86	*Satoru Komiyama*	8.00
87	*So Taguchi*	15.00
88	*Jorge Padilla*	8.00
89	*Rene Reyes*	8.00
90	*Jorge Nunez*	8.00
91	*Ron Calloway*	8.00
92	*Kazuhisa Ishii*	15.00
93	Dewon Brazelton	8.00
94	Angel Berroa	8.00
95	*Felix Escalona*	8.00
96	Sean Burroughs	10.00
97	Brandon Duckworth	8.00
98	Hank Blalock	12.00
99	Eric Hinske	10.00
100	Carlos Pena	8.00
101	Morgan Ensberg	8.00
102	Ryan Ludwick	10.00
103	*Chris Snelling*	20.00
104	Jason Lane	8.00
105	Drew Henson	15.00
106	Bobby Kielty	5.00
107	*Earl Snyder*	5.00
108	*Nate Field*	5.00
109	Juan Diaz	5.00
110	Ryan Anderson	5.00
111	Esteban German	5.00
112	*Takahito Nomura*	5.00
113	David Kelton	5.00
114	*Steve Kent*	5.00
115	Colby Lewis	5.00
116	*Jason Simontacchi*	12.00
117	*Rodrigo Rosario*	8.00
118	*Ben Howard*	6.00
119	*Hansel Izquierdo*	5.00
120	*John Ennis*	6.00
121	*Anderson Machado*	5.00
122	*Luis Ugueto*	5.00
123	*Anastacio Martinez*	5.00
124	*Reed Johnson*	6.00
125	Juan Cruz	5.00

2002 Fleer Hot Prospects Co-Stars

		MT
Complete Set (15):		40.00
Common Card:		1.50
Inserted 1:6		
1CS	Barry Bonds, Alex Rodriguez	6.00
2CS	Derek Jeter, Nomar Garciaparra	8.00
3CS	Andruw Jones, Chipper Jones	4.00
4CS	Juan Gonzalez, Jim Thome	2.00
5CS	Pedro J. Martinez, Randy Johnson	2.50
6CS	Adam Dunn, Pat Burrell	1.50
7CS	Frank Thomas, Manny Ramirez	2.00
8CS	Jeff Bagwell, Lance Berkman	2.00
9CS	So Taguchi, Kazuhisa Ishii	6.00
10CS	Jimmy Rollins, Miguel Tejada	2.00
11CS	Morgan Ensberg, Carlos Pena	1.50
12CS	Adam Dunn, Austin Kearns	2.00
13CS	Vladimir Guerrero, Scott Rolen	3.00
14CS	Drew Henson, Xavier Nady	1.50
15CS	Mike Piazza, Ivan Rodriguez	5.00

2002 Fleer Hot Prospects Future Swatch Autograph

		MT
Common Auto.		
Production 100		
83	Mark Prior	
87	So Taguchi	
89	Rene Reyes	
105	Drew Henson	

2002 Fleer Hot Prospects Inside Barry Bonds

		MT
Common Bonds:		15.00
1BB	Barry Bonds/ pants/1,000	20.00
2BB	Barry Bonds/ pants/900	20.00
3BB	Barry Bonds/ jsy/800	20.00
4BB	Barry Bonds/ bat/700	20.00
5BB	Barry Bonds/ base/600	15.00
6BB	Barry Bonds/ cleat/500	25.00
7BB	Barry Bonds/ glove/400	25.00
8BB	Barry Bonds/ cap/300	30.00

2002 Fleer Hot Prospects Jerseygraphs

		MT
Common Player:		10.00
Inserted 1:186		
1J	Derek Jeter/108	250.00
2J	Barry Bonds/65	
3J	Chipper Jones/ 100	80.00
4J	Drew Henson	40.00
5J	So Taguchi/100	25.00
6J	David Espinosa	10.00
7J	Dane Sardinha	10.00
8J	Adrian Beltre/169	20.00
9J	Kazuhisa Ishii/40	

2002 Fleer Hot Prospects MLB Hot Materials

		MT
Common Player:		6.00
Inserted 1:9		
Red Hots:		1-2X
Production 50 sets		
1HM	Adam Dunn	15.00
2HM	Alex Rodriguez	15.00
3HM	Bret Boone	6.00
4HM	Barry Bonds	20.00
5HM	Brandon Duckworth	6.00
6HM	Brian Giles	10.00
7HM	Bernie Williams	10.00
8HM	Carlos Delgado	6.00
9HM	Cristian Guzman	10.00
10HM	Carlos Pena	8.00
11HM	Corey Patterson	6.00
12HM	Curt Schilling	12.00
13HM	Frank Thomas	10.00
14HM	Gabe Kapler	6.00
15HM	Greg Maddux	15.00
16HM	Gary Sheffield	6.00
17HM	Ivan Rodriguez	10.00
18HM	Josh Beckett	8.00
19HM	Jeff Bagwell/108	20.00
20HM	Juan Gonzalez	10.00
21HM	Jim Thome	12.00
22HM	Juan Uribe	6.00
23HM	Lance Berkman	10.00
24HM	Mark Mulder	8.00
25HM	Moises Alou	6.00
26HM	Mike Piazza	20.00
27HM	Mike Sweeney	6.00
28HM	Nick Johnson	10.00
29HM	Paul LoDuca	6.00
30HM	Pedro J. Martinez	12.00
31HM	Rafael Furcal	6.00
32HM	Roy Oswalt	8.00
33HM	Rafael Palmeiro	10.00
34HM	Sean Burroughs/ 350	12.00
35HM	Shawn Green	10.00
36HM	Tony Armas Jr.	6.00
37HM	Torii Hunter	6.00
38HM	Tino Martinez	10.00
39HM	Vernon Wells	6.00
40HM	Kazuhisa Ishii/70	
41HM	Todd Helton	10.00
42HM	Magglio Ordonez	10.00
43HM	Freddy Garcia	6.00
44HM	So Taguchi	10.00

2002 Fleer Hot Prospects MLB Hot Tandems

		MT
Common Card:		10.00
Production 100 sets		
Red Hots 10 sets no pricing		
1HT	Adam Dunn, Lance Berkman	30.00
2HT	Alex Rodriguez, Ivan Rodriguez	30.00
3HT	Bret Boone, Freddy Garcia	10.00
4HT	Barry Bonds, Kazuhisa Ishii	40.00
5HT	Brandon Duckworth, Roy Oswalt	15.00
6HT	Bernie Williams, Jorge Posada	15.00
7HT	Carlos Delgado, Vernon Wells	10.00
8HT	Cristian Guzman, Torii Hunter	25.00
9HT	Carlos Pena, Corey Patterson	10.00
10HT	Curt Schilling, Greg Maddux	40.00
11HT	Frank Thomas, Magglio Ordonez	15.00
12HT	Gabe Kapler, Rafael Palmeiro	12.00
13HT	Gary Sheffield, Rafael Furcal	10.00
14HT	Josh Beckett, Roy Oswalt	10.00
15HT	Brandon Duckworth, Josh Beckett	10.00
16HT	Jeff Bagwell, Lance Berkman	30.00
17HT	Juan Gonzalez, Rafael Palmeiro	15.00
18HT	Jim Thome, Shawn Green	15.00
19HT	Paul LoDuca, Shawn Green	10.00
20HT	Juan Uribe, Miguel Tejada	15.00
21HT	Mark Mulder, Miguel Tejada	15.00
22HT	Moises Alou, Magglio Ordonez	10.00
23HT	Jorge Posada, Mike Piazza	30.00
24HT	Mike Sweeney, Todd Helton	15.00
25HT	Carlos Pena, Nick Johnson	10.00
26HT	Curt Schilling, Pedro J. Martinez	30.00
27HT	Tony Armas Jr., Freddy Garcia	10.00
28HT	Tino Martinez, Todd Helton	15.00
29HT	Barry Bonds, Derek Jeter	60.00
30HT	Kazuhisa Ishii, Derek Jeter	40.00
31HT	Juan Uribe, Cristian Guzman	10.00
32HT	Kazuhisa Ishii, So Taguchi	40.00
33HT	Adam Dunn, Corey Patterson	10.00
34HT	Bernie Williams, Nick Johnson	10.00
35HT	Bret Boone, Torii Hunter	20.00
36HT	Greg Maddux, Pedro J. Martinez	30.00
37HT	Sean Burroughs, Drew Henson	20.00
38HT	Kazuhisa Ishii, Satoru Komiyama	35.00
39HT	Kazuhisa Ishii, Mark Prior	45.00
40HT	Hank Blalock, Austin Kearns	25.00
41HT	Hank Blalock, Joe Teixeira	10.00
42HT	Marlon Byrd, Jorge Padilla	10.00
43HT	Marlon Byrd, Austin Kearns	15.00
44HT	Gabe Kapler, Juan Gonzalez	15.00
45HT	Jeff Bagwell, Mike Piazza	30.00

2002 Fleer Hot Prospects We're Number One

		MT
Complete Set (10):		40.00
Common Player:		2.00
Inserted 1:15		
1WN	Derek Jeter	10.00
2WN	Barry Bonds	8.00
3WN	Ken Griffey Jr.	6.00
4WN	Roger Clemens	5.00
5WN	Alex Rodriguez	8.00
6WN	J.D. Drew	2.00
7WN	Chipper Jones	5.00
8WN	Manny Ramirez	3.00
9WN	Nomar Garciaparra	6.00
10WN	Todd Helton	2.00

2002 Fleer Hot Prospects We're Number One Memorabilia

	MT
Common Player:	2.00
Inserted 1:25	
Derek Jeter/jsy	25.00
Barry Bonds/jsy	20.00
Ken Griffey Jr/ base	15.00
Alex Rodriguez/ jsy	15.00
J.D. Drew/jsy	10.00
Chipper Jones/jsy	15.00
Manny Ramirez/ jsy	12.00
Nomar Garciaparra/ jsy	20.00
Todd Helton/jsy	10.00

2002 Fleer Hot Prospects We're Number One Autograph

	MT
Common Player:	2.00
Derek Jeter/92	
Barry Bonds/85	

2002 Fleer Maximum

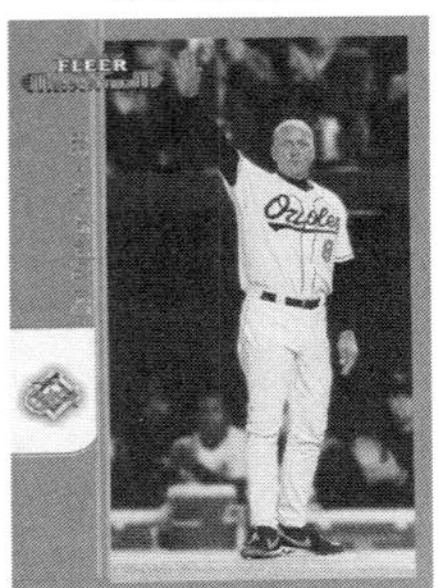

		MT
Complete Set (270):		NA
Common Player:		.15
Common (201-250):		8.00
Production 500		
Common (251-270):		.50
Inserted 1:hobby pack		
Pack (15):		4.00
Box (16):		55.00
1	Barry Bonds	1.50
2	Alex Rodriguez	2.00
3	Jim Edmonds	.25
4	Manny Ramirez	.75
5	Jeff Bagwell	.75
6	Kazuhiro Sasaki	.25
7	Jason Giambi	.60
8	J.D. Drew	.30
9	Barry Larkin	.30
10	Chipper Jones	1.50
11	Rafael Palmeiro	.40
12	Roberto Alomar	.60
13	Randy Johnson	.75
14	Juan Gonzalez	.75
15	Gary Sheffield	.30
16	Larry Walker	.25
17	Todd Helton	.75
18	Ivan Rodriguez	.75
19	Greg Maddux	1.50
20	Mike Piazza	2.00
21	Tsuyoshi Shinjo	.25
22	Luis Gonzalez	.50
23	Pedro Martinez	.75
24	Albert Pujols	1.50
25	Jose Canseco	.40
26	Edgar Martinez	.15
27	Moises Alou	.20
28	Vladimir Guerrero	.75
29	Shawn Green	.30
30	Miguel Tejada	.25
31	Bernie Williams	.60
32	Frank Thomas	.75
33	Jim Thome	.40
34	Derek Jeter	3.00
35	Julio Lugo	.15
36	Mo Vaughn	.20
37	Steve Cox	.15
38	Brad Radke	.15
39	Brian Jordan	.15
40	Garret Anderson	.15
41	Ichiro Suzuki	3.00
42	Mike Lieberthal	.15
43	Preston Wilson	.15
44	Bud Smith	.25
45	Curt Schilling	.30
46	Eric Chavez	.25
47	Javier Vazquez	.15
48	Jose Ortiz	.15
49	Mike Sweeney	.15
50	Travis Fryman	.25
51	Brady Anderson	.20
52	Chan Ho Park	.25
53	C.C. Sabathia	.15
54	Jack Wilson	.15
55	Joe Crede	.15
56	Mike Mussina	.60
57	Sean Casey	.40
58	Bobby Abreu	.15
59	Joe Randa	.15
60	Jose Vidro	.15
61	Juan Uribe	.15
62	Mark Grace	.40
63	Matt Morris	.25
64	Omar Vizquel	.25
65	Darryl Kile	.15
66	Dee Brown	.15
67	Fernando Tatis	.15
68	Jeff Cirillo	.15
69	Johnny Damon	.15
70	Milton Bradley	.15
71	Reggie Sanders	.15
72	Al Leiter	.25
73	Andres Galarraga	.25
74	Ellis Burks	.15
75	Jermaine Dye	.15
76	Juan Pierre	.15
77	Junior Spivey	.15
78	Mark Quinn	.15
79	Ben Sheets	.15
80	Brad Fullmer	.15
81	Bubba Trammell	.15
82	Dante Bichette	.15
83	Ken Griffey Jr.	2.50
84	Paul O'Neill	.40
85	Robert Fick	.15
86	Bret Boone	.15
87	Raul Mondesi	.15
88	Josh Beckett	.25
89	Geoff Jenkins	.25
90	Ramon Ortiz	.15
91	Robin Ventura	.25
92	Tom Glavine	.40
93	Jimmy Rollins	.15
94	Jamie Moyer	.15
95	Magglio Ordonez	.25
96	Mike Lowell	.15
97	Ryan Dempster	.15
98	Scott Schoeneweis	.15
99	Todd Zeile	.15
100	A.J. Burnett	.15
101	Aaron Sele	.15
102	Cal Ripken Jr.	3.00
103	Carlos Beltran	.15
104	David Eckstein	.15
105	Jason Marquis	.15
106	Matt Lawton	.15
107	Ben Grieve	.15
108	Brian Giles	.25
109	Josh Towers	.15
110	Lance Berkman	.30
111	Sammy Sosa	1.50
112	Torii Hunter	.15
113	Aubrey Huff	.15
114	Craig Biggio	.25
115	Doug Mientkiewicz	.15
116	Fred McGriff	.25
117	Jason Johnson	.15
118	Pat Burrell	.25
119	Aaron Boone	.15
120	Carlos Delgado	.50
121	Nomar Garciaparra	2.00
122	Richie Sexson	.15
123	Russ Ortiz	.15
124	Tim Hudson	.40
125	Tony Clark	.15
126	Jeromy Burnitz	.15
127	Jose Cruz	.15
128	Juan Encarnacion	.15
129	Mark Mulder	.25
130	Mike Hampton	.15
131	Rich Aurilia	.15
132	Trot Nixon	.15
133	Greg Vaughn	.15
134	Jacque Jones	.15
135	Jason Kendall	.15
136	Jay Gibbons	.15
137	Mark Buehrle	.15
138	Richard Hidalgo	.25
139	Rondell White	.25
140	Cristian Guzman	.15
141	Andy Pettitte	.40
142	Chris Richard	.15
143	Paul LoDuca	.15
144	Phil Nevin	.25
145	Ray Durham	.15
146	Todd Walker	.15
147	Bartolo Colon	.25
148	Ben Petrick	.15
149	Freddy Garcia	.15
150	Jon Lieber	.15
151	Jose Hernandez	.15
152	Matt Williams	.30
153	Shannon Stewart	.15
154	Adrian Beltre	.25
155	Carlos Lee	.15
156	Frank Catalanotto	.15
157	Jorge Posada	.30
158	Pokey Reese	.15
159	Ryan Klesko	.15
160	Ugueth Urbina	.15
161	Adam Dunn	.75
162	Alfonso Soriano	.30
163	Ben Davis	.15
164	Paul Konerko	.15
165	Eric Karros	.25
166	Jeff Weaver	.15
167	Ruben Sierra	.15
168	Bobby Higginson	.15
169	Eric Milton	.15
170	Kerry Wood	.40
171	Roy Oswalt	.30
172	Scott Rolen	.30
173	Tim Salmon	.25
174	Aramis Ramirez	.25
175	Jason Tyner	.15
176	Juan Cruz	.15
177	Keith Foulke	.15
178	Kevin Brown	.25
179	Roger Clemens	1.25
180	Tony Batista	.15
181	Andruw Jones	.40
182	Cliff Floyd	.15
183	Darin Erstad	.25
184	Joe Mays	.15
185	Mike Cameron	.15
186	Robert Person	.15
187	Jeff Kent	.25
188	Gabe Kapler	.25
189	Jason Jennings	.15
190	Jason Varitek	.15
191	Barry Zito	.25
192	Rickey Henderson	.40
193	Tino Martinez	.25
194	Brandon Duckworth	.25
195	Corey Koskie	.15
196	Derrek Lee	.15
197	Javy Lopez	.25
198	John Olerud	.30
199	Terrance Long	.15
200	Troy Glaus	.60
201	Scott MacRae	8.00
202	Scott Chiasson	8.00
203	Bart Miadich	8.00
204	Brian Bowles	8.00
205	David Williams	8.00
206	Victor Zambrano	8.00
207	Joe Beimel	8.00
208	Scott Stewart	8.00
209	Bob File	8.00
210	Ryan Jensen	8.00
211	Jason Karnuth	8.00
212	Brandon Knight	8.00
213	*Andy Shibilo*	12.00
214	*Chad Ricketts*	8.00
215	Mark Prior	20.00
216	Chad Paronto	8.00
217	Corky Miller	8.00
218	Luis Pineda	8.00
219	Ramon Vazquez	8.00
220	Tony Cogan	8.00
221	Roy Smith	8.00
222	Mark Lukasiewicz	8.00
223	Mike Rivera	8.00
224	Brad Voyles	8.00
225	*Jamie Burke*	10.00
226	Justin Duchscherer	8.00
227	*Eric Cyr*	8.00
228	Mark Lukasiewicz	8.00
229	Marlon Byrd	15.00
230	*Chris Piersoll*	8.00
231	Ramon Vazquez	8.00
232	Tony Cogan	8.00
233	Roy Smith	8.00
234	*Franklin Nunez*	8.00
235	Corky Miller	8.00
236	*Jorge Nunez*	12.00
237	Joe Beimel	8.00
238	Eric Knott	8.00
239	Victor Zambrano	8.00
240	Jason Karnuth	8.00
241	Jason Middlebrook	8.00
242	Scott Stewart	8.00
243	Tim Spooneybarger	8.00
244	David Williams	8.00
245	Bart Miadich	8.00
246	Mike Koplove	8.00
247	Ryan Jensen	8.00
248	Jeremy Fikac	8.00
249	Bob File	8.00
250	Craig Monroe	8.00
251	Albert Pujols	2.00
252	Ichiro Suzuki	5.00
253	Nomar Garciaparra	2.50
254	Barry Bonds	2.00
255	Jason Giambi	1.00
256	Derek Jeter	4.00
257	Roberto Alomar	.75
258	Roger Clemens	1.50
259	Mike Piazza	2.50
260	Vladimir Guerrero	1.00
261	Todd Helton	1.00
262	Shawn Green	.50
263	Chipper Jones	2.00
264	Pedro Martinez	1.00
265	Pat Burrell	.50
266	Sammy Sosa	2.00
267	Ken Griffey Jr.	3.00
268	Cal Ripken Jr.	4.00
269	Kerry Wood	.75
270	Alex Rodriguez	2.50

2002 Fleer Maximum To The Max

	MT
Stars (1-200):	4-8X
Print Run 200-500	
Stars (1-200):	5-10X
Print Run 121-199	
Stars (1-200):	8-15X
Print Run 75-120	
Stars (1-200):	15-25X
Print Run 40-75	
Stars (1-200):	20-40X
Print Run 20-39	
Rookies (201-250):	.5-1X
Production 100	
Impact (251-270):	2-5X
Production 200-400	

2002 Fleer Maximum Americas Game Jersey

		MT
Common Player:		8.00
Inserted 1:24 H, 1:72 R		
1	Jeff Bagwell	20.00
2	Craig Biggio	15.00
3	Barry Bonds	30.00
4	Carlos Delgado	10.00
5	J.D. Drew	10.00
6	Jason Giambi	20.00
7	Tom Glavine	10.00
8	Luis Gonzalez	10.00
9	Todd Helton	15.00
10	Reggie Jackson	20.00
11	Randy Johnson	15.00
12	Chipper Jones	20.00
13	Greg Maddux	20.00
14	Edgar Martinez	8.00
15	Pedro Martinez	20.00
16	Rafael Palmeiro	12.00
17	Chan Ho Park	10.00
18	Mike Piazza	25.00
19	Albert Pujols	25.00
20	Kazuhiro Sasaki	10.00
21	Miguel Tejada	10.00
22	Frank Thomas	15.00
23	Larry Walker	10.00
24	Dave Winfield	15.00

2002 Fleer Maximum Americas Game Stars and Stripes

		MT
Common Player:		
Production 25 sets		
SS1	Mike Piazza	
SS2	Chipper Jones	
SS3	Barry Bonds	
SS4	Luis Gonzalez	
SS5	Ivan Rodriguez	
SS6	Jason Giambi	
SS7	Randy Johnson	
SS8	Edgar Martinez	
SS9	Todd Helton	

2002 Fleer Maximum Coverage

		MT
Common Player:		20.00
Production 100 sets		
1	Roberto Alomar Bat	30.00
2	Jeff Bagwell Jsy	40.00
3	Barry Bonds Bat	50.00
4	Jose Canseco Bat	40.00
5	J.D. Drew Bat	40.00
6	Jim Edmonds Bat	20.00
7	Jason Giambi Bat	35.00
8	Juan Gonzalez Bat	30.00
9	Luis Gonzalez Jsy	30.00
10	Todd Helton Jsy	40.00
11	Randy Johnson Jsy	40.00
12	Chipper Jones Bat	50.00
13	Greg Maddux Jsy	60.00
14	Pedro Martinez Jsy	40.00
15	Rafael Palmeiro Pants	25.00
16	Albert Pujols Jsy	60.00
17	Manny Ramirez Bat	30.00
18	Alex Rodriguez Bat	30.00
19	Ivan Rodriguez Bat	25.00
20	Kazuhiro Sasaki Jsy	40.00
21	Gary Sheffield Bat	20.00
22	Tsuyoshi Shinjo Bat	40.00

2002 Fleer Maximum Coverage Autographs

		MT
Quantity produced listed		
1	Barry Bonds Pants/50	
2	J.D. Drew Bat/100	65.00
3	Jim Edmonds Bat/100	60.00
4	Drew Henson Bat/100	
5	Chipper Jones Bat/50	
6	Albert Pujols Jsy/100	140.00
7	Gary Sheffield Bat/100	35.00

2002 Fleer Maximum Derek Jeter Legacy Collection

		MT
Inserted 1:236		
DJ	Derek Jeter/bat	50.00
DJ	Derek Jeter/Bat Auto/222	200.00
DJ	Derek Jeter/jersey	70.00
DJ	Derek Jeter/jersey Auto	275.00

2002 Fleer Maximum Maximum Power

	MT
Common Player:	10.00
Inserted 1:24 H	
Golds:	4-6X
Production 25 sets	
Luis Gonzalez	15.00
Larry Walker	10.00
Frank Thomas	15.00
Manny Ramirez	15.00
Barry Bonds	25.00
Jim Thome	10.00
Tsuyoshi Shinjo	20.00
Bernie Williams/175	25.00
Chipper Jones	20.00
Shawn Green	10.00
Juan Gonzalez	15.00
Jim Edmonds	10.00
Moises Alou	10.00
Roberto Alomar	10.00
Jose Canseco	15.00
Ivan Rodriguez	12.00
Barry Larkin/50	40.00
Mike Piazza	25.00
Gary Sheffield	10.00
J.D. Drew/200	35.00
Alex Rodriguez	20.00
Jason Giambi	15.00
Todd Helton	15.00

2002 Fleer Platinum

		MT
Complete Set (302):		NA
Common Player:		.20
Common (251-260):		2.00
Common (261-302):		1.50
Inserted 1:3 H, 1:6 Retail		
Hobby Pack (10):		2.75
Hobby Box (24):		55.00
1	Garrett Anderson	.20
2	Randy Johnson	.75
3	Chipper Jones	1.25
4	David Cone	.20
5	Corey Patterson	.30
6	Carlos Lee	.20
7	Barry Larkin	.40
8	Jim Thome	.40
9	Larry Walker	.40
10	Randall Simon	.20
11	Charles Johnson	.20
12	Richard Hidalgo	.20
13	Mark Quinn	.20
14	Paul LoDuca	.20
15	Cristian Guzman	.20
16	Orlando Cabrera	.20
17	Al Leiter	.30
18	Nick Johnson	.30
19	Eric Chavez	.30
20	Miguel Tejada	.30
21	Mike Lieberthal	.20
22	Robert Mackowiak	.20
23	Ryan Klesko	.20
24	Jeff Kent	.20
25	Edgar Martinez	.20
26	Steve Kline	.20
27	Toby Hall	.20
28	Rusty Greer	.20
29	Jose Cruz Jr.	.20
30	Darin Erstad	.40
31	Reggie Sanders	.20
32	Javy Lopez	.20
33	Carl Everett	.20
34	Sammy Sosa	1.25
35	Magglio Ordonez	.30
36	Todd Walker	.20
37	Omar Vizquel	.20
38	Matt Anderson	.20
39	Jeff Weaver	.20
40	Derrek Lee	.20
41	Julio Lugo	.20
42	Joe Randa	.20
43	Chan Ho Park	.20
44	Torii Hunter	.20
45	Vladimir Guerrero	.75
46	Rey Ordonez	.20
47	Tino Martinez	.30
48	Johnny Damon	.20
49	Barry Zito	.30
50	Robert Person	.20
51	Aramis Ramirez	.20
52	Mark Kotsay	.20
53	Jason Schmidt	.20
54	Jamie Moyer	.20
55	David Justice	.40
56	Aubrey Huff	.20
57	Rick Helling	.20
58	Carlos Delgado	.40
59	Troy Glaus	.50
60	Curt Schilling	.40
61	Greg Maddux	1.25
62	Nomar Garciaparra	1.50
63	Kerry Wood	.40
64	Frank Thomas	.75
65	Dmitri Young	.20
66	Alex Ochoa	.20
67	Jose Macias	.20
68	Antonio Alfonseca	.20
69	Mike Lowell	.20
70	Wade Miller	.20
71	Mike Sweeney	.20
72	Gary Sheffield	.30
73	Corey Koskie	.20
74	Lee Stevens	.20
75	Jay Payton	.20
76	Mike Mussina	.50
77	Jermaine Dye	.20
78	Bobby Abreu	.20
79	Scott Rolen	.40
80	Todd Ritchie	.20
81	D'Angelo Jimenez	.20
82	Rob Nenn	.20
83	John Olerud	.40
84	Matt Morris	.20
85	Joe Kennedy	.20
86	Gabe Kapler	.20
87	Chris Carpenter	.20
88	David Eckstein	.20
89	Matt Williams	.30
90	John Smoltz	.20
91	Pedro J. Martinez	.75
92	Eric Young	.20
93	Jose Valentin	.20
94	Erubiel Durazo	.20
95	Jeff Cirillo	.20
96	Brandon Inge	.20
97	Josh Beckett	.40
98	Preston Wilson	.20
99	Damian Jackson	.20
100	Adrian Beltre	.30
101	Jeromy Burnitz	.20
102	Joe Mays	.20
103	Michael Barrett	.20
104	Mike Piazza	1.50
105	Brady Anderson	.20
106	Jason Giambi	.60
107	Marlon Anderson	.20
108	Jimmy Rollins	.20
109	Jack Wilson	.20
110	Brian Lawrence	.20
111	Russ Ortiz	.20
112	Kazuhiro Sasaki	.20
113	Placido Polanco	.20
114	Damian Rolls	.20
115	Rafael Palmeiro	.40
116	Brad Fullmer	.20
117	Tim Salmon	.30
118	Tony Womack	.20
119	Tony Batista	.20
120	Trot Nixon	.20
121	Mark Buehrle	.20
122	Derek Jeter	2.50
123	Ellis Burks	.20
124	Mike Hampton	.20
125	Roger Cedeno	.20
126	A.J. Burnett	.20
127	Moises Alou	.30
128	Billy Wagner	.20
129	Kevin Brown	.30
130	Jose Hernandez	.20
131	Doug Mientkiewicz	.20
132	Javier Vazquez	.20
133	Tsuyoshi Shinjo	.20
134	Andy Pettitte	.40
135	Tim Hudson	.40
136	Pat Burrell	.40
137	Brian Giles	.40
138	Kevin Young	.20
139	Xavier Nady	.20
140	J.T. Snow	.20
141	Aaron Sele	.20
142	Albert Pujols	1.25
143	Jason Tyner	.20
144	Ivan Rodriguez	.60
145	Raul Mondesi	.30
146	Matt Lawton	.20
147	Rafael Furcal	.20
148	Jeff Conine	.20
149	Hideo Nomo	.50
150	Jose Canseco	.40
151	Aaron Boone	.20
152	Bartolo Colon	.20
153	Todd Helton	.75
154	Tony Clark	.20
155	Pablo Ozuna	.20
156	Jeff Bagwell	.75
157	Carlos Beltran	.20
158	Shawn Green	.30
159	Geoff Jenkins	.30
160	Eric Milton	.20
161	Jose Vidro	.20
162	Robin Ventura	.30
163	Jorge Posada	.30
164	Terrence Long	.20
165	Brandon Duckworth	.20
166	Chad Hermansen	.20
167	Ben Davis	.20
168	Phil Nevin	.20
169	Bret Boone	.20
170	J.D. Drew	.40
171	Edgar Renteria	.20
172	Randy Winn	.20
173	Alex Rodriguez	1.50
174	Shannon Stewart	.20
175	Steve Finley	.20
176	Marcus Giles	.20
177	Jay Gibbons	.20
178	Manny Ramirez	.75
179	Ray Durham	.20
180	Sean Casey	.40
181	Travis Fryman	.20
182	Denny Neagle	.20
183	Deivi Cruz	.20
184	Luis Castillo	.20
185	Lance Berkman	.50
186	Dee Brown	.20
187	Jeff Shaw	.20
188	Mark Loretta	.20
189	David Ortiz	.20
190	Edgardo Alfonzo	.20
191	Roger Clemens	1.00
192	Mariano Rivera	.40
193	Jeremy Giambi	.20
194	Johnny Estrada	.20
195	Craig Wilson	.20
196	Adam Eaton	.20
197	Rich Aurilia	.20
198	Mike Cameron	.20
199	Jim Edmonds	.40
200	Fernando Vina	.20
201	Greg Vaughn	.20
202	Mike Young	.20
203	Vernon Wells	.20
204	Luis Gonzalez	.50
205	Tom Glavine	.40
206	Chris Richard	.20
207	Jon Lieber	.20
208	Keith Foulke	.20
209	Rondell White	.20
210	Bernie Williams	.50

211 Juan Pierre .20
212 Juan Encarnacion .20
213 Ryan Dempster .20
214 Tim Redding .20
215 Jeff Suppan .20
216 Mark Grudzielanek .20
217 Richie Sexson .40
218 Brad Radke .20
219 Armando Benitez .20
220 Orlando Hernandez .40
221 Alfonso Soriano .75
222 Mark Mulder .20
223 Travis Lee .20
224 Jason Kendall .20
225 Trevor Hoffman .20
226 Barry Bonds 1.25
227 Freddy Garcia .20
228 Darryl Kile .20
229 Ben Grieve .20
230 Frank Catalanotto .20
231 Ruben Sierra .20
232 Homer Bush .20
233 Mark Grace .40
234 Andruw Jones .50
235 Brian Roberts .20
236 Fred McGriff .40
237 Paul Konerko .20
238 Ken Griffey Jr. 1.50
239 John Burkett .20
240 Juan Uribe .20
241 Bobby Higginson .20
242 Cliff Floyd .30
243 Craig Biggio .30
244 Neifi Perez .20
245 Eric Karros .20
246 Ben Sheets .30
247 Tony Armas Jr. .20
248 Mo Vaughn .40
249 David Wells .20
250 Juan Gonzalez .75
251 Barry Bonds 4.00
252 Sammy Sosa 4.00
253 Ken Griffey Jr. 5.00
254 Roger Clemens 3.00
255 Greg Maddux 4.00
256 Chipper Jones 4.00
257 Alex Rodriguez, Derek Jeter, Nomar Garciaparra 8.00
258 Roberto Alomar 2.00
259 Jeff Bagwell 2.00
260 Mike Piazza 5.00
261 Mark Teixeira 3.00
262 Mark Prior 4.00
263 Alex Escobar 1.50
264 C.C. Sabathia 1.50
265 Drew Henson 3.00
266 Wilson Betemit 2.00
267 Roy Oswalt 2.50
268 Adam Dunn 4.00
269 Bud Smith 1.50
270 Dewon Brazelton 1.50
271 *Brandon Backe*, Jason Standridge 1.50
272 Wilfredo Rodriguez, Carlos Hernandez 1.50
273 Geronimo Gil, Luis Rivera 1.50
274 Carlos Pena, Jovanny Cedeno 3.00
275 Austin Kearns, Ben Broussard 2.50
276 *Jorge De La Rosa*, Kenny Kelly 1.50
277 Ryan Drese, Victor Martinez 1.50
278 Joel Pinero, Nate Cornejo 1.50
279 David Kelton, Carlos Zambrano 1.50
281 Donnie Bridges, Wilkin Ruan 1.50
282 Wily Mo Pena, Brandon Claussen 2.00
283 Jason Jennings *Rene Reyes* 1.50
284 Steve Green, Alfredo Amezaga 1.50
285 Eric Hinske, Felipe Lopez 1.50
286 *Anderson Machado*, Brad Baisley 1.50
287 Carlos Garcia, Sean Douglass 1.50
288 Pat Strange, Jae Weong Seo 1.50
289 Marcus Thames, Alex Graman 1.50
290 *Matt Childers*, *Hansel Izquierdo* 1.50
291 *Ron Calloway*, *Adam Walker* 1.50
292 J.R. House, J.J. Davis 1.50
293 Ryan Anderson, Rafael Soriano 1.50
294 Mike Bynum, Dennis Tankersley 1.50
295 Kurt Ainsworth, Carlos Valderrama 1.50
296 Billy Hall, Cristian Guerrero 1.50
297 Miguel Olivo, Danny Wright 1.50
298 Marlon Byrd, *Jorge Padilla* 1.50
299 Juan Cruz, Ben Christensen 1.50
300 Adam Johnson, Michael Restovich 1.50
301 *So Taguchi* 5.00
302 *Kazuhisa Ishii* 10.00

2002 Fleer Platinum Edition

MT
Stars (1-250): 4-8X
Production 202
Cards 251-302 not priced
Production 22

2002 Fleer Platinum Barry Bonds RC Autograph

MT
73 cards autographed
1BBRCABarry Bonds 300.00

2002 Fleer Platinum Buy Back Autographs

MT
261BBMark Teixeira
262BBMark Prior
263BBAlex Escobar
264BBC.C. Sabathia
265BBDrew Henson
266BBWilson Betemit
267BBRoy Oswalt
268BBAdam Dunn
269BBBud Smith
270BBDewon Brazelton

2002 Fleer Platinum Clubhouse Collection - Dual

MT
Common Card: 10.00
Inserted 1:96
Edgardo Alfonzo 10.00
Rick Ankiel 12.00
Craig Biggio
Adrian Beltre 10.00
Barry Bonds 40.00
Sean Casey 20.00
Eric Chavez 10.00
Roger Clemens 30.00
Carlos Delgado 20.00
J.D. Drew 20.00
Darin Erstad 20.00
Jim Thome 20.00
Juan Gonzalez 20.00
Nomar Garciaparra 40.00
Todd Helton
Derek Jeter 70.00
Randy Johnson 25.00
Andruw Jones 20.00
Jason Kendall
Johnny Damon 10.00
Paul LoDuca 10.00
Greg Maddux 35.00
Pedro J. Martinez 20.00
Raul Mondesi
Magglio Ordonez 20.00
Mike Piazza 40.00
Manny Ramirez 20.00
Mariano Rivera 20.00
Ivan Rodriguez 20.00
Alex Rodriguez 25.00
Scott Rolen 20.00
Kazuhiro Sasaki 20.00
Curt Schilling 20.00
Gary Sheffield 10.00
Frank Thomas 20.00
Jim Thome 20.00
37CCDOmar Vizquel 10.00

2002 Fleer Platinum Clubhouse Collection Memorabilia

MT
Common Player: 8.00
Inserted 1:32
Edgardo Alfonzo/jsy 8.00
Rick Ankiel/jsy 10.00
Craig Biggio/bat 10.00
Adrian Beltre/jsy 8.00
Sean Casey/jsy 10.00
Barry Bonds/jsy 30.00
Scott Rolen/jsy 12.00
Eric Chavez/jsy 8.00
Roger Clemens/jsy 25.00
Carlos Delgado/jsy 10.00
J.D. Drew/jsy 12.00
Darin Erstad/jsy 10.00
Jim Thome/bat 15.00
Juan Gonzalez/bat 12.00
Nomar Garciaparra/jsy 25.00
Todd Helton/jsy 12.00
Derek Jeter/pants 50.00
Randy Johnson/jsy 15.00
Andruw Jones/jsy 10.00
Tim Hudson/jsy 10.00
Jason Kendall/jsy 8.00
Johnny Damon/bat 8.00
Paul LoDuca/jsy 8.00
Greg Maddux/jsy 25.00
Pedro Martinez/jsy 12.00
Raul Mondesi/bat 8.00
Magglio Ordonez/jsy 12.00
Mike Piazza/jsy 25.00
Manny Ramirez/jsy 12.00
Mariano Rivera/jsy 12.00
Ivan Rodriguez/jsy 10.00
Alex Rodriguez/jsy 20.00
Kazuhiro Sasaki/jsy 12.00
Frank Thomas/jsy 12.00
Curt Schilling/jsy 12.00
Gary Sheffield/bat 8.00
Omar Vizquel/jsy 8.00

2002 Fleer Platinum Cornerstones

MT
Complete Set (44):
Common Player:
1CSGUBill Terry
2CSGUJohnny Mize
3CSGUEddie Murray
4CSGUCal Ripken Jr.
5CSGUEddie Matthews
6CSGUChipper Jones
7CSGUTony Perez
8CSGUSean Casey
9CSGUJimmie Foxx
10CSGUScott Rolen
11CSGUWade Boggs
12CSGUGeorge Brett
13CSGUJeff Bagwell
14CSGURafael Palmeiro
15CSGUBrooks Robinson
16CSGUCal Ripken Jr.
17CSGUTed Kluszewski
18CSGUTony Perez
19CSGUJimmie Foxx
20CSGUHank Greenberg
21CSGUJim Thome
22CSGUTravis Fryman
23CSGUTed Kluszewski
24CSGUSean Casey
25CSGUDon Mattingly
26CSGUWade Boggs
27CSGUGeorge Brett
28CSGUPaul Molitor
29CSGUBill Terry
30CSGUWillie McCovey
31CSGUGeorge Brett
32CSGUMike Sweeney
33CSGUDon Mattingly
34CSGUPaul Molitor
35CSGUFrank Thomas
36CSGUCarlos Delgado
37CSGUJeff Bagwell
38CSGUTodd Helton
39CSGUWade Boggs
40CSGUCal Ripken Jr.
41CSGUWillie McCovey
42CSGUOrlando Cepeda
43CSGUMark Grace
44CSGUJohn Olerud

2002 Fleer Platinum Fencebusters

MT
Common Player: 6.00
1FB Derek Jeter 25.00
2FB J.D. Drew 10.00
3FB Brian Giles 6.00
4FB Moises Alou 6.00
5FB Rafael Palmeiro 6.00
6FB Jeff Bagwell 10.00
7FB Mike Piazza 15.00
8FB Manny Ramirez 10.00
9FB Tino Martinez 6.00
10FB Jim Thome 8.00
11FB Andruw Jones 6.00
12FB Shawn Green 6.00
13FB Frank Thomas 10.00
14FB Miguel Tejada 6.00
15FB Luis Gonzalez 6.00
16FB Alex Rodriguez 15.00
17FB Larry Walker 6.00
18FB Barry Bonds 15.00
19FB Todd Helton 8.00
20FB Chipper Jones 15.00
21FB Roberto Alomar 8.00
22FB Jim Edmonds 6.00

2002 Fleer Platinum Fencebusters Autographed

MT
Common Autograph:
Derek Jeter/21
Jeff Bagwell/39
Miguel Tejada/31
Barry Bonds/73

2002 Fleer Platinum National Patch Time

	MT
Common Player:	30.00
Barry Bonds/75	100.00
Todd Helton/110	50.00
Ivan Rodriguez/225	40.00
Kazuhiro Sasaki/310	65.00
Derek Jeter/65	125.00
Cal Ripken Jr/350	80.00
Darin Erstad/315	30.00
Jose Canseco/150	60.00
Miguel Tejada/55	40.00
Greg Maddux/775	30.00
Juan Gonzalez/50	65.00
J.D. Drew/210	40.00
Manny Ramirez/100	45.00
Pedro Martinez/45	80.00
Carlos Delgado/70	40.00
Magglio Ordonez/85	40.00
Pat Burrell/285	30.00
Adam Dunn/75	60.00
Alex Rodriguez/325	50.00

2002 Fleer Platinum Wheelhouse

	MT
Complete Set (20):	50.00
Common Player:	1.50
Inserted 1:12	
1WH Derek Jeter	8.00
2WH Barry Bonds	4.00
3WH Luis Gonzalez	1.50
4WH Jason Giambi	2.00
5WH Ivan Rodriguez	1.50
6WH Mike Piazza	6.00
7WH Troy Glaus	1.50
8WH Nomar Garciaparra	5.00
9WH Juan Gonzalez	2.00
10WHSammy Sosa	4.00
11WHAlbert Pujols	4.00
12WHKen Griffey Jr.	5.00
13WHScott Rolen	1.50
14WHJeff Bagwell	2.00
15WHIchiro Suzuki	8.00
16WHTodd Helton	2.00
17WHChipper Jones	4.00
18WHAlex Rodriguez	5.00
19WHVladimir Guerrero	2.00
20WHManny Ramirez	2.00

A player's name in *italic* type indicates a rookie card.

2002 Fleer Premium

		MT
Complete Set (240):		50.00
Common Player:		.20
Common SP (201-240):		.50
Inserted 1:2		
Pack (8):		3.75
Box (24):		75.00
1	Garret Anderson	.20
2	Derek Jeter	3.00
3	Ken Griffey Jr.	2.50
4	Luis Castillo	.20
5	Richie Sexson	.30
6	Mike Mussina	.60
7	Ricky Henderson	.40
8	Bud Smith	.20
9	David Eckstein	.20
10	Nomar Garciaparra	2.00
11	Barry Larkin	.40
12	Cliff Floyd	.20
13	Ben Sheets	.30
14	Jorge Posada	.40
15	Phil Nevin	.20
16	Fernando Vina	.20
17	Darin Erstad	.30
18	Shea Hillenbrand	.20
19	Todd Walker	.20
20	Charles Johnson	.20
21	Cristian Guzman	.20
22	Mariano Rivera	.40
23	Bubba Trammell	.20
24	Brent Abernathy	.20
25	Troy Glaus	.50
26	Pedro J. Martinez	.75
27	Dmitri Young	.20
28	Derrek Lee	.20
29	Torii Hunter	.20
30	Alfonso Soriano	.50
31	Rich Aurilia	.20
32	Ben Grieve	.20
33	Tim Salmon	.20
34	Trot Nixon	.20
35	Roberto Alomar	.50
36	Mike Lowell	.20
37	Jacque Jones	.20
38	Bernie Williams	.50
39	Barry Bonds	1.25
40	Toby Hall	.20
41	Mo Vaughn	.30
42	Hideo Nomo	.40
43	Travis Fryman	.20
44	Preston Wilson	.20
45	Corey Koskie	.20
46	Eric Chavez	.40
47	Andres Galarraga	.20
48	Greg Vaughn	.20
49	Shawn Wooten	.20
50	Manny Ramirez	.75
51	Juan Gonzalez	.75
52	Moises Alou	.20
53	Joe Mays	.20
54	Johnny Damon	.20
55	Jeff Kent	.20
56	Frank Catalanotto	.20
57	Steve Finley	.20
58	Jason Varitek	.20
59	Kenny Lofton	.25
60	Jeff Bagwell	.75
61	Doug Mientkiewicz	.20
62	Jermaine Dye	.20
63	John Vander Wal	.20
64	Gabe Kapler	.20
65	Luis Gonzalez	.50
66	Jon Lieber	.20
67	C.C. Sabathia	.20
68	Lance Berkman	.40
69	Eric Milton	.20
70	Jason Giambi	.75
71	Ichiro Suzuki	3.00
72	Rafael Palmeiro	.40
73	Mark Grace	.40
74	Fred McGriff	.30
75	Jim Thome	.40
76	Craig Biggio	.30
77	A.J. Pierzynski	.20
78	Ramon Hernandez	.20
79	Paul Abbott	.20
80	Alex Rodriguez	2.00
81	Randy Johnson	.75
82	Corey Patterson	.20
83	Omar Vizquel	.20
84	Richard Hidalgo	.20
85	Luis Rivas	.20
86	Tim Hudson	.40
87	Bret Boone	.20
88	Ivan Rodriguez	.60
89	Junior Spivey	.20
90	Sammy Sosa	1.50
91	Jeff Cirillo	.20
92	Roy Oswalt	.40
93	Orlando Cabrera	.20
94	Terrence Long	.20
95	Mike Cameron	.20
96	Homer Bush	.20
97	Reggie Sanders	.20
98	Rondell White	.20
99	Mike Hampton	.20
100	Carlos Beltran	.20
101	Vladimir Guerrero	.75
102	Miguel Tejada	.40
103	Freddy Garcia	.20
104	Jose Cruz Jr.	.20
105	Curt Schilling	.40
106	Kerry Wood	.40
107	Todd Helton	.75
108	Neifi Perez	.20
109	Javier Vazquez	.20
110	Barry Zito	.30
111	Edgar Martinez	.20
112	Carlos Delgado	.50
113	Matt Williams	.30
114	Eric Young	.20
115	Alex Ochoa	.20
116	Mark Quinn	.20
117	Jose Vidro	.20
118	Bobby Abreu	.30
119	David Bell	.20
120	Brad Fullmer	.20
121	Rafael Furcal	.20
122	Ray Durham	.20
123	Jose Ortiz	.20
124	Joe Randa	.20
125	Edgardo Alfonzo	.20
126	Marlon Anderson	.20
127	Jamie Moyer	.20
128	Alex Gonzalez	.20
129	Marcus Giles	.20
130	Keith Foulke	.20
131	Juan Pierre	.20
132	Mike Sweeney	.20
133	Matt Lawton	.20
134	Pat Burrell	.40
135	John Olerud	.40
136	Raul Mondesi	.30
137	Tom Glavine	.40
138	Paul Konerko	.20
139	Larry Walker	.40
140	Adrian Beltre	.30
141	Al Leiter	.30
142	Mike Lieberthal	.20
143	Kazuhiro Sasaki	.20
144	Shannon Stewart	.20
145	Andruw Jones	.40
146	Carlos Lee	.20
147	Roger Cedeno	.20
148	Kevin Brown	.20
149	Jay Payton	.20
150	Scott Rolen	.40
151	J.D. Drew	.40
152	Chipper Jones	1.50
153	Magglio Ordonez	.40
154	Tony Clark	.20
155	Shawn Green	.40
156	Mike Piazza	2.00
157	Jimmy Rollins	.20
158	Jim Edmonds	.40
159	Javy Lopez	.20
160	Chris Singleton	.20
161	Juan Encarnacion	.20
162	Eric Karros	.20
163	Tsuyoshi Shinjo	.20
164	Brian Giles	.30
165	Darryl Kile	.20
166	Greg Maddux	1.50
167	Frank Thomas	.75
168	Shane Halter	.20
169	Paul LoDuca	.20
170	Robin Ventura	.20
171	Jason Kendall	.20
172	Jason Hart	.20
173	Brady Anderson	.20
174	Jose Valentin	.20
175	Bobby Higginson	.20
176	Gary Sheffield	.40
177	Roger Clemens	1.00
178	Aramis Ramirez	.20
179	Matt Morris	.40
180	Jeff Conine	.20
181	Aaron Boone	.20
182	Jose Macias	.20
183	Jeromy Burnitz	.20
184	Carl Everett	.20
185	Trevor Hoffman	.20
186	Placido Polanco	.20
187	Jay Gibbons	.20
188	Sean Casey	.40
189	Josh Beckett	.40
190	Jeffrey Hammonds	.20
191	Chuck Knoblauch	.20
192	Ryan Klesko	.20
193	Albert Pujols	1.50
194	Chris Richard	.20
195	Adam Dunn	.75
196	A.J. Burnett	.20
197	Geoff Jenkins	.40
198	Tino Martinez	.20
199	Ray Lankford	.20
200	Edgar Renteria	.20
201	*Eric Cyr*	1.00
202	Travis Phelps	.50
203	Rick Bauer	.50
204	Mark Prior	4.00
205	Wilson Betemit	.75
206	Dewon Brazelton	.50
207	Cody Ransom	.50
208	Donnie Bridges	.50
209	Justin Duchscherer	.50
210	Nate Cornejo	.50
211	Jason Romano	.50
212	Juan Cruz	.75
213	Pedro Santana	.50
214	Ryan Drese	.50
215	Bert Snow	.50
216	Nate Frese	.50
217	Rafael Soriano	.50
218	*Franklin Nunez*	5.00
219	Tim Spooneybarger	.50
220	Willie Harris	.50
221	Billy Sylvester	.50
222	Carlos Hernandez	.50
223	Mark Teixeira	5.00
224	Adrian Hernandez	.50
225	Andres Torres	.50
226	Marlon Byrd	.50
227	Juan Rivera	.50
228	Adam Johnson	.50
229	Justin Kaye	.50
230	Kyle Kessel	.50
231	Horacio Ramirez	.50
232	Brandon Larson	.50
233	Luis Lopez	.50
234	Robert Mackowiak	.50
235	Henry Mateo	.50
236	Corky Miller	.50
237	Greg Miller	.50
238	Dustan Mohr	.50
239	Bill Ortega	.50
240	Billy Hall	.50

2002 Fleer Premium Diamond Stars

		MT
Complete Set (20):		100.00
Common Player:		2.50
Inserted 1:72		
1DS	Pedro J. Martinez	4.00
2DS	Derek Jeter	15.00
3DS	Sammy Sosa	8.00
4DS	Ken Griffey Jr.	12.00
5DS	Chipper Jones	8.00
6DS	Roger Clemens	6.00
7DS	Ichiro Suzuki	15.00

	MT
8DS Jeff Bagwell	4.00
9DS Luis Gonzalez	2.50
10DSManny Ramirez	3.00
11DSAlex Rodriguez	10.00
12DSKazuhiro Sasaki	2.50
13DSMike Piazza	10.00
14DSVladimir Guerrero	4.00
15DSRandy Johnson	4.00
16DSIvan Rodriguez	3.00
17DSNomar Garciaparra	10.00
18DSBarry Bonds	8.00
19DSTodd Helton	3.00
20DSGreg Maddux	8.00

2002 Fleer Premium Diamond Stars Game-Used

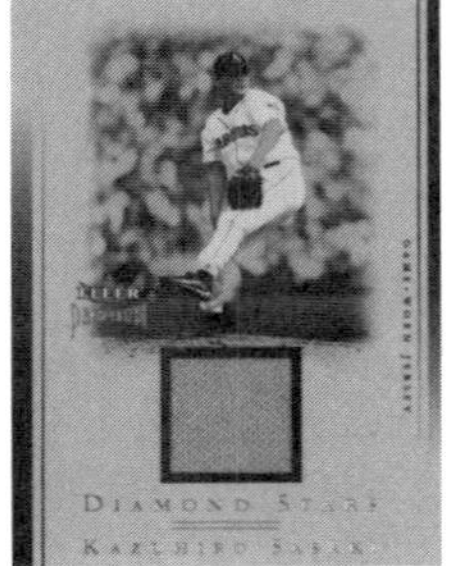

	MT
Common Player:	12.00
Inserted 1:105	
Barry Bonds/jsy	35.00
Manny Ramirez/jsy	15.00
Ivan Rodriguez/jsy	12.00
Kazuhiro Sasaki/jsy	15.00
Roger Clemens	25.00
Alex Rodriguez	20.00
Derek Jeter	50.00
Chipper Jones	20.00
Todd Helton	15.00
Luis Gonzalez	15.00
Mike Piazza	30.00
Nomar Garciaparra	40.00

2002 Fleer Premium Diamond Stars Game-Used Premium

	MT
Production 75 sets	
1DSGPBarry Bonds	70.00
2DSGPRoger Clemens	60.00
3DSGPTodd Helton	30.00
4DSGPChipper Jones	50.00
5DSGPManny Ramirez	30.00
6DSGPAlex Rodriguez	50.00
7DSGPIvan Rodriguez	25.00
8DSGPLuis Gonzalez	25.00
9DSGPMike Piazza	65.00
10DSGPKazuhiro Sasaki	25.00

2002 Fleer Premium Diamond Stars Dual Game-Used

	MT
Numbered to 100	
Barry Bonds	50.00
Todd Helton	25.00
Derek Jeter	100.00
Chipper Jones	50.00
Mike Piazza	50.00
Manny Ramirez	25.00
Alex Rodriguez	40.00

2002 Fleer Premium Diamond Stars Dual Game-Used Premium

	MT
Complete Set (5):	
Common Player:	
Barry Bonds	
Chipper Jones	
Manny Ramirez	
Mike Piazza	
Alex Rodriguez	

2002 Fleer Premium Diamond Stars Autograph

	MT
Numbered to 100	
1DSDJDerek Jeter	150.00

2002 Fleer Premium International Pride

	MT
Complete Set (15):	12.00
Common Player:	.50
Inserted 1:6	
1IP Larry Walker	.50
2IP Albert Pujols	2.00
3IP Juan Gonzalez	1.00
4IP Ichiro Suzuki	4.00
5IP Rafael Palmeiro	.50
6IP Carlos Delgado	.75
7IP Kazuhiro Sasaki	.50
8IP Vladimir Guerrero	1.00
9IP Bobby Abreu	.50
10IP Ivan Rodriguez	1.00
11IP Tsuyoshi Shinjo	.50
12IP Pedro J. Martinez	1.00
13IP Andruw Jones	.50
14IP Sammy Sosa	2.00
15IP Chan Ho Park	.50

2002 Fleer Premium International Pride Game-Used

	MT
Common Player:	10.00
Inserted 1:90	
Carlos Delgado/jsy	10.00
Juan Gonzalez/jsy	15.00
Andruw Jones/jsy	10.00
Pedro Martinez/jsy	15.00
Rafael Palmeiro/jsy	10.00
Chan Ho Park/jsy	15.00
Albert Pujols/jsy	30.00
Ivan Rodriguez/bat	12.00
Kazuhiro Sasaki/jsy	15.00
Tsuyoshi Shinjo/jsy	20.00

2002 Fleer Premium International Pride Premium

	MT
Production 75 sets	
1IPGPCarlos Delgado	25.00
2IPGPJuan Gonzalez	25.00
3IPGPAndruw Jones	25.00
4IPGPPedro J. Martinez	50.00
5IPGPChan Ho Park	25.00
6IPGPIvan Rodriguez	25.00
7IPGPTsuyoshi Shinjo	75.00
8IPGPRafael Palmeiro	25.00
9IPGPAlbert Pujols	40.00
10IPGPKazuhiro Sasaki	25.00

2002 Fleer Premium Legendary Dynasties

	MT
Complete Set (36):	140.00
Common Player:	1.50
Inserted 1:18	
1LD Honus Wagner	6.00
2LD Christy Mathewson	5.00
3LD Lou Gehrig	10.00
4LD Babe Ruth	12.00
5LD Jimmie Foxx	5.00
6LD Lefty Grove	3.00
7LD Al Simmons	1.50
8LD Bill Dickey	1.50
9LD Stan Musial	6.00
10LD Enos Slaughter	1.50
11LD Johnny Mize	2.00
12LD Yogi Berra	6.00
13LD Whitey Ford	5.00
14LD Jackie Robinson	10.00
15LD Duke Snider	5.00
16LD Roger Maris	8.00
17LD Jim Palmer	3.00
18LD Don Drysdale	4.00
19LD Brooks Robinson	4.00
20LD Rollie Fingers	1.50
21LD Reggie Jackson	5.00
22LD Joe Morgan	4.00
23LD Johnny Bench	6.00
24LD Thurman Munson	6.00
25LD Jose Canseco	2.50
26LD Tom Glavine	2.00
27LD Chipper Jones	8.00
28LD Greg Maddux	8.00
29LD Roberto Alomar	4.00
30LD David Cone	1.50
31LD Jim Thome	2.00
32LD Manny Ramirez	4.00
33LD Roger Clemens	6.00
34LD Derek Jeter	12.00
35LD Bernie Williams	2.50
36LD Alfonso Soriano	2.50

2002 Fleer Premium Legendary Dynasties Game-Used

	MT
Common Player:	15.00
Inserted 1:120	
Roberto Alomar/jsy	20.00
Johnny Bench/jsy	35.00
Yogi Berra/bat/SP	75.00
Roger Clemens/jsy	25.00
Bill Dickey/bat	25.00
Rollie Fingers/jsy	15.00
Whitey Ford	
Reggie Jackson/bat	25.00
Derek Jeter/bat	50.00
Chipper Jones/jsy	20.00
Roger Maris/pants/SP	60.00
Johnny Mize/bat	15.00
Joe Morgan/bat	15.00
Thurman Munson/bat	35.00
Jim Palmer/jsy	20.00
Manny Ramirez/jsy	15.00
Brooks Robinson/bat	50.00
Jackie Robinson	
Babe Ruth/bat	275.00
Duke Snider/bat	35.00
Alfonso Soriano/bat	20.00
Bernie Williams/jsy	15.00

2002 Fleer Premium Legendary Dynasties Premium

	MT
1LDGPRollie Fingers	15.00
2LDGPRoger Clemens	50.00
3LDGPRoger Maris	80.00
4LDGPRoberto Alomar	25.00
5LDGPReggie Jackson	30.00
6LDGPManny Ramirez	30.00
7LDGPJohnny Bench	40.00
8LDGPJim Palmer	20.00
9LDGPDerek Jeter	120.00
10LDGPAlfonso Soriano	50.00
11LDGPChipper Jones	35.00
12LDGPBernie Williams	20.00

2002 Fleer Premium Legendary Dynasties Autographs

	MT
#'d to World Series Year	
Johnny Bench	80.00
Yogi Berra	60.00
Rollie Fingers	
Tom Glavine	
Reggie Jackson	60.00
Derek Jeter	160.00
Greg Maddux	
Jim Palmer	
Brooks Robinson	

A card number in parentheses ( ) indicates the set is unnumbered.

2002 Fleer Premium On Base!

	MT
Complete Set (30):	180.00
Common Player:	3.00
#'d to 2001 OBP	
1OB Frank Thomas/316	6.00
2OB Ivan Rodriguez/347	5.00
3OB Nomar Garciaparra/352	15.00
4OB Ken Griffey Jr/365	18.00
5OB Juan Gonzalez/370	6.00
6OB Shawn Green/372	3.00
7OB Vladimir Guerrero/377	6.00
8OB Derek Jeter/377	20.00
9OB Scott Rolen/378	5.00
10OBIchiro Suzuki/381	20.00
11OBMike Piazza/384	15.00
12OBBernie Williams/395	5.00
13OBMoises Alou/396	3.00
14OBJeff Bagwell/397	6.00
15OBAlex Rodriguez/399	10.00
16OBAlbert Pujols/403	10.00
17OBManny Ramirez/405	6.00
18OBCarlos Delgado/408	5.00
19OBJim Edmonds/410	3.00
20OBRoberto Alomar/415	5.00
21OBJim Thome/416	4.00
22OBGary Sheffield/417	4.00
23OBChipper Jones/427	10.00
24OBLuis Gonzalez/429	5.00
25OBLance Berkman/430	5.00
26OBTodd Helton/432	5.00
27OBSammy Sosa/437	10.00
28OBLarry Walker/449	4.00
29OBJason Giambi/477	5.00
30OBBarry Bonds/515	8.00

2002 Fleer Premium On Base! Game-Used

	MT
Common Player:	5.00
Production 100 sets	
Roberto Alomar	20.00
Moises Alou	5.00
Jeff Bagwell	10.00
Lance Berkman	10.00
Barry Bonds	20.00
Carlos Delgado	10.00
Jim Edmonds	5.00
Nomar Garciaparra	20.00
Jason Giambi	10.00
Juan Gonzalez	10.00
Luis Gonzalez	10.00
Shawn Green	8.00
Ken Griffey Jr.	30.00
Vladimir Guerrero	10.00
Todd Helton	10.00
Derek Jeter	35.00
Chipper Jones	20.00
Mike Piazza	25.00
Albert Pujols	20.00
Manny Ramirez	10.00
Alex Rodriguez	25.00
Ivan Rodriguez	10.00
Scott Rolen	20.00
Gary Sheffield	6.00
Sammy Sosa	20.00
Ichiro Suzuki	35.00
Frank Thomas	10.00
Jim Thome	8.00
Larry Walker	8.00
Bernie Williams	8.00

2002 Fleer Showcase

		MT
Complete Set (166):		225.00
Common Player:		.25
Common (136-141):		8.00
Production 500		
Common (141-166		5.00
Production 1,500		
Pack (5):		4.50
Box (24):		90.00
1	Albert Pujols	1.50
2	Pedro J. Martinez	1.00
3	Frank Thomas	.75
4	Gary Sheffield	.40
5	Roberto Alomar	.50
6	Luis Gonzalez	.50
7	Bobby Abreu	.25
8	Carlos Lee	.25
9	Preston Wilson	.25
10	Todd Helton	.75
11	Juan Gonzalez	.75
12	Chuck Knoblauch	.25
13	Jason Kendall	.25
14	Aaron Sele	.25
15	Greg Vaughn	.25
16	Fred McGriff	.40
17	Doug Mientkiewicz	.25
18	Richard Hidalgo	.25
19	Alfonso Soriano	1.50
20	Matt Williams	.40
21	Bobby Higginson	.25
22	Mo Vaughn	.50
23	Andruw Jones	.50
24	Omar Vizquel	.40
25	Bret Boone	.25
26	Bernie Williams	.50
27	Rafael Furcal	.25
28	Jeff Bagwell	.75
29	Marty Cardova	.25
30	Lance Berkman	.75
31	Vernon Wells	.25
32	Garret Anderson	.25
33	Larry Bigbie	.25
34	Steve Finley	.25
35	Barry Bonds	1.50
36	Eric Chavez	.50
37	Tony Clark	.25
38	Roger Clemens	1.00
39	Adam Dunn	.75
40	Roger Cedeno	.25
41	Carlos Delgado	.50
42	Jermaine Dye	.25
43	Brian Jordan	.25
44	Darin Erstad	.50
45	Paul LoDuca	.25
46	Jim Edmonds	.50
47	Tom Glavine	.50
48	Cliff Floyd	.25
49	Jon Lieber	.25
50	Adrian Beltre	.50
51	Joel Pineiro	.25
52	Jim Thome	.50
53	Jimmy Rollins	.50
54	Pat Burrell	.50
55	Jeromy Burnitz	.25
56	Larry Walker	.40
57	Damon Minor	.25
58	John Olerud	.50
59	Carlos Beltran	.25
60	Vladimir Guerrero	.75
61	David Justice	.50
62	Phil Nevin	.25
63	Tino Martinez	.40
64	Curt Schilling	.75
65	Corey Patterson	.25
66	Aubrey Huff	.25
67	Mark Grace	.50
68	Rafael Palmeiro	.50
69	Jorge Posada	.50
70	Craig Biggio	.40
71	Manny Ramirez	.75
72	Mark Quinn	.25
73	Raul Mondesi	.25
74	Shawn Green	.50
75	Brian Giles	.50
76	Paul Konerko	.50
77	Troy Glaus	.50
78	Mike Mussina	.50
79	Greg Maddux	1.50
80	Edgar Martinez	.25
81	Jose Vidro	.25
82	Scott Rolen	.50
83	Ben Grieve	.25
84	Jeff Kent	.40
85	Magglio Ordonez	.50
86	Freddy Garcia	.25
87	Ivan Rodriguez	.50
88	Pokey Reese	.25
89	Shannon Stewart	.25
90	Randy Johnson	.75
91	Cristian Guzman	.25
92	Tsuyoshi Shinjo	.50
93	Steve Cox	.25
94	Mike Sweeney	.25
95	Robert Fick	.25
96	Sean Casey	.25
97	Tim Hudson	.50
98	Bud Smith	.25
99	Corey Koskie	.25
100	Richie Sexson	.50
101	Aramis Ramirez	.25
102	Barry Larkin	.50
103	Rich Aurilia	.25
104	Charles Johnson	.25
105	Ryan Klesko	.25
106	Ben Sheets	.40
107	J.D. Drew	.40
108	Jay Gibbons	.25
109	Kerry Wood	.50
110	C.C. Sabathia	.25
111	Eric Munson	.25
112	Josh Beckett	.25
113	Javier Vasquez	.25
114	Barry Zito	.25
115	Kazuhiro Sasaki	.25
116	Bubba Trammell	.25
117	Russell Branyan	.25
118	Todd Walker	.25
119	Mike Hampton	.25
120	Jeff Weaver	.25
121	Geoff Jenkins	.50
122	Edgardo Alfonzo	.25
123	Mike Lieberthal	.25
124	Mike Lowell	.25
125	Kevin Brown	.40
126	Derek Jeter	8.00
127	Ichiro Suzuki	6.00
128	Nomar Garciaparra	5.00
129	Ken Griffey Jr.	5.00
130	Jason Giambi	3.00
131	Alex Rodriguez	6.00
132	Chipper Jones	4.00
133	Mike Piazza	6.00
134	Sammy Sosa	4.00
135	Hideo Nomo	3.00
136	*Kazuhisa Ishii*	40.00
137	*Satoru Komiyama*	15.00
138	*So Taguchi*	15.00
139	*Jorge Padilla*	15.00
140	*Rene Reyes*	10.00
141	*Jorge Nunez*	8.00
142	*Nelson Castro*	5.00
143	*Anderson Machado*	5.00
144	*Edwin Almonte*	5.00
145	*Luis Ugueto*	5.00
146	*Felix Escalona*	5.00
147	*Ron Calloway*	5.00
148	*Hansel Izquierdo*	5.00
149	Mark Teixeira	8.00
150	Orlando Hudson	5.00
151	*Aaron Cook*	10.00
152	Aaron Taylor	5.00
153	*Takahito Nomura*	5.00
154	Matt Thornton	5.00
155	Mark Prior	15.00
156	*Reed Johnson*	5.00
157	Doug DeVore	5.00
158	*Ben Howard*	10.00
159	*Francis Beltran*	5.00
160	*Brian Mallette*	5.00
161	Sean Burroughs	5.00
162	Michael Restovich	5.00
163	Austin Kearns	8.00
164	Marlon Byrd	8.00
165	Hank Blalock	5.00
166	Mike Rivera	5.00

2002 Fleer Showcase Baseball's Best

	MT
Complete Set (20):	40.00
Common Player:	1.00
Inserted 1:8	
1BBI Derek Jeter	6.00
2BBI Barry Bonds	4.00
3BBI Mike Piazza	4.00
4BBI Alex Rodriguez	4.00
5BBI Pat Burrell	1.00
6BBI Rafael Palmeiro	1.00
7BBI Nomar Garciaparra	4.00
8BBI Todd Helton	1.50
9BBI Roger Clemens	2.00
10BBIShawn Green	1.00
11BBIChipper Jones	3.00
12BBIPedro J. Martinez	1.50
13BBILuis Gonzalez	1.00
14BBIRandy Johnson	1.50
15BBIIchiro Suzuki	5.00
16BBIKen Griffey Jr.	4.00
17BBIVladimir Guerrero	1.50
18BBISammy Sosa	3.00
19BBIJason Giambi	2.00
20BBIAlbert Pujols	3.00

2002 Fleer Showcase Baseball's Best Memorabilia

	MT
Common Player:	8.00
Inserted 1:24	

Golds: 1-2X
Production 100 sets
1BBI Derek Jeter/jsy 30.00
2BBI Barry Bonds/jsy 20.00
3BBI Mike Piazza/jsy 15.00
4BBI Alex Rodriguez/bat 15.00
5BBI Pat Burrell
6BBI Rafael Palmeiro/jsy 8.00
7BBI Nomar Garciaparra/jsy 15.00
8BBI Todd Helton/bat 10.00
9BBI Roger Clemens/jsy 15.00
10BBI Shawn Green/jsy 8.00
11BBI Chipper Jones/jsy 12.00
12BBI Pedro Martinez/jsy 12.00
13BBI Luis Gonzalez/jsy 8.00
14BBI Randy Johnson/jsy 10.00
15BBI Ichiro Suzuki/base 20.00
16BBI Ken Griffey Jr./base 15.00
17BBI Vladimir Guerrero/base 8.00
18BBI Sammy Sosa/base 10.00
19BBI Jason Giambi/base 10.00
20BBI Albert Pujols/base 10.00

2002 Fleer Showcase Baseball's Best Silver Auto

MT
Serial numbered to 400
Derek Jeter
Barry Bonds

2002 Fleer Showcase Baseball's Best Gold Auto

MT
Serial numbered to 100
Derek Jeter
Barry Bonds

2002 Fleer Showcase Derek Jeter's Legacy Collection

MT
Complete Set (22): 150.00
Common Jeter: 8.00
Production 1,000 sets
1DJL Derek Jeter 8.00
2DJL Derek Jeter 8.00
3DJL Derek Jeter 8.00
4DJL Derek Jeter 8.00
5DJL Derek Jeter 8.00
6DJL Derek Jeter 8.00
7DJL Derek Jeter 8.00
8DJL Derek Jeter 8.00
9DJL Derek Jeter 8.00
10DJL Derek Jeter 8.00
11DJL Derek Jeter 8.00
12DJL Derek Jeter 8.00
13DJL Derek Jeter 8.00
14DJL Derek Jeter 8.00
15DJL Derek Jeter 8.00
16DJL Derek Jeter 8.00
17DJL Derek Jeter 8.00
18DJL Derek Jeter 8.00
19DJL Derek Jeter 8.00
20DJL Derek Jeter 8.00
21DJL Derek Jeter 8.00
22DJL Derek Jeter 8.00

2002 Fleer Showcase Sweet Sigs

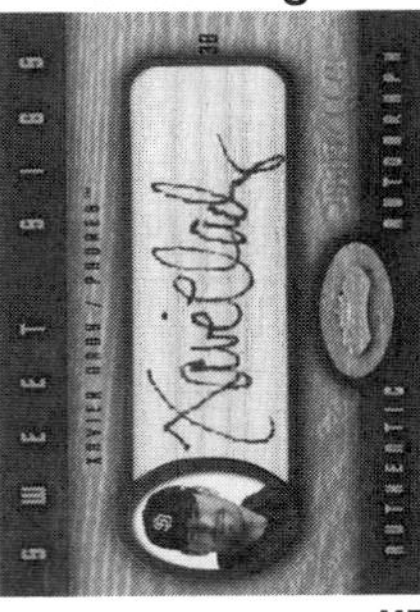

MT
Varying quantities produced
1SS Bobby Abreu/310 12.00
2SS Wilson Betemit
3SS Russell Branyan/315 8.00
4SS Pat Burrell/185 50.00
5SS Sean Casey
6SS Eric Chavez/360 15.00
7SS Rafael Furcal/825 10.00
8SS Nomar Garciaparra/55 125.00
9SS Elpidio Guzman
10SS Brandon Inge/835 10.00
11SS Jackson Melian/815 10.00
12SS Xavier Nady/1,175 10.00
13SS Jose Ortiz/680 8.00
14SS Ben Sheets/665 15.00
15SS Mike Sweeney/965 15.00

2002 Fleer Tradition

MT
Complete Set (500): 175.00
Common Player: .15
Common SP (1-100): 1.50
Inserted 1:2
Pack (10): 1.25
Box (36): 40.00
1 Barry Bonds 8.00
2 Cal Ripken Jr. 12.00
3 Tony Gwynn 5.00
4 Brad Radke 1.50
5 Jose Ortiz 1.50
6 Mark Mudler 2.00
7 Jon Lieber 1.50
8 John Olerud 3.00
9 Phil Nevin 1.50
10 Craig Biggio 2.50
11 Pedro Martinez 5.00
12 Fred McGriff 3.00
13 Vladimir Guerrero 4.00
14 Jason Giambi 5.00
15 Mark Kotsay 1.50
16 Bud Smith 5.00
17 Kevin Brown 4.00
18 Darin Erstad 3.00
19 Julio Franco 1.50
20 C.C. Sabathia 2.00
21 Larry Walker 3.00
22 Doug Mientkiewicz 1.50
23 Luis Gonzalez 3.00
24 Albert Pujols 6.00
25 Brian Lawrence 1.50
26 Al Leiter 3.00
27 Mike Sweeney 1.50
28 Jeff Weaver 1.50
29 Matt Morris 2.00
30 Hideo Nomo 3.00
31 Tom Glavine 3.00
32 Magglio Ordonez 3.00
33 Roberto Alomar 5.00
34 Roger Cedeno 1.50
35 Greg Vaughn 1.50
36 Chan Ho Park 3.00
37 Rich Aurilia 1.50
38 Tsuyoshi Shinjo 3.00
39 Eric Young 1.50
40 Bobby Higginson 1.50
41 Marlon Anderson 1.50
42 Mark Grace 3.00
43 Steve Cox 1.50
44 Cliff Floyd 1.50
45 Brian Roberts 1.50
46 Paul Konerko 2.00
47 Brandon Duckworth 3.00
48 Josh Beckett 3.00
49 David Ortiz 1.50
50 Geoff Jenkins 3.00
51 Ruben Sierra 2.00
52 John Franco 1.50
53 Einar Diaz 1.50
54 Luis Castillo 1.50
55 Mark Quinn 1.50
56 Shea Hillenbrand 1.50
57 Rafael Palmeiro 4.00
58 Paul O'Neill 4.00
59 Andruw Jones 3.00
60 Lance Berkman 3.00
61 Jimmy Rollins 3.00
62 Jose Hernandez 1.50
63 Rusty Greer 1.50
64 Wade Miller 1.50
65 David Eckstein 1.50
66 Jose Valentin 1.50
67 Javier Vazquez 1.50
68 Roger Clemens 8.00
69 Omar Vizquel 2.50
70 Roy Oswalt 2.50
71 Shannon Stewart 1.50
72 Byung-Hyun Kim 1.50
73 Jay Gibbons 2.00
74 Barry Larkin 4.00
75 Brian Giles 3.00
76 Andres Galarraga 2.50
77 Sammy Sosa 6.00
78 Manny Ramirez 6.00
79 Carlos Delgado 3.00
80 Jorge Posada 3.00
81 Todd Ritchie 1.50
82 Russ Ortiz 1.50
83 Brent Mayne 1.50
84 Mike Mussina 5.00
85 Raul Mondesi 1.50
86 Mark Loretta 1.50
87 Tim Raines 1.50
88 Ichiro Suzuki 10.00
89 Juan Pierre 1.50
90 Adam Dunn 8.00
91 Jason Tyner 1.50
92 Miguel Tejada 3.00
93 Elpidio Guzman 1.50
94 Freddy Garcia 2.50
95 Marcus Giles 1.50
96 Junior Spivey 1.50
97 Aramis Ramirez 2.50
98 Jose Rijo 1.50
99 Paul LoDuca 1.50
100 Mike Cameron 1.50
101 Alex Hernandez .15
102 Benji Gil .15
103 Benito Santiago .15
104 Bobby Abreu .25
105 Brad Penny .15
106 Calvin Murray .15
107 Chad Durbin .15
108 Chris Singleton .15
109 Chris Carpenter .15
110 David Justice .30
111 Eric Chavez .25
112 Fernando Tatis .15
113 Frank Castillo .15
114 Jason LaRue .15
115 Jim Edmonds .25
116 Joe Kennedy .15
117 Jose Jimenez .15
118 Josh Towers .15
119 Junior Herndon .15
120 Luke Prokopec .15
121 Mac Suzuki .15
122 Mark DeRosa .15
123 Marty Cordova .15
124 Michael Tucker .15
125 Michael Young .15
126 Robin Ventura .25
127 Shane Halter .15
128 Shane Reynolds .15
129 Tony Womack .15
130 A.J. Pierzynski .15
131 Aaron Rowand .15
132 Antonio Alfonseca .15
133 Arthur Rhodes .15
134 Bob Wickman .15
135 Brady Clark .15
136 Chad Hermansen .15
137 Marlon Byrd .15
138 Dan Wilson .15
139 David Cone .15
140 Dean Palmer .15
141 Denny Neagle .15
142 Derek Jeter 2.50
143 Erubiel Durazo .15
144 Felix Rodriguez .15
145 Jason Hart .15
146 Jay Bell .15
147 Jeff Suppan .15
148 Jeff Zimmerman .15
149 Kerry Wood .30
150 Kerry Robinson .15
151 Kevin Appier .15
152 Michael Barrett .15
153 Mo Vaughn .25
154 Rafael Furcal .25
155 Sidney Ponson .15
156 Terry Adams .15
157 Tim Redding .15
158 Toby Hall .15
159 Aaron Sele .15
160 Bartolo Colon .25
161 Brad Ausmus .15
162 Carlos Pena .15
163 Jace Brewer .15
164 David Wells .15
165 David Segui .15
166 Derek Lowe .15
167 Derek Bell .15
168 Jason Grabowski .15
169 Johnny Damon .15
170 Jose Mesa .15
171 Juan Encarnacion .15
172 Ken Caminiti .15
173 Ken Griffey Jr. 2.00
174 Luis Rivas .15
175 Mariano Rivera .25
176 Mark Grudzielanek .15
177 Mark McGwire 2.00
178 Mike Bordick .15
179 Mike Hampton .25
180 Nick Bierbrodt .15
181 Paul Byrd .15
182 Robb Nen .15
183 Ryan Dempster .15
184 Ryan Klesko .15
185 Scott Spiezio .15
186 Scott Strickland .15
187 Todd Zeile .15
188 Tom Gordon .15
189 Troy Glaus .50
190 Matt Williams .30
191 Wes Helms .15
192 Jerry Hairston Jr. .15
193 Brook Fordyce .15
194 Nomar Garciaparra 2.00
195 Kevin Tapani .15
196 Mark Buehrle .15
197 Dmitri Young .15
198 John Rocker .15
199 Juan Uribe .15
200 Matt Anderson .15
201 Alex Gonzalez .15
202 Julio Lugo .15
203 Roberto Hernandez .15
204 Richie Sexson .15
205 Corey Koskie .15
206 Tony Armas Jr. .15
207 Rey Ordonez .15
208 Orlando Hernandez .15
209 Pokey Reese .15
210 Mike Lieberthal .15
211 Kris Benson .15
212 Jermaine Dye .15

213 Livan Hernandez .15
214 Bret Boone .15
215 Dustin Hermanson .15
216 Placido Polanco .15
217 Jesus Colome .15
218 Alex Gonzalez .15
219 Adam Everett .15
220 Adam Piatt .15
221 Brad Fullmer .15
222 Brian Buchanan .15
223 Chipper Jones 1.25
224 Chuck Finley .15
225 David Bell .15
226 Jack Wilson .15
227 Jason Bere .15
228 Jeff Conine .15
229 Jeff Bagwell .60
230 Joe McEwing .15
231 Kip Wells .15
232 Mike Lansing .15
233 Neifi Perez .15
234 Omar Daal .15
235 Reggie Sanders .15
236 Shawn Wooten .15
237 Shawn Chacon .15
238 Shawn Estes .15
239 Steve Sparks .15
240 Steve Kline .15
241 Tino Martinez .25
242 Tyler Houston .15
243 Xavier Nady .15
244 Bengie Molina .15
245 Ben Davis .15
246 Casey Fossum .15
247 Chris Stynes .15
248 Danny Graves .15
249 Pedro Feliz .15
250 Darren Oliver .15
251 Dave Veres .15
252 Deivi Cruz .15
253 Desi Relaford .15
254 Devon White .15
255 Edgar Martinez .25
256 Eric Munson .15
257 Eric Karros .15
258 Homer Bush .15
259 Jason Kendall .15
260 Javy Lopez .25
261 Keith Foulke .15
262 Keith Ginter .15
263 Nick Johnson .15
264 Pat Burrell .30
265 Ricky Gutierrez .15
266 Russ Johnson .15
267 Steve Finley .15
268 Terrence Long .15
269 Tony Batista .15
270 Torii Hunter .15
271 Vinny Castilla .15
272 A.J. Burnett .15
273 Adrian Beltre .25
274 Alex Rodriguez 1.50
275 Armando Benitez .15
276 Billy Koch .15
277 Brady Anderson .15
278 Brian Jordan .15
279 Carlos Febles .15
280 Daryle Ward .15
281 Eli Marrero .15
282 Garret Anderson .15
283 Jack Cust .15
284 Jacque Jones .15
285 Jamie Moyer .15
286 Jeffrey Hammonds .15
287 Jim Thome .30
288 Jon Garland .15
289 Jose Offerman .15
290 Matt Stairs .15
291 Orlando Cabrera .15
292 Ramiro Mendoza .15
293 Ray Durham .15
294 Rickey Henderson .25
295 Rob Mackowiak .15
296 Scott Rolen .30
297 Tim Hudson .25
298 Todd Helton .60
299 Tony Clark .15
300 B.J. Surhoff .15
301 Bernie Williams .50
302 Bill Mueller .15
303 Chris Richard .15
304 Craig Paquette .15
305 Curt Schilling .25
306 Damian Jackson .15
307 Derrek Lee .15
308 Eric Milton .15
309 Frank Catalanotto .15
310 J.T. Snow .15
311 Jared Sandberg .15
312 Jason Varitek .15
313 Jeff Cirillo .15
314 Jeromy Burnitz .15
315 Joe Crede .15
316 Joel Pineiro .15
317 Jose Cruz Jr. .15
318 Kevin Young .15
319 Marquis Grissom .15
320 Moises Alou .20
321 Randall Simon .15
322 Royce Clayton .15
323 Tim Salmon .15
324 Travis Fryman .20
325 Travis Lee .15
326 Vance Wilson .15
327 Jarrod Washburn .15
328 Ben Petrick .15
329 Ben Grieve .15
330 Carl Everett .15
331 Eric Byrnes .15
332 Doug Glanville .15
333 Edgardo Alfonzo .15
334 Ellis Burks .15
335 Gabe Kapler .20
336 Gary Sheffield .25
337 Greg Maddux 1.25
338 J.D. Drew .30
339 Jamey Wright .15
340 Jeff Kent .20
341 Jeremy Giambi .15
342 Joe Randa .15
343 Joe Mays .15
344 Jose Macias .15
345 Kazuhiro Sasaki .15
346 Mike Kinkade .15
347 Mike Lowell .15
348 Randy Johnson .60
349 Randy Wolf .15
350 Richard Hidalgo .20
351 Ron Coomer .15
352 Sandy Alomar .15
353 Sean Casey .25
354 Trevor Hoffman .15
355 Adam Eaton .15
356 Alfonso Soriano .40
357 Barry Zito .15
358 Billy Wagner .15
359 Brent Abernathy .15
360 Bret Prinz .15
361 Carlos Beltran .15
362 Carlos Guillen .15
363 Charles Johnson .15
364 Cristian Guzman .15
365 Damion Easley .15
366 Darryl Kile .15
367 Delino DeShields .15
368 Eric Davis .15
369 Frank Thomas .60
370 Ivan Rodriguez .60
371 Jay Payton .15
372 Jeff D'Amico .15
373 John Burkett .15
374 Melvin Mora .15
375 Ramon Ortiz .15
376 Robert Person .15
377 Russell Branyan .15
378 Shawn Green .25
379 Todd Hollandsworth .15
380 Tony McKnight .15
381 Trot Nixon .15
382 Vernon Wells .15
383 Troy Percival .15
384 Albie Lopez .15
385 Alex Ochoa .15
386 Andy Pettitte .25
387 Brandon Inge .15
388 Bubba Trammell .15
389 Corey Patterson .15
390 Damian Rolls .15
391 Dee Brown .15
392 Edgar Renteria .15
393 Eric Gagne .15
394 Jason Johnson .15
395 Jeff Nelson .15
396 John Vander Wal .15
397 Johnny Estrada .15
398 Jose Canseco .30
399 Juan Gonzalez .60
400 Kevin Millwood .15
401 Lee Stevens .15
402 Matt Lawton .15
403 Mike Lamb .15
404 Octavio Dotel .15
405 Ramon Hernandez .15
406 Ruben Quevedo .15
407 Todd Walker .15
408 Troy O'Leary .15
409 Wascar Serrano .15
410 Aaron Boone .15
411 Aubrey Huff .15
412 Ben Sheets .15
413 Carlos Lee .15
414 Chuck Knoblauch .15
415 Steve Karsay .15
416 Dante Bichette .15
417 David Dellucci .15
418 Esteban Loaiza .15
419 Fernando Vina .15
420 Ismael Valdes .15
421 Jason Isringhausen .15
422 Jeff Shaw .15
423 John Smoltz .15
424 Jose Vidro .15
425 Kenny Lofton .25
426 Mark Little .15
427 Mark McLemore .15
428 Marvin Benard .15
429 Mike Piazza 1.50
430 Pat Hentgen .15
431 Preston Wilson .15
432 Rick Helling .15
433 Robert Fick .15
434 Rondell White .15
435 Adam Kennedy .15
436 David Espinosa .15
437 Dewon Brazelton .15
438 Drew Henson .40
439 Juan Cruz .25
440 Jason Jennings .15
441 Carlos Garcia .15
442 Carlos Hernandez .15
443 Wilkin Ruan .15
444 Wilson Betemit .25
445 Horacio Ramirez .15
446 Danys Baez .15
447 Abraham Nunez .15
448 Josh Hamilton .25
449 Chris George .15
450 Rick Bauer .15
451 Donnie Bridges .15
452 Erick Almonte .15
453 Cory Aldridge .15
454 Ryan Drese .15
455 Jason Romano .15
456 Corky Miller .15
457 Rafael Soriano .15
458 Mark Prior .75
459 Mark Teixeira 1.00
460 Adrian Hernandez .15
461 Tim Spooneybarger .15
462 Bill Ortega .15
463 D'Angelo Jimenez .15
464 Andres Torres .15
465 Alexis Gomez .15
466 Angel Berroa .15
467 Henry Mateo .15
468 Endy Chavez .15
469 Billy Sylvester .15
470 Nate Frese .15
471 Luis Gonzalez .25
472 Barry Bonds .75
473 Rich Aurilia .15
474 Albert Pujols .50
475 Todd Helton .40
476 Moises Alou .15
477 Lance Berkman .15
478 Brian Giles .15
479 Cliff Floyd .15
480 Sammy Sosa .60
481 Shawn Green .15
482 Jon Lieber .15
483 Matt Morris .15
484 Curt Schilling .15
485 Randy Johnson .30
486 Manny Ramirez .30
487 Ichiro Suzuki 1.00
488 Juan Gonzalez .30
489 Derek Jeter 1.25
490 Alex Rodriguez .75
491 Bret Boone .15
492 Roberto Alomar .30
493 Jason Giambi .30
494 Rafael Palmeiro .20
495 Doug Mientkiewicz .15
496 Jim Thome .25
497 Freddy Garcia .15
498 Mark Buehrle .15
499 Mark Mulder .15
500 Roger Clemens .50

2002 Fleer Tradition Diamond Tributes

MT
Complete Set (15): 18.00
Common Player: .50
Inserted 1:6
1DT Cal Ripken Jr. 3.00
2DT Tony Gwynn .75
3DT Derek Jeter 3.00
4DT Pedro Martinez .75
5DT Mark McGwire 2.50
6DT Sammy Sosa 1.50
7DT Barry Bonds 1.50
8DT Roger Clemens 1.25
9DT Mike Piazza 2.00
10DT Alex Rodriguez 2.00
11DT Randy Johnson .75
12DT Chipper Jones 1.50
13DT Nomar Garciaparra 2.00
14DT Ichiro Suzuki 3.00
15DT Jason Giambi .50

2002 Fleer Tradition Grass Roots

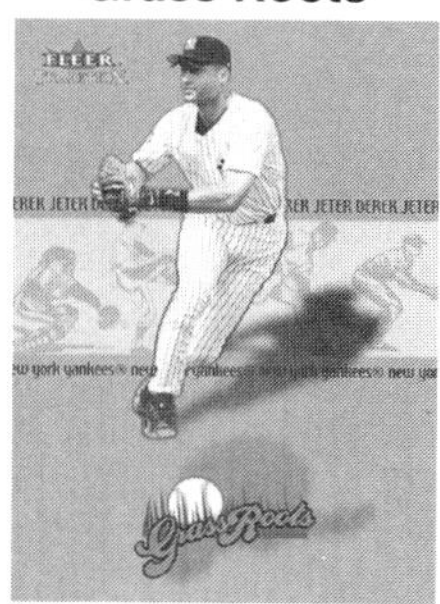

MT
Complete Set (10): 15.00
Common Player: .75
Inserted 1:18
1GR Barry Bonds 2.50
2GR Alex Rodriguez 3.00
3GR Derek Jeter 5.00
4GR Greg Maddux 2.50
5GR Ivan Rodriguez 1.25
6GR Cal Ripken Jr. 5.00
7GR Bernie Williams 1.00
8GR Jeff Bagwell 1.25
9GR Scott Rolen .75
10GR Larry Walker .75

2002 Fleer Tradition Grass Roots Patch (game-worn)

MT
Common Player:
Production 50 sets
1GRP Barry Bonds 75.00
2GRP Alex Rodriguez 60.00

3GRP Derek Jeter	
4GRP Greg Maddux	50.00
5GRP Ivan Rodriguez	30.00
6GRP Cal Ripken Jr.	150.00
7GRP Bernie Williams	40.00
8GRP Jeff Bagwell	40.00
9GRP Scott Rolen	20.00
10GRP Larry Walker	

2002 Fleer Tradition Heads Up

	MT
Complete Set (10):	45.00
Common Player:	1.00
Inserted 1:36	
1HU Derek Jeter	8.00
2HU Ichiro Suzuki	8.00
3HU Sammy Sosa	4.00
4HU Mike Piazza	5.00
5HU Ken Griffey Jr.	6.00
6HU Alex Rodriguez	5.00
7HU Barry Bonds	4.00
8HU Nomar Garciaparra	5.00
9HU Mark McGwire	6.00
10HU Cal Ripken Jr.	8.00

2002 Fleer Tradition Lumber Company

	MT
Complete Set (30):	40.00
Common Player:	1.00
Inserted 1:12	
1LC Moises Alou	1.00
2LC Luis Gonzalez	1.50
3LC Todd Helton	2.00
4LC Mike Piazza	5.00
5LC J.D. Drew	1.00
6LC Albert Pujols	4.00
7LC Chipper Jones	4.00
8LC Manny Ramirez	2.00
9LC Miguel Tejada	1.00
10LC Curt Schilling	1.00
11LC Alex Rodriguez	5.00
12LC Barry Larkin	1.00
13LC Nomar Garciaparra	5.00
14LC Cliff Floyd	1.00
15LC Alfonso Soriano	1.50
16LC Sean Casey	1.00
17LC Scott Rolen	1.00
18LC Jose Ortiz	1.00
19LC Corey Patterson	1.00
20LC Joe Crede	1.00
21LC Jace Brewer	1.00
22LC Derek Jeter	8.00
23LC Jim Thome	1.50
24LC Frank Thomas	2.00
25LC Shawn Green	1.00
26LC Drew Henson	1.50
27LC Jimmy Rollins	1.00
28LC Dave Justice	1.00
29LC Roberto Alomar	1.50
30LC Bernie Williams	1.50

2002 Fleer Tradition Lumber Company (game-used)

	MT
Common Player:	6.00
Inserted 1:72	
1LCG Moises Alou	6.00
2LCG Luis Gonzalez	10.00
3LCG Todd Helton	15.00
4LCG Mike Piazza	30.00
5LCG J.D. Drew	15.00
6LCG Albert Pujols	30.00
7LCG Chipper Jones	20.00
8LCG Manny Ramirez	15.00
9LCG Miguel Tejada	8.00
10LCG Curt Schilling	10.00
11LCG Alex Rodriguez	20.00
12LCG Barry Larkin	12.00
13LCG Nomar Garciaparra	40.00
14LCG Cliff Floyd	6.00
15LCG Alfonso Soriano	15.00
16LCG Sean Casey	12.00
17LCG Scott Rolen	12.00
18LCG Jose Ortiz	8.00
19LCG Corey Patterson	15.00
20LCG Joe Crede	8.00
21LCG Jace Brewer	6.00
22LCG Derek Jeter	40.00
23LCG Jim Thome	15.00
24LCG Frank Thomas	15.00
25LCG Shawn Green	10.00
26LCG Drew Henson	20.00
27LCG Jimmy Rollins	12.00
28LCG Dave Justice	10.00
29LCG Roberto Alomar	10.00
30LCG Bernie Williams	15.00

2002 Fleer Tradition This Day in History

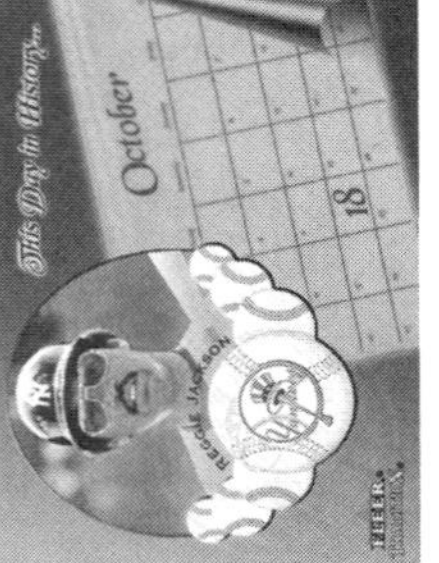

	MT
Complete Set (29):	120.00
Common Player:	2.00
Inserted 1:18	
1TDH Cal Ripken Jr.	12.00
2TDH Barry Bonds	6.00
3TDH George Brett	6.00
4TDH Tony Gwynn	3.00
5TDH Nolan Ryan	12.00
6TDH Reggie Jackson	3.00
7TDH Paul Molitor	3.00
8TDH Ichiro Suzuki	12.00
9TDH Alex Rodriguez	8.00
10TDH Don Mattingly	8.00
11TDH Sammy Sosa	6.00
12TDH Mark McGwire	10.00
13TDH Derek Jeter	12.00
14TDH Roger Clemens	6.00
15TDH Jim "Catfish" Hunter	2.00
16TDH Greg Maddux	6.00
17TDH Ken Griffey Jr.	10.00
18TDH Gil Hodges	2.00
19TDH Edgar Martinez	2.00
20TDH Mike Piazza	8.00
21TDH Jimmie Foxx	3.00
22TDH Albert Pujols	5.00
23TDH Chipper Jones	6.00
24TDH Jeff Bagwell	3.00
25TDH Nomar Garciaparra	8.00
26TDH Randy Johnson	3.00
27TDH Todd Helton	3.00
28TDH Ted Kluszewski	2.00
29TDH Ivan Rodriguez	3.00

2002 Fleer Tradition Update

	MT
Complete Set (400):	75.00
Common Player:	.20
Common SP (1-100):	.50
Inserted 1:1	
Pack (10):	2.00
Box (36):	50.00
1 *P.J. Bevis*	.50
2 Michael Crudale	.50
3 *Ben Howard*	.75
4 *Travis Driskill*	.50
5 *Reed Johnson*	.50
6 *Kyle Kane*	.75
7 Deivis Santos	.50
8 *Tim Kalita*	.75
9 *Brandon Puffer*	.50
10 *Chris Snelling*	2.50
11 *Juan Brito*	.50
12 *Tyler Yates*	.50
13 *Victor Alvarez*	.75
14 *Takahito Nomura*	.50
15 *Ron Calloway*	.50
16 *Satoru Komiyama*	.50
17 *Julius Matos*	.50
18 Jorge Nunez	.50
19 *Anderson Machado*	1.00
20 *Scotty Layfield*	.50
21 *Aaron Cook*	1.00
22 *Alex Pelaez*	.50
23 *Corey Thurman*	.50
24 Nelson Castro	.50
25 *Jeff Austin*	.50
26 *Felix Escalona*	.50
27 *Luis Ugueto*	.50
28 Jaime Cerda	.50
29 *J.J. Trujillo*	.50
30 *Rodrigo Rosario*	1.00
31 *Jorge Padilla*	1.00
32 *Shawn Sedlacek*	.50
33 Nate Field	.50
34 *Earl Snyder*	.75
35 *Miguel Asencio*	.50
36 Ken Huckaby	.50
37 Valentino Pascucci	.50
38 *So Taguchi*	1.50
39 *Brian Mallette*	.50
40 *Kazuhisa Ishii*	2.50
41 Matt Thornton	.50
42 Mark Corey	.50
43 Kirk Saarloos	3.00
44 Brandon Bracke	.50
45 *Hansel Izquierdo*	.50
46 *Rene Reyes*	.50
47 Luis Garcia	.50
48 *Jason Simontacchi*	2.50
49 *John Ennis*	.75
50 *Franklyn German*	.50
51 *Aaron Guiel*	.75
52 *Howie Clark*	.50
53 *David Ross*	.50
54 Walt McKeel	.50
55 *Francis Beltran*	.50
56 *Barry Wesson*	.50
57 *Runelvys Hernandez*	.50
58 *Oliver Perez*	4.00
59 Ryan Bukvich	.50
60 *Steve Kent*	.50
61 *Julio Mateo*	.50
62 Jason Jimenez	.50
63 *Jayson Durocher*	.75
64 *Kevin Frederick*	.50
65 *Kevin Gryboski*	.50
66 *Edwin Almonte*	.50
67 *John Foster*	.50
68 *Doug Devore*	1.00
69 *Tom Shearn*	.50
70 *Colin Young*	.50
71 Jon Adkins	.50
72 *Wilbert Nieves*	.50
73 Matt Duff	.50
74 Carl Sadler	.50
75 Jason Kershner	.50
76 Brandon Backe	.50
77 Wilson Valdez	.50
78 *Chris Baker*	.50
79 Ryan Jamison	.50
80 *Steve Bechler*	.75
81 *Allan Simpson*	.50
82 *Aaron Taylor*	.50
83 *Kevin Cash*	1.00
84 *Chone Figgins*	.50
85 *Clay Condrey*	.50
86 *Shane Nance*	.50
87 *Freddy Sanchez*	1.50
88 *Jim Rushford*	.50
89 *Jeriome Robertson*	.50
90 *Trey Lunsford*	.50
91 *Cody McKay*	.50
92 *Trey Hodges*	.50
93 Hee Seop Choi	1.00
94 Joe Borchard	1.00
95 Orlando Hudson	.50
96 Carl Crawford	.50
97 Mark Prior	3.00
98 Brett Myers	.75
99 Kenny Lofton	.50
100 Cliff Floyd	.50
101 Randy Winn	.20
102 Ryan Dempster	.20
103 Josh Phelps	.50
104 Marcus Giles	.20
105 Rickey Henderson	.75
106 Jose Leon	.20
107 Tino Martinez	.40
108 Greg Norton	.20
109 Odalis Perez	.20
110 J.C. Romero	.20
111 Gary Sheffield	.40
112 Ismael Valdes	.20
113 Juan Acevedo	.20
114 Ben Broussard	.20
115 Deivi Cruz	.20
116 Geronimo Gil	.20
117 Eric Hinske	.40
118 Ted Lilly	.20
119 Quinton McCracken	.20
120 Antonio Alfonseca	.20
121 Brent Abernathy	.20
122 Johnny Damon	.20
123 Francisco Cordova	.20
124 Sterling Hitchcock	.20
125 Vladimir Nunez	.20
126 Andres Galarraga	.20
127 Timoniel Perez	.20
128 Tsuyoshi Shinjo	.40
129 Joe Girardi	.20
130 Roberto Alomar	.60
131 Ellis Burks	.20
132 Mike DeJean	.20
133 Alex Gonzalez	.20
134 Johan Santana	.20
135 Kenny Lofton	.20
136 Juan Encarnacion	.20
137 Dewon Brazelton	.20
138 Jeromy Burnitz	.20
139 Elmer Dessens	.20
140 Juan Gonzalez	.75
141 Todd Hundley	.20
142 Tomokazu Ohka	.20
143 Robin Ventura	.20
144 Rodrigo Lopez	.20
145 Ruben Sierra	.20
146 Jason Phillips	.20
147 Ryan Rupe	.20
148 Kevin Appier	.20
149 Sean Burroughs	.20
150 Masato Yoshii	.20
151 Juan Diaz	.20

152 Tony Graffanino .20
153 Raul Ibanez .20
154 Kevin Mench .20
155 Pedro Astacio .20
156 Brent Butler .20
157 Kirk Rueter .20
158 Eddie Guardado .20
159 Hideki Irabu .20
160 Wendell Magee .20
161 Antonio Osuna .20
162 Jose Vizcaino .20
163 Danny Bautista .20
164 Vinny Castilla .20
165 Chris Singleton .20
166 Mark Redman .20
167 Olmedo Saenz .20
168 Scott Erickson .20
169 Ty Wigginton .20
170 Jason Isringhausen .20
171 Lou Merloni .20
172 Chris Magruder .20
173 Brandon Berger .20
174 Roger Cedeno .20
175 Kelvim Escobar .20
176 Jose Guillen .20
177 Damian Jackson .20
178 Eric Owens .20
179 Angel Berroa .20
180 Alex Cintron .20
181 Jeff Weaver .20
182 Damon Minor .20
183 Bobby Estalella .20
184 David Justice .40
185 Roy Halladay .20
186 Brian Jordan .20
187 Mike Maroth .20
188 Pokey Reese .20
189 Rey Sanchez .20
190 Hank Blalock .40
191 Jeff Cirillo .20
192 Dmitri Young .20
193 Carl Everett .20
194 Joey Hamilton .20
195 Jorge Julio .20
196 Pablo Ozuna .20
197 Jason Marquis .20
198 Dustan Mohr .20
199 Joe Borowski .20
200 Tony Clark .20
201 David Wells .20
202 Josh Fogg .20
203 Aaron Harang .20
204 John McDonald .20
205 John Stephens .20
206 Chris Reitsma .20
207 Alex Sanchez .20
208 Milton Bradley .20
209 Matt Clement .20
210 Brad Fullmer .20
211 Shigetoshi Hasegawa .20
212 Austin Kearns .50
213 Damaso Marte .20
214 Vicente Padilla .20
215 Raul Mondesi .20
216 Russell Branyan .20
217 Bartolo Colon .20
218 Moises Alou .20
219 Scott Hatteberg .20
220 Bobby Kielty .20
221 Kip Wells .20
222 Scott Stewart .20
223 Victor Martinez .50
224 Marty Cordova .20
225 Desi Relaford .20
226 Reggie Sanders .20
227 Jason Giambi .75
228 Jimmy Haynes .20
229 Billy Koch .20
230 Damian Moss .20
231 Chan Ho Park .20
232 Cliff Floyd .20
233 Todd Zeile .20
234 Jeremy Giambi .20
235 Rick Helling .20
236 Matt Lawton .20
237 Ramon Martinez .20
238 Rondell White .20
239 Scott Sullivan .20
240 Hideo Nomo .40
241 Todd Ritchie .20
242 Ramon Santiago .20
243 Jake Peavy .20
244 Brad Wilkerson .20
245 Reggie Taylor .20
246 Carlos Pena .20
247 Willis Roberts .20
248 Jason Schmidt .20
249 Mike Williams .20
250 Alan Zinter .20
251 Michael Tejera .20
252 Dave Roberts .20
253 Scott Schoeneweis .20
254 Woody Williams .20
255 John Thomson .20
256 Ricardo Rodriguez .20
257 Aaron Sele .20
258 Paul Wilson .20
259 Brett Tomko .20
260 Kenny Rogers .20
261 Mo Vaughn .20
262 John Burkett .20
263 Dennis Stark .20
264 Ray Durham .20
265 Scott Rolen .40
266 Gabe Kapler .20
267 Todd Hollandsworth .20
268 Bud Smith .20
269 Jay Payton .20
270 Tyler Houston .20
271 Brian Moehler .20
272 David Espinosa .20
273 Placido Polanco .20
274 John Patterson .20
275 Adam Hyzdu .20
276 Albert Pujols .75
277 Larry Walker .30
278 Magglio Ordonez .30
279 Ryan Klesko .20
280 Darin Erstad .20
281 Jeff Kent .20
282 Paul LoDuca .20
283 Jim Edmonds .20
284 Chipper Jones .75
285 Bernie Williams .40
286 Pat Burrell .40
287 Cliff Floyd .20
288 Troy Glaus .40
289 Brian Giles .20
290 Jim Thome .40
291 Greg Maddux .75
292 Roberto Alomar .30
293 Jeff Bagwell .40
294 Rafael Furcal .20
295 Josh Beckett .20
296 Carlos Delgado .20
297 Ken Griffey Jr. .75
298 Jason Giambi .75
299 Paul Konerko .20
300 Mike Sweeney .20
301 Alfonso Soriano .75
302 Shea Hillenbrand .20
303 Tony Batista .20
304 Robin Ventura .20
305 Alex Rodriguez .75
306 Nomar Garciaparra .75
307 Derek Jeter 1.00
308 Miguel Tejada .30
309 Omar Vizquel .20
310 Jorge Posada .20
311 A.J. Pierzynski .20
312 Ichiro Suzuki .75
313 Manny Ramirez .40
314 Torii Hunter .20
315 Garret Anderson .20
316 Robert Fick .20
317 Randy Winn .20
318 Mark Buerhle .20
319 Freddy Garcia .20
320 Eddie Guardado .20
321 Roy Halladay .20
322 Derek Lowe .20
323 Pedro J. Martinez .50
324 Mariano Rivera .20
325 Kazuhiro Sasaki .20
326 Barry Zito .20
327 Johnny Damon .20
328 Ugueth Urbina .20
329 Todd Helton .30
330 Richie Sexson .20
331 Jose Vidro .20
332 Luis Castillo .20
333 Junior Spivey .20
334 Scott Rolen .30
335 Mike Lowell .20
336 Jimmy Rollins .20
337 Jose Hernandez .20
338 Mike Piazza .75
339 Benito Santiago .20
340 Sammy Sosa .75
341 Barry Bonds .75
342 Vladimir Guerrero .50
343 Lance Berkman .30
344 Adam Dunn .40
345 Shawn Green .20
346 Luis Gonzalez .25
347 Eric Gagne .20
348 Tom Glavine .30
349 Trevor Hoffman .20
350 Randy Johnson .50
351 Byung-Hyun Kim .20
352 Matt Morris .20
353 Odalis Perez .20
354 Curt Schilling .40
355 John Smoltz .20
356 Mike Williams .20
357 Andruw Jones .30
358 Vicente Padilla .20
359 Mike Remlinger .20
360 Robb Nen .20
361 Shawn Green .20
362 Derek Jeter 1.00
363 Troy Glaus .40
364 Ken Griffey Jr. .75
365 Mike Piazza .75
366 Jason Giambi .75
367 Greg Maddux .75
368 Albert Pujols .75
369 Pedro J. Martinez .50
370 Barry Zito .20
371 Ichiro Suzuki .75
372 Nomar Garciaparra .75
373 Vladimir Guerrero .50
374 Randy Johnson .50
375 Barry Bonds .75
376 Sammy Sosa .75
377 Hideo Nomo .40
378 Jeff Bagwell .40
379 Curt Schilling .20
380 Jim Thome .40
381 Todd Helton .30
382 Roger Clemens .50
383 Chipper Jones .50
384 Alex Rodriguez .75
385 Manny Ramirez .40
386 Barry Bonds .75
387 Jim Thome .40
388 Adam Dunn .40
389 Alex Rodriguez .75
390 Shawn Green .20
391 Jason Giambi .75
392 Lance Berkman .40
393 Pat Burrell .40
394 Eric Chavez .20
395 Mike Piazza .75
396 Vladimir Guerrero .50
397 Paul Konerko .20
398 Sammy Sosa .75
399 Richie Sexson .20
400 Torii Hunter .20

2002 Fleer Tradition Update Glossy

	MT
Stars (1-100):	1-2X
Cards (101-400):	4-10X
Production 200 sets	

2002 Fleer Tradition Update Diamond Debuts

		MT
Complete Set (15):		10.00
Common Player:		.50
Inserted 1:6		
1DD	Mark Prior	2.50
2DD	Eric Hinske	.50
3DD	Kazuhisa Ishii	1.00
4DD	Ben Broussard	.50
5DD	Sean Burroughs	.50
6DD	Austin Kearns	1.50
7DD	Hee Seop Choi	1.00
8DD	Kirk Saarloos	1.50
9DD	Orlando Hudson	.50
10DD	So Taguchi	.75
11DD	Kevin Mench	.50
12DD	Carl Crawford	.50
13DD	John Patterson	.50
14DD	Hank Blalock	1.50
15DD	Brett Myers	.75

2002 Fleer Tradition Update Grass Roots

		MT
Complete Set (10):		15.00
Common Player:		1.00
Inserted 1:24		
1GR	Alfonso Soriano	4.00
2GR	Torii Hunter	1.00
3GR	Andruw Jones	1.50
4GR	Jim Edmonds	1.00
5GR	Shawn Green	1.00
6GR	Todd Helton	1.50
7GR	Nomar Garciaparra	4.00
8GR	Roberto Alomar	1.50
9GR	Vladimir Guerrero	2.00
10GR	Ichiro Suzuki	4.00

2002 Fleer Tradition Update Grass Patch

	MT
Common Player:	20.00
Production 50 sets	
Alfonso Soriano	50.00
Torii Hunter	30.00
Andruw Jones	30.00
Jim Edmonds	20.00
Shawn Green	30.00
Todd Helton	30.00
Nomar Garciaparra	50.00
Roberto Alomar	35.00

2002 Fleer Tradition Update Heads Up

		MT
Complete Set (10):		30.00
Common Player:		2.00
Inserted 1:48		
1HU	Roger Clemens	6.00
2HU	Adam Dunn	3.00
3HU	Kazuhisa Ishii	4.00
4HU	Barry Zito	2.00
5HU	Pedro J. Martinez	4.00
6HU	Alfonso Soriano	6.00
7HU	Mark Prior	3.00
8HU	Chipper Jones	5.00
9HU	Randy Johnson	4.00
10HU	Lance Berkman	2.00

2002 Fleer Tradition Update Heads Up Game-Used

	MT
Common Player:	12.00
Production 150 sets	
Roger Clemens	30.00

Adam Dunn 20.00
Kazuhisa Ishii 15.00
Barry Zito 20.00
Alfonso Soriano 30.00
Mark Prior 20.00
Chipper Jones 20.00
Randy Johnson 30.00
Lance Berkman 12.00
Mike Piazza 35.00
Barry Bonds 50.00

2002 Fleer Tradition Update New York's Finest

MT
Complete Set (15): 75.00
Common Player: 3.00
Inserted 1:83
1NYFEdgardo Alfonzo 3.00
2NYFRoberto Alomar 4.00
3NYFJeromy Burnitz 3.00
4NYFSatoru Komiyama 3.00
5NYFRey Ordonez 3.00
6NYFMike Piazza 12.00
7NYFMo Vaughn 4.00
8NYFRoger Clemens 8.00
9NYFJason Giambi 8.00
10NYFDerek Jeter 15.00
11NYFMike Mussina 5.00
12NYFJorge Posada 4.00
13NYFAlfonso Soriano 10.00
14NYFRobin Ventura 3.00
15NYFBernie Williams 5.00

2002 Fleer Tradition Update N.Y.'s Finest Single Swatch

MT
Common Card: 5.00
Inserted 1:112
Derek Jeter/jsy, Rey Ordonez 25.00
Alfonso Soriano/jsy, Roberto Alomar 15.00
Roger Clemens/jsy, Mike Piazza 15.00
Mike Mussina/jsy, Mo Vaughn 8.00
Bernie Williams/jsy, Jeromy Burnitz 8.00
Derek Jeter/jsy, Satoru Komiyama 25.00
Robin Ventura/jsy, Edgardo Alfonzo 8.00
Jorge Posada/jsy, Mike Piazza 8.00
Jason Giambi/base, Mo Vaughn 8.00
Alfonso Soriano/jsy, Edgardo Alfonzo 15.00
Derek Jeter, Rey Ordonez/jsy 5.00
Alfonso Soriano, Roberto Alomar/jsy 8.00
Roger Clemens, Mike Piazza/jsy 15.00
Mike Mussina, Mo Vaughn/jsy 6.00
Bernie Williams, Jeromy Burnitz/jsy 5.00
Derek Jeter, Satoru Komiyama/bat 8.00
Robin Ventura, Edgardo Alfonzo/jsy 5.00
Jorge Posada, Mike Piazza/jsy 15.00
Jason Giambi, Mo Vaughn/jsy 6.00
Alfonso Soriano, Edgardo Alfonzo/jsy 5.00

2002 Fleer Tradition Update N.Y.'s Finest Dual Swatch

MT
Common Card:
Production 100 sets
Derek Jeter, Rey Ordonez 75.00
Alfonso Soriano, Roberto Alomar 50.00
Roger Clemens, Mike Piazza 65.00
Mike Mussina, Mo Vaughn 30.00
Bernie Williams, Jeromy Burnitz 20.00
Robin Ventura, Edgardo Alfonzo 12.00

2002 Fleer Tradition Update Plays of the Week

MT
Complete Set (30): 40.00
Common Player: 1.00
Inserted 1:12
1PW Troy Glaus 1.50
2PW Andruw Jones 1.00
3PW Curt Schilling 1.00
4PW Manny Ramirez 1.50
5PW Sammy Sosa 4.00
6PW Magglio Ordonez 1.00
7PW Ken Griffey Jr. 4.00
8PW Jim Thome 1.50
9PW Larry Walker 1.00
10PWRobert Fick 1.00
11PWJosh Beckett 1.00
12PWRoy Oswalt 1.00
13PWMike Sweeney 1.00
14PWShawn Green 1.00
15PWTorii Hunter 1.00
16PWVladimir Guerrero 2.00
17PWMike Piazza 4.00
18PWJason Giambi 3.00
19PWEric Chavez 1.00
20PWPat Burrell 1.50
21PWBrian Giles 1.00
22PWRyan Klesko 1.00
23PWBarry Bonds 5.00
24PWMike Cameron 1.00
25PWAlbert Pujols 2.00
26PWAlex Rodriguez 5.00
27PWCarlos Delgado 1.00
28PWRichie Sexson 1.00
29PWJay Gibbons 1.00
30PWRandy Winn 1.00

2002 Fleer Tradition Update This Day in History

MT
Complete Set (25): 50.00
Common Player: 1.00
1TDHShawn Green 1.00
2TDHOzzie Smith 2.50
3TDHDerek Lowe 1.00
4TDHKen Griffey Jr. 4.00
5TDHBarry Bonds 5.00
6TDHJuan Gonzalez 1.50
7TDHWade Boggs 1.50
8TDHMark Prior 1.50
9TDHThurman Munson 2.00
10TDHCurt Schilling 1.50
11TDHJason Giambi 3.00
12TDHCal Ripken Jr. 6.00
13TDHCraig Biggio 1.00
14TDHDrew Henson 1.00
15TDHSteve Carlton 1.50
16TDHGreg Maddux 3.00
17TDHAdam Dunn 1.50
18TDHVladimir Guerrero 2.00
19TDHAlex Rodriguez 5.00
20TDHCarlton Fisk 1.50
21TDHIchiro Suzuki 4.00
22TDHJohnny Bench 3.00
23TDHKazuhisa Ishii 1.50
24TDHDerek Jeter 6.00
25TDHJim Thome 1.50

2002 Fleer Tradition Update This Day in History Auto.

MT
Inserted 1:582
Barry Bonds/150 110.00
Mark Prior/64
Cal Ripken Jr/35
Drew Henson 25.00
Greg Maddux/99
Derek Jeter 120.00

2002 Fleer Tradition Update This Day in History Memor.

MT
Common Player: 6.00
Inserted 1:24
Shawn Green/jsy 6.00
Ozzie Smith/jsy 10.00
Barry Bonds/bat 15.00
Barry Bonds/jsy 15.00
Juan Gonzalez/bat 6.00
Wade Boggs/jsy 6.00
Wade Boggs/pants 6.00
Thurman Munson/jsy/40
Curt Schilling/jsy 6.00
Craig Biggio/jsy 6.00
Craig Biggio/bat/80
Adam Dunn/jsy 10.00
Alex Rodriguez/bat 10.00
Alex Rodriguez/jsy 10.00
Carlton Fisk/bat 8.00
Kazuhisa Ishii/bat 8.00
Derek Jeter/pants 20.00
Jim Thome/bat/120
Jim Thome/jsy 8.00
Greg Maddux/jsy 10.00

2002 Fleer Triple Crown

MT
Complete Set (270): 30.00
Common Player: .15
1 Mo Vaughn .25
2 Derek Jeter 2.50
3 Ken Griffey Jr. 2.00
4 Charles Johnson .15
5 Geoff Jenkins .25
6 Chuck Knoblauch .15
7 Jason Kendall .15
8 Jim Edmonds .25
9 David Eckstein .15
10 Carl Everett .15
11 Barry Larkin .25
12 Cliff Floyd .15
13 Ben Sheets .25
14 Jeff Conine .15
15 Brian Giles .15
16 Darryl Kile .15
17 Troy Glaus .50
18 Trot Nixon .15
19 Jim Thome .40
20 Preston Wilson .15
21 Roger Clemens 1.00
22 Chad Hermansen .15
23 Matt Morris .25
24 Shawn Wooten .15
25 Manny Ramirez .60
26 Roberto Alomar .50
27 Josh Beckett .25
28 Jose Hernandez .15
29 Mike Mussina .50
30 Jack Wilson .15
31 Bud Smith .25
32 Garret Anderson .15
33 Pedro J. Martinez .60
34 Travis Fryman .15
35 Jeff Bagwell .60
36 Doug Mientkiewicz .15
37 Andy Pettitte .30
38 Ryan Klesko .15
39 Edgar Renteria .15
40 Mariano Rivera .25
41 Darin Erstad .25
42 Hideo Nomo .30
43 Ellis Burks .15
44 Craig Biggio .25
45 Corey Koskie .15
46 Jason Varitek .15
47 Xavier Nady .15

48	Aubrey Huff	.15
49	Tim Salmon	.25
50	Nomar Garciaparra	1.50
51	Juan Gonzalez	.60
52	Moises Alou	.25
53	A.J. Pierzynski	.15
54	Bernie Williams	.50
55	Phil Nevin	.25
56	Ben Grieve	.15
57	Mark Grace	.25
58	Mike Lansing	.15
59	Kenny Lofton	.25
60	Lance Berkman	.25
61	David Ortiz	.15
62	Jason Giambi	.50
63	Mark Kotsay	.15
64	Greg Vaughn	.15
65	Junior Spivey	.15
66	Fred McGriff	.25
67	C.C. Sabathia	.15
68	Richard Hidalgo	.15
69	Torii Hunter	.15
70	Jason Hart	.15
71	Bubba Trammell	.15
72	Jace Brewer	.15
73	Matt Williams	.25
74	Matt Stairs	.15
75	Omar Vizquel	.25
76	Daryle Ward	.15
77	Joe Mays	.15
78	Eric Chavez	.25
79	Andres Galarraga	.20
80	Rafael Palmeiro	.30
81	Steve Finley	.15
82	Eric Young	.15
83	Todd Helton	.60
84	Roy Oswalt	.30
85	Eric Milton	.15
86	Ramon Hernandez	.15
87	Jeff Kent	.25
88	Ivan Rodriguez	.50
89	Luis Gonzalez	.40
90	Corey Patterson	.25
91	Jose Ortiz	.15
92	Mike Sweeney	.15
93	Cristian Guzman	.15
94	Johnny Damon	.15
95	Barry Bonds	1.00
96	Rusty Greer	.15
97	Reggie Sanders	.15
98	Sammy Sosa	1.25
99	Jeff Cirillo	.15
100	Carlos Febles	.15
101	Jose Vidro	.15
102	Jermaine Dye	.15
103	Rich Aurilia	.15
104	Gabe Kapler	.15
105	Randy Johnson	.60
106	Rondell White	.15
107	Ben Petrick	.15
108	Joe Randa	.15
109	Fernando Tatis	.15
110	Tim Hudson	.25
111	John Olerud	.25
112	Alex Rodriguez	1.50
113	Curt Schilling	.25
114	Kerry Wood	.30
115	Alex Ochoa	.15
116	Carlos Beltran	.15
117	Vladimir Guerrero	.60
118	Mark Mulder	.25
119	Bret Boone	.15
120	Carlos Delgado	.50
121	Marcus Giles	.15
122	Paul Konerko	.15
123	Juan Pierre	.15
124	Mark Quinn	.15
125	Edgardo Alfonzo	.15
126	Barry Zito	.25
127	Dan Wilson	.15
128	Jose Cruz Jr.	.15
129	Chipper Jones	1.25
130	Ray Durham	.15
131	Larry Walker	.30
132	Neifi Perez	.15
133	Robin Ventura	.25
134	Miguel Tejada	.25
135	Edgar Martinez	.25
136	Raul Mondesi	.25
137	Javy Lopez	.15
138	Jose Canseco	.25
139	Mike Hampton	.15
140	Eric Karros	.15
141	Mike Piazza	2.00
142	Travis Lee	.15
143	Ichiro Suzuki	2.50
144	Shannon Stewart	.15
145	Andruw Jones	.40
146	Frank Thomas	.60
147	Tony Clark	.15
148	Adrian Beltre	.25
149	Matt Lawton	.15
150	Marlon Anderson	.15
151	Freddy Garcia	.20
152	Brian Jordan	.15
153	Carlos Lee	.15
154	Eric Munson	.15
155	Paul LoDuca	.15
156	Jay Payton	.15
157	Scott Rolen	.40
158	Jamie Moyer	.15
159	Tom Glavine	.25
160	Magglio Ordonez	.25
161	Brandon Inge	.15
162	Shawn Green	.30
163	Tsuyoshi Shinjo	.15
164	Mike Lieberthal	.15
165	Kazuhiro Sasaki	.25
166	Greg Maddux	1.25
167	Chris Singleton	.15
168	Juan Encarnacion	.15
169	Gary Sheffield	.25
170	Nick Johnson	.15
171	Bobby Abreu	.15
172	Aaron Boone	.15
173	Rafael Furcal	.15
174	Mark Buerhle	.15
175	Bobby Higginson	.15
176	Kevin Brown	.15
177	Tino Martinez	.20
178	Pat Burrell	.30
179	Fernando Vina	.15
180	Jay Gibbons	.15
181	Jose Valentin	.15
182	Derrek Lee	.15
183	Richie Sexson	.15
184	Alfonso Soriano	.25
185	Jimmy Rollins	.15
186	Albert Pujols	1.00
187	Brady Anderson	.15
188	Sean Casey	.20
189	Luis Castillo	.15
190	Jeromy Burnitz	.15
191	Jorge Posada	.25
192	Kevin Young	.15
193	Eli Marrero	.15
194	Shea Hillenbrand	.15
195	Adam Dunn	.50
196	Mike Lowell	.15
197	Jeffrey Hammonds	.15
198	David Justice	.25
199	Aramis Ramirez	.15
200	J.D. Drew	.25
201	Pedro Santana	.15
202	Endy Chavez	.15
203	Donnie Bridges	.15
204	Travis Phelps	.15
205	Drew Henson	.75
206	Angel Berroa	.15
207	George Perez	.15
208	Billy Sylvester	.15
209	Juan Cruz	.30
210	Horacio Ramirez	.15
211	J.J. Davis	.15
212	Cody Ransom	.15
213	Mark Teixeira	1.50
214	Nate Frese	.15
215	Brian Rogers	.15
216	Dewon Brazelton	.15
217	Carlos Hernandez	.15
218	Juan Rivera	.15
219	Luis Lopez	.15
220	Benito Baez	.15
221	Bill Ortega	.15
222	Dustan Mohr	.15
223	Corky Miller	.15
224	Tyler Walker	.15
225	Rick Bauer	.15
226	Mark Prior	1.00
227	Rafael Soriano	.15
228	Greg Miller	.15
229	Dave Williams	.15
230	Bert Snow	.15
231	Barry Bonds	.75
232	Rickey Henderson	.25
233	Alex Rodriguez	.75
234	Luis Gonzalez	.30
235	Derek Jeter	1.00
236	Bud Smith	.15
237	Sammy Sosa	.75
238	Jeff Bagwell	.50
239	Jim Thome	.40
240	Hideo Nomo	.40
241	Greg Maddux	.75
242	Ken Griffey Jr.	1.00
243	Curt Schilling	.25
244	Arizona Diamondbacks	.15
245	Ichiro Suzuki	1.00
246	Albert Pujols	.75
247	Ichiro Suzuki	1.00
248	Barry Bonds	.75
249	Roger Clemens	.50
250	Randy Johnson	.40
251	Todd Helton	.40
252	Rafael Palmeiro	.30
253	Mike Piazza	.75
254	Alex Rodriguez	.75
255	Manny Ramirez	.40
256	Ken Griffey Jr.	1.00
257	Jason Giambi	.40
258	Chipper Jones	.60
259	Larry Walker	.25
260	Sammy Sosa	.75
261	Vladimir Guerrero	.40
262	Nomar Garciaparra	.75
263	Randy Johnson	.40
264	Roger Clemens	.50
265	Ichiro Suzuki	1.00
266	Barry Bonds	.75
267	Paul LoDuca	.15
268	Albert Pujols	.75
269	Derek Jeter	1.00
270	Adam Dunn	.40

2002 Fleer Triple Crown Batting Average Parallel

	MT
Stars:	4-8X

Numbered to 2001 batting avg.

(See 2002 Fleer Triple Crown for checklist and base card values.)

2002 Fleer Triple Crown RBI parallel

	MT
Stars Print Run 101-200:	5-10X
Stars P/R 76-100:	6-12X
Stars P/R 51-75:	8-15X
Stars P/R 25-50:	10-20X

Numbered to 2001 RBI total

(See 2002 Fleer Triple Crown for checklist and base card values.)

2002 Fleer Triple Crown Home Run parallel

	MT
Stars Print Run 50-75:	10-20X
Stars P/R 31-50:	15-25X
Stars P/R 21-30:	20-40X

Numbered to 2001 HR total

2002 Fleer Triple Crown Diamond Immortality

		MT
Complete Set (10):		30.00
Common Player:		1.00
Inserted 1:12		
1DI	Derek Jeter	6.00
2DI	Barry Bonds	2.50
3DI	Ricky Henderson	1.00
4DI	Roger Clemens	2.00
5DI	Alex Rodriguez	4.00
6DI	Albert Pujols	3.00
7DI	Nomar Garciaparra	4.00
8DI	Ichiro Suzuki	6.00
9DI	Chipper Jones	3.00
10DI	Ken Griffey Jr.	5.00

2002 Fleer Triple Crown Diamond Immortality Game-Used

	MT
Common Player:	15.00
Inserted 1:129	
Barry Bonds/jsy	25.00
Roger Clemens/jsy	20.00
Nomar Garciaparra/jsy/sp	40.00
Ricky Henderson/bat	15.00
Derek Jeter/bat	45.00
Chipper Jones/bat	20.00
Albert Pujols/jsy	25.00
Alex Rodriguez/jsy	35.00

2002 Fleer Triple Crown Home Run Kings

		MT
Complete Set (25):		100.00
Common Player:		2.00
Inserted 1:24		
1HRK	Ted Williams	12.00
2HRK	Todd Helton	4.00

3HRK Eddie Murray 2.00
4HRK Jeff Bagwell 4.00
5HRK Babe Ruth 15.00
6HRK Eddie Mathews 5.00
7HRK Alex Rodriguez 10.00
8HRK Juan Gonzalez 4.00
9HRK Chipper Jones 8.00
10HRK Luis Gonzalez 3.00
11HRK Johnny Bench 6.00
12HRK Frank Thomas 4.00
13HRK Ernie Banks 3.00
14HRK Jimmie Foxx 4.00
15HRK Ken Griffey Jr. 10.00
16HRK Rafael Palmeiro 3.00
17HRK Sammy Sosa 8.00
18HRK Reggie Jackson 4.00
19HRK Barry Bonds 6.00
20HRK Willie McCovey 2.00
21HRK Manny Ramirez 4.00
22HRK Larry Walker 2.50
23HRK Jason Giambi 4.00
24HRK Mike Piazza 12.00
25HRK Jose Canseco 2.00

2002 Fleer Triple Crown Home Run Kings Game-Used

MT
Common Player: 10.00
Inserted 1:155
Jeff Bagwell/jsy 15.00
Johnny Bench/bat/sp 60.00
Barry Bonds/jsy 25.00
Jimmie Foxx/bat 40.00
Jason Giambi/jsy 15.00
Reggie Jackson/bat 20.00
Eddie Mathews/bat 35.00
Eddie Murray/bat 25.00
Rafael Palmeiro/bat 10.00
Mike Piazza/jsy 25.00
Manny Ramirez/bat/sp 50.00
Todd Helton/bat 12.00
Alex Rodriguez/bat 20.00
Babe Ruth/bat/27
Larry Walker/bat 10.00
Ted Williams/jsy 180.00

2002 Fleer Triple Crown Home Run Kings Autograph

MT
Common Player:
Johnny Bench/45
Barry Bonds/73
Alex Rodriguez/52

2002 Fleer Triple Crown RBI Kings

MT
Complete Set (15): 150.00
Common Player: 5.00
Inserted 1:144
1RBIK Sammy Sosa 15.00
2RBIK Todd Helton 8.00
3RBIK Albert Pujols 20.00
4RBIK Manny Ramirez 8.00
5RBIK Luis Gonzalez 6.00
6RBIK Shawn Green 5.00
7RBIK Barry Bonds 12.00
8RBIK Ken Griffey Jr. 25.00
9RBIK Alex Rodriguez 20.00
10RBIK Jason Giambi 8.00
11RBIK Jeff Bagwell 8.00
12RBIK Vladimir Guerrero 8.00
13RBIK Juan Gonzalez 8.00
14RBIK Chipper Jones 15.00
15RBIK Mike Piazza 20.00

2002 Fleer Triple Crown RBI Kings Game-Used

MT
Common Player: 10.00
Inserted 1:70
Jeff Bagwell/jsy 15.00
Barry Bonds/jsy 30.00
Jason Giambi/jsy 15.00
Luis Gonzalez/bat 10.00
Juan Gonzalez/bat 15.00
Shawn Green/jsy 10.00
Todd Helton/jsy 15.00
Mike Piazza/jsy 35.00
Albert Pujols/bat/sp 70.00
Manny Ramirez/bat 15.00
Alex Rodriguez/shoe 30.00

2002 Fleer Triple Crown Season Crowns

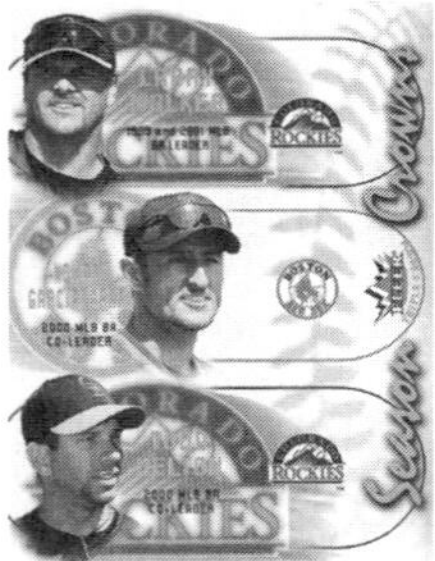

MT
Complete Set (10): 40.00
Common Card: 2.50
Inserted 1:12
1SC Barry Bonds, Sammy Sosa, Luis Gonzalez 4.00
2SC Larry Walker, Nomar Garciaparra, Todd Helton 4.00
3SC Sammy Sosa, Todd Helton, Manny Ramirez 4.00
4SC Pedro J. Martinez, Derek Jeter, Cal Ripken Jr. 8.00
5SC Jose Canseco, Barry Bonds, Alex Rodriguez 5.00
6SC Barry Bonds, Jeff Kent, Chipper Jones 4.00
7SC Ichiro Suzuki, Jason Giambi, Ivan Rodriguez 8.00
8SC Curt Schilling, Tom Glavine, Pedro J. Martinez 2.50
9SC Randy Johnson, Pedro J. Martinez, Greg Maddux 4.00
10SC Randy Johnson, Curt Schilling, John Smoltz 2.50

2002 Fleer Triple Crown Season Crowns Autograph

MT
Jeter #'d to 160
1SCDJ Derek Jeter/160 190.00
1SCBB Barry Bonds/77

2002 Fleer Triple Crown Season Crowns Game-Used

MT
Common Player: 10.00
Inserted 1:90
Barry Bonds/jsy 25.00
Sammy Sosa/base 15.00
Larry Walker/bat 10.00
Nomar Garciaparra/jsy 35.00
Todd Helton/jsy 15.00
Sammy Sosa/base 15.00
Todd Helton/jsy 15.00
Manny Ramirez/jsy 15.00
Pedro Martinez/jsy 20.00
Derek Jeter/pants 40.00
Cal Ripken Jr/bat 75.00
Jose Canseco/jsy 25.00
Barry Bonds/jsy 25.00
Alex Rodriguez/sy 20.00
Barry Bonds/jsy 25.00
Jeff Kent/jsy 8.00
Ichiro Suzuki/base 40.00
Jason Giambi/jsy 12.00
Ivan Rodriguez/jsy 15.00
Curt Schilling/jsy 15.00
Tom Glavine/jsy 10.00
Pedro Martinez jsy 20.00
Randy Johnson/jsy 15.00
Pedro Martinez/jsy 20.00
Greg Maddux/jsy 20.00
Randy Johnson /jsy 20.00
Curt Schilling/jsy 15.00
John Smoltz/jsy 10.00

2002 Fleer Triple Crown Season Crowns Triple Swatch

MT
Production 100 sets
Barry Bonds, Sammy Sosa, Luis Gonzalez 100.00
Larry Walker, Nomar Garciaparra, Todd Helton 80.00
Sammy Sosa, Todd Helton, Manny Ramirez 50.00
Barry Bonds, Jeff Kent, Chipper Jones 80.00
Ichiro Suzuki, Jason Giambi, Ivan Rodriguez 125.00
Curt Schilling, Tom Glavine, Pedro J. Martinez 50.00
Randy Johnson, Pedro J. Martinez, Greg Maddux 60.00
Randy Johnson, Curt Schilling, John Smoltz 50.00

L

1990 Leaf Previews

This 12-card set was produced for dealer distribution to introduce Leaf as Donruss' premium-quality brand in mid-1990. Cards have the same format as the regular-issue versions with metallic silver ink highlights on front and back. The preview cards have a white undertype on back over the stats and career highlights. It reads "Special Preview Card".

		MT
Complete Set (12):		750.00
Common Player:		20.00
1	Steve Sax	20.00
2	Joe Carter	35.00
3	Dennis Eckersley	45.00
4	Ken Griffey, Jr.	400.00
5	Barry Larkin	50.00
6	Mark Langston	20.00
7	Eric Anthony	20.00
8	Robin Ventura	60.00
9	Greg Vaughn	20.00
10	Bobby Bonilla	20.00
11	Gary Gaetti	20.00
12	Ozzie Smith	200.00

1990 Leaf

This 528-card set was issued in two 264-card series. The cards were printed on heavy quality stock and both the card fronts and backs have full color player photos. Cards also have an ultra-glossy finish on both the fronts and the backs. A high-tech foil Hall of Fame puzzle features former Yankee great Yogi Berra.

	MT
Complete Set (528):	120.00
Complete Series 1 (264):	75.00
Complete Series 2 (264):	45.00
Common Player:	.15
Complete Yogi Berra Puzzle:	2.00
Series 1 Foil Pack (15):	8.00
Series 1 Foil Wax Box (36):	240.00
Series 2 Foil Pack (15):	3.75
Series 2 Foil Wax Box (36):	125.00

1	Introductory card	.15
2	Mike Henneman	.15
3	Steve Bedrosian	.15
4	Mike Scott	.15
5	Allan Anderson	.15
6	Rick Sutcliffe	.15
7	Gregg Olson	.15
8	Kevin Elster	.15
9	Pete O'Brien	.15
10	Carlton Fisk	.75
11	Joe Magrane	.15
12	Roger Clemens	3.00
13	Tom Glavine	.30
14	Tom Gordon	.15
15	Todd Benzinger	.15
16	Hubie Brooks	.15
17	Roberto Kelly	.15
18	Barry Larkin	.30
19	Mike Boddicker	.15
20	Roger McDowell	.15
21	Nolan Ryan	6.00
22	John Farrell	.15
23	Bruce Hurst	.15
24	Wally Joyner	.15
25	Greg Maddux	5.00
26	Chris Bosio	.15
27	John Cerutti	.15
28	Tim Burke	.15
29	Dennis Eckersley	.25
30	Glenn Davis	.15
31	Jim Abbott	.15
32	Mike LaValliere	.15
33	Andres Thomas	.15
34	Lou Whitaker	.15
35	Alvin Davis	.15
36	Melido Perez	.15
37	Craig Biggio	.30
38	Rick Aguilera	.15
39	Pete Harnisch	.15
40	David Cone	.25
41	Scott Garrelts	.15
42	Jay Howell	.15
43	Eric King	.15
44	Pedro Guerrero	.15
45	Mike Bielecki	.15
46	Bob Boone	.15
47	Kevin Brown	.50
48	Jerry Browne	.15
49	Mike Scioscia	.15
50	Chuck Cary	.15
51	Wade Boggs	1.00
52	Von Hayes	.15
53	Tony Fernandez	.15
54	Dennis Martinez	.15
55	Tom Candiotti	.15
56	Andy Benes	.15
57	Rob Dibble	.15
58	Chuck Crim	.15
59	John Smoltz	.20
60	Mike Heath	.15
61	Kevin Gross	.15
62	Mark McGwire	6.00
63	Bert Blyleven	.15
64	Bob Walk	.15
65	Mickey Tettleton	.15
66	Sid Fernandez	.15
67	Terry Kennedy	.15
68	Fernando Valenzuela	.15
69	Don Mattingly	3.00
70	Paul O'Neill	.15
71	Robin Yount	1.00
72	Bret Saberhagen	.15
73	Geno Petralli	.15
74	Brook Jacoby	.15
75	Roberto Alomar	2.50
76	Devon White	.15
77	Jose Lind	.15
78	Pat Combs	.15
79	Dave Steib	.15
80	Tim Wallach	.15
81	Dave Stewart	.15
82	*Eric Anthony*	.15
83	Randy Bush	.15
84	Checklist	.15
85	Jaime Navarro	.15
86	Tommy Gregg	.15
87	Frank Tanana	.15
88	Omar Vizquel	.15
89	Ivan Calderon	.15
90	Vince Coleman	.15
91	Barry Bonds	3.00
92	Randy Milligan	.15
93	Frank Viola	.15
94	Matt Williams	.75
95	Alfredo Griffin	.15
96	Steve Sax	.15
97	Gary Gaetti	.15
98	Ryne Sandberg	2.00
99	Danny Tartabull	.15
100	Rafael Palmeiro	1.00
101	Jesse Orosco	.15
102	Garry Templeton	.15
103	Frank DiPino	.15
104	Tony Pena	.15
105	Dickie Thon	.15
106	Kelly Gruber	.15
107	*Marquis Grissom*	2.00
108	Jose Canseco	1.00
109	Mike Blowers	.15
110	Tom Browning	.15
111	Greg Vaughn	.20
112	Oddibe McDowell	.15
113	Gary Ward	.15
114	Jay Buhner	.15
115	Eric Show	.15
116	Bryan Harvey	.15
117	Andy Van Slyke	.15
118	Jeff Ballard	.15
119	Barry Lyons	.15
120	Kevin Mitchell	.15
121	Mike Gallego	.15
122	Dave Smith	.15
123	Kirby Puckett	3.00
124	Jerome Walton	.15
125	Bo Jackson	.50
126	Harold Baines	.15
127	Scott Bankhead	.15
128	Ozzie Guillen	.15
129	Jose Oquendo	.15
130	John Dopson	.15
131	Charlie Hayes	.15
132	Fred McGriff	.15
133	Chet Lemon	.15
134	Gary Carter	.50
135	Rafael Ramirez	.15
136	Shane Mack	.15
137	Mark Grace	.75
138	Phil Bradley	.15
139	Dwight Gooden	.15
140	Harold Reynolds	.15
141	Scott Fletcher	.15
142	Ozzie Smith	2.50
143	Mike Greenwell	.15
144	Pete Smith	.15
145	Mark Gubicza	.15
146	Chris Sabo	.15
147	Ramon Martinez	.15
148	Tim Leary	.15
149	Randy Myers	.15
150	Jody Reed	.15
151	Bruce Ruffin	.15
152	Jeff Russell	.15
153	Doug Jones	.15
154	Tony Gwynn	3.00
155	Mark Langston	.15
156	Mitch Williams	.15
157	Gary Sheffield	1.00
158	Tom Henke	.15
159	Oil Can Boyd	.15
160	Rickey Henderson	.75
161	Bill Doran	.15
162	Chuck Finley	.15
163	Jeff King	.15
164	Nick Esasky	.15
165	Cecil Fielder	.15
166	Dave Valle	.15
167	Robin Ventura	.30
168	Jim Deshaies	.15
169	Juan Berenguer	.15
170	Craig Worthington	.15
171	Gregg Jefferies	.15
172	Will Clark	.50
173	Kirk Gibson	.15
174	Checklist	.15
175	Bobby Thigpen	.15
176	John Tudor	.15
177	Andre Dawson	.35
178	George Brett	3.00
179	Steve Buechele	.15
180	Albert Belle	.50
181	Eddie Murray	.75
182	Bob Geren	.15
183	Rob Murphy	.15
184	Tom Herr	.15
185	George Bell	.15
186	Spike Owen	.15
187	Cory Snyder	.15
188	Fred Lynn	.15
189	Eric Davis	.15
190	Dave Parker	.15
191	Jeff Blauser	.15
192	Matt Nokes	.15
193	*Delino DeShields*	.50
194	Scott Sanderson	.15
195	Lance Parrish	.15
196	Bobby Bonilla	.15
197	Cal Ripken, Jr.	6.00
198	Kevin McReynolds	.15
199	Robby Thompson	.15
200	Tim Belcher	.15
201	Jesse Barfield	.15
202	Mariano Duncan	.15
203	Bill Spiers	.15
204	Frank White	.15
205	Julio Franco	.15
206	Greg Swindell	.15
207	Benito Santiago	.15
208	Johnny Ray	.15
209	Gary Redus	.15
210	Jeff Parrett	.15
211	Jimmy Key	.15
212	Tim Raines	.15
213	Carney Lansford	.15
214	Gerald Young	.15
215	Gene Larkin	.15
216	Dan Plesac	.15
217	Lonnie Smith	.15
218	Alan Trammell	.15
219	Jeffrey Leonard	.15
220	*Sammy Sosa*	75.00
221	Todd Zeile	.15
222	Bill Landrum	.15
223	Mike Devereaux	.15
224	Mike Marshall	.15
225	Jose Uribe	.15
226	Juan Samuel	.15
227	Mel Hall	.15
228	Kent Hrbek	.15
229	Shawon Dunston	.15
230	Kevin Seitzer	.15
231	Pete Incaviglia	.15
232	Sandy Alomar	.15
233	Bip Roberts	.15
234	Scott Terry	.15
235	Dwight Evans	.15
236	Ricky Jordan	.15
237	*John Olerud*	6.00
238	Zane Smith	.15
239	Walt Weiss	.15
240	Alvaro Espinoza	.15
241	Billy Hatcher	.15
242	Paul Molitor	1.00
243	Dale Murphy	.30
244	Dave Bergman	.15
245	Ken Griffey, Jr.	6.00
246	Ed Whitson	.15
247	Kirk McCaskill	.15
248	Jay Bell	.15
249	*Ben McDonald*	.50
250	Darryl Strawberry	.15
251	Brett Butler	.15
252	Terry Steinbach	.15
253	Ken Caminiti	.15
254	Dan Gladden	.15
255	Dwight Smith	.15
256	Kurt Stillwell	.15
257	Ruben Sierra	.15
258	Mike Schooler	.15
259	Lance Johnson	.15
260	Terry Pendleton	.15
261	Ellis Burks	.15
262	Len Dykstra	.15
263	Mookie Wilson	.15
264	Checklist (Nolan Ryan)	.15
265	Nolan Ryan (No-Hit King)	2.00
266	Brian DuBois	.15
267	Don Robinson	.15
268	Glenn Wilson	.15
269	*Kevin Tapani*	.75
270	Marvell Wynne	.15
271	Billy Ripken	.15
272	Howard Johnson	.15
273	Brian Holman	.15
274	Dan Pasqua	.15
275	Ken Dayley	.15
276	Jeff Reardon	.15
277	Jim Presley	.15
278	Jim Eisenreich	.15
279	Danny Jackson	.15
280	Orel Hershiser	.15
281	Andy Hawkins	.15
282	Jose Rijo	.15
283	Luis Rivera	.15
284	John Kruk	.15
285	Jeff Huson	.15
286	Joel Skinner	.15
287	Jack Clark	.15
288	Chili Davis	.15
289	Joe Girardi	.15
290	B.J. Surhoff	.15
291	Luis Sojo	.15
292	Tom Foley	.15
293	Mike Moore	.15
294	Ken Oberkfell	.15
295	Luis Polonia	.15
296	Doug Drabek	.15
297	*Dave Justice*	5.00
298	Paul Gibson	.15
299	Edgar Martinez	.15
300	*Frank Thomas*	25.00
301	Eric Yelding	.15
302	Greg Gagne	.15
303	Brad Komminsk	.15
304	Ron Darling	.15
305	Kevin Bass	.15
306	Jeff Hamilton	.15
307	Ron Karkovice	.15
308	Milt Thompson	.15
309	Mike Harkey	.15
310	Mel Stottlemyre	.15
311	Kenny Rogers	.15
312	Mitch Webster	.15
313	Kal Daniels	.15
314	Matt Nokes	.15
315	Dennis Lamp	.15
316	Ken Howell	.15
317	Glenallen Hill	.15
318	Dave Martinez	.15
319	Chris James	.15
320	Mike Pagliarulo	.15
321	Hal Morris	.15
322	Rob Deer	.15
323	Greg Olson	.15
324	Tony Phillips	.15
325	*Larry Walker*	8.00
326	Ron Hassey	.15
327	Jack Howell	.15
328	John Smiley	.15
329	Steve Finley	.15
330	Dave Magadan	.15
331	Greg Litton	.15
332	Mickey Hatcher	.15
333	Lee Guetterman	.15
334	Norm Charlton	.15
335	Edgar Diaz	.15
336	Willie Wilson	.15
337	Bobby Witt	.15
338	Candy Maldonado	.15
339	Craig Lefferts	.15
340	Dante Bichette	.15
341	Wally Backman	.15
342	Dennis Cook	.15
343	Pat Borders	.15
344	Wallace Johnson	.15
345	Willie Randolph	.15
346	Danny Darwin	.15
347	Al Newman	.15
348	Mark Knudson	.15
349	Joe Boever	.15
350	Larry Sheets	.15
351	Mike Jackson	.15
352	Wayne Edwards	.15
353	*Bernard Gilkey*	1.50
354	Don Slaught	.15
355	Joe Orsulak	.15
356	John Franco	.15
357	Jeff Brantley	.15
358	Mike Morgan	.15
359	Deion Sanders	.30
360	Terry Leach	.15
361	Les Lancaster	.15
362	Storm Davis	.15
363	Scott Coolbaugh	.15
364	Checklist	.15
365	Cecilio Guante	.15

366	Joey Cora	.15
367	Willie McGee	.15
368	Jerry Reed	.15
369	Darren Daulton	.15
370	Manny Lee	.15
371	Mark Gardner	.15
372	Rick Honeycutt	.15
373	Steve Balboni	.15
374	Jack Armstrong	.15
375	Charlie O'Brien	.15
376	Ron Gant	.15
377	Lloyd Moseby	.15
378	Gene Harris	.15
379	Joe Carter	.15
380	Scott Bailes	.15
381	R.J. Reynolds	.15
382	Bob Melvin	.15
383	Tim Teufel	.15
384	John Burkett	.15
385	Felix Jose	.15
386	Larry Andersen	.15
387	David West	.15
388	Luis Salazar	.15
389	Mike Macfarlane	.15
390	Charlie Hough	.15
391	Greg Briley	.15
392	Donn Pall	.15
393	Bryn Smith	.15
394	Carlos Quintana	.15
395	Steve Lake	.15
396	*Mark Whiten*	.25
397	Edwin Nunez	.15
398	Rick Parker	.15
399	Mark Portugal	.15
400	Roy Smith	.15
401	Hector Villanueva	.15
402	Bob Milacki	.15
403	Alejandro Pena	.15
404	Scott Bradley	.15
405	Ron Kittle	.15
406	Bob Tewksbury	.15
407	Wes Gardner	.15
408	Ernie Whitt	.15
409	Terry Shumpert	.15
410	Tim Layana	.15
411	Chris Gwynn	.15
412	Jeff Robinson	.15
413	Scott Scudder	.15
414	Kevin Romine	.15
415	Jose DeJesus	.15
416	Mike Jeffcoat	.15
417	Rudy Seanez	.15
418	Mike Dunne	.15
419	Dick Schofield	.15
420	Steve Wilson	.15
421	Bill Krueger	.15
422	Junior Felix	.15
423	Drew Hall	.15
424	Curt Young	.15
425	Franklin Stubbs	.15
426	Dave Winfield	.75
427	Rick Reed	.15
428	Charlie Leibrandt	.15
429	Jeff Robinson	.15
430	Erik Hanson	.15
431	Barry Jones	.15
432	Alex Trevino	.15
433	John Moses	.15
434	Dave Johnson	.15
435	Mackey Sasser	.15
436	Rick Leach	.15
437	Lenny Harris	.15
438	Carlos Martinez	.15
439	Rex Hudler	.15
440	Domingo Ramos	.15
441	Gerald Perry	.15
442	John Russell	.15
443	*Carlos Baerga*	.50
444	Checklist	.15
445	Stan Javier	.15
446	*Kevin Maas*	.15
447	Tom Brunansky	.15
448	Carmelo Martinez	.15
449	*Willie Blair*	.15
450	Andres Galarraga	.15
451	Bud Black	.15
452	Greg Harris	.15
453	Joe Oliver	.15
454	Greg Brock	.15
455	Jeff Treadway	.15
456	Lance McCullers	.15
457	Dave Schmidt	.15
458	Todd Burns	.15
459	Max Venable	.15
460	Neal Heaton	.15
461	Mark Williamson	.15
462	Keith Miller	.15
463	Mike LaCoss	.15
464	*Jose Offerman*	.50
465	*Jim Leyritz*	.50
466	Glenn Braggs	.15
467	Ron Robinson	.15
468	Mark Davis	.15
469	Gary Pettis	.15
470	Keith Hernandez	.15
471	Dennis Rasmussen	.15
472	Mark Eichhorn	.15
473	Ted Power	.15
474	Terry Mulholland	.15
475	Todd Stottlemyre	.15
476	Jerry Goff	.15
477	Gene Nelson	.15
478	Rich Gedman	.15
479	Brian Harper	.15
480	Mike Felder	.15
481	Steve Avery	.15
482	Jack Morris	.15
483	Randy Johnson	2.50
484	Scott Radinsky	.15
485	Jose DeLeon	.15
486	*Stan Belinda*	.15
487	Brian Holton	.15
488	Mark Carreon	.15
489	Trevor Wilson	.15
490	Mike Sharperson	.15
491	*Alan Mills*	.15
492	John Candelaria	.15
493	Paul Assenmacher	.15
494	Steve Crawford	.15
495	Brad Arnsberg	.15
496	Sergio Valdez	.15
497	Mark Parent	.15
498	Tom Pagnozzi	.15
499	Greg Harris	.15
500	Randy Ready	.15
501	Duane Ward	.15
502	Nelson Santovenia	.15
503	Joe Klink	.15
504	Eric Plunk	.15
505	Jeff Reed	.15
506	Ted Higuera	.15
507	Joe Hesketh	.15
508	Dan Petry	.15
509	Matt Young	.15
510	Jerald Clark	.15
511	*John Orton*	.15
512	Scott Ruskin	.15
513	*Chris Hoiles*	.75
514	Daryl Boston	.15
515	Francisco Oliveras	.15
516	Ozzie Canseco	.15
517	*Xavier Hernandez*	.40
518	Fred Manrique	.15
519	Shawn Boskie	.15
520	Jeff Montgomery	.15
521	Jack Daugherty	.15
522	Keith Comstock	.15
523	*Greg Hibbard*	.25
524	Lee Smith	.15
525	Dana Kiecker	.15
526	Darrel Akerfelds	.15
527	Greg Myers	.15
528	Checklist	.15

1991 Leaf Previews

Cello packs of four cards previewing the 1991 Leaf set were included in each 1991 Donruss hobby factory set. The cards are identical in format to the regular 1991 Leafs, except there is a notation, "1991 PREVIEW CARD" in white print beneath the statistics and career information on the back.

		MT
Complete Set (26):		27.00
Common Player:		.50
1	Dave Justice	1.00
2	Ryne Sandberg	2.50
3	Barry Larkin	.75
4	Craig Biggio	.50
5	Ramon Martinez	.50
6	Tim Wallach	.50
7	Dwight Gooden	.50
8	Len Dykstra	.50
9	Barry Bonds	3.00
10	Ray Lankford	.50
11	Tony Gwynn	3.00
12	Will Clark	1.00
13	Leo Gomez	.50
14	Wade Boggs	1.75
15	Chuck Finley	.50
16	Carlton Fisk	1.50
17	Sandy Alomar, Jr.	.50
18	Cecil Fielder	.50
19	Bo Jackson	.75
20	Paul Molitor	1.75
21	Kirby Puckett	3.00
22	Don Mattingly	4.00
23	Rickey Henderson	1.50
24	Tino Martinez	.75
25	Nolan Ryan	6.00
26	Dave Steib	.50

1991 Leaf

Silver borders and black insets surround the color action photos on the 1991 Leaf cards. The set was once again released in two series. Series I consists of cards 1-264. Card backs feature an additional player photo, biographical information, statistics and career highlights. The 1991 issue is not considered as scarce as the 1990 release.

		MT
Complete Set (528):		15.00
Common Player:		.05
Complete Harmon Killebrew Puzzle:		1.00
Series 1 or 2 Pack (15):		.50
Series 1 or 2 Wax Box (36):		15.00
1	The Leaf Card	.05
2	Kurt Stillwell	.05
3	Bobby Witt	.05
4	Tony Phillips	.05
5	Scott Garrelts	.05
6	Greg Swindell	.05
7	Billy Ripken	.05
8	Dave Martinez	.05
9	Kelly Gruber	.05
10	Juan Samuel	.05
11	Brian Holman	.05
12	Craig Biggio	.10
13	Lonnie Smith	.05
14	Ron Robinson	.05
15	Mike LaValliere	.05
16	Mark Davis	.05
17	Jack Daugherty	.05
18	Mike Henneman	.05
19	Mike Greenwell	.05
20	Dave Magadan	.05
21	Mark Williamson	.05
22	Marquis Grissom	.05
23	Pat Borders	.05
24	Mike Scioscia	.05
25	Shawon Dunston	.05
26	Randy Bush	.05
27	John Smoltz	.10
28	Chuck Crim	.05
29	Don Slaught	.05
30	Mike Macfarlane	.05
31	Wally Joyner	.05
32	Pat Combs	.05
33	Tony Pena	.05
34	Howard Johnson	.05
35	Leo Gomez	.05
36	Spike Owen	.05
37	Eric Davis	.05
38	Roberto Kelly	.05
39	Jerome Walton	.05
40	Shane Mack	.05
41	Kent Mercker	.05
42	B.J. Surhoff	.05
43	Jerry Browne	.05
44	Lee Smith	.05
45	Chuck Finley	.05
46	Terry Mulholland	.05
47	Tom Bolton	.05
48	Tom Herr	.05
49	Jim Deshaies	.05
50	Walt Weiss	.05
51	Hal Morris	.05
52	Lee Guetterman	.05
53	Paul Assenmacher	.05
54	Brian Harper	.05
55	Paul Gibson	.05
56	John Burkett	.05
57	Doug Jones	.05
58	Jose Oquendo	.05
59	Dick Schofield	.05
60	Dickie Thon	.05
61	Ramon Martinez	.05
62	Jay Buhner	.05
63	Mark Portugal	.05
64	Bob Welch	.05
65	Chris Sabo	.05
66	Chuck Cary	.05
67	Mark Langston	.05
68	Joe Boever	.05
69	Jody Reed	.05
70	Alejandro Pena	.05
71	Jeff King	.05
72	Tom Pagnozzi	.05
73	Joe Oliver	.05
74	Mike Witt	.05
75	Hector Villanueva	.05
76	Dan Gladden	.05
77	Dave Justice	.10
78	Mike Gallego	.05
79	Tom Candiotti	.05
80	Ozzie Smith	1.00
81	Luis Polonia	.05
82	Randy Ready	.05
83	Greg Harris	.05
84	Checklist (Dave Justice)	.05
85	Kevin Mitchell	.05
86	Mark McLemore	.05
87	Terry Steinbach	.05
88	Tom Browning	.05
89	Matt Nokes	.05
90	Mike Harkey	.05
91	Omar Vizquel	.05
92	Dave Bergman	.05
93	Matt Williams	.20
94	Steve Olin	.05
95	Craig Wilson	.05
96	Dave Stieb	.05
97	Ruben Sierra	.05
98	Jay Howell	.05
99	Scott Bradley	.05
100	Eric Yelding	.05
101	Rickey Henderson	.40
102	Jeff Reed	.05
103	Jimmy Key	.05
104	Terry Shumpert	.05
105	Kenny Rogers	.05
106	Cecil Fielder	.05

No.	Player	Value
107	Robby Thompson	.05
108	Alex Cole	.05
109	Randy Milligan	.05
110	Andres Galarraga	.05
111	Bill Spiers	.05
112	Kal Daniels	.05
113	Henry Cotto	.05
114	Casy Candaele	.05
115	Jeff Blauser	.05
116	Robin Yount	.75
117	Ben McDonald	.05
118	Bret Saberhagen	.05
119	Juan Gonzalez	1.00
120	Lou Whitaker	.05
121	Ellis Burks	.05
122	Charlie O'Brien	.05
123	John Smiley	.05
124	Tim Burke	.05
125	John Olerud	.05
126	Eddie Murray	.40
127	Greg Maddux	1.50
128	Kevin Tapani	.05
129	Ron Gant	.05
130	Jay Bell	.05
131	Chris Hoiles	.05
132	Tom Gordon	.05
133	Kevin Seitzer	.05
134	Jeff Huson	.05
135	Jerry Don Gleaton	.05
136	Jeff Brantley	.05
137	Felix Fermin	.05
138	Mike Devereaux	.05
139	Delino DeShields	.05
140	David Wells	.10
141	Tim Crews	.05
142	Erik Hanson	.05
143	Mark Davidson	.05
144	Tommy Gregg	.05
145	Jim Gantner	.05
146	Jose Lind	.05
147	Danny Tartabull	.05
148	Geno Petralli	.05
149	Travis Fryman	.05
150	Tim Naehring	.05
151	Kevin McReynolds	.05
152	Joe Orsulak	.05
153	Steve Frey	.05
154	Duane Ward	.05
155	Stan Javier	.05
156	Damon Berryhill	.05
157	Gene Larkin	.05
158	Greg Olson	.05
159	Mark Knudson	.05
160	Carmelo Martinez	.05
161	Storm Davis	.05
162	Jim Abbott	.05
163	Len Dykstra	.05
164	Tom Brunansky	.05
165	Dwight Gooden	.05
166	Jose Mesa	.05
167	Oil Can Boyd	.05
168	Barry Larkin	.10
169	Scott Sanderson	.05
170	Mark Grace	.25
171	Mark Guthrie	.05
172	Tom Glavine	.10
173	Gary Sheffield	.25
174	Checklist (Roger Clemens)	.20
175	Chris James	.05
176	Milt Thompson	.05
177	Donnie Hill	.05
178	Wes Chamberlain	.05
179	John Marzano	.05
180	Frank Viola	.05
181	Eric Anthony	.05
182	Jose Canseco	.50
183	Scott Scudder	.05
184	Dave Eiland	.05
185	Luis Salazar	.05
186	Pedro Munoz	.05
187	Steve Searcy	.05
188	Don Robinson	.05
189	Sandy Alomar	.05
190	Jose DeLeon	.05
191	John Orton	.05
192	Darren Daulton	.05
193	Mike Morgan	.05
194	Greg Briley	.05
195	Karl Rhodes	.05
196	Harold Baines	.05
197	Bill Doran	.05
198	Alvaro Espinoza	.05
199	Kirk McCaskill	.05
200	Jose DeJesus	.05
201	Jack Clark	.05
202	Daryl Boston	.05
203	Randy Tomlin	.05
204	Pedro Guerrero	.05
205	Billy Hatcher	.05
206	Tim Leary	.05
207	Ryne Sandberg	1.00
208	Kirby Puckett	1.00
209	Charlie Leibrandt	.05
210	Rick Honeycutt	.05
211	Joel Skinner	.05
212	Rex Hudler	.05
213	Bryan Harvey	.05
214	Charlie Hayes	.05
215	Matt Young	.05
216	Terry Kennedy	.05
217	Carl Nichols	.05
218	Mike Moore	.05
219	Paul O'Neill	.05
220	Steve Sax	.05
221	Shawn Boskie	.05
222	Rich DeLucia	.05
223	Lloyd Moseby	.05
224	Mike Kingery	.05
225	Carlos Baerga	.05
226	Bryn Smith	.05
227	Todd Stottlemyre	.05
228	Julio Franco	.05
229	Jim Gott	.05
230	Mike Schooler	.05
231	Steve Finley	.05
232	Dave Henderson	.05
233	Luis Quinones	.05
234	Mark Whiten	.05
235	Brian McRae	.05
236	Rich Gossage	.05
237	Rob Deer	.05
238	Will Clark	.25
239	Albert Belle	.25
240	Bob Melvin	.05
241	Larry Walker	.25
242	Dante Bichette	.05
243	Orel Hershiser	.05
244	Pete O'Brien	.05
245	Pete Harnisch	.05
246	Jeff Treadway	.05
247	Julio Machado	.05
248	Dave Johnson	.05
249	Kirk Gibson	.05
250	Kevin Brown	.05
251	Milt Cuyler	.05
252	Jeff Reardon	.05
253	David Cone	.05
254	Gary Redus	.05
255	Junior Noboa	.05
256	Greg Myers	.05
257	Dennis Cook	.05
258	Joe Girardi	.05
259	Allan Anderson	.05
260	Paul Marak	.05
261	Barry Bonds	1.00
262	Juan Bell	.05
263	Russ Morman	.05
264	Checklist (George Brett)	.20
265	Jerald Clark	.05
266	Dwight Evans	.05
267	Roberto Alomar	.50
268	Danny Jackson	.05
269	Brian Downing	.05
270	John Cerutti	.05
271	Robin Ventura	.05
273	Wade Boggs	.50
274	Dennis Martinez	.05
275	Andy Benes	.05
276	Tony Fossas	.05
277	Franklin Stubbs	.05
278	John Kruk	.05
279	Kevin Gross	.05
280	Von Hayes	.05
281	Frank Thomas	1.50
282	Rob Dibble	.05
283	Mel Hall	.05
284	Rick Mahler	.05
285	Dennis Eckersley	.05
286	Bernard Gilkey	.05
287	Dan Plesac	.05
288	Jason Grimsley	.05
289	Mark Lewis	.05
290	Tony Gwynn	1.00
291	Jeff Russell	.05
292	Curt Schilling	.10
293	Pascual Perez	.05
294	Jack Morris	.05
295	Hubie Brooks	.05
296	Alex Fernandez	.10
297	Harold Reynolds	.05
298	Craig Worthington	.05
299	Willie Wilson	.05
300	Mike Maddux	.05
301	Dave Righetti	.05
302	Paul Molitor	.50
303	Gary Gaetti	.05
304	Terry Pendleton	.05
305	Kevin Elster	.05
306	Scott Fletcher	.05
307	Jeff Robinson	.05
308	Jesse Barfield	.05
309	Mike LaCoss	.05
310	Andy Van Slyke	.05
311	Glenallen Hill	.05
312	Bud Black	.05
313	Kent Hrbek	.05
314	Tim Teufel	.05
315	Tony Fernandez	.05
316	Beau Allred	.05
317	Curtis Wilkerson	.05
318	Bill Sampen	.05
319	Randy Johnson	.40
320	Mike Heath	.05
321	Sammy Sosa	2.00
322	Mickey Tettleton	.05
323	Jose Vizcaino	.05
324	John Candelaria	.05
325	David Howard	.05
326	Jose Rijo	.05
327	Todd Zeile	.05
328	Gene Nelson	.05
329	Dwayne Henry	.05
330	Mike Boddicker	.05
331	Ozzie Guillen	.05
332	Sam Horn	.05
333	Wally Whitehurst	.05
334	Dave Parker	.05
335	George Brett	.50
336	Bobby Thigpen	.05
337	Ed Whitson	.05
338	Ivan Calderon	.05
339	Mike Pagliarulo	.05
340	Jack McDowell	.05
341	Dana Kiecker	.05
342	Fred McGriff	.05
343	Mark Lee	.05
344	Alfredo Griffin	.05
345	Scott Bankhead	.05
346	Darrin Jackson	.05
347	Rafael Palmeiro	.25
348	Steve Farr	.05
349	Hensley Meulens	.05
350	Danny Cox	.05
351	Alan Trammell	.05
352	Edwin Nunez	.05
353	Joe Carter	.05
354	Eric Show	.05
355	Vance Law	.05
356	Jeff Gray	.05
357	Bobby Bonilla	.05
358	Ernest Riles	.05
359	Ron Hassey	.05
360	Willie McGee	.05
361	Mackey Sasser	.05
362	Glenn Braggs	.05
363	Mario Diaz	.05
364	Checklist (Barry Bonds)	.25
365	Kevin Bass	.05
366	Pete Incaviglia	.05
367	Luis Sojo	.05
368	Lance Parrish	.05
369	Mark Leonard	.05
370	Heathcliff Slocumb	.05
371	Jimmy Jones	.05
372	Ken Griffey, Jr.	2.00
373	Chris Hammond	.05
374	Chili Davis	.05
375	Joey Cora	.05
376	Ken Hill	.05
377	Darryl Strawberry	.05
378	Ron Darling	.05
379	Sid Bream	.05
380	Bill Swift	.05
381	Shawn Abner	.05
382	Eric King	.05
383	Mickey Morandini	.05
384	Carlton Fisk	.30
385	Steve Lake	.05
386	Mike Jeffcoat	.05
387	Darren Holmes	.05
388	Tim Wallach	.05
389	George Bell	.05
390	Craig Lefferts	.05
391	Ernie Whitt	.05
392	Felix Jose	.05
393	Kevin Maas	.05
394	Devon White	.05
395	Otis Nixon	.05
396	Chuck Knoblauch	.05
397	Scott Coolbaugh	.05
398	Glenn Davis	.05
399	Manny Lee	.05
400	Andre Dawson	.15
401	Scott Chiamparino	.05
402	Bill Gullickson	.05
403	Lance Johnson	.05
404	Juan Agosto	.05
405	Danny Darwin	.05
406	Barry Jones	.05
407	Larry Andersen	.05
408	Luis Rivera	.05
409	Jaime Navarro	.05
410	Roger McDowell	.05
411	Brett Butler	.05
412	Dale Murphy	.15
413	Tim Raines	.05
414	Norm Charlton	.05
415	Greg Cadaret	.05
416	Chris Nabholz	.05
417	Dave Stewart	.05
418	Rich Gedman	.05
419	Willie Randolph	.05
420	Mitch Williams	.05
421	Brook Jacoby	.05
422	Greg Harris	.05
423	Nolan Ryan	2.00
424	Dave Rohde	.05
425	Don Mattingly	1.00
426	Greg Gagne	.05
427	Vince Coleman	.05
428	Dan Pasqua	.05
429	Alvin Davis	.05
430	Cal Ripken, Jr.	2.00
431	Jamie Quirk	.05
432	Benito Santiago	.05
433	Jose Uribe	.05
434	Candy Maldonado	.05
435	Junior Felix	.05
436	Deion Sanders	.10
437	John Franco	.05
438	Greg Hibbard	.05
439	Floyd Bannister	.05
440	Steve Howe	.05
441	Steve Decker	.05
442	Vicente Palacios	.05
443	Pat Tabler	.05
444	Checklist (Darryl Strawberry)	.05
445	Mike Felder	.05
446	Al Newman	.05
447	Chris Donnels	.05
448	Rich Rodriguez	.05
449	Turner Ward	.05
450	Bob Walk	.05
451	Gilberto Reyes	.05
452	Mike Jackson	.05
453	Rafael Belliard	.05
454	Wayne Edwards	.05
455	Andy Allanson	.05
456	Dave Smith	.05
457	Gary Carter	.30
458	Warren Cromartie	.05
459	Jack Armstrong	.05
460	Bob Tewksbury	.05
461	Joe Klink	.05
462	Xavier Hernandez	.05
463	Scott Radinsky	.05
464	Jeff Robinson	.05
465	Gregg Jefferies	.05
466	Denny Neagle	.05
467	Carmelo Martinez	.05
468	Donn Pall	.05
469	Bruce Hurst	.05
470	Eric Bullock	.05
471	Rick Aguilera	.05
472	Charlie Hough	.05
473	Carlos Quintana	.05
474	Marty Barrett	.05
475	Kevin Brown	.10
476	Bobby Ojeda	.05
477	Edgar Martinez	.05
478	Bip Roberts	.05
479	Mike Flanagan	.05
480	John Habyan	.05
481	Larry Casian	.05
482	Wally Backman	.05
483	Doug Dascenzo	.05
484	Rick Dempsey	.05
485	Ed Sprague	.05
486	Steve Chitren	.05
487	Mark McGwire	3.00

488	Roger Clemens	.75
489	Orlando Merced	.05
490	Rene Gonzales	.05
491	Mike Stanton	.05
492	Al Osuna	.05
493	Rick Cerone	.05
494	Mariano Duncan	.05
495	Zane Smith	.05
496	John Morris	.05
497	Frank Tanana	.05
498	Junior Ortiz	.05
499	Dave Winfield	.50
500	Gary Varsho	.05
501	Chico Walker	.05
502	Ken Caminiti	.05
503	Ken Griffey, Sr.	.05
504	Randy Myers	.05
505	Steve Bedrosian	.05
506	Cory Snyder	.05
507	Cris Carpenter	.05
508	Tim Belcher	.05
509	Jeff Hamilton	.05
510	Steve Avery	.05
511	Dave Valle	.05
512	Tom Lampkin	.05
513	Shawn Hillegas	.05
514	Reggie Jefferson	.05
515	Ron Karkovice	.05
516	Doug Drabek	.05
517	Tom Henke	.05
518	Chris Bosio	.05
519	Gregg Olson	.05
520	Bob Scanlan	.05
521	Alonzo Powell	.05
522	Jeff Ballard	.05
523	Ray Lankford	.05
524	Tommy Greene	.05
525	Mike Timlin	.05
526	Juan Berenguer	.05
527	Scott Erickson	.05
528	Checklist (Sandy Alomar Jr.)	.05

1991 Leaf Gold Rookies

Special gold rookie and gold bonus cards were randomly inserted in 1991 Leaf packs. Backs have a design similar to the regular-issue cards, but have gold, rather than silver background. Fronts have gold-foil highlights. Card numbers of the issued version have a "BC" prefix, but there is a much rarer second version of the Series 1 cards, which carry card numbers between 265-276.

		MT
Complete Set (26):		15.00
Common Player:		.25
1	Scott Leius	.25
2	Luis Gonzalez	2.00
3	Wil Cordero	.25
4	Gary Scott	.25
5	Willie Banks	.25
6	Arthur Rhodes	.25
7	Mo Vaughn	2.00
8	Henry Rodriguez	.25
9	Todd Van Poppel	.25
10	Reggie Sanders	.40
11	Rico Brogna	.25
12	Mike Mussina	4.00
13	Kirk Dressendorfer	.25
14	Jeff Bagwell	6.00
15	Pete Schourek	.25
16	Wade Taylor	.25
17	Pat Kelly	.25
18	Tim Costo	.25
19	Roger Salkeld	.25
20	Andujar Cedeno	.25
21	Ryan Klesko	.50
22	Mike Huff	.25
23	Anthony Young	.25
24	Eddie Zosky	.25
25	Nolan Ryan (7th no-hitter)	2.50
26	Rickey Henderson (record steal)	1.00
265	Scott Leius	4.00
266	Luis Gonzalez	20.00
267	Wil Cordero	4.00
268	Gary Scott	4.00
269	Willie Banks	4.00
270	Arthur Rhodes	4.00
271	Mo Vaughn	20.00
272	Henry Rodriguez	4.00
273	Todd Van Poppel	4.00
274	Reggie Sanders	4.00
275	Rico Brogna	4.00
276	Mike Mussina	30.00

1992 Leaf Previews

In a format identical to the regular-issue 1992 Leaf cards, this 26-card preview set was issued as a bonus in packs of four cards in each 1992 Donruss hobby factory set.

		MT
Complete Set (26):		60.00
Common Player:		.50
1	Steve Avery	.50
2	Ryne Sandberg	4.00
3	Chris Sabo	.50
4	Jeff Bagwell	6.00
5	Darryl Strawberry	.50
6	Bret Barberie	.50
7	Howard Johnson	.50
8	John Kruk	.50
9	Andy Van Slyke	.50
10	Felix Jose	.50
11	Fred McGriff	.50
12	Will Clark	1.00
13	Cal Ripken, Jr.	10.00
14	Phil Plantier	.50
15	Lee Stevens	.50
16	Frank Thomas	6.00
17	Mark Whiten	.50
18	Cecil Fielder	.50
19	George Brett	6.00
20	Robin Yount	3.00
21	Scott Erickson	.50
22	Don Mattingly	6.00
23	Jose Canseco	3.00
24	Ken Griffey, Jr.	10.00
25	Nolan Ryan	10.00
26	Joe Carter	.50

1992 Leaf

Two 264-card series comprise this 528-card set. The cards feature action photos on both the front and the back. Silver borders surround the photo on the card front. Each leaf card was also produced in a gold foil version. One gold card was issued per pack and a complete Leaf Gold Edition set can be assembled. Traded players and free agents are shown in uniform with their new teams.

		MT
Complete Set (528):		10.00
Common Player:		.05
Complete Rod Carew Puzzle:		1.00
Gold Stars/Rookies:		3X
Series 1 or 2 Pack (15):		.50
Series 1 or 2 Wax Box (36):		10.00
1	Jim Abbott	.05
2	Cal Eldred	.05
3	Bud Black	.05
4	Dave Howard	.05
5	Luis Sojo	.05
6	Gary Scott	.05
7	Joe Oliver	.05
8	Chris Gardner	.05
9	Sandy Alomar	.05
10	Greg Harris	.05
11	Doug Drabek	.05
12	Darryl Hamilton	.05
13	Mike Mussina	.60
14	Kevin Tapani	.05
15	Ron Gant	.05
16	Mark McGwire	2.00
17	Robin Ventura	.05
18	Pedro Guerrero	.05
19	Roger Clemens	.65
20	Steve Farr	.05
21	Frank Tanana	.05
22	Joe Hesketh	.05
23	Erik Hanson	.05
24	Greg Cadaret	.05
25	Rex Hudler	.05
26	Mark Grace	.20
27	Kelly Gruber	.05
28	Jeff Bagwell	.75
29	Darryl Strawberry	.05
30	Dave Smith	.05
31	Kevin Appier	.05
32	Steve Chitren	.05
33	Kevin Gross	.05
34	Rick Aguilera	.05
35	Juan Guzman	.05
36	Joe Orsulak	.05
37	Tim Raines	.05
38	Harold Reynolds	.05
39	Charlie Hough	.05
40	Tony Phillips	.05
41	Nolan Ryan	2.00
42	Vince Coleman	.05
43	Andy Van Slyke	.05
44	Tim Burke	.05
45	Luis Polonia	.05
46	Tom Browning	.05
47	Willie McGee	.05
48	Gary DiSarcina	.05
49	Mark Lewis	.05
50	Phil Plantier	.05
51	Doug Dascenzo	.05
52	Cal Ripken, Jr.	2.00
53	Pedro Munoz	.05
54	Carlos Hernandez	.05
55	Jerald Clark	.05
56	Jeff Brantley	.05
57	Don Mattingly	.75
58	Roger McDowell	.05
59	Steve Avery	.05
60	John Olerud	.05
61	Bill Gullickson	.05
62	Juan Gonzalez	.75
63	Felix Jose	.05
64	Robin Yount	.35
65	Greg Briley	.05
66	Steve Finley	.05
67	Checklist	.05
68	Tom Gordon	.05
69	Rob Dibble	.05
70	Glenallen Hill	.05
71	Calvin Jones	.05
72	Joe Girardi	.05
73	Barry Larkin	.10
74	Andy Benes	.05
75	Milt Cuyler	.05
76	Kevin Bass	.05
77	Pete Harnisch	.05
78	Wilson Alvarez	.05
79	Mike Devereaux	.05
80	Doug Henry	.05
81	Orel Hershiser	.05
82	Shane Mack	.05
83	Mike Macfarlane	.05
84	Thomas Howard	.05
85	Alex Fernandez	.05
86	Reggie Jefferson	.05
87	Leo Gomez	.05
88	Mel Hall	.05
89	Mike Greenwell	.05
90	Jeff Russell	.05
91	Steve Buechele	.05
92	David Cone	.05
93	Kevin Reimer	.05
94	Mark Lemke	.05
95	Bob Tewksbury	.05
96	Zane Smith	.05
97	Mark Eichhorn	.05
98	Kirby Puckett	.75
99	Paul O'Neill	.05
100	Dennis Eckersley	.05
101	Duane Ward	.05
102	Matt Nokes	.05
103	Mo Vaughn	.30
104	Pat Kelly	.05
105	Ron Karkovice	.05
106	Bill Spiers	.05
107	Gary Gaetti	.05
108	Mackey Sasser	.05
109	Robby Thompson	.05
110	Marvin Freeman	.05
111	Jimmy Key	.05
112	Dwight Gooden	.05
113	Charlie Leibrandt	.05
114	Devon White	.05
115	Charles Nagy	.05
116	Rickey Henderson	.35
117	Paul Assenmacher	.05
118	Junior Felix	.05
119	Julio Franco	.05
120	Norm Charlton	.05
121	Scott Servais	.05
122	Gerald Perry	.05
123	Brian McRae	.05
124	Don Slaught	.05
125	Juan Samuel	.05
126	Harold Baines	.05
127	Scott Livingstone	.05
128	Jay Buhner	.05
129	Darrin Jackson	.05
130	Luis Mercedes	.05
131	Brian Harper	.05
132	Howard Johnson	.05
133	Checklist	.05
134	Dante Bichette	.05
135	Dave Righetti	.05
136	Jeff Montgomery	.05
137	Joe Grahe	.05
138	Delino DeShields	.05
139	Jose Rijo	.05
140	Ken Caminiti	.05
141	Steve Olin	.05

No.	Player	Value
142	Kurt Stillwell	.05
143	Jay Bell	.05
144	Jaime Navarro	.05
145	Ben McDonald	.05
146	Greg Gagne	.05
147	Jeff Blauser	.05
148	Carney Lansford	.05
149	Ozzie Guillen	.05
150	Milt Thompson	.05
151	Jeff Reardon	.05
152	Scott Sanderson	.05
153	Cecil Fielder	.05
154	Greg Harris	.05
155	Rich DeLucia	.05
156	Roberto Kelly	.05
157	Bryn Smith	.05
158	Chuck McElroy	.05
159	Tom Henke	.05
160	Luis Gonzalez	.25
161	Steve Wilson	.05
162	Shawn Boskie	.05
163	Mark Davis	.05
164	Mike Moore	.05
165	Mike Scioscia	.05
166	Scott Erickson	.05
167	Todd Stottlemyre	.05
168	Alvin Davis	.05
169	Greg Hibbard	.05
170	David Valle	.05
171	Dave Winfield	.35
172	Alan Trammell	.05
173	Kenny Rogers	.05
174	John Franco	.05
175	Jose Lind	.05
176	Pete Schourek	.05
177	Von Hayes	.05
178	Chris Hammond	.05
179	John Burkett	.05
180	Dickie Thon	.05
181	Joel Skinner	.05
182	Scott Cooper	.05
183	Andre Dawson	.15
184	Billy Ripken	.05
185	Kevin Mitchell	.05
186	Brett Butler	.05
187	Tony Fernandez	.05
188	Cory Snyder	.05
189	John Habyan	.05
190	Dennis Martinez	.05
191	John Smoltz	.10
192	Greg Myers	.05
193	Rob Deer	.05
194	Ivan Rodriguez	.40
195	Ray Lankford	.05
196	Bill Wegman	.05
197	Edgar Martinez	.05
198	Darryl Kile	.05
199	Checklist	.05
200	Brent Mayne	.05
201	Larry Walker	.15
202	Carlos Baerga	.05
203	Russ Swan	.05
204	Mike Morgan	.05
205	Hal Morris	.05
206	Tony Gwynn	.75
207	Mark Leiter	.05
208	Kirt Manwaring	.05
209	Al Osuna	.05
210	Bobby Thigpen	.05
211	Chris Hoiles	.05
212	B.J. Surhoff	.05
213	Lenny Harris	.05
214	Scott Leius	.05
215	Gregg Jefferies	.05
216	Bruce Hurst	.05
217	Steve Sax	.05
218	Dave Otto	.05
219	Sam Horn	.05
220	Charlie Hayes	.05
221	Frank Viola	.05
222	Jose Guzman	.05
223	Gary Redus	.05
224	Dave Gallagher	.05
225	Dean Palmer	.05
226	Greg Olson	.05
227	Jose DeLeon	.05
228	Mike LaValliere	.05
229	Mark Langston	.05
230	Chuck Knoblauch	.05
231	Bill Doran	.05
232	Dave Henderson	.05
233	Roberto Alomar	.50
234	Scott Fletcher	.05
235	Tim Naehring	.05
236	Mike Gallego	.05
237	Lance Johnson	.05
238	Paul Molitor	.30
239	Dan Gladden	.05
240	Willie Randolph	.05
241	Will Clark	.15
242	Sid Bream	.05
243	Derek Bell	.05
244	Bill Pecota	.05
245	Terry Pendleton	.05
246	Randy Ready	.05
247	Jack Armstrong	.05
248	Todd Van Poppel	.05
249	Shawon Dunston	.05
250	Bobby Rose	.05
251	Jeff Huson	.05
252	Bip Roberts	.05
253	Doug Jones	.05
254	Lee Smith	.05
255	George Brett	.50
256	Randy Tomlin	.05
257	Todd Benzinger	.05
258	Dave Stewart	.05
259	Mark Carreon	.05
260	Pete O'Brien	.05
261	Tim Teufel	.05
262	Bob Milacki	.05
263	Mark Guthrie	.05
264	Darrin Fletcher	.05
265	Omar Vizquel	.05
266	Chris Bosio	.05
267	Jose Canseco	.25
268	Mike Boddicker	.05
269	Lance Parrish	.05
270	Jose Vizcaino	.05
271	Chris Sabo	.05
272	Royce Clayton	.05
273	Marquis Grissom	.05
274	Fred McGriff	.05
275	Barry Bonds	1.00
276	Greg Vaughn	.05
277	Gregg Olson	.05
278	Dave Hollins	.05
279	Tom Glavine	.15
280	Bryan Hickerson	.05
281	Scott Radinsky	.05
282	Omar Olivares	.05
283	Ivan Calderon	.05
284	Kevin Maas	.05
285	Mickey Tettleton	.05
286	Wade Boggs	.25
287	Stan Belinda	.05
288	Bret Barberie	.05
289	Jose Oquendo	.05
290	Frank Castillo	.05
291	Dave Stieb	.05
292	Tommy Greene	.05
293	Eric Karros	.05
294	Greg Maddux	1.50
295	Jim Eisenreich	.05
296	Rafael Palmeiro	.15
297	Ramon Martinez	.05
298	Tim Wallach	.05
299	Jim Thome	.05
300	Chito Martinez	.05
301	Mitch Williams	.05
302	Randy Johnson	.30
303	Carlton Fisk	.30
304	Travis Fryman	.05
305	Bobby Witt	.05
306	Dave Magadan	.05
307	Alex Cole	.05
308	Bobby Bonilla	.05
309	Bryan Harvey	.05
310	Rafael Belliard	.05
311	Mariano Duncan	.05
312	Chuck Crim	.05
313	John Kruk	.05
314	Ellis Burks	.05
315	Craig Biggio	.10
316	Glenn Davis	.05
317	Ryne Sandberg	.45
318	Mike Sharperson	.05
319	Rich Rodriguez	.05
320	Lee Guetterman	.05
321	Benito Santiago	.05
322	Jose Offerman	.05
323	Tony Pena	.05
324	Pat Borders	.05
325	Mike Henneman	.05
326	Kevin Brown	.15
327	Chris Nabholz	.05
328	Franklin Stubbs	.05
329	Tino Martinez	.05
330	Mickey Morandini	.05
331	Checklist	.05
332	Mark Gubicza	.05
333	Bill Landrum	.05
334	Mark Whiten	.05
335	Darren Daulton	.05
336	Rick Wilkins	.05
337	*Brian Jordan*	1.50
338	Kevin Ward	.05
339	Ruben Amaro	.05
340	Trevor Wilson	.05
341	Andujar Cedeno	.05
342	Michael Huff	.05
343	Brady Anderson	.05
344	Craig Grebeck	.05
345	Bobby Ojeda	.05
346	Mike Pagliarulo	.05
347	Terry Shumpert	.05
348	Dann Bilardello	.05
349	Frank Thomas	1.50
350	Albert Belle	.25
351	Jose Mesa	.05
352	Rich Monteleone	.05
353	Bob Walk	.05
354	Monty Fariss	.05
355	Luis Rivera	.05
356	Anthony Young	.05
357	Geno Petralli	.05
358	Otis Nixon	.05
359	Tom Pagnozzi	.05
360	Reggie Sanders	.05
361	Lee Stevens	.05
362	Kent Hrbek	.05
363	Orlando Merced	.05
364	Mike Bordick	.05
365	Dion James	.05
366	Jack Clark	.05
367	Mike Stanley	.05
368	Randy Velarde	.05
369	Dan Pasqua	.05
370	Pat Listach	.05
371	Mike Fitzgerald	.05
372	Tom Foley	.05
373	Matt Williams	.15
374	Brian Hunter	.05
375	Joe Carter	.05
376	Bret Saberhagen	.05
377	Mike Stanton	.05
378	Hubie Brooks	.05
379	Eric Bell	.05
380	Walt Weiss	.05
381	Danny Jackson	.05
382	Manuel Lee	.05
383	Ruben Sierra	.05
384	Greg Swindell	.05
385	Ryan Bowen	.05
386	Kevin Ritz	.05
387	Curtis Wilkerson	.05
388	Gary Varsho	.05
389	Dave Hansen	.05
390	Bob Welch	.05
391	Lou Whitaker	.05
392	Ken Griffey, Jr.	1.50
393	Mike Maddux	.05
394	Arthur Rhodes	.05
395	Chili Davis	.05
396	Eddie Murray	.25
397	Checklist	.05
398	Dave Cochrane	.05
399	Kevin Seitzer	.05
400	Ozzie Smith	.45
401	Paul Sorrento	.05
402	Les Lancaster	.05
403	Junior Noboa	.05
404	Dave Justice	.15
405	Andy Ashby	.05
406	Danny Tartabull	.05
407	Bill Swift	.05
408	Craig Lefferts	.05
409	Tom Candiotti	.05
410	Lance Blankenship	.05
411	Jeff Tackett	.05
412	Sammy Sosa	1.50
413	Jody Reed	.05
414	Bruce Ruffin	.05
415	Gene Larkin	.05
416	John Vanderwal	.05
417	Tim Belcher	.05
418	Steve Frey	.05
419	Dick Schofield	.05
420	Jeff King	.05
421	Kim Batiste	.05
422	Jack McDowell	.05
423	Damon Berryhill	.05
424	Gary Wayne	.05
425	Jack Morris	.05
426	Moises Alou	.10
427	Mark McLemore	.05
428	Juan Guerrero	.05
429	Scott Scudder	.05
430	Eric Davis	.05
431	Joe Slusarski	.05
432	Todd Zeile	.05
433	Dwayne Henry	.05
434	Cliff Brantley	.05
435	Butch Henry	.05
436	Todd Worrell	.05
437	Bob Scanlan	.05
438	Wally Joyner	.05
439	John Flaherty	.05
440	Brian Downing	.05
441	Darren Lewis	.05
442	Gary Carter	.30
443	Wally Ritchie	.05
444	Chris Jones	.05
445	Jeff Kent	.10
446	Gary Sheffield	.15
447	Ron Darling	.05
448	Deion Sanders	.10
449	Andres Galarraga	.05
450	Chuck Finley	.05
451	Derek Lilliquist	.05
452	Carl Willis	.05
453	Wes Chamberlain	.05
454	Roger Mason	.05
455	Spike Owen	.05
456	Thomas Howard	.05
457	Dave Martinez	.05
458	Pete Incaviglia	.05
459	Keith Miller	.05
460	Mike Fetters	.05
461	Paul Gibson	.05
462	George Bell	.05
463	Checklist	.05
464	Terry Mulholland	.05
465	Storm Davis	.05
466	Gary Pettis	.05
467	Randy Bush	.05
468	Ken Hill	.05
469	Rheal Cormier	.05
470	Andy Stankiewicz	.05
471	Dave Burba	.05
472	Henry Cotto	.05
473	Dale Sveum	.05
474	Rich Gossage	.05
475	William Suero	.05
476	Doug Strange	.05
477	Bill Krueger	.05
478	John Wetteland	.05
479	Melido Perez	.05
480	Lonnie Smith	.05
481	Mike Jackson	.05
482	Mike Gardiner	.05
483	David Wells	.10
484	Barry Jones	.05
485	Scott Bankhead	.05
486	Terry Leach	.05
487	Vince Horsman	.05
488	Dave Eiland	.05
489	Alejandro Pena	.05
490	Julio Valera	.05
491	Joe Boever	.05
492	Paul Miller	.05
493	*Arci Cianfrocco*	.05
494	Dave Fleming	.05
495	Kyle Abbott	.05
496	Chad Kreuter	.05
497	Chris James	.05
498	Donnie Hill	.05
499	Jacob Brumfield	.05
500	Ricky Bones	.05
501	Terry Steinbach	.05
502	Bernard Gilkey	.05
503	Dennis Cook	.05
504	Len Dykstra	.05
505	Mike Bielecki	.05
506	Bob Kipper	.05
507	Jose Melendez	.05
508	Rick Sutcliffe	.05
509	Ken Patterson	.05
510	Andy Allanson	.05
511	Al Newman	.05
512	Mark Gardner	.05
513	Jeff Schaefer	.05
514	Jim McNamara	.05
515	Peter Hoy	.05
516	Curt Schilling	.10
517	Kirk McCaskill	.05
518	Chris Gwynn	.05
519	Sid Fernandez	.05
520	Jeff Parrett	.05
521	Scott Ruskin	.05
522	Kevin McReynolds	.05
523	Rick Cerone	.05
524	Jesse Orosco	.05
525	Troy Afenir	.05

526	John Smiley	.05
527	Dale Murphy	.15
528	Leaf Set Card	.05

1992 Leaf Gold Previews

In the same format as the chase cards which would be included in the regular 1992 Leaf packs, this preview set was produced for distribution to the Donruss dealer network. Cards feature the same black borders and gold highlights as the regular-issue Leaf Gold cards, but are numbered "X of 33" on the back.

		MT
Complete Set (33):		55.00
Common Player:		1.00
1	Steve Avery	1.00
2	Ryne Sandberg	3.00
3	Chris Sabo	1.00
4	Jeff Bagwell	3.00
5	Darryl Strawberry	1.00
6	Bret Barbarie	1.00
7	Howard Johnson	1.00
8	John Kruk	1.00
9	Andy Van Slyke	1.00
10	Felix Jose	1.00
11	Fred McGriff	1.00
12	Will Clark	2.00
13	Cal Ripken, Jr.	5.00
14	Phil Plantier	1.00
15	Lee Stevens	1.00
16	Frank Thomas	3.25
17	Mark Whiten	1.00
18	Cecil Fielder	1.00
19	George Brett	4.00
20	Robin Yount	2.50
21	Scott Erickson	1.00
22	Don Mattingly	4.00
23	Jose Canseco	2.50
24	Ken Griffey, Jr.	4.00
25	Nolan Ryan	5.00
26	Joe Carter	1.00
27	Deion Sanders	2.00
28	Dean Palmer	1.00
29	Andy Benes	1.00
30	Gary DiSarcina	1.00
31	Chris Hoiles	1.00
32	Mark McGwire	5.00
33	Reggie Sanders	1.00

1992 Leaf Gold Edition

This set is a parallel version of Leaf's regular 1992 set. Card fronts do not have silver borders like the regular cards do; black borders and gold foil highlights are seen instead. A Gold Edition card was inserted in each 15-card 1992 Leaf foil pack.

	MT
Complete Set (528):	50.00
Common Player:	.10
Stars/Rookies:	3X

(See 1992 Leaf for checklist and base card values)

1992 Leaf Gold Rookies

Two dozen of the major leagues' most promising players are featured in this insert set. Cards 1-12 were randomly included in Series I foil packs, while cards 13-24 were in Series II packs. Cards, numbered with a BC prefix, are standard size and enhanced with gold foil.

		MT
Complete Set (24):		9.00
Common Player:		.25
1	Chad Curtis	.25
2	Brent Gates	.25
3	Pedro Martinez	2.00
4	Kenny Lofton	.50
5	Turk Wendell	.25
6	Mark Hutton	.25
7	Todd Hundley	.75
8	Matt Stairs	.25
9	Ed Taubensee	.25
10	David Nied	.25
11	Salomon Torres	.25
12	Bret Boone	.75
13	John Ruffin	.25
14	Ed Martel	.25
15	Rick Trlicek	.25
16	Raul Mondesi	2.00
17	Pat Mahomes	.25
18	Dan Wilson	.25
19	Donovan Osborne	.25
20	Dave Silvestri	.25
21	Gary DiSarcina	.25
22	Denny Neagle	.25
23	Steve Hosey	.25
24	John Doherty	.25

1993 Leaf

Leaf issued this set in three series: two 220-card series and a 110-card update set. Card fronts have full-bleed action photos and players' names stamped in gold foil. Color-coded slate corners are used to differentiate teams. Backs have player photos against cityscapes or landmarks from the team's home city, a holographic embossed team logo and 1992 and career statistics. Players from the National League's expansion teams, the Colorado Rockies and Florida Marlins, along with the Cincinnati Reds, California Angels and Seattle Mariners were featured in Series II packs so they could be pictured in their new uniforms. The Update series included a specially numbered "DW" insert card honoring Dave Winfield's 3,000-hit landmark, plus 3,500 special Frank Thomas autographed cards.

		MT
Complete Set (550):		25.00
Common Player:		.10
Series 1 or 2 Pack (14):		.50
Series 1 or 2 Wax Box (36):		20.00
Update Pack (14):		1.00
Update Wax Box (36):		30.00
1	Ben McDonald	.10
2	Sid Fernandez	.10
3	Juan Guzman	.10
4	Curt Schilling	.15
5	Ivan Rodriguez	.60
6	Don Slaught	.10
7	Terry Steinbach	.10
8	Todd Zeile	.10
9	Andy Stankiewicz	.10
10	Tim Teufel	.10
11	Marvin Freeman	.10
12	Jim Austin	.10
13	Bob Scanlan	.10
14	Rusty Meacham	.10
15	Casey Candaele	.10
16	Travis Fryman	.10
17	Jose Offerman	.10
18	Albert Belle	.20
19	John Vander Wahl (Vander Wal)	.10
20	Dan Pasqua	.10
21	Frank Viola	.10
22	Terry Mulholland	.10
23	Gregg Olson	.10
24	Randy Tomlin	.10
25	Todd Stottlemyre	.10
26	Jose Oquendo	.10
27	Julio Franco	.10
28	Tony Gwynn	1.25
29	Ruben Sierra	.10
30	Bobby Thigpen	.10
31	Jim Bullinger	.10
32	Rick Aguilera	.10
33	Scott Servais	.10
34	Cal Eldred	.10
35	Mike Piazza	2.00
36	Brent Mayne	.10
37	Wil Cordero	.10
38	Milt Cuyler	.10
39	Howard Johnson	.10
40	Kenny Lofton	.10
41	Alex Fernandez	.10
42	Denny Neagle	.10
43	Tony Pena	.10
44	Bob Tewksbury	.10
45	Glenn Davis	.10
46	Fred McGriff	.10
47	John Olerud	.10
48	Steve Hosey	.10
49	Rafael Palmeiro	.20
50	Dave Justice	.20
51	Pete Harnisch	.10
52	Sam Militello	.10
53	Orel Hershiser	.10
54	Pat Mahomes	.10
55	Greg Colbrunn	.10
56	Greg Vaughn	.10
57	Vince Coleman	.10
58	Brian McRae	.10
59	Len Dykstra	.10
60	Dan Gladden	.10
61	Ted Power	.10
62	Donovan Osborne	.10
63	Ron Karkovice	.10
64	Frank Seminara	.10
65	Bob Zupcic	.10
66	Kirt Manwaring	.10
67	Mike Devereaux	.10
68	Mark Lemke	.10
69	Devon White	.10
70	Sammy Sosa	1.50
71	Pedro Astacio	.10
72	Dennis Eckersley	.10
73	Chris Nabholz	.10
74	Melido Perez	.10
75	Todd Hundley	.10
76	Kent Hrbek	.10
77	Mickey Morandini	.10
78	Tim McIntosh	.10
79	Andy Van Slyke	.10
80	Kevin McReynolds	.10
81	Mike Henneman	.10
82	Greg Harris	.10
83	Sandy Alomar Jr.	.10
84	Mike Jackson	.10
85	Ozzie Guillen	.10
86	Jeff Blauser	.10
87	John Valentin	.10
88	Rey Sanchez	.10
89	Rick Sutcliffe	.10
90	Luis Gonzalez	.25
91	Jeff Fassero	.10
92	Kenny Rogers	.10
93	Bret Saberhagen	.10
94	Bob Welch	.10
95	Darren Daulton	.10
96	Mike Gallego	.10
97	Orlando Merced	.10
98	Chuck Knoblauch	.10
99	Bernard Gilkey	.10
100	Billy Ashley	.10
101	Kevin Appier	.10
102	Jeff Brantley	.10
103	Bill Gullickson	.10
104	John Smoltz	.10
105	Paul Sorrento	.10
106	Steve Buechele	.10
107	Steve Sax	.10
108	Andujar Cedeno	.10
109	Billy Hatcher	.10
110	Checklist	.10
111	Alan Mills	.10
112	John Franco	.10
113	Jack Morris	.10
114	Mitch Williams	.10
115	Nolan Ryan	2.50
116	Jay Bell	.10
117	Mike Bordick	.10
118	Geronimo Pena	.10
119	Danny Tartabull	.10
120	Checklist	.10
121	Steve Avery	.10
122	Ricky Bones	.10
123	Mike Morgan	.10
124	Jeff Montgomery	.10
125	Jeff Bagwell	.75
126	Tony Phillips	.10
127	Lenny Harris	.10

No.	Player	Price
128	Glenallen Hill	.10
129	Marquis Grissom	.10
130	Gerald Williams (photo, stats actually Bernie Williams)	.60
131	Greg Harris	.10
132	Tommy Greene	.10
133	Chris Hoiles	.10
134	Bob Walk	.10
135	Duane Ward	.10
136	Tom Pagnozzi	.10
137	Jeff Huson	.10
138	Kurt Stillwell	.10
139	Dave Henderson	.10
140	Darrin Jackson	.10
141	Frank Castillo	.10
142	Scott Erickson	.10
143	Darryl Kile	.10
144	Bill Wegman	.10
145	Steve Wilson	.10
146	George Brett	1.00
147	Moises Alou	.15
148	Lou Whitaker	.10
149	Chico Walker	.10
150	Jerry Browne	.10
151	Kirk McCaskill	.10
152	Zane Smith	.10
153	Matt Young	.10
154	Lee Smith	.10
155	Leo Gomez	.10
156	Dan Walters	.10
157	Pat Borders	.10
158	Matt Williams	.15
159	Dean Palmer	.10
160	John Patterson	.10
161	Doug Jones	.10
162	John Habyan	.10
163	Pedro Martinez	.35
164	Carl Willis	.10
165	Darrin Fletcher	.10
166	B.J. Surhoff	.10
167	Eddie Murray	.40
168	Keith Miller	.10
169	Ricky Jordan	.10
170	Juan Gonzalez	.75
171	Charles Nagy	.10
172	Mark Clark	.10
173	Bobby Thigpen	.10
174	Tim Scott	.10
175	Scott Cooper	.10
176	Royce Clayton	.10
177	Brady Anderson	.10
178	Sid Bream	.10
179	Derek Bell	.10
180	Otis Nixon	.10
181	Kevin Gross	.10
182	Ron Darling	.10
183	John Wetteland	.10
184	Mike Stanley	.10
185	Jeff Kent	.10
186	Brian Harper	.10
187	Mariano Duncan	.10
188	Robin Yount	.50
189	Al Martin	.10
190	Eddie Zosky	.10
191	Mike Munoz	.10
192	Andy Benes	.10
193	Dennis Cook	.10
194	Bill Swift	.10
195	Frank Thomas	1.50
196	Damon Berryhill	.10
197	Mike Greenwell	.10
198	Mark Grace	.20
199	Darryl Hamilton	.10
200	Derrick May	.10
201	Ken Hill	.10
202	Kevin Brown	.15
203	Dwight Gooden	.10
204	Bobby Witt	.10
205	Juan Bell	.10
206	Kevin Maas	.10
207	Jeff King	.10
208	Scott Leius	.10
209	Rheal Cormier	.10
210	Darryl Strawberry	.10
211	Tom Gordon	.10
212	Bud Black	.10
213	Mickey Tettleton	.10
214	Pete Smith	.10
215	Felix Fermin	.10
216	Rick Wilkins	.10
217	George Bell	.10
218	Eric Anthony	.10
219	Pedro Munoz	.10
220	Checklist	.10
221	Lance Blankenship	.10
222	Deion Sanders	.15
223	Craig Biggio	.15
224	Ryne Sandberg	.60
225	Ron Gant	.10
226	Tom Brunansky	.10
227	Chad Curtis	.10
228	Joe Carter	.10
229	Brian Jordan	.10
230	Brett Butler	.10
231	Frank Bolick	.10
232	Rod Beck	.10
233	Carlos Baerga	.10
234	Eric Karros	.10
235	Jack Armstrong	.10
236	Bobby Bonilla	.10
237	Don Mattingly	1.50
238	Jeff Gardner	.10
239	Dave Hollins	.10
240	Steve Cooke	.10
241	Jose Canseco	.25
242	Ivan Calderon	.10
243	Tim Belcher	.10
244	Freddie Benavides	.10
245	Roberto Alomar	.50
246	Rob Deer	.10
247	Will Clark	.15
248	Mike Felder	.10
249	Harold Baines	.10
250	David Cone	.10
251	Mark Guthrie	.10
252	Ellis Burks	.10
253	Jim Abbott	.10
254	Chili Davis	.10
255	Chris Bosio	.10
256	Bret Barberie	.10
257	Hal Morris	.10
258	Dante Bichette	.10
259	Storm Davis	.10
260	Gary DiSarcina	.10
261	Ken Caminiti	.10
262	Paul Molitor	.50
263	Joe Oliver	.10
264	Pat Listach	.10
265	Gregg Jefferies	.10
266	Jose Guzman	.10
267	Eric Davis	.10
268	Delino DeShields	.10
269	Barry Bonds	1.00
270	Mike Bielecki	.10
271	Jay Buhner	.10
272	*Scott Pose*	.10
273	Tony Fernandez	.10
274	Chito Martinez	.10
275	Phil Plantier	.10
276	Pete Incaviglia	.10
277	Carlos Garcia	.10
278	Tom Henke	.10
279	Roger Clemens	1.00
280	Rob Dibble	.10
281	Daryl Boston	.10
282	Greg Gagne	.10
283	Cecil Fielder	.10
284	Carlton Fisk	.30
285	Wade Boggs	.45
286	Damion Easley	.10
287	Norm Charlton	.10
288	Jeff Conine	.10
289	Roberto Kelly	.10
290	Jerald Clark	.10
291	Rickey Henderson	.40
292	Chuck Finley	.10
293	Doug Drabek	.10
294	Dave Stewart	.10
295	Tom Glavine	.15
296	Jaime Navarro	.10
297	Ray Lankford	.10
298	Greg Hibbard	.10
299	Jody Reed	.10
300	Dennis Martinez	.10
301	Dave Martinez	.10
302	Reggie Jefferson	.10
303	*John Cummings*	.25
304	Orestes Destrade	.10
305	Mike Maddux	.10
306	David Segui	.10
307	Gary Sheffield	.30
308	Danny Jackson	.10
309	Criag Lefferts	.10
310	Andre Dawson	.15
311	Barry Larkin	.15
312	Alex Cole	.10
313	Mark Gardner	.10
314	Kirk Gibson	.10
315	Shane Mack	.10
316	Bo Jackson	.15
317	Jimmy Key	.10
318	Greg Myers	.10
319	Ken Griffey, Jr.	2.00
320	Monty Fariss	.10
321	Kevin Mitchell	.10
322	Andres Galarraga	.10
323	Mark McGwire	2.50
324	Mark Langston	.10
325	Steve Finley	.10
326	Greg Maddux	1.50
327	Dave Nilsson	.10
328	Ozzie Smith	.65
329	Candy Maldonado	.10
330	Checklist	.10
331	*Tim Pugh*	.10
332	Joe Girardi	.10
333	Junior Feliz	.10
334	Greg Swindell	.10
335	Ramon Martinez	.10
336	Sean Berry	.10
337	Joe Orsulak	.10
338	Wes Chamberlain	.10
339	Stan Belinda	.10
340	Checklist	.10
341	Bruce Hurst	.10
342	John Burkett	.10
343	Mike Mussina	.60
344	Scott Fletcher	.10
345	Rene Gonzales	.10
346	Roberto Hernandez	.10
347	Carlos Martinez	.10
348	Bill Krueger	.10
349	Felix Jose	.10
350	John Jaha	.10
351	Willie Banks	.10
352	Matt Nokes	.10
353	Kevin Seitzer	.10
354	Erik Hanson	.10
355	*David Hulse*	.10
356	*Domingo Martinez*	.10
357	Greg Olson	.10
358	Randy Myers	.10
359	Tom Browning	.10
360	Charlie Hayes	.10
361	Bryan Harvey	.10
362	Eddie Taubensee	.10
363	Tim Wallach	.10
364	Mel Rojas	.10
365	Frank Tanana	.10
366	John Kruk	.10
367	*Tim Laker*	.10
368	Rich Rodriguez	.10
369	Darren Lewis	.10
370	Harold Reynolds	.10
371	Jose Melendez	.10
372	Joe Grahe	.10
373	Lance Johnson	.10
374	Jose Mesa	.10
375	Scott Livingstone	.10
376	Wally Joyner	.10
377	Kevin Reimer	.10
378	Kirby Puckett	1.00
379	Paul O'Neill	.10
380	Randy Johnson	.40
381	Manuel Lee	.10
382	Dick Schofield	.10
383	Darren Holmes	.10
384	Charlie Hough	.10
385	John Orton	.10
386	Edgar Martinez	.10
387	Terry Pendleton	.10
388	Dan Plesac	.10
389	Jeff Reardon	.10
390	David Nied	.10
391	Dave Magadan	.10
392	Larry Walker	.25
393	Ben Rivera	.10
394	Lonnie Smith	.10
395	Craig Shipley	.10
396	Willie McGee	.10
397	Arthur Rhodes	.10
398	Mike Stanton	.10
399	Luis Polonia	.10
400	Jack McDowell	.10
401	Mike Moore	.10
402	Jose Lind	.10
403	Bill Spiers	.10
404	Kevin Tapani	.10
405	Spike Owen	.10
406	Tino Martinez	.10
407	Charlie Leibrandt	.10
408	Ed Sprague	.10
409	Bryn Smith	.10
410	Benito Santiago	.10
411	Jose Rijo	.10
412	Pete O'Brien	.10
413	Willie Wilson	.10
414	Bip Roberts	.10
415	Eric Young	.10
416	Walt Weiss	.10
417	Milt Thompson	.10
418	Chris Sabo	.10
419	Scott Sanderson	.10
420	Tim Raines	.10
421	Alan Trammell	.10
422	Mike Macfarlane	.10
423	Dave Winfield	.50
424	Bob Wickman	.10
425	David Valie	.10
426	Gary Redus	.10
427	Turner Ward	.10
428	Reggie Sanders	.10
429	Todd Worrell	.10
430	Julio Valera	.10
431	Cal Ripken, Jr.	2.50
432	Mo Vaughn	.50
433	John Smiley	.10
434	Omar Vizquel	.10
435	Billy Ripken	.10
436	Cory Snyder	.10
437	Carlos Quintana	.10
438	Omar Olivares	.10
439	Robin Ventura	.10
440	Checklist	.10
441	Kevin Higgins	.10
442	Carlos Hernandez	.10
443	Dan Peltier	.10
444	Derek Lilliquist	.10
445	Tim Salmon	.25
446	*Sherman Obando*	.10
447	Pat Kelly	.10
448	Todd Van Poppel	.10
449	Mark Whiten	.10
450	Checklist	.10
451	Pat Meares	.10
452	*Tony Tarasco*	.10
453	Chris Gwynn	.10
454	Armando Reynoso	.10
455	Danny Darwin	.10
456	Willie Greene	.10
457	Mike Blowers	.10
458	*Kevin Roberson*	.15
459	*Graeme Lloyd*	.10
460	David West	.10
461	Joey Cora	.10
462	Alex Arias	.10
463	Chad Kreuter	.10
464	Mike Lansing	.10
465	Mike Timlin	.10
466	Paul Wagner	.10
467	Mark Portugal	.10
468	Jim Leyritz	.10
469	Ryan Klesko	.10
470	Mario Diaz	.10
471	Guillermo Velasquez	.10
472	Fernando Valenzuela	.10
473	Raul Mondesi	.50
474	Mike Pagliarulo	.10
475	Chris Hammond	.10
476	Torey Lovullo	.10
477	Trevor Wilson	.10
478	*Marcos Armas*	.10
479	Dave Gallagher	.10
480	Jeff Treadway	.10
481	Jeff Branson	.10
482	Dickie Thon	.10
483	Eduardo Perez	.10
484	David Wells	.15
485	Brian Williams	.10
486	Domingo Cedeno	.10
487	Tom Candiotti	.10
488	Steve Frey	.10
489	Greg McMichael	.10
490	Marc Newfield	.10
491	Larry Andersen	.10
492	Damon Buford	.10
493	Ricky Gutierrez	.10
494	Jeff Russell	.10
495	Vinny Castilla	.10
496	Wilson Alvarez	.10
497	Scott Bullett	.10
498	Larry Casian	.10
499	Jose Vizcaino	.10
500	*J.T. Snow*	.75
501	Bryan Hickerson	.10
502	Jeremy Hernandez	.10
503	Jeromy Burnitz	.10
504	Steve Farr	.10
505	J. Owens	.10
506	Craig Paquette	.10
507	Jim Eisenreich	.10
508	Matt Whiteside	.10

509	Luis Aquino	.10
510	Mike LaValliere	.10
511	Jim Gott	.10
512	Mark McLemore	.10
513	Randy Milligan	.10
514	Gary Gaetti	.10
515	Lou Frazier	.10
516	Rich Amaral	.10
517	Gene Harris	.10
518	Aaron Sele	.10
519	Mark Wohlers	.10
520	Scott Kamieniecki	.10
521	Kent Mercker	.10
522	Jim Deshaies	.10
523	Kevin Stocker	.10
524	Jason Bere	.10
525	Tim Bogar	.10
526	Brad Pennington	.10
527	*Curt Leskanic*	.15
528	Wayne Kirby	.10
529	Tim Costo	.10
530	Doug Henry	.10
531	Trevor Hoffman	.10
532	Kelly Gruber	.10
533	Mike Harkey	.10
534	John Doherty	.10
535	Erik Pappas	.10
536	Brent Gates	.10
537	Roger McDowell	.10
538	Chris Haney	.10
539	Blas Minor	.10
540	Pat Hentgen	.10
541	Chuck Carr	.10
542	Doug Strange	.10
543	Xavier Hernandez	.10
544	Paul Quantrill	.10
545	Anthony Young	.10
546	Bret Boone	.15
547	Dwight Smith	.10
548	Bobby Munoz	.10
549	Russ Springer	.10
550	Roger Pavlik	.10
----	Dave Winfield (3000 Hits)	2.00

1993 Leaf Fasttrack

This 20-card insert set was released in two series; cards 1-10 were randomly included in Leaf Series I retail packs, while 11-20 were in Series II packs. Card fronts and backs are similar with a player photo and a diagonal white strip with "on the Fasttrack" printed in black and red. Fronts have the gold embossed Leaf logo, backs have the silver holographic team logo.

		MT
Complete Set (20):		22.50
Common Player:		.75
1	Frank Thomas	5.00
2	Tim Wakefield	.75
3	Kenny Lofton	.75
4	Mike Mussina	2.00
5	Juan Gonzalez	4.00
6	Chuck Knoblauch	.75
7	Eric Karros	.75
8	Ray Lankford	.75
9	Juan Guzman	.75
10	Pat Listach	.75
11	Carlos Baerga	.75
12	Felix Jose	.75
13	Steve Avery	.75
14	Robin Ventura	.75
15	Ivan Rodriguez	2.00
16	Cal Eldred	.75
17	Jeff Bagwell	4.00
18	Dave Justice	1.00
19	Travis Fryman	.75
20	Marquis Grissom	.75

1993 Leaf Gold All-Stars

Cards 1-10 in this insert set were randomly inserted one per Leaf Series I jumbo packs, while cards 11-20 were in Series II jumbo packs. Cards feature two players per card, one on each side. Only one side is numbered, but both sides have gold foil.

		MT
Complete Set (20):		20.00
Common Player:		.25
1	Ivan Rodriguez, Darren Daulton	.75
2	Don Mattingly, Fred McGriff	1.50
3	Cecil Fielder, Jeff Bagwell	1.00
4	Carlos Baerga, Ryne Sandberg	1.00
5	Chuck Knoblauch, Delino DeShields	.25
6	Robin Ventura, Terry Pendleton	.25
7	Ken Griffey, Jr., Andy Van Slyke	3.00
8	Joe Carter, Dave Justice	.40
9	Jose Canseco, Tony Gwynn	1.50
10	Dennis Eckersley, Rob Dibble	.25
11	Mark McGwire, Will Clark	3.00
12	Frank Thomas, Mark Grace	2.50
13	Roberto Alomar, Craig Biggio	.75
14	Barry Larkin, Cal Ripken, Jr.	3.00
15	Gary Sheffield, Edgar Martinez	.50
16	Juan Gonzalez, Barry Bonds	1.50
17	Kirby Puckett, Marquis Grissom	1.00
18	Jim Abbott, Tom Glavine	.40
19	Nolan Ryan, Greg Maddux	3.00
20	Roger Clemens, Doug Drabek	1.00

1993 Leaf Gold Rookies

These cards, numbered 1 of 20 etc., feature 1993 rookies and were randomly inserted into hobby foil packs, 10 players per series. Card fronts feature action photos, while the backs show a player photo against a landmark from his team's city.

		MT
Complete Set (20):		12.00
Common Player:		.25
1	Kevin Young	.25
2	Wil Cordero	.25
3	Mark Kiefer	.25
4	Gerald Williams	.25
5	Brandon Wilson	.25
6	Greg Gohr	.25
7	Ryan Thompson	.25
8	Tim Wakefield	.25
9	Troy Neel	.25
10	Tim Salmon	2.00
11	Kevin Rogers	.25
12	Rod Bolton	.25
13	Ken Ryan	.25
14	Phil Hiatt	.25
15	Rene Arocha	.25
16	Nigel Wilson	.25
17	J.T. Snow	1.00
18	Benji Gil	.25
19	Chipper Jones	5.00
20	Darrell Sherman	.25

1993 Leaf Heading for the Hall

Ten players on the way to the Baseball Hall of Fame are featured in this insert set. Series I Leaf packs had cards 1-5 randomly included; Series II packs had cards 6-10.

		MT
Complete Set (10):		12.50
Common Player:		.75
1	Nolan Ryan	3.00
2	Tony Gwynn	1.50
3	Robin Yount	1.00
4	Eddie Murray	.75
5	Cal Ripken, Jr.	3.00
6	Roger Clemens	1.50
7	George Brett	1.50
8	Ryne Sandberg	1.00
9	Kirby Puckett	2.00
10	Ozzie Smith	1.50

1993 Leaf Frank Thomas

Leaf signed Frank Thomas as its spokesman for 1993, and honored him with a 10-card insert set. Cards 1-5 were randomly included in Series I packs; cards 6-10 were in Series II packs. A custom designed "Frank" logo in a holographic foil stamp is featured on each card front which includes a one-word character trait. On back is a color portrait photo of Thomas superimposed on a Chicago skyline. A paragraph on back describes how the character trait on front applies to Thomas.

		MT
Complete Set (10):		8.00
Common Card:		1.00
Autographed Card:		30.00
1	Aggressive (Frank Thomas)	1.00
2	Serious (Frank Thomas)	1.00
3	Intense (Frank Thomas)	1.00
4	Confident (Frank Thomas)	1.00
5	Assertive (Frank Thomas)	1.00
6	Power (Frank Thomas)	1.00
7	Control (Frank Thomas)	1.00
8	Strength (Frank Thomas)	1.00
9	Concentration (Frank Thomas)	1.00
10	Preparation (Frank Thomas)	1.00

1993 Leaf Update Gold All-Stars

These 10 cards, featuring 20 all-stars, were randomly inserted in Leaf Update packs. Each card features two players, one on each side. Cards are distinguished from the regular Gold All-Stars by indicating on the front the card is number X of 10, with a tiny white "Update" in the red stripe above the card number.

		MT
Complete Set (10):		9.00
Common Player:		.25
1	Mark Langston, Terry Mulholland	.25
2	Ivan Rodriguez, Darren Daulton	.50
3	John Olerud, John Kruk	.25
4	Roberto Alomar, Ryne Sandberg	1.00
5	Wade Boggs, Gary Sheffield	.50
6	Cal Ripken, Jr., Barry Larkin	3.00
7	Kirby Puckett, Barry Bonds	2.00
8	Marquis Grissom, Ken Griffey Jr.	3.00
9	Joe Carter, Dave Justice	.35
10	Mark Grace, Paul Molitor	.75

1993 Leaf Update Gold Rookies

These five cards were randomly inserted in Leaf Update packs. Cards are similiar in design to the regular Gold Rookies cards, except the logo on the back indicates they are from the Update series.

		MT
Complete Set (5):		5.00
Common Player:		.50
1	Allen Watson	.50
2	Jeffrey Hammonds	.50
3	David McCarty	.50
4	Mike Piazza	4.00
5	Roberto Meija	.50

1993 Leaf Update Frank Thomas Super

This 10-card insert set features Leaf's 1993 spokesman, Frank Thomas. Cards, which measure 5" x 7", were included one per every Leaf Update foil box and are identical to the inserts found in Series I and II except in size. Cards are individually numbered. Thomas autographed 3,500 cards.

		MT
Complete Set (10):		27.50
Common Card:		3.00
1	Aggressive (Frank Thomas)	3.00
2	Serious (Frank Thomas)	3.00
3	Intense (Frank Thomas)	3.00
4	Confident (Frank Thomas)	3.00
5	Assertive (Frank Thomas)	3.00
6	Power (Frank Thomas)	3.00
7	Control (Frank Thomas)	3.00
8	Strength (Frank Thomas)	3.00
9	Concentration (Frank Thomas)	3.00
10	Preparation (Frank Thomas)	3.00

1993 Leaf Update Frank Thomas Autograph

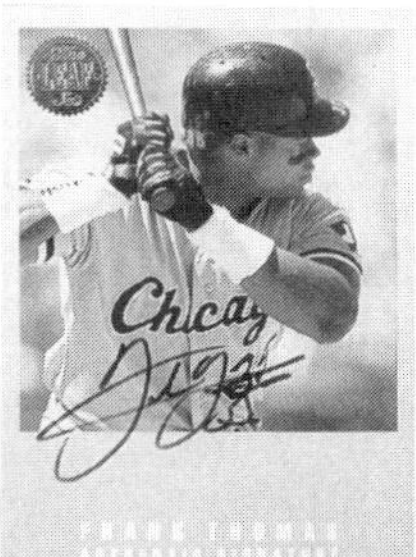

This card was a random insert in '93 Leaf Update packs and features a genuine Frank Thomas autograph on front. Unlike the other cards in the set, this has a silver-gray border on front and back. Front has a gold-foil seal in upper-left. Back has a photo of Thomas in his batting follow-through. At bottom on back is a white strip bearing the card's individual serial number from within an edition of 3,500.

		MT
FT	Frank Thomas	35.00

1994 Leaf Promos

Identical in format to the regular issue, this nine-card set was produced as a preview for the 1994 Leaf cards. The only differences on the promo cards are a large, black "Promotional Sample" notice overprinted diagonally on both the front and back of the cards. Instead of the regular card numbers, the promos are numbered "X of 9" at top to the left of the team logo hologram.

		MT
Complete Set (9):		22.50
Common Player:		1.00
1	Roberto Alomar	2.00
2	Darren Daulton	1.00
3	Ken Griffey, Jr.	5.00
4	David Justice	2.00
5	Don Mattingly	4.00
6	Mike Piazza	4.00
7	Cal Ripken, Jr.	5.00
8	Ryne Sandberg	3.00
9	Frank Thomas	4.00

1994 Leaf

Donruss returned its premium-brand Leaf set in 1994 with an announced 25% production cut from the previous season - fewer than 20,000 20-box cases of each 220-card series. Game-action photos dominate the fronts of the cards, borderless at the top and sides. At bottom are team color-coded faux-marble borders with the player's name (last name in gold foil) and team. Backs have a background of the player's home stadium with another action photo superimposed. In a ticket-stub device at upper-left is a portrait photo and a few personal numbers. Previous season and career stats are in white stripes at bottom. The team logo is presented in holographic foil at upper-right. To feature 1994's new stadiums and uniforms, cards of the Indians, Rangers, Brewers and Astros were included only in the second series. Seven different types of insert cards were produced and distributed among the various types of Leaf packaging.

		MT
Complete Set (440):		20.00
Complete Series 1 (220):		10.00
Complete Series 2 (220):		10.00
Common Player:		.10
Series 1 or 2 Pack (12):		.75
Series 1 or 2 Wax Box (36):		20.00
1	Cal Ripken, Jr.	2.50
2	Tony Tarasco	.10
3	Joe Girardi	.10
4	Bernie Williams	.30
5	Chad Kreuter	.10
6	Troy Neel	.10
7	Tom Pagnozzi	.10
8	Kirk Rueter	.10
9	Chris Bosio	.10
10	Dwight Gooden	.10
11	Mariano Duncan	.10
12	Jay Bell	.10
13	Lance Johnson	.10
14	Richie Lewis	.10
15	Dave Martinez	.10
16	Orel Hershiser	.10
17	Rob Butler	.10
18	Glenallen Hill	.10
19	Chad Curtis	.10
20	Mike Stanton	.10
21	Tim Wallach	.10
22	Milt Thompson	.10
23	Kevin Young	.10
24	John Smiley	.10
25	Jeff Montgomery	.10
26	Robin Ventura	.10
27	Scott Lydy	.10
28	Todd Stottlemyre	.10
29	Mark Whiten	.10
30	Robby Thompson	.10
31	Bobby Bonilla	.10
32	Andy Ashby	.10
33	Greg Myers	.10
34	Billy Hatcher	.10
35	Brad Holman	.10
36	Mark McLemore	.10
37	Scott Sanders	.10
38	Jim Abbott	.10
39	David Wells	.15
40	Roberto Kelly	.10
41	Jeff Conine	.10
42	Sean Berry	.10
43	Mark Grace	.25
44	Eric Young	.10
45	Rick Aguilera	.10
46	Chipper Jones	1.50
47	Mel Rojas	.10
48	Ryan Thompson	.10
49	Al Martin	.10
50	Cecil Fielder	.10
51	Pat Kelly	.10
52	Kevin Tapani	.10
53	Tim Costo	.10
54	Dave Hollins	.10
55	Kirt Manwaring	.10

No.	Player	Price
56	Gregg Jefferies	.10
57	Ron Darling	.10
58	Bill Haselman	.10
59	Phil Plantier	.10
60	Frank Viola	.10
61	Todd Zeile	.10
62	Bret Barberie	.10
63	Roberto Mejia	.10
64	Chuck Knoblauch	.10
65	Jose Lind	.10
66	Brady Anderson	.10
67	Ruben Sierra	.10
68	Jose Vizcaino	.10
69	Joe Grahe	.10
70	Kevin Appier	.10
71	Wilson Alvarez	.10
72	Tom Candiotti	.10
73	John Burkett	.10
74	Anthony Young	.10
75	Scott Cooper	.10
76	Nigel Wilson	.10
77	John Valentin	.10
78	Dave McCarty	.10
79	Archi Cianfrocco	.10
80	Lou Whitaker	.10
81	Dante Bichette	.10
82	Mark Dewey	.10
83	Danny Jackson	.10
84	Harold Baines	.10
85	Todd Benzinger	.10
86	Damion Easley	.10
87	Danny Cox	.10
88	Jose Bautista	.10
89	Mike Lansing	.10
90	Phil Hiatt	.10
91	Tim Pugh	.10
92	Tino Martinez	.10
93	Raul Mondesi	.30
94	Greg Maddux	1.50
95	Al Leiter	.10
96	Benito Santiago	.10
97	Len Dykstra	.10
98	Sammy Sosa	1.50
99	Tim Bogar	.10
100	Checklist	.10
101	Deion Sanders	.15
102	Bobby Witt	.10
103	Wil Cordero	.10
104	Rich Amaral	.10
105	Mike Mussina	.45
106	Reggie Sanders	.10
107	Ozzie Guillen	.10
108	Paul O'Neill	.10
109	Tim Salmon	.30
110	Rheal Cormier	.10
111	Billy Ashley	.10
112	Jeff Kent	.10
113	Derek Bell	.10
114	Danny Darwin	.10
115	Chip Hale	.10
116	Tim Raines	.10
117	Ed Sprague	.10
118	Darrin Fletcher	.10
119	Darren Holmes	.10
120	Alan Trammell	.10
121	Don Mattingly	1.50
122	Greg Gagne	.10
123	Jose Offerman	.10
124	Joe Orsulak	.10
125	Jack McDowell	.10
126	Barry Larkin	.20
127	Ben McDonald	.10
128	Mike Bordick	.10
129	Devon White	.10
130	Mike Perez	.10
131	Jay Buhner	.10
132	Phil Leftwich	.10
133	Tommy Greene	.10
134	Charlie Hayes	.10
135	Don Slaught	.10
136	Mike Gallego	.10
137	Dave Winfield	.75
138	Steve Avery	.10
139	Derrick May	.10
140	Bryan Harvey	.10
141	Wally Joyner	.10
142	Andre Dawson	.15
143	Andy Benes	.10
144	John Franco	.10
145	Jeff King	.10
146	Joe Oliver	.10
147	Bill Gullickson	.10
148	Armando Reynoso	.10
149	Dave Fleming	.10
150	Checklist	.10
151	Todd Van Poppel	.10
152	Bernard Gilkey	.10
153	Kevin Gross	.10
154	Mike Devereaux	.10
155	Tim Wakefield	.10
156	Andres Galarraga	.10
157	Pat Meares	.10
158	Jim Leyritz	.10
159	Mike Macfarlane	.10
160	Tony Phillips	.10
161	Brent Gates	.10
162	Mark Langston	.10
163	Allen Watson	.10
164	Randy Johnson	.75
165	Doug Brocail	.10
166	Rob Dibble	.10
167	Roberto Hernandez	.10
168	Felix Jose	.10
169	Steve Cooke	.10
170	Darren Daulton	.10
171	Eric Karros	.10
172	Geronimo Pena	.10
173	Gary DiSarcina	.10
174	Marquis Grissom	.10
175	Joey Cora	.10
176	Jim Eisenreich	.10
177	Brad Pennington	.10
178	Terry Steinbach	.10
179	Pat Borders	.10
180	Steve Buechele	.10
181	Jeff Fassero	.10
182	Mike Greenwell	.10
183	Mike Henneman	.10
184	Ron Karkovice	.10
185	Pat Hentgen	.10
186	Jose Guzman	.10
187	Brett Butler	.10
188	Charlie Hough	.10
189	Terry Pendleton	.10
190	Melido Perez	.10
191	Orestes Destrade	.10
192	Mike Morgan	.10
193	Joe Carter	.10
194	Jeff Blauser	.10
195	Chris Hoiles	.10
196	Ricky Gutierrez	.10
197	Mike Moore	.10
198	Carl Willis	.10
199	Aaron Sele	.10
200	Checklist	.10
201	Tim Naehring	.10
202	Scott Livingstone	.10
203	Luis Alicea	.10
204	*Torey Lovullo*	.10
205	Jim Gott	.10
206	Bob Wickman	.10
207	Greg McMichael	.10
208	Scott Brosius	.10
209	Chris Gwynn	.10
210	Steve Sax	.10
211	Dick Schofield	.10
212	Robb Nen	.10
213	Ben Rivera	.10
214	Vinny Castilla	.10
215	Jamie Moyer	.10
216	Wally Whitehurst	.10
217	Frank Castillo	.10
218	Mike Blowers	.10
219	Tim Scott	.10
220	Paul Wagner	.10
221	Jeff Bagwell	.75
222	Ricky Bones	.10
223	Sandy Alomar Jr.	.10
224	Rod Beck	.10
225	Roberto Alomar	.60
226	Jack Armstrong	.10
227	Scott Erickson	.10
228	Rene Arocha	.10
229	Eric Anthony	.10
230	Jeromy Burnitz	.10
231	Kevin Brown	.15
232	Tim Belcher	.10
233	Bret Boone	.10
234	Dennis Eckersley	.10
235	Tom Glavine	.15
236	Craig Biggio	.15
237	Pedro Astacio	.10
238	Ryan Bowen	.10
239	Brad Ausmus	.10
240	Vince Coleman	.10
241	Jason Bere	.10
242	Ellis Burks	.10
243	Wes Chamberlain	.10
244	Ken Caminiti	.10
245	Willie Banks	.10
246	Sid Fernandez	.10
247	Carlos Baerga	.10
248	Carlos Garcia	.10
249	Jose Canseco	.40
250	Alex Diaz	.10
251	Albert Belle	.30
252	Moises Alou	.15
253	Bobby Ayala	.10
254	Tony Gwynn	1.00
255	Roger Clemens	1.00
256	Eric Davis	.10
257	Wade Boggs	.40
258	Chili Davis	.10
259	Rickey Henderson	.40
260	Andujar Cedeno	.10
261	Cris Carpenter	.10
262	Juan Guzman	.10
263	Dave Justice	.20
264	Barry Bonds	1.00
265	Pete Incaviglia	.10
266	Tony Fernandez	.10
267	Cal Eldred	.10
268	Alex Fernandez	.10
269	Kent Hrbek	.10
270	Steve Farr	.10
271	Doug Drabek	.10
272	Brian Jordan	.10
273	Xavier Hernandez	.10
274	David Cone	.10
275	Brian Hunter	.10
276	Mike Harkey	.10
277	Delino DeShields	.10
278	David Hulse	.10
279	Mickey Tettleton	.10
280	Kevin McReynolds	.10
281	Darryl Hamilton	.10
282	Ken Hill	.10
283	Wayne Kirby	.10
284	Chris Hammond	.10
285	Mo Vaughn	.45
286	Ryan Klesko	.10
287	Rick Wilkins	.10
288	Bill Swift	.10
289	Rafael Palmeiro	.40
290	Brian Harper	.10
291	Chris Turner	.10
292	Luis Gonzalez	.20
293	Kenny Rogers	.10
294	Kirby Puckett	1.00
295	Mike Stanley	.10
296	Carlos Reyes	.10
297	Charles Nagy	.10
298	Reggie Jefferson	.10
299	Bip Roberts	.10
300	Darrin Jackson	.10
301	Mike Jackson	.10
302	Dave Nilsson	.10
303	Ramon Martinez	.10
304	Bobby Jones	.10
305	Johnny Ruffin	.10
306	Brian McRae	.10
307	Bo Jackson	.15
308	Dave Stewart	.10
309	John Smoltz	.15
310	Dennis Martinez	.10
311	Dean Palmer	.10
312	David Nied	.10
313	Eddie Murray	.35
314	Darryl Kile	.10
315	Rick Sutcliffe	.10
316	Shawon Dunston	.10
317	John Jaha	.10
318	Salomon Torres	.10
319	Gary Sheffield	.20
320	Curt Schilling	.15
321	Greg Vaughn	.10
322	Jay Howell	.10
323	Todd Hundley	.10
324	Chris Sabo	.10
325	Stan Javier	.10
326	Willie Greene	.10
327	Hipolito Pichardo	.10
328	Doug Strange	.10
329	Dan Wilson	.10
330	Checklist	.10
331	Omar Vizquel	.10
332	Scott Servais	.10
333	Bob Tewksbury	.10
334	Matt Williams	.30
335	Tom Foley	.10
336	Jeff Russell	.10
337	Scott Leius	.10
338	Ivan Rodriguez	.60
339	Kevin Seitzer	.10
340	Jose Rijo	.10
341	Eduardo Perez	.10
342	Kirk Gibson	.10
343	Randy Milligan	.10
344	Edgar Martinez	.10
345	Fred McGriff	.10
346	Kurt Abbott	.10
347	John Kruk	.10
348	Mike Felder	.10
349	Dave Staton	.10
350	Kenny Lofton	.10
351	Graeme Lloyd	.10
352	David Segui	.10
353	Danny Tartabull	.10
354	Bob Welch	.10
355	Duane Ward	.10
356	Tuffy Rhodes	.10
357	Lee Smith	.10
358	Chris James	.10
359	Walt Weiss	.10
360	Pedro Munoz	.10
361	Paul Sorrento	.10
362	Todd Worrell	.10
363	Bob Hamelin	.10
364	Julio Franco	.10
365	Roberto Petagine	.10
366	Willie McGee	.10
367	Pedro Martinez	.75
368	Ken Griffey, Jr.	2.50
369	B.J. Surhoff	.10
370	Kevin Mitchell	.10
371	John Doherty	.10
372	Manuel Lee	.10
373	Terry Mulholland	.10
374	Zane Smith	.10
375	Otis Nixon	.10
376	Jody Reed	.10
377	Doug Jones	.10
378	John Olerud	.10
379	Greg Swindell	.10
380	Checklist	.10
381	Royce Clayton	.10
382	Jim Thome	.10
383	Steve Finley	.10
384	Ray Lankford	.10
385	Henry Rodriguez	.10
386	Dave Magadan	.10
387	Gary Redus	.10
388	Orlando Merced	.10
389	Tom Gordon	.10
390	Luis Polonia	.10
391	Mark McGwire	2.50
392	Mark Lemke	.10
393	Doug Henry	.10
394	Chuck Finley	.10
395	Paul Molitor	.40
396	Randy Myers	.10
397	Larry Walker	.20
398	Pete Harnisch	.10
399	Darren Lewis	.10
400	Frank Thomas	1.00
401	Jack Morris	.10
402	Greg Hibbard	.10
403	Jeffrey Hammonds	.10
404	Will Clark	.25
405	Travis Fryman	.10
406	Scott Sanderson	.10
407	Gene Harris	.10
408	Chuck Carr	.10
409	Ozzie Smith	1.00
410	Kent Mercker	.10
411	Andy Van Slyke	.10
412	Jimmy Key	.10
413	Pat Mahomes	.10
414	John Wetteland	.10
415	Todd Jones	.10
416	Greg Harris	.10
417	Kevin Stocker	.10
418	Juan Gonzalez	.75
419	Pete Smith	.10
420	Pat Listach	.10
421	Trevor Hoffman	.10
422	Scott Fletcher	.10
423	Mark Lewis	.10
424	Mickey Morandini	.10
425	Ryne Sandberg	.75
426	Erik Hanson	.10
427	Gary Gaetti	.10
428	Harold Reynolds	.10
429	Mark Portugal	.10
430	David Valle	.10
431	Mitch Williams	.10
432	Howard Johnson	.10
433	Hal Morris	.10
434	Tom Henke	.10
435	Shane Mack	.10
436	Mike Piazza	2.00
437	Bret Saberhagen	.10
438	Jose Mesa	.10
439	Jaime Navarro	.10
440	Checklist	.10

1994 Leaf Clean-Up Crew

The number four spot in the line-up is featured on this 12-card insert set (six per series) found only in magazine distributor packaging. Fronts are gold-foil enhanced; backs feature an action photo set against a background of a lineup card on which the player is pencilled into the #4 spot. His 1993 stats when batting clean-up are presented.

		MT
Complete Set (12):		15.00
Common Player:		1.00
1	Larry Walker	2.50
2	Andres Galarraga	1.00
3	Dave Hollins	1.00
4	Bobby Bonilla	1.00
5	Cecil Fielder	1.00
6	Danny Tartabull	1.00
7	Juan Gonzalez	4.00
8	Joe Carter	1.00
9	Fred McGriff	1.00
10	Matt Williams	2.00
11	Albert Belle	2.00
12	Harold Baines	1.00

1994 Leaf 5th Anniversary

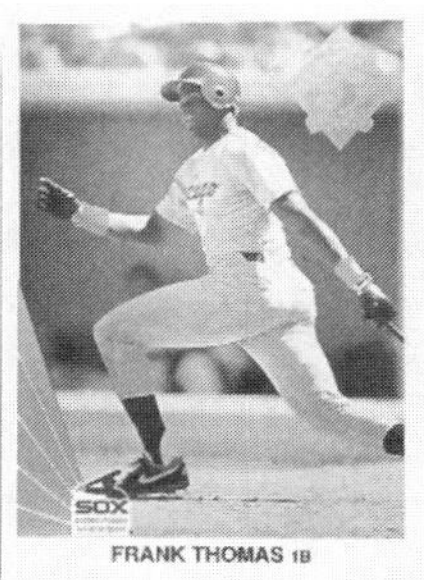

The card which insured the success of the Leaf brand name when it was re-introduced in 1990, the Frank Thomas rookie card, was re-issued in a 5th anniversary commemorative form as an insert in the 1994 set. On the chase card, silver foil rays emanate from the White Sox logo at lower-left, while a silver-foil 5th anniversary logo at upper-right replaces the Leaf script on the 1990 version. The card back carries a 1994 copyright. The Thomas anniversary card is found on average of once every 36 Series I hobby packs.

		MT
300	Frank Thomas	2.50

1994 Leaf Gamers

Leaf jumbo packs are the exclusive venue for the six cards of this insert set which were issued in each series.

		MT
Complete Set (12):		40.00
Common Player:		1.00
1	Ken Griffey, Jr.	8.00
2	Len Dykstra	1.00
3	Juan Gonzalez	4.00
4	Don Mattingly	6.00
5	Dave Justice	2.00
6	Mark Grace	2.50
7	Frank Thomas	6.00
8	Barry Bonds	5.00
9	Kirby Puckett	5.00
10	Will Clark	2.00
11	John Kruk	1.00
12	Mike Piazza	7.50

1994 Leaf Gold Rookies

A gold-foil rendered stadium background and huge black "94 Gold Leaf Rookie" serve as a backdrop for a player photo on these insert cards found at the rate of about one per 18 foil packs. The player's name and team are in silver at bottom. Horizontal backs have a ghosted action photo of the player in the background. A portrait photo is in the upper-right corner, above some personal data and stats. Cards are numbered "X of 20".

		MT
Complete Set (20):		12.00
Common Player:		.25
1	Javier Lopez	.50
2	Rondell White	2.00
3	Butch Huskey	.50
4	Midre Cummings	.25
5	Scott Ruffcorn	.25
6	Manny Ramirez	4.00
7	Danny Bautista	.25
8	Russ Davis	.25
9	Steve Karsay	.25
10	Carlos Delgado	3.00
11	Bob Hamelin	.25
12	Marcus Moore	.25
13	Miguel Jimenez	.25
14	Matt Walbeck	.25
15	James Mouton	.25
16	Rich Becker	.25
17	Brian Anderson	.25
18	Cliff Floyd	.50
19	Steve Trachsel	.40
20	Hector Carrasco	.25

1994 Leaf Gold Stars

The "Cadillac" of 1994 Leaf inserts, this 15-card series (#1-8 in Series 1; 9-15 in Series 2) is found on average of one card per 90 packs. The edition of 10,000 of each player's card is serially numbered. Fronts feature a rather small photo in a diamond-shaped frame against a green marble-look background. The border, facsimile autograph and several other graphic elements are presented in prismatic foil. The back repeats the basic front design with a few sentences about the player and a serial number strip at bottom.

		MT
Complete Set (15):		55.00
Common Player:		2.50
1	Roberto Alomar	3.50
2	Barry Bonds	6.00
3	Dave Justice	3.00
4	Ken Griffey, Jr.	10.00
5	Len Dykstra	2.50
6	Don Mattingly	7.50
7	Andres Galarraga	2.50
8	Greg Maddux	8.00
9	Carlos Baerga	2.50
10	Paul Molitor	4.00
11	Frank Thomas	7.50
12	John Olerud	2.50
13	Juan Gonzalez	5.00
14	Fred McGriff	2.50
15	Jack McDowell	2.50

1994 Leaf MVP Contenders

Found on an average of about once per 36-pack foil box, these inserts were produced in an edition of 10,000 each. Cards found in packs were marked "Silver Collection" on the horizontal fronts, and featured a silver-foil Leaf seal and other enhancements. Persons holding cards of the players selected as N.L. and A.L. MVPs could trade in their Contender card for an individually numbered 5" x 7" card of Leaf spokesman Frank Thomas and be entered in a drawing for one of 5,000 Gold Collection MVP Contender 28-card sets. Winning cards were punch-cancelled and returned to the winner along with his prize.

		MT
Complete Set, Silver (30):		75.00
Complete Set, Gold (30):		100.00
Common Player, Silver:		.50
Common Player, Gold:		1.00
AMERICAN LEAGUE		4.00
1a	Albert Belle (silver)	1.00
1b	Albert Belle (gold)	2.00
2a	Jose Canseco (silver)	1.50
2b	Jose Canseco (gold)	3.00
3a	Joe Carter (silver)	.50
3b	Joe Carter (gold)	1.00
4a	Will Clark (silver)	1.00
4b	Will Clark (gold)	2.00
5a	Cecil Fielder (silver)	.50
5b	Cecil Fielder (gold)	1.00
6a	Juan Gonzalez (silver)	4.00
6b	Juan Gonzalez (gold)	7.50
7a	Ken Griffey, Jr. (silver)	12.50
7b	Ken Griffey, Jr. (gold)	25.00
8a	Paul Molitor (silver)	2.00
8b	Paul Molitor (gold)	4.00
9a	Rafael Palmeiro (silver)	1.00
9b	Rafael Palmeiro (gold)	2.00
10a	Kirby Puckett (silver)	4.00
10b	Kirby Puckett (gold)	7.50
11a	Cal Ripken, Jr. (silver)	12.50
11b	Cal Ripken, Jr. (gold)	25.00
12a	Frank Thomas (silver)	6.00
12b	Frank Thomas (gold)	12.00

13a	Mo Vaughn (silver)	.75
13b	Mo Vaughn (gold)	1.50
14a	Carlos Baerga (silver)	.50
14b	Carlos Baerga (gold)	1.00
15	AL Bonus Card (silver)	.50
NATIONAL LEAGUE		
1a	Gary Sheffield (silver)	1.00
1b	Gary Sheffield (gold)	2.00
2a	Jeff Bagwell (silver)	6.00
2b	Jeff Bagwell (gold)	12.00
3a	Dante Bichette (silver)	.50
3b	Dante Bichette (gold)	1.00
4a	Barry Bonds (silver)	3.00
4b	Barry Bonds (gold)	6.00
5a	Darren Daulton (silver)	.50
5b	Darren Daulton (gold)	1.00
6a	Andres Galarraga (silver)	.50
6b	Andres Galarraga (gold)	1.00
7a	Gregg Jefferies (silver)	.50
7b	Gregg Jefferies (gold)	1.00
8a	Dave Justice (silver)	.75
8b	Dave Justice (gold)	1.50
9a	Ray Lankford (silver)	.50
9b	Ray Lankford (gold)	1.00
10a	Fred McGriff (silver)	.50
10b	Fred McGriff (gold)	.10
11a	Barry Larkin (silver)	.65
11b	Barry Larkin (gold)	1.25
12a	Mike Piazza (silver)	8.00
12b	Mike Piazza (gold)	15.00
13a	Deion Sanders (silver)	.75
13b	Deion Sanders (gold)	1.50
14a	Matt Williams (silver)	.75
14b	Matt Williams (gold)	1.50
15	NL Bonus Card (silver)	.50

1994 Leaf Power Brokers

This insert set was unique to Leaf Series 2 and features top sluggers. Horizontal fronts have a player photo at left, depicting his power stroke. A fireworks display is featured in the large letters of "POWER" at top. Other gold and silver foil highlights are featured on the black background. Backs have pie charts showing home run facts along with another player photo and a few stats. Stated odds of finding a Power Brokers insert card were one per dozen packs, on average.

		MT
Complete Set (10):		12.00
Common Player:		.50
1	Frank Thomas	2.00
2	Dave Justice	.75
3	Barry Bonds	1.50
4	Juan Gonzalez	1.25
5	Ken Griffey, Jr.	4.00
6	Mike Piazza	3.00
7	Cecil Fielder	.50
8	Fred McGriff	.50
9	Joe Carter	.50
10	Albert Belle	1.00

1994 Leaf Slide Show

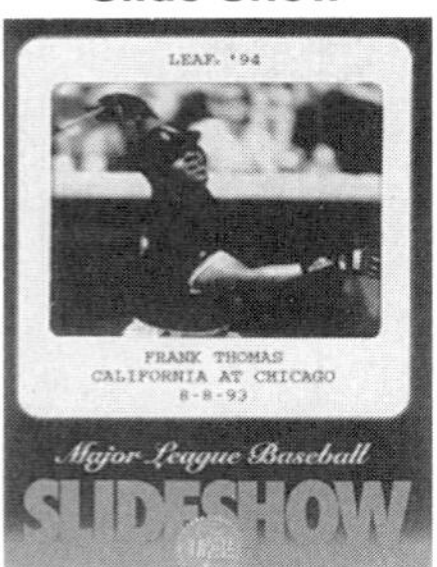

A new level of high-tech insert card production values was reached with the creation of Leaf's "Slide Show" cards, featuring a printed acetate center sandwiched between cardboard front and back. The see-through portion of the card is bordered in white to give it the appearance of a slide. The player's name, location and date of the photo are printed on the front of the "slide," with the card number on back. The pseudo-slide is bordered in black (Series 1) or white (Series 2), with a blue "Slide Show" logo at bottom and a silver-foil Leaf logo. Backs of the Slide Show inserts have a few sentences about the featured player from Frank Thomas, Leaf's official spokesman again in 1994. The first five cards were released in Series 1; cards 6-10 in Series 2. Stated odds of finding a Slide Show insert are one per 54 packs.

		MT
Complete Set (10):		16.00
Common Player:		.35
1	Frank Thomas	2.50
2	Mike Piazza	3.50
3	Darren Daulton	.35
4	Ryne Sandberg	1.75
5	Roberto Alomar	1.25
6	Barry Bonds	2.00
7	Juan Gonzalez	1.75
8	Tim Salmon	.75
9	Ken Griffey, Jr.	5.00
10	Dave Justice	.35

1994 Leaf Statistical Standouts

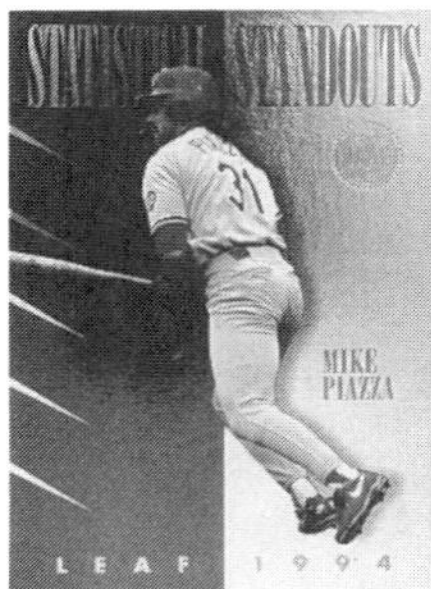

Significant statistical achievements of the 1993 season are marked in this insert set found in both retail and hobby packs at a rate of about once every 12 packs. Fronts feature player action photos set against a foil background of silver at right and a team color at left. A gold embossed Leaf seal is at upper-left. Backs are bordered in the complementary team color at right, silver at left and have a vertical player photo along with the statistical achievement. Cards are numbered "X-10".

		MT
Complete Set (10):		12.50
Common Player:		.50
1	Frank Thomas	1.50
2	Barry Bonds	1.50
3	Juan Gonzalez	1.00
4	Mike Piazza	2.50
5	Greg Maddux	2.00
6	Ken Griffey, Jr.	3.00
7	Joe Carter	.50
8	Dave Winfield	.75
9	Tony Gwynn	2.00
10	Cal Ripken, Jr.	3.00

1994 Leaf/Limited

Leaf Limited is a 160-card super-premium set printed on the highest quality board stock ever used by Donruss. Production was limited to 3,000 20-box case equivalents, making this the most limited product up to that point from Donruss. Fronts feature silver holographic Spectra Tech foiling and a silhouetted player action photo over full silver foil. The team name and logo in silver and player name in black are at the bottom of the card. Leaf Limited appears in silver at the top. Backs are dull gray with a quote from a baseball personality and a player picture in the top-right corner.

		MT
Complete Set (160):		30.00
Common Player:		.25
Pack (5):		2.00
Wax Box (20):		50.00
1	Jeffrey Hammonds	.25
2	Ben McDonald	.25
3	Mike Mussina	2.00
4	Rafael Palmeiro	1.00
5	Cal Ripken, Jr.	6.00
6	Lee Smith	.25
7	Roger Clemens	4.00
8	Scott Cooper	.25
9	Andre Dawson	.75
10	Mike Greenwell	.25
11	Aaron Sele	.25
12	Mo Vaughn	1.50
13	*Brian Anderson*	1.50
14	Chad Curtis	.25
15	Chili Davis	.25
16	Gary DiSarcina	.25
17	Mark Langston	.25
18	Tim Salmon	.75
19	Wilson Alvarez	.25
20	Jason Bere	.25
21	Julio Franco	.25
22	Jack McDowell	.25
23	Tim Raines	.25
24	Frank Thomas	4.00
25	Robin Ventura	.25
26	Carlos Baerga	.25
27	Albert Belle	1.00
28	Kenny Lofton	.25
29	Eddie Murray	1.00
30	Manny Ramirez	3.00
31	Cecil Fielder	.25
32	Travis Fryman	.25
33	Mickey Tettleton	.25
34	Alan Trammell	.25
35	Lou Whitaker	.25
36	David Cone	.25
37	Gary Gaetti	.25
38	Greg Gagne	.25
39	Bob Hamelin	.25
40	Wally Joyner	.25
41	Brian McRae	.25
42	Ricky Bones	.25
43	Brian Harper	.25
44	John Jaha	.25
45	Pat Listach	.25
46	Dave Nilsson	.25
47	Greg Vaughn	.25
48	Kent Hrbek	.25
49	Chuck Knoblauch	.25
50	Shane Mack	.25
51	Kirby Puckett	3.00
52	Dave Winfield	1.50
53	Jim Abbott	.25
54	Wade Boggs	1.50
55	Jimmy Key	.25
56	Don Mattingly	3.00
57	Paul O'Neill	.25
58	Danny Tartabull	.25
59	Dennis Eckersley	.25
60	Rickey Henderson	1.00
61	Mark McGwire	6.00
62	Troy Neel	.25
63	Ruben Sierra	.25
64	Eric Anthony	.25
65	Jay Buhner	.25
66	Ken Griffey, Jr.	6.00
67	Randy Johnson	2.50
68	Edgar Martinez	.25
69	Tino Martinez	.25
70	Jose Canseco	1.50
71	Will Clark	.75
72	Juan Gonzalez	2.50
73	Dean Palmer	.25
74	Ivan Rodriguez	2.00

75	Roberto Alomar	1.50
76	Joe Carter	.25
77	Carlos Delgado	2.00
78	Paul Molitor	1.50
79	John Olerud	.25
80	Devon White	.25
81	Steve Avery	.25
82	Tom Glavine	.40
83	Dave Justice	.75
84	Roberto Kelly	.25
85	Ryan Klesko	.25
86	Javier Lopez	.25
87	Greg Maddux	4.00
88	Fred McGriff	.25
89	Shawon Dunston	.25
90	Mark Grace	.75
91	Derrick May	.25
92	Sammy Sosa	5.00
93	Rick Wilkins	.25
94	Bret Boone	.25
95	Barry Larkin	.50
96	Kevin Mitchell	.25
97	Hal Morris	.25
98	Deion Sanders	.50
99	Reggie Sanders	.25
100	Dante Bichette	.25
101	Ellis Burks	.25
102	Andres Galarraga	.25
103	Joe Girardi	.25
104	Charlie Hayes	.25
105	Chuck Carr	.25
106	Jeff Conine	.25
107	Bryan Harvey	.25
108	Benito Santiago	.25
109	Gary Sheffield	.75
110	Jeff Bagwell	3.00
111	Craig Biggio	.50
112	Ken Caminiti	.25
113	Andujar Cedeno	.25
114	Doug Drabek	.25
115	Luis Gonzalez	.50
116	Brett Butler	.25
117	Delino DeShields	.25
118	Eric Karros	.25
119	Raul Mondesi	.75
120	Mike Piazza	5.00
121	Henry Rodriguez	.25
122	Tim Wallach	.25
123	Moises Alou	.50
124	Cliff Floyd	.25
125	Marquis Grissom	.25
126	Ken Hill	.25
127	Larry Walker	.75
128	John Wetteland	.25
129	Bobby Bonilla	.25
130	John Franco	.25
131	Jeff Kent	.25
132	Bret Saberhagen	.25
133	Ryan Thompson	.25
134	Darren Daulton	.25
135	Mariano Duncan	.25
136	Len Dykstra	.25
137	Danny Jackson	.25
138	John Kruk	.25
139	Jay Bell	.25
140	Jeff King	.25
141	Al Martin	.25
142	Orlando Merced	.25
143	Andy Van Slyke	.25
144	Bernard Gilkey	.25
145	Gregg Jefferies	.25
146	Ray Lankford	.25
147	Ozzie Smith	2.50
148	Mark Whiten	.25
149	Todd Zeile	.25
150	Derek Bell	.25
151	Andy Benes	.25
152	Tony Gwynn	3.00
153	Phil Plantier	.25
154	Bip Roberts	.25
155	Rod Beck	.25
156	Barry Bonds	4.00
157	John Burkett	.25
158	Royce Clayton	.25
159	Bill Swift	.25
160	Matt Williams	.75

1994 Leaf/Limited Gold

Leaf Limited Gold was an 18-card insert set randomly packed into Leaf Limited. All cards are individually numbered and feature the starting line-ups at each position in both the National League and American League for the 1994 All-Star Game. There were only 10,000 cards of each player produced in this insert set.

		MT
Complete Set (18):		60.00
Common Player:		.50
1	Frank Thomas	6.00
2	Gregg Jefferies	.50
3	Roberto Alomar	3.00
4	Mariano Duncan	.50
5	Wade Boggs	3.00
6	Matt Williams	1.50
7	Cal Ripken, Jr.	10.00
8	Ozzie Smith	4.00
9	Kirby Puckett	5.00
10	Barry Bonds	5.00
11	Ken Griffey, Jr.	10.00
12	Tony Gwynn	6.00
13	Joe Carter	.50
14	Dave Justice	1.50
15	Ivan Rodriguez	3.00
16	Mike Piazza	7.50
17	Jimmy Key	.50
18	Greg Maddux	6.00

1994 Leaf/Limited Rookies

Similar in format to the super-premium Leaf Limited issue, this separate issue features 80 of baseball's brightest young talents. Total production was reported as 30,000 serial numbered 20-pack foil boxes.

		MT
Complete Set (80):		30.00
Common Player:		.25
Pack (5):		4.00
Wax Box (20):		80.00
1	Charles Johnson	1.00
2	Rico Brogna	.25
3	Melvin Nieves	.25
4	Rich Becker	.25
5	Russ Davis	.25
6	Matt Mieske	.25
7	Paul Shuey	.25
8	Hector Carrasco	.25
9	J.R. Phillips	.25
10	Scott Ruffcorn	.25
11	Kurt Abbott	.25
12	Danny Bautista	.25
13	Rick White	.25
14	Steve Dunn	.25
15	Joe Ausanio	.25
16	Salomon Torres	.25
17	Rick Bottalico	.75
18	Johnny Ruffin	.25
19	Kevin Foster	.25
20	*W. Van Landingham*	.50
21	Troy O'Leary	.25
22	Mark Acre	.25
23	Norberto Martin	.25
24	*Jason Jacome*	.25
25	Steve Trachsel	.75
26	Denny Hocking	.25
27	Mike Lieberthal	.50
28	Gerald Williams	.25
29	John Mabry	.25
30	Greg Blosser	.25
31	Carl Everett	.75
32	Steve Karsay	.25
33	Jose Valentin	.25
34	Jon Lieber	.50
35	Chris Gomez	.25
36	Jesus Tavarez	.25
37	Tony Longmire	.25
38	Luis Lopez	.25
39	Matt Walbeck	.25
40	Rikkert Faneyte	.25
41	Shane Reynolds	.45
42	Joey Hamilton	1.00
43	Ismael Valdes	1.00
44	Danny Miceli	.25
45	Darren Bragg	.25
46	Alex Gonzalez	1.00
47	Rick Helling	.25
48	Jose Oliva	.25
49	Jim Edmonds	3.00
50	Miguel Jimenez	.25
51	Tony Eusebio	.45
52	Shawn Green	5.00
53	Billy Ashley	.25
54	Rondell White	3.00
55	Cory Bailey	.45
56	Tim Davis	.25
57	John Hudek	.25
58	Darren Hall	.25
59	Darren Dreifort	.25
60	Mike Kelly	.25
61	Marcus Moore	.25
62	Garret Anderson	1.00
63	Brian Hunter	.25
64	Mark Smith	.25
65	Garey Ingram	.25
66	*Rusty Greer*	1.50
67	Marc Newfield	.25
68	Gar Finnvold	.25
69	Paul Spoljaric	.25
70	Ray McDavid	.25
71	Orlando Miller	.75
72	Jorge Fabregas	.25
73	Ray Holbert	.25
74	Armando Benitez	.50
75	Ernie Young	.25
76	James Mouton	.25
77	*Robert Perez*	.45
78	*Chan Ho Park*	6.00
79	Roger Salkeld	.25
80	Tony Tarasco	.25

1994 Leaf/Limited Rookies Rookie Phenoms

Similar in format to the other Leaf Limited cards for 1994, these Phenom inserts feature gold-foil background and graphics, rather than silver. Each card is numbered from within an edition of 5,000 of each player.

		MT
Complete Set (10):		95.00
Common Player:		1.00
1	Raul Mondesi	3.00
2	Bob Hamelin	1.00
3	Midre Cummings	1.00
4	Carlos Delgado	8.00
5	Cliff Floyd	1.50
6	Jeffrey Hammonds	1.00
7	Ryan Klesko	1.00
8	Javier Lopez	1.00
9	Manny Ramirez	10.00
10	Alex Rodriguez	100.00

1994 Leaf Frank Thomas Super

An edition of 20,000 super-size versions of Frank Thomas' 1994 Leaf card was produced for inclusion in Series II hobby boxes as a bonus. Except for its 5" x 7" format and a white strip on back bearing a serial number, the card is identical to the normal-size issue.

		MT
400	Frank Thomas	6.00

1994 Leaf Frank Thomas Poster

This large (24" x 28") poster was distributed by

Leaf in a mail-in promotional offer. The blank-back sheet is printed on heavy gloss paper. A black-and-white photo of Thomas dominates the piece. In the bottom border is an embossed gold-foil Leaf seal.

	MT
Frank Thomas	15.00

1994 Leaf/Limited Promo

A single, unlabeled promo card was issued by Leaf to preview its Limited brand. The front is printed on a matte finish background as opposed to the shiny silver of the issued versions, but is otherwise identical. On back there are subtle differences in the cropping of the background photo, and a Total Bases stat is provided instead of Slugging Percentage as on the issued card. The principal difference is the use of card number 1 on the promo; the issued card is #24.

		MT
1	Frank Thomas	150.00

1995 Leaf

Two series of 200 basic cards each, plus numerous insert sets, are featured in 1995 Leaf. The basic card design has a borderless action photo on front, with a small portrait photo printed at upper-left on holographic silver foil. The team name is printed in the same foil in large letters down the left side. A script rendition of the player's name is at bottom-right, with the Leaf logo under the portrait photo; both elements are in gold foil. Backs have a couple more player photos. The card number is in white in a silver-foil seal at upper-right. Previous season and career stats are at lower-left. Several of the inserts sets are unique to various package configurations, while others are found in all types of packs.

	MT
Complete Set (400):	30.00
Complete Series 1 (200):	10.00
Complete Series 2 (200):	20.00
Common Player:	.10
Series 1 or 2 Pack (12):	.75
Series 1 or 2 Wax Box (36):	25.00

1	Frank Thomas	1.00
2	Carlos Garcia	.10
3	Todd Hundley	.10
4	Damion Easley	.10
5	Roberto Mejia	.10
6	John Mabry	.10
7	Aaron Sele	.10
8	Kenny Lofton	.10
9	John Doherty	.10
10	Joe Carter	.10
11	Mike Lansing	.10
12	John Valentin	.10
13	Ismael Valdes	.10
14	Dave McCarty	.10
15	Melvin Nieves	.10
16	Bobby Jones	.10
17	Trevor Hoffman	.10
18	John Smoltz	.15
19	Leo Gomez	.10
20	Roger Pavlik	.10
21	Dean Palmer	.10
22	Rickey Henderson	.30
23	Eddie Taubensee	.10
24	Damon Buford	.10
25	Mark Wohlers	.10
26	Jim Edmonds	.15
27	Wilson Alvarez	.10
28	Matt Williams	.30
29	Jeff Montgomery	.10
30	Shawon Dunston	.10
31	Tom Pagnozzi	.10
32	Jose Lind	.10
33	Royce Clayton	.10
34	Cal Eldred	.10
35	Chris Gomez	.10
36	Henry Rodriguez	.10
37	Dave Fleming	.10
38	Jon Lieber	.10
39	Scott Servais	.10
40	Wade Boggs	.30
41	John Olerud	.10
42	Eddie Williams	.10
43	Paul Sorrento	.10
44	Ron Karkovice	.10
45	Kevin Foster	.10
46	Miguel Jimenez	.10
47	Reggie Sanders	.10
48	Rondell White	.10
49	Scott Leius	.10
50	Jose Valentin	.10
51	William Van Landingham	.10
52	Denny Hocking	.10
53	Jeff Fassero	.10
54	Chris Hoiles	.10
55	Walt Weiss	.10
56	Geronimo Berroa	.10
57	Rich Rowland	.10
58	Dave Weathers	.10
59	Sterling Hitchcock	.10
60	Raul Mondesi	.40
61	Rusty Greer	.10
62	Dave Justice	.25
63	Cecil Fielder	.10
64	Brian Jordan	.10
65	Mike Lieberthal	.10
66	Rick Aguilera	.10
67	Chuck Finley	.10
68	Andy Ashby	.10
69	Alex Fernandez	.10
70	Ed Sprague	.10
71	Steve Buechele	.10
72	Willie Greene	.10
73	Dave Nilsson	.10
74	Bret Saberhagen	.10
75	Jimmy Key	.10
76	Darren Lewis	.10
77	Steve Cooke	.10
78	Kirk Gibson	.10
79	Ray Lankford	.10
80	Paul O'Neill	.10
81	Mike Bordick	.10
82	Wes Chamberlain	.10
83	Rico Brogna	.10
84	Kevin Appier	.10
85	Juan Guzman	.10
86	Kevin Seitzer	.10
87	Mickey Morandini	.10
88	Pedro Martinez	.45
89	Matt Mieske	.10
90	Tino Martinez	.10
91	Paul Shuey	.10
92	Bip Roberts	.10
93	Chili Davis	.10
94	Deion Sanders	.20
95	Darrell Whitmore	.10
96	Joe Orsulak	.10
97	Bret Boone	.10
98	Kent Mercker	.10
99	Scott Livingstone	.10
100	Brady Anderson	.10
101	James Mouton	.10
102	Jose Rijo	.10
103	Bobby Munoz	.10
104	Ramon Martinez	.10
105	Bernie Williams	.40
106	Troy Neel	.10
107	Ivan Rodriguez	.50
108	Salomon Torres	.10
109	Johnny Ruffin	.10
110	Darryl Kile	.10
111	Bobby Ayala	.10
112	Ron Darling	.10
113	Jose Lima	.10
114	Joey Hamilton	.10
115	Greg Maddux	1.50
116	Greg Colbrunn	.10
117	Ozzie Guillen	.10
118	Brian Anderson	.10
119	Jeff Bagwell	1.00
120	Pat Listach	.10
121	Sandy Alomar	.10
122	Jose Vizcaino	.10
123	Rick Helling	.10
124	Allen Watson	.10
125	Pedro Munoz	.10
126	Craig Biggio	.15
127	Kevin Stocker	.10
128	Wil Cordero	.10
129	Rafael Palmeiro	.25
130	Gar Finnvold	.10
131	Darren Hall	.10
132	Heath Slocumb	.10
133	Darrin Fletcher	.10
134	Cal Ripken Jr.	2.50
135	Dante Bichette	.10
136	Don Slaught	.10
137	Pedro Astacio	.10
138	Ryan Thompson	.10
139	Greg Gohr	.10
140	Javier Lopez	.10
141	Lenny Dykstra	.10
142	Pat Rapp	.10
143	Mark Kiefer	.10
144	Greg Gagne	.10
145	Eduardo Perez	.10
146	Felix Fermin	.10
147	Jeff Frye	.10
148	Terry Steinbach	.10
149	Jim Eisenreich	.10
150	Brad Ausmus	.10
151	Randy Myers	.10
152	Rick White	.10
153	Mark Portugal	.10
154	Delino DeShields	.10
155	Scott Cooper	.10
156	Pat Hentgen	.10
157	Mark Gubicza	.10
158	Carlos Baerga	.10
159	Joe Girardi	.10
160	Rey Sanchez	.10
161	Todd Jones	.10
162	Luis Polonia	.10
163	Steve Trachsel	.10
164	Roberto Hernandez	.10
165	John Patterson	.10
166	Rene Arocha	.10
167	Will Clark	.30
168	Jim Leyritz	.10
169	Todd Van Poppel	.10
170	Robb Nen	.10
171	Midre Cummings	.10
172	Jay Buhner	.10
173	Kevin Tapani	.10
174	Mark Lemke	.10
175	Marcus Moore	.10
176	Wayne Kirby	.10
177	Rich Amaral	.10
178	Lou Whitaker	.10
179	Jay Bell	.10
180	Rick Wilkins	.10
181	Paul Molitor	.50
182	Gary Sheffield	.40
183	Kirby Puckett	1.00
184	Cliff Floyd	.10
185	Darren Oliver	.10
186	Tim Naehring	.10
187	John Hudek	.10
188	Eric Young	.10
189	Roger Salkeld	.10
190	Kirt Manwaring	.10
191	Kurt Abbott	.10
192	David Nied	.10
193	Todd Zeile	.10
194	Wally Joyner	.10
195	Dennis Martinez	.10
196	Billy Ashley	.10
197	Ben McDonald	.10
198	Bob Hamelin	.10
199	Chris Turner	.10
200	Lance Johnson	.10
201	Willie Banks	.10
202	Juan Gonzalez	.75
203	Scott Sanders	.10
204	Scott Brosius	.10
205	Curt Schilling	.15
206	Alex Gonzalez	.15
207	Travis Fryman	.10
208	Tim Raines	.10
209	Steve Avery	.10
210	Hal Morris	.10
211	Ken Griffey Jr.	2.50
212	Ozzie Smith	.75
213	Chuck Carr	.10
214	Ryan Klesko	.10
215	Robin Ventura	.10
216	Luis Gonzalez	.25
217	Ken Ryan	.10
218	Mike Piazza	1.50
219	Matt Walbeck	.10
220	Jeff Kent	.10
221	Orlando Miller	.10
222	Kenny Rogers	.10
223	J.T. Snow	.10
224	Alan Trammell	.10
225	John Franco	.10
226	Gerald Williams	.10
227	Andy Benes	.10
228	Dan Wilson	.10
229	Dave Hollins	.10
230	Vinny Castilla	.10
231	Devon White	.10
232	Fred McGriff	.10
233	Quilvio Veras	.10
234	Tom Candiotti	.10
235	Jason Bere	.10
236	Mark Langston	.10
237	Mel Rojas	.10
238	Chuck Knoblauch	.10
239	Bernard Gilkey	.10
240	Mark McGwire	3.00
241	Kirk Rueter	.10
242	Pat Kelly	.10
243	Ruben Sierra	.10
244	Randy Johnson	.40
245	Shane Reynolds	.10
246	Danny Tartabull	.10
247	Darryl Hamilton	.10
248	Danny Bautista	.10
249	Tom Gordon	.10
250	Tom Glavine	.15
251	Orlando Merced	.10
252	Eric Karros	.10
253	Benji Gil	.10
254	Sean Bergman	.10
255	Roger Clemens	1.00

256	Roberto Alomar	.60
257	Benito Santiago	.10
258	Robby Thompson	.10
259	Marvin Freeman	.10
260	Jose Offerman	.10
261	Greg Vaughn	.10
262	David Segui	.10
263	Geronimo Pena	.10
264	Tim Salmon	.20
265	Eddie Murray	.45
266	Mariano Duncan	.10
267	*Hideo Nomo*	2.00
268	Derek Bell	.10
269	Mo Vaughn	.50
270	Jeff King	.10
271	Edgar Martinez	.10
272	Sammy Sosa	1.50
273	Scott Ruffcorn	.10
274	Darren Daulton	.10
275	John Jaha	.10
276	Andres Galarraga	.10
277	Mark Grace	.20
278	Mike Moore	.10
279	Barry Bonds	1.00
280	Manny Ramirez	1.00
281	Ellis Burks	.10
282	Greg Swindell	.10
283	Barry Larkin	.15
284	Albert Belle	.30
285	Shawn Green	.20
286	John Roper	.10
287	Scott Erickson	.10
288	Moises Alou	.15
289	Mike Blowers	.10
290	Brent Gates	.10
291	Sean Berry	.10
292	Mike Stanley	.10
293	Jeff Conine	.10
294	Tim Wallach	.10
295	Bobby Bonilla	.10
296	Bruce Ruffin	.10
297	Chad Curtis	.10
298	Mike Greenwell	.10
299	Tony Gwynn	1.00
300	Russ Davis	.10
301	Danny Jackson	.10
302	Pete Harnisch	.10
303	Don Mattingly	1.00
304	Rheal Cormier	.10
305	Larry Walker	.20
306	Hector Carrasco	.10
307	Jason Jacome	.10
308	Phil Plantier	.10
309	Harold Baines	.10
310	Mitch Williams	.10
311	Charles Nagy	.10
312	Ken Caminiti	.10
313	Alex Rodriguez	3.00
314	Chris Sabo	.10
315	Gary Gaetti	.10
316	Andre Dawson	.15
317	Mark Clark	.10
318	Vince Coleman	.10
319	Brad Clontz	.10
320	Steve Finley	.10
321	Doug Drabek	.10
322	Mark McLemore	.10
323	Stan Javier	.10
324	Ron Gant	.10
325	Charlie Hayes	.10
326	Carlos Delgado	.50
327	Ricky Bottalico	.10
328	Rod Beck	.10
329	Mark Acre	.10
330	Chris Bosio	.10
331	Tony Phillips	.10
332	Garret Anderson	.15
333	Pat Meares	.10
334	Todd Worrell	.10
335	Marquis Grissom	.10
336	Brent Mayne	.10
337	Lee Tinsley	.10
338	Terry Pendleton	.10
339	David Cone	.10
340	Tony Fernandez	.10
341	Jim Bullinger	.10
342	Armando Benitez	.10
343	John Smiley	.10
344	Dan Miceli	.10
345	Charles Johnson	.10
346	Lee Smith	.10
347	Brian McRae	.10
348	Jim Thome	.10
349	Jose Oliva	.10
350	Terry Mulholland	.10
351	Tom Henke	.10
352	Dennis Eckersley	.10
353	Sid Fernandez	.10
354	Paul Wagner	.10
355	John Dettmer	.10
356	John Wetteland	.10
357	John Burkett	.10
358	Marty Cordova	.10
359	Norm Charlton	.10
360	Mike Devereaux	.10
361	Alex Cole	.10
362	Brett Butler	.10
363	Mickey Tettleton	.10
364	Al Martin	.10
365	Tony Tarasco	.10
366	Pat Mahomes	.10
367	Gary DiSarcina	.10
368	Bill Swift	.10
369	Chipper Jones	1.50
370	Orel Hershiser	.10
371	Kevin Gross	.10
372	Dave Winfield	.45
373	Andujar Cedeno	.10
374	Jim Abbott	.10
375	Glenallen Hill	.10
376	Otis Nixon	.10
377	Roberto Kelly	.10
378	Chris Hammond	.10
379	Mike Macfarlane	.10
380	J.R. Phillips	.10
381	Luis Alicea	.10
382	Bret Barberie	.10
383	Tom Goodwin	.10
384	Mark Whiten	.10
385	Jeffrey Hammonds	.10
386	Omar Vizquel	.10
387	Mike Mussina	.35
388	Rickey Bones	.10
389	Steve Ontiveros	.10
390	Jeff Blauser	.10
391	Jose Canseco	.25
392	Bob Tewksbury	.10
393	Jacob Brumfield	.10
394	Doug Jones	.10
395	Ken Hill	.10
396	Pat Borders	.10
397	Carl Everett	.15
398	Gregg Jefferies	.10
399	Jack McDowell	.10
400	Denny Neagle	.10

1995 Leaf Checklists

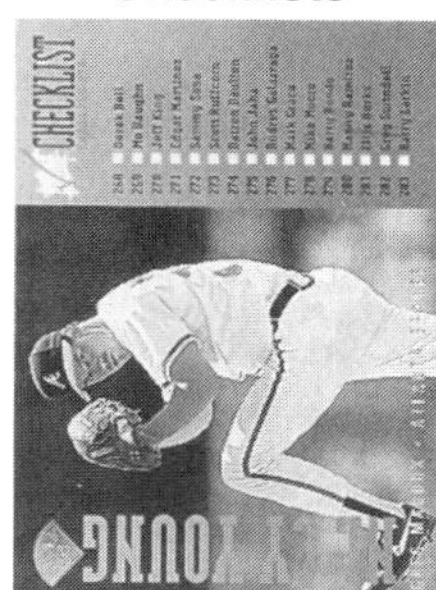

Honoring the major 1994 award winners in the American (Series I) and National (Series II) Leagues, checklists for the 1995 Leaf set are not numbered among the regular issue. Horizontal cards have a player action photo at left with his name and team in gold foil at bottom. The award is printed vertically at left with the checklist beginning on the right. Backs continue the checklist on a graduated purple background with the checklist number in a silver-foil seal at top-right.

		MT
	Complete Set (8):	2.00
	Common Player:	.25
1	Checklist 1-67 (Bob Hamelin) (Rookie of the Year)	.25
2	Checklist 68-134 (David Cone) (Cy Young)	.25
3	Checklist 135-200 (Frank Thomas) (MVP)	.50
4	Series II inserts checklist (Paul O'Neill) (Batting title)	.25
5	Checklist 201-267 (Raul Mondesi) (Rookie of the Year)	.35
6	Checklist 268-334 (Greg Maddux) (Cy Young)	.50
7	Checklist 335-400 (Jeff Bagwell) (MVP)	.45
8	Series 2 inserts checklist (Tony Gwynn) (Batting title)	.45

1995 Leaf Cornerstones

Cornerstones, six of the best first baseman-third baseman combos in baseball, are a six-card insert series found, on average, once every 18 packs in Series I Leaf. Card fronts are horizontally oriented and have a silver prismatic border and player names. Player defensive action photos are set against a background resembling their team logo chiseled into a stone block. Backs have player batting photos at each end with offensive and defensive stats from 1994, and a few words about the duo.

		MT
	Complete Set (6):	5.00
	Common Player:	.50
1	Frank Thomas, Robin Ventura	2.00
2	Cecil Fielder, Travis Fryman	.50
3	Don Mattingly, Wade Boggs	2.00
4	Jeff Bagwell, Ken Caminiti	1.00
5	Will Clark, Dean Palmer	.75
6	J.R. Phillips, Matt Williams	.50

1995 Leaf Gold Stars

Once again the toughest pull among the Leaf inserts are the Gold Leaf Stars found in both series. Found on average of one card per 90-270 packs, depending on pack card count, each of these chase cards is numbered on back within an edition of 10,000. Cards have fronts printed on metallic foil with the player name at top, the series title at bottom and a vertical stars and stripe device at right all printed in gold foil. A die-cut star appears at bottom-left. Backs are coventionally printed with another player photo and a few sentences about the star. The serial number is in gold foil in a white strip at top.

		MT
	Complete Set (14):	60.00
	Common Player:	2.00
1	Jeff Bagwell	6.00
2	Albert Belle	3.00
3	Tony Gwynn	7.00
4	Ken Griffey Jr.	9.00
5	Barry Bonds	5.00
6	Don Mattingly	7.50
7	Raul Mondesi	2.50
8	Joe Carter	2.00
9	Greg Maddux	7.50
10	Frank Thomas	6.00
11	Mike Piazza	8.00
12	Jose Canseco	3.50
13	Kirby Puckett	7.50
14	Matt Williams	2.00

1995 Leaf Gold Rookies

Every other pack of Series I Leaf Series I is seeded with a Gold Leaf Rookie card. Fronts have a largely white background with a large player photo at left-center and a smaller picture in a rectangle at upper-right. A team-color stripe is at left, while a smaller gray stripe is at top-right. The team name is printed in large gray letters across the center of the card, with the player name in a team color beneath that and above the gold-foil Leaf logo at lower-left. "Gold Leaf Rookies" is printed in gold foil down the right side. Backs repeat the team-color motif with a large action photo of the player in a single color and a smaller color portrait. Full career stats are at bottom.

		MT
Complete Set (16):		5.00
Common Player:		.15
1	Alex Rodriguez	2.50
2	Garret Anderson	.25
3	Shawn Green	.75
4	Armando Benitez	.25
5	Darren Dreifort	.15
6	Orlando Miller	.15
7	Jose Oliva	.15
8	Ricky Bottalico	.15
9	Charles Johnson	.15
10	Brian Hunter	.15
11	Ray McDavid	.15
12	Chan Ho Park	.75
13	Mike Kelly	.15
14	Cory Bailey	.15
15	Alex Gonzalez	.50
16	Andrew Lorraine	.15

1995 Leaf Frank Thomas

The Big Hurt's six seasons in the major leagues are chronicled in this flashy insert set. Silver and gold foil squares are the background for a photo of Thomas on front. Backs repeat the motif with standard print technology and another photo, along with a few words about Thomas' season. The Frank Thomas inserts are found in all types of Series II packs, with odds varying from one in 42 packs to one in 14 packs, depending on card count per pack.

		MT
Complete Set (6):		15.00
Common Card:		3.00
1	The Rookie	3.00
2	Sophomore Stardom	3.00
3	Super Star	3.00
4	AL MVP	3.00
5	Back-To-Back	3.00
6	The Big Hurt	3.00

1995 Leaf Great Gloves

While the stated emphasis is on fielding prowess in this Series II chase set, players who don't also swing a big stick are ignored. Found as frequently as one per two packs, cards have a detail photo of a glove at left, with an action photo at right. The player name in the Great Gloves logo at bottom-right is in gold foil, as are the Leaf logo at top-left and the team name vertically at right. Backs repeat the glove photo and series logo as background for another player photo and a few words and stats about the player's defense.

		MT
Complete Set (16):		4.00
Common Player:		.15
1	Jeff Bagwell	.35
2	Roberto Alomar	.25
3	Barry Bonds	.50
4	Wade Boggs	.25
5	Andres Galarraga	.15
6	Ken Griffey Jr.	1.50
7	Marquis Grissom	.15
8	Kenny Lofton	.15
9	Barry Larkin	.15
10	Don Mattingly	.75
11	Greg Maddux	.75
12	Kirby Puckett	.50
13	Ozzie Smith	.45
14	Cal Ripken Jr.	1.50
15	Matt Williams	.15
16	Ivan Rodriguez	.25

1995 Leaf Heading For The Hall

Series 2 hobby packs were the home of this scarce (one per 75 packs, average) chase set. Eight players deemed to be sure shots for Cooperstown are pictured in a semblance of the famed tombstone-shaped plaque they will someday adorn at the Hall of Fame; in fact the cards are die-cut to that shape. Backs have a sepia-toned photo, career stats and a serial number placing the card within an edition of 5,000.

		MT
Complete Set (8):		100.00
Common Player:		8.00
1	Frank Thomas	12.00
2	Ken Griffey Jr.	30.00
3	Jeff Bagwell	10.00
4	Barry Bonds	12.00
5	Kirby Puckett	15.00
6	Cal Ripken Jr.	30.00
7	Tony Gwynn	12.00
8	Paul Molitor	8.00

1995 Leaf Slideshow

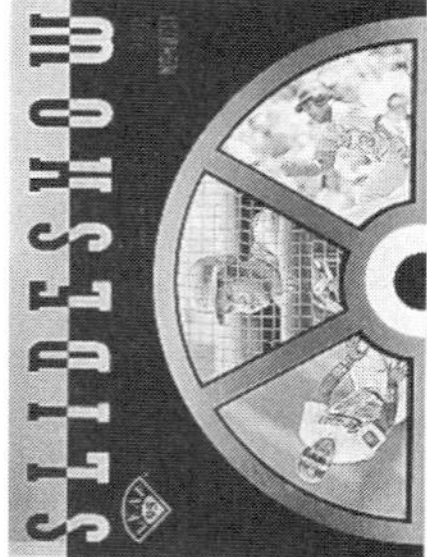

The hold-to-light technology which Leaf debuted with its 1994 Slideshow inserts continued in 1995 with a cross-series concept. The same eight players are featured on these cards in both Series I and II. Each has three clear photos at center, between the spokes of a silver-foil wheel. When both the player's cards are placed side-by-side, the six-picture see-through photo device is complete. Silver-foil and black borders surround the photo wheel on each side of the card. The Slideshow inserts are found on average of just over one per box among all types of pack configurations. Cards were issued with a peelable plastic protector on the front.

		MT
Complete Set (16):		35.00
Complete Series 1 (1a-8a):		20.00
Complete Series 2 (1b-8b):		20.00
Same CL and prices for both series		
Common Player:		1.75
1a	Raul Mondesi	2.00
1b	Raul Mondesi	2.00
2a	Frank Thomas	3.50
2b	Frank Thomas	3.50
3a	Fred McGriff	1.75
3b	Fred McGriff	1.75
4a	Cal Ripken Jr.	5.00
4b	Cal Ripken Jr.	5.00
5a	Jeff Bagwell	3.00
5b	Jeff Bagwell	3.00
6a	Will Clark	1.75
6b	Will Clark	1.75
7a	Matt Williams	1.75
7b	Matt Williams	1.75
8a	Ken Griffey Jr.	5.00
8b	Ken Griffey Jr.	5.00

1995 Leaf Statistical Standouts

Embossed red stitches on the large baseball background make the Statistical Standouts chase cards stand out among the inserts in Series I hobby packs (one per 70, average). The leather surface of the ball is also lightly textured, as is the player action photo at center. Printed in gold foil on front are the series name at top, the player's facsimile autograph at lower-center and the Leaf logo and team name at bottom. Backs have a graduated black background with a large team logo at bottom, and a circular player portrait at center. A few words explain why the player's stats stand out among his peers.

		MT
Complete Set (9):		80.00
Common Player:		2.50
1	Joe Carter	2.50
2	Ken Griffey Jr.	20.00
3	Don Mattingly	15.00
4	Fred McGriff	2.50
5	Paul Molitor	7.50
6	Kirby Puckett	15.00
7	Cal Ripken Jr.	25.00
8	Frank Thomas	15.00
9	Matt Williams	2.50

1995 Leaf 300 Club

Issued in both Series I and II Leaf, but only in the retail and magazine packs, at a rate of one per 12-30 packs, depending on pack configuration, 300 Club inserts feature the 18 active players with lifetime .300+ batting averages in a minimum of 1,000 AB. Fronts have color player photos with a large white "300" in the background and "club" in gold foil near the bottom. The player name is in gold foil in an arc above the silver Leaf logo at bottom-center. Large embossed silver triangles in each bottom corner have the team name and player position (left) and career BA (right). Backs have another player photo and highlight his place on the list of .300+ batters.

		MT
Complete Set (18):		35.00
Common Player:		.50
1	Frank Thomas	5.00
2	Paul Molitor	2.00
3	Mike Piazza	6.50
4	Moises Alou	.75
5	Mike Greenwell	.50
6	Will Clark	1.00
7	Hal Morris	.50
8	Edgar Martinez	.50
9	Carlos Baerga	.50
10	Ken Griffey Jr.	7.50
11	Wade Boggs	1.50
12	Jeff Bagwell	3.50
13	Tony Gwynn	4.50
14	John Kruk	.50
15	Don Mattingly	5.00
16	Mark Grace	1.50
17	Kirby Puckett	4.50
18	Kenny Lofton	.50

1995 Leaf/ Opening Day

Issued in celebration of the 1995's season's delayed debut, this set was only available via a mail-in offer for $2 and eight wrappers. Cards were advertised as featuring front and back photos shot on opening day. Fronts have a player photo bordered on the left with a vertical "1995 Opening Day" stripe featuring exploding fireworks at the bottom. The player's name and position appear in a silver-foil strip at bottom; a silver-foil Leaf logo is at upper-right. Backs have a player action photo set against a background of exploding fireworks and a re-cap of the player's 1995 Opening Day performance.

		MT
Complete Set (8):		4.00
Common Player:		.25
1	Frank Thomas	.75
2	Jeff Bagwell	.60
3	Barry Bonds	.75
5	Ken Griffey Jr.	1.50
5	Mike Piazza	1.00
6	Cal Ripken Jr.	1.50
7	Jose Canseco	.25
8	Larry Walker	.25

1995 Leaf/Limited

Issued in two series of 96 basic cards each, plus inserts, Leaf Limited was a hobby-only product limited to 90,000 numbered 20-pack boxes. Five-card packs had a suggested retail price of $4.99. Fronts of the basic cards have a player action photo on a background of silver holographic foil highlighted with team colors and a gold-foil Leaf Limited logo. Horizontal-format backs have two more player photos, career stats and holographic foil team logos and card numbers.

		MT
Complete Set (192):		20.00
Complete Series 1 (96):		10.00
Complete Series 2 (96):		10.00
Common Player:		.15
Series 1 or 2 Pack (5):		2.00
Series 1 or 2 Wax Box (20):		30.00
1	Frank Thomas	2.50
2	Geronimo Berroa	.15
3	Tony Phillips	.15
4	Roberto Alomar	1.25
5	Steve Avery	.15
6	Darryl Hamilton	.15
7	Scott Cooper	.15
8	Mark Grace	.65
9	Billy Ashley	.15
10	Wil Cordero	.15
11	Barry Bonds	2.50
12	Kenny Lofton	.15
13	Jay Buhner	.15
14	Alex Rodriguez	3.00
15	Bobby Bonilla	.15
16	Brady Anderson	.15
17	Ken Caminiti	.15
18	Charlie Hayes	.15
19	Jay Bell	.15
20	Will Clark	.45
21	Jose Canseco	.50
22	Bret Boone	.15
23	Dante Bichette	.15
24	Kevin Appier	.15
25	Chad Curtis	.15
26	Marty Cordova	.15
27	Jason Bere	.15
28	Jimmy Key	.15
29	Rickey Henderson	.45
30	Tim Salmon	.50
31	Joe Carter	.15
32	Tom Glavine	.30
33	Pat Listach	.15
34	Brian Jordan	.15
35	Brian McRae	.15
36	Eric Karros	.15
37	Pedro Martinez	.65
38	Royce Clayton	.15
39	Eddie Murray	.75
40	Randy Johnson	1.00
41	Jeff Conine	.15
42	Brett Butler	.15
43	Jeffrey Hammonds	.15
44	Andujar Cedeno	.15
45	Dave Hollins	.15
46	Jeff King	.15
47	Benji Gil	.15
48	Roger Clemens	2.00
49	Barry Larkin	.30
50	Joe Girardi	.15
51	Bob Hamelin	.15
52	Travis Fryman	.15
53	Chuck Knoblauch	.15
54	Ray Durham	.15
55	Don Mattingly	2.50
56	Ruben Sierra	.15
57	J.T. Snow	.25
58	Derek Bell	.15
59	David Cone	.15
60	Marquis Grissom	.15
61	Kevin Seitzer	.15
62	Ozzie Smith	1.50
63	Rick Wilkins	.15
64	*Hideo Nomo*	3.50
65	Tony Tarasco	.15
66	Manny Ramirez	2.00
67	Charles Johnson	.15
68	Craig Biggio	.25
69	Bobby Jones	.15
70	Mike Mussina	.75
71	Alex Gonzalez	.25
72	Gregg Jefferies	.15
73	Rusty Greer	.15
74	Mike Greenwell	.15
75	Hal Morris	.15
76	Paul O'Neill	.15
77	Luis Gonzalez	.40
78	Chipper Jones	3.00
79	Mike Piazza	3.00
80	Rondell White	.25
81	Glenallen Hill	.15
82	Shawn Green	.60
83	Bernie Williams	.50
84	Jim Thome	.15
85	Terry Pendleton	.15
86	Rafael Palmeiro	.45
87	Tony Gwynn	2.00
88	Mickey Tettleton	.15
89	John Valentin	.15
90	Deion Sanders	.50
91	Larry Walker	.60
92	Michael Tucker	.15
93	Alan Trammell	.15
94	Tim Raines	.15
95	Dave Justice	.50
96	Tino Martinez	.15
97	Cal Ripken Jr.	5.00
98	Deion Sanders	.35
99	Darren Daulton	.15
100	Paul Molitor	1.00
101	Randy Myers	.15
102	Wally Joyner	.15
103	Carlos Perez	.15
104	Brian Hunter	.15
105	Wade Boggs	.75
106	*Bobby Higginson*	3.00
107	Jeff Kent	.15
108	Jose Offerman	.15
109	Dennis Eckersley	.15
110	Dave Nilsson	.15
111	Chuck Finley	.15
112	Devon White	.15
113	Bip Roberts	.15
114	Ramon Martinez	.15
115	Greg Maddux	3.00
116	Curtis Goodwin	.15
117	John Jaha	.15
118	Ken Griffey Jr.	4.00
119	Geronimo Pena	.15
120	Shawon Dunston	.15
121	Ariel Prieto	.15
122	Kirby Puckett	2.00
123	Carlos Baerga	.15
124	Todd Hundley	.15
125	Tim Naehring	.15
126	Gary Sheffield	.45
127	Dean Palmer	.15
128	Rondell White	.25
129	Greg Gagne	.15
130	Jose Rijo	.15
131	Ivan Rodriguez	.65
132	Jeff Bagwell	1.50
133	Greg Vaughn	.15
134	Chili Davis	.15
135	Al Martin	.15
136	Kenny Rogers	.15
137	Aaron Sele	.15
138	Raul Mondesi	.35
139	Cecil Fielder	.15
140	Tim Wallach	.15
141	Andres Galarraga	.15
142	Lou Whitaker	.15
143	Jack McDowell	.15
144	Matt Williams	.45
145	Ryan Klesko	.15
146	Carlos Garcia	.15
147	Albert Belle	.50
148	Ryan Thompson	.15
149	Roberto Kelly	.15
150	Edgar Martinez	.15
151	Robby Thompson	.15
152	Mo Vaughn	.65
153	Todd Zeile	.15
154	Harold Baines	.15
155	Phil Plantier	.15
156	Mike Stanley	.15
157	Ed Sprague	.15
158	Moises Alou	.30
159	Quilvio Veras	.15
160	Reggie Sanders	.15
161	Delino DeShields	.15
162	Rico Brogna	.15
163	Greg Colbrunn	.15
164	Steve Finley	.15
165	Orlando Merced	.15
166	Mark McGwire	5.00
167	Garret Anderson	.15
168	Paul Sorrento	.15
169	Mark Langston	.15
170	Danny Tartabull	.15
171	Vinny Castilla	.15
172	Javier Lopez	.15
173	Bret Saberhagen	.15
174	Eddie Williams	.15
175	Scott Leius	.15
176	Juan Gonzalez	1.50
177	Gary Gaetti	.15
178	Jim Edmonds	.25
179	John Olerud	.15
180	Lenny Dykstra	.15
181	Ray Lankford	.15
182	Ron Gant	.15
183	Doug Drabek	.15
184	Fred McGriff	.15
185	Andy Benes	.15
186	Kurt Abbott	.15
187	Bernard Gilkey	.15
188	Sammy Sosa	3.00
189	Lee Smith	.15
190	Dennis Martinez	.15
191	Ozzie Guillen	.15
192	Robin Ventura	.15

1995 Leaf/Limited Gold

Seeded one per pack in Series I only, this insert set follows the format of the basic Leaf Limited cards, but is distinguished by the presence of gold, rather than silver, holographic foil.

		MT
Complete Set (24):		25.00
Common Player:		.50
1	Frank Thomas	1.50
2	Jeff Bagwell	1.00
3	Raul Mondesi	.75
4	Barry Bonds	1.50
5	Albert Belle	.75
6	Ken Griffey Jr.	3.00
7	Cal Ripken Jr.	3.00
8	Will Clark	.75
9	Jose Canseco	.75
10	Larry Walker	.75
11	Kirby Puckett	1.50
12	Don Mattingly	1.50
13	Tim Salmon	.50
14	Roberto Alomar	1.00
15	Greg Maddux	1.50
16	Mike Piazza	2.00
17	Matt Williams	.50
18	Kenny Lofton	.50
19	Alex Rodriquez (Rodriguez)	3.00
20	Tony Gwynn	1.50
21	Mo Vaughn	1.00
22	Chipper Jones	2.00
23	Manny Ramirez	1.50
24	Deion Sanders	.50

1995 Leaf/Limited Lumberjacks

Lumberjacks inserts are found in both Series 1 and 2 Leaf Limited at a rate of one per 23 packs on average (less than one per box). Fronts are printed on woodgrain veneer with a large team logo behind a batting action photo of the game's top sluggers. Backs have another photo against a background of tree trunks. A white stripe at bottom carries each card's unique serial number within an edition of 5,000.

		MT
Complete Set (16):		100.00
Common Player:		4.00
1	Albert Belle	4.00
2	Barry Bonds	6.00
3	Juan Gonzalez	7.50
4	Ken Griffey Jr.	20.00
5	Fred McGriff	4.00
6	Mike Piazza	15.00
7	Kirby Puckett	7.50
8	Mo Vaughn	5.00
9	Frank Thomas	10.00
10	Jeff Bagwell	7.50
11	Matt Williams	4.00
12	Jose Canseco	5.00
13	Raul Mondesi	4.00
14	Manny Ramirez	7.50
15	Cecil Fielder	4.00
16	Cal Ripken Jr.	20.00

1995 Leaf/Limited Bat Patrol

Yet another insert of the game's top veteran hitters was featured as chase cards in Series 2 Leaf Limited. The cards have player action photos on front with large silver-foil "BAT / PATROL" lettering at lower-left. Backs are printed on a silver background and include career stats plus another color player photo. The cards were seeded at the rate of one per pack.

		MT
Complete Set (24):		22.50
Common Player:		.25
1	Frank Thomas	2.50
2	Tony Gwynn	2.00
3	Wade Boggs	.75
4	Larry Walker	.60
5	Ken Griffey Jr.	4.00
6	Jeff Bagwell	2.00
7	Manny Ramirez	1.50
8	Mark Grace	.60
9	Kenny Lofton	.25
10	Mike Piazza	3.00
11	Will Clark	.50
12	Mo Vaughn	.75
13	Carlos Baerga	.25
14	Rafael Palmeiro	.50
15	Barry Bonds	1.50
16	Kirby Puckett	2.00
17	Roberto Alomar	1.00
18	Barry Larkin	.35
19	Eddie Murray	.75
20	Tim Salmon	.45
21	Don Mattingly	2.00
22	Fred McGriff	.25
23	Albert Belle	.75
24	Dante Bichette	.25

1996 Leaf

Reverting to a single-series issue of 220 basic cards, plus numerous insert set bells and whistles, this was the final Leaf set under Donruss' ownership. Regular cards offer large action photos on front and back with a side and bottom border subdued through darkening (front) or lightening (back). Fronts feature silver prismatic-foil graphic highlights while the back includes a circular portrait photo with vital data around. Leaf was sold in both hobby and retail versions, each with some unique inserts. Basic unit was the 12-card foil pack, with suggested retail of $2.49.

		MT
Complete Set (220):		10.00
Common Player:		.10
Complete Gold Set (220):		800.00
Common Golds:		4.00
Gold Press Proofs:		20X
Complete Silver Set (220):		400.00
Common Silvers:		2.50
Silver Press Proofs:		10X
Complete Bronze Set (220):		200.00
Common Bronze:		1.00
Bronze Press Proofs:		7X
Pack (12):		1.50
Wax Box (30):		40.00
1	John Smoltz	.15
2	Dennis Eckersley	.10
3	Delino DeShields	.10
4	Cliff Floyd	.10
5	Chuck Finley	.10
6	Cecil Fielder	.10
7	Tim Naehring	.10
8	Carlos Perez	.10
9	Brad Ausmus	.10
10	*Matt Lawton*	.75
11	Alan Trammell	.10
12	Steve Finley	.10
13	Paul O'Neill	.10
14	Gary Sheffield	.35
15	Mark McGwire	2.50
16	Bernie Williams	.35
17	Jeff Montgomery	.10
18	Chan Ho Park	.25
19	Greg Vaughn	.10
20	Jeff Kent	.10
21	Cal Ripken Jr.	2.50
22	Charles Johnson	.10
23	Eric Karros	.10
24	Alex Rodriguez	2.00
25	Chris Snopek	.10
26	Jason Isringhausen	.10
27	Chili Davis	.10
28	Chipper Jones	2.00
29	Bret Saberhagen	.10
30	Tony Clark	.10
31	Marty Cordova	.10
32	Dwayne Hosey	.10
33	Fred McGriff	.10
34	Deion Sanders	.15
35	Orlando Merced	.10
36	Brady Anderson	.10
37	Ray Lankford	.10
38	Manny Ramirez	1.00
39	Alex Fernandez	.10
40	Greg Colbrunn	.10
41	Ken Griffey Jr.	2.50
42	Mickey Morandini	.10
43	Chuck Knoblauch	.10
44	Quinton McCracken	.10
45	Tim Salmon	.25
46	Jose Mesa	.10
47	Marquis Grissom	.10
48	Checklist	.10
49	Raul Mondesi	.25
50	Mark Grudzielanek	.10
51	Ray Durham	.10
52	Matt Williams	.25
53	Bob Hamelin	.10
54	Lenny Dykstra	.10
55	Jeff King	.10
56	LaTroy Hawkins	.10
57	Terry Pendleton	.10
58	Kevin Stocker	.10
59	Ozzie Timmons	.10
60	David Justice	.20
61	Ricky Bottalico	.10
62	Andy Ashby	.10
63	Larry Walker	.25
64	Jose Canseco	.30
65	Bret Boone	.10
66	Shawn Green	.25
67	Chad Curtis	.10
68	Travis Fryman	.10
69	Roger Clemens	.75
70	David Bell	.10
71	Rusty Greer	.10
72	Bob Higginson	.10
73	Joey Hamilton	.10
74	Kevin Seitzer	.10
75	Julian Tavarez	.10
76	Troy Percival	.10
77	Kirby Puckett	1.25
78	Barry Bonds	1.00
79	Michael Tucker	.10
80	Paul Molitor	.35
81	Carlos Garcia	.10
82	Johnny Damon	.25
83	Mike Hampton	.10
84	Ariel Prieto	.10
85	Tony Tarasco	.10
86	Pete Schourek	.10
87	Tom Glavine	.20
88	Rondell White	.15
89	Jim Edmonds	.10
90	Robby Thompson	.10
91	Wade Boggs	.35
92	Pedro Martinez	.30
93	Gregg Jefferies	.10
94	Albert Belle	.30
95	Benji Gil	.10
96	Denny Neagle	.10
97	Mark Langston	.10
98	Sandy Alomar	.10
99	Tony Gwynn	1.25
100	Todd Hundley	.10
101	Dante Bichette	.10
102	Eddie Murray	.45
103	Lyle Mouton	.10
104	John Jaha	.10
105	Checklist	.10
106	Jon Nunnally	.10
107	Juan Gonzalez	.75
108	Kevin Appier	.10
109	Brian McRae	.10
110	Lee Smith	.10
111	Tim Wakefield	.10
112	Sammy Sosa	1.50
113	Jay Buhner	.15
114	Garret Anderson	.10
115	Edgar Martinez	.10
116	Edgardo Alfonzo	.15
117	Billy Ashley	.10
118	Joe Carter	.10
119	Javy Lopez	.10
120	Bobby Bonilla	.10
121	Ken Caminiti	.10
122	Barry Larkin	.15
123	Shannon Stewart	.10
124	Orel Hershiser	.10
125	Jeff Conine	.10

126	Mark Grace	.25
127	Kenny Lofton	.10
128	Luis Gonzalez	.20
129	Rico Brogna	.10
130	Mo Vaughn	.45
131	Brad Radke	.15
132	Jose Herrera	.10
133	Rick Aguilera	.10
134	Gary DiSarcina	.10
135	Andres Galarraga	.10
136	Carl Everett	.15
137	Steve Avery	.10
138	Vinny Castilla	.10
139	Dennis Martinez	.10
140	John Wetteland	.10
141	Alex Gonzalez	.15
142	Brian Jordan	.10
143	Todd Hollandsworth	.10
144	Terrell Wade	.10
145	Wilson Alvarez	.10
146	Reggie Sanders	.10
147	Will Clark	.25
148	Hideo Nomo	.75
149	J.T. Snow	.10
150	Frank Thomas	1.50
151	Ivan Rodriguez	.45
152	Jay Bell	.10
153	Checklist	.10
154	David Cone	.10
155	Roberto Alomar	.60
156	Carlos Delgado	.50
157	Carlos Baerga	.10
158	Geronimo Berroa	.10
159	Joe Vitiello	.10
160	Terry Steinbach	.10
161	Doug Drabek	.10
162	David Segui	.10
163	Ozzie Smith	1.00
164	Kurt Abbott	.10
165	Randy Johnson	.50
166	John Valentin	.10
167	Mickey Tettleton	.10
168	Ruben Sierra	.10
169	Jim Thome	.10
170	Mike Greenwell	.10
171	Quilvio Veras	.10
172	Robin Ventura	.10
173	Bill Pulsipher	.10
174	Rafael Palmeiro	.20
175	Hal Morris	.10
176	Ryan Klesko	.10
177	Eric Young	.10
178	Shane Andrews	.10
179	Brian Hunter	.10
180	Brett Butler	.10
181	John Olerud	.10
182	Moises Alou	.10
183	Glenallen Hill	.10
184	Ismael Valdes	.10
185	Andy Pettitte	.25
186	Yamil Benitez	.10
187	Jason Bere	.10
188	Dean Palmer	.10
189	Jimmy Haynes	.10
190	Trevor Hoffman	.10
191	Mike Mussina	.35
192	Greg Maddux	1.50
193	Ozzie Guillen	.10
194	Pat Listach	.10
195	Derek Bell	.10
196	Darren Daulton	.10
197	John Mabry	.10
198	Ramon Martinez	.10
199	Jeff Bagwell	1.00
200	Mike Piazza	2.00
201	Al Martin	.10
202	Aaron Sele	.10
203	Ed Sprague	.10
204	Rod Beck	.10
205	Checklist	.10
206	Mike Lansing	.10
207	Craig Biggio	.15
208	Jeffrey Hammonds	.10
209	Dave Nilsson	.10
210	Checklist, Inserts (Dante Bichette, Albert Belle)	.10
211	Derek Jeter	2.00
212	Alan Benes	.10
213	Jason Schmidt	.10
214	Alex Ochoa	.10
215	Ruben Rivera	.15
216	Roger Cedeno	.20
217	Jeff Suppan	.10
218	Billy Wagner	.10
219	Mark Loretta	.10
220	Karim Garcia	.20

1996 Leaf Press Proofs

Carrying the parallel edition concept to its inevitable next level, '96 Leaf offered the Press Proof insert cards in three degrees of scarcity, each highlighted with appropriate holographic foil. Like the other '96 Leaf inserts, these are individually serially numbered within its edition limit. At the top of the line are Gold Press Proofs in an edition of only 500 of each card. Silver and Bronze versions were produced in editions of 1,000 and 2,000, respectively. Press Proofs are inserted into both hobby and retail packs at an average rate of one card per 10 packs.

	MT
Complete Set, Gold (220):	800.00
Complete Set, Silver (220):	400.00
Complete Set, Bronze (220):	200.00
Common Player, Gold:	4.00
Common Player, Silver:	2.50
Common Player, Bronze:	1.00

(Press Proof stars valued as follows in comparison to regular-issue '96 Leaf - Gold: 20X; Silver: 10X; Bronze: 7X.)

1996 Leaf All-Star MVP Contenders

A surprise insert in Leaf boxes was this interactive redemption issue. Twenty leading candidates for MVP honors at the 1996 All-Star Game in Philadelphia were presented in a silver-foil highlighted horizontal format. The player's league logo serves as a background to the color action photo on front. Backs have details of the redemption offer which expired Aug. 15, 1996. The first 5,000 persons who sent in the Mike Piazza card for redemption received a gold version of the set and had their Piazza card punch-cancelled and returned.

		MT
Complete Set (20):		30.00
Common Card:		.50
Golds:		1.5X
1	Frank Thomas	2.50
2	Mike Piazza	3.50
2c	Mike Piazza (redeemed and punch-cancelled)	2.50
3	Sammy Sosa	2.50
4	Cal Ripken Jr.	4.00
5	Jeff Bagwell	1.50
6	Reggie Sanders	.50
7	Mo Vaughn	1.00
8	Tony Gwynn	2.00
9	Dante Bichette	.60
10	Tim Salmon	.75
11	Chipper Jones	3.50
12	Kenny Lofton	.50
13	Manny Ramirez	1.50
14	Barry Bonds	1.75
15	Raul Mondesi	.60
16	Kirby Puckett	1.50
17	Albert Belle	.75
18	Ken Griffey Jr.	4.00
19	Greg Maddux	2.00
20	Bonus card	.50

1996 Leaf Frank Thomas The Big Heart

In one of several specialty card charitable endeavors, Frank Thomas and Leaf teamed up to issue this set as a fund raiser for "The Big Hurt's" charitable foundation. Each of the cards was available in an edition limited to 3,500 each for a $20 donation. Cards are standard 2-1/2" x 3-1/2" with posed photos on front and "THE BIG HEART", a play on his nickname. Backs have information on the foundation.

		MT
Complete Set (4):		35.00
Common Card:		10.00
(1)	Frank Thomas (bat on shoulder)	10.00
(2)	Frank Thomas (holding glove)	10.00
(3)	Frank Thomas (horizontal)	10.00
(4)	Frank Thomas (seated)	10.00

1996 Leaf Frank Thomas' Greatest Hits

Die-cut plastic with a background of prismatic foil to simulate a segment of a compact disc is the format for this insert issue chronicling the career-to-date of Frank Thomas. Backs include a few stats and a portrait photo, plus a gold-foil serial number from within an edition of 5,000. Cards #1-4 are found only in hobby packs; cards #5-7 are exclusive to retail packs (average insertion rate one per 210 packs) and card #8 could be had only through a wrapper redemption.

		MT
Complete Set (8):		35.00
Common Card:		5.00
1	1990	5.00
2	1991	5.00
3	1992	5.00
4	1993	5.00
5	1994	5.00
6	1995	5.00
7	Career	5.00
8	MVP	5.00

1996 Leaf Gold Leaf Stars

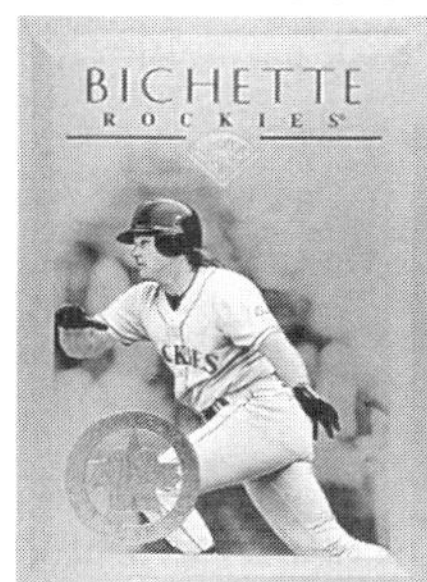

A vignetted background of embossed gold metallic cardboard and a Gold Leaf Stars logo in 22-karat gold foil are featured on this limited (2,500 of each) edition insert. Backs include a second color photo of the player and a serial number from within the edition. Gold Leaf Stars were included in both hobby and retail packaging, with an average insertion rate of one per 210 packs.

		MT
Complete Set (15):		135.00
Common Player:		3.00
1	Frank Thomas	12.50
2	Dante Bichette	3.00
3	Sammy Sosa	12.50

4	Ken Griffey Jr.	25.00
5	Mike Piazza	20.00
6	Tim Salmon	3.00
7	Hideo Nomo	10.00
8	Cal Ripken Jr.	25.00
9	Chipper Jones	12.50
10	Albert Belle	6.00
11	Tony Gwynn	12.00
12	Mo Vaughn	6.00
13	Barry Larkin	5.00
14	Manny Ramirez	10.00
15	Greg Maddux	12.50

1996 Leaf Hats Off

The most technically innovative inserts of 1996 have to be the Hats Off series exclusive to Leaf retail packs. Front player photos are on a background that is both flocked to simulate the cloth of a baseball cap, plus enhanced with a stiched team logo. The graphics are all in raised textured gold foil. Backs are conventionally printed and include a gold-foil serial number placing each card within an edition of 5,000 per player.

		MT
Complete Set (8):		35.00
Common Player:		2.00
1	Cal Ripken Jr.	10.00
2	Barry Larkin	2.00
3	Frank Thomas	6.50
4	Mo Vaughn	3.00
5	Ken Griffey Jr.	10.00
6	Hideo Nomo	5.00
7	Albert Belle	3.00
8	Greg Maddux	6.50

1996 Leaf Picture Perfect

Leaf calls the glossy central area of these inserts "pearlized foil," which allows the player action photo to stand out in contrast to the actual wood veneer background. Gold-foil highlights complete the design. Backs are conventionally printed and include a gold-foil serial number from within the edition of 5,000 of each player's card. Cards #1-6 are hobby-only inserts, while #7-12 are found in retail packs. Average insertion rate is one per 140 packs. A promo version of each card was also issued.

		MT
Complete Set (12):		55.00
Common Player:		2.00
Promos:		1X
1	Frank Thomas	6.00
2	Cal Ripken Jr.	10.00
3	Greg Maddux	6.00
4	Manny Ramirez	4.00
5	Chipper Jones	7.50
6	Tony Gwynn	4.00
7	Ken Griffey Jr.	9.00
8	Albert Belle	2.00
9	Jeff Bagwell	4.00
10	Mike Piazza	8.00
11	Mo Vaughn	2.00
12	Barry Bonds	5.00

1996 Leaf Statistical Standouts

The feel of leather complements the game-used baseball background on these hobby-only inserts featuring the game's top names. Backs offer statistical data and a gold-foil serial number placing the card within an edition of 2,500 for each player. Average insertion rate is one per 210 packs.

		MT
Complete Set (8):		55.00
Common Player:		2.50
1	Cal Ripken Jr.	15.00
2	Tony Gwynn	7.00
3	Frank Thomas	8.00
4	Ken Griffey Jr.	12.50
5	Hideo Nomo	6.00
6	Greg Maddux	9.00
7	Albert Belle	2.50
8	Chipper Jones	10.00

1996 Leaf Total Bases

Total-base leaders from 1991-95 are featured in this hobby-only insert set. Card fronts are printed on textured canvas to simulate a base. Fronts are highlighted with gold foil. Backs have stats ranking the player in this category plus a gold-foil serial number from an edition of 5,000 of each player. Total Bases inserts are seeded at an average rate of one per 72 packs. Each player can also be found in a promo card version, marked as such on each side.

		MT
Complete Set (12):		30.00
Common Player:		1.00
Promos:		1X
1	Frank Thomas	5.00
2	Albert Belle	2.00
3	Rafael Palmeiro	1.50
4	Barry Bonds	3.00
5	Kirby Puckett	4.00
6	Joe Carter	1.00
7	Paul Molitor	2.00
8	Fred McGriff	1.00
9	Ken Griffey Jr.	8.00
10	Carlos Baerga	1.00
11	Juan Gonzalez	2.50
12	Cal Ripken Jr.	8.00

1996 Leaf/Limited

Leaf Limited contains 90 of the top rookies and stars. There is also a 100-card Limited Gold parallel set which includes the 90 base cards, plus 10 Limited Rookies inserts. The gold parallel cards are seeded one per 11 packs. Regular Limited Rookies inserts were seeded one per seven packs. Other insert sets were two versions of Lumberjacks and Pennant Craze.

		MT
Complete Set (90):		20.00
Common Player:		.15
Gold Set (90):		64.00
Gold Stars/Rookies:		4X
Pack (5):		1.50
Wax Box (14):		20.00
1	Ivan Rodriguez	.60
2	Roger Clemens	2.50
3	Gary Sheffield	.40
4	Tino Martinez	.15
5	Sammy Sosa	2.50
6	Reggie Sanders	.15
7	Ray Lankford	.15
8	Manny Ramirez	2.00
9	Jeff Bagwell	1.50
10	Greg Maddux	2.50
11	Ken Griffey Jr.	3.25
12	Rondell White	.15
13	Mike Piazza	3.25
14	Marc Newfield	.15
15	Cal Ripken Jr.	4.00
16	Carlos Delgado	.40
17	Tim Salmon	.40
18	Andres Galarraga	.15
19	Chuck Knoblauch	.15
20	Matt Williams	.40
21	Mark McGwire	4.00
22	Ben McDonald	.15
23	Frank Thomas	2.50
24	Johnny Damon	.20
25	Gregg Jefferies	.15
26	Travis Fryman	.15
27	Chipper Jones	4.00
28	David Cone	.15
29	Kenny Lofton	.15
30	Mike Mussina	.60
31	Alex Rodriguez	3.25
32	Carlos Baerga	.15
33	Brian Hunter	.15
34	Juan Gonzalez	1.50
35	Bernie Williams	.50
36	Wally Joyner	.15
37	Fred McGriff	.15
38	Randy Johnson	.60
39	Marty Cordova	.15
40	Garret Anderson	.15
41	Albert Belle	.40
42	Edgar Martinez	.15
43	Barry Larkin	.25
44	Paul O'Neill	.15
45	Cecil Fielder	.15
46	Rusty Greer	.15
47	Mo Vaughn	.60
48	Dante Bichette	.15
49	Ryan Klesko	.15
50	Roberto Alomar	.75
51	Raul Mondesi	.40
52	Robin Ventura	.15
53	Tony Gwynn	2.00
54	Mark Grace	.40
55	Jim Thome	.15
56	Jason Giambi	.35
57	Tom Glavine	.20
58	Jim Edmonds	.25
59	Pedro Martinez	.45
60	Charles Johnson	.15
61	Wade Boggs	.75
62	Orlando Merced	.15
63	Craig Biggio	.20
64	Brady Anderson	.15
65	Hideo Nomo	.75
66	Ozzie Smith	1.25
67	Eddie Murray	.60
68	Will Clark	.35
69	Jay Buhner	.15
70	Kirby Puckett	2.50
71	Barry Bonds	2.00
72	Ray Durham	.15
73	Sterling Hitchcock	.15
74	John Smoltz	.20
75	Andre Dawson	.30
76	Joe Carter	.15
77	Ryne Sandberg	1.25
78	Rickey Henderson	.60
79	Brian Jordan	.15
80	Greg Vaughn	.15
81	Andy Pettitte	.40
82	Dean Palmer	.15
83	Paul Molitor	.75
84	Rafael Palmeiro	.40
85	Henry Rodriguez	.15
86	Larry Walker	.50
87	Ismael Valdes	.15
88	Derek Bell	.15
89	J.T. Snow	.15
90	Jack McDowell	.15

1996 Leaf/Limited Lumberjacks

Lumberjacks inserts returned to Leaf Limited, but the 1996 versions feature an improved maple stock that puts wood grains on both sides of the card. Ten different Lumberjacks are available in two different versions. Regular versions are serial numbered to 5,000, while a special black-bordered Limited Edition version is numbered to 500. Each Lumberjacks card was also produced in a promo card version, appropriately marked on each side.

		MT
Complete Set (10):		40.00
Common Player:		1.50
Lumberjack Blacks (500):		2X
Promos:		1X
1	Ken Griffey Jr.	6.00
2	Sammy Sosa	5.00
3	Cal Ripken Jr.	7.50
4	Frank Thomas	3.50
5	Alex Rodriguez	6.00
6	Mo Vaughn	1.50
7	Chipper Jones	5.00
8	Mike Piazza	5.00
9	Jeff Bagwell	3.00
10	Mark McGwire	7.50

1996 Leaf/Limited Pennant Craze

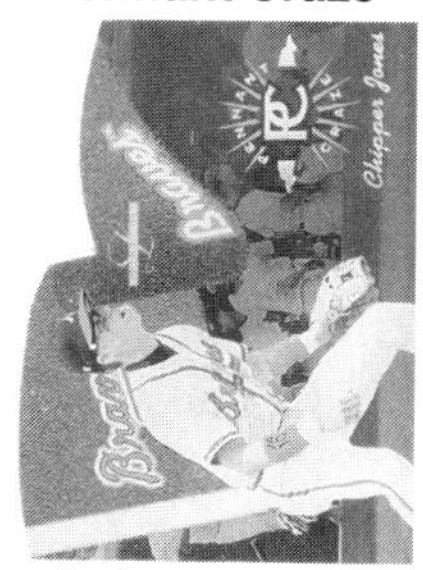

Each card in this insert set is sequentially numbered to 2,500 in silver foil on the back. The top-front of the cards have a die-cut pennant shape and is felt-textured.

		MT
Complete Set (10):		60.00
Common Player:		3.00
1	Juan Gonzalez	4.00
2	Cal Ripken Jr.	12.00
3	Frank Thomas	7.50
4	Ken Griffey Jr.	12.00
5	Albert Belle	3.00
6	Greg Maddux	7.50
7	Paul Molitor	3.50
8	Alex Rodriguez	12.00
9	Barry Bonds	5.50
10	Chipper Jones	10.00

1996 Leaf/Limited Rookies

There are two versions of this 1996 Limited insert set. The cards are reprinted as part of a Limited Gold parallel set, which also includes the regular issue's 90 cards. The gold cards are seeded one per every 11 packs. The top young players are also featured on regular Limited Rookies inserts; these versions are seeded one per every seven packs.

		MT
Complete Set (10):		25.00
Common Player:		1.00
Limited Gold:		4X
1	Alex Ochoa	1.00
2	Darin Erstad	6.50
3	Ruben Rivera	1.00
4	Derek Jeter	10.00
5	Jermaine Dye	1.00
6	Jason Kendall	1.50
7	Mike Grace	1.00
8	Andruw Jones	6.50
9	Rey Ordonez	3.50
10	George Arias	1.00

1996 Leaf/ Preferred

Leaf Preferred consists of 150 cards, a Press Proof parallel set and three insert sets, one of which has its own parallel set, too. While no individual odds are given for insert sets, the overall odds of getting an insert card are one per 10 packs. The Press Proof inserts replace the silver foil name and strip down the left side of the card with gold foil. Press Proof parallels were limited to 250 sets. Another insert set, Silver Leaf Steel, has a card seeded one per pack. This insert set is paralleled by a Gold Leaf Steel set, which appears in much more limited numbers. The two other insert sets are Steel Power and Staremaster.

		MT
Complete Set (150):		25.00
Common Player:		.15
Press Proofs:		15X
Pack (6):		2.25
Wax Box (24):		40.00
1	Ken Griffey Jr.	2.00
2	Rico Brogna	.15
3	Gregg Jefferies	.15
4	Reggie Sanders	.15
5	Manny Ramirez	1.00
6	Shawn Green	.35
7	Tino Martinez	.15
8	Jeff Bagwell	.75
9	Marc Newfield	.15
10	Ray Lankford	.15
11	Jay Bell	.15
12	Greg Maddux	1.50
13	Frank Thomas	1.00
14	Travis Fryman	.15
15	Mark McGwire	2.50
16	Chuck Knoblauch	.15
17	Sammy Sosa	1.50
18	Matt Williams	.25
19	Roger Clemens	1.00
20	Rondell White	.15
21	Ivan Rodriguez	.75
22	Cal Ripken Jr.	2.50
23	Ben McDonald	.15
24	Kenny Lofton	.15
25	Mike Piazza	2.00
26	David Cone	.15
27	Gary Sheffield	.30
28	Tim Salmon	.30
29	Andres Galarraga	.15
30	Johnny Damon	.20
31	Ozzie Smith	1.00
32	Carlos Baerga	.15
33	Raul Mondesi	.20
34	Moises Alou	.20
35	Alex Rodriguez	2.50
36	Mike Mussina	.60
37	Jason Isringhausen	.20
38	Barry Larkin	.25
39	Bernie Williams	.45
40	Chipper Jones	1.50
41	Joey Hamilton	.15
42	Charles Johnson	.15
43	Juan Gonzalez	.75
44	Greg Vaughn	.15
45	Robin Ventura	.15
46	Albert Belle	.30
47	Rafael Palmeiro	.35
48	Brian Hunter	.15
49	Mo Vaughn	.30
50	Paul O'Neill	.15
51	Mark Grace	.30
52	Randy Johnson	.60
53	Pedro Martinez	.75
54	Marty Cordova	.15
55	Garret Anderson	.15
56	Joe Carter	.15
57	Jim Thome	.15
58	Edgardo Alfonzo	.20
59	Dante Bichette	.15
60	Darryl Hamilton	.15
61	Roberto Alomar	.50
62	Fred McGriff	.15
63	Kirby Puckett	1.00
64	Hideo Nomo	.75
65	Alex Fernandez	.15
66	Ryan Klesko	.15
67	Wade Boggs	.40
68	Eddie Murray	.40
69	Eric Karros	.15
70	Jim Edmonds	.25
71	Edgar Martinez	.15
72	Andy Pettitte	.30
73	Mark Grudzielanek	.15
74	Tom Glavine	.25
75	Ken Caminiti	.15
76	Will Clark	.30
77	Craig Biggio	.20
78	Brady Anderson	.15
79	Tony Gwynn	1.00
80	Larry Walker	.25
81	Brian Jordan	.15
82	Lenny Dykstra	.15
83	Butch Huskey	.15
84	Jack McDowell	.15
85	Cecil Fielder	.15
86	Jose Canseco	.30
87	Jason Giambi	.50
88	Rickey Henderson	.45
89	Kevin Seitzer	.15
90	Carlos Delgado	.50
91	Ryne Sandberg	.75
92	Dwight Gooden	.15
93	Michael Tucker	.15
94	Barry Bonds	1.50
95	Eric Young	.15
96	Dean Palmer	.15
97	Henry Rodriguez	.15
98	John Mabry	.15
99	J.T. Snow	.15
100	Andre Dawson	.20
101	Ismael Valdes	.15
102	Charles Nagy	.15
103	Jay Buhner	.15
104	Derek Bell	.15
105	Paul Molitor	.50
106	Hal Morris	.15
107	Ray Durham	.15
108	Bernard Gilkey	.15
109	John Valentin	.15
110	Melvin Nieves	.15
111	John Smoltz	.20
112	Terrell Wade	.15
113	Chad Mottola	.15
114	Tony Clark	.15
115	John Wasdin	.15
116	Derek Jeter	2.00
117	Rey Ordonez	.15
118	Jason Thompson	.15
119	*Robin Jennings*	.15
120	*Rocky Coppinger*	.15
121	Billy Wagner	.15
122	Steve Gibralter	.15
123	Jermaine Dye	.15
124	Jason Kendall	.15
125	*Mike Grace*	.15
126	Jason Schmidt	.15
127	Paul Wilson	.15
128	Alan Benes	.15
129	Justin Thompson	.15
130	Brooks Kieschnick	.15
131	George Arias	.15
132	*Osvaldo Fernandez*	.20
133	Todd Hollandsworth	.15
134	Eric Owens	.15
135	Chan Ho Park	.25
136	Mark Loretta	.15
137	Ruben Rivera	.15
138	Jeff Suppan	.15
139	Ugueth Urbina	.15
140	LaTroy Hawkins	.15
141	Chris Snopek	.15
142	Edgar Renteria	.15
143	Raul Casanova	.15
144	Jose Herrera	.15
145	*Matt Lawton*	.75
146	*Ralph Milliard*	.15
147	Checklist	.15
148	Checklist	.15
149	Checklist	.15
150	Checklist	.15

1996 Leaf/ Preferred Press Proofs

Inserted at a rate of about one per 48 packs, Press Proof parallels of the 150 cards in Leaf Preferred are identifiable only by the use of gold foil, rather than silver, on the card fronts, and gold ink on back. The cards are not otherwise marked or numbered. It is believed the issue was limited to 250-500 of each card.

	MT
Complete Set (150):	400.00
Common Player:	2.00
Stars/Rookies:	15X

(See 1996 Leaf Preferred for checklist and base card values.)

1996 Leaf/ Preferred Leaf Steel Gold Promos

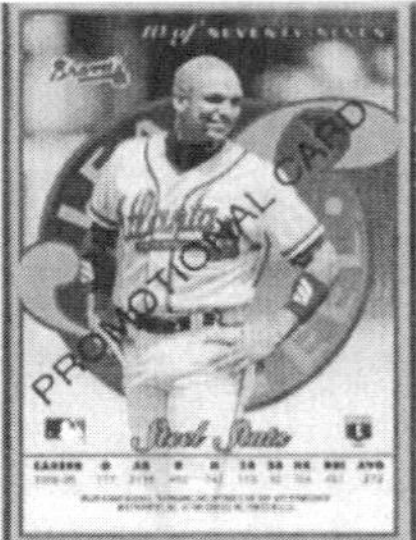

Each of the 77 gold cards in the Preferred Steel set can also be found in a promo card version. The samples differ from the issued versions only in an overprint diagonally on the back which reads "PROMOTIONAL CARD". This parallel promo edition represents one of the largest promo card issues of the mid-1990s. Cards were reportedly distributed to dealers on the basis of one per three-case order. A bronze version, also marked "PROMOTIONAL CARD" on back, was created, but never officially released, though examples have found their way into the market.

		MT
Complete Set (77):		275.00
Common Player:		2.00
Bronze: VALUES UNDETERMINED		
1	Frank Thomas	8.00
2	Paul Molitor	6.00
3	Kenny Lofton	2.00
4	Travis Fryman	2.00
5	Jeff Conine	2.00
6	Barry Bonds	13.00
7	Gregg Jefferies	2.00
8	Alex Rodriguez	16.00
9	Wade Boggs	5.00
10	David Justice	3.00
11	Hideo Nomo	5.00
12	Roberto Alomar	3.50
13	Todd Hollandsworth	2.00
14	Mark McGwire	17.50
15	Rafael Palmeiro	3.00
16	Will Clark	3.00
17	Cal Ripken Jr.	17.50
18	Derek Bell	2.00
19	Gary Sheffield	4.00
20	Juan Gonzalez	8.00
21	Garret Anderson	2.00
22	Mo Vaughn	4.00
23	Robin Ventura	2.00
24	Carlos Baerga	2.00
25	Tim Salmon	3.00
26	Matt Williams	3.00
27	Fred McGriff	2.00
28	Rondell White	2.00
29	Ray Lankford	2.00
30	Lenny Dykstra	2.00
31	J.T. Snow	2.00
32	Sammy Sosa	7.50
33	Chipper Jones	14.00
34	Bobby Bonilla	2.00
35	Paul Wilson	2.00
36	Darren Daulton	2.00
37	Larry Walker	3.00
38	Raul Mondesi	3.00
39	Jeff Bagwell	8.00
40	Derek Jeter	12.50
41	Kirby Puckett	10.00
42	Jason Isringhausen	2.00
43	Vinny Castilla	2.00
44	Jim Edmonds	3.00
45	Ron Gant	2.00
46	Carlos Delgado	3.00
47	Jose Canseco	4.00
48	Tony Gwynn	10.00
49	Mike Mussina	4.00
50	Charles Johnson	2.00
51	Mike Piazza	14.00
52	Ken Griffey Jr.	16.00
53	Greg Maddux	12.00
54	Mark Grace	4.00
55	Ryan Klesko	2.00
56	Dennis Eckersley	2.00
57	Rickey Henderson	4.00
58	Michael Tucker	2.00
59	Joe Carter	2.00
60	Randy Johnson	5.00
61	Brian Jordan	2.00
62	Shawn Green	3.50
63	Roger Clemens	8.00
64	Andres Galarraga	2.00
65	Johnny Damon	3.00
66	Ryne Sandberg	6.00
67	Alan Benes	2.00
68	Albert Belle	3.00
69	Barry Larkin	2.50
70	Marty Cordova	2.50
71	Dante Bichette	2.00
72	Craig Biggio	2.50
73	Reggie Sanders	2.00
74	Moises Alou	2.00
75	Chuck Knoblauch	2.00
76	Cecil Fielder	2.00
77	Manny Ramirez	5.00

1996 Leaf/ Preferred Leaf Steel

This 77-card insert set has two versions - a silver one and a much more limited gold one. A Silver Leaf Steel card is included in every pack; the parallel versions appear about one per 24 packs.

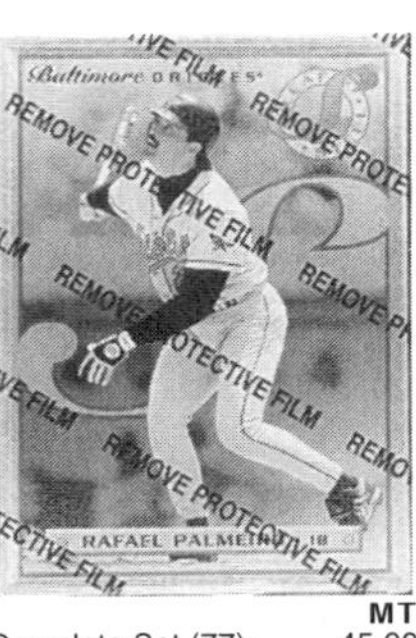

		MT
Complete Set (77):		45.00
Common Player:		.25
Gold:		2X
1	Frank Thomas	2.50
2	Paul Molitor	1.00
3	Kenny Lofton	.25
4	Travis Fryman	.25
5	Jeff Conine	.25
6	Barry Bonds	3.00
7	Gregg Jefferies	.25
8	Alex Rodriguez	4.00
9	Wade Boggs	1.00
10	David Justice	.75
11	Hideo Nomo	1.00
12	Roberto Alomar	1.25
13	Todd Hollandsworth	.25
14	Mark McGwire	5.00
15	Rafael Palmeiro	.60
16	Will Clark	.40
17	Cal Ripken Jr.	5.00
18	Derek Bell	.25
19	Gary Sheffield	.40
20	Juan Gonzalez	1.50
21	Garret Anderson	.25
22	Mo Vaughn	.55
23	Robin Ventura	.25
24	Carlos Baerga	.25
25	Tim Salmon	.40
26	Matt Williams	.40
27	Fred McGriff	.25
28	Rondell White	.25
29	Ray Lankford	.25
30	Lenny Dykstra	.25
31	J.T. Snow	.25
32	Sammy Sosa	3.00
33	Chipper Jones	3.50
34	Bobby Bonilla	.25
35	Paul Wilson	.25
36	Darren Daulton	.25
37	Larry Walker	.35
38	Raul Mondesi	.35
39	Jeff Bagwell	1.50
40	Derek Jeter	4.00
41	Kirby Puckett	2.00
42	Jason Isringhausen	.25
43	Vinny Castilla	.25
44	Jim Edmonds	.35
45	Ron Gant	.25
46	Carlos Delgado	1.00
47	Jose Canseco	.75
48	Tony Gwynn	2.00
49	Mike Mussina	1.00
50	Charles Johnson	.25
51	Mike Piazza	4.00
52	Ken Griffey Jr.	4.00
53	Greg Maddux	3.00
54	Mark Grace	.55
55	Ryan Klesko	.25
56	Dennis Eckersley	.25
57	Rickey Henderson	.75
58	Michael Tucker	.25
59	Joe Carter	.25
60	Randy Johnson	1.25
61	Brian Jordan	.25
62	Shawn Green	.60
63	Roger Clemens	2.00
64	Andres Galarraga	.25
65	Johnny Damon	.35
66	Ryne Sandberg	1.25
67	Alan Benes	.25
68	Albert Belle	.65
69	Barry Larkin	.40
70	Marty Cordova	.25
71	Dante Bichette	.25
72	Craig Biggio	.35
73	Reggie Sanders	.25
74	Moises Alou	.35
75	Chuck Knoblauch	.25
76	Cecil Fielder	.25
77	Manny Ramirez	1.50

1996 Leaf/ Preferred Staremaster

These 1996 Leaf Preferred inserts provide a photographic tribute to the stares of 12 top players. Each card is printed on silver holographic card stock and is numbered up to 2,500.

		MT
Complete Set (12):		175.00
Common Player:		7.50
1	Chipper Jones	20.00
2	Alex Rodriguez	22.50
3	Derek Jeter	20.00
4	Tony Gwynn	16.00
5	Frank Thomas	15.00
6	Ken Griffey Jr.	25.00
7	Cal Ripken Jr.	25.00
8	Greg Maddux	17.50
9	Albert Belle	7.50
10	Barry Bonds	10.00
11	Jeff Bagwell	10.00
12	Mike Piazza	22.50

1996 Leaf/ Preferred Steel Power

This eight-card Leaf Steel insert set combines micro-etched foil with interior die-cutting to honor the game's top power hitters. Each insert card carries a serial number up to 5,000.

		MT
Complete Set (8):		45.00
Common Player:		2.50
1	Albert Belle	2.50
2	Mo Vaughn	3.00
3	Ken Griffey Jr.	10.00

4	Cal Ripken Jr.	12.50
5	Mike Piazza	9.00
6	Barry Bonds	6.00
7	Jeff Bagwell	5.00
8	Frank Thomas	7.50

1996 Leaf/ Signature Series

The base set which rode along with the autographed cards of more than 250 Major League players in Leaf's Signature Series (at least one authentic signature is guaranteed in every pack) feature action photos with silver-foil highlights. Horizontal backs have a large photo along with a few stats and bits of personal data. One out of every 48 packs is a super pack containing nothing but autographed cards. The 150-card base set is paralleled in Gold and Platinum Press Proof insert sets. The gold version is seeded one per 12 packs in Series 1 and one per eight in the Extended Series. Platinums were issued in an edition of 150 of each of the 150 cards and are found only in the Extended Series at the rate of one per 24 packs. Four-card packs of Leaf Signature Series carried a suggested retail price at issue of $9.99.

	MT
Complete Set (150):	60.00
Complete 1st Series (100):	40.00
Complete Extended Series (50):	20.00
Common Player:	.15
Gold PP Stars/Rookies:	10X
Platinum PP Stars/Rookies:	20X
Pack (4):	5.25
Wax Box (12):	50.00

1	Mike Piazza	2.00
2	Juan Gonzalez	1.00
3	Greg Maddux	2.00
4	Marc Newfield	.15
5	Wade Boggs	.65
6	Ray Lankford	.15
7	Frank Thomas	1.50
8	Rico Brogna	.15
9	Tim Salmon	.25
10	Ken Griffey Jr.	2.50
11	Manny Ramirez	1.00
12	Cecil Fielder	.15
13	Gregg Jefferies	.15
14	Rondell White	.25
15	Cal Ripken Jr.	3.00
16	Alex Rodriguez	2.50
17	Bernie Williams	.50
18	Andres Galarraga	.15
19	Mike Mussina	.65
20	Chuck Knoblauch	.15
21	Joe Carter	.15
22	Jeff Bagwell	1.00
23	Mark McGwire	3.00
24	Sammy Sosa	1.50
25	Reggie Sanders	.15
26	Chipper Jones	2.00
27	Jeff Cirillo	.15
28	Roger Clemens	.75
29	Craig Biggio	.25
30	Gary Sheffield	.35
31	Paul O'Neill	.15
32	Johnny Damon	.25
33	Jason Isringhausen	.15
34	Jay Bell	.15
35	Henry Rodriguez	.15
36	Matt Williams	.25
37	Randy Johnson	.60
38	Fred McGriff	.15
39	Jason Giambi	.40
40	Ivan Rodriguez	.60
41	Raul Mondesi	.25
42	Barry Larkin	.25
43	Ryan Klesko	.15
44	Joey Hamilton	.15
45	Todd Hundley	.15
46	Jim Edmonds	.25
47	Dante Bichette	.15
48	Roberto Alomar	.75
49	Mark Grace	.40
50	Brady Anderson	.15
51	Hideo Nomo	.75
52	Ozzie Smith	1.00
53	Robin Ventura	.15
54	Andy Pettitte	.45
55	Kenny Lofton	.15
56	John Mabry	.15
57	Paul Molitor	.55
58	Rey Ordonez	.15
59	Albert Belle	.50
60	Charles Johnson	.15
61	Edgar Martinez	.15
62	Derek Bell	.15
63	Carlos Delgado	.50
64	Raul Casanova	.15
65	Ismael Valdes	.15
66	J.T. Snow	.15
67	Derek Jeter	2.50
68	Jason Kendall	.15
69	John Smoltz	.25
70	Chad Mottola	.15
71	Jim Thome	.15
72	Will Clark	.35
73	Mo Vaughn	.60
74	John Wasdin	.15
75	Rafael Palmeiro	.35
76	Mark Grudzielanek	.15
77	Larry Walker	.25
78	Alan Benes	.15
79	Michael Tucker	.15
80	Billy Wagner	.15
81	Paul Wilson	.15
82	Greg Vaughn	.15
83	Dean Palmer	.15
84	Ryne Sandberg	.75
85	Eric Young	.15
86	Jay Buhner	.15
87	Tony Clark	.15
88	Jermaine Dye	.15
89	Barry Bonds	1.50
90	Ugueth Urbina	.15
91	Charles Nagy	.15
92	Ruben Rivera	.15
93	Todd Hollandsworth	.15
94	*Darin Erstad*	4.00
95	Brooks Kieschnick	.15
96	Edgar Renteria	.15
97	Lenny Dykstra	.15
98	Tony Gwynn	1.50
99	Kirby Puckett	1.00
100	Checklist	.15
101	Andruw Jones	1.00
102	Alex Ochoa	.15
103	David Cone	.15
104	Rusty Greer	.15
105	Jose Canseco	.35
106	Ken Caminiti	.15
107	Mariano Rivera	.40
108	Ron Gant	.15
109	Darryl Strawberry	.15
110	Vladimir Guerrero	1.00
111	George Arias	.15
112	Jeff Conine	.15
113	Bobby Higginson	.15
114	Eric Karros	.15
115	Brian Hunter	.15
116	Eddie Murray	.45
117	Todd Walker	.25
118	Chan Ho Park	.25
119	John Jaha	.15
120	David Justice	.30
121	Makoto Suzuki	.15
122	Scott Rolen	1.00
123	Tino Martinez	.15
124	Kimera Bartee	.15
125	Garret Anderson	.15
126	Brian Jordan	.15
127	Andre Dawson	.25
128	Javier Lopez	.15
129	Bill Pulsipher	.15
130	Dwight Gooden	.15
131	Al Martin	.15
132	Terrell Wade	.15
133	Steve Gibralter	.15
134	Tom Glavine	.25
135	Kevin Appier	.15
136	Tim Raines	.15
137	Curtis Pride	.15
138	Todd Greene	.15
139	Bobby Bonilla	.15
140	Trey Beamon	.15
141	Marty Cordova	.15
142	Rickey Henderson	.50
143	Ellis Burks	.15
144	Dennis Eckersley	.15
145	Kevin Brown	.25
146	Carlos Baerga	.15
147	Brett Butler	.15
148	Marquis Grissom	.15
149	Karim Garcia	.25
150	Checklist	.15

1996 Leaf/ Signature Series Press Proofs

The 150-card base set of Leaf/Signature was paralleled in a pair of Press Proof versions. Identical in format to the regular issue, the Press Proofs have an embossed gold- or platinum-foil oval seal at left and "PRESS PROOF" vertically at right in the same color foil. Backs are identical to the regular version. Gold Press Proofs were inserted one per 12 packs of Series 1 and one per eight packs of Extended. Platinum Proofs are found only in Extended Series packs, at an average rate of one per 24. Total production of Platinum Press proofs was 150 of each card.

	MT
Common Gold:	2.00
Gold Stars:	10X
Common Platinum:	4.00
Platinum Stars:	20X

(See 1996 Leaf/Signature Series for checklist and base card values.)

1996 Leaf/ Signature Series Autographs Promos

To introduce its Autograph Series, Leaf sent dealers one of two promo card versions of the Frank Thomas card. Most received a card with a pre-printed facsimile autograph, duly noted in small type beneath the signature. Others (500) received a genuine Frank Thomas autograph on their promo. All of the cards are marked "PROMOTIONAL CARD" diagonally on both front and back.

	MT
Frank Thomas (facsimile signature)	5.00
Frank Thomas (genuine autograph)	50.00

1996 Leaf/ Signature Series Autographs

Every pack of 1996 Leaf Signature Series includes at least one authentically signed card from one of over 250 players. There were 240 players who signed three versions in these quantities: 500 Gold, 1,000 Silver and 3,500 Bronze. There are also short-printed autographs for 10 players in quantities of 100 Gold, 200 Silver and 700 Bronze. The short-printed players are designated with an "SP" in the checklist. Cards are numbered alphabetically in the checklist since the autographed cards are unnumbered. Each major leaguer signed a notarized affidavit to guarantee each signature was authentic. Series 1 cards of Carlos Delgado, Brian Hunter, Phil Plantier, Jim Thome, Terrell Wade and Ernie Young were signed too late for inclusion in Series 1 packs, and were inserted with Extended. No Bronze cards of Thome were signed.

MT
Complete Bronze Set (251): 800.00
Common Bronze Player: 1.00
Silver: 2X
Gold: 3X-4X
SPs: 100 Gold, 200 Silver, 700 Bronze

(1) Kurt Abbott 2.00
(2) Juan Acevedo 1.00
(3) Terry Adams 1.00
(4) Manny Alexander 1.00
(5) Roberto Alomar (SP) 50.00
(6) Moises Alou 10.00
(7) Wilson Alvarez 2.00
(8) Garret Anderson 2.00
(9) Shane Andrews 2.00
(10) Andy Ashby 2.00
(11) Pedro Astacio 2.00
(12) Brad Ausmus 1.00
(13) Bobby Ayala 1.00
(14) Carlos Baerga 1.00
(15) Harold Baines 5.00
(16) Jason Bates 1.00
(17) Allen Battle 1.00
(18) Rich Becker 1.00
(19) David Bell 1.00
(20) Rafael Belliard 1.00
(21) Andy Benes 2.00
(22) Armando Benitez 1.00
(23) Jason Bere 1.00
(24) Geronimo Berroa 1.00
(25) Willie Blair 1.00
(26) Mike Blowers 1.00
(27) Wade Boggs (SP) 60.00
(28) Ricky Bones 1.00
(29) Mike Bordick 1.00
(30) Toby Borland 1.00
(31) Ricky Bottalico 1.00
(32) Darren Bragg 1.00
(33) Jeff Branson 1.00
(34) Tilson Brito 1.00
(35) Rico Brogna 1.00
(36) Scott Brosius 2.00
(37) Damon Buford 2.00
(38) Mike Busby 1.00
(39) Tom Candiotti 1.00
(40) Frank Castillo 1.00
(41) Andujar Cedeno 1.00
(42) Domingo Cedeno 1.00
(43) Roger Cedeno 3.00
(44) Norm Charlton 1.00
(45) Jeff Cirillo 2.00
(46) Will Clark 10.00
(47) Jeff Conine 3.00
(48) Steve Cooke 2.00
(49) Joey Cora 1.00
(50) Marty Cordova 3.00
(51) Rheal Cormier 1.00
(52) Felipe Crespo 1.00
(53) Chad Curtis 2.00
(54) Johnny Damon 10.00
(55) Russ Davis 1.00
(56) Andre Dawson 15.00
(57a) Carlos Delgado (black autograph) 10.00
(57b) Carlos Delgado (blue autograph) 10.00
(58) Doug Drabek 3.00
(59) Darren Dreifort 2.00
(60) Shawon Dunston 2.00
(61) Ray Durham 3.00
(62) Jim Edmonds 7.50
(63) Joey Eischen 1.00
(64) Jim Eisenreich 1.50
(65) Sal Fasano 1.00
(66) Jeff Fassero 1.00
(67) Alex Fernandez 3.00
(68) Darrin Fletcher 1.00
(69) Chad Fonville 1.00
(70) Kevin Foster 1.00
(71) John Franco 1.00
(72) Julio Franco 1.50
(73) Marvin Freeman 1.00
(74) Travis Fryman 3.00
(75) Gary Gaetti 2.00
(76) Carlos Garcia 3.00
(77) Jason Giambi 17.50
(78) Benji Gil 1.00
(79) Greg Gohr 1.00
(80) Chris Gomez 1.00
(81) Leo Gomez 1.00
(82) Tom Goodwin 2.00
(83) Mike Grace 1.00
(84) Mike Greenwell 4.00
(85) Rusty Greer 2.00
(86) Mark Grudzielanek 1.00
(87) Mark Gubicza 3.00
(88) Juan Guzman 2.00
(89) Darryl Hamilton 1.50
(90) Joey Hamilton 2.00
(91) Chris Hammond 1.00
(92) Mike Hampton 5.00
(93) Chris Haney 1.00
(94) Todd Haney 1.00
(95) Erik Hanson 1.00
(96) Pete Harnisch 1.50
(97) LaTroy Hawkins 1.00
(98) Charlie Hayes 1.00
(99) Jimmy Haynes 1.00
(100) Roberto Hernandez 2.00
(101) Bobby Higginson 6.00
(102) Glenallen Hill 1.00
(103) Ken Hill 1.00
(104) Sterling Hitchcock 2.00
(105) Trevor Hoffman 5.00
(106) Dave Hollins 2.00
(107) Dwayne Hosey 1.00
(108) Thomas Howard 1.00
(109) Steve Howe 6.00
(110) John Hudek 1.00
(111) Rex Hudler 1.00
(112) Brian Hunter 1.00
(113) Butch Huskey 4.00
(114) Mark Hutton 1.00
(115) Jason Jacome 1.00
(116) John Jaha 1.00
(117) Reggie Jefferson 1.00
(118) Derek Jeter (SP) 100.00
(119) Bobby Jones 2.00
(120) Todd Jones 1.00
(121) Brian Jordan 2.00
(122) Kevin Jordan 1.00
(123) Jeff Juden 1.00
(124) Ron Karkovice 1.00
(125) Roberto Kelly 1.50
(126) Mark Kiefer 1.00
(127) Brooks Kieschnick 1.00
(128) Jeff King 4.00
(129) Mike Lansing 4.00
(130) Matt Lawton 4.00
(131) Al Leiter 2.00
(132) Mark Leiter 1.00
(133) Curtis Leskanic 2.00
(134) Darren Lewis 1.00
(135) Mark Lewis 1.00
(136) Felipe Lira 1.00
(137) Pat Listach 1.00
(138) Keith Lockhart 1.00
(139) Kenny Lofton (SP) 15.00
(140) John Mabry 1.00
(141) Mike Macfarlane 1.00
(142) Kirt Manwaring 1.00
(143) Al Martin 2.00
(144) Norberto Martin 1.00
(145) Dennis Martinez 5.00
(146) Pedro Martinez 45.00
(147) Sandy Martinez 1.00
(148) Mike Matheny 1.00
(149) T.J. Mathews 1.00
(150) David McCarty 1.00
(151) Ben McDonald 2.00
(152) Pat Meares 1.00
(153) Orlando Merced 2.00
(154) Jose Mesa 3.00
(155) Matt Mieske 2.00
(156) Orlando Miller 2.00
(157) Mike Mimbs 1.00
(158) Paul Molitor (SP) 30.00
(159) Raul Mondesi (SP) 15.00
(160) Jeff Montgomery 2.00
(161) Mickey Morandini 1.00
(162) Lyle Mouton 1.00
(163) James Mouton 1.00
(164) Jamie Moyer 1.00
(165) Rodney Myers 1.00
(166) Denny Neagle 1.00
(167) Robb Nen 1.00
(168) Marc Newfield 1.00
(169) Dave Nilsson 1.00
(170) Jon Nunnally 2.00
(171) Chad Ogea 1.00
(172) Troy O'Leary 1.00
(173) Rey Ordonez 7.50
(174) Jayhawk Owens 1.00
(175) Tom Pagnozzi 1.00
(176) Dean Palmer 2.00
(177) Roger Pavlik 1.00
(178) Troy Percival 2.00
(179) Carlos Perez 1.00
(180) Robert Perez 1.00
(181) Andy Pettitte 15.00
(182) Phil Plantier 1.00
(183) Mike Potts 1.00
(184) Curtis Pride 1.50
(185) Ariel Prieto 1.00
(186) Bill Pulsipher 1.00
(187) Brad Radke 6.00
(188) Manny Ramirez (SP) 25.00
(189) Joe Randa 1.00
(190) Pat Rapp 1.00
(191) Bryan Rekar 1.00
(192) Shane Reynolds 2.00
(193) Arthur Rhodes 1.00
(194) Mariano Rivera 17.50
(195a) Alex Rodriguez (SP, black autograph) 60.00
(195b) Alex Rodriguez (SP, blue autograph) 60.00
(196) Frank Rodriguez 1.00
(197) Mel Rojas 1.00
(198) Ken Ryan 1.00
(199) Bret Saberhagen 4.00
(200) Tim Salmon 4.00
(201) Rey Sanchez 2.00
(202) Scott Sanders 1.00
(203) Steve Scarsone 1.00
(204) Curt Schilling 6.00
(205) Jason Schmidt 1.00
(206) David Segui 1.00
(207) Kevin Seitzer 1.00
(208) Scott Servais 1.00
(209) Don Slaught 1.00
(210) Zane Smith 1.00
(211) Paul Sorrento 1.00
(212) Scott Stahoviak 1.00
(213) Mike Stanley 1.00
(214) Terry Steinbach 1.00
(215) Kevin Stocker 1.00
(216) Jeff Suppan 1.00
(217) Bill Swift 1.00
(218) Greg Swindell 1.00
(219) Kevin Tapani 2.00
(220) Danny Tartabull 1.00
(221) Julian Tavarez 1.00
(222a) Frank Thomas (SP) (blue autograph) 50.00
(222b) Frank Thomas (SP) (black autograph) 50.00
(223) Jim Thome (SP) (Silver) 20.00
(224) Ozzie Timmons 1.00
(225a) Michael Tucker (black autograph) 2.00
(225b) Michael Tucker (blue autograph) 2.00
(226) Ismael Valdez 2.00
(227) Jose Valentin 1.00
(228) Todd Van Poppel 2.00
(229) Mo Vaughn (SP) 30.00
(230) Quilvio Veras 1.00
(231) Fernando Vina 1.00
(232) Joe Vitiello 1.50
(233) Jose Vizcaino 1.00
(234) Omar Vizquel 5.00
(235) Terrell Wade 1.00
(236) Paul Wagner 1.00
(237) Matt Walbeck 1.00
(238) Jerome Walton 1.00
(239) Turner Ward 1.00
(240) Allen Watson 1.00
(241) David Weathers 1.00
(242) Walt Weiss 1.00
(244) Turk Wendell 2.00
(244) Rondell White 3.00
(245) Brian Williams 1.00
(246) George Williams 1.00
(247) Paul Wilson 1.00
(248) Bobby Witt 1.00
(249) Bob Wolcott 1.00
(250) Eric Young 1.50
(251) Ernie Young 1.00
(252) Greg Zaun 1.00
--- Frank Thomas (Autographed jumbo edition of 1,500) 30.00

1996 Leaf/ Signature Series Extended Autographs

Signature Series Exended Autograph cards comprise 30 short-printed stars and top prospects, and 187 other major leaguers. Most players signed 5,000 cards each, while other signees' totals are listed in parentheses. Signature cards for Alex Rodriguez, Juan Gonzalez and Andruw Jones were only available through mail-in redemption. Autographed cards were a different design from Series 1 and were seeded two per pack in Extended. The unnumbered cards are checklisted here in alphabetical order.

MT
Complete Set (217): 1000.
Common Player: 1.00
Extended Box: 150.00

(1) Scott Aldred 1.00
(2) Mike Aldrete 1.00
(3) Rich Amaral 1.00
(4) Alex Arias 1.00
(5) Paul Assenmacher 1.00
(6) Roger Bailey 1.00
(7) Erik Bennett 1.00
(8) Sean Bergman 1.00
(9) Doug Bochtler 1.00
(10) Tim Bogar 1.00
(11) Pat Borders 1.00
(12) Pedro Borbon 1.00
(13) Shawn Boskie 1.00
(14) Rafael Bournigal 1.00
(15) Mark Brandenburg 1.00
(16) John Briscoe 1.00
(17) Jorge Brito 1.00
(18) Doug Brocail 1.00
(19) Jay Buhner (SP, 1000) 10.00
(20) Scott Bullett 1.00
(21) Dave Burba 1.00

(22) Ken Caminiti (SP, 1000) 10.00
(23) John Cangelosi 1.00
(24) Cris Carpenter 1.00
(25) Chuck Carr 1.00
(26) Larry Casian 1.00
(27) Tony Castillo 1.00
(28) Jason Christiansen 1.00
(29) Archi Cianfrocco 3.00
(30) Mark Clark 1.00
(31) Terry Clark 1.00
(32) Roger Clemens (SP, 1000) 40.00
(33) Jim Converse 1.00
(34) Dennis Cook 2.00
(35) Francisco Cordova 2.00
(36) Jim Corsi 1.00
(37) Tim Crabtree 1.00
(38) Doug Creek (SP, 1950) 3.00
(39) John Cummings 1.00
(40) Omar Daal 2.50
(41) Rich DeLucia 1.00
(42) Mark Dewey 1.00
(43) Alex Diaz 1.00
(44) Jermaine Dye (SP, 2500) 6.00
(45) Ken Edenfield 1.00
(46) Mark Eichhorn 1.00
(47) John Ericks 1.00
(48) Darin Erstad 10.00
(49) Alvaro Espinoza 1.00
(50) Jorge Fabregas 1.00
(51) Mike Fetters 1.00
(52) John Flaherty 1.00
(53) Bryce Florie 1.00
(54) Tony Fossas 1.00
(55) Lou Frazier 1.00
(56) Mike Gallego 1.00
(57) Karim Garcia (SP, 2500) 10.00
(58) Jason Giambi 15.00
(59) Ed Giovanola 1.00
(60) Tom Glavine (SP, 1250) 15.00
(61) Juan Gonzalez (SP, 1000) 30.00
(61) Juan Gonzalez (redemption card) 5.00
(62) Craig Grebeck 1.00
(63) Buddy Groom 1.00
(64) Kevin Gross 1.00
(65) Eddie Guardado 1.00
(66) Mark Guthrie 1.00
(67) Tony Gwynn (SP, 1000) 35.00
(68) Chip Hale 1.00
(69) Darren Hall 1.00
(70) Lee Hancock 1.00
(71) Dave Hansen 1.00
(72) Bryan Harvey 1.00
(73) Bill Haselman 1.00
(74) Mike Henneman 1.00
(75) Doug Henry 1.00
(76) Gil Heredia 1.00
(77) Carlos Hernandez 1.00
(78) Jose Hernandez 1.00
(79) Darren Holmes 1.00
(80) Mark Holzemer 1.00
(81) Rick Honeycutt 1.00
(82) Chris Hook 1.00
(83) Chris Howard 1.00
(84) Jack Howell 1.00
(85) David Hulse 1.00
(86) Edwin Hurtado 1.00
(87) Jeff Huson 1.00
(88) Mike James 1.00
(89) Derek Jeter (SP, 1000) 100.00
(90) Brian Johnson 1.00
(91) Randy Johnson (SP, 1000) 25.00
(92) Mark Johnson 1.00
(93) Andruw Jones (SP, 2000) 15.00
(93) Andruw Jones (redemption card) 5.00
(94) Chris Jones 1.00
(95) Ricky Jordan 1.00
(96) Matt Karchner 1.00
(97) Scott Karl 1.00
(98) Jason Kendall (SP, 2500) 7.50
(99) Brian Keyser 1.00
(100) Mike Kingery 1.00
(101) Wayne Kirby 1.00
(102) Ryan Klesko (SP, 1000) 6.00
(103) Chuck Knoblauch (SP, 1000) 10.00
(104) Chad Kreuter 1.00
(105) Tom Lampkin 1.00
(106) Scott Leius 1.00
(107) Jon Lieber 2.00
(108) Nelson Liriano 1.00
(109) Scott Livingstone 1.00
(110) Graeme Lloyd 1.00
(111) Kenny Lofton (SP, 1000) 10.00
(112) Luis Lopez 1.00
(113) Torey Lovullo 1.00
(114) Greg Maddux (SP, 500) 125.00
(115) Mike Maddux 1.00
(116) Dave Magadan 1.00
(117) Mike Magnante 1.00
(118) Joe Magrane 1.00
(119) Pat Mahomes 1.00
(120) Matt Mantei 1.00
(121) John Marzano 1.00
(122) Terry Matthews 1.00
(123) Chuck McElroy 1.00
(124) Fred McGriff (SP, 1000) 10.00
(125) Mark McLemore 1.00
(126) Greg McMichael 1.00
(127) Blas Minor 1.00
(128) Dave Mlicki 1.00
(129) Mike Mohler 1.00
(130) Paul Molitor (SP, 1000) 25.00
(131) Steve Montgomery 1.00
(132) Mike Mordecai 1.00
(133) Mike Morgan 1.00
(134) Mike Munoz 1.00
(135) Greg Myers 1.00
(136) Jimmy Myers 1.00
(137) Mike Myers 1.00
(138) Bob Natal 1.00
(139) Dan Naulty 1.00
(140) Jeff Nelson 1.00
(141) Warren Newson 1.00
(142) Chris Nichting 1.00
(143) Melvin Nieves 1.00
(144) Charlie O'Brien 1.00
(145) Alex Ochoa 3.00
(146) Omar Olivares 1.00
(147) Joe Oliver 1.00
(148) Lance Painter 1.00
(149) Rafael Palmeiro (SP, 2000) 10.00
(150) Mark Parent 1.00
(151) Steve Parris (SP, 1800) 6.00
(152) Bob Patterson 1.00
(153) Tony Pena 1.00
(154) Eddie Perez 1.00
(155) Yorkis Perez 1.00
(156) Robert Person 3.00
(157) Mark Petkovsek 2.00
(158) Andy Pettitte (SP, 1000) 25.00
(159) J.R. Phillips 1.00
(160) Hipolito Pichardo 1.00
(161) Eric Plunk 1.00
(162) Jimmy Poole 1.00
(163) Kirby Puckett (SP, 1000) 45.00
(164) Paul Quantrill 1.00
(165) Tom Quinlan 1.00
(166) Jeff Reboulet 1.00
(167) Jeff Reed 1.00
(168) Steve Reed 1.00
(169) Carlos Reyes 1.00
(170) Bill Risley 1.00
(171) Kevin Ritz 1.00
(172) Kevin Roberson 1.00
(173) Rich Robertson 1.00
(174) Alex Rodriguez (SP, 500) 150.00
(174) Alex Rodriguez (redemption card) 20.00
(175) Ivan Rodriguez (SP, 1250) 25.00
(176) Bruce Ruffin 1.00
(177) Juan Samuel 1.00
(178) Tim Scott 1.00
(179) Kevin Sefcik 1.00
(180) Jeff Shaw 4.00
(181) Danny Sheaffer 1.00
(182) Craig Shipley 1.00
(183) Dave Silvestri 1.00
(184) Aaron Small 1.00
(185) John Smoltz (SP, 1000) 10.00
(186) Luis Sojo 1.00
(187) Sammy Sosa (SP, 1000) 250.00
(188) Steve Sparks 1.00
(189) Tim Spehr 1.00
(190) Russ Springer 1.00
(191) Matt Stairs 1.00
(192) Andy Stankiewicz 1.00
(193) Mike Stanton 1.00
(194) Kelly Stinnett 1.00
(195) Doug Strange 1.00
(196) Mark Sweeney 1.00
(197) Jeff Tabaka 1.00
(198) Jesus Tavarez 1.00
(199) Frank Thomas (SP, 1000) 50.00
(200) Larry Thomas 1.00
(201) Mark Thompson 1.00
(202) Mike Timlin 1.00
(203) Steve Trachsel 2.00
(204) Tom Urbani 1.00
(205) Julio Valera 1.00
(206) Dave Valle 1.00
(207) William VanLandingham 1.00
(208) Mo Vaughn (SP, 1000) 25.00
(209) Dave Veres 1.00
(210) Ed Vosberg 1.00
(211) Don Wengert 1.00
(212) Matt Whiteside 1.00
(213) Bob Wickman 1.00
(214) Matt Williams (SP, 1250) 10.00
(215) Mike Williams 1.00
(216) Woody Williams 1.00
(217) Craig Worthington 1.00
--- Frank Thomas (Autographed jumbo edition of 1,500) 50.00

1996 Leaf/ Signature Extended Autographs - Century Marks

Century Marks represent the first 100 autographs by the 30 short-printed stars and prospects, plus Alex Ochoa. These are designated with a blue holographic foil "Century Marks" logo. Cards of Gonzalez, Jeter, Andruw Jones, Palmeiro and Alex Rodriguez were available only via mail-in redemption cards.

	MT
Common Player:	10.00
(1) Jay Buhner	10.00
(2) Ken Caminiti	10.00
(3) Roger Clemens	75.00
(4) Jermaine Dye	10.00
(5) Darin Erstad	20.00
(6) Karim Garcia	10.00
(7) Jason Giambi	25.00
(8) Tom Glavine	12.50
(9) Juan Gonzalez	35.00
(9) Juan Gonzalez (redemption card)	12.50
(10) Tony Gwynn	65.00
(11) Derek Jeter	125.00
(11) Derek Jeter (redemption card)	15.00
(12) Randy Johnson	40.00
(13) Andruw Jones	50.00
(13) Andruw Jones (redemption card)	7.50
(14) Jason Kendall	10.00
(15) Ryan Klesko	10.00
(16) Chuck Knoblauch	10.00
(17) Kenny Lofton	10.00
(18) Greg Maddux	100.00
(19) Fred McGriff	10.00
(20) Paul Molitor	30.00
(21) Alex Ochoa	10.00
(22) Rafael Palmeiro	10.00
(22) Rafael Palmeiro (redemption card)	2.50
(23) Andy Pettitte	12.50
(24) Kirby Puckett	65.00
(25) Alex Rodriguez	135.00
(25) Alex Rodriguez (redemption card)	20.00
(26) Ivan Rodriguez	30.00
(27) John Smoltz	12.50
(28) Sammy Sosa	200.00
(29) Frank Thomas	45.00
(30) Mo Vaughn	20.00
(31) Matt Williams	15.00

1997 Leaf

Leaf produced a 400-card set in two series in 1997. The cards feature a grey border with the player photo vignetted at center. The player's name, team and a Leaf logo are displayed at bottom in silver foil. A team logo is in the upper-right corner. Besides the base cards, 10-card packs retailing for $2.99 could contain one of the following inserts: Banner Season, Dress for Success, Get-A-Grip, Knot-hole Gang, Statistical Standouts, Fractal Matrix or Fractal Matrix Die-cut.

	MT
Complete Set (400):	40.00
Common Player:	.10
Jackie Robinson 1948 Leaf Reprint:	12.00
Series 1 Pack (12):	2.00
Series 1 Wax Box (18):	30.00
Series 2 Pack (12):	2.00
Series 2 Wax Box (24):	40.00
1 Wade Boggs	.45
2 Brian McRae	.10
3 Jeff D'Amico	.10
4 George Arias	.10
5 Billy Wagner	.10
6 Ray Lankford	.10
7 Will Clark	.25

No.	Player	Value
8	Edgar Renteria	.10
9	Alex Ochoa	.10
10	Roberto Hernandez	.10
11	Joe Carter	.10
12	Gregg Jefferies	.10
13	Mark Grace	.30
14	Roberto Alomar	.75
15	Joe Randa	.10
16	Alex Rodriguez	3.00
17	Tony Gwynn	1.25
18	Steve Gibralter	.10
19	Scott Stahoviak	.10
20	Matt Williams	.25
21	Quinton McCracken	.10
22	Ugueth Urbina	.10
23	Jermaine Allensworth	.10
24	Paul Molitor	.40
25	Carlos Delgado	.40
26	Bob Abreu	.10
27	John Jaha	.10
28	Rusty Greer	.10
29	Kimera Bartee	.10
30	Ruben Rivera	.10
31	Jason Kendall	.10
32	Lance Johnson	.10
33	Robin Ventura	.10
34	Kevin Appier	.10
35	John Mabry	.10
36	Ricky Otero	.10
37	Mike Lansing	.10
38	Mark McGwire	3.00
39	Tim Naehring	.10
40	Tom Glavine	.20
41	Rey Ordonez	.15
42	Tony Clark	.10
43	Rafael Palmeiro	.25
44	Pedro Martinez	.30
45	Keith Lockhart	.10
46	Dan Wilson	.10
47	John Wetteland	.10
48	Chan Ho Park	.25
49	Gary Sheffield	.40
50	Shawn Estes	.10
51	Royce Clayton	.10
52	Jaime Navarro	.10
53	Raul Casanova	.10
54	Jeff Bagwell	1.00
55	Barry Larkin	.20
56	Charles Nagy	.10
57	Ken Caminiti	.10
58	Todd Hollandsworth	.10
59	Pat Hentgen	.10
60	Jose Valentin	.10
61	Frank Rodriguez	.10
62	Mickey Tettleton	.10
63	Marty Cordova	.10
64	Cecil Fielder	.10
65	Barry Bonds	1.25
66	Scott Servais	.10
67	Ernie Young	.10
68	Wilson Alvarez	.10
69	Mike Grace	.10
70	Shane Reynolds	.10
71	Henry Rodriguez	.10
72	Eric Karros	.10
73	Mark Langston	.10
74	Scott Karl	.10
75	Trevor Hoffman	.10
76	Orel Hershiser	.10
77	John Smoltz	.15
78	Raul Mondesi	.25
79	Jeff Brantley	.10
80	Donne Wall	.10
81	Joey Cora	.10
82	Mel Rojas	.10
83	Chad Mottola	.10
84	Omar Vizquel	.10
85	Greg Maddux	2.00
86	Jamey Wright	.10
87	Chuck Finley	.10
88	Brady Anderson	.10
89	Alex Gonzalez	.15
90	Andy Benes	.10
91	Reggie Jefferson	.10
92	Paul O'Neill	.10
93	Javier Lopez	.10
94	Mark Grudzielanek	.10
95	Marc Newfield	.10
96	Kevin Ritz	.10
97	Fred McGriff	.10
98	Dwight Gooden	.10
99	Hideo Nomo	.75
100	Steve Finley	.10
101	Juan Gonzalez	1.00
102	Jay Buhner	.10
103	Paul Wilson	.10
104	Alan Benes	.10
105	Manny Ramirez	1.00
106	Kevin Elster	.10
107	Frank Thomas	1.50
108	Orlando Miller	.10
109	Ramon Martinez	.10
110	Kenny Lofton	.10
111	Bernie Williams	.35
112	Robby Thompson	.10
113	Bernard Gilkey	.10
114	Ray Durham	.10
115	Jeff Cirillo	.10
116	Brian Jordan	.10
117	Rich Becker	.10
118	Al Leiter	.10
119	Mark Johnson	.10
120	Ellis Burks	.10
121	Sammy Sosa	1.50
122	Willie Greene	.10
123	Michael Tucker	.10
124	Eddie Murray	.40
125	Joey Hamilton	.10
126	Antonio Osuna	.10
127	Bobby Higginson	.10
128	Tomas Perez	.10
129	Tim Salmon	.20
130	Mark Wohlers	.10
131	Charles Johnson	.10
132	Randy Johnson	.50
133	Brooks Kieschnick	.10
134	Al Martin	.10
135	Dante Bichette	.10
136	Andy Pettitte	.40
137	Jason Giambi	.25
138	James Baldwin	.10
139	Ben McDonald	.10
140	Shawn Green	.20
141	Geronimo Berroa	.10
142	Jose Offerman	.10
143	Curtis Pride	.10
144	Terrell Wade	.10
145	Ismael Valdes	.10
146	Mike Mussina	.60
147	Mariano Rivera	.30
148	Ken Hill	.10
149	Darin Erstad	1.00
150	Jay Bell	.10
151	Mo Vaughn	.50
152	Ozzie Smith	1.00
153	Jose Mesa	.10
154	Osvaldo Fernandez	.10
155	Vinny Castilla	.10
156	Jason Isringhausen	.15
157	B.J. Surhoff	.10
158	Robert Perez	.10
159	Ron Coomer	.10
160	Darren Oliver	.10
161	Mike Mohler	.10
162	Russ Davis	.10
163	Bret Boone	.15
164	Ricky Bottalico	.10
165	Derek Jeter	2.50
166	Orlando Merced	.10
167	John Valentin	.10
168	Andruw Jones	1.00
169	Angel Echevarria	.10
170	Todd Walker	.25
171	Desi Relaford	.10
172	Trey Beamon	.10
173	*Brian Giles*	1.50
174	Scott Rolen	.75
175	Shannon Stewart	.10
176	Dmitri Young	.10
177	Justin Thompson	.10
178	Trot Nixon	.10
179	Josh Booty	.10
180	Robin Jennings	.10
181	Marvin Benard	.10
182	Luis Castillo	.10
183	Wendell Magee	.10
184	Vladimir Guerrero	1.00
185	Nomar Garciaparra	1.50
186	Ryan Hancock	.10
187	Mike Cameron	.10
188	Cal Ripken Jr. (Legacy)	1.50
189	Chipper Jones (Legacy)	1.00
190	Albert Belle (Legacy)	.25
191	Mike Piazza (Legacy)	1.00
192	Chuck Knoblauch (Legacy)	.10
193	Ken Griffey Jr. (Legacy)	1.50
194	Ivan Rodriguez (Legacy)	.25
195	Jose Canseco (Legacy)	.20
196	Ryne Sandberg (Legacy)	.35
197	Jim Thome (Legacy)	.10
198	Andy Pettitte (Checklist)	.25
199	Andruw Jones (Checklist)	.50
200	Derek Jeter (Checklist)	.60
201	Chipper Jones	2.00
202	Albert Belle	.50
203	Mike Piazza	2.00
204	Ken Griffey Jr.	3.00
205	Ryne Sandberg	.75
206	Jose Canseco	.35
207	Chili Davis	.10
208	Roger Clemens	1.00
209	Deion Sanders	.15
210	Darryl Hamilton	.10
211	Jermaine Dye	.10
212	Matt Williams	.25
213	Kevin Elster	.10
214	John Wetteland	.10
215	Garret Anderson	.10
216	Kevin Brown	.10
217	Matt Lawton	.10
218	Cal Ripken Jr.	3.00
219	Moises Alou	.15
220	Chuck Knoblauch	.10
221	Ivan Rodriguez	.60
222	Travis Fryman	.10
223	Jim Thome	.10
224	Eddie Murray	.40
225	Eric Young	.10
226	Ron Gant	.10
227	Tony Phillips	.10
228	Reggie Sanders	.10
229	Johnny Damon	.15
230	Bill Pulsipher	.10
231	Jim Edmonds	.10
232	Melvin Nieves	.10
233	Ryan Klesko	.10
234	David Cone	.10
235	Derek Bell	.10
236	Julio Franco	.10
237	Juan Guzman	.10
238	Larry Walker	.25
239	Delino DeShields	.10
240	Troy Percival	.10
241	Andres Galarraga	.10
242	Rondell White	.15
243	John Burkett	.10
244	J.T. Snow	.10
245	Alex Fernandez	.10
246	Edgar Martinez	.10
247	Craig Biggio	.15
248	Todd Hundley	.10
249	Jimmy Key	.10
250	Cliff Floyd	.10
251	Jeff Conine	.10
252	Curt Schilling	.15
253	Jeff King	.10
254	Tino Martinez	.10
255	Carlos Baerga	.10
256	Jeff Fassero	.10
257	Dean Palmer	.10
258	Robb Nen	.10
259	Sandy Alomar Jr.	.10
260	Carlos Perez	.10
261	Rickey Henderson	.45
262	Bobby Bonilla	.10
263	Darren Daulton	.10
264	Jim Leyritz	.10
265	Dennis Martinez	.10
266	Butch Huskey	.10
267	Joe Vitiello	.10
268	Steve Trachsel	.10
269	Glenallen Hill	.10
270	Terry Steinbach	.10
271	Mark McLemore	.10
272	Devon White	.10
273	Jeff Kent	.10
274	Tim Raines	.10
275	Carlos Garcia	.10
276	Hal Morris	.10
277	Gary Gaetti	.10
278	John Olerud	.10
279	Wally Joyner	.10
280	Brian Hunter	.10
281	Steve Karsay	.10
282	Denny Neagle	.10
283	Jose Herrera	.10
284	Todd Stottlemyre	.10
285	Bip Roberts	.10
286	Kevin Seitzer	.10
287	Benji Gil	.10
288	Dennis Eckersley	.10
289	Brad Ausmus	.10
290	Otis Nixon	.10
291	Darryl Strawberry	.10
292	Marquis Grissom	.10
293	Darryl Kile	.10
294	Quilvio Veras	.10
295	Tom Goodwin	.10
296	Benito Santiago	.10
297	Mike Bordick	.10
298	Roberto Kelly	.10
299	David Justice	.20
300	Carl Everett	.15
301	Mark Whiten	.10
302	Aaron Sele	.10
303	Darren Dreifort	.10
304	Bobby Jones	.10
305	Fernando Vina	.10
306	Ed Sprague	.10
307	Andy Ashby	.10
308	Tony Fernandez	.10
309	Roger Pavlik	.10
310	Mark Clark	.10
311	Mariano Duncan	.10
312	Tyler Houston	.10
313	Eric Davis	.10
314	Greg Vaughn	.10
315	David Segul	.10
316	Dave Nilsson	.10
317	F.P. Santangelo	.10
318	Wilton Guerrero	.10
319	Jose Guillen	.50
320	Kevin Orie	.10
321	Derrek Lee	.10
322	*Bubba Trammell*	.50
323	Pokey Reese	.10
324	*Hideki Irabu*	.50
325	Scott Spiezio	.10
326	Bartolo Colon	.10
327	Damon Mashore	.10
328	Ryan McGuire	.10
329	Chris Carpenter	.10
330	*Jose Cruz Jr.*	.75
331	Todd Greene	.10
332	Brian Moehler	.10
333	Mike Sweeney	.10
334	Neifi Perez	.10
335	Matt Morris	.10
336	Marvin Benard	.10
337	Karim Garcia	.10
338	Jason Dickson	.10
339	Brant Brown	.10
340	Jeff Suppan	.10
341	*Deivi Cruz*	.50
342	Antone Williamson	.10
343	Curtis Goodwin	.10
344	Brooks Kieschnick	.10
345	*Tony Womack*	.50
346	Rudy Pemberton	.10
347	Todd Dunwoody	.10
348	Frank Thomas (Legacy)	.75
349	Andruw Jones (Legacy)	.50
350	Alex Rodriguez (Legacy)	1.50
351	Greg Maddux (Legacy)	1.00
352	Jeff Bagwell (Legacy)	.50
353	Juan Gonzalez (Legacy)	.40
354	Barry Bonds (Legacy)	.75
355	Mark McGwire (Legacy)	1.50
356	Tony Gwynn (Legacy)	.60
357	Gary Sheffield (Legacy)	.20
358	Derek Jeter (Legacy)	1.25
359	Manny Ramirez (Legacy)	.50
360	Hideo Nomo (Legacy)	.35
361	Sammy Sosa (Legacy)	.75
362	Paul Molitor (Legacy)	.20
363	Kenny Lofton (Legacy)	.10
364	Eddie Murray (Legacy)	.20

365 Barry Larkin (Legacy) .10
366 Roger Clemens (Legacy) .50
367 John Smoltz (Legacy) .10
368 Alex Rodriguez (Gamers) 1.50
369 Frank Thomas (Gamers) .75
370 Cal Ripken Jr. (Gamers) 1.50
371 Ken Griffey Jr. (Gamers) 1.50
372 Greg Maddux (Gamers) 1.00
373 Mike Piazza (Gamers) 1.00
374 Chipper Jones (Gamers) 1.00
375 Albert Belle (Gamers) .25
376 Chuck Knoblauch (Gamers) .10
377 Brady Anderson (Gamers) .10
378 David Justice (Gamers) .10
379 Randy Johnson (Gamers) .20
380 Wade Boggs (Gamers) .15
381 Kevin Brown (Gamers) .10
382 Tom Glavine (Gamers) .10
383 Raul Mondesi (Gamers) .10
384 Ivan Rodriguez (Gamers) .30
385 Larry Walker (Gamers) .10
386 Bernie Williams (Gamers) .15
387 Rusty Greer (Gamers) .10
388 Rafael Palmeiro (Gamers) .10
389 Matt Williams (Gamers) .15
390 Eric Young (Gamers) .10
391 Fred McGriff (Gamers) .10
392 Ken Caminiti (Gamers) .10
393 Roberto Alomar (Gamers) .30
394 Brian Jordan (Gamers) .10
395 Mark Grace (Gamers) .10
396 Jim Edmonds (Gamers) .10
397 Deion Sanders (Gamers) .10
398 Checklist (Vladimir Guerrero) .50
399 Checklist (Darin Erstad) .40
400 Checklist (Nomar Garciaparra) .75

1997 Leaf Fractal Matrix

Leaf introduced Fractal Matrix inserts, a 400-card parallel set broken down into three colors and three unique die-cuts. One "fracture" breaks the insert set down by foil background color (80 Gold, 120 Silver and 200 Bronze). A second fracture breaks those cards down into X, Y and Z "axis" variations. There are no markings on the cards to segregate the X, Y and Z groups, though that information was printed on the box bottoms. No production numbers or insert ratios were released for either fracture. Each player is available in only one color/axis combination. The incredibly convoluted nature of the issue insured that virtually nobody understood the concept, putting a damper on collector interest.

	MT
Common Bronze:	.50
Common Silver:	.75
Common Gold:	2.00

1 Wade Boggs G/Y 7.50
2 Brian McRae B/Y .50
3 Jeff D'Amico B/Y .50
4 George Arias S/Y .75
5 Billy Wagner S/Y .75
6 Ray Lankford B/Z .50
7 Will Clark S/Y 1.25
8 Edgar Renteria S/Y .75
9 Alex Ochoa S/Y .75
10 Roberto Hernandez B/X 1.00
11 Joe Carter S/Y .75
12 Gregg Jefferies B/Y .50
13 Mark Grace S/Y 1.50
14 Roberto Alomar G/Y 12.00
15 Joe Randa B/X .50
16 Alex Rodriguez G/Z 15.00
17 Tony Gwynn G/Z 8.00
18 Steve Gibralter B/Y .50
19 Scott Stahoviak B/X .50
20 Matt Williams S/Z 1.25
21 Quinton McCracken B/Y .50
22 Ugueth Urbina B/X .50
23 Jermaine Allensworth S/X .75
24 Paul Molitor G/X 9.00
25 Carlos Delgado S/Y 1.50
26 Bob Abreu S/Y 1.00
27 John Jaha S/Y .75
28 Rusty Greer S/Z .75
29 Kimera Bartee B/X .50
30 Ruben Rivera S/Y .75
31 Jason Kendall S/Y 1.00
32 Lance Johnson B/X .50
33 Robin Ventura B/Y .50
34 Kevin Appier S/X .75
35 John Mabry S/Y .75
36 Ricky Otero B/X .50
37 Mike Lansing B/X .50
38 Mark McGwire G/Z 17.00
39 Tim Naehring B/X .50
40 Tom Glavine S/Z 1.25
41 Rey Ordonez S/Y 1.25
42 Tony Clark S/Y 1.50
43 Rafael Palmeiro S/Z 1.25
44 Pedro Martinez B/X 1.00
45 Keith Lockhart B/X .50
46 Dan Wilson B/Y .50
47 John Wetteland B/Y .50
48 Chan Ho Park B/X .75
49 Gary Sheffield G/Z 3.00
50 Shawn Estes B/X .50
51 Royce Clayton B/X .50
52 Jaime Navarro B/X .50
53 Raul Casanova B/X .50
54 Jeff Bagwell G/Z 7.00
55 Barry Larkin G/X 3.00
56 Charles Nagy B/Y .50
57 Ken Caminiti G/Y 2.50
58 Todd Hollandsworth S/Z .75
59 Pat Hentgen S/X .75
60 Jose Valentin B/X .50
61 Frank Rodriguez B/X .50
62 Mickey Tettleton B/X .50
63 Marty Cordova G/X 3.00
64 Cecil Fielder S/X .75
65 Barry Bonds G/Z 10.00
66 Scott Servais B/X .50
67 Ernie Young B/X .50
68 Wilson Alvarez B/X .50
69 Mike Grace B/X .50
70 Shane Reynolds S/X .75
71 Henry Rodriguez S/Y .75
72 Eric Karros B/X .50
73 Mark Langston B/X .50
74 Scott Karl B/X .50
75 Trevor Hoffman B/X .50
76 Orel Hershiser S/X .75
77 John Smoltz G/Y 5.00
78 Raul Mondesi G/Z 3.00
79 Jeff Brantley B/X .50
80 Donne Wall B/X .50
81 Joey Cora B/X .50
82 Mel Rojas B/X .50
83 Chad Mottola B/X .50
84 Omar Vizquel B/X .50
85 Greg Maddux G/Z 13.50
86 Jamey Wright S/Y 1.00
87 Chuck Finley B/X .50
88 Brady Anderson G/Y 4.00
89 Alex Gonzalez S/X 1.00
90 Andy Benes B/X .50
91 Reggie Jefferson B/X .50
92 Paul O'Neill B/Y .50
93 Javier Lopez S/X .75
94 Mark Grudzielanek S/X .75
95 Marc Newfield B/X .50
96 Kevin Ritz B/X .50
97 Fred McGriff G/Y 4.00
98 Dwight Gooden S/X .75
99 Hideo Nomo S/Y 4.00
100 Steve Finley B/X .50
101 Juan Gonzalez G/Z 7.00
102 Jay Buhner S/Z .75
103 Paul Wilson S/Y .75
104 Alan Benes B/Y .50
105 Manny Ramirez G/Z 5.00
106 Kevin Elster B/X .50
107 Frank Thomas G/Z 7.00
108 Orlando Miller B/X .50
109 Ramon Martinez B/X .50
110 Kenny Lofton G/Z 2.00
111 Bernie Williams G/Y 10.00
112 Robby Thompson B/X .50
113 Bernard Gilkey B/Z .50
114 Ray Durham B/X .50
115 Jeff Cirillo S/Z .75
116 Brian Jordan G/Z 2.00
117 Rich Becker S/Y .75
118 Al Leiter B/X .50
119 Mark Johnson B/X .50
120 Ellis Burks B/Y .50
121 Sammy Sosa G/Z 9.00
122 Willie Greene B/X .50
123 Michael Tucker B/X .50
124 Eddie Murray G/Y 9.00
125 Joey Hamilton S/Y .75
126 Antonio Osuna B/X .50
127 Bobby Higginson S/Y .75
128 Tomas Perez B/X .50
129 Tim Salmon G/Z 2.50
130 Mark Wohlers B/X .50
131 Charles Johnson S/X .75
132 Randy Johnson S/Y 2.50
133 Brooks Kieschnick S/X .75
134 Al Martin S/Y .75
135 Dante Bichette B/X 1.00
136 Andy Pettitte G/Z 7.00
137 Jason Giambi G/Y 10.00
138 James Baldwin S/X .75
139 Ben McDonald B/X .50
140 Shawn Green S/X 2.00
141 Geronimo Berroa B/Y .50
142 Jose Offerman B/X .50
143 Curtis Pride B/X .50
144 Terrell Wade B/X .50
145 Ismael Valdes S/X .75
146 Mike Mussina S/Y 4.00
147 Mariano Rivera S/X 5.00
148 Ken Hill B/Y .50
149 Darin Erstad G/Z 8.00
150 Jay Bell B/X .50
151 Mo Vaughn G/Z 5.00
152 Ozzie Smith G/Y 12.00
153 Jose Mesa B/X .50
154 Osvaldo Fernandez B/X .50
155 Vinny Castilla B/Y .50
156 Jason Isringhausen S/Y 1.00
157 B.J. Surhoff B/X .50
158 Robert Perez B/X .50
159 Ron Coomer B/X .50
160 Darren Oliver B/X .50
161 Mike Mohler B/X .50
162 Russ Davis B/X .50
163 Bret Boone B/X .50
164 Ricky Bottalico B/X .50
165 Derek Jeter G/Z 12.00
166 Orlando Merced B/X .50
167 John Valentin B/X .50
168 Andruw Jones G/Z 10.00
169 Angel Echevarria B/X .50
170 Todd Walker G/Z 3.00
171 Desi Relaford B/Y .50
172 Trey Beamon S/X .75
173 Brian Giles S/Y 1.00
174 Scott Rolen G/Z 7.00
175 Shannon Stewart S/Z .75
176 Dmitri Young G/Z 2.00
177 Justin Thompson B/X .50
178 Trot Nixon S/Y .75
179 Josh Booty S/Y .75
180 Robin Jennings B/X .50
181 Marvin Benard B/X .50
182 Luis Castillo B/Y .50
183 Wendell Magee B/X .50
184 Vladimir Guerrero G/X 8.00
185 Nomar Garciaparra G/X 11.00
186 Ryan Hancock B/X .50
187 Mike Cameron S/X 1.00
188 Cal Ripken Jr. B/Z (Legacy) 6.50
189 Chipper Jones S/Z (Legacy) 6.00
190 Albert Belle S/Z (Legacy) 2.50
191 Mike Piazza B/Z (Legacy) 5.50
192 Chuck Knoblauch S/Y (Legacy) .75
193 Ken Griffey Jr. B/Z (Legacy) 6.50
194 Ivan Rodriguez G/Z (Legacy) 3.50
195 Jose Canseco S/X (Legacy) 2.50
196 Ryne Sandberg S/X (Legacy) 5.00
197 Jim Thome G/Y (Legacy) 2.00
198 Checklist (Andy Pettitte B/Y) 2.00
199 Checklist (Andruw Jones B/Y) 4.00
200 Checklist (Derek Jeter S/Y) 7.50
201 Chipper Jones G/X 11.00
202 Albert Belle G/Y 4.00
203 Mike Piazza G/Y 40.00
204 Ken Griffey Jr. G/X 25.00
205 Ryne Sandberg G/Z 3.00
206 Jose Canseco S/Y 1.00
207 Chili Davis B/X .50
208 Roger Clemens G/Z 4.00

209 Deion Sanders G/Z 2.00
210 Darryl Hamilton B/X .50
211 Jermaine Dye S/X .75
212 Matt Williams G/Y 2.50
213 Kevin Elster B/X .50
214 John Wetteland S/X .75
215 Garret Anderson G/Z 2.00
216 Kevin Brown G/Y 2.50
217 Matt Lawton S/Y .75
218 Cal Ripken Jr. G/X 22.50
219 Moises Alou G/Y 4.00
220 Chuck Knoblauch G/Z 2.00
221 Ivan Rodriguez G/Y 8.00
222 Travis Fryman B/Y .50
223 Jim Thome G/Z 2.00
224 Eddie Murray S/Z 2.00
225 Eric Young G/Z 2.00
226 Ron Gant S/X .75
227 Tony Phillips B/X .50
228 Reggie Sanders B/Y .50
229 Johnny Damon S/Z .75
230 Bill Pulsipher B/X .50
231 Jim Edmonds G/Z 3.00
232 Melvin Nieves B/X .50
233 Ryan Klesko G/Z 2.00
234 David Cone S/X .75
235 Derek Bell B/Y .50
236 Julio Franco S/X .75
237 Juan Guzman B/X .50
238 Larry Walker G/Z 2.50
239 Delino DeShields B/X .50
240 Troy Percival B/Y .50
241 Andres Galarraga G/Z 2.00
242 Rondell White G/Z 2.00
243 John Burkett B/X .50
244 J.T. Snow B/Y .50
245 Alex Fernandez S/Y .75
246 Edgar Martinez G/Z 2.00
247 Craig Biggio G/Z 2.00
248 Todd Hundley G/Y 2.50
249 Jimmy Key S/X .75
250 Cliff Floyd B/Y .50
251 Jeff Conine B/Y .50
252 Curt Schilling B/X .65
253 Jeff King B/X .50
254 Tino Martinez G/Z 2.00
255 Carlos Baerga S/Y .75
256 Jeff Fassero B/Y .50
257 Dean Palmer S/Y .75
258 Robb Nen B/X .50
259 Sandy Alomar Jr. S/Y .75
260 Carlos Perez B/X .50
261 Rickey Henderson S/Y 2.00
262 Bobby Bonilla S/Y .75
263 Darren Daulton B/X .50
264 Jim Leyritz B/X .50
265 Dennis Martinez B/X .50
266 Butch Huskey B/X .50
267 Joe Vitiello S/Y .75
268 Steve Trachsel B/X .50
269 Glenallen Hill B/X .50
270 Terry Steinbach B/X .50
271 Mark McLemore B/X .50
272 Devon White B/X .50
273 Jeff Kent B/X .50
274 Tim Raines B/X .50
275 Carlos Garcia B/X .50
276 Hal Morris B/X .50
277 Gary Gaetti B/X .50
278 John Olerud S/Y .75
279 Wally Joyner B/X .50
280 Brian Hunter S/X .75
281 Steve Karsay B/X .50
282 Denny Neagle S/X .75
283 Jose Herrera B/X .50
284 Todd Stottlemyre B/X .50
285 Bip Roberts S/X .75
286 Kevin Seitzer B/X .50
287 Benji Gil B/X .50
288 Dennis Eckersley S/X .75
289 Brad Ausmus B/X .50
290 Otis Nixon B/X .50
291 Darryl Strawberry B/X .50
292 Marquis Grissom S/Y .75
293 Darryl Kile B/X .50
294 Quilvio Veras B/X .50
295 Tom Goodwin B/X .50
296 Benito Santiago B/X .50
297 Mike Bordick B/X .50
298 Roberto Kelly B/X .50
299 David Justice G/Z 2.50
300 Carl Everett B/X .65
301 Mark Whiten B/X .50
302 Aaron Sele B/X .50
303 Darren Dreifort B/X .50
304 Bobby Jones B/X .50
305 Fernando Vina B/X .50
306 Ed Sprague B/X .50
307 Andy Ashby S/X .75
308 Tony Fernandez B/X .50
309 Roger Pavlik B/X .50
310 Mark Clark B/X .50
311 Mariano Duncan B/X .50
312 Tyler Houston B/X .50
313 Eric Davis S/Y .75
314 Greg Vaughn B/Y .50
315 David Segui S/Y .75
316 Dave Nilsson S/X .75
317 F.P. Santangelo S/X .75
318 Wilton Guerrero G/Z 2.00
319 Jose Guillen G/Z 2.50
320 Kevin Orie S/Y .75
321 Derrek Lee G/Z 2.00
322 Bubba Trammell S/Y 2.00
323 Pokey Reese G/Z 2.00
324 Hideki Irabu G/X 3.00
325 Scott Spiezio S/Z .75
326 Bartolo Colon G/Z 2.00
327 Damon Mashore S/Y .75
328 Ryan McGuire S/Y .75
329 Chris Carpenter B/X .50
330 Jose Cruz, Jr. G/X 3.50
331 Todd Greene S/Z 1.00
332 Brian Moehler B/X .50
333 Mike Sweeney B/Y .50
334 Neifi Perez G/Z 2.00
335 Matt Morris S/Y 1.00
336 Marvin Benard B/Y .50
337 Karim Garcia S/Z .75
338 Jason Dickson S/Y .75
339 Brant Brown S/Y .75
340 Jeff Suppan S/Z .75
341 Deivi Cruz B/X .50
342 Antone Williamson G/Z 2.00
343 Curtis Goodwin B/X .50
344 Brooks Kieschnick S/Y .75
345 Tony Womack B/X .50
346 Rudy Pemberton B/X .50
347 Todd Dunwoody B/X .50
348 Frank Thomas S/Y (Legacy) 3.00
349 Andruw Jones S/X (Legacy) 3.00
350 Alex Rodriguez B/Y (Legacy) 6.50
351 Greg Maddux S/Y (Legacy) 5.00
352 Jeff Bagwell B/Y (Legacy) 4.50
353 Juan Gonzalez S/Y (Legacy) 3.00
354 Barry Bonds B/Y (Legacy) 5.00
355 Mark McGwire B/Y (Legacy) 6.50
356 Tony Gwynn B/Y (Legacy) 4.50
357 Gary Sheffield B/X (Legacy) 1.00
358 Derek Jeter S/X (Legacy) 5.00
359 Manny Ramirez S/Y (Legacy) 2.00
360 Hideo Nomo G/Z (Legacy) 4.00
361 Sammy Sosa B/X (Legacy) 5.00
362 Paul Molitor S/Z (Legacy) 1.00
363 Kenny Lofton B/Y (Legacy) .50
364 Eddie Murray B/X (Legacy) 1.25
365 Barry Larkin S/Z (Legacy) .75
366 Roger Clemens S/Y (Legacy) 2.50
367 John Smoltz B/Z (Legacy) .50
368 Alex Rodriguez S/X (Gamers) 5.00
369 Frank Thomas B/X (Gamers) 3.50
370 Cal Ripken Jr. S/Y (Gamers) 6.00
371 Ken Griffey Jr. S/Y (Gamers) 5.00
372 Greg Maddux B/X (Gamers) 4.00
373 Mike Piazza S/X (Gamers) 4.00
374 Chipper Jones B/Y (Gamers) 4.50
375 Albert Belle B/X (Gamers) 1.00
376 Chuck Knoblauch B/X (Gamers) .50
377 Brady Anderson B/Z (Gamers) .50
378 David Justice S/X (Gamers) 1.00
379 Randy Johnson B/Z (Gamers) 1.75
380 Wade Boggs B/X (Gamers) 1.00
381 Kevin Brown B/X (Gamers) .50
382 Tom Glavine G/Y (Gamers) 2.50
383 Raul Mondesi S/X (Gamers) .75
384 Ivan Rodriguez S/X (Gamers) 1.25
385 Larry Walker B/Y (Gamers) 1.00
386 Bernie Williams B/Z (Gamers) .75
387 Rusty Greer G/Y (Gamers) 2.50
388 Rafael Palmeiro G/Y (Gamers) 2.50
389 Matt Williams B/X (Gamers) 1.00
390 Eric Young B/X (Gamers) .50
391 Fred McGriff B/X (Gamers) .50
392 Ken Caminiti B/X (Gamers) .50
393 Roberto Alomar B/Z (Gamers) 1.75
394 Brian Jordan B/X (Gamers) .50
395 Mark Grace G/Z (Gamers) 2.50
396 Jim Edmonds B/Y (Gamers) .65
397 Deion Sanders S/Y (Gamers) .75
398 Checklist (Vladimir Guerrero S/Z) 2.00
399 Checklist (Darin Erstad S/Y) 2.50
400 Checklist (Nomar Garciaparra S/Z) 3.00

1997 Leaf Fractal Matrix Die-Cut

A second parallel set to the Leaf product, the Fractal Matrix Die-Cuts offer three different die-cut designs with three colors for each. The Axis-X die-cuts comprise 200 players (150 Bronze, 40 Silver and 10 Gold), the Axis-Y die-cuts has 120 players (60 Silver, 40 Bronze, 20 Gold), and the Axis-Z die-cuts consist of 80 players (50 Gold, 20 Silver, 10 Bronze). Odds of finding any of these inserts are 1:6 packs. Each player was issued in only one color/cut combination.

	MT
Common X-Axis:	1.00
Common Y-Axis:	1.25
Common Z-Axis:	2.00

1 Wade Boggs G/Y 7.00
2 Brian McRae B/Y 1.25
3 Jeff D'Amico B/Y 1.25
4 George Arias S/Y 1.25
5 Billy Wagner S/Y 1.25
6 Ray Lankford B/Z 2.00
7 Will Clark S/Y 2.00
8 Edgar Renteria S/Y 1.25
9 Alex Ochoa S/Y 1.25
11 Joe Carter S/Y 1.25
12 Gregg Jefferies B/Y 1.25
13 Mark Grace S/Y 2.00
14 Roberto Alomar G/Y 7.00
15 Joe Randa B/X 1.00
16 Alex Rodriguez G/Z 25.00
17 Tony Gwynn G/Z 15.00
18 Steve Gibralter B/Y 1.25
19 Scott Stahoviak B/X 1.00
20 Matt Williams S/Z 3.00
21 Quinton McCracken B/Y 1.25
22 Ugueth Urbina B/X 1.00
23 Jermaine Allensworth S/X 1.00
24 Paul Molitor G/X 4.50
25 Carlos Delgado S/Y 2.00
26 Bob Abreu S/Y 1.25
27 John Jaha S/Y 1.25
28 Rusty Greer S/Z 2.00
29 Kimera Bartee B/X 1.00
30 Ruben Rivera S/Y 1.25
31 Jason Kendall S/Y 1.25
32 Lance Johnson B/X 1.00
33 Robin Ventura B/Y 1.25
34 Kevin Appier S/X 1.00
35 John Mabry S/Y 1.25
36 Ricky Otero B/X 1.00
37 Mike Lansing B/X 1.00
38 Mark McGwire G/Z 25.00
39 Tim Naehring B/X 1.00
40 Tom Glavine S/Z 2.50
41 Rey Ordonez S/Y 1.25
42 Tony Clark S/Y 1.25
43 Rafael Palmeiro S/Z 2.50
44 Pedro Martinez B/X 3.00
45 Keith Lockhart B/X 1.00
46 Dan Wilson B/Y 1.25
47 John Wetteland B/Y 1.25
48 Chan Ho Park B/X 2.50
49 Gary Sheffield G/Z 6.00
50 Shawn Estes B/X 1.00
51 Royce Clayton B/X 1.00
52 Jaime Navarro B/X 1.00
53 Raul Casanova B/X 1.00
54 Jeff Bagwell G/Z 15.00
55 Barry Larkin G/X 3.00
56 Charles Nagy B/Y 1.25
57 Ken Caminiti G/Y 2.00
58 Todd Hollandsworth S/Z 2.00
59 Pat Hentgen S/X 1.00
60 Jose Valentin B/X 1.00
61 Frank Rodriguez B/X 1.00
62 Mickey Tettleton B/X 1.00
63 Marty Cordova G/X 2.00
64 Cecil Fielder S/X 1.00
65 Barry Bonds G/Z 12.00

66 Scott Servais B/X 1.00
67 Ernie Young B/X 1.00
68 Wilson Alvarez B/X 1.00
69 Mike Grace B/X 1.00
70 Shane Reynolds S/X 1.00
71 Henry Rodriguez S/Y 1.25
72 Eric Karros B/X 1.00
73 Mark Langston B/X 1.00
74 Scott Karl B/X 1.00
75 Trevor Hoffman B/X 1.00
76 Orel Hershiser S/X 1.00
77 John Smoltz G/Y 4.00
78 Raul Mondesi G/Z 2.50
79 Jeff Brantley B/X 1.00
80 Donne Wall B/X 1.00
81 Joey Cora B/X 1.00
82 Mel Rojas B/X 1.00
83 Chad Mottola B/X 1.00
84 Omar Vizquel B/X 1.00
85 Greg Maddux G/Z 18.00
86 Jamey Wright S/Y 1.25
87 Chuck Finley B/X 1.00
88 Brady Anderson G/Y 1.25
89 Alex Gonzalez S/X 1.50
90 Andy Benes B/X 1.00
91 Reggie Jefferson B/X 1.00
92 Paul O'Neill B/Y 1.25
93 Javier Lopez S/X 1.00
94 Mark Grudzielanek S/X 1.00
95 Marc Newfield B/X 1.00
96 Kevin Ritz B/X 1.00
97 Fred McGriff G/Y 2.00
98 Dwight Gooden S/X 1.00
99 Hideo Nomo S/Y 5.00
100 Steve Finley B/X 1.00
101 Juan Gonzalez G/Z 12.00
102 Jay Buhner S/Z 2.00
103 Paul Wilson S/Y 1.25
104 Alan Benes B/Y 1.25
105 Manny Ramirez G/Z 6.00
106 Kevin Elster B/X 1.00
107 Frank Thomas G/Z 15.00
108 Orlando Miller B/X 1.00
109 Ramon Martinez B/X 1.00
110 Kenny Lofton G/Z 2.00
111 Bernie Williams G/Y 5.00
112 Robby Thompson B/X 1.00
113 Bernard Gilkey B/Z 2.00
114 Ray Durham B/X 1.00
115 Jeff Cirillo S/Z 2.00
116 Brian Jordan G/Z 2.00
117 Rich Becker S/Y 1.25
118 Al Leiter B/X 1.00
119 Mark Johnson B/X 1.00
120 Ellis Burks B/Y 1.25
121 Sammy Sosa G/Z 15.00
122 Willie Greene B/X 1.00
123 Michael Tucker B/X 1.00
124 Eddie Murray G/Y 4.00
125 Joey Hamilton S/Y 1.25
126 Antonio Osuna B/X 1.00
127 Bobby Higginson S/Y 1.25
128 Tomas Perez B/X 1.00
129 Tim Salmon G/Z 4.00
130 Mark Wohlers B/X 1.00
131 Charles Johnson S/X 1.00
132 Randy Johnson S/Y 4.00
133 Brooks Kieschnick S/X 1.00
134 Al Martin S/Y 1.25
135 Dante Bichette B/X 1.50
136 Andy Pettitte G/Z 4.00
137 Jason Giambi G/Y 5.00
138 James Baldwin S/X 1.00
139 Ben McDonald B/X 1.00
140 Shawn Green S/X 2.50
141 Geronimo Berroa B/Y 1.25
142 Jose Offerman B/X 1.00
143 Curtis Pride B/X 1.00
144 Terrell Wade B/X 1.00
145 Ismael Valdes S/X 1.00
146 Mike Mussina S/Y 4.00
147 Mariano Rivera S/X 3.00
148 Ken Hill B/Y 1.25
149 Darin Erstad G/Z 10.00
150 Jay Bell B/X 1.00
151 Mo Vaughn G/Z 5.00
152 Ozzie Smith G/Y 8.00
153 Jose Mesa B/X 1.00
154 Osvaldo Fernandez B/X 1.00
155 Vinny Castilla B/Y 1.25
156 Jason Isringhausen S/Y 1.50
157 B.J. Surhoff B/X 1.00
158 Robert Perez B/X 1.00
159 Ron Coomer B/X 1.00
160 Darren Oliver B/X 1.00
161 Mike Mohler B/X 1.00
162 Russ Davis B/X 1.00
163 Bret Boone B/X 1.00
164 Ricky Bottalico B/X 1.00
165 Derek Jeter G/Z 20.00
166 Orlando Merced B/X 1.00
167 John Valentin B/X 1.00
168 Andruw Jones G/Z 12.00
169 Angel Echevarria B/X 1.00
170 Todd Walker G/Z 2.50
171 Desi Relaford B/Y 1.25
172 Trey Beamon S/X 1.00
173 Brian Giles S/Y 1.25
174 Scott Rolen G/Z 6.00
175 Shannon Stewart S/Z 2.00
176 Dmitri Young G/Z 2.00
177 Justin Thompson B/X 1.00
178 Trot Nixon S/Y 1.25
179 Josh Booty S/Y 1.25
180 Robin Jennings B/X 1.00
181 Marvin Benard B/X 1.00
182 Luis Castillo B/Y 1.25
183 Wendell Magee B/X 1.00
184 Vladimir Guerrero G/X 5.00
185 Nomar Garciaparra G/X 8.00
186 Ryan Hancock B/X 1.00
187 Mike Cameron S/X 1.00
188 Cal Ripken Jr. B/Z (Legacy) 25.00
189 Chipper Jones S/Z (Legacy) 20.00
190 Albert Belle S/Z (Legacy) 3.00
191 Mike Piazza B/Z (Legacy) 20.00
192 Chuck Knoblauch S/Y (Legacy) 1.25
193 Ken Griffey Jr. B/Z (Legacy) 25.00
194 Ivan Rodriguez G/Z (Legacy) 4.00
195 Jose Canseco S/X (Legacy) 2.00
196 Ryne Sandberg S/X (Legacy) 4.00
197 Jim Thome G/Y (Legacy) 2.00
198 Checklist (Andy Pettitte B/Y) 4.00
199 Checklist (Andruw Jones B/Y) 4.00
200 Checklist (Derek Jeter S/Y) 12.00
201 Chipper Jones G/X 12.00
202 Albert Belle G/Y 4.00
203 Mike Piazza G/Y 20.00
204 Ken Griffey Jr. G/X 20.00
205 Ryne Sandberg G/Z 8.00
206 Jose Canseco S/Y 2.00
207 Chili Davis B/X 1.00
208 Roger Clemens G/Z 10.00
209 Deion Sanders G/Z 2.50
210 Darryl Hamilton B/X 1.00
211 Jermaine Dye S/X 1.00
212 Matt Williams G/Y 3.50
213 Kevin Elster B/X 1.00
214 John Wetteland S/X 1.00
215 Garret Anderson G/Z 2.00
216 Kevin Brown G/Y 1.25
217 Matt Lawton S/Y 1.25
218 Cal Ripken Jr. G/X 20.00
219 Moises Alou G/Y 1.50
220 Chuck Knoblauch G/Z 2.00
221 Ivan Rodriguez G/Y 5.00
222 Travis Fryman B/Y 1.25
223 Jim Thome G/Z 2.00
224 Eddie Murray S/Z 5.00
225 Eric Young G/Z 2.00
226 Ron Gant S/X 1.00
227 Tony Phillips B/X 1.00
228 Reggie Sanders B/Y 1.25
229 Johnny Damon S/Z 2.00
230 Bill Pulsipher B/X 1.00
231 Jim Edmonds G/Z 4.50
232 Melvin Nieves B/X 1.00
233 Ryan Klesko G/Z 2.00
234 David Cone S/X 1.00
235 Derek Bell B/Y 1.25
236 Julio Franco S/X 1.00
237 Juan Guzman B/X 1.00
238 Larry Walker G/Z 4.00
239 Delino DeShields B/X 1.00
240 Troy Percival B/Y 1.25
241 Andres Galarraga G/Z 2.00
242 Rondell White G/Z 2.00
243 John Burkett B/X 1.00
244 J.T. Snow B/Y 1.25
245 Alex Fernandez S/Y 1.25
246 Edgar Martinez G/Z 2.00
247 Craig Biggio G/Z 3.00
248 Todd Hundley G/Y 3.00
249 Jimmy Key S/X 1.00
250 Cliff Floyd B/Y 1.25
251 Jeff Conine B/Y 1.25
252 Curt Schilling B/X 1.25
253 Jeff King B/X 1.00
254 Tino Martinez G/Z 2.00
255 Carlos Baerga S/Y 1.25
256 Jeff Fassero B/Y 1.25
257 Dean Palmer S/Y 1.25
258 Robb Nen B/X 1.00
259 Sandy Alomar Jr. S/Y 1.25
260 Carlos Perez B/X 1.00
261 Rickey Henderson S/Y 3.00
262 Bobby Bonilla S/Y 1.25
263 Darren Daulton B/X 1.00
264 Jim Leyritz B/X 1.00
265 Dennis Martinez B/X 1.00
266 Butch Huskey B/X 1.00
267 Joe Vitiello S/Y 1.25
268 Steve Trachsel B/X 1.00
269 Glenallen Hill B/X 1.00
270 Terry Steinbach B/X 1.00
271 Mark McLemore B/X 1.00
272 Devon White B/X 1.00
273 Jeff Kent B/X 1.00
274 Tim Raines B/X 1.00
275 Carlos Garcia B/X 1.00
276 Hal Morris B/X 1.00
277 Gary Gaetti B/X 1.00
278 John Olerud S/Y 1.25
279 Wally Joyner B/X 1.00
280 Brian Hunter S/X 1.00
281 Steve Karsay B/X 1.00
282 Denny Neagle S/X 1.00
283 Jose Herrera B/X 1.00
284 Todd Stottlemyre B/X 1.00
285 Bip Roberts S/X 1.00
286 Kevin Seitzer B/X 1.00
287 Benji Gil B/X 1.00
288 Dennis Eckersley S/X 1.00
289 Brad Ausmus B/X 1.00
290 Otis Nixon B/X 1.00
291 Darryl Strawberry B/X 1.00
292 Marquis Grissom S/Y 1.25
293 Darryl Kile B/X 1.00
294 Quilvio Veras B/X 1.00
295 Tom Goodwin B/X 1.00
296 Benito Santiago B/X 1.00
297 Mike Bordick B/X 1.00
298 Roberto Kelly B/X 1.00
299 David Justice G/Z 4.50
300 Carl Everett B/X 1.25
301 Mark Whiten B/X 1.00
302 Aaron Sele B/X 1.00
303 Darren Dreifort B/X 1.00
304 Bobby Jones B/X 1.00
305 Fernando Vina B/X 1.00
306 Ed Sprague B/X 1.00
307 Andy Ashby S/X 1.00
308 Tony Fernandez B/X 1.00
309 Roger Pavlik B/X 1.00
310 Mark Clark B/X 1.00
311 Mariano Duncan B/X 1.00
312 Tyler Houston B/X 1.00
313 Eric Davis S/Y 1.25
314 Greg Vaughn B/Y 1.25
315 David Segui S/Y 1.25
316 Dave Nilsson S/X 1.00
317 F.P. Santangelo S/X 1.00
318 Wilton Guerrero G/Z 2.00
319 Jose Guillen G/Z 7.00
320 Kevin Orie S/Y 1.25
321 Derrek Lee G/Z 2.00
322 Bubba Trammell S/Y 3.00
323 Pokey Reese G/Z 2.00
324 Hideki Irabu G/X 4.00
325 Scott Spiezio S/Z 2.00
326 Bartolo Colon G/Z 3.00
327 Damon Mashore S/Y 1.25
328 Ryan McGuire S/Y 1.25
329 Chris Carpenter B/X 1.00
330 Jose Cruz, Jr. G/X 4.50
331 Todd Greene S/Z 3.00
332 Brian Moehler B/X 1.00
333 Mike Sweeney B/Y 1.25
334 Neifi Perez G/Z 2.00
335 Matt Morris S/Y 1.50
336 Marvin Benard B/Y 1.25
337 Karim Garcia S/Z 2.00
338 Jason Dickson S/Y 1.25
339 Brant Brown S/Y 1.25
340 Jeff Suppan S/Z 2.00
341 Deivi Cruz B/X 1.00
342 Antone Williamson G/Z 2.00
343 Curtis Goodwin B/X 1.00
344 Brooks Kieschnick S/Y 1.25
345 Tony Womack B/X 1.00
346 Rudy Pemberton B/X 1.00
347 Todd Dunwoody B/X 1.00
348 Frank Thomas S/Y (Legacy) 7.00
349 Andruw Jones S/X (Legacy) 4.00
350 Alex Rodriguez B/Y (Legacy) 12.00
351 Greg Maddux S/Y (Legacy) 10.00
352 Jeff Bagwell B/Y (Legacy) 7.00
353 Juan Gonzalez S/Y (Legacy) 5.00
354 Barry Bonds B/Y (Legacy) 5.00
355 Mark McGwire B/Y (Legacy) 15.00
356 Tony Gwynn B/Y (Legacy) 7.00
357 Gary Sheffield B/X (Legacy) 1.25
358 Derek Jeter S/X (Legacy) 7.50
359 Manny Ramirez S/Y (Legacy) 4.50
360 Hideo Nomo G/Z (Legacy) 5.00
361 Sammy Sosa B/X (Legacy) 5.00
362 Paul Molitor S/Z (Legacy) 3.00

363	Kenny Lofton B/Y (Legacy)	1.25
364	Eddie Murray B/X (Legacy)	1.50
365	Barry Larkin S/Z (Legacy)	2.00
366	Roger Clemens S/Y (Legacy)	5.00
367	John Smoltz B/Z (Legacy)	2.00
368	Alex Rodriguez S/X (Gamers)	7.00
369	Frank Thomas B/X (Gamers)	4.00
370	Cal Ripken Jr. S/Y (Gamers)	12.00
371	Ken Griffey Jr. S/Y (Gamers)	15.00
372	Greg Maddux B/X (Gamers)	4.00
373	Mike Piazza S/X (Gamers)	7.00
374	Chipper Jones B/Y (Gamers)	10.00
375	Albert Belle B/X (Gamers)	1.50
376	Chuck Knoblauch B/X (Gamers)	1.00
377	Brady Anderson B/Z (Gamers)	2.00
378	David Justice S/X (Gamers)	1.25
379	Randy Johnson B/Z (Gamers)	4.00
380	Wade Boggs B/X (Gamers)	1.50
381	Kevin Brown B/X (Gamers)	1.25
382	Tom Glavine G/Y (Gamers)	3.00
383	Raul Mondesi S/X (Gamers)	1.25
384	Ivan Rodriguez S/X (Gamers)	3.00
385	Larry Walker B/Y (Gamers)	2.00
386	Bernie Williams B/Z (Gamers)	3.00
387	Rusty Greer G/Y (Gamers)	2.00
388	Rafael Palmeiro G/Y (Gamers)	1.50
389	Matt Williams B/X (Gamers)	1.25
390	Eric Young B/X (Gamers)	1.00
391	Fred McGriff B/X (Gamers)	1.00
392	Ken Caminiti B/X (Gamers)	1.00
393	Roberto Alomar B/Z (Gamers)	4.00
394	Brian Jordan B/X (Gamers)	1.00
395	Mark Grace G/Z (Gamers)	4.50
396	Jim Edmonds B/Y (Gamers)	1.75
397	Deion Sanders S/Y (Gamers)	1.75
398	Checklist (Vladimir Guerrero S/Z)	3.00
399	Checklist (Darin Erstad S/Y)	3.00
400	Checklist (Nomar Garciaparra S/Z)	4.00

1997 Leaf Banner Season

Banner Season was a 15-card insert set that was die-cut and printed on a canvas card stock. Only 2,500 individually numbered sets were produced, with cards only found in pre-priced packs.

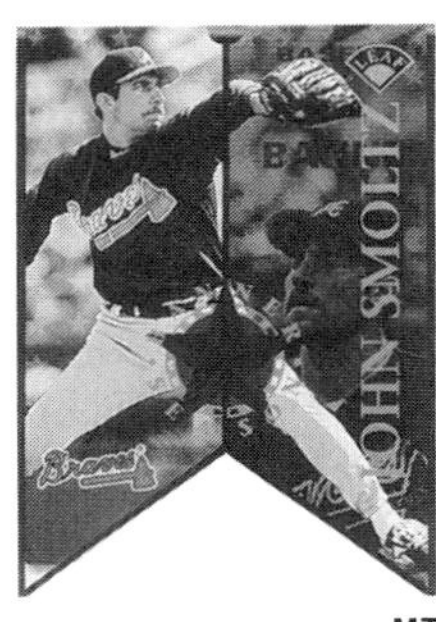

		MT
Complete Set (15):		110.00
Common Player:		1.50
1	Jeff Bagwell	12.00
2	Ken Griffey Jr.	30.00
3	Juan Gonzalez	9.00
4	Frank Thomas	12.00
5	Alex Rodriguez	25.00
6	Kenny Lofton	1.50
7	Chuck Knoblauch	1.50
8	Mo Vaughn	4.00
9	Chipper Jones	20.00
10	Ken Caminiti	1.50
11	Craig Biggio	3.00
12	John Smoltz	2.00
13	Pat Hentgen	1.50
14	Derek Jeter	15.00
15	Todd Hollandsworth	1.50

1997 Leaf Dress for Success

Exclusive to retail packs was an insert called Dress for Success. It included 18 players printed on nylon and flocking card stock. Dress for Success was limited to 3,500 individually numbered sets.

		MT
Complete Set (18):		30.00
Common Player:		.60
1	Greg Maddux	2.50
2	Cal Ripken Jr.	5.00
3	Albert Belle	1.00
4	Frank Thomas	2.50
5	Dante Bichette	.60
6	Gary Sheffield	1.00
7	Jeff Bagwell	2.00
8	Mike Piazza	3.50
9	Mark McGwire	6.00
10	Ken Caminiti	.60
11	Alex Rodriguez	5.00
12	Ken Griffey Jr.	5.00
13	Juan Gonzalez	2.00
14	Brian Jordan	.60
15	Mo Vaughn	1.25
16	Ivan Rodriguez	1.00
17	Andruw Jones	2.00
18	Chipper Jones	3.50

1997 Leaf Get-A-Grip

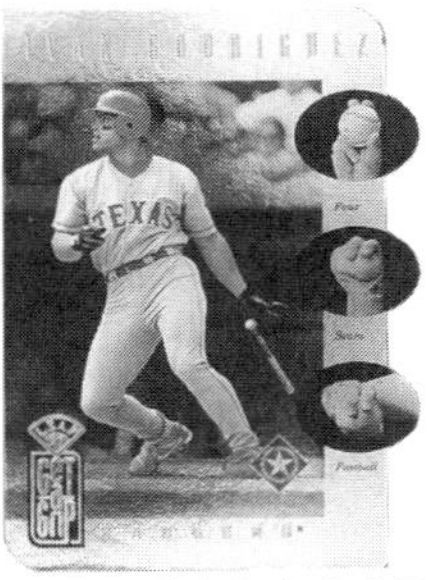

Get a Grip included 16 double-sided cards, with a star hitter on one side and a star pitcher on the other. The card slated the two stars against each other and explained how the hitter would hit against the pitcher, while featuring the pitcher's top pitch. This insert was printed on silver foilboard with the right side die-cut, and limited to 3,500 numbered sets found only in hobby packs.

		MT
Complete Set (16):		50.00
Common Player:		1.25
1	Ken Griffey Jr., Greg Maddux	6.50
2	John Smoltz, Frank Thomas	4.00
3	Mike Piazza, Andy Pettitte	6.50
4	Randy Johnson, Chipper Jones	6.00
5	Tom Glavine, Alex Rodriguez	6.50
6	Pat Hentgen, Jeff Bagwell	2.50
7	Kevin Brown, Juan Gonzalez	2.50
8	Barry Bonds, Mike Mussina	4.00
9	Hideo Nomo, Albert Belle	2.00
10	Troy Percival, Andruw Jones	2.50
11	Roger Clemens, Brian Jordan	4.00
12	Paul Wilson, Ivan Rodriguez	2.00
13	Andy Benes, Mo Vaughn	1.25
14	Al Leiter, Derek Jeter	6.50
15	Bill Pulsipher, Cal Ripken Jr.	7.50
16	Mariano Rivera, Ken Caminiti	1.75

1997 Leaf Knot-Hole Gang

Knot-Hole Gang pictures 12 hitters viewed through a wood picket fence. Cards are die-cut along the top of the fence and printed on a wood stock. Production was limited to 5,000 numbered sets. A "SAMPLE" marked promo card exists for each.

		MT
Complete Set (12):		18.00
Common Player:		.50
Promos:		2X
1	Chuck Knoblauch	.50
2	Ken Griffey Jr.	3.50
3	Frank Thomas	2.50
4	Tony Gwynn	2.00
5	Mike Piazza	3.00
6	Jeff Bagwell	2.00
7	Rusty Greer	.50
8	Cal Ripken Jr.	4.00
9	Chipper Jones	3.00
10	Ryan Klesko	.50
11	Barry Larkin	.75
12	Paul Molitor	1.00

1997 Leaf Leagues of the Nation

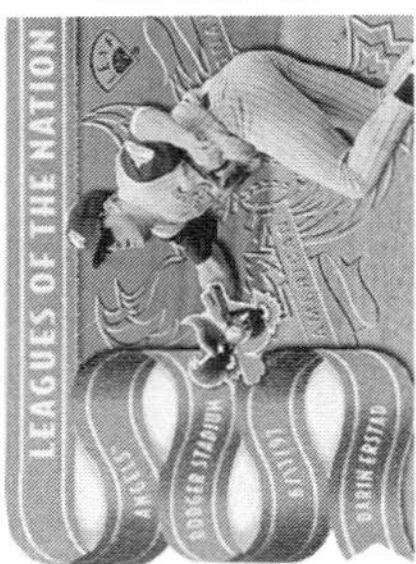

A 15-card insert set featuring a double-sided die-cut design. The players on each card represent matchups from the initial rounds of inter-league play. Cards were numbered to 2,500 and feature a flocked texture.

		MT
Complete Set (15):		110.00
Common Player:		3.00
1	Juan Gonzalez, Barry Bonds	10.00
2	Cal Ripken Jr., Chipper Jones	17.50
3	Mark McGwire, Ken Caminiti	17.50
4	Derek Jeter, Kenny Lofton	15.00
5	Ivan Rodriguez, Mike Piazza	15.00
6	Ken Griffey Jr., Larry Walker	15.00
7	Frank Thomas, Sammy Sosa	15.00
8	Paul Molitor, Barry Larkin	5.00
9	Albert Belle, Deion Sanders	4.00
10	Matt Williams, Jeff Bagwell	7.50
11	Mo Vaughn, Gary Sheffield	4.00

12	Alex Rodriguez, Tony Gwynn	17.50
13	Tino Martinez, Scott Rolen	3.00
14	Darin Erstad, Wilton Guerrero	4.00
15	Tony Clark, Vladimir Guerrero	3.00

1997 Leaf Statistical Standouts

Statistical Standouts were limited to only 1,000 individually numbered sets. Inserts were printed on leather and die-cut. The set included 15 top stars who excelled beyond their competition in many statistical categories.

		MT
Complete Set (15):		130.00
Common Player:		3.25
1	Albert Belle	4.00
2	Juan Gonzalez	5.00
3	Ken Griffey Jr.	17.50
4	Alex Rodriguez	20.00
5	Frank Thomas	10.00
6	Chipper Jones	15.00
7	Greg Maddux	12.00
8	Mike Piazza	15.00
9	Cal Ripken Jr.	20.00
10	Mark McGwire	20.00
11	Barry Bonds	7.50
12	Derek Jeter	15.00
13	Ken Caminiti	3.00
14	John Smoltz	3.00
15	Paul Molitor	4.50

1997 Leaf Thomas Collection

This six-card insert from Series II features pieces of various game-used Frank Thomas items built into the texture of each card. Jerseys, bats, hats, batting gloves and sweatbands are all featured on the various cards, which are numbered to 100 each.

		MT
Complete Set (6):		450.00
Common Card:		75.00
1	Frank Thomas Hat	75.00
2	Frank Thomas Home Jersey	100.00
3	Frank Thomas Batting Glove	75.00
4	Frank Thomas Bat	75.00
5	Frank Thomas Sweatband	75.00
6	Frank Thomas Away Jersey	100.00

1997 Leaf Warning Track

A 12-card insert printed on embossed canvas depicting players who are known for making tough catches. Cards were numbered to 3,500.

		MT
Complete Set (18):		50.00
Common Player:		1.00
1	Ken Griffey Jr.	12.50
2	Albert Belle	2.00
3	Barry Bonds	6.00
4	Andruw Jones	4.00
5	Kenny Lofton	1.00
6	Tony Gwynn	7.50
7	Manny Ramirez	5.00
8	Rusty Greer	1.00
9	Bernie Williams	2.00
10	Gary Sheffield	2.50
11	Juan Gonzalez	4.00
12	Raul Mondesi	2.00
13	Brady Anderson	1.00
14	Rondell White	1.00
15	Sammy Sosa	10.00
16	Deion Sanders	1.50
17	David Justice	1.50
18	Jim Edmonds	1.50

1997 Leaf 22kt Gold Stars

A 36-card insert from Series II Leaf, each card features a special 22kt. gold foil embossed stamp on front which is printed on gold foil cardboard. Horizontal backs have a portrait photo on a dark background and are serially numbered to a limit of 2,500 each.

		MT
Complete Set (36):		290.00
Common Player:		2.50
1	Frank Thomas	15.00
2	Alex Rodriguez	25.00
3	Ken Griffey Jr.	25.00
4	Andruw Jones	10.00
5	Chipper Jones	20.00
6	Jeff Bagwell	12.50
7	Derek Jeter	17.50
8	Deion Sanders	2.50
9	Ivan Rodriguez	7.50
10	Juan Gonzalez	12.50
11	Greg Maddux	15.00
12	Andy Pettitte	5.00
13	Roger Clemens	12.50
14	Hideo Nomo	6.00
15	Tony Gwynn	12.50
16	Barry Bonds	12.50
17	Kenny Lofton	2.50
18	Paul Molitor	6.00
19	Jim Thome	2.50
20	Albert Belle	5.00
21	Cal Ripken Jr.	25.00
22	Mark McGwire	25.00
23	Barry Larkin	3.00
24	Mike Piazza	20.00
25	Darin Erstad	10.00
26	Chuck Knoblauch	2.50
27	Vladimir Guerrero	10.00
28	Tony Clark	2.50
29	Scott Rolen	10.00
30	Nomar Garciaparra	15.00
31	Eric Young	2.50
32	Ryne Sandberg	10.00
33	Roberto Alomar	6.00
34	Eddie Murray	4.00
35	Rafael Palmeiro	3.00
36	Jose Guillen	2.50

1998 Leaf

The 50th Anniversary edition of Leaf Baseball consists of a 200-card base set with three subsets, three parallels and four inserts. The base set has 148 regular cards, a 10-card Curtain Calls subset, Gold Leaf Stars subset (20 cards), Gold Leaf Rookies subset (20 cards) and three checklists. The subsets cards #148-197 are short-printed in relation to the rest of the set. Card #42 does not exist because Leaf retired the number in honor of Jackie Robinson. The base set was paralleled in Fractal Matrix, Fractal Matrix Die-Cuts and Fractal Diamond Axis. Inserts include Crusade, Heading for the Hall, State Representatives and Statistical Standouts.

		MT
Complete Set (200):		200.00
Common Player:		.10
Diamond Axis Stars:		50X
SP Diamond Axis (148-177):		12X
Pack (10):		2.50
Wax Box (24):		50.00
1	Rusty Greer	.10
2	Tino Martinez	.10
3	Bobby Bonilla	.10
4	Jason Giambi	.25
5	Matt Morris	.15
6	Craig Counsell	.10
7	Reggie Jefferson	.10
8	Brian Rose	.10
9	Ruben Rivera	.10
10	Shawn Estes	.10
11	Tony Gwynn	.75
12	Jeff Abbott	.10
13	Jose Cruz Jr.	.20
14	Francisco Cordova	.10
15	Ryan Klesko	.10
16	Tim Salmon	.20
17	Brett Tomko	.10
18	Matt Williams	.25
19	Joe Carter	.10
20	Harold Baines	.10
21	Gary Sheffield	.25
22	Charles Johnson	.10
23	Aaron Boone	.10
24	Eddie Murray	.25
25	Matt Stairs	.10
26	David Cone	.10
27	Jon Nunnally	.10
28	Chris Stynes	.10
29	Enrique Wilson	.10
30	Randy Johnson	.50
31	Garret Anderson	.10
32	Manny Ramirez	.75
33	Jeff Suppan	.10
34	Rickey Henderson	.40
35	Scott Spiezio	.10
36	Rondell White	.10
37	Todd Greene	.20
38	Delino DeShields	.10
39	Kevin Brown	.20
40	Chili Davis	.10
41	Jimmy Key	.10
42	NOT ISSUED	
43	Mike Mussina	.75
44	Joe Randa	.10
45	Chan Ho Park	.25
46	Brad Radke	.15
47	Geronimo Berroa	.10
48	Wade Boggs	.40
49	Kevin Appier	.10
50	Moises Alou	.15
51	David Justice	.25
52	Ivan Rodriguez	.60
53	J.T. Snow	.10
54	Brian Giles	.10
55	Will Clark	.25
56	Justin Thompson	.10
57	Javier Lopez	.10
58	Hideki Irabu	.10
59	Mark Grudzielanek	.10
60	Abraham Nunez	.10
61	Todd Hollandsworth	.10
62	Jay Bell	.10
63	Nomar Garciaparra	1.00
64	Vinny Castilla	.10
65	Lou Collier	.10
66	Kevin Orie	.10
67	John Valentin	.10
68	Robin Ventura	.10
69	Denny Neagle	.10
70	Tony Womack	.10
71	Dennis Reyes	.10
72	Wally Joyner	.10
73	Kevin Brown	.15
74	Ray Durham	.10
75	Mike Cameron	.10
76	Dante Bichette	.10
77	Jose Guillen	.15
78	Carlos Delgado	.50
79	Paul Molitor	.50
80	Jason Kendall	.10

81 Mark Belhorn .10
82 Damian Jackson .10
83 Bill Mueller .10
84 Kevin Young .10
85 Curt Schilling .15
86 Jeffrey Hammonds .10
87 Sandy Alomar Jr. .10
88 Bartolo Colon .10
89 Wilton Guerrero .10
90 Bernie Williams .35
91 Deion Sanders .15
92 Mike Piazza 1.50
93 Butch Huskey .10
94 Edgardo Alfonzo .10
95 Alan Benes .10
96 Craig Biggio .15
97 Mark Grace .20
98 Shawn Green .25
99 Derrek Lee .15
100 Ken Griffey Jr. 2.00
101 Tim Raines .10
102 Pokey Reese .10
103 Lee Stevens .10
104 Shannon Stewart .10
105 John Smoltz .15
106 Frank Thomas 1.00
107 Jeff Fassero .10
108 Jay Buhner .10
109 Jose Canseco .25
110 Omar Vizquel .10
111 Travis Fryman .10
112 Dave Nilsson .10
113 John Olerud .10
114 Larry Walker .20
115 Jim Edmonds .15
116 Bobby Higginson .15
117 Todd Hundley .10
118 Paul O'Neill .10
119 Bip Roberts .10
120 Ismael Valdes .10
121 Pedro Martinez .25
122 Jeff Cirillo .10
123 Andy Benes .10
124 Bobby Jones .10
125 Brian Hunter .10
126 Darryl Kile .10
127 Pat Hentgen .10
128 Marquis Grissom .10
129 Eric Davis .10
130 Chipper Jones 1.50
131 Edgar Martinez .10
132 Andy Pettitte .25
133 Cal Ripken Jr. 2.50
134 Scott Rolen .75
135 Ron Coomer .10
136 Luis Castillo .10
137 Fred McGriff .10
138 Neifi Perez .10
139 Eric Karros .10
140 Alex Fernandez .10
141 Jason Dickson .10
142 Lance Johnson .10
143 Ray Lankford .10
144 Sammy Sosa 1.50
145 Eric Young .10
146 Bubba Trammell .20
147 Todd Walker .20
148 Mo Vaughn (Curtain Calls) 1.50
149 Jeff Bagwell (Curtain Calls) 2.50
150 Kenny Lofton (Curtain Calls) .75
151 Raul Mondesi (Curtain Calls) .75
152 Mike Piazza (Curtain Calls) 5.00
153 Chipper Jones (Curtain Calls) 4.00
154 Larry Walker (Curtain Calls) .75
155 Greg Maddux (Curtain Calls) 5.00
156 Ken Griffey Jr. (Curtain Calls) 6.00
157 Frank Thomas (Curtain Calls) 3.00
158 Darin Erstad (Gold Leaf Stars) 1.50
159 Roberto Alomar (Gold Leaf Stars) 1.00
160 Albert Belle (Gold Leaf Stars) 1.00
161 Jim Thome (Gold Leaf Stars) .75
162 Tony Clark (Gold Leaf Stars) .75
163 Chuck Knoblauch (Gold Leaf Stars) .75
164 Derek Jeter (Gold Leaf Stars) 4.00
165 Alex Rodriguez (Gold Leaf Stars) 4.00
166 Tony Gwynn (Gold Leaf Stars) 3.00
167 Roger Clemens (Gold Leaf Stars) 3.00
168 Barry Larkin (Gold Leaf Stars) .75
169 Andres Galarraga (Gold Leaf Stars) .75
170 Vladimir Guerrero (Gold Leaf Stars) 2.00
171 Mark McGwire (Gold Leaf Stars) 6.00
172 Barry Bonds (Gold Leaf Stars) 2.50
173 Juan Gonzalez (Gold Leaf Stars) 2.50
174 Andruw Jones (Gold Leaf Stars) 2.00
175 Paul Molitor (Gold Leaf Stars) 1.00
176 Hideo Nomo (Gold Leaf Stars) 1.50
177 Cal Ripken Jr. (Gold Leaf Stars) 6.00
178 Brad Fullmer (Gold Leaf Rookies) .75
179 Jaret Wright (Gold Leaf Rookies) 3.00
180 Bobby Estalella (Gold Leaf Rookies) .75
181 Ben Grieve (Gold Leaf Rookies) 2.00
182 Paul Konerko (Gold Leaf Rookies) 1.00
183 David Ortiz (Gold Leaf Rookies) .75
184 Todd Helton (Gold Leaf Rookies) 1.50
185 Juan Encarnacion (Gold Leaf Rookies) .75
186 Miguel Tejada (Gold Leaf Rookies) 1.50
187 Jacob Cruz (Gold Leaf Rookies) .75
188 Mark Kotsay (Gold Leaf Rookies) .75
189 Fernando Tatis (Gold Leaf Rookies) .75
190 Ricky Ledee (Gold Leaf Rookies) .75
191 Richard Hidalgo (Gold Leaf Rookies) 1.00
192 Richie Sexson (Gold Leaf Rookies) .75
193 Luis Ordaz (Gold Leaf Rookies) .75
194 Eli Marrero (Gold Leaf Rookies) .75
195 Livan Hernandez (Gold Leaf Rookies) .75
196 Homer Bush (Gold Leaf Rookies) .75
197 Raul Ibanez (Gold Leaf Rookies) .75
198 Checklist (Nomar Garciaparra) .35
199 Checklist (Scott Rolen) .25
200 Checklist (Jose Cruz Jr.) .10
201 Al Martin .10

1998 Leaf Fractal Matrix

Fractal Matrix is a parallel insert set to 1998 Leaf. Cards have a metallic finish, with 100 done in bronze, 60 in silver and 40 in gold, and each color having some cards in X, Y and Z axis. Stated print runs are: Bronze: X - 1,600; Y - 1,800; Z - 1,900. Silver: X - 600; Y - 800; Z - 900. Gold: X - 100; Y - 300; Z - 400. Each player is found only in a single color/axis combination.

MT

Complete Set (200): 750.00
Common Bronze: .75
Common Silver: 2.50
Common Gold: 5.00
1 Rusty Greer G/Z 5.00
2 Tino Martinez G/Z 5.00
3 Bobby Bonilla S/Y 2.50
4 Jason Giambi S/Y 6.00
5 Matt Morris S/Y 3.00
6 Craig Counsell B/X .75
7 Reggie Jefferson B/X .75
8 Brian Rose S/Y 2.50
9 Ruben Rivera B/X .75
10 Shawn Estes S/Y 2.50
11 Tony Gwynn G/Z 20.00
12 Jeff Abbott B/Y .75
13 Jose Cruz Jr. G/Z 6.50
14 Francisco Cordova B/X .75
15 Ryan Klesko B/X .75
16 Tim Salmon G/Y 7.50
17 Brett Tomko B/X .75
18 Matt Williams S/Y 3.00
19 Joe Carter B/X .75
20 Harold Baines B/X .75
21 Gary Sheffield S/Z 5.00
22 Charles Johnson S/X 2.50
23 Aaron Boone B/X .75
24 Eddie Murray G/Y 7.50
25 Matt Stairs B/X .75
26 David Cone B/X .75
27 Jon Nunnally B/X .75
28 Chris Stynes B/X .75
29 Enrique Wilson B/Y .75
30 Randy Johnson S/Z 7.50
31 Garret Anderson S/Y 2.50
32 Manny Ramirez G/Z 12.50
33 Jeff Suppan S/X 2.50
34 Rickey Henderson B/X 2.00
35 Scott Spiezio B/X .75
36 Rondell White S/Y 2.50
37 Todd Greene S/Z 3.00
38 Delino DeShields B/X .75
39 Kevin Brown S/X 3.00
40 Chili Davis B/X .75
41 Jimmy Key B/X .75
42 NOT ISSUED
43 Mike Mussina G/Y 12.50
44 Joe Randa B/X .75
45 Chan Ho Park S/Z 4.00
46 Brad Radke B/X .75
47 Geronimo Berroa B/X .75
48 Wade Boggs S/Y 7.00
49 Kevin Appier B/X .75
50 Moises Alou S/Y 3.00
51 David Justice G/Y 7.00
52 Ivan Rodriguez G/Z 10.00
53 J.T. Snow B/X .75
54 Brian Giles B/X .75
55 Will Clark B/Y 1.25
56 Justin Thompson S/Y 2.50
57 Javier Lopez S/X 2.50
58 Hideki Irabu B/Z .75
59 Mark Grudzielanek B/X .75
60 Abraham Nunez S/X 2.50
61 Todd Hollandsworth B/X .75
62 Jay Bell B/X .75
63 Nomar Garciaparra G/Z 20.00
64 Vinny Castilla B/Y .75
65 Lou Collier B/Y .75
66 Kevin Orie S/X 2.50
67 John Valentin B/X .75
68 Robin Ventura B/X .75
69 Denny Neagle B/X .75
70 Tony Womack S/Y 2.50
71 Dennis Reyes S/Y 2.50
72 Wally Joyner B/X .75
73 Kevin Brown B/Y 1.00
74 Ray Durham B/X .75
75 Mike Cameron S/Z 2.50
76 Dante Bichette B/X .75
77 Jose Guillen G/Y 6.00
78 Carlos Delgado B/Y 1.50
79 Paul Molitor G/Z 7.50
80 Jason Kendall B/X .75
81 Mark Belhorn B/X .75
82 Damian Jackson B/X .75
83 Bill Mueller B/X .75
84 Kevin Young B/X .75
85 Curt Schilling B/X 1.00
86 Jeffrey Hammonds B/X .75
87 Sandy Alomar Jr. S/Y 2.50
88 Bartolo Colon B/Y .75
89 Wilton Guerrero B/Y .75
90 Bernie Williams G/Y 8.00
91 Deion Sanders S/Y 3.00
92 Mike Piazza G/X 75.00
93 Butch Huskey B/X .75
94 Edgardo Alfonzo S/X 2.50
95 Alan Benes S/Y 2.50
96 Craig Biggio S/Y 3.00
97 Mark Grace S/Y 4.00
98 Shawn Green S/Y 5.00
99 Derrek Lee S/Y 2.50
100 Ken Griffey Jr. G/Z 30.00
101 Tim Raines B/X .75
102 Pokey Reese S/X 2.50
103 Lee Stevens B/X .75
104 Shannon Stewart S/Y 2.50
105 John Smoltz S/Y 3.00
106 Frank Thomas G/X 45.00
107 Jeff Fassero B/X .75
108 Jay Buhner B/Y .75
109 Jose Canseco B/X 1.50
110 Omar Vizquel B/X .75
111 Travis Fryman B/X .75
112 Dave Nilsson B/X .75
113 John Olerud B/X .75
114 Larry Walker G/Z 6.00
115 Jim Edmonds S/Y 2.50
116 Bobby Higginson S/X 2.50
117 Todd Hundley S/X 2.50
118 Paul O'Neill B/X .75
119 Bip Roberts B/X .75
120 Ismael Valdes B/X .75
121 Pedro Martinez S/Y 6.00
122 Jeff Cirillo B/X .75
123 Andy Benes B/X .75
124 Bobby Jones B/X .75
125 Brian Hunter B/X .75
126 Darryl Kile B/X .75
127 Pat Hentgen B/X .75
128 Marquis Grissom B/X .75
129 Eric Davis B/X .75
130 Chipper Jones G/Z 25.00
131 Edgar Martinez S/Z 2.50
132 Andy Pettitte G/Z 7.50
133 Cal Ripken Jr. G/X 90.00
134 Scott Rolen G/Z 15.00
135 Ron Coomer B/X .75
136 Luis Castillo B/Y .75
137 Fred McGriff B/Y .75
138 Neifi Perez S/Y 2.50

139 Eric Karros B/X .75
140 Alex Fernandez B/X .75
141 Jason Dickson B/X .75
142 Lance Johnson B/X .75
143 Ray Lankford B/Y .75
144 Sammy Sosa G/Y 20.00
145 Eric Young B/Y .75
146 Bubba Trammell S/Y 2.50
147 Todd Walker S/Y 2.50
148 Mo Vaughn S/X (Curtain Calls) 5.00
149 Jeff Bagwell S/X (Curtain Calls) 7.50
150 Kenny Lofton S/X (Curtain Calls) 2.50
151 Raul Mondesi S/X (Curtain Calls) 3.00
152 Mike Piazza S/X (Curtain Calls) 12.50
153 Chipper Jones S/X (Curtain Calls) 12.50
154 Larry Walker S/X (Curtain Calls) 3.00
155 Greg Maddux S/X (Curtain Calls) 10.00
156 Ken Griffey Jr. S/X (Curtain Calls) 15.00
157 Frank Thomas S/X (Curtain Calls) 8.50
158 Darin Erstad B/Z (Gold Leaf Stars) 2.00
159 Roberto Alomar B/Y (Gold Leaf Stars) 1.50
160 Albert Belle G/Y (Gold Leaf Stars) 6.00
161 Jim Thome G/Y (Gold Leaf Stars) 6.00
162 Tony Clark G/Y (Gold Leaf Stars) 6.00
163 Chuck Knoblauch B/Y (Gold Leaf Stars) .75
164 Derek Jeter G/Z (Gold Leaf Stars) 25.00
165 Alex Rodriguez G/Z (Gold Leaf Stars) 25.00
166 Tony Gwynn B/X (Gold Leaf Stars) 6.00
167 Roger Clemens G/Z (Gold Leaf Stars) 7.50
168 Barry Larkin B/Y (Gold Leaf Stars) 1.00
169 Andres Galarraga B/Y (Gold Leaf Stars) .75
170 Vladimir Guerrero G/Z (Gold Leaf Stars) 6.00
171 Mark McGwire B/Z (Gold Leaf Stars) 7.50
172 Barry Bonds B/Z (Gold Leaf Stars) 3.00
173 Juan Gonzalez G/Z (Gold Leaf Stars) 15.00
174 Andruw Jones G/Z (Gold Leaf Stars) 12.50
175 Paul Molitor B/X (Gold Leaf Stars) 1.50
176 Hideo Nomo B/Z (Gold Leaf Stars) 2.50
177 Cal Ripken Jr. B/X (Gold Leaf Stars) 7.50
178 Brad Fullmer S/Z (Gold Leaf Rookies) 2.50
179 Jaret Wright G/Z (Gold Leaf Rookies) 12.50
180 Bobby Estalella B/Y (Gold Leaf Rookies) .75
181 Ben Grieve G/X (Gold Leaf Rookies) 20.00
182 Paul Konerko G/Z (Gold Leaf Rookies) 7.50
183 David Ortiz G/Z (Gold Leaf Rookies) 10.00
184 Todd Helton G/X (Gold Leaf Rookies) 20.00
185 Juan Encarnacion G/Z (Gold Leaf Rookies) 6.00
186 Miguel Tejada G/Z (Gold Leaf Rookies) 6.00
187 Jacob Cruz B/Y (Gold Leaf Rookies) .75
188 Mark Kotsay G/Z (Gold Leaf Rookies) 5.00
189 Fernando Tatis S/Z (Gold Leaf Rookies) 2.50
190 Ricky Ledee S/Y (Gold Leaf Rookies) 2.50
191 Richard Hidalgo S/Y (Gold Leaf Rookies) 3.00
192 Richie Sexson S/Y (Gold Leaf Rookies) 2.50
193 Luis Ordaz B/X (Gold Leaf Rookies) .75
194 Eli Marrero S/Z (Gold Leaf Rookies) 2.50
195 Livan Hernandez S/Z (Gold Leaf Rookies) 2.50
196 Homer Bush B/X (Gold Leaf Rookies) .75
197 Raul Ibanez B/X (Gold Leaf Rookies) .75
198 Checklist (Nomar Garciaparra B/X) 2.00
199 Checklist (Scott Rolen B/X) 1.50
200 Checklist (Jose Cruz Jr. B/X) 1.50
201 Al Martin B/X .75

1998 Leaf Fractal Matrix Die-Cut

This parallel set adds a die-cut to the Fractal Matrix set. Three different die-cut versions were created: X-axis, Y-axis and Z-axis. An X-axis die-cut was added to 75 bronze, 20 silver and 5 gold cards. A Y-axis die-cut was added to 20 bronze, 30 silver and 10 gold cards. Of the 40 Z-axis cards, 5 are bronze, 10 silver and 25 gold. Stated print runs were 400 of each X-axis card; 200 Y and 100 Z.

	MT
Complete Set (200):	1400.
Common X-Axis:	2.50
Common Y-Axis:	4.00
Common Z-Axis:	7.50

1 Rusty Greer G/Z 7.50
2 Tino Martinez G/Z 7.50
3 Bobby Bonilla S/Y 4.00
4 Jason Giambi S/Y 10.00
5 Matt Morris S/Y 5.00
6 Craig Counsell B/X 2.50
7 Reggie Jefferson B/X 2.50
8 Brian Rose S/Y 4.00
9 Ruben Rivera B/X 2.50
10 Shawn Estes S/Y 4.00
11 Tony Gwynn G/Z 55.00
12 Jeff Abbott B/Y 4.00
13 Jose Cruz Jr. G/Z 10.00
14 Francisco Cordova B/X 2.50
15 Ryan Klesko B/X 2.50
16 Tim Salmon G/Y 6.00
17 Brett Tomko B/X 2.50
18 Matt Williams S/Y 6.00
19 Joe Carter B/X 2.50
20 Harold Baines B/X 2.50
21 Gary Sheffield S/Z 15.00
22 Charles Johnson S/X 2.50
23 Aaron Boone B/X 2.50
24 Eddie Murray G/Y 7.50
25 Matt Stairs B/X 2.50
26 David Cone B/X 2.50
27 Jon Nunnally B/X 2.50
28 Chris Stynes B/X 2.50
29 Enrique Wilson B/Y 4.00
30 Randy Johnson S/Z 20.00
31 Garret Anderson S/Y 4.00
32 Manny Ramirez G/Z 22.50
33 Jeff Suppan S/X 2.50
34 Rickey Henderson B/X 6.50
35 Scott Spiezio B/X 2.50
36 Rondell White S/Y 4.00
37 Todd Greene S/Z 7.50
38 Delino DeShields B/X 2.50
39 Kevin Brown S/X 3.00
40 Chili Davis B/X 2.50
41 Jimmy Key B/X 2.50
42 NOT ISSUED
43 Mike Mussina G/Y 15.00
44 Joe Randa B/X 2.50
45 Chan Ho Park S/Z 12.50
46 Brad Radke B/X 3.00
47 Geronimo Berroa B/X 2.50
48 Wade Boggs S/Y 9.00
49 Kevin Appier B/X 2.50
50 Moises Alou S/Y 5.00
51 David Justice G/Y 7.50
52 Ivan Rodriguez G/Z 30.00
53 J.T. Snow B/X 2.50
54 Brian Giles B/X 2.50
55 Will Clark B/Y 7.50
56 Justin Thompson S/Y 4.00
57 Javier Lopez S/X 2.50
58 Hideki Irabu B/Z 7.50
59 Mark Grudzielanek B/X 2.50
60 Abraham Nunez S/X 2.50
61 Todd Hollandsworth B/X 2.50
62 Jay Bell B/X 2.50
63 Nomar Garciaparra G/Z 65.00
64 Vinny Castilla B/Y 4.00
65 Lou Collier B/Y 4.00
66 Kevin Orie S/X 2.50
67 John Valentin B/X 2.50
68 Robin Ventura B/X 2.50
69 Denny Neagle B/X 2.50
70 Tony Womack S/Y 4.00
71 Dennis Reyes S/Y 4.00
72 Wally Joyner B/X 2.50
73 Kevin Brown B/Y 5.00
74 Ray Durham B/X 2.50
75 Mike Cameron S/Z 7.50
76 Dante Bichette B/X 2.50
77 Jose Guillen G/Y 6.00
78 Carlos Delgado B/Y 6.00
79 Paul Molitor G/Z 22.50
80 Jason Kendall B/X 2.50
81 Mark Belhorn B/X 2.50
82 Damian Jackson B/X 2.50
83 Bill Mueller B/X 2.50
84 Kevin Young B/X 2.50
85 Curt Schilling B/X 3.50
86 Jeffrey Hammonds B/X 2.50
87 Sandy Alomar Jr. S/Y 4.00
88 Bartolo Colon B/Y 4.00
89 Wilton Guerrero B/Y 4.00
90 Bernie Williams G/Y 12.00
91 Deion Sanders S/Y 5.00
92 Mike Piazza G/X 30.00
93 Butch Huskey B/X 2.50
94 Edgardo Alfonzo S/X 2.50
95 Alan Benes S/Y 4.00
96 Craig Biggio S/Y 5.00
97 Mark Grace S/Y 8.00
98 Shawn Green S/Y 7.50
99 Derrek Lee S/Y 4.00
100 Ken Griffey Jr. G/Z 90.00
101 Tim Raines B/X 2.50
102 Pokey Reese S/X 2.50
103 Lee Stevens B/X 2.50
104 Shannon Stewart S/Y 4.00
105 John Smoltz S/Y 5.00
106 Frank Thomas G/X 20.00
107 Jeff Fassero B/X 2.50
108 Jay Buhner B/Y 4.00
109 Jose Canseco B/X 4.00
110 Omar Vizquel B/X 2.50
111 Travis Fryman B/X 2.50
112 Dave Nilsson B/X 2.50
113 John Olerud B/X 2.50
114 Larry Walker G/Z 15.00
115 Jim Edmonds S/Y 6.00
116 Bobby Higginson S/X 2.50
117 Todd Hundley S/X 2.50
118 Paul O'Neill B/X 2.50
119 Bip Roberts B/X 2.50
120 Ismael Valdes B/X 2.50
121 Pedro Martinez S/Y 10.00
122 Jeff Cirillo B/X 2.50
123 Andy Benes B/X 2.50
124 Bobby Jones B/X 2.50
125 Brian Hunter B/X 2.50
126 Darryl Kile B/X 2.50
127 Pat Hentgen B/X 2.50
128 Marquis Grissom B/X 2.50
129 Eric Davis B/X 2.50
130 Chipper Jones G/Z 75.00
131 Edgar Martinez S/Z 4.00
132 Andy Pettitte G/Z 15.00
133 Cal Ripken Jr. G/X 35.00
134 Scott Rolen G/Z 45.00
135 Ron Coomer B/X 2.50
136 Luis Castillo B/Y 4.00
137 Fred McGriff B/Y 4.00
138 Neifi Perez S/Y 4.00
139 Eric Karros B/X 2.50
140 Alex Fernandez B/X 2.50
141 Jason Dickson B/X 2.50
142 Lance Johnson B/X 2.50
143 Ray Lankford B/Y 4.00
144 Sammy Sosa G/Y 30.00
145 Eric Young B/Y 4.00
146 Bubba Trammell S/Y 5.00
147 Todd Walker S/Y 5.00
148 Mo Vaughn S/X (Curtain Calls) 5.00
149 Jeff Bagwell S/X (Curtain Calls) 9.00
150 Kenny Lofton S/X (Curtain Calls) 2.50
151 Raul Mondesi S/X (Curtain Calls) 3.00
152 Mike Piazza S/X (Curtain Calls) 15.00
153 Chipper Jones S/X (Curtain Calls) 15.00
154 Larry Walker S/X (Curtain Calls) 3.00
155 Greg Maddux S/X (Curtain Calls) 12.50
156 Ken Griffey Jr. S/X (Curtain Calls) 25.00
157 Frank Thomas S/X (Curtain Calls) 12.50
158 Darin Erstad B/Z (Gold Leaf Stars) 15.00
159 Roberto Alomar B/Y (Gold Leaf Stars) 7.50
160 Albert Belle G/Y (Gold Leaf Stars) 6.00
161 Jim Thome G/Y (Gold Leaf Stars) 4.00
162 Tony Clark G/Y (Gold Leaf Stars) 4.00
163 Chuck Knoblauch B/Y (Gold Leaf Stars) 4.00
164 Derek Jeter G/Z (Gold Leaf Stars) 75.00
165 Alex Rodriguez G/Z (Gold Leaf Stars) 75.00
166 Tony Gwynn B/X (Gold Leaf Stars) 10.00
167 Roger Clemens G/Z (Gold Leaf Stars) 27.50

168	Barry Larkin B/Y (Gold Leaf Stars)	5.00
169	Andres Galarraga B/Y (Gold Leaf Stars)	4.00
170	Vladimir Guerrero G/Z (Gold Leaf Stars)	17.50
171	Mark McGwire B/Z (Gold Leaf Stars)	75.00
172	Barry Bonds B/Z (Gold Leaf Stars)	35.00
173	Juan Gonzalez G/Z (Gold Leaf Stars)	20.00
174	Andruw Jones G/Z (Gold Leaf Stars)	25.00
175	Paul Molitor B/X (Gold Leaf Stars)	7.50
176	Hideo Nomo B/Z (Gold Leaf Stars)	22.50
177	Cal Ripken Jr. B/X (Gold Leaf Stars)	20.00
178	Brad Fullmer S/Z (Gold Leaf Rookies)	7.50
179	Jaret Wright G/Z (Gold Leaf Rookies)	15.00
180	Bobby Estalella B/Y (Gold Leaf Rookies)	4.00
181	Ben Grieve G/X (Gold Leaf Rookies)	5.00
182	Paul Konerko G/Z (Gold Leaf Rookies)	7.50
183	David Ortiz G/Z (Gold Leaf Rookies)	9.00
184	Todd Helton G/X (Gold Leaf Rookies)	5.00
185	Juan Encarnacion G/Z (Gold Leaf Rookies)	9.00
186	Miguel Tejada G/Z (Gold Leaf Rookies)	15.00
187	Jacob Cruz B/Y (Gold Leaf Rookies)	4.00
188	Mark Kotsay G/Z (Gold Leaf Rookies)	7.50
189	Fernando Tatis S/Z (Gold Leaf Rookies)	7.50
190	Ricky Ledee S/Y (Gold Leaf Rookies)	4.00
191	Richard Hidalgo S/Y (Gold Leaf Rookies)	6.00
192	Richie Sexson S/Y (Gold Leaf Rookies)	4.00
193	Luis Ordaz B/X (Gold Leaf Rookies)	2.50
194	Eli Marrero S/Z (Gold Leaf Rookies)	7.50
195	Livan Hernandez S/Z (Gold Leaf Rookies)	7.50
196	Homer Bush B/X (Gold Leaf Rookies)	2.50
197	Raul Ibanez B/X (Gold Leaf Rookies)	2.50
198	Checklist (Nomar Garciaparra B/X)	4.00
199	Checklist (Scott Rolen B/X)	3.00
200	Checklist (Jose Cruz Jr. B/X)	3.00
201	Al Martin B/X	2.50

1998 Leaf Crusade

Thirty cards from the cross-brand Crusade insert appear in 1998 Leaf. The cards had Green (250 sets), Purple (100 sets) and Red (25 sets) versions. Forty Crusade cards were in 1998 Donruss and 30 each in 1998 Donruss Update and Leaf Rookies & Stars.

		MT
Complete Set (30):		285.00
Common Player:		3.00
Purples:		1.5X
Reds:		6X
3	Jim Edmonds	4.50
4	Darin Erstad	15.00
11	Mike Mussina	17.50
15	Albert Belle	7.50
18	Manny Ramirez	15.00
19	Jim Thome	3.00
24	Bubba Trammell	4.50
26	Bobby Higginson	3.00
28	Paul Molitor	12.00
30	Todd Walker	4.50
34	Andy Pettitte	10.00
35	Wade Boggs	15.00
40	Alex Rodriguez	45.00
41	Randy Johnson	12.00
46	Ivan Rodriguez	20.00
48	Roger Clemens	30.00
54	John Smoltz	4.50
56	Andruw Jones	27.50
58	Javier Lopez	3.00
59	Fred McGriff	3.00
64	Pokey Reese	3.00
66	Andres Galarraga	3.00
70	Eric Young	3.00
73	Moises Alou	4.00
76	Ben Grieve	12.50
79	Mike Piazza	45.00
91	Jason Kendall	3.00
95	Alan Benes	3.00
97	Tony Gwynn	42.50
98	Ken Caminiti	3.00

1998 Leaf Heading for the Hall

This 20-card insert features players destined for the Hall of Fame. The set is sequentially numbered to 3,500. Each card is also found in a "SAMPLE" marked edition with no serial number.

		MT
Complete Set (20):		55.00
Common Player:		1.50
Samples:		1X
1	Roberto Alomar	2.00
2	Jeff Bagwell	3.50
3	Albert Belle	2.00
4	Wade Boggs	2.00
5	Barry Bonds	3.50
6	Roger Clemens	3.50
7	Juan Gonzalez	2.50
8	Ken Griffey Jr.	7.50
9	Tony Gwynn	4.00
10	Barry Larkin	1.50
11	Kenny Lofton	1.50
12	Greg Maddux	5.00
13	Mark McGwire	7.50
14	Paul Molitor	2.00
15	Eddie Murray	2.00
16	Mike Piazza	6.00
17	Cal Ripken Jr.	7.50
18	Ivan Rodriguez	2.00
19	Ryne Sandberg	2.50
20	Frank Thomas	3.50

1998 Leaf Statistical Standouts

This 24-card insert features players with impressive statistics. The cards have a horizontal layout and the feel of leather. The background has a ball and glove with the player's facsimile signature on the ball. Statistical Standouts is numbered to 2,500. A parallel die-cut version of each card comprises the first 250 numbered cards.

		MT
Complete Set (24):		100.00
Common Player:		2.00
Die-Cuts:		2X
1	Frank Thomas	5.00
2	Ken Griffey Jr.	10.00
3	Alex Rodriguez	12.00
4	Mike Piazza	9.00
5	Greg Maddux	6.50
6	Cal Ripken Jr.	12.50
7	Chipper Jones	7.00
8	Juan Gonzalez	3.50
9	Jeff Bagwell	3.50
10	Mark McGwire	12.50
11	Tony Gwynn	4.00
12	Mo Vaughn	3.00
13	Nomar Garciaparra	6.50
14	Jose Cruz Jr.	2.50
15	Vladimir Guerrero	3.00
16	Scott Rolen	3.00
17	Andy Pettitte	2.50
18	Randy Johnson	3.50
19	Larry Walker	2.50
20	Kenny Lofton	2.00
21	Tony Clark	2.00
22	David Justice	3.00
23	Derek Jeter	9.00
24	Barry Bonds	4.00

1998 Leaf Fractal Foundation

Fractal Foundations is a stand-alone product but it parallels the 1998 Leaf set. It contains the Curtain Calls, Gold Leaf Stars and Gold Leaf Rookies subsets and is missing card #42 which Leaf retired in honor of Jackie Robinson. The set was printed on foil board and each card is numbered to 3,999. The set is paralleled in Fractal Materials, Fractal Materials Die-Cuts and Fractal Materials Z2 Axis.

		MT
Complete Set (200):		250.00
Common Player:		.50
Semistars:		1.50
Unlisted Stars:		2.50
Pack (3):		5.00
Wax Box (18):		80.00
1	Rusty Greer	.50
2	Tino Martinez	.50
3	Bobby Bonilla	.50
4	Jason Giambi	1.00
5	Matt Morris	.75
6	Craig Counsell	.50
7	Reggie Jefferson	.50
8	Brian Rose	.50
9	Ruben Rivera	.50
10	Shawn Estes	.50
11	Tony Gwynn	2.00
12	Jeff Abbott	.50
13	Jose Cruz Jr.	.75
14	Francisco Cordova	.50
15	Ryan Klesko	.50
16	Tim Salmon	1.00
17	Brett Tomko	.50
18	Matt Williams	1.00
19	Joe Carter	.50
20	Harold Baines	.50
21	Gary Sheffield	1.00
22	Charles Johnson	.50
23	Aaron Boone	.50
24	Eddie Murray	1.25
25	Matt Stairs	.50
26	David Cone	.50
27	Jon Nunnally	.50
28	Chris Stynes	.50
29	Enrique Wilson	.50
30	Randy Johnson	1.50
31	Garret Anderson	.50
32	Manny Ramirez	1.50
33	Jeff Suppan	.50
34	Rickey Henderson	1.50
35	Scott Spiezio	.50
36	Rondell White	.50
37	Todd Greene	.75
38	Delino DeShields	.50
39	Kevin Brown	.75
40	Chili Davis	.50
41	Jimmy Key	.50
42	NOT ISSUED	
43	Mike Mussina	1.50
44	Joe Randa	.50
45	Chan Ho Park	1.00
46	Brad Radke	.65
47	Geronimo Berroa	.50
48	Wade Boggs	1.50
49	Kevin Appier	.50
50	Moises Alou	.75
51	David Justice	1.00
52	Ivan Rodriguez	1.50
53	J.T. Snow	.50
54	Brian Giles	.50
55	Will Clark	1.00
56	Justin Thompson	.50
57	Javier Lopez	.50
58	Hideki Irabu	.50
59	Mark Grudzielanek	.50
60	Abraham Nunez	.50
61	Todd Hollandsworth	.50
62	Jay Bell	.50
63	Nomar Garciaparra	2.00
64	Vinny Castilla	.50
65	Lou Collier	.50

66 Kevin Orie .50
67 John Valentin .50
68 Robin Ventura .50
69 Denny Neagle .50
70 Tony Womack .50
71 Dennis Reyes .50
72 Wally Joyner .50
73 Kevin Brown 1.00
74 Ray Durham .50
75 Mike Cameron .50
76 Dante Bichette .50
77 Jose Guillen .75
78 Carlos Delgado 1.50
79 Paul Molitor 1.50
80 Jason Kendall .50
81 Mark Belhorn .50
82 Damian Jackson .50
83 Bill Mueller .50
84 Kevin Young .50
85 Curt Schilling .75
86 Jeffrey Hammonds .50
87 Sandy Alomar Jr. .50
88 Bartolo Colon .50
89 Wilton Guerrero .50
90 Bernie Williams 1.00
91 Deion Sanders .75
92 Mike Piazza 3.00
93 Butch Huskey .50
94 Edgardo Alfonzo .50
95 Alan Benes .50
96 Craig Biggio .75
97 Mark Grace 1.25
98 Shawn Green 1.00
99 Derrek Lee .75
100 Ken Griffey Jr. 4.00
101 Tim Raines .50
102 Pokey Reese .50
103 Lee Stevens .50
104 Shannon Stewart .50
105 John Smoltz .75
106 Frank Thomas 2.50
107 Jeff Fassero .50
108 Jay Buhner .50
109 Jose Canseco 1.25
110 Omar Vizquel .50
111 Travis Fryman .50
112 Dave Nilsson .50
113 John Olerud .50
114 Larry Walker 1.00
115 Jim Edmonds 1.00
116 Bobby Higginson 1.00
117 Todd Hundley .50
118 Paul O'Neill .50
119 Bip Roberts .50
120 Ismael Valdes .50
121 Pedro Martinez 1.50
122 Jeff Cirillo .50
123 Andy Benes .50
124 Bobby Jones .50
125 Brian Hunter .50
126 Darryl Kile .50
127 Pat Hentgen .50
128 Marquis Grissom .50
129 Eric Davis .50
130 Chipper Jones 3.00
131 Edgar Martinez .50
132 Andy Pettitte 1.00
133 Cal Ripken Jr. 6.00
134 Scott Rolen 1.50
135 Ron Coomer .50
136 Luis Castillo .50
137 Fred McGriff .50
138 Neifi Perez .50
139 Eric Karros .50
140 Alex Fernandez .50
141 Jason Dickson .50
142 Lance Johnson .50
143 Ray Lankford .50
144 Sammy Sosa 2.00
145 Eric Young .50
146 Bubba Trammell .75
147 Todd Walker 1.00
148 Mo Vaugh (Curtain Calls) 1.00
149 Jeff Bagwell (Curtain Calls) 2.00
150 Kenny Lofton (Curtain Calls) .50
151 Raul Mondesi (Curtain Calls) 1.00
152 Mike Piazza (Curtain Calls) 3.00
153 Chipper Jones (Curtain Calls) 3.00
154 Larry Walker (Curtain Calls) 1.00
155 Greg Maddux (Curtain Calls) 2.50
156 Ken Griffey Jr. (Curtain Calls) 4.00
157 Frank Thomas (Curtain Calls) 2.50
158 Darin Erstad (Gold Leaf Stars) 1.50
159 Roberto Alomar (Gold Leaf Stars) 1.50
160 Albert Belle (Gold Leaf Stars) 1.00
161 Jim Thome (Gold Leaf Stars) .50
162 Tony Clark (Gold Leaf Stars) .50
163 Chuck Knoblauch (Gold Leaf Stars) .50
164 Derek Jeter (Gold Leaf Stars) 3.00
165 Alex Rodriguez (Gold Leaf Stars) 3.00
166 Tony Gwynn (Gold Leaf Stars) 2.00
167 Roger Clemens (Gold Leaf Stars) 2.00
168 Barry Larkin (Gold Leaf Stars) .75
169 Andres Galarraga (Gold Leaf Stars) .50
170 Vladimir Guerrero (Gold Leaf Stars) 1.50
171 Mark McGwire (Gold Leaf Stars) 6.00
172 Barry Bonds (Gold Leaf Stars) 2.50
173 Juan Gonzalez (Gold Leaf Stars) 1.50
174 Andruw Jones (Gold Leaf Stars) 1.50
175 Paul Molitor (Gold Leaf Stars) 1.50
176 Hideo Nomo (Gold Leaf Stars) 1.50
177 Cal Ripken Jr. (Gold Leaf Stars) 6.00
178 Brad Fullmer (Gold Leaf Rookies) .50
179 Jaret Wright (Gold Leaf Rookies) 1.00
180 Bobby Estalella (Gold Leaf Rookies) .50
181 Ben Grieve (Gold Leaf Rookies) .75
182 Paul Konerko (Gold Leaf Rookies) .50
183 David Ortiz (Gold Leaf Rookies) .75
184 Todd Helton (Gold Leaf Rookies) 1.50
185 Juan Encarnacion (Gold Leaf Rookies) .50
186 Miguel Tejada (Gold Leaf Rookies) 1.00
187 Jacob Cruz (Gold Leaf Rookies) .50
188 Mark Kotsay (Gold Leaf Rookies) .75
189 Fernando Tatis (Gold Leaf Rookies) .75
190 Ricky Ledee (Gold Leaf Rookies) .50
191 Richard Hidalgo (Gold Leaf Rookies) 1.00
192 Richie Sexson (Gold Leaf Rookies) .50
193 Luis Ordaz (Gold Leaf Rookies) .50
194 Eli Marrero (Gold Leaf Rookies) .50
195 Livan Hernandez (Gold Leaf Rookies) .50
196 Homer Bush (Gold Leaf Rookies) .50
197 Raul Ibanez (Gold Leaf Rookies) .50
198 Checklist (Nomar Garciaparra) .75
199 Checklist (Scott Rolen) .75
200 Checklist (Jose Cruz Jr.) .50

1998 Leaf Fractal Foundation Z2 Axis

This 200-card set parallels Leaf Fractal Materials and was numbered to 20 sets.

	MT
Common Player:	15.00
Z2 Stars:	15-20X

Production 20 sets
(See 1998 Leaf Fractal Foundation for checklist and base card prices.)

1998 Leaf Fractal Materials

The Fractal Materials set fully parallels Fractal Foundations. Each of the inserts is sequentially numbered. The 200 card chase set was printed on four different materials: 100 plastic cards (numbered to 3,250), 50 leather (1,000), 30 nylon (500) and 20 wood (250). These parallels were inserted one per pack of Fractal Foundations.

	MT
Complete Set (200):	550.00
Complete Plastic Set (100):	95.00
Common Plastic (3,250):	.50
Complete Leather Set (50):	80.00
Common Leather (1,000):	1.00
Complete Nylon Set (30):	90.00
Common Nylon (500):	2.00
Complete Wood Set (20):	310.00
Common Wood (250):	7.50
Wax Box:	120.00

1 Rusty Greer N 2.00
2 Tino Martinez W 7.50
3 Bobby Bonilla N 2.00
4 Jason Giambi N 5.00
5 Matt Morris L 1.50
6 Craig Counsell P .50
7 Reggie Jefferson P .50
8 Brian Rose P .50
9 Ruben Rivera L 1.00
10 Shawn Estes L 1.00
11 Tony Gwynn W 30.00
12 Jeff Abbott P .50
13 Jose Cruz Jr. W 9.50
14 Francisco Cordova P .50
15 Ryan Klesko L 1.00
16 Tim Salmon W 9.50
17 Brett Tomko L 1.00
18 Matt Williams N 3.00
19 Joe Carter P .50
20 Harold Baines P .50
21 Gary Sheffield N 3.50
22 Charles Johnson L 1.00
23 Aaron Boone P .50
24 Eddie Murray N 5.00
25 Matt Stairs P .50
26 David Cone P .50
27 Jon Nunnally P .50
28 Chris Stynes P .50
29 Enrique Wilson P .50
30 Randy Johnson W 13.00
31 Garret Anderson N 3.00
32 Manny Ramirez W 16.00
33 Jeff Suppan L 1.00
34 Rickey Henderson N 6.00
35 Scott Spiezio P .50
36 Rondell White L 1.00
37 Todd Greene N 3.00
38 Delino DeShields P .50
39 Kevin Brown L 2.00
40 Chili Davis P .50
41 Jimmy Key P .50
42 NOT ISSUED
43 Mike Mussina N 7.50
44 Joe Randa P .50
45 Chan Ho Park N 4.00
46 Brad Radke P .75
47 Geronimo Berroa P .50
48 Wade Boggs N 6.00
49 Kevin Appier P .50
50 Moises Alou N 3.00
51 David Justice N 4.00
52 Ivan Rodriguez W 15.00
53 J.T. Snow L 1.00
54 Brian Giles P .50
55 Will Clark L 2.00
56 Justin Thompson N 2.00
57 Javier Lopez P .50
58 Hideki Irabu L 1.00
59 Mark Grudzielanek P .50
60 Abraham Nunez P .50
61 Todd Hollandsworth P .50
62 Jay Bell P .50
63 Nomar Garciaparra W 35.00
64 Vinny Castilla P .50
65 Lou Collier P .50
66 Kevin Orie L 1.00
67 John Valentin P .50
68 Robin Ventura P .50
69 Denny Neagle P .50
70 Tony Womack L 1.50
71 Dennis Reyes L 1.00
72 Wally Joyner P .50
73 Kevin Brown P .75
74 Ray Durham P .50
75 Mike Cameron N 2.00
76 Dante Bichette L 1.00
77 Jose Guillen N 3.00
78 Carlos Delgado L 3.00
79 Paul Molitor W 10.00
80 Jason Kendall P .50
81 Mark Belhorn L 1.00
82 Damian Jackson P .50
83 Bill Mueller P .50
84 Kevin Young P .50
85 Curt Schilling P .75
86 Jeffrey Hammonds P .50
87 Sandy Alomar Jr. L 1.00
88 Bartolo Colon P .65
89 Wilton Guerrero L 1.00
90 Bernie Williams N 4.00
91 Deion Sanders N 3.00
92 Mike Piazza W 40.00
93 Butch Huskey L 1.00
94 Edgardo Alfonzo L 1.00
95 Alan Benes L 1.00
96 Craig Biggio N 3.00
97 Mark Grace L 2.50

98 Shawn Green L 3.00
99 Derrek Lee L 1.00
100 Ken Griffey Jr. W 45.00
101 Tim Raines P .50
102 Pokey Reese P .50
103 Lee Stevens P .50
104 Shannon Stewart N 3.00
105 John Smoltz L 1.50
106 Frank Thomas W 25.00
107 Jeff Fassero P .50
108 Jay Buhner L 1.00
109 Jose Canseco L 2.50
110 Omar Vizquel P .50
111 Travis Fryman P .50
112 Dave Nilsson P .50
113 John Olerud P .50
114 Larry Walker W 10.00
115 Jim Edmonds N 3.00
116 Bobby Higginson L 1.50
117 Todd Hundley L 1.00
118 Paul O'Neill P .50
119 Bip Roberts P .50
120 Ismael Valdes P .50
121 Pedro Martinez N 6.00
122 Jeff Cirillo P .50
123 Andy Benes P .50
124 Bobby Jones P .50
125 Brian Hunter P .50
126 Darryl Kile P .50
127 Pat Hentgen P .50
128 Marquis Grissom P .50
129 Eric Davis P .50
130 Chipper Jones W 40.00
131 Edgar Martinez N 2.00
132 Andy Pettitte W 12.50
133 Cal Ripken Jr. W 50.00
134 Scott Rolen W 15.00
135 Ron Coomer P .50
136 Luis Castillo L 1.00
136 Luis Castillo ("SAMPLE" overprint on back) 1.50
137 Fred McGriff L 1.00
138 Neifi Perez L 1.00
139 Eric Karros P .50
140 Alex Fernandez P .50
141 Jason Dickson P .50
142 Lance Johnson P .50
143 Ray Lankford P .50
144 Sammy Sosa N 10.00
145 Eric Young P .50
146 Bubba Trammell L 1.50
147 Todd Walker L 1.50
148 Mo Vaughn P (Curtain Calls) 1.00
149 Jeff Bagwell P (Curtain Calls) 3.00
150 Kenny Lofton P (Curtain Calls) .50
151 Raul Mondesi P (Curtain Calls) 1.00
152 Mike Piazza P (Curtain Calls) 6.50
153 Chipper Jones P (Curtain Calls) 6.50
154 Larry Walker P (Curtain Calls) 1.00
155 Greg Maddux P (Curtain Calls) 6.00
156 Ken Griffey Jr. P (Curtain Calls) 9.00
157 Frank Thomas P (Curtain Calls) 6.00
158 Darin Erstad L (Gold Leaf Stars) 6.00
159 Roberto Alomar P (Gold Leaf Stars) 2.50
160 Albert Belle L (Gold Leaf Stars) 2.00
161 Jim Thome L (Gold Leaf Stars) 1.00
162 Tony Clark L (Gold Leaf Stars) 1.00
163 Chuck Knoblauch L (Gold Leaf Stars) 1.00
164 Derek Jeter P (Gold Leaf Stars) 6.50
165 Alex Rodriguez P (Gold Leaf Stars) 8.00
166 Tony Gwynn P (Gold Leaf Stars) 4.00
167 Roger Clemens L (Gold Leaf Stars) 7.50
168 Barry Larkin P (Gold Leaf Stars) .50
169 Andres Galarraga P (Gold Leaf Stars) .50
170 Vladimir Guerrero L (Gold Leaf Stars) 5.00
171 Mark McGwire L (Gold Leaf Stars) 15.00
172 Barry Bonds L (Gold Leaf Stars) 10.00
173 Juan Gonzalez P (Gold Leaf Stars) 3.00
174 Andruw Jones P (Gold Leaf Stars) 2.50
175 Paul Molitor P (Gold Leaf Stars) 2.50
176 Hideo Nomo L (Gold Leaf Stars) 5.00
177 Cal Ripken Jr. P (Gold Leaf Stars) 10.00
178 Brad Fullmer P (Gold Leaf Rookies) .50
179 Jaret Wright N (Gold Leaf Rookies) 3.00
180 Bobby Estalella P (Gold Leaf Rookies) .50
181 Ben Grieve W (Gold Leaf Rookies) 10.00
182 Paul Konerko W (Gold Leaf Rookies) 7.50
183 David Ortiz N (Gold Leaf Rookies) 4.00
184 Todd Helton W (Gold Leaf Rookies) 12.50
185 Juan Encarnacion N (Gold Leaf Rookies) 3.00
186 Miguel Tejada N (Gold Leaf Rookies) 4.00
187 Jacob Cruz P (Gold Leaf Rookies) .50
188 Mark Kotsay N (Gold Leaf Rookies) 3.00
189 Fernando Tatis L (Gold Leaf Rookies) 1.50
190 Ricky Ledee P (Gold Leaf Rookies) .50
191 Richard Hidalgo P (Gold Leaf Rookies) .75
192 Richie Sexson P (Gold Leaf Rookies) .50
193 Luis Ordaz P (Gold Leaf Rookies) .60
194 Eli Marrero L (Gold Leaf Rookies) 1.00
195 Livan Hernandez L (Gold Leaf Rookies) 1.00
196 Homer Bush P (Gold Leaf Rookies) .50
197 Raul Ibanez P (Gold Leaf Rookies) .50
198 Checklist (Nomar Garciaparra P) .75
199 Checklist (Scott Rolen P) .50
200 Checklist (Jose Cruz Jr. P) .50
201 Al Martin L 1.00

1998 Leaf Fractal Materials Die-Cut

This parallel set adds a die-cut to the Fractal Materials set. The first 200 of 75 plastic, 15 leather, 5 nylon and 5 wood cards have an x-axis die-cut. The first 100 of 20 plastic, 25 leather, 10 nylon and 5 wood cards have a y-axis die-cut. The first 50 of 5 plastic, 10 leather, 15 nylon and 10 wood cards have a z-axis die-cut. The serial numbers on the backs of the die-cut cards are meaningless because they were printed prior to the die-cut fracture. This compounds the confusion engendered among collectors which has had a significant dampening effect on demand and, thus, market values.

MT
Common X (200 of each): 2.00
Common Y (100): 5.00
Common Z (50): 10.00
1 Rusty Greer Z 10.00
2 Tino Martinez Y 5.00
3 Bobby Bonilla Y 5.00
4 Jason Giambi Z 30.00
5 Matt Morris Y 7.50
6 Craig Counsell X 2.00
7 Reggie Jefferson X 2.00
8 Brian Rose X 2.00
9 Ruben Rivera Y 5.00
10 Shawn Estes Y 5.00
11 Tony Gwynn X 22.50
12 Jeff Abbott Y 5.00
13 Jose Cruz Jr. Z 15.00
14 Francisco Cordova Y 5.00
15 Ryan Klesko X 2.00
16 Tim Salmon Y 7.50
17 Brett Tomko Y 5.00
18 Matt Williams Y 7.50
19 Joe Carter X 2.00
20 Harold Baines X 2.00
21 Gary Sheffield Z 15.00
22 Charles Johnson Y 5.00
23 Aaron Boone Y 5.00
24 Eddie Murray Y 12.00
25 Matt Stairs X 2.00
26 David Cone X 2.00
27 Jon Nunnally X 2.00
28 Chris Stynes X 2.00
29 Enrique Wilson Y 5.00
30 Randy Johnson Y 12.50
31 Garret Anderson Y 5.00
32 Manny Ramirez Y 15.00
33 Jeff Suppan Y 5.00
34 Rickey Henderson X 5.00
35 Scott Spiezio Y 5.00
36 Rondell White Y 5.00
37 Todd Greene Z 12.50
38 Delino DeShields Y 5.00
39 Kevin Brown X 3.50
40 Chili Davis X 2.00
41 Jimmy Key X 2.00
42 NOT ISSUED
43 Mike Mussina Z 30.00
44 Joe Randa X 2.00
45 Chan Ho Park Y 8.00
46 Brad Radke X 3.00
47 Geronimo Berroa X 2.00
48 Wade Boggs Y 10.00
49 Kevin Appier X 2.00
50 Moises Alou X 3.00
51 David Justice Z 17.50
52 Ivan Rodriguez X 9.00
53 J.T. Snow X 2.00
54 Brian Giles Y 5.00
55 Will Clark X 5.00
56 Justin Thompson Y 5.00
57 Javier Lopez Y 5.00
58 Hideki Irabu X 2.00
59 Mark Grudzielanek X 2.00
60 Abraham Nunez Z 10.00
61 Todd Hollandsworth X 2.00
62 Jay Bell X 2.00
63 Nomar Garciaparra Z 85.00
64 Vinny Castilla Y 5.00
65 Lou Collier Y 5.00
66 Kevin Orie X 2.00
67 John Valentin X 2.00
68 Robin Ventura X 2.00
69 Denny Neagle X 2.00
70 Tony Womack X 2.00
71 Dennis Reyes Y 5.00
72 Wally Joyner X 2.00
73 Kevin Brown X 2.50
74 Ray Durham X 2.00
75 Mike Cameron Y 5.00
76 Dante Bichette X 2.00
77 Jose Guillen Z 12.50
78 Carlos Delgado Y 10.00
79 Paul Molitor X 10.00
80 Jason Kendall X 2.00
81 Mark Belhorn X 2.00
82 Damian Jackson Y 5.00
83 Bill Mueller X 2.00
84 Kevin Young X 2.00
85 Curt Schilling X 4.00
86 Jeffrey Hammonds X 2.00
87 Sandy Alomar Jr. Y 5.00
88 Bartolo Colon Y 5.00
89 Wilton Guerrero Y 5.00
90 Bernie Williams Z 15.00
91 Deion Sanders Y 6.50
92 Mike Piazza Z 100.00
93 Butch Huskey X 2.00
94 Edgardo Alfonzo Y 5.00
95 Alan Benes Z 10.00
96 Craig Biggio X 3.00
97 Mark Grace Y 12.50
98 Shawn Green Y 9.00
99 Derrek Lee Y 5.00
100 Ken Griffey Jr. Z 125.00
101 Tim Raines X 2.00
102 Pokey Reese Y 5.00
103 Lee Stevens X 2.00
104 Shannon Stewart X 3.00
105 John Smoltz Y 6.50
106 Frank Thomas Z 65.00
107 Jeff Fassero X 2.00
108 Jay Buhner Y 5.00
109 Jose Canseco X 5.00
110 Omar Vizquel X 2.00
111 Travis Fryman X 2.00
112 Dave Nilsson X 2.00
113 John Olerud X 2.00
114 Larry Walker X 5.00
115 Jim Edmonds Z 12.50
116 Bobby Higginson Y 5.00
117 Todd Hundley Z 10.00
118 Paul O'Neill X 2.00
119 Bip Roberts X 2.00
120 Ismael Valdes X 2.00
121 Pedro Martinez X 6.00
122 Jeff Cirillo X 2.00
123 Andy Benes X 2.00
124 Bobby Jones X 2.00
125 Brian Hunter X 2.00
126 Darryl Kile X 2.00
127 Pat Hentgen X 2.00
128 Marquis Grissom X 2.00
129 Eric Davis X 2.00
130 Chipper Jones Z 100.00
131 Edgar Martinez Z 10.00
132 Andy Pettitte Y 10.00
133 Cal Ripken Jr. Z 125.00
134 Scott Rolen X 10.00
135 Ron Coomer X 2.00
136 Luis Castillo X 2.00
137 Fred McGriff Y 2.00
138 Neifi Perez Y 5.00
139 Eric Karros X 2.00
140 Alex Fernandez X 2.00
141 Jason Dickson X 2.00
142 Lance Johnson X 2.00
143 Ray Lankford Y 5.00
144 Sammy Sosa Y 25.00
145 Eric Young Y 5.00
146 Bubba Trammell Z 10.00
147 Todd Walker Z 12.50
148 Mo Vaughn X (Curtain Calls) 6.00
149 Jeff Bagwell X (Curtain Calls) 15.00
150 Kenny Lofton X (Curtain Calls) 2.00
151 Raul Mondesi X (Curtain Calls) 3.00
152 Mike Piazza X (Curtain Calls) 30.00
153 Chipper Jones X (Curtain Calls) 30.00
154 Larry Walker X

(Curtain Calls) 4.00
155 Greg Maddux X (Curtain Calls) 25.00
156 Ken Griffey Jr. X (Curtain Calls) 32.50
157 Frank Thomas X (Curtain Calls) 20.00
158 Darin Erstad Y (Gold Leaf Stars) 12.50
159 Roberto Alomar X (Gold Leaf Stars) 10.00
160 Albert Belle X (Gold Leaf Stars) 4.00
161 Jim Thome X (Gold Leaf Stars) 2.00
162 Tony Clark Z (Gold Leaf Stars) 10.00
163 Chuck Knoblauch Z (Gold Leaf Stars) 10.00
164 Derek Jeter X (Gold Leaf Stars) 30.00
165 Alex Rodriguez Y (Gold Leaf Stars) 45.00
166 Tony Gwynn X (Gold Leaf Stars) 20.00
167 Roger Clemens Y (Gold Leaf Stars) 25.00
168 Barry Larkin Y (Gold Leaf Stars) 7.50
169 Andres Galarraga Y (Gold Leaf Stars) 5.00
170 Vladimir Guerrero Y (Gold Leaf Stars) 12.00
171 Mark McGwire Z (Gold Leaf Stars) 125.00
172 Barry Bonds Y (Gold Leaf Stars) 17.50
173 Juan Gonzalez Y (Gold Leaf Stars) 15.00
174 Andruw Jones X (Gold Leaf Stars) 10.00
175 Paul Molitor X (Gold Leaf Stars) 9.00
176 Hideo Nomo Z (Gold Leaf Stars) 25.00
177 Cal Ripken Jr. X (Gold Leaf Stars) 35.00
178 Brad Fullmer Z (Gold Leaf Rookies) 10.00
179 Jaret Wright Z (Gold Leaf Rookies) 20.00
180 Bobby Estalella Y (Gold Leaf Rookies) 5.00
181 Ben Grieve Z (Gold Leaf Rookies) 15.00
182 Paul Konerko Z (Gold Leaf Rookies) 10.00
183 David Ortiz Z (Gold Leaf Rookies) 15.00
184 Todd Helton Z (Gold Leaf Rookies) 25.00
185 Juan Encarnacion Z (Gold Leaf Rookies) 10.00
186 Miguel Tejada Z (Gold Leaf Rookies) 20.00
187 Jacob Cruz X (Gold Leaf Rookies) 2.00
188 Mark Kotsay Z (Gold Leaf Rookies) 10.00
189 Fernando Tatis Y (Gold Leaf Rookies) 5.00
190 Ricky Ledee X (Gold Leaf Rookies) 2.00
191 Richard Hidalgo Z (Gold Leaf Rookies) 12.50
192 Richie Sexson Z (Gold Leaf Rookies) 10.00
193 Luis Ordaz X (Gold Leaf Rookies) 2.00
194 Eli Marrero Z (Gold Leaf Rookies) 10.00
195 Livan Hernandez Z (Gold Leaf Rookies) 10.00
196 Homer Bush X (Gold Leaf Rookies) 2.00
197 Raul Ibanez X (Gold Leaf Rookies) 2.00
198 Checklist (Nomar Garciaparra X) 7.50
199 Checklist (Scott Rolen Z) 10.00
200 Checklist (Jose Cruz Jr. X) 3.00
201 Al Martin Y 5.00

1998 Leaf Rookies & Stars

This 339-card set consists of three subsets: Power Tools, Lineup Card and Rookies. Fronts feature full-bleed photos and silver-foil graphics.Backs have complete year-by-year statistics and a small photo. The base set has short-printed base cards, numbers 131-230, 301-339, which are seeded 1:2 packs. Rookies and Stars has two parallels to the base set: True Blue and Longevity. True Blue's feature blue foil stamping and are each numbered "1 0f 500" on the card back. Longevity's are printed on a full-foiled card front with gold foil stamping and limited to 50 serially numbered sets.

	MT
Complete Set (339):	500.00
Common Player:	.10
Common SP (131-230):	.40
Common SP (301-339):	1.00
Inserted 1:2	
True Blues:	8-12X
SP True Blues:	2X
Production 500 sets	
Longevitys:	40-60X
SP Longevitys:	10-15X
Production 50 sets	
Pack (9):	13.00
Wax Box (24):	200.00

1 Andy Pettitte .30
2 Roberto Alomar .45
3 Randy Johnson .45
4 Manny Ramirez .75
5 Paul Molitor .50
6 Mike Mussina .50
7 Jim Thome .10
8 Tino Martinez .10
9 Gary Sheffield .15
10 Chuck Knoblauch .10
11 Bernie Williams .25
12 Tim Salmon .15
13 Sammy Sosa 1.25
14 Wade Boggs .35
15 Andres Galarraga .10
16 Pedro Martinez .30
17 David Justice .20
18 Chan Ho Park .25
19 Jay Buhner .10
20 Ryan Klesko .10
21 Barry Larkin .15
22 Will Clark .20
23 Raul Mondesi .15
24 Rickey Henderson .40
25 Jim Edmonds .15
26 Ken Griffey Jr. 1.50
27 Frank Thomas 1.00
28 Cal Ripken Jr. 2.00
29 Alex Rodriguez 1.50
30 Mike Piazza 1.25
31 Greg Maddux 1.00
32 Chipper Jones 1.25
33 Tony Gwynn 1.00
34 Derek Jeter 1.50
35 Jeff Bagwell .75
36 Juan Gonzalez .75
37 Nomar Garciaparra 1.00
38 Andruw Jones .45
39 Hideo Nomo .25
40 Roger Clemens .75
41 Mark McGwire 1.50
42 Scott Rolen .60
43 Vladimir Guerrero .75
44 Barry Bonds 1.00
45 Darin Erstad .45
46 Albert Belle .35
47 Kenny Lofton .10
48 Mo Vaughn .45
49 Ivan Rodriguez .45
50 Jose Cruz Jr. .30
51 Tony Clark .10
52 Larry Walker .25
53 Mark Grace .25
54 Edgar Martinez .10
55 Fred McGriff .10
56 Rafael Palmeiro .15
57 Matt Williams .15
58 Craig Biggio .15
59 Ken Caminiti .10
60 Jose Canseco .25
61 Brady Anderson .10
62 Moises Alou .15
63 Justin Thompson .10
64 John Smoltz .15
65 Carlos Delgado .60
66 J.T. Snow .10
67 Jason Giambi .25
68 Garret Anderson .10
69 Rondell White .10
70 Eric Karros .10
71 Javier Lopez .10
72 Pat Hentgen .10
73 Dante Bichette .10
74 Charles Johnson .10
75 Tom Glavine .15
76 Rusty Greer .10
77 Travis Fryman .10
78 Todd Hundley .10
79 Ray Lankford .10
80 Denny Neagle .10
81 Henry Rodriguez .10
82 Sandy Alomar Jr. .10
83 Robin Ventura .10
84 John Olerud .10
85 Omar Vizquel .10
86 Darren Dreifort .10
87 Kevin Brown .15
88 Curt Schilling .15
89 Francisco Cordova .10
90 Brad Radke .15
91 David Cone .10
92 Paul O'Neill .10
93 Vinny Castilla .10
94 Marquis Grissom .10
95 Brian Hunter .10
96 Kevin Appier .10
97 Bobby Bonilla .10
98 Eric Young .10
99 Jason Kendall .10
100 Shawn Green .20
101 Edgardo Alfonzo .10
102 Alan Benes .10
103 Bobby Higginson .10
104 Todd Greene .10
105 Jose Guillen .15
106 Neifi Perez .10
107 Edgar Renteria .10
108 Chris Stynes .10
109 Todd Walker .15
110 Brian Jordan .10
111 Joe Carter .10
112 Ellis Burks .10
113 Brett Tomko .10
114 Mike Cameron .10
115 Shannon Stewart .10
116 Kevin Orie .10
117 Brian Giles .10
118 Hideki Irabu .10
119 Delino DeShields .10
120 David Segui .10
121 Dustin Hermanson .10
122 Kevin Young .10
123 Jay Bell .10
124 Doug Glanville .10
125 *John Roskos* .10
126 *Damon Hollins* .10
127 Matt Stairs .10
128 Cliff Floyd .10
129 Derek Bell .10
130 Darryl Strawberry .10
131 Ken Griffey Jr. (Power Tools) 3.00
132 Tim Salmon (Power Tools) .75
133 Manny Ramirez (Power Tools) 1.25
134 Paul Konerko (Power Tools) .40
135 Frank Thomas (Power Tools) 2.00
136 Todd Helton (Power Tools) 1.25
137 Larry Walker (Power Tools) .75
138 Mo Vaughn (Power Tools) .75
139 Travis Lee (Power Tools) .60
140 Ivan Rodriguez (Power Tools) 1.25
141 Ben Grieve (Power Tools) .60
142 Brad Fullmer (Power Tools) .50
143 Alex Rodriguez (Power Tools) 3.00
144 Mike Piazza (Power Tools) 3.00
145 Greg Maddux (Power Tools) 2.00
146 Chipper Jones (Power Tools) 3.00
147 Kenny Lofton (Power Tools) .40
148 Albert Belle (Power Tools) .75
149 Barry Bonds (Power Tools) 2.00
150 Vladimir Guerrero (Power Tools) 1.25
151 Tony Gwynn (Power Tools) 1.75
152 Derek Jeter (Power Tools) 3.00
153 Jeff Bagwell (Power Tools) 1.25
154 Juan Gonzalez (Power Tools) 1.25
155 Nomar Garciaparra (Power Tools) 1.50
156 Andruw Jones (Power Tools) 1.00
157 Hideo Nomo (Power Tools) 1.00
158 Roger Clemens (Power Tools) 1.75
159 Mark McGwire (Power Tools) 4.00
160 Scott Rolen (Power Tools) .75
161 Travis Lee (Team Line-Up) .60
162 Ben Grieve (Team Line-Up) .75
163 Jose Guillen (Team Line-Up) .50
164 John Olerud (Team Line-Up) .40
165 Kevin Appier (Team Line-Up) .40
166 Marquis Grissom (Team Line-Up) .40
167 Rusty Greer (Team Line-Up) .40
168 Ken Caminiti (Team Line-Up) .40
169 Craig Biggio (Team Line-Up) .45
170 Ken Griffey Jr. (Team Line-Up) 3.00
171 Larry Walker (Team Line-Up) .75
172 Barry Larkin (Team Line-Up) .60
173 Andres Galarraga (Team Line-Up) .40
174 Wade Boggs (Team Line-Up) .75
175 Sammy Sosa (Team Line-Up) 3.00
176 Mike Piazza (Team Line-Up) 3.00
177 Jim Thome (Team Line-Up) .40

178 Paul Molitor (Team Line-Up) 1.00
179 Tony Clark (Team Line-Up) .40
180 Jose Cruz Jr. (Team Line-Up) .50
181 Darin Erstad (Team Line-Up) 1.00
182 Barry Bonds (Team Line-Up) 2.00
183 Vladimir Guerrero (Team Line-Up) 1.25
184 Scott Rolen (Team Line-Up) .75
185 Mark McGwire (Team Line-Up) 4.00
186 Nomar Garciaparra (Team Line-Up) 1.50
187 Gary Sheffield (Team Line-Up) .60
188 Cal Ripken Jr. (Team Line-Up) 4.00
189 Frank Thomas (Team Line-Up) 1.50
190 Andy Petitte (Team Line-Up) .60
191 Paul Konerko .60
192 Todd Helton 2.50
193 Mark Kotsay .40
194 Brad Fullmer .40
195 *Kevin Millwood* 10.00
196 David Ortiz .50
197 Kerry Wood 3.00
198 Miguel Tejada 2.00
199 Fernando Tatis .45
200 Jaret Wright 1.00
201 Ben Grieve .75
202 Travis Lee .75
203 Wes Helms .40
204 Geoff Jenkins 2.50
205 Russell Branyan .40
206 *Esteban Yan* 2.00
207 *Ben Ford* 2.00
208 *Rich Butler* 2.00
209 *Ryan Jackson* 1.50
210 A.J. Hinch .40
211 *Magglio Ordonez* 30.00
212 *David Dellucci* 2.50
213 Billy McMillon .40
214 *Mike Lowell* 15.00
215 *Todd Erdos* 1.00
216 *Carlos Mendoza* 1.00
217 *Frank Catalanotto* 1.50
218 *Julio Ramirez* 2.00
219 *John Halama* 1.50
220 Wilson Delgado .40
221 *Mike Judd* 2.50
222 *Rolando Arrojo* 4.00
223 *Jason LaRue* 2.50
224 *Manny Aybar* 1.00
225 Jorge Velandia .40
226 *Mike Kinkade* 1.50
227 *Carlos Lee* 15.00
228 Bobby Hughes .40
229 *Ryan Christenson* 1.50
230 *Masato Yoshii* 2.00
231 Richard Hidalgo .15
232 Rafael Medina .10
233 Damian Jackson .10
234 Derek Lowe .10
235 Mario Valdez .10
236 Eli Marrero .10
237 Juan Encarnacion .10
238 Livan Hernandez .10
239 Bruce Chen .10
240 Eric Milton .15
241 Jason Varitek .10
242 Scott Elarton .10
243 *Manuel Barrios* .20
244 Mike Caruso .10
245 Tom Evans .10
246 Pat Cline .10
247 Matt Clement .10
248 Karim Garcia .10
249 Richie Sexson .10
250 Sidney Ponson .10
251 Randall Simon .10
252 Tony Saunders .10
253 Javier Valentin .10
254 Danny Clyburn .10
255 Michael Coleman .10
256 *Hanley Frias* .15
257 Miguel Cairo .10
258 *Rob Stanifer* .10
259 Lou Collier .10
260 Abraham Nunez .10
261 Ricky Ledee .10
262 Carl Pavano .15
263 Derrek Lee .10
264 Jeff Abbott .10
265 Bob Abreu .15
266 Bartolo Colon .15
267 Mike Drumright .10
268 Daryle Ward .10
269 Gabe Alvarez .10
270 Josh Booty .10
271 Damian Moss .10
272 Brian Rose .10
273 Jarrod Washburn .10
274 Bobby Estalella .10
275 Enrique Wilson .10
276 Derrick Gibson .10
277 Ken Cloude .10
278 Kevin Witt .10
279 Donnie Sadler .10
280 Sean Casey .15
281 Jacob Cruz .10
282 Ron Wright .10
283 Jeremi Gonzalez .10
284 Desi Relaford .10
285 Bobby Smith .10
286 Javier Vazquez .10
287 *Steve Woodard* .20
288 Greg Norton .10
289 Cliff Politte .10
290 Felix Heredia .10
291 Braden Looper .10
292 Felix Martinez .10
293 Brian Meadows .10
294 Edwin Diaz .10
295 Pat Watkins .10
296 *Marc Pisciotta* .10
297 Rick Gorecki .10
298 DaRond Stovall .10
299 Andy Larkin .10
300 Felix Rodriguez .10
301 Blake Stein 1.00
302 *John Rocker* 9.00
303 *Justin Baughman* 1.00
304 *Jesus Sanchez* 2.00
305 Randy Winn 1.00
306 Lou Merloni 1.00
307 *Jim Parque* 4.00
308 Dennis Reyes 1.00
309 *Orlando Hernandez* 15.00
310 Jason Johnson 1.00
311 Torii Hunter 1.00
312 Mike Piazza 9.00
313 *Mike Frank* 2.50
314 *Troy Glaus* 150.00
315 *Jin Cho* 1.50
316 *Ruben Mateo* 15.00
317 *Ryan Minor* 12.50
318 Aramis Ramirez 1.50
319 Adrian Beltre 2.00
320 *Matt Anderson* 2.00
321 *Gabe Kapler* 20.00
322 *Jeremy Giambi* 6.00
323 Carlos Beltran 1.00
324 Dermal Brown 1.00
325 Ben Davis 1.00
326 Eric Chavez 2.00
327 *Bob Howry* 2.00
328 Roy Halladay 1.00
329 George Lombard 1.00
330 Michael Barrett 1.00
331 *Fernando Seguignol* 4.00
332 *J.D. Drew* 60.00
333 *Odalis Perez* 4.00
334 *Alex Cora* 2.00
335 *Placido Polanco* 7.00
336 *Armando Rios* 1.00
337 Sammy Sosa (HR commemorative) 10.00
338 Mark McGwire (HR commemorative) 15.00
339 Sammy Sosa, Mark McGwire (Checklist) 15.00

1998 Leaf Rookies & Stars True Blue

This parallel edition of the Rookies & Stars base set is labeled at top-back "1 of 500". The parallels feature blue foil graphic highlights on front with TRUE BLUE at top.

	MT
Complete Set (339):	650.00
Common Player:	1.00
Stars:	8-12X
SP Stars (131-230; 301-339):	2X

(See 1998 Leaf Rookies & Stars for checklist and base card values.)

1998 Leaf Rookies & Stars Longevity

Only 50 sets of this parallel edition were issued. Each card is serially numbered on back. Fronts are printed with gold foil background and have LONGEVITY printed at top. Special Longevity holographic 1 of 1 cards exist, but cannot be priced due to rarity.

	MT
Common Player:	7.50
Stars:	40-60X
SP Stars (131-230):	10-15X
SP Stars (301-339):	5-7X

(See 1998 Leaf Rookies & Stars for checklist and base card values.)

1998 Leaf Rookies & Stars Cross Training

This 10-card insert set highlights players who excel at multiple aspects of the game. Card fronts are full-foiled and sequentially numbered on the card back to 1,000.

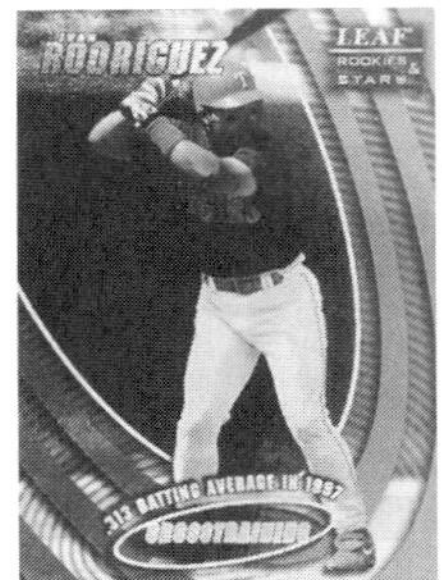

		MT
Complete Set (10):		45.00
Common Player:		2.00
Production 1,000 sets		
1	Kenny Lofton	2.00
2	Ken Griffey Jr.	8.00
3	Alex Rodriguez	10.00
4	Greg Maddux	6.50
5	Barry Bonds	4.00
6	Ivan Rodriguez	3.00
7	Chipper Jones	7.50
8	Jeff Bagwell	3.00
9	Nomar Garciaparra	6.50
10	Derek Jeter	10.00

1998 Leaf Rookies & Stars Crusade

This 30-card set is a continuation of this cross-brand insert. Cards are printed on a holographic green foil front and limited to 250 serial numbered sets. Two parallels are also randomly seeded: Purple and Red. Purples have purple holographic foil fronts and limited to 100 serial numbered sets. Reds are printed on red holographic foil fronts and limited to 25 serial numbered sets.

		MT
Complete Green Set (30):		200.00
Common Player:		4.00
Production 250 sets		
Purples (100 sets):		1.5X
Reds (25 sets):		6X
101	Richard Hidalgo	6.00
102	Paul Konerko	6.00
103	Miguel Tejada	12.50
104	Fernando Tatis	5.00
105	Travis Lee	15.00
106	Wes Helms	4.00
107	Rich Butler	4.00
108	Mark Kotsay	4.00
109	Eli Marrero	4.00
110	David Ortiz	5.00
111	Juan Encarnacion	6.00

112 Jaret Wright 15.00
113 Livan Hernandez 4.00
114 Ron Wright 4.00
115 Ryan Christenson 4.00
116 Eric Milton 4.00
117 Brad Fullmer 4.00
118 Karim Garcia 4.00
119 Abraham Nunez 4.00
120 Ricky Ledee 4.00
121 Carl Pavano 4.00
122 Derrek Lee 4.00
123 A.J. Hinch 4.00
124 Brian Rose 4.00
125 Bobby Estalella 4.00
126 Kevin Millwood 25.00
127 Kerry Wood 25.00
128 Sean Casey 12.50
129 Russell Branyan 5.00
130 Magglio Ordonez 20.00

1998 Leaf Rookies & Stars Extreme Measures

These inserts are printed on a full-foiled card front. Each card highlights an outstanding statistic for the featured player and is sequentially numbered to 1,000, minus the number of die-cut versions produced for each.

		MT
Complete Set (10):		75.00
Common Player:		5.00
Die-Cuts:		2X
1	Ken Griffey Jr. (944)	12.50
2	Frank Thomas (653)	10.00
3	Tony Gwynn (628)	7.50
4	Mark McGwire (942)	12.50
5	Larry Walker (280)	5.00
6	Mike Piazza (960)	12.50
7	Roger Clemens (708)	7.50
8	Greg Maddux (980)	10.00
9	Jeff Bagwell (873)	5.00
10	Nomar Garciaparra (989)	10.00

1998 Leaf Rookies & Stars Extreme Measures Die-Cuts

Each card highlights an outstanding statistic for each featured player, is die-cut and serially numbered to the limit of the particular statistic as shown.

		MT
Complete Set (10):		415.00
Common Player:		2.50
1	Ken Griffey Jr. (56)	65.00
2	Frank Thomas (347)	11.00
3	Tony Gwynn (372)	13.50
4	Mark McGwire (58)	110.00
5	Larry Walker (720)	2.50
6	Mike Piazza (40)	60.00
7	Roger Clemens (292)	11.00
8	Greg Maddux (20)	110.00
9	Jeff Bagwell (127)	20.00
10	Nomar Garciaparra (11)	145.00

1998 Leaf Rookies & Stars Freshman Orientation

Card fronts are printed on holographic foil with silver foil stamping and feature top prospects. Card backs highlight the date of the featured player's Major League debut, have a small photo and are serially numbered to 5,000 sets. Each card was also issued in an appropriately labeled sample version.

		MT
Complete Set (20):		22.50
Common Player:		.75
Production 5,000 sets		
Samples:		1X
1	Todd Helton	4.00
2	Ben Grieve	1.50
3	Travis Lee	1.00
4	Paul Konerko	.75
5	Jaret Wright	1.00
6	Livan Hernandez	.75
7	Brad Fullmer	.75
8	Carl Pavano	.75
9	Richard Hidalgo	1.50
10	Miguel Tejada	1.50
11	Mark Kotsay	.75
12	David Ortiz	1.00
13	Juan Encarnacion	1.00
14	Fernando Tatis	1.00
15	Kevin Millwood	2.00
16	Kerry Wood	2.00
17	Magglio Ordonez	5.00
18	Derrek Lee	.75
19	Jose Cruz Jr.	1.00
20	A.J. Hinch	.75

1998 Leaf Rookies & Stars Great American Heroes

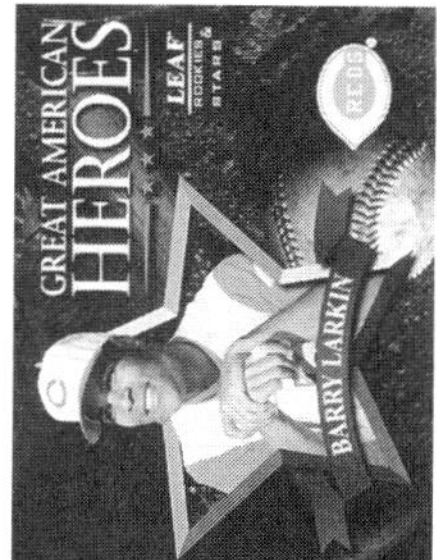

Card fronts are stamped with a holographic silver foil and done on a horizontal format. Card backs have a photo and are serially numbered to 2,500. Each card was also produced in an appropriately marked sample version.

		MT
Complete Set (20):		35.00
Common Player:		.75
Production 2,500 sets		
Samples:		1X
1	Frank Thomas	2.00
2	Cal Ripken Jr.	5.00
3	Ken Griffey Jr.	4.00
4	Alex Rodriguez	4.50
5	Greg Maddux	3.25
6	Mike Piazza	3.75
7	Chipper Jones	3.75
8	Tony Gwynn	2.00
9	Jeff Bagwell	1.50
10	Juan Gonzalez	1.50
11	Hideo Nomo	1.00
12	Roger Clemens	2.00
13	Mark McGwire	5.00
14	Barry Bonds	2.00
15	Kenny Lofton	.75
16	Larry Walker	.75
17	Paul Molitor	1.25
18	Wade Boggs	1.25
19	Barry Larkin	.75
20	Andres Galarraga	.75

1998 Leaf Rookies & Stars Greatest Hits

These inserts feature holographic silver foil stamping on the card front done on a horizontal format. Card backs have a photo and are serially numbered to 2,500.

		MT
Complete Set (20):		45.00
Common Player:		1.00
Production 2,500 sets		
1	Ken Griffey Jr.	5.00
2	Frank Thomas	2.50
3	Cal Ripken Jr.	6.00
4	Alex Rodriguez	5.00
5	Ben Grieve	1.00
6	Mike Piazza	4.00
7	Chipper Jones	4.00
8	Tony Gwynn	2.50
9	Derek Jeter	4.00
10	Jeff Bagwell	2.00
11	Tino Martinez	1.00
12	Juan Gonzalez	2.00
13	Nomar Garciaparra	3.00
14	Mark McGwire	6.00
15	Scott Rolen	1.50
16	David Justice	1.00
17	Darin Erstad	2.00
18	Mo Vaughn	1.00
19	Ivan Rodriguez	2.00
20	Travis Lee	1.00

1998 Leaf Rookies & Stars Home Run Derby

This 20-card set spotlights the top home run hitters on a bronze full-foiled card front. Card backs have a portrait photo and are serially numbered to 2,500.

		MT
Complete Set (20):		75.00
Common Player:		2.00
Production 2,500 sets		
1	Tino Martinez	2.00
2	Jim Thome	2.00
3	Larry Walker	2.50
4	Tony Clark	2.00
5	Jose Cruz Jr.	2.50
6	Barry Bonds	5.00
7	Scott Rolen	3.00
8	Paul Konerko	2.00
9	Travis Lee	2.00
10	Todd Helton	3.00
11	Mark McGwire	15.00
12	Andruw Jones	3.00
13	Nomar Garciaparra	8.00
14	Juan Gonzalez	4.00
15	Jeff Bagwell	4.00
16	Chipper Jones	8.00

17	Mike Piazza	10.00
18	Frank Thomas	6.00
19	Ken Griffey Jr.	10.00
20	Albert Belle	2.50

1998 Leaf Rookies & Stars MVPs

This 20-card set is printed on a full silver-foil card stock and sequentially numbered to 5,000. The first 500 of each card is treated with a "Pennant Edition" logo and unique color coating.

		MT
Complete Set (20):		30.00
Common Player:		.50
Production 4,500 sets		
Pennant Editions: 2X		
Production 500 sets		
1	Frank Thomas	2.50
2	Chuck Knoblauch	.50
3	Cal Ripken Jr.	4.00
4	Alex Rodriguez	4.00
5	Ivan Rodriguez	1.25
6	Albert Belle	.50
7	Ken Griffey Jr.	4.00
8	Juan Gonzalez	1.25
9	Roger Clemens	2.00
10	Mo Vaughn	1.00
11	Jeff Bagwell	1.25
12	Craig Biggio	.50
13	Chipper Jones	3.00
14	Barry Larkin	.50
15	Mike Piazza	3.00
16	Barry Bonds	1.50
17	Andruw Jones	1.00
18	Tony Gwynn	1.50
19	Greg Maddux	2.50
20	Mark McGwire	4.00

1998 Leaf Rookies & Stars ML Hard Drives

Card fronts are stamped with silver holographic foil. Card backs detail to which field (left, center and right) the featured player hit each of his singles, doubles, triples and homeruns. Each card is serially numbered to 2,500. Each card was also produced in an appropriately marked sample version.

		MT
Complete Set (20):		90.00
Common Player:		2.00
Production 2,500 sets		
Samples:		1X
1	Jeff Bagwell	4.00
2	Juan Gonzalez	4.00
3	Nomar Garciaparra	8.00
4	Ken Griffey Jr.	10.00
5	Frank Thomas	6.00
6	Cal Ripken Jr.	12.50
7	Alex Rodriguez	12.00
8	Mike Piazza	10.00
9	Chipper Jones	8.00
10	Tony Gwynn	5.00
11	Derek Jeter	12.00
12	Mo Vaughn	2.00
13	Ben Grieve	2.00
14	Manny Ramirez	4.00
15	Vladimir Guerrero	3.50
16	Scott Rolen	2.50
17	Darin Erstad	3.50
18	Kenny Lofton	2.00
19	Brad Fullmer	2.00
20	David Justice	2.00

1998 Leaf Rookies & Stars Standing Ovation

Card fronts are stamped with silver holographic foil and card backs have a small photo of the featured player and are serially numbered to 5,000. Each card was also produced in an appropriately labeled sample version.

		MT
Complete Set (10):		27.50
Common Player:		1.50
Production 5,000 sets		
Samples:		1X
1	Barry Bonds	2.50
2	Mark McGwire	6.00
3	Ken Griffey Jr.	5.00
4	Frank Thomas	3.00
5	Tony Gwynn	3.00
6	Cal Ripken Jr.	6.00
7	Greg Maddux	3.50
8	Roger Clemens	2.50
9	Paul Molitor	1.50
10	Ivan Rodriguez	1.50

1998 Leaf Rookies & Stars Ticket Masters

Card fronts are printed on a full-foiled card stock with silver foil stamping and have a photo of one of the two players featured from the same team. Card backs have a photo of the other featured player and are serially numbered to 2,500. The first 250 of each card are die-cut.

		MT
Complete Set (20):		65.00
Common Player:		1.00
Production 2,250 sets		
Die-Cuts:		2X
Production 250 sets		
1	Ken Griffey Jr., Alex Rodriguez	9.00
2	Frank Thomas, Albert Belle	5.00
3	Cal Ripken Jr., Roberto Alomar	7.00
4	Greg Maddux, Chipper Jones	7.00
5	Tony Gwynn, Ken Caminiti	4.50
6	Derek Jeter, Andy Pettitte	7.00
7	Jeff Bagwell, Craig Biggio	2.50
8	Juan Gonzalez, Ivan Rodriguez	3.00
9	Nomar Garciaparra, Mo Vaughn	5.50
10	Vladimir Guerrero, Brad Fullmer	3.00
11	Andruw Jones, Andres Galarraga	2.50
12	Tino Martinez, Chuck Knoblauch	1.00
13	Raul Mondesi, Paul Konerko	1.00
14	Roger Clemens, Jose Cruz Jr.	4.50
15	Mark McGwire, Brian Jordan	10.00
16	Kenny Lofton, Manny Ramirez	3.00
17	Larry Walker, Todd Helton	2.50
18	Darin Erstad, Tim Salmon	2.50
19	Travis Lee, Matt Williams	1.00
20	Ben Grieve, Jason Giambi	2.00

2001 Leaf Certified Materials

		MT
Complete Set (160):		
Common Player:		.40
Common SP (111-160):		15.00
Production 200		
Pack (5):		12.00
Box (12):		125.00
1	Alex Rodriguez	5.00
2	Barry Bonds	4.00
3	Cal Ripken Jr.	6.00
4	Chipper Jones	4.00
5	Derek Jeter	6.00
6	Troy Glaus	2.00
7	Frank Thomas	2.00
8	Greg Maddux	4.00
9	Ivan Rodriguez	2.00
10	Jeff Bagwell	2.00
11	Eric Karros	.40
12	Todd Helton	2.00
13	Ken Griffey Jr.	5.00
14	Manny Ramirez	2.00
15	Mark McGwire	5.00
16	Mike Piazza	5.00
17	Nomar Garciaparra	4.00
18	Pedro Martinez	2.50
19	Randy Johnson	2.00
20	Rick Ankiel	.75
21	Rickey Henderson	.75
22	Roger Clemens	3.00
23	Sammy Sosa	4.00
24	Tony Gwynn	2.50
25	Vladimir Guerrero	2.00
26	Kazuhiro Sasaki	.40
27	Roberto Alomar	1.50
28	Barry Zito	.60
29	Pat Burrell	.75
30	Harold Baines	.40
31	Carlos Delgado	1.00
32	J.D. Drew	1.00
33	Jim Edmonds	.60
34	Darin Erstad	.75
35	Jason Giambi	1.50
36	Tom Glavine	.75
37	Juan Gonzalez	2.00
38	Mark Grace	1.00
39	Shawn Green	.75
40	Tim Hudson	.75
41	Andruw Jones	1.00
42	Jeff Kent	.40
43	Barry Larkin	.75
44	Rafael Furcal	.40
45	Mike Mussina	1.50
46	Hideo Nomo	.75
47	Rafael Palmeiro	1.00
48	Scott Rolen	.75
49	Gary Sheffield	.60
50	Bernie Williams	1.50
51	Bobby Abreu	.40
52	Edgardo Alfonzo	.40
53	Edgar Martinez	.40
54	Magglio Ordonez	.40
55	Kerry Wood	.75
56	Adrian Beltre	.40
57	Lance Berkman	.40
58	Kevin Brown	.40
59	Sean Casey	.60
60	Eric Chavez	.60
61	Bartolo Colon	.40
62	Johnny Damon	.40
63	Jermaine Dye	.40
64	Juan Encarnacion	.40
65	Carl Everett	.40
66	Brian Giles	.40
67	Mike Hampton	.40
68	Richard Hidalgo	.40
69	Geoff Jenkins	.60
70	Jacque Jones	.40
71	Jason Kendall	.40
72	Ryan Klesko	.40
73	Chan Ho Park	.40
74	Richie Sexson	.40
75	Mike Sweeney	.40
76	Fernando Tatis	.40
77	Miguel Tejada	.75
78	Jose Vidro	.40
79	Larry Walker	.75
80	Preston Wilson	.40
81	Craig Biggio	.40
82	Fred McGriff	.60
83	Jim Thome	.75
84	Garret Anderson	.40
85	Russell Branyan	.40
86	Tony Batista	.40
87	Terrence Long	.40
88	Deion Sanders	.40
89	Rusty Greer	.40
90	Orlando Hernandez	.40
91	Gabe Kapler	.40
92	Paul Konerko	.40

93	Carlos Lee	.40
94	Kenny Lofton	.60
95	Raul Mondesi	.40
96	Jorge Posada	.75
97	Tim Salmon	.40
98	Greg Vaughn	.40
99	Mo Vaughn	.60
100	Omar Vizquel	.40
101	Ray Durham	.40
102	Jeff Cirillo	.40
103	Dean Palmer	.40
104	Ryan Dempster	.40
105	Carlos Beltran	.40
106	Timo Perez	.40
107	Robin Ventura	.40
108	Andy Pettitte	.75
109	Aramis Ramirez	.40
110	Phil Nevin	.40
111	Alex Escobar	20.00
112	*Johnny Estrada*	25.00
113	Pedro Feliz	15.00
114	*Nate Frese*	15.00
115	*Joe Kennedy*	15.00
116	*Brandon Larson*	15.00
117	*Alexis Gomez*	15.00
118	Jason Hart	15.00
119	*Jason Michaels*	20.00
120	Marcus Giles	20.00
121	*Christian Parker*	15.00
122	*Jackson Melian*	20.00
123	*Donaldo Mendez*	15.00
124	*Adrian Hernandez*	25.00
125	*Bud Smith*	20.00
126	*Jose Mieses*	15.00
127	Roy Oswalt	25.00
128	Eric Munson	15.00
129	Xavier Nady	15.00
130	*Horacio Ramirez*	15.00
131	Abraham Nunez	15.00
132	Jose Ortiz	15.00
133	*Jeremy Owens*	15.00
134	*Claudio Vargas*	20.00
135	*Ricardo Rodriguez*	15.00
136	Aubrey Huff	15.00
137	Ben Sheets	20.00
138	Adam Dunn	50.00
139	*Andres Torres*	15.00
140	*Elpidio Guzman*	15.00
141	*Jay Gibbons*	25.00
142	*Wilkin Ruan*	15.00
143	*Tsuyoshi Shinjo*	40.00
144	Alfonso Soriano	25.00
145	*Josh Towers*	15.00
146	*Ichiro Suzuki*	200.00
147	*Juan Uribe*	20.00
148	Joe Crede	15.00
149	*Carlos Valderrama*	15.00
150	*Matt White*	25.00
151	Dee Brown	15.00
152	*Juan Cruz*	25.00
153	*Cory Aldridge*	15.00
154	Wilmy Caceres	15.00
155	Josh Beckett	25.00
156	*Wilson Betemit*	35.00
157	Corey Patterson	20.00
158	*Albert Pujols*	100.00
159	*Rafael Soriano*	20.00
160	*Jack Wilson*	20.00

2001 Leaf Certified Materials Fabric of the Game

		MT
Common Player:		10.00
1	Lou Gehrig/184	300.00
1	Lou Gehrig/23	475.00
2	Babe Ruth/136	350.00
2	Babe Ruth/60	450.00
3	Stan Musial/177	50.00
3	Stan Musial/39	100.00
4	Nolan Ryan	50.00
5	Roberto Clemente/166	110.00
6	Al Kaline/137	60.00
7	Brooks Robinson	25.00
7	Brooks Robinson/68	50.00
8	Mel Ott	50.00
8	Mel Ott/72	60.00
9	Dave Winfield/88	25.00
10	Eddie Mathews/115	40.00
10	Eddie Mathews/72	50.00
11	Ernie Banks/50	75.00
11	Ernie Banks/47	75.00
12	Frank Robinson	25.00
13	George Brett/137	50.00
14	Hank Aaron	40.00
14	Hank Aaron/98	50.00
14	Hank Aaron/47	75.00
15	Harmon Killebrew	40.00
15	Harmon Killebrew/49	75.00
16	Joe Morgan	20.00
16	Joe Morgan/96	25.00
17	Johnny Bench	25.00
17	Johnny Bench/68	40.00
18	Kirby Puckett/134	60.00
19	Mike Schmidt	40.00
19	Mike Schmidt/59	75.00
20	Phil Rizzuto/149	40.00
21	Reggie Jackson	25.00
21	Reggie Jackson/44	50.00
22	Catfish Hunter	20.00
22	Catfish Hunter/42	40.00
23	Rod Carew/92	40.00
23	Rod Carew/100	40.00
24	Bob Feller	30.00
24	Bob Feller/44	40.00
25	Lou Brock	20.00
25	Lou Brock/141	25.00
26	Tom Seaver	30.00
26	Tom Seaver/61	50.00
27	Paul Molitor	25.00
27	Paul Molitor/114	40.00
27		40.00
28	Willie McCovey/126	25.00
29	Yogi Berra	30.00
29	Yogi Berra/49	60.00
30	Don Drysdale	20.00
30	Don Drysdale/49	50.00
31	Duke Snider	35.00
31	Duke Snider/99	60.00
33	Orlando Cepeda/46	30.00
34	Casey Stengel	25.00
34	Casey Stengel/103	30.00
35	Robin Yount	30.00
35	Robin Yount/126	50.00
36	Eddie Murray	20.00
36	Eddie Murray/35	80.00
37	Jim Palmer	25.00
38	Juan Marichal	20.00
38	Juan Marichal/52	30.00
39	Willie Stargell	20.00
39	Willie Stargell/55	40.00
40	Ted Williams	350.00
41	Cal Ripken Jr.	40.00
41	Cal Ripken/75	60.00
41	Cal Ripken/277	50.00
42	Vladimir Guerrero/322	20.00
42	Vladimir Guerrero/44	50.00
43	Greg Maddux	20.00
43	Greg Maddux/240	30.00
44	Barry Bonds	30.00
44	Barry Bonds/289	40.00
45	Pedro Martinez	15.00
45	Pedro Martinez/268	20.00
46	Ivan Rodriguez	15.00
46	Ivan Rodriguez/304	20.00
47	Roger Maris	50.00
47	Roger Maris/275	60.00
48	Randy Johnson	20.00
48	Randy Johnson/179	25.00
49	Roger Clemens	25.00
49	Roger Clemens/260	40.00
50	Todd Helton	20.00
50	Todd Helton/334	25.00
51	Tony Gwynn	20.00
51	Tony Gwynn/119	25.00
51	Tony Gwynn/134	25.00
52	Troy Glaus	15.00
52	Troy Glaus/47	35.00
52	Troy Glaus/256	15.00
53	Phil Niekro	15.00
53	Phil Niekro/245	15.00
54	Don Sutton	15.00
54	Don Sutton/178	15.00
55	Frank Thomas	15.00
55	Frank Thomas/321	20.00
56	Jeff Bagwell	20.00
56	Jeff Bagwell/305	25.00
57	Rickey Henderson	20.00
57	Rickey Henderson/282	25.00
58	Darin Erstad/301	15.00
59	Andruw Jones	15.00
59	Andruw Jones/272	15.00
60	Roberto Alomar	15.00
60	Roberto Alomar/120	20.00
60	Roberto Alomar/170	20.00
61	Mike Piazza	40.00
61	Mike Piazza/328	40.00
62	Chipper Jones	20.00
62	Chipper Jones/189	25.00
63	Shawn Green	10.00
63	Shawn Green/143	15.00
64	Don Mattingly	60.00
64	Don Mattingly/145	75.00
64	Don Mattingly/222	75.00
65	Rafael Palmeiro	10.00
66	Wade Boggs	15.00
66	Wade Boggs/116	25.00
66	Wade Boggs/89	30.00
67	Hoyt Wilhelm	10.00
67	Hoyt Wilhelm/143	15.00
68	Andre Dawson	10.00
68	Andre Dawson/49	20.00
68	Andre Dawson/314	15.00
69	Ryne Sandberg	30.00
69	Ryne Sandberg/282	35.00
70	Nomar Garciaparra/333	40.00
71	Tom Glavine	10.00
71	Tom Glavine/208	15.00
71	Tom Glavine/247	15.00
72	Magglio Ordonez	10.00
72	Magglio Ordonez/301	10.00
72	Magglio Ordonez/126	15.00
73	Bernie Williams	20.00
73	Bernie Williams/304	25.00
74	Jim Edmonds	10.00
74	Jim Edmonds/108	15.00
74	Jim Edmonds/291	10.00
75	Hideo Nomo	40.00
75	Hideo Nomo/69	70.00
76	Barry Larkin	15.00
76	Barry Larkin/300	15.00
77	Scott Rolen	10.00
77	Scott Rolen/284	10.00
78	Miguel Tejada	10.00
78	Miguel Tejada/253	10.00
79	Freddy Garcia	10.00
79	Freddy Garcia/170	15.00
79	Freddy Garcia/249	10.00
80	Edgar Martinez	10.00
80	Edgar Martinez/320	10.00
81	Edgardo Alfonzo	10.00
81	Edgardo Alfonzo/108	15.00
81	Edgardo Alfonzo/296	10.00
82	Steve Garvey	10.00
82	Steve Garvey/272	15.00
83	Larry Walker	10.00
83	Larry Walker/311	10.00
83	Larry Walker/49	20.00
84	A.J. Burnett	10.00
84	A.J. Burnett/90	10.00
85	Richie Sexson	10.00
85	Richie Sexson/242	10.00
85	Richie Sexson/116	10.00
86	Mark Mulder	10.00
86	Mark Mulder/88	15.00
87	Kerry Wood	15.00
87	Kerry Wood/233	15.00
88	Sean Casey	10.00
88	Sean Casey/312	10.00
89	Jermaine Dye	10.00
89	Jermaine Dye/118	10.00
89	Jermaine Dye/286	10.00
90	Kevin Brown	10.00
90	Kevin Brown/170	10.00
90	Kevin Brown/257	10.00
91	Craig Biggio	15.00
91	Craig Biggio/88	25.00
91	Craig Biggio/291	15.00
92	Mike Sweeney	10.00
92	Mike Sweeney/302	10.00
92	Mike Sweeney/144	10.00
93	Jim Thome	15.00
93	Jim Thome/233	15.00
93	Jim Thome/40	40.00
94	Al Leiter	10.00
94	Al Leiter/247	15.00
94	Al Leiter/106	15.00
95	Barry Zito	15.00
95	Barry Zito/272	20.00
95	Barry Zito/78	25.00
96	Rafael Furcal	10.00
96	Rafael Furcal/295	10.00
97	J.D. Drew	15.00
97	J.D. Drew/276	20.00
98	Andres Galarraga	10.00
98	Andres Galarraga/150	10.00
98	Andres Galarraga/291	10.00
99	Kazuhiro Sasaki	15.00
99	Kazuhiro Sasaki/266	20.00
100	Chan Ho Park	15.00
100	Chan Ho Park/65	30.00
100	Chan Ho Park/217	15.00
101	Eric Milton	10.00
101	Eric Milton/163	10.00
102	Carlos Lee	10.00
102	Carlos Lee/297	10.00
103	Preston Wilson	10.00
103	Preston Wilson/266	10.00
104	Adrian Beltre	10.00
104	Adrian Beltre/85	15.00
104	Adrian Beltre/272	10.00
105	Luis Gonzalez	15.00
105	Luis Gonzalez/281	20.00
105	Luis Gonzalez/114	25.00
106	Kenny Lofton	10.00
106	Kenny Lofton/306	10.00
107	Shannon Stewart	10.00
107	Shannon Stewart/297	10.00
108	Javy Lopez	10.00
108	Javy Lopez/290	10.00
108	Javy Lopez/106	10.00
109	Raul Mondesi	10.00
109	Raul Mondesi/286	10.00
110	Mark Grace	15.00
110	Mark Grace/51	25.00
110	Mark Grace/308	15.00
111	Curt Schilling	15.00
111	Curt Schilling/235	15.00
111	Curt Schilling/110	25.00
112	Cliff Floyd	10.00
112	Cliff Floyd/275	10.00
113	Moises Alou	10.00
113	Moises Alou/124	10.00
113	Moises Alou/303	10.00
114	Aaron Sele	10.00
114	Aaron Sele/92	10.00
115	Jose Cruz Jr.	10.00
115	Jose Cruz Jr/245	10.00
116	John Olerud	10.00
116	John Olerud/186	15.00
116	John Olerud/107	15.00
117	Jose Vidro	10.00
117	Jose Vidro/296	10.00
118	John Smoltz	10.00
118	John Smoltz/334	10.00

2001 Leaf Limited

	MT
Complete Set (375):	NA
Common Player:	.75
Common Lumberjack (151-200):	6.00
#'d to 100, 250 or 500	
Common Rk (201-300):	8.00
Production 1,500	
Common Auto (301-325):	10.00

Production 1,000
Pack (3): 6.00
Box (18): 100.00
1 Curt Schilling .75
2 Craig Biggio .75
3 Brian Giles .75
4 Scott Brosius .75
5 Barry Larkin 1.00
6 Bartolo Colon .75
7 John Olerud 1.00
8 Cal Ripken Jr. 6.00
9 Moises Alou .75
10 Barry Zito .75
11 Ken Griffey Jr. 4.00
12 Garret Anderson .75
13 Andy Pettitte .75
14 Jim Edmonds .75
15 Tom Glavine 1.00
16 Jose Canseco 1.00
17 Fred McGriff .75
18 Robin Ventura .75
19 Tony Gwynn 1.50
20 Jeff Cirillo .75
21 Brad Radke .75
22 Ellis Burks .75
23 Scott Rolen 1.00
24 Rickey Henderson 1.00
25 Edgar Martinez .75
26 Kerry Wood 1.00
27 Al Leiter .75
28 Jose Cruz Jr. .75
29 Sean Casey .75
30 Eric Chavez .75
31 Jarrod Washburn .75
32 Gary Sheffield 1.00
33 Jermaine Dye .75
34 Bernie Williams 1.00
35 Tony Armas Jr. .75
36 Carlos Beltran .75
37 Geoff Jenkins .75
38 Shawn Green 1.00
39 Ryan Klesko .75
40 Richie Sexson .75
41 Pat Burrell 1.00
42 J.D. Drew 1.00
43 Larry Walker 1.00
44 Andres Galarraga .75
45 Tino Martinez .75
46 Rafael Furcal .75
47 Cristian Guzman .75
48 Omar Vizquel .75
49 Bret Boone .75
50 Wade Miller .75
51 Eric Milton .75
52 Gabe Kapler .75
53 Johnny Damon .75
54 Shannon Stewart .75
55 Kenny Lofton .75
56 Raul Mondesi .75
57 Jorge Posada .75
58 Mark Grace 1.00
59 Robert Fick .75
60 Phil Nevin .75
61 Mike Mussina 1.00
62 Joe Mays .75
63 Todd Helton 1.50
64 Tim Hudson 1.00
65 Manny Ramirez 1.50
66 Sammy Sosa 3.00
67 Darin Erstad 1.00
68 Roberto Alomar 1.00
69 Jeff Bagwell 1.50
70 Mark McGwire 5.00
71 Jason Giambi 1.00
72 Cliff Floyd .75
73 Barry Bonds 3.00
74 Juan Gonzalez 1.50
75 Jeremy Giambi .75
76 Carlos Lee .75
77 Randy Johnson 1.50
78 Frank Thomas 1.50
79 Carlos Delgado 1.00
80 Pedro Martinez 1.50
81 Rusty Greer .75
82 Brian Jordan .75
83 Vladimir Guerrero 1.50
84 Mike Sweeney .75
85 Jose Vidro .75
86 Paul LoDuca .75
87 Matt Morris .75
88 Adrian Beltre .75
89 Aramis Ramirez .75
90 Derek Jeter 6.00
91 Rich Aurilia .75
92 Freddy Garcia .75
93 Preston Wilson .75
94 Greg Maddux 3.00
95 Miguel Tejada .75
96 Luis Gonzalez 1.25
97 Torii Hunter .75
98 Nomar Garciaparra 4.00
99 Jamie Moyer .75
100 Javier Vazquez .75
101 Ben Grieve .75
102 Mike Piazza 4.00
103 Paul O'Neill 1.00
104 Terrence Long .75
105 Charles Johnson .75
106 Rafael Palmeiro 1.00
107 David Cone .75
108 Alex Rodriguez 4.00
109 John Burkett .75
110 Chipper Jones 3.00
111 Ryan Dempster .75
112 Bobby Abreu .75
113 Brad Fullmer .75
114 Kazuhiro Sasaki .75
115 Mariano Rivera 1.00
116 Edgardo Alfonzo .75
117 Ray Durham .75
118 Richard Hidalgo .75
119 Jeff Weaver .75
120 Paul Konerko .75
121 Jon Lieber .75
122 Mike Hampton .75
123 Mike Cameron .75
124 Kevin Brown .75
125 Doug Mientkiewicz .75
126 Jim Thome 1.00
127 Corey Koskie .75
128 Trot Nixon .75
129 Darryl Kile .75
130 Ivan Rodriguez 1.50
131 Carl Everett .75
132 Jeff Kent .75
133 Rondell White .75
134 Chan Ho Park .75
135 Robert Person .75
136 Troy Glaus 1.50
137 Aaron Sele .75
138 Roger Clemens 2.50
139 Tony Clark .75
140 Mark Buehrle .75
141 David Justice 1.00
142 Magglio Ordonez .75
143 Bobby Higginson .75
144 Hideo Nomo 1.00
145 Tim Salmon .75
146 Mark Mulder .75
147 Troy Percival .75
148 Lance Berkman .75
149 Russ Ortiz .75
150 Andruw Jones 1.00
151 Mike Piazza 30.00
152 Manny Ramirez 20.00
153 Bernie Williams 15.00
154 Nomar Garciaparra 30.00
155 Andres Galarraga 6.00
156 Kenny Lofton 6.00
157 Scott Rolen 10.00
158 Jim Thome 15.00
159 Darin Erstad 8.00
160 Garret Anderson 6.00
161 Andruw Jones 10.00
162 Juan Gonzalez 15.00
163 Rafael Palmeiro 10.00
164 Magglio Ordonez 6.00
165 Jeff Bagwell 30.00
166 Eric Chavez 12.00
167 Brian Giles 8.00
168 Adrian Beltre 6.00
169 Tony Gwynn 25.00
170 Shawn Green 6.00
171 Todd Helton 15.00
172 Troy Glaus 60.00
173 Lance Berkman 8.00
174 Ivan Rodriguez 15.00
175 Sean Casey 10.00
176 Aramis Ramirez 6.00
177 J.D. Drew 20.00
178 Barry Bonds 40.00
179 Barry Larkin 20.00
180 Cal Ripken Jr. 50.00
181 Frank Thomas 15.00
182 Craig Biggio 15.00
183 Carlos Lee 8.00
184 Chipper Jones 20.00
185 Miguel Tejada 15.00
186 Jose Vidro 8.00
187 Terrence Long 8.00
188 Moises Alou 8.00
189 Trot Nixon 30.00
190 Shannon Stewart 6.00
191 Ryan Klesko 8.00
192 Carlos Beltran 10.00
193 Vladimir Guerrero 15.00
194 Edgar Martinez 15.00
195 Luis Gonzalez 15.00
196 Richard Hidalgo 8.00
197 Roberto Alomar 10.00
198 Mike Sweeney 6.00
199 Bobby Abreu 10.00
200 Cliff Floyd 10.00
201 *Jackson Melian* 10.00
202 Jason Jennings 8.00
203 Toby Hall 10.00
204 *Jason Karnuth* 8.00
205 *Jason Smith* 8.00
206 *Mike Maroth* 8.00
207 *Sean Douglass* 8.00
208 Adam Johnson 8.00
209 *Luke Hudson* 8.00
210 *Nick Maness* 8.00
211 *Les Walrond* 8.00
212 *Travis Phelps* 8.00
213 *Carlos Garcia* 8.00
214 Bill Ortega 8.00
215 *Gene Altman* 8.00
216 Nate Frese 8.00
217 *Bob File* 8.00
218 *Steve Green* 8.00
219 *Kris Keller* 8.00
220 *Matt White* 8.00
221 *Nate Teut* 8.00
222 Nick Johnson 8.00
223 *Jeremy Fikac* 8.00
224 Abraham Nunez 8.00
225 *Mike Penney* 8.00
226 *Roy Smith* 8.00
227 *Tim Christman* 8.00
228 Carlos Pena 15.00
229 *Joe Beimel* 8.00
230 *Mike Koplove* 8.00
231 *Scott MacRae* 8.00
232 *Kyle Lohse* 15.00
233 *Jerrod Riggan* 8.00
234 *Scott Podsednik* 8.00
235 *Winston Abreu* 8.00
236 *Ryan Freel* 8.00
237 *Ken Vining* 8.00
238 *Bret Prinz* 8.00
239 *Paul Phillips* 8.00
240 *Josh Fogg* 10.00
241 *Saul Rivera* 8.00
242 *Esix Snead* 8.00
243 *John Grabow* 8.00
244 *Tony Cogan* 8.00
245 *Pedro Santana* 8.00
246 Jack Cust 8.00
247 Joe Crede 8.00
248 *Juan Moreno* 8.00
249 *Kevin Joseph* 8.00
250 *Scott Stewart* 8.00
251 *Rob Mackowiak* 8.00
252 *Luis Pineda* 8.00
253 *Bert Snow* 8.00
254 *Dustan Mohr* 8.00
255 *Justin Kaye* 8.00
256 *Chad Paronto* 8.00
257 *Nick Punto* 8.00
258 *Brian Roberts* 8.00
259 *Eric Hinske* 12.00
260 *Victor Zambrano* 8.00
261 Juan Pena 8.00
262 *Rick Bauer* 8.00
263 *Jorge Julio* 8.00
264 *Craig Monroe* 8.00
265 *Stubby Clapp* 8.00
266 *Martin Vargas* 8.00
267 *Josue Perez* 8.00
268 *Cody Ransom* 8.00
269 *Will Ohman* 8.00
270 *Juan Diaz* 8.00
271 *Ramon Vazquez* 8.00
272 *Grant Balfour* 8.00
273 *Ryan Jensen* 8.00
274 *Benito Baez* 8.00
275 *Angel Santos* 8.00
276 *Brian Reith* 8.00
277 *Brandon Lyon* 8.00
278 *Erik Hiljus* 8.00
279 *Brandon Knight* 8.00
280 *Jose Acevedo* 8.00
281 *Cesar Crespo* 8.00
282 *Kevin Olsen* 8.00
283 *Duaner Sanchez* 8.00
284 *Endy Chavez* 8.00
285 *Blaine Neal* 8.00
286 *Brett Jodie* 8.00
287 *Brad Voyles* 8.00
288 *Doug Nickle* 8.00
289 *Junior Spivey* 8.00
290 *Henry Mateo* 8.00
291 Xavier Nady 8.00
292 *Lance Davis* 8.00
293 *Willie Harris* 8.00
294 *Mark Lukasiewicz* 8.00
295 *Ryan Drese* 8.00
296 *Morgan Ensberg* 12.00
297 *Jose Mieses* 8.00
298 *Jason Michaels* 10.00
299 *Kris Foster* 8.00
300 *Justin Duchscherer* 8.00
301 *Elpidio Guzman* 10.00
302 *Cory Aldridge* 10.00
303 *Angel Berroa* 35.00
304 *Travis Hafner* 15.00
305 *Horacio Ramirez* 10.00
306 *Juan Uribe* 15.00
307 *Mark Prior* 120.00
308 *Brandon Larson* 10.00
309 Nick Neugebauer 20.00
310 *Zach Day* 15.00
311 *Jeremy Owens* 10.00
312 *Dewon Brazelton* 20.00
313 *Brandon Duckworth* 25.00
314 *Adrian Hernandez* 15.00
315 *Mark Teixeira* 90.00
316 *Brian Rogers* 10.00
317 *David Brous* 10.00
318 *Geronimo Gil* 10.00
319 *Erick Almonte* 15.00
320 *Claudio Vargas* 10.00
321 *Wilkin Ruan* 10.00
322 *David Williams* 10.00
323 *Alexis Gomez* 10.00
324 *Mike Rivera* 10.00
325 *Brandon Berger* 30.00
326 Keith Ginter
327 Brandon Inge/700 10.00
328 Brent Abernathy/700 10.00
329 *Billy Sylvester/700* 10.00
330 *Bart Miadich/500* 10.00
331 *Tsuyoshi Shinjo/500* 35.00
332 Eric Valent
333 Dee Brown/500 10.00
334 *Andres Torres/125* 60.00
335 Timo Perez/700 10.00
336 Cesar Izturis/650 10.00
337 Pedro Feliz
338 Jason Hart/200 20.00
339 *Greg Miller/700* 10.00
340 Eric Munson/700 15.00
341 Aubrey Huff/450 10.00
342 *Wilmy Caceres/700* 10.00
343 Alex Escobar/650 15.00
344 *Brian Lawrence/700* 15.00
345 *Adam Pettyjohn/650* 10.00
346 *Donaldo Mendez/700* 10.00
347 *Carlos Valderrama*
348 *Christian Parker/650* 10.00
349 *Corky Miller/500* 12.00
350 Michael Cuddyer/500 15.00
351 Adam Dunn/500 40.00
352 Josh Beckett/650 20.00
353 *Juan Cruz/500* 35.00
354 Ben Sheets/400 15.00
355 Roy Oswalt/100 40.00
356 *Rafael Soriano/650* 15.00
357 *Ricardo Rodriguez/650* 10.00
358 Jimmy Rollins/300 15.00
359 C.C. Sabathia
360 *Bud Smith/500* 30.00
361 Jose Ortiz
362 Marcus Giles/400 15.00
363 *Jack Wilson*
364 *Wilson Betemit/100* 90.00
365 Corey Patterson/650 15.00
366 *Jay Gibbons*
367 *Albert Pujols/250* 60.00
368 *Joe Kennedy*
369 Alfonso Soriano 60.00
370 *Delvin James/650* 10.00
371 *Josh Towers/500* 15.00

372 *Jeremy Affeldt/650* 15.00
373 Tim Redding/500 20.00
374 *Ichiro Suzuki/100* 250.00
375 *Johnny Estrada*

2001 Leaf Rookies & Stars

	MT
Complete Set (300):	NA
Common Player:	.15
Common (101-200):	2.00
Inserted 1:4	
Common (201-300):	
Inserted 1:24	8.00
Pack (5):	3.00
Box (24):	55.00

1 Alex Rodriguez 2.00
2 Derek Jeter 3.00
3 Aramis Ramirez .15
4 Cliff Floyd .15
5 Nomar Garciaparra 2.00
6 Craig Biggio .25
7 Ivan Rodriguez .75
8 Cal Ripken Jr. 3.00
9 Fred McGriff .25
10 Chipper Jones 1.50
11 Roberto Alomar .60
12 Moises Alou .25
13 Freddy Garcia .15
14 Bobby Abreu .15
15 Shawn Green .25
16 Jason Giambi .40
17 Todd Helton .60
18 Robert Fick .15
19 Tony Gwynn .75
20 Luis Gonzalez .40
21 Sean Casey .25
22 Roger Clemens 1.00
23 Brian Giles .25
24 Manny Ramirez .75
25 Barry Bonds 1.50
26 Richard Hidalgo .15
27 Vladimir Guerrero .75
28 Kevin Brown .15
29 Mike Sweeney .15
30 Ken Griffey Jr. 2.00
31 Mike Piazza 2.00
32 Richie Sexson .15
33 Matt Morris .15
34 Jorge Posada .25
35 Eric Chavez .25
36 Mark Buehrle .15
37 Jeff Bagwell .75
38 Curt Schilling .25
39 Bartolo Colon .15
40 Mark Quinn .15
41 Tony Clark .15
42 Brad Radke .15
43 Gary Sheffield .25
44 Doug Mientkiewicz .15
45 Pedro Martinez .75
46 Carlos Lee .15
47 Troy Glaus .50
48 Preston Wilson .15
49 Phil Nevin .15
50 Chan Ho Park .15
51 Randy Johnson .75
52 Jermaine Dye .15
53 Terrence Long .15
54 Joe Mays .15
55 Scott Rolen .40
56 Miguel Tejada .25
57 Jim Thome .40
58 Jose Vidro .15
59 Gabe Kapler .25
60 Darin Erstad .25
61 Jim Edmonds .25
62 Jarrod Washburn .15
63 Tom Glavine .30
64 Adrian Beltre .25
65 Sammy Sosa 1.50
66 Juan Gonzalez .75
67 Rafael Furcal .25
68 Mike Mussina .60
69 Mark McGwire 2.50
70 Ryan Klesko .15
71 Raul Mondesi .15
72 Trot Nixon .15
73 Barry Larkin .30
74 Rafael Palmeiro .40
75 Mark Mulder .25
76 Carlos Delgado .40
77 Mike Hampton .15
78 Carl Everett .15
79 Paul Konerko .15
80 Larry Walker .35
81 Kerry Wood .30
82 Frank Thomas .75
83 Andruw Jones .50
84 Eric Milton .15
85 Ben Grieve .15
86 Carlos Beltran .15
87 Tim Hudson .25
88 Hideo Nomo .40
89 Greg Maddux 1.50
90 Edgar Martinez .15
91 Lance Berkman .25
92 Pat Burrell .25
93 Jeff Kent .25
94 Magglio Ordonez .15
95 Cristian Guzman .15
96 Jose Canseco .30
97 J.D. Drew .30
98 Bernie Williams .50
99 Kazuhiro Sasaki .15
100 Rickey Henderson .30
101 *Wilson Guzman* 2.00
102 Nick Neugebauer 2.00
103 *Lance Davis* 2.00
104 Felipe Lopez 2.00
105 Toby Hall 2.00
106 Jack Cust 2.00
107 Jason Kamuth 2.00
108 *Bart Miadich* 2.00
109 *Brian Roberts* 2.00
110 *Brandon Larson* 2.00
111 *Sean Douglass* 3.00
112 Joe Crede 2.00
113 Tim Redding 2.00
114 Adam Johnson 2.00
115 Marcus Giles 2.00
116 Jose Ortiz 2.00
117 *Jose Mieses* 3.00
118 *Nick Maness* 2.00
119 *Les Walrond* 2.00
120 *Travis Phelps* 2.00
121 *Troy Mattes* 2.00
122 Carlos Garcia 2.00
123 Bill Ortega 2.00
124 *Gene Altman* 2.00
125 Nate Frese 2.00
126 Alfonso Soriano 3.00
127 Jose Nunez 2.00
128 *Bob File* 2.00
129 Dan Wright 2.00
130 Nick Johnson 2.00
131 Brent Abernathy 2.00
132 *Steve Green* 2.00
133 *Billy Sylvester* 2.00
134 *Scott MacRae* 2.00
135 *Kris Keller* 2.00
136 *Scott Stewart* 2.00
137 *Henry Mateo* 2.00
138 Timoniel Perez 2.00
139 *Nate Teut* 2.00
140 *Jason Michaels* 2.00
141 *Junior Spivey* 2.00
142 Carlos Pena 2.00
143 *Wilmy Caceres* 2.00
144 David Lundquist 2.00
145 *Jack Wilson* 2.00
146 *Jeremy Fikac* 2.00
147 Alex Escobar 2.00
148 Abraham Nunez 2.00
149 Xavier Nady 2.00
150 Michael Cuddyer 2.00
151 *Greg Miller* 2.00
152 Eric Munson 2.00
153 Aubrey Huff 2.00
154 *Tim Christman* 2.00
155 *Erick Almonte* 4.00
156 Mike Penny 2.00
157 *Delvin James* 2.00
158 Ben Sheets 2.00
159 Jason Hart 2.00
160 *Jose Acevedo* 2.00
161 *Will Ohman* 2.00
162 *Erik Hiljus* 2.00
163 *Juan Moreno* 2.00
164 *Mike Koplove* 2.00
165 *Pedro Santana* 2.00
166 Jimmy Rollins 2.00
167 *Matt White* 2.00
168 *Cesar Crespo* 2.00
169 Carlos Hernandez 2.00
170 Chris George 2.00
171 *Brad Voyles* 2.00
172 *Luis Pineda* 2.00
173 Carlos Zambrano 2.00
174 Nate Comejo 2.00
175 *Jason Smith* 2.00
176 *Craig Monroe* 3.00
177 *Cody Ransom* 2.00
178 *John Grabow* 2.00
179 Pedro Feliz 2.00
180 *Jeremy Owens* 2.00
181 Kurt Ainsworth 2.00
182 Luis Lopez 2.00
183 *Stubby Clapp* 2.00
184 *Ryan Freel* 2.00
185 *Duaner Sanchez* 2.00
186 Jason Jennings 2.00
187 *Kyle Lohse* 4.00
188 *Jerrod Riggan* 2.00
189 *Joe Beimel* 2.00
190 *Nick Punto* 2.00
191 *Willie Harris* 2.00
192 *Ryan Jensen* 2.00
193 *Adam Pettyjohn* 2.00
194 *Donaldo Mendez* 2.00
195 *Bret Prinz* 2.00
196 *Paul Phillips* 2.00
197 *Brian Lawrence* 3.00
198 Cesar Izturis 2.00
199 *Blaine Neal* 2.00
200 *Josh Fogg* 5.00
201 *Josh Towers* 12.00
202 *Tim Spooneybarger* 8.00
203 *Mike Rivera* 8.00
204 *Juan Cruz* 15.00
205 *Albert Pujols* 50.00
206 Josh Beckett 8.00
207 Roy Oswalt 10.00
208 *Elpidio Guzman* 8.00
209 *Horacio Ramirez* 8.00
210 Corey Patterson 8.00
211 *Geronimo Gil* 8.00
212 *Jay Gibbons* 12.00
213 Orlando Woodwards 8.00
214 David Espinosa 8.00
215 *Angel Berroa* 8.00
216 *Brandon Duckworth* 15.00
217 *Brian Reith* 8.00
218 *David Brous* 8.00
219 *Bud Smith* 10.00
220 *Ramon Vazquez* 8.00
221 *Mark Teixeira* 40.00
222 *Justin Atchley* 8.00
223 *Tony Cogan* 8.00
224 *Grant Balfour* 8.00
225 *Ricardo Rodriguez* 8.00
226 *Brian Rogers* 8.00
227 Adam Dunn 20.00
228 *Wilson Betemit* 25.00
229 *Juan Diaz* 8.00
230 *Jackson Melian* 8.00
231 *Claudio Vargas* 8.00
232 *Wilkin Ruan* 8.00
233 *Justin Duchscherer* 8.00
234 *Kevin Olsen* 8.00
235 Tony Fiore 8.00
236 *Jeremy Affeldt* 8.00
237 *Mike Maroth* 8.00
238 C.C. Sabathia 8.00
239 *Cory Aldridge* 8.00
240 *Zach Day* 8.00
241 *Brett Jodie* 8.00
242 *Winston Abreu* 8.00
243 *Travis Hafner* 10.00
244 *Joe Kennedy* 8.00
245 *Rick Bauer* 8.00
246 Mike Young 8.00
247 *Ken Vining* 8.00
248 *Doug Nickle* 8.00
249 Pablo Ozuno 8.00
250 *Dustan Mohr* 8.00
251 *Ichiro Suzuki* 65.00
252 *Ryan Drese* 10.00
253 *Morgan Ensberg* 12.00
254 *George Perez* 8.00
255 *Roy Smith* 8.00
256 *Juan Uribe* 12.00
257 *Dewon Brazelton* 15.00
258 *Endy Chavez* 8.00
259 *Kris Foster* 8.00
260 *Eric Knott* 8.00
261 *Corky Miller* 8.00
262 Larry Bigbie 8.00
263 *Andres Torres* 8.00
264 *Adrian Hernandez* 8.00
265 *Johnny Estrada* 12.00
266 *David Williams* 8.00
267 Steve Lomasney 8.00
268 *Victor Zambrano* 8.00
269 Keith Ginter 8.00
270 *Casey Fossum* 12.00
271 *Josue Perez* 8.00
272 Josh Phelps 8.00
273 *Mark Prior* 70.00
274 *Brandon Berger* 8.00
275 *Scott Podsednik* 8.00
276 *Jorge Julio* 8.00
277 *Esix Snead* 8.00
278 *Brandon Knight* 8.00
279 *Saul Rivera* 8.00
280 *Benito Baez* 8.00
281 *Robert Mackowiak* 8.00
282 *Eric Hinske* 15.00
283 Juan Rivera 8.00
284 *Kevin Joseph* 8.00
285 Juan Pena 8.00
286 *Brandon Lyon* 8.00
287 Adam Everett 8.00
288 Eric Valent 8.00
289 Ken Harvey 8.00
290 *Bert Snow* 8.00
291 Wily Mo Pena 8.00
292 *Rafael Soriano* 8.00
293 *Carlos Valderrama* 8.00
294 *Christian Parker* 8.00
295 *Tsuyoshi Shinjo* 20.00
296 *Martin Vargas* 8.00
297 *Luke Hudson* 8.00
298 Dee Brown 8.00
299 *Alexis Gomez* 8.00
300 *Angel Santos* 8.00

2001 Leaf Rookies & Stars Longevity

	MT
Stars (1-100):	10-25X
Production 50	
#'s 101-300 production 25	

2001 Leaf Rookies & Stars Autographs

	MT
Common Player:	8.00

107 Jason Karnuth 8.00
110 Brandon Larson/100 10.00
117 Jose Mieses 8.00
118 Nick Maness 8.00
119 Les Walrond 8.00
122 Carlos Garcia 8.00
123 Bill Ortega 8.00
124 Gene Altman 8.00
125 Nate Frese 8.00
130 Nick Johnson/100 8.00
133 Billy Sylvester 8.00
135 Kris Keller 8.00
139 Nate Teut 8.00
140 Jason Michaels 8.00
143 Wilmy Caceres 8.00
145 Jack Wilson/100 12.00
151 Greg Miller 8.00
155 Erick Almonte 8.00
156 Mike Penney 8.00
157 Delvin James 8.00
161 Will Ohman 8.00
167 Matt White 8.00
180 Jeremy Owens 8.00
184 Ryan Freel 8.00

185	Duaner Sanchez	8.00
193	Adam Pettyjohn/100	8.00
194	Donaldo Mendez/100	10.00
196	Paul Phillips	8.00
197	Brian Lawrence/100	10.00
199	Blaine Neal	8.00
201	Josh Towers/100	20.00
203	Michael Rivera	8.00
204	Juan Cruz/100	50.00
205	Albert Pujols SP	
207	Roy Oswalt SP	
208	Elpidio Guzman/100	8.00
209	Horacio Ramirez	8.00
210	Corey Patterson SP	25.00
211	Geronimo Gil	8.00
212	Jay Gibbons/100	35.00
213	Orlando Woodards	8.00
215	Angel Berroa/100	20.00
216	Brandon Duckworth/100	35.00
218	David Brous	8.00
219	Bud Smith SP	70.00
221	Mark Teixeira/100	160.00
223	Tony Cogan	8.00
225	Ricardo Rodriguez	8.00
226	Brian Rogers	8.00
227	Adam Dunn SP	
228	Wilson Betemit/100	50.00
231	Claudio Vargas	8.00
232	Wilkin Ruan	8.00
234	Kevin Olsen	8.00
236	Jeremy Affeldt	8.00
237	Mike Maroth	8.00
238	C.C. Sabathia SP	
239	Cory Aldridge	8.00
240	Zach Day	8.00
243	Travis Hafner	12.00
244	Joe Kennedy/100	35.00
254	George Perez	8.00
256	Juan Uribe	12.00
257	Dewon Brazelton/100	35.00
261	Corky Miller/100	25.00
263	Andres Torres/100	8.00
265	Johnny Estrada/100	25.00
266	David Williams	10.00
270	Casey Fossum	8.00
273	Mark Prior/100	320.00
274	Brandon Berger	10.00
277	Esix Snead	8.00
282	Eric Hinske	25.00
292	Rafael Soriano	10.00
293	Carlos Valderrama	8.00
299	Alexis Gomez	8.00

2001 Leaf Rookies & Stars Dress For Success

		MT
Common Player:		10.00
Inserted 1:96		
1	Cal Ripken Jr.	60.00
2	Mike Piazza	50.00
3	Barry Bonds	40.00
4	Frank Thomas	20.00
5	Nomar Garciaparra	40.00
6	Richie Sexson	15.00
7	Brian Giles	10.00
8	Todd Helton	20.00
9	Ivan Rodriguez	20.00
10	Andruw Jones	15.00
11	Juan Gonzalez	20.00
12	Vladimir Guerrero	20.00
13	Greg Maddux	40.00
14	Tony Gwynn	30.00
15	Randy Johnson	20.00
16	Jeff Bagwell	25.00
17	Kerry Wood	25.00
18	Roberto Alomar	20.00
19	Chipper Jones	25.00
20	Pedro Martinez	25.00
21	Shawn Green	15.00
22	Magglio Ordonez	10.00
23	Darin Erstad	
24	Rafael Palmeiro	20.00
25	Edgar Martinez	15.00

2001 Leaf Rookies & Stars Dress For Success Autographs

MT

VALUES UNDETERMINED

DFS-6	Richie Sexson
DFS-7	Brian Giles
DFS-8	Todd Helton
DFS-12	Vladimir Guerrero
DFS-13	Greg Maddux
DFS-16	Jeff Bagwell
DFS-17	Kerry Wood
DFS-19	Chipper Jones
DFS-21	Shawn Green
DFS-25	Edgar Martinez

2001 Leaf Rookies & Stars Freshman Orientation

		MT
Common Player:		10.00
Inserted 1:96		
1	Adam Dunn	50.00
2	Josh Towers	20.00
3	Vernon Wells	10.00
4	Corey Patterson	10.00
5	Albert Pujols	
6	Ben Sheets	15.00
7	Pedro Feliz	10.00
8	Keith Ginter	10.00
9	Luis Rivas	10.00
10	Andres Torres	10.00
11	Carlos Valderrama	10.00
12	Brandon Inge	10.00
13	Jay Gibbons	40.00
14	Cesar Izturis	10.00
15	Marcus Giles	10.00
16	Tsuyoshi Shinjo	30.00
17	Eric Valent	10.00
18	David Espinosa	10.00
19	Aubrey Huff	10.00
20	Wilmy Caceres	10.00
21	Bud Smith	35.00
22	Ricardo Rodriguez	15.00
23	Wes Helms	10.00
24	Jason Hart	10.00
25	Dee Brown	10.00

2001 Leaf Rookies & Stars Freshman Orientation Auto.

MT

VALUES UNDETERMINED

FO-1	Adam Dunn Bat SP
FO-2	Josh Towers Pants SP
FO-4	Corey Patterson Pants SP
FO-5	Albert Pujols Jsy SP
FO-6	Ben Sheets Jsy SP
FO-7	Pedro Feliz Bat
FO-8	Keith Ginter Bat
FO-9	Luis Rivas Bat
FO-10	Andres Torres Bat
FO-11	Carlos Valderrama Jsy
FO-13	Jay Gibbons Cap
FO-14	Cesar Izturis Bat
FO-15	Marcus Giles Jsy
FO-17	Eric Valent Bat
FO-18	David Espinosa Bat
FO-19	Aubrey Huff Jsy
FO-20	Wilmy Caceres Jsy
FO-21	Bud Smith Jsy SP
FO-22	Ricardo Rodriguez Pants
FO-24	Jason Hart Bat
FO-25	Dee Brown Jsy

2001 Leaf Rookies & Stars Great American Treasures

		MT
Inserted 1:1,120		
1	Barry Bonds	75.00
2	Magglio Ordonez	40.00
3	Derek Jeter	125.00
4	Nolan Ryan	650.00
5	Sammy Sosa	
6	Tom Glavine	
7	Ivan Rodriguez	40.00
8	Pedro Martinez	60.00
9	Mark McGwire	
10	Ted Williams	
11	Ryne Sandberg	60.00
12	Barry Bonds	
13	Hideo Nomo	
14	Roger Maris	
15	Ty Cobb	
16	Harmon Killebrew	
17	Magglio Ordonez	
18	Wade Boggs	50.00
19	Hank Aaron	
20	David Cone	

2001 Leaf Rookies & Stars Great American Treasures Auto

MT

VALUES UNDETERMINED

GT-6	Tom Glavine 96 WS Jsy
GT-11	Ryne Sandberg 91 AS Bat
GT-16	Harmon Killebrew 570 HR Bat
GT-18	Wade Boggs WS Bat

2001 Leaf Rookies & Stars Player's Collection

		MT
Common Player:		50.00
Singles #'d to 100		
1	Tony Gwynn bat	50.00
2	Tony Gwynn jsy	50.00
3	Tony Gwynn pants	50.00
4	Tony Gwynn shoe	50.00
5	Tony Gwynn quad/25	
6	Cal Ripken jsy	100.00
7	Cal Ripken bat	100.00
8	Cal Ripken glove	100.00
9	Cal Ripken jsy	100.00
10	Cal Ripken quad/25	
11	Barry Bonds jsy	75.00
12	Barry Bonds shoe	75.00
13	Barry Bonds pants	75.00
14	Barry Bonds bat	75.00
15	Barry Bonds quad/25	

2001 Leaf Rookies & Stars Slideshow

		MT
Common Player:		15.00
Production 100 sets		
1	Cal Ripken Jr.	100.00
2	Chipper Jones	40.00
3	Jeff Bagwell	30.00
4	Larry Walker	15.00
5	Greg Maddux	60.00
6	Ivan Rodriguez	25.00
7	Andruw Jones	20.00
8	Lance Berkman	20.00
9	Luis Gonzalez	25.00
10	Tony Gwynn	50.00
11	Troy Glaus	25.00
12	Todd Helton	30.00
13	Roberto Alomar	25.00
14	Barry Bonds	60.00
15	Vladimir Guerrero	30.00
16	Sean Casey	20.00
17	Curt Schilling	25.00
18	Frank Thomas	30.00
19	Pedro Martinez	30.00
20	Juan Gonzalez	25.00
21	Randy Johnson	30.00
22	Kerry Wood	25.00
23	Mike Sweeney	15.00
24	Magglio Ordonez	20.00
25	Kazuhiro Sasaki	20.00
26	Manny Ramirez	35.00
27	Roger Clemens	60.00
28	Albert Pujols	60.00
29	Hideo Nomo	75.00
30	Miguel Tejada	15.00

2001 Leaf Rookies & Stars Slideshow Autographs

MT

Complete Set:

Common Player:

VALUES UNDETERMINED

S-2	Chipper Jones
S-5	Greg Maddux
S-7	Andruw Jones
S-8	Lance Berkman
S-9	Luis Gonzalez
S-11	Troy Glaus
S-15	Vladimir Guerrero
S-16	Sean Casey
S-17	Curt Schilling
S-22	Kerry Wood
S-28	Albert Pujols
S-30	Miguel Tejada

2001 Leaf Rookies & Stars Statistical Standouts

		MT
1	Ichiro Suzuki	75.00
2	Barry Bonds	40.00
3	Ivan Rodriguez	10.00
4	Jeff Bagwell	15.00
5	Vladimir Guerrero	20.00
6	Mike Sweeney	8.00
7	Miguel Tejada	8.00
8	Mike Piazza	50.00
9	Darin Erstad	8.00
10	Alex Rodriguez	25.00
11	Jason Giambi	15.00
12	Cal Ripken Jr.	50.00
13	Albert Pujols	40.00
14	Carlos Delgado	10.00
15	Rafael Palmeiro	10.00
16	Lance Berkman	8.00
17	Luis Gonzalez	20.00
18	Sammy Sosa	40.00
19	Andruw Jones	20.00
20	Derek Jeter	50.00
21	Edgar Martinez	10.00
22	Troy Glaus	8.00
23	Magglio Ordonez	8.00
24	Mark McGwire	40.00
25	Manny Ramirez	15.00

2001 Leaf Rookies & Stars Statistical Standouts Auto.

MT

VALUES UNDETERMINED
SS-3 Ivan Rodriguez
SS-4 Jeff Bagwell
SS-5 Vladimir Guerrero
SS-7 Miguel Tejada
SS-11 Jason Giambi
SS-13 Albert Pujols
SS-16 Lance Berkman
SS-17 Luis Gonzalez
SS-19 Andruw Jones
SS-22 Troy Glaus

2001 Leaf Rookies & Stars Triple Threads

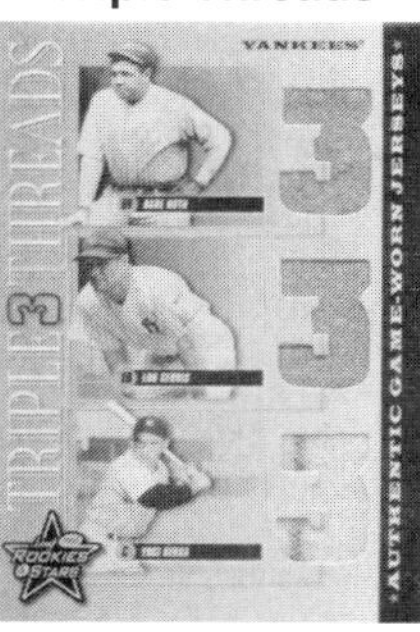

		MT
	Numbered to 100	
TT-1	Pedro Martinez, Manny Ramirez, Nomar Garciaparra	150.00
TT-2	Frank Robinson, Cal Ripken Jr., Brooks Robinson	450.00
TT-3	Yogi Berra, Lou Gehrig, Babe Ruth	750.00
TT-4	Andre Dawson, Ryne Sandberg, Ernie Banks	200.00
TT-5	Warren Spahn, Hank Aaron, Eddie Mathews	400.00
TT-6	Greg Maddux, Chipper Jones, Andruw Jones	150.00
TT-7	Nolan Ryan, Ivan Rodriguez, Juan Gonzalez	250.00
TT-8	Lance Berkman, Jeff Bagwell, Craig Biggio	100.00
TT-9	Rod Carew, Harmon Killebrew, Kirby Puckett	100.00
TT-10	Luis Gonzalez, Curt Schilling, Randy Johnson	100.00

2002 Leaf

		MT
	Complete Set (1-200):	120.00
	Common Player:	.15
	Common (151-200):	1.50
	Inserted 1:6	
	Pack (4):	3.00
	Box (24):	65.00
1	Tim Salmon	.20
2	Troy Glaus	.60
3	Curt Schilling	.40
4	Luis Gonzalez	.50
5	Mark Grace	.50
6	Matt Williams	.40
7	Randy Johnson	.75
8	Tom Glavine	.40
9	Brady Anderson	.15
10	Hideo Nomo	.40
11	Pedro Martinez	.75
12	Corey Patterson	.15
13	Paul Konerko	.15
14	Jon Lieber	.15
15	Carlos Lee	.15
16	Magglio Ordonez	.15
17	Adam Dunn	.50
18	Ken Griffey Jr.	2.50
19	C.C. Sabathia	.15
20	Jim Thome	.40
21	Juan Gonzalez	.75
22	Kenny Lofton	.15
23	Juan Encarnacion	.15
24	Tony Clark	.15
25	A.J. Burnett	.15
26	Josh Beckett	.25
27	Lance Berkman	.25
28	Eric Karros	.25
29	Shawn Green	.25
30	Brad Radke	.15
31	Joe Mays	.15
32	Javier Vazquez	.15
33	Alfonso Soriano	.40
34	Jorge Posada	.25
35	Eric Chavez	.25
36	Mark Mulder	.25
37	Miguel Tejada	.25
38	Tim Hudson	.40
39	Bobby Abreu	.25
40	Pat Burrell	.40
41	Ryan Klesko	.15
43	John Olerud	.30
44	Ellis Burks	.15
45	Mike Cameron	.15
46	Jim Edmonds	.25
47	Ben Grieve	.15
48	Carlos Pena	.15
49	Alex Rodriguez	2.00
50	Raul Mondesi	.15
51	Billy Koch	.15
52	Manny Ramirez	.75
53	Darin Erstad	.25
54	Troy Percival	.15
55	Andruw Jones	.40
56	Chipper Jones	1.50
57	David Segui	.15
58	Chris Stynes	.15
59	Trot Nixon	.15
60	Sammy Sosa	1.50
61	Kerry Wood	.40
62	Frank Thomas	.75
63	Barry Larkin	.40
64	Bartolo Colon	.15
65	Kazuhiro Sasaki	.15
66	Roberto Alomar	.60
67	Mike Hampton	.20
68	Roger Cedeno	.15
69	Cliff Floyd	.15
70	Mike Lowell	.15
71	Billy Wagner	.15
72	Craig Biggio	.25
73	Jeff Bagwell	.75
74	Carlos Beltran	.15
75	Mark Quinn	.15
76	Mike Sweeney	.15
77	Gary Sheffield	.30
78	Kevin Brown	.25
79	Paul LoDuca	.15
80	Ben Sheets	.15
81	Jeromy Burnitz	.15
82	Richie Sexson	.15
83	Corey Koskie	.15
84	Eric Milton	.15
85	Jose Vidro	.15
86	Mike Piazza	2.00
87	Robin Ventura	.25
88	Andy Pettitte	.25
89	Mike Mussina	.60
90	Orlando Hernandez	.15
91	Roger Clemens	1.25
92	Barry Zito	.15
93	Jermaine Dye	.15
94	Jimmy Rollins	.15
95	Jason Kendall	.15
96	Rickey Henderson	.40
97	Andres Galarraga	.25
98	Bret Boone	.15
99	Freddy Garcia	.15
100	J.D. Drew	.40
101	Jose Cruz Jr.	.15
102	Greg Maddux	1.50
103	Javy Lopez	.15
104	Nomar Garciaparra	2.00
105	Fred McGriff	.25
106	Keith Foulke	.15
107	Ray Durham	.15
108	Sean Casey	.30
109	Todd Walker	.15
110	Omar Vizquel	.25
111	Travis Fryman	.25
112	Larry Walker	.40
113	Todd Helton	.75
114	Bobby Higginson	.15
115	Charles Johnson	.15
116	Moises Alou	.20
117	Richard Hidalgo	.20
118	Roy Oswalt	.25
119	Neifi Perez	.15
120	Adrian Beltre	.25
121	Chan Ho Park	.25
122	Geoff Jenkins	.25
123	Doug Mientkiewicz	.15
124	Torii Hunter	.15
125	Vladimir Guerrero	.75
126	Matt Lawton	.15
127	Tsuyoshi Shinjo	.25
128	Bernie Williams	.60
129	Derek Jeter	3.00
130	Mariano Rivera	.25
131	Tino Martinez	.25
132	Jason Giambi	.60
133	Scott Rolen	.40
134	Brian Giles	.25
135	Phil Nevin	.25
136	Trevor Hoffman	.15
137	Barry Bonds	1.50
138	Jeff Kent	.15
139	Shannon Stewart	.15
140	Shawn Estes	.15
141	Edgar Martinez	.20
142	Ichiro Suzuki	3.00
143	Albert Pujols	1.50
144	Bud Smith	.25
145	Matt Morris	.15
146	Frank Catalanotto	.15
147	Gabe Kapler	.25
148	Ivan Rodriguez	.75
149	Rafael Palmeiro	.40
150	Carlos Delgado	.50
151	Marlon Byrd	4.00
152	Alex Herrera	1.50
153	*Brandon Backe*	3.00
154	*Jorge De La Rosa*	4.00
155	Corky Miller	1.50
156	Dennis Tankersley	3.00
157	*Kyle Kane*	8.00
158	Justin Duchscherer	1.50
159	*Brian Mallette*	6.00
160	Eric Hinske	1.50
161	Jason Lane	1.50
162	Hee Seop Choi	3.00
163	Juan Cruz	3.00
164	*Rodrigo Rosario*	2.00
165	Matt Guerrier	1.50
166	*Anderson Machado*	3.00
167	Geronimo Gil	1.50
168	Dewon Brazelton	1.50
169	Mark Prior	6.00
170	Bill Hall	1.50
171	*Jorge Padilla*	4.00
172	Josh Pearce	1.50
173	*Allan Simpson*	3.00
174	*Doug Devore*	4.00
175	Morgan Ensberg	1.50
176	Angel Berroa	1.50
177	*Steve Bechler*	3.00
178	Antonio Perez	1.50
179	Mark Teixeira	8.00
180	Mark Ellis	1.50
181	Michael Cuddyer	1.50
182	Mike Rivera	1.50
183	*Raul Chavez*	4.00
184	Juan Pena	1.50
185	Austin Kearns	3.00
186	Ryan Ludwick	1.50
187	Ed Rogers	1.50
188	Wilson Betemit	3.00
189	Nick Neugebauer	1.50
190	*Tom Shearn*	4.00
191	*Eric Cyr*	4.00
192	Victor Martinez	1.50
193	Brandon Berger	1.50
194	Erik Bedard	1.50
195	*Franklin German*	4.00
196	Joe Thurston	1.50
197	John Buck	1.50
198	*Jeff Deardorff*	4.00
199	*Ryan Jamison*	3.00
200	Alfredo Amezaga	1.50
201	*So Taguchi/500*	15.00
202	*Kazuhisa Ishii/250*	40.00

2002 Leaf Lineage

	MT
1999 Lineage (1-50):	2-5X
Inserted 1:12	

2000 Lineage (51-100): 2-5X
Inserted 1:12
2001 Lineage (101-150): 2-5X
Inserted 1:12
Silver Holofoils: 8-15X
Production 100

2002 Leaf Burn n' Turn

		MT
Complete Set (10):		50.00
Common Player:		4.00
Inserted 1:96		
1	Fernando Vina, Edgar Renteria	6.00
2	Alex Rodriguez, Mike Young	10.00
3	Derek Jeter, Alfonso Soriano	20.00
4	Carlos Guillen, Bret Boone	4.00
5	Jose Vidro, Orlando Cabrera	4.00
6	Barry Larkin, Todd Walker	6.00
7	Carlos Febles, Neifi Perez	4.00
8	Jeff Kent, Rich Aurilia	4.00
9	Craig Biggio, Julio Lugo	5.00
10	Miguel Tejada, Mark Ellis	4.00

2002 Leaf Clean Up Crew

		MT
Complete Set (15):		90.00
Common Player:		4.00
1	Barry Bonds	12.00
2	Sammy Sosa	12.00
3	Luis Gonzalez	5.00
4	Richie Sexson	4.00
5	Jim Thome	5.00
6	Chipper Jones	12.00
7	Alex Rodriguez	15.00
8	Troy Glaus	5.00
9	Rafael Palmeiro	5.00
10	Lance Berkman	4.00
11	Mike Piazza	18.00
12	Jason Giambi	5.00
13	Todd Helton	6.00
14	Shawn Green	5.00
15	Carlos Delgado	5.00

2002 Leaf Clubhouse Signatures

MT

Prices & #'s for some Bronze cards Golds & Silvers not priced yet

	MT
Rich Aurilia	
Josh Beckett	
Wilson Betemit	
Marlon Byrd/200	40.00
Sean Casey	
Eric Chavez	
Roger Clemens	
Joe Crede/200	20.00
Andre Dawson	
J.D. Drew	
Adam Dunn/200	50.00
Jermaine Dye/125	25.00
Mark Ellis/300	15.00
Johnny Estrada/250	20.00
Bob Feller/225	25.00
Robert Fick/300	15.00
Steve Garvey/200	35.00
Luis Gonzalez	
Vladimir Guerrero	
Todd Helton	
Orel Hershiser	
Austin Kearns/300	40.00
Jason Lane	
Paul LoDuca/300	40.00
Terrence Long/250	12.00
Edgar Martinez	
Don Mattingly	
Joe Mays/200	15.00
Mark Mulder	
Xavier Nady	
Roy Oswalt/300	30.00
Chan Ho Park	
Kirby Puckett	
Aramis Ramirez/250	15.00
Tim Redding/300	15.00
Cal Ripken Jr.	
Phil Rizzuto	
Ryne Sandberg	
Ron Santo/300	40.00
Mike Schmidt	
Bud Smith/200	40.00
Ozzie Smith	
Alfonso Soriano	
Miguel Tejada	
Alan Trammell	
Javier Vazquez	
Billy Williams/150	20.00
Barry Zito/100	25.00

2002 Leaf Cornerstones

		MT
Production 50 sets		
Some not priced yet		
1	Andruw Jones, Chipper Jones	150.00
2	Craig Biggio, Jeff Bagwell	
3	Ivan Rodriguez, Rafael Palmeiro	
4	Curt Schilling, Randy Johnson	75.00
5	Gary Sheffield, Shawn Green	
6	Larry Walker, Todd Helton	40.00
7	Carlos Delgado, Shannon Stewart	40.00
8	Omar Vizquel, Jim Thome	
9	Vladimir Guerrero, Jose Vidro	
10	Bernie Williams, Roger Clemens	100.00

2002 Leaf Gold Leaf Rookies

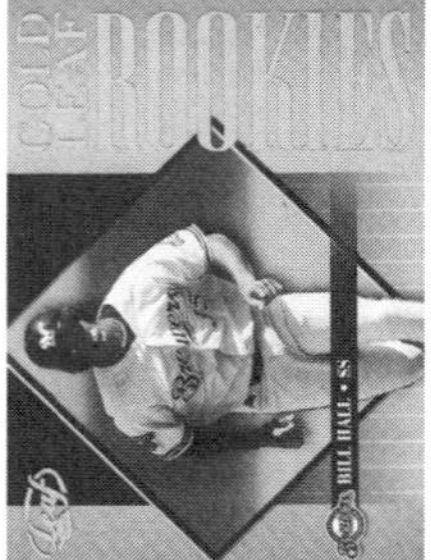

		MT
Complete Set (10):		20.00
Common Player:		2.00
Inserted 1:24		
1	Josh Beckett	4.00
2	Marlon Byrd	4.00
3	Dennis Tankersley	2.00
4	Jason Lane	2.00
5	Dewon Brazelton	2.00
6	Mark Prior	5.00
7	Bill Hall	2.00
8	Angel Berroa	2.00
9	Mark Teixeira	6.00
10	John Buck	2.00

2002 Leaf Future 500 Club

		MT
Complete Set (10):		50.00
Common Player:		3.00
Inserted 1:64		
1	Sammy Sosa	8.00
2	Mike Piazza	10.00
3	Alex Rodriguez	10.00
4	Chipper Jones	8.00
5	Jeff Bagwell	4.00
6	Carlos Delgado	3.00
7	Shawn Green	3.00
8	Ken Griffey Jr.	12.00
9	Rafael Palmeiro	3.00
10	Vladimir Guerrero	4.00

2002 Leaf Heading For The Hall

		MT
Complete Set (10):		90.00
Common Player:		4.00
Inserted 1:64		
1	Greg Maddux	15.00
2	Ozzie Smith	15.00
3	Andre Dawson	4.00
4	Dennis Eckersley	4.00
5	Roberto Alomar	8.00
6	Cal Ripken Jr.	25.00
7	Roger Clemens	12.00
8	Tony Gwynn	10.00
9	Alex Rodriguez	15.00
10	Jeff Bagwell	8.00

2002 Leaf League of Nations

		MT
Complete Set (10):		40.00
Common Player:		3.00
Inserted 1:60		
1	Ichiro Suzuki	20.00
2	Tsuyoshi Shinjo	5.00
3	Chan Ho Park	4.00
4	Larry Walker	4.00
5	Andruw Jones	4.00
6	Hideo Nomo	4.00
7	Byung-Hyun Kim	3.00
8	Sun-Woo Kim	3.00
9	Orlando Hernandez	3.00
10	Luke Prokopec	3.00

2002 Leaf Rookie Reprints

	MT
Complete Set (6):	40.00
Common Player:	3.00

#'d to year of issue

1	Roger Clemens/1,985	10.00
2	Kirby Puckett/1,985	12.00
3	Andres Galarraga/1,986	3.00
4	Fred McGriff/1,986	4.00
5	Sammy Sosa/1,990	15.00
6	Frank Thomas/1,990	10.00

2002 Leaf Shirt Off My Back

		MT
Common Player:		8.00
Inserted 1:29		
Patch variations:		3-5X
RA	Roberto Alomar	20.00
JB	Jeff Bagwell	30.00
MB	Michael Barrett	8.00
CB	Carlos Beltran	15.00
LB	Lance Berkman	20.00
GB	George Brett	50.00
KB	Kevin Brown	10.00
MB	Mark Buehrle	12.00
AB	A.J. Burnett	15.00
JBU	Jeromy Burnitz	10.00
CD	Carlos Delgado	15.00
RD	Ryan Dempster	10.00
DE	Darin Erstad	30.00
CF	Cliff Floyd	8.00
FG	Freddy Garcia	15.00
NG	Nomar Garciaparra	60.00
TGL	Troy Glaus	20.00
TGL	Tom Glavine	15.00
LG	Luis Gonzalez	15.00
TG	Tony Gwynn	20.00
MH	Mike Hampton	10.00
TH	Todd Helton	15.00
THU	Tim Hudson	15.00
BJA	Bo Jackson	40.00
RJ	Randy Johnson	40.00
CJ	Chipper Jones	30.00
AK	Al Kaline	75.00
EK	Eric Karros	10.00
BL	Barry Larkin	15.00
CL	Carlos Lee	8.00
JL	Javy Lopez	10.00
GM	Greg Maddux/patch	125.00
EM	Edgar Martinez	12.00
PM	Pedro Martinez	30.00
DM	Don Mattingly	70.00
KM	Kevin Millwood	10.00
HN	Hideo Nomo	60.00
JO	John Olerud	10.00
MO	Magglio Ordonez	15.00
RP	Rafael Palmeiro	15.00
CHP	Chan Ho Park	20.00
TP	Troy Percival	8.00
AP	Andy Pettitte	
MP	Mike Piazza	40.00
KP	Kirby Puckett	75.00
BR	Brad Radke	10.00
MR	Manny Ramirez	25.00
CR	Cal Ripken Jr.	
AR	Alex Rodriguez	35.00
SR	Scott Rolen	15.00
KS	Kazuhiro Sasaki/patch	100.00
CS	Curt Schilling	15.00
RS	Richie Sexson	12.00
TS	Tsuyoshi Shinjo	
JS	John Smoltz	15.00

MS Mike Sweeney 12.00
MT Miguel Tejada 15.00
LW Larry Walker
MW Matt Williams 15.00
DW Dave Winfield 30.00

2002 Leaf Certified

MT
Complete Set (200): NA
Common Player: .75
Common (151-200): 8.00
Production 500
Pack (5): 10.00
Box (16): 135.00
1 Alex Rodriguez 5.00
2 Luis Gonzalez 1.00
3 Javier Vazquez .75
4 Juan Uribe .75
5 Ben Sheets .75
6 George Brett 4.00
7 Magglio Ordonez 1.00
8 Randy Johnson 1.50
9 Joe Kennedy .75
10 Richie Sexson 1.00
11 Larry Walker 1.00
12 Lance Berkman 1.50
13 Jose Cruz Jr. .75
14 Doug Davis .75
15 Cliff Floyd .75
16 Ryan Klesko .75
17 Troy Glaus 1.00
18 Robert Person .75
19 Bartolo Colon 1.00
20 Adam Dunn 1.50
21 Kevin Brown .75
22 John Smoltz .75
23 Edgar Martinez .75
24 Eric Karros .75
25 Tony Gwynn 1.50
26 Mark Mulder 1.00
27 Don Mattingly 5.00
28 Brandon Duckworth .75
29 C.C. Sabathia .75
30 Nomar Garciaparra 4.00
31 Adam Johnson .75
32 Miguel Tejada 1.50
33 Ryne Sandberg 3.00
34 Roger Clemens 3.00
35 Edgardo Alfonzo .75
36 Jason Jennings .75
37 Todd Helton 1.00
38 Nolan Ryan 6.00
39 Paul LoDuca .75
40 Cal Ripken Jr. 6.00
41 Terrence Long .75
42 Mike Sweeney .75
43 Carlos Lee .75
44 Ben Grieve .75
45 Tony Armas Jr. .75
46 Joe Mays .75
47 Jeff Kent 1.00
48 Andy Pettitte 1.00
49 Kirby Puckett 4.00
50 Aramis Ramirez .75
51 Tim Redding .75
52 Freddy Garcia .75
53 Javy Lopez .75
54 Mike Schmidt 3.00
55 Wade Miller .75
56 Ramon Ortiz .75
57 Ray Durham .75
58 J.D. Drew 1.00
59 Bret Boone .75
60 Mark Buehrle .75
61 Geoff Jenkins .75
62 Greg Maddux 3.00
63 Mark Grace 1.00
64 Toby Hall .75
65 A.J. Burnett .75
66 Bernie Williams 1.00
67 Roy Oswalt 1.00
68 Shannon Stewart .75
69 Barry Zito 1.00
70 Juan Pierre .75
71 Preston Wilson .75
72 Rafael Furcal .75
73 Sean Casey .75
74 John Olerud 1.00
75 Paul Konerko .75
76 Vernon Wells .75
77 Juan Gonzalez 1.50
78 Ellis Burks .75
79 Jim Edmonds 1.00
80 Robert Fick .75
81 Michael Cuddyer .75
82 Tim Hudson 1.00
83 Phil Nevin .75
84 Curt Schilling 1.50
85 Juan Cruz .75
86 Jeff Bagwell 1.50
87 Raul Mondesi .75
88 Bud Smith .75
89 Omar Vizquel .75
90 Vladimir Guerrero 2.00
91 Garret Anderson 1.00
92 Mike Piazza 4.00
93 Josh Beckett .75
94 Carlos Delgado 1.00
95 Kazuhiro Sasaki .75
96 Chipper Jones 3.00
97 Jacque Jones .75
98 Pedro J. Martinez 2.00
99 Marcus Giles .75
100 Craig Biggio 1.00
101 Orlando Cabrera .75
102 Al Leiter .75
103 Michael Barrett .75
104 Hideo Nomo 1.00
105 Mike Mussina 1.00
106 Jeremy Giambi .75
107 Cristian Guzman .75
108 Frank Thomas 1.50
109 Carlos Beltran .75
110 Jorge Posada 1.00
111 Roberto Alomar 1.00
112 Bobby Abreu 1.00
113 Robin Ventura 1.00
114 Pat Burrell 1.25
115 Kenny Lofton .75
116 Adrian Beltre 1.00
117 Gary Sheffield 1.00
118 Jermaine Dye .75
119 Manny Ramirez 1.50
120 Brian Giles 1.00
121 Tsuyoshi Shinjo 1.00
122 Rafael Palmeiro 1.00
123 Mo Vaughn 1.00
124 Kerry Wood 1.00
125 Moises Alou .75
126 Rickey Henderson 1.00
127 Corey Patterson .75
128 Jim Thome 1.50
129 Richard Hidalgo .75
130 Darin Erstad 1.00
131 Johnny Damon .75
132 Juan Encarnacion .75
133 Scott Rolen 1.00
134 Tom Glavine 1.00
135 Ivan Rodriguez 1.00
136 Jay Gibbons .75
137 Trot Nixon .75
138 Nick Neugebauer .75
139 Barry Larkin 1.00
140 Andruw Jones 1.00
141 Shawn Green 1.00
142 Jose Vidro .75
143 Derek Jeter 6.00
144 Ichiro Suzuki 4.00
145 Ken Griffey Jr. 4.00
146 Barry Bonds 5.00
147 Albert Pujols 3.00
148 Sammy Sosa 3.00
149 Jason Giambi 3.00
150 Alfonso Soriano 4.00
151 Drew Henson/bat 15.00
152 Luis Garcia/bat 8.00
153 Geronimo Gil/jsy 8.00
154 Corky Miller/jsy 8.00
155 Mike Rivera/bat 8.00
156 Mark Ellis/jsy 12.00
157 Josh Pearce/bat 8.00
158 Ryan Ludwick/bat 8.00
159 *So Taguchi/bat* 12.00
160 Cody Ransom/jsy 8.00
161 Jeff Deardorff/bat 10.00
162 *Franklyn German/bat* 8.00
163 Ed Rogers/jsy 10.00
164 *Eric Cyr/jsy* 8.00
165 *Victor Alvarez/jsy* 8.00
166 Victor Martinez/jsy 15.00
167 Brandon Berger/jsy 8.00
168 Juan Diaz/jsy 8.00
169 *Kevin Frederick/jsy* 8.00
170 *Earl Snyder/bat* 12.00
171 Morgan Ensberg/bat 8.00
172 *Ryan Jamison/jsy* 8.00
173 *Rodrigo Rosario/jsy* 8.00
174 Willie Harris/bat 8.00
175 Ramon Vazquez/bat 8.00
176 *Kazuhisa Ishii/bat* 15.00
177 Hank Blalock/jsy 12.00
178 Mark Prior/bat 20.00
179 Dewon Brazelton/jsy 8.00
180 *Doug Devore/jsy* 8.00
181 *Jorge Padilla/bat* 10.00
182 Mark Teixeira/jsy 15.00
183 Orlando Hudson/bat 10.00
184 John Buck/jsy 10.00
185 Erik Bedard/jsy 8.00
186 *Allan Simpson/jsy* 8.00
187 Travis Hafner/jsy 10.00
188 Jason Lane/jsy 10.00
189 Marlon Byrd/jsy 15.00
190 Joe Thurston/jsy 12.00
191 *Brandon Backe/jsy* 8.00
192 Josh Phelps/jsy 15.00
193 Bill Hall/bat 8.00
194 *Chris Snelling/bat* 12.00
195 Austin Kearns/jsy 20.00
196 Antonio Perez/bat 8.00
197 Angel Berroa/bat 8.00
198 *Anderson Machado/jsy* 10.00
199 Alfredo Amezaga/jsy 8.00
200 Eric Hinske/bat 15.00

2002 Leaf Certified Mirror Red

MT
Common (1-200): 5.00
Cards (151-200): .5-1X base .75
Production 150 sets
Mirror Blues (1-200): .5-1.5X
Production 75 sets
Mirror Golds not priced
Production 25 sets
Mirror Emerald five sets produced
Mirror Black one set produced
1 Alex Rodriguez/jsy 25.00
2 Luis Gonzalez/jsy 15.00
3 Javier Vazquez/bat 5.00
4 Juan Uribe/jsy 5.00
5 Ben Sheets/jsy 8.00
6 George Brett/jsy 40.00
7 Magglio Ordonez/jsy 12.00
8 Randy Johnson/jsy 15.00
9 Joe Kennedy/jsy 6.00
10 Richie Sexson/jsy 10.00
11 Larry Walker/jsy 10.00
12 Lance Berkman/jsy 15.00
13 Jose Cruz Jr/jsy 8.00
14 Doug Davis/jsy 6.00
15 Cliff Floyd/jsy 8.00
16 Ryan Klesko/bat 8.00
17 Troy Glaus/jsy 12.00
18 Robert Person/jsy 6.00
19 Bartolo Colon/jsy 6.00
20 Adam Dunn/jsy 15.00
21 Kevin Brown/jsy 8.00
22 John Smoltz/jsy 8.00
23 Edgar Martinez/jsy 8.00
24 Eric Karros/jsy 6.00
25 Tony Gwynn/jsy 20.00
26 Mark Mulder/jsy 8.00
27 Don Mattingly/jsy 40.00
28 Brandon Duckworth/jsy 8.00
29 C.C. Sabathia/jsy 6.00
30 Nomar Garciaparra/jsy 25.00
31 Adam Johnson/jsy 6.00
32 Miguel Tejada/jsy 15.00
33 Ryne Sandberg/jsy 45.00
34 Roger Clemens/jsy 25.00
35 Edgardo Alfonzo/jsy 6.00
36 Jason Jennings/jsy 8.00
37 Todd Helton/jsy 10.00
38 Nolan Ryan/jsy 60.00
39 Paul LoDuca/jsy 8.00
40 Cal Ripken Jr/jsy 55.00
41 Terrence Long/jsy 6.00
42 Mike Sweeney/jsy 8.00
43 Carlos Lee/jsy 6.00
44 Ben Grieve/jsy 6.00
45 Tony Armas Jr/jsy 6.00
46 Joe Mays/jsy 6.00
47 Jeff Kent/jsy 10.00
48 Andy Pettitte/jsy 12.00
49 Kirby Puckett/jsy 40.00
50 Aramis Ramirez/jsy 6.00
51 Tim Redding/jsy 6.00
52 Freddy Garcia/jsy 8.00
53 Javy Lopez/jsy 6.00
54 Mike Schmidt/jsy 35.00
55 Wade Miller/jsy 6.00
56 Ramon Ortiz/jsy 6.00
57 Ray Durham/jsy 6.00
58 J.D. Drew/jsy 10.00
59 Bret Boone/jsy 6.00
60 Mark Buehrle/jsy 8.00
61 Geoff Jenkins/jsy 6.00
62 Greg Maddux/jsy 20.00
63 Mark Grace/jsy 15.00
64 Toby Hall/jsy 6.00
65 A.J. Burnett/jsy 8.00
66 Bernie Williams/jsy 12.00
67 Roy Oswalt/jsy 12.00
68 Shannon Stewart/jsy 6.00
69 Barry Zito/jsy 12.00
70 Juan Pierre/jsy 6.00
71 Preston Wilson/jsy 6.00
72 Rafael Furcal/jsy 8.00
73 Sean Casey/jsy 8.00
74 John Olerud/jsy 12.00
75 Paul Konerko/jsy 8.00
76 Vernon Wells/jsy 6.00
77 Juan Gonzalez/jsy 10.00
78 Ellis Burks/jsy 6.00
79 Jim Edmonds/jsy 8.00
80 Robert Fick/jsy 6.00
81 Michael Cuddyer/jsy 10.00
82 Tim Hudson/jsy 8.00
83 Phil Nevin/jsy 6.00
84 Curt Schilling/jsy 12.00
85 Juan Cruz/jsy 8.00
86 Jeff Bagwell/jsy 10.00
87 Raul Mondesi/jsy 8.00
88 Bud Smith/jsy 6.00
89 Omar Vizquel/jsy 12.00
90 Vladimir Guerrero/jsy 20.00
91 Garret Anderson/jsy 8.00
92 Mike Piazza/jsy 20.00
93 Josh Beckett/jsy 10.00
94 Carlos Delgado/jsy 8.00
95 Kazuhiro Sasaki/jsy 15.00
96 Chipper Jones/jsy 18.00

97 Jacque Jones/jsy 10.00
98 Pedro Martinez/jsy 15.00
99 Marcus Giles/jsy 6.00
100 Craig Biggio/jsy 10.00
101 Orlando Cabrera/jsy 6.00
102 Al Leiter/jsy 8.00
103 Michael Barrett/jsy 6.00
104 Hideo Nomo/jsy 45.00
105 Mike Mussina/jsy 12.00
106 Jeremy Giambi/jsy 6.00
107 Cristian Guzman/jsy 6.00
108 Frank Thomas/jsy 10.00
109 Carlos Beltran/bat 6.00
110 Jorge Posada/bat 15.00
111 Roberto Alomar/bat 12.00
112 Bobby Abreu/bat 10.00
113 Robin Ventura/bat 10.00
114 Pat Burrell/bat 18.00
115 Kenny Lofton/bat 6.00
116 Adrian Beltre/bat 8.00
117 Gary Sheffield/bat 6.00
118 Jermaine Dye/bat 6.00
119 Manny Ramirez/bat 12.00
120 Brian Giles/bat 12.00
121 Tsuyoshi Shinjo/bat 12.00
122 Rafael Palmeiro/bat 10.00
123 Mo Vaughn/bat 10.00
124 Kerry Wood/bat 10.00
125 Moises Alou/bat 6.00
126 Rickey Henderson/bat 20.00
127 Corey Patterson/bat 8.00
128 Jim Thome/bat 25.00
129 Richard Hidalgo/bat 6.00
130 Darin Erstad/jsy 8.00
131 Johnny Damon/bat 10.00
132 Juan Encarnacion/bat 6.00
133 Scott Rolen/bat 10.00
134 Tom Glavine/bat 10.00
135 Ivan Rodriguez/bat 12.00
136 Jay Gibbons/bat 8.00
137 Trot Nixon/bat 8.00
138 Nick Neugebauer/bat 15.00
139 Barry Larkin/jsy 10.00
140 Andruw Jones/bat 12.00
141 Shawn Green/bat 10.00
142 Jose Vidro/jsy 6.00
143 Derek Jeter/base 35.00
144 Ichiro Suzuki/base 25.00
145 Ken Griffey Jr/base 15.00
146 Barry Bonds/base 20.00
147 Albert Pujols/base 15.00
148 Sammy Sosa/base 15.00
149 Jason Giambi/base 12.00
150 Alfonso Soriano/jsy 25.00
151 Drew Henson/bat 15.00
152 Luis Garcia/bat 6.00
153 Geronimo Gil/jsy 6.00
154 Corky Miller/jsy 6.00
155 Mike Rivera/bat 6.00
156 Mark Ellis/jsy 12.00
157 Josh Pearce/bat 6.00
158 Ryan Ludwick/bat 6.00
159 So Taguchi/bat 12.00
160 Cody Ransom/jsy 6.00
161 Jeff Deardorff/bat 10.00
162 Franklyn German/bat 6.00
163 Ed Rogers/jsy 10.00
164 Eric Cyr/jsy 6.00
165 Victor Alvarez/jsy 6.00
166 Victor Martinez/jsy 10.00
167 Brandon Berger/jsy 6.00
168 Juan Diaz/jsy 6.00
169 Kevin Frederick/jsy 6.00
170 Earl Snyder/bat 10.00
171 Morgan Ensberg/bat 6.00
172 Ryan Jamison/jsy 6.00
173 Rodrigo Rosario/jsy 6.00
174 Willie Harris/bat 6.00
175 Ramon Vazquez/bat 6.00
176 Kazuhisa Ishii/bat 15.00
177 Hank Blalock/jsy 10.00
178 Mark Prior/bat 15.00
179 Dewon Brazelton/jsy 6.00
180 Doug Devore/jsy 6.00
181 Jorge Padilla/bat 8.00
182 Mark Teixeira/jsy 12.00
183 Orlando Hudson/bat 8.00
184 John Buck/jsy 8.00
185 Erik Bedard/jsy 6.00
186 Allan Simpson/jsy 6.00
187 Travis Hafner/jsy 8.00
188 Jason Lane/jsy 8.00
189 Marlon Byrd/jsy 12.00
190 Joe Thurston/jsy 10.00
191 Brandon Backe/jsy 6.00
192 Josh Phelps/jsy 12.00
193 Bill Hall/bat 6.00
194 Chris Snelling/bat 10.00
195 Austin Kearns/jsy 20.00
196 Antonio Perez/bat 6.00
197 Angel Berroa/bat 6.00
198 Anderson Machado/jsy 6.00
199 Alfredo Amezaga/jsy 6.00
200 Eric Hinske/bat 10.00

2002 Leaf Certified All Certified Team

MT
Complete Set (25): 80.00
Common Player: 2.00
Inserted 1:17
Mirror Blues: 2-4X
Production 50 sets
Mirror Reds: 1.5-3X
Production 75 sets
Golds not priced 25 sets produced
1 Ichiro Suzuki 6.00
2 Alex Rodriguez 8.00
3 Sammy Sosa 5.00
4 Jeff Bagwell 2.50
5 Greg Maddux 5.00
6 Todd Helton 2.00
7 Nomar Garciaparra 6.00
8 Ken Griffey Jr. 6.00
9 Roger Clemens 5.00
10 Adam Dunn 2.50
11 Chipper Jones 5.00
12 Hideo Nomo 2.00
13 Lance Berkman 2.50
14 Barry Bonds 8.00
15 Manny Ramirez 2.50
16 Jason Giambi 5.00
17 Rickey Henderson 2.00
18 Randy Johnson 2.50
19 Derek Jeter 10.00
20 Kazuhisa Ishii 2.00
21 Frank Thomas 2.50
22 Mike Piazza 6.00
23 Albert Pujols 5.00
24 Pedro J. Martinez 3.00
25 Vladimir Guerrero 3.00

2002 Leaf Certified Certified Skills

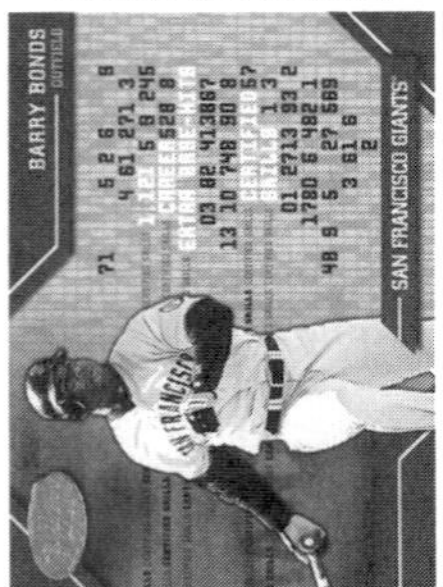

MT
Complete Set (20): 75.00
Common Player: 2.00
Inserted 1:17
Mirror Blues: 1.5-2.5X
Production 75 sets
Mirror Reds: 1-2X
Production 150 sets
Mirror Golds not priced 25 sets
1 Barry Bonds 8.00
2 Greg Maddux 5.00
3 Rickey Henderson 2.00
4 Ichiro Suzuki 6.00
5 Pedro J. Martinez 3.00
6 Kazuhisa Ishii 2.00
7 Alex Rodriguez 8.00
8 Mike Piazza 6.00
9 Sammy Sosa 5.00
10 Derek Jeter 10.00
11 Albert Pujols 5.00
12 Roger Clemens 5.00
13 Mark Prior 2.00
14 Chipper Jones 5.00
15 Ken Griffey Jr. 6.00
16 Frank Thomas 2.50
17 Randy Johnson 2.50
18 Vladimir Guerrero 3.00
19 Nomar Garciaparra 6.00
20 Jeff Bagwell 2.50

2002 Leaf Rookies & Stars

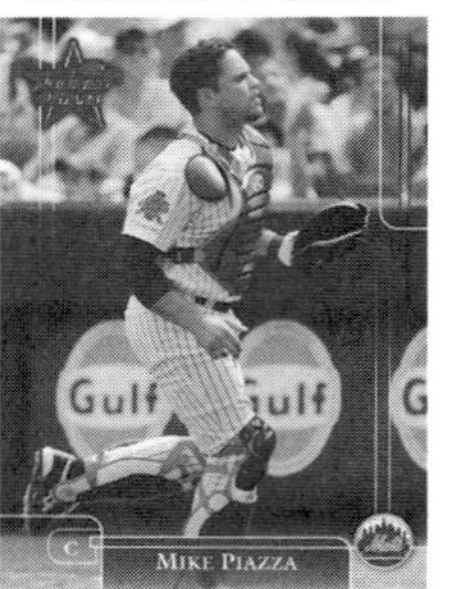

MT
Complete Set (400): NA
Common Player: .15
Common SP (1-300): .75
Common (301-400): .40
Inserted 1:2
Pack (6): 3.00
Box (24): 60.00
1 Darin Erstad .25
2 Garret Anderson .25
3 Troy Glaus .60
4 David Eckstein .15
5 Adam Kennedy .15
6 Kevin Appier .15
6 Kevin Appier/SP/Mets .75
6 Kevin Appier/SP/Royals .75
7 Jarrod Washburn .15
8 David Segui .15
9 Jay Gibbons .15
10 Tony Batista .15
11 Scott Erickson .15
12 Jeff Conine .15
13 Melvin Mora .15
14 Shea Hillenbrand .15
15 Manny Ramirez .60
15 Manny Ramirez/SP/Indians 2.00
16 Pedro J. Martinez .75
16 Pedro J. Martinez/SP/Dodgers 2.50
16 Pedro J. Martinez/SP/Expos 2.50
17 Nomar Garciaparra 1.50
18 Rickey Henderson .50
18 Rickey Henderson/SP/Angels 3.00
18 Rickey Henderson/SP/A's 3.00
18 Rickey Henderson/SP/Blue Jays 3.00
18 Rickey Henderson/SP/M's 3.00
18 Rickey Henderson/SP/Mets 3.00
18 Rickey Henderson/SP/Padres 3.00
18 Rickey Henderson/SP/Yankees 3.00
19 Johnny Damon .15
19 Johnny Damon/SP/A's .75
19 Johnny Damon/SP/Royals .75
20 Trot Nixon .15
21 Derek Lowe .15
22 Jason Varitek .15
23 Tim Wakefield .15
24 Frank Thomas .60
25 Kenny Lofton .15
25 Kenny Lofton/SP/Indians .75
26 Magglio Ordonez .25
27 Ray Durham .15
28 Mark Buehrle .15
29 Paul Konerko .15
29 Paul Konerko/SP/Dodgers 1.00
29 Paul Konerko/SP/Reds 1.00
30 Jose Valentin .15
31 C.C. Sabathia .15
32 Ellis Burks .15
32 Ellis Burks/SP/Giants .75
32 Ellis Burks/SP/Red Sox .75
32 Ellis Burks/SP/Rockies .75
33 Omar Vizquel .25
33 Omar Vizquel/SP/Mariners 1.00
34 Jim Thome .60
35 Matt Lawton .15
36 Travis Fryman .15
36 Travis Fryman/SP/Tigers .75
37 Robert Fick .15
38 Bobby Higginson .15
39 Steve Sparks .15
40 Mike Rivera .15
41 Wendell Magee .15
42 Randall Simon .15
43 Carlos Pena .15
43 Carlos Pena/SP/A's .75
43 Carlos Pena/SP/Rangers .75
44 Mike Sweeney .15
45 Chuck Knoblauch .15
46 Carlos Beltran .15
47 Joe Randa .15
48 Paul Byrd .15
49 Mac Suzuki .15
50 Torii Hunter .15
51 Jacque Jones .15
52 David Ortiz .15
53 Corey Koskie .15
54 Brad Radke .15
55 Doug Mientkiewicz .15
56 A.J. Pierzynski .15
57 Dustan Mohr .15
58 Derek Jeter 2.50
59 Bernie Williams .50
60 Roger Clemens 1.25
60 Roger Clemens/SP/Blue Jays 4.00
60 Roger Clemens/SP/Red Sox 4.00
61 Mike Mussina .50
61 Mike Mussina/SP/Orioles 1.50
62 Jorge Posada .25
63 Alfonso Soriano 1.50
64 Jason Giambi 1.25
64 Jason Giambi/SP/A's 3.00
65 Robin Ventura .15
65 Robin Ventura/SP/Mets .75
65 Robin Ventura/SP/White Sox .75
66 Andy Pettitte .25
67 David Wells .15
67 David Wells/SP/Blue Jays .75
67 David Wells/SP/Tigers .75
68 Nick Johnson .15
69 Jeff Weaver .15
69 Jeff Weaver/SP/Tigers .75
70 Raul Mondesi .15
70 Raul Mondesi/SP/Blue Jays .75

70 Raul Mondesi/SP/Dodgers .75
71 Tim Hudson .25
72 Barry Zito .25
73 Mark Mulder .25
74 Miguel Tejada .50
75 Eric Chavez .25
76 Billy Koch .15
76 Billy Koch/SP/Blue Jays .75
77 Jermaine Dye .15
77 Jermaine Dye/SP/Royals .75
78 Scott Hatteberg .15
79 Ichiro Suzuki 1.50
80 Edgar Martinez .15
81 Mike Cameron .15
81 Mike Cameron/SP/White Sox .75
82 John Olerud .25
82 John Olerud/SP/Blue Jays .75
82 John Olerud/SP/Mets .75
83 Bret Boone .15
84 Dan Wilson .15
85 Freddy Garcia .15
86 Jamie Moyer .15
87 Carlos Guillen .15
88 Ruben Sierra .15
89 Kazuhiro Sasaki .15
90 Mark McLemore .15
91 Ben Grieve .15
92 Aubrey Huff .15
93 Steve Cox .15
94 Toby Hall .15
95 Randy Winn .15
96 Brent Abernathy .15
97 Chan Ho Park .15
97 Chan Ho Park/SP/Dodgers .75
98 Alex Rodriguez 2.00
98 Alex Rodriguez/SP/Mariners 4.00
99 Juan Gonzalez .50
99 Juan Gonzalez/SP/Indians 1.50
99 Juan Gonzalez/SP/Tigers 1.50
100 Rafael Palmeiro .40
100 Rafael Palmeiro/SP/Cubs 1.00
100 Rafael Palmeiro/SP/Orioles 1.00
101 Ivan Rodriguez .50
102 Rusty Greer .15
103 Kenny Rogers .15
103 Kenny Rogers/SP/A's .75
103 Kenny Rogers/SP/Yankees .75
104 Hank Blalock .15
105 Mark Teixeira .15
106 Carlos Delgado .40
107 Shannon Stewart .15
108 Eric Hinske .15
109 Roy Halladay .15
110 Felipe Lopez .15
111 Vernon Wells .15
112 Curt Schilling .50
112 Curt Schilling/SP/Phillies 1.50
113 Randy Johnson .75
113 Randy Johnson/SP/Astros 3.00
113 Randy Johnson/SP/Expos 3.00
113 Randy Johnson/SP/Mariners 3.00
114 Luis Gonzalez .25
114 Luis Gonzalez/SP/Astros 1.00
114 Luis Gonzalez/SP/Cubs 1.00
115 Mark Grace .40
115 Mark Grace/SP/Cubs 1.50
116 Junior Spivey .15
117 Tony Womack .15
118 Matt Williams .15
118 Matt Williams/SP/Giants 1.00
118 Matt Williams/SP/Indians 1.00
119 Danny Bautista .15
120 Byung-Hyun Kim .15
121 Craig Counsell .15
122 Greg Maddux 1.25
122 Greg Maddux/SP/Cubs 4.00
123 Tom Glavine .40
124 John Smoltz .15
124 John Smoltz/SP/Tigers .75
125 Chipper Jones 1.25
126 Gary Sheffield .25
127 Andruw Jones .40
128 Vinny Castilla .15
129 Damian Moss .15
130 Rafael Furcal .15
131 Kerry Wood .25
132 Fred McGriff .25
132 Fred McGriff/SP/Blue Jays 1.00
132 Fred McGriff/SP/Braves 1.00
132 Fred McGriff/SP/Devil Rays 1.00
132 Fred McGriff/SP/Padres 1.00
133 Sammy Sosa 1.25
133 Sammy Sosa/SP/Rangers 4.00
133 Sammy Sosa/SP/White Sox 4.00
134 Alex Gonzalez .15
135 Corey Patterson .15
136 Moises Alou .15
137 Mark Prior .75
138 Jon Lieber .15
139 Matt Clement .15
140 Ken Griffey Jr. 1.50
140 Ken Griffey Jr./SP/Mariners 4.00
141 Barry Larkin .40
142 Adam Dunn .60
143 Sean Casey .15
143 Sean Casey/SP/Indians .75
144 Jose Rijo .15
145 Elmer Dessens .15
146 Austin Kearns .40
147 Corky Miller .15
148 Todd Walker .15
148 Todd Walker/SP/Rockies .75
148 Todd Walker/SP/Expos .75
149 Chris Reitsma .15
150 Ryan Dempster .15
151 Larry Walker .25
152 Todd Helton .50
153 Juan Uribe .15
154 Juan Pierre .15
155 Mike Hampton .15
156 Todd Zeile .15
157 Josh Beckett .15
158 Mike Lowell .15
158 Mike Lowell/SP/Yankees .75
159 Derrek Lee .15
160 A.J. Burnett .15
161 Luis Castillo .15
162 Tim Raines .15
163 Preston Wilson .15
164 Juan Encarnacion .15
165 Jeff Bagwell .60
166 Craig Biggio .25
167 Lance Berkman .50
168 Wade Miller .15
169 Roy Oswalt .25
170 Richard Hidalgo .15
171 Carlos Hernandez .15
172 Daryle Ward .15
173 Shawn Green .25
173 Shawn Green/SP/Blue Jays 1.00
174 Adrian Beltre .25
175 Paul LoDuca .15
176 Eric Karros .15
177 Kevin Brown .15
178 Hideo Nomo .40
178 Hideo Nomo/SP/Brewers 1.50
178 Hideo Nomo/SP/Mets 1.50
178 Hideo Nomo/SP/Red Sox 1.50
178 Hideo Nomo/SP/Tigers 1.50
179 Odalis Perez .15
180 Eric Gagne .15
181 Brian Jordan .15
182 Cesar Izturis .15
183 Geoff Jenkins .15
184 Richie Sexson .25
184 Richie Sexson/SP/Indians 1.00
185 Jose Hernandez .15
186 Ben Sheets .15
187 Ruben Quevedo .15
188 Jeffrey Hammonds .15
189 Alex Sanchez .15
190 Vladimir Guerrero .75
191 Jose Vidro .15
192 Orlando Cabrera .15
193 Michael Barrett .15
194 Javier Vazquez .15
195 Tony Armas Jr. .15
196 Andres Galarraga .25
197 Tomokazu Ohka .15
198 Bartolo Colon .15
198 Bartolo Colon/SP/Indians .75
199 Cliff Floyd .15
199 Cliff Floyd/SP/Marlins .75
200 Mike Piazza 1.50
200 Mike Piazza/SP/Dodgers 4.00
200 Mike Piazza/SP/Marlins 4.00
201 Jeromy Burnitz .15
202 Roberto Alomar .50
202 Roberto Alomar/SP/Blue Jays 1.50
202 Roberto Alomar/SP/Indians 1.50
202 Roberto Alomar/SP/Orioles 1.50
202 Roberto Alomar/SP/Padres 1.50
203 Mo Vaughn .25
203 Mo Vaughn/SP/Angels 1.00
203 Mo Vaughn/SP/Red Sox 1.00
204 Al Leiter .15
204 Al Leiter/SP/Blue Jays .75
205 Pedro Astacio .15
206 Edgardo Alfonzo .15
207 Armando Benitez .15
208 Scott Rolen .50
209 Pat Burrell .50
210 Bobby Abreu .25
210 Bobby Abreu/SP/Astros .75
211 Mike Lieberthal .15
212 Brandon Duckworth .15
213 Jimmy Rollins .15
214 Jeremy Giambi .15
215 Vicente Padilla .15
216 Travis Lee .15
217 Jason Kendall .15
218 Brian Giles .25
218 Brian Giles/SP/Indians 1.00
219 Aramis Ramirez .15
220 Pokey Reese .15
221 Kip Wells .15
222 Josh Fogg .15
222 Josh Fogg/SP/White Sox .75
223 Mike Williams .15
224 Ryan Klesko .25
224 Ryan Klesko/SP/Braves .75
225 Phil Nevin .15
225 Phil Nevin/SP/Tigers .75
226 Brian Lawrence .15
227 Mark Kotsay .15
228 Brett Tomko .15
229 Trevor Hoffman .15
229 Trevor Hoffman/SP/Marlins .75
230 Barry Bonds 2.00
230 Barry Bonds/SP/Pirates 5.00
231 Jeff Kent .25
231 Jeff Kent/SP/Blue Jays 1.00
232 Rich Aurilia .15
233 Tsuyoshi Shinjo .15
233 Tsuyoshi Shinjo/SP/Mets 1.00
234 Benito Santiago .15
234 Benito Santiago/SP/Padres .75
235 Kirk Rueter .15
236 Kurt Ainsworth .15
237 Livan Hernandez .15
238 Russ Ortiz .15
239 David Bell .15
240 Jason Schmidt .15
241 Reggie Sanders .15
242 Jim Edmonds .25
242 Jim Edmonds/SP/Angels 1.00
243 J.D. Drew .25
244 Albert Pujols 1.00
245 Fernando Vina .15
246 Tino Martinez .25
246 Tino Martinez/SP/Mariners 1.00
246 Tino Martinez/SP/Yankees 1.00
247 Edgar Renteria .15
248 Matt Morris .15
249 Woody Williams .15
250 Jason Isringhausen .15
250 Jason Isringhausen/SP/A's .75
251 Cal Ripken Jr. 2.00
252 Cal Ripken Jr. 2.00
253 Cal Ripken Jr. 2.00
254 Cal Ripken Jr. 2.00
255 Ryne Sandberg .75
256 Don Mattingly 1.00
257 Don Mattingly 1.00
258 Roger Clemens .75
259 Roger Clemens .75
260 Roger Clemens .75
261 Roger Clemens .75
262 Roger Clemens .75
263 Roger Clemens .75
264 Roger Clemens .75
265 Rickey Henderson .40
266 Rickey Henderson .40
267 Jose Canseco .40
268 Barry Bonds 1.50
269 Barry Bonds 1.50
270 Barry Bonds 1.50
271 Barry Bonds 1.50
272 Jeff Bagwell .50
273 Kirby Puckett 1.00
274 Kirby Puckett 1.00
275 Greg Maddux 1.00
276 Greg Maddux 1.00
277 Greg Maddux 1.00
278 Greg Maddux 1.00
279 Ken Griffey Jr. 1.00
280 Mike Piazza 1.50
281 Kirby Puckett 1.00
282 Mike Piazza 1.50
283 Frank Thomas .50
284 Hideo Nomo .40
285 Randy Johnson .75
286 Juan Gonzalez .50
287 Derek Jeter 2.00
288 Derek Jeter 2.00
289 Derek Jeter 2.00
290 Nomar Garciaparra 1.50
291 Pedro J. Martinez .75
292 Kerry Wood .25
293 Sammy Sosa 1.00
294 Chipper Jones 1.00
295 Ivan Rodriguez .40
296 Ivan Rodriguez .40
297 Albert Pujols .75
298 Ichiro Suzuki 1.50
299 Ichiro Suzuki 1.50
300 Ichiro Suzuki 1.50
301 *So Taguchi* 1.00
302 *Kazuhisa Ishii* 2.50
303 *Jeremy Lambert* .50
304 Sean Burroughs .40
305 *P.J. Bevis* .50
306 Jon Rauch .40
307 *Scotty Layfield* .50
308 Miguel Ascencio .40
309 *Franklyn German* .50
310 *Luis Ugueto* .50
311 *Jorge Sosa* .50
312 *Felix Escalona* .50
313 *Jose Valverde* .50
314 *Jeremy Ward* .50
315 *Kevin Gryboski* .50
316 *Francis Beltran* .50
317 Joe Thurston .40
318 *Cliff Lee* 1.00
319 *Takahito Nomura* .50
320 Bill Hall .40
321 Marlon Byrd .50
322 *Andy Shibilo* .50
323 *Edwin Almonte* .50
324 Brandon Backe .40
325 *Chone Figgins* .50
326 *Brian Mallette* .50
327 *Rodrigo Rosario* .50
328 *Anderson Machado* 1.00
329 *Jorge Padilla* .75
330 *Allan Simpson* .50
331 *Doug Devore* .50
332 Drew Henson 1.00
333 *Raul Chavez* .50

334	*Tom Shearn*	.50
335	*Ben Howard*	.50
336	*Chris Baker*	.50
337	*Travis Hughes*	.75
338	Kevin Mench	.40
339	Brian Tallet	.40
340	*Mike Moriarty*	.50
341	*Corey Thurman*	.50
342	*Terry Pearson*	.50
343	*Steve Kent*	.50
344	*Satoru Komiyama*	.50
345	Jason Lane	.40
346	*Freddy Sanchez*	1.00
347	*Brandon Puffer*	.50
348	*Clay Condrey*	.50
349	*Rene Reyes*	.50
350	Hee Seop Choi	1.00
351	Rodrigo Lopez	.40
352	*Colin Young*	.50
353	*Jason Simontacchi*	2.00
354	*Oliver Perez*	3.00
355	Kirk Saarloos	2.50
356	Marcus Thames	.40
357	*Jeff Austin*	.50
358	Justin Kaye	.40
359	*Julio Mateo*	.50
360	*Mike Smith*	.50
361	*Chris Snelling*	2.00
362	Dennis Tankersley	.40
363	*Runelvys Hernandez*	.50
364	*Aaron Cook*	.75
365	Joe Borchard	.40
366	*Earl Snyder*	.75
367	*Shane Nance*	.50
368	*Aaron Guiel*	.75
369	*Steve Bechler*	.50
370	*Tim Kalita*	.50
371	*Shawn Sedlacek*	.50
372	*Eric Good*	.50
373	*Eric Junge*	.50
374	Matt Thornton	.40
375	*Travis Driskill*	.50
376	*Mitch Wylie*	.50
377	*John Ennis*	.50
378	*Reed Johnson*	.50
379	*Juan Brito*	.50
380	*Ron Calloway*	.50
381	*Adrian Burnside*	.50
382	*Josh Bard*	.50
383	*Matt Childers*	.50
384	*Gustavo Chacin*	.50
385	*Luis Martinez*	.50
386	*Trey Hodges*	.50
387	*Hansel Izquierdo*	.50
388	*Jeriome Robertson*	.50
389	*Victor Alvarez*	.50
390	*David Ross*	.50
391	Ron Chiavacci	.40
392	*Adam Walker*	.50
393	*Mike Gonzalez*	.50
394	*John Foster*	.50
395	*Kyle Kane*	.50
396	*Cam Esslinger*	.50
397	*Kevin Frederick*	.50
398	*Franklin Nunez*	.50
399	*Todd Donovan*	.50
400	*Kevin Cash*	.75

2002 Leaf Rookies & Stars Longevity

	MT
Stars (1-300):	5-10X
SP's (1-300):	1-3X
Production 100	
Rookies (301-400): Not Priced	
Production 25	

2002 Leaf Rookies & Stars BLC Homers

		MT
Common Player:		25.00
Production 25 sets		
1	Luis Gonzalez	40.00
2	Luis Gonzalez	40.00
3	Luis Gonzalez	40.00
4	Todd Helton	50.00
5	Todd Helton	50.00
6	Todd Helton	50.00
7	Todd Helton	50.00
8	Todd Helton	50.00
9	Todd Helton	50.00
10	Todd Helton	50.00
11	Todd Helton	50.00
12	Jim Thome	50.00
13	Jim Thome	50.00
14	Jim Thome	50.00
15	Rafael Palmeiro	40.00
16	Rafael Palmeiro	40.00
17	Rafael Palmeiro	40.00
18	Rafael Palmeiro	40.00
19	Rafael Palmeiro	40.00
20	Troy Glaus	50.00
21	Troy Glaus	50.00
22	Troy Glaus	50.00
23	Gary Sheffield	25.00
24	Gary Sheffield	25.00
25	Gary Sheffield	25.00
26	Mike Piazza	80.00
27	Mike Piazza	80.00
28	Mike Piazza	80.00
29	Mike Piazza	80.00
30	Mike Piazza	80.00

2002 Leaf Rookies & Stars Dress For Success

		MT
Common Player:		8.00
Production 250 sets		
Prime Cuts: Not Priced		
Production 25 sets		
1	Mike Piazza	20.00
2	Cal Ripken Jr.	30.00
3	Carlos Delgado	8.00
4	Chipper Jones	15.00
5	Bernie Williams	10.00
6	Carlos Beltran	10.00
7	Curt Schilling	15.00
8	Greg Maddux	15.00
9	Ivan Rodriguez	10.00
10	Alex Rodriguez	15.00
11	Roger Clemens	15.00
12	Todd Helton	12.00
13	Jim Edmonds	10.00
14	Manny Ramirez	12.00
15	Mark Buehrle	12.00

2002 Leaf Rookies & Stars Freshman Orientation

		MT
Common Player:		
Inserted 1:142		
Class Officer parallel:		1.5-2X
Production 50 sets		
1	Andres Torres/bat	8.00
2	Mark Ellis/jsy	10.00
3	Erik Bedard/bat	8.00
4	Delvin James/jsy	6.00
5	Austin Kearns/bat	15.00
6	Josh Pearce/bat	8.00
7	Rafael Soriano/jsy	10.00
8	Jason Lane/bat	8.00
9	Mark Prior/jsy	20.00
10	Alfredo Amezaga/bat	8.00
11	Ryan Ludwick/bat	6.00
12	So Taguchi/bat	10.00
13	Duaner Sanchez/bat	6.00
14	Kazuhisa Ishii/jsy	20.00
15	Zach Day/jsy	8.00
16	Eric Cyr/bat	8.00
17	Francis Beltran/jsy	8.00
18	Joe Borchard/jsy	15.00
19	Jeremy Affeldt/shoe	15.00
20	Alexis Gomez/jsy	8.00

2002 Leaf Rookies & Stars Great American Signings

	MT
Common Autograph:	6.00
Inserted 1:56	
Brent Abernathy/175	6.00
Bobby Abreu/25	
Brandon Backe/175	6.00
Chris Baker/175	6.00
Francis Beltran/175	6.00
Raul Chavez/175	6.00
Roger Clemens/10	
Doug Devore/175	6.00
Adam Dunn/25	
Felix Escalona/100	8.00
Franklyn German/175	6.00
Jay Gibbons/150	10.00
Geronimo Gil	
Vladimir Guerrero/15	
Bill Hall/175	6.00
Rickey Henderson/20	
Drew Henson/50	35.00
Eric Hinske/175	25.00
Ben Howard/175	6.00
Aubrey Huff/175	8.00
Travis Hughes/175	6.00
Kazuhisa Ishii/25	
Cesar Izturis/175	6.00
Nick Johnson/175	15.00
Austin Kearns/75	25.00
Satoru Komiyama/75	60.00
Jason Lane/150	12.00
Barry Larkin/25	
Brian Lawrence/175	6.00
Anderson Machado/175	8.00
Don Mattingly/25	
Roy Oswalt/100	15.00
Jorge Padilla/175	8.00
Oliver Perez/175	40.00
Albert Pujols/25	
Rene Reyes/175	6.00
Mike Rivera/175	6.00
Rodrigo Rosario/175	8.00
Tom Shearn/175	6.00
Chris Snelling/175	25.00
Alfonso Soriano/25	
Mac Suzuki/100	40.00
So Taguchi/50	40.00
Dennis Tankersley/175	8.00
Corey Thurman/175	8.00
Luis Ugueto/175	6.00
Kip Wells/175	6.00
Bernie Williams/15	
Kerry Wood/25	

2002 Leaf Rookies & Stars Statistical Standouts

		MT
Complete Set (50):		160.00
Common Player:		2.00
Inserted 1:12		
1	Adam Dunn	4.00
2	Alex Rodriguez	12.00
3	Andruw Jones	3.00
4	Brian Giles	2.50
5	Chipper Jones	8.00
6	Cliff Floyd	2.00
7	Craig Biggio	2.00
8	Frank Thomas	4.00
9	Fred McGriff	2.00
10	Garret Anderson	2.00
11	Greg Maddux	8.00
12	Luis Gonzalez	2.50
13	Magglio Ordonez	2.00
14	Ivan Rodriguez	3.00
15	Ken Griffey Jr.	8.00
16	Ichiro Suzuki	10.00
17	Jason Giambi	8.00
18	Derek Jeter	15.00
19	Sammy Sosa	8.00
20	Albert Pujols	5.00
21	J.D. Drew	3.00
22	Jeff Bagwell	4.00
23	Jim Edmonds	2.00
24	Jose Vidro	2.00
25	Juan Encarnacion	2.00
26	Kerry Wood	3.00
27	Al Leiter	2.00
28	Curt Schilling	3.00
29	Manny Ramirez	4.00
30	Lance Berkman	3.00
31	Miguel Tejada	3.00
32	Mike Piazza	10.00
33	Nomar Garciaparra	10.00
34	Omar Vizquel	2.00
35	Pat Burrell	3.00
36	Paul Konerko	2.00
37	Rafael Palmeiro	3.00
38	Randy Johnson	5.00
39	Richie Sexson	2.00
40	Roger Clemens	8.00
41	Shawn Green	2.00
42	Todd Helton	3.00
43	Tom Glavine	2.50
44	Troy Glaus	4.00
45	Vladimir Guerrero	5.00
46	Mike Sweeney	2.00
47	Alfonso Soriano	8.00
48	Barry Zito	2.50
49	John Smoltz	2.00
50	Ellis Burks	2.00

2002 Leaf Rookies & Stars Stat. Standouts Materials

		MT
Common Player:		5.00
Inserted 1:69		
Super Materials: Not Priced		
Production 25 sets		
1	Adam Dunn/bat/200	15.00

2 Alex Rodriguez/bat/200 15.00
3 Andruw Jones/bat/200 10.00
4 Brian Giles/bat 8.00
5 Chipper Jones/bat/200 15.00
6 Cliff Floyd/jsy 6.00
7 Craig Biggio/jsy 10.00
8 Frank Thomas/jsy/125 12.00
9 Fred McGriff/bat 10.00
10 Garret Anderson/bat 8.00
11 Greg Maddux/jsy/200 25.00
12 Luis Gonzalez/jsy 10.00
13 Magglio Ordonez/bat/150 10.00
14 Ivan Rodriguez/jsy/100 12.00
15 Ken Griffey Jr/base/100 15.00
16 Ichiro Suzuki/base/100 40.00
17 Jason Giambi/base 12.00
18 Derek Jeter/base/100 35.00
19 Sammy Sosa/base/100 15.00
20 Albert Pujols/base/100 15.00
21 J.D. Drew/bat/150 12.00
22 Jeff Bagwell/jsy/150 15.00
23 Jim Edmonds/bat 8.00
24 Jose Vidro/bat 6.00
25 Juan Encarnacion/bat 5.00
26 Kerry Wood/jsy/200 12.00
27 Al Leiter/jsy 8.00
28 Curt Schilling/jsy/225 12.00
29 Manny Ramirez/bat/100 15.00
30 Lance Berkman/bat/150 12.00
31 Miguel Tejada/jsy 10.00
32 Mike Piazza/bat/200 20.00
33 Nomar Garciaparra/bat/200 20.00
34 Omar Vizquel/jsy 8.00
35 Pat Burrell/bat 12.00
36 Paul Konerko/jsy 6.00
37 Rafael Palmeiro/bat 10.00
38 Randy Johnson/jsy/200 15.00
39 Richie Sexson/jsy 10.00
40 Roger Clemens/jsy/200 20.00
41 Shawn Green/jsy 10.00
42 Todd Helton/jsy/175 10.00
43 Tom Glavine/jsy/125 10.00
44 Troy Glaus/jsy 10.00
45 Vladimir Guerrero/jsy 12.00
46 Mike Sweeney/bat 6.00
47 Alfonso Soriano/jsy/200 20.00
48 Barry Zito/jsy/100 12.00
49 John Smoltz/jsy 8.00
50 Ellis Burks/jsy 8.00

2002 Leaf Rookies & Stars Triple Threads

MT
Common Card: 40.00
Production 100 sets
1 Reggie Jackson, Alfonso Soriano, Don Mattingly 100.00
2 Alex Rodriguez, Rafael Palmeiro, Ivan Rodriguez 40.00
3 Mike Piazza, Gary Carter, Rickey Henderson 50.00
4 Dale Murphy, Andruw Jones, Chipper Jones 50.00
5 Mike Schmidt, Steve Carlton, Scott Rolen 85.00
6 Rickey Henderson 75.00
7 Johnny Bench, Joe Morgan, Tom Seaver 70.00
8 Randy Johnson, Pedro J. Martinez, Vladimir Guerrero 40.00
9 Nolan Ryan, Rod Carew, Troy Glaus 100.00
10 Lou Brock, J.D. Drew, Stan Musial 65.00

2002 Leaf Rookies & Stars View Masters

MT
Common Player: 10.00
Production 100 sets
Slideshows: Not Priced
Production 25 sets
1 Carlos Delgado 10.00
2 Todd Helton 15.00
3 Tony Gwynn 35.00
4 Bernie Williams 15.00
5 Luis Gonzalez 15.00
6 Larry Walker 10.00
7 Troy Glaus 15.00
8 Alfonso Soriano 30.00
9 Curt Schilling 15.00
10 Chipper Jones 20.00
11 Vladimir Guerrero 20.00
12 Adam Dunn 20.00
13 Rickey Henderson 30.00
14 Miguel Tejada 15.00
15 Kazuhisa Ishii 25.00
16 Greg Maddux 35.00
17 Pedro J. Martinez 20.00
18 Nomar Garciaparra 30.00
19 Mike Piazza 35.00
20 Lance Berkman 15.00

1996 Metal Universe

Certainly one of the most unusual baseball card issues of its era, Fleer's Metal Universe set is distinguished by its colored, textured metallic-foil backgrounds created by comic book illustrators. The effects range from gaudy to grotesque. Glossy player action photos are featured on front, with a steel-colored metallic strip at bottom carrying set and player ID. Conventionally printed backs have a heavy-metal theme with a color player portrait photo at top and a few stats and person data around. The issue was sold in hobby and retail packaging with the basic hobby pack containing eight cards at a suggested retail price of $2.49. Several insert sets were included, along with a platinum parallel edition of the player cards.

MT
Complete Set (250): 25.00
Common Player: .10
Platinum Set (250): 100.00
Common Platinum: .25
Platinums: 5X
Pack (8): 1.50
Wax Box (24): 30.00
1 Roberto Alomar .50
2 Brady Anderson .10
3 Bobby Bonilla .10
4 Chris Holles .10
5 Ben McDonald .10
6 Mike Mussina .60
7 Randy Myers .10
8 Rafael Palmeiro .30
9 Cal Ripken Jr. 2.50
10 B.J. Surhoff .10
11 Luis Alicea .10
12 Jose Canseco .40
13 Roger Clemens 1.00
14 Wil Cordero .10
15 Tom Gordon .10
16 Mike Greenwell .10
17 Tim Naehring .10
18 Troy O'Leary .10
19 Mike Stanley .10
20 John Valentin .10
21 Mo Vaughn .40
22 Tim Wakefield .10
23 Garret Anderson .15
24 Chili Davis .10
25 Gary DiSarcina .10
26 Jim Edmonds .20
27 Chuck Finley .10
28 Todd Greene .10
29 Mark Langston .10
30 Troy Percival .10
31 Tony Phillips .10
32 Tim Salmon .25
33 Lee Smith .10
34 J.T. Snow .10
35 Ray Durham .10
36 Alex Fernandez .10
37 Ozzie Guillen .10
38 Roberto Hernandez .10
39 Lyle Mouton .10
40 Frank Thomas 1.00
41 Robin Ventura .10
42 Sandy Alomar .10
43 Carlos Baerga .10
44 Albert Belle .25
45 Orel Hershiser .10
46 Kenny Lofton .10
47 Dennis Martinez .10
48 Jack McDowell .10
49 Jose Mesa .10
50 Eddie Murray .40
51 Charles Nagy .10
52 Manny Ramirez .75
53 Julian Tavarez .10
54 Jim Thome .10
55 Omar Vizquel .10
56 Chad Curtis .10
57 Cecil Fielder .10
58 John Flaherty .10
59 Travis Fryman .10
60 Chris Gomez .10
61 Felipe Lira .10
62 Kevin Appier .10
63 Johnny Damon .15
64 Tom Goodwin .10
65 Mark Gubicza .10
66 Jeff Montgomery .10
67 Jon Nunnally .10
68 Ricky Bones .10
69 Jeff Cirillo .10
70 John Jaha .10
71 Dave Nilsson .10
72 Joe Oliver .10
73 Kevin Seitzer .10
74 Greg Vaughn .10
75 Marty Cordova .15
76 Chuck Knoblauch .10
77 Pat Meares .10
78 Paul Molitor .50
79 Pedro Munoz .10
80 Kirby Puckett 1.00
81 Brad Radke .15
82 Scott Stahoviak .10
83 Matt Walbeck .10
84 Wade Boggs .75
85 David Cone .10
86 Joe Girardi .10
87 Derek Jeter 2.00
88 Jim Leyritz .10
89 Tino Martinez .10
90 Don Mattingly 1.00
91 Paul O'Neill .10
92 Andy Pettitte .30
93 Tim Raines .10
94 Kenny Rogers .10
95 Ruben Sierra .10
96 John Wetteland .10
97 Bernie Williams .50
98 Geronimo Berroa .10
99 Dennis Eckersley .10
100 Brent Gates .10
101 Mark McGwire 2.50
102 Steve Ontiveros .10
103 Terry Steinbach .10
104 Jay Buhner .10
105 Vince Coleman .10
106 Joey Cora .10
107 Ken Griffey Jr. 2.00
108 Randy Johnson .75
109 Edgar Martinez .10
110 Alex Rodriguez 2.50
111 Paul Sorrento .10
112 Will Clark .30
113 Juan Gonzalez .75
114 Rusty Greer .10
115 Dean Palmer .10
116 Ivan Rodriguez .60
117 Mickey Tettleton .10
118 Joe Carter .10
119 Alex Gonzalez .15
120 Shawn Green .20
121 Erik Hanson .10
122 Pat Hentgen .10
123 *Sandy Martinez* .10
124 Otis Nixon .10
125 John Olerud .10
126 Steve Avery .10
127 Tom Glavine .25
128 Marquis Grissom .15
129 Chipper Jones 2.00
130 David Justice .30
131 Ryan Klesko .10
132 Mark Lemke .10
133 Javier Lopez .10
134 Greg Maddux 1.50
135 Fred McGriff .10
136 John Smoltz .20
137 Mark Wohlers .10
138 Frank Castillo .10
139 Shawon Dunston .10
140 Luis Gonzalez .30
141 Mark Grace .35
142 Brian McRae .10
143 Jaime Navarro .10
144 Rey Sanchez .10
145 Ryne Sandberg .75
146 Sammy Sosa 1.50
147 Bret Boone .10
148 Curtis Goodwin .10
149 Barry Larkin .15
150 Hal Morris .10
151 Reggie Sanders .10
152 Pete Schourek .10
153 John Smiley .10
154 Dante Bichette .10
155 Vinny Castilla .10
156 Andres Galarraga .10
157 Bret Saberhagen .10
158 Bill Swift .10
159 Larry Walker .30
160 Walt Weiss .10

161	Kurt Abbott	.10
162	John Burkett	.10
163	Greg Colbrunn	.10
164	Jeff Conine	.10
165	Chris Hammond	.10
166	Charles Johnson	.10
167	Al Leiter	.10
168	Pat Rapp	.10
169	Gary Sheffield	.30
170	Quilvio Veras	.10
171	Devon White	.10
172	Jeff Bagwell	.75
173	Derek Bell	.10
174	Sean Berry	.10
175	Craig Biggio	.15
176	Doug Drabek	.10
177	Tony Eusebio	.10
178	Brian Hunter	.10
179	Orlando Miller	.10
180	Shane Reynolds	.10
181	Mike Blowers	.10
182	Roger Cedeno	.10
183	Eric Karros	.10
184	Ramon Martinez	.10
185	Raul Mondesi	.25
186	Hideo Nomo	.75
187	Mike Piazza	2.00
188	Moises Alou	.15
189	Yamil Benitez	.10
190	Darrin Fletcher	.10
191	Cliff Floyd	.10
192	Pedro Martinez	.75
193	Carlos Perez	.10
194	David Segul	.10
195	Tony Tarasco	.10
196	Rondell White	.15
197	Edgardo Alfonzo	.15
198	Rico Brogna	.10
199	Carl Everett	.15
200	Todd Hundley	.10
201	Jason Isringhausen	.10
202	Lance Johnson	.10
203	Bobby Jones	.10
204	Jeff Kent	.10
205	Bill Pulsipher	.10
206	Jose Vizcaino	.10
207	Ricky Bottalico	.10
208	Darren Daulton	.10
209	Lenny Dykstra	.10
210	Jim Eisenreich	.10
211	Gregg Jefferies	.10
212	Mickey Morandini	.10
213	Heathcliff Slocumb	.10
214	Jay Bell	.10
215	Carlos Garcia	.10
216	Jeff King	.10
217	Al Martin	.10
218	Orlando Merced	.10
219	Dan Miceli	.10
220	Denny Neagle	.10
221	Andy Benes	.10
222	Royce Clayton	.10
223	Gary Gaetti	.10
224	Ron Gant	.10
225	Bernard Gilkey	.10
226	Brian Jordan	.10
227	Ray Lankford	.10
228	John Mabry	.10
229	Ozzie Smith	.75
230	Todd Stottlemyre	.10
231	Andy Ashby	.10
232	Brad Ausmus	.10
233	Ken Caminiti	.10
234	Steve Finley	.10
235	Tony Gwynn	1.00
236	Joey Hamilton	.10
237	Rickey Henderson	.30
238	Trevor Hoffman	.10
239	Wally Joyner	.10
240	Rod Beck	.10
241	Barry Bonds	1.00
242	Glenallen Hill	.10
243	Stan Javier	.10
244	Mark Leiter	.10
245	Deion Sanders	.20
246	William VanLandingham	.10
247	Matt Williams	.25
248	Checklist	.10
249	Checklist	.10
250	Checklist	.10

1996 Metal Universe Platinum Edition

One of the eight cards in each pack of Fleer Metal baseball is a Platinum Edition parallel insert. Each of the 247 player cards (no checklists) in this special version has the textured foil background rendered only in silver. The second line of the logo/ID strip at bottom also identifies the card as part of the Platinum Edition.

	MT
Complete Set (247):	100.00
Common Player:	.50
Stars:	5X

(See 1996 Metal Universe for checklist and base card values.)

1996 Metal Universe Heavy Metal

Some of the game's biggest hitters are included in this insert set. Action photos of players at bat are set on a silver-foil background on front. Backs have a close-up photo down one side, with praise for the player's power potential down the other. The Heavy Metal inserts can be expected to turn up at an average rate of one per eight packs.

		MT
Complete Set (10):		8.00
Common Player:		.50
1	Albert Belle	.50
2	Barry Bonds	1.00
3	Juan Gonzalez	.75
4	Ken Griffey Jr.	2.00
5	Mark McGwire	2.00
6	Mike Piazza	1.50
7	Sammy Sosa	1.00
8	Frank Thomas	1.00
9	Mo Vaughn	.50
10	Matt Williams	.50

1996 Metal Universe Mining for Gold

Available only in retail packs, at an average rate of one per dozen packs, the Mining for Gold insert series focuses on 1995's top rookies. Fronts have player action photos frame and backgrounded with several different gold tones in etched metal foil. Backs are conventionally printed, carrying on the same format with a portrait photo and a few words about the player.

		MT
Complete Set (12):		35.00
Common Player:		1.00
1	Yamil Benitez	1.00
2	Marty Cordova	2.00
3	Shawn Green	4.00
4	Todd Greene	1.00
5	Brian Hunter	1.00
6	Derek Jeter	10.00
7	Charles Johnson	1.00
8	Chipper Jones	8.00
9	Hideo Nomo	7.50
10	Alex Ochoa	1.00
11	Andy Pettitte	6.00
12	Quilvio Veras	1.00

1996 Metal Universe Mother Lode

Medieval designs rendered in textured silver-foil on a plain white background are the setting for the color player photos in this hobby-only insert. Backs also have a silver and white background along with another player photo and some kind words about his skills. The cards are found at an average rate of one per 12 packs.

		MT
Complete Set (12):		40.00
Common Player:		1.50
1	Barry Bonds	4.00
2	Jim Edmonds	2.00
3	Ken Griffey Jr.	10.00
4	Kenny Lofton	1.50
5	Raul Mondesi	1.50
6	Rafael Palmeiro	1.50
7	Manny Ramirez	5.00
8	Cal Ripken Jr.	10.00
9	Tim Salmon	1.50
10	Ryne Sandberg	4.00
11	Frank Thomas	6.00
12	Matt Williams	1.50

1996 Metal Universe Platinum Portraits

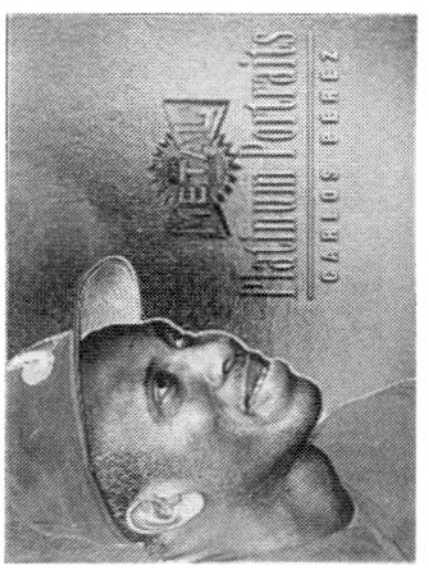

Close-up color photos on a plain metallic-foil background are featured in this insert set. The checklist is heavy in rookie and sophomore players, who are featured in an action photo on back, with a few career details. Platinum Portraits inserts are found in every fourth pack, on average.

		MT
Complete Set (10):		7.50
Common Player:		.50
1	Garret Anderson	.50
2	Marty Cordova	.50
3	Jim Edmonds	.75
4	Jason Isringhausen	.50
5	Chipper Jones	3.00
6	Ryan Klesko	.50
7	Hideo Nomo	1.50
8	Carlos Perez	.50
9	Manny Ramirez	2.00
10	Rondell White	.50

1996 Metal Universe Titanium

A huge purple-highlighted silver baseball in a star-studded night sky is the background for the action photos of the game's biggest names in this insert series. Backs have a second, more up-close, photo and a few words about the player. Titanium inserts are found in Metal Universe packs at an average rate of one per 24 packs.

		MT
Complete Set (10):		25.00
Common Player:		1.00
1	Albert Belle	1.00
2	Barry Bonds	3.00
3	Ken Griffey Jr.	6.50
4	Tony Gwynn	2.50
5	Greg Maddux	3.00
6	Mike Piazza	5.00
7	Cal Ripken Jr.	6.50
8	Frank Thomas	2.50
9	Mo Vaughn	1.00
10	Matt Williams	1.00

1997 Metal Universe

Metal Universe Baseball arrived in a 250-card set, including three checklists. Each card is printed on 100-percent etched foil with "comic book" art full-bleed backgrounds, with the player's name, team, position and the Metal Universe logo near the bottom of the card. Backs contain another player photo and key statistics. Metal Universe sold in eight-card packs and contained six different insert sets. They included: Blast Furnace, Magnetic Field, Mining for Gold, Mother Lode, Platinum Portraits and Titanium.

		MT
Complete Set (250):		30.00
Common Player:		.10
Pack (8):		1.50
Wax Box (24):		30.00
1	Roberto Alomar	.60
2	Brady Anderson	.10
3	Rocky Coppinger	.10
4	Chris Hoiles	.10
5	Eddie Murray	.40
6	Mike Mussina	.50
7	Rafael Palmeiro	.30
8	Cal Ripken Jr.	2.50
9	B.J. Surhoff	.10
10	Brant Brown	.10
11	Mark Grace	.40
12	Brian McRae	.10
13	Jaime Navarro	.10
14	Ryne Sandberg	.75
15	Sammy Sosa	1.50
16	Amaury Telemaco	.10
17	Steve Trachsel	.10
18	Darren Bragg	.10
19	Jose Canseco	.40
20	Roger Clemens	1.00
21	Nomar Garciaparra	1.50
22	Tom Gordon	.10
23	Tim Naehring	.10
24	Mike Stanley	.10
25	John Valentin	.10
26	Mo Vaughn	.40
27	Jermaine Dye	.10
28	Tom Glavine	.25
29	Marquis Grissom	.10
30	Andruw Jones	.75
31	Chipper Jones	1.50
32	Ryan Klesko	.10
33	Greg Maddux	1.00
34	Fred McGriff	.10
35	John Smoltz	.15
36	Garret Anderson	.10
37	George Arias	.10
38	Gary DiSarcina	.10
39	Jim Edmonds	.20
40	Darin Erstad	.75
41	Chuck Finley	.10
42	Troy Percival	.10
43	Tim Salmon	.20
44	Bret Boone	.10
45	Jeff Brantley	.10
46	Eric Davis	.10
47	Barry Larkin	.20
48	Hal Morris	.10
49	Mark Portugal	.10
50	Reggie Sanders	.10
51	John Smiley	.10
52	Wilson Alvarez	.10
53	Harold Baines	.10
54	James Baldwin	.10
55	Albert Belle	.30
56	Mike Cameron	.10
57	Ray Durham	.10
58	Alex Fernandez	.10
59	Roberto Hernandez	.10
60	Tony Phillips	.10
61	Frank Thomas	1.00
62	Robin Ventura	.10
63	Jeff Cirillo	.10
64	Jeff D'Amico	.10
65	John Jaha	.10
66	Scott Karl	.10
67	Ben McDonald	.10
68	Marc Newfield	.10
69	Dave Nilsson	.10
70	Jose Valentin	.10
71	Dante Bichette	.10
72	Ellis Burks	.10
73	Vinny Castilla	.10
74	Andres Galarraga	.10
75	Kevin Ritz	.10
76	Larry Walker	.30
77	Walt Weiss	.10
78	Jamey Wright	.10
79	Eric Young	.10
80	Julio Franco	.10
81	Orel Hershiser	.10
82	Kenny Lofton	.10
83	Jack McDowell	.10
84	Jose Mesa	.10
85	Charles Nagy	.10
86	Manny Ramirez	.75
87	Jim Thome	.10
88	Omar Vizquel	.10
89	Matt Williams	.25
90	Kevin Appier	.10
91	Johnny Damon	.15
92	Chili Davis	.10
93	Tom Goodwin	.10
94	Keith Lockhart	.10
95	Jeff Montgomery	.10
96	Craig Paquette	.10
97	Jose Rosado	.10
98	Michael Tucker	.10
99	Wilton Guerrero	.10
100	Todd Hollandsworth	.10
101	Eric Karros	.10
102	Ramon Martinez	.10
103	Raul Mondesi	.25
104	Hideo Nomo	.75
105	Mike Piazza	2.00
106	Ismael Valdes	.10
107	Todd Worrell	.10
108	Tony Clark	.10
109	Travis Fryman	.10
110	Bob Higginson	.10
111	Mark Lewis	.10
112	Melvin Nieves	.10
113	Justin Thompson	.10
114	Wade Boggs	.40
115	David Cone	.10
116	Cecil Fielder	.10
117	Dwight Gooden	.10
118	Derek Jeter	2.00
119	Tino Martinez	.10
120	Paul O'Neill	.10
121	Andy Pettitte	.30
122	Mariano Rivera	.25
123	Darryl Strawberry	.10
124	John Wetteland	.10
125	Bernie Williams	.40
126	Tony Batista	.10
127	Geronimo Berroa	.10
128	Scott Brosius	.10
129	Jason Giambi	.45
130	Jose Herrera	.10
131	Mark McGwire	2.50
132	John Wasdin	.10
133	Bob Abreu	.20
134	Jeff Bagwell	.75
135	Derek Bell	.10
136	Craig Biggio	.15
137	Brian Hunter	.10
138	Darryl Kile	.10
139	Orlando Miller	.10
140	Shane Reynolds	.10
141	Billy Wagner	.10
142	Donne Wall	.10
143	Jay Buhner	.10
144	Jeff Fassero	.10
145	Ken Griffey Jr.	2.00
146	Sterling Hitchcock	.10
147	Randy Johnson	.75
148	Edgar Martinez	.10
149	Alex Rodriguez	2.50
149p	Alex Rodriguez ("PROMOTIONAL SAMPLE")	2.00
150	Paul Sorrento	.10
151	Dan Wilson	.10
152	Moises Alou	.15
153	Darrin Fletcher	.10
154	Cliff Floyd	.10
155	Mark Grudzielanek	.10
156	Vladimir Guerrero	.75
157	Mike Lansing	.10
158	Pedro Martinez	.75
159	Henry Rodriguez	.10
160	Rondell White	.10
161	Will Clark	.30
162	Juan Gonzalez	.75
163	Rusty Greer	.10
164	Ken Hill	.10
165	Mark McLemore	.10
166	Dean Palmer	.10
167	Roger Pavlik	.10
168	Ivan Rodriguez	.60
169	Mickey Tettleton	.10
170	Bobby Bonilla	.10
171	Kevin Brown	.15
172	Greg Colbrunn	.10
173	Jeff Conine	.10
174	Jim Eisenreich	.10
175	Charles Johnson	.10
176	Al Leiter	.10
177	Robb Nen	.10
178	Edgar Renteria	.10
179	Gary Sheffield	.35
180	Devon White	.10
181	Joe Carter	.10
182	Carlos Delgado	.60
183	Alex Gonzalez	.15
184	Shawn Green	.35
185	Juan Guzman	.10
186	Pat Hentgen	.10
187	Orlando Merced	.10
188	John Olerud	.10
189	Robert Perez	.10
190	Ed Sprague	.10
191	Mark Clark	.10
192	John Franco	.10
193	Bernard Gilkey	.10
194	Todd Hundley	.10
195	Lance Johnson	.10
196	Bobby Jones	.10
197	Alex Ochoa	.10
198	Rey Ordonez	.10
199	Paul Wilson	.10
200	Ricky Bottalico	.10
201	Gregg Jefferies	.10
202	Wendell Magee Jr.	.10
203	Mickey Morandini	.10
204	Ricky Otero	.10
205	Scott Rolen	.50
206	Benito Santiago	.10
207	Curt Schilling	.20
208	Rich Becker	.10
209	Marty Cordova	.10
210	Chuck Knoblauch	.10
211	Pat Meares	.10
212	Paul Molitor	.50
213	Frank Rodriguez	.10
214	Terry Steinbach	.10
215	Todd Walker	.10
216	Andy Ashby	.10
217	Ken Caminiti	.10
218	Steve Finley	.10
219	Tony Gwynn	1.00
220	Joey Hamilton	.10
221	Rickey Henderson	.50
222	Trevor Hoffman	.10
223	Wally Joyner	.10
224	Scott Sanders	.10
225	Fernando Valenzuela	.10
226	Greg Vaughn	.10
227	Alan Benes	.10
228	Andy Benes	.10
229	Dennis Eckersley	.10
230	Ron Gant	.10
231	Brian Jordan	.10
232	Ray Lankford	.10
233	John Mabry	.10
234	Tom Pagnozzi	.10
235	Todd Stottlemyre	.10
236	Jermaine Allensworth	.10
237	Francisco Cordova	.10
238	Jason Kendall	.10
239	Jeff King	.10
240	Al Martin	.10
241	Rod Beck	.10
242	Barry Bonds	1.50
243	Shawn Estes	.10
244	Mark Gardner	.10
245	Glenallen Hill	.10
246	Bill Mueller	.10
247	J.T. Snow	.10
248	Checklist	.10
249	Checklist	.10
250	Checklist	.10

1997 Metal Universe Blast Furnace

Blast Furnace inserts were found only in hobby packs, at a rate of one per 48 packs. The 12-card set was printed on a red-tinted plastic, with the words "Blast Furnace" near the bottom in gold foil with a fire-like border.

		MT
Complete Set (12):		70.00
Common Player:		2.00
1	Jeff Bagwell	8.00
2	Albert Belle	3.00

3	Barry Bonds	6.00
4	Andres Galarraga	2.00
5	Juan Gonzalez	5.00
6	Ken Griffey Jr.	15.00
7	Todd Hundley	2.00
8	Mark McGwire	15.00
9	Mike Piazza	12.00
10	Alex Rodriguez	12.50
11	Frank Thomas	7.50
12	Mo Vaughn	3.00

1997 Metal Universe Emerald Autographs

Six different young stars were featured in this insert, which was found every 480 hobby packs of Metal Universe. The cards are similar to regular-issue cards, but have a green foil finish and autograph on the front. Redemption cards are numbered AU1-AU6, the autographed cards have a notation on back, "Certified Emerald Autograph Card".

		MT
Complete Set (6):		75.00
Common Autograph:		6.00
1	Darin Erstad	9.00
2	Todd Hollandsworth	6.00
3	Alex Ochoa	6.00
4	Alex Rodriguez	40.00
5	Scott Rolen	30.00
6	Todd Walker	6.00

1997 Metal Universe Emerald Autograph Redemption

Six different young stars were featured in this insert, which was found every 480 hobby packs of Metal Universe. The cards are similar to regular-issue cards, but have green foil highlights. Redemption cards are numbered AU1-AU6. The redemption period expired Jan. 15, 1998.

		MT
Complete Set (6):		12.00
Common Player:		1.00
1	Darin Erstad	2.50
2	Todd Hollandsworth	1.00
3	Alex Ochoa	1.00
4	Alex Rodriguez	7.50
5	Scott Rolen	2.50
6	Todd Walker	1.00

1997 Metal Universe Magnetic Field

Magnetic Field inserts are printed in a horizontal format with prismatic foil backgrounds. This 10-card insert was found every 12 packs of Metal Universe.

		MT
Complete Set (10):		22.50
Common Player:		1.00
1	Roberto Alomar	1.25
2	Jeff Bagwell	2.00
3	Barry Bonds	3.00
4	Ken Griffey Jr.	5.00
5	Derek Jeter	4.00
6	Kenny Lofton	1.00
7	Edgar Renteria	1.00
8	Cal Ripken Jr.	5.00
9	Alex Rodriguez	5.00
10	Matt Williams	1.00

1997 Metal Universe Mining for Gold

Mining for Gold was a 10-card insert that featured some of baseball's brightest stars on a die-cut "ingot" design with pearlized gold coating. This insert was found every nine packs.

		MT
Complete Set (10):		13.50
Common Player:		.75
1	Bob Abreu	1.50
2	Kevin Brown	.75
3	Nomar Garciaparra	4.00
4	Vladimir Guerrero	3.00
5	Wilton Guerrero	.75
6	Andruw Jones	3.00
7	Curt Lyons	.75
8	Neifi Perez	.75
9	Scott Rolen	2.50
10	Todd Walker	.75

1997 Metal Universe Mother Lode

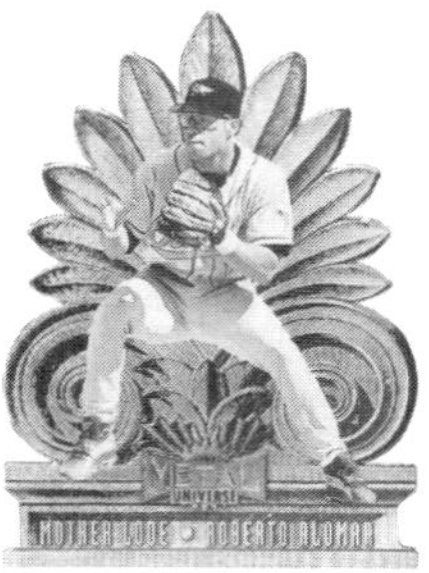

Mother lode was the most difficult insert out of Metal Universe with a one per 288 pack insertion ratio. Each card in this 10-card inert was printed on etched foil with a plant-type monument in back of the player.

		MT
Complete Set (12):		70.00
Common Player:		2.00
1	Roberto Alomar	3.00
2	Jeff Bagwell	5.00
3	Barry Bonds	7.50
4	Ken Griffey Jr.	13.50
5	Andruw Jones	4.00
6	Chipper Jones	10.00
7	Kenny Lofton	2.00
8	Mike Piazza	10.00
9	Cal Ripken Jr.	15.00
10	Alex Rodriguez	12.50
11	Frank Thomas	7.50
12	Matt Williams	2.00

1997 Metal Universe Platinum Portraits

Each card in the Platinum Portraits insert is printed on a background of platinum-colored etched foil. The 10-card set includes some of the top prospects and rising stars in baseball, and is included every 36 packs.

		MT
Complete Set (10):		10.00
Common Player:		.35
1	James Baldwin	.35
2	Jermaine Dye	.35
3	Todd Hollandsworth	.35
4	Derek Jeter	3.00
5	Chipper Jones	3.00
6	Jason Kendall	.35
7	Rey Ordonez	.75
8	Andy Pettitte	1.00
9	Edgar Renteria	.75
10	Alex Rodriguez	4.00

1997 Metal Universe Titanium

These retail exclusive inserts include 10 cards and were found every 24 packs. Each card is die-cut on the top-left and bottom-right corner with a silver foil background. Titanium includes some of the most popular players in baseball on cards that are also embossed.

		MT
Complete Set (10):		30.00
Common Player:		1.50
1	Jeff Bagwell	2.50
2	Albert Belle	1.50
3	Ken Griffey Jr.	5.00
4	Chipper Jones	4.00
5	Greg Maddux	3.00
6	Mark McGwire	5.00
7	Mike Piazza	4.00
8	Cal Ripken Jr.	5.00
9	Alex Rodriguez	4.00
10	Frank Thomas	3.00

1998 Metal Universe

This 220-card single series release captured

players over a foil etched, art background that related in some way to them or the city they played in. Metal Universe included a 15-card Hardball Galaxy subset and dealers and media were given an Alex Rodriguez promo card that was identical the base card except for the words "Promotional Sample" written across the back. The set arrived with a parallel called Precious Metal Gems, and included the following insert sets: All-Galactic Team, Diamond Heroes, Platinum Portraits, Titanium and Universal Language.

		MT
Complete Set (220):		25.00
Common Player:		.10
Pack (8):		1.50
Wax Box (24):		25.00
1	Jose Cruz Jr.	.15
2	Jeff Abbott	.10
3	Rafael Palmeiro	.30
4	Ivan Rodriguez	.65
5	Jaret Wright	.20
6	Derek Bell	.10
7	Chuck Finley	.10
8	Travis Fryman	.10
9	Randy Johnson	.75
10	Derrek Lee	.10
11	Bernie Williams	.30
12	Carlos Baerga	.10
13	Ricky Bottalico	.10
14	Ellis Burks	.10
15	Russ Davis	.10
16	Nomar Garciaparra	1.50
17	Joey Hamilton	.10
18	Jason Kendall	.10
19	Darryl Kile	.10
20	Edgardo Alfonzo	.10
21	Moises Alou	.20
22	Bobby Bonilla	.10
23	Jim Edmonds	.20
24	Jose Guillen	.15
25	Chuck Knoblauch	.10
26	Javy Lopez	.10
27	Billy Wagner	.10
28	Kevin Appier	.10
29	Joe Carter	.10
30	Todd Dunwoody	.10
31	Gary Gaetti	.10
32	Juan Gonzalez	.75
33	Jeffrey Hammonds	.10
34	Roberto Hernandez	.10
35	Dave Nilsson	.10
36	Manny Ramirez	.75
37	Robin Ventura	.10
38	Rondell White	.10
39	Vinny Castilla	.10
40	Will Clark	.30
41	Scott Hatteberg	.10
42	Russ Johnson	.10
43	Ricky Ledee	.10
44	Kenny Lofton	.10
45	Paul Molitor	.65
46	Justin Thompson	.10
47	Craig Biggio	.15
48	Damion Easley	.10
49	Brad Radke	.15
50	Ben Grieve	.40
51	Mark Bellhorn	.10
52	*Henry Blanco*	.10
53	Mariano Rivera	.25
54	Reggie Sanders	.10
55	Paul Sorrento	.10
56	Terry Steinbach	.10
57	Mo Vaughn	.30
58	Brady Anderson	.10
59	Tom Glavine	.25
60	Sammy Sosa	2.00
61	Larry Walker	.30
62	Rod Beck	.10
63	Jose Canseco	.40
64	Steve Finley	.10
65	Pedro Martinez	.75
66	John Olerud	.10
67	Scott Rolen	.50
68	Ismael Valdes	.10
69	Andrew Vessel	.10
70	Mark Grudzielanek	.10
71	Eric Karros	.10
72	Jeff Shaw	.10
73	Lou Collier	.10
74	Edgar Martinez	.10
75	Vladimir Guerrero	.60
76	Paul Konerko	.15
77	Kevin Orie	.10
78	Kevin Polcovich	.10
79	Brett Tomko	.10
80	Jeff Bagwell	.75
81	Barry Bonds	1.00
82	David Justice	.30
83	Hideo Nomo	.75
84	Ryne Sandberg	.75
85	Shannon Stewart	.10
86	Derek Wallace	.10
87	Tony Womack	.10
88	Jason Giambi	.40
89	Mark Grace	.30
90	Pat Hentgen	.10
91	Raul Mondesi	.25
92	Matt Morris	.10
93	Matt Perisho	.10
94	Tim Salmon	.25
95	Jeremi Gonzalez	.10
96	Shawn Green	.25
97	Todd Greene	.10
98	Ruben Rivera	.10
99	Deion Sanders	.20
100	Alex Rodriguez	2.00
101	Will Cunnane	.10
102	Ray Lankford	.10
103	Ryan McGuire	.10
104	Charles Nagy	.10
105	Rey Ordonez	.10
106	Mike Piazza	2.00
107	Tony Saunders	.10
108	Curt Schilling	.25
109	Fernando Tatis	.10
110	Mark McGwire	2.50
111	*David Dellucci*	.25
112	Garret Anderson	.10
113	Shane Bowers	.10
114	David Cone	.10
115	Jeff King	.10
116	Matt Williams	.25
117	Aaron Boone	.10
118	Dennis Eckersley	.10
119	Livan Hernandez	.10
120	Richard Hidalgo	.15
121	Bobby Higginson	.10
122	Tino Martinez	.10
123	Tim Naehring	.10
124	Jose Vidro	.10
125	John Wetteland	.10
126	Jay Bell	.10
127	Albert Belle	.40
128	Marty Cordova	.10
129	Chili Davis	.10
130	Jason Dickson	.10
131	Rusty Greer	.10
132	Hideki Irabu	.10
133	Greg Maddux	1.50
134	Billy Taylor	.10
135	Jim Thome	.10
136	Gerald Williams	.10
137	Jeff Cirillo	.10
138	Delino DeShields	.10
139	Andres Galarraga	.10
140	Willie Greene	.10
141	John Jaha	.10
142	Charles Johnson	.10
143	Ryan Klesko	.10
144	Paul O'Neill	.10
145	Robinson Checo	.10
146	Roberto Alomar	.50
147	Wilson Alvarez	.10
148	Bobby Jones	.10
149	Raul Casanova	.10
150	Andruw Jones	.60
151	Mike Lansing	.10
152	Mickey Morandini	.10
153	Neifi Perez	.10
154	Pokey Reese	.10
155	Edgar Renteria	.10
156	Eric Young	.10
157	Darin Erstad	.60
158	Kelvim Escobar	.10
159	Carl Everett	.15
160	Tom Gordon	.10
161	Ken Griffey Jr.	2.50
162	Al Martin	.10
163	Bubba Trammell	.10
164	Carlos Delgado	.50
165	Kevin Brown	.20
166	Ken Caminiti	.10
167	Roger Clemens	1.00
168	Ron Gant	.10
169	Jeff Kent	.10
170	Mike Mussina	.50
171	Dean Palmer	.10
172	Henry Rodriguez	.10
173	Matt Stairs	.10
174	Jay Buhner	.10
175	Frank Thomas	1.00
176	Mike Cameron	.10
177	Johnny Damon	.15
178	Tony Gwynn	1.00
179	John Smoltz	.20
180	B.J. Surhoff	.10
181	Antone Williamson	.10
182	Alan Benes	.10
183	Jeromy Burnitz	.10
184	Tony Clark	.10
185	Shawn Estes	.10
186	Todd Helton	.50
187	Todd Hundley	.10
188	Chipper Jones	1.50
189	Mark Kotsay	.10
190	Barry Larkin	.20
191	Mike Lieberthal	.10
192	Andy Pettitte	.25
193	Gary Sheffield	.30
194	Jeff Suppan	.10
195	Mark Wohlers	.10
196	Dante Bichette	.10
197	Trevor Hoffman	.10
198	J.T. Snow	.10
199	Derek Jeter	2.00
200	Cal Ripken Jr.	2.50
201	*Steve Woodard*	.25
202	Ray Durham	.10
203	Barry Bonds (Hardball Galaxy)	.50
204	Tony Clark (Hardball Galaxy)	.10
205	Roger Clemens (Hardball Galaxy)	.50
206	Ken Griffey Jr. (Hardball Galaxy)	1.00
207	Tony Gwynn (Hardball Galaxy)	.50
208	Derek Jeter (Hardball Galaxy)	1.00
209	Randy Johnson (Hardball Galaxy)	.40
210	Mark McGwire (Hardball Galaxy)	1.25
211	Hideo Nomo (Hardball Galaxy)	.50
212	Mike Piazza (Hardball Galaxy)	1.00
213	Cal Ripken Jr. (Hardball Galaxy)	1.25
214	Alex Rodriguez (Hardball Galaxy)	1.00
215	Frank Thomas (Hardball Galaxy)	.50
216	Mo Vaughn (Hardball Galaxy)	.20
217	Larry Walker (Hardball Galaxy)	.15
218	Checklist (Ken Griffey Jr.)	.60
219	Checklist (Alex Rodriguez)	.60
220	Checklist (Frank Thomas)	.50

1998 Metal Universe Precious Metal Gems

Precious Metal Gems includes 217 (no checklists) player cards from Metal Universe and are serial numbered to 50 sets. Because there were five Ultimate Metal Gems redemption cards (good for a complete set of Metal Gems) available, only serial numberes 1-45 were found in packs (46-50 were held back for the exchage program).

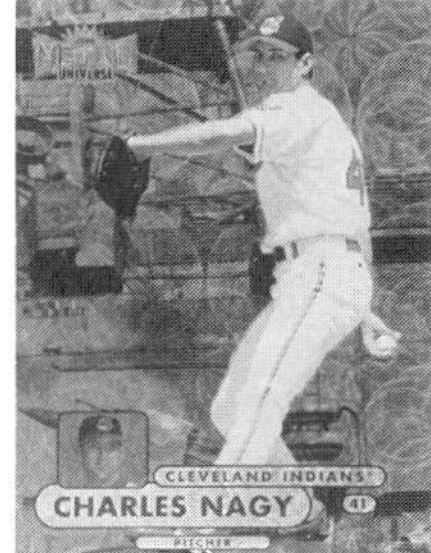

	MT
Common Player:	5.00
Stars:	20X
Production 50 sets	

(See 1998 Metal Universe for checklist and base card values.)

1998 Metal Universe All-Galactic Team

This 18-card insert captures players over a planet holofoil background. Cards were inserted one per 192 packs.

		MT
Complete Set (18):		130.00
Common Player:		3.00
Inserted 1:192		
1	Ken Griffey Jr.	17.50
2	Frank Thomas	8.00
3	Chipper Jones	12.50
4	Albert Belle	3.00
5	Juan Gonzalez	5.00
6	Jeff Bagwell	5.00
7	Andruw Jones	4.00
8	Cal Ripken Jr.	20.00
9	Derek Jeter	15.00
10	Nomar Garciaparra	10.00
11	Darin Erstad	5.00
12	Greg Maddux	8.00
13	Alex Rodriguez	15.00
14	Mike Piazza	12.50
15	Vladimir Guerrero	6.00
16	Jose Cruz Jr.	3.00
17	Mark McGwire	20.00
18	Scott Rolen	3.00

1998 Metal Universe Diamond Heroes

Diamond Heroes displayed six players in a comic book setting. This insert was seeded one per 18 packs and contained a foil etched image of a Marvel comic in the background.

		MT
Complete Set (6):		10.00
Common Player:		.70
Inserted 1:18		
1	Ken Griffey Jr.	3.00
2	Frank Thomas	2.00
3	Andruw Jones	1.50
4	Alex Rodriguez	2.50
5	Jose Cruz Jr.	.75
6	Cal Ripken Jr.	3.00

1998 Metal Universe Platinum Portraits

This 12-card insert set featured color portraits of top players highlighted with a platinum-colored etched foil frame over it. Platinum Portraits are seeded one per 360 packs of Metal Universe.

		MT
Complete Set (12):		150.00
Common Player:		7.50
Inserted 1:360		
1	Ken Griffey Jr.	25.00
2	Frank Thomas	12.00
3	Chipper Jones	20.00
4	Jose Cruz Jr.	7.50
5	Andruw Jones	7.50
6	Cal Ripken Jr.	25.00
7	Derek Jeter	20.00
8	Darin Erstad	7.50
9	Greg Maddux	15.00
10	Alex Rodriguez	22.50
11	Mike Piazza	20.00
12	Vladimir Guerrero	10.00

1998 Metal Universe Titanium

This die-cut 15-card insert contained color photos printed on embossed, sculpted cards on etched foil. Titanium inserts were seeded one per 96 packs.

		MT
Complete Set (15):		60.00
Common Player:		3.00
Inserted 1:96		
1	Ken Griffey Jr.	8.00
2	Frank Thomas	4.50
3	Chipper Jones	6.50
4	Jose Cruz Jr.	3.00
5	Juan Gonzalez	3.00
6	Scott Rolen	3.00
7	Andruw Jones	3.00
8	Cal Ripken Jr.	8.00
9	Derek Jeter	6.50
10	Nomar Garciaparra	5.00
11	Darin Erstad	3.00
12	Greg Maddux	4.50
13	Alex Rodriguez	7.50
14	Mike Piazza	6.50
15	Vladimir Guerrero	3.00

1998 Metal Universe Universal Language

This 20-card insert features illustration and copy done in the player's native language. Cards were die-cut and inserted one per six packs.

		MT
Complete Set (20):		20.00
Common Player:		.50
Inserted 1:6		
1	Ken Griffey Jr.	2.50
2	Frank Thomas	1.50
3	Chipper Jones	2.00
4	Albert Belle	.75
5	Juan Gonzalez	1.25
6	Jeff Bagwell	1.25
7	Andruw Jones	1.00
8	Cal Ripken Jr.	2.50
9	Derek Jeter	2.00
10	Nomar Garciaparra	1.75
11	Darin Erstad	1.00
12	Greg Maddux	1.50
13	Alex Rodriguez	2.00
14	Mike Piazza	2.00
15	Vladimir Guerrero	1.00
16	Jose Cruz Jr.	.75
17	Hideo Nomo	1.00
18	Kenny Lofton	.50
19	Tony Gwynn	1.50
20	Scott Rolen	1.00

1999 Metal Universe

The 300-card base set offers 232 player cards and three subsets: Building Blocks, M.L.P.D. and Caught on the Fly. Base cards feature an action photo framed in an ethed-foil and metallic, embossed name plate. Packs consist of eight cards with a S.R.P. of $2.69. There are two parallels, Precious Metal Gems and Gem Masters. Metal Gems are numbered to 50 with gold-foil etching. Gem Masters are limited to only one set, with silver foil etching and serial numbered "one of one".

		MT
Complete Set (300):		40.00
Common Player:		.10
Pack (8):		2.00
Wax Box (24):		40.00
1	Mark McGwire	2.50
2	Jim Edmonds	.15
3	Travis Fryman	.10
4	Tom Gordon	.10
5	Jeff Bagwell	.75
6	Rico Brogna	.10
7	Tom Evans	.10
8	John Franco	.10
9	Juan Gonzalez	.75
10	Paul Molitor	.50
11	Roberto Alomar	.50
12	Mike Hampton	.10
13	Orel Hershiser	.10
14	Todd Stottlemyre	.10
15	Robin Ventura	.10
16	Todd Walker	.10
17	Bernie Williams	.30
18	Shawn Estes	.10
19	Richie Sexson	.10
20	Kevin Millwood	.10
21	David Ortiz	.10
22	Mariano Rivera	.25
23	Ivan Rodriguez	.60
24	Mike Sirotka	.10
25	David Justice	.30
26	Carl Pavano	.10
27	Albert Belle	.30
28	Will Clark	.30
29	Jose Cruz Jr.	.15
30	Trevor Hoffman	.10
31	Dean Palmer	.10
32	Edgar Renteria	.10
33	David Segui	.10
34	B.J. Surhoff	.10
35	Miguel Tejada	.25
36	Bob Wickman	.10
37	Charles Johnson	.10
38	Andruw Jones	.50
39	Mike Lieberthal	.10
40	Eli Marrero	.10
41	Neifi Perez	.10
42	Jim Thome	.10
43	Barry Bonds	1.00
44	Carlos Delgado	.50
45	Chuck Finley	.10
46	Brian Meadows	.10
47	Tony Gwynn	1.00
48	Jose Offerman	.10
49	Cal Ripken Jr.	2.50
50	Alex Rodriguez	2.00
51	Esteban Yan	.10
52	Matt Stairs	.10
53	Fernando Vina	.10
54	Rondell White	.10
55	Kerry Wood	.40
56	Dmitri Young	.10
57	Ken Caminiti	.10
58	Alex Gonzalez	.15
59	Matt Mantei	.10
60	Tino Martinez	.10
61	Hal Morris	.10
62	Rafael Palmeiro	.30
63	Troy Percival	.10
64	Bobby Smith	.10
65	Ed Sprague	.10
66	Brett Tomko	.10
67	Steve Trachsel	.10
68	Ugueth Urbina	.10
69	Jose Valentin	.10
70	Kevin Brown	.15
71	Shawn Green	.25
72	Dustin Hermanson	.10
73	Livan Hernandez	.10
74	Geoff Jenkins	.10
75	Jeff King	.10
76	Chuck Knoblauch	.10
77	Edgar Martinez	.10
78	Fred McGriff	.10
79	Mike Mussina	.50
80	Dave Nilsson	.10
81	Kenny Rogers	.10
82	Tim Salmon	.20
83	Reggie Sanders	.10
84	Wilson Alvarez	.10
85	Rod Beck	.10
86	Jose Guillen	.10
87	Bob Higginson	.10
88	Gregg Olson	.10
89	Jeff Shaw	.10
90	Masato Yoshii	.10
91	Todd Helton	.50
92	David Dellucci	.10
93	Johnny Damon	.15
94	Cliff Floyd	.10
95	Ken Griffey Jr.	2.50
96	Juan Guzman	.10
97	Derek Jeter	2.00
98	Barry Larkin	.20
99	Quinton McCracken	.10
100	Sammy Sosa	2.00
101	Kevin Young	.10
102	Jay Bell	.10
103	Jay Buhner	.10
104	Jeff Conine	.10
105	Ryan Jackson	.10
106	Sidney Ponson	.10
107	Jeromy Burnitz	.10
108	Roberto Hernandez	.10
109	A.J. Hinch	.10
110	Hideki Irabu	.10
111	Paul Konerko	.10
112	Henry Rodriguez	.10
113	Shannon Stewart	.10
114	Tony Womack	.10
115	Wilton Guerrero	.10
116	Andy Benes	.10
117	Jeff Cirillo	.10
118	Chili Davis	.10
119	Eric Davis	.10
120	Vladimir Guerrero	.50
121	Dennis Reyes	.10
122	Rickey Henderson	.45
123	Mickey Morandini	.10
124	Jason Schmidt	.10
125	J.T. Snow	.10
126	Justin Thompson	.10
127	Billy Wagner	.10
128	Armando Benitez	.10
129	Sean Casey	.15
130	Brad Fullmer	.10
131	Ben Grieve	.25
132	Robb Nen	.10
133	Shane Reynolds	.10
134	Todd Zeile	.10
135	Brady Anderson	.10

136 Aaron Boone .10
137 Orlando Cabrera .10
138 Jason Giambi .40
139 Randy Johnson .75
140 Jeff Kent .10
141 John Wetteland .10
142 Rolando Arrojo .10
143 Scott Brosius .10
144 Mark Grace .30
145 Jason Kendall .10
146 Travis Lee .10
147 Gary Sheffield .30
148 David Cone .10
149 Jose Hernandez .10
150 Todd Jones .10
151 Al Martin .10
152 Ismael Valdes .10
153 Wade Boggs .50
154 Garret Anderson .10
155 Bobby Bonilla .10
156 Darryl Kile .10
157 Ryan Klesko .10
158 Tim Wakefield .10
159 Kenny Lofton .10
160 Jose Canseco .40
161 Doug Glanville .10
162 Todd Hundley .10
163 Brian Jordan .10
164 Steve Finley .10
165 Tom Glavine .25
166 Al Leiter .10
167 Raul Mondesi .20
168 Desi Relaford .10
169 Bret Saberhagen .10
170 Omar Vizquel .10
171 Larry Walker .30
172 Bobby Abreu .20
173 Moises Alou .15
174 Mike Caruso .10
175 Royce Clayton .10
176 Bartolo Colon .15
177 Marty Cordova .10
178 Darin Erstad .50
179 Nomar Garciaparra 1.50
180 Andy Ashby .10
181 Dan Wilson .10
182 Larry Sutton .10
183 Tony Clark .10
184 Andres Galarraga .10
185 Ray Durham .10
186 Hideo Nomo .50
187 Steve Woodard .10
188 Scott Rolen .50
189 Mike Stanley .10
190 Jaret Wright .10
191 Vinny Castilla .10
192 Jason Christiansen .10
193 Paul Bako .10
194 Carlos Perez .10
195 Mike Piazza 2.00
196 Fernando Tatis .10
197 Mo Vaughn .40
198 Devon White .10
199 Ricky Gutierrez .10
200 Charlie Hayes .10
201 Brad Radke .10
202 Rick Helling .10
203 John Smoltz .20
204 Frank Thomas 1.00
205 David Wells .10
206 Roger Clemens 1.00
207 Mark Grudzielanek .10
208 Chipper Jones 2.00
209 Ray Lankford .10
210 Pedro Martinez .75
211 Manny Ramirez .75
212 Greg Vaughn .10
213 Craig Biggio .15
214 Rusty Greer .10
215 Greg Maddux 1.50
216 Rick Aguilera .10
217 Andy Pettitte .20
218 Dante Bichette .10
219 Damion Easley .10
220 Matt Morris .10
221 John Olerud .10
222 Chan Ho Park .25
223 Curt Schilling .25
224 John Valentin .10
225 Matt Williams .30
226 Ellis Burks .10
227 Tom Goodwin .10
228 Javy Lopez .10
229 Eric Milton .10
230 Paul O'Neill .10
231 Magglio Ordonez .15
232 Derrek Lee .10
233 Ken Griffey Jr. (Caught on the Fly) 1.00
234 Randy Johnson (Caught on the Fly) .30
235 Alex Rodriguez (Caught on the Fly) 1.00
236 Darin Erstad (Caught on the Fly) .40
237 Juan Gonzalez (Caught on the Fly) .40
238 Derek Jeter (Caught on the Fly) 1.00
239 Tony Gwynn (Caught on the Fly) .50
240 Kerry Wood (Caught on the Fly) .25
241 Cal Ripken Jr. (Caught on the Fly) 1.00
242 Sammy Sosa (Caught on the Fly) 1.00
243 Greg Maddux (Caught on the Fly) .50
244 Mark McGwire (Caught on the Fly) 1.00
245 Chipper Jones (Caught on the Fly) .75
246 Barry Bonds (Caught on the Fly) .75
247 Ben Grieve (Caught on the Fly) .25
248 Ben Davis (Building Blocks) .10
249 Robert Fick (Building Blocks) .10
250 Carlos Guillen (Building Blocks) .10
251 Mike Frank (Building Blocks) .10
252 Ryan Minor (Building Blocks) .10
253 Troy Glaus (Building Blocks) 1.00
254 Matt Anderson (Building Blocks) .10
255 Josh Booty (Building Blocks) .10
256 Gabe Alvarez (Building Blocks) .10
257 Gabe Kapler (Building Blocks) .25
258 Enrique Wilson (Building Blocks) .10
259 Alex Gonzalez (Building Blocks) .10
260 Preston Wilson (Building Blocks) .15
261 Eric Chavez (Building Blocks) .25
262 Adrian Beltre (Building Blocks) .30
263 Corey Koskie (Building Blocks) .10
264 *Robert Machado* (Building Blocks) .10
265 Orlando Hernandez (Building Blocks) .40
266 Matt Clement (Building Blocks) .10
267 Luis Ordaz (Building Blocks) .10
268 Jeremy Giambi (Building Blocks) .20
269 J.D. Drew (Building Blocks) .35
269a J.D. Drew (Building Blocks "Sample" autographed edition of 35) 40.00
270 Cliff Politte (Building Blocks) .10
271 Carlton Loewer (Building Blocks) .10
272 Aramis Ramirez (Building Blocks) .10
273 Ken Griffey Jr. (M.L.P.D.) 1.00
274 Randy Johnson (M.L.P.D.) .40
275 Alex Rodriguez (M.L.P.D.) 1.00
276 Darin Erstad (M.L.P.D.) .40
277 Scott Rolen (M.L.P.D.) .40
278 Juan Gonzalez (M.L.P.D.) .40
279 Jeff Bagwell (M.L.P.D.) .40
280 Mike Piazza (M.L.P.D.) 1.00
281 Derek Jeter (M.L.P.D.) 1.00
282 Travis Lee (M.L.P.D.) .15
283 Tony Gwynn (M.L.P.D.) .50
284 Kerry Wood (M.L.P.D.) .25
285 Albert Belle (M.L.P.D.) .20
286 Sammy Sosa (M.L.P.D.) 1.00
287 Mo Vaughn (M.L.P.D.) .20
288 Nomar Garciaparra (M.L.P.D.) .75
289 Frank Thomas (M.L.P.D.) .50
290 Cal Ripken Jr. (M.L.P.D.) 1.00
291 Greg Maddux (M.L.P.D.) .75
292 Chipper Jones (M.L.P.D.) .75
293 Ben Grieve (M.L.P.D.) .20
294 Andruw Jones (M.L.P.D.) .40
295 Mark McGwire (M.L.P.D.) 1.00
296 Roger Clemens (M.L.P.D.) .50
297 Barry Bonds (M.L.P.D.) .75
298 Ken Griffey Jr.-Checklist (M.L.P.D.) 1.00
299 Kerry Wood-Checklist (M.L.P.D.) .25
300 Alex Rodriguez-Checklist (M.L.P.D.) 1.00

1999 Metal Universe Precious Metal Gems

A 300-card parallel of the base set, these cards feature gold-foil etching and are inserted exclusively in hobby packs. Each card is serially numbered to 50. A Gem Master 1 of 1 parallel was also issued, but is too rare to value.

	MT
Common Player:	5.00
Stars:	20X
Gem Master 1 of 1: (Value undetermined)	

(See 1999 Metal Universe for checklist and base card values.)

1999 Metal Universe Boyz With The Wood

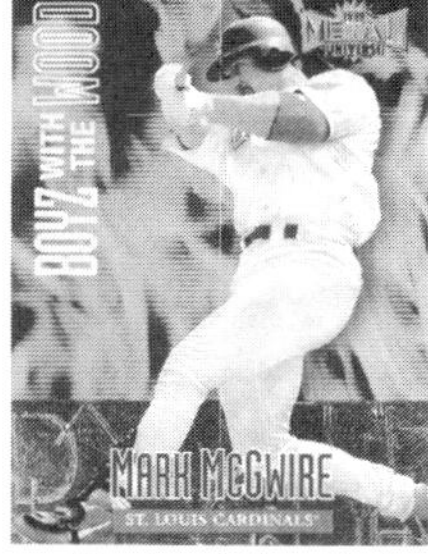

The top hitters in the game are featured on these folded cards with four sides. These are inserted 1:18.

		MT
Complete Set (15):		40.00
Common Player:		1.00
Inserted 1:18		
1	Ken Griffey Jr.	6.00
2	Frank Thomas	3.00
3	Jeff Bagwell	2.00
4	Juan Gonzalez	2.00
5	Mark McGwire	6.00
6	Scott Rolen	1.50
7	Travis Lee	1.00
8	Tony Gwynn	3.00
9	Mike Piazza	4.00
10	Chipper Jones	4.00
11	Nomar Garciaparra	3.50
12	Derek Jeter	4.00
13	Cal Ripken Jr.	6.00
14	Andruw Jones	1.50
15	Alex Rodriguez	5.00

1999 Metal Universe Diamond Soul

Utilizing lenticular technology these inserts showcase a soulful "galactic" design. The set consists of 15 cards which are seeded at 1:72 packs.

		MT
Complete Set (15):		50.00
Common Player:		1.00
Inserted 1:72		
1	Cal Ripken Jr.	6.50
2	Alex Rodriguez	5.00
3	Chipper Jones	5.00
4	Derek Jeter	6.50
5	Frank Thomas	3.00
6	Greg Maddux	4.00
7	Juan Gonzalez	2.00
8	Ken Griffey Jr.	6.50

9 Kerry Wood 1.50
10 Mark McGwire 6.50
11 Mike Piazza 5.00
12 Nomar Garciaparra 4.00
13 Scott Rolen 1.50
14 Tony Gwynn 2.50
15 Travis Lee 1.00

1999 Metal Universe Linchpins

This 10-card set features a laser die-cut background and highlights key players who hold their teams together on the field and in the clubhouse. These are seeded 1:360 packs.

		MT
Complete Set (10):		110.00
Common Player:		6.00
Inserted 1:360		
1	Mike Piazza	15.00
2	Mark McGwire	20.00
3	Kerry Wood	6.00
4	Ken Griffey Jr.	17.50
5	Greg Maddux	12.00
6	Frank Thomas	12.00
7	Derek Jeter	15.00
8	Chipper Jones	15.00
9	Cal Ripken Jr.	20.00
10	Alex Rodriguez	17.50

1999 Metal Universe Neophytes

This 15-card insert set showcases young stars like J.D. Drew and Troy Glaus. The cards feature silver foil stamping on a horizontal format, found on an average of 1:6 packs.

		MT
Complete Set (15):		11.00
Common Player:		.35
Inserted 1:6		
1	Troy Glaus	3.00
2	Travis Lee	1.00
3	Scott Elarton	.35
4	Ricky Ledee	.35
5	Richard Hidalgo	.50
6	J.D. Drew	1.00
7	Paul Konerko	.50
8	Orlando Hernandez	3.00
9	Mike Caruso	.35
10	Mike Frank	.35
11	Miguel Tejada	.75
12	Matt Anderson	.35
13	Kerry Wood	1.00
14	Gabe Alvarez	.35
15	Adrian Beltre	1.00

1999 Metal Universe Planet Metal

These die-cut cards feature a metallic view of the planet behind pop-out action photography. The 15-card set features the top players in the game and are seeded 1:36 packs.

		MT
Complete Set (15):		40.00
Common Player:		.75
Inserted 1:36		
1	Alex Rodriguez	6.00
2	Andruw Jones	1.25
3	Cal Ripken Jr.	6.50
4	Chipper Jones	4.50
5	Darin Erstad	1.00
6	Derek Jeter	5.00
7	Frank Thomas	3.00
8	Travis Lee	.75
9	Scott Rolen	1.00
10	Nomar Garciaparra	3.50
11	Mike Piazza	5.00
12	Mark McGwire	6.50
13	Ken Griffey Jr.	5.50
14	Juan Gonzalez	1.75
15	Jeff Bagwell	1.75

2000 Metal

		MT
Complete Set (250):		40.00
Common Player:		.10
Common Prospect (201-250):		.75
Inserted 1:2		
Pack (10):		2.00
Wax Box (28):		30.00
1	Tony Gwynn	1.00
2	Derek Jeter	2.00
3	Johnny Damon	.15
4	Javy Lopez	.10
5	Preston Wilson	.15
6	Derek Bell	.10
7	Richie Sexson	.10
8	Vinny Castilla	.10
9	Billy Wagner	.10
10	Carlos Beltran	.10
11	Chris Singleton	.10
12	Nomar Garciaparra	1.50
13	Carlos Febles	.10
14	Jason Varitek	.10
15	Luis Gonzalez	.25
16	Jon Lieber	.10
17	Mo Vaughn	.40
18	Dave Burba	.10
19	Brady Anderson	.10
20	Carlos Lee	.10
21	Chuck Finley	.10
22	Alex Gonzalez	.15
23	Matt Williams	.20
24	Chipper Jones	2.00
25	Pokey Reese	.10
26	Todd Helton	.50
27	Mike Mussina	.50
28	Butch Huskey	.10
29	Jeff Bagwell	.75
30	Juan Encarnacion	.10
31	A.J. Burnett	.10
32	Micah Bowie	.10
33	Brian Jordan	.10
34	Scott Erickson	.10
35	Sean Casey	.15
36	John Smoltz	.15
37	Edgard Clemente	.10
38	Mike Hampton	.10
39	Tom Glavine	.15
40	Albert Belle	.30
41	Jim Thome	.10
42	Jermaine Dye	.10
43	Sammy Sosa	2.00
44	Pedro Martinez	.65
45	Paul Konerko	.10
46	Damion Easley	.10
47	Cal Ripken Jr.	2.50
48	Jose Lima	.10
49	Mike Lowell	.10
50	Randy Johnson	.75
51	Dean Palmer	.10
52	Tim Salmon	.25
53	Kevin Millwood	.15
54	Mark Grace	.25
55	Aaron Boone	.10
56	Omar Vizquel	.10
57	Moises Alou	.15
58	Travis Fryman	.10
59	Erubiel Durazo	.10
60	Carl Everett	.15
61	Charles Johnson	.10
62	Trot Nixon	.10
63	Andres Galarraga	.10
64	Magglio Ordonez	.15
65	Pedro Astacio	.10
66	Roberto Alomar	.40
67	Pete Harnisch	.10
68	Scott Williamson	.10
69	Alex Fernandez	.10
70	Robin Ventura	.10
71	Chad Allen	.10
72	Darin Erstad	.30
73	Ron Coomer	.10
74	Ellis Burks	.10
75	Kent Bottenfield	.10
76	Ken Griffey Jr.	2.50
77	Mike Piazza	2.00
78	Jorge Posada	.10
79	Dante Bichette	.10
80	Adrian Beltre	.15
81	Andruw Jones	.50
82	Wilson Alvarez	.10
83	Edgardo Alfonzo	.15
84	Brian Giles	.10
85	Gary Sheffield	.25
86	Matt Stairs	.10
87	Bret Boone	.10
88	Kenny Rogers	.10
89	Barry Bonds	1.00
90	Scott Rolen	.50
91	Edgar Renteria	.10
92	Larry Walker	.25
93	Roger Cedeno	.10
94	Kevin Brown	.15
95	Lee Stevens	.10
96	Brad Radke	.15
97	Andy Pettitte	.25
98	Bobby Higginson	.10
99	Eric Chavez	.25
100	Alex Rodriguez	2.25
100s	Alex Rodriguez (overprinted "PROMOTIONAL SAMPLE")	3.00
101	Shannon Stewart	.10
102	Ryan Rupe	.10
103	Freddy Garcia	.15
104	John Jaha	.10
105	Greg Maddux	1.50
106	Hideki Irabu	.10
107	Rey Ordonez	.10
108	Troy O'Leary	.10
109	Frank Thomas	1.00
110	Corey Koskie	.10
111	Bernie Williams	.30
112	Barry Larkin	.15
113	Kevin Appier	.10
114	Curt Schilling	.25
115	Bartolo Colon	.10
116	Edgar Martinez	.10
117	Ray Lankford	.10
118	Todd Walker	.10
119	John Wetteland	.10
120	David Nilsson	.10
121	Tino Martinez	.10
122	Phil Nevin	.10
123	Ben Grieve	.15
124	Ron Gant	.10
125	Jeff Kent	.10
126	Rick Helling	.10
127	Russ Ortiz	.10
128	Troy Glaus	.60
129	Chan Ho Park	.25
130	Jeromy Burnitz	.10
131	Aaron Sele	.10
132	Mike Sirotka	.10
133	Brad Ausmus	.10
134	Jose Rosado	.10
135	Mariano Rivera	.25
136	Jason Giambi	.40
137	Mike Lieberthal	.10
138	Chris Carpenter	.10
139	Henry Rodriguez	.10
140	Mike Sweeney	.10
141	Vladimir Guerrero	.50
142	Charles Nagy	.10
143	Jason Kendall	.10
144	Matt Lawton	.10
145	Michael Barrett	.10
146	David Cone	.10
147	Bobby Abreu	.10
148	Fernando Tatis	.10
149	Jose Canseco	.40
150	Craig Biggio	.15
151	Matt Mantei	.10
152	Jacque Jones	.10
153	John Halama	.10
154	Trevor Hoffman	.10
155	Rondell White	.10
156	Reggie Sanders	.10
157	Steve Finley	.10
158	Roberto Hernandez	.10
159	Geoff Jenkins	.10
160	Chris Widger	.10
161	Orel Hershiser	.10
162	Tim Hudson	.10
163	Kris Benson	.10
164	Kevin Young	.10
165	Rafael Palmeiro	.30
166	David Wells	.10
167	Ben Davis	.10
168	Jamie Moyer	.10
169	Randy Wolf	.10
170	Jeff Cirillo	.10
171	Warren Morris	.10
172	Billy Koch	.10
173	Marquis Grissom	.10
174	Geoff Blum	.10
175	Octavio Dotel	.10
176	Orlando Hernandez	.30
177	J.D. Drew	.25
178	Carlos Delgado	.50
179	Sterling Hitchcock	.10
180	Shawn Green	.30
181	Tony Clark	1.00
182	Joe McEwing	.10
183	Fred McGriff	.10
184	Tony Batista	1.00
185	Al Leiter	.10
186	Roger Clemens	1.00
187	Al Martin	.10

#	Player	MT
188	Eric Milton	.10
189	Bobby Smith	.10
190	Rusty Greer	.10
191	Shawn Estes	.10
192	Ken Caminiti	1.00
193	Eric Karros	.10
194	Manny Ramirez	.75
195	Jim Edmonds	.15
196	Paul O'Neill	.10
197	Rico Brogna	.10
198	Ivan Rodriguez	.60
199	Doug Glanville	.10
200	Mark McGwire	2.50
201	Mark Quinn (Prospect)	.75
202	Norm Hutchins (Prospect)	.75
203	Ramon Ortiz (Prospect)	.75
204	Brett Laxton (Prospect)	.75
205	Jimmy Anderson (Prospect)	.75
206	Calvin Murray (Prospect)	.75
207	Wilton Veras (Prospect)	.75
208	Chad Hermansen (Prospect)	.75
209	Nick Johnson (Prospect)	.75
210	Kevin Barker (Prospect)	.75
211	Casey Blake (Prospect)	.75
212	Chad Meyers (Prospect)	.75
213	Kip Wells (Prospect)	.75
214	Eric Munson (Prospect)	1.00
215	Lance Berkman (Prospect)	1.00
216	Wily Pena (Prospect)	1.00
217	Gary Matthews Jr. (Prospect)	.75
218	Travis Dawkins (Prospect)	1.00
219	Josh Beckett (Prospect)	1.00
220	Tony Armas Jr. (Prospect)	1.00
221	Alfonso Soriano (Prospect)	1.00
222	Pat Burrell (Prospect)	2.50
223	*Danys Baez* (Prospect)	1.00
224	Adam Kennedy (Prospect)	1.00
225	Ruben Mateo (Prospect)	.75
226	Vernon Wells (Prospect)	.75
227	Brian Cooper (Prospect)	.75
228	*Jeff DaVanon* (Prospect)	.75
229	Glen Barker (Prospect)	.75
230	Robinson Cancel (Prospect)	.75
231	D'Angelo Jimenez (Prospect)	.75
232	Adam Piatt (Prospect)	1.00
233	Buddy Carlyle (Prospect)	.75
234	Chad Hutchinson (Prospect)	.75
235	Matt Riley (Prospect)	.75
236	Cole Liniak (Prospect)	.75
237	Ben Petrick (Prospect)	.75
238	Peter Bergeron (Prospect)	.75
239	Cesar King (Prospect)	.75
240	Aaron Myette (Prospect)	.75
241	Eric Gagne (Prospect)	.75
242	Joe Nathan (Prospect)	.75
243	Bruce Chen (Prospect)	.75
244	Rob Bell (Prospect)	.75
245	*Juan Sosa* (Prospect)	.75
246	Julio Ramirez (Prospect)	.75
247	Wade Miller (Prospect)	.75
248	*Trace Coquillette* (Prospect)	.75
249	Robert Ramsay (Prospect)	.75
250	Rick Ankiel (Prospect)	1.00

2000 Metal Emerald

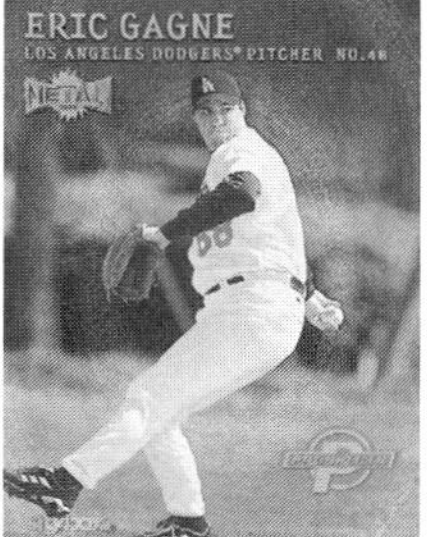

A green tone at the top 1/4 or so of the card fronts, and a small circled "E" at top-right on back differentiates these parallels from the regular-issue cards. The first 200 cards in the set are found in this version about one every four packs. The odds double for the Prospects cards (#201-250) which are short-printed in the regular version, as well.

	MT
Common Player:	.25
Stars:	2X
Inserted 1:4	
Prospects (201-250):	2X
Inserted 1:8	

2000 Metal Autographics

	MT
Common Player:	5.00
Bobby Abreu	10.00
Chad Allen	5.00
Marlon Anderson	7.50
Rick Ankiel	12.50
Glen Barker	5.00
Rob Bell	5.00
Mark Bellhorn	5.00
Peter Bergeron	10.00
Lance Berkman	10.00
Wade Boggs	30.00
Barry Bonds	60.00
Kent Bottenfield	5.00
Pat Burrell	25.00
Miguel Cairo	5.00
Mike Cameron	7.50
Chris Carpenter	5.00
Roger Cedeno	7.50
Mike Darr	5.00
Einar Diaz	5.00
J.D. Drew	20.00
Erubiel Durazo	10.00
Ray Durham	5.00
Damion Easley	5.00
Scott Elarton	5.00
Jeremy Giambi	7.50
Doug Glanville	5.00
Shawn Green	25.00
Jerry Hairston Jr.	5.00
Bob Howry	5.00
Norm Hutchins	5.00
Randy Johnson	30.00
Jacque Jones	7.50
Gabe Kapler	10.00
Cesar King	5.00
Mark Kotsay	7.50
Cole Liniak	5.00
Greg Maddux	60.00
Pedro Martinez	50.00
Ruben Mateo	7.50
Warren Morris	7.50
Heath Murray	5.00
Joe Nathan	5.00
Jim Parque	5.00
Angel Pena	5.00
Cal Ripken Jr.	100.00
Alex Rodriguez	75.00
Ryan Rupe	5.00
Randall Simon	5.00
Chris Singleton	7.50
Mike Sweeney	10.00
Wilton Veras	5.00
Scott Williamson	7.50
Randy Wolf	7.50
Tony Womack	7.50

2000 Metal Base Shredders

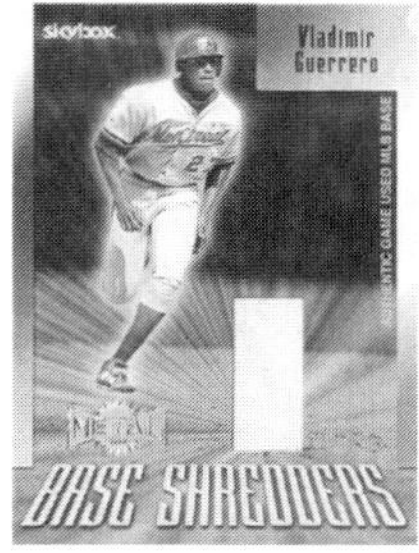

	MT
Complete Set (18):	165.00
Common Player:	6.00
Inserted 1:288	
Roberto Alomar	12.00
Michael Barrett	6.00
Tony Clark	6.00
Ben Davis	6.00
Erubiel Durazo	6.00
Troy Glaus	12.00
Ben Grieve	10.00
Vladimir Guerrero	20.00
Tony Gwynn	25.00
Todd Helton	20.00
Eric Munson	8.00
Rafael Palmeiro	10.00
Manny Ramirez	20.00
Ivan Rodriguez	15.00
Miguel Tejada	8.00
Mo Vaughn	8.00
Larry Walker	8.00
Matt Williams	8.00

2000 Metal Fusion

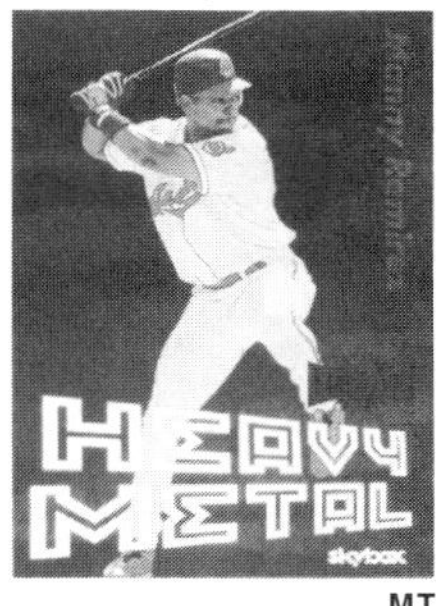

#	Players	MT
	Complete Set (15):	17.50
	Common Player:	.50
	Inserted 1:4	
1	Ken Griffey Jr., Alex Rodriguez	2.50
2	Mark McGwire, Rick Ankiel	2.50
3	Scott Rolen, Curt Schilling	.75
4	Pedro Martinez, Nomar Garciaparra	2.00
5	Carlos Beltran, Carlos Febles	.50
6	Sammy Sosa, Mark Grace	2.00
7	Vladimir Guerrero, Ugueth Urbina	1.00
8	Roger Clemens, Derek Jeter	2.00
9	Jeff Bagwell, Craig Biggio	.75
10	Chipper Jones, Andruw Jones	1.50
11	Cal Ripken Jr., Mike Mussina	2.50
12	Manny Ramirez, Roberto Alomar	.75
13	Sean Casey, Barry Larkin	.50
14	Ivan Rodriguez, Rafael Palmeiro	.75
15	Mike Piazza, Robin Ventura	1.50

2000 Metal Heavy Metal

#	Player	MT
	Complete Set (10):	11.00
	Common Player:	.75
	Inserted 1:20	
1	Sammy Sosa	1.50
2	Mark McGwire	2.00
3	Ken Griffey Jr.	2.00
4	Mike Piazza	1.50
5	Nomar Garciaparra	1.25
6	Alex Rodriguez	2.00
7	Manny Ramirez	.75
8	Jeff Bagwell	.75
9	Chipper Jones	1.50
10	Vladimir Guerrero	.75

2000 Metal Hit Machines

#	Player	MT
	Complete Set (10):	16.00
	Common Player:	.75
	Inserted 1:20	
1	Ken Griffey Jr.	3.50
2	Mark McGwire	4.00

3 Frank Thomas 1.50
4 Tony Gwynn 1.50
5 Rafael Palmeiro .75
6 Bernie Williams .75
7 Derek Jeter 2.50
8 Sammy Sosa 2.00
9 Mike Piazza 2.50
10 Chipper Jones 2.50

2000 Metal Platinum Portraits

MT
Complete Set (10): 7.50
Common Player: .25
Inserted 1:8
1 Carlos Beltran .25
2 Vladimir Guerrero 1.25
3 Manny Ramirez .75
4 Ivan Rodriguez .60
5 Sean Casey .40
6 Alex Rodriguez 2.50
7 Derek Jeter 2.00
8 Nomar Garciaparra 1.50
9 Vernon Wells .25
10 Shawn Green .50

2000 Metal Talent Show

MT
Complete Set (15): 3.50
Common Player: .15
Inserted 1:4
1 Rick Ankiel .50
2 Matt Riley .15
3 Chad Hermansen .15
4 Ruben Mateo .25
5 Eric Munson .40
6 Alfonso Soriano .40
7 Wilton Veras .15
8 Vernon Wells .25
9 Erubiel Durazo .15
10 Pat Burrell .75
11 Ben Davis .15
12 A.J. Burnett .25
13 Peter Bergeron .25
14 Mark Quinn .25
15 Ben Petrick .150

P

1993 Pacific

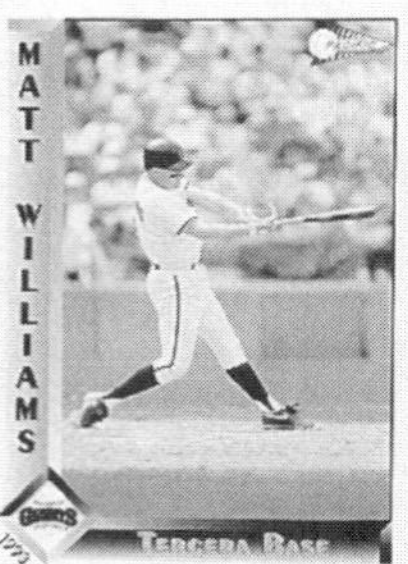

This set marks the first time a major league set was designed entirely for the Spanish-speaking market. Distribution areas included retail markets in the United States, Mexico, South America and the Caribbean. The cards are glossy and feature Spanish text on both sides. Cards are numbered in alphabetical order by team, beginning with Atlanta. Insert sets are: Prism (20 cards featuring Spanish players and their accomplishments), Beisbol De Estralla (Stars of Baseball), Hot Players and Amigos (a 30-card set which features two or more players per card).

MT
Complete Set (660): 20.00
Common Player: .05
1 Rafael Belliard .05
2 Sid Bream .05
3 Francisco Cabrera .05
4 Marvin Freeman .05
5 Ron Gant .05
6 Tom Glavine .15
7 Brian Hunter .05
8 Dave Justice .25
9 Ryan Klesko .05
10 Melvin Nieves .05
11 Deion Sanders .15
12 John Smoltz .15
13 Mark Wohlers .05
14 Brady Anderson .05
15 Glenn Davis .05
16 Mike Devereaux .05
17 Leo Gomez .05
18 Chris Hoiles .05
19 Chito Martinez .05
20 Ben McDonald .05
21 Mike Mussina .35
22 Gregg Olson .05
23 Joe Orsulak .05
24 Cal Ripken, Jr. 1.50
25 David Segui .05
26 Rick Sutcliffe .05
27 Wade Boggs .40
28 Tom Brunansky .05
29 Ellis Burks .05
30 Roger Clemens .50
31 John Dopson .05
32 John Flaherty .05
33 Mike Greenwell .05
34 Tony Pena .05
35 Carlos Quintana .05
36 Luis Rivera .05
37 Mo Vaughn .25
38 Frank Viola .05
39 Matt Young .05
40 Scott Bailes .05
41 Bert Blyleven .05
42 Chad Curtis .05
43 Gary DiSarcina .05
44 Chuck Finley .05
45 Mike Fitzgerald .05
46 Gary Gaetti .05
47 Rene Gonzales .05
48 Mark Langston .05
49 Scott Lewis .05
50 Luis Polonia .05
51 Tim Salmon .25
52 Lee Stevens .05
53 Steve Buechele .05
54 Frank Castillo .05
55 Doug Dascenzo .05
56 Andre Dawson .15
57 Shawon Dunston .05
58 Mark Grace .20
59 Mike Morgan .05
60 Luis Salazar .05
61 Rey Sanchez .05
62 Ryne Sandberg .50
63 Dwight Smith .05
64 Jerome Walton .05
65 Rick Wilkins .05
66 Wilson Alvarez .05
67 George Bell .05
68 Joey Cora .05
69 Alex Fernandez .05
70 Carlton Fisk .25
71 Craig Grebeck .05
72 Ozzie Guillen .05
73 Jack McDowell .05
74 Scott Radinsky .05
75 Tim Raines .05
76 Bobby Thigpen .05
77 Frank Thomas .75
78 Robin Ventura .05
79 Tom Browning .05
80 Jacob Brumfield .05
81 Rob Dibble .05
82 Bill Doran .05
83 Billy Hatcher .05
84 Barry Larkin .10
85 Hal Morris .05
86 Joe Oliver .05
87 Jeff Reed .05
88 Jose Rijo .05
89 Bip Roberts .05
90 Chris Sabo .05
91 Sandy Alomar, Jr. .05
92 Brad Arnsberg .05
93 Carlos Baerga .05
94 Albert Belle .15
95 Felix Fermin .05
96 Mark Lewis .05
97 Kenny Lofton .05
98 Carlos Martinez .05
99 Rod Nicholos .05
100 Dave Rohde .05
101 Scott Scudder .05
102 Paul Sorrento .05
103 Mark Whiten .05
104 Mark Carreon .05
105 Milt Cuyler .05
106 Rob Deer .05
107 Cecil Fielder .05
108 Travis Fryman .05
109 Dan Gladden .05
110 Bill Gullickson .05
111 Les Lancaster .05
112 Mark Leiter .05
113 Tony Phillips .05
114 Mickey Tettleton .05
115 Alan Trammell .05
116 Lou Whitaker .05
117 Jeff Bagwell .50
118 Craig Biggio .10
119 Joe Boever .05
120 Casey Candaele .05
121 Andujar Cedeno .05
122 Steve Finley .05
123 Luis Gonzalez .20
124 Pete Harnisch .05
125 Jimmy Jones .05
126 Mark Portugal .05
127 Rafael Ramirez .05
128 Mike Simms .05
129 Eric Yelding .05
130 Luis Aquino .05
131 Kevin Appier .05
132 Mike Boddicker .05
133 George Brett .60
134 Tom Gordon .05
135 Mark Gubicza .05
136 David Howard .05
137 Gregg Jefferies .05
138 Wally Joyner .05
139 Brian McRae .05
140 Jeff Montgomery .05
141 Terry Shumpert .05
142 Curtis Wilkerson .05
143 Brett Butler .05
144 Eric Davis .05
145 Kevin Gross .05
146 Dave Hansen .05
147 Lenny Harris .05
148 Carlos Hernandez .05
149 Orel Hershiser .05
150 Jay Howell .05
151 Eric Karros .05
152 Ramon Martinez .05
153 Jose Offerman .05
154 Mike Sharperson .05
155 Darryl Strawberry .05
156 Jim Gantner .05
157 Darryl Hamilton .05
158 Doug Henry .05
159 John Jaha .05
160 Pat Listach .05
161 Jaime Navarro .05
162 Dave Nilsson .05
163 Jesse Orosco .05
164 Kevin Seitzer .05
165 B.J. Surhoff .05
166 Greg Vaughn .05
167 Robin Yount .35
168 Rick Aguilera .05
169 Scott Erickson .05
170 Mark Guthrie .05
171 Kent Hrbek .05
172 Chuck Knoblauch .05
173 Gene Larkin .05
174 Shane Mack .05
175 Pedro Munoz .05
176 Mike Pagliarulo .05
177 Kirby Puckett .60
178 Kevin Tapani .05
179 Gary Wayne .05
180 Moises Alou .10
181 Brian Barnes .05
182 Archie Cianfrocco .05
183 Delino DeShields .05
184 Darrin Fletcher .05
185 Marquis Grissom .05
186 Ken Hill .05
187 Dennis Martinez .05
188 Bill Sampen .05
189 John VanderWal .05
190 Larry Walker .15
191 Tim Wallach .05
192 Bobby Bonilla .05
193 Daryl Boston .05
194 Vince Coleman .05
195 Kevin Elster .05
196 Sid Fernandez .05
197 John Franco .05
198 Dwight Gooden .05
199 Howard Johnson .05
200 Willie Randolph .05
201 Bret Saberhagen .05
202 Dick Schofield .05
203 Pete Schourek .05
204 Greg Cadaret .05
205 John Habyan .05
206 Pat Kelly .05
207 Kevin Maas .05
208 Don Mattingly .75
209 Matt Nokes .05
210 Melido Perez .05
211 Scott Sanderson .05
212 Andy Stankiewicz .05
213 Danny Tartabull .05
214 Randy Velarde .05
215 Bernie Williams .20
216 Harold Baines .05
217 Mike Bordick .05
218 Scott Brosius .05
219 Jerry Browne .05
220 Ron Darling .05
221 Dennis Eckersley .10
222 Rickey Henderson .35
223 Rick Honeycutt .05
224 Mark McGwire 1.50
225 Ruben Sierra .05
226 Terry Steinbach .05
227 Bob Welch .05

228 Willie Wilson .05
229 Ruben Amaro .05
230 Kim Batiste .05
231 Juan Bell .05
232 Wes Chamberlain .05
233 Darren Daulton .05
234 Mariano Duncan .05
235 Len Dykstra .05
236 Dave Hollins .05
237 Stan Javier .05
238 John Kruk .05
239 Mickey Morandini .05
240 Terry Mulholland .05
241 Mitch Williams .05
242 Stan Belinda .05
243 Jay Bell .05
244 Carlos Garcia .05
245 Jeff King .05
246 Mike LaValliere .05
247 Lloyd McClendon .05
248 Orlando Merced .05
249 Paul Miller .05
250 Gary Redus .05
251 Don Slaught .05
252 Zane Smith .05
253 Andy Van Slyke .05
254 Tim Wakefield .05
255 Andy Benes .05
256 Dann Bilardello .05
257 Tony Gwynn .50
258 Greg Harris .05
259 Darrin Jackson .05
260 Mike Maddux .05
261 Fred McGriff .05
262 Rich Rodriguez .05
263 Benito Santiago .05
264 Gary Sheffield .20
265 Kurt Stillwell .05
266 Tim Teufel .05
267 Bud Black .05
268 John Burkett .05
269 Will Clark .15
270 Royce Calyton .05
271 Bryan Hickerson .05
272 Chris James .05
273 Darren Lewis .05
274 Willie McGee .05
275 Jim McNamara .05
276 Francisco Oliveras .05
277 Robby Thompson .05
278 Matt Williams .15
279 Trevor Wilson .05
280 Bret Boone .10
281 Greg Briley .05
282 Jay Buhner .05
283 Henry Cotto .05
284 Rich DeLucia .05
285 Dave Fleming .05
286 Ken Griffey, Jr. 1.50
287 Erik Hanson .05
288 Randy Johnson .50
289 Tino Martinez .05
290 Edgar Martinez .05
291 Dave Valle .05
292 Omar Vizquel .05
293 Luis Alicea .05
294 Bernard Gilkey .05
295 Felix Jose .05
296 Ray Lankford .05
297 Omar Olivares .05
298 Jose Oquendo .05
299 Tom Pagnozzi .05
300 Geronimo Pena .05
301 Gerald Perry .05
302 Ozzie Smith .50
303 Lee Smith .05
304 Bob Tewksbury .05
305 Todd Zeile .05
306 Kevin Brown .10
307 Todd Burns .05
308 Jose Canseco .35
309 Hector Fajardo .05
310 Julio Franco .05
311 Juan Gonzalez .50
312 Jeff Huson .05
313 Rob Maurer .05
314 Rafael Palmeiro .25
315 Dean Palmer .05
316 Ivan Rodriguez .40
317 Nolan Ryan 1.50
318 Dickie Thon .05
319 Roberto Alomar .40
320 Derek Bell .05
321 Pat Borders .05
322 Joe Carter .05
323 Kelly Gruber .05
324 Juan Guzman .05
325 Manny Lee .05
326 Jack Morris .05
327 John Olerud .05
328 Ed Sprague .05
329 Todd Stottlemyre .05
330 Duane Ward .05
331 Steve Avery .05
332 Damon Berryhill .05
333 Jeff Blauser .05
334 Mark Lemke .05
335 Greg Maddux .75
336 Kent Mercker .05
337 Otis Nixon .05
338 Greg Olson .05
339 Bill Pecota .05
340 Terry Pendleton .05
341 Mike Stanton .05
342 Todd Frohwirth .05
343 Tim Hulett .05
344 Mark McLemore .05
345 Luis Mercedes .05
346 Alan Mills .05
347 Sherman Obando .05
348 Jim Poole .05
349 Harold Reynolds .05
350 Arthur Rhodes .05
351 Jeff Tackett .05
352 Fernando Valenzuela .05
353 Scott Bankhead .05
354 Ivan Calderon .05
355 Scott Cooper .05
356 Danny Darwin .05
357 Scott Fletcher .05
358 Tony Fossas .05
359 Greg Harris .05
360 Joe Hesketh .05
361 Jose Melendez .05
362 Paul Quantrill .05
363 John Valentin .05
364 Mike Butcher .05
365 Chuck Crim .05
366 Chili Davis .05
367 Damion Easley .05
368 Steve Frey .05
369 Joe Grahe .05
370 Greg Myers .05
371 John Orton .05
372 J.T. Snow .05
373 Ron Tingley .05
374 Julio Valera .05
375 Paul Assenmacher .05
376 Jose Bautista .05
377 Jose Guzman .05
378 Greg Hibbard .05
379 Candy Maldonado .05
380 Derrick May .05
381 Dan Plesac .05
382 Tommy Shields .05
383 Sammy Sosa 1.00
384 Jose Vizcaino .05
385 Greg Walbeck .05
386 Ellis Burks .05
387 Roberto Hernandez .05
388 Mike Huff .05
389 Bo Jackson .15
390 Lance Johnson .05
391 Ron Karkovice .05
392 Kirk McCaskill .05
393 Donn Pall .05
394 Dan Pasqua .05
395 Steve Sax .05
396 Dave Stieb .05
397 Bobby Ayala .05
398 Tim Belcher .05
399 Jeff Branson .05
400 Cesar Hernandez .05
401 Roberto Kelly .05
402 Randy Milligan .05
403 Kevin Mitchell .05
404 Juan Samuel .05
405 Reggie Sanders .05
406 John Smiley .05
407 Dan Wilson .05
408 Mike Christopher .05
409 Dennis Cook .05
410 Alvaro Espinoza .05
411 Glenallen Hill .05
412 Reggie Jefferson .05
413 Derek Lilliquist .05
414 Jose Mesa .05
415 Charles Nagy .10
416 Junior Ortiz .05
417 Eric Plunk .05
418 Ted Power .05
419 Scott Aldred .05
420 Andy Ashby .05
421 Freddie Benavides .05
422 Dante Bichette .05
423 Willie Blair .05
424 Vinny Castilla .05
425 Jerald Clark .05
426 Alex Cole .05
427 Andres Galarraga .05
428 Joe Girardi .05
429 Charlie Hayes .05
430 Butch Henry .05
431 Darren Holmes .05
432 Dale Murphy .15
433 David Nied .05
434 Jeff Parrett .05
435 *Steve Reed* .05
436 Armando Reynoso .05
437 Bruce Ruffin .05
438 Bryn Smith .05
439 Jim Tatum .05
440 Eric Young .05
441 Skeeter Barnes .05
442 Tom Bolton .05
443 Kirk Gibson .05
444 Chad Krueter .05
445 Bill Krueger .05
446 Scott Livingstone .05
447 Bob MacDonald .05
448 Mike Moore .05
449 Mike Munoz .05
450 Gary Thurman .05
451 David Wells .10
452 Alex Arias .05
453 Jack Armstrong .05
454 Bret Barberie .05
455 Ryan Bowen .05
456 Cris Carpenter .05
457 Chuck Carr .05
458 Jeff Conine .05
459 Steve Decker .05
460 Orestes Destrade .05
461 Monty Fariss .05
462 Junior Felix .05
463 Bryan Harvey .05
464 Trevor Hoffman .10
465 Charlie Hough .05
466 Dave Magadan .05
467 Bob McClure .05
468 Rob Natal .05
469 Scott Pose .05
470 Rich Renteria .05
471 Benito Santiago .05
472 Matt Turner .05
473 Walt Weiss .05
474 Eric Anthony .05
475 Chris Donnels .05
476 Doug Drabek .05
477 Xavier Hernandez .05
478 Doug Jones .05
479 Darryl Kile .10
480 Scott Servais .05
481 Greg Swindell .05
482 Eddie Taubensee .05
483 Jose Uribe .05
484 Brian Williams .05
485 Billy Brewer .05
486 David Cone .05
487 Greg Gagne .05
488 Phil Hiatt .05
489 Jose Lind .05
490 Brent Mayne .05
491 Kevin McReynolds .05
492 Keith Miller .05
493 Hipolito Pichardo .05
494 Harvey Pulliam .05
495 Rico Rossay .05
496 Pedro Astacio .05
497 Tom Candiotti .05
498 Tom Goodwin .05
499 Jim Gott .05
500 Pedro Martinez .40
501 Roger McDowell .05
502 Mike Piazza 1.00
503 Jody Reed .05
504 Rick Trlicek .05
505 Mitch Weber .05
506 Steve Wilson .05
507 James Austin .05
508 Ricky Bones .05
509 Alex Diaz .05
510 Mike Fetters .05
511 Teddy Higuera .05
512 Graeme Lloyd .05
513 Carlos Maldonado .05
514 Josias Manzanillo .05
515 Kevin Reimer .05
516 Bill Spiers .05
517 Bill Wegman .05
518 Willie Banks .05
519 J.T. Bruett .05
520 Brian Harper .05
521 Terry Jorgensen .05
522 Scott Leius .05
523 Pat Mahomes .05
524 Dave McCarty .05
525 Jeff Reboulet .05
526 Mike Trombley .05
527 Carl Willis .05
528 Dave Winfield .35
529 Sean Berry .05
530 Frank Bolick .05
531 Kent Bottenfield .05
532 Wil Cordero .05
533 Jeff Fassero .05
534 Tim Laker .05
535 Mike Lansing .05
536 Chris Nabholz .05
537 Mel Rojas .05
538 John Wetteland .05
539 Ted Wood (Front photo actually Frank Bollick) .05
540 Mike Draper .05
541 Tony Fernandez .05
542 Todd Hundley .10
543 Jeff Innis .05
544 Jeff McKnight .05
545 Eddie Murray .35
546 Charlie O'Brien .05
547 Frank Tanana .05
548 Ryan Thompson .05
549 Chico Walker .05
550 Anthony Young .05
551 Jim Abbott .05
552 Wade Boggs .40
553 Steve Farr .05
554 Neal Heaton .05
555 Steve Howe .05
556 Dion James .05
557 Scott Kamieniecki .05
558 Jimmy Key .05
559 Jim Leyritz .05
560 Paul O'Neill .05
561 Spike Owen .05
562 Lance Blankenship .05
563 Joe Boever .05
564 Storm Davis .05
565 Kelly Downs .05
566 Eric Fox .05
567 Rich Gossage .05
568 Dave Henderson .05
569 Shawn Hillegas .05
570 *Mike Mohler* .05
571 Troy Neel .05
572 Dale Sveum .05
573 Larry Anderson .05
574 Bob Ayrault .05
575 Jose DeLeon .05
576 Jim Eisenreich .05
577 Pete Incaviglia .05
578 Danny Jackson .05
579 Ricky Jordan .05
580 Ben Rivera .05
581 Curt Schilling .15
582 Milt Thompson .05
583 David West .05
584 John Candelaria .05
585 Steve Cooke .05
586 Tom Foley .05
587 Al Martin .05
588 Blas Minor .05
589 Dennis Moeller .05
590 Denny Neagle .05
591 Tom Prince .05
592 Randy Tomlin .05
593 Bob Walk .05
594 Kevin Young .05
595 Pat Gomez .05
596 Ricky Gutierrez .05
597 Gene Harris .05
598 Jeremy Hernandez .05
599 Phil Plantier .05
600 Tim Scott .05
601 Frank Seminara .05
602 Darrell Sherman .05
603 Craig Shipley .05
604 Guillermo Velasquez .05
605 Dan Walters .05
606 Mike Benjamin .05
607 Barry Bonds .75
608 Jeff Brantley .05

609	Dave Burba	.05
610	Craig Colbert	.05
611	Mike Jackson	.05
612	Kirt Manwaring	.05
613	Dave Martinez	.05
614	Dave Righetti	.05
615	Kevin Rogers	.05
616	Bill Swift	.05
617	Rich Amaral	.05
618	Mike Blowers	.05
619	Chris Bosio	.05
620	Norm Charlton	.05
621	John Cummings	.05
622	Mike Felder	.05
623	Bill Haselman	.05
624	Tim Leary	.05
625	Pete O'Brien	.05
626	Russ Swan	.05
627	Fernando Vina	.05
628	Rene Arocha	.05
629	Rod Brewer	.05
630	Ozzie Canseco	.05
631	Rheal Cormier	.05
632	Brian Jordan	.05
633	Joe Magrane	.05
634	Donovan Osborne	.05
635	Mike Perez	.05
636	Stan Royer	.05
637	Hector Villanueva	.05
638	Tracy Woodson	.05
639	Benji Gil	.05
640	Tom Henke	.05
641	David Hulse	.05
642	Charlie Leibrandt	.05
643	Robb Nen	.05
644	Dan Peltier	.05
645	Billy Ripken	.05
646	Kenny Rogers	.05
647	John Russell	.05
648	Dan Smith	.05
649	Matt Whiteside	.05
650	William Canate	.05
651	Darnell Coles	.05
652	Al Leiter	.05
653	Dominigo Martinez	.05
654	Paul Molitor	.35
655	Luis Sojo	.05
656	Dave Stewart	.05
657	Mike Timlin	.05
658	Turner Ward	.05
659	Devon White	.10
660	Eddie Zosky	.05

1993 Pacific Beisbol Amigos

In groups of two, three or more, and generally from the same team, Latin players are paired in this second series insert set. The cards feature player photos (sometimes posed, sometimes superimposed) on a background of red, white and black baseballs. The players' last names and a card title are printed in Spanish on front and repeated on back. Also on back a few career highlights and stats are printed in red on a marbled background - again all in Spanish.

		MT
Complete Set (30):		12.00
Common Player:		.50
1	Edgar Martinez	.50
2	Luis Polonia, Stan Javier	.50
3	George Bell, Julio Franco	.50
4	Ozzie Guillen, Ivan Rodriguez	.75
5	Carlos Baerga, Sandy Alomar Jr.	.50
6	Sandy Alomar Jr., Alvaro Espinoza, Paul Sorrento, Carlos Baerga, Felix Fermin, Junior Ortiz, Jose Mesa, Carlos Martinez	.50
7	Sandy Alomar Jr., Roberto Alomar	1.50
8	Jose Lind, Felix Jose	.50
9	Ricky Bones, Jaime Navarro	.50
10	Jaime Navarro, Jesse Orosco	.50
11	Tino Martinez, Edgar Martinez	.50
12	Juan Gonzalez, Ivan Rodriguez	1.50
13	Juan Gonzalez, Julio Franco	.75
14	Julio Franco, Jose Canseco, Rafael Palmeiro	.60
15	Juan Gonzalez, Jose Canseco	1.50
16	Ivan Rodriguez, Benji Gil	.60
17	Jose Guzman, Frank Castillo	.50
18	Rey Sanchez, Jose Vizcaino	.50
19	Derrick May, Sammy Sosa	2.00
20	Sammy Sosa, Candy Maldonado	2.00
21	Jose Rijo, Juan Samuel	.50
22	Freddie Benavides, Andres Galarraga	.50
23	Guillermo Velasquez, Benito Santiago	.50
24	Luis Gonzalez, Andujar Cedeno	.75
25	Wil Cordero, Dennis Martinez	.50
26	Moises Alou, Wil Cordero	.50
27	Ozzie Canseco, Jose Canseco	.75
28	Jose Oquendo, Luis Alicea	.50
29	Luis Alicea, Rene Arocha	.50
30	Geronimo Pena, Luis Alicea	.50

1993 Pacific Estrellas de Beisbol

Pacific produced a gold-foil "Stars of Baseball" set of 20 that was randomly inserted as part of the company's first series Spanish language major league set in 1993. Each card features a color action photo on the front surrounded by a gold-foil border. Production was limited to 10,000 of each card.

		MT
Complete Set (20):		13.50
Common Player:		.50
1	Moises Alou	1.50
2	Bobby Bonilla	.50
3	Tony Fernandez	.50
4	Felix Jose	.50
5	Dennis Martinez	.50
6	Orlando Merced	.50
7	Jose Oquendo	.50
8	Geronimo Pena	.50
9	Jose Rijo	.50
10	Benito Santiago	.50
11	Sandy Alomar Jr.	.50
12	Carlos Baerga	.50
13	Jose Canseco	2.00
14	Juan "Igor" Gonzalez	4.00
15	Juan Guzman	.50
16	Edgar Martinez	.50
17	Rafael Palmeiro	1.50
18	Ruben Sierra	.50
19	Danny Tartabull	.50
20	Omar Vizquel	.50

1993 Pacific Jugadores Calientes

Three dozen "hot players" with a decidedly Hispanic predominance are featured in this glittery Series 2 insert set. Player action photos appear in front of a silver prismatic foil background. Names appear at bottom in boldly styled but hard to read letters in bright colors. Horizontal backs have a pair of player photos and a large team logo, along with a few stats, all printed in Spanish.

		MT
Complete Set (36):		25.00
Common Player:		.50
1	Rich Amaral	.50
2	George Brett	2.00
3	Jay Buhner	.50
4	Roger Clemens	1.25
5	Kirk Gibson	.50
6	Juan Gonzalez	1.50
7	Ken Griffey Jr.	2.50
8	Bo Jackson	.50
9	Kenny Lofton	.50
10	Mark McGwire	2.50
11	Sherman Obando	.50
12	John Olerud	.50
13	Carlos Quintana	.50
14	Ivan Rodriguez	.75
15	Nolan Ryan	2.50
16	J.T. Snow	.50
17	Fernando Valenzuela	.50
18	Dave Winfield	1.25
19	Moises Alou	.50
20	Jeff Bagwell	1.25
21	Barry Bonds	1.50
22	Bobby Bonilla	.50
23	Vinny Castilla	.50
24	Andujar Cedeno	.50
25	Orestes Destrade	.50
26	Andres Galarraga	.50
27	Mark Grace	.75
28	Tony Gwynn	1.25
29	Roberto Kelly	.50
30	John Kruk	.50
31	Dave Magadan	.50
32	Derrick May	.50
33	Orlando Merced	.50
34	Mike Piazza	2.00
35	Armadno Reynoso	.50
36	Jose Vizcaino	.50

1993 Pacific Prism Insert

Pacific produced a prism card that was randomly inserted in its Series 1 Spanish-language set in 1993. Each of the 20 cards has a color photo of a star Latino player on the front superimposed over a prismatic silver-foil background. Card backs contain an action photo and a brief player biography on a marbled background. Production was limited to 10,000 of each card.

		MT
Complete Set (20):		75.00
Common Player:		4.00
1	Francisco Cabrera	4.00
2	Jose Lind	4.00
3	Dennis Martinez	4.00
4	Ramon Martinez	4.00
5	Jose Rijo	4.00
6	Benito Santiago	4.00
7	Roberto Alomar	8.00
8	Sandy Alomar Jr.	4.00
9	Carlos Baerga	4.00
10	George Bell	4.00
11	Jose Canseco	6.00
12	Alex Fernandez	4.00
13	Julio Franco	4.00
14	Igor (Juan) Gonzalez	12.00
15	Ozzie Guillen	4.00
16	Teddy Higuera	4.00
17	Edgar Martinez	4.00
18	Hipolito Pichardo	4.00
19	Luis Polonia	4.00
20	Ivan Rodriguez	7.50

1994 Pacific Crown Promos

Virtually identical in format to the regular 1994

Pacific Crown issue, the eight cards in the promo set have a "P-" prefix to the card number. Each side has a large "For Promotional Use Only" printed diagonally in black. The cards were sent to dealers as a preview to Pacific's 1994 bilingual issue.

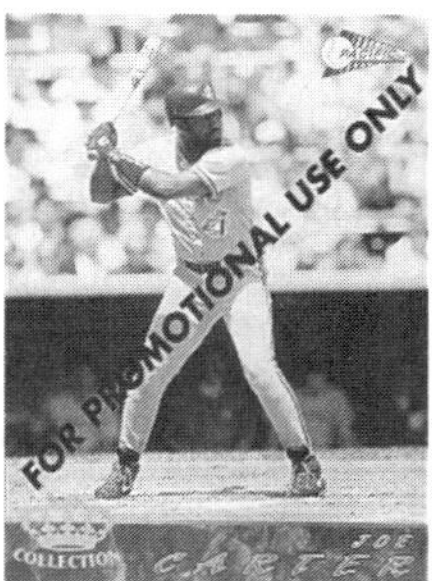

		MT
Complete Set (8):		12.50
Common Player:		1.50
1	Carlos Baerga	1.50
2	Joe Carter	1.50
3	Juan Gonzalez	2.00
4	Ken Griffey, Jr.	3.00
5	Greg Maddux	2.00
6	Mike Piazza	2.50
7	Tim Salmon	2.00
8	Frank Thomas	2.50

1994 Pacific Crown

Following its 1993 Spanish-language set, Pacific's 1994 "Crown Collection" offering is bilingual, featuring both English and Spanish for most of the back printing. Fronts have an action photo which is borderless at the top and sides. A gold-foil line separates the bottom of the photo from a marbled strip that is color-coded by team. The player's name appears in two lines at the left of the strip, a gold-foil crown logo is at left. A Pacific logo appears in one of the upper corners of the photo. Backs have a photo, again borderless at top and sides, with a Pacific logo in one upper corner and the card number and MLB logos in the lower corners. At bottom is a gray marble strip with a few biographical details, 1993 and career stats and a ghost-image color team logo. The 660 cards in the set were issued in a single series.

		MT
Complete Set (660):		35.00
Common Player:		.05
Pack (12):		1.00
Wax Box (36):		25.00
1	Steve Avery	.05
2	Steve Bedrosian	.05
3	Damon Beryhill	.05
4	Jeff Blauser	.05
5	Sid Bream	.05
6	Francisco Cabrera	.05
7	Ramon Caraballo	.05
8	Ron Gant	.05
9	Tom Glavine	.15
10	Chipper Jones	1.50
11	Dave Justice	.20
12	Ryan Klesko	.05
13	Mark Lemke	.05
14	Javier Lopez	.05
15	Greg Maddux	1.25
16	Fred McGriff	.05
17	Greg McMichael	.05
18	Kent Mercker	.05
19	Otis Nixon	.05
20	Terry Pendleton	.05
21	Deion Sanders	.15
22	John Smoltz	.15
23	Tony Tarasco	.05
24	Manny Alexander	.05
25	Brady Anderson	.05
26	Harold Baines	.05
27	Damion Buford (Damon)	.05
28	Paul Carey	.05
29	Mike Devereaux	.05
30	Todd Frohwirth	.05
31	Leo Gomez	.05
32	Jeffrey Hammonds	.05
33	Chris Hoiles	.05
34	Tim Hullett	.05
35	Ben McDonald	.05
36	Mark McLemore	.05
37	Alan Mills	.05
38	Mike Mussina	.20
39	Sherman Obando	.05
40	Gregg Olson	.05
41	Mike Pagliarulo	.05
42	Jim Poole	.05
43	Harold Reynolds	.05
44	Cal Ripken, Jr.	2.00
45	David Segui	.05
46	Fernando Valenzuela	.05
47	Jack Voight	.05
48	Scott Bankhead	.05
49	Roger Clemens	.75
50	Scott Cooper	.05
51	Danny Darwin	.05
52	Andre Dawson	.10
53	John Dopson	.05
54	Scott Fletcher	.05
55	Tony Fossas	.05
56	Mike Greenwell	.05
57	Billy Hatcher	.05
58	Jeff McNeely	.05
59	Jose Melendez	.05
60	Tim Naehring	.05
61	Tony Pena	.05
62	Carlos Quintana	.05
63	Paul Quantrill	.05
64	Luis Rivera	.05
65	Jeff Russell	.05
66	Aaron Sele	.05
67	John Valentin	.05
68	Mo Vaughn	.30
69	Frank Viola	.05
70	Bob Zupcic	.05
71	Mike Butcher	.05
72	Ron Correia	.05
73	Chad Curtis	.05
74	Chili Davis	.05
75	Gary DiSarcina	.05
76	Damion Easley	.05
77	John Farrell	.05
78	Chuck Finley	.05
79	Joe Grahe	.05
80	Stan Javier	.05
81	Mark Langston	.05
82	Phil Leftwich	.05
83	Torey Lovullo	.05
84	Joe Magrane	.05
85	Greg Myers	.05
86	Eduardo Perez	.05
87	Luis Polonia	.05
88	Tim Salmon	.20
89	J.T. Snow	.05
90	Kurt Stillwell	.05
91	Ron Tingley	.05
92	Chris Turner	.05
93	Julio Valera	.05
94	Jose Bautista	.05
95	Shawn Boskie	.05
96	Steve Buechele	.05
97	Frank Castillo	.05
98	Mark Grace	.20
99	Jose Guzman	.05
100	Mike Harkey	.05
101	Greg Hibbard	.05
102	Doug Jennings	.05
103	Derrick May	.05
104	Mike Morgan	.05
105	Randy Myers	.05
106	Karl Rhodes	.05
107	Kevin Robinson	.05
108	Rey Sanchez	.05
109	Ryne Sandberg	.50
110	Tommy Shields	.05
111	Dwight Smith	.05
112	Sammy Sosa	1.00
113	Jose Vizcaino	.05
114	Turk Wendell	.05
115	Rick Wilkins	.05
116	Willie Wilson	.05
117	Eddie Zambrano	.05
118	Wilson Alvarez	.05
119	Tim Belcher	.05
120	Jason Bere	.05
121	Rodney Bolton	.05
122	Ellis Burks	.05
123	Joey Cora	.05
124	Alex Fernandez	.05
125	Ozzie Guillen	.05
126	Craig Grebeck	.05
127	Roberto Hernandez	.05
128	Bo Jackson	.15
129	Lance Johnson	.05
130	Ron Karkovice	.05
131	Mike Lavalliere	.05
132	Norberto Martin	.05
133	Kirk McCaskill	.05
134	Jack McDowell	.05
135	Scott Radinsky	.05
136	Tim Raines	.05
137	Steve Sax	.05
138	Frank Thomas	1.00
139	Dan Pasqua	.05
140	Robin Ventura	.05
141	Jeff Branson	.05
142	Tom Browning	.05
143	Jacob Brumfield	.05
144	Tim Costo	.05
145	Rob Dibble	.05
146	Brian Dorsett	.05
147	Steve Foster	.05
148	Cesar Hernandez	.05
149	Roberto Kelly	.05
150	Barry Larkin	.10
151	Larry Luebbers	.05
152	Kevin Mitchell	.05
153	Joe Oliver	.05
154	Tim Pugh	.05
155	Jeff Reardon	.05
156	Jose Rijo	.05
157	Bip Roberts	.05
158	Chris Sabo	.05
159	Juan Samuel	.05
160	Reggie Sanders	.05
161	John Smiley	.05
162	Jerry Spradlin	.05
163	Gary Varsho	.05
164	Sandy Alomar Jr.	.05
165	Carlos Baerga	.05
166	Albert Belle	.15
167	Mark Clark	.05
168	Alvaro Espinoza	.05
169	Felix Fermin	.05
170	Reggie Jefferson	.05
171	Wayne Kirby	.05
172	Tom Kramer	.05
173	Jesse Levis	.05
174	Kenny Lofton	.05
175	Candy Maldonado	.05
176	Carlos Martinez	.05
177	Jose Mesa	.05
178	Jeff Mutis	.05
179	Charles Nagy	.05
180	Bob Ojeda	.05
181	Junior Ortiz	.05
182	Eric Plunk	.05
183	Manny Ramirez	.75
184	Paul Sorrento	.05
185	Jeff Treadway	.05
186	Bill Wertz	.05
187	Freddie Benavides	.05
188	Dante Bichette	.05
189	Willie Blair	.05
190	Daryl Boston	.05
191	Pedro Castellano	.05
192	Vinny Castilla	.05
193	Jerald Clark	.05
194	Alex Cole	.05
195	Andres Galarraga	.10
196	Joe Girardi	.05
197	Charlie Hayes	.05
198	Darren Holmes	.05
199	Chris Jones	.05
200	Curt Leskanic	.05
201	Roberto Mejia	.05
202	David Nied	.05
203	J. Owens	.05
204	Steve Reed	.05
205	Armando Reynoso	.05
206	Bruce Ruffin	.05
207	Keith Shepherd	.05
208	Jim Tatum	.05
209	Eric Young	.05
210	Skeeter Barnes	.05
211	Danny Bautista	.05
212	Tom Bolton	.05
213	Eric Davis	.05
214	Storm Davis	.05
215	Cecil Fielder	.05
216	Travis Fryman	.05
217	Kirk Gibson	.05
218	Dan Gladden	.05
219	John Doherty	.05
220	Chris Gomez	.05
221	David Haas	.05
222	Bill Krueger	.05
223	Chad Kreuter	.05
224	Mark Leiter	.05
225	Bob MacDonald	.05
226	Mike Moore	.05
227	Tony Phillips	.05
228	Rich Rowland	.05
229	Mickey Tettleton	.05
230	Alan Trammell	.05
231	David Wells	.10
232	Lou Whitaker	.05
233	Luis Aquino	.05
234	Alex Arias	.05
235	Jack Armstrong	.05
236	Ryan Bowen	.05
237	Chuck Carr	.05
238	Matias Carrillo	.05
239	Jeff Conine	.05
240	Henry Cotto	.05
241	Orestes Destrade	.05
242	Chris Hammond	.05
243	Bryan Harvey	.05
244	Charlie Hough	.05
245	Richie Lewis	.05
246	Mitch Lyden	.05
247	Dave Magadan	.05
248	Bob Natal	.05
249	Benito Santiago	.05
250	Gary Sheffield	.20
251	Matt Turner	.05
252	David Weathers	.05
253	Walt Weiss	.05
254	Darrell Whitmore	.05
255	Nigel Wilson	.05
256	Eric Anthony	.05
257	Jeff Bagwell	.75
258	Kevin Bass	.05
259	Craig Biggio	.10
260	Ken Caminiti	.05
261	Andujar Cedeno	.05
262	Chris Donnels	.05
263	Doug Drabek	.05
264	Tom Edens	.05
265	Steve Finley	.05
266	Luis Gonzalez	.25
267	Pete Harnisch	.05
268	Xavier Hernandez	.05
269	Todd Jones	.05
270	Darryl Kile	.05
271	Al Osuna	.05

272 Rick Parker .05
273 Mark Portugal .05
274 Scott Servais .05
275 Greg Swindell .05
276 Eddie Taubensee .05
277 Jose Uribe .05
278 Brian Williams .05
279 Kevin Appier .05
280 Billy Brewer .05
281 David Cone .05
282 Greg Gagne .05
283 Tom Gordon .05
284 Chris Gwynn .05
285 John Habyan .05
286 Chris Haney .05
287 Phil Hiatt .05
288 David Howard .05
289 Felix Jose .05
290 Wally Joyner .05
291 Kevin Koslofski .05
292 Jose Lind .05
293 Brent Mayne .05
294 Mike Mcfarlane .05
295 Brian McRae .05
296 Kevin McReynolds .05
297 Keith Miller .05
298 Jeff Montgomery .05
299 Hipolito Pichardo .05
300 Rico Rossy .05
301 Curtis Wilkerson .05
302 Pedro Astacio .05
303 Rafael Bournigal .05
304 Brett Butler .05
305 Tom Candiotti .05
306 Omar Daal .05
307 Jim Gott .05
308 Kevin Gross .05
309 Dave Hansen .05
310 Carlos Hernandez .05
311 Orel Hershiser .05
312 Eric Karros .05
313 Pedro Martinez .35
314 Ramon Martinez .05
315 Roger McDowell .05
316 Raul Mondesi .15
317 Jose Offerman .05
318 Mike Piazza 1.50
319 Jody Reed .05
320 Henry Rodriguez .05
321 Cory Snyder .05
322 Darryl Strawberry .05
323 Tim Wallach .05
324 Steve Wilson .05
325 Juan Bell .05
326 Ricky Bones .05
327 Alex Diaz .05
328 Cal Eldred .05
329 Darryl Hamilton .05
330 Doug Henry .05
331 John Jaha .05
332 Pat Listach .05
333 Graeme Lloyd .05
334 Carlos Maldonado .05
335 Angel Miranda .05
336 Jaime Navarro .05
337 Dave Nilsson .05
338 Rafael Novoa .05
339 Troy O'Leary .05
340 Jesse Orosco .05
341 Kevin Seitzer .05
342 Bill Spiers .05
343 William Suero .05
344 B.J. Surhoff .05
345 Dickie Thon .05
346 Jose Valentin .05
347 Greg Vaughn .05
348 Robin Yount .45
349 Willie Banks .05
350 Bernardo Brito .05
351 Scott Erickson .05
352 Mark Guthrie .05
353 Chip Hale .05
354 Brian Harper .05
355 Kent Hrbek .05
356 Terry Jorgenson .05
357 Chuck Knoblauch .05
358 Gene Larkin .05
359 Scott Leius .05
360 Shane Mack .05
361 David McCarty .05
362 Pat Meares .05
363 Pedro Munoz .05
364 Derek Parks .05
365 Kirby Puckett 1.00
366 Jeff Reboulet .05
367 Kevin Tapani .05
368 Mike Trombley .05
369 George Tsamis .05
370 Carl Willis .05
371 Dave Winfield .50
372 Moises Alou .10
373 Brian Barnes .05
374 Sean Berry .05
375 Frank Bolick .05
376 Wil Cordero .05
377 Delino DeShields .05
378 Jeff Fassero .05
379 Darren Fletcher .05
380 Cliff Floyd .05
381 Lou Frazier .05
382 Marquis Grissom .05
383 Gil Heredia .05
384 Mike Lansing .05
385 Oreste Marrero .05
386 Dennis Martinez .05
387 Curtis Pride .05
388 Mel Rojas .05
389 Kirk Rueter .05
390 Joe Siddall .05
391 John Vander Wal .05
392 Larry Walker .20
393 John Wetteland .05
394 Rondell White .10
395 Tom Bogar .05
396 Bobby Bonilla .05
397 Jeromy Burnitz .05
398 Mike Draper .05
399 Sid Fernandez .05
400 John Franco .05
401 Dave Gallagher .05
402 Dwight Gooden .05
403 Eric Hillman .05
404 Todd Hundley .10
405 Butch Huskey .05
406 Jeff Innis .05
407 Howard Johnson .05
408 Jeff Kent .05
409 Ced Landrum .05
410 Mike Maddux .05
411 Josias Manzanillo .05
412 Jeff McKnight .05
413 Eddie Murray .30
414 Tito Navarro .05
415 Joe Orsulak .05
416 Bret Saberhagen .05
417 Dave Telgheder .05
418 Ryan Thompson .05
419 Chico Walker .05
420 Jim Abbott .05
421 Wade Boggs .40
422 Mike Gallego .05
423 Mark Hutton .05
424 Dion James .05
425 Domingo Jean .05
426 Pat Kelly .05
427 Jimmy Key .05
428 Jim Leyritz .05
429 Kevin Maas .05
430 Don Mattingly 1.00
431 Bobby Munoz .05
432 Matt Nokes .05
433 Paul O'Neill .05
434 Spike Owen .05
435 Melido Perez .05
436 Lee Smith .05
437 Andy Stankiewicz .05
438 Mike Stanley .05
439 Danny Tartabull .05
440 Randy Velarde .05
441 Bernie Williams .35
442 Gerald Williams .05
443 Mike Witt .05
444 Marcos Armas .05
445 Lance Blankenship .05
446 Mike Bordick .05
447 Ron Darling .05
448 Dennis Eckersley .10
449 Brent Gates .05
450 Goose Gossage .05
451 Scott Hemond .05
452 Dave Henderson .05
453 Shawn Hillegas .05
454 Rick Honeycutt .05
455 Scott Lydy .05
456 Mark McGwire 2.00
457 Henry Mercedes .05
458 Mike Mohler .05
459 Troy Neel .05
460 Edwin Nunez .05
461 Craig Paquette .05
462 Ruben Sierra .05
463 Terry Steinbach .05
464 Todd Van Poppel .05
465 Bob Welch .05
466 Bobby Witt .05
467 Ruben Amaro .05
468 Larry Anderson .05
469 Kim Batiste .05
470 Wes Chamberlain .05
471 Darren Daulton .05
472 Mariano Duncan .05
473 Len Dykstra .05
474 Jim Eisenreich .05
475 Tommy Greene .05
476 Dave Hollins .05
477 Pete Incaviglia .05
478 Danny Jackson .05
479 John Kruk .05
480 Tony Longmire .05
481 Jeff Manto .05
482 Mike Morandini .05
483 Terry Mulholland .05
484 Todd Pratt .05
485 Ben Rivera .05
486 Curt Schilling .10
487 Kevin Stocker .05
488 Milt Thompson .05
489 David West .05
490 Mitch Williams .05
491 Jeff Ballard .05
492 Jay Bell .05
493 Scott Bullett .05
494 Dave Clark .05
495 Steve Cooke .05
496 Midre Cummings .05
497 Mark Dewey .05
498 Carlos Garcia .05
499 Jeff King .05
500 Al Martin .05
501 Lloyd McClendon .05
502 Orlando Merced .05
503 Blas Minor .05
504 Denny Neagle .05
505 Tom Prince .05
506 Don Slaught .05
507 Zane Smith .05
508 Randy Tomlin .05
509 Andy Van Slyke .05
510 Paul Wagner .05
511 Tim Wakefield .05
512 Bob Walk .05
513 John Wehner .05
514 Kevin Young .05
515 Billy Bean .05
516 Andy Benes .05
517 Derek Bell .05
518 Doug Brocail .05
519 Jarvis Brown .05
520 Phil Clark .05
521 Mark Davis .05
522 Jeff Gardner .05
523 Pat Gomez .05
524 Ricky Gutierrez .05
525 Tony Gwynn .60
526 Gene Harris .05
527 Kevin Higgins .05
528 Trevor Hoffman .05
529 Luis Lopez .05
530 Pedro A. Martinez .05
531 Melvin Nieves .05
532 Phil Plantier .05
533 Frank Seminara .05
534 Craig Shipley .05
535 Tim Tuefel .05
536 Guillermo Velasquez .05
537 Wally Whitehurst .05
538 Rod Beck .05
539 Todd Benzinger .05
540 Barry Bonds 1.00
541 Jeff Brantley .05
542 Dave Burba .05
543 John Burkett .05
544 Will Clark .15
545 Royce Clayton .05
546 Brian Hickerson
(Bryan) .05
547 Mike Jackson .05
548 Darren Lewis .05
549 Kirt Manwaring .05
550 Dave Martinez .05
551 Willie McGee .05
552 Jeff Reed .05
553 Dave Righetti .05
554 Kevin Rogers .05
555 Steve Scarsone .05
556 Bill Swift .05
557 Robby Thompson .05
558 Salomon Torres .05
559 Matt Williams .15
560 Trevor Wilson .05
561 Rich Amaral .05
562 Mike Blowers .05
563 Chris Bosio .05
564 Jay Buhner .05
565 Norm Charlton .05
566 Jim Converse .05
567 Rich DeLucia .05
568 Mike Felder .05
569 Dave Fleming .05
570 Ken Griffey, Jr. 2.00
571 Bill Haselman .05
572 Dwayne Henry .05
573 Brad Holman .05
574 Randy Johnson .25
575 Greg Litton .05
576 Edgar Martinez .05
577 Tino Martinez .05
578 Jeff Nelson .05
579 Mark Newfield .05
580 Roger Salkeld .05
581 Mackey Sasser .05
582 Brian Turang .05
583 Omar Vizquel .05
584 Dave Valle .05
585 Luis Alicea .05
586 Rene Arocha .05
587 Rheal Cormier .05
588 Tripp Cromer .05
589 Bernard Gilkey .05
590 Lee Guetterman .05
591 Gregg Jefferies .05
592 Tim Jones .05
593 Paul Kilgus .05
594 Les Lancaster .05
595 Omar Olivares .05
596 Jose Oquendo .05
597 Donovan Osborne .05
598 Tom Pagnozzi .05
599 Erik Pappas .05
600 Geronimo Pena .05
601 Mike Perez .05
602 Gerald Perry .05
603 Stan Royer .05
604 Ozzie Smith .50
605 Bob Tewksbury .05
606 Allen Watson .05
607 Mark Whiten .05
608 Todd Zeile .05
609 Jeff Bronkey .05
610 Kevin Brown .10
611 Jose Canseco .35
612 Doug Dascenzo .05
613 Butch Davis .05
614 Mario Diaz .05
615 Julio Franco .05
616 Benji Gil .05
617 Juan Gonzalez .75
618 Tom Henke .05
619 Jeff Huson .05
620 David Hulse .05
621 Craig Lefferts .05
622 Rafael Palmeiro .15
623 Dean Palmer .05
624 Bob Patterson .05
625 Roger Pavlik .05
626 Gary Redus .05
627 Ivan Rodriguez .40
628 Kenny Rogers .05
629 Jon Shave .05
630 Doug Strange .05
631 Matt Whiteside .05
632 Roberto Alomar .45
633 Pat Borders .05
634 Scott Brow .05
635 Rob Butler .05
636 Joe Carter .05
637 Tony Castillo .05
638 Mark Eichhorn .05
639 Tony Fernandez .05
640 *Huck Flener* .05
641 Alfredo Griffin .05
642 Juan Guzman .05
643 Rickey Henderson .40
644 Pat Hentgen .05
645 Randy Knorr .05
646 Al Leiter .05
647 Dominigo Martinez .05
648 Paul Molitor .40
649 Jack Morris .05
650 John Olerud .05
651 Ed Sprague .05
652 Dave Stewart .05
653 Devon White .10
654 Woody Williams .05

655 Barry Bonds (MVP) .50
656 Greg Maddux (CY) .65
657 Jack McDowell (CY) .05
658 Mike Piazza (ROY) .75
659 Tim Salmon (ROY) .15
660 Frank Thomas (MVP) .50

1994 Pacific Crown All Latino All-Star Team

Latino All-Stars is the theme of the third insert set found randomly packed in Pacific Spanish for 1994. Cards feature a player action photo on front, with a gold foil pinstripe around the sides and top. The player's name appears in gold script at bottom and there is a baseball logo in the corner. On backs a portrait photo of the player is set against a background of his native flag. Season highlights of 1993 are presented in English and Spanish. Eight thousand sets were produced.

		MT
Complete Set (20):		13.00
Common Player:		.50
1	Benito Santiago	.50
2	Dave Magadan	.50
3	Andres Galarraga	.50
4	Luis Gonzalez	2.00
5	Jose Offerman	.50
6	Bobby Bonilla	.50
7	Dennis Martinez	.50
8	Mariano Duncan	.50
9	Orlando Merced	.50
10	Jose Rijo	.50
11	Danny Tartabull	.50
12	Ruben Sierra	.50
13	Ivan Rodriguez	2.00
14	Juan Gonzalez	4.00
15	Jose Canseco	1.50
16	Rafael Palmeiro	1.00
17	Roberto Alomar	2.00
18	Eduardo Perez	.50
19	Alex Fernandez	.50
20	Omar Vizquel	.50

1994 Pacific Crown Homerun Leaders

A gold prismatic background behind a color action player photo is the featured design on this Pacific insert set. Backs have another player photo against a ballfield backdrop. A huge baseball is overprinted with the player's name and number of 1993 homers. A league designation is among the logos featured on back. A total of 8,000 of these inserts sets was the announced production.

		MT
Complete Set (20):		30.00
Common Player:		1.00
1	Juan Gonzalez	2.50
2	Ken Griffey, Jr.	6.00
3	Frank Thomas	3.00
4	Albert Belle	1.50
5	Rafael Palmeiro	1.50
6	Joe Carter	1.00
7	Dean Palmer	1.00
8	Mickey Tettleton	1.00
9	Tim Salmon	1.50
10	Danny Tartabull	1.00
11	Barry Bonds	3.00
12	Dave Justice	1.50
13	Matt Williams	1.25
14	Fred McGriff	1.00
15	Ron Gant	1.00
16	Mike Piazza	4.50
17	Bobby Bonilla	1.00
18	Phil Plantier	1.00
19	Sammy Sosa	5.00
20	Rick Wilkins	1.00

1994 Pacific Crown Jewels of the Crown

One of three inserts into 1994 Pacific Spanish foil packs. The design features a player action photo set against a silver prismatic background. On back is another color player photo against a background of colored silk and a large jewel. Season highlight stats and awards won are presented in both English and Spanish. The announced production run of these inserts was 8,000 sets.

		MT
Complete Set (36):		60.00
Common Player:		1.00
1	Robin Yount	2.00
2	Juan Gonzalez	4.00
3	Rafael Palmeiro	1.50
4	Paul Molitor	2.50
5	Roberto Alomar	2.50
6	John Olerud	1.00
7	Randy Johnson	2.50
8	Ken Griffey, Jr.	6.00
9	Wade Boggs	2.50
10	Don Mattingly	5.00
11	Kirby Puckett	4.00
12	Tim Salmon	1.50
13	Frank Thomas	4.00
14	Fernando Valenzuela (Comeback Player)	1.00
15	Cal Ripken, Jr.	6.00
16	Carlos Baerga	1.00
17	Kenny Lofton	1.00
18	Cecil Fielder	1.00
19	John Burkett	1.00
20	Andres Galarraga (Comeback Player)	1.00
21	Charlie Hayes	1.00
22	Orestes Destrade	1.00
23	Jeff Conine	1.00
24	Jeff Bagwell	3.00
25	Mark Grace	1.50
26	Ryne Sandberg	2.50
27	Gregg Jefferies	1.00
28	Barry Bonds	4.00
29	Mike Piazza	5.00
30	Greg Maddux	4.00
31	Darren Daulton	1.00
32	John Kruk	1.00
33	Len Dykstra	1.00
34	Orlando Merced	1.00
35	Tony Gwynn	4.00
36	Robby Thompson	1.00

1994 Pacific Crown Jewels of the Crown - Retail

Using the same design, photos, graphics and card numbers, the retail version of the Jewels of the Crown insert set varies only in the silver prismatic foil background on front. While the scarcer hobby version has a diamond-shaped pattern to the foil, the retail version has numerous circles as a background pattern. The retail cards were inserted one per pack of retail product and are thus much more common than the hobby version.

		MT
Complete Set (36):		50.00
Common Player:		.75
1	Robin Yount	1.50
2	Juan Gonzalez	2.25
3	Rafael Palmeiro	1.00
4	Paul Molitor	1.50
5	Roberto Alomar	2.00
6	John Olerud	.75
7	Randy Johnson	1.50
8	Ken Griffey, Jr.	4.50
9	Wade Boggs	1.50
10	Don Mattingly	3.50
11	Kirby Puckett	3.50
12	Tim Salmon	1.00
13	Frank Thomas	3.50
14	Fernando Valenzuela (Comeback Player)	.75
15	Cal Ripken, Jr.	4.50
16	Carlos Baerga	.75
17	Kenny Lofton	.75
18	Cecil Fielder	.75
19	John Burkett	.75
20	Andres Galarraga (Comeback Player)	.75
21	Charlie Hayes	.75
22	Orestes Destrade	.75
23	Jeff Conine	.75
24	Jeff Bagwell	2.25
25	Mark Grace	1.25
26	Ryne Sandberg	2.00
27	Gregg Jefferies	.75
28	Barry Bonds	3.00
29	Mike Piazza	4.50
30	Greg Maddux	3.50
31	Darren Daulton	.75
32	John Kruk	.75
33	Len Dykstra	.75
34	Orlando Merced	.75
35	Tony Gwynn	3.50
36	Robby Thompson	.75

1995 Pacific Prism

The rainbow prismatic foil which is the background ot the action photos on the card fronts provides the visual punch to Pacific's premium brand cards. In a throwback to the 1950s, the cards were sold in single-card packs for $1.75. Production was limited to 2,999 cases of 36-pack boxes. Backs have a large portrait photo on a conventionally printed rainbow background. In keeping with the company's license, the 1994 season summary printed at bottom on back is in both English and Spanish. One checklist, team or Pacific logo was inserted into each pack to protect the Prism card.

		MT
Complete Set (144):		75.00
Common Player:		.25
Pack (2):		.75
Wax Box (36):		20.00
1	Dave Justice	.50
2	Ryan Klesko	.25
3	Javier Lopez	.25
4	Greg Maddux	4.00
5	Fred McGriff	.25
6	Tony Tarasco	.25

7 Jeffrey Hammonds .25
8 Mike Mussina 1.00
9 Rafael Palmeiro .50
10 Cal Ripken Jr. 6.00
11 Lee Smith .25
12 Roger Clemens 1.50
13 Scott Cooper .25
14 Mike Greenwell .25
15 Carlos Rodriguez .25
16 Mo Vaughn 1.00
17 Chili Davis .25
18 Jim Edmonds .35
19 Jorge Fabregas .25
20 Bo Jackson .40
21 Tim Salmon .40
22 Mark Grace .50
23 Jose Guzman .25
24 Randy Myers .25
25 Rey Sanchez .25
26 Sammy Sosa 4.00
27 Wilson Alvarez .25
28 Julio Franco .25
29 Ozzie Guillen .25
30 Jack McDowell .25
31 Frank Thomas 3.50
32 Bret Boone .25
33 Barry Larkin .50
34 Hal Morris .25
35 Jose Rijo .25
36 Deion Sanders .50
37 Carlos Baerga .25
38 Albert Belle .75
39 Kenny Lofton .25
40 Dennis Martinez .25
41 Manny Ramirez 2.00
42 Omar Vizquel .25
43 Dante Bichette .25
44 Marvin Freeman .25
45 Andres Galarraga .25
46 Mike Kingery .25
47 Danny Bautista .25
48 Cecil Fielder .25
49 Travis Fryman .25
50 Tony Phillips .25
51 Alan Trammell .25
52 Lou Whitaker .25
53 Alex Arias .25
54 Bret Barberie .25
55 Jeff Conine .25
56 Charles Johnson .25
57 Gary Sheffield 1.00
58 Jeff Bagwell 3.00
59 Craig Biggio .25
60 Doug Drabek .25
61 Tony Eusebio .25
62 Luis Gonzalez .75
63 David Cone .25
64 Bob Hamelin .25
65 Felix Jose .25
66 Wally Joyner .25
67 Brian McRae .25
68 Brett Butler .25
69 Garey Ingram .25
70 Ramon Martinez .25
71 Raul Mondesi .50
72 Mike Piazza 5.00
73 Henry Rodriguez .25
74 Ricky Bones .25
75 Pat Listach .25
76 Dave Nilsson .25
77 Jose Valentin .25
78 Rick Aguilera .25
79 Denny Hocking .25
80 Shane Mack .25
81 Pedro Munoz .25
82 Kirby Puckett 3.00
83 Dave Winfield 1.00
84 Moises Alou .35
85 Wil Cordero .25
86 Cliff Floyd .25
87 Marquis Grissom .25
88 Pedro Martinez .75
89 Larry Walker .50
90 Bobby Bonilla .25
91 Jeremy Burnitz .25
92 John Franco .25
93 Jeff Kent .25
94 Jose Vizcaino .25
95 Wade Boggs 1.00
96 Jimmy Key .25
97 Don Mattingly 4.00
98 Paul O'Neill .25
99 Luis Polonia .25
100 Danny Tartabull .25
101 Geronimo Berroa .25
102 Rickey Henderson .75
103 Ruben Sierra .25
104 Terry Steinbach .25
105 Darren Daulton .25
106 Mariano Duncan .25
107 Lenny Dykstra .25
108 Mike Lieberthal .25
109 Tony Longmire .25
110 Tom Marsh .25
111 Jay Bell .25
112 Carlos Garcia .25
113 Orlando Merced .25
114 Andy Van Slyke .25
115 Derek Bell .25
116 Tony Gwynn 3.00
117 Luis Lopez .25
118 Bip Roberts .25
119 Rod Beck .25
120 Barry Bonds 3.00
121 Darryl Strawberry .25
122 Bill Van Landingham .25
123 Matt Williams .50
124 Jay Buhner .25
125 Felix Fermin .25
126 Ken Griffey Jr. 6.00
127 Randy Johnson .75
128 Edgar Martinez .25
129 Alex Rodriguez 6.00
130 Rene Arocha .25
131 Gregg Jefferies .25
132 Mike Perez .25
133 Ozzie Smith 2.00
134 Jose Canseco 1.00
135 Will Clark .75
136 Juan Gonzalez 2.00
137 Ivan Rodriguez 1.50
138 Roberto Alomar 1.50
139 Joe Carter .25
140 Carlos Delgado .75
141 Alex Gonzalez .50
142 Juan Guzman .25
143 Paul Molitor 1.50
144 John Olerud .25

1995 Pacific Prism Team Logos

Inserted one card per pack to provide some protection to the Prism card was a checklist, team or Pacific logo card. The large color logos are on a background of a playing field. Backs have a short English/Spanish history of the team.

		MT
Complete Set (31):		2.00
Common Player:		.10
1	Baltimore Orioles	.10
2	Boston Red Sox	.10
3	California Angels	.10
4	Chicago White Sox	.10
5	Cleveland Indians	.10
6	Detroit Tigers	.10
7	Kansas City Royals	.10
8	Milwaukee Brewers	.10
9	Minnesota Twins	.10
10	New York Yankees	.10
11	Oakland Athletics	.10
12	Seattle Mariners	.10
13	Texas Rangers	.10
14	Toronto Blue Jays	.10
15	Atlanta Braves	.10
16	Chicago Cubs	.10
17	Cincinnati Reds	.10
18	Colorado Rockies	.10
19	Florida Marlins	.10
20	Houston Astros	.10
21	Los Angeles Dodgers	.10
22	Montreal Expos	.10
23	New York Mets	.10
24	Philadelphia Phillies	.10
25	Pittsburgh Pirates	.10
26	St. Louis Cardinals	.10
27	San Diego Padres	.10
28	San Francisco Giants	.10
1	Checklist 1-72	.05
2	Checklist 73-144	.05
---	Pacific logo card	.05

1995 Pacific

The base cards in Pacific's Crown Collection baseball issue for 1995 feature borderless color action photos on front, graphically highlighted by the player name at bottom in gold foil and a color team logo in a baseball at lower-left. Backs have a playing field design in the background with a portrait photo at left. At right are 1994 stats, career highlights and a ghosted image of the team logo. Most back printing is in both English and Spanish. The 450 cards in the series are arranged alphabetically within team, with the teams arranged in city-alpha order. Several chase cards series are found in the 12-card foil packs.

		MT
Complete Set (450):		22.00
Common Player:		.05
Unlisted Stars: .25 to .50		
Pack (12):		1.50
Wax Box (36):		45.00
1	Steve Avery	.05
2	Rafael Belliard	.05
3	Jeff Blauser	.05
4	Tom Glavine	.10
5	Dave Justice	.25
6	Mike Kelly	.05
7	Roberto Kelly	.05
8	Ryan Klesko	.05
9	Mark Lemke	.05
10	Javier Lopez	.05
11	Greg Maddux	1.25
12	Fred McGriff	.05
13	Greg McMichael	.05
14	Jose Oliva	.05
15	John Smoltz	.10
16	Tony Tarasco	.05
17	Brady Anderson	.05
18	Harold Baines	.05
19	Armando Benitez	.05
20	Mike Devereaux	.05
21	Leo Gomez	.05
22	Jeffrey Hammonds	.05
23	Chris Hoiles	.05
24	Ben McDonald	.05
25	Mark McLemore	.05
26	Jamie Moyer	.05
27	Mike Mussina	.25
28	Rafael Palmeiro	.15
29	Jim Poole	.05
30	Cal Ripken Jr.	2.50
31	Lee Smith	.05
32	Mark Smith	.05
33	Jose Canseco	.35
34	Roger Clemens	.60
35	Scott Cooper	.05
36	Andre Dawson	.10
37	Tony Fossas	.05
38	Mike Greenwell	.05
39	Chris Howard	.05
40	Jose Melendez	.05
41	Nate Minchey	.05
42	Tim Naehring	.05
43	Otis Nixon	.05
44	Carlos Rodriguez	.05
45	Aaron Sele	.05
46	Lee Tinsley	.05
47	Sergio Valdez	.05
48	John Valentin	.05
49	Mo Vaughn	.30
50	Brian Anderson	.05
51	Garret Anderson	.05
52	Rod Correia	.05
53	Chad Curtis	.05
54	Mark Dalesandro	.05
55	Chili Davis	.05
56	Gary DiSarcina	.05
57	Damion Easley	.05
58	Jim Edmonds	.10
59	Jorge Fabregas	.05
60	Chuck Finley	.05
61	Bo Jackson	.10
62	Mark Langston	.05
63	Eduardo Perez	.05
64	Tim Salmon	.15
65	J.T. Snow	.05
66	Willie Banks	.05
67	Jose Bautista	.05
68	Shawon Dunston	.05
69	Kevin Foster	.05
70	Mark Grace	.25
71	Jose Guzman	.05
72	Jose Hernandez	.05
73	Blaise Ilsley	.05
74	Derrick May	.05
75	Randy Myers	.05
76	Karl Rhodes	.05
77	Kevin Roberson	.05
78	Rey Sanchez	.05
79	Sammy Sosa	1.00
80	Steve Trachsel	.05
81	Eddie Zambrano	.05
82	Wilson Alvarez	.05
83	Jason Bere	.05
84	Joey Cora	.05
85	Jose DeLeon	.05
86	Alex Fernandez	.05
87	Julio Franco	.05
88	Ozzie Guillen	.05
89	Joe Hall	.05
90	Roberto Hernandez	.05
91	Darrin Jackson	.05
92	Lance Johnson	.05
93	Norberto Martin	.05
94	Jack McDowell	.05
95	Tim Raines	.05
96	Olmedo Saenz	.05
97	Frank Thomas	1.00
98	Robin Ventura	.05
99	Bret Boone	.10
100	Jeff Brantley	.05
101	Jacob Brumfield	.05
102	Hector Carrasco	.05
103	Brian Dorsett	.05
104	Tony Fernandez	.05
105	Willie Greene	.05
106	Erik Hanson	.05
107	Kevin Jarvis	.05
108	Barry Larkin	.10
109	Kevin Mitchell	.05
110	Hal Morris	.05
111	Jose Rijo	.05
112	Johnny Ruffin	.05
113	Deion Sanders	.15

114 Reggie Sanders .05
115 Sandy Alomar Jr. .05
116 Ruben Amaro .05
117 Carlos Baerga .05
118 Albert Belle .15
119 Alvaro Espinoza .05
120 Rene Gonzales .05
121 Wayne Kirby .05
122 Kenny Lofton .05
123 Candy Maldonado .05
124 Dennis Martinez .05
125 Eddie Murray .30
126 Charles Nagy .05
127 Tony Pena .05
128 Manny Ramirez .50
129 Paul Sorrento .05
130 Jim Thome .05
131 Omar Vizquel .05
132 Dante Bichette .05
133 Ellis Burks .05
134 Vinny Castilla .05
135 Marvin Freeman .05
136 Andres Galarraga .05
137 Joe Girardi .05
138 Charlie Hayes .05
139 Mike Kingery .05
140 Nelson Liriano .05
141 Roberto Mejia .05
142 David Nied .05
143 Steve Reed .05
144 Armando Reynoso .05
145 Bruce Ruffin .05
146 John Vander Wal .05
147 Walt Weiss .05
148 Skeeter Barnes .05
149 Tim Belcher .05
150 Junior Felix .05
151 Cecil Fielder .05
152 Travis Fryman .05
153 Kirk Gibson .05
154 Chris Gomez .05
155 Buddy Groom .05
156 Chad Kreuter .05
157 Mike Moore .05
158 Tony Phillips .05
159 Juan Samuel .05
160 Mickey Tettleton .05
161 Alan Trammell .05
162 David Wells .10
163 Lou Whitaker .05
164 Kurt Abbott .05
165 Luis Aquino .05
166 Alex Arias .05
167 Bret Barberie .05
168 Jerry Browne .05
169 Chuck Carr .05
170 Matias Carrillo .05
171 Greg Colbrunn .05
172 Jeff Conine .05
173 Carl Everett .10
174 Robb Nen .05
175 Yorkis Perez .05
176 Pat Rapp .05
177 Benito Santiago .05
178 Gary Sheffield .15
179 Darrell Whitmore .05
180 Jeff Bagwell .75
181 Kevin Bass .05
182 Craig Biggio .10
183 Andujar Cedeno .05
184 Doug Drabek .05
185 Tony Eusebio .05
186 Steve Finley .05
187 Luis Gonzalez .25
188 Pete Harnisch .05
189 John Hudek .05
190 Orlando Miller .05
191 James Mouton .05
192 Roberto Petagine .05
193 Shane Reynolds .05
194 Greg Swindell .05
195 Dave Veres .05
196 Kevin Appier .05
197 Stan Belinda .05
198 Vince Coleman .05
199 David Cone .05
200 Gary Gaetti .05
201 Greg Gagne .05
202 Mark Gubicza .05
203 Bob Hamelin .05
204 Dave Henderson .05
205 Felix Jose .05
206 Wally Joyner .05
207 Jose Lind .05
208 Mike Macfarlane .05
209 Brian McRae .05
210 Jeff Montgomery .05
211 Hipolito Pichardo .05
212 Pedro Astacio .05
213 Brett Butler .05
214 Omar Daal .05
215 Delino DeShields .05
216 Darren Dreifort .05
217 Carlos Hernandez .05
218 Orel Hershiser .05
219 Garey Ingram .05
220 Eric Karros .05
221 Ramon Martinez .05
222 Raul Mondesi .25
223 Jose Offerman .05
224 Mike Piazza 1.50
225 Henry Rodriguez .05
226 Ismael Valdes .05
227 Tim Wallach .05
228 Jeff Cirillo .05
229 Alex Diaz .05
230 Cal Eldred .05
231 Mike Fetters .05
232 Brian Harper .05
233 Ted Higuera .05
234 John Jaha .05
235 Graeme Lloyd .05
236 Jose Mercedes .05
237 Jaime Navarro .05
238 Dave Nilsson .05
239 Jesse Orosco .05
240 Jody Reed .05
241 Jose Valentin .05
242 Greg Vaughn .05
243 Turner Ward .05
244 Rick Aguilera .05
245 Rich Becker .05
246 Jim Deshaies .05
247 Steve Dunn .05
248 Scott Erickson .05
249 Kent Hrbek .05
250 Chuck Knoblauch .05
251 Scott Leius .05
252 David McCarty .05
253 Pat Meares .05
254 Pedro Munoz .05
255 Kirby Puckett .75
256 Carlos Pulido .05
257 Kevin Tapani .05
258 Matt Walbeck .05
259 Dave Winfield .50
260 Moises Alou .10
261 Juan Bell .05
262 Freddie Benavides .05
263 Sean Berry .05
264 Wil Cordero .05
265 Jeff Fassero .05
266 Darrin Fletcher .05
267 Cliff Floyd .05
268 Marquis Grissom .05
269 Gil Heredia .05
270 Ken Hill .05
271 Pedro Martinez .25
272 Mel Rojas .05
273 Larry Walker .25
274 John Wetteland .05
275 Rondell White .10
276 Tim Bogar .05
277 Bobby Bonilla .05
278 Rico Brogna .05
279 Jeromy Burnitz .05
280 John Franco .05
281 Eric Hillman .05
282 Todd Hundley .10
283 Jeff Kent .05
284 Mike Maddux .05
285 Joe Orsulak .05
286 Luis Rivera .05
287 Bret Saberhagen .05
288 David Segui .05
289 Ryan Thompson .05
290 Fernando Vina .05
291 Jose Vizcaino .05
292 Jim Abbott .05
293 Wade Boggs .40
294 Russ Davis .05
295 Mike Gallego .05
296 Xavier Hernandez .05
297 Steve Howe .05
298 Jimmy Key .05
299 Don Mattingly 1.00
300 Terry Mulholland .05
301 Paul O'Neill .05
302 Luis Polonia .05
303 Mike Stanley .05
304 Danny Tartabull .05
305 Randy Velarde .05
306 Bob Wickman .05
307 Bernie Williams .25
308 Mark Acre .05
309 Geronimo Berroa .05
310 Mike Bordick .05
311 Dennis Eckersley .05
312 Rickey Henderson .40
313 Stan Javier .05
314 Miguel Jimenez .05
315 Francisco Matos .05
316 Mark McGwire 2.50
317 Troy Neel .05
318 Steve Ontiveros .05
319 Carlos Reyes .05
320 Ruben Sierra .05
321 Terry Steinbach .05
322 Bob Welch .05
323 Bobby Witt .05
324 Larry Andersen .05
325 Kim Batiste .05
326 Darren Daulton .05
327 Mariano Duncan .05
328 Lenny Dykstra .05
329 Jim Eisenreich .05
330 Danny Jackson .05
331 John Kruk .05
332 Tony Longmire .05
333 Tom Marsh .05
334 Mickey Morandini .05
335 Bobby Munoz .05
336 Todd Pratt .05
337 Tom Quinlan .05
338 Kevin Stocker .05
339 Fernando Valenzuela .05
340 Jay Bell .05
341 Dave Clark .05
342 Steve Cooke .05
343 Carlos Garcia .05
344 Jeff King .05
345 Jon Lieber .05
346 Ravelo Manzanillo .05
347 Al Martin .05
348 Orlando Merced .05
349 Denny Neagle .05
350 Alejandro Pena .05
351 Don Slaught .05
352 Zane Smith .05
353 Andy Van Slyke .05
354 Rick White .05
355 Kevin Young .05
356 Andy Ashby .05
357 Derek Bell .05
358 Andy Benes .05
359 Phil Clark .05
360 Donnie Elliott .05
361 Ricky Gutierrez .05
362 Tony Gwynn .75
363 Trevor Hoffman .05
364 Tim Hyers .05
365 Luis Lopez .05
366 Jose Martinez .05
367 Pedro A. Martinez .05
368 Phil Plantier .05
369 Bip Roberts .05
370 A.J. Sager .05
371 Jeff Tabaka .05
372 Todd Benzinger .05
373 Barry Bonds .75
374 John Burkett .05
375 Mark Carreon .05
376 Royce Clayton .05
377 Pat Gomez .05
378 Erik Johnson .05
379 Darren Lewis .05
380 Kirt Manwaring .05
381 Dave Martinez .05
382 John Patterson .05
383 Mark Portugal .05
384 Darryl Strawberry .05
385 Salomon Torres .05
386 Bill Van Landingham .05
387 Matt Williams .15
388 Rich Amaral .05
389 Bobby Ayala .05
390 Mike Blowers .05
391 Chris Bosio .05
392 Jay Buhner .05
393 Jim Converse .05
394 Tim Davis .05
395 Felix Fermin .05
396 Dave Fleming .05
397 Goose Gossage .05
398 Ken Griffey Jr. 2.50
399 Randy Johnson .50
400 Edgar Martinez .05
401 Tino Martinez .05
402 Alex Rodriguez 2.00
403 Dan Wilson .05
404 Luis Alicea .05
405 Rene Arocha .05
406 Bernard Gilkey .05
407 Gregg Jefferies .05
408 Ray Lankford .05
409 Terry McGriff .05
410 Omar Olivares .05
411 Jose Oquendo .05
412 Vicente Palacios .05
413 Geronimo Pena .05
414 Mike Perez .05
415 Gerald Perry .05
416 Ozzie Smith .75
417 Bob Tewksbury .05
418 Mark Whiten .05
419 Todd Zeile .05
420 Esteban Beltre .05
421 Kevin Brown .10
422 Cris Carpenter .05
423 Will Clark .15
424 Hector Fajardo .05
425 Jeff Frye .05
426 Juan Gonzalez .65
427 Rusty Greer .05
428 Rick Honeycutt .05
429 David Hulse .05
430 Manny Lee .05
431 Junior Ortiz .05
432 Dean Palmer .05
433 Ivan Rodriguez .45
434 Dan Smith .05
435 Roberto Alomar .40
436 Pat Borders .05
437 Scott Brow .05
438 Rob Butler .05
439 Joe Carter .05
440 Tony Castillo .05
441 Domingo Cedeno .05
442 Brad Cornett .05
443 Carlos Delgado .25
444 Alex Gonzalez .10
445 Juan Guzman .05
446 Darren Hall .05
447 Paul Molitor .50
448 John Olerud .05
449 Robert Perez .05
450 Devon White .05

1995 Pacific Gold Crown Die-cut

A die-cut gold holographic foil crown in the background is featured in this chase set. The player's name at bottom is rendered in the same foil. Backs have a dark blue background, a portrait photo and a 1994 season recap.

		MT
Complete Set (20):		65.00
Common Player:		1.00
1	Greg Maddux	8.00
2	Fred McGriff	1.00
3	Rafael Palmeiro	1.50
4	Cal Ripken Jr.	10.00
5	Jose Canseco	2.00

6	Frank Thomas	4.00
7	Albert Belle	2.00
8	Manny Ramirez	3.50
9	Andres Galarraga	1.00
10	Jeff Bagwell	5.00
11	Chan Ho Park	1.50
12	Raul Mondesi	1.25
13	Mike Piazza	9.00
14	Kirby Puckett	5.00
15	Barry Bonds	4.00
16	Ken Griffey Jr.	10.00
17	Alex Rodriguez	10.00
18	Juan Gonzalez	3.50
19	Roberto Alomar	2.50
20	Carlos Delgado	2.00

1995 Pacific Hot Hispanics

Acknowledging its bilingual card license and market niche, this insert set of Latinos Destacados (Hot Hispanics) features top Latin players in the majors. The series logo and a gold-foil holographic player name rise from a row of flames at bottom-front. On the reverse is another player photo, on an inferno background, along with 1994 season highlights and a large team logo.

		MT
Complete Set (36):		50.00
Common Player:		.75
1	Roberto Alomar	3.50
2	Moises Alou	1.25
3	Wilson Alvarez	.75
4	Carlos Baerga	.75
5	Geronimo Berroa	.75
6	Jose Canseco	2.50
7	Hector Carrasco	.75
8	Wil Cordero	.75
9	Carlos Delgado	1.50
10	Damion Easley	.75
11	Tony Eusebio	.75
12	Hector Fajardo	.75
13	Andres Galarraga	.75
14	Carlos Garcia	.75
15	Chris Gomez	.75
16	Alex Gonzalez	1.00
17	Juan Gonzalez	6.00
18	Luis Gonzalez	2.00
19	Felix Jose	.75
20	Javier Lopez	.75
21	Luis Lopez	.75
22	Dennis Martinez	.75
23	Orlando Miller	.75
24	Raul Mondesi	1.25
25	Jose Oliva	.75
26	Rafael Palmeiro	1.25
27	Yorkis Perez	.75
28	Manny Ramirez	6.00
29	Jose Rijo	.75
30	Alex Rodriguez	10.00
31	Ivan Rodriguez	4.00
32	Carlos Rodriguez	.75
33	Sammy Sosa	7.50
34	Tony Tarasco	.75
35	Ismael Valdes	.75
36	Bernie Williams	2.00

1995 Pacific Marquee Prism

Etched gold holographic foil is the background to the action photos in this insert set. Player names at bottom-front are shadowed in team colors. Backs repeat the front photo in miniature version in a box at one side that offers career stats and a highlight. On the other end is a portrait photo on a background of baseballs.

		MT
Complete Set (36):		80.00
Common Player:		1.00
1	Jose Canseco	2.00
2	Gregg Jefferies	1.00
3	Fred McGriff	1.00
4	Joe Carter	1.00
5	Tim Salmon	1.50
6	Wade Boggs	3.00
7	Dave Winfield	3.00
8	Bob Hamelin	1.00
9	Cal Ripken Jr.	10.00
10	Don Mattingly	6.00
11	Juan Gonzalez	4.00
12	Carlos Delgado	1.50
13	Barry Bonds	5.00
14	Albert Belle	2.00
15	Raul Mondesi	1.50
16	Jeff Bagwell	4.00
17	Mike Piazza	7.00
18	Rafael Palmeiro	1.50
19	Frank Thomas	5.00
20	Matt Williams	1.50
21	Ken Griffey Jr.	10.00
22	Will Clark	1.50
23	Bobby Bonilla	1.00
24	Kenny Lofton	1.00
25	Paul Molitor	4.00
26	Kirby Puckett	4.00
27	Dave Justice	1.25
28	Jeff Conine	1.00
29	Bret Boone	1.00
30	Larry Walker	1.50
31	Cecil Fielder	1.00
32	Manny Ramirez	4.00
33	Javier Lopez	1.00
34	Jimmy Key	1.00
35	Andres Galarraga	1.00
36	Tony Gwynn	4.00

1996 Pacific Crown Collection

Pacific's base set for 1996 features 450 gold-foil enhanced cards. Fronts have borderless game-action photos with the issuer's logo in an upper corner and the player's name at bottom center in gold. Horizontal backs have a portrait photo at right, career highlights in both English and Spanish at left, and 1995 stats at top. Cards were sold in 12-card foil packs which could include one of six types of insert cards.

		MT
Complete Set (450):		30.00
Common Player:		.05
Pack (12):		2.00
Wax Box (36):		45.00
1	Steve Avery	.05
2	Ryan Klesko	.05
3	Pedro Borbon	.05
4	Chipper Jones	2.00
5	Kent Mercker	.05
6	Greg Maddux	1.50
7	Greg McMichael	.05
8	Mark Wohlers	.05
9	Fred McGriff	.05
10	John Smoltz	.10
11	Rafael Belliard	.05
12	Mark Lemke	.05
13	Tom Glavine	.10
14	Javier Lopez	.05
15	Jeff Blauser	.05
16	Dave Justice	.25
17	Marquis Grissom	.05
18	Greg Maddux (NL Cy Young)	.75
19	Randy Myers	.05
20	Scott Servais	.05
21	Sammy Sosa	1.50
22	Kevin Foster	.05
23	Jose Hernandez	.05
24	Jim Bullinger	.05
25	Mike Perez	.05
26	Shawon Dunston	.05
27	Rey Sanchez	.05
28	Frank Castillo	.05
29	Jaime Navarro	.05
30	Brian McRae	.05
31	Mark Grace	.20
32	Roberto Rivera	.05
33	Luis Gonzalez	.25
34	Hector Carrasco	.05
35	Bret Boone	.10
36	Thomas Howard	.05
37	Hal Morris	.05
38	John Smiley	.05
39	Jeff Brantley	.05
40	Barry Larkin	.10
41	Mariano Duncan	.05
42	Xavier Hernandez	.05
43	Pete Schourek	.05
44	Reggie Sanders	.05
45	Dave Burba	.05
46	Jeff Branson	.05
47	Mark Portugal	.05
48	Ron Gant	.05
49	Benito Santiago	.05
50	Barry Larkin (NL MVP)	.05
51	Steve Reed	.05
52	Kevin Ritz	.05
53	Dante Bichette	.05
54	Darren Holmes	.05
55	Ellis Burks	.05
56	Walt Weiss	.05
57	Armando Reynoso	.05
58	Vinny Castilla	.05
59	Jason Bates	.05
60	Mike Kingery	.05
61	Bryan Rekar	.05
62	Curtis Leskanic	.05
63	Bret Saberhagen	.05
64	Andres Galarraga	.05
65	Larry Walker	.25
66	Joe Girardi	.05
67	Quilvio Veras	.05
68	Robb Nen	.05
69	Mario Diaz	.05
70	Chuck Carr	.05
71	Alex Arias	.05
72	Pat Rapp	.05
73	Rich Garces	.05
74	Kurt Abbott	.05
75	Andre Dawson	.10
76	Greg Colbrunn	.05
77	John Burkett	.05
78	Terry Pendleton	.05
79	Jesus Tavarez	.05
80	Charles Johnson	.05
81	Yorkis Perez	.05
82	Jeff Conine	.05
83	Gary Sheffield	.35
84	Brian Hunter	.05
85	Derrick May	.05
86	Greg Swindell	.05
87	Derek Bell	.05
88	Dave Veres	.05
89	Jeff Bagwell	.75
90	Todd Jones	.05
91	Orlando Miller	.05
92	Pedro A. Martinez	.05
93	Tony Eusebio	.05
94	Craig Biggio	.10
95	Shane Reynolds	.05
96	James Mouton	.05
97	Doug Drabek	.05
98	Dave Magadan	.05
99	Ricky Gutierrez	.05
100	Hideo Nomo	.75
101	Delino DeShields	.05
102	Tom Candiotti	.05
103	Mike Piazza	2.00
104	Ramon Martinez	.05
105	Pedro Astacio	.05
106	Chad Fonville	.05
107	Raul Mondesi	.20
108	Ismael Valdes	.05
109	Jose Offerman	.05
110	Todd Worrell	.05
111	Eric Karros	.05
112	Brett Butler	.05
113	Juan Castro	.05
114	Roberto Kelly	.05
115	Omar Daal	.05
116	Antonio Osuna	.05
117	Hideo Nomo (NL Rookie of Year)	.50
118	Mike Lansing	.05
119	Mel Rojas	.05
120	Sean Berry	.05
121	David Segui	.05
122	Tavo Alvarez	.05
123	Pedro Martinez	.25
124	*F.P. Santangelo*	.05
125	Rondell White	.10
126	Cliff Floyd	.05
127	Henry Rodriguez	.05
128	Tony Tarasco	.05
129	Yamil Benitez	.05
130	Carlos Perez	.05
131	Wil Cordero	.05
132	Jeff Fassero	.05
133	Moises Alou	.10
134	John Franco	.05
135	Rico Brogna	.05
136	Dave Mlicki	.05
137	Bill Pulsipher	.05
138	Jose Vizcaino	.05
139	Carl Everett	.10
140	Edgardo Alfonzo	.10
141	Bobby Jones	.05
142	Alberto Castillo	.05
143	Joe Orsulak	.05
144	Jeff Kent	.05
145	Ryan Thompson	.05
146	Jason Isringhausen	.10
147	Todd Hundley	.05
148	Alex Ochoa	.05
149	Charlie Hayes	.05
150	Michael Mimbs	.05
151	Darren Daulton	.05
152	Toby Borland	.05
153	Andy Van Slyke	.05
154	Mickey Morandini	.05
155	Sid Fernandez	.05

#	Player	MT
156	Tom Marsh	.05
157	Kevin Stocker	.05
158	Paul Quantrill	.05
159	Gregg Jefferies	.05
160	Ricky Bottalico	.05
161	Lenny Dykstra	.05
162	Mark Whiten	.05
163	Tyler Green	.05
164	Jim Eisenreich	.05
165	Heathcliff Slocumb	.05
166	Esteban Loaiza	.05
167	Rich Aude	.05
168	Jason Christiansen	.05
169	Ramon Morel	.05
170	Orlando Merced	.05
171	Paul Wagner	.05
172	Jeff King	.05
173	Jay Bell	.05
174	Jacob Brumfield	.05
175	Nelson Liriano	.05
176	Dan Miceli	.05
177	Carlos Garcia	.05
178	Denny Neagle	.05
179	Angelo Encarnacion	.05
180	Al Martin	.05
181	Midre Cummings	.05
182	Eddie Williams	.05
183	Roberto Petagine	.05
184	Tony Gwynn	.75
185	Andy Ashby	.05
186	Melvin Nieves	.05
187	Phil Clark	.05
188	Brad Ausmus	.05
189	Bip Roberts	.05
190	Fernando Valenzuela	.05
191	Marc Newfield	.05
192	Steve Finley	.05
193	Trevor Hoffman	.05
194	Andujar Cedeno	.05
195	Jody Reed	.05
196	Ken Caminiti	.05
197	Joey Hamilton	.05
198	Tony Gwynn (NL Batting Champ)	.30
199	Shawn Barton	.05
200	Deion Sanders	.10
201	Rikkert Faneyte	.05
202	Barry Bonds	1.00
203	Matt Williams	.15
204	Jose Bautista	.05
205	Mark Leiter	.05
206	Mark Carreon	.05
207	Robby Thompson	.05
208	Terry Mulholland	.05
209	Rod Beck	.05
210	Royce Clayton	.05
211	J.R. Phillips	.05
212	Kirt Manwaring	.05
213	Glenallen Hill	.05
214	William Van Landingham	.05
215	Scott Cooper	.05
216	Bernard Gilkey	.05
217	Allen Watson	.05
218	Donovan Osborne	.05
219	Ray Lankford	.05
220	Tony Fossas	.05
221	Tom Pagnozzi	.05
222	John Mabry	.05
223	Tripp Cromer	.05
224	Mark Petkovsek	.05
225	Mike Morgan	.05
226	Ozzie Smith	.75
227	Tom Henke	.05
228	Jose Oquendo	.05
229	Brian Jordan	.05
230	Cal Ripken Jr.	2.50
231	Scott Erickson	.05
232	Harold Baines	.05
233	Jeff Manto	.05
234	Jesse Orosco	.05
235	Jeffrey Hammonds	.05
236	Brady Anderson	.05
237	Manny Alexander	.05
238	Chris Hoiles	.05
239	Rafael Palmeiro	.15
240	Ben McDonald	.05
241	Curtis Goodwin	.05
242	Bobby Bonilla	.05
243	Mike Mussina	.50
244	Kevin Brown	.10
245	Armando Benitez	.05
246	Jose Canseco	.35
247	Erik Hanson	.05
248	Mo Vaughn	.45
249	Tim Naehring	.05
250	Vaughn Eshelman	.05
251	Mike Greenwell	.05
252	Troy O'Leary	.05
253	Tim Wakefield	.05
254	Dwayne Hosey	.05
255	John Valentin	.05
256	Rick Aguilera	.05
257	Mike MacFarlane	.05
258	Roger Clemens	.75
259	Luis Alicea	.05
260	Mo Vaughn (AL MVP)	.20
261	Mark Langston	.05
262	Jim Edmonds	.10
263	Rod Correia	.05
264	Tim Salmon	.15
265	J.T. Snow	.05
266	Orlando Palmeiro	.05
267	Jorge Fabregas	.05
268	Jim Abbott	.05
269	Eduardo Perez	.05
270	Lee Smith	.05
271	Gary DiSarcina	.05
272	Damion Easley	.05
273	Tony Phillips	.05
274	Garret Anderson	.05
275	Chuck Finley	.05
276	Chili Davis	.05
277	Lance Johnson	.05
278	Alex Fernandez	.05
279	Robin Ventura	.05
280	Chris Snopek	.05
281	Brian Keyser	.05
282	Lyle Mouton	.05
283	*Luis Andujar*	.05
284	Tim Raines	.05
285	Larry Thomas	.05
286	Ozzie Guillen	.05
287	Frank Thomas	1.50
288	Roberto Hernandez	.05
289	Dave Martinez	.05
290	Ray Durham	.05
291	Ron Karkovice	.05
292	Wilson Alvarez	.05
293	Omar Vizquel	.05
294	Eddie Murray	.40
295	Sandy Alomar	.05
296	Orel Hershiser	.05
297	Jose Mesa	.05
298	Julian Tavarez	.05
299	Dennis Martinez	.05
300	Carlos Baerga	.05
301	Manny Ramirez	.75
302	Jim Thome	.05
303	Kenny Lofton	.05
304	Tony Pena	.05
305	Alvaro Espinoza	.05
306	Paul Sorrento	.05
307	Albert Belle	.25
308	Danny Bautista	.05
309	Chris Gomez	.05
310	Jose Lima	.05
311	Phil Nevin	.05
312	Alan Trammell	.05
313	Chad Curtis	.05
314	John Flaherty	.05
315	Travis Fryman	.05
316	Todd Steverson	.05
317	Brian Bohanon	.05
318	Lou Whitaker	.05
319	Bobby Higginson	.10
320	Steve Rodriguez	.05
321	Cecil Fielder	.05
322	Felipe Lira	.05
323	Juan Samuel	.05
324	Bob Hamelin	.05
325	Tom Goodwin	.05
326	Johnny Damon	.10
327	Hipolito Pichardo	.05
328	Dilson Torres	.05
329	Kevin Appier	.05
330	Mark Gubicza	.05
331	Jon Nunnally	.05
332	Gary Gaetti	.05
333	Brent Mayne	.05
334	Brent Cookson	.05
335	Tom Gordon	.05
336	Wally Joyner	.05
337	Greg Gagne	.05
338	Fernando Vina	.05
339	Joe Oliver	.05
340	John Jaha	.05
341	Jeff Cirillo	.05
342	Pat Listach	.05
343	Dave Nilsson	.05
344	Steve Sparks	.05
345	Ricky Bones	.05
346	David Hulse	.05
347	Scott Karl	.05
348	Darryl Hamilton	.05
349	B.J. Surhoff	.05
350	Angel Miranda	.05
351	Sid Roberson	.05
352	Matt Mieske	.05
353	*Jose Valentin*	.05
354	*Matt Lawton*	.25
355	Eddie Guardado	.05
356	Brad Radke	.05
357	Pedro Munoz	.05
358	Scott Stahoviak	.05
359	Erik Schullstrom	.05
360	Pat Meares	.05
361	Marty Cordova	.05
362	Scott Leius	.05
363	Matt Walbeck	.05
364	Rich Becker	.05
365	Kirby Puckett	.75
366	Oscar Munoz	.05
367	Chuck Knoblauch	.05
368	Marty Cordova (AL Rookie of Year)	.05
369	Bernie Williams	.20
370	Mike Stanley	.05
371	Andy Pettitte	.30
372	Jack McDowell	.05
373	Sterling Hitchcock	.05
374	David Cone	.05
375	Randy Velarde	.05
376	Don Mattingly	1.00
377	Melido Perez	.05
378	Wade Boggs	.30
379	Ruben Sierra	.05
380	Tony Fernandez	.05
381	John Wetteland	.05
382	Mariano Rivera	.15
383	Derek Jeter	2.00
384	Paul O'Neill	.05
385	Mark McGwire	2.50
386	Scott Brosius	.05
387	Don Wengert	.05
388	Terry Steinbach	.05
389	Brent Gates	.05
390	Craig Paquette	.05
391	Mike Bordick	.05
392	Ariel Prieto	.05
393	Dennis Eckersley	.05
394	Carlos Reyes	.05
395	Todd Stottlemyre	.05
396	Rickey Henderson	.40
397	Geronimo Berroa	.05
398	Steve Ontiveros	.05
399	Mike Gallego	.05
400	Stan Javier	.05
401	Randy Johnson	.45
402	Norm Charlton	.05
403	Mike Blowers	.05
404	Tino Martinez	.05
405	Dan Wilson	.05
406	Andy Benes	.05
407	Alex Diaz	.05
408	Edgar Martinez	.05
409	Chris Bosio	.05
410	Ken Griffey Jr.	2.50
411	Luis Sojo	.05
412	Bob Wolcott	.05
413	Vince Coleman	.05
414	Rich Amaral	.05
415	Jay Buhner	.05
416	Alex Rodriguez	2.50
417	Joey Cora	.05
418	Randy Johnson (AL Cy Young)	.20
419	Edgar Martinez (AL Batting Champ)	.05
420	Ivan Rodriguez	.40
421	Mark McLemore	.05
422	Mickey Tettleton	.05
423	Juan Gonzalez	.75
424	Will Clark	.15
425	Kevin Gross	.05
426	Dean Palmer	.05
427	Kenny Rogers	.05
428	Bob Tewksbury	.05
429	Benji Gil	.05
430	Jeff Russell	.05
431	Rusty Greer	.05
432	Roger Pavlik	.05
433	Esteban Beltre	.05
434	Otis Nixon	.05
435	Paul Molitor	.60
436	Carlos Delgado	.25
437	Ed Sprague	.05
438	Juan Guzman	.05
439	Domingo Cedeno	.05
440	Pat Hentgen	.05
441	Tomas Perez	.05
442	John Olerud	.05
443	Shawn Green	.20
444	Al Leiter	.05
445	Joe Carter	.05
446	Robert Perez	.05
447	Devon White	.05
448	Tony Castillo	.05
449	Alex Gonzalez	.10
450	Roberto Alomar	.60
450p	Roberto Alomar (unmarked promo card, "Games: 128" on back)	3.00

1996 Pacific Crown Cramer's Choice

One of the most unusually shaped baseball cards of all time is the Cramer's Choice insert set from the 1996 Pacific Crown Collection. The set features the 10 best players as chosen by Pacific founder and president Mike Cramer. Cards are in a die-cut pyramidal design 3-1/2" tall and 2-1/2" at the base. The player picture on front is set against a silver-foil background, while the player name and other information is in gold foil on a faux marble base at bottom; the effect is a simulation of a trophy. Backs repeat the marbled background and have a bi-lingual justification from Cramer concerning his choice of the player as one of the 10 best. Average insertion rate is one card per case (720 packs). Cards are numbered with a "CC" prefix.

		MT
Complete Set (10):		225.00
Common Player:		10.00
1	Roberto Alomar	15.00
2	Wade Boggs	15.00
3	Cal Ripken Jr.	50.00
4	Greg Maddux	30.00
5	Frank Thomas	25.00
6	Tony Gwynn	25.00
7	Mike Piazza	40.00
8	Ken Griffey Jr.	50.00
9	Manny Ramirez	20.00
10	Edgar Martinez	10.00

1996 Pacific Crown Estrellas Latinas

Three dozen of the best contemporary Latino ballplayers are honored in this chase set. Cards feature action photos silhouetted on a black background shot through with gold-foil streaks and stars. The player name, set and insert set logos are in gold at left. Backs have a player portrait photo and English/Spanish career summary. The Latino Stars insert cards are inserted at an average rate of one per nine packs; about four per foil box. Cards are numbered with an "EL" prefix.

		MT
Complete Set (36):		16.00
Common Player:		.25
1	Roberto Alomar	1.00
2	Moises Alou	.30
3	Carlos Baerga	.25
4	Geronimo Berroa	.25
5	Ricky Bones	.25
6	Bobby Bonilla	.25
7	Jose Canseco	.50
8	Vinny Castilla	.25
9	Pedro Martinez	.50
10	John Valentin	.25
11	Andres Galarraga	.25
12	Juan Gonzalez	1.75
13	Ozzie Guillen	.25
14	Esteban Loaiza	.25
15	Javier Lopez	.25
16	Dennis Martinez	.25
17	Edgar Martinez	.25
18	Tino Martinez	.25
19	Orlando Merced	.25
20	Jose Mesa	.25
21	Raul Mondesi	.35
22	Jaime Navarro	.25
23	Rafael Palmeiro	.35
24	Carlos Perez	.25
25	Manny Ramirez	1.75
26	Alex Rodriguez	3.50
27	Ivan Rodriguez	1.50
28	David Segui	.25
29	Ruben Sierra	.25
30	Sammy Sosa	2.50
31	Julian Tavarez	.25
32	Ismael Valdes	.25
33	Fernando Valenzuela	.25
34	Quilvio Veras	.25
35	Omar Vizquel	.25
36	Bernie Williams	.50

1996 Pacific Crown Gold Crown Die-Cuts

One of Pacific's most popular inserts of the previous year returns in 1996. The Gold Crown die-cuts have the top of the card cut away to form a gold-foil crown design with an action photo below. The player's name is also in gold foil. Backs repeat the gold crown design at top, have a portrait photo at lower-right and a few words about the player, in both English and Spanish. Insertion rate was advertised as one per 37 packs, on average. Cards are numbered with a "DC" prefix.

		MT
Complete Set (36):		60.00
Common Player:		.75
1	Roberto Alomar	1.50
2	Will Clark	1.25
3	Johnny Damon	1.25
4	Don Mattingly	4.00
5	Edgar Martinez	.75
6	Manny Ramirez	2.00
7	Mike Piazza	5.00
8	Quilvio Veras	.75
9	Rickey Henderson	1.50
10	Jeff Bagwell	2.00
11	Andres Galarraga	.75
12	Tim Salmon	1.25
13	Ken Griffey Jr.	6.50
14	Sammy Sosa	5.00
15	Cal Ripken Jr.	6.50
16	Raul Mondesi	1.25
17	Jose Canseco	1.50
18	Frank Thomas	3.00
19	Hideo Nomo	2.00
20	Wade Boggs	2.00
21	Reggie Sanders	.75
22	Carlos Baerga	.75
23	Mo Vaughn	1.50
24	Ivan Rodriguez	1.50
25	Kirby Puckett	2.00
26	Albert Belle	1.00
27	Vinny Castilla	.75
28	Greg Maddux	4.00
29	Dante Bichette	.75
30	Deion Sanders	1.00
31	Chipper Jones	4.00
32	Cecil Fielder	.75
33	Randy Johnson	1.50
34	Mark McGwire	6.50
35	Tony Gwynn	3.00
36	Barry Bonds	2.00

1996 Pacific Crown Hometown of the Players

The hometown roots of 20 top players are examined in this chase set. Fronts have action photos with large areas of the background replaced with textured gold foil, including solid and outline versions of the player's name. Backs have a portrait photo, a representation of the player's native flag and a few words about his hometown. Card numbers have an "HP" prefix and are inserted at an average rate of one per 18 packs; about two per box.

		MT
Complete Set (20):		35.00
Common Player:		1.00
1	Mike Piazza	4.00
2	Greg Maddux	3.00
3	Tony Gwynn	2.00
4	Carlos Baerga	1.00
5	Don Mattingly	3.50
6	Cal Ripken Jr.	5.00
7	Chipper Jones	4.00
8	Andres Galarraga	1.00
9	Manny Ramirez	1.75
10	Roberto Alomar	1.50
11	Ken Griffey Jr.	5.00
12	Jose Canseco	1.50
13	Frank Thomas	2.00
14	Vinny Castilla	1.00
15	Roberto Kelly	1.00
16	Dennis Martinez	1.00
17	Kirby Puckett	2.00
18	Raul Mondesi	1.25
19	Hideo Nomo	1.75
20	Edgar Martinez	1.00

1996 Pacific Crown Milestones

A textured metallic blue-foil background is featured in this insert set. Behind the player action photo is a spider's web design with flying baseballs, team logo and a number representing the milestone. The player's name is in purple foil, outlined in white, vertically at right. Backs have a portrait photo and bi-lingual description of the milestone. Average insertion rate for this insert series is one per 37 packs. Cards are numbered with a "M" prefix.

		MT
Complete Set (10):		12.00
Common Player:		.50
1	Albert Belle	1.00
2	Don Mattingly	2.00
3	Tony Gwynn	1.75
4	Jose Canseco	1.00
5	Marty Cordova	.50
6	Wade Boggs	1.00
7	Greg Maddux	2.00
8	Eddie Murray	1.00
9	Ken Griffey Jr.	3.00
10	Cal Ripken Jr.	3.00

1996 Pacific Crown October Moments

Post-season baseball has never been better represented on a card than in Pacific's "October Moments" chase set. Color action photos are set again a background of a stadium decked in the traditional Fall Classic bunting, all rendered in metallic copper foil. At bottom is a textured silver strip with the player name in copper and a swirl of fallen leaves. Backs have a repeat of the leaves and bunting themes with a player portrait at center and English/Spanish description of his October heroics. These cards are found at an average rate of once per 37 packs. Cards are numbered with an "OM" prefix.

		MT
Complete Set (20):		45.00
Common Player:		1.00
1	Carlos Baerga	1.00
2	Albert Belle	2.00
3	Dante Bichette	1.00
4	Jose Canseco	1.50
5	Tom Glavine	1.25
6	Ken Griffey Jr.	8.00
7	Randy Johnson	3.50
8	Chipper Jones	7.00
9	Dave Justice	1.25
10	Ryan Klesko	1.00
11	Kenny Lofton	1.00
12	Javier Lopez	1.00
13	Greg Maddux	6.00
14	Edgar Martinez	1.00
15	Don Mattingly	6.00
16	Hideo Nomo	3.50
17	Mike Piazza	7.00
18	Manny Ramirez	4.00
19	Reggie Sanders	1.00
20	Jim Thome	1.00

1996 Pacific Prism

Only the best in baseball make the cut for the Prism checklist. Sold in one-card foil packs the cards feature action photos set against an etched silver-foil background highlighted by slashes approximating team colors. Backs are conventionally printed in a horizontal format with a player portrait photo at left center on a purple background. A short 1995 season recap is feature in both English and Spanish. Card numbers are prefixed with a "P".

		MT
Complete Set (144):		150.00
Common Player:		1.00
Unlisted Stars: 2.00		
Golds:		2X
Pack (2):		1.50
Wax Box (36):		40.00
1	Tom Glavine	1.50
2	Chipper Jones	10.00
3	David Justice	1.50
4	Ryan Klesko	1.00
5	Javier Lopez	1.00
6	Greg Maddux	7.00
7	Fred McGriff	1.00
8	Frank Castillo	1.00
9	Luis Gonzalez	2.50
10	Mark Grace	1.50
11	Brian McRae	1.00
12	Jaime Navarro	1.00
13	Sammy Sosa	9.00
14	Bret Boone	1.00
15	Ron Gant	1.00
16	Barry Larkin	1.50
17	Reggie Sanders	1.00
18	Benito Santiago	1.00
19	Dante Bichette	1.00
20	Vinny Castilla	1.00
21	Andres Galarraga	1.00
22	Bryan Rekar	1.00
23	Roberto Alomar	3.00
23p	Roberto Alomar ("Azulejos" rather than "Los Azulajos" on back, unmarked promo card)	4.00
24	Jeff Conine	1.00
25	Andre Dawson	1.00
26	Charles Johnson	1.00
27	Gary Sheffield	2.00
28	Quilvio Veras	1.00
29	Jeff Bagwell	4.00
30	Derek Bell	1.00
31	Craig Biggio	1.50
32	Tony Eusebio	1.00
33	Karim Garcia	1.00
34	Eric Karros	1.00
35	Ramon Martinez	1.00
36	Raul Mondesi	1.50
37	Hideo Nomo	3.00
38	Mike Piazza	10.00
39	Ismael Valdes	1.00
40	Moises Alou	1.00
41	Wil Cordero	1.00
42	Pedro Martinez	4.00
43	Mel Rojas	1.00
44	David Segui	1.00
45	Edgardo Alfonzo	1.00
46	Rico Brogna	1.00
47	John Franco	1.00
48	Jason Isringhausen	1.00
49	Jose Vizcaino	1.00
50	Ricky Bottalico	1.00
51	Darren Daulton	1.00
52	Lenny Dykstra	1.00
53	Tyler Green	1.00
54	Gregg Jefferies	1.00
55	Jay Bell	1.00
56	Jason Christiansen	1.00
57	Carlos Garcia	1.00
58	Esteban Loaiza	1.00
59	Orlando Merced	1.00
60	Andujar Cedeno	1.00
61	Tony Gwynn	5.00
62	Melvin Nieves	1.00
63	Phil Plantier	1.00
64	Fernando Valenzuela	1.00
65	Barry Bonds	6.00
66	J.R. Phillips	1.00
67	Deion Sanders	1.50
68	Matt Williams	1.50
69	Bernard Gilkey	1.00
70	Tom Henke	1.00
71	Brian Jordan	1.00
72	Ozzie Smith	4.00
73	Manny Alexander	1.00
74	Bobby Bonilla	1.00
75	Mike Mussina	3.00
76	Rafael Palmeiro	2.00
77	Cal Ripken Jr.	12.00
78	Jose Canseco	2.50
79	Roger Clemens	5.00
80	John Valentin	1.00
81	Mo Vaughn	2.50
82	Tim Wakefield	1.00
83	Garret Anderson	1.00
84	Damion Easley	1.00
85	Jim Edmonds	1.50
86	Tim Salmon	1.50
87	Wilson Alvarez	1.00
88	Alex Fernandez	1.00
89	Ozzie Guillen	1.00
90	Roberto Hernandez	1.00
91	Frank Thomas	5.00
92	Robin Ventura	1.00
93	Carlos Baerga	1.00
94	Albert Belle	2.00
95	Kenny Lofton	1.00
96	Dennis Martinez	1.00
97	Eddie Murray	3.00
98	Manny Ramirez	4.00
99	Omar Vizquel	1.00
100	Chad Curtis	1.00
101	Cecil Fielder	1.00
102	Felipe Lira	1.00
103	Alan Trammell	1.00
104	Kevin Appier	1.00
105	Johnny Damon	1.00
106	Gary Gaetti	1.00
107	Wally Joyner	1.00
108	Ricky Bones	1.00
109	John Jaha	1.00
110	B.J. Surhoff	1.00
111	Jose Valentin	1.00
112	Fernando Vina	1.00
113	Marty Cordova	1.00
114	Chuck Knoblauch	1.00
115	Scott Leius	1.00
116	Pedro Munoz	1.00
117	Kirby Puckett	6.00
118	Wade Boggs	3.00
119	Don Mattingly	8.00
120	Jack McDowell	1.00
121	Paul O'Neill	1.00
122	Ruben Rivera	1.00
123	Bernie Williams	2.00
124	Geronimo Berroa	1.00
125	Rickey Henderson	3.00
126	Mark McGwire	12.00
127	Terry Steinbach	1.00
128	Danny Tartabull	1.00
129	Jay Buhner	1.00
130	Joey Cora	1.00
131	Ken Griffey Jr.	12.00
132	Randy Johnson	4.00
133	Edgar Martinez	1.00
134	Tino Martinez	1.00
135	Will Clark	2.00
136	Juan Gonzalez	4.00
137	Dean Palmer	1.00
138	Ivan Rodriguez	3.00
139	Mickey Tettleton	1.00
140	Larry Walker	1.50
141	Joe Carter	1.00
142	Carlos Delgado	3.00
143	Alex Gonzalez	1.00
144	Paul Molitor	3.00

1996 Pacific Prism Gold

Exactly paralleling the cards in the regular Prism set, this chase card insert replaces the silver foil on front with gold foil. All else remains the same. Stated odds of picking a Gold Prism parallel card are about one per 18 packs, on average (two per box).

	MT
Complete Set (144):	300.00
Common Player:	2.00
Stars:	2X

(See 1996 Pacific Prism for checklist and base card values.)

1996 Pacific Prism Fence Busters

Home run heroes are featured in this insert set. The player's big swing is photographed in the foreground while a baseball flies out of the etched metallic foil stadium background. The player's name is in blue foil. Backs have another player photo and details of his 1995 season home run output, in both English and Spanish. Cards are numbered with an FB prefix. Stated odds of finding a Fence Busters insert are one per 37 packs, on average.

		MT
Complete Set (19):		75.00
Common Player:		2.00
1	Albert Belle	2.50
2	Dante Bichette	2.00
3	Barry Bonds	5.00
4	Jay Buhner	2.00
5	Jose Canseco	3.00
6	Ken Griffey Jr.	12.00
7	Chipper Jones	9.00
8	David Justice	2.50
9	Eric Karros	2.00
10	Edgar Martinez	2.00
11	Mark McGwire	12.00
12	Eddie Murray	3.00
13	Mike Piazza	9.00
14	Kirby Puckett	4.50
15	Cal Ripken Jr.	12.00
16	Tim Salmon	2.50
17	Sammy Sosa	7.00
18	Frank Thomas	4.50
19	Mo Vaughn	2.50

1996 Pacific Prism Flame Throwers

Burning baseballs are the background for the game's best pitchers in this die-cut insert set. The gold-foil highlighted flames have their tails die-cut at the card's left end. The featured pitcher is shown in action in the foreground. The name at bottom and company logo are in gold foil. Backs are conventionally printed with another action photo and 1995 highlight printed in both English and Spanish. Card numbers carry an FT prefix. Stated odds of finding a Flame Throwers card are one in 73 boxes, about every two boxes.

		MT
Complete Set (10):		35.00
Common Player:		2.00
1	Roger Clemens	9.00
2	David Cone	2.00
3	Tom Glavine	3.00
4	Randy Johnson	6.00
5	Greg Maddux	10.00
6	Ramon Martinez	2.00
7	Jose Mesa	2.00
8	Mike Mussina	5.00
9	Hideo Nomo	6.00
10	Jose Rijo	2.00

1996 Pacific Prism Red Hot Stars

Bright red metallic foil provides the background for these inserts. Color action photos are in the foreground, while player name and multiple team logos are worked into the background. Backs are conventionally printed with another player photo and a few words - in both English and Spanish - about the player's 1995 season. Card numbers have an RH prefix. Stated odds of finding a Red Hot Stars insert are one per 37 packs.

		MT
Complete Set (19):		70.00
Common Player:		1.00
1	Roberto Alomar	2.50
2	Jeff Bagwell	5.00
3	Albert Belle	3.00
4	Wade Boggs	2.00
5	Barry Bonds	5.00
6	Jose Canseco	2.00
7	Ken Griffey Jr.	10.00
8	Tony Gwynn	5.00
9	Randy Johnson	2.50
10	Chipper Jones	7.50
11	Greg Maddux	6.00
12	Edgar Martinez	1.00
13	Don Mattingly	6.50
14	Mike Piazza	7.50
15	Kirby Puckett	5.00
16	Manny Ramirez	4.00
17	Cal Ripken Jr.	10.00
18	Tim Salmon	2.00
19	Frank Thomas	5.00

1997 Pacific Crown

The 450-card, regular-sized set was available in 12-card packs. The card fronts feature the player's name in gold foil along the left border with the team logo in the bottom right corner. The card backs feature a head shot of the player in the lower left quadrant with a short highlight in both Spanish and English. Inserted in packs were: Card-Supials, Cramer's Choice, Latinos Of The Major Leagues, Fireworks Die-Cuts, Gold Crown Die-Cuts and Triple Crown Die-Cuts. A parallel silver version (67 sets) was available.

		MT
Complete Set (450):		30.00
Common Player:		.05
Pack (12):		1.50
Wax Box (36):		35.00
1	Garret Anderson	.05
2	George Arias	.05
3	Chili Davis	.05
4	Gary DiSarcina	.05
5	Jim Edmonds	.10
6	Darin Erstad	.75
7	Jorge Fabregas	.05
8	Chuck Finley	.05
9	Rex Hudler	.05
10	Mark Langston	.05
11	Orlando Palmeiro	.05
12	Troy Percival	.05
13	Tim Salmon	.15
14	J.T. Snow	.05
15	Randy Velarde	.05
16	Manny Alexander	.05
17	Roberto Alomar	.50
18	Brady Anderson	.05
19	Armando Benitez	.05
20	Bobby Bonilla	.05
21	Rocky Coppinger	.05
22	Scott Erickson	.05
23	Jeffrey Hammonds	.05
24	Chris Hoiles	.05
25	Eddie Murray	.35
26	Mike Mussina	.60
27	Randy Myers	.05
28	Rafael Palmeiro	.20
29	Cal Ripken Jr.	2.50
30	B.J. Surhoff	.05
31	Tony Tarasco	.05
32	Esteban Beltre	.05
33	Darren Bragg	.05
34	Jose Canseco	.40
35	Roger Clemens	1.00
36	Wil Cordero	.05
37	Alex Delgado	.05
38	Jeff Frye	.05
39	Nomar Garciaparra	1.50
40	Tom Gordon	.05
41	Mike Greenwell	.05
42	Reggie Jefferson	.05
43	Tim Naehring	.05
44	Troy O'Leary	.05
45	Heathcliff Slocumb	.05
46	Lee Tinsley	.05
47	John Valentin	.05
48	Mo Vaughn	.30
49	Wilson Alvarez	.05
50	Harold Baines	.05
51	Ray Durham	.05
52	Alex Fernandez	.05
53	Ozzie Guillen	.05
54	Roberto Hernandez	.05
55	Ron Karkovice	.05
56	Darren Lewis	.05
57	Norberto Martin	.05
58	Dave Martinez	.05
59	Lyle Mouton	.05
60	Jose Munoz	.05
61	Tony Phillips	.05
62	Rich Sauveur	.05
63	Danny Tartabull	.05
64	Frank Thomas	1.00
65	Robin Ventura	.05
66	Sandy Alomar Jr.	.05
67	Albert Belle	.15
68	Julio Franco	.05
69	*Brian Giles*	1.50
70	Danny Graves	.05
71	Orel Hershiser	.05
72	Jeff Kent	.05
73	Kenny Lofton	.05
74	Dennis Martinez	.05
75	Jack McDowell	.05
76	Jose Mesa	.05
77	Charles Nagy	.05
78	Manny Ramirez	.75
79	Julian Tavarez	.05
80	Jim Thome	.05
81	Jose Vizcaino	.05
82	Omar Vizquel	.05
83	Brad Ausmus	.05
84	Kimera Bartee	.05
85	Raul Casanova	.05
86	Tony Clark	.05
87	Travis Fryman	.05
88	Bobby Higginson	.10
89	Mark Lewis	.05
90	Jose Lima	.05
91	Felipe Lira	.05
92	Phil Nevin	.05
93	Melvin Nieves	.05
94	Curtis Pride	.05
95	Ruben Sierra	.05
96	Alan Trammell	.05
97	Kevin Appier	.05
98	Tim Belcher	.05
99	Johnny Damon	.15
100	Tom Goodwin	.05
101	Bob Hamelin	.05
102	David Howard	.05
103	Jason Jacome	.05
104	Keith Lockhart	.05
105	Mike Macfarlane	.05
106	Jeff Montgomery	.05
107	Jose Offerman	.05
108	Hipolito Pichardo	.05
109	Joe Randa	.05
110	Bip Roberts	.05
111	Chris Stynes	.05
112	Mike Sweeney	.05
113	Joe Vitiello	.05
114	Jeromy Burnitz	.05
115	Chuck Carr	.05
116	Jeff Cirillo	.05
117	Mike Fetters	.05
118	David Hulse	.05
119	John Jaha	.05
120	Scott Karl	.05
121	Jesse Levis	.05
122	Mark Loretta	.05
123	Mike Matheny	.05
124	Ben McDonald	.05
125	Matt Mieske	.05
126	Angel Miranda	.05
127	Dave Nilsson	.05
128	Jose Valentin	.05
129	Fernando Vina	.05
130	Ron Villone	.05
131	Gerald Williams	.05
132	Rick Aguilera	.05
133	Rich Becker	.05
134	Ron Coomer	.05
135	Marty Cordova	.05
136	Eddie Guardado	.05
137	Denny Hocking	.05
138	Roberto Kelly	.05
139	Chuck Knoblauch	.05
140	Matt Lawton	.05
141	Pat Meares	.05
142	Paul Molitor	.50
143	Greg Myers	.05
144	Jeff Reboulet	.05
145	Scott Stahoviak	.05
146	Todd Walker	.10
147	Wade Boggs	.25
148	David Cone	.05
149	Mariano Duncan	.05
150	Cecil Fielder	.05
151	Dwight Gooden	.05
152	Derek Jeter	2.00
153	Jim Leyritz	.05
154	Tino Martinez	.05
155	Paul O'Neill	.05
156	Andy Pettitte	.15
157	Tim Raines	.05
158	Mariano Rivera	.15
159	Ruben Rivera	.05
160	Kenny Rogers	.05
161	Darryl Strawberry	.05
162	John Wetteland	.05
163	Bernie Williams	.30
164	Tony Batista	.05
165	Geronimo Berroa	.05
166	Mike Bordick	.05
167	Scott Brosius	.05
168	Brent Gates	.05
169	Jason Giambi	.30
170	Jose Herrera	.05
171	Brian Lesher	.05
172	*Damon Mashore*	.05
173	Mark McGwire	2.50
174	Ariel Prieto	.05
175	Carlos Reyes	.05
176	Matt Stairs	.05
177	Terry Steinbach	.05
178	John Wasdin	.05
179	Ernie Young	.05
180	Rich Amaral	.05
181	Bobby Ayala	.05
182	Jay Buhner	.05
183	Rafael Carmona	.05
184	Norm Charlton	.05
185	Joey Cora	.05
186	Ken Griffey Jr.	2.50
187	Sterling Hitchcock	.05
188	Dave Hollins	.05
189	Randy Johnson	.75
190	Edgar Martinez	.05
191	Jamie Moyer	.05
192	Alex Rodriguez	2.50
193	Paul Sorrento	.05
194	Salomon Torres	.05
195	Bob Wells	.05
196	Dan Wilson	.05
197	Will Clark	.15
198	Kevin Elster	.05
199	Rene Gonzales	.05
200	Juan Gonzalez	.75
201	Rusty Greer	.05
202	Darryl Hamilton	.05
203	Mike Henneman	.05
204	Ken Hill	.05
205	Mark McLemore	.05
206	Darren Oliver	.05
207	Dean Palmer	.05
208	Roger Pavlik	.05
209	Ivan Rodriguez	.60
210	Kurt Stillwell	.05
211	Mickey Tettleton	.05
212	Bobby Witt	.05
213	Tilson Brito	.05
214	Jacob Brumfield	.05
215	Miguel Cairo	.05
216	Joe Carter	.05
217	Felipe Crespo	.05
218	Carlos Delgado	.35
219	Alex Gonzalez	.10
220	Shawn Green	.20
221	Juan Guzman	.05
222	Pat Hentgen	.05
223	Charlie O'Brien	.05
224	John Olerud	.05
225	Robert Perez	.05
226	Tomas Perez	.05
227	Juan Samuel	.05
228	Ed Sprague	.05
229	Mike Timlin	.05
230	Rafael Belliard	.05
231	Jermaine Dye	.05
232	Tom Glavine	.10
233	Marquis Grissom	.05
234	Andruw Jones	.75
235	Chipper Jones	1.50
236	David Justice	.20
237	Ryan Klesko	.05
238	Mark Lemke	.05
239	Javier Lopez	.05
240	Greg Maddux	1.00
241	Fred McGriff	.05
242	Denny Neagle	.05
243	Eddie Perez	.05
244	John Smoltz	.10
245	Mark Wohlers	.05
246	Brant Brown	.05
247	Scott Bullett	.05
248	Leo Gomez	.05
249	Luis Gonzalez	.25
250	Mark Grace	.15
251	Jose Hernandez	.05
252	Brooks Kieschnick	.05
253	Brian McRae	.05
254	Jaime Navarro	.05
255	Mike Perez	.05
256	Rey Sanchez	.05
257	Ryne Sandberg	.75
258	Scott Servais	.05
259	Sammy Sosa	1.50
260	*Pedro Valdes*	.05
261	Turk Wendell	.05
262	Bret Boone	.10
263	Jeff Branson	.05
264	Jeff Brantley	.05
265	Dave Burba	.05
266	Hector Carrasco	.05
267	Eric Davis	.05
268	Willie Greene	.05
269	Lenny Harris	.05
270	Thomas Howard	.05
271	Barry Larkin	.10
272	Hal Morris	.05
273	Joe Oliver	.05
274	Eric Owens	.05
275	Jose Rijo	.05
276	Reggie Sanders	.05

277 Eddie Taubensee .05
278 Jason Bates .05
279 Dante Bichette .05
280 Ellis Burks .05
281 Vinny Castilla .05
282 Andres Galarraga .05
283 Quinton McCracken .05
284 Jayhawk Owens .05
285 Jeff Reed .05
286 Bryan Rekar .05
287 Armando Reynoso .05
288 Kevin Ritz .05
289 Bruce Ruffin .05
290 John Vander Wal .05
291 Larry Walker .25
292 Walt Weiss .05
293 Eric Young .05
294 Kurt Abbott .05
295 Alex Arias .05
296 Miguel Batista .05
297 Kevin Brown .10
298 Luis Castillo .05
299 Greg Colbrunn .05
300 Jeff Conine .05
301 Charles Johnson .05
302 Al Leiter .05
303 Robb Nen .05
304 Joe Orsulak .05
305 Yorkis Perez .05
306 Edgar Renteria .05
307 Gary Sheffield .25
308 Jesus Tavarez .05
309 Quilvio Veras .05
310 Devon White .05
311 Jeff Bagwell .75
312 Derek Bell .05
313 Sean Berry .05
314 Craig Biggio .10
315 Doug Drabek .05
316 Tony Eusebio .05
317 Ricky Gutierrez .05
318 Xavier Hernandez .05
319 Brian L. Hunter .05
320 Darryl Kile .05
321 Derrick May .05
322 Orlando Miller .05
323 James Mouton .05
324 Bill Spiers .05
325 Pedro Astacio .05
326 Brett Butler .05
327 Juan Castro .05
328 Roger Cedeno .05
329 Delino DeShields .05
330 Karim Garcia .10
331 Todd Hollandsworth .05
332 Eric Karros .05
333 Oreste Marrero .05
334 Ramon Martinez .05
335 Raul Mondesi .15
336 Hideo Nomo .50
337 Antonio Osuna .05
338 Chan Ho Park .15
339 Mike Piazza 2.00
340 Ismael Valdes .05
341 Moises Alou .10
342 Omar Daal .05
343 Jeff Fassero .05
344 Cliff Floyd .05
345 Mark Grudzielanek .05
346 Mike Lansing .05
347 Pedro Martinez .75
348 Sherman Obando .05
349 Jose Paniagua .05
350 Henry Rodriguez .05
351 Mel Rojas .05
352 F.P. Santangelo .05
353 Dave Segui .05
354 Dave Silvestri .05
355 Ugueth Urbina .05
356 Rondell White .10
357 Edgardo Alfonzo .10
358 Carlos Baerga .05
359 Tim Bogar .05
360 Rico Brogna .05
361 Alvaro Espinoza .05
362 Carl Everett .10
363 John Franco .05
364 Bernard Gilkey .05
365 Todd Hundley .05
366 Butch Huskey .05
367 Jason Isringhausen .10
368 Bobby Jones .05
369 Lance Johnson .05
370 Brent Mayne .05
371 Alex Ochoa .05
372 Rey Ordonez .10
373 Ron Blazier .05
374 Ricky Bottalico .05
375 David Doster .05
376 Lenny Dykstra .05
377 Jim Eisenreich .05
378 Bobby Estalella .05
379 Gregg Jefferies .05
380 Kevin Jordan .05
381 Ricardo Jordan .05
382 Mickey Morandini .05
383 Ricky Otero .05
384 Benito Santiago .05
385 Gene Schall .05
386 Curt Schilling .15
387 Kevin Sefcik .05
388 Kevin Stocker .05
389 Jermaine Allensworth .05
390 Jay Bell .05
391 Jason Christiansen .05
392 Francisco Cordova .05
393 Mark Johnson .05
394 Jason Kendall .10
395 Jeff King .05
396 Jon Lieber .05
397 Nelson Liriano .05
398 Esteban Loaiza .05
399 Al Martin .05
400 Orlando Merced .05
401 Ramon Morel .05
402 Luis Alicea .05
403 Alan Benes .05
404 Andy Benes .05
405 Terry Bradshaw .05
406 Royce Clayton .05
407 Dennis Eckersley .05
408 Gary Gaetti .05
409 Mike Gallego .05
410 Ron Gant .05
411 Brian Jordan .05
412 Ray Lankford .05
413 John Mabry .05
414 Willie McGee .05
415 Tom Pagnozzi .05
416 Ozzie Smith .50
417 Todd Stottlemyre .05
418 Mark Sweeney .05
419 Andy Ashby .05
420 Ken Caminiti .05
421 Archi Cianfrocco .05
422 Steve Finley .05
423 Chris Gomez .05
424 Tony Gwynn 1.00
425 Joey Hamilton .05
426 Rickey Henderson .30
427 Trevor Hoffman .05
428 Brian Johnson .05
429 Wally Joyner .05
430 Scott Livingstone .05
431 Jody Reed .05
432 Craig Shipley .05
433 Fernando Valenzuela .05
434 Greg Vaughn .05
435 Rich Aurilia .05
436 Kim Batiste .05
437 Jose Bautista .05
438 Rod Beck .05
439 Marvin Benard .05
440 Barry Bonds 1.00
441 Shawon Dunston .05
442 Shawn Estes .05
443 Osvaldo Fernandez .05
444 Stan Javier .05
445 David McCarty .05
446 *Bill Mueller* .10
447 Steve Scarsone .05
448 Robby Thompson .05
449 Rick Wilkins .05
450 Matt Williams .15

1997 Pacific Crown Silver

This parallel insert was produced in an edition of only 67 cards per player. Following the format of the regular-issue, they use silver foil, rather than the standard gold. Silver parallels were inserted at an advertised rate of one per 73 packs. Silver inserts should not be confused with the much more common light blue inserts which are visually similar.

	MT
Common Player:	2.00
Stars/Rookies:	50X

(See 1997 Pacific Crown for checklist and base card values.)

1997 Pacific Crown Light Blue

This parallel insert was produced exclusively for insertion in Wal-Mart/Sam's jumbo packs at the rate of one per pack. Following the format of the regular-issue, they use light blue foil, rather than the standard gold. Light blue inserts should not be confused with the much scarcer silver inserts which are visually similar.

	MT
Complete Set (450):	150.00
Common Player:	.25
Stars:	2X

(See 1997 Pacific Crown for checklist and base card values.)

1997 Pacific Crown Card-Supials

The 36-card, regular-sized set was inserted every 37 packs of 1997 Pacific Crown baseball. The card fronts feature a gold-foil spiral with the player's name printed along a curve on the bottom edge. The team logo appears in the lower right corner. The card backs feature an action shot and are numbered "x of 36." The cards come with a mini (1-1/4" x 1-3/4") card that slides into a pocket on the back. The mini cards are of a different player, but depict the same action shot as the larger card backs.

		MT
Complete Set (72):		125.00
Complete Large Set (36):		85.00
Complete Small Set (36):		45.00
Common Large:		1.00
Small Cards: 50%		
1	Roberto Alomar	2.00
2	Brady Anderson	1.00
3	Eddie Murray	2.00
4	Cal Ripken Jr.	6.50
5	Jose Canseco	2.00
6	Mo Vaughn	2.00
7	Frank Thomas	4.00
8	Albert Belle	3.00
9	Omar Vizquel	1.00
10	Chuck Knoblauch	1.00
11	Paul Molitor	2.00
12	Wade Boggs	2.00
13	Derek Jeter	5.00
14	Andy Pettitte	2.00
15	Mark McGwire	6.50
16	Jay Buhner	1.00
17	Ken Griffey Jr.	6.00
18	Alex Rodriguez	6.00
19	Juan Gonzalez	3.00
20	Ivan Rodriguez	2.00
21	Andruw Jones	3.50
22	Chipper Jones	5.00
23	Ryan Klesko	1.00
24	Greg Maddux	4.00
25	Ryne Sandberg	3.00
26	Andres Galarraga	1.00
27	Gary Sheffield	1.50
28	Jeff Bagwell	3.50
29	Todd Hollandsworth	1.00
30	Hideo Nomo	2.50
31	Mike Piazza	5.00
32	Todd Hundley	1.00
33	Dennis Eckersley	1.00
34	Ken Caminiti	1.00
35	Tony Gwynn	3.50
36	Barry Bonds	4.00

1997 Pacific Crown Cramer's Choice Awards

The 10-card, regular-sized set was inserted every 721 packs and features a die-cut pyramid design. A color player photo is imaged over silver foil with the player's name and position in gold foil over a green marble background along the bottom. The card backs feature a headshot with a brief career highlight in both Spanish and English. The cards are numbered with a "CC" prefix.

		MT
Complete Set (10):		125.00
Common Player:		6.00
1	Roberto Alomar	8.00
2	Frank Thomas	15.00
3	Albert Belle	6.00
4	Andy Pettitte	6.00
5	Ken Griffey Jr.	30.00
6	Alex Rodriguez	30.00
7	Chipper Jones	25.00
8	John Smoltz	6.00
9	Mike Piazza	25.00
10	Tony Gwynn	13.50

1997 Pacific Crown Fireworks Die-Cuts

The 20-card, regular-sized, die-cut set was inserted every 73 packs of 1997 Crown. The card fronts feature a color action shot with generic fireworks over a stadium on the upper half. The horizontal card backs contain close-up shots with highlights in Spanish and English. The cards are numbered with the "FW" prefix.

		MT
Complete Set (20):		70.00
Common Player:		1.00
1	Roberto Alomar	2.50
2	Brady Anderson	1.00
3	Eddie Murray	2.50
4	Cal Ripken Jr.	9.00
5	Frank Thomas	5.00
6	Albert Belle	2.00
7	Derek Jeter	6.50
8	Andy Pettitte	2.00
9	Bernie Williams	2.00
10	Mark McGwire	9.00
11	Ken Griffey Jr.	9.00
12	Alex Rodriguez	8.00
13	Juan Gonzalez	3.00
14	Andruw Jones	3.00
15	Chipper Jones	6.50
16	Hideo Nomo	3.00
17	Mike Piazza	6.50
18	Henry Rodriguez	1.00
19	Tony Gwynn	4.00
20	Barry Bonds	5.00

1997 Pacific Crown Gold Crown Die-Cuts

The 36-card, regular-sized, die-cut set was inserted every 37 packs. The card fronts feature a die-cut, gold-foil crown on the top border and the player's name appears in gold along the bottom edge. The card backs contain a headshot and a Spanish/English highlight and are numbered with the "GC" prefix.

		MT
Complete Set (36):		100.00
Common Player:		1.00
1	Roberto Alomar	2.00
2	Brady Anderson	1.00
3	Mike Mussina	2.00
4	Eddie Murray	2.25
5	Cal Ripken Jr.	10.00
6	Jose Canseco	2.50
7	Frank Thomas	6.00
8	Albert Belle	2.00
9	Omar Vizquel	1.00
10	Wade Boggs	2.50
11	Derek Jeter	7.50
12	Andy Pettitte	2.00
13	Mariano Rivera	2.50
14	Bernie Williams	2.00
15	Mark McGwire	10.00
16	Ken Griffey Jr.	10.00
17	Edgar Martinez	1.00
18	Alex Rodriquez	9.00
19	Juan Gonzalez	4.00
20	Ivan Rodriguez	3.00
21	Andruw Jones	4.00
22	Chipper Jones	7.50
23	Ryan Klesko	1.00
24	John Smoltz	1.50
25	Ryne Sandberg	4.00
26	Andres Galarraga	1.00
27	Edgar Renteria	1.00
28	Jeff Bagwell	5.00
29	Todd Hollandsworth	1.00
30	Hideo Nomo	3.00
31	Mike Piazza	7.50
32	Todd Hundley	1.00
33	Brian Jordan	1.00
34	Ken Caminiti	1.00
35	Tony Gwynn	5.00
36	Barry Bonds	4.00

1997 Pacific Crown Latinos of the Major Leagues

The 36-card, regular-sized set was inserted twice every 37 packs. The card fronts feature a color action shot over the player's name in gold foil. The card backs have another action shot and a Spanish/English highlight.

		MT
Complete Set (36):		55.00
Common Player:		1.00
1	George Arias	1.00
2	Roberto Alomar	2.50
3	Rafael Palmeiro	2.00
4	Bobby Bonilla	1.00
5	Jose Canseco	2.00
6	Wilson Alvarez	1.00
7	Dave Martinez	1.00
8	Julio Franco	1.00
9	Manny Ramirez	4.00
10	Omar Vizquel	1.00
11	Marty Cordova	1.00
12	Roberto Kelly	1.00
13	Tino Martinez	1.00
14	Mariano Rivera	2.50
15	Ruben Rivera	1.00
16	Bernie Williams	2.00
17	Geronimo Berroa	1.00
18	Joey Cora	1.00
19	Edgar Martinez	1.00
20	Alex Rodriguez	8.50
21	Juan Gonzalez	4.00
22	Ivan Rodriguez	5.00
23	Andruw Jones	4.00
24	Javier Lopez	1.00
25	Sammy Sosa	7.00
26	Vinny Castilla	1.00
27	Andres Galarraga	1.00
28	Ramon Martinez	1.00
29	Raul Mondesi	2.00
30	Ismael Valdes	1.00
31	Pedro Martinez	4.00
32	Henry Rodriguez	1.00
33	Carlos Baerga	1.00
34	Rey Ordonez	1.00
35	Fernando Valenzuela	1.00
36	Osvaldo Fernandez	1.00

1997 Pacific Crown Triple Crown Die-Cuts

The 20-card, regular-sized, die-cut set was inserted every 145 packs of Crown baseball. The horizontal card fronts feature the same gold-foil, die-cut crown as on the Gold Crown Die-Cut inserts. The card backs feature a headshot, Spanish/English text and are numbered with the "TC" prefix.

		MT
Complete Set (20):		120.00
Common Player:		2.50
1	Brady Anderson	2.50
2	Rafael Palmeiro	4.00
3	Mo Vaughn	4.00
4	Frank Thomas	7.50
5	Albert Belle	3.00
6	Jim Thome	2.50
7	Cecil Fielder	2.50
8	Mark McGwire	25.00
9	Ken Griffey Jr.	22.50
10	Alex Rodriguez	20.00
11	Juan Gonzalez	6.00
12	Andruw Jones	6.00
13	Chipper Jones	15.00
14	Dante Bichette	2.50
15	Ellis Burks	2.50
16	Andres Galarraga	2.50
17	Jeff Bagwell	6.00
18	Mike Piazza	15.00
19	Ken Caminiti	2.50
20	Barry Bonds	7.50

1997 Pacific Invincible

The 1997 Pacific Invincible 150-card set was sold in three-card packs. The card fronts feature gold foil parallel lines with a color action shot. The bottom right quadrant contains a transparent cel headshot. The card backs have Spanish/English text and another color action shot. The reverse cel has the player's hat team logo air-brushed off to prevent reverse print. Insert sets are: Sluggers & Hurlers, Sizzling Lumber, Gate Attractions, Gems of the Diamond (2:1), and Light

Blue (retail only) and Platinum (hobby) parallel sets of the 150 baseb cards.

		MT
Complete Set (150):		70.00
Common Player:		.50
Light Blues:		2X
Platinums:		2X
Pack (3):		1.50
Wax Box (36):		35.00
1	Chili Davis	.50
2	Jim Edmonds	1.00
3	Darin Erstad	1.50
4	Orlando Palmeiro	.50
5	Tim Salmon	1.00
6	J.T. Snow	.50
7	Roberto Alomar	2.00
8	Brady Anderson	.50
9	Eddie Murray	1.50
10	Mike Mussina	2.00
11	Rafael Palmeiro	1.00
12	Cal Ripken Jr.	8.00
13	Jose Canseco	1.50
14	Roger Clemens	3.00
15	Nomar Garciaparra	4.00
16	Reggie Jefferson	.50
17	Mo Vaughn	1.00
18	Wilson Alvarez	.50
19	Harold Baines	.50
20	Alex Fernandez	.50
21	Danny Tartabull	.50
22	Frank Thomas	3.00
23	Robin Ventura	.50
24	Sandy Alomar Jr.	.50
25	Albert Belle	1.00
26	Kenny Lofton	.50
27	Jim Thome	.50
28	Omar Vizquel	.50
29	Raul Casanova	.50
30	Tony Clark	.50
31	Travis Fryman	.50
32	Bobby Higginson	.50
33	Melvin Nieves	.50
34	Justin Thompson	.50
35	Johnny Damon	.50
36	Tom Goodwin	.50
37	Jeff Montgomery	.50
38	Jose Offerman	.50
39	John Jaha	.50
40	Jeff Cirillo	.50
41	Dave Nilsson	.50
42	Jose Valentin	.50
43	Fernando Vina	.50
44	Marty Cordova	.50
45	Roberto Kelly	.50
46	Chuck Knoblauch	.50
47	Paul Molitor	1.50
48	Todd Walker	.50
49	Wade Boggs	2.00
50	Cecil Fielder	.50
51	Derek Jeter	6.00
52	Tino Martinez	.50
53	Andy Pettitte	1.00
54	Mariano Rivera	1.50
55	Bernie Williams	1.25
56	Tony Batista	.50
57	Geronimo Berroa	.50
58	Jason Giambi	1.50
59	Mark McGwire	8.00
60	Terry Steinbach	.50
61	Jay Buhner	.50
62	Joey Cora	.50
63	Ken Griffey Jr.	7.00
64	Edgar Martinez	.50
65	Alex Rodriguez	6.50
66	Paul Sorrento	.50
67	Will Clark	1.00
68	Juan Gonzalez	2.50
69	Rusty Greer	.50
70	Dean Palmer	.50
71	Ivan Rodriguez	2.00
72	Joe Carter	.50
73	Carlos Delgado	1.50
74	Juan Guzman	.50
75	Pat Hentgen	.50
76	Ed Sprague	.50
77	Jermaine Dye	.50
78	Andruw Jones	2.50
79	Chipper Jones	6.00
80	Ryan Klesko	.50
81	Javier Lopez	.50
82	Greg Maddux	5.00
83	John Smoltz	1.00
84	Mark Grace	1.50
85	Luis Gonzalez	.50
86	Brooks Kieschnick	.50
87	Jaime Navarro	.50
88	Ryne Sandberg	2.50
89	Sammy Sosa	5.00
90	Bret Boone	.50
91	Jeff Brantley	.50
92	Eric Davis	.50
93	Barry Larkin	1.00
94	Reggie Sanders	.50
95	Ellis Burks	.50
96	Dante Bichette	.50
97	Vinny Castilla	.50
98	Andres Galarraga	.50
99	Eric Young	.50
100	Kevin Brown	1.00
101	Jeff Conine	.50
102	Charles Johnson	.50
103	Edgar Renteria	.50
104	Gary Sheffield	1.50
105	Jeff Bagwell	2.50
106	Derek Bell	.50
107	Sean Berry	.50
108	Craig Biggio	1.00
109	Shane Reynolds	.50
110	Karim Garcia	.50
111	Todd Hollandsworth	.50
112	Ramon Martinez	.50
113	Raul Mondesi	1.00
114	Hideo Nomo	2.50
115	Mike Piazza	6.00
116	Ismael Valdes	.50
117	Moises Alou	.50
118	Mark Grudzielanek	.50
119	Pedro Martinez	2.00
120	Henry Rodriguez	.50
121	F.P. Santangelo	.50
122	Carlos Baerga	.50
123	Bernard Gilkey	.50
124	Todd Hundley	.50
125	Lance Johnson	.50
126	Alex Ochoa	.50
127	Rey Ordonez	.50
128	Lenny Dykstra	.50
129	Gregg Jefferies	.50
130	Ricky Otero	.50
131	Benito Santiago	.50
132	Jermaine Allensworth	.50
133	Francisco Cordova	.50
134	Carlos Garcia	.50
135	Jason Kendall	.50
136	Al Martin	.50
137	Dennis Eckersley	.50
138	Ron Gant	.50
139	Brian Jordan	.50
140	John Mabry	.50
141	Ozzie Smith	2.50
142	Ken Caminiti	.50
143	Steve Finley	.50
144	Tony Gwynn	3.00
145	Wally Joyner	.50
146	Fernando Valenzuela	.50
147	Barry Bonds	4.00
148	Jacob Cruz	.50
149	Osvaldo Fernandez	.50
150	Matt Williams	1.00

1997 Pacific Invincible Gate Attractions

The 32-card, regular-sized set was inserted every 73 packs of Pacific Invincible baseball. The card fronts feature a generic baseball glove background with the player's name and position in a gold-foil circle. The center of the card is a cel action shot within a common baseball image. The player's team logo appears in the upper right corner. The card backs contain a headshot in the upper left corner with highlights in Spanish and English. The player's image in the cel is etched in gray in reverse. The cards are numbered with the "GA" prefix.

		MT
Complete Set (32):		100.00
Common Player:		1.00
1	Roberto Alomar	2.00
2	Brady Anderson	1.00
3	Cal Ripken Jr.	10.00
4	Frank Thomas	6.00
5	Kenny Lofton	1.00
6	Omar Vizquel	1.00
7	Paul Molitor	2.50
8	Wade Boggs	2.50
9	Derek Jeter	8.00
10	Andy Pettitte	2.00
11	Bernie Williams	1.50
12	Geronimo Berroa	1.00
13	Mark McGwire	10.00
14	Ken Griffey Jr.	10.00
15	Alex Rodriguez	9.00
16	Juan Gonzalez	4.00
17	Andruw Jones	5.00
18	Chipper Jones	8.00
19	Greg Maddux	7.00
20	Ryne Sandberg	3.00
21	Sammy Sosa	6.00
22	Andres Galarraga	1.00
23	Jeff Bagwell	5.00
24	Todd Hollandsworth	1.00
25	Hideo Nomo	2.50
26	Mike Piazza	8.00
27	Todd Hundley	1.00
28	Lance Johnson	1.00
29	Ozzie Smith	3.00
30	Ken Caminiti	1.00
31	Tony Gwynn	6.00
32	Barry Bonds	5.00

1997 Pacific Invincible Gems of the Diamond

Essentially the base set for 1997 Pacific Prism Invincible, these cards are found two per three-card pack. Fronts of the 2-1/2" x 3-1/2" cards have action photos with earth-tone borders and a color team logo at bottom. Backs have a large player portrait photos in a diamond at right-center and are numbered with a "GD-" prefix.

		MT
Complete Set (220):		20.00
Common Player:		.15
1	Jim Abbott	.15
2	Shawn Boskie	.15
3	Gary DiSarcina	.15
4	Jim Edmonds	.25
5	Todd Greene	.15
6	Jack Howell	.15
7	Jeff Schmidt	.15
8	Shad Williams	.15
9	Roberto Alomar	.50
10	Cesar Devarez	.15
11	Alan Mills	.15
12	Eddie Murray	.25
13	Jesse Orosco	.15
14	Arthur Rhodes	.15
15	Bill Ripken	.15
16	Cal Ripken Jr.	2.50
17	Mark Smith	.15
18	Roger Clemens	1.00
19	Vaughn Eshelman	.15
20	Rich Garces	.15
21	Bill Haselman	.15
22	Dwayne Hosey	.15
23	Mike Maddux	.15
24	Jose Malave	.15
25	Aaron Sele	.15
26	James Baldwin	.15
27	Pat Borders	.15
28	Mike Cameron	.15
29	Tony Castillo	.15
30	Domingo Cedeno	.15
31	Greg Norton	.15
32	Frank Thomas	1.00
33	Albert Belle	.40
34	Einar Diaz	.15
35	Alan Embree	.15
36	Albie Lopez	.15
37	Chad Ogea	.15
38	Tony Pena	.15
39	Joe Roa	.15
40	Fausto Cruz	.15
41	Joey Eischen	.15
42	Travis Fryman	.30
43	Mike Myers	.15
44	A.J. Sager	.15
45	Duane Singleton	.15
46	Justin Thompson	.15
47	Jeff Granger	.15
48	Les Norman	.15
49	Jon Nunnally	.15
50	Craig Paquette	.15
51	Michael Tucker	.15
52	Julio Valera	.15
53	Kevin Young	.15
54	Cal Eldred	.15
55	Ramon Garcia	.15
56	Marc Newfield	.15
57	Al Reyes	.15
58	Tim Unroe	.15
59	Tim Vanegmond	.15
60	Turner Ward	.15
61	Bob Wickman	.15
62	Chuck Knoblauch	.25
63	Paul Molitor	.50
64	Kirby Puckett	.75
65	Tom Quinlan	.15
66	Rich Robertson	.15
67	Dave Stevens	.15
68	Matt Walbeck	.15
69	Wade Boggs	.50
70	Tony Fernandez	.15
71	Andy Fox	.15
72	Joe Girardi	.15
73	Charlie Hayes	.15
74	Pat Kelly	.15
75	Jeff Nelson	.15
76	Melido Perez	.15
77	Mark Acre	.15
78	Allen Battle	.15
79	Rafael Bournigal	.15
80	Mark McGwire	3.00
81	Pedro Munoz	.15
82	Scott Spiezio	.15
83	Don Wengert	.15
84	Steve Wojciechowski	.15
85	Alex Diaz	.15
86	Ken Griffey Jr.	2.00
87	Raul Ibanez	.15
88	Mike Jackson	.15

89	John Marzano	.15
90	Greg McCarthy	.15
91	Alex Rodriguez	2.50
92	Andy Sheets	.15
93	Makoto Suzuki	.15
94	Benji Gil	.15
95	Juan Gonzalez	.75
96	Kevin Gross	.15
97	Gil Heredia	.15
98	Luis Ortiz	.15
99	Jeff Russell	.15
100	Dave Valle	.15
101	Marty Janzen	.15
102	Sandy Martinez	.15
103	Julio Mosquera	.15
104	Otis Nixon	.15
105	Paul Spoljaric	.15
106	Shannon Stewart	.15
107	Woody Williams	.15
108	Steve Avery	.15
109	Mike Bielecki	.15
110	Pedro Borbon	.15
111	Ed Giovanola	.15
112	Chipper Jones	1.50
113	Greg Maddux	1.50
114	Mike Mordecai	.15
115	Terrell Wade	.15
116	Terry Adams	.15
117	Brian Dorsett	.15
118	Doug Glanville	.15
119	Tyler Houston	.15
120	Robin Jennings	.15
121	Ryne Sandberg	.75
122	Terry Shumpert	.15
123	Amaury Telemaco	.15
124	Steve Trachsel	.15
125	Curtis Goodwin	.15
126	Mike Kelly	.15
127	Chad Mottola	.15
128	Mark Portugal	.15
129	Roger Salkeld	.15
130	John Smiley	.15
131	Lee Smith	.15
132	Roger Bailey	.15
133	Andres Galarraga	.25
134	Darren Holmes	.15
135	Curtis Leskanic	.15
136	Mike Munoz	.15
137	Jeff Reed	.15
138	Mark Thompson	.15
139	Jamey Wright	.15
140	Andre Dawson	.20
141	Craig Grebeck	.15
142	Matt Mantei	.15
143	Billy McMillon	.15
144	Kurt Miller	.15
145	Ralph Milliard	.15
146	Bob Natal	.15
147	Joe Siddall	.15
148	Bob Abreu	.25
149	Doug Brocail	.15
150	Danny Darwin	.15
151	Mike Hampton	.15
152	Todd Jones	.15
153	Kirt Manwaring	.15
154	Alvin Morman	.15
155	Billy Ashley	.15
156	Tom Candiotti	.15
157	Darren Dreifort	.15
158	Greg Gagne	.15
159	Wilton Guerrero	.15
160	Hideo Nomo	.50
161	Mike Piazza	2.00
162	Tom Prince	.15
163	Todd Worrell	.15
164	Moises Alou	.20
165	Shane Andrews	.15
166	Derek Aucoin	.15
167	Raul Chavez	.15
168	Darrin Fletcher	.15
169	Mark Leiter	.15
170	Henry Rodriguez	.15
171	Dave Veres	.15
172	Paul Byrd	.15
173	Alberto Castillo	.15
174	Mark Clark	.15
175	Rey Ordonez	.20
176	Roberto Petagine	.15
177	Andy Tomberlin	.15
178	Derek Wallace	.15
179	Paul Wilson	.15
180	Ruben Amaro, Jr.	.15
181	Toby Borland	.15
182	Rich Hunter	.15
183	Tony Longmire	.15
184	Wendell Magee Jr.	.15
185	Bobby Munoz	.15
186	Scott Rolen	.50
187	Mike Williams	.15
188	Trey Beamon	.15
189	Jason Christiansen	.15
190	Elmer Dessens	.15
191	Angelo Encarnacion	.15
192	Carlos Garcia	.15
193	Mike Kingery	.15
194	Chris Peters	.15
195	Tony Womack	.20
196	Brian Barber	.15
197	David Bell	.15
198	Tony Fossas	.15
199	Rick Honeycutt	.15
200	T.J. Mathews	.15
201	Miguel Mejia	.15
202	Donovan Osborne	.15
203	Ozzie Smith	.50
204	Andres Berumen	.15
205	Ken Caminiti	.20
206	Chris Gwynn	.15
207	Tony Gwynn	1.00
208	Rickey Henderson	.30
209	Scott Sanders	.15
210	Jason Thompson	.15
211	Fernando Valenzuela	.15
212	Tim Worrell	.15
213	Barry Bonds	1.00
214	Jay Canizaro	.15
215	Doug Creek	.15
216	Jacob Cruz	.15
217	Glenallen Hill	.15
218	Tom Lampkin	.15
219	Jim Poole	.15
220	Desi Wilson	.15

1997 Pacific Invincible Sizzling Lumber

The 36-card, regular-sized, die-cut set was inserted every 37 packs of Ivincible. The cards have die-cut flames along the right border with a bat running parallel. The player's name appears in gold foil along the top border with his position in English and Spanish in gold foil along the bottom. The card backs feature a headshot in the upper half and contain Spanish and English text. The cards are numbered with the "SL" prefix.

		MT
Complete Set (36):		65.00
Common Player:		.75
1A	Cal Ripken Jr.	6.50
1B	Rafael Palmeiro	1.25
1C	Roberto Alomar	1.25
2A	Frank Thomas	4.00
2B	Robin Ventura	.75
2C	Harold Baines	.75
3A	Albert Belle	2.00
3B	Manny Ramirez	3.00
3C	Kenny Lofton	.75
4A	Derek Jeter	5.00
4B	Bernie Williams	1.25
4C	Wade Boggs	2.00
5A	Mark McGwire	6.50
5B	Jason Giambi	2.00
5C	Geronimo Berroa	.75
6A	Ken Griffey Jr.	6.50
6B	Alex Rodriguez	6.00
6C	Jay Buhner	.75
7A	Juan Gonzalez	3.50
7B	Dean Palmer	.75
7C	Ivan Rodriguez	2.50
8A	Ryan Klesko	.75
8B	Chipper Jones	5.00
8C	Andruw Jones	3.50
9A	Dante Bichette	.75
9B	Andres Galarraga	.75
9C	Vinny Castilla	.75
10A	Jeff Bagwell	4.00
10B	Craig Biggio	.75
10C	Derek Bell	.75
11A	Mike Piazza	5.00
11B	Raul Mondesi	1.25
11C	Karim Garcia	1.00
12A	Tony Gwynn	4.00
12B	Ken Caminiti	.75
12C	Greg Vaughn	.75

1997 Pacific Invincible Sluggers & Hurlers

The 24-card, regular-sized set was inserted every 145 packs of Pacific Invincible baseball. The cards are numbered with an "SH-xA" or "SH-xaB." Each "A" card is the left half of a two-card set with the two players from the same team having their logo in the fit-together center. Each card has the player's name printed in gold foil along the bottom border with gold-foil swirls around the team logo. The card backs have a circular headshot with text in English and Spanish.

		MT
Complete Set (24):		160.00
Common Player:		3.00
SH-1a	Cal Ripken Jr.	20.00
SH-1b	Mike Mussina	7.50
SH-2a	Jose Canseco	4.00
SH-2b	Roger Clemens	9.00
SH-3a	Frank Thomas	12.50
SH-3b	Wilson Alvarez	3.00
SH-4a	Kenny Lofton	3.00
SH-4b	Orel Hershiser	3.00
SH-5a	Derek Jeter	15.00
SH-5b	Andy Pettitte	4.00
SH-6a	Ken Griffey Jr.	20.00
SH-6b	Randy Johnson	5.00
SH-7a	Alex Rodriguez	17.50
SH-7b	Jamie Moyer	3.00
SH-8a	Andruw Jones	7.50
SH-8b	Greg Maddux	12.50
SH-9a	Chipper Jones	15.00
SH-9b	John Smoltz	3.50
SH-10a	Jeff Bagwell	10.00
SH-10b	Shane Reynolds	3.00
SH-11a	Mike Piazza	15.00
SH-11b	Hideo Nomo	5.00
SH-12a	Tony Gwynn	10.00
SH-12b	Fernando Valenzuela	3.00

1998 Pacific

Pacific Baseball for 1998 is a 450-card, bilingual set. The base set features full-bleed photos with the Pacific Crown Collection logo in the upper-left and the player's name, position and team at the bottom. Inserts include Cramer's Choice Awards, In The Cage Laser-Cuts, Home Run Hitters, Team Checklist Laser-Cuts, Gold Crown Die-Cuts and Latinos of the Major Leagues. Three foil-color parallels were issued: Reds were found one per Wal-Mart exclusive retail pack; Silvers were found one per Hobby pack. Platinum Blues, numbered to 67 each, were found one per 73 packs.

		MT
Complete Set (450):		40.00
Common Player:		.05
Pack (12):		1.50
Wax Box (36):		45.00
1	Luis Alicea	.05
2	Garret Anderson	.05
3	Jason Dickson	.05
4	Gary DiSarcina	.05
5	Jim Edmonds	.15
6	Darin Erstad	.50
7	Chuck Finley	.05
8	Shigetosi Hasegawa	.05
9	Rickey Henderson	.30
10	Dave Hollins	.05
11	Mark Langston	.05

No.	Player	Price
12	Orlando Palmeiro	.05
13	Troy Percival	.05
14	Tony Phillips	.05
15	Tim Salmon	.25
16	Allen Watson	.05
17	Roberto Alomar	.60
18	Brady Anderson	.05
19	Harold Baines	.05
20	Armando Benitez	.05
21	Geronimo Berroa	.05
22	Mike Bordick	.05
23	Eric Davis	.05
24	Scott Erickson	.05
25	Chris Hoiles	.05
26	Jimmy Key	.05
27	Aaron Ledesma	.05
28	Mike Mussina	.50
29	Randy Myers	.05
30	Jesse Orosco	.05
31	Rafael Palmeiro	.20
32	Jeff Reboulet	.05
33	Cal Ripken Jr.	2.50
34	B.J. Surhoff	.05
35	Steve Avery	.05
36	Darren Bragg	.05
37	Wil Cordero	.05
38	Jeff Frye	.05
39	Nomar Garciaparra	1.50
40	Tom Gordon	.05
41	Bill Haselman	.05
42	Scott Hatteberg	.05
43	Butch Henry	.05
44	Reggie Jefferson	.05
45	Tim Naehring	.05
46	Troy O'Leary	.05
47	Jeff Suppan	.05
48	John Valentin	.05
49	Mo Vaughn	.30
50	Tim Wakefield	.05
51	James Baldwin	.05
52	Albert Belle	.20
53	Tony Castillo	.05
54	Doug Drabek	.05
55	Ray Durham	.05
56	Jorge Fabregas	.05
57	Ozzie Guillen	.05
58	Matt Karchner	.05
59	Norberto Martin	.05
60	Dave Martinez	.05
61	Lyle Mouton	.05
62	Jaime Navarro	.05
63	Frank Thomas	1.00
64	Mario Valdez	.05
65	Robin Ventura	.05
66	Sandy Alomar Jr.	.05
67	Paul Assenmacher	.05
68	Tony Fernandez	.05
69	Brian Giles	.10
70	Marquis Grissom	.05
71	Orel Hershiser	.05
72	Mike Jackson	.05
73	David Justice	.30
74	Albie Lopez	.05
75	Jose Mesa	.05
76	Charles Nagy	.05
77	Chad Ogea	.05
78	Manny Ramirez	.75
79	Jim Thome	.05
80	Omar Vizquel	.05
81	Matt Williams	.20
82	Jaret Wright	.15
83	Willie Blair	.05
84	Raul Casanova	.05
85	Tony Clark	.05
86	Deivi Cruz	.05
87	Damion Easley	.05
88	Travis Fryman	.05
89	Bobby Higginson	.10
90	Brian Hunter	.05
91	Todd Jones	.05
92	Dan Miceli	.05
93	Brian Moehler	.05
94	Melvin Nieves	.05
95	Jody Reed	.05
96	Justin Thompson	.05
97	Bubba Trammell	.05
98	Kevin Appier	.05
99	Jay Bell	.05
100	Yamil Benitez	.05
101	Johnny Damon	.10
102	Chili Davis	.05
103	Jermaine Dye	.05
104	Jed Hansen	.05
105	Jeff King	.05
106	Mike Macfarlane	.05
107	Felix Martinez	.05
108	Jeff Montgomery	.05
109	Jose Offerman	.05
110	Dean Palmer	.05
111	Hipolito Pichardo	.05
112	Jose Rosado	.05
113	Jeromy Burnitz	.05
114	Jeff Cirillo	.05
115	Cal Eldred	.05
116	John Jaha	.05
117	Doug Jones	.05
118	Scott Karl	.05
119	Jesse Levis	.05
120	Mark Loretta	.05
121	Ben McDonald	.05
122	Jose Mercedes	.05
123	Matt Mieske	.05
124	Dave Nilsson	.05
125	Jose Valentin	.05
126	Fernando Vina	.05
127	Gerald Williams	.05
128	Rick Aguilera	.05
129	Rich Becker	.05
130	Ron Coomer	.05
131	Marty Cordova	.05
132	Eddie Guardado	.05
133	LaTroy Hawkins	.05
134	Denny Hocking	.05
135	Chuck Knoblauch	.05
136	Matt Lawton	.05
137	Pat Meares	.05
138	Paul Molitor	.50
139	David Ortiz	.05
140	Brad Radke	.10
141	Terry Steinbach	.05
142	Bob Tewksbury	.05
143	Javier Valentin	.05
144	Wade Boggs	.40
145	David Cone	.05
146	Chad Curtis	.05
147	Cecil Fielder	.05
148	Joe Girardi	.05
149	Dwight Gooden	.05
150	Hideki Irabu	.10
151	Derek Jeter	2.00
152	Tino Martinez	.05
153	Ramiro Mendoza	.05
154	Paul O'Neill	.05
155	Andy Pettitte	.20
156	Jorge Posada	.10
157	Mariano Rivera	.25
158	Rey Sanchez	.05
159	Luis Sojo	.05
160	David Wells	.05
161	Bernie Williams	.30
162	Rafael Bournigal	.05
163	Scott Brosius	.05
164	Jose Canseco	.40
165	Jason Giambi	.75
166	Ben Grieve	.25
167	Dave Magadan	.05
168	Brent Mayne	.05
169	Jason McDonald	.05
170	Izzy Molina	.05
171	Ariel Prieto	.05
172	Carlos Reyes	.05
173	Scott Spiezio	.05
174	Matt Stairs	.05
175	Bill Taylor	.05
176	Dave Telgheder	.05
177	Steve Wojciechowski	.05
178	Rich Amaral	.05
179	Bobby Ayala	.05
180	Jay Buhner	.05
181	Rafael Carmona	.05
182	Ken Cloude	.05
183	Joey Cora	.05
184	Russ Davis	.05
185	Jeff Fassero	.05
186	Ken Griffey Jr.	2.25
187	Raul Ibanez	.05
188	Randy Johnson	.75
189	Roberto Kelly	.05
190	Edgar Martinez	.05
191	Jamie Moyer	.05
192	Omar Olivares	.05
193	Alex Rodriguez	2.00
194	Heathcliff Slocumb	.05
195	Paul Sorrento	.05
196	Dan Wilson	.05
197	Scott Bailes	.05
198	John Burkett	.05
199	Domingo Cedeno	.05
200	Will Clark	.20
201	*Hanley Frias*	.05
202	Juan Gonzalez	.75
203	Tom Goodwin	.05
204	Rusty Greer	.05
205	Wilson Heredia	.05
206	Darren Oliver	.05
207	Billy Ripken	.05
208	Ivan Rodriguez	.60
209	Lee Stevens	.05
210	Fernando Tatis	.10
211	John Wetteland	.05
212	Bobby Witt	.05
213	Jacob Brumfield	.05
214	Joe Carter	.05
215	Roger Clemens	1.00
216	Felipe Crespo	.05
217	Jose Cruz Jr.	.30
218	Carlos Delgado	.50
219	Mariano Duncan	.05
220	Carlos Garcia	.05
221	Alex Gonzalez	.10
222	Juan Guzman	.05
223	Pat Hentgen	.05
224	Orlando Merced	.05
225	Tomas Perez	.05
226	Paul Quantrill	.05
227	Benito Santiago	.05
228	Woody Williams	.05
229	Rafael Belliard	.05
230	Jeff Blauser	.05
231	Pedro Borbon	.05
232	Tom Glavine	.10
233	Tony Graffanino	.05
234	Andruw Jones	.75
235	Chipper Jones	2.00
236	Ryan Klesko	.05
237	Mark Lemke	.05
238	Kenny Lofton	.05
239	Javier Lopez	.05
240	Fred McGriff	.05
241	Greg Maddux	1.00
242	Denny Neagle	.05
243	John Smoltz	.10
244	Michael Tucker	.05
245	Mark Wohlers	.05
246	Manny Alexander	.05
247	Miguel Batista	.05
248	Mark Clark	.05
249	Doug Glanville	.05
250	Jeremi Gonzalez	.05
251	Mark Grace	.25
252	Jose Hernandez	.05
253	Lance Johnson	.05
254	Brooks Kieschnick	.05
255	Kevin Orie	.05
256	Ryne Sandberg	.75
257	Scott Servais	.05
258	Sammy Sosa	2.00
259	Kevin Tapani	.05
260	Ramon Tatis	.05
261	Bret Boone	.05
262	Dave Burba	.05
263	Brook Fordyce	.05
264	Willie Greene	.05
265	Barry Larkin	.10
266	Pedro A. Martinez	.05
267	Hal Morris	.05
268	Joe Oliver	.05
269	Eduardo Perez	.05
270	Pokey Reese	.05
271	Felix Rodriguez	.05
272	Deion Sanders	.10
273	Reggie Sanders	.05
274	Jeff Shaw	.05
275	Scott Sullivan	.05
276	Brett Tomko	.05
277	Roger Bailey	.05
278	Dante Bichette	.05
279	Ellis Burks	.05
280	Vinny Castilla	.05
281	Frank Castillo	.05
282	*Mike DeJean*	.05
283	Andres Galarraga	.05
284	Darren Holmes	.05
285	Kirt Manwaring	.05
286	Quinton McCracken	.05
287	Neifi Perez	.05
288	Steve Reed	.05
289	John Thomson	.05
290	Larry Walker	.30
291	Walt Weiss	.05
292	Kurt Abbott	.05
293	Antonio Alfonseca	.05
294	Moises Alou	.10
295	Alex Arias	.05
296	Bobby Bonilla	.05
297	Kevin Brown	.10
298	Craig Counsell	.05
299	Darren Daulton	.05
300	Jim Eisenreich	.05
301	Alex Fernandez	.05
302	Felix Heredia	.05
303	Livan Hernandez	.05
304	Charles Johnson	.05
305	Al Leiter	.05
306	Robb Nen	.05
307	Edgar Renteria	.05
308	Gary Sheffield	.30
309	Devon White	.05
310	Bob Abreu	.10
311	Brad Ausmus	.05
312	Jeff Bagwell	.75
313	Derek Bell	.05
314	Sean Berry	.05
315	Craig Biggio	.10
316	Ramon Garcia	.05
317	Luis Gonzalez	.25
318	Ricky Gutierrez	.05
319	Mike Hampton	.05
320	Richard Hidalgo	.10
321	Thomas Howard	.05
322	Darryl Kile	.05
323	Jose Lima	.05
324	Shane Reynolds	.05
325	Bill Spiers	.05
326	Tom Candiotti	.05
327	Roger Cedeno	.05
328	Greg Gagne	.05
329	Karim Garcia	.05
330	Wilton Guerrero	.05
331	Todd Hollandsworth	.05
332	Eric Karros	.05
333	Ramon Martinez	.05
334	Raul Mondesi	.20
335	Otis Nixon	.05
336	Hideo Nomo	.75
337	Antonio Osuna	.05
338	Chan Ho Park	.20
339	Mike Piazza	2.00
340	Dennis Reyes	.05
341	Ismael Valdes	.05
342	Todd Worrell	.05
343	Todd Zeile	.05
344	Darrin Fletcher	.05
345	Mark Grudzielanek	.05
346	Vladimir Guerrero	.75
347	Dustin Hermanson	.05
348	Mike Lansing	.05
349	Pedro Martinez	.75
350	Ryan McGuire	.05
351	Jose Paniagua	.05
352	Carlos Perez	.05
353	Henry Rodriguez	.05
354	F.P. Santangelo	.05
355	David Segui	.05
356	Ugueth Urbina	.05
357	Marc Valdes	.05
358	Jose Vidro	.05
359	Rondell White	.10
360	Juan Acevedo	.05
361	Edgardo Alfonzo	.10
362	Carlos Baerga	.05
363	Carl Everett	.10
364	John Franco	.05
365	Bernard Gilkey	.05
366	Todd Hundley	.10
367	Butch Huskey	.05
368	Bobby Jones	.05
369	Takashi Kashiwada	.05
370	Greg McMichael	.05
371	Brian McRae	.05
372	Alex Ochoa	.05
373	John Olerud	.05
374	Rey Ordonez	.10
375	Turk Wendell	.05
376	Ricky Bottalico	.05
377	Rico Brogna	.05
378	Lenny Dykstra	.05
379	Bobby Estalella	.05
380	Wayne Gomes	.05
381	Tyler Green	.05
382	Gregg Jefferies	.05
383	Mark Leiter	.05
384	Mike Lieberthal	.05
385	Mickey Morandini	.05
386	Scott Rolen	.50
387	Curt Schilling	.20
388	Kevin Stocker	.05
389	Danny Tartabull	.05
390	Jermaine Allensworth	.05
391	Adrian Brown	.05
392	Jason Christiansen	.05
393	Steve Cooke	.05

394	Francisco Cordova	.05
395	Jose Guillen	.15
396	Jason Kendall	.05
397	Jon Lieber	.05
398	Esteban Loaiza	.05
399	Al Martin	.05
400	*Kevin Polcovich*	.15
401	Joe Randa	.05
402	Ricardo Rincon	.05
403	Tony Womack	.05
404	Kevin Young	.05
405	Andy Benes	.05
406	Royce Clayton	.05
407	Delino DeShields	.05
408	Mike Difelice	.05
409	Dennis Eckersley	.05
410	John Frascatore	.05
411	Gary Gaetti	.05
412	Ron Gant	.05
413	Brian Jordan	.05
414	Ray Lankford	.05
415	Willie McGee	.05
416	Mark McGwire	2.50
417	Matt Morris	.05
418	Luis Ordaz	.05
419	Todd Stottlemyre	.05
420	Andy Ashby	.05
421	Jim Bruske	.05
422	Ken Caminiti	.05
423	Will Cunnane	.05
424	Steve Finley	.05
425	John Flaherty	.05
426	Chris Gomez	.05
427	Tony Gwynn	1.00
428	Joey Hamilton	.05
429	Carlos Hernandez	.05
430	Sterling Hitchcock	.05
431	Trevor Hoffman	.05
432	Wally Joyner	.05
433	Greg Vaughn	.05
434	Quilvio Veras	.05
435	Wilson Alvarez	.05
436	Rod Beck	.05
437	Barry Bonds	1.00
438	Jacob Cruz	.05
439	Shawn Estes	.05
440	Darryl Hamilton	.05
441	Roberto Hernandez	.05
442	Glenallen Hill	.05
443	Stan Javier	.05
444	Brian Johnson	.05
445	Jeff Kent	.05
446	Bill Mueller	.05
447	Kirk Rueter	.05
448	J.T. Snow	.05
449	Julian Tavarez	.05
450	Jose Vizcaino	.05

1998 Pacific Red/Silver/Blue

Red, Silver and Platinum Blue parallels were printed for all 450 cards in Pacific, with the gold foil found on base cards being replaced by one of those foils. Red foil versions were inserted one per Wal-Mart pack (retail). Silver versions were inserted one per hobby pack. Platinum Blues, limited to 67 sets, were a one per 73 pack insert.

	MT
Reds:	4X
Silvers:	3X
Platinum Blues:	40X

(See 1998 Pacific for checklist and base card values.)

1998 Pacific Cramer's Choice

Cramer's Choice Awards is a 10-card die-cut insert. The cards feature the top player at each position as selected by Pacific CEO Mike Cramer. Each card is shaped like a trophy.

		MT
Complete Set (10):		225.00
Common Player:		10.00
Inserted 1:721		
1	Greg Maddux	25.00
2	Roberto Alomar	15.00
3	Cal Ripken Jr.	50.00
4	Nomar Garciaparra	30.00
5	Larry Walker	10.00
6	Mike Piazza	35.00
7	Mark McGwire	50.00
8	Tony Gwynn	20.00
9	Ken Griffey Jr.	40.00
10	Roger Clemens	20.00

1998 Pacific Gold Crown Die-Cuts

Gold Crown Die-Cuts is a 36-card insert seeded one per 37 packs. Each card has a holographic silver foil background and gold etching. The cards are die-cut around a crown design at the top.

		MT
Complete Set (36):		200.00
Common Player:		3.00
1	Chipper Jones	15.00
2	Greg Maddux	10.00
3	Denny Neagle	3.00
4	Roberto Alomar	4.50
5	Rafael Palmeiro	3.50
6	Cal Ripken Jr.	18.00
7	Nomar Garciaparra	12.50
8	Mo Vaughn	3.50
9	Frank Thomas	8.00
10	Sandy Alomar Jr.	3.00
11	David Justice	3.50
12	Manny Ramirez	6.00
13	Andres Galarraga	3.00
14	Larry Walker	3.50
15	Moises Alou	3.00
16	Livan Hernandez	3.00
17	Gary Sheffield	3.50
18	Jeff Bagwell	6.00
19	Raul Mondesi	3.00
20	Hideo Nomo	5.00
21	Mike Piazza	15.00
22	Derek Jeter	15.00
23	Tino Martinez	3.00
24	Bernie Williams	4.00
25	Ben Grieve	3.50
26	Mark McGwire	18.00
27	Tony Gwynn	7.50
28	Barry Bonds	8.00
29	Ken Griffey Jr.	16.50
30	Randy Johnson	6.00
31	Edgar Martinez	3.00
32	Alex Rodriguez	16.50
33	Juan Gonzalez	6.00
34	Ivan Rodriguez	5.00
35	Roger Clemens	7.50
36	Jose Cruz Jr.	3.50

1998 Pacific Home Run Hitters

This 20-card set was inserted one per 73 packs. The full-foil cards feature a color player photo with their home run total from 1997 embossed in the background.

		MT
Complete Set (20):		110.00
Common Player:		2.00
1	Rafael Palmeiro	3.00
2	Mo Vaughn	4.00
3	Sammy Sosa	10.00
4	Albert Belle	4.00
5	Frank Thomas	10.00
6	David Justice	3.00
7	Jim Thome	2.00
8	Matt Williams	2.00
9	Vinny Castilla	2.00
10	Andres Galarraga	2.00
11	Larry Walker	3.00
12	Jeff Bagwell	7.50
13	Mike Piazza	12.50
14	Tino Martinez	2.00
15	Mark McGwire	20.00
16	Barry Bonds	9.00
17	Jay Buhner	2.00
18	Ken Griffey Jr.	17.50
19	Alex Rodriguez	17.50
20	Juan Gonzalez	6.00

1998 Pacific In the Cage

This 20-card insert features top players in a die-cut batting cage. The netting on the cage is laser-cut. In The Cage laser-cuts were inserted one per 145 packs.

		MT
Complete Set (20):		180.00
Common Player:		3.50
1	Chipper Jones	18.00
2	Roberto Alomar	5.00
3	Cal Ripken Jr.	25.00
4	Nomar Garciaparra	16.00
5	Frank Thomas	16.00
6	Sandy Alomar Jr.	3.50
7	David Justice	4.50
8	Larry Walker	4.50
9	Bobby Bonilla	3.50
10	Mike Piazza	18.00
11	Tino Martinez	3.50
12	Bernie Williams	4.50
13	Mark McGwire	25.00
14	Tony Gwynn	15.00
15	Barry Bonds	15.00
16	Ken Griffey Jr.	22.50
17	Edgar Martinez	3.50
18	Alex Rodriguez	22.50
19	Juan Gonzalez	7.50
20	Ivan Rodriguez	5.00

1998 Pacific Latinos of the Major Leagues

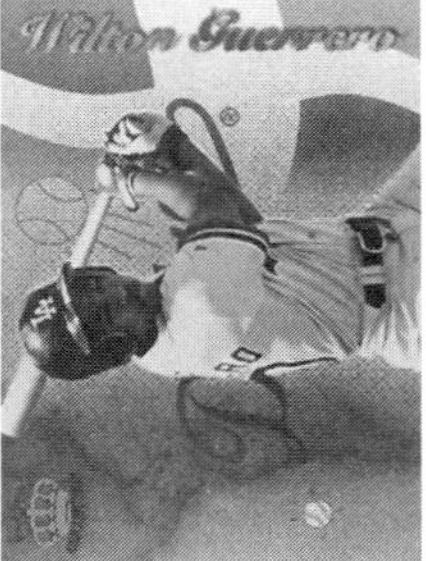

This 36-card set features Major League players of Hispanic descent. The background has a world map on the left, the player's team logo in the center and an American flag on the right.

		MT
Complete Set (36):		40.00
Common Player:		.75
Inserted 2:37		
1	Andruw Jones	3.50
2	Javier Lopez	.75
3	Roberto Alomar	2.00
4	Geronimo Berroa	.75
5	Rafael Palmeiro	1.00
6	Nomar Garciaparra	4.00
7	Sammy Sosa	4.50
8	Ozzie Guillen	.75
9	Sandy Alomar Jr.	.75
10	Manny Ramirez	3.50
11	Omar Vizquel	.75
12	Vinny Castilla	.75
13	Andres Galarraga	.75
14	Moises Alou	.75
15	Bobby Bonilla	.75
16	Livan Hernandez	.75
17	Edgar Renteria	.75
18	Wilton Guerrero	.75
19	Raul Mondesi	1.25
20	Ismael Valdes	.75
21	Fernando Vina	.75
22	Pedro Martinez	3.00
23	Edgardo Alfonzo	.75
24	Carlos Baerga	.75
25	Rey Ordonez	.75
26	Tino Martinez	.75
27	Mariano Rivera	2.00
28	Bernie Williams	2.00
29	Jose Canseco	1.50
30	Joey Cora	.75
31	Roberto Kelly	.75
32	Edgar Martinez	.75
33	Alex Rodriguez	5.00
34	Juan Gonzalez	3.50
35	Ivan Rodriguez	2.50
36	Jose Cruz Jr.	1.50

1998 Pacific Team Checklists

Team Checklists is a 30-card insert in the bilingual Pacific Baseball set. One card was created for each team. A player photo is featured on the right with the team logo laser-cut into a bat barrel design on the left.

		MT
Complete Set (30):		100.00
Common Player:		1.00
1	Tim Salmon, Jim Edmonds	1.50
2	Cal Ripken Jr., Roberto Alomar	10.00
3	Nomar Garciaparra Mo Vaughn	8.00
4	Frank Thomas, Albert Belle	8.00
5	Sandy Alomar Jr., Manny Ramirez	3.50
6	Justin Thompson, Tony Clark	1.00
7	Johnny Damon, Jermaine Dye	1.00
8	Dave Nilsson, Jeff Cirillo	1.00
9	Paul Molitor, Chuck Knoblauch	1.50
10	Tino Martinez, Derek Jeter	5.00
11	Ben Grieve, Jose Canseco	4.50
12	Ken Griffey Jr., Alex Rodriguez	10.00
13	Juan Gonzalez, Ivan Rodriguez	4.50
14	Jose Cruz Jr., Roger Clemens	2.00
15	Greg Maddux, Chipper Jones	9.00
16	Sammy Sosa, Mark Grace	8.00
17	Barry Larkin, Deion Sanders	1.50
18	Larry Walker, Andres Galarraga	1.50
19	Moises Alou, Bobby Bonilla	1.00
20	Jeff Bagwell, Craig Biggio	6.00
21	Mike Piazza, Hideo Nomo	10.00
22	Pedro Martinez, Henry Rodriguez	1.50
23	Rey Ordonez, Carlos Baerga	1.00
24	Curt Schilling, Scott Rolen	4.00
25	Al Martin, Tony Womack	1.00
26	Mark McGwire, Dennis Eckersley	10.00
27	Tony Gwynn, Wally Joyner	6.00
28	Barry Bonds, J.T. Snow	4.00
29	Matt Williams, Jay Bell	1.00
30	Fred McGriff, Roberto Hernandez	1.00

1998 Pacific Aurora

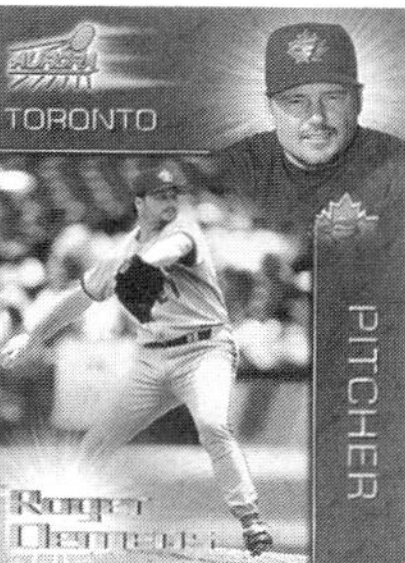

The Aurora base set consists of 200 cards printed on 24-point board. The cards have a color photo bordered on two sides by a thick green (National League) or red (A.L.) border. A portrait photo appears in the upper-right corner. Back has another portrait photo, 1997 and career stats, career highlights and personal data. Aurora was sold in six-card foil packs. Inserts include Pennant Fever (with three parallels), Hardball Cel-Fusions, Kings of the Major Leagues, On Deck Laser-Cuts and Pacific Cubes.

		MT
Complete Set (200):		35.00
Common Player:		.10
Pack (6):		2.00
Wax Box (36):		50.00
1	Garret Anderson	.10
2	Jim Edmonds	.20
3	Darin Erstad	.75
4	Cecil Fielder	.10
5	Chuck Finley	.10
6	Todd Greene	.10
7	Ken Hill	.10
8	Tim Salmon	.25
9	Roberto Alomar	.60
10	Brady Anderson	.10
11	Joe Carter	.10
12	Mike Mussina	.60
13	Rafael Palmeiro	.25
14	Cal Ripken Jr.	2.50
15	B.J. Surhoff	.10
16	Steve Avery	.10
17	Nomar Garciaparra	1.50
18	Pedro Martinez	.75
19	John Valentin	.10
20	Jason Varitek	.10
21	Mo Vaughn	.35
22	Albert Belle	.30
23	Ray Durham	.10
24	*Magglio Ordonez*	1.00
25	Frank Thomas	1.00
26	Robin Ventura	.10
27	Sandy Alomar Jr.	.10
28	Travis Fryman	.10
29	Dwight Gooden	.10
30	David Justice	.30
31	Kenny Lofton	.10
32	Manny Ramirez	.75
33	Jim Thome	.10
34	Omar Vizquel	.10
35	Enrique Wilson	.10
36	Jaret Wright	.15
37	Tony Clark	.10
38	Bobby Higginson	.10
39	Brian Hunter	.10
40	Bip Roberts	.10
41	Justin Thompson	.10
42	Jeff Conine	.10
43	Johnny Damon	.15
44	Jermaine Dye	.10
45	Jeff King	.10
46	Jeff Montgomery	.10
47	Hal Morris	.10
48	Dean Palmer	.10
49	Terry Pendleton	.10
50	Rick Aguilera	.10
51	Marty Cordova	.10
52	Paul Molitor	.60
53	Otis Nixon	.10
54	Brad Radke	.15
55	Terry Steinbach	.10
56	Todd Walker	.10
57	Chili Davis	.10
58	Derek Jeter	2.00
59	Chuck Knoblauch	.10
60	Tino Martinez	.10
61	Paul O'Neill	.10
62	Andy Pettitte	.25
63	Mariano Rivera	.25
64	Bernie Williams	.35
65	Jason Giambi	.75
66	Ben Grieve	.25
67	Rickey Henderson	.40
68	A.J. Hinch	.10
69	Kenny Rogers	.10
70	Jay Buhner	.10
71	Joey Cora	.10
72	Ken Griffey Jr.	2.25
73	Randy Johnson	.75
74	Edgar Martinez	.10
75	Jamie Moyer	.10
76	Alex Rodriguez	2.25
77	David Segui	.10
78	*Rolando Arrojo*	.40
79	Wade Boggs	.60
80	Roberto Hernandez	.10
81	Dave Martinez	.10
82	Fred McGriff	.10
83	Paul Sorrento	.10
84	Kevin Stocker	.10
85	Will Clark	.30
86	Juan Gonzalez	.75
87	Tom Goodwin	.10
88	Rusty Greer	.10
89	Ivan Rodriguez	.60
90	John Wetteland	.10
91	Jose Canseco	.45
92	Roger Clemens	1.00
93	Jose Cruz Jr.	.25
94	Carlos Delgado	.50
95	Pat Hentgen	.10
96	Jay Bell	.10
97	Andy Benes	.10
98	Karim Garcia	.10
99	Travis Lee	.15
100	Devon White	.10
101	Matt Williams	.30
102	Andres Galarraga	.10
103	Tom Glavine	.20
104	Andruw Jones	.75
105	Chipper Jones	2.00
106	Ryan Klesko	.10
107	Javy Lopez	.10
108	Greg Maddux	1.00
109	Walt Weiss	.10
110	Rod Beck	.10
111	Jeff Blauser	.10
112	Mark Grace	.40
113	Lance Johnson	.10
114	Mickey Morandini	.10
115	Henry Rodriguez	.10
116	Sammy Sosa	1.50
117	Kerry Wood	.50
118	Lenny Harris	.10
119	Damian Jackson	.10
120	Barry Larkin	.15
121	Reggie Sanders	.10
122	Brett Tomko	.10
123	Dante Bichette	.10
124	Ellis Burks	.10
125	Vinny Castilla	.10
126	Todd Helton	.75
127	Darryl Kile	.10
128	Larry Walker	.30
129	Bobby Bonilla	.10
130	Livan Hernandez	.10
131	Charles Johnson	.10
132	Derrek Lee	.10
133	Edgar Renteria	.10
134	Gary Sheffield	.30
135	Moises Alou	.15
136	Jeff Bagwell	.75
137	Derek Bell	.10
138	Craig Biggio	.15
139	*John Halama*	.40
140	Mike Hampton	.10
141	Richard Hidalgo	.15
142	Wilton Guerrero	.10
143	Todd Hollandsworth	.10
144	Eric Karros	.10
145	Paul Konerko	.10
146	Raul Mondesi	.25
147	Hideo Nomo	.75
148	Chan Ho Park	.35
149	Mike Piazza	2.00
150	Jeromy Burnitz	.10
151	Todd Dunn	.10
152	Marquis Grissom	.10
153	John Jaha	.10
154	Dave Nilsson	.10
155	Fernando Vina	.10
156	Mark Grudzielanek	.10
157	Vladimir Guerrero	.75
158	F.P. Santangelo	.10
159	Jose Vidro	.15
160	Rondell White	.15
161	Edgardo Alfonzo	.15
162	Carlos Baerga	.10
163	John Franco	.10
164	Todd Hundley	.10
165	Brian McRae	.10
166	John Olerud	.10
167	Rey Ordonez	.10
168	*Masato Yoshii*	.50
169	Ricky Bottalico	.10
170	Doug Glanville	.10
171	Gregg Jefferies	.10
172	Desi Relaford	.10
173	Scott Rolen	.50
174	Curt Schilling	.25
175	Jose Guillen	.10
176	Jason Kendall	.10
177	Al Martin	.10
178	Abraham Nunez	.10
179	Kevin Young	.10
180	Royce Clayton	.10
181	Delino DeShields	.10
182	Gary Gaetti	.10
183	Ron Gant	.10
184	Brian Jordan	.10
185	Ray Lankford	.10
186	Willie McGee	.10
187	Mark McGwire	2.50
188	Kevin Brown	.20
189	Ken Caminiti	.10
190	Steve Finley	.10
191	Tony Gwynn	.75
192	Wally Joyner	.10
193	Ruben Rivera	.10
194	Quilvio Veras	.10
195	Barry Bonds	1.00
196	Shawn Estes	.10
197	Orel Hershiser	.10
198	Jeff Kent	.10
199	Robb Nen	.10
200	J.T. Snow	.10

1998 Pacific Aurora Cubes

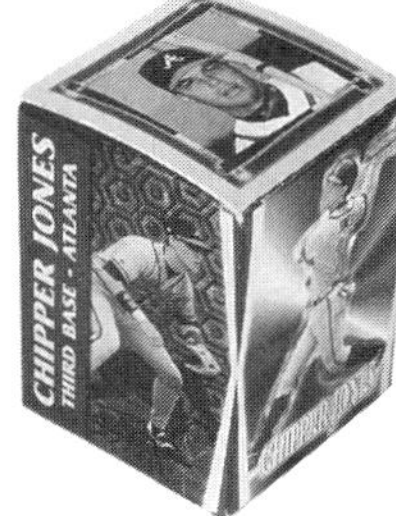

A cardboard cube presenting player photos on top and three sides, plus a side of stats was created as a hobby-only insert for Pacific Aurora. The assembled, shrink-wrapped cubes were packed one per box.

	MT
Complete Set (20):	50.00
Common Player:	1.00
Inserted 1:box	

1	Travis Lee	1.00
2	Chipper Jones	5.00
3	Greg Maddux	3.50
4	Cal Ripken Jr.	6.00
5	Nomar Garciaparra	4.00
6	Frank Thomas	2.50
7	Manny Ramirez	2.00
8	Larry Walker	1.00
9	Hideo Nomo	1.75
10	Mike Piazza	5.00
11	Derek Jeter	5.00
12	Ben Grieve	1.00
13	Mark McGwire	6.00
14	Tony Gwynn	2.00
15	Barry Bonds	3.00
16	Ken Griffey Jr.	5.50
17	Alex Rodriguez	5.50
18	Wade Boggs	1.50
19	Juan Gonzalez	2.00
20	Jose Cruz Jr.	1.00

1998 Pacific Aurora Hardball Cel-Fusion

Hardball Cel-Fusions is a 20-card insert featuring a die-cut celluloid baseball fused to a foiled and etched card.

		MT
Complete Set (20):		175.00
Common Player:		4.00
Inserted 1:73		
1	Travis Lee	5.00
2	Chipper Jones	16.00
3	Greg Maddux	12.00
4	Cal Ripken Jr.	20.00
5	Nomar Garciaparra	13.50
6	Frank Thomas	10.00
7	David Justice	4.00
8	Jeff Bagwell	8.00
9	Hideo Nomo	7.50
10	Mike Piazza	16.00
11	Derek Jeter	16.00
12	Ben Grieve	4.00
13	Scott Rolen	6.00
14	Mark McGwire	20.00
15	Tony Gwynn	11.00
16	Ken Griffey Jr.	20.00
17	Alex Rodriguez	20.00
18	Ivan Rodriguez	6.00
19	Roger Clemens	8.00
20	Jose Cruz Jr.	4.00

1998 Pacific Aurora Kings of the Major Leagues

This 10-card insert features star players on fully-foiled cards. A marble-look semi-circular panel at bottom has the player identification. The action photo at center is set against a bronze orb and concentric circles of gold-foil repeat the "Kings of the Major Leagues" title. Backs have a color portrait on a red and black background along with a few sentences about the player.

		MT
Complete Set (10):		240.00
Common Player:		20.00
Inserted 1:361		
1	Chipper Jones	30.00
2	Greg Maddux	20.00
3	Cal Ripken Jr.	40.00
4	Nomar Garciaparra	20.00
5	Frank Thomas	20.00
6	Mike Piazza	30.00
7	Mark McGwire	40.00
8	Tony Gwynn	20.00
9	Ken Griffey Jr.	35.00
10	Alex Rodriguez	35.00

1998 Pacific Aurora On Deck Laser-Cut

On Deck Laser-Cuts is a 20-card insert in packs of 1998 Pacific Aurora Baseball. Fronts have an action pphoto at top, with an intricately die-cut pattern in gold foil below. Backs feature a portrait photo.

		MT
Complete Set (20):		75.00
Common Player:		1.00
Inserted 1:9		
1	Travis Lee	2.00
2	Chipper Jones	6.00
3	Greg Maddux	5.00
4	Cal Ripken Jr.	10.00
5	Nomar Garciaparra	5.00
6	Frank Thomas	5.00
7	Manny Ramirez	4.00
8	Larry Walker	1.00
9	Hideo Nomo	3.00
10	Mike Piazza	6.00
11	Derek Jeter	6.00
12	Ben Grieve	4.00
13	Mark McGwire	10.00
14	Tony Gwynn	4.00
15	Barry Bonds	4.00
16	Ken Griffey Jr.	9.00
17	Alex Rodriguez	8.00
18	Wade Boggs	1.50
19	Juan Gonzalez	4.00
20	Jose Cruz Jr.	1.00

1998 Pacific Aurora Pennant Fever

Pennant Fever is a 50-card insert seeded one per pack. Each card is fully foiled and etched. The color player image is duplicated in the upper-left corner with an image stamped in gold foil. Pennant Fever has four parallels. Red cards are a 1:4 retail insert. The Silver retail parallel is numbered to 250, Platinum Blue is numbered to 100 and the Copper hobby parallel is numbered to 20. Tony Gwynn signed his card serially numbered one in each insert.

		MT
Complete Set (50):		25.00
Common Player:		.25
Inserted 1:1		
Reds (1:4 Retail):		2X
Silvers (250 sets):		5X
Platinum Blues (100 sets):		10X
Coppers (20 sets):		40X
1	Tony Gwynn	1.00
2	Derek Jeter	1.50
3	Alex Rodriguez	2.00
4	Paul Molitor	.50
5	Nomar Garciaparra	1.25
6	Jeff Bagwell	.75
7	Ivan Rodriguez	.60
8	Cal Ripken Jr.	2.50
9	Matt Williams	.35
10	Chipper Jones	1.50
11	Edgar Martinez	.25
12	Wade Boggs	.50
13	Paul Konerko	.25
14	Ben Grieve	.50
15	Sandy Alomar Jr.	.25
16	Travis Lee	.50
17	Scott Rolen	.60
18	Ryan Klesko	.25
19	Juan Gonzalez	.75
20	Albert Belle	.50
21	Roger Clemens	1.00
22	Javy Lopez	.25
23	Jose Cruz Jr.	.40
24	Ken Griffey Jr.	2.25
25	Mark McGwire	2.50
26	Brady Anderson	.25
27	Jaret Wright	.50
28	Roberto Alomar	.50
29	Joe Carter	.25
30	Hideo Nomo	.60
31	Mike Piazza	1.50
32	Andres Galarraga	.25
33	Larry Walker	.35
34	Tim Salmon	.35
35	Frank Thomas	1.00
36	Moises Alou	.25
37	David Justice	.40
38	Manny Ramirez	.75
39	Jim Edmonds	.25
40	Barry Bonds	1.00
41	Jim Thome	.25
42	Mo Vaughn	.50
43	Rafael Palmeiro	.35
44	Darin Erstad	.65
45	Pedro Martinez	.50
46	Greg Maddux	1.00
47	Jose Canseco	.40
48	Vladimir Guerrero	.75
49	Bernie Williams	.40
50	Randy Johnson	.50

1998 Pacific Crown Royale

The Crown Royale base set consists of 144 die-cut cards. The cards have a horizontal layout and are die-cut around a crown design at the top. The cards are double-foiled and etched. Inserts include Diamond Knights, Pillars of the Game, Race to the Record, All-Star Die-Cuts, Firestone on Baseball and Cramer's Choice Awards.

		MT
Complete Set (144):		100.00
Common Player:		.25
Pack (6):		3.00
Wax Box (24):		60.00
1	Garret Anderson	.25
2	Jim Edmonds	.40
3	Darin Erstad	1.50
4	Tim Salmon	.50
5	Jarrod Washburn	.25
6	David Dellucci	.25
7	Travis Lee	.50
8	Devon White	.25
9	Matt Williams	.50
10	Andres Galarraga	.25
11	Tom Glavine	.40
12	Andruw Jones	1.50
13	Chipper Jones	5.00
14	Ryan Klesko	.25
15	Javy Lopez	.25
16	Greg Maddux	4.00
17	Walt Weiss	.25
18	Roberto Alomar	1.50
19	Harold Baines	.25
20	Eric Davis	.25
21	Mike Mussina	2.00
22	Rafael Palmeiro	.50
23	Cal Ripken Jr.	6.00
24	Nomar Garciaparra	4.00
25	Pedro Martinez	2.50
26	Troy O'Leary	.25
27	Mo Vaughn	1.00
28	Tim Wakefield	.25
29	Mark Grace	1.25
30	Mickey Morandini	.25
31	Sammy Sosa	4.50
32	Kerry Wood	1.50
33	Albert Belle	1.00
34	Mike Caruso	.25

35	Ray Durham	.25
36	Frank Thomas	3.50
37	Robin Ventura	.25
38	Bret Boone	.25
39	Sean Casey	.60
40	Barry Larkin	.50
41	Reggie Sanders	.25
42	Sandy Alomar Jr.	.25
43	David Justice	.50
44	Kenny Lofton	.25
45	Manny Ramirez	2.50
46	Jim Thome	.25
47	Omar Vizquel	.25
48	Jaret Wright	.60
49	Dante Bichette	.25
50	Ellis Burks	.25
51	Vinny Castilla	.25
52	Todd Helton	1.50
53	Larry Walker	.50
54	Tony Clark	.25
55	Damion Easley	.25
56	Bobby Higginson	.25
57	Cliff Floyd	.25
58	Livan Hernandez	.25
59	Derrek Lee	.25
60	Edgar Renteria	.25
61	Moises Alou	.35
62	Jeff Bagwell	2.50
63	Derek Bell	.25
64	Craig Biggio	.35
65	Johnny Damon	.25
66	Jeff King	.25
67	Hal Morris	.25
68	Dean Palmer	.25
69	Bobby Bonilla	.25
70	Eric Karros	.25
71	Raul Mondesi	.50
72	Gary Sheffield	.60
73	Jeromy Burnitz	.25
74	Jeff Cirillo	.25
75	Marquis Grissom	.25
76	Fernando Vina	.25
77	Marty Cordova	.25
78	Pat Meares	.25
79	Paul Molitor	1.50
80	Terry Steinbach	.25
81	Todd Walker	.25
82	Brad Fullmer	.25
83	Vladimir Guerrero	1.50
84	Carl Pavano	.25
85	Rondell White	.35
86	Carlos Baerga	.25
87	Hideo Nomo	1.00
88	John Olerud	.25
89	Rey Ordonez	.25
90	Mike Piazza	5.00
91	*Masato Yoshii*	1.50
92	*Orlando Hernandez*	5.00
93	Hideki Irabu	.25
94	Derek Jeter	5.00
95	Chuck Knoblauch	.25
96	Ricky Ledee	.25
97	Tino Martinez	.25
98	Paul O'Neill	.25
99	Bernie Williams	1.50
100	Jason Giambi	1.50
101	Ben Grieve	.50
102	Rickey Henderson	1.50
103	Matt Stairs	.25
104	Bob Abreu	.25
105	Doug Glanville	.25
106	Scott Rolen	1.50
107	Curt Schilling	.50
108	Jose Guillen	.25
109	Jason Kendall	.25
110	Jason Schmidt	.25
111	Kevin Young	.25
112	Delino DeShields	.25
113	Brian Jordan	.25
114	Ray Lankford	.25
115	Mark McGwire	6.00
116	Tony Gwynn	2.50
117	Wally Joyner	.25
118	Ruben Rivera	.25
119	Greg Vaughn	.25
120	Rich Aurilia	.25
121	Barry Bonds	4.00
122	Bill Mueller	.25
123	Robb Nen	.25
124	Jay Buhner	.25
125	Ken Griffey Jr.	5.50
126	Edgar Martinez	.25
127	Shane Monahan	.25
128	Alex Rodriguez	5.50
129	David Segui	.25
130	*Rolando Arrojo*	1.50
131	Wade Boggs	.75
132	Quinton McCracken	.25
133	Fred McGriff	.25
134	Bobby Smith	.25
135	Will Clark	.50
136	Juan Gonzalez	2.50
137	Rusty Greer	.25
138	Ivan Rodriguez	2.00
139	Aaron Sele	.25
140	John Wetteland	.25
141	Jose Canseco	1.50
142	Roger Clemens	4.00
143	Carlos Delgado	1.50
144	Shawn Green	.75

1998 Pacific Crown Royale All-Stars

This 20-card insert was seeded one per 25 packs. The featured players all participated in the 1998 All-Star Game. The background features the sun rising over a mountain with a die-cut at the top of the card.

		MT
Complete Set (20):		160.00
Common Player:		2.50
Inserted 1:25		
1	Roberto Alomar	5.00
2	Cal Ripken Jr.	20.00
3	Kenny Lofton	2.50
4	Jim Thome	2.50
5	Derek Jeter	15.00
6	David Wells	3.00
7	Ken Griffey Jr.	17.50
8	Alex Rodriguez	17.50
9	Juan Gonzalez	7.50
10	Ivan Rodriguez	6.00
11	Gary Sheffield	3.00
12	Chipper Jones	15.00
13	Greg Maddux	12.50
14	Walt Weiss	2.50
15	Larry Walker	3.00
16	Craig Biggio	2.50
17	Mike Piazza	15.00
18	Mark McGwire	20.00
19	Tony Gwynn	12.50
20	Barry Bonds	8.00

1998 Pacific Crown Royale Cramer's Choice Awards

Premium-sized Cramer's Choice Awards were inserted one per box. The ten players in the set are featured on a die-cut card designed to resemble a trophy. Pacific CEO Mike Cramer signed and hand-numbered ten sets of Cramer's Choice Awards.

		MT
Complete Set (10):		80.00
Common Player:		5.00
Inserted 1:box		
1	Cal Ripken Jr.	15.00
2	Ken Griffey Jr.	13.50
3	Alex Rodriguez	13.50
4	Juan Gonzalez	7.50
5	Travis Lee	5.00
6	Chipper Jones	12.00
7	Greg Maddux	10.00
8	Kerry Wood	6.00
9	Mark McGwire	15.00
10	Tony Gwynn	9.00

1998 Pacific Crown Royale Diamond Knights

Diamond Knights is a 25-card, one per pack insert. Each card features a color action photo and the player's name, team and position listed in a Medieval-type border at the bottom.

		MT
Complete Set (25):		40.00
Common Player:		.75
Inserted 1:1		
1	Andres Galarraga	.75
2	Chipper Jones	3.00
3	Greg Maddux	2.50
4	Cal Ripken Jr.	5.00
5	Nomar Garciaparra	2.50
6	Mo Vaughn	1.00
7	Kerry Wood	1.50
8	Frank Thomas	2.50
9	Vinny Castilla	.75
10	Jeff Bagwell	1.50
11	Craig Biggio	.75
12	Paul Molitor	1.00
13	Mike Piazza	3.00
14	Orlando Hernandez	2.50
15	Derek Jeter	3.00
16	Ricky Ledee	.75
17	Mark McGwire	5.00
18	Tony Gwynn	2.50
19	Barry Bonds	2.50
20	Ken Griffey Jr.	4.00
21	Alex Rodriguez	4.00
22	Wade Boggs	1.25
23	Juan Gonzalez	1.50
24	Ivan Rodriguez	1.25
25	Jose Canseco	1.00

1998 Pacific Crown Royale Firestone on Baseball

This 26-card insert features star players with commentary by sports personality Roy Firestone. The fronts have a color photo of the player and a portrait of Firestone in the lower-right corner. The card backs have text by Firestone on what makes the featured player great. Firestone signed a total of 300 cards in this insert.

		MT
Complete Set (26):		85.00
Common Player:		1.00
Firestone Autographed Card:		15.00
Inserted 1:12		
1	Travis Lee	1.50
2	Chipper Jones	7.50
3	Greg Maddux	6.00
4	Cal Ripken Jr.	10.00
5	Nomar Garciaparra	6.00
6	Mo Vaughn	2.00
7	Kerry Wood	2.50
8	Frank Thomas	5.00
9	Manny Ramirez	3.00
10	Larry Walker	1.50
11	Gary Sheffield	1.00
12	Paul Molitor	2.00
13	Hideo Nomo	2.00
14	Mike Piazza	7.50
15	Ben Grieve	1.50
16	Mark McGwire	10.00
17	Tony Gwynn	6.00
18	Barry Bonds	4.00
19	Ken Griffey Jr.	9.00
20	Randy Johnson	2.50
21	Alex Rodriquez	9.00
22	Wade Boggs	1.50
23	Juan Gonzalez	3.00
24	Ivan Rodriguez	2.00
25	Roger Clemens	5.00
26	Roy Firestone	1.00

1998 Pacific Crown Royale Pillars of the Game

This 25-card insert was seeded one per pack. Each card features a star player with a background of holographic silver foil.

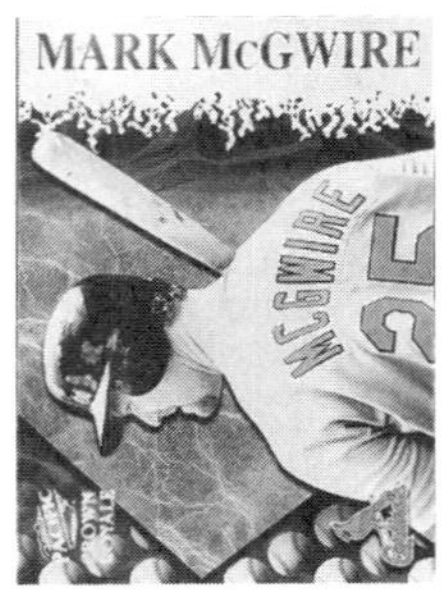

		MT
Complete Set (25):		40.00
Common Player:		.75
Inserted 1:1		
1	Jim Edmonds	.75
2	Travis Lee	1.00
3	Chipper Jones	3.00
4	Tom Glavine, John Smoltz, Greg Maddux	2.00
5	Cal Ripken Jr.	5.00
6	Nomar Garciaparra	2.00
7	Mo Vaughn	1.25
8	Sammy Sosa	3.00
9	Kerry Wood	1.50
10	Frank Thomas	2.50
11	Jim Thome	.75
12	Larry Walker	1.00
13	Moises Alou	.75
14	Raul Mondesi	1.00
15	Mike Piazza	3.00
16	Hideki Irabu	.75
17	Bernie Williams	1.00
18	Ben Grieve	1.00
19	Scott Rolen	1.50
20	Mark McGwire	5.00
21	Tony Gwynn	2.00
22	Ken Griffey Jr.	4.00
23	Alex Rodriguez	4.00
24	Juan Gonzalez	2.00
25	Roger Clemens	2.00

1998 Pacific Crown Royale Home Run Fever

Home Run Fever (10 cards, 1:73) features players who had a shot at breaking Roger Maris' home run record in 1998. The card fronts have a player photo on the left and a blackboard with numbers from 1 to 60 on the right. Ten circles featuring disappearing ink contained numbers 61 through 70. Collectors could rub the circles to reveal the player's potential record home run total.

		MT
Complete Set (10):		70.00
Common Player:		2.50
Inserted 1:73		
1	Andres Galarraga	2.50
2	Sammy Sosa	15.00
3	Albert Belle	3.00
4	Jim Thome	2.50
5	Mark McGwire	20.00
6	Greg Vaughn	2.50
7	Ken Griffey Jr.	18.00
8	Alex Rodriguez	18.00
9	Juan Gonzalez	5.00
10	Jose Canseco	3.00

1998 Pacific Invincible

Invincible Baseball consists of a 150-card base set. The base cards have a horizontal layout and feature a player photo on the left and a headshot in a cel window on the right. The regular cards were inserted one per five-card pack. Silver (2:37) and Platinum Blue (1:73) parallels were also created. Inserts include Moments in Time, Team Checklists, Photoengravings, Interleague Players, Gems of the Diamond and Cramer's Choice Awards.

		MT
Complete Set (150):		60.00
Common Player:		.25
Silvers:		2X
Inserted 2:37		
Platinum Blues:		4X
Inserted 1:73		
Pack (5):		1.50
Wax Box (36):		40.00
1	Garret Anderson	.25
2	Jim Edmonds	.35
3	Darin Erstad	1.00
4	Chuck Finley	.25
5	Tim Salmon	.50
6	Roberto Alomar	1.00
7	Brady Anderson	.25
8	Geronimo Berroa	.25
9	Eric Davis	.25
10	Mike Mussina	1.00
11	Rafael Palmeiro	.75
12	Cal Ripken Jr.	8.00
13	Steve Avery	.25
14	Nomar Garciaparra	5.00
15	John Valentin	.25
16	Mo Vaughn	.50
17	Albert Belle	.50
18	Ozzie Guillen	.25
19	Norberto Martin	.25
20	Frank Thomas	2.00
21	Robin Ventura	.25
22	Sandy Alomar Jr.	.25
23	David Justice	.75
24	Kenny Lofton	.25
25	Manny Ramirez	1.50
26	Jim Thome	.25
27	Omar Vizquel	.25
28	Matt Williams	.75
29	Jaret Wright	.50
30	Raul Casanova	.25
31	Tony Clark	.25
32	Deivi Cruz	.25
33	Bobby Higginson	.25
34	Justin Thompson	.25
35	Yamil Benitez	.25
36	Johnny Damon	.25
37	Jermaine Dye	.25
38	Jed Hansen	.25
39	Larry Sutton	.25
40	Jeromy Burnitz	.25
41	Jeff Cirillo	.25
42	Dave Nilsson	.25
43	Jose Valentin	.25
44	Fernando Vina	.25
45	Marty Cordova	.25
46	Chuck Knoblauch	.25
47	Paul Molitor	1.00
48	Brad Radke	.25
49	Terry Steinbach	.25
50	Wade Boggs	1.00
51	Hideki Irabu	.25
52	Derek Jeter	5.50
53	Tino Martinez	.25
54	Andy Pettitte	.75
55	Mariano Rivera	.65
56	Bernie Williams	.75
57	Jose Canseco	1.00
58	Jason Giambi	1.50
59	Ben Grieve	.50
60	Aaron Small	.25
61	Jay Buhner	.25
62	Ken Cloude	.25
63	Joey Cora	.25
64	Ken Griffey Jr.	6.50
65	Randy Johnson	1.50
66	Edgar Martinez	.25
67	Alex Rodriguez	6.50
68	Will Clark	.75
69	Juan Gonzalez	1.50
70	Rusty Greer	.25
71	Ivan Rodriguez	1.25
72	Joe Carter	.25
73	Roger Clemens	3.00
74	Jose Cruz Jr.	.45
75	Carlos Delgado	.75
76	Andruw Jones	1.00
77	Chipper Jones	5.50
78	Ryan Klesko	.25
79	Javier Lopez	.25
80	Greg Maddux	3.00
81	Miguel Batista	.25
82	Jeremi Gonzalez	.25
83	Mark Grace	.75
84	Kevin Orie	.25
85	Sammy Sosa	3.00
86	Barry Larkin	.40
87	Deion Sanders	.35
88	Reggie Sanders	.25
89	Chris Stynes	.25
90	Dante Bichette	.25
91	Vinny Castilla	.25
92	Andres Galarraga	.25
93	Neifi Perez	.25
94	Larry Walker	.65
95	Moises Alou	.25
96	Bobby Bonilla	.25
97	Kevin Brown	.40
98	Craig Counsell	.25
99	Livan Hernandez	.25
100	Edgar Renteria	.25
101	Gary Sheffield	.65
102	Jeff Bagwell	1.50
103	Craig Biggio	.40
104	Luis Gonzalez	1.00
105	Darryl Kile	.25
106	Wilton Guerrero	.25
107	Eric Karros	.25
108	Ramon Martinez	.25
109	Raul Mondesi	.50
110	Hideo Nomo	1.25
111	Chan Ho Park	.65
112	Mike Piazza	5.50
113	Mark Grudzielanek	.25
114	Vladimir Guerrero	1.00
115	Pedro Martinez	2.00
116	Henry Rodriguez	.25
117	David Segui	.25
118	Edgardo Alfonzo	.25
119	Carlos Baerga	.25
120	John Franco	.25
121	John Olerud	.25
122	Rey Ordonez	.25
123	Ricky Bottalico	.25
124	Gregg Jefferies	.25
125	Mickey Morandini	.25
126	Scott Rolen	.75
127	Curt Schilling	.50
128	Jose Guillen	.40
129	Esteban Loaiza	.25
130	Al Martin	.25
131	Tony Womack	.25
132	Dennis Eckersley	.25
133	Gary Gaetti	.25
134	Curtis King	.25
135	Ray Lankford	.25
136	Mark McGwire	8.00
137	Ken Caminiti	.25
138	Steve Finley	.25
139	Tony Gwynn	2.00
140	Carlos Hernandez	.25
141	Wally Joyner	.25
142	Barry Bonds	3.00
143	Jacob Cruz	.25
144	Shawn Estes	.25
145	Stan Javier	.25
146	J.T. Snow	.25
147	Nomar Garciaparra (ROY)	3.00
148	Scott Rolen (ROY)	1.00
149	Ken Griffey Jr. (MVP)	4.00
150	Larry Walker (MVP)	.50

1998 Pacific Invincible Cramer's Choice

The 10-card Cramer's Choice Awards insert features top players on cards with a die-cut trophy design. This set has six different foil variations, each with a different production number. Green (99 hand-numbered sets), Dark Blue (80), Light Blue (50), Red (25), Gold (15) and Purple (10) versions were included in Invincible.

		MT
Complete Green Set (10):		475.00
Common Green (99 sets):		25.00
Dark Blues (80 sets):		1X
Light Blues (50 sets):		1.5X
Reds (25 sets):		2X
Golds (15 sets):		3X
Purples (10 sets):		5X
1	Greg Maddux	60.00
2	Roberto Alomar	25.00
3	Cal Ripken Jr.	100.00
4	Nomar Garciaparra	60.00
5	Larry Walker	25.00
6	Mike Piazza	75.00
7	Mark McGwire	100.00
8	Tony Gwynn	50.00
9	Ken Griffey Jr.	85.00
10	Roger Clemens	50.00

1998 Pacific Invincible Gems of the Diamond

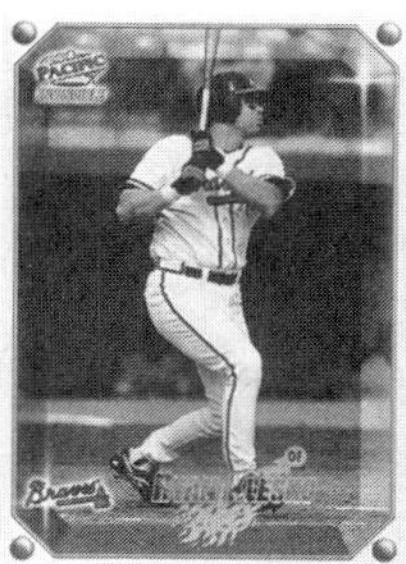

Gems of the Diamond is a 220-card insert seeded four per pack. The cards feature a color photo inside a white border.

		MT
Complete Set (220):		30.00
Common Player:		.10
1	Jim Edmonds	.15
2	Todd Greene	.10
3	Ken Hill	.10
4	Mike Holtz	.10
5	Mike James	.10
6	Chad Kreuter	.10
7	Tim Salmon	.25
8	Roberto Alomar	.60
9	Brady Anderson	.10
10	David Dellucci	.10
11	Jeffrey Hammonds	.10
12	Mike Mussina	.60
13	Rafael Palmeiro	.25
14	Arthur Rhodes	.10
15	Cal Ripken Jr.	2.50
16	Nerio Rodriguez	.10
17	Tony Tarasco	.10
18	Lenny Webster	.10
19	Mike Benjamin	.10
20	Rich Garces	.10
21	Nomar Garciaparra	1.50
22	Shane Mack	.10
23	Jose Malave	.10
24	Jesus Tavarez	.10
25	Mo Vaughn	.50
26	John Wasdin	.10
27	Jeff Abbott	.10
28	Albert Belle	.35
29	Mike Cameron	.10
30	Al Levine	.10
31	Robert Machado	.10
32	Greg Norton	.10
33	Magglio Ordonez	.35
34	Mike Sirotka	.10
35	Frank Thomas	1.00
36	Mario Valdez	.10
37	Sandy Alomar Jr.	.10
38	David Justice	.25
39	Jack McDowell	.10
40	Eric Plunk	.10
41	Manny Ramirez	.75
42	Kevin Seitzer	.10
43	Paul Shuey	.10
44	Omar Vizquel	.10
45	Kimera Bartee	.10
46	Glenn Dishman	.10
47	Orlando Miller	.10
48	Mike Myers	.10
49	Phil Nevin	.10
50	A.J. Sager	.10
51	Ricky Bones	.10
52	Scott Cooper	.10
53	Shane Halter	.10
54	David Howard	.10
55	Glendon Rusch	.10
56	Joe Vitiello	.10
57	Jeff D'Amico	.10
58	Mike Fetters	.10
59	Mike Matheny	.10
60	Jose Mercedes	.10
61	Ron Villone	.10
62	Jack Voigt	.10
63	Brent Brede	.10
64	Chuck Knoblauch	.10
65	Paul Molitor	.65
66	Todd Ritchie	.10
67	Frankie Rodriguez	.10
68	Scott Stahoviak	.10
69	Greg Swindell	.10
70	Todd Walker	.10
71	Wade Boggs	.35
72	Hideki Irabu	.10
73	Derek Jeter	2.00
74	Pat Kelly	.10
75	Graeme Lloyd	.10
76	Tino Martinez	.10
77	Jeff Nelson	.10
78	Scott Pose	.10
79	Mike Stanton	.10
80	Darryl Strawberry	.10
81	Bernie Williams	.35
82	Tony Batista	.10
83	Mark Bellhorn	.10
84	Ben Grieve	.25
85	Pat Lennon	.10
86	Brian Lesher	.10
87	Miguel Tejada	.25
88	George Williams	.10
89	Joey Cora	.10
90	Rob Ducey	.10
91	Ken Griffey Jr.	2.25
92	Randy Johnson	.60
93	Edgar Martinez	.10
94	John Marzano	.10
95	Greg McCarthy	.10
96	Alex Rodriguez	2.00
97	Andy Sheets	.10
98	Mike Timlin	.10
99	Lee Tinsley	.10
100	Damon Buford	.10
101	Alex Diaz	.10
102	Benji Gil	.10
103	Juan Gonzalez	.75
104	Eric Gunderson	.10
105	Danny Patterson	.10
106	Ivan Rodriguez	.60
107	Mike Simms	.10
108	Luis Andujar	.10
109	Joe Carter	.10
110	Roger Clemens	1.00
111	Jose Cruz Jr.	.40
112	Shawn Green	.20
113	Robert Perez	.10
114	Juan Samuel	.10
115	Ed Sprague	.10
116	Shannon Stewart	.10
117	Danny Bautista	.10
118	Chipper Jones	2.00
119	Ryan Klesko	.10
120	Keith Lockhart	.10
121	Javier Lopez	.10
122	Greg Maddux	1.50
123	Kevin Millwood	.50
124	Mike Mordecai	.10
125	Eddie Perez	.10
126	Randall Simon	.10
127	Miguel Cairo	.10
128	Dave Clark	.10
129	Kevin Foster	.10
130	Mark Grace	.25
131	Tyler Houston	.10
132	Mike Hubbard	.10
133	Kevin Orie	.10
134	Ryne Sandberg	.75
135	Sammy Sosa	1.50
136	Lenny Harris	.10
137	Kent Mercker	.10
138	Mike Morgan	.10
139	Deion Sanders	.15
140	Chris Stynes	.10
141	Gabe White	.10
142	Jason Bates	.10
143	Vinny Castilla	.10
144	Andres Galarraga	.10
145	Curtis Leskanic	.10
146	Jeff McCurry	.10
147	Mike Munoz	.10
148	Larry Walker	.25
149	Jamey Wright	.10
150	Moises Alou	.20
151	Bobby Bonilla	.10
152	Kevin Brown	.15
153	John Cangelosi	.10
154	Jeff Conine	.10
155	Cliff Floyd	.10
156	Jay Powell	.10
157	Edgar Renteria	.10
158	Tony Saunders	.10
159	Gary Sheffield	.25
160	Jeff Bagwell	.75
161	Tim Bogar	.10
162	Tony Eusebio	.10
163	Chris Holt	.10
164	Ray Montgomery	.10
165	Luis Rivera	.10
166	Eric Anthony	.10
167	Brett Butler	.10
168	Juan Castro	.10
169	Tripp Cromer	.10
170	Raul Mondesi	.25
171	Hideo Nomo	.75
172	Mike Piazza	2.00
173	Tom Prince	.10
174	Adam Riggs	.10
175	Shane Andrews	.10
176	Shayne Bennett	.10
177	Raul Chavez	.10
178	Pedro Martinez	.50
179	Sherman Obando	.10
180	Andy Stankiewicz	.10
181	Alberto Castillo	.10
182	Shawn Gilbert	.10
183	Luis Lopez	.10
184	Roberto Petagine	.10
185	Armando Reynoso	.10
186	Midre Cummings	.10
187	Kevin Jordan	.10
188	Desi Relaford	.10
189	Scott Rolen	.50
190	Ken Ryan	.10
191	Kevin Sefcik	.10
192	Emil Brown	.10
193	Lou Collier	.10
194	Francisco Cordova	.10
195	Kevin Elster	.10
196	Mark Smith	.10
197	Marc Wilkins	.10
198	Manny Aybar	.10
199	Jose Bautista	.10
200	David Bell	.10
201	Rigo Beltran	.10
202	Delino DeShields	.10
203	Dennis Eckersley	.10
204	John Mabry	.10
205	Eli Marrero	.10
206	Willie McGee	.10
207	Mark McGwire	2.50
208	Ken Caminiti	.20
209	Tony Gwynn	1.00
210	Chris Jones	.10
211	Craig Shipley	.10
212	Pete Smith	.10
213	Jorge Velandia	.10
214	Dario Veras	.10
215	Rich Aurilia	.10
216	Damon Berryhill	.10
217	Barry Bonds	1.50
218	Osvaldo Fernandez	.10
219	Dante Powell	.10
220	Rich Rodriguez	.10

1998 Pacific Invincible Interleague Players

Interleague Players is a 30-card insert featuring 15 sets of players - one National League and one American League player. The dark blue backgrounds have red lightning bolts and the white borders are made of a leather-like material. When a set of players is placed next to each other, they form the MLB Interleague logo in the center. Interleague Players cards were inserted one per 73 packs.

		MT
Complete Set (30):		185.00
Common Player:		2.00
Inserted 1:73		
1A	Roberto Alomar	5.00
1N	Craig Biggio	2.00
2A	Cal Ripken Jr.	20.00
2N	Chipper Jones	15.00
3A	Nomar Garciaparra	12.50
3N	Scott Rolen	8.00
4A	Mo Vaughn	4.00
4N	Andres Galarraga	2.00
5A	Frank Thomas	10.00
5N	Tony Gwynn	12.00
6A	Albert Belle	4.00
6N	Barry Bonds	8.00
7A	Hideki Irabu	2.00
7N	Hideo Nomo	6.00
8A	Derek Jeter	15.00
8N	Rey Ordonez	2.00
9A	Tino Martinez	2.00
9N	Mark McGwire	20.00
10A	Alex Rodriguez	17.50
10N	Edgar Renteria	2.00
11A	Ken Griffey Jr.	17.50
11N	Larry Walker	3.00
12A	Randy Johnson	5.00
12N	Greg Maddux	12.00
13A	Ivan Rodriguez	6.00
13N	Mike Piazza	15.00
14A	Roger Clemens	10.00
14N	Pedro Martinez	4.00
15A	Jose Cruz Jr.	2.50
15N	Wilton Guerrero	2.00

1998 Pacific Invincible Moments in Time

Moments in Time (20 cards, 1:145) is designed as a baseball scoreboard. The cards have a horizontal layout with the date of an important game in the player's career at the top. The player's stats from the game are featured and a picture is located on the scoreboard screen.

		MT
Complete Set (20):		230.00
Common Player:		5.00
Inserted 1:145		
1	Chipper Jones	25.00
2	Cal Ripken Jr.	35.00
3	Frank Thomas	17.50
4	David Justice	6.00
5	Andres Galarraga	5.00
6	Larry Walker	7.50
7	Livan Hernandez	5.00
8	Wilton Guerrero	5.00
9	Hideo Nomo	12.50
10	Mike Piazza	25.00
11	Pedro Martinez	10.00

12	Bernie Williams	5.00
13	Ben Grieve	7.50
14	Scott Rolen	7.50
15	Mark McGwire	35.00
16	Tony Gwynn	17.50
17	Ken Griffey Jr.	30.00
18	Alex Rodriguez	30.00
19	Juan Gonzalez	12.50
20	Jose Cruz Jr.	6.00

1998 Pacific Invincible Photoengravings

Photoengravings is an 18-card insert seeded one per 37 packs. Each card has a unique "old-style" design with a player photo in a frame in the center.

		MT
Complete Set (18):		60.00
Common Player:		1.00
Inserted 1:37		
1	Greg Maddux	4.00
2	Cal Ripken Jr.	7.50
3	Nomar Garciaparra	4.00
4	Frank Thomas	4.00
5	Larry Walker	2.00
6	Mike Piazza	5.00
7	Hideo Nomo	3.50
8	Pedro Martinez	3.00
9	Derek Jeter	5.00
10	Tino Martinez	1.00
11	Mark McGwire	7.50
12	Tony Gwynn	4.00
13	Barry Bonds	3.50
14	Ken Griffey Jr.	6.00
15	Alex Rodriguez	6.00
16	Ivan Rodriguez	2.50
17	Roger Clemens	3.50
18	Jose Cruz Jr.	1.50

1998 Pacific Invincible Team Checklists

Team Checklists is a 30-card insert seeded 2:37. The fronts feature a player collage with the team logo in the background. The back has a complete checklist for that team in Invincible and more player photos.

		MT
Complete Set (30):		135.00
Common Player:		2.00
Inserted 2:37		
1	Anaheim Angels (Jim Edmonds, Tim Salmon, Darin Erstad, Garret Anderson, Rickey Henderson)	5.00
2	Atlanta Braves (Greg Maddux, Chipper Jones, Javy Lopez, Ryan Klesko, Andruw Jones)	12.50
3	Baltimore Orioles (Cal Ripken Jr., Roberto Alomar, Brady Anderson, Mike Mussina, Rafael Palmeiro)	13.50
4	Boston Red Sox (Nomar Garciaparra, Mo Vaughn, Steve Avery, John Valentin)	10.00
5	Chicago Cubs (Sammy Sosa, Mark Grace, Ryne Sandberg, Jeremi Gonzalez)	7.50
6	Chicago White Sox (Frank Thomas, Albert Belle, Robin Ventura, Ozzie Guillen)	10.00
7	Cincinnati Reds (Barry Larkin, Deion Sanders, Reggie Sanders, Brett Tomko)	2.00
8	Cleveland Indians (Sandy Alomar Jr., Manny Ramirez, David Justice, Jim Thome, Omar Vizquel)	3.50
9	Colorado Rockies (Andres Galarraga, Larry Walker, Vinny Castilla, Dante Bichette, Ellis Burks)	2.50
10	Detroit Tigers (Jason Thompson, Tony Clark, Deivi Cruz, Bobby Higginson)	3.00
11	Florida Marlins (Gary Sheffield, Edgar Renteria, Livan Hernandez, Charles Johnson, Bobby Bonilla)	2.50
12	Houston Astros (Jeff Bagwell, Craig Biggio, Richard Hidalgo, Darryl Kile)	6.50
13	Kansas City Royals (Johnny Damon, Jermaine Dye, Chili Davis, Jose Rosado)	2.00
14	Los Angeles Dodgers (Mike Piazza, Wilton Guerrero, Raul Mondesi, Hideo Nomo, Ramon Martinez)	12.50
15	Milwaukee Brewers (David Nilsson, Fernando Vina, Jeromy Burnitz, Julio Franco, Jeff Cirillo)	2.00
16	Minnesota Twins (Paul Molitor, Chuck Knoblauch, Brad Radke, Terry Steinbach, Marty Cordova)	3.00
17	Montreal Expos (Henry Rodriguez, Vladimir Guerrero, Pedro Martinez, David Segui, Mark Grudzielanek)	4.00
18	New York Mets (Carlos Baerga, Todd Hundley, Rey Ordonez, John Olerud, Edgardo Alfonzo)	2.00
19	New York Yankees (Derek Jeter, Tino Martinez, Bernie Williams, Andy Pettite, Mariano Rivera)	12.50
20	Oakland Athletics (Jose Canseco, Ben Grieve, Jason Giambi, Matt Stairs)	6.50
21	Philadelphia Phillies (Curt Schilling, Scott Rolen, Gregg Jefferies, Lenny Dykstra, Ricky Bottalico)	6.00
22	Pittsburgh Pirates (Al Martin, Tony Womack, Jose Guillen, Esteban Loiaza)	2.00
23	St. Louis Cardinals (Mark McGwire, Dennis Eckersley, Delino DeShields, Willie McGee, Ray Lankford)	7.50
24	San Diego Padres (Tony Gwynn, Ken Caminiti, Wally Joyner, Steve Finley)	7.50
25	San Francisco Giants (Barry Bonds, J.T. Snow, Stan Javier, Rod Beck, Jose Vizcaino)	4.00
26	Seattle Mariners (Ken Griffey Jr., Alex Rodriguez, Edgar Martinez, Randy Johnson, Jay Buhner)	15.00
27	Texas Rangers (Juan Gonzalez, Ivan Rodriguez, Will Clark, John Wetteland, Rusty Greer)	7.50
28	Toronto Blue Jays (Jose Cruz Jr., Roger Clemens, Pat Hentgen, Joe Carter)	7.50
29	Arizona Diamondbacks (Yamil Benitez, Devon White, Matt Williams, Jay Bell)	3.00
30	Tampa Bay Devil Rays (Wade Boggs, Paul Sorrento, Fred McGriff, Roberto Hernandez)	3.00

1998 Pacific Omega

The Omega base set consists of 250 three-image cards. The horizontal cards feature a color player photo in the center with the image duplicated in foil on the right. Another color photo is on the left. The photos are divided by a baseball seam design. Red-foil parallels were a 1:4 pack insert in Wal-Mart exclusive packaging.

		MT
Complete Set (250):		25.00
Common Player:		.10
Reds:		3X
Pack (6):		1.00
Wax Box (36):		30.00
1	Garret Anderson	.10
2	Gary DiSarcina	.10
3	Jim Edmonds	.20
4	Darin Erstad	.75
5	Cecil Fielder	.10
6	Chuck Finley	.10
7	Shigetosi Hasegawa	.10
8	Tim Salmon	.20
9	Brian Anderson	.10
10	Jay Bell	.10
11	Andy Benes	.10
12	Yamil Benitez	.10
13	Jorge Fabregas	.10
14	Travis Lee	.50
15	Devon White	.10
16	Matt Williams	.20
17	Andres Galarraga	.10
18	Tom Glavine	.20
19	Andruw Jones	.75
20	Chipper Jones	2.00
21	Ryan Klesko	.10
22	Javy Lopez	.10
23	Greg Maddux	1.50
24	*Kevin Millwood*	2.50
25	Denny Neagle	.10
26	John Smoltz	.20
27	Roberto Alomar	.60
28	Brady Anderson	.10
29	Joe Carter	.10
30	Eric Davis	.10
31	Jimmy Key	.10
32	Mike Mussina	.60
33	Rafael Palmeiro	.25
34	Cal Ripken Jr.	3.00
35	B.J. Surhoff	.10
36	Dennis Eckersley	.10
37	Nomar Garciaparra	1.50
38	Reggie Jefferson	.10
39	Derek Lowe	.10
40	Pedro Martinez	.50
41	Brian Rose	.10
42	John Valentin	.10
43	Jason Varitek	.10
44	Mo Vaughn	.45
45	Jeff Blauser	.10
46	Jeremi Gonzalez	.10
47	Mark Grace	.25
48	Lance Johnson	.10
49	Kevin Orie	.10
50	Henry Rodriguez	.10
51	Sammy Sosa	1.50
52	Kerry Wood	.75
53	Albert Belle	.35
54	Mike Cameron	.10
55	Mike Caruso	.10
56	Ray Durham	.10
57	Jaime Navarro	.10
58	Greg Norton	.10
59	*Magglio Ordonez*	1.00
60	Frank Thomas	1.50
61	Robin Ventura	.10
62	Bret Boone	.10
63	Willie Greene	.10
64	Barry Larkin	.15
65	Jon Nunnally	.10
66	Eduardo Perez	.10
67	Reggie Sanders	.10
68	Brett Tomko	.10
69	Sandy Alomar Jr.	.10
70	Travis Fryman	.10
71	David Justice	.25
72	Kenny Lofton	.10
73	Charles Nagy	.10
74	Manny Ramirez	.75
75	Jim Thome	.10
76	Omar Vizquel	.10
77	Enrique Wilson	.10
78	Jaret Wright	.50
79	Dante Bichette	.10
80	Ellis Burks	.10
81	Vinny Castilla	.10
82	Todd Helton	.75
83	Darryl Kile	.10
84	Mike Lansing	.10
85	Neifi Perez	.10
86	Larry Walker	.25
87	Raul Casanova	.10
88	Tony Clark	.10
89	Luis Gonzalez	.25
90	Bobby Higginson	.10
91	Brian Hunter	.10
92	Bip Roberts	.10
93	Justin Thompson	.10

94	Josh Booty	.10
95	Craig Counsell	.10
96	Livan Hernandez	.10
97	*Ryan Jackson*	.50
98	Mark Kotsay	.10
99	Derrek Lee	.10
100	Mike Piazza	2.00
101	Edgar Renteria	.10
102	Cliff Floyd	.10
103	Moises Alou	.20
104	Jeff Bagwell	.75
105	Derrick Bell	.10
106	Sean Berry	.10
107	Craig Biggio	.15
108	*John Halama*	.25
109	Richard Hidalgo	.15
110	Shane Reynolds	.10
111	Tim Belcher	.10
112	Brian Bevil	.10
113	Jeff Conine	.10
114	Johnny Damon	.10
115	Jeff King	.10
116	Jeff Montgomery	.10
117	Dean Palmer	.10
118	Terry Pendleton	.10
119	Bobby Bonilla	.10
120	Wilton Guerrero	.10
121	Todd Hollandsworth	.10
122	Charles Johnson	.10
123	Eric Karros	.10
124	Paul Konerko	.10
125	Ramon Martinez	.10
126	Raul Mondesi	.20
127	Hideo Nomo	.65
128	Gary Sheffield	.30
129	Ismael Valdes	.10
130	Jeromy Burnitz	.10
131	Jeff Cirillo	.10
132	Todd Dunn	.10
133	Marquis Grissom	.10
134	John Jaha	.10
135	Scott Karl	.10
136	Dave Nilsson	.10
137	Jose Valentin	.10
138	Fernando Vina	.10
139	Rick Aguilera	.10
140	Marty Cordova	.10
141	Pat Meares	.10
142	Paul Molitor	.60
143	David Ortiz	.10
144	Brad Radke	.10
145	Terry Steinbach	.10
146	Todd Walker	.10
147	Shane Andrews	.10
148	Brad Fullmer	.10
149	Mark Grudzielanek	.10
150	Vladimir Guerrero	.75
151	F.P. Santangelo	.10
152	Jose Vidro	.15
153	Rondell White	.10
154	Carlos Baerga	.10
155	Bernard Gilkey	.10
156	Todd Hundley	.10
157	Butch Huskey	.10
158	Bobby Jones	.10
159	Brian McRae	.10
160	John Olerud	.20
161	Rey Ordonez	.10
162	*Masato Yoshii*	.50
163	David Cone	.10
164	Hideki Irabu	.10
165	Derek Jeter	2.00
166	Chuck Knoblauch	.10
167	Tino Martinez	.10
168	Paul O'Neill	.10
169	Andy Pettitte	.35
170	Mariano Rivera	.20
171	Darryl Strawberry	.10
172	David Wells	.10
173	Bernie Williams	.25
174	*Ryan Christenson*	.20
175	Jason Giambi	.25
176	Ben Grieve	.50
177	Rickey Henderson	.35
178	A.J. Hinch	.10
179	Kenny Rogers	.10
180	Ricky Bottalico	.10
181	Rico Brogna	.10
182	Doug Glanville	.10
183	Gregg Jefferies	.10
184	Mike Lieberthal	.10
185	Scott Rolen	.65
186	Curt Schilling	.20
187	Jermaine Allensworth	.10
188	Lou Collier	.10
189	Jose Guillen	.15
190	Jason Kendall	.10
191	Al Martin	.10
192	Tony Womack	.10
193	Kevin Young	.10
194	Royce Clayton	.10
195	Delino DeShields	.10
196	Gary Gaetti	.10
197	Ron Gant	.10
198	Brian Jordan	.10
199	Ray Lankford	.10
200	Mark McGwire	3.00
201	Todd Stottlemyre	.10
202	Kevin Brown	.20
203	Ken Caminiti	.10
204	Steve Finley	.10
205	Tony Gwynn	1.50
206	Carlos Hernandez	.10
207	Wally Joyner	.10
208	Greg Vaughn	.10
209	Barry Bonds	1.00
210	Shawn Estes	.10
211	Orel Hershiser	.10
212	Stan Javier	.10
213	Jeff Kent	.10
214	Bill Mueller	.10
215	Robb Nen	.10
216	J.T. Snow	.10
217	Jay Buhner	.10
218	Ken Cloude	.10
219	Joey Cora	.10
220	Ken Griffey Jr.	2.25
221	Glenallen Hill	.10
222	Randy Johnson	.60
223	Edgar Martinez	.10
224	Jamie Moyer	.10
225	Alex Rodriguez	2.50
226	David Segui	.10
227	Dan Wilson	.10
228	*Rolando Arrojo*	.40
229	Wade Boggs	.35
230	Miguel Cairo	.10
231	Roberto Hernandez	.10
232	Quinton McCracken	.10
233	Fred McGriff	.10
234	Paul Sorrento	.10
235	Kevin Stocker	.10
236	Will Clark	.30
237	Juan Gonzalez	.75
238	Rusty Greer	.10
239	Rick Helling	.10
240	Roberto Kelly	.10
241	Ivan Rodriguez	.75
242	Aaron Sele	.10
243	John Wetteland	.10
244	Jose Canseco	.30
245	Roger Clemens	1.00
246	Jose Cruz Jr.	.15
247	Carlos Delgado	.30
248	Alex Gonzalez	.15
249	Ed Sprague	.10
250	Shannon Stewart	.15

1998 Pacific Omega EO Portraits

EO Portraits is a 20-card insert seeded 1:73. Each card has a color action photo with a player portrait laser-cut into the card. A "1-of-1" parallel features a laser-cut number on the card as well. The "EO" stands for "Electro Optical" technology.

		MT
Complete Set (20):		125.00
Common Player:		2.50
Inserted 1:73		
1	Cal Ripken Jr.	15.00
2	Nomar Garciaparra	10.00
3	Mo Vaughn	3.00
4	Frank Thomas	7.50
5	Manny Ramirez	6.50
6	Ben Grieve	3.00
7	Ken Griffey Jr.	12.50
8	Alex Rodriguez	12.50
9	Juan Gonzalez	6.50
10	Ivan Rodriguez	5.00
11	Travis Lee	3.00
12	Greg Maddux	10.00
13	Chipper Jones	12.00
14	Kerry Wood	5.00
15	Larry Walker	2.50
16	Jeff Bagwell	6.50
17	Mike Piazza	12.00
18	Mark McGwire	15.00
19	Tony Gwynn	8.50
20	Barry Bonds	7.00

1998 Pacific Omega Face to Face

Face to Face features two star players on each card. It is a 10-card insert seeded one per 145 packs.

		MT
Complete Set (10):		100.00
Common Player:		4.00
Inserted 1:145		
1	Alex Rodriguez, Nomar Garciaparra	17.50
2	Mark McGwire, Ken Griffey Jr.	25.00
3	Mike Piazza, Sandy Alomar Jr.	15.00
4	Kerry Wood, Roger Clemens	12.50
5	Cal Ripken Jr., Paul Molitor	17.50
6	Tony Gwynn, Wade Boggs	10.00
7	Frank Thomas, Chipper Jones	10.00
8	Travis Lee, Ben Grieve	4.00
9	Hideo Nomo, Hideki Irabu	7.50
10	Juan Gonzalez, Manny Ramirez	7.50

1998 Pacific Omega Online

Online is a 36-card insert seeded about one per nine packs. The foiled and etched cards feature a color player photo in front of a hi-tech designed background. The card fronts also include the internet address for the player's web site on bigleaguers.com.

		MT
Complete Set (36):		60.00
Common Player:		.50
Inserted 1:9		
1	Cal Ripken Jr.	6.00
2	Nomar Garciaparra	3.00
3	Pedro Martinez	1.00
4	Mo Vaughn	1.00
5	Frank Thomas	3.00
6	Sandy Alomar Jr.	.50
7	Manny Ramirez	2.50
8	Jaret Wright	.75
9	Paul Molitor	1.50
10	Derek Jeter	4.00
11	Bernie Williams	.75
12	Ben Grieve	.75
13	Ken Griffey Jr.	5.00
14	Edgar Martinez	.50
15	Alex Rodriguez	5.00
16	Wade Boggs	1.00
17	Juan Gonzalez	2.50
18	Ivan Rodriguez	1.50
19	Roger Clemens	2.50
20	Travis Lee	.75
21	Matt Williams	.50
22	Andres Galarraga	.50
23	Chipper Jones	4.00
24	Greg Maddux	3.00
25	Sammy Sosa	2.50
26	Kerry Wood	1.50
27	Barry Larkin	.50
28	Larry Walker	.75
29	Derrek Lee	.50
30	Jeff Bagwell	2.50
31	Hideo Nomo	1.00
32	Mike Piazza	4.00
33	Scott Rolen	2.00
34	Mark McGwire	6.00
35	Tony Gwynn	2.50
36	Barry Bonds	2.50

1998 Pacific Omega Prism

This 20-card insert was seeded one per 37 packs. Horizontal card fronts feature prismatic foil technology.

		MT
Complete Set (20):		50.00
Common Player:		1.00
Inserted 1:37		
1	Cal Ripken Jr.	6.00
2	Nomar Garciaparra	3.00
3	Pedro Martinez	2.00
4	Frank Thomas	3.00
5	Manny Ramirez	2.50
6	Brian Giles	1.00
7	Derek Jeter	4.00
8	Ben Grieve	1.00
9	Ken Griffey Jr.	5.00
10	Alex Rodriguez	5.00
11	Juan Gonzalez	2.50
12	Travis Lee	1.00
13	Chipper Jones	4.00
14	Greg Maddux	3.00
15	Kerry Wood	2.00
16	Larry Walker	1.50
17	Hideo Nomo	3.00
18	Mike Piazza	4.00
19	Mark McGwire	6.00
20	Tony Gwynn	2.50

1998 Pacific Omega Rising Stars

Rising Stars is a multi-tiered hobby-only insert. The 20 base cards are found about 1:9 packs. Each card has two or three prospects from the same team. Five tiers of partial parallels of the insert are sequentially numbered. Tier One cards are numbered to 100, Tier Two to 75, Tier Three to 50, Tier 4 to 25 and Tier 5, with only one card of each.

		MT
Complete Set (30):		20.00
Common Player:		.50
Inserted 1:9		
1	Nerio Rodriguez, Sidney Ponson	.50
2	Frank Catalanotto, Roberto Duran, Sean Runyan	.50
3	Kevin L. Brown, Carlos Almanzar	.50
4	Aaron Boone, Pat Watkins, Scott Winchester	.50
5	Brian Meadows, Andy Larkin, Antonio Alfonseca	.50
6	DaRond Stovall, Trey Moore, Shayne Bennett	.50
7	Felix Martinez, Larry Sutton, Brian Bevil	.50
8	Homer Bush, Mike Buddie	.50
9	Rich Butler, Esteban Yan	.50
10	Damon Hollins, Brian Edmondson	.50
11	Lou Collier, Jose Silva, Javier Martinez	.50
12	Steve Sinclair, Mark Dalesandro	.50
13	Jason Varitek, Brian Rose, Brian Shouse	.75
14	Mike Caruso, Jeff Abbott, Tom Fordham	.50
15	Jason Johnson, Bobby Smith	.50
16	Dave Berg, Mark Kotsay, Jesus Sanchez	.50
17	Richard Hidalgo, John Halama, Trever Miller	1.00
18	Geoff Jenkins, Bobby Hughes, Steve Woodard	.75
19	Eli Marrero, Cliff Politte, Mike Busby	.75
20	Desi Relaford, Darrin Winston	.50
21	Todd Helton, Bobby Jones	1.50
22	Rolando Arrojo, Miguel Cairo, Dan Carlson	.75
23	David Ortiz, Javier Valentin, Eric Milton	.75
24	Magglio Ordonez, Greg Norton	1.50
25	Brad Fullmer, Javier Vazquez, Rick DeHart	.75
26	Paul Konerko, Matt Luke	1.50
27	Derrek Lee, Ryan Jackson, John Roskos	.75
28	Ben Grieve, A.J. Hinch, Ryan Christenson	1.50
29	Travis Lee, Karim Garcia, David Dellucci	2.00
30	Kerry Wood, Marc Pisciotta	2.00

1998 Pacific Online

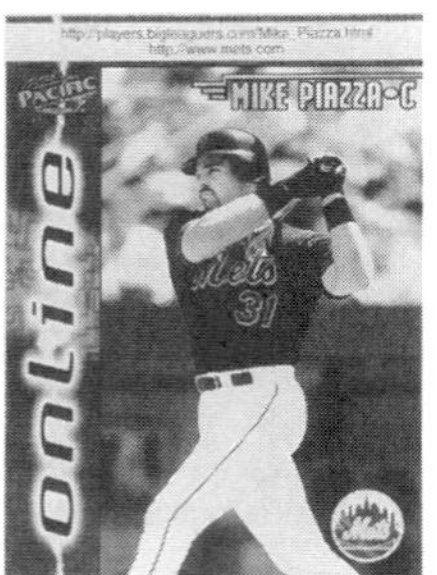

Online Baseball consists of an 800-card base set featuring 750 players on cards that list the internet address of the player's home page on the bigleaguers.com web site. Twenty players have two cards, each with different front and back photos but sharing a card number. Each of the 30 teams has a checklist that lists the team's web site. The Web Cards set parallels the 750 player cards. It has a serial number that can be entered at the bigleaguers.com web site to determine if a prize has been won. Red-foil versions of each card were produced for retail-only jumbo packs; they may carry a modest premium.

		MT
Complete Set (800):		75.00
Common Player:		.05
Web Stars/RCs:		2X
Inserted 1:1		
Pack (9):		1.00
Wax Box (36):		35.00
1	Garret Anderson	.05
2	*Rich DeLucia*	.30
3	Jason Dickson	.05
4	Gary DiSarcina	.05
5	Jim Edmonds	.10
6	Darin Erstad	.75
7	Cecil Fielder	.05
8	Chuck Finley	.05
9	Carlos Carcia	.05
10	Shigetosi Hasegawa	.05
11	Ken Hill	.05
12	Dave Hollins	.05
13	Mike Holtz	.05
14	Mike James	.05
15	Norberto Martin	.05
16	Damon Mashore	.05
17	Jack McDowell	.05
18	Phil Nevin	.05
19	Omar Olivares	.05
20	Troy Percival	.05
21	Rich Robertson	.05
22	Tim Salmon	.15
23	Craig Shipley	.05
24	Matt Walbeck	.05
25	Allen Watson	.05
26	Jim Edmonds (Angels checklist)	.05
27	Brian Anderson	.05
28	Tony Batista	.05
29	Jay Bell	.05
30	Andy Benes	.05
31	Yamil Benitez	.05
32	Willie Blair	.05
33	Brent Brede	.05
34	Scott Brow	.05
35	Omar Daal	.05
36	David Dellucci	.05
37	Edwin Diaz	.05
38	Jorge Fabregas	.05
39	Andy Fox	.05
40	Karim Garcia	.10
41a	Travis Lee (batting)	.50
41b	Travis Lee (fielding)	.50
42	Barry Manuel	.05
43	Gregg Olson	.05
44	Felix Rodriguez	.05
45	Clint Sodowsky	.05
46	Russ Springer	.05
47	Andy Stankiewicz	.05
48	Kelly Stinnett	.05
49	Jeff Suppan	.05
50	Devon White	.05
51	Matt Williams	.15
52	Travis Lee (Diamondbacks checklist)	.10
53	Danny Bautista	.05
54	Rafael Belliard	.05
55	*Adam Butler*	.10
56	Mike Cather	.05
57	Brian Edmondson	.05
58	Alan Embree	.05
59	Andres Galarraga	.05
60	Tom Glavine	.15
61	Tony Graffanino	.05
62	Andruw Jones	.75
63a	Chipper Jones (batting)	2.00
63b	Chipper Jones (fielding)	2.00
64	Ryan Klesko	.05
65	Keith Lockhart	.05
66	Javy Lopez	.05
67a	Greg Maddux (batting)	1.50
67b	Greg Maddux (pitching)	1.50
68	Dennis Martinez	.05
69	*Kevin Millwood*	2.50
70	Denny Neagle	.05
71	Eddie Perez	.05
72	Curtis Pride	.05
73	John Smoltz	.15
74	Michael Tucker	.05
75	Walt Weiss	.05
76	Gerald Williams	.05
77	Mark Wohlers	.05
78	Chipper Jones (Braves checklist)	1.25
79	Roberto Alomar	.40
80	Brady Anderson	.05
81	Harold Baines	.05
82	Armando Benitez	.05
83	Mike Bordick	.05
84	Joe Carter	.05
85	Norm Charlton	.05
86	Eric Davis	.05
87	Doug Drabek	.05
88	Scott Erickson	.05
89	Jeffrey Hammonds	.05
90	Chris Hoiles	.05
91	Scott Kamieniecki	.05
92	Jimmy Key	.05
93	Terry Mathews	.05
94	Alan Mills	.05
95	Mike Mussina	.75
96	Jesse Orosco	.05
97	Rafael Palmeiro	.25
98	Sidney Ponson	.05
99	Jeff Reboulet	.05
100	Arthur Rhodes	.05
101a	Cal Ripken Jr. (batting)	3.00
101b	Cal Ripken Jr. (batting, close-up)	3.00
102	Nerio Rodriguez	.05
103	B.J. Surhoff	.05
104	Lenny Webster	.05
105	Cal Ripken Jr. (Orioles checklist)	1.50
106	Steve Avery	.05
107	Mike Benjamin	.05
108	Darren Bragg	.05
109	Damon Buford	.05
110	Jim Corsi	.05
111	Dennis Eckersley	.05
112	Rich Garces	.05
113a	Nomar Garciaparra (batting)	2.00
113b	Nomar Garciaparra (fielding)	2.00
114	Tom Gordon	.05
115	Scott Hatteberg	.05
116	Butch Henry	.05
117	Reggie Jefferson	.05
118	Mark Lemke	.05
119	Darren Lewis	.05
120	Jim Leyritz	.05
121	Derek Lowe	.05
122	Pedro Martinez	.75
123	Troy O'Leary	.05
124	Brian Rose	.05
125	Bret Saberhagen	.05
126	Donnie Sadler	.05
127	Brian Shouse	.05
128	John Valentin	.05
129	Jason Varitek	.05
130	Mo Vaughn	.35
131	Tim Wakefield	.05
132	John Wasdin	.05
133	Nomar Garciaparra (Red Sox checklist)	1.00
134	Terry Adams	.05
135	Manny Alexander	.05
136	Rod Beck	.05
137	Jeff Blauser	.05
138	Brant Brown	.05
139	Mark Clark	.05
140	Jeremi Gonzalez	.05
141	Mark Grace	.25
142	Jose Hernandez	.05
143	Tyler Houston	.05
144	Lance Johnson	.05
145	Sandy Martinez	.05
146	Matt Mieske	.05
147	Mickey Morandini	.05
148	Terry Mulholland	.05
149	Kevin Orie	.05
150	Bob Patterson	.05
151	Marc Pisciotta	.05
152	Henry Rodriguez	.05
153	Scott Servais	.05
154	Sammy Sosa	2.00
155	Kevin Tapani	.05
156	Steve Trachsel	.05
157a	Kerry Wood (pitching)	.75
157b	Kerry Wood (pitching, close-up)	.75
158	Kerry Wood (Cubs checklist)	.35
159	Jeff Abbott	.05
160	James Baldwin	.05
161	Albert Belle	.25
162	Jason Bere	.05
163	Mike Cameron	.05

164 Mike Caruso .05
165 Carlos Castillo .05
166 Tony Castillo .05
167 Ray Durham .05
168 Scott Eyre .05
169 Tom Fordham .05
170 Keith Foulke .05
171 Lou Frazier .05
172 Matt Karchner .05
173 Chad Kreuter .05
174 Jaime Navarro .05
175 Greg Norton .05
176 Charlie O'Brien .05
177 Magglio Ordonez .25
178 Ruben Sierra .05
179 Bill Simas .05
180 Mike Sirotka .05
181 Chris Snopek .05
182a Frank Thomas (in batter's box) 1.50
182b Frank Thomas (swinging) 1.50
183 Robin Ventura .05
184 Frank Thomas (White Sox checklist) .50
185 Stan Belinda .05
186 Aaron Boone .05
187 Bret Boone .10
188 Brook Fordyce .05
189 Willie Greene .05
190 Pete Harnisch .05
191 Lenny Harris .05
192 Mark Hutton .05
193 Damian Jackson .05
194 Ricardo Jordan .05
195 Barry Larkin .15
196 Eduardo Perez .05
197 Pokey Reese .05
198 Mike Remlinger .05
199 Reggie Sanders .05
200 Jeff Shaw .05
201 Chris Stynes .05
202 Scott Sullivan .05
203 Eddie Taubensee .05
204 Brett Tomko .05
205 Pat Watkins .05
206 David Weathers .05
207 Gabe White .05
208 Scott Winchester .05
209 Barry Larkin (Reds checklist) .05
210 Sandy Alomar Jr. .05
211 Paul Assenmacher .05
212 Geronimo Berroa .05
213 Pat Borders .05
214 Jeff Branson .05
215 Dave Burba .05
216 Bartolo Colon .15
217 Shawon Dunston .05
218 Travis Fryman .05
219 Brian Giles .05
220 Dwight Gooden .05
221 Mike Jackson .05
222 David Justice .25
223 Kenny Lofton .05
224 Jose Mesa .05
225 Alvin Morman .05
226 Charles Nagy .05
227 Chad Ogea .05
228 Eric Plunk .05
229 Manny Ramirez 1.00
230 Paul Shuey .05
231 Jim Thome .05
232 Ron Villone .05
233 Omar Vizquel .05
234 Enrique Wilson .05
235 Jaret Wright .50
236 Manny Ramirez (Indians checklist) .50
237 Pedro Astacio .05
238 Jason Bates .05
239 Dante Bichette .05
240 Ellis Burks .05
241 Vinny Castilla .05
242 Greg Colbrunn .05
243 Mike DeJean .05
244 Jerry Dipoto .05
245 Curtis Goodwin .05
246 Todd Helton .75
247 Bobby Jones .05
248 Darryl Kile .05
249 Mike Lansing .05
250 Curtis Leskanic .05
251 Nelson Liriano .05
252 Kirt Manwaring .05
253 Chuck McElroy .05
254 Mike Munoz .05
255 Neifi Perez .05
256 Jeff Reed .05
257 Mark Thompson .05
258 John Vander Wal .05
259 Dave Veres .05
260a Larry Walker (batting) .25
260b Larry Walker (batting, close-up) .25
261 Jamey Wright .05
262 Larry Walker (Rockies checklist) .10
263 Kimera Bartee .05
264 Doug Brocail .05
265 Raul Casanova .05
266 Frank Castillo .05
267 Frank Catalanotto .05
268 Tony Clark .05
269 Deivi Cruz .05
270 Roberto Duran .05
271 Damion Easley .05
272 Bryce Florie .05
273 Luis Gonzalez .25
274 Bob Higginson .10
275 Brian Hunter .05
276 Todd Jones .05
277 Greg Keagle .05
278 Jeff Manto .05
279 Brian Moehler .05
280 Joe Oliver .05
281 Joe Randa .05
282 Billy Ripken .05
283 Bip Roberts .05
284 Sean Runyan .05
285 A.J. Sager .05
286 Justin Thompson .05
287 Tony Clark (Tigers checklist) .05
288 Antonio Alfonseca .05
289 Dave Berg .05
290 Josh Booty .05
291 John Cangelosi .05
292 Craig Counsell .05
293 Vic Darensbourg .05
294 Cliff Floyd .05
295 Oscar Henriquez .05
296 Felix Heredia .05
297 *Ryan Jackson* .05
298 Mark Kotsay .05
299 Andy Larkin .05
300 Derrek Lee .05
301 Brian Meadows .05
302 Rafael Medina .05
303 Jay Powell .05
304 Edgar Renteria .05
305 *Jesus Sanchez* .10
306 Rob Stanifer .05
307 Greg Zaun .05
308 Derrek Lee (Marlins checklist) .05
309 Moises Alou .10
310 Brad Ausmus .05
311a Jeff Bagwell (batting) 1.00
311b Jeff Bagwell (fielding) 1.00
312 Derek Bell .05
313 Sean Bergman .05
314 Sean Berry .05
315 Craig Biggio .10
316 Tim Bogar .05
317 Jose Cabrera .05
318 Dave Clark .05
319 Tony Eusebio .05
320 Carl Everett .10
321 Ricky Gutierrez .05
322 John Halama .05
323 Mike Hampton .10
324 Doug Henry .05
325 Richard Hidalgo .05
326 Jack Howell .05
327 Jose Lima .05
328 Mike Magnante .05
329 Trever Miller .05
330 C.J. Nitkowski .05
331 Shane Reynolds .05
332 Bill Spiers .05
333 Billy Wagner .10
334 Jeff Bagwell (Astros checklist) .50
335 Tim Belcher .05
336 Brian Bevil .05
337 Johnny Damon .10
338 Jermaine Dye .05
339 Sal Fasano .05
340 Shane Halter .05
341 Chris Haney .05
342 Jed Hansen .05
343 Jeff King .05
344 Jeff Montgomery .05
345 Hal Morris .05
346 Jose Offerman .05
347 Dean Palmer .05
348 Terry Pendleton .05
349 Hipolito Pichardo .05
350 Jim Pittsley .05
351 Pat Rapp .05
352 Jose Rosado .05
353 Glendon Rusch .05
354 Scott Service .05
355 Larry Sutton .05
356 Mike Sweeney .05
357 Joe Vitiello .05
358 Matt Whisenant .05
359 Ernie Young .05
360 Jeff King (Royals checklist) .05
361 Bobby Bonilla .05
362 Jim Bruske .05
363 Juan Castro .05
364 Roger Cedeno .05
365 Mike Devereaux .05
366 Darren Dreifort .05
367 Jim Eisenreich .05
368 Wilton Guerrero .05
369 Mark Guthrie .05
370 Darren Hall .05
371 Todd Hollandsworth .05
372 Thomas Howard .05
373 Trenidad Hubbard .05
374 Charles Johnson .05
375 Eric Karros .05
376 Paul Konerko .10
377 Matt Luke .05
378 Ramon Martinez .05
379 Raul Mondesi .20
380 Hideo Nomo .75
381 Antonio Osuna .05
382 Chan Ho Park .30
383 Tom Prince .05
384 Scott Radinsky .05
385 Gary Sheffield .25
386 Ismael Valdes .05
387 Jose Vizcaino .05
388 Eric Young .05
389 Gary Sheffield (Dodgers checklist) .10
390 Jeromy Burnitz .05
391 Jeff Cirillo .05
392 Cal Eldred .05
393 Chad Fox .05
394 Marquis Grissom .05
395 Bob Hamelin .05
396 Bobby Hughes .05
397 Darrin Jackson .05
398 John Jaha .05
399 Geoff Jenkins .05
400 Doug Jones .05
401 Jeff Juden .05
402 Scott Karl .05
403 Jesse Levis .05
404 Mark Loretta .05
405 Mike Matheny .05
406 Jose Mercedes .05
407 Mike Myers .05
408 Marc Newfield .05
409 Dave Nilsson .05
410 Al Reyes .05
411 Jose Valentin .05
412 Fernando Vina .05
413 Paul Wagner .05
414 Bob Wickman .05
415 Steve Woodard .05
416 Marquis Grissom (Brewers checklist) .05
417 Rick Aguilera .05
418 Ron Coomer .05
419 Marty Cordova .05
420 Brent Gates .05
421 Eddie Guardado .05
422 Denny Hocking .05
423 Matt Lawton .05
424 Pat Meares .05
425 Orlando Merced .05
426 Eric Milton .05
427 Paul Molitor .60
428 Mike Morgan .05
429 Dan Naulty .05
430 Otis Nixon .05
431 Alex Ochoa .05
432 David Ortiz .05
433 Brad Radke .10
434 Todd Ritchie .05
435 Frank Rodriguez .05
436 Terry Steinbach .05
437 Greg Swindell .05
438 Bob Tewksbury .05
439 Mike Trombley .05
440 Javier Valentin .05
441 Todd Walker .10
442 Paul Molitor (Twins checklist) .40
443 Shane Andrews .05
444 Miguel Batista .05
445 Shayne Bennett .05
446 Rick DeHart .05
447 Brad Fullmer .10
448 Mark Grudzielanek .05
449 Vladimir Guerrero .75
450 Dustin Hermanson .05
451 Steve Kline .05
452 Scott Livingstone .05
453 Mike Maddux .05
454 Derrick May .05
455 Ryan McGuire .05
456 Trey Moore .05
457 Mike Mordecai .05
458 Carl Pavano .05
459 Carlos Perez .05
460 F.P. Santangelo .05
461 DaRond Stovall .05
462 Anthony Telford .05
463 Ugueth Urbina .05
464 Marc Valdes .05
465 Jose Vidro .05
466 Rondell White .10
467 Chris Widger .05
468 Vladimir Guerrero (Expos checklist) .40
469 Edgardo Alfonzo .05
470 Carlos Baerga .05
471 Rich Becker .05
472 Brian Bohanon .05
473 Alberto Castillo .05
474 Dennis Cook .05
475 John Franco .05
476 Matt Franco .05
477 Bernard Gilkey .05
478 John Hudek .05
479 Butch Huskey .05
480 Bobby Jones .05
481 Al Leiter .05
482 Luis Lopez .05
483 Brian McRae .05
484 Dave Mlicki .05
485 John Olerud .05
486 Rey Ordonez .05
487 Craig Paquette .05
488a Mike Piazza (batting) 2.00
488b Mike Piazza (batting, close-up) 2.00
489 Todd Pratt .05
490 Mel Rojas .05
491 Tim Spehr .05
492 Turk Wendell .05
493 *Masato Yoshii* .40
494 Mike Piazza (Mets checklist) 1.00
495 Willie Banks .05
496 Scott Brosius .05
497 Mike Buddie .05
498 Homer Bush .05
499 David Cone .05
500 Chad Curtis .05
501 Chili Davis .05
502 Joe Girardi .05
503 Darren Holmes .05
504 Hideki Irabu .10
505a Derek Jeter (batting) 2.00
505b Derek Jeter (fielding) 2.00
506 Chuck Knoblauch .05
507 Graeme Lloyd .05
508 Tino Martinez .05
509 Ramiro Mendoza .05
510 Jeff Nelson .05
511 Paul O'Neill .05
512 Andy Pettitte .20
513 Jorge Posada .15
514 Tim Raines .05
515 Mariano Rivera .25
516 Luis Sojo .05
517 Mike Stanton .05
518 Darryl Strawberry .05
519 Dale Sveum .05
520 David Wells .10

521 Bernie Williams .35
522 Bernie Williams (Yankees checklist) .20
523 Kurt Abbott .05
524 Mike Blowers .05
525 Rafael Bournigal .05
526 Tom Candiotti .05
527 Ryan Christenson .05
528 Mike Fetters .05
529 Jason Giambi .25
530a Ben Grieve (batting) .25
530b Ben Grieve (running) .25
531 Buddy Groom .05
532 Jimmy Haynes .05
533 Rickey Henderson .35
534 A.J. Hinch .05
535 Mike Macfarlane .05
536 Dave Magadan .05
537 T.J. Mathews .05
538 Jason McDonald .05
539 Kevin Mitchell .05
540 Mike Mohler .05
541 Mike Oquist .05
542 Ariel Prieto .05
543 Kenny Rogers .05
544 Aaron Small .05
545 Scott Spiezio .05
546 Matt Stairs .05
547 Bill Taylor .05
548 Dave Telgheder .05
549 Jack Voigt .05
550 Ben Grieve (A's checklist) .10
551 Bob Abreu .05
552 Ruben Amaro .05
553 Alex Arias .05
554 Matt Beech .05
555 Ricky Bottalico .05
556 Billy Brewer .05
557 Rico Brogna .05
558 Doug Glanville .05
559 Wayne Gomes .05
560 Mike Grace .05
561 Tyler Green .05
562 Rex Hudler .05
563 Gregg Jefferies .05
564 Kevin Jordan .05
565 Mark Leiter .05
566 Mark Lewis .05
567 Mike Lieberthal .05
568 Mark Parent .05
569 Yorkis Perez .05
570 Desi Relaford .05
571 Scott Rolen .75
572 Curt Schilling .25
573 Kevin Sefcik .05
574 Jerry Spradlin .05
575 Garrett Stephenson .05
576 Darrin Winston .05
577 Scott Rolen (Phillies checklist) .40
578 Jermaine Allensworth .05
579 Jason Christiansen .05
580 Lou Collier .05
581 Francisco Cordova .05
582 Elmer Dessens .05
583 Freddy Garcia .10
584 Jose Guillen .15
585 Jason Kendall .05
586 Jon Lieber .05
587 Esteban Loaiza .05
588 Al Martin .05
589 Javier Martinez .05
590 *Chris Peters* .05
591 Kevin Polcovich .05
592 Ricardo Rincon .05
593 Jason Schmidt .05
594 Jose Silva .05
595 Mark Smith .05
596 Doug Strange .05
597 Turner Ward .05
598 Marc Wilkins .05
599 Mike Williams .05
600 Tony Womack .05
601 Kevin Young .05
602 Tony Womack (Pirates checklist) .05
603 Manny Aybar .05
604 Kent Bottenfield .05
605 Jeff Brantley .05
606 Mike Busby .05
607 Royce Clayton .05
608 Delino DeShields .05
609 John Frascatore .05
610 Gary Gaetti .05
611 Ron Gant .05
612 David Howard .05
613 Brian Hunter .05
614 Brian Jordan .05
615 Tom Lampkin .05
616 Ray Lankford .05
617 Braden Looper .05
618 John Mabry .05
619 Eli Marrero .05
620 Willie McGee .05
621a Mark McGwire (batting) 3.00
621b Mark McGwire (fielding) 3.00
622 Kent Mercker .05
623 Matt Morris .10
624 Donovan Osborne .05
625 Tom Pagnozzi .05
626 Lance Painter .05
627 Mark Petkovsek .05
628 Todd Stottlemyre .05
629 Mark McGwire (Cardinals checklist) 1.50
630 Andy Ashby .05
631 Brian Boehringer .05
632 Kevin Brown .15
633 Ken Caminiti .05
634 Steve Finley .05
635 Ed Giovanola .05
636 Chris Gomez .05
637a Tony Gwynn (blue jersey) 1.00
637b Tony Gwynn (white jersey) 1.00
SAMPLE Tony Gwynn (SAMPLE overprint on back) 1.00
638 Joey Hamilton .05
639 Carlos Hernandez .05
640 Sterling Hitchcock .05
641 Trevor Hoffman .05
642 Wally Joyner .05
643 Dan Miceli .05
644 James Mouton .05
645 Greg Myers .05
646 Carlos Reyes .05
647 Andy Sheets .05
648 Pete Smith .05
649 Mark Sweeney .05
650 Greg Vaughn .05
651 Quilvio Veras .05
652 Tony Gwynn (Padres checklist) .50
653 Rich Aurilla .05
654 Marvin Benard .05
655a Barry Bonds (batting) 1.00
655b Barry Bonds (batting, close-up) 1.00
656 Danny Darwin .05
657 Shawn Estes .05
658 Mark Gardner .05
659 Darryl Hamilton .05
660 Charlie Hayes .05
661 Orel Hershiser .05
662 Stan Javier .05
663 Brian Johnson .05
664 John Johnstone .05
665 Jeff Kent .05
666 Brent Mayne .05
667 Bill Mueller .05
668 Robb Nen .05
669 Jim Poole .05
670 Steve Reed .05
671 Rich Rodriguez .05
672 Kirk Rueter .05
673 Rey Sanchez .05
674 J.T. Snow .05
675 Julian Tavarez .05
676 Barry Bonds (Giants checklist) .50
677 Rich Amaral .05
678 Bobby Ayala .05
679 Jay Buhner .05
680 Ken Cloude .05
681 Joey Cora .05
682 Russ Davis .05
683 Rob Ducey .05
684 Jeff Fassero .05
685 Tony Fossas .05
686a Ken Griffey Jr. (batting) 2.50
686b Ken Griffey Jr. (fielding) 2.50
687 Glenallen Hill .05
688 Jeff Huson .05
689 Randy Johnson .75
690 Edgar Martinez .05
691 John Marzano .05
692 Jamie Moyer .05
693a Alex Rodriguez (batting) 2.50
693b Alex Rodriguez (fielding) 2.50
694 David Segui .05
695 Heathcliff Slocumb .05
696 Paul Spoljaric .05
697 Bill Swift .05
698 Mike Timlin .05
699 Bob Wells .05
700 Dan Wilson .05
701 Ken Griffey Jr. (Mariners checklist) 1.50
702 Wilson Alvarez .05
703 *Rolando Arrojo* .75
704a Wade Boggs (batting) .50
704b Wade Boggs (fielding) .50
705 Rich Butler .05
706 Miguel Cairo .05
707 Mike Difelice .05
708 John Flaherty .05
709 Roberto Hernandez .05
710 Mike Kelly .05
711 Aaron Ledesma .05
712 Albie Lopez .05
713 Dave Martinez .05
714 Quinton McCracken .05
715 Fred McGriff .05
716 Jim Mecir .05
717 Tony Saunders .05
718 Bobby Smith .05
719 Paul Sorrento .05
720 Dennis Springer .05
721 Kevin Stocker .05
722 Ramon Tatis .05
723 Bubba Trammell .05
724 Esteban Yan .05
725 Wade Boggs (Devil Rays checklist) .20
726 Luis Alicea .05
727 Scott Bailes .05
728 John Burkett .05
729 Domingo Cedeno .05
730 Will Clark .15
731 Kevin Elster .05
732a Juan Gonzalez (bat) 1.00
732b Juan Gonzalez (no bat) 1.00
733 Tom Goodwin .05
734 Rusty Greer .05
735 Eric Gunderson .05
736 Bill Haselman .05
737 Rick Helling .05
738 Roberto Kelly .05
739 Mark McLemore .05
740 Darren Oliver .05
741 Danny Patterson .05
742 Roger Pavlik .05
743a Ivan Rodriguez (batting) .60
743b Ivan Rodriguez (fielding) .60
744 Aaron Sele .05
745 Mike Simms .05
746 Lee Stevens .05
747 Fernando Tatis .10
748 John Wetteland .05
749 Bobby Witt .05
750 Juan Gonzalez (Rangers checklist) .50
751 Carlos Almanzar .05
752 Kevin Brown .10
753 Jose Canseco .40
754 Chris Carpenter .05
755 Roger Clemens 1.25
756 Felipe Crespo .05
757 Jose Cruz Jr. .20
758 Mark Dalesandro .05
759 Carlos Delgado .40
760 Kelvim Escobar .05
761 Tony Fernandez .05
762 Darrin Fletcher .05
763 Alex Gonzalez .10
764 Craig Grebeck .05
765 Shawn Green .25
766 Juan Guzman .05
767 Erik Hanson .05
768 Pat Hentgen .05
769 Randy Myers .05
770 Robert Person .05
771 Dan Plesac .05
772 Paul Quantrill .05
773 Bill Risley .05
774 Juan Samuel .05
775 Steve Sinclair .05
776 Ed Sprague .05
777 Mike Stanley .05
778 Shannon Stewart .10
779 Woody Williams .05
780 Roger Clemens (Blue Jays checklist) .50

1998 Pacific Online Web Cards

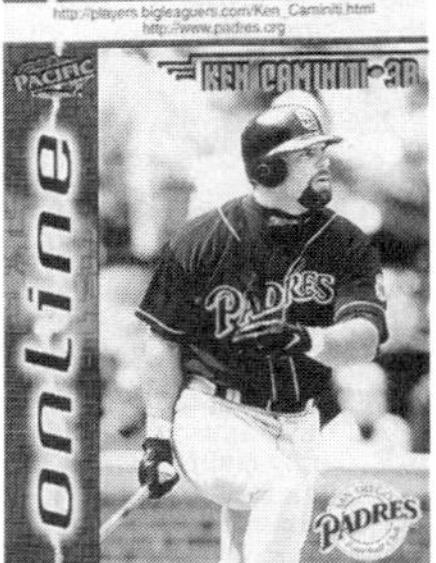

This 800-card parallel set allowed collectors to use Pacific's web site to find out the prize they had won. The cards used gold foil on the front instead of the silver foil used on base cards, and contained an eight-digit code on the back that was the claim number. These were inserted one per pack in Online Baseball.

	MT
Web Stars/RCs:	2X
Inserted 1:1	

(See 1998 Pacific Online for checklist and base card values.)

1998 Pacific Paramount

Paramount was Pacific's first fully-licensed baseball card product. The 250 base cards feature full-bleed photos with the player's name and team listed at the bottom. The base set is paralleled three times. Gold retail (1:1), Copper hobby (1:1) and Platinum Blue (1:73) versions were included. Inserts in the product are Special Delivery Die-Cuts, Team Checklist Die-Cuts, Cooperstown Bound, Fielder's Choice Laser-Cuts and Inaugural Issue.

		MT
Complete Set (250):		20.00
Common Player:		.10
Pack (6):		1.50
Wax Box (36):		40.00
1	Garret Anderson	.10
2	Gary DiSarcina	.10
3	Jim Edmonds	.15
4	Darin Erstad	.65
5	Cecil Fielder	.10
6	Chuck Finley	.10
7	Todd Greene	.15
8	Shigetosi Hasegawa	.10
9	Tim Salmon	.30
10	Roberto Alomar	.50
11	Brady Anderson	.10
12	Joe Carter	.10
13	Eric Davis	.10
14	Ozzie Guillen	.10
15	Mike Mussina	.60
16	Rafael Palmeiro	.30
17	Cal Ripken Jr.	2.50
18	B.J. Surhoff	.10
19	Steve Avery	.10
20	Nomar Garciaparra	1.00
21	Reggie Jefferson	.10
22	Pedro Martinez	.50
23	Tim Naehring	.10
24	John Valentin	.10
25	Mo Vaughn	.40
26	James Baldwin	.10
27	Albert Belle	.35
28	Ray Durham	.10
29	Benji Gil	.10
30	Jaime Navarro	.10
31	*Magglio Ordonez*	1.00
32	Frank Thomas	1.00
33	Robin Ventura	.10
34	Sandy Alomar Jr.	.10
35	Geronimo Berroa	.10
36	Travis Fryman	.10
37	David Justice	.25
38	Kenny Lofton	.10
39	Charles Nagy	.10
40	Manny Ramirez	.75
41	Jim Thome	.10
42	Omar Vizquel	.10
43	Jaret Wright	.50
44	Raul Casanova	.10
45	*Frank Catalanotto*	.20
46	Tony Clark	.10
47	Bobby Higginson	.10
48	Brian Hunter	.10
49	Todd Jones	.10
50	Bip Roberts	.10
51	Justin Thompson	.10
52	Kevin Appier	.10
53	Johnny Damon	.15
54	Jermaine Dye	.10
55	Jeff King	.10
56	Jeff Montgomery	.10
57	Dean Palmer	.10
58	Jose Rosado	.10
59	Larry Sutton	.10
60	Rick Aguilera	.10
61	Marty Cordova	.10
62	Pat Meares	.10
63	Paul Molitor	.50
64	Otis Nixon	.10
65	Brad Radke	.10
66	Terry Steinbach	.10
67	Todd Walker	.25
68	Hideki Irabu	.10
69	Derek Jeter	1.50
70	Chuck Knoblauch	.10
71	Tino Martinez	.10
72	Paul O'Neill	.10
73	Andy Pettitte	.20
74	Mariano Rivera	.25
75	Bernie Williams	.35
76	Mark Bellhorn	.10
77	Tom Candiotti	.10
78	Jason Giambi	.30
79	Ben Grieve	.35
80	Rickey Henderson	.40
81	Jason McDonald	.10
82	Aaron Small	.10
83	Miguel Tejada	.10
84	Jay Buhner	.10
85	Joey Cora	.10
86	Jeff Fassero	.10
87	Ken Griffey Jr.	2.00
88	Randy Johnson	.50
89	Edgar Martinez	.10
90	Alex Rodriguez	2.00
91	David Segui	.10
92	Dan Wilson	.10
93	Wilson Alvarez	.10
94	Wade Boggs	.35
95	Miguel Cairo	.10
96	John Flaherty	.10
97	Dave Martinez	.10
98	Quinton McCracken	.10
99	Fred McGriff	.10
100	Paul Sorrento	.10
101	Kevin Stocker	.10
102	John Burkett	.10
103	Will Clark	.25
104	Juan Gonzalez	.75
105	Rusty Greer	.10
106	Roberto Kelly	.10
107	Ivan Rodriguez	.60
108	Fernando Tatis	.10
109	John Wetteland	.10
110	Jose Canseco	.35
111	Roger Clemens	1.00
112	Jose Cruz Jr.	.20
113	Carlos Delgado	.20
114	Alex Gonzalez	.15
115	Pat Hentgen	.10
116	Ed Sprague	.10
117	Shannon Stewart	.10
118	Brian Anderson	.10
119	Jay Bell	.10
120	Andy Benes	.10
121	Yamil Benitez	.10
122	Jorge Fabregas	.10
123	Travis Lee	.25
124	Devon White	.10
125	Matt Williams	.25
126	Bob Wolcott	.10
127	Andres Galarraga	.10
128	Tom Glavine	.20
129	Andruw Jones	.75
130	Chipper Jones	1.50
131	Ryan Klesko	.10
132	Javy Lopez	.10
133	Greg Maddux	1.00
134	Denny Neagle	.10
135	John Smoltz	.20
136	Rod Beck	.10
137	Jeff Blauser	.10
138	Mark Grace	.25
139	Lance Johnson	.10
140	Mickey Morandini	.10
141	Kevin Orie	.10
142	Sammy Sosa	1.00
143	Aaron Boone	.10
144	Bret Boone	.10
145	Dave Burba	.10
146	Lenny Harris	.10
147	Barry Larkin	.15
148	Reggie Sanders	.10
149	Brett Tomko	.10
150	Pedro Astacio	.10
151	Dante Bichette	.10
152	Ellis Burks	.10
153	Vinny Castilla	.10
154	Todd Helton	.75
155	Darryl Kile	.10
156	Jeff Reed	.10
157	Larry Walker	.30
158	Bobby Bonilla	.10
159	Todd Dunwoody	.15
160	Livan Hernandez	.10
161	Charles Johnson	.10
162	Mark Kotsay	.10
163	Derrek Lee	.10
164	Edgar Renteria	.10
165	Gary Sheffield	.30
166	Moises Alou	.15
167	Jeff Bagwell	.75
168	Derek Bell	.10
169	Craig Biggio	.15
170	Mike Hampton	.10
171	Richard Hidalgo	.15
172	Chris Holt	.10
173	Shane Reynolds	.10
174	Wilton Guerrero	.10
175	Eric Karros	.10
176	Paul Konerko	.15
177	Ramon Martinez	.10
178	Raul Mondesi	.20
179	Hideo Nomo	.50
180	Chan Ho Park	.25
181	Mike Piazza	1.50
182	Ismael Valdes	.10
183	Jeromy Burnitz	.10
184	Jeff Cirillo	.10
185	Todd Dunn	.10
186	Marquis Grissom	.10
187	John Jaha	.10
188	Doug Jones	.10
189	Dave Nilsson	.10
190	Jose Valentin	.10
191	Fernando Vina	.10
192	Orlando Cabrera	.10
193	Steve Falteisek	.10
194	Mark Grudzielanek	.10
195	Vladimir Guerrero	.75
196	Carlos Perez	.10
197	F.P. Santangelo	.10
198	Jose Vidro	.10
199	Rondell White	.15
200	Edgardo Alfonzo	.15
201	Carlos Baerga	.10
202	John Franco	.10
203	Bernard Gilkey	.10
204	Todd Hundley	.10
205	Butch Huskey	.10
206	Bobby Jones	.10
207	Brian McRae	.10
208	John Olerud	.10
209	Rey Ordonez	.15
210	Ricky Bottalico	.10
211	Bobby Estalella	.10
212	Doug Glanville	.10
213	Gregg Jefferies	.10
214	Mike Lieberthal	.10
215	Desi Relaford	.10
216	Scott Rolen	.75
217	Curt Schilling	.25
218	Adrian Brown	.10
219	Emil Brown	.10
220	Francisco Cordova	.10
221	Jose Guillen	.15
222	Al Martin	.10
223	Abraham Nunez	.10
224	Tony Womack	.10
225	Kevin Young	.10
226	Alan Benes	.10
227	Royce Clayton	.10
228	Gary Gaetti	.10
229	Ron Gant	.10
230	Brian Jordan	.10
231	Ray Lankford	.10
232	Mark McGwire	2.50
233	Todd Stottlemyre	.10
234	Kevin Brown	.10
235	Ken Caminiti	.10
236	Steve Finley	.10
237	Tony Gwynn	1.00
238	Wally Joyner	.10
239	Ruben Rivera	.10
240	Greg Vaughn	.10
241	Quilvio Veras	.10
242	Barry Bonds	1.00
243	Jacob Cruz	.10
244	Shawn Estes	.10
245	Orel Hershiser	.10
246	Stan Javier	.10
247	Brian Johnson	.10
248	Jeff Kent	.10
249	Robb Nen	.10
250	J.T. Snow	.10

1998 Pacific Paramount Gold/Copper/Red

Gold, Copper and Red foil versions of all 250 cards in Paramount were reprinted and inserted at a rate of one per pack. Gold versions were retail exclusive, Copper versions were hobby exclusive and Red versions were ANCO pack exclusive. The only difference is these parallels use a different color foil than the base cards.

	MT
Common Gold/Copper Player:	.25
Gold/Copper Stars:	2X
Inserted 1:1	
Common Red Player:	.30
Red Stars:	3X
Inserted 1:ANCO pack	

(See 1998 Pacific Paramount for checklist and base card values.)

1998 Pacific Paramount Platinum Blue

This paralled set reprinted all 250 cards in Paramount using blue foil stamping on the card front. These were inserted one per 73 packs.

	MT
Common Platinum Blue Player:	2.00
Platinum Blue Stars:	15-30X
Inserted 1:73	

(See 1998 Pacific Paramount for checklist and base card values.)

1998 Pacific Paramount Holographic Silver

Holographics Silver parallel cards were issued for all 250 cards in the Paramount set. These were inserted into hobby packs, while only 99 sets were produced.

	MT
Common Player:	3.00
Holographic Silver Stars:	40-60X
Production 99 sets	

(See 1998 Pacific Paramount for checklist and base card values.)

1998 Pacific Paramount Cooperstown Bound

Cooperstown Bound is a 10-card insert seeded

one per 361 packs. Each card features a color player photo with a silver foil column on the left. The cards are fully foiled and etched.

		MT
Complete Set (10):		130.00
Common Player:		7.50
Inserted 1:361		
Pacific Proofs:		6X
Production 20 sets		
1	Greg Maddux	15.00
2	Cal Ripken Jr.	30.00
3	Frank Thomas	12.50
4	Mike Piazza	25.00
5	Paul Molitor	7.50
6	Mark McGwire	30.00
7	Tony Gwynn	12.50
8	Barry Bonds	15.00
9	Ken Griffey Jr.	27.50
10	Wade Boggs	7.50

1998 Pacific Paramount Fielder's Choice

Fielder's Choice Laser-Cuts is a 20-card insert seeded one per 73 packs. Each card is die-cut around a baseball glove that appears in the background. The webbing of the glove is laser-cut.

		MT
Complete Set (20):		90.00
Common Player:		2.00
Inserted 1:73		
1	Chipper Jones	9.00
2	Greg Maddux	6.50
3	Cal Ripken Jr.	10.00
4	Nomar Garciaparra	8.00
5	Frank Thomas	5.00
6	David Justice	2.00
7	Larry Walker	2.00
8	Jeff Bagwell	4.00
9	Hideo Nomo	3.00
10	Mike Piazza	9.00
11	Derek Jeter	9.00
12	Ben Grieve	2.00
13	Mark McGwire	10.00
14	Tony Gwynn	5.00
15	Barry Bonds	7.00
16	Ken Griffey Jr.	9.50
17	Alex Rodriguez	9.50
18	Wade Boggs	3.00
19	Ivan Rodriguez	3.00
20	Jose Cruz Jr.	2.00

1998 Pacific Paramount Inaugural Issue

A special edition of Pacific's premiere Paramount issue was created to mark the new brand's introduction on May 27 at the debut SportsFest '98 show in Philadelphia. Each of the cards from the Paramount issue was printed with a gold-foil "INAUGURAL ISSUE May 27, 1998" logo, was embossed with Pacific and SportsFest logos at center and hand-numbered at bottom from within an edition of just 20 cards each.

	MT
Common Player:	3.00
(Stars and rookies valued at 50-75X regular Paramount version.)	

1998 Pacific Paramount Special Delivery

Special Delivery cards are die-cut to resemble a postage stamp. Each card front is foiled and etched and features three photos of the player. Special Delivery is a 20-card insert seeded one per 37 packs.

		MT
Complete Set (20):		100.00
Common Player:		2.00
Inserted 1:37		
1	Chipper Jones	9.00
2	Greg Maddux	7.50
3	Cal Ripken Jr.	12.50
4	Nomar Garciaparra	7.50
5	Pedro Martinez	3.00
6	Frank Thomas	7.50
7	David Justice	2.00
8	Larry Walker	2.00
9	Jeff Bagwell	6.00
10	Hideo Nomo	3.00
11	Mike Piazza	9.00
12	Vladimir Guerrero	5.00
13	Derek Jeter	9.00
14	Ben Grieve	4.00
15	Mark McGwire	12.50
16	Tony Gwynn	6.50
17	Barry Bonds	6.00
18	Ken Griffey Jr.	10.00
19	Alex Rodriguez	10.00
20	Jose Cruz Jr.	2.00

1998 Pacific Paramount Team Checklists

Team Checklists (30 cards, 2:37) feature a player photo surrounded by two bats. The card is die-cut around the photo and the bats at the top. The bottom has the player's name, position and team.

		MT
Complete Set (30):		75.00
Common Player:		.75
Inserted 1:18		
1	Tim Salmon	1.00
2	Cal Ripken Jr.	10.00
3	Nomar Garciaparra	6.00
4	Frank Thomas	5.00
5	Manny Ramirez	4.00
6	Tony Clark	.75
7	Dean Palmer	.75
8	Paul Molitor	1.50
9	Derek Jeter	7.50
10	Ben Grieve	1.00
11	Ken Griffey Jr.	8.00
12	Wade Boggs	1.50
13	Ivan Rodriguez	3.00
14	Roger Clemens	4.00
15	Matt Williams	1.00
16	Chipper Jones	7.50
17	Sammy Sosa	5.00
18	Barry Larkin	.75
19	Larry Walker	1.00
20	Livan Hernandez	.75
21	Jeff Bagwell	4.00
22	Mike Piazza	7.50
23	John Jaha	.75
24	Vladimir Guerrero	2.50
25	Todd Hundley	.75
26	Scott Rolen	2.50
27	Kevin Young	.75
28	Mark McGwire	10.00
29	Tony Gwynn	4.00
30	Barry Bonds	3.50

1998 Pacific Revolution

Pacific Revolution Baseball consists of a 150-card base set. The base cards are dual-foiled, etched and embossed. Inserts include Showstoppers, Prime Time Performers Laser-Cuts, Foul Pole Laser-Cuts, Major League Icons and Shadow Series.

		MT
Complete Set (150):		75.00
Common Player:		.25
Pack (3):		2.50
Wax Box (24):		50.00
1	Garret Anderson	.25
2	Jim Edmonds	.35
3	Darin Erstad	1.00
4	Chuck Finley	.25
5	Tim Salmon	.50
6	Jay Bell	.25
7	Travis Lee	.65
8	Devon White	.25
9	Matt Williams	.50
10	Andres Galarraga	.25
11	Tom Glavine	.35
12	Andruw Jones	1.00
13	Chipper Jones	6.00
14	Ryan Klesko	.25
15	Javy Lopez	.25
16	Greg Maddux	4.50
17	Walt Weiss	.25
18	Roberto Alomar	2.00
19	Joe Carter	.25
20	Mike Mussina	2.00
21	Rafael Palmeiro	.75
22	Cal Ripken Jr.	10.00
23	B.J. Surhoff	.25
24	Nomar Garciaparra	4.50
25	Reggie Jefferson	.25
26	Pedro Martinez	2.00
27	Troy O'Leary	.25
28	Mo Vaughn	1.50
29	Mark Grace	.75
30	Mickey Morandini	.25
31	Henry Rodriguez	.25
32	Sammy Sosa	5.00
33	Kerry Wood	2.00
34	Albert Belle	.75
35	Ray Durham	.25
36	*Magglio Ordonez*	4.00
37	Frank Thomas	5.00
38	Robin Ventura	.25
39	Bret Boone	.25
40	Barry Larkin	.35
41	Reggie Sanders	.25
42	Brett Tomko	.25
43	Sandy Alomar	.25
44	David Justice	.75
45	Kenny Lofton	.25
46	Manny Ramirez	3.00
47	Jim Thome	.25
48	Omar Vizquel	.25
49	Jaret Wright	.75
50	Dante Bichette	.25
51	Ellis Burks	.25
52	Vinny Castilla	.25
53	Todd Helton	1.00
54	Larry Walker	.75
55	Tony Clark	.25
56	Deivi Cruz	.25
57	Damion Easley	.25
58	Bobby Higginson	.25
59	Brian Hunter	.25
60	Cliff Floyd	.25
61	Livan Hernandez	.25
62	Derrek Lee	.25
63	Edgar Renteria	.25
64	Moises Alou	.35
65	Jeff Bagwell	3.00
66	Derek Bell	.25
67	Craig Biggio	.35
68	Richard Hidalgo	.25
69	Johnny Damon	.25
70	Jeff King	.25
71	Hal Morris	.25
72	Dean Palmer	.25
73	Bobby Bonilla	.25
74	Charles Johnson	.25
75	Paul Konerko	.35
76	Raul Mondesi	.50
77	Gary Sheffield	.75
78	Jeromy Burnitz	.25
79	Marquis Grissom	.25
80	Dave Nilsson	.25
81	Fernando Vina	.25

82	Marty Cordova	.25
83	Pat Meares	.25
84	Paul Molitor	2.00
85	Brad Radke	.25
86	Terry Steinbach	.25
87	Todd Walker	.75
88	Brad Fullmer	.25
89	Vladimir Guerrero	1.00
90	Carl Pavano	.25
91	Rondell White	.25
92	Bernard Gilkey	.25
93	Hideo Nomo	1.50
94	John Olerud	.25
95	Rey Ordonez	.25
96	Mike Piazza	6.00
97	*Masato Yoshii*	1.50
98	Hideki Irabu	.25
99	Derek Jeter	6.00
100	Chuck Knoblauch	.25
101	Tino Martinez	.25
102	Paul O'Neill	.25
103	Darryl Strawberry	.25
104	Bernie Williams	.65
105	Jason Giambi	.75
106	Ben Grieve	1.00
107	Rickey Henderson	1.00
108	Matt Stairs	.25
109	Doug Glanville	.25
110	Desi Relaford	.25
111	Scott Rolen	1.00
112	Curt Schilling	.75
113	Jason Kendall	.35
114	Al Martin	.25
115	Jason Schmidt	.25
116	Kevin Young	.25
117	Delino DeShields	.25
118	Gary Gaetti	.25
119	Brian Jordan	.25
120	Ray Lankford	.25
121	Mark McGwire	10.00
122	Kevin Brown	.40
123	Steve Finley	.25
124	Tony Gwynn	4.50
125	Wally Joyner	.25
126	Greg Vaughn	.25
127	Barry Bonds	4.00
128	Orel Hershiser	.25
129	Jeff Kent	.25
130	Bill Mueller	.25
131	Jay Buhner	.20
132	Ken Griffey Jr.	8.00
133	Randy Johnson	2.00
134	Edgar Martinez	.25
135	Alex Rodriguez	8.00
136	David Segui	.25
137	*Rolando Arrojo*	3.00
138	Wade Boggs	1.00
139	Quinton McCracken	.25
140	Fred McGriff	.25
141	Will Clark	.75
142	Juan Gonzalez	3.00
143	Tom Goodwin	.25
144	Ivan Rodriguez	2.50
145	Aaron Sele	.25
146	John Wetteland	.25
147	Jose Canseco	.60
148	Roger Clemens	3.00
149	Jose Cruz Jr.	.40
150	Carlos Delgado	1.00

1998 Pacific Revolution Shadows

Shadows is a full parallel of the Revolution base set. Limited to 99 sequentially numbered sets, each card is embossed with a special "Shadow Series" stamp.

	MT
Common Player:	5.00
Veteran Stars:	12X
Young Stars:	8X

(See 1998 Pacific Revolution for checklist and base card values.)

1998 Pacific Revolution Foul Pole

Foul Pole Laser-Cuts is a 20-card insert seeded one per 49 packs. Each card features a color player photo on the left and a foul pole on the right. The foul pole design includes netting that is laser cut.

		MT
Complete Set (20):		80.00
Common Player:		1.50
Inserted 1:49		
1	Cal Ripken Jr.	12.50
2	Nomar Garciaparra	6.00
3	Mo Vaughn	2.00
4	Frank Thomas	5.00
5	Manny Ramirez	3.50
6	Bernie Williams	2.00
7	Ben Grieve	2.00
8	Ken Griffey Jr.	10.00
9	Alex Rodriguez	10.00
10	Juan Gonzalez	3.50
11	Ivan Rodriguez	3.00
12	Travis Lee	2.00
13	Chipper Jones	7.50
14	Sammy Sosa	6.00
15	Vinny Castilla	1.50
16	Moises Alou	1.50
17	Gary Sheffield	2.00
18	Mike Piazza	7.50
19	Mark McGwire	12.50
20	Barry Bonds	5.00

1998 Pacific Revolution Major League Icons

Major League Icons is a 10-card insert seeded one per 121 packs. Each card features a player photo on a die-cut shield, with the shield on a flaming stand.

		MT
Complete Set (10):		150.00
Common Player:		10.00
Inserted 1:121		
1	Cal Ripken Jr.	30.00
2	Nomar Garciaparra	15.00
3	Frank Thomas	15.00
4	Ken Griffey Jr.	25.00
5	Alex Rodriguez	25.00
6	Chipper Jones	20.00
7	Kerry Wood	10.00
8	Mike Piazza	20.00
9	Mark McGwire	30.00
10	Tony Gwynn	12.50

1998 Pacific Revolution Prime Time Performers

Prime Time Performers is a 20-card insert seeded one per 25 packs. The cards are designed like a TV program guide with the team logo laser-cut on the TV screen. The color player photo is located on the left.

		MT
Complete Set (20):		60.00
Common Player:		1.25
Inserted 1:25		
1	Cal Ripken Jr.	6.50
2	Nomar Garciaparra	4.50
3	Frank Thomas	4.50
4	Jim Thome	1.25
5	Hideki Irabu	1.25
6	Derek Jeter	5.50
7	Ben Grieve	1.50
8	Ken Griffey Jr.	6.00
9	Alex Rodriguez	6.00
10	Juan Gonzalez	3.50
11	Ivan Rodriguez	2.50
12	Travis Lee	1.25
13	Chipper Jones	5.50
14	Greg Maddux	4.50
15	Kerry Wood	1.50
16	Larry Walker	1.25
17	Jeff Bagwell	3.50
18	Mike Piazza	5.50
19	Mark McGwire	6.50
20	Tony Gwynn	4.50

1998 Pacific Revolution Rookies and Hardball Heroes

This hobby-only insert combines 20 hot prospects with 10 veteran stars. Horizontal cards have action photos on a flashy metallic-foil background. A portrait photo is on back. The first 20 cards in the set, the youngsters, are paralleled in a gold edition which was limited to just 50 cards of each.

		MT
Complete Set (30):		75.00
Common Player:		.50
Inserted 1:6		
Gold (1-20):		10X
Production 50 sets		
1	Justin Baughman	.50
2	Jarrod Washburn	.50
3	Travis Lee	1.50
4	Kerry Wood	6.00
5	Magglio Ordonez	1.00
6	Todd Helton	1.50
7	Derrek Lee	.50
8	Richard Hidalgo	1.00
9	Mike Caruso	.50
10	David Ortiz	.50
11	Brad Fullmer	.50
12	Masato Yoshii	.50
13	Orlando Hernandez	6.00
14	Ricky Ledee	.50
15	Ben Grieve	1.50
16	Carlton Loewer	.50
17	Desi Relaford	.50
18	Ruben Rivera	.50
19	Rolando Arrojo	2.00
20	Matt Perisho	.50
21	Chipper Jones	7.00
22	Greg Maddux	6.00
23	Cal Ripken Jr.	10.00
24	Nomar Garciaparra	6.00
25	Frank Thomas	6.00
26	Mark McGwire	10.00
27	Tony Gwynn	5.00
28	Ken Griffey Jr.	8.00
29	Alex Rodriguez	8.00
30	Juan Gonzalez	4.00

1998 Pacific Revolution Showstoppers

This 36-card insert was seeded two per 25 packs. The cards feature holographic foil. The color photo is centered above the team logo and the Showstoppers logo.

		MT
Complete Set (36):		110.00
Common Player:		1.00
Inserted 1:12		
1	Cal Ripken Jr.	10.00
2	Nomar Garciaparra	6.00
3	Pedro Martinez	2.50
4	Mo Vaughn	1.50
5	Frank Thomas	5.00
6	Manny Ramirez	4.00
7	Jim Thome	1.00
8	Jaret Wright	1.50
9	Paul Molitor	2.00
10	Orlando Hernandez	6.00
11	Derek Jeter	7.50
12	Bernie Williams	1.50
13	Ben Grieve	1.50
14	Ken Griffey Jr.	8.50
15	Alex Rodriguez	8.50
16	Wade Boggs	2.00
17	Juan Gonzalez	4.00
18	Ivan Rodriguez	3.00
19	Jose Canseco	1.50
20	Roger Clemens	5.00
21	Travis Lee	1.50
22	Andres Galarraga	1.00

23 Chipper Jones 7.50
24 Greg Maddux 6.00
25 Sammy Sosa 5.00
26 Kerry Wood 3.00
27 Vinny Castilla 1.00
28 Larry Walker 1.50
29 Moises Alou 1.00
30 Raul Mondesi 1.50
31 Gary Sheffield 1.50
32 Hideo Nomo 2.50
33 Mike Piazza 7.50
34 Mark McGwire 10.00
35 Tony Gwynn 4.00
36 Barry Bonds 5.00

1999 Pacific

The 450-card base set features full bleed fronts enhanced with silver foil stamping. Card backs have year-by-year statistics, a small photo and a brief career highlight caption. There are two parallels, Platinum Blues and Reds. Platinum Blues have blue foil stamping and are seeded 1:73 packs. Reds are retail exclusive with red foil stamping and are seeded one per retail pack.

	MT
Complete Set (500):	35.00
Common Player:	.10
Platinum Blues (1:73):	20X
Reds (1:1R):	2X
Pack (10):	1.50
Wax Box (36):	45.00

1 Garret Anderson .10
2 Jason Dickson .10
3 Gary DiSarcina .10
4 Jim Edmonds .20
5 Darin Erstad .75
6 Chuck Finley .10
7 Shigetosi Hasegawa .10
8 Ken Hill .10
9 Dave Hollins .10
10 Phil Nevin .10
11 Troy Percival .10
12a Tim Salmon (action) .25
12b Tim Salmon (portrait) .25
13 Brian Anderson .10
14 Tony Batista .10
15 Jay Bell .10
16 Andy Benes .10
17 Yamil Benitez .10
18 Omar Daal .10
19 David Dellucci .10
20 Karim Garcia .15
21 Bernard Gilkey .10
22a Travis Lee (action) .25
22b Travis Lee (portrait) .25
23 Aaron Small .10
24 Kelly Stinnett .10
25 Devon White .10
26 Matt Williams .25
27a Bruce Chen (action) .10
27b Bruce Chen (portrait) .10
28a Andres Galarraga (action) .10
28b Andres Galarraga (portrait) .10
29 Tom Glavine .20
30 Ozzie Guillen .10
31 Andruw Jones .75
32a Chipper Jones (action) 2.00
32b Chipper Jones (portrait) 2.00
33 Ryan Klesko .10
34 George Lombard .10
35 Javy Lopez .10
36a Greg Maddux (action) 1.50
36b Greg Maddux (portrait) 1.50
37a Marty Malloy (action) .10
37b Marty Malloy (portrait) .10
38 Dennis Martinez .10
39 Kevin Millwood .25
40a Alex Rodriguez (action) 2.50
40b Alex Rodriguez (portrait) 2.50
41 Denny Neagle .10
42 John Smoltz .20
43 Michael Tucker .10
44 Walt Weiss .10
45a Roberto Alomar (action) .50
45b Roberto Alomar (portrait) .50
46 Brady Anderson .10
47 Harold Baines .10
48 Mike Bordick .10
49a Danny Clyburn (action) .10
49b Danny Clyburn (portrait) .10
50 Eric Davis .10
51 Scott Erickson .10
52 Chris Hoiles .10
53 Jimmy Key .10
54a Ryan Minor (action) .25
54b Ryan Minor (portrait) .25
55 Mike Mussina .50
56 Jesse Orosco .10
57a Rafael Palmeiro (action) .25
57b Rafael Palmeiro (portrait) .25
58 Sidney Ponson .10
59 Arthur Rhodes .10
60a Cal Ripken Jr. (action) 3.00
60b Cal Ripken Jr. (portrait) 3.00
61 B.J. Surhoff .10
62 Steve Avery .10
63 Darren Bragg .10
64 Dennis Eckersley .10
65a Nomar Garciaparra (action) 1.50
65b Nomar Garciaparra (portrait) 1.50
66a Sammy Sosa (action) 1.75
66b Sammy Sosa (portrait) 1.75
67 Tom Gordon .10
68 Reggie Jefferson .10
69 Darren Lewis .10
70a Mark McGwire (action) 3.00
70b Mark McGwire (portrait) 3.00
71 Pedro Martinez .50
72 Troy O'Leary .10
73 Bret Saberhagen .10
74 Mike Stanley .10
75 John Valentin .10
76 Jason Varitek .10
77 Mo Vaughn .40
78 Tim Wakefield .10
79 Manny Alexander .10
80 Rod Beck .10
81 Brant Brown .10
82 Mark Clark .10
83 Gary Gaetti .10
84 Mark Grace .25
85 Jose Hernandez .10
86 Lance Johnson .10
87a Jason Maxwell (action) .10
87b Jason Maxwell (portrait) .10
88 Mickey Morandini .10
89 Terry Mulholland .10
90 Henry Rodriguez .10
91 Scott Servais .10
92 Kevin Tapani .10
93 Pedro Valdes .10
94 Kerry Wood .75
95 Jeff Abbott .10
96 James Baldwin .10
97 Albert Belle .35
98 Mike Cameron .10
99 Mike Caruso .10
100 Wil Cordero .10
101 Ray Durham .10
102 Jaime Navarro .10
103 Greg Norton .10
104 Magglio Ordonez .20
105 Mike Sirotka .10
106a Frank Thomas (action) 1.25
106b Frank Thomas (portrait) 1.25
107 Robin Ventura .10
108 Craig Wilson .10
109 Aaron Boone .10
110 Bret Boone .10
111 Sean Casey .20
112 Pete Harnisch .10
113 John Hudek .10
114 Barry Larkin .15
115 Eduardo Perez .10
116 Mike Remlinger .10
117 Reggie Sanders .10
118 Chris Stynes .10
119 Eddie Taubensee .10
120 Brett Tomko .10
121 Pat Watkins .10
122 Dmitri Young .10
123 Sandy Alomar Jr. .10
124 Dave Burba .10
125 Bartolo Colon .15
126 Joey Cora .10
127 Brian Giles .10
128 Dwight Gooden .10
129 Mike Jackson .10
130 David Justice .25
131 Kenny Lofton .10
132 Charles Nagy .10
133 Chad Ogea .10
134a Manny Ramirez (action) 1.00
134b Manny Ramirez (portrait) 1.00
135 Richie Sexson .10
136a Jim Thome (action) .10
136b Jim Thome (portrait) .10
137 Omar Vizquel .10
138 Jaret Wright .25
139 Pedro Astacio .10
140 Jason Bates .10
141a Dante Bichette (action) .10
141b Dante Bichette (portrait) .10
142a Vinny Castilla (action) .10
142b Vinny Castilla (portrait) .10
143a Edgar Clemente (action) .10
143b Edgar Clemente (portrait) .10
144a Derrick Gibson (action) .10
144b Derrick Gibson (portrait) .10
145 Curtis Goodwin .10
146a Todd Helton (action) .75
146b Todd Helton (portrait) .75
147 Bobby Jones .10
148 Darryl Kile .10
149 Mike Lansing .10
150 Chuck McElroy .10
151 Neifi Perez .10
152 Jeff Reed .10
153 John Thomson .10
154a Larry Walker (action) .30
154b Larry Walker (portrait) .30
155 Jamey Wright .10
156 Kimera Bartee .10
157 Geronimo Berroa .10
158 Raul Casanova .10
159 Frank Catalanotto .10
160 Tony Clark .10
161 Deivi Cruz .10
162 Damion Easley .10
163 Juan Encarnacion .10
164 Luis Gonzalez .25
165 Seth Greisinger .10
166 Bob Higginson .10
167 Brian Hunter .10
168 Todd Jones .10
169 Justin Thompson .10
170 Antonio Alfonseca .10
171 Dave Berg .10
172 John Cangelosi .10
173 Craig Counsell .10
174 Todd Dunwoody .10
175 Cliff Floyd .10
176 Alex Gonzalez .10
177 Livan Hernandez .10
178 Ryan Jackson .10
179 Mark Kotsay .10
180 Derrek Lee .10
181 Matt Mantei .10
182 Brian Meadows .10
183 Edgar Renteria .10
184a Moises Alou (action) .15
184b Moises Alou (portrait) .15
185 Brad Ausmus .10
186a Jeff Bagwell (action) 1.00
186b Jeff Bagwell (portrait) 1.00
187 Derek Bell .10
188 Sean Berry .10
189 Craig Biggio .15
190 Carl Everett .15
191 Ricky Gutierrez .10
192 Mike Hampton .10
193 Doug Henry .10
194 Richard Hidalgo .15
195 Randy Johnson .50
196a Russ Johnson (action) .10
196b Russ Johnson (portrait) .10
197 Shane Reynolds .10
198 Bill Spiers .10
199 Kevin Appier .10
200 Tim Belcher .10
201 Jeff Conine .10
202 Johnny Damon .15
203 Jermaine Dye .10
204a Jeremy Giambi (batting stance) .15
204b Jeremy Giambi (follow-through) .15
205 Jeff King .10
206 Shane Mack .10
207 Jeff Montgomery .10
208 Hal Morris .10
209 Jose Offerman .10
210 Dean Palmer .10
211 Jose Rosado .10
212 Glendon Rusch .10
213 Larry Sutton .10
214 Mike Sweeney .10
215 Bobby Bonilla .10
216 Alex Cora .10
217 Darren Dreifort .10
218 Mark Grudzielanek .10
219 Todd Hollandsworth .10
220 Trenidad Hubbard .10
221 Charles Johnson .10
222 Eric Karros .10
223 Matt Luke .10
224 Ramon Martinez .10
225 Raul Mondesi .25
226 Chan Ho Park .25
227 Jeff Shaw .10
228 Gary Sheffield .25
229 Eric Young .10

230 Jeromy Burnitz .10
231 Jeff Cirillo .10
232 Marquis Grissom .10
233 Bobby Hughes .10
234 John Jaha .10
235 Geoff Jenkins .10
236 Scott Karl .10
237 Mark Loretta .10
238 Mike Matheny .10
239 Mike Myers .10
240 Dave Nilsson .10
241 Bob Wickman .10
242 Jose Valentin .10
243 Fernando Vina .10
244 Rick Aguilera .10
245 Ron Coomer .10
246 Marty Cordova .10
247 Denny Hocking .10
248 Matt Lawton .10
249 Pat Meares .10
250a Paul Molitor (action) .50
250b Paul Molitor (portrait) .50
251 Otis Nixon .10
252 Alex Ochoa .10
253 David Ortiz .10
254 A.J. Pierzynski .10
255 Brad Radke .15
256 Terry Steinbach .10
257 Bob Tewksbury .10
258 Todd Walker .25
259 Shane Andrews .10
260 Shayne Bennett .10
261 Orlando Cabrera .10
262 Brad Fullmer .10
263 Vladimir Guerrero .75
264 Wilton Guerrero .10
265 Dustin Hermanson .10
266 Terry Jones .10
267 Steve Kline .10
268 Carl Pavano .10
269 F.P. Santangelo .10
270a Fernando Seguignol (action) .10
270b Fernando Seguignol (portrait) .10
271 Ugueth Urbina .10
272 Jose Vidro .10
273 Chris Widger .10
274 Edgardo Alfonzo .15
275 Carlos Baerga .10
276 John Franco .10
277 Todd Hundley .10
278 Butch Huskey .10
279 Bobby Jones .10
280 Al Leiter .10
281 Greg McMichael .10
282 Brian McRae .10
283 Hideo Nomo .50
284 John Olerud .10
285 Rey Ordonez .15
286a Mike Piazza (action) 2.00
286b Mike Piazza (portrait) 2.00
287 Turk Wendell .10
288 Masato Yoshii .10
289 David Cone .10
290 Chad Curtis .10
291 Joe Girardi .10
292 Orlando Hernandez 1.00
293a Hideki Irabu (action) .10
293b Hideki Irabu (portrait) .10
294a Derek Jeter (action) 2.00
294b Derek Jeter (portrait) 2.00
295 Chuck Knoblauch .10
296a Mike Lowell (action) .10
296b Mike Lowell (portrait) .10
297 Tino Martinez .10
298 Ramiro Mendoza .10
299 Paul O'Neill .10
300 Andy Pettitte .35
301 Jorge Posada .15
302 Tim Raines .10
303 Mariano Rivera .25
304 David Wells .10
305a Bernie Williams (action) .35
305b Bernie Williams (portrait) .35
306 Mike Blowers .10
307 Tom Candiotti .10
308a Eric Chavez (action) .40
308b Eric Chavez (portrait) .40
309 Ryan Christenson .10
310 Jason Giambi .30
311a Ben Grieve (action) .25
311b Ben Grieve (portrait) .25
312 Rickey Henderson .40
313 A.J. Hinch .10
314 Jason McDonald .10
315 Bip Roberts .10
316 Kenny Rogers .10
317 Scott Spiezio .10
318 Matt Stairs .10
319 Miguel Tejada .25
320 Bob Abreu .10
321 Alex Arias .10
322a *Gary Bennett* (action) .15
322b *Gary Bennett* (portrait) .15
323 Ricky Bottalico .10
324 Rico Brogna .10
325 Bobby Estalella .10
326 Doug Glanville .10
327 Kevin Jordan .10
328 Mark Leiter .10
329 Wendell Magee .10
330 Mark Portugal .10
331 Desi Relaford .10
332 Scott Rolen .75
333 Curt Schilling .20
334 Kevin Sefcik .10
335 Adrian Brown .10
336 Emil Brown .10
337 Lou Collier .10
338 Francisco Cordova .10
339 Freddy Garcia .10
340 Jose Guillen .20
341 Jason Kendall .15
342 Al Martin .10
343 Abraham Nunez .10
344 Aramis Ramirez .15
345 Ricardo Rincon .10
346 Jason Schmidt .10
347 Turner Ward .10
348 Tony Womack .10
349 Kevin Young .10
350 Juan Acevedo .10
351 Delino DeShields .10
352a J.D. Drew (action) .25
352b J.D. Drew (portrait) .25
353 Ron Gant .10
354 Brian Jordan .10
355 Ray Lankford .10
356 Eli Marrero .10
357 Kent Mercker .10
358 Matt Morris .10
359 Luis Ordaz .10
360 Donovan Osborne .10
361 Placido Polanco .10
362 Fernando Tatis .10
363 Andy Ashby .10
364 Kevin Brown .20
365 Ken Caminiti .10
366 Steve Finley .10
367 Chris Gomez .10
368a Tony Gwynn (action) 1.25
368b Tony Gwynn (portrait) 1.25
369 Joey Hamilton .10
370 Carlos Hernandez .10
371 Trevor Hoffman .10
372 Wally Joyner .10
373 Jim Leyritz .10
374 Ruben Rivera .10
375 Greg Vaughn .10
376 Quilvio Veras .10
377 Rich Aurilla .10
378a Barry Bonds (action) 1.25
378b Barry Bonds (portrait) 1.25
379 Ellis Burks .10
380 Joe Carter .10
381 Stan Javier .10
382 Brian Johnson .10
383 Jeff Kent .10
384 Jose Mesa .10
385 Bill Mueller .10
386 Robb Nen .10
387a Armando Rios (action) .10
387b Armando Rios (portrait) .10
388 Kirk Rueter .10
389 Rey Sanchez .10
390 J.T. Snow .10
391 David Bell .10
392 Jay Buhner .10
393 Ken Cloude .10
394 Russ Davis .10
395 Jeff Fassero .10
396a Ken Griffey Jr. (action) 3.00
396b Ken Griffey Jr. (portrait) 3.00
397 *Giomar Guevara* .10
398 Carlos Guillen .10
399 Edgar Martinez .10
400 Shane Monahan .10
401 Jamie Moyer .10
402 David Segui .10
403 Makoto Suzuki .10
404 Mike Timlin .10
405 Dan Wilson .10
406 Wilson Alvarez .10
407 Rolando Arrojo .15
408 Wade Boggs .45
409 Miguel Cairo .10
410 Roberto Hernandez .10
411 Mike Kelly .10
412 Aaron Ledesma .10
413 Albie Lopez .10
414 Dave Martinez .10
415 Quinton McCracken .10
416 Fred McGriff .10
417 Bryan Rekar .10
418 Paul Sorrento .10
419 Randy Winn .10
420 John Burkett .10
421 Will Clark .25
422 Royce Clayton .10
423a Juan Gonzalez (action) 1.00
423b Juan Gonzalez (portrait) 1.00
424 Tom Goodwin .10
425 Rusty Greer .10
426 Rick Helling .10
427 Roberto Kelly .10
428 Mark McLemore .10
429a Ivan Rodriguez (action) .90
429b Ivan Rodriguez (portrait) .90
430 Aaron Sele .10
431 Lee Stevens .10
432 Todd Stottlemyre .10
433 John Wetteland .10
434 Todd Zeile .10
435 Jose Canseco .40
436a Roger Clemens (action) 1.50
436b Roger Clemens (portrait) 1.50
437 Felipe Crespo .10
438a Jose Cruz Jr. (action) .20
438b Jose Cruz Jr. (portrait) .20
439 Carlos Delgado .40
440a Tom Evans (action) .10
440b Tom Evans (portrait) .10
441 Tony Fernandez .10
442 Darrin Fletcher .10
443 Alex Gonzalez .15
444 Shawn Green .20
445 Roy Halladay .15
446 Pat Hentgen .10
447 Juan Samuel .10
448 Benito Santiago .10
449 Shannon Stewart .10
450 Woody Williams .10

1999 Pacific Cramer's Choice

Pacific CEO/President Michael Cramer personally chose this 10-card set. Die-cut into a trophy shape, the cards are enhanced with silver holographic etching and gold foil stamping across the card bottom. These are seeded 1:721 packs.

		MT
Complete Set (10):		200.00
Common Player:		20.00
Inserted 1:721		
1	Cal Ripken Jr.	35.00
2	Nomar Garciaparra	20.00
3	Frank Thomas	20.00
4	Ken Griffey Jr.	30.00
5	Alex Rodriguez	30.00
6	Greg Maddux	20.00
7	Sammy Sosa	25.00
8	Kerry Wood	20.00
9	Mark McGwire	35.00
10	Tony Gwynn	20.00

1999 Pacific Dynagon Diamond

Dynagon Diamond captures 20 of baseball's biggest stars in action against a mirror-patterned full-foil background. These are seeded about 1:9. A Titanium parallel with each card numbered to 99 was exclusive to hobby packs.

		MT
Complete Set (20):		37.50
Common Player:		.75
Inserted 1:9		
Titanium (99 Sets):		8X
1	Cal Ripken Jr.	5.00
2	Nomar Garciaparra	3.00
3	Frank Thomas	2.50
4	Derek Jeter	3.50
5	Ben Grieve	.75
6	Ken Griffey Jr.	4.00
7	Alex Rodriguez	4.00
8	Juan Gonzalez	1.50
9	Travis Lee	.75
10	Chipper Jones	3.50
11	Greg Maddux	2.50
12	Sammy Sosa	3.00
13	Kerry Wood	1.00
14	Jeff Bagwell	1.50
15	Hideo Nomo	1.00
16	Mike Piazza	3.50
17	J.D. Drew	1.00
18	Mark McGwire	5.00
19	Tony Gwynn	2.00
20	Barry Bonds	1.75

1999 Pacific Gold Crown Die-Cuts

This 36-card die-cut set is shaped like a crown at the top and features dual foiling, 24-pt. stock and gold foil stamping. These are seeded 1:37 packs.

		MT
Complete Set (36):		150.00
Common Player:		1.50
Inserted 1:37		
1	Darin Erstad	2.00
2	Cal Ripken Jr.	15.00
3	Nomar Garciaparra	8.00
4	Pedro Martinez	3.50
5	Mo Vaughn	2.00
6	Frank Thomas	8.00
7	Kenny Lofton	1.50
8	Manny Ramirez	5.00
9	Jaret Wright	2.00
10	Paul Molitor	3.50
11	Derek Jeter	10.00
12	Bernie Williams	1.50
13	Ben Grieve	2.00
14	Ken Griffey Jr.	12.50
15	Alex Rodriguez	12.00
16	Rolando Arrojo	1.50
17	Wade Boggs	2.50
18	Juan Gonzalez	5.00
19	Ivan Rodriguez	4.00
20	Roger Clemens	8.00
21	Travis Lee	2.00
22	Chipper Jones	10.00
23	Greg Maddux	8.00
24	Sammy Sosa	9.00
25	Kerry Wood	3.00
26	Todd Helton	2.00
27	Jeff Bagwell	5.00
28	Craig Biggio	1.50
29	Vladimir Guerrero	2.00
30	Hideo Nomo	2.50
31	Mike Piazza	10.00
32	Scott Rolen	2.00
33	J.D. Drew	2.00
34	Mark McGwire	15.00
35	Tony Gwynn	7.50
36	Barry Bonds	5.00

1999 Pacific Hot Cards

This dealer-only 10-card set was awarded to any dealer that had sold any packs/boxes that produced a card for the Pacific Hot Cards Registry Program. Fronts have a metallic foil background. Backs have a portrait photo and are serial numbered within an edition of 500 each.

		MT
Complete Set (10):		100.00
Common Player:		4.00
1	Alex Rodriguez	17.50
2	Tony Gwynn	10.00
3	Ken Griffey Jr.	17.50
4	Sammy Sosa	12.50
5	Ivan Rodriguez	5.00
6	Derek Jeter	15.00
7	Cal Ripken Jr.	20.00
8	Mark McGwire	20.00
9	J.D. Drew	7.50
10	Bernie Williams	4.00

1999 Pacific Team Checklists

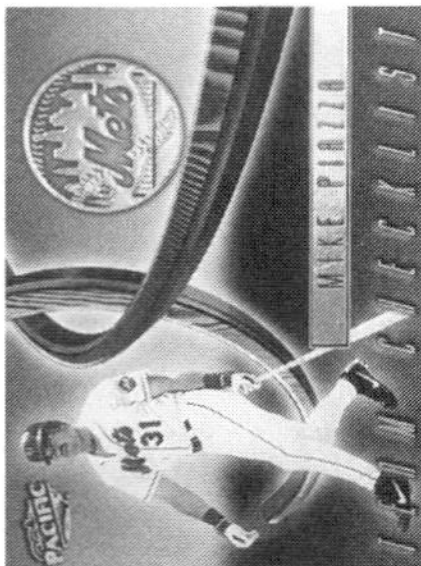

This 30-card horizontal insert set features a star player from each team on the card front, with each team's complete checklist on the card back. Fronts feature a holographic silver-foiled and embossed logo of the player's respective team. These are seeded 2:37 packs.

		MT
Complete Set (30):		60.00
Common Player:		.75
Inserted 1:18		
1	Darin Erstad	1.50
2	Cal Ripken Jr.	7.50
3	Nomar Garciaparra	4.00
4	Frank Thomas	2.50
5	Manny Ramirez	1.75
6	Damion Easley	.75
7	Jeff King	.75
8	Paul Molitor	1.50
9	Derek Jeter	5.00
10	Ben Grieve	1.00
11	Ken Griffey Jr.	6.00
12	Wade Boggs	1.50
13	Juan Gonzalez	2.00
14	Roger Clemens	3.00
15	Travis Lee	1.00
16	Chipper Jones	5.00
17	Sammy Sosa	5.00
18	Barry Larkin	.75
19	Todd Helton	1.25
20	Mark Kotsay	.75
21	Jeff Bagwell	1.75
22	Raul Mondesi	.75
23	Jeff Cirillo	.75
24	Vladimir Guerrero	1.50
25	Mike Piazza	5.00
26	Scott Rolen	1.50
27	Jason Kendall	.75
28	Mark McGwire	7.50
29	Tony Gwynn	2.25
30	Barry Bonds	2.50

1999 Pacific Timelines

Timelines features 20 superstars, giving a chronological history of each player complete with photos from early in their careers. Three photos of the player are on the card front. Inserted exclusively in hobby packs these are limited to 199 serially numbered sets.

		MT
Complete Set (20):		525.00
Common Player:		10.00
Inserted 1:181 H		
1	Cal Ripken Jr.	75.00
2	Frank Thomas	35.00
3	Jim Thome	10.00
4	Paul Molitor	12.50
5	Bernie Williams	10.00
6	Derek Jeter	50.00
7	Ken Griffey Jr.	65.00
8	Alex Rodriguez	60.00
9	Wade Boggs	15.00
10	Jose Canseco	12.50
11	Roger Clemens	40.00
12	Andres Galarraga	10.00
13	Chipper Jones	50.00
14	Greg Maddux	40.00
15	Sammy Sosa	40.00
16	Larry Walker	10.00
17	Randy Johnson	15.00
18	Mike Piazza	50.00
19	Mark McGwire	75.00
20	Tony Gwynn	35.00

1999 Pacific Aurora

The 200-card set features two photos on the card front and one on the back. Card backs also have '98 and career stats along with personal information. The player's name and Aurora logo are stamped with gold foil.

		MT
Complete Set (200):		40.00
Common Player:		.10
Pack (6):		1.50
Wax Box (36):		50.00
1	Garret Anderson	.10
2	Jim Edmonds	.20
3	Darin Erstad	.75
4	Matt Luke	.10
5	Tim Salmon	.25
6	Mo Vaughn	.40
7	Jay Bell	.10
8	David Dellucci	.10
9	Steve Finley	.10
10	Bernard Gilkey	.10
11	Randy Johnson	1.00
12	Travis Lee	.15
13	Matt Williams	.40
14	Andres Galarraga	.10
15	Tom Glavine	.15
16	Andruw Jones	1.00
17	Chipper Jones	3.00
18	Brian Jordan	.10
19	Javy Lopez	.10
20	Greg Maddux	2.00
21	Albert Belle	.30
22	Will Clark	.30
23	Scott Erickson	.10
24	Mike Mussina	.75
25	Cal Ripken Jr.	4.00
26	B.J. Surhoff	.10
27	Nomar Garciaparra	2.50
28	Reggie Jefferson	.10
29	Darren Lewis	.10
30	Pedro Martinez	.75
31	John Valentin	.10
32	Rod Beck	.10
33	Mark Grace	.40
34	Lance Johnson	.10
35	Mickey Morandini	.10
36	Sammy Sosa	2.50
37	Kerry Wood	.40
38	James Baldwin	.10
39	Mike Caruso	.10
40	Ray Durham	.10
41	Magglio Ordonez	.15
42	Frank Thomas	1.75
43	Aaron Boone	.10
44	Sean Casey	.30
45	Barry Larkin	.15
46	Hal Morris	.10
47	Denny Neagle	.10
48	Greg Vaughn	.10
49	Pat Watkins	.10
50	Roberto Alomar	.60
51	Sandy Alomar Jr.	.10
52	David Justice	.30
53	Kenny Lofton	.10
54	Manny Ramirez	1.00
55	Richie Sexson	.10
56	Jim Thome	.10
57	Omar Vizquel	.10
58	Dante Bichette	.10
59	Vinny Castilla	.10
60	*Edgard Clemente*	.15
61	Derrick Gibson	.10
62	Todd Helton	.75
63	Darryl Kile	.10
64	Larry Walker	.30
65	Tony Clark	.10
66	Damion Easley	.10
67	Bob Higginson	.10
68	Brian Hunter	.10
69	Dean Palmer	.10
70	Justin Thompson	.10
71	Craig Counsell	.10
72	Todd Dunwoody	.10
73	Cliff Floyd	.10
74	Alex Gonzalez	.10
75	Livan Hernandez	.10
76	Mark Kotsay	.10
77	Derrek Lee	.10
78	Moises Alou	.15
79	Jeff Bagwell	1.00
80	Derek Bell	.10
81	Craig Biggio	.15
82	Ken Caminiti	.10
83	Richard Hidalgo	.15
84	Shane Reynolds	.10
85	Jeff Conine	.10
86	Johnny Damon	.15
87	Jermaine Dye	.10
88	Jeff King	.10
89	Jeff Montgomery	.10
90	Mike Sweeney	.10
91	Kevin Brown	.25
92	Mark Grudzielanek	.10
93	Eric Karros	.10
94	Raul Mondesi	.25
95	Chan Ho Park	.30
96	Gary Sheffield	.40
97	Jeromy Burnitz	.10
98	Jeff Cirillo	.10
99	Marquis Grissom	.10
100	Geoff Jenkins	.10
101	Dave Nilsson	.10
102	Jose Valentin	.10
103	Fernando Vina	.10
104	Marty Cordova	.10
105	Matt Lawton	.10
106	David Ortiz	.10
107	Brad Radke	.15
108	Todd Walker	.10
109	Shane Andrews	.10
110	Orlando Cabrera	.10
111	Brad Fullmer	.10
112	Vladimir Guerrero	.75
113	Wilton Guerrero	.10
114	Carl Pavano	.10
115	Fernando Seguignol	.10
116	Ugueth Urbina	.10
117	Edgardo Alfonzo	.15

118	Bobby Bonilla	.10
119	Rickey Henderson	.65
120	Hideo Nomo	.65
121	John Olerud	.10
122	Rey Ordonez	.15
123	Mike Piazza	3.00
124	Masato Yoshii	.10
125	Scott Brosius	.10
126	Orlando Hernandez	.35
127	Hideki Irabu	.10
128	Derek Jeter	3.00
129	Chuck Knoblauch	.10
130	Tino Martinez	.10
131	Jorge Posada	.25
132	Bernie Williams	.25
133	Eric Chavez	.25
134	Ryan Christenson	.10
135	Jason Giambi	.50
136	Ben Grieve	.25
137	A.J. Hinch	.10
138	Matt Stairs	.10
139	Miguel Tejada	.30
140	Bob Abreu	.10
141	*Gary Bennett*	.15
142	Desi Relaford	.10
143	Scott Rolen	.75
144	Curt Schilling	.20
145	Kevin Sefcik	.10
146	Brian Giles	.15
147	Jose Guillen	.10
148	Jason Kendall	.15
149	Aramis Ramirez	.10
150	Tony Womack	.10
151	Kevin Young	.10
152	Eric Davis	.10
153	J.D. Drew	.25
154	Ray Lankford	.10
155	Eli Marrero	.10
156	Mark McGwire	4.00
157	Luis Ordaz	.10
158	Edgar Renteria	.10
159	Andy Ashby	.10
160	Tony Gwynn	1.50
161	Trevor Hoffman	.10
162	Wally Joyner	.10
163	Jim Leyritz	.10
164	Ruben Rivera	.10
165	Reggie Sanders	.10
166	Quilvio Veras	.10
167	Rich Aurilia	.10
168	Marvin Benard	.10
169	Barry Bonds	1.75
170	Ellis Burks	.10
171	Jeff Kent	.10
172	Bill Mueller	.10
173	J.T. Snow	.10
174	Jay Buhner	.10
175	Jeff Fassero	.10
176	Ken Griffey Jr.	3.50
177	Carlos Guillen	.10
178	Edgar Martinez	.10
179	Alex Rodriguez	3.50
180	David Segui	.10
181	Dan Wilson	.10
182	Rolando Arrojo	.10
183	Wade Boggs	.75
184	Jose Canseco	.65
185	Aaron Ledesma	.10
186	Dave Martinez	.10
187	Quinton McCracken	.10
188	Fred McGriff	.10
189	Juan Gonzalez	1.00
190	Tom Goodwin	.10
191	Rusty Greer	.10
192	Roberto Kelly	.10
193	Rafael Palmeiro	.50
194	Ivan Rodriguez	.85
195	Roger Clemens	1.50
196	Jose Cruz Jr.	.25
197	Carlos Delgado	.75
198	Alex Gonzalez	.15
199	Roy Halladay	.10
200	Pat Hentgen	.10

1999 Pacific Aurora Complete Players

The 10 players featured in this serial numbered 20-card set each have two cards, designed to fit together. Card fronts feature a red border on the top and bottom with the rest of the card done in gold foil etching. Each card is serially numbered to 299.

		MT
Complete Set (10):		130.00
Common Player:		10.00
Production 299 sets		
1	Cal Ripken Jr.	25.00
2	Nomar Garciaparra	15.00
3	Sammy Sosa	15.00
4	Kerry Wood	10.00
5	Frank Thomas	10.00
6	Mike Piazza	17.50
7	Mark McGwire	25.00
8	Tony Gwynn	10.00
9	Ken Griffey Jr.	20.00
10	Alex Rodriguez	20.00

1999 Pacific Aurora Kings of the Major Leagues

The full foiled card fronts also utilize gold foil stamping. Pacific's crown as well as the featured player's team are shadow boxed in the background with the player's image in the foreground. These are seeded 1:361.

		MT
Complete Set (10):		275.00
Common Player:		25.00
Inserted 1:361		
1	Cal Ripken Jr.	50.00
2	Nomar Garciaparra	30.00
3	Sammy Sosa	30.00
4	Kerry Wood	25.00
5	Frank Thomas	30.00
6	Mike Piazza	35.00
7	Mark McGwire	50.00
8	Tony Gwynn	25.00
9	Ken Griffey Jr.	45.00
10	Alex Rodriguez	40.00

1999 Pacific Aurora On Deck

Twenty of the game's hottest players are featured in this laser-cut and silver foil stamped set. The player's team logo is laser cut into the bottom half of the card beneath the player photo. These are seeded 4:37 packs.

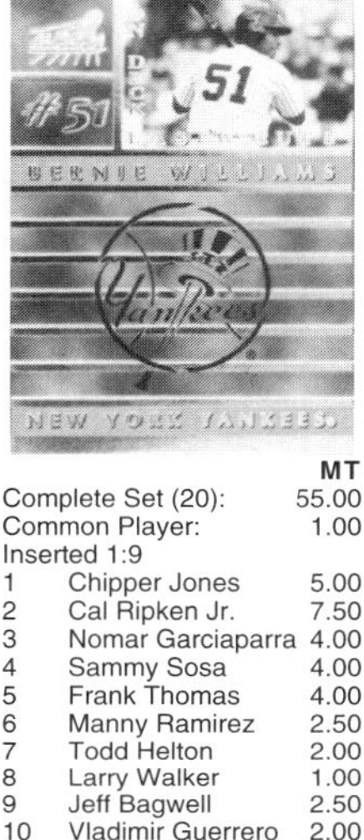

		MT
Complete Set (20):		55.00
Common Player:		1.00
Inserted 1:9		
1	Chipper Jones	5.00
2	Cal Ripken Jr.	7.50
3	Nomar Garciaparra	4.00
4	Sammy Sosa	4.00
5	Frank Thomas	4.00
6	Manny Ramirez	2.50
7	Todd Helton	2.00
8	Larry Walker	1.00
9	Jeff Bagwell	2.50
10	Vladimir Guerrero	2.00
11	Mike Piazza	5.00
12	Derek Jeter	5.00
13	Bernie Williams	1.00
14	J.D. Drew	1.50
15	Mark McGwire	7.50
16	Tony Gwynn	3.00
17	Ken Griffey Jr.	6.00
18	Alex Rodriguez	6.00
19	Juan Gonzalez	2.50
20	Ivan Rodriguez	1.50

1999 Pacific Aurora Pennant Fever

Regular Pennant Fever inserts feature gold foil stamping of 20 of the hottest players in the hobby. These are seeded 4:37 packs. There are also three parallel versions which consist of: Platinum Blue, Silver and Copper. Platinum Blues are limited to 100 serial numbered sets, Silvers are retail exclusive and limited to 250 numbered sets and Coppers are hobby exclusive and limited to 20 numbered sets. Pacific spokesman Tony Gwynn autographed 97 regular Pennent Fever cards and one each of the Silver, Blue and Copper.

		MT
Complete Set (20):		75.00
Common Player:		1.00
Silver (250 Sets):		2X
Platinum Blue (100):		6X
Copper (20):		20X
Tony Gwynn Autograph:		50.00
1	Chipper Jones	6.00
2	Greg Maddux	5.00
3	Cal Ripken Jr.	10.00
4	Nomar Garciaparra	5.00
5	Sammy Sosa	5.00
6	Kerry Wood	2.50
7	Frank Thomas	5.00
8	Manny Ramirez	3.00
9	Todd Helton	2.00
10	Jeff Bagwell	3.00
11	Mike Piazza	6.00
12	Derek Jeter	6.00
13	Bernie Williams	2.00
14	J.D. Drew	2.50
15	Mark McGwire	10.00
16	Tony Gwynn	4.00
17	Ken Griffey Jr.	8.00
18	Alex Rodriguez	7.50
19	Juan Gonzalez	3.00
20	Ivan Rodriguez	2.50

1999 Pacific Aurora Styrotechs

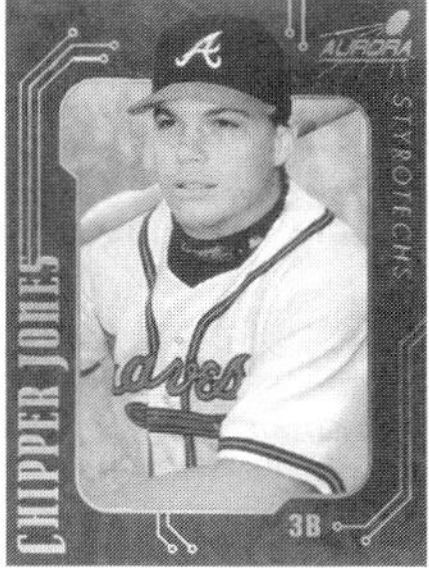

This 20-card set features styrene stock, making the cards more resilient. Fronts have a black border highlighted with gold foil. Backs have a photo and brief career highlights. These are seeded 1:37 packs.

		MT
Complete Set (20):		100.00
Common Player:		2.00
Inserted 1:37		
1	Chipper Jones	9.00
2	Greg Maddux	6.00
3	Cal Ripken Jr.	12.50
4	Nomar Garciaparra	7.00
5	Sammy Sosa	7.00
6	Kerry Wood	2.50
7	Frank Thomas	5.00
8	Manny Ramirez	3.50
9	Larry Walker	2.00
10	Jeff Bagwell	3.50
11	Mike Piazza	9.00
12	Derek Jeter	9.00
13	Bernie Williams	2.00
14	J.D. Drew	2.50
15	Mark McGwire	12.50
16	Tony Gwynn	4.00
17	Ken Griffey Jr.	10.00
18	Alex Rodriguez	10.00
19	Juan Gonzalez	3.50
20	Ivan Rodriguez	3.00

1999 Pacific Crown Collection

Released in one series the 300-card set has white borders and gold-foil highlights on front. Backs have a small photo along with English and Spanish narrative. A Platinum Blue parallel to the base set utilizes platinum blue holographic foil and is seeded 1:73 packs. Twelve-card packs had an S.R.P. of $2.49.

		MT
Complete Set (300):		30.00
Common Player:		.10
Platinum Blue Stars:		30X
Inserted 1:73		
Pack (12):		1.50
Wax Box (36):		50.00
1	Garret Anderson	.10
2	Gary DiSarcina	.10
3	Jim Edmonds	.15
4	Darin Erstad	.40
5	Shigetosi Hasegawa	.10
6	Norberto Martin	.10
7	Omar Olivares	.10
8	Orlando Palmeiro	.10
9	Tim Salmon	.25
10	Randy Velarde	.10
11	Tony Batista	.10
12	Jay Bell	.10
13	Yamil Benitez	.10
14	Omar Daal	.10
15	David Dellucci	.10
16	Karim Garcia	.10
17	Travis Lee	.15
18	Felix Rodriguez	.10
19	Devon White	.10
20	Matt Williams	.25
21	Andres Galarraga	.10
22	Tom Glavine	.20
23	Ozzie Guillen	.10
24	Andruw Jones	.60
25	Chipper Jones	2.00
26	Ryan Klesko	.10
27	Javy Lopez	.10
28	Greg Maddux	1.50
29	Dennis Martinez	.10
30	Odaliz Perez	.10
31	Rudy Seanez	.10
32	John Smoltz	.15
33	Roberto Alomar	.50
34	Armando Benitez	.10
35	Scott Erickson	.10
36	Juan Guzman	.10
37	Mike Mussina	.50
38	Jesse Orosco	.10
39	Rafael Palmeiro	.30
40	Sidney Ponson	.10
41	Cal Ripken Jr.	3.00
42	B.J. Surhoff	.10
43	Lenny Webster	.10
44	Dennis Eckersley	.10
45	Nomar Garciaparra	2.00
46	Darren Lewis	.10
47	Pedro Martinez	.65
48	Troy O'Leary	.10
49	Bret Saberhagen	.10
50	John Valentin	.10
51	Mo Vaughn	.35
52	Tim Wakefield	.10
53	Manny Alexander	.10
54	Rod Beck	.10
55	Gary Gaetti	.10
56	Mark Grace	.25
57	Felix Heredia	.10
58	Jose Hernandez	.10
59	Henry Rodriguez	.10
60	Sammy Sosa	2.00
61	Kevin Tapani	.10
62	Kerry Wood	.40
63	James Baldwin	.10
64	Albert Belle	.30
65	Mike Caruso	.10
66	Carlos Castillo	.10
67	Wil Cordero	.10
68	Jaime Navarro	.10
69	Magglio Ordonez	.20
70	Frank Thomas	1.25
71	Robin Ventura	.10
72	Bret Boone	.10
73	Sean Casey	.25
74	*Guillermo Garcia*	.10
75	Barry Larkin	.15
76	Melvin Nieves	.10
77	Eduardo Perez	.10
78	Roberto Petagine	.10
79	Reggie Sanders	.10
80	Eddie Taubensee	.10
81	Brett Tomko	.10
82	Sandy Alomar Jr.	.10
83	Bartolo Colon	.15
84	Joey Cora	.10
85	Einar Diaz	.10
86	David Justice	.30
87	Kenny Lofton	.10
88	Manny Ramirez	.75
89	Jim Thome	.10
90	Omar Vizquel	.10
91	Enrique Wilson	.10
92	Pedro Astacio	.10
93	Dante Bichette	.10
94	Vinny Castilla	.10
95	*Edgard Clemente*	.15
96	Todd Helton	.60
97	Darryl Kile	.10
98	Mike Munoz	.10
99	Neifi Perez	.10
100	Jeff Reed	.10
101	Larry Walker	.25
102	Gabe Alvarez	.10
103	Kimera Bartee	.10
104	Frank Castillo	.10
105	Tony Clark	.10
106	Deivi Cruz	.10
107	Damion Easley	.10
108	Luis Gonzalez	.30
109	Marino Santana	.10
110	Justin Thompson	.10
111	Antonio Alfonseca	.10
112	Alex Fernandez	.10
113	Cliff Floyd	.10
114	Alex Gonzalez	.10
115	Livan Hernandez	.10
116	Mark Kotsay	.10
117	Derrek Lee	.10
118	Edgar Renteria	.10
119	Jesus Sanchez	.10
120	Moises Alou	.15
121	Jeff Bagwell	.75
122	Derek Bell	.10
123	Craig Biggio	.15
124	Tony Eusebio	.10
125	Ricky Gutierrez	.10
126	Richard Hidalgo	.15
127	Randy Johnson	.75
128	Jose Lima	.10
129	Shane Reynolds	.10
130	Johnny Damon	.15
131	Carlos Febles	.10
132	Jeff King	.10
133	Mendy Lopez	.10
134	Hal Morris	.10
135	Jose Offerman	.10
136	Jose Rosado	.10
137	Jose Santiago	.10
138	Bobby Bonilla	.10
139	Roger Cedeno	.10
140	Alex Cora	.10
141	Eric Karros	.10
142	Raul Mondesi	.20
143	Antonio Osuna	.10
144	Chan Ho Park	.25
145	Gary Sheffield	.25
146	Ismael Valdes	.10
147	Jeromy Burnitz	.10
148	Jeff Cirillo	.10
149	Valerio de los Santos	.10
150	Marquis Grissom	.10
151	Scott Karl	.10
152	Dave Nilsson	.10
153	Al Reyes	.10
154	Rafael Roque	.10
155	Jose Valentin	.10
156	Fernando Vina	.10
157	Rick Aguilera	.10
158	Hector Carrasco	.10
159	Marty Cordova	.10
160	Eddie Guardado	.10
161	Paul Molitor	.50
162	Otis Nixon	.10
163	Alex Ochoa	.10
164	David Ortiz	.10
165	Frank Rodriguez	.10
166	Todd Walker	.10
167	Miguel Batista	.10
168	Orlando Cabrera	.10
169	Vladimir Guerrero	.60
170	Wilton Guerrero	.10
171	Carl Pavano	.10
172	Robert Perez	.10
173	F.P. Santangelo	.10
174	Fernando Seguignol	.10
175	Ugueth Urbina	.10
176	Javier Vazquez	.10
177	Edgardo Alfonzo	.15
178	Carlos Baerga	.10
179	John Franco	.10
180	Luis Lopez	.10
181	Hideo Nomo	.60
182	John Olerud	.10
183	Rey Ordonez	.15
184	Mike Piazza	2.00
185	Armando Reynoso	.10
186	Masato Yoshii	.10
187	David Cone	.10
188	Orlando Hernandez	.35
189	Hideki Irabu	.10
190	Derek Jeter	2.50
191	Ricky Ledee	.10
192	Tino Martinez	.10
193	Ramiro Mendoza	.10
194	Paul O'Neill	.10
195	Jorge Posada	.15
196	Mariano Rivera	.20
197	Luis Sojo	.10
198	Bernie Williams	.30
199	Rafael Bournigal	.10
200	Eric Chavez	.25
201	Ryan Christenson	.10
202	Jason Giambi	.40
203	Ben Grieve	.25
204	Rickey Henderson	.40
205	A.J. Hinch	.10
206	Kenny Rogers	.10
207	Miguel Tejada	.20
208	Jorge Velandia	.10
209	Bobby Abreu	.10
210	Marlon Anderson	.10
211	Alex Arias	.10
212	Bobby Estalella	.10
213	Doug Glanville	.10
214	Scott Rolen	.50
215	Curt Schilling	.20
216	Kevin Sefcik	.10
217	Adrian Brown	.10
218	Francisco Cordova	.10
219	Freddy Garcia	.10
220	Jose Guillen	.10
221	Jason Kendall	.10
222	Al Martin	.10
223	Abraham Nunez	.10
224	Aramis Ramirez	.10
225	Ricardo Rincon	.10
226	Kevin Young	.10
227	J.D. Drew	.25
228	Ron Gant	.10
229	Jose Jimenez	.10
230	Brian Jordan	.10
231	Ray Lankford	.10
232	Eli Marrero	.10
233	Mark McGwire	3.00
234	Luis Ordaz	.10
235	Placido Polanco	.10
236	Fernando Tatis	.10
237	Andy Ashby	.10
238	Kevin Brown	.15
239	Ken Caminiti	.10
240	Steve Finley	.10
241	Chris Gomez	.10
242	Tony Gwynn	1.25
243	Carlos Hernandez	.10
244	Trevor Hoffman	.10
245	Wally Joyner	.10
246	Ruben Rivera	.10
247	Greg Vaughn	.10
248	Quilvio Veras	.10
249	Rich Aurilia	.10
250	Barry Bonds	1.50
251	Stan Javier	.10
252	Jeff Kent	.10
253	Ramon Martinez	.10
254	Jose Mesa	.10
255	Armando Rios	.10
256	Rich Rodriguez	.10
257	Rey Sanchez	.10
258	J.T. Snow	.10
259	Julian Tavarez	.10
260	Jeff Fassero	.10
261	Ken Griffey Jr.	2.75
262	*Giomar Guevara*	.10
263	Carlos Guillen	.10
264	Raul Ibanez	.10
265	Edgar Martinez	.10
266	Jamie Moyer	.10
267	Alex Rodriguez	2.75
268	David Segui	.10
269	Makoto Suzuki	.10
270	Wilson Alvarez	.10
271	Rolando Arrojo	.10
272	Wade Boggs	.40
273	Miguel Cairo	.10
274	Roberto Hernandez	.10
275	Aaron Ledesma	.10
276	Albie Lopez	.10
277	Quinton McCracken	.10
278	Fred McGriff	.10
279	Esteban Yan	.10
280	Luis Alicea	.10
281	Will Clark	.30
282	Juan Gonzalez	.75
283	Rusty Greer	.10
284	Rick Helling	.10
285	Xavier Hernandez	.10
286	Roberto Kelly	.10
287	Esteban Loaiza	.10
288	Ivan Rodriguez	.60
289	Aaron Sele	.10
290	John Wetteland	.10
291	Jose Canseco	.50
292	Roger Clemens	1.25
293	Felipe Crespo	.10
294	Jose Cruz Jr.	.20
295	Carlos Delgado	.50
296	Kelvim Escobar	.10
297	Tony Fernandez	.10
298	Alex Gonzalez	.15
299	Tomas Perez	.10
300	Juan Samuel	.10

1999 Pacific Crown Collection In The Cage

These die-cut inserts have a netting like background with laser cutting, giving the look that the player is hitting in a batting cage. These are seeded 1:145 packs.

		MT
Complete Set (20):		235.00
Common Player:		5.00
Inserted 1:145		
1	Chipper Jones	22.50
2	Cal Ripken Jr.	30.00
3	Nomar Garciaparra	20.00
4	Sammy Sosa	20.00
5	Frank Thomas	15.00
6	Manny Ramirez	10.00
7	Todd Helton	7.50
8	Moises Alou	5.00
9	Vladimir Guerrero	10.00

10	Mike Piazza	22.50
11	Derek Jeter	22.50
12	Ben Grieve	7.50
13	J.D. Drew	6.00
14	Mark McGwire	30.00
15	Tony Gwynn	12.50
16	Ken Griffey Jr.	25.00
17	Edgar Martinez	5.00
18	Alex Rodriguez	25.00
19	Juan Gonzalez	10.00
20	Ivan Rodriguez	7.50

1999 Pacific Crown Collection Latinos/Major Leagues

This 36-card set salutes the many latino players in the major league including Roberto Alomar, Manny Ramirez and Juan Gonzalez. These are seeded 2:37 packs.

		MT
Complete Set (36):		70.00
Common Player:		1.00
Inserted 1:18		
1	Roberto Alomar	2.50
2	Rafael Palmeiro	1.50
3	Nomar Garciaparra	8.00
4	Pedro Martinez	3.50
5	Magglio Ordonez	1.50
6	Sandy Alomar Jr.	1.00
7	Bartolo Colon	1.25
8	Manny Ramirez	5.00
9	Omar Vizquel	1.00
10	Enrique Wilson	1.00
11	David Ortiz	1.00
12	Orlando Hernandez	8.00
13	Tino Martinez	1.00
14	Mariano Rivera	2.50
15	Bernie Williams	1.00
16	Edgar Martinez	1.00
17	Alex Rodriguez	12.00
18	David Segui	1.00
19	Rolando Arrojo	1.50
20	Juan Gonzalez	5.00
21	Ivan Rodriguez	3.50
22	Jose Canseco	2.00
23	Jose Cruz Jr.	1.25
24	Andres Galarraga	1.00
25	Andruw Jones	3.00
26	Javy Lopez	1.00
27	Sammy Sosa	10.00
28	Vinny Castilla	1.00
29	Alex Gonzalez	1.00
30	Moises Alou	1.00
31	Bobby Bonilla	1.00
32	Raul Mondesi	1.00
33	Fernando Vina	1.00
34	Vladimir Guerrero	4.00
35	Carlos Baerga	1.00
36	Rey Ordonez	1.00

1999 Pacific Crown Collection Pacific Cup

These die-cut inserts are shaped like a trophy with the featured player's photo in the foreground. These are seeded 1:721 packs.

		MT
Complete Set (10):		100.00
Common Player:		6.00
Inserted 1:721		
1	Cal Ripken Jr.	20.00
2	Nomar Garciaparra	12.00
3	Frank Thomas	10.00
4	Ken Griffey Jr.	15.00
5	Alex Rodriguez	15.00
6	Greg Maddux	12.00
7	Sammy Sosa	12.00
8	Kerry Wood	6.00
9	Mark McGwire	20.00
10	Tony Gwynn	7.50

1999 Pacific Crown Collection Players Choice

In conjunction with the annual Players Choice Awards ceremonies, Pacific produced a special edition of the cards of some of the players involved. Cards have a "Players Choice" foil stamp on front. Quantities produced were in the range of 25-40 of each.

		MT
Complete Set (6):		60.00
Common Player:		5.00
10	Randy Velarde	5.00
41	Cal Ripken Jr.	35.00
47	Pedro Martinez	12.00
88	Manny Ramirez	12.00
112	Alex Fernandez	5.00
128	Jose Lima	5.00

1999 Pacific Crown Collection Tape Measure

This 20-card insert set is fully foiled in platinum blue with rainbow highlights in the background of the player photo. Saluting the top power hitters in the game today, these are seeded 1:73 packs.

		MT
Complete Set (20):		105.00
Common Player:		2.50
Inserted 1:73		
1	Andres Galarraga	2.50
2	Chipper Jones	10.00
3	Nomar Garciaparra	8.00
4	Sammy Sosa	14.00
5	Frank Thomas	6.00
6	Manny Ramirez	5.00
7	Vinny Castilla	2.50
8	Moises Alou	2.50
9	Jeff Bagwell	5.00
10	Raul Mondesi	2.50
11	Vladimir Guerrero	4.00
12	Mike Piazza	10.00
13	J.D. Drew	3.00
14	Mark McGwire	18.00
15	Greg Vaughn	2.50
16	Ken Griffey Jr.	16.00
17	Alex Rodriguez	14.00
18	Juan Gonzalez	5.00
19	Ivan Rodriguez	4.00
20	Jose Canseco	3.00

1999 Pacific Crown Collection Team Checklists

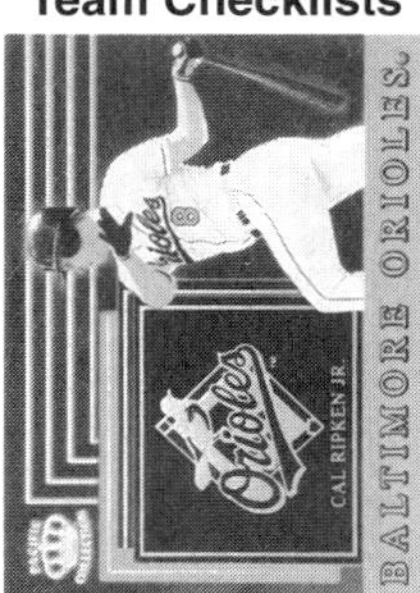

This 30-card set features is highlighted with holographic silver foil stamping and done in a horizontal format. The backs have a complete team checklist for the featured player's team. These have an insertion rate of 1:37 packs.

		MT
Complete Set (30):		85.00
Common Player:		1.00
Inserted 1:37		
1	Darin Erstad	1.50
2	Travis Lee	1.00
3	Chipper Jones	8.00
4	Cal Ripken Jr.	10.00
5	Nomar Garciaparra	6.00
6	Sammy Sosa	7.00
7	Frank Thomas	6.00
8	Barry Larkin	1.00
9	Manny Ramirez	3.50
10	Larry Walker	1.00
11	Bob Higginson	1.00
12	Livan Hernandez	1.00
13	Moises Alou	1.00
14	Jeff King	1.00
15	Raul Mondesi	1.00
16	Marquis Grissom	1.00
17	David Ortiz	1.00
18	Vladimir Guerrero	3.00
19	Mike Piazza	8.00
20	Derek Jeter	8.00
21	Ben Grieve	1.50
22	Scott Rolen	1.50
23	Jason Kendall	1.00
24	Mark McGwire	10.00
25	Tony Gwynn	4.50
26	Barry Bonds	3.50
27	Ken Griffey Jr.	9.00
28	Wade Boggs	2.00
29	Juan Gonzalez	3.50
30	Jose Canseco	1.50

1999 Pacific Crown Royale

The Crown Royale 144-card base set has a horizontal format die-cut around a crown design at the top. The cards are double foiled and etched. There are 18 short-printed rookies and prospects cards, which were inserted at a rate of about one per eight packs. There are two parallels: Limited Series and Opening Day. Limited Series is produced on 24-point stock with silver foil and limited to 99 numbered sets. Opening Day is limited to 72 numbered sets.

		MT
Complete Set (144):		150.00
Common Player:		.25
Common SP:		4.00
Limited Series (99 Sets):		8X
SPs:		2X
Opening Day (72 Sets):		15X
SPs:		3X
Pack (6):		3.50
Wax Box (24):		65.00
1	Jim Edmonds	.35
2	Darin Erstad	1.00
3	Troy Glaus	2.00
4	Tim Salmon	.50
5	Mo Vaughn	1.00
6	Jay Bell	.25
7	Steve Finley	.25
8	Randy Johnson	2.00
9	Travis Lee	.25
10	Matt Williams	.50
11	Andruw Jones	1.00
12	Chipper Jones	5.00
13	Brian Jordan	.25
14	Ryan Klesko	.25
15	Javy Lopez	.25
16	Greg Maddux	4.00
17	Randall Simon (SP)	1.00
18	Albert Belle	.75
19	Will Clark	.75
20	Delino DeShields	.25
21	Mike Mussina	1.50
22	Cal Ripken Jr.	8.00
23	Nomar Garciaparra	5.00
24	Pedro Martinez	2.00
25	Jose Offerman	.25
26	John Valentin	.25
27	Mark Grace	1.00
28	Lance Johnson	.25
29	Henry Rodriguez	.25
30	Sammy Sosa	5.00
31	Kerry Wood	1.00
32	Mike Caruso	.25
33	Ray Durham	.25
34	Magglio Ordonez	.50
35	Brian Simmons (SP)	1.00
36	Frank Thomas	3.00
37	Mike Cameron	.25
38	Barry Larkin	.35
39	Greg Vaughn	.25
40	Dmitri Young	.25
41	Roberto Alomar	1.00
42	Sandy Alomar Jr.	.25
43	David Justice	.65
44	Kenny Lofton	.25
45	Manny Ramirez	2.00
46	Jim Thome	.25
47	Dante Bichette	.25
48	Vinny Castilla	.25
49	Todd Helton	1.00
50	Larry Walker	.65
51	Tony Clark	.25
52	Damion Easley	.25

53	Bob Higginson	.25
54	Brian Hunter	.25
55	Gabe Kapler (SP)	4.00
56	*Jeff Weaver* (SP)	10.00
57	Cliff Floyd	.25
58	Alex Gonzalez (SP)	1.00
59	Mark Kotsay	.25
60	Derrek Lee	.25
61	Preston Wilson (SP)	4.00
62	Moises Alou	.35
63	Jeff Bagwell	2.00
64	Derek Bell	.25
65	Craig Biggio	.35
66	Ken Caminiti	.25
67	Carlos Beltran (SP)	4.00
68	Johnny Damon	.25
69	Carlos Febles (SP)	4.00
70	Jeff King	.25
71	Kevin Brown	.50
72	Todd Hundley	.25
73	Eric Karros	.25
74	Raul Mondesi	.50
75	Gary Sheffield	.75
76	Jeromy Burnitz	.25
77	Jeff Cirillo	.25
78	Marquis Grissom	.25
79	Fernando Vina	.25
80	*Chad Allen* (SP)	2.00
81	Matt Lawton	.25
82	Doug Mientkiewicz (SP)	3.00
83	Brad Radke	.25
84	Todd Walker	.25
85	Michael Barrett (SP)	3.00
86	Brad Fullmer	.25
87	Vladimir Guerrero	1.00
88	Wilton Guerrero	.25
89	Ugueth Urbina	.25
90	Bobby Bonilla	.25
91	Rickey Henderson	2.00
92	Rey Ordonez	.25
93	Mike Piazza	6.00
94	Robin Ventura	.25
95	Roger Clemens	3.00
96	Orlando Hernandez	2.00
97	Derek Jeter	6.00
98	Chuck Knoblauch	.25
99	Tino Martinez	.25
100	Bernie Williams	1.00
101	Eric Chavez (SP)	5.00
102	Jason Giambi	.60
103	Ben Grieve	.50
104	Tim Raines	.25
105	Marlon Anderson (SP)	3.00
106	Doug Glanville	.25
107	Scott Rolen	1.00
108	Curt Schilling	.75
109	Brian Giles	.25
110	Jose Guillen	.25
111	Jason Kendall	.25
112	Kevin Young	.25
113	J.D. Drew (SP)	5.00
114	Jose Jimenez (SP)	3.00
115	Ray Lankford	.25
116	Mark McGwire	8.00
117	Fernando Tatis	.25
118	Matt Clement (SP)	3.00
119	Tony Gwynn	3.00
120	Trevor Hoffman	.25
121	Wally Joyner	.25
122	Reggie Sanders	.25
123	Barry Bonds	3.00
124	Ellis Burks	.25
125	Jeff Kent	.25
126	J.T. Snow	.25
127	*Freddy Garcia* (SP)	15.00
128	Ken Griffey Jr.	7.00
129	Edgar Martinez	.25
130	Alex Rodriguez	7.00
131	David Segui	.25
132	Rolando Arrojo	.25
133	Wade Boggs	1.50
134	Jose Canseco	.75
135	Quinton McCracken	.25
136	Fred McGriff	.25
137	Juan Gonzalez	2.00
138	Rusty Greer	.25
139	Rafael Palmeiro	.60
140	Ivan Rodriguez	1.50
141	Jose Cruz Jr.	.50
142	Carlos Delgado	.75
143	Shawn Green	.75
144	Roy Halladay (SP)	4.00

1999 Pacific Crown Royale Century 21

This 10-card set features some of baseball's most dominating players, on a full silver foil front. These are seeded 1:25 packs.

		MT
Complete Set (10):		100.00
Common Player:		5.00
Inserted 1:25		
1	Cal Ripken Jr.	20.00
2	Nomar Garciaparra	12.00
3	Sammy Sosa	12.00
4	Frank Thomas	10.00
5	Mike Piazza	12.50
6	J.D. Drew	5.00
7	Mark McGwire	20.00
8	Tony Gwynn	7.50
9	Ken Griffey Jr.	17.50
10	Alex Rodriguez	15.00

1999 Pacific Crown Royale Cramer's Choice Premiums

This enlarged 10-card set is die-cut into a trophy shape. Cards are enhanced with silver holographic fronts with silver holographic etching and gold-foil stamping across the bottom. They are found one per box. Six serially numbered parallels were randomly seeded: Dark Blue (35 each), Green (30), Red (25), Light Blue (20), Gold (10) and Purple (1).

		MT
Complete Set (10):		75.00
Common Player:		5.00
Inserted 1:box		
Dark Blue (35 Sets):		5X
Green (30):		6X
Red (25):		8X
Light Blue (20):		10X
Gold (10):		15X
Purple (1): Value Undetermined		
1	Cal Ripken Jr.	15.00
2	Nomar Garciaparra	7.50
3	Sammy Sosa	7.50
4	Frank Thomas	6.00
5	Mike Piazza	10.00
6	Derek Jeter	10.00
7	J.D. Drew	5.00
8	Mark McGwire	15.00
9	Tony Gwynn	6.00
10	Ken Griffey Jr.	12.00

1999 Pacific Crown Royale Gold Crown Die-Cut Premiums

This enlarged six-card set is identical to Crown Die-cuts except for their jumbo. These were limited to 1,036 numbered sets, found less than once every other box.

		MT
Complete Set (6):		22.50
Common Player:		2.50
Inserted 6:10 boxes		
1	Cal Ripken Jr.	6.50
2	Mike Piazza	4.00
3	Ken Griffey Jr.	5.00
4	Tony Gwynn	3.00
5	Mark McGwire	6.50
6	J.D. Drew	2.50

1999 Pacific Crown Royale Living Legends

This 10-card set spotlights baseball's top stars on a fully foiled card front. These are serial numbered to 375 sets.

		MT
Complete Set (10):		110.00
Common Player:		10.00
Production 375 sets		
1	Greg Maddux	12.00
2	Cal Ripken Jr.	20.00
3	Nomar Garciaparra	12.50
4	Sammy Sosa	12.50
5	Frank Thomas	10.00
6	Mike Piazza	14.00
7	Mark McGwire	20.00
8	Tony Gwynn	10.00
9	Ken Griffey Jr.	17.50
10	Alex Rodriguez	15.00

1999 Pacific Crown Royale Master Performers

This 20-card set features a full foiled front with the player photo in a frame like border. Master Performers are seeded 2:25 packs.

		MT
Complete Set (20):		125.00
Common Player:		2.00
Inserted 2:25		
1	Chipper Jones	12.00
2	Greg Maddux	8.00
3	Cal Ripken Jr.	15.00
4	Nomar Garciaparra	9.00
5	Sammy Sosa	9.00
6	Frank Thomas	9.00
7	Raul Mondesi	2.00
8	Vladimir Guerrero	4.00
9	Mike Piazza	12.00
10	Roger Clemens	8.00
11	Derek Jeter	12.00
12	Scott Rolen	4.00
13	J.D. Drew	2.00
14	Mark McGwire	15.00
15	Tony Gwynn	8.00
16	Barry Bonds	6.00
17	Ken Griffey Jr.	13.50
18	Alex Rodriguez	12.50
19	Juan Gonzalez	6.00
20	Ivan Rodriguez	3.00

1999 Pacific Crown Royale Pillars of the Game

This 25-card set features holographic silver foil fronts on a horizontal format. These are seeded one per pack.

		MT
Complete Set (25):		27.50
Common Player:		.50
Inserted 1:1		
1	Mo Vaughn	.75
2	Chipper Jones	2.00
3	Greg Maddux	1.25
4	Albert Belle	.75
5	Cal Ripken Jr.	3.50

6	Nomar Garciaparra	1.50
7	Sammy Sosa	1.50
8	Frank Thomas	1.50
9	Manny Ramirez	1.00
10	Jeff Bagwell	.75
11	Raul Mondesi	.50
12	Vladimir Guerrero	1.00
13	Mike Piazza	2.00
14	Roger Clemens	1.25
15	Derek Jeter	2.00
16	Bernie Williams	.50
17	Ben Grieve	.50
18	J.D. Drew	.75
19	Mark McGwire	3.50
20	Tony Gwynn	1.25
21	Barry Bonds	1.25
22	Ken Griffey Jr.	3.00
23	Alex Rodriguez	2.50
24	Juan Gonzalez	1.00
25	Ivan Rodriguez	.60

1999 Pacific Crown Royale Pivotal Players

This 25-card set features holographic silver foil fronts with a flame in the background of the player photo. These are seeded one per pack.

		MT
Complete Set (25):		25.00
Common Player:		.45
Inserted 1:1		
1	Mo Vaughn	.60
2	Chipper Jones	2.25
3	Greg Maddux	1.75
4	Albert Belle	.60
5	Cal Ripken Jr.	3.00
6	Nomar Garciaparra	1.75
7	Sammy Sosa	1.75
8	Frank Thomas	1.75
9	Manny Ramirez	.90
10	Craig Biggio	.45
11	Raul Mondesi	.45
12	Vladimir Guerrero	.60
13	Mike Piazza	2.25
14	Roger Clemens	1.25
15	Derek Jeter	2.25
16	Bernie Williams	.45
17	Ben Grieve	.45
18	Scott Rolen	.60
19	J.D. Drew	.60
20	Mark McGwire	3.00
21	Tony Gwynn	1.25
22	Ken Griffey Jr.	2.50
23	Alex Rodriguez	2.50
24	Juan Gonzalez	.90
25	Ivan Rodriguez	.50

1999 Pacific Invincible

The base set consists of 150 base cards and feature a player photo and a headshot in a cel window on the bottom right portion of the card. There are also two parallels to the base set: Opening Day and Platinum Blue. Both parallels are limited to 67 serial numbered sets.

		MT
Complete Set (150):		100.00
Common Player:		.50
Opening Day (69 Sets):		6X
Platinum Blues (67):		6X
Pack (3):		2.00
Wax Box (24):		50.00
1	Jim Edmonds	.65
2	Darin Erstad	2.00
3	Troy Glaus	2.50
4	Tim Salmon	1.00
5	Mo Vaughn	2.00
6	Steve Finley	.50
7	Randy Johnson	2.50
8	Travis Lee	1.00
9	Dante Powell	.50
10	Matt Williams	1.00
11	Bret Boone	.50
12	Andruw Jones	2.00
13	Chipper Jones	8.00
14	Brian Jordan	.50
15	Ryan Klesko	.50
16	Javy Lopez	.50
17	Greg Maddux	6.00
18	Brady Anderson	.50
19	Albert Belle	1.00
20	Will Clark	1.00
21	Mike Mussina	2.00
22	Cal Ripken Jr.	10.00
23	Nomar Garciaparra	7.00
24	Pedro Martinez	2.50
25	Trot Nixon	.50
26	Jose Offerman	.50
27	Donnie Sadler	.50
28	John Valentin	.50
29	Mark Grace	1.25
30	Lance Johnson	.50
31	Henry Rodriguez	.50
32	Sammy Sosa	7.00
33	Kerry Wood	2.50
34	McKay Christensen	.50
35	Ray Durham	.50
36	Jeff Liefer	.50
37	Frank Thomas	7.00
38	Mike Cameron	.50
39	Barry Larkin	.75
40	Greg Vaughn	.50
41	Dmitri Young	.50
42	Roberto Alomar	2.00
43	Sandy Alomar Jr.	.50
44	David Justice	1.00
45	Kenny Lofton	.50
46	Manny Ramirez	4.00
47	Jim Thome	.50
48	Dante Bichette	.50
49	Vinny Castilla	.50
50	Darryl Hamilton	.50
51	Todd Helton	2.00
52	Neifi Perez	.50
53	Larry Walker	1.00
54	Tony Clark	.50
55	Damion Easley	.50
56	Bob Higginson	.50
57	Brian Hunter	.50
58	Gabe Kapler	2.00
59	Cliff Floyd	.50
60	Alex Gonzalez	.50
61	Mark Kotsay	.50
62	Derrek Lee	.50
63	Braden Looper	.50
64	Moises Alou	.75
65	Jeff Bagwell	4.00
66	Craig Biggio	.75
67	Ken Caminiti	.50
68	Scott Elarton	.50
69	Mitch Meluskey	.50
70	Carlos Beltran	.50
71	Johnny Damon	.75
72	Carlos Febles	1.00
73	Jeremy Giambi	.50
74	Kevin Brown	.75
75	Todd Hundley	.50
76	Paul LoDuca	.50
77	Raul Mondesi	.75
78	Gary Sheffield	1.00
79	Geoff Jenkins	.50
80	Jeromy Burnitz	.50
81	Marquis Grissom	.50
82	Jose Valentin	.50
83	Fernando Vina	.50
84	Corey Koskie	.50
85	Matt Lawton	.50
86	Christian Guzman	.50
87	Torii Hunter	.50
88	Doug Mientkiewicz	.50
89	Michael Barrett	.50
90	Brad Fullmer	.50
91	Vladimir Guerrero	2.00
92	Fernando Seguignol	.50
93	Ugueth Urbina	.50
94	Bobby Bonilla	.50
95	Rickey Henderson	2.50
96	Rey Ordonez	.50
97	Mike Piazza	8.00
98	Robin Ventura	.50
99	Roger Clemens	5.00
100	Derek Jeter	8.00
101	Chuck Knoblauch	.50
102	Tino Martinez	.50
103	Paul O'Neill	.50
104	Bernie Williams	1.00
105	Eric Chavez	2.00
106	Ryan Christenson	.50
107	Jason Giambi	1.00
108	Ben Grieve	1.50
109	Miguel Tejada	.75
110	Marlon Anderson	.50
111	Doug Glanville	.50
112	Scott Rolen	2.00
113	Curt Schilling	.75
114	Brian Giles	.50
115	Warren Morris	.50
116	Jason Kendall	.50
117	Kris Benson	.50
118	J.D. Drew	.75
119	Ray Lankford	.50
120	Mark McGwire	10.00
121	Matt Clement	.50
122	Tony Gwynn	6.00
123	Trevor Hoffman	.50
124	Wally Joyner	.50
125	Reggie Sanders	.50
126	Barry Bonds	5.00
127	Ellis Burks	.50
128	Jeff Kent	.50
129	Stan Javier	.50
130	J.T. Snow	.50
131	Jay Buhner	.50
132	*Freddy Garcia*	3.00
133	Ken Griffey Jr.	8.50
134	Russ Davis	.50
135	Edgar Martinez	.50
136	Alex Rodriguez	8.50
137	David Segui	.50
138	Rolando Arrojo	.50
139	Wade Boggs	2.00
140	Jose Canseco	2.00
141	Quinton McCracken	.50
142	Fred McGriff	.50
143	Juan Gonzalez	4.00
144	Tom Goodwin	.50
145	Rusty Greer	.50
146	Ivan Rodriguez	3.00
147	Jose Cruz Jr.	.75
148	Carlos Delgado	1.50
149	Shawn Green	1.00
150	Roy Halladay	1.00

1999 Pacific Invincible Diamond Magic

This 10-card set features a horizontal format with silver foil stamping on the front. Diamond Magic's are seeded 1:49 packs.

		MT
Complete Set (10):		55.00
Common Player:		4.00
Inserted 1:49		
1	Cal Ripken Jr.	10.00
2	Nomar Garciaparra	6.00
3	Sammy Sosa	6.00
4	Frank Thomas	5.00
5	Mike Piazza	7.00
6	J.D. Drew	4.00
7	Mark McGwire	10.00
8	Tony Gwynn	5.00
9	Ken Griffey Jr.	9.00
10	Alex Rodriguez	8.00

1999 Pacific Invincible Flash Point

This 20-card set features gold etching and gold foil stamping on the card front. These were seeded 1:25 packs.

		MT
Complete Set (20):		125.00
Common Player:		3.00
Inserted 1:25		
1	Mo Vaughn	3.00
2	Chipper Jones	10.00
3	Greg Maddux	7.00
4	Cal Ripken Jr.	17.50
5	Nomar Garciaparra	8.00
6	Sammy Sosa	8.00
7	Frank Thomas	8.00
8	Manny Ramirez	5.00
9	Vladimir Guerrero	4.00
10	Mike Piazza	10.00
11	Roger Clemens	7.00
12	Derek Jeter	10.00
13	Ben Grieve	3.00
14	Scott Rolen	3.00
15	J.D. Drew	3.00
16	Mark McGwire	17.50
17	Tony Gwynn	7.00
18	Ken Griffey Jr.	15.00
19	Alex Rodriguez	12.50
20	Juan Gonzalez	5.00

1999 Pacific Invincible Giants of the Game

This jumbo mail-in redemption set of baseball's top stars is limited to 10 serially numbered specimens of each card.

		MT
Complete Set (10):		550.00
Common Player:		40.00
Production 10 sets		
1	Cal Ripken Jr.	100.00
2	Nomar Garciaparra	60.00
3	Sammy Sosa	60.00
4	Frank Thomas	60.00
5	Mike Piazza	75.00
6	J.D. Drew	40.00
7	Mark McGwire	100.00
8	Tony Gwynn	50.00
9	Ken Griffey Jr.	85.00
10	Alex Rodriguez	80.00

1999 Pacific Invincible Sandlot Heroes

Sandlot Heroes salutes baseball's top players on a horizontal format with holographic silver foil stamping on front. These were inserted one per pack. A special version, serially numbered to 10 of each and overprinted with a SportsFest logo, were created for use as a redemption prize at Pacific's booth at the show.

		MT
Complete Set (20):		25.00
Common Player:		.75
Inserted 1:1		
SportsFest (10 Sets):		25X
1	Mo Vaughn	.75
2	Chipper Jones	2.00
3	Greg Maddux	1.25
4	Cal Ripken Jr.	4.00
5	Nomar Garciaparra	1.50
6	Sammy Sosa	1.50
7	Frank Thomas	1.50
8	Manny Ramirez	1.00
9	Vladimir Guerrero	1.00
10	Mike Piazza	2.00
11	Roger Clemens	1.00
12	Derek Jeter	2.00
13	Eric Chavez	.75
14	Ben Grieve	.75
15	J.D. Drew	.75
16	Mark McGwire	4.00
17	Tony Gwynn	1.25
18	Ken Griffey Jr.	3.00
19	Alex Rodriguez	2.50
20	Juan Gonzalez	1.00

1999 Pacific Invincible Seismic Force

This 20-card set has a dot pattern behind the featured player with the left side and bottom of the card in a gold border. These were seeded one per pack. A specially marked SportsFest version was created for use as a redemption prize at Pacific's booth at the show. These are serially numbered to just 20 apiece.

		MT
Complete Set (20):		25.00
Common Player:		.75
Inserted 1:1		
SportsFest (20 Sets):		15X
1	Mo Vaughn	.75
2	Chipper Jones	2.00
3	Greg Maddux	1.25
4	Cal Ripken Jr.	4.00
5	Nomar Garciaparra	1.50
6	Sammy Sosa	1.50
7	Frank Thomas	1.50
8	Manny Ramirez	1.00
9	Vladimir Guerrero	1.00
10	Mike Piazza	2.00
11	Bernie Williams	.75
12	Derek Jeter	2.00
13	Ben Grieve	.75
14	J.D. Drew	.75
15	Mark McGwire	4.00
16	Tony Gwynn	1.25
17	Ken Griffey Jr.	3.00
18	Alex Rodriguez	2.50
19	Juan Gonzalez	1.00
20	Ivan Rodriguez	.75

1999 Pacific Invincible Thunder Alley

Thunder Alley focuses on baseball's top power hitters. These were inserted 1:121 packs.

		MT
Complete Set (20):		195.00
Common Player:		5.00
Inserted 1:121		
1	Mo Vaughn	5.00
2	Chipper Jones	17.50
3	Cal Ripken Jr.	25.00
4	Nomar Garciaparra	15.00
5	Sammy Sosa	15.00
6	Frank Thomas	12.50
7	Manny Ramirez	10.00
8	Todd Helton	6.00
9	Vladimir Guerrero	7.50
10	Mike Piazza	17.50
11	Derek Jeter	17.50
12	Ben Grieve	5.00
13	Scott Rolen	6.00
14	J.D. Drew	5.00
15	Mark McGwire	25.00
16	Tony Gwynn	12.50
17	Ken Griffey Jr.	22.50
18	Alex Rodriguez	20.00
19	Juan Gonzalez	7.50
20	Ivan Rodriguez	6.00

1999 Pacific Omega

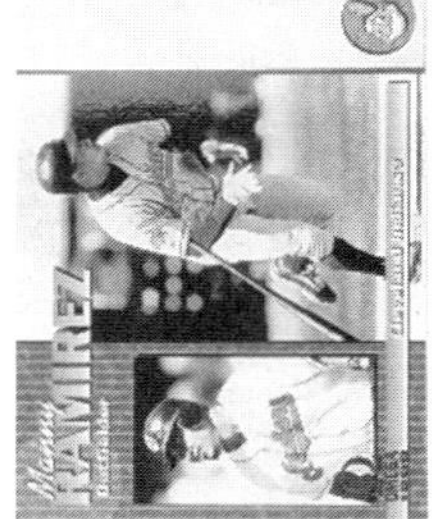

This single-series product features both portrait and action photos on front in an horizontal format. Four parallel versions distinguished by the color of foil highlights were random inserts in the six-card packs. Gold parallels are serially numbered to 299 each; Copper to 99; Platinum Blue to 75 and Premiere Date to 50.

		MT
Complete Set (250):		35.00
Common Player:		.10
Gold (299 Sets):		12X
Copper (99):		20X
Platinum Blue (75):		25X
Premire Date (50):		25X
Wax Pack (6):		1.50
Wax Box (36):		45.00
1	Garret Anderson	.10
2	Jim Edmonds	.15
3	Darin Erstad	.40
4	Chuck Finley	.10
5	Troy Glaus	.75
6	Troy Percival	.10
7	Chris Pritchett	.10
8	Tim Salmon	.25
9	Mo Vaughn	.50
10	Jay Bell	.10
11	Steve Finley	.10
12	Luis Gonzalez	.25
13	Randy Johnson	.65
14	*Byung-Hyun Kim*	2.00
15	Travis Lee	.25
16	Matt Williams	.30
17	Tony Womack	.10
18	Bret Boone	.10
19	Mark DeRosa	.10
20	Tom Glavine	.20
21	Andruw Jones	.75
22	Chipper Jones	2.00
23	Brian Jordan	.10
24	Ryan Klesko	.10
25	Javy Lopez	.10
26	Greg Maddux	1.25
27	John Smoltz	.20
28	Bruce Chen, Odalis Perez	.10
29	Brady Anderson	.10
30	Harold Baines	.10
31	Albert Belle	.30
32	Will Clark	.30
33	Delino DeShields	.10
34	Jerry Hairston Jr.	.10
35	Charles Johnson	.10
36	Mike Mussina	.60
37	Cal Ripken Jr.	3.00
38	B.J. Surhoff	.10
39	Jin Ho Cho	.10
40	Nomar Garciaparra	1.50
41	Pedro Martinez	.75
42	Jose Offerman	.10
43	Troy O'Leary	.10
44	John Valentin	.10
45	Jason Varitek	.10
46	*Juan Pena,* Brian Rose	.10
47	Mark Grace	.25
48	Glenallen Hill	.10
49	Tyler Houston	.10
50	Mickey Morandini	.10
51	Henry Rodriguez	.10
52	Sammy Sosa	1.50
53	Kevin Tapani	.10
54	Mike Caruso	.10
55	Ray Durham	.10
56	Paul Konerko	.10
57	Carlos Lee	.10
58	Magglio Ordonez	.15
59	Mike Sirotka	.10
60	Frank Thomas	1.25
61	Mark L. Johnson, Chris Singleton	.10
62	Mike Cameron	.10
63	Sean Casey	.25
64	Pete Harnisch	.10
65	Barry Larkin	.15
66	Pokey Reese	.10
67	Greg Vaughn	.10
68	Scott Williamson	.10
69	Dmitri Young	.10
70	Roberto Alomar	.50
71	Sandy Alomar Jr.	.10
72	Travis Fryman	.10
73	David Justice	.20
74	Kenny Lofton	.10
75	Manny Ramirez	1.00
76	Richie Sexson	.10
77	Jim Thome	.10
78	Omar Vizquel	.10
79	Jaret Wright	.15
80	Dante Bichette	.10
81	Vinny Castilla	.10
82	Todd Helton	.60
83	Darryl Hamilton	.10
84	Darryl Kile	.10
85	Neifi Perez	.10
86	Larry Walker	.25
87	Tony Clark	.10
88	Damion Easley	.10
89	Juan Encarnacion	.15
90	Bobby Higginson	.10
91	Gabe Kapler	.50
92	Dean Palmer	.10
93	Justin Thompson	.10
94	*Masao Kida* *Jeff Weaver*	1.00
95	Bruce Aven	.10
96	Luis Castillo	.10
97	Alex Fernandez	.10
98	Cliff Floyd	.10
99	Alex Gonzalez	.10
100	Mark Kotsay	.10
101	Preston Wilson	.15
102	Moises Alou	.15
103	Jeff Bagwell	1.00
104	Derek Bell	.10
105	Craig Biggio	.15
106	Mike Hampton	.10
107	Richard Hidalgo	.15
108	Jose Lima	.10
109	Billy Wagner	.10
110	Russ Johnson, Daryle Ward	.10
111	Carlos Beltran	.20
112	Johnny Damon	.15
113	Jermaine Dye	.10
114	Carlos Febles	.40
115	Jeremy Giambi	.10
116	Joe Randa	.10
117	Mike Sweeney	.10
118	*Orber Moreno,* Jose Santiago	.10
119	Kevin Brown	.20

120 Todd Hundley .10
121 Eric Karros .10
122 Raul Mondesi .20
123 Chan Ho Park .25
124 Angel Pena .10
125 Gary Sheffield .25
126 Devon White .10
127 Eric Young .10
128 Ron Belliard .10
129 Jeromy Burnitz .10
130 Jeff Cirillo .10
131 Marquis Grissom .10
132 Geoff Jenkins .10
133 David Nilsson .10
134 Hideo Nomo .50
135 Fernando Vina .10
136 Ron Coomer .10
137 Marty Cordova .10
138 Corey Koskie .10
139 Brad Radke .15
140 Todd Walker .10
141 *Chad Allen*, Torii Hunter .10
142 Cristian Guzman, Jacque Jones .10
143 Michael Barrett .20
144 Orlando Cabrera .10
145 Vladimir Guerrero .75
146 Wilton Guerrero .10
147 Ugueth Urbina .10
148 Rondell White .15
149 Chris Widger .10
150 Edgardo Alfonzo .10
151 Roger Cedeno .10
152 Octavio Dotel .10
153 Rickey Henderson .40
154 John Olerud .10
155 Rey Ordonez .10
156 Mike Piazza 2.00
157 Robin Ventura .10
158 Scott Brosius .10
159 Roger Clemens 1.00
160 David Cone .10
161 Chili Davis .10
162 Orlando Hernandez .50
163 Derek Jeter 2.00
164 Chuck Knoblauch .10
165 Tino Martinez .10
166 Paul O'Neill .10
167 Bernie Williams .30
168 Jason Giambi .40
169 Ben Grieve .25
170 *Chad Harville* .10
171 *Tim Hudson* 2.00
172 Tony Phillips .10
173 Kenny Rogers .10
174 Matt Stairs .10
175 Miguel Tejada .20
176 Eric Chavez .25
177 Bobby Abreu .10
178 Ron Gant .10
179 Doug Glanville .10
180 Mike Lieberthal .10
181 Desi Relaford .10
182 Scott Rolen .75
183 Curt Schilling .25
184 Marlon Anderson, Randy Wolf .10
185 Brant Brown .10
186 Brian Giles .10
187 Jason Kendall .10
188 Al Martin .10
189 Ed Sprague .10
190 Kevin Young .10
191 Kris Benson, Warren Morris .10
192 Kent Bottenfield .10
193 Eric Davis .10
194 J.D. Drew .25
195 Ray Lankford .10
196 *Joe McEwing* .50
197 Mark McGwire 3.00
198 Edgar Renteria .10
199 Fernando Tatis .10
200 Andy Ashby .10
201 Ben Davis .15
202 Tony Gwynn 1.25
203 Trevor Hoffman .10
204 Wally Joyner .10
205 Gary Matthews Jr. .10
206 Ruben Rivera .10
207 Reggie Sanders .10
208 Rich Aurilia .10
209 Marvin Benard .10
210 Barry Bonds 1.00
211 Ellis Burks .10
212 Stan Javier .10
213 Jeff Kent .10
214 Robb Nen .10
215 J.T. Snow .10
216 David Bell .10
217 Jay Buhner .10
218 *Freddy Garcia* 3.00
219 Ken Griffey Jr. 2.75
220 Brian Hunter .10
221 Butch Huskey .10
222 Edgar Martinez .10
223 Jamie Moyer .10
224 Alex Rodriguez 2.50
225 David Segui .10
226 Rolando Arrojo .10
227 Wade Boggs .65
228 Miguel Cairo .10
229 Jose Canseco .50
230 Dave Martinez .10
231 Fred McGriff .10
232 Kevin Stocker .10
233 *Mike Duvall*, David Lamb .10
234 Royce Clayton .10
235 Juan Gonzalez 1.00
236 Rusty Greer .10
237 Ruben Mateo .15
238 Rafael Palmeiro .35
239 Ivan Rodriguez .75
240 John Wetteland .10
241 Todd Zeile .10
242 Jeff Zimmerman .10
243 Homer Bush .10
244 Jose Cruz Jr. .25
245 Carlos Delgado .45
246 Tony Fernandez .10
247 Shawn Green .25
248 Shannon Stewart .15
249 David Wells .15
250 Roy Halladay, Billy Koch .15

1999 Pacific Omega Debut Duos

The careers of two players who made their major league debuts the same season are compared in this scarce (1:145) insert series. Fronts feature action photos of the pair, backs have portraits.

		MT
Complete Set (10):		120.00
Common Player:		5.00
Inserted 1:145		
1	Nomar Garciaparra, Vladimir Guerrero	15.00
2	Derek Jeter, Andy Pettitte	17.50
3	Garret Anderson, Alex Rodriguez	15.00
4	Chipper Jones, Raul Mondesi	15.00
5	Pedro Martinez, Mike Piazza	17.50
6	Mo Vaughn, Bernie Williams	5.00
7	Juan Gonzalez, Ken Griffey Jr.	20.00
8	Sammy Sosa, Larry Walker	12.50
9	Barry Bonds, Mark McGwire	25.00
10	Wade Boggs, Tony Gwynn	12.50

1999 Pacific Omega Diamond Masters

		MT
Complete Set (36):		55.00
Common Player:		1.00
Inserted 1:9		
1	Darin Erstad	1.50
2	Mo Vaughn	1.00
3	Matt Williams	1.00
4	Andruw Jones	1.50
5	Chipper Jones	3.00
6	Greg Maddux	2.00
7	Cal Ripken Jr.	6.00
8	Nomar Garciaparra	2.50
9	Pedro Martinez	1.50
10	Sammy Sosa	2.50
11	Frank Thomas	2.00
12	Kenny Lofton	1.00
13	Manny Ramirez	1.50
14	Larry Walker	1.00
15	Gabe Kapler	1.00
16	Jeff Bagwell	1.50
17	Craig Biggio	1.00
18	Raul Mondesi	1.00
19	Vladimir Guerrero	1.50
20	Mike Piazza	3.00
21	Roger Clemens	2.00
22	Derek Jeter	3.00
23	Bernie Williams	1.00
24	Scott Rolen	1.00
25	J.D. Drew	1.50
26	Mark McGwire	6.00
27	Fernando Tatis	1.00
28	Tony Gwynn	2.00
29	Barry Bonds	2.50
30	Ken Griffey Jr.	4.50
31	Alex Rodriguez	4.50
32	Jose Canseco	1.25
33	Juan Gonzalez	2.00
34	Ruben Mateo	1.00
35	Ivan Rodriguez	1.50
36	Rusty Greer	1.00

1999 Pacific Omega EO Portraits

		MT
Complete Set (20):		165.00
Common Player:		3.00
Inserted 1:73		
1	Mo Vaughn	3.00
2	Chipper Jones	12.50
3	Greg Maddux	10.00
4	Cal Ripken Jr.	20.00
5	Nomar Garciaparra	11.00
6	Sammy Sosa	11.00
7	Frank Thomas	10.00
8	Manny Ramirez	7.50
9	Jeff Bagwell	7.50
10	Mike Piazza	12.50
11	Roger Clemens	10.00
12	Derek Jeter	12.50
13	Scott Rolen	6.00
14	Mark McGwire	20.00
15	Tony Gwynn	10.00
16	Barry Bonds	8.00
17	Ken Griffey Jr.	17.50
18	Alex Rodriguez	15.00
19	Jose Canseco	5.00
20	Juan Gonzalez	7.50

1999 Pacific Omega 5-Tool Talents

		MT
Complete Set (30):		115.00
Common Player:		1.00
Inserted 4:37		
1	Randy Johnson	2.00
2	Carlos Lee	1.00
3	Chipper Jones	8.00
4	Nomar Garciaparra	6.00
5	Barry Bonds	5.00
6	Jeff Bagwell	4.00
7	Greg Maddux	6.00
8	Gabe Kapler	2.00
9	Manny Ramirez	4.00
10	Frank Thomas	5.00
11	Ivan Rodriguez	3.00
12	Ken Griffey Jr.	12.00
13	Pedro Martinez	3.00
14	Carlos Beltran	1.00
15	Mark McGwire	15.00
16	Larry Walker	1.50
17	Cal Ripken Jr.	15.00
18	Derek Jeter	8.00
19	Kevin Brown	1.00
20	J.D. Drew	1.00
21	Sammy Sosa	7.00
22	Tony Gwynn	6.00
23	Alex Rodriguez	10.00
24	Jose Canseco	3.00
25	Roger Clemens	5.00
26	Ruben Mateo	1.50
27	Vladimir Guerrero	4.00
28	Mike Piazza	8.00
29	Scott Rolen	1.50
30	Juan Gonzalez	4.00

1999 Pacific Omega 5-Tool Talents Tiered

A parallel of the 5-Tool Talents inserts is fractured into five tiers of increasing scarcity, differentiated by the color of foil highlights and the serially numbered limited edition. The breakdown is: Tier 1, blue, 100 sets; Tier 2, red, 75 sets; Tier 3, green, 50 sets; Tier

4, purple, 25 sets; Tier 5, gold, 1 set. The unique gold cards are not priced due to their rarity.

		MT
	TIER 1 (BLUE, 100 SETS)	
1	Randy Johnson	7.50
6	Carlos Lee	3.00
11	Chipper Jones	15.00
18	Nomar Garciaparra	12.00
21	Jeff Bagwell	9.00
28	Barry Bonds	10.00
	TIER 2 (RED, 75 SETS)	
2	Greg Maddux	15.00
7	Gabe Kapler	5.00
13	Manny Ramirez	12.50
16	Ken Griffey Jr.	30.00
19	Frank Thomas	15.00
30	Ivan Rodriguez	12.50
	TIER 3 (GREEN, 50 SETS)	
3	Pedro Martinez	25.00
8	Carlos Beltran	10.00
15	Mark McGwire	75.00
20	Larry Walker	10.00
25	Cal Ripken Jr.	75.00
26	Derek Jeter	60.00
	TIER 4 (PURPLE, 25 SETS)	
4	Kevin Brown	15.00
9	J.D. Drew	25.00
12	Sammy Sosa	60.00
17	Jose Canseco	40.00
23	Tony Gwynn	50.00
29	Alex Rodriguez	75.00
	TIER 5 (GOLD 1 SET)	
5	Roger Clemens	
10	Ruben Mateo	
14	Vladimir Guerrero	
22	Mike Piazza	
24	Juan Gonzalez	
27	Scott Rolen	

1999 Pacific Omega Hit Machine 3000

Within days of Tony Gwynn's 3,000 hit on Aug. 6, Pacific had rushed into production a special insert set honoring the achievement of its long-time spokesman. A total of 3,000 serially numbered sets of 20 cards were issued as random packs inserts in Omega. Fronts feature various game-action and studio photos of Gwynn, and are highlighted in silver foil. Backs have two more color photos of Gwynn and a few sentences about the player. A serial number in printed on front.

		MT
Complete Set (20):		75.00
Common Card:		7.50
1	The Hitting Machine	7.50
2	The Eyes Have It	7.50
3	The Art of Hitting	7.50
4	Solid as a Rock	7.50
5	Seeing Doubles	7.50
6	Pithcer's Worst Nightmare	7.50
7	Portrait of an All-Star	7.50
8	An American Hero	7.50
9	Fan Favorite	7.50
10	Mr. Batting Title	7.50
11	4-for-5!	7.50
12	Mission Accomplished	7.50
13	One Hit Away	7.50
14	A Tip of the Hat	7.50
15	It's a Base Hit!	7.50
16	2997th - Grand Slam!	7.50
17	2998th Hit	7.50
18	2999th Hit - 2-Run Double	7.50
19	3000th Hit!	7.50
20	3000 Hits, 887 4 At-Bats, 18 Years	7.50

1999 Pacific Omega HR '99

		MT
Complete Set (20):		30.00
Common Player:		.60
Inserted 1:37		
1	Mo Vaughn	.60
2	Matt Williams	.60
3	Chipper Jones	3.00
4	Albert Belle	.60
5	Nomar Garciaparra	2.00
6	Sammy Sosa	2.50
7	Frank Thomas	1.50
8	Manny Ramirez	1.25
9	Jeff Bagwell	1.25
10	Raul Mondesi	.60
11	Vladimir Guerrero	1.00
12	Mike Piazza	3.00
13	Derek Jeter	3.00
14	Mark McGwire	5.00
15	Fernando Tatis	.60
16	Barry Bonds	2.50
17	Ken Griffey Jr.	4.00
18	Alex Rodriguez	3.50
19	Jose Canseco	1.00
20	Juan Gonzalez	1.25

1999 Pacific Paramount

The 250-card base set is highlighted by silver foil stamping and a white border. Card backs have a small photo along with 1998 statistics and career totals and a a brief career note. There are six parallels to the base set: Copper, Platinum Blue, Holographic Silver, Opening Day Issue, Gold and Holographic Gold. Each parallel is enhanced with the appropriate foil color. Coppers are found exclusively in hobby packs at a rate of one per pack. Platinum Blues are seeded one per 73 packs, Holographic Silvers are hobby only and limited to 99 serial numbered sets. Opening Day Issue is limited to 74 numbered sets. Golds are found one per retail pack. Holographic Golds are limited to 199 numbered sets.

		MT
Complete Set (250):		35.00
Common Player:		.10
Copper (1:1H):		3X
Gold (1:1R):		4X
Red (1:1R):		4X
Platinum Blue (1:73):		20X
Holographic Gold (199):		20X
Holographic Silver (99 Sets):		30X
Opening Day (74):		30X
Pack (6):		1.00
Wax Box (36):		35.00
1	Garret Anderson	.10
2	Gary DiSarcina	.10
3	Jim Edmonds	.15
4	Darin Erstad	.60
5	Chuck Finley	.10
6	Troy Glaus	.75
7	Troy Percival	.10
8	Tim Salmon	.25
9	Mo Vaughn	.40
10	Tony Batista	.10
11	Jay Bell	.10
12	Andy Benes	.10
13	Steve Finley	.10
14	Luis Gonzalez	.35
15	Randy Johnson	.60
16	Travis Lee	.25
17	Todd Stottlemyre	.10
18	Matt Williams	.25
19	David Dellucci	.10
20	Bret Boone	.10
21	Andres Galarraga	.10
22	Tom Glavine	.20
23	Andruw Jones	.75
24	Chipper Jones	1.50
25	Brian Jordan	.10
26	Ryan Klesko	.10
27	Javy Lopez	.10
28	Greg Maddux	1.00
29	John Smoltz	.20
30	Brady Anderson	.10
31	Albert Belle	.30
32	Will Clark	.30
33	Delino DeShields	.10
34	Charles Johnson	.10
35	Mike Mussina	.75
36	Cal Ripken Jr.	3.00
37	B.J. Surhoff	.10
38	Nomar Garciaparra	1.25
39	Reggie Jefferson	.10
40	Darren Lewis	.10
41	Pedro Martinez	.65
42	Troy O'Leary	.10
43	Jose Offerman	.10
44	Donnie Sadler	.10
45	John Valentin	.10
46	Rod Beck	.10
47	Gary Gaetti	.10
48	Mark Grace	.25
49	Lance Johnson	.10
50	Mickey Morandini	.10
51	Henry Rodriguez	.10
52	Sammy Sosa	1.25
53	Kerry Wood	.60
54	Mike Caruso	.10
55	Ray Durham	.10
56	Paul Konerko	.10
57	Jaime Navarro	.10
58	Greg Norton	.10
59	Magglio Ordonez	.15
60	Frank Thomas	1.00
61	Aaron Boone	.10
62	Mike Cameron	.10
63	Barry Larkin	.15
64	Hal Morris	.10
65	Pokey Reese	.10
66	Brett Tomko	.10
67	Greg Vaughn	.10
68	Dmitri Young	.10
69	Roberto Alomar	.50
70	Sandy Alomar Jr.	.10
71	Bartolo Colon	.15
72	Travis Fryman	.10
73	David Justice	.25
74	Kenny Lofton	.10
75	Manny Ramirez	.75
76	Richie Sexson	.10
77	Jim Thome	.10
78	Omar Vizquel	.10
79	Dante Bichette	.10
80	Vinny Castilla	.10
81	Darryl Hamilton	.10
82	Todd Helton	.50
83	Darryl Kile	.10
84	Mike Lansing	.10
85	Neifi Perez	.10
86	Larry Walker	.30
87	Tony Clark	.10
88	Damion Easley	.10
89	Bob Higginson	.10
90	Brian Hunter	.10
91	Dean Palmer	.10
92	Justin Thompson	.10
93	Todd Dunwoody	.10
94	Cliff Floyd	.10
95	Alex Gonzalez	.10
96	Livan Hernandez	.10
97	Mark Kotsay	.10
98	Derrek Lee	.10
99	Kevin Orie	.10
100	Moises Alou	.15
101	Jeff Bagwell	.75
102	Derek Bell	.10
103	Craig Biggio	.15
104	Ken Caminiti	.10
105	Ricky Gutierrez	.10
106	Richard Hidalgo	.15
107	Billy Wagner	.15
108	Jeff Conine	.10
109	Johnny Damon	.15
110	Carlos Febles	.20
111	Jeremy Giambi	.10
112	Jeff King	.10
113	Jeff Montgomery	.10
114	Joe Randa	.10
115	Kevin Brown	.20
116	Mark Grudzielanek	.10
117	Todd Hundley	.10
118	Eric Karros	.10
119	Raul Mondesi	.20
120	Chan Ho Park	.25
121	Gary Sheffield	.25
122	Devon White	.10
123	Eric Young	.10
124	Jeromy Burnitz	.10
125	Jeff Cirillo	.10
126	Marquis Grissom	.10
127	Geoff Jenkins	.10
128	Dave Nilsson	.10
129	Jose Valentin	.10
130	Fernando Vina	.10
131	Rick Aguilera	.10
132	Ron Coomer	.10
133	Marty Cordova	.10
134	Matt Lawton	.10
135	David Ortiz	.10
136	Brad Radke	.15
137	Terry Steinbach	.10
138	Javier Valentin	.10

139	Todd Walker	.10
140	Orlando Cabrera	.10
141	Brad Fullmer	.10
142	Vladimir Guerrero	.75
143	Wilton Guerrero	.10
144	Carl Pavano	.10
145	Ugueth Urbina	.10
146	Rondell White	.15
147	Chris Widger	.10
148	Edgardo Alfonzo	.15
149	Bobby Bonilla	.10
150	Rickey Henderson	.40
151	Brian McRae	.10
152	Hideo Nomo	.60
153	John Olerud	.10
154	Rey Ordonez	.15
155	Mike Piazza	1.50
156	Robin Ventura	.10
157	Masato Yoshii	.10
158	Roger Clemens	1.00
159	David Cone	.10
160	Orlando Hernandez	.75
161	Hideki Irabu	.10
162	Derek Jeter	1.50
163	Chuck Knoblauch	.10
164	Tino Martinez	.10
165	Paul O'Neill	.10
166	Darryl Strawberry	.10
167	Bernie Williams	.30
168	Eric Chavez	.40
169	Ryan Christenson	.10
170	Jason Giambi	.35
171	Ben Grieve	.25
172	Tony Phillips	.10
173	Tim Raines	.10
174	Scott Spiezio	.10
175	Miguel Tejada	.25
176	Bobby Abreu	.10
177	Rico Brogna	.10
178	Ron Gant	.10
179	Doug Glanville	.10
180	Desi Relaford	.10
181	Scott Rolen	.75
182	Curt Schilling	.25
183	Brant Brown	.10
184	Brian Giles	.15
185	Jose Guillen	.10
186	Jason Kendall	.10
187	Al Martin	.10
188	Ed Sprague	.10
189	Kevin Young	.10
190	Eric Davis	.10
191	J.D. Drew	.25
192	Ray Lankford	.10
193	Eli Marrero	.10
194	Mark McGwire	3.00
195	Edgar Renteria	.10
196	Fernando Tatis	.15
197	Andy Ashby	.10
198	Tony Gwynn	1.00
199	Carlos Hernandez	.10
200	Trevor Hoffman	.10
201	Wally Joyner	.10
202	Jim Leyritz	.10
203	Ruben Rivera	.10
204	Matt Clement	.10
205	Quilvio Veras	.10
206	Rich Aurilia	.10
207	Marvin Benard	.10
208	Barry Bonds	1.50
209	Ellis Burks	.10
210	Jeff Kent	.10
211	Bill Mueller	.10
212	Robb Nen	.10
213	J.T. Snow	.10
214	Jay Buhner	.10
215	Jeff Fassero	.10
216	Ken Griffey Jr.	2.50
217	Carlos Guillen	.10
218	Butch Huskey	.10
219	Edgar Martinez	.10
220	Alex Rodriguez	2.50
221	David Segui	.10
222	Dan Wilson	.10
223	Rolando Arrojo	.10
224	Wade Boggs	.40
225	Jose Canseco	.50
226	Roberto Hernandez	.10
227	Dave Martinez	.10
228	Quinton McCracken	.10
229	Fred McGriff	.10
230	Kevin Stocker	.10
231	Randy Winn	.10
232	Royce Clayton	.10
233	Juan Gonzalez	.75
234	Tom Goodwin	.10
235	Rusty Greer	.10
236	Rick Helling	.10
237	Rafael Palmeiro	.25
238	Ivan Rodriguez	.60
239	Aaron Sele	.10
240	John Wetteland	.10
241	Todd Zeile	.10
242	Jose Cruz Jr.	.20
243	Carlos Delgado	.40
244	Tony Fernandez	.10
245	Cecil Fielder	.10
246	Alex Gonzalez	.15
247	Shawn Green	.25
248	Roy Halladay	.15
249	Shannon Stewart	.15
250	David Wells	.10

1999 Pacific Paramount Cooperstown Bound

This 10-card set focuses on players who seem destined for the Hall of Fame. These inserts feature silver foil stamping and are seeded 1:361 packs.

		MT
Complete Set (10):		240.00
Common Player:		20.00
Inserted 1:361		
1	Greg Maddux	25.00
2	Cal Ripken Jr.	40.00
3	Nomar Garciaparra	30.00
4	Sammy Sosa	30.00
5	Frank Thomas	20.00
6	Mike Piazza	35.00
7	Mark McGwire	40.00
8	Tony Gwynn	25.00
9	Ken Griffey Jr.	35.00
10	Alex Rodriguez	35.00

1999 Pacific Paramount Fielder's Choice

This 20-card set is die-cut into a glove shape and enhanced with gold foil stamping. These are seeded 1:73 packs.

		MT
Complete Set (20):		235.00
Common Player:		5.00
Inserted 1:73		
1	Chipper Jones	20.00
2	Greg Maddux	15.00
3	Cal Ripken Jr.	30.00
4	Nomar Garciaparra	17.50
5	Sammy Sosa	17.50
6	Kerry Wood	7.50
7	Frank Thomas	15.00
8	Manny Ramirez	10.00
9	Todd Helton	5.00
10	Jeff Bagwell	10.00
11	Mike Piazza	20.00
12	Derek Jeter	20.00
13	Bernie Williams	5.00
14	J.D. Drew	5.50
15	Mark McGwire	30.00
16	Tony Gwynn	15.00
17	Ken Griffey Jr.	27.50
18	Alex Rodriguez	25.00
19	Juan Gonzalez	10.00
20	Ivan Rodriguez	6.50

1999 Pacific Paramount Personal Bests

This 36-card set features holographic silver foil stamping on the card front. Card backs include a close-up photo of the featured player and a career note. These are seeded 1:37 packs.

		MT
Complete Set (36):		250.00
Common Player:		2.00
Inserted 1:37		
1	Darin Erstad	4.00
2	Mo Vaughn	4.00
3	Travis Lee	3.00
4	Chipper Jones	17.50
5	Greg Maddux	13.50
6	Albert Belle	3.00
7	Cal Ripken Jr.	25.00
8	Nomar Garciaparra	14.00
9	Sammy Sosa	15.00
10	Kerry Wood	6.00
11	Frank Thomas	13.50
12	Greg Vaughn	2.00
13	Manny Ramirez	10.00
14	Todd Helton	4.00
15	Larry Walker	4.00
16	Jeff Bagwell	10.00
17	Craig Biggio	2.00
18	Raul Mondesi	2.00
19	Vladimir Guerrero	8.00
20	Hideo Nomo	8.00
21	Mike Piazza	17.50
22	Roger Clemens	12.50
23	Derek Jeter	17.50
24	Bernie Williams	3.00
25	Eric Chavez	3.00
26	Ben Grieve	3.00
27	Scott Rolen	5.00
28	J.D. Drew	2.50
29	Mark McGwire	25.00
30	Tony Gwynn	13.50
31	Barry Bonds	12.00
32	Ken Griffey Jr.	22.50
33	Alex Rodriguez	20.00
34	Jose Canseco	4.00
35	Juan Gonzalez	10.00
36	Ivan Rodriguez	6.00

1999 Pacific Paramount Team Checklists

This 30-card set features gold foil etching and stamping on the card front. Card backs feature the featured player's team checklist for the main set. These were seeded 2:37 packs.

		MT
Complete Set (30):		100.00
Common Player:		1.00
Inserted 2:37		
1	Mo Vaughn	2.50
2	Travis Lee	1.50
3	Chipper Jones	8.00
4	Cal Ripken Jr.	12.50
5	Nomar Garciaparra	6.50
6	Sammy Sosa	8.00
7	Frank Thomas	6.50
8	Greg Vaughn	1.00
9	Manny Ramirez	4.00
10	Larry Walker	1.50
11	Damion Easley	1.00
12	Mark Kotsay	1.00
13	Jeff Bagwell	4.00
14	Jeremy Giambi	1.00
15	Raul Mondesi	1.00
16	Marquis Grissom	1.00
17	Brad Radke	1.00
18	Vladimir Guerrero	5.00
19	Mike Piazza	8.00
20	Roger Clemens	6.00
21	Ben Grieve	2.00
22	Scott Rolen	2.00
23	Brian Giles	1.00
24	Mark McGwire	12.50
25	Tony Gwynn	6.00
26	Barry Bonds	4.00
27	Ken Griffey Jr.	10.00
28	Jose Canseco	2.50
29	Juan Gonzalez	4.00
30	Jose Cruz Jr.	1.25

1999 Pacific Prism

This 150-card base set has a full, holographic silver card front. Card backs feature two more player photos along with 1998 and career statistics. Hobby packs consist of five cards. There are also five parallels including Holographic Gold, Holographic Mirror, Holographic Blue, Holographic Purple and Red. Golds are limited to 480 serial numbered sets, Mirrors 160 sets, Blues 80 numbered sets, and, Purples 320 sets. Red parallels are a retail-only insert and are seeded at a rate of one per 12.5 packs.

		MT
Complete Set (150):		80.00
Common Player:		.25
Red (2:25R):		3X
HoloGold (480 Sets):		5X
HoloPurple (320):		6X
HoloMirror (160):		10X
HoloBlue (80):		20X
Retail Pack (3):		2.00
Hobby Pack (5):		3.00
Wax Box (24):		50.00
1	Garret Anderson	.25
2	Jim Edmonds	.35
3	Darin Erstad	1.00
4	Chuck Finley	.25
5	Tim Salmon	.45
6	Jay Bell	.25
7	David Dellucci	.25
8	Travis Lee	.40
9	Matt Williams	.50
10	Andres Galarraga	.25
11	Tom Glavine	.35
12	Andruw Jones	1.50
13	Chipper Jones	4.00
14	Ryan Klesko	.25
15	Javy Lopez	.25
16	Greg Maddux	2.50
17	Roberto Alomar	1.00
18	Ryan Minor	.25
19	Mike Mussina	.75
20	Rafael Palmeiro	.75
21	Cal Ripken Jr.	6.00
22	Nomar Garciaparra	3.00
23	Pedro Martinez	1.00
24	John Valentin	.25
25	Mo Vaughn	.75
26	Tim Wakefield	.25
27	Rod Beck	.25
28	Mark Grace	.75
29	Lance Johnson	.25
30	Sammy Sosa	3.00
31	Kerry Wood	1.50
32	Albert Belle	.75
33	Mike Caruso	.25
34	Magglio Ordonez	.50
35	Frank Thomas	3.00
36	Robin Ventura	.25
37	Aaron Boone	.25
38	Barry Larkin	.35
39	Reggie Sanders	.25
40	Brett Tomko	.25
41	Sandy Alomar Jr.	.25
42	Bartolo Colon	.25
43	David Justice	.75
44	Kenny Lofton	.25
45	Manny Ramirez	2.00
46	Richie Sexson	.25
47	Jim Thome	.25
48	Omar Vizquel	.25
49	Dante Bichette	.25
50	Vinny Castilla	.25
51	*Edgard Clemente*	.35
52	Todd Helton	1.00
53	Quinton McCracken	.25
54	Larry Walker	.75
55	Tony Clark	.25
56	Damion Easley	.25
57	Luis Gonzalez	.75
58	Bob Higginson	.25
59	Brian Hunter	.25
60	Cliff Floyd	.25
61	Alex Gonzalez	.25
62	Livan Hernandez	.25
63	Derrek Lee	.25
64	Edgar Renteria	.25
65	Moises Alou	.35
66	Jeff Bagwell	2.00
67	Derek Bell	.25
68	Craig Biggio	.35
69	Randy Johnson	1.00
70	Johnny Damon	.25
71	Jeff King	.25
72	Hal Morris	.25
73	Dean Palmer	.25
74	Eric Karros	.25
75	Raul Mondesi	.35
76	Chan Ho Park	.60
77	Gary Sheffield	.75
78	Jeromy Burnitz	.25
79	Jeff Cirillo	.25
80	Marquis Grissom	.25
81	Jose Valentin	.25
82	Fernando Vina	.25
83	Paul Molitor	1.00
84	Otis Nixon	.25
85	David Ortiz	.25
86	Todd Walker	.25
87	Vladimir Guerrero	1.50
88	Carl Pavano	.25
89	Fernando Seguignol	.25
90	Ugueth Urbina	.25
91	Carlos Baerga	.25
92	Bobby Bonilla	.25
93	Hideo Nomo	.85
94	John Olerud	.25
95	Rey Ordonez	.25
96	Mike Piazza	4.00
97	David Cone	.25
98	Orlando Hernandez	1.50
99	Hideki Irabu	.25
100	Derek Jeter	4.00
101	Tino Martinez	.25
102	Bernie Williams	.75
103	Eric Chavez	.25
104	Jason Giambi	.75
105	Ben Grieve	.50
106	Rickey Henderson	1.00
107	Bob Abreu	.25
108	Doug Glanville	.25
109	Scott Rolen	1.00
110	Curt Schilling	.50
111	Emil Brown	.25
112	Jose Guillen	.25
113	Jason Kendall	.25
114	Al Martin	.25
115	Aramis Ramirez	.25
116	Kevin Young	.25
117	J.D. Drew	.50
118	Ron Gant	.25
119	Brian Jordan	.25
120	Eli Marrero	.25
121	Mark McGwire	6.00
122	Kevin Brown	.40
123	Tony Gwynn	2.50
124	Trevor Hoffman	.25
125	Wally Joyner	.25
126	Greg Vaughn	.25
127	Barry Bonds	3.00
128	Ellis Burks	.25
129	Jeff Kent	.25
130	Robb Nen	.25
131	J.T. Snow	.25
132	Jay Buhner	.25
133	Ken Griffey Jr.	5.00
134	Edgar Martinez	.25
135	Alex Rodriguez	5.00
136	David Segui	.25
137	Rolando Arrojo	.25
138	Wade Boggs	1.00
139	Aaron Ledesma	.25
140	Fred McGriff	.25
141	Will Clark	.75
142	Juan Gonzalez	2.00
143	Rusty Greer	.25
144	Ivan Rodriguez	1.00
145	Aaron Sele	.25
146	Jose Canseco	.75
147	Roger Clemens	2.00
148	Jose Cruz Jr.	.45
149	Carlos Delgado	1.00
150	Alex Gonzalez	.35

1999 Pacific Prism Ahead of the Game

Each card features full gold foil and etching with a close- up photo of baseball's top 20 stars. These are seeded 1:49 packs.

		MT
Complete Set (20):		90.00
Common Player:		2.00
Inserted 1:49		
1	Darin Erstad	3.00
2	Travis Lee	2.00
3	Chipper Jones	8.00
4	Cal Ripken Jr.	12.50
5	Nomar Garciaparra	6.50
6	Sammy Sosa	6.50
7	Kerry Wood	2.50
8	Frank Thomas	6.00
9	Manny Ramirez	4.00
10	Todd Helton	2.00
11	Jeff Bagwell	4.00
12	Mike Piazza	8.00
13	Derek Jeter	8.00
14	Bernie Williams	2.00
15	J.D. Drew	2.50
16	Mark McGwire	12.50
17	Tony Gwynn	5.00
18	Ken Griffey Jr.	10.00
19	Alex Rodriguez	10.00
20	Ivan Rodriguez	3.00

1999 Pacific Prism Ballpark Legends

This 10 card set salutes baseball's biggest stars. These inserts feature silver foil stamping and etching with an image of a ballpark in the background of the player photo. These are seeded 1:193 packs.

		MT
Complete Set (10):		95.00
Common Player:		5.00
Inserted 1:193		
1	Cal Ripken Jr.	20.00
2	Nomar Garciaparra	12.50
3	Frank Thomas	10.00
4	Ken Griffey Jr.	17.50
5	Alex Rodriguez	15.00
6	Greg Maddux	10.00
7	Sammy Sosa	12.50
8	Kerry Wood	5.00
9	Mark McGwire	20.00
10	Tony Gwynn	10.00

1999 Pacific Prism Diamond Glory

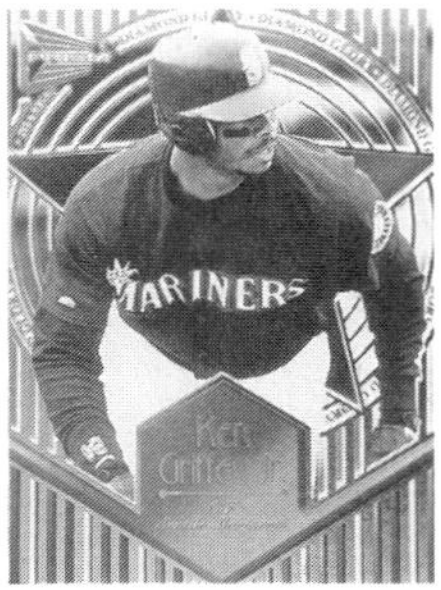

Card fronts feature full copper foil stamping with a star in the background of the player's photo. The 20-card set features 20 of baseball's most exciting players including several top 1999 rookies. These are seeded 2:25 packs.

		MT
Complete Set (20):		100.00
Common Player:		2.00
Inserted 2:25		
1	Darin Erstad	2.00
2	Travis Lee	2.00
3	Chipper Jones	10.00
4	Greg Maddux	6.00
5	Cal Ripken Jr.	12.00
6	Nomar Garciaparra	8.00
7	Sammy Sosa	8.00
8	Kerry Wood	4.00
9	Frank Thomas	8.00
10	Todd Helton	2.00
11	Jeff Bagwell	4.00
12	Mike Piazza	10.00
13	Derek Jeter	10.00
14	Bernie Williams	2.00
15	J.D. Drew	3.00
16	Mark McGwire	12.00
17	Tony Gwynn	6.00
18	Ken Griffey Jr.	11.50
19	Alex Rodriguez	11.00
20	Juan Gonzalez	4.00

1999 Pacific Prism Epic Performers

This hobby-only set features the 10 of the top hobby favorites and seeded at 1:97 packs.

		MT
Complete Set (10):		175.00
Common Player:		10.00
Inserted 1:97 H		
1	Cal Ripken Jr.	35.00
2	Nomar Garciaparra	20.00
3	Frank Thomas	20.00
4	Ken Griffey Jr.	30.00

5	Alex Rodriguez	25.00
6	Greg Maddux	15.00
7	Sammy Sosa	25.00
8	Kerry Wood	10.00
9	Mark McGwire	35.00
10	Tony Gwynn	15.00

1999 Pacific Private Stock

The premiere issue of Private Stock base cards features holographic silver foil on 30-pt. cardboard. Card backs have selected box scores from the '98 season, with a brief commentary on the player. Packs consist of six cards.

		MT
Complete Set (150):		50.00
Common Player:		.15
Pack (6):		2.00
Wax Box (24):		30.00
Wax Box (36):		35.00
1	Jeff Bagwell	1.50
2	Roger Clemens	1.50
3	J.D. Drew	.25
4	Nomar Garciaparra	2.00
5	Juan Gonzalez	1.50
6	Ken Griffey Jr.	3.50
7	Tony Gwynn	1.75
8	Derek Jeter	2.50
9	Chipper Jones	2.50
10	Travis Lee	.45
11	Greg Maddux	1.75
12	Mark McGwire	4.00
13	Mike Piazza	2.50
14	Manny Ramirez	1.50
15	Cal Ripken Jr.	4.00
16	Alex Rodriguez	3.00
17	Ivan Rodriguez	1.25
18	Sammy Sosa	2.00
19	Frank Thomas	2.00
20	Kerry Wood	.65
21	Roberto Alomar	.75
22	Moises Alou	.25
23	Albert Belle	.50
24	Craig Biggio	.25
25	Wade Boggs	1.00
26	Barry Bonds	2.00
27	Jose Canseco	.75
28	Jim Edmonds	.25
29	Darin Erstad	.75
30	Andres Galarraga	.15
31	Tom Glavine	.25
32	Ben Grieve	.50
33	Vladimir Guerrero	.75
34	Wilton Guerrero	.15
35	Todd Helton	.75
36	Andruw Jones	.75
37	Ryan Klesko	.15
38	Kenny Lofton	.15
39	Javy Lopez	.15
40	Pedro Martinez	.75
41	Paul Molitor	.75
42	Raul Mondesi	.25
43	Rafael Palmeiro	.50
44	Tim Salmon	.25
45	Jim Thome	.15
46	Mo Vaughn	.50
47	Larry Walker	.50
48	David Wells	.15
49	Bernie Williams	.50
50	Jaret Wright	.50
51	Bobby Abreu	.15
52	Garret Anderson	.15
53	Rolando Arrojo	.15
54	Tony Batista	.15
55	Rod Beck	.15
56	Derek Bell	.15
57	Marvin Benard	.15
58	Dave Berg	.15
59	Dante Bichette	.15
60	Aaron Boone	.15
61	Bret Boone	.15
62	Scott Brosius	.15
63	Brant Brown	.15
64	Kevin Brown	.40
65	Jeromy Burnitz	.15
66	Ken Caminiti	.15
67	Mike Caruso	.15
68	Sean Casey	.40
69	Vinny Castilla	.15
70	Eric Chavez	.50
71	Ryan Christenson	.15
72	Jeff Cirillo	.15
73	Tony Clark	.15
74	Will Clark	.50
75	*Edgard Clemente*	.25
76	David Cone	.15
77	Marty Cordova	.15
78	Jose Cruz Jr.	.25
79	Eric Davis	.15
80	Carlos Delgado	.65
81	David Dellucci	.15
82	Delino DeShields	.15
83	Gary DiSarcina	.15
84	Damion Easley	.15
85	Dennis Eckersley	.15
86	Cliff Floyd	.15
87	Jason Giambi	.65
88	Doug Glanville	.15
89	Alex Gonzalez	.15
90	Mark Grace	.50
91	Rusty Greer	.15
92	Jose Guillen	.25
93	Carlos Guillen	.15
94	Jeffrey Hammonds	.15
95	Rick Helling	.15
96	Bob Henley	.15
97	Livan Hernandez	.15
98	Orlando Hernandez	1.00
99	Bob Higginson	.15
100	Trevor Hoffman	.15
101	Randy Johnson	.75
102	Brian Jordan	.15
103	Wally Joyner	.15
104	Eric Karros	.15
105	Jason Kendall	.15
106	Jeff Kent	.15
107	Jeff King	.15
108	Mark Kotsay	.15
109	Ray Lankford	.15
110	Barry Larkin	.25
111	Mark Loretta	.15
112	Edgar Martinez	.15
113	Tino Martinez	.15
114	Quinton McCracken	.15
115	Fred McGriff	.15
116	Ryan Minor	.25
117	Hal Morris	.15
118	Bill Mueller	.15
119	Mike Mussina	.75
120	Dave Nilsson	.15
121	Otis Nixon	.15
122	Hideo Nomo	1.00
123	Paul O'Neill	.15
124	Jose Offerman	.15
125	John Olerud	.15
126	Rey Ordonez	.15
127	David Ortiz	.15
128	Dean Palmer	.15
129	Chan Ho Park	.50
130	Aramis Ramirez	.15
131	Edgar Renteria	.15
132	Armando Rios	.15
133	Henry Rodriguez	.15
134	Scott Rolen	.65
135	Curt Schilling	.35
136	David Segui	.15
137	Richie Sexson	.15
138	Gary Sheffield	.45
139	John Smoltz	.25
140	Matt Stairs	.15
141	Justin Thompson	.15
142	Greg Vaughn	.15
143	Omar Vizquel	.15
144	Tim Wakefield	.15
145	Todd Walker	.15
146	Devon White	.15
147	Rondell White	.15
148	Matt Williams	.45
149	*Enrique Wilson*	.25
150	Kevin Young	.15

1999 Pacific Private Stock Platinum Series

Another partial parallel of the first 50 cards in the base set. Cards have a platinum holographic sheen to them with a Platinum stamp on the front. These are limited to 199 numbered sets.

		MT
Complete Set (50):		265.00
Common Player:		3.00
Production 199 sets		
1	Jeff Bagwell	16.00
2	Roger Clemens	20.00
3	J.D. Drew	4.00
4	Nomar Garciaparra	25.00
5	Juan Gonzalez	16.00
6	Ken Griffey Jr.	40.00
7	Tony Gwynn	20.00
8	Derek Jeter	30.00
9	Chipper Jones	30.00
10	Travis Lee	5.00
11	Greg Maddux	20.00
12	Mark McGwire	45.00
13	Mike Piazza	30.00
14	Manny Ramirez	16.00
15	Cal Ripken Jr.	45.00
16	Alex Rodriguez	35.00
17	Ivan Rodriguez	13.50
18	Sammy Sosa	25.00
19	Frank Thomas	20.00
20	Kerry Wood	12.00
21	Roberto Alomar	6.00
22	Moises Alou	3.00
23	Albert Belle	9.00
24	Craig Biggio	4.00
25	Wade Boggs	10.00
26	Barry Bonds	12.00
27	Jose Canseco	6.00
28	Jim Edmonds	3.50
29	Darin Erstad	6.00
30	Andres Galarraga	3.00
31	Tom Glavine	3.50
32	Ben Grieve	5.00
33	Vladimir Guerrero	12.50
34	Wilton Guerrero	3.00
35	Todd Helton	6.00
36	Andruw Jones	12.00
37	Ryan Klesko	3.00
38	Kenny Lofton	3.00
39	Javy Lopez	3.00
40	Pedro Martinez	10.00
41	Paul Molitor	10.00
42	Raul Mondesi	4.00
43	Rafael Palmeiro	5.00
44	Tim Salmon	3.50
45	Jim Thome	3.00
46	Mo Vaughn	6.00
47	Larry Walker	6.00
48	David Wells	3.00
49	Bernie Williams	6.00
50	Jaret Wright	6.00

1999 Pacific Private Stock Exclusive Series

This 20-card set is a partial parallel to the base set. Taking the first 20 cards from the set and serially numbering them to 299 sets. These are inserted exclusively in hobby packs.

		MT
Complete Set (20):		105.00
Common Player:		2.00
Production: 299 sets H		
1	Jeff Bagwell	4.00
2	Roger Clemens	6.00
3	J.D. Drew	2.50
4	Nomar Garciaparra	8.00
5	Juan Gonzalez	4.00
6	Ken Griffey Jr.	11.00
7	Tony Gwynn	7.00
8	Derek Jeter	9.00
9	Chipper Jones	9.00
10	Travis Lee	2.00
11	Greg Maddux	7.00
12	Mark McGwire	12.00
13	Mike Piazza	9.00
14	Manny Ramirez	4.00
15	Cal Ripken Jr.	12.00
16	Alex Rodriguez	10.00
17	Ivan Rodriguez	3.50
18	Sammy Sosa	8.00
19	Frank Thomas	7.00
20	Kerry Wood	3.50

1999 Pacific Private Stock Homerun History

This holographic silver foiled commemorative set honors Mark McGwire and Sammy Sosa's historic '98 seasons. Two cards were added to the end of the set, which are Silver Crown Die-Cuts honoring Ripken Jr.'s consecutive games streak and McGwire's 70 home runs. These are inserted 2:25 packs.

		MT
Complete Set (22):		100.00
Common McGwire:		6.00
Common Sosa:		4.00
Inserted 1:12		
1	Home Run #61 (Mark McGwire)	7.50
2	Home Run #59 (Sammy Sosa)	5.00
3	Home Run #62 (Mark McGwire)	7.50
4	Home Run #60 (Sammy Sosa)	5.00
5	Home Run #63 (Mark McGwire)	7.50
6	Home Run #61 (Sammy Sosa)	5.00
7	Home Run #64 (Mark McGwire)	7.50
8	Home Run #62 (Sammy Sosa)	5.00
9	Home Run #65 (Mark McGwire)	7.50
10	Home Run #63 (Sammy Sosa)	5.00
11	Home Run #67 (Mark McGwire)	7.50
12	Home Run #64 (Sammy Sosa)	5.00
13	Home Run #68 (Mark McGwire)	7.50
14	Home Run #65 (Sammy Sosa)	5.00
15	Home Run #70 (Mark McGwire)	7.50
16	Home Run #66 (Sammy Sosa)	5.00
17	A Season of Celebration (Mark McGwire)	7.50
18	A Season of Celebration (Sammy Sosa)	5.00
19	Awesome Power (Sammy Sosa, Mark McGwire)	7.50
20	Transcending Sports (Mark McGwire, Sammy Sosa)	7.50
21	Crown Die-Cut (Mark McGwire)	7.50
22	Crown Die-Cut (Cal Ripken Jr.)	5.00

1999 Pacific Private Stock Preferred Series

Another partial parallel of the first 20 base cards. Each card is stamped with a holographic Preferred logo and are numbered to 399 sets.

		MT
Complete Set (20):		70.00
Common Player:		1.00
Production: 399 sets		
1	Jeff Bagwell	2.50
2	Roger Clemens	4.00
3	J.D. Drew	1.00
4	Nomar Garciaparra	5.00
5	Juan Gonzalez	2.50
6	Ken Griffey Jr.	9.00
7	Tony Gwynn	3.50
8	Derek Jeter	6.00
9	Chipper Jones	6.00
10	Travis Lee	1.00
11	Greg Maddux	3.50
12	Mark McGwire	10.00
13	Mike Piazza	6.00
14	Manny Ramirez	2.50
15	Cal Ripken Jr.	10.00
16	Alex Rodriguez	8.00
17	Ivan Rodriguez	1.50
18	Sammy Sosa	5.00
19	Frank Thomas	4.00
20	Kerry Wood	1.00

1999 Pacific Private Stock PS-206

This 150-card set takes reverent reach back into collecting history with its smaller format (1.5" x 2.5"). Card fronts have a white border with silver foil stamping and a blue back, these are found one per pack. A parallel also exists with a red back, which are seeded 1:25 packs.

		MT
Complete Set (150):		25.00
Common Player:		.25
Inserted 1:1		
Red Parallels:		4X
Inserted 1:25		
1	Jeff Bagwell	.75
2	Roger Clemens	1.00
3	J.D. Drew	.40
4	Nomar Garciaparra	1.50
5	Juan Gonzalez	.75
6	Ken Griffey Jr.	3.00
7	Tony Gwynn	1.00
8	Derek Jeter	2.00
9	Chipper Jones	2.00
10	Travis Lee	.50
11	Greg Maddux	1.00
12	Mark McGwire	3.50
13	Mike Piazza	2.00
14	Manny Ramirez	.75
15	Cal Ripken Jr.	3.50
16	Alex Rodriguez	2.50
17	Ivan Rodriguez	.60
18	Sammy Sosa	1.50
19	Frank Thomas	1.50
20	Kerry Wood	.60
21	Roberto Alomar	.50
22	Moises Alou	.25
23	Albert Belle	.50
24	Craig Biggio	.35
25	Wade Boggs	.60
26	Barry Bonds	1.00
27	Jose Canseco	.40
28	Jim Edmonds	.35
29	Darin Erstad	.65
30	Andres Galarraga	.25
31	Tom Glavine	.35
32	Ben Grieve	.50
33	Vladimir Guerrero	.60
34	Wilton Guerrero	.25
35	Todd Helton	.60
36	Andruw Jones	.60
37	Ryan Klesko	.25
38	Kenny Lofton	.25
39	Javy Lopez	.25
40	Pedro Martinez	.60
41	Paul Molitor	.50
42	Raul Mondesi	.35
43	Rafael Palmeiro	.35
44	Tim Salmon	.35
45	Jim Thome	.25
46	Mo Vaughn	.60
47	Larry Walker	.40
48	David Wells	.25
49	Bernie Williams	.50
50	Jaret Wright	.50
51	Bobby Abreu	.25
52	Garret Anderson	.25
53	Rolando Arrojo	.25
54	Tony Batista	.25
55	Rod Beck	.25
56	Derek Bell	.25
57	Marvin Benard	.25
58	Dave Berg	.25
59	Dante Bichette	.25
60	Aaron Boone	.25
61	Bret Boone	.25
62	Scott Brosius	.25
63	Brant Brown	.25
64	Kevin Brown	.35
65	Jeromy Burnitz	.25
66	Ken Caminiti	.25
67	Mike Caruso	.25
68	Sean Casey	.35
69	Vinny Castilla	.25
70	Eric Chavez	.50
71	Ryan Christenson	.25
72	Jeff Cirillo	.25
73	Tony Clark	.25
74	Will Clark	.40
75	Edgard Clemente	.25
76	David Cone	.25
77	Marty Cordova	.25
78	Jose Cruz Jr.	.35
79	Eric Davis	.25
80	Carlos Delgado	.50
81	David Dellucci	.25
82	Delino DeShields	.25
83	Gary DiSarcina	.25
84	Damion Easley	.25
85	Dennis Eckersley	.25
86	Cliff Floyd	.25
87	Jason Giambi	.50
88	Doug Glanville	.25
89	Alex Gonzalez	.25
90	Mark Grace	.50
91	Rusty Greer	.25
92	Jose Guillen	.25
93	Carlos Guillen	.25
94	Jeffrey Hammonds	.25
95	Rick Helling	.25
96	Bob Henley	.25
97	Livan Hernandez	.25
98	Orlando Hernandez	.65
99	Bob Higginson	.25
100	Trevor Hoffman	.25
101	Randy Johnson	.65
102	Brian Jordan	.25
103	Wally Joyner	.25
104	Eric Karros	.25
105	Jason Kendall	.25
106	Jeff Kent	.25
107	Jeff King	.25
108	Mark Kotsay	.25
109	Ray Lankford	.25
110	Barry Larkin	.35
111	Mark Loretta	.25
112	Edgar Martinez	.25
113	Tino Martinez	.25
114	Quinton McCracken	.25
115	Fred McGriff	.25
116	Ryan Minor	.25
117	Hal Morris	.25
118	Bill Mueller	.25
119	Mike Mussina	.65
120	Dave Nilsson	.25
121	Otis Nixon	.25
122	Hideo Nomo	.65
123	Paul O'Neill	.25
124	Jose Offerman	.25
125	John Olerud	.25
126	Rey Ordonez	.25
127	David Ortiz	.25
128	Dean Palmer	.25
129	Chan Ho Park	.40
130	Aramis Ramirez	.25
131	Edgar Renteria	.25
132	Armando Rios	.25
133	Henry Rodriguez	.25
134	Scott Rolen	.60
135	Curt Schilling	.35
136	David Segui	.25
137	Richie Sexson	.25
138	Gary Sheffield	.40
139	John Smoltz	.35
140	Matt Stairs	.25
141	Justin Thompson	.25
142	Greg Vaughn	.25
143	Omar Vizquel	.25
144	Tim Wakefield	.25
145	Todd Walker	.25
146	Devon White	.25
147	Rondell White	.25
148	Matt Williams	.40
149	Enrique Wilson	.25
150	Kevin Young	.25

1999 Pacific Private Stock Vintage Series

This insert set is a partial parallel of the first 50 cards in the base set and have a Vintage holograpic stamp on the card fronts. These are limited to 99 numbered sets.

		MT
Complete Set (50):		750.00
Common Player:		5.00
Production: 99 sets		
1	Jeff Bagwell	25.00
2	Roger Clemens	35.00
3	J.D. Drew	10.00
4	Nomar Garciaparra	40.00
5	Juan Gonzalez	25.00
6	Ken Griffey Jr.	55.00
7	Tony Gwynn	35.00
8	Derek Jeter	50.00
9	Chipper Jones	50.00
10	Travis Lee	7.50
11	Greg Maddux	35.00
12	Mark McGwire	60.00
13	Mike Piazza	50.00
14	Manny Ramirez	25.00
15	Cal Ripken Jr.	60.00
16	Alex Rodriguez	55.00
17	Ivan Rodriguez	20.00
18	Sammy Sosa	40.00
19	Frank Thomas	40.00
20	Kerry Wood	10.00
21	Roberto Alomar	17.50
22	Moises Alou	5.00
23	Albert Belle	10.00
24	Craig Biggio	7.50
25	Wade Boggs	12.50
26	Barry Bonds	25.00
27	Jose Canseco	10.00
28	Jim Edmonds	6.00
29	Darin Erstad	10.00
30	Andres Galarraga	5.00
31	Tom Glavine	7.50
32	Ben Grieve	7.50
33	Vladimir Guerrero	15.00
34	Wilton Guerrero	5.00
35	Todd Helton	10.00
36	Andruw Jones	15.00
37	Ryan Klesko	5.00
38	Kenny Lofton	5.00
39	Javy Lopez	5.00
40	Pedro Martinez	12.50
41	Paul Molitor	12.50
42	Raul Mondesi	5.00
43	Rafael Palmeiro	6.50
44	Tim Salmon	6.00
45	Jim Thome	5.00
46	Mo Vaughn	5.00
47	Larry Walker	5.00
48	David Wells	5.00
49	Bernie Williams	6.00
50	Jaret Wright	6.50

1999 Pacific Revolution

The 150-card set features dual foiled etching and embossing enhanced by gold-foil stamping. Card backs have year-by-year statistics along with a close-up photo. There are 25 short-printed rookie and prospect cards, which were inserted at a rate of about one per four packs. There are three parallels to the base set: Premiere Date, Red and Shadow. Reds are retail exclusive and are limited to 299 numbered sets. Shadows have light blue foil stamping and are limited to 99 numbered sets. Premiere Date are seeded exclusively in hobby packs at a rate of 1:25 packs.

		MT
Complete Set (150):		125.00
Common Player:		.25
Shadow (99 Sets H):		6X
SP:		3X
Red (299 R):		3X
SP:		1.5X
Premiere Date (49 H):		15X
SP:		6X
Wax Pack (3):		5.00
1	Jim Edmonds	.35
2	Darin Erstad	1.50
3	Troy Glaus	3.00
4	Tim Salmon	.50
5	Mo Vaughn	1.50
6	Steve Finley	.25
7	Luis Gonzalez	.75
8	Randy Johnson	2.00
9	Travis Lee	.50
10	Matt Williams	.75
11	Andruw Jones	2.00
12	Chipper Jones	6.00
13	Brian Jordan	.25
14	Javy Lopez	.25
15	Greg Maddux	4.00
16	*Kevin McGlinchy* (SP)	2.00
17	John Smoltz	.35
18	Brady Anderson	.25
19	Albert Belle	1.25
20	Will Clark	.75
21	*Willis Otanez* (SP)	1.00
23	*Calvin Pickering* (SP)	1.50
23	Cal Ripken Jr.	10.00
24	Nomar Garciaparra	5.00
25	Pedro Martinez	2.00
26	Troy O'Leary	.25
27	Jose Offerman	.25
28	Mark Grace	1.00
29	Mickey Morandini	.25
30	Henry Rodriguez	.25
31	Sammy Sosa	5.00
32	Ray Durham	.25
33	Carlos Lee (SP)	1.00
34	*Jeff Liefer* (SP)	1.00
35	Magglio Ordonez	.50
36	Frank Thomas	5.00
37	Mike Cameron	.25
38	Sean Casey	.75
39	Barry Larkin	.35
40	Greg Vaughn	.25
41	Roberto Alomar	2.00
42	Sandy Alomar Jr.	.25
43	David Justice	.75
44	Kenny Lofton	.25
45	Manny Ramirez	3.00
46	Richie Sexson	.25
47	Jim Thome	.25
48	Dante Bichette	.25
49	Vinny Castilla	.25
50	Darryl Hamilton	.25
51	Todd Helton	1.50
52	Larry Walker	.75
53	Tony Clark	.25
54	Damion Easley	.25
55	Bob Higginson	.25
56	Gabe Kapler (SP)	3.00
57	*Alex Gonzalez* (SP)	1.00
58	Mark Kotsay	.25
59	Kevin Orie	.25
60	Preston Wilson (SP)	2.00
61	Jeff Bagwell	3.00
62	Derek Bell	.25
63	Craig Biggio	.35
64	Ken Caminiti	.25
65	Carlos Beltran (SP)	1.50
66	Johnny Damon	.25
67	Jermaine Dye	.25
68	Carlos Febles (SP)	2.00
69	Kevin Brown	.50
70	Todd Hundley	.25
71	Eric Karros	.25
72	Raul Mondesi	.45
73	Gary Sheffield	.65
74	Jeromy Burnitz	.25
75	Jeff Cirillo	.25
76	Marquis Grissom	.25
77	Fernando Vina	.25
78	*Chad Allen* (SP)	2.00
79	*Corey Koskie* (SP)	3.00
80	*Doug Mientkiewicz* (SP)	3.00
81	Brad Radke	.25
82	Todd Walker	.25
83	*Michael Barrett* (SP)	3.00
84	Vladimir Guerrero	2.00
85	Wilton Guerrero	.25
86	*Guillermo Mota* (SP)	2.00
87	Rondell White	.35
88	Edgardo Alfonzo	.25
89	Rickey Henderson	1.50
90	John Olerud	.25
91	Mike Piazza	6.00
92	Robin Ventura	.25
93	Roger Clemens	4.00
94	Chili Davis	.25
95	Derek Jeter	6.00
96	Chuck Knoblauch	.25
97	Tino Martinez	.25
98	Paul O'Neill	.25
99	Bernie Williams	.50
100	Eric Chavez (SP)	2.00
101	Jason Giambi	.75
102	Ben Grieve	1.00
103	John Jaha	.25
104	*Olmedo Saenz* (SP)	2.00
105	Bobby Abreu	.25
106	Doug Glanville	.25
107	Desi Relaford	.25
108	Scott Rolen	2.00
109	Curt Schilling	.50
110	Brian Giles	.25
111	Jason Kendall	.25
112	Pat Meares	.25
113	Kevin Young	.25
114	J.D. Drew (SP)	3.00
115	Ray Lankford	.25
116	Eli Marrero	.25
117	*Joe McEwing* (SP)	3.00
118	Mark McGwire	10.00
119	Fernando Tatis	.25
120	Tony Gwynn	4.00
121	Trevor Hoffman	.25
122	Wally Joyner	.25
123	Reggie Sanders	.25
124	Barry Bonds	4.00
125	Ellis Burks	.25
126	Jeff Kent	.25
127	*Ramon Martinez* (SP)	1.00
128	*Joe Nathan* (SP)	3.00
129	*Freddy Garcia* (SP)	10.00
130	Ken Griffey Jr.	9.00
131	Brian Hunter	.25
132	Edgar Martinez	.25
133	Alex Rodriguez	8.00
134	David Segui	.25
135	Wade Boggs	1.50
136	Jose Canseco	1.00
137	Quinton McCracken	.25
138	Fred McGriff	.25
139	*Kelly Dransfeldt* (SP)	2.00
140	Juan Gonzalez	3.00
141	Rusty Greer	.25
142	Rafael Palmeiro	.75
143	Ivan Rodriguez	2.00
144	Lee Stevens	.25
145	Jose Cruz Jr.	.40
146	Carlos Delgado	1.00
147	Shawn Green	.75
148	*Roy Halladay* (SP)	5.00
149	Shannon Stewart	.35
150	*Kevin Witt* (SP)	1.00

1999 Pacific Revolution Shadow

This hobby-only parallel insert features blue metallic-foil background and graphics on front. Backs are identical to the base version except they include a dot-matrix applied serial number at left within an edition of 99.

	MT
Common Player:	4.00
Stars:	6X
SPs:	3X

(See 1999 Pacific Revolution for checklist and base card values.)

1999 Pacific Revolution Diamond Legacy

This 36-card set features a holographic patterned foil card front. Card backs have a small close-up photo along with a career note. These were seeded 2:25 packs.

		MT
Complete Set (36):		275.00
Common Player:		2.00
Inserted 2:25		
1	Troy Glaus	8.00
2	Mo Vaughn	4.00
3	Matt Williams	3.00
4	Chipper Jones	17.50
5	Andruw Jones	8.00
6	Greg Maddux	13.50
7	Albert Belle	4.00
8	Cal Ripken Jr.	25.00
9	Nomar Garciaparra	15.00
10	Sammy Sosa	15.00
11	Frank Thomas	15.00
12	Manny Ramirez	12.00
13	Todd Helton	6.00
14	Larry Walker	4.00
15	Gabe Kapler	7.50
16	Jeff Bagwell	12.00
17	Craig Biggio	3.00
18	Raul Mondesi	2.00
19	Vladimir Guerrero	8.00
20	Mike Piazza	17.50
21	Roger Clemens	13.50
22	Derek Jeter	17.50
23	Bernie Williams	3.00
24	Ben Grieve	4.00
25	Scott Rolen	6.00
26	J.D. Drew	2.00
27	Mark McGwire	25.00
28	Fernando Tatis	2.00
29	Tony Gwynn	13.50
30	Barry Bonds	12.00
31	Ken Griffey Jr.	22.50
32	Alex Rodriguez	20.00
33	Jose Canseco	4.00
34	Juan Gonzalez	12.00
35	Ivan Rodriguez	6.00
36	Shawn Green	5.00

1999 Pacific Revolution Foul Pole

This 20-card set features netting down the right side of each card, with the player photo on the left side. The player name, position and logo are stamped with gold foil. These were seeded 1:49 packs.

		MT
Complete Set (20):		150.00
Common Player:		3.00
Inserted 1:49		
1	Chipper Jones	12.00
2	Andruw Jones	6.00
3	Cal Ripken Jr.	20.00
4	Nomar Garciaparra	10.00
5	Sammy Sosa	10.00
6	Frank Thomas	10.00
7	Manny Ramirez	8.00
8	Jeff Bagwell	8.00
9	Raul Mondesi	3.00
10	Vladimir Guerrero	6.00
11	Mike Piazza	12.00
12	Derek Jeter	12.00
13	Bernie Williams	3.00
14	Scott Rolen	6.00
15	J.D. Drew	4.00
16	Mark McGwire	20.00
17	Tony Gwynn	9.00
18	Ken Griffey Jr.	17.50
19	Alex Rodriguez	15.00
20	Juan Gonzalez	8.00

1999 Pacific Revolution Icons

This 10-card set spotlights the top players, each card is die-cut in the shape of a shield with silver foil etching and stamping. These were seeded 1:121 packs.

		MT
Complete Set (10):		180.00
Common Player:		20.00
Inserted 1:121		
1	Cal Ripken Jr.	30.00
2	Nomar Garciaparra	20.00
3	Sammy Sosa	20.00
4	Frank Thomas	20.00
5	Mike Piazza	22.50
6	Derek Jeter	22.50
7	Mark McGwire	30.00
8	Tony Gwynn	20.00
9	Ken Griffey Jr.	27.50
10	Alex Rodriguez	25.00

1999 Pacific Revolution Thorn in the Side

This 20-card set features full holographic silver foil and is die-cut in the upper right portion. Card backs analyzes the featured player's success against a certain opponent over the years. These were seeded 1:25 packs.

		MT
Complete Set (20):		150.00
Common Player:		3.00
Inserted 1:25		
1	Mo Vaughn	3.00
2	Chipper Jones	12.00
3	Greg Maddux	8.00
4	Cal Ripken Jr.	20.00
5	Nomar Garciaparra	10.00
6	Sammy Sosa	10.00
7	Frank Thomas	10.00
8	Manny Ramirez	6.00
9	Jeff Bagwell	6.00
10	Mike Piazza	12.00
11	Derek Jeter	12.00
12	Bernie Williams	3.00
13	J.D. Drew	4.00
14	Mark McGwire	20.00
15	Tony Gwynn	8.00
16	Barry Bonds	8.00
17	Ken Griffey Jr.	17.50
18	Alex Rodriguez	15.00
19	Juan Gonzalez	6.00
20	Ivan Rodriguez	5.00

1999 Pacific Revolution Tripleheader

This 30-card set features spotted gold foil blotching around the player image with the name, postion, team and logo stamped in gold foil. These were seeded 4:25 hobby packs. The set is also broken down into three separate tiers of 10 cards. Tier 1 (cards 1-10) are limited to 99 numbered sets. Tier 2 (11-20) 199 numbered sets and Tier 3 (21-30) 299 numbered sets.

		MT
Complete Set (30):		120.00
Common Player:		1.00
Inserted 4:25 H		
Tier 1 (1-10):		6X
Production 99 sets H		
Tier 2 (11-20):		3X
Production 199 sets H		
Tier 3 (21-30):		1.5X
Production 299 sets H		
1	Greg Maddux	6.00
2	Cal Ripken Jr.	12.50
3	Nomar Garciaparra	8.00
4	Sammy Sosa	8.00
5	Frank Thomas	8.00
6	Mike Piazza	9.00
7	Mark McGwire	12.50
8	Tony Gwynn	6.00
9	Ken Griffey Jr.	12.00
10	Alex Rodriguez	10.00
11	Mo Vaughn	2.00
12	Chipper Jones	9.00
13	Manny Ramirez	4.00
14	Larry Walker	1.00
15	Jeff Bagwell	4.00
16	Vladimir Guerrero	3.00
17	Derek Jeter	9.00
18	J.D. Drew	1.50
19	Barry Bonds	7.00
20	Juan Gonzalez	4.00
21	Troy Glaus	3.00
22	Andruw Jones	3.00
23	Matt Williams	1.00
24	Craig Biggio	1.00
25	Raul Mondesi	1.00
26	Roger Clemens	6.00
27	Bernie Williams	1.00
28	Scott Rolen	3.00
29	Jose Canseco	1.50
30	Ivan Rodriguez	3.00

2000 Pacific

The base set consists of 500-cards with the Pacific logo and player name stamped in silver foil on the card front. Card backs have a small photo along with complete career statistics and a brief career highlight. 50 players in the base set also have another version and are priced equally.

		MT
Complete Set (500):		60.00
Common Player:		.10
Pack (12):		2.50
Wax Box (24):		55.00
1	Garret Anderson	.10
2	Tim Belcher	.10
3	Gary DiSarcina	.10
4	Trent Durrington	.10
5	Jim Edmonds	.10
6	Darin Erstad	.25
6b	Darin Erstad	.25
7	Chuck Finley	.10
8	Troy Glaus	.75
9	Todd Greene	.10
10	Bret Hemphill	.10
11	Ken Hill	.10
12	Ramon Ortiz	.10
13	Troy Percival	.10
14	Mark Petkovsek	.10
15	Tim Salmon	.20
16	Mo Vaughn	.50
16b	Mo Vaughn	.50
17	Jay Bell	.10
18	Omar Daal	.10
19	Erubiel Durazo	.10
20	Steve Finley	.10
21	Bernard Gilkey	.10
22	Luis Gonzalez	.20
23	Randy Johnson	.50
24	Byung-Hyun Kim	.10
25	Travis Lee	.25
26	Matt Mantei	.10
27	Armando Reynoso	.10
28	Rob Ryan	.10
29	Kelly Stinnett	.10
30	Todd Stottlemyre	.10
31	Matt Williams	.30
31b	Matt Williams	.30
32	Tony Womack	.10
33	Bret Boone	.10
34	Andres Galarraga	.40
35	Tom Glavine	.25
36	Ozzie Guillen	.10
37	Andruw Jones	.40
37b	Andruw Jones	.40
38	Chipper Jones	1.50
38b	Chipper Jones	1.50
39	Brian Jordan	.10
40	Ryan Klesko	.20
41	Javy Lopez	.20
42	Greg Maddux	1.50
42b	Greg Maddux	1.50
43	Kevin Millwood	.10
44	John Rocker	.10
45	Randall Simon	.10
46	John Smoltz	.20
47	Gerald Williams	.10
48	Brady Anderson	.20
49	Albert Belle	.60
49b	Albert Belle	.60
50	Mike Bordick	.10
51	Will Clark	.25
52	Jeff Conine	.10
53	Delino DeShields	.10
54	Jerry Hairston Jr.	.10
55	Charles Johnson	.10
56	Eugene Kingsale	.10
57	Ryan Minor	.20
58	Mike Mussina	.50
59	Sidney Ponson	.10
60	Cal Ripken Jr.	2.00
60b	Cal Ripken Jr.	2.00
61	B.J. Surhoff	.10
62	Mike Timlin	.10
63	Rod Beck	.10
64	Nomar Garciaparra	2.00
64b	Nomar Garciaparra	2.00
65	Tom Gordon	.10
66	Butch Huskey	.10
67	Derek Lowe	.10
68	Pedro Martinez	.75
68b	Pedro Martinez	.75
69	Trot Nixon	.10
70	Jose Offerman	.10
71	Troy O'Leary	.10
72	Pat Rapp	.10
73	Donnie Sadler	.10
74	Mike Stanley	.10
75	John Valentin	.10
76	Jason Varitek	.10
77	Wilton Veras	.25
78	Tim Wakefield	.10
79	Rick Aguilera	.10
80	Manny Alexander	.10
81	Roosevelt Brown	.10
82	Mark Grace	.20
83	Glenallen Hill	.10
84	Lance Johnson	.10
85	Jon Lieber	.10
86	Cole Liniak	.10
87	Chad Meyers	.10
88	Mickey Morandini	.10
89	Jose Nieves	.10
90	Henry Rodriguez	.10
91	Sammy Sosa	2.00
91b	Sammy Sosa	2.00
92	Kevin Tapani	.10
93	Kerry Wood	.40
94	Mike Caruso	.10
95	Ray Durham	.10
96	Brook Fordyce	.10
97	Bobby Howry	.10
98	Paul Konerko	.10
99	Carlos Lee	.10
100	Aaron Myette	.10
101	Greg Norton	.10
102	Magglio Ordonez	.25
103	Jim Parque	.10
104	Liu Rodriguez	.10
105	Chris Singleton	.10
106	Mike Sirotka	.10
107	Frank Thomas	.75
107b	Frank Thomas	.75
108	Kip Wells	.10
109	Aaron Boone	.10
110	Mike Cameron	.10
111	Sean Casey	.40
111b	Sean Casey	.40
112	Jeffrey Hammonds	.10
113	Pete Harnisch	.10
114	Barry Larkin	.40
114b	Barry Larkin	.40
115	Jason LaRue	.10
116	Denny Neagle	.10
117	Pokey Reese	.10
118	Scott Sullivan	.10
119	Eddie Taubensee	.10
120	Greg Vaughn	.20
121	Scott Williamson	.10
122	Dmitri Young	.10
123	Roberto Alomar	.50
123b	Roberto Alomar	.50
124	Sandy Alomar Jr.	.10
125	Harold Baines	.10
126	Russell Branyan	.10
127	Dave Burba	.10
128	Bartolo Colon	.10
129	Travis Fryman	.20
130	Mike Jackson	.10
131	David Justice	.25
132	Kenny Lofton	.50
132b	Kenny Lofton	.50
133	Charles Nagy	.10
134	Manny Ramirez	.75
134b	Manny Ramirez	.75
135	Dave Roberts	.10
136	Richie Sexson	.10
137	Jim Thome	.40
138	Omar Vizquel	.10
139	Jaret Wright	.10
140	Pedro Astacio	.10
141	Dante Bichette	.25
142	Brian Bohanon	.10
143	Vinny Castilla	.10
143b	Vinny Castilla	.10
144	Edgard Clemente	.10
145	Derrick Gibson	.10
146	Todd Helton	.75
147	Darryl Kile	.10
148	Mike Lansing	.10
149	Kirt Manwaring	.10
150	Neifi Perez	.10
151	Ben Petrick	.10
152	*Juan Sosa*	.40
153	Dave Veres	.10
154	Larry Walker	.50
154b	Larry Walker	.50
155	Brad Ausmus	.10
156	Dave Borkowski	.10
157	Tony Clark	.25
158	Francisco Cordero	.10
159	Deivi Cruz	.10
160	Damion Easley	.10
161	Juan Encarnacion	.10
162	Robert Fick	.10
163	Bobby Higginson	.10
164	Gabe Kapler	.25
165	Brian Moehler	.10

166 Dean Palmer .10
167 Luis Polonia .10
168 Justin Thompson .10
169 Jeff Weaver .10
170 Antonio Alfonseca .10
171 Bruce Aven .10
172 A.J. Burnett .25
173 Luis Castillo .10
174 Ramon Castro .10
175 Ryan Dempster .10
176 Alex Fernandez .10
177 Cliff Floyd .10
178 Amaury Garcia .10
179 Alex Gonzalez .10
180 Mark Kotsay .10
181 Mike Lowell .10
182 Brian Meadows .10
183 Kevin Orie .10
184 Julio Ramirez .10
185 Preston Wilson .10
186 Moises Alou .20
187 Jeff Bagwell .75
187b Jeff Bagwell .75
188 Glen Barker .10
189 Derek Bell .10
190 Craig Biggio .40
190b Craig Biggio .40
191 Ken Caminiti .20
192 Scott Elarton .10
193 Carl Everett .10
194 Mike Hampton .10
195 Carlos Hernandez .10
196 Richard Hidalgo .10
197 Jose Lima .10
198 Shane Reynolds .20
199 Bill Spiers .10
200 Billy Wagner .10
201 Carlos Beltran .20
201b Carlos Beltran .20
202 Dermal Brown .10
203 Johnny Damon .10
204 Jermaine Dye .10
205 Carlos Febles .10
206 Jeremy Giambi .10
207 Mark Quinn .10
208 Joe Randa .10
209 Dan Reichert .10
210 Jose Rosado .10
211 Rey Sanchez .10
212 Jeff Suppan .10
213 Mike Sweeney .10
214 Kevin Brown .20
214b Kevin Brown .20
215 Darren Dreifort .10
216 Eric Gagne .10
217 Mark Grudzielanek .10
218 Todd Hollandsworth .10
219 Todd Hundley .10
220 Eric Karros .20
221 Raul Mondesi .20
222 Chan Ho Park .20
223 Jeff Shaw .10
224 Gary Sheffield .25
224b Gary Sheffield .25
225 Ismael Valdes .10
226 Devon White .10
227 Eric Young .10
228 Kevin Barker .10
229 Ron Belliard .10
230 Jeromy Burnitz .10
230b Jeromy Burnitz .10
231 Jeff Cirillo .10
232 Marquis Grissom .10
233 Geoff Jenkins .10
234 Mark Loretta .10
235 David Nilsson .10
236 Hideo Nomo .10
237 Alex Ochoa .10
238 Kyle Peterson .10
239 Fernando Vina .10
240 Bob Wickman .10
241 Steve Woodard .10
242 Chad Allen .10
243 Ron Coomer .10
244 Marty Cordova .10
245 Cristian Guzman .10
246 Denny Hocking .10
247 Jacque Jones .10
248 Corey Koskie .10
249 Matt Lawton .10
250 Joe Mays .10
251 Eric Milton .10
252 Brad Radke .10
253 Mark Redman .10
254 Terry Steinbach .10
255 Todd Walker .10
256 Tony Armas Jr. .10
257 Michael Barrett .10
258 Peter Bergeron .10
259 Geoff Blum .10
260 Orlando Cabrera .10
261 *Trace Coquillette* .25
262 Brad Fullmer .10
263 Vladimir Guerrero 1.25
263b Vladimir Guerrero 1.25
264 Wilton Guerrero .10
265 Dustin Hermanson .10
266 Manny Martinez .10
267 Ryan McGuire .10
268 Ugueth Urbina .10
269 Jose Vidro .10
270 Rondell White .20
271 Chris Widger .10
272 Edgardo Alfonzo .25
273 Armando Benitez .10
274 Roger Cedeno .10
275 Dennis Cook .10
276 Octavio Dotel .10
277 John Franco .10
278 Darryl Hamilton .10
279 Rickey Henderson .25
280 Orel Hershiser .10
281 Al Leiter .20
282 John Olerud .25
282b John Olerud .25
283 Rey Ordonez .10
284 Mike Piazza 2.00
284b Mike Piazza 2.00
285 Kenny Rogers .10
286 Jorge Toca .10
287 Robin Ventura .20
288 Scott Brosius .10
289 Roger Clemens 1.00
289b Roger Clemens 1.00
290 David Cone .20
291 Chili Davis .10
292 Orlando Hernandez .25
293 Hideki Irabu .10
294 Derek Jeter 2.00
294b Derek Jeter 2.00
295 Chuck Knoblauch .25
296 Ricky Ledee .10
297 Jim Leyritz .10
298 Tino Martinez .40
299 Paul O'Neill .25
300 Andy Pettitte .25
301 Jorge Posada .10
302 Mariano Rivera .25
303 Alfonso Soriano .50
304 Bernie Williams .50
304b Bernie Williams .50
305 Ed Yarnall .10
306 Kevin Appier .10
307 Rich Becker .10
308 Eric Chavez .10
309 Jason Giambi .10
310 Ben Grieve .25
311 Ramon Hernandez .10
312 Tim Hudson .40
313 John Jaha .10
314 Doug Jones .10
315 Omar Olivares .10
316 Mike Oquist .10
317 Matt Stairs .10
318 Miguel Tejada .10
319 Randy Velarde .10
320 Bobby Abreu .10
321 Marlon Anderson .10
322 Alex Arias .10
323 Rico Brogna .10
324 Paul Byrd .10
325 Ron Gant .10
326 Doug Glanville .10
327 Wayne Gomes .10
328 Mike Lieberthal .10
329 Robert Person .10
330 Desi Relaford .10
331 Scott Rolen .75
331b Scott Rolen .75
332 Curt Schilling .20
332b Curt Schilling .20
333 Kris Benson .10
334 Adrian Brown .10
335 Brant Brown .10
336 Brian Giles .10
337 Chad Hermansen .10
338 Jason Kendall .20
339 Al Martin .10
340 Pat Meares .10
341 Warren Morris .10
341b Warren Morris .10
342 Todd Ritchie .10
343 Jason Schmidt .10
344 Ed Sprague .10
345 Mike Williams .10
346 Kevin Young .10
347 Rick Ankiel .40
348 Ricky Bottalico .10
349 Kent Bottenfield .10
350 Darren Bragg .10
351 Eric Davis .20
352 J.D. Drew .25
352b J.D. Drew .25
353 Adam Kennedy .10
354 Ray Lankford .10
355 Joe McEwing .10
356 Mark McGwire 3.00
356b Mark McGwire 3.00
357 Matt Morris .10
358 Darren Oliver .10
359 Edgar Renteria .10
360 Fernando Tatis .25
361 Andy Ashby .10
362 Ben Davis .10
363 Tony Gwynn 1.50
363b Tony Gwynn 1.50
364 Sterling Hitchcock .10
365 Trevor Hoffman .10
366 Damian Jackson .10
367 Wally Joyner .10
368 Dave Magadan .10
369 Gary Matthews Jr. .10
370 Phil Nevin .10
371 Eric Owens .10
372 Ruben Rivera .10
373 Reggie Sanders .10
373b Reggie Sanders .10
374 Quilvio Veras .10
375 Rich Aurilia .10
376 Marvin Benard .10
377 Barry Bonds 1.00
377b Barry Bonds 1.00
378 Ellis Burks .10
379 Shawn Estes .10
380 Livan Hernandez .10
381 Jeff Kent .10
381b Jeff Kent .10
382 Brent Mayne .10
383 Bill Mueller .10
384 Calvin Murray .10
385 Robb Nen .10
386 Russ Ortiz .10
387 Kirk Rueter .10
388 J.T. Snow .10
389 David Bell .10
390 Jay Buhner .20
391 Russ Davis .10
392 Freddy Garcia .25
392b Freddy Garcia .25
393 Ken Griffey Jr. 2.50
393b Ken Griffey Jr. 2.50
394 Carlos Guillen .10
395 John Halama .10
396 Brian Hunter .10
397 Ryan Jackson .10
398 Edgar Martinez .10
399 Gil Meche .10
400 Jose Mesa .10
401 Jamie Moyer .10
402 Alex Rodriguez 2.50
402b Alex Rodriguez 2.50
403 Dan Wilson .10
404 Wilson Alvarez .10
405 Rolando Arrojo .10
406 Wade Boggs .25
406b Wade Boggs .25
407 Miguel Cairo .10
408 Jose Canseco .75
408b Jose Canseco .75
409 John Flaherty .10
410 Jose Guillen .10
411 Roberto Hernandez .10
412 Terrell Lowery .10
413 Dave Martinez .10
414 Quinton McCracken .10
415 Fred McGriff .25
415b Fred McGriff .25
416 Ryan Rupe .10
417 Kevin Stocker .10
418 Bubba Trammell .10
419 Royce Clayton .10
420 Juan Gonzalez .75
420b Juan Gonzalez .75
421 Tom Goodwin .10
422 Rusty Greer .10
423 Rick Helling .10
424 Roberto Kelly .10
425 Ruben Mateo .10
426 Mark McLemore .10
427 Mike Morgan .10
428 Rafael Palmeiro .40
429 Ivan Rodriguez .75
429b Ivan Rodriguez .75
430 Aaron Sele .10
431 Lee Stevens .10
432 John Wetteland .10
433 Todd Zeile .10
434 Jeff Zimmerman .10
435 Tony Batista .10
436 Casey Blake .10
437 Homer Bush .10
438 Chris Carpenter .10
439 Jose Cruz Jr. .10
440 Carlos Delgado .50
440b Carlos Delgado .50
441 Tony Fernandez .10
442 Darrin Fletcher .10
443 Alex Gonzalez .10
444 Shawn Green .50
444b Shawn Green .50
445 Roy Halladay .10
446 Billy Koch .10
447 David Segui .10
448 Shannon Stewart .10
449 David Wells .10
450 Vernon Wells .10

2000 Pacific Copper

Coppers are a parallel set to the 500-card base set and are identical to the base cards besides the copper foil stamping. Inserted exclusively in hobby packs Coppers are limited to 99 serial numbered sets.

	MT
Common Copper:	5.00
Stars:	8x to 15x
Yng. Stars & RCs:	5x to 10x
Production 99 sets	

2000 Pacific Platinum Blue

A parallel to the 500-card base set these have identical photos as the regular cards besides platinum blue foil stamping. A total of 75 serial numbered sets were produced.

	MT
Common Player:	8.00
Stars:	10x to 20x
Yng Stars & RCs:	8x to 15x
Production 75 sets	

2000 Pacific Premiere Date

A parallel to the 500-card base set these are sequentially numbered to 37 sets.

	MT
Common Player:	15.00
Stars:	20x to 40x
Yng Stars & RCs:	15x to 30x
Production 37 sets	

2000 Pacific Ruby Red (Seven-11)

This parallel to the base set of 2000 Pacific was available only in 10-card retail "Jewel Collection" packs at Seven-11 convenience stores. Other than the use of red metallic foil for the player name and Pacific logo, the cards are identical to the regular-issue version.

	MT
Complete Set (500):	75.00
Common Player:	.15
Stars/Rookies	1.5X

(See 2000 Pacific for checklist and base card values.)

2000 Pacific Command Performers

		MT
Complete Set (20):		
Common Player:		
1	Chipper Jones	
2	Greg Maddux	
3	Cal Ripken Jr.	
4	Nomar Garciaparra	
5	Sammy Sosa	
6	Sean Casey	
7	Manny Ramirez	
8	Larry Walker	
9	Jeff Bagwell	
10	Vladimir Guerrero	
11	Mike Piazza	
12	Roger Clemens	
13	Derek Jeter	
14	Mark McGwire	
15	Tony Gwynn	
16	Barry Bonds	
17	Ken Griffey Jr.	
18	Alex Rodriguez	
19	Ivan Rodriguez	
20	Shawn Green	

2000 Pacific Cramer's Choice Awards

This die-cut set is shaped in a trophy-like design on a holographic silver foil design. Cramer's Choice are seeded 1:721 packs.

		MT
Complete Set (10):		420.00
Common Player:		25.00
Inserted 1:721		
1	Chipper Jones	35.00
2	Cal Ripken Jr.	60.00
3	Nomar Garciaparra	50.00
4	Sammy Sosa	40.00
5	Mike Piazza	50.00
6	Derek Jeter	60.00
7	Mark McGwire	50.00
8	Tony Gwynn	35.00
9	Ken Griffey Jr.	50.00
10	Alex Rodriguez	50.00

2000 Pacific Diamond Leaders

Designed on a horizontal format each card features three statistical leaders from the 1999 season for each respective team. Card fronts have gold holofoil stamping while card backs give statistical leaders for eight categories for the featured team. These were seeded 2:25 packs.

		MT
Complete Set (30):		60.00
Common Player:		1.00
Inserted 2:25		
1	Anaheim Angels (Garret Anderson, Chuck Finley, Troy Percival, Mo Vaughn)	2.00
2	Baltimore Orioles (Albert Belle, Mike Mussina, B.J. Surhoff)	2.00
3	Boston Red Sox (Nomar Garciaparra, Pedro J. Martinez, Troy O'Leary)	6.00
4	Chicago White Sox (Ray Durham, Magglio Ordonez, Frank Thomas)	2.50
5	Cleveland Indians (Bartolo Colon, Manny Ramirez, Omar Vizquel)	2.50
6	Detroit Tigers (Deivi Cruz, Dave Mlicki, David Palmer)	1.00
7	Kansas City Royals (Johnny Damon, Jermaine Dye, Jose Rosado, Mike Sweeney)	1.00
8	Minnesota Twins (Corey Koskie, Eric Milton, Brad Radke)	1.00
9	New York Yankees (Orlando Hernandez, Derek Jeter, Mariano Rivera, Bernie Williams)	6.00
10	Oakland Athletics (Jeremy Giambi, Tim Hudson, Matt Stairs)	1.00
11	Seattle Mariners (Freddy Garcia, Ken Griffey Jr., Edgar Martinez)	8.00
12	Tampa Bay Devil Rays (Jose Canseco , Roberto Hernandez, Fred McGriff)	2.00
13	Texas Rangers (Rafael Palmeiro, Ivan Rodriguez, John Wetteland)	2.50
14	Toronto Blue Jays (Carlos Delgado, Shannon Stewart, David Wells)	1.50
15	Arizona Diamondbacks (Luis Gonzalez, Randy Johnson, Matt Williams)	2.00
16	Atlanta Braves (Chipper Jones, Brian Jordan, Greg Maddux)	5.00
17	Chicago Cubs (Mark Grace, Jon Lieber, Sammy Sosa)	6.00
18	Cincinnati Reds (Sean Casey, Pete Harnisch, Greg Vaughn)	1.00
19	Colorado Rockies (Pedro Astacio, Dante Bichette, Larry Walker)	2.00
20	Florida Marlins (Luis Castillo, Alex Fernandez, Preston Wilson)	1.00
21	Houston Astros (Jeff Bagwell, Mike Hampton, Billy Wagner)	2.50
22	Los Angeles Dodgers (Kevin Brown, Mark Grudzielanek, Eric Karros)	1.00
23	Milwaukee Brewers (Jeromy Burnitz, Jeff Cirillo, Marquis Grissom, Hideo Nomo)	1.00
24	Montreal Expos (Vladimir Guerrero, Dustin Hermanson, Ugueth Urbina)	3.00
25	New York Mets (Roger Cedeno, Rickey Henderson, Mike Piazza)	6.00
26	Philadelphia Phillies (Bobby Abreu, Mike Lieberthal, Curt Schilling)	1.00
27	Pittsburgh Pirates (Brian Giles, Jason Kendall, Kevin Young)	1.00
28	St. Louis Cardinals (Kent Bottenfield, Ray Lankford, Mark McGwire)	10.00
29	San Diego Padres (Tony Gwynn, Trevor Hoffman, Reggie Sanders)	5.00
30	San Francisco Giants (Barry Bonds, Jeff Kent, Russ Ortiz)	3.00

2000 Pacific Gold Crown Die-Cuts

Printed on a 24-point stock this set features Pacific's classic crown shaped design on a dual foiled holographic gold and silver stock. These were seeded 1:25 packs.

		MT
Complete Set (36):		250.00
Common Player:		3.00
Inserted 1:25		
1	Mo Vaughn	5.00
2	Matt Williams	4.00
3	Andruw Jones	4.00
4	Chipper Jones	12.00
5	Greg Maddux	12.00
6	Cal Ripken Jr.	20.00
7	Nomar Garciaparra	12.00
8	Pedro Martinez	6.00
9	Sammy Sosa	15.00
10	Magglio Ordonez	4.00
11	Frank Thomas	6.00
12	Sean Casey	4.00
13	Roberto Alomar	5.00
14	Manny Ramirez	6.00
15	Larry Walker	5.00
16	Jeff Bagwell	6.00
17	Craig Biggio	4.00
18	Carlos Beltran	3.00
19	Vladimir Guerrero	8.00
20	Mike Piazza	15.00
21	Roger Clemens	10.00
22	Derek Jeter	20.00
23	Bernie Williams	5.00
24	Scott Rolen	6.00
25	Warren Morris	3.00
26	J.D. Drew	3.00
27	Mark McGwire	20.00
28	Tony Gwynn	10.00
29	Barry Bonds	8.00
30	Ken Griffey Jr.	20.00
31	Alex Rodriguez	20.00
32	Jose Canseco	6.00
33	Juan Gonzalez	6.00
34	Rafael Palmeiro	5.00
35	Ivan Rodriguez	6.00
36	Shawn Green	4.00

2000 Pacific Ornaments

This 20-card set features a number of different

Christmas patterned die-cut shapes, including ornaments, wreaths and Christmas trees. Each card comes with a string intended to hang from a tree on a holographic foil design. These were seeded 2:25 packs.

		MT
Complete Set (20):		100.00
Common Player:		3.00
Inserted 2:25		
1	Mo Vaughn	3.00
2	Chipper Jones	8.00
3	Greg Maddux	8.00
4	Cal Ripken Jr.	12.00
5	Nomar Garciaparra	8.00
6	Sammy Sosa	10.00
7	Frank Thomas	5.00
8	Manny Ramirez	5.00
9	Larry Walker	3.00
10	Jeff Bagwell	5.00
11	Mike Piazza	10.00
12	Roger Clemens	6.00
13	Derek Jeter	12.00
14	Scott Rolen	5.00
15	J.D. Drew	3.00
16	Mark McGwire	10.00
17	Tony Gwynn	6.00
18	Ken Griffey Jr.	10.00
19	Alex Rodriguez	10.00
20	Ivan Rodriguez	5.00

2000 Pacific Past & Present

Inserted exclusively in hobby packs at a rate of 1:49, these inserts have a silver prism front and a cardboard textured back. The fronts have a current photo of the player while the backs have a photo taken years before.

		MT
Complete Set (20):		150.00
Common Player:		4.00
Inserted 1:49 H		
1	Chipper Jones	10.00
2	Greg Maddux	12.00
3	Cal Ripken Jr.	20.00
4	Nomar Garciaparra	12.00
5	Pedro Martinez	6.00
6	Sammy Sosa	12.00
7	Frank Thomas	6.00
8	Manny Ramirez	6.00
9	Larry Walker	4.00
10	Jeff Bagwell	6.00
11	Mike Piazza	12.00
12	Roger Clemens	8.00
13	Derek Jeter	20.00
14	Mark McGwire	15.00
15	Tony Gwynn	8.00
16	Barry Bonds	8.00
17	Ken Griffey Jr.	15.00
18	Alex Rodriguez	15.00
19	Wade Boggs	4.00
20	Ivan Rodriguez	5.00

2000 Pacific Reflections

This 20-card die-cut set features a unique sunglasses-on- cap design utilizing cel technology for added effect on the sunglasses portion of the insert. The backs have a small photo of the featured player. These were seeded 1:97 packs.

		MT
Complete Set (20):		275.00
Common Player:		8.00
Inserted 1:97		
1	Andruw Jones	8.00
2	Chipper Jones	25.00
3	Cal Ripken Jr.	35.00
4	Nomar Garciaparra	25.00
5	Sammy Sosa	25.00
6	Frank Thomas	10.00
7	Manny Ramirez	10.00
8	Jeff Bagwell	10.00
9	Vladimir Guerrero	10.00
10	Mike Piazza	25.00
11	Derek Jeter	35.00
12	Bernie Williams	8.00
13	Scott Rolen	6.00
14	J.D. Drew	6.00
15	Mark McGwire	30.00
16	Tony Gwynn	15.00
17	Ken Griffey Jr.	30.00
18	Alex Rodriguez	30.00
19	Juan Gonzalez	10.00
20	Ivan Rodriguez	8.00

2000 Pacific Aurora

		MT
Complete Set (151):		50.00
Common Player:		.15
Pack (10):		3.00
Wax Box (24):		65.00
1	Darin Erstad	.25
2	Troy Glaus	1.00
3	Tim Salmon	.40
4	Mo Vaughn	.75
5	Jay Bell	.15
6	Erubiel Durazo	.50
7	Luis Gonzalez	.15
8	Randy Johnson	.75
9	Matt Williams	.50
10	Tom Glavine	.40
11	Andruw Jones	.75
12	Chipper Jones	2.00
13	Brian Jordan	.15
14	Greg Maddux	2.00
15	Kevin Millwood	.25
16	Albert Belle	.75
17	Will Clark	.50
18	Mike Mussina	.75
19	Cal Ripken Jr.	3.00
20	B.J. Surhoff	.15
21	Nomar Garciaparra	2.50
22	Pedro Martinez	1.00
23	Troy O'Leary	.15
24	Wilton Veras	.40
25	Mark Grace	.40
26	Henry Rodriguez	.15
27	Sammy Sosa	2.50
28	Kerry Wood	.40
29	Ray Durham	.15
30	Paul Konerko	.25
31	Carlos Lee	.15
32	Magglio Ordonez	.40
33	Chris Singleton	.15
34	Frank Thomas	1.25
35	Mike Cameron	.15
36	Sean Casey	.40
37	Barry Larkin	.50
38	Pokey Reese	.15
39	Eddie Taubensee	.15
40	Roberto Alomar	.75
41	David Justice	.40
42	Kenny Lofton	.50
43	Manny Ramirez	1.00
44	Richie Sexson	.15
45	Jim Thome	.50
46	Omar Vizquel	.15
47	Todd Helton	.75
48	Mike Lansing	.15
49	Neifi Perez	.15
50	Ben Petrick	.15
51	Larry Walker	.75
52	Tony Clark	.40
53	Damion Easley	.15
54	Juan Encarnacion	.15
55	Juan Gonzalez	1.25
56	Dean Palmer	.15
57	Luis Castillo	.15
58	Cliff Floyd	.15
59	Alex Gonzalez	.15
60	Mike Lowell	.15
61	Preston Wilson	.15
62	Jeff Bagwell	1.00
63	Craig Biggio	.50
64	Ken Caminiti	.25
65	Jose Lima	.15
66	Billy Wagner	.15
67	Carlos Beltran	.20
68	Johnny Damon	.15
69	Jermaine Dye	.15
70	Mark Quinn	.15
71	Mike Sweeney	.15
72	Kevin Brown	.25
73	Shawn Green	.75
74	Eric Karros	.25
75	Chan Ho Park	.15
76	Gary Sheffield	.40
77	Ron Belliard	.15
78	Jeromy Burnitz	.15
79	Marquis Grissom	.15
80	Geoff Jenkins	.15
81	David Nilsson	.15
82	Ron Coomer	.15
83	Jacque Jones	.15
84	Brad Radke	.15
85	Todd Walker	.15
86	Michael Barrett	.15
87	Peter Bergeron	.15
88	Vladimir Guerrero	1.50
89	Jose Vidro	.15
90	Rondell White	.25
91	Edgardo Alfonzo	.25
92	Darryl Hamilton	.15
93	Rey Ordonez	.15
94	Mike Piazza	2.50
95	Robin Ventura	.25
96	Roger Clemens	1.50
97	Orlando Hernandez	.50
98	Derek Jeter	2.50
99	Tino Martinez	.40
100	Mariano Rivera	.25
101	Bernie Williams	.75
102	Eric Chavez	.40
103	Jason Giambi	.15
104	Ben Grieve	.40
105	Tim Hudson	.50
106	John Jaha	.15
107	Matt Stairs	.15
108	Bobby Abreu	.15
109	Doug Glanville	.15
110	Mike Lieberthal	.15
111	Scott Rolen	1.00
112	Curt Schilling	.25
113	Brian Giles	.15
114	Chad Hermansen	.15
115	Jason Kendall	.25
116	Warren Morris	.15
117	Kevin Young	.15
118	Rick Ankiel	.40
119	J.D. Drew	.25
120	Ray Lankford	.15
121	Mark McGwire	4.00
122	Edgar Renteria	.15
123	Fernando Tatis	.25
124	Ben Davis	.15
125	Tony Gwynn	2.00
126	Trevor Hoffman	.15
127	Phil Nevin	.15
128	Barry Bonds	1.25
129	Ellis Burks	.15
130	Jeff Kent	.15
131	J.T. Snow	.15
132	Freddy Garcia	.40
133	Ken Griffey Jr.	3.00
133a	Ken Griffey Jr. Reds	5.00
134	Edgar Martinez	.15
135	Alex Rodriguez	3.00
136	Dan Wilson	.15
137	Jose Canseco	1.00
138	Roberto Hernandez	.15
139	Dave Martinez	.15
140	Fred McGriff	.40
141	Rusty Greer	.15
142	Ruben Mateo	.40
143	Rafael Palmeiro	.75
144	Ivan Rodriguez	1.00
145	Jeff Zimmerman	.15
146	Homer Bush	.15
147	Carlos Delgado	.75
148	Raul Mondesi	.40
149	Shannon Stewart	.15
150	Vernon Wells	.25

2000 Pacific Aurora Copper

	MT
Stars:	3x-6x
Yng. Stars & Rookies:	2x-4x
Production 399 sets	

2000 Pacific Aurora Silver

	MT
Stars:	4x-8x
Yng. Stars & RCs:	3x-6x
Production 199 sets	

2000 Pacific Aurora Platinum Blue

	MT
Stars:	15x-25x
Yng. Stars & RCs:	8x-15x
Production 67 sets	

2000 Pacific Aurora Pinstripes

	MT
Complete Set (50):	200.00
Common Player:	1.00
Premiere Date:	4x-8x

Production 51 sets

4	Mo Vaughn	2.00
8	Randy Johnson	2.50
9	Matt Williams	2.50
11	Andruw Jones	2.50
12	Chipper Jones	6.00
14	Greg Maddux	6.00
19	Cal Ripken Jr.	10.00
21	Nomar Garciaparra	8.00
22	Pedro Martinez	4.00
27	Sammy Sosa	8.00
32	Magglio Ordonez	1.00
34	Frank Thomas	4.00
36	Sean Casey	1.50
37	Barry Larkin	2.00
42	Kenny Lofton	1.50
43	Manny Ramirez	3.00
45	Jim Thome	2.50
47	Todd Helton	2.00
51	Larry Walker	2.00
55	Juan Gonzalez	4.00
62	Jeff Bagwell	3.00
63	Craig Biggio	2.00
67	Carlos Beltran	2.00
73	Shawn Green	3.00
76	Gary Sheffield	1.50
78	Jeromy Burnitz	1.00
88	Vladimir Guerrero	4.00
91	Edgardo Alfonzo	2.00
94	Mike Piazza	8.00
96	Roger Clemens	5.00
97	Orlando Hernandez	1.50
98	Derek Jeter	8.00
101	Bernie Williams	2.00
102	Eric Chavez	1.00
105	Tim Hudson	1.50
111	Scott Rolen	3.00
112	Curt Schilling	1.50
113	Brian Giles	1.00
114	Rick Ankiel	2.00
121	Mark McGwire	12.00
125	Tony Gwynn	6.00
128	Barry Bonds	3.00
130	Jeff Kent	1.00
133	Ken Griffey Jr.	1.50
135	Alex Rodriguez	8.00
137	Jose Canseco	3.00
140	Fred McGriff	2.00
143	Rafael Palmeiro	2.00
144	Ivan Rodriguez	3.00
147	Carlos Delgado	2.50

2000 Pacific Aurora At-Bat Styrotechs

		MT
Complete Set (20):		250.00
Common Player:		4.00
Production 299 sets		
1	Chipper Jones	20.00
2	Cal Ripken Jr.	30.00
3	Nomar Garciaparra	20.00
4	Sammy Sosa	20.00
5	Frank Thomas	8.00
6	Manny Ramirez	8.00
7	Larry Walker	4.00
8	Jeff Bagwell	8.00
9	Carlos Beltran	4.00
10	Vladimir Guerrero	8.00
11	Mike Piazza	25.00
12	Derek Jeter	30.00
13	Bernie Williams	6.00
14	Mark McGwire	25.00
15	Tony Gwynn	12.00
16	Barry Bonds	12.00
17	Ken Griffey Jr.	25.00
18	Alex Rodriguez	25.00
19	Jose Canseco	6.00
20	Ivan Rodriguez	6.00

2000 Pacific Aurora Dugout View Net-Fusions

		MT
Complete Set (20):		125.00
Common Player:		3.00
Inserted 1:37		
1	Mo Vaughn	4.00
2	Chipper Jones	10.00
3	Cal Ripken Jr.	15.00
4	Nomar Garciaparra	10.00
5	Sammy Sosa	10.00
6	Manny Ramirez	6.00
7	Larry Walker	4.00
8	Juan Gonzalez	6.00
9	Jeff Bagwell	6.00
10	Craig Biggio	3.00
11	Shawn Green	3.00
12	Vladimir Guerrero	6.00
13	Mike Piazza	10.00
14	Derek Jeter	15.00
15	Scott Rolen	5.00
16	Mark McGwire	8.00
17	Tony Gwynn	6.00
18	Ken Griffey Jr.	12.00
19	Alex Rodriguez	12.00
20	Rafael Palmeiro	4.00

2000 Pacific Aurora Pennant Fever

		MT
Complete Set (20):		50.00
Common Player:		1.00
T. Gwynn Auto./147		100.00
Inserted 4:37		
1	Andruw Jones	1.50
2	Chipper Jones	4.00
3	Greg Maddux	4.00
4	Cal Ripken Jr.	6.00
5	Nomar Garciaparra	4.00
6	Pedro Martinez	2.00
7	Sammy Sosa	4.00
8	Manny Ramirez	2.00
9	Jim Thome	1.00
10	Jeff Bagwell	2.00
11	Mike Piazza	5.00
12	Roger Clemens	2.50
13	Derek Jeter	5.00
14	Bernie Williams	1.50
15	Mark McGwire	5.00
16	Tony Gwynn	3.00
17	Ken Griffey Jr.	5.00
18	Alex Rodriguez	5.00
19	Rafael Palmeiro	1.00
20	Ivan Rodriguez	2.00

A player's name in *italic* type indicates a rookie card.

2000 Pacific Aurora Star Factor

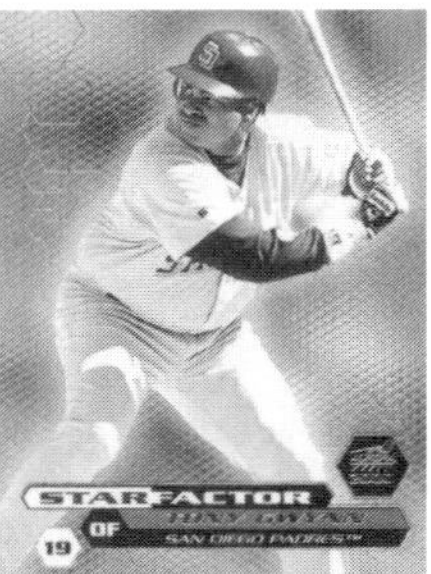

		MT
Complete Set (10):		375.00
Common Player:		25.00
Inserted 1:361		
1	Chipper Jones	40.00
2	Cal Ripken Jr.	50.00
3	Nomar Garciaparra	40.00
4	Sammy Sosa	40.00
5	Mike Piazza	40.00
6	Derek Jeter	50.00
7	Mark McGwire	40.00
8	Tony Gwynn	30.00
9	Ken Griffey Jr.	40.00
10	Alex Rodriguez	40.00

2000 Pacific Crown Collection

This 300-card base set has a white bordered design with the logo, player name and team stamped in gold foil. Card backs have a small close-up photo, a brief career highlight and 1999 statistics along with career totals.

		MT
Complete Set (300):		35.00
Common Player:		.10
Pack (10):		2.50
Wax Box (36):		70.00
1	Garret Anderson	.10
2	Darin Erstad	.25
3	Ben Molina	.10
4	(Ramon Ortiz)	.10
5	Orlando Palmeiro	.10
6	Troy Percival	.10
7	Tim Salmon	.20
8	Mo Vaughn	.50
9	Checklist (Mo Vaughn)	.25
10	Jay Bell	.10
11	Omar Daal	.10
12	Erubiel Durazo	.25
13	Steve Finley	.10
14	Hanley Frias	.10
15	Luis Gonzalez	.10
16	Randy Johnson	.50
17	Matt Williams	.40
18	Checklist (Matt Williams)	.20
19	Andres Galarraga	.40
20	Tom Glavine	.20
21	Andruw Jones	.40
22	Chipper Jones	1.50
23	Brian Jordan	.10
24	Javy Lopez	.10
25	Greg Maddux	1.50
26	Kevin Millwood	.20
27	Eddie Perez	.10
28	John Smoltz	.20
29	Checklist (Chipper Jones)	.75
30	Albert Belle	.50
31	Jesse Garcia	.10
32	Jerry Hairston Jr.	.10
33	Charles Johnson	.10
34	Mike Mussina	.50
35	Sidney Ponson	.10
36	Cal Ripken Jr.	2.00
37	B.J. Surhoff	.10
38	Checklist (Cal Ripken Jr.)	1.00
39	Nomar Garciaparra	2.00
40	Pedro Martinez	.75
41	Ramon Martinez	.10
42	Trot Nixon	.10
43	Jose Offerman	.10
44	Troy O'Leary	.10
45	John Valentin	.10
46	Wilton Veras	.10
47	Checklist (Nomar Garciaparra)	1.00
48	Mark Grace	.20
49	Felix Heredia	.10
50	Jose Molina	.10
51	Jose Nieves	.10
52	Henry Rodriguez	.10
53	Sammy Sosa	2.00
54	Kerry Wood	.40
55	Checklist (Sammy Sosa)	1.00
56	Mike Caruso	.10
57	Carlos Castillo	.10
58	Jason Dellaero	.10
59	Carlos Lee	.10
60	Magglio Ordonez	.25
61	Jesus Pena	.10
62	Liu Rodriguez	.10
63	Frank Thomas	1.00
64	Checklist (Magglio Ordonez)	.15
65	Aaron Boone	.10
66	Mike Cameron	.10
67	Sean Casey	.40
68	Juan Guzman	.10
69	Barry Larkin	.40
70	Pokey Reese	.10
71	Eddie Taubensee	.10
72	Greg Vaughn	.25
73	Checklist (Sean Casey)	.20
74	Roberto Alomar	.25
75	Sandy Alomar Jr.	.15
76	Bartolo Colon	.10
77	Jacob Cruz	.10
78	Einar Diaz	.10
79	David Justice	.20
80	Kenny Lofton	.50
81	Manny Ramirez	.75
82	Richie Sexson	.10
83	Jim Thome	.40
84	Omar Vizquel	.10
85	Enrique Wilson	.10
86	Checklist (Manny Ramirez)	.40
87	Pedro Astacio	.10
88	Henry Blanco	.10
89	Vinny Castilla	.20
90	Edgard Clemente	.10
91	Todd Helton	.75
92	Neifi Perez	.10
93	Terry Shumpert	.10
94	*Juan Sosa*	.40
95	Larry Walker	.50
96	Checklist (Vinny Castilla)	.10
97	Tony Clark	.25
98	Deivi Cruz	.10
99	Damion Easley	.10
100	Juan Encarnacion	.10
101	Karim Garcia	.10
102	Luis Garcia	.10
103	Juan Gonzalez	1.00

104 Jose Macias .10
105 Dean Palmer .10
106 Checklist (Juan Encarnacion) .10
107 Antonio Alfonseca .10
108 Armando Almanza .10
109 Bruce Aven .10
110 Luis Castillo .10
111 Ramon Castro .10
112 Alex Fernandez .10
113 Cliff Floyd .10
114 Alex Gonzalez .10
115 *Michael Tejera* .10
116 Preston Wilson .10
117 Checklist (Luis Castillo) .10
118 Jeff Bagwell .75
119 Craig Biggio .50
120 Jose Cabrera .10
121 Tony Eusebio .10
122 Carl Everett .10
123 Ricky Gutierrez .10
124 Mike Hampton .10
125 Richard Hidalgo .10
126 Jose Lima .10
127 Billy Wagner .10
128 Checklist (Jeff Bagwell) .40
129 Carlos Beltran .20
130 Johnny Damon .10
131 Jermaine Dye .10
132 Carlos Febles .10
133 Jeremy Giambi .10
134 Jose Rosado .10
135 Rey Sanchez .10
136 Jose Santiago .10
137 Checklist (Carlos Beltran) .10
138 Kevin Brown .20
139 Craig Counsell .10
140 Shawn Green .40
141 Eric Karros .20
142 Angel Pena .10
143 Gary Sheffield .25
144 Ismael Valdes .10
145 Jose Vizcaino .10
146 Devon White .10
147 Checklist (Eric Karros) .10
148 Ron Belliard .10
149 Jeromy Burnitz .10
150 Jeff Cirillo .10
151 Marquis Grissom .10
152 Geoff Jenkins .10
153 Dave Nilsson .10
154 Rafael Roque .10
155 Jose Valentin .10
156 Fernando Vina .10
157 Jeromy Burnitz .10
158 Chad Allen .10
159 Ron Coomer .10
160 Eddie Guardado .10
161 Cristian Guzman .10
162 Jacque Jones .10
163 Javier Valentin .10
164 Todd Walker .10
165 Checklist (Ron Coomer) .10
166 Michael Barrett .10
167 Miguel Batista .10
168 Vladimir Guerrero 1.25
169 Wilton Guerrero .10
170 Fernando Seguignol .10
171 Ugueth Urbina .10
172 Javier Vazquez .10
173 Jose Vidro .10
174 Rondell White .20
175 Checklist (Vladimir Guerrero) .60
176 Edgardo Alfonzo .25
177 Armando Benitez .10
178 Roger Cedeno .10
179 Octavio Dotel .10
180 Melvin Mora .10
181 Rey Ordonez .10
182 Mike Piazza 2.00
183 Jorge Toca .10
184 Robin Ventura .25
185 Checklist (Edgardo Alfonzo) .15
186 Roger Clemens 1.00
187 David Cone .20
188 Orlando Hernandez .25
189 Derek Jeter 2.00
190 Ricky Ledee .10
191 Tino Martinez .25
192 Ramiro Mendoza .10
193 Jorge Posada .20
194 Mariano Rivera .25
195 Alfonso Soriano .75
196 Bernie Williams .50
197 Checklist (Derek Jeter) 1.00
198 Eric Chavez .10
199 Jason Giambi .10
200 Ben Grieve .25
201 Ramon Hernandez .10
202 Tim Hudson .40
203 John Jaha .10
204 Omar Olivares .10
205 Olmedo Saenz .10
206 Matt Stairs .10
207 Miguel Tejada .10
208 Checklist (Tim Hudson) .25
209 Rico Brogna .10
210 Bobby Abreu .10
211 Marlon Anderson .10
212 Alex Arias .10
213 Doug Glanville .10
214 Robert Person .10
215 Scott Rolen .75
216 Curt Schilling .20
217 Checklist (Scott Rolen) .40
218 Francisco Cordova .10
219 Brian Giles .10
220 Jason Kendall .20
221 Warren Morris .10
222 Abraham Nunez .10
223 Aramis Ramirez .10
224 Jose Silva .10
225 Kevin Young .10
226 Checklist (Brian Giles) .10
227 Rick Ankiel .40
228 Ricky Bottalico .10
229 J.D. Drew .25
230 Ray Lankford .10
231 Mark McGwire 3.00
232 Eduardo Perez .10
233 Placido Polanco .10
234 Edgar Renteria .10
235 Fernando Tatis .10
236 Checklist (Mark McGwire) 1.50
237 Carlos Almanzar .10
238 Wiki Gonzalez .10
239 Tony Gwynn 1.50
240 Trevor Hoffman .10
241 Damian Jackson .10
242 Wally Joyner .10
243 Ruben Rivera .10
244 Reggie Sanders .10
245 Quilvio Veras .10
246 Checklist (Tony Gwynn) .75
247 Rich Aurilia .10
248 Marvin Benard .10
249 Barry Bonds 1.00
250 Ellis Burks .10
251 Miguel Del Toro .10
252 Edwards Guzman .10
253 Livan Hernandez .10
254 Jeff Kent .10
255 Russ Ortiz .10
256 Armando Rios .10
257 Checklist (Barry Bonds) .50
258 Rafael Bournigal .10
259 Freddy Garcia .50
260 Ken Griffey Jr. 2.50
261 Carlos Guillen .10
262 Raul Ibanez .10
263 Edgar Martinez .20
264 Jose Mesa .10
265 Jamie Moyer .10
266 John Olerud .25
267 Jose Paniagua .10
268 Alex Rodriguez 2.50
269 Checklist (Alex Rodriguez) 1.25
270 Wilson Alvarez .10
271 Rolando Arrojo .10
272 Wade Boggs .40
273 Miguel Cairo .10
274 Jose Canseco .75
275 Jose Guillen .10
276 Roberto Hernandez .10
277 Albie Lopez .10
278 Fred McGriff .25
279 Esteban Yan .10
280 Checklist (Jose Canseco) .40
281 Rusty Greer .10
282 Roberto Kelly .10
283 Esteban Loaiza .10
284 Ruben Mateo .25
285 Rafael Palmeiro .50
286 Ivan Rodriguez .75
287 Aaron Sele .10
288 John Wetteland .10
289 Checklist (Ivan Rodriguez) .40
290 Tony Batista .10
291 Jose Cruz Jr. .10
292 Carlos Delgado .50
293 Kelvim Escobar .10
294 Tony Fernandez .10
295 Billy Koch .10
296 Raul Mondesi .20
297 Willis Otanez .10
298 David Segui .10
299 David Wells .10
300 Checklist (Carlos Delgado) .25

2000 Pacific Crown Collection Holographic Purple

A parallel to the 300-card base set, holographic purple stamping replaces the gold foil to differentiate these from the base cards. These are limited to 199 numbered sets.

	MT
Stars:	5x-10x
Yng Stars:	4x-8x
Production 199 sets	

2000 Pacific Crown Collection Platinum Blue

A parallel to the 300-card base set, these have blue foil stamping in place of gold foil and are limited to 67 serial numbered sets.

	MT
Stars:	15x-25x
Yng Stars & RCs:	8x-15x
Production 67 sets	

2000 Pacific Crown Collection In The Cage

These inserts have a die-cut design around an image of a batting cage, with net-fusion technology used to mimic the netting in a batting cage. These were inserted 1:145 packs.

		MT
Complete Set (20):		340.00
Common Player:		8.00
Inserted 1:145		
1	Mo Vaughn	8.00
2	Chipper Jones	25.00
3	Cal Ripken Jr.	40.00
4	Nomar Garciaparra	25.00
5	Sammy Sosa	25.00
6	Frank Thomas	15.00
7	Roberto Alomar	10.00
8	Manny Ramirez	12.00
9	Larry Walker	8.00
10	Jeff Bagwell	12.00
11	Vladimir Guerrero	15.00
12	Mike Piazza	30.00
13	Derek Jeter	40.00
14	Bernie Williams	10.00
15	Mark McGwire	30.00
16	Tony Gwynn	15.00
17	Ken Griffey Jr.	30.00
18	Alex Rodriguez	30.00
19	Rafael Palmeiro	8.00
20	Ivan Rodriguez	10.00

2000 Pacific Crown Coll. Latinos of the Major Leagues

This set salutes major leagues who have a latino heritage. These were seeded 2:37 packs and have a horizontal format with two images of the featured player on the card front.

		MT
Complete Set (36):		80.00
Common Player:		1.50
Inserted 2:37		
Parallel:		2-3X
Production 99 sets		
1	Erubiel Durazo	1.50
2	Luis Gonzalez	1.50
3	Andruw Jones	3.00
4	Nomar Garciaparra	10.00
5	Pedro Martinez	4.00
6	Sammy Sosa	10.00
7	Carlos Lee	1.50
8	Magglio Ordonez	2.50
9	Roberto Alomar	3.00
10	Manny Ramirez	4.00
11	Omar Vizquel	1.50
12	Vinny Castilla	1.50
13	Juan Gonzalez	4.00
14	Luis Castillo	1.50
15	Jose Lima	1.50
16	Carlos Beltran	1.50
17	Vladimir Guerrero	5.00
18	Edgardo Alfonzo	1.50
19	Roger Cedeno	1.50
20	Rey Ordonez	1.50
21	Orlando Hernandez	1.50
22	Tino Martinez	1.50
23	Mariano Rivera	1.50
24	Bernie Williams	3.00
25	Miguel Tejada	1.50
26	Bobby Abreu	1.50
27	Fernando Tatis	1.50
28	Freddy Garcia	1.50

29 Edgar Martinez 1.50
30 Alex Rodriguez 12.00
31 Jose Canseco 2.50
32 Ruben Mateo 1.50
33 Rafael Palmeiro 2.50
34 Ivan Rodriguez 4.00
35 Carlos Delgado 4.00
36 Raul Mondesi 2.00

2000 Pacific Crown Collection Moment of Truth

These inserts feature gold foil stamping and a shadow image of the player in the background of the player photo. These were inserted 1:37 packs.

MT
Complete Set (30): 160.00
Common Player: 2.00
Inserted 1:37
1 Mo Vaughn 3.00
2 Chipper Jones 10.00
3 Greg Maddux 10.00
4 Albert Belle 2.00
5 Cal Ripken Jr. 15.00
6 Nomar Garciaparra 10.00
7 Pedro Martinez 5.00
8 Sammy Sosa 10.00
9 Frank Thomas 5.00
10 Barry Larkin 3.00
11 Kenny Lofton 2.00
12 Manny Ramirez 5.00
13 Larry Walker 3.00
14 Juan Gonzalez 5.00
15 Jeff Bagwell 5.00
16 Craig Biggio 3.00
17 Carlos Beltran 2.00
18 Vladimir Guerrero 5.00
19 Mike Piazza 12.00
20 Roger Clemens 6.00
21 Derek Jeter 15.00
22 Bernie Williams 4.00
23 Mark McGwire 12.00
24 Tony Gwynn 5.00
25 Barry Bonds 8.00
26 Ken Griffey Jr. 12.00
27 Alex Rodriguez 12.00
28 Rafael Palmeiro 4.00
29 Ivan Rodriguez 8.00
30 Carlos Delgado 4.00

2000 Pacific Crown Collection Pacific Cup

Pacific Cup's have a horizontal format with gold foil stamping and an image of a trophy cup beside the player photo. These were inserted 1:721 packs.

MT
Complete Set (10): 300.00
Inserted 1:721
1 Cal Ripken Jr. 50.00
2 Nomar Garciaparra 30.00
3 Pedro Martinez 20.00
4 Sammy Sosa 30.00
5 Vladimir Guerrero 20.00
6 Derek Jeter 50.00
7 Mark McGwire 40.00
8 Tony Gwynn 20.00
9 Ken Griffey Jr. 40.00
10 Alex Rodriguez 40.00

2000 Pacific Crown Collection Timber 2000

These 1:73 pack inserts have a horizontal format highlighted by gold foil stamping. A black bat is in the background of the player image with 2000 written in the bat head.

MT
Complete Set (20): 160.00
Common Player: 4.00
Inserted 1:73
1 Chipper Jones 15.00
2 Nomar Garciaparra 15.00
3 Sammy Sosa 15.00
4 Magglio Ordonez 5.00
5 Manny Ramirez 8.00
6 Vinny Castilla 4.00
7 Juan Gonzalez 8.00
8 Jeff Bagwell 8.00
9 Shawn Green 5.00
10 Vladimir Guerrero 8.00
11 Mike Piazza 20.00
12 Derek Jeter 25.00
13 Bernie Williams 6.00
14 Mark McGwire 20.00
15 Ken Griffey Jr. 20.00
16 Alex Rodriguez 20.00
17 Jose Canseco 6.00
18 Rafael Palmeiro 5.00
19 Ivan Rodriguez 6.00
20 Carlos Delgado 6.00

2000 Pacific Crown Royale

The Crown Royale 144-card base set has a horizontal format die-cut around a crown design at the top. The cards are double foiled with gold and silver foil etching.

MT
Complete Set (144): 150.00
Common Player: .25
Common SP: 1.50
Pack (6): 5.00
Box (24): 110.00
1 Darin Erstad .50
2 Troy Glaus 2.00
3 Adam Kennedy SP 2.00
4 *Derrick Turnbow SP* 1.50
5 Mo Vaughn 1.50
6 Erubiel Durazo .50
7 Steve Finley .25
8 Randy Johnson 2.00
9 Travis Lee .25
10 Matt Williams .75
11 Rafael Furcal SP 1.50
12 Andres Galarraga 1.00
13 Andruw Jones .75
14 Chipper Jones 4.00
15 Javy Lopez .25
16 Greg Maddux 4.00
17 Albert Belle 1.50
18 Will Clark 1.00
19 Mike Mussina 1.00
20 Cal Ripken Jr. 6.00
21 Carl Everett .25
22 Nomar Garciaparra 5.00
23 Pedro Martinez 2.00
24 Jason Varitek .25
25 *Scott Downs SP* 2.00
26 Mark Grace .50
27 Sammy Sosa 5.00
28 Kerry Wood .75
29 Ray Durham .25
30 Paul Konerko .25
31 Carlos Lee .25
32 Magglio Ordonez .50
33 Frank Thomas 3.00
34 Rob Bell SP 1.50
35 Sean Casey .25
36 Ken Griffey Jr. 6.00
37 Barry Larkin 1.00
38 Pokey Reese .25
39 Roberto Alomar 1.50
40 David Justice .50
41 Kenny Lofton 1.00
42 Manny Ramirez 2.00
43 Richie Sexson .25
44 Jim Thome 1.00
45 Rolando Arrojo .25
46 Jeff Cirillo .25
47 Tom Goodwin .25
48 Todd Helton 2.00
49 Larry Walker 1.00
50 Tony Clark .25
51 Juan Encarnacion .50
52 Juan Gonzalez 2.00
53 Hideo Nomo .25
54 Dean Palmer .25
55 Cliff Floyd .25
56 Alex Gonzalez .25
57 Mike Lowell .25
58 Brad Penny SP 1.50
59 Preston Wilson .25
60 Moises Alou .25
61 Jeff Bagwell 2.00
62 Craig Biggio .75
63 Roger Cedeno .25
64 Julio Lugo SP 1.50
65 Carlos Beltran .25
66 Johnny Damon .25
67 Jermaine Dye .25
68 Carlos Febles .25
69 Mark Quinn SP 1.50
70 Kevin Brown .50
71 Shawn Green 1.50
72 Eric Karros .50
73 Gary Sheffield .75
74 Kevin Barker SP 2.00
75 Ron Belliard .25
76 Jeromy Burnitz .25
77 Geoff Jenkins .50
78 Jacque Jones .25
79 Corey Koskie .25
80 Matt LeCroy SP 1.50
81 Brad Radke .25
82 Peter Bergeron SP 2.00
83 Matt Blank SP 1.50
84 Vladimir Guerrero 4.00
85 Hideki Irabu .25
86 Rondell White .50
87 Edgardo Alfonzo .50
88 Mike Hampton .25
89 Rickey Henderson .50
90 Rey Ordonez .25
91 Jay Payton SP 1.50
92 Mike Piazza 5.00
93 Roger Clemens 2.50
94 Orlando Hernandez .75
95 Derek Jeter 5.00
96 Tino Martinez .50
97 Alfonso Soriano SP 3.00
98 Bernie Williams 1.50
99 Eric Chavez .50
100 Jason Giambi .50
101 Ben Grieve .50
102 Tim Hudson .50
103 Terrence Long SP 1.50
104 Mark Mulder SP 1.50
105 Adam Piatt SP 1.50
106 Bobby Abreu .25
107 Doug Glanville .25
108 Mike Lieberthal .25
109 Scott Rolen 1.50
110 Brian Giles .25
111 Chad Hermansen SP 1.50
112 Jason Kendall .50
113 Warren Morris .25
114 Rick Ankiel SP 3.00
115 *Justin Brunette SP* 1.50
116 J.D. Drew .40
117 Mark McGwire 8.00
118 Fernando Tatis .50
119 Wiki Gonzalez SP 1.50
120 Tony Gwynn 3.00
121 Trevor Hoffman .25
122 Ryan Klesko .25
123 Barry Bonds 2.50
124 Ellis Burks .25
125 Jeff Kent .25
126 Calvin Murray SP 1.50
127 J.T. Snow .25
128 Freddy Garcia .25
129 John Olerud .50
130 Alex Rodriguez 6.00
131 *Kazuhiro Sasaki SP* 6.00
132 Jose Canseco 1.00
133 Vinny Castilla .25
134 Fred McGriff .50
135 Greg Vaughn .25
136 Gabe Kapler .50
137 *Mike Lamb SP* 2.00
138 Ruben Mateo SP 1.00
139 Rafael Palmeiro 1.00
140 Ivan Rodriguez 2.00
141 Tony Batista .25
142 Carlos Delgado 1.50
143 Raul Mondesi .50
144 Shannon Stewart .25

2000 Pacific Crown Royale Platinum Blue

A parallel to the 144-card base set these have blue foil in place of gold foil to differentiate them from regular cards. They are limited to 75 serial numbered sets.

MT
Stars: 3-6X
Production 75 sets

2000 Pacific Crown Royale Limited Series

A parallel to the 144-card base set, silver foil replaces gold foil to differentiate these from regular cards. They are also limited to 144 serial numbered sets.

MT
Stars: 2-4X
Production 144 sets

2000 Pacific Crown Royale Premiere Date

A parallel to the 144-card base set these are found exclusively in hobby packs and are limited to 144 serial numbered sets.

	MT
Stars:	2-4X
Production 121 sets	

2000 Pacific Crown Royale Red

Identical in design to the base set, these have red foil instead of gold and are the base cards in retail packaging.

	MT
All singles:	1X
base cards in retail packs	

2000 Pacific Crown Royale Cramer's Choice Jumbo

This enlarged 10-card set is die-cut into a trophy shape. The jumbo cards are enhanced with a silver holo-foiled front with gold foil stamping and etching across the bottom portion. These were found one per box exclusively in hobby boxes. Six parallels also were randomly inserted with each individual color replacing the gold foil stamping. Aqua's are limited to 20 numbered sets, Blue's 35 sets, Gold's 10 sets, Green's 30 sets, Purple's one set and Red's 25 sets.

		MT
Complete Set (10):		100.00
Common Player:		5.00
Inserted 1:box H		
Aqua:		5-10X
Production 20 sets		
Blue:		2-5X
Production 35 sets		
Gold:		10-20X
Production 10 sets		
Green:		3-6X
Production 30 sets		
Red:		4-8X
Production 25 sets		
1	Cal Ripken Jr.	15.00
2	Nomar Garciaparra	12.00
3	Ken Griffey Jr.	15.00
4	Sammy Sosa	12.00
5	Mike Piazza	12.00
6	Derek Jeter	12.00
7	Rick Ankiel	5.00
8	Mark McGwire	15.00
9	Tony Gwynn	8.00
10	Alex Rodriguez	15.00

2000 Pacific Crown Royale Feature Attractions

This 25-card set has a horizontal format with the featured players achievements on a billboard in the background. These were seeded 1 per hobby pack and one per two retail packs. An Exclusive Showing parallel is also randomly inserted and is limited to 20 serial numbered sets.

		MT
Complete Set (25):		25.00
Common Player:		.25
Inserted 1:1		
Exclusive Showing:		30-50X
Production 20 sets		
1	Erubiel Durazo	.25
2	Chipper Jones	1.50
3	Greg Maddux	1.50
4	Cal Ripken Jr.	2.50
5	Nomar Garciaparra	2.00
6	Pedro Martinez	.75
7	Sammy Sosa	2.00
8	Frank Thomas	1.00
9	Ken Griffey Jr.	2.50
10	Manny Ramirez	1.00
11	Larry Walker	.40
12	Juan Gonzalez	.75
13	Jeff Bagwell	.75
14	Carlos Beltran	.25
15	Shawn Green	.50
16	Vladimir Guerrero	1.50
17	Mike Piazza	2.00
18	Roger Clemens	1.00
19	Derek Jeter	2.00
20	Ben Grieve	.25
21	Rick Ankiel	.50
22	Mark McGwire	3.00
23	Tony Gwynn	1.50
24	Alex Rodriguez	2.00
25	Ivan Rodriguez	.75

2000 Pacific Crown Royale Final Numbers

These inserts are found one per hobby pack and one per two retail packs. The logo, player name and team are stamped in silver foil and has "Final Numbers" written down the right hand portion of the front. A Holographic parallel limited to 10 serial numbered sets is also randomly inserted.

		MT
Complete Set (25):		25.00
Common Player:		.25
Inserted 1:1		
1	Randy Johnson	.75
2	Andruw Jones	.50
3	Chipper Jones	1.50
4	Cal Ripken Jr.	2.50
5	Nomar Garciaparra	2.00
6	Pedro Martinez	.75
7	Sammy Sosa	2.00
8	Ken Griffey Jr.	2.50
9	Sean Casey	.25
10	Manny Ramirez	1.00
11	Larry Walker	.50
12	Jeff Bagwell	.75
13	Craig Biggio	.40
14	Shawn Green	.50
15	Vladimir Guerrero	1.50
16	Mike Piazza	2.00
17	Derek Jeter	2.00
18	Bernie Williams	.50
19	Scott Rolen	.50
20	Mark McGwire	3.00
21	Tony Gwynn	1.00
22	Barry Bonds	1.00
23	Alex Rodriguez	2.50
24	Jose Canseco	.50
25	Ivan Rodriguez	.75

2000 Pacific Crown Royale Jumbo

These jumbo cards are identical in design to the base cards besides their enlarged size. These were found exclusively in hobby boxes and were found as a box topper in 6:10 boxes.

		MT
Complete Set (6):		75.00
Common Player:		5.00
Inserted 6:10 boxes H		
1	Cal Ripken Jr.	15.00
2	Nomar Garciaparra	12.00
3	Ken Griffey Jr.	15.00
4	Derek Jeter	12.00
5	Mark McGwire	20.00
6	Alex Rodriguez	15.00

2000 Pacific Crown Royale Proofs

Proofs are the actual printer's proofs used to produce this set. The inserts are transparent and have a coal black tint. These were inserted 1:25 packs. A parallel is also randomly inserted and is limited to 50 serial numbered sets.

		MT
Complete Set (36):		200.00
Common Player:		3.00
Inserted 1:25		
Proofs:		2-3X
1	Erubiel Durazo	3.00
2	Randy Johnson	6.00
3	Chipper Jones	10.00
4	Greg Maddux	10.00
5	Cal Ripken Jr.	20.00
6	Nomar Garciaparra	12.00
7	Pedro Martinez	6.00
8	Sammy Sosa	12.00
9	Frank Thomas	6.00
10	Sean Casey	4.00
11	Ken Griffey Jr.	15.00
12	Manny Ramirez	6.00
13	Jim Thome	4.00
14	Larry Walker	4.00
15	Juan Gonzalez	6.00
16	Jeff Bagwell	6.00
17	Craig Biggio	3.00
18	Carlos Beltran	3.00
19	Shawn Green	4.00
20	Vladimir Guerrero	6.00
21	Edgardo Alfonzo	3.00
22	Mike Piazza	15.00
23	Roger Clemens	8.00
24	Derek Jeter	20.00
25	Alfonso Soriano	5.00
26	Bernie Williams	5.00
27	Ben Grieve	3.00
28	Rick Ankiel	4.00
29	Mark McGwire	15.00
30	Tony Gwynn	6.00
31	Barry Bonds	8.00
32	Alex Rodriguez	15.00
33	Jose Canseco	4.00
34	Vinny Castilla	3.00
35	Ivan Rodriguez	5.00
36	Rafael Palmeiro	4.00

2000 Pacific Crown Royale Sweet Spot Signatures

These die-cut autographed cards are done on a horizontal format with an image of a baseball beside the player photo. The signature is on the "sweet spot" of the baseball image. Red foil stamping is used on the seams of the baseball and the player name. No insertion ratio was announced.

		MT
Common Player:		8.00
1	Adam Kennedy	8.00
2	Trot Nixon	10.00
3	Magglio Ordonez	20.00
4	Sean Casey	15.00
5	Travis Dawkins	8.00
6	Todd Helton	25.00
7	Ben Petrick	10.00
8	Jeff Weaver	10.00
9	Preston Wilson	10.00
10	Lance Berkman	25.00
11	Roger Cedeno	10.00
12	Eric Gagne	8.00
13	Kevin Barker	8.00
14	Kyle Peterson	8.00
15	Tony Armas Jr.	10.00
16	Peter Bergeron	8.00
17	Alfonso Soriano	25.00
18	Ben Grieve	12.00
19	Ramon Hernandez	8.00
20	Brian Giles	15.00
21	Chad Hermansen	8.00
22	Warren Morris	8.00
23	Ben Davis	8.00
24	Rick Ankiel	15.00
25	Chad Hutchinson	8.00
26	Freddy Garcia	20.00
27	Gabe Kapler	12.00
28	Ruben Mateo	8.00
29	Billy Koch	8.00
30	Vernon Wells	10.00

2000 Pacific Crown Royale Team Card-Supials

These inserts feature a superstar's regular sized card paired with a top prospect teammate's smaller card. The standard sized card has a horizontal format with gold foil stamping, the small prospect card has gold foil stamping on a vertical format. These were seeded 2:25 packs.

		MT
Complete Set (20):		90.00
Common Card:		2.00
Inserted 2:25		
1	Randy Johnson, Erubiel Durazo	4.00
2	Chipper Jones, Andruw Jones	8.00
3	Cal Ripken Jr., Matt Riley	10.00
4	Nomar Garciaparra, Jason Varitek	8.00
5	Sammy Sosa, Kerry Wood	8.00
6	Frank Thomas, Magglio Ordonez	4.00
7	Ken Griffey Jr., Sean Casey	8.00
8	Manny Ramirez, Richie Sexson	4.00
9	Larry Walker, Ben Petrick	2.00
10	Juan Gonzalez, Juan Encarnacion	4.00
11	Jeff Bagwell, Lance Berkman	4.00
12	Shawn Green, Eric Gagne	2.00
13	Vladimir Guerrero, Peter Bergeron	4.00
14	Mike Piazza, Edgardo Alfonzo	8.00
15	Derek Jeter, Alfonso Soriano	10.00
16	Scott Rolen, Bobby Abreu	3.00
17	Mark McGwire, Rick Ankiel	8.00
18	Tony Gwynn, Ben Davis	6.00
19	Alex Rodriguez, Freddy Garcia	8.00
20	Ivan Rodriguez, Ruben Mateo	3.00

2000 Pacific Invincible

The base set consists of 150 cards. The player image is on an acetate stock with a blue sky background. The rest of the card is on standard UV coated stock and has the player name stamped in gold foil.

		MT
Complete Set (150):		120.00
Common Player:		.50
Pack (3):		3.00
Box (36):		85.00
1	Darin Erstad	1.00
2	Troy Glaus	2.00
3	Ramon Ortiz	.50
4	Tim Salmon	.75
5	Mo Vaughn	1.00
6	Erubiel Durazo	.50
7	Luis Gonzalez	.50
8	Randy Johnson	2.00
9	Matt Williams	.75
10	Rafael Furcal	.50
11	Andres Galarraga	1.50
12	Tom Glavine	.75
13	Andruw Jones	.75
14	Chipper Jones	4.00
15	Greg Maddux	4.00
16	Kevin Millwood	.50
17	Albert Belle	1.00
18	Will Clark	.75
19	Mike Mussina	1.00
20	Matt Riley	.50
21	Cal Ripken Jr.	6.00
22	Carl Everett	.50
23	Nomar Garciaparra	5.00
24	Steve Lomasney	.50
25	Pedro Martinez	2.00
26	*Tomo Ohka*	.50
27	Wilton Veras	.50
28	Mark Grace	.75
29	Sammy Sosa	5.00
30	Kerry Wood	.75
31	Eric Young	.50
32	*Julio Zuleta*	.50
33	Paul Konerko	.50
34	Carlos Lee	.50
35	Magglio Ordonez	.75
36	Josh Paul	.50
37	Frank Thomas	3.00
38	Rob Bell	.50
39	Dante Bichette	.75
40	Sean Casey	.50
41	Ken Griffey Jr.	6.00
42	Barry Larkin	1.00
43	Pokey Reese	.50
44	Roberto Alomar	1.50
45	Manny Ramirez	2.00
46	Richie Sexson	.50
47	Jim Thome	1.00
48	Omar Vizquel	.50
49	Jeff Cirillo	.75
50	Todd Helton	2.00
51	Neifi Perez	.50
52	Larry Walker	1.00
53	Tony Clark	.50
54	Juan Encarnacion	.50
55	Juan Gonzalez	2.00
56	Hideo Nomo	.50
57	Luis Castillo	.50
58	Alex Gonzalez	.50
59	Brad Penny	.50
60	Preston Wilson	.50
61	Moises Alou	.50
62	Jeff Bagwell	2.00
63	Lance Berkman	.50
64	Craig Biggio	.75
65	Roger Cedeno	.50
66	Jose Lima	.50
67	Carlos Beltran	.50
68	Johnny Damon	.50
69	*Chad Durbin*	.50
70	Jermaine Dye	.50
71	Carlos Febles	.50
72	Mark Quinn	.50
73	Kevin Brown	.75
74	Eric Gagne	.50
75	Shawn Green	1.50
76	Eric Karros	.75
77	Gary Sheffield	1.00
78	Kevin Barker	.50
79	Ron Belliard	.50
80	Jeromy Burnitz	.50
81	Geoff Jenkins	.75
82	Jacque Jones	.50
83	Corey Koskie	.50
84	Matt LeCroy	.50
85	David Ortiz	.50
86	*Johan Santana*	.50
87	Todd Walker	.50
88	Peter Bergeron	.50
89	Vladimir Guerrero	3.00
90	Jose Vidro	.50
91	Rondell White	.50
92	Edgardo Alfonzo	.75
93	Derek Bell	.50
94	Mike Hampton	.50
95	Rey Ordonez	.50
96	Mike Piazza	5.00
97	Robin Ventura	.75
98	Roger Clemens	3.00
99	Orlando Hernandez	.75
100	Derek Jeter	5.00
101	Alfonso Soriano	1.00
102	Bernie Williams	1.50
103	Eric Chavez	.50
104	Jason Giambi	.75
105	Ben Grieve	.75
106	Tim Hudson	.75
107	Miguel Tejada	.50
108	Bobby Abreu	.50
109	Doug Glanville	.50
110	Mike Lieberthal	.50
111	Scott Rolen	1.50
112	Brian Giles	.50
113	Chad Hermansen	.50
114	Jason Kendall	.50
115	Warren Morris	.50
116	Aramis Ramirez	.50
117	Rick Ankiel	.75
118	J.D. Drew	.50
119	Mark McGwire	8.00
120	Fernando Tatis	.50
121	Fernando Vina	.50
122	Bret Boone	.50
123	Ben Davis	.50
124	Tony Gwynn	3.00
125	Trevor Hoffman	.50
126	Ryan Klesko	.50
127	Rich Aurilia	.50
128	Barry Bonds	3.00
129	Ellis Burks	.50
130	Jeff Kent	.75
131	Freddy Garcia	.50
132	Carlos Guillen	.50
133	Edgar Martinez	.50
134	John Olerud	.75
135	Robert Ramsay	.50
136	Alex Rodriguez	6.00
137	*Kazuhiro Sasaki*	4.00
138	Jose Canseco	1.50
139	Vinny Castilla	.50
140	Fred McGriff	.75
141	Greg Vaughn (front photo is Mo Vaughn)	.75
142	Dan Wheeler	.50
143	Gabe Kapler	.75
144	Ruben Mateo	.50
145	Rafael Palmeiro	1.00
146	Ivan Rodriguez	2.00
147	Tony Batista	.75
148	Carlos Delgado	1.50
149	Raul Mondesi	.75
150	Vernon Wells	.50

2000 Pacific Invincible Holographic Purple

A parallel to the 150-card set, holographic purple stamping replaces the gold foil from the base cards. These are limited to 299 serial numbered sets.

	MT
Stars:	2-3X
Production 299 sets	

2000 Pacific Invincible Platinum Blue

A parallel to the 150-card base set these differ only from the regular cards in that blue foil stamping replaces gold. Each card is also serially numbered on the card front in an edition of 67 sets.

	MT
Stars:	6-10X
Production 67 sets	

2000 Pacific Invincible Diamond Aces

This 20-card set highlights the top pitchers in the game. Silver foil stamping is used on the card fronts and are designed to duplicate the look of an Ace in a playing deck of cards. These were seeded 1 per pack. A parallel version limited to 399 serial numbered sets is also randomly seeded.

		MT
Complete Set (20):		8.00
Common Player:		.40
Inserted 1:1		
Edition of 399 Parallel:		2-3X
1	Randy Johnson	.75
2	Greg Maddux	1.50
3	Tom Glavine	.40
4	John Smoltz	.40
5	Mike Mussina	.50
6	Pedro Martinez	.75
7	Kerry Wood	.40
8	Bartolo Colon	.40
9	Brad Penny	.40
10	Billy Wagner	.40
11	Kevin Brown	.40
12	Mike Hampton	.40
13	Roger Clemens	1.00
14	David Cone	.40
15	Orlando Hernandez	.40
16	Mariano Rivera	.40
17	Tim Hudson	.40
18	Trevor Hoffman	.40
19	Rick Ankiel	.50
20	Freddy Garcia	.40

2000 Pacific Invincible Eyes of the World

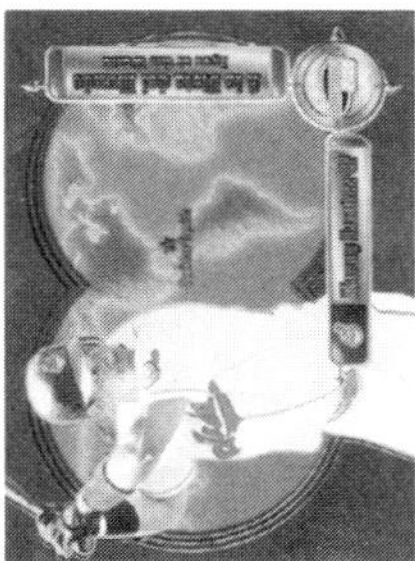

This 20-card set has a horizontal format with gold foil stamping. The background of the player photo has a partial globe with a star and the country the featured player is from stamped in gold foil. These were inserted 1:25 packs.

		MT
Complete Set (20):		90.00
Common Player:		2.00
Inserted 1:25		
1	Erubiel Durazo	2.00
2	Andruw Jones	4.00
3	Cal Ripken Jr.	15.00
4	Nomar Garciaparra	10.00
5	Pedro Martinez	5.00
6	Sammy Sosa	10.00
7	Ken Griffey Jr.	12.00
8	Manny Ramirez	5.00
9	Larry Walker	3.00
10	Juan Gonzalez	5.00
11	Carlos Beltran	2.00
12	Vladimir Guerrero	5.00
13	Orlando Hernandez	2.00
14	Derek Jeter	15.00
15	Mark McGwire	12.00
16	Tony Gwynn	5.00
17	Freddy Garcia	3.00
18	Alex Rodriguez	12.00
19	Jose Canseco	4.00
20	Ivan Rodriguez	4.00

A card number in parentheses ( ) indicates the set is unnumbered.

2000 Pacific Invincible Game Gear

		MT
Common Card:		12.00
1	Jeff Bagwell Jsy/1000	35.00
2	Tom Glavine Jsy/1000	20.00
3	Mark Grace Jsy/1000	25.00
4	Eric Karros Jsy/1000	15.00
5	Edgar Martinez Jsy/800	20.00
6	Manny Ramirez Jsy/975	35.00
7	Cal Ripken Jr. Jsy/1000	60.00
8	Alex Rodriguez Jsy/900	50.00
9	Ivan Rodriguez Jsy/675	40.00
10	Mo Vaughn Jsy/1000	12.00
11	Edgar Martinez Bat-Jsy/200	35.00
12	Manny Ramirez Jsy/145	60.00
13	Alex Rodriguez Bat-Jsy/200	125.00
14	Ivan Rodriguez Bat-Jsy/200	60.00
15	Edgar Martinez Bat/200	30.00
16	Manny Ramirez Bat/200	40.00
17	Ivan Rodriguez Bat/200	60.00
18	Alex Rodriguez Bat/200	120.00
19	Jeff Bagwell Patch/125	75.00
20	Tom Glavine Patch/110	65.00
21	Mark Grace Patch/125	65.00
22	Tony Gwynn Patch/65	180.00
23	Chipper Jones Patch/80	125.00
24	Eric Karros Patch/125	40.00
25	Greg Maddux Patch/80	150.00
26	Edgar Martinez Patch/125	60.00
27	Manny Ramirez Patch/125	100.00
28	Cal Ripken Jr. Patch/125	160.00
29	Alex Rodriguez Patch/125	180.00
30	Ivan Rodriguez Patch/125	100.00
31	Frank Thomas Patch/125	100.00
32	Mo Vaughn Patch/125	40.00

2000 Pacific Invincible Kings of the Diamond

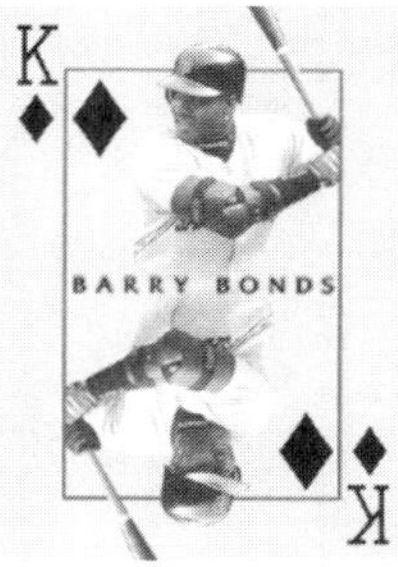

Twenty of the top hitters in the game are featured on a design intended to duplicate the look of a King card in a playing deck of cards. These were seeded 1 per pack. A parallel version limited to 299 serial numbered sets is also randomly seeded.

		MT
Complete Set (30):		25.00
Common Player:		.40
Inserted 1:1		
1	Mo Vaughn	.50
2	Erubiel Durazo	.40
3	Andruw Jones	.50
4	Chipper Jones	1.50
5	Cal Ripken Jr.	2.50
6	Nomar Garciaparra	2.00
7	Sammy Sosa	2.00
8	Frank Thomas	1.00
9	Sean Casey	.40
10	Ken Griffey Jr.	2.50
11	Manny Ramirez	.75
12	Larry Walker	.50
13	Juan Gonzalez	.75
14	Jeff Bagwell	.75
15	Craig Biggio	.50
16	Carlos Beltran	.40
17	Shawn Green	.50
18	Vladimir Guerrero	1.25
19	Mike Piazza	2.00
20	Derek Jeter	2.00
21	Bernie Williams	.50
22	Ben Grieve	.40
23	Scott Rolen	.50
24	Mark McGwire	3.00
25	Tony Gwynn	1.50
26	Barry Bonds	.75
27	Alex Rodriguez	2.50
28	Jose Canseco	.50
29	Rafael Palmeiro	.50
30	Ivan Rodriguez	.75

2000 Pacific Invincible Lighting The Fire

These full foiled inserts are die-cut in the shape of a flame, with an image of a baseball at the core of the fiery image. These were inserted 1:49 packs.

		MT
Complete Set (20):		200.00
Common Player:		5.00
Inserted 1:49		
1	Chipper Jones	15.00
2	Greg Maddux	15.00
3	Cal Ripken Jr.	25.00
4	Nomar Garciaparra	15.00
5	Pedro Martinez	8.00
6	Ken Griffey Jr.	20.00
7	Sammy Sosa	15.00
8	Manny Ramirez	8.00
9	Juan Gonzalez	8.00
10	Jeff Bagwell	8.00
11	Shawn Green	6.00
12	Vladimir Guerrero	8.00
13	Mike Piazza	20.00
14	Roger Clemens	10.00
15	Derek Jeter	25.00
16	Mark McGwire	20.00
17	Tony Gwynn	8.00
18	Alex Rodriguez	20.00
19	Jose Canseco	6.00
20	Ivan Rodriguez	6.00

2000 Pacific Invincible Ticket To Stardom

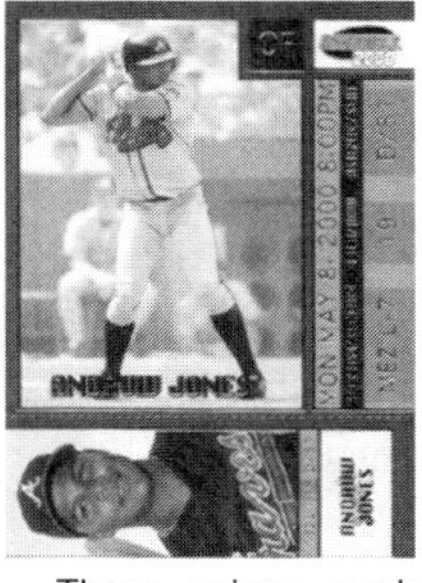

These unique cards have a design intended to replicate a ticket stub. Two images of the featured player are on the front, the bigger primary photo is vertical, while the smaller photo is horizontal. Silver foil stamping is used throughout. These are found 1:121 packs.

		MT
Complete Set (20):		375.00
Common Player:		8.00
Inserted 1:121		
1	Andruw Jones	10.00
2	Chipper Jones	30.00
3	Cal Ripken Jr.	50.00
4	Nomar Garciaparra	30.00
5	Pedro Martinez	15.00
6	Ken Griffey Jr.	40.00
7	Sammy Sosa	30.00
8	Manny Ramirez	15.00
9	Jeff Bagwell	15.00
10	Shawn Green	8.00
11	Vladimir Guerrero	15.00
12	Mike Piazza	40.00
13	Derek Jeter	50.00
14	Alfonso Soriano	10.00
15	Scott Rolen	10.00
16	Rick Ankiel	8.00
17	Mark McGwire	40.00
18	Tony Gwynn	15.00
19	Alex Rodriguez	40.00
20	Ivan Rodriguez	10.00

2000 Pacific Omega

		MT
Complete Set (255):		900.00
Common Player:		.10
Common (151-255):		8.00
Production 999 sets		
1	Garret Anderson	.10
2	Darin Erstad	.40
3	Troy Glaus	.75
4	Tim Salmon	.25
5	Mo Vaughn	.40
6	Jay Bell	.10
7	Steve Finley	.10
8	Luis Gonzalez	.10
9	Randy Johnson	.75
10	Matt Williams	.25
11	Andres Galarraga	.25
12	Andruw Jones	.50
13	Chipper Jones	1.50
14	Brian Jordan	.10
15	Greg Maddux	1.50
16	B.J. Surhoff	.10
17	Brady Anderson	.20
18	Albert Belle	.40
19	Mike Mussina	.50
20	Cal Ripken Jr.	2.50
21	Carl Everett	.10
22	Nomar Garciaparra	2.00
23	Pedro Martinez	.75
24	Jason Varitek	.10
25	Mark Grace	.20
26	Sammy Sosa	2.00
27	Rondell White	.10
28	Kerry Wood	.25
29	Eric Young	.10
30	Ray Durham	.10
31	Carlos Lee	.10
32	Magglio Ordonez	.25
33	Frank Thomas	1.00
34	Sean Casey	.10
35	Ken Griffey Jr.	2.00
36	Barry Larkin	.40
37	Pokey Reese	.10
38	Roberto Alomar	.60
39	Kenny Lofton	.30
40	Manny Ramirez	.75
41	David Segui	.10
42	Jim Thome	.40
43	Omar Vizquel	.10
44	Jeff Cirillo	.10
45	Jeffrey Hammonds	.10
46	Todd Helton	.75
47	Todd Hollandsworth	.10
48	Larry Walker	.30
49	Tony Clark	.20
50	Juan Encarnacion	.10
51	Juan Gonzalez	.75
52	Bobby Higginson	.10
53	Hideo Nomo	.40
54	Dean Palmer	.10
55	Luis Castillo	.10
56	Cliff Floyd	.10
57	Derrek Lee	.10
58	Mike Lowell	.10
59	Henry Rodriguez	.10
60	Preston Wilson	.10
61	Moises Alou	.20
62	Jeff Bagwell	.75
63	Craig Biggio	.20
64	Ken Caminiti	.20
65	Richard Hidalgo	.10
66	Carlos Beltran	.10
67	Johnny Damon	.10
68	Jermaine Dye	.10
69	Joe Randa	.10
70	Mike Sweeney	.10
71	Adrian Beltre	.20
72	Kevin Brown	.20
73	Shawn Green	.25
74	Eric Karros	.20
75	Chan Ho Park	.10
76	Gary Sheffield	.30
77	Ron Belliard	.10
78	Jeromy Burnitz	.10
79	Geoff Jenkins	.20
80	Richie Sexson	.10
81	Ron Coomer	.10
82	Jacque Jones	.10
83	Corey Koskie	.10
84	Matt Lawton	.10
85	Vladimir Guerrero	1.00
86	Lee Stevens	.10
87	Jose Vidro	.10
88	Edgardo Alfonzo	.20
89	Derek Bell	.10
90	Mike Bordick	.10
91	Mike Piazza	2.00
92	Robin Ventura	.20
93	Jose Canseco	.40
94	Roger Clemens	1.00
95	Orlando Hernandez	.10
96	Derek Jeter	2.50
97	David Justice	.30
98	Tino Martinez	.20
99	Jorge Posada	.20
100	Bernie Williams	.60
101	Eric Chavez	.20
102	Jason Giambi	.40
103	Ben Grieve	.20
104	Miguel Tejada	.10
105	Bobby Abreu	.10
106	Doug Glanville	.10
107	Travis Lee	.10
108	Mike Lieberthal	.10
109	Scott Rolen	.50
110	Brian S. Giles	.20
111	Jason Kendall	.10
112	Warren Morris	.10
113	Kevin Young	.10
114	Will Clark	.30
115	J.D. Drew	.25
116	Jim Edmonds	.25
117	Mark McGwire	3.00
118	Edgar Renteria	.10
119	Fernando Tatis	.10
120	Fernando Vina	.10
121	Bret Boone	.10
122	Tony Gwynn	1.00
123	Trevor Hoffman	.10
124	Phil Nevin	.10
125	Eric Owens	.10
126	Barry Bonds	1.00
127	Ellis Burks	.10
128	Jeff Kent	.10
129	J.T. Snow	.10
130	Jay Buhner	.10
131	Mike Cameron	.10
132	Rickey Henderson	.30
133	Edgar Martinez	.10
134	John Olerud	.20
135	Alex Rodriguez	2.50
136	*Kazuhiro Sasaki*	2.00
137	Fred McGriff	.25
138	Greg Vaughn	.10
139	Gerald Williams	.10
140	Rusty Greer	.10
141	Gabe Kapler	.10
142	Ricky Ledee	.10
143	Rafael Palmeiro	.40
144	Ivan Rodriguez	.75
145	Tony Batista	.10
146	Jose Cruz Jr.	.10
147	Carlos Delgado	.60
148	Brad Fullmer	.10
149	Shannon Stewart	.10
150	David Wells	.10
151	Juan Alvarez, Jeff DaVanon	8.00
152	Seth Etherton, Adam Kennedy	8.00
153	Ramon Ortiz, Lou Pote	8.00
154	*Derrick Turnbow*, Eric Weaver	8.00
155	Rod Barajas, Jason Conti	8.00
156	Byung-Hyun Kim, Rob Ryan	8.00
157	David Cortes, George Lombard	8.00
158	Ivanon Coffie, Melvin Mora	8.00
159	*Ryan Kohlmeier, Luis Matos*	10.00
160	Willie Morales, *John Parrish*	8.00
161	*Chris Richard, Jay Spurgeon*	15.00
162	Israel Alcantara, *Tomokazu Ohka*	10.00
163	*Paxton Crawford, Sang-Hoon Lee*	8.00
164	Mike Mahoney, Wilton Veras	8.00
165	*Daniel Garibay, Ross Gload*	8.00
166	Gary Matthews Jr., Phil Norton	8.00
167	Roosevelt Brown, Ruben Quevedo	8.00
168	*Lorenzo Barcelo, Rocky Biddle*	8.00
169	*Mark Buehrle*, John Garland	8.00
170	Aaron Myette, Josh Paul	8.00
171	Kip Wells, Kelly Wunsch	8.00
172	Rob Bell, Travis Dawkins	8.00
173	*Hector Mercado ,John Riedling*	8.00
174	Russell Branyan, Sean DePaula	8.00
175	Tim Drew, Mark Watson	8.00
176	*Craig House*, Ben Petrick	8.00
177	Robert Fick, Jose Macias	8.00
178	*Javier Cardona*, Brandon Villafuerte	8.00
179	Armando Almanza, A.J. Burnett	8.00
180	Ramon Castro, Pablo Ozuna	8.00
181	Lance Berkman, Jason Green	8.00
182	Julio Lugo, Tony McKnight	8.00
183	Mitch Meluskey, Wade Miller	8.00
184	*Chad Durbin, Hector Ortiz*	8.00
185	Dermal Brown, Mark Quinn	8.00
186	Eric Gagne, Mike Judd	8.00
187	*Kane Davis*, Valerio de los Santos	8.00
188	Santiago Perez, *Paul Rigdon*	8.00
189	Matt Kinney, Matt LeCroy	8.00
190	Jason Maxwell, A.J. Pierzynski	8.00
191	*J.C. Romero ,Johan Santana*	8.00
192	Tony Armas Jr., Peter Bergeron	8.00
193	Matt Blank, Milton Bradley	8.00
194	Tomas De La Rossa, Scott Forster	8.00
195	*Yovanny Lara,Talmadge Nunnari*	8.00
196	Brian Schneider, Andy Tracy	8.00
197	Scott Strickland, T.J. Tucker	8.00
198	Eric Cammack, *Jim Mann*	8.00
199	Grant Roberts, Jorge Toca	8.00
200	Alfonso Soriano, Jay Tessmer	8.00
201	Terrence Long, Mark Mulder	10.00
202	Pat Burrell, Cliff Politte	15.00
203	Jimmy Anderson, Bronson Arroyo	8.00
204	Mike Darr, Kory DeHaan	8.00
205	Adam Eaton, Wiki Gonzalez	8.00
206	*Brandon Kolb*, Kevin Walker	8.00
207	Damon Minor, Calvin Murray	8.00
208	Kevin Hodges, *Joel Pineiro*	10.00
209	*Rob Ramsay, Kazuhiro Sasaki*	20.00
210	Rick Ankiel, Mike Matthews	10.00
211	Steve Cox, Travis Harper	8.00
212	*Kenny Kelly, Damian Rolls*	10.00
213	Doug Davis, Scott Sheldon	8.00
214	Brian Sikorski, Pedro Valdes	8.00
215	Francisco Cordero, B.J. Waszgis	8.00
216	Matt DeWitt *,Josh Phelps*	20.00
217	Vernon Wells, Dewayne Wise	8.00
218	*Geraldo Guzman*, Jason Marquis	8.00
219	Rafael Furcal, *Steve Sisco*	10.00
220	B.J. Ryan, Kevin Beirne	8.00
221	*Matt Ginter*, Brad Penny	8.00
222	*Julio Zuleta*, Eric Munson	10.00
223	Dan Reichert, Jeff Williams	8.00
224	Jason LaRue, Danny Ardoin	8.00
225	Ray King, Mark Redman	8.00
226	Joe Crede, Mike Bell	10.00
227	*Juan Pierre*, Jay Payton	15.00
228	Wayne Franklin, *Randy Choate*	8.00
229	Chris Truby, Adam Piatt	12.00
230	Kevin Nicholson, Chris Woodward	8.00
231	*Barry Zito*, Jason Boyd	25.00
232	*Brian O'Connor*, Miguel Del Toro	8.00
233	Carlos Guillen, Aubrey Huff	8.00
234	Chad Hermansen, Jason Tyner	8.00
235	Aaron Fultz, Ryan Vogelsong	10.00
236	Shawn Wooten, Vance Wilson	8.00
237	Danny Klassen, *Mike Lamb*	10.00
238	Chad Bradford, *Gene Stechschulte*	8.00
239	Ismael Villegas, Hector Ramirez, Matt T. Williams, Luis Vizcaino	8.00
240	Mike Garcia, Domingo Guzman, *Justin Brunette, Pasqual Coco*	8.00
241	Frank Charles, *Keith McDonald*	8.00
242	*Carlos Casimiro, Morgan Burkhart*	8.00
243	*Raul Gonzalez*, Shawn Gilbert	8.00
244	Darrell Einertson, *Jeff Sparks*	8.00
245	*Augie Ojeda*, Brady Clark, Todd Belitz, *Eric Byrnes*	8.00
246	*Leo Estrella*, Charlie Greene	8.00
247	Trace Coquillette, *Pedro Feliz*	10.00
248	*Tike Redman*, David Newhan	8.00
249	*Rodrigo Lopez*, John Bales	8.00
250	Corey Patterson *,Jose Ortiz*	25.00
251	*Britt Reames, Oswaldo Mairena*	8.00
252	*Xavier Nady, Timoniel Perez*	25.00
253	Tom Jacquez, Vicente Padilla	8.00
254	*Elvis Pena, Adam Melhuse*	8.00
255	Ben Weber, *Alex Cabrera*	12.00

2000 Pacific Omega Copper

	MT
Stars (1-150):	20-40X
Production 45 sets	

2000 Pacific Omega Platinum Blue

	MT
Stars (1-150):	15-35X
Production 55 sets	

2000 Pacific Omega Premiere Date

	MT
Stars (1-150):	15-30X
Production 77 sets	

2000 Pacific Omega Gold

	MT
Stars (1-150):	8-15X
Production 120 sets	
(Retail only, one per box)	

2000 Pacific Omega EO Portraits

		MT
Complete Set (20):		250.00
Common Player:		4.00
Inserted 1:73		
1	Chipper Jones	15.00
2	Greg Maddux	15.00
3	Cal Ripken Jr.	30.00
4	Pedro Martinez	8.00
5	Nomar Garciaparra	20.00
6	Sammy Sosa	20.00
7	Frank Thomas	8.00
8	Ken Griffey Jr.	25.00
9	Gary Sheffield	4.00
10	Vladimir Guerrero	8.00
11	Mike Piazza	25.00
12	Roger Clemens	10.00
13	Derek Jeter	30.00
14	Pat Burrell	6.00
15	Tony Gwynn	10.00
16	Barry Bonds	10.00
17	Alex Rodriguez	25.00
18	Rick Ankiel	4.00
19	Mark McGwire	25.00
20	Ivan Rodriguez	6.00

2000 Pacific Omega Full Court

		MT
Complete Set (36):		60.00
Common Player:		.75
Inserted 4:37 H		
1	Magglio Ordonez	1.00
2	Manny Ramirez	2.00
3	Todd Helton	2.00
4	David Justice	1.00
5	Bernie Williams	1.50
6	Jason Giambi	1.50
7	Scott Rolen	1.50
8	Jeff Kent	.75
9	Edgar Martinez	.75
10	Randy Johnson	2.00
11	Greg Maddux	4.00
12	Mike Mussina	1.50
13	Pedro Martinez	2.00
14	Chuck Finley	.75
15	Kevin Brown	.75
16	Roger Clemens	3.00
17	Tim Hudson	1.00
18	Rick Ankiel	1.00
19	Troy Glaus	1.50
20	Chipper Jones	4.00
21	Nomar Garciaparra	5.00
22	Jeff Bagwell	2.00
23	Shawn Green	1.00
24	Vladimir Guerrero	2.00
25	Mike Piazza	6.00
26	Jim Edmonds	.75
27	Rafael Palmeiro	1.50
28	Cal Ripken Jr.	8.00
29	Sammy Sosa	5.00
30	Frank Thomas	2.50
31	Ken Griffey Jr.	6.00
32	Gary Sheffield	1.00
33	Barry Bonds	2.50
34	Alex Rodriguez	6.00
35	Mark McGwire	6.00
36	Carlos Delgado	1.50

2000 Pacific Omega AL Contenders

		MT
Complete Set (18):		50.00
Common Player:		1.00
Inserted 2:37		
1	Darin Erstad	1.50
2	Troy Glaus	2.50
3	Mo Vaughn	1.50
4	Albert Belle	1.00
5	Cal Ripken Jr.	10.00
6	Nomar Garciaparra	6.00
7	Pedro Martinez	2.50
8	Frank Thomas	3.00
9	Manny Ramirez	2.50
10	Jim Thome	1.50
11	Juan Gonzalez	2.50
12	Roger Clemens	3.00
13	Derek Jeter	10.00
14	Bernie Williams	2.00
15	Jason Giambi	2.00
16	Alex Rodriguez	8.00
17	Edgar Martinez	1.00
18	Carlos Delgado	2.00

2000 Pacific Omega NL Contenders

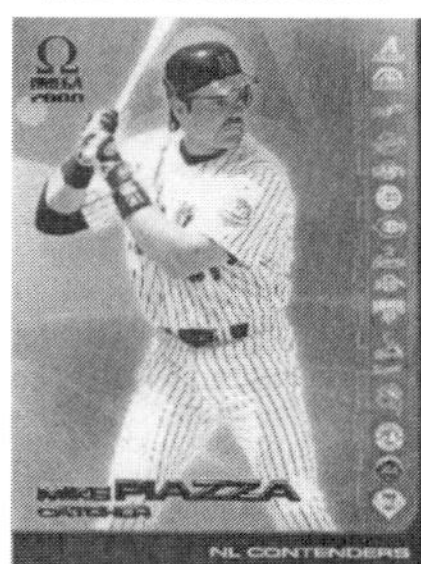

		MT
Complete Set (18):		50.00
Common Player:		1.00
Inserted 2:37		
1	Randy Johnson	2.50
2	Chipper Jones	5.00
3	Greg Maddux	5.00
4	Sammy Sosa	6.00
5	Sean Casey	1.50
6	Ken Griffey Jr.	8.00
7	Todd Helton	2.50
8	Jeff Bagwell	2.50
9	Shawn Green	1.50
10	Gary Sheffield	1.00
11	Vladimir Guerrero	2.50
12	Mike Piazza	8.00
13	Scott Rolen	2.00
14	Barry Bonds	4.00
15	Rick Ankiel	1.00
16	J.D. Drew	1.50
17	Jim Edmonds	1.00
18	Mark McGwire	8.00

2000 Pacific Omega MLB Generations

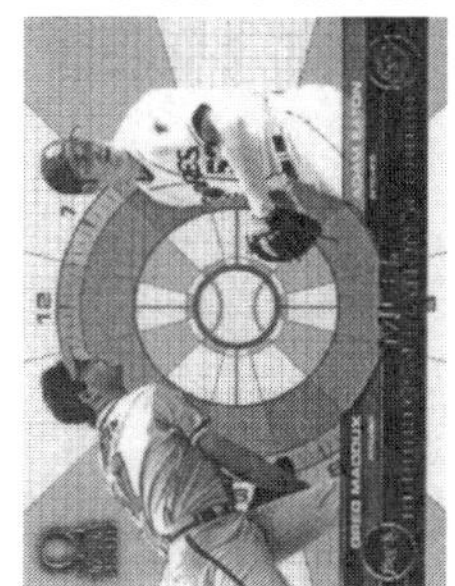

		MT
Complete Set (20):		275.00
Common Card:		6.00
Inserted 1:145		
1	Mark McGwire, Pat Burrell	35.00
2	Cal Ripken Jr., Alex Rodriguez	40.00
3	Randy Johnson, Rick Ankiel	8.00
4	Tony Gwynn, Darin Erstad	15.00
5	Barry Bonds, Magglio Ordonez	15.00
6	Frank Thomas, Jason Giambi	15.00
7	Roger Clemens, Kerry Wood	20.00
8	Mike Piazza, Mitch Meluskey	30.00
9	Ken Griffey Jr., Andruw Jones	30.00
10	Bernie Williams, J.D. Drew	8.00
11	Chipper Jones, Troy Glaus	20.00
12	Andres Galarraga, Todd Helton	8.00
13	Juan Gonzalez, Vladimir Guerrero	10.00
14	Craig Biggio, Rafael Furcal	6.00
15	Sammy Sosa, Jermaine Dye	20.00
16	Larry Walker, Richard Hidalgo	6.00
17	Greg Maddux, Adam Eaton	20.00
18	Barry Larkin, Derek Jeter	35.00
19	Roberto Alomar, Jose Vidro	8.00
20	Jeff Kent, Edgardo Alfonzo	6.00

2000 Pacific Omega Omega Signatures

		MT
Common Player:		10.00
1	Darin Erstad	25.00
2	Nomar Garciaparra	125.00
3	Cal Eldred	10.00
4	Magglio Ordonez	20.00
5	Frank Thomas	50.00
6	Brady Clark	10.00
7	Richard Hidalgo	15.00
8	Gary Sheffield	20.00
9	Pat Burrell	30.00
10	Jim Edmonds	25.00

2000 Pacific Omega Stellar Performers

		MT
Complete Set (20):		100.00
Common Player:		3.00
Inserted 1:37		
1	Darin Erstad	2.00
2	Chipper Jones	8.00
3	Greg Maddux	8.00
4	Cal Ripken Jr.	15.00
5	Pedro Martinez	4.00
6	Nomar Garciaparra	8.00
7	Sammy Sosa	10.00
8	Frank Thomas	4.00
9	Ken Griffey Jr.	12.00
10	Todd Helton	4.00
11	Jeff Bagwell	4.00
12	Vladimir Guerrero	4.00
13	Mike Piazza	10.00
14	Derek Jeter	15.00
15	Roger Clemens	5.00
16	Tony Gwynn	4.00
17	Barry Bonds	6.00
18	Alex Rodriguez	12.00
19	Mark McGwire	12.00
20	Ivan Rodriguez	3.00

A player's name in *italic* type indicates a rookie card.

2000 Pacific Paramount

	MT
Complete Set (250):	35.00
Common Player:	.10
Pack (6):	1.75
Wax Box (36):	50.00

No.	Player	MT
1	Garret Anderson	.10
2	Jim Edmonds	.10
3	Darin Erstad	.20
4	Chuck Finley	.10
5	Troy Glaus	.75
6	Troy Percival	.10
7	Tim Salmon	.20
8	Mo Vaughn	.40
9	Jay Bell	.10
10	Erubiel Durazo	.20
11	Steve Finley	.10
12	Luis Gonzalez	.10
13	Randy Johnson	.40
14	Travis Lee	.20
15	Matt Mantei	.10
16	Matt Williams	.25
17	Tony Womack	.10
18	Bret Boone	.10
19	Tom Glavine	.20
20	Andruw Jones	.40
21	Chipper Jones	1.00
22	Brian Jordan	.10
23	Javy Lopez	.15
24	Greg Maddux	1.00
25	Kevin Millwood	.20
26	John Rocker	.10
27	John Smoltz	.15
28	Brady Anderson	.15
29	Albert Belle	.40
30	Will Clark	.25
31	Charles Johnson	.10
32	Mike Mussina	.40
33	Cal Ripken Jr.	1.25
34	B.J. Surhoff	.10
35	Nomar Garciaparra	1.25
36	Derek Lowe	.10
37	Pedro Martinez	.50
38	Trot Nixon	.10
39	Troy O'Leary	.10
40	Jose Offerman	.10
41	John Valentin	.10
42	Jason Varitek	.10
43	Mark Grace	.20
44	Glenallen Hill	.10
45	Jon Lieber	.10
46	Cole Liniak	.10
47	Jose Nieves	.10
48	Henry Rodriguez	.10
49	Sammy Sosa	1.25
50	Kerry Wood	.40
51	Jason Dellaero	.10
52	Ray Durham	.10
53	Paul Konerko	.10
54	Carlos Lee	.10
55	Greg Norton	.10
56	Magglio Ordonez	.25
57	Chris Singleton	.10
58	Frank Thomas	.60
59	Aaron Boone	.10
60	Mike Cameron	.10
61	Sean Casey	.40
62	Pete Harnisch	.10
63	Barry Larkin	.25
64	Pokey Reese	.10
65	Greg Vaughn	.25
66	Scott Williamson	.10
67	Roberto Alomar	.40
68	*Sean DePaula*	.25
69	Travis Fryman	.20
70	David Justice	.20
71	Kenny Lofton	.40
72	Manny Ramirez	.50
73	Richie Sexson	.10
74	Jim Thome	.25
75	Omar Vizquel	.10
76	Pedro Astacio	.10
77	Vinny Castilla	.15
78	Derrick Gibson	.10
79	Todd Helton	.75
80	Neifi Perez	.10
81	Ben Petrick	.10
82	Larry Walker	.40
83	Brad Ausmus	.10
84	Tony Clark	.20
85	Deivi Cruz	.10
86	Damion Easley	.10
87	Juan Encarnacion	.10
88	Juan Gonzalez	.50
89	Bobby Higginson	.10
90	Dave Mlicki	.10
91	Dean Palmer	.15
92	Bruce Aven	.10
93	Luis Castillo	.10
94	Ramon Castro	.10
95	Cliff Floyd	.10
96	Alex Gonzalez	.10
97	Mike Lowell	.10
98	Preston Wilson	.10
99	Jeff Bagwell	.50
100	Derek Bell	.10
101	Craig Biggio	.30
102	Ken Caminiti	.15
103	Carl Everett	.15
104	Mike Hampton	.10
105	Jose Lima	.10
106	Billy Wagner	.10
107	Daryle Ward	.10
108	Carlos Beltran	.15
109	Johnny Damon	.10
110	Jermaine Dye	.10
111	Carlos Febles	.10
112	Mark Quinn	.10
113	Joe Randa	.10
114	Jose Rosado	.10
115	Mike Sweeney	.10
116	Kevin Brown	.15
117	Shawn Green	.40
118	Mark Grudzielanek	.10
119	Todd Hollandsworth	.10
120	Eric Karros	.15
121	Chan Ho Park	.15
122	Gary Sheffield	.25
123	Devon White	.10
124	Eric Young	.10
125	Kevin Barker	.10
126	Ron Belliard	.10
127	Jeromy Burnitz	.10
128	Jeff Cirillo	.10
129	Marquis Grissom	.10
130	Geoff Jenkins	.10
131	David Nilsson	.10
132	Chad Allen	.10
133	Ron Coomer	.10
134	Jacque Jones	.10
135	Corey Koskie	.10
136	Matt Lawton	.10
137	Brad Radke	.10
138	Todd Walker	.10
139	Michael Barrett	.10
140	Peter Bergeron	.10
141	Brad Fullmer	.10
142	Vladimir Guerrero	.75
143	Ugueth Urbina	.10
144	Jose Vidro	.10
145	Rondell White	.15
146	Edgardo Alfonzo	.20
147	Armando Benitez	.10
148	Roger Cedeno	.10
149	Rickey Henderson	.30
150	Melvin Mora	.10
151	John Olerud	.25
152	Rey Ordonez	.10
153	Mike Piazza	1.25
154	Jorge Toca	.10
155	Robin Ventura	.20
156	Roger Clemens	.75
157	David Cone	.20
158	Orlando Hernandez	.20
159	Derek Jeter	1.25
160	Chuck Knoblauch	.25
161	Ricky Ledee	.10
162	Tino Martinez	.25
163	Paul O'Neill	.20
164	Mariano Rivera	.20
165	Alfonso Soriano	.50
166	Bernie Williams	.40
167	Eric Chavez	.10
168	Jason Giambi	.10
169	Ben Grieve	.20
170	Tim Hudson	.20
171	John Jaha	.10
172	Matt Stairs	.10
173	Miguel Tejada	.10
174	Randy Velarde	.10
175	Bobby Abreu	.10
176	Marlon Anderson	.10
177	Rico Brogna	.10
178	Ron Gant	.20
179	Doug Glanville	.10
180	Mike Lieberthal	.10
181	Scott Rolen	.50
182	Curt Schilling	.15
183	Brian Giles	.10
184	Chad Hermansen	.10
185	Jason Kendall	.10
186	Al Martin	.10
187	Pat Meares	.10
188	Warren Morris	.10
189	Ed Sprague	.10
190	Kevin Young	.10
191	Rick Ankiel	.40
192	Kent Bottenfield	.10
193	Eric Davis	.20
194	J.D. Drew	.25
195	Adam Kennedy	.10
196	Ray Lankford	.10
197	Joe McEwing	.10
198	Mark McGwire	2.00
199	Edgar Renteria	.10
200	Fernando Tatis	.20
201	Mike Darr	.10
202	Ben Davis	.10
203	Tony Gwynn	1.00
204	Trevor Hoffman	.10
205	Damian Jackson	.10
206	Phil Nevin	.10
207	Reggie Sanders	.10
208	Quilvio Veras	.10
209	Rich Aurilia	.10
210	Marvin Benard	.10
211	Barry Bonds	.75
212	Ellis Burks	.10
213	Livan Hernandez	.10
214	Jeff Kent	.10
215	Russ Ortiz	.10
216	J.T. Snow	.10
217	Paul Abbott	.10
218	David Bell	.10
219	Freddy Garcia	.25
220	Ken Griffey Jr.	1.50
221	Carlos Guillen	.10
222	Brian Hunter	.10
223	Edgar Martinez	.15
224	Jamie Moyer	.10
225	Alex Rodriguez	1.50
226	Wade Boggs	.25
227	Miguel Cairo	.10
228	Jose Canseco	.50
229	Roberto Hernandez	.10
230	Dave Martinez	.10
231	Quinton McCracken	.10
232	Fred McGriff	.20
233	Kevin Stocker	.10
234	Royce Clayton	.10
235	Rusty Greer	.10
236	Ruben Mateo	.10
237	Rafael Palmeiro	.30
238	Ivan Rodriguez	.50
239	Aaron Sele	.10
240	John Wetteland	.10
241	Todd Zeile	.10
242	Tony Batista	.10
243	Homer Bush	.10
244	Carlos Delgado	.40
245	Tony Fernandez	.10
246	Billy Koch	.10
247	Raul Mondesi	.20
248	Shannon Stewart	.10
249	David Wells	.10
250	Vernon Wells	.10

2000 Pacific Paramount Premiere Date

	MT
Stars:	30x to 60x
Yng Stars & RCs:	15x to 40x

Production 50 sets

2000 Pacific Paramount Copper

	MT
Stars:	2x to 4x
Yng Stars & RCs:	1x to 2x

Inserted 1:1 H

2000 Pacific Paramount Holographic Silver

	MT
Stars:	20x to 40x
Yng Stars & RCs:	10x to 20x

Production 99 sets

2000 Pacific Paramount Platinum Blue

	MT
Stars:	25x to 50x
Yng Stars & RCs:	20x to 40x

Production 67 sets

2000 Pacific Paramount Ruby Red

	MT
Stars:	1-2X
RCs:	1X

Inserted 9 per 7-11 pack

2000 Pacific Paramount Holographic Gold

	MT
Stars:	10-20X
Young Stars/RCs:	5-10X

Production 199 sets

2000 Pacific Paramount Cooperstown Bound

	MT
Complete Set (10):	550.00
Common Player:	30.00

Inserted 1:361

No.	Player	MT
1	Greg Maddux	50.00
2	Cal Ripken Jr.	70.00

3	Nomar Garciaparra	60.00
4	Sammy Sosa	60.00
5	Roger Clemens	40.00
6	Derek Jeter	60.00
7	Mark McGwire	100.00
8	Tony Gwynn	50.00
9	Ken Griffey Jr.	80.00
10	Alex Rodriguez	70.00

2000 Pacific Paramount Double Vision

		MT
Complete Set (36):		350.00
Common Player:		3.00
Inserted 1:37		
1	Chipper Jones	15.00
2	Cal Ripken Jr.	15.00
3	Nomar Garciaparra	15.00
4	Pedro Martinez	6.00
5	Sammy Sosa	15.00
6	Manny Ramirez	6.00
7	Jeff Bagwell	6.00
8	Craig Biggio	3.00
9	Vladimir Guerrero	10.00
10	Mike Piazza	15.00
11	Roger Clemens	10.00
12	Derek Jeter	15.00
13	Mark McGwire	25.00
14	Tony Gwynn	12.00
15	Ken Griffey Jr.	20.00
16	Alex Rodriguez	20.00
17	Rafael Palmeiro	4.00
18	Ivan Rodriguez	6.00
19	Chipper Jones	12.00
20	Cal Ripken Jr.	15.00
21	Nomar Garciaparra	15.00
22	Pedro Martinez	6.00
23	Sammy Sosa	15.00
24	Manny Ramirez	6.00
25	Jeff Bagwell	6.00
26	Craig Biggio	3.00
27	Vladimir Guerrero	10.00
28	Mike Piazza	15.00
29	Roger Clemens	10.00
30	Derek Jeter	15.00
31	Mark McGwire	25.00
32	Tony Gwynn	12.00
33	Ken Griffey Jr.	20.00
34	Alex Rodriguez	20.00
35	Rafael Palmeiro	4.00
36	Ivan Rodriguez	6.00

Figure values of lower-grade cards from 1981-date as:
Near Mint (NM) 75%
Excellent (EX) 40%
of the listed Mint price

For cards through 1980, values should be figured as:
Excellent (EX) 50%
Very Good (VG) 30%
of the listed
Near Mint price

2000 Pacific Paramount Fielder's Choice

		MT
Complete Set (20):		400.00
Common Player:		8.00
Inserted 1:73		
1	Andruw Jones	10.00
2	Chipper Jones	25.00
3	Greg Maddux	25.00
4	Cal Ripken Jr.	30.00
5	Nomar Garciaparra	30.00
6	Sammy Sosa	30.00
7	Sean Casey	8.00
8	Manny Ramirez	15.00
9	Larry Walker	12.00
10	Jeff Bagwell	15.00
11	Mike Piazza	30.00
12	Derek Jeter	30.00
13	Bernie Williams	12.00
14	Scott Rolen	15.00
15	Mark McGwire	50.00
16	Tony Gwynn	25.00
17	Barry Bonds	15.00
18	Ken Griffey Jr.	40.00
19	Alex Rodriguez	35.00
20	Ivan Rodriguez	15.00

2000 Pacific Paramount Season in Review

		MT
Complete Set (30):		125.00
Common Player:		2.00
Inserted 2:37		
1	Randy Johnson	3.00
2	Matt Williams	2.00
3	Chipper Jones	8.00
4	Greg Maddux	8.00
5	Cal Ripken Jr.	10.00
6	Nomar Garciaparra	10.00
7	Pedro Martinez	4.00
8	Sammy Sosa	10.00
9	Manny Ramirez	4.00
10	Larry Walker	3.00
11	Jeff Bagwell	4.00
12	Craig Biggio	2.00
13	Carlos Beltran	2.00
14	Mark Quinn	2.00
15	Vladimir Guerrero	6.00
16	Mike Piazza	10.00
17	Robin Ventura	2.00
18	Roger Clemens	5.00
19	David Cone	2.00
20	Derek Jeter	10.00
21	Mark McGwire	15.00
22	Fernando Tatis	2.00
23	Tony Gwynn	8.00
24	Barry Bonds	4.00
25	Ken Griffey Jr.	12.00
26	Alex Rodriguez	12.00
27	Wade Boggs	2.50
28	Jose Canseco	4.00
29	Rafael Palmeiro	3.00
30	Ivan Rodriguez	4.00

2000 Pacific Prism

		MT
Complete Set (150):		70.00
Common Player:		.40
Pack (5):		4.00
Wax Box (24):		80.00
1	*Jeff DaVanon*	.50
2	Troy Glaus	1.50
3	Tim Salmon	.75
4	Mo Vaughn	1.00
5	Jay Bell	.40
6	Erubiel Durazo	1.00
7	Luis Gonzalez	.50
8	Randy Johnson	1.25
9	Matt Williams	1.00
10	Andres Galarraga	1.00
11	Andruw Jones	1.00
12	Chipper Jones	3.00
13	Brian Jordan	.40
14	Greg Maddux	3.00
15	Kevin Millwood	.75
16	John Smoltz	.50
17	Albert Belle	1.00
18	Mike Mussina	1.25
19	Calvin Pickering	.40
20	Cal Ripken Jr.	5.00
21	B.J. Surhoff	.50
22	Nomar Garciaparra	4.00
23	Pedro Martinez	1.50
24	Troy O'Leary	.50
25	John Valentin	.40
26	Jason Varitek	.40
27	Mark Grace	.75
28	Henry Rodriguez	.50
29	Sammy Sosa	4.00
30	Kerry Wood	1.00
31	Ray Durham	.40
32	Carlos Lee	.40
33	Magglio Ordonez	.75
34	Chris Singleton	.40
35	Frank Thomas	2.00
36	Sean Casey	.75
37	Travis Dawkins	.40
38	Barry Larkin	1.00
39	Pokey Reese	.40
40	Scott Williamson	.40
41	Roberto Alomar	1.25
42	Bartolo Colon	.50
43	David Justice	.75
44	Manny Ramirez	1.50
45	Richie Sexson	.40
46	Jim Thome	1.00
47	Omar Vizquel	.60
48	Pedro Astacio	.40
49	Todd Helton	1.50
50	Neifi Perez	.40
51	Ben Petrick	.40
52	Larry Walker	1.00
53	Tony Clark	.75
54	Damion Easley	.40
55	Juan Gonzalez	1.50
56	Dean Palmer	.40
57	A.J. Burnett	.40
58	Luis Castillo	.40
59	Cliff Floyd	.40
60	Alex Gonzalez	.40
61	Preston Wilson	.40
62	Jeff Bagwell	1.50
63	Craig Biggio	1.00
64	Ken Caminiti	.60
65	Jose Lima	.40
66	Billy Wagner	.40
67	Carlos Beltran	.40
68	Johnny Damon	.40
69	Jermaine Dye	.50
70	Carlos Febles	.40
71	Mike Sweeney	.40
72	Kevin Brown	.75
73	Shawn Green	1.00
74	Eric Karros	.75
75	Chan Ho Park	.75
76	Gary Sheffield	.75
77	Ron Belliard	.40
78	Jeromy Burnitz	.50
79	Marquis Grissom	.40
80	Geoff Jenkins	.50
81	Mark Loretta	.40
82	Ron Coomer	.40
83	Jacque Jones	.40
84	Corey Koskie	.40
85	Brad Radke	.40
86	Todd Walker	.40
87	Michael Barrett	.40
88	Peter Bergeron	.40
89	Vladimir Guerrero	3.00
90	Jose Vidro	.40
91	Rondell White	.60
92	Edgardo Alfonzo	.60
93	Rickey Henderson	.75
94	Rey Ordonez	.40
95	Mike Piazza	4.00
96	Robin Ventura	.75
97	Roger Clemens	2.50
98	Orlando Hernandez	1.00
99	Derek Jeter	4.00
100	Tino Martinez	.75
101	Mariano Rivera	.75
102	Alfonso Soriano	1.50
103	Bernie Williams	1.00
104	Eric Chavez	.50
105	Jason Giambi	.50
106	Ben Grieve	.75
107	Tim Hudson	.75
108	John Jaha	.40
109	Bobby Abreu	.75
110	Doug Glanville	.40
111	Mike Lieberthal	.40
112	Scott Rolen	1.50
113	Curt Schilling	.75
114	Brian Giles	.50
115	Jason Kendall	.75
116	Warren Morris	.40
117	Kevin Young	.40
118	Rick Ankiel	.75
119	J.D. Drew	.50
120	Chad Hutchinson	.40
121	Ray Lankford	.40
122	Mark McGwire	6.00
123	Fernando Tatis	.50
124	Bret Boone	.40
125	Ben Davis	.40
126	Tony Gwynn	3.00
127	Trevor Hoffman	.40
128	Barry Bonds	1.50
129	Ellis Burks	.40
130	Jeff Kent	.40
131	J.T. Snow	.40
132	Freddy Garcia	.75
133	Ken Griffey Jr.	6.00
134	Edgar Martinez	.40
135	John Olerud	.75
136	Alex Rodriguez	5.00
137	Jose Canseco	1.50
138	Vinny Castilla	.50
139	Roberto Hernandez	.50
140	Fred McGriff	.75
141	Rusty Greer	.50
142	Ruben Mateo	.75
143	Rafael Palmeiro	1.00
144	Ivan Rodriguez	1.50
145	Lee Stevens	.40
146	Tony Batista	.50
147	Carlos Delgado	1.00
148	Shannon Stewart	.40
149	David Wells	.40
150	Vernon Wells	.50

2000 Pacific Prism Holographic Blue

	MT
Stars:	8x-15x
Production 80 sets	

2000 Pacific Prism Holographic Mirror

	MT
Stars:	4x-8x
Production 160 sets	

2000 Pacific Prism Holographic Gold

	MT
Stars:	1x-2x
Production 480 sets	

2000 Pacific Prism Silver Drops

	MT
Stars:	1X-2X
Yng. Stars & RCs:	1X

2000 Pacific Prism Holographic Purple

	MT
Stars:	6X-10X
Production 99 sets	

2000 Pacific Prism Premiere Date

	MT
Stars:	8X-15X
Production 61 sets	

2000 Pacific Prism Rapture Silver

	MT
Stars:	1X-2X
Yng. Stars & RCs:	1X

2000 Pacific Prism A.L. Legends

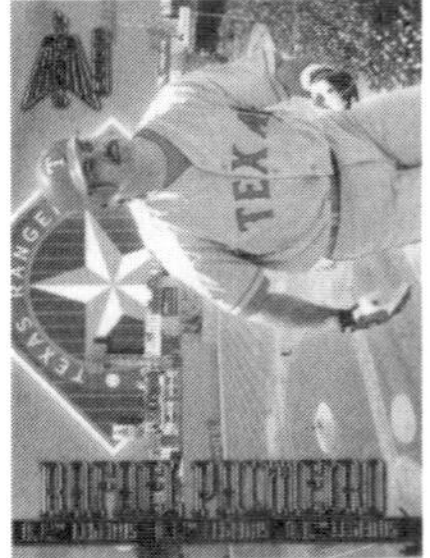

		MT
Complete Set (10):		40.00
Common Player:		1.50
Inserted 1:25		
1	Mo Vaughn	1.50
2	Cal Ripken Jr.	10.00
3	Nomar Garciaparra	6.00
4	Manny Ramirez	3.00
5	Roger Clemens	4.00
6	Derek Jeter	10.00
7	Ken Griffey Jr.	8.00
8	Alex Rodriguez	8.00
9	Jose Canseco	2.00
10	Rafael Palmeiro	2.00

2000 Pacific Prism N.L. Legends

		MT
Complete Set (10):		35.00
Common Player:		1.50
Inserted 1:25		
1	Chipper Jones	5.00
2	Greg Maddux	5.00
3	Sammy Sosa	6.00
4	Larry Walker	1.50
5	Jeff Bagwell	3.00
6	Vladimir Guerrero	3.00
7	Mike Piazza	6.00
8	Mark McGwire	8.00
9	Tony Gwynn	3.00
10	Barry Bonds	4.00

2000 Pacific Prism Center Stage

		MT
Complete Set (20):		100.00
Common Player:		1.50
Inserted 1:25		
1	Chipper Jones	8.00
2	Cal Ripken Jr.	15.00
3	Nomar Garciaparra	10.00
4	Pedro Martinez	4.00
5	Sammy Sosa	10.00
6	Sean Casey	2.50
7	Manny Ramirez	4.00
8	Jim Thome	2.50
9	Jeff Bagwell	4.00
10	Carlos Beltran	1.50
11	Vladimir Guerrero	4.00
12	Mike Piazza	10.00
13	Derek Jeter	15.00
14	Bernie Williams	3.00
15	Scott Rolen	3.00
16	Mark McGwire	12.00
17	Tony Gwynn	5.00
18	Ken Griffey Jr.	12.00
19	Alex Rodriguez	12.00
20	Ivan Rodriguez	3.00

A card number in parentheses ( ) indicates the set is unnumbered.

2000 Pacific Prism Diamond Dial-A-Stats

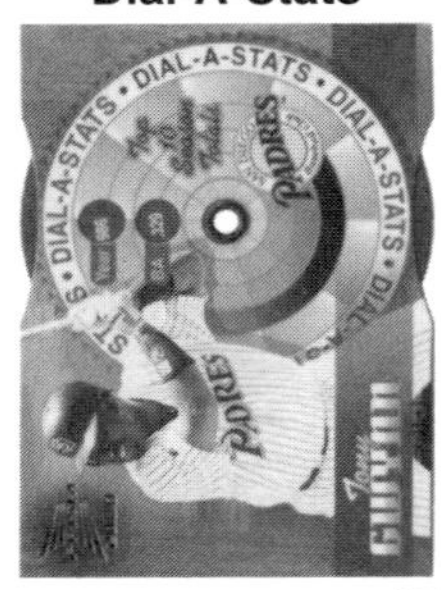

		MT
Complete Set (10):		200.00
Common Player:		10.00
Inserted 1:193		
1	Chipper Jones	20.00
2	Greg Maddux	20.00
3	Cal Ripken Jr.	40.00
4	Sammy Sosa	25.00
5	Mike Piazza	25.00
6	Roger Clemens	15.00
7	Mark McGwire	30.00
8	Tony Gwynn	15.00
9	Ken Griffey Jr.	30.00
10	Alex Rodriguez	30.00

2000 Pacific Prism Prospects

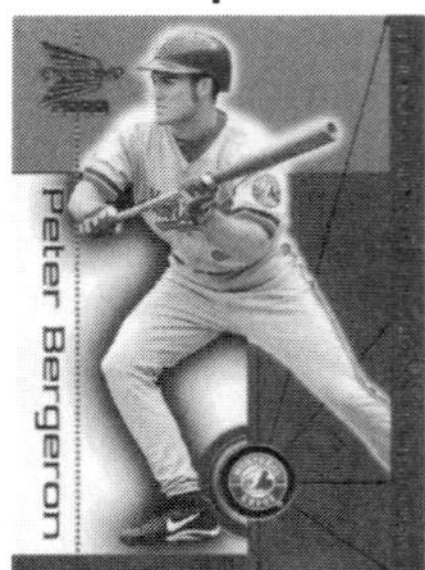

		MT
Complete Set (10):		35.00
Common Player:		4.00
Inserted 1:97		
1	Erubiel Durazo	4.00
2	Wilton Veras	4.00
3	Ben Petrick	4.00
4	Mark Quinn	4.00
5	Peter Bergeron	4.00
6	Alfonso Soriano	8.00
7	Tim Hudson	6.00
8	Chad Hermansen	4.00
9	Rick Ankiel	6.00
10	Ruben Mateo	4.00

2000 Pacific Private Stock

This base set consists of 150-cards, each card image uses an artist's computer generated brush strokes. Short-printed prospects are seeded 1:4 packs. The logo, player name and team are stamped in gold foil.

		MT
Complete Set (150):		125.00
Common Player:		.25
Common SP Prospect:		2.00
Inserted 1:4		
Pack (7):		4.00
Wax Box (24):		85.00
1	Darin Erstad	.50
2	Troy Glaus	1.50
3	Tim Salmon	.40
4	Mo Vaughn	1.00
5	Jay Bell	.25
6	Luis Gonzalez	.25
7	Randy Johnson	1.00
8	Matt Williams	.75
9	Andruw Jones	1.00
10	Chipper Jones	2.50
11	Brian Jordan	.25
12	Greg Maddux	2.50
13	Kevin Millwood	.50
14	Albert Belle	1.00
15	Mike Mussina	1.00
16	Cal Ripken Jr.	3.00
17	B.J. Surhoff	.25
18	Nomar Garciaparra	3.00
19	Butch Huskey	.25
20	Pedro Martinez	1.50
21	Troy O'Leary	.25
22	Mark Grace	.50
23	Bo Porter (SP)	2.00
24	Henry Rodriguez	.25
25	Sammy Sosa	3.00
26	Kerry Wood	.75
27	Jason Dellaero (SP)	3.00
28	Ray Durham	.25
29	Paul Konerko	.25
30	Carlos Lee	.25
31	Magglio Ordonez	.50
32	Frank Thomas	1.50
33	Mike Cameron	.25
34	Sean Casey	.75
35	Barry Larkin	.75
36	Greg Vaughn	.50
37	Roberto Alomar	1.00
38	Russell Branyan (SP)	3.00
39	Kenny Lofton	1.00
40	Manny Ramirez	1.50
41	Richie Sexson	.25
42	Jim Thome	.75
43	Omar Vizquel	.25
44	Dante Bichette	.50
45	Vinny Castilla	.40
46	Todd Helton	1.00
47	Ben Petrick (SP)	3.00
48	Juan Sosa (SP)	3.00
49	Larry Walker	1.00
50	Tony Clark	.50
51	Damion Easley	.25
52	Juan Encarnacion	.25
53	Robert Fick (SP)	2.00
54	Dean Palmer	.25
55	A.J. Burnett (SP)	4.00
56	Luis Castillo	.25
57	Alex Gonzalez	.25
58	Julio Ramirez (SP)	3.00
59	Preston Wilson	.25
60	Jeff Bagwell	1.50
61	Craig Biggio	.75
62	Ken Caminiti	.40
63	Carl Everett	.25
64	Mike Hampton	.25
65	Billy Wagner	.25
66	Carlos Beltran	.25
67	Dermal Brown (SP)	2.00
68	Jermaine Dye	.25

69	Carlos Febles	.25
70	Mark Quinn (SP)	4.00
71	Mike Sweeney	.25
72	Kevin Brown	.40
73	Eric Gagne (SP)	2.00
74	Eric Karros	.40
75	Raul Mondesi	.40
76	Gary Sheffield	.50
77	Jeromy Burnitz	.25
78	Jeff Cirillo	.25
79	Geoff Jenkins	.25
80	David Nilsson	.25
81	Ron Coomer	.25
82	Jacque Jones	.25
83	Corey Koskie	.25
84	Brad Radke	.25
85	Tony Armas Jr. (SP)	3.00
86	Peter Bergeron (SP)	3.00
87	Vladimir Guerrero	2.00
88	Jose Vidro	.25
89	Rondell White	.40
90	Edgardo Alfonzo	.50
91	Roger Cedeno	.25
92	Rickey Henderson	.75
93	Jay Payton (SP)	2.00
94	Mike Piazza	3.00
95	Jorge Toca (SP)	4.00
96	Robin Ventura	.50
97	Roger Clemens	2.00
98	David Cone	.40
99	Derek Jeter	3.00
100	D'Angelo Jimenez (SP)	2.00
101	Tino Martinez	.50
102	Alfonso Soriano (SP)	8.00
103	Bernie Williams	1.00
104	Jason Giambi	.25
105	Ben Grieve	.50
106	Tim Hudson	.50
107	Matt Stairs	.25
108	Bobby Abreu	.25
109	Doug Glanville	.25
110	Scott Rolen	1.50
111	Curt Schilling	.40
112	Brian Giles	.25
113	Chad Hermansen (SP)	3.00
114	Jason Kendall	.25
115	Warren Morris	.25
116	Rick Ankiel (SP)	6.00
117	J.D. Drew	.25
118	Adam Kennedy (SP)	2.00
119	Ray Lankford	.25
120	Mark McGwire	5.00
121	Fernando Tatis	.50
122	Mike Darr (SP)	2.00
123	Ben Davis	.25
124	Tony Gwynn	2.50
125	Trevor Hoffman	.25
126	Reggie Sanders	.25
127	Barry Bonds	2.00
128	Ellis Burks	.25
129	Jeff Kent	.25
130	J.T. Snow	.25
131	Freddy Garcia	.75
132	Ken Griffey Jr.	4.00
133	Carlos Guillen (SP)	2.00
134	Edgar Martinez	.25
135	Alex Rodriguez	4.00
136	Miguel Cairo	.25
137	Jose Canseco	1.00
138	Steve Cox (SP)	2.00
139	Roberto Hernandez	.25
140	Fred McGriff	.50
141	Juan Gonzalez	1.50
142	Rusty Greer	.25
143	Ruben Mateo (SP)	3.00
144	Rafael Palmeiro	.75
145	Ivan Rodriguez	1.50
146	Carlos Delgado	.75
147	Tony Fernandez	.25
148	Shawn Green	1.00
149	Shannon Stewart	.25
150	Vernon Wells (SP)	3.00

2000 Pacific Private Stock Premiere Date

A parallel to the 150-card base set these are limited to 34 serial numbered sets.

	MT
Stars:	20x to 40x
Prospects:	3x to 5x
Inserted 1:24	

2000 Pacific Private Stock Silver Portraits

A parallel to the 150-card base set. These have a silver foiled border. Found exclusively in retail packs, these are limited to 199 serial numbered sets.

	MT
Stars:	5x to 10x
Prospects:	1x to 2x
Production 199 sets	

2000 Pacific Private Stock Extreme Action

The focus of this 20-card set is the action photography, hence the name Extreme Action. They are seeded 2:25 packs.

		MT
Complete Set (20):		70.00
Common Player:		1.50
Inserted 2:25		
1	Andruw Jones	2.00
2	Chipper Jones	5.00
3	Cal Ripken Jr.	10.00
4	Nomar Garciaparra	6.00
5	Sammy Sosa	6.00
6	Frank Thomas	3.00
7	Roberto Alomar	2.00
8	Manny Ramirez	3.00
9	Larry Walker	1.50
10	Jeff Bagwell	3.00
11	Vladimir Guerrero	3.00
12	Mike Piazza	6.00
13	Derek Jeter	10.00
14	Bernie Williams	2.00
15	Scott Rolen	2.00
16	Mark McGwire	8.00
17	Tony Gwynn	3.00
18	Ken Griffey Jr.	8.00
19	Alex Rodriguez	8.00
20	Ivan Rodriguez	2.00

2000 Pacific Private Stock Gold Portraits

A parallel to the 150-card base set these have a gold foiled border. These are found exclusively in hobby packs and are limited to 99 serial numbered sets.

	MT
Stars:	10x to 20x
Prospects:	1.5x to 3x
Production 99 sets	

2000 Pacific Private Stock Private Stock Canvas

This 20-card set is printed on real artist's canvas and have the look of a miniature piece of art. They are seeded 1:49 packs.

		MT
Complete Set (20):		300.00
Common Player:		6.00
Inserted 1:49		
1	Chipper Jones	20.00
2	Greg Maddux	20.00
3	Cal Ripken Jr.	40.00
4	Nomar Garciaparra	25.00
5	Sammy Sosa	25.00
6	Frank Thomas	10.00
7	Manny Ramirez	10.00
8	Larry Walker	6.00
9	Jeff Bagwell	10.00
10	Vladimir Guerrero	10.00
11	Mike Piazza	30.00
12	Roger Clemens	15.00
13	Derek Jeter	40.00
14	Mark McGwire	35.00
15	Tony Gwynn	15.00
16	Barry Bonds	15.00
17	Ken Griffey Jr.	35.00
18	Alex Rodriguez	30.00
19	Juan Gonzalez	10.00
20	Ivan Rodriguez	8.00

2000 Pacific Private Stock PS-2000

This miniature 60-card set has a white border with gold foil stamping and are seeded 2 per pack.

		MT
Complete Set (60):		40.00
Common Player:		.25
Inserted 2:pack		
1	Mo Vaughn	.75
2	Greg Maddux	2.00
3	Andruw Jones	.75
4	Chipper Jones	2.00
5	Cal Ripken Jr.	2.50
6	Nomar Garciaparra	2.50
7	Pedro Martinez	1.00
8	Sammy Sosa	2.50
9	Jason Dellaero	.25
10	Magglio Ordonez	.25
11	Frank Thomas	1.00
12	Sean Casey	.50
13	Russell Branyan	.25
14	Manny Ramirez	1.00
15	Richie Sexson	.25
16	Ben Petrick	.25
17	Juan Sosa	.25
18	Larry Walker	.75
19	Robert Fick	.25
20	Craig Biggio	.50
21	Jeff Bagwell	1.00
22	Carlos Beltran	.25
23	Dermal Brown	.25
24	Mark Quinn	.25
25	Eric Gagne	.25
26	Jeromy Burnitz	.25
27	Tony Armas Jr.	.25
28	Peter Bergeron	.25
29	Vladimir Guerrero	1.50
30	Edgardo Alfonzo	.50
31	Mike Piazza	2.50
32	Jorge Toca	.25
33	Roger Clemens	1.50
34	Alfonso Soriano	1.00
35	Bernie Williams	.75
36	Derek Jeter	2.50
37	Tim Hudson	.50
38	Bobby Abreu	.25
39	Scott Rolen	1.00
40	Brian Giles	.25
41	Chad Hermansen	.25
42	Warren Morris	.25
43	Rick Ankiel	1.00
44	J.D. Drew	.50
45	Adam Kennedy	.25
46	Mark McGwire	4.00
47	Mike Darr	.25
48	Tony Gwynn	2.00
49	Barry Bonds	1.00
50	Ken Griffey Jr.	3.00
51	Carlos Guillen	.25
52	Alex Rodriguez	3.00
53	Juan Gonzalez	1.00
54	Ruben Mateo	.50
55	Ivan Rodriguez	1.00
56	Rafael Palmeiro	.50
57	Jose Canseco	1.00
58	Steve Cox	.25
59	Shawn Green	.75
60	Vernon Wells	.25

2000 Pacific Private Stock PS-2000 Stars

This miniature 20-card set is limited to 299 serial numbered sets.

		MT
Complete Set (20):		100.00
Common Player:		3.00
Production 299 sets		
1	Mo Vaughn	3.00
2	Greg Maddux	10.00
3	Cal Ripken Jr.	20.00
4	Pedro Martinez	5.00
5	Sammy Sosa	12.00
6	Frank Thomas	5.00
7	Larry Walker	3.00
8	Craig Biggio	3.00
9	Jeff Bagwell	5.00
10	Mike Piazza	12.00
11	Roger Clemens	8.00
12	Bernie Williams	4.00
13	Mark McGwire	15.00
14	Tony Gwynn	6.00
15	Barry Bonds	6.00
16	Ken Griffey Jr.	15.00
17	Juan Gonzalez	5.00
18	Ivan Rodriguez	4.00
19	Rafael Palmeiro	3.00
20	Jose Canseco	4.00

2000 Pacific Private Stock PS-2000 New Wave

This miniature 20-card set has copper foil stamping and is limited to 199 serial numbered sets.

		MT
Complete Set (20):		160.00
Common Player:		3.00
Production 199 sets		
1	Andruw Jones	8.00
2	Chipper Jones	20.00
3	Nomar Garciaparra	30.00
4	Magglio Ordonez	5.00
5	Sean Casey	8.00
6	Manny Ramirez	12.00
7	Richie Sexson	3.00
8	Carlos Beltran	3.00
9	Jeromy Burnitz	3.00
10	Vladimir Guerrero	15.00
11	Edgardo Alfonzo	5.00
12	Derek Jeter	30.00
13	Tim Hudson	3.00
14	Bobby Abreu	3.00
15	Scott Rolen	12.00
16	Brian Giles	3.00
17	Warren Morris	3.00
18	J.D. Drew	4.00
19	Alex Rodriguez	35.00
20	Shawn Green	8.00

2000 Pacific Private Stock PS-2000 Rookies

This miniature 20-card set has holographic silver foil stamping and is limited to 99 serial numbered sets.

		MT
Complete Set (20):		90.00
Common Player:		6.00
Inserted 99 sets		
1	Jason Dellaero	6.00
2	Russell Branyan	6.00
3	Ben Petrick	6.00
4	Juan Sosa	6.00
5	Robert Fick	6.00
6	Dermal Brown	6.00
7	Mark Quinn	8.00
8	Eric Gagne	6.00
9	Tony Armas Jr.	6.00
10	Peter Bergeron	6.00
11	Jorge Toca	6.00
12	Alfonso Soriano	15.00
13	Chad Hermansen	6.00
14	Rick Ankiel	8.00
15	Adam Kennedy	6.00
16	Mike Darr	6.00
17	Carlos Guillen	6.00
18	Steve Cox	6.00
19	Ruben Mateo	6.00
20	Vernon Wells	8.00

2000 Pacific Private Stock Reserve

Found exclusively in hobby packs these have a paper thin stock, enhanced with gold foil stamping. These are seeded 1:25 packs.

		MT
Complete Set (20):		150.00
Common Player:		2.50
Inserted 1:25		
1	Chipper Jones	10.00
2	Greg Maddux	10.00
3	Cal Ripken Jr.	20.00
4	Nomar Garciaparra	12.00
5	Sammy Sosa	12.00
6	Frank Thomas	6.00
7	Manny Ramirez	5.00
8	Larry Walker	3.00
9	Jeff Bagwell	5.00
10	Vladimir Guerrero	5.00
11	Mike Piazza	15.00
12	Roger Clemens	8.00
13	Derek Jeter	20.00
14	Mark McGwire	15.00
15	Tony Gwynn	6.00
16	Barry Bonds	6.00
17	Ken Griffey Jr.	15.00
18	Alex Rodriguez	15.00
19	Ivan Rodriguez	4.00
20	Shawn Green	2.50

2000 Pacific Revolution

The base set consists of 150 cards with silver holofoil throughout the card front. "Revolution" is embossed on the left portion and the logo is stamped in gold foil. Twenty- five short-printed prospects are seeded 1:4 packs.

		MT
Complete Set (150):		150.00
Common Player:		.50
Common SP:		2.00
Pack (3):		4.00
Box:		80.00
1	Darin Erstad	.75
2	Troy Glaus	2.00
3	Adam Kennedy SP	2.00
4	Mo Vaughn	1.00
5	Erubiel Durazo	.50
6	Steve Finley	.50
7	Luis Gonzalez	.75
8	Randy Johnson	2.00
9	Travis Lee	.50
10	Vicente Padilla SP	2.00
11	Matt Williams	.75
12	Rafael Furcal SP	2.00
13	Andres Galarraga	1.00
14	Andruw Jones	1.00
15	Chipper Jones	4.00
16	Greg Maddux	4.00
17	Luis Rivera SP	2.00
18	Albert Belle	1.00
19	Mike Bordick	.50
20	Will Clark	.75
21	Mike Mussina	1.00
22	Cal Ripken Jr.	6.00
23	B.J. Surhoff	.50
24	Carl Everett	.50
25	Nomar Garciaparra	5.00
26	Pedro Martinez	2.00
27	Jason Varitek	.50
28	Wilton Veras SP	3.00
29	Shane Andrews	.50
30	*Scott Downs SP*	2.00
31	Mark Grace	.75
32	Sammy Sosa	5.00
33	Kerry Wood	.75
34	Ray Durham	.50
35	Paul Konerko	.50
36	Carlos Lee	.50
37	Magglio Ordonez	.75
38	Frank Thomas	3.00
39	Rob Bell SP	2.00
40	Sean Casey	.50
41	Ken Griffey Jr.	6.00
42	Barry Larkin	1.00
43	Pokey Reese	.50
44	Roberto Alomar	1.50
45	David Justice	.75
46	Kenny Lofton	.75
47	Manny Ramirez	2.00
48	Richie Sexson	.50
49	Jim Thome	1.00
50	Jeff Cirillo	.75
51	Jeffrey Hammonds	.50
52	Todd Helton	2.00
53	Larry Walker	1.00
54	Tony Clark	.50
55	Juan Gonzalez	2.00
56	Hideo Nomo	.50
57	Dean Palmer	.50
58	Alex Gonzalez	.50
59	Mike Lowell	.50
60	Pablo Ozuna SP	2.00
61	Brad Penny SP	2.00
62	Preston Wilson	.50
63	Moises Alou	.50
64	Jeff Bagwell	2.00
65	Craig Biggio	.75
66	Ken Caminiti	.50
67	Julio Lugo SP	2.00
68	Carlos Beltran	.50
69	Johnny Damon	.50
70	Jermaine Dye	.50
71	Carlos Febles	.50
72	Mark Quinn SP	3.00
73	Kevin Brown	.75
74	Shawn Green	1.00
75	Chan Ho Park	.50
76	Gary Sheffield	1.00
77	Kevin Barker SP	3.00
78	Ron Belliard	.50
79	Jeromy Burnitz	.50
80	Geoff Jenkins	.75
81	Cristian Guzman	.50
82	Jacque Jones	.50
83	Corey Koskie	.50
84	Matt Lawton	.50
85	Peter Bergeron SP	3.00
86	Vladimir Guerrero	3.00
87	Andy Tracy SP	2.00
88	Jose Vidro	.50
89	Rondell White	.50
90	Edgardo Alfonzo	.75
91	Derek Bell	.50
92	Eric Cammack SP	2.00
93	Mike Piazza	5.00
94	Robin Ventura	.75
95	Roger Clemens	3.00
96	Orlando Hernandez	.75
97	Derek Jeter	5.00
98	Tino Martinez	.75
99	Alfonso Soriano SP	5.00
100	Bernie Williams	1.50
101	Eric Chavez	.50
102	Jason Giambi	.75
103	Ben Grieve	.75
104	Terrence Long SP	2.00
105	Mark Mulder SP	2.00
106	Adam Piatt SP	5.00
107	Bobby Abreu	.50
108	Rico Brogna	.50
109	Doug Glanville	.50
110	Mike Lieberthal	.50
111	Scott Rolen	1.50
112	Brian Giles	.50
113	Chad Hermansen SP	2.00
114	Jason Kendall	.50
115	Warren Morris	.50
116	Rick Ankiel SP	4.00
117	J.D. Drew	.50
118	Jim Edmonds	.75
119	Mark McGwire	8.00
120	Fernando Tatis	.50
121	Fernando Vina	.50
122	Tony Gwynn	3.00
123	Trevor Hoffman	.50
124	Ryan Klesko	.50
125	Eric Owens	.50
126	Barry Bonds	3.00
127	Ellis Burks	.50
128	Bobby Estalella	.50
129	Jeff Kent	.75
130	*Scott Linebrink SP*	2.00
131	Jay Buhner	.50
132	Stan Javier	.50
133	Edgar Martinez	.50
134	John Olerud	.75
135	Alex Rodriguez	6.00
136	*Kazuhiro Sasaki SP*	8.00
137	Jose Canseco	1.00
138	Vinny Castilla	.50
139	Fred McGriff	.75
140	Greg Vaughn	.75
141	Gabe Kapler	.75
142	*Mike Lamb SP*	3.00
143	Ruben Mateo	.50
144	Rafael Palmeiro	1.00
145	Ivan Rodriguez	2.00
146	Tony Batista	.50
147	Jose Cruz Jr.	.50
148	Carlos Delgado	1.50
149	Brad Fullmer	.50
150	Raul Mondesi	.75

2000 Pacific Revolution Red

A parallel to the 150-card base set these insert have red foil in place of the gold from the base version. These are also serial numbered on the card front, limited to 299 sets.

	MT
Stars:	1-2X
SPs:	1X
Production 299 sets	

2000 Pacific Revolution Shadow

This parallel to the 150-card base set replaces the gold foil highlights with blue foil on front and has an embossed box at center which reads "SHADOW SERIES". Backs have a serial number ink-jetted from within an edition of 99 each.

	MT
Stars:	3-6X
SPs:	2-3X
Production 99 sets	

2000 Pacific Revolution Foul Pole Net-Fusions

These inserts utilize net-fusion technology, with netting infused in the left and right portion. The player name and logo are stamped in gold foil. These are found on the average of 1:49 packs.

		MT
Complete Set (20):		250.00
Common Player:		4.00
Inserted 1:49		
1	Chipper Jones	15.00
2	Cal Ripken Jr.	25.00
3	Nomar Garciaparra	20.00
4	Pedro Martinez	8.00
5	Sammy Sosa	20.00
6	Frank Thomas	10.00
7	Ken Griffey Jr.	25.00
8	Manny Ramirez	8.00
9	Jeff Bagwell	8.00
10	Shawn Green	5.00
11	Vladimir Guerrero	10.00
12	Mike Piazza	20.00
13	Derek Jeter	25.00
14	Bernie Williams	6.00
15	Rick Ankiel	6.00
16	Mark McGwire	25.00
17	Tony Gwynn	10.00
18	Barry Bonds	10.00
19	Alex Rodriguez	25.00
20	Ivan Rodriguez	6.00

2000 Pacific Revolution Game-Ball Signatures

This 25-card autographed set has a piece of baseball leather embedded into the front on which the player penned his signature.

		MT
Common Player:		8.00
1	Adam Kennedy	8.00
2	Randy Johnson	40.00
3	Rafael Furcal	15.00
4	Greg Maddux	90.00
5	Shane Andrews	8.00
6	Sean Casey	15.00
7	Travis Dawkins	8.00
8	Alex Gonzalez	10.00
9	Brad Penny	10.00
10	Shane Reynolds	10.00
11	Mark Quinn	10.00
12	Eric Gagne	8.00
13	Kevin Barker	8.00
14	Eric Milton	10.00
15	Alfonso Soriano	30.00
16	Mark Mulder	12.00
17	Adam Piatt	8.00
18	Brian Giles	10.00
19	Warren Morris	8.00
20	Rick Ankiel	15.00
21	Fernando Tatis	8.00
22	Barry Bonds	80.00
23	Alex Rodriguez	125.00
24	Ruben Mateo	8.00
25	Billy Koch	10.00

2000 Pacific Revolution Icons

These die-cut cards feature silver foil stamping and the player's team logo in the background. These are found on the average of 1:121 packs.

		MT
Complete Set (20):		400.00
Common Player:		8.00
Inserted 1:121		
1	Randy Johnson	12.00
2	Chipper Jones	25.00
3	Greg Maddux	25.00
4	Cal Ripken Jr.	50.00
5	Nomar Garciaparra	30.00
6	Pedro Martinez	12.00
7	Sammy Sosa	30.00
8	Frank Thomas	12.00
9	Ken Griffey Jr.	40.00
10	Juan Gonzalez	12.00
11	Jeff Bagwell	12.00
12	Vladimir Guerrero	12.00
13	Mike Piazza	40.00
14	Roger Clemens	20.00
15	Derek Jeter	50.00
16	Mark McGwire	40.00
17	Tony Gwynn	15.00
18	Barry Bonds	15.00
19	Alex Rodriguez	40.00
20	Ivan Rodriguez	8.00

2000 Pacific Revolution On Deck

These inserts have a die-cut rounded bottom and feature the player in a simulated on-deck circle enhanced by green foil stamping. These are seeded 1:25 packs.

		MT
Complete Set (20):		130.00
Common Player:		3.00
Inserted 1:25		
1	Chipper Jones	10.00
2	Cal Ripken Jr.	20.00
3	Nomar Garciaparra	12.00
4	Sammy Sosa	12.00
5	Frank Thomas	6.00
6	Ken Griffey Jr.	15.00
7	Manny Ramirez	5.00
8	Larry Walker	3.00
9	Juan Gonzalez	5.00
10	Jeff Bagwell	5.00
11	Shawn Green	3.00
12	Vladimir Guerrero	6.00
13	Mike Piazza	12.00
14	Derek Jeter	15.00
15	Scott Rolen	4.00
16	Mark McGwire	15.00
17	Tony Gwynn	6.00
18	Alex Rodriguez	15.00
19	Jose Canseco	3.00
20	Ivan Rodriguez	4.00

2000 Pacific Revolution Season Opener

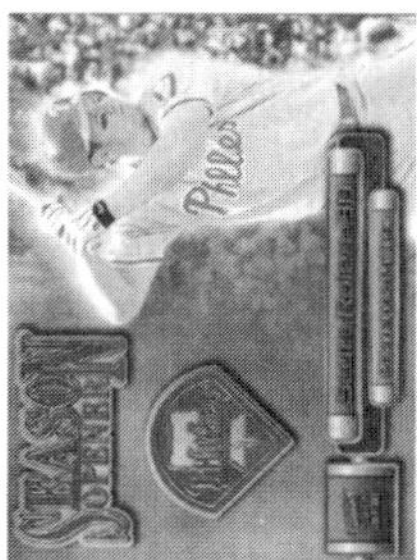

This 36-card set has a horizontal format with the set name, team logo, player name and Revolution logo stamped in gold foil. These are seeded 2:25 packs.

		MT
Complete Set (36):		140.00
Common Player:		1.50
Inserted 2:25		
1	Erubiel Durazo	1.50
2	Randy Johnson	4.00
3	Andruw Jones	3.00
4	Chipper Jones	8.00
5	Greg Maddux	8.00
6	Cal Ripken Jr.	15.00
7	Nomar Garciaparra	10.00
8	Pedro Martinez	4.00
9	Sammy Sosa	10.00
10	Frank Thomas	4.00
11	Magglio Ordonez	2.00
12	Ken Griffey Jr.	12.00
13	Barry Larkin	2.00
14	Kenny Lofton	1.50
15	Manny Ramirez	4.00
16	Jim Thome	2.50
17	Larry Walker	2.50
18	Juan Gonzalez	4.00
19	Jeff Bagwell	4.00
20	Craig Biggio	2.00
21	Carlos Beltran	1.50
22	Shawn Green	2.50
23	Vladimir Guerrero	4.00
24	Mike Piazza	12.00
25	Orlando Hernandez	1.50
26	Derek Jeter	12.00
27	Bernie Williams	3.00
28	Eric Chavez	2.00
29	Scott Rolen	3.00
30	Jim Edmonds	1.50
31	Tony Gwynn	5.00
32	Barry Bonds	5.00
33	Alex Rodriguez	12.00
34	Jose Canseco	3.00
35	Ivan Rodriguez	3.00
36	Rafael Palmeiro	2.50

2000 Pacific Revolution Triple Header

This 30-card set is broken down into three tiers with cards 1-10 spotlighting batting average leaders, 11-20 home run leaders and 21-30 strikeout leaders. The base versions are seeded 4:25 packs. A parallel version for each of the three groups is also inserted. Cards 1-20 are limited to 99 serial numbered sets while cards 21-30 are limited to 599 serial numbered sets.

		MT
Complete Set (30):		50.00
Common Player:		1.00
Inserted 4:25		
Parallel (1-10):		4-6X
99 sets produced		
Parallel (11-20):		4-6X
99 sets produced		
Parallel (21-30):		1-2X
599 sets produced		
1	Chipper Jones	4.00
2	Cal Ripken Jr.	6.00
3	Nomar Garciaparra	4.00
4	Frank Thomas	1.50
5	Larry Walker	.75
6	Vladimir Guerrero	1.50
7	Mike Piazza	5.00
8	Derek Jeter	5.00
9	Tony Gwynn	2.00
10	Ivan Rodriguez	1.00
11	Sammy Sosa	4.00
12	Ken Griffey Jr.	5.00
13	Manny Ramirez	1.50
14	Jeff Bagwell	1.50
15	Shawn Green	.75
16	Mark McGwire	5.00
17	Barry Bonds	2.00
18	Alex Rodriguez	5.00

19	Jose Canseco	1.00
20	Rafael Palmeiro	1.00
21	Randy Johnson	1.50
22	Tom Glavine	.75
23	Greg Maddux	4.00
24	Mike Mussina	1.00
25	Pedro Martinez	1.50
26	Kerry Wood	1.00
27	Chuck Finley	1.00
28	Kevin Brown	1.00
29	Roger Clemens	2.00
30	Rick Ankiel	.75

2000 Pacific Vanguard

		MT
Complete Set (100):		75.00
Common Player:		.25
Pack (4):		4.00
Wax Box (24):		85.00
1	Troy Glaus	1.25
2	Tim Salmon	.40
3	Mo Vaughn	.75
4	Albert Belle	.75
5	Mike Mussina	1.00
6	Cal Ripken Jr.	4.00
7	Nomar Garciaparra	3.00
8	Pedro Martinez	1.50
9	Troy O'Leary	.25
10	Wilton Veras	.25
11	Magglio Ordonez	.25
12	Chris Singleton	.25
13	Frank Thomas	1.50
14	Roberto Alomar	1.00
15	Russell Branyan	.25
16	Manny Ramirez	1.25
17	Jim Thome	.75
18	Omar Vizquel	.40
19	Tony Clark	.40
20	Juan Gonzalez	1.25
21	Dean Palmer	.25
22	Carlos Beltran	.25
23	Johnny Damon	.25
24	Jermaine Dye	.25
25	Mark Quinn	.25
26	Jacque Jones	.25
27	Corey Koskie	.25
28	Brad Radke	.25
29	Roger Clemens	2.00
30	Derek Jeter	3.00
31	Alfonso Soriano	.75
32	Bernie Williams	1.00
33	Eric Chavez	.25
34	Jason Giambi	.40
35	Ben Grieve	.40
36	Tim Hudson	.40
37	Mike Cameron	.25
38	Freddy Garcia	.25
39	Edgar Martinez	.25
40	Alex Rodriguez	4.00
41	Jose Canseco	1.25
42	Vinny Castilla	.40
43	Fred McGriff	.40
44	Rusty Greer	.25
45	Ruben Mateo	.40
46	Rafael Palmeiro	1.00
47	Ivan Rodriguez	1.25
48	Carlos Delgado	1.00
49	Shannon Stewart	.25
50	Vernon Wells	.25
51	Erubiel Durazo	.50
52	Randy Johnson	1.00
53	Matt Williams	.75
54	Andruw Jones	.75
55	Chipper Jones	2.50
56	Greg Maddux	2.50
57	Mark Grace	.50
58	Sammy Sosa	3.00
59	Kerry Wood	.75
60	Sean Casey	.75
61	Ken Griffey Jr.	4.00
62	Barry Larkin	.75
63	Todd Helton	1.25
64	Ben Petrick	.25
65	Larry Walker	1.00
66	Luis Castillo	.25
67	Alex Gonzalez	.25
68	Preston Wilson	.25
69	Jeff Bagwell	1.25
70	Craig Biggio	.75
71	Billy Wagner	.25
72	Kevin Brown	.50
73	Shawn Green	1.00
74	Gary Sheffield	.50
75	Kevin Barker	.25
76	Ron Belliard	.25
77	Jeromy Burnitz	.40
78	Michael Barrett	.25
79	Peter Bergeron	.25
80	Vladimir Guerrero	2.00
81	Edgardo Alfonzo	.50
82	Rey Ordonez	.25
83	Mike Piazza	3.00
84	Robin Ventura	.40
85	Bobby Abreu	.40
86	Mike Lieberthal	.25
87	Scott Rolen	1.25
88	Brian Giles	.40
89	Chad Hermansen	.25
90	Jason Kendall	.40
91	Rick Ankiel	.50
92	J.D. Drew	.30
93	Mark McGwire	5.00
94	Fernando Tatis	.50
95	Ben Davis	.25
96	Tony Gwynn	2.50
97	Trevor Hoffman	.25
98	Barry Bonds	1.50
99	Ellis Burks	.25
100	Jeff Kent	.25

2000 Pacific Vanguard Green

	MT
A.L. (1-50):	5-10X
Production 99 sets	
N.L. (51-100):	3-6X
Production 199 sets	

2000 Pacific Vanguard Gold

	MT
A.L. (1-50):	3-6X
Production 199 sets R	
N.L. (51-100):	5-10X
Production 99 sets R	

2000 Pacific Vanguard Premiere Date

	MT
Stars:	4-8X
Production 135 sets H	

2000 Pacific Vanguard Purple

MT

Production 10 sets

2000 Pacific Vanguard A.L. Vanguard Press

		MT
Complete Set (10):		18.00
Common Player:		1.00
Inserted 2:25		
1	Cal Ripken Jr.	5.00
2	Nomar Garciaparra	3.00
3	Pedro Martinez	1.50
4	Manny Ramirez	1.50
5	Carlos Beltran	1.00
6	Roger Clemens	2.00
7	Derek Jeter	4.00
8	Alex Rodriguez	4.00
9	Rafael Palmeiro	1.25
10	Ivan Rodriguez	1.25

2000 Pacific Vanguard N.L. Vanguard Press

		MT
Complete Set (10):		20.00
Common Player:		1.00
Inserted 2:37		
1	Chipper Jones	3.00
2	Greg Maddux	3.00
3	Sammy Sosa	3.00
4	Ken Griffey Jr.	4.00
5	Larry Walker	1.00
6	Jeff Bagwell	1.50
7	Vladimir Guerrero	2.00
8	Mike Piazza	4.00
9	Mark McGwire	4.00
10	Tony Gwynn	2.00

2000 Pacific Vanguard Cosmic Force

		MT
Complete Set (10):		100.00
Common Player:		6.00
Inserted 1:73		
1	Chipper Jones	10.00
2	Cal Ripken Jr.	20.00
3	Nomar Garciaparra	12.00
4	Sammy Sosa	12.00
5	Ken Griffey Jr.	15.00
6	Mike Piazza	15.00
7	Derek Jeter	20.00
8	Mark McGwire	15.00
9	Tony Gwynn	6.00
10	Alex Rodriguez	15.00

A card number in parentheses ( ) indicates the set is unnumbered.

2000 Pacific Vanguard Diamond Architects

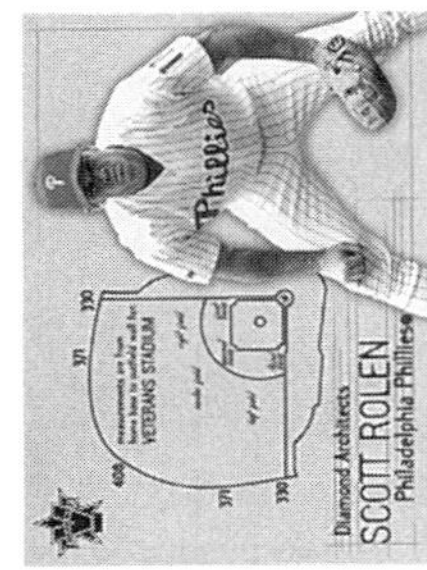

		MT
Complete Set (20):		90.00
Common Player:		2.00
Inserted 1:25		
1	Chipper Jones	6.00
2	Greg Maddux	6.00
3	Cal Ripken Jr.	12.00
4	Nomar Garciaparra	8.00
5	Sammy Sosa	8.00
6	Ken Griffey Jr.	10.00
7	Manny Ramirez	3.00
8	Larry Walker	2.00
9	Jeff Bagwell	3.00
10	Vladimir Guerrero	3.00
11	Mike Piazza	10.00
12	Roger Clemens	4.00
13	Derek Jeter	12.00
14	Bernie Williams	2.50
15	Scott Rolen	2.00
16	Mark McGwire	10.00
17	Tony Gwynn	4.00
18	Alex Rodriguez	10.00
19	Rafael Palmeiro	2.00
20	Ivan Rodriguez	2.50

2000 Pacific Vanguard Game Worn Jersey

		MT
Inserted 1:120		
1	Greg Maddux	20.00
2	Tony Gwynn	15.00
3	Alex Rodriguez	25.00
4	Frank Thomas	15.00
5	Chipper Jones	20.00

2000 Pacific Vanguard High Voltage

		MT
Complete Set (36):		30.00
Common Player:		.40
Inserted 1:1		
1	Mo Vaughn	.50
2	Erubiel Durazo	.40
3	Randy Johnson	.60
4	Andruw Jones	.60
5	Chipper Jones	1.50

6	Greg Maddux	1.50
7	Cal Ripken Jr.	2.50
8	Nomar Garciaparra	2.00
9	Pedro Martinez	.75
10	Sammy Sosa	2.00
11	Frank Thomas	1.00
12	Sean Casey	.50
13	Ken Griffey Jr.	2.50
14	Barry Larkin	.50
15	Manny Ramirez	.75
16	Jim Thome	.50
17	Larry Walker	.50
18	Jeff Bagwell	.75
19	Craig Biggio	.50
20	Carlos Beltran	.40
21	Shawn Green	.60
22	Vladimir Guerrero	1.00
23	Edgardo Alfonzo	.50
24	Mike Piazza	2.00
25	Roger Clemens	1.00
26	Derek Jeter	2.00
27	Bernie Williams	.60
28	Scott Rolen	.75
29	Brian Giles	.40
30	Rick Ankiel	.75
31	Mark McGwire	3.00
32	Tony Gwynn	1.50
33	Barry Bonds	1.00
34	Alex Rodriguez	2.50
35	Rafael Palmeiro	.50
36	Ivan Rodriguez	.75

2001 Pacific

	MT
Complete Set (500):	50.00
Common Player:	.10
Pack (12):	2.50
Box (36):	75.00

1	Garret Anderson	.10
2	Gary DiSarcina	.10
3	Darin Erstad	.40
4	Seth Etherton	.10
5	Ron Gant	.20
6	Troy Glaus	.75
7	Shigetosi Hasegawa	.10
8	Adam Kennedy	.10
9	Ben Molina	.10
10	Ramon Ortiz	.10
11	Troy Percival	.10
12	Tim Salmon	.25
13	Scott Schoeneweis	.10
14	Mo Vaughn	.40
15	Jarrod Washburn	.10
16	Brian Anderson	.10
17	Danny Bautista	.10
18	Jay Bell	.10
19	Greg Colbrunn	.10
20	Erubiel Durazo	.10
21	Steve Finley	.10
22	Luis Gonzalez	.10
23	Randy Johnson	.75
24	Byung-Hyun Kim	.10
25	Matt Mantei	.10
26	Armando Reynoso	.10
27	Todd Stottlemyre	.10
28	Matt Williams	.25
29	Tony Womack	.10
30	Andy Ashby	.10
31	Bobby Bonilla	.10
32	Rafael Furcal	.25
33	Andres Galarraga	.25
34	Tom Glavine	.25
35	Andruw Jones	.50
36	Chipper Jones	1.50
37	Brian Jordan	.10
38	Wally Joyner	.10
39	Keith Lockhart	.10
40	Javy Lopez	.20
41	Greg Maddux	1.50
42	Kevin Millwood	.10
43	John Rocker	.10
44	Reggie Sanders	.10
45	John Smoltz	.10
46	B.J. Surhoff	.10
47	Quilvio Veras	.10
48	Walt Weiss	.10
49	Brady Anderson	.20
50	Albert Belle	.40
51	Jeff Conine	.10
52	Delino DeShields	.10
53	Brook Fordyce	.10
54	Jerry Hairston Jr.	.10
55	Mark Lewis	.10
56	Luis Matos	.10
57	Melvin Mora	.10
58	Mike Mussina	.40
59	Chris Richard	.10
60	Cal Ripken Jr.	2.50
61	Manny Alexander	.10
62	Rolando Arrojo	.10
63	Midre Cummings	.10
64	Carl Everett	.10
65	Nomar Garciaparra	2.00
66	Mike Lansing	.10
67	Darren Lewis	.10
68	Derek Lowe	.10
69	Pedro Martinez	.75
70	Ramon Martinez	.10
71	Trot Nixon	.10
72	Troy O'Leary	.10
73	Jose Offerman	.10
74	Tomo Ohka	.10
75	Jason Varitek	.10
76	Rick Aguilera	.10
77	Shane Andrews	.10
78	Brant Brown	.10
79	Damon Buford	.10
80	Joe Girardi	.10
81	Mark Grace	.25
82	Willie Greene	.10
83	Ricky Gutierrez	.10
84	Jon Lieber	.10
85	Sammy Sosa	2.00
86	Kevin Tapani	.10
87	Rondell White	.20
88	Kerry Wood	.25
89	Eric Young	.10
90	Harold Baines	.10
91	James Baldwin	.10
92	Ray Durham	.10
93	Cal Eldred	.10
94	Keith Foulke	.10
95	Charles Johnson	.10
96	Paul Konerko	.10
97	Carlos Lee	.10
98	Magglio Ordonez	.25
99	Jim Parque	.10
100	Herbert Perry	.10
101	Chris Singleton	.10
102	Mike Sirotka	.10
103	Frank Thomas	1.00
104	Jose Valentin	.10
105	Rob Bell	.10
106	Aaron Boone	.10
107	Sean Casey	.20
108	Danny Graves	.10
109	Ken Griffey Jr.	2.00
110	Pete Harnisch	.10
111	Brian L. Hunter	.10
112	Barry Larkin	.40
113	Pokey Reese	.10
114	Benito Santiago	.10
115	Chris Stynes	.10
116	Michael Tucker	.10
117	Ron Villone	.10
118	Scott Williamson	.10
119	Dmitri Young	.10
120	Roberto Alomar	.60
121	Sandy Alomar Jr.	.10
122	Russell Branyan	.10
123	Dave Burba	.10
124	Bartolo Colon	.10
125	Wil Cordero	.10
126	Einar Diaz	.10
127	Chuck Finley	.10
128	Travis Fryman	.20
129	Kenny Lofton	.30
130	Charles Nagy	.10
131	Manny Ramirez	.75
132	David Segui	.10
133	Jim Thome	.40
134	Omar Vizquel	.20
135	Brian Bohanon	.10
136	Jeff Cirillo	.10
137	Jeff Frye	.10
138	Jeffrey Hammonds	.10
139	Todd Helton	.75
140	Todd Hollandsworth	.10
141	Jose Jimenez	.10
142	Brent Mayne	.10
143	Neifi Perez	.10
144	Ben Petrick	.10
145	Juan Pierre	.10
146	Larry Walker	.30
147	Todd Walker	.10
148	Masato Yoshii	.10
149	Brad Ausmus	.10
150	Rich Becker	.10
151	Tony Clark	.20
152	Deivi Cruz	.10
153	Damion Easley	.10
154	Juan Encarnacion	.10
155	Robert Fick	.10
156	Juan Gonzalez	.75
157	Bobby Higginson	.10
158	Todd Jones	.10
159	Wendell Magee Jr.	.10
160	Brian Moehler	.10
161	Hideo Nomo	.40
162	Dean Palmer	.10
163	Jeff Weaver	.10
164	Antonio Alfonseca	.10
165	David Berg	.10
166	A.J. Burnett	.10
167	Luis Castillo	.10
168	Ryan Dempster	.10
169	Cliff Floyd	.10
170	Alex Gonzalez	.10
171	Mark Kotsay	.10
172	Derrek Lee	.10
173	Mike Lowell	.10
174	Mike Redmond	.10
175	Henry Rodriguez	.10
176	Jesus Sanchez	.10
177	Preston Wilson	.10
178	Moises Alou	.10
179	Jeff Bagwell	.75
180	Glen Barker	.10
181	Lance Berkman	.15
182	Craig Biggio	.20
183	Tim Bogar	.10
184	Ken Caminiti	.10
185	Roger Cedeno	.10
186	Scott Elarton	.10
187	Tony Eusebio	.10
188	Richard Hidalgo	.10
189	Jose Lima	.10
190	Mitch Meluskey	.10
191	Shane Reynolds	.10
192	Bill Spiers	.10
193	Billy Wagner	.10
194	Daryle Ward	.10
195	Carlos Beltran	.10
196	Ricky Bottalico	.10
197	Johnny Damon	.10
198	Jermaine Dye	.10
199	Jorge Fabregas	.10
200	David McCarty	.10
201	Mark Quinn	.10
202	Joe Randa	.10
203	Jeff Reboulet	.10
204	Rey Sanchez	.10
205	Blake Stein	.10
206	Jeff Suppan	.10
207	Mac Suzuki	.10
208	Mike Sweeney	.10
209	Greg Zaun	.10
210	Adrian Beltre	.20
211	Kevin Brown	.20
212	Alex Cora	.10
213	Darren Dreifort	.10
214	Tom Goodwin	.10
215	Shawn Green	.30
216	Mark Grudzielanek	.10
217	Todd Hundley	.10
218	Eric Karros	.20
219	Chad Kreuter	.10
220	Jim Leyritz	.10
221	Chan Ho Park	.20
222	Jeff Shaw	.10
223	Gary Sheffield	.30
224	Devon White	.10
225	Ron Belliard	.10
226	Henry Blanco	.10
227	Jeromy Burnitz	.10
228	Jeff D'Amico	.10
229	Marquis Grissom	.10
230	Charlie Hayes	.10
231	Jimmy Haynes	.10
232	Tyler Houston	.10
233	Geoff Jenkins	.25
234	Mark Loretta	.10
235	James Mouton	.10
236	Richie Sexson	.10
237	Jamey Wright	.10
238	Jay Canizaro	.10
239	Ron Coomer	.10
240	Cristian Guzman	.10
241	Denny Hocking	.10
242	Torii Hunter	.10
243	Jacque Jones	.10
244	Corey Koskie	.10
245	Matt Lawton	.10
246	Matt LeCroy	.10
247	Eric Milton	.10
248	David Ortiz	.10
249	Brad Radke	.10
250	Mark Redman	.10
251	Michael Barrett	.10
252	Peter Bergeron	.10
253	Milton Bradley	.10
254	Orlando Cabrera	.10
255	Vladimir Guerrero	1.00
256	Wilton Guerrero	.10
257	Dustin Hermanson	.10
258	Hideki Irabu	.10
259	Fernando Seguignol	.10
260	Lee Stevens	.10
261	Andy Tracy	.10
262	Javier Vazquez	.10
263	Jose Vidro	.10
264	Edgardo Alfonzo	.20
265	Derek Bell	.10
266	Armando Benitez	.10
267	Mike Bordick	.10
268	John Franco	.10
269	Darryl Hamilton	.10
270	Mike Hampton	.10
271	Lenny Harris	.10
272	Al Leiter	.20
273	Joe McEwing	.10
274	Rey Ordonez	.10
275	Jay Payton	.10
276	Mike Piazza	2.00
277	Glendon Rusch	.10
278	Bubba Trammell	.10
279	Robin Ventura	.20
280	Todd Zeile	.10
281	Scott Brosius	.10
282	Jose Canseco	.40
283	Roger Clemens	1.00
284	David Cone	.10
285	Dwight Gooden	.10
286	Orlando Hernandez	.10
287	Glenallen Hill	.10
288	Derek Jeter	2.50
289	David Justice	.40
290	Chuck Knoblauch	.20
291	Tino Martinez	.20
292	Denny Neagle	.10
293	Paul O'Neill	.20
294	Andy Pettitte	.20
295	Jorge Posada	.20
296	Mariano Rivera	.20
297	Luis Sojo	.10
298	Jose Vizcaino	.10
299	Bernie Williams	.60
300	Kevin Appier	.10
301	Eric Chavez	.20
302	Ryan Christenson	.10
303	Jason Giambi	.40
304	Jeremy Giambi	.10
305	Ben Grieve	.20
306	Gil Heredia	.10
307	Ramon Hernandez	.10
308	Tim Hudson	.20
309	Jason Isringhausen	.10
310	Terrence Long	.10
311	Mark Mulder	.10
312	Adam Piatt	.20
313	Matt Stairs	.10
314	Miguel Tejada	.10
315	Randy Velarde	.10
316	Alex Arias	.10
317	Pat Burrell	.50
318	Omar Daal	.10
319	Travis Lee	.10
320	Mike Lieberthal	.10
321	Randy Wolf	.10
322	Bobby Abreu	.10
323	Jeff Brantley	.10
324	Bruce Chen	.10
325	Doug Glanville	.10
326	Kevin Jordan	.10
327	Robert Person	.10
328	Scott Rolen	.50
329	Jimmy Anderson	.10
330	Mike Benjamin	.10
331	Kris Benson	.10
332	Adam Brown	.10
333	Brian Giles	.20
334	Jason Kendall	.10
335	Pat Meares	.10
336	Warren Morris	.10
337	Aramis Ramirez	.10
338	Todd Ritchie	.10
339	Jason Schmidt	.10
340	John Vander Wal	.10
341	Mike Williams	.10
342	Enrique Wilson	.10
343	Kevin Young	.10
344	Rick Ankiel	.25

345 Andy Benes .10
346 Will Clark .40
347 Eric Davis .20
348 J.D. Drew .25
349 Shawon Dunston .10
350 Jim Edmonds .25
351 Pat Hentgen .10
352 Darryl Kile .10
353 Ray Lankford .10
354 Mike Matheny .10
355 Mark McGwire 3.00
356 Craig Paquette .10
357 Edgar Renteria .10
358 Garrett Stephenson .10
359 Fernando Tatis .10
360 Dave Veres .10
361 Fernando Vina .10
362 Bret Boone .10
363 Matt Clement .10
364 Ben Davis .10
365 Adam Eaton .10
366 Wiki Gonzalez .10
367 Tony Gwynn 1.00
368 Damian Jackson .10
369 Ryan Klesko .20
370 John Mabry .10
371 Dave Magadan .10
372 Phil Nevin .10
373 Eric Owens .10
374 Desi Relaford .10
375 Ruben Rivera .10
376 Woody Williams .10
377 Rich Aurilia .10
378 Marvin Bernard .10
379 Barry Bonds 1.00
380 Ellis Burks .10
381 Bobby Estalella .10
382 Shawn Estes .10
383 Mark Gardner .10
384 Livan Hernandez .10
385 Jeff Kent .10
386 Bill Mueller .10
387 Robb Nen .10
388 Russ Ortiz .10
389 Armando Rios .10
390 Kirk Rueter .10
391 J.T. Snow .10
392 David Bell .10
393 Jay Buhner .10
394 Mike Cameron .10
395 Freddy Garcia .10
396 Carlos Guillen .10
397 John Halama .10
398 Rickey Henderson .30
399 Al Martin .10
400 Edgar Martinez .10
401 Mark McLemore .10
402 Jamie Moyer .10
403 John Olerud .20
404 Joe Oliver .10
405 Alex Rodriguez 2.50
406 Kazuhiro Sasaki .25
407 Aaron Sele .10
408 Dan Wilson .10
409 Miguel Cairo .10
410 Vinny Castilla .10
411 Steve Cox .10
412 John Flaherty .10
413 Jose Guillen .10
414 Roberto Hernandez .10
415 Russ Johnson .10
416 Felix Martinez .10
417 Fred McGriff .25
418 Greg Vaughn .10
419 Gerald Williams .10
420 Luis Alicea .10
421 Frank Catalanotto .10
422 Royce Clayton .10
423 Chad Curtis .10
424 Rusty Greer .10
425 Bill Haselman .10
426 Rick Helling .10
427 Gabe Kapler .20
428 Mike Lamb .10
429 Ricky Ledee .10
430 Ruben Mateo .10
431 Rafael Palmeiro .40
432 Ivan Rodriguez .75
433 Kenny Rogers .10
434 John Wetteland .10
435 Jeff Zimmerman .10
436 Tony Batista .10
437 Homer Bush .10
438 Chris Carpenter .10
439 Marty Cordova .10
440 Jose Cruz Jr. .10
441 Carlos Delgado .60
442 Darrin Fletcher .10
443 Brad Fullmer .10
444 Alex S. Gonzalez .10
445 Billy Koch .10
446 Raul Mondesi .25
447 Mickey Morandini .10
448 Shannon Stewart .10
449 Steve Trachsel .10
450 David Wells .10
451 Juan Alvarez .10
452 Shawn Wooten .10
453 Ismael Villegas .10
454 Carlos Casimiro .10
455 Morgan Burkhart .10
456 Paxton Crawford .10
457 Dernell Stenson .10
458 Ross Gload .10
459 Raul Gonzalez .10
460 Corey Patterson .25
461 Julio Zuleta .10
462 Rocky Biddle .10
463 Joe Crede .10
464 Matt Ginter .10
465 Aaron Myette .10
466 Mike Bell .10
467 Travis Dawkins .10
468 Mark Watson .10
469 Elvis Pena .10
470 Eric Munson .10
471 Pablo Ozuna .10
472 Frank Charles .10
473 Mike Judd .10
474 Hector Ramirez .10
475 Jack Cressend .10
476 Talmadge Nunnari .10
477 Jorge Toca .10
478 Alfonso Soriano .25
479 Jay Tessmer .10
480 Jake Westbrook .10
481 Todd Belitz .10
482 Eric Byrnes .10
483 Jose Ortiz .10
484 Tike Redman .10
485 Domingo Guzman .10
486 Rodrigo Lopez .10
487 Pedro Feliz .10
488 Damon Minor .10
489 Ryan Vogelsong .10
490 Joel Pineiro .10
491 Justin Brunette .10
492 Keith McDonald .10
493 Aubrey Huff .10
494 Kenny Kelly .10
495 Damian Rolls .10
496 John Bale .10
497 Pasqual Coco .10
498 Matt DeWitt .10
499 Leo Estrella .10
500 Josh Phelps .10

2001 Pacific Premiere Date

MT
Stars: 25-50X
Production 35 sets

2001 Pacific Hobby parallel

MT
Stars: 15-25X
Production 70 sets

2001 Pacific Cramer's Choice Awards

MT
Complete Set (10): 575.00
Common Player: 25.00
Inserted 1:721
Styrene & Canvas pricing unavailable
1 Cal Ripken Jr. 80.00
2 Nomar Garciaparra 60.00
3 Sammy Sosa 60.00
4 Frank Thomas 30.00
5 Ken Griffey Jr. 70.00
6 Mike Piazza 60.00
7 Derek Jeter 80.00
8 Mark McGwire 100.00
9 Barry Bonds 30.00
10 Alex Rodriguez 80.00

2001 Pacific Extreme

MT
Stars: 20-40X
Production 45 sets

2001 Pacific AL Decade's Best

MT
Complete Set (18): 80.00
Common Player: 1.50
Inserted 2:37
1 Rickey Henderson 2.00
2 Rafael Palmeiro 2.50
3 Cal Ripken Jr. 12.00
4 Jose Canseco 2.50
5 Juan Gonzalez 4.00
6 Frank Thomas 5.00
7 Albert Belle 2.50
8 Edgar Martinez 1.50
9 Mo Vaughn 2.50
10 Derek Jeter 12.00
11 Mark McGwire 15.00
12 Alex Rodriguez 12.00
13 Ken Griffey Jr. 10.00
14 Nomar Garciaparra 10.00
15 Roger Clemens 5.00
16 Bernie Williams 3.00
17 Ivan Rodriguez 4.00
18 Pedro Martinez 4.00

2001 Pacific NL Decade's Best

MT
Complete Set (18): 75.00
Common Player: 1.50
Inserted 2:37
1 Barry Bonds 4.00
2 Jeff Bagwell 4.00
3 Tom Glavine 2.00
4 Gary Sheffield 2.50
5 Fred McGriff 2.00
6 Greg Maddux 8.00
7 Mike Piazza 10.00
8 Tony Gwynn 5.00
9 Hideo Nomo 2.00
10 Andres Galarraga 2.00
11 Larry Walker 2.00
12 Scott Rolen 3.00
13 Pedro Martinez 4.00
14 Sammy Sosa 10.00
15 Mark McGwire 15.00
16 Kerry Wood 1.50
17 Chipper Jones 8.00
18 Mark Grace 1.50

2001 Pacific Gold Crown Die-Cuts

MT
Complete Set (36): 400.00
Common Player: 4.00
Inserted 1:73
1 Darin Erstad 5.00
2 Troy Glaus 10.00
3 Randy Johnson 10.00
4 Rafael Furcal 4.00
5 Andruw Jones 8.00
6 Chipper Jones 20.00
7 Greg Maddux 20.00
8 Cal Ripken Jr. 30.00
9 Nomar Garciaparra 25.00
10 Pedro Martinez 10.00
11 Sammy Sosa 25.00
12 Kerry Wood 4.00
13 Frank Thomas 15.00
14 Ken Griffey Jr. 25.00
15 Manny Ramirez 10.00
16 Todd Helton 10.00
17 Jeff Bagwell 10.00
18 Shawn Green 6.00
19 Gary Sheffield 6.00
20 Vladimir Guerrero 12.00
21 Mike Piazza 25.00
22 Jose Canseco 6.00
23 Roger Clemens 15.00
24 Derek Jeter 30.00
25 Jason Giambi 6.00
26 Pat Burrell 8.00
27 Rick Ankiel 4.00
28 Jim Edmonds 5.00
29 Mark McGwire 40.00
30 Tony Gwynn 15.00
31 Barry Bonds 10.00
32 Rickey Henderson 5.00
33 Edgar Martinez 4.00
34 Alex Rodriguez 30.00
35 Ivan Rodriguez 10.00
36 Carlos Delgado 8.00

2001 Pacific On The Horizon

MT
Complete Set (10): 100.00
Common Player: 5.00
Inserted 1:145
1 Rafael Furcal 8.00
2 Corey Patterson 15.00
3 Russell Branyan 5.00
4 Juan Pierre 5.00
5 Mark Quinn 5.00
6 Alfonso Soriano 4.00
7 Adam Piatt 10.00
8 Pat Burrell 20.00
9 Kazuhiro Sasaki 10.00
10 Aubrey Huff 5.00

2001 Pacific Ornaments

MT
Complete Set (20): 120.00
Common Player: 2.00
Inserted 2:37
1 Rafael Furcal 2.00
2 Chipper Jones 8.00
3 Greg Maddux 8.00
4 Cal Ripken Jr. 12.00
5 Nomar Garciaparra 10.00
6 Pedro Martinez 4.00
7 Sammy Sosa 10.00
8 Frank Thomas 5.00
9 Ken Griffey Jr. 10.00
10 Manny Ramirez 4.00
11 Todd Helton 4.00
12 Vladimir Guerrero 5.00
13 Mike Piazza 10.00
14 Roger Clemens 5.00
15 Derek Jeter 12.00
16 Pat Burrell 3.00
17 Rick Ankiel 3.00
18 Mark McGwire 15.00
19 Barry Bonds 4.00
20 Alex Rodriguez 12.00

2001 Pacific Private Stock

MT
Complete Set (150): 150.00
Common Player: .25
Common (126-150): 3.00
Inserted 1:4
Hobby Pack (7): 22.00

Hobby Box (10): 220.00
1 Darin Erstad .75
2 Troy Glaus 1.25
3 Tim Salmon .50
4 Mo Vaughn .50
5 Steve Finley .25
6 Luis Gonzalez .40
7 Randy Johnson 1.25
8 Matt Williams .50
9 Rafael Furcal .25
10 Andres Galarraga .50
11 Tom Glavine .50
12 Andruw Jones 1.00
13 Chipper Jones 2.50
14 Greg Maddux 2.50
15 B.J. Surhoff .25
16 Brady Anderson .40
17 Albert Belle .75
18 Mike Mussina 1.00
19 Cal Ripken Jr. 4.00
20 Carl Everett .25
21 Nomar Garciaparra 3.00
22 Pedro Martinez 1.25
23 Mark Grace .50
24 Sammy Sosa 2.50
25 Kerry Wood .50
26 Carlos Lee .25
27 Magglio Ordonez .40
28 Frank Thomas 1.50
29 Sean Casey .40
30 Ken Griffey Jr. 3.00
31 Barry Larkin .75
32 Pokey Reese .25
33 Roberto Alomar 1.00
34 Kenny Lofton .50
35 Manny Ramirez 1.25
36 Jim Thome .75
37 Omar Vizquel .50
38 Jeff Cirillo .25
39 Jeffrey Hammonds .25
40 Todd Helton 1.25
41 Larry Walker .75
42 Tony Clark .40
43 Juan Encarnacion .25
44 Juan Gonzalez 1.25
45 Hideo Nomo .75
46 Cliff Floyd .25
47 Derrek Lee .25
48 Henry Rodriguez .25
49 Preston Wilson .25
50 Jeff Bagwell 1.25
51 Craig Biggio .40
52 Richard Hidalgo .40
53 Moises Alou .25
54 Carlos Beltran .25
55 Johnny Damon .25
56 Jermaine Dye .25
57 Mac Suzuki .25
58 Mike Sweeney .25
59 Adrian Beltre .40
60 Kevin Brown .40
61 Shawn Green .50
62 Eric Karros .25
63 Chan Ho Park .40
64 Gary Sheffield .75
65 Jeromy Burnitz .25
66 Geoff Jenkins .40
67 Richie Sexson .25
68 Jacque Jones .25
69 Matt Lawton .25
70 Eric Milton .25
71 Vladimir Guerrero 1.50
72 Jose Vidro .25
73 Edgardo Alfonzo .40
74 Mike Hampton .40
75 Mike Piazza 3.00
76 Robin Ventura .40
77 Jose Canseco .75
78 Roger Clemens 1.50
79 Derek Jeter 4.00
80 David Justice .75
81 Jorge Posada .40
82 Bernie Williams 1.00
83 Jason Giambi .75
84 Ben Grieve .50
85 Tim Hudson .25
86 Terrence Long .25
87 Miguel Tejada .25
88 Bobby Abreu .25
89 Pat Burrell .75
90 Mike Lieberthal .25
91 Scott Rolen 1.00
92 Kris Benson .25
93 Brian Giles .40
94 Jason Kendall .25
95 Aramis Ramirez .25
96 Rick Ankiel .50
97 Will Clark .75
98 J.D. Drew .50
99 Jim Edmonds .50
100 Mark McGwire 4.00
101 Fernando Tatis .25
102 Adam Eaton .25
103 Tony Gwynn 1.50
104 Phil Nevin .25
105 Eric Owens .25
106 Barry Bonds 1.50
107 Jeff Kent .40
108 J.T. Snow .25
109 Rickey Henderson .75
110 Edgar Martinez .25
111 John Olerud .40
112 Alex Rodriguez 3.00
113 Kazuhiro Sasaki .75
114 Vinny Castilla .25
115 Fred McGriff .50
116 Greg Vaughn .25
117 Gabe Kapler .25
118 Ruben Mateo .25
119 Rafael Palmeiro .75
120 Ivan Rodriguez 1.25
121 Tony Batista .25
122 Jose Cruz Jr. .25
123 Carlos Delgado 1.00
124 Shannon Stewart .25
125 David Wells .25
126 Shawn Wooten 4.00
127 George Lombard 3.00
128 Morgan Burkhart 3.00
129 Ross Gload 3.00
130 Corey Patterson 4.00
131 Julio Zuleta 4.00
132 Joe Crede 8.00
133 Matt Ginter 4.00
134 Travis Dawkins 3.00
135 Eric Munson 4.00
136 Dee Brown 3.00
137 Luke Prokopec 3.00
138 Timoniel Perez 6.00
139 Alfonso Soriano 4.00
140 Jake Westbrook 4.00
141 Eric Byrnes 3.00
142 Adam Hyzdu 3.00
143 Jimmy Rollins 3.00
144 Xavier Nady 15.00
145 Ryan Vogelsong 3.00
146 Joel Pineiro 8.00
147 Aubrey Huff 3.00
148 Kenny Kelly 3.00
149 Josh Phelps 3.00
150 Vernon Wells 3.00

2001 Pacific Private Stock Silver

MT
Stars: .5-1.5X
SP's: .5-1X
Base cards in retail

2001 Pacific Private Stock Premiere Date

MT
Stars: 8-15X
SP's: 1-2X
Production 90 sets

2001 Pacific Private Stock Gold Portraits

MT
Stars: 10-15X
SP's (126-150): 1-2X
Production 75 sets H

2001 Pacific Private Stock Silver Portraits

MT
Stars: 3-6X
SP's: .75-1X
Production 290 sets R

2001 Pacific Private Stock Artist's Canvas

MT
Complete Set (20): 300.00
Common Player: 5.00
Inserted 1:21
1 Randy Johnson 10.00
2 Chipper Jones 20.00
3 Greg Maddux 20.00
4 Cal Ripken Jr. 30.00
5 Nomar Garciaparra 25.00
6 Pedro Martinez 10.00
7 Sammy Sosa 20.00
8 Frank Thomas 15.00
9 Ken Griffey Jr. 25.00
10 Manny Ramirez 10.00
11 Vladimir Guerrero 15.00
12 Mike Piazza 25.00
13 Roger Clemens 15.00
14 Derek Jeter 30.00
15 Jason Giambi 5.00
16 Rick Ankiel 5.00
17 Mark McGwire 30.00
18 Barry Bonds 10.00
19 Alex Rodriguez 25.00
20 Ivan Rodriguez 10.00

2001 Pacific Private Stock Extreme Action

MT
Complete Set (20): 125.00
Common Player: 2.00
Inserted 1:11
1 Troy Glaus 5.00
2 Rafael Furcal 2.00
3 Chipper Jones 10.00
4 Cal Ripken Jr. 15.00
5 Nomar Garciaparra 12.00
6 Sammy Sosa 10.00
7 Ken Griffey Jr. 12.00
8 Manny Ramirez 5.00
9 Todd Helton 5.00
10 Jeff Bagwell 5.00
11 Vladimir Guerrero 6.00
12 Derek Jeter 15.00
13 Mike Piazza 12.00
14 Pat Burrell 4.00
15 Jim Edmonds 2.00
16 Mark McGwire 15.00
17 Barry Bonds 5.00
18 Alex Rodriguez 12.00
19 Ivan Rodriguez 5.00
20 Carlos Delgado 4.00

2001 Pacific Private Stock Game Gear

MT
Common Player: 8.00
Inserted 1:1 H
1 Garret Anderson Bat 8.00
2 Darin Erstad Jsy 20.00
3 Ron Gant Bat 8.00
4 Troy Glaus Jsy 25.00
5 Tim Salmon Bat 15.00
6 Mo Vaughn Jsy Grey 12.00
7 Mo Vaughn Jsy White 12.00
8 Mo Vaughn Bat 10.00
9 Jay Bell Jsy 8.00
10 Jay Bell Bat 8.00
11 Erubiel Durazo Jsy Black 8.00
12 Erubiel Durazo Jsy White 8.00
13 Erubiel Durazo Bat 8.00
14 Steve Finley Bat 8.00
15 Randy Johnson Jsy 30.00
16 Byung-Hyun Kim Jsy White 15.00
17 Byung-Hyun Kim Jsy Grey 15.00
18 Matt Williams Jsy Grey 20.00
19 Matt Williams Jsy White 20.00
20 Matt Williams Jsy Purple 20.00
21 Bobby Bonilla Jsy 8.00
22 Rafael Furcal Bat 15.00
23 Andruw Jones Bat 20.00
24 Chipper Jones Jsy 40.00
25 Chipper Jones Bat 30.00
26 Brian Jordan Jsy 10.00
27 Javier Lopez Bat 10.00
28 Greg Maddux Jsy 40.00
29 Greg Maddux Bat 30.00
30 Brady Anderson Bat 8.00
31 Albert Belle Bat 10.00
32 Nomar Garciaparra Bat 80.00
33 Pedro Martinez Bat 40.00
34 Jose Offerman Bat 8.00
35 Damon Buford Jsy 8.00
36 Jose Nieves Bat 8.00
38 Kerry Wood Bat 20.00
39 James Baldwin Jsy 8.00
40 Ray Durham Jsy 8.00
41 Ray Durham Bat 8.00
42 Carlos Lee Bat 15.00
43 Magglio Ordonez Jsy 20.00
44 Magglio Ordonez Bat 15.00
45 Chris Singleton Jsy 8.00
46 Aaron Boone Bat 8.00
47 Sean Casey Bat 12.00
48 Barry Larkin Jsy 30.00
49 Pokey Reese Jsy 15.00
50 Pokey Reese Bat 8.00
51 Dmitri Young Bat 12.00
52 Roberto Alomar Bat 20.00
53 Einar Diaz Bat 8.00
54 Kenny Lofton Jsy 15.00
55 David Segui Bat 8.00
56 Omar Vizquel Jsy 15.00
57 Luis Castillo Jsy 8.00
58 Jeff Cirillo Jsy 8.00
59 Jeff Frye Bat 8.00
60 Todd Helton Jsy 25.00
61 Todd Helton Bat 20.00
62 Neifi Perez Bat 8.00
63 Larry Walker Jsy 15.00
64 Larry Walker Bat 12.00
65 Masato Yoshii Jsy 25.00
66 Brad Ausmus Jsy 8.00
67 Rich Becker Bat 8.00
68 Tony Clark Bat 8.00
69 Deivi Cruz Bat 8.00
70 Juan Gonzalez Bat 20.00
71 Dean Palmer Bat 8.00
72 Cliff Floyd Jsy White 8.00
73 Cliff Floyd Jsy Teal 8.00
74 Cliff Floyd Bat 8.00
75 Alex Gonzalez Jsy 8.00
76 Alex Gonzalez Marlins Bat 8.00
77 Mark Kotsay Bat 8.00
78 Derrek Lee Bat 8.00
79 Pablo Ozuna Jsy 8.00
80 Craig Biggio Bat 20.00
81 Ken Caminiti Bat 8.00
82 Roger Cedeno Bat 8.00
83 Ricky Bottalico Bat 8.00

84 Dee Brown Bat 8.00
85 Jermaine Dye Bat 15.00
86 David McCarty Bat 10.00
87 Hector Ortiz Bat 8.00
88 Joe Randa Bat 8.00
89 Adrian Beltre Jsy 10.00
90 Kevin Brown Jsy 10.00
91 Alex Cora Bat 8.00
92 Darren Dreifort Bat 8.00
93 Shawn Green Jsy White 20.00
94 Shawn Green Jsy Grey 20.00
95 Shawn Green Bat 15.00
96 Todd Hundley Jsy 8.00
97 Eric Karros Bat 8.00
98 Chan Ho Park Jsy 20.00
99 Chan Ho Park Bat 15.00
101 Gary Sheffield Bat 15.00
102 Ismael Valdes Bat 8.00
103 Jeromy Burnitz Bat 8.00
104 Marquis Grissom Bat 8.00
105 Matt Lawton Bat 8.00
106 Fernando Seguignol Bat 8.00
107 Edgardo Alfonzo White Swing 15.00
108 Edgardo Alfonzo Jsy White Drop 15.00
109 Edgardo Alfonzo Jsy Black 15.00
110 Derek Bell Jsy White 8.00
111 Derek Bell Jsy Black 8.00
112 Armando Benitez Bat 8.00
113 Al Leiter Bat 8.00
114 Rey Ordonez Jsy Grey Field 12.00
115 Rey Ordonez Jsy White 12.00
116 Rey Ordonez Jsy Grey Bunt 12.00
117 Rey Ordonez Bat 10.00
118 Jay Payton Bat 12.00
119 Mike Piazza Jsy 60.00
120 Robin Ventura Jsy Black Hit 15.00
121 Robin Ventura Jsy Black Field 15.00
122 Robin Ventura Jsy White 15.00
123 Luis Polonia Bat 8.00
124 Bernie Williams Bat 20.00
125 Eric Chavez Jsy 15.00
126 Jason Giambi Jsy 20.00
127 Jason Giambi Bat 15.00
128 Ben Grieve Jsy 15.00
129 Ben Grieve Bat 10.00
130 Ramon Hernandez Bat 8.00
131 Tim Hudson Jsy 15.00
132 Terrence Long Bat 10.00
133 Mark Mulder Jsy 8.00
134 Adam Piatt Jsy 10.00
135 Olmedo Saenz Bat 8.00
136 Matt Stairs Bat 8.00
137 Mike Stanley Bat 8.00
138 Miguel Tejada Bat 15.00
139 Travis Lee Bat 8.00
140 Brian Giles Bat 15.00
141 Jason Kendall Jsy 15.00
142 Will Clark Bat 30.00
143 J.D. Drew Bat 20.00
144 Jim Edmonds Bat 20.00
145 Mark McGwire Bat 200.00
146 Edgar Renteria Bat 8.00
147 Garrett Stephenson Jsy 8.00
148 Tony Gwynn Jsy 30.00
149 Ruben Rivera Bat 8.00
150 Barry Bonds Jsy 40.00
151 Barry Bonds Bat 30.00
152 Ellis Burks Jsy 8.00
153 J.T. Snow Bat 10.00
154 Jay Buhner Jsy 15.00
155 Jay Buhner Bat 10.00
156 Carlos Guillen Jsy 8.00
157 Carlos Guillen Bat 8.00
158 Rickey Henderson Bat 20.00
159 Edgar Martinez Bat 15.00
160 Gil Meche Jsy 8.00
161 John Olerud Bat 15.00
162 Joe Oliver Bat 8.00
163 Alex Rodriguez Jsy 80.00
164 Kazuhiro Sasaki Jsy 60.00
165 Dan Wilson Jsy 8.00
166 Dan Wilson Bat 8.00
167 Vinny Castilla Bat 8.00
168 Jose Guillen Bat 8.00
169 Fred McGriff Jsy 15.00
170 Rusty Greer Bat 10.00
171 Mike Lamb Bat 8.00
172 Ruben Mateo Jsy 15.00
173 Ruben Mateo Bat 10.00
174 Rafael Palmeiro Jsy 20.00
175 Rafael Palmeiro Bat 15.00
178 Tony Batista Bat 8.00
179 Marty Cordova Bat 8.00
180 Jose Cruz Jr. Bat 8.00
181 Alex Gonzalez Blue Jays Bat 8.00
182 Raul Mondesi Bat 8.00

2001 Pacific Private Stock Game Jersey Patch

MT
Common Player: 30.00
2 Darin Erstad 60.00
4 Troy Glaus 120.00
6 Mo Vaughn Grey 50.00
7 Mo Vaughn White 50.00
9 Jay Bell 30.00
11 Erubiel Durazo Black 30.00
12 Erubiel Durazo White 30.00
15 Randy Johnson 150.00
16 Byung-Hyun Kim White 50.00
17 Byung-Hyun Kim Grey 50.00
18 Matt Williams Grey 70.00
19 Matt Williams White 70.00
20 Matt Williams Purple 70.00
21 Bobby Bonilla 30.00
24 Chipper Jones 150.00
26 Brian Jordan 40.00
28 Greg Maddux 180.00
35 Damon Buford 30.00
39 James Baldwin 30.00
40 Ray Durham 30.00
43 Magglio Ordonez 80.00
45 Chris Singleton 30.00
48 Barry Larkin 100.00
49 Pokey Reese 60.00
54 Kenny Lofton 60.00
56 Omar Vizquel 60.00
57 Luis Castillo 30.00
58 Jeff Cirillo 30.00
60 Todd Helton 100.00
63 Larry Walker 60.00
65 Masato Yoshii 100.00
66 Brad Ausmus 30.00
72 Cliff Floyd White 30.00
73 Cliff Floyd Teal 30.00
75 Alex Gonzalez 30.00
79 Pablo Ozuna 30.00
89 Adrian Beltre 40.00
90 Kevin Brown 40.00
93 Shawn Green White 70.00
94 Shawn Green Grey 70.00
96 Todd Hundley 30.00
98 Chan Ho Park 80.00
107 Edgardo Alfonzo White Swing 60.00
108 Edgardo Alfonzo White Drop 60.00
109 Edgardo Alfonzo Black 60.00
110 Derek Bell White 30.00
111 Derek Bell Black 30.00
114 Rey Ordonez Grey Field 50.00
115 Rey Ordonez White 50.00
116 Rey Ordonez Grey Bunt 50.00
119 Mike Piazza 200.00
120 Robin Ventura Black Hit 60.00
121 Robin Ventura Black Field 60.00
122 Robin Ventura White 60.00
125 Eric Chavez 60.00
126 Jason Giambi 80.00
128 Ben Grieve 60.00
131 Tim Hudson 60.00
133 Mark Mulder 30.00
134 Adam Piatt 40.00
141 Jason Kendall 60.00
147 Garrett Stephenson 30.00
148 Tony Gwynn 120.00
150 Barry Bonds 160.00
152 Ellis Burks 30.00
154 Jay Buhner 50.00
156 Carlos Guillen 30.00
160 Gil Meche 30.00
163 Alex Rodriguez 30.00
164 Kazuhiro Sasaki 300.00
165 Dan Wilson 30.00
169 Fred McGriff 60.00
172 Ruben Mateo 60.00
174 Rafael Palmeiro 80.00

2001 Pacific Private Stock PS-206 Stars

MT
Complete Set (20): 300.00
Common Player: 6.00
Inserted 3:hobby case
1 Chipper Jones 20.00
2 Greg Maddux 20.00
3 Cal Ripken Jr. 30.00
4 Nomar Garciaparra 25.00
5 Pedro Martinez 10.00
6 Sammy Sosa 20.00
7 Frank Thomas 15.00
8 Ken Griffey Jr. 25.00
9 Manny Ramirez 10.00
10 Jeff Bagwell 10.00
11 Gary Sheffield 6.00
12 Mike Piazza 25.00
13 Roger Clemens 15.00
14 Derek Jeter 30.00
15 Rick Ankiel 6.00
16 Mark McGwire 30.00
17 Tony Gwynn 15.00
18 Barry Bonds 10.00
19 Alex Rodriguez 25.00
20 Ivan Rodriguez 10.00

2001 Pacific Private Stock PS-206 Action

MT
Complete Set (60): 30.00
Common Player: .25
Inserted 2:pack
1 Darin Erstad .50
2 Troy Glaus .75
3 Randy Johnson .75
4 Rafael Furcal .25
5 Tom Glavine .40
6 Andruw Jones .50
7 Chipper Jones 1.50
8 Greg Maddux 1.50
9 Albert Belle .40
10 Mike Mussina .50
11 Cal Ripken Jr. 2.50
12 Nomar Garciaparra 2.00
13 Pedro Martinez .75
14 Mark Grace .40
15 Sammy Sosa 1.50
16 Kerry Wood .25
17 Magglio Ordonez .25
18 Frank Thomas 1.00
19 Ken Griffey Jr. 2.00
20 Barry Larkin .40
21 Roberto Alomar .50
22 Manny Ramirez .75
23 Jim Thome .40
24 Jeff Cirillo .25
25 Todd Helton .75
26 Larry Walker .40
27 Juan Gonzalez .75
28 Hideo Nomo .40
29 Preston Wilson .25
30 Jeff Bagwell .75
31 Craig Biggio .40
32 Johnny Damon .25
33 Jermaine Dye .25
34 Shawn Green .40
35 Gary Sheffield .40
36 Vladimir Guerrero 1.00
37 Mike Piazza 2.00
38 Jose Canseco .50
39 Roger Clemens 1.00
40 Derek Jeter 2.50
41 Bernie Williams .60
42 Jason Giambi .40
43 Ben Grieve .25
44 Pat Burrell .50
45 Scott Rolen .50
46 Rick Ankiel .40
47 J.D. Drew .40
48 Jim Edmonds .25
49 Mark McGwire 2.50
50 Tony Gwynn 1.50
51 Barry Bonds .75
52 Jeff Kent .25
53 Edgar Martinez .25
54 Alex Rodriguez 2.00
55 Kazuhiro Sasaki .50
56 Fred McGriff .40
57 Rafael Palmeiro .50
58 Ivan Rodriguez .75
59 Tony Batista .25
60 Carlos Delgado .50

2001 Pacific Private Stock PS-206 New Wave

MT
Complete Set (20): 150.00
Common Player: 5.00
Inserted 2:hobby case
1 Darin Erstad 8.00
2 Troy Glaus 12.00
3 Rafael Furcal 5.00
4 Andruw Jones 10.00
5 Magglio Ordonez 6.00
6 Carlos Lee 5.00
7 Todd Helton 12.00
8 Johnny Damon 5.00
9 Jermaine Dye 5.00
10 Vladimir Guerrero 15.00
11 Jason Giambi 8.00
12 Ben Grieve 6.00
13 Pat Burrell 10.00
14 Rick Ankiel 6.00
15 J.D. Drew 6.00
16 Adam Eaton 5.00
17 Kazuhiro Sasaki 10.00
18 Ruben Mateo 6.00
19 Tony Batista 5.00
20 Carlos Delgado 8.00

2001 Pacific Private Stock PS-206 Rookies

MT
Complete Set (20): 180.00
Common Player: 8.00
Inserted 1:case
1 George Lombard 8.00
2 Morgan Burkhart 8.00
3 Corey Patterson 15.00
4 Julio Zuleta 8.00
5 Joe Crede 15.00
6 Matt Ginter 10.00
7 Aaron Myette 8.00
8 Travis Dawkins 8.00
9 Eric Munson 10.00
10 Dee Brown 8.00
11 Luke Prokopec 8.00
12 Jorge Toca 8.00
13 Alfonso Soriano 10.00

14	Eric Byrnes	8.00
15	Adam Hyzdu	8.00
16	Jimmy Rollins	8.00
17	Joel Pineiro	12.00
18	Aubrey Huff	8.00
19	Kenny Kelly	8.00
20	Vernon Wells	8.00

2001 Pacific Private Stock Reserve

		MT
Complete Set (20):		180.00
Common Player:		4.00
Inserted 1:21 H		
1	Randy Johnson	6.00
2	Chipper Jones	12.00
3	Greg Maddux	12.00
4	Cal Ripken Jr.	20.00
5	Nomar Garciaparra	15.00
6	Pedro Martinez	6.00
7	Sammy Sosa	12.00
8	Frank Thomas	8.00
9	Ken Griffey Jr.	15.00
10	Todd Helton	6.00
11	Vladimir Guerrero	8.00
12	Mike Piazza	15.00
13	Roger Clemens	8.00
14	Derek Jeter	20.00
15	Rick Ankiel	4.00
16	Mark McGwire	20.00
17	Tony Gwynn	8.00
18	Barry Bonds	6.00
19	Alex Rodriguez	18.00
20	Ivan Rodriguez	6.00

1992 Pinnacle

Score entered the high-end card market with the release of this 620-card set. The cards feature black borders surrounding a white frame with a full-color action photo inside. The player extends beyond the natural background. The backs are horizontal and feature a closeup photo, statistics, team logo, biographical information and career notes. Several subsets can be found within the set including "Idols, Sidelines, Grips, Shades" and "Technicians".

		MT
Complete Set (620):		30.00
Common Player:		.05
Foil Pack (16):		.50
Foil Box (36):		20.00
Jumbo Pack (24+3):		1.50
Jumbo Box (12):		15.00
1	Frank Thomas	1.50
2	Benito Santiago	.05
3	Carlos Baerga	.05
4	Cecil Fielder	.05
5	Barry Larkin	.10
6	Ozzie Smith	1.00
7	Willie McGee	.05
8	Paul Molitor	.65
9	Andy Van Slyke	.05
10	Ryne Sandberg	.75
11	Kevin Seitzer	.05
12	Len Dykstra	.05
13	Edgar Martinez	.05
14	Ruben Sierra	.05
15	Howard Johnson	.05
16	Dave Henderson	.05
17	Devon White	.05
18	Terry Pendleton	.05
19	Steve Finley	.05
20	Kirby Puckett	1.00
21	Orel Hershiser	.05
22	Hal Morris	.05
23	Don Mattingly	.75
24	Delino DeShields	.05
25	Dennis Eckersley	.05
26	Ellis Burks	.05
27	Jay Buhner	.05
28	Matt Williams	.15
29	Lou Whitaker	.05
30	Alex Fernandez	.05
31	Albert Belle	.25
32	Todd Zeile	.05
33	Tony Pena	.05
34	Jay Bell	.05
35	Rafael Palmeiro	.20
36	Wes Chamberlain	.05
37	George Bell	.05
38	Robin Yount	.65
39	Vince Coleman	.05
40	Bruce Hurst	.05
41	Harold Baines	.05
42	Chuck Finley	.05
43	Ken Caminiti	.05
44	Ben McDonald	.05
45	Roberto Alomar	.60
46	Chili Davis	.05
47	Bill Doran	.05
48	Jerald Clark	.05
49	Jose Lind	.05
50	Nolan Ryan	2.00
51	Phil Plantier	.05
52	Gary DiSarcina	.05
53	Kevin Bass	.05
54	Pat Kelly	.05
55	Mark Wohlers	.05
56	Walt Weiss	.05
57	Lenny Harris	.05
58	Ivan Calderon	.05
59	Harold Reynolds	.05
60	George Brett	1.00
61	Gregg Olson	.05
62	Orlando Merced	.05
63	Steve Decker	.05
64	John Franco	.05
65	Greg Maddux	1.00
66	Alex Cole	.05
67	Dave Hollins	.05
68	Kent Hrbek	.05
69	Tom Pagnozzi	.05
70	Jeff Bagwell	.75
71	Jim Gantner	.05
72	Matt Nokes	.05
73	Brian Harper	.05
74	Andy Benes	.05
75	Tom Glavine	.10
76	Terry Steinbach	.05
77	Dennis Martinez	.05
78	John Olerud	.05
79	Ozzie Guillen	.05
80	Darryl Strawberry	.05
81	Gary Gaetti	.05
82	Dave Righetti	.05
83	Chris Hoiles	.05
84	Andujar Cedeno	.05
85	Jack Clark	.05
86	David Howard	.05
87	Bill Gullickson	.05
88	Bernard Gilkey	.05
89	Kevin Elster	.05
90	Kevin Maas	.05
91	Mark Lewis	.05
92	Greg Vaughn	.05
93	Bret Barberie	.05
94	Dave Smith	.05
95	Roger Clemens	.75
96	Doug Drabek	.05
97	Omar Vizquel	.05
98	Jose Guzman	.05
99	Juan Samuel	.05
100	Dave Justice	.20
101	Tom Browning	.05
102	Mark Gubicza	.05
103	Mickey Morandini	.05
104	Ed Whitson	.05
105	Lance Parrish	.05
106	Scott Erickson	.05
107	Jack McDowell	.05
108	Dave Stieb	.05
109	Mike Moore	.05
110	Travis Fryman	.05
111	Dwight Gooden	.05
112	Fred McGriff	.05
113	Alan Trammell	.05
114	Roberto Kelly	.05
115	Andre Dawson	.15
116	Bill Landrum	.05
117	Brian McRae	.05
118	B.J. Surhoff	.05
119	Chuck Knoblauch	.05
120	Steve Olin	.05
121	Robin Ventura	.05
122	Will Clark	.15
123	Tino Martinez	.05
124	Dale Murphy	.25
125	Pete O'Brien	.05
126	Ray Lankford	.05
127	Juan Gonzalez	.75
128	Ron Gant	.05
129	Marquis Grissom	.05
130	Jose Canseco	.40
131	Mike Greenwell	.05
132	Mark Langston	.05
133	Brett Butler	.05
134	Kelly Gruber	.05
135	Chris Sabo	.05
136	Mark Grace	.25
137	Tony Fernandez	.05
138	Glenn Davis	.05
139	Pedro Munoz	.05
140	Craig Biggio	.10
141	Pete Schourek	.05
142	Mike Boddicker	.05
143	Robby Thompson	.05
144	Mel Hall	.05
145	Bryan Harvey	.05
146	Mike LaValliere	.05
147	John Kruk	.05
148	Joe Carter	.05
149	Greg Olson	.05
150	Julio Franco	.05
151	Darryl Hamilton	.05
152	Felix Fermin	.05
153	Jose Offerman	.05
154	Paul O'Neill	.05
155	Tommy Greene	.05
156	Ivan Rodriguez	.60
157	Dave Stewart	.05
158	Jeff Reardon	.05
159	Felix Jose	.05
160	Doug Dascenzo	.05
161	Tim Wallach	.05
162	Dan Plesac	.05
163	Luis Gonzalez	.20
164	Mike Henneman	.05
165	Mike Devereaux	.05
166	Luis Polonia	.05
167	Mike Sharperson	.05
168	Chris Donnels	.05
169	Greg Harris	.05
170	Deion Sanders	.10
171	Mike Schooler	.05
172	Jose DeJesus	.05
173	Jeff Montgomery	.05
174	Milt Cuyler	.05
175	Wade Boggs	.60
176	Kevin Tapani	.05
177	Bill Spiers	.05
178	Tim Raines	.05
179	Randy Milligan	.05
180	Rob Dibble	.05
181	Kirt Manwaring	.05
182	Pascual Perez	.05
183	Juan Guzman	.05
184	John Smiley	.05
185	David Segui	.05
186	Omar Olivares	.05
187	Joe Slusarski	.05
188	Erik Hanson	.05
189	Mark Portugal	.05
190	Walt Terrell	.05
191	John Smoltz	.10
192	Wilson Alvarez	.05
193	Jimmy Key	.05
194	Larry Walker	.25
195	Lee Smith	.05
196	Pete Harnisch	.05
197	Mike Harkey	.05
198	Frank Tanana	.05
199	Terry Mulholland	.05
200	Cal Ripken, Jr.	2.00
201	Dave Magadan	.05
202	Bud Black	.05
203	Terry Shumpert	.05
204	Mike Mussina	.60
205	Mo Vaughn	.45
206	Steve Farr	.05
207	Darrin Jackson	.05
208	Jerry Browne	.05
209	Jeff Russell	.05
210	Mike Scioscia	.05
211	Rick Aguilera	.05
212	Jaime Navarro	.05
213	Randy Tomlin	.05
214	Bobby Thigpen	.05
215	Mark Gardner	.05
216	Norm Charlton	.05
217	Mark McGwire	2.00
218	Skeeter Barnes	.05
219	Bob Tewksbury	.05
220	Junior Felix	.05
221	Sam Horn	.05
222	Jody Reed	.05
223	Luis Sojo	.05
224	Jerome Walton	.05
225	Darryl Kile	.10
226	Mickey Tettleton	.05
227	Dan Pasqua	.05
228	Jim Gott	.05
229	Bernie Williams	.15
230	Shane Mack	.05
231	Steve Avery	.05
232	Dave Valle	.05
233	Mark Leonard	.05
234	Spike Owen	.05
235	Gary Sheffield	.20
236	Steve Chitren	.05
237	Zane Smith	.05
238	Tom Gordon	.05
239	Jose Oquendo	.05
240	Todd Stottlemyre	.05
241	Darren Daulton	.05
242	Tim Naehring	.05
243	Tony Phillips	.05
244	Shawon Dunston	.05
245	Manuel Lee	.05
246	Mike Pagliarulo	.05
247	Jim Thome (Rookie Prospect)	.50
248	Luis Mercedes (Rookie Prospect)	.05
249	Cal Eldred (Rookie Prospect)	.05
250	Derek Bell (Rookie Prospect)	.05
251	Arthur Rhodes (Rookie Prospect)	.10
252	Scott Cooper (Rookie Prospect)	.05
253	Roberto Hernandez (Rookie Prospect)	.10
254	Mo Sanford (Rookie Prospect)	.05
255	Scott Servais (Rookie Prospect)	.05
256	Eric Karros (Rookie Prospect)	.05
257	Andy Mota	.05
258	Keith Mitchell	.05
259	Joel Johnston (Rookie Prospect)	.05
260	John Wehner (Rookie Prospect)	.05
261	Gino Minutelli (Rookie Prospect)	.05
262	Greg Gagne	.05
263	Stan Royer (Rookie Prospect)	.05
264	Carlos Garcia (Rookie Prospect)	.10
265	Andy Ashby (Rookie Prospect)	.10
266	Kim Batiste (Rookie Prospect)	.05
267	Julio Valera (Rookie Prospect)	.05
268	Royce Clayton (Rookie Prospect)	.05
269	Gary Scott (Rookie Prospect)	.05
270	Kirk Dressendorfer (Rookie Prospect)	.05
271	Sean Berry (Rookie Prospect)	.05

272 Lance Dickson (Rookie Prospect) .10
273 Rob Maurer (Rookie Prospect) .05
274 Scott Brosius (Rookie Prospect) .05
275 Dave Fleming (Rookie Prospect) .05
276 Lenny Webster (Rookie Prospect) .05
277 Mike Humphreys .05
278 Freddie Benavides (Rookie Prospect) .05
279 Harvey Pulliam (Rookie Prospect) .05
280 Jeff Carter (Rookie Prospect) .05
281 Jim Abbott, Nolan Ryan (Idols) .25
282 Wade Boggs, George Brett (Idols) .25
283 Ken Griffey Jr., Rickey Henderson (Idols) .50
284 Dale Murphy, Wally Joyner (Idols) .15
285 Chuck Knoblauch, Ozzie Smith (Idols) .15
286 Robin Ventura, Lou Gehrig (Idols) .25
287 Robin Yount (Sidelines - Motocross) .30
288 Bob Tewksbury (Sidelines - Cartoonist) .05
289 Kirby Puckett (Sidelines - Pool Player) .40
290 Kenny Lofton (Sidelines - Basketball Player) .05
291 Jack McDowell (Sidelines - Guitarist) .05
292 John Burkett (Sidelines - Bowler) .05
293 Dwight Smith (Sidelines - Singer) .05
294 Nolan Ryan (Sidelines - Cattle Rancher) 1.00
295 *Manny Ramirez* (1st Round Draft Pick) 3.00
296 *Cliff Floyd* (1st Round Draft Pick) .75
297 *Al Shirley* (1st Round Draft Pick) .05
298 *Brian Barber* (1st Round Draft Pick) .15
299 *Jon Farrell* (1st Round Draft Pick) .05
300 *Scott Ruffcorn* (1st Round Draft Pick) .05
301 *Tyrone Hill* (1st Round Draft Pick) .05
302 *Benji Gil* (1st Round Draft Pick) .15
303 *Tyler Green* (1st Round Draft Pick) .10
304 Allen Watson (Shades) .05
305 Jay Buhner (Shades) .05
306 Roberto Alomar (Shades) .35
307 Chuck Knoblauch (Shades) .05
308 Darryl Strawberry (Shades) .05
309 Danny Tartabull (Shades) .05
310 Bobby Bonilla (Shades) .05
311 Mike Felder .05
312 Storm Davis .05
313 Tim Teufel .05
314 Tom Brunansky .05
315 Rex Hudler .05
316 Dave Otto .05
317 Jeff King .05
318 Dan Gladden .05
319 Bill Pecota .05
320 Franklin Stubbs .05
321 Gary Carter .25
322 Melido Perez .05
323 Eric Davis .05
324 Greg Myers .05
325 Pete Incaviglia .05
326 Von Hayes .05
327 Greg Swindell .05
328 Steve Sax .05
329 Chuck McElroy .05
330 Gregg Jefferies .05
331 Joe Oliver .05
332 Paul Faries .05
333 David West .05
334 Craig Grebeck .05
335 Chris Hammond .05
336 Billy Ripken .05
337 Scott Sanderson .05
338 Dick Schofield .05
339 Bob Milacki .05
340 Kevin Reimer .05
341 Jose DeLeon .05
342 Henry Cotto .05
343 Daryl Boston .05
344 Kevin Gross .05
345 Milt Thompson .05
346 Luis Rivera .05
347 Al Osuna .05
348 Rob Deer .05
349 Tim Leary .05
350 Mike Stanton .05
351 Dean Palmer .05
352 Trevor Wilson .05
353 Mark Eichhorn .05
354 Scott Aldred .05
355 Mark Whiten .05
356 Leo Gomez .05
357 Rafael Belliard .05
358 Carlos Quintana .05
359 Mark Davis .05
360 Chris Nabholz .05
361 Carlton Fisk .50
362 Joe Orsulak .05
363 Eric Anthony .05
364 Greg Hibbard .05
365 Scott Leius .05
366 Hensley Meulens .05
367 Chris Bosio .05
368 Brian Downing .05
369 Sammy Sosa 1.50
370 Stan Belinda .05
371 Joe Grahe .05
372 Luis Salazar .05
373 Lance Johnson .05
374 Kal Daniels .05
375 Dave Winfield .75
376 Brook Jacoby .05
377 Mariano Duncan .05
378 Ron Darling .05
379 Randy Johnson .50
380 Chito Martinez .05
381 Andres Galarraga .05
382 Willie Randolph .05
383 Charles Nagy .05
384 Tim Belcher .05
385 Duane Ward .05
386 Vicente Palacios .05
387 Mike Gallego .05
388 Rich DeLucia .05
389 Scott Radinsky .05
390 Damon Berryhill .05
391 Kirk McCaskill .05
392 Pedro Guerrero .05
393 Kevin Mitchell .05
394 Dickie Thon .05
395 Bobby Bonilla .05
396 Bill Wegman .05
397 Dave Martinez .05
398 Rick Sutcliffe .05
399 Larry Andersen .05
400 Tony Gwynn .75
401 Rickey Henderson .65
402 Greg Cadaret .05
403 Keith Miller .05
404 Bip Roberts .05
405 Kevin Brown .10
406 Mitch Williams .05
407 Frank Viola .05
408 Darren Lewis .05
409 Bob Walk .05
410 Bob Walk .05
411 Todd Frohwirth .05
412 Brian Hunter .05
413 Ron Karkovice .05
414 Mike Morgan .05
415 Joe Hesketh .05
416 Don Slaught .05
417 Tom Henke .05
418 Kurt Stillwell .05
419 Hector Villanueva .05
420 Glenallen Hill .05
421 Pat Borders .05
422 Charlie Hough .05
423 Charlie Leibrandt .05
424 Eddie Murray .45
425 Jesse Barfield .05
426 Mark Lemke .05
427 Kevin McReynolds .05
428 Gilberto Reyes .05
429 Ramon Martinez .05
430 Steve Buechele .05
431 David Wells .10
432 Kyle Abbott (Rookie Prospect) .10
433 John Habyan .05
434 Kevin Appier .05
435 Gene Larkin .05
436 Sandy Alomar, Jr. .05
437 Mike Jackson .05
438 Todd Benzinger .05
439 Teddy Higuera .05
440 Reggie Sanders (Rookie Prospect) .05
441 Mark Carreon .05
442 Bret Saberhagen .05
443 Gene Nelson .05
444 Jay Howell .05
445 Roger McDowell .05
446 Sid Bream .05
447 Mackey Sasser .05
448 Bill Swift .05
449 Hubie Brooks .05
450 David Cone .15
451 Bobby Witt .05
452 Brady Anderson .05
453 Lee Stevens .05
454 Luis Aquino .05
455 Carney Lansford .05
456 Carlos Hernandez (Rookie Prospect) .15
457 Danny Jackson .05
458 Gerald Young .05
459 Tom Candiotti .05
460 Billy Hatcher .05
461 John Wetteland .05
462 Mike Bordick .05
463 Don Robinson .05
464 Jeff Johnson .05
465 Lonnie Smith .05
466 Paul Assenmacher .05
467 Alvin Davis .05
468 Jim Eisenreich .05
469 Brent Mayne .05
470 Jeff Brantley .05
471 Tim Burke .05
472 *Pat Mahomes* (Rookie Prospect) .10
473 Ryan Bowen .05
474 Bryn Smith .05
475 Mike Flanagan .05
476 Reggie Jefferson (Rookie Prospect) .05
477 Jeff Blauser .05
478 Craig Lefferts .05
479 Todd Worrell .05
480 Scott Scudder .05
481 Kirk Gibson .05
482 Kenny Rogers .05
483 Jack Morris .05
484 Russ Swan .05
485 Mike Huff .05
486 Ken Hill .05
487 Geronimo Pena .05
488 Charlie O'Brien .05
489 Mike Maddux .05
490 Scott Livingstone (Rookie Prospect) .05
491 Carl Willis .05
492 Kelly Downs .05
493 Dennis Cook .05
494 Joe Magrane .05
495 Bob Kipper .05
496 Jose Mesa .05
497 Charlie Hayes .05
498 Joe Girardi .05
499 Doug Jones .05
500 Barry Bonds 1.00
501 Bill Krueger .05
502 Glenn Braggs .05
503 Eric King .05
504 Frank Castillo .05
505 Mike Gardiner .05
506 Cory Snyder .05
507 Steve Howe .05
508 Jose Rijo .05
509 Sid Fernandez .05
510 *Archi Cianfrocco* (Rookie Prospect) .10
511 Mark Guthrie .05
512 Bob Ojeda .05
513 John Doherty (Rookie Prospect) .05
514 Dante Bichette .05
515 Juan Berenguer .05
516 Jeff Robinson .05
517 Mike MacFarlane .05
518 Matt Young .05
519 Otis Nixon .05
520 Brian Holman .05
521 Chris Haney .05
522 *Jeff Kent* (Rookie Prospect) .75
523 *Chad Curtis* (Rookie Prospect) .25
524 Vince Horsman .05
525 Rod Nichols .05
526 *Peter Hoy* (Rookie Prospect) .05
527 Shawn Boskie .05
528 Alejandro Pena .05
529 Dave Burba (Rookie Prospect) .05
530 Ricky Jordan .05
531 David Silvestri (Rookie Prospect) .05
532 John Patterson (Rookie Prospect) .05
533 Jeff Branson (Rookie Prospect) .05
534 Derrick May (Rookie Prospect) .05
535 Esteban Beltre (Rookie Prospect) .05
536 Jose Melendez .05
537 Wally Joyner .05
538 Eddie Taubensee (Rookie Prospect) .05
539 Jim Abbott .05
540 *Brian Williams* (Rookie Prospect) .05
541 Donovan Osborne (Rookie Prospect) .05
542 Patrick Lennon (Rookie Prospect) .05
543 *Mike Groppuso* (Rookie Prospect) .05
544 *Jarvis Brown* (Rookie Prospect) .05
545 *Shawn Livesy* (1st Round Draft Pick) .10
546 Jeff Ware (1st Round Draft Pick) .15
547 Danny Tartabull .05
548 *Bobby Jones* (1st Round Draft Pick) .50
549 Ken Griffey, Jr. 2.00
550 *Rey Sanchez* (Rookie Prospect) .15
551 *Pedro Astacio* (Rookie Prospect) .25
552 *Juan Guerrero* (Rookie Prospect) .05
553 *Jacob Brumfield* (Rookie Prospect) .05
554 *Ben Rivera* (Rookie Prospect) .05
555 *Brian Jordan* (Rookie Prospect) .75
556 Denny Neagle (Rookie Prospect) .05
557 Cliff Brantley (Rookie Prospect) .05
558 Anthony Young (Rookie Prospect) .05
559 *John VanderWal* (Rookie Prospect) .15
560 *Monty Fariss* (Rookie Prospect) .05
561 *Russ Springer* (Rookie Prospect) .20
562 *Pat Listach* (Rookie Prospect) .10
563 Pat Hentgen (Rookie Prospect) .05
564 Andy Stankiewicz (Rookie Prospect) .05
565 Mike Perez (Rookie Prospect) .05
566 Mike Bielecki .05
567 Butch Henry (Rookie Prospect) .05
568 *Dave Nilsson* (Rookie Prospect) .10
569 *Scott Hatteberg* (Rookie Prospect) .20
570 Ruben Amaro, Jr. (Rookie Prospect) .05
571 Todd Hundley (Rookie Prospect) .10

572	Moises Alou (Rookie Prospect)	.20
573	Hector Fajardo (Rookie Prospect)	.05
574	Todd Van Poppel (Rookie Prospect)	.05
575	Willie Banks (Rookie Prospect)	.05
576	Bob Zupcic (Rookie Prospect)	.05
577	*J.J. Johnson* (1st Round Draft Pick)	.05
578	John Burkett	.05
579	Trever Miller (1st Round Draft Pick)	.05
580	Scott Bankhead	.05
581	Rich Amaral (Rookie Prospect)	.05
582	Kenny Lofton (Rookie Prospect)	.05
583	Matt Stairs (Rookie Prospect)	.10
584	Don Mattingly, Rod Carew (Idols)	.25
585	Jack Morris, Steve Avery (Idols)	.05
586	Roberto Alomar, Sandy Alomar (Idols)	.25
587	Scott Sanderson, Catfish Hunter (Idols)	.05
588	Dave Justice, Willie Stargell (Idols)	.20
589	Rex Hudler, Roger Staubach (Idols)	.05
590	David Cone, Jackie Gleason (Idols)	.05
591	Willie Davis, Tony Gwynn (Idols)	.15
592	Orel Hershiser (Sidelines)	.05
593	John Wetteland (Sidelines)	.05
594	Tom Glavine (Sidelines)	.05
595	Randy Johnson (Sidelines)	.25
596	Jim Gott (Sidelines)	.05
597	Donald Harris	.05
598	*Shawn Hare*	.15
599	Chris Gardner	.05
600	Rusty Meacham	.05
601	Benito Santiago (Shades)	.05
602	Eric Davis (Shades)	.05
603	Jose Lind (Shades)	.05
604	Dave Justice (Shades)	.20
605	Tim Raines (Shades)	.05
606	Randy Tomlin (Grips)	.05
607	Jack McDowell (Grips)	.05
608	Greg Maddux (Grips)	.30
609	Charles Nagy (Grips)	.05
610	Tom Candiotti (Grips)	.05
611	David Cone (Grips)	.05
612	Steve Avery (Grips)	.05
613	*Rod Beck*	.30
614	Rickey Henderson (Technician)	.25
615	Benito Santiago (Technician)	.05
616	Ruben Sierra (Technician)	.05
617	Ryne Sandberg (Technician)	.40
618	Nolan Ryan (Technician)	1.00
619	Brett Butler (Technician)	.05
620	Dave Justice (Technician)	.20

1992 Pinnacle Rookie Idols

Carrying on with the Idols subset theme in the regular issue, these Series 2 foil-pack inserts feature 18 young prospects sharing cards with their baseball heroes. Both front and back are horizontal in format and include photos of both the rookie and his idol.

		MT
Complete Set (18):		20.00
Common Player:		.50
1	Reggie Sanders, Eric Davis	.50
2	Hector Fajardo, Jim Abbott	.50
3	Gary Cooper, George Brett	2.50
4	Mark Wohlers, Roger Clemens	2.50
5	Luis Mercedes, Julio Franco	.50
6	Willie Banks, Dwight Gooden	.50
7	Kenny Lofton, Rickey Henderson	1.50
8	Keith Mitchell, Dave Henderson	.50
9	Kim Batiste, Barry Larkin	.50
10	Thurman Munson, Todd Hundley	1.50
11	Eddie Zosky, Cal Ripken Jr.	4.50
12	Todd Van Poppel, Nolan Ryan	4.50
13	Ryne Sandberg, Jim Thome	2.00
14	Dave Fleming, Bobby Murcer	.50
15	Royce Clayton, Ozzie Smith	2.00
16	Don Harris, Darryl Strawberry	.50
17	Alan Trammell, Chad Curtis	.50
18	Derek Bell, Dave Winfield	2.00

1992 Pinnacle Slugfest

Each specially marked Slugfest jumbo pack of '92 Pinnacle contained one of these horizontal-format cards of the game's top hitters. The player's name is printed in gold foil at the bottom of the card, along with a red and white Slugfest logo. Backs, which are vertical, have a color player photo, a career summary and a few lifetime stats.

		MT
Complete Set (15):		20.00
Common Player:		.30
1	Cecil Fielder	.30
2	Mark McGwire	4.50
3	Jose Canseco	1.50
4	Barry Bonds	2.50
5	Dave Justice	1.00
6	Bobby Bonilla	.30
7	Ken Griffey, Jr.	3.00
8	Ron Gant	.30
9	Ryne Sandberg	2.00
10	Ruben Sierra	.30
11	Frank Thomas	2.50
12	Will Clark	.75
13	Kirby Puckett	2.00
14	Cal Ripken, Jr.	3.00
15	Jeff Bagwell	2.00

1992 Pinnacle Team Pinnacle

The most sought-after of the 1992 Pinnacle inserts is this 12-piece set of "two-headed" cards. An American and a National League superstar at each position are featured on each card, with two cards each for starting and relief pitchers. The ultra-realistic artwork of Chris Greco is featured on the cards, which were inserted into Series 1 foil packs.

		MT
Complete Set (12):		20.00
Common Player:		.75
1	Roger Clemens, Ramon Martinez	2.50
2	Jim Abbott, Steve Avery	.75
3	Benito Santiago, Ivan Rodriguez	1.50
4	Frank Thomas, Will Clark	3.00
5	Roberto Alomar, Ryne Sandberg	3.00
6	Robin Ventura, Matt Williams	1.00
7	Cal Ripken, Jr., Barry Larkin	4.00
8	Danny Tartabull, Barry Bonds	2.00
9	Brett Butler, Ken Griffey Jr.	4.00
10	Ruben Sierra, Dave Justice	1.00
11	Dennis Eckersley, Rob Dibble	.75
12	Scott Radinsky, John Franco	.75

1992 Pinnacle Team 2000

Young stars projected to be the superstars of the 2000 season were chosen for this insert set found three at a time in jumbo packs. Cards #1-40 were included in Series 1 packaging, while cards #41-80 were inserted with Series 2 Pinnacle. Cards feature gold foil highlights on both front and back.

		MT
Complete Set (80):		10.00
Common Player:		.05
1	Mike Mussina	.40
2	Phil Plantier	.05
3	Frank Thomas	1.50
4	Travis Fryman	.05
5	Kevin Appier	.05
6	Chuck Knoblauch	.05
7	Pat Kelly	.05
8	Ivan Rodriguez	.40
9	Dave Justice	.15
10	Jeff Bagwell	.75
11	Marquis Grissom	.05
12	Andy Benes	.05
13	Gregg Olson	.05
14	Kevin Morton	.05
15	Tim Naehring	.05
16	Dave Hollins	.05
17	Sandy Alomar Jr.	.05
18	Albert Belle	.25
19	Charles Nagy	.05
20	Brian McRae	.05
21	Larry Walker	.20
22	Delino DeShields	.05
23	Jeff Johnson	.05
24	Bernie Williams	.25
25	Jose Offerman	.05
26	Juan Gonzalez	.75
27	Juan Guzman	.05
28	Eric Anthony	.05
29	Brian Hunter	.05
30	John Smoltz	.10
31	Deion Sanders	.10
32	Greg Maddux	1.00
33	Andujar Cedeno	.05
34	Royce Clayton	.05
35	Kenny Lofton	.05
36	Cal Eldred	.05
37	Jim Thome	.05
38	Gary DiSarcina	.05
39	Brian Jordan	.05
40	Chad Curtis	.05
41	Ben McDonald	.05
42	Jim Abbott	.05
43	Robin Ventura	.05
44	Milt Cuyler	.05
45	Gregg Jefferies	.05
46	Scott Radinsky	.05
47	Ken Griffey, Jr.	2.00
48	Roberto Alomar	.40
49	Ramon Martinez	.05
50	Bret Barberie	.05
51	Ray Lankford	.05
52	Leo Gomez	.05
53	Tommy Greene	.05
54	Mo Vaughn	.25
55	Sammy Sosa	1.50

56	Carlos Baerga	.05
57	Mark Lewis	.05
58	Tom Gordon	.05
59	Gary Sheffield	.20
60	Scott Erickson	.05
61	Pedro Munoz	.05
62	Tino Martinez	.05
63	Darren Lewis	.05
64	Dean Palmer	.05
65	John Olerud	.05
66	Steve Avery	.05
67	Pete Harnisch	.05
68	Luis Gonzalez	.25
69	Kim Batiste	.05
70	Reggie Sanders	.05
71	Luis Mercedes	.05
72	Todd Van Poppel	.05
73	Gary Scott	.05
74	Monty Fariss	.05
75	Kyle Abbott	.05
76	Eric Karros	.05
77	Mo Sanford	.05
78	Todd Hundley	.05
79	Reggie Jefferson	.05
80	Pat Mahomes	.05

1992 Pinnacle Rookies

Styled after the regular 1992 Pinnacle cards, this 30-card boxed set features the year's top rookies. The cards have a game-action photo which is borderless on the top and sides. Beneath the photo a team color-coded strip carries the player's name in gold foil, with a gold-bordered team logo at left. A black strip at bottom has the notation "1992 Rookie". Horizontal backs follow a similar design and include a bit of player information, Pinnacle's anti-counterfeiting strip and some gold-foil enhancements.

		MT
Complete Set (30):		4.00
Common Player:		.10
1	Luis Mercedes	.10
2	Scott Cooper	.10
3	Kenny Lofton	.25
4	John Doherty	.10
5	Pat Listach	.10
6	Andy Stankiewicz	.10
7	Derek Bell	.35
8	Gary DiSarcina	.10
9	Roberto Hernandez	.25
10	Joel Johnston	.10
11	Pat Mahomes	.10
12	Todd Van Poppel	.10
13	Dave Fleming	.10
14	Monty Fariss	.10
15	Gary Scott	.10
16	Moises Alou	1.00
17	Todd Hundley	.40
18	Kim Batiste	.10
19	Denny Neagle	.10
20	Donovan Osborne	.10
21	Mark Wohlers	.10
22	Reggie Sanders	.20
23	Brian Williams	.10
24	Eric Karros	.25
25	Frank Seminara	.10
26	Royce Clayton	.10
27	Dave Nilsson	.10
28	Matt Stairs	.15
29	Chad Curtis	.25
30	Carlos Hernandez	.15

1993 Pinnacle

This set offers many of the same features which made the debut Pinnacle set so popular in 1992. Subsets are titled Rookies, Now & Then (which shows the player as he looked as a rookie and in 1993), Idols (active players and their heroes on the same card), Hometown Heroes (players who are playing with their hometown team), Draft Picks and Rookies. More than 100 rookies and 10 draft picks are featured. All regular cards have an action photo, a black border and the Pinnacle name in gold foil. Series 1 cards feature portraits of players on the two new expansion teams; Series 2 cards feature action shots of them. Team Pinnacle insert cards returned, while Rookie Team Pinnacle cards made their debut. Other insert sets are titled Team 2001, Slugfest and Tribute, which features five cards each of Nolan Ryan and George Brett.

		MT
Complete Set (620):		30.00
Complete Series 1 (310):		7.50
Complete Series 2 (310):		22.50
Common Player:		.05
Series 1 Pack (15):		1.00
Series 1 Foil Box (36):		20.00
Series 2 Pack (15):		2.50
Series 2 Foil Box (36):		45.00
1	Gary Sheffield	.20
2	Cal Eldred	.05
3	Larry Walker	.25
4	Deion Sanders	.15
5	Dave Fleming	.05
6	Carlos Baerga	.05
7	Bernie Williams	.25
8	John Kruk	.05
9	Jimmy Key	.05
10	Jeff Bagwell	.75
11	Jim Abbott	.05
12	Terry Steinbach	.05
13	Bob Tewksbury	.05
14	Eric Karros	.05
15	Ryne Sandberg	.75
16	Will Clark	.15
17	Edgar Martinez	.05
18	Eddie Murray	.40
19	Andy Van Slyke	.05
20	Cal Ripken, Jr.	2.50
21	Ivan Rodriguez	.60
22	Barry Larkin	.10
23	Don Mattingly	1.00
24	Gregg Jefferies	.05
25	Roger Clemens	.75
26	Cecil Fielder	.05
27	Kent Hrbek	.05
28	Robin Ventura	.05
29	Rickey Henderson	.45
30	Roberto Alomar	.60
31	Luis Polonia	.05
32	Andujar Cedeno	.05
33	Pat Listach	.05
34	Mark Grace	.25
35	Otis Nixon	.05
36	Felix Jose	.05
37	Mike Sharperson	.05
38	Dennis Martinez	.05
39	Willie McGee	.05
40	Kenny Lofton	.05
41	Randy Johnson	.40
42	Andy Benes	.05
43	Bobby Bonilla	.05
44	Mike Mussina	.60
45	Len Dykstra	.05
46	Ellis Burks	.05
47	Chris Sabo	.05
48	Jay Bell	.05
49	Jose Canseco	.35
50	Craig Biggio	.10
51	Wally Joyner	.05
52	Mickey Tettleton	.05
53	Tim Raines	.05
54	Brian Harper	.05
55	Rene Gonzales	.05
56	Mark Langston	.05
57	Jack Morris	.05
58	Mark McGwire	2.50
59	Ken Caminiti	.05
60	Terry Pendleton	.05
61	Dave Nilsson	.05
62	Tom Pagnozzi	.05
63	Mike Morgan	.05
64	Darryl Strawberry	.05
65	Charles Nagy	.05
66	Ken Hill	.05
67	Matt Williams	.15
68	Jay Buhner	.05
69	Vince Coleman	.05
70	Brady Anderson	.05
71	Fred McGriff	.05
72	Ben McDonald	.05
73	Terry Mulholland	.05
74	Randy Tomlin	.05
75	Nolan Ryan	2.50
76	Frank Viola	.05
77	Jose Rijo	.05
78	Shane Mack	.05
79	Travis Fryman	.05
80	Jack McDowell	.05
81	Mark Gubicza	.05
82	Matt Nokes	.05
83	Bert Blyleven	.05
84	Eric Anthony	.05
85	Mike Bordick	.05
86	John Olerud	.05
87	B.J. Surhoff	.05
88	Bernard Gilkey	.05
89	Shawon Dunston	.05
90	Tom Glavine	.10
91	Brett Butler	.05
92	Moises Alou	.15
93	Albert Belle	.25
94	Darren Lewis	.05
95	Omar Vizquel	.05
96	Dwight Gooden	.05
97	Gregg Olson	.05
98	Tony Gwynn	.75
99	Darren Daulton	.05
100	Dennis Eckersley	.05
101	Rob Dibble	.05
102	Mike Greenwell	.05
103	Jose Lind	.05
104	Julio Franco	.05
105	Tom Gordon	.05
106	Scott Livingstone	.05
107	Chuck Knoblauch	.05
108	Frank Thomas	1.50
109	Melido Perez	.05
110	Ken Griffey, Jr.	2.00
111	Harold Baines	.05
112	Gary Gaetti	.05
113	Pete Harnisch	.05
114	David Wells	.10
115	Charlie Leibrandt	.05
116	Ray Lankford	.05
117	Kevin Seitzer	.05
118	Robin Yount	.50
119	Lenny Harris	.05
120	Chris James	.05
121	Delino DeShields	.05
122	Kirt Manwaring	.05
123	Glenallen Hill	.05
124	Hensley Meulens	.05
125	Darrin Jackson	.05
126	Todd Hundley	.05
127	Dave Hollins	.05
128	Sam Horn	.05
129	Roberto Hernandez	.05
130	Vicente Palacios	.05
131	George Brett	.75
132	Dave Martinez	.05
133	Kevin Appier	.05
134	Pat Kelly	.05
135	Pedro Munoz	.05
136	Mark Carreon	.05
137	Lance Johnson	.05
138	Devon White	.05
139	Julio Valera	.05
140	Eddie Taubensee	.05
141	Willie Wilson	.05
142	Stan Belinda	.05
143	John Smoltz	.10
144	Darryl Hamilton	.05
145	Sammy Sosa	1.50
146	Carlos Hernandez	.05
147	Tom Candiotti	.05
148	Mike Felder	.05
149	Rusty Meacham	.05
150	Ivan Calderon	.05
151	Pete O'Brien	.05
152	Erik Hanson	.05
153	Billy Ripken	.05
154	Kurt Stillwell	.05
155	Jeff Kent	.05
156	Mickey Morandini	.05
157	Randy Milligan	.05
158	Reggie Sanders	.05
159	Luis Rivera	.05
160	Orlando Merced	.05
161	Dean Palmer	.05
162	Mike Perez	.05
163	Scott Erikson	.05
164	Kevin McReynolds	.05
165	Kevin Maas	.05
166	Ozzie Guillen	.05
167	Rob Deer	.05
168	Danny Tartabull	.05
169	Lee Stevens	.05
170	Dave Henderson	.05
171	Derek Bell	.05
172	Steve Finley	.05
173	Greg Olson	.05
174	Geronimo Pena	.05
175	Paul Quantrill	.05
176	Steve Buechele	.05
177	Kevin Gross	.05
178	Tim Wallach	.05
179	Dave Valle	.05
180	Dave Silvestri	.05
181	Bud Black	.05
182	Henry Rodriguez	.05
183	Tim Teufel	.05
184	Mark McLemore	.05
185	Bret Saberhagen	.05
186	Chris Hoiles	.05
187	Ricky Jordan	.05
188	Don Slaught	.05
189	Mo Vaughn	.40
190	Joe Oliver	.05
191	Juan Gonzalez	.75
192	Scott Leius	.05
193	Milt Cuyler	.05
194	Chris Haney	.05
195	Ron Karkovice	.05
196	Steve Farr	.05
197	John Orton	.05
198	Kelly Gruber	.05
199	Ron Darling	.05
200	Ruben Sierra	.05
201	Chuck Finley	.05
202	Mike Moore	.05
203	Pat Borders	.05

204 Sid Bream .05
205 Todd Zeile .05
206 Rick Wilkins .05
207 Jim Gantner .05
208 Frank Castillo .05
209 Dave Hansen .05
210 Trevor Wilson .05
211 Sandy Alomar, Jr. .05
212 Sean Berry .05
213 Tino Martinez .05
214 Chito Martinez .05
215 Dan Walters .05
216 John Franco .05
217 Glenn Davis .05
218 Mariano Duncan .05
219 Mike LaValliere .05
220 Rafael Palmeiro .20
221 Jack Clark .05
222 Hal Morris .05
223 Ed Sprague .05
224 John Valentin .05
225 Sam Militello .05
226 Bob Wickman .05
227 Damion Easley .05
228 John Jaha .05
229 Bob Ayrault .05
230 Mo Sanford (Expansion Draft) .05
231 Walt Weiss (Expansion Draft) .05
232 Dante Bichette (Expansion Draft) .10
233 Steve Decker (Expansion Draft) .05
234 Jerald Clark (Expansion Draft) .05
235 Bryan Harvey (Expansion Draft) .05
236 Joe Girardi (Expansion Draft) .10
237 Dave Magadan (Expansion Draft) .05
238 David Nied (Rookie Prospect) .05
239 *Eric Wedge* (Rookie Prospect) .05
240 Rico Brogna (Rookie Prospect) .05
241 J.T. Bruett (Rookie Prospect) .05
242 Jonathan Hurst (Rookie Prospect) .05
243 Bret Boone (Rookie Prospect) .25
244 Manny Alexander (Rookie Prospect) .05
245 Scooter Tucker (Rookie Prospect) .05
246 Troy Neel (Rookie Prospect) .05
247 Eddie Zosky (Rookie Prospect) .05
248 Melvin Nieves (Rookie Prospect) .05
249 Ryan Thompson (Rookie Prospect) .05
250 Shawn Barton (Rookie Prospect) .05
251 Ryan Klesko (Rookie Prospect) .05
252 Mike Piazza (Rookie Prospect) 2.00
253 Steve Hosey (Rookie Prospect) .05
254 Shane Reynolds (Rookie Prospect) .10
255 Dan Wilson (Rookie Prospect) .10
256 Tom Marsh (Rookie Prospect) .05
257 Barry Manuel (Rookie Prospect) .05
258 Paul Miller (Rookie Prospect) .05
259 Pedro Martinez (Rookie Prospect) .25
260 Steve Cooke (Rookie Prospect) .05
261 Johnny Guzman (Rookie Prospect) .05
262 Mike Butcher (Rookie Prospect) .05
263 Bien Figueroa (Rookie Prospect) .05
264 Rich Rowland (Rookie Prospect) .05
265 Shawn Jeter (Rookie Prospect) .05
266 Gerald Williams (Rookie Prospect) .05
267 Derek Parks (Rookie Prospect) .05
268 Henry Mercedes (Rookie Prospect) .05
269 *David Hulse* (Rookie Prospect) .05
270 *Tim Pugh* (Rookie Prospect) .05
271 William Suero (Rookie Prospect) .05
272 Ozzie Canseco (Rookie Prospect) .05
273 Fernando Ramsey (Rookie Prospect) .05
274 Bernardo Brito (Rookie Prospect) .05
275 Dave Mlicki (Rookie Prospect) .05
276 Tim Salmon (Rookie Prospect) .25
277 Mike Raczka (Rookie Prospect) .05
278 *Ken Ryan* (Rookie Prospect) .20
279 Rafael Bournigal (Rookie Prospect) .05
280 Wil Cordero (Rookie Prospect) .05
281 Billy Ashley (Rookie Prospect) .05
282 Paul Wagner (Rookie Prospect) .05
283 Blas Minor (Rookie Prospect) .05
284 Rick Trlicek (Rookie Prospect) .05
285 Willie Greene (Rookie Prospect) .05
286 Ted Wood (Rookie Prospect) .05
287 Phil Clark (Rookie Prospect) .05
288 Jesse Levis (Rookie Prospect) .05
289 Tony Gwynn (Now & Then) .40
290 Nolan Ryan (Now & Then) 1.25
291 Dennis Martinez (Now & Then) .05
292 Eddie Murray (Now & Then) .20
293 Robin Yount (Now & Then) .30
294 George Brett (Now & Then) .40
295 Dave Winfield (Now & Then) .25
296 Bert Blyleven (Now & Then) .05
297 Jeff Bagwell (Idols - Carl Yastrzemski) .40
298 John Smoltz (Idols - Jack Morris) .05
299 Larry Walker (Idols - Mike Bossy) .05
300 Gary Sheffield (Idols - Barry Larkin) .10
301 Ivan Rodriguez (Idols - Carlton Fisk) .30
302 Delino DeShields (Idols - Malcolm X) .05
303 Tim Salmon (Idols - Dwight Evans) .10
304 Bernard Gilkey (Hometown Heroes) .05
305 Cal Ripken, Jr. (Hometown Heroes) 1.25
306 Barry Larkin (Hometown Heroes) .05
307 Kent Hrbek (Hometown Heroes) .05
308 Rickey Henderson (Hometown Heroes) .20
309 Darryl Strawberry (Hometown Heroes) .05
310 John Franco (Hometown Heroes) .05
311 Todd Stottlemyre .05
312 Luis Gonzalez .25
313 Tommy Greene .05
314 Randy Velarde .05
315 Steve Avery .05
316 Jose Oquendo .05
317 Rey Sanchez .05
318 Greg Vaughn .05
319 Orel Hershiser .05
320 Paul Sorrento .05
321 Royce Clayton .05
322 John Vander Wal .05
323 Henry Cotto .05
324 Pete Schourek .05
325 David Segui .05
326 Arthur Rhodes .05
327 Bruce Hurst .05
328 Wes Chamberlain .05
329 Ozzie Smith .65
330 Scott Cooper .05
331 Felix Fermin .05
332 Mike Macfarlane .05
333 Dan Gladden .05
334 Kevin Tapani .05
335 Steve Sax .05
336 Jeff Montgomery .05
337 Gary DiSarcina .05
338 Lance Blankenship .05
339 Brian Williams .05
340 Duane Ward .05
341 Chuck McElroy .05
342 Joe Magrane .05
343 Jaime Navarro .05
344 Dave Justice .20
345 Jose Offerman .05
346 Marquis Grissom .05
347 Bill Swift .05
348 Jim Thome .05
349 Archi Cianfrocco .05
350 Anthony Young .05
351 Leo Gomez .05
352 Bill Gullickson .05
353 Alan Trammell .05
354 Dan Pasqua .05
355 Jeff King .05
356 Kevin Brown .10
357 Tim Belcher .05
358 Bip Roberts .05
359 Brent Mayne .05
360 Rheal Cormier .05
361 Mark Guthrie .05
362 Craig Grebeck .05
363 Andy Stankiewicz .05
364 Juan Guzman .05
365 Bobby Witt .05
366 Mark Portugal .05
367 Brian McRae .05
368 Mark Lemke .05
369 Bill Wegman .05
370 Donovan Osborne .05
371 Derrick May .05
372 Carl Willis .05
373 Chris Nabholz .05
374 Mark Lewis .05
375 John Burkett .05
376 Luis Mercedes .05
377 Ramon Martinez .05
378 Kyle Abbott .05
379 Mark Wohlers .05
380 Bob Walk .05
381 Kenny Rogers .05
382 Tim Naehring .05
383 Alex Fernandez .05
384 Keith Miller .05
385 Mike Henneman .05
386 Rick Aguilera .05
387 George Bell .05
388 Mike Gallego .05
389 Howard Johnson .05
390 Kim Batiste .05
391 Jerry Browne .05
392 Damon Berryhill .05
393 Ricky Bones .05
394 Omar Olivares .05
395 Mike Harkey .05
396 Pedro Astacio .05
397 John Wetteland .05
398 Rod Beck .05
399 Thomas Howard .05
400 Mike Devereaux .05
401 Tim Wakefield .05
402 Curt Schilling .10
403 Zane Smith .05
404 Bob Zupcic .05
405 Tom Browning .05
406 Tony Phillips .05
407 John Doherty .05
408 Pat Mahomes .05
409 John Habyan .05
410 Steve Olin .05
411 Chad Curtis .05
412 Joe Grahe .05
413 John Patterson .05
414 Brian Hunter .05
415 Doug Henry .05
416 Lee Smith .05
417 Bob Scanlan .05
418 Kent Mercker .05
419 Mel Rojas .05
420 Mark Whiten .05
421 Carlton Fisk .50
422 Candy Maldonado .05
423 Doug Drabek .05
424 Wade Boggs .50
425 Mark Davis .05
426 Kirby Puckett .75
427 Joe Carter .05
428 Paul Molitor .60
429 Eric Davis .05
430 Darryl Kile .05
431 Jeff Parrett (Expansion Draft) .05
432 Jeff Blauser .05
433 Dan Plesac .05
434 Andres Galarraga (Expansion Draft) .10
435 Jim Gott .05
436 Jose Mesa .05
437 Ben Rivera .05
438 Dave Winfield .50
439 Norm Charlton .05
440 Chris Bosio .05
441 Wilson Alvarez .05
442 Dave Stewart .05
443 Doug Jones .05
444 Jeff Russell .05
445 Ron Gant .05
446 Paul O'Neill .05
447 Charlie Hayes (Expansion Draft) .05
448 Joe Hesketh .05
449 Chris Hammond .05
450 Hipolito Pichardo .05
451 Scott Radinsky .05
452 Bobby Thigpen .05
453 Xavier Hernandez .05
454 Lonnie Smith .05
455 *Jamie Arnold* (1st Draft Pick) .05
456 B.J. Wallace (1st Draft Pick) .05
457 *Derek Jeter* (Rookie Prospect) 12.50
458 *Jason Kendall* (Rookie Prospect) 2.00
459 Rick Helling (Rookie Prospect) .05
460 *Derek Wallace* (Rookie Prospect) .05
461 *Sean Lowe* (Rookie Prospect) .05
462 *Shannon Stewart* (Rookie Prospect) 1.00
463 *Benji Grigsby* (Rookie Prospect) .05
464 *Todd Steverson* (Rookie Prospect) .05
465 *Dan Serafini* (Rookie Prospect) .05
466 Michael Tucker (Rookie Prospect) .05
467 Chris Roberts (Rookie Prospect) .05
468 *Pete Janicki* (1st Draft Pick) .05
469 *Jeff Schmidt* (1st Draft Pick) .05
470 Don Mattingly (Now & Then) .50
471 Cal Ripken, Jr. (Now & Then) 1.25
472 Jack Morris (Now & Then) .05
473 Terry Pendleton (Now & Then) .05
474 Dennis Eckersley (Now & Then) .05
475 Carlton Fisk (Now & Then) .20
476 Wade Boggs (Now & Then) .25
477 Len Dykstra (Idols - Ken Stabler) .05
478 Danny Tartabull (Idols - Jose Tartabull) .05
479 Jeff Conine (Idols - Dale Murphy) .10

480 Gregg Jefferies (Idols - Ron Cey) .05
481 Paul Molitor (Idols - Harmon Killebrew) .25
482 John Valentin (Idols - Dave Concepcion) .05
483 Alex Arias (Idols - Dave Winfield) .10
484 Barry Bonds (Hometown Heroes) 1.00
485 Doug Drabek (Hometown Heroes) .05
486 Dave Winfield (Hometown Heroes) .25
487 Brett Butler (Hometown Heroes) .05
488 Harold Baines (Hometown Heroes) .05
489 David Cone (Hometown Heroes) .05
490 Willie McGee (Hometown Heroes) .05
491 Robby Thompson .05
492 Pete Incaviglia .05
493 Manuel Lee .05
494 Rafael Belliard .05
495 Scott Fletcher .05
496 Jeff Frye .05
497 Andre Dawson .15
498 Mike Scioscia .05
499 Spike Owen .05
500 Sid Fernandez .05
501 Joe Orsulak .05
502 Benito Santiago (Expansion Draft) .05
503 Dale Murphy .15
504 Barry Bonds 1.00
505 Jose Guzman .05
506 Tony Pena .05
507 Greg Swindell .05
508 Mike Pagliarulo .05
509 Lou Whitaker .05
510 Greg Gagne .05
511 Butch Henry (Expansion Draft) .05
512 Jeff Brantley .05
513 Jack Armstrong (Expansion Draft) .05
514 Danny Jackson .05
515 Junior Felix (Expansion Draft) .05
516 Milt Thompson .05
517 Greg Maddux 1.00
518 Eric Young (Expansion Draft) .05
519 Jody Reed .05
520 Roberto Kelly .05
521 Darren Holmes (Expansion Draft) .05
522 Craig Lefferts .05
523 Charlie Hough (Expansion Draft) .05
524 Bo Jackson .15
525 Bill Spiers .05
526 Orestes Destrade (Expansion Draft) .05
527 Greg Hibbard .05
528 Roger McDowell .05
529 Cory Snyder .05
530 Harold Reynolds .05
531 Kevin Reimer .05
532 Rick Sutcliffe .05
533 Tony Fernandez .05
534 Tom Brunansky .05
535 Jeff Reardon .05
536 Chili Davis .05
537 Bob Ojeda .05
538 Greg Colbrunn .05
539 Phil Plantier .05
540 Brian Jordan .05
541 Pete Smith .05
542 Frank Tanana .05
543 John Smiley .05
544 David Cone .05
545 Daryl Boston (Expansion Draft) .05
546 Tom Henke .05
547 Bill Krueger .05
548 Freddie Benavides (Expansion Draft) .05
549 Randy Myers .05
550 Reggie Jefferson .05
551 Kevin Mitchell .05
552 Dave Stieb .05
553 Bret Barberie (Expansion Draft) .05
554 Tim Crews .05
555 Doug Dascenzo .05
556 Alex Cole (Expansion Draft) .05
557 Jeff Innis .05
558 Carlos Garcia .05
559 Steve Howe .05
560 Kirk McCaskill .05
561 Frank Seminara .05
562 Cris Carpenter (Expansion Draft) .05
563 Mike Stanley .05
564 Carlos Quintana .05
565 Mitch Williams .05
566 Juan Bell .05
567 Eric Fox .05
568 Al Leiter .05
569 Mike Stanton .05
570 Scott Kamieniecki .05
571 Ryan Bowen (Expansion Draft) .05
572 Andy Ashby (Expansion Draft) .10
573 Bob Welch .05
574 Scott Sanderson .05
575 Joe Kmak (Rookie Prospect) .05
576 Scott Pose (Rookie Prospect/ Expansion Draft) .05
577 Ricky Gutierrez (Rookie Prospect) .15
578 Mike Trombley (Rookie Prospect) .05
579 *Sterling Hitchcock* (Rookie Prospect) .25
580 Rodney Bolton (Rookie Prospect) .05
581 Tyler Green (Rookie Prospect) .05
582 Tim Costo (Rookie Prospect) .05
583 *Tim Laker* (Rookie Prospect) .05
584 *Steve Reed* (Rookie Prospect/ Expansion Draft) .10
585 *Tom Kramer* (Rookie Prospect) .05
586 Robb Nen (Rookie Prospect) .05
587 *Jim Tatum* (Rookie Prospect) .05
588 Frank Bolick (Rookie Prospect) .05
589 Kevin Young (Rookie Prospect) .05
590 *Matt Whiteside* (Rookie Prospect) .10
591 Cesar Hernandez (Rookie Prospect) .05
592 *Mike Mohler* (Rookie Prospect) .05
593 Alan Embree (Rookie Prospect) .05
594 Terry Jorgensen (Rookie Prospect) .05
595 *John Cummings* (Rookie Prospect) .20
596 Domingo Martinez (Rookie Prospect) .05
597 Benji Gil (Rookie Prospect) .05
598 *Todd Pratt* (Rookie Prospect) .10
599 *Rene Arocha* (Rookie Prospect) .05
600 Dennis Moeller (Rookie Prospect) .05
601 Jeff Conine (Rookie Prospect/ Expansion Draft) .25
602 Trevor Hoffman (Rookie Prospect/ Expansion Draft) .15
603 Daniel Smith (Rookie Prospect) .05
604 Lee Tinsley (Rookie Prospect) .05
605 Dan Peltier (Rookie Prospect) .05
606 Billy Brewer (Rookie Prospect) .05
607 *Matt Walbeck* (Rookie Prospect) .20
608 Richie Lewis (Rookie Prospect/ Expansion Draft) .05
609 *J.T. Snow* (Rookie Prospect) .75
610 *Pat Gomez* (Rookie Prospect) .05
611 Phil Hiatt (Rookie Prospect) .05
612 Alex Arias (Rookie Prospect/ Expansion Draft) .10
613 Kevin Rogers (Rookie Prospect) .05
614 Al Martin (Rookie Prospect) .05
615 Greg Gohr (Rookie Prospect) .05
616 *Grame Lloyd* (Rookie Prospect) .05
617 Kent Bottenfield (Rookie Prospect) .05
618 Chuck Carr (Rookie Prospect/ Expansion Draft) .05
619 *Darrell Sherman* (Rookie Prospect) .05
620 *Mike Lansing* (Rookie Prospect) .25

1993 Pinnacle Expansion Opening Day

This nine-card set features 18 players for the two N.L. expansion teams: Florida Marlins and Colorado Rockies. Each "two-headed" card shows a projected Opening Day starter for each team. Cards were available one per Series 2 hobby box. Complete sets were available through a special mail-in offer.

		MT
Complete Set (9):		4.50
Common Player:		.50
1	Charlie Hough, David Nied	.50
2	Benito Santiago, Joe Girardi	.75
3	Orestes Destrade, Andres Galarraga	1.50
4	Bret Barberie, Eric Young	.50
5	Dave Magadan, Charlie Hayes	.50
6	Walt Weiss, Freddie Benevides	.50
7	Jeff Conine, Jerald Clark	1.00
8	Scott Pose, Alex Cole	.50
9	Junior Felix, Dante Bichette	.75

1993 Pinnacle Rookie Team Pinnacle

These 10 cards were randomly inserted into Series 2 packs. Rookie Team Pinnacle is printed in gold foil on both sides of the card. Cards are numbered 1 of 10, etc., and use the special Dufex process. Each card shows two players painted by artist Christopher Greco. Stated odds of finding a Rookie Team Pinnacle insert were one in 90 packs.

		MT
Complete Set (10):		50.00
Common Player:		3.00
1	Pedro Martinez, Mike Trombley	10.00
2	Kevin Rogers, Sterling Hitchcock	3.00
3	Mike Piazza, Jesse Levis	25.00
4	Ryan Klesko, J.T. Snow	3.00
5	John Patterson, Bret Boone	5.00
6	Domingo Martinez, Kevin Young	3.00
7	Wil Cordero, Manny Alexander	3.00
8	Steve Hosey, Tim Salmon	7.50
9	Ryan Thompson, Gerald Williams	3.00
10	Melvin Nieves, David Hulse	3.00

1993 Pinnacle Slugfest

Baseball's top sluggers are featured in this 30-card insert set. Cards were available one per Series 2 jumbo pack. Slugfest is printed in gold foil on the card front.

		MT
Complete Set (30):		20.00
Common Player:		.25
1	Juan Gonzalez	1.00
2	Mark McGwire	4.00
3	Cecil Fielder	.25
4	Joe Carter	.25

5 Fred McGriff .25
6 Barry Bonds 2.00
7 Gary Sheffield .50
8 Dave Hollins .25
9 Frank Thomas 2.00
10 Danny Tartabull .25
11 Albert Belle .50
12 Ruben Sierra .25
13 Larry Walker .50
14 Jeff Bagwell 1.00
15 Dave Justice .50
16 Kirby Puckett 1.50
17 John Kruk .25
18 Howard Johnson .25
19 Darryl Strawberry .25
20 Will Clark .50
21 Kevin Mitchell .25
22 Mickey Tettleton .25
23 Don Mattingly 2.00
24 Jose Canseco .75
25 Sam Millitello .25
26 Andre Dawson .50
27 Ryne Sandberg 2.00
28 Ken Griffey, Jr. 3.00
29 Carlos Baerga .25
30 Travis Fryman .25

1993 Pinnacle Team Pinnacle

These cards were randomly inserted in Series 1 at a rate of about one in every 24 packs. Each card features two players painted by artist Christopher Greco. An eleventh card, featuring relief pitchers, was available only via a mail-in offer.

MT
Complete Set (11): 45.00
Common Player: 1.50
1 Greg Maddux, Mike Mussina 10.00
2 Tom Glavine, John Smiley 2.00
3 Darren Daulton, Ivan Rodriguez 4.00
4 Fred McGriff, Frank Thomas 10.00
5 Delino DeShields, Carlos Baerga 1.50
6 Gary Sheffield, Edgar Martinez 3.00
7 Ozzie Smith, Pat Listach 5.00
8 Barry Bonds, Juan Gonzalez 7.50
9 Kirby Puckett, Andy Van Slyke 6.00
10 Larry Walker, Joe Carter 2.50
11 Rick Aguilera, Rob Dibble 3.00

1993 Pinnacle Team 2001

This insert set features 30 players who are expected to be stars in the year 2001. Cards were randomly inserted into 27-card jumbo packs from Series 1.

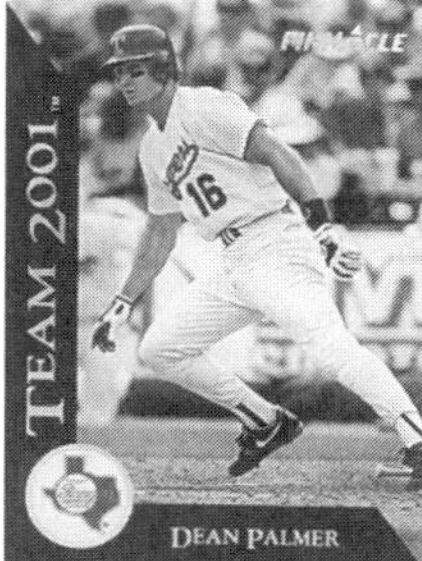

MT
Complete Set (30): 17.50
Common Player: .30
1 Wil Cordero .30
2 Cal Eldred .30
3 Mike Mussina 2.00
4 Chuck Knoblauch .30
5 Melvin Nieves .30
6 Tim Wakefield .30
7 Carlos Baerga .30
8 Bret Boone .45
9 Jeff Bagwell 3.00
10 Travis Fryman .30
11 Royce Clayton .30
12 Delino DeShields .30
13 Juan Gonzalez 3.00
14 Pedro Martinez 1.50
15 Bernie Williams .75
16 Billy Ashley .30
17 Marquis Grissom .30
18 Kenny Lofton .30
19 Ray Lankford .30
20 Tim Salmon .75
21 Steve Hosey .30
22 Charles Nagy .30
23 Dave Fleming .30
24 Reggie Sanders .30
25 Sam Millitello .30
26 Eric Karros .30
27 Ryan Klesko .30
28 Dean Palmer .30
29 Ivan Rodriguez 2.50
30 Sterling Hitchcock .30

1993 Pinnacle Tribute

These Hall of Famers each have five-card sets devoted to their career achievements. Each card commemorates a career milestone. Cards were random inserts in Series 2, about one every 24 packs. Fronts have a gold-foil stamped "Tribute" vertically at right.

MT
Complete Set (10): 30.00
George Brett Card (1-5): 2.50
Nolan Ryan Card (6-10): 5.00
1 Kansas City Royalty (George Brett) 3.00
2 The Chase for .400 (George Brett) 3.00
3 Pine Tar Pandemonium - "The Bat" 3.00
4 MVP and a World Series, Too (George Brett) 3.00
5 3,000 or Bust (George Brett) 3.00
6 The Rookie (Nolan Ryan) 5.00
7 Angel of No Merc (Nolan Ryan) 5.00
8 Astronomical Success (Nolan Ryan) 5.00
9 5,000 Ks (Nolan Ryan) 5.00
10 No-Hitter No. 7 (Nolan Ryan) 5.00

1994 Pinnacle

Pinnacle's 1994 mid-priced brand features full bleed photos, gold-foil graphics and UV coating. On front, player and team names appear in a shield-and-bar motif in the lower-left corner. On horizontal backs, the front photo is reproduced as a subdued background photo, over which are printed recent stats and a few biographical details. A different player photo is featured at left, while the brand's optical-variable anti-counterfeiting device is at bottom center. Subsets include major award winners, Rookie Prospects and Draft Picks which are appropriately noted with gold-foil lettering on front. The issue was produced in two series of 270 cards each.

MT
Complete Set (540): 20.00
Complete Series 1 (270): 12.00
Complete Series 2 (270): 8.00
Common Player: .05
Artist's Proof Stars/Rookies: 15X
Museum Stars/Rookies: 6X
Series 1 or 2 Pack (14): 1.00
Series 1 or 2 Wax Box (24): 20.00
1 Frank Thomas 1.25
2 Carlos Baerga .05
3 Sammy Sosa 1.50
4 Tony Gwynn 1.00
5 John Olerud .05
6 Ryne Sandberg .75
7 Moises Alou .15
8 Steve Avery .05
9 Tim Salmon .25
10 Cecil Fielder .05
11 Greg Maddux 1.00
12 Barry Larkin .10
13 Mike Devereaux .05
14 Charlie Hayes .05
15 Albert Belle .25
16 Andy Van Slyke .05
17 Mo Vaughn .35
18 Brian McRae .05
19 Cal Eldred .05
20 Craig Biggio .10
21 Kirby Puckett 1.00
22 Derek Bell .05
23 Don Mattingly 1.00
24 John Burkett .05
25 Roger Clemens 1.00
26 Barry Bonds 1.00
27 Paul Molitor .40
28 Mike Piazza 2.00
29 Robin Ventura .05
30 Jeff Conine .05
31 Wade Boggs .45
32 Dennis Eckersley .05
33 Bobby Bonilla .05
34 Len Dykstra .05
35 Manny Alexander .05
36 Ray Lankford .05
37 Greg Vaughn .05
38 Chuck Finley .05
39 Todd Benzinger .05
40 Dave Justice .40
41 Rob Dibble .05
42 Tom Henke .05
43 David Nied .05
44 Sandy Alomar Jr. .05
45 Pete Harnisch .05
46 Jeff Russell .05
47 Terry Mulholland .05
48 Kevin Appier .05
49 Randy Tomlin .05
50 Cal Ripken, Jr. 2.50
51 Andy Benes .05
52 Jimmy Key .05
53 Kirt Manwaring .05
54 Kevin Tapani .05
55 Jose Guzman .05
56 Todd Stottlemyre .05
57 Jack McDowell .05
58 Orel Hershiser .05
59 Chris Hammond .05
60 Chris Nabholz .05
61 Ruben Sierra .05
62 Dwight Gooden .05
63 John Kruk .05
64 Omar Vizquel .05
65 Tim Naehring .05
66 Dwight Smith .05
67 Mickey Tettleton .05
68 J.T. Snow .05
69 Greg McMichael .05
70 Kevin Mitchell .05
71 Kevin Brown .10
72 Scott Cooper .05
73 Jim Thome .05
74 Joe Girardi .05
75 Eric Anthony .05
76 Orlando Merced .05
77 Felix Jose .05
78 Tommy Greene .05
79 Bernard Gilkey .05
80 Phil Plantier .05
81 Danny Tartabull .05
82 Trevor Wilson .05
83 Chuck Knoblauch .05
84 Rick Wilkins .05
85 Devon White .05
86 Lance Johnson .05
87 Eric Karros .15
88 Gary Sheffield .25
89 Wil Cordero .05
90 Ron Darling .05
91 Darren Daulton .05
92 Joe Orsulak .05
93 Steve Cooke .05
94 Darryl Hamilton .05
95 Aaron Sele .05
96 John Doherty .05
97 Gary DiSarcina .05
98 Jeff Blauser .05
99 John Smiley .05
100 Ken Griffey, Jr. 2.50
101 Dean Palmer .05

102	Felix Fermin	.05
103	Jerald Clark	.05
104	Doug Drabek	.05
105	Curt Schilling	.15
106	Jeff Montgomery	.05
107	Rene Arocha	.05
108	Carlos Garcia	.05
109	Wally Whitehurst	.05
110	Jim Abbott	.05
111	Royce Clayton	.05
112	Chris Hoiles	.05
113	Mike Morgan	.05
114	Joe Magrane	.05
115	Tom Candiotti	.05
116	Ron Karkovice	.05
117	Ryan Bowen	.05
118	Rod Beck	.05
119	John Wetteland	.05
120	Terry Steinbach	.05
121	Dave Hollins	.05
122	Jeff Kent	.05
123	Ricky Bones	.05
124	Brian Jordan	.05
125	Chad Kreuter	.05
126	John Valentin	.05
127	Billy Hathaway	.05
128	Wilson Alvarez	.05
129	Tino Martinez	.05
130	Rodney Bolton	.05
131	David Segui	.05
132	Wayne Kirby	.05
133	Eric Young	.05
134	Scott Servais	.05
135	Scott Radinsky	.05
136	Bret Barberie	.05
137	John Roper	.05
138	Ricky Gutierrez	.05
139	Bernie Williams	.20
140	Bud Black	.05
141	Jose Vizcaino	.05
142	Gerald Williams	.05
143	Duane Ward	.05
144	Danny Jackson	.05
145	Allen Watson	.05
146	Scott Fletcher	.05
147	Delino DeShields	.05
148	Shane Mack	.05
149	Jim Eisenreich	.05
150	Troy Neel	.05
151	Jay Bell	.05
152	B.J. Surhoff	.05
153	Mark Whiten	.05
154	Mike Henneman	.05
155	Todd Hundley	.05
156	Greg Myers	.05
157	Ryan Klesko	.05
158	Dave Fleming	.05
159	Mickey Morandini	.05
160	Blas Minor	.05
161	Reggie Jefferson	.05
162	David Hulse	.05
163	Greg Swindell	.05
164	Roberto Hernandez	.05
165	Brady Anderson	.05
166	Jack Armstrong	.05
167	Phil Clark	.05
168	Melido Perez	.05
169	Darren Lewis	.05
170	Sam Horn	.05
171	Mike Harkey	.05
172	Juan Guzman	.05
173	Bob Natal	.05
174	Deion Sanders	.10
175	Carlos Quintana	.05
176	Mel Rojas	.05
177	Willie Banks	.05
178	Ben Rivera	.05
179	Kenny Lofton	.05
180	Leo Gomez	.05
181	Roberto Mejia	.05
182	Mike Perez	.05
183	Travis Fryman	.05
184	Ben McDonald	.05
185	Steve Frey	.05
186	Kevin Young	.05
187	Dave Magadan	.05
188	Bobby Munoz	.05
189	Pat Rapp	.05
190	Jose Offerman	.05
191	Vinny Castilla	.05
192	Ivan Calderon	.05
193	Ken Caminiti	.05
194	Benji Gil	.05
195	Chuck Carr	.05
196	Derrick May	.05
197	Pat Kelly	.05
198	Jeff Brantley	.05
199	Jose Lind	.05
200	Steve Buechele	.05
201	Wes Chamberlain	.05
202	Eduardo Perez	.05
203	Bret Saberhagen	.05
204	Gregg Jefferies	.05
205	Darrin Fletcher	.05
206	Kent Hrbek	.05
207	Kim Batiste	.05
208	Jeff King	.05
209	Donovan Osborne	.05
210	Dave Nilsson	.05
211	Al Martin	.05
212	Mike Moore	.05
213	Sterling Hitchcock	.05
214	Geronimo Pena	.05
215	Kevin Higgins	.05
216	Norm Charlton	.05
217	Don Slaught	.05
218	Mitch Williams	.05
219	Derek Lilliquist	.05
220	Armando Reynoso	.05
221	Kenny Rogers	.05
222	Doug Jones	.05
223	Luis Aquino	.05
224	Mike Oquist	.05
225	Darryl Scott	.05
226	Kurt Abbott	.05
227	Andy Tomberlin	.05
228	Norberto Martin	.05
229	Pedro Castellano	.05
230	*Curtis Pride*	.10
231	Jeff McNeely	.05
232	Scott Lydy	.05
233	Darren Oliver	.05
234	Danny Bautista	.05
235	Butch Huskey	.05
236	Chipper Jones	2.00
237	Eddie Zambrano	.05
238	Jean Domingo	.05
239	Javier Lopez	.05
240	Nigel Wilson	.05
241	*Drew Denson*	.05
242	Raul Mondesi	.20
243	Luis Ortiz	.05
244	Manny Ramirez	.75
245	Greg Blosser	.05
246	Rondell White	.20
247	Steve Karsay	.05
248	Scott Stahoviak	.05
249	Jose Valentin	.05
250	Marc Newfield	.05
251	Keith Kessinger	.05
252	Carl Everett	.10
253	John O'Donoghue	.05
254	Turk Wendell	.05
255	Scott Ruffcorn	.05
256	Tony Tarasco	.05
257	Andy Cook	.05
258	Matt Mieske	.05
259	Luis Lopez	.05
260	Ramon Caraballo	.05
261	Salomon Torres	.05
262	*Brooks Kieschnick*	.05
263	*Daron Kirkreit*	.05
264	*Bill Wagner*	.40
265	*Matt Drews*	.05
266	Scott Christman	.05
267	*Torii Hunter*	.50
268	*Jamey Wright*	.15
269	Jeff Granger	.05
270	*Trot Nixon*	.75
271	Randy Myers	.05
272	Trevor Hoffman	.05
273	Bob Wickman	.05
274	Willie McGee	.05
275	Hipolito Pichardo	.05
276	Bobby Witt	.05
277	Gregg Olson	.05
278	Randy Johnson	.60
279	Robb Nen	.05
280	Paul O'Neill	.05
281	Lou Whitaker	.05
282	Chad Curtis	.05
283	Doug Henry	.05
284	Tom Glavine	.10
285	Mike Greenwell	.05
286	Roberto Kelly	.05
287	Roberto Alomar	.60
288	Charlie Hough	.05
289	Alex Fernandez	.05
290	Jeff Bagwell	.75
291	Wally Joyner	.05
292	Andujar Cedeno	.05
293	Rick Aguilera	.05
294	Darryl Strawberry	.05
295	Mike Mussina	.50
296	Jeff Gardner	.05
297	Chris Gwynn	.05
298	Matt Williams	.15
299	Brent Gates	.05
300	Mark McGwire	2.50
301	Jim Deshaies	.05
302	Edgar Martinez	.05
303	Danny Darwin	.05
304	Pat Meares	.05
305	Benito Santiago	.05
306	Jose Canseco	.40
307	Jim Gott	.05
308	Paul Sorrento	.05
309	Scott Kamieniecki	.05
310	Larry Walker	.25
311	Mark Langston	.05
312	John Jaha	.05
313	Stan Javier	.05
314	Hal Morris	.05
315	Robby Thompson	.05
316	Pat Hentgen	.05
317	Tom Gordon	.05
318	Joey Cora	.05
319	Luis Alicea	.05
320	Andre Dawson	.20
321	Darryl Kile	.05
322	Jose Rijo	.05
323	Luis Gonzalez	.25
324	Billy Ashley	.05
325	David Cone	.05
326	Bill Swift	.05
327	Phil Hiatt	.05
328	Craig Paquette	.05
329	Bob Welch	.05
330	Tony Phillips	.05
331	Archi Cianfrocco	.05
332	Dave Winfield	.50
333	David McCarty	.05
334	Al Leiter	.05
335	Tom Browning	.05
336	Mark Grace	.20
337	Jose Mesa	.05
338	Mike Stanley	.05
339	Roger McDowell	.05
340	Damion Easley	.05
341	Angel Miranda	.05
342	John Smoltz	.10
343	Jay Buhner	.05
344	Bryan Harvey	.05
345	Joe Carter	.05
346	Dante Bichette	.05
347	Jason Bere	.05
348	Frank Viola	.05
349	Ivan Rodriguez	.60
350	Juan Gonzalez	.75
351	Steve Finley	.05
352	Mike Felder	.05
353	Ramon Martinez	.05
354	Greg Gagne	.05
355	Ken Hill	.05
356	Pedro Munoz	.05
357	Todd Van Poppel	.05
358	Marquis Grissom	.05
359	Milt Cuyler	.05
360	Reggie Sanders	.05
361	Scott Erickson	.05
362	Billy Hatcher	.05
363	Gene Harris	.05
364	Rene Gonzales	.05
365	Kevin Rogers	.05
366	Eric Plunk	.05
367	Todd Zeile	.05
368	John Franco	.05
369	Brett Butler	.05
370	Bill Spiers	.05
371	Terry Pendleton	.05
372	Chris Bosio	.05
373	Orestes Destrade	.05
374	Dave Stewart	.05
375	Darren Holmes	.05
376	Doug Strange	.05
377	Brian Turang	.05
378	Carl Willis	.05
379	Mark McLemore	.05
380	Bobby Jones	.05
381	Scott Sanders	.05
382	Kirk Rueter	.05
383	Randy Velarde	.05
384	Fred McGriff	.05
385	Charles Nagy	.05
386	Rich Amaral	.05
387	Geronimo Berroa	.05
388	Eric Davis	.05
389	Ozzie Smith	.75
390	Alex Arias	.05
391	Brad Ausmus	.05
392	Cliff Floyd	.10
393	Roger Salkeld	.05
394	Jim Edmonds	.10
395	Jeromy Burnitz	.05
396	Dave Staton	.05
397	Rob Butler	.05
398	Marcos Armas	.05
399	Darrell Whitmore	.05
400	Ryan Thompson	.05
401	*Ross Powell*	.05
402	Joe Oliver	.05
403	Paul Carey	.05
404	Bob Hamelin	.05
405	Chris Turner	.05
406	Nate Minchey	.05
407	*Lonnie Maclin*	.05
408	Harold Baines	.05
409	Brian Williams	.05
410	Johnny Ruffin	.05
411	*Julian Tavarez*	.10
412	Mark Hutton	.05
413	Carlos Delgado	.50
414	Chris Gomez	.05
415	Mike Hampton	.05
416	Alex Diaz	.05
417	Jeffrey Hammonds	.05
418	Jayhawk Owens	.05
419	J.R. Phillips	.05
420	*Cory Bailey*	.10
421	Denny Hocking	.05
422	Jon Shave	.05
423	Damon Buford	.05
424	Troy O'Leary	.05
425	Tripp Cromer	.05
426	Albie Lopez	.05
427	Tony Fernandez	.05
428	Ozzie Guillen	.05
429	Alan Trammell	.05
430	*John Wasdin*	.10
431	Marc Valdes	.05
432	*Brian Anderson*	.40
433	*Matt Brunson*	.05
434	*Wayne Gomes*	.10
435	*Jay Powell*	.10
436	*Kirk Presley*	.05
437	*Jon Ratliff*	.10
438	*Derrek Lee*	.50
439	Tom Pagnozzi	.05
440	Kent Mercker	.05
441	*Phil Leftwich*	.05
442	Jamie Moyer	.05
443	John Flaherty	.05
444	Mark Wohlers	.05
445	Jose Bautista	.05
446	Andres Galarraga	.05
447	Mark Lemke	.05
448	Tim Wakefield	.05
449	Pat Listach	.05
450	Rickey Henderson	.40
451	Mike Gallego	.05
452	Bob Tewksbury	.05
453	Kirk Gibson	.05
454	Pedro Astacio	.05
455	Mike Lansing	.05
456	Sean Berry	.05
457	Bob Walk	.05
458	Chili Davis	.05
459	Ed Sprague	.05
460	Kevin Stocker	.05
461	Mike Stanton	.05
462	Tim Raines	.05
463	Mike Bordick	.05
464	David Wells	.10
465	Tim Laker	.05
466	Cory Snyder	.05
467	Alex Cole	.05
468	Pete Incaviglia	.05
469	Roger Pavlik	.05
470	Greg W. Harris	.05
471	Xavier Hernandez	.05
472	Erik Hanson	.05
473	Jesse Orosco	.05
474	Greg Colbrunn	.05
475	Harold Reynolds	.05
476	Greg Harris	.05
477	Pat Borders	.05
478	Melvin Nieves	.05
479	Mariano Duncan	.05
480	Greg Hibbard	.05
481	Tim Pugh	.05
482	Bobby Ayala	.05
483	Sid Fernandez	.05
484	Tim Wallach	.05
485	Randy Milligan	.05

486	Walt Weiss	.05
487	Matt Walbeck	.05
488	Mike Macfarlane	.05
489	Jerry Browne	.05
490	Chris Sabo	.05
491	Tim Belcher	.05
492	Spike Owen	.05
493	Rafael Palmeiro	.20
494	Brian Harper	.05
495	Eddie Murray	.45
496	Ellis Burks	.05
497	Karl Rhodes	.05
498	Otis Nixon	.05
499	Lee Smith	.05
500	Bip Roberts	.05
501	Pedro Martinez	.05
502	Brian L. Hunter	.05
503	Tyler Green	.05
504	Bruce Hurst	.05
505	Alex Gonzalez	.15
506	Mark Portugal	.05
507	Bob Ojeda	.05
508	Dave Henderson	.05
509	Bo Jackson	.10
510	Bret Boone	.10
511	Mark Eichhorn	.05
512	Luis Polonia	.05
513	Will Clark	.15
514	Dave Valle	.05
515	Dan Wilson	.05
516	Dennis Martinez	.05
517	Jim Leyritz	.05
518	Howard Johnson	.05
519	Jody Reed	.05
520	Julio Franco	.05
521	Jeff Reardon	.05
522	Willie Greene	.05
523	Shawon Dunston	.05
524	Keith Mitchell	.05
525	Rick Helling	.05
526	Mark Kiefer	.05
527	*Chan Ho Park*	1.50
528	Tony Longmire	.05
529	Rich Becker	.05
530	Tim Hyers	.05
531	Darrin Jackson	.05
532	Jack Morris	.05
533	Rick White	.05
534	Mike Kelly	.05
535	James Mouton	.05
536	Steve Trachsel	.05
537	Tony Eusebio	.05
538	Kelly Stinnett	.05
539	Paul Spoljaric	.05
540	Darren Dreifort	.05

1994 Pinnacle Artist's Proof

A specially designated version of the regular Pinnacle set, described as the first day's production of the first 1,000 of each card, was issued as a random pack insert. Cards feature a small gold-foil "Artist's Proof" rectangle embossed above the player/team name shield on front. In all other respects the cards are identical to the regular-issue versions.

	MT
Complete Set (540):	400.00
Common Player:	2.00
Stars/Rookies:	15X

(See 1994 Pinnacle for checklist and base card values.)

1994 Pinnacle Museum Collection

Each card in the 1994 Pinnacle set was produced in a parallel "Museum Collection" version. The inserts were produced utilizing the company's Dufex foil-printing technology on front, with rays emanating from the Pinnacle logo. Backs are identical to the regular-issue version except for the substitution of a "1994 Museum Collection" logo for the optical-variable anti-counterfeiting bar at bottom-center. Museums were random package inserts, appearing at the rate of about once per four packs.

	MT
Complete Set (540):	125.00
Common Player:	1.00
Stars/Rookies:	6X

(See 1994 Pinnacle for checklist and base card values.)

1994 Pinnacle Rookie Team Pinnacle

The popular Rookie Team Pinnacle insert card tradition continued in 1994 with a series of nine "two-headed" cards featuring the top prospect from each league at each position. The cards again feature the ultra-realistic artwork of Chris Greco. Each side is enhanced with gold-foil presentations of the player's name, the Pinnacle logo and the Rookie Team Pinnacle logo. The inserts were packaged, on average, one per 90 packs of hobby foil only.

		MT
Complete Set (9):		20.00
Common Player:		1.00
1	Carlos Delgado, Javier Lopez	5.00
2	Bob Hamelin, J.R. Phillips	1.00
3	Jon Shave, Keith Kessinger	1.00
4	Butch Huskey, Luis Ortiz	1.00
5	Chipper Jones, Kurt Abbott	7.50
6	Rondell White, Manny Ramirez	6.00
7	Cliff Floyd, Jeffrey Hammonds	2.00
8	Marc Newfield, Nigel Wilson	1.00
9	Salomon Torres, Mark Hutton	1.00

1994 Pinnacle Run Creators

This insert set, exclusive to Pinnacle jumbo packaging, features the top 44 performers of the previous season in the arcane statistic of "runs created." Fronts have an action photo on which the stadium background has been muted in soft-focus red or blue. The player's last name appears at right in gold foil; the logo, "The Run Creators" is in one of the lower corners. Backs are printed in teal with a color team logo at center, beneath the stats that earned the player's inclusion in the series. The player's runs created are in gold foil above the write-up. Cards are numbered with an "RC" prefix.

		MT
Complete Set (44):		15.00
Common Player:		.25
1	John Olerud	.25
2	Frank Thomas	1.00
3	Ken Griffey, Jr.	2.00
4	Paul Molitor	.50
5	Rafael Palmeiro	.35
6	Roberto Alomar	.60
7	Juan Gonzalez	.75
8	Albert Belle	.50
9	Travis Fryman	.25
10	Rickey Henderson	.50
11	Tony Phillips	.25
12	Mo Vaughn	.50
13	Tim Salmon	.35
14	Kenny Lofton	.25
15	Carlos Baerga	.25
16	Greg Vaughn	.25
17	Jay Buhner	.25
18	Chris Hoiles	.25
19	Mickey Tettleton	.25
20	Kirby Puckett	.85
21	Danny Tartabull	.25
22	Devon White	.25
23	Barry Bonds	1.00
24	Lenny Dykstra	.25
25	John Kruk	.25
26	Fred McGriff	.25
27	Gregg Jefferies	.25
28	Mike Piazza	1.50
29	Jeff Blauser	.25
30	Andres Galarraga	.25
31	Darren Daulton	.25
32	Dave Justice	.50
33	Craig Biggio	.25
34	Mark Grace	.40
35	Tony Gwynn	.85
36	Jeff Bagwell	.75
37	Jay Bell	.25
38	Marquis Grissom	.25
39	Matt Williams	.35
40	Charlie Hayes	.25
41	Dante Bichette	.25
42	Bernard Gilkey	.25
43	Brett Butler	.25
44	Rick Wilkins	.25

1994 Pinnacle Team Pinnacle

The double-sided Team Pinnacle insert set features 18 of the top players in the game. They were inserted into Series 2 at a rate of one every 90 packs.

		MT
Complete Set (9):		30.00
Common Player:		1.00
1	Jeff Bagwell, Frank Thomas	4.50
2	Carlos Baerga, Robby Thompson	1.00
3	Matt Williams, Dean Palmer	2.00
4	Cal Ripken, Jr., Jay Bell	8.00
5	Ivan Rodriguez, Mike Piazza	6.50
6	Len Dykstra, Ken Griffey, Jr.	7.50
7	Juan Gonzalez, Barry Bonds	4.50
8	Tim Salmon, Dave Justice	2.00
9	Greg Maddux, Jack McDowell	4.50

1994 Pinnacle Tribute

A hobby-only insert set, found approximately one per 18 foil packs, this nine-card series honors players who reached significant season or career milestones or otherwise had special achievements in 1993. Fronts feature full-bleed action photos. At left is a black strip with "TRIBUTE" in gold foil. A colored strip at bottom has the player name in gold foil and a short description of why he is being feted beneath. The Pinnacle logo is in gold foil at top. The same gold-foil enhancements are found on back, along with a portrait photo. In a black box at bottom are details of the tribute. The Pinnacle optical-variable anti-counterfeiting device is at bottom center. Card numbers are prefixed with "TR".

		MT
Complete Set (18):		16.00
Common Player:		.35
1	Paul Molitor	1.00
2	Jim Abbott	.25
3	Dave Winfield	1.00
4	Bo Jackson	.35
5	Dave Justice	.50
6	Len Dykstra	.25
7	Mike Piazza	2.50
8	Barry Bonds	1.50
9	Randy Johnson	1.00
10	Ozzie Smith	1.00
11	Mark Whiten	.25
12	Greg Maddux	1.50
13	Cal Ripken, Jr.	3.50
14	Frank Thomas	1.50
15	Juan Gonzalez	1.00
16	Roberto Alomar	.65
17	Ken Griffey, Jr.	3.00
18	Lee Smith	.25

1995 Pinnacle

The 1995 Pinnacle set was produced in two series of 225 base cards each, plus inserts. Fronts have borderless photos with a large embossed gold foil "wave" at bottom containing the player's last name and team logo. Horizontal backs have a portrait photo at left, an action photo at right and a few sentences about the player at center. Stats at the bottom offer previous year, career and career-best numbers. Subsets with the base cards include rookie specials in both Series 1 and 2 have a design featuring a green stripe at one side or bottom with the player's name in gold and a special round gold-foil logo. A similar design, with red stripes, is used for Series 1 cards featuring Draft Picks. In Series 2, a 30-card Swing Men subset has a blue vortex background design and special gold-foil identifier. Basic pack configurations offered 12-card ($2.49) and 15-card ($2.99) counts in both retail and hobby versions, each with some unique inserts.

		MT
Complete Set (450):		30.00
Common Player:		.10
Hobby Pack (12):		1.50
Hobby Wax Box (24):		32.00
Retail Pack (12):		1.50
Retail Wax Box (36):		35.00
1	Jeff Bagwell	.75
2	Roger Clemens	.75
3	Mark Whiten	.10
4	Shawon Dunston	.10
5	Bobby Bonilla	.10
6	Kevin Tapani	.10
7	Eric Karros	.10
8	Cliff Floyd	.10
9	Pat Kelly	.10
10	Jeffrey Hammonds	.10
11	Jeff Conine	.10
12	Fred McGriff	.10
13	Chris Bosio	.10
14	Mike Mussina	.40
15	Danny Bautista	.10
16	Mickey Morandini	.10
17	Chuck Finley	.10
18	Jim Thome	.10
19	Luis Ortiz	.10
20	Walt Weiss	.10
21	Don Mattingly	1.00
22	Bob Hamelin	.10
23	Melido Perez	.10
24	Kevin Mitchell	.10
25	John Smoltz	.15
26	Hector Carrasco	.10
27	Pat Hentgen	.10
28	Derrick May	.10
29	Mike Kingery	.10
30	Chuck Carr	.10
31	Billy Ashley	.10
32	Todd Hundley	.10
33	Luis Gonzalez	.35
34	Marquis Grissom	.10
35	Jeff King	.10
36	Eddie Williams	.10
37	Tom Pagnozzi	.10
38	Chris Hoiles	.10
39	Sandy Alomar	.10
40	Mike Greenwell	.10
41	Lance Johnson	.10
42	Junior Felix	.10
43	Felix Jose	.10
44	Scott Leius	.10
45	Ruben Sierra	.10
46	Kevin Seitzer	.10
47	Wade Boggs	.50
48	Reggie Jefferson	.10
49	Jose Canseco	.40
50	Dave Justice	.20
51	John Smiley	.10
52	Joe Carter	.10
53	Rick Wilkins	.10
54	Ellis Burks	.10
55	Dave Weathers	.10
56	Pedro Astacio	.10
57	Ryan Thompson	.10
58	James Mouton	.10
59	Mel Rojas	.10
60	Orlando Merced	.10
61	Matt Williams	.30
62	Bernard Gilkey	.10
63	J.R. Phillips	.10
64	Lee Smith	.10
65	Jim Edmonds	.15
66	Darrin Jackson	.10
67	Scott Cooper	.10
68	Ron Karkovice	.10
69	Chris Gomez	.10
70	Kevin Appier	.10
71	Bobby Jones	.10
72	Doug Drabek	.10
73	Matt Mieske	.10
74	Sterling Hitchcock	.10
75	John Valentin	.10
76	Reggie Sanders	.10
77	Wally Joyner	.10
78	Turk Wendell	.10
79	Wendell Hayes	.10
80	Bret Barberie	.10
81	Troy Neel	.10
82	Ken Caminiti	.10
83	Milt Thompson	.10
84	Paul Sorrento	.10
85	Trevor Hoffman	.10
86	Jay Bell	.10
87	Mark Portugal	.10
88	Sid Fernandez	.10
89	Charles Nagy	.10
90	Jeff Montgomery	.10
91	Chuck Knoblauch	.10
92	Jeff Frye	.10
93	Tony Gwynn	.75
94	John Olerud	.10
95	David Nied	.10
96	Chris Hammond	.10
97	Edgar Martinez	.10
98	Kevin Stocker	.10
99	Jeff Fassero	.10
100	Curt Schilling	.15
101	Dave Clark	.10
102	Delino DeShields	.10
103	Leo Gomez	.10
104	Dave Hollins	.10
105	Tim Naehring	.10
106	Otis Nixon	.10
107	Ozzie Guillen	.10
108	Jose Lind	.10
109	Stan Javier	.10
110	Greg Vaughn	.10
111	Chipper Jones	2.00
112	Ed Sprague	.10
113	Mike Macfarlane	.10
114	Steve Finley	.10
115	Ken Hill	.10
116	Carlos Garcia	.10
117	Lou Whitaker	.10
118	Todd Zeile	.10
119	Gary Sheffield	.40
120	Ben McDonald	.10
121	Pete Harnisch	.10
122	Ivan Rodriguez	.60
123	Wilson Alvarez	.10
124	Travis Fryman	.10
125	Pedro Munoz	.10
126	Mark Lemke	.10
127	Jose Valentin	.10
128	Ken Griffey Jr.	2.50
129	Omar Vizquel	.10
130	Milt Cuyler	.10
131	Steve Traschel	.10
132	Alex Rodriguez	2.50
133	Garret Anderson	.15
134	Armando Benitez	.10
135	Shawn Green	.20
136	Jorge Fabregas	.10
137	Orlando Miller	.10
138	Rikkert Faneyte	.10
139	Ismael Valdes	.10
140	Jose Oliva	.10
141	Aaron Small	.10
142	Tim Davis	.10
143	Ricky Bottalacio	.10
144	Mike Matheny	.10
145	Roberto Petagine	.10
146	Fausto Cruz	.10
147	Bryce Florie	.10
148	Jose Lima	.10
149	John Hudek	.10
150	Duane Singleton	.10
151	John Mabry	.10
152	Robert Eenhoorn	.10
153	Jon Lieber	.10
154	Garey Ingram	.10
155	Paul Shuey	.10
156	Mike Lieberthal	.10
157	Steve Dunn	.10
158	Charles Johnson	.10
159	Ernie Young	.10
160	Jose Martinez	.10
161	Kurt Miller	.10
162	Joey Eischen	.10
163	Dave Stevens	.10
164	Brian Hunter	.10
165	Jeff Cirillo	.10
166	Mark Smith	.10
167	*McKay Christensen*	.10
168	C.J. Nitkowski	.10
169	*Antone Williamson*	.10
170	Paul Konerko	.25
171	*Scott Elarton*	.25
172	Jacob Shumate	.10
173	Terrence Long	.10
174	*Mark Johnson*	.15
175	Ben Grieve	.50
176	*Jayson Peterson*	.10
177	Checklist	.10
178	Checklist	.10
179	Checklist	.10
180	Checklist	.10
181	Brian Anderson	.10
182	Steve Buechele	.10
183	Mark Clark	.10
184	Cecil Fielder	.10
185	Steve Avery	.10
186	Devon White	.10
187	Craig Shipley	.10
188	Brady Anderson	.10
189	Kenny Lofton	.10
190	Alex Cole	.10
191	Brent Gates	.10
192	Dean Palmer	.10
193	Alex Gonzalez	.15
194	Steve Cooke	.10
195	Ray Lankford	.10
196	Mark McGwire	2.50
197	Marc Newfield	.10
198	Pat Rapp	.10
199	Darren Lewis	.10
200	Carlos Baerga	.10
201	Rickey Henderson	.50
202	Kurt Abbott	.10
203	Kirt Manwaring	.10
204	Cal Ripken Jr.	2.50
205	Darren Daulton	.10
206	Greg Colbrunn	.10
207	Darryl Hamilton	.10
208	Bo Jackson	.15
209	Tony Phillips	.10
210	Geronimo Berroa	.10
211	Rich Becker	.10
212	Tony Tarasco	.10
213	Karl Rhodes	.10
214	Phil Plantier	.10
215	J.T. Snow	.10
216	Mo Vaughn	.50
217	Greg Gagne	.10
218	Rickey Bones	.10
219	Mike Bordick	.10
220	Chad Curtis	.10
221	Royce Clayton	.10
222	Roberto Alomar	.60
223	Jose Rijo	.10
224	Ryan Klesko	.10
225	Mark Langston	.10
226	Frank Thomas	1.50
227	Juan Gonzalez	.75
228	Ron Gant	.10
229	Javier Lopez	.10
230	Sammy Sosa	1.50

No.	Player	Value
231	Kevin Brown	.15
232	Gary DiSarcina	.10
233	Albert Belle	.40
234	Jay Buhner	.10
235	Pedro Martinez	.35
236	Bob Tewksbury	.10
237	Mike Piazza	2.00
238	Darryl Kile	.10
239	Bryan Harvey	.10
240	Andres Galarraga	.10
241	Jeff Blauser	.10
242	Jeff Kent	.10
243	Bobby Munoz	.10
244	Greg Maddux	1.50
245	Paul O'Neill	.10
246	Lenny Dykstra	.10
247	Todd Van Poppel	.10
248	Bernie Williams	.40
249	Glenallen Hill	.10
250	Duane Ward	.10
251	Dennis Eckersley	.10
252	Pat Mahomes	.10
253	Rusty Greer (photo actually Jeff Frye)	.10
254	Roberto Kelly	.10
255	Randy Myers	.10
256	Scott Ruffcorn	.10
257	Robin Ventura	.10
258	Eduardo Perez	.10
259	Aaron Sele	.10
260	Paul Molitor	.60
261	Juan Guzman	.10
262	Darren Oliver	.10
263	Mike Stanley	.10
264	Tom Glavine	.15
265	Rico Brogna	.10
266	Craig Biggio	.15
267	Darrell Whitmore	.10
268	Jimmy Key	.10
269	Will Clark	.30
270	David Cone	.10
271	Brian Jordan	.10
272	Barry Bonds	.75
273	Danny Tartabull	.10
274	Ramon Martinez	.10
275	Al Martin	.10
276	Fred McGriff (Swing Men)	.10
277	Carlos Delgado (Swing Men)	.40
278	Juan Gonzalez (Swing Men)	.40
279	Shawn Green (Swing Men)	.15
280	Carlos Baerga (Swing Men)	.10
281	Cliff Floyd (Swing Men)	.10
282	Ozzie Smith (Swing Men)	.40
283	Alex Rodriguez (Swing Men)	1.50
284	Kenny Lofton (Swing Men)	.10
285	Dave Justice (Swing Men)	.20
286	Tim Salmon (Swing Men)	.15
287	Manny Ramirez (Swing Men)	.50
288	Will Clark (Swing Men)	.20
289	Garret Anderson (Swing Men)	.10
290	Billy Ashley (Swing Men)	.10
291	Tony Gwynn (Swing Men)	.50
292	Raul Mondesi (Swing Men)	.25
293	Rafael Palmeiro (Swing Men)	.15
294	Matt Williams (Swing Men)	.10
295	Don Mattingly (Swing Men)	.75
296	Kirby Puckett (Swing Men)	.50
297	Paul Molitor (Swing Men)	.30
298	Albert Belle (Swing Men)	.25
299	Barry Bonds (Swing Men)	.65
300	Mike Piazza (Swing Men)	1.00
301	Jeff Bagwell (Swing Men)	.50
302	Frank Thomas (Swing Men)	1.00
303	Chipper Jones (Swing Men)	1.00
304	Ken Griffey Jr. (Swing Men)	1.50
305	Cal Ripken Jr. (Swing Men)	1.50
306	Eric Anthony	.10
307	Todd Benzinger	.10
308	Jacob Brumfield	.10
309	Wes Chamberlain	.10
310	Tino Martinez	.10
311	Roberto Mejia	.10
312	Jose Offerman	.10
313	David Segui	.10
314	Eric Young	.10
315	Rey Sanchez	.10
316	Raul Mondesi	.35
317	Bret Boone	.10
318	Andre Dawson	.15
319	Brian McRae	.10
320	Dave Nilsson	.10
321	Moises Alou	.15
322	Don Slaught	.10
323	Dave McCarty	.10
324	Mike Huff	.10
325	Rick Aguilera	.10
326	Rod Beck	.10
327	Kenny Rogers	.10
328	Andy Benes	.10
329	Allen Watson	.10
330	Randy Johnson	.35
331	Willie Greene	.10
332	Hal Morris	.10
333	Ozzie Smith	.75
334	Jason Bere	.10
335	Scott Erickson	.10
336	Dante Bichette	.10
337	Willie Banks	.10
338	Eric Davis	.10
339	Rondell White	.20
340	Kirby Puckett	.75
341	Deion Sanders	.15
342	Eddie Murray	.50
343	Mike Harkey	.10
344	Joey Hamilton	.10
345	Roger Salkeld	.10
346	Wil Cordero	.10
347	John Wetteland	.10
348	Geronimo Pena	.10
349	Kirk Gibson	.10
350	Manny Ramirez	.75
351	William Van Landingham	.10
352	B.J. Surhoff	.10
353	Ken Ryan	.10
354	Terry Steinbach	.10
355	Bret Saberhagen	.10
356	John Jaha	.10
357	Joe Girardi	.10
358	Steve Karsay	.10
359	Alex Fernandez	.10
360	Salomon Torres	.10
361	John Burkett	.10
362	Derek Bell	.10
363	Tom Henke	.10
364	Gregg Jefferies	.10
365	Jack McDowell	.10
366	Andujar Cedeno	.10
367	Dave Winfield	.50
368	Carl Everett	.15
369	Danny Jackson	.10
370	Jeromy Burnitz	.10
371	Mark Grace	.20
372	Larry Walker	.25
373	Bill Swift	.10
374	Dennis Martinez	.10
375	Mickey Tettleton	.10
376	Mel Nieves	.10
377	Cal Eldred	.10
378	Orel Hershiser	.10
379	David Wells	.15
380	Gary Gaetti	.10
381	Tim Raines	.10
382	Barry Larkin	.15
383	Jason Jacome	.10
384	Tim Wallach	.10
385	Robby Thompson	.10
386	Frank Viola	.10
387	Dave Stewart	.10
388	Bip Roberts	.10
389	Ron Darling	.10
390	Carlos Delgado	.35
391	Tim Salmon	.20
392	Alan Trammell	.10
393	Kevin Foster	.10
394	Jim Abbott	.10
395	John Kruk	.10
396	Andy Van Slyke	.10
397	Dave Magadan	.10
398	Rafael Palmeiro	.25
399	Mike Devereaux	.10
400	Benito Santiago	.10
401	Brett Butler	.10
402	John Franco	.10
403	Matt Walbeck	.10
404	Terry Pendleton	.10
405	Chris Sabo	.10
406	Andrew Lorraine	.10
407	Dan Wilson	.10
408	Mike Lansing	.10
409	Ray McDavid	.10
410	Shane Andrews	.10
411	Tom Gordon	.10
412	Chad Ogea	.10
413	James Baldwin	.10
414	Russ Davis	.10
415	Ray Holbert	.10
416	Ray Durham	.10
417	Matt Nokes	.10
418	Rodney Henderson	.10
419	Gabe White	.10
420	Todd Hollandsworth	.10
421	Midre Cummings	.10
422	Harold Baines	.10
423	Troy Percival	.10
424	Joe Vitiello	.10
425	Andy Ashby	.10
426	Michael Tucker	.10
427	Mark Gubicza	.10
428	Jim Bullinger	.10
429	Jose Malave	.10
430	Pete Schourek	.10
431	Bobby Ayala	.10
432	Marvin Freeman	.10
433	Pat Listach	.10
434	Eddie Taubensee	.10
435	Steve Howe	.10
436	Kent Mercker	.10
437	Hector Fajardo	.10
438	Scott Kamieniecki	.10
439	Robb Nen	.10
440	Mike Kelly	.10
441	Tom Candiotti	.10
442	Albie Lopez	.10
443	Jeff Granger	.10
444	Rich Aude	.10
445	Luis Polonia	.10
446	A.L. Checklist (Frank Thomas)	.40
447	A.L. Checklist (Ken Griffey Jr.)	.75
448	N.L. Checklist (Mike Piazza)	.50
449	N.L. Checklist (Jeff Bagwell)	.40
450	Insert Checklist (Frank Thomas, Ken Griffey Jr., Mike Piazza, Jeff Bagwell)	.40

1995 Pinnacle Artist's Proof

Said to represent the first 1,000 of each card printed, the Artist's Proof chase set is a parallel issue with a counterpart for each of the regular-issue cards. The proofs differ in the use of silver, rather than gold foil for front graphic highlights, and the inclusion of a rectangular silver-foil "ARTIST'S PROOF" logo on front. The AP inserts were reported seeded at an average rate of one per 26 packs.

	MT
Complete Set (450):	600.00
Common Player:	2.00
Stars/Rookies:	10X

(See 1995 Pinnacle for checklist and base card values.)

1995 Pinnacle Museum Collection

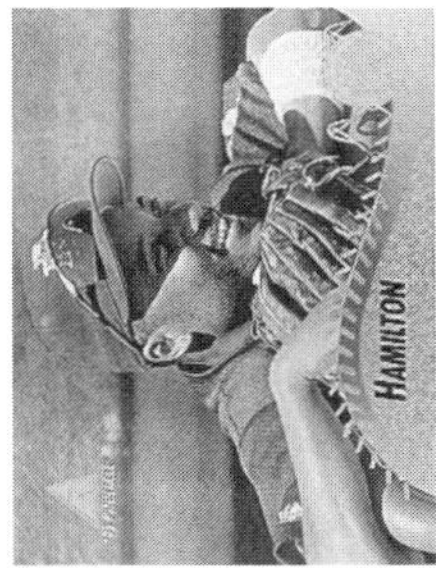

Pinnacle's Dufex foil-printing technology on the card fronts differentiates this parallel insert from the corresponding cards in the regular issue. Backs have a rectangular "1995 Museum Collection" logo at lower-left. Museum inserts are found at an average rate of one per four packs. Because of production difficulties, trade cards had to be issued in place of seven of the rookie cards in Series 2. Those redemption cards were valid only through Dec. 31, 1995.

	MT
Complete Set (450):	350.00
Common Player:	.75
Stars/Rookies:	6X

(See 1995 Pinnacle for checklist and base card values.)

Redemption card	.50

1995 Pinnacle E.T.A. '95

This hobby-only chase set identifies six players picked to arrive in the major leagues for a 1995 debut. Both sides have borderless action photos on which the background has been subdued and posterized. Gold-foil headlines on each side of the card give the player's credentials. These inserts are found on average of once per 24 packs.

		MT
Complete Set (6):		12.00
Common Player:		1.00
1	Ben Grieve	8.00
2	Alex Ochoa	1.00
3	Joe Vitiello	1.00
4	Johnny Damon	4.00
5	Trey Beamon	1.00
6	Brooks Kieschnick	1.00

1995 Pinnacle Gate Attraction

Series 2 jumbo packs are the exclusive source for this chase set. Printed on metallic foil, the cards have a color photo at top and a second photo at bottom that is shown in gold tones only. A "Gate Attraction" seal is in the lower-left corner. Backs have a large portrait photo on a color-streaked background, plus a few words about the player.

		MT
Complete Set (18):		20.00
Common Player:		.35
1	Ken Griffey Jr.	3.50
2	Frank Thomas	2.50
3	Cal Ripken Jr.	3.50
4	Jeff Bagwell	1.50
5	Mike Piazza	3.00
6	Barry Bonds	2.00
7	Kirby Puckett	2.00
8	Albert Belle	1.00
9	Tony Gwynn	2.00
10	Raul Mondesi	.50
11	Will Clark	.50
12	Don Mattingly	2.50
13	Roger Clemens	2.00
14	Paul Molitor	1.00
15	Matt Williams	.50
16	Greg Maddux	2.00
17	Kenny Lofton	.35
18	Cliff Floyd	.35

1995 Pinnacle New Blood

Both hobby and retail packs of Series 2 hide this insert set of young stars, at an average rate of one card per 90 packs. A player photo appears in the red and silver foil-printed background, and there is a color action photo in the foreground. Conventionally printed backs feature the same photos, but with their prominence reversed. A few words of text describe the player's star potential.

		MT
Complete Set (9):		27.50
Common Player:		1.00
1	Alex Rodriguez	12.50
2	Shawn Green	5.00
3	Brian Hunter	1.00
4	Garret Anderson	1.50
5	Charles Johnson	1.00
6	Chipper Jones	10.00
7	Carlos Delgado	2.00
8	Billy Ashley	1.00
9	J.R. Phillips	1.00

1995 Pinnacle Performers

Series 1 jumbos were the only place to find this chase set. Fronts have a deep red background with a golden pyramid at center and a silver apex, all in foil printing. A color player action photo is in the center foreground. The reverse repeats the front photo in the background, in one color, and has a second color photo, along with a few words about the player.

		MT
Complete Set (18):		60.00
Common Player:		1.00
1	Frank Thomas	7.50
2	Albert Belle	3.00
3	Barry Bonds	7.50
4	Juan Gonzalez	6.00
5	Andres Galarraga	1.00
6	Raul Mondesi	1.50
7	Paul Molitor	5.00
8	Tim Salmon	2.00
9	Mike Piazza	10.00
10	Gregg Jefferies	1.00
11	Will Clark	2.00
12	Greg Maddux	7.50
13	Manny Ramirez	6.00
14	Kirby Puckett	7.50
15	Shawn Green	4.00
16	Rafael Palmeiro	2.00
17	Paul O'Neill	1.00
18	Jason Bere	1.00

1995 Pinnacle Red Hot

These Series 2 inserts are found at an average rate of one per 16 packs and feature top veteran stars. Fronts have a large action photo on right, over a background of foil-printed red and yellow flames. A vertical strip at left of graduated red tones has a player portrait photo and the "RED HOT" flame logo, again printed on foil. Backs are conventionally printed and have a black background with large flaming "RED HOT" letters and a color player photo.

		MT
Complete Set (25):		30.00
Common Player:		.50
1	Cal Ripken Jr.	4.00
2	Ken Griffey Jr.	4.00
3	Frank Thomas	2.50
4	Jeff Bagwell	1.50
5	Mike Piazza	3.00
6	Barry Bonds	2.00
7	Albert Belle	1.00
8	Tony Gwynn	2.00
9	Kirby Puckett	2.00
10	Don Mattingly	2.50
11	Matt Williams	.75
12	Greg Maddux	2.00
13	Raul Mondesi	.75
14	Paul Molitor	1.50
15	Manny Ramirez	1.50
16	Joe Carter	.50
17	Will Clark	.75
18	Roger Clemens	2.00
19	Tim Salmon	.75
20	Dave Justice	.75
21	Kenny Lofton	.50
22	Deion Sanders	.75
23	Roberto Alomar	1.00
24	Cliff Floyd	.50
25	Carlos Baerga	.50

1995 Pinnacle White Hot

Similar in format to the Red Hot inserts, and featuring the same players, the hobby-only White Hot cards are a chase set of a chase set. Seeded once per 36 packs on average (more than twice as scarce as the Red Hots), the White Hot cards have fronts totally printed in the Dufex process, with predominantly blue and white background colors, while the backs are highlighted by blue foil printing in the "WHITE HOT" background lettering on black background.

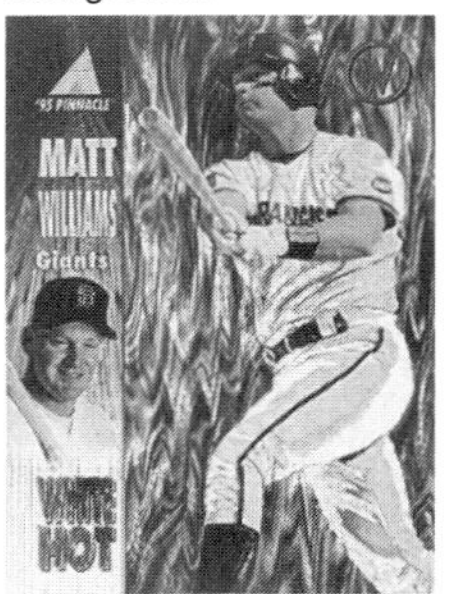

		MT
Complete Set (25):		100.00
Common Player:		2.00
1	Cal Ripken Jr.	12.50
2	Ken Griffey Jr.	12.50
3	Frank Thomas	7.50
4	Jeff Bagwell	6.00
5	Mike Piazza	10.00
6	Barry Bonds	7.50
7	Albert Belle	4.00
8	Tony Gwynn	7.50
9	Kirby Puckett	7.50
10	Don Mattingly	7.50
11	Matt Williams	3.00
12	Greg Maddux	7.50
13	Raul Mondesi	3.00
14	Paul Molitor	6.00
15	Manny Ramirez	6.00
16	Joe Carter	2.00
17	Will Clark	3.00
18	Roger Clemens	7.50
19	Tim Salmon	3.00
20	Dave Justice	3.00
21	Kenny Lofton	2.00
22	Deion Sanders	3.00
23	Roberto Alomar	5.00
24	Cliff Floyd	2.00
25	Carlos Baerga	2.00

1995 Pinnacle Team Pinnacle

This nine-card Series 1 insert set becomes an 18-card challenge if the collector decides to hunt for both versions of each card. As in the past the Team Pinnacle cards picture National and American League counterparts at each position on different sides of the same card. In 1995 each card is printed with one side in Pinnacle's Dufex foil technology, and the other side conventionally printed. Thus card #1 can be found with Mike Mussina in Dufex and Greg Maddux conventionally printed, or with Maddux in Dufex and Mussina conventional. Team Pinnacle cards are found inserted at an average rate of only one per 90 packs. Card numbers have a "TP" prefix.

		MT
Complete Set (9):		40.00
Common Player:		1.50
1	Mike Mussina, Greg Maddux	6.00
2	Carlos Delgado, Mike Piazza	6.00
3	Frank Thomas, Jeff Bagwell	6.00
4	Roberto Alomar, Craig Biggio	2.50
5	Cal Ripken Jr., Ozzie Smith	7.50
6	Travis Fryman, Matt Williams	1.50
7	Ken Griffey Jr., Barry Bonds	7.50
8	Albert Belle, Dave Justice	1.50
9	Kirby Puckett, Tony Gwynn	6.00

1995 Pinnacle Team Pinnacle Pin Trade Cards

In one of the hobby's first major attempts to cross-promote pin- and card-collecting, Series 2 Pinnacle packs offered a special insert set of cards which could be redeemed for a collector's pin of the same player. Seeded at the rate of one per 48 regular packs and one per 36 jumbo packs, the pin redemption cards were valid until Nov. 15, 1995. Payment of $2 handling fee was required for redemption.

		MT
Complete Set (18):		75.00
Common Player:		2.00
1	Greg Maddux	5.00
2	Mike Mussina	4.00
3	Mike Piazza	7.50
4	Carlos Delgado	3.00
5	Jeff Bagwell	4.00
6	Frank Thomas	5.00
7	Craig Biggio	2.00
8	Roberto Alomar	3.00
9	Ozzie Smith	5.00
10	Cal Ripken Jr.	10.00
11	Matt Williams	3.00
12	Travis Fryman	2.00
13	Barry Bonds	5.00
14	Ken Griffey Jr.	10.00
15	Dave Justice	2.50
16	Albert Belle	3.00
17	Tony Gwynn	5.00
18	Kirby Puckett	5.00

1995 Pinnacle Team Pinnacle Collector Pins

Redemption cards in Series 2 packs could be traded in (until Nov. 15, 1995) for an enameled pin of the player pictured on the trade card. Pins are about 1-3/8" x 1-1/4". A raised relief portrait of the player is at center with his name in pennants above and his team logo at bottom, along with the Pinnacle logo. Backs are goldtone with a post-and-button style of pinback. The unnumbered pins are listed here in the same sequence as the redemption cards.

		MT
Complete Set (18):		125.00
Common Player:		4.00
(1)	Greg Maddux	10.00
(2)	Mike Mussina	7.50
(3)	Mike Piazza	12.00
(4)	Carlos Delgado	5.00
(5)	Jeff Bagwell	8.00
(6)	Frank Thomas	10.00
(7)	Craig Biggio	4.00
(8)	Roberto Alomar	6.00
(9)	Ozzie Smith	10.00
(10)	Cal Ripken Jr.	15.00
(11)	Matt Williams	6.00
(12)	Travis Fryman	4.00
(13)	Barry Bonds	10.00
(14)	Ken Griffey Jr.	15.00
(15)	Dave Justice	5.00
(16)	Albert Belle	5.00
(17)	Tony Gwynn	10.00
(18)	Kirby Puckett	10.00

1995 Pinnacle Upstarts

The most dominant young players in the game were featured in this insert series. Cards are printed with most of the photo's background covered by the legs of a large blue-and-gold star device, which includes the team logo at its red center. A blue circular "'95 UPSTARTS" logo at bottom-left has the player name in gold. These cards are exclusive to Series 1, found at an average rate of one per eight packs.

		MT
Complete Set (30):		30.00
Common Player:		.40
1	Frank Thomas	6.00
2	Roberto Alomar	2.50
3	Mike Piazza	7.50
4	Javier Lopez	.40
5	Albert Belle	.75
6	Carlos Delgado	1.50
7	Rusty Greer	.40
8	Tim Salmon	.60
9	Raul Mondesi	.60
10	Juan Gonzalez	4.00
11	Manny Ramirez	4.00
12	Sammy Sosa	6.00
13	Jeff Kent	.40
14	Melvin Nieves	.40
15	Rondell White	.60
16	Shawn Green	1.50
17	Bernie Williams	1.50
18	Aaron Sele	.40
19	Jason Bere	.40
20	Joey Hamilton	.40
21	Mike Kelly	.40
22	Wil Cordero	.40
23	Moises Alou	.50
24	Roberto Kelly	.40
25	Deion Sanders	.75
26	Steve Karsay	.40
27	Bret Boone	.40
28	Willie Greene	.40
29	Billy Ashley	.40
30	Brian Anderson	.40

1996 Pinnacle

Pinnacle's 400-card regular-issue set has borderless front photos highlighted by prismatic gold-foil graphics in a triangle at bottom. Backs have another photo along with stats and data. Parallel Starburst and Starburst Artist's Proof sets contain only 200 of the cards in the base issue. Series 1 inserts include a Cal Ripken Jr. "Tribute" card, numbered "1 of 1", along with Team Pinnacle, Pinnacle Power, Team Tomorrow, Essence of the Game and First Rate. Series 2 inserts are Christie Brinkley Collection, Project Stardom, Skylines, Slugfest and Team Spirit. Pinnacle was sold in 10-card hobby and retail foil packs, and 18-card jumbo packs.

		MT
Complete Set (400):		25.00
Common Player:		.10
Series 1 or 2 Pack (10):		1.50
Series 1 or 2 Wax Box (24):		30.00
1	Greg Maddux	1.50
2	Bill Pulsipher	.10
3	Dante Bichette	.10
4	Mike Piazza	2.00
5	Garret Anderson	.10
6	Steve Finley	.10
7	Andy Benes	.10
8	Chuck Knoblauch	.10
9	Tom Gordon	.10
10	Jeff Bagwell	.75
11	Wil Cordero	.10
12	John Mabry	.10
13	Jeff Frye	.10
14	Travis Fryman	.10
15	John Wetteland	.10
16	Jason Bates	.10
17	Danny Tartabull	.10
18	Charles Nagy	.10
19	Robin Ventura	.10
20	Reggie Sanders	.10
21	Dave Clark	.10
22	Jaime Navarro	.10
23	Joey Hamilton	.10
24	Al Leiter	.10
25	Deion Sanders	.20
26	Tim Salmon	.20
27	Tino Martinez	.10
28	Mike Greenwell	.10
29	Phil Plantier	.10
30	Bobby Bonilla	.10
31	Kenny Rogers	.10
32	Chili Davis	.10
33	Joe Carter	.10
34	Mike Mussina	.50
35	Matt Mieske	.10
36	Jose Canseco	.40
37	Brad Radke	.10
38	Juan Gonzalez	.75
39	David Segui	.10
40	Alex Fernandez	.10
41	Jeff Kent	.10
42	Todd Zeile	.10
43	Darryl Strawberry	.10
44	Jose Rijo	.10
45	Ramon Martinez	.10
46	Manny Ramirez	.75
47	Gregg Jefferies	.10
48	Bryan Rekar	.10
49	Jeff King	.10
50	John Olerud	.10
51	Marc Newfield	.10
52	Charles Johnson	.10
53	Robby Thompson	.10
54	Brian Hunter	.10
55	Mike Blowers	.10
56	Keith Lockhart	.10
57	Ray Lankford	.10
58	Tim Wallach	.10
59	Ivan Rodriguez	.60
60	Ed Sprague	.10
61	Paul Molitor	.50
62	Eric Karros	.10
63	Glenallen Hill	.10
64	Jay Bell	.10
65	Tom Pagnozzi	.10
66	Greg Colbrunn	.10
67	Edgar Martinez	.10

68	Paul Sorrento	.10
69	Kirt Manwaring	.10
70	Pete Schourek	.10
71	Orlando Merced	.10
72	Shawon Dunston	.10
73	Ricky Bottalico	.10
74	Brady Anderson	.10
75	Steve Ontiveros	.10
76	Jim Abbott	.10
77	Carl Everett	.15
78	Mo Vaughn	.35
79	Pedro Martinez	.50
80	Harold Baines	.10
81	Alan Trammell	.10
82	Steve Avery	.10
83	Jeff Cirillo	.10
84	John Valentin	.10
85	Bernie Williams	.30
86	Andre Dawson	.20
87	Dave Winfield	.75
88	B.J. Surhoff	.10
89	Jeff Blauser	.10
90	Barry Larkin	.15
91	Cliff Floyd	.15
92	Sammy Sosa	1.50
93	Andres Galarraga	.10
94	Dave Nilsson	.10
95	James Mouton	.10
96	Marquis Grissom	.10
97	Matt Williams	.25
98	John Jaha	.10
99	Don Mattingly	1.50
100	Tim Naehring	.10
101	Kevin Appier	.10
102	Bobby Higginson	.15
103	Andy Pettitte	.30
104	Ozzie Smith	1.50
105	Kenny Lofton	.10
106	Ken Caminiti	.10
107	Walt Weiss	.10
108	Jack McDowell	.10
109	Brian McRae	.10
110	Gary Gaetti	.10
111	Curtis Goodwin	.10
112	Dennis Martinez	.10
113	Omar Vizquel	.10
114	Chipper Jones	2.00
115	Mark Gubicza	.10
116	Ruben Sierra	.10
117	Eddie Murray	.75
118	Chad Curtis	.10
119	Hal Morris	.10
120	Ben McDonald	.10
121	Marty Cordova	.10
122	Ken Griffey Jr.	2.50
123	Gary Sheffield	.20
124	Charlie Hayes	.10
125	Shawn Green	.30
126	Jason Giambi	.30
127	Mark Langston	.10
128	Mark Whiten	.10
129	Greg Vaughn	.10
130	Mark McGwire	2.50
131	Hideo Nomo	.50
132	Eric Karros, Raul Mondesi, Hideo Nomo, Mike Piazza	.50
133	Jason Bere	.10
134	Ken Griffey Jr. (The Naturals)	1.25
135	Frank Thomas (The Naturals)	.75
136	Cal Ripken Jr. (The Naturals)	1.25
137	Albert Belle (The Naturals)	.20
138	Mike Piazza (The Naturals)	1.00
139	Dante Bichette (The Naturals)	.10
140	Sammy Sosa (The Naturals)	.75
141	Mo Vaughn (The Naturals)	.20
142	Tim Salmon (The Naturals)	.15
143	Reggie Sanders (The Naturals)	.10
144	Cecil Fielder (The Naturals)	.10
145	Jim Edmonds (The Naturals)	.10
146	Rafael Palmeiro (The Naturals)	.10
147	Edgar Martinez (The Naturals)	.10
148	Barry Bonds (The Naturals)	.75
149	Manny Ramirez (The Naturals)	.35
150	Larry Walker (The Naturals)	.15
151	Jeff Bagwell (The Naturals)	.35
152	Ron Gant (The Naturals)	.10
153	Andres Galarraga (The Naturals)	.10
154	Eddie Murray (The Naturals)	.25
155	Kirby Puckett (The Naturals)	.75
156	Will Clark (The Naturals)	.15
157	Don Mattingly (The Naturals)	.75
158	Mark McGwire (The Naturals)	1.25
159	Dean Palmer (The Naturals)	.10
160	Matt Williams (The Naturals)	.15
161	Fred McGriff (The Naturals)	.10
162	Joe Carter (The Naturals)	.10
163	Juan Gonzalez (The Naturals)	.35
164	Alex Ochoa	.10
165	Ruben Rivera	.10
166	Tony Clark	.10
167	Brian Barber	.10
168	Matt Lawton	.10
169	Terrell Wade	.10
170	Johnny Damon	.20
171	Derek Jeter	2.00
172	Phil Nevin	.10
173	Robert Perez	.10
174	C.J. Nitkowski	.10
175	Joe Vitiello	.10
176	Roger Cedeno	.10
177	Ron Coomer	.10
178	Chris Widger	.10
179	Jimmy Haynes	.10
180	*Mike Sweeney*	.50
181	Howard Battle	.10
182	John Wasdin	.10
183	Jim Pittsley	.10
184	Bob Wolcott	.10
185	LaTroy Hawkins	.10
186	Nigel Wilson	.10
187	Dustin Hermanson	.15
188	Chris Snopek	.10
189	Mariano Rivera	.30
190	Jose Herrera	.10
191	Chris Stynes	.10
192	Larry Thomas	.10
193	David Bell	.10
194	(Frank Thomas) (checklist)	.50
195	(Ken Griffey Jr.) (checklist)	.75
196	(Cal Ripken Jr.) (checklist)	.75
197	(Jeff Bagwell) (checklist)	.25
198	(Mike Piazza) (checklist)	.75
199	(Barry Bonds) (checklist)	.75
200	(Garrett Anderson, Chipper Jones) (checklist)	.25
201	Frank Thomas	1.50
202	Michael Tucker	.10
203	Kirby Puckett	1.25
204	Alex Gonzalez	.15
205	Tony Gwynn	1.25
206	Moises Alou	.15
207	Albert Belle	.30
208	Barry Bonds	1.25
209	Fred McGriff	.10
210	Dennis Eckersley	.10
211	Craig Biggio	.10
212	David Cone	.10
213	Will Clark	.25
214	Cal Ripken Jr.	2.50
215	Wade Boggs	.50
216	Pete Schourek	.10
217	Darren Daulton	.10
218	Carlos Baerga	.10
219	Larry Walker	.30
220	Denny Neagle	.10
221	Jim Edmonds	.15
222	Lee Smith	.10
223	Jason Isringhausen	.15
224	Jay Buhner	.10
225	John Olerud	.10
226	Jeff Conine	.10
227	Dean Palmer	.10
228	Jim Abbott	.10
229	Raul Mondesi	.25
230	Tom Glavine	.15
231	Kevin Seitzer	.10
232	Lenny Dykstra	.10
233	Brian Jordan	.10
234	Rondell White	.15
235	Bret Boone	.15
236	Randy Johnson	.50
237	Paul O'Neill	.10
238	Jim Thome	.10
239	Edgardo Alfonzo	.10
240	Terry Pendleton	.10
241	Harold Baines	.10
242	Roberto Alomar	.60
243	Mark Grace	.25
244	Derek Bell	.10
245	Vinny Castilla	.10
246	Cecil Fielder	.10
247	Roger Clemens	1.25
248	Orel Hershiser	.10
249	J.T. Snow	.10
250	Rafael Palmeiro	.25
251	Bret Saberhagen	.10
252	Todd Hollandsworth	.10
253	Ryan Klesko	.10
254	Greg Maddux (Hardball Heroes)	.75
255	Ken Griffey Jr. (Hardball Heroes)	1.25
256	Hideo Nomo (Hardball Heroes)	.35
257	Frank Thomas (Hardball Heroes)	.75
258	Cal Ripken Jr. (Hardball Heroes)	1.25
259	Jeff Bagwell (Hardball Heroes)	.35
260	Barry Bonds (Hardball Heroes)	.75
261	Mo Vaughn (Hardball Heroes)	.20
262	Albert Belle (Hardball Heroes)	.20
263	Sammy Sosa (Hardball Heroes)	.75
264	Reggie Sanders (Hardball Heroes)	.10
265	Mike Piazza (Hardball Heroes)	1.00
266	Chipper Jones (Hardball Heroes)	1.00
267	Tony Gwynn (Hardball Heroes)	.60
268	Kirby Puckett (Hardball Heroes)	.75
269	Wade Boggs (Hardball Heroes)	.25
270	Will Clark (Hardball Heroes)	.15
271	Gary Sheffield (Hardball Heroes)	.15
272	Dante Bichette (Hardball Heroes)	.10
273	Randy Johnson (Hardball Heroes)	.30
274	Matt Williams (Hardball Heroes)	.15
275	Alex Rodriguez (Hardball Heroes)	2.50
276	Tim Salmon (Hardball Heroes)	.10
277	Johnny Damon (Hardball Heroes)	.15
278	Manny Ramirez (Hardball Heroes)	.35
279	Derek Jeter (Hardball Heroes)	1.00
280	Eddie Murray (Hardball Heroes)	.20
281	Ozzie Smith (Hardball Heroes)	.50
282	Garret Anderson (Hardball Heroes)	.10
283	Raul Mondesi (Hardball Heroes)	.10
284	Terry Steinbach	.10
285	Carlos Garcia	.10
286	Dave Justice	.25
287	Eric Anthony	.10
288	Benji Gil	.10
289	Bob Hamelin	.10
290	Dwayne Hosey	.10
291	Andy Pettitte	.25
292	Rod Beck	.10
293	Shane Andrews	.10
294	Julian Tavarez	.10
295	Willie Greene	.10
296	Ismael Valdes	.10
297	Glenallen Hill	.10
298	Troy Percival	.10
299	Ray Durham	.10
300	Jeff Conine (.300 Series)	.10
301.8	Ken Griffey Jr. (.300 Series)	1.50
302	Will Clark (.300 Series)	.20
303	Mike Greenwell (.300 Series)	.10
304.9	Carlos Baerga (.300 Series)	.10
305.3	Paul Molitor (.300 Series)	.25
305.6	Jeff Bagwell (.300 Series)	.35
306	Mark Grace (.300 Series)	.20
307	Don Mattingly (.300 Series)	.75
308	Hal Morris (.300 Series)	.10
309	Butch Huskey	.10
310	Ozzie Guillen	.10
311	Erik Hanson	.10
312	Kenny Lofton (.300 Series)	.10
313	Edgar Martinez (.300 Series)	.10
314	Kurt Abbott	.10
315	John Smoltz	.15
316	Ariel Prieto	.10
317	Mark Carreon	.10
318	Kirby Puckett (.300 Series)	.65
319	Carlos Perez	.10
320	Gary DiSarcina	.10
321	Trevor Hoffman	.10
322	Mike Piazza (.300 Series)	1.00
323	Frank Thomas (.300 Series)	.75
324	Juan Acevedo	.10
325	Bip Roberts	.10
326	Javier Lopez	.10
327	Benito Santiago	.10
328	Mark Lewis	.10
329	Royce Clayton	.10
330	Tom Gordon	.10
331	Ben McDonald	.10
332	Dan Wilson	.10
333	Ron Gant	.10
334	Wade Boggs (.300 Series)	.25
335	Paul Molitor	.50
336	Tony Gwynn (.300 Series)	.60
337	Sean Berry	.10
338	Rickey Henderson	.50
339	Wil Cordero	.10
340	Kent Mercker	.10
341	Kenny Rogers	.10
342	Ryne Sandberg	.75
343	Charlie Hayes	.10
344	Andy Benes	.10
345	Sterling Hitchcock	.10
346	Bernard Gilkey	.10
347	Julio Franco	.10
348	Ken Hill	.10
349	Russ Davis	.10
350	Mike Blowers	.10
351	B.J. Surhoff	.10
352	Lance Johnson	.10
353	Darryl Hamilton	.10
354	Shawon Dunston	.10
355	Rick Aguilera	.10
356	Danny Tartabull	.10
357	Todd Stottlemyre	.10
358	Mike Bordick	.10
359	Jack McDowell	.10
360	Todd Zeile	.10
361	Tino Martinez	.10
362	Greg Gagne	.10
363	Mike Kelly	.10
364	Tim Raines	.10

365 Ernie Young .10
366 Mike Stanley .10
367 Wally Joyner .10
368 Karim Garcia .10
369 Paul Wilson .10
370 Sal Fasano .10
371 Jason Schmidt .10
372 *Livan Hernandez* .25
373 George Arias .10
374 Steve Gibralter .10
375 Jermaine Dye .10
376 Jason Kendall .10
377 Brooks Kieschnick .10
378 Jeff Ware .10
379 Alan Benes .10
380 Rey Ordonez .10
381 Jay Powell .10
382 *Osvaldo Fernandez* .15
383 *Wilton Guerrero* .25
384 Eric Owens .10
385 George Williams .10
386 Chan Ho Park .25
387 Jeff Suppan .10
388 *F.P. Santangelo* .25
389 Terry Adams .10
390 Bob Abreu .20
391 *Quinton McCracken* .10
392 *Mike Busby* .10
393 (Cal Ripken Jr.) (checklist) .75
394 (Ken Griffey Jr.) (checklist) .75
395 (Frank Thomas) (checklist) .50
396 (Chipper Jones) (checklist) .75
397 (Greg Maddux) (checklist) .50
398 (Mike Piazza) (checklist) .75
399 (Ken Griffey Jr., Frank Thomas, Cal Ripken Jr., Greg Maddux, Chipper Jones, Mike Piazza) (checklist) .50

1996 Pinnacle Starburst

For 1996 Pinnacle abbreviated its parallel insert set to just half of the cards from the base issue. Only 200 select players are included in the Starburst Dufex-printed parallel set found on average of once per seven hobby packs and once per 10 retail packs.

	MT
Complete Set (200):	200.00
Common Player:	.50
Common Artist's Proof:	2.00
Artist's Proofs:	3X

1 Greg Maddux 4.50
2 Bill Pulsipher .50
3 Dante Bichette .50
4 Mike Piazza 6.00
5 Garret Anderson .50
6 Chuck Knoblauch .50
7 Jeff Bagwell 2.50
8 Wil Cordero .50
9 Travis Fryman .50
10 Reggie Sanders .50
11 Deion Sanders .75
12 Tim Salmon 1.00
13 Tino Martinez .50
14 Bobby Bonilla .50
15 Joe Carter .50
16 Mike Mussina 1.50
17 Jose Canseco 1.50
18 Manny Ramirez 2.50
19 Gregg Jefferies .50
20 Charles Johnson .50
21 Brian Hunter .50
22 Ray Lankford .50
23 Ivan Rodriguez 2.00
24 Paul Molitor 2.50
25 Eric Karros .50
26 Edgar Martinez .50
27 Shawon Dunston .50
28 Mo Vaughn 1.00
29 Pedro Martinez 1.00
30 Marty Cordova .50
31 Ken Caminiti .50
32 Gary Sheffield .75
33 Shawn Green .75
34 Cliff Floyd .50
35 Andres Galarraga .50
36 Matt Williams 1.00
37 Don Mattingly 3.00
38 Kevin Appier .50
39 Ozzie Smith 3.00
40 Kenny Lofton .50
41 Ken Griffey Jr. 7.50
42 Jack McDowell .50
43 Gary Gaetti .50
44 Dennis Martinez .50
45 Chipper Jones 6.00
46 Eddie Murray 2.00
47 Bernie Williams 1.25
48 Andre Dawson .75
49 Dave Winfield 1.50
50 B.J. Surhoff .50
51 Barry Larkin .50
52 Alan Trammell .50
53 Sammy Sosa 5.00
54 Hideo Nomo 2.00
55 Mark McGwire 7.50
56 Jay Bell .50
57 Juan Gonzalez 2.50
58 Chili Davis .50
59 Robin Ventura .50
60 John Mabry .50
61 Ken Griffey Jr. (Naturals) 4.00
62 Frank Thomas (Naturals) 2.00
63 Cal Ripken Jr. (Naturals) 4.00
64 Albert Belle (Naturals) .75
65 Mike Piazza (Naturals) 3.00
66 Dante Bichette (Naturals) .50
67 Sammy Sosa (Naturals) 2.50
68 Mo Vaughn (Naturals) .75
69 Tim Salmon (Naturals) .65
70 Reggie Sanders (Naturals) .50
71 Cecil Fielder (Naturals) .50
72 Jim Edmonds (Naturals) .50
73 Rafael Palmeiro (Naturals) .50
74 Edgar Martinez (Naturals) .50
75 Barry Bonds (Naturals) 2.00
76 Manny Ramirez (Naturals) 1.50
77 Larry Walker (Naturals) .50
78 Jeff Bagwell (Naturals) 1.50
79 Ron Gant (Naturals) .50
80 Andres Galarraga (Naturals) .50
81 Eddie Murray (Naturals) .75
82 Kirby Puckett (Naturals) 2.00
83 Will Clark (Naturals) .75
84 Don Mattingly (Naturals) 2.00
85 Mark McGwire (Naturals) 4.00
86 Dean Palmer (Naturals) .50
87 Matt Williams (Naturals) .75
88 Fred McGriff (Naturals) .50
89 Joe Carter (Naturals) .50
90 Juan Gonzalez (Naturals) 1.50
91 Alex Ochoa .50
92 Ruben Rivera .50
93 Tony Clark .50
94 Pete Schourek .50
95 Terrell Wade .50
96 Johnny Damon .50
97 Derek Jeter 6.00
98 Phil Nevin .50
99 Robert Perez .50
100 Dustin Hermanson .50
101 Frank Thomas 3.00
102 Michael Tucker .50
103 Kirby Puckett 3.00
104 Alex Gonzalez .50
105 Tony Gwynn 4.50
106 Moises Alou .50
107 Albert Belle 1.50
108 Barry Bonds 3.00
109 Fred McGriff .50
110 Dennis Eckersley .50
111 Craig Biggio .50
112 David Cone .50
113 Will Clark 1.00
114 Cal Ripken Jr. 7.50
115 Wade Boggs 2.00
116 Pete Schourek .50
117 Darren Daulton .50
118 Carlos Baerga .50
119 Larry Walker 1.00
120 Denny Neagle .50
121 Jim Edmonds .50
122 Lee Smith .50
123 Jason Isringhausen .50
124 Jay Buhner .50
125 John Olerud .50
126 Jeff Conine .50
127 Dean Palmer .50
128 Jim Abbott .50
129 Raul Mondesi .75
130 Tom Glavine .50
131 Kevin Seitzer .50
132 Lenny Dykstra .50
133 Brian Jordan .50
134 Rondell White .50
135 Bret Boone .50
136 Randy Johnson 2.00
137 Paul O'Neill .50
138 Jim Thome .50
139 Edgardo Alfonzo .50
140 Terry Pendleton .50
141 Harold Baines .50
142 Roberto Alomar 2.00
143 Mark Grace 1.00
144 Derek Bell .50
145 Vinny Castilla .50
146 Cecil Fielder .50
147 Roger Clemens 3.00
148 Orel Hershiser .50
149 J.T. Snow .50
150 Rafael Palmeiro .75
151 Bret Saberhagen .50
152 Todd Hollandsworth .50
153 Ryan Klesko .50
154 Greg Maddux (Hardball Heroes) 2.50
155 Ken Griffey Jr. (Hardball Heroes) 4.00
156 Hideo Nomo (Hardball Heroes) 1.50
157 Frank Thomas (Hardball Heroes) 2.00
158 Cal Ripken Jr. (Hardball Heroes) 4.00
159 Jeff Bagwell (Hardball Heroes) 1.50
160 Barry Bonds (Hardball Heroes) 2.00
161 Mo Vaughn (Hardball Heroes) .75
162 Albert Belle (Hardball Heroes) .75
163 Sammy Sosa (Hardball Heroes) 2.50
164 Reggie Sanders (Hardball Heroes) .50
165 Mike Piazza (Hardball Heroes) 3.00
166 Chipper Jones (Hardball Heroes) 3.00
167 Tony Gwynn (Hardball Heroes) 2.00
168 Kirby Puckett (Hardball Heroes) 2.00
169 Wade Boggs (Hardball Heroes) .75
170 Will Clark (Hardball Heroes) .75
171 Gary Sheffield (Hardball Heroes) .75
172 Dante Bichette (Hardball Heroes) .50
173 Randy Johnson (Hardball Heroes) 1.00
174 Matt Williams (Hardball Heroes) .50
175 Alex Rodrigue z (Hardball Heroes) 6.00
176 Tim Salmon (Hardball Heroes) .50
177 Johnny Damon (Hardball Heroes) .50
178 Manny Ramirez (Hardball Heroes) 1.50
179 Derek Jeter (Hardball Heroes) 3.00
180 Eddie Murray (Hardball Heroes) 1.00
181 Ozzie Smith (Hardball Heroes) 2.00
182 Garret Anderson (Hardball Heroes) .50
183 Raul Mondesi (Hardball Heroes) .50
184 Jeff Conine (.300 Series) .50
185 Ken Griffey Jr. (.300 Series) 4.00
186 Will Clark (.300 Series) .75
187 Mike Greenwell (.300 Series) .50
188 Carlos Baerga (.300 Series) .50
189 Paul Molitor (.300 Series) 1.00
190 Jeff Bagwell (.300 Series) 1.50
191 Mark Grace (.300 Series) .75
192 Don Mattingly (.300 Series) 2.00
193 Hal Morris (.300 Series) .50
194 Kenny Lofton (.300 Series) .50
195 Edgar Martinez (.300 Series) .50
196 Kirby Puckett (.300 Series) 2.00
197 Mike Piazza (.300 Series) 3.00
198 Frank Thomas (.300 Series) 2.00
199 Wade Boggs (.300 Series) 1.00
200 Tony Gwynn (.300 Series) 2.00

1996 Pinnacle Artist's Proof

AP is a parallel to the Starburst partial parallel of '96 Pinnacle. Like Starburst, the Artist's Proof cards are printed in Dufex technology on front, with the AP cards having the words "ARTIST'S PROOF" repeated throughout the background. AP backs are identical to Starburst. Stated insertion rate for the Artist's Proofs was one per 47 packs in hobby and one per 67 retail packs.

	MT
Common Artist's Proof:	2.00
Stars:	3X

(See 1996 Pinnacle Starburst for checklist and base card values.)

1996 Pinnacle Foil Series 2

The 200 cards from Series 2 were paralleled in a special foil edition which was sold at retail outlets only in five-card $2.99 packs. Fronts have a metallic foil background to differentiate them from the regular-issue Series 2 version.

	MT
Complete Set (200):	15.00
Common Player:	.15
Stars:	1.5X

(See 1996 Pinnacle #201-399 for checklist and base card values.)

1996 Pinnacle Cal Ripken Tribute

A special Cal Ripken Tribute card was issued in Series 1 Pinnacle packs at a rate of 1:150. Front features an etched metallic foil background, a gold-foil facsimile autograph and a "2,131+ Consecutive Games Played" starburst. Back has a photo of the scoreboard on that historic occasion, and a photo of Ripken being driven around Camden Yards in a red Corvette. The card is numbered "1 of 1", but it is not unique.

		MT
1 of 1	Cal Ripken Jr.	6.00

1996 Pinnacle Christie Brinkley Collection

Supermodel Christie Brinkley took the photos for these 1996 Pinnacle Series 2 inserts. The cards capture players from the 1995 World Series participants during a spring training photo session. Cards were seeded one per every 23 hobby packs or 32 retail packs.

		MT
Complete Set (16):		27.50
Common Player:		1.00
1	Greg Maddux	6.00
2	Ryan Klesko	1.00
3	Dave Justice	2.00
4	Tom Glavine	2.00
5	Chipper Jones	7.50
6	Fred McGriff	1.00
7	Javier Lopez	1.00
8	Marquis Grissom	1.00
9	Jason Schmidt	1.00
10	Albert Belle	3.00
11	Manny Ramirez	4.50
12	Carlos Baerga	1.00
13	Sandy Alomar	1.00
14	Jim Thome	1.00
15	Julio Franco	1.00
16	Kenny Lofton	1.00

1996 Pinnacle Essence of the Game

Essence of the Game is an 18-card insert set found only in hobby packs at a one per 23 packs rate in Series 1. Cards are printed on clear plastic with the front photo also appearing in an inverted fashion on back. Micro-etched Dufex printing technology is utilized on the front.

		MT
Complete Set (18):		35.00
Common Player:		.75
1	Cal Ripken Jr.	6.00
2	Greg Maddux	2.50
3	Frank Thomas	2.50
4	Matt Williams	1.00
5	Chipper Jones	4.00
6	Reggie Sanders	.75
7	Ken Griffey Jr.	6.00
8	Kirby Puckett	2.50
9	Hideo Nomo	1.50
10	Mike Piazza	4.00
11	Jeff Bagwell	2.00
12	Mo Vaughn	1.50
13	Albert Belle	1.50
14	Tim Salmon	1.00
15	Don Mattingly	2.50
16	Will Clark	1.00
17	Eddie Murray	1.50
18	Barry Bonds	2.00

1996 Pinnacle First Rate

Retail-exclusive First Rate showcases former first round draft picks playing in the majors. Printed in Dufex foil throughout, a red swirl pattern covers the left 2/3 of the front. Backs show the player again, within a large numeral "1". These inserts are found at an average rate of one per 23 packs in Series 1.

		MT
Complete Set (18):		50.00
Common Player:		1.00
1	Ken Griffey Jr.	8.00
2	Frank Thomas	4.00
3	Mo Vaughn	2.00
4	Chipper Jones	6.00
5	Alex Rodriguez	8.00
6	Kirby Puckett	3.50
7	Gary Sheffield	1.50
8	Matt Williams	1.50
9	Barry Bonds	3.50
10	Craig Biggio	1.00
11	Robin Ventura	1.00
12	Michael Tucker	1.00
13	Derek Jeter	6.00
14	Manny Ramirez	3.00
15	Barry Larkin	1.00
16	Shawn Green	2.00
17	Will Clark	1.50
18	Mark McGwire	8.00

1996 Pinnacle Pinnacle Power

Pinnacle Power inserts are seeded at the rate of one per 47 packs in both hobby and retail Series 1. The sluggers are featured on a two-layered front. The bottom layer is silver Dufex foil with solid black on top; a color action photo of the player is at center, giving the card a die-cut appearance.

		MT
Complete Set (20):		35.00
Common Player:		.75
1	Frank Thomas	4.00
2	Mo Vaughn	1.50
2p	Mo Vaughn (promo)	1.50
3	Ken Griffey Jr.	6.00
4	Matt Williams	1.00
5	Barry Bonds	3.50
6	Reggie Sanders	.75
7	Mike Piazza	5.00
8	Jim Edmonds	.75
9	Dante Bichette	.75
10	Sammy Sosa	4.00
11	Jeff Bagwell	3.00
12	Fred McGriff	.75
13	Albert Belle	1.50
14	Tim Salmon	.75
15	Joe Carter	.75
16	Manny Ramirez	3.00
17	Eddie Murray	2.00
18	Cecil Fielder	.75
19	Larry Walker	1.00
20	Juan Gonzalez	3.00

1996 Pinnacle Project Stardom

These inserts feature young players on their way to stardom. The cards, which use Dufex technology, are seeded one per every 35 packs of Series 2 hobby packs.

		MT
Complete Set (18):		40.00
Common Player:		1.00
1	Paul Wilson	1.00
2	Derek Jeter	8.00
3	Karim Garcia	1.00
4	Johnny Damon	1.50
5	Alex Rodriguez	10.00
6	Chipper Jones	8.00
7	Todd Walker	1.00
8	Bob Abreu	2.00
9	Alan Benes	1.00
10	Richard Hidalgo	1.50
11	Brooks Kieschnick	1.00
12	Garret Anderson	1.00
13	Livan Hernandez	1.00
14	Manny Ramirez	6.00

15	Jermaine Dye	1.00
16	Todd Hollandsworth	1.00
17	Raul Mondesi	2.00
18	Ryan Klesko	1.00

1996 Pinnacle Skylines

These inserts feature player portraits looming over the city skyline where they play their home games. Printed on a clear plastic stock, the cards were seeded one per every 29 Series 2 magazine packs, and one per 50 retail packs.

		MT
Complete Set (18):		200.00
Common Player:		5.00
1	Ken Griffey Jr.	30.00
2	Frank Thomas	15.00
3	Greg Maddux	15.00
4	Cal Ripken Jr.	30.00
5	Albert Belle	10.00
6	Mo Vaughn	10.00
7	Mike Piazza	20.00
8	Wade Boggs	13.50
9	Will Clark	5.00
10	Barry Bonds	15.00
11	Gary Sheffield	5.00
12	Hideo Nomo	15.00
13	Tony Gwynn	13.50
14	Kirby Puckett	15.00
15	Chipper Jones	20.00
16	Jeff Bagwell	12.50
17	Manny Ramirez	12.50
18	Raul Mondesi	5.00

1996 Pinnacle Slugfest

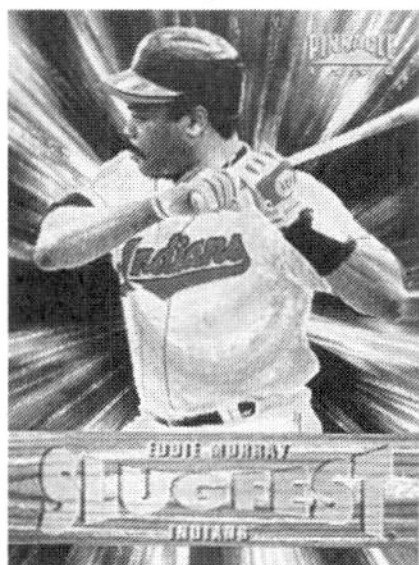

These Series 2 inserts feature the game's heaviest hitters on all-foil Dufex cards. The cards were seeded one per every 35 retail packs.

		MT
Complete Set (18):		50.00
Common Player:		1.00
1	Frank Thomas	6.00
2	Ken Griffey Jr.	10.00
3	Jeff Bagwell	5.00
4	Barry Bonds	5.00
5	Mo Vaughn	2.50
6	Albert Belle	2.50
7	Mike Piazza	8.00
8	Matt Williams	2.00
9	Dante Bichette	1.00
10	Sammy Sosa	7.50
11	Gary Sheffield	2.00
12	Reggie Sanders	1.00
13	Manny Ramirez	5.00
14	Eddie Murray	2.00
15	Juan Gonzalez	5.00
16	Dean Palmer	1.00
17	Rafael Palmeiro	1.50
18	Cecil Fielder	1.00

1996 Pinnacle Team Pinnacle

Team Pinnacle inserts offer 18 players in a double-sided nine-card set. Each card can be found with Dufex printing on one side and regular gold-foil printing on the other. Inserted one per 72 packs of Series 1, Team Pinnacle pairs up an American League player and a National Leaguer at the same position on each card.

		MT
Complete Set (9):		47.50
Common Player:		2.50
1	Frank Thomas, Jeff Bagwell	7.50
2	Chuck Knoblauch, Craig Biggio	2.50
3	Jim Thome, Matt Williams	2.50
4	Barry Larkin, Cal Ripken Jr.	10.00
5	Barry Bonds, Tim Salmon	6.00
6	Ken Griffey Jr., Reggie Sanders	10.00
7	Albert Belle, Sammy Sosa	7.50
8	Ivan Rodriguez, Mike Piazza	7.50
9	Greg Maddux, Randy Johnson	7.50

1996 Pinnacle Team Spirit

One in every 72 Series 2 hobby packs or every 103 retail packs has one of these die-cut insert cards. Each card has a holographic baseball design behind an embossed glossy action photo of the player on a flat black background. Backs are conventionally printed.

		MT
Complete Set (12):		70.00
Common Player:		3.00
1	Greg Maddux	8.50
2	Ken Griffey Jr.	12.00
3	Derek Jeter	10.00
4	Mike Piazza	10.00
5	Cal Ripken Jr.	12.00
6	Frank Thomas	8.50
7	Jeff Bagwell	6.00
8	Mo Vaughn	3.00
9	Albert Belle	3.00
10	Chipper Jones	10.00
11	Johnny Damon	3.00
12	Barry Bonds	7.50

1996 Pinnacle Team Tomorrow

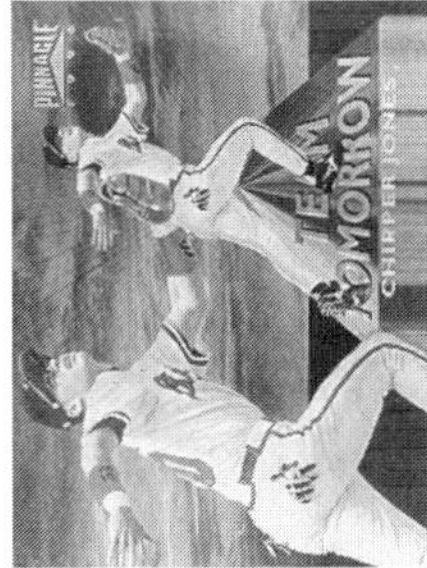

Team Tomorrow showcases young superstars on a horizontal Dufex design. While the player appears twice on the card front, the left side is merely a close-up of the same shot appearing on the right. These inserts are exclusive to Series 1 jumbo packs, found on average at the rate of one per 19 packs.

		MT
Complete Set (10):		35.00
Common Player:		1.00
1	Ruben Rivera	1.00
2	Johnny Damon	1.50
3	Raul Mondesi	1.50
4	Manny Ramirez	6.00
5	Hideo Nomo	5.00
6	Chipper Jones	10.00
7	Garret Anderson	1.00
8	Alex Rodriguez	12.50
9	Derek Jeter	10.00
10	Karim Garcia	1.00

1996 Pinnacle/ Aficionado

Pinnacle's 1996 Aficionado set gives every card the look of maple woodgrain. The 200 regular issue cards include 160 cards in an antique-look sepia-tone finish. The horizontal front also has a rainbow holographic foil image of the player. The back has comparison statistics that show how the player compares with the league average at that position and the league average at that position in different eras. There are also 60 four-color cards, which include 25 rookie cards, and a 10-card Global Reach subset. This subset, which honors baseball's international flavor, features Aficionado's new heliogram printing process. Artist's Proof parallel cards, seeded about one per 35 packs, were also created. These cards mirror the regular issue and use a unique gold foil stamp. There were three insert sets: Slick Picks, Rivals and Magic Numbers.

		MT
Complete Set (200):		40.00
Common Player:		.20
Common Artist's Proof:		.50
Artist's Proof Stars:		5X
Pack (5):		1.50
Wax Box (16):		22.50
1	Jack McDowell	.20
2	Jay Bell	.20
3	Rafael Palmeiro	.35
4	Wally Joyner	.20
5	Ozzie Smith	2.00
6	Mark McGwire	4.00
7	Kevin Seitzer	.20
8	Fred McGriff	.20
9	Roger Clemens	2.00
9s	Roger Clemens (marked "SAMPLE")	3.00
10	Randy Johnson	1.00
11	Cecil Fielder	.20
12	David Cone	.20
13	Chili Davis	.20
14	Andres Galarraga	.20
15	Joe Carter	.20
16	Ryne Sandberg	2.00
17	Paul O'Neill	.20
18	Cal Ripken Jr.	4.00
19	Wade Boggs	1.00
20	Greg Gagne	.20
21	Edgar Martinez	.20
22	Greg Maddux	2.50
23	Ken Caminiti	.20
24	Kirby Puckett	2.00
25	Craig Biggio	.20
26	Will Clark	.40
27	Ron Gant	.20
28	Eddie Murray	1.00
29	Lance Johnson	.20
30	Tony Gwynn	2.50
31	Dante Bichette	.20

32	Darren Daulton	.20
33	Danny Tartabull	.20
34	Jeff King	.20
35	Tom Glavine	.35
36	Rickey Henderson	1.00
37	Jose Canseco	.50
38	Barry Larkin	.35
39	Dennis Martinez	.20
40	Ruben Sierra	.20
41	Bobby Bonilla	.20
42	Jeff Conine	.20
43	Lee Smith	.20
44	Charlie Hayes	.20
45	Walt Weiss	.20
46	Jay Buhner	.20
47	Kenny Rogers	.20
48	Paul Molitor	1.00
49	Hal Morris	.20
50	Todd Stottlemyre	.20
51	Mike Stanley	.20
52	Mark Grace	.50
53	Lenny Dykstra	.20
54	Andre Dawson	.35
55	Dennis Eckersley	.20
56	Ben McDonald	.20
57	Ray Lankford	.20
58	Mo Vaughn	1.00
59	Frank Thomas	2.50
60	Julio Franco	.20
61	Jim Abbott	.20
62	Greg Vaughn	.20
63	Marquis Grissom	.20
64	Tino Martinez	.20
65	Kevin Appier	.20
66	Matt Williams	.40
67	Sammy Sosa	2.50
68	Larry Walker	.60
69	Ivan Rodriguez	.75
70	Eric Karros	.20
71	Bernie Williams	.50
72	Carlos Baerga	.20
73	Jeff Bagwell	1.50
74	Pete Schourek	.20
75	Ken Griffey Jr.	4.00
76	Bernard Gilkey	.20
77	Albert Belle	.75
78	Chuck Knoblauch	.20
79	John Smoltz	.35
80	Barry Bonds	2.00
81	Vinny Castilla	.20
82	John Olerud	.20
83	Mike Mussina	1.25
84	Alex Fernandez	.20
85	Shawon Dunston	.20
86	Travis Fryman	.20
87	Moises Alou	.35
88	Dean Palmer	.20
89	Gregg Jefferies	.20
90	Jim Thome	.20
91	Dave Justice	.40
92	B.J. Surhoff	.20
93	Ramon Martinez	.20
94	Gary Sheffield	.50
95	Andy Benes	.20
96	Reggie Sanders	.20
97	Roberto Alomar	1.25
98	Omar Vizquel	.20
99	Juan Gonzalez	1.50
100	Robin Ventura	.20
101	Jason Isringhausen	.20
102	Greg Colbrunn	.20
103	Brian Jordan	.20
104	Shawn Green	.40
105	Brian Hunter	.20
106	Rondell White	.35
107	Ryan Klesko	.20
107s	Ryan Klesko (marked "SAMPLE")	1.00
108	Sterling Hitchcock	.20
109	Manny Ramirez	1.50
110	Bret Boone	.20
111	Michael Tucker	.20
112	Julian Tavarez	.20
113	Benji Gil	.20
114	Kenny Lofton	.20
115	Mike Kelly	.20
116	Ray Durham	.20
117	Trevor Hoffman	.20
118	Butch Huskey	.20
119	Phil Nevin	.20
120	Pedro Martinez	.75
121	Wil Cordero	.20
122	Tim Salmon	.35
123	Jim Edmonds	.20
124	Mike Piazza	3.00
125	Rico Brogna	.20
126	John Mabry	.20
127	Chipper Jones	3.00
128	Johnny Damon	.20
129	Raul Mondesi	.35
130	Denny Neagle	.20
131	Marc Newfield	.20
132	Hideo Nomo	1.50
133	Joe Vitiello	.20
134	Garret Anderson	.20
135	Dave Nilsson	.20
136	Alex Rodriguez	3.50
137	Russ Davis	.20
138	Frank Rodriguez	.20
139	Royce Clayton	.20
140	John Valentin	.20
141	Marty Cordova	.20
142	Alex Gonzalez	.20
143	Carlos Delgado	.50
144	Willie Greene	.20
145	Cliff Floyd	.20
146	Bobby Higginson	.35
147	J.T. Snow	.20
148	Derek Bell	.20
149	Edgardo Alfonzo	.20
150	Charles Johnson	.20
151	Hideo Nomo (Global Reach)	.50
152	Larry Walker (Global Reach)	.20
153	Bob Abreu (Global Reach)	.20
154	Karim Garcia (Global Reach)	.20
155	Dave Nilsson (Global Reach)	.20
156	Chan Ho Park (Global Reach)	.35
157	Dennis Martinez (Global Reach)	.20
158	Sammy Sosa (Global Reach)	1.00
159	Rey Ordonez (Global Reach)	.20
160	Roberto Alomar (Global Reach)	.50
161	George Arias	.20
162	Jason Schmidt	.20
163	Derek Jeter	3.00
164	Chris Snopek	.20
165	Todd Hollandsworth	.20
166	Sal Fasano	.20
167	Jay Powell	.20
168	Paul Wilson	.20
169	Jim Pittsley	.20
170	LaTroy Hawkins	.20
171	Bob Abreu	.35
172	*Mike Grace*	.20
173	Karim Garcia	.35
174	Richard Hidalgo	.20
175	Felipe Crespo	.20
176	Terrell Wade	.20
177	Steve Gibralter	.20
178	Jermaine Dye	.20
179	Alan Benes	.20
180	*Wilton Guerrero*	.20
181	Brooks Kieschnick	.20
182	Roger Cedeno	.20
183	*Osvaldo Fernandez*	.20
184	*Matt Lawton*	1.00
185	George Williams	.20
186	Jimmy Haynes	.20
187	*Mike Busby*	.20
188	Chan Ho Park	.50
189	Marc Barcelo	.20
190	Jason Kendall	.20
191	Rey Ordonez	.20
192	Tyler Houston	.20
193	John Wasdin	.20
194	Jeff Suppan	.20
195	Jeff Ware	.20
196	Checklist	.20
197	Checklist	.20
198	Checklist	.20
199	Checklist	.20
200	Checklist	.20

1996 Pinnacle/ Aficionado First Pitch Previews

This parallel set differs from the regularly issued version in that there is a "FIRST PITCH / PREVIEW" label printed on the front on the end opposite the heliogram player portrait. Also, whereas on the regular cards, the player portrait is in silver metallic composition, the First Pitch Preview cards have the portrait in gold. These cards were most often obtained by visiting Pinnacle's site on the Internet and answering a trivia question.

	MT
Complete Set (200):	450.00
Common Player:	2.50

(Star cards valued at 8X-10X regular Aficionado edition.)

1996 Pinnacle/ Aficionado Magic Numbers

This insert set focuses on 10 of the game's best players, printing them on a wooden stock which carries the distinct grain and color of natural wood. The cards, seeded one every 72 packs, compares current players with others who have worn the same uniform number. Each card can also be found with a large black "SAMPLE" printed on back.

		MT
Complete Set (10):		45.00
Common Player:		2.00
Samples:		2X
1	Ken Griffey Jr.	10.00
2	Greg Maddux	6.00
3	Frank Thomas	6.00
4	Mo Vaughn	2.50
5	Jeff Bagwell	4.00
6	Chipper Jones	8.00
7	Albert Belle	2.00
8	Cal Ripken Jr.	10.00
9	Matt Williams	2.00
10	Sammy Sosa	6.00

1996 Pinnacle/ Aficionado Rivals

These inserts concentrate on the many matchups and rivalries that make baseball fun. Each card uses spot embossing. The cards are seeded one per every 24 packs.

		MT
Complete Set (24):		100.00
Common Player:		3.00
1	Ken Griffey Jr., Frank Thomas	8.00
2	Frank Thomas, Cal Ripken Jr.	8.50
3	Cal Ripken Jr., Mo Vaughn	6.00
4	Mo Vaughn, Ken Griffey Jr.	6.00
5	Ken Griffey Jr., Cal Ripken Jr.	10.00
6	Frank Thomas, Mo Vaughn	6.00
7	Cal Ripken Jr., Ken Griffey Jr.	10.00
8	Mo Vaughn, Frank Thomas	3.50
9	Ken Griffey Jr., Mo Vaughn	6.00
10	Frank Thomas, Ken Griffey Jr.	8.00
11	Cal Ripken Jr., Frank Thomas	8.50
12	Mo Vaughn, Cal Ripken Jr.	5.00
13	Mike Piazza, Jeff Bagwell	4.00
14	Jeff Bagwell, Barry Bonds	3.50
15	Jeff Bagwell, Mike Piazza	4.00
16	Tony Gwynn, Mike Piazza	4.00
17	Mike Piazza, Barry Bonds	5.00
18	Jeff Bagwell, Tony Gwynn	3.00
19	Barry Bonds, Mike Piazza	5.00
20	Tony Gwynn, Jeff Bagwell	3.00
21	Mike Piazza, Tony Gwynn	4.00
22	Barry Bonds, Jeff Bagwell	3.50
23	Tony Gwynn, Barry Bonds	3.50
24	Barry Bonds, Tony Gwynn	3.50

1996 Pinnacle/ Aficionado Slick Picks

This insert set pictures 32 of the best players in baseball on cards which use Spectroetch printing. Each card notes where that player was selected in the annual draft, emphasizing that there are numerous bargains available throughout the amateur draft. The cards were seeded one per 10 packs, making them the easiest to obtain of the set's insert cards.

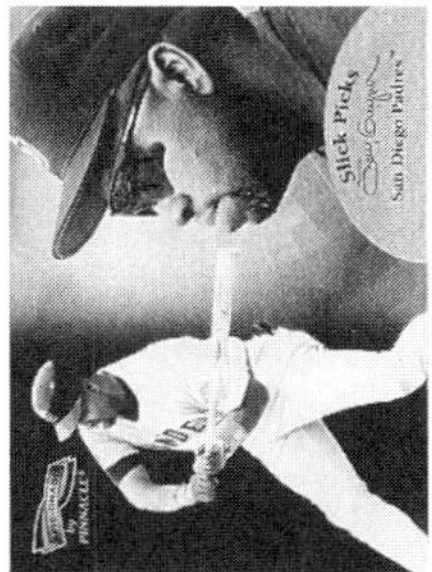

		MT
Complete Set (32):		80.00
Common Player:		1.00
1	Mike Piazza	6.00
2	Cal Ripken Jr.	7.50
3	Ken Griffey Jr.	7.50
4	Paul Wilson	1.00
5	Frank Thomas	5.00
6	Mo Vaughn	1.50
7	Barry Bonds	4.00
8	Albert Belle	2.50
9	Jeff Bagwell	4.00
10	Dante Bichette	1.00
11	Hideo Nomo	2.50
12	Raul Mondesi	1.50
13	Manny Ramirez	4.00
14	Greg Maddux	5.00
15	Tony Gwynn	4.50
16	Ryne Sandberg	4.00
17	Reggie Sanders	1.00
18	Derek Jeter	6.00
19	Johnny Damon	1.00
20	Alex Rodriguez	7.00
21	Ryan Klesko	1.00
22	Jim Thome	1.00
23	Kenny Lofton	1.00
24	Tino Martinez	1.00
25	Randy Johnson	3.00
26	Wade Boggs	2.00
27	Juan Gonzalez	4.00
28	Kirby Puckett	4.50
29	Tim Salmon	1.50
30	Chipper Jones	6.00
31	Garret Anderson	1.00
32	Eddie Murray	2.50

1997 Pinnacle

Pinnacle baseball consists of 200 base cards. Fronts have the player's name stamped within a foil baseball-diamond shape at the bottom of each card. Backs contain summaries of the players' 1996 and lifetime statistics. Included within the base set is a 30-card Rookies subset, a 12-card Clout subset and three checklists. Inserts include two parallel sets (Artist's Proof and Museum Collection), Passport to the Majors, Shades, Team Pinnacle, Cardfrontations, and Home/Away. Cards were sold in 10-card packs for $2.49 each.

		MT
Complete Set (200):		15.00
Common Player:		.10
Pack (10):		1.25
Wax Box (24):		25.00
Wax Retail Box (16):		20.00
1	Cecil Fielder	.10
2	Garret Anderson	.10
3	Charles Nagy	.10
4	Darryl Hamilton	.10
5	Greg Myers	.10
6	Eric Davis	.10
7	Jeff Frye	.10
8	Marquis Grissom	.10
9	Curt Schilling	.15
10	Jeff Fassero	.10
11	Alan Benes	.10
12	Orlando Miller	.10
13	Alex Fernandez	.10
14	Andy Pettitte	.30
15	Andre Dawson	.20
16	Mark Grudzielanek	.10
17	Joe Vitiello	.10
18	Juan Gonzalez	.75
19	Mark Whiten	.10
20	Lance Johnson	.10
21	Trevor Hoffman	.10
22	Marc Newfield	.10
23	Jim Eisenreich	.10
24	Joe Carter	.10
25	Jose Canseco	.40
26	Bill Swift	.10
27	Ellis Burks	.10
28	Ben McDonald	.10
29	Edgar Martinez	.10
30	Jamie Moyer	.10
31	Chan Ho Park	.25
32	Carlos Delgado	.50
33	Kevin Mitchell	.10
34	Carlos Garcia	.10
35	Darryl Strawberry	.10
36	Jim Thome	.10
37	Jose Offerman	.10
38	Ryan Klesko	.10
39	Ruben Sierra	.10
40	Devon White	.10
41	Brian Jordan	.10
42	Tony Gwynn	1.00
43	Rafael Palmeiro	.30
44	Dante Bichette	.10
45	Scott Stahoviak	.10
46	Roger Cedeno	.10
47	Ivan Rodriguez	.60
48	Bob Abreu	.10
49	Darryl Kile	.10
50	Darren Dreifort	.10
51	Shawon Dunston	.10
52	Mark McGwire	2.50
53	Tim Salmon	.15
54	Gene Schall	.10
55	Roger Clemens	1.00
56	Rondell White	.20
57	Ed Sprague	.10
58	Craig Paquette	.10
59	David Segui	.10
60	Jaime Navarro	.10
61	Tom Glavine	.15
62	Jeff Brantley	.10
63	Kimera Bartee	.10
64	Fernando Vina	.10
65	Eddie Murray	.50
66	Lenny Dykstra	.10
67	Kevin Elster	.10
68	Vinny Castilla	.10
69	Todd Greene	.10
70	Brett Butler	.10
71	Robby Thompson	.10
72	Reggie Jefferson	.10
73	Todd Hundley	.10
74	Jeff King	.10
75	Ernie Young	.10
76	Jeff Bagwell	.75
77	Dan Wilson	.10
78	Paul Molitor	.35
79	Kevin Seitzer	.10
80	Kevin Brown	.15
81	Ron Gant	.10
82	Dwight Gooden	.10
83	Todd Stottlemyre	.10
84	Ken Caminiti	.10
85	James Baldwin	.10
86	Jermaine Dye	.10
87	Harold Baines	.10
88	Pat Hentgen	.10
89	Frank Rodriguez	.10
90	Mark Johnson	.10
91	Jason Kendall	.10
92	Alex Rodriguez	2.50
93	Alan Trammell	.10
94	Scott Brosius	.10
95	Delino DeShields	.10
96	Chipper Jones	2.00
97	Barry Bonds	1.00
98	Brady Anderson	.10
99	Ryne Sandberg	.75
100	Albert Belle	.30
101	Jeff Cirillo	.10
102	Frank Thomas	1.00
103	Mike Piazza	2.00
104	Rickey Henderson	.65
105	Rey Ordonez	.10
106	Mark Grace	.25
107	Terry Steinbach	.10
108	Ray Durham	.10
109	Barry Larkin	.10
110	Tony Clark	.10
111	Bernie Williams	.40
112	John Smoltz	.15
113	Moises Alou	.15
114	Alex Gonzalez	.10
115	Rico Brogna	.10
116	Eric Karros	.10
117	Jeff Conine	.10
118	Todd Hollandsworth	.10
119	Troy Percival	.10
120	Paul Wilson	.10
121	Orel Hershiser	.10
122	Ozzie Smith	1.00
123	Dave Hollins	.10
124	Ken Hill	.10
125	Rick Wilkins	.10
126	Scott Servais	.10
127	Fernando Valenzuela	.10
128	Mariano Rivera	.20
129	Mark Loretta	.10
130	Shane Reynolds	.10
131	Darren Oliver	.10
132	Steve Trachsel	.10
133	Darren Bragg	.10
134	Jason Dickson	.10
135	Darren Fletcher	.10
136	Gary Gaetti	.10
137	Joey Cora	.10
138	Terry Pendleton	.10
139	Derek Jeter	2.50
140	Danny Tartabull	.10
141	John Flaherty	.10
142	B.J. Surhoff	.10
143	Mark Sweeney	.10
144	Chad Mottola	.10
145	Andujar Cedeno	.10
146	Tim Belcher	.10
147	Mark Thompson	.10
148	Rafael Bournigal	.10
149	Marty Cordova	.10
150	Osvaldo Fernandez	.10
151	Mike Stanley	.10
152	Ricky Bottalico	.10
153	Donnie Wall	.10
154	Omar Vizquel	.10
155	Mike Mussina	.50
156	Brant Brown	.10
157	F.P. Santangelo	.10
158	Ryan Hancock	.10
159	Jeff D'Amico	.10
160	Luis Castillo	.10
161	Darin Erstad	.50
162	Ugueth Urbina	.10
163	Andruw Jones	.75
164	Steve Gibralter	.10
165	Robin Jennings	.10
166	Mike Cameron	.10
167	George Arias	.10
168	Chris Stynes	.10
169	Justin Thompson	.10
170	Jamey Wright	.10
171	Todd Walker	.10
172	Nomar Garciaparra	1.50
173	Jose Paniagua	.10
174	Marvin Benard	.10
175	Rocky Coppinger	.10
176	Quinton McCracken	.10
177	Amaury Telemaco	.10
178	Neifi Perez	.10
179	Todd Greene	.10
180	Jason Thompson	.10
181	Wilton Guerrero	.10
182	Edgar Renteria	.10
183	Billy Wagner	.10
184	Alex Ochoa	.10
185	Billy McMillon	.10
186	Kenny Lofton	.10
187	Andres Galarraga (Clout)	.10
188	Chuck Knoblauch (Clout)	.10
189	Greg Maddux (Clout)	1.50
190	Mo Vaughn (Clout)	.40
191	Cal Ripken Jr. (Clout)	2.50
192	Hideo Nomo (Clout)	.75
193	Ken Griffey Jr. (Clout)	2.50
194	Sammy Sosa (Clout)	1.50
195	Jay Buhner (Clout)	.10
196	Manny Ramirez (Clout)	.75
197	Matt Williams (Clout)	.25
198	Andruw Jones (Checklist)	.35
199	Darin Erstad (Checklist)	.20
200	Trey Beamon (Checklist)	.10

1997 Pinnacle Museum Collection

Each of the 200 cards in 1997 Pinnacle Series 1 was also issued in a graphically enhanced Museum Collection parallel set. The Museum cards utilize basically the same design as the regular-issue Pinnacle cards, but the front is printed in the company's Dufex gold-foil technology. On back, a small rectangular logo verifies the card's special status.

	MT
Complete Set (200):	200.00
Common Player:	1.00
Stars/Rookies:	8X

(See 1997 Pinnacle for checklist and regular-issue card values.)

1997 Pinnacle Artist's Proofs

Artist's Proofs parallels for 1997 Pinnacle were issued in a "fractured" set form. That is, three levels of scarcity were created, with each card available in only one of those levels. For 125 of the players, bronze is the scarcity level; 50 of the players have a silver-level scarcity and 25 players are found in the top-shelf gold level, with a reported production of 300 each. Stated odds of finding an AP parallel were 1:47 in hobby and retail packs, and 1:55 in magazine packs.

	MT
Common Bronze (125):	2.00
Bronze Stars:	30X
Common Silver (50):	5.00
Silver Stars:	12X
Common Gold:	7.50
Gold Stars:	10X

(See 1997 Pinnacle for checklist and base card values.)

1997 Pinnacle Cardfrontations

This hobby-only set was inserted every 23 packs of 1997 Pinnacle baseball. Fronts depict a player portrait imaged over a foil rainbow background. The same player is then pictured in action shots with the "Cardfrontation" logo in gold foil in the lower right half. The player's name appears in gold foil below the gold-foil team logo. Backs depict another player's portrait with text describing interaction between the two players. The cards are numbered as "x of 20."

		MT
Complete Set (20):		90.00
Common Player:		1.50
1	Greg Maddux, Mike Piazza	10.00
2	Tom Glavine, Ken Caminiti	1.50
3	Randy Johnson, Cal Ripken Jr.	12.50
4	Kevin Appier, Mark McGwire	12.50
5	Andy Pettitte, Juan Gonzalez	4.00
6	Pat Hentgen, Albert Belle	1.50
7	Hideo Nomo, Chipper Jones	10.00
8	Ismael Valdes, Sammy Sosa	7.50
9	Manny Ramirez	5.00
10	David Cone, Jay Buhner	1.50
11	Mark Wohlers, Gary Sheffield	1.50
12	Alan Benes, Barry Bonds	4.00
13	Roger Clemens Ivan Rodriguez	5.00
14	Mariano Rivera, Ken Griffey Jr.	12.00
15	Dwight Gooden, Frank Thomas	5.00
16	John Wetteland, Darin Erstad	1.50
17	John Smoltz, Brian Jordan	1.50
18	Kevin Brown, Jeff Bagwell	4.00
19	Jack McDowell, Alex Rodriguez	12.00
20	Charles Nagy, Bernie Williams	1.50

1997 Pinnacle Home/Away

The 24-card, shirt-shaped, die-cut set was inserted every 33 retail packs. The background on front and back is a facsimile of the player's home or road jersey. A color action photo is on front with gold-foil graphics. Backs have a few words about the player.

		MT
Complete Set (24):		150.00
Common Player:		2.50
1	Chipper Jones	10.00
2	Ken Griffey Jr.	12.50
3	Mike Piazza	10.00
4	Frank Thomas	7.50
5	Jeff Bagwell	6.00
6	Alex Rodriguez	12.00
7	Barry Bonds	7.00
8	Mo Vaughn	4.00
9	Derek Jeter	10.00
10	Mark McGwire	12.50
11	Cal Ripken Jr.	12.50
12	Albert Belle	4.00

1997 Pinnacle Passport to the Majors

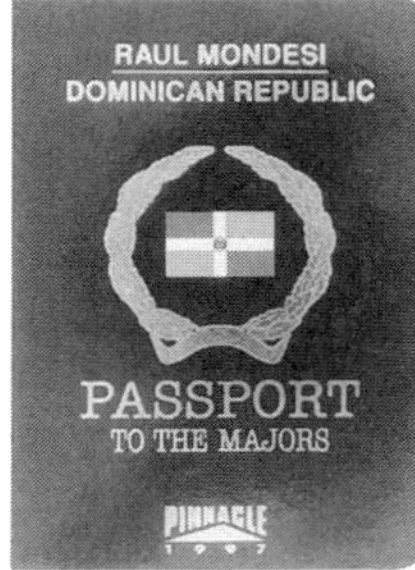

The 25-card, regular-sized set was inserted every 36 packs of 1997 Pinnacle baseball. The cards fold out and resemble a mini passport.

		MT
Complete Set (25):		70.00
Common Player:		1.00
1	Greg Maddux	6.00
1s	Greg Maddux ("SAMPLE" overprint)	2.50
2	Ken Griffey Jr.	9.00
3	Frank Thomas	4.00
4	Cal Ripken Jr.	10.00
5	Mike Piazza	7.50
6	Alex Rodriguez	9.00
7	Mo Vaughn	2.00
8	Chipper Jones	6.00
9	Roberto Alomar	2.50
10	Edgar Martinez	1.00
11	Javier Lopez	1.00
12	Ivan Rodriguez	2.50
13	Juan Gonzalez	3.00
14	Carlos Baerga	1.00
15	Sammy Sosa	6.00
16	Manny Ramirez	3.00
17	Raul Mondesi	1.50
18	Henry Rodriguez	1.00
19	Rafael Palmeiro	1.50
20	Rey Ordonez	1.00
21	Hideo Nomo	4.00
22	Makoto Suzuki	1.00
23	Chan Ho Park	2.50
24	Larry Walker	2.00
25	Ruben Rivera	1.00

1997 Pinnacle Shades

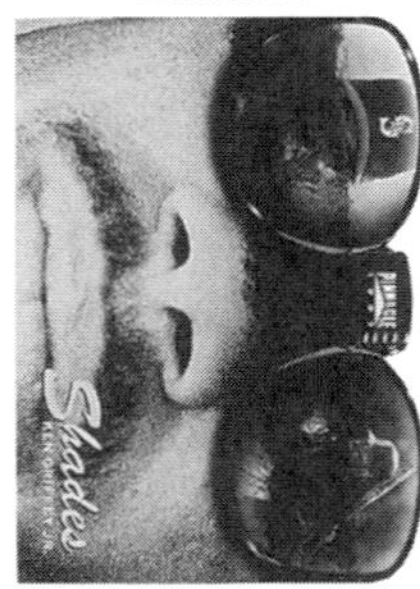

This set was inserted every 23 retail packs of Pinnacle baseball. The horizontal cards are die-cut at the top of a pair of sunglasses whose lenses contain color portrait and action pictures of the player. The player face beneath the shades is printed on silver foil stock. Backs have a mirror-image of the front photos in the lenses and a baseball diamond in the background.

		MT
Complete Set (10):		30.00
Common Player:		1.50
1	Ken Griffey Jr.	7.50
2	Juan Gonzalez	2.50
3	John Smoltz	1.50
4	Gary Sheffield	1.50
5	Cal Ripken Jr.	7.50
6	Mo Vaughn	1.50
7	Brian Jordan	1.50
8	Mike Piazza	6.00
9	Frank Thomas	5.00
10	Alex Rodriguez	7.00

1997 Pinnacle Team Pinnacle

This insert features top National League players from a position on one side with the best American League players on the other. One side of the card is in Dufex printing and there is actually two versions of each card, as either side can feature the Dufex foil. Team Pinnacle is inserted every 90 packs.

		MT
Complete Set (10):		30.00
Common Player:		1.50
1	Frank Thomas, Jeff Bagwell	5.00
2	Chuck Knoblauch, Eric Young	1.50
3	Ken Caminiti, Jim Thome	1.50
4	Alex Rodriguez, Chipper Jones	6.50
5	Mike Piazza, Ivan Rodriguez	6.00
6	Albert Belle, Barry Bonds	4.00
7	Ken Griffey Jr., Ellis Burks	6.50
8	Juan Gonzalez, Gary Sheffield	3.00
9	John Smoltz, Andy Pettitte	2.00
10	All Players	1.50

1997 New Pinnacle

In lieu of a second series of Pinnacle Baseball, the company offered collectors New Pinnacle, a 200-card set sold in 10-card packs for $2.99. Two parallel versions of the 200-card set exist in Museum Collection and Artist's Proofs. Other inserts include Press Plates, Spellbound, Keeping the Pace and Interleague Encounter. Collectors who obtained four Press Plates of the same player's card back or front were eligible to win cash prizes.

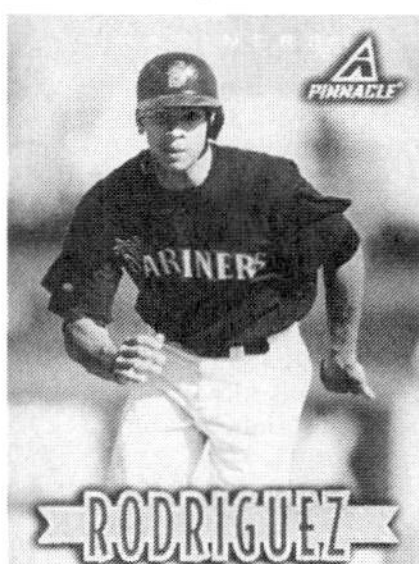

	MT
Complete Set (200):	25.00
Common Player:	.10
Common Museum:	1.00
Museum Stars:	10X
Pack (10):	1.50
Wax Box (18):	25.00

1	Ken Griffey Jr.	2.50
2	Sammy Sosa	1.50
3	Greg Maddux	1.50
4	Matt Williams	.30
5	Jason Isringhausen	.10
6	Gregg Jefferies	.10
7	Chili Davis	.10
8	Paul O'Neill	.10
9	Larry Walker	.30
10	Ellis Burks	.10
11	Cliff Floyd	.10
12	Albert Belle	.30
13	Javier Lopez	.10
14	David Cone	.10
15	Jose Canseco	.40
16	Todd Zeile	.10
17	Bernard Gilkey	.10
18	Andres Galarraga	.10
19	Chris Snopek	.10
20	Tim Salmon	.20
21	Roger Clemens	1.00
22	Reggie Sanders	.10
23	John Jaha	.10
24	Andy Pettitte	.30
25	Kenny Lofton	.10
26	Robb Nen	.10
27	John Wetteland	.10
28	Bobby Bonilla	.10
29	Hideo Nomo	.75
30	Cecil Fielder	.10
31	Garret Anderson	.10
32	Pat Hentgen	.10
33	David Justice	.30
34	Billy Wagner	.10
35	Al Leiter	.10
36	Mark Wohlers	.10
37	Rondell White	.15
38	Charles Johnson	.10
39	Mark Grace	.25
40	Pedro Martinez	.60
41	Tom Goodwin	.10
42	Manny Ramirez	.75
43	Greg Vaughn	.10
44	Brian Jordan	.10
45	Mike Piazza	2.00
46	Roberto Hernandez	.10
47	Wade Boggs	.50
48	Scott Sanders	.10
49	Alex Gonzalez	.10
50	Kevin Brown	.15
51	Bob Higginson	.10
52	Ken Caminiti	.10
53	Derek Jeter	2.50
54	Carlos Baerga	.10
55	Jay Buhner	.10
56	Tim Naehring	.10
57	Jeff Bagwell	.75
58	Steve Finley	.10
59	Kevin Appier	.10
60	Jay Bell	.10
61	Ivan Rodriguez	.60
62	Terrell Wade	.10
63	Rusty Greer	.10
64	Juan Guzman	.10
65	Fred McGriff	.10
66	Tino Martinez	.10
67	Ray Lankford	.10
68	Juan Gonzalez	.75
69	Ron Gant	.10
70	Jack McDowell	.10
71	Tony Gwynn	1.00
72	Joe Carter	.10
73	Wilson Alvarez	.10
74	Jason Giambi	.40
75	Brian Hunter	.10
76	Michael Tucker	.10
77	Andy Benes	.10
78	Brady Anderson	.10
79	Ramon Martinez	.10
80	Troy Percival	.10
81	Alex Rodriguez	2.50
82	Jim Thome	.10
83	Denny Neagle	.10
84	Rafael Palmeiro	3.00
85	Jose Valentin	.10
86	Marc Newfield	.10
87	Mariano Rivera	.25
88	Alan Benes	.10
89	Jimmy Key	.10
90	Joe Randa	.10
91	Cal Ripken Jr.	2.50
92	Craig Biggio	.10
93	Dean Palmer	.10
94	Gary Sheffield	.30
95	Ismael Valdez	.10
96	John Valentin	.10
97	Johnny Damon	.15
98	Mo Vaughn	.40
99	Paul Sorrento	.10
100	Randy Johnson	.65
101	Raul Mondesi	.20
102	Roberto Alomar	.60
103	Royce Clayton	.10
104	Mark Grudzielanek	.10
105	Wally Joyner	.10
106	Wil Cordero	.10
107	Will Clark	.30
108	Chuck Knoblauch	.10
109	Derek Bell	.10
110	Henry Rodriguez	.10
111	Edgar Renteria	.10
112	Travis Fryman	.10
113	Eric Young	.10
114	Sandy Alomar Jr.	.10
115	Darin Erstad	.50
116	Barry Larkin	.15
117	Barry Bonds	1.00
118	Frank Thomas	1.00
119	Carlos Delgado	.50
120	Jason Kendall	.10
121	Todd Hollandsworth	.10
122	Jim Edmonds	.20
123	Chipper Jones	2.00
124	Jeff Fassero	.10
125	Deion Sanders	.20
126	Matt Lawton	.10
127	Ryan Klesko	.10
128	Mike Mussina	.60
129	Paul Molitor	.60
130	Dante Bichette	.10
131	Bill Pulsipher	.10
132	Todd Hundley	.10
133	J.T. Snow	.10
134	Chuck Finley	.10
135	Shawn Green	.20
136	Charles Nagy	.10
137	Willie Greene	.10
138	Marty Cordova	.10
139	Eddie Murray	.40
140	Ryne Sandberg	.75
141	Alex Fernandez	.10
142	Mark McGwire	2.50
143	Eric Davis	.10
144	Jermaine Dye	.10
145	Ruben Sierra	.10
146	Damon Buford	.10
147	John Smoltz	.15
148	Alex Ochoa	.10
149	Moises Alou	.15
150	Rico Brogna	.10
151	Terry Steinbach	.10
152	Jeff King	.10
153	Carlos Garcia	.10
154	Tom Glavine	.15
155	Edgar Martinez	.10
156	Kevin Elster	.10
157	Darryl Hamilton	.10
158	Jason Dickson	.10
159	Kevin Orie	.10
160	*Bubba Trammell*	.25
161	Jose Guillen	.10
162	Brant Brown	.10
163	Wendell Magee	.10
164	Scott Spiezio	.10
165	Todd Walker	.10
166	*Rod Myers*	.10
167	Damon Mashore	.10
168	Wilton Guerrero	.10
169	Vladimir Guerrero	.75
170	Nomar Garciaparra	1.50
171	Shannon Stewart	.10
172	Scott Rolen	.50
173	Bob Abreu	.10
174	*Danny Patterson*	.20
175	Andruw Jones	.50
176	*Brian Giles*	1.50
177	Dmitri Young	.10
178	Cal Ripken Jr. (East Meets West)	1.25
179	Chuck Knoblauch (East Meets West)	.10
180	Alex Rodriguez (East Meets West)	1.25
181	Andres Galarraga (East Meets West)	.10
182	Pedro Martinez (East Meets West)	.30
183	Brady Anderson (East Meets West)	.10
184	Barry Bonds (East Meets West)	.50
185	Ivan Rodriguez (East Meets West)	.30
186	Gary Sheffield (East Meets West)	.15
187	Denny Neagle (East Meets West)	.10
188	Mark McGwire (Aura)	1.25
189	Ellis Burks (Aura)	.10
190	Alex Rodriguez (Aura)	1.25
191	Mike Piazza (Aura)	1.00
192	Barry Bonds (Aura)	.50
193	Albert Belle (Aura)	.20
194	Chipper Jones (Aura)	1.00
195	Juan Gonzalez (Aura)	.40
196	Brady Anderson (Aura)	.10
197	Frank Thomas (Aura)	.50
198	Checklist (Vladimir Guerrero)	.35
199	Checklist (Todd Walker)	.10
200	Checklist (Scott Rolen)	.25

1997 New Pinnacle Artist's Proof

This 200-card parallel set features a special AP seal and foil treatment and is fractured into three levels of scarcity - Red (125 cards), Blue (50 cards) and Green (25 cards). Cards were inserted at a rate of 1:39 packs. "Artist's Proof" is stamped along the lower edge.

	MT
Common Red Artist's Proof:	3.00
Red Artist's Proofs:	10X
Common Blue Artist's Proof:	9.00
Blue Artist's Proofs:	50X
Common Green Artist's Proof:	18.00
Green Artist's Proofs:	35X

(See 1997 New Pinnacle for checklist and base values.)

1997 New Pinnacle Museum Collection

Dufex printing on gold-foil backgrounds differentiates the Musuem Collection parallel of New Pinnacle from the regular-issue cards. Museums were inserted at an average rate of one per nine packs.

	MT
Complete Set (200):	200.00
Common Player:	1.00
Stars/Rookies:	10X

(See 1997 New Pinnacle for checklist and base card values.)

1997 New Pinnacle Press Plates

Just when collectors thought they had seen every type of insert card imaginable, New Pinnacle proved them wrong by cutting up and inserting into packs (about one per 1,250) the metal plates used to print the set. There are black, blue, red and yellow plates for the front and back of each card. Rather than touting the collector value of the plates, Pinnacle created a treasure hunt by offering $20,000-35,000 to anybody assembling a complete set of four plates for either the front or back of any card. The $35,000, which would have been awarded for completion prior to Aug. 22, was unclaimed. The amount decreased to $20,000 for any set redeemed by the end of 1997.

MT

(Because of the unique nature of each press plate, no current market value can be quoted.)

1997 New Pinnacle Interleague Encounter

Inserted 1:240 packs, this 10-card sets showcases 20 American League and National League rivals with the date of their first interleague match-up on double-sided mirror mylar cards.

		MT
Complete Set (10):		165.00
Common Player:		10.00
1	Albert Belle, Brian Jordan	10.00
2	Andruw Jones, Brady Anderson	15.00
3	Ken Griffey Jr., Tony Gwynn	30.00
4	Cal Ripken Jr., Chipper Jones	30.00
5	Mike Piazza, Ivan Rodriguez	25.00
6	Derek Jeter, Vladimir Guerrero	25.00
7	Greg Maddux, Mo Vaughn	20.00
8	Alex Rodriguez, Hideo Nomo	30.00
9	Juan Gonzalez, Barry Bonds	17.50
10	Frank Thomas, Jeff Bagwell	20.00

1997 New Pinnacle Keeping the Pace

Top sluggers who were considered candidates to break Roger Maris' single-season record of 61 home runs were featured in this insert set. Cards feature Dot Matrix holographic borders and backgrounds on front. Backs present career stats of an all-time great and project future numbers for the current player. The cards were inserted 1:89 packs.

		MT
Complete Set (18):		175.00
Common Player:		2.00
1	Juan Gonzalez	10.00
2	Greg Maddux	15.00
3	Ivan Rodriguez	7.50
4	Ken Griffey Jr.	25.00
5	Alex Rodriguez	25.00
6	Barry Bonds	12.50
7	Frank Thomas	15.00
8	Chuck Knoblauch	2.00
9	Derek Jeter	20.00
10	Roger Clemens	12.50
11	Kenny Lofton	2.00
12	Tony Gwynn	12.50
13	Troy Percival	2.00
14	Cal Ripken Jr.	30.00
15	Andy Pettitte	5.00
16	Hideo Nomo	7.50
17	Randy Johnson	7.50
18	Mike Piazza	20.00

1997 New Pinnacle Spellbound

Each of the 50 cards in this insert features a letter of the alphabet as the basic card design. The letters can be used to spell out the names of nine players featured in the set. Cards feature micro-etched foil and are inserted 1:19 packs. Cards of Griffey, Ripken and the Jones were inserted only in hobby packs; retail packs have cards of Belle, Thomas, Piazza and the Rodriguezes. Values shown are per card; multiply by number of cards to determine a player's set value.

	MT
Complete Set (50):	350.00
1-5AB Albert Belle	4.00
1-6AJ Andruw Jones	6.50
1-4AR Alex Rodriguez	12.50
1-7CJ Chipper Jones	9.00
1-6CR Cal Ripken Jr.	15.00
1-5FT Frank Thomas	7.50
1-5IR Ivan Rodriguez	5.00
1-6KG Ken Griffey Jr.	15.00
1-6MP Mike Piazza	9.00

1997 Pinnacle Certified

This 150-card base features a mirror-like mylar finish and a peel-off protector on each card front. Backs feature the player's 1996 statistics against each opponent. There are four different parallel sets, each with varying degrees of scarcity: Certified Red (1:5), Mirror Red (1:99), Mirror Blue (1:199) and Mirror Gold (1:299). Other inserts include Lasting Impressions, Certified Team, and Certified Gold Team. Cards were sold in six-card packs for a suggested price of $4.99.

		MT
Complete Set (150):		30.00
Common Player:		.15
Jose Cruz Jr. Redemption:		3.00
Pack (6):		2.00
Wax Box (20):		35.00
1	Barry Bonds	1.00
2	Mo Vaughn	.50
3	Matt Williams	.35
4	Ryne Sandberg	1.00
5	Jeff Bagwell	.75
6	Alan Benes	.15
7	John Wetteland	.15
8	Fred McGriff	.15
9	Craig Biggio	.15
10	Bernie Williams	.35
11	Brian L. Hunter	.15
12	Sandy Alomar Jr.	.15
13	Ray Lankford	.15
14	Ryan Klesko	.15
15	Jermaine Dye	.15
16	Andy Benes	.15
17	Albert Belle	.50
18	Tony Clark	.15
19	Dean Palmer	.15
20	Bernard Gilkey	.15
21	Ken Caminiti	.15
22	Alex Rodriguez	3.00
23	Tim Salmon	.35
24	Larry Walker	.35
25	Barry Larkin	.25
26	Mike Piazza	2.50
27	Brady Anderson	.15
28	Cal Ripken Jr.	3.00
29	Charles Nagy	.15
30	Paul Molitor	.60
31	Darin Erstad	.75
32	Rey Ordonez	.15
33	Wally Joyner	.15
34	David Cone	.15
35	Sammy Sosa	2.00
36	Dante Bichette	.15
37	Eric Karros	.15
38	Omar Vizquel	.15
39	Roger Clemens	1.50
40	Joe Carter	.15
41	Frank Thomas	1.50
42	Javier Lopez	.15
43	Mike Mussina	.50
44	Gary Sheffield	.35
45	Tony Gwynn	1.50
46	Jason Kendall	.15
47	Jim Thome	.15
48	Andres Galarraga	.15
49	Mark McGwire	3.00
50	Troy Percival	.15
51	Derek Jeter	2.50
52	Todd Hollandsworth	.15
53	Ken Griffey Jr.	3.00
54	Randy Johnson	.75
55	Pat Hentgen	.15
56	Rusty Greer	.15
57	John Jaha	.15
58	Kenny Lofton	.15
59	Chipper Jones	2.50
60	Robb Nen	.15
61	Rafael Palmeiro	.35
62	Mariano Rivera	.45
63	Hideo Nomo	.75
64	Greg Vaughn	.15
65	Ron Gant	.15
66	Eddie Murray	.60
67	John Smoltz	.20
68	Manny Ramirez	.75
69	Juan Gonzalez	.75
70	F.P. Santangelo	.15
71	Moises Alou	.25
72	Alex Ochoa	.15
73	Chuck Knoblauch	.15
74	Raul Mondesi	.30
75	J.T. Snow	.15
76	Rickey Henderson	.75
77	Bobby Bonilla	.15
78	Wade Boggs	.60
79	Ivan Rodriguez	.60
80	Brian Jordan	.15
81	Al Leiter	.15
82	Jay Buhner	.15
83	Greg Maddux	2.00
84	Edgar Martinez	.15
85	Kevin Brown	.20
86	Eric Young	.15
87	Todd Hundley	.15
88	Ellis Burks	.15
89	Marquis Grissom	.15
90	Jose Canseco	.50
91	Henry Rodriguez	.15
92	Andy Pettitte	.40
93	Mark Grudzielanek	.15
94	Dwight Gooden	.15
95	Roberto Alomar	.60
96	Paul Wilson	.15
97	Will Clark	.35
98	Rondell White	.25
99	Charles Johnson	.15
100	Jim Edmonds	.15
101	Jason Giambi	.75
102	Billy Wagner	.15
103	Edgar Renteria	.15
104	Johnny Damon	.20
105	Jason Isringhausen	.15
106	Andruw Jones	.75
107	Jose Guillen	.15
108	Kevin Orie	.15
109	*Brian Giles*	2.50
110	Danny Patterson	.15
111	Vladimir Guerrero	.75
112	Scott Rolen	.60
113	Damon Mashore	.15
114	Nomar Garciaparra	2.00
115	Todd Walker	.15
116	Wilton Guerrero	.15
117	Bob Abreu	.15
118	Brooks Kieschnick	.15
119	Pokey Reese	.15
120	Todd Greene	.15
121	Dmitri Young	.15
122	Raul Casanova	.15
123	Glendon Rusch	.15
124	Jason Dickson	.15
125	Jorge Posada	.15
126	*Rod Myers*	.15
127	*Bubba Trammell*	.50
128	Scott Spiezio	.15
129	*Hideki Irabu*	.75
130	Wendell Magee	.15
131	Bartolo Colon	.15
132	Chris Holt	.15
133	Calvin Maduro	.15
134	Ray Montgomery	.15
135	Shannon Stewart	.15
136	Ken Griffey Jr. (Certified Stars)	1.50
137	Vladimir Guerrero (Certified Stars)	.60
138	Roger Clemens (Certified Stars)	.75
139	Mark McGwire (Certified Stars)	2.00
140	Albert Belle (Certified Stars)	.25
141	Derek Jeter (Certified Stars)	1.50
142	Juan Gonzalez (Certified Stars)	.50
143	Greg Maddux (Certified Stars)	1.00
144	Alex Rodriguez (Certified Stars)	1.50

145	Jeff Bagwell (Certified Stars)	.50
146	Cal Ripken Jr. (Certified Stars)	1.50
147	Tony Gwynn (Certified Stars)	.75
148	Frank Thomas (Certified Stars)	.75
149	Hideo Nomo (Certified Stars)	.75
150	Andruw Jones (Certified Stars)	.50

1997 Pinnacle Certified Red

This parallel set features a red tint to the triangular mylar background left and right of the photo on front. "CERTIFIED RED" is printed vertically on both edges. Backs are identical to regular Certified cards. A peel-off protection coating is on the front of the card. Cards were inserted 1:5 packs.

	MT
Common Certified Red:	1.00
Certified Red Stars:	5X

(See 1997 Pinnacle Certified for checklist and base values.)

1997 Pinnacle Certified Mirror Red

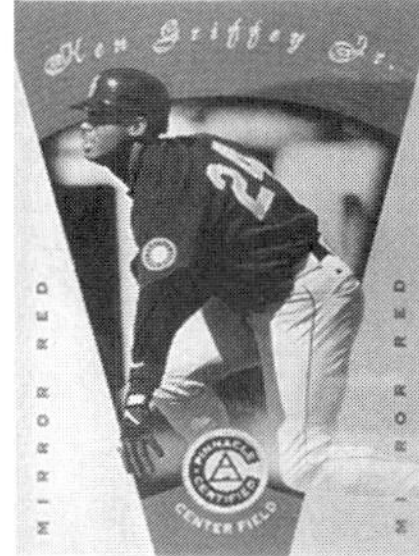

This parallel set features a red design element on the front of each card. Cards were inserted 1:99 packs.

	MT
Common Mirror Red:	4.00
Mirror Red Stars:	15X

(See 1997 Pinnacle Certified for checklist and base values.)

1997 Pinnacle Certified Mirror Blue

This parallel set features a blue design element on the front of each card. Cards were inserted 1:199 packs.

	MT
Common Mirror Blue:	4.00
Mirror Blue Stars:	20X

(See 1997 Pinnacle Certified for checklist and base values.)

1997 Pinnacle Certified Mirror Gold

This parallel set features a holographic gold design on the front of each card. Cards were inserted 1:299 packs.

	MT
Common Mirror Gold:	10.00
Mirror Gold Stars:	50X

(See 1997 Pinnacle Certified for checklist and base values.)

1997 Pinnacle Certified Mirror Black

The exact nature of these cards is undetermined. They may have been intentionally created and "secretly" seeded in packs as an insert or they may have been test cards which were mistakenly inserted. They are not marked in any fashion. The cards are said to reflect in bright green under direct light. It is commonly believed that each "Mirror Black" card exists in only a single piece, but that has not been verified. Neither is it confirmed that a Mirror Black parallel exists for each of the 151 cards in the base set. Even the most undistinguished player's card can sell for $100 or more due to the scarcity of the type.

	MT
Common Player:	100.00

(Star cards valued at 150-250X base value.)

1997 Pinnacle Certified Lasting Impression

This insert features an hour-glass die-cut design and a mirror mylar finish and pictures some of baseball's top veteran stars. Backs are conventionally printed and include a color portrait photo and a few words about the player. Cards were inserted 1:19 packs.

		MT
Complete Set (20):		50.00
Common Player:		1.00
1	Cal Ripken Jr.	7.50
2	Ken Griffey Jr.	7.50
3	Mo Vaughn	1.50
4	Brian Jordan	1.00
5	Mark McGwire	7.50
6	Chuck Knoblauch	1.00
7	Sammy Sosa	4.50
8	Brady Anderson	1.00
9	Frank Thomas	4.50
10	Tony Gwynn	4.50
11	Roger Clemens	4.00
12	Alex Rodriguez	6.00
13	Paul Molitor	2.00
14	Kenny Lofton	1.00
15	John Smoltz	1.00
16	Roberto Alomar	2.00
17	Randy Johnson	2.00
18	Ryne Sandberg	3.00
19	Manny Ramirez	4.00
20	Mike Mussina	2.00

1997 Pinnacle Certified Team

The top 20 players in the game are honored on cards with frosted silver mylar printing. Cards were inserted 1:19 packs. A parallel version of this set, Certified Gold Team, has a gold mylar design with each card numbered to 500; while a super-premium parallel, Mirror Gold, is numbered to 25.

		MT
Complete Set (20):		85.00
Common Player:		1.00
Gold:		1.5X
Mirror Gold:		8X
1	Frank Thomas	5.00
2	Jeff Bagwell	4.00
3	Derek Jeter	6.50
4	Chipper Jones	6.50
5	Alex Rodriguez	7.00
6	Ken Caminiti	1.00
7	Cal Ripken Jr.	7.50
8	Mo Vaughn	2.00
9	Ivan Rodriguez	3.00
10	Mike Piazza	6.50
11	Juan Gonzalez	4.00
12	Barry Bonds	35.00
13	Ken Griffey Jr.	7.50
14	Andruw Jones	3.00
15	Albert Belle	2.50
16	Gary Sheffield	1.50
17	Andy Pettitte	1.50
18	Hideo Nomo	2.50
19	Greg Maddux	5.00
19s	Greg Maddux (Gold Team "SAMPLE")	2.50
20	John Smoltz	1.00

1997 Pinnacle Inside

The first baseball card set to be sold within a sealed tin can, Inside Baseball consists of a 150-card base set featuring both a color and black-and-white photo of the player on front. Included in the base set are 20 Rookies cards and three checklists. Inserts include the Club Edition and Diamond Edition parallel sets, Dueling Dugouts and Forty-something. In addition, 24 different cans, each featuring a different player, were available. Cans containing one pack of 10 cards were sold for $2.99 each.

		MT
Complete Set (150):		35.00
Common Player:		.10
Common Club Edition:		.75
Club Edition Stars:		5X
Common Diamond Edition:		5.00
Diamond Edition Stars:		25X
Unopened Can (10):		2.00
Case Cans (48):		80.00
1	David Cone	.10
2	Sammy Sosa	1.50
3	Joe Carter	.10
4	Juan Gonzalez	1.00
5	Hideo Nomo	.75
6	Moises Alou	.15
7	Marc Newfield	.10
8	Alex Rodriguez	2.50
9	Kimera Bartee	.10
10	Chuck Knoblauch	.10
11	Jason Isringhausen	.10
12	Jermaine Allensworth	.10
13	Frank Thomas	1.50
14	Paul Molitor	.75
15	John Mabry	.10
16	Greg Maddux	1.50
17	Rafael Palmeiro	.30
18	Brian Jordan	.10
19	Ken Griffey Jr.	2.50
20	Brady Anderson	.10
21	Ruben Sierra	.10
22	Travis Fryman	.10
23	Cal Ripken Jr.	3.00
24	Will Clark	.30

25	Todd Hollandsworth	.10
26	Kevin Brown	.15
27	Mike Piazza	2.00
28	Craig Biggio	.10
29	Paul Wilson	.10
30	Andres Galarraga	.10
31	Chipper Jones	2.00
32	Jason Giambi	.75
33	Ernie Young	.10
34	Marty Cordova	.10
35	Albert Belle	.30
36	Roger Clemens	1.50
37	Ryne Sandberg	1.00
38	Henry Rodriguez	.10
39	Jay Buhner	.10
40	Raul Mondesi	.20
41	Jeff Fassero	.10
42	Edgar Martinez	.10
43	Trey Beamon	.10
44	Mo Vaughn	.50
45	Gary Sheffield	.35
46	Ray Durham	.10
47	Brett Butler	.10
48	Ivan Rodriguez	.75
49	Fred McGriff	.10
50	Dean Palmer	.10
51	Rickey Henderson	.65
52	Andy Pettitte	.40
53	Bobby Bonilla	.10
54	Shawn Green	.25
55	Tino Martinez	.10
56	Tony Gwynn	1.50
57	Tom Glavine	.15
58	Eric Young	.10
59	Kevin Appier	.10
60	Barry Bonds	1.25
61	Wade Boggs	.65
62	Jason Kendall	.10
63	Jeff Bagwell	1.00
64	Jeff Conine	.10
65	Greg Vaughn	.10
66	Eric Karros	.10
67	Manny Ramirez	1.00
68	John Smoltz	.15
69	Terrell Wade	.10
70	John Wetteland	.10
71	Kenny Lofton	.10
72	Jim Thome	.10
73	Bill Pulsipher	.10
74	Darryl Strawberry	.10
75	Roberto Alomar	.75
76	Bobby Higginson	.10
77	James Baldwin	.10
78	Mark McGwire	3.00
79	Jose Canseco	.50
80	Mark Grudzielanek	.10
81	Ryan Klesko	.10
82	Javier Lopez	.10
83	Ken Caminiti	.10
84	Dave Nilsson	.10
85	Tim Salmon	.20
86	Cecil Fielder	.10
87	Derek Jeter	2.00
88	Garret Anderson	.10
89	Dwight Gooden	.10
90	Carlos Delgado	.75
91	Ugueth Urbina	.10
92	Chan Ho Park	.25
93	Eddie Murray	.55
94	Alex Ochoa	.10
95	Rusty Greer	.10
96	Mark Grace	.25
97	Pat Hentgen	.10
98	John Jaha	.10
99	Charles Johnson	.10
100	Jermaine Dye	.10
101	Quinton McCracken	.10
102	Troy Percival	.10
103	Shane Reynolds	.10
104	Rondell White	.15
105	Charles Nagy	.10
106	Alan Benes	.10
107	Tom Goodwin	.10
108	Ron Gant	.10
109	Dan Wilson	.10
110	Darin Erstad	.50
111	Matt Williams	.30
112	Barry Larkin	.15
113	Mariano Rivera	.45
114	Larry Walker	.30
115	Jim Edmonds	.10
116	Michael Tucker	.10
117	Todd Hundley	.10
118	Alex Fernandez	.10
119	J.T. Snow	.10
120	Ellis Burks	.10
121	Steve Finley	.10
122	Mike Mussina	.75
123	Curtis Pride	.10
124	Derek Bell	.10
125	Dante Bichette	.10
126	Terry Steinbach	.10
127	Randy Johnson	.75
128	Andruw Jones	1.00
129	Vladimir Guerrero	1.00
130	Ruben Rivera	.10
131	Billy Wagner	.10
132	Scott Rolen	.75
133	Rey Ordonez	.10
134	Karim Garcia	.10
135	George Arias	.10
136	Todd Greene	.10
137	Robin Jennings	.10
138	Raul Casanova	.10
139	Josh Booty	.10
140	Edgar Renteria	.10
141	Chad Mottola	.10
142	Dmitri Young	.10
143	Tony Clark	.10
144	Todd Walker	.10
145	Kevin Brown	.15
146	Nomar Garciaparra	1.50
147	Neifi Perez	.10
148	Derek Jeter, Todd Hollandsworth	.40
149	Pat Hentgen, John Smoltz	.10
150	Juan Gonzalez, Ken Caminiti	.25

1997 Pinnacle Inside Club Edition

A 150-card parallel set featuring a special silver foil design and "CLUB EDITION" notation on back, these cards were inserted 1:7 can of Inside.

	MT
Complete Club Edition Set (150):	300.00
Common Club Edition:	.75
Stars:	5X

(See 1997 Pinnacle Inside for checklist and base values.)

1997 Pinnacle Inside Diamond Edition

A second parallel set, this time featuring a special die-cut design and gold holographic stamping. Cards were inserted 1:63 packs.

	MT
Common Diamond Edition:	5.00
Stars:	25X

(See 1997 Pinnacle Inside for checklist and base values.)

1997 Pinnacle Inside Cans

In addition to the cards, collectors had the option of collecting the 24 different player cans which are the "packs" in which the cards were sold. About the size of a can of peas (3" diameter, 4-1/2" tall), the cans feature several color and black-and-white reproductions of the player's Inside card. The package had to be opened with a can opener to access the cards. Values shown are for empty cans which have been opened from the bottom; top-opened cans have little collectible value.

		MT
Complete Set (24):		20.00
Common Can:		.50
Sealed Cans:		2X
1	Ken Griffey Jr.	2.00
2	Juan Gonzalez	1.00
3	Frank Thomas	1.00
4	Cal Ripken Jr.	2.00
5	Derek Jeter	1.50
6	Andruw Jones	.75
7	Alex Rodriguez	2.00
8	Mike Piazza	1.50
9	Mo Vaughn	.75
10	Jeff Bagwell	1.00
11	Ken Caminiti	.50
12	Andy Pettitte	.50
13	Barry Bonds	1.50
14	Mark McGwire	2.00
15	Ryan Klesko	.50
16	Manny Ramirez	1.00
17	Ivan Rodriguez	.75
18	Chipper Jones	1.50
19	Albert Belle	.75
20	Tony Gwynn	1.00
21	Kenny Lofton	.50
22	Greg Maddux	1.00
23	Hideo Nomo	.65
24	John Smoltz	.50

1997 Pinnacle Inside Dueling Dugouts

This 20-card insert set features a veteran player on one side, a rising star on the other, and a spinning wheel that reveals their respective achievements in various statistical categories. Cards were inserted 1:23 packs.

		MT
Complete Set (20):		140.00
Common Player:		3.00
1	Alex Rodriguez, Cal Ripken Jr.	20.00
2	Jeff Bagwell, Ken Caminiti	7.50
3	Barry Bonds, Albert Belle	10.00
4	Mike Piazza, Ivan Rodriguez	15.00
5	Chuck Knoblauch, Roberto Alomar	3.00
6	Ken Griffey Jr., Andruw Jones	15.00
7	Chipper Jones, Jim Thome	12.00
8	Frank Thomas, Mo Vaughn	10.00
9	Fred McGriff, Mark McGwire	17.50
10	Brian Jordan, Tony Gwynn	6.00
11	Barry Larkin, Derek Jeter	12.00
12	Kenny Lofton, Bernie Williams	3.00
13	Juan Gonzalez, Manny Ramirez	10.00
14	Will Clark, Rafael Palmeiro	3.00
15	Greg Maddux, Roger Clemens	12.00
16	John Smoltz, Andy Pettitte	3.00
17	Mariano Rivera, John Wetteland	3.00
18	Hideo Nomo, Mike Mussina	6.00
19	Todd Hollandsworth, Darin Erstad	4.50
20	Vladimir Guerrero, Karim Garcia	6.00

1997 Pinnacle Inside Fortysomething

The top home run hitters in the game are pictured in this 16-card set. Cards were inserted 1:47 packs.

	MT
Complete Set (16):	80.00
Common Player:	2.00

1	Juan Gonzalez	7.50
2	Barry Bonds	10.00
3	Ken Caminiti	2.00
4	Mark McGwire	20.00
5	Todd Hundley	2.00
6	Albert Belle	4.00
7	Ellis Burks	2.00
8	Jay Buhner	2.00
9	Brady Anderson	2.00
10	Vinny Castilla	2.00
11	Mo Vaughn	4.50
12	Ken Griffey Jr.	15.00
13	Sammy Sosa	12.00
14	Andres Galarraga	2.00
15	Gary Sheffield	3.00
16	Frank Thomas	12.00

1997 Pinnacle Mint Collection

The 30-card Mint Collection set came in three-card packs that also contained two coins. Cards come in two versions: die-cut and foil. Three foil versions appear with Bronze as the "common." Silver (1:15) and Gold (1:48) parallels also appear. The coins that come with each pack arrive in brass, silver and gold and can be matched up with the corresponding player's die-cut card. Fronts feature a player action shot on the left side with a shadowed portrait at right. On the die-cut versions, the coin-size hole is in the lower-right; the foil team stamp for the common cards is in the same location. Backs are numbered as "x of 30" and deliver a short text.

		MT
Complete Set (30):		24.00
Common Player:		.25
Bronze Cards:		2X
Silver Cards:		3X
Gold Cards:		7X
Wax Box (24):		25.00
1	Ken Griffey Jr.	2.50
2	Frank Thomas	1.50
3	Alex Rodriguez	2.50
4	Cal Ripken Jr.	2.50
5	Mo Vaughn	.50
6	Juan Gonzalez	1.00
7	Mike Piazza	2.00
8	Albert Belle	.50
9	Chipper Jones	2.00
10	Andruw Jones	1.00
11	Greg Maddux	1.50
12	Hideo Nomo	.50
13	Jeff Bagwell	1.00
14	Manny Ramirez	1.00
15	Mark McGwire	2.50
16	Derek Jeter	2.00
17	Sammy Sosa	1.50
18	Barry Bonds	1.50
19	Chuck Knoblauch	.25
20	Dante Bichette	.25
21	Tony Gwynn	1.25
22	Ken Caminiti	.25
23	Gary Sheffield	.40
24	Tim Salmon	.35
25	Ivan Rodriguez	.50
26	Henry Rodriguez	.25
27	Barry Larkin	.25
28	Ryan Klesko	.25
29	Brian Jordan	.25
30	Jay Buhner	.25

1997 Pinnacle Mint Collection Coins

Two coins from the 30-coin set were included in each three-card pack of 1997 Pinnacle Mint Collection. Brass coins are common while nickel-silver coins were inserted every 20 packs and gold-plated coins were inserted every 48 packs. Redemption cards for solid silver coins were found every 2,300 packs and a redemption card for a solid gold coin was inserted one per 47,200 packs. Only one of each 24K gold coin was produced. The front of the coins feature the player's portrait while the backs have a baseball diamond with "Limited Edition, Pinnacle Mint Collection 1997" printed.

		MT
Complete Set (30):		35.00
Common Brass Coin:		.25
Nickel Coins:		2X
Gold Plated Coins:		6X
Silver Coins:		50X
24K Gold Coins: Value undetermined		
1	Ken Griffey Jr.	4.00
2	Frank Thomas	2.00
3	Alex Rodriguez	4.00
4	Cal Ripken Jr.	4.00
5	Mo Vaughn	.75
6	Juan Gonzalez	1.50
7	Mike Piazza	3.00
8	Albert Belle	.75
9	Chipper Jones	3.00
10	Andruw Jones	1.50
11	Greg Maddux	2.00
12	Hideo Nomo	1.00
13	Jeff Bagwell	1.50
14	Manny Ramirez	1.50
15	Mark McGwire	4.00
16	Derek Jeter	3.00
17	Sammy Sosa	2.00
18	Barry Bonds	2.00
19	Chuck Knoblauch	.25
20	Dante Bichette	.25
21	Tony Gwynn	2.00
22	Ken Caminiti	.25
23	Gary Sheffield	.45
24	Tim Salmon	.35
25	Ivan Rodriguez	1.00
26	Henry Rodriguez	.25
27	Barry Larkin	.25
28	Ryan Klesko	.25
29	Brian Jordan	.25
30	Jay Buhner	.25

1997 Pinnacle X-Press

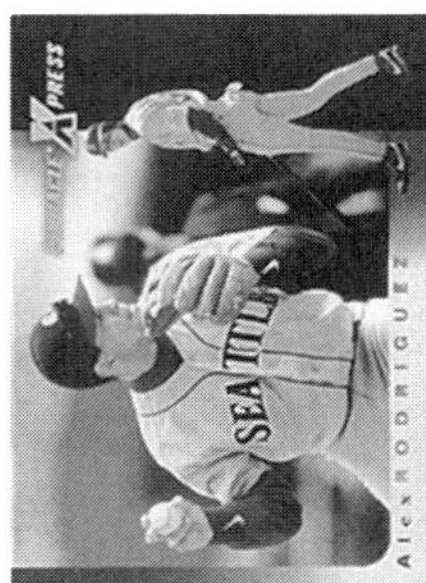

The 150-card set features 115 base cards, a 22-card Rookies subset, 10 Peak Performers and three checklist cards. Each of the regular cards features a horizontal design with two photos of each player on front. Inserts include Swing for the Fences (regular player cards as well as base and booster cards that can be used to accumulate points for a sweepstakes), Men of Summer, Far & Away, Melting Pot, and Metal Works Silver and Gold redemptions. Cards were sold in eight-card packs for $1.99. X-Press Metal Works boxes were also available for $14.99 and contained a regular pack, one metal card and a master deck used to play the Swing for the Fences game.

		MT
Complete Set (150):		10.00
Common Player:		.05
Pack (8):		1.00
Wax Box (24):		20.00
1	Larry Walker	.20
2	Andy Pettitte	.20
3	Matt Williams	.15
4	Juan Gonzalez	.65
5	Frank Thomas	1.00
6	Kenny Lofton	.05
7	Ken Griffey Jr.	2.00
8	Andres Galarraga	.05
9	Greg Maddux	1.00
10	Hideo Nomo	.50
11	Cecil Fielder	.05
12	Jose Canseco	.40
13	Tony Gwynn	.75
14	Eddie Murray	.40
15	Alex Rodriguez	1.75
16	Mike Piazza	1.50
17	Ken Hill	.05
18	Chuck Knoblauch	.05
19	Ellis Burks	.05
20	Rafael Palmeiro	.20
21	Vinny Castilla	.05
22	Rusty Greer	.05
23	Chipper Jones	1.50
24	Rey Ordonez	.05
25	Mariano Rivera	.20
26	Garret Anderson	.05
27	Edgar Martinez	.05
28	Dante Bichette	.05
29	Todd Hundley	.05
30	Barry Bonds	.75
31	Barry Larkin	.10
32	Derek Jeter	1.50
33	Marquis Grissom	.05
34	David Justice	.25
35	Ivan Rodriguez	.50
36	Jay Buhner	.05
37	Fred McGriff	.05
38	Brady Anderson	.05
39	Tony Clark	.05
40	Eric Young	.05
41	Charles Nagy	.05
42	Mark McGwire	2.00
43	Paul O'Neill	.05
44	Tino Martinez	.05
45	Ryne Sandberg	.65
46	Bernie Williams	.30
47	Albert Belle	.20
48	Jeff Cirillo	.05
49	Tim Salmon	.15
50	Steve Finley	.05
51	Lance Johnson	.05
52	John Smoltz	.10
53	Javier Lopez	.05
54	Roger Clemens	.75
55	Kevin Appier	.05
56	Ken Caminiti	.05
57	Cal Ripken Jr.	2.00
58	Moises Alou	.10
59	Marty Cordova	.05
60	David Cone	.05
61	Manny Ramirez	.65
62	Ray Durham	.05
63	Jermaine Dye	.05
64	Craig Biggio	.10
65	Will Clark	.15
66	Omar Vizquel	.05
67	Bernard Gilkey	.05
68	Greg Vaughn	.05
69	Wade Boggs	.40
70	Dave Nilsson	.05
71	Mark Grace	.25
72	Dean Palmer	.05
73	Sammy Sosa	1.25
74	Mike Mussina	.50
75	Alex Fernandez	.05
76	Henry Rodriguez	.05
77	Travis Fryman	.05
78	Jeff Bagwell	.65
79	Pat Hentgen	.05
80	Gary Sheffield	.20
81	Jim Edmonds	.10
82	Darin Erstad	.30
83	Mark Grudzielanek	.05
84	Jim Thome	.05
85	Bobby Higginson	.10
86	Al Martin	.05
87	Jason Giambi	.40
88	Mo Vaughn	.30
89	Jeff Conine	.05
90	Edgar Renteria	.05
91	Andy Ashby	.05
92	Ryan Klesko	.05
93	John Jaha	.05
94	Paul Molitor	.50
95	Brian Hunter	.05
96	Randy Johnson	.50
97	Joey Hamilton	.05
98	Billy Wagner	.05
99	John Wetteland	.05
100	Jeff Fassero	.05
101	Rondell White	.15
102	Kevin Brown	.15
103	Andy Benes	.05
104	Raul Mondesi	.15
105	Todd Hollandsworth	.05
106	Alex Ochoa	.05
107	Bobby Bonilla	.05
108	Brian Jordan	.05
109	Tom Glavine	.10
110	Ron Gant	.05
111	Jason Kendall	.05
112	Roberto Alomar	.50
113	Troy Percival	.05
114	Michael Tucker	.05
115	Joe Carter	.05
116	Andruw Jones	.65
117	Nomar Garciaparra	1.25
118	Todd Walker	.05
119	Jose Guillen	.05
120	*Bubba Trammell*	.20
121	Wilton Guerrero	.05
122	Bob Abreu	.10
123	Vladimir Guerrero	.65
124	Dmitri Young	.05
125	Kevin Orie	.05
126	Glendon Rusch	.05
127	Brooks Kieschnick	.05

128	Scott Spiezio	.05
129	*Brian Giles*	1.50
130	Jason Dickson	.05
131	Damon Mashore	.05
132	Wendell Magee	.05
133	Matt Morris	.05
134	Scott Rolen	.50
135	Shannon Stewart	.10
136	*Deivi Cruz*	.25
137	*Hideki Irabu*	.25
138	Larry Walker (Peak Performers)	.10
139	Ken Griffey Jr. (Peak Performers)	.75
140	Frank Thomas (Peak Performers)	.50
141	Ivan Rodriguez (Peak Performers)	.20
142	Randy Johnson (Peak Performers)	.20
143	Mark McGwire (Peak Performers)	1.00
144	Tino Martinez (Peak Performers)	.05
145	Tony Clark (Peak Performers)	.05
146	Mike Piazza (Peak Performers)	.75
147	Alex Rodriguez (Peak Performers)	1.00
148	Checklist (Roger Clemens)	.25
149	Checklist (Greg Maddux)	.35
150	Checklist (Hideo Nomo)	.35

1997 Pinnacle X-Press Men of Summer

This parallel set of the 150 cards in the base X-Press issue differs in that the fronts are printed on foil backgrounds and the backs have a notation "MEN OF SUMMER" printed in gold vertically at top.

	MT
Complete Set (150):	50.00
Common Player:	.25

(See 1997 Pinnacle X-Press for checklist and base card values.)

1997 Pinnacle X-Press Far & Away

This 18-card insert highlights the top home run hitters in baseball and is printed with Dufex technology. Cards were inserted 1:19 packs.

		MT
Complete Set (18):		40.00
Common Player:		.60
1	Albert Belle	1.50
2	Mark McGwire	7.50
3	Frank Thomas	4.00
4	Mo Vaughn	2.00
5	Jeff Bagwell	3.00
6	Juan Gonzalez	2.50
7	Mike Piazza	5.00
8	Andruw Jones	3.00
9	Chipper Jones	5.00
10	Gary Sheffield	1.00
11	Sammy Sosa	4.00
12	Darin Erstad	2.50
13	Jay Buhner	.60
14	Ken Griffey Jr.	6.00
15	Ken Caminiti	.60
16	Brady Anderson	.60
17	Manny Ramirez	3.00
18	Alex Rodriguez	6.00

1997 Pinnacle X-Press Melting Pot

This insert showcases the talents of major leaguers from various countries. Fronts have color player photos on a background which combines shiny silver foil and textured foil in the design of the player's native flag. Backs have another photo and are ink-jet numbered in a white stripe at bottom in an edition of 500 each. Stated insertion rate was one per 288 packs. Each card can also be found in a promo card version overprinted "SAMPLE".

		MT
Complete Set (20):		150.00
Common Player:		2.00
Samples:		1X
1	Jose Guillen	3.00
2	Vladimir Guerrero	10.00
3	Andruw Jones	10.00
4	Larry Walker	4.00
5	Manny Ramirez	10.00
6	Ken Griffey Jr.	20.00
7	Alex Rodriguez	20.00
8	Frank Thomas	15.00
9	Juan Gonzalez	10.00
10	Ivan Rodriguez	6.00
11	Hideo Nomo	8.00
12	Rafael Palmeiro	3.00
13	Dave Nilsson	2.00
14	Nomar Garciaparra	15.00
15	Wilton Guerrero	2.00
16	Sammy Sosa	15.00
17	Edgar Renteria	2.00
18	Cal Ripken Jr.	25.00
19	Derek Jeter	17.50
20	Rey Ordonez	3.00

1997 Pinnacle X-Press Metal Works

Each Home Plate Box of X-Press contains one heavy bronze Metal Works "card." The 2-3/8" x 3-1/2" slabs have a player portrait on front. Backs have a few words about the player. Redemption cards for silver-plated parallels were inserted 1:470 packs, while a silver slab was found 1:54 Home Plate Boxes. Silver Metal Works are serially numbered to 400 each. Gold-plated Metal Works were produced in an edition of 200 each, with redemption cards inserted 1:950 packs or one per 108 Home Plate Boxes.

		MT
Complete Set (20):		75.00
Common Player:		1.50
Silver:		4X
Gold:		8X
1	Ken Griffey Jr.	9.00
2	Frank Thomas	4.00
3	Andruw Jones	2.50
4	Alex Rodriguez	7.50
5	Derek Jeter	6.00
6	Cal Ripken Jr.	7.50
7	Mike Piazza	6.00
8	Chipper Jones	6.00
9	Juan Gonzalez	3.00
10	Greg Maddux	5.00
11	Tony Gwynn	4.50
12	Jeff Bagwell	2.50
13	Albert Belle	1.50
14	Mark McGwire	10.00
15	Nomar Garciaparra	5.00
16	Mo Vaughn	1.50
17	Andy Pettitte	1.50
18	Manny Ramirez	3.00
19	Kenny Lofton	1.50
20	Roger Clemens	3.00

1997 Pinnacle X-Press Swing for the Fences

These inserts allow collectors to play an interactive game based on the number of home runs hit by the home run champion of each league. Cards feature 60 different players and were inserted 1:2 packs. Base cards feature a number between 20-42 printed on them and are found one in every master deck. Booster cards feature a plus-or-minus point total (i.e. +7, -2) that can be used to add or subtract points to get to the winning home run total. Booster cards are found 1:2 packs. Collectors who accumulated the winning home run totals were eligible to win prizes ranging from autographs to a trip to the 1998 All-Star Game. The unnumbered cards are checklisted here in alphabetical order.

		MT
Complete Set (60):		40.00
Common Player:		.25
(1)	Sandy Alomar Jr.	.25
(2)	Moises Alou	.25
(3)	Brady Anderson	.25
(4)	Jeff Bagwell	1.50
(5)	Derek Bell	.25
(6)	Jay Bell	.25
(7)	Albert Belle	.75
(8)	Geronimo Berroa	.25
(9)	Dante Bichette	.25
(10)	Barry Bonds	1.50
(11)	Bobby Bonilla	.25
(12)	Jay Buhner	.25
(13)	Ellis Burks	.25
(14)	Ken Caminiti	.25
(15)	Jose Canseco	.75
(16)	Joe Carter	.25
(17)	Vinny Castilla	.25
(18)	Tony Clark	.25
(19)	Carlos Delgado	.50
(20)	Jim Edmonds	.25
(21)	Cecil Fielder	.25
(22)	Andres Galarraga	.25
(23)	Ron Gant	.25
(24)	Bernard Gilkey	.25
(25)	Juan Gonzalez	1.50
(26)	Ken Griffey Jr. (AL WINNER)	8.00
(27)	Vladimir Guerrero	1.50
(28)	Todd Hundley	.25
(29)	John Jaha	.25
(30)	Andruw Jones	1.50
(31)	Chipper Jones	2.50
(32)	David Justice	.45
(33)	Jeff Kent	.25

(34)	Ryan Klesko	.25
(35)	Barry Larkin	.25
(36)	Mike Lieberthal	.25
(37)	Javy Lopez	.25
(38)	Edgar Martinez	.25
(39)	Tino Martinez	.25
(40)	Fred McGriff	.25
(41)	Mark McGwire (AL/NL WINNER)	8.00
(42)	Raul Mondesi	.35
(43)	Tim Naehring	.25
(44)	Dave Nillson	.25
(45)	Rafael Palmeiro	.35
(46)	Dean Palmer	.25
(47)	Mike Piazza	2.50
(48)	Cal Ripken Jr.	4.00
(49)	Henry Rodriguez	.25
(50)	Tim Salmon	.35
(51)	Gary Sheffield	.45
(52)	Sammy Sosa	2.50
(53)	Terry Steinbach	.25
(54)	Frank Thomas	2.50
(55)	Jim Thome	.25
(56)	Mo Vaughn	.45
(57)	Larry Walker (NL Winner)	3.00
(58)	Rondell White	.35
(59)	Matt Williams	.35
(60)	Todd Zeile	.25

1997 Pinnacle X-Press Swing/Fences Gold

Collectors who correctly matched Swing for the Fences insert game cards of the final 1997 season American and National home run champions with proper point cards equal to the number of home runs each hit could exchange them for a random assortment of 10 upgraded cards featuring gold-foil highlights and a premium card stock. The first 1,000 redemptions received an autographed Andruw Jones gold card. The redemption period ended March 1, 1998.

	MT
Complete Set (60):	150.00
Common Player:	1.00
Stars:	4X
Andruw Jones Autograph:	75.00

(See 1997 Pinnacle X-Press Swing for the Fences for checklist and base values.)

1997 Totally Certified Platinum Red

Totally Certified doesn't have a true base set. Instead, the product consists of three different 150-card parallel sets. Packs consisted of three cards for $6.99 each. The first of three parallels is the Platinum Red set, inserted two per pack, and featuring micro-etched holographic mylar stock with red accents and foil stamping. Each card in the Red set is sequentially-numbered to 3,999.

		MT
Complete Set (150):		200.00
Common Player:		.75
Pack (3):		7.50
Wax Box (20):		120.00
1	Barry Bonds	4.50
2	Mo Vaughn	2.50
3	Matt Williams	1.25
4	Ryne Sandberg	4.50
5	Jeff Bagwell	4.50
6	Alan Benes	.75
7	John Wetteland	.75
8	Fred McGriff	.75
9	Craig Biggio	.75
10	Bernie Williams	2.00
11	Brian Hunter	.75
12	Sandy Alomar Jr.	.75
13	Ray Lankford	.75
14	Ryan Klesko	.75
15	Jermaine Dye	.75
16	Andy Benes	.75
17	Albert Belle	2.00
18	Tony Clark	.75
19	Dean Palmer	.75
20	Bernard Gilkey	.75
21	Ken Caminiti	.75
22	Alex Rodriguez	10.00
23	Tim Salmon	1.25
24	Larry Walker	2.00
25	Barry Larkin	1.25
26	Mike Piazza	8.00
27	Brady Anderson	.75
28	Cal Ripken Jr.	12.00
29	Charles Nagy	.75
30	Paul Molitor	3.00
31	Darin Erstad	4.00
32	Rey Ordonez	.75
33	Wally Joyner	.75
34	David Cone	.75
35	Sammy Sosa	6.00
36	Dante Bichette	.75
37	Eric Karros	.75
38	Omar Vizquel	.75
39	Roger Clemens	6.00
40	Joe Carter	.75
41	Frank Thomas	6.00
42	Javier Lopez	.75
43	Mike Mussina	3.00
44	Gary Sheffield	1.50
45	Tony Gwynn	6.00
46	Jason Kendall	.75
47	Jim Thome	.75
48	Andres Galarraga	.75
49	Mark McGwire	12.00
50	Troy Percival	.75
51	Derek Jeter	8.00
52	Todd Hollandsworth	.75
53	Ken Griffey Jr.	10.00
54	Randy Johnson	2.50
55	Pat Hentgen	.75
56	Rusty Greer	.75
57	John Jaha	.75
58	Kenny Lofton	.75
59	Chipper Jones	8.00
60	Robb Nen	.75
61	Rafael Palmeiro	1.50
62	Mariano Rivera	2.00
63	Hideo Nomo	3.00
64	Greg Vaughn	.75
65	Ron Gant	.75
66	Eddie Murray	2.50
67	John Smoltz	1.25
68	Manny Ramirez	4.50
69	Juan Gonzalez	4.50
70	F.P. Santangelo	.75
71	Moises Alou	1.25
72	Alex Ochoa	.75
73	Chuck Knoblauch	.75
74	Raul Mondesi	1.25
75	J.T. Snow	.75
76	Rickey Henderson	2.50
77	Bobby Bonilla	.75
78	Wade Boggs	3.00
79	Ivan Rodriguez	3.50
80	Brian Jordan	.75
81	Al Leiter	.75
82	Jay Buhner	.75
83	Greg Maddux	6.00
84	Edgar Martinez	.75
85	Kevin Brown	.75
86	Eric Young	.75
87	Todd Hundley	.75
88	Ellis Burks	.75
89	Marquis Grissom	.75
90	Jose Canseco	2.00
91	Henry Rodriguez	.75
92	Andy Pettitte	1.50
93	Mark Grudzielanek	.75
94	Dwight Gooden	.75
95	Roberto Alomar	2.50
96	Paul Wilson	.75
97	Will Clark	1.25
98	Rondell White	1.25
99	Charles Johnson	.75
100	Jim Edmonds	.75
101	Jason Giambi	2.00
102	Billy Wagner	.75
103	Edgar Renteria	.75
104	Johnny Damon	.90
105	Jason Isringhausen	.75
106	Andruw Jones	4.50
107	Jose Guillen	.75
108	Kevin Orie	.75
109	*Brian Giles*	8.00
110	Danny Patterson	.75
111	Vladimir Guerrero	4.50
112	Scott Rolen	4.50
113	Damon Mashore	.75
114	Nomar Garciaparra	6.00
115	Todd Walker	.75
116	Wilton Guerrero	.75
117	Bob Abreu	.75
118	Brooks Kieschnick	.75
119	Pokey Reese	.75
120	Todd Greene	.75
121	Dmitri Young	.75
122	Raul Casanova	.75
123	Glendon Rusch	.75
124	Jason Dickson	.75
125	Jorge Posada	.75
126	Rod Myers	.75
127	Bubba Trammell	1.25
128	Scott Spiezio	.75
129	Hideki Irabu	.75
130	Wendell Magee	.75
131	Bartolo Colon	.75
132	Chris Holt	.75
133	Calvin Maduro	.75
134	Ray Montgomery	.75
135	Shannon Stewart	.75
136	Ken Griffey Jr. (Certified Stars)	5.00
137	Vladimir Guerrero (Certified Stars)	2.50
138	Roger Clemens (Certified Stars)	2.50
139	Mark McGwire (Certified Stars)	6.00
140	Albert Belle (Certified Stars)	1.50
141	Derek Jeter (Certified Stars)	4.00
142	Juan Gonzalez (Certified Stars)	2.50
143	Greg Maddux (Certified Stars)	3.50
144	Alex Rodriguez (Certified Stars)	5.00
145	Jeff Bagwell (Certified Stars)	2.50
146	Cal Ripken Jr. (Certified Stars)	5.00
147	Tony Gwynn (Certified Stars)	3.50
148	Frank Thomas (Certified Stars)	2.50
149	Hideo Nomo (Certified Stars)	1.50
150	Andruw Jones (Certified Stars)	3.00

1997 Totally Certified Platinum Blue

Featuring blue accents and foil stamping, the Platinum Blue cards are sequentially numbered on back in gold foil to 1,999 and inserted per pack.

	MT
Complete Set (150):	400.00
Common Player:	1.00
Platinum Blue Stars:	1.5X

(See 1997 Totally Certified Platinum Red for checklist and base card values.)

1997 Totally Certified Platinum Gold

The most difficult to find of the Totally Certified cards, the Platinum Gold versions are sequentially-numbered to 30 per card and inserted 1:79 packs.

	MT
Common Player:	15.00
Platinum Gold Stars:	35X

(See 1997 Totally Certified Platinum Red for checklist and base card values.)

1998 Pinnacle

Pinnacle's 200-card base set features full-bleed photos on front. Three different backs were produced for each card #1-157: home stats, away stats and seasonal stats. The set also includes cards, 24 Rookies, six Field of Vision, 10 Goin' Jake cards and three checklists. Parallel sets include Artist's Proofs, Press Plates and Museum Collection. Inserts include Epix, Hit it Here, Spellbound and Uncut.

		MT
	Complete Set (200):	15.00
	Common Player:	.05
	Pack (10):	1.50
	Wax Box (18):	24.00
1	Tony Gwynn (All-Star)	1.00
2	Pedro Martinez (All-Star)	.75
3	Kenny Lofton (All-Star)	.05
4	Curt Schilling (All-Star)	.10
5	Shawn Estes (All-Star)	.05
6	Tom Glavine (All-Star)	.10
7	Mike Piazza (All-Star)	2.00
8	Ray Lankford (All-Star)	.05
9	Barry Larkin (All-Star)	.10
10	Tony Womack (All-Star)	.05
11	Jeff Blauser (All-Star)	.05
12	Rod Beck (All-Star)	.05
13	Larry Walker (All-Star)	.25
14	Greg Maddux (All-Star)	1.50
15	Mark Grace (All-Star)	.20
16	Ken Caminiti (All-Star)	.05
17	Bobby Jones (All-Star)	.05
18	Chipper Jones (All-Star)	2.00
19	Javier Lopez (All-Star)	.05
20	Moises Alou (All-Star)	.05
21	Royce Clayton (All-Star)	.05
22	Darryl Kile (All-Star)	.05
23	Barry Bonds (All-Star)	1.00
24	Steve Finley (All-Star)	.05
25	Andres Galarraga (All-Star)	.05
26	Denny Neagle (All-Star)	.05
27	Todd Hundley (All-Star)	.05
28	Jeff Bagwell	.75
29	Andy Pettitte	.25
30	Darin Erstad	.50
31	Carlos Delgado	.50
32	Matt Williams	.15
33	Will Clark	.15
34	Vinny Castilla	.05
35	Brad Radke	.10
36	John Olerud	.05
37	Andruw Jones	.75
38	Jason Giambi	.40
39	Scott Rolen	.60
40	Gary Sheffield	.25
41	Jimmy Key	.05
42	Kevin Appier	.05
43	Wade Boggs	.45
44	Hideo Nomo	.75
45	Manny Ramirez	.75
46	Wilton Guerrero	.05
47	Travis Fryman	.05
48	Chili Davis	.05
49	Jeromy Burnitz	.05
50	Craig Biggio	.10
51	Tim Salmon	.25
52	Jose Cruz Jr.	.15
53	Sammy Sosa	1.50
54	Hideki Irabu	.10
55	Chan Ho Park	.20
56	Robin Ventura	.05
57	Jose Guillen	.05
58	Deion Sanders	.15
59	Jose Canseco	.50
60	Jay Buhner	.05
61	Rafael Palmeiro	.25
62	Vladimir Guerrero	.75
63	Mark McGwire	2.50
64	Derek Jeter	2.00
65	Bobby Bonilla	.05
66	Raul Mondesi	.20
67	Paul Molitor	.50
68	Joe Carter	.05
69	Marquis Grissom	.05
70	Juan Gonzalez	.75
71	Kevin Orie	.05
72	Rusty Greer	.05
73	Henry Rodriguez	.05
74	Fernando Tatis	.10
75	John Valentin	.05
76	Matt Morris	.05
77	Ray Durham	.05
78	Geronimo Berroa	.05
79	Scott Brosius	.05
80	Willie Greene	.05
81	Rondell White	.15
82	Doug Drabek	.05
83	Derek Bell	.05
84	Butch Huskey	.05
85	Doug Jones	.05
86	Jeff Kent	.05
87	Jim Edmonds	.15
88	Mark McLemore	.05
89	Todd Zeile	.05
90	Edgardo Alfonzo	.05
91	Carlos Baerga	.05
92	Jorge Fabregas	.05
93	Alan Benes	.05
94	Troy Percival	.05
95	Edgar Renteria	.05
96	Jeff Fassero	.05
97	Reggie Sanders	.05
98	Dean Palmer	.05
99	J.T. Snow	.05
100	Dave Nilsson	.05
101	Dan Wilson	.05
102	Robb Nen	.05
103	Damion Easley	.05
104	Kevin Foster	.05
105	Jose Offerman	.05
106	Steve Cooke	.05
107	Matt Stairs	.05
108	Darryl Hamilton	.05
109	Steve Karsay	.05
110	Gary DiSarcina	.05
111	Dante Bichette	.05
112	Billy Wagner	.05
113	David Segui	.05
114	Bobby Higginson	.05
115	Jeffrey Hammonds	.05
116	Kevin Brown	.15
117	Paul Sorrento	.05
118	Mark Leiter	.05
119	Charles Nagy	.05
120	Danny Patterson	.05
121	Brian McRae	.05
122	Jay Bell	.05
123	Jamie Moyer	.05
124	Carl Everett	.15
125	Greg Colbrunn	.05
126	Jason Kendall	.05
127	Luis Sojo	.05
128	Mike Lieberthal	.05
129	Reggie Jefferson	.05
130	Cal Eldred	.05
131	Orel Hershiser	.05
132	Doug Glanville	.05
133	Willie Blair	.05
134	Neifi Perez	.05
135	Sean Berry	.05
136	Chuck Finley	.05
137	Alex Gonzalez	.10
138	Dennis Eckersley	.05
139	Kenny Rogers	.05
140	Troy O'Leary	.05
141	Roger Bailey	.05
142	Yamil Benitez	.05
143	Wally Joyner	.05
144	Bobby Witt	.05
145	Pete Schourek	.05
146	Terry Steinbach	.05
147	B.J. Surhoff	.05
148	Esteban Loaiza	.05
149	Heathcliff Slocumb	.05
150	Ed Sprague	.05
151	Gregg Jefferies	.05
152	Scott Erickson	.05
153	Jaime Navarro	.05
154	David Wells	.10
155	Alex Fernandez	.05
156	Tim Belcher	.05
157	Mark Grudzielanek	.05
158	Scott Hatteberg	.05
159	Paul Konerko	.10
160	Ben Grieve	.25
161	Abraham Nunez	.10
162	Shannon Stewart	.10
163	Jaret Wright	.10
164	Derrek Lee	.05
165	Todd Dunwoody	.05
166	*Steve Woodard*	.25
167	Ryan McGuire	.05
168	Jeremi Gonzalez	.05
169	Mark Kotsay	.05
170	Brett Tomko	.05
171	Bobby Estalella	.05
172	Livan Hernandez	.05
173	Todd Helton	.75
174	Garrett Stephenson	.05
175	Pokey Reese	.05
176	Tony Saunders	.05
177	Antone Williamson	.05
178	Bartolo Colon	.15
179	Karim Garcia	.05
180	Juan Encarnacion	.05
181	Jacob Cruz	.05
182	Alex Rodriguez (Field of Vision)	2.50
183	Cal Ripken Jr., Roberto Alomar (Field of Vision)	1.00
184	Roger Clemens (Field of Vision)	1.00
185	Derek Jeter (Field of Vision)	1.00
186	Frank Thomas (Field of Vision)	1.00
187	Ken Griffey Jr. (Field of Vision)	2.50
188	Mark McGwire (Goin' Jake)	1.25
189	Tino Martinez (Goin' Jake)	.05
190	Larry Walker (Goin' Jake)	.10
191	Brady Anderson (Goin' Jake)	.05
192	Jeff Bagwell (Goin' Jake)	.40
193	Ken Griffey Jr. (Goin' Jake)	1.25
194	Chipper Jones (Goin' Jake)	1.00
195	Ray Lankford (Goin' Jake)	.05
196	Jim Thome (Goin' Jake)	.05
197	Nomar Garciaparra (Goin' Jake)	1.00
198	Checklist (1997 HR Contest)	.05
199	Checklist (1997 HR Contest Winner)	.05
200	Checklist (Overall View of the Park)	.05
9	Ken Griffey Jr. (All-Star, overprinted "SAMPLE" on back)	2.00
24	Frank Thomas (All-Star, overprinted "SAMPLE" on back)	1.50

1998 Pinnacle Artist's Proofs

Artist's Proofs is a 100-card partial parallel of the Pinnacle base set. The gold-foil Dufex cards were renumbered with a "PP" prefix and inserted one per 39 packs. A red AP seal appears on front.

		MT
	Complete Set (100):	265.00
	Common Artist's Proof:	1.00
1	Tony Gwynn (All-Star)	9.00
2	Pedro Martinez (All-Star)	7.50
3	Kenny Lofton (All-Star)	1.00
4	Curt Schilling (All-Star)	1.50
5	Shawn Estes (All-Star)	1.00
6	Tom Glavine (All-Star)	1.50
7	Mike Piazza (All-Star)	13.50
8	Ray Lankford (All-Star)	1.00
9	Barry Larkin (All-Star)	1.00
10	Tony Womack (All-Star)	1.00
11	Jeff Blauser (All-Star)	1.00
12	Rod Beck (All-Star)	1.00
13	Larry Walker (All-Star)	1.50
14	Greg Maddux (All-Star)	10.00
15	Mark Grace (All-Star)	2.50
16	Ken Caminiti (All-Star)	1.00
17	Bobby Jones (All-Star)	1.00
18	Chipper Jones (All-Star)	13.50
19	Javier Lopez (All-Star)	1.00
20	Moises Alou (All-Star)	1.50
21	Royce Clayton (All-Star)	1.00
22	Darryl Kile (All-Star)	1.00
23	Barry Bonds (All-Star)	10.00
24	Steve Finley (All-Star)	1.00
25	Andres Galarraga (All-Star)	1.00
26	Denny Neagle (All-Star)	1.00
27	Todd Hundley (All-Star)	1.00
28	Jeff Bagwell	6.50

29 Andy Pettitte 1.50
30 Darin Erstad 5.00
31 Carlos Delgado 1.50
32 Matt Williams 1.50
33 Will Clark 1.50
34 Brad Radke 1.00
35 John Olerud 1.00
36 Andruw Jones 6.50
37 Scott Rolen 6.00
38 Gary Sheffield 1.50
39 Jimmy Key 1.00
40 Wade Boggs 4.00
41 Hideo Nomo 6.00
42 Manny Ramirez 6.50
43 Wilton Guerrero 1.00
44 Travis Fryman 1.00
45 Craig Biggio 1.00
46 Tim Salmon 1.50
47 Jose Cruz Jr. 1.50
48 Sammy Sosa 12.00
49 Hideki Irabu 1.50
50 Jose Guillen 1.00
51 Deion Sanders 1.50
52 Jose Canseco 2.50
53 Jay Buhner 1.00
54 Rafael Palmeiro 1.50
55 Vladimir Guerrero 6.50
56 Mark McGwire 15.00
57 Derek Jeter 13.50
58 Bobby Bonilla 1.00
59 Raul Mondesi 1.50
60 Paul Molitor 5.00
61 Joe Carter 1.00
62 Marquis Grissom 1.00
63 Juan Gonzalez 6.50
64 Dante Bichette 1.00
65 Shannon Stewart (Rookie) 1.50
66 Jaret Wright (Rookie) 4.00
67 Derrek Lee (Rookie) 1.50
68 Todd Dunwoody (Rookie) 1.00
69 Steve Woodard (Rookie) 1.00
70 Ryan McGuire (Rookie) 1.00
71 Jeremi Gonzalez (Rookie) 1.00
72 Mark Kotsay (Rookie) 1.00
73 Brett Tomko (Rookie) 1.00
74 Bobby Estalella (Rookie) 1.00
75 Livan Hernandez (Rookie) 1.00
76 Todd Helton (Rookie) 6.50
77 Garrett Stephenson (Rookie) 1.00
78 Pokey Reese (Rookie) 1.00
79 Tony Saunders (Rookie) 1.00
80 Antone Williamson (Rookie) 1.00
81 Bartolo Colon (Rookie) 2.00
82 Karim Garcia (Rookie) 1.00
83 Juan Encarnacion (Rookie) 1.00
84 Jacob Cruz (Rookie) 1.00
85 Alex Rodriguez (Field of Vision) 15.00
86 Cal Ripken Jr., Roberto Alomar (Field of Vision) 8.00
87 Roger Clemens (Field of Vision) 9.00
88 Derek Jeter (Field of Vision) 7.00
89 Frank Thomas (Field of Vision) 9.00
90 Ken Griffey Jr. (Field of Vision) 13.50
91 Mark McGwire (Goin' Jake) 7.50
92 Tino Martinez (Goin' Jake) 1.00
93 Larry Walker (Goin' Jake) 1.50
94 Brady Anderson (Goin' Jake) 1.00
95 Jeff Bagwell (Goin' Jake) 3.50
96 Ken Griffey Jr. (Goin' Jake) 7.00
97 Chipper Jones (Goin' Jake) 6.00
98 Ray Lankford (Goin' Jake) 1.00
99 Jim Thome (Goin' Jake) 1.00
100 Nomar Garciaparra (Goin' Jake) 12.00

1998 Pinnacle Museum Collection

Museum Collection is a 100-card partial parallel of the Pinnacle base set. The silver-foil Dufex cards were renumbered with a "PP" prefix. Backs have a small "Musuem Collection" logo at bottom-center. The cards were inserted one per nine packs.

MT
Complete Museum Set (100): 130.00
Common Museum: .35
1 Tony Gwynn (All-Star) 4.50
2 Pedro Martinez (All-Star) 3.50
3 Kenny Lofton (All-Star) .50
4 Curt Schilling (All-Star) .65
5 Shawn Estes (All-Star) .50
6 Tom Glavine (All-Star) .75
7 Mike Piazza (All-Star) 6.00
8 Ray Lankford (All-Star) .50
9 Barry Larkin (All-Star) .50
10 Tony Womack (All-Star) .50
11 Jeff Blauser (All-Star) .50
12 Rod Beck (All-Star) .50
13 Larry Walker (All-Star) 1.50
14 Greg Maddux (All-Star) 4.50
15 Mark Grace (All-Star) 1.00
16 Ken Caminiti (All-Star) .50
17 Bobby Jones (All-Star) .50
18 Chipper Jones (All-Star) 6.00
19 Javier Lopez (All-Star) .50
20 Moises Alou (All-Star) .75
21 Royce Clayton (All-Star) .50
22 Darryl Kile (All-Star) .50
23 Barry Bonds (All-Star) 4.50
24 Steve Finley (All-Star) .50
25 Andres Galarraga (All-Star) .50
26 Denny Neagle (All-Star) .50
27 Todd Hundley (All-Star) .50
28 Jeff Bagwell 3.50
29 Andy Pettitte 1.00
30 Darin Erstad 2.00
31 Carlos Delgado 1.00
32 Matt Williams .75
33 Will Clark .75
34 Brad Radke .50
35 John Olerud .50
36 Andruw Jones 3.50
37 Scott Rolen 3.00
38 Gary Sheffield 1.00
39 Jimmy Key .50
40 Wade Boggs 2.00
41 Hideo Nomo 2.50
42 Manny Ramirez 3.50
43 Wilton Guerrero .50
44 Travis Fryman .50
45 Craig Biggio .50
46 Tim Salmon .75
47 Jose Cruz Jr. .75
48 Sammy Sosa 5.00
49 Hideki Irabu .60
50 Jose Guillen .50
51 Deion Sanders .75
52 Jose Canseco 2.00
53 Jay Buhner .50
54 Rafael Palmeiro .75
55 Vladimir Guerrero 3.50
56 Mark McGwire 7.50
57 Derek Jeter 6.00
58 Bobby Bonilla .50
59 Raul Mondesi .75
60 Paul Molitor 2.50
61 Joe Carter .50
62 Marquis Grissom .50
63 Juan Gonzalez 3.50
64 Dante Bichette .50
65 Shannon Stewart (Rookie) .65
66 Jaret Wright (Rookie) 1.50
67 Derrek Lee (Rookie) .65
68 Todd Dunwoody (Rookie) .50
69 Steve Woodard (Rookie) .50
70 Ryan McGuire (Rookie) .50
71 Jeremi Gonzalez (Rookie) .50
72 Mark Kotsay (Rookie) .50
73 Brett Tomko (Rookie) .50
74 Bobby Estalella (Rookie) .50
75 Livan Hernandez (Rookie) .50
76 Todd Helton (Rookie) 3.00
77 Garrett Stephenson (Rookie) .50
78 Pokey Reese (Rookie) .50
79 Tony Saunders (Rookie) .50
80 Antone Williamson (Rookie) .50
81 Bartolo Colon (Rookie) 1.00
82 Karim Garcia (Rookie) .65
83 Juan Encarnacion (Rookie) .50
84 Jacob Cruz (Rookie) .50
85 Alex Rodriguez (Field of Vision) 7.00
86 Cal Ripken Jr., Roberto Alomar (Field of Vision) 4.50
87 Roger Clemens (Field of Vision) 4.00
88 Derek Jeter (Field of Vision) 3.00
89 Frank Thomas (Field of Vision) 5.00
90 Ken Griffey Jr. (Field of Vision) 7.00
91 Mark McGwire (Goin' Jake) 4.00
92 Tino Martinez (Goin' Jake) .50
93 Larry Walker (Goin' Jake) .65
94 Brady Anderson (Goin' Jake) .50
95 Jeff Bagwell (Goin' Jake) 1.75
96 Ken Griffey Jr. (Goin' Jake) 4.00
97 Chipper Jones (Goin' Jake) 3.00
98 Ray Lankford (Goin' Jake) .50
99 Jim Thome (Goin' Jake) .50
100 Nomar Garciaparra (Goin' Jake) 5.00

1998 Pinnacle Epix

This cross-brand insert was included in Pinnacle, Score, Pinnacle Certified and Zenith. Twenty-four cards were seeded in Pinnacle packs (1:21). The four-tiered set highlights a memorable Game, Season, Moment and Play in a player's career. The holographic foil cards came in three colors: orange, purple and emerald.

MT
Complete Set (24): 160.00
Common Player: 2.00
Purples: 1X
Emeralds: 2X
1 Ken Griffey Jr. G 15.00
2 Juan Gonzalez G 5.00
3 Jeff Bagwell G 5.00
4 Ivan Rodriguez G 7.00
5 Nomar Garciaparra G 10.00
6 Ryne Sandberg G 8.00
7 Frank Thomas S 9.00
8 Derek Jeter S 12.50
9 Tony Gwynn S 8.00
10 Albert Belle S 2.00
11 Scott Rolen S 5.00
12 Barry Larkin S 2.00
13 Alex Rodriguez M 15.00
14 Cal Ripken Jr. M 20.00
15 Chipper Jones M 12.50
16 Roger Clemens M 9.00
17 Mo Vaughn M 4.00
18 Mark McGwire M 20.00
19 Mike Piazza P 12.50
20 Andruw Jones P 5.00
21 Greg Maddux P 9.00
22 Barry Bonds P 9.00
23 Paul Molitor P 6.00
24 Eddie Murray P 3.00

1998 Pinnacle Hit It Here

Hit it Here is seeded one per 17 packs. The micro-etched silver foil cards feature a color player photo with a red "Hit it Here" target at left. Each card has a serial number. If the pictured player hit for the cycle on Opening Day 1998, the collector with the correct serially numbered card would have won $1 million. Each card was also produced in a promo version without serial number and with a large black "SAMPLE" overprint on back.

		MT
Complete Set (10):		20.00
Common Player:		.50
Inserted 1:17		
Samples:		1X
1	Larry Walker	1.00
2	Ken Griffey Jr.	4.00
3	Mike Piazza	3.50
4	Frank Thomas	3.00
5	Barry Bonds	2.50
6	Albert Belle	1.00
7	Tino Martinez	.50
8	Mark McGwire	5.00
9	Juan Gonzalez	2.00
10	Jeff Bagwell	2.00

1998 Pinnacle Spellbound

Spellbound is a 50-card insert seeded one per 17 packs. Nine players are featured in the set. The cards feature a photo of the player with a letter from his first or last name in the background. Each player has enough cards to spell his first or last name or a nickname. Values shown are per card and should be multiplied by the number of cards in a player name to arrive at a value for a complete-player set.

		MT
Complete Set (50):		55.00
Common Card:		.50
Inserted 1:17		
1	Mark McGwire (M)	3.00
2	Mark McGwire (C)	3.00
3	Mark McGwire (G)	3.00
4	Mark McGwire (W)	3.00
5	Mark McGwire (I)	3.00
6	Mark McGwire (R)	3.00
7	Mark McGwire (E)	3.00
8	Roger Clemens (R)	1.00
9	Roger Clemens (O)	1.00
10	Roger Clemens (C)	1.00
11	Roger Clemens (K)	1.00
12	Roger Clemens (E)	1.00
13	Roger Clemens (T)	1.00
14	Frank Thomas (B)	1.00
15	Frank Thomas (I)	1.00
16	Frank Thomas (G)	1.00
17	Frank Thomas (H)	1.00
18	Frank Thomas (U)	1.00
19	Frank Thomas (R)	1.00
20	Frank Thomas (T)	1.00
21	Scott Rolen (R)	.50
22	Scott Rolen (O)	.50
23	Scott Rolen (L)	.50
24	Scott Rolen (E)	.50
25	Scott Rolen (N)	.50
26	Ken Griffey Jr. (G)	2.00
27	Ken Griffey Jr. (R)	2.00
28	Ken Griffey Jr. (I)	2.00
29	Ken Griffey Jr. (F)	2.00
30	Ken Griffey Jr. (F)	2.00
31	Ken Griffey Jr. (E)	2.00
32	Ken Griffey Jr. (Y)	2.00
33	Larry Walker (W)	.50
34	Larry Walker (A)	.50
35	Larry Walker (L)	.50
36	Larry Walker (K)	.50
37	Larry Walker (E)	.50
38	Larry Walker (R)	.50
39	Nomar Garciaparra (N)	1.00
40	Nomar Garciaparra (O)	1.00
41	Nomar Garciaparra (M)	1.00
42	Nomar Garciaparra (A)	1.00
43	Nomar Garciaparra (R)	1.00
44	Cal Ripken Jr. (C)	3.00
45	Cal Ripken Jr. (A)	3.00
46	Cal Ripken Jr. (L)	3.00
47	Tony Gwynn (T)	.75
48	Tony Gwynn (O)	.75
49	Tony Gwynn (N)	.75
50	Tony Gwynn (Y)	.75

1998 Pinnacle Inside

Pinnacle Inside features cards in a can. The 150 base cards have full-bleed photos on front with stats on the right and the player's name and position at bottom. The Club Edition parallel (1:7) is printed on silver foil board and the Diamond Edition parallel (1:67) is printed on prismatic foil board. Each pack of cards was packaged inside a collectible can. Inserts include Behind the Numbers and Stand Up Guys.

		MT
Complete Set (150):		20.00
Common Player:		.10
Can (10):		2.00
Box (48):		75.00
1	Darin Erstad	.65
2	Derek Jeter	2.50
3	Alex Rodriguez	2.75
4	Bobby Higginson	.10
5	Nomar Garciaparra	2.00
6	Kenny Lofton	.10
7	Ivan Rodriguez	.60
8	Cal Ripken Jr.	3.00
9	Todd Hundley	.10
10	Chipper Jones	2.50
11	Barry Larkin	.15
12	Roberto Alomar	.60
13	Mo Vaughn	.45
14	Sammy Sosa	2.00
15	Sandy Alomar Jr.	.10
16	Albert Belle	.30
17	Scott Rolen	.65
18	Pokey Reese	.10
19	Ryan Klesko	.10
20	Andres Galarraga	.10
21	Justin Thompson	.10
22	Gary Sheffield	.30
23	David Justice	.30
24	Ken Griffey Jr.	2.75
25	Andruw Jones	.75
26	Jeff Bagwell	.75
27	Vladimir Guerrero	.75
28	Mike Piazza	2.50
29	Chuck Knoblauch	.10
30	Rondell White	.20
31	Greg Maddux	1.50
32	Andy Pettitte	.30
33	Larry Walker	.30
34	Bobby Estalella	.10
35	Frank Thomas	1.50
36	Tony Womack	.10
37	Tony Gwynn	1.25
38	Barry Bonds	1.50
39	Randy Johnson	.75
40	Mark McGwire	3.00
41	Juan Gonzalez	.75
42	Tim Salmon	.30
43	John Smoltz	.15
44	Rafael Palmeiro	.30
45	Mark Grace	.30
46	Mike Cameron	.10
47	Jim Thome	.10
48	Neifi Perez	.10
49	Kevin Brown	.15
50	Craig Biggio	.10
51	Bernie Williams	.30
52	Hideo Nomo	.75
53	Bob Abreu	.10
54	Edgardo Alfonzo	.10
55	Wade Boggs	1.00
56	Jose Guillen	.10
57	Ken Caminiti	.10
58	Paul Molitor	.60
59	Shawn Estes	.10
60	Edgar Martinez	.10
61	Livan Hernandez	.10
62	Ray Lankford	.10
63	Rusty Greer	.10
64	Jim Edmonds	.15
65	Tom Glavine	.15
66	Alan Benes	.10
67	Will Clark	.30
68	Garret Anderson	.10
69	Javier Lopez	.10
70	Mike Mussina	.60
71	Kevin Orie	.10
72	Matt Williams	.30
73	Bobby Bonilla	.10
74	Ruben Rivera	.10
75	Jason Giambi	.50
76	Todd Walker	.10
77	Tino Martinez	.10
78	Matt Morris	.10
79	Fernando Tatis	.10
80	Todd Greene	.10
81	Fred McGriff	.10
82	Brady Anderson	.10
83	Mark Kotsay	.10
84	Raul Mondesi	.20
85	Moises Alou	.20
86	Roger Clemens	1.25
87	Wilton Guerrero	.10
88	Shannon Stewart	.15
89	Chan Ho Park	.25
90	Carlos Delgado	.60
91	Jose Cruz Jr.	.25
92	Shawn Green	.25
93	Robin Ventura	.10
94	Reggie Sanders	.10
95	Orel Hershiser	.10
96	Dante Bichette	.10
97	Charles Johnson	.10
98	Pedro Martinez	.75
99	Mariano Rivera	.25
100	Joe Randa	.10
101	Jeff Kent	.10
102	Jay Buhner	.10
103	Brian Jordan	.10
104	Jason Kendall	.10
105	Scott Spiezio	.10
106	Desi Relaford	.10
107	Bernard Gilkey	.10
108	Manny Ramirez	.75
109	Tony Clark	.10
110	Eric Young	.10
111	Johnny Damon	.15
112	Glendon Rusch	.10
113	Ben Grieve	.30
114	Homer Bush	.10
115	Miguel Tejada	.25
116	Lou Collier	.10
117	Derrek Lee	.10
118	Jacob Cruz	.10
119	Raul Ibanez	.10
120	Ryan McGuire	.10
121	Antone Williamson	.10
122	Abraham Nunez	.10
123	Jeff Abbott	.10
124	Brett Tomko	.10
125	Richie Sexson	.10
126	Todd Helton	.65
127	Juan Encarnacion	.10
128	Richard Hidalgo	.15
129	Paul Konerko	.10
130	Brad Fullmer	.10
131	Jeremi Gonzalez	.10
132	Jaret Wright	.15
133	Derek Jeter (Inside Tips)	1.00
134	Frank Thomas (Inside Tips)	.75
135	Nomar Garciaparra (Inside Tips)	.75
136	Kenny Lofton (Inside Tips)	.10
137	Jeff Bagwell (Inside Tips)	.40
138	Todd Hundley (Inside Tips)	.10
139	Alex Rodriguez (Inside Tips)	1.50
140	Ken Griffey Jr. (Inside Tips)	1.25
141	Sammy Sosa (Inside Tips)	.75
142	Greg Maddux (Inside Tips)	.75
143	Albert Belle (Inside Tips)	.20
144	Cal Ripken Jr. (Inside Tips)	1.50
145	Mark McGwire (Inside Tips)	1.50
146	Chipper Jones (Inside Tips)	1.00
147	Charles Johnson (Inside Tips)	.10
148	Checklist (Ken Griffey Jr.)	.75
149	Checklist (Jose Cruz Jr.)	.15
150	Checklist (Larry Walker)	.20

1998 Pinnacle Inside Club Edition

This parallel set is virtually identical to the regular Inside cards, except for the addition of a "CLUB EDITION" notice to the right of the player's first name, and the use of gold foil highlights instead of silver on front.

	MT
Complete Set (150):	75.00
Common Player:	1.00
Stars:	2X
Inserted 1:7	

(See 1998 Pinnacle Inside for checklist and base card values.)

1998 Pinnacle Inside Diamond Edition

Diamond Edition cards parallel all 150 cards in Pinnacle Inside. The fronts have the insert name. These are printed on prismatic foil board and inserted one per 67 cans.

	MT
Common Card:	4.00
Stars:	7X
Inserted 1:67	

(See 1998 Pinnacle Inside for checklist and base card values.)

1998 Pinnacle Inside Behind the Numbers

Behind the Numbers is seeded one per 23 cans. Fronts feature an action photo printed in front of the player's number. The card is die-cut around the large metallic foil numerals. The back has a portrait photo and text explaining why the player wears that number.

		MT
Complete Set (20):		70.00
Common Player:		1.00
Inserted 1:23		
1	Ken Griffey Jr.	7.50
2	Cal Ripken Jr.	8.00
3	Alex Rodriguez	7.50
4	Jose Cruz Jr.	1.00
5	Mike Piazza	6.50
6	Nomar Garciaparra	5.00
7	Scott Rolen	2.00
8	Andruw Jones	2.50
9	Frank Thomas	4.50
10	Mark McGwire	8.00
11	Ivan Rodriguez	2.00
12	Greg Maddux	4.50
13	Roger Clemens	4.50
14	Derek Jeter	6.50
15	Tony Gwynn	4.00
16	Ben Grieve	1.00
17	Jeff Bagwell	3.00
18	Chipper Jones	6.50
19	Hideo Nomo	3.00
20	Sandy Alomar Jr.	1.00

1998 Pinnacle Inside Cans

Ten-card packs of Pinnacle Inside were packaged in collectible cans. The 24 cans featured a player photo or team logo. Cans were created to honor the Florida Marlins' world championship and the expansion Arizona and Tampa Bay teams. Gold parallel versions of the cans were found one every 47 cans. Vales shown are for bottom-opened cans; cans opened from the top have little collectible value.

		MT
Complete Set (23):		22.50
Common Can:		.50
Gold Cans:		2X
1	Ken Griffey Jr.	2.00
2	Frank Thomas	1.50
3	Alex Rodriguez	2.00
4	Andruw Jones	1.00
5	Mike Piazza	1.75
6	Ben Grieve	.75
7	Hideo Nomo	1.50
8	Vladimir Guerrero	1.00
9	Roger Clemens	1.50
10	Tony Gwynn	1.00
11	Mark McGwire	2.50
12	Cal Ripken Jr.	2.50
13	Jose Cruz Jr.	.50
14	Greg Maddux	1.50
15	Chipper Jones	1.75
16	Derek Jeter	1.75
17	Juan Gonzalez	1.00
18	Nomar Garciaparra (AL ROY)	1.50
19	Scott Rolen (NL ROY)	1.00
20	Florida Marlins World Series Winner	.50
21	Larry Walker (NL MVP)	.50
22	Tampa Bay Devil Rays	.50
23	Arizona Diamondbacks	.50

1998 Pinnacle Inside Stand Up Guys

This 50-card insert was seeded one per can. Each card has a match; the two cards join together in the center to form a stand-up collectible featuring four Major League players. Each card can also be found in a promo edition with a large "SAMPLE" overprint.

	MT
Complete Set (50):	30.00
Common Card:	.25
Sample:	3X
1-A/BKen Griffey Jr., Cal Ripken Jr.	2.00
1-C/DTony Gwynn, Mike Piazza	1.25
2-A/BAndruw Jones, Alex Rodriguez	1.50
2-C/DScott Rolen, Nomar Garciaparra	1.00
3-A/BAndruw Jones, Greg Maddux	1.00
3-C/DJavy Lopez, Chipper Jones	1.00
4-A/BJay Buhner, Randy Johnson	.50
4-C/DKen Griffey Jr., Alex Rodriguez	2.00
5-A/BFrank Thomas, Jeff Bagwell	1.00
5-C/DMark McGwire, Mo Vaughn	1.50
6-A/BNomar Garciaparra, Derek Jeter	1.50
6-C/DAlex Rodriguez, Barry Larkin	1.50
7-A/BMike Piazza, Ivan Rodriguez	1.25
7-C/DCharles Johnson, Javy Lopez	.25
8-A/BCal Ripken Jr., Chipper Jones	1.75
8-C/DKen Caminiti, Scott Rolen	.25
9-A/BJose Cruz Jr., Vladimir Guerrero	.75
9-C/DAndruw Jones, Jose Guillen	.50
10-A/BLarry Walker, Dante Bichette	.25
10-C/DEllis Burks, Neifi Perez	.25
11-A/BJuan Gonzalez, Sammy Sosa	1.25
11-C/DVladimir Guerrero, Manny Ramirez	.75
12-A/BGreg Maddux, Roger Clemens	1.25
12-C/DHideo Nomo, Randy Johnson	1.25
13-A/BBen Grieve, Paul Konerko	.50
13-C/DJose Cruz Jr., Fernando Tatis	.25
14-A/BRyne Sandberg, Chuck Knoblauch	.35
14-C/DRoberto Alomar, Craig Biggio	.30
15-A/BCal Ripken Jr., Brady Anderson	1.50
15-C/DRafael Palmeiro, Roberto Alomar	.30
16-A/BDarin Erstad, Jim Edmonds	.45
16-C/DTim Salmon, Garret Anderson	.25
17-A/BMike Piazza, Hideo Nomo	1.50
17-C/DRaul Mondesi, Eric Karros	.45
18-A/BIvan Rodriguez, Juan Gonzalez	.50
18-C/DWill Clark, Rusty Greer	.35
19-A/BDerek Jeter, Bernie Williams	1.25
19-C/DTino Martinez, Andy Pettitte	.25
20-A/BKenny Lofton, Ken Griffey Jr.	1.25
20-C/DBrady Anderson, Bernie Williams	.25
21-A/BPaul Molitor, Eddie Murray	.45
21-C/DRyne Sandberg, Rickey Henderson	.50
22-A/BTony Clark, Frank Thomas	.50
22-C/DJeff Bagwell, Mark McGwire	1.50
23-A/BManny Ramirez, Jim Thome	.50
23-C/DDavid Justice, Sandy Alomar Jr.	.25
24-A/BBarry Bonds, Albert Belle	.50
24-C/DJeff Bagwell, Dante Bichette	.35
25-A/BKen Griffey Jr., Frank Thomas	2.00
25-C/DAlex Rodriguez, Andruw Jones	1.50

1998 Pinnacle Mint Collection

Mint Collection consists of 30 cards and 30 matching coins with numerous parallels of each. The cards come in four different versions. The base card features a player photo at left with a circular bronze foil team logo at right. The base cards were inserted one per hobby pack and two per retail pack. Die-cut versions removed the team logo and were inserted two per hobby and one per retail packs. Silver Mint Team (1:15 hobby, 1:23 retail) and Gold Mint Team (1:47 hobby, 1:71 retail) parallels were printed on silver foil and gold foil board, respectively.

		MT
Complete Set (30):		15.00
Common Die-Cut:		.25
Bronze (1:1H):		1X
Silver (1:15H):		2X
Gold (1:47):		6X
Pack (1):		2.00
Wax Box (21):		40.00
1	Jeff Bagwell	1.00
2	Albert Belle	.50
3	Barry Bonds	1.00
4	Tony Clark	.25
5	Roger Clemens	1.00
6	Juan Gonzalez	.75
7	Ken Griffey Jr.	2.00
8	Tony Gwynn	1.00
9	Derek Jeter	1.50
10	Randy Johnson	.65
11	Chipper Jones	1.50
12	Greg Maddux	1.00
13	Tino Martinez	.25
14	Mark McGwire	2.00
15	Hideo Nomo	.75
16	Andy Pettitte	.35
17	Mike Piazza	1.50
18	Cal Ripken Jr.	2.00
19	Alex Rodriguez	2.00
20	Ivan Rodriguez	.60
21	Sammy Sosa	1.00
22	Frank Thomas	1.00
23	Mo Vaughn	.40
24	Larry Walker	.40
25	Jose Cruz Jr.	.35
26	Nomar Garciaparra	1.00
27	Vladimir Guerrero	.75
28	Livan Hernandez	.25
29	Andruw Jones	.75
30	Scott Rolen	.60

1998 Pinnacle Mint Collection Coins

Two base coins were included in each pack of Mint Collection. The coins feature the player's image, name and number on the front along with his team's name and logo. The back has the Mint Collection logo. Seven parallels were included: Nickel-Silver (1:41), Brass Proof (numbered to 500), Nickel Proof (numbered to 250), Gold Proof (numbered to 100), Gold-Plated (1:199), Solid Silver (1:288 hobby, 1:960 retail) and Solid Gold by redemption (1-of-1).

		MT
Complete Set (30):		45.00
Common Brass Coin:		.35
Brass Proof (500):		5X
Nickel (1:41):		3X
Nickel Proof (250):		8X
Silver:		12X
Inserted 1:288 H, 1:960 R		
Gold Plated (1:199):		15X
Gold Proof (100):		20X
1	Jeff Bagwell	2.00
2	Albert Belle	1.00
3	Barry Bonds	2.50
4	Tony Clark	.35
5	Roger Clemens	2.25
6	Juan Gonzalez	2.00
7	Ken Griffey Jr.	4.00
8	Tony Gwynn	2.25
9	Derek Jeter	3.00
10	Randy Johnson	1.25
11	Chipper Jones	3.00
12	Greg Maddux	2.50
13	Tino Martinez	.35
14	Mark McGwire	4.00
15	Hideo Nomo	1.25
16	Andy Pettitte	.75
17	Mike Piazza	3.00
18	Cal Ripken Jr.	4.00
19	Alex Rodriguez	3.50
20	Ivan Rodriguez	1.50
21	Sammy Sosa	2.50
22	Frank Thomas	2.50
23	Mo Vaughn	1.25
24	Larry Walker	.75
25	Jose Cruz Jr.	.60
26	Nomar Garciaparra	2.50
27	Vladimir Guerrero	2.00
28	Livan Hernandez	.35
29	Andruw Jones	2.00
30	Scott Rolen	2.00

1998 Pinnacle Mint Collection Mint Gems

Mint Gems is a six-card insert printed on silver foil board. The cards were inserted 1:31 hobby packs and 1:47 retail. The oversized Mint Gems coins are twice the size of the regular coins. The six coins were inserted 1:31 hobby packs.

		MT
Complete Set (6)		40.00
Common Player:		4.00
Coins:		1X
1	Ken Griffey Jr.	15.00
2	Larry Walker	4.00
3	Roger Clemens	10.00
4	Pedro Martinez	6.00
5	Nomar Garciaparra	12.00
6	Scott Rolen	8.00

1998 Pinnacle Performers

Pinnacle Performers consists of a 150-card base set. The Peak Performers parallel adds silver foil to the base cards and was inserted 1:7. Inserts in the home run-themed product include Big Bang, Launching Pad, Player's Card and Power Trip.

		MT
Complete Set (150):		15.00
Common Player:		.10
Peak Performers (1:7):		4X
Pack (10):		1.00
Wax Box (48):		30.00
1	Ken Griffey Jr.	1.50
2	Frank Thomas	1.00
3	Cal Ripken Jr.	1.50
4	Alex Rodriguez	1.50
5	Greg Maddux	1.00
6	Mike Piazza	1.25
7	Chipper Jones	1.25
8	Tony Gwynn	.75
9	Derek Jeter	1.25
10	Jeff Bagwell	.60
11	Juan Gonzalez	.60
12	Nomar Garciaparra	1.00
13	Andruw Jones	.50
14	Hideo Nomo	.60
15	Roger Clemens	.75
16	Mark McGwire	1.50
17	Scott Rolen	.40
18	Vladimir Guerrero	.60
19	Barry Bonds	.75
20	Darin Erstad	.40
21	Albert Belle	.30
22	Kenny Lofton	.10
23	Mo Vaughn	.30
24	Tony Clark	.10
25	Ivan Rodriguez	.50
26	Jose Cruz Jr.	.20
27	Larry Walker	.25
28	Jaret Wright	.10
29	Andy Pettitte	.20
30	Roberto Alomar	.40
31	Randy Johnson	.50
32	Manny Ramirez	.60
33	Paul Molitor	.50
34	Mike Mussina	.50
35	Jim Thome	.10
36	Tino Martinez	.10
37	Gary Sheffield	.25
38	Chuck Knoblauch	.10
39	Bernie Williams	.30
40	Tim Salmon	.20
41	Sammy Sosa	1.00
42	Wade Boggs	.65
43	Will Clark	.25
44	Andres Galarraga	.10
45	Raul Mondesi	.20
46	Rickey Henderson	.50
47	Jose Canseco	.30
48	Pedro Martinez	.50
49	Jay Buhner	.10
50	Ryan Klesko	.10
51	Barry Larkin	.15
52	Charles Johnson	.10
53	Tom Glavine	.15
54	Edgar Martinez	.10
55	Fred McGriff	.10
56	Moises Alou	.15
57	Dante Bichette	.15
58	Jim Edmonds	.10
59	Mark Grace	.25
60	Chan Ho Park	.20
61	Justin Thompson	.10
62	John Smoltz	.15
63	Craig Biggio	.10
64	Ken Caminiti	.10
65	Richard Hidalgo	.10
66	Carlos Delgado	.40
67	David Justice	.25
68	J.T. Snow	.10
69	Jason Giambi	.50
70	Garret Anderson	.10
71	Rondell White	.15
72	Matt Williams	.25
73	Brady Anderson	.10
74	Eric Karros	.10
75	Javier Lopez	.10
76	Pat Hentgen	.10
77	Todd Hundley	.10
78	Ray Lankford	.10
79	Denny Neagle	.10
80	Sandy Alomar Jr.	.10
81	Jason Kendall	.10
82	Omar Vizquel	.10
83	Kevin Brown	.15
84	Kevin Appier	.10
85	Al Martin	.10
86	Rusty Greer	.10
87	Bobby Bonilla	.10
88	Shawn Estes	.10
89	Rafael Palmeiro	.30
90	Edgar Renteria	.10
91	Alan Benes	.10
92	Bobby Higginson	.10
93	Mark Grudzielanek	.10
94	Jose Guillen	.10
95	Neifi Perez	.10
96	Jeff Abbott	.10
97	Todd Walker	.10
98	Eric Young	.10
99	Brett Tomko	.10
100	Mike Cameron	.10
101	Karim Garcia	.10
102	Brian Jordan	.10
103	Jeff Suppan	.10
104	Robin Ventura	.10
105	Henry Rodriguez	.10
106	Shannon Stewart	.10
107	Kevin Orie	.10
108	Bartolo Colon	.10
109	Bob Abreu	.10
110	Vinny Castilla	.10
111	Livan Hernandez	.10
112	Derrek Lee	.10
113	Mark Kotsay	.10
114	Todd Greene	.10
115	Edgardo Alfonzo	.10
116	A.J. Hinch	.10
117	Paul Konerko	.10
118	Todd Helton	.35
119	Miguel Tejada	.25
120	Fernando Tatis	.10
121	Ben Grieve	.20
122	Travis Lee	.10
123	Kerry Wood	.20
124	Eli Marrero	.10
125	David Ortiz	.10
126	Juan Encarnacion	.10
127	Brad Fullmer	.10
128	Richie Sexson	.10
129	Aaron Boone	.10
130	Enrique Wilson	.10
131	Javier Valentin	.10
132	Abraham Nunez	.10
133	Ricky Ledee	.10
134	Carl Pavano	.10
135	Bobby Estalella	.10
136	Homer Bush	.10
137	Brian Rose	.10
138	Ken Griffey Jr . (Far and Away)	.75
139	Frank Thomas (Far and Away)	.40
140	Cal Ripken Jr. (Far and Away)	.75
141	Alex Rodriguez (Far and Away)	.65
142	Greg Maddux (Far and Away)	.40
143	Chipper Jones (Far and Away)	.50
144	Mike Piazza (Far and Away)	.50

145	Tony Gwynn (Far and Away)	.40
146	Derek Jeter (Far and Away)	.50
147	Jeff Bagwell (Far and Away)	.35
148	Checklist (Hideo Nomo)	.25
149	Checklist (Roger Clemens)	.25
150	Checklist (Greg Maddux)	.25

1998 Pinnacle Performers Peak Performers

This 150-card parallel set is printed on silver foil vs. the white cardboard stock used on regular-issue cards. The parallel set name is printed down the right side in gold letters. They were seeded one per seven packs.

	MT
Complete Set (150):	100.00
Common Player:	.50
Stars:	4X
Inserted 1:7	

(See 1998 Pinnacle Performers for checklist and base card values.)

1998 Pinnacle Performers Big Bang

This 20-card insert features top power hitters. The micro-etched cards are sequentially numbered to 2,500. Each player has a Seasonal Outburst parallel, with a red overlay and numbered to that player's best seasonal home run total. Each card is also found in a promo edition with a large black "SAMPLE" overprinted on back.

		MT
Complete Set (20):		55.00
Common Player:		1.00
Production 2,500 sets		
Sample:		1X
1	Ken Griffey Jr.	6.50
2	Frank Thomas	4.00
3	Mike Piazza	5.00
4	Chipper Jones	5.00
5	Alex Rodriguez	6.00
6	Nomar Garciaparra	4.00
7	Jeff Bagwell	3.50
8	Cal Ripken Jr.	6.50
9	Albert Belle	1.50
10	Mark McGwire	6.50
11	Juan Gonzalez	3.50
12	Larry Walker	1.25
13	Tino Martinez	1.00
14	Jim Thome	1.00
15	Manny Ramirez	3.50
16	Barry Bonds	3.50
17	Mo Vaughn	2.00
18	Jose Cruz Jr.	1.25
19	Tony Clark	1.00
20	Andruw Jones	2.50

1998 Pinnacle Performers Big Bang Season Outburst

Season Outburst parallels the Big Bang insert. The cards have a red overlay and are sequentially numbered to each player's season-high home run total. Unnumbered versions of the cards, likely leaked into the market after Pinnacle went bankrupt in mid-1998, have been seen; their value is much lower than the issued version.

		MT
Complete Set (20):		500.00
Common Player:		10.00
#'d to player's 1997 HR total		
Unnumbered: 25%		
1	Ken Griffey Jr. (56)	50.00
2	Frank Thomas (35)	20.00
3	Mike Piazza (40)	35.00
4	Chipper Jones (21)	65.00
5	Alex Rodriguez (23)	75.00
6	Nomar Garciaparra (30)	40.00
7	Jeff Bagwell (43)	20.00
8	Cal Ripken Jr. (17)	100.00
9	Albert Belle (30)	12.50
10	Mark McGwire (58)	60.00
11	Juan Gonzalez (42)	20.00
12	Larry Walker (49)	10.00
13	Tino Martinez (44)	10.00
14	Jim Thome (40)	10.00
15	Manny Ramirez (26)	25.00
16	Barry Bonds (40)	25.00
17	Mo Vaughn (35)	15.00
18	Jose Cruz Jr. (26)	12.50
19	Tony Clark (32)	10.00
20	Andruw Jones (18)	25.00

1998 Pinnacle Performers Launching Pad

Launching Pad is a 20-card insert seeded one per nine packs. It features top sluggers on foil-on-foil cards with an outer space background.

		MT
Complete Set (20):		45.00
Common Player:		1.00
Inserted 1:9		
1	Ben Grieve	1.00
2	Ken Griffey Jr.	5.00
3	Derek Jeter	4.00
4	Frank Thomas	2.50
5	Travis Lee	1.00
6	Vladimir Guerrero	2.00
7	Tony Gwynn	2.50
8	Jose Cruz Jr.	1.00
9	Cal Ripken Jr.	7.50
10	Chipper Jones	4.00
11	Scott Rolen	1.50
12	Andruw Jones	2.00
13	Ivan Rodriguez	1.50
14	Todd Helton	1.50
15	Nomar Garciaparra	3.50
16	Mark McGwire	7.50
17	Gary Sheffield	1.00
18	Bernie Williams	1.00
19	Alex Rodriguez	5.00
20	Mike Piazza	4.00

1998 Pinnacle Performers Power Trip

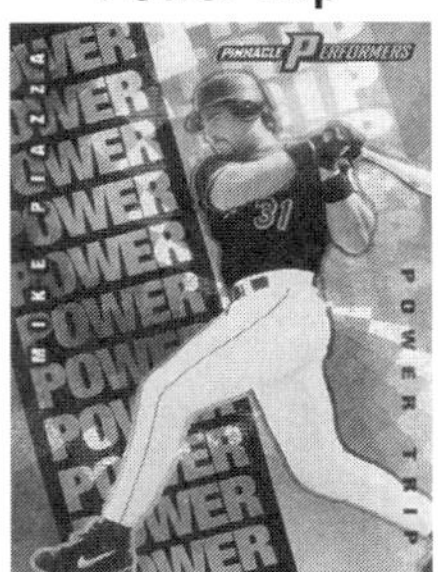

This 10-card insert was seeded 1:21. Printed on silver foil, each card is sequentially-numbered to 10,000. Cards backs have details about one of the player's power-hitting highlights of the previous season.

		MT
Complete Set (10):		32.50
Common Player:		2.00
Production 10,000 sets		
1	Frank Thomas	3.00
2	Alex Rodriguez	5.00
3	Nomar Garciaparra	4.00
4	Jeff Bagwell	2.00
5	Cal Ripken Jr.	6.00
6	Mike Piazza	4.50
7	Chipper Jones	4.50
8	Ken Griffey Jr.	5.50
9	Mark McGwire	6.00
10	Juan Gonzalez	2.00

1998 Pinnacle Performers Swing for the Fences

Pinnacle Performers included the "Swing for the Fences" sweepstakes. Fifty players were featured on cards with numbers on an all-red background. Fifty Home Run Points cards were also inserted, with each card featuring a point total on the front. Collectors who found the player cards of the AL and NL home run leaders, as well as enough point cards to match each of their season totals, were eligible to win prizes. A player or point card was inserted in each pack.

		MT
Complete Set (50):		27.50
Common Player:		.25
Inserted 1:1		
1	Brady Anderson	.25
2	Albert Belle	.50
3	Jay Buhner	.25
4	Jose Canseco	.60
5	Tony Clark	.25
6	Jose Cruz Jr.	.45
7	Jim Edmonds	.25
8	Cecil Fielder	.25
9	Travis Fryman	.25
10	Nomar Garciaparra	1.50
11	Juan Gonzalez	1.00
12	Ken Griffey Jr.	3.00
13	David Justice	.40
14	Travis Lee	.40
15	Edgar Martinez	.25
16	Tino Martinez	.25
17	Rafael Palmeiro	.40
18	Manny Ramirez	1.00
19	Cal Ripken Jr.	2.50
20	Alex Rodriguez	2.50
21	Tim Salmon	.40
22	Frank Thomas	1.50
23	Jim Thome	.25
24	Mo Vaughn	.45
25	Bernie Williams	.45
26	Fred McGriff	.25
27	Jeff Bagwell	1.00
28	Dante Bichette	.25
29	Barry Bonds	1.50
30	Ellis Burks	.25
31	Ken Caminiti	.25
32	Vinny Castilla	.25
33	Andres Galarraga	.25
34	Vladimir Guerrero	.75
35	Todd Helton	.60
36	Todd Hundley	.25
37	Andruw Jones	.75
38	Chipper Jones	2.00
39	Eric Karros	.25

40 Ryan Klesko .25
41 Ray Lankford .25
42 Mark McGwire 3.50
43 Raul Mondesi .40
44 Mike Piazza 2.00
45 Scott Rolen .65
46 Gary Sheffield .40
47 Sammy Sosa 1.50
48 Larry Walker .50
49 Matt Williams .40
50 WILDCARD .25

1998 Pinnacle Plus

Pinnacle Plus consists of a 200-card base set. Five subsets are included: Field of Vision, Naturals, All-Stars, Devil Rays and Diamondbacks. Artist's Proof is a 60-card partial parallel of the base set, inserted 1:35 packs. Gold Artist's Proof cards are numbered to 100 and Mirror Artist's Proofs are 1-of-1 inserts. Inserts include Lasting Memories, Yardwork, A Piece of the Game, All-Star Epix, Team Pinnacle, Gold Team Pinnacle, Pinnabilia and Certified Souvenir.

MT
Complete Set (200): 25.00
Common Player: .10
1 Roberto Alomar (All-star) .60
2 Sandy Alomar Jr. (All-star) .10
3 Brady Anderson (All-star) .10
4 Albert Belle (All-star) .30
5 Jeff Cirillo (All-star) .10
6 Roger Clemens (All-star) 1.25
7 David Cone (All-star) .10
8 Nomar Garciaparra (All-star) 1.50
9 Ken Griffey Jr. (All-star) 2.25
10 Jason Dickson (All-star) .10
11 Edgar Martinez (All-star) .10
12 Tino Martinez (All-star) .10
13 Randy Johnson (All-star) .60
14 Mark McGwire (All-star) 2.50
15 David Justice (All-star) .25
16 Mike Mussina (All-star) .60
17 Chuck Knoblauch (All-star) .10
18 Joey Cora (All-star) .10
19 Pat Hentgen (All-star) .10
20 Randy Myers (All-star) .10
21 Cal Ripken Jr. (All-star) 2.50
22 Mariano Rivera (All-star) .25
23 Jose Rosado (All-star) .10
24 Frank Thomas (All-star) 1.25
25 Alex Rodriguez (All-star) 2.50
26 Justin Thompson (All-star) .10
27 Ivan Rodriguez (All-star) .60
28 Bernie Williams (All-star) .25
29 Pedro Martinez .60
30 Tony Clark .10
31 Garret Anderson .10
32 Travis Fryman .10
33 Mike Piazza 2.00
34 Carl Pavano .10
35 *Kevin Millwood* 2.50
36 Miguel Tejada .25
37 Willie Blair .10
38 Devon White .10
39 Andres Galarraga .10
40 Barry Larkin .15
41 Al Leiter .10
42 Moises Alou .20
43 Eric Young .10
44 John Jaha .10
45 Bernard Gilkey .10
46 Freddy Garcia .20
47 Ruben Rivera .10
48 Robb Nen .10
49 Ray Lankford .10
50 Kenny Lofton .10
51 Joe Carter .10
52 Jason McDonald .10
53 Quinton McCracken .10
54 Kerry Wood .65
55 Mike Lansing .10
56 Chipper Jones 2.00
57 Barry Bonds 1.00
58 Brad Fullmer .10
59 Jeff Bagwell .75
60 Rondell White .20
61 Geronimo Berroa .10
62 *Magglio Ordonez* 1.00
63 Dwight Gooden .10
64 Brian Hunter .10
65 Todd Walker .10
66 *Frank Catalanotto* .20
67 Tony Saunders .10
68 Travis Lee .15
69 Michael Tucker .10
70 Reggie Sanders .10
71 Derrek Lee .10
72 Larry Walker .25
73 Marquis Grissom .10
74 Craig Biggio .10
75 Kevin Brown .15
76 J.T. Snow .10
77 Eric Davis .10
78 Jeff Abbott .10
79 Jermaine Dye .10
80 Otis Nixon .10
81 Curt Schilling .20
82 Enrique Wilson .10
83 Tony Gwynn 1.25
84 Orlando Cabrera .15
85 Ramon Martinez .10
86 Greg Vaughn .10
87 Alan Benes .10
88 Dennis Eckersley .10
89 Jim Thome .10
90 Juan Encarnacion .10
91 Jeff King .10
92 Shannon Stewart .10
93 Roberto Hernandez .10
94 Raul Ibanez .10
95 Darryl Kile .10
96 Charles Johnson .10
97 Rich Becker .10
98 Hal Morris .10
99 Ismael Valdes .10
100 Orel Hershiser .10
101 Mo Vaughn .45
102 Aaron Boone .10
103 Jeff Conine .10
104 Paul O'Neill .10
105 Tom Candiotti .10
106 Wilson Alvarez .10
107 Mike Stanley .10
108 Carlos Delgado .30
109 Tony Batista .10
110 Dante Bichette .10
111 Henry Rodriguez .10
112 Karim Garcia .10
113 Shane Reynolds .10
114 Ken Caminiti .10
115 Jose Silva .10
116 Juan Gonzalez .75
117 Brian Jordan .10
118 Jim Leyritz .10
119 Manny Ramirez .75
120 Fred McGriff .10
121 Brooks Kieschnick .10
122 Sean Casey .25
123 John Smoltz .15
124 Rusty Greer .10
125 Cecil Fielder .10
126 Mike Cameron .10
127 Reggie Jefferson .10
128 Bobby Higginson .10
129 Kevin Appier .10
130 Robin Ventura .10
131 Ben Grieve .30
132 Wade Boggs .75
133 Jose Cruz Jr. .15
134 Jeff Suppan .10
135 Vinny Castilla .10
136 Sammy Sosa 1.50
137 Mark Wohlers .10
138 Jay Bell .10
139 Brett Tomko .10
140 Gary Sheffield .25
141 Tim Salmon .25
142 Jaret Wright .30
143 Kenny Rogers .10
144 Brian Anderson .10
145 Darrin Fletcher .10
146 John Flaherty .10
147 Dmitri Young .10
148 Andruw Jones .75
149 Matt Williams .25
150 Bobby Bonilla .10
151 Mike Hampton .10
152 Al Martin .10
153 Mark Grudzielanek .10
154 Dave Nilsson .10
155 Roger Cedeno .10
156 Greg Maddux 1.25
157 Mark Kotsay .10
158 Steve Finley .10
159 Wilson Delgado .10
160 Ron Gant .10
161 Jim Edmonds .10
162 Jeff Blauser .10
163 Dave Burba .10
164 Pedro Astacio .10
165 Livan Hernandez .10
166 Neifi Perez .10
167 Ryan Klesko .10
168 Fernando Tatis .10
169 Richard Hidalgo .10
170 Carlos Perez .10
171 Bob Abreu .10
172 Francisco Cordova .10
173 Todd Helton .60
174 Doug Glanville .10
175 Brian Rose .10
176 Yamil Benitez .10
177 Darin Erstad .60
178 Scott Rolen .60
179 John Wetteland .10
180 Paul Sorrento .10
181 Walt Weiss .10
182 Vladimir Guerrero .75
183 Ken Griffey Jr. (The Naturals) 1.50
184 Alex Rodriguez (The Naturals) 1.25
185 Cal Ripken Jr. (The Naturals) 1.50
186 Frank Thomas (The Naturals) .65
187 Chipper Jones (The Naturals) 1.00
188 Hideo Nomo (The Naturals) .75
189 Nomar Garciaparra (The Naturals) .65
190 Mike Piazza (The Naturals) 1.00
191 Greg Maddux (The Naturals) .60
192 Tony Gwynn (The Naturals) .60
193 Mark McGwire (The Naturals) 1.50
194 Roger Clemens (The Naturals) .65
195 Mike Piazza (Field of Vision) 1.00
196 Mark McGwire (Field of Vision) 1.50
197 Chipper Jones (Field of Vision) 1.00
198 Larry Walker (Field of Vision) .20
199 Hideo Nomo (Field of Vision) .75
200 Barry Bonds (Field of Vision) 1.00

1998 Pinnacle Plus Artist's Proofs

Artist's Proofs is a 60-card partial parallel of the Pinnacle Plus base set. The dot matrix hologram cards were inserted 1:35. Gold Artist's Proofs added a gold finish and are sequentially numbered to 100. Mirror Artist's Proofs are a "1-of-1" insert. Card numbers have an "AP" prefix.

MT
Complete Set (60): 225.00
Common Player: 1.00
Inserted 1:35
Golds: 15X
Production 100 sets
1 Roberto Alomar (All-Star) 4.50
2 Albert Belle (All-Star) 2.00
3 Roger Clemens (All-Star) 10.00
4 Nomar Garciaparra (All-Star) 13.50
5 Ken Griffey Jr. (All-Star) 17.50
6 Tino Martinez (All-Star) 1.00
7 Randy Johnson (All-Star) 4.00
8 Mark McGwire (All-Star) 20.00
9 David Justice (All-Star) 1.50
10 Chuck Knoblauch (All-Star) 1.00
11 Cal Ripken Jr. (All-Star) 20.00
12 Frank Thomas (All-Star) 12.00
13 Alex Rodriguez (All-Star) 17.50
14 Ivan Rodriguez (All-Star) 6.00
15 Bernie Williams (All-Star) 2.00
16 Pedro Martinez 4.00
17 Tony Clark 1.00
18 Mike Piazza 16.00
19 Miguel Tejada 2.00
20 Andres Galarraga 1.00
21 Barry Larkin 1.00
22 Kenny Lofton 1.00
23 Chipper Jones 16.00
24 Barry Bonds 10.00
25 Brad Fullmer 1.00
26 Jeff Bagwell 7.50

27	Todd Walker	1.00
28	Travis Lee	1.50
29	Larry Walker	1.50
30	Craig Biggio	1.00
31	Tony Gwynn	10.00
32	Jim Thome	1.00
33	Juan Encarnacion	1.00
34	Mo Vaughn	3.00
35	Karim Garcia	1.00
36	Ken Caminiti	1.00
37	Juan Gonzalez	7.50
38	Manny Ramirez	7.50
39	Fred McGriff	1.00
40	Rusty Greer	1.00
41	Bobby Higginson	1.00
42	Ben Grieve	1.50
43	Wade Boggs	4.00
44	Jose Cruz Jr.	1.50
45	Sammy Sosa	12.50
46	Gary Sheffield	1.50
47	Tim Salmon	1.50
48	Jaret Wright	2.00
49	Andruw Jones	6.00
50	Matt Williams	1.50
51	Greg Maddux	12.00
52	Jim Edmonds	1.00
53	Livan Hernandez	1.00
54	Neifi Perez	1.00
55	Fernando Tatis	1.00
56	Richard Hidalgo	1.00
57	Todd Helton	4.00
58	Darin Erstad	4.50
59	Scott Rolen	4.50
60	Vladimir Guerrero	6.50

1998 Pinnacle Plus A Piece of the Game

Inserted 1:17 hoby packs (1:19 retail), this 10-card insert features baseball's top players on micro-etched foil cards.

		MT
Complete Set (10):		25.00
Common Player:		1.00
Inserted 1:19		
1	Ken Griffey Jr.	5.00
2	Frank Thomas	2.50
3	Alex Rodriguez	4.00
4	Chipper Jones	3.50
5	Cal Ripken Jr.	5.00
6	Mike Piazza	3.50
7	Greg Maddux	2.50
8	Juan Gonzalez	1.50
9	Nomar Garciaparra	3.00
10	Larry Walker	1.00

1998 Pinnacle Plus All-Star Epix Game

The All-Star Epix insert is part of the cross-brand Epix set. This 24-card set honors the All-Star Game achievements of baseball's stars on cards with dot matrix holograms. All-Star Epix was seeded 1:21.

		MT
Complete Set (24):		150.00
Common Player:		2.00
Purples:		1.5X
Emeralds:		2.5X
Overall Odds 1:21		
1	Ken Griffey Jr.	13.50
2	Juan Gonzalez	6.50
3	Jeff Bagwell	6.50
4	Ivan Rodriguez	5.00
5	Nomar Garciaparra	10.00
6	Ryne Sandberg	9.00
7	Frank Thomas	9.00
8	Derek Jeter	12.00
9	Tony Gwynn	8.00
10	Albert Belle	3.00
11	Scott Rolen	3.50
12	Barry Larkin	2.00
13	Alex Rodriguez	13.50
14	Cal Ripken Jr.	15.00
15	Chipper Jones	12.00
16	Roger Clemens	9.00
17	Mo Vaughn	2.50
18	Mark McGwire	15.00
19	Mike Piazza	12.00
20	Andruw Jones	6.00
21	Greg Maddux	9.00
22	Barry Bonds	10.00
23	Paul Molitor	5.00
24	Hideo Nomo	5.00

1998 Pinnacle Plus Lasting Memories

Lasting Memories is a 30-card insert seeded 1:5. Printed on foil board, the cards feature a player photo with a sky background.

		MT
Complete Set (30):		20.00
Common Player:		.25
Inserted 1:5		
1	Nomar Garciaparra	1.50
2	Ken Griffey Jr.	2.00
3	Livan Hernandez	.25
4	Hideo Nomo	.60
5	Ben Grieve	.35
6	Scott Rolen	.50
7	Roger Clemens	1.00
8	Cal Ripken Jr.	2.50
9	Mo Vaughn	.40
10	Frank Thomas	1.25
11	Mark McGwire	2.50
12	Barry Larkin	.25
13	Matt Williams	.25
14	Jose Cruz Jr.	.35
15	Andruw Jones	.50
16	Mike Piazza	1.75
17	Jeff Bagwell	.60
18	Chipper Jones	1.75
19	Juan Gonzalez	.60
20	Kenny Lofton	.25
21	Greg Maddux	1.25
22	Ivan Rodriguez	.50
23	Alex Rodriguez	2.00
24	Derek Jeter	1.75
25	Albert Belle	.35
26	Barry Bonds	1.25
27	Larry Walker	.40
28	Sammy Sosa	1.50
29	Tony Gwynn	1.00
30	Randy Johnson	.50

1998 Pinnacle Plus Team Pinnacle

Team Pinnacle is a 15-card, double-sided insert. Printed on mirror-mylar, the cards were inserted 1:71. The hobby-only Gold Team Pinnacle parallel was inserted 1:199 packs.

		MT
Complete Set (15):		75.00
Common Player:		2.50
Inserted 1:71		
Golds:		1.5X
Inserted 1:199		
1	Mike Piazza, Ivan Rodriguez	7.50
2	Mark McGwire, Mo Vaughn	12.50
3	Roberto Alomar, Craig Biggio	2.50
4	Alex Rodriguez, Barry Larkin	10.00
5	Cal Ripken Jr., Chipper Jones	10.00
6	Ken Griffey Jr., Larry Walker	12.50
7	Juan Gonzalez, Tony Gwynn	5.00
8	Albert Belle, Barry Bonds	4.00
9	Kenny Lofton, Andruw Jones	2.50
10	Tino Martinez, Jeff Bagwell	3.50
11	Frank Thomas, Andres Galarraga	5.00
12	Roger Clemens, Greg Maddux	7.50
13	Pedro Martinez, Hideo Nomo	6.50
14	Nomar Garciaparra, Scott Rolen	6.50
15	Ben Grieve, Paul Konerko	3.50

1998 Pinnacle Plus Yardwork

Yardwork is a 15-card insert seeded one per 19 packs. It features the top home run hitters in Major League Baseball.

		MT
Complete Set (15):		20.00
Common Player:		.50
Inserted 1:9		
1	Mo Vaughn	.75
2	Frank Thomas	2.00
3	Albert Belle	.50
4	Nomar Garciaparra	2.00
5	Tony Clark	.50
6	Tino Martinez	.50
7	Ken Griffey Jr.	3.00
8	Juan Gonzalez	1.50
9	Sammy Sosa	2.50
10	Jose Cruz Jr.	.50
11	Jeff Bagwell	1.50
12	Mike Piazza	2.50
13	Larry Walker	.50
14	Mark McGwire	3.00
15	Barry Bonds	2.50

1998 Pinnacle Snapshots

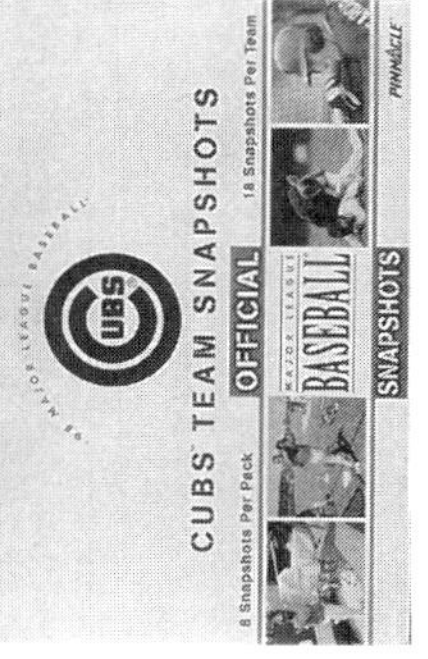

One of Pinnacle's last issues was a team-oriented presentation of large-format (4" x 6") cards called Snapshots. Like their namesake, the focus on this issue is on candid photos rather than posed portraits or game-action pictures. The cards are printed on thin high-gloss cardboard stock resembling photo paper. Fronts, many of them horizontally formatted, are borderless and have no graphic enhancement. Backs are lightly printed with Pinnacle and licensor logos and a card number expressed "x of 18". The player's name is nowhere to be found. Snapshots were sold regionally in single-team boxes of 25 packs with eight cards each.

MT

(See individual teams for checklists and values.)

A card number in parentheses ( ) indicates the set is unnumbered.

1998 Pinnacle Snapshots Angels

		MT
Complete Set (18):		14.00
Common Player:		.50
1	Jason Dickson	.75
2	Gary DiSarcina	.50
3	Garret Anderson	.75
4	Shigetosi Hasegawa	.75
5	Ken Hill	.50
6	Todd Greene	.75
7	Tim Salmon	2.00
8	Jim Edmonds	2.00
9	Garret Anderson	.75
10	Dave Hollins	.50
11	Todd Greene	.75
12	Troy Percival	.50
13	Gary DiSarcina	.50
14	Cecil Fielder	.75
15	Darin Erstad	3.00
16	Chuck Finley	.75
17	Jim Edmonds	2.00
18	Jason Dickson	.75

1998 Pinnacle Snapshots Braves

		MT
Complete Set (18):		20.00
Common Player:		.50
1	Ryan Klesko	.75
2	Walt Weiss	.50
3	Tom Glavine	2.00
4	Randall Simon	.50
5	John Smoltz	2.00
6	Chipper Jones	4.00
7	Javier Lopez	1.50
8	Greg Maddux	3.00
9	Andruw Jones	2.50
10	Michael Tucker	.50
11	Andres Galarraga	.75
12	Andres Galarraga	.75
13	Greg Maddux	3.00
14	Wes Helms	.50
15	Bruce Chen	.50
16	Denny Neagle	.50
17	Mark Wohlers	.50
18	Kevin Millwood	2.50

1998 Pinnacle Snapshots Cardinals

		MT
Complete Set (18):		16.50
Common Player:		.50
1	Alan Benes	.50
2	Ron Gant	1.00
3	Donovan Osborne	.50
4	Eli Marrero	.50
5	Mark McGwire	5.00
6	Delino DeShields	.50
7	Tom Pagnozzi	.50
8	Delino DeShields	.50
9	Mark McGwire	5.00
10	Royce Clayton	.50
11	Brian Jordan	2.00
12	Ray Lankford	.75
13	Brian Jordan	1.00
14	Matt Morris	1.00
15	John Mabry	.50
16	Luis Ordaz	.50
17	Ron Gant	1.00
18	Todd Stottlemyre	.75

1998 Pinnacle Snapshots Cubs

		MT
Complete Set (18):		16.50
Common Player:		.50
1	Mark Grace	2.00
2	Manny Alexander	.50
3	Jeremi Gonzalez	.75
4	Brant Brown	.75
5	Mark Grace	2.00
6	Lance Johnson	.50
7	Mark Clark	.50
8	Kevin Foster	.50
9	Brant Brown	.75
10	Kevin Foster	.50
11	Kevin Tapani	.50
12	Sammy Sosa	5.00
13	Sammy Sosa	5.00
14	Pat Cline	.50
15	Kevin Orie	.50
16	Steve Trachsel	.50
17	Lance Johnson	.50
18	Robin Jennings	.50

1998 Pinnacle Snapshots Devil Rays

		MT
Complete Set (18):		11.00
Common Player:		.50
1	Kevin Stocker	.50
2	Paul Sorrento	.50
3	John Flaherty	.50
4	Wade Boggs	4.00
5	Rich Butler	.50
6	Wilson Alvarez	.50
7	Bubba Trammell	.75
8	David Martinez	.50
9	Brooks Kieschnick	.50
10	Tony Saunders	.50
11	Esteban Yan	.50
12	Quinton McCracken	.50
13	Albie Lopez	.50
14	Roberto Hernandez	.75
15	Fred McGriff	1.50
16	Bubba Trammell	.75
17	Brooks Kieschnick	.50
18	Fred McGriff	1.50

1998 Pinnacle Snapshots Diamondbacks

		MT
Complete Set (18):		13.00
Common Player:		.50
1	Travis Lee	2.00
2	Matt Williams	1.50
3	Jay Bell	1.00
4	Devon White	.75
5	Andy Benes	.50
6	Tony Batista	.50
7	Jay Bell	1.00
8	Edwin Diaz	.50
9	Devon White	.75
10	Bob Wolcott	.50
11	Karim Garcia	1.50
12	Yamil Benitez	.50
13	Jorge Fabregas	.50
14	Jeff Suppan	.50
15	Ben Ford	.50
16	Brian Anderson	1.00
17	Travis Lee	2.00
18	Matt Williams	1.50

1998 Pinnacle Snapshots Dodgers

		MT
Complete Set (18):		17.50
Common Player:		.50
1	Mike Piazza	4.00
2	Eric Karros	1.00
3	Raul Mondesi	1.25
4	Wilton Guerrero	.50
5	Darren Dreifort	.50
6	Roger Cedeno	.75
7	Todd Zeile	.50
8	Paul Konerko	1.00
9	Todd Hollandsworth	.50
10	Ismael Valdes	.50
11	Hideo Nomo	3.00
12	Ramon Martinez	.50
13	Chan Ho Park	2.00
14	Eric Young	.50
15	Dennis Reyes	.50
16	Eric Karros	1.00
17	Mike Piazza	4.00
18	Raul Mondesi	1.25

1998 Pinnacle Snapshots Indians

		MT
Complete Set (18):		15.00
Common Player:		.50
1	Manny Ramirez	3.00
2	Travis Fryman	.75
3	Jaret Wright	3.00
4	Brian Giles	1.00
5	Bartolo Colon	1.00
6	Kenny Lofton	1.00
7	David Justice	1.50
8	Brian Giles	1.00
9	Sandy Alomar Jr.	1.00
10	Jose Mesa	.50
11	Jim Thome	1.00
12	Sandy Alomar Jr.	1.00
13	Omar Vizquel	.75
14	Geronimo Berroa	.50
15	John Smiley	.50
16	Chad Ogea	.50
17	Charles Nagy	.75
18	Enrique Wilson	.75

1998 Pinnacle Snapshots Mariners

		MT
Complete Set (18):		18.00
Common Player:		.50
1	Alex Rodriguez	4.00
2	Jay Buhner	.75
3	Russ Davis	.50
4	Joey Cora	.50
5	Joey Cora	.50
6	Jay Buhner	.75
7	Ken Griffey Jr.	5.00
8	Raul Ibanez	.50
9	Rich Amaral	.50
10	Shane Monahan	.50
11	Alex Rodriguez	4.00
12	Dan Wilson	.50
13	Bob Wells	.50
14	Randy Johnson	2.00
15	Randy Johnson	2.00
16	Jeff Fassero	.50
17	Ken Cloude	.50
18	Edgar Martinez	.50

1998 Pinnacle Snapshots Mets

		MT
Complete Set (18):		12.00
Common Player:		.50
1	Rey Ordonez	2.00
2	Todd Hundley	.75
3	Preston Wilson	1.00
4	Rich Becker	.50
5	Bernard Gilkey	.50
6	Rey Ordonez	2.00
7	Butch Huskey	.50
8	Carlos Baerga	.50
9	Edgardo Alfonzo	2.00
10	Bill Pulsipher	.50
11	John Franco	.50
12	Todd Pratt	.50
13	Brian McRae	.50
14	Bobby Jones	.50
15	John Olerud	1.50
16	Todd Hundley	.75
17	Jay Payton	.75
18	Paul Wilson	.75

A player's name in *italic* type indicates a rookie card.

1998 Pinnacle Snapshots Orioles

		MT
Complete Set (18):		20.00
Common Player:		.50
1	Cal Ripken Jr.	5.00
2	Rocky Coppinger	.50
3	Eric Davis	.75
4	Chris Hoiles	.50
5	Mike Mussina	2.50
6	Joe Carter	.75
7	Rafael Palmeiro	1.50
8	B.J. Surhoff	.75
9	Jimmy Key	.50
10	Scott Erickson	.50
11	Armando Benitez	.50
12	Roberto Alomar	2.00
13	Cal Ripken Jr.	5.00
14	Mike Bordick	.50
15	Roberto Alomar	2.00
16	Jeffrey Hammonds	.50
17	Rafael Palmeiro	1.50
18	Brady Anderson	1.00

1998 Pinnacle Snapshots Rangers

		MT
Complete Set (18):		12.50
Common Player:		.50
1	Ivan Rodriguez	2.50
2	Fernando Tatis	1.00
3	Danny Patterson	.50
4	Will Clark	1.50
5	Kevin Elster	.50
6	Rusty Greer	.75
7	Darren Oliver	.50
8	John Burkett	.50
9	Tom Goodwin	.50
10	Roberto Kelly	.50
11	Aaron Sele	.75
12	Rick Helling	.50
13	Mark McLemore	.50
14	Lee Stevens	.50
15	John Wetteland	.50
16	Will Clark	1.50
17	Juan Gonzalez	3.00
18	Roger Pavlik	.50

1998 Pinnacle Snapshots Red Sox

		MT
Complete Set (18):		13.50
Common Player:		.50
1	Tim Naehring	.50
2	Brian Rose	.50
3	Darren Bragg	.50
4	Pedro Martinez	2.00
5	Mo Vaughn	1.50
6	Jim Leyritz	.50
7	Troy O'Leary	.50
8	Mo Vaughn	1.50
9	Nomar Garciaparra	3.00
10	Michael Coleman	.50
11	Tom Gordon	.50
12	Tim Naehring	.50
13	Nomar Garciaparra	3.00
14	John Valentin	.75
15	Steve Avery	.50
16	Damon Buford	.50
17	Troy O'Leary	.50
18	Bret Saberhagen	.75

1998 Pinnacle Snapshots Rockies

		MT
Complete Set (18):		12.00
Common Player:		.50
1	Larry Walker	2.00
2	Pedro Astacio	.50
3	Jamey Wright	.50
4	Darryl Kile	.75
5	Kirt Manwaring	.50
6	Todd Helton	2.50
7	Mike Lansing	.50
8	Neifi Perez	.50
9	Dante Bichette	1.00
10	Derrick Gibson	.50
11	Neifi Perez	.50
12	Darryl Kile	.75
13	Larry Walker	2.00
14	Roger Bailey	.50
15	Ellis Burks	.75
16	Dante Bichette	1.00
17	Derrick Gibson	.50
18	Ellis Burks	.75

1998 Pinnacle Snapshots Yankees

		MT
Complete Set (18):		18.00
Common Player:		.75
1	Andy Pettitte	1.50
2	Darryl Strawberry	.75
3	Joe Girardi	.75
4	Derek Jeter	4.00
5	Andy Pettitte	1.50
6	Tim Raines	.75
7	Mariano Rivera	1.50
8	Tino Martinez	.75
9	Derek Jeter	4.00
10	Hideki Irabu	.75
11	Tino Martinez	.75
12	David Cone	1.00
13	Bernie Williams	1.50
14	David Cone	1.00
15	Bernie Williams	1.50
16	Chuck Knoblauch	.75
17	Paul O'Neill	.75
18	David Wells	.75

2001 Playoff Absolute Memorabilia

		MT
Complete Set (200):		NA
Common Player:		.50
Common SP (151-200):		15.00
Production 700		
Pack (6):		8.00
Box (18) w/baseball:		160.00
1	Alex Rodriguez	5.00
2	Barry Bonds	3.00
3	Cal Ripken Jr.	6.00
4	Chipper Jones	4.00
5	Derek Jeter	6.00
6	Troy Glaus	2.00
7	Frank Thomas	2.00
8	Greg Maddux	4.00
9	Ivan Rodriguez	2.00
10	Jeff Bagwell	2.50
11	Ryan Dempster	.50
12	Todd Helton	2.00
13	Ken Griffey Jr.	5.00
14	Manny Ramirez	2.00
15	Mark McGwire	6.00
16	Mike Piazza	5.00
17	Nomar Garciaparra	5.00
18	Pedro Martinez	2.50
19	Randy Johnson	2.00
20	Rick Ankiel	.50
21	Rickey Henderson	.75
22	Roger Clemens	3.00
23	Sammy Sosa	4.00
24	Tony Gwynn	2.50
25	Vladimir Guerrero	2.50
26	Kazuhiro Sasaki	.50
27	Roberto Alomar	1.50
28	Barry Zito	.50
29	Pat Burrell	1.00
30	Harold Baines	.50
31	Carlos Delgado	1.50
32	J.D. Drew	.75
33	Jim Edmonds	.50
34	Darin Erstad	.75
35	Jason Giambi	1.50
36	Tom Glavine	.75
37	Juan Gonzalez	2.00
38	Mark Grace	1.00
39	Shawn Green	.50
40	Tim Hudson	.50
41	Andruw Jones	1.50
42	David Justice	1.00
43	Jeff Kent	.50
44	Barry Larkin	.75
45	Rafael Furcal	.75
46	Mike Mussina	1.00
47	Hideo Nomo	1.00
48	Rafael Palmeiro	1.00
49	Adam Piatt	1.00
50	Scott Rolen	1.00
51	Gary Sheffield	.75
52	Bernie Williams	1.50
53	Bob Abreu	.50
54	Edgardo Alfonzo	.50
55	Edgar Renteria	.50
56	Phil Nevin	.50
57	Craig Biggio	.75
58	Andres Galarraga	.75
59	Edgar Martinez	.50
60	Fred McGriff	.75
61	Magglio Ordonez	.75
62	Jim Thome	.75
63	Matt Williams	.75
64	Kerry Wood	.75
65	Moises Alou	.50
66	Brady Anderson	.50
67	Garret Anderson	.50
68	Russell Branyan	.50
69	Tony Batista	.50
70	Vernon Wells	.50
71	Carlos Beltran	.50
72	Adrian Beltre	.50
73	Kris Benson	.50
74	Lance Berkman	.75
75	Kevin Brown	.50
76	Dee Brown	.50
77	Jeromy Burnitz	.50
78	Timoniel Perez	.50
79	Sean Casey	.75
80	Luis Castillo	.50
81	Eric Chavez	.75
82	Jeff Cirillo	.50
83	Bartolo Colon	.50
84	David Cone	.50
85	Freddy Garcia	.50
86	Johnny Damon	.50
87	Ray Durham	.50
88	Jermaine Dye	.50
89	Juan Encarnacion	.50
90	Terrence Long	.50
91	Carl Everett	.50
92	Steve Finley	.50
93	Cliff Floyd	.50
94	Brad Fullmer	.50
95	Brian Giles	.50
96	Luis Gonzalez	1.00
97	Rusty Greer	.50
98	Jeffrey Hammonds	.50
99	Mike Hampton	.50
100	Orlando Hernandez	.50
101	Richard Hidalgo	.75
102	Geoff Jenkins	.75
103	Jacque Jones	.50
104	Brian Jordan	.50
105	Gabe Kapler	.75
106	Eric Karros	.50
107	Jason Kendall	.50
108	Adam Kennedy	.50
109	Deion Sanders	.50
110	Ryan Klesko	.50
111	Chuck Knoblauch	.50
112	Paul Konerko	.50
113	Carlos Lee	.50
114	Kenny Lofton	.75
115	Javy Lopez	.50
116	Tino Martinez	.50
117	Ruben Mateo	.50
118	Kevin Millwood	.50
119	Jimmy Rollins	.50
120	Raul Mondesi	.50
121	Trot Nixon	.50
122	John Olerud	1.00
123	Paul O'Neill	.75
124	Chan Ho Park	.75
125	Andy Pettitte	.75
126	Jorge Posada	.75
127	Mark Quinn	.50
128	Aramis Ramirez	.50
129	Mariano Rivera	.75
130	Tim Salmon	.75
131	Curt Schilling	.75
132	Richie Sexson	.50
133	John Smoltz	.50
134	J.T. Snow	.50
135	Jay Payton	.50
136	Shannon Stewart	.50
137	B.J. Surhoff	.50
138	Mike Sweeney	.50
139	Fernando Tatis	.50
140	Miguel Tejada	.75
141	Jason Varitek	.50
142	Greg Vaughn	.50
143	Mo Vaughn	.50
144	Robin Ventura	.50
145	Jose Vidro	.50
146	Omar Vizquel	.50
147	Larry Walker	1.00
148	David Wells	.50
149	Rondell White	.50
150	Preston Wilson	.50
151	*Eddie Oropesa*	15.00
		.50
152	*Cory Aldridge*	15.00
153	*Wilmy Caceres*	15.00
154	Josh Beckett	15.00
155	*Wilson Betemit*	35.00
156	*Jason Michaels*	15.00
157	*Albert Pujols*	100.00
158	*Andres Torres*	15.00
159	*Jack Wilson*	15.00
160	Alex Escobar	20.00
161	Ben Sheets	30.00
162	*Rafael Soriano*	15.00
163	*Nate Frese*	15.00
164	*Carlos Garcia*	15.00
165	*Brandon Larson*	15.00
166	*Alexis Gomez*	15.00
167	Jason Hart	20.00
168	Nick Johnson	20.00
169	*Donaldo Mendez*	15.00
170	*Christian Parker*	15.00
171	*Jackson Melian*	30.00
172	Jack Cust	15.00
173	*Adrian Hernandez*	20.00
174	Joe Crede	15.00
175	*Jose Mieses*	15.00
176	Roy Oswalt	20.00
177	Eric Munson	15.00
178	Xavier Nady	20.00
179	*Horacio Ramirez*	15.00
180	Abraham Nunez	15.00
181	Jose Ortiz	15.00
182	*Jeremy Owens*	15.00
183	*Claudio Vargas*	15.00
184	Marcus Giles	15.00

185	Aubrey Huff	15.00
186	C.C. Sabathia	20.00
187	Adam Dunn	50.00
188	*Adam Pettyjohn*	15.00
189	*Elpidio Guzman*	15.00
190	*Jay Gibbons*	15.00
191	*Wilkin Ruan*	15.00
192	*Tsuyoshi Shinjo*	25.00
193	Alfonso Soriano	25.00
194	Corey Patterson	25.00
195	*Ichiro Suzuki*	150.00
196	*Billy Sylvester*	15.00
197	*Juan Uribe*	20.00
198	*Johnny Estrada*	15.00
199	*Carlos Valderrama*	15.00
200	*Matt White*	20.00

2001 Playoff Absolute Memorabilia Spectrum

	MT
Stars (1-150):	
Production 10	
Rk's (151-200):	2-4X
Production 25	

2001 Playoff Absolute Memorabilia Ballpark Souvenirs

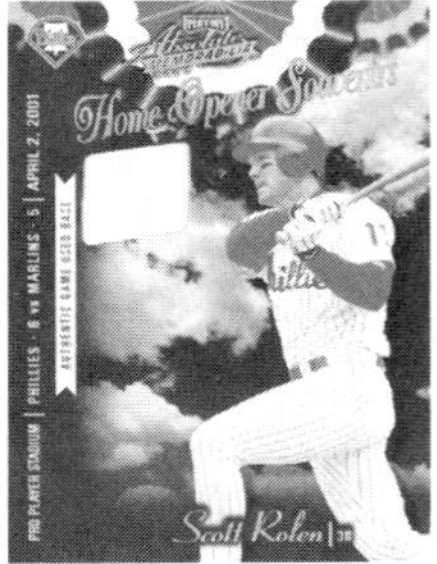

		MT
Common Player:		10.00
Production 400 sets		
Doubles:		1-1.5X
Production 200 sets		
Triples:		1.5-3X
Production 75 sets		
Home Runs:		3-5X
Production 25 sets		
1	Barry Bonds	30.00
2	Cal Ripken Jr.	50.00
3	Pedro Martinez	25.00
4	Troy Glaus	15.00
5	Frank Thomas	20.00
6	Alex Rodriguez	30.00
7	Ivan Rodriguez	15.00
8	Jeff Bagwell	20.00
9	Mark McGwire	50.00
10	Todd Helton	20.00
11	Gary Sheffield	10.00
12	Manny Ramirez	20.00
13	Mike Piazza	30.00
14	Sammy Sosa	25.00
15	Preston Wilson	10.00
16	Tony Gwynn	25.00
17	Vladimir Guerrero	20.00
18	Carlos Delgado	15.00
19	Roberto Alomar	20.00
20	Todd Helton	20.00
21	Albert Pujols	70.00
22	Jason Giambi	15.00
23	Sammy Sosa	25.00
24	Ken Griffey Jr.	30.00
25	Darin Erstad	15.00
26	Mark McGwire	50.00
27	Carlos Delgado	15.00
28	Juan Gonzalez	15.00
29	Mike Sweeney	10.00
30	Alex Rodriguez	30.00
31	Roger Clemens	25.00
32	Tsuyoshi Shinjo	30.00
33	Ben Grieve	10.00
34	Jeff Kent	10.00
35	Vladimir Guerrero	20.00
36	Shawn Green	15.00
37	Rafael Palmeiro	15.00
38	Tony Gwynn	25.00
39	Scott Rolen	15.00
40	Ken Griffey Jr.	30.00
41	Albert Pujols	70.00
42	Barry Bonds	30.00
43	Mark Grace	20.00
44	Bernie Williams	15.00
45	Frank Thomas	20.00
46	Jermaine Dye	10.00
47	Mike Piazza	30.00
48	Chipper Jones	20.00
49	Richie Sexson	10.00
50	Magglio Ordonez	10.00

2001 Playoff Absolute Memorabilia Ball Hoggs

		MT
Common Player:		20.00
Production 75 unless noted		
1	Vladimir Guerrero	30.00
2	Troy Glaus	30.00
3	Tony Gwynn	40.00
4	Cal Ripken/125	100.00
5	Todd Helton	30.00
6	Jacque Jones/125	20.00
7	Shawn Green/100	20.00
8	Ichiro Suzuki	400.00
9	Scott Rolen	20.00
10	Roger Clemens	50.00
11	Ken Griffey/25	125.00
14	Sammy Sosa	50.00
15	J.D. Drew	25.00
16	Barry Bonds	50.00
17	Pat Burrell	25.00
18	Mark McGwire/100	160.00
19	Mike Piazza	60.00
20	Magglio Ordonez	20.00
21	Miguel Tejada	20.00
22	Albert Pujols/100	150.00
23	Derek Jeter	100.00
24	Johnny Damon	20.00
25	Mike Sweeney	20.00
26	Ben Grieve	20.00
27	Jeff Kent	20.00
28	Andres Galarraga	20.00
29	Richie Sexson	20.00
30	Juan Encarnacion	20.00
31	Ruben Mateo	20.00
33	Manny Ramirez	30.00
35	Ivan Rodriguez	30.00
36	Darin Erstad	25.00
37	Carlos Delgado	25.00
38	Jeff Bagwell	30.00
39	Jermaine Dye	20.00
40	Jose Ortiz	20.00
41	Gary Sheffield	20.00
42	Eric Chavez	20.00
43	Mark Grace	40.00
44	Rafael Palmeiro	25.00
45	Tsuyoshi Shinjo/100	90.00
46	Terrence Long	20.00
47	Carlos Delgado/25	40.00
48	Frank Thomas	40.00
49	Chipper Jones/25	75.00
50	Jason Giambi	30.00

2001 Playoff Absolute Memorabilia Boss Hoggs

		MT
Common Player:		30.00
Production 25 sets		
4	Cal Ripken	175.00
6	Jacque Jones	40.00
7	Shawn Green	40.00
8	Ichiro Suzuki	600.00
9	Scott Rolen	40.00
11	Ken Griffey	125.00
14	Sammy Sosa	80.00
15	J.D. Drew	40.00
16	Barry Bonds	80.00
17	Pat Burrell	40.00
18	Mark McGwire	240.00
19	Mike Piazza	125.00
20	Magglio Ordonez	30.00
21	Miguel Tejada	30.00
23	Derek Jeter	150.00
24	Johnny Damon	30.00
25	Mike Sweeney	30.00
26	Ben Grieve	30.00
27	Jeff Kent	30.00
28	Andres Galarraga	30.00
29	Richie Sexson	30.00
30	Juan Encarnacion	30.00
31	Ruben Mateo	30.00
33	Manny Ramirez	30.00
35	Ivan Rodriguez	50.00
36	Darin Erstad	35.00
37	Carlos Delgado	40.00
38	Jeff Bagwell	50.00
39	Jermaine Dye	30.00
40	Jose Ortiz	30.00
42	Eric Chavez	30.00
43	Mark Grace	75.00
44	Rafael Palmeiro	40.00
45	Tsuyoshi Shinjo	100.00
46	Terrence Long	30.00
47	Carlos Delgado	40.00
48	Frank Thomas	60.00
50	Jason Giambi	40.00

2001 Playoff Absolute Memorabilia Rookie Premiere Autos

		MT
Common Autograph:		30.00
Production 25 sets		
151	Eddie Oropesa	30.00
152	Cory Aldridge	40.00
154	Josh Beckett	40.00
155	Wilson Betemit	
157	Albert Pujols	350.00
158	Andres Torres	40.00
160	Alex Escobar	40.00
161	Ben Sheets	
162	Rafael Soriano	
164	Carlos Garcia	30.00
165	Brandon Larson	40.00
167	Jason Hart	50.00
168	Nick Johnson	50.00
169	Donaldo Mendez	30.00
170	Christian Parker	30.00
171	Jackson Melian	
173	Adrian Hernandez	30.00
174	Joe Crede	40.00
175	Jose Mieses	40.00
176	Roy Oswalt	
178	Xavier Nady	40.00
179	Horacio Ramirez	30.00
180	Abraham Nunez	30.00
181	Jose Ortiz	40.00
182	Jeremy Owens	30.00
183	Claudio Vargas	30.00
184	Marcus Giles	40.00
186	C.C. Sabathia	50.00
187	Adam Dunn	
188	Adam Pettyjohn	30.00
190	Jay Gibbons	40.00
191	Wilkin Ruan	30.00
193	Alfonso Soriano	
194	Corey Patterson	75.00
196	Billy Sylvester	30.00
197	Juan Uribe	40.00
198	Johnny Estrada	30.00
199	Carlos Valderrama	30.00
200	Matt White	30.00

2001 Playoff Absolute Memor. Signing Bonus Baseball

	MT
Common Auto. Baseball:	20.00
Inserted 1:box	
Al Oliver/500	25.00
Andre Dawson/550	40.00
Barry Bonds/25	
Bill Madlock/525	20.00
Bill Mazeroski/25	100.00
Billy Williams/325	35.00
Bob Feller/550	40.00
Bob Gibson/25	125.00
Bobby Doerr/300	40.00
Bobby Richardson/500	30.00
Boog Powell/500	30.00
Brian Jordan/25	
Bucky Dent/500	20.00
Charles Johnson/25	50.00
Chipper Jones/25	
Clete Boyer/500	35.00
Dale Murphy/25	
Dave Concepcion/500	20.00
Dave Kingman/500	20.00
Don Larsen/200	50.00
Don Newcombe/500	25.00
Don Zimmer/500	40.00
Duke Snider/25	150.00
Earl Weaver/300	40.00
Enos Slaughter/525	30.00
Fergie Jenkins/1000	20.00
Frank Howard/500	25.00
Frank Robinson/25	150.00
Frank Thomas/25	150.00
Gary Carter/200	50.00
Gaylord Perry/1000	25.00
George Foster/500	25.00
George Kell/300	40.00
Goose Gossage/500	25.00
Greg Maddux/25	
Hank Aaron/25	
Hank Bauer/500	25.00
Harmon Killebrew/200	75.00
Henry Rodriguez/400	20.00
Herb Score/500	20.00
Hoyt Wilhelm/500	25.00
J.D. Drew/75	
Javy Lopez/25	60.00
Jim Edmonds/25	75.00
Jim Palmer/500	40.00
Joe Pepitone/500	40.00
Johnny Bench/25	200.00
Johnny Podres/500	35.00
Juan Marichal/485	40.00
Kirby Puckett/25	
Larry Doby/300	40.00
Lou Brock/25	
Luis Tiant/500	20.00
Magglio Ordonez/200	40.00
Manny Ramirez/25	
Maury Wills/500	30.00
Mike Schmidt/25	
Minnie Minoso/1000	20.00
Monte Irvin/500	30.00
Moose Skowron/500	25.00
Nolan Ryan/25	400.00
Ozzie Smith/25	150.00
Phil Rizzuto/25	
Ralph Kiner/100	50.00
Randy Johnson/25	200.00
Red Schoendienst/500	35.00
Reggie Jackson/25	
Rickey Henderson/25	150.00
Robin Roberts/500	40.00
Roger Clemens/25	
Rollie Fingers/575	25.00
Ryne Sandberg/25	150.00

Sean Casey/25
Stan Musial/25
Steve Carlton/25
Steve Garvey/ 1000 25.00
Todd Helton/25 150.00
Tom Glavine/25 100.00
Tom Seaver/25
Tommy John/ 1000 20.00
Tony Gwynn/25
Tony Perez/400 40.00
Wade Boggs/25 125.00
Warren Spahn/ 500 50.00
Whitey Ford/25 150.00
Willie Mays/25 400.00
Willie McCovey/ 25 125.00
Willie Stargell/25
Yogi Berra/25

2001 Playoff Absolute Memorabilia Tools Of The Trade

MT

Common Player: 15.00
Jerseys (1-20):
Production 300
Bats (21-40):
Production 125
Batting Glove (41-45):
Production 50
Hat (46-50):
Production 100

1 Vladimir Guerrero 25.00
2 Troy Glaus 25.00
3 Tony Gwynn 35.00
4 Todd Helton 25.00
5 Scott Rolen 20.00
6 Roger Clemens 40.00
7 Pedro Martinez 50.00
8 Richie Sexson 15.00
9 Magglio Ordonez 15.00
10 Ben Grieve 15.00
11 Jeff Bagwell 25.00
12 Edgar Martinez 15.00
13 Greg Maddux 40.00
15 Frank Thomas 25.00
16 Edgardo Alfonzo 15.00
17 Cal Ripken Jr. 75.00
18 Jose Vidro 15.00
19 Andruw Jones 20.00
21 Barry Bonds 75.00
22 Juan Gonzalez 40.00
23 Andruw Jones 35.00
24 Cal Ripken Jr. 125.00
25 Greg Maddux 75.00
26 Manny Ramirez 40.00
27 Roberto Alomar
28 Shawn Green 30.00
29 Edgardo Alfonzo 25.00
30 Rafael Palmeiro 40.00
31 Hideo Nomo 250.00
32 Andres Galarraga 35.00
33 Todd Helton 40.00
34 Darin Erstad 25.00
35 Ivan Rodriguez 40.00
36 Sean Casey 30.00
37 Vladimir Guerrero 50.00
39 Troy Glaus
40 Jeff Bagwell 50.00
41 Barry Bonds 150.00
42 Cal Ripken Jr. 180.00
43 Roberto Alomar 70.00
44 Sean Casey 50.00
45 Tony Gwynn
46 Bernie Williams 40.00
47 Barry Zito 30.00
48 Greg Maddux
49 Tom Glavine
50 Troy Glaus

A card number in parentheses ( ) indicates the set is unnumbered.

2002 Playoff Absolute Memorabilia

MT

Complete Set (200): NA
Common Player: .50
Common Rk/Prospect (151-200): 5.00
Production 1,000
Spectrum (1-150): 3-5X
Spectrum (151-200): .5-1.5X
Pack (6): 5.00
Box + 8X10: 175.00

1 David Eckstein .50
2 Darin Erstad .75
3 Troy Glaus .75
4 Garret Anderson .75
5 Tim Salmon .75
6 Curt Schilling 1.00
7 Randy Johnson 1.50
8 Luis Gonzalez .75
9 Mark Grace .75
10 Tom Glavine .75
11 Greg Maddux 2.00
12 Chipper Jones 2.00
13 Gary Sheffield .75
14 John Smoltz .50
15 Andruw Jones .75
16 Wilson Betemit .50
17 Tony Batista .50
18 Javier Vazquez .50
19 Scott Erickson .50
20 Josh Towers .50
21 Pedro J. Martinez 1.50
22 Johnny Damon .50
23 Manny Ramirez 1.00
24 Rickey Henderson .75
25 Trot Nixon .50
26 Nomar Garciaparra 3.00
27 Juan Cruz .50
28 Kerry Wood .75
29 Fred McGriff .75
30 Moises Alou .50
31 Sammy Sosa 2.50
32 Corey Patterson .50
33 Mark Buehrle .50
34 Keith Foulke .50
35 Frank Thomas 1.00
36 Kenny Lofton .50
37 Magglio Ordonez .50
38 Barry Larkin .75
39 Ken Griffey Jr. 2.00
40 Adam Dunn 1.00
41 Juan Encarnacion .50
42 Sean Casey .50
43 Bartolo Colon .50
44 C.C. Sabathia .50
45 Travis Fryman .50
46 Jim Thome 1.00
47 Omar Vizquel .50
48 Ellis Burks .50
49 Russell Branyan .50
50 Mike Hampton .50
51 Todd Helton .75
52 Jose Ortiz .50
53 Juan Uribe .50
54 Juan Pierre .50
55 Larry Walker .75
56 Mike Rivera .50
57 Robert Fick .50
58 Bobby Higginson .50
59 Josh Beckett .50
60 Richard Hidalgo .50
61 Cliff Floyd .50
62 Mike Lowell .50
63 Roy Oswalt .75
64 Morgan Ensberg .50
65 Jeff Bagwell 1.00
66 Craig Biggio .75
67 Lance Berkman 1.00
68 Carlos Beltran .50
69 Mike Sweeney .50
70 Neifi Perez .50
71 Kevin Brown .50
72 Hideo Nomo .75
73 Paul LoDuca .50
74 Adrian Beltre .50
75 Shawn Green .75
76 Eric Karros .50
77 Brad Radke .50
78 Corey Koskie .50
79 Doug Mientkiewicz .50
80 Torii Hunter .50
81 Jacque Jones .50
82 Ben Sheets .50
83 Richie Sexson .75
84 Geoff Jenkins .50
85 Tony Armas .50
86 Michael Barrett .50
87 Jose Vidro .50
88 Vladimir Guerrero 1.25
89 Roger Clemens 2.00
90 Derek Jeter 4.00
91 Bernie Williams .75
92 Jason Giambi 2.00
93 Jorge Posada .75
94 Mike Mussina .75
95 Andy Pettitte .75
96 Nick Johnson .75
97 Alfonso Soriano 4.00
98 Shawn Estes .50
99 Al Leiter .75
100 Mike Piazza 3.00
101 Roberto Alomar .75
102 Mo Vaughn .50
103 Jeromy Burnitz .50
104 Tim Hudson .75
105 Barry Zito .75
106 Mark Mulder .75
107 Eric Chavez .75
108 Miguel Tejada .75
109 Jeremy Giambi .50
110 Jermaine Dye .50
111 Mike Lieberthal .50
112 Scott Rolen .75
113 Pat Burrell .75
114 Brandon Duckworth .50
115 Bobby Abreu .50
116 Jason Kendall .50
117 Aramis Ramirez .50
118 Brian Giles .75
119 Pokey Reese .50
120 Phil Nevin .50
121 Ryan Klesko .50
122 Carlos Pena .50
123 Trevor Hoffman .50
124 Barry Bonds 3.00
125 Rich Aurilia .50
126 Jeff Kent .75
127 Tsuyoshi Shinjo .50
128 Ichiro Suzuki 3.00
129 Edgar Martinez .50
130 Freddy Garcia .50
131 Bret Boone .50
132 Matt Morris .50
133 Tino Martinez .50
134 Albert Pujols 2.00
135 J.D. Drew .75
136 Jim Edmonds .75
137 Gabe Kapler .50
138 Paul Wilson .50
139 Ben Grieve .50
140 Wade Miller .50
141 Chan Ho Park .50
142 Alex Rodriguez 4.00
143 Rafael Palmeiro .75
144 Juan Gonzalez .75
145 Ivan Rodriguez .75
146 Carlos Delgado .75
147 Jose Cruz Jr. .50
148 Shannon Stewart .50
149 Raul Mondesi .50
150 Vernon Wells .50
151 *So Taguchi* 8.00
152 *Kazuhisa Ishii* 10.00
153 Hank Blalock 8.00
154 Sean Burroughs 6.00
155 Geronimo Gil 5.00
156 Jon Rauch 5.00
157 Fernando Rodney 5.00
158 *Miguel Asencio* 5.00
159 *Franklyn German* 5.00
160 *Luis Ugueto* 5.00
161 *Jorge Sosa* 5.00
162 *Felix Escalona* 5.00
163 Colby Lewis 5.00
164 Mark Teixeira 8.00
165 Mark Prior 15.00
166 *Francis Beltran* 5.00
167 Joe Thurston 5.00
168 *Earl Snyder* 5.00
169 *Takahito Nomura* 5.00
170 Bill Hall 5.00
171 Marlon Byrd 5.00
172 Dave Williams 5.00
173 Yorvit Torrealba 5.00
174 *Brandon Backe* 8.00
175 Jorge de la Rosa 5.00
176 *Brian Mallette* 8.00
177 *Rodrigo Rosario* 6.00
178 *Anderson Machado* 5.00
179 *Jorge Padilla* 8.00
180 *Allan Simpson* 5.00
181 *Doug Devore* 8.00
182 *Steve Bechler* 8.00
183 Raul Chavez 5.00
184 *Tom Shearn* 5.00
185 *Ben Howard* 5.00
186 *Chris Baker* 5.00
187 *Travis Hughes* 5.00
188 Kevin Mench 5.00
189 Drew Henson 5.00
190 *Mike Moriarty* 20.00
191 *Corey Thurman* 5.00
192 Bobby Hill 5.00
193 *Steve Kent* 8.00
194 *Satoru Komiyama* 5.00
195 Jason Lane 5.00
196 Angel Berroa 5.00
197 *Brandon Puffer* 8.00
198 *Brian Fitzgerald* 5.00
199 *Rene Reyes* 8.00
200 Hee Seop Choi 8.00

2002 Playoff Absolute Memorabilia Absolutely Ink

MT

Common Autograph: 6.00
Inserted 1:27
Gold Parallel #'d to 25 not priced
Jsy Parallel #'d to Jsy # not priced

Adrian Beltre 10.00
Alex Rodriguez/50
Ben Sheets 10.00
Bernie Williams/25
Bobby Doerr 15.00
Blaine Neal 6.00
Carlos Beltran 8.00
Carlos Pena 10.00
Corey Patterson/150
Curt Schilling/15
Dave Parker 12.00
David Justice/65 25.00
Don Mattingly/75
Duaner Sanchez 6.00
Eric Chavez/100
Freddy Garcia 15.00
Gary Carter 30.00
Gary Sheffield/25
George Brett/25
Greg Maddux/25

Ivan Rodriguez/50
J.D. Drew/100 35.00
Jack Cust 8.00
Jason Michaels 6.00
Jermaine Dye/125 15.00
Jose Vidro 8.00
Josh Towers 6.00
Kerry Wood/50
Kirby Puckett/50
Luis Gonzalez/75 25.00
Luis Rivera 6.00
Manny Ramirez/50 50.00
Marcus Giles 10.00
Mark Prior/100 60.00
Mark Teixeira/100 35.00
Marlon Byrd/250 25.00
Matt Ginter 6.00
Moises Alou/150 10.00
Nate Frese 6.00
Nick Johnson 20.00
Nomar Garciaparra/15
Pablo Ozuna 6.00
Paul LoDuca/200 20.00
Richie Sexson 12.00
Roberto Alomar/100 45.00
Roy Oswalt/300 25.00
Ryan Klesko/75 20.00
Sean Casey/125 15.00
Shannon Stewart 8.00
So Taguchi 25.00
Terrence Long 8.00
Timoniel Perez 8.00
Todd Helton/25
Tony Gwynn/50
Troy Glaus/300 20.00
Vladimir Guerrero/225 40.00
Wade Miller 15.00
Wilson Betemit 12.00

2002 Playoff Absolute Memorabilia Signing Bonus

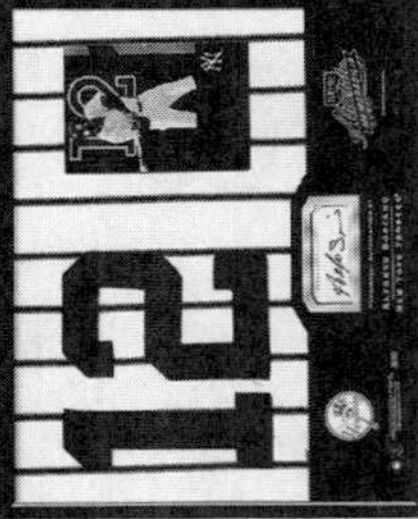

MT

Common Player:
Bobby Abreu/53
Grover Alexander/1
Roberto Alomar/12
Roberto Alomar/100 60.00
Moises Alou/18
Moises Alou/250 40.00
Jeff Bagwell/5
Carlos Beltran/15
Carlos Beltran/50
Adrian Beltre/29
Adrian Beltre/150 35.00
Lance Berkman/17
Angel Berroa/4
Angel Berroa/50
Angel Berroa/100 30.00
Wilson Betemit/250 30.00
Craig Biggio/7
Hank Blalock/12
Hank Blalock/50
Hank Blalock/100 50.00
George Brett/5
Lou Brock/100 60.00
Lou Brock/200 60.00
Kevin Brown/27
Kevin Brown/100
Kevin Brown/150
Mark Buehrle/56
Mark Buehrle/200 50.00
Sean Burroughs/21
Marlon Byrd/61
Steve Carlton/100 85.00
Steve Carlton/150
Sean Casey/21
Sean Casey/100
Eric Chavez/3
Eric Chavez/25
Eric Chavez/28
Roger Clemens/10
Ty Cobb/6
Eddie Collins/1
Juan Cruz/51
J.D. Drew/7
J.D. Drew/100 65.00
Brandon Duckworth/56
Brandon Duckworth/150 35.00
Adam Dunn/10
Adam Dunn/44
Jermaine Dye/100 40.00
Jermaine Dye/250 40.00
Morgan Ensberg/100 40.00
Darin Erstad/5
Darin Erstad/17
Cliff Floyd/200 40.00
Jimmie Foxx/1
Freddy Garcia/34
Freddy Garcia/125 35.00
Nomar Garciaparra/5
Troy Glaus/50
Troy Glaus/100
Tom Glavine/25
Tom Glavine/200 75.00
Luis Gonzalez/20
Luis Gonzalez/125 85.00
Hank Greenberg/1
Vladimir Guerrero/27
Vladimir Guerrero/150 150.00
Tony Gwynn/19
Richard Hidalgo/15
Richard Hidalgo/100 30.00
Richard Hidalgo/135 30.00
Richard Hidalgo/150 30.00
Rogers Hornsby/1
Tim Hudson/15
Tim Hudson/50
Tim Hudson/100 65.00
Kazuhisa Ishii/17
Reggie Jackson/44
Nick Johnson/200 55.00
Walter Johnson/4
Andruw Jones/25
Andruw Jones/75
Chipper Jones/10
Al Kaline/6
Al Kaline/250
Gabe Kapler/18
Gabe Kapler/125 35.00
Gabe Kapler/175 35.00
Ryan Klesko/30
Nap Lajoie/1
Jason Lane/100 35.00
Barry Larkin/11
Barry Larkin/50
Barry Larkin/100
Paul LoDuca/16
Paul LoDuca/50
Fred Lynn/150 40.00
Fred Lynn/250 40.00
Connie Mack/2
Greg Maddux/31
Roger Maris/3
Edgar Martinez/11
Edgar Martinez/150 55.00
Pedro J. Martinez/5
Pedro J. Martinez/45
Don Mattingly/100 175.00
Willie McCovey/190 70.00
Willie McCovey/250 60.00
Wade Miller/52
Wade Miller/150 35.00
Wade Miller/250 35.00
Paul Molitor/75 60.00
Paul Molitor/100 60.00
Paul Molitor/125 60.00
Mark Mulder/20
Mark Mulder/40
Mike Mussina/5
Jose Ortiz/125 25.00
Roy Oswalt/44
Roy Oswalt/100
Mel Ott/3
Rafael Palmeiro/25
Jim Palmer/150 40.00
Jim Palmer/250 40.00
Dave Parker/150 45.00
Corey Patterson/20
Corey Patterson/250 40.00
Carlos Pena/19
Carlos Pena/150 40.00
Carlos Pena/250 40.00
Tony Perez/24 65.00
Tony Perez/250 50.00
Juan Pierre/75
Mark Prior/22
Mark Prior/50
Mark Prior/75
Mark Prior/125
Kirby Puckett/34
Albert Pujols/5
Albert Pujols/100 135.00
Aramis Ramirez/16
Aramis Ramirez/50
Aramis Ramirez/125 40.00
Manny Ramirez/5
Manny Ramirez/24
Phil Rizzuto/10 265.00
Phil Rizzuto/250 70.00
Brooks Robinson/150 70.00
Brooks Robinson/250 60.00
Jackie Robinson/3
Alex Rodriguez/3
Alex Rodriguez/15
Ivan Rodriguez/7
Scott Rolen/17
Babe Ruth/8
Nolan Ryan/30
Nolan Ryan/34
C.C. Sabathia/10
C.C. Sabathia/15
Ryne Sandberg/23
Ryne Sandberg/50
Curt Schilling/5
Curt Schilling/10
Mike Schmidt/100 100.00
Richie Sexson/100 40.00
Ben Sheets/100 40.00
Ben Sheets/150 40.00
Gary Sheffield/11
George Sisler/3
Alfonso Soriano/12
Alfonso Soriano/100 180.00
Tris Speaker/1
Shannon Stewart/24
Shannon Stewart/100 40.00
Shannon Stewart/150 40.00
Mike Sweeney/100
So Taguchi/99 35.00
Mark Teixeira/23
Mark Teixeira/100 55.00
Miguel Tejada/4
Miguel Tejada/40
Miguel Tejada/50
Frank Thomas/10
Frank Thomas/35
Juan Uribe/4
Juan Uribe/25
Javier Vazquez/125 35.00
Jose Vidro/150 35.00
Honus Wagner/11
Bernie Williams/15
Ted Williams/1
Hack Wilson/1
Dave Winfield/25
Kerry Wood/34
Cy Young/2
Barry Zito/25
Barry Zito/50

2002 Playoff Absolute Memorabilia Team Quads

		MT
Complete Set (20):		125.00
Common Card:		3.00
Inserted 1:18		
Golds:		2X
Inserted 1:72		
1	Troy Glaus, Darin Erstad, Garret Anderson, Troy Percival	3.00
2	Curt Schilling, Randy Johnson, Luis Gonzalez, Mark Grace	6.00
3	Chipper Jones, Andruw Jones, Greg Maddux, Tom Glavine	10.00
4	Nomar Garciaparra, Manny Ramirez, Trot Nixon, Pedro J. Martinez	12.00
5	Kerry Wood, Sammy Sosa, Fred McGriff, Moises Alou	10.00
6	Frank Thomas, Magglio Ordonez, Mark Buehrle, Kenny Lofton	5.00
7	Ken Griffey Jr., Barry Larkin, Juan Encarnacion, Sean Casey	10.00
8	C.C. Sabathia, Jim Thome, Bartolo Colon, Russell Branyan	5.00
9	Todd Helton, Larry Walker, Juan Pierre, Mike Hampton	4.00
10	Jeff Bagwell, Craig Biggio, Lance Berkman, Richard Hidalgo	6.00
11	Shawn Green, Adrian Beltre, Hideo Nomo, Paul LoDuca	4.00
12	Mike Piazza, Roberto Alomar, Mo Vaughn, Roger Cedeno	12.00
13	Roger Clemens, Derek Jeter, Jason Giambi, Mike Mussina	20.00
14	Barry Zito, Tim Hudson, Eric Chavez, Miguel Tejada	8.00
15	Pat Burrell, Scott Rolen, Bobby Abreu, Marlon Byrd	4.00
16	Bernie Williams, Jorge Posada, Alfonso Soriano, Andy Pettitte	15.00
17	Barry Bonds, Rich Aurilia, Tsuyoshi Shinjo, Jeff Kent	15.00
18	Ichiro Suzuki, Kazuhiro Sasaki, Bret Boone, Edgar Martinez	10.00
19	Albert Pujols, J.D. Drew, Jim Edmonds, Tino Martinez	10.00
20	Alex Rodriguez, Ivan Rodriguez, Juan Gonzalez, Rafael Palmeiro	12.00

2002 Playoff Absolute Memorabilia Team Quads Game Used

MT

Numbered to 100
Prime Parallel #'d to 25 not priced

1 Troy Glaus, Darin Erstad, Garret Anderson, Troy Percival 25.00
2 Curt Schilling, Randy Johnson, Luis Gonzalez, Mark Grace 40.00
3 Chipper Jones, Andruw Jones, Greg Maddux, Tom Glavine 60.00
4 Nomar Garciaparra, Manny Ramirez, Trot Nixon, Pedro J. Martinez 50.00
5 Kerry Wood, Sammy Sosa, Fred McGriff, Moises Alou 35.00
6 Frank Thomas, Magglio Ordonez, Mark Buehrle, Kenny Lofton
7 Ken Griffey Jr., Barry Larkin, Juan Encarnacion, Sean Casey
8 C.C. Sabathia, Jim Thome, Bartolo Colon, Russell Branyan 40.00
9 Todd Helton, Larry Walker, Juan Pierre, Mike Hampton 30.00
10 Jeff Bagwell, Craig Biggio, Lance Berkman, Richard Hidalgo 40.00
11 Shawn Green, Adrian Beltre, Hideo Nomo, Paul LoDuca 45.00
12 Mike Piazza, Roberto Alomar, Mo Vaughn, Roger Cedeno 50.00
13 Roger Clemens, Derek Jeter, Jason Giambi, Mike Mussina 140.00
14 Barry Zito, Tim Hudson, Eric Chavez, Miguel Tejada 30.00
15 Pat Burrell, Scott Rolen, Bobby Abreu, Marlon Byrd 35.00
16 Bernie Williams, Jorge Posada, Alfonso Soriano, Andy Pettitte 40.00
17 Barry Bonds, Rich Aurilia, Tsuyoshi Shinjo, Jeff Kent 25.00
18 Ichiro Suzuki, Kazuhiro Sasaki, Bret Boone, Edgar Martinez 50.00
19 Albert Pujols, J.D. Drew, Jim Edmonds, Tino Martinez 30.00
20 Alex Rodriguez, Ivan Rodriguez, Juan Gonzalez, Rafael Palmeiro 50.00

2002 Playoff Absolute Memorabilia Team Tandems

MT

Complete Set (40): 95.00
Common Card: 1.50
Inserted 1:12
Golds: 2-3X
Inserted 1:72

1 Troy Glaus, Darin Erstad 1.50
2 Curt Schilling, Randy Johnson 3.00
3 Chipper Jones, Andruw Jones 5.00
4 Greg Maddux, Tom Glavine 5.00
5 Nomar Garciaparra, Manny Ramirez 6.00
6 Pedro J. Martinez, Trot Nixon 4.00
7 Kerry Wood, Sammy Sosa 5.00
8 Frank Thomas, Magglio Ordonez 2.50
9 Ken Griffey Jr., Barry Larkin 5.00
10 C.C. Sabathia, Jim Thome 2.50
11 Todd Helton, Larry Walker 2.00
12 Bobby Higginson, Shane Halter 1.50
13 Cliff Floyd, Brad Penny 1.50
14 Jeff Bagwell, Craig Biggio 2.50
15 Shawn Green, Adrian Beltre 1.50
16 Ben Sheets, Richie Sexson 1.50
17 Vladimir Guerrero, Jose Vidro 3.00
18 Mike Piazza, Roberto Alomar 6.00
19 Roger Clemens, Mike Mussina 6.00
20 Derek Jeter, Jason Giambi 10.00
21 Barry Zito, Tim Hudson 2.00
22 Eric Chavez, Miguel Tejada 2.00
23 Pat Burrell, Scott Rolen 2.00
24 Brian Giles, Aramis Ramirez 1.50
25 Ryan Klesko, Phil Nevin 1.50
26 Barry Bonds, Rich Aurilia 6.00
27 Ichiro Suzuki, Kazuhiro Sasaki 6.00
28 Albert Pujols, J.D. Drew 5.00
29 Alex Rodriguez , Ivan Rodriguez 8.00
30 Carlos Delgado, Shannon Stewart 1.50
31 Mo Vaughn, Roger Cedeno 1.50
32 Carlos Beltran, Mike Sweeney 1.50
33 Edgar Martinez, Bret Boone 1.50
34 Juan Gonzalez, Rafael Palmeiro 2.00
35 Johnny Damon, Rickey Henderson 1.50
36 Sean Casey, Adam Dunn 2.00
37 Jeff Kent, Tsuyoshi Shinjo 1.50
38 Lance Berkman, Richard Hidalgo 2.00
39 So Taguchi, Tino Martinez 1.50
40 Hideo Nomo, Kazuhisa Ishii 3.00

2002 Playoff Absolute Memorabilia Team Tandems GameUsed

MT

Common Card: 6.00
Inserted 1:33
Golds: 2-4X
Production 50

1 Troy Glaus, Darin Erstad 8.00
2 Curt Schilling, Randy Johnson 15.00
3 Chipper Jones, Andruw Jones 12.00
4 Greg Maddux, Tom Glavine 20.00
5 Nomar Garciaparra, Manny Ramirez 30.00
6 Pedro J. Martinez, Trot Nixon 15.00
7 Kerry Wood, Sammy Sosa 15.00
8 Frank Thomas, Magglio Ordonez 10.00
9 Ken Griffey Jr., Barry Larkin 15.00
10 C.C. Sabathia, Jim Thome 12.00
11 Todd Helton, Larry Walker 8.00
12 Bobby Higginson, Shane Halter 8.00
13 Cliff Floyd, Brad Penny 6.00
14 Jeff Bagwell, Craig Biggio 15.00
15 Shawn Green, Adrian Beltre 8.00
16 Ben Sheets, Richie Sexson 8.00
17 Vladimir Guerrero, Jose Vidro 12.00
18 Mike Piazza, Roberto Alomar 20.00
19 Roger Clemens, Mike Mussina 50.00
20 Derek Jeter, Jason Giambi 40.00
21 Barry Zito, Tim Hudson 15.00
22 Eric Chavez, Miguel Tejada 10.00
23 Pat Burrell, Scott Rolen 15.00
24 Brian Giles, Aramis Ramirez 12.00
25 Ryan Klesko, Phil Nevin 8.00
26 Barry Bonds, Rich Aurilia 12.00
27 Ichiro Suzuki, Kazuhiro Sasaki
28 Albert Pujols, J.D. Drew 15.00
29 Alex Rodriguez Ivan Rodriguez 15.00
30 Carlos Delgado, Shannon Stewart 8.00
31 Mo Vaughn, Roger Cedeno 6.00
32 Carlos Beltran, Mike Sweeney 6.00
33 Edgar Martinez, Bret Boone 6.00
34 Juan Gonzalez, Rafael Palmeiro 12.00
35 Johnny Damon, Rickey Henderson 20.00
36 Sean Casey, Adam Dunn 25.00
37 Jeff Kent, Tsuyoshi Shinjo 15.00
38 Lance Berkman, Richard Hidalgo 8.00
39 So Taguchi, Tino Martinez 15.00
40 Hideo Nomo, Kazuhisa Ishii 35.00

A player's name in *italic* type indicates a rookie card.

2002 Playoff Absolute Memorabilia Tools of the Trade

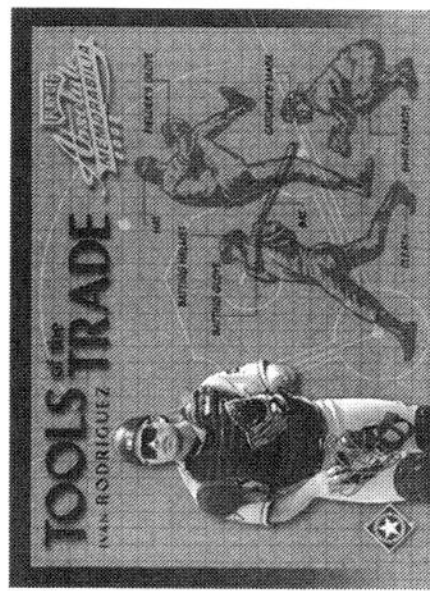

MT

Complete Set (95): 120.00
Common Player: 1.00
Inserted 1:9
Golds: 2-3X
Inserted 1:45

1 Mike Mussina 2.00
2 Rickey Henderson 2.00
3 Raul Mondesi 1.00
4 Nomar Garciaparra 8.00
5 Randy Johnson 3.00
6 Roger Clemens 5.00
7 Shawn Green 1.00
8 Todd Helton 2.00
9 Aramis Ramirez 1.00
10 Barry Larkin 1.50
11 Byung-Hyun Kim 1.00
12 C.C. Sabathia 1.00
13 Curt Schilling 2.50
14 Darin Erstad 1.50
15 Eric Karros 1.00
16 Freddy Garcia 1.00
17 Greg Maddux 5.00
18 Jason Kendall 1.00
19 Jim Thome 2.50
20 Juan Gonzalez 2.00
21 Kazuhiro Sasaki 1.00
22 Kerry Wood 2.00
23 Luis Gonzalez 1.50
24 Mark Mulder 1.00
25 Rich Aurilia 1.00
26 Ray Durham 1.00
27 Ben Grieve 1.00
28 Bret Boone 1.00
29 Edgar Martinez 1.00
30 Ivan Rodriguez 2.00
31 Jorge Posada 2.00
32 Mike Piazza 8.00
33 Pat Burrell 2.00
34 Robin Ventura 1.00
35 Trot Nixon 1.00
36 Adrian Beltre 1.00
37 Bernie Williams 2.00
38 Bobby Abreu 1.00
39 Carlos Delgado 1.50
40 Craig Biggio 1.50
41 Garret Anderson 1.00
42 Jermaine Dye 1.00
43 Johnny Damon 1.00
44 Tim Salmon 1.00
45 Tino Martinez 1.00
46 Fred McGriff 1.50
47 Gary Sheffield 1.00
48 Adam Dunn 2.50
49 Joe Mays 1.00
50 Kenny Lofton 1.00
51 Josh Beckett 1.00
52 Bud Smith 1.00
53 Johnny Estrada 1.00
54 Charles Johnson 1.00
55 Craig Wilson 1.00
56 Terrence Long 1.00
57 Andy Pettitte 1.50
58 Brian Giles 2.00
59 Juan Pierre 1.00
60 Cliff Floyd 1.00
61 Ivan Rodriguez 2.00
62 Andruw Jones 2.00
63 Lance Berkman 2.00
64 Mark Buehrle 1.00
65 Miguel Tejada 2.00
66 Wade Miller 1.00
67 Johnny Estrada 1.00

68	Tsuyoshi Shinjo	1.00
69	Scott Rolen	2.00
70	Roberto Alomar	2.00
71	Mark Grace	2.00
72	Larry Walker	1.50
73	Jim Edmonds	1.50
74	Jeff Kent	1.50
75	Frank Thomas	2.50
76	Carlos Beltran	1.00
77	Barry Zito	1.50
78	Alex Rodriguez	8.00
79	Troy Glaus	1.50
80	Ryan Klesko	1.00
81	Tom Glavine	1.50
82	Ben Sheets	1.00
83	Manny Ramirez	2.50
84	Shannon Stewart	1.00
85	Vladimir Guerrero	4.00
86	Chipper Jones	5.00
87	Jeff Bagwell	2.50
88	Richie Sexson	1.50
89	Sean Casey	1.00
90	Tim Hudson	1.50
91	J.D. Drew	1.00
92	Ivan Rodriguez	2.00
93	Magglio Ordonez	1.00
94	John Buck	1.00
95	Paul LoDuca	1.00

2002 Playoff Absolute Memorabilia Tools of Trade G-U

		MT
Common Player:		5.00
Jerseys #'d to 300		
Bats #'d to 250		
Shoes #'d to 150		
Shin Guard #'d to 150		
Glove #'d to 125		
Mask #'d to 100		
Hat #'d to 50		
Doubles #'d to 200		
Triples #'d to 75		
Quads #'d to 50		
1	Mike Mussina/jsy	10.00
2	Rickey Henderson/ jsy	35.00
3	Raul Mondesi/jsy	8.00
4	Nomar Garciaparra/ jsy	20.00
5	Randy Johnson/ jsy	10.00
6	Roger Clemens/ jsy	20.00
7	Shawn Green/jsy	8.00
8	Todd Helton/jsy	8.00
9	Aramis Ramirez/jsy	5.00
10	Barry Larkin/jsy	10.00
11	Byung-Hyun Kim/ jsy	10.00
12	C.C. Sabathia/jsy	8.00
13	Curt Schilling/jsy	12.00
14	Darin Erstad/jsy	8.00
15	Eric Karros/jsy	5.00
16	Freddy Garcia/jsy	5.00
17	Greg Maddux/jsy	15.00
18	Jason Kendall/jsy	5.00
19	Jim Thome/jsy	12.00
20	Juan Gonzalez/jsy	8.00
21	Kazuhiro Sasaki/jsy	5.00
22	Kerry Wood/jsy	10.00
23	Luis Gonzalez/jsy	8.00
24	Mark Mulder/jsy	12.00
25	Rich Aurilia/jsy	5.00
26	Ray Durham/jsy	5.00
27	Ben Grieve/jsy	5.00
28	Bret Boone/jsy	5.00
29	Edgar Martinez/jsy	5.00
30	Ivan Rodriguez/jsy	8.00
31	Jorge Posada/jsy	12.00
32	Mike Piazza/jsy	20.00
33	Pat Burrell/bat	15.00
34	Robin Ventura/bat	6.00
35	Trot Nixon/bat	10.00
36	Adrian Beltre/bat	5.00
37	Bernie Williams/ bat	10.00
38	Bobby Abreu/bat	6.00
39	Carlos Delgado/bat	6.00
40	Craig Biggio/bat	8.00
41	Garret Anderson/ bat	5.00
42	Jermaine Dye/bat	5.00
43	Johnny Damon/bat	8.00
44	Tim Salmon/bat	8.00
45	Tino Martinez/bat	10.00
46	Fred McGriff/bat	8.00
47	Gary Sheffield/bat	5.00
48	Adam Dunn/shoe	30.00
49	Joe Mays/shoe	8.00
50	Kenny Lofton/ shoe	10.00
51	Josh Beckett/shoe	10.00
52	Bud Smith/shoe	8.00
53	Johnny Estrada/ shin	15.00
54	Charles Johnson/ shin	8.00
55	Craig Wilson/shin	8.00
56	Terrence Long/ glove	10.00
57	Andy Pettitte/ glove	20.00
58	Brian Giles/glove	15.00
59	Juan Pierre/glove	10.00
60	Cliff Floyd/glove	10.00
61	Ivan Rodriguez/jsy	10.00
62	Andruw Jones/hat	20.00
63	Lance Berkman	
64	Mark Buehrle/hat	15.00
65	Miguel Tejada/hat	20.00
66	Wade Miller/hat	10.00
67	Johnny Estrada/ shin	15.00
68	T. Shinjo/bat/shoe	25.00
69	S. Rolen/bat/jsy	20.00
70	R. Alomar/ bat/shoe	25.00
71	M. Grace/glv/jsy	25.00
72	L. Walker/jsy/bat	15.00
73	J. Edmonds/ jsy/bat	20.00
74	J. Kent/jsy/bat	10.00
75	F. Thomas/jsy/bat	20.00
76	C. Beltran/jsy/bat	10.00
77	B. Zito/shoe/jsy	25.00
78	A. Rodriguez/ jsy/bat	30.00
79	T. Glaus/dualjsy	15.00
80	R. Klesko/bat/glv	12.00
81	T. Glavine/ jsy/shoe	25.00
82	B. Sheets/bat/jsy	10.00
83	M. Ramirez/shoe/ glv/jsy	40.00
84	S. Stewart/hat/ jsy/bat	15.00
85	V. Guerrero/glv/ bat/jsy	45.00
86	C. Jones/ glv/bat/jsy	50.00
87	J. Bagwell/ jsy/hat/bat	50.00
88	R. Sexson/ bat/jsy/glv/shoe	40.00
89	S. Casey/ jsy/hat/shoe/bat	35.00
90	T Hudson/ shoe/hat/glv/jsy	75.00
91	JD Drew/ shoe/jsy/hat/bat	65.00
92	I Rodriguez/ jsy/mask/chst/glv	60.00
93	M Ordonez/ hat/glv/jsy/shoe	40.00
94	J Buck/ glv/chst/shin/msk	25.00
95	P LoDuca/ jsy/chst/shin/msk	50.00

S

1988 Score

A fifth member joined the group of nationally distributed baseball cards in 1988. Titled "Score," the cards are characterized by extremely sharp color photography and printing. Card backs are full-color also and carry a player portrait along with a brief biography, player data and statistics. The 660 cards in the set are standard 2-1/2" x 3-1/2" format. The fronts come with one of six different border colors which are equally divided at 110 cards per color. The Score set was produced by Major League Marketing, the same company that marketed the "triple-action" Sportflics card sets.

		MT
Complete Set (660):		8.00
Factory Set (660):		10.00
Common Player:		.05
Plastic Pack (17):		.50
Plastic Wax Box (36):		10.00
1	Don Mattingly	.50
2	Wade Boggs	.35
3	Tim Raines	.05
4	Andre Dawson	.15
5	Mark McGwire	1.00
6	Kevin Seitzer	.05
7	Wally Joyner	.05
8	Jesse Barfield	.05
9	Pedro Guerrero	.05
10	Eric Davis	.05
11	George Brett	.40
12	Ozzie Smith	.45
13	Rickey Henderson	.35
14	Jim Rice	.10
15	*Matt Nokes*	.05
16	Mike Schmidt	.40
17	Dave Parker	.05
18	Eddie Murray	.30
19	Andres Galarraga	.05
20	Tony Fernandez	.05
21	Kevin McReynolds	.05
22	B.J. Surhoff	.05
23	Pat Tabler	.05
24	Kirby Puckett	.45
25	Benny Santiago	.05
26	Ryne Sandberg	.40
27	Kelly Downs	.05
28	Jose Cruz	.05
29	Pete O'Brien	.05
30	Mark Langston	.05
31	Lee Smith	.05
32	Juan Samuel	.05
33	Kevin Bass	.05
34	R.J. Reynolds	.05
35	Steve Sax	.05
36	John Kruk	.05
37	Alan Trammell	.05
38	Chris Bosio	.05
39	Brook Jacoby	.05
40	Willie McGee	.05
41	Dave Magadan	.05
42	Fred Lynn	.05
43	Kent Hrbek	.05
44	Brian Downing	.05
45	Jose Canseco	.35
46	Jim Presley	.05
47	Mike Stanley	.05
48	Tony Pena	.05
49	David Cone	.05
50	Rick Sutcliffe	.05
51	Doug Drabek	.05
52	Bill Doran	.05
53	Mike Scioscia	.05
54	Candy Maldonado	.05
55	Dave Winfield	.35
56	Lou Whitaker	.05
57	Tom Henke	.05
58	Ken Gerhart	.05
59	Glenn Braggs	.05
60	Julio Franco	.05
61	Charlie Leibrandt	.05
62	Gary Gaetti	.05
63	Bob Boone	.05
64	*Luis Polonia*	.10
65	Dwight Evans	.05
66	Phil Bradley	.05
67	Mike Boddicker	.05
68	Vince Coleman	.05
69	Howard Johnson	.05
70	Tim Wallach	.05
71	Keith Moreland	.05
72	Barry Larkin	.10
73	Alan Ashby	.05
74	Rick Rhoden	.05
75	Darrell Evans	.10
76	Dave Stieb	.05
77	Dan Plesac	.05
78	Will Clark	.15
79	Frank White	.05
80	Joe Carter	.05
81	Mike Witt	.05
82	Terry Steinbach	.05
83	Alvin Davis	.05
84	Tom Herr	.05
85	Vance Law	.05
86	Kal Daniels	.05
87	Rick Honeycutt	.05
88	Alfredo Griffin	.05
89	Bret Saberhagen	.10
90	Bert Blyleven	.05
91	Jeff Reardon	.05
92	Cory Snyder	.05
93	Greg Walker	.05
94	*Joe Magrane*	.10
95	Rob Deer	.05
96	Ray Knight	.05
97	Casey Candaele	.05
98	John Cerutti	.05
99	Buddy Bell	.05
100	Jack Clark	.05
101	Eric Bell	.05
102	Willie Wilson	.05
103	Dave Schmidt	.05
104	Dennis Eckersley	.10
105	Don Sutton	.20
106	Danny Tartabull	.05
107	Fred McGriff	.05
108	*Les Straker*	.05
109	Lloyd Moseby	.05
110	Roger Clemens	.35
111	Glenn Hubbard	.05
112	*Ken Williams*	.05
113	Ruben Sierra	.05
114	Stan Jefferson	.05
115	Milt Thompson	.05
116	Bobby Bonilla	.05
117	Wayne Tolleson	.05
118	Matt Williams	.15
119	Chet Lemon	.05
120	Dale Sveum	.05
121	Dennis Boyd	.05
122	Brett Butler	.05
123	Terry Kennedy	.05
124	Jack Howell	.05
125	Curt Young	.05
126a	Dale Valle (first name incorrect)	.25
126b	Dave Valle (correct spelling)	.05

No.	Player	Price
127	Curt Wilkerson	.05
128	Tim Teufel	.05
129	Ozzie Virgil	.05
130	Brian Fisher	.05
131	Lance Parrish	.05
132	Tom Browning	.05
133a	Larry Anderson (incorrect spelling)	.25
133b	Larry Andersen (correct spelling)	.05
134a	Bob Brenley (incorrect spelling)	.25
134b	Bob Brenly (correct spelling)	.05
135	Mike Marshall	.05
136	Gerald Perry	.05
137	Bobby Meacham	.05
138	Larry Herndon	.05
139	*Fred Manrique*	.05
140	Charlie Hough	.05
141	Ron Darling	.05
142	Herm Winningham	.05
143	Mike Diaz	.05
144	*Mike Jackson*	.05
145	Denny Walling	.05
146	Rob Thompson	.05
147	Franklin Stubbs	.05
148	Albert Hall	.05
149	Bobby Witt	.05
150	Lance McCullers	.05
151	Scott Bradley	.05
152	Mark McLemore	.05
153	Tim Laudner	.05
154	Greg Swindell	.05
155	Marty Barrett	.05
156	Mike Heath	.05
157	Gary Ward	.05
158a	Lee Mazilli (incorrect spelling)	.25
158b	Lee Mazzilli (correct spelling)	.05
159	Tom Foley	.05
160	Robin Yount	.25
161	Steve Bedrosian	.05
162	Bob Walk	.05
163	Nick Esasky	.05
164	*Ken Caminiti*	.50
165	Jose Uribe	.05
166	Dave Anderson	.05
167	Ed Whitson	.05
168	Ernie Whitt	.05
169	Cecil Cooper	.05
170	Mike Pagliarulo	.05
171	Pat Sheridan	.05
172	Chris Bando	.05
173	Lee Lacy	.05
174	Steve Lombardozzi	.05
175	Mike Greenwell	.05
176	Greg Minton	.05
177	Moose Haas	.05
178	Mike Kingery	.05
179	Greg Harris	.05
180	Bo Jackson	.10
181	Carmelo Martinez	.05
182	Alex Trevino	.05
183	Ron Oester	.05
184	Danny Darwin	.05
185	Mike Krukow	.05
186	Rafael Palmeiro	.20
187	Tim Burke	.05
188	Roger McDowell	.05
189	Garry Templeton	.05
190	Terry Pendleton	.05
191	Larry Parrish	.05
192	Rey Quinones	.05
193	Joaquin Andujar	.05
194	Tom Brunansky	.05
195	Donnie Moore	.05
196	Dan Pasqua	.05
197	Jim Gantner	.05
198	Mark Eichhorn	.05
199	John Grubb	.05
200	*Bill Ripken*	.05
201	*Sam Horn*	.05
202	Todd Worrell	.05
203	Terry Leach	.05
204	Garth Iorg	.05
205	Brian Dayett	.05
206	Bo Diaz	.05
207	Craig Reynolds	.05
208	Brian Holton	.05
209	Marvelle Wynne (Marvell)	.05
210	Dave Concepcion	.05
211	Mike Davis	.05
212	Devon White	.10
213	Mickey Brantley	.05
214	Greg Gagne	.05
215	Oddibe McDowell	.05
216	Jimmy Key	.05
217	Dave Bergman	.05
218	Calvin Schiraldi	.05
219	Larry Sheets	.05
220	Mike Easler	.05
221	Kurt Stillwell	.05
222	*Chuck Jackson*	.05
223	Dave Martinez	.05
224	Tim Leary	.05
225	Steve Garvey	.15
226	Greg Mathews	.05
227	Doug Sisk	.05
228	Dave Henderson	.05
229	Jimmy Dwyer	.05
230	Larry Owen	.05
231	Andre Thornton	.05
232	Mark Salas	.05
233	Tom Brookens	.05
234	Greg Brock	.05
235	Rance Mulliniks	.05
236	Bob Brower	.05
237	Joe Niekro	.05
238	Scott Bankhead	.05
239	Doug DeCinces	.05
240	Tommy John	.10
241	Rich Gedman	.05
242	Ted Power	.05
243	*Dave Meads*	.05
244	Jim Sundberg	.05
245	Ken Oberkfell	.05
246	Jimmy Jones	.05
247	Ken Landreaux	.05
248	Jose Oquendo	.05
249	*John Mitchell*	.05
250	Don Baylor	.10
251	Scott Fletcher	.05
252	Al Newman	.05
253	Carney Lansford	.05
254	Johnny Ray	.05
255	Gary Pettis	.05
256	Ken Phelps	.05
257	Rick Leach	.05
258	Tim Stoddard	.05
259	Ed Romero	.05
260	Sid Bream	.05
261a	Tom Neidenfuer (incorrect spelling)	.25
261b	Tom Niedenfuer (correct spelling)	.05
262	Rick Dempsey	.05
263	Lonnie Smith	.05
264	Bob Forsch	.05
265	Barry Bonds	.50
266	Willie Randolph	.05
267	Mike Ramsey	.05
268	Don Slaught	.05
269	Mickey Tettleton	.05
270	Jerry Reuss	.05
271	Marc Sullivan	.05
272	Jim Morrison	.05
273	Steve Balboni	.05
274	Dick Schofield	.05
275	John Tudor	.05
276	*Gene Larkin*	.05
277	Harold Reynolds	.05
278	Jerry Browne	.05
279	Willie Upshaw	.05
280	Ted Higuera	.05
281	Terry McGriff	.05
282	Terry Puhl	.05
283	*Mark Wasinger*	.05
284	Luis Salazar	.05
285	Ted Simmons	.05
286	John Shelby	.05
287	*John Smiley*	.15
288	Curt Ford	.05
289	Steve Crawford	.05
290	Dan Quisenberry	.05
291	Alan Wiggins	.05
292	Randy Bush	.05
293	John Candelaria	.05
294	Tony Phillips	.05
295	Mike Morgan	.05
296	Bill Wegman	.05
297a	Terry Franconia (incorrect spelling)	.25
297b	Terry Francona (correct spelling)	.05
298	Mickey Hatcher	.05
299	Andres Thomas	.05
300	Bob Stanley	.05
301	*Alfredo Pedrique*	.05
302	Jim Lindeman	.05
303	Wally Backman	.05
304	Paul O'Neill	.05
305	Hubie Brooks	.05
306	Steve Buechele	.05
307	Bobby Thigpen	.05
308	George Hendrick	.05
309	John Moses	.05
310	Ron Guidry	.10
311	Bill Schroeder	.05
312	*Jose Nunez*	.05
313	Bud Black	.05
314	Joe Sambito	.05
315	Scott McGregor	.05
316	Rafael Santana	.05
317	Frank Williams	.05
318	Mike Fitzgerald	.05
319	Rick Mahler	.05
320	Jim Gott	.05
321	Mariano Duncan	.05
322	Jose Guzman	.05
323	Lee Guetterman	.05
324	Dan Gladden	.05
325	Gary Carter	.15
326	Tracy Jones	.05
327	Floyd Youmans	.05
328	Bill Dawley	.05
329	*Paul Noce*	.05
330	Angel Salazar	.05
331	Goose Gossage	.10
332	George Frazier	.05
333	Ruppert Jones	.05
334	Billy Jo Robidoux	.05
335	Mike Scott	.05
336	Randy Myers	.05
337	Bob Sebra	.05
338	Eric Show	.05
339	Mitch Williams	.05
340	Paul Molitor	.30
341	Gus Polidor	.05
342	Steve Trout	.05
343	Jerry Don Gleaton	.05
344	Bob Knepper	.05
345	Mitch Webster	.05
346	John Morris	.05
347	Andy Hawkins	.05
348	Dave Leiper	.05
349	Ernest Riles	.05
350	Dwight Gooden	.05
351	Dave Righetti	.05
352	Pat Dodson	.05
353	John Habyan	.05
354	Jim Deshaies	.05
355	Butch Wynegar	.05
356	Bryn Smith	.05
357	Matt Young	.05
358	*Tom Pagnozzi*	.05
359	Floyd Rayford	.05
360	Darryl Strawberry	.05
361	Sal Butera	.05
362	Domingo Ramos	.05
363	Chris Brown	.05
364	Jose Gonzalez	.05
365	Dave Smith	.05
366	Andy McGaffigan	.05
367	Stan Javier	.05
368	Henry Cotto	.05
369	Mike Birkbeck	.05
370	Len Dykstra	.05
371	Dave Collins	.05
372	Spike Owen	.05
373	Geno Petralli	.05
374	Ron Karkovice	.05
375	Shane Rawley	.05
376	*DeWayne Buice*	.05
377	*Bill Pecota*	.05
378	Leon Durham	.05
379	Ed Olwine	.05
380	Bruce Hurst	.05
381	Bob McClure	.05
382	Mark Thurmond	.05
383	Buddy Biancalana	.05
384	Tim Conroy	.05
385	Tony Gwynn	.40
386	Greg Gross	.05
387	*Barry Lyons*	.05
388	Mike Felder	.05
389	Pat Clements	.05
390	Ken Griffey	.05
391	Mark Davis	.05
392	Jose Rijo	.05
393	Mike Young	.05
394	Willie Fraser	.05
395	Dion James	.05
396	*Steve Shields*	.05
397	Randy St. Claire	.05
398	Danny Jackson	.05
399	Cecil Fielder	.05
400	Keith Hernandez	.05
401	Don Carman	.05
402	*Chuck Crim*	.05
403	Rob Woodward	.05
404	Junior Ortiz	.05
405	Glenn Wilson	.05
406	Ken Howell	.05
407	Jeff Kunkel	.05
408	Jeff Reed	.05
409	Chris James	.05
410	Zane Smith	.05
411	Ken Dixon	.05
412	Ricky Horton	.05
413	Frank DiPino	.05
414	*Shane Mack*	.05
415	Danny Cox	.05
416	Andy Van Slyke	.05
417	Danny Heep	.05
418	John Cangelosi	.05
419a	John Christiansen (incorrect spelling)	.25
419b	John Christensen (correct spelling)	.05
420	*Joey Cora*	.10
421	Mike LaValliere	.05
422	Kelly Gruber	.05
423	Bruce Benedict	.05
424	Len Matuszek	.05
425	Kent Tekulve	.05
426	Rafael Ramirez	.05
427	Mike Flanagan	.05
428	Mike Gallego	.05
429	Juan Castillo	.05
430	Neal Heaton	.05
431	Phil Garner	.05
432	*Mike Dunne*	.05
433	Wallace Johnson	.05
434	Jack O'Connor	.05
435	Steve Jeltz	.05
436	*Donnell Nixon*	.05
437	Jack Lazorko	.05
438	*Keith Comstock*	.05
439	Jeff Robinson	.05
440	Graig Nettles	.10
441	Mel Hall	.05
442	*Gerald Young*	.05
443	Gary Redus	.05
444	Charlie Moore	.05
445	Bill Madlock	.05
446	Mark Clear	.05
447	Greg Booker	.05
448	Rick Schu	.05
449	Ron Kittle	.05
450	Dale Murphy	.15
451	Bob Dernier	.05
452	Dale Mohorcic	.05
453	Rafael Belliard	.05
454	Charlie Puleo	.05
455	Dwayne Murphy	.05
456	Jim Eisenreich	.05
457	David Palmer	.05
458	Dave Stewart	.05
459	Pascual Perez	.05
460	Glenn Davis	.05
461	Dan Petry	.05
462	Jim Winn	.05
463	Darrell Miller	.05
464	Mike Moore	.05
465	Mike LaCoss	.05
466	Steve Farr	.05
467	Jerry Mumphrey	.05
468	Kevin Gross	.05
469	Bruce Bochy	.05
470	Orel Hershiser	.05
471	Eric King	.05
472	*Ellis Burks*	.30
473	Darren Daulton	.05
474	Mookie Wilson	.05
475	Frank Viola	.05
476	Ron Robinson	.05
477	Bob Melvin	.05
478	Jeff Musselman	.05
479	Charlie Kerfeld	.05
480	Richard Dotson	.05
481	Kevin Mitchell	.05
482	Gary Roenicke	.05
483	Tim Flannery	.05
484	Rich Yett	.05
485	Pete Incaviglia	.05
486	Rick Cerone	.05
487	Tony Armas	.05
488	Jerry Reed	.05
489	Davey Lopes	.05
490	Frank Tanana	.05
491	Mike Loynd	.05

492	Bruce Ruffin	.05
493	Chris Speier	.05
494	Tom Hume	.05
495	Jesse Orosco	.05
496	*Robby Wine, Jr.*	.05
497	*Jeff Montgomery*	.20
498	Jeff Dedmon	.05
499	Luis Aguayo	.05
500	Reggie Jackson (1968-75)	.20
501	Reggie Jackson (1976)	.20
502	Reggie Jackson (1977-81)	.20
503	Reggie Jackson (1982-86)	.20
504	Reggie Jackson (1987)	.20
505	Billy Hatcher	.05
506	Ed Lynch	.05
507	Willie Hernandez	.05
508	Jose DeLeon	.05
509	Joel Youngblood	.05
510	Bob Welch	.05
511	Steve Ontiveros	.05
512	Randy Ready	.05
513	Juan Nieves	.05
514	Jeff Russell	.05
515	Von Hayes	.05
516	Mark Gubicza	.05
517	Ken Dayley	.05
518	Don Aase	.05
519	Rick Reuschel	.05
520	*Mike Henneman*	.15
521	Rick Aguilera	.05
522	Jay Howell	.05
523	Ed Correa	.05
524	Manny Trillo	.05
525	Kirk Gibson	.05
526	*Wally Ritchie*	.05
527	Al Nipper	.05
528	Atlee Hammaker	.05
529	Shawon Dunston	.05
530	Jim Clancy	.05
531	Tom Paciorek	.05
532	Joel Skinner	.05
533	Scott Garrelts	.05
534	Tom O'Malley	.05
535	John Franco	.05
536	*Paul Kilgus*	.05
537	Darrell Porter	.05
538	Walt Terrell	.05
539	*Bill Long*	.05
540	George Bell	.05
541	Jeff Sellers	.05
542	*Joe Boever*	.05
543	Steve Howe	.05
544	Scott Sanderson	.05
545	Jack Morris	.05
546	*Todd Benzinger*	.10
547	Steve Henderson	.05
548	Eddie Milner	.05
549	*Jeff Robinson*	.05
550	Cal Ripken, Jr.	.75
551	Jody Davis	.05
552	Kirk McCaskill	.05
553	Craig Lefferts	.05
554	Darnell Coles	.05
555	Phil Niekro	.25
556	Mike Aldrete	.05
557	Pat Perry	.05
558	Juan Agosto	.05
559	Rob Murphy	.05
560	Dennis Rasmussen	.05
561	Manny Lee	.05
562	*Jeff Blauser*	.10
563	Bob Ojeda	.05
564	Dave Dravecky	.05
565	Gene Garber	.05
566	Ron Roenicke	.05
567	*Tommy Hinzo*	.05
568	*Eric Nolte*	.05
569	Ed Hearn	.05
570	*Mark Davidson*	.05
571	*Jim Walewander*	.05
572	Donnie Hill	.05
573	Jamie Moyer	.05
574	Ken Schrom	.05
575	Nolan Ryan	.75
576	Jim Acker	.05
577	Jamie Quirk	.05
578	*Jay Aldrich*	.05
579	Claudell Washington	.05
580	Jeff Leonard	.05
581	Carmen Castillo	.05
582	Daryl Boston	.05
583	*Jeff DeWillis*	.05
584	*John Marzano*	.05
585	Bill Gullickson	.05
586	Andy Allanson	.05
587	Lee Tunnell	.05
588	Gene Nelson	.05
589	Dave LaPoint	.05
590	Harold Baines	.05
591	Bill Buckner	.05
592	Carlton Fisk	.30
593	Rick Manning	.05
594	*Doug Jones*	.10
595	Tom Candiotti	.05
596	Steve Lake	.05
597	*Jose Lind*	.10
598	*Ross Jones*	.05
599	Gary Matthews	.05
600	Fernando Valenzuela	.05
601	Dennis Martinez	.05
602	*Les Lancaster*	.05
603	Ozzie Guillen	.05
604	Tony Bernazard	.05
605	Chili Davis	.05
606	Roy Smalley	.05
607	Ivan Calderon	.05
608	Jay Tibbs	.05
609	Guy Hoffman	.05
610	Doyle Alexander	.05
611	Mike Bielecki	.05
612	*Shawn Hillegas*	.05
613	Keith Atherton	.05
614	Eric Plunk	.05
615	Sid Fernandez	.05
616	Dennis Lamp	.05
617	Dave Engle	.05
618	Harry Spilman	.05
619	Don Robinson	.05
620	*John Farrell*	.05
621	*Nelson Liriano*	.05
622	Floyd Bannister	.05
623	*Randy Milligan*	.10
624	*Kevin Elster*	.10
625	*Jody Reed*	.15
626	*Shawn Abner*	.05
627	*Kirt Manwaring*	.10
628	*Pete Stanicek*	.05
629	*Rob Ducey*	.05
630	Steve Kiefer	.05
631	*Gary Thurman*	.05
632	*Darrel Akerfelds*	.05
633	Dave Clark	.05
634	*Roberto Kelly*	.15
635	*Keith Hughes*	.05
636	*John Davis*	.05
637	*Mike Devereaux*	.10
638	*Tom Glavine*	1.00
639	*Keith Miller*	.05
640	*Chris Gwynn*	.05
641	*Tim Crews*	.05
642	*Mackey Sasser*	.05
643	*Vicente Palacios*	.05
644	Kevin Romine	.05
645	*Gregg Jefferies*	.25
646	*Jeff Treadway*	.05
647	*Ron Gant*	.25
648	Rookie Sluggers (Mark McGwire, Matt Nokes)	.50
649	Speed and Power (Tim Raines, Eric Davis)	.05
650	Game Breakers (Jack Clark, Don Mattingly)	.20
651	Super Shortstops (Tony Fernandez, Cal Ripken, Jr., Alan Trammell)	.25
652	Vince Coleman (Highlight)	.05
653	Kirby Puckett (Highlight)	.30
654	Benito Santiago (Highlight)	.05
655	Juan Nieves (Highlight)	.05
656	Steve Bedrosian (Highlight)	.05
657	Mike Schmidt (Highlight)	.20
658	Don Mattingly (Highlight)	.40
659	Mark McGwire (Highlight)	.50
660	Paul Molitor (Highlight)	.15

1988 Score Glossy

With production of a reported 5,000 sets, there is a significant premium attached to the glossy version of Score's debut baseball card issue. The specially packaged collector's edition features cards with a high-gloss front finish and was sold only as a complete set.

	MT
Complete Set (660):	125.00
Common Player:	.25
Stars:	15X

(See 1988 Score for checklist and base card values.)

1988 Score Traded/Rookie

This 110-card set featuring rookies and traded veterans is similar in design to the 1988 Score set, except for a change in border color. Individual standard-size player cards (2-1/2" x 3-1/2") feature a bright orange border framing action photos highlighted by a thin white outline. The player name (in white) is centered in the bottom margin, flanked by three yellow stars lower left and a yellow Score logo lower right. The backs carry full-color player portraits on a cream-colored background, plus team name and logo, personal information and a purple stats chart that lists year-by-year and major league totals. A brief player profile follows the stats chart and, on some cards, information is included about the player's trade or acquisition. The boxed update set also includes 10 Magic Motion 3-D trivia cards. The cards are numbered with a "T" suffix.

		MT
Complete Set (110):		25.00
Common Player:		.10
1	Jack Clark	.10
2	Danny Jackson	.10
3	Brett Butler	.10
4	Kurt Stillwell	.10
5	Tom Brunansky	.10
6	Dennis Lamp	.10
7	Jose DeLeon	.10
8	Tom Herr	.10
9	Keith Moreland	.10
10	Kirk Gibson	.10
11	Bud Black	.10
12	Rafael Ramirez	.10
13	Luis Salazar	.10
14	Goose Gossage	.15
15	Bob Welch	.10
16	Vance Law	.10
17	Ray Knight	.10
18	Dan Quisenberry	.10
19	Don Slaught	.10
20	Lee Smith	.15
21	Rick Cerone	.10
22	Pat Tabler	.10
23	Larry McWilliams	.10
24	Rick Horton	.10
25	Graig Nettles	.10
26	Dan Petry	.10
27	Jose Rijo	.10
28	Chili Davis	.10
29	Dickie Thon	.10
30	Mackey Sasser	.10
31	Mickey Tettleton	.10
32	Rick Dempsey	.10
33	Ron Hassey	.10
34	Phil Bradley	.10
35	Jay Howell	.10
36	Bill Buckner	.10
37	Alfredo Griffin	.10
38	Gary Pettis	.10
39	Calvin Schiraldi	.10
40	John Candelaria	.10
41	Joe Orsulak	.10
42	Willie Upshaw	.10
43	Herm Winningham	.10
44	Ron Kittle	.10
45	Bob Dernier	.10
46	Steve Balboni	.10
47	Steve Shields	.10
48	Henry Cotto	.10
49	Dave Henderson	.10
50	Dave Parker	.10
51	Mike Young	.10
52	Mark Salas	.10
53	Mike Davis	.10
54	Rafael Santana	.10
55	Don Baylor	.35
56	Dan Pasqua	.10
57	Ernest Riles	.10
58	Glenn Hubbard	.10
59	Mike Smithson	.10
60	Richard Dotson	.10
61	Jerry Reuss	.10
62	Mike Jackson	.10
63	Floyd Bannister	.10
64	Jesse Orosco	.10
65	Larry Parrish	.10
66	Jeff Bittiger	.10
67	Ray Hayward	.10
68	*Ricky Jordan*	.15
69	Tommy Gregg	.10
70	*Brady Anderson*	3.00
71	Jeff Montgomery	.10
72	Darryl Hamilton	.10
73	Cecil Espy	.10
74	Greg Briley	.10
75	Joey Meyer	.10
76	*Mike Macfarlane*	.50
77	Oswald Peraza	.10
78	Jack Armstrong	.10
79	Don Heinkel	.10
80	*Mark Grace*	7.00
81	Steve Curry	.10
82	Damon Berryhill	.10
83	Steve Ellsworth	.10
84	Pete Smith	.10
85	*Jack McDowell*	.75
86	Rob Dibble	.10
87	Bryan Harvey	.10
88	John Dopson	.10
89	Dave Gallagher	.10
90	*Todd Stottlemyre*	.50
91	Mike Schooler	.10
92	Don Gordon	.10
93	Sil Campusano	.10
94	Jeff Pico	.10
95	*Jay Buhner*	3.00
96	Nelson Santovenia	.10
97	Al Leiter	.10
98	Luis Alicea	.10
99	Pat Borders	.10
100	*Chris Sabo*	.50
101	Tim Belcher	.10
102	Walt Weiss	.10
103	*Craig Biggio*	6.00

104	Don August	.10
105	*Roberto Alomar*	12.50
106	Todd Burns	.10
107	John Costello	.10
108	Melido Perez	.10
109	Darrin Jackson	.10
110	Orestes Destrade	.10

1988 Score Traded/Rookie Glossy

Among the scarcest of the major card companies' high-gloss collector's editions of the late 1980s is the 1988 Score Rookie/Traded issue. Production of the regular-finish set was limited in itself and the glossy version is moreso, adding a significant premium value.

	MT
Complete Set (110):	140.00
Common Player:	.25
Stars:	3X

(See 1988 Score Traded/Rookie for checklist and base card values.)

1988 Score Young Superstar Series 1

This 40-card set of 2-1/2" x 3-1/2" cards is divided into five separate 8-card subsets. Similar to the company's regular issue, these cards are distinguished by excellent full-color photography on both front and back. The glossy player photos are centered on a white background and framed by a vivid blue and green border. A player name banner beneath the photo includes the name, position and uniform number. The card backs feature color player portraits beneath a hot pink player name/Score logo banner. Hot pink also frames the personal stats (in green), career stats (in black) and career biography (in blue). The backs also include quotes from well-known baseball authorities discussing player performance. This set was distributed via a write-in offer printed on 1988 Score 17-card package wrappers.

		MT
Complete Set (40):		6.00
Common Player:		.10
1	Mark McGwire	3.00
2	Benito Santiago	.10
3	Sam Horn	.10
4	Chris Bosio	.10
5	Matt Nokes	.10
6	Ken Williams	.10
7	Dion James	.10
8	B.J. Surhoff	.10
9	Joe Margrane	.10
10	Kevin Seitzer	.10
11	Stanley Jefferson	.10
12	Devon White	.25
13	Nelson Liriano	.10
14	Chris James	.10
15	Mike Henneman	.10
16	Terry Steinbach	.10
17	John Kruk	.10
18	Matt Williams	.35
19	Kelly Downs	.10
20	Bill Ripken	.10
21	Ozzie Guillen	.10
22	Luis Polonia	.10
23	Dave Magadan	.10
24	Mike Greenwell	.10
25	Will Clark	.25
26	Mike Dunne	.10
27	Wally Joyner	.10
28	Robby Thompson	.10
29	Ken Caminiti	.10
30	Jose Canseco	1.00
31	Todd Benzinger	.10
32	Pete Incaviglia	.10
33	John Farrell	.10
34	Casey Candaele	.10
35	Mike Aldrete	.10
36	Ruben Sierra	.10
37	Ellis Burks	.10
38	Tracy Jones	.10
39	Kal Daniels	.10
40	Cory Snyder	.10

1988 Score Young Superstar Series 2

This set of 40 standard-size cards and five Magic trivia cards is part of a double series issued by Score. Each series is divided into five smaller sets of eight baseball cards and one trivia card. The design on both series is similar, except for border color. Series I has blue and green borders. Series II has red and blue borders framing full-color player photos. Backs carry color portrait photos and stats in a variety of colors. Young Superstar series were offered via a write-in offer on '88 Score wrappers. For each 8-card subset, collectors were instructed to send two Score wrappers and $1. Complete sets were offered by a number of hobby dealers nationwide.

		MT
Complete Set (40):		7.00
Common Player:		.10
1	Don Mattingly	2.50
2	Glenn Braggs	.10
3	Dwight Gooden	.10
4	Jose Lind	.10
5	Danny Tartabull	.10
6	Tony Fernandez	.10
7	Julio Franco	.10
8	Andres Galarraga	.10
9	Bobby Bonilla	.10
10	Eric Davis	.10
11	Gerald Young	.10
12	Barry Bonds	2.00
13	Jerry Browne	.10
14	Jeff Blauser	.10
15	Mickey Brantley	.10
16	Floyd Youmans	.10
17	Bret Saberhagen	.10
18	Shawon Dunston	.10
19	Len Dykstra	.10
20	Darryl Strawberry	.10
21	Rick Aguilera	.10
22	Ivan Calderon	.10
23	Roger Clemens	1.50
24	Vince Coleman	.10
25	Gary Thurman	.10
26	Jeff Treadway	.10
27	Oddibe McDowell	.10
28	Fred McGriff	.10
29	Mark McLemore	.10
30	Jeff Musselman	.10
31	Mitch Williams	.10
32	Dan Plesac	.10
33	Juan Nieves	.10
34	Barry Larkin	.10
35	Greg Mathews	.10
36	Shane Mack	.10
37	Scott Bankhead	.10
38	Eric Bell	.10
39	Greg Swindell	.10
40	Kevin Elster	.10

1989 Score

This set of 660 cards plus 56 Magic Motion trivia cards is the second annual basic issue from Score. Full-color player photos highlight 651 individual players and 9 season highlights, including the first Wrigley Field night game. Action photos are framed by thin brightly colored borders (green, cyan blue, purple, orange, red, royal blue) with a baseball diamond logo/player name beneath the photo. Full-color player close-ups (1-5/16" x 1-5/8") are printed on the pastel-colored backs, along with personal information, stats and career highlights. The cards measure 2-1/2" x 3-1/2".

		MT
Complete Set (660):		8.00
Factory Set (660):		10.00
Common Player:		.05
Plastic Pack (16):		.50
Wax Box (36):		10.00
1	Jose Canseco	.25
2	Andre Dawson	.15
3	Mark McGwire	.75
4	Benny Santiago	.05
5	Rick Reuschel	.05
6	Fred McGriff	.05
7	Kal Daniels	.05
8	Gary Gaetti	.05
9	Ellis Burks	.05
10	Darryl Strawberry	.05
11	Julio Franco	.05
12	Lloyd Moseby	.05
13	*Jeff Pico*	.05
14	Johnny Ray	.05
15	Cal Ripken, Jr.	.75
16	Dick Schofield	.05
17	Mel Hall	.05
18	Bill Ripken	.05
19	Brook Jacoby	.05
20	Kirby Puckett	.65
21	Bill Doran	.05
22	Pete O'Brien	.05
23	Matt Nokes	.05
24	Brian Fisher	.05
25	Jack Clark	.05
26	Gary Pettis	.05
27	Dave Valle	.05
28	Willie Wilson	.05
29	Curt Young	.05
30	Dale Murphy	.15
31	Barry Larkin	.10
32	Dave Stewart	.05
33	Mike LaValliere	.05
34	Glenn Hubbard	.05
35	Ryne Sandberg	.25
36	Tony Pena	.05
37	Greg Walker	.05
38	Von Hayes	.05
39	Kevin Mitchell	.05
40	Tim Raines	.05
41	Keith Hernandez	.05
42	Keith Moreland	.05
43	Ruben Sierra	.05
44	Chet Lemon	.05
45	Willie Randolph	.05
46	Andy Allanson	.05
47	Candy Maldonado	.05
48	Sid Bream	.05
49	Denny Walling	.05
50	Dave Winfield	.30
51	Alvin Davis	.05
52	Cory Snyder	.05
53	Hubie Brooks	.05
54	Chili Davis	.05
55	Kevin Seitzer	.05
56	Jose Uribe	.05
57	Tony Fernandez	.05
58	Tim Teufel	.05
59	Oddibe McDowell	.05
60	Les Lancaster	.05
61	Billy Hatcher	.05
62	Dan Gladden	.05
63	Marty Barrett	.05
64	Nick Esasky	.05
65	Wally Joyner	.05
66	Mike Greenwell	.05
67	Ken Williams	.05
68	Bob Horner	.05
69	Steve Sax	.05
70	Rickey Henderson	.40
71	Mitch Webster	.05
72	Rob Deer	.05
73	Jim Presley	.05
74	Albert Hall	.05
75a	George Brett ("At age 33 ...")	1.00
75b	George Brett ("At age 35 ...")	.50
76	Brian Downing	.05
77	Dave Martinez	.05
78	Scott Fletcher	.05
79	Phil Bradley	.05
80	Ozzie Smith	.50
81	Larry Sheets	.05

No.	Player	Price
82	Mike Aldrete	.05
83	Darnell Coles	.05
84	Len Dykstra	.05
85	Jim Rice	.10
86	Jeff Treadway	.05
87	Jose Lind	.05
88	Willie McGee	.05
89	Mickey Brantley	.05
90	Tony Gwynn	.50
91	R.J. Reynolds	.05
92	Milt Thompson	.05
93	Kevin McReynolds	.05
94	Eddie Murray	.25
95	Lance Parrish	.05
96	Ron Kittle	.05
97	Gerald Young	.05
98	Ernie Whitt	.05
99	Jeff Reed	.05
100	Don Mattingly	.65
101	Gerald Perry	.05
102	Vance Law	.05
103	John Shelby	.05
104	Chris Sabo	.05
105	Danny Tartabull	.05
106	Glenn Wilson	.05
107	Mark Davidson	.05
108	Dave Parker	.05
109	Eric Davis	.05
110	Alan Trammell	.05
111	Ozzie Virgil	.05
112	Frank Tanana	.05
113	Rafael Ramirez	.05
114	Dennis Martinez	.05
115	Jose DeLeon	.05
116	Bob Ojeda	.05
117	Doug Drabek	.05
118	Andy Hawkins	.05
119	Greg Maddux	.50
120	Cecil Fielder } (reversed negative)	.10
121	Mike Scioscia	.05
122	Dan Petry	.05
123	Terry Kennedy	.05
124	Kelly Downs	.05
125	Greg Gross	.05
126	Fred Lynn	.05
127	Barry Bonds	.60
128	Harold Baines	.05
129	Doyle Alexander	.05
130	Kevin Elster	.05
131	Mike Heath	.05
132	Teddy Higuera	.05
133	Charlie Leibrandt	.05
134	Tim Laudner	.05
135a	Ray Knight (photo reversed)	.40
135b	Ray Knight (correct photo)	.05
136	Howard Johnson	.05
137	Terry Pendleton	.05
138	Andy McGaffigan	.05
139	Ken Oberkfell	.05
140	Butch Wynegar	.05
141	Rob Murphy	.05
142	*Rich Renteria*	.05
143	Jose Guzman	.05
144	Andres Galarraga	.05
145	Rick Horton	.05
146	Frank DiPino	.05
147	Glenn Braggs	.05
148	John Kruk	.05
149	Mike Schmidt	.50
150	Lee Smith	.05
151	Robin Yount	.25
152	Mark Eichhorn	.05
153	DeWayne Buice	.05
154	B.J. Surhoff	.05
155	Vince Coleman	.05
156	Tony Phillips	.05
157	Willie Fraser	.05
158	Lance McCullers	.05
159	Greg Gagne	.05
160	Jesse Barfield	.05
161	Mark Langston	.05
162	Kurt Stillwell	.05
163	Dion James	.05
164	Glenn Davis	.05
165	Walt Weiss	.05
166	Dave Concepcion	.05
167	Alfredo Griffin	.05
168	*Don Heinkel*	.05
169	Luis Rivera	.05
170	Shane Rawley	.05
171	Darrell Evans	.10
172	Robby Thompson	.05
173	Jody Davis	.05
174	Andy Van Slyke	.05
175	Wade Boggs	.25
176	Garry Templeton	.05
177	Gary Redus	.05
178	Craig Lefferts	.05
179	Carney Lansford	.05
180	Ron Darling	.05
181	Kirk McCaskill	.05
182	Tony Armas	.05
183	Steve Farr	.05
184	Tom Brunansky	.05
185	*Bryan Harvey*	.10
186	Mike Marshall	.05
187	Bo Diaz	.05
188	Willie Upshaw	.05
189	Mike Pagliarulo	.05
190	Mike Krukow	.05
191	Tommy Herr	.05
192	Jim Pankovits	.05
193	Dwight Evans	.05
194	Kelly Gruber	.05
195	Bobby Bonilla	.05
196	Wallace Johnson	.05
197	Dave Stieb	.05
198	*Pat Borders*	.25
199	Rafael Palmeiro	.15
200	Dwight Gooden	.05
201	Pete Incaviglia	.05
202	Chris James	.05
203	Marvell Wynne	.05
204	Pat Sheridan	.05
205	Don Baylor	.10
206	Paul O'Neill	.05
207	Pete Smith	.05
208	Mark McLemore	.05
209	Henry Cotto	.05
210	Kirk Gibson	.05
211	Claudell Washington	.05
212	Randy Bush	.05
213	Joe Carter	.05
214	Bill Buckner	.05
215	Bert Blyleven	.05
216	Brett Butler	.05
217	Lee Mazzilli	.05
218	Spike Owen	.05
219	Bill Swift	.05
220	Tim Wallach	.05
221	David Cone	.05
222	Don Carman	.05
223	Rich Gossage	.05
224	Bob Walk	.05
225	Dave Righetti	.05
226	Kevin Bass	.05
227	Kevin Gross	.05
228	Tim Burke	.05
229	Rick Mahler	.05
230	Lou Whitaker	.05
231	*Luis Alicea*	.10
232	Roberto Alomar	.30
233	Bob Boone	.05
234	Dickie Thon	.05
235	Shawon Dunston	.05
236	Pete Stanicek	.05
237	Craig Biggio	.25
238	Dennis Boyd	.05
239	Tom Candiotti	.05
240	Gary Carter	.20
241	Mike Stanley	.05
242	Ken Phelps	.05
243	Chris Bosio	.05
244	Les Straker	.05
245	Dave Smith	.05
246	John Candelaria	.05
247	Joe Orsulak	.05
248	Storm Davis	.05
249	Floyd Bannister	.05
250	Jack Morris	.05
251	Bret Saberhagen	.05
252	Tom Niedenfuer	.05
253	Neal Heaton	.05
254	Eric Show	.05
255	Juan Samuel	.05
256	Dale Sveum	.05
257	Jim Gott	.05
258	Scott Garrelts	.05
259	Larry McWilliams	.05
260	Steve Bedrosian	.05
261	Jack Howell	.05
262	Jay Tibbs	.05
263	Jamie Moyer	.05
264	Doug Sisk	.05
265	Todd Worrell	.05
266	John Farrell	.05
267	Dave Collins	.05
268	Sid Fernandez	.05
269	Tom Brookens	.05
270	Shane Mack	.05
271	Paul Kilgus	.05
272	Chuck Crim	.05
273	Bob Knepper	.05
274	Mike Moore	.05
275	Guillermo Hernandez	.05
276	Dennis Eckersley	.05
277	Graig Nettles	.05
278	Rich Dotson	.05
279	Larry Herndon	.05
280	Gene Larkin	.05
281	Roger McDowell	.05
282	Greg Swindell	.05
283	Juan Agosto	.05
284	Jeff Robinson	.05
285	Mike Dunne	.05
286	Greg Mathews	.05
287	Kent Tekulve	.05
288	Jerry Mumphrey	.05
289	Jack McDowell	.05
290	Frank Viola	.05
291	Mark Gubicza	.05
292	Dave Schmidt	.05
293	Mike Henneman	.05
294	Jimmy Jones	.05
295	Charlie Hough	.05
296	Rafael Santana	.05
297	Chris Speier	.05
298	Mike Witt	.05
299	Pascual Perez	.05
300	Nolan Ryan	.75
301	Mitch Williams	.05
302	Mookie Wilson	.05
303	Mackey Sasser	.05
304	John Cerutti	.05
305	Jeff Reardon	.05
306	Randy Myers	.05
307	Greg Brock	.05
308	Bob Welch	.05
309	Jeff Robinson	.05
310	Harold Reynolds	.05
311	Jim Walewander	.05
312	Dave Magadan	.05
313	Jim Gantner	.05
314	Walt Terrell	.05
315	Wally Backman	.05
316	Luis Salazar	.05
317	Rick Rhoden	.05
318	Tom Henke	.05
319	Mike Macfarlane	.05
320	Dan Plesac	.05
321	Calvin Schiraldi	.05
322	Stan Javier	.05
323	Devon White	.05
324	Scott Bradley	.05
325	Bruce Hurst	.05
326	Manny Lee	.05
327	Rick Aguilera	.05
328	Bruce Ruffin	.05
329	Ed Whitson	.05
330	Bo Jackson	.15
331	Ivan Calderon	.05
332	Mickey Hatcher	.05
333	Barry Jones	.05
334	Ron Hassey	.05
335	Bill Wegman	.05
336	Damon Berryhill	.05
337	Steve Ontiverso	.05
338	Dan Pasqua	.05
339	Bill Pecota	.05
340	Greg Cadaret	.05
341	Scott Bankhead	.05
342	Ron Guidry	.10
343	Danny Heep	.05
344	Bob Brower	.05
345	Rich Gedman	.05
346	*Nelson Santovenia*	.05
347	George Bell	.05
348	Ted Power	.05
349	Mark Grant	.05
350a	Roger Clemens (778 wins)	2.00
350b	Roger Clemens (78 wins)	.30
351	Bill Long	.05
352	Jay Bell	.15
353	Steve Balboni	.05
354	Bob Kipper	.05
355	Steve Jeltz	.05
356	Jesse Orosco	.05
357	Bob Dernier	.05
358	Mickey Tettleton	.05
359	Duane Ward	.05
360	Darrin Jackson	.05
361	Rey Quinones	.05
362	Mark Grace	.25
363	Steve Lake	.05
364	Pat Perry	.05
365	Terry Steinbach	.05
366	Alan Ashby	.05
367	Jeff Montgomery	.05
368	Steve Buechele	.05
369	Chris Brown	.05
370	Orel Hershiser	.05
371	Todd Benzinger	.05
372	Ron Gant	.05
373	Paul Assenmacher	.05
374	Joey Meyer	.05
375	Neil Allen	.05
376	Mike Davis	.05
377	Jeff Parrett	.05
378	Jay Howell	.05
379	Rafael Belliard	.05
380	Luis Polonia	.05
381	Keith Atherton	.05
382	Kent Hrbek	.05
383	Bob Stanley	.05
384	Dave LaPoint	.05
385	Rance Mulliniks	.05
386	Melido Perez	.05
387	Doug Jones	.05
388	Steve Lyons	.05
389	Alejandro Pena	.05
390	Frank White	.05
391	Pat Tabler	.05
392	Eric Plunk	.05
393	Mike Maddux	.05
394	Allan Anderson	.05
395	Bob Brenly	.05
396	Rick Cerone	.05
397	Scott Terry	.05
398	Mike Jackson	.05
399	Bobby Thigpen	.05
400	Don Sutton	.20
401	Cecil Espy	.05
402	Junior Ortiz	.05
403	Mike Smithson	.05
404	Bud Black	.05
405	Tom Foley	.05
406	Andres Thomas	.05
407	Rick Sutcliffe	.05
408	Brian Harper	.05
409	John Smiley	.05
410	Juan Nieves	.05
411	Shawn Abner	.05
412	Wes Gardner	.05
413	Darren Daulton	.05
414	Juan Berenguer	.05
415	Charles Hudson	.05
416	Rick Honeycutt	.05
417	Greg Booker	.05
418	Tim Belcher	.05
419	Don August	.05
420	Dale Mohorcic	.05
421	Steve Lombardozzi	.05
422	Atlee Hammaker	.05
423	Jerry Don Gleaton	.05
424	Scott Bailes	.05
425	Bruce Sutter	.05
426	Randy Ready	.05
427	Jerry Reed	.05
428	Bryn Smith	.05
429	Tim Leary	.05
430	Mark Clear	.05
431	Terry Leach	.05
432	John Moses	.05
433	Ozzie Guillen	.05
434	Gene Nelson	.05
435	Gary Ward	.05
436	Luis Aguayo	.05
437	Fernando Valenzuela	.05
438	Jeff Russell	.05
439	Cecilio Guante	.05
440	Don Robinson	.05
441	Rick Anderson	.05
442	Tom Glavine	.25
443	Daryl Boston	.05
444	Joe Price	.05
445	Stewart Cliburn	.05
446	Manny Trillo	.05
447	Joel Skinner	.05
448	Charlie Puleo	.05
449	Carlton Fisk	.25
450	Will Clark	.15
451	Otis Nixon	.05
452	Rick Schu	.05
453	Todd Stottlemyre	.05
454	Tim Birtsas	.05
455	*Dave Gallagher*	.05
456	Barry Lyons	.05

457 Fred Manrique .05
458 Ernest Riles .05
459 *Doug Jennings* .05
460 Joe Magrane .05
461 Jamie Quirk .05
462 *Jack Armstrong* .05
463 Bobby Witt .05
464 Keith Miller .05
465 *Todd Burns* .05
466 *John Dopson* .05
467 Rich Yett .05
468 Craig Reynolds .05
469 Dave Bergman .05
470 Rex Hudler .05
471 Eric King .05
472 Joaquin Andujar .05
473 *Sil Campusano* .05
474 Terry Mulholland .05
475 Mike Flanagan .05
476 Greg Harris .05
477 Tommy John .10
478 Dave Anderson .05
479 Fred Toliver .05
480 Jimmy Key .05
481 Donell Nixon .05
482 Mark Portugal .05
483 Tom Pagnozzi .05
484 Jeff Kunkel .05
485 Frank Williams .05
486 Jody Reed .05
487 Roberto Kelly .05
488 Shawn Hillegas .05
489 Jerry Reuss .05
490 Mark Davis .05
491 Jeff Sellers .05
492 Zane Smith .05
493 Al Newman .05
494 Mike Young .05
495 Larry Parrish .05
496 Herm Winningham .05
497 Carmen Castillo .05
498 Joe Hesketh .05
499 Darrell Miller .05
500 Mike LaCoss .05
501 Charlie Lea .05
502 Bruce Benedict .05
503 Chuck Finley .05
504 Brad Wellman .05
505 Tim Crews .05
506 Ken Gerhart .05
507a Brian Holton (Born: 1/25/65, Denver) .15
507b Brian Holton (Born: 11/29/59, McKeesport) .05
508 Dennis Lamp .05
509 Bobby Meacham .05
510 Tracy Jones .05
511 Mike Fitzgerald .05
512 *Jeff Bittiger* .05
513 Tim Flannery .05
514 Ray Hayward .05
515 Dave Leiper .05
516 Rod Scurry .05
517 Carmelo Martinez .05
518 Curtis Wilkerson .05
519 Stan Jefferson .05
520 Dan Quisenberry .05
521 Lloyd McClendon .05
522 Steve Trout .05
523 Larry Andersen .05
524 Don Aase .05
525 Bob Forsch .05
526 Geno Petralli .05
527 Angel Salazar .05
528 *Mike Schooler* .05
529 Jose Oquendo .05
530 Jay Buhner .15
531 Tom Bolton .05
532 Al Nipper .05
533 Dave Henderson .05
534 *John Costello* .05
535 Donnie Moore .05
536 Mike Laga .05
537 Mike Gallego .05
538 Jim Clancy .05
539 Joel Youngblood .05
540 Rick Leach .05
541 Kevin Romine .05
542 Mark Salas .05
543 Greg Minton .05
544 Dave Palmer .05
545 Dwayne Murphy .05
546 Jim Deshaies .05
547 Don Gordon .05
548 Ricky Jordan .05
549 Mike Boddicker .05
550 Mike Scott .05
551 Jeff Ballard .05
552a Jose Rijo (uniform number #24 on card back) .15
552b Jose Rijo (uniform number #27 on card back) .10
553 Danny Darwin .05
554 Tom Browning .05
555 Danny Jackson .05
556 Rick Dempsey .05
557 Jeffrey Leonard .05
558 Jeff Musselman .05
559 Ron Robinson .05
560 John Tudor .05
561 Don Slaught .05
562 Dennis Rasmussen .05
563 Brady Anderson .05
564 Pedro Guerrero .05
565 Paul Molitor .35
566 *Terry Clark* .05
567 Terry Puhl .05
568 Mike Campbell .05
569 Paul Mirabella .05
570 Jeff Hamilton .05
571 *Oswald Peraza* .05
572 Bob McClure .05
573 *Jose Bautista* .05
574 Alex Trevino .05
575 John Franco .05
576 *Mark Parent* .05
577 Nelson Liriano .05
578 Steve Shields .05
579 Odell Jones .05
580 Al Leiter .05
581 Dave Stapleton .05
582 1988 World Series (Jose Canseco, Kirk Gibson, Orel Hershiser, Dave Stewart) .10
583 Donnie Hill .05
584 Chuck Jackson .05
585 Rene Gonzales .05
586 Tracy Woodson .05
587 Jim Adduci .05
588 Mario Soto .05
589 Jeff Blauser .05
590 Jim Traber .05
591 Jon Perlman .05
592 Mark Williamson .05
593 Dave Meads .05
594 Jim Eisenreich .05
595a *Paul Gibson* (player in background adjusting cup) .15
595b *Paul Gibson* (hand airbrushed away) .05
596 Mike Birkbeck .05
597 Terry Francona .05
598 Paul Zuvella .05
599 Franklin Stubbs .05
600 Gregg Jefferies .05
601 John Cangelosi .05
602 Mike Sharperson .05
603 Mike Diaz .05
604 *Gary Varsho* .05
605 *Terry Blocker* .05
606 Charlie O'Brien .05
607 Jim Eppard .05
608 John Davis .05
609 Ken Griffey, Sr. .05
610 Buddy Bell .05
611 Ted Simmons .05
612 Matt Williams .15
613 Danny Cox .05
614 Al Pedrique .05
615 Ron Oester .05
616 John Smoltz .10
617 Bob Melvin .05
618 *Rob Dibble* .15
619 Kirt Manwaring .05
620 Felix Fermin .05
621 *Doug Dascenzo* .05
622 *Bill Brennan* .05
623 *Carlos Quintana* .05
624 *Mike Harkey* .05
625 *Gary Sheffield* 1.00
626 *Tom Prince* .05
627 *Steve Searcy* .05
628 *Charlie Hayes* .25
629 *Felix Jose* .05
630 *Sandy Alomar* .75
631 *Derek Lilliquist* .05
632 Geronimo Berroa .05
633 *Luis Medina* .05
634 *Tom Gordon* .25
635 *Ramon Martinez* .50
636 *Craig Worthington* .05
637 Edgar Martinez .15
638 *Chad Krueter* .05
639 *Ron Jones* .05
640 *Van Snider* .05
641 *Lance Blankenship* .10
642 *Dwight Smith* .05
643 *Cameron Drew* .05
644 *Jerald Clark* .10
645 *Randy Johnson* 3.00
646 *Norm Charlton* .10
647 Todd Frohwirth .05
648 *Luis de los Santos* .05
649 *Tim Jones* .05
650 *Dave West* .10
651 *Bob Milacki* .10
652 1988 Highlight (Wrigley Field) .05
653 1988 Highlight (Orel Hershiser) .05
654a 1988 Highlight (Wade Boggs) ("...sixth consecutive seaason..." on back) 2.00
654b 1988 Highlight (Wade Boggs) ("season" corrected) .10
655 1988 Highlight (Jose Canseco) .15
656 1988 Highlight (Doug Jones) .05
657 1988 Highlight (Rickey Henderson) .10
658 1988 Highlight (Tom Browning) .05
659 1988 Highlight (Mike Greenwell) .05
660 1988 Highlight (Joe Morgan) (A.L. Win Streak) .05

1989 Score Traded

Score issued its second consecutive traded set in 1989 to supplement and update its regular set. The 110-card traded set features the same basic card design as the regular 1989 Score set. The set consists of rookies and traded players pictured with correct teams. The set was sold by hobby dealers in a special box that included an assortment of "Magic Motion" trivia cards. Cards are numbered with a "T" suffix.

MT
Complete Set (110): 17.50
Common Player: .05
1 Rafael Palmeiro .20
2 Nolan Ryan 3.00
3 Jack Clark .05
4 Dave LaPoint .05
5 Mike Moore .05
6 Pete O'Brien .05
7 Jeffrey Leonard .05
8 Rob Murphy .05
9 Tom Herr .05
10 Claudell Washington .05
11 Mike Pagliarulo .05
12 Steve Lake .05
13 Spike Owen .05
14 Andy Hawkins .05
15 Todd Benzinger .05
16 Mookie Wilson .05
17 Bert Blyleven .05
18 Jeff Treadway .05
19 Bruce Hurst .05
20 Steve Sax .05
21 Juan Samuel .05
22 Jesse Barfield .05
23 Carmelo Castillo .05
24 Terry Leach .05
25 Mark Langston .05
26 Eric King .05
27 Steve Balboni .05
28 Len Dykstra .05
29 Keith Moreland .05
30 Terry Kennedy .05
31 Eddie Murray .30
32 Mitch Williams .05
33 Jeff Parrett .05
34 Wally Backman .05
35 Julio Franco .05
36 Lance Parrish .05
37 Nick Esasky .05
38 Luis Polonia .05
39 Kevin Gross .05
40 John Dopson .05
41 Willie Randolph .05
42 Jim Clancy .05
43 Tracy Jones .05
44 Phil Bradley .05
45 Milt Thompson .05
46 Chris James .05
47 Scott Fletcher .05
48 Kal Daniels .05
49 Steve Bedrosian .05
50 Rickey Henderson .40
51 Dion James .05
52 Tim Leary .05
53 Roger McDowell .05
54 Mel Hall .05
55 Dickie Thon .05
56 Zane Smith .05
57 Danny Heep .05
58 Bob McClure .05
59 Brian Holton .05
60 Randy Ready .05
61 Bob Melvin .05
62 Harold Baines .05
63 Lance McCullers .05
64 Jody Davis .05
65 Darrell Evans .05
66 Joel Youngblood .05
67 Frank Viola .05
68 Mike Aldrete .05
69 Greg Cadaret .05
70 John Kruk .05
71 Pat Sheridan .05
72 Oddibe McDowell .05
73 Tom Brookens .05
74 Bob Boone .05
75 Walt Terrell .05
76 Joel Skinner .05
77 Randy Johnson 3.00
78 Felix Fermin .05
79 Rick Mahler .05
80 Rich Dotson .05
81 Cris Carpenter .05
82 Bill Spiers .05
83 Junior Felix .05
84 Joe Girardi .15
85 Jerome Walton .05
86 Greg Litton .05
87 Greg Harris .05
88 Jim Abbott .10
89 Kevin Brown .25
90 *John Wetteland* .25
91 Gary Wayne .05
92 Rich Monteleone .05
93 Bob Geren .05
94 Clay Parker .05
95 Steve Finley .25
96 Gregg Olson .05
97 Ken Patterson .05
98 Ken Hill .05
99 Scott Scudder .05
100 *Ken Griffey, Jr.* 10.00
101 Jeff Brantley .05
102 Donn Pall .05
103 Carlos Martinez .05

104	Joe Oliver	.05
105	Omar Vizquel	.25
106	*Albert Belle*	1.00
107	*Kenny Rogers*	.25
108	Mark Carreon	.05
109	Rolando Roomes	.05
110	Pete Harnisch	.05

1989 Score Young Superstars Series 1

These standard-size cards (2-1/2" x 3-1/2") display color action photos with a high-gloss finish. Fronts feature a red and blue border surrounding the photo with the team logo in the lower right. A red band beneath the photo provides the setting for the player ID including name, position, and uniform number. Backs feature a red "Young Superstar" headline above a portrait photo. Above the headline appears the player's personal information and statistics in orange and black. To the right photo a condensed scouting report and career hightlights are revealed. The card number and related logos appear on the bottom portion. Five trivia cards featuring "A Year to Remember" accompanied the series. Each trivia card relates to a highlight from the past 56 years. This set was distributed via a write-in offer with Score card wrappers.

		MT
Complete Set (42):		5.00
Common Player:		.10
1	Gregg Jefferies	.10
2	Jody Reed	.10
3	Mark Grace	.50
4	Dave Gallagher	.10
5	Bo Jackson	.15
6	Jay Buhner	.10
7	Melido Perez	.10
8	Bobby Witt	.10
9	David Cone	.10
10	Chris Sabo	.10
11	Pat Borders	.10
12	Mark Grant	.10
13	Mike Macfarlane	.10
14	Mike Jackson	.10
15	Ricky Jordan	.10
16	Ron Gant	.10
17	Al Leiter	.10
18	Jeff Parrett	.10
19	Pete Smith	.10
20	Walt Weiss	.10
21	Doug Drabek	.10
22	Kirt Manwaring	.10
23	Keith Miller	.10
24	Damon Berryhill	.10
25	Gary Sheffield	.25
26	Brady Anderson	.10
27	Mitch Williams	.10
28	Roberto Alomar	.35
29	Bobby Thigpen	.10
30	Bryan Harvey	.10
31	Jose Rijo	.10
32	Dave West	.10
33	Joey Meyer	.10
34	Allan Anderson	.10
35	Rafael Palmeiro	.20
36	Tim Belcher	.10
37	John Smiley	.10
38	Mackey Sasser	.10
39	Greg Maddux	1.00
40	Ramon Martinez	.10
41	Randy Myers	.10
42	Scott Bankhead	.10

1989 Score Young Superstars Series 2

Score followed up with a second series of Young Superstars in 1989. The second series also included 42 cards and featured the same design as the first series. The set was also distributed via a write-in offer with Score card wrappers.

		MT
Complete Set (42):		25.00
Common Player:		.10
1	Sandy Alomar	.35
2	Tom Gordon	.10
3	Ron Jones	.10
4	Todd Burns	.10
5	Paul O'Neill	.10
6	Gene Larkin	.10
7	Eric King	.10
8	Jeff Robinson	.10
9	Bill Wegman	.10
10	Cecil Espy	.10
11	Jose Guzman	.10
12	Kelly Gruber	.10
13	Duane Ward	.10
14	Mark Gubicza	.10
15	Norm Charlton	.10
16	Jose Oquendo	.10
17	Geronimo Berroa	.10
18	Ken Griffey Jr.	20.00
19	Lance McCullers	.10
20	Todd Stottlemyre	.10
21	Craig Worthington	.10
22	Mike Devereaux	.10
23	Tom Glavine	.20
24	Dale Sveum	.10
25	Roberto Kelly	.10
26	Luis Medina	.10
27	Steve Searcy	.10
28	Don August	.10
29	Shawn Hillegas	.10
30	Mike Campbell	.10
31	Mike Harkey	.10
32	Randy Johnson	.50
33	Craig Biggio	.25
34	Mike Schooler	.10
35	Andres Thomas	.10
36	Jerome Walton	.10
37	Cris Carpenter	.10
38	Kevin Mitchell	.10
39	Eddie Williams	.10
40	Chad Kreuter	.10
41	Danny Jackson	.10
42	Kurt Stillwell	.10

1990 Score

The regular Score set increased to 704 cards in 1990. Included were a series of cards picturing first-round draft picks, an expanded subset of rookie cards, four World Series specials, five Highlight cards, and a 13-card "Dream Team" series featuring the game's top players pictured on old tobacco-style cards. For the first time in a Score set, team logos are displayed on the card fronts Card backs include a full-color portrait photo with player data. A one-paragraph write-up of each player was again provided by former Sports Illustrated editor Les Woodcock. The Score set was again distributed with "Magic Motion" trivia cards, this year using "Baseball's Most Valuable Players" as its theme.

		MT
Complete Set (704):		8.00
Factory Set (704):		10.00
Common Player:		.05
Plastic Pack (16):		.60
Plastic Wax Box (36):		15.00
1	Don Mattingly	.60
2	Cal Ripken, Jr.	.75
3	Dwight Evans	.05
4	Barry Bonds	.50
5	Kevin McReynolds	.05
6	Ozzie Guillen	.05
7	Terry Kennedy	.05
8	Bryan Harvey	.05
9	Alan Trammell	.05
10	Cory Snyder	.05
11	Jody Reed	.05
12	Roberto Alomar	.35
13	Pedro Guerrero	.05
14	Gary Redus	.05
15	Marty Barrett	.05
16	Ricky Jordan	.05
17	Joe Magrane	.05
18	Sid Fernandez	.05
19	Rich Dotson	.05
20	Jack Clark	.05
21	Bob Walk	.05
22	Ron Karkovice	.05
23	Lenny Harris	.05
24	Phil Bradley	.05
25	Andres Galarraga	.05
26	Brian Downing	.05
27	Dave Martinez	.05
28	Eric King	.05
29	Barry Lyons	.05
30	Dave Schmidt	.05
31	Mike Boddicker	.05
32	Tom Foley	.05
33	Brady Anderson	.05
34	Jim Presley	.05
35	Lance Parrish	.05
36	Von Hayes	.05
37	Lee Smith	.05
38	Herm Winningham	.05
39	Alejandro Pena	.05
40	Mike Scott	.05
41	Joe Orsulak	.05
42	Rafael Ramirez	.05
43	Gerald Young	.05
44	Dick Schofield	.05
45	Dave Smith	.05
46	Dave Magadan	.05
47	Dennis Martinez	.05
48	Greg Minton	.05
49	Milt Thompson	.05
50	Orel Hershiser	.05
51	Bip Roberts	.05
52	Jerry Browne	.05
53	Bob Ojeda	.05
54	Fernando Valenzuela	.05
55	Matt Nokes	.05
56	Brook Jacoby	.05
57	Frank Tanana	.05
58	Scott Fletcher	.05
59	Ron Oester	.05
60	Bob Boone	.05
61	Dan Gladden	.05
62	Darnell Coles	.05
63	Gregg Olson	.05
64	Todd Burns	.05
65	Todd Benzinger	.05
66	Dale Murphy	.15
67	Mike Flanagan	.05
68	Jose Oquendo	.05
69	Cecil Espy	.05
70	Chris Sabo	.05
71	Shane Rawley	.05
72	Tom Brunansky	.05
73	Vance Law	.05
74	B.J. Surhoff	.05
75	Lou Whitaker	.05
76	Ken Caminiti	.05
77	Nelson Liriano	.05
78	Tommy Gregg	.05
79	Don Slaught	.05
80	Eddie Murray	.30
81	Joe Boever	.05
82	Charlie Leibrandt	.05
83	Jose Lind	.05
84	Tony Phillips	.05
85	Mitch Webster	.05
86	Dan Plesac	.05
87	Rick Mahler	.05
88	Steve Lyons	.05
89	Tony Fernandez	.05
90	Ryne Sandberg	.40
91	Nick Esasky	.05
92	Luis Salazar	.05
93	Pete Incaviglia	.05
94	Ivan Calderon	.05
95	Jeff Treadway	.05
96	Kurt Stillwell	.05
97	Gary Sheffield	.25
98	Jeffrey Leonard	.05
99	Andres Thomas	.05
100	Roberto Kelly	.05
101	Alvaro Espinoza	.05
102	Greg Gagne	.05
103	John Farrell	.05
104	Willie Wilson	.05
105	Glenn Braggs	.05
106	Chet Lemon	.05
107	Jamie Moyer	.05
108	Chuck Crim	.05
109	Dave Valle	.05
110	Walt Weiss	.05
111	Larry Sheets	.05
112	Don Robinson	.05
113	Danny Heep	.05
114	Carmelo Martinez	.05
115	Dave Gallagher	.05
116	Mike LaValliere	.05
117	Bob McClure	.05
118	Rene Gonzales	.05
119	Mark Parent	.05
120	Wally Joyner	.05
121	Mark Gubicza	.05

No.	Player	Price
122	Tony Pena	.05
123	Carmen Castillo	.05
124	Howard Johnson	.05
125	Steve Sax	.05
126	Tim Belcher	.05
127	Tim Burke	.05
128	Al Newman	.05
129	Dennis Rasmussen	.05
130	Doug Jones	.05
131	Fred Lynn	.05
132	Jeff Hamilton	.05
133	German Gonzalez	.05
134	John Morris	.05
135	Dave Parker	.05
136	Gary Pettis	.05
137	Dennis Boyd	.05
138	Candy Maldonado	.05
139	Rick Cerone	.05
140	George Brett	.50
141	Dave Clark	.05
142	Dickie Thon	.05
143	Junior Ortiz	.05
144	Don August	.05
145	Gary Gaetti	.05
146	Kirt Manwaring	.05
147	Jeff Reed	.05
148	Jose Alvarez	.05
149	Mike Schooler	.05
150	Mark Grace	.25
151	Geronimo Berroa	.05
152	Barry Jones	.05
153	Geno Petralli	.05
154	Jim Deshaies	.05
155	Barry Larkin	.10
156	Alfredo Griffin	.05
157	Tom Henke	.05
158	Mike Jeffcoat	.05
159	Bob Welch	.05
160	Julio Franco	.05
161	Henry Cotto	.05
162	Terry Steinbach	.05
163	Damon Berryhill	.05
164	Tim Crews	.05
165	Tom Browning	.05
166	Frd Manrique	.05
167	Harold Reynolds	.05
168a	Ron Hassey (uniform #27 on back)	.05
168b	Ron Hassey (uniform #24 on back)	.50
169	Shawon Dunston	.05
170	Bobby Bonilla	.05
171	Tom Herr	.05
172	Mike Heath	.05
173	Rich Gedman	.05
174	Bill Ripken	.05
175	Pete O'Brien	.05
176a	Lloyd McClendon (uniform number 1 on back)	.50
176b	Lloyd McClendon (uniform number 10 on back)	.05
177	Brian Holton	.05
178	Jeff Blauser	.05
179	Jim Eisenreich	.05
180	Bert Blyleven	.05
181	Rob Murphy	.05
182	Bill Doran	.05
183	Curt Ford	.05
184	Mike Henneman	.05
185	Eric Davis	.05
186	Lance McCullers	.05
187	*Steve Davis*	.05
188	Bill Wegman	.05
189	Brian Harper	.05
190	Mike Moore	.05
191	Dale Mohorcic	.05
192	Tim Wallach	.05
193	Keith Hernandez	.05
194	Dave Righetti	.05
195a	Bret Saberhagen ("joke" on card back)	.10
195b	Bret Saberhagen ("joker" on card back)	.30
196	Paul Kilgus	.05
197	Bud Black	.05
198	Juan Samuel	.05
199	Kevin Seitzer	.05
200	Darryl Strawberry	.05
201	Dave Steib	.05
202	Charlie Hough	.05
203	Jack Morris	.05
204	Rance Mulliniks	.05
205	Alvin Davis	.05
206	Jack Howell	.05
207	Ken Patterson	.05
208	Terry Pendleton	.05
209	Craig Lefferts	.05
210	Kevin Brown	.05
211	Dan Petry	.05
212	Dave Leiper	.05
213	Daryl Boston	.05
214	Kevin Hickey	.05
215	Mike Krukow	.05
216	Terry Francona	.05
217	Kirk McCaskill	.05
218	Scott Bailes	.05
219	Bob Forsch	.05
220	Mike Aldrete	.05
221	Steve Buechele	.05
222	Jesse Barfield	.05
223	Juan Berenguer	.05
224	Andy McGaffigan	.05
225	Pete Smith	.05
226	Mike Witt	.05
227	Jay Howell	.05
228	Scott Bradley	.05
229	*Jerome Walton*	.05
230	Greg Swindell	.05
231	Atlee Hammaker	.05
232a	Mike Devereaux (RF)	.05
232b	Mike Devereaux (CF)	.05
233	Ken Hill	.05
234	Craig Worthington	.05
235	Scott Terry	.05
236	Brett Butler	.05
237	Doyle Alexander	.05
238	Dave Anderson	.05
239	Bob Milacki	.05
240	Dwight Smith	.05
241	Otis Nixon	.05
242	Pat Tabler	.05
243	Derek Lilliquist	.05
244	Danny Tartabull	.05
245	Wade Boggs	.45
246	Scott Garrelts	.05
247	Spike Owen	.05
248	Norm Charlton	.05
249	Gerald Perry	.05
250	Nolan Ryan	.75
251	Kevin Gross	.05
252	Randy Milligan	.05
253	Mike LaCoss	.05
254	Dave Bergman	.05
255	Tony Gwynn	.45
256	Felix Fermin	.05
257	Greg Harris	.05
258	*Junior Felix*	.05
259	Mark Davis	.05
260	Vince Coleman	.05
261	Paul Gibson	.05
262	Mitch Williams	.05
263	Jeff Russell	.05
264	Omar Vizquel	.05
265	Andre Dawson	.15
266	Storm Davis	.05
267	Guillermo Hernandez	.05
268	Mike Felder	.05
269	Tom Candiotti	.05
270	Bruce Hurst	.05
271	Fred McGriff	.05
272	Glenn Davis	.05
273	John Franco	.05
274	Rich Yett	.05
275	Craig Biggio	.10
276	Gene Larkin	.05
277	Rob Dibble	.05
278	Randy Bush	.05
279	Kevin Bass	.05
280a	Bo Jackson ("Watham" on back)	.15
280b	Bo Jackson ("Wathan" on back)	.50
281	Wally Backman	.05
282	Larry Andersen	.05
283	Chris Bosio	.05
284	Juan Agosto	.05
285	Ozzie Smith	.45
286	George Bell	.05
287	Rex Hudler	.05
288	Pat Borders	.05
289	Danny Jackson	.05
290	Carlton Fisk	.25
291	Tracy Jones	.05
292	Allan Anderson	.05
293	Johnny Ray	.05
294	Lee Guetterman	.05
295	Paul O'Neill	.05
296	Carney Lansford	.05
297	Tom Brookens	.05
298	Claudell Washington	.05
299	Hubie Brooks	.05
300	Will Clark	.15
301	Kenny Rogers	.05
302	Darrell Evans	.05
303	Greg Briley	.05
304	Donn Pall	.05
305	Teddy Higuera	.05
306	Dan Pasqua	.05
307	Dave Winfield	.40
308	Dennis Powell	.05
309	Jose DeLeon	.05
310	Roger Clemens	.45
311	Melido Perez	.05
312	Devon White	.10
313	Dwight Gooden	.05
314	*Carlos Martinez*	.10
315	Dennis Eckersley	.05
316	Clay Parker	.05
317	Rick Honeycutt	.05
318	Tim Laudner	.05
319	Joe Carter	.05
320	Robin Yount	.30
321	Felix Jose	.05
322	Mickey Tettleton	.05
323	Mike Gallego	.05
324	Edgar Martinez	.05
325	Dave Henderson	.05
326	Chili Davis	.05
327	Steve Balboni	.05
328	Jody Davis	.05
329	Shawn Hillegas	.05
330	Jim Abbott	.05
331	John Dopson	.05
332	Mark Williamson	.05
333	Jeff Robinson	.05
334	John Smiley	.05
335	Bobby Thigpen	.05
336	Garry Templeton	.05
337	Marvell Wynne	.05
338a	Ken Griffey, Sr. (uniform #25 on card back)	.05
338b	Ken Griffey, Sr. (uniform #30 on card back)	1.00
339	Steve Finley	.05
340	Ellis Burks	.05
341	Frank Williams	.05
342	Mike Morgan	.05
343	Kevin Mitchell	.05
344	Joel Youngblood	.05
345	Mike Greenwell	.05
346	Glenn Wilson	.05
347	John Costello	.05
348	Wes Gardner	.05
349	Jeff Ballard	.05
350	Mark Thurmond	.05
351	Randy Myers	.05
352	Shawn Abner	.05
353	Jesse Orosco	.05
354	Greg Walker	.05
355	Pete Harnisch	.05
356	Steve Farr	.05
357	Dave LaPoint	.05
358	Willie Fraser	.05
359	Mickey Hatcher	.05
360	Rickey Henderson	.35
361	Mike Fitzgerald	.05
362	Bill Schroeder	.05
363	Mark Carreon	.05
364	Ron Jones	.05
365	Jeff Montgomery	.05
366	Bill Krueger	.05
367	John Cangelosi	.05
368	Jose Gonzalez	.05
369	*Greg Hibbard*	.10
370	John Smoltz	.10
371	*Jeff Brantley*	.05
372	Frank White	.05
373	Ed Whitson	.05
374	Willie McGee	.05
375	Jose Canseco	.25
376	Randy Ready	.05
377	Don Aase	.05
378	Tony Armas	.05
379	Steve Bedrosian	.05
380	Chuck Finley	.05
381	Kent Hrbek	.05
382	Jim Gantner	.05
383	Mel Hall	.05
384	Mike Marshall	.05
385	Mark McGwire	.75
386	Wayne Tolleson	.05
387	Brian Holton	.05
388	John Wetteland	.05
389	Darren Daulton	.05
390	Rob Deer	.05
391	John Moses	.05
392	Todd Worrell	.05
393	Chuck Cary	.05
394	Stan Javier	.05
395	Willie Randolph	.05
396	Bill Buckner	.05
397	Robby Thompson	.05
398	Mike Scioscia	.05
399	Lonnie Smith	.05
400	Kirby Puckett	.30
401	Mark Langston	.05
402	Danny Darwin	.05
403	Greg Maddux	.45
404	Lloyd Moseby	.05
405	Rafael Palmeiro	.20
406	Chad Kreuter	.05
407	Jimmy Key	.05
408	Tim Birtsas	.05
409	Tim Raines	.05
410	Dave Stewart	.05
411	*Eric Yelding*	.15
412	*Kent Anderson*	.05
413	Les Lancaster	.05
414	Rick Dempsey	.05
415	Randy Johnson	.25
416	Gary Carter	.15
417	Rolando Roomes	.05
418	Dan Schatzeder	.05
419	Bryn Smith	.05
420	Ruben Sierra	.05
421	Steve Jeltz	.05
422	Ken Oberkfell	.05
423	Sid Bream	.05
424	Jim Clancy	.05
425	Kelly Gruber	.05
426	Rick Leach	.05
427	Len Dykstra	.05
428	Jeff Pico	.05
429	John Cerutti	.05
430	David Cone	.05
431	Jeff Kunkel	.05
432	Luis Aquino	.05
433	Ernie Whitt	.05
434	Bo Diaz	.05
435	Steve Lake	.05
436	Pat Perry	.05
437	Mike Davis	.05
438	Cecilio Guante	.05
439	Duane Ward	.05
440	Andy Van Slyke	.05
441	Gene Nelson	.05
442	Luis Polonia	.05
443	Kevin Elster	.05
444	Keith Moreland	.05
445	Roger McDowell	.05
446	Ron Darling	.05
447	Ernest Riles	.05
448	Mookie Wilson	.05
449a	*Bill Spiers* (66 missing for year of birth)	.50
449b	*Bill Spiers* (1966 for birth year)	.05
450	Rick Sutcliffe	.05
451	Nelson Santovenia	.05
452	Andy Allanson	.05
453	Bob Melvin	.05
454	Benny Santiago	.05
455	Jose Uribe	.05
456	Bill Landrum	.05
457	Bobby Witt	.05
458	Kevin Romine	.05
459	Lee Mazzilli	.05
460	Paul Molitor	.30
461	Ramon Martinez	.05
462	Frank DiPino	.05
463	Walt Terrell	.05
464	*Bob Geren*	.05
465	Rick Reuchel	.05
466	Mark Grant	.05
467	John Kruk	.05
468	Gregg Jefferies	.05
469	R.J. Reynolds	.05
470	Harold Baines	.05
471	Dennis Lamp	.05
472	Tom Gordon	.05
473	Terry Puhl	.05
474	Curtis Wilkerson	.05
475	Dan Quisenberry	.05
476	Oddibe McDowell	.05
477a	Zane Smith (Career ERA 3.93)	.50
477b	Zane Smith	.05
478	Franklin Stubbs	.05
479	Wallace Johnson	.05
480	Jay Tibbs	.05
481	Tom Glavine	.10

482 Manny Lee .05
483 Joe Hesketh .05
484 Mike Bielecki .05
485 Greg Brock .05
486 Pascual Perez .05
487 Kirk Gibson .05
488 Scott Sanderson .05
489 Domingo Ramos .05
490 Kal Daniels .05
491a David Wells (reversed negative on back photo) 1.50
491b David Wells (corrected) .10
492 Jerry Reed .05
493 Eric Show .05
494 Mike Pagliarulo .05
495 Ron Robinson .05
496 Brad Komminsk .05
497 *Greg Litton* .05
498 Chris James .05
499 Luis Quinones .05
500 Frank Viola .05
501 Tim Teufel .05
502 Terry Leach .05
503 Matt Williams .15
504 Tim Leary .05
505 Doug Drabek .05
506 Mariano Duncan .05
507 Charlie Hayes .05
508 Albert Belle .20
509 Pat Sheridan .05
510 Mackey Sasser .05
511 Jose Rijo .05
512 Mike Smithson .05
513 Gary Ward .05
514 Dion James .05
515 Jim Gott .05
516 Drew Hall .05
517 Doug Bair .05
518 *Scott Scudder* .10
519 Rick Aguilera .05
520 Rafael Belliard .05
521 Jay Buhner .05
522 Jeff Reardon .05
523 Steve Rosenberg .05
524 Randy Velarde .05
525 Jeff Musselman .05
526 Bill Long .05
527 *Gary Wayne* .05
528 *Dave Johnson* .05
529 Ron Kittle .05
530 Erik Hanson .05
531 Steve Wilson .05
532 Joey Meyer .05
533 Curt Young .05
534 Kelly Downs .05
535 Joe Girardi .05
536 Lance Blankenship .05
537 Greg Mathews .05
538 Donell Nixon .05
539 Mark Knudson .05
540 *Jeff Wetherby* .05
541 Darrin Jackson .05
542 Terry Mulholland .05
543 Eric Hetzel .05
544 *Rick Reed* .05
545 Dennis Cook .05
546 Mike Jackson .05
547 Brian Fisher .05
548 *Gene Harris* .05
549 Jeff King .10
550 Dave Dravecky (Salute) .10
551 Randy Kutcher .05
552 Mark Portugal .05
553 *Jim Corsi* .05
554 Todd Stottlemyre .05
555 Scott Bankhead .05
556 Ken Dayley .05
557 *Rick Wrona* .15
558 *Sammy Sosa* 3.00
559 Keith Miller .05
560 Ken Griffey, Jr. .75
561a Ryne Sandberg (Highlight, 3B on front) 2.00
561b Ryne Sandberg (Highlight, no position) .20
562 Billy Hatcher .05
563 Jay Bell .05
564 *Jack Daugherty* .05
565 *Rich Monteleone* .05
566 Bo Jackson (All-Star MVP) .10
567 *Tony Fossas* .05
568 *Roy Smith* .05
569 *Jaime Navarro* .05
570 Lance Johnson .05
571 *Mike Dyer* .05
572 *Kevin Ritz* .05
573 Dave West .05
574 *Gary Mielke* .05
575 Scott Lusader .05
576 Joe Oliver .05
577 Sandy Alomar, Jr. .05
578 Andy Benes .05
579 Tim Jones .05
580 *Randy McCament* .05
581 Curt Schilling .25
582 *John Orton* .05
583a *Milt Cuyler* (998 games) 1.00
583b *Milt Cuyler* (98 games) .10
584 *Eric Anthony* .25
585 *Greg Vaughn* .30
586 Deion Sanders .10
587 Jose DeJesus .05
588 *Chip Hale* .05
589 *John Olerud* .50
590 *Steve Olin* .10
591 *Marquis Grissom* .40
592 *Moises Alou* .40
593 Mark Lemke .05
594 *Dean Palmer* .25
595 Robin Ventura .05
596 Tino Martinez .05
597 *Mike Huff* .05
598 *Scott Hemond* .05
599 *Wally Whitehurst* .05
600 *Todd Zeile* .15
601 Glenallen Hill .05
602 Hal Morris .05
603 Juan Bell .05
604 *Bobby Rose* .05
605 *Matt Merullo* .05
606 *Kevin Maas* .05
607 *Randy Nosek* .05
608a *Billy Bates* ("12 triples" mentioned in second-last line) .05
608b Billy Bates (triples not mentioned) .50
609 *Mike Stanton* .05
610 *Goose Gozzo* .05
611 *Charles Nagy* .40
612 *Scott Coolbaugh* .05
613 *Jose Vizcaino* .25
614 *Greg Smith* .05
615 *Jeff Huson* .05
616 *Mickey Weston* .05
617 *John Pawlowski* .05
618a *Joe Skalski* (uniform #27 on card back) .15
618b *Joe Skalski* (uniform #67 on card back) 1.00
619 *Bernie Williams* 1.50
620 *Shawn Holman* .05
621 *Gary Eave* .05
622 *Darrin Fletcher* .15
623 *Pat Combs* .05
624 *Mike Blowers* .05
625 Kevin Appier .05
626 *Pat Austin* .05
627 *Kelly Mann* .05
628 *Matt Kinzer* .05
629 *Chris Hammond* .15
630 *Dean Wilkins* .05
631 *Larry Walker* .50
632 *Blaine Beatty* .05
633a Tom Barrett (uniform #29 on card back) .05
633b Tom Barrett (uniform #14 on card back) 1.00
634 *Stan Belinda* .10
635 *Tex Smith* .05
636 *Hensley Meulens* .10
637 *Juan Gonzalez* 2.00
638 *Lenny Webster* .10
639 *Mark Gardner* .05
640 *Tommy Greene* .05
641 *Mike Hartley* .05
642 *Phil Stephenson* .05
643 *Kevin Mmahat* .05
644 *Ed Whited* .05
645 *Delino DeShields* .25
646 Kevin Blankenship .10
647 *Paul Sorrento* .15
648 *Mike Roesler* .05
649 *Jason Grimsley* .10
650 *Dave Justice* 1.00
651 *Scott Cooper* .05
652 Dave Eiland .05
653 *Mike Munoz* .05
654 *Jeff Fischer* .05
655 *Terry Jorgenson* .05
656 *George Canale* .05
657 *Brian DuBois* .05
658 Carlos Quintana .05
659 Luis de los Santos .05
660 Jerald Clark .05
661 *Donald Harris* (1st Round Pick) .10
662 *Paul Coleman* (1st Round Pick) .05
663 *Frank Thomas* (1st Round Pick) 2.50
664 *Brent Mayne* (1st Round Pick) .10
665 *Eddie Zosky* (1st Round Pick) .10
666 *Steve Hosey* (1st Round Pick) .15
667 *Scott Bryant* (1st Round Pick) .05
668 *Tom Goodwin* (1st Round Pick) .10
669 *Cal Eldred* (1st Round Pick) .25
670 *Earl Cunningham* (1st Round Pick) .05
671 *Alan Zinter* (1st Round Pick) .15
672 *Chuck Knoblauch* (1st Round Pick) .40
672 (a)Chuck Knoblauch (3,000 autographed cards with a special hologram on back were inserted into 1992 rack packs) 10.00
673 *Kyle Abbott* (1st Round Pick) .10
674 *Roger Salkeld* (1st Round Pick) .15
675 *Mo Vaughn* (1st Round Pick) .50
676 *Kiki Jones* (1st Round Pick) .05
677 *Tyler Houston* (1st Round Pick) .10
678 *Jeff Jackson* (1st Round Pick) .05
679 *Greg Gohr* (1st Round Pick) .05
680 *Ben McDonald* (1st Round Pick) .25
681 *Greg Blosser* (1st Round Pick) .15
682 *Willie Green* (Greene) 1st Round Pick) .15
683 Wade Boggs (Dream Team) .20
684 Will Clark (Dream Team) .10
685 Tony Gwynn (Dream Team) .20
686 Rickey Henderson (Dream Team) .20
687 Bo Jackson (Dream Team) .15
688 Mark Langston (Dream Team) .05
689 Barry Larkin (Dream Team) .05
690 Kirby Puckett (Dream Team) .25
691 Ryne Sandberg (Dream Team) .25
692 Mike Scott (Dream Team) .05
693 Terry Steinbach (Dream Team) .05
694 Bobby Thigpen (Dream Team) .05
695 Mitch Williams (Dream Team) .05
696 Nolan Ryan (Highlight) .50
697 Bo Jackson (FB/BB) .25
698 Rickey Henderson (ALCS MVP) .15
699 Will Clark (NLCS MVP) .10
700 World Series Games 1-2 .05
701 Lights Out: Candlestick .15
702 World Series Game 3 .05
703 World Series Wrap-up .05
704 Wade Boggs (Highlight) .10

1990 Score Rookie Dream Team

This 10-card "Rookie Dream Team" set, in the same format as those found in the regular-issue 1990 Score, was available only in factory sets for the hobby trade. Factory sets for general retail outlets did not include these cards, nor were they available in Score packs. Cards carry a "B" prefix to their numbers.

		MT
Complete Set (10):		2.50
Common Player:		.25
1	A. Bartlett Giamatti	.25
2	Pat Combs	.25
3	Todd Zeile	.30
4	Luis de los Santos	.25
5	Mark Lemke	.25
6	Robin Ventura	1.50
7	Jeff Huson	.25
8	Greg Vaughn	.75
9	Marquis Grissom	1.00
10	Eric Anthony	.25

1990 Score Traded

This 110-card set features players with new teams as well as 1990 Major League rookies. The cards feature full-color action photos framed in yellow with an orange border. The player's ID appears in green below the photo. The team logo is displayed next to the player's name. The card backs feature posed player photos and follow the style of the regular 1990 Score issue. The cards are numbered 1T-110T. Young hockey phenom Eric Lindros is featured trying out for the Toronto Blue Jays.

		MT
Complete Set (110):		5.00
Common Player:		.05
1	Dave Winfield	.40
2	Kevin Bass	.05
3	Nick Esasky	.05
4	Mitch Webster	.05
5	Pascual Perez	.05
6	Gary Pettis	.05
7	Tony Pena	.05
8	Candy Maldonado	.05
9	Cecil Fielder	.05
10	Carmelo Martinez	.05
11	Mark Langston	.05
12	Dave Parker	.05
13	Don Slaught	.05
14	Tony Phillips	.05
15	John Franco	.05
16	Randy Myers	.05
17	Jeff Reardon	.05
18	Sandy Alomar, Jr.	.05
19	Joe Carter	.05
20	Fred Lynn	.05
21	Storm Davis	.05
22	Craig Lefferts	.05
23	Pete O'Brien	.05
24	Dennis Boyd	.05
25	Lloyd Moseby	.05
26	Mark Davis	.05
27	Tim Leary	.05
28	Gerald Perry	.05
29	Don Aase	.05
30	Ernie Whitt	.05
31	Dale Murphy	.35
32	Alejandro Pena	.05
33	Juan Samuel	.05
34	Hubie Brooks	.05
35	Gary Carter	.20
36	Jim Presley	.05
37	Wally Backman	.05
38	Matt Nokes	.05
39	Dan Petry	.05
40	Franklin Stubbs	.05
41	Jeff Huson	.05
42	Billy Hatcher	.05
43	Terry Leach	.05
44	Phil Bradley	.05
45	Claudell Washington	.05
46	Luis Polonia	.05
47	Daryl Boston	.05
48	Lee Smith	.05
49	Tom Brunansky	.05
50	Mike Witt	.05
51	Willie Randolph	.05
52	Stan Javier	.05
53	Brad Komminsk	.05
54	John Candelaria	.05
55	Bryn Smith	.05
56	Glenn Braggs	.05
57	Keith Hernandez	.05
58	Ken Oberkfell	.05
59	Steve Jeltz	.05
60	Chris James	.05
61	Scott Sanderson	.05
62	Bill Long	.05
63	Rick Cerone	.05
64	Scott Bailes	.05
65	Larry Sheets	.05
66	Junior Ortiz	.05
67	Francisco Cabrera	.05
68	Gary DiSarcina	.05
69	Greg Olson	.05
70	Beau Allred	.05
71	Oscar Azocar	.05
72	Kent Mercker	.05
73	John Burkett	.05
74	Carlos Baerga	.10
75	Dave Hollins	.05
76	*Todd Hundley*	.50
77	Rick Parker	.05
78	Steve Cummings	.05
79	Bill Sampen	.05
80	Jerry Kutzler	.05
81	Derek Bell	.05
82	Kevin Tapani	.05
83	*Jim Leyritz*	.15
84	*Ray Lankford*	.50
85	Wayne Edwards	.05
86	Frank Thomas	3.00
87	Tim Naehring	.05
88	Willie Blair	.05
89	*Alan Mills*	.05
90	Scott Radinsky	.05
91	Howard Farmer	.05
92	Julio Machado	.05
93	Rafael Valdez	.05
94	*Shawn Boskie*	.05
95	David Segui	.15
96	Chris Hoiles	.05
97	D.J. Dozier	.05
98	Hector Villanueva	.05
99	Eric Gunderson	.05
100	*Eric Lindros*	1.00
101	Dave Otto	.05
102	Dana Kiecker	.05
103	Tim Drummond	.05
104	Mickey Pina	.05
105	Craig Grebeck	.05
106	*Bernard Gilkey*	.35
107	Tim Layana	.05
108	Scott Chiamparino	.05
109	Steve Avery	.05
110	Terry Shumpert	.05

1990 Score Young Superstars Set 1

For the third consecutive year, Score produced Young Superstars boxed sets. The 1990 versions contain 42 player cards plus five Magic-Motion trivia cards. The cards are similar to previous Young Superstar sets, with action photography on the front and a glossy finish. Card backs have a color portrait, major league statistics and scouting reports. Besides the boxed set, cards from Set I were inserted into rack packs.

		MT
Complete Set (42):		5.00
Common Player:		.15
1	Bo Jackson	.25
2	Dwight Smith	.15
3	Joey Belle	.25
4	Gregg Olson	.15
5	Jim Abbott	.15
6	Felix Fermin	.15
7	Brian Holman	.15
8	Clay Parker	.15
9	Junior Felix	.15
10	Joe Oliver	.15
11	Steve Finley	.15
12	Greg Briley	.15
13	Greg Vaughn	.15
14	Bill Spiers	.15
15	Eric Yelding	.15
16	Jose Gonzalez	.15
17	Mark Carreon	.15
18	Greg Harris	.15
19	Felix Jose	.15
20	Bob Milacki	.15
21	Kenny Rogers	.15
22	Rolando Roomes	.15
23	Bip Roberts	.15
24	Jeff Brantley	.15
25	Jeff Ballard	.15
26	John Dopson	.15
27	Ken Patterson	.15
28	Omar Vizquel	.15
29	Kevin Brown	.25
30	Derek Lilliquist	.15
31	David Wells	.25
32	Ken Hill	.15
33	Greg Litton	.15
34	Rob Ducey	.15
35	Carlos Martinez	.15
36	John Smoltz	.45
37	Lenny Harris	.15
38	Charlie Hayes	.15
39	Tommy Gregg	.15
40	John Wetteland	.15
41	Jeff Huson	.15
42	Eric Anthony	.15

1990 Score Young Superstars Set 2

Available only as a boxed set via a mail-order offer, Set II of 1990 Score Young Superstars is identical in format to Set I, with the exception that the graphic elements on the front of Set II cards are in red and green, while in Set I they are in blue and magenta.

		MT
Complete Set (42):		7.50
Common Player:		.15
1	Todd Zeile	.15
2	Ben McDonald	.15
3	Delino DeShields	.15
4	Pat Combs	.15
5	John Olerud	.30
6	Marquis Grissom	.15
7	Mike Stanton	.15
8	Robin Ventura	.30
9	Larry Walker	.50
10	Dante Bichette	.15
11	Jack Armstrong	.15
12	Jay Bell	.15
13	Andy Benes	.15
14	Joey Cora	.15
15	Rob Dibble	.15
16	Jeff King	.15
17	Jeff Hamilton	.15
18	Erik Hanson	.15
19	Pete Harnisch	.15
20	Greg Hibbard	.15
21	Stan Javier	.15
22	Mark Lemke	.15
23	Steve Olin	.15
24	Tommy Greene	.15
25	Sammy Sosa	5.00
26	Gary Wayne	.15
27	Deion Sanders	.25
28	Steve Wilson	.15
29	Joe Girardi	.15
30	John Orton	.15
31	Kevin Tapani	.15
32	Carlos Baerga	.15
33	Glenallen Hill	.15
34	Mike Blowers	.15
35	Dave Hollins	.15
36	Lance Blankenship	.15
37	Hal Morris	.15
38	Lance Johnson	.15
39	Chris Gwynn	.15
40	Doug Dascenzo	.15
41	Jerald Clark	.15
42	Carlos Quintana	.15

1991 Score

Score introduced a two series format in 1991. The first series includes cards 1-441. Score cards once again feature multiple border colors within the set, several subsets (Master Blaster, K-Man, Highlights and Riflemen), full-color action photos on the front and portraits on the flip side. Score eliminated display of the player's uniform number on the 1991 cards. Black-and-white Dream Team cards, plus Prospects and #1 Draft Picks highlight the 1991 set. The second series was released in February of 1991.

		MT
Complete Set (893):		6.00
Factory Set (900):		8.00
Common Player:		.05
Pack (16):		.40
Wax Box Series 1 (36):		8.00
Wax Box Series 2 (36):		12.00
1	Jose Canseco	.35
2	Ken Griffey, Jr.	.75
3	Ryne Sandberg	.40
4	Nolan Ryan	.75
5	Bo Jackson	.15
6	Bret Saberhagen	.05
7	Will Clark	.15
8	Ellis Burks	.05
9	Joe Carter	.05
10	Rickey Henderson	.35
11	Ozzie Guillen	.05
12	Wade Boggs	.40
13	Jerome Walton	.05
14	John Franco	.05
15	Ricky Jordan	.05
16	Wally Backman	.05
17	Rob Dibble	.05
18	Glenn Braggs	.05
19	Cory Snyder	.05
20	Kal Daniels	.05
21	Mark Langston	.05
22	Kevin Gross	.05
23	Don Mattingly	.75
24	Dave Righetti	.05
25	Roberto Alomar	.35
26	Robby Thompson	.05
27	Jack McDowell	.05
28	Bip Roberts	.05
29	Jay Howell	.05
30	Dave Steib	.05
31	Johnny Ray	.05

No.	Player	Price
32	Steve Sax	.05
33	Terry Mulholland	.05
34	Lee Guetterman	.05
35	Tim Raines	.05
36	Scott Fletcher	.05
37	Lance Parrish	.05
38	Tony Phillips	.05
39	Todd Stottlemyre	.05
40	Alan Trammell	.05
41	Todd Burns	.05
42	Mookie Wilson	.05
43	Chris Bosio	.05
44	Jeffrey Leonard	.05
45	Doug Jones	.05
46	Mike Scott	.05
47	Andy Hawkins	.05
48	Harold Reynolds	.05
49	Paul Molitor	.35
50	John Farrell	.05
51	Danny Darwin	.05
52	Jeff Blauser	.05
53	John Tudor	.05
54	Milt Thompson	.05
55	Dave Justice	.30
56	*Greg Olson*	.05
57	*Willie Blair*	.05
58	*Rick Parker*	.05
59	Shawn Boskie	.05
60	Kevin Tapani	.05
61	Dave Hollins	.05
62	*Scott Radinsky*	.10
63	Francisco Cabrera	.05
64	*Tim Layana*	.05
65	Jim Leyritz	.05
66	Wayne Edwards	.05
67	Lee Stevens	.10
68	*Bill Sampen*	.05
69	*Craig Grebeck*	.10
70	John Burkett	.05
71	*Hector Villanueva*	.05
72	*Oscar Azocar*	.05
73	Alan Mills	.05
74	Carlos Baerga	.05
75	Charles Nagy	.05
76	Tim Drummond	.05
77	*Dana Kiecker*	.05
78	*Tom Edens*	.05
79	Kent Mercker	.05
80	Steve Avery	.05
81	Lee Smith	.05
82	Dave Martinez	.05
83	Dave Winfield	.40
84	Bill Spiers	.05
85	Dan Pasqua	.05
86	Randy Milligan	.05
87	Tracy Jones	.05
88	Greg Myers	.05
89	Keith Hernandez	.05
90	Todd Benzinger	.05
91	Mike Jackson	.05
92	Mike Stanley	.05
93	Candy Maldonado	.05
94	John Kruk	.05
95	Cal Ripken, Jr.	.75
96	Willie Fraser	.05
97	Mike Felder	.05
98	Bill Landrum	.05
99	Chuck Crim	.05
100	Chuck Finley	.05
101	Kirt Manwaring	.05
102	Jaime Navarro	.05
103	Dickie Thon	.05
104	Brian Downing	.05
105	Jim Abbott	.05
106	Tom Brookens	.05
107	Darryl Hamilton	.05
108	Bryan Harvey	.05
109	Greg Harris	.05
110	Greg Swindell	.05
111	Juan Berenguer	.05
112	Mike Heath	.05
113	Scott Bradley	.05
114	Jack Morris	.05
115	Barry Jones	.05
116	Kevin Romine	.05
117	Garry Templeton	.05
118	Scott Sanderson	.05
119	Roberto Kelly	.05
120	George Brett	.50
121	Oddibe McDowell	.05
122	Jim Acker	.05
123	Bill Swift	.05
124	Eric King	.05
125	Jay Buhner	.05
126	Matt Young	.05
127	Alvaro Espinoza	.05
128	Greg Hibbard	.05
129	Jeff Robinson	.05
130	Mike Greenwell	.05
131	Dion James	.05
132	Donn Pall	.05
133	Lloyd Moseby	.05
134	Randy Velarde	.05
135	Allan Anderson	.05
136	Mark Davis	.05
137	Eric Davis	.05
138	Phil Stephenson	.05
139	Felix Fermin	.05
140	Pedro Guerrero	.05
141	Charlie Hough	.05
142	Mike Henneman	.05
143	Jeff Montgomery	.05
144	Lenny Harris	.05
145	Bruce Hurst	.05
146	Eric Anthony	.05
147	Paul Assenmacher	.05
148	Jesse Barfield	.05
149	Carlos Quintana	.05
150	Dave Stewart	.05
151	Roy Smith	.05
152	Paul Gibson	.05
153	Mickey Hatcher	.05
154	Jim Eisenreich	.05
155	Kenny Rogers	.05
156	Dave Schmidt	.05
157	Lance Johnson	.05
158	Dave West	.05
159	Steve Balboni	.05
160	Jeff Brantley	.05
161	Craig Biggio	.10
162	Brook Jacoby	.05
163	Dan Gladden	.05
164	Jeff Reardon	.05
165	Mark Carreon	.05
166	Mel Hall	.05
167	Gary Mielke	.05
168	Cecil Fielder	.05
169	Darrin Jackson	.05
170	Rick Aguilera	.05
171	Walt Weiss	.05
172	Steve Farr	.05
173	Jody Reed	.05
174	Mike Jeffcoat	.05
175	Mark Grace	.20
176	Larry Sheets	.05
177	Bill Gullickson	.05
178	Chris Gwynn	.05
179	Melido Perez	.05
180	Sid Fernandez	.05
181	Tim Burke	.05
182	Gary Pettis	.05
183	Rob Murphy	.05
184	Craig Lefferts	.05
185	Howard Johnson	.05
186	Ken Caminiti	.05
187	Tim Belcher	.05
188	Greg Cadaret	.05
189	Matt Williams	.15
190	Dave Magadan	.05
191	Geno Petralli	.05
192	Jeff Robinson	.05
193	Jim Deshaies	.05
194	Willie Randolph	.05
195	George Bell	.05
196	Hubie Brooks	.05
197	Tom Gordon	.05
198	Mike Fitzgerald	.05
199	Mike Pagliarulo	.05
200	Kirby Puckett	.50
201	Shawon Dunston	.05
202	Dennis Boyd	.05
203	Junior Felix	.05
204	Alejandro Pena	.05
205	Pete Smith	.05
206	Tom Glavine	.10
207	Luis Salazar	.05
208	John Smoltz	.10
209	Doug Dascenzo	.05
210	Tim Wallach	.05
211	Greg Gagne	.05
212	Mark Gubicza	.05
213	Mark Parent	.05
214	Ken Oberkfell	.05
215	Gary Carter	.20
216	Rafael Palmeiro	.20
217	Tom Niedenfuer	.05
218	Dave LaPoint	.05
219	Jeff Treadway	.05
220	Mitch Williams	.05
221	Jose DeLeon	.05
222	Mike LaValliere	.05
223	Darrel Akerfelds	.05
224	Kent Anderson	.05
225	Dwight Evans	.05
226	Gary Redus	.05
227	Paul O'Neill	.05
228	Marty Barrett	.05
229	Tom Browning	.05
230	Terry Pendleton	.05
231	Jack Armstrong	.05
232	Mike Boddicker	.05
233	Neal Heaton	.05
234	Marquis Grissom	.05
235	Bert Blyleven	.05
236	Curt Young	.05
237	Don Carman	.05
238	Charlie Hayes	.05
239	Mark Knudson	.05
240	Todd Zeile	.05
241	Larry Walker	.25
242	Jerald Clark	.05
243	Jeff Ballard	.05
244	Jeff King	.05
245	Tom Brunansky	.05
246	Darren Daulton	.05
247	Scott Terry	.05
248	Rob Deer	.05
249	Brady Anderson	.05
250	Len Dykstra	.05
251	Greg Harris	.05
252	Mike Hartley	.05
253	Joey Cora	.05
254	Ivan Calderon	.05
255	Ted Power	.05
256	Sammy Sosa	.60
257	Steve Buechele	.05
258	Mike Devereaux	.05
259	Brad Komminsk	.05
260	Teddy Higuera	.05
261	Shawn Abner	.05
262	Dave Valle	.05
263	Jeff Huson	.05
264	Edgar Martinez	.05
265	Carlton Fisk	.25
266	Steve Finley	.05
267	John Wetteland	.05
268	Kevin Appier	.05
269	Steve Lyons	.05
270	Mickey Tettleton	.05
271	Luis Rivera	.05
272	Steve Jeltz	.05
273	R.J. Reynolds	.05
274	Carlos Martinez	.05
275	Dan Plesac	.05
276	Mike Morgan	.05
277	Jeff Russell	.05
278	Pete Incaviglia	.05
279	Kevin Seitzer	.05
280	Bobby Thigpen	.05
281	Stan Javier	.05
282	Henry Cotto	.05
283	Gary Wayne	.05
284	Shane Mack	.05
285	Brian Holman	.05
286	Gerald Perry	.05
287	Steve Crawford	.05
288	Nelson Liriano	.05
289	Don Aase	.05
290	Randy Johnson	.35
291	Harold Baines	.05
292	Kent Hrbek	.05
293	Les Lancaster	.05
294	Jeff Musselman	.05
295	Kurt Stillwell	.05
296	Stan Belinda	.05
297	Lou Whitaker	.05
298	Glenn Wilson	.05
299	Omar Vizquel	.05
300	Ramon Martinez	.05
301	Dwight Smith	.05
302	Tim Crews	.05
303	Lance Blankenship	.05
304	Sid Bream	.05
305	Rafael Ramirez	.05
306	Steve Wilson	.05
307	Mackey Sasser	.05
308	Franklin Stubbs	.05
309	Jack Daugherty	.05
310	Eddie Murray	.30
311	Bob Welch	.05
312	Brian Harper	.05
313	Lance McCullers	.05
314	Dave Smith	.05
315	Bobby Bonilla	.05
316	Jerry Don Gleaton	.05
317	Greg Maddux	.60
318	Keith Miller	.05
319	Mark Portugal	.05
320	Robin Ventura	.05
321	Bob Ojeda	.05
322	Mike Harkey	.05
323	Jay Bell	.05
324	Mark McGwire	.75
325	Gary Gaetti	.05
326	Jeff Pico	.05
327	Kevin McReynolds	.05
328	Frank Tanana	.05
329	Eric Yelding	.05
330	Barry Bonds	.60
331	*Brian McRae*	.05
332	*Pedro Munoz*	.05
333	*Daryl Irvine*	.05
334	Chris Hoiles	.05
335	*Thomas Howard*	.05
336	*Jeff Schulz*	.05
337	Jeff Manto	.05
338	Beau Allred	.05
339	*Mike Bordick*	.15
340	Todd Hundley	.05
341	*Jim Vatcher*	.05
342	Luis Sojo	.05
343	*Jose Offerman*	.15
344	*Pete Coachman*	.05
345	Mike Benjamin	.05
346	*Ozzie Canseco*	.05
347	Tim McIntosh	.05
348	*Phil Plantier*	.05
349	*Terry Shumpert*	.05
350	Darren Lewis	.05
351	*David Walsh*	.05
352	*Scott Chiamparino*	.05
353	*Julio Valera*	.05
354	*Anthony Telford*	.05
355	Kevin Wickander	.05
356	*Tim Naehring*	.05
357	*Jim Poole*	.05
358	*Mark Whiten*	.05
359	*Terry Wells*	.05
360	*Rafael Valdez*	.05
361	*Mel Stottlemyre*	.05
362	*David Segui*	.10
363	Paul Abbott	.05
364	*Steve Howard*	.05
365	*Karl Rhodes*	.10
366	*Rafael Novoa*	.05
367	*Joe Grahe*	.05
368	*Darren Reed*	.05
369	Jeff McKnight	.05
370	Scott Leius	.05
371	*Mark Dewey*	.05
372	*Mark Lee*	.05
373	*Rosario Rodriguez*	.05
374	Chuck McElroy	.05
375	*Mike Bell*	.05
376	Mickey Morandini	.05
377	*Bill Haselman*	.05
378	*Dave Pavlas*	.05
379	Derrick May	.05
380	*Jeromy Burnitz* (1st Draft Pick)	.25
381	*Donald Peters* (1st Draft Pick)	.05
382	*Alex Fernandez* (1st Draft Pick)	.05
383	*Mike Mussina* (1st Draft Pick)	1.50
384	*Daniel Smith* (1st Draft Pick)	.05
385	*Lance Dickson* (1st Draft Pick)	.15
386	*Carl Everett* (1st Draft Pick)	.75
387	*Thomas Nevers* (1st Draft Pick)	.15
388	*Adam Hyzdu* (1st Draft Pick)	.10
389	*Todd Van Poppel* (1st Draft Pick)	.10
390	*Rondell White* (1st Draft Pick)	1.00
391	*Marc Newfield* (1st Draft Pick)	.05
392	Julio Franco (AS)	.05
393	Wade Boggs (AS)	.15
394	Ozzie Guillen (AS)	.05
395	Cecil Fielder (AS)	.05
396	Ken Griffey, Jr. (AS)	.50
397	Rickey Henderson (AS)	.20
398	Jose Canseco (AS)	.15
399	Roger Clemens (AS)	.25
400	Sandy Alomar,Jr. (AS)	.05
401	Bobby Thigpen (AS)	.05

402 Bobby Bonilla (Master Blaster) .05
403 Eric Davis (Master Blaster) .05
404 Fred McGriff (Master Blaster) .05
405 Glenn Davis (Master Blaster) .05
406 Kevin Mitchell (Master Blaster) .05
407 Rob Dibble (K-Man) .05
408 Ramon Martinez (K-Man) .05
409 David Cone (K-Man) .05
410 Bobby Witt (K-Man) .05
411 Mark Langston (K-Man) .05
412 Bo Jackson (Rifleman) .10
413 Shawon Dunston (Rifleman) .05
414 Jesse Barfield (Rifleman) .05
415 Ken Caminiti (Rifleman) .05
416 Benito Santiago (Rifleman) .05
417 Nolan Ryan (Highlight) .35
418 Bobby Thigpen (HL) .05
419 Ramon Martinez (HL) .05
420 Bo Jackson (HL) .10
421 Carlton Fisk (HL) .15
422 Jimmy Key .05
423 Junior Noboa .05
424 Al Newman .05
425 Pat Borders .05
426 Von Hayes .05
427 Tim Teufel .05
428 Eric Plunk .05
429 John Moses .05
430 Mike Witt .05
431 Otis Nixon .05
432 Tony Fernandez .05
433 Rance Mulliniks .05
434 Dan Petry .05
435 Bob Geren .05
436 Steve Frey .05
437 Jamie Moyer .05
438 Junior Ortiz .05
439 Tom O'Malley .05
440 Pat Combs .05
441 Jose Canseco (Dream Team) .20
442 Alfredo Griffin .05
443 Andres Galarraga .05
444 Bryn Smith .05
445 Andre Dawson .20
446 Juan Samuel .05
447 Mike Aldrete .05
448 Ron Gant .05
449 Fernando Valenzuela .05
450 Vince Coleman .05
451 Kevin Mitchell .05
452 Spike Owen .05
453 Mike Bielecki .05
454 Dennis Martinez .05
455 Brett Butler .05
456 Ron Darling .05
457 Dennis Rasmussen .05
458 Ken Howell .05
459 Steve Bedrosian .05
460 Frank Viola .05
461 Jose Lind .05
462 Chris Sabo .05
463 Dante Bichette .05
464 Rick Mahler .05
465 John Smiley .05
466 Devon White .05
467 John Orton .05
468 Mike Stanton .05
469 Billy Hatcher .05
470 Wally Joyner .05
471 Gene Larkin .05
472 Doug Drabek .05
473 Gary Sheffield .20
474 David Wells .10
475 Andy Van Slyke .05
476 Mike Gallego .05
477 B.J. Surhoff .05
478 Gene Nelson .05
479 Mariano Duncan .05
480 Fred McGriff .05
481 Jerry Browne .05
482 Alvin Davis .05
483 Bill Wegman .05
484 Dave Parker .05
485 Dennis Eckersley .05
486 Erik Hanson .05
487 Bill Ripken .05
488 Tom Candiotti .05
489 Mike Schooler .05
490 Gregg Olson .05
491 Chris James .05
492 Pete Harnisch .05
493 Julio Franco .05
494 Greg Briley .05
495 Ruben Sierra .05
496 Steve Olin .05
497 Mike Fetters .05
498 Mark Williamson .05
499 Bob Tewksbury .05
500 Tony Gwynn .45
501 Randy Myers .05
502 Keith Comstock .05
503 Craig Worthington .05
504 Mark Eichhorn .05
505 Barry Larkin .10
506 Dave Johnson .05
507 Bobby Witt .05
508 Joe Orsulak .05
509 Pete O'Brien .05
510 Brad Arnsberg .05
511 Storm Davis .05
512 Bob Milacki .05
513 Bill Pecota .05
514 Glenallen Hill .05
515 Danny Tartabull .05
516 Mike Moore .05
517 Ron Robinson .05
518 Mark Gardner .05
519 Rick Wrona .05
520 Mike Scioscia .05
521 Frank Wills .05
522 Greg Brock .05
523 Jack Clark .05
524 Bruce Ruffin .05
525 Robin Yount .25
526 Tom Foley .05
527 Pat Perry .05
528 Greg Vaughn .05
529 Wally Whitehurst .05
530 Norm Charlton .05
531 Marvell Wynne .05
532 Jim Gantner .05
533 Greg Litton .05
534 Manny Lee .05
535 Scott Bailes .05
536 Charlie Leibrandt .05
537 Roger McDowell .05
538 Andy Benes .05
539 Rick Honeycutt .05
540 Dwight Gooden .05
541 Scott Garrelts .05
542 Dave Clark .05
543 Lonnie Smith .05
544 Rick Rueschel .05
545 Delino DeShields .05
546 Mike Sharperson .05
547 Mike Kingery .05
548 Terry Kennedy .05
549 David Cone .05
550 Orel Hershiser .05
551 Matt Nokes .05
552 Eddie Williams .05
553 Frank DiPino .05
554 Fred Lynn .05
555 Alex Cole .05
556 Terry Leach .05
557 Chet Lemon .05
558 Paul Mirabella .05
559 Bill Long .05
560 Phil Bradley .05
561 Duane Ward .05
562 Dave Bergman .05
563 Eric Show .05
564 Xavier Hernandez .05
565 Jeff Parrett .05
566 Chuck Cary .05
567 Ken Hill .05
568 Bob Welch .05
569 John Mitchell .05
570 Travis Fryman .05
571 Derek Lilliquist .05
572 Steve Lake .05
573 *John Barfield* .05
574 Randy Bush .05
575 Joe Magrane .05
576 Edgar Diaz .05
577 Casy Candaele .05
578 Jesse Orosco .05
579 Tom Henke .05
580 Rick Cerone .05
581 Drew Hall .05
582 Tony Castillo .05
583 Jimmy Jones .05
584 Rick Reed .05
585 Joe Girardi .05
586 *Jeff Gray* .05
587 Luis Polonia .05
588 Joe Klink .05
589 Rex Hudler .05
590 Kirk McCaskill .05
591 Juan Agosto .05
592 Wes Gardner .05
593 *Rich Rodriguez* .05
594 Mitch Webster .05
595 Kelly Gruber .05
596 Dale Mohorcic .05
597 Willie McGee .05
598 Bill Krueger .05
599 Bob Walk .05
600 Kevin Maas .05
601 Danny Jackson .05
602 Craig McMurtry .05
603 Curtis Wilkerson .05
604 Adam Peterson .05
605 Sam Horn .05
606 Tommy Gregg .05
607 Ken Dayley .05
608 Carmelo Castillo .05
609 John Shelby .05
610 Don Slaught .05
611 Calvin Schiraldi .05
612 Dennis Lamp .05
613 Andres Thomas .05
614 Jose Gonzales .05
615 Randy Ready .05
616 Kevin Bass .05
617 Mike Marshall .05
618 Daryl Boston .05
619 Andy McGaffigan .05
620 Joe Oliver .05
621 Jim Gott .05
622 Jose Oquendo .05
623 Jose DeJesus .05
624 Mike Brumley .05
625 John Olerud .05
626 Ernest Riles .05
627 Gene Harris .05
628 Jose Uribe .05
629 Darnell Coles .05
630 Carney Lansford .05
631 Tim Leary .05
632 Tim Hulett .05
633 Kevin Elster .05
634 Tony Fossas .05
635 Francisco Oliveras .05
636 Bob Patterson .05
637 Gary Ward .05
638 Rene Gonzales .05
639 Don Robinson .05
640 Darryl Strawberry .05
641 Dave Anderson .05
642 Scott Scudder .05
643 *Reggie Harris* .05
644 Dave Henderson .05
645 Ben McDonald .05
646 Bob Kipper .05
647 Hal Morris .05
648 Tim Birtsas .05
649 Steve Searcy .05
650 Dale Murphy .15
651 Ron Oester .05
652 Mike LaCoss .05
653 Ron Jones .05
654 Kelly Downs .05
655 Roger Clemens .50
656 Herm Winningham .05
657 Trevor Wilson .05
658 Jose Rijo .05
659 Dann Bilardello .05
660 Gregg Jefferies .05
661 Doug Drabek (All-Star) .05
662 Randy Myers (AS) .05
663 Benito Santiago (AS) .05
664 Will Clark (AS) .10
665 Ryne Sandberg (AS) .15
666 Barry Larkin (AS) .05
667 Matt Williams (AS) .05
668 Barry Bonds (AS) .40
669 Eric Davis .05
670 Bobby Bonilla (AS) .05
671 *Chipper Jones* (1st Draft Pick) 2.00
672 *Eric Christopherson* (1st Draft Pick) .05
673 *Robbie Beckett* (1st Draft Pick) .05
674 *Shane Andrews* (1st Draft Pick) .15
675 *Steve Karsay* (1st Draft Pick) .15
676 *Aaron Holbert* (1st Draft Pick) .05
677 *Donovan Osborne* (1st Draft Pick) .05
678 *Todd Ritchie* (1st Draft Pick) .15
679 *Ron Walden* (1st Draft Pick) .05
680 *Tim Costo* (1st Draft Pick) .05
681 *Dan Wilson* (1st Draft Pick) .15
682 *Kurt Miller* (1st Draft Pick) .05
683 *Mike Lieberthal* (1st Draft Pick) .25
684 Roger Clemens (K-Man) .20
685 Dwight Gooden (K-Man) .05
686 Nolan Ryan (K-Man) .30
687 Frank Viola (K-Man) .05
688 Erik Hanson (K-Man) .05
689 Matt Williams (Master Blaster) .05
690 Jose Canseco (Master Blaster) .15
691 Darryl Strawberry (Master Blaster) .05
692 Bo Jackson (Master Blaster) .10
693 Cecil Fielder (Master Blaster) .05
694 Sandy Alomar, Jr. (Rifleman) .05
695 Cory Snyder (Rifleman) .05
696 Eric Davis (Rifleman) .05
697 Ken Griffey, Jr. (Rifleman) .50
698 Andy Van Slyke (Rifleman) .05
699 Mark Langston, Mike Witt (No-hitter) .05
700 Randy Johnson (No-hitter) .20
701 Nolan Ryan (No-hitter) .30
702 Dave Stewart (No-hitter) .05
703 Fernando Valenzuela (No-hitter) .05
704 Andy Hawkins (No-hitter) .05
705 Melido Perez (No-hitter) .05
706 Terry Mulholland (No-hitter) .05
707 Dave Stieb (No-hitter) .05
708 *Brian Barnes* .05
709 Bernard Gilkey .05
710 *Steve Decker* .05
711 *Paul Faries* .05
712 *Paul Marak* .05
713 *Wes Chamberlain* .05
714 *Kevin Belcher* .05
715 Dan Boone .05
716 *Steve Adkins* .05
717 *Geronimo Pena* .05
718 *Howard Farmer* .05
719 *Mark Leonard* .05
720 Tom Lampkin .05
721 *Mike Gardiner* .05
722 *Jeff Conine* .40
723 *Efrain Valdez* .05
724 Chuck Malone .05
725 *Leo Gomez* .05
726 *Paul McClellan* .05
727 *Mark Leiter* .05
728 *Rich DeLucia* .05
729 Mel Rojas .05
730 *Hector Wagner* .05
731 Ray Lankford .05
732 *Turner Ward* .05
733 *Gerald Alexander* .05
734 *Scott Anderson* .05
735 Tony Perezchica .05
736 Jimmy Kremers .05

737	American Flag	.25
738	*Mike York*	.05
739	Mike Rochford	.05
740	Scott Aldred	.05
741	*Rico Brogna*	.10
742	*Dave Burba*	.10
743	*Ray Stephens*	.05
744	*Eric Gunderson*	.05
745	*Troy Afenir*	.05
746	Jeff Shaw	.50
747	*Orlando Merced*	.15
748	*Omar Oliveras*	.05
749	Jerry Kutzler	.05
750	Mo Vaughn	.30
751	*Matt Stark*	.05
752	*Randy Hennis*	.05
753	*Andujar Cedeno*	.05
754	Kelvin Torve	.05
755	Joe Kraemer	.05
756	*Phil Clark*	.05
757	*Ed Vosberg*	.05
758	*Mike Perez*	.05
759	*Scott Lewis*	.05
760	*Steve Chitren*	.05
761	*Ray Young*	.05
762	*Andres Santana*	.05
763	*Rodney McCray*	.05
764	*Sean Berry*	.10
765	Brent Mayne	.05
766	*Mike Simms*	.05
767	*Glenn Sutko*	.05
768	Gary Disarcina	.05
769	George Brett (HL)	.20
770	Cecil Fielder (HL)	.05
771	Jim Presley	.05
772	John Dopson	.05
773	Bo Jackson (Breaker)	.10
774	Brent Knackert	.05
775	Bill Doran	.05
776	Dick Schofield	.05
777	Nelson Santovenia	.05
778	Mark Guthrie	.05
779	Mark Lemke	.05
780	Terry Steinbach	.05
781	Tom Bolton	.05
782	*Randy Tomlin*	.05
783	Jeff Kunkel	.05
784	Felix Jose	.05
785	Rick Sutcliffe	.05
786	John Cerutti	.05
787	Jose Vizcaino	.05
788	Curt Schilling	.20
789	Ed Whitson	.05
790	Tony Pena	.05
791	John Candelaria	.05
792	Carmelo Martinez	.05
793	Sandy Alomar, Jr.	.05
794	*Jim Neidlinger*	.05
795	Red's October (Barry Larkin, Chris Sabo)	.10
796	Paul Sorrento	.05
797	Tom Pagnozzi	.05
798	Tino Martinez	.05
799	Scott Ruskin	.05
800	Kirk Gibson	.05
801	Walt Terrell	.05
802	John Russell	.05
803	Chili Davis	.05
804	Chris Nabholz	.05
805	Juan Gonzalez	.40
806	Ron Hassey	.05
807	Todd Worrell	.05
808	Tommy Greene	.05
809	Joel Skinner	.05
810	Benito Santiago	.05
811	Pat Tabler	.05
812	*Scott Erickson*	.05
813	Moises Alou	.15
814	Dale Sveum	.05
815	Ryne Sandberg (Man of the Year)	.20
816	Rick Dempsey	.05
817	Scott Bankhead	.05
818	Jason Grimsley	.05
819	Doug Jennings	.05
820	Tom Herr	.05
821	Rob Ducey	.05
822	Luis Quinones	.05
823	Greg Minton	.05
824	Mark Grant	.05
825	Ozzie Smith	.50
826	Dave Eiland	.05
827	Danny Heep	.05
828	Hensley Meulens	.05
829	Charlie O'Brien	.05
830	Glenn Davis	.05
831	John Marzano	.05
832	Steve Ontiveros	.05
833	Ron Karkovice	.05
834	Jerry Goff	.05
835	Ken Griffey, Sr.	.05
836	Kevin Reimer	.05
837	Randy Kutcher	.05
838	Mike Blowers	.05
839	Mike Macfarlane	.05
840	Frank Thomas	.75
841	Ken Griffey Sr., Ken Griffey Jr.	.50
842	Jack Howell	.05
843	Mauro Gozzo	.05
844	Gerald Young	.05
845	Zane Smith	.05
846	Kevin Brown	.05
847	Sil Campusano	.05
848	Larry Andersen	.05
849	Cal Ripken, Jr. (Franchise)	.25
850	Roger Clemens (Franchise)	.15
851	Sandy Alomar, Jr. (Franchise)	.05
852	Alan Trammell (Franchise)	.05
853	George Brett (Franchise)	.20
854	Robin Yount (Franchise)	.10
855	Kirby Puckett (Franchise)	.15
856	Don Mattingly (Franchise)	.20
857	Rickey Henderson (Franchise)	.10
858	Ken Griffey, Jr. (Franchise)	.50
859	Ruben Sierra (Franchise)	.05
860	John Olerud (Franchise)	.05
861	Dave Justice (Franchise)	.10
862	Ryne Sandberg (Franchise)	.15
863	Eric Davis (Franchise)	.05
864	Darryl Strawberry (Franchise)	.05
865	Tim Wallach (Franchise)	.05
866	Dwight Gooden (Franchise)	.05
867	Len Dykstra (Franchise)	.05
868	Barry Bonds (Franchise)	.35
869	Todd Zeile (Franchise)	.05
870	Benito Santiago (Franchise)	.05
871	Will Clark (Franchise)	.10
872	Craig Biggio (Franchise)	.05
873	Wally Joyner (Franchise)	.05
874	Frank Thomas (Franchise)	.45
875	Rickey Henderson (MVP)	.10
876	Barry Bonds (MVP)	.35
877	Bob Welch (Cy Young)	.05
878	Doug Drabek (Cy Young)	.05
879	Sandy Alomar, Jr. (ROY)	.05
880	Dave Justice (ROY)	.20
881	Damon Berryhill	.05
882	Frank Viola (Dream Team)	.05
883	Dave Stewart (Dream Team)	.05
884	Doug Jones (Dream Team)	.05
885	Randy Myers (Dream Team)	.05
886	Will Clark (Dream Team)	.10
887	Roberto Alomar (Dream Team)	.50
888	Barry Larkin (Dream Team)	.05
889	Wade Boggs (Dream Team)	.20
890	Rickey Henderson (Dream Team)	.20
891	Kirby Puckett (Dream Team)	.40
892	Ken Griffey, Jr. (Dream Team)	.50
893	Benito Santiago (Dream Team)	.05

1991 Score Cooperstown

This seven-card set was included as an insert in every factory set. The card fronts are white, with an oval-vignetted player portrait. The backs have green borders surrounding a yellow background which contains a summary of the player's career.

		MT
Complete Set (7):		5.00
Common Player:		.25
B1	Wade Boggs	.75
B2	Barry Larkin	.25
B3	Ken Griffey, Jr.	2.00
B4	Rickey Henderson	.45
B5	George Brett	1.00
B6	Will Clark	.25
B7	Nolan Ryan	2.00

1991 Score Hot Rookies

These standard-size cards were inserted one per every 100-card 1991 Score blister pack. Action photos with white borders are featured on the front, and "Hot Rookie" is written in yellow at the top. The background is shaded from yellow to orange. The backs are numbered and each has a color mug shot and a career summary.

		MT
Complete Set (10):		5.00
Common Player:		.25
1	Dave Justice	1.00
2	Kevin Maas	.25
3	Hal Morris	.25
4	Frank Thomas	2.50
5	Jeff Conine	.45
6	Sandy Alomar Jr.	.35
7	Ray Lankford	.25
8	Steve Decker	.25
9	Juan Gonzalez	1.50
10	Jose Offerman	.25

1991 Score Mickey Mantle

This special set recalls Mickey Mantle's career as a Yankee. Card fronts are glossy and have red and white borders. The card's caption appears at the bottom in a blue stripe. The backs have a photo and a summary of the caption, plus the card number and serial number. Dealers and media members received the sets, which were limited to 5,000, in a fin-fold plastic wrapper. A total of 2,500 of the cards were numbered and autographed.

		MT
Complete Set (7):		65.00
Common Card:		12.00
Autographed Card:		250.00
1	The Rookie	12.00
2	Triple Crown	12.00
3	World Series	12.00
4	Going, Going, Gone	12.00
5	Speed and Grace	12.00
6	A True Yankee	12.00
7	Twilight	12.00

1991 Score Traded

This 110-card set features players with new teams as well as 1991 Major League rookies.

The cards are designed in the same style as the regular 1991 Score issue. The cards once again feature a "T" designation along with the card number. The complete set was sold at hobby shops in a special box.

		MT
Complete Set (110):		4.00
Common Player:		.05
1	Bo Jackson	.10
2	Mike Flanagan	.05
3	Pete Incaviglia	.05
4	Jack Clark	.05
5	Hubie Brooks	.05
6	Ivan Calderon	.05
7	Glenn Davis	.05
8	Wally Backman	.05
9	Dave Smith	.05
10	Tim Raines	.05
11	Joe Carter	.05
12	Sid Bream	.05
13	George Bell	.05
14	Steve Bedrosian	.05
15	Willie Wilson	.05
16	Darryl Strawberry	.05
17	Danny Jackson	.05
18	Kirk Gibson	.05
19	Willie McGee	.05
20	Junior Felix	.05
21	Steve Farr	.05
22	Pat Tabler	.05
23	Brett Butler	.05
24	Danny Darwin	.05
25	Mickey Tettleton	.05
26	Gary Carter	.20
27	Mitch Williams	.05
28	Candy Maldonado	.05
29	Otis Nixon	.05
30	Brian Downing	.05
31	Tom Candiotti	.05
32	John Candelaria	.05
33	Rob Murphy	.05
34	Deion Sanders	.15
35	Willie Randolph	.05
36	Pete Harnisch	.05
37	Dante Bichette	.05
38	Garry Templeton	.05
39	Gary Gaetti	.05
40	John Cerutti	.05
41	Rick Cerone	.05
42	Mike Pagliarulo	.05
43	Ron Hassey	.05
44	Roberto Alomar	.35
45	Mike Boddicker	.05
46	Bud Black	.05
47	Rob Deer	.05
48	Devon White	.05
49	Luis Sojo	.05
50	Terry Pendleton	.05
51	Kevin Gross	.05
52	Mike Huff	.05
53	Dave Righetti	.05
54	Matt Young	.05
55	Ernest Riles	.05
56	Bill Gullickson	.05
57	Vince Coleman	.05
58	Fred McGriff	.05
59	Franklin Stubbs	.05
60	Eric King	.05
61	Cory Snyder	.05
62	Dwight Evans	.05
63	Gerald Perry	.05
64	Eric Show	.05
65	Shawn Hillegas	.05
66	Tony Fernandez	.05
67	Tim Teufel	.05
68	Mitch Webster	.05
69	Mike Heath	.05
70	Chili Davis	.05
71	Larry Andersen	.05
72	Gary Varsho	.05
73	Juan Berenguer	.05
74	Jack Morris	.05
75	Barry Jones	.05
76	Rafael Belliard	.05
77	Steve Buechele	.05
78	Scott Sanderson	.05
79	Bob Ojeda	.05
80	Curt Schilling	.25
81	Brian Drahman	.05
82	*Ivan Rodriguez*	2.00
83	David Howard	.05
84	Heath Slocumb	.05
85	Mike Timlin	.05
86	Darryl Kile	.10
87	Pete Schourek	.05
88	Bruce Walton	.05
89	Al Osuna	.05
90	Gary Scott	.05
91	Doug Simons	.05
92	Chris Jones	.05
93	Chuck Knoblauch	.05
94	Dana Allison	.05
95	Erik Pappas	.05
96	*Jeff Bagwell*	2.50
97	Kirk Dressendorfer	.05
98	Freddie Benavides	.05
99	*Luis Gonzalez*	2.00
100	Wade Taylor	.05
101	Ed Sprague	.05
102	Bob Scanlan	.05
103	Rick Wilkins	.05
104	Chris Donnels	.05
105	Joe Slusarski	.05
106	Mark Lewis	.05
107	Pat Kelly	.05
108	John Briscoe	.05
109	Luis Lopez	.05
110	Jeff Johnson	.05

1992 Score

Score used a two series format for the second consecutive year in 1992. Cards 1-442 are featured in the first series. Fronts feature full-color game action photos. Backs feature color head shots of the players, team logo and career stats. Several subsets are included in 1992, including a five-card Joe DiMaggio set. DiMaggio autographed cards were also inserted into random packs. Cards 736-772 can be found with or without a "Rookie Prospects" banner on the card front. Rack packs could be found with random inserts of 1991 Rookie of the Year Chuck Knoblauch's 1990 Score #1 Draft Pick card in a special autographed editon of 3,000. Factory sets contain 17 bonus cards not found in any other packaging.

		MT
Complete Set (893):		9.00
Factory Set (910):		12.00
Common Player:		.05
Wax Pack (16):		.50
Wax Box (36):		10.00
1	Ken Griffey, Jr.	1.00
2	Nolan Ryan	1.00
3	Will Clark	.15
4	Dave Justice	.20
5	Dave Henderson	.05
6	Bret Saberhagen	.05
7	Fred McGriff	.05
8	Erik Hanson	.05
9	Darryl Strawberry	.05
10	Dwight Gooden	.05
11	Juan Gonzalez	.50
12	Mark Langston	.05
13	Lonnie Smith	.05
14	Jeff Montgomery	.05
15	Roberto Alomar	.25
16	Delino DeShields	.05
17	Steve Bedrosian	.05
18	Terry Pendleton	.05
19	Mark Carreon	.05
20	Mark McGwire	1.00
21	Roger Clemens	.50
22	Chuck Crim	.05
23	Don Mattingly	.75
24	Dickie Thon	.05
25	Ron Gant	.05
26	Milt Cuyler	.05
27	Mike Macfarlane	.05
28	Dan Gladden	.05
29	Melido Perez	.05
30	Willie Randolph	.05
31	Albert Belle	.25
32	Dave Winfield	.35
33	Jimmy Jones	.05
34	Kevin Gross	.05
35	Andres Galarraga	.05
36	Mike Devereaux	.05
37	Chris Bosio	.05
38	Mike LaValliere	.05
39	Gary Gaetti	.05
40	Felix Jose	.05
41	Alvaro Espinoza	.05
42	Rick Aguilera	.05
43	Mike Gallego	.05
44	Eric Davis	.05
45	George Bell	.05
46	Tom Brunansky	.05
47	Steve Farr	.05
48	Duane Ward	.05
49	David Wells	.10
50	Cecil Fielder	.05
51	Walt Weiss	.05
52	Todd Zeile	.05
53	Doug Jones	.05
54	Bob Walk	.05
55	Rafael Palmeiro	.15
56	Rob Deer	.05
57	Paul O'Neill	.05
58	Jeff Reardon	.05
59	Randy Ready	.05
60	Scott Erickson	.05
61	Paul Molitor	.25
62	Jack McDowell	.05
63	Jim Acker	.05
64	Jay Buhner	.05
65	Travis Fryman	.05
66	Marquis Grissom	.05
67	Mike Harkey	.05
68	Luis Polonia	.05
69	Ken Caminiti	.05
70	Chris Sabo	.05
71	Gregg Olson	.05
72	Carlton Fisk	.30
73	Juan Samuel	.05
74	Todd Stottlemyre	.05
75	Andre Dawson	.20
76	Alvin Davis	.05
77	Bill Doran	.05
78	B.J. Surhoff	.05
79	Kirk McCaskill	.05
80	Dale Murphy	.15
81	Jose DeLeon	.05
82	Alex Fernandez	.05
83	Ivan Calderon	.05
84	Brent Mayne	.05
85	Jody Reed	.05
86	Randy Tomlin	.05
87	Randy Milligan	.05
88	Pascual Perez	.05
89	Hensley Meulens	.05
90	Joe Carter	.05
91	Mike Moore	.05
92	Ozzie Guillen	.05
93	Shawn Hillegas	.05
94	Chili Davis	.05
95	Vince Coleman	.05
96	Jimmy Key	.05
97	Billy Ripken	.05
98	Dave Smith	.05
99	Tom Bolton	.05
100	Barry Larkin	.10
101	Kenny Rogers	.05
102	Mike Boddicker	.05
103	Kevin Elster	.05
104	Ken Hill	.05
105	Charlie Leibrandt	.05
106	Pat Combs	.05
107	Hubie Brooks	.05
108	Julio Franco	.05
109	Vicente Palacios	.05
110	Kal Daniels	.05
111	Bruce Hurst	.05
112	Willie McGee	.05
113	Ted Power	.05
114	Milt Thompson	.05
115	Doug Drabek	.05
116	Rafael Belliard	.05
117	Scott Garrelts	.05
118	Terry Mulholland	.05
119	Jay Howell	.05
120	Danny Jackson	.05
121	Scott Ruskin	.05
122	Robin Ventura	.05
123	Bip Roberts	.05
124	Jeff Russell	.05
125	Hal Morris	.05
126	Teddy Higuera	.05
127	Luis Sojo	.05
128	Carlos Baerga	.05
129	Jeff Ballard	.05
130	Tom Gordon	.05
131	Sid Bream	.05
132	Rance Mulliniks	.05
133	Andy Benes	.05
134	Mickey Tettleton	.05
135	Rich DeLucia	.05
136	Tom Pagnozzi	.05
137	Harold Baines	.05
138	Danny Darwin	.05
139	Kevin Bass	.05
140	Chris Nabholz	.05
141	Pete O'Brien	.05
142	Jeff Treadway	.05
143	Mickey Morandini	.05
144	Eric King	.05
145	Danny Tartabull	.05
146	Lance Johnson	.05
147	Casey Candaele	.05
148	Felix Fermin	.05
149	Rich Rodriguez	.05
150	Dwight Evans	.05
151	Joe Klink	.05
152	Kevin Reimer	.05
153	Orlando Merced	.05
154	Mel Hall	.05
155	Randy Myers	.05
156	Greg Harris	.05
157	Jeff Brantley	.05
158	Jim Eisenreich	.05
159	Luis Rivera	.05
160	Cris Carpenter	.05
161	Bruce Ruffin	.05
162	Omar Vizquel	.05
163	Gerald Alexander	.05
164	Mark Guthrie	.05
165	Scott Lewis	.05
166	Bill Sampen	.05
167	Dave Anderson	.05
168	Kevin McReynolds	.05
169	Jose Vizcaino	.05
170	Bob Geren	.05
171	Mike Morgan	.05
172	Jim Gott	.05
173	Mike Pagliarulo	.05
174	Mike Jeffcoat	.05
175	Craig Lefferts	.05
176	Steve Finley	.05
177	Wally Backman	.05
178	Kent Mercker	.05
179	John Cerutti	.05
180	Jay Bell	.05
181	Dale Sveum	.05
182	Greg Gagne	.05
183	Donnie Hill	.05
184	Rex Hudler	.05
185	Pat Kelly	.05
186	Jeff Robinson	.05
187	Jeff Gray	.05
188	Jerry Willard	.05
189	Carlos Quintana	.05
190	Dennis Eckersley	.05
191	Kelly Downs	.05
192	Gregg Jefferies	.05
193	Darrin Fletcher	.05
194	Mike Jackson	.05
195	Eddie Murray	.35
196	Billy Landrum	.05
197	Eric Yelding	.05

198	Devon White	.05
199	Larry Walker	.20
200	Ryne Sandberg	.40
201	Dave Magadan	.05
202	Steve Chitren	.05
203	Scott Fletcher	.05
204	Dwayne Henry	.05
205	Scott Coolbaugh	.05
206	Tracy Jones	.05
207	Von Hayes	.05
208	Bob Melvin	.05
209	Scott Scudder	.05
210	Luis Gonzalez	.20
211	Scott Sanderson	.05
212	Chris Donnels	.05
213	Heath Slocumb	.05
214	Mike Timlin	.05
215	Brian Harper	.05
216	Juan Berenguer	.05
217	Mike Henneman	.05
218	Bill Spiers	.05
219	Scott Terry	.05
220	Frank Viola	.05
221	Mark Eichhorn	.05
222	Ernest Riles	.05
223	Ray Lankford	.05
224	Pete Harnisch	.05
225	Bobby Bonilla	.05
226	Mike Scioscia	.05
227	Joel Skinner	.05
228	Brian Holman	.05
229	Gilberto Reyes	.05
230	Matt Williams	.15
231	Jaime Navarro	.05
232	Jose Rijo	.05
233	Atlee Hammaker	.05
234	Tim Teufel	.05
235	John Kruk	.05
236	Kurt Stillwell	.05
237	Dan Pasqua	.05
238	Tim Crews	.05
239	Dave Gallagher	.05
240	Leo Gomez	.05
241	Steve Avery	.05
242	Bill Gullickson	.05
243	Mark Portugal	.05
244	Lee Guetterman	.05
245	Benny Santiago	.05
246	Jim Gantner	.05
247	Robby Thompson	.05
248	Terry Shumpert	.05
249	*Mike Bell*	.05
250	Harold Reynolds	.05
251	Mike Felder	.05
252	Bill Pecota	.05
253	Bill Krueger	.05
254	Alfredo Griffin	.05
255	Lou Whitaker	.05
256	Roy Smith	.05
257	Jerald Clark	.05
258	Sammy Sosa	.60
259	Tim Naehring	.05
260	Dave Righetti	.05
261	Paul Gibson	.05
262	Chris James	.05
263	Larry Andersen	.05
264	Storm Davis	.05
265	Jose Lind	.05
266	Greg Hibbard	.05
267	Norm Charlton	.05
268	Paul Kilgus	.05
269	Greg Maddux	.60
270	Ellis Burks	.05
271	Frank Tanana	.05
272	Gene Larkin	.05
273	Ron Hassey	.05
274	Jeff Robinson	.05
275	Steve Howe	.05
276	Daryl Boston	.05
277	Mark Lee	.05
278	*Jose Segura*	.05
279	Lance Blankenship	.05
280	Don Slaught	.05
281	Russ Swan	.05
282	Bob Tewksbury	.05
283	Geno Petralli	.05
284	Shane Mack	.05
285	Bob Scanlan	.05
286	Tim Leary	.05
287	John Smoltz	.10
288	Pat Borders	.05
289	Mark Davidson	.05
290	Sam Horn	.05
291	Lenny Harris	.05
292	Franklin Stubbs	.05
293	Thomas Howard	.05
294	Steve Lyons	.05
295	Francisco Oliveras	.05
296	Terry Leach	.05
297	Barry Jones	.05
298	Lance Parrish	.05
299	Wally Whitehurst	.05
300	Bob Welch	.05
301	Charlie Hayes	.05
302	Charlie Hough	.05
303	Gary Redus	.05
304	Scott Bradley	.05
305	Jose Oquendo	.05
306	Pete Incaviglia	.05
307	Marvin Freeman	.05
308	Gary Pettis	.05
309	Joe Slusarski	.05
310	Kevin Seitzer	.05
311	Jeff Reed	.05
312	Pat Tabler	.05
313	Mike Maddux	.05
314	Bob Milacki	.05
315	Eric Anthony	.05
316	Dante Bichette	.05
317	Steve Decker	.05
318	Jack Clark	.05
319	Doug Dascenzo	.05
320	Scott Leius	.05
321	Jim Lindeman	.05
322	Bryan Harvey	.05
323	Spike Owen	.05
324	Roberto Kelly	.05
325	Stan Belinda	.05
326	Joey Cora	.05
327	Jeff Innis	.05
328	Willie Wilson	.05
329	Juan Agosto	.05
330	Charles Nagy	.05
331	Scott Bailes	.05
332	Pete Schourek	.05
333	Mike Flanagan	.05
334	Omar Olivares	.05
335	Dennis Lamp	.05
336	Tommy Greene	.05
337	Randy Velarde	.05
338	Tom Lampkin	.05
339	John Russell	.05
340	Bob Kipper	.05
341	Todd Burns	.05
342	Ron Jones	.05
343	Dave Valle	.05
344	Mike Heath	.05
345	John Olerud	.05
346	Gerald Young	.05
347	Ken Patterson	.05
348	Les Lancaster	.05
349	Steve Crawford	.05
350	John Candelaria	.05
351	Mike Aldrete	.05
352	Mariano Duncan	.05
353	Julio Machado	.05
354	Ken Williams	.05
355	Walt Terrell	.05
356	Mitch Williams	.05
357	Al Newman	.05
358	Bud Black	.05
359	Joe Hesketh	.05
360	Paul Assenmacher	.05
361	Bo Jackson	.10
362	Jeff Blauser	.05
363	Mike Brumley	.05
364	Jim Deshaies	.05
365	Brady Anderson	.05
366	Chuck McElroy	.05
367	Matt Merullo	.05
368	Tim Belcher	.05
369	Luis Aquino	.05
370	Joe Oliver	.05
371	Greg Swindell	.05
372	Lee Stevens	.05
373	Mark Knudson	.05
374	Bill Wegman	.05
375	Jerry Don Gleaton	.05
376	Pedro Guerrero	.05
377	Randy Bush	.05
378	Greg Harris	.05
379	Eric Plunk	.05
380	Jose DeJesus	.05
381	Bobby Witt	.05
382	Curtis Wilkerson	.05
383	Gene Nelson	.05
384	Wes Chamberlain	.05
385	Tom Henke	.05
386	Mark Lemke	.05
387	Greg Briley	.05
388	Rafael Ramirez	.05
389	Tony Fossas	.05
390	Henry Cotto	.05
391	Tim Hulett	.05
392	Dean Palmer	.05
393	Glenn Braggs	.05
394	Mark Salas	.05
395	*Rusty Meacham*	.10
396	*Andy Ashby*	.25
397	*Jose Melendez*	.05
398	*Warren Newson*	.05
399	*Frank Castillo*	.05
400	*Chito Martinez*	.05
401	Bernie Williams	.20
402	Derek Bell	.05
403	*Javier Ortiz*	.05
404	*Tim Sherrill*	.05
405	*Rob MacDonald*	.05
406	Phil Plantier	.05
407	Troy Afenir	.05
408	*Gino Minutelli*	.05
409	*Reggie Jefferson*	.05
410	*Mike Remlinger*	.10
411	*Carlos Rodriguez*	.05
412	*Joe Redfield*	.05
413	Alonzo Powell	.05
414	*Scott Livingstone*	.05
415	*Scott Kamieniecki*	.05
416	*Tim Spehr*	.05
417	*Brian Hunter*	.05
418	*Ced Landrum*	.05
419	*Bret Barberie*	.05
420	Kevin Morton	.05
421	*Doug Henry*	.05
422	*Doug Piatt*	.05
423	*Pat Rice*	.05
424	Juan Guzman	.05
425	Nolan Ryan (No-Hit)	.30
426	Tommy Greene (No-Hit)	.05
427	Bob Milacki, Mike Flanagan, Mark Williamson, Gregg Olson (No-Hit)	.05
428	Wilson Alvarez (No-Hit)	.05
429	Otis Nixon (Highlight)	.05
430	Rickey Henderson (Highlight)	.15
431	Cecil Fielder (All-Star)	.05
432	Julio Franco (AS)	.05
433	Cal Ripken, Jr. (AS)	.35
434	Wade Boggs (AS)	.15
435	Joe Carter (AS)	.05
436	Ken Griffey, Jr. (AS)	.35
437	Ruben Sierra (AS)	.05
438	Scott Erickson (AS)	.05
439	Tom Henke (AS)	.05
440	Terry Steinbach (AS)	.05
441	Rickey Henderson (Dream Team)	.15
442	Ryne Sandberg (Dream Team)	.25
443	Otis Nixon	.05
444	Scott Radinsky	.05
445	Mark Grace	.20
446	Tony Pena	.05
447	Billy Hatcher	.05
448	Glenallen Hill	.05
449	Chris Gwynn	.05
450	Tom Glavine	.10
451	John Habyan	.05
452	Al Osuna	.05
453	Tony Phillips	.05
454	Greg Cadaret	.05
455	Rob Dibble	.05
456	Rick Honeycutt	.05
457	Jerome Walton	.05
458	Mookie Wilson	.05
459	Mark Gubicza	.05
460	Craig Biggio	.10
461	Dave Cochrane	.05
462	Keith Miller	.05
463	Alex Cole	.05
464	Pete Smith	.05
465	Brett Butler	.05
466	Jeff Huson	.05
467	Steve Lake	.05
468	Lloyd Moseby	.05
469	Tim McIntosh	.05
470	Dennis Martinez	.05
471	Greg Myers	.05
472	Mackey Sasser	.05
473	Junior Ortiz	.05
474	Greg Olson	.05
475	Steve Sax	.05
476	Ricky Jordan	.05
477	Max Venable	.05
478	Brian McRae	.05
479	Doug Simons	.05
480	Rickey Henderson	.35
481	Gary Varsho	.05
482	Carl Willis	.05
483	Rick Wilkins	.05
484	Donn Pall	.05
485	Edgar Martinez	.05
486	Tom Foley	.05
487	Mark Williamson	.05
488	Jack Armstrong	.05
489	Gary Carter	.20
490	Ruben Sierra	.05
491	Gerald Perry	.05
492	Rob Murphy	.05
493	Zane Smith	.05
494	Darryl Kile	.10
495	Kelly Gruber	.05
496	Jerry Browne	.05
497	Darryl Hamilton	.05
498	Mike Stanton	.05
499	Mark Leonard	.05
500	Jose Canseco	.30
501	Dave Martinez	.05
502	Jose Guzman	.05
503	Terry Kennedy	.05
504	Ed Sprague	.05
505	Frank Thomas	.60
506	Darren Daulton	.05
507	Kevin Tapani	.05
508	Luis Salazar	.05
509	Paul Faries	.05
510	Sandy Alomar, Jr.	.05
511	Jeff King	.05
512	Gary Thurman	.05
513	Chris Hammond	.05
514	*Pedro Munoz*	.05
515	Alan Trammell	.05
516	Geronimo Pena	.05
517	Rodney McCray	.05
518	Manny Lee	.05
519	Junior Felix	.05
520	Kirk Gibson	.05
521	Darrin Jackson	.05
522	John Burkett	.05
523	Jeff Johnson	.05
524	Jim Corsi	.05
525	Robin Yount	.25
526	Jamie Quirk	.05
527	Bob Ojeda	.05
528	Mark Lewis	.05
529	Bryn Smith	.05
530	Kent Hrbek	.05
531	Dennis Boyd	.05
532	Ron Karkovice	.05
533	Don August	.05
534	Todd Frohwirth	.05
535	Wally Joyner	.05
536	Dennis Rasmussen	.05
537	Andy Allanson	.05
538	Rich Gossage	.05
539	John Marzano	.05
540	Cal Ripken, Jr.	1.00
541	Bill Swift	.05
542	Kevin Appier	.05
543	Dave Bergman	.05
544	Bernard Gilkey	.05
545	Mike Greenwell	.05
546	Jose Uribe	.05
547	Jesse Orosco	.05
548	Bob Patterson	.05
549	Mike Stanley	.05
550	Howard Johnson	.05
551	Joe Orsulak	.05
552	Dick Schofield	.05
553	Dave Hollins	.05
554	David Segui	.05
555	Barry Bonds	.65
556	Mo Vaughn	.25
557	Craig Wilson	.05
558	Bobby Rose	.05
559	Rod Nichols	.05
560	Len Dykstra	.05
561	Craig Grebeck	.05
562	Darren Lewis	.05
563	Todd Benzinger	.05
564	Ed Whitson	.05
565	Jesse Barfield	.05
566	Lloyd McClendon	.05
567	Dan Plesac	.05
568	Danny Cox	.05
569	Skeeter Barnes	.05
570	Bobby Thigpen	.05
571	Deion Sanders	.10
572	Chuck Knoblauch	.05

573 Matt Nokes .05
574 Herm Winningham .05
575 Tom Candiotti .05
576 Jeff Bagwell .50
577 Brook Jacoby .05
578 Chico Walker .05
579 Brian Downing .05
580 Dave Stewart .05
581 Francisco Cabrera .05
582 Rene Gonzales .05
583 Stan Javier .05
584 Randy Johnson .25
585 Chuck Finley .05
586 Mark Gardner .05
587 Mark Whiten .05
588 Garry Templeton .05
589 Gary Sheffield .20
590 Ozzie Smith .50
591 Candy Maldonado .05
592 Mike Sharperson .05
593 Carlos Martinez .05
594 Scott Bankhead .05
595 Tim Wallach .05
596 Tino Martinez .05
597 Roger McDowell .05
598 Cory Snyder .05
599 Andujar Cedeno .05
600 Kirby Puckett .60
601 Rick Parker .05
602 Todd Hundley .05
603 Greg Litton .05
604 Dave Johnson .05
605 John Franco .05
606 Mike Fetters .05
607 Luis Alicea .05
608 Trevor Wilson .05
609 Rob Ducey .05
610 Ramon Martinez .05
611 Dave Burba .05
612 Dwight Smith .05
613 Kevin Maas .05
614 John Costello .05
615 Glenn Davis .05
616 Shawn Abner .05
617 Scott Hemond .05
618 Tom Prince .05
619 Wally Ritchie .05
620 Jim Abbott .05
621 Charlie O'Brien .05
622 Jack Daugherty .05
623 Tommy Gregg .05
624 Jeff Shaw .05
625 Tony Gwynn .60
626 Mark Leiter .05
627 Jim Clancy .05
628 Tim Layana .05
629 Jeff Schaefer .05
630 Lee Smith .05
631 Wade Taylor .05
632 Mike Simms .05
633 Terry Steinbach .05
634 Shawon Dunston .05
635 Tim Raines .10
636 Kirt Manwaring .05
637 Warren Cromartie .05
638 Luis Quinones .05
639 Greg Vaughn .05
640 Kevin Mitchell .05
641 Chris Hoiles .05
642 Tom Browning .05
643 Mitch Webster .05
644 Steve Olin .05
645 Tony Fernandez .05
646 Juan Bell .05
647 Joe Boever .05
648 Carney Lansford .05
649 Mike Benjamin .05
650 George Brett .60
651 Tim Burke .05
652 Jack Morris .05
653 Orel Hershiser .05
654 Mike Schooler .05
655 Andy Van Slyke .05
656 Dave Stieb .05
657 Dave Clark .05
658 Ben McDonald .05
659 John Smiley .05
660 Wade Boggs .40
661 Eric Bullock .05
662 Eric Show .05
663 Lenny Webster .05
664 Mike Huff .05
665 Rick Sutcliffe .05
666 Jeff Manto .05
667 Mike Fitzgerald .05
668 Matt Young .05
669 Dave West .05
670 Mike Hartley .05
671 Curt Schilling .15
672 Brian Bohanon .05
673 Cecil Espy .05
674 Joe Grahe .05
675 Sid Fernandez .05
676 Edwin Nunez .05
677 Hector Villanueva .05
678 Sean Berry .05
679 Dave Eiland .05
680 David Cone .05
681 Mike Bordick .05
682 Tony Castillo .05
683 John Barfield .05
684 Jeff Hamilton .05
685 Ken Dayley .05
686 Carmelo Martinez .05
687 Mike Capel .05
688 Scott Chiamparino .05
689 Rich Gedman .05
690 Rich Monteleone .05
691 Alejandro Pena .05
692 Oscar Azocar .05
693 Jim Poole .05
694 Mike Gardiner .05
695 Steve Buechele .05
696 Rudy Seanez .05
697 Paul Abbott .05
698 Steve Searcy .05
699 Jose Offerman .05
700 Ivan Rodriguez .30
701 Joe Girardi .05
702 Tony Perezchica .05
703 Paul McClellan .05
704 *David Howard* .05
705 Dan Petry .05
706 Jack Howell .05
707 Jose Mesa .05
708 Randy St. Claire .05
709 Kevin Brown .10
710 Ron Darling .05
711 Jason Grimsley .05
712 John Orton .05
713 Shawn Boskie .05
714 Pat Clements .05
715 Brian Barnes .05
716 *Luis Lopez* .05
717 Bob McClure .05
718 Mark Davis .05
719 Dann Billardello .05
720 Tom Edens .05
721 Willie Fraser .05
722 Curt Young .05
723 Neal Heaton .05
724 Craig Worthington .05
725 Mel Rojas .05
726 Daryl Irvine .05
727 Roger Mason .05
728 Kirk Dressendorfer .05
729 Scott Aldred .05
730 Willie Blair .05
731 Allan Anderson .05
732 Dana Kiecker .05
733 Jose Gonzalez .05
734 Brian Drahman .05
735 Brad Komminsk .05
736 *Arthur Rhodes* .10
737 *Terry Mathews* .05
738 *Jeff Fassero* .05
739 *Mike Magnante* .05
740 *Kip Gross* .05
741 *Jim Hunter* .05
742 *Jose Mota* .05
743 Joe Bitker .05
744 *Tim Mauser* .05
745 *Ramon Garcia* .05
746 *Rod Beck* .15
747 *Jim Austin* .05
748 *Keith Mitchell* .05
749 *Wayne Rosenthal* .05
750 *Bryan Hickerson* .05
751 *Bruce Egloff* .05
752 *John Wehner* .05
753 Darren Holmes .05
754 Dave Hansen .05
755 Mike Mussina .40
756 *Anthony Young* .05
757 Ron Tingley .05
758 *Ricky Bones* .05
759 *Mark Wohlers* .05
760 Wilson Alvarez .05
761 *Harvey Pulliam* .05
762 *Ryan Bowen* .05
763 Terry Bross .05
764 *Joel Johnston* .05
765 *Terry McDaniel* .05
766 *Esteban Beltre* .05
767 *Rob Maurer* .05
768 Ted Wood .05
769 *Mo Sanford* .05
770 *Jeff Carter* .05
771 *Gil Heredia* .10
772 Monty Fariss .05
773 Will Clark (AS) .10
774 Ryne Sandberg (AS) .20
775 Barry Larkin (AS) .10
776 Howard Johnson (AS) .05
777 Barry Bonds (AS) .35
778 Brett Butler (AS) .05
779 Tony Gwynn (AS) .15
780 Ramon Martinez (AS) .05
781 Lee Smith (AS) .05
782 Mike Scioscia (AS) .05
783 Dennis Martinez (Highlight) .05
784 Dennis Martinez (No-Hit) .05
785 Mark Gardner (No-Hit) .05
786 Bret Saberhagen (No-Hit) .05
787 Kent Mercker, Mark Wohlers, Alejandro Pena (No-Hit) .05
788 Cal Ripken (MVP) .40
789 Terry Pendleton (MVP) .05
790 Roger Clemens (CY) .25
791 Tom Glavine (CY) .05
792 Chuck Knoblauch (ROY) .10
793 Jeff Bagwell (ROY) .25
794 Cal Ripken, Jr. (Man of the Year) .40
795 David Cone (Highlight) .05
796 Kirby Puckett (Highlight) .20
797 Steve Avery (Highlight) .05
798 Jack Morris (Highlight) .05
799 *Allen Watson* .10
800 *Manny Ramirez* 3.00
801 *Cliff Floyd* .50
802 *Al Shirley* .05
803 *Brian Barber* .05
804 *Jon Farrell* .05
805 *Brent Gates* .05
806 *Scott Ruffcorn* .05
807 *Tyrone Hill* .05
808 *Benji Gil* .10
809 *Aaron Sele* .30
810 *Tyler Green* .05
811 Chris Jones .05
812 Steve Wilson .05
813 *Cliff Young* .05
814 *Don Wakamatsu* .05
815 *Mike Humphreys* .05
816 *Scott Servais* .05
817 *Rico Rossy* .05
818 *John Ramos* .05
819 Rob Mallicoat .05
820 *Milt Hill* .05
821 Carlos Garcia .05
822 Stan Royer .05
823 *Jeff Plympton* .05
824 *Braulio Castillo* .05
825 *David Haas* .05
826 *Luis Mercedes* .05
827 Eric Karros .05
828 *Shawn Hare* .05
829 Reggie Sanders .05
830 Tom Goodwin .05
831 *Dan Gakeler* .05
832 *Stacy Jones* .05
833 *Kim Batiste* .05
834 Cal Eldred .05
835 *Chris George* .05
836 *Wayne Housie* .05
837 *Mike Ignasiak* .05
838 *Josias Manzanillo* .05
839 *Jim Olander* .05
840 *Gary Cooper* .05
841 Royce Clayton .05
842 Hector Fajardo .05
843 Blaine Beatty .05
844 *Jorge Pedre* .05
845 Kenny Lofton .05
846 Scott Brosius .05
847 *Chris Cron* .05
848 Denis Boucher .05
849 Kyle Abbott .05
850 Bob Zupcic .05
851 *Rheal Cormier* .10
852 *Jim Lewis* .05
853 Anthony Telford .05
854 *Cliff Brantley* .05
855 *Kevin Campbell* .05
856 *Craig Shipley* .05
857 Chuck Carr .05
858 *Tony Eusebio* .15
859 Jim Thome .05
860 *Vinny Castilla* .75
861 Dann Howitt .05
862 *Kevin Ward* .05
863 *Steve Wapnick* .05
864 Rod Brewer .05
865 Todd Van Poppel .05
866 *Jose Hernandez* .05
867 *Amalio Carreno* .05
868 *Calvin Jones* .05
869 *Jeff Gardner* .05
870 *Jarvis Brown* .05
871 *Eddie Taubensee* .10
872 *Andy Mota* .05
873 Chris Haney (Front photo actually Scott Ruskin) .05
874 Roberto Hernandez .05
875 *Laddie Renfroe* .05
876 Scott Cooper .05
877 *Armando Reynoso* .05
878 Ty Cobb (Memorabilia) .30
879 Babe Ruth (Memorabilia) .40
880 Honus Wagner (Memorabilia) .30
881 Lou Gehrig (Memorabilia) .30
882 Satchel Paige (Memorabilia) .20
883 Will Clark (Dream Team) .15
884 Cal Ripken, Jr. (Dream Team) .50
885 Wade Boggs (Dream Team) .30
886 Kirby Puckett (Dream Team) .30
887 Tony Gwynn (Dream Team) .30
888 Craig Biggio (Dream Team) .10
889 Scott Erickson (Dream Team) .05
890 Tom Glavine (Dream Team) .10
891 Rob Dibble (Dream Team) .05
892 Mitch Williams (Dream Team) .05
893 Frank Thomas (Dream Team) .40

1992 Score Hot Rookies

This 10-card rookie issue was produced as an insert in special blister packs of 1992 Score cards sold at retail outlets. Action photos on front and portraits on back are set against white backgrounds with orange highlights. Cards are standard 2-1/2" x 3-1/2".

		MT
Complete Set (10):		7.00
Common Player:		.50
1	Cal Eldred	.50
2	Royce Clayton	.50
3	Kenny Lofton	2.00
4	Todd Van Poppel	.50
5	Scott Cooper	.50
6	Todd Hundley	1.00
7	Tino Martinez	2.00
8	Anthony Telford	.50
9	Derek Bell	1.00
10	Reggie Jefferson	.50

1992 Score Impact Players

Jumbo packs of 1992 Score Series 1 and 2 contained five of these special inserts labeled "90's Impact Players". Front action photos contrast with portrait photos on the backs, which are color-coded by team. Cards #1-45 were packaged with Series 1, cards #46-90 were included in Series 2 packs.

		MT
Complete Set (90):		10.00
Common Player:		.05
1	Chuck Knoblauch	.10
2	Jeff Bagwell	.50
3	Juan Guzman	.05
4	Milt Cuyler	.05
5	Ivan Rodriguez	.35
6	Rich DeLucia	.05
7	Orlando Merced	.05
8	Ray Lankford	.10
9	Brian Hunter	.05
10	Roberto Alomar	.30
11	Wes Chamberlain	.05
12	Steve Avery	.05
13	Scott Erickson	.05
14	Jim Abbott	.08
15	Mark Whiten	.05
16	Leo Gomez	.05
17	Doug Henry	.05
18	Brent Mayne	.05
19	Charles Nagy	.08
20	Phil Plantier	.05
21	Mo Vaughn	.30
22	Craig Biggio	.10
23	Derek Bell	.10
24	Royce Clayton	.08
25	Gary Cooper	.05
26	Scott Cooper	.05
27	Juan Gonzalez	.45
28	Ken Griffey, Jr.	1.00
29	Larry Walker	.25
30	John Smoltz	.10
31	Todd Hundley	.08
32	Kenny Lofton	.10
33	Andy Mota	.05
34	Todd Zeile	.05
35	Arthur Rhodes	.05
36	Jim Thome	.10
37	Todd Van Poppel	.05
38	Mark Wohlers	.05
39	Anthony Young	.05
40	Sandy Alomar Jr.	.08
41	John Olerud	.10
42	Robin Ventura	.10
43	Frank Thomas	.65
44	Dave Justice	.25
45	Hal Morris	.05
46	Ruben Sierra	.05
47	Travis Fryman	.05
48	Mike Mussina	.25
49	Tom Glavine	.08
50	Barry Larkin	.10
51	Will Clark	.15
52	Jose Canseco	.30
53	Bo Jackson	.15
54	Dwight Gooden	.08
55	Barry Bonds	.65
56	Fred McGriff	.10
57	Roger Clemens	.50
58	Benito Santiago	.05
59	Darryl Strawberry	.08
60	Cecil Fielder	.08
61	John Franco	.05
62	Matt Williams	.15
63	Marquis Grissom	.08
64	Danny Tartabull	.05
65	Ron Gant	.10
66	Paul O'Neill	.08
67	Devon White	.05
68	Rafael Palmeiro	.20
69	Tom Gordon	.05
70	Shawon Dunston	.05
71	Rob Dibble	.05
72	Eddie Zosky	.05
73	Jack McDowell	.05
74	Len Dykstra	.05
75	Ramon Martinez	.08
76	Reggie Sanders	.10
77	Greg Maddux	.65
78	Ellis Burks	.10
79	John Smiley	.05
80	Roberto Kelly	.05
81	Ben McDonald	.05
82	Mark Lewis	.05
83	Jose Rijo	.05
84	Ozzie Guillen	.05
85	Lance Dickson	.05
86	Kim Batiste	.05
87	Gregg Olson	.05
88	Andy Benes	.08
89	Cal Eldred	.05
90	David Cone	.08

1992 Score Joe DiMaggio

Colorized vintage photos are featured on the front and back of each of five Joe DiMaggio tribute cards which were issued as random inserts in 1992 Score Series 1 packs. It was reported at the time that 30,000 of eacg card were produced. A limited number (from an edition of 2,500) of each card were autographed.

		MT
Complete Set (5):		25.00
Common Card:		8.00
Autographed Card:		350.00
1	Joe DiMaggio (The Minors)	8.00
2	Joe DiMaggio (The Rookie)	8.00
3	Joe DiMaggio (The MVP)	8.00
4	Joe DiMaggio (The Streak)	8.00
5	Joe DiMaggio (The Legend)	8.00

1992 Score The Franchise

This four-card set, in both autographed and unautographed form, was a random insert in various premium packaging of Score's 1992 Series II cards. Each of the four cards was produced in an edition of 150,000, with 2,000 of each player's card being autographed and 500 of the triple-player card carrying the autographs of all three superstars.

		MT
Complete Set (4):		12.00
Common Player:		2.50
Musial Autograph:		50.00
Mantle Autograph:		150.00
Yastrzemski Autograph:		35.00
Triple Autograph:		350.00
1	Stan Musial	3.00
2	Mickey Mantle	5.00
3	Carl Yastrzemski	2.50
4	Stan Musial, Mickey Mantle, Carl Yastrzemski	3.00

1992 Score Factory Set Inserts - Cooperstown

Available exclusively in factory sets, these bonus cards have posterized color portraits vignetted on a white background. Blue-bordered backs have a yellow "tombstone" at center with career highlights and a quote or two about the player.

		MT
Complete Set (4):		2.00
Common Player:		.50
B8	Carlton Fisk	.50
B9	Ozzie Smith	1.00
B10	Dave Winfield	.65
B11	Robin Yount	.50

1992 Score Factory Set Inserts - DiMaggio

Available exclusively in factory sets, these bonus cards honor Joe DiMaggio career. Fronts have black-and-white photos with silver borders. Color backs have quotes from the Clipper or other ballplayers, plus detailed career highlights.

		MT
Complete Set (3):		2.00
Common Card:		1.00
B12	Joe DiMaggio (The Hard Hitter)	1.00
B13	Joe DiMaggio (The Stylish Fielder)	1.00
B14	Joe DiMaggio (The Championship Player)	1.00

1992 Score Factory Set Inserts - World Series

Available exclusively in factory sets 17 bonus cards are divided into four subsets commemorating the 1991 World Series, potential Hall of Famers, the career of Joe DiMaggio and Carl Yastrzemski's 1967 Triple Crown season. Cards carry a "B" prefix to the card number.

		MT
Complete Set (7):		1.50
Common Card:		.15
1	World Series Game 1 (Greg Gagne)	.15
2	World Series Game 2 (Scott Leius)	.15
3	World Series Game 3 (David Justice, Brian Harper)	.20
4	World Series Game 4 (Lonnie Smith, Brian Harper)	.15
5	World Series Game 5 (David Justice)	.30
6	World Series Game 6 (Kirby Puckett)	.75
7	World Series Game 7 (Gene Larkin)	.15

1992 Score Factory Set Inserts - Yastrzemski

Available exclusively in factory sets, these bonus cards honor Carl Yastrzemski's 1967 Triple Crown season. Fronts have game-action photos with silver borders and a silver 25 Years logo. Color backs have quotes from Yaz or teammates, plus details of the season's highlights.

		MT
Complete Set (3):		2.00
Common Card:		1.00
B15	Carl Yastrzemski (The Impossible Dream)	1.00
B16	Carl Yastrzemski (The Triple Crown)	1.00
B17	Carl Yastrzemski (The World Series)	1.00

1992 Score Rookie & Traded

This 110-card set features traded players, free agents and top rookies from 1992. The cards are styled after the regular 1992 Score cards. Cards 80-110 feature the rookies. The set was released as a boxed set and was available only through hobby dealers.

		MT
Complete Set (110):		9.00
Common Player:		.05
1	Gary Sheffield	.20
2	Kevin Seitzer	.05
3	Danny Tartabull	.05
4	Steve Sax	.05
5	Bobby Bonilla	.05
6	Frank Viola	.05
7	Dave Winfield	.50
8	Rick Sutcliffe	.05
9	Jose Canseco	.45
10	Greg Swindell	.05
11	Eddie Murray	.50
12	Randy Myers	.05
13	Wally Joyner	.05
14	Kenny Lofton	.05
15	Jack Morris	.05
16	Charlie Hayes	.05
17	Pete Incaviglia	.05
18	Kevin Mitchell	.05
19	Kurt Stillwell	.05
20	Bret Saberhagen	.05
21	Steve Buechele	.05
22	John Smiley	.05
23	Sammy Sosa	3.00
24	George Bell	.05
25	Curt Schilling	.20
26	Dick Schofield	.05
27	David Cone	.05
28	Dan Gladden	.05
29	Kirk McCaskill	.05
30	Mike Gallego	.05
31	Kevin McReynolds	.05
32	Bill Swift	.05
33	Dave Martinez	.05
34	Storm Davis	.05
35	Willie Randolph	.05
36	Melido Perez	.05
37	Mark Carreon	.05
38	Doug Jones	.05
39	Gregg Jefferies	.05
40	Mike Jackson	.05
41	Dickie Thon	.05
42	Eric King	.05
43	Herm Winningham	.05
44	Derek Lilliquist	.05
45	Dave Anderson	.05
46	Jeff Reardon	.05
47	Scott Bankhead	.05
48	Cory Snyder	.05
49	Al Newman	.05
50	Keith Miller	.05
51	Dave Burba	.05
52	Bill Pecota	.05
53	Chuck Crim	.05
54	Mariano Duncan	.05
55	Dave Gallagher	.05
56	Chris Gwynn	.05
57	Scott Ruskin	.05
58	Jack Armstrong	.05
59	Gary Carter	.15
60	Andres Galarraga	.05
61	Ken Hill	.05
62	Eric Davis	.05
63	Ruben Sierra	.05
64	Darrin Fletcher	.05
65	Tim Belcher	.05
66	Mike Morgan	.05
67	Scott Scudder	.05
68	Tom Candiotti	.05
69	Hubie Brooks	.05
70	Kal Daniels	.05
71	Bruce Ruffin	.05
72	Billy Hatcher	.05
73	Bob Melvin	.05
74	Lee Guetterman	.05
75	Rene Gonzales	.05
76	Kevin Bass	.05
77	Tom Bolton	.05
78	John Wetteland	.05
79	Bip Roberts	.05
80	Pat Listach	.05
81	John Doherty	.05
82	Sam Militello	.05
83	Brian Jordan	.05
84	Jeff Kent	.25
85	Dave Fleming	.05
86	Jeff Tackett	.05
87	Chad Curtis	.25
88	Eric Fox	.05
89	Denny Neagle	.05
90	Donovan Osborne	.05
91	Carlos Hernandez	.05
92	Tim Wakefield	.05
93	Tim Salmon	.25
94	Dave Nilsson	.05
95	Mike Perez	.05
96	Pat Hentgen	.05
97	Frank Seminara	.05
98	Ruben Amaro, Jr.	.05
99	Archi Cianfrocco	.05
100	Andy Stankiewicz	.05
101	Jim Bullinger	.05
102	Pat Mahomes	.05
103	Hipolito Pichardo	.05
104	Bret Boone	.10
105	John Vander Wal	.05
106	Vince Horsman	.05
107	James Austin	.05
108	Brian Williams	.05
109	Dan Walters	.05
110	Wil Cordero	.05

1993 Score

Score's 1993 cards have white borders surrounding color action photographs. The player's name is at the bottom of the card, while his team's name and position appears on the left side in a color band. Backs have color portraits, statistics and text. Subsets feature rookies, award winners, draft picks, highlights, World Series highlights, all-star caricatures, dream team players, and the Man of the Year (Kirby Puckett). Insert sets include: Boys of Summer, the Franchise and Stat Leaders, which feature Select's card design.

		MT
Complete Set (660):		25.00
Common Player:		.05
Pack (16):		.75
Wax Box (36):		25.00
1	Ken Griffey, Jr.	1.00
2	Gary Sheffield	.20
3	Frank Thomas	.65
4	Ryne Sandberg	.50
5	Larry Walker	.20
6	Cal Ripken, Jr.	1.00
7	Roger Clemens	.65
8	Bobby Bonilla	.05
9	Carlos Baerga	.05
10	Darren Daulton	.05
11	Travis Fryman	.05
12	Andy Van Slyke	.05
13	Jose Canseco	.30
14	Roberto Alomar	.35
15	Tom Glavine	.10
16	Barry Larkin	.10
17	Gregg Jefferies	.05
18	Craig Biggio	.10
19	Shane Mack	.05
20	Brett Butler	.05
21	Dennis Eckersley	.05
22	Will Clark	.15
23	Don Mattingly	.75
24	Tony Gwynn	.65
25	Ivan Rodriguez	.40
26	Shawon Dunston	.05
27	Mike Mussina	.35
28	Marquis Grissom	.05
29	Charles Nagy	.05
30	Len Dykstra	.05
31	Cecil Fielder	.05
32	Jay Bell	.05
33	B.J. Surhoff	.05
34	Bob Tewksbury	.05
35	Danny Tartabull	.05
36	Terry Pendleton	.05
37	Jack Morris	.05
38	Hal Morris	.05
39	Luis Polonia	.05
40	Ken Caminiti	.05
41	Robin Ventura	.05
42	Darryl Strawberry	.05
43	Wally Joyner	.05
44	Fred McGriff	.05
45	Kevin Tapani	.05
46	Matt Williams	.15
47	Robin Yount	.35
48	Ken Hill	.05
49	Edgar Martinez	.05
50	Mark Grace	.20
51	Juan Gonzalez	.50
52	Curt Schilling	.20
53	Dwight Gooden	.05
54	Chris Hoiles	.05
55	Frank Viola	.05
56	Ray Lankford	.05
57	George Brett	.50
58	Kenny Lofton	.05
59	Nolan Ryan	1.00
60	Mickey Tettleton	.05
61	John Smoltz	.10
62	Howard Johnson	.05
63	Eric Karros	.05
64	Rick Aguilera	.05
65	Steve Finley	.05
66	Mark Langston	.05
67	Bill Swift	.05
68	John Olerud	.05
69	Kevin McReynolds	.05
70	Jack McDowell	.05
71	Rickey Henderson	.35
72	Brian Harper	.05
73	Mike Morgan	.05
74	Rafael Palmeiro	.20
75	Dennis Martinez	.05
76	Tino Martinez	.05
77	Eddie Murray	.35
78	Ellis Burks	.05
79	John Kruk	.05
80	Gregg Olson	.05
81	Bernard Gilkey	.05
82	Milt Cuyler	.05
83	Mike LaValliere	.05
84	Albert Belle	.20
85	Bip Roberts	.05
86	Melido Perez	.05
87	Otis Nixon	.05
88	Bill Spiers	.05
89	Jeff Bagwell	.50
90	Orel Hershiser	.05
91	Andy Benes	.05
92	Devon White	.05
93	Willie McGee	.05
94	Ozzie Guillen	.05
95	Ivan Calderon	.05
96	Keith Miller	.05
97	Steve Buechele	.05
98	Kent Hrbek	.05
99	Dave Hollins	.05
100	Mike Bordick	.05
101	Randy Tomlin	.05
102	Omar Vizquel	.05
103	Lee Smith	.05
104	Leo Gomez	.05
105	Jose Rijo	.05
106	Mark Whiten	.05
107	Dave Justice	.20
108	Eddie Taubensee	.05
109	Lance Johnson	.05
110	Felix Jose	.05
111	Mike Harkey	.05
112	Randy Milligan	.05
113	Anthony Young	.05

No.	Player	Price
114	Rico Brogna	.05
115	Bret Saberhagen	.05
116	Sandy Alomar, Jr.	.05
117	Terry Mulholland	.05
118	Darryl Hamilton	.05
119	Todd Zeile	.05
120	Bernie Williams	.30
121	Zane Smith	.05
122	Derek Bell	.05
123	Deion Sanders	.10
124	Luis Sojo	.05
125	Joe Oliver	.05
126	Craig Grebeck	.05
127	Andujar Cedeno	.05
128	Brian McRae	.05
129	Jose Offerman	.05
130	Pedro Munoz	.05
131	Bud Black	.05
132	Mo Vaughn	.30
133	Bruce Hurst	.05
134	Dave Henderson	.05
135	Tom Pagnozzi	.05
136	Erik Hanson	.05
137	Orlando Merced	.05
138	Dean Palmer	.05
139	John Franco	.05
140	Brady Anderson	.05
141	Ricky Jordan	.05
142	Jeff Blauser	.05
143	Sammy Sosa	.65
144	Bob Walk	.05
145	Delino DeShields	.05
146	Kevin Brown	.10
147	Mark Lemke	.05
148	Chuck Knoblauch	.05
149	Chris Sabo	.05
150	Bobby Witt	.05
151	Luis Gonzalez	.20
152	Ron Karkovice	.05
153	Jeff Brantley	.05
154	Kevin Appier	.05
155	Darrin Jackson	.05
156	Kelly Gruber	.05
157	Royce Clayton	.05
158	Chuck Finley	.05
159	Jeff King	.05
160	Greg Vaughn	.05
161	Geronimo Pena	.05
162	Steve Farr	.05
163	Jose Oquendo	.05
164	Mark Lewis	.05
165	John Wetteland	.05
166	Mike Henneman	.05
167	Todd Hundley	.05
168	Wes Chamberlain	.05
169	Steve Avery	.05
170	Mike Devereaux	.05
171	Reggie Sanders	.05
172	Jay Buhner	.05
173	Eric Anthony	.05
174	John Burkett	.05
175	Tom Candiotti	.05
176	Phil Plantier	.05
177	Doug Henry	.05
178	Scott Leius	.05
179	Kirt Manwaring	.05
180	Jeff Parrett	.05
181	Don Slaught	.05
182	Scott Radinsky	.05
183	Luis Alicea	.05
184	Tom Gordon	.05
185	Rick Wilkins	.05
186	Todd Stottlemyre	.05
187	Moises Alou	.15
188	Joe Grahe	.05
189	Jeff Kent	.05
190	Bill Wegman	.05
191	Kim Batiste	.05
192	Matt Nokes	.05
193	Mark Wohlers	.05
194	Paul Sorrento	.05
195	Chris Hammond	.05
196	Scott Livingstone	.05
197	Doug Jones	.05
198	Scott Cooper	.05
199	Ramon Martinez	.05
200	Dave Valle	.05
201	Mariano Duncan	.05
202	Ben McDonald	.05
203	Darren Lewis	.05
204	Kenny Rogers	.05
205	Manuel Lee	.05
206	Scott Erickson	.05
207	Dan Gladden	.05
208	Bob Welch	.05
209	Greg Olson	.05
210	Dan Pasqua	.05
211	Tim Wallach	.05
212	Jeff Montgomery	.05
213	Derrick May	.05
214	Ed Sprague	.05
215	David Haas	.05
216	Darrin Fletcher	.05
217	Brian Jordan	.05
218	Jaime Navarro	.05
219	Randy Velarde	.05
220	Ron Gant	.05
221	Paul Quantrill	.05
222	Damion Easley	.05
223	Charlie Hough	.05
224	*Brad Brink*	.05
225	*Barry Manual*	.05
226	*Kevin Koslofski*	.05
227	*Ryan Thompson*	.05
228	*Mike Munoz*	.05
229	*Dan Wilson*	.10
230	*Peter Hoy*	.05
231	*Pedro Astacio*	.10
232	*Matt Stairs*	.10
233	*Jeff Reboulet*	.05
234	*Manny Alexander*	.05
235	*Willie Banks*	.05
236	*John Jaha*	.05
237	*Scooter Tucker*	.05
238	*Russ Springer*	.05
239	*Paul Miller*	.05
240	*Dan Peltier*	.05
241	*Ozzie Canseco*	.05
242	*Ben Rivera*	.05
243	*John Valentin*	.10
244	Henry Rodriguez	.05
245	*Derek Parks*	.05
246	*Carlos Garcia*	.10
247	*Tim Pugh*	.05
248	*Melvin Nieves*	.05
249	*Rich Amaral*	.05
250	*Willie Greene*	.05
251	*Tim Scott*	.05
252	*Dave Silvestri*	.05
253	*Rob Mallicoat*	.05
254	*Donald Harris*	.05
255	*Craig Colbert*	.05
256	Jose Guzman	.05
257	*Domingo Martinez*	.05
258	*William Suero*	.05
259	*Juan Guerrero*	.05
260	*J.T. Snow*	.50
261	Tony Pena	.05
262	*Tim Fortugno*	.05
263	*Tom Marsh*	.05
264	*Kurt Knudsen*	.05
265	*Tim Costo*	.05
266	*Steve Shifflett*	.05
267	*Billy Ashley*	.05
268	Jerry Nielsen	.05
269	*Pete Young*	.05
270	*Johnny Guzman*	.05
271	*Greg Colbrunn*	.05
272	Jeff Nelson	.05
273	*Kevin Young*	.05
274	Jeff Frye	.05
275	*J.T. Bruett*	.05
276	*Todd Pratt*	.05
277	*Mike Butcher*	.05
278	*John Flaherty*	.05
279	*John Patterson*	.05
280	*Eric Hillman*	.05
281	*Bien Figueros*	.05
282	*Shane Reynolds*	.05
283	*Rich Rowland*	.05
284	*Steve Foster*	.05
285	*Dave Mlicki*	.05
286	Mike Piazza	.75
287	*Mike Trombley*	.05
288	*Jim Pena*	.05
289	*Bob Ayrault*	.05
290	*Henry Mercedes*	.05
291	Bob Wickman	.05
292	*Jacob Brumfield*	.05
293	*David Hulse*	.05
294	Ryan Klesko	.05
295	Doug Linton	.05
296	Steve Cooke	.05
297	Eddie Zosky	.05
298	*Gerald Williams*	.05
299	*Jonathan Hurst*	.05
300	*Larry Carter*	.05
301	*William Pennyfeather*	.05
302	*Cesar Hernandez*	.05
303	*Steve Hosey*	.05
304	*Blas Minor*	.05
305	*Jeff Grotewold*	.05
306	*Bernardo Brito*	.05
307	*Rafael Bournigal*	.05
308	*Jeff Branson*	.05
309	*Tom Quinlan*	.05
310	*Pat Gomez*	.05
311	*Sterling Hitchcock*	.10
312	Kent Bottenfield	.05
313	Alan Trammell	.05
314	*Cris Colon*	.05
315	*Paul Wagner*	.05
316	*Matt Maysey*	.05
317	Mike Stanton	.05
318	*Rick Trlicek*	.05
319	*Kevin Rogers*	.05
320	*Mark Clark*	.05
321	Pedro Martinez	.35
322	*Al Martin*	.05
323	Mike Macfarlane	.05
324	*Rey Sanchez*	.10
325	*Roger Pavlik*	.05
326	Troy Neel	.05
327	*Kerry Woodson*	.05
328	*Wayne Kirby*	.05
329	*Ken Ryan*	.05
330	*Jesse Levis*	.05
331	James Austin	.05
332	Dan Walters	.05
333	Brian Williams	.05
334	Wil Cordero	.05
335	Bret Boone	.10
336	Hipolito Pichardo	.05
337	Pat Mahomes	.05
338	Andy Stankiewicz	.05
339	Jim Bullinger	.05
340	Archi Cianfrocco	.05
341	Ruben Amaro, Jr.	.05
342	Frank Seminara	.05
343	Pat Hentgen	.05
344	Dave Nilsson	.05
345	Mike Perez	.05
346	Tim Salmon	.20
347	*Tim Wakefield*	.10
348	Carlos Hernandez	.05
349	Donovan Osborne	.05
350	Denny Naegle	.05
351	Sam Militello	.05
352	Eric Fox	.05
353	John Doherty	.05
354	Chad Curtis	.05
355	Jeff Tackett	.05
356	Dave Fleming	.05
357	Pat Listach	.05
358	Kevin Wickander	.05
359	John VanderWal	.05
360	Arthur Rhodes	.05
361	Bob Scanlan	.05
362	Bob Zupcic	.05
363	Mel Rojas	.05
364	Jim Thome	.05
365	Bill Pecota	.05
366	Mark Carreon	.05
367	Mitch Williams	.05
368	Cal Eldred	.05
369	Stan Belinda	.05
370	Pat Kelly	.05
371	Pheal Cormier	.05
372	Juan Guzman	.05
373	Damon Berryhill	.05
374	Gary DiSarcina	.05
375	Norm Charlton	.05
376	Roberto Hernandez	.05
377	Scott Kamieniecki	.05
378	Rusty Meacham	.05
379	Kurt Stillwell	.05
380	Lloyd McClendon	.05
381	Mark Leonard	.05
382	Jerry Browne	.05
383	Glenn Davis	.05
384	Randy Johnson	.40
385	Mike Greenwell	.05
386	Scott Chiamparino	.05
387	George Bell	.05
388	Steve Olin	.05
389	Chuck McElroy	.05
390	Mark Gardner	.05
391	Rod Beck	.05
392	Dennis Rasmussen	.05
393	Charlie Leibrandt	.05
394	Julio Franco	.05
395	Pete Harnisch	.05
396	Sid Bream	.05
397	Milt Thompson	.05
398	Glenallen Hill	.05
399	Chico Walker	.05
400	Alex Cole	.05
401	Trevor Wilson	.05
402	Jeff Conine	.05
403	Kyle Abbott	.05
404	Tom Browning	.05
405	Jerald Clark	.05
406	Vince Horsman	.05
407	Kevin Mitchell	.05
408	Pete Smith	.05
409	Jeff Innis	.05
410	Mike Timlin	.05
411	Charlie Hayes	.05
412	Alex Fernandez	.05
413	Jeff Russell	.05
414	Jody Reed	.05
415	Mickey Morandini	.05
416	Darnell Coles	.05
417	Xavier Hernandez	.05
418	Steve Sax	.05
419	Joe Girardi	.05
420	Mike Fetters	.05
421	Danny Jackson	.05
422	Jim Gott	.05
423	Tim Belcher	.05
424	Jose Mesa	.05
425	Junior Felix	.05
426	Thomas Howard	.05
427	Julio Valera	.05
428	Dante Bichette	.05
429	Mike Sharperson	.05
430	Darryl Kile	.05
431	Lonnie Smith	.05
432	Monty Fariss	.05
433	Reggie Jefferson	.05
434	Bob McClure	.05
435	Craig Lefferts	.05
436	Duane Ward	.05
437	Shawn Abner	.05
438	Roberto Kelly	.05
439	Paul O'Neill	.05
440	Alan Mills	.05
441	Roger Mason	.05
442	Gary Pettis	.05
443	Steve Lake	.05
444	Gene Larkin	.05
445	Larry Anderson	.05
446	Doug Dascenzo	.05
447	Daryl Boston	.05
448	John Candelaria	.05
449	Storm Davis	.05
450	Tom Edens	.05
451	Mike Maddux	.05
452	Tim Naehring	.05
453	John Orton	.05
454	Joey Cora	.05
455	Chuck Crim	.05
456	Dan Plesac	.05
457	Mike Bielecki	.05
458	*Terry Jorgensen*	.05
459	John Habyan	.05
460	Pete O'Brien	.05
461	Jeff Treadway	.05
462	Frank Castillo	.05
463	Jimmy Jones	.05
464	Tommy Greene	.05
465	Tracy Woodson	.05
466	Rich Rodriguez	.05
467	Joe Hesketh	.05
468	Greg Myers	.05
469	Kirk McCaskill	.05
470	Ricky Bones	.05
471	Lenny Webster	.05
472	Francisco Cabrera	.05
473	Turner Ward	.05
474	Dwayne Henry	.05
475	Al Osuna	.05
476	Craig Wilson	.05
477	Chris Nabholz	.05
478	Rafael Belliard	.05
479	Terry Leach	.05
480	Tim Teufel	.05
481	Dennis Eckersley (Award Winner)	.05
482	Barry Bonds (Award Winner)	.35
483	Dennis Eckersley (Award Winner)	.05
484	Greg Maddux (Award Winner)	.30
485	Pat Listach (ROY)	.05
486	Eric Karros (ROY)	.05
487	*Jamie Arnold*	.05
488	B.J. Wallace	.05
489	*Derek Jeter*	7.50
490	*Jason Kendall*	.50
491	Rick Helling	.05
492	*Derek Wallace*	.05
493	*Sean Lowe*	.05
494	*Shannon Stewart*	.75
495	*Benji Grigsby*	.05
496	*Todd Steverson*	.05
497	*Dan Serafini*	.05

498	Michael Tucker	.05
499	Chris Roberts (Draft Pick)	.05
500	*Pete Janicki* (Draft Pick)	.05
501	*Jeff Schmidt*	.05
502	Edgar Martinez (All-Star)	.05
503	Omar Vizquel (AS)	.05
504	Ken Griffey, Jr. (AS)	.50
505	Kirby Puckett (AS)	.30
506	Joe Carter (AS)	.05
507	Ivan Rodriguez (AS)	.15
508	Jack Morris (AS)	.05
509	Dennis Eckersley (AS)	.05
510	Frank Thomas (AS)	.40
511	Roberto Alomar (AS)	.15
512	Mickey Morandini (Highlight)	.05
513	Dennis Eckersley (Highlight)	.05
514	Jeff Reardon (Highlight)	.05
515	Danny Tartabull (Highlight)	.05
516	Bip Roberts (Highlight)	.05
517	George Brett (Highlight)	.20
518	Robin Yount (Highlight)	.15
519	Kevin Gross (Highlight)	.05
520	Ed Sprague (World Series Highlight)	.05
521	Dave Winfield (World Series Highlight)	.10
522	Ozzie Smith (AS)	.25
523	Barry Bonds (AS)	.30
524	Andy Van Slyke (AS)	.05
525	Tony Gwynn (AS)	.30
526	Darren Daulton (AS)	.05
527	Greg Maddux (AS)	.30
528	Fred McGriff (AS)	.05
529	Lee Smith (AS)	.05
530	Ryne Sandberg (AS)	.25
531	Gary Sheffield (AS)	.10
532	Ozzie Smith (Dream Team)	.25
533	Kirby Puckett (Dream Team)	.30
534	Gary Sheffield (Dream Team)	.10
535	Andy Van Slyke (Dream Team)	.05
536	Ken Griffey, Jr. (Dream Team)	.50
537	Ivan Rodriguez (Dream Team)	.10
538	Charles Nagy (Dream Team)	.05
539	Tom Glavine (Dream Team)	.10
540	Dennis Eckersley (Dream Team)	.05
541	Frank Thomas (Dream Team)	.40
542	Roberto Alomar (Dream Team)	.10
543	Sean Barry	.05
544	Mike Schooler	.05
545	Chuck Carr	.05
546	Lenny Harris	.05
547	Gary Scott	.05
548	Derek Lilliquist	.05
549	Brian Hunter	.05
550	Kirby Puckett (MOY)	.30
551	Jim Eisenreich	.05
552	Andre Dawson	.15
553	David Nied	.05
554	Spike Owen	.05
555	Greg Gagne	.05
556	Sid Fernandez	.05
557	Mark McGwire	1.00
558	Bryan Harvey	.05
559	Harold Reynolds	.05
560	Barry Bonds	.65
561	*Eric Wedge*	.05
562	Ozzie Smith	.50
563	Rick Sutcliffe	.05
564	Jeff Reardon	.05
565	*Alex Arias*	.05
566	Greg Swindell	.05
567	Brook Jacoby	.05
568	Pete Incaviglia	.05
569	*Butch Henry*	.05
570	Eric Davis	.05
571	Kevin Seitzer	.05
572	Tony Fernandez	.05
573	*Steve Reed*	.05
574	Cory Snyder	.05
575	Joe Carter	.05
576	Greg Maddux	.65
577	Bert Blyleven	.05
578	Kevin Bass	.05
579	Carlton Fisk	.40
580	Doug Drabek	.05
581	Mark Gubicza	.05
582	Bobby Thigpen	.05
583	Chili Davis	.05
584	Scott Bankhead	.05
585	Harold Baines	.05
586	*Eric Young*	.15
587	Lance Parrish	.05
588	Juan Bell	.05
589	Bob Ojeda	.05
590	Joe Orsulak	.05
591	Benito Santiago	.05
592	Wade Boggs	.40
593	Robby Thompson	.05
594	Erik Plunk	.05
595	Hensley Meulens	.05
596	Lou Whitaker	.05
597	Dale Murphy	.15
598	Paul Molitor	.35
599	Greg W. Harris	.05
600	Darren Holmes	.05
601	Dave Martinez	.05
602	Tom Henke	.05
603	Mike Benjamin	.05
604	Rene Gonzales	.05
605	Roger McDowell	.05
606	Kirby Puckett	.65
607	Randy Myers	.05
608	Ruben Sierra	.05
609	Wilson Alvarez	.05
610	Dave Segui	.05
611	Juan Samuel	.05
612	Tom Brunansky	.05
613	Willie Randolph	.05
614	Tony Phillips	.05
615	Candy Maldonado	.05
616	Chris Bosio	.05
617	Bret Barberie	.05
618	Scott Sanderson	.05
619	Ron Darling	.05
620	Dave Winfield	.40
621	Mike Felder	.05
622	Greg Hibbard	.05
623	Mike Scioscia	.05
624	John Smiley	.05
625	Alejandro Pena	.05
626	Terry Steinbach	.05
627	Freddie Benavides	.05
628	Kevin Reimer	.05
629	Braulio Castillo	.05
630	Dave Stieb	.05
631	Dave Magadan	.05
632	Scott Fletcher	.05
633	Cris Carpenter	.05
634	Kevin Maas	.05
635	Todd Worrell	.05
636	Rob Deer	.05
637	Dwight Smith	.05
638	Chito Martinez	.05
639	Jimmy Key	.05
640	Greg Harris	.05
641	Mike Moore	.05
642	Pat Borders	.05
643	Bill Gullickson	.05
644	Gary Gaetti	.05
645	David Howard	.05
646	Jim Abbott	.05
647	Willie Wilson	.05
648	David Wells	.10
649	Andres Galarraga	.05
650	Vince Coleman	.05
651	Rob Dibble	.05
652	Frank Tanana	.05
653	Steve Decker	.05
654	David Cone	.05
655	Jack Armstrong	.05
656	Dave Stewart	.05
657	Billy Hatcher	.05
658	Tim Raines	.05
659	Walt Weiss	.05
660	Jose Lind	.05

1993 Score Boys of Summer

These cards were available as inserts only in Score 35-card Super Packs, about one in every four packs. Borderless fronts have a color action photo of the player superimposed over the sun. The player's name is in black script in a green strip at bottom, along with a subset logo. On back is a player portrait, again with the sun as a background. Subset, company, team and major league logos are in color on the right, and there is a short career summary on the green background at bottom.

		MT
Complete Set (30):		25.00
Common Player:		.40
1	Billy Ashley	.40
2	Tim Salmon	3.00
3	Pedro Martinez	5.00
4	Luis Mercedes	.40
5	Mike Piazza	12.00
6	Troy Neel	.40
7	Melvin Nieves	.40
8	Ryan Klesko	.40
9	Ryan Thompson	.40
10	Kevin Young	.40
11	Gerald Williams	.40
12	Willie Greene	.40
13	John Patterson	.40
14	Carlos Garcia	.40
15	Eddie Zosky	.40
16	Sean Berry	.40
17	Rico Brogna	.40
18	Larry Carter	.40
19	Bobby Ayala	.40
20	Alan Embree	.40
21	Donald Harris	.40
22	Sterling Hitchcock	.40
23	David Nied	.40
24	Henry Mercedes	.40
25	Ozzie Canseco	.40
26	David Hulse	.40
27	Al Martin	.40
28	Dan Wilson	.40
29	Paul Miller	.40
30	Rich Rowland	.40

1993 Score The Franchise

These glossy inserts have full-bleed color action photos against a darkened background so that the player stands out. Cards could be found in 16-card packs only; odds of finding one are 1 in every 24 packs. The fronts have gold-foil highlights.

		MT
Complete Set (28):		50.00
Common Player:		.50
1	Cal Ripken, Jr.	12.50
2	Roger Clemens	5.00
3	Mark Langston	.50
4	Frank Thomas	7.50
5	Carlos Baerga	.50
6	Cecil Fielder	.50
7	Gregg Jefferies	.50
8	Robin Yount	3.50
9	Kirby Puckett	6.00
10	Don Mattingly	6.00
11	Dennis Eckersley	.50
12	Ken Griffey, Jr.	12.00
13	Juan Gonzalez	4.00
14	Roberto Alomar	2.00
15	Terry Pendleton	.50
16	Ryne Sandberg	3.50
17	Barry Larkin	1.50
18	Jeff Bagwell	6.00
19	Brett Butler	.50
20	Larry Walker	2.00
21	Bobby Bonilla	.50
22	Darren Daulton	.50
23	Andy Van Slyke	.50
24	Ray Lankford	.50
25	Gary Sheffield	1.50
26	Will Clark	1.00
27	Bryan Harvey	.50
28	David Nied	.50

1993 Score Dream Team

This set which features most of the players in street clothes in sepia-toned photos on a white background, has gold-foil graphics and was available only via a mail-in offer.

		MT
Complete Set (12):		6.00
Common Player:		.25
1	Ozzie Smith	1.00
2	Kirby Puckett	1.25
3	Gary Sheffield	.35
4	Andy Van Slyke	.25
5	Ken Griffey, Jr.	2.00
6	Ivan Rodriguez	.50
7	Charles Nagy	.25
8	Tom Glavine	.35
9	Dennis Eckersley	.25
10	Frank Thomas	1.50
11	Roberto Alomar	.40
---	Header card	.05

1994 Score

Score's 1994 set, with a new design and UV coating, was issued in two series of 330 cards each. The cards, which use more action photos than before, have dark blue borders with the player's name in a team color-coded strip at the bottom. A special Gold Rush card, done for each card in the set, is included in every pack. Series 1 includes American League checklists, which are printed on the backs of cards depicting panoramic views of each team's ballpark. Series 2 has the National League team checklists. Insert sets include Dream Team players, and National (Series 1 packs) and American League Gold Stars (Series 2 packs), which use the Gold Rush process and appear once every 18 packs.

		MT
Complete Set (660):		15.00
Common Player:		.05
Gold Rush:		2X
Wax Pack (14):		.50
Wax Box (36):		15.00
1	Barry Bonds	.65
2	John Olerud	.05
3	Ken Griffey, Jr.	1.00
4	Jeff Bagwell	.50
5	John Burkett	.05
6	Jack McDowell	.05
7	Albert Belle	.20
8	Andres Galarraga	.05
9	Mike Mussina	.25
10	Will Clark	.15
11	Travis Fryman	.05
12	Tony Gwynn	.60
13	Robin Yount	.30
14	Dave Magadan	.05
15	Paul O'Neill	.05
16	Ray Lankford	.05
17	Damion Easley	.05
18	Andy Van Slyke	.05
19	Brian McRae	.05
20	Ryne Sandberg	.50
21	Kirby Puckett	.60
22	Dwight Gooden	.05
23	Don Mattingly	.75
24	Kevin Mitchell	.05
25	Roger Clemens	.60
26	Eric Karros	.05
27	Juan Gonzalez	.45
28	John Kruk	.05
29	Gregg Jefferies	.05
30	Tom Glavine	.10
31	Ivan Rodriguez	.35
32	Jay Bell	.05
33	Randy Johnson	.40
34	Darren Daulton	.05
35	Rickey Henderson	.30
36	Eddie Murray	.25
37	Brian Harper	.05
38	Delino DeShields	.05
39	Jose Lind	.05
40	Benito Santiago	.05
41	Frank Thomas	.60
42	Mark Grace	.20
43	Roberto Alomar	.25
44	Andy Benes	.05
45	Luis Polonia	.05
46	Brett Butler	.05
47	Terry Steinbach	.05
48	Craig Biggio	.10
49	Greg Vaughn	.05
50	Charlie Hayes	.05
51	Mickey Tettleton	.05
52	Jose Rijo	.05
53	Carlos Baerga	.05
54	Jeff Blauser	.05
55	Leo Gomez	.05
56	Bob Tewksbury	.05
57	Mo Vaughn	.25
58	Orlando Merced	.05
59	Tino Martinez	.05
60	Len Dykstra	.05
61	Jose Canseco	.25
62	Tony Fernandez	.05
63	Donovan Osborne	.05
64	Ken Hill	.05
65	Kent Hrbek	.05
66	Bryan Harvey	.05
67	Wally Joyner	.05
68	Derrick May	.05
69	Lance Johnson	.05
70	Willie McGee	.05
71	Mark Langston	.05
72	Terry Pendleton	.05
73	Joe Carter	.05
74	Barry Larkin	.10
75	Jimmy Key	.05
76	Joe Girardi	.05
77	B.J. Surhoff	.05
78	Pete Harnisch	.05
79	Lou Whitaker	.05
80	Cory Snyder	.05
81	Kenny Lofton	.05
82	Fred McGriff	.05
83	Mike Greenwell	.05
84	Mike Perez	.05
85	Cal Ripken, Jr.	1.00
86	Don Slaught	.05
87	Omar Vizquel	.05
88	Curt Schilling	.15
89	Chuck Knoblauch	.05
90	Moises Alou	.10
91	Greg Gagne	.05
92	Bret Saberhagen	.05
93	Ozzie Guillen	.05
94	Matt Williams	.15
95	Chad Curtis	.05
96	Mike Harkey	.05
97	Devon White	.05
98	Walt Weiss	.05
99	Kevin Brown	.10
100	Gary Sheffield	.15
101	Wade Boggs	.40
102	Orel Hershiser	.05
103	Tony Phillips	.05
104	Andujar Cedeno	.05
105	Bill Spiers	.05
106	Otis Nixon	.05
107	Felix Fermin	.05
108	Bip Roberts	.05
109	Dennis Eckersley	.05
110	Dante Bichette	.05
111	Ben McDonald	.05
112	Jim Poole	.05
113	John Dopson	.05
114	Rob Dibble	.05
115	Jeff Treadway	.05
116	Ricky Jordan	.05
117	Mike Henneman	.05
118	Willie Blair	.05
119	Doug Henry	.05
120	Gerald Perry	.05
121	Greg Myers	.05
122	John Franco	.05
123	Roger Mason	.05
124	Chris Hammond	.05
125	Hubie Brooks	.05
126	Kent Mercker	.05
127	Jim Abbott	.05
128	Kevin Bass	.05
129	Rick Aguilera	.05
130	Mitch Webster	.05
131	Eric Plunk	.05
132	Mark Carreon	.05
133	Dave Stewart	.05
134	Willie Wilson	.05
135	Dave Fleming	.05
136	Jeff Tackett	.05
137	Geno Petralli	.05
138	Gene Harris	.05
139	Scott Bankhead	.05
140	Trevor Wilson	.05
141	Alvaro Espinoza	.05
142	Ryan Bowen	.05
143	Mike Moore	.05
144	Bill Pecota	.05
145	Jaime Navarro	.05
146	Jack Daugherty	.05
147	Bob Wickman	.05
148	Chris Jones	.05
149	Todd Stottlemyre	.05
150	Brian Williams	.05
151	Chuck Finley	.05
152	Lenny Harris	.05
153	Alex Fernandez	.05
154	Candy Maldonado	.05
155	Jeff Montgomery	.05
156	David West	.05
157	Mark Williamson	.05
158	Milt Thompson	.05
159	Ron Darling	.05
160	Stan Belinda	.05
161	Henry Cotto	.05
162	Mel Rojas	.05
163	Doug Strange	.05
164	Rene Arocha (1993 Rookie)	.05
165	Tim Hulett	.05
166	Steve Avery	.05
167	Jim Thome	.05
168	Tom Browning	.05
169	Mario Diaz	.05
170	Steve Reed (1993 Rookie)	.05
171	Scott Livingstone	.05
172	Chris Donnels	.05
173	John Jaha	.05
174	Carlos Hernandez	.05
175	Dion James	.05
176	Bud Black	.05
177	Tony Castillo	.05
178	Jose Guzman	.05
179	Torey Lovullo	.05
180	John Vander Wal	.05
181	Mike LaValliere	.05
182	Sid Fernandez	.05
183	Brent Mayne	.05
184	Terry Mulholland	.05
185	Willie Banks	.05
186	Steve Cooke (1993 Rookie)	.05
187	Brent Gates (1993 Rookie)	.05
188	Erik Pappas (1993 Rookie)	.05
189	Bill Haselman (1993 Rookie)	.05
190	Fernando Valenzuela	.05
191	Gary Redus	.05
192	Danny Darwin	.05
193	Mark Portugal	.05
194	Derek Lilliquist	.05
195	Charlie O'Brien	.05
196	Matt Nokes	.05
197	Danny Sheaffer	.05
198	Bill Gullickson	.05
199	Alex Arias (1993 Rookie)	.05
200	Mike Fetters	.05
201	Brian Jordan	.05
202	Joe Grahe	.05
203	Tom Candiotti	.05
204	Jeremy Stanton	.05
205	Mike Stanton	.05
206	David Howard	.05
207	Darren Holmes	.05
208	Rick Honeycutt	.05
209	Danny Jackson	.05
210	Rich Amaral (1993 Rookie)	.05
211	Blas Minor (1993 Rookie)	.05
212	Kenny Rogers	.05
213	Jim Leyritz	.05
214	Mike Morgan	.05
215	Dan Gladden	.05
216	Randy Velarde	.05
217	Mitch Williams	.05
218	Hipolito Pichardo	.05
219	Dave Burba	.05
220	Wilson Alvarez	.05
221	Bob Zupcic	.05
222	Francisco Cabrera	.05
223	Julio Valera	.05
224	Paul Assenmacher	.05
225	Jeff Branson	.05
226	Todd Frohwirth	.05
227	Armando Reynoso	.05
228	Rich Rowland (1993 Rookie)	.05
229	Freddie Benavides	.05
230	Wayne Kirby (1993 Rookie)	.05
231	Darryl Kile	.05
232	Skeeter Barnes	.05
233	Ramon Martinez	.05
234	Tom Gordon	.05
235	Dave Gallagher	.05
236	Ricky Bones	.05
237	Larry Andersen	.05
238	Pat Meares (1993 Rookie)	.05
239	Zane Smith	.05
240	Tim Leary	.05
241	Phil Clark	.05
242	Danny Cox	.05
243	Mike Jackson	.05
244	Mike Gallego	.05
245	Lee Smith	.05
246	Todd Jones (1993 Rookie)	.05
247	Steve Bedrosian	.05
248	Troy Neel	.05
249	Jose Bautista	.05
250	Steve Frey	.05
251	Jeff Reardon	.05
252	Stan Javier	.05
253	Mo Sanford (1993 Rookie)	.05
254	Steve Sax	.05
255	Luis Aquino	.05
256	Domingo Jean (1993 Rookie)	.05
257	Scott Servais	.05
258	Brad Pennington (1993 Rookie)	.05
259	Dave Hansen	.05
260	Goose Gossage	.05
261	Jeff Fassero	.05
262	Junior Ortiz	.05
263	Anthony Young	.05
264	Chris Bosio	.05
265	Ruben Amaro, Jr.	.05
266	Mark Eichhorn	.05
267	Dave Clark	.05
268	Gary Thurman	.05
269	Les Lancaster	.05
270	Jamie Moyer	.05
271	Ricky Gutierrez (1993 Rookie)	.05
272	Greg Harris	.05
273	Mike Benjamin	.05
274	Gene Nelson	.05
275	Damon Berryhill	.05
276	Scott Radinsky	.05
277	Mike Aldrete	.05
278	Jerry DiPoto (1993 Rookie)	.05
279	Chris Haney	.05
280	Richie Lewis (1993 Rookie)	.05
281	Jarvis Brown	.05
282	Juan Bell	.05
283	Joe Klink	.05
284	Graeme Lloyd (1993 Rookie)	.05
285	Casey Candaele	.05
286	Bob MacDonald	.05
287	Mike Sharperson	.05
288	Gene Larkin	.05
289	Brian Barnes	.05
290	David McCarty (1993 Rookie)	.05
291	Jeff Innis	.05
292	Bob Patterson	.05
293	Ben Rivera	.05
294	John Habyan	.05
295	Rich Rodriguez	.05
296	Edwin Nunez	.05
297	Rod Brewer	.05
298	Mike Timlin	.05
299	Jesse Orosco	.05
300	Gary Gaetti	.05
301	Todd Benzinger	.05

302 Jeff Nelson .05
303 Rafael Belliard .05
304 Matt Whiteside .05
305 Vinny Castilla .05
306 Matt Turner .05
307 Eduardo Perez .05
308 Joel Johnston .05
309 Chris Gomez .05
310 Pat Rapp .05
311 Jim Tatum .05
312 Kirk Rueter .05
313 John Flaherty .05
314 Tom Kramer .05
315 Mark Whiten (Highlights) .05
316 Chris Bosio (Highlights) .05
317 Orioles Checklist .05
318 Red Sox Checklist .05
319 Angels Checklist .05
320 White Sox Checklist .05
321 Indians Checklist .05
322 Tigers Checklist .05
323 Royals Checklist .05
324 Brewers Checklist .05
325 Twins Checklist .05
326 Yankees Checklist .05
327 Athletics Checklist .05
328 Mariners Checklist .05
329 Rangers Checklist .05
330 Blue Jays Checklist .05
331 Frank Viola .05
332 Ron Gant .05
333 Charles Nagy .05
334 Roberto Kelly .05
335 Brady Anderson .05
336 Alex Cole .05
337 Alan Trammell .05
338 Derek Bell .05
339 Bernie Williams .20
340 Jose Offerman .05
341 Bill Wegman .05
342 Ken Caminiti .05
343 Pat Borders .05
344 Kirt Manwaring .05
345 Chili Davis .05
346 Steve Buechele .05
347 Robin Ventura .05
348 Teddy Higuera .05
349 Jerry Browne .05
350 Scott Kamieniecki .05
351 Kevin Tapani .05
352 Marquis Grissom .05
353 Jay Buhner .05
354 Dave Hollins .05
355 Dan Wilson .05
356 Bob Walk .05
357 Chris Hoiles .05
358 Todd Zeile .05
359 Kevin Appier .05
360 Chris Sabo .05
361 David Segui .05
362 Jerald Clark .05
363 Tony Pena .05
364 Steve Finley .05
365 Roger Pavlik .05
366 John Smoltz .10
367 Scott Fletcher .05
368 Jody Reed .05
369 David Wells .10
370 Jose Vizcaino .05
371 Pat Listach .05
372 Orestes Destrade .05
373 Danny Tartabull .05
374 Greg W. Harris .05
375 Juan Guzman .05
376 Larry Walker .20
377 Gary DiSarcina .05
378 Bobby Bonilla .05
379 Tim Raines .05
380 Tommy Greene .05
381 Chris Gwynn .05
382 Jeff King .05
383 Shane Mack .05
384 Ozzie Smith .50
385 *Eddie Zambrano* .05
386 Mike Devereaux .05
387 Erik Hanson .05
388 Scott Cooper .05
389 Dean Palmer .05
390 John Wetteland .05
391 Reggie Jefferson .05
392 Mark Lemke .05
393 Cecil Fielder .05
394 Reggie Sanders .05
395 Darryl Hamilton .05
396 Daryl Boston .05
397 Pat Kelly .05
398 Joe Orsulak .05
399 Ed Sprague .05
400 Eric Anthony .05
401 Scott Sanderson .05
402 Jim Gott .05
403 Ron Karkovice .05
404 Phil Plantier .05
405 David Cone .05
406 Robby Thompson .05
407 Dave Winfield .35
408 Dwight Smith .05
409 Ruben Sierra .05
410 Jack Armstrong .05
411 Mike Felder .05
412 Wil Cordero .05
413 Julio Franco .05
414 Howard Johnson .05
415 Mark McLemore .05
416 Pete Incaviglia .05
417 John Valentin .05
418 Tim Wakefield .05
419 Jose Mesa .05
420 Bernard Gilkey .05
421 Kirk Gibson .05
422 Dave Justice .15
423 Tom Brunansky .05
424 John Smiley .05
425 Kevin Maas .05
426 Doug Drabek .05
427 Paul Molitor .30
428 Darryl Strawberry .05
429 Tim Naehring .05
430 Bill Swift .05
431 Ellis Burks .05
432 Greg Hibbard .05
433 Felix Jose .05
434 Bret Barberie .05
435 Pedro Munoz .05
436 Darrin Fletcher .05
437 Bobby Witt .05
438 Wes Chamberlain .05
439 Mackey Sasser .05
440 Mark Whiten .05
441 Harold Reynolds .05
442 Greg Olson .05
443 Billy Hatcher .05
444 Joe Oliver .05
445 Sandy Alomar Jr. .05
446 Tim Wallach .05
447 Karl Rhodes .05
448 Royce Clayton .05
449 Cal Eldred .05
450 Rick Wilkins .05
451 Mike Stanley .05
452 Charlie Hough .05
453 Jack Morris .05
454 *Jon Ratliff* .05
455 Rene Gonzales .05
456 Eddie Taubensee .05
457 Roberto Hernandez .05
458 Todd Hundley .05
459 Mike MacFarlane .05
460 Mickey Morandini .05
461 Scott Erickson .05
462 Lonnie Smith .05
463 Dave Henderson .05
464 Ryan Klesko .05
465 Edgar Martinez .05
466 Tom Pagnozzi .05
467 Charlie Leibrandt .05
468 *Brian Anderson* .10
469 Harold Baines .05
470 Tim Belcher .05
471 Andre Dawson .15
472 Eric Young .05
473 Paul Sorrento .05
474 Luis Gonzalez .20
475 Rob Deer .05
476 Mike Piazza .75
477 Kevin Reimer .05
478 Jeff Gardner .05
479 Melido Perez .05
480 Darren Lewis .05
481 Duane Ward .05
482 Rey Sanchez .05
483 Mark Lewis .05
484 Jeff Conine .05
485 Joey Cora .05
486 *Trot Nixon* .25
487 Kevin McReynolds .05
488 Mike Lansing .05
489 Mike Pagliarulo .05
490 Mariano Duncan .05
491 Mike Bordick .05
492 Kevin Young .05
493 Dave Valle .05
494 *Wayne Gomes* .10
495 Rafael Palmeiro .20
496 Deion Sanders .10
497 Rick Sutcliffe .05
498 Randy Milligan .05
499 Carlos Quintana .05
500 Chris Turner .05
501 Thomas Howard .05
502 Greg Swindell .05
503 Chad Kreuter .05
504 Eric Davis .05
505 Dickie Thon .05
506 *Matt Drews* .05
507 Spike Owen .05
508 Rod Beck .05
509 Pat Hentgen .05
510 Sammy Sosa .60
511 J.T. Snow .05
512 Chuck Carr .05
513 Bo Jackson .10
514 Dennis Martinez .05
515 Phil Hiatt .05
516 Jeff Kent .05
517 *Brooks Kieschnick* .05
518 *Kirk Presley* .05
519 Kevin Seitzer .05
520 Carlos Garcia .05
521 Mike Blowers .05
522 Luis Alicea .05
523 David Hulse .05
524 Greg Maddux .60
525 Gregg Olson .05
526 Hal Morris .05
527 Daron Kirkreit .05
528 David Nied .05
529 Jeff Russell .05
530 Kevin Gross .05
531 John Doherty .05
532 *Matt Brunson* .05
533 Dave Nilsson .05
534 Randy Myers .05
535 Steve Farr .05
536 *Billy Wagner* .20
537 Darnell Coles .05
538 Frank Tanana .05
539 Tim Salmon .10
540 Kim Batiste .05
541 George Bell .05
542 Tom Henke .05
543 Sam Horn .05
544 Doug Jones .05
545 Scott Leius .05
546 Al Martin .05
547 Bob Welch .05
548 *Scott Christman* .05
549 Norm Charlton .05
550 Mark McGwire 1.00
551 Greg McMichael .05
552 Tim Costo .05
553 Rodney Bolton .05
554 Pedro Martinez .40
555 Marc Valdes .05
556 Darrell Whitmore .05
557 Tim Bogar .05
558 Steve Karsay .05
559 Danny Bautista .05
560 Jeffrey Hammonds .05
561 Aaron Sele .05
562 Russ Springer .05
563 Jason Bere .05
564 Billy Brewer .05
565 Sterling Hitchcock .05
566 Bobby Munoz .05
567 Craig Paquette .05
568 Bret Boone .10
569 Dan Peltier .05
570 Jeromy Burnitz .05
571 *John Wasdin* .10
572 Chipper Jones .75
573 *Jamey Wright* .05
574 Jeff Granger .05
575 *Jay Powell* .05
576 Ryan Thompson .05
577 Lou Frazier .05
578 Paul Wagner .05
579 Brad Ausmus .05
580 Jack Voigt .05
581 Kevin Rogers .05
582 Damon Buford .05
583 Paul Quantrill .05
584 Marc Newfield .05
585 *Derrek Lee* .20
586 Shane Reynolds .05
587 Cliff Floyd .05
588 Jeff Schwarz .05
589 *Ross Powell* .05
590 Gerald Williams .05
591 Mike Trombley .05
592 Ken Ryan .05
593 John O'Donoghue .05
594 Rod Correia .05
595 Darrell Sherman .05
596 Steve Scarsone .05
597 Sherman Obando .05
598 Kurt Abbott .05
599 Dave Telgheder .05
600 Rick Trlicek .05
601 Carl Everett .10
602 Luis Ortiz .05
603 *Larry Luebbers* .05
604 Kevin Roberson .05
605 Butch Huskey .05
606 Benji Gil .05
607 Todd Van Poppel .05
608 Mark Hutton .05
609 Chip Hale .05
610 Matt Maysey .05
611 Scott Ruffcorn .05
612 Hilly Hathaway .05
613 Allen Watson .05
614 Carlos Delgado .20
615 Roberto Mejia .05
616 Turk Wendell .05
617 Tony Tarasco .05
618 Raul Mondesi .20
619 Kevin Stocker .05
620 Javier Lopez .05
621 *Keith Kessinger* .05
622 Bob Hamelin .05
623 John Roper .05
624 Len Dykstra (World Series) .05
625 Joe Carter (World Series) .05
626 Jim Abbott (Highlight) .05
627 Lee Smith (Highlight) .05
628 Ken Griffey, Jr. (HL) .50
629 Dave Winfield (Highlight) .05
630 Darryl Kile (Highlight) .05
631 Frank Thomas (MVP) .45
632 Barry Bonds (MVP) .30
633 Jack McDowell (Cy Young) .05
634 Greg Maddux (Cy Young) .30
635 Tim Salmon (ROY) .10
636 Mike Piazza (ROY) .40
637 *Brian Turang* .05
638 Rondell White .15
639 Nigel Wilson .05
640 *Torii Hunter* .50
641 Salomon Torres .05
642 Kevin Higgins .05
643 Eric Wedge .05
644 Roger Salkeld .05
645 Manny Ramirez .50
646 Jeff McNeely .05
647 Braves Checklist .05
648 Cubs Checklist .05
649 Reds Checklist .05
650 Rockies Checklist .05
651 Marlins Checklist .05
652 Astros Checklist .05
653 Dodgers Checklist .05
654 Expos Checklist .05
655 Mets Checklist .05
656 Phillies Checklist .05
657 Pirates Checklist .05
658 Cardinals Checklist .05
659 Padres Checklist .05
660 Giants Checklist .05

1994 Score Gold Rush

Opting to include one insert card in each pack of its 1994 product, Score created a "Gold Rush" version of each card in its regular set. Gold Rush cards are basically the same as their counterparts with a few enhancements. Card fronts are printed on foil with a gold border and a Score

Gold Rush logo in one of the upper corners. The background of the photo has been metalized, allowing the color player portion to stand out in sharp contrast. Backs are identical to the regular cards except for the appearance of a large Gold Rush logo under the typography.

	MT
Complete Set (660):	50.00
Common Player:	.15
Stars:	2X

(See 1994 Score for checklist and base card values.)

1994 Score Boys of Summer

A heavy emphasis on rookies and recent rookies is noted in this insert set. Released in two series, cards #1-30 are found in Series 1, with #31-60 packaged with Series 2. Fronts feature a color action photo on which the background has been rendered in a blurred watercolor effect. A hot-color aura separates the player from the background. The player's name appears vertically in gold foil. Backs have the background in reds and orange with a portrait-style player photo on one side and a large "Boys of Summer" logo on the other. A short description of the player's talents appears at center.

		MT
Complete Set (60):		25.00
Common Player:		.25
1	Jeff Conine	.25
2	Aaron Sele	.25
3	Kevin Stocker	.25
4	Pat Meares	.25
5	Jeromy Burnitz	.25
6	Mike Piazza	5.00
7	Allen Watson	.25
8	Jeffrey Hammonds	.25
9	Kevin Roberson	.25
10	Hilly Hathaway	.25
11	Kirk Reuter	.25
12	Eduardo Perez	.25
13	Ricky Gutierrez	.25
14	Domingo Jean	.25
15	David Nied	.25
16	Wayne Kirby	.25
17	Mike Lansing	.25
18	Jason Bere	.25
19	Brent Gates	.25
20	Javier Lopez	.25
21	Greg McMichael	.25
22	David Hulse	.25
23	Roberto Mejia	.25
24	Tim Salmon	.75
25	Rene Arocha	.25
26	Bret Boone	.40
27	David McCarty	.25
28	Todd Van Poppel	.25
29	Lance Painter	.25
30	Erik Pappas	.25
31	Chuck Carr	.25
32	Mark Hutton	.25
33	Jeff McNeely	.25
34	Willie Greene	.25
35	Nigel Wilson	.25
36	Rondell White	.60
37	Brian Turang	.25
38	Manny Ramirez	4.00
39	Salomon Torres	.25
40	Melvin Nieves	.25
41	Ryan Klesko	.25
42	Keith Kessinger	.25
43	Eric Wedge	.25
44	Bob Hamelin	.25
45	Carlos Delgado	2.00
46	Marc Newfield	.25
47	Raul Mondesi	1.00
48	Tim Costo	.25
49	Pedro Martinez	3.00
50	Steve Karsay	.25
51	Danny Bautista	.25
52	Butch Huskey	.25
53	Kurt Abbott	.25
54	Darrell Sherman	.25
55	Damon Buford	.25
56	Ross Powell	.25
57	Darrell Whitmore	.25
58	Chipper Jones	5.00
59	Jeff Granger	.25
60	Cliff Floyd	.25

1994 Score Dream Team

Score's 1994 "Dream Team," one top player at each position, was featured in a 10-card insert set. The stars were decked out in vintage uniforms and equipment for the photos. Green and black bars at top and bottom frame the photo, and all printing on the front is in gold foil. Backs have a white background with green highlights. A color player portrait photo is featured, along with a brief justification for the player's selection to the squad. Cards are UV coated on both sides. Stated odds of finding a Dream Team insert were given as one per 72 packs.

		MT
Complete Set (10):		25.00
Common Player:		1.00
1	Mike Mussina	4.00
2	Tom Glavine	2.00
3	Don Mattingly	10.00
4	Carlos Baerga	1.00
5	Barry Larkin	1.50
6	Matt Williams	1.50
7	Juan Gonzalez	7.50
8	Andy Van Slyke	1.00
9	Larry Walker	2.00
10	Mike Stanley	1.00

1994 Score Gold Stars

Limited to inclusion in hobby packs, Score's 60-card "Gold Stars" insert set features 30 National League players, found in Series I packs, and 30 American Leaguers inserted with Series II. Stated odds of finding a Gold Stars card were listed on the wrapper as one in 18 packs. A notation on the cards' back indicates that no more than 6,500 sets of Gold Stars were produced. The high-tech cards feature a color player action photo, the full-bleed background of which has been converted to metallic tones. Backs have a graduated gold background with a portrait-style color player photo.

		MT
Complete Set (60):		60.00
Common Player:		.25
1	Barry Bonds	4.00
2	Orlando Merced	.25
3	Mark Grace	1.00
4	Darren Daulton	.25
5	Jeff Blauser	.25
6	Deion Sanders	.40
7	John Kruk	.25
8	Jeff Bagwell	2.50
9	Gregg Jefferies	.25
10	Matt Williams	.50
11	Andres Galarraga	.25
12	Jay Bell	.25
13	Mike Piazza	5.00
14	Ron Gant	.25
15	Barry Larkin	.35
16	Tom Glavine	.40
17	Len Dykstra	.25
18	Fred McGriff	.25
19	Andy Van Slyke	.25
20	Gary Sheffield	.60
21	John Burkett	.25
22	Dante Bichette	.25
23	Tony Gwynn	3.50
24	Dave Justice	.45
25	Marquis Grissom	.25
26	Bobby Bonilla	.25
27	Larry Walker	.50
28	Brett Butler	.25
29	Robby Thompson	.25
30	Jeff Conine	.25
31	Joe Carter	.25
32	Ken Griffey, Jr.	6.00
33	Juan Gonzalez	2.50
34	Rickey Henderson	2.00
35	Bo Jackson	.40
36	Cal Ripken, Jr.	6.00
37	John Olerud	.25
38	Carlos Baerga	.25
39	Jack McDowell	.25
40	Cecil Fielder	.25
41	Kenny Lofton	.25
42	Roberto Alomar	1.50
43	Randy Johnson	2.50
44	Tim Salmon	.40
45	Frank Thomas	4.00
46	Albert Belle	1.50
47	Greg Vaughn	.25
48	Travis Fryman	.25
49	Don Mattingly	4.00
50	Wade Boggs	1.50
51	Mo Vaughn	1.50
52	Kirby Puckett	3.50
53	Devon White	.25
54	Tony Phillips	.25
55	Brian Harper	.25
56	Chad Curtis	.25
57	Paul Molitor	2.00
58	Ivan Rodriguez	2.00
59	Rafael Palmeiro	.50
60	Brian McRae	.25

1994 Score The Cycle

Leaders in the previous season's production of singles, doubles, triples and home runs are featured in this insert set which was packaged with Series II Score. Player action photos pop out of a circle at center and are surrounded by dark blue borders. "The Cycle" in printed in green at top. The player's name is in gold foil at bottom, printed over an infield diagram in a green strip. The stat which earned the player inclusion in the set is in gold foil at bottom right. On back are the rankings for the statistical category. Cards are numbered with a "TC" prefix.

		MT
Complete Set (20):		30.00
Common Player:		1.00
1	Brett Butler	1.00
2	Kenny Lofton	1.00
3	Paul Molitor	2.50
4	Carlos Baerga	1.00
5	Gregg Jefferies, Tony Phillips	1.00
6	John Olerud	1.00
7	Charlie Hayes	1.00
8	Len Dykstra	1.00
9	Dante Bichette	1.00
10	Devon White	1.00
11	Lance Johnson	1.00
12	Joey Cora, Steve Finley	1.00
13	Tony Fernandez	1.00
14	David Hulse, Brett Butler	1.00
15	Jay Bell, Brian McRae, Mickey Morandini	1.00
16	Juan Gonzalez, Barry Bonds	5.00
17	Ken Griffey, Jr.	10.00
18	Frank Thomas	5.00
19	Dave Justice	1.50
20	Matt Williams, Albert Belle	2.00

1994 Score Rookie/Traded

Score Rookie & Traded completed the 1994 baseball season with a 165-card update set. These were available in both retail and hobby packs. Score issued Super Rookies and Changing Places insert sets, as well as a Traded Redemption card and a parallel Gold Rush set. Basic cards features red front borders. Team logos are in a bottom corner in a gold polygon. One of the upper corners contains a green polygon with a gold Score logo. Most cards #71-163 feature a square multi-colored "Rookie '94" logo in a lower corner. Backs of all cards have a purple background. Traded players' card backs are vertical and contain two additional photos. Backs of the rookie cards are horizontal and feature a portrait photo at left. The "Rookie '94" logo is repeated in the upper-right corner. This is in reverse of the fronts, on which traded players have a single photo and rookie cards have both portrait and action photos. Card numbers have an "RT" prefix.

		MT
Complete Set (165):		6.00
Common Player:		.05
Pack (10):		.50
Wax Box (36):		15.00
1	Will Clark	.15
2	Lee Smith	.05
3	Bo Jackson	.10
4	Ellis Burks	.05
5	Eddie Murray	.40
6	Delino DeShields	.05
7	Erik Hanson	.05
8	Rafael Palmeiro	.20
9	Luis Polonia	.05
10	Omar Vizquel	.05
11	Kurt Abbott	.05
12	Vince Coleman	.05
13	Rickey Henderson	.75
14	Terry Mulholland	.05
15	Greg Hibbard	.05
16	Walt Weiss	.05
17	Chris Sabo	.05
18	Dave Henderson	.05
19	Rick Sutcliffe	.05
20	Harold Reynolds	.05
21	Jack Morris	.05
22	Dan Wilson	.05
23	Dave Magadan	.05
24	Dennis Martinez	.05
25	Wes Chamberlain	.05
26	Otis Nixon	.05
27	Eric Anthony	.05
28	Randy Milligan	.05
29	Julio Franco	.05
30	Kevin McReynolds	.05
31	Anthony Young	.05
32	Brian Harper	.05
33	Lenny Harris	.05
34	Eddie Taubensee	.05
35	David Segui	.05
36	Stan Javier	.05
37	Felix Fermin	.05
38	Darrin Jackson	.05
39	Tony Fernandez	.05
40	Jose Vizcaino	.05
41	Willie Banks	.05
42	Brian Hunter	.05
43	Reggie Jefferson	.05
44	Junior Felix	.05
45	Jack Armstrong	.05
46	Bip Roberts	.05
47	Jerry Browne	.05
48	Marvin Freeman	.05
49	Jody Reed	.05
50	Alex Cole	.05
51	Sid Fernandez	.05
52	Pete Smith	.05
53	Xavier Hernandez	.05
54	Scott Sanderson	.05
55	Turner Ward	.05
56	Rex Hudler	.05
57	Deion Sanders	.10
58	Sid Bream	.05
59	Tony Pena	.05
60	Bret Boone	.10
61	Bobby Ayala	.05
62	Pedro Martinez	1.00
63	Howard Johnson	.05
64	Mark Portugal	.05
65	Roberto Kelly	.05
66	Spike Owen	.05
67	Jeff Treadway	.05
68	Mike Harkey	.05
69	Doug Jones	.05
70	Steve Farr	.05
71	Billy Taylor	.05
72	Manny Ramirez	1.50
73	Bob Hamelin	.05
74	Steve Karsay	.05
75	Ryan Klesko	.05
76	Cliff Floyd	.05
77	Jeffrey Hammonds	.05
78	Javier Lopez	.05
79	Roger Salkeld	.05
80	Hector Carrasco	.05
81	Gerald Williams	.05
82	Raul Mondesi	.50
83	Sterling Hitchcock	.05
84	Danny Bautista	.05
85	Chris Turner	.05
86	Shane Reynolds	.05
87	Rondell White	.20
88	Salomon Torres	.05
89	Turk Wendell	.05
90	Tony Tarasco	.05
91	Shawn Green	.50
92	Greg Colbrunn	.05
93	Eddie Zambrano	.05
94	Rich Becker	.05
95	Chris Gomez	.05
96	John Patterson	.05
97	Derek Parks	.05
98	Rich Rowland	.05
99	James Mouton	.05
100	Tim Hyers	.05
101	Jose Valentin	.05
102	Carlos Delgado	.75
103	Robert Esenhoorn	.05
104	John Hudek	.05
105	Domingo Cedeno	.05
106	Denny Hocking	.05
107	Greg Pirkl	.05
108	Mark Smith	.05
109	Paul Shuey	.05
110	Jorge Fabregas	.05
111	Rikkert Faneyte	.05
112	Rob Butler	.05
113	Darren Oliver	.05
114	Troy O'Leary	.05
115	Scott Brow	.05
116	Tony Eusebio	.05
117	Carlos Reyes	.05
118	J.R. Phillips	.05
119	Alex Diaz	.05
120	Charles Johnson	.05
121	Nate Minchey	.05
122	Scott Sanders	.05
123	Daryl Boston	.05
124	Joey Hamilton	.05
125	Brian Anderson	.05
126	Dan Miceli	.05
127	Tom Brunansky	.05
128	Dave Staton	.05
129	Mike Oquist	.05
130	John Mabry	.05
131	Norberto Martin	.05
132	Hector Fajardo	.05
133	Mark Hutton	.05
134	Fernando Vina	.05
135	Lee Tinsley	.05
136	*Chan Ho Park*	2.50
137	Paul Spoljaric	.05
138	Matias Carrillo	.05
139	Mark Kiefer	.05
140	Stan Royer	.05
141	Bryan Eversgerd	.05
143	Joe Hall	.05
144	Johnny Ruffin	.05
145	Alex Gonzalez	.15
146	Keith Lockhart	.05
147	Tom Marsh	.05
148	Tony Longmire	.05
149	Keith Mitchell	.05
150	Melvin Nieves	.05
151	Kelly Stinnett	.05
152	Miguel Jimenez	.05
153	Jeff Juden	.05
154	Matt Walbeck	.05
155	Marc Newfield	.05
156	Matt Mieske	.05
157	Marcus Moore	.05
158	*Jose Lima*	2.00
159	Mike Kelly	.05
160	Jim Edmonds	.25
161	Steve Trachsel	.05
162	Greg Blosser	.05
163	Mark Acre	.05
164	AL Checklist	.05
165	NL Checklist	.05

1994 Score Rookie/Traded Gold Rush

Each pack of Score Rookie and Traded cards included one Gold Rush parallel version of one of the set's cards. The insert cards feature fronts that are printed directly on gold foil and include a Gold Rush logo in an upper corner.

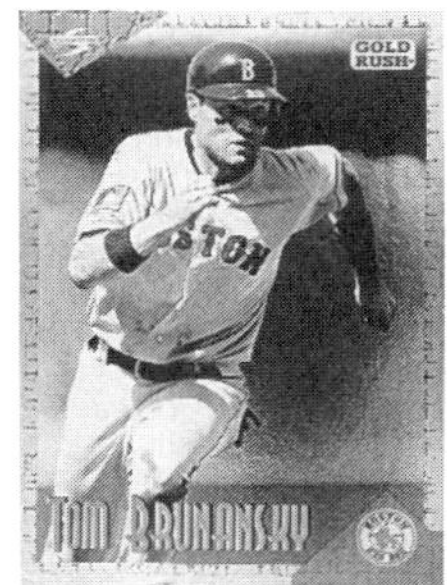

	MT
Complete Set (165):	20.00
Common Player:	.15
Stars:	2X

(See 1994 Score Rookie/Traded for checklist and base card values.)

1994 Score Rookie/Traded Changing Places

Changing Places documents the relocation of 10 veteran stars. Cards were inserted into one of every 36 retail or hobby packs. Fronts have a color photo of the player in his new uniform and are enhanced with red foil. Backs have a montage of color and black-and-white photos and a few words about the trade. Card numbers have a "CP" prefix.

		MT
Complete Set (10):		7.00
Common Player:		.50
1	Will Clark	1.50
2	Rafael Palmeiro	2.00
3	Roberto Kelly	.50
4	Bo Jackson	.75
5	Otis Nixon	.50
6	Rickey Henderson	2.50
7	Ellis Burks	.50
8	Lee Smith	.50
9	Delino DeShields	.50
10	Deion Sanders	1.50

1994 Score Rookie/Traded Super Rookies

Super Rookies is an 18-card set honoring baseball's brightest young stars.

They appear only in hobby packs at a rate of one every 36 packs. Fronts are printed on foil, with a multi-colored border. Backs feature another photo, most of which is rendered in single-color blocks, along with a few words about the player and a large Super Rookie logo. Cards are numbered with an "SU" prefix.

		MT
Complete Set (18):		22.50
Common Player:		1.00
1	Carlos Delgado	2.50
2	Manny Ramirez	7.50
3	Ryan Klesko	1.00
4	Raul Mondesi	3.50
5	Bob Hamelin	1.00
6	Steve Karsay	1.00
7	Jeffrey Hammonds	1.00
8	Cliff Floyd	1.00
9	Kurt Abbott	1.00
10	Marc Newfield	1.00
11	Javier Lopez	1.00
12	Rich Becker	1.00
13	Greg Pirkl	1.00
14	Rondell White	2.50
15	James Mouton	1.00
16	Tony Tarasco	1.00
17	Brian Anderson	1.00
18	Jim Edmonds	1.25

1994 Score Rookie/Traded Redemption Card

The Score Rookie and Traded Redemption card was inserted at a rate of one every 240 packs. It gave collectors a chance to mail in for the best rookie in the annual September call-up: Alex Rodriguez

	MT
September Call-Up redemption card (expired)	2.00
Alex Rodriguez	300.00

1995 Score

Score 1995 Baseball is composed of 605 cards, issued in two series; the first comprising 330 cards, the second, 275. Basic cards have photos placed on a dirt-like background with a green strip running up each side. The player's name, position, and team logo is given in white letters on a blue strip across the bottom. Backs resemble the fronts, except with a smaller, portrait photo of the player, which leaves room for statistics and biographical information. Score had a parallel set of Gold Rush cards, along with several other series of inserts. Eleven players in Series 2 can be found in two team variations as the result of a redemption program for updated cards.

		MT
Complete Set (605):		12.50
Common Player:		.05
Platinums:		4X
Wax Pack (12):		.50
Wax Box (36):		15.00
1	Frank Thomas	.65
2	Roberto Alomar	.40
3	Cal Ripken, Jr.	1.50
4	Jose Canseco	.25
5	Matt Williams	.15
6	Esteban Beltre	.05
7	Domingo Cedeno	.05
8	John Valentin	.05
9	Glenallen Hill	.05
10	Rafael Belliard	.05
11	Randy Myers	.05
12	Mo Vaughn	.30
13	Hector Carrasco	.05
14	Chili Davis	.05
15	Dante Bichette	.05
16	Darren Jackson	.05
17	Mike Piazza	.75
18	Junior Felix	.05
19	Moises Alou	.10
20	Mark Gubicza	.05
21	Bret Saberhagen	.05
22	Len Dykstra	.05
23	Steve Howe	.05
24	Mark Dewey	.05
25	Brian Harper	.05
26	Ozzie Smith	.65
27	Scott Erickson	.05
28	Tony Gwynn	.65
29	Bob Welch	.05
30	Barry Bonds	.65
31	Leo Gomez	.05
32	Greg Maddux	.65
33	Mike Greenwell	.05
34	Sammy Sosa	.65
35	Darnell Coles	.05
36	Tommy Greene	.05
37	Will Clark	.15
38	Steve Ontiveros	.05
39	Stan Javier	.05
40	Bip Roberts	.05
41	Paul O'Neill	.05
42	Bill Haselman	.05
43	Shane Mack	.05
44	Orlando Merced	.05
45	Kevin Seitzer	.05
46	Trevor Hoffman	.05
47	Greg Gagne	.05
48	Jeff Kent	.05
49	Tony Phillips	.05
50	Ken Hill	.05
51	Carlos Baerga	.05
52	Henry Rodriguez	.05
53	Scott Sanderson	.05
54	Jeff Conine	.05
55	Chris Turner	.05
56	Ken Caminiti	.05
57	Harold Baines	.05
58	Charlie Hayes	.05
59	Roberto Kelly	.05
60	John Olerud	.05
61	Tim Davis	.05
62	Rich Rowland	.05
63	Rey Sanchez	.05
64	Junior Ortiz	.05
65	Ricky Gutierrez	.05
66	Rex Hudler	.05
67	Johnny Ruffin	.05
68	Jay Buhner	.05
69	Tom Pagnozzi	.05
70	Julio Franco	.05
71	Eric Young	.05
72	Mike Bordick	.05
73	Don Slaught	.05
74	Goose Gossage	.05
75	Lonnie Smith	.05
76	Jimmy Key	.05
77	Dave Hollins	.05
78	Mickey Tettleton	.05
79	Luis Gonzalez	.15
80	Dave Winfield	.40
81	Ryan Thompson	.05
82	Felix Jose	.05
83	Rusty Meacham	.05
84	Darryl Hamilton	.05
85	John Wetteland	.05
86	Tom Brunansky	.05
87	Mark Lemke	.05
88	Spike Owen	.05
89	Shawon Dunston	.05
90	Wilson Alvarez	.05
91	Lee Smith	.05
92	Scott Kamieniecki	.05
93	Jacob Brumfield	.05
94	Kirk Gibson	.05
95	Joe Girardi	.05
96	Mike Macfarlane	.05
97	Greg Colbrunn	.05
98	Ricky Bones	.05
99	Delino DeShields	.05
100	Pat Meares	.05
101	Jeff Fassero	.05
102	Jim Leyritz	.05
103	Gary Redus	.05
104	Terry Steinbach	.05
105	Kevin McReynolds	.05
106	Felix Fermin	.05
107	Danny Jackson	.05
108	Chris James	.05
109	Jeff King	.05
110	Pat Hentgen	.05
111	Gerald Perry	.05
112	Tim Raines	.05
113	Eddie Williams	.05
114	Jamie Moyer	.05
115	Bud Black	.05
116	Chris Gomez	.05
117	Luis Lopez	.05
118	Roger Clemens	.65
119	Javier Lopez	.05
120	Dave Nilsson	.05
121	Karl Rhodes	.05
122	Rick Aguilera	.05
123	Tony Fernandez	.05
124	Bernie Williams	.30
125	James Mouton	.05
126	Mark Langston	.05
127	Mike Lansing	.05
128	Tino Martinez	.05
129	Joe Orsulak	.05
130	David Hulse	.05
131	Pete Incaviglia	.05
132	Mark Clark	.05
133	Tony Eusebio	.05
134	Chuck Finley	.05
135	Lou Frazier	.05
136	Craig Grebeck	.05
137	Kelly Stinnett	.05
138	Paul Shuey	.05
139	David Nied	.05
140	Billy Brewer	.05
141	Dave Weathers	.05
142	Scott Leius	.05
143	Brian Jordan	.05
144	Melido Perez	.05
145	Tony Tarasco	.05
146	Dan Wilson	.05
147	Rondell White	.10
148	Mike Henneman	.05
149	Brian Johnson	.05
150	Tom Henke	.05
151	John Patterson	.05
152	Bobby Witt	.05
153	Eddie Taubensee	.05
154	Pat Borders	.05
155	Ramon Martinez	.05
156	Mike Kingery	.05
157	Zane Smith	.05
158	Benito Santiago	.05
159	Matias Carrillo	.05
160	Scott Brosius	.05
161	Dave Clark	.05
162	Mark McLemore	.05
163	Curt Schilling	.15
164	J.T. Snow	.05
165	Rod Beck	.05
166	Scott Fletcher	.05
167	Bob Tewksbury	.05
168	Mike LaValliere	.05
169	Dave Hansen	.05
170	Pedro Martinez	.40
171	Kirk Rueter	.05
172	Jose Lind	.05
173	Luis Alicea	.05
174	Mike Moore	.05
175	Andy Ashby	.05
176	Jody Reed	.05
177	Darryl Kile	.05
178	Carl Willis	.05
179	Jeromy Burnitz	.05
180	Mike Gallego	.05
181	*W. Van Landingham*	.10
182	Sid Fernandez	.05
183	Kim Batiste	.05
184	Greg Myers	.05
185	Steve Avery	.05
186	Steve Farr	.05
187	Robb Nen	.05
188	Dan Pasqua	.05
189	Bruce Ruffin	.05
190	Jose Valentin	.05
191	Willie Banks	.05
192	Mike Aldrete	.05
193	Randy Milligan	.05
194	Steve Karsay	.05
195	Mike Stanley	.05
196	Jose Mesa	.05
197	Tom Browning	.05
198	John Vander Wal	.05
199	Kevin Brown	.10
200	Mike Oquist	.05
201	Greg Swindell	.05
202	Eddie Zambrano	.05
203	Joe Boever	.05
204	Gary Varsho	.05
205	Chris Gwynn	.05
206	David Howard	.05
207	Jerome Walton	.05
208	Danny Darwin	.05
209	Darryl Strawberry	.05
210	Todd Van Poppel	.05
211	Scott Livingstone	.05
212	Dave Fleming	.05
213	Todd Worrell	.05
214	Carlos Delgado	.30
215	Bill Pecota	.05
216	Jim Lindeman	.05
217	Rick White	.05
218	Jose Oquendo	.05
219	Tony Castillo	.05
220	Fernando Vina	.05
221	Jeff Bagwell	.50
222	Randy Johnson	.50
223	Albert Belle	.20
224	Chuck Carr	.05
225	Mark Leiter	.05
226	Hal Morris	.05
227	Robin Ventura	.05
228	Mike Munoz	.05
229	Jim Thome	.05
230	Mario Diaz	.05

231 John Doherty .05
232 Bobby Jones .05
233 Raul Mondesi .20
234 Ricky Jordan .05
235 John Jaha .05
236 Carlos Garcia .05
237 Kirby Puckett .65
238 Orel Hershiser .05
239 Don Mattingly .75
240 Sid Bream .05
241 Brent Gates .05
242 Tony Longmire .05
243 Robby Thompson .05
244 Rick Sutcliffe .05
245 Dean Palmer .05
246 Marquis Grissom .05
247 Paul Molitor .40
248 Mark Carreon .05
249 Jack Voight .05
250 Greg McMichael (photo on front is Mike Stanton) .05
251 Damon Berryhill .05
252 Brian Dorsett .05
253 Jim Edmonds .10
254 Barry Larkin .10
255 Jack McDowell .05
256 Wally Joyner .05
257 Eddie Murray .35
258 Lenny Webster .05
259 Milt Cuyler .05
260 Todd Benzinger .05
261 Vince Coleman .05
262 Todd Stottlemyre .05
263 Turner Ward .05
264 Ray Lankford .05
265 Matt Walbeck .05
266 Deion Sanders .10
267 Gerald Williams .05
268 Jim Gott .05
269 Jeff Frye .05
270 Jose Rijo .05
271 Dave Justice .20
272 Ismael Valdes .10
273 Ben McDonald .05
274 Darren Lewis .05
275 Graeme Lloyd .05
276 Luis Ortiz .05
277 Julian Tavarez .05
278 Mark Dalesandro .05
279 Brett Merriman .05
280 Ricky Bottalico .05
281 Robert Eenhoorn .05
282 Rikkert Faneyte .05
283 Mike Kelly .05
284 Mark Smith .05
285 Turk Wendell .05
286 Greg Blosser .05
287 Garey Ingram .05
288 Jorge Fabregas .05
289 Blaise Ilsley .05
290 Joe Hall .05
291 Orlando Miller .05
292 Jose Lima .10
293 Greg O'Halloran .05
294 Mark Kiefer .05
295 Jose Oliva .05
296 Rich Becker .05
297 Brian Hunter .05
298 Dave Silvestri .05
299 *Armando Benitez* .15
300 Darren Dreifort .05
301 John Mabry .05
302 Greg Pirkl .05
303 J.R. Phillips .05
304 Shawn Green .20
305 Roberto Petagine .05
306 Keith Lockhart .05
307 Jonathon Hurst .05
308 Paul Spoljaric .05
309 Mike Lieberthal .10
310 Garret Anderson .10
311 John Johnston .05
312 Alex Rodriguez 1.00
313 Kent Mercker .05
314 John Valentin .05
315 Kenny Rogers .05
316 Fred McGriff .05
317 Atlanta Braves, Baltimore Orioles .05
318 Chicago Cubs, Boston Red Sox .05
319 Cincinnati Reds, California Angels .05
320 Colorado Rockies, Chicago White Sox .05
321 Cleveland Indians, Florida Marlins .05
322 Houston Astros, Detroit Tigers .05
323 Los Angels Dodgers, Kansas City Royals .05
324 Montreal Expos, Milwaukee Brewers .05
325 New York Mets, Minnesota Twins .05
326 Philadelphia Phillies, New York Yankees .05
327 Pittsburgh Pirates, Oakland Athletics .05
328 San Diego Padres, Seattle Mariners .05
329 San Francisco Giants, Texas Rangers .05
330 St. Louis Cardinals, Toronto Blue Jays .05
331 Pedro Munoz .05
332 Ryan Klesko .05
333a Andre Dawson (Red Sox) .25
333b Andre Dawson (Marlins) .35
334 Derrick May .05
335 Aaron Sele .05
336 Kevin Mitchell .05
337 Steve Traschel .05
338 Andres Galarraga .05
339a Terry Pendleton (Braves) .05
339b Terry Pendleton (Marlins) .25
340 Gary Sheffield .25
341 Travis Fryman .05
342 Bo Jackson .10
343 Gary Gaetti .05
344a Brett Butler (Dodgers) .05
344b Brett Butler (Mets) .25
345 B. J. Surhoff .05
346a Larry Walker (Expos) .25
346b Larry Walker (Rockies) .50
347 Kevin Tapani .05
348 Rick Wilkins .05
349 Wade Boggs .35
350 Mariano Duncan .05
351 Ruben Sierra .05
352a Andy Van Slyke (Pirates) .05
352b Andy Van Slyke (Orioles) .25
353 Reggie Jefferson .05
354 Gregg Jefferies .05
355 Tim Naehring .05
356 John Roper .05
357 Joe Carter .05
358 Kurt Abbott .05
359 Lenny Harris .05
360 Lance Johnson .05
361 Brian Anderson .05
362 Jim Eisenreich .05
363 Jerry Browne .05
364 Mark Grace .25
365 Devon White .05
366 Reggie Sanders .05
367 Ivan Rodriguez .35
368 Kirt Manwaring .05
369 Pat Kelly .05
370 Ellis Burks .05
371 Charles Nagy .05
372 Kevin Bass .05
373 Lou Whitaker .05
374 Rene Arocha .05
375 Derrick Parks .05
376 Mark Whiten .05
377 Mark McGwire 1.50
378 Doug Drabek .05
379 Greg Vaughn .05
380 Al Martin .05
381 Ron Darling .05
382 Tim Wallach .05
383 Alan Trammell .05
384 Randy Velarde .05
385 Chris Sabo .05
386 Wil Cordero .05
387 Darrin Fletcher .05
388 David Segui .05
389 Steve Buechele .05
390 Otis Nixon .05
391 Jeff Brantley .05
392a Chad Curtis (Angels) .05
392b Chad Curtis (Tigers) .25
393 Cal Eldred .05
394 Jason Bere .05
395 Bret Barberie .05
396 Paul Sorrento .05
397 Steve Finley .05
398 Cecil Fielder .05
399 Eric Karros .05
400 Jeff Montgomery .05
401 Cliff Floyd .05
402 Matt Mieske .05
403 Brian Hunter .05
404 Alex Cole .05
405 Kevin Stocker .05
406 Eric Davis .05
407 Marvin Freeman .05
408 Dennis Eckersley .05
409 Todd Zeile .05
410 Keith Mitchell .05
411 Andy Benes .05
412 Juan Bell .05
413 Royce Clayton .05
414 Ed Sprague .05
415 Mike Mussina .25
416 Todd Hundley .05
417 Pat Listach .05
418 Joe Oliver .05
419 Rafael Palmeiro .20
420 Tim Salmon .15
421 Brady Anderson .05
422 Kenny Lofton .05
423 Craig Biggio .10
424 Bobby Bonilla .05
425 Kenny Rogers .05
426 Derek Bell .05
427a Scott Cooper (Red Sox) .05
427b Scott Cooper (Cardinals) .25
428 Ozzie Guillen .05
429 Omar Vizquel .05
430 Phil Plantier .05
431 Chuck Knoblauch .05
432 Darren Daulton .05
433 Bob Hamelin .05
434 Tom Glavine .10
435 Walt Weiss .05
436 Jose Vizcaino .05
437 Ken Griffey Jr. 1.25
438 Jay Bell .05
439 Juan Gonzalez .50
440 Jeff Blauser .05
441 Rickey Henderson .40
442 Bobby Ayala .05
443a David Cone (Royals) .05
443b David Cone (Blue Jays) .35
444 Pedro Martinez .05
445 Manny Ramirez .50
446 Mark Portugal .05
447 Damion Easley .05
448 Gary DiSarcina .05
449 Roberto Hernandez .05
450 Jeffrey Hammonds .05
451 Jeff Treadway .05
452a Jim Abbott (Yankees) .05
452b Jim Abbott (White Sox) .25
453 Carlos Rodriguez .05
454 Joey Cora .05
455 Bret Boone .10
456 Danny Tartabull .05
457 John Franco .05
458 Roger Salkeld .05
459 Fred McGriff .05
460 Pedro Astacio .05
461 Jon Lieber .05
462 Luis Polonia .05
463 Geronimo Pena .05
464 Tom Gordon .05
465 Brad Ausmus .05
466 Willie McGee .05
467 Doug Jones .05
468 John Smoltz .10
469 Troy Neel .05
470 Luis Sojo .05
471 John Smiley .05
472 Rafael Bournigal .05
473 Billy Taylor .05
474 Juan Guzman .05
475 Dave Magadan .05
476 Mike Devereaux .05
477 Andujar Cedeno .05
478 Edgar Martinez .05
479 Troy Neel .05
480 Allen Watson .05
481 Ron Karkovice .05
482 Joey Hamilton .05
483 Vinny Castilla .05
484 Kevin Gross .05
485 Bernard Gilkey .05
486 John Burkett .05
487 Matt Nokes .05
488 Mel Rojas .05
489 Craig Shipley .05
490 Chip Hale .05
491 Bill Swift .05
492 Pat Rapp .05
493a Brian McRae (Royals) .05
493b Brian McRae (Cubs) .25
494 Mickey Morandini .05
495 Tony Pena .05
496 Danny Bautista .05
497 Armando Reynoso .05
498 Ken Ryan .05
499 Billy Ripken .05
500 Pat Mahomes .05
501 Mark Acre .05
502 Geronimo Berroa .05
503 Norberto Martin .05
504 Chad Kreuter .05
505 Howard Johnson .05
506 Eric Anthony .05
507 Mark Wohlers .05
508 Scott Sanders .05
509 Pete Harnisch .05
510 Wes Chamberlain .05
511 Tom Candiotti .05
512 Albie Lopez .05
513 Denny Neagle .05
514 Sean Berry .05
515 Billy Hatcher .05
516 Todd Jones .05
517 Wayne Kirby .05
518 Butch Henry .05
519 Sandy Alomar Jr. .05
520 Kevin Appier .05
521 Robert Mejia .05
522 Steve Cooke .05
523 Terry Shumpert .05
524 Mike Jackson .05
525 Kent Mercker .05
526 David Wells .10
527 Juan Samuel .05
528 Salomon Torres .05
529 Duane Ward .05
530a Rob Dibble (Reds) .05
530b Rob Dibble (White Sox) .25
531 Mike Blowers .05
532 Mark Eichhorn .05
533 Alex Diaz .05
534 Dan Miceli .05
535 Jeff Branson .05
536 Dave Stevens .05
537 Charlie O'Brien .05
538 Shane Reynolds .05
539 Rich Amaral .05
540 Rusty Greer .05
541 Alex Arias .05
542 Eric Plunk .05
543 John Hudek .05
544 Kirk McCaskill .05
545 Jeff Reboulet .05
546 Sterling Hitchcock .05
547 Warren Newson .05
548 Bryan Harvey .05
549 Mike Huff .05
550 Lance Parrish .05
551 Ken Griffey Jr. (Hitters Inc.) .65
552 Matt Williams (Hitters Inc.) .10
553 Roberto Alomar (Hitters Inc.) .15
554 Jeff Bagwell (Hitters Inc.) .25
555 Dave Justice (Hitters Inc.) .10
556 Cal Ripken Jr. (Hitters Inc.) .75
557 Albert Belle (Hitters Inc.) .10
558 Mike Piazza (Hitters Inc.) .40
559 Kirby Puckett (Hitters Inc.) .30
560 Wade Boggs (Hitters Inc.) .20
561 Tony Gwynn (Hitters Inc.) .30
562 Barry Bonds (Hitters Inc.) .35

563	Mo Vaughn (Hitters Inc.)	.10
564	Don Mattingly (Hitters Inc.)	.40
565	Carlos Baerga (Hitters Inc.)	.05
566	Paul Molitor (Hitters Inc.)	.15
567	Raul Mondesi (Hitters Inc.)	.10
568	Manny Ramirez (Hitters Inc.)	.25
569	Alex Rodriguez (Hitters Inc.)	.50
570	Will Clark (Hitters Inc.)	.10
571	Frank Thomas (Hitters Inc.)	.35
572	Moises Alou (Hitters Inc.)	.05
573	Jeff Conine (Hitters Inc.)	.05
574	Joe Ausanio	.05
575	Charles Johnson	.05
576	Ernie Young	.05
577	Jeff Granger	.05
578	Robert Perez	.05
579	Melvin Nieves	.05
580	Gar Finnvold	.05
581	Duane Singleton	.05
582	Chan Ho Park	.15
583	Fausto Cruz	.05
584	Dave Staton	.05
585	Denny Hocking	.05
586	Nate Minchey	.05
587	Marc Newfield	.05
588	Jayhawk Owens	.05
589	Darren Bragg	.05
590	Kevin King	.05
591	Kurt Miller	.05
592	Aaron Small	.05
593	Troy O'Leary	.05
594	Phil Stidham	.05
595	Steve Dunn	.05
596	Cory Bailey	.05
597	Alex Gonzalez	.10
598	Jim Bowie	.05
599	Jeff Cirillo	.05
600	Mark Hutton	.05
601	Russ Davis	.05
602	Checklist #331-400	.05
603	Checklist #401-469	.05
604	Checklist #470-537	.05
605	Checklist #538-605	.05
----	"You Trade 'em" redemption card (Expired Dec. 31, 1995)	.25

1995 Score Gold Rush

Besides being collectible in their own right, the gold-foil printed parallel versions of the Score regular-issue cards could be collected into team sets and exchanged with a trade card for platinum versions. The deadline for redemption of Series I was July 1, 1995; Oct. 1, 1995, for Series II. Gold Rush cards were found either one or two per pack, depending on pack card count. Gold Rush versions exist for each card in the Score set and have fronts that are identical to the regular cards except they are printed on foil and have gold borders. Backs of the Gold Rush cards have a small rectangular "GOLD RUSH" logo overprinted.

	MT
Complete Set (605):	45.00
Common Player:	.15
Gold Rush Stars:	2X

(See 1995 Score for checklist and base card values.)

1995 Score Airmail

Young ballplayers with a propensity for hitting the long ball are featured in this insert set found only in Series II jumbo packs. Cards have a player batting action photo set in sky-and-clouds background. A gold-foil stamp in the upper-left corner identifies the series. Backs have a background photo of sunset and dark clouds, with a player portrait photo in the foreground. A few stats and sentences describe the player's power hitting potential. Cards have an AM prefix to the number. Stated odds for insertion rate are an average of one Airmail chase card per 24 packs.

		MT
Complete Set (18):		16.00
Common Player:		.40
1	Bob Hamelin	.40
2	John Mabry	.40
3	Marc Newfield	.40
4	Jose Oliva	.40
5	Charles Johnson	.50
6	Russ Davis	.40
7	Ernie Young	.40
8	Billy Ashley	.40
9	Ryan Klesko	.40
10	J.R. Phillips	.40
11	Cliff Floyd	.40
12	Carlos Delgado	2.50
13	Melvin Nieves	.40
14	Raul Mondesi	1.50
15	Manny Ramirez	3.50
16	Mike Kelly	.40
17	Alex Rodriguez	8.00
18	Rusty Greer	.40

1995 Score Double Gold Champions

A dozen veteran players, who have won at least two of the game's top awards are designated as "Double Gold Champs," in this Series II hobby insert set. Fronts have horizontal action photos at top, with a speckled red border at bottom. Vertical backs have a portrait photo and a list of the major awards won by the player. Cards have a GC prefix to the number. These chase cards were reportedly inserted at an average rate of one per 36.

		MT
Complete Set (12):		36.00
Common Player:		1.00
1	Frank Thomas	5.00
2	Ken Griffey Jr.	8.00
3	Barry Bonds	3.50
4	Tony Gwynn	3.50
5	Don Mattingly	5.00
6	Greg Maddux	3.50
7	Roger Clemens	3.50
8	Kenny Lofton	1.00
9	Jeff Bagwell	2.50
10	Matt Williams	1.00
11	Kirby Puckett	3.50
12	Cal Ripken Jr.	8.00

1995 Score Draft Picks

These cards were randomly included in 1995 Score hobby packs at a rate of one per every 36 packs. The cards showcase 18 of baseball's potential superstars and document their professional beginnings. The card front has the player's team logo and name in the lower-right corner. " '94 Draft Pick" appears in the upper-right corner. The front also has a mug shot and an action shot of the player. The card back has a portrait and career summary and is numbered with a DP prefix.

		MT
Complete Set (18):		10.00
Common Player:		.50
1	McKay Christensen	.50
2	Brett Wagner	.50
3	Paul Wilson	.50
4	C.J. Nitkowski	.50
5	Josh Booty	.75
6	Antone Williamson	.50
7	Paul Konerko	2.00
8	Scott Elarton	.50
9	Jacob Shumate	.50
10	Terrence Long	.75
11	Mark Johnson	.50
12	Ben Grieve	3.00
13	Doug Million	.50
14	Jayson Peterson	.50
15	Dustin Hermanson	.75
16	Matt Smith	.50
17	Kevin Witt	.50
18	Brian Buchanon	.50

1995 Score Dream Team Gold

The Major Leagues' top players at each position are featured in this Series I insert set. Fronts are printed entirely on rainbow holographic foil and feature a large and a small player action photo. Backs have a single-color version of one of the front photos as well as a color portrait photo in a circle at center, all in conventional printing technology. Card numbers have a DG prefix.

		MT
Complete Set (12):		45.00
Common Player:		.75
1	Frank Thomas	6.50
2	Roberto Alomar	3.00
3	Cal Ripken Jr.	10.00
4	Matt Williams	1.50
5	Mike Piazza	7.50
6	Albert Belle	1.50
7	Ken Griffey Jr.	10.00
8	Tony Gwynn	6.00
9	Paul Molitor	3.00
10	Jimmy Key	.75
11	Greg Maddux	6.00
12	Lee Smith	.75

1995 Score Hall of Gold

Hall of Gold inserts picture 110 of the top players on gold foil cards. Each card front has the Hall of Gold logo in an upper corner, plus a color action photo of the player, and his name and team logo at the bottom. The card back is numbered using an "HG" prefix and includes another color photo of the player, his team's name, his position, and a career summary. Cards were inserted one per every six regular 1995 Score packs and one per every two jumbo packs. Updated versions of five traded players were issued in Series II, available only via mail-in offer with a trade card found randomly inserted in packs.

		MT
Complete Set (110):		35.00
Common Player:		.10
1	Ken Griffey Jr.	2.00
2	Matt Williams	.25
3	Roberto Alomar	.45
4	Jeff Bagwell	1.00
5	Dave Justice	.25
6	Cal Ripken Jr.	2.00
7	Randy Johnson	.25
8	Barry Larkin	.15
9	Albert Belle	.35
10	Mike Piazza	1.50
11	Kirby Puckett	1.25
12	Moises Alou	.15
13	Jose Canseco	.25
14	Tony Gwynn	12.50
15	Roger Clemens	1.25
16	Barry Bonds	1.25
17	Mo Vaughn	.40
18	Greg Maddux	1.25
19	Dante Bichette	.10
20	Will Clark	.30
21	Len Dykstra	.10
22	Don Mattingly	1.50
23	Carlos Baerga	.10
24	Ozzie Smith	1.00
25	Paul Molitor	.45
26	Paul O'Neill	.10
27	Deion Sanders	.15
28	Jeff Conine	.10
29	John Olerud	.10
30	Jose Rijo	.10
31	Sammy Sosa	1.25
32	Robin Ventura	.10
33	Raul Mondesi	.20
34	Eddie Murray	.45
35	Marquis Grissom	.10
36	Darryl Strawberry	.10
37	Dave Nilsson	.10
38	Manny Ramirez	1.00
39	Delino DeShields	.10
40	Lee Smith	.10
41	Alex Rodriguez	1.75
42	Julio Franco	.10
43	Bret Saberhagen	.10
44	Ken Hill	.10
45	Roberto Kelly	.10
46	Hal Morris	.10
47	Jimmy Key	.10
48	Terry Steinbach	.10
49	Mickey Tettleton	.10
50	Tony Phillips	.10
51	Carlos Garcia	.10
52	Jim Edmonds	.15
53	Rod Beck	.10
54	Shane Mack	.10
55	Ken Caminiti	.10
56	Frank Thomas	1.25
57	Kenny Lofton	.10
58	Jack McDowell	.10
59	Jason Bere	.10
60	Joe Carter	.10
61	Gary Sheffield	.20
62	Andres Galarraga	.10
63	Gregg Jefferies	.10
64	Bobby Bonilla	.10
65	Tom Glavine	.10
66	John Smoltz	.10
67	Fred McGriff	.10
68	Craig Biggio	.10
69	Reggie Sanders	.10
70	Kevin Mitchell	.10
71a	Larry Walker (Expos)	.15
71b	Larry Walker (Rockies)	.75
72	Carlos Delgado	.15
73	Andujar Cedeno	.10
74	Ivan Rodriguez	.30
75	Ryan Klesko	.10
76a	John Kruk (Phillies)	.10
76b	John Kruk (White Sox)	.20
77a	Brian McRae (Royals)	.10
77b	Brian McRae (Cubs)	.20
78	Tim Salmon	.15
79	Travis Fryman	.10
80	Chuck Knoblauch	.10
81	Jay Bell	.10
82	Cecil Fielder	.10
83	Cliff Floyd	.10
84	Ruben Sierra	.10
85	Mike Mussina	.45
86	Mark Grace	.25
87	Dennis Eckersley	.10
88	Dennis Martinez	.10
89	Rafael Palmeiro	.20
90	Ben McDonald	.10
91	Dave Hollins	.10
92	Steve Avery	.10
93a	David Cone (Royals)	.10
93b	David Cone (Blue Jays)	.20
94	Darren Daulton	.10
95	Bret Boone	.10
96	Wade Boggs	.40
97	Doug Drabek	.10
98	Derek Bell	.10
99	Jim Thome	.10
100	Chili Davis	.10
101	Jeffrey Hammonds	.10
102	Rickey Henderson	.40
103	Brett Butler	.10
104	Tim Wallach	.10
105	Wil Cordero	.10
106	Mark Whiten	.10
107	Bob Hamelin	.10
108	Rondell White	.10
109	Devon White	.10
110a	Tony Tarasco (Braves)	.10
110b	Tony Tarasco (Expos)	.20
----	Redemption trade card (Expired Dec. 31, 1995)	.10

1995 Score Rookie Dream Team

These Series II inserts feature a dozen of 1995's best rookie prospects. Fronts are printed on a silver-foil background. The words "ROOKIE DREAM TEAM" are formed of sky-and-cloud images within the letters. Horizontal backs repeat the motif and include another player photo in a vignette at center. Card numbers have an RDT prefix.

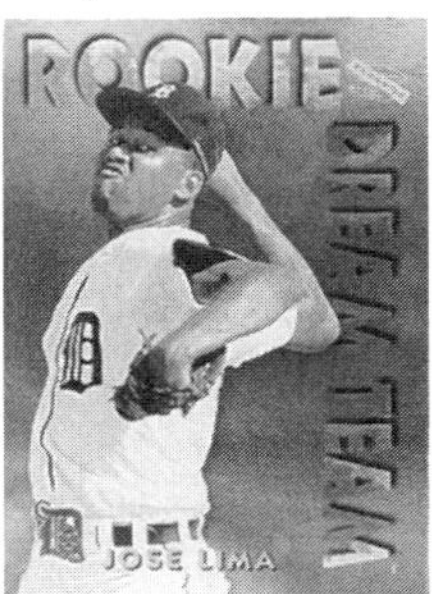

		MT
Complete Set (12):		16.00
Common Player:		.50
1	J.R. Phillips	.50
2	Alex Gonzalez	2.50
3	Alex Rodriguez	8.00
4	Jose Oliva	.50
5	Charles Johnson	1.00
6	Shawn Green	2.50
7	Brian Hunter	.50
8	Garret Anderson	1.00
9	Julian Tavarez	.50
10	Jose Lima	2.00
11	Armando Benitez	.50
12	Ricky Bottalico	1.00

1995 Score Rookie Greatness

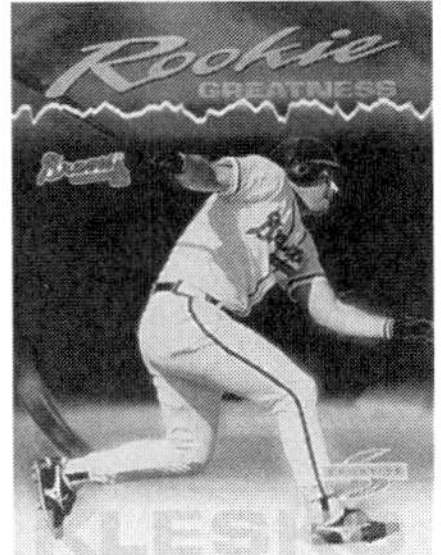

This single-card insert set is the toughest pull among the 1995 Score chase cards. Honoring slugging Braves star Ryan Klesko, the card is inserted at the rate of one per 720 retail packs. An even scarcer autographed version of the card in an edition of just over 6,000 was also created for insertion into hobby packs.

		MT
RG1	Ryan Klesko	2.00
SG1	Ryan Klesko (autographed)	10.00

1995 Score Score Rules

Series I jumbo packs were the only sources for "Score Rules" insert set of rookie and veteran stars. A color player photo at left has a team logo toward the bottom, beneath which is a gold-foil "tie tack" device with the league initials and position. At top-right is a baseball which appears to be dripping orange and green goop down the card. The player's last name is presented vertically with a sepia photo of the player within the letters. Backs repeat the green baseball and ooze motif, with three progressive color proof versions of the sepia front photo and a few sentences about the star. Cards are numbered with an "SR" prefix.

		MT
Complete Set (30):		35.00
Common Player:		.40
1	Ken Griffey, Jr.	3.50
2	Frank Thomas	2.50
3	Mike Piazza	3.00
4	Jeff Bagwell	2.00
5	Alex Rodriguez	3.25
6	Albert Belle	1.00
7	Matt Williams	.65
8	Roberto Alomar	1.00
9	Barry Bonds	2.50
10	Raul Mondesi	.60
11	Jose Canseco	1.50
12	Kirby Puckett	2.50
13	Fred McGriff	.40
14	Kenny Lofton	.40
15	Greg Maddux	2.50
16	Juan Gonzalez	2.00
17	Cliff Floyd	.40
18	Cal Ripken, Jr.	3.50
19	Will Clark	.75
20	Tim Salmon	.60
21	Paul O'Neill	.40
22	Jason Bere	.40
23	Tony Gwynn	2.50
24	Manny Ramirez	2.00
25	Don Mattingly	2.75
26	Dave Justice	.65
27	Javier Lopez	.40
28	Ryan Klesko	.40
29	Carlos Delgado	.65
30	Mike Mussina	1.50

1996 Score

Large, irregularly shaped action photos are featured on the fronts of the basic cards in the 1996 Score issue. Backs feature a portrait photo (in most cases) at left and a full slate of major and minor league stats at right, along with a few words about the player. Slightly different design details and a "ROOKIE" headline identify that subset within the regular issue. A wide variety of insert cards was produced, most of them exclusive to one type of packaging.

		MT
Complete Set (510):		10.00
Complete Series 1 (275):		6.00
Complete Series 2 (235):		4.00
Common Player:		.05
Wax Pack (10):		.50
Wax Box (36):		17.50
1	Will Clark	.15
2	Rich Becker	.05
3	Ryan Klesko	.05
4	Jim Edmonds	.10
5	Barry Larkin	.10
6	Jim Thome	.05
7	Raul Mondesi	.15
8	Don Mattingly	1.00
9	Jeff Conine	.05
10	Rickey Henderson	.35
11	Chad Curtis	.05
12	Darren Daulton	.05
13	Larry Walker	.20
14	Carlos Garcia	.05
15	Carlos Baerga	.05
16	Tony Gwynn	.60
17	Jon Nunally	.05
18	Deion Sanders	.10
19	Mark Grace	.20
20	Alex Rodriguez	1.50
21	Frank Thomas	.75
22	Brian Jordan	.05
23	J.T. Snow	.05
24	Shawn Green	.15
25	Tim Wakefield	.05
26	Curtis Goodwin	.05
27	John Smoltz	.10
28	Devon White	.05
29	Brian Hunter	.05
30	Rusty Greer	.05
31	Rafael Palmeiro	.20
32	Bernard Gilkey	.05
33	John Valentin	.05
34	Randy Johnson	.40
35	Garret Anderson	.10
36	Rikkert Faneyte	.05
37	Ray Durham	.05
38	Bip Roberts	.05
39	Jaime Navarro	.05
40	Mark Johnson	.05
41	Darren Lewis	.05
42	Tyler Green	.05
43	Bill Pulsipher	.05
44	Jason Giambi	.25
45	Kevin Ritz	.05
46	Jack McDowell	.05
47	Felipe Lira	.05
48	Rico Brogna	.05
49	Terry Pendleton	.05
50	Rondell White	.10
51	Andre Dawson	.15
52	Kirby Puckett	.65
53	Wally Joyner	.05
54	B.J. Surhoff	.05
55	Chan Ho Park	.15
56	Greg Vaughn	.05
57	Roberto Alomar	.35
58	Dave Justice	.20
59	Kevin Seitzer	.05
60	Cal Ripken Jr.	1.50
61	Ozzie Smith	.60
62	Mo Vaughn	.35
63	Ricky Bones	.05
64	Gary DiSarcina	.05
65	Matt Williams	.15
66	Wilson Alvarez	.05
67	Lenny Dykstra	.05
68	Brian McRae	.05
69	Todd Stottlemyre	.05
70	Bret Boone	.10
71	Sterling Hitchcock	.05
72	Albert Belle	.20
73	Todd Hundley	.05
74	Vinny Castilla	.05
75	Moises Alou	.10
76	Cecil Fielder	.05
77	Brad Radke	.05
78	Quilvio Veras	.05
79	Eddie Murray	.35
80	James Mouton	.05
81	Pat Listach	.05
82	Mark Gubicza	.05
83	Dave Winfield	.40
84	Fred McGriff	.05
85	Darryl Hamilton	.05
86	Jeffrey Hammonds	.05
87	Pedro Munoz	.05
88	Craig Biggio	.10
89	Cliff Floyd	.05
90	Tim Naehring	.05
91	Brett Butler	.05
92	Kevin Foster	.05
93	Patrick Kelly	.05
94	John Smiley	.05
95	Terry Steinbach	.05
96	Orel Hershiser	.05
97	Darrin Fletcher	.05
98	Walt Weiss	.05
99	John Wetteland	.05
100	Alan Trammell	.05
101	Steve Avery	.05
102	Tony Eusebio	.05
103	Sandy Alomar	.05
104	Joe Girardi	.05
105	Rick Aguilera	.05
106	Tony Tarasco	.05
107	Chris Hammond	.05
108	Mike McFarlane	.05
109	Doug Drabek	.05
110	Derek Bell	.05
111	Ed Sprague	.05
112	Todd Hollandsworth	.05
113	Otis Nixon	.05
114	Keith Lockhart	.05
115	Donovan Osborne	.05
116	Dave Magadan	.05
117	Edgar Martinez	.05
118	Chuck Carr	.05
119	J.R. Phillips	.05
120	Sean Bergman	.05
121	Andujar Cedeno	.05
122	Eric Young	.05
123	Al Martin	.05
124	Ken Hill	.05
125	Jim Eisenreich	.05
126	Benito Santiago	.05
127	Ariel Prieto	.05
128	Jim Bullinger	.05
129	Russ Davis	.05
130	Jim Abbott	.05
131	Jason Isringhausen	.05
132	Carlos Perez	.05
133	David Segui	.05
134	Troy O'Leary	.05
135	Pat Meares	.05
136	Chris Hoiles	.05
137	Ismael Valdes	.05
138	Jose Oliva	.05
139	Carlos Delgado	.30
140	Tom Goodwin	.05
141	Bob Tewksbury	.05
142	Chris Gomez	.05
143	Jose Oquendo	.05
144	Mark Lewis	.05
145	Salomon Torres	.05
146	Luis Gonzalez	.20
147	Mark Carreon	.05
148	Lance Johnson	.05
149	Melvin Nieves	.05
150	Lee Smith	.05
151	Jacob Brumfield	.05
152	Armando Benitez	.05
153	Curt Schilling	.15
154	Javier Lopez	.05
155	Frank Rodriguez	.05
156	Alex Gonzalez	.10
157	Todd Worrell	.05
158	Benji Gil	.05
159	Greg Gagne	.05
160	Tom Henke	.05
161	Randy Myers	.05
162	Joey Cora	.05
163	Scott Ruffcorn	.05
164	William VanLandingham	.05
165	Tony Phillips	.05
166	Eddie Williams	.05
167	Bobby Bonilla	.05
168	Denny Neagle	.05
169	Troy Percival	.05
170	Billy Ashley	.05
171	Andy Van Slyke	.05
172	Jose Offerman	.05
173	Mark Parent	.05
174	Edgardo Alfonzo	.05
175	Trevor Hoffman	.05
176	David Cone	.05
177	Dan Wilson	.05
178	Steve Ontiveros	.05
179	Dean Palmer	.05
180	Mike Kelly	.05
181	Jim Leyritz	.05
182	Ron Karkovice	.05
183	Kevin Brown	.10
184	*Jose Valentin*	.05
185	Jorge Fabregas	.05
186	Jose Mesa	.05
187	Brent Mayne	.05
188	Carl Everett	.10
189	Paul Sorrento	.05
190	Pete Shourek	.05
191	Scott Kamieniecki	.05
192	Roberto Hernandez	.05
193	Randy Johnson (Radar Rating)	.10
194	Greg Maddux (Radar Rating)	.30
195	Hideo Nomo (Radar Rating)	.25
196	David Cone (Radar Rating)	.05
197	Mike Mussina (Radar Rating)	.20
198	Andy Benes (Radar Rating)	.05
199	Kevin Appier (Radar Rating)	.05
200	John Smoltz (Radar Rating)	.05
201	John Wetteland (Radar Rating)	.05
202	Mark Wohlers (Radar Rating)	.05
203	Stan Belinda	.05
204	Brian Anderson	.05
205	Mike Devereaux	.05
206	Mark Wohlers	.05
207	Omar Vizquel	.05
208	Jose Rijo	.05
209	Willie Blair	.05
210	Jamie Moyer	.05
211	Craig Shipley	.05
212	Shane Reynolds	.05
213	Chad Fonville	.05
214	Jose Vizcaino	.05
215	Sid Fernandez	.05
216	Andy Ashby	.05
217	Frank Castillo	.05
218	Kevin Tapani	.05
219	Kent Mercker	.05
220	Karim Garcia	.05
221	Chris Snopek	.05
222	Tim Unroe	.05
223	Johnny Damon	.20
224	LaTroy Hawkins	.05
225	Mariano Rivera	.25
226	Jose Alberro	.05
227	Angel Martinez	.05
228	Jason Schmidt	.05
229	Tony Clark	.05
230	Kevin Jordan	.05
231	Mark Thompson	.05
232	Jim Dougherty	.05
333	Roger Cedeno	.05
234	Ugueth Urbina	.05
235	Ricky Otero	.05
236	Mark Smith	.05
237	Brian Barber	.05
238	Marc Kroon	.05
239	Joe Rosselli	.05
240	Derek Jeter	1.25
241	Michael Tucker	.05
242	*Joe Borowski*	.05
243	Joe Vitiello	.05
244	Orlando Palmeiro	.05
245	James Baldwin	.05
246	Alan Embree	.05
247	Shannon Penn	.05
248	Chris Stynes	.05
249	Oscar Munoz	.05
250	Jose Herrera	.05
251	Scott Sullivan	.05
252	Reggie Williams	.05
253	Mark Grudzielanek	.05
254	Kevin Jordan	.05
255	Terry Bradshaw	.05
256	*F.P. Santangelo*	.05
257	Doug Johns	.05
258	George Williams	.05
259	Larry Thomas	.05
260	Rudy Pemberton	.05
261	Jim Pittsley	.05
262	Les Norman	.05
263	Ruben Rivera	.05
264	*Cesar Devarez*	.05
265	Greg Zaun	.05
266	Eric Owens	.05
267	John Frascatore	.05
268	Shannon Stewart	.10
269	Checklist	.05
270	Checklist	.05
271	Checklist	.05
272	Checklist	.05
273	Checklist	.05
274	Checklist	.05
275	Checklist	.05
276	Greg Maddux	.65
277	Pedro Martinez	.35
278	Bobby Higginson	.05
279	Ray Lankford	.05
280	Shawon Dunston	.05
281	Gary Sheffield	.20
282	Ken Griffey Jr.	1.50
283	Paul Molitor	.35
284	Kevin Appier	.05
285	Chuck Knoblauch	.05
286	Alex Fernandez	.05
287	Steve Finley	.05
288	Jeff Blauser	.05
289	Charles Johnson	.05
290	John Franco	.05
291	Mark Langston	.05
292	Bret Saberhagen	.05
293	John Mabry	.05
294	Ramon Martinez	.05
295	Mike Blowers	.05
296	Paul O'Neill	.05
297	Dave Nilsson	.05
298	Dante Bichette	.05
299	Marty Cordova	.05
300	Jay Bell	.05
301	Mike Mussina	.40
302	Ivan Rodriguez	.35
303	Jose Canseco	.30
304	Jeff Bagwell	.50
305	Manny Ramirez	.50
306	Dennis Martinez	.05
307	Charlie Hayes	.05
308	Joe Carter	.05
309	Travis Fryman	.05
310	Mark McGwire	1.50
311	Reggie Sanders	.05
312	Julian Tavarez	.05
313	Jeff Montgomery	.05
314	Andy Benes	.05
315	John Jaha	.05
316	Jeff Kent	.05
317	Mike Piazza	1.25
318	Erik Hanson	.05
319	Kenny Rogers	.05
320	Hideo Nomo	.40
321	Gregg Jefferies	.05
322	Chipper Jones	1.25
323	Jay Buhner	.05
324	Dennis Eckersley	.05
325	Kenny Lofton	.05
326	Robin Ventura	.05
327	Tom Glavine	.10
328	Tim Salmon	.10
329	Andres Galarraga	.05
330	Hal Morris	.05
331	Brady Anderson	.05
332	Chili Davis	.05
333	Roger Clemens	.65
334	Marquis Grissom	.05
335	Jeff (Mike) Greenwell	.05
336	Sammy Sosa	.75
337	Ron Gant	.05
338	Ken Caminiti	.05
339	Danny Tartabull	.05
340	Barry Bonds	.65

341	Ben McDonald	.05
342	Ruben Sierra	.05
343	Bernie Williams	.30
344	Wil Cordero	.05
345	Wade Boggs	.40
346	Gary Gaetti	.05
347	Greg Colbrunn	.05
348	Juan Gonzalez	.50
349	Marc Newfield	.05
350	Charles Nagy	.05
351	Robby Thompson	.05
352	Roberto Petagine	.05
353	Darryl Strawberry	.05
354	Tino Martinez	.05
355	Eric Karros	.05
356	Cal Ripken Jr. (Star Struck)	.75
357	Cecil Fielder (Star Struck)	.05
358	Kirby Puckett (Star Struck)	.30
359	Jim Edmonds (Star Struck)	.05
360	Matt Williams (Star Struck)	.05
361	Alex Rodriguez (Star Struck)	.75
362	Barry Larkin (Star Struck)	.05
363	Rafael Palmeiro (Star Struck)	.10
364	David Cone (Star Struck)	.05
365	Roberto Alomar (Star Struck)	.20
366	Eddie Murray (Star Struck)	.20
367	Randy Johnson (Star Struck)	.20
368	Ryan Klesko (Star Struck)	.05
369	Raul Mondesi (Star Struck)	.05
370	Mo Vaughn (Star Struck)	.15
371	Will Clark (Star Struck)	.05
372	Carlos Baerga (Star Struck)	.05
373	Frank Thomas (Star Struck)	.40
374	Larry Walker (Star Struck)	.10
375	Garret Anderson (Star Struck)	.05
376	Edgar Martinez (Star Struck)	.05
377	Don Mattingly (Star Struck)	.50
378	Tony Gwynn (Star Struck)	.30
379	Albert Belle (Star Struck)	.10
380	Jason Isringhausen (Star Struck)	.05
381	Ruben Rivera (Star Struck)	.05
382	Johnny Damon (Star Struck)	.05
383	Karim Garcia (Star Struck)	.05
384	Derek Jeter (Star Struck)	.60
385	David Justice (Star Struck)	.05
386	Royce Clayton	.05
387	Mark Whiten	.05
388	Mickey Tettleton	.05
389	Steve Trachsel	.05
390	Danny Bautista	.05
391	Midre Cummings	.05
392	Scott Leius	.05
393	Manny Alexander	.05
394	Brent Gates	.05
395	Rey Sanchez	.05
396	Andy Pettitte	.15
397	Jeff Cirillo	.05
398	Kurt Abbott	.05
399	Lee Tinsley	.05
400	Paul Assenmacher	.05
401	Scott Erickson	.05
402	Todd Zeile	.05
403	Tom Pagnozzi	.05
404	Ozzie Guillen	.05
405	Jeff Frye	.05
406	Kirt Manwaring	.05
407	Chad Ogea	.05
408	Harold Baines	.05
409	Jason Bere	.05
410	Chuck Finley	.05
411	Jeff Fassero	.05
412	Joey Hamilton	.05
413	John Olerud	.05
414	Kevin Stocker	.05
415	Eric Anthony	.05
416	Aaron Sele	.05
417	Chris Bosio	.05
418	Michael Mimbs	.05
419	Orlando Miller	.05
420	Stan Javier	.05
421	Matt Mieske	.05
422	Jason Bates	.05
423	Orlando Merced	.05
424	John Flaherty	.05
425	Reggie Jefferson	.05
426	Scott Stahoviak	.05
427	John Burkett	.05
428	Rod Beck	.05
429	Bill Swift	.05
430	Scott Cooper	.05
431	Mel Rojas	.05
432	Todd Van Poppel	.05
433	Bobby Jones	.05
434	Mike Harkey	.05
435	Sean Berry	.05
436	Glenallen Hill	.05
437	Ryan Thompson	.05
438	Luis Alicea	.05
439	Esteban Loaiza	.05
440	Jeff Reboulet	.05
441	Vince Coleman	.05
442	Ellis Burks	.05
443	Allen Battle	.05
444	Jimmy Key	.05
445	Ricky Bottalico	.05
446	Delino DeShields	.05
447	Albie Lopez	.05
448	Mark Petkovsek	.05
449	Tim Raines	.05
450	Bryan Harvey	.05
451	Pat Hentgen	.05
452	Tim Laker	.05
453	Tom Gordon	.05
454	Phil Plantier	.05
455	Ernie Young	.05
456	Pete Harnisch	.05
457	Roberto Kelly	.05
458	Mark Portugal	.05
459	Mark Leiter	.05
460	Tony Pena	.05
461	Roger Pavlik	.05
462	Jeff King	.05
463	Bryan Rekar	.05
464	Al Leiter	.05
465	Phil Nevin	.05
466	Jose Lima	.05
467	Mike Stanley	.05
468	David McCarty	.05
469	Herb Perry	.05
470	Geronimo Berroa	.05
471	David Wells	.10
472	Vaughn Eshelman	.05
473	Greg Swindell	.05
474	Steve Sparks	.05
475	Luis Sojo	.05
476	Derrick May	.05
477	Joe Oliver	.05
478	Alex Arias	.05
479	Brad Ausmus	.05
480	Gabe White	.05
481	Pat Rapp	.05
482	Damon Buford	.05
483	Turk Wendell	.05
484	Jeff Brantley	.05
485	Curtis Leskanic	.05
486	Robb Nen	.05
487	Lou Whitaker	.05
488	Melido Perez	.05
489	Luis Polonia	.05
490	Scott Brosius	.05
491	Robert Perez	.05
492	*Mike Sweeney*	1.00
493	Mark Loretta	.05
494	Alex Ochoa	.05
495	*Matt Lawton*	.50
496	Shawn Estes	.05
497	John Wasdin	.05
498	Marc Kroon	.05
499	Chris Snopek	.05
500	Jeff Suppan	.05
501	Terrell Wade	.05
502	*Marvin Benard*	.10
503	Chris Widger	.05
504	Quinton McCracken	.05
505	Bob Wolcott	.05
506	C.J. Nitkowski	.05
507	Aaron Ledesma	.05
508	Scott Hatteberg	.05
509	Jimmy Haynes	.05
510	Howard Battle	.05

1996 Score Dugout Collection

The concept of a partial parallel set, including the stars and rookies but not the journeymen and bench warmers, was initiated with Score's "Dugout Collection," with fewer than half of the cards from the regular series chosen for inclusion. The white borders of the regular cards are replaced with copper-foil and background printing is also done on foil in this special version. On back is a special "Dugout Collection '96" logo. Advertised insertion rate of the copper-version cards is one per three packs.

		MT
Complete Set (220):		60.00
Complete Series 1 (1-110):		30.00
Complete Series 2 (1-110):		30.00
Common Player:		.20
	SERIES 1	
1	(Will Clark)	.40
2	(Rich Becker)	.20
3	(Ryan Klesko)	.20
4	(Jim Edmonds)	.25
5	(Barry Larkin)	.20
6	(Jim Thome)	.20
7	(Raul Mondesi)	.30
8	(Don Mattingly)	1.00
9	(Jeff Conine)	.20
10	(Rickey Henderson)	.45
11	(Chad Curtis)	.20
12	(Darren Daulton)	.20
13	(Larry Walker)	.30
14	(Carlos Baerga)	.20
15	(Tony Gwynn)	1.25
16	(Jon Nunnally)	.20
17	(Deion Sanders)	.25
18	(Mark Grace)	.30
19	(Alex Rodriguez)	2.50
20	(Frank Thomas)	1.50
21	(Brian Jordan)	.20
22	(J.T. Snow)	.20
23	(Shawn Green)	.30
24	(Tim Wakefield)	.20
25	(Curtis Goodwin)	.20
26	(John Smoltz)	.20
27	(Devon White)	.20
28	(Brian Hunter)	.20
29	(Rusty Greer)	.20
30	(Rafael Palmeiro)	.25
31	(Bernard Gilkey)	.20
32	(John Valentin)	.20
33	(Randy Johnson)	.35
34	(Garret Anderson)	.20
35	(Ray Durham)	.20
36	(Bip Roberts)	.20
37	(Tyler Green)	.20
38	(Bill Pulsipher)	.20
39	(Jason Giambi)	.35
40	(Jack McDowell)	.20
41	(Rico Brogna)	.20
42	(Terry Pendleton)	.20
43	(Rondell White)	.25
44	(Andre Dawson)	.25
45	(Kirby Puckett)	1.25
46	(Wally Joyner)	.20
47	(B.J. Surhoff)	.20
48	(Randy Velarde)	.20
49	(Greg Vaughn)	.20
50	(Roberto Alomar)	.40
51	(David Justice)	.30
52	(Cal Ripken Jr.)	3.00
53	(Ozzie Smith)	1.00
54	(Mo Vaughn)	.45
55	(Gary DiSarcina)	.20
56	(Matt Williams)	.30
57	(Lenny Dykstra)	.20
58	(Bret Boone)	.20
59	(Albert Belle)	.50
60	(Vinny Castilla)	.20
61	(Moises Alou)	.20
62	(Cecil Fielder)	.20
63	(Brad Radke)	.20
64	(Quilvio Veras)	.20
65	(Eddie Murray)	.40
66	(Dave Winfield)	.50
67	(Fred McGriff)	.20
68	(Craig Biggio)	.20
69	(Cliff Floyd)	.20
70	(Tim Naehring)	.20
71	(John Wetteland)	.20
72	(Alan Trammell)	.20
73	(Steve Avery)	.20
74	(Rick Aguilera)	.20
75	(Derek Bell)	.20
76	(Todd Hollandsworth)	.20
77	(Edgar Martinez)	.20
78	(Mark Lemke)	.20
79	(Ariel Prieto)	.20
80	(Russ Davis)	.20
81	(Jim Abbott)	.20
82	(Jason Isringhausen)	.20
83	(Carlos Perez)	.20
84	(David Segui)	.20
85	(Troy O'Leary)	.20
86	(Ismael Valdes)	.20
87	(Carlos Delgado)	.25
88	(Lee Smith)	.20
89	(Javy Lopez)	.20
90	(Frank Rodriguez)	.20
91	(Alex Gonzalez)	.20
92	(Benji Gil)	.20
93	(Greg Gagne)	.20
94	(Randy Myers)	.20
95	(Bobby Bonilla)	.20
96	(Billy Ashley)	.20
97	(Andy Van Slyke)	.20
98	(Edgardo Alfonzo)	.20
99	(David Cone)	.20
100	(Dean Palmer)	.20
101	(Jose Mesa)	.20
102	(Karim Garcia)	.30
103	(Johnny Damon)	.25
104	(LaTroy Hawkins)	.20
105	(Mark Smith)	.20
106	(Derek Jeter)	2.00
107	(Michael Tucker)	.20
108	(Joe Vitiello)	.20
109	(Ruben Rivera)	.20
110	(Greg Zaun)	.20
	SERIES 2	
1	Greg Maddux	1.00
2	Pedro Martinez	.35
3	Bobby Higginson	.20
4	Ray Lankford	.20
5	Shawon Dunston	.20
6	Gary Sheffield	.45
7	Ken Griffey Jr.	2.50
8	Paul Molitor	.75
9	Kevin Appier	.20
10	Chuck Knoblauch	.20
11	Alex Fernandez	.20
12	Steve Finley	.20
13	Jeff Blauser	.20
14	Charles Johnson	.20

15	John Franco	.20
16	Mark Langston	.20
17	Bret Saberhagen	.20
18	John Mabry	.20
19	Ramon Martinez	.20
20	Mike Blowers	.20
21	Paul O'Neill	.20
22	Dave Nilsson	.20
23	Dante Bichette	.20
24	Marty Cordova	.20
25	Jay Bell	.20
26	Mike Mussina	.40
27	Ivan Rodriguez	.35
28	Jose Canseco	.35
29	Jeff Bagwell	.60
30	Manny Ramirez	.60
31	Dennis Martinez	.20
32	Charlie Hayes	.20
33	Joe Carter	.20
34	Travis Fryman	.20
35	Mark McGwire	3.00
36	Reggie Sanders	.20
37	Julian Tavarez	.20
38	Jeff Montgomery	.20
39	Andy Benes	.20
40	John Jaha	.20
41	Jeff Kent	.20
42	Mike Piazza	2.00
43	Erik Hanson	.20
44	Kenny Rogers	.20
45	Hideo Nomo	.75
46	Gregg Jefferies	.20
47	Chipper Jones	2.00
48	Jay Buhner	.20
49	Dennis Eckersley	.20
50	Kenny Lofton	.20
51	Robin Ventura	.20
52	Tom Glavine	.20
53	Tim Salmon	.25
54	Andres Galarraga	.20
55	Hal Morris	.20
56	Brady Anderson	.20
57	Chili Davis	.20
58	Roger Clemens	.65
59	Marquis Grissom	.20
60	Mike Greenwell	.20
61	Sammy Sosa	1.50
62	Ron Gant	.20
63	Ken Caminiti	.20
64	Danny Tartabull	.20
65	Barry Bonds	1.50
66	Ben McDonald	.20
67	Ruben Sierra	.20
68	Bernie Williams	.35
69	Wil Cordero	.20
70	Wade Boggs	.50
71	Gary Gaetti	.20
72	Greg Colbrunn	.20
73	Juan Gonzalez	.60
74	Marc Newfield	.20
75	Charles Nagy	.20
76	Robby Thompson	.20
77	Roberto Petagine	.20
78	Darryl Strawberry	.20
79	Tino Martinez	.20
80	Eric Karros	.20
81	Cal Ripken Jr. (Star Struck)	1.50
82	Cecil Fielder (Star Struck)	.20
83	Kirby Puckett (Star Struck)	.75
84	Jim Edmonds (Star Struck)	.20
85	Matt Williams (Star Struck)	.20
86	Alex Rodriguez (Star Struck)	1.25
87	Barry Larkin (Star Struck)	.20
88	Rafael Palmeiro (Star Struck)	.20
89	David Cone (Star Struck)	.20
90	Roberto Alomar (Star Struck)	.25
91	Eddie Murray (Star Struck)	.25
92	Randy Johnson (Star Struck)	.25
93	Ryan Klesko (Star Struck)	.20
94	Raul Mondesi (Star Struck)	.20
95	Mo Vaughn (Star Struck)	.25
96	Will Clark (Star Struck)	.25
97	Carlos Baerga (Star Struck)	.20
98	Frank Thomas (Star Struck)	1.00
99	Larry Walker (Star Struck)	.25
100	Garret Anderson (Star Struck)	.20
101	Edgar Martinez (Star Struck)	.20
102	Don Mattingly (Star Struck)	.75
103	Tony Gwynn (Star Struck)	.60
104	Albert Belle (Star Struck)	.35
105	Jason Isringhausen (Star Struck)	.20
106	Ruben Rivera (Star Struck)	.20
107	Johnny Damon (Star Struck)	.20
108	Karim Garcia (Star Struck)	.20
109	Derek Jeter (Star Struck)	1.25
110	David Justice (Star Struck)	.25

1996 Score Dugout Collection Artist's Proofs

A parallel set within a parallel set, the Artist's Proof logo added to the copper-foil design of the Dugout Collection cards raises the odds of finding one to just once in 36 packs.

MT

(Artist's Proofs stars valued at 3X-5X of regular Dugout Collection versions)

	MT
Complete Set (220):	450.00
Common Player:	1.00
Artist's Proof Stars:	5X

(See 1996 Score Dugout Collection for checklist and base card values.)

1996 Score All-Stars

An exclusive insert found only in 20-card Series 2 jumbo packs at an average rate of one per nine packs, these inserts feature the game's top stars printed in a rainbow holographic-foil technology.

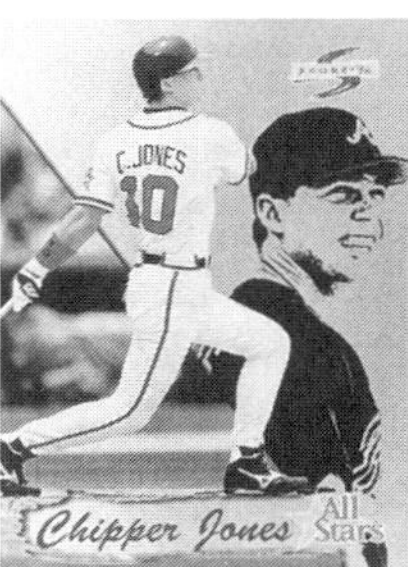

		MT
Complete Set (20):		22.50
Common Player:		.30
1	Frank Thomas	2.50
2	Albert Belle	1.00
3	Ken Griffey Jr.	3.50
4	Cal Ripken Jr.	3.50
5	Mo Vaughn	1.00
6	Matt Williams	.50
7	Barry Bonds	2.00
8	Dante Bichette	.30
9	Tony Gwynn	2.00
10	Greg Maddux	2.00
11	Randy Johnson	1.00
12	Hideo Nomo	1.00
13	Tim Salmon	.50
14	Jeff Bagwell	1.50
15	Edgar Martinez	.30
16	Reggie Sanders	.30
17	Larry Walker	.50
18	Chipper Jones	3.00
19	Manny Ramirez	1.50
20	Eddie Murray	.75

1996 Score Big Bats

Gold-foil printing highlights cards of 20 of the game's top hitters found in this retail-packaging exclusive insert set. Stated odds of picking a Big Bats card are one in 31 packs.

		MT
Complete Set (20):		25.00
Common Player:		.50
1	Cal Ripken Jr.	3.50
2	Ken Griffey Jr.	3.50
3	Frank Thomas	2.50
4	Jeff Bagwell	2.00
5	Mike Piazza	3.00
6	Barry Bonds	2.50
7	Matt Williams	.75
8	Raul Mondesi	.75
9	Tony Gwynn	2.50
10	Albert Belle	1.00
11	Manny Ramirez	2.00
12	Carlos Baerga	.50
13	Mo Vaughn	1.50
14	Derek Bell	.50
15	Larry Walker	.75
16	Kenny Lofton	.50
17	Edgar Martinez	.50
18	Reggie Sanders	.50
19	Eddie Murray	1.50
20	Chipper Jones	3.00

1996 Score Cal Ripken Tribute

The toughest pick among the 1996 Score inserts is this special card marking Cal Ripken's 2,131st consecutive game. The insertion rate is one per 300 packs hobby and retail, one per 150 jumbo packs.

		MT
2131	Cal Ripken Jr. (Tribute)	5.00

1996 Score Diamond Aces

Thirty of the top veterans and young stars are included in this jumbo-only insert set, seeded at a rate of one per eight packs.

		MT
Complete Set (30):		45.00
Common Player:		.75
1	Hideo Nomo	1.50
2	Brian Hunter	.75
3	Ray Durham	.75
4	Frank Thomas	3.50
5	Cal Ripken Jr.	5.00
6	Barry Bonds	3.00
7	Greg Maddux	3.00
8	Chipper Jones	4.00
9	Raul Mondesi	1.00
10	Mike Piazza	4.00
11	Derek Jeter	4.00
12	Bill Pulsipher	.75
13	Larry Walker	1.00
14	Ken Griffey Jr.	4.50
15	Alex Rodriguez	4.50
16	Manny Ramirez	2.00
17	Mo Vaughn	1.50
18	Reggie Sanders	.75
19	Derek Bell	.75
20	Jim Edmonds	.75
21	Albert Belle	1.00
22	Eddie Murray	1.50
23	Tony Gwynn	3.00
24	Jeff Bagwell	2.00

25	Carlos Baerga	.75
26	Matt Williams	1.00
27	Garret Anderson	.75
28	Todd Hollandsworth	.75
29	Johnny Damon	1.00
30	Tim Salmon	1.00

1996 Score Dream Team

The hottest player at each position is honored in the Dream Team insert set. Once again featured on holographic foil printing technology, the cards are found in all types of Score packaging at a rate of once per 72 packs.

		MT
Complete Set (9):		18.50
Common Player:		.75
1	Cal Ripken Jr.	5.00
2	Frank Thomas	3.00
3	Carlos Baerga	.75
4	Matt Williams	1.00
5	Mike Piazza	3.50
6	Barry Bonds	3.00
7	Ken Griffey Jr.	4.00
8	Manny Ramirez	1.50
9	Greg Maddux	2.50

1996 Score Future Franchise

Future Franchise is the most difficult insert to pull from packs of Series 2, at the rate of once per 72 packs, on average. Sixteen young stars are showcased on holographic gold-foil printing in the set.

		MT
Complete Set (16):		27.50
Common Player:		.75
1	Jason Isringhausen	.75
2	Chipper Jones	6.00
3	Derek Jeter	6.00
4	Alex Rodriguez	8.00
5	Alex Ochoa	.75
6	Manny Ramirez	3.50
7	Johnny Damon	1.00
8	Ruben Rivera	.75
9	Karim Garcia	1.00
10	Garret Anderson	.75
11	Marty Cordova	.75
12	Bill Pulsipher	.75
13	Hideo Nomo	1.50
14	Marc Newfield	.75
15	Charles Johnson	.75
16	Raul Mondesi	1.00

1996 Score Gold Stars

Appearing once in every 15 packs of Series 2, Gold Stars are labeled with a stamp in the upper-left corner. The set contains 30 top current stars printed on gold-foil and seeded at the average rate of one per 15 packs.

		MT
Complete Set (30):		35.00
Common Player:		.45
1	Ken Griffey Jr.	4.00
2	Frank Thomas	3.00
3	Reggie Sanders	.45
4	Tim Salmon	.60
5	Mike Piazza	3.50
6	Tony Gwynn	2.50
7	Gary Sheffield	.60
8	Matt Williams	.60
9	Bernie Williams	.60
10	Jason Isringhausen	.45
11	Albert Belle	1.00
12	Chipper Jones	3.50
13	Edgar Martinez	.45
14	Barry Larkin	.50
15	Barry Bonds	2.50
16	Jeff Bagwell	2.00
17	Greg Maddux	2.50
18	Mo Vaughn	1.25
19	Ryan Klesko	.45
20	Sammy Sosa	3.00
21	Darren Daulton	.45
22	Ivan Rodriguez	1.25
23	Dante Bichette	.45
24	Hideo Nomo	1.00
25	Cal Ripken Jr.	4.50
26	Rafael Palmeiro	.60
27	Larry Walker	.60
28	Carlos Baerga	.45
29	Randy Johnson	1.50
30	Manny Ramirez	2.00

1996 Score Numbers Game

Some of the 1995 season's most impressive statistical accomplishments are featured in this chase set. Cards are enhanced with gold foil and found in all types of Score packs at an average rate of one per 15 packs.

		MT
Complete Set (30):		24.00
Common Player:		.25
1	Cal Ripken Jr.	2.50
2	Frank Thomas	1.75
3	Ken Griffey Jr.	2.25
4	Mike Piazza	2.00
5	Barry Bonds	1.50
6	Greg Maddux	1.50
7	Jeff Bagwell	1.00
8	Derek Bell	.25
9	Tony Gwynn	1.50
10	Hideo Nomo	.75
11	Raul Mondesi	.35
12	Manny Ramirez	1.00
13	Albert Belle	.50
14	Matt Williams	.35
15	Jim Edmonds	.35
16	Edgar Martinez	.25
17	Mo Vaughn	.60
18	Reggie Sanders	.25
19	Chipper Jones	2.00
20	Larry Walker	.35
21	Juan Gonzalez	1.00
22	Kenny Lofton	.25
23	Don Mattingly	1.50
24	Ivan Rodriguez	.75
25	Randy Johnson	.75
26	Derek Jeter	2.00
27	J.T. Snow	.25
28	Will Clark	.35
29	Rafael Palmeiro	.50
30	Alex Rodriguez	2.25

1996 Score Power Pace

Power Pace is exclusive to retail packs in Series 2, where they are found on average every 31 packs. Eighteen top power hitters are featured in this issue in a gold-foil design.

		MT
Complete Set (18):		24.00
Common Player:		.50
1	Mark McGwire	5.00
2	Albert Belle	1.00
3	Jay Buhner	.50
4	Frank Thomas	3.00
5	Matt Williams	.75
6	Gary Sheffield	.75
7	Mike Piazza	4.00
8	Larry Walker	.75
9	Mo Vaughn	1.00
10	Rafael Palmeiro	.75
11	Dante Bichette	.50
12	Ken Griffey Jr.	4.50
13	Barry Bonds	3.00
14	Manny Ramirez	1.50
15	Sammy Sosa	3.00
16	Tim Salmon	.65
17	Dave Justice	.65
18	Eric Karros	.50

1996 Score Reflexions

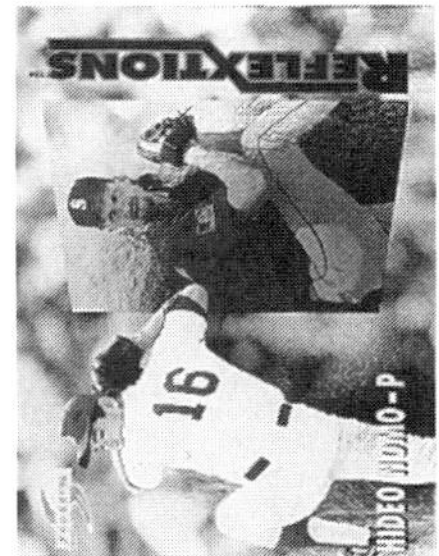

Appearing only in hobby packs this insert set pairs 20 veteran stars with 20 up-and-coming players in a foil-printed format. Odds of finding a Reflexions insert are stated as one per 31 packs.

		MT
Complete Set (20):		30.00
Common Player:		.35
1	Cal Ripken Jr., Chipper Jones	5.00
2	Ken Griffey Jr., Alex Rodriguez	4.00
3	Frank Thomas, Mo Vaughn	2.50
4	Kenny Lofton, Brian Hunter	.35
5	Don Mattingly, J.T. Snow	2.50
6	Manny Ramirez, Raul Mondesi	1.50
7	Tony Gwynn, Garret Anderson	1.75
8	Roberto Alomar, Carlos Baerga	.75
9	Andre Dawson, Larry Walker	.50
10	Barry Larkin, Derek Jeter	3.50
11	Barry Bonds, Reggie Sanders	2.00
12	Mike Piazza, Albert Belle	3.50
13	Wade Boggs, Edgar Martinez	.50
14	David Cone, John Smoltz	.35
15	Will Clark, Jeff Bagwell	1.50
16	Mark McGwire, Cecil Fielder	6.00
17	Greg Maddux, Mike Mussina	3.00
18	Randy Johnson, Hideo Nomo	2.00
19	Jim Thome, Dean Palmer	.35
20	Chuck Knoblauch, Craig Biggio	.35

1996 Score Titantic Taters

One of the more creative names in the 1996 insert lineup, Titanic Taters are found one in every 31 packs of Series 2 hobby. Gold-foil fronts feature 18 of the game's heaviest hitters.

		MT
Complete Set (18):		24.00
Common Player:		.50
1	Albert Belle	1.00
2	Frank Thomas	3.00
3	Mo Vaughn	1.50
4	Ken Griffey Jr.	4.00
5	Matt Williams	.75
6	Mark McGwire	4.00
7	Dante Bichette	.50
8	Tim Salmon	.75
9	Jeff Bagwell	2.00
10	Rafael Palmeiro	.75
11	Mike Piazza	3.50
12	Cecil Fielder	.50
13	Larry Walker	.75
14	Sammy Sosa	3.00
15	Manny Ramirez	2.00
16	Gary Sheffield	.75
17	Barry Bonds	3.00
18	Jay Buhner	.50

1997 Score

A total of 551 cards make up the base set, with 330 cards sold in Series I and 221 making up Series II. The basic card design features a color action photo surrounded by a white border. The player's name is above the photo, with the team name underneath. Backs feature text and statistics against a white background with the image of the team logo ghosted into the background. Two parallel insert sets - Artist's Proof and Showcase Series - were part of each series. Other inserts in Series I were Pitcher Perfect, The Franchise, The Glowing Franchise, Titanic Taters (retail exclusive), Stellar Season (magazine packs only), and The Highlight Zone (hobby exclusive). Series II inserts were Blastmasters, Heart of the Order and Stand and Deliver. Cards were sold in 10-card packs for 99 cents each.

		MT
Complete Set (551):		25.00
Factory Tin-Box Set (551):		27.50
Complete Series 1 Set (330):		15.00
Complete Series 2 Set (221):		10.00
Common Player:		.05
Wax Pack (10):		.50
Wax Box (36):		15.00
1	Jeff Bagwell	.50
2	Mickey Tettleton	.05
3	Johnny Damon	.15
4	Jeff Conine	.05
5	Bernie Williams	.30
6	Will Clark	.15
7	Ryan Klesko	.05
8	Cecil Fielder	.05
9	Paul Wilson	.05
10	Gregg Jefferies	.05
11	Chili Davis	.05
12	Albert Belle	.25
13	Ken Hill	.05
14	Cliff Floyd	.05
15	Jaime Navarro	.05
16	Ismael Valdes	.05
17	Jeff King	.05
18	Chris Bosio	.05
19	Reggie Sanders	.05
20	Darren Daulton	.05
21	Ken Caminiti	.05
22	Mike Piazza	1.25
23	Chad Mottola	.05
24	Darin Erstad	.40
25	Dante Bichette	.05
26	Frank Thomas	1.00
27	Ben McDonald	.05
28	Raul Casanova	.05
29	Kevin Ritz	.05
30	Garret Anderson	.05
31	Jason Kendall	.05
32	Billy Wagner	.05
33	David Justice	.25
34	Marty Cordova	.05
35	Derek Jeter	1.25
36	Trevor Hoffman	.05
37	Geronimo Berroa	.05
38	Walt Weiss	.05
39	Kirt Manwaring	.05
40	Alex Gonzalez	.10
41	Sean Berry	.05
42	Kevin Appier	.05
43	Rusty Greer	.05
44	Pete Incaviglia	.05
45	Rafael Palmeiro	.20
46	Eddie Murray	.35
47	Moises Alou	.10
48	Mark Lewis	.05
49	Hal Morris	.05
50	Edgar Renteria	.05
51	Rickey Henderson	.40
52	Pat Listach	.05
53	John Wasdin	.05
54	James Baldwin	.05
55	Brian Jordan	.05
56	Edgar Martinez	.05
57	Wil Cordero	.05
58	Danny Tartabull	.05
59	Keith Lockhart	.05
60	Rico Brogna	.05
61	Ricky Bottalico	.05
62	Terry Pendleton	.05
63	Bret Boone	.10
64	Charlie Hayes	.05
65	Marc Newfield	.05
66	Sterling Hitchcock	.05
67	Roberto Alomar	.40
68	John Jaha	.05
69	Greg Colbrunn	.05
70	Sal Fasano	.05
71	Brooks Kieschnick	.05
72	Pedro Martinez	.50
73	Kevin Elster	.05
74	Ellis Burks	.05
75	Chuck Finley	.05
76	John Olerud	.05
77	Jay Bell	.05
78	Allen Watson	.05
79	Darryl Strawberry	.05
80	Orlando Miller	.05
81	Jose Herrera	.05
82	Andy Pettitte	.15
83	Juan Guzman	.05
84	Alan Benes	.05
85	Jack McDowell	.05
86	Ugueth Urbina	.05
87	Rocky Coppinger	.05
88	Jeff Cirillo	.05
89	Tom Glavine	.10
90	Robby Thompson	.05
91	Barry Bonds	1.00
92	Carlos Delgado	.20
93	Mo Vaughn	.35
94	Ryne Sandberg	.65
95	Alex Rodriguez	1.50
96	Brady Anderson	.05
97	Scott Brosius	.05
98	Dennis Eckersley	.05
99	Brian McRae	.05
100	Rey Ordonez	.05
101	John Valentin	.05
102	Brett Butler	.05
103	Eric Karros	.05
104	Harold Baines	.05
105	Javier Lopez	.05
106	Alan Trammell	.05
107	Jim Thome	.05
108	Frank Rodriguez	.05
109	Bernard Gilkey	.05
110	Reggie Jefferson	.05
111	Scott Stahoviak	.05
112	Steve Gibralter	.05
113	Todd Hollandsworth	.05
114	Ruben Rivera	.05
115	Dennis Martinez	.05
116	Mariano Rivera	.25
117	John Smoltz	.10
118	John Mabry	.05
119	Tom Gordon	.05
120	Alex Ochoa	.05
121	Jamey Wright	.05
122	Dave Nilsson	.05
123	Bobby Bonilla	.05
124	Al Leiter	.05
125	Rick Aguilera	.05
126	Jeff Brantley	.05
127	Kevin Brown	.10
128	George Arias	.05
129	Darren Oliver	.05
130	Bill Pulsipher	.05
131	Roberto Hernandez	.05
132	Delino DeShields	.05
133	Mark Grudzielanek	.05
134	John Wetteland	.05
135	Carlos Baerga	.05
136	Paul Sorrento	.05
137	Leo Gomez	.05
138	Andy Ashby	.05
139	Julio Franco	.05
140	Brian Hunter	.05
141	Jermaine Dye	.05
142	Tony Clark	.05
143	Ruben Sierra	.05
144	Donovan Osborne	.05
145	Mark McLemore	.05
146	Terry Steinbach	.05
147	Bob Wells	.05
148	Chan Ho Park	.15
149	Tim Salmon	.15
150	Paul O'Neill	.05
151	Cal Ripken Jr.	2.00
152	Wally Joyner	.05
153	Omar Vizquel	.05
154	Mike Mussina	.50
155	Andres Galarraga	.05
156	Ken Griffey Jr.	1.50
157	Kenny Lofton	.05
158	Ray Durham	.05
159	Hideo Nomo	.40
160	Ozzie Guillen	.05
161	Roger Pavlik	.05
162	Manny Ramirez	.50
163	Mark Lemke	.05
164	Mike Stanley	.05
165	Chuck Knoblauch	.05
166	Kimera Bartee	.05
167	Wade Boggs	.45
168	Jay Buhner	.05
169	Eric Young	.05
170	Jose Canseco	.35
171	Dwight Gooden	.05
172	Fred McGriff	.05
173	Sandy Alomar Jr.	.05
174	Andy Benes	.05
175	Dean Palmer	.05
176	Larry Walker	.25
177	Charles Nagy	.05
178	David Cone	.05
179	Mark Grace	.20
180	Robin Ventura	.05
181	Roger Clemens	.75
182	Bobby Witt	.05
183	Vinny Castilla	.05
184	Gary Sheffield	.20
185	Dan Wilson	.05
186	Roger Cedeno	.05
187	Mark McGwire	2.00
188	Darren Bragg	.05
189	Quinton McCracken	.05
190	Randy Myers	.05
191	Jeromy Burnitz	.05
192	Randy Johnson	.50
193	Chipper Jones	1.25
194	Greg Vaughn	.05
195	Travis Fryman	.05
196	Tim Naehring	.05
197	B.J. Surhoff	.05
198	Juan Gonzalez	.50
199	Terrell Wade	.05
200	Jeff Frye	.05
201	Joey Cora	.05
202	Raul Mondesi	.15
203	Ivan Rodriguez	.40
204	Armando Reynoso	.05
205	Jeffrey Hammonds	.05
206	Darren Dreifort	.05
207	Kevin Seitzer	.05
208	Tino Martinez	.05
209	Jim Bruske	.05
210	Jeff Suppan	.05
211	Mark Carreon	.05
212	Wilson Alvarez	.05
213	John Burkett	.05
214	Tony Phillips	.05
215	Greg Maddux	1.00
216	Mark Whiten	.05
217	Curtis Pride	.05
218	Lyle Mouton	.05
219	Todd Hundley	.05
220	Greg Gagne	.05
221	Rich Amaral	.05
222	Tom Goodwin	.05
223	Chris Hoiles	.05
224	Jayhawk Owens	.05
225	Kenny Rogers	.05
226	Mike Greenwell	.05
227	Mark Wohlers	.05
228	Henry Rodriguez	.05
229	Robert Perez	.05
230	Jeff Kent	.05
231	Darryl Hamilton	.05
232	Alex Fernandez	.05
233	Ron Karkovice	.05
234	Jimmy Haynes	.05
235	Craig Biggio	.10
236	Ray Lankford	.05
237	Lance Johnson	.05
238	Matt Williams	.15
239	Chad Curtis	.05
240	Mark Thompson	.05
241	Jason Giambi	.25
242	Barry Larkin	.10
243	Paul Molitor	.40
244	Sammy Sosa	1.00
245	Kevin Tapani	.05
246	Marquis Grissom	.05
247	Joe Carter	.05
248	Ramon Martinez	.05
249	Tony Gwynn	1.00
250	Andy Fox	.05
251	Troy O'Leary	.05
252	Warren Newson	.05
253	Troy Percival	.05
254	Jamie Moyer	.05
255	Danny Graves	.05
256	David Wells	.10
257	Todd Zeile	.05
258	Raul Ibanez	.05
259	Tyler Houston	.05
260	LaTroy Hawkins	.05
261	Joey Hamilton	.05
262	Mike Sweeney	.05
263	Brant Brown	.05
264	Pat Hentgen	.05
265	Mark Johnson	.05
266	Robb Nen	.05
267	Justin Thompson	.05

268 Ron Gant .05
269 Jeff D'Amico .05
270 Shawn Estes .05
271 Derek Bell .05
272 Fernando Valenzuela .05
273 Luis Castillo .05
274 Ray Montgomery .05
275 Ed Sprague .05
276 F.P. Santangelo .05
277 Todd Greene .05
278 Butch Huskey .05
279 Steve Finley .05
280 Eric Davis .05
281 Shawn Green .15
282 Al Martin .05
283 Michael Tucker .05
284 Shane Reynolds .05
285 Matt Mieske .05
286 Jose Rosado .05
287 Mark Langston .05
288 Ralph Milliard .05
289 Mike Lansing .05
290 Scott Servais .05
291 Royce Clayton .05
292 Mike Grace .05
293 James Mouton .05
294 Charles Johnson .05
295 Gary Gaetti .05
296 Kevin Mitchell .05
297 Carlos Garcia .05
298 Desi Relaford .05
299 Jason Thompson .05
300 Osvaldo Fernandez .05
301 Fernando Vina .05
302 Jose Offerman .05
303 Yamil Benitez .05
304 J.T. Snow .05
305 Rafael Bournigal .05
306 Jason Isringhausen .05
307 Bob Higginson .05
308 *Nerio Rodriguez* .05
309 *Brian Giles* 1.50
310 Andruw Jones .50
311 Billy McMillon .05
312 Arquimedez Pozo .05
313 Jermaine Allensworth .05
314 Luis Andujar .05
315 Angel Echevarria .05
316 Karim Garcia .05
317 Trey Beamon .05
318 Makoto Suzuki .05
319 Robin Jennings .05
320 Dmitri Young .05
321 *Damon Mashore* .05
322 Wendell Magee .05
323 *Dax Jones* .05
324 Todd Walker .05
325 Marvin Benard .05
326 *Brian Raabe* .05
327 Marcus Jensen .05
328 Checklist .05
329 Checklist .05
330 Checklist .05
331 Norm Charlton .05
332 Bruce Ruffin .05
333 John Wetteland .05
334 Marquis Grissom .05
335 Sterling Hitchcock .05
336 John Olerud .05
337 David Wells .10
338 Chili Davis .05
339 Mark Lewis .05
340 Kenny Lofton .05
341 Alex Fernandez .05
342 Ruben Sierra .05
343 Delino DeShields .05
344 John Wasdin .05
345 Dennis Martinez .05
346 Kevin Elster .05
347 Bobby Bonilla .05
348 Jaime Navarro .05
349 Chad Curtis .05
350 Terry Steinbach .05
351 Ariel Prieto .05
352 Jeff Kent .05
353 Carlos Garcia .05
354 Mark Whiten .05
355 Todd Zelle .05
356 Eric Davis .05
357 Greg Colbrunn .05
358 Moises Alou .10
359 Allen Watson .05
360 Jose Canseco .35
361 Matt Williams .15
362 Jeff King .05
363 Darryl Hamilton .05
364 Mark Clark .05
365 J.T. Snow .05
366 Kevin Mitchell .05
367 Orlando Miller .05
368 Rico Brogna .05
369 Mike James .05
370 Brad Ausmus .05
371 Darryl Kile .05
372 Edgardo Alfonzo .05
373 Julian Tavarez .05
374 Darren Lewis .05
375 Steve Karsay .05
376 Lee Stevens .05
377 Albie Lopez .05
378 Orel Hershiser .05
379 Lee Smith .05
380 Rick Helling .05
381 Carlos Perez .05
382 Tony Tarasco .05
383 Melvin Nieves .05
384 Benji Gil .05
385 Devon White .05
386 Armando Benitez .05
387 Bill Swift .05
388 John Smiley .05
389 Midre Cummings .05
390 Tim Belcher .05
391 Tim Raines .05
392 Todd Worrell .05
393 Quilvio Veras .05
394 Matt Lawton .05
395 Aaron Sele .05
396 Bip Roberts .05
397 Denny Neagle .05
398 Tyler Green .05
399 Hipolito Pichardo .05
400 Scott Erickson .05
401 Bobby Jones .05
402 Jim Edmonds .10
403 Chad Ogea .05
404 Cal Eldred .05
405 Pat Listach .05
406 Todd Stottlemyre .05
407 Phil Nevin .05
408 Otis Nixon .05
409 Billy Ashley .05
410 Jimmy Key .05
411 Mike Timlin .05
412 Joe Vitiello .05
413 Rondell White .10
414 Jeff Fassero .05
415 Rex Hudler .05
416 Curt Schilling .15
417 Rich Becker .05
418 William VanLandingham .05
419 Chris Snopek .05
420 David Segui .05
421 Eddie Murray .35
422 Shane Andrews .05
423 Gary DiSarcina .05
424 Brian Hunter .05
425 Willie Greene .05
426 Felipe Crespo .05
427 Jason Bates .05
428 Albert Belle .25
429 Rey Sanchez .05
430 Roger Clemens .75
431 Deion Sanders .10
432 Ernie Young .05
433 Jay Bell .05
434 Jeff Blauser .05
435 Lenny Dykstra .05
436 Chuck Carr .05
437 Russ Davis .05
438 Carl Everett .10
439 Damion Easley .05
440 Pat Kelly .05
441 Pat Rapp .05
442 David Justice .25
443 Graeme Lloyd .05
444 Damon Buford .05
445 Jose Valentin .05
446 Jason Schmidt .05
447 Dave Martinez .05
448 Danny Tartabull .05
449 Jose Vizcaino .05
450 Steve Avery .05
451 Mike Devereaux .05
452 Jim Eisenreich .05
453 Mark Leiter .05
454 Roberto Kelly .05
455 Benito Santiago .05
456 Steve Trachsel .05
457 Gerald Williams .05
458 Pete Schourek .05
459 Esteban Loaiza .05
460 Mel Rojas .05
461 Tim Wakefield .05
462 Tony Fernandez .05
463 Doug Drabek .05
464 Joe Girardi .05
465 Mike Bordick .05
466 Jim Leyritz .05
467 Erik Hanson .05
468 Michael Tucker .05
469 *Tony Womack* .25
470 Doug Glanville .05
471 Rudy Pemberton .05
472 Keith Lockhart .05
473 Nomar Garciaparra 1.00
474 Scott Rolen .40
475 Jason Dickson .05
476 Glendon Rusch .05
477 Todd Walker .05
478 Dmitri Young .05
479 *Rod Myers* .05
480 Wilton Guerrero .05
481 Jorge Posada .05
482 Brant Brown .05
483 *Bubba Trammell* .25
484 Jose Guillen .05
485 Scott Spiezio .05
486 Bob Abreu .10
487 Chris Holt .05
488 *Deivi Cruz* .25
489 Vladimir Guerrero .50
490 Julio Santana .05
491 Ray Montgomery .05
492 Kevin Orie .05
493 Todd Hundley (Goin' Yard) .05
494 Tim Salmon (Goin' Yard) .10
495 Albert Belle (Goin' Yard) .20
496 Manny Ramirez (Goin' Yard) .25
497 Rafael Palmeiro (Goin' Yard) .10
498 Juan Gonzalez (Goin' Yard) .25
499 Ken Griffey Jr. (Goin' Yard) .75
500 Andruw Jones (Goin' Yard) .25
501 Mike Piazza (Goin' Yard) .60
502 Jeff Bagwell (Goin' Yard) .25
503 Bernie Williams (Goin' Yard) .15
504 Barry Bonds (Goin' Yard) .50
505 Ken Caminiti (Goin' Yard) .05
506 Darin Erstad (Goin' Yard) .20
507 Alex Rodriguez (Goin' Yard) .65
508 Frank Thomas (Goin' Yard) .50
509 Chipper Jones (Goin' Yard) .60
510 Mo Vaughn (Goin' Yard) .20
511 Mark McGwire (Goin' Yard) 1.00
512 Fred McGriff (Goin' Yard) .05
513 Jay Buhner (Goin' Yard) .05
514 Jim Thome (Goin' Yard) .05
515 Gary Sheffield (Goin' Yard) .10
516 Dean Palmer (Goin' Yard) .05
517 Henry Rodriguez (Goin' Yard) .05
518 Andy Pettitte (Rock & Fire) .10
519 Mike Mussina (Rock & Fire) .20
520 Greg Maddux (Rock & Fire) .50
521 John Smoltz (Rock & Fire) .05
522 Hideo Nomo (Rock & Fire) .25
523 Troy Percival (Rock & Fire) .05
524 John Wetteland (Rock & Fire) .05
525 Roger Clemens (Rock & Fire) .40
526 Charles Nagy (Rock & Fire) .05
527 Mariano Rivera (Rock & Fire) .10
528 Tom Glavine (Rock & Fire) .05
529 Randy Johnson (Rock & Fire) .20
530 Jason Isringhausen (Rock & Fire) .05
531 Alex Fernandez (Rock & Fire) .05
532 Kevin Brown (Rock & Fire) .05
533 Chuck Knoblauch (True Grit) .05
534 Rusty Greer (True Grit) .05
535 Tony Gwynn (True Grit) .50
536 Ryan Klesko (True Grit) .05
537 Ryne Sandberg (True Grit) .40
538 Barry Larkin (True Grit) .05
539 Will Clark (True Grit) .10
540 Kenny Lofton (True Grit) .05
541 Paul Molitor (True Grit) .20
542 Roberto Alomar (True Grit) .20
543 Rey Ordonez (True Grit) .05
544 Jason Giambi (True Grit) .15
545 Derek Jeter (True Grit) .60
546 Cal Ripken Jr. (True Grit) .75
547 Ivan Rodriguez (True Grit) .20
548 Checklist (Ken Griffey Jr.) .50
549 Checklist (Frank Thomas) .35
550 Checklist (Mike Piazza) .50
551a *Hideki Irabu* (SP) (English on back; factory sets/retail packs) .50
551b *Hideki Irabu* (SP) (Japanese back; Hobby Reserve packs) .50

1997 Score Premium Stock

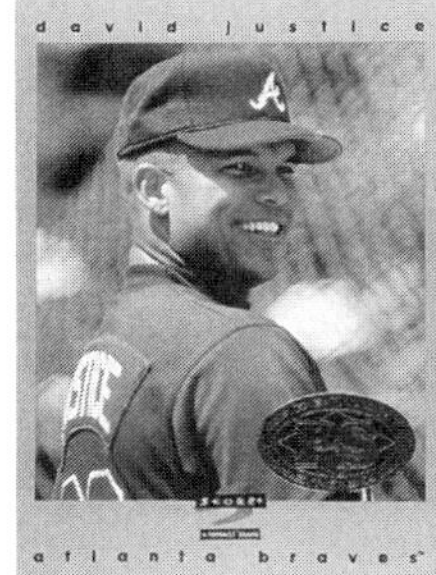

This is an upscale version of Score's regular Series 1 1997 issue, designated for hobby sales only. The cards are basically the same as the regular issue, except for the use of gray borders on front and an embossed gold-foil "Premium Stock" logo.

	MT
Complete Set (330):	25.00
Common Player:	.10
Premium Stock Stars:	3X

(See 1997 Score #1-330 for checklist and base card values.)

1997 Score Showcase

A silver metallic-foil background distinguishes the cards in this parallel set, inserted at a rate of about one per seven packs of both hobby and retail.

	MT
Complete Set (551):	250.00
Common Player:	.50
Showcase Stars:	4X

(See 1997 Score for checklist and base card values.)

1997 Score Showcase Artist's Proofs

This is a parallel of the Showcase parallel set covering all 551 cards of the base '97 Score set. The Artist's Proofs cards carry over the silver foil background of the Showcase cards on front with a rainbow-wave effect, and are marked with a round red "ARTIST'S PROOF" logo.

	MT
Complete Set (551):	600.00
Common Player:	1.50
Showcase AP Stars:	15X

(See 1997 Score for checklist and base card values.)

1997 Score Reserve Collection

This was a hobby-only parallel version of Score Series 2, Cards are similar to regular Series 2 Score except for the use of a textured ray-like silver-foil background on front and a Reserve Collection underprint on back. Cards are numbered with an "HR" prefix. Average insertion rate was one per 11 packs.

	MT
Complete Set (221):	450.00
Common Player:	2.00
Reserve Collection Stars:	10X

(See 1997 Score #331-551 for checklist and base card values.)

1997 Score Hobby Reserve

This is a hobby-only parallel version of Score Series 2, similar in concept to the Series 1 Premium Stock. Cards are identical to the regular Series 2 cards except for the addition of a gold Hobby Reserve foil seal on front.

	MT
Complete Set (221):	45.00
Common Player:	.10
Hobby Reserve Stars:	3X

(See 1997 Score #331-551 for checklist and base card values.)

1997 Score Blast Masters

This 18-card set was inserted into every 35 Series II retail packs and every 23 hobby packs. The set displays the top power hitters in the game over a prismatic gold foil background. The word "Blast" is printed across the top, while "Master" is printed across the bottom, both in red. Backs are predominantly black with a color player photo at center.

		MT
Complete Set (18):		35.00
Common Player:		.50
1	Mo Vaughn	1.50
2	Mark McGwire	6.00
3	Juan Gonzalez	2.50
4	Albert Belle	1.50
5	Barry Bonds	3.00
6	Ken Griffey Jr.	5.00
7	Andruw Jones	2.50
8	Chipper Jones	4.00
9	Mike Piazza	4.00
10	Jeff Bagwell	2.50
11	Dante Bichette	.50
12	Alex Rodriguez	5.00
13	Gary Sheffield	.75
14	Ken Caminiti	.50
15	Sammy Sosa	3.50
16	Vladimir Guerrero	2.50
17	Brian Jordan	.50
18	Tim Salmon	.75

1997 Score Heart of the Order

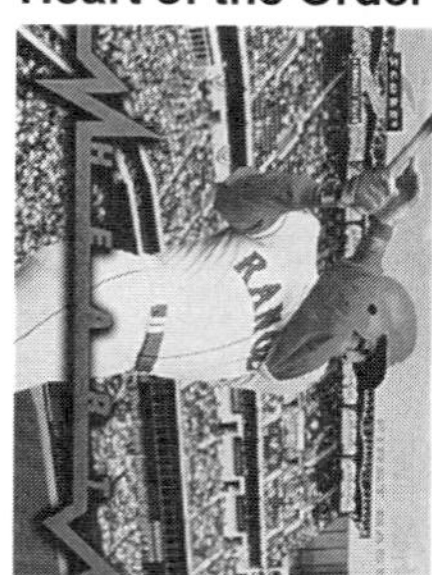

This 36-card set was distributed in Series II retail and hobby packs, with cards 1-18 in retail (one per 23 packs) and cards 19-36 in hobby (one per 15). The cards are printed in a horizontal format, with some of the top hitters in the game included in the insert. Fronts are highlighted in red metallic foil. Backs have a color portrait photo and a few words about the player.

		MT
Complete Set (36):		60.00
Complete Retail Set (1-18):		35.00
Complete Hobby Set (19-36):		25.00
Common Player:		.75
1	Ivan Rodriguez	2.00
2	Will Clark	1.00
3	Juan Gonzalez	3.00
4	Frank Thomas	3.00
5	Albert Belle	2.00
6	Robin Ventura	.75
7	Alex Rodriguez	6.00
8	Ken Griffey Jr.	5.00
9	Jay Buhner	.75
10	Roberto Alomar	2.00
11	Rafael Palmeiro	1.00
12	Cal Ripken Jr.	6.00
13	Manny Ramirez	3.00
14	Matt Williams	1.00
15	Jim Thome	.75
16	Derek Jeter	6.00
17	Wade Boggs	2.00
18	Bernie Williams	1.00
19	Chipper Jones	4.00
20	Andruw Jones	2.00
21	Ryan Klesko	.75
22	Wilton Guerrero	.75
23	Mike Piazza	5.00
24	Raul Mondesi	1.00
25	Tony Gwynn	3.00
26	Ken Caminiti	.75
27	Greg Vaughn	.75
28	Brian Jordan	.75
29	Ron Gant	.75
30	Dmitri Young	.75
31	Darin Erstad	2.00
32	Jim Edmonds	.75
33	Tim Salmon	1.00
34	Chuck Knoblauch	.75
35	Paul Molitor	2.00
36	Todd Walker	.75

1997 Score Highlight Zone

Exclusive to 1997 Score Series I hobby packs are these Highlight Zone inserts, seeded one per every 35 packs. Within the 18-card set, card numbers 1-9 are in regular hobby packs, while numbers 10-18 are found only in premium stock packs.

		MT
Complete Set (18):		40.00
Common Player:		.75
1	Frank Thomas	3.00
2	Ken Griffey Jr.	6.00
3	Mo Vaughn	1.50
4	Albert Belle	1.00
5	Mike Piazza	4.00
6	Barry Bonds	3.00
7	Greg Maddux	2.50
8	Sammy Sosa	3.00
9	Jeff Bagwell	2.00
10	Alex Rodriguez	5.00
11	Chipper Jones	4.00
12	Brady Anderson	.75
13	Ozzie Smith	3.00
14	Edgar Martinez	.75
15	Cal Ripken Jr.	6.00
16	Ryan Klesko	.75
17	Randy Johnson	2.00
18	Eddie Murray	1.50

1997 Score Pitcher Perfect

PITCHER PERFECT
CAL RIPKEN JR. and ALEX RODRIGUEZ

Seattle Mariners' star pitcher and accomplished photographer Randy Johnson makes his picks for the top talent in this 1997 Score Series I insert set. Fronts have player photos with a gold-foil filmstrip graphic at bottom featuring player names and a portrait of The Big Unit. Backs have additional color photos in a filmstrip design and a few words about the player.

		MT
Complete Set (15):		25.00
Common Player:		.50
1	Cal Ripken Jr.	4.00
2	Alex Rodriguez	4.00
3	Cal Ripken Jr., Alex Rodriguez	3.00
4	Edgar Martinez	.50
5	Ivan Rodriguez	1.25
6	Mark McGwire	4.00
7	Tim Salmon	.75
8	Chili Davis	.50
9	Joe Carter	.50
10	Frank Thomas	2.00
11	Will Clark	.75
12	Mo Vaughn	1.00
13	Wade Boggs	1.50
14	Ken Griffey Jr.	4.00
15	Randy Johnson	1.50

1997 Score Stand & Deliver

This 24-card insert was printed on a silver foil background, with the series name and team logo in gold foil across the bottom. Cards were found in Series 2 packs one per 71 retail, one per 41 hobby. Card numbers 21-24 (Florida Marlins) were designated as the winning group, meaning the first 225 collectors that mailed in the complete four card set received a gold upgrade version of the set framed in glass. The gold cards have a gold foil background and red foil highlights.

		MT
Complete Set (24):		90.00
Common Player:		1.00
Gold:		4X
1	Andruw Jones	4.00
2	Greg Maddux	8.00
3	Chipper Jones	8.00
4	John Smoltz	1.50
5	Ken Griffey Jr.	10.00
6	Alex Rodriguez	10.00
7	Jay Buhner	1.00
8	Randy Johnson	5.00
9	Derek Jeter	12.00
10	Andy Pettitte	2.00
11	Bernie Williams	2.00
12	Mariano Rivera	2.50
13	Mike Piazza	9.00
14	Hideo Nomo	4.00
15	Raul Mondesi	1.50
16	Todd Hollandsworth	1.00
17	Manny Ramirez	4.00
18	Jim Thome	1.00
19	David Justice	2.00
20	Matt Williams	1.50
21	Juan Gonzalez	4.00
22	Jeff Bagwell	4.00
23	Cal Ripken Jr.	12.00
24	Frank Thomas	6.00

1997 Score Stellar Season

These 1997 Score Series I inserts were seeded one per every 17 magazine packs.

		MT
Complete Set (18):		17.50
Common Player:		.50
1	Juan Gonzalez	1.00
2	Chuck Knoblauch	.50
3	Jeff Bagwell	1.00
4	John Smoltz	.60
5	Mark McGwire	3.00
6	Ken Griffey Jr.	3.00
7	Frank Thomas	2.00
8	Alex Rodriguez	3.00
9	Mike Piazza	2.50
10	Albert Belle	.60
11	Roberto Alomar	.75
12	Sammy Sosa	2.00
13	Mo Vaughn	.75
14	Brady Anderson	.50
15	Henry Rodriguez	.50
16	Eric Young	.50
17	Gary Sheffield	.75
18	Ryan Klesko	.50

1997 Score The Franchise

There were two versions made for these 1997 Score Series 1 inserts - regular and The Glowing Franchise, which has glow-in-the-dark highlights. The regular version is seeded one per 72 packs; glow-in-the-dark cards are seeded one per 240 packs. Each regular card can also be found in a promo version with a large, black "SAMPLE" on front and back.

		MT
Complete Set (9):		17.50
Common Player:		.50
Glowing:		1X
Samples:		1X
1	Ken Griffey Jr.	5.00
2	John Smoltz	.50
3	Cal Ripken Jr.	5.00
4	Chipper Jones	3.00
5	Mike Piazza	3.00
6	Albert Belle	.50
7	Frank Thomas	2.00
8	Sammy Sosa	2.50
9	Roberto Alomar	1.00

1997 Score Titanic Taters

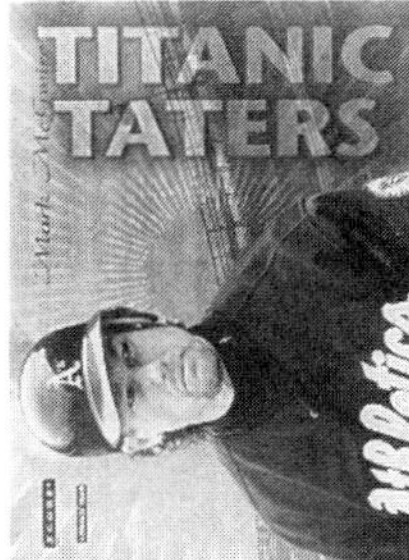

Some of the game's most powerful hitters are featured on these 1997 Score Series I inserts. The cards were seeded one per every 35 retail packs.

		MT
Complete Set (18):		32.50
Common Player:		.50
1	Mark McGwire	6.00
2	Mike Piazza	4.00
3	Ken Griffey Jr.	5.00
4	Juan Gonzalez	1.50
5	Frank Thomas	3.00
6	Albert Belle	1.00
7	Sammy Sosa	3.50
8	Jeff Bagwell	1.50
9	Todd Hundley	.50
10	Ryan Klesko	.50
11	Brady Anderson	.50
12	Mo Vaughn	1.00
13	Jay Buhner	.50
14	Chipper Jones	4.00
15	Barry Bonds	2.50
16	Gary Sheffield	1.00
17	Alex Rodriguez	5.00
18	Cecil Fielder	.50

1997 Score Team Collection

Team sets consisting of 15 players each were produced for 10 different teams. Each card is similar in design to the regular 1997 Score set except for a special foil stamping at the bottom of the card that corresponds with team colors. In a parallel "Platinum" version, seeded one per six packs, the background and team foil on front are replaced with silver prismatic foil. A top of the line parallel set, "Premier" utilizes gold foil highlights on fronts and is found one per 31 packs. Team Collection was sold in five-card, single-team packs with a suggested retail price of about $1.29. It was reported that 100 cases of each team were issued.

		MT
Complete Set (150):		40.00
Common Player:		.15
Braves Wax Box:		40.00
Orioles Wax Box:		35.00
Red Sox Wax Box:		30.00
White Sox Wax Box:		35.00
Indians Wax Box:		35.00
Rockies Wax Box:		25.00
Dodgers Wax Box:		35.00
Yankees Wax Box:		40.00
Mariners Wax Box:		60.00
Rangers Wax Box:		30.00
	Atlanta Braves	7.50
1	Ryan Klesko	.15
2	David Justice	.40
3	Terry Pendleton	.15
4	Tom Glavine	.25
5	Javier Lopez	.15
6	John Smoltz	.25
7	Jermaine Dye	.15
8	Mark Lemke	.15
9	Fred McGriff	.15
10	Chipper Jones	2.50
11	Terrell Wade	.15
12	Greg Maddux	2.00
13	Mark Wohlers	.15
14	Marquis Grissom	.15
15	Andruw Jones	1.50

Baltimore Orioles 7.00
1 Rafael Palmeiro .35
2 Eddie Murray .75
3 Roberto Alomar 1.00
4 Rocky Coppinger .15
5 Brady Anderson .15
6 Bobby Bonilla .15
7 Cal Ripken Jr. 3.00
8 Mike Mussina 1.00
9 Nerio Rodriguez .15
10 Randy Myers .15
11 B.J. Surhoff .15
12 Jeffrey Hammonds .15
13 Chris Hoiles .15
14 Jimmy Haynes .15
15 David Wells .15
Boston Red Sox 4.50
1 Wil Cordero .15
2 Mo Vaughn 1.00
3 John Valentin .15
4 Reggie Jefferson .15
5 Tom Gordon .15
6 Mike Stanley .15
7 Jose Canseco .50
8 Roger Clemens 2.00
9 Darren Bragg .15
10 Jeff Frye .15
11 Jeff Suppan .15
12 Mike Greenwell .15
13 Arquimedez Pozo .15
14 Tim Naehring .15
15 Troy O'Leary .15
Chicago White Sox 3.50
1 Frank Thomas 2.00
2 James Baldwin .15
3 Danny Tartabull .15
4 Jeff Darwin .15
5 Harold Baines .15
6 Roberto Hernandez .15
7 Ray Durham .15
8 Robin Ventura .15
9 Wilson Alvarez .15
10 Lyle Mouton .15
11 Alex Fernandez .15
12 Ron Karkovice .15
13 Kevin Tapani .15
14 Tony Phillips .15
15 Mike Cameron .15
Cleveland Indians 3.50
1 Albert Belle .50
2 Jack McDowell .15
3 Jim Thome .15
4 Dennis Martinez .15
5 Julio Franco .15
6 Omar Vizquel .15
7 Kenny Lofton .15
8 Manny Ramirez 1.50
9 Sandy Alomar Jr. .15
10 Charles Nagy .15
11 Kevin Seitzer .15
12 Mark Carreon .15
13 Jeff Kent .15
14 Danny Graves .15
15 Brian Giles .15
Colorado Rockies 2.50
1 Dante Bichette .15
2 Kevin Ritz .15
3 Walt Weiss .15
4 Ellis Burks .15
5 Jamey Wright .15
6 Andres Galarraga .15
7 Eric Young .15
8 Larry Walker .50
9 Vinny Castilla .15
10 Quinton McCracken .15
11 Armando Reynoso .15
12 Jayhawk Owens .15
13 Mark Thompson .15
14 John Burke .15
15 Bruce Ruffin .15
Los Angeles Dodgers 6.00
1 Ismael Valdez .15
2 Mike Piazza 2.50
3 Todd Hollandsworth .15
4 Delino DeShields .15
5 Chan Ho Park .45
6 Roger Cedeno .15
7 Raul Mondesi .40
8 Darren Dreifort .15
9 Jim Bruske .15
10 Greg Gagne .15
11 Chad Curtis .15
12 Ramon Martinez .15
13 Brett Butler .15
14 Eric Karros .15
15 Hideo Nomo 1.50
New York Yankees 6.50
1 Bernie Williams .45
2 Cecil Fielder .15
3 Derek Jeter 2.50
4 Darryl Strawberry .15
5 Andy Pettitte .35
6 Ruben Rivera .15
7 Mariano Rivera .75
8 John Wetteland .15
9 Paul O'Neill .15
10 Wade Boggs 1.50
11 Dwight Gooden .15
12 David Cone .15
13 Tino Martinez .15
14 Kenny Rogers .15
15 Andy Fox .15
Seattle Mariners 8.00
1 Chris Bosio .15
2 Edgar Martinez .15
3 Alex Rodriguez 3.00
4 Paul Sorrento .15
5 Bob Wells .15
6 Ken Griffey Jr. 3.00
7 Jay Buhner .15
8 Dan Wilson .15
9 Randy Johnson 1.00
10 Joey Cora .15
11 Mark Whiten .15
12 Rich Amaral .15
13 Raul Ibanez .15
14 Jamie Moyer .15
15 Makoto Suzuki .15
Texas Rangers 3.50
1 Mickey Tettleton .15
2 Will Clark .40
3 Ken Hill .15
4 Rusty Greer .15
5 Kevin Elster .15
6 Darren Oliver .15
7 Mark McLemore .15
8 Roger Pavlik .15
9 Dean Palmer .15
10 Bobby Witt .15
11 Juan Gonzalez 1.50
12 Ivan Rodriguez .45
13 Darryl Hamilton .15
14 John Burkett .15
15 Warren Newson .15

1997 Score Team Collection Platinum Team

Team sets consisting of 15 players each were produced for 10 different teams. Each card is similar in design to the regular 1997 Score set except for a special foil stamping at the bottom of the card that corresponds with team colors. In a parallel "Platinum" version, seeded one per six packs, the background and team foil on front are replaced with silver prismatic foil. Backs are overprinted in gold script, "Platinum Team." Team Collection was sold in five-card, single-team packs with a suggested retail price of about $1.29. It was reported that 100 cases of each team were issued.

	MT
Complete Set (150):	250.00
Common Player:	2.00
Platinum Stars:	4X

(See 1997 Score Team Collection for checklists and base card values.)

1997 Score Team Collection Premier Club

Team sets consisting of 15 players each were produced for 10 different teams. Each card is similar in design to the regular 1997 Score set except for a special foil stamping at the bottom of the card that corresponds with team colors. In a top of the line parallel "Premier Club" version, seeded one per 31 packs, the background and team foil on front are replaced with gold prismatic foil, and backs are overprinted "Premier Club" in gold script. Team Collection was sold in five-card, single-team packs with a suggested retail price of about $1.29. It was reported that 100 cases of each team were issued.

	MT
Complete Set (150):	900.00
Common Player:	5.00
Premier Club Stars:	15X

(See 1997 Score Team Collection for checklists and base card values.)

1998 Score

The cards in the 270-card base set feature a color photo inside a black and white border. The player's name is printed in the left border. The entire base set is paralleled in the silver-foil Showcase Series (1:5). The Artist's Proof partial parallel gives a prismatic foil treatment to 165 base cards and was seeded 1:23. Inserts included All-Stars, Complete Players and Epix.

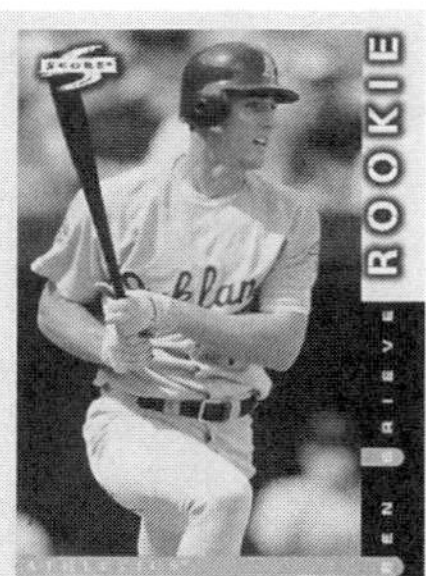

	MT
Complete Set (270):	25.00
Common Player:	.05
Showcases:	3X
Pack (10):	1.00
Wax Box (36):	20.00

1 Andruw Jones .50
2 Dan Wilson .05
3 Hideo Nomo .40
4 Chuck Carr .05
5 Barry Bonds .75
6 Jack McDowell .05
7 Albert Belle .25
8 Francisco Cordova .05
9 Greg Maddux .75
10 Alex Rodriguez 1.25
11 Steve Avery .05
12 Chuck McElroy .05
13 Larry Walker .20
14 Hideki Irabu .05
15 Roberto Alomar .40
16 Neifi Perez .05
17 Jim Thome .05
18 Rickey Henderson .35
19 Andres Galarraga .05
20 Jeff Fassero .05
21 Kevin Young .05
22 Derek Jeter 1.00
23 Andy Benes .05
24 Mike Piazza 1.00
25 Todd Stottlemyre .05
26 Michael Tucker .05
27 Denny Neagle .05
28 Javier Lopez .05
29 Aaron Sele .05
30 Ryan Klesko .05
31 Dennis Eckersley .05
32 Quinton McCracken .05
33 Brian Anderson .05
34 Ken Griffey Jr. 1.25
35 Shawn Estes .05
36 Tim Wakefield .05
37 Jimmy Key .05
38 Jeff Bagwell .50
39 Edgardo Alfonzo .05
40 Mike Cameron .05
41 Mark McGwire 1.50
42 Tino Martinez .05
43 Cal Ripken Jr. 1.50
44 Curtis Goodwin .05
45 Bobby Ayala .05
46 Sandy Alomar Jr. .05
47 Bobby Jones .05
48 Omar Vizquel .05
49 Roger Clemens .75
50 Tony Gwynn .75
51 Chipper Jones 1.00
52 Ron Coomer .05
53 Dmitri Young .05
54 Brian Giles .05
55 Steve Finley .05
56 David Cone .05
57 Andy Pettitte .15
58 Wilton Guerrero .05
59 Deion Sanders .10
60 Carlos Delgado .25
61 Jason Giambi .25
62 Ozzie Guillen .05
63 Jay Bell .05
64 Barry Larkin .10
65 Sammy Sosa .75
66 Bernie Williams .30
67 Terry Steinbach .05

68 Scott Rolen .40
69 Melvin Nieves .05
70 Craig Biggio .10
71 Todd Greene .05
72 Greg Gagne .05
73 Shigetosi Hasegawa .05
74 Mark McLemore .05
75 Darren Bragg .05
76 Brett Butler .05
77 Ron Gant .05
78 Mike Difelice .05
79 Charles Nagy .05
80 Scott Hatteberg .05
81 Brady Anderson .05
82 Jay Buhner .05
83 Todd Hollandsworth .05
84 Geronimo Berroa .05
85 Jeff Suppan .05
86 Pedro Martinez .40
87 Roger Cedeno .05
88 Ivan Rodriguez .35
89 Jaime Navarro .05
90 Chris Hoiles .05
91 Nomar Garciaparra .75
92 Rafael Palmeiro .20
93 Darin Erstad .40
94 Kenny Lofton .05
95 Mike Timlin .05
96 Chris Clemons .05
97 Vinny Castilla .05
98 Charlie Hayes .05
99 Lyle Mouton .05
100 Jason Dickson .05
101 Justin Thompson .05
102 Pat Kelly .05
103 Chan Ho Park .15
104 Ray Lankford .05
105 Frank Thomas .75
106 Jermaine Allensworth .05
107 Doug Drabek .05
108 Todd Hundley .05
109 Carl Everett .10
110 Edgar Martinez .05
111 Robin Ventura .05
112 John Wetteland .05
113 Mariano Rivera .20
114 Jose Rosado .05
115 Ken Caminiti .05
116 Paul O'Neill .05
117 Tim Salmon .20
118 Eduardo Perez .05
119 Mike Jackson .05
120 John Smoltz .10
121 Brant Brown .05
122 John Mabry .05
123 Chuck Knoblauch .05
124 Reggie Sanders .05
125 Ken Hill .05
126 Mike Mussina .40
127 Chad Curtis .05
128 Todd Worrell .05
129 Chris Widger .05
130 Damon Mashore .05
131 Kevin Brown .10
132 Bip Roberts .05
133 Tim Naehring .05
134 Dave Martinez .05
135 Jeff Blauser .05
136 David Justice .20
137 Dave Hollins .05
138 Pat Hentgen .05
139 Darren Daulton .05
140 Ramon Martinez .05
141 Raul Casanova .05
142 Tom Glavine .10
143 J.T. Snow .05
144 Tony Graffanino .05
145 Randy Johnson .50
146 Orlando Merced .05
147 Jeff Juden .05
148 Darryl Kile .05
149 Ray Durham .05
150 Alex Fernandez .05
151 Joey Cora .05
152 Royce Clayton .05
153 Randy Myers .05
154 Charles Johnson .05
155 Alan Benes .05
156 Mike Bordick .05
157 Heathcliff Slocumb .05
158 Roger Bailey .05
159 Reggie Jefferson .05
160 Ricky Bottalico .05
161 Scott Erickson .05
162 Matt Williams .15
163 Robb Nen .05
164 Matt Stairs .05
165 Ismael Valdes .05
166 Lee Stevens .05
167 Gary DiSarcina .05
168 Brad Radke .05
169 Mike Lansing .05
170 Armando Benitez .05
171 Mike James .05
172 Russ Davis .05
173 Lance Johnson .05
174 Joey Hamilton .05
175 John Valentin .05
176 David Segui .05
177 David Wells .10
178 Delino DeShields .05
179 Eric Karros .05
180 Jim Leyritz .05
181 Raul Mondesi .15
182 Travis Fryman .05
183 Todd Zeile .05
184 Brian Jordan .05
185 Rey Ordonez .05
186 Jim Edmonds .10
187 Terrell Wade .05
188 Marquis Grissom .05
189 Chris Snopek .05
190 Shane Reynolds .05
191 Jeff Frye .05
192 Paul Sorrento .05
193 James Baldwin .05
194 Brian McRae .05
195 Fred McGriff .05
196 Troy Percival .05
197 Rich Amaral .05
198 Juan Guzman .05
199 Cecil Fielder .05
200 Willie Blair .05
201 Chili Davis .05
202 Gary Gaetti .05
203 B.J. Surhoff .05
204 Steve Cooke .05
205 Chuck Finley .05
206 Jeff Kent .05
207 Ben McDonald .05
208 Jeffrey Hammonds .05
209 Tom Goodwin .05
210 Billy Ashley .05
211 Wil Cordero .05
212 Shawon Dunston .05
213 Tony Phillips .05
214 Jamie Moyer .05
215 John Jaha .05
216 Troy O'Leary .05
217 Brad Ausmus .05
218 Garret Anderson .05
219 Wilson Alvarez .05
220 Kent Mercker .05
221 Wade Boggs .35
222 Mark Wohlers .05
223 Kevin Appier .05
224 Tony Fernandez .05
225 Ugueth Urbina .05
226 Gregg Jefferies .05
227 Mo Vaughn .35
228 Arthur Rhodes .05
229 Jorge Fabregas .05
230 Mark Gardner .05
231 Shane Mack .05
232 Jorge Posada .05
233 Jose Cruz Jr. .10
234 Paul Konerko .15
235 Derrek Lee .05
236 *Steve Woodard* .15
237 Todd Dunwoody .05
238 Fernando Tatis .05
239 Jacob Cruz .05
240 *Pokey Reese* .25
241 Mark Kotsay .05
242 Matt Morris .05
243 *Antone Williamson* .05
244 Ben Grieve .20
245 Ryan McGuire .05
246 *Lou Collier* .05
247 Shannon Stewart .10
248 *Brett Tomko* .10
249 Bobby Estalella .05
250 *Livan Hernandez* .15
251 Todd Helton .30
252 Jaret Wright .05
253 Darryl Hamilton (Interleague Moments) .05
254 Stan Javier (Interleague Moments) .05
255 Glenallen Hill (Interleague Moments) .05
256 Mark Gardner (Interleague Moments) .05
257 Cal Ripken Jr. (Interleague Moments) .75
258 Mike Mussina (Interleague Moments) .20
259 Mike Piazza (Interleague Moments) .60
260 Sammy Sosa (Interleague Moments) .50
261 Todd Hundley (Interleague Moments) .05
262 Eric Karros (Interleague Moments) .05
263 Denny Neagle (Interleague Moments) .05
264 Jeromy Burnitz (Interleague Moments) .05
265 Greg Maddux (Interleague Moments) .50
266 Tony Clark (Interleague Moments) .05
267 Vladimir Guerrero (Interleague Moments) .25
268 Checklist .05
269 Checklist .05
270 Checklist .05

1998 Score Artist's Proofs

This partial parallel reprinted 160 of the 270 cards in Score Baseball on a foil background with an Artist's Proof logo on the front. The cards were renumbered within the 160-card set and inserted one per 35 packs. Cards have a "PP" prefix to the number on back.

MT
Complete Set (160): 300.00
Common Player: 1.50
Inserted 1:35
1 Andruw Jones 6.00
2 Dan Wilson 1.50
3 Hideo Nomo 6.00
4 Neifi Perez 1.50
5 Jim Thome 1.50
6 Jeff Fassero 1.50
7 Derek Jeter 10.00
8 Andy Benes 1.50
9 Michael Tucker 1.50
10 Ryan Klesko 1.50
11 Dennis Eckersley 1.50
12 Jimmy Key 1.50
13 Edgardo Alfonzo 1.50
14 Mike Cameron 1.50
15 Omar Vizquel 1.50
16 Ron Coomer 1.50
17 Dmitri Young 1.50
18 Brian Giles 1.50
19 Steve Finley 1.50
20 Andy Pettitte 2.50
21 Wilton Guerrero 1.50
22 Deion Sanders 1.50
23 Carlos Delgado 3.00
24 Jason Giambi 2.50
25 David Cone 1.50
26 Jay Bell 1.50
27 Sammy Sosa 8.50
28 Barry Larkin 1.50
29 Scott Rolen 4.00
30 Todd Greene 1.50
31 Bernie Williams 2.50
32 Brett Butler 1.50
33 Ron Gant 1.50
34 Brady Anderson 1.50
35 Craig Biggio 1.50
36 Charles Nagy 1.50
37 Jay Buhner 1.50
38 Geronimo Berroa 1.50
39 Jeff Suppan 1.50
40 Rafael Palmeiro 2.50
41 Darin Erstad 3.00
42 Mike Timlin 1.50
43 Vinny Castilla 1.50
44 Carl Everett 2.00
45 Robin Ventura 1.50
46 John Wetteland 1.50
47 Paul O'Neill 1.50
48 Tim Salmon 2.00
49 Mike Jackson 1.50
50 John Smoltz 1.50
51 Brant Brown 1.50
52 Reggie Sanders 1.50
53 Ken Hill 1.50
54 Todd Worrell 1.50
55 Bip Roberts 1.50
56 Tim Naehring 1.50
57 Darren Daulton 1.50
58 Ramon Martinez 1.50
59 Raul Casanova 1.50
60 J.T. Snow 1.50
61 Jeff Juden 1.50
62 Royce Clayton 1.50
63 Charles Johnson 1.50
64 Alan Benes 1.50
65 Reggie Jefferson 1.50
66 Ricky Bottalico 1.50
67 Scott Erickson 1.50
68 Matt Williams 2.00
69 Robb Nen 1.50
70 Matt Stairs 1.50
71 Ismael Valdes 1.50
72 Brad Radke 1.50
73 Armando Benitez 1.50
74 Russ Davis 1.50
75 Lance Johnson 1.50
76 Joey Hamilton 1.50
77 John Valentin 1.50
78 David Segui 1.50
79 David Wells 1.50
80 Eric Karros 1.50
81 Raul Mondesi 2.00
82 Travis Fryman 1.50
83 Todd Zeile 1.50
84 Brian Jordan 1.50
85 Rey Ordonez 1.50
86 Jim Edmonds 1.50
87 Marquis Grissom 1.50
88 Shane Reynolds 1.50
89 Paul Sorrento 1.50
90 Brian McRae 1.50
91 Fred McGriff 1.50
92 Troy Percival 1.50
93 Juan Guzman 1.50
94 Cecil Fielder 1.50
95 Chili Davis 1.50
96 B.J. Surhoff 1.50
97 Chuck Finley 1.50
98 Jeff Kent 1.50
99 Ben McDonald 1.50
100 Jeffrey Hammonds 1.50
101 Tom Goodwin 1.50
102 Wil Cordero 1.50
103 Tony Phillips 1.50
104 John Jaha 1.50
105 Garret Anderson 1.50
106 Wilson Alvarez 1.50
107 Wade Boggs 7.50
108 Mark Wohlers 1.50
109 Kevin Appier 1.50
110 Mo Vaughn 2.50
111 Ray Durham 1.50
112 Alex Fernandez 1.50
113 Barry Bonds 8.50
114 Albert Belle 3.00
115 Greg Maddux 7.50
116 Alex Rodriguez 12.00
117 Larry Walker 2.50
118 Roberto Alomar 4.00
119 Andres Galarraga 1.50
120 Mike Piazza 10.00
121 Denny Neagle 1.50
122 Javier Lopez 1.50
123 Ken Griffey Jr. 12.00

124	Shawn Estes	2.00
125	Jeff Bagwell	6.00
126	Mark McGwire	12.50
127	Tino Martinez	1.50
128	Cal Ripken Jr.	12.50
129	Sandy Alomar Jr.	1.50
130	Bobby Jones	1.50
131	Roger Clemens	7.50
132	Tony Gwynn	7.50
133	Chipper Jones	10.00
134	Orlando Merced	1.50
135	Todd Stottlemyre	1.50
136	Delino DeShields	1.50
137	Pedro Martinez	3.00
138	Ivan Rodriguez	4.00
139	Nomar Garciaparra	8.50
140	Kenny Lofton	1.50
141	Jason Dickson	1.50
142	Justin Thompson	1.50
143	Ray Lankford	1.50
144	Frank Thomas	8.00
145	Todd Hundley	1.50
146	Edgar Martinez	1.50
147	Mariano Rivera	2.50
148	Jose Rosado	1.50
149	Ken Caminiti	1.50
150	Chuck Knoblauch	1.50
151	Mike Mussina	3.50
152	Kevin Brown	1.50
153	Jeff Blauser	1.50
154	David Justice	2.00
155	Pat Hentgen	1.50
156	Tom Glavine	2.00
157	Randy Johnson	4.00
158	Darryl Kile	1.50
159	Joey Cora	1.50
160	Randy Myers	1.50

1998 Score All Score Team

For its 10th anniversary Score selected an all-star team and issued this insert set. Cards have player action photos on a silver-foil background with an anniversary logo at bottom. Backs have a portrait photo and a career summary. The cards were inserted one per 35 packs.

		MT
Complete Set (20):		30.00
Common Player:		.50
Inserted 1:35		
1	Mike Piazza	3.00
2	Ivan Rodriguez	1.50
3	Frank Thomas	2.50
4	Mark McGwire	4.00
5	Ryne Sandberg	2.00
6	Roberto Alomar	1.50
7	Cal Ripken Jr.	4.00
8	Barry Larkin	.50
9	Paul Molitor	1.50
10	Travis Fryman	.50
11	Kirby Puckett	2.50
12	Tony Gwynn	2.50
13	Ken Griffey Jr.	4.00
14	Juan Gonzalez	2.00
15	Barry Bonds	2.50
16	Andruw Jones	1.50
17	Roger Clemens	2.50
18	Randy Johnson	1.50
19	Greg Maddux	2.50
20	Dennis Eckersley	.50

1998 Score Complete Players

Complete Players is a 30-card insert featuring 10 players who can do it all. Each player had three cards displaying their variety of skills. The cards feature holographic foil highlights on fronts. Backs form a three-piece vertical picture of the player. The cards were inserted about one per 23 packs. Cards can be found with either gold or silver holographic foil.

		MT
Complete Set (30):		45.00
Common Player:		.50
Inserted 1:23		
1A	Ken Griffey Jr.	3.00
1B	Ken Griffey Jr.	3.00
1C	Ken Griffey Jr.	3.00
2A	Mark McGwire	3.00
2B	Mark McGwire	3.00
2C	Mark McGwire	3.00
3A	Derek Jeter	2.50
3B	Derek Jeter	2.50
3C	Derek Jeter	2.50
4A	Cal Ripken Jr.	3.00
4B	Cal Ripken Jr.	3.00
4C	Cal Ripken Jr.	3.00
5A	Mike Piazza	2.50
5B	Mike Piazza	2.50
5C	Mike Piazza	2.50
6A	Darin Erstad	.50
6B	Darin Erstad	.50
6C	Darin Erstad	.50
7A	Frank Thomas	2.00
7B	Frank Thomas	2.00
7C	Frank Thomas	2.00
8A	Andruw Jones	1.00
8B	Andruw Jones	1.00
8C	Andruw Jones	1.00
9A	Nomar Garciaparra	2.00
9B	Nomar Garciaparra	2.00
9C	Nomar Garciaparra	2.00
10A	Manny Ramirez	1.00
10B	Manny Ramirez	1.00
10C	Manny Ramirez	1.00

1998 Score Epix

Epix is a cross-brand insert, with 24 cards appearing in Score. The cards are printed on 20-point stock with holographic foil technology. The cards honor the top Play, Game, Season and Moment in a player's career and come in Orange, Purple and Emerald versions. Game cards were inserted 1:141, Plays 1:171, Seasons 1:437 and Moments 1:757.

		MT
Common Card:		2.00
Purple:		1.5X
Emeralds:		2.5X
1	Ken Griffey Jr. P	12.00
2	Juan Gonzalez P	2.50
3	Jeff Bagwell P	2.50
4	Ivan Rodriguez P	2.00
5	Nomar Garciaparra P	6.00
6	Ryne Sandberg P	2.50
7	Frank Thomas G	6.00
8	Derek Jeter G	10.00
9	Tony Gwynn G	7.50
10	Albert Belle G	1.50
11	Scott Rolen G	2.00
12	Barry Larkin G	2.00
13	Alex Rodriguez S	12.00
14	Cal Ripken Jr. S	15.00
15	Chipper Jones S	10.00
16	Roger Clemens S	8.50
17	Mo Vaughn S	2.50
18	Mark McGwire S	15.00
19	Mike Piazza M	10.00
20	Andruw Jones M	5.00
21	Greg Maddux M	8.50
22	Barry Bonds M	8.50
23	Paul Molitor M	4.00
24	Eddie Murray M	4.00

1998 Score First Pitch

These inserts were a 1:11 pack find in Score's All-Star edition. Fronts have portrait photos printed in the center of textured foil background of red and silver. The basic design is repeated on back, with career highlights and team logo instead of a photo.

		MT
Complete Set (20):		45.00
Common Player:		1.00
Inserted 1:11 All-Star Edition		
1	Ken Griffey Jr.	5.00
2	Frank Thomas	3.00
3	Alex Rodriguez	5.00
4	Cal Ripken Jr.	6.00
5	Chipper Jones	4.00
6	Juan Gonzalez	2.00
7	Derek Jeter	4.00
8	Mike Piazza	4.00
9	Andruw Jones	2.00
10	Nomar Garciaparra	3.00
11	Barry Bonds	3.00
12	Jeff Bagwell	2.00
13	Scott Rolen	1.50
14	Hideo Nomo	1.50
15	Roger Clemens	3.00
16	Mark McGwire	6.00
17	Greg Maddux	3.00
18	Albert Belle	1.00
19	Ivan Rodriguez	1.50
20	Mo Vaughn	1.00

1998 Score Loaded Lineup

This insert series was packaged on average of one card per 45 packs of Score's All-Star edition. Fronts have action photos printed on a copper and silver textured metallic-foil background. Backs have a portrait photo, career highlights, the Loaded Lineup batting order and stats for the player's best season. Cards have an "LL" prefix to their number.

		MT
Complete Set (10):		50.00
Common Player:		2.00
Inserted 1:45 All-Star Edition		
LL1	Chuck Knoblauch	2.00
LL2	Tony Gwynn	6.00
LL3	Frank Thomas	7.50
LL4	Ken Griffey Jr.	9.00
LL5	Mike Piazza	7.50
LL6	Barry Bonds	7.00
LL7	Cal Ripken Jr.	10.00
LL8	Paul Molitor	4.00
LL9	Nomar Garciaparra	7.00
LL10	Greg Maddux	6.00

1998 Score New Season

Found only in Score All-Star Edition, at an average rate of one per 23 packs, this insert series mixes veteran stars with hot young players. Fronts have a large portrait photo. Horizontal backs have an action photo.

		MT
Complete Set (15):		55.00
Common Player:		2.00
Inserted 1:23 All-Star Edition		
NS1	Kenny Lofton	2.00
NS2	Nomar Garciaparra	7.00
NS3	Todd Helton	2.50

NS4 Miguel Tejada 2.00
NS5 Jaret Wright 2.00
NS6 Alex Rodriguez 9.00
NS7 Vladimir Guerrero 5.00
NS8 Ken Griffey Jr. 9.00
NS9 Ben Grieve 3.00
NS10 Travis Lee 2.00
NS11 Jose Cruz Jr. 2.00
NS12 Paul Konerko 2.00
NS13 Frank Thomas 7.00
NS14 Chipper Jones 8.00
NS15 Cal Ripken Jr. 10.00

1998 Score Rookie & Traded

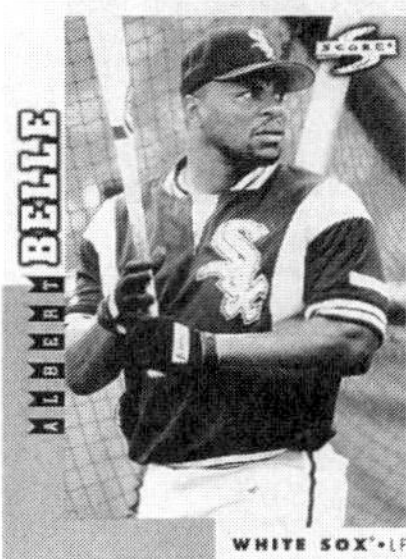

Score Rookie/Traded consists of a 270-card base set. The base cards have a white and gray border with the player's name on the left. Cards are printed on a slightly glossier stock. The Showcase Series parallels 110 base cards and was inserted 1:7. Artist's Proofs is a 50-card partial parallel done on prismatic foil and inserted 1:35. Inserts included All-Star Epix, Complete Players and Star Gazing.

	MT
Complete Set (270):	25.00
Common SP (1-50):	.25
Common Player (51-270):	.10
Paul Konerko Auto. (500):	25.00
Pack (10):	.50
Wax Box (36):	15.00

1 Tony Clark .25
2 Juan Gonzalez .75
3 Frank Thomas 1.50
4 Greg Maddux 1.50
5 Barry Larkin .30
6 Derek Jeter 2.00
7 Randy Johnson .75
8 Roger Clemens 1.50
9 Tony Gwynn 1.50
10 Barry Bonds 1.50
11 Jim Edmonds .30
12 Bernie Williams .40
13 Ken Griffey Jr. 2.50
14 Tim Salmon .40
15 Mo Vaughn .60
16 David Justice .40
17 Jose Cruz Jr. .35
18 Andruw Jones .75
19 Sammy Sosa 1.50
20 Jeff Bagwell 1.00
21 Scott Rolen 1.00
22 Darin Erstad .75
23 Andy Pettitte .40
24 Mike Mussina .65
25 Mark McGwire 2.50
26 Hideo Nomo .75
27 Chipper Jones 2.00
28 Cal Ripken Jr. 2.50
29 Chuck Knoblauch .25
30 Alex Rodriguez 2.50
31 Jim Thome .25
32 Mike Piazza 2.00
33 Ivan Rodriguez .65
34 Roberto Alomar .65
35 Nomar Garciaparra 1.50
36 Albert Belle .50
37 Vladimir Guerrero .75
38 Raul Mondesi .30
39 Larry Walker .40
40 Manny Ramirez 1.00
41 Tino Martinez .25
42 Craig Biggio .25
43 Jay Buhner .25
44 Kenny Lofton .25
45 Pedro Martinez .60
46 Edgar Martinez .25
47 Gary Sheffield .40
48 Jose Guillen .25
49 Ken Caminiti .25
50 Bobby Higginson .25
51 Alan Benes .10
52 Shawn Green .15
53 Ron Coomer .10
54 Charles Nagy .10
55 Steve Karsay .10
56 Matt Morris .10
57 Bobby Jones .10
58 Jason Kendall .10
59 Jeff Conine .10
60 Joe Girardi .10
61 Mark Kotsay .10
62 Eric Karros .10
63 Bartolo Colon .15
64 Mariano Rivera .25
65 Alex Gonzalez .15
66 Scott Spiezio .10
67 Luis Castillo .10
68 Joey Cora .10
69 Mark McLemore .10
70 Reggie Jefferson .10
71 Lance Johnson .10
72 Damian Jackson .10
73 Jeff D'Amico .10
74 David Ortiz .10
75 J.T. Snow .10
76 Todd Hundley .10
77 Billy Wagner .10
78 Vinny Castilla .10
79 Ismael Valdes .10
80 Neifi Perez .10
81 Derek Bell .10
82 Ryan Klesko .10
83 Rey Ordonez .10
84 Carlos Garcia .10
85 Curt Schilling .20
86 Robin Ventura .10
87 Pat Hentgen .10
88 Glendon Rusch .10
89 Hideki Irabu .10
90 Antone Williamson .10
91 Denny Neagle .10
92 Kevin Orie .10
93 Reggie Sanders .10
94 Brady Anderson .10
95 Andy Benes .10
96 John Valentin .10
97 Bobby Bonilla .10
98 Walt Weiss .10
99 Robin Jennings .10
100 Marty Cordova .10
101 Brad Ausmus .10
102 Brian Rose .10
103 Calvin Maduro .10
104 Raul Casanova .10
105 Jeff King .10
106 Sandy Alomar .10
107 Tim Naehring .10
108 Mike Cameron .10
109 Omar Vizquel .10
110 Brad Radke .10
111 Jeff Fassero .10
112 Deivi Cruz .10
113 Dave Hollins .10
114 Dean Palmer .10
115 Esteban Loaiza .10
116 Brian Giles .10
117 Steve Finley .10
118 Jose Canseco .35
119 Al Martin .10
120 Eric Young .10
121 Curtis Goodwin .10
122 Ellis Burks .10
123 Mike Hampton .10
124 Lou Collier .10
125 John Olerud .10
126 Ramon Martinez .10
127 Todd Dunwoody .10
128 Jermaine Allensworth .10
129 Eduardo Perez .10
130 Dante Bichette .10
131 Edgar Renteria .10
132 Bob Abreu .10
133 Rondell White .15
134 Michael Coleman .10
135 Jason Giambi .35
136 Brant Brown .10
137 Michael Tucker .10
138 Dave Nilsson .10
139 Benito Santiago .10
140 Ray Durham .10
141 Jeff Kent .10
142 Matt Stairs .10
143 Kevin Young .10
144 Eric Davis .10
145 John Wetteland .10
146 Esteban Yan .10
147 Wilton Guerrero .10
148 Moises Alou .15
149 Edgardo Alfonzo .10
150 Andy Ashby .10
151 Todd Walker .10
152 Jermaine Dye .10
153 Brian Hunter .10
154 Shawn Estes .10
155 Bernard Gilkey .10
156 Tony Womack .10
157 John Smoltz .10
158 Delino DeShields .10
159 Jacob Cruz .10
160 Javier Valentin .10
161 Chris Hoiles .10
162 Garret Anderson .10
163 Dan Wilson .10
164 Paul O'Neill .10
165 Matt Williams .25
166 Travis Fryman .10
167 Javier Lopez .10
168 Ray Lankford .10
169 Bobby Estalella .10
170 Henry Rodriguez .10
171 Quinton McCracken .10
172 Jaret Wright .10
173 Darryl Kile .10
174 Wade Boggs .40
175 Orel Hershiser .10
176 B.J. Surhoff .10
177 Fernando Tatis .10
178 Carlos Delgado .25
179 Jorge Fabregas .10
180 Tony Saunders .10
181 Devon White .10
182 Dmitri Young .10
183 Ryan McGuire .10
184 Mark Bellhorn .10
185 Joe Carter .10
186 Kevin Stocker .10
187 Mike Lansing .10
188 Jason Dickson .10
189 Charles Johnson .10
190 Will Clark .25
191 Shannon Stewart .15
192 Johnny Damon .15
193 Todd Greene .10
194 Carlos Baerga .10
195 David Cone .10
196 Pokey Reese .10
197 Livan Hernandez .10
198 Tom Glavine .10
199 Geronimo Berroa .10
200 Darryl Hamilton .10
201 Terry Steinbach .10
202 Robb Nen .10
203 Ron Gant .10
204 Rafael Palmeiro .25
205 Rickey Henderson .40
206 Justin Thompson .10
207 Jeff Suppan .10
208 Kevin Brown .15
209 Jimmy Key .10
210 Brian Jordan .10
211 Aaron Sele .10
212 Fred McGriff .10
213 Jay Bell .10
214 Andres Galarraga .10
215 Mark Grace .25
216 Brett Tomko .10
217 Francisco Cordova .10
218 Rusty Greer .10
219 Bubba Trammell .10
220 Derrek Lee .10
221 Brian Anderson .10
222 Mark Grudzielanek .10
223 Marquis Grissom .10
224 Gary DiSarcina .10
225 Jim Leyritz .10
226 Jeffrey Hammonds .10
227 Karim Garcia .15
228 Chan Ho Park .30
229 Brooks Kieschnick .10
230 Trey Beamon .10
231 Kevin Appier .10
232 Wally Joyner .10
233 Richie Sexson .10
234 *Frank Catalanotto* .20
235 Rafael Medina .10
236 Travis Lee .10
237 Eli Marrero .10
238 Carl Pavano .10
239 Enrique Wilson .10
240 Richard Hidalgo .10
241 Todd Helton .25
242 Ben Grieve .25
243 Mario Valdez .10
244 *Magglio Ordonez* 1.50
245 Juan Encarnacion .10
246 Russell Branyan .10
247 Sean Casey .25
248 Abraham Nunez .10
249 Brad Fullmer .10
250 Paul Konerko .15
251 Miguel Tejada .20
252 *Mike Lowell* .40
253 Ken Griffey Jr. (Spring Training) 1.00
254 Frank Thomas (Spring Training) .60
255 Alex Rodriguez (Spring Training) .75
256 Jose Cruz Jr. (Spring Training) .10
257 Jeff Bagwell (Spring Training) .30
258 Chipper Jones (Spring Training) .60
259 Mo Vaughn (Spring Training) .20
260 Nomar Garciaparra (Spring Training) .60
261 Jim Thome (Spring Training) .10
262 Derek Jeter (Spring Training) .60
263 Mike Piazza (Spring Training) .60
264 Tony Gwynn (Spring Training) .50
265 Scott Rolen (Spring Training) .20
266 Andruw Jones (Spring Training) .25
267 Cal Ripken Jr. (Spring Training) 1.00
268 Checklist (Ken Griffey Jr.) .60
269 Checklist (Cal Ripken Jr.) .60
270 Checklist (Jose Cruz Jr.) .10

1998 Score Rookie & Traded Showcase Series

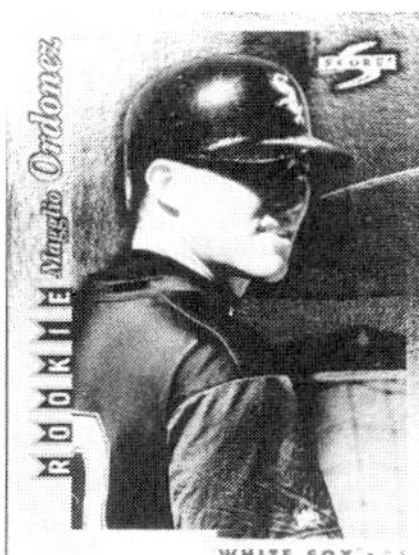

The Showcase Series is a partial parallel reprint of 160 of the 270 cards in Rookie & Traded. The cards are printed on a silver-foil surface, marked on the back and renumbered (with an "RTPP" prefix) within the 160-card set. Showcase parallels were inserted one per seven packs.

		MT
Complete Set (160):		84.00
Common Player:		.50
1	Tony Clark	.50
2	Juan Gonzalez	2.50
3	Frank Thomas	3.00
4	Greg Maddux	3.00
5	Barry Larkin	.60
6	Derek Jeter	4.00
7	Randy Johnson	1.00
8	Roger Clemens	3.00
9	Tony Gwynn	3.00
10	Barry Bonds	3.00
11	Jim Edmonds	.50
12	Bernie Williams	.75
13	Ken Griffey Jr.	4.50
14	Tim Salmon	.75
15	Mo Vaughn	1.00
16	David Justice	.75
17	Jose Cruz Jr.	.50
18	Andruw Jones	2.00
19	Sammy Sosa	3.00
20	Jeff Bagwell	2.50
21	Scott Rolen	2.00
22	Darin Erstad	.75
23	Andy Pettitte	.75
24	Mike Mussina	1.00
25	Mark McGwire	5.00
26	Hideo Nomo	1.00
27	Chipper Jones	4.00
28	Cal Ripken Jr.	5.00
29	Chuck Knoblauch	.50
30	Alex Rodriguez	4.50
31	Jim Thome	.50
32	Mike Piazza	4.00
33	Ivan Rodriguez	1.50
34	Roberto Alomar	1.25
35	Nomar Garciaparra	3.00
36	Albert Belle	.75
37	Vladimir Guerrero	1.25
38	Raul Mondesi	.65
39	Larry Walker	1.00
40	Manny Ramirez	2.50
41	Tino Martinez	.50
42	Craig Biggio	.50
43	Jay Buhner	.50
44	Kenny Lofton	.50
45	Pedro Martinez	1.25
46	Edgar Martinez	.50
47	Gary Sheffield	.65
48	Jose Guillen	.50
49	Ken Caminiti	.50
50	Bobby Higginson	.50
51	Alan Benes	.50
52	Shawn Green	.75
53	Matt Morris	.50
54	Jason Kendall	.50
55	Mark Kotsay	.50
56	Bartolo Colon	.50
57	Damian Jackson	.50
58	David Ortiz	.50
59	J.T. Snow	.50
60	Todd Hundley	.50
61	Neifi Perez	.50
62	Ryan Klesko	.50
63	Robin Ventura	.50
64	Pat Hentgen	.50
65	Antone Williamson	.50
66	Kevin Orie	.50
67	Brady Anderson	.50
68	Bobby Bonilla	.50
69	Brian Rose	.50
70	Sandy Alomar Jr.	.50
71	Mike Cameron	.50
72	Omar Vizquel	.50
73	Steve Finley	.50
74	Jose Canseco	1.00
75	Al Martin	.50
76	Eric Young	.50
77	Ellis Burks	.50
78	Todd Dunwoody	.50
79	Dante Bichette	.50
80	Edgar Renteria	.50
81	Bobby Abreu	.50
82	Rondell White	.65
83	Michael Coleman	.50
84	Jason Giambi	1.00
85	Wilton Guerrero	.50
86	Moises Alou	.60
87	Todd Walker	.50
88	Shawn Estes	.50
89	John Smoltz	.50
90	Jacob Cruz	.50
91	Javier Valentin	.50
92	Garret Anderson	.50
93	Paul O'Neill	.50
94	Matt Williams	.75
95	Travis Fryman	.50
96	Javier Lopez	.50
97	Ray Lankford	.50
98	Bobby Estalella	.50
99	Jaret Wright	.50
100	Wade Boggs	1.25
101	Fernando Tatis	.50
102	Carlos Delgado	.75
103	Joe Carter	.50
104	Jason Dickson	.50
105	Charles Johnson	.50
106	Will Clark	.75
107	Shannon Stewart	.50
108	Todd Greene	.50
109	Pokey Reese	.50
110	Livan Hernandez	.50
111	Tom Glavine	.50
112	Rafael Palmeiro	.75
113	Justin Thompson	.50
114	Jeff Suppan	.50
115	Kevin Brown	.75
116	Brian Jordan	.50
117	Fred McGriff	.50
118	Andres Galarraga	.50
119	Mark Grace	1.00
120	Rusty Greer	.50
121	Bubba Trammell	.50
122	Derrek Lee	.50
123	Brian Anderson	.50
124	Karim Garcia	.50
125	Chan Ho Park	.60
126	Richie Sexson	.50
127	Frank Catalanotto	.50
128	Rafael Medina	.50
129	Travis Lee	.65
130	Eli Marrero	.50
131	Carl Pavano	.50
132	Enrique Wilson	.50
133	Richard Hidalgo	.50
134	Todd Helton	.50
135	Ben Grieve	.75
136	Mario Valdez	.50
137	Magglio Ordonez	.50
138	Juan Encarnacion	.50
139	Russell Branyan	.50
140	Sean Casey	.75
141	Abraham Nunez	.50
142	Brad Fullmer	.50
143	Paul Konerko	.75
144	Miguel Tejada	.75
145	Mike Lowell	.50
146	Ken Griffey Jr. (Spring Training)	1.75
147	Frank Thomas (Spring Training)	1.00
148	Alex Rodriguez (Spring Training)	1.50
149	Jose Cruz Jr. (Spring Training)	.50
150	Jeff Bagwell (Spring Training)	.75
151	Chipper Jones (Spring Training)	1.25
152	Mo Vaughn (Spring Training)	.75
153	Nomar Garciaparra (Spring Training)	1.00
154	Jim Thome (Spring Training)	.50
155	Derek Jeter (Spring Training)	1.25
156	Mike Piazza (Spring Training)	1.25
157	Tony Gwynn (Spring Training)	1.00
158	Scott Rolen (Spring Training)	.75
159	Andruw Jones (Spring Training)	.75
160	Cal Ripken Jr. (Spring Training)	1.75

1998 Score Rookie & Traded Artist's Proofs

This partial parallel reprints 160 (the same cards as the Showcase Series) of the 270 cards in Score Rookie & Traded. The cards are printed on a foil surface and feature an Artist's Proof logo on front. The cards were renumbered within the 160-card set and inserted one per 35 packs.

	MT
Complete Set (160):	400.00
Common Player:	1.50
AP Stars:	3X

(See 1998 Score Rookie & Traded Showcase for checklist and base card values.)

1998 Score Rookie & Traded All-Star Epix Moment

All-Star Epix is a 1:61 insert. The cards honor the top All-Star Game moments of 12 star players. The dot matrix hologram cards were printed in orange, purple and emerald versions.

		MT
Complete Set (12):		150.00
Common Player:		5.00
Purples:		1.5X
Emeralds:		2.5X
1	Ken Griffey Jr.	25.00
2	Juan Gonzalez	8.50
3	Jeff Bagwell	10.00
4	Ivan Rodriguez	8.00
5	Nomar Garciaparra	20.00
6	Ryne Sandberg	8.50
7	Frank Thomas	16.50
8	Derek Jeter	20.00
9	Tony Gwynn	15.00
10	Albert Belle	6.00
11	Scott Rolen	10.00
12	Barry Larkin	5.00
13	Alex Rodriguez	12.00
14	Cal Ripken Jr.	15.00
15	Chipper Jones	10.00
16	Roger Clemens	8.50
17	Mo Vaughn	2.50
18	Mark McGwire	15.00
19	Mike Piazza	10.00
20	Andruw Jones	5.00
21	Greg Maddux	8.50
22	Barry Bonds	8.50
23	Paul Molitor	4.00
24	Eddie Murray	4.00

1998 Score Rookie & Traded Complete Players

Complete Players is a 30-card insert seeded one per 11 packs. The set highlights 10 players who can do it all on the field. Each player has three cards showcasing one of their talents. The cards feature holographic foil stamping. Each card can also be found in a promo version with a large, black "SAMPLE" overprinted on front and back.

		MT
Complete Set (30):		45.00
Common Player:		.75
Inserted 1:11		
1A	Ken Griffey Jr.	3.50
1B	Ken Griffey Jr.	3.50
1C	Ken Griffey Jr.	3.50
2A	Larry Walker	.75
2B	Larry Walker	.75
2C	Larry Walker	.75
3A	Alex Rodriguez	3.50
3B	Alex Rodriguez	3.50
3C	Alex Rodriguez	3.50
4A	Jose Cruz Jr.	.75
4B	Jose Cruz Jr.	.75
4C	Jose Cruz Jr.	.75
5A	Jeff Bagwell	1.50
5B	Jeff Bagwell	1.50
5C	Jeff Bagwell	1.50
6A	Greg Maddux	2.00
6B	Greg Maddux	2.00
6C	Greg Maddux	2.00
7A	Ivan Rodriguez	1.25
7B	Ivan Rodriguez	1.25
7C	Ivan Rodriguez	1.25
8A	Roger Clemens	2.00
8B	Roger Clemens	2.00
8C	Roger Clemens	2.00
9A	Chipper Jones	2.50
9B	Chipper Jones	2.50
9C	Chipper Jones	2.50
10A	Hideo Nomo	1.00
10B	Hideo Nomo	1.00
10C	Hideo Nomo	1.00

1998 Score Rookie & Traded Star Gazing

Printed on micro-etched foil board, Star Gazing features 20 top players and was seeded 1:35.

		MT
Complete Set (20):		45.00
Common Player:		1.00
Inserted 1:35		
1	Ken Griffey Jr.	4.50
2	Frank Thomas	3.00
3	Chipper Jones	4.00
4	Mark McGwire	5.00
5	Cal Ripken Jr.	5.00
6	Mike Piazza	4.00
7	Nomar Garciaparra	3.50
8	Derek Jeter	4.00
9	Juan Gonzalez	2.50
10	Vladimir Guerrero	2.00
11	Alex Rodriguez	4.50
12	Tony Gwynn	3.00
13	Andruw Jones	2.00
14	Scott Rolen	1.50
15	Jose Cruz Jr.	1.00
16	Mo Vaughn	1.00
17	Bernie Williams	1.00
18	Greg Maddux	3.00
19	Tony Clark	1.00
20	Ben Grieve	1.50

1993 Select Promos

Zeroes in the career stats line on the back of the card distinguish the promo cards for Score's premiere issue of its Select brand name. The promo cards were distributed to introduce dealers and collectors to the new mid-range set.

		MT
Complete Set (8):		22.50
Common Player:		1.00
22	Robin Yount	7.50
24	Don Mattingly	10.00
26	Sandy Alomar Jr.	1.00
41	Gary Sheffield	4.00
56	Brady Anderson	1.00
65	Rob Dibble	1.00
75	John Smiley	1.00
79	Mitch Williams	1.00

1993 Select

This 400-card set from Score is designed for the mid-priced card market. The card fronts feature green borders on two sides of the card with the photo filling the remaining portion of the card front. The backs feature an additional photo, player information and statistics. Cards numbered 271-360 are devoted to rookies and draft picks.

		MT
Complete Set (405):		20.00
Common Player:		.05
Pack (15):		.75
Wax Box (36):		20.00
1	Barry Bonds	1.00
2	Ken Griffey, Jr.	1.50
3	Will Clark	.15
4	Kirby Puckett	1.00
5	Tony Gwynn	.75
6	Frank Thomas	1.00
7	Tom Glavine	.10
8	Roberto Alomar	.40
9	Andre Dawson	.15
10	Ron Darling	.05
11	Bobby Bonilla	.05
12	Danny Tartabull	.05
13	Darren Daulton	.05
14	Roger Clemens	.75
15	Ozzie Smith	1.00
16	Mark McGwire	2.00
17	Terry Pendleton	.05
18	Cal Ripken, Jr.	2.00
19	Fred McGriff	.05
20	Cecil Fielder	.05
21	Darryl Strawberry	.05
22	Robin Yount	.40
23	Barry Larkin	.10
24	Don Mattingly	1.00
25	Craig Biggio	.10
26	Sandy Alomar Jr.	.05
27	Larry Walker	.30
28	Junior Felix	.05
29	Eddie Murray	.35
30	Robin Ventura	.05
31	Greg Maddux	.75
32	Dave Winfield	.40
33	John Kruk	.05
34	Wally Joyner	.05
35	Andy Van Slyke	.05
36	Chuck Knoblauch	.05
37	Tom Pagnozzi	.05
38	Dennis Eckersley	.05
39	Dave Justice	.25
40	Juan Gonzalez	.50
41	Gary Sheffield	.35
42	Paul Molitor	.40
43	Delino DeShields	.05
44	Travis Fryman	.05
45	Hal Morris	.05
46	Gregg Olson	.05
47	Ken Caminiti	.05
48	Wade Boggs	.50
49	Orel Hershiser	.05
50	Albert Belle	.25
51	Bill Swift	.05
52	Mark Langston	.05
53	Joe Girardi	.05
54	Keith Miller	.05
55	Gary Carter	.20
56	Brady Anderson	.05
57	Dwight Gooden	.05
58	Julio Franco	.05
59	Len Dykstra	.05
60	Mickey Tettleton	.05
61	Randy Tomlin	.05
62	B.J. Surhoff	.05
63	Todd Zeile	.05
64	Roberto Kelly	.05
65	Rob Dibble	.05
66	Leo Gomez	.05
67	Doug Jones	.05
68	Ellis Burks	.05
69	Mike Scioscia	.05
70	Charles Nagy	.05
71	Cory Snyder	.05
72	Devon White	.05
73	Mark Grace	.20
74	Luis Polonia	.05
75	John Smiley	.05
76	Carlton Fisk	.40
77	Luis Sojo	.05
78	George Brett	1.00
79	Mitch Williams	.05
80	Kent Hrbek	.05
81	Jay Bell	.05
82	Edgar Martinez	.05
83	Lee Smith	.05
84	Deion Sanders	.10
85	Bill Gullickson	.05
86	Paul O'Neill	.05
87	Kevin Seitzer	.05
88	Steve Finley	.05
89	Mel Hall	.05
90	Nolan Ryan	2.00
91	Eric Davis	.05
92	Mike Mussina	.40
93	Tony Fernandez	.05
94	Frank Viola	.05
95	Matt Williams	.15
96	Joe Carter	.05
97	Ryne Sandberg	.75
98	Jim Abbott	.05
99	Marquis Grissom	.05
100	George Bell	.05
101	Howard Johnson	.05
102	Kevin Appier	.05
103	Dale Murphy	.15
104	Shane Mack	.05
105	Jose Lind	.05
106	Rickey Henderson	.35
107	Bob Tewksbury	.05
108	Kevin Mitchell	.05
109	Steve Avery	.05
110	Candy Maldonado	.05
111	Bip Roberts	.05
112	Lou Whitaker	.05
113	Jeff Bagwell	.50
114	Dante Bichette	.05
115	Brett Butler	.05
116	Melido Perez	.05
117	Andy Benes	.05
118	Randy Johnson	.50
119	Willie McGee	.05
120	Jody Reed	.05
121	Shawon Dunston	.05
122	Carlos Baerga	.05
123	Bret Saberhagen	.05
124	John Olerud	.05
125	Ivan Calderon	.05
126	Bryan Harvey	.05
127	Terry Mulholland	.05
128	Ozzie Guillen	.05
129	Steve Buechele	.05
130	Kevin Tapani	.05
131	Felix Jose	.05
132	Terry Steinbach	.05
133	Ron Gant	.05
134	Harold Reynolds	.05
135	Chris Sabo	.05
136	Ivan Rodriguez	.40
137	Eric Anthony	.05
138	Mike Henneman	.05
139	Robby Thompson	.05
140	Scott Fletcher	.05
141	Bruce Hurst	.05
142	Kevin Maas	.05
143	Tom Candiotti	.05
144	Chris Hoiles	.05
145	Mike Morgan	.05
146	Mark Whiten	.05
147	Dennis Martinez	.05
148	Tony Pena	.05
149	Dave Magadan	.05
150	Mark Lewis	.05
151	Mariano Duncan	.05
152	Gregg Jefferies	.05
153	Doug Drabek	.05
154	Brian Harper	.05
155	Ray Lankford	.05
156	Carney Lansford	.05
157	Mike Sharperson	.05
158	Jack Morris	.05
159	Otis Nixon	.05
160	Steve Sax	.05
161	Mark Lemke	.05
162	Rafael Palmeiro	.20
163	Jose Rijo	.05
164	Omar Vizquel	.05
165	Sammy Sosa	1.00
166	Milt Cuyler	.05
167	John Franco	.05
168	Darryl Hamilton	.05
169	Ken Hill	.05
170	Mike Devereaux	.05
171	Don Slaught	.05
172	Steve Farr	.05
173	Bernard Gilkey	.05
174	Mike Fetters	.05
175	Vince Coleman	.05
176	Kevin McReynolds	.05
177	John Smoltz	.10
178	Greg Gagne	.05
179	Greg Swindell	.05
180	Juan Guzman	.05
181	Kal Daniels	.05
182	Rick Sutcliffe	.05
183	Orlando Merced	.05
184	Bill Wegman	.05
185	Mark Gardner	.05
186	Rob Deer	.05
187	Dave Hollins	.05
188	Jack Clark	.05
189	Brian Hunter	.05
190	Tim Wallach	.05
191	Tim Belcher	.05
192	Walt Weiss	.05
193	Kurt Stillwell	.05
194	Charlie Hayes	.05
195	Willie Randolph	.05
196	Jack McDowell	.05
197	Jose Offerman	.05
198	Chuck Finley	.05
199	Darrin Jackson	.05
200	Kelly Gruber	.05
201	John Wetteland	.05
202	Jay Buhner	.05
203	Mike LaValliere	.05
204	Kevin Brown	.10
205	Luis Gonzalez	.20
206	Rick Aguilera	.05
207	Norm Charlton	.05
208	Mike Bordick	.05
209	Charlie Leibrandt	.05
210	Tom Brunansky	.05
211	Tom Henke	.05
212	Randy Milligan	.05
213	Ramon Martinez	.05
214	Mo Vaughn	.35
215	Randy Myers	.05
216	Greg Hibbard	.05
217	Wes Chamberlain	.05
218	Tony Phillips	.05
219	Pete Harnisch	.05
220	Mike Gallego	.05
221	Bud Black	.05
222	Greg Vaughn	.05
223	Milt Thompson	.05
224	Ben McDonald	.05
225	Billy Hatcher	.05
226	Paul Sorrento	.05
227	Mark Gubicza	.05
228	Mike Greenwell	.05
229	Curt Schilling	.15
230	Alan Trammell	.05
231	Zane Smith	.05
232	Bobby Thigpen	.05
233	Greg Olson	.05
234	Joe Orsulak	.05
235	Joe Oliver	.05
236	Tim Raines	.05
237	Juan Samuel	.05
238	Chili Davis	.05
239	Spike Owen	.05
240	Dave Stewart	.05
241	Jim Eisenreich	.05
242	Phil Plantier	.05
243	Sid Fernandez	.05
244	Dan Gladden	.05
245	Mickey Morandini	.05
246	Tino Martinez	.05
247	Kirt Manwaring	.05
248	Dean Palmer	.05
249	Tom Browning	.05

250	Brian McRae	.05
251	Scott Leius	.05
252	Bert Blyleven	.05
253	Scott Erickson	.05
254	Bob Welch	.05
255	Pat Kelly	.05
256	Felix Fermin	.05
257	Harold Baines	.05
258	Duane Ward	.05
259	Bill Spiers	.05
260	Jaime Navarro	.05
261	Scott Sanderson	.05
262	Gary Gaetti	.05
263	Bob Ojeda	.05
264	Jeff Montgomery	.05
265	Scott Bankhead	.05
266	Lance Johnson	.05
267	Rafael Belliard	.05
268	Kevin Reimer	.05
269	Benito Santiago	.05
270	Mike Moore	.05
271	Dave Fleming	.05
272	Moises Alou	.15
273	Pat Listach	.05
274	Reggie Sanders	.05
275	Kenny Lofton	.05
276	Donovan Osborne	.05
277	Rusty Meacham	.05
278	Eric Karros	.05
279	Andy Stankiewicz	.05
280	Brian Jordan	.05
281	Gary DiSarcina	.05
282	Mark Wohlers	.05
283	Dave Nilsson	.05
284	Anthony Young	.05
285	Jim Bullinger	.05
286	Derek Bell	.05
287	Brian Williams	.05
288	Julio Valera	.05
289	Dan Walters	.05
290	Chad Curtis	.05
291	Michael Tucker	.05
292	Bob Zupcic	.05
293	Todd Hundley	.05
294	Jeff Tackett	.05
295	Greg Colbrunn	.05
296	Cal Eldred	.05
297	Chris Roberts	.05
298	John Doherty	.05
299	Denny Neagle	.05
300	Arthur Rhodes	.05
301	Mark Clark	.05
302	Scott Cooper	.05
303	*Jamie Arnold*	.05
304	Jim Thome	.05
305	Frank Seminara	.05
306	Kurt Knudsen	.05
307	Tim Wakefield	.05
308	John Jaha	.05
309	Pat Hentgen	.05
310	B.J. Wallace	.05
311	Roberto Hernandez	.05
312	Hipolito Pichardo	.05
313	Eric Fox	.05
314	Willie Banks	.05
315	Sam Millitello	.05
316	Vince Horsman	.05
317	Carlos Hernandez	.05
318	Jeff Kent	.05
319	Mike Perez	.05
320	Scott Livingstone	.05
321	Jeff Conine	.05
322	James Austin	.05
323	John Vander Wal	.05
324	Pat Mahomes	.05
325	Pedro Astacio	.05
326	Bret Boone	.10
327	Matt Stairs	.05
328	Damion Easley	.05
329	Ben Rivera	.05
330	Reggie Jefferson	.05
331	Luis Mercedes	.05
332	Kyle Abbott	.05
333	Eddie Taubensee	.05
334	Tim McIntosh	.05
335	Phil Clark	.05
336	Wil Cordero	.05
337	Russ Springer	.05
338	Craig Colbert	.05
339	Tim Salmon	.20
340	Braulio Castillo	.05
341	Donald Harris	.05
342	Eric Young	.05
343	Bob Wickman	.05
344	John Valentin	.05
345	Dan Wilson	.05
346	Steve Hosey	.05
347	Mike Piazza	1.25
348	Willie Greene	.05
349	Tom Goodwin	.05
350	Eric Hillman	.05
351	*Steve Reed*	.05
352	*Dan Serafini*	.05
353	*Todd Steverson*	.05
354	Benji Grigsby	.05
355	*Shannon Stewart*	1.00
356	Sean Lowe	.05
357	Derek Wallace	.05
358	Rick Helling	.05
359	*Jason Kendall*	1.50
360	*Derek Jeter*	10.00
361	David Cone	.05
362	Jeff Reardon	.05
363	Bobby Witt	.05
364	Jose Canseco	.35
365	Jeff Russell	.05
366	Ruben Sierra	.05
367	Alan Mills	.05
368	Matt Nokes	.05
369	Pat Borders	.05
370	Pedro Munoz	.05
371	Danny Jackson	.05
372	Geronimo Pena	.05
373	Craig Lefferts	.05
374	Joe Grahe	.05
375	Roger McDowell	.05
376	Jimmy Key	.05
377	Steve Olin	.05
378	Glenn Davis	.05
379	Rene Gonzales	.05
380	Manuel Lee	.05
381	Ron Karkovice	.05
382	Sid Bream	.05
383	Gerald Williams	.05
384	Lenny Harris	.05
385	*J.T. Snow*	1.00
386	Dave Stieb	.05
387	Kirk McCaskill	.05
388	Lance Parrish	.05
389	Craig Greback	.05
390	Rick Wilkins	.05
391	Manny Alexander	.05
392	Mike Schooler	.05
393	Bernie Williams	.25
394	Kevin Koslofski	.05
395	Willie Wilson	.05
396	Jeff Parrett	.05
397	Mike Harkey	.05
398	Frank Tanana	.05
399	Doug Henry	.05
400	Royce Clayton	.05
401	Eric Wedge	.05
402	Derrick May	.05
403	Carlos Garcia	.05
404	Henry Rodriguez	.05
405	Ryan Klesko	.05

1993 Select Aces

Cards from this set feature 24 of the top pitchers from 1992 and were included one per every 27-card Super Pack. The fronts have a picture of the player in action against an Ace card background. Backs have text and a portrait in the middle of a card suit for an Ace.

		MT
Complete Set (24):		17.00
Common Player:		.50
1	Roger Clemens	4.00
2	Tom Glavine	1.00
3	Jack McDowell	.50
4	Greg Maddux	4.00
5	Jack Morris	.50
6	Dennis Martinez	.50
7	Kevin Brown	.50
8	Dwight Gooden	.50
9	Kevin Appier	.50
10	Mike Morgan	.50
11	Juan Guzman	.50
12	Charles Nagy	.50
13	John Smiley	.50
14	Ken Hill	.50
15	Bob Tewksbury	.50
16	Doug Drabek	.50
17	John Smoltz	1.00
18	Greg Swindell	.50
19	Bruce Hurst	.50
20	Mike Mussina	3.00
21	Cal Eldred	.50
22	Melido Perez	.50
23	Dave Fleming	.50
24	Kevin Tapani	.50

1993 Select Rookies

Top newcomers in 1992 are featured in this 21-card insert set. Cards were randomly inserted in 15-card hobby packs. The fronts, printed on metallic foil, have a Score Select Rookies logo on the front. The backs have text and a player portrait.

		MT
Complete Set (21):		15.00
Common Player:		.50
1	Pat Listach	.50
2	Moises Alou	1.50
3	Reggie Sanders	1.00
4	Kenny Lofton	1.00
5	Eric Karros	1.00
6	Brian Williams	.50
7	Donovan Osborne	.50
8	Sam Militello	.50
9	Chad Curtis	.50
10	Bob Zupcic	.50
11	Tim Salmon	4.00
12	Jeff Conine	1.25
13	Pedro Astacio	.50
14	Arthur Rhodes	.50
15	Cal Eldred	.50
16	Tim Wakefield	.50
17	Andy Stankiewicz	.50
18	Wil Cordero	.50
19	Todd Hundley	1.00
20	Dave Fleming	.50
21	Bret Boone	2.00

1993 Select Stars

The top 24 players from 1992 are featured in this insert set. Cards were randomly inserted in 15-card retail packs. Fronts are printed on metallic foil.

		MT
Complete Set (24):		37.50
Common Player:		.50
1	Fred McGriff	.50
2	Ryne Sandberg	3.00
3	Ozzie Smith	3.50
4	Gary Sheffield	1.00
5	Darren Daulton	.50
6	Andy Van Slyke	.50
7	Barry Bonds	4.00
8	Tony Gwynn	3.50
9	Greg Maddux	3.50
10	Tom Glavine	.75
11	John Franco	.50
12	Lee Smith	.50
13	Cecil Fielder	.50
14	Roberto Alomar	2.00
15	Cal Ripken, Jr.	6.00
16	Edgar Martinez	.50
17	Ivan Rodriguez	2.00
18	Kirby Puckett	3.50
19	Ken Griffey, Jr.	6.00
20	Joe Carter	.50
21	Roger Clemens	3.50
22	Dave Fleming	.50
22s	Dave Fleming (blank-back sample card)	2.00
23	Paul Molitor	2.00
24	Dennis Eckersley	.50

1993 Select Stat Leaders

This 90-card set features 1992 American League and National League leaders in various statistical categories. Each card front indicates the league and the category in which the player finished at or near the top. The backs have a list of the leaders; the pictured player's name is in larger type size. Cards were inserted one per foil pack.

	MT
Complete Set (90):	10.00
Common Player:	.10

1	Edgar Martinez	.10
2	Kirby Puckett	.60
3	Frank Thomas	.60
4	Gary Sheffield	.20
5	Andy Van Slyke	.10
6	John Kruk	.10
7	Kirby Puckett	.60
8	Carlos Baerga	.10
9	Paul Molitor	.25
10	Andy Van Slyke, Terry Pendleton	.10
11	Ryne Sandberg	.50
12	Mark Grace	.20
13	Frank Thomas	.60
14	Don Mattingly	.65
15	Ken Griffey, Jr.	.75
16	Andy Van Slyke	.10
17	Mariano Duncan, Jerald Clark, Ray Lankford	.10
18	Marquis Grissom, Terry Pendleton	.10
19	Lance Johnson	.10
20	Mike Devereaux	.10
21	Brady Anderson	.10
22	Deion Sanders	.10
23	Steve Finley	.10
24	Andy Van Slyke	.10
25	Juan Gonzalez	.40
26	Mark McGwire	.75
27	Cecil Fielder	.10
28	Fred McGriff	.10
29	Barry Bonds	.65
30	Gary Sheffield	.20
31	Cecil Fielder	.10
32	Joe Carter	.10
33	Frank Thomas	.60
34	Darren Daulton	.10
35	Terry Pendleton	.10
36	Fred McGriff	.10
37	Tony Phillips	.10
38	Frank Thomas	.60
39	Roberto Alomar	.25
40	Barry Bonds	.65
41	Dave Hollins	.10
42	Andy Van Slyke	.10
43	Mark McGwire	.75
44	Edgar Martinez	.10
45	Frank Thomas	.60
46	Barry Bonds	.65
47	Gary Sheffield	.20
48	Fred McGriff	.10
49	Frank Thomas	.60
50	Danny Tartabull	.10
51	Roberto Alomar	.25
52	Barry Bonds	.65
53	John Kruk	.10
54	Brett Butler	.10
55	Kenny Lofton	.10
56	Pat Listach	.10
57	Brady Anderson	.10
58	Marquis Grissom	.10
59	Delino DeShields	.10
60	Steve Finley, Bip Roberts	.10
61	Jack McDowell	.10
62	Kevin Brown	.10
63	Melido Perez	.10
64	Terry Mulholland	.10
65	Curt Schilling	.15
66	John Smoltz, Doug Drabek, Greg Maddux	.10
67	Dennis Eckersley	.10
68	Rick Aguilera	.10
69	Jeff Montgomery	.10
70	Lee Smith	.10
71	Randy Myers	.10
72	John Wetteland	.10
73	Randy Johnson	.25
74	Melido Perez	.10
75	Roger Clemens	.50
76	John Smoltz	.10
77	David Cone	.10
78	Greg Maddux	.60
79	Roger Clemens	.50
80	Kevin Appier	.10
81	Mike Mussina	.40
82	Bill Swift	.10
83	Bob Tewksbury	.10
84	Greg Maddux	.60
85	Kevin Brown	.10
86	Jack McDowell	.10
87	Roger Clemens	.50
88	Tom Glavine	.10
89	Ken Hill, Bob Tewksbury	.10
90	Dennis Martinez, Mike Morgan	.10

1993 Select Triple Crown

This three-card set commemorates the Triple Crown seasons of Hall of Famers Mickey Mantle, Frank Robinson and Carl Yastrzemski. Cards were randomly inserted in 15-card hobby packs. Card fronts have a green metal-lic-look textured border, with the player's name at top in gold, and "Triple Crown" in gold at bottom. There are other silver and green highlights around the photo, which feature the player set against a metallized background. Dark green backs have a player photo and information on his Triple Crown season.

		MT
Complete Set (3):		25.00
Common Player:		6.00
1	Mickey Mantle	20.00
2	Frank Robinson	6.00
3	Carl Yastrzemski	7.50

1993 Select Rookie/Traded

Production of this 150-card set was limited to 1,950 numbered cases. Several future Hall of Famers and six dozen top rookies are featured in the set. Cards were available in packs rather than collated sets and include randomly inserted FX cards, which feature Nolan Ryan (two per 24-box case), Tim Salmon and Mike Piazza (one per 576 packs) and All-Star Rookie Team members (one per 58 packs).

		MT
Complete Set (150):		15.00
Common Player:		.10
Pack (12):		1.50
Wax Box (24):		25.00
1	Rickey Henderson	.45
2	Rob Deer	.10
3	Tim Belcher	.10
4	Gary Sheffield	.40
5	Fred McGriff	.10
6	Mark Whiten	.10
7	Jeff Russell	.10
8	Harold Baines	.10
9	Dave Winfield	.40
10	Ellis Burks	.10
11	Andre Dawson	.20
12	Gregg Jefferies	.10
13	Jimmy Key	.10
14	Harold Reynolds	.10
15	Tom Henke	.10
16	Paul Molitor	.75
17	Wade Boggs	.45
18	David Cone	.10
19	Tony Fernandez	.10
20	Roberto Kelly	.10
21	Paul O'Neill	.10
22	Jose Lind	.10
23	Barry Bonds	3.00
24	Dave Stewart	.10
25	Randy Myers	.10
26	Benito Santiago	.10
27	Tim Wallach	.10
28	Greg Gagne	.10
29	Kevin Mitchell	.10
30	Jim Abbott	.10
31	Lee Smith	.10
32	*Bobby Munoz*	.10
33	*Mo Sanford*	.10
34	John Roper	.10
35	*David Hulse*	.10
36	Pedro Martinez	2.00
37	*Chuck Carr*	.10
38	*Armando Reynoso*	.25
39	Ryan Thompson	.10
40	*Carlos Garcia*	.10
41	Matt Whiteside	.10
42	Benji Gil	.10
43	*Rodney Bolton*	.10
44	J.T. Snow	.10
45	David McCarty	.10
46	*Paul Quantrill*	.10
47	Al Martin	.10
48	Lance Painter	.10
49	*Lou Frazier*	.10
50	Eduardo Perez	.10
51	Kevin Young	.10
52	Mike Trombley	.10
53	*Sterling Hitchcock*	.35
54	*Tim Bogar*	.10
55	*Hilly Hathaway*	.10
56	*Wayne Kirby*	.10
57	*Craig Paquette*	.10
58	Bret Boone	.15
59	*Greg McMichael*	.10
60	*Mike Lansing*	.35
61	Brent Gates	.10
62	Rene Arocha	.10
63	Ricky Gutierrez	.10
64	*Kevin Rogers*	.10
65	*Ken Ryan*	.10
66	Phil Hiatt	.10
67	*Pat Meares*	.10
68	Troy Neel	.10
69	Steve Cooke	.10
70	*Sherman Obando*	.10
71	*Blas Minor*	.10
72	*Angel Miranda*	.10
73	*Tom Kramer*	.10
74	*Chip Hale*	.10
75	*Brad Pennington*	.10
76	*Graeme Lloyd*	.10
77	*Darrell Whitmore*	.10
78	David Nied	.10
79	Todd Van Poppel	.10
80	*Chris Gomez*	.15
81	Jason Bere	.10
82	Jeffrey Hammonds	.10
83	*Brad Ausmus*	.15
84	Kevin Stocker	.10
85	Jeromy Burnitz	.10
86	Aaron Sele	.10
87	*Roberto Mejia*	.10
88	*Kirk Rueter*	.25
89	*Kevin Roberson*	.10
90	*Allen Watson*	.10
91	Charlie Leibrandt	.10
92	Eric Davis	.10
93	Jody Reed	.10
94	Danny Jackson	.10
95	Gary Gaetti	.10
96	Norm Charlton	.10
97	Doug Drabek	.10
98	Scott Fletcher	.10
99	Greg Swindell	.10
100	John Smiley	.10
101	Kevin Reimer	.10
102	Andres Galarraga	.10
103	Greg Hibbard	.10
104	Chris Hammond	.10
105	Darnell Coles	.10
106	Mike Felder	.10
107	Jose Guzman	.10
108	Chris Bosio	.10
109	Spike Owen	.10
110	Felix Jose	.10
111	Cory Snyder	.10
112	Craig Lefferts	.10
113	David Wells	.15
114	Pete Incaviglia	.10
115	Mike Pagliarulo	.10
116	Dave Magadan	.10
117	Charlie Hough	.10
118	Ivan Calderon	.10
119	Manuel Lee	.10
120	Bob Patterson	.10
121	Bob Ojeda	.10
122	Scott Bankhead	.10
123	Greg Maddux	3.00
124	Chili Davis	.10
125	Milt Thompson	.10
126	Dave Martinez	.10
127	Frank Tanana	.10
128	Phil Plantier	.10
129	Juan Samuel	.10
130	Eric Young	.10
131	Joe Orsulak	.10
132	Derek Bell	.10
133	Darrin Jackson	.10
134	Tom Brunansky	.10
135	Jeff Reardon	.10
136	*Kevin Higgins*	.10
137	*Joel Johnston*	.10
138	*Rick Trlicek*	.10
139	*Richie Lewis*	.10
140	*Jeff Gardner*	.10
141	*Jack Voigt*	.10
142	*Rod Correia*	.10
143	*Billy Brewer*	.10
144	*Terry Jorgensen*	.10
145	*Rich Amaral*	.15
146	*Sean Berry*	.10
147	*Dan Peltier*	.10
148	*Paul Wagner*	.10
149	*Damon Buford*	.50
150	Wil Cordero	.10

1993 Select Rookie/Traded All-Star Rookies

These cards were randomly inserted into the Score Select Rookie/Traded packs, making them among the scarcest of the year's many "chase"

cards. Card fronts feature metallic foil printing. Backs have a few words about the player. Stated odds of finding an All-Star Rookie Team insert card are one per 58 packs.

		MT
Complete Set (10):		50.00
Common Player:		1.50
1	Jeff Conine	2.50
2	Brent Gates	1.50
3	Mike Lansing	2.50
4	Kevin Stocker	1.50
5	Mike Piazza	35.00
6	Jeffrey Hammonds	1.50
7	David Hulse	1.50
8	Tim Salmon	10.00
9	Rene Arocha	1.50
10	Greg McMichael	1.50

1993 Select Rookie/Traded Inserts

Three cards honoring the 1993 Rookies of the Year and retiring superstar Nolan Ryan were issued as random inserts in the Select Rookie/Traded packs. Cards are printed with metallic foil front backgrounds. Stated odds of finding a Piazza or Salmon card are about one per 24-box case; Ryan cards are found on average two per case.

		MT
Complete Set (3):		75.00
Common Player:		10.00
1NR	Nolan Ryan	45.00
1ROY	Tim Salmon	10.00
2ROY	Mike Piazza	35.00

1994 Select Promos

To introduce its 1994 offering to dealers and collectors, Score Select created an eight-card promo set. Cards are identical in format to regular-issue cards with the exception of the word "SAMPLE" overprinted diagonally on front and back. The promos included five of the regular-run cards, a Rookie Prospect card and one each of its Rookie Surge '94 and Crown Contenders insert sets. The promos were cello-packaged with a header card describing the set and chase cards.

		MT
Complete Set (8):		10.00
Common Player:		.75
3	Paul Molitor	1.50
17	Kirby Puckett	2.50
19	Randy Johnson	1.50
24	John Kruk	.75
51	Jose Lind	.75
197	Ryan Klesko (Rookie Prospect)	1.00
1CC	Lenny Dykstra (Crown Contenders)	1.00
1RS	Cliff Floyd (Rookie Surge '94)	1.50
----	Header card	.05

1994 Select

Both series of this premium brand from the Score/Pinnacle lineup offered 210 regular cards for a combined 420 cards, and seven insert sets. The announced press run for each series was 4,950 20-box cases. Cards have a horizontal format with a color action photo at right and a second photo at left done in a single team color-coded hue. The player's last name is dropped out of a vertical gold-foil strip between the two photos, with his first name in white at top-center. Backs are vertical with yet another color action photo at center. In a vertical bar at right, matching the color-coding on front and printed over the photo are 1993 and career stats, a "Select Stat," and a few sentences about the player. The appropriate logos and Pinnacle's optical-variable anti-counterfeiting device are at bottom-center. Thirty of the final 33 cards in the first series are a "1994 Rookie Prospect" subset, so noted in a special gold-foil logo on front.

		MT
Complete Set (420):		20.00
Common Player:		.10
Wax Pack (12):		.75
Wax Box (24):		15.00
1	Ken Griffey, Jr.	2.25
2	Greg Maddux	1.00
3	Paul Molitor	.60
4	Mike Piazza	2.00
5	Jay Bell	.10
6	Frank Thomas	1.50
7	Barry Larkin	.15
8	Paul O'Neill	.10
9	Darren Daulton	.10
10	Mike Greenwell	.10
11	Chuck Carr	.10
12	Joe Carter	.10
13	Lance Johnson	.10
14	Jeff Blauser	.10
15	Chris Hoiles	.10
16	Rick Wilkins	.10
17	Kirby Puckett	1.00
18	Larry Walker	.35
19	Randy Johnson	.75
20	Bernard Gilkey	.10
21	Devon White	.10
22	Randy Myers	.10
23	Don Mattingly	1.25
24	John Kruk	.10
25	Ozzie Guillen	.10
26	Jeff Conine	.10
27	Mike Macfarlane	.10
28	Dave Hollins	.10
29	Chuck Knoblauch	.10
30	Ozzie Smith	1.00
31	Harold Baines	.10
32	Ryne Sandberg	.85
33	Ron Karkovice	.10
34	Terry Pendleton	.10
35	Wally Joyner	.10
36	Mike Mussina	.60
37	Felix Jose	.10
38	Derrick May	.10
39	Scott Cooper	.10
40	Jose Rijo	.10
41	Robin Ventura	.10
42	Charlie Hayes	.10
43	Jimmy Key	.10
44	Eric Karros	.10
45	Ruben Sierra	.10
46	Ryan Thompson	.10
47	Brian McRae	.10
48	Pat Hentgen	.10
49	John Valentin	.10
50	Al Martin	.10
51	Jose Lind	.10
52	Kevin Stocker	.10
53	Mike Gallego	.10
54	Dwight Gooden	.10
55	Brady Anderson	.10
56	Jeff King	.10
57	Mark McGwire	2.50
58	Sammy Sosa	1.50
59	Ryan Bowen	.10
60	Mark Lemke	.10
61	Roger Clemens	1.00
62	Brian Jordan	.10
63	Andres Galarraga	.10
64	Kevin Appier	.10
65	Don Slaught	.10
66	Mike Blowers	.10
67	Wes Chamberlain	.10
68	Troy Neel	.10
69	John Wetteland	.10
70	Joe Girardi	.10
71	Reggie Sanders	.10
72	Edgar Martinez	.10
73	Todd Hundley	.10
74	Pat Borders	.10
75	Roberto Mejia	.10
76	David Cone	.10
77	Tony Gwynn	1.00
78	Jim Abbott	.10
79	Jay Buhner	.10
80	Mark McLemore	.10
81	Wil Cordero	.10
82	Pedro Astacio	.10
83	Bob Tewksbury	.10
84	Dave Winfield	.50
85	Jeff Kent	.10
86	Todd Van Poppel	.10
87	Steve Avery	.10
88	Mike Lansing	.10
89	Len Dykstra	.10
90	Jose Guzman	.10
91	Brian Hunter	.10
92	Tim Raines	.10
93	Andre Dawson	.20
94	Joe Orsulak	.10
95	Ricky Jordan	.10
96	Billy Hatcher	.10
97	Jack McDowell	.10
98	Tom Pagnozzi	.10
99	Darryl Strawberry	.10
100	Mike Stanley	.10
101	Bret Saberhagen	.10
102	Willie Greene	.10
103	Bryan Harvey	.10
104	Tim Bogar	.10
105	Jack Voight	.10
106	Brad Ausmus	.10
107	Ramon Martinez	.10
108	Mike Perez	.10
109	Jeff Montgomery	.10
110	Danny Darwin	.10
111	Wilson Alvarez	.10
112	Kevin Mitchell	.10
113	David Nied	.10
114	Rich Amaral	.10
115	Stan Javier	.10
116	Mo Vaughn	.50
117	Ben McDonald	.10
118	Tom Gordon	.10
119	Carlos Garcia	.10
120	Phil Plantier	.10
121	Mike Morgan	.10
122	Pat Meares	.10
123	Kevin Young	.10
124	Jeff Fassero	.10
125	Gene Harris	.10
126	Bob Welch	.10
127	Walt Weiss	.10
128	Bobby Witt	.10
129	Andy Van Slyke	.10
130	Steve Cooke	.10
131	Mike Devereaux	.10
132	Joey Cora	.10
133	Bret Barberie	.10
134	Orel Hershiser	.10
135	Ed Sprague	.10
136	Shawon Dunston	.10
137	Alex Arias	.10
138	Archi Cianfrocco	.10
139	Tim Wallach	.10
140	Bernie Williams	.30
141	Karl Rhodes	.10
142	Pat Kelly	.10
143	Dave Magadan	.10
144	Kevin Tapani	.10
145	Eric Young	.10
146	Derek Bell	.10
147	Dante Bichette	.10
148	Geronimo Pena	.10
149	Joe Oliver	.10
150	Orestes Destrade	.10
151	Tim Naehring	.10
152	Ray Lankford	.10
153	Phil Clark	.10
154	David McCarty	.10
155	Tommy Greene	.10
156	Wade Boggs	.75
157	Kevin Gross	.10
158	Hal Morris	.10
159	Moises Alou	.15
160	Rick Aguilera	.10
161	Curt Schilling	.15
162	Chip Hale	.10
163	Tino Martinez	.10
164	Mark Whiten	.10
165	Dave Stewart	.10
166	Steve Buechele	.10
167	Bobby Jones	.10
168	Darrin Fletcher	.10
169	John Smiley	.10
170	Cory Snyder	.10
171	Scott Erickson	.10
172	Kirk Rueter	.10
173	Dave Fleming	.10
174	John Smoltz	.10
175	Ricky Gutierrez	.10
176	Mike Bordick	.10
177	*Chan Ho Park*	2.00
178	Alex Gonzalez	.10
179	Steve Karsay	.10

No.	Player	Price
180	Jeffrey Hammonds	.10
181	Manny Ramirez	.75
182	Salomon Torres	.10
183	Raul Mondesi	.30
184	James Mouton	.10
185	Cliff Floyd	.10
186	Danny Bautista	.10
187	*Kurt Abbott*	.15
188	Javier Lopez	.10
189	John Patterson	.10
190	Greg Blosser	.10
191	Bob Hamelin	.10
192	Tony Eusebio	.10
193	Carlos Delgado	.30
194	Chris Gomez	.10
195	Kelly Stinnett	.10
196	Shane Reynolds	.10
197	Ryan Klesko	.10
198	Jim Edmonds	.15
199	James Hurst	.10
200	Dave Staton	.10
201	Rondell White	.30
202	Keith Mitchell	.10
203	Darren Oliver	.10
204	Mike Matheny	.10
205	Chris Turner	.10
206	Matt Mieske	.10
207	N.L. team checklist	.10
208	N.L. team checklist	.10
209	A.L. team checklist	.10
210	A.L. team checklist	.10
211	Barry Bonds	1.50
212	Juan Gonzalez	.75
213	Jim Eisenreich	.10
214	Ivan Rodriguez	.60
215	Tony Phillips	.10
216	John Jaha	.10
217	Lee Smith	.10
218	Bip Roberts	.10
219	Dave Hansen	.10
220	Pat Listach	.10
221	Willie McGee	.10
222	Damion Easley	.10
223	Dean Palmer	.10
224	Mike Moore	.10
225	Brian Harper	.10
226	Gary DiSarcina	.10
227	Delino DeShields	.10
228	Otis Nixon	.10
229	Roberto Alomar	.60
230	Mark Grace	.30
231	Kenny Lofton	.10
232	Gregg Jefferies	.10
233	Cecil Fielder	.10
234	Jeff Bagwell	.75
235	Albert Belle	.25
236	Dave Justice	.35
237	Tom Henke	.10
238	Bobby Bonilla	.10
239	John Olerud	.10
240	Robby Thompson	.10
241	Dave Valle	.10
242	Marquis Grissom	.10
243	Greg Swindell	.10
244	Todd Zeile	.10
245	Dennis Eckersley	.10
246	Jose Offerman	.10
247	Greg McMichael	.10
248	Tim Belcher	.10
249	Cal Ripken, Jr.	2.50
250	Tom Glavine	.10
251	Luis Polonia	.10
252	Bill Swift	.10
253	Juan Guzman	.10
254	Rickey Henderson	.50
255	Terry Mulholland	.10
256	Gary Sheffield	.30
257	Terry Steinbach	.10
258	Brett Butler	.10
259	Jason Bere	.10
260	Doug Strange	.10
261	Kent Hrbek	.10
262	Graeme Lloyd	.10
263	Lou Frazier	.10
264	Charles Nagy	.10
265	Bret Boone	.10
266	Kirk Gibson	.10
267	Kevin Brown	.15
269	Matt Williams	.35
270	Greg Gagne	.10
271	Mariano Duncan	.10
272	Jeff Russell	.10
273	Eric Davis	.10
274	Shane Mack	.10
275	Jose Vizcaino	.10
276	Jose Canseco	.40
277	Roberto Hernandez	.10
278	Royce Clayton	.10
279	Carlos Baerga	.10
280	Pete Incaviglia	.10
281	Brent Gates	.10
282	Jeromy Burnitz	.10
283	Chili Davis	.10
284	Pete Harnisch	.10
285	Alan Trammell	.10
286	Eric Anthony	.10
287	Ellis Burks	.10
288	Julio Franco	.10
289	Jack Morris	.10
290	Erik Hanson	.10
291	Chuck Finley	.10
292	Reggie Jefferson	.10
293	Kevin McReynolds	.10
294	Greg Hibbard	.10
295	Travis Fryman	.10
296	Craig Biggio	.10
297	Kenny Rogers	.10
298	Dave Henderson	.10
299	Jim Thome	.10
300	Rene Arocha	.10
301	Pedro Munoz	.10
302	David Hulse	.10
303	Greg Vaughn	.10
304	Darren Lewis	.10
305	Deion Sanders	.10
306	Danny Tartabull	.10
307	Darryl Hamilton	.10
308	Andujar Cedeno	.10
309	Tim Salmon	.30
310	Tony Fernandez	.10
311	Alex Fernandez	.10
312	Roberto Kelly	.10
313	Harold Reynolds	.10
314	Chris Sabo	.10
315	Howard Johnson	.10
316	Mark Portugal	.10
317	Rafael Palmeiro	.30
318	Pete Smith	.10
319	Will Clark	.30
320	Henry Rodriguez	.10
321	Omar Vizquel	.10
322	David Segui	.10
323	Lou Whitaker	.10
324	Felix Fermin	.10
325	Spike Owen	.10
326	Darryl Kile	.10
327	Chad Kreuter	.10
328	Rod Beck	.10
329	Eddie Murray	.45
330	B.J. Surhoff	.10
331	Mickey Tettleton	.10
332	Pedro Martinez	.60
333	Roger Pavlik	.10
334	Eddie Taubensee	.10
335	John Doherty	.10
336	Jody Reed	.10
337	Aaron Sele	.10
338	Leo Gomez	.10
339	Dave Nilsson	.10
340	Rob Dibble	.10
341	John Burkett	.10
342	Wayne Kirby	.10
343	Dan Wilson	.10
344	Armando Reynoso	.10
345	Chad Curtis	.10
346	Dennis Martinez	.10
347	Cal Eldred	.10
348	Luis Gonzalez	.25
349	Doug Drabek	.10
350	Jim Leyritz	.10
351	Mark Langston	.10
352	Darrin Jackson	.10
353	Sid Fernandez	.10
354	Benito Santiago	.10
355	Kevin Seitzer	.10
356	Bo Jackson	.15
357	David Wells	.10
358	Paul Sorrento	.10
359	Ken Caminiti	.10
360	Eduardo Perez	.10
361	Orlando Merced	.10
362	Steve Finley	.10
363	Andy Benes	.10
364	Manuel Lee	.10
365	Todd Benzinger	.10
366	Sandy Alomar Jr.	.10
367	Rex Hudler	.10
368	Mike Henneman	.10
369	Vince Coleman	.10
370	Kirt Manwaring	.10
371	Ken Hill	.10
372	Glenallen Hill	.10
373	Sean Berry	.10
374	Geronimo Berroa	.10
375	Duane Ward	.10
376	Allen Watson	.10
377	Marc Newfield	.10
378	Dan Miceli	.10
379	Denny Hocking	.10
380	Mark Kiefer	.10
381	Tony Tarasco	.10
382	Tony Longmire	.10
383	*Brian Anderson*	.40
384	Fernando Vina	.10
385	Hector Carrasco	.10
386	Mike Kelly	.10
387	Greg Colbrunn	.10
388	Roger Salkeld	.10
389	Steve Trachsel	.10
390	Rich Becker	.10
391	*Billy Taylor*	.10
392	Rich Rowland	.10
393	Carl Everett	.15
394	Johnny Ruffin	.10
395	*Keith Lockhart*	.10
396	J.R. Phillips	.10
397	Sterling Hitchcock	.10
398	Jorge Fabregas	.10
399	Jeff Granger	.10
400	*Eddie Zambrano*	.10
401	*Rikkert Faneyte*	.10
402	Gerald Williams	.10
403	Joey Hamilton	.10
404	*Joe Hall*	.10
405	*John Hudek*	.10
406	Roberto Petagine	.10
407	Charles Johnson	.10
408	Mark Smith	.10
409	Jeff Juden	.10
410	*Carlos Pulido*	.10
411	Paul Shuey	.10
412	Rob Butler	.10
413	Mark Acre	.10
414	Greg Pirkl	.10
415	Melvin Nieves	.10
416	*Tim Hyers*	.10
417	N.L. checklist	.10
418	N.L. checklist	.10
419	A.L. checklist	.10
420	A.L. checklist	.10

1994 Select Crown Contenders

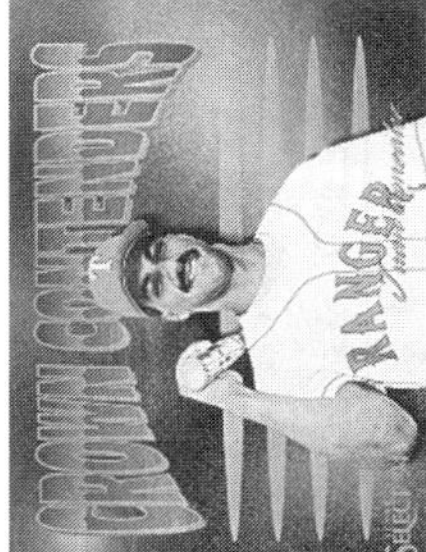

Candidates for the major baseball annual awards are featured in this subset. Horizontal-format cards have a color player photo printed on a holographic foil background. Backs are vertically oriented with a player portrait photo and justification for the player's inclusion in the set. Cards are numbered with a "CC" prefix and feature a special optical-variable anti-counterfeiting device at bottom-center. According to stated odds of one card on average in every 24 packs it has been estimated that fewer than 12,000 of each Crown Contenders card was produced.

		MT
Complete Set (10):		20.00
Common Player:		.50
1	Len Dykstra	.50
2	Greg Maddux	2.50
3	Roger Clemens	2.50
4	Randy Johnson	2.00
5	Frank Thomas	2.00
6	Barry Bonds	3.00
7	Juan Gonzalez	2.00
8	John Olerud	.50
9	Mike Piazza	4.00
10	Ken Griffey, Jr.	5.00

1994 Select MVP

Paul Molitor was the 1994 Select MVP and is featured in this one card set. Molitor is pictured in front of three distinct foil designs across the rest of the card.

		MT
MVP1	Paul Molitor	5.00

1994 Select Rookie of the Year

Carlos Delgado was the 1994 Select Rookie of the Year. Delgado is pictured on top of a glowing foil background with his initials in large capital letters in the background and Rookie of the Year printed across the bottom.

		MT
RY1	Carlos Delgado	4.00

1994 Select Rookie Surge

Each series of 1994 Score Select offered a

chase card set of nine top rookies. Fronts feature action photos set against a rainbow-colored metallic foil background. Backs have a portrait photo and a few words about the player. Cards are numbered with an "RS" prefix and were inserted at an average rate of one per 48 packs.

		MT
Complete Set (18):		15.00
Common Player:		.50
1	Cliff Floyd	1.00
2	Bob Hamelin	.50
3	Ryan Klesko	1.00
4	Carlos Delgado	4.00
5	Jeffrey Hammonds	.50
6	Rondell White	1.50
7	Salomon Torres	.50
8	Steve Karsay	.50
9	Javier Lopez	1.00
10	Manny Ramirez	5.00
11	Tony Tarasco	.50
12	Kurt Abbott	.50
13	Chan Ho Park	2.00
14	Rich Becker	.50
15	James Mouton	.50
16	Alex Gonzalez	1.00
17	Raul Mondesi	1.00
18	Steve Trachsel	.50

1994 Select Salute

With odds of finding one of these cards stated at one per 360 packs, it is estimated that only about 4,000 of each of this two-card chase set were produced.

		MT
Complete Set (2):		20.00
1	Cal Ripken, Jr.	15.00
2	Dave Winfield	5.00

1994 Select Skills

Select Skills is a 10-card insert that was randomly inserted into every 24 packs. Ten specific skills were designated and matched with the player whom, in the opinion of Select officials, demonstrated that particular skill the best in baseball. Each card is printed on a foil background with the player name running along the lower right side of the card and the skill that they are being featured for along the bottom.

		MT
Complete Set (10):		15.00
Common Player:		1.00
1	Randy Johnson	3.00
2	Barry Larkin	1.00
3	Len Dykstra	1.00
4	Kenny Lofton	1.00
5	Juan Gonzalez	3.00
6	Barry Bonds	5.00
7	Marquis Grissom	1.00
8	Ivan Rodriguez	3.00
9	Larry Walker	1.50
10	Travis Fryman	1.00

1995 Select Samples

Pinnacle's hobby-only Select brand issue for 1995 was previewed with this four-card cello-packed sample set. Three player cards are in the basic format of the regular-issue Select cards, except they have a large white "SAMPLE" printed diagonally across the front and back. The fourth card in the sample pack is a header card advertising the features of the issue.

		MT
Complete Set (4):		6.00
Common Player:		1.50
34	Roberto Alomar	1.50
37	Jeff Bagwell	2.00
241	Alex Rodriguez	4.00
--	Header card	.05

1995 Select

The 250 regular-issue cards in Pinnacle's mid-price brand feature three basic formats. Veteran players' cards are presented horizontally and feature an action photo at left. At right is a portrait in a trapezoidal gold-foil frame set against a team color-coordinated marbled background. The team logo beneath the portrait and the player's name below that are printed in gold foil. Backs feature a black-and-white photo with a few career highlights, 1994 and career stats, and a "Select Stat" printed in red. The colored marble effect is carried over from the front. The Select Rookie cards which are grouped toward the end of the set are vertical in format and feature a borderless player photo with a gold-foil band at bottom which includes the player name and team logo, along with waves of gold emanating from the logo. Backs have a small, narrow color photo at left, with a large sepia version of the same photo ghosted at center and overprinted with a career summary. At bottom are 1994 and career stats. Ending the set are a series of "Show Time" cards of top prospects. Cards feature large gold-foil "Show Time" and team logos at bottom, with a facsimile autograph printed above. The player photo is shown as if at a curtain raising, with spotlight effects behind. Backs repeat the curtain and spotlight motif and feature another player photo, with autograph above. Production of this hobby-only product was stated as 4,950 cases, which translates to about 110,000 of each regular-issue card. A special card (#251) of Hideo Nomo was added to the set later. It was not issued in foil packs, but distributed to dealers who had purchased Select cases.

		MT
Complete Set (251):		10.00
Common Player:		.10
Pack (12):		1.00
Wax Box (24):		15.00
1	Cal Ripken Jr.	1.50
2	Robin Ventura	.10
3	Al Martin	.10
4	Jeff Frye	.10
5	Darryl Strawberry	.10
6	Chan Ho Park	.25
7	Steve Avery	.10
8	Bret Boone	.10
9	Danny Tartabull	.10
10	Dante Bichette	.10
11	Rondell White	.15
12	Dave McCarty	.10
13	Bernard Gilkey	.10
14	Mark McGwire	1.50
15	Ruben Sierra	.10
16	Wade Boggs	.50
17	Mike Piazza	1.25
18	Jeffrey Hammonds	.10
19	Mike Mussina	.35
20	Darryl Kile	.10
21	Greg Maddux	.75
22	Frank Thomas	1.00
23	Kevin Appier	.10
24	Jay Bell	.10
25	Kirk Gibson	.10
26	Pat Hentgen	.10
27	Joey Hamilton	.10
28	Bernie Williams	.30
29	Aaron Sele	.10
30	Delino DeShields	.10
31	Danny Bautista	.10
32	Jim Thome	.10
33	Rikkert Faneyte	.10
34	Roberto Alomar	.40
35	Paul Molitor	.40
36	Allen Watson	.10
37	Jeff Bagwell	.50
38	Jay Buhner	.10
39	Marquis Grissom	.10
40	Jim Edmonds	.15
41	Ryan Klesko	.10
42	Fred McGriff	.10
43	Tony Tarasco	.10
44	Darren Daulton	.10
45	Marc Newfield	.10
46	Barry Bonds	1.00
47	Bobby Bonilla	.10
48	Greg Pirkl	.10
49	Steve Karsay	.10
50	Bob Hamelin	.10
51	Javier Lopez	.10
52	Barry Larkin	.10
53	Kevin Young	.10
54	Sterling Hitchcock	.10
55	Tom Glavine	.10
56	Carlos Delgado	.25
57	Darren Oliver	.10
58	Cliff Floyd	.10
59	Tim Salmon	.20
60	Albert Belle	.25
61	Salomon Torres	.10
62	Gary Sheffield	.30
63	Ivan Rodriguez	.40
64	Charles Nagy	.10
65	Eduardo Perez	.10
66	Terry Steinbach	.10
67	Dave Justice	.25
68	Jason Bere	.10
69	Dave Nilsson	.10
70	Brian Anderson	.10
71	Billy Ashley	.10
72	Roger Clemens	.75
73	Jimmy Key	.10
74	Wally Joyner	.10
75	Andy Benes	.10
76	Ray Lankford	.10
77	Jeff Kent	.10
78	Moises Alou	.15
79	Kirby Puckett	.75
80	Joe Carter	.10
81	Manny Ramirez	.50
82	J.R. Phillips	.10
83	Matt Mieske	.10
84	John Olerud	.10
85	Andres Galarraga	.10

86	Juan Gonzalez	.50
87	Pedro Martinez	.45
88	Dean Palmer	.10
89	Ken Griffey Jr.	1.50
90	Brian Jordan	.10
91	Hal Morris	.10
92	Lenny Dykstra	.10
93	Wil Cordero	.10
94	Tony Gwynn	.75
95	Alex Gonzalez	.10
96	Cecil Fielder	.10
97	Mo Vaughn	.30
98	John Valentin	.10
99	Will Clark	.25
100	Geronimo Pena	.10
101	Don Mattingly	1.00
102	Charles Johnson	.10
103	Raul Mondesi	.15
104	Reggie Sanders	.10
105	Royce Clayton	.10
106	Reggie Jefferson	.10
107	Craig Biggio	.10
108	Jack McDowell	.10
109	James Mouton	.10
110	Mike Greenwell	.10
111	David Cone	.10
112	Matt Williams	.25
113	Garret Anderson	.10
114	Carlos Garcia	.10
115	Alex Fernandez	.10
116	Deion Sanders	.10
117	Chili Davis	.10
118	Mike Kelly	.10
119	Jeff Conine	.10
120	Kenny Lofton	.10
121	Rafael Palmeiro	.20
122	Chuck Knoblauch	.10
123	Ozzie Smith	.75
124	Carlos Baerga	.10
125	Brett Butler	.10
126	Sammy Sosa	1.00
127	Ellis Burks	.10
128	Bret Saberhagen	.10
129	Doug Drabek	.10
130	Dennis Martinez	.10
131	Paul O'Neill	.10
132	Travis Fryman	.10
133	Brent Gates	.10
134	Rickey Henderson	.40
135	Randy Johnson	.45
136	Mark Langston	.10
137	Greg Colbrunn	.10
138	Jose Rijo	.10
139	Bryan Harvey	.10
140	Dennis Eckersley	.10
141	Ron Gant	.10
142	Carl Everett	.10
143	Jeff Granger	.10
144	Ben McDonald	.10
145	Kurt Abbott	.10
146	Jim Abbott	.10
147	Jason Jacome	.10
148	Rico Brogna	.10
149	Cal Eldred	.10
150	Rich Becker	.10
151	Pete Harnisch	.10
152	Roberto Petagine	.10
153	Jacob Brumfield	.10
154	Todd Hundley	.15
155	Roger Cedeno	.10
156	Harold Baines	.10
157	Steve Dunn	.10
158	Tim Belk	.10
159	Marty Cardova	.10
160	Russ Davis	.10
161	Jose Malave	.10
162	Brian Hunter	.10
163	Andy Pettitte	.15
164	Brooks Kieschnick	.10
165	Midre Cummings	.10
166	Frank Rodriguez	.10
167	Chad Mottola	.10
168	Brian Barber	.10
169	Tim Unroe	.10
170	Shane Andrews	.10
171	Kevin Flora	.10
172	Ray Durham	.10
173	Chipper Jones	1.25
174	Butch Huskey	.10
175	Ray McDavid	.10
176	Jeff Cirillo	.10
177	Terry Pendleton	.10
178	Scott Ruffcorn	.10
179	Ray Holbert	.10
180	Joe Randa	.10
181	Jose Oliva	.10
182	Andy Van Slyke	.10
183	Albie Lopez	.10
184	Chad Curtis	.10
185	Ozzie Guillen	.10
186	Chad Ogea	.10
187	Dan Wilson	.10
188	Tony Fernandez	.10
189	John Smoltz	.10
190	Willie Greene	.10
191	Darren Lewis	.10
192	Orlando Miller	.10
193	Kurt Miller	.10
194	Andrew Lorraine	.10
195	Ernie Young	.10
196	Jimmy Haynes	.10
197	*Raul Casanova*	.15
198	Joe Vitiello	.10
199	Brad Woodall	.10
200	Juan Acevedo	.10
201	Michael Tucker	.10
202	Shawn Green	.25
203	Alex Rodriguez	1.50
204	Julian Tavarez	.10
205	Jose Lima	.10
206	Wilson Alvarez	.10
207	Rich Aude	.10
208	Armando Benitez	.10
209	Dwayne Hosey	.10
210	Gabe White	.10
211	Joey Eischen	.10
212	Bill Pulsipher	.10
213	Robby Thompson	.10
214	Toby Borland	.10
215	Rusty Greer	.10
216	Fausto Cruz	.10
217	Luis Ortiz	.10
218	Duane Singleton	.10
219	Troy Percival	.10
220	Gregg Jefferies	.10
221	Mark Grace	.25
222	Mickey Tettleton	.10
223	Phil Plantier	.10
224	Larry Walker	.25
225	Ken Caminiti	.10
226	Dave Winfield	.50
227	Brady Anderson	.10
228	Kevin Brown	.15
229	Andujar Cedeno	.10
230	Roberto Kelly	.10
231	Jose Canseco	.35
231	(Scott Ruffcorn) (Showtime)	.10
232	Billy Ashley (Showtime)	.10
234	J.R. Phillips (Showtime)	.10
235	Chipper Jones (Showtime)	.60
236	Charles Johnson (Showtime)	.10
237	Midre Cummings (Showtime)	.10
238	Brian Hunter (Showtime)	.10
239	Garret Anderson (Showtime)	.10
240	Shawn Green (Showtime)	.20
241	Alex Rodriguez (Showtime)	.75
242	Checklist #1 (Frank Thomas)	.40
243	Checklist #2 (Ken Griffey Jr.)	.50
244	Checklist #3 (Albert Belle)	.20
245	Checklist #4 (Cal Ripken Jr.)	.50
246	Checklist #5 (Barry Bonds)	.40
247	Checklist #6 (Raul Mondesi)	.10
248	Checklist #7 (Mike Piazza)	.40
249	Checklist #8 (Jeff Bagwell)	.25
250	Checklist #9 (Jeff Bagwell, Frank Thomas, Ken Griffey Jr., Mike Piazza)	.35
251	Hideo Nomo	1.00

1995 Select Artist's Proofs

Among the scarcest and most valuable of 1995's baseball card inserts are the Select Artist's Proof parallel set. While an AP card is found on average once per 24 packs, the limited print run of the basic Select set means that only about 475 of each of the 250 regular-issue cards in the Select set were made in this edition. The AP inserts have a gold-foil "ARTIST'S PROOF" line at bottom, and other gold-foil highlights are embossed, rather than merely stamped on, as on regular Select cards.

	MT
Complete Set (250):	300.00
Common Player:	1.50
AP Stars:	12X

(See 1995 Select for checklist and base card values.)

1995 Select Big Sticks

With fronts printed in what Pinnacle describes as "holographic Gold Rush technology," the Big Sticks chase card issue offers a dozen of the game's big hitters in action photos superimposed over their team logo. Conventionally printed backs have another player photo, along with a summary of career highlights and description of the player's power potential. Stated odds of pulling a Big Sticks chase card are one per 48 packs, on average. Cards are numbered with a "BS" prefix.

		MT
Complete Set (12):		35.00
Common Player:		1.50
1	Frank Thomas	4.00
2	Ken Griffey Jr.	7.50
3	Cal Ripken Jr.	7.50
4	Mike Piazza	6.00
5	Don Mattingly	5.00
6	Will Clark	1.50
7	Tony Gwynn	3.00
8	Jeff Bagwell	2.00
9	Barry Bonds	4.00
10	Paul Molitor	2.00
11	Matt Williams	1.50
12	Albert Belle	2.00

1995 Select Can't Miss

A mix of rookies and sophomore standouts, along with a few players of slightly longer service are presented in this chase set. Cards feature color player action photos printed on a metallic red background, with their last name in gold foil at lower-left. An umpire on the "Can't Miss" logo is at upper-left. Backs repeat the logo, have a tall, narrow player photo, a few biographical details and a paragraph of career summary. Cards are numbered with a "CM" prefix.

		MT
Complete Set (12):		20.00
Common Player:		.50
1	Cliff Floyd	.75
2	Ryan Klesko	.50
3	Charles Johnson	.60
4	Raul Mondesi	.75
5	Manny Ramirez	3.00
6	Billy Ashley	.50
7	Alex Gonzalez	.75
8	Carlos Delgado	1.00
9	Garret Anderson	.75
10	Alex Rodriguez	6.50
11	Chipper Jones	5.00
12	Shawn Green	1.00

1995 Select Sure Shots

Ten of Select's picks for future stardom are featured in this chase set, the toughest find of any of the 1995 Select inserts, at an average rate of one per 90 packs. Card fronts feature player action photos set against a gold "Dufex" foil printed background with a Sure Shots logo vertically at left. Backs have a blue background with a few words about the player and a portrait photo at left. Cards are numbered with a "SS" prefix.

		MT
Complete Set (10):		4.00
Common Player:		.25
1	Ben Grieve	2.00
2	Kevin Witt	.25
3	Mark Farris	.25
4	Paul Konerko	1.00
5	Dustin Hermanson	.35
6	Ramon Castro	.25
7	McKay Christensen	.25
8	Brian Buchanan	.25
9	Paul Wilson	.25
10	Terrence Long	.50

1995 Select Certified Samples

Pinnacle's hobby-only Select brand issue for 1995 was previewed with this four-card cello-packed sample set. Three player cards are in the basic format of the regular-issue Select cards, except they have a large which "SAMPLE" printed diagonally across the front and back. The fourth card in the sample pack is a header card advertising the features of the issue.

		MT
Complete Set (8):		16.00
Common Player:		1.00
2	Reggie Sanders	1.00
10	Mo Vaughn	2.00
39	Mike Piazza	3.50
50	Mark McGwire	4.50
75	Roberto Alomar	2.00
89	Larry Walker	2.00
110	Ray Durham	1.00
3 of 12	Cal Ripken Jr. (Gold Team)	4.50

1995 Select Certified

The concepts of hobby-only distribution and limited production which were the hallmarks of Pinnacle's Select brand were carried a step further with the post-season release of Select Certified baseball. Printed on double-thich cardboard stock card fronts feature all metallic-foil printing protected by a double laminated gloss coat. Backs have key player stats against each team in the league. The final 44 cards in the set are distinguished with a special Rookie logo and with gold added to the silver foil in the photo background.

		MT
Complete Set (135):		20.00
Common Player:		.10
Pack (6):		2.50
Wax Box (20):		45.00
1	Barry Bonds	2.50
2	Reggie Sanders	.10
3	Terry Steinbach	.10
4	Eduardo Perez	.10
5	Frank Thomas	2.50
6	Wil Cordero	.10
7	John Olerud	.10
8	Deion Sanders	.10
9	Mike Mussina	1.00
10	Mo Vaughn	.75
11	Will Clark	.30
12	Chili Davis	.10
13	Jimmy Key	.10
14	Eddie Murray	.75
15	Bernard Gilkey	.10
16	David Cone	.10
17	Tim Salmon	.30
18	(Not issued, see #2131)	
19	Steve Ontiveros	.10
20	Andres Galarraga	.10
21	Don Mattingly	2.50
22	Kevin Appier	.10
23	Paul Molitor	.75
24	Edgar Martinez	.10
25	Andy Benes	.10
26	Rafael Palmeiro	.35
27	Barry Larkin	.10
28	Gary Sheffield	.35
29	Wally Joyner	.10
30	Wade Boggs	.65
31	Rico Brogna	.10
32	Eddie Murray (Murray Tribute)	.40
33	Kirby Puckett	2.00
34	Bobby Bonilla	.10
35	Hal Morris	.10
36	Moises Alou	.15
37	Javier Lopez	.10
38	Chuck Knoblauch	.10
39	Mike Piazza	3.00
40	Travis Fryman	.10
41	Rickey Henderson	.50
42	Jim Thome	.10
43	Carlos Baerga	.10
44	Dean Palmer	.10
45	Kirk Gibson	.10
46	Bret Saberhagen	.10
47	Cecil Fielder	.10
48	Manny Ramirez	1.50
49	Derek Bell	.10
50	Mark McGwire	4.00
51	Jim Edmonds	.10
52	Robin Ventura	.10
53	Ryan Klesko	.10
54	Jeff Bagwell	1.50
55	Ozzie Smith	2.00
56	Albert Belle	.30
57	Darren Daulton	.10
58	Jeff Conine	.10
59	Greg Maddux	2.00
60	Lenny Dykstra	.10
61	Randy Johnson	1.50
62	Fred McGriff	.10
63	Ray Lankford	.10
64	Dave Justice	.40
65	Paul O'Neill	.10
66	Tony Gwynn	2.00
67	Matt Williams	.30
68	Dante Bichette	.10
69	Craig Biggio	.10
70	Ken Griffey Jr.	3.00
71	J.T. Snow	.10
72	Cal Ripken Jr.	4.00
73	Jay Bell	.10
74	Joe Carter	.10
75	Roberto Alomar	1.00
76	Benji Gil	.10
77	Ivan Rodriguez	1.00
78	Raul Mondesi	.25
79	Cliff Floyd	.10
80	Eric Karros, Mike Piazza, Raul Mondesi (Dodger Dynasty)	.60
81	Royce Clayton	.10
82	Billy Ashley	.10
83	Joey Hamilton	.10
84	Sammy Sosa	2.50
85	Jason Bere	.10
86	Dennis Martinez	.10
87	Greg Vaughn	.10
88	Roger Clemens	2.00
89	Larry Walker	.40
90	Mark Grace	.40
91	Kenny Lofton	.10
92	*Carlos Perez*	.10
93	Roger Cedeno	.10
94	Scott Ruffcorn	.10
95	Jim Pittsley	.10
96	Andy Pettitte	.30
97	James Baldwin	.10
98	*Hideo Nomo*	3.00
99	Ismael Valdes	.10
100	Armando Benitez	.10
101	Jose Malave	.10
102	*Bobby Higginson*	1.50
103	LaTroy Hawkins	.10
104	Russ Davis	.10
105	Shawn Green	.35
106	Joe Vitiello	.10
107	Chipper Jones	3.00
108	Shane Andrews	.10
109	Jose Oliva	.10
110	Ray Durham	.10
111	Jon Nunnally	.10
112	Alex Gonzalez	.10
113	Vaughn Eshelman	.10
114	Marty Cordova	.10
115	*Mark Grudzielanek*	.50
116	Brian Hunter	.10
117	Charles Johnson	.10
118	Alex Rodriguez	3.50
119	David Bell	.10
120	Todd Hollandsworth	.10
121	Joe Randa	.10
122	Derek Jeter	3.00
123	Frank Rodriguez	.10
124	Curtis Goodwin	.10
125	Bill Pulsipher	.10
126	John Mabry	.10
127	Julian Tavarez	.10
128	Edgardo Alfonzo	.10
129	Orlando Miller	.10
130	Juan Acevedo	.10
131	Jeff Cirillo	.10
132	Roberto Petagine	.10
133	Antonio Osuna	.10
134	Michael Tucker	.10
135	Garret Anderson	.10
2131	Cal Ripken Jr. (Consecutive Game Record)	2.50

1995 Select Certified Mirror Gold

Inserted at an average rate of one per nine packs, this parallel set is a gold-foil version of the regular Select Certified set. Backs have a "MIRROR GOLD" notation at bottom.

	MT
Complete Set (135):	250.00
Common Player:	1.50
Mirror Gold Stars:	7X

(See 1995 Select Certified for checklist and base card values.)

1995 Select Certified Checklists

The seven checklists issued with Select Certified are not numbered as part of the set. They are found one per foil pack and are printed on much thinner card stock than the regular-issue cards.

		MT
Complete Set (7):		2.00
Common Player:		.35
1	Ken Griffey Jr. (A.L., #3-41)	.65
2	Frank Thomas (A.L., #42-95)	.50
3	Cal Ripken Jr. (A.L., #96-135)	.65
4	Jeff Bagwell (N.L., #1-58)	.40
5	Mike Piazza (N.L., #59-92)	.50
6	Barry Bonds (N.L., #93-133)	.50
7	Manny Ramirez, Raul Mondesi (Chase cards)	.40

1995 Select Certified Future

A striking new all-metal, brushed-foil printing technology was used in the production of this chase set of 10 rookie players with "unlimited future potential." Stated odds of finding a Certified Future insert card were one in 19 packs.

		MT
Complete Set (10):		20.00
Common Player:		.75
1	Chipper Jones	5.00
2	Curtis Goodwin	.75
3	Hideo Nomo	2.50
4	Shawn Green	2.50
5	Ray Durham	1.00
6	Todd Hollandsworth	.75
7	Brian Hunter	.75
8	Carlos Delgado	2.50
9	Michael Tucker	.75
10	Alex Rodriguez	7.50

1995 Select Certified Gold Team

A dozen of the top position players in the league were selected for appearance in this insert set. Cards are printed in a special double-sided, all-gold Dufex technology. An action photo is featured on the front, a portrait on back. Odds of picking a Gold Team card were stated as one in 41 packs.

		MT
Complete Set (12):		65.00
Common Player:		2.50
1	Ken Griffey Jr.	12.00
2	Frank Thomas	8.00
3	Cal Ripken Jr.	12.00
4	Jeff Bagwell	6.50
5	Mike Piazza	10.00
6	Barry Bonds	7.00
7	Matt Williams	2.50
8	Don Mattingly	7.50
9	Will Clark	2.50
10	Tony Gwynn	7.00
11	Kirby Puckett	7.50
12	Jose Canseco	2.50

1995 Select Certified Potential Unlimited

Dufex printing with textured foil highlights and transparent inks is featured in this chase set which was produced in an edition of no more the 1,975 sets, as witnessed by the numbering on card backs. Approximate odds of finding a Potential Unlimited card are one per 29 packs. A super-scarce edition of 903 cards each featuring "microetch" foil printing technology was issued at the rate of one per 70 packs.

		MT
Complete Set (20):		70.00
Common Player:		2.00
903s:		1.5X
1	Cliff Floyd	2.00
2	Manny Ramirez	10.00
3	Raul Mondesi	2.50
4	Scott Ruffcorn	2.00
5	Billy Ashley	2.00
6	Alex Gonzalez	3.00
7	Midre Cummings	2.00
8	Charles Johnson	2.00
9	Garret Anderson	2.00
10	Hideo Nomo	7.50
11	Chipper Jones	15.00
12	Curtis Goodwin	2.00
13	Frank Rodriguez	2.00
14	Shawn Green	4.00
15	Ray Durham	2.00
16	Todd Hollandsworth	2.00
17	Brian Hunter	2.00
18	Carlos Delgado	3.50
19	Michael Tucker	2.00
20	Alex Rodriguez	20.00

1996 Select

Select's 1996 baseball set has 200 cards in it, including 35 rookies, five checklists and 10 Lineup Leaders subset cards. All 200 cards are also reprinted as part of an Artist's Proof parallel set, using a holographic Artist's Proof logo. Cards were seeded one per every 35 packs; there were approximately 435 sets produced. Three insert sets were also created: Claim to Fame, En Fuego and Team Nucleus.

		MT
Complete Set (200):		10.00
Common Player:		.10
Pack (10):		1.00
Wax Box (24):		20.00
1	Wade Boggs	.50
2	Shawn Green	.20
3	Andres Galarraga	.10
4	Bill Pulsipher	.10
5	Chuck Knoblauch	.10
6	Ken Griffey Jr.	2.25
7	Greg Maddux	1.25
8	Manny Ramirez	1.00
9	Ivan Rodriguez	.50
10	Tim Salmon	.25
11	Frank Thomas	1.50
12	Jeff Bagwell	1.00
13	Travis Fryman	.10
14	Kenny Lofton	.10
15	Matt Williams	.25
16	Jay Bell	.10
17	Ken Caminiti	.10
18	Ray Lankford	.10
19	Cal Ripken Jr.	2.50
20	Roger Clemens	1.00
21	Carlos Baerga	.10
22	Mike Piazza	2.00
23	Gregg Jefferies	.10
24	Reggie Sanders	.10
25	Rondell White	.15
26	Sammy Sosa	1.50
27	Kevin Appier	.10
28	Kevin Seitzer	.10
29	Gary Sheffield	.30
30	Mike Mussina	.40
31	Mark McGwire	2.50
32	Barry Larkin	.10
33	Marc Newfield	.10
34	Ismael Valdes	.10
35	Marty Cordova	.10
36	Albert Belle	.30
37	Johnny Damon	.25
38	Garret Anderson	.10
39	Cecil Fielder	.10
40	John Mabry	.10
41	Chipper Jones	2.00
42	Omar Vizquel	.10
43	Jose Rijo	.10
44	Charles Johnson	.10
45	Alex Rodriquez	2.25
46	Rico Brogna	.10
47	Joe Carter	.10
48	Mo Vaughn	.40
49	Moises Alou	.15
50	Raul Mondesi	.25
51	Robin Ventura	.10
52	Jim Thome	.10
53	Dave Justice	.20
54	Jeff King	.10
55	Brian Hunter	.10
56	Juan Gonzalez	.75
57	John Olerud	.10
58	Rafael Palmeiro	.20
59	Tony Gwynn	1.25
60	Eddie Murray	.45
61	Jason Isringhausen	.10
62	Dante Bichette	.10
63	Randy Johnson	.45
64	Kirby Puckett	1.25
65	Jim Edmonds	.10
66	David Cone	.10
67	Ozzie Smith	.75
68	Fred McGriff	.10
69	Darren Daulton	.10
70	Edgar Martinez	.10
71	J.T. Snow	.10
72	Butch Huskey	.10
73	Hideo Nomo	.40
74	Pedro Martinez	.35
75	Bobby Bonilla	.10
76	Jeff Conine	.10
77	Ryan Klesko	.10
78	Bernie Williams	.30
79	Andre Dawson	.20
80	Trevor Hoffman	.10
81	Mark Grace	.20
82	Benji Gil	.10
83	Eric Karros	.10
84	Pete Schourek	.10
85	Edgardo Alfonzo	.10
86	Jay Buhner	.10
87	Vinny Castilla	.10
88	Bret Boone	.10
89	Ray Durham	.10
90	Brian Jordan	.10
91	Jose Canseco	.35
92	Paul O'Neill	.10
93	Chili Davis	.10
94	Tom Glavine	.10
95	Julian Tavarez	.10
96	Derek Bell	.10
97	Will Clark	.25
98	Larry Walker	.25
99	Denny Neagle	.10
100	Alex Fernandez	.10
101	Barry Bonds	1.25
102	Ben McDonald	.10
103	Andy Pettitte	.35
104	Tino Martinez	.10
105	Sterling Hitchcock	.10
106	Royce Clayton	.10
107	Jim Abbott	.10
108	Rickey Henderson	.50
109	Ramon Martinez	.10
110	Paul Molitor	.40
111	Dennis Eckersley	.10
112	Alex Gonzalez	.10
113	Marquis Grissom	.10
114	Greg Vaughn	.10
115	Lance Johnson	.10
116	Todd Stottlemyre	.10
117	Jack McDowell	.10
118	Ruben Sierra	.10
119	Brady Anderson	.10
120	Julio Franco	.10
121	Brooks Kieshnick	.10
122	Roberto Alomar	.50
123	Greg Gagne	.10
124	Wally Joyner	.10
125	John Smoltz	.10
126	John Valentin	.10
127	Russ Davis	.10
128	Joe Vitiello	.10
129	Shawon Dunston	.10
130	Frank Rodriguez	.10
131	Charlie Hayes	.10
132	Andy Benes	.10
133	B.J. Surhoff	.10
134	Dave Nilsson	.10
135	Carlos Delgado	.30
136	Walt Weiss	.10
137	Mike Stanley	.10
138	Greg Colbrunn	.10
139	Mike Kelly	.10
140	Ryne Sandberg	.75
141	Lee Smith	.10
142	Dennis Martinez	.10
143	Bernard Gilkey	.10
144	Lenny Dykstra	.10
145	Danny Tartabull	.10
146	Dean Palmer	.10
147	Craig Biggio	.10
148	Juan Acevedo	.10
149	Michael Tucker	.10
150	Bobby Higginson	.10
151	Ken Griffey Jr. (Line Up Leaders)	1.00
152	Frank Thomas (Line Up Leaders)	.65
153	Cal Ripken Jr. (Line Up Leaders)	1.00
154	Albert Belle (Line Up Leaders)	.15
155	Mike Piazza (Line Up Leaders)	.75
156	Barry Bonds (Line Up Leaders)	.65

157	Sammy Sosa (Line Up Leaders)	.75
158	Mo Vaughn (Line Up Leaders)	.20
159	Greg Maddux (Line Up Leaders)	.65
160	Jeff Bagwell (Line Up Leaders)	.40
161	Derek Jeter	2.00
162	Paul Wilson	.10
163	Chris Snopek	.10
164	Jason Schmidt	.10
165	Jimmy Haynes	.10
166	George Arias	.10
167	Steve Gibralter	.10
168	Bob Wolcott	.10
169	Jason Kendall	.10
170	Greg Zaun	.10
171	Quinton McCracken	.10
172	Alan Benes	.10
173	Rey Ordonez	.10
174	Ugueth Urbina	.10
175	*Osvaldo Fernandez*	.20
176	Marc Barcelo	.10
177	Sal Fasano	.10
178	*Mike Grace*	.10
179	Chan Ho Park	.30
180	Robert Perez	.10
181	Todd Hollandsworth	.10
182	*Wilton Guerrero*	.25
183	John Wasdin	.10
184	Jim Pittsley	.10
185	LaTroy Hawkins	.10
186	Jay Powell	.10
187	Felipe Crespo	.10
188	Jermaine Dye	.10
189	Bob Abreu	.10
190	*Matt Luke*	.10
191	Richard Hidalgo	.10
192	Karim Garcia	.10
193	Tavo Alvarez	.10
194	*Andy Fox*	.10
195	Terrell Wade	.10
196	Frank Thomas (checklist)	.50
197	Ken Griffey Jr. (checklist)	.75
198	Greg Maddux (checklist)	.60
199	Mike Piazza (checklist)	.60
200	Cal Ripken Jr. (checklist)	.75

1996 Select Artist's Proofs

Approximately once per 35 packs, a card from this parallel chase set is encountered among 1996 Select. Reported production was 435 sets. The Artist's Proof cards are distinguished by a holographic logo testifying to their status on the front of the card.

	MT
Complete Set (200):	300.00
Common Player:	1.00
AP Stars:	15X

(See 1996 Select for checklist and base card values.)

1996 Select Claim to Fame

Twenty different stars are featured on these 1996 Select insert cards. Each card is numbered "1 of 2100" and uses an external die-cut design. The cards were seeded one per every 72 packs.

		MT
Complete Set (20):		85.00
Common Player:		1.00
1	Cal Ripken Jr.	12.50
2	Greg Maddux	6.00
3	Ken Griffey Jr.	12.00
4	Frank Thomas	7.50
5	Mo Vaughn	2.50
6	Albert Belle	1.50
7	Jeff Bagwell	4.00
8	Sammy Sosa	7.50
8s	Sammy Sosa (overprinted "SAMPLE")	5.00
9	Reggie Sanders	1.00
10	Hideo Nomo	3.50
11	Chipper Jones	9.00
12	Mike Piazza	9.00
13	Matt Williams	1.50
14	Tony Gwynn	6.00
15	Johnny Damon	1.50
16	Dante Bichette	1.00
17	Kirby Puckett	6.00
18	Barry Bonds	7.00
19	Randy Johnson	4.00
20	Eddie Murray	3.00

1996 Select En Fuego

ESPN announcer Dan Patrick is featured on his own card in this set, inspired by his Sportscenter catch phrase "en fuego," which means "on fire." Patrick's teammate, Keith Olberman, wrote the card backs. The 25 cards, printed on all-foil Dufex stock, are seeded one per every 48 packs of 1996 Select baseball.

		MT
Complete Set (25):		90.00
Common Player:		1.50
1	Ken Griffey Jr.	9.00
2	Frank Thomas	6.50
3	Cal Ripken Jr.	10.00
4	Greg Maddux	6.00
5	Jeff Bagwell	5.00
6	Barry Bonds	6.50
7	Mo Vaughn	2.50
8	Albert Belle	2.50
9	Sammy Sosa	6.50
10	Reggie Sanders	1.50
11	Mike Piazza	7.50
12	Chipper Jones	7.50
13	Tony Gwynn	6.00
14	Kirby Puckett	6.00
15	Wade Boggs	3.50
16	Dan Patrick	1.50
17	Gary Sheffield	2.00
18	Dante Bichette	1.50
19	Randy Johnson	4.00
20	Matt Williams	1.50
21	Alex Rodriguez	8.50
22	Tim Salmon	2.00
23	Johnny Damon	1.50
24	Manny Ramirez	5.00
25	Hideo Nomo	3.50

1996 Select Team Nucleus

This 1996 Select insert set pays tribute to the three top players from each Major League Baseball team; each card features the three teammates on it. The cards are printed on a clear plastic, utilizing a holographic micro-etched design. They are seeded one per every 18 packs.

		MT
Complete Set (28):		100.00
Common Player:		2.00
1	Albert Belle, Manny Ramirez, Carlos Baerga	5.00
2	Ray Lankford, Brian Jordan, Ozzie Smith	4.00
3	Jay Bell, Jeff King, Denny Neagle	2.00
4	Dante Bichette, Andres Galarraga, Larry Walker	3.00
5	Mark McGwire, Mike Bordick, Terry Steinbach	10.00
6	Bernie Williams, Wade Boggs, David Cone	5.00
7	Joe Carter, Alex Gonzalez, Shawn Green	3.00
8	Roger Clemens, Mo Vaughn, Jose Canseco	5.00
9	Ken Griffey Jr., Edgar Martinez, Randy Johnson	10.00
10	Gregg Jefferies, Darren Daulton, Lenny Dykstra	2.00
11	Mike Piazza, Raul Mondesi, Hideo Nomo	9.00
12	Greg Maddux, Chipper Jones, Ryan Klesko	9.00
13	Cecil Fielder, Travis Fryman, Phil Nevin	2.00
14	Ivan Rodriguez, Will Clark, Juan Gonzalez	4.00
15	Ryne Sandberg, Sammy Sosa, Mark Grace	10.00
16	Gary Sheffield, Charles Johnson, Andre Dawson	3.00
17	Johnny Damon, Michael Tucker, Kevin Appier	2.00
18	Barry Bonds, Matt Williams, Rod Beck	4.00
19	Kirby Puckett, Chuck Knoblauch, Marty Cordova	4.00
20	Cal Ripken Jr., Bobby Bonilla, Mike Mussina	9.00
21	Jason Isringhausen, Bill Pulsipher, Rico Brogna	2.50
22	Tony Gwynn, Ken Caminiti, Marc Newfield	5.00
23	Tim Salmon, Garret Anderson, Jim Edmonds	2.50
24	Moises Alou, Rondell White, Cliff Floyd	2.50
25	Barry Larkin, Reggie Sanders, Bret Boone	2.00
26	Jeff Bagwell, Craig Biggio, Derek Bell	7.50
27	Frank Thomas, Robin Ventura, Alex Fernandez	6.00
28	John Jaha, Greg Vaughn, Kevin Seitzer	2.00

1996 Select Certified

This hobby-exclusive set has 144 cards in its regular issue, plus six parallel versions and two insert sets. The parallel sets are: Certified Red (one per five packs), Certified Blue (one per 50), Artist's Proofs (one per 12), Mirror Red (one per 100), Mirror Blue (one per 200), and Mirror Gold (one per 300). Breaking down the numbers, there are 1,800 Certified Red sets, 180 Certified Blue, 500 Artist's Proofs, 90 Mirror Red 45 Mirror Blue and 30 Mirror Gold sets. The insert sets are Interleague Preview cards and Select Few. Cards #135-144 are a "Pastime Power" subset.

		MT
Complete Set (144):		40.00
Common Player:		.20
Pack (6):		3.00
Wax Box (20):		50.00
1	Frank Thomas	1.50
2	Tino Martinez	.20
3	Gary Sheffield	.45
4	Kenny Lofton	.20
5	Joe Carter	.20
6	Alex Rodriguez	3.00
7	Chipper Jones	2.00
8	Roger Clemens	1.25
9	Jay Bell	.20
10	Eddie Murray	.60
11	Will Clark	.50
12	Mike Mussina	.85
13	Hideo Nomo	.85
14	Andres Galarraga	.20
15	Marc Newfield	.20
16	Jason Isringhausen	.20
17	Randy Johnson	.85
18	Chuck Knoblauch	.20
19	J.T. Snow	.20
20	Mark McGwire	3.50
21	Tony Gwynn	1.25
22	Albert Belle	.50
23	Gregg Jefferies	.20
24	Reggie Sanders	.20
25	Bernie Williams	.40
26	Ray Lankford	.20
27	Johnny Damon	.20
28	Ryne Sandberg	1.25
29	Rondell White	.30
30	Mike Piazza	2.00
31	Barry Bonds	1.50
32	Greg Maddux	1.25
33	Craig Biggio	.20
34	John Valentin	.20
35	Ivan Rodriguez	.85
36	Rico Brogna	.20
37	Tim Salmon	.30
38	Sterling Hitchcock	.20
39	Charles Johnson	.20
40	Travis Fryman	.20
41	Barry Larkin	.20
42	Tom Glavine	.20
43	Marty Cordova	.20
44	Shawn Green	.35
45	Ben McDonald	.20
46	Robin Ventura	.20
47	Ken Griffey Jr.	3.00
48	Orlando Merced	.20
49	Paul O'Neill	.20
50	Ozzie Smith	1.25
51	Manny Ramirez	1.00
52	Ismael Valdes	.20
53	Cal Ripken Jr.	3.50
54	Jeff Bagwell	1.00
55	Greg Vaughn	.20
56	Juan Gonzalez	1.00
57	Raul Mondesi	.35
58	Carlos Baerga	.20
59	Sammy Sosa	1.50
60	Mike Kelly	.20
61	Edgar Martinez	.20
62	Kirby Puckett	1.25
63	Cecil Fielder	.20
64	David Cone	.20
65	Moises Alou	.35
66	Fred McGriff	.20
67	Mo Vaughn	.75
68	Edgardo Alfonzo	.20
69	Jim Thome	.20
70	Rickey Henderson	.65
71	Dante Bichette	.20
72	Lenny Dykstra	.20
73	Benji Gil	.20
74	Wade Boggs	.75
75	Jim Edmonds	.20
76	Michael Tucker	.20
77	Carlos Delgado	.35
78	Butch Huskey	.20
79	Billy Ashley	.20
80	Dean Palmer	.20
81	Paul Molitor	.50
82	Ryan Klesko	.20
83	Brian Hunter	.20
84	Jay Buhner	.20
85	Larry Walker	.50
86	Mike Bordick	.20
87	Matt Williams	.45
88	Jack McDowell	.20
89	Hal Morris	.20
90	Brian Jordan	.20
91	Andy Pettitte	.40
92	Melvin Nieves	.20
93	Pedro Martinez	.75
94	Mark Grace	.40
95	Garret Anderson	.20
96	Andre Dawson	.30
97	Ray Durham	.20
98	Jose Canseco	.60
99	Roberto Alomar	.85
100	Derek Jeter	2.00
101	Alan Benes	.20
102	Karim Garcia	.20
103	*Robin Jennings*	.20
104	Bob Abreu	.20
105	Sal Fasano (Card front has Livan Hernandez' name)	.20
106	Steve Gibralter	.20
107	Jermaine Dye	.20
108	Jason Kendall	.20
109	*Mike Grace*	.20
110	Jason Schmidt	.20
111	Paul Wilson	.20
112	Rey Ordonez	.20
113	*Wilton Guerrero*	.50
114	Brooks Kieschnick	.20
115	George Arias	.20
116	*Osvaldo Fernandez*	.20
117	Todd Hollandsworth	.20
118	John Wasdin	.20
119	Eric Owens	.20
120	Chan Ho Park	.45
121	Mark Loretta	.20
122	Richard Hidalgo	.20
123	Jeff Suppan	.20
124	Jim Pittsley	.20
125	LaTroy Hawkins	.20
126	Chris Snopek	.20
127	Justin Thompson	.20
128	Jay Powell	.20
129	Alex Ochoa	.20
130	Felipe Crespo	.20
131	*Matt Lawton*	.20
132	Jimmy Haynes	.20
133	Terrell Wade	.20
134	Ruben Rivera	.20
135	Frank Thomas (Pastime Power)	.75
136	Ken Griffey Jr. (Pastime Power)	1.25
137	Greg Maddux (Pastime Power)	.65
138	Mike Piazza (Pastime Power)	1.00
139	Cal Ripken Jr. (Pastime Power)	1.50
140	Albert Belle (Pastime Power)	.30
141	Mo Vaughn (Pastime Power)	.40
142	Chipper Jones (Pastime Power)	1.00
143	Hideo Nomo (Pastime Power)	.50
144	Ryan Klesko (Pastime Power)	.20

1996 Select Certified Artist's Proofs

Only 500 cards each of this parallel issue were produced, seeded one in every dozen packs. The cards are identical to the regular-issue Select Certified except for the presence on front of a prismatic gold Artist's Proof logo.

	MT
Complete Set (144):	500.00
Common Player:	1.00
AP Stars:	10X

(See 1996 Select Certified for checklist and base card values.)

1996 Select Certified Red, Blue

These 1996 Select Certified insert cards were the most common of the parallel cards issued; they were seeded one per five packs. There were 1,800 Certified Red sets produced, with the number of Certified Blue sets at 180. Cards are essentially the same as regular-issue Select Certified except for the color of the foil background on front.

	MT
Common Red:	1.00
Red Stars:	3X
Common Blue:	5.00
Blue Stars:	20X

(See 1996 Select Certified for checklist and base card values.)

1996 Select Certified Mirror Red, Blue, Gold

These 1996 Select Certified inserts are the scarcest of the set. Only 30 Mirror Gold sets were made, with 60 Mirror Blue sets and 90 Mirror Red. Due to the improbability of completing the collection, no complete set price is given.

	MT
Common Mirror Red:	6.00
Mirror Red Stars:	25X
Common Mirror Blue:	12.50
Mirror Blue Stars:	40X
Common Mirror Gold:	30.00
Mirror Gold Stars:	120X

(See 1996 Select Certified for checklist and base card values.)

1996 Select Certified Interleague Preview

These 1996 Select Certified insert cards feature 21 prospective match-ups from interleague play's beginnings. The cards were seeded one per 42 packs. Each card can also be found in a promo version with a large, black "SAMPLE" overprint on front and back.

		MT
Complete Set (25):		60.00
Common Player:		1.00
1	Ken Griffey Jr., Hideo Nomo	6.50
2	Greg Maddux, Mo Vaughn	5.00
3	Frank Thomas, Sammy Sosa	7.50
4	Mike Piazza, Jim Edmonds	6.00
5	Ryan Klesko, Roger Clemens	3.50
6	Derek Jeter, Rey Ordonez	5.00
7	Johnny Damon, Ray Lankford	1.00
8	Manny Ramirez, Reggie Sanders	2.50
9	Barry Bonds, Jay Buhner	2.50
10	Jason Isringhausen, Wade Boggs	1.50
11	David Cone, Chipper Jones	5.00
12	Jeff Bagwell, Will Clark	2.00
13	Tony Gwynn, Randy Johnson	3.50
14	Cal Ripken Jr., Tom Glavine	6.50
15	Kirby Puckett, Alan Benes	2.00
16	Gary Sheffield, Mike Mussina	1.50
17	Raul Mondesi, Tim Salmon	1.00
18	Rondell White, Carlos Delgado	1.00
19	Cecil Fielder, Ryne Sandberg	2.00

20	Kenny Lofton, Brian Hunter	1.00
21	Paul Wilson, Paul O'Neill	1.00
22	Ismael Valdes, Edgar Martinez	1.00
23	Matt Williams, Mark McGwire	6.50
24	Albert Belle, Barry Larkin	1.00
25	Brady Anderson, Marquis Grissom	1.00

1996 Select Certified Select Few

Eighteen top players are featured on these 1996 Select Certified inserts, which utilize holographic technology with a dot matrix hologram. Cards were seeded one per every 60 packs.

		MT
Complete Set (18):		70.00
Common Player:		1.50
1	Sammy Sosa	7.00
2	Derek Jeter	8.00
3	Ken Griffey Jr.	9.00
4	Albert Belle	3.00
5	Cal Ripken Jr.	10.00
6	Greg Maddux	6.00
7	Frank Thomas	7.00
8	Mo Vaughn	4.00
9	Chipper Jones	8.00
10	Mike Piazza	8.00
11	Ryan Klesko	1.50
12	Hideo Nomo	4.00
13	Alan Benes	1.50
14	Manny Ramirez	4.00
15	Gary Sheffield	2.50
16	Barry Bonds	6.00
17	Matt Williams	1.50
18	Johnny Damon	1.50

1997 Select Samples

The 1997 edition of Select was previewed with the issue of several regular-issue cards carrying a large black "SAMPLE" overprint on front and back. The Rodriguez sample, untrimmed and larger than standard size, was not distributed in the three-card cello packs with the other cards.

		MT
Complete Set (5):		15.00
Common Player:		2.50
3	Tony Gwynn	2.50
8	Frank Thomas	1.50
23	Greg Maddux	2.00
47	Ken Griffey Jr.	4.50
53	Alex Rodriguez	6.00

1997 Select

The Series 1 base set is made up of 150 cards printed on a thick 16-point stock. Each card features a distinctive silver-foil treatment and either red (100 cards) or blue (50 cards) foil accent. Blue-foiled cards were short-printed at a ratio of 1:2 compared to the red-foil cards. Blue-foil cards are indicated with a (B) in the checklist. Subsets include 40 Rookies, eight Super Stars and two checklists. Inserts include two parallel sets, (Artist's Proof and Registered Gold), Tools of the Trade, Mirror Blue Tools of the Trade, and Rookie Revolution. The cards were sold only at hobby shops in six-card packs for $2.99 each. A high-number series was issued with each card bearing a "Select Company" notation.

		MT
Complete Set (200):		65.00
Series 1 (#1-150):		40.00
Common Red Player:		.10
Common Blue Player:		.25
Common High Series:		.25
Pack (6):		1.50
Wax Box (24):		30.00
1	Juan Gonzalez (B)	1.50
2	Mo Vaughn (B)	1.00
3	Tony Gwynn	1.50
4	Manny Ramirez (B)	1.50
5	Jose Canseco	.50
6	David Cone	.10
7	Chan Ho Park	.25
8	Frank Thomas (B)	2.50
9	Todd Hollandsworth	.10
10	Marty Cordova	.10
11	Gary Sheffield (B)	.65
12	John Smoltz (B)	.25
13	Mark Grudzielanek	.10
14	Sammy Sosa (B)	3.50
15	Paul Molitor	.40
16	Kevin Brown	.15
17	Albert Belle (B)	.75
18	Eric Young	.10
19	John Wetteland	.10
20	Ryan Klesko (B)	.25
21	Joe Carter	.10
22	Alex Ochoa	.10
23	Greg Maddux (B)	3.00
24	Roger Clemens (B)	3.00
25	Ivan Rodriguez (B)	1.25
26	Barry Bonds (B)	3.50
27	Kenny Lofton (B)	.25
28	Javy Lopez	.10
29	Hideo Nomo (B)	1.50
30	Rusty Greer	.10
31	Rafael Palmeiro	.30
32	Mike Piazza (B)	4.00
33	Ryne Sandberg	.75
34	Wade Boggs	.75
35	Jim Thome (B)	.25
36	Ken Caminiti (B)	.25
37	Mark Grace	.30
38	Brian Jordan (B)	.25
39	Craig Biggio	.10
40	Henry Rodriguez	.10
41	Dean Palmer	.10
42	Jason Kendall	.10
43	Bill Pulsipher	.10
44	Tim Salmon (B)	.40
45	Marc Newfield	.10
46	Pat Hentgen	.10
47	Ken Griffey Jr. (B)	4.50
48	Paul Wilson	.10
49	Jay Buhner (B)	.25
50	Rickey Henderson	.75
51	Jeff Bagwell (B)	1.50
52	Cecil Fielder	.10
53	Alex Rodriguez (B)	4.50
54	John Jaha	.10
55	Brady Anderson (B)	.25
56	Andres Galarraga	.10
57	Raul Mondesi	.30
58	Andy Pettitte	.30
59	Roberto Alomar (B)	1.25
60	Derek Jeter (B)	4.00
61	Charles Johnson	.10
62	Travis Fryman	.10
63	Chipper Jones (B)	4.00
64	Edgar Martinez	.10
65	Bobby Bonilla	.10
66	Greg Vaughn	.10
67	Bobby Higginson	.10
68	Garret Anderson	.10
69	Chuck Knoblauch (B)	.25
70	Jermaine Dye	.10
71	Cal Ripken Jr. (B)	5.00
72	Jason Giambi	.25
73	Trey Beamon	.10
74	Shawn Green	.30
75	Mark McGwire (B)	5.00
76	Carlos Delgado	.20
77	Jason Isringhausen	.10
78	Randy Johnson (B)	1.25
79	Troy Percival (B)	.25
80	Ron Gant	.10
81	Ellis Burks	.10
82	Mike Mussina (B)	1.25
83	Todd Hundley	.10
84	Jim Edmonds	.10
85	Charles Nagy	.10
86	Dante Bichette (B)	.25
87	Mariano Rivera	.25
88	Matt Williams (B)	.50
89	Rondell White	.15
90	Steve Finley	.10
91	Alex Fernandez	.10
92	Barry Larkin	.10
93	Tom Goodwin	.10
94	Will Clark	.30
95	Michael Tucker	.10
96	Derek Bell	.10
97	Larry Walker	.35
98	Alan Benes	.10
99	Tom Glavine	.10
100	Darin Erstad (B)	1.50
101	Andruw Jones (B)	1.50
102	Scott Rolen	1.00
103	Todd Walker (B)	.25
104	Dmitri Young	.10
105	Vladimir Guerrero (B)	1.50
106	Nomar Garciaparra	2.00
107	*Danny Patterson*	.25
108	Karim Garcia	.10
109	Todd Greene	.10
110	Ruben Rivera	.10
111	Raul Casanova	.10
112	Mike Cameron	.10
113	Bartolo Colon	.10
114	*Rod Myers*	.10
115	Todd Dunn	.10
116	Torii Hunter	.10
117	Jason Dickson	.10
118	*Gene Kingsale*	.10
119	Rafael Medina	.10
120	Raul Ibanez	.10
121	*Bobby Henley*	.10
122	Scott Spiezio	.10
123	*Bobby Smith*	.10
124	J.J. Johnson	.10
125	*Bubba Trammell*	1.00
126	Jeff Abbott	.10
127	Neifi Perez	.10
128	Derrek Lee	.10
129	*Kevin Brown*	.10
130	Mendy Lopez	.10
131	Kevin Orie	.10
132	Ryan Jones	.10
133	Juan Encarnacion	.10
134	Jose Guillen (B)	.25
135	Greg Norton	.10
136	Richie Sexson	.10
137	Jay Payton	.10
138	Bob Abreu	.10
139	*Ronnie Belliard*	.25
140	Wilton Guerrero (B)	.25
141	Alex Rodriguez (Select Stars) (B)	1.50
142	Juan Gonzalez (Select Stars) (B)	.75
143	Ken Caminiti (Select Stars) (B)	.25
144	Frank Thomas (Select Stars) (B)	1.00
145	Ken Griffey Jr. (Select Stars) (B)	1.50
146	John Smoltz (Select Stars) (B)	.25
147	Mike Piazza (Select Stars) (B)	1.25
148	Derek Jeter (Select Stars) (B)	1.25
149	Frank Thomas (checklist)	.75
150	Ken Griffey Jr. (checklist)	1.00
151	*Jose Cruz Jr.*	1.50
152	Moises Alou	1.50
153	*Hideki Irabu*	.50
154	Glendon Rusch	.25
155	Ron Coomer	.25
156	*Jeremi Gonzalez*	.50
157	*Fernando Tatis*	1.00
158	John Olerud	.25
159	Rickey Henderson	.75
160	Shannon Stewart	.50
161	Kevin Polcovich	.25
162	Jose Rosado	.25
163	Ray Lankford	.25
164	David Justice	.45
165	*Mark Kotsay*	.60
166	*Deivi Cruz*	.50
167	Billy Wagner	.35
168	Jacob Cruz	.25
169	Matt Morris	.35
170	Brian Banks	.25
171	Brett Tomko	.25
172	Todd Helton	.50
173	Eric Young	.25
174	Bernie Williams	.50
175	Jeff Fassero	.25
176	Ryan McGuire	.25
177	Darryl Kile	.25
178	*Kelvim Escobar*	.50
179	Dave Nilsson	.25
180	Geronimo Berroa	.25
181	Livan Hernandez	.25
182	*Tony Womack*	.50
183	Deion Sanders	.25
184	Jeff Kent	.25
185	Brian Hunter	.25
186	Jose Malave	.25
187	*Steve Woodard*	.50
188	Brad Radke	.40
189	Todd Dunwoody	.25
190	Joey Hamilton	.25
191	Denny Naegle	.25
192	Bobby Jones	.25
193	Tony Clark	.25
194	*Jaret Wright*	2.00
195	Matt Stairs	.25

196	Francisco Cordova	.25
197	Justin Thompson	.25
198	Pokey Reese	.25
199	Garrett Stephenson	.25
200	Carl Everett	.35

1997 Select Artist's Proofs

Featuring a holographic foil background and special Artist's Proof logo on front, this parallel of the 150-card Series 1 Select was a random pack insert at an average pull rate of 1:71 for reds and 1:355 for blues.

	MT
Complete Set (150):	750.00
Common Red:	2.00
Red Stars:	10X
Common Blue:	4.00
Blue Stars:	2.5X

(See 1997 Select #1-150 for checklist and base card values.)

1997 Select Registered Gold

This parallel insert set, like the regular issue, can be found with 100 red-foil and 50 blue-foil enhanced cards. They differ from the regular issue in the use of gold foil instead of silver on the right side of the front. Also, the inserts have "Registered Gold" printed vertically on the right side of the photo. Backs are identical to the regular issue. Red-foil Registered Gold cards are found on average of once every 11 packs; blue-foiled cards are a 1-in-47 pick.

	MT
Complete Set (150):	600.00
Common Red Gold:	1.00
Common Blue Gold:	2.00

(See 1997 Select #1-150 for checklist and base card values.)

1997 Select Autographs

Four top candidates for the 1997 Rookie of the Year Award - Wilton Guerrero, Jose Guillen, Andruw Jones and Todd Walker - each signed a limited number of their Select Rookie cards. Jones signed 2,500 cards while each of the other players signed 3,000 each.

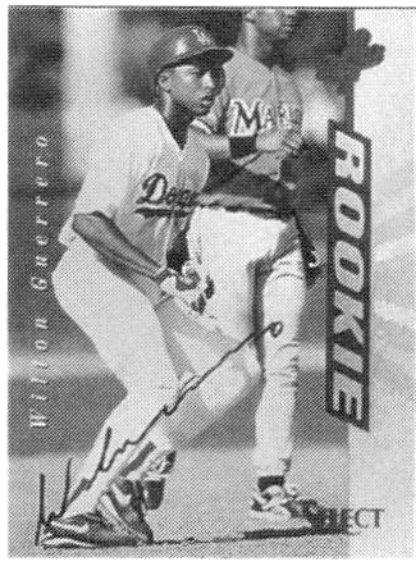

		MT
Complete Set (4):		25.00
Common Autograph:		5.00
AU1	Wilton Guerrero	5.00
AU2	Jose Guillen	5.00
AU3	Andruw Jones	20.00
AU4	Todd Walker	5.00

1997 Select Company

Select Company was intended to be a one-per-pack parallel found in '97 high series. The cards have the front background photo replaced with textured silver metallic foil and "Select Company" printed vertically at right-center. While all high-number (151-200) cards have the "Select Company" notation erroneously printed on front, only those cards with silver-foil backgrounds are true parallels.

	MT
Complete Set (200):	150.00
Common Player:	.50
Red Stars:	3X
Blue Stars:	1.5X
High-Series Stars:	1.5X

(See 1997 Select for checklist and base card values.)

1997 Select Rookie Revolution

This 20-card insert highlights some of the top young stars in the game. Cards feature a silver micro-etched mylar design on front. Backs are sequentially numbered and contain a few words about the player. Odds of finding a card are 1:56 packs.

		MT
Complete Set (20):		25.00
Common Player:		.50
1	Andruw Jones	3.50
2	Derek Jeter	6.00
3	Todd Hollandsworth	.50
4	Edgar Renteria	.50
5	Jason Kendall	1.50
6	Rey Ordonez	1.00
7	F.P. Santangelo	.50
8	Jermaine Dye	.75
9	Alex Ochoa	.50
10	Vladimir Guerrero	3.50
11	Dmitri Young	.50
12	Todd Walker	.50
13	Scott Rolen	3.00
14	Nomar Garciaparra	5.00
15	Ruben Rivera	.50
16	Darin Erstad	3.00
17	Todd Greene	.50
18	Mariano Rivera	4.00
19	Trey Beamon	.50
20	Karim Garcia	.50

1997 Select Tools of the Trade

A 25-card insert featuring a double-front design salutes a top veteran player on one side and a promising youngster on the other. Cards feature a silver-foil card stock with gold-foil stamping. Cards were inserted 1:9 packs. A parallel to this set - Blue Mirror Tools of the Trade - features blue-foil stock with an insert ratio of 1:240 packs.

		MT
Complete Set (25):		50.00
Common Player:		.75
Mirror Blues:		1.5X
1	Ken Griffey Jr., Andruw Jones	4.75
2	Greg Maddux, Andy Pettitte	3.50
3	Cal Ripken Jr., Chipper Jones	5.00
4	Mike Piazza, Jason Kendall	3.50
5	Albert Belle, Karim Garcia	2.00
6	Mo Vaughn, Dmitri Young	1.25
7	Juan Gonzalez, Vladimir Guerrero	2.50
8	Tony Gwynn, Jermaine Dye	2.50
9	Barry Bonds, Alex Ochoa	2.00
10	Jeff Bagwell, Jason Giambi	2.00
11	Kenny Lofton, Darin Erstad	2.00
12	Gary Sheffield, Manny Ramirez	2.00
13	Tim Salmon, Todd Hollandsworth	1.00
14	Sammy Sosa, Ruben Rivera	3.50
15	Paul Molitor, George Arias	1.50
16	Jim Thome, Todd Walker	.75
17	Wade Boggs, Scott Rolen	2.50
18	Ryne Sandberg, Chuck Knoblauch	2.00
19	Mark McGwire, Frank Thomas	6.00
20	Ivan Rodriguez, Charles Johnson	1.50
21	Brian Jordan, Trey Beamon	.75
22	Roger Clemens, Troy Percival	2.00
23	John Smoltz, Mike Mussina	1.50
24	Alex Rodriguez, Rey Ordonez	4.50
25	Derek Jeter, Nomar Garciaparra	4.50

1998 Select Selected Samples

Selected promos were released in two-card cello packs prior to Pinnacle's bankruptcy. Fronts have color action photos on bright metallic-foil backgrounds was a large "S". Backs have a smaller version of the front photo along with career highlights and a large overprinted "SAMPLE".

		MT
Complete Set (10):		30.00
Common Player:		3.00
1	Vladimir Guerrero	4.00
2	Nomar Garciaparra	5.00
3	Ben Grieve	3.00
4	Travis Lee	3.00
5	Jose Cruz Jr.	3.00
6	Alex Rodriguez	8.00
7	Todd Helton	3.00
8	Derek Jeter	6.00
9	Scott Rolen	3.00
10	Jaret Wright	3.00

1995 SkyBox E-Motion Promo

To introduce its new super-premium baseball card line, SkyBox debuted a Cal Ripken promo card at the 1995 National Sports Collectors Convention. The card is virtually identical to Ripken's card in the regular issue, except for diagonal overprinting on each side which reads, "Promotional Sample".

		MT
8	Cal Ripken Jr. (Class)	2.50

1995 SkyBox E-Motion

This is a super-premium debut issue from the newly merged Fleer/SkyBox company. Printed on double-thick cardboard, card fronts have borderless photos marred by the presence of four gold-foil "viewfinder" corner marks. The player's last name and team are printed in gold foil near the bottom. On each card there is a large silver-foil word printed in block letters; either a nickname or an emotion or attribute associated with the player. Backs have two more player photos, 1994 and career stats and a few biographical bits. Eight-cards packs were issued with a suggested retail price of $4.99.

		MT
Complete Set (200):		35.00
Common Player:		.10
Pack (8):		1.00
Wax Box (36):		30.00
1	Brady Anderson	.10
2	Kevin Brown	.25
3	Curtis Goodwin	.10
4	Jeffrey Hammonds	.10
5	Ben McDonald	.10
6	Mike Mussina	.60
7	Rafael Palmeiro	.30
8	Cal Ripken Jr.	2.50
9	Jose Canseco	.40
10	Roger Clemens	1.25
11	Vaughn Eshelman	.10
12	Mike Greenwell	.10
13	Erik Hanson	.10
14	Tim Naehring	.10
15	Aaron Sele	.10
16	John Valentin	.10
17	Mo Vaughn	.40
18	Chili Davis	.10
19	Gary DiSarcina	.10
20	Chuck Finley	.10
21	Tim Salmon	.30
22	Lee Smith	.10
23	J.T. Snow	.10
24	Jim Abbott	.10
25	Jason Bere	.10
26	Ray Durham	.10
27	Ozzie Guillen	.10
28	Tim Raines	.10
29	Frank Thomas	1.50
30	Robin Ventura	.10
31	Carlos Baerga	.10
32	Albert Belle	.40
33	Orel Hershiser	.10
34	Kenny Lofton	.10
35	Dennis Martinez	.10
36	Eddie Murray	.55
37	Manny Ramirez	1.00
38	Julian Tavarez	.10
39	Jim Thome	.10
40	Dave Winfield	.65
41	Chad Curtis	.10
42	Cecil Fielder	.10
43	Travis Fryman	.10
44	Kirk Gibson	.10
45	*Bob Higginson*	1.50
46	Alan Trammell	.10
47	Lou Whitaker	.10
48	Kevin Appier	.10
49	Gary Gaetti	.10
50	Jeff Montgomery	.10
51	Jon Nunnally	.10
52	Ricky Bones	.10
53	Cal Eldred	.10
54	Joe Oliver	.10
55	Kevin Seitzer	.10
56	Marty Cordova	.10
57	Chuck Knoblauch	.10
58	Kirby Puckett	1.25
59	Wade Boggs	.65
60	Derek Jeter	2.00
61	Jimmy Key	.10
62	Don Mattingly	1.75
63	Jack McDowell	.10
64	Paul O'Neill	.10
65	Andy Pettitte	.30
66	Ruben Rivera	.10
67	Mike Stanley	.10
68	John Wetteland	.10
69	Geronimo Berroa	.10
70	Dennis Eckersley	.10
71	Rickey Henderson	.60
72	Mark McGwire	2.50
73	Steve Ontiveros	.10
74	Ruben Sierra	.10
75	Terry Steinbach	.10
76	Jay Buhner	.10
77	Ken Griffey Jr.	2.50
78	Randy Johnson	.75
79	Edgar Martinez	.10
80	Tino Martinez	.10
81	Marc Newfield	.10
82	Alex Rodriguez	2.50
83	Will Clark	.40
84	Benji Gil	.10
85	Juan Gonzalez	1.00
86	Rusty Greer	.10
87	Dean Palmer	.10
88	Ivan Rodriguez	.75
89	Kenny Rogers	.10
90	Roberto Alomar	.60
91	Joe Carter	.10
92	David Cone	.10
93	Alex Gonzalez	.10
94	Shawn Green	.30
95	Pat Hentgen	.10
96	Paul Molitor	.60
97	John Olerud	.10
98	Devon White	.10
99	Steve Avery	.10
100	Tom Glavine	.10
101	Marquis Grissom	.10
102	Chipper Jones	2.00
103	Dave Justice	.35
104	Ryan Klesko	.10
105	Javier Lopez	.10
106	Greg Maddux	1.25
107	Fred McGriff	.10
108	John Smoltz	.10
109	Shawon Dunston	.10
110	Mark Grace	.30
111	Brian McRae	.10
112	Randy Myers	.10
113	Sammy Sosa	1.50
114	Steve Trachsel	.10
115	Bret Boone	.10
116	Ron Gant	.10
117	Barry Larkin	.10
118	Deion Sanders	.15
119	Reggie Sanders	.10
120	Pete Schourek	.10
121	John Smiley	.10
122	Jason Bates	.10
123	Dante Bichette	.10
124	Vinny Castilla	.10
125	Andres Galarraga	.10
126	Larry Walker	.40
127	Greg Colbrunn	.10
128	Jeff Conine	.10
129	Andre Dawson	.25
130	Chris Hammond	.10
131	Charles Johnson	.10
132	Gary Sheffield	.45
133	Quilvio Veras	.10
134	Jeff Bagwell	1.00
135	Derek Bell	.10
136	Craig Biggio	.10
137	Jim Dougherty	.10
138	John Hudek	.10
139	Orlando Miller	.10
140	Phil Plantier	.10
141	Eric Karros	.10
142	Ramon Martinez	.10
143	Raul Mondesi	.30
144	*Hideo Nomo*	2.00
145	Mike Piazza	2.00
146	Ismael Valdes	.10
147	Todd Worrell	.10
148	Moises Alou	.15
149	*Yamil Benitez*	.15
150	Wil Cordero	.10
151	Jeff Fassero	.10
152	Cliff Floyd	.10
153	Pedro Martinez	.60
154	*Carlos Perez*	.10
155	Tony Tarasco	.10
156	Rondell White	.15
157	Edgardo Alfonzo	.10
158	Bobby Bonilla	.10
159	Rico Brogna	.10
160	Bobby Jones	.10
161	Bill Pulsipher	.10
162	Bret Saberhagen	.10
163	Ricky Bottalico	.10
164	Darren Daulton	.10
165	Lenny Dykstra	.10
166	Charlie Hayes	.10
167	Dave Hollins	.10
168	Gregg Jefferies	.10
169	*Michael Mimbs*	.10
170	Curt Schilling	.15
171	Heathcliff Slocumb	.10
172	Jay Bell	.10
173	*Micah Franklin*	.10
174	*Mark Johnson*	.10
175	Jeff King	.10
176	Al Martin	.10
177	Dan Miceli	.10
178	Denny Neagle	.10
179	Bernard Gilkey	.10
180	Ken Hill	.10
181	Brian Jordan	.10
182	Ray Lankford	.10
183	Ozzie Smith	1.25
184	Andy Benes	.10
185	Ken Caminiti	.10
186	Steve Finley	.10
187	Tony Gwynn	1.25
188	Joey Hamilton	.10
189	Melvin Nieves	.10
190	Scott Sanders	.10
191	Rod Beck	.10
192	Barry Bonds	1.50
193	Royce Clayton	.10
194	Glenallen Hill	.10
195	Darren Lewis	.10
196	Mark Portugal	.10
197	Matt Williams	.40
198	Checklist	.05
199	Checklist	.05
200	Checklist	.05

1995 SkyBox E-Motion Cal Ripken Jr. Timeless

A white background with a clockface and gold-foil "TIMELESS" logo are the standard elements of this insert tribute to Cal Ripken, Jr. Each card front features a large color photo and a smaller sepia photo contemporary to some phase of his career. The first 10 cards in the set chronicle Ripken's career through 1994. A special mail-in offer provided five more cards featuring highlights of his 1995 season.

		MT
Complete Set (15):		30.00
Common Player:		2.50
1	High School Pitcher	2.50
2	Role Model	2.50
3	Rookie of the Year	2.50
4	1st MVP Season	2.50
5	95 Consecutive Errorless Games	2.50
6	All-Star MVP	2.50
7	Conditioning	2.50
8	Shortstop HR Record	2.50
9	Literacy Work	2.50
10	2000th Consecutive Game	2.50
11	All-Star Selection	3.00
12	Record-tying Game	3.00
13	Record-breaking Game	3.00
14	2,153 and Counting	3.00
15	Birthday	3.00

1995 SkyBox E-Motion Masters

Ten of the game's top veterans are featured in this chase card set. A large close-up photo in a single team-related color in the background, with a color action photo in the foreground. Backs have a borderless color photo and a top to bottom color bar with some good words about the player. The Masters inserts are found at an average rate of one per eight packs.

		MT
Complete Set (10):		16.00
Common Player:		1.00
1	Barry Bonds	2.00
2	Juan Gonzalez	1.50
3	Ken Griffey Jr.	3.50
4	Tony Gwynn	2.00
5	Kenny Lofton	1.00
6	Greg Maddux	2.00
7	Raul Mondesi	1.00
8	Cal Ripken Jr.	4.00
9	Frank Thomas	2.50
10	Matt Williams	1.00

1995 SkyBox E-Motion N-Tense

A colored wave-pattern printed on metallic foil is the background for the action photo of one of baseball's top sluggers in this chase card set. A huge rainbow prismatic foil "N" appears in an upper corner. The player's name and team are at lower-right in gold foil. Backs are conventionally printed and repeat the front's patterned background, with another color player photo and a shaded box with a few career highlights.

		MT
Complete Set (12):		27.50
Common Player:		.75
1	Jeff Bagwell	2.00
2	Albert Belle	1.50
3	Barry Bonds	3.00
4	Cecil Fielder	.75
5	Ron Gant	.75
6	Ken Griffey Jr.	6.00
7	Mark McGwire	7.50
8	Mike Piazza	4.50
9	Manny Ramirez	2.00
10	Frank Thomas	3.50
11	Mo Vaughn	2.00
12	Matt Williams	1.50

1995 SkyBox E-Motion Rookies

A bold colored background with outline white letters repeating the word "ROOKIE" is the frame for the central action photo in this insert series. The top of the photo is vignetted with a white circle that has the player's name in gold at left, and his team in white at right. Backs repeat the front background and include a player portrait photo and a few sentences about his potential. Rookie inserts are found at an average rate of one per five packs.

		MT
Complete Set (10):		12.00
Common Player:		.50
1	Edgardo Alfonzo	1.00
2	Jason Bates	.50
3	Marty Cordova	.50
4	Ray Durham	.75
5	Alex Gonzalez	1.00
6	Shawn Green	1.50
7	Charles Johnson	.75
8	Chipper Jones	3.00
9	Hideo Nomo	2.50
10	Alex Rodriguez	4.00

1996 SkyBox E-Motion XL

Each card in SkyBox's 1996 E-Motion XL Baseball arrives on two layers of stock - a die-cut matte frame over a UV-coated card. The frames come in three colors - blue, green and maroon (but each player has only one color version). The 300-card set also includes four insert sets: Legion of Boom, D-Fense, N-Tense and Rare Breed.

		MT
Complete Set (300):		40.00
Common Player:		.15
Pack (7):		2.00
Wax Box (24):		40.00
1	Roberto Alomar	1.00
2	Brady Anderson	.15
3	Bobby Bonilla	.15
4	Jeffrey Hammonds	.15
5	Chris Hoiles	.15
6	Mike Mussina	1.00
7	Randy Myers	.15
8	Rafael Palmeiro	.45
9	Cal Ripken Jr.	4.00
10	B.J. Surhoff	.15
11	Jose Canseco	.60
12	Roger Clemens	2.00
13	Wil Cordero	.15
14	Mike Greenwell	.15
15	Dwayne Hosey	.15
16	Tim Naehring	.15
17	Troy O'Leary	.15
18	Mike Stanley	.15
19	John Valentin	.15
20	Mo Vaughn	.50
21	Jim Abbott	.15
22	Garret Anderson	.15
23	George Arias	.15
24	Chili Davis	.15
25	Jim Edmonds	.15
26	Chuck Finley	.15
27	Todd Greene	.15
28	Mark Langston	.15
29	Troy Percival	.15
30	Tim Salmon	.30
31	Lee Smith	.15
32	J.T. Snow	.15
33	Harold Baines	.15
34	Jason Bere	.15
35	Ray Durham	.15
36	Alex Fernandez	.15
37	Ozzie Guillen	.15
38	Darren Lewis	.15
39	Lyle Mouton	.15
40	Tony Phillips	.15
41	Danny Tartabull	.15
42	Frank Thomas	2.25
43	Robin Ventura	.15
44	Sandy Alomar	.15
45	Carlos Baerga	.15
46	Albert Belle	.50
47	Julio Franco	.15
48	Orel Hershiser	.15
49	Kenny Lofton	.15
50	Dennis Martinez	.15
51	Jack McDowell	.15
52	Jose Mesa	.15
53	Eddie Murray	.75
54	Charles Nagy	.15
55	Manny Ramirez	1.50
55p	Manny Ramirez (overprinted "PROMOTIONAL SAMPLE")	2.50
56	Jim Thome	.15
57	Omar Vizquel	.15
58	Chad Curtis	.15
59	Cecil Fielder	.15
60	Travis Fryman	.15
61	Chris Gomez	.15
62	Felipe Lira	.15
63	Alan Trammell	.15
64	Kevin Appier	.15
65	Johnny Damon	.25
66	Tom Goodwin	.15
67	Mark Gubicza	.15
68	Jeff Montgomery	.15
69	Jon Nunnally	.15
70	Bip Roberts	.15
71	Ricky Bones	.15
72	Chuck Carr	.15
73	John Jaha	.15
74	Ben McDonald	.15
75	Matt Mieske	.15
76	Dave Nilsson	.15
77	Kevin Seitzer	.15
78	Greg Vaughn	.15
79	Rick Aguilera	.15
80	Marty Cordova	.15
81	Roberto Kelly	.15
82	Chuck Knoblauch	.15
83	Pat Meares	.15
84	Paul Molitor	1.00
85	Kirby Puckett	2.00
86	Brad Radke	.15
87	Wade Boggs	.75
88	David Cone	.15
89	Dwight Gooden	.15
90	Derek Jeter	3.00
91	Tino Martinez	.15
92	Paul O'Neill	.15
93	Andy Pettitte	.30
94	Tim Raines	.15
95	Ruben Rivera	.15
96	Kenny Rogers	.15
97	Ruben Sierra	.15
98	John Wetteland	.15
99	Bernie Williams	.45
100	Allen Battle	.15
101	Geronimo Berroa	.15
102	Brent Gates	.15
103	Doug Johns	.15
104	Mark McGwire	4.00
105	Pedro Munoz	.15
106	Ariel Prieto	.15
107	Terry Steinbach	.15
108	Todd Van Poppel	.15
109	Chris Bosio	.15
110	Jay Buhner	.15
111	Joey Cora	.15
112	Russ Davis	.15
113	Ken Griffey Jr.	3.50
114	Sterling Hitchcock	.15
115	Randy Johnson	1.25
116	Edgar Martinez	.15
117	Alex Rodriguez	3.50
118	Paul Sorrento	.15
119	Dan Wilson	.15
120	Will Clark	.45
121	Juan Gonzalez	1.50
122	Rusty Greer	.15
123	Kevin Gross	.15
124	Ken Hill	.15
125	Dean Palmer	.15
126	Roger Pavlik	.15
127	Ivan Rodriguez	1.00
128	Mickey Tettleton	.15
129	Joe Carter	.15
130	Carlos Delgado	.75
131	Alex Gonzalez	.15
132	Shawn Green	.30
133	Erik Hanson	.15
134	Pat Hentgen	.15
135	Otis Nixon	.15
136	John Olerud	.15
137	Ed Sprague	.15
138	Steve Avery	.15
139	Jermaine Dye	.15
140	Tom Glavine	.15
141	Marquis Grissom	.15
142	Chipper Jones	2.50
143	David Justice	.40
144	Ryan Klesko	.15
145	Javier Lopez	.15
146	Greg Maddux	2.00
147	Fred McGriff	.15
148	Jason Schmidt	.15
149	John Smoltz	.15
150	Mark Wohlers	.15
151	Jim Bullinger	.15
152	Frank Castillo	.15
153	Kevin Foster	.15
154	Luis Gonzalez	.40
155	Mark Grace	.40
156	Brian McRae	.15
157	Jaime Navarro	.15
158	Rey Sanchez	.15
159	Ryne Sandberg	1.50
160	Sammy Sosa	2.25
161	Bret Boone	.15
162	Jeff Brantley	.15
163	Vince Coleman	.15
164	Steve Gibralter	.15
165	Barry Larkin	.15
166	Hal Morris	.15
167	Mark Portugal	.15
168	Reggie Sanders	.15
169	Pete Schourek	.15
170	John Smiley	.15
171	Jason Bates	.15
172	Dante Bichette	.15
173	Ellis Burks	.15
174	Vinny Castilla	.15
175	Andres Galarraga	.15
176	Kevin Ritz	.15
177	Bill Swift	.15
178	Larry Walker	.45
179	Walt Weiss	.15
180	Eric Young	.15
181	Kurt Abbott	.15
182	Kevin Brown	.25
183	John Burkett	.15
184	Greg Colbrunn	.15
185	Jeff Conine	.15
186	Chris Hammond	.15

187 Charles Johnson .15
188 Terry Pendleton .15
189 Pat Rapp .15
190 Gary Sheffield .60
191 Quilvio Veras .15
192 Devon White .15
193 Jeff Bagwell 1.50
194 Derek Bell .15
195 Sean Berry .15
196 Craig Biggio .15
197 Doug Drabek .15
198 Tony Eusebio .15
199 Mike Hampton .15
200 Brian Hunter .15
201 Derrick May .15
202 Orlando Miller .15
203 Shane Reynolds .15
204 Mike Blowers .15
205 Tom Candiotti .15
206 Delino DeShields .15
207 Greg Gagne .15
208 Karim Garcia .15
209 Todd Hollandsworth .15
210 Eric Karros .15
211 Ramon Martinez .15
212 Raul Mondesi .30
213 Hideo Nomo 1.50
214 Chan Ho Park .50
215 Mike Piazza 3.00
216 Ismael Valdes .15
217 Todd Worrell .15
218 Moises Alou .25
219 Yamil Benitez .15
220 Jeff Fassero .15
221 Darrin Fletcher .15
222 Cliff Floyd .15
223 Pedro Martinez 1.25
224 Carlos Perez .15
225 Mel Rojas .15
226 David Segui .15
227 Rondell White .25
228 Rico Brogna .15
229 Carl Everett .25
230 John Franco .15
231 Bernard Gilkey .15
232 Todd Hundley .15
233 Jason Isringhausen .15
234 Lance Johnson .15
235 Bobby Jones .15
236 Jeff Kent .15
237 Rey Ordonez .15
238 Bill Pulsipher .15
239 Jose Vizcaino .15
240 Paul Wilson .15
241 Ricky Bottalico .15
242 Darren Daulton .15
243 Lenny Dykstra .15
244 Jim Eisenreich .15
245 Sid Fernandez .15
246 Gregg Jefferies .15
247 Mickey Morandini .15
248 Benito Santiago .15
249 Curt Schilling .25
250 Mark Whiten .15
251 Todd Zeile .15
252 Jay Bell .15
253 Carlos Garcia .15
254 Charlie Hayes .15
255 Jason Kendall .15
256 Jeff King .15
257 Al Martin .15
258 Orlando Merced .15
259 Dan Miceli .15
260 Denny Neagle .15
261 Alan Benes .15
262 Andy Benes .15
263 Royce Clayton .15
264 Dennis Eckersley .15
265 Gary Gaetti .15
266 Ron Gant .15
267 Brian Jordan .15
268 Ray Lankford .15
269 John Mabry .15
270 Tom Pagnozzi .15
271 Ozzie Smith 2.00
272 Todd Stottlemyre .15
273 Andy Ashby .15
274 Brad Ausmus .15
275 Ken Caminiti .15
276 Steve Finley .15
277 Tony Gwynn 2.00
278 Joey Hamilton .15
279 Rickey Henderson .65
280 Trevor Hoffman .15
281 Wally Joyner .15
282 Jody Reed .15
283 Bob Tewksbury .15
284 Fernando Valenzuela .15
285 Rod Beck .15
286 Barry Bonds 2.25
287 Mark Carreon .15
288 Shawon Dunston .15
289 *Osvaldo Fernandez* .30
290 Glenallen Hill .15
291 Stan Javier .15
292 Mark Leiter .15
293 Kirt Manwaring .15
294 Robby Thompson .15
295 William VanLandingham .15
296 Allen Watson .15
297 Matt Williams .45
298 Checklist .10
299 Checklist .10
300 Checklist .10

1996 SkyBox E-Motion XL D-Fense

Ten top defensive players are featured on these 1996 SkyBox E-Motion XL insert cards. The cards were seeded at a rate of one per every four packs.

	MT
Complete Set (10):	12.50
Common Player:	.50
1 Roberto Alomar	.75
2 Barry Bonds	2.00
3 Mark Grace	.65
4 Ken Griffey Jr.	3.50
5 Kenny Lofton	.50
6 Greg Maddux	2.50
7 Raul Mondesi	.50
8 Cal Ripken Jr.	3.50
9 Ivan Rodriguez	1.00
10 Matt Williams	.50

1996 SkyBox E-Motion XL Legion of Boom

The top power hitters in baseball are featured on these 1996 SkyBox E-Motion XL insert cards. The cards, exclusive to hobby packs at a ratio of one per every 36 packs, have translucent card backs.

	MT
Complete Set (12):	55.00
Common Player:	2.50
1 Albert Belle	2.50
2 Barry Bonds	6.00
3 Juan Gonzalez	4.50
4 Ken Griffey Jr.	13.50
5 Mark McGwire	15.00
6 Mike Piazza	11.00
7 Manny Ramirez	4.50
8 Tim Salmon	2.50
9 Sammy Sosa	9.00
10 Frank Thomas	6.00
11 Mo Vaughn	2.50
12 Matt Williams	2.50

1996 SkyBox E-Motion XL N-Tense

Ten top clutch performers are featured on these 1996 SkyBox E-Motion XL insert cards. The cards, which use an N-shaped die-cut design, were included one per every 12 packs.

	MT
Complete Set (10):	25.00
Common Player:	1.00
1 Albert Belle	1.50
2 Barry Bonds	3.50
3 Jose Canseco	2.00
4 Ken Griffey Jr.	6.00
5 Tony Gwynn	3.00
6 Randy Johnson	2.50
7 Greg Maddux	3.00
8 Cal Ripken Jr.	6.00
9 Frank Thomas	4.50
10 Matt Williams	1.00

1996 SkyBox E-Motion XL Rare Breed

These 1996 E-Motion XL inserts are the most difficult to find; they are seeded one per every 100 packs. The cards showcase top young stars on 3-D lenticular design, similar to the Hot Numbers in Fleer Flair basketball.

	MT
Complete Set (10):	25.00
Common Player:	1.50
1 Garret Anderson	1.50
2 Marty Cordova	1.50
3 Brian Hunter	1.50
4 Jason Isringhausen	1.50
5 Charles Johnson	1.50
6 Chipper Jones	9.00
7 Raul Mondesi	2.00
8 Hideo Nomo	4.50
9 Manny Ramirez	7.50
10 Rondell White	2.00

1997 SkyBox E-X2000 Sample

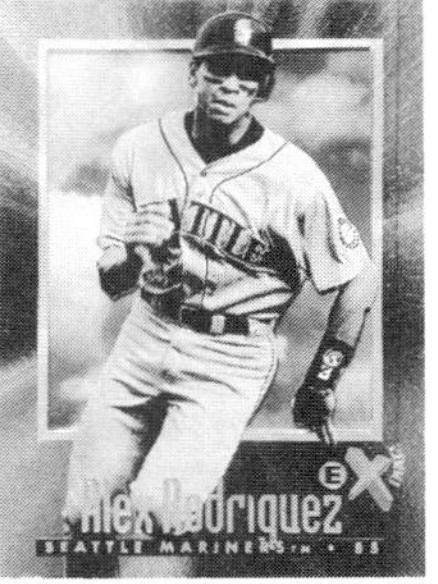

To introduce its innovative high-tech premium brand, SkyBox released this promo card. It is identical in format to the issued version, except it carries a "SAMPLE" notation instead of a card number on back.

	MT
Alex Rodriguez	5.00

1997 SkyBox E-X2000

The premiere issue of E-X2000 consists of 100 base cards designed with "SkyView" technology, utilizing a die-cut holofoil border and the player silhouetted in front of a transparent "window" featuring a variety of sky patterns. Inserts include two sequentially-numbered parallel sets - Credentials

(1:50 packs) and Essential Credentials (1:200 packs) - as well as Emerald Autograph Exchange Cards, A Cut Above, Hall of Nothing, and Star Date. Cards were sold in two-card packs for $3.99 each.

		MT
Complete Set (100):		40.00
Common Player:		.15
Pack (2):		2.00
Wax Box (24):		40.00
1	Jim Edmonds	.15
2	Darin Erstad	1.50
3	Eddie Murray	1.00
4	Roberto Alomar	1.25
5	Brady Anderson	.15
6	Mike Mussina	1.25
7	Rafael Palmeiro	.45
8	Cal Ripken Jr.	4.00
9	Steve Avery	.15
10	Nomar Garciaparra	2.50
11	Mo Vaughn	.60
12	Albert Belle	.50
13	Mike Cameron	.15
14	Ray Durham	.15
15	Frank Thomas	2.50
16	Robin Ventura	.15
17	Manny Ramirez	1.50
18	Jim Thome	.15
19	Matt Williams	.45
20	Tony Clark	.15
21	Travis Fryman	.15
22	Bob Higginson	.15
23	Kevin Appier	.15
24	Johnny Damon	.25
25	Jermaine Dye	.15
26	Jeff Cirillo	.15
27	Ben McDonald	.15
28	Chuck Knoblauch	.15
29	Paul Molitor	1.00
30	Todd Walker	.15
31	Wade Boggs	1.50
32	Cecil Fielder	.15
33	Derek Jeter	4.00
34	Andy Pettitte	.40
35	Ruben Rivera	.15
36	Bernie Williams	.45
37	Jose Canseco	1.00
38	Mark McGwire	4.00
39	Jay Buhner	.15
40	Ken Griffey Jr.	3.50
41	Randy Johnson	1.50
42	Edgar Martinez	.15
43	Alex Rodriguez	3.50
44	Dan Wilson	.15
45	Will Clark	.45
46	Juan Gonzalez	1.50
47	Ivan Rodriguez	1.25
48	Joe Carter	.15
49	Roger Clemens	2.00
50	Juan Guzman	.15
51	Pat Hentgen	.15
52	Tom Glavine	.15
53	Andruw Jones	1.50
54	Chipper Jones	3.00
55	Ryan Klesko	.15
56	Kenny Lofton	.15
57	Greg Maddux	2.00
58	Fred McGriff	.15
59	John Smoltz	.15
60	Mark Wohlers	.15
61	Mark Grace	.45
62	Ryne Sandberg	1.50
63	Sammy Sosa	2.50
64	Barry Larkin	.15
65	Deion Sanders	.15
66	Reggie Sanders	.15
67	Dante Bichette	.15
68	Ellis Burks	.15
69	Andres Galarraga	.15
70	Moises Alou	.25
71	Kevin Brown	.25
72	Cliff Floyd	.15
73	Edgar Renteria	.15
74	Gary Sheffield	.60
75	Bob Abreu	.15
76	Jeff Bagwell	1.50
77	Craig Biggio	.15
78	Todd Hollandsworth	.15
79	Eric Karros	.15
80	Raul Mondesi	.25
81	Hideo Nomo	1.25
82	Mike Piazza	3.00
83	Vladimir Guerrero	1.50
84	Henry Rodriguez	.15
85	Todd Hundley	.15
86	Rey Ordonez	.15
87	Alex Ochoa	.15
88	Gregg Jefferies	.15
89	Scott Rolen	1.25
90	Jermaine Allensworth	.15
91	Jason Kendall	.15
92	Ken Caminiti	.15
93	Tony Gwynn	2.00
94	Rickey Henderson	.75
95	Barry Bonds	2.50
96	J.T. Snow	.15
97	Dennis Eckersley	.15
98	Ron Gant	.15
99	Brian Jordan	.15
100	Ray Lankford	.15

1997 SkyBox E-X2000 Essential Credentials

A sequentially-numbered parallel set, found one per 200 packs, and limited to 99 total sets.

	MT
Common Player:	4.00
Essential Credentials Stars:	12X

(See 1997 SkyBox E-X2000 for checklist and base card values.)

1997 SkyBox E-X2000 Credentials

This parallel set features different colored foils from the base cards, as well as different images on the "window." Cards are sequentially numbered on back within an issue of 299. Cards were inserted 1:50 packs.

	MT
Common Player:	2.00
Credentials Stars:	7X

(See E-X2000 for checklist, base card values)

1997 SkyBox E-X2000 A Cut Above

Some of the game's elite players are featured in this 1:288 pack insert that features a die-cut design resembling a saw blade. Printed on silver-foil stock, the player's name and Cut Above logo are embossed on front. On back is another color photo and a few words about the player.

		MT
Complete Set (10):		55.00
Common Player:		2.50
1	Frank Thomas	8.00
2	Ken Griffey Jr.	12.50
3	Alex Rodriguez	12.50
4	Albert Belle	3.50
5	Juan Gonzalez	5.00
6	Mark McGwire	15.00
7	Mo Vaughn	4.00
8	Manny Ramirez	5.00
9	Barry Bonds	6.50
10	Fred McGriff	2.50

1997 SkyBox E-X2000 Alex Rodriguez Jumbo

This 8" x 10" version of A-Rod's SkyBox E-X2000 card was given to dealers who ordered case quantities of the new product. The card is identical in design to the standard-sized issued version, but is numbered on back from within an edition of 3,000.

	MT
Alex Rodriguez	15.00

1997 SkyBox E-X2000 Emerald Autographs

These authentically autographed versions of the players' E-X2000 cards were available (until May 1, 1998) by a mail-in exchange of redemption cards. The autographed cards are authenticated by the presence of an embossed SkyBox logo seal.

		MT
Complete Set (6):		90.00
Common Player:		4.00
2	Darin Erstad	25.00
30	Todd Walker	5.00
43	Alex Rodriguez	50.00
78	Todd Hollandsworth	4.00
86	Alex Ochoa	4.00
89	Scott Rolen	20.00

1997 SkyBox E-X2000 Emerald Autograph Redemptions

Inserted 1:480 packs, these cards could be exchanged by mail prior to May 1, 1998, for autographed cards or memorabilia from one of six major leaguers.

		MT
Complete Set (6):		20.00
Common Player:		1.00
(1)	Darin Erstad	5.00
(2)	Todd Hollandsworth	1.00
(3)	Alex Ochoa	1.00
(4)	Alex Rodriguez	12.50
(5)	Scott Rolen	5.00
(6)	Todd Walker	1.00

1997 SkyBox E-X2000 Hall or Nothing

This 20-card insert, featuring players who are candidates for the Hall of Fame, utilizes a die-cut design on plastic stock. Stately architectural details and brush bronze highlights frame the player picture on front. The player silhouette on back contains career information. Cards were inserted 1:20 packs.

		MT
Complete Set (20):		60.00
Common Player:		.75
1	Frank Thomas	3.00
2	Ken Griffey Jr.	6.00
3	Eddie Murray	1.50
4	Cal Ripken Jr.	8.00
5	Ryne Sandberg	4.00
6	Wade Boggs	2.50
7	Roger Clemens	4.00
8	Tony Gwynn	3.00
9	Alex Rodriguez	6.00
10	Mark McGwire	8.00
11	Barry Bonds	4.00
12	Greg Maddux	4.00
13	Juan Gonzalez	2.00
14	Albert Belle	1.00
15	Mike Piazza	6.00

16	Jeff Bagwell	2.00
17	Dennis Eckersley	.75
18	Mo Vaughn	1.50
19	Roberto Alomar	1.25
20	Kenny Lofton	.75

1997 SkyBox E-X2000 Star Date 2000

A 15-card set highlighting young stars that are likely to be the game's top players in the year 2000. Cards were inserted 1:9 packs.

		MT
Complete Set (15):		25.00
Common Player:		1.00
1	Alex Rodriguez	5.00
2	Andruw Jones	2.50
3	Andy Pettitte	1.50
4	Brooks Kieschnick	1.00
5	Chipper Jones	5.00
6	Darin Erstad	2.00
7	Derek Jeter	6.00
8	Jason Kendall	1.00
9	Jermaine Dye	1.00
10	Neifi Perez	1.00
11	Scott Rolen	2.00
12	Todd Hollandsworth	1.00
13	Todd Walker	1.00
14	Tony Clark	1.00
15	Vladimir Guerrero	3.00

1998 SkyBox E-X2001 Sample

To preview its high-tech E-X2001 brand for 1998, SkyBox issued this sample card of A-Rod. Similar in format to the issued version, it is numbered "SAMPLE" on back and has a "PROMOTIONAL SAMPLE" overprint on back.

	MT
Alex Rodriguez	3.50

1998 SkyBox E-X2001

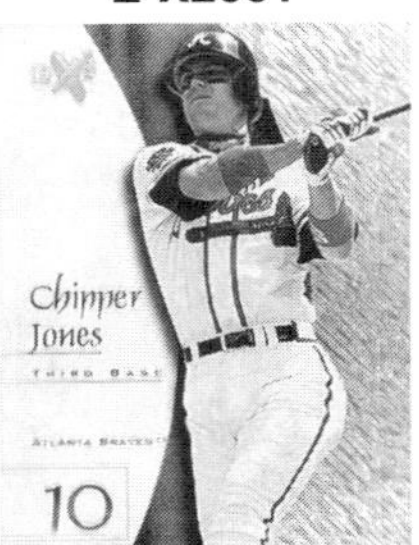

This super-premium set featured 100 players on a layered, die-cuct design utilizing mirror-image silhouetted photography and etched holofoil treatment over a clear, 20-point plastic card.

		MT
Complete Set (100):		50.00
Common Player:		.25
Pack (2):		2.00
Wax Box (24):		40.00
1	Alex Rodriguez	3.50
2	Barry Bonds	2.50
3	Greg Maddux	2.00
4	Roger Clemens	2.00
5	Juan Gonzalez	1.50
6	Chipper Jones	3.00
7	Derek Jeter	3.00
8	Frank Thomas	2.50
9	Cal Ripken Jr.	4.00
10	Ken Griffey Jr.	3.50
11	Mark McGwire	4.00
12	Hideo Nomo	1.25
13	Tony Gwynn	2.00
14	Ivan Rodriguez	1.25
15	Mike Piazza	3.00
16	Roberto Alomar	1.25
17	Jeff Bagwell	1.50
18	Andruw Jones	1.50
19	Albert Belle	.75
20	Mo Vaughn	1.00
21	Kenny Lofton	.25
22	Gary Sheffield	.75
23	Tony Clark	.25
24	Mike Mussina	1.50
25	Barry Larkin	.25
26	Moises Alou	.25
27	Brady Anderson	.25
28	Andy Pettitte	.50
29	Sammy Sosa	2.50
30	Raul Mondesi	.25
31	Andres Galarraga	.25
32	Chuck Knoblauch	.25
33	Jim Thome	.25
34	Craig Biggio	.25
35	Jay Buhner	.25
36	Rafael Palmeiro	.65
37	Curt Schilling	.25
38	Tino Martinez	.25
39	Pedro Martinez	1.50
40	Jose Canseco	1.00
41	Jeff Cirillo	.25
42	Dean Palmer	.25
43	Tim Salmon	.50
44	Jason Giambi	1.00
45	Bobby Higginson	.25
46	Jim Edmonds	.25
47	David Justice	1.00
48	John Olerud	.25
49	Ray Lankford	.25
50	Al Martin	.25
51	Mike Lieberthal	.25
52	Henry Rodriguez	.25
53	Edgar Renteria	.25
54	Eric Karros	.25
55	Marquis Grissom	.25
56	Wilson Alvarez	.25
57	Darryl Kile	.25
58	Jeff King	.25
59	Shawn Estes	.25
60	Tony Womack	.25
61	Willie Greene	.25
62	Ken Caminiti	.25
63	Vinny Castilla	.25
64	Mark Grace	.75
65	Ryan Klesko	.25
66	Robin Ventura	.25
67	Todd Hundley	.25
68	Travis Fryman	.25
69	Edgar Martinez	.25
70	Matt Williams	.75
71	Paul Molitor	1.00
72	Kevin Brown	.50
73	Randy Johnson	1.50
74	Bernie Williams	.75
75	Manny Ramirez	1.50
76	Fred McGriff	.25
77	Tom Glavine	.25
78	Carlos Delgado	.75
79	Larry Walker	1.00
80	Hideki Irabu	.25
81	Ryan McGuire	.25
82	Justin Thompson	.25
83	Kevin Orie	.25
84	Jon Nunnally	.25
85	Mark Kotsay	.25
86	Todd Walker	.25
87	Jason Dickson	.25
88	Fernando Tatis	.25
89	Karim Garcia	.25
90	Ricky Ledee	.25
91	Paul Konerko	.25
92	Jaret Wright	.25
93	Darin Erstad	1.25
94	Livan Hernandez	.25
95	Nomar Garciaparra	2.50
96	Jose Cruz Jr.	.25
97	Scott Rolen	1.25
98	Ben Grieve	.50
99	Vladimir Guerrero	1.50
100	Travis Lee	.25

1998 SkyBox E-X2001 Essential Credentials Now

Essential Credentials Now parallels all 100 cards in the E-X2001 base set. Production for each card was limited to that player's card number, as shown in parentheses.

		MT
Common Player:		7.00
1	Alex Rodriguez (1)	1200.
2	Barry Bonds (2)	750.00
3	Greg Maddux (3)	250.00
4	Roger Clemens (4)	250.00
5	Juan Gonzalez (5)	210.00
6	Chipper Jones (6)	225.00
7	Derek Jeter (7)	225.00
8	Frank Thomas (8)	200.00
9	Cal Ripken Jr. (9)	300.00
10	Ken Griffey Jr. (10)	300.00
11	Mark McGwire (11)	300.00
12	Hideo Nomo (12)	125.00
13	Tony Gwynn (13)	105.00
14	Ivan Rodriguez (14)	75.00
15	Mike Piazza (15)	125.00
16	Roberto Alomar (16)	75.00
17	Jeff Bagwell (17)	80.00
18	Andruw Jones (18)	70.00
19	Albert Belle (19)	40.00
20	Mo Vaughn (20)	60.00
21	Kenny Lofton (21)	30.00
22	Gary Sheffield (22)	50.00
23	Tony Clark (23)	35.00
24	Mike Mussina (24)	60.00
25	Barry Larkin (25)	35.00
26	Moises Alou (26)	30.00
27	Brady Anderson (27)	30.00
28	Andy Pettitte (28)	30.00
29	Sammy Sosa (29)	175.00
30	Raul Mondesi (30)	25.00
31	Andres Galarraga (31)	20.00
32	Chuck Knoblauch (32)	20.00
33	Jim Thome (33)	20.00
34	Craig Biggio (34)	20.00
35	Jay Buhner (35)	20.00
36	Rafael Palmeiro (36)	30.00
37	Curt Schilling (37)	30.00
38	Tino Martinez (38)	25.00
39	Pedro Martinez (39)	50.00
40	Jose Canseco (40)	40.00
41	Jeff Cirillo (41)	12.50
42	Dean Palmer (42)	12.50
43	Tim Salmon (43)	25.00
44	Jason Giambi (44)	35.00
45	Bobby Higginson (45)	15.00
46	Jim Edmonds (46)	15.00
47	David Justice (47)	25.00
48	John Olerud (48)	22.50
49	Ray Lankford (49)	9.00
50	Al Martin (50)	7.00
51	Mike Lieberthal (51)	9.00
52	Henry Rodriguez (52)	7.00
53	Edgar Renteria (53)	7.00
54	Eric Karros (54)	7.00
55	Marquis Grissom (55)	7.00
56	Wilson Alvarez (56)	7.00
57	Darryl Kile (57)	7.00
58	Jeff King (58)	7.00
59	Shawn Estes (59)	7.00
60	Tony Womack (60)	7.00
61	Willie Greene (61)	7.00
62	Ken Caminiti (62)	7.00
63	Vinny Castilla (63)	7.00
64	Mark Grace (64)	20.00
65	Ryan Klesko (65)	7.00
66	Robin Ventura (66)	7.00
67	Todd Hundley (67)	7.00
68	Travis Fryman (68)	7.00
69	Edgar Martinez (69)	7.00
70	Matt Williams (70)	12.50
71	Paul Molitor (71)	25.00
72	Kevin Brown (72)	12.50
73	Randy Johnson (73)	25.00
74	Bernie Williams (74)	10.00
75	Manny Ramirez (75)	35.00
76	Fred McGriff (76)	7.00
77	Tom Glavine (77)	12.50
78	Carlos Delgado (78)	12.50
79	Larry Walker (79)	25.00
80	Hideki Irabu (80)	10.00
81	Ryan McGuire (81)	7.00
82	Justin Thompson (82)	7.00
83	Kevin Orie (83)	7.00
84	Jon Nunnally (84)	7.00
85	Mark Kotsay (85)	10.00
86	Todd Walker (86)	10.00
87	Jason Dickson (87)	10.00
88	Fernando Tatis (88)	10.00
89	Karim Garcia (89)	10.00
90	Ricky Ledee (90)	7.00
91	Paul Konerko (91)	15.00
92	Jaret Wright (92)	15.00
93	Darin Erstad (93)	25.00
94	Livan Hernandez (94)	7.00
95	Nomar Garciaparra (95)	55.00
96	Jose Cruz Jr. (96)	12.50
97	Scott Rolen (97)	35.00
98	Ben Grieve (98)	25.00
99	Vladimir Guerrero (99)	35.00
100	Travis Lee (100)	10.00

1998 SkyBox E-X2001 Essential Credentials Future

Essential Credentials Future, along with Essential Credentials Now, paralleled all 100 cards in the base set. Production varied depending on the card number, with the exact production number of each player determined by subtracting his card number from 101. Number issued for each card is shown in parentheses.

		MT
Common Player:		7.00
1	Alex Rodriguez (100)	95.00
2	Barry Bonds (99)	75.00
3	Greg Maddux (98)	55.00
4	Roger Clemens (97)	55.00
5	Juan Gonzalez (96)	45.00
6	Chipper Jones (95)	70.00
7	Derek Jeter (94)	90.00
8	Frank Thomas (93)	60.00
9	Cal Ripken Jr. (92)	90.00
10	Ken Griffey Jr. (91)	85.00
11	Mark McGwire (90)	90.00
12	Hideo Nomo (89)	35.00
13	Tony Gwynn (88)	35.00
14	Ivan Rodriguez (87)	35.00
15	Mike Piazza (86)	80.00
16	Roberto Alomar (85)	35.00
17	Jeff Bagwell (84)	35.00
18	Andruw Jones (83)	30.00
19	Albert Belle (82)	15.00
20	Mo Vaughn (81)	25.00
21	Kenny Lofton (80)	12.50
22	Gary Sheffield (79)	17.50
23	Tony Clark (78)	12.50
24	Mike Mussina (77)	40.00
25	Barry Larkin (76)	15.00
26	Moises Alou (75)	15.00
27	Brady Anderson (74)	15.00
28	Andy Pettitte (73)	20.00
29	Sammy Sosa (72)	85.00
30	Raul Mondesi (71)	15.00
31	Andres Galarraga (70)	15.00
32	Chuck Knoblauch (69)	15.00
33	Jim Thome (68)	15.00
34	Craig Biggio (67)	20.00
35	Jay Buhner (66)	15.00
36	Rafael Palmeiro (65)	35.00
37	Curt Schilling (64)	40.00
38	Tino Martinez (63)	17.50
39	Pedro Martinez (62)	60.00
40	Jose Canseco (61)	45.00
41	Jeff Cirillo (60)	12.50
42	Dean Palmer (59)	12.50
43	Tim Salmon (58)	25.00
44	Jason Giambi (57)	45.00
45	Bobby Higginson (56)	20.00
46	Jim Edmonds (55)	20.00
47	David Justice (54)	25.00
48	John Olerud (53)	22.50
49	Ray Lankford (52)	12.50
50	Al Martin (51)	12.50
51	Mike Lieberthal (50)	17.50
52	Henry Rodriguez (49)	10.00
53	Edgar Renteria (48)	12.50
54	Eric Karros (47)	12.50
55	Marquis Grissom (46)	12.50
56	Wilson Alvarez (45)	10.00
57	Darryl Kile (44)	9.00
58	Jeff King (43)	7.00
59	Shawn Estes (42)	7.00
60	Tony Womack (41)	7.00
61	Willie Greene (40)	7.00
62	Ken Caminiti (39)	9.00
63	Vinny Castilla (38)	10.00
64	Mark Grace (37)	50.00
65	Ryan Klesko (36)	15.00
66	Robin Ventura (35)	20.00
67	Todd Hundley (34)	20.00
68	Travis Fryman (33)	20.00
69	Edgar Martinez (32)	20.00
70	Matt Williams (31)	30.00
71	Paul Molitor (30)	55.00
72	Kevin Brown (29)	35.00
73	Randy Johnson (28)	55.00
74	Bernie Williams (27)	45.00
75	Manny Ramirez (26)	85.00
76	Fred McGriff (25)	30.00
77	Tom Glavine (24)	35.00
78	Carlos Delgado (23)	50.00
79	Larry Walker (22)	50.00
80	Hideki Irabu (21)	35.00
81	Ryan McGuire (20)	10.00
82	Justin Thompson (19)	7.00
83	Kevin Orie (18)	7.50
84	Jon Nunnally (17)	7.00
85	Mark Kotsay (16)	25.00
86	Todd Walker (15)	20.00
87	Jason Dickson (14)	20.00
88	Fernando Tatis (13)	35.00
89	Karim Garcia (12)	35.00
90	Ricky Ledee (11)	25.00
91	Paul Konerko (10)	25.00
92	Jaret Wright (9)	35.00
93	Darin Erstad (8)	70.00
94	Livan Hernandez (7)	25.00
95	Nomar Garciaparra (6)	250.00
96	Jose Cruz Jr. (5)	50.00
97	Scott Rolen (4)	175.00
98	Ben Grieve (3)	175.00
99	Vladimir Guerrero (2)	600.00
100	Travis Lee (1)	400.00

1998 SkyBox E-X2001 Cheap Seat Treats

This 20-card die-cut insert arrived in the shape of a stadium seat. Inserted at one per 24 packs, Cheap Seat Treats included some of the top home run hitters and were numbered with a "CS" prefix.

		MT
Complete Set (20):		36.00
Common Player:		1.00
Inserted 1:24		
1	Frank Thomas	3.50
2	Ken Griffey Jr.	6.00
3	Mark McGwire	7.50
4	Tino Martinez	1.00
5	Larry Walker	1.50
6	Juan Gonzalez	2.50
7	Mike Piazza	5.00
8	Jeff Bagwell	2.50
9	Tony Clark	1.00
10	Albert Belle	1.50
11	Andres Galarraga	1.00
12	Jim Thome	1.00
13	Mo Vaughn	1.50
14	Barry Bonds	3.50
15	Vladimir Guerrero	2.00
16	Scott Rolen	2.00
17	Travis Lee	1.00
18	David Justice	1.50
19	Jose Cruz Jr.	1.00
20	Andruw Jones	2.00

1998 SkyBox E-X2001 Destination: Cooperstown

Destination: Cooperstown captures a mixture of rising young stars and top veterans on die-cut cards that were inserted one per 720 packs. Cards resemble a luggage tag and have a string through a hole at top. Fronts have an action photo, backs have a portrait. Cards are numbered with a "DC" prefix.

		MT
Complete Set (15):		400.00
Common Player:		8.00
Inserted 1:720		
1	Alex Rodriguez	40.00
2	Frank Thomas	25.00
3	Cal Ripken Jr.	50.00
4	Roger Clemens	30.00
5	Greg Maddux	30.00
6	Chipper Jones	40.00
7	Ken Griffey Jr.	45.00
8	Mark McGwire	50.00
9	Tony Gwynn	30.00
10	Mike Piazza	40.00
11	Jeff Bagwell	20.00
12	Jose Cruz Jr.	8.00
13	Derek Jeter	50.00
14	Hideo Nomo	15.00
15	Ivan Rodriguez	15.00

1998 SkyBox E-X2001 Kerry Wood

In an effort to get rookie pitching phenom Kerry Wood into its E-X2001 set, SkyBox created a cardboard, rather than plastic, trade card and inserted it at a rate of one per 50 packs. The trade card could be exchanged bu mail for a plastic version.

		MT
Complete Set (2):		2.00
---	Kerry Wood (cardboard trade card)	1.00
101	Kerry Wood (plastic redemption card)	1.00

1998 SkyBox E-X2001 Signature 2001

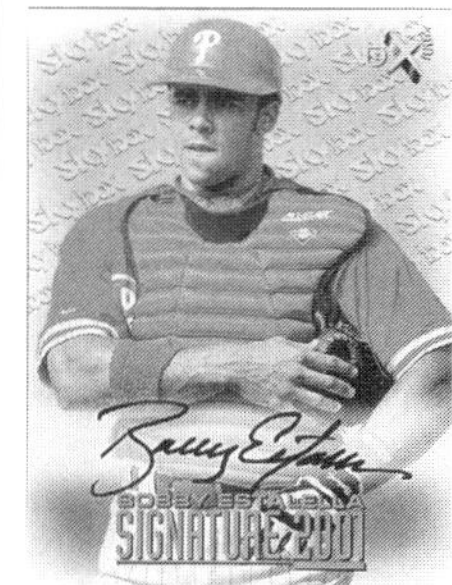

Seventeen top young and future stars signed cards for Signature 2001 inserts in E-X2001. The cards featured the player over a blue and white, sky-like background, with an embossed SkyBox seal of authenticity. Backs were horizontal and also included a Certificate of Authenticity. These cards were unnumbered and inserted one per 60 packs.

		MT
Complete Set (17):		175.00
Common Player:		4.00
Inserted 1:60		
1	Ricky Ledee	4.00
2	Derrick Gibson	4.00
3	Mark Kotsay	7.50
4	Kevin Millwood	15.00
5	Brad Fullmer	4.00
6	Todd Walker	6.00
7	Ben Grieve	10.00
8	Tony Clark	6.00
9	Jaret Wright	5.00
10	Randall Simon	4.00
11	Paul Konerko	6.00
12	Todd Helton	15.00
13	David Ortiz	6.00
14	Alex Gonzalez	6.00
15	Bobby Estalella	4.00
16	Alex Rodriguez	80.00
17	Mike Lowell	5.00

1998 SkyBox E-X2001 Star Date 2001

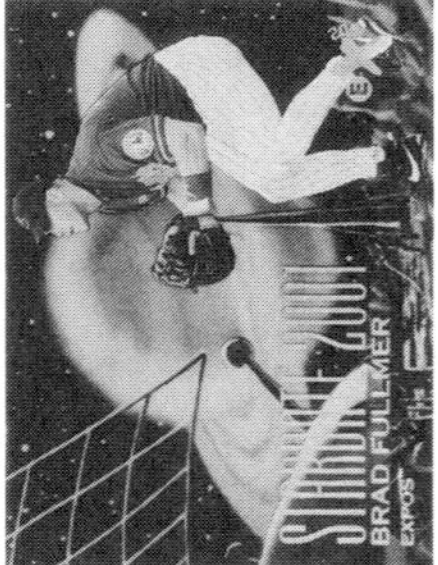

Star Date 2001 displays 15 of the top rising stars on an acetate space/planet background with gold-foil printing on front. This insert was seeded one per 12 packs and was numbered with a "SD" suffix.

		MT
Complete Set (15):		12.00
Common Player:		.50
Inserted 1:12		
1	Travis Lee	.65
2	Jose Cruz Jr.	.75
3	Paul Konerko	.75
4	Bobby Estalella	.50
5	Magglio Ordonez	3.00
6	Juan Encarnacion	.75
7	Richard Hidalgo	.75
8	Abraham Nunez	.50
9	Sean Casey	1.50
10	Todd Helton	2.50
11	Brad Fullmer	.50
12	Ben Grieve	1.50
13	Livan Hernandez	.50
14	Jaret Wright	.50
15	Todd Dunwoody	.50

1998 SkyBox Dugout Axcess

Dugout Axcess was a 150-card set that attempted to provide collectors with an inside look at baseball. The cards were printed on "playing card" quality stock and used unique information and photography. The product arrived in 12-card packs with an Inside Axcess parallel set that was individually numbered to 50 sets. Six different inserts sets were available, including Double Header, Frequent Flyers, Dishwashers, Superheroes, Gronks and Autograph Redemptions.

		MT
Complete Set (150):		15.00
Common Player:		.10
Pack (12):		1.00
Wax Box (36):		30.00
1	Travis Lee	.15
2	Matt Williams	.25
3	Andy Benes	.10
4	Chipper Jones	1.00
5	Ryan Klesko	.10
6	Greg Maddux	.60
7	Sammy Sosa	.75
8	Henry Rodriguez	.10
9	Mark Grace	.25
10	Barry Larkin	.15
11	Bret Boone	.10
12	Reggie Sanders	.10
13	Vinny Castilla	.10
14	Larry Walker	.25
15	Darryl Kile	.10
16	Charles Johnson	.10
17	Edgar Renteria	.10
18	Gary Sheffield	.25
19	Jeff Bagwell	.50
20	Craig Biggio	.15
21	Moises Alou	.15
22	Mike Piazza	1.00
23	Hideo Nomo	.40
24	Raul Mondesi	.15
25	John Jaha	.10
26	Jeff Cirillo	.10
27	Jeromy Burnitz	.10
28	Mark Grudzielanek	.10
29	Vladimir Guerrero	.50
30	Rondell White	.15
31	Edgardo Alfonzo	.10
32	Rey Ordonez	.10
33	Bernard Gilkey	.10
34	Scott Rolen	.40
35	Curt Schilling	.20
36	Ricky Bottalico	.10
37	Tony Womack	.10
38	Al Martin	.10
39	Jason Kendall	.10
40	Ron Gant	.10
41	Mark McGwire	1.50
42	Ray Lankford	.10
43	Tony Gwynn	.60
44	Ken Caminiti	.10
45	Kevin Brown	.15
46	Barry Bonds	.75
47	J.T. Snow	.10
48	Shawn Estes	.10
49	Jim Edmonds	.10
50	Tim Salmon	.20
51	Jason Dickson	.10
52	Cal Ripken Jr.	1.50
53	Mike Mussina	.40
54	Roberto Alomar	.40
55	Mo Vaughn	.25
56	Pedro Martinez	.50
57	Nomar Garciaparra	.75
58	Albert Belle	.20
59	Frank Thomas	.75
60	Robin Ventura	.10
61	Jim Thome	.10
62	Sandy Alomar Jr.	.10
63	Jaret Wright	.10
64	Bobby Higginson	.10
65	Tony Clark	.10
66	Justin Thompson	.10
67	Dean Palmer	.10
68	Kevin Appier	.10
69	Johnny Damon	.10
70	Paul Molitor	.30
71	Marty Cordova	.10
72	Brad Radke	.10
73	Derek Jeter	1.00
74	Bernie Williams	.30
75	Andy Pettitte	.20
76	Matt Stairs	.10
77	Ben Grieve	.20
78	Jason Giambi	.40
79	Randy Johnson	.50
80	Ken Griffey Jr.	1.25
81	Alex Rodriguez	1.25
82	Fred McGriff	.10
83	Wade Boggs	.50
84	Wilson Alvarez	.10
85	Juan Gonzalez	.50
86	Ivan Rodriguez	.40
87	Fernando Tatis	.10
88	Roger Clemens	.60
89	Jose Cruz Jr.	.15
90	Shawn Green	.20
91	Jeff Suppan (Little Dawgs)	.10
92	Eli Marrero (Little Dawgs)	.10
93	*Mike Lowell* (Little Dawgs)	.40
94	Ben Grieve (Little Dawgs)	.15
95	Cliff Politte (Little Dawgs)	.10
96	*Rolando Arrojo* (Little Dawgs)	.25
97	Mike Caruso (Little Dawgs)	.10
98	Miguel Tejada (Little Dawgs)	.15
99	Rod Myers (Little Dawgs)	.10
100	Juan Encarnacion (Little Dawgs)	.10
101	Enrique Wilson (Little Dawgs)	.10
102	Brian Giles (Little Dawgs)	.10
103	*Magglio Ordonez* (Little Dawgs)	.75
104	Brian Rose (Little Dawgs)	.10
105	*Ryan Jackson* (Little Dawgs)	.10
106	Mark Kotsay (Little Dawgs)	.10
107	Desi Relaford (Little Dawgs)	.10
108	A.J. Hinch (Little Dawgs)	.10
109	Eric Milton (Little Dawgs)	.10
110	Ricky Ledee (Little Dawgs)	.10
111	Karim Garcia (Little Dawgs)	.10
112	Derrek Lee (Little Dawgs)	.10
113	Brad Fullmer (Little Dawgs)	.10
114	Travis Lee (Little Dawgs)	.10
115	Greg Norton (Little Dawgs)	.10
116	Rich Butler (Little Dawgs)	.10
117	*Masato Yoshii* (Little Dawgs)	.25
118	Paul Konerko (Little Dawgs)	.20
119	Richard Hidalgo (Little Dawgs)	.10
120	Todd Helton (Little Dawgs)	.50
121	Nomar Garciaparra (7th Inning Sketch)	.35
122	Scott Rolen (7th Inning Sketch)	.20
123	Cal Ripken Jr. (7th Inning Sketch)	.75
124	Derek Jeter (7th Inning Sketch)	.50
125	Mike Piazza (7th Inning Sketch)	.50
126	Tony Gwynn (7th Inning Sketch)	.40
127	Mark McGwire (7th Inning Sketch)	.75
128	Kenny Lofton (7th Inning Sketch)	.10
129	Greg Maddux (7th Inning Sketch)	.40
130	Jeff Bagwell (7th Inning Sketch)	.25
131	Randy Johnson (7th Inning Sketch)	.25
132	Alex Rodriguez (7th Inning Sketch)	.65
133	Mo Vaughn (Name Plates)	.20
134	Chipper Jones (Name Plates)	.50
135	Juan Gonzalez (Name Plates)	.30
136	Tony Clark (Name Plates)	.10
137	Fred McGriff (Name Plates)	.10
138	Roger Clemens (Name Plates)	.40
139	Ken Griffey Jr. (Name Plates)	.60
140	Ivan Rodriguez (Name Plates)	.25
141	Vinny Castilla (Trivia Card)	.10
142	Livan Hernandez (Trivia Card)	.10
143	Jose Cruz Jr. (Trivia Card)	.10
144	Andruw Jones (Trivia Card)	.20
145	Rafael Palmeiro (Trivia Card)	.10
146	Chuck Knoblauch (Trivia Card)	.10
147	Jay Buhner (Trivia Card)	.10
148	Andres Galarraga (Trivia Card)	.10
149	Frank Thomas (Trivia Card)	.30
150	Todd Hundley (Trivia Card)	.10

1998 SkyBox Dugout Axcess Inside Axcess

This 150-card parallel set was sequentially numbered to 50 sets, with each card containing a stamped logo on the front and serial numbering on the back.

	MT
Common Player:	4.00
Inside Axcess Stars:	60X

(See 1998 SkyBox Dugout Access for checklist and base card values.)

1998 SkyBox Dugout Axcess Autograph Redemption Cards

These scarce - one per 96 packs - inserts were redeemable (until March 31, 1999) for autographed baseballs or gloves from more than a dozen established stars and promising youngsters. Because the cards do not picture the player involved, having a generic photo of a person's arm signing an autograph, the exchange cards don't have tremendous collector value now that the redemption period has expired. The autographed balls and gloves would be valued according to supply and demand in the memorabilia marketplace.

		MT
Complete Set (15):		37.00
Common Card:		1.50
(1)	Jay Buhner (Ball)	1.50
(2)	Roger Clemens (Ball)	2.50
(3)	Jose Cruz Jr. (Ball)	2.25
(4)	Darin Erstad (Glove)	4.50
(5)	Nomar Garciaparra (Ball)	3.00
(6)	Tony Gwynn (Ball)	2.50
(7)	Roberto Hernandez (Ball)	1.50
(8)	Todd Hollandsworth (Glove)	3.00
(9)	Greg Maddux (Ball)	3.00
(10)	Alex Ochoa (Glove)	3.00
(11)	Alex Rodriguez (Ball)	4.00
(12)	Scott Rolen (Glove)	4.50
(13)	Scott Rolen (Ball)	2.50
(14)	Todd Walker (Glove)	3.00
(15)	Tony Womack (Ball)	1.50

1998 SkyBox Dugout Axcess Dishwashers

This 10-card set was a tribute to the game's best pitchers who "clean the home plate of opposing batters." Cards were inserted one per eight packs.

		MT
Complete Set (10):		6.00
Common Player:		.50
Inserted 1:8		
D1	Greg Maddux	2.50
D2	Kevin Brown	.50
D3	Pedro Martinez	.75
D4	Randy Johnson	1.25
D5	Curt Schilling	.75
D6	John Smoltz	.50
D7	Darryl Kile	.50
D8	Roger Clemens	2.50
D9	Andy Pettitte	.60
D10	Mike Mussina	.75

1998 SkyBox Dugout Axcess Double Header

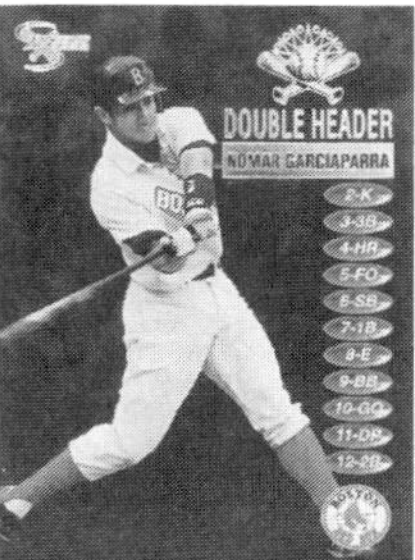

Double Header featured 20 players on cards that doubled as game pieces. The game instructions were on the card and required two dice to play. These were inserted at a rate of two per pack.

		MT
Complete Set (20):		4.00
Common Player:		.15
Inserted 2:1		
DH1	Jeff Bagwell	.25
DH2	Albert Belle	.20
DH3	Barry Bonds	.45
DH4	Derek Jeter	.50
DH5	Tony Clark	.15
DH6	Nomar Garciaparra	.45
DH7	Juan Gonzalez	.25
DH8	Ken Griffey Jr.	.65
DH9	Chipper Jones	.50
DH10	Kenny Lofton	.15
DH11	Mark McGwire	.75
DH12	Mo Vaughn	.25
DH13	Mike Piazza	.50
DH14	Cal Ripken Jr.	.75
DH15	Ivan Rodriguez	.25
DH16	Scott Rolen	.25
DH17	Frank Thomas	.45
DH18	Tony Gwynn	.35
DH19	Travis Lee	.20
DH20	Jose Cruz Jr.	.15

1998 SkyBox Dugout Axcess Frequent Flyers

The game's top 10 base stealers were included in Frequent Flyers. This insert was designed to look like airline frequent flyer cards and was inserted one per four packs. Fronts have player action photos on a metallic-foil background of a cloudy sky. Backs have a portrait photo and a few words about the player's base-stealing ability. Cards are numbered with an "FF" prefix.

		MT
Complete Set (10):		2.50
Common Player:		.25
Inserted 1:4		
FF1	Brian Hunter	.25
FF2	Kenny Lofton	.25
FF3	Chuck Knoblauch	.25
FF4	Tony Womack	.25
FF5	Marquis Grissom	.25
FF6	Craig Biggio	.25
FF7	Barry Bonds	1.00
FF8	Tom Goodwin	.25
FF9	Delino DeShields	.25
FF10	Eric Young	.25

1998 SkyBox Dugout Axcess Gronks

Gronks featured 10 of the top home run hitters and was a hobby exclusive insert. The name of the insert originated from shortstop Greg Gagne, and the cards were inserted in one per 72 packs.

		MT
Complete Set (10):		70.00
Common Player:		3.00
Inserted 1:72		
G1	Jeff Bagwell	8.50
G2	Albert Belle	5.00
G3	Juan Gonzalez	8.50
G4	Ken Griffey Jr.	17.50
G5	Mark McGwire	20.00
G6	Mike Piazza	15.50
G7	Frank Thomas	12.50
G8	Mo Vaughn	3.00
G9	Ken Caminiti	3.00
G10	Tony Clark	3.00

1998 SkyBox Dugout Axcess SuperHeroes

SuperHeroes combined 10 top superstars with the Marvel Comics superhero with whom they share a common trait in this 10-card insert set. Cards were inserted at a rate of one per 20 packs.

		MT
Complete Set (10):		12.50
Common Player:		.50
Inserted 1:20		
SH1	Barry Bonds	1.50
SH2	Andres Galarraga	.50
SH3	Ken Griffey Jr.	2.50
SH4	Chipper Jones	2.00
SH5	Andruw Jones	1.00
SH6	Hideo Nomo	1.00
SH7	Cal Ripken Jr.	3.00
SH8	Alex Rodriguez	3.00
SH9	Frank Thomas	1.50
SH10	Mo Vaughn	.75

1999 SkyBox E-X Century

The 120-card base set features a clear plastic stock with the player name, logo and position stamped in holographic foil. Card backs have the featured player's vital information along with his '98 statistics and his major league totals. Cards 91-120 are part of a prospects subset and are short-printed seeded 1:2 packs. Three-card packs have a SRP of $5.99.

		MT
Complete Set (120):		45.00
Common Player:		.25
Common SP (91-120):		.60
Inserted 1:2		
Pack (3):		2.50
Wax Box (18):		40.00
1	Scott Rolen	1.25
2	Nomar Garciaparra	2.75
3	Mike Piazza	3.25
4	Tony Gwynn	2.25
5	Sammy Sosa	2.75
6	Alex Rodriguez	3.50
7	Vladimir Guerrero	1.50
8	Chipper Jones	3.25
9	Derek Jeter	3.25
10	Kerry Wood	.50
11	Juan Gonzalez	1.50
12	Frank Thomas	2.75
13	Mo Vaughn	.50
14	Greg Maddux	2.25

15	Jeff Bagwell	1.50
16	Mark McGwire	4.00
17	Ken Griffey Jr.	3.50
18	Roger Clemens	2.25
19	Cal Ripken Jr.	4.00
20	Travis Lee	.25
21	Todd Helton	1.25
22	Darin Erstad	1.25
23	Pedro Martinez	1.25
24	Barry Bonds	2.50
25	Andruw Jones	1.50
26	Larry Walker	.45
27	Albert Belle	.45
28	Ivan Rodriguez	1.25
29	Magglio Ordonez	.25
30	Andres Galarraga	.25
31	Mike Mussina	1.00
32	Randy Johnson	1.25
33	Tom Glavine	.25
34	Barry Larkin	.25
35	Jim Thome	.25
36	Gary Sheffield	.45
37	Bernie Williams	.65
38	Carlos Delgado	.60
39	Rafael Palmeiro	.60
40	Edgar Renteria	.25
41	Brad Fullmer	.25
42	David Wells	.25
43	Dante Bichette	.25
44	Jaret Wright	.25
45	Ricky Ledee	.25
46	Ray Lankford	.25
47	Mark Grace	.40
48	Jeff Cirillo	.25
49	Rondell White	.25
50	Jeromy Burnitz	.25
51	Sean Casey	.50
52	Rolando Arrojo	.25
53	Jason Giambi	.60
54	John Olerud	.25
55	Will Clark	.45
56	Raul Mondesi	.35
57	Scott Brosius	.25
58	Bartolo Colon	.25
59	Steve Finley	.25
60	Javy Lopez	.25
61	Tim Salmon	.30
62	Roberto Alomar	1.00
63	Vinny Castilla	.25
64	Craig Biggio	.25
65	Jose Guillen	.25
66	Greg Vaughn	.25
67	Jose Canseco	.60
68	Shawn Green	.40
69	Curt Schilling	.35
70	Orlando Hernandez	.35
71	Jose Cruz Jr.	.25
72	Alex Gonzalez	.25
73	Tino Martinez	.25
74	Todd Hundley	.25
75	Brian Giles	.25
76	Cliff Floyd	.25
77	Paul O'Neill	.25
78	Ken Caminiti	.25
79	Ron Gant	.25
80	Juan Encarnacion	.25
81	Ben Grieve	.50
82	Brian Jordan	.25
83	Rickey Henderson	.60
84	Tony Clark	.25
85	Shannon Stewart	.25
86	Robin Ventura	.25
87	Todd Walker	.25
88	Kevin Brown	.40
89	Moises Alou	.30
90	Manny Ramirez	1.50
91	Gabe Alvarez	.60
92	Jeremy Giambi	.60
93	Adrian Beltre	.60
94	George Lombard	.60
95	Ryan Minor	.60
96	Kevin Witt	.60
97	*Scott Hunter*	.60
98	Carlos Guillen	.60
99	Derrick Gibson	.60
100	Trot Nixon	.60
101	Troy Glaus	3.00
102	Armando Rios	.60
103	Preston Wilson	1.25
104	*Pat Burrell*	5.00
105	J.D. Drew	1.25
106	Bruce Chen	.60
107	Matt Clement	.60
108	Carlos Beltran	.60
109	Carlos Febles	.60
110	Rob Fick	.60
111	Russell Branyan	.60
112	*Roosevelt Brown*	1.00
113	Corey Koskie	.60
114	Mario Encarnacion	.60
115	*Peter Tucci*	.60
116	Eric Chavez	.75
117	Gabe Kapler	.60
118	Marlon Anderson	.60
119	*A.J. Burnett*	.75
120	Ryan Bradley	.60
---	Checklist 1-96	.05
---	Checklist 97-120/ Inserts	.05

1999 SkyBox E-X Century Essential Credentials Future

A glossy silver design replaces the clear plastic portions seen on the base cards. Production varied depending on the card number, with the exact production number of each player determined by subtracting his card number from 121. Quantity issued is listed in parentheses.

		MT
Common Player:		7.50
1	Scott Rolen (120)	30.00
2	Nomar Garciaparra (119)	60.00
3	Mike Piazza (118)	65.00
4	Tony Gwynn (117)	50.00
5	Sammy Sosa (116)	65.00
6	Alex Rodriguez (115)	70.00
7	Vladimir Guerrero (114)	30.00
8	Chipper Jones (113)	60.00
9	Derek Jeter (112)	60.00
10	Kerry Wood (111)	25.00
11	Juan Gonzalez (110)	25.00
12	Frank Thomas (109)	35.00
13	Mo Vaughn (108)	25.00
14	Greg Maddux (107)	40.00
15	Jeff Bagwell (106)	30.00
16	Mark McGwire (105)	85.00
17	Ken Griffey Jr. (104)	75.00
18	Roger Clemens (103)	40.00
19	Cal Ripken Jr. (102)	85.00
20	Travis Lee (101)	15.00
21	Todd Helton (100)	20.00
22	Darin Erstad (99)	15.00
23	Pedro Martinez (98)	30.00
24	Barry Bonds (97)	40.00
25	Andruw Jones (96)	25.00
26	Larry Walker (95)	20.00
27	Albert Belle (94)	17.50
28	Ivan Rodriguez (93)	20.00
29	Magglio Ordonez (92)	20.00
30	Andres Galarraga (91)	9.00
31	Mike Mussina (90)	30.00
32	Randy Johnson (89)	30.00
33	Tom Glavine (88)	20.00
34	Barry Larkin (87)	12.50
35	Jim Thome (86)	9.00
36	Gary Sheffield (85)	15.00
37	Bernie Williams (84)	25.00
38	Carlos Delgado (83)	20.00
39	Rafael Palmeiro (82)	20.00
40	Edgar Renteria (81)	7.50
41	Brad Fullmer (80)	7.50
42	David Wells (79)	9.00
43	Dante Bichette (78)	7.50
44	Jaret Wright (77)	12.50
45	Ricky Ledee (76)	9.00
46	Ray Lankford (75)	7.50
47	Mark Grace (74)	20.00
48	Jeff Cirillo (73)	7.50
49	Rondell White (72)	10.00
50	Jeromy Burnitz (71)	7.50
51	Sean Casey (70)	25.00
52	Rolando Arrojo (69)	7.50
53	Jason Giambi (68)	30.00
54	John Olerud (67)	9.00
55	Will Clark (66)	15.00
56	Raul Mondesi (65)	12.50
57	Scott Brosius (64)	7.50
58	Bartolo Colon (63)	9.00
59	Steve Finley (62)	7.50
60	Javy Lopez (61)	7.50
61	Tim Salmon (60)	12.50
62	Roberto Alomar (59)	37.50
63	Vinny Castilla (58)	7.50
64	Craig Biggio (57)	9.00
65	Jose Guillen (56)	7.50
66	Greg Vaughn (55)	7.50
67	Jose Canseco (54)	30.00
68	Shawn Green (53)	15.00
69	Curt Schilling (52)	25.00
70	Orlando Hernandez (51)	35.00
71	Jose Cruz Jr. (50)	15.00
72	Alex Gonzalez (49)	15.00
73	Tino Martinez (48)	20.00
74	Todd Hundley (47)	10.00
75	Brian Giles (46)	10.00
76	Cliff Floyd (45)	10.00
77	Paul O'Neill (44)	10.00
78	Ken Caminiti (43)	10.00
79	Ron Gant (42)	10.00
80	Juan Encarnacion (41)	15.00
81	Ben Grieve (40)	25.00
82	Brian Jordan (39)	10.00
83	Rickey Henderson (38)	30.00
84	Tony Clark (37)	15.00
85	Shannon Stewart (36)	10.00
86	Robin Ventura (35)	12.50
87	Todd Walker (34)	10.00
88	Kevin Brown (33)	12.50
89	Moises Alou (32)	17.50
90	Manny Ramirez (31)	60.00
91	Gabe Alvarez (30)	12.50
92	Jeremy Giambi (29)	12.50
93	Adrian Beltre (28)	20.00
94	George Lombard (27)	12.50
95	Ryan Minor (26)	12.50
96	Kevin Witt (25)	12.50
97	Scott Hunter (24)	12.50
98	Carlos Guillen (23)	12.50
99	Derrick Gibson (22)	12.50
100	Trot Nixon (21)	15.00
101	Troy Glaus (20)	60.00
102	Armando Rios (19)	12.50
103	Preston Wilson (18)	20.00
104	Pat Burrell (17)	100.00
105	J.D. Drew (16)	100.00
106	Bruce Chen (15)	15.00
107	Matt Clement (14)	12.50
108	Carlos Beltran (13)	60.00
109	Carlos Febles (12)	20.00
110	Rob Fick (11)	20.00
111	Russell Branyan (10)	30.00
112	Roosevelt Brown (9)	50.00
113	Corey Koskie (8)	25.00
114	Mario Encarnacion (7)	25.00
115	Peter Tucci (6)	35.00
116	Eric Chavez (5)	65.00
117	Gabe Kapler (4)	65.00
118	Marlon Anderson (3)	75.00
119	A.J. Burnett (2)	75.00
120	Ryan Bradley (1)	90.00

1999 SkyBox E-X Century Essential Credentials Now

Like Future, this is a parallel of the base set, with production of each card limited to that player's card number. These cards have a glossy gold look.

		MT
Common Player:		7.50
1	Scott Rolen (1)	200.00
2	Nomar Garciaparra (2)	250.00
3	Mike Piazza (3)	300.00
4	Tony Gwynn (4)	125.00
5	Sammy Sosa (5)	225.00
6	Alex Rodriguez (6)	225.00
7	Vladimir Guerrero (7)	100.00
8	Chipper Jones (8)	150.00
9	Derek Jeter (9)	150.00
10	Kerry Wood (10)	115.00
11	Juan Gonzalez (11)	110.00
12	Frank Thomas (12)	125.00
13	Mo Vaughn (13)	75.00
14	Greg Maddux (14)	100.00
15	Jeff Bagwell (15)	85.00
16	Mark McGwire (16)	400.00
17	Ken Griffey Jr. (17)	325.00
18	Roger Clemens (18)	100.00
19	Cal Ripken Jr. (19)	350.00
20	Travis Lee (20)	30.00

21 Todd Helton (21) 40.00
22 Darin Erstad (22) 30.00
23 Pedro Martinez (23) 40.00
24 Barry Bonds (24) 75.00
25 Andruw Jones (25) 60.00
26 Larry Walker (26) 40.00
27 Albert Belle (27) 40.00
28 Ivan Rodriguez (28) 50.00
29 Magglio Ordonez (29) 25.00
30 Andres Galarraga (30) 15.00
31 Mike Mussina (31) 50.00
32 Randy Johnson (32) 50.00
33 Tom Glavine (33) 30.00
34 Barry Larkin (34) 12.50
35 Jim Thome (35) 10.00
36 Gary Sheffield (36) 15.00
37 Bernie Williams (37) 30.00
38 Carlos Delgado (38) 25.00
39 Rafael Palmeiro (39) 30.00
40 Edgar Renteria (40) 12.50
41 Brad Fullmer (41) 10.00
42 David Wells (42) 12.50
43 Dante Bichette (43) 12.50
44 Jaret Wright (44) 12.50
45 Ricky Ledee (45) 10.00
46 Ray Lankford (46) 7.50
47 Mark Grace (47) 20.00
48 Jeff Cirillo (48) 7.50
49 Rondell White (49) 12.50
50 Jeromy Burnitz (50) 7.50
51 Sean Casey (51) 25.00
52 Rolando Arrojo (52) 7.50
53 Jason Giambi (53) 35.00
54 John Olerud (54) 10.00
55 Will Clark (55) 15.00
56 Raul Mondesi (56) 15.00
57 Scott Brosius (57) 7.50
58 Bartolo Colon (58) 10.00
59 Steve Finley (59) 7.50
60 Javy Lopez (60) 7.50
61 Tim Salmon (61) 10.00
62 Roberto Alomar (62) 40.00
63 Vinny Castilla (63) 7.50
64 Craig Biggio (64) 9.00
65 Jose Guillen (65) 7.50
66 Greg Vaughn (66) 7.50
67 Jose Canseco (67) 30.00
68 Shawn Green (68) 12.50
69 Curt Schilling (69) 15.00
70 Orlando Hernandez (70) 20.00
71 Jose Cruz Jr. (71) 9.00
72 Alex Gonzalez (72) 9.00
73 Tino Martinez (73) 9.00
74 Todd Hundley (74) 9.00
75 Brian Giles (75) 7.50
76 Cliff Floyd (76) 7.50
77 Paul O'Neill (77) 7.50
78 Ken Caminiti (78) 7.50
79 Ron Gant (79) 7.50
80 Juan Encarnacion (80) 7.50
81 Ben Grieve (81) 10.00
82 Brian Jordan (82) 7.50
83 Rickey Henderson (83) 25.00
84 Tony Clark (84) 9.00
85 Shannon Stewart (85) 10.00
86 Robin Ventura (86) 10.00
87 Todd Walker (87) 7.50
88 Kevin Brown (88) 15.00
89 Moises Alou (89) 10.00
90 Manny Ramirez (90) 30.00
91 Gabe Alvarez (91) 7.50
92 Jeremy Giambi (92) 7.50
93 Adrian Beltre (93) 12.50
94 George Lombard (94) 7.50
95 Ryan Minor (95) 7.50
96 Kevin Witt (96) 7.50
97 Scott Hunter (97) 7.50
98 Carlos Guillen (98) 7.50
99 Derrick Gibson (99) 7.50
100 Trot Nixon (100) 7.50
101 Troy Glaus (101) 20.00
102 Armando Rios (102) 7.50
103 Preston Wilson (103) 10.00
104 Pat Burrell (104) 30.00
105 J.D. Drew (105) 30.00
106 Bruce Chen (106) 7.50
107 Matt Clement (107) 7.50
108 Carlos Beltran (108) 15.00
109 Carlos Febles (109) 9.00
110 Rob Fick (110) 7.50
111 Russell Branyan (111) 10.00
112 Roosevelt Brown (112) 10.00
113 Corey Koskie (113) 10.00
114 Mario Encarnacion (114) 7.50
115 Peter Tucci (115) 7.50
116 Eric Chavez (116) 15.00
117 Gabe Kapler (117) 15.00
118 Marlon Anderson (118) 12.50
119 A.J. Burnett (119) 12.50
120 Ryan Bradley (120) 7.50

1999 SkyBox E-X Century Authen-Kicks

Authen-Kicks is a game-used insert that embeds game-worn shoe swatches from the featured player. Each is done in a horizontal format and is sequentially hand-numbered. The number of swatch cards differs from player to player, and is indicated here in parentheses. Autographed versions of two colors of J.D. Drew shoes were also produced.

MT
Complete Set (11): 350.00
Common Player: 5.00
(1) J.D. Drew (160) 35.00
(1ab) J.D. Drew (autographed black) (8) 150.00
(1ar) J.D. Drew (autographed red) (8) 150.00
(2) Travis Lee (175) 5.00
(3) Kevin Millwood (160) 10.00
(4) Bruce Chen (205) 5.00
(5) Troy Glaus (205) 60.00
(6) Todd Helton (205) 10.00
(7) Ricky Ledee (180) 5.00
(8) Scott Rolen (205) 25.00
(9) Jeremy Giambi (205) 5.00

1999 SkyBox E-X Century E-X Quisite

15 of baseball's top young players are showcased, with a black background and interior die-cutting around the player image. These are seeded 1:18 packs.

MT
Complete Set (15): 50.00
Common Player: 2.00
Inserted 1:18
1 Troy Glaus 12.50
2 J.D. Drew 5.00
3 Pat Burrell 12.50
4 Russell Branyan 2.00
5 Kerry Wood 5.00
6 Eric Chavez 7.50
7 Ben Grieve 2.00
8 Gabe Kapler 6.00
9 Adrian Beltre 4.00
10 Todd Helton 6.00
11 Roosevelt Brown 3.00
12 Marlon Anderson 2.00
13 Jeremy Giambi 2.00
14 Magglio Ordonez 4.00
15 Travis Lee 5.00

1999 SkyBox E-X Century Favorites for Fenway

This 20-card set pays tribute to one of baseball's favorite ballparks, Fenway Park the venue for the 1999 All-Star Game. These have a photo of the featured player with an image of Fenway Park in the background on a horizontal format. These are seeded 1:36 packs.

MT
Complete Set (20): 165.00
Common Player: 3.00
Inserted 1:36
1 Mo Vaughn 3.00
2 Nomar Garciaparra 12.50
3 Frank Thomas 12.50
4 Ken Griffey Jr. 17.50
5 Roger Clemens 8.00
6 Alex Rodriguez 17.50
7 Derek Jeter 15.00
8 Juan Gonzalez 6.00
9 Cal Ripken Jr. 20.00
10 Ivan Rodriguez 5.00
11 J.D. Drew 4.00
12 Barry Bonds 10.00
13 Tony Gwynn 8.00
14 Vladimir Guerrero 6.00
15 Chipper Jones 15.00
16 Kerry Wood 5.00
17 Mike Piazza 15.00
18 Sammy Sosa 12.50
19 Scott Rolen 5.00
20 Mark McGwire 20.00

1999 SkyBox E-X Century Milestones of the Century

This 10-card set spotlights the top statistical performances from the 1998 season, sequentially numbered to that performance in a multi-layered design.

MT
Complete Set (10): 375.00
Common Player: 5.00
Numbered to featured milestone
1 Kerry Wood (20) 25.00
2 Mark McGwire (70) 80.00
3 Sammy Sosa (66) 40.00
4 Ken Griffey Jr. (350) 17.50
5 Roger Clemens (98) 25.00
6 Cal Ripken Jr. (17) 165.00
7 Alex Rodriguez (40) 70.00
8 Barry Bonds (400) 8.00
9 N.Y. Yankees (114) 35.00
10 Travis Lee (98) 5.00

1999 SkyBox Molten Metal Xplosion Sample

This sample card was issued to preview SkyBox's Xplosion metal inserts. Etched and printed on metal stock, the card is identical in format to the issued versions, except for sample notations on back.

	MT
Kerry Wood	6.00

1999 SkyBox Molten Metal

Distributed exclusively to the hobby, the 150-card set consists of three subsets: Metal Smiths, Heavy Metal and Supernatural. Metal Smiths (1-100) show baseball's top players, Heavy Metal (101-130) focus on power hitters and Supernatural (131-150) focus on rookies. Base cards feature silver foil stamping on a 24-point stock with holofoil and wet-laminate overlays. Molten Metal was released in six-card packs with a SRP of $4.99. A special version of the issue was sold only at the 20th Nat'l Sports Collectors Convention in Atlanta, July 19-24. The show version includes autograph redemption cards for show guests and a die-cut series of 30 current and former Braves favorites. Each of the show version cards has a small National Convention logo printed on back; they currently carry no premium.

	MT
Complete Set (150):	90.00
Common Metalsmiths (1-100):	.25
Inserted 4:1	
Common Heavy Metal (101-130):	.40
Inserted 1:1	
Common Supernatural (131-150):	.75
Inserted 1:2	
Pack (6):	2.00
Wax Box (24):	45.00

1	Larry Walker	.75
2	Jose Canseco	1.00
3	Brian Jordan	.25
4	Rafael Palmeiro	.75
5	Edgar Renteria	.25
6	Dante Bichette	.25
7	Mark Kotsay	.25
8	Denny Neagle	.25
9	Ellis Burks	.25
10	Paul O'Neill	.25
11	Miguel Tejada	.50
12	Ken Caminiti	.25
13	David Cone	.25
14	Jason Kendall	.25
15	Ruben Rivera	.25
16	Todd Walker	.25
17	Bobby Higginson	.25
18	Derrek Lee	.25
19	Rondell White	.35
20	Pedro J. Martinez	1.00
21	Jeff Kent	.25
22	Randy Johnson	1.00
23	Matt Williams	.50
24	Sean Casey	.40
25	Eric Davis	.25
26	Ryan Klesko	.25
27	Curt Schilling	.35
28	Geoff Jenkins	.25
29	Armand Abreu	.25
30	Vinny Castilla	.25
31	Will Clark	.50
32	Ray Durham	.25
33	Ray Lankford	.25
34	Richie Sexson	.25
35	Derrick Gibson	.25
36	Mark Grace	.50
37	Greg Vaughn	.25
38	Bartolo Colon	.25
39	Steve Finley	.25
40	Chuck Knoblauch	.25
41	Ricky Ledee	.25
42	John Smoltz	.25
43	Moises Alou	.35
44	Jim Edmonds	.25
45	Cliff Floyd	.25
46	Javy Lopez	.25
47	Jim Thome	.25
48	J.T. Snow	.25
49	Sandy Alomar Jr.	.25
50	Andy Pettitte	.35
51	Juan Encarnacion	.25
52	Travis Fryman	.25
53	Eli Marrero	.25
54	Jeff Cirillo	.25
55	Brady Anderson	.25
56	Jose Cruz Jr.	.35
57	Edgar Martinez	.25
58	Garret Anderson	.25
59	Paul Konerko	.25
60	Eric Milton	.25
61	Jason Giambi	.65
62	Tom Glavine	.25
63	Justin Thompson	.25
64	Brad Fullmer	.25
65	Marquis Grissom	.25
66	Fernando Tatis	.25
67	Carlos Beltran	.25
68	Charles Johnson	.25
69	Raul Mondesi	.35
70	Richard Hildalgo	.25
71	Barry Larkin	.25
72	David Wells	.25
73	Jay Buhner	.25
74	Matt Clement	.25
75	Eric Karros	.25
76	Carl Pavano	.25
77	Mariano Rivera	.50
78	Livan Hernandez	.25
79	A.J. Hinch	.25
80	Tino Martinez	.25
81	Rusty Greer	.25
82	Jose Guillen	.25
83	Robin Ventura	.25
84	Kevin Brown	.35
85	Chan Ho Park	.40
86	John Olerud	.25
87	Johnny Damon	.25
88	Todd Hundley	.25
89	Fred McGriff	.25
90	Wade Boggs	.75
91	Mike Cameron	.25
92	Gary Sheffield	.50
93	Rickey Henderson	.75
94	Pat Hentgen	.25
95	Omar Vizquel	.25
96	Craig Biggio	.25
97	Mike Caruso	.25
98	Neifi Perez	.25
99	Mike Mussina	.75
100	Carlos Delgado	.45
101	Andruw Jones (Heavy Metal)	1.50
102	*Pat Burrell* (Heavy Metal)	5.00
103	Orlando Hernandez (Heavy Metal)	1.50
104	Darin Erstad (Heavy Metal)	1.25
105	Roberto Alomar (Heavy Metal)	1.25
106	Tim Salmon (Heavy Metal)	.75
107	Albert Belle (Heavy Metal)	1.00
108	*Chad Allen* (Heavy Metal)	.75
109	Travis Lee (Heavy Metal)	.75
110	*Jesse Garcia* (Heavy Metal)	.40
111	Tony Clark (Heavy Metal)	.40
112	Ivan Rodriguez (Heavy Metal)	1.50
113	Troy Glaus (Heavy Metal)	1.50
114	*A.J. Burnett* (Heavy Metal)	1.50
115	David Justice (Heavy Metal)	.75
116	Adrian Beltre (Heavy Metal)	.75
117	Eric Chavez (Heavy Metal)	.75
118	Kenny Lofton (Heavy Metal)	.40
119	Michael Barrett (Heavy Metal)	.40
120	*Jeff Weaver* (Heavy Metal)	4.00
121	Manny Ramirez (Heavy Metal)	2.00
122	Barry Bonds (Heavy Metal)	2.50
123	Bernie Williams (Heavy Metal)	.75
124	*Freddy Garcia* (Heavy Metal)	6.00
125	*Scott Hunter* (Heavy Metal)	.50
126	Jeremy Giambi (Heavy Metal)	.40
127	*Masao Kida* (Heavy Metal)	.40
128	Todd Helton (Heavy Metal)	1.00
129	Mike Figga (Heavy Metal)	.40
130	Mo Vaughn (Heavy Metal)	.75
131	J.D. Drew (Supernaturals)	.75
132	Cal Ripken Jr. (Supernaturals)	4.00
133	Ken Griffey Jr. (Supernaturals)	3.50
134	Mark McGwire (Supernaturals)	4.00
135	Nomar Garciaparra (Supernaturals)	2.50
136	Greg Maddux (Supernaturals)	2.00
137	Mike Piazza (Supernaturals)	3.00
138	Alex Rodriguez (Supernaturals)	3.50
139	Frank Thomas (Supernaturals)	2.50
140	Juan Gonzalez (Supernaturals)	1.00
141	Tony Gwynn (Supernaturals)	2.00
142	Derek Jeter (Supernaturals)	3.00
143	Chipper Jones (Supernaturals)	3.00
144	Scott Rolen (Supernaturals)	1.00
145	Sammy Sosa (Supernaturals)	2.50
146	Kerry Wood (Supernaturals)	1.00
147	Roger Clemens (Supernaturals)	2.00
148	Jeff Bagwell (Supernaturals)	1.50
149	Vladimir Guerrero (Supernaturals)	1.50
150	Ben Grieve (Supernaturals)	.75

1999 SkyBox Molten Metal Fusion - Sterling

Sterling Fusions are limited to 500 numbered sets with each card laser die-cut on a blue background with blue foil graphic highlights. A special version of the issue was sold only at the 20th Nat'l Sports Collectors Convention in Atlanta, July 19-24. Each of the show-version cards has a small National Convention logo printed on back; they currently carry no premium.

	MT
Complete Set (50):	250.00
Common Player:	1.50
Sterling Stars:	1.5X

(See 1999 Molten Metal Fusion for checklist and base card values.)

1999 SkyBox Molten Metal Fusion - Titanium

Titanium Fusions are limited to 50 sequentially numbered sets with gold background and enhanced with gold foil highlights. A special version of the issue was sold only at the 20th Nat'l Sports Collectors Convention in Atlanta, July 19-24. Each of the show-version cards has a small National Convention logo printed on back; they currently carry no premium.

	MT
Common Player:	4.00
Titanium Stars:	4X

(See 1999 SkyBox Molten Metal Fusion for checklist and base card values.)

1999 SkyBox Molten Metal Fusion

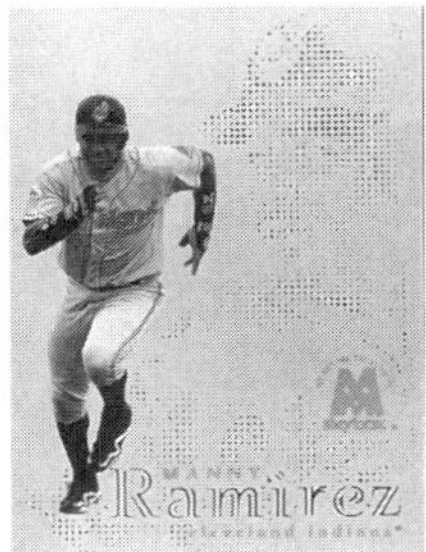

Fusion is a 50-card partial parallel that is paralleled three times: Fusion, Sterling Fusion and Titanium Fusion. The three parallels consist of the two subsets Heavy Metal and Supernatural. Fusion Heavy Metals (1-30) are seeded 1:12 packs and Supernatural Fusions are seeded 1:24 packs. Fusions are laser die-cut with additional silver-foil stamping. Sterling Fusions are limited to 500 numbered sets with each card laser die-cut on a blue background with blue foil stamping. Titanium Fusions are limited to 50 sequentially numbered sets with gold background and enhanced with gold foil highlights.

		MT
Complete Set (50):		140.00
Common Heavy Metal (1-30):		1.00
Inserted 1:12		
Common Supernatural (31-50):		2.50
Inserted 1:24		
Sterling (31-50):		1.5X
Production 500 sets		
Titanium (31-50):		4X
Production 50 sets		
1	Andruw Jones	2.50
2	Pat Burrell	5.00
3	Orlando Hernandez	2.00
4	Darin Erstad	2.00
5	Roberto Alomar	2.00
6	Tim Salmon	1.50
7	Albert Belle	1.50
8	Chad Allen	1.00
9	Travis Lee	1.50
10	Jesse Garcia	1.00
11	Tony Clark	1.00
12	Ivan Rodriguez	2.00
13	Troy Glaus	4.00
14	A.J. Burnett	1.50
15	David Justice	1.50
16	Adrian Beltre	1.50
17	Eric Chavez	1.50
18	Kenny Lofton	1.00
19	Michael Barrett	1.00
20	Jeff Weaver	2.00
21	Manny Ramirez	3.00
22	Barry Bonds	5.00
23	Bernie Williams	1.50
24	Freddy Garcia	3.00
25	Scott Hunter	1.00
26	Jeremy Giambi	1.00
27	Masao Kida	1.00
28	Todd Helton	2.00
29	Mike Figga	1.00
30	Mo Vaughn	1.00
31	J.D. Drew	2.50
32	Cal Ripken Jr.	10.00
33	Ken Griffey Jr.	9.00
34	Mark McGwire	10.00
35	Nomar Garciaparra	7.00
36	Greg Maddux	6.00
37	Mike Piazza	8.00
38	Alex Rodriguez	9.00
39	Frank Thomas	7.00
40	Juan Gonzalez	5.00
41	Tony Gwynn	6.00
42	Derek Jeter	8.00
43	Chipper Jones	8.00
44	Scott Rolen	4.00
45	Sammy Sosa	7.00
46	Kerry Wood	3.00
47	Roger Clemens	6.00
48	Jeff Bagwell	5.00
49	Vladimir Guerrero	5.00
50	Ben Grieve	2.50

1999 SkyBox Molten Metal Oh Atlanta!

This 30-card set features players who are either current or former Atlanta Braves like Chipper Jones and Dave Justice. These inserts are seeded one per pack and was produced in conjunction with the 20th annual National Sports Collectors Convention in Atlanta.

		MT
Complete Set (30):		50.00
Common Player:		1.00
Inserted 1:1		
1	Kenny Lofton	1.00
2	Kevin Millwood	6.00
3	Bret Boone	1.50
4	Otis Nixon	1.00
5	Vinny Castilla	1.00
6	Brian Jordan	1.00
7	Chipper Jones	12.00
8	Dave Justice	3.00
9	Micah Bowie	1.00
10	Fred McGriff	1.00
11	Ron Gant	1.00
12	Andruw Jones	6.00
13	Kent Mercker	1.00
14	Greg McMichael	1.00
15	Steve Avery	1.00
16	Marquis Grissom	1.00
17	Jason Schmidt	1.00
18	Ryan Klesko	1.00
19	Charlie O'Brien	1.00
20	Terry Pendleton	1.00
21	Denny Neagle	1.00
22	Greg Maddux	9.00
23	Tom Glavine	1.50
24	Javy Lopez	1.00
25	John Rocker	1.00
26	Walt Weiss	1.00
27	John Smoltz	1.50
28	Michael Tucker	1.00
29	Odalis Perez	1.00
30	Andres Galarraga	1.00

1999 SkyBox Molten Metal Xplosion

This is a 150-card parallel set, which is seeeded 1:2 packs. These are made of actual metal that have added etching and some foil stamping.

	MT
Complete Set (150):	450.00
Common Player:	1.00
Stars:	3X
Inserted 1:2	

(See 1999 SkyBox Molten Metal for checklist and base card values.)

1999 SkyBox Premium

The base set consists of 300 cards, base cards feature full bleed fronts with gold-foil stamped player and team names. Card backs have complete year-by-year stats along with a close-up photo. The Rookie subset (223-272) also have a short-printed parallel version as well. Different photos are used but they have the same card number and card back. The short-print versions are seeded 1:8 packs and have an action photo front while the non-seeded cards have a close-up photo.

		MT
Complete Set (300):		20.00
Complete Set w/sp's (350):		135.00
Common Player:		.10
Common SP (223-272):		.75
SPs inserted 1:8		
Pack (8):		2.00
Wax Box (24):		40.00
1	Alex Rodriguez	2.50
2	Sidney Ponson	.10
3	Shawn Green	.20
4	Dan Wilson	.10
5	Rolando Arrojo	.10
6	Roberto Alomar	.40
7	Matt Anderson	.10
8	David Segui	.10
9	Alex Gonzalez	.10
10	Edgar Renteria	.10
11	Benito Santiago	.10
12	Todd Stottlemyre	.10
13	Rico Brogna	.10
14	Troy Glaus	.50
15	Al Leiter	.10
16	Pedro J. Martinez	.75
17	Paul O'Neill	.10
18	Manny Ramirez	.50
19	Scott Rolen	.50
20	Curt Schilling	.25
21	Bobby Abreu	.10
22	Robb Nen	.10
23	Andy Pettitte	.25
24	John Wetteland	.10
25	Bobby Bonilla	.10
26	Darin Erstad	.40
27	Shawn Estes	.10
28	John Franco	.10
29	Nomar Garciaparra	1.50
30	Rick Helling	.10
31	David Justice	.30
32	Chuck Knoblauch	.10
33	Quinton McCracken	.10
34	Kenny Rogers	.10
35	Brian Giles	.10
36	Armando Benitez	.10
37	Trevor Hoffman	.10
38	Charles Johnson	.10
39	Travis Lee	.10
40	Tom Glavine	.10
41	Rondell White	.15
42	Orlando Hernandez	.25
43	Mickey Morandini	.10
44	Darryl Kile	.10
45	Greg Vaughn	.10
46	Gregg Jefferies	.10
47	Mark McGwire	2.50
48	Kerry Wood	.25
49	Jeromy Burnitz	.10
50	Ron Gant	.10
51	Vinny Castilla	.10
52	Doug Glanville	.10
53	Juan Guzman	.10
54	Dustin Hermanson	.10
55	Jose Hernandez	.10
56	Bob Higginson	.10
57	A.J. Hinch	.10
58	Randy Johnson	.50
59	Eli Marrero	.10
60	Rafael Palmeiro	.30
61	Carl Pavano	.10
62	Brett Tomko	.10
63	Jose Guillen	.10
64	Mike Lieberthal	.10
65	Jim Abbott	.10
66	Dante Bichette	.10
67	Jeff Cirillo	.10
68	Eric Davis	.10
69	Delino DeShields	.10
70	Steve Finley	.10
71	Mark Grace	.20
72	Jason Kendall	.10
73	Jeff Kent	.10
74	Desi Relaford	.10
75	Ivan Rodriguez	.40
76	Shannon Stewart	.15
77	Geoff Jenkins	.10
78	Ben Grieve	.25
79	Cliff Floyd	.10
80	Jason Giambi	.45
81	Rod Beck	.10

82 Derek Bell .10
83 Will Clark .25
84 David Dellucci .10
85 Joey Hamilton .10
86 Livan Hernandez .10
87 Barry Larkin .15
88 Matt Mantei .10
89 Dean Palmer .10
90 Chan Ho Park .20
91 Jim Thome .10
92 Miguel Tejada .15
93 Justin Thompson .10
94 David Wells .10
95 Bernie Williams .30
96 Jeff Bagwell .50
97 Derrek Lee .10
98 Devon White .10
99 Jeff Shaw .15
100 Brad Radke .10
101 Mark Grudzielanek .10
102 Javy Lopez .10
103 Mike Sirotka .10
104 Robin Ventura .10
105 Andy Ashby .10
106 Juan Gonzalez .50
107 Albert Belle .25
108 Andy Benes .10
109 Jay Buhner .10
110 Ken Caminiti .10
111 Roger Clemens 1.00
112 Mike Hampton .10
113 Pete Harnisch .10
114 Mike Piazza 2.00
115 J.T. Snow .10
116 John Olerud .10
117 Tony Womack .10
118 Todd Zeile .10
119 Tony Gwynn 1.00
120 Brady Anderson .10
121 Sean Casey .15
122 Jose Cruz Jr. .15
123 Carlos Delgado .20
124 Edgar Martinez .10
125 Jose Mesa .10
126 Shane Reynolds .10
127 John Valentin .10
128 Mo Vaughn .30
129 Kevin Young .10
130 Jay Bell .10
131 Aaron Boone .10
132 John Smoltz .10
133 Mike Stanley .10
134 Bret Saberhagen .10
135 Tim Salmon .20
136 Mariano Rivera .25
137 Ken Griffey Jr. 2.50
138 Jose Offerman .10
139 Troy Percival .10
140 Greg Maddux 1.00
141 Frank Thomas 1.50
142 Steve Avery .10
143 Kevin Millwood .15
144 Sammy Sosa 1.50
145 Larry Walker .25
146 Matt Williams .25
147 Mike Caruso .10
148 Todd Helton .50
149 Andruw Jones .50
150 Ray Lankford .10
151 Craig Biggio .15
152 Ugueth Urbina .10
153 Wade Boggs .50
154 Derek Jeter 2.50
155 Wally Joyner .10
156 Mike Mussina .45
157 Gregg Olson .10
158 Henry Rodriguez .10
159 Reggie Sanders .10
160 Fernando Tatis .10
161 Dmitri Young .10
162 Rick Aguilera .10
163 Marty Cordova .10
164 Johnny Damon .10
165 Ray Durham .10
166 Brad Fullmer .10
167 Chipper Jones 2.00
168 Bobby Smith .10
169 Omar Vizquel .10
170 Todd Hundley .10
171 David Cone .10
172 Royce Clayton .10
173 Ryan Klesko .10
174 Jeff Montgomery .10
175 Maggio Ordonez .10
176 Billy Wagner .10
177 Masato Yoshii .10
178 Jason Christiansen .10
179 Chuck Finley .10
180 Tom Gordon .10
181 Wilton Guerrero .10
182 Rickey Henderson .40
183 Sterling Hitchcock .10
184 Kenny Lofton .10
185 Tino Martinez .10
186 Fred McGriff .10
187 Matt Stairs .10
188 Neifi Perez .10
189 Bob Wickman .10
190 Barry Bonds 1.25
191 Jose Canseco .35
192 Damion Easley .10
193 Jim Edmonds .10
194 Juan Encarnacion .10
195 Travis Fryman .10
196 Tom Goodwin .10
197 Rusty Greer .10
198 Roberto Hernandez .10
199 B.J. Surhoff .10
200 Scott Brosius .10
201 Brian Jordan .10
202 Paul Konerko .10
203 Ismael Valdes .10
204 Eric Milton .10
205 Adrian Beltre .15
206 Tony Clark .10
207 Bartolo Colon .10
208 Cal Ripken Jr. 2.50
209 Moises Alou .15
210 Wilson Alvarez .10
211 Kevin Brown .15
212 Orlando Cabrera .10
213 Vladimir Guerrero .75
214 Jose Rosado .10
215 Raul Mondesi .15
216 Dave Nilsson .10
217 Carlos Perez .10
218 Jason Schmidt .10
219 Richie Sexson .10
220 Gary Sheffield .25
221 Fernando Vina .10
222 Todd Walker .10
223 *Scott Sauerbeck* .15
223 *Scott Sauerbeck (sp)* .75
224 *Pascual Matos* .10
224 *Pascual Matos (sp)* .75
225 *Kyle Farnsworth* .15
225 *Kyle Farnsworth (sp)* .75
226 *Freddy Garcia* .75
226 *Freddy Garcia (sp)* 3.00
227 *David Lundquist* .10
227 *David Lundquist (sp)* .75
228 *Jolbert Cabrera* .10
228 *Jolbert Cabrera (sp)* .75
229 *Dan Perkins* .10
229 *Dan Perkins (sp)* .75
230 Warren Morris .10
230 Warren Morris (sp) .75
231 Carlos Febles .10
231 Carlos Febles (sp) .75
232 *Brett Hinchliffe* .10
232 *Brett Hinchliffe (sp)* .75
233 *Jason Phillips* .10
233 *Jason Phillips (sp)* .75
234 *Glen Barker* .10
234 *Glen Barker (sp)* .75
235 *Jose Macias* .25
235 *Jose Macias (sp)* 1.00
236 *Joe Mays* .10
236 *Joe Mays (sp)* .75
237 *Chad Allen* .10
237 *Chad Allen (sp)* .75
238 *Miguel Del Toro* .10
238 *Miguel Del Toro (sp)* .75
239 Chris Singleton .10
239 Chris Singleton (sp) .75
240 *Jesse Garcia* .10
240 *Jesse Garcia (sp)* .75
241 Kris Benson .10
241 Kris Benson (sp) .75
242 *Clay Bellinger* .10
242 *Clay Bellinger (sp)* .75
243 Scott Williamson .10
243 Scott Williamson (sp) .75
244 *Masao Kida* .10
244 *Masao Kida (sp)* .75
245 *Guillermo Garcia* .10
245 *Guillermo Garcia (sp)* .75
246 *A.J. Burnett* .25
246 *A.J. Burnett (sp)* 1.25
247 *Bo Porter* .10
247 *Bo Porter (sp)* .75
248 *Pat Burrell* 2.00
248 *Pat Burrell (sp)* 9.00
249 Carlos Lee .10
249 Carlos Lee (sp) .75
250 *Jeff Weaver* 1.50
250 *Jeff Weaver (sp)* 5.00
251 Ruben Mateo .10
251 Ruben Mateo (sp) .75
252 J.D. Drew .40
252 J.D. Drew (sp) 2.00
253 Jeremy Giambi .10
253 Jeremy Giambi (sp) .75
254 *Gary Bennett* .10
254 *Gary Bennett (sp)* .75
255 *Edwards Guzman* .10
255 *Edwards Guzman (sp)* .75
256 Ramon Martinez .10
256 Ramon Martinez (sp) .75
257 *Giomar Guevara* .10
257 *Giomar Guevara (sp)* .75
258 *Joe McEwing* .25
258 *Joe McEwing (sp)* 1.00
259 *Tom Davey* .10
259 *Tom Davey (sp)* .75
260 Gabe Kapler .20
260 Gabe Kapler (sp) 1.00
261 *Ryan Rupe* .10
261 *Ryan Rupe (sp)* .75
262 *Kelly Dransfeldt* .10
262 *Kelly Dransfeldt (sp)* .75
263 Michael Barrett .10
263 Michael Barrett (sp) .75
264 Eric Chavez .15
264 Eric Chavez (sp) .75
265 *Orber Moreno* .15
265 *Orber Moreno (sp)* .75
266 Marlon Anderson .10
266 Marlon Anderson (sp) .75
267 Carlos Beltran .10
267 Carlos Beltran (sp) .75
268 Doug Mientkiewicz .10
268 Doug Mientkiewicz (sp) .75
269 Roy Halladay .10
269 Roy Halladay (sp) .75
270 Torii Hunter .10
270 Torii Hunter (sp) .75
271 Stan Spencer .10
271 Stan Spencer (sp) .75
272 Alex Gonzalez .10
272 Alex Gonzalez (sp) .75
273 Mark McGwire (Spring Fling) 1.25
274 Scott Rolen (Spring Fling) .25
275 Jeff Bagwell (Spring Fling) .25
276 Derek Jeter (Spring Fling) 1.00
277 Tony Gwynn (Spring Fling) .40
278 Frank Thomas (Spring Fling) .60
279 Sammy Sosa (Spring Fling) .60
280 Nomar Garciaparra (Spring Fling) .60
281 Cal Ripken Jr. (Spring Fling) 1.25
282 Albert Belle (Spring Fling) .25
283 Kerry Wood (Spring Fling) .10
284 Greg Maddux (Spring Fling) .40
285 Barry Bonds (Spring Fling) .50
286 Juan Gonzalez (Spring Fling) .25
287 Ken Griffey Jr. (Spring Fling) 1.00
288 Alex Rodriguez (Spring Fling) 1.00
289 Ben Grieve (Spring Fling) .20
290 Travis Lee (Spring Fling) .10
291 Mo Vaughn (Spring Fling) .20
292 Mike Piazza (Spring Fling) .75
293 Roger Clemens (Spring Fling) .40
294 J.D. Drew (Spring Fling) .25
295 Randy Johnson (Spring Fling) .15
296 Chipper Jones (Spring Fling) .75
297 Vladimir Guerrero (Spring Fling) .40
298 Checklist (Nomar Garciaparra) .40
299 Checklist (Ken Griffey Jr.) .50
300 Checklist (Mark McGwire) .60

1999 SkyBox Premium Star Rubies

Star Rubies are a parallel of the base set and are limited to 50 sequentially numbered sets. SP Rookie parallels are limited to 15 numbered sets. Rubies feature a complete prism foil front with red-foil stamping.

	MT
Star Rubies:	50X
Production 50 sets	
SP Star Rubies:	15X
Production 15 sets	

(See 1999 SkyBox Premium for checklist and base card values.)

1999 SkyBox Premium Autographics

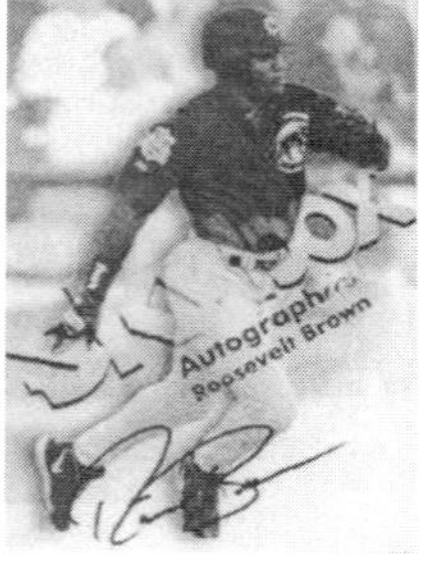

This 54-card autographed set feature an embossed SkyBox Seal of Authenticity stamp and are seeded 1:68 packs. Cards are commonly found signed in black ink. Blue-ink versions, serially numbered to 50 each, were also produced.

	MT
Common Player:	4.00
Inserted 1:68	

Blue Ink: 1.5X
Production 50 sets

	Roberto Alomar	25.00
	Paul Bako	4.00
	Michael Barrett	4.00
	Kris Benson	6.00
	Micah Bowie	4.00
	Roosevelt Brown	4.00
	A.J. Burnett	7.50
	Pat Burrell	12.50
	Ken Caminiti	5.00
	Royce Clayton	4.00
	Edgard Clemente	4.00
	Bartolo Colon	5.00
	J.D. Drew	35.00
	Damion Easley	4.00
	Derrin Ebert	4.00
	Mario Encarnacion	4.00
	Juan Encarnacion	5.00
	Troy Glaus	15.00
	Tom Glavine	12.50
	Juan Gonzalez	30.00
	Shawn Green	12.50
	Wilton Guerrero	4.00
	Jose Guillen	4.00
	Tony Gwynn	25.00
	Mark Harriger	4.00
	Bobby Higginson	5.00
	Todd Hollandsworth	4.00
	Scott Hunter	4.00
	Gabe Kapler	5.00
	Scott Karl	4.00
	Mike Kinkade	4.00
	Ray Lankford	5.00
	Barry Larkin	25.00
	Matt Lawton	4.00
	Ricky Ledee	5.00
	Travis Lee	5.00
	Eli Marrero	4.00
	Ruben Mateo	4.00
	Joe McEwing	4.00
	Doug Mientkiewicz	6.00
	Russ Ortiz	4.00
	Jim Parque	4.00
	Robert Person	4.00
	Alex Rodriguez	100.00
	Scott Rolen	10.00
	Benj Sampson	4.00
	Luis Saturria	4.00
	Curt Schilling	15.00
	David Segui	4.00
	Fernando Tatis	4.00
	Peter Tucci	4.00
	Javier Vasquez	15.00
	Robin Ventura	6.00

1999 SkyBox Premium Diamond Debuts

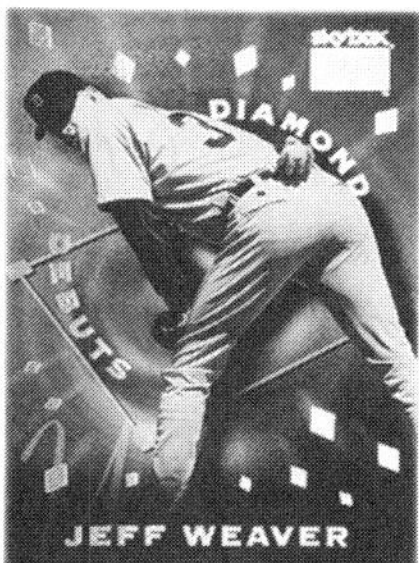

This 15-card set features the best rookies of 1999 on a silver rainbow holo-foil card stock. These are seeded 1:49 packs. Card backs are numbered with a "DD" suffix.

		MT
Complete Set (15):		26.00
Common Player:		2.00
Inserted 1:49		
1	Eric Chavez	3.50
2	Kyle Farnsworth	2.00
3	Ryan Rupe	2.00
4	Jeremy Giambi	2.00
5	Marlon Anderson	2.00
6	J.D. Drew	4.00
7	Carlos Febles	2.00
8	Joe McEwing	2.00
9	Jeff Weaver	2.00
10	Alex Gonzalez	2.00
11	Chad Allen	2.00
12	Michael Barrett	2.00
13	Gabe Kapler	3.00
14	Carlos Lee	2.00
15	Edwards Guzman	2.00

1999 SkyBox Premium Intimidation Nation

This 15-card set highlights the top performers in baseball and features gold rainbow holo-foil stamping. These are limited to 99 sequentially numbered sets. Card backs are numbered with a "IN" suffix.

		MT
Complete Set (15):		290.00
Common Player:		10.00
Production 99 sets		
1	Cal Ripken Jr.	40.00
2	Tony Gwynn	20.00
3	Nomar Garciaparra	25.00
4	Frank Thomas	25.00
5	Mike Piazza	30.00
6	Mark McGwire	40.00
7	Scott Rolen	10.00
8	Chipper Jones	30.00
9	Greg Maddux	20.00
10	Ken Griffey Jr.	35.00
11	Juan Gonzalez	12.50
12	Derek Jeter	30.00
13	J.D. Drew	10.00
14	Roger Clemens	20.00
15	Alex Rodriguez	35.00

1999 SkyBox Premium Live Bats

This 15-card set spotlights baseball's top hitters and feature red foil stamping. Card backs are numbered with a "LB" suffix and are seeded 1:7 packs.

		MT
Complete Set (15):		11.00
Common Player:		.25
Inserted 1:7		
1	Juan Gonzalez	.50
2	Mark McGwire	2.00
3	Jeff Bagwell	.50
4	Frank Thomas	1.00
5	Mike Piazza	1.25
6	Nomar Garciaparra	1.00
7	Alex Rodriguez	1.50
8	Scott Rolen	.40
9	Travis Lee	.25
10	Tony Gwynn	.75
11	Derek Jeter	1.25
12	Ben Grieve	.25
13	Chipper Jones	1.25
14	Ken Griffey Jr.	1.50
15	Cal Ripken Jr.	2.00

1999 SkyBox Premium Show Business

This 15-card set features some of the best players in the "show" on double foil-stamped card fronts. Card backs are numbered with a "SB" suffix and are seeded 1:70 packs.

		MT
Complete Set (15):		75.00
Common Player:		3.00
Inserted 1:70		
1	Mark McGwire	10.00
2	Tony Gwynn	4.00
3	Nomar Garciaparra	6.00
4	Juan Gonzalez	3.50
5	Roger Clemens	4.00
6	Chipper Jones	8.00
7	Cal Ripken Jr.	10.00
8	Alex Rodriguez	9.00
9	Orlando Hernandez	3.00
10	Greg Maddux	4.00
11	Mike Piazza	8.00
12	Frank Thomas	6.00
13	Ken Griffey Jr.	9.00
14	Scott Rolen	3.00
15	Derek Jeter	8.00

1999 SkyBox Premium Soul of The Game

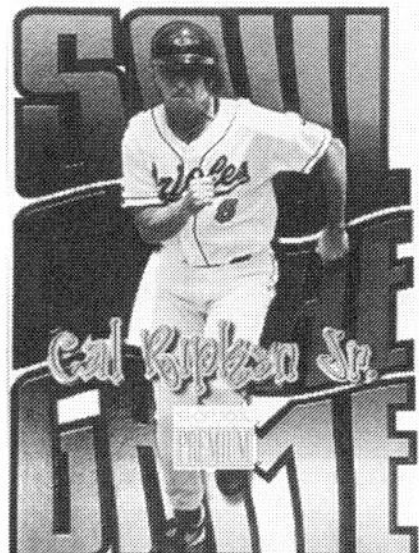

This 15-card set features rainbow foil stamping and the name Soul of the Game prominently stamped, covering the entire card behind the player photo. Card backs are numbered with a "SG" suffix and are seeded 1:14 packs.

		MT
Complete Set (15):		27.50
Common Player:		1.00
Inserted 1:14		
1	Alex Rodriguez	3.50
2	Vladimir Guerrero	1.00
3	Chipper Jones	3.00
4	Derek Jeter	3.00
5	Tony Gwynn	1.50
6	Scott Rolen	1.00
7	Juan Gonzalez	1.00
8	Mark McGwire	4.00
9	Ken Griffey Jr.	3.50
10	Jeff Bagwell	1.00
11	Cal Ripken Jr.	4.00
12	Frank Thomas	2.50
13	Mike Piazza	3.00
14	Nomar Garciaparra	2.50
15	Sammy Sosa	2.50

1999 SkyBox Thunder

Skybox Thunder consists of a 300-card base set with three pa rallels and six inserts. The base set is inserted at varying odds. In hobby packs, regular-player cards #1-140 come 4-5 per pack, veteran stars on cards #141-240 come two per pack, and superstars on cards #241-300 are seeded one per pack. For retail packs the odds were: #1-141 (3-4 per pack), #141-240 (two per pack), and #241-300 (one per pack). Parallels include Rave (numbered to 150 sets) and Super Rave (25 sets), which are both hobby exclusive. The Rant parallel set is retail exclusive (1:2). The inserts are Unleashed (1:6), www.batterz.com (1:18), In Depth (1:24), Hip-No-Tized (1:36), Turbo-Charged (1:72), and Dial "1" (1:300).

		MT
Complete Set (300):		35.00
Common Player (1-140):		.10
Common Player (141-240):		.15
Common Player (241-300):		.25
Raves:		20X
Production 150 sets		
SuperRaves:		50X
Production 25 sets		
Rants:		10X
Inserted 1:2 R		
Pack (8):		1.00
Wax Box (36):		25.00
1	John Smoltz	.15
2	Garret Anderson	.10
3	Matt Williams	.25
4	Daryle Ward	.10
5	Andy Ashby	.10
6	Miguel Tejada	.20
7	Dmitri Young	.10
8	Roberto Alomar	.50
9	Kevin Brown	.15
10	Eric Young	.10
11	Odalis Perez	.10
12	Preston Wilson	.10
13	Jeff Abbott	.10
14	Bret Boone	.15
15	Mendy Lopez	.10
16	B.J. Surhoff	.10
17	Steve Woodard	.10
18	Ron Coomer	.10
19	Rondell White	.20
20	Edgardo Alfonzo	.10
21	Kevin Millwood	.15
22	Jose Canseco	.40
23	Blake Stein	.10
24	Quilvio Veras	.10
25	Chuck Knoblauch	.10
26	David Segui	.10

27 Eric Davis .10
28 Francisco Cordova .10
29 Randy Winn .10
30 Will Clark .25
31 Billy Wagner .10
32 Kevin Witt .10
33 Jim Edmonds .10
34 Todd Stottlemyre .10
35 Shane Andrews .10
36 Michael Tucker .10
37 Sandy Alomar Jr. .10
38 Neifi Perez .10
39 Jaret Wright .10
40 Devon White .10
41 Edgar Renteria .10
42 Shane Reynolds .10
43 Jeff King .10
44 Darren Dreifort .10
45 Fernando Vina .10
46 Marty Cordova .10
47 Ugueth Urbina .10
48 Bobby Bonilla .10
49 Omar Vizquel .10
50 Tom Gordon .10
51 Ryan Christenson .10
52 Aaron Boone .10
53 Jamie Moyer .10
54 Brian Giles .10
55 Kevin Tapani .10
56 Scott Brosius .10
57 Ellis Burks .10
58 Al Leiter .10
59 Royce Clayton .10
60 Chris Carpenter .10
61 Bubba Trammell .10
62 Tom Glavine .15
63 Shannon Stewart .15
64 Todd Zeile .10
65 J.T. Snow .10
66 Matt Clement .10
67 Matt Stairs .10
68 Ismael Valdes .10
69 Todd Walker .10
70 Jose Lima .10
71 Mike Caruso .10
72 Brett Tomko .10
73 Mike Lansing .10
74 Justin Thompson .10
75 Damion Easley .10
76 Derrek Lee .10
77 Derek Bell .10
78 Brady Anderson .10
79 Charles Johnson .10
80 *Rafael Roque* .10
81 Corey Koskie .10
82 Fernando Seguignol .10
83 Jay Tessmer .10
84 Jason Giambi .40
85 Mike Lieberthal .10
86 Jose Guillen .10
87 Jim Leyritz .10
88 Shawn Estes .10
89 Ray Lankford .10
90 Paul Sorrento .10
91 Javy Lopez .10
92 John Wetteland .10
93 Sean Casey .15
94 Chuck Finley .10
95 Trot Nixon .10
96 Ray Durham .10
97 Reggie Sanders .10
98 Bartolo Colon .10
99 Henry Rodriguez .10
100 Rolando Arrojo .10
101 Geoff Jenkins .10
102 Darryl Kile .10
103 Mark Kotsay .10
104 Craig Biggio .15
105 Omar Daal .10
106 Carlos Febles .10
107 Eric Karros .10
108 Matt Lawton .10
109 Carl Pavano .10
110 Brian McRae .10
111 Mariano Rivera .20
112 Jay Buhner .10
113 Doug Glanville .10
114 Jason Kendall .10
115 Wally Joyner .10
116 Jeff Kent .10
117 Shane Monahan .10
118 Eli Marrero .10
119 Bobby Smith .10
120 Shawn Green .15
121 Kirk Rueter .10
122 Tom Goodwin .10
123 Andy Benes .10
124 Ed Sprague .10
125 Mike Mussina .50
126 Jose Offerman .10
127 Mickey Morandini .10
128 Paul Konerko .10
129 Denny Neagle .10
130 Travis Fryman .10
131 John Rocker .10
132 *Rob Fick* .10
133 Livan Hernandez .10
134 Ken Caminiti .10
135 Johnny Damon .10
136 Jeff Kubenka .10
137 Marquis Grissom .10
138 Doug Mientkiewicz .10
139 Dustin Hermanson .15
140 Carl Everett .15
141 Hideo Nomo .40
142 Jorge Posada .15
143 Rickey Henderson .50
144 Robb Nen .15
145 Ron Gant .15
146 Aramis Ramirez .15
147 Trevor Hoffman .15
148 Bill Mueller .15
149 Edgar Martinez .15
150 Fred McGriff .15
151 Rusty Greer .15
152 Tom Evans .15
153 Todd Greene .15
154 Jay Bell .15
155 Mike Lowell .15
156 Orlando Cabrera .15
157 Troy O'Leary .15
158 Jose Hernandez .15
159 Magglio Ordonez .15
160 Barry Larkin .20
161 David Justice .40
162 Derrick Gibson .15
163 Luis Gonzalez .40
164 Alex Gonzalez .20
165 Scott Elarton .15
166 Dermal Brown .15
167 Eric Milton .15
168 Raul Mondesi .25
169 Jeff Cirillo .15
170 Benj Sampson .15
171 John Olerud .15
172 Andy Pettitte .35
173 A.J. Hinch .15
174 Rico Brogna .15
175 Jason Schmidt .15
176 Dean Palmer .15
177 Matt Morris .15
178 Quinton McCracken .15
179 Rick Helling .15
180 Walt Weiss .15
181 Troy Percival .15
182 Tony Batista .15
183 Brian Jordan .15
184 Jerry Hairston Jr. .15
185 Bret Saberhagen .15
186 Mark Grace .30
187 Brian Simmons .15
188 Pete Harnisch .15
189 Kenny Lofton .15
190 Vinny Castilla .15
191 Bobby Higginson .15
192 Joey Hamilton .15
193 Cliff Floyd .15
194 Andres Galarraga .15
195 Chan Ho Park .30
196 Jeromy Burnitz .15
197 David Ortiz .15
198 Wilton Guerrero .15
199 Rey Ordonez .15
200 Paul O'Neill .15
201 Kenny Rogers .15
202 Marlon Anderson .15
203 Tony Womack .15
204 Robin Ventura .15
205 Russ Ortiz .15
206 Mike Frank .15
207 Fernando Tatis .15
208 Miguel Cairo .15
209 Ivan Rodriguez .65
210 Carlos Delgado .50
211 Tim Salmon .30
212 Brian Anderson .15
213 Ryan Klesko .15
214 Scott Erickson .15
215 Mike Stanley .15
216 Brant Brown .15
217 Rod Beck .15
218 *Guillermo Garcia* .15
219 David Wells .15
220 Dante Bichette .15
221 Armando Benitez .15
222 Todd Dunwoody .15
223 Kelvim Escobar .15
224 Richard Hidalgo .15
225 Angel Pena .15
226 Ronnie Belliard .15
227 Brad Radke .15
228 Brad Fullmer .15
229 Jay Payton .15
230 Tino Martinez .15
231 Scott Spiezio .15
232 Bobby Abreu .15
233 John Valentin .15
234 Kevin Young .15
235 Steve Finley .15
236 David Cone .15
237 Armando Rios .15
238 Russ Davis .15
239 Wade Boggs .65
240 Aaron Sele .15
241 Jose Cruz Jr. .25
242 George Lombard .25
243 Todd Helton .75
244 Andruw Jones .75
245 Troy Glaus 1.00
246 Manny Ramirez .75
247 Ben Grieve .40
247p Ben Grieve ("PROMOTIONAL SAMPLE") 2.00
248 Richie Sexson .25
249 Juan Encarnacion .25
250 Randy Johnson .75
251 Gary Sheffield .45
252 Rafael Palmeiro .40
253 Roy Halladay .25
254 Mike Piazza 2.00
255 Tony Gwynn 1.00
256 Juan Gonzalez .75
257 Jeremy Giambi .25
258 Ben Davis .25
259 Russ Branyan .25
260 Pedro Martinez .75
261 Frank Thomas 1.50
262 Calvin Pickering .25
263 Chipper Jones 2.00
264 Ryan Minor .25
265 Roger Clemens 1.00
266 Sammy Sosa 1.50
267 Mo Vaughn .50
268 Carlos Beltran .25
269 Jim Thome .25
270 Mark McGwire 3.00
271 Travis Lee .25
272 Darin Erstad .75
273 Derek Jeter 2.00
274 Greg Maddux 1.00
275 Ricky Ledee .25
276 Alex Rodriguez 2.50
277 Vladimir Guerrero .75
278 Greg Vaughn .25
279 Scott Rolen .65
280 Carlos Guillen .25
281 Jeff Bagwell .75
282 Bruce Chen .25
283 Tony Clark .25
284 Albert Belle .40
285 Cal Ripken Jr. 3.00
286 Barry Bonds 1.50
287 Curt Schilling .50
288 Eric Chavez .40
289 Larry Walker .40
290 Orlando Hernandez .50
291 Moises Alou .40
292 Ken Griffey Jr. 2.50
293 Kerry Wood .40
294 Nomar Garciaparra 1.50
295 Gabe Kapler .40
296 Bernie Williams .60
297 Matt Anderson .25
298 Adrian Beltre .40
299 J.D. Drew .40
300 Ryan Bradley .25

1999 SkyBox Thunder Rant

A retail-only parallel of the 300-card base set, Rant substitutes purple metallic foil highlights for the regular-issue's silver on front, and a has a "RANT" notation at upper-right on back, also in purple. The stated insertion rate for the parallel is one per two retail packs.

	MT
Common Player:	.50
Rant Stars:	10X

(See 1999 SkyBox Thunder for checklist and base card values.)

1999 SkyBox Thunder Dial "1"

Designed to look like a mobile phone, this insert set featur ed 10 cards of long distance hitters. The set consisted of b lack plastic cards with rounded corners, and were seeded one card per every 300 packs.

		MT
Complete Set (10):		65.00
Common Player:		2.50
Inserted 1:300		
1D	Nomar Garciaparra	7.50
2D	Juan Gonzalez	5.00
3D	Ken Griffey Jr.	12.50
4D	Chipper Jones	9.00
5D	Mark McGwire	15.00
6D	Mike Piazza	9.00
7D	Manny Ramirez	5.00
8D	Alex Rodriguez	12.50
9D	Sammy Sosa	7.50
10D	Mo Vaughn	2.50

1999 SkyBox Thunder Hip-No-Tized

This insert set consisted of 15 cards, featuring both hitters and pitchers. The cards were seeded one card in every 36 packs, and consist of mesmerizing patterned holofoil stamping.

		MT
Complete Set (15):		40.00
Common Player:		1.00
Inserted 1:36		
1H	J.D. Drew	2.00
2H	Nomar Garciaparra	3.00
3H	Juan Gonzalez	2.00
4H	Ken Griffey Jr.	5.00
5H	Derek Jeter	4.00
6H	Randy Johnson	2.00
7H	Chipper Jones	4.00
8H	Mark McGwire	6.00
9H	Mike Piazza	4.00
10H	Cal Ripken Jr.	6.00
11H	Alex Rodriguez	5.00
12H	Sammy Sosa	3.00
13H	Frank Thomas	3.00
14H	Jim Thome	1.00
15H	Kerry Wood	1.50

1999 SkyBox Thunder In Depth

This insert set consists of 10 cards, featuring baseball's elite players. The cards are highlighted with gold rainbow holo-foil and gold metallic ink. The insertion rate for this insert was one card in every 24 packs.

		MT
Complete Set (10):		7.50
Common Player:		.50
Inserted 1:24		
1ID	Albert Belle	.50
2ID	Barry Bonds	1.00
3ID	Roger Clemens	.75
4ID	Juan Gonzalez	.65
5ID	Ken Griffey Jr.	1.50
6ID	Mark McGwire	2.00
7ID	Mike Piazza	1.25
8ID	Sammy Sosa	1.00
9ID	Mo Vaughn	.50
10ID	Kerry Wood	.50

1999 SkyBox Thunder Todd Helton Autograph

An unknown number of Helton's regular card (#243) were autographed and received an embossed seal of authenticity for use in various promotional endeavors.

		MT
243	Todd Helton	10.00

1999 SkyBox Thunder Turbo Charged

This 10-card insert set consisted of the top home run hitters. The players were featured on platic see-through cards with rainbow holofoil. One card was included in every 72 packs.

		MT
Complete Set (10):		22.50
Common Player:		1.00
Inserted 1:72		
1TC	Jose Canseco	1.50
2TC	Juan Gonzalez	2.00
3TC	Ken Griffey Jr.	4.00
4TC	Vladimir Guerrero	1.50
5TC	Mark McGwire	5.00
6TC	Mike Piazza	3.00
7TC	Manny Ramirez	2.00
8TC	Alex Rodriguez	4.00
9TC	Sammy Sosa	2.50
10TC	Mo Vaughn	1.00

1999 SkyBox Thunder Unleashed

This insert set contained 15 cards designed to resemble a cereal box. The players featured included the best young talent in baseball. The cards were silver-foil stamped, and offered facsimile signatures of each player. One card was included with every six packs.

		MT
Complete Set (15):		17.50
Common Player:		.75
Inserted 1:6		
1U	Carlos Beltran	.75
2U	Adrian Beltre	1.00
3U	Eric Chavez	2.00
4U	J.D. Drew	1.50
5U	Juan Encarnacion	1.00
6U	Jeremy Giambi	.75
7U	Troy Glaus	2.50
8U	Ben Grieve	1.00
9U	Todd Helton	2.00
10U	Orlando Hernandez	2.50
11U	Gabe Kapler	2.00
12U	Travis Lee	1.50
13U	Calvin Pickering	.75
14U	Richie Sexson	.75
15U	Kerry Wood	1.00

1999 SkyBox Thunder www.Batterz.com

www.batterz.com is a 10 card insert set that was seeded one card per every 18 packs. The game's best hitters are in ther e own home site in this computer-inspired set.

		MT
Complete Set (10):		15.00
Common Player:		.75
Inserted 1:18		
1WB	J.D. Drew	1.00
2WB	Nomar Garciaparra	2.25
3WB	Ken Griffey Jr.	2.75
4WB	Tony Gwynn	1.50
5WB	Derek Jeter	2.50
6WB	Mark McGwire	3.00
7WB	Alex Rodriguez	2.75
8WB	Scott Rolen	1.00
9WB	Sammy Sosa	2.00
10WB	Bernie Williams	.75

A player's name in *italic* type indicates a rookie card.

2000 SkyBox Dominion

		MT
Complete Set (300):		35.00
Common Player:		.10
Pack (10):		1.25
Wax Box (36):		35.00
1	Mark McGwire, Ken Griffey Jr. (League Leaders)	.50
2	Mark McGwire, Manny Ramirez (League Leaders)	.50
3	Larry Walker, Nomar Garciaparra (League Leaders)	.25
4	Tony Womack, Brian Hunter (League Leaders)	.10
5	Mike Hampton, Pedro Martinez (League Leaders)	.25
6	Randy Johnson, Pedro Martinez (League Leaders)	.25
7	Randy Johnson, Pedro Martinez (League Leaders)	.25
8	Ugueth Urbina, Mariano Rivera (League Leaders)	.10
9	Vinny Castilla (Highlights)	.10
10	Orioles host Cuban National Team (Highlights)	.10
11	Jose Canseco (Highlights)	.25
12	Fernando Tatis (Highlights)	.10
13	Robin Ventura (Highlights)	.10
14	Roger Clemens (Highlights)	.40
15	Jose Jimenez (Highlights)	.10
16	David Cone (Highlights)	.10
17	Mark McGwire (Highlights)	.75
18	Cal Ripken Jr. (Highlights)	.50
19	Tony Gwynn (Highlights)	.25
20	Wade Boggs (Highlights)	.10
21	Ivan Rodriguez (Highlights)	.25
22	Chuck Finley (Highlights)	.10
23	Eric Milton (Highlights)	.10
24	Adrian Beltre (Highlights)	.10
25	Brad Radke	.10
26	Derek Bell	.10
27	Garret Anderson	.10
28	Ivan Rodriguez	.50
29	Jeff Kent	.10
30	Jeremy Giambi	.10
31	John Franco	.10
32	Jose Hernandez	.10
33	Jose Offerman	.10
34	Jose Rosado	.10
35	Kevin Appier	.10
36	Kris Benson	.10
37	Mark McGwire	2.00
38	Matt Williams	.25

#	Player	Price
39	Paul O'Neill	.20
40	Rickey Henderson	.25
41	Todd Greene	.10
42	Russ Ortiz	.10
43	Sean Casey	.25
44	Tony Womack	.10
45	Troy O'Leary	.10
46	Ugueth Urbina	.10
47	Tom Glavine	.20
48	Mike Mussina	.40
49	Carlos Febles	.10
50	Jon Lieber	.10
51	Juan Gonzalez	.50
52	Matt Clement	.10
53	Moises Alou	.10
54	Ray Durham	.10
55	Robb Nen	.10
56	Tino Martinez	.25
57	Troy Glaus	.50
58	Curt Schilling	.15
59	Mike Sweeney	.10
60	Steve Finley	.10
61	Roger Cedeno	.10
62	Bobby Jones	.10
63	John Smoltz	.15
64	Darin Erstad	.20
65	Carlos Delgado	.25
66	Ray Lankford	.10
67	Todd Stottlemyre	.10
68	Andy Ashby	.10
69	Bobby Abreu	.10
70	Chuck Finley	.10
71	Damion Easley	.10
72	Dustin Hermanson	.10
73	Frank Thomas	.60
74	Kevin Brown	.15
75	Kevin Millwood	.20
76	Mark Grace	.15
77	Matt Stairs	.10
78	Mike Hampton	.10
79	Omar Vizquel	.10
80	Preston Wilson	.10
81	Robin Ventura	.15
82	Todd Helton	.50
83	Tony Clark	.20
84	Al Leiter	.15
85	Alex Fernandez	.10
86	Bernie Williams	.40
87	Edgar Martinez	.15
88	Edgar Renteria	.10
89	Fred McGriff	.20
90	Jermaine Dye	.10
91	Joe McEwing	.10
92	John Halama	.10
93	Lee Stevens	.10
94	Matt Lawton	.10
95	Mike Piazza	1.25
96	Pete Harnisch	.10
97	Scott Karl	.10
98	Tony Fernandez	.10
99	Sammy Sosa	1.25
100	Bobby Higginson	.10
101	Tony Gwynn	1.00
102	J.D. Drew	.25
103	Roberto Hernandez	.20
104	Rondell White	.15
105	David Nilsson	.10
106	Shane Reynolds	.15
107	Jaret Wright	.10
108	Jeff Bagwell	.50
109	Jay Bell	.10
110	Kevin Tapani	.10
111	Michael Barrett	.10
112	Neifi Perez	.10
113	Pat Hentgen	.10
114	Roger Clemens	.75
115	Travis Fryman	.15
116	Aaron Sele	.10
117	Eric Davis	.15
118	Trevor Hoffman	.10
119	Chris Singleton	.10
120	Ryan Klesko	.15
121	Scott Rolen	.50
122	Jorge Posada	.15
123	Abraham Nunez	.10
124	Alex Gonzalez	.10
125	B.J. Surhoff	.10
126	Barry Bonds	.50
127	Billy Koch	.10
128	Billy Wagner	.10
129	Brad Ausmus	.10
130	Bret Boone	.10
131	Cal Ripken Jr.	1.25
132	Chad Allen	.10
133	Chris Carpenter	.10
134	Craig Biggio	.25
135	Dante Bichette	.15
136	Dean Palmer	.10
137	Derek Jeter	1.50
138	Ellis Burks	.10
139	Freddy Garcia	.10
140	Gabe Kapler	.10
141	Greg Maddux	1.00
142	Greg Vaughn	.25
143	Jason Kendall	.15
144	Jim Parque	.10
145	John Valentin	.10
146	Jose Vidro	.10
147	Ken Griffey Jr.	1.50
148	Kenny Lofton	.40
149	Kenny Rogers	.10
150	Kent Bottenfield	.10
151	Chuck Knoblauch	.20
152	Larry Walker	.40
153	Manny Ramirez	.50
154	Mickey Morandini	.10
155	Mike Cameron	.10
156	Mike Lieberthal	.10
157	Mo Vaughn	.40
158	Randy Johnson	.40
159	Rey Ordonez	.10
160	Roberto Alomar	.40
161	Scott Williamson	.10
162	Shawn Estes	.10
163	Tim Wakefield	.10
164	Tony Batista	.10
165	Will Clark	.25
166	Wade Boggs	.25
167	David Cone	.15
168	Doug Glanville	.10
169	Jeff Cirillo	.10
170	John Jaha	.10
171	Mariano Rivera	.20
172	Tom Gordon	.10
173	Wally Joyner	.10
174	Alex Gonzalez	.10
175	Andruw Jones	.25
176	Barry Larkin	.25
177	Bartolo Colon	.10
178	Brian Giles	.10
179	Carlos Lee	.10
180	Darren Dreifort	.10
181	Eric Chavez	.10
182	Henry Rodriguez	.10
183	Ismael Valdes	.10
184	Jason Giambi	.10
185	John Wetteland	.10
186	Juan Encarnacion	.10
187	Luis Gonzalez	.10
188	Reggie Sanders	.10
189	Richard Hidalgo	.10
190	Ryan Rupe	.10
191	Sean Berry	.10
192	Rick Helling	.10
193	Randy Wolf	.10
194	Cliff Floyd	.10
195	Jose Lima	.10
196	Chipper Jones	1.00
197	Charles Johnson	.10
198	Nomar Garciaparra	1.25
199	Magglio Ordonez	.20
200	Shawn Green	.40
201	Travis Lee	.15
202	Jose Canseco	.40
203	Fernando Tatis	.10
204	Bruce Aven	.10
205	Johnny Damon	.10
206	Gary Sheffield	.20
207	Ken Caminiti	.15
208	Ben Grieve	.20
209	Sidney Ponson	.10
210	Vinny Castilla	.10
211	Alex Rodriguez	1.50
212	Chris Widger	.10
213	Carl Pavano	.10
214	J.T. Snow	.10
215	Jim Thome	.25
216	Kevin Young	.10
217	Mike Sirotka	.10
218	Rafael Palmeiro	.25
219	Rico Brogna	.10
220	Todd Walker	.10
221	Todd Zelle	.10
222	Brian Rose	.10
223	Chris Fussell	.10
224	Corey Koskie	.10
225	Rich Aurilla	.10
226	Geoff Jenkins	.10
227	Pedro Martinez	.50
228	Todd Hundley	.10
229	Brian Jordan	.10
230	Cristian Guzman	.10
231	Raul Mondesi	.15
232	Tim Hudson	.10
233	Albert Belle	.40
234	Andy Pettitte	.20
235	Brady Anderson	.15
236	Brian Bohannon	.10
237	Carlos Beltran	.15
238	Doug Mientkiewicz	.10
239	Jason Schmidt	.10
240	Jeff Zimmerman	.10
241	John Olerud	.20
242	Paul Byrd	.10
243	Vladimir Guerrero	.75
244	Warren Morris	.10
245	Eric Karros	.10
246	Jeff Weaver	.10
247	Jeromy Burnitz	.10
248	David Bell	.10
249	Rusty Greer	.10
250	Kevin Stocker	.10
251	Shea Hillenbrand (Prospect)	.20
252	Alfonso Soriano (Prospect)	.50
253	Micah Bowie (Prospect)	.20
254	Gary Matthews Jr. (Prospect)	.20
255	Lance Berkman (Prospect)	.20
256	Pat Burrell (Prospect)	1.00
257	Ruben Mateo (Prospect)	.25
258	Kip Wells (Prospect)	.25
259	Wilton Veras (Prospect)	.50
260	Ben Davis (Prospect)	.20
261	Eric Munson (Prospect)	.40
262	Ramon Hernandez (Prospect)	.20
263	Tony Armas Jr. (Prospect)	.25
264	Erubiel Durazo (Prospect)	.25
265	Chad Meyers (Prospect)	.25
266	Rick Ankiel (Prospect)	1.00
267	Ramon Ortiz (Prospect)	.25
268	Adam Kennedy (Prospect)	.20
269	Vernon Wells (Prospect)	.20
270	Chad Hermansen (Prospect)	.20
271	Norm Hutchins, Trent Durrington (Prospects)	.25
272	Gabe Molina, B.J. Ryan (Prospects)	.25
273	Juan Pena, *Tomokazu Ohka* (Prospects)	.25
274	Pat Daneker, Aaron Myette (Prospects)	.25
275	Jason Rakers, Russell Branyan (Prospects)	.25
276	Beiker Graterol, Dave Borkowski (Prospects)	.25
277	Mark Quinn, Dan Reichert (Prospects)	.50
278	Mark Redman, Jacque Jones (Prospects)	.25
279	Ed Yarnall, Wily Pena (Prospects)	1.00
280	Chad Harville, Brett Laxton (Prospects)	.25
281	Aaron Scheffer, Gil Meche (Prospects)	.25
282	Jim Morris, Dan Wheeler (Prospects)	.25
283	Danny Kolb, Kelly Dransfeldt (Prospects)	.25
284	Peter Munro, Casey Blake (Prospects)	.25
285	Rob Ryan, Byung-Hyun Kim (Prospects)	.25
286	Derrin Ebert, Pascual Matos (Prospects)	.50
287	Richard Barker, Kyle Farnsworth (Prospects)	.25
288	Jason LaRue, Travis Dawkins (Prospects)	.50
289	Chris Sexton, Edgard Clemente (Prospects)	.25
290	Amaury Garcia, A.J. Burnett (Prospects)	.50
291	Carlos Hernandez, Daryle Ward (Prospects)	.50
292	Eric Gagne, Jeff Williams (Prospects)	.25
293	Kyle Peterson, Kevin Barker (Prospects)	.25
294	Fernando Seguignol, Guillermo Mota (Prospects)	.25
295	Melvin Mora, Octavio Dotel (Prospects)	.25
296	Anthony Shumaker, Cliff Politte (Prospects)	.25
297	Yamid Haad, Jimmy Anderson (Prospects)	.25
298	Rick Heiserman, Chad Hutchinson (Prospects)	.25
299	Mike Darr, Wiki Gonzalez (Prospects)	.25
300	Joe Nathan, Calvin Murray (Prospects)	.25

2000 SkyBox Dominion Autographics

		MT
Common Player:		10.00
Inserted 1:144		
1	Rick Ankiel	20.00
2	Peter Bergeron	10.00
3	Wade Boggs	50.00
4	Barry Bonds	80.00
5	Pat Burrell	25.00
6	Miguel Cairo	10.00
7	Mike Cameron	10.00
8	Ben Davis	10.00
9	Russ Davis	10.00
10	Einar Diaz	10.00
11	Scott Elarton	10.00
12	Jeremy Giambi	10.00
13	Todd Greene	10.00
14	Vladimir Guerrero	40.00
15	Tony Gwynn	50.00
16	Bobby Howry	10.00
17	Tim Hudson	25.00
18	Randy Johnson	60.00
19	Andruw Jones	25.00
20	Jacque Jones	10.00
21	Jason LaRue	10.00
22	Matt Lawton	10.00
23	Greg Maddux	60.00
24	Pedro Martinez	75.00
25	Pokey Reese	10.00
26	Alex Rodriguez	75.00
27	Ryan Rupe	10.00
28	J.T. Snow	10.00
29	Jose Vidro	10.00
30	Tony Womack	10.00
31	Ed Yarnall	10.00
32	Kevin Young	10.00

2000 SkyBox Dominion Double Play

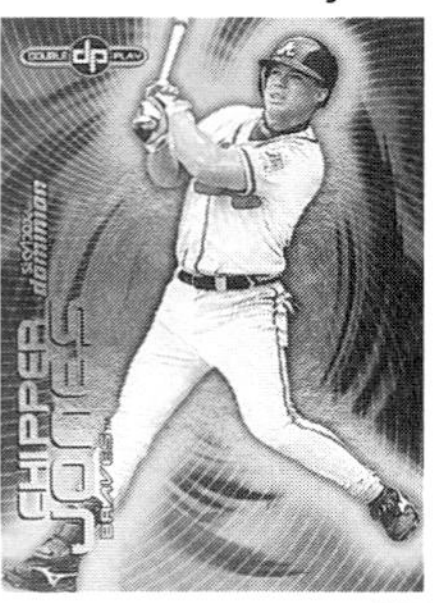

	MT
Complete Set (10):	25.00
Common Player:	1.50
Inserted 1:9	
Plus:	2x-4x
Inserted 1:90	
WarpTek:	12x to 20x

Inserted 1:900

1	Nomar Garciaparra	4.00
2	Pedro Martinez	1.50
3	Chipper Jones	3.00
4	Mark McGwire	6.00
5	Cal Ripken Jr.	4.00
6	Roger Clemens	2.00
7	Juan Gonzalez	1.50
8	Tony Gwynn	3.00
9	Sammy Sosa	4.00
10	Mike Piazza	4.00

2000 SkyBox Dominion Eye on October

		MT
Complete Set (15):		75.00
Common Player:		2.00
Inserted 1:24		
Plus:		2x to 5x
Inserted 1:240		
1	Ken Griffey Jr.	10.00
2	Mark McGwire	12.00
3	Derek Jeter	10.00
4	Juan Gonzalez	3.00
5	Chipper Jones	6.00
6	Sammy Sosa	8.00
7	Greg Maddux	6.00
8	Frank Thomas	3.00
9	Nomar Garciaparra	8.00
10	Shawn Green	2.00
11	Cal Ripken Jr.	8.00
12	Manny Ramirez	3.00
13	Scott Rolen	3.00
14	Mike Piazza	8.00
15	Alex Rodriguez	10.00

2000 SkyBox Dominion Hats Off

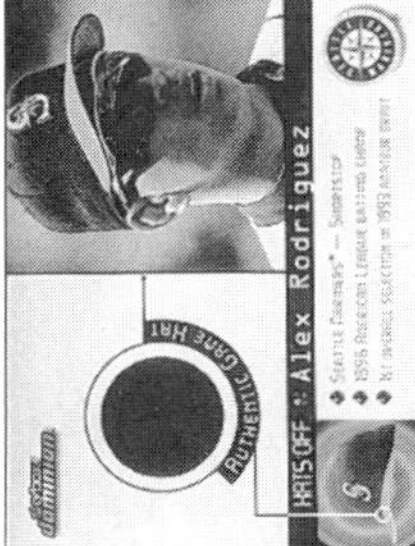

		MT
Common Player:		15.00
Inserted 1:468 H		
1	Wade Boggs	25.00
2	Barry Bonds	75.00
3	J.D. Drew	20.00
4	Shawn Green	15.00
5	Vladimir Guerrero	25.00
6	Randy Johnson	30.00
7	Andruw Jones	20.00
8	Greg Maddux	40.00
9	Pedro Martinez	30.00
10	Mike Mussina	20.00
11	Rafael Palmeiro	20.00
12	Alex Rodriguez	50.00
13	Scott Rolen	15.00
14	Tim Salmon	15.00
15	Robin Ventura	15.00

2000 SkyBox Dominion Milestones

		MT
Complete Set (6):		450.00
Common Player:		50.00
Inserted 1:1,999		
1	Mark McGwire	150.00
2	Roger Clemens	75.00
3	Tony Gwynn	75.00
4	Wade Boggs	40.00
5	Cal Ripken Jr.	120.00
6	Jose Canseco	60.00

2000 SkyBox Dominion New Era

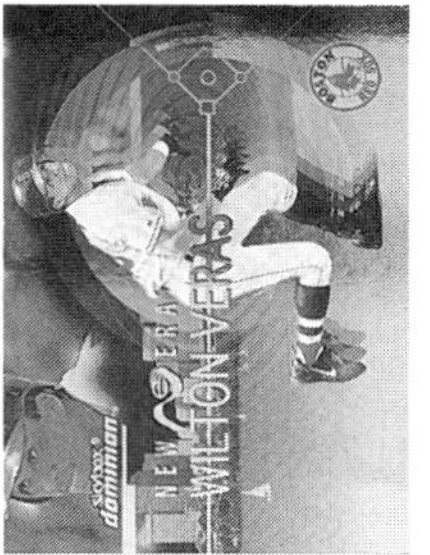

		MT
Complete Set (20):		15.00
Common Player:		.50
Inserted 1:3		
Plus:		2x to 4x
Inserted 1:30		
WarpTek:		5x to 10x
Inserted 1:300		
1	Pat Burrell	2.00
2	Ruben Mateo	.50
3	Wilton Veras	.50
4	Eric Munson	.75
5	Jeff Weaver	.75
6	Tim Hudson	.75
7	Carlos Beltran	.50
8	Chris Singleton	.50
9	Lance Berkman	.50
10	Freddy Garcia	1.00
11	Erubiel Durazo	.75
12	Randy Wolf	.50
13	Shea Hillenbrand	.50
14	Kip Wells	.50
15	Alfonso Soriano	2.00
16	Rick Ankiel	2.00
17	Ramon Ortiz	.50
18	Adam Kennedy	.50
19	Vernon Wells	.50
20	Chad Hermansen	.50

2000 SkyBox

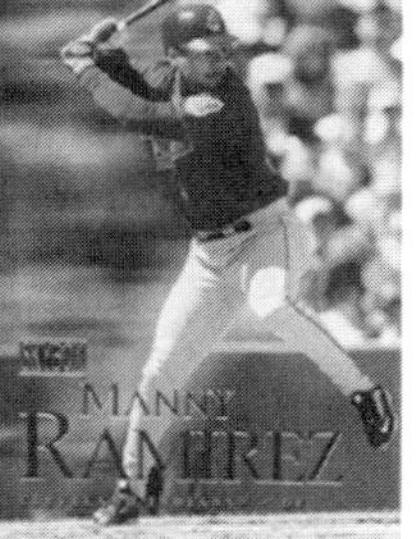

		MT
Complete Set (250):		40.00
Comp. Set w/SPs (300):		140.00
Common Player:		.10
Common SP (201-240):		2.00
Inserted 1:8		
Common SP (241-250):		1.00
Inserted 1:12		
Pack (10):		2.50
Wax Box (24):		55.00
1	Cal Ripken Jr.	2.50
2	Ivan Rodriguez	.75
3	Chipper Jones	1.50
4	Dean Palmer	.10
5	Devon White	.10
6	Ugueth Urbina	.10
7	Doug Glanville	.10
8	Damian Jackson	.10
9	Jose Canseco	.50
10	Billy Koch	.10
11	Brady Anderson	.20
12	Vladimir Guerrero	1.50
13	Dan Wilson	.10
14	Kevin Brown	.10
15	Eddie Taubensee	.10
16	Jose Lima	.10
17	Greg Maddux	1.50
18	Manny Ramirez	.75
19	Brad Fullmer	.10
20	Ron Gant	.10
21	Edgar Martinez	.20
22	Pokey Reese	.10
23	Jason Varitek	.10
24	Neifi Perez	.10
25	Shane Reynolds	.10
26	Robin Ventura	.20
27	Scott Rolen	.75
28	Trevor Hoffman	.10
29	John Valentin	.10
30	Shannon Stewart	.10
31	Troy Glaus	.75
32	Kerry Wood	.30
33	Jim Thome	.40
34	Rafael Roque	.10
35	Tino Martinez	.25
36	Jeffrey Hammonds	.10
37	Orlando Hernandez	.25
38	Kris Benson	.10
39	Fred McGriff	.25
40	Brian Jordan	.10
41	Trot Nixon	.10
42	Matt Clement	.10
43	Ray Durham	.10
44	Johnny Damon	.10
45	Todd Hollandsworth	.10
46	Edgardo Alfonzo	.20
47	Tim Hudson	.25
48	Tony Gwynn	1.00
49	Barry Bonds	1.00
50	Andruw Jones	.50
51	Pedro Martinez	.75
52	Mike Hampton	.10
53	Miguel Tejada	.10
54	Kevin Young	.10
55	J.T. Snow	.10
56	Carlos Delgado	.50
57	Bobby Howry	.10
58	Andres Galarraga	.40
59	Paul Konerko	.10
60	Mike Cameron	.10
61	Jeremy Giambi	.10
62	Todd Hundley	.10
63	Al Leiter	.20
64	Matt Stairs	.10
65	Edgar Renteria	.10
66	Jeff Kent	.10
67	John Wetteland	.10
68	Nomar Garciaparra	2.00
69	Jeff Weaver	.10
70	Matt Williams	.40
71	Kyle Farnsworth	.10
72	Brad Radke	.10
73	Eric Chavez	.10
74	J.D. Drew	.25
75	Steve Finley	.10
76	Pete Harnisch	.10
77	Chad Kreuter	.10
78	Todd Pratt	.10
79	John Jaha	.10
80	Armando Rios	.10
81	Luis Gonzalez	.10
82	Ryan Minor	.10
83	Juan Gonzalez	.75
84	Rickey Henderson	.25
85	Jason Giambi	.20
86	Shawn Estes	.10
87	Chad Curtis	.10
88	Jeff Cirillo	.10
89	Juan Encarnacion	.10
90	Tony Womack	.10
91	Mike Mussina	.50
92	Jeff Bagwell	.75
93	Rey Ordonez	.10
94	Joe McEwing	.10
95	Robb Nen	.10
96	Will Clark	.40
97	Chris Singleton	.10
98	Jason Kendall	.10
99	Ken Griffey Jr.	2.50
100	Rusty Greer	.10
101	Charles Johnson	.10
102	Carlos Lee	.10
103	Brad Ausmus	.10
104	Preston Wilson	.10
105	Ronnie Belliard	.10
106	Mike Lieberthal	.10
107	Alex Rodriguez	2.50
108	Jay Bell	.10
109	Frank Thomas	1.00
110	Adrian Beltre	.20
111	Ron Coomer	.10
112	Ben Grieve	.20
113	Darryl Kile	.10
114	Erubiel Durazo	.10
115	Magglio Ordonez	.25
116	Gary Sheffield	.40
117	Joe Mays	.10
118	Fernando Tatis	.25
119	David Wells	.10
120	Tim Salmon	.20
121	Troy O'Leary	.10
122	Roberto Alomar	.50
123	Damion Easley	.10
124	Brant Brown	.10
125	Carlos Beltran	.10
126	Eric Karros	.20
127	Geoff Jenkins	.20
128	Roger Clemens	1.00
129	Warren Morris	.10
130	Eric Owens	.10
131	Jose Cruz Jr.	.10
132	Mo Vaughn	.50
133	Eric Young	.10
134	Kenny Lofton	.40
135	Marquis Grissom	.10
136	A.J. Burnett	.10
137	Bernie Williams	.50
138	Javy Lopez	.20
139	Jose Offerman	.10
140	Sean Casey	.10
141	Alex Gonzalez	.10
142	Carlos Febles	.10
143	Mike Piazza	2.00
144	Curt Schilling	.20
145	Ben Davis	.10
146	Rafael Palmeiro	.40
147	Scott Williamson	.10
148	Darin Erstad	.25
149	Joe Girardi	.10
150	Gerald Williams	.10
151	Richie Sexson	.10
152	Corey Koskie	.10
153	Paul O'Neill	.20
154	Chad Hermansen	.10
155	Randy Johnson	.75
156	Henry Rodriguez	.10
157	Bartolo Colon	.10
158	Tony Clark	.20
159	Mike Lowell	.10
160	Moises Alou	.20
161	Todd Walker	.10
162	Mariano Rivera	.20
163	Mark McGwire	3.00
164	Roberto Hernandez	.10
165	Larry Walker	.30
166	Albert Belle	.50
167	Barry Larkin	.30
168	Rolando Arrojo	.10
169	Mark Kotsay	.10
170	Ken Caminiti	.10
171	Dermal Brown	.10
172	Michael Barrett	.10
173	Jay Buhner	.20
174	Ruben Mateo	.10
175	Jim Edmonds	.20
176	Sammy Sosa	2.00
177	Omar Vizquel	.10
178	Todd Helton	.75
179	Kevin Barker	.10
180	Derek Jeter	2.00
181	Brian Giles	.10
182	Greg Vaughn	.20
183	Roy Halladay	.10
184	Tom Glavine	.25

185 Craig Biggio .25
186 Jose Vidro .10
187 Andy Ashby .10
188 Freddy Garcia .10
189 Garret Anderson .10
190 Mark Grace .25
191 Travis Fryman .20
192 Jeromy Burnitz .10
193 Jacque Jones .10
194 David Cone .20
195 Ryan Rupe .10
196 John Smoltz .10
197 Daryle Ward .10
198 Rondell White .20
199 Bobby Abreu .20
200 Justin Thompson .10
201 Norm Hutchins (Prospect) .10
201 Norm Hutchins SP 2.00
202 Ramon Ortiz (Prospect) .10
202 Ramon Ortiz SP 2.00
203 Dan Wheeler (Prospect) .10
203 Dan Wheeler SP 2.00
204 Matt Riley (Prospect) .40
204 Matt Riley SP 3.00
205 Steve Lomasney (Prospect) .10
205 Steve Lomasney SP 2.00
206 Chad Meyers (Prospect) .10
206 Chad Meyers SP 2.00
207 *Gary Glover*
207Gary Glover SP 2.00
208 Joe Crede (Prospect) .10
208 Joe Crede SP 2.00
209 Kip Wells (Prospect) .10
209 Kip Wells SP 2.00
210 Travis Dawkins (Prospect) .10
210 Travis Dawkins SP 2.00
211 *Denny Stark* (Prospect) .25
211 Denny Stark SP 2.00
212 Ben Petrick (Prospect) .10
212 Ben Petrick SP 2.00
213 Eric Munson (Prospect) .75
213 Eric Munson SP 4.00
214 Josh Beckett (Prospect) .75
214 Josh Beckett SP 4.00
215 Pablo Ozuna (Prospect) .10
215 Pablo Ozuna SP 2.00
216 Brad Penny (Prospect) .10
216 Brad Penny SP 2.00
217 Julio Ramirez (Prospect) .10
217 Julio Ramirez SP 2.00
218 Danny Peoples (Prospect) .10
218 Danny Peoples SP 2.00
219 *Wilfredo Rodriguez* (Prospect) .10
219 *Wilfredo Rodriguez SP* 3.00
220 Julio Lugo (Prospect) .10
220 Julio Lugo SP 2.00
221 Mark Quinn (Prospect) .10
221 Mark Quinn SP 2.00
222 Eric Gagne (Prospect) .10
222 Eric Gagne SP 2.00
223 Chad Green (Prospect) .10
223 Chad Green SP 2.00
224 Tony Armas Jr. (Prospect) .10
224 Tony Armas Jr. SP 2.00
225 Milton Bradley (Prospect) .10
225 Milton Bradley SP 3.00
226 Rob Bell (Prospect) .10
226 Rob Bell SP 2.00
227 Alfonso Soriano (Prospect) .40
227 Alfonso Soriano SP 4.00
228 Wily Pena (Prospect) .10
228 Wily Pena SP 5.00
229 Nick Johnson (Prospect) .10
229 Nick Johnson SP 4.00
230 Ed Yarnall (Prospect) .10
230 Ed Yarnall SP 2.00
231 Ryan Bradley (Prospect) .10
231 Ryan Bradley SP 2.00
232 Adam Piatt (Prospect) .10
232 Adam Piatt SP 4.00
233 Chad Harville (Prospect) .10
233 Chad Harville SP 2.00
234 Alex Sanchez (Prospect) .10
234 Alex Sanchez SP 2.00
235 Michael Coleman (Prospect) .10
235 Michael Coleman SP 2.00
236 Pat Burrell (Prospect) .40
236 Pat Burrell SP 8.00
237 *Wascar Serrano* (Prospect) .10
237 *Wascar Serrano SP* 3.00
238 Rick Ankiel (Prospect) .10
238 Rick Ankiel SP 2.00
239 *Mike Lamb* (Prospect) .10
239 *Mike Lamb SP* 5.00
240 Vernon Wells (Prospect) .10
240 Vernon Wells SP 2.00
241 Jorge Toca, Goefrey Tomlinson (Premium Pairs) .10
241 Jorge Toca, Goefrey Tomlinson SP 1.00
242 Shea Hillenbrand *,Josh Phelps* (Premium Pairs) 3.00
242 Shea Hillenbrand, *Josh Phelps SP* 8.00
243 Aaron Myette, Doug Davis (Premium Pairs) .10
243 Aaron Myette, Doug Davis SP 1.00
244 Brett Laxton, Robert Ramsay (Premium Pairs) .10
244 Brett Laxton, Robert Ramsay SP 1.00
245 B.J. Ryan, Corey Lee (Premium Pairs) .10
245 B.J. Ryan, Corey Lee SP 1.00
246 Chris Haas, Wilton Veras (Premium Pairs) .50
246 Chris Haas, Wilton Veras SP 2.00
247 Jimmy Anderson, Kyle Peterson (Premium Pairs) .10
247 Jimmy Anderson, Kyle Peterson SP 1.00
248 Jason Dewey, Giuseppe Chiaramonte (Premium Pairs) .10
248 Jason Dewey, Giuseppe Chiaramonte SP 1.00
249 Guillermo Mota, Orber Moreno (Premium Pairs) .10
249 Guillermo Mota, Orber Moreno SP 1.00
250 Steve Cox,*Julio Zuleta* (Premium Pairs) .25
250 Steve Cox, *Julio Zuleta SP* 1.50

2000 SkyBox Star Rubies

This parallel of the 250-card SkyBox base set shares the same format and photos. On front, however, the player identification and SkyBox logo are in red foil. On back, an SR has been added beneath the card number. Insertion rate was one per 12 packs.

	MT
Common Player (1-200):	.50
Common SP Prospect (201-250):	3.00
Stars:	6X
Star SPs:	4X

(See 2000 SkyBox for checklist and base card values.)

2000 SkyBox Star Rubies Extreme

This parallel of the 250-card SkyBox base set shares the same format and photos. On front, however, the player identification and SkyBox logo are in red foil, and the metallic-foil background has an optical variable layer of stars. On back, an SRE has been added beneath the card number, as well as a strip with a red-foil serial number from within an edition of 50 cards each.

	MT
Common Player (1-200):	3.00
Common SP Prospect (201-250):	4.50
Stars:	35X
Star SPs:	25X

(See 2000 SkyBox for checklist and base card values.)

2000 SkyBox Autographics

	MT
Common Player	10.00
Rick Ankiel	20.00
Michael Barrett	10.00
Josh Beckett	20.00
Rob Bell	10.00
Adrian Beltre	15.00
Peter Bergeron	10.00
Lance Berkman	15.00
Rico Brogna	10.00
Pat Burrell	25.00
Orlando Cabrera	10.00
Mike Cameron	10.00
Roger Cedeno	10.00
Eric Chavez	15.00
Bruce Chen	10.00
Johnny Damon	15.00
Ben Davis	10.00
Jason Dewey	10.00
Octavio Dotel	10.00
J.D. Drew	30.00
Erubiel Durazo	10.00
Jason Giambi	25.00
Doug Glanville	10.00
Troy Glaus	30.00
Alex Gonzalez	10.00
Shawn Green	20.00
Jason Grilli	10.00
Tony Gwynn	50.00
Mike Hampton	15.00
Tim Hudson	25.00
Norm Hutchins	10.00
John Jaha	10.00
Derek Jeter	100.00
D'Angelo Jimenez	10.00
Randy Johnson	60.00
Andruw Jones	25.00
Gabe Kapler	15.00
Jason Kendall	15.00
Adam Kennedy	10.00
Cesar King	10.00
Paul Konerko	15.00
Mark Kotsay	10.00
Carlos Lee	10.00
Mike Lieberthal	10.00
Steve Lomasney	10.00
Greg Maddux	60.00
Edgar Martinez	20.00
Aaron McNeal	10.00
Kevin Millwood	10.00
Raul Mondesi	15.00
Joe Nathan	10.00
Magglio Ordonez	20.00
Eric Owens	10.00
Rafael Palmeiro	25.00
Angel Pena	10.00
Wily Pena	10.00
Cal Ripken Jr.	100.00
Scott Rolen	25.00
Jimmy Rollins	10.00
B.J. Ryan	10.00
Tim Salmon	20.00
Chris Singleton	10.00
J.T. Snow	10.00
Mike Sweeney	10.00
Jose Vidro	10.00
Rondell White	15.00
Jaret Wright	10.00

2000 SkyBox E-Ticket

		MT
Complete Set (14):		25.00
Common Player:		.50
Inserted 1:4		
Star Ruby:		10-20X
Production 100 sets		
1	Alex Rodriguez	3.00
2	Derek Jeter	2.50
3	Nomar Garciaparra	2.50
4	Cal Ripken Jr.	3.00
5	Sean Casey	.50
6	Mark McGwire	4.00
7	Sammy Sosa	2.50
8	Ken Griffey Jr.	3.00
9	Tony Gwynn	2.00

10	Pedro Martinez	1.00
11	Chipper Jones	2.00
12	Vladimir Guerrero	2.00
13	Roger Clemens	1.50
14	Mike Piazza	2.50

2000 SkyBox Genuine Coverage HOBBY

		MT
Common Player:		10.00
Inserted 1:144		
1	Ivan Rodriguez	10.00
2	Jose Canseco	10.00
3	Frank Thomas	15.00
4	Manny Ramirez	15.00

2000 SkyBox Genuine Coverage

		MT
Common Player:		8.00
Inserted 1:399		
1	Troy Glaus	15.00
2	Cal Ripken Jr.	40.00
3	Alex Rodriguez	30.00
4	Mike Mussina	15.00
5	J.D. Drew	10.00
6	Robin Ventura	8.00
7	Matt Williams	8.00

2000 SkyBox Higher Level

		MT
Complete Set (10):		70.00
Common Player:		3.00
Inserted 1:24		
Star Ruby:		6-12X
Production 50 sets		
1	Cal Ripken Jr.	10.00
2	Derek Jeter	8.00
3	Nomar Garciaparra	8.00
4	Chipper Jones	6.00
5	Mike Piazza	8.00
6	Ivan Rodriguez	3.00
7	Ken Griffey Jr.	10.00
8	Sammy Sosa	8.00
9	Alex Rodriguez	10.00
10	Mark McGwire	12.00

2000 SkyBox Hobby Bullpen Embossed

At "Meet the Manufacturer Night" events held in various locations around the country by Fleer, special versions of ShyBox cards featured a red foil-embossed "Fleer / Hobby Bullpen" logo were given to retailers present. The cards are otherwise identical to the regularly issued 2000 SkyBox. It is unknown how many different regional stars were used in this promotional program.

		MT
49	Barry Bonds	6.00

2000 SkyBox Preeminence

		MT
Complete Set (10):		60.00
Common Player:		2.00
Inserted 1:24		
Star Ruby:		6-12X
Production 50 sets		
1	Pedro Martinez	3.00
2	Derek Jeter	8.00
3	Nomar Garciaparra	8.00
4	Alex Rodriguez	10.00
5	Mark McGwire	12.00
6	Sammy Sosa	8.00
7	Sean Casey	2.00
8	Mike Piazza	8.00
9	Chipper Jones	6.00
10	Ivan Rodriguez	3.00

2000 SkyBox SkyLines

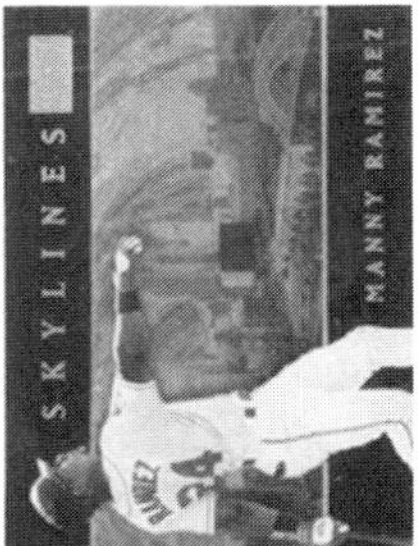

		MT
Complete Set (10):		35.00
Common Player:		1.00
Inserted 1:11		
Star Ruby:		15-25X
Production 50 sets		
1	Cal Ripken Jr.	5.00
2	Mark McGwire	6.00
3	Alex Rodriguez	5.00
4	Sammy Sosa	4.00
5	Derek Jeter	4.00
6	Mike Piazza	4.00
7	Nomar Garciaparra	4.00
8	Chipper Jones	3.00
9	Ken Griffey Jr.	5.00
10	Manny Ramirez	1.50

2000 SkyBox Speed Merchants

		MT
Complete Set (10):		20.00
Common Player:		.75
Inserted 1:8		
Star Ruby:		8-15X
Production 100 sets		
1	Derek Jeter	3.00
2	Sammy Sosa	3.00
3	Nomar Garciaparra	3.00
4	Alex Rodriguez	4.00
5	Randy Johnson	1.25
6	Ken Griffey Jr.	4.00
7	Pedro Martinez	1.25
8	Pat Burrell	2.00
9	Barry Bonds	1.50
10	Mark McGwire	5.00

2000 SkyBox The Technique

		MT
Complete Set (15):		60.00
Common Player:		1.00
Inserted 1:11		
Star Ruby:		10-18X
Production 50 sets		
1	Alex Rodriguez	6.00
2	Tony Gwynn	3.00
3	Sean Casey	1.00
4	Mark McGwire	8.00
5	Sammy Sosa	5.00
6	Ken Griffey Jr.	6.00
7	Mike Piazza	5.00
8	Nomar Garciaparra	5.00
9	Derek Jeter	5.00
10	Vladimir Guerrero	4.00
11	Cal Ripken Jr.	6.00
12	Chipper Jones	4.00
13	Frank Thomas	3.00
14	Manny Ramirez	2.00
15	Jeff Bagwell	2.00

1993 SP

Upper Deck's first super-premium baseball card issue features 290 cards in the single-series set; 252 are individual player cards, while the remainder includes a Premier Prospects subset featuring top prospects (20 cards), 18 All-Stars and a Platinum Power insert set of 20 top home run hitters. Cards, which were available in 12-card foil packs, feature borderless color photos and UV coating on the front, plus a special logo using lenticular printing. Foil is also used intricately in the design. Backs have a large color photo and statistics. Cards are numbered and color-coded by team.

		MT
Complete Set (290):		125.00
Common Player:		.15
Pack (12):		15.00
Wax Box (24):		400.00
1	Roberto Alomar	2.00
2	Wade Boggs	2.00
3	Joe Carter	.15
4	Ken Griffey, Jr.	5.00
5	Mark Langston	.15
6	John Olerud	.15
7	Kirby Puckett	3.00
8	Cal Ripken, Jr.	6.00
9	Ivan Rodriguez	2.00
10	Barry Bonds	3.50
11	Darren Daulton	.15
12	Marquis Grissom	.15
13	Dave Justice	.75
14	John Kruk	.15
15	Barry Larkin	.25
16	Terry Mulholland	.15
17	Ryne Sandberg	2.00
18	Gary Sheffield	.75
19	Chad Curtis	.15
20	Chili Davis	.15
21	Gary DiSarcina	.15
22	Damion Easley	.15
23	Chuck Finley	.15
24	Luis Polonia	.15
25	Tim Salmon	.40
26	*J.T. Snow*	1.00
27	Russ Springer	.15
28	Jeff Bagwell	2.50
29	Craig Biggio	.25
30	Ken Caminiti	.15
31	Andujar Cedeno	.15
32	Doug Drabek	.15
33	Steve Finley	.15
34	Luis Gonzalez	.60
35	Pete Harnisch	.15
36	Darryl Kile	.15
37	Mike Bordick	.15
38	Dennis Eckersley	.15
39	Brent Gates	.15
40	Rickey Henderson	1.00
41	Mark McGwire	6.00
42	Craig Paquette	.15
43	Ruben Sierra	.15
44	Terry Steinbach	.15
45	Todd Van Poppel	.15

46 Pat Borders .15
47 Tony Fernandez .15
48 Juan Guzman .15
49 Pat Hentgen .15
50 Paul Molitor 2.00
51 Jack Morris .15
52 Ed Sprague .15
53 Duane Ward .15
54 Devon White .15
55 Steve Avery .15
56 Jeff Blauser .15
57 Ron Gant .15
58 Tom Glavine .25
59 Greg Maddux 3.00
60 Fred McGriff .15
61 Terry Pendleton .15
62 Deion Sanders .25
63 John Smoltz .25
64 Cal Eldred .15
65 Darryl Hamilton .15
66 John Jaha .15
67 Pat Listach .15
68 Jaime Navarro .15
69 Kevin Reimer .15
70 B.J. Surhoff .15
71 Greg Vaughn .15
72 Robin Yount 2.00
73 *Rene Arocha* .15
74 Bernard Gilkey .15
75 Gregg Jefferies .15
76 Ray Lankford .15
77 Tom Pagnozzi .15
78 Lee Smith .15
79 Ozzie Smith 3.00
80 Bob Tewksbury .15
81 Mark Whiten .15
82 Steve Buechele .15
83 Mark Grace .50
84 Jose Guzman .15
85 Derrick May .15
86 Mike Morgan .15
87 Randy Myers .15
88 *Kevin Roberson* .15
89 Sammy Sosa 3.50
90 Rick Wilkins .15
91 Brett Butler .15
92 Eric Davis .15
93 Orel Hershiser .15
94 Eric Karros .15
95 Ramon Martinez .15
96 Raul Mondesi .50
97 Jose Offerman .15
98 Mike Piazza 4.00
99 Darryl Strawberry .15
100 Moises Alou .35
101 Wil Cordero .15
102 Delino DeShields .15
103 Darrin Fletcher .15
104 Ken Hill .15
105 *Mike Lansing* .40
106 Dennis Martinez .15
107 Larry Walker .75
108 John Wetteland .15
109 Rod Beck .15
110 John Burkett .15
111 Will Clark .50
112 Royce Clayton .15
113 Darren Lewis .15
114 Willie McGee .15
115 Bill Swift .15
116 Robby Thompson .15
117 Matt Williams .50
118 Sandy Alomar Jr. .15
119 Carlos Baerga .15
120 Albert Belle .50
121 Reggie Jefferson .15
122 Kenny Lofton .15
123 Wayne Kirby .15
124 Carlos Martinez .15
125 Charles Nagy .15
126 Paul Sorrento .15
127 Rich Amaral .15
128 Jay Buhner .15
129 Norm Charlton .15
130 Dave Fleming .15
131 Erik Hanson .15
132 Randy Johnson 2.00
133 Edgar Martinez .15
134 Tino Martinez .15
135 Omar Vizquel .15
136 Bret Barberie .15
137 Chuck Carr .15
138 Jeff Conine .15
139 Orestes Destrade .15
140 Chris Hammond .15
141 Bryan Harvey .15
142 Benito Santiago .15
143 Walt Weiss .15
144 *Darrell Whitmore* .15
145 *Tim Bolger* .15
146 Bobby Bonilla .15
147 Jeromy Burnitz .15
148 Vince Coleman .15
149 Dwight Gooden .15
150 Todd Hundley .15
151 Howard Johnson .15
152 Eddie Murray 1.00
153 Bret Saberhagen .15
154 Brady Anderson .15
155 Mike Devereaux .15
156 Jeffrey Hammonds .15
157 Chris Hoiles .15
158 Ben McDonald .15
159 Mark McLemore .15
160 Mike Mussina 2.00
161 Gregg Olson .15
162 David Segui .15
163 Derek Bell .15
164 Andy Benes .15
165 Archi Cianfrocco .15
166 Ricky Gutierrez .15
167 Tony Gwynn 3.00
168 Gene Harris .15
169 Trevor Hoffman .15
170 *Ray McDavid* .15
171 Phil Plantier .15
172 Mariano Duncan .15
173 Len Dykstra .15
174 Tommy Greene .15
175 Dave Hollins .15
176 Pete Incaviglia .15
177 Mickey Morandini .15
178 Curt Schilling .40
179 Kevin Stocker .15
180 Mitch Williams .15
181 Stan Belinda .15
182 Jay Bell .15
183 Steve Cooke .15
184 Carlos Garcia .15
185 Jeff King .15
186 Orlando Merced .15
187 Don Slaught .15
188 Andy Van Slyke .15
189 Kevin Young .15
190 Kevin Brown .35
191 Jose Canseco .75
192 Julio Franco .15
193 Benji Gil .15
194 Juan Gonzalez 2.50
195 Tom Henke .15
196 Rafael Palmeiro .50
197 Dean Palmer .15
198 Nolan Ryan 6.00
199 Roger Clemens 3.00
200 Scott Cooper .15
201 Andre Dawson .30
202 Mike Greenwell .15
203 Carlos Quintana .15
204 Jeff Russell .15
205 Aaron Sele .15
206 Mo Vaughn .75
207 Frank Viola .15
208 Rob Dibble .15
209 Roberto Kelly .15
210 Kevin Mitchell .15
211 Hal Morris .15
212 Joe Oliver .15
213 Jose Rijo .15
214 Bip Roberts .15
215 Chris Sabo .15
216 Reggie Sanders .15
217 Dante Bichette .15
218 Jerald Clark .15
219 Alex Cole .15
220 Andres Galarraga .15
221 Joe Girardi .15
222 Charlie Hayes .15
223 *Robert Mejia* .15
224 Armando Reynoso .15
225 Eric Young .15
226 Kevin Appier .15
227 George Brett 3.00
228 David Cone .15
229 Phil Hiatt .15
230 Felix Jose .15
231 Wally Joyner .15
232 Mike Macfarlane .15
233 Brian McRae .15
234 Jeff Montgomery .15
235 Rob Deer .15
236 Cecil Fielder .15
237 Travis Fryman .15
238 Mike Henneman .15
239 Tony Phillips .15
240 Mickey Tettleton .15
241 Alan Trammell .15
242 David Wells .15
243 Lou Whitaker .15
244 Rick Aguilera .15
245 Scott Erickson .15
246 Brian Harper .15
247 Kent Hrbek .15
248 Chuck Knoblauch .15
249 Shane Mack .15
250 David McCarty .15
251 Pedro Munoz .15
252 Dave Winfield 2.50
253 Alex Fernandez .15
254 Ozzie Guillen .15
255 Bo Jackson .25
256 Lance Johnson .15
257 Ron Karkovice .15
258 Jack McDowell .15
259 Tim Raines .15
260 Frank Thomas 3.50
261 Robin Ventura .15
262 Jim Abbott .15
263 Steve Farr .15
264 Jimmy Key .15
265 Don Mattingly 3.50
266 Paul O'Neill .15
267 Mike Stanley .15
268 Danny Tartabull .15
269 Bob Wickman .15
270 Bernie Williams 1.00
271 Jason Bere .15
272 *Roger Cedeno* 4.00
273 *Johnny Damon* 7.50
274 *Russ Davis* .50
275 Carlos Delgado 2.00
276 Carl Everett .50
277 Cliff Floyd .15
278 Alex Gonzalez .25
279 *Derek Jeter* 100.00
280 Chipper Jones 4.00
281 Javier Lopez .15
282 *Chad Mottola* .15
283 Marc Newfield .15
284 Eduardo Perez .15
285 Manny Ramirez 3.00
286 *Todd Steverson* .15
287 Michael Tucker .15
288 Allen Watson .15
289 Rondell White .50
290 Dmitri Young .15

1993 SP Platinum Power

This 20-card insert set features 20 of the game's top home run hitters. The top of each insert card features a special die cut treatment. Backs are numbered with a PP prefix.

MT
Complete Set (20): 30.00
Common Player: .75
1 Albert Belle 1.00
2 Barry Bonds 3.00
3 Joe Carter .75
4 Will Clark 1.00
5 Darren Daulton .75
6 Cecil Fielder .75
7 Ron Gant .75
8 Juan Gonzalez 2.00
9 Ken Griffey, Jr. 5.00
10 Dave Hollins .75
11 Dave Justice 1.50
12 Fred McGriff .75
13 Mark McGwire 6.00
14 Dean Palmer .75
15 Mike Piazza 4.00
16 Tim Salmon 1.00
17 Ryne Sandberg 2.00
18 Gary Sheffield 1.00
19 Frank Thomas 3.25
20 Matt Williams 1.00

1994 SP Promo

Virtually identical to the issued version of Ken Griffey, Jr.'s card in the regular SP set (#105) this differs in the card number on the back (#24) and the inclusion on front and back of the notice, "For Promotional Use Only".

MT
24 Ken Griffey Jr. 5.00

1994 SP

The second edition of Upper Deck's top-shelf SP brand features each card with a front background printed on metallic foil; the first 20 cards in the set, a series of "Prospects," have front backgrounds of textured metallic foil. Backs are printed with standard processes and include a color player photo a few stats and typical copyright notice and logos. Each foil pack contains one card featuring a special die-cut treatment at top.

MT
Complete Set (200): 125.00
Common Player: .15
Pack (8): 9.00
Wax Box (32): 350.00

1	*Mike Bell*	.25
2	D.J. Boston	.15
3	Johnny Damon	.30
4	*Brad Fullmer*	4.00
5	Joey Hamilton	.15
6	Todd Hollandsworth	.15
7	Brian Hunter	.15
8	*LaTroy Hawkins*	.75
9	*Brooks Kieschnick*	.25
10	*Derrek Lee*	1.50
11	*Trot Nixon*	3.00
12	Alex Ochoa	.15
13	*Chan Ho Park*	3.00
14	*Kirk Presley*	.15
15	*Alex Rodriguez*	100.00
16	*Jose Silva*	.25
17	*Terrell Wade*	.15
18	*Billy Wagner*	1.00
19	*Glenn Williams*	.25
20	Preston Wilson	.25
21	Brian Anderson	.15
22	Chad Curtis	.15
23	Chili Davis	.15
24	Bo Jackson	.25
25	Mark Langston	.15
26	Tim Salmon	.40
27	Jeff Bagwell	1.00
28	Craig Biggio	.25
29	Ken Caminiti	.15
30	Doug Drabek	.15
31	John Hudek	.15
32	Greg Swindell	.15
33	Brent Gates	.15
34	Rickey Henderson	1.00
35	Steve Karsay	.15
36	Mark McGwire	3.00
37	Ruben Sierra	.15
38	Terry Steinbach	.15
39	Roberto Alomar	.75
40	Joe Carter	.15
41	Carlos Delgado	.40
42	Alex Gonzalez	.25
43	Juan Guzman	.15
44	Paul Molitor	.75
45	John Olerud	.15
46	Devon White	.15
47	Steve Avery	.15
48	Jeff Blauser	.15
49	Tom Glavine	.25
50	Dave Justice	.50
51	Roberto Kelly	.15
52	Ryan Klesko	.15
53	Javier Lopez	.15
54	Greg Maddux	1.50
55	Fred McGriff	.15
56	Ricky Bones	.15
57	Cal Eldred	.15
58	Brian Harper	.15
59	Pat Listach	.15
60	B.J. Surhoff	.15
61	Greg Vaughn	.15
62	Bernard Gilkey	.15
63	Gregg Jefferies	.15
64	Ray Lankford	.15
65	Ozzie Smith	1.50
66	Bob Tewksbury	.15
67	Mark Whiten	.15
68	Todd Zeile	.15
69	Mark Grace	.30
70	Randy Myers	.15
71	Ryne Sandberg	1.50
72	Sammy Sosa	2.00
73	Steve Trachsel	.15
74	Rick Wilkins	.15
75	Brett Butler	.15
76	Delino DeShields	.15
77	Orel Hershiser	.15
78	Eric Karros	.15
79	Raul Mondesi	.40
80	Mike Piazza	2.25
81	Tim Wallach	.15
82	Moises Alou	.25
83	Cliff Floyd	.15
84	Marquis Grissom	.15
85	Pedro Martinez	1.00
86	Larry Walker	.40
87	John Wetteland	.15
88	Rondell White	.35
89	Rod Beck	.15
90	Barry Bonds	2.00
91	John Burkett	.15
92	Royce Clayton	.15
93	Billy Swift	.15
94	Robby Thompson	.15
95	Matt Williams	.45
96	Carlos Baerga	.15
97	Albert Belle	.50
98	Kenny Lofton	.15
99	Dennis Martinez	.15
100	Eddie Murray	.60
101	Manny Ramirez	1.00
102	Eric Anthony	.15
103	Chris Bosio	.15
104	Jay Buhner	.15
105	Ken Griffey, Jr.	2.50
106	Randy Johnson	1.00
107	Edgar Martinez	.15
108	Chuck Carr	.15
109	Jeff Conine	.15
110	Carl Everett	.25
111	Chris Hammond	.15
112	Bryan Harvey	.15
113	Charles Johnson	.15
114	Gary Sheffield	.50
115	Bobby Bonilla	.15
116	Dwight Gooden	.15
117	Todd Hundley	.15
118	Bobby Jones	.15
119	Jeff Kent	.15
120	Bret Saberhagen	.15
121	Jeffrey Hammonds	.15
122	Chris Hoiles	.15
123	Ben McDonald	.15
124	Mike Mussina	.75
125	Rafael Palmeiro	.30
126	Cal Ripken, Jr.	3.00
127	Lee Smith	.15
128	Derek Bell	.15
129	Andy Benes	.15
130	Tony Gwynn	1.50
131	Trevor Hoffman	.15
132	Phil Plantier	.15
133	Bip Roberts	.15
134	Darren Daulton	.15
135	Len Dykstra	.15
136	Dave Hollins	.15
137	Danny Jackson	.15
138	John Kruk	.15
139	Kevin Stocker	.15
140	Jay Bell	.15
141	Carlos Garcia	.15
142	Jeff King	.15
143	Orlando Merced	.15
144	Andy Van Slyke	.15
145	Paul Wagner	.15
146	Jose Canseco	.50
147	Will Clark	.45
148	Juan Gonzalez	1.00
149	Rick Helling	.15
150	Dean Palmer	.15
151	Ivan Rodriguez	1.00
152	Roger Clemens	1.50
153	Scott Cooper	.15
154	Andre Dawson	.30
155	Mike Greenwell	.15
156	Aaron Sele	.15
157	Mo Vaughn	.50
158	Bret Boone	.25
159	Barry Larkin	.25
160	Kevin Mitchell	.15
161	Jose Rijo	.15
162	Deion Sanders	.25
163	Reggie Sanders	.15
164	Dante Bichette	.15
165	Ellis Burks	.15
166	Andres Galarraga	.15
167	Charlie Hayes	.15
168	David Nied	.15
169	Walt Weiss	.15
170	Kevin Appier	.15
171	David Cone	.15
172	Jeff Granger	.15
173	Felix Jose	.15
174	Wally Joyner	.15
175	Brian McRae	.15
176	Cecil Fielder	.15
177	Travis Fryman	.15
178	Mike Henneman	.15
179	Tony Phillips	.15
180	Mickey Tettleton	.15
181	Alan Trammell	.15
182	Rick Aguilera	.15
183	Rich Becker	.15
184	Scott Erickson	.15
185	Chuck Knoblauch	.15
186	Kirby Puckett	1.50
187	Dave Winfield	1.00
188	Wilson Alvarez	.15
189	Jason Bere	.15
190	Alex Fernandez	.15
191	Julio Franco	.15
192	Jack McDowell	.15
193	Frank Thomas	2.00
194	Robin Ventura	.15
195	Jim Abbott	.15
196	Wade Boggs	.75
197	Jimmy Key	.15
198	Don Mattingly	2.00
199	Paul O'Neill	.15
200	Danny Tartabull	.15

1994 SP Die-Cut

Upper Deck SP Die-cuts are a 200-card parallel set inserted at the rate of one per foil pack. Each card has a die-cut top instead of the flat-top found on regular SP cards. Die-cuts also have a silver-foil Upper Deck hologram logo on back, in contrast to the gold-tone hologram found on regular SP; this is an effort to prevent fraudulent replication by any crook with a pair of scissors.

	MT
Complete Set (200):	125.00
Common Player:	.25

(Star cards valued at 1.5-3X corresponding cards in regular SP issue)

1994 SP Holoview Blue

Holoview F/X Blue is a 38-card set utilizing Holoview printing technology, which features 200 frames of video to produce a true, three-dimensional image on the bottom third of each card. The hologram is bordered in blue and there is a blue stripe running down the right side of the card. Backs are done with a blue background and feature a player photo over top of bold letters reading "Holo-View FX". This insert could be found in one per five packs of SP baseball.

		MT
Complete Set (38):		100.00
Common Player:		1.00
1	Roberto Alomar	2.50
2	Kevin Appier	1.00
3	Jeff Bagwell	3.00
4	Jose Canseco	2.50
5	Roger Clemens	4.00
6	Carlos Delgado	1.50
7	Cecil Fielder	1.00
8	Cliff Floyd	1.00
9	Travis Fryman	1.00
10	Andres Galarraga	1.00
11	Juan Gonzalez	3.00
12	Ken Griffey, Jr.	8.00
13	Tony Gwynn	3.00
14	Jeffrey Hammonds	1.00
15	Bo Jackson	1.25
16	Michael Jordan	15.00
17	Dave Justice	1.50
18	Steve Karsay	1.00
19	Jeff Kent	1.00
20	Brooks Kieschnick	1.00
21	Ryan Klesko	1.00
22	John Kruk	1.00
23	Barry Larkin	1.00
24	Pat Listach	1.00
25	Don Mattingly	4.00
26	Mark McGwire	10.00
27	Raul Mondesi	1.50
28	Trot Nixon	1.00
29	Mike Piazza	6.00
30	Kirby Puckett	4.00
31	Manny Ramirez	3.00
32	Cal Ripken, Jr.	10.00
33	Alex Rodriguez	35.00
34	Tim Salmon	1.50
35	Gary Sheffield	1.50
36	Ozzie Smith	3.00
37	Sammy Sosa	5.00
38	Andy Van Slyke	1.00

1994 SP Holoview Red

HoloView F/X Red is a parallel set to the Blue insert. Once again, this 38-card set utilizes Holoview printing technology. However, these cards have a red border surrounding the hologram and along the right side, as well as a red background on the back and a large "SPECIAL FX" under the player photo. Holoview red cards also have die-cut tops. Red cards are much scarcer than blue; the red being inserted once per 75 packs of SP baseball.

		MT
Complete Set (38):		575.00
Common Player:		2.50
1	Roberto Alomar	12.00
2	Kevin Appier	2.50

3	Jeff Bagwell	15.00
4	Jose Canseco	12.00
5	Roger Clemens	25.00
6	Carlos Delgado	4.00
7	Cecil Fielder	2.50
8	Cliff Floyd	2.50
9	Travis Fryman	2.50
10	Andres Galarraga	2.50
11	Juan Gonzalez	15.00
12	Ken Griffey, Jr.	40.00
13	Tony Gwynn	25.00
14	Jeffrey Hammonds	2.50
15	Bo Jackson	3.50
16	Michael Jordan	60.00
17	Dave Justice	7.50
18	Steve Karsay	2.50
19	Jeff Kent	2.50
20	Brooks Kieschnick	2.50
21	Ryan Klesko	2.50
22	John Kruk	2.50
23	Barry Larkin	2.50
24	Pat Listach	2.50
25	Don Mattingly	30.00
26	Mark McGwire	45.00
27	Raul Mondesi	4.00
28	Trot Nixon	2.50
29	Mike Piazza	35.00
30	Kirby Puckett	25.00
31	Manny Ramirez	15.00
32	Cal Ripken, Jr.	45.00
33	Alex Rodriguez	275.00
34	Tim Salmon	4.00
35	Gary Sheffield	7.50
36	Ozzie Smith	25.00
37	Sammy Sosa	30.00
38	Andy Van Slyke	2.50

1995 SP

Foil highlights and die-cut specialty cards are once again featured in Upper Deck's premium-brand SP baseball card issue. The 207-card set opens with four die-cut tribute cards, followed by 20 Premier Prospect die-cuts printed on metallic foil backgrounds with copper-foil highlights. Three checklists follow, also die-cut. The regular player cards in the set are arranged in team-alphabetical order within league. Card fronts feature photos which are borderless at top, bottom and right. On the left is a gold-highlighted metallic foil border of blue for N.L., red for A.L. Backs have a large photo at top, with a few stats and career highlights at bottom, along with a gold infield-shaped hologram. The SP insert program consists of a "SuperbaFoil" parallel set, in which each card's normal foil highlights are replaced with silver foil; a 48-card Special F/X set utilizing holographic portraits, and, a 20-card Platinum Power set. The hobby-only SP was issued in eight-card foil packs with a $3.99 suggested retail price.

		MT
	Complete Set (207):	20.00
	Common Player:	.10
	Pack (8):	2.00
	Wax Box (32):	40.00
1	Cal Ripken Jr. (Salute)	2.50
2	Nolan Ryan (Salute)	2.50
3	George Brett (Salute)	1.00
4	Mike Schmidt (Salute)	1.00
5	Dustin Hermanson (Premier Prospects)	.15
6	Antonio Osuna (Premier Prospects)	.10
7	*Mark Grudzielanek* (Premier Prospects)	.75
8	Ray Durham (Premier Prospects)	.15
9	Ugueth Urbina (Premier Prospects)	.10
10	Ruben Rivera (Premier Prospects)	.10
11	Curtis Goodwin (Premier Prospects)	.10
12	Jimmy Hurst (Premier Prospects)	.10
13	Jose Malave (Premier Prospects)	.10
14	*Hideo Nomo* (Premier Prospects)	2.00
15	Juan Acevedo (Premier Prospects)	.10
16	Tony Clark (Premier Prospects)	.10
17	Jim Pittsley (Premier Prospects)	.10
18	*Freddy Garcia* (Premier Prospects)	2.00
19	*Carlos Perez* (Premier Prospects)	.25
20	*Raul Casanova* (Premier Prospects)	.50
21	Quilvio Veras (Premier Prospects)	.10
22	Edgardo Alfonzo (Premier Prospects)	.15
23	Marty Cordova (Premier Prospects)	.10
24	C.J. Nitkowski (Premier Prospects)	.10
25	Checklist 1-69 (Wade Boggs)	.25
26	Checklist 70-138 (Dave Winfield)	.25
27	Checklist 139-207 (Eddie Murray)	.15
28	Dave Justice	.40
29	Marquis Grissom	.10
30	Fred McGriff	.10
31	Greg Maddux	1.50
32	Tom Glavine	.15
33	Steve Avery	.10
34	Chipper Jones	2.00
35	Sammy Sosa	1.75
36	Jaime Navarro	.10
37	Randy Myers	.10
38	Mark Grace	.30
39	Todd Zeile	.10
40	Brian McRae	.10
41	Reggie Sanders	.10
42	Ron Gant	.10
43	Deion Sanders	.15
44	Barry Larkin	.15
45	Bret Boone	.15
46	Jose Rijo	.10
47	Jason Bates	.10
48	Andres Galarraga	.10
49	Bill Swift	.10
50	Larry Walker	.40
51	Vinny Castilla	.10
52	Dante Bichette	.10
53	Jeff Conine	.10
54	John Burkett	.10
55	Gary Sheffield	.40
56	Andre Dawson	.25
57	Terry Pendleton	.10
58	Charles Johnson	.10
59	Brian L. Hunter	.10
60	Jeff Bagwell	1.25
61	Craig Biggio	.15
62	Phil Nevin	.10
63	Doug Drabek	.10
64	Derek Bell	.10
65	Raul Mondesi	.25
66	Eric Karros	.10
67	Roger Cedeno	.10
68	Delino DeShields	.10
69	Ramon Martinez	.10
70	Mike Piazza	2.00
71	Billy Ashley	.10
72	Jeff Fassero	.10
73	Shane Andrews	.10
74	Wil Cordero	.10
75	Tony Tarasco	.10
76	Rondell White	.25
77	Pedro Martinez	.40
78	Moises Alou	.20
79	Rico Brogna	.10
80	Bobby Bonilla	.10
81	Jeff Kent	.10
82	Brett Butler	.10
83	Bobby Jones	.10
84	Bill Pulsipher	.10
85	Bret Saberhagen	.10
86	Gregg Jefferies	.10
87	Lenny Dykstra	.10
88	Dave Hollins	.10
89	Charlie Hayes	.10
90	Darren Daulton	.10
91	Curt Schilling	.40
92	Heathcliff Slocumb	.10
93	Carlos Garcia	.10
94	Denny Neagle	.10
95	Jay Bell	.10
96	Orlando Merced	.10
97	Dave Clark	.10
98	Bernard Gilkey	.10
99	Scott Cooper	.10
100	Ozzie Smith	1.50
100	Ken Griffey Jr. (promo card)	5.00
101	Tom Henke	.10
102	Ken Hill	.10
103	Brian Jordan	.10
104	Ray Lankford	.10
105	Tony Gwynn	1.50
106	Andy Benes	.10
107	Ken Caminiti	.10
108	Steve Finley	.10
109	Joey Hamilton	.10
110	Bip Roberts	.10
111	Eddie Williams	.10
112	Rod Beck	.10
113	Matt Williams	.30
114	Glenallen Hill	.10
115	Barry Bonds	1.75
116	Robby Thompson	.10
117	Mark Portugal	.10
118	Brady Anderson	.10
119	Mike Mussina	.75
120	Rafael Palmeiro	.30
121	Chris Hoiles	.10
122	Harold Baines	.10
123	Jeffrey Hammonds	.10
124	Tim Naehring	.10
125	Mo Vaughn	.60
126	Mike Macfarlane	.10
127	Roger Clemens	1.50
128	John Valentin	.10
129	Aaron Sele	.10
130	Jose Canseco	.40
131	J.T. Snow	.10
132	Mark Langston	.10
133	Chili Davis	.10
134	Chuck Finley	.10
135	Tim Salmon	.25
136	Tony Phillips	.10
137	Jason Bere	.10
138	Robin Ventura	.10
139	Tim Raines	.10
140a	Frank Thomas (5-yr. BA .326)	1.75
140b	Frank Thomas (5-yr. BA .303)	2.00
141	Alex Fernandez	.10
142	Jim Abbott	.10
143	Wilson Alvarez	.10
144	Carlos Baerga	.10
145	Albert Belle	.50
146	Jim Thome	.10
147	Dennis Martinez	.10
148	Eddie Murray	.60
149	Dave Winfield	1.25
150	Kenny Lofton	.10
151	Manny Ramirez	1.25
152	Chad Curtis	.10
153	Lou Whitaker	.10
154	Alan Trammell	.10
155	Cecil Fielder	.10
156	Kirk Gibson	.10
157	Michael Tucker	.10
158	Jon Nunnally	.10
159	Wally Joyner	.10
160	Kevin Appier	.10
161	Jeff Montgomery	.10
162	Greg Gagne	.10
163	Ricky Bones	.10
164	Cal Eldred	.10
165	Greg Vaughn	.10
166	Kevin Seitzer	.10
167	Jose Valentin	.10
168	Joe Oliver	.10
169	Rick Aguilera	.10
170	Kirby Puckett	1.50
171	Scott Stahoviak	.10
172	Kevin Tapani	.10
173	Chuck Knoblauch	.10
174	Rich Becker	.10
175	Don Mattingly	1.75
176	Jack McDowell	.10
177	Jimmy Key	.10
178	Paul O'Neill	.10
179	John Wetteland	.10
180	Wade Boggs	.65
181	Derek Jeter	3.00
182	Rickey Henderson	.75
183	Terry Steinbach	.10
184	Ruben Sierra	.10
185	Mark McGwire	2.50
186	Todd Stottlemyre	.10
187	Dennis Eckersley	.10
188	Alex Rodriguez	2.25
189	Randy Johnson	.65
190	Ken Griffey Jr.	2.25
191	Tino Martinez	.10
192	Jay Buhner	.10
193	Edgar Martinez	.10
194	Mickey Tettleton	.10
195	Juan Gonzalez	1.25
196	Benji Gil	.10
197	Dean Palmer	.10
198	Ivan Rodriguez	.75
199	Kenny Rogers	.10
200	Will Clark	.30
201	Roberto Alomar	.75
202	David Cone	.10
203	Paul Molitor	.75
204	Shawn Green	.25
205	Joe Carter	.10
206	Alex Gonzalez	.15
207	Pat Hentgen	.10

1995 SP SuperbaFoil

This chase set parallels the 207 regular cards in the SP issue. Cards were found at the rate of one per eight-card foil pack. SuperbaFoil cards feature a silver-rainbow metallic foil in place of the gold, copper, red or blue foil highlights on regular-issue SP cards. On back, the SuperbaFoil inserts have a silver hologram instead of the gold version found on standard cards.

	MT
Complete Set (207):	40.00
Common Player:	.15
SuperbaFoil Stars:	1.5X

(See 1995 SP for checklist and base values.)

1995 SP Platinum Power

This die-cut insert set features the game's top power hitters in color action photos set against a background of two-toned gold rays emanating from the SP logo at lower-right. Player name, team and position are printed in white in a black band at bottom. Backs repeat the golden ray effect in the background and have a color photo at center. Career and 1994 stats are presented. An infield-shaped gold foil hologram is at lower-right. Cards have a "PP" prefix. Stated odds of finding one of the 20 Platinum Power inserts are one per five packs.

		MT
Complete Set (20):		10.00
Common Player:		.20
1	Jeff Bagwell	.75
2	Barry Bonds	1.00
3	Ron Gant	.20
4	Fred McGriff	.20
5	Raul Mondesi	.25
6	Mike Piazza	1.00
7	Larry Walker	.30
8	Matt Williams	.30
9	Albert Belle	.40
10	Cecil Fielder	.20
11	Juan Gonzalez	.75
12	Ken Griffey Jr.	1.25
13	Mark McGwire	1.50
14	Eddie Murray	.40
15	Manny Ramirez	.75
16	Cal Ripken Jr.	1.50
17	Tim Salmon	.25
18	Frank Thomas	.75
19	Jim Thome	.20
20	Mo Vaughn	.40

1995 SP Special F/X

By far the preferred pick of the '95 SP insert program is the Special F/X set of 48. The cards have a color action photo on front, printed on a metallic foil background. A 3/4" square holographic portrait is printed on the front. Backs are printed in standard technology and include another photo and a few stats and career highlights. Stated odds of finding a Special F/X card are 1 per 75 packs, or about one per two boxes.

		MT
Complete Set (48):		225.00
Common Player:		1.50
1	Jose Canseco	5.00
2	Roger Clemens	12.00
3	Mo Vaughn	6.00
4	Tim Salmon	2.50
5	Chuck Finley	1.50
6	Robin Ventura	1.50
7	Jason Bere	1.50
8	Carlos Baerga	1.50
9	Albert Belle	4.00
10	Kenny Lofton	1.50
11	Manny Ramirez	8.00
12	Jeff Montgomery	1.50
13	Kirby Puckett	12.00
14	Wade Boggs	6.00
15	Don Mattingly	15.00
16	Cal Ripken Jr.	25.00
17	Ruben Sierra	1.50
18	Ken Griffey Jr.	25.00
19	Randy Johnson	8.00
20	Alex Rodriguez	20.00
21	Will Clark	3.00
22	Juan Gonzalez	8.00
23	Roberto Alomar	7.00
24	Joe Carter	1.50
25	Alex Gonzalez	1.50
26	Paul Molitor	8.00
27	Ryan Klesko	1.50
28	Fred McGriff	1.50
29	Greg Maddux	12.00
30	Sammy Sosa	15.00
31	Bret Boone	2.00
32	Barry Larkin	1.50
33	Reggie Sanders	1.50
34	Dante Bichette	1.50
35	Andres Galarraga	1.50
36	Charles Johnson	1.50
37	Gary Sheffield	3.00
38	Jeff Bagwell	8.00
39	Craig Biggio	2.00
40	Eric Karros	1.50
41	Billy Ashley	1.50
42	Raul Mondesi	2.00
43	Mike Piazza	20.00
44	Rondell White	2.00
45	Bret Saberhagen	1.50
46	Tony Gwynn	10.00
47	Melvin Nieves	1.50
48	Matt Williams	3.00

1995 SP/ Championship

Championship was a version of Upper Deck's popular SP line designed for sale in retail outlets. The first 20 cards in the set are a "Diamond in the Rough" subset featuring hot rookies printed on textured metallic foil background. Regular player cards are arranged by team within league, alphabetically by city name. Each team set is led off with a "Pro Files" card of a star player; those card backs feature team season and post-season results. Each of the regular player cards has a borderless action photo on front, highlighted with a gold-foil SP Championship logo. The team name is in a blue-foil oval on National Leaguers' cards; red on American Leaguers. Backs have a portrait photo, a few stats and career highlights. Situated between the N.L. and A.L. cards in the checklist are a subset of 15 October Legends. A parallel set of cards with die-cut tops was inserted into the six-card foil packs at the rate of one per pack. A special card honoring Cal Ripken's consecutive-game record was issued as a super-scarce insert.

		MT
Complete Set (200):		35.00
Common Player:		.15
Pack (6):		1.50
Wax Box (44):		65.00
1	*Hideo Nomo* (Diamonds in the Rough)	2.00
2	Roger Cedeno (Diamonds in the Rough)	.15
3	Curtis Goodwin (Diamonds in the Rough)	.15
4	Jon Nunnally (Diamonds in the Rough)	.15
5	Bill Pulsipher (Diamonds in the Rough)	.15
6	C.J. Nitkowski (Diamonds in the Rough)	.15
7	Dustin Hermanson (Diamonds in the Rough)	.15
8	Marty Cordova (Diamonds in the Rough)	.15
9	Ruben Rivera (Diamonds in the Rough)	.15
10	*Ariel Prieto* (Diamonds in the Rough)	.25
11	Edgardo Alfonzo (Diamonds in the Rough)	.15
12	Ray Durham (Diamonds in the Rough)	.15
13	Quilvio Veras (Diamonds in the Rough)	.15
14	Ugueth Urbina (Diamonds in the Rough)	.15
15	*Carlos Perez* (Diamonds in the Rough)	.25
16	*Glenn Dishman* (Diamonds in the Rough)	.15
17	Jeff Suppan (Diamonds in the Rough)	.15
18	Jason Bates (Diamonds in the Rough)	.15
19	Jason Isringhausen (Diamonds in the Rough)	.25
20	Derek Jeter (Diamonds in the Rough)	2.50
21	Fred McGriff (Major League ProFiles)	.15
22	Marquis Grissom	.15
23	Fred McGriff	.15
24	Tom Glavine	.20
25	Greg Maddux	1.50
26	Chipper Jones	2.00
27	Sammy Sosa (Major League ProFiles)	1.00
28	Randy Myers	.15
29	Mark Grace	.30
30	Sammy Sosa	1.75
31	Todd Zeile	.15
32	Brian McRae	.15
33	Ron Gant (Major League ProFiles)	.15
34	Reggie Sanders	.15
35	Ron Gant	.15
36	Barry Larkin	.15
37	Bret Boone	.20
38	John Smiley	.15
39	Larry Walker (Major League ProFiles)	.25
40	Andres Galarraga	.15
41	Bill Swift	.15
42	Larry Walker	.35
43	Vinny Castilla	.15
44	Dante Bichette	.15
45	Jeff Conine (Major League ProFiles)	.15
46	Charles Johnson	.15
47	Gary Sheffield	.35
48	Andre Dawson	.25
49	Jeff Conine	.15
50	Jeff Bagwell (Major League ProFiles)	.40
51	Phil Nevin	.15
52	Craig Biggio	.20
53	Brian L. Hunter	.15
54	Doug Drabek	.15
55	Jeff Bagwell	1.25
56	Derek Bell	.15
57	Mike Piazza (Major League ProFiles)	1.00
58	Raul Mondesi	.30
59	Eric Karros	.15
60	Mike Piazza	2.00
61	Ramon Martinez	.15
62	Billy Ashley	.15
63	Rondell White (Major League ProFiles)	.20
64	Jeff Fassero	.15
65	Moises Alou	.25
66	Tony Tarasco	.15
67	Rondell White	.30
68	Pedro Martinez	.50
69	Bobby Jones (Major League ProFiles)	.15
70	Bobby Bonilla	.15
71	Bobby Jones	.15
72	Bret Saberhagen	.15
73	Darren Daulton (Major League ProFiles)	.15
74	Darren Daulton	.15
75	Gregg Jefferies	.15
76	Tyler Green	.15
77	Heathcliff Slocumb	.15
78	Lenny Dykstra	.15
79	Jay Bell (Major League ProFiles)	.15
80	Denny Neagle	.15
81	Orlando Merced	.15
82	Jay Bell	.15
83	Ozzie Smith (Major League ProFiles)	.50
84	Ken Hill	.15
85	Ozzie Smith	1.50
86	Bernard Gilkey	.15
87	Ray Lankford	.15
88	Tony Gwynn (Major League ProFiles)	.75

89 Ken Caminiti .15
90 Tony Gwynn 1.50
91 Joey Hamilton .15
92 Bip Roberts .15
93 Deion Sanders (Major League ProFiles) .20
94 Glenallen Hill .15
95 Matt Williams .30
96 Barry Bonds 1.75
97 Rod Beck .15
98 Eddie Murray (Checklist) .25
99 Cal Ripken Jr. (Checklist) 1.25
100 Roberto Alomar (October Legends) .30
101 George Brett (October Legends) .75
102 Joe Carter (Ocober Legends) .15
103 Will Clark (October Legends) .15
104 Dennis Eckersley (October Legends) .15
105 Whitey Ford (October Legends) .30
106 Steve Garvey (October Legends) .15
107 Kirk Gibson (October Legends) .15
108 Orel Hershiser (October Legends) .15
109 Reggie Jackson (October Legends) .50
110 Paul Molitor (October Legends) .25
111 Kirby Puckett (October Legends) .75
112 Mike Schmidt (October Legends) .50
113 Dave Stewart (October Legends) .15
114 Alan Trammell (October Legends) .15
115 Cal Ripken Jr. (Major League ProFiles) 1.25
116 Brady Anderson .15
117 Mike Mussina .65
118 Rafael Palmeiro .30
119 Chris Hoiles .15
120 Cal Ripken Jr. 2.50
121 Mo Vaughn (Major League ProFiles) .35
122 Roger Clemens 1.50
123 Tim Naehring .15
124 John Valentin .15
125 Mo Vaughn .60
126 Tim Wakefield .15
127 Jose Canseco .40
128 Rick Aguilera .15
129 Chili Davis (Major League ProFiles) .15
130 Lee Smith .15
131 Jim Edmonds .15
132 Chuck Finley .15
133 Chili Davis .15
134 J.T. Snow .15
135 Tim Salmon .30
136 Frank Thomas (Major League ProFiles) .75
137 Jason Bere .15
138 Robin Ventura .15
139 Tim Raines .15
140 Frank Thomas 1.75
141 Alex Fernandez .15
142 Eddie Murray (Major League ProFiles) .25
143 Carlos Baerga .15
144 Eddie Murray .60
145 Albert Belle .60
146 Jim Thome .15
147 Dennis Martinez .15
148 Dave Winfield 1.25
149 Kenny Lofton .15
150 Manny Ramirez 1.25
151 Cecil Fielder (Major League ProFiles) .15
152 Lou Whitaker .15
153 Alan Trammell .15
154 Kirk Gibson .15
155 Cecil Fielder .15
156 *Bobby Higginson* 1.50
157 Kevin Appier (Major League ProFiles) .15
158 Wally Joyner .15
159 Jeff Montgomery .15
160 Kevin Appier .15
161 Gary Gaetti .15
162 Greg Gagne .15
163 Ricky Bones (Major League ProFiles) .15
164 Greg Vaughn .15
165 Kevin Seitzer .15
166 Ricky Bones .15
167 Kirby Puckett (Major League ProFiles) .50
168 Pedro Munoz .15
169 Chuck Knoblauch .15
170 Kirby Puckett 1.50
171 Don Mattingly (Major League ProFiles) .75
172 Wade Boggs .65
173 Paul O'Neill .15
174 John Wetteland .15
175 Don Mattingly 1.75
176 Jack McDowell .15
177 Mark McGwire (Major League ProFiles) 1.25
178 Rickey Henderson .60
179 Terry Steinbach .15
180 Ruben Sierra .15
181 Mark McGwire 2.50
182 Dennis Eckersley .15
183 Ken Griffey Jr. (Major League ProFiles) 1.00
184 Alex Rodriguez 2.25
185 Ken Griffey Jr. 2.25
186 Randy Johnson .60
187 Jay Buhner .15
188 Edgar Martinez .15
189 Will Clark (Major League ProFiles) .25
190 Juan Gonzalez 1.25
191 Benji Gil .15
192 Ivan Rodriguez .50
193 Kenny Rogers .15
194 Will Clark .30
195 Paul Molitor (Major League ProFiles) .35
196 Roberto Alomar .60
197 David Cone .15
198 Paul Molitor .65
199 Shawn Green .25
200 Joe Carter .15
CR1 Cal Ripken Jr. (2,131 games tribute) 5.00
CR1 Cal Ripken Jr. die-cut 15.00

1995 SP/ Championship Die-Cuts

Each of the 200 cards in the regular SP championship issue, plus the 20 insert cards, can also be found in a parallel chase card set with die-cut tops. One die-cut card was found in each six-card foil pack, making them five times scarcer than the regular cards. To prevent regular cards from being fraudulently cut, factory-issue die-cuts have the Upper Deck hologram on back in silver tone, rather than the gold holograms found on regular cards.

	MT
Complete Set (200):	75.00
Common Player:	.25
Die-Cut Stars:	1.5X

(See 1995 SP/Championship for checklist and base values.)

1995 SP/ Championship Classic Performances

Vintage action photos are featured in this chase set marking great post-season performances of modern times. The cards have a wide red strip at top with "CLASSIC PERFORMANCES" in gold-foil; the player's name, team and the SP Championship embossed logo at bottom are also in gold. Backs have a portrait photo and description of the highlight along with stats from that series. Regular Classic Performances cards are found at a stated rate of one per 15 foil packs, with die-cut versions in every 75 packs, on average. The die-cuts have silver UD holograms on back as opposed to the gold hologram found on regular versions of the chase cards.

	MT
Complete Set (10):	16.00
Common Player:	1.00
Complete Die-Cut Set (10):	32.00
Common Die-Cuts:	2.00

CP1 Reggie Jackson (Game 6 of '77 WS) 1.25
CP1 Reggie Jackson (die-cut) 2.50
CP2 Nolan Ryan (Game 3 of '69 WS) 8.00
CP2 Nolan Ryan (die-cut) 16.00
CP3 Kirk Gibson (Game 1 of '88 WS) 1.00
CP3 Kirk Gibson (die-cut) 2.00
CP4 Joe Carter (Game 6 of '93 WS) 1.00
CP4 Joe Carter (die-cut) 2.00
CP5 George Brett (Game 3 of '80 ALCS) 2.50
CP5 George Brett (die-cut) 5.00
CP6 Roberto Alomar (Game 4 of '92 ALCS) 1.50
CP6 Roberto Alomar (die-cut) 3.00
CP7 Ozzie Smith (Game 5 of '85 NLCS) 1.50
CP7 Ozzie Smith (die-cut) 3.00
CP8 Kirby Puckett (Game 6 of '91 WS) 2.50
CP8 Kirby Puckett (die-cut) 5.00
CP9 Bret Saberhagen (Game 7 of '85 WS) 1.00
CP9 Bret Saberhagen (die-cut) 2.00
CP10 Steve Garvey (Game 4 of '84 NLCS) 1.00
CP10 Steve Garvey (die-cut) 2.00

1995 SP/C hampionship Destination: Fall Classic

Colored foil background printing and copper-foil graphic highlights are featured on this insert set picturing players who, for the most part, had yet to make a post-season appearance prior to 1995's expanded playoffs. Found at a stated average rate of one per 40 foil packs, the cards have short career summaries and another photo on back. A die-cut version of the cards was also issued, with a silver UD hologram on back rather than the gold found on the standard chase cards. The die-cut Fall Classic cards were inserted at a rate of one per 75 packs.

	MT
Complete Set (9):	32.50
Common Player:	1.50
Complete Die-Cut Set (9):	65.00
Common Die-Cut:	1.00

1 Ken Griffey Jr. 8.00
1 Ken Griffey Jr. (die-cut) 16.00
2 Frank Thomas 5.00
2 Frank Thomas (die-cut) 10.00
3 Albert Belle 2.00
3 Albert Belle (die-cut) 4.00
4 Mike Piazza 6.00
4 Mike Piazza (die-cut) 12.00
5 Don Mattingly 5.00
5 Don Mattingly (die-cut) 10.00
6 Hideo Nomo 2.50
6 Hideo Nomo (die-cut) 5.00
7 Greg Maddux 4.00
7 Greg Maddux (die-cut) 8.00
8 Fred McGriff 1.00

8	Fred McGriff (die-cut)	2.00
9	Barry Bonds	5.00
9	Barry Bonds (die-cut)	10.00

1995 SP/ Championship Ripken Tribute Jumbo

A special super-size (3" x 5") version of the SP/Championship edition Cal Ripken Jr. 2,131 Games tribute card insert was created for sale by Upper Deck Authentic on home shopping programs. The card is die-cut and serially numbered on back from within an edition of 2,131 pieces.

		MT
CR1	Cal Ripken Jr.	12.00

1996 SP

This 188-card set, distributed through hobby-only channels, features tremendous photography, including two photos on the front, and six insert sets. The inserts sets are Heroes, Marquee Matchups Blue and Die-Cut Marquee Matchups Red, Holoview Special F/X Blue and Die-Cut Holoview Special F/X Red, and the continuation of the Cal Ripken Collection.

		MT
Complete Set (188):		30.00
Common Player:		.10
Pack (8):		2.00
Wax Box (30):		45.00
1	Rey Ordonez (Premier Prospects)	.25
2	George Arias (Premier Prospects)	.10
3	*Osvaldo Fernandez* (Premier Prospects)	.30
4	*Darin Erstad* (Premier Prospects)	8.00
5	Paul Wilson (Premier Prospects)	.10
6	Richard Hidalgo (Premier Prospects)	.15
7	Bob Wolcott (Premier Prospects)	.10
8	Jimmy Haynes (Premier Prospects)	.10
9	Edgar Renteria (Premier Prospects)	.10
10	Alan Benes (Premier Prospects)	.10
11	Chris Snopek (Premier Prospects)	.10
12	Billy Wagner (Premier Prospects)	.10
13	*Mike Grace* (Premier Prospects)	.10
14	Todd Greene (Premier Prospects)	.10
15	Karim Garcia (Premier Prospects)	.15
16	John Wasdin (Premier Prospects)	.10
17	Jason Kendall (Premier Prospects)	.10
18	Bob Abreu (Premier Prospects)	.15
19	Jermaine Dye (Premier Prospects)	.10
20	Jason Schmidt (Premier Prospects)	.10
21	Javy Lopez	.10
22	Ryan Klesko	.10
23	Tom Glavine	.15
24	John Smoltz	.15
25	Greg Maddux	2.00
26	Chipper Jones	2.50
27	Fred McGriff	.10
28	David Justice	.40
29	Roberto Alomar	.75
30	Cal Ripken Jr.	3.00
31	Jeffrey Hammonds	.10
32	Bobby Bonilla	.10
33	Mike Mussina	.75
34	Randy Myers	.10
35	Rafael Palmeiro	.30
36	Brady Anderson	.10
37	Tim Naehring	.10
38	Jose Canseco	.50
39	Roger Clemens	2.00
40	Mo Vaughn	.50
41	*Jose Valentin*	.10
42	Kevin Mitchell	.10
43	Chili Davis	.10
44	Garret Anderson	.10
45	Tim Salmon	.30
46	Chuck Finley	.10
47	Mark Langston	.10
48	Jim Abbott	.10
49	J.T. Snow	.10
50	Jim Edmonds	.10
51	Sammy Sosa	2.25
52	Brian McRae	.10
53	Ryne Sandberg	2.00
54	Mark Grace	.30
55	Jaime Navarro	.10
56	Harold Baines	.10
57	Robin Ventura	.10
58	Tony Phillips	.10
59	Alex Fernandez	.10
60	Frank Thomas	2.25
61	Ray Durham	.10
62	Bret Boone	.15
63	Barry Larkin	.15
64	Pete Schourek	.10
65	Reggie Sanders	.10
66	John Smiley	.10
67	Carlos Baerga	.10
68	Jim Thome	.10
69	Eddie Murray	.60
70	Albert Belle	.35
71	Dennis Martinez	.10
72	Jack McDowell	.10
73	Kenny Lofton	.10
74	Manny Ramirez	1.50
75	Dante Bichette	.10
76	Vinny Castilla	.10
77	Andres Galarraga	.10
78	Walt Weiss	.10
79	Ellis Burks	.10
80	Larry Walker	.30
81	Cecil Fielder	.10
82	Melvin Nieves	.10
83	Travis Fryman	.10
84	Chad Curtis	.10
85	Alan Trammell	.10
86	Gary Sheffield	.40
87	Charles Johnson	.10
88	Andre Dawson	.30
89	Jeff Conine	.10
90	Greg Colbrunn	.10
91	Derek Bell	.10
92	Brian Hunter	.10
93	Doug Drabek	.10
94	Craig Biggio	.15
95	Jeff Bagwell	1.50
96	Kevin Appier	.10
97	Jeff Montgomery	.10
98	Michael Tucker	.10
99	Bip Roberts	.10
100	Johnny Damon	.15
101	Eric Karros	.10
102	Raul Mondesi	.30
103	Ramon Martinez	.10
104	Ismael Valdes	.10
105	Mike Piazza	2.50
106	Hideo Nomo	.75
107	Chan Ho Park	.25
108	Ben McDonald	.10
109	Kevin Seitzer	.10
110	Greg Vaughn	.10
111	Jose Valentin	.10
112	Rick Aguilera	.10
113	Marty Cordova	.10
114	Brad Radke	.10
115	Kirby Puckett	2.00
116	Chuck Knoblauch	.10
117	Paul Molitor	.75
118	Pedro Martinez	1.00
119	Mike Lansing	.10
120	Rondell White	.15
121	Moises Alou	.20
122	Mark Grudzielanek	.10
123	Jeff Fassero	.10
124	Rico Brogna	.10
125	Jason Isringhausen	.10
126	Jeff Kent	.10
127	Bernard Gilkey	.10
128	Todd Hundley	.10
129	David Cone	.10
130	Andy Pettitte	.40
131	Wade Boggs	.50
132	Paul O'Neill	.10
133	Ruben Sierra	.10
134	John Wetteland	.10
135	Derek Jeter	2.50
136	Geronimo Pena	.10
137	Terry Steinbach	.10
138	Ariel Prieto	.10
139	Scott Brosius	.10
140	Mark McGwire	3.00
141	Lenny Dykstra	.10
142	Todd Zeile	.10
143	Benito Santiago	.10
144	Mickey Morandini	.10
145	Gregg Jefferies	.10
146	Denny Neagle	.10
147	Orlando Merced	.10
148	Charlie Hayes	.10
149	Carlos Garcia	.10
150	Jay Bell	.10
151	Ray Lankford	.10
152	Alan Benes	.10
153	Dennis Eckersley	.10
154	Gary Gaetti	.10
155	Ozzie Smith	2.00
156	Ron Gant	.10
157	Brian Jordan	.10
158	Ken Caminiti	.10
159	Rickey Henderson	.65
160	Tony Gwynn	2.00
161	Wally Joyner	.10
162	Andy Ashby	.10
163	Steve Finley	.10
164	Glenallen Hill	.10
165	Matt Williams	.30
166	Barry Bonds	2.50
167	William VanLandingham	.10
168	Rod Beck	.10
169	Randy Johnson	1.00
170	Ken Griffey Jr.	2.75
170p	Ken Griffey Jr. (unmarked promo; bio on back says, ". . . against Cleveland" as opposed to ". . . against the Indians")	8.00
171	Alex Rodriguez	2.75
172	Edgar Martinez	.10
173	Jay Buhner	.10
174	Russ Davis	.10
175	Juan Gonzalez	1.50
176	Mickey Tettleton	.10
177	Will Clark	.30
178	Ken Hill	.10
179	Dean Palmer	.10
180	Ivan Rodriguez	.75
181	Carlos Delgado	.30
182	Alex Gonzalez	.15
183	Shawn Green	.30
184	Erik Hanson	.10
185	Joe Carter	.10
186	Checklist (Hideo Nomo)	.35
187	Checklist (Cal Ripken Jr.)	1.50
188	Checklist (Ken Griffey Jr.)	1.25

1996 SP Baseball Heroes

This 1996 insert set is a continuation of the series which began in 1990. These cards, numbered 81-90, feature nine of today's top stars, plus a Ken Griffey Jr. header card (#81). The cards were seeded one per every 96 packs.

		MT
Complete Set (10):		80.00
Common Player:		5.00
81	Ken Griffey Jr. Header	12.00
82	Frank Thomas	8.00
83	Albert Belle	5.00
84	Barry Bonds	10.00
85	Chipper Jones	12.00
86	Hideo Nomo	8.00
87	Mike Piazza	12.00
88	Manny Ramirez	8.00
89	Greg Maddux	10.00
90	Ken Griffey Jr.	15.00

1996 SP Marquee Matchups Blue

This 20-card Upper Deck SP insert set contains cards that allow collectors to match up the game's top players against each other, such as Greg Maddux against Cal Ripken Jr. The design and stadiums in the background match together when the two cards are next to each other. Blue versions are seeded one per every five packs. Red versions, with die-cut tops but otherwise identical to the blue, are found on average of once in 61 packs. Cards are numbered with a "MM" prefix.

		MT
Complete Set (20):		40.00
Common Player:		.75
1	Ken Griffey Jr.	4.00
2	Hideo Nomo	1.25
3	Derek Jeter	4.00
4	Rey Ordonez	1.00
5	Tim Salmon	1.00
6	Mike Piazza	3.50
7	Mark McGwire	4.00
8	Barry Bonds	3.00
9	Cal Ripken Jr.	4.00
10	Greg Maddux	3.00
11	Albert Belle	1.00
12	Barry Larkin	.75
13	Jeff Bagwell	2.00
14	Juan Gonzalez	2.00
15	Frank Thomas	2.00
16	Sammy Sosa	3.00
17	Mike Mussina	1.50
18	Chipper Jones	3.00
19	Roger Clemens	3.00
20	Fred McGriff	.75

1996 SP Marquee Matchups Red

A parallel set to the blue Marquee Matchups, the red cards are found on average of one per 61 packs. Besides the red background printing, this version is distinguished from the more common blue version by the die-cutting around the top. Cards are numbered with a "MM" prefix.

		MT
Complete Set (20):		90.00
Common Player:		1.25
1	Ken Griffey Jr.	7.50
2	Hideo Nomo	2.00
3	Derek Jeter	6.50
4	Rey Ordonez	1.25
5	Tim Salmon	1.50
6	Mike Piazza	6.50
7	Mark McGwire	8.00
8	Barry Bonds	6.00
9	Cal Ripken Jr.	8.00
10	Greg Maddux	5.00
11	Albert Belle	1.50
12	Barry Larkin	1.25
13	Jeff Bagwell	3.50
14	Juan Gonzalez	3.50
15	Frank Thomas	6.00
16	Sammy Sosa	6.00
17	Mike Mussina	2.00
18	Chipper Jones	6.50
19	Roger Clemens	5.00
20	Fred McGriff	1.25

1996 SP Ripken Collection

The last five cards of the Cal Ripken Jr. Collection, which began in Collector's Choice Series I, are featured in this Upper Deck SP product. These five cards, numbered 18-22, cover Ripken's early days, including his 1982 Rookie of the Year Award, his Major League debut, and photos of him playing third base. Ripken Collection inserts are found one per every 45 packs.

		MT
Complete Set (5):		45.00
Common Card:		10.00
18	Cal Ripken Jr.	10.00
19	Cal Ripken Jr.	10.00
20	Cal Ripken Jr.	10.00
21	Cal Ripken Jr.	10.00
22	Cal Ripken Jr.	20.00

1996 SP SpecialFX

These 48 cards capture Upper Deck Holoview technology. Blue versions were seeded one per every five packs of 1996 Upper Deck SP baseball.

		MT
Complete Set (48):		75.00
Common Player:		.75
1	Greg Maddux	3.00
2	Eric Karros	.75
3	Mike Piazza	5.00
4	Raul Mondesi	.75
5	Hideo Nomo	1.50
6	Jim Edmonds	.75
7	Jason Isringhausen	.75
8	Jay Buhner	.75
9	Barry Larkin	.75
10	Ken Griffey Jr.	6.00
11	Gary Sheffield	1.25
12	Craig Biggio	.75
13	Paul Wilson	.75
14	Rondell White	1.00
15	Chipper Jones	4.00
16	Kirby Puckett	3.00
17	Ron Gant	.75
18	Wade Boggs	2.00
19	Fred McGriff	.75
20	Cal Ripken Jr.	6.00
21	Jason Kendall	.75
22	Johnny Damon	.75
23	Kenny Lofton	.75
24	Roberto Alomar	1.50
25	Barry Bonds	4.00
26	Dante Bichette	.75
27	Mark McGwire	6.00
28	Rafael Palmeiro	1.00
29	Juan Gonzalez	3.00
30	Albert Belle	1.00
31	Randy Johnson	1.50
32	Jose Canseco	1.50
33	Sammy Sosa	4.00
34	Eddie Murray	1.50
35	Frank Thomas	3.00
36	Tom Glavine	.75
37	Matt Williams	1.00
38	Roger Clemens	3.00
39	Paul Molitor	1.50
40	Tony Gwynn	3.00
41	Mo Vaughn	1.50
42	Tim Salmon	1.00
43	Manny Ramirez	3.00
44	Jeff Bagwell	3.00
45	Edgar Martinez	.75
46	Rey Ordonez	.75
47	Osvaldo Fernandez	.75
48	Derek Jeter	6.00

1996 SP SpecialFX Red

These 1996 Upper Deck SP red die-cut cards use Upper Deck's Holoview technology. They are scarcer than the blue versions; these being seeded one per every 75 packs.

		MT
Complete Set (48):		180.00
Common Player:		2.00
1	Greg Maddux	10.00
2	Eric Karros	1.50
3	Mike Piazza	15.00
4	Raul Mondesi	2.00
5	Hideo Nomo	3.00
6	Jim Edmonds	1.50
7	Jason Isringhausen	1.50
8	Jay Buhner	1.50
9	Barry Larkin	1.50
10	Ken Griffey Jr.	15.00
11	Gary Sheffield	2.50
12	Craig Biggio	1.50
13	Paul Wilson	1.50
14	Rondell White	2.00
15	Chipper Jones	12.00
16	Kirby Puckett	8.00
17	Ron Gant	1.50
18	Wade Boggs	3.00
19	Fred McGriff	1.50
20	Cal Ripken Jr.	20.00
21	Jason Kendall	1.50
22	Johnny Damon	1.50
23	Kenny Lofton	1.50
24	Roberto Alomar	4.00
25	Barry Bonds	10.00
26	Dante Bichette	1.50
27	Mark McGwire	20.00
28	Rafael Palmeiro	2.50
29	Juan Gonzalez	5.00
30	Albert Belle	2.00
31	Randy Johnson	5.00
32	Jose Canseco	2.50
33	Sammy Sosa	10.00
34	Eddie Murray	2.50
35	Frank Thomas	8.00
36	Tom Glavine	1.50
37	Matt Williams	2.00
38	Roger Clemens	8.00
39	Paul Molitor	4.00
40	Tony Gwynn	8.00
41	Mo Vaughn	2.50
42	Tim Salmon	2.00
43	Manny Ramirez	5.00
44	Jeff Bagwell	5.00
45	Edgar Martinez	1.50
46	Rey Ordonez	1.50
47	Osvaldo Fernandez	1.50
48	Derek Jeter	20.00

1996 SPx

Upper Deck's 1996 SPX set has 60 players in it, which are each paralleled as a Gold version (one per every seven packs). Base cards feature a new look with a different perimeter die-cut design from those used in the past for basketball and football sets. A 10-card insert set, Bound for Glory, was also produced. Tribute cards were also made for Ken Griffey Jr. and Mike Piazza, with scarcer autographed versions also produced for each player.

	MT
Complete Set (60):	35.00
Common Player:	.50
Complete Gold Set (60):	100.00
Golds:	2.5X
Pack (1):	2.00
Wax Box (36):	65.00

1	Greg Maddux	2.50
2	Chipper Jones	4.00
3	Fred McGriff	.50
4	Tom Glavine	.75
5	Cal Ripken Jr.	6.00
6	Roberto Alomar	1.50
7	Rafael Palmeiro	1.00
8	Jose Canseco	1.50
9	Roger Clemens	2.50
10	Mo Vaughn	1.50
11	Jim Edmonds	.50
12	Tim Salmon	1.00
13	Sammy Sosa	3.00
14	Ryne Sandberg	2.50
15	Mark Grace	1.00
16	Frank Thomas	3.00
17	Barry Larkin	.50
18	Kenny Lofton	.50
19	Albert Belle	1.00
20	Eddie Murray	1.50
21	Manny Ramirez	2.00
22	Dante Bichette	.50
23	Larry Walker	1.00
24	Vinny Castilla	.50
25	Andres Galarraga	.50
26	Cecil Fielder	.50
27	Gary Sheffield	1.25
28	Craig Biggio	.50
29	Jeff Bagwell	2.00
30	Derek Bell	.50
31	Johnny Damon	.50
32	Eric Karros	.50
33	Mike Piazza	4.00
34	Raul Mondesi	.50
35	Hideo Nomo	2.00
36	Kirby Puckett	2.50
37	Paul Molitor	1.50
38	Marty Cordova	.50
39	Rondell White	.65
40	Jason Isringhausen	.50
41	Paul Wilson	.50
42	Rey Ordonez	.50
43	Derek Jeter	4.00
44	Wade Boggs	2.00
45	Mark McGwire	6.00
46	Jason Kendall	.50
47	Ron Gant	.50
48	Ozzie Smith	2.50
49	Tony Gwynn	2.50
50	Ken Caminiti	.50
51	Barry Bonds	3.00
52	Matt Williams	.50
53	*Osvaldo Fernandez*	1.00
54	Jay Buhner	.50
55	Ken Griffey Jr.	5.00
55p	Ken Griffey Jr. (overprinted "For Promotional Use Only")	3.50
56	Randy Johnson	2.00
57	Alex Rodriguez	5.00
58	Juan Gonzalez	2.00
59	Joe Carter	.50
60	Carlos Delgado	1.00

1996 SPx Bound for Glory

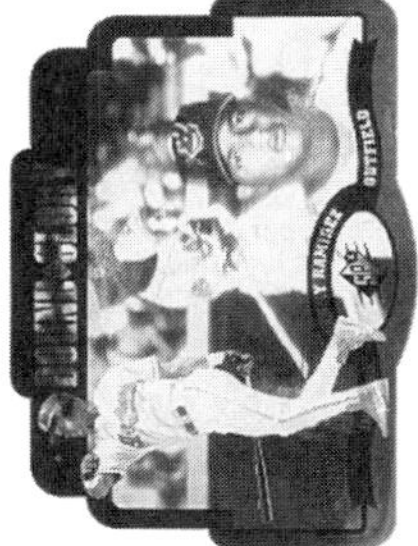

Some of baseball's best players are highlighted on these 1996 Upper Deck SPX insert cards. The cards were seeded one per every 24 packs. Fronts of the die-cut cards feature a color photograph on a background of silver-foil holographic portrait and action photos. Backs have another portrait photo, stats, career highlights and logos.

		MT
Complete Set (10):		35.00
Common Player:		2.50
1	Ken Griffey Jr.	6.00
2	Frank Thomas	4.00
3	Barry Bonds	4.00
4	Cal Ripken Jr.	7.50
5	Greg Maddux	3.50
6	Chipper Jones	5.00
7	Roberto Alomar	2.50
8	Manny Ramirez	3.00
9	Tony Gwynn	3.50
10	Mike Piazza	5.00

1996 SPx Ken Griffey Jr. Commemorative

Seattle Mariners' star Ken Griffey Jr. has this tribute card in Upper Deck's 1996 SPX set. The card was seeded one per every 75 packs. Autographed versions were also produced; these cards were seeded one per every 2,000 packs.

		MT
		10.00
KG1	Ken Griffey Jr.	5.00
KGA1	Ken Griffey Jr./ autograph	175.00

1996 SPx Mike Piazza Tribute

Los Angeles Dodgers' star catcher Mike Piazza is featured on this 1996 Upper Deck SPX insert card. Normal versions of the card are found one per every 95 packs, making it scarcer than the Ken Griffey Jr. inserts. Autographed Piazza cards are seeded one per every 2,000 packs.

		MT
		8.00
MP1	Mike Piazza	6.00
MP1	Mike Piazza/ autograph	160.00

1997 SP Sample

To preview its SP brand for 1997, Upper Deck issued a sample card of Ken Griffey, Jr. Similar in format to the issued cards, the promo bears card number 1 and is overprinted "SAMPLE" on back.

		MT
1	Ken Griffey Jr.	4.00

1997 SP

The fifth anniversary edition of SP Baseball features 184 regular cards sold in eight-card packs for $4.39. Card fronts feature the player's name in gold foil-stamping at bottom. Team name and position are vertically at one edge. Backs have two more photos along with "Best Year" and career stats. Inserts include Marquee Matchups, Special FX, Inside Info, Baseball Heroes, Game Film, SPx Force, and Autographed Vintage SP Cards.

		MT
Complete Set (184):		30.00
Common Player:		.10
Pack (8):		2.50
Wax Box (30):		60.00
1	Andruw Jones (Great Futures)	2.00
2	Kevin Orie (Great Futures)	.10
3	Nomar Garciaparra (Great Futures)	2.50
4	Jose Guillen (Great Futures)	1.00
5	Todd Walker (Great Futures)	.10
6	Derrick Gibson (Great Futures)	.10
7	Aaron Boone (Great Futures)	.15
8	Bartolo Colon (Great Futures)	.10
9	Derrek Lee (Great Futures)	.10
10	Vladimir Guerrero (Great Futures)	2.00
11	Wilton Guerrero (Great Futures)	.10
12	Luis Castillo (Great Futures)	.10
13	Jason Dickson (Great Futures)	.10
14	*Bubba Trammell* (Great Futures)	1.50
15	*Jose Cruz Jr.* (Great Futures)	2.50
16	Eddie Murray	.75
17	Darin Erstad	1.00
18	Garret Anderson	.10
19	Jim Edmonds	.10
20	Tim Salmon	.15
21	Chuck Finley	.10
22	John Smoltz	.15
23	Greg Maddux	2.25
24	Kenny Lofton	.10
25	Chipper Jones	3.00
26	Ryan Klesko	.10
27	Javier Lopez	.10
28	Fred McGriff	.10
29	Roberto Alomar	.75
30	Rafael Palmeiro	.30
31	Mike Mussina	.75
32	Brady Anderson	.10
33	Rocky Coppinger	.10
34	Cal Ripken Jr.	4.00
35	Mo Vaughn	.60
36	Steve Avery	.10
37	Tom Gordon	.10
38	Tim Naehring	.10
39	Troy O'Leary	.10
40	Sammy Sosa	2.50
41	Brian McRae	.10
42	Mel Rojas	.10
43	Ryne Sandberg	2.00
44	Mark Grace	.30
45	Albert Belle	1.00
46	Robin Ventura	.10
47	Roberto Hernandez	.10
48	Ray Durham	.10
49	Harold Baines	.10
50	Frank Thomas	2.50
51	Bret Boone	.15
52	Reggie Sanders	.10
53	Deion Sanders	.15
54	Hal Morris	.10
55	Barry Larkin	.10
56	Jim Thome	.10
57	Marquis Grissom	.10
58	David Justice	.40
59	Charles Nagy	.10
60	Manny Ramirez	2.00
61	Matt Williams	.30
62	Jack McDowell	.10
63	Vinny Castilla	.10
64	Dante Bichette	.10
65	Andres Galarraga	.10
66	Ellis Burks	.10
67	Larry Walker	.30
68	Eric Young	.10
69	Brian L. Hunter	.10
70	Travis Fryman	.10
71	Tony Clark	.10
72	Bobby Higginson	.15
73	Melvin Nieves	.10
74	Jeff Conine	.10
75	Gary Sheffield	.40
76	Moises Alou	.15
77	Edgar Renteria	.10
78	Alex Fernandez	.10
79	Charles Johnson	.10
80	Bobby Bonilla	.10
81	Darryl Kile	.10

82	Derek Bell	.10
83	Shane Reynolds	.10
84	Craig Biggio	.15
85	Jeff Bagwell	2.00
86	Billy Wagner	.10
87	Chili Davis	.10
88	Kevin Appier	.10
89	Jay Bell	.10
90	Johnny Damon	.15
91	Jeff King	.10
92	Hideo Nomo	.65
93	Todd Hollandsworth	.10
94	Eric Karros	.10
95	Mike Piazza	3.00
96	Ramon Martinez	.10
97	Todd Worrell	.10
98	Raul Mondesi	.30
99	Dave Nilsson	.10
100	John Jaha	.10
101	Jose Valentin	.10
102	Jeff Cirillo	.10
103	Jeff D'Amico	.10
104	Ben McDonald	.10
105	Paul Molitor	.75
106	Rich Becker	.10
107	Frank Rodriguez	.10
108	Marty Cordova	.10
109	Terry Steinbach	.10
110	Chuck Knoblauch	.10
111	Mark Grudzielanek	.10
112	Mike Lansing	.10
113	Pedro Martinez	.40
114	Henry Rodriguez	.10
115	Rondell White	.25
116	Rey Ordonez	.10
117	Carlos Baerga	.10
118	Lance Johnson	.10
119	Bernard Gilkey	.10
120	Todd Hundley	.10
121	John Franco	.10
122	Bernie Williams	.30
123	David Cone	.10
124	Cecil Fielder	.10
125	Derek Jeter	3.00
126	Tino Martinez	.10
127	Mariano Rivera	.25
128	Andy Pettitte	.30
129	Wade Boggs	.75
130	Mark McGwire	4.00
131	Jose Canseco	.50
132	Geronimo Berroa	.10
133	Jason Giambi	.35
134	Ernie Young	.10
135	Scott Rolen	1.50
136	Ricky Bottalico	.10
137	Curt Schilling	.20
138	Gregg Jefferies	.10
139	Mickey Morandini	.10
140	Jason Kendall	.10
141	Kevin Elster	.10
142	Al Martin	.10
143	Joe Randa	.10
144	Jason Schmidt	.10
145	Ray Lankford	.10
146	Brian Jordan	.10
147	Andy Benes	.10
148	Alan Benes	.10
149	Gary Gaetti	.10
150	Ron Gant	.10
151	Dennis Eckersley	.10
152	Rickey Henderson	.55
153	Joey Hamilton	.10
154	Ken Caminiti	.10
155	Tony Gwynn	2.25
156	Steve Finley	.10
157	Trevor Hoffman	.10
158	Greg Vaughn	.10
159	J.T. Snow	.10
160	Barry Bonds	2.50
161	Glenallen Hill	.10
162	William VanLandingham	.10
163	Jeff Kent	.10
164	Jay Buhner	.10
165	Ken Griffey Jr.	3.50
166	Alex Rodriguez	3.50
167	Randy Johnson	.75
168	Edgar Martinez	.10
169	Dan Wilson	.10
170	Ivan Rodriguez	.65
171	Roger Pavlik	.10
172	Will Clark	.30
173	Dean Palmer	.10
174	Rusty Greer	.10
175	Juan Gonzalez	2.00
176	John Wetteland	.10
177	Joe Carter	.10
178	Ed Sprague	.10
179	Carlos Delgado	.30
180	Roger Clemens	2.25
181	Juan Guzman	.10
182	Pat Hentgen	.10
183	Ken Griffey Jr. (checklist)	1.50
184	*Hideki Irabu*	.75

1997 SP Buy-Back Autographed Inserts

To celebrate the fifth anniversary of its premium SP brand, Upper Deck went into the hobby market to buy nearly 3,000 previous years' cards for a special insert program in 1997 SP packs. Various SP cards from 1993-96 issues and inserts were autographed by star players and a numbered holographic seal added on back. The number of each particular card signed ranged widely from fewer than 10 to more than 100. Numbers in parentheses in the checklist are the quantity reported signed for that card. All cards were inserted into foil packs except those of Mo Vaughn, which were a mail-in redemption.

		MT
Common Autograph:		7.50
	1993 SP	
4	Ken Griffey Jr. (16)	600.00
28	Jeff Bagwell (7)	
167	Tony Gwynn (17)	250.00
280	Chipper Jones (34)	200.00
	1993 SP Platinum Power	
PP9	Ken Griffey Jr. (5)	800.00
	1994 SP	
6	Todd Hollandsworth (167)	7.50
15	Alex Rodriguez (94)	900.00
105	Ken Griffey Jr. (103)	200.00
114	Gary Sheffield (130)	15.00
130	Tony Gwynn (367)	40.00
	1994 SP Holoview Blue	
13	Tony Gwynn (31)	200.00
	1994 SP Holoview Red	
35	Gary Sheffield (4)	30.00
	1995 SP	
34	Chipper Jones (60)	125.00
60	Jeff Bagwell (173)	60.00
75	Gary Sheffield (221)	20.00
105	Tony Gwynn (64)	150.00
188	Alex Rodriguez (63)	200.00
190	Ken Griffey Jr. (38)	375.00
195	Jay Buhner (57)	15.00
	1996 SP	
1	Rey Ordonez (111)	12.00
18	Gary Sheffield (58)	40.00
26	Chipper Jones (102)	100.00
40	Mo Vaughn (250)	15.00
95	Jeff Bagwell (292)	50.00
160	Tony Gwynn (20)	250.00
170	Ken Griffey Jr. (312)	90.00
171	Alex Rodriguez (73)	120.00
173	Jay Buhner (79)	25.00
	1996 SP Marquee Matchups	
MM13	Jeff Bagwell (23)	150.00
MM4	Rey Ordonez (40)	25.00
	1996 SP Special F/X	
8	Jay Buhner (27)	30.00

1997 SP Game Film

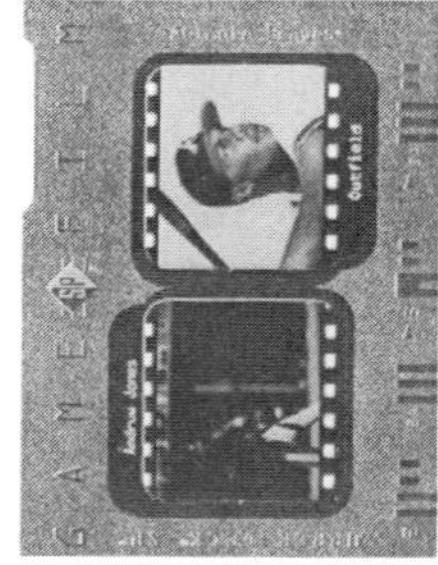

A 10-card insert utilizing pieces of actual game footage to highlight the top stars in the game. Only 500 of each card were available. Cards are numbered with a "GF" prefix.

		MT
Complete Set (10):		135.00
Common Player:		8.00
1	Alex Rodriguez	20.00
2	Frank Thomas	12.00
3	Andruw Jones	8.00
4	Cal Ripken Jr.	25.00
5	Mike Piazza	17.50
6	Derek Jeter	25.00
7	Mark McGwire	25.00
8	Chipper Jones	17.50
9	Barry Bonds	12.00
10	Ken Griffey Jr.	20.00

1997 SP Griffey Baseball Heroes

First started in 1990, this single-player insert continues with a salute to Ken Griffey Jr. Each card in the set is numbered to 2,000.

		MT
Complete Set (10):		65.00
Common Griffey Jr.:		9.00
91	Ken Griffey Jr.	9.00
92	Ken Griffey Jr.	9.00
93	Ken Griffey Jr.	9.00
94	Ken Griffey Jr.	9.00
95	Ken Griffey Jr.	9.00
96	Ken Griffey Jr.	9.00
97	Ken Griffey Jr.	9.00
98	Ken Griffey Jr.	9.00
99	Ken Griffey Jr.	9.00
100	Ken Griffey Jr.	9.00

1997 SP Inside Info

Each of the 25 cards in this insert feature a pull-out panel describing the player's major accomplishments. Both front and back are printed on metallic-foil stock. Cards were inserted one per box.

		MT
Complete Set (25):		95.00
Common Player:		1.00
1	Ken Griffey Jr.	6.50
2	Mark McGwire	8.00
3	Kenny Lofton	1.00
4	Paul Molitor	2.00
5	Frank Thomas	4.50
6	Greg Maddux	4.00
7	Mo Vaughn	1.50
8	Cal Ripken Jr.	8.00
9	Jeff Bagwell	3.00
10	Alex Rodriguez	6.50
11	John Smoltz	1.00
12	Manny Ramirez	3.00
13	Sammy Sosa	4.50
14	Vladimir Guerrero	3.00
15	Albert Belle	1.50
16	Mike Piazza	5.00
17	Derek Jeter	5.00
18	Scott Rolen	1.50
19	Tony Gwynn	4.00
20	Barry Bonds	4.50
21	Ken Caminiti	1.00
22	Chipper Jones	5.00
23	Juan Gonzalez	3.00
24	Roger Clemens	4.00
25	Andruw Jones	3.00

1997 SP Marquee Matchups

A 20-card die-cut set designed to highlight top interleague matchups. When the matching cards are put together, a third player is highlighted in the background. Cards were inserted 1:5 packs.

	MT
Complete Set (30):	20.00
Common Player:	.25
MM1 Ken Griffey Jr.	2.50
MM2 Andres Galarraga	.25
MM2 Juan Gonzalez	.75
MM3 Barry Bonds	1.25
MM4 Mark McGwire	2.50
MM4 Jose Canseco	.60
MM5 Mike Piazza	2.00
MM6 Tim Salmon	.40
MM6 Hideo Nomo	.50
MM7 Tony Gwynn	1.00
MM8 Alex Rodriguez	2.50
MM8 Ken Caminiti	.25
MM9 Chipper Jones	1.50
MM10Derek Jeter	3.00
MM10Andruw Jones	.75
MM11Manny Ramirez	.75
MM12Jeff Bagwell	.75
MM12Matt Williams	.30
MM13Greg Maddux	1.00
MM14Cal Ripken Jr.	3.00
MM14Brady Anderson	.25
MM15Mo Vaughn	.40
MM16Gary Sheffield	.40
MM16Vladimir Guerrero	.75
MM17Jim Thome	.25
MM18Barry Larkin	.25
MM18Deion Sanders	.25
MM19Frank Thomas	1.00
MM20Sammy Sosa	1.50
MM20Albert Belle	.50

1997 SP Special FX

Color 3-D motion portraits are front and center on these cards that also feature a die-cut design. The rest of the front includes color action photos printed on silver-foil stock. Backs have another color photo. One of the Alex Rodriguez cards (#49) features the 1996 die-cut design. Special FX were inserted 1:9 packs.

		MT
Complete Set (48):		120.00
Common Player:		1.00
1	Ken Griffey Jr.	8.00
2	Frank Thomas	4.00
3	Barry Bonds	5.00
4	Albert Belle	1.50
5	Mike Piazza	6.00
6	Greg Maddux	5.00
7	Chipper Jones	6.00
8	Cal Ripken Jr.	8.00
9	Jeff Bagwell	3.00
10	Alex Rodriguez	6.00
11	Mark McGwire	8.00
12	Kenny Lofton	1.00
13	Juan Gonzalez	3.00
14	Mo Vaughn	2.00
15	John Smoltz	1.00
16	Derek Jeter	8.00
17	Tony Gwynn	4.50
18	Ivan Rodriguez	2.50
19	Barry Larkin	1.00
20	Sammy Sosa	5.00
21	Mike Mussina	2.50
22	Gary Sheffield	1.50
23	Brady Anderson	1.00
24	Roger Clemens	4.50
25	Ken Caminiti	1.00
26	Roberto Alomar	2.50
27	Hideo Nomo	2.50
28	Bernie Williams	2.00
29	Todd Hundley	1.00
30	Manny Ramirez	3.00
31	Eric Karros	1.00
32	Tim Salmon	1.50
33	Jay Buhner	1.00
34	Andy Pettitte	1.50
35	Jim Thome	1.00
36	Ryne Sandberg	3.00
37	Matt Williams	1.00
38	Ryan Klesko	1.00
39	Jose Canseco	2.00
40	Paul Molitor	2.00
41	Eddie Murray	2.50
42	Darin Erstad	2.50
43	Todd Walker	1.00
44	Wade Boggs	2.50
45	Andruw Jones	2.50
46	Scott Rolen	2.00
47	Vladimir Guerrero	3.00
48	NOT ISSUED	
49	Alex Rodriguez (1996 design)	6.00

1997 SP SPx Force

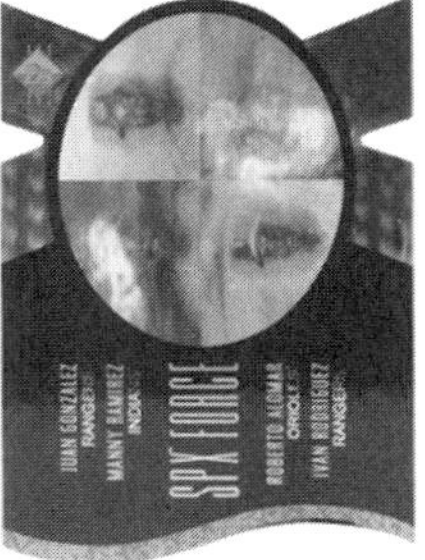

Each of the 10 cards in this set feature four different players. Cards are individually numbered to 500. In addition, a number of players signed 100 versions of their SPx Force cards that are also randomly inserted into packs.

		MT
Complete Set (10):		135.00
Common Player:		12.00
1	Ken Griffey Jr., Jay Buhner, Andres Galarraga, Dante Bichette	20.00
2	Albert Belle, Brady Anderson, Mark McGwire, Cecil Fielder	25.00
3	Mo Vaughn, Ken Caminiti, Frank Thomas, Jeff Bagwell	12.00
4	Gary Sheffield, Sammy Sosa, Barry Bonds, Jose Canseco	20.00
5	Greg Maddux, Roger Clemens, John Smoltz, Randy Johnson	15.00
6	Alex Rodriguez, Derek Jeter, Chipper Jones, Rey Ordonez	30.00
7	Todd Hollandsworth, Mike Piazza, Raul Mondesi, Hideo Nomo	20.00
8	Juan Gonzalez, Manny Ramirez, Roberto Alomar, Ivan Rodriguez	12.00
9	Tony Gwynn, Wade Boggs, Eddie Murray, Paul Molitor	12.00
10	Andruw Jones, Vladimir Guerrero, Todd Walker, Scott Rolen	12.00

1997 SP SPx Force Autographs

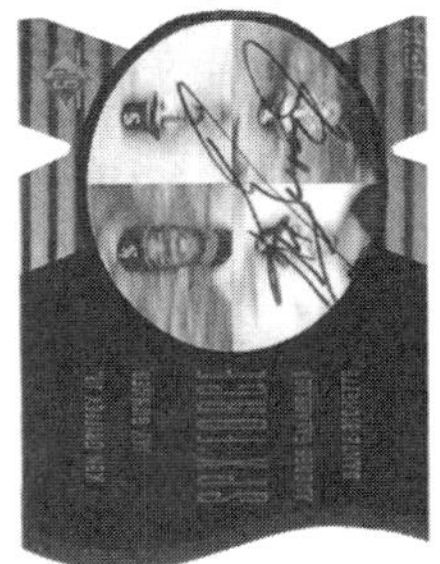

Ten players signed cards for this insert, which was serially numbered to 100. The cards were randomly seeded in packs except the Mo Vaughn card which was available by redemption.

		MT
Common Player:		16.50
1	Ken Griffey Jr.	200.00
2	Albert Belle	25.00
3	Mo Vaughn	20.00
4	Gary Sheffield	16.50
5	Greg Maddux	125.00
6	Alex Rodriguez	140.00
7	Todd Hollandsworth	20.00
8	Roberto Alomar	75.00
9	Tony Gwynn	120.00
10	Andruw Jones	40.00

1997 SPx

Fifty cards, each featuring a perimeter die-cut design and a 3-D holoview photo, make up the SPx base set. Five different parallel sets - Steel (1:1 pack), Bronze (1:1), Silver (1:1), Gold (1:17) and Grand Finale (50 per card) - are found as inserts, as are Cornerstones of the Game, Bound for Glory and Bound for Glory Signature cards. Packs contain three cards and carried a suggested retail price of $5.99.

		MT
Complete Set (50):		40.00
Common Player:		.50
Steel:		1.5X
Bronze:		1.5X
Silver:		2X
Gold:		2.5X
Pack (3):		2.75
Wax Box (18):		45.00
1	Eddie Murray	1.25
2	Darin Erstad	2.00
3	Tim Salmon	1.00
4	Andruw Jones	2.50
5	Chipper Jones	4.00
6	John Smoltz	.75
7	Greg Maddux	3.00
8	Kenny Lofton	.50
9	Roberto Alomar	1.25
10	Rafael Palmeiro	.75
11	Brady Anderson	.50
12	Cal Ripken Jr.	6.00
13	Nomar Garciaparra	3.00
14	Mo Vaughn	1.50
15	Ryne Sandberg	2.50
16	Sammy Sosa	3.50
17	Frank Thomas	3.50
18	Albert Belle	1.25
19	Barry Larkin	.50
20	Deion Sanders	.50
21	Manny Ramirez	2.50
22	Jim Thome	.50
23	Dante Bichette	.50
24	Andres Galarraga	.50
25	Larry Walker	1.00
26	Gary Sheffield	1.00
27	Jeff Bagwell	2.50
28	Raul Mondesi	.75
29	Hideo Nomo	1.50
30	Mike Piazza	4.00
31	Paul Molitor	1.25
32	Todd Walker	.50
33	Vladimir Guerrero	2.50
34	Todd Hundley	.50
35	Andy Pettitte	1.00
36	Derek Jeter	4.00
37	Jose Canseco	1.25
38	Mark McGwire	6.00
39	Scott Rolen	2.00
40	Ron Gant	.50
41	Ken Caminiti	.50
42	Tony Gwynn	3.00
43	Barry Bonds	3.50
44	Jay Buhner	.50
45	Ken Griffey Jr.	5.00
45s	Ken Griffey Jr. (overprinted SAMPLE on back)	3.50
46	Alex Rodriguez	5.00
47	*Jose Cruz Jr.*	2.00
48	Juan Gonzalez	2.00
49	Ivan Rodriguez	1.25
50	Roger Clemens	3.00

1997 SPx Bound for Glory

A 20-card insert utilizing holoview technology and sequentially numbered to 1,500 per card. Five players (Andruw Jones, Gary Sheffield, Alex Rodriguez, Ken Griffey Jr. and Jeff Bagwell) signed versions of their cards as part of the Bound For Glory Supreme Signatures set.

		MT
Complete Set (20):		110.00
Common Player:		2.50
1	Andruw Jones	5.00
2	Chipper Jones	10.00
3	Greg Maddux	8.00
4	Kenny Lofton	2.50
5	Cal Ripken Jr.	15.00
6	Mo Vaughn	3.00
7	Frank Thomas	6.00
8	Albert Belle	3.00
9	Manny Ramirez	6.00
10	Gary Sheffield	3.00
11	Jeff Bagwell	6.00
12	Mike Piazza	12.00
13	Derek Jeter	15.00
14	Mark McGwire	12.00
15	Tony Gwynn	8.00
16	Ken Caminiti	2.50
17	Barry Bonds	8.00
18	Alex Rodriguez	12.00
19	Ken Griffey Jr.	12.00
20	Juan Gonzalez	6.00

1997 SPx Bound for Glory Supreme Signatures

This five-card set featured autographs from the players and was sequentially numbered to 250.

		MT
Complete Set (5):		300.00
Common Player:		30.00
1	Jeff Bagwell	80.00
2	Ken Griffey Jr.	150.00
3	Andruw Jones	60.00
4	Alex Rodriguez	120.00
5	Gary Sheffield	30.00

1997 SPx Cornerstones of the Game

A 20-card insert utilizing a double-front design highlighting 40 of the top players in the game. Each card is sequentially numbered to 500.

		MT
Complete Set (10):		190.00
Common Player:		15.00
1	Ken Griffey Jr., Barry Bonds	35.00
2	Frank Thomas, Albert Belle	15.00
3	Chipper Jones, Greg Maddux	25.00
4	Tony Gwynn, Paul Molitor	20.00
5	Andruw Jones, Vladimir Guerrero	15.00
6	Jeff Bagwell, Ryne Sandberg	15.00
7	Mike Piazza, Ivan Rodriguez	25.00
8	Cal Ripken Jr., Eddie Murray	30.00
9	Mo Vaughn, Mark McGwire	35.00
10	Alex Rodriguez, Derek Jeter	35.00

1998 SP Authentic Sample

This card of Upper Deck spokesman Ken Griffey, Jr., was issued to preview the new SP Authentic line. Design is similar to the issued version but the sample displays different photos, a different the card number and the word "SAMPLE" printed in large letters on back.

	MT
Ken Griffey Jr.	4.00

1998 SP Authentic

The SP Authentic base set consists of 198 cards, including the 30-card Future Watch subset and one checklist card. The base cards have a color photo inside a thick white border. Inserts include Chirography, Sheer Dominance and SP Authentics.

		MT
Complete Set (198):		40.00
Common Player:		.15
Pack (5):		3.00
Wax Box (24):		65.00
1	Travis Lee (Future Watch)	.25
2	Mike Caruso (Future Watch)	.15
3	Kerry Wood (Future Watch)	1.00
4	Mark Kotsay (Future Watch)	.15
5	*Magglio Ordonez* (Future Watch)	6.00
6	Scott Elarton (Future Watch)	.15
7	Carl Pavano (Future Watch)	.15
8	A.J. Hinch (Future Watch)	.15
9	*Rolando Arrojo* (Future Watch)	.75
10	Ben Grieve (Future Watch)	.25
11	Gabe Alvarez (Future Watch)	.15
12	*Mike Kinkade* (Future Watch)	.75
13	Bruce Chen (Future Watch)	.15
14	Juan Encarnacion (Future Watch)	.20
15	Todd Helton (Future Watch)	1.00
16	Aaron Boone (Future Watch)	.15
17	Sean Casey (Future Watch)	.40
18	Ramon Hernandez (Future Watch)	.15
19	Daryle Ward (Future Watch)	.15
20	Paul Konerko (Future Watch)	.25
21	David Ortiz (Future Watch)	.15
22	Derrek Lee (Future Watch)	.15
23	Brad Fullmer (Future Watch)	.30
24	Javier Vazquez (Future Watch)	.25
25	Miguel Tejada (Future Watch)	.35
26	David Dellucci (Future Watch)	.15
27	Alex Gonzalez (Future Watch)	.20
28	Matt Clement (Future Watch)	.15
29	Eric Milton (Future Watch)	.15
30	Russell Branyan (Future Watch)	.20
31	Chuck Finley	.15
32	Jim Edmonds	.15
33	Darren Erstad	1.00
34	Jason Dickson	.15
35	Tim Salmon	.40
36	Cecil Fielder	.15
37	Todd Greene	.15
38	Andy Benes	.15
39	Jay Bell	.15
40	Matt Williams	.45
41	Brian Anderson	.15
42	Karim Garcia	.15
43	Javy Lopez	.15
44	Tom Glavine	.20
45	Greg Maddux	2.00
46	Andruw Jones	1.50
47	Chipper Jones	3.00
48	Ryan Klesko	.15
49	John Smoltz	.20
50	Andres Galarraga	.15
51	Rafael Palmeiro	.30
52	Mike Mussina	1.00
53	Roberto Alomar	1.00
54	Joe Carter	.15
55	Cal Ripken Jr.	4.00
56	Brady Anderson	.15
57	Mo Vaughn	.85
58	John Valentin	.15
59	Dennis Eckersley	.15
60	Nomar Garciaparra	2.50
61	Pedro J. Martinez	1.00
62	Jeff Blauser	.15
63	Kevin Orie	.15
64	Henry Rodriguez	.15
65	Mark Grace	.50
66	Albert Belle	.45
67	Mike Cameron	.15
68	Robin Ventura	.15
69	Frank Thomas	1.50
70	Barry Larkin	.20
71	Brett Tomko	.15
72	Willie Greene	.15
73	Reggie Sanders	.15
74	Sandy Alomar Jr.	.15
75	Kenny Lofton	.15
76	Jaret Wright	.15
77	David Justice	.40
78	Omar Vizquel	.15
79	Manny Ramirez	1.50
80	Jim Thome	.15
81	Travis Fryman	.15
82	Neifi Perez	.15
83	Mike Lansing	.15
84	Vinny Castilla	.15
85	Larry Walker	.45
86	Dante Bichette	.15
87	Darryl Kile	.15
88	Justin Thompson	.15
89	Damion Easley	.15
90	Tony Clark	.15
91	Bobby Higginson	.20
92	Brian L. Hunter	.15
93	Edgar Renteria	.15
94	Craig Counsell	.15
95	Mike Piazza	3.00
96	Livan Hernandez	.15
97	Todd Zeile	.15
98	Richard Hidalgo	.15
99	Moises Alou	.25
100	Jeff Bagwell	1.50
101	Mike Hampton	.15
102	Craig Biggio	.20
103	Dean Palmer	.15
104	Tim Belcher	.15
105	Jeff King	.15
106	Jeff Conine	.15
107	Johnny Damon	.20
108	Hideo Nomo	1.00
109	Raul Mondesi	.25
110	Gary Sheffield	.60
111	Ramon Martinez	.15
112	Chan Ho Park	.50
113	Eric Young	.15
114	Charles Johnson	.15
115	Eric Karros	.15
116	Bobby Bonilla	.15
117	Jeromy Burnitz	.15
118	Carl Eldred	.15
119	Jeff D'Amico	.15
120	Marquis Grissom	.15
121	Dave Nilsson	.15
122	Brad Radke	.15
123	Marty Cordova	.15
124	Ron Coomer	.15
125	Paul Molitor	1.00
126	Todd Walker	.15
127	Rondell White	.30
128	Mark Grudzielanek	.15
129	Carlos Perez	.15
130	Vladimir Guerrero	1.50
131	Dustin Hermanson	.15
132	Butch Huskey	.15
133	John Franco	.15
134	Rey Ordonez	.15
135	Todd Hundley	.15
136	Edgardo Alfonzo	.15
137	Bobby Jones	.15
138	John Olerud	.15
139	Chili Davis	.15
140	Tino Martinez	.15
141	Andy Pettitte	.60
142	Chuck Knoblauch	.15
143	Bernie Williams	.60
144	David Cone	.15
145	Derek Jeter	4.00
146	Paul O'Neill	.15
147	Rickey Henderson	1.00
148	Jason Giambi	.40
149	Kenny Rogers	.15
150	Scott Rolen	1.25
151	Curt Schilling	.40

152 Ricky Bottalico .15
153 Mike Lieberthal .15
154 Francisco Cordova .15
155 Jose Guillen .15
156 Jason Schmidt .15
157 Jason Kendall .15
158 Kevin Young .15
159 Delino DeShields .15
160 Mark McGwire 4.00
161 Ray Lankford .15
162 Brian Jordan .15
163 Ron Gant .15
164 Todd Stottlemyre .15
165 Ken Caminiti .15
166 Kevin Brown .25
167 Trevor Hoffman .15
168 Steve Finley .15
169 Wally Joyner .15
170 Tony Gwynn 1.50
171 Shawn Estes .15
172 J.T. Snow .15
173 Jeff Kent .15
174 Robb Nen .15
175 Barry Bonds 2.50
176 Randy Johnson 1.00
177 Edgar Martinez .15
178 Jay Buhner .15
179 Alex Rodriguez 3.50
180 Ken Griffey Jr. 3.50
181 Ken Cloude .15
182 Wade Boggs 1.00
183 Tony Saunders .15
184 Wilson Alvarez .15
185 Fred McGriff .15
186 Roberto Hernandez .15
187 Kevin Stocker .15
188 Fernando Tatis .15
189 Will Clark .45
190 Juan Gonzalez 1.50
191 Rusty Greer .15
192 Ivan Rodriguez 1.25
193 Jose Canseco .65
194 Carlos Delgado .40
195 Roger Clemens 2.00
196 Pat Hentgen .15
197 Randy Myers .15
198 Checklist (Ken Griffey Jr.) 1.25

1998 SP Authentic Chirography

Chirography is a 30-card insert seeded one per 25 packs. The featured player signed his cards in the white border at the bottom.

MT
Common Card: 5.00
Inserted 1:25
RA Roberto Alomar 20.00
RB Russell Branyan 6.00
SC Sean Casey 15.00
TC Tony Clark 6.00
RC Roger Clemens 75.00
JC Jose Cruz Jr. 6.00
DE Darin Erstad 15.00
NG Nomar Garciaparra 100.00
BG Ben Grieve 10.00
KG Ken Griffey Jr. 100.00
VG Vladimir Guerrero 20.00
TG Tony Gwynn 40.00
TH Todd Helton 20.00
LH Livan Hernandez 5.00
CJ Charles Johnson 6.00
AJ Andruw Jones 15.00
CHIP Chipper Jones 35.00
PK Paul Konerko 6.00
MK Mark Kotsay 5.00
RL Ray Lankford 5.00
TL Travis Lee 7.00
PM Paul Molitor 15.00
MM Mike Mussina 20.00
AR Alex Rodriguez 50.00
IR Ivan Rodriguez 15.00
SR Scott Rolen 10.00
DL Gary Sheffield 10.00
MT Miguel Tejada 12.00
JW Jaret Wright 6.00
MV Mo Vaughn 10.00

1998 SP Authentic Jersey Swatch

These 5" x 7" redemption cards were issued in exchange for Trade Cards found as random foil-packs inserts. Fronts have a player action photo on a white background. Backs have a congratulatory message of authenticity. Sandwiched between in a swatch of that player's uniform jersey. The large-format jersey cards were available in limited editions which are listed in parentheses, though all might not have been redeemed prior to the Aug. 1, 1999, cut-off date.

MT
Complete Set (6): 400.00
Common Player: 25.00
(1) Jay Buhner (125) 25.00
(2) Ken Griffey Jr. (125) 175.00
(3) Tony Gwynn (415) 50.00
(4) Greg Maddux (125) 100.00
(5) Alex Rodriguez (125) 150.00
(6) Gary Sheffield (125) 35.00

1998 SP Authentic Ken Griffey Jr. 300th HR Redemption

This 5" x 7" version of Ken Griffey Jr.'s SP Authentic card was issued as a redemption for one of the 1000 Trade Cards which were foil-pack inserts.

MT
KG300Ken Griffey Jr. 30.00

1998 SP Authentic Sheer Dominance

Sheer Dominance is a 42-card insert. The base set is inserted one per three packs. The Sheer Dominance Gold parallel is sequentially numbered to 2,000 and the Titanium parallel is numbered to 100. The cards feature a player photo inside a white border. The background color corresponds to the level of the insert.

MT
Complete Set (42): 35.00
Common Player: .35
Inserted 1:3
SD1 Ken Griffey Jr. 2.75
SD2 Rickey Henderson .75
SD3 Jaret Wright .35
SD4 Craig Biggio .35
SD5 Travis Lee .35
SD6 Kenny Lofton .35
SD7 Raul Mondesi .50
SD8 Cal Ripken Jr. 3.00
SD9 Matt Williams .50
SD10Mark McGwire 3.00
SD11Alex Rodriguez 2.75
SD12Fred McGriff .35
SD13Scott Rolen 1.00
SD14Paul Molitor .75
SD15Nomar Garciaparra 2.25
SD16Vladimir Guerrero 1.50
SD17Andruw Jones 1.50
SD18Manny Ramirez 1.50
SD19Tony Gwynn 2.00
SD20Barry Bonds 2.50
SD21Ben Grieve .50
SD22Ivan Rodriguez 1.00
SD23Jose Cruz Jr. .45
SD24Pedro J. Martinez 1.00
SD25Chipper Jones 2.50
SD26Albert Belle .50
SD27Todd Helton .75
SD28Paul Konerko .35
SD29Sammy Sosa 2.25
SD30Frank Thomas 2.25
SD31Greg Maddux 2.00
SD32Randy Johnson .75
SD33Larry Walker .50
SD34Roberto Alomar .75
SD35Roger Clemens 2.00
SD36Mo Vaughn .50
SD37Jim Thome .35
SD38Jeff Bagwell 1.50
SD39Tino Martinez .35
SD40Mike Piazza 2.50
SD41Derek Jeter 2.50
SD42Juan Gonzalez 1.50

1998 SP Authentic Sheer Dominance Gold

Identical in format and using the same photos as the Silver version, the scarcer Sheer Dominance Gold card differs on front in its use of a gold-metallic foil background within the white border. Backs of the gold version are individually serial numbered within an edition of 2,000 each.

MT
Complete Set (42): 125.00
Common Player: 1.00
Gold Stars : 2X
(See 1998 SP Authentic Sheer Dominance for checklist and base card values.)

1998 SP Authentic Sheer Dominance Titanium

Sheer Dominance Titanium is a parallel of the 42-card Sheer Dominance insert. The cards are numbered to 100 and have a gray background with "Titanium" printed across it.

MT
Common Player: 10.00
Titanium Stars: 12X
(See 1998 SP Authentic Sheer Dominance for checklist and base card values.)

1998 SP Authentic Trade Cards

Cards which could be traded (prior to the Aug. 1, 1999 cut-off) for special cards and autographed memorabilia were inserted into SP Authentic foil packs at an announced rate of one per 291 packs. Trade cards have a white background on front with a color player action photo and the name of the redemption item. Backs gives details for redemption. In some cases, because of their insertion-rate rarity, the cards are worth more than the redemption items. The unnumbered cards are listed here alphabetically.

MT
Common Card: 5.00
(1) Roberto Alomar (autographed ball 100) 15.00
(2) Albert Belle (autographed ball 100) 7.50
(3) Jay Buhner (jersey card 125) 5.00
(4) Ken Griffey Jr. (autographed glove 30) 200.00
(5) Ken Griffey Jr. (autographed jersey 30) 200.00
(6) Ken Griffey Jr. (jersey card 125) 40.00
(7) Ken Griffey Jr. (standee 200) 15.00
(8) Ken Griffey Jr. (300th HR card 1000) 5.00
(9) Tony Gwynn (jersey card 415) 15.00
(10) Brian Jordan (autographed ball 50) 10.00

(11) Greg Maddux (jersey card 125) 20.00
(12) Raul Mondesi (autographed ball 100) 5.00
(13) Alex Rodriguez (jersey card 125) 25.00
(14) Gary Sheffield (jersey card 125) 5.00
(15) Robin Ventura (autographed ball 50) 10.00

1998 SPx Finite Sample

This card was issued to promote SPx's all-numbered Finite issue. The serial number on the card's back is "0000/0000". The card is overprinted "SAMPLE" on back.

		MT
1	Ken Griffey Jr.	4.00

1998 SPx Finite

SPx Finite is an all-sequentially numbered set issued in two 180-card series. The Series 1 base set consists of five subsets: 90 regular cards (numbered to 9,000), 30 Star Focus (7,000), 30 Youth Movement (5,000), 20 Power Explosion (4,000) and 10 Heroes of the Game (2,000). The set is paralleled in the Radiance and Spectrum sets. Radiance regular cards are numbered to 4,500, Star Focus to 3,500, Youth Movement to 2,500, Power Explosion to 1,000 and Heroes of the Game to 100. Spectrum regular cards are numbered to 2,250, Star Focus to 1,750, Youth Movement to 1,250, Power Explosion to 50 and Heroes of the Game to 1. The Series 2 base set has 90 regular cards (numbered to 9,000), 30 Power Passion (7,000), 30 Youth Movement (5,000), 20 Tradewinds (4,000) and 10 Cornerstones of the Game (2,000). Series 2 also has Radiance and Spectrum parallels. Radiance regular cards are numbered to 4,500, Power Passion to 3,500, Youth Movement to 2,500, Tradewinds to 1,000 and Cornerstones of the Game to 100. Spectrum regular cards are numbered to 2,250, Power Passion to 1,750, Youth Movement to 1,250, Tradewinds to 50 and Cornerstones of the Game to 1. The only insert is Home Run Hysteria.

	MT
Complete Set (360):	500.00
Common Youth Movement (#1-30, 181-210):	.75
Radiance YM (2,500):	1.5X
Spectrum YM (1,250):	2X
Common Power Explosion (#31-50):	1.00
Radiance PE (1,000):	2X
Spectrum PE (50):	25X
Common Base Card (#51-140, 241-330):	.50
Radiance Base Card (4,500):	1X
Spectrum Base Card (2,250):	2X
Common Star Focus (#141-170):	.75
Radiance SF (3,500):	1X
Spectrum SF (1,750):	2X
Common Heroes of the Game (#171-180):	5.00
Radiance HG (100):	15X
Spectrum HG (1):	VALUE UNDETERMINED
Common Power Passion (#211-240):	.75
Radiance PP (3,500)	1X
Spectrum PP (1,750)	2X
Common Tradewinds (#331-350):	1.00
Radiance TW (1,000)	2X
Spectrum TW (50):	25X
Common Cornerstones/Game (#351-360):	5.00
Radiance CG (100):	15X
Spectrum CG (1):	VALUE UNDETERMINED
Pack:	3.00
Wax Box:	65.00

1	Nomar Garciaparra (Youth Movement)	5.00
2	Miguel Tejada (Youth Movement)	1.50
3	Mike Cameron (Youth Movement)	.75
4	Ken Cloude (Youth Movement)	.75
5	Jaret Wright (Youth Movement)	1.00
6	Mark Kotsay (Youth Movement)	.75
7	Craig Counsell (Youth Movement)	.75
8	Jose Guillen (Youth Movement)	.75
9	Neifi Perez (Youth Movement)	.75
10	Jose Cruz Jr. (Youth Movement)	1.00
11	Brett Tomko (Youth Movement)	.75
12	Matt Morris (Youth Movement)	1.00
13	Justin Thompson (Youth Movement)	.75
14	Jeremi Gonzalez (Youth Movement)	.75
15	Scott Rolen (Youth Movement)	2.00
16	Vladimir Guerrero (Youth Movement)	2.50
17	Brad Fullmer (Youth Movement)	1.00
18	Brian Giles (Youth Movement)	.75
19	Todd Dunwoody (Youth Movement)	.75
20	Ben Grieve (Youth Movement)	1.50
21	Juan Encarnacion (Youth Movement)	1.00
22	Aaron Boone (Youth Movement)	.75
23	Richie Sexson (Youth Movement)	.75
24	Richard Hidalgo (Youth Movement)	1.00
25	Andruw Jones (Youth Movement)	2.50
26	Todd Helton (Youth Movement)	2.00
27	Paul Konerko (Youth Movement)	1.00
28	Dante Powell (Youth Movement)	.75
29	Elieser Marrero (Youth Movement)	.75
30	Derek Jeter (Youth Movement)	3.00
31	Mike Piazza (Power Explosion)	4.00
32	Tony Clark (Power Explosion)	1.00
33	Larry Walker (Power Explosion)	1.25
34	Jim Thome (Power Explosion)	1.00
35	Juan Gonzalez (Power Explosion)	2.00
36	Jeff Bagwell (Power Explosion)	2.00
37	Jay Buhner (Power Explosion)	1.00
38	Tim Salmon (Power Explosion)	1.25
39	Albert Belle (Power Explosion)	1.25
40	Mark McGwire (Power Explosion)	5.00
41	Sammy Sosa (Power Explosion)	3.00
42	Mo Vaughn (Power Explosion)	1.50
43	Manny Ramirez (Power Explosion)	2.00
44	Tino Martinez (Power Explosion)	1.00
45	Frank Thomas (Power Explosion)	3.00
46	Nomar Garciaparra (Power Explosion)	3.00
47	Alex Rodriguez (Power Explosion)	4.50
48	Chipper Jones (Power Explosion)	4.00
49	Barry Bonds (Power Explosion)	3.00
50	Ken Griffey Jr. (Power Explosion)	4.50
51	Jason Dickson	.50
52	Jim Edmonds	.50
53	Darin Erstad	1.50
54	Tim Salmon	.75
55	Chipper Jones	4.00
56	Ryan Klesko	.75
57	Tom Glavine	.65
58	Denny Neagle	.50
59	John Smoltz	.65
60	Javy Lopez	.50
61	Roberto Alomar	1.50
62	Rafael Palmeiro	1.25
63	Mike Mussina	1.50
64	Cal Ripken Jr.	5.00
65	Mo Vaughn	1.25
66	Tim Naehring	.50
67	John Valentin	.50
68	Mark Grace	.75
69	Kevin Orie	.50
70	Sammy Sosa	3.00
71	Albert Belle	.75
72	Frank Thomas	3.00
73	Robin Ventura	.50
74	David Justice	.75
75	Kenny Lofton	.50
76	Omar Vizquel	.50
77	Manny Ramirez	2.00
78	Jim Thome	.50
79	Dante Bichette	.50
80	Larry Walker	1.00
81	Vinny Castilla	.50
82	Ellis Burks	.50
83	Bobby Higginson	.75
84	Brian L. Hunter	.50
85	Tony Clark	.50
86	Mike Hampton	.50
87	Jeff Bagwell	2.00
88	Craig Biggio	.65
89	Derek Bell	.50
90	Mike Piazza	4.00
91	Ramon Martinez	.50
92	Raul Mondesi	1.00
93	Hideo Nomo	2.00
94	Eric Karros	.50
95	Paul Molitor	2.00
96	Marty Cordova	.50
97	Brad Radke	.50
98	Mark Grudzielanek	.50
99	Carlos Perez	.50
100	Rondell White	.65
101	Todd Hundley	.50
102	Edgardo Alfonzo	.50
103	John Franco	.50
104	John Olerud	.50
105	Tino Martinez	.50
106	David Cone	.50
107	Paul O'Neill	.50
108	Andy Pettitte	1.00
109	Bernie Williams	1.00
110	Rickey Henderson	2.00
111	Jason Giambi	2.00
112	Matt Stairs	.50
113	Gregg Jefferies	.50
114	Rico Brogna	.50
115	Curt Schilling	1.00
116	Jason Schmidt	.50
117	Jose Guillen	.50
118	Kevin Young	.50
119	Ray Lankford	.50
120	Mark McGwire	5.00
121	Delino DeShields	.50
122	Ken Caminiti	.50
123	Tony Gwynn	2.50
124	Trevor Hoffman	.50
125	Barry Bonds	3.00
126	Jeff Kent	.50
127	Shawn Estes	.50
128	J.T. Snow	.50
129	Jay Buhner	.50
130	Ken Griffey Jr.	4.50
131	Dan Wilson	.50
132	Edgar Martinez	.50
133	Alex Rodriguez	4.50
134	Rusty Greer	.50
135	Juan Gonzalez	2.00
136	Fernando Tatis	.50
137	Ivan Rodriguez	1.50
138	Carlos Delgado	1.00
139	Pat Hentgen	.50
140	Roger Clemens	2.50
141	Chipper Jones (Star Focus)	5.00
142	Greg Maddux (Star Focus)	3.00
143	Rafael Palmeiro (Star Focus)	1.00
144	Mike Mussina (Star Focus)	2.00
145	Cal Ripken Jr. (Star Focus)	6.00
146	Nomar Garciaparra (Star Focus)	4.00
147	Mo Vaughn (Star Focus)	1.50
148	Sammy Sosa (Star Focus)	4.00
149	Albert Belle (Star Focus)	1.50
150	Frank Thomas (Star Focus)	4.00
151	Jim Thome (Star Focus)	.75
152	Kenny Lofton (Star Focus)	.75
153	Manny Ramirez (Star Focus)	2.50
154	Larry Walker (Star Focus)	1.00
155	Jeff Bagwell (Star Focus)	2.50
156	Craig Biggio (Star Focus)	.75
157	Mike Piazza (Star Focus)	5.00
158	Paul Molitor (Star Focus)	1.50
159	Derek Jeter (Star Focus)	5.00
160	Tino Martinez (Star Focus)	.75
161	Curt Schilling (Star Focus)	1.00

162 Mark McGwire (Star Focus) 6.00
163 Tony Gwynn (Star Focus) 3.00
164 Barry Bonds (Star Focus) 4.00
165 Ken Griffey Jr. (Star Focus) 5.50
166 Randy Johnson (Star Focus) 1.00
167 Alex Rodriguez (Star Focus) 5.50
168 Juan Gonzalez (Star Focus) 2.50
169 Ivan Rodriguez (Star Focus) 1.50
170 Roger Clemens (Star Focus) 3.00
171 Greg Maddux (Heroes of the Game) 5.00
172 Cal Ripken Jr. (Heroes of the Game) 15.00
173 Frank Thomas (Heroes of the Game) 7.50
174 Jeff Bagwell (Heroes of the Game) 5.00
175 Mike Piazza (Heroes of the Game) 10.00
176 Mark McGwire (Heroes of the Game) 15.00
177 Barry Bonds (Heroes of the Game) 7.50
178 Ken Griffey Jr. (Heroes of the Game) 12.50
179 Alex Rodriguez (Heroes of the Game) 12.50
180 Roger Clemens (Heroes of the Game) 5.00
181 Mike Caruso (Youth Movement) .75
182 David Ortiz (Youth Movement) .75
183 Gabe Alvarez (Youth Movement) .75
184 Gary Matthews Jr. (Youth Movement) .75
185 Kerry Wood (Youth Movement) 3.00
186 Carl Pavano (Youth Movement) .75
187 Alex Gonzalez (Youth Movement) 1.00
188 Masato Yoshii (Youth Movement) 2.00
189 Larry Sutton (Youth Movement) .75
190 Russell Branyan (Youth Movement) 1.00
191 Bruce Chen (Youth Movement) .75
192 Rolando Arrojo (Youth Movement) 1.00
193 Ryan Christenson (Youth Movement) .75
194 Cliff Politte (Youth Movement) .75
195 A.J. Hinch (Youth Movement) 1.00
196 Kevin Witt (Youth Movement) .75
197 Daryle Ward (Youth Movement) .75
198 Corey Koskie (Youth Movement) 1.00
199 Mike Lowell (Youth Movement) .75
200 Travis Lee (Youth Movement) 1.00
201 *Kevin Millwood* (Youth Movement) 4.00
202 Robert Smith (Youth Movement) .75
203 *Magglio Ordonez* (Youth Movement) 12.00
204 Eric Milton (Youth Movement) .75
205 Geoff Jenkins (Youth Movement) .75
206 Rich Butler (Youth Movement) .75
207 *Mike Kinkade* (Youth Movement) 1.00
208 Braden Looper (Youth Movement) .75
209 Matt Clement (Youth Movement) .75
210 Derrek Lee (Youth Movement) .75
211 Randy Johnson (Power Passion) 1.50
212 John Smoltz (Power Passion) 1.00
213 Roger Clemens (Power Passion) 2.50
214 Curt Schilling (Power Passion) 1.25
215 Pedro J. Martinez (Power Passion) 1.50
216 Vinny Castilla (Power Passion) .75
217 Jose Cruz Jr. (Power Passion) 1.00
218 Jim Thome (Power Passion) .75
219 Alex Rodriguez (Power Passion) 5.50
220 Frank Thomas (Power Passion) 4.00
221 Tim Salmon (Power Passion) 1.00
222 Larry Walker (Power Passion) 1.00
223 Albert Belle (Power Passion) 1.00
224 Manny Ramirez (Power Passion) 2.00
225 Mark McGwire (Power Passion) 6.00
226 Mo Vaughn (Power Passion) 1.50
227 Andres Galarraga (Power Passion) .75
228 Scott Rolen (Power Passion) 1.50
229 Travis Lee (Power Passion) .75
230 Mike Piazza (Power Passion) 5.00
231 Nomar Garciaparra (Power Passion) 4.00
232 Andruw Jones (Power Passion) 2.00
233 Barry Bonds (Power Passion) 4.00
234 Jeff Bagwell (Power Passion) 2.00
235 Juan Gonzalez (Power Passion) 2.00
236 Tino Martinez (Power Passion) .75
237 Vladimir Guerrero (Power Passion) 2.00
238 Rafael Palmeiro (Power Passion) 1.00
239 Russell Branyan (Power Passion) .75
240 Ken Griffey Jr. (Power Passion) 5.50
241 Cecil Fielder .50
242 Chuck Finley .50
243 Jay Bell .50
244 Andy Benes .50
245 Matt Williams .75
246 Brian Anderson .50
247 David Dellucci .50
248 Andres Galarraga .50
249 Andruw Jones 2.00
250 Greg Maddux 2.50
251 Brady Anderson .50
252 Joe Carter .50
253 Eric Davis .50
254 Pedro J. Martinez 1.50
255 Nomar Garciaparra 3.00
256 Dennis Eckersley .50
257 Henry Rodriguez .50
258 Jeff Blauser .50
259 Jaime Navarro .50
260 Ray Durham .50
261 Chris Stynes .50
262 Willie Greene .50
263 Reggie Sanders .50
264 Bret Boone .65
265 Barry Larkin .50
266 Travis Fryman .50
267 Charles Nagy .50
268 Sandy Alomar Jr. .50
269 Darryl Kile .50
270 Mike Lansing .50
271 Pedro Astacio .50
272 Damion Easley .50
273 Joe Randa .50
274 Luis Gonzalez 1.25
275 Mike Piazza 4.00
276 Todd Zeile .50
277 Edgar Renteria .50
278 Livan Hernandez .50
279 Cliff Floyd .50
280 Moises Alou .75
281 Billy Wagner .50
282 Jeff King .50
283 Hal Morris .50
284 Johnny Damon .75
285 Dean Palmer .50
286 Tim Belcher .50
287 Eric Young .50
288 Bobby Bonilla .50
289 Gary Sheffield 1.00
290 Chan Ho Park 1.00
291 Charles Johnson .50
292 Jeff Cirillo .50
293 Jeromy Burnitz .50
294 Jose Valentin .50
295 Marquis Grissom .50
296 Todd Walker .50
297 Terry Steinbach .50
298 Rick Aguilera .50
299 Vladimir Guerrero 2.00
300 Rey Ordonez .50
301 Butch Huskey .50
302 Bernard Gilkey .50
303 Mariano Rivera 1.25
304 Chuck Knoblauch .50
305 Derek Jeter 5.00
306 Ricky Bottalico .50
307 Bob Abreu .75
308 Scott Rolen 1.50
309 Al Martin .50
310 Jason Kendall .50
311 Brian Jordan .50
312 Ron Gant .50
313 Todd Stottlemyre .50
314 Greg Vaughn .50
315 J. Kevin Brown .75
316 Wally Joyner .50
317 Robb Nen .50
318 Orel Hershiser .50
319 Russ Davis .50
320 Randy Johnson 1.50
321 Quinton McCracken .50
322 Tony Saunders .50
323 Wilson Alvarez .50
324 Wade Boggs 1.75
325 Fred McGriff .50
326 Lee Stevens .50
327 John Wetteland .50
328 Jose Canseco 1.50
329 Randy Myers .50
330 Jose Cruz Jr. 1.00
331 Matt Williams (Tradewinds) 1.25
332 Andres Galarraga (Tradewinds) 1.00
333 Walt Weiss (Tradewinds) 1.00
334 Joe Carter (Tradewinds) 1.00
335 Pedro J. Martinez (Tradewinds) 1.75
336 Henry Rodriguez (Tradewinds) 1.00
337 Travis Fryman (Tradewinds) 1.00
338 Darryl Kile (Tradewinds) 1.00
339 Mike Lansing (Tradewinds) 1.00
340 Mike Piazza (Tradewinds) 4.00
341 Moises Alou (Tradewinds) 1.00
342 Charles Johnson (Tradewinds) 1.00
343 Chuck Knoblauch (Tradewinds) 1.00
344 Rickey Henderson (Tradewinds) 1.50
345 J. Kevin Brown (Tradewinds) 1.00
346 Orel Hershiser (Tradewinds) 1.00
347 Wade Boggs (Tradewinds) 1.75
348 Fred McGriff (Tradewinds) 1.00
349 Jose Canseco (Tradewinds) 1.50
350 Gary Sheffield (Tradewinds) 1.25
351 Travis Lee (Cornerstones) 5.00
352 Nomar Garciaparra (Cornerstones) 7.50
353 Frank Thomas (Cornerstones) 7.50
354 Cal Ripken Jr. (Cornerstones) 15.00
355 Mark McGwire (Cornerstones) 15.00
356 Mike Piazza (Cornerstones) 10.00
357 Alex Rodriguez (Cornerstones) 12.50
358 Barry Bonds (Cornerstones) 7.50
359 Tony Gwynn (Cornerstones) 5.00
360 Ken Griffey Jr. (Cornerstones) 12.50

1998 SPx Finite Home Run Hysteria

Home Run Hysteria is a 10-card insert in SPx Finite Series Two. The cards were sequentially numbered to 62.

	MT
Complete Set (10):	450.00
Common Player:	20.00
Production 62 sets	
HR1 Ken Griffey Jr.	100.00
HR2 Mark McGwire	125.00
HR3 Sammy Sosa	60.00
HR4 Albert Belle	20.00
HR5 Alex Rodriguez	100.00
HR6 Greg Vaughn	20.00
HR7 Andres Galarraga	20.00
HR8 Vinny Castilla	20.00
HR9 Juan Gonzalez	30.00
HR10Chipper Jones	75.00

1999 SP Authentic Sample

UD spokesman Ken Griffey Jr. is featured on the promo card for '99 SP

Authentic. In the same format as the issued version, the sample card has different photos on front and back, a different season summary on back and a large, black "SAMPLE" overprint on back.

		MT
1	Ken Griffey Jr.	4.00

1999 SP Authentic

SP Authentic Baseball was a 135-card set that sold in packs of 5 cards for $4.99 per pack. The set included a 30-card Future Watch subset and a 15-card Season to Remember subset. Both subsets were shorted-printed, with each card sequentially numbered to 2,700. The insert lineup included Ernie Banks 500 Club 'Piece of History' Bat cards. Each card features a piece of a Ernie Banks game-used bat. Only 350 of the cards were produced. Fourteen more of the cards were produced and autographed by Ernie Banks. Other insert sets included SP Chirography, The Home Run Chronicles, Epic Figures, Reflections, and SP Authentics.

	MT
Complete Set (135):	150.00
Common Player (1-90):	.25
Common Future Watch (91-120):	1.00
Production: (2,700)	
Common Season to Remember (121-135):	1.00
Production: (2,700)	
Pack (5):	4.00
Wax Box (24):	90.00

1	Mo Vaughn	.75
2	Jim Edmonds	.25
3	Darin Erstad	1.00
4	Travis Lee	.25
5	Matt Williams	.60
6	Randy Johnson	1.00
7	Chipper Jones	2.00
8	Greg Maddux	1.50
9	Andruw Jones	1.00
10	Andres Galarraga	.25
11	Tom Glavine	.25
12	Cal Ripken Jr.	3.00
13	Brady Anderson	.25
14	Albert Belle	.50
15	Nomar Garciaparra	1.75
16	Donnie Sadler	.25
17	Pedro Martinez	.75
18	Sammy Sosa	1.75
19	Kerry Wood	.75
20	Mark Grace	.45
21	Mike Caruso	.25
22	Frank Thomas	1.75
23	Paul Konerko	.25
24	Sean Casey	.35
25	Barry Larkin	.25
26	Kenny Lofton	.25
27	Manny Ramirez	1.00
28	Jim Thome	.25
29	Bartolo Colon	.25
30	Jaret Wright	.25
31	Larry Walker	.50
32	Todd Helton	.75
33	Tony Clark	.25
34	Dean Palmer	.25
35	Mark Kotsay	.25
36	Cliff Floyd	.25
37	Ken Caminiti	.25
38	Craig Biggio	.25
39	Jeff Bagwell	1.00
40	Moises Alou	.35
41	Johnny Damon	.35
42	Larry Sutton	.25
43	Kevin Brown	.35
44	Gary Sheffield	.45
45	Raul Mondesi	.35
46	Jeromy Burnitz	.25
47	Jeff Cirillo	.25
48	Todd Walker	.25
49	David Ortiz	.25
50	Brad Radtke	.25
51	Vladimir Guerrero	1.00
52	Rondell White	.40
53	Brad Fullmer	.25
54	Mike Piazza	2.00
55	Robin Ventura	.25
56	John Olerud	.25
57	Derek Jeter	2.00
58	Tino Martinez	.25
59	Bernie Williams	.50
60	Roger Clemens	1.50
61	Ben Grieve	.35
62	Miguel Tejada	.35
63	A.J. Hinch	.25
64	Scott Rolen	.75
65	Curt Schilling	.50
66	Doug Glanville	.25
67	Aramis Ramirez	.25
68	Tony Womack	.25
69	Jason Kendall	.25
70	Tony Gwynn	1.50
71	Wally Joyner	.25
72	Greg Vaughn	.25
73	Barry Bonds	1.75
74	Ellis Burks	.25
75	Jeff Kent	.25
76	Ken Griffey Jr.	2.50
77	Alex Rodriguez	2.50
78	Edgar Martinez	.25
79	Mark McGwire	3.00
80	Eli Marrero	.25
81	Matt Morris	.25
82	Rolando Arrojo	.25
83	Quinton McCracken	.25
84	Jose Canseco	.75
85	Ivan Rodriguez	.85
86	Juan Gonzalez	1.00
87	Royce Clayton	.25
88	Shawn Green	.50
89	Jose Cruz Jr.	.35
90	Carlos Delgado	.50
91	Troy Glaus (Future Watch)	6.00
92	George Lombard (Future Watch)	1.00
93	Ryan Minor (Future Watch)	1.00
94	Calvin Pickering (Future Watch)	1.00
95	Jin Ho Cho (Future Watch)	2.50
96	Russ Branyon (Future Watch)	1.50
97	Derrick Gibson (Future Watch)	1.00
98	Gabe Kapler (Future Watch)	1.50
99	Matt Anderson (Future Watch)	1.00
100	Preston Wilson (Future Watch)	1.50
101	Alex Gonzalez (Future Watch)	1.50
102	Carlos Beltran (Future Watch)	1.50
103	Dee Brown (Future Watch)	1.00
104	Jeremy Giambi (Future Watch)	1.00
105	Angel Pena (Future Watch)	1.00
106	Geoff Jenkins (Future Watch)	1.00
107	Corey Koskie (Future Watch)	1.50
108	A.J. Pierzynski (Future Watch)	1.00
109	Michael Barrett (Future Watch)	1.00
110	Fernando Seguignol (Future Watch)	1.00
111	Mike Kinkade (Future Watch)	1.00
112	Ricky Ledee (Future Watch)	1.00
113	Mike Lowell (Future Watch)	1.00
114	Eric Chavez (Future Watch)	2.00
115	Matt Clement (Future Watch)	1.00
116	Shane Monahan (Future Watch)	1.00
117	J.D. Drew (Future Watch)	3.50
118	Bubba Trammell (Future Watch)	1.25
119	Kevin Witt (Future Watch)	1.00
120	Roy Halladay (Future Watch)	1.25
121	Mark McGwire (Season to Remember)	8.00
122	Mark McGwire, Sammy Sosa (Season to Remember)	8.00
123	Sammy Sosa (Season to Remember)	6.00
124	Ken Griffey Jr. (Season to Remember)	7.00
125	Cal Ripken Jr. (Season to Remember)	8.00
126	Juan Gonzalez (Season to Remember)	3.00
127	Kerry Wood (Season to Remember)	3.00
128	Trevor Hoffman (Season to Remember)	1.00
129	Barry Bonds (Season to Remember)	5.00
130	Alex Rodriguez (Season to Remember)	7.00
131	Ben Grieve (Season to Remember)	2.00
132	Tom Glavine (Season to Remember)	1.00
133	David Wells (Season to Remember)	1.00
134	Mike Piazza (Season to Remember)	6.00
135	Scott Brosius (Season to Remember)	1.00

1999 SP Authentic Chirography

Baseball's top players and future stars are included in this 39-card autograph insert set. The set was split into Level 1 and Level 2 versions. Level 1 cards are not numbered, and were inserted one card per 24 packs. Level 2 cards are sequentially numbered to the featured player's jersey number.

		MT
Common Player:		3.00
Inserted 1:24		
EC	Eric Chavez	10.00
GK	Gabe Kapler	7.00
GMj	Gary Matthews Jr.	5.00
CP	Calvin Pickering	3.00
CK	Corey Koskie	6.00
SM	Shane Monahan	3.00
RH	Richard Hidalgo	8.00
MK	Mike Kinkade	3.00
CB	Carlos Beltran	3.00
AG	Alex Gonzalez	6.00
BC	Bruce Chen	3.00
MA	Matt Anderson	4.00
RM	Ryan Minor	3.00
RL	Ricky Ledee	3.00
RR	Ruben Rivera	3.00
BF	Brad Fullmer	6.00
RB	Russ Branyon	5.00
ML	Mike Lowell	4.00
JG	Jeremy Giambi	3.00
GL	George Lombard	3.00
KW	Kevin Witt	3.00
TW	Todd Walker	4.50
SR	Scott Rolen	10.00
KW	Kerry Wood	15.00
BG	Ben Grieve	8.00
JR	Ken Griffey Jr.	90.00
CJ	Chipper Jones	40.00
IR	Ivan Rodriguez	25.00
TGl	Troy Glaus	20.00
TL	Travis Lee	5.00
VG	Vladimir Guerrero	25.00
GV	Greg Vaughn	5.00
JT	Jim Thome	10.00
JD	J.D. Drew	20.00
TH	Todd Helton	15.00
GM	Greg Maddux	60.00
NG	Nomar Garciaparra	100.00
TG	Tony Gwynn	20.00
CR	Cal Ripken Jr.	125.00

1999 SP Authentic Chirography Gold

These Chirography parallels can be identified by the gold tint on the card front and their sequential numbering; each featured player signed to his jersey number.

		MT
Common Player:		5.00
Inserted 1:24		
EC	Eric Chavez (30)	40.00
GK	Gabe Kapler (51)	10.00
GMj	Gary Matthews Jr. (68)	5.00
CP	Calvin Pickering (6)	40.00
CK	Corey Koskie (47)	12.50
SM	Shane Monahan (12)	20.00

RH	Richard Hidalgo (15)	40.00
MK	Mike Kinkade (33)	12.50
CB	Carlos Beltran (36)	17.50
AG	Alex Gonzalez (22)	20.00
BC	Bruce Chen (48)	10.00
MA	Matt Anderson (14)	20.00
RM	Ryan Minor (10)	35.00
RL	Ricky Ledee (38)	10.00
RR	Ruben Rivera (28)	10.00
BF	Brad Fullmer (20)	10.00
RB	Russ Branyon (66)	10.00
ML	Mike Lowell (60)	10.00
JG	Jeremy Giambi (15)	20.00
GL	George Lombard (26)	10.00
KW	Kevin Witt (6)	20.00
TW	Todd Walker (12)	40.00
SR	Scott Rolen (17)	75.00
KW	Kerry Wood (34)	45.00
BG	Ben Grieve (14)	35.00
JR	Ken Griffey Jr. (24)	400.00
CJ	Chipper Jones (10)	250.00
IR	Ivan Rodriguez (7)	125.00
TGI	Troy Glaus (14)	90.00
TL	Travis Lee (16)	35.00
VG	Vladimir Guerrero (27)	45.00
GV	Greg Vaughn (23)	10.00
JT	Jim Thome (25)	30.00
JD	J.D. Drew (8)	125.00
TH	Todd Helton (17)	75.00
GM	Greg Maddux (31)	125.00
NG	Nomar Garciaparra (5)	375.00
TG	Tony Gwynn (19)	125.00
CR	Cal Ripken Jr. (8)	750.00

1999 SP Authentic Epic Figures

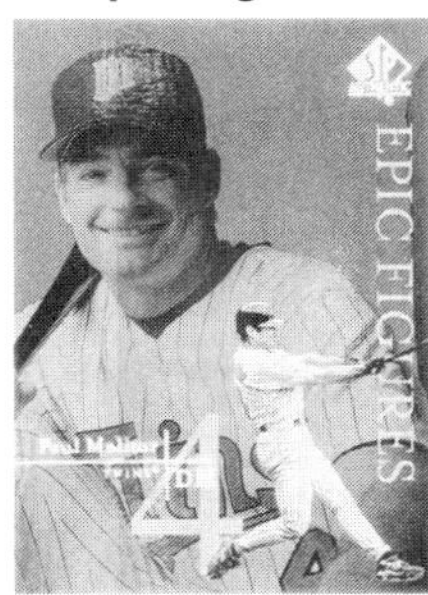

This 30-card set highlights baseball's biggest talents, including Mark McGwire and Derek Jeter. The card fronts have two photos, with the larger photo done with a shadow look in the background. Fronts also feature a holographic look, while the card backs feature the player's career highlights. These are seeded one per seven packs.

		MT
Complete Set (30):		42.50
Common Player:		.50
Inserted 1:7		
E01	Mo Vaughn	.75
E02	Travis Lee	.60
E03	Andres Galarraga	.50
E04	Andruw Jones	1.50
E05	Chipper Jones	3.00
E06	Greg Maddux	2.00
E07	Cal Ripken Jr.	5.00
E08	Nomar Garciaparra	2.50
E09	Sammy Sosa	2.50
E10	Frank Thomas	2.50
E11	Kerry Wood	1.00
E12	Kenny Lofton	.50
E13	Manny Ramirez	1.50
E14	Larry Walker	.60
E15	Jeff Bagwell	1.50
E16	Paul Molitor	1.00
E17	Vladimir Guerrero	1.50
E18	Derek Jeter	3.00
E19	Tino Martinez	.50
E20	Mike Piazza	3.00
E21	Ben Grieve	.60
E22	Scott Rolen	1.00
E23	Mark McGwire	5.00
E24	Tony Gwynn	2.00
E25	Barry Bonds	2.50
E26	Ken Griffey Jr.	4.00
E27	Alex Rodriguez	4.00
E28	J.D. Drew	.75
E29	Juan Gonzalez	1.50
E30	Kevin Brown	.50

1999 SP Authentic Home Run Chronicles

This two-tiered 70-card set focuses on the amazing seasons of McGwire and Sammy Sosa. Other players help round out the 70-card set, but special emphasis has been placed on the duo. These are seeded one per pack. A die-cut version also exists, with each card serially numbered to 70.

		MT
Complete Set (70):		120.00
Common Player:		.50
Inserted 1:1		
Die-Cuts:		6X
Production 70 sets		
HR01	Mark McGwire	4.00
HR02	Sammy Sosa	2.50
HR03	Ken Griffey Jr.	2.50
HR04	Mark McGwire	4.00
HR05	Mark McGwire	4.00
HR06	Albert Belle	.75
HR07	Jose Canseco	.50
HR08	Juan Gonzalez	1.00
HR09	Manny Ramirez	1.00
HR10	Rafael Palmeiro	.50
HR11	Mo Vaughn	.50
HR12	Carlos Delgado	.50
HR13	Nomar Garciaparra	1.50
HR14	Barry Bonds	1.50
HR15	Alex Rodriguez	2.50
HR16	Tony Clark	.50
HR17	Jim Thome	.50
HR18	Edgar Martinez	.50
HR19	Frank Thomas	1.50
HR20	Greg Vaughn	.50
HR21	Vinny Castilla	.50
HR22	Andres Galarraga	.50
HR23	Moises Alou	.50
HR24	Jeromy Burnitz	.50
HR25	Vladimir Guerrero	1.00
HR26	Jeff Bagwell	1.00
HR27	Chipper Jones	2.00
HR28	Javier Lopez	.50
HR29	Mike Piazza	2.00
HR30	Andruw Jones	1.00
HR31	Henry Rodriguez	.50
HR32	Jeff Kent	.50
HR33	Ray Lankford	.50
HR34	Scott Rolen	.75
HR35	Raul Mondesi	.50
HR36	Ken Caminiti	.50
HR37	J.D. Drew	1.00
HR38	Troy Glaus	1.50
HR39	Gabe Kapler	.75
HR40	Alex Rodriguez	2.50
HR41	Ken Griffey Jr.	2.50
HR42	Sammy Sosa	2.50
HR43	Mark McGwire	4.00
HR44	Sammy Sosa	2.50
HR45	Mark McGwire	4.00
HR46	Vinny Castilla	.50
HR47	Sammy Sosa	2.50
HR48	Mark McGwire	4.00
HR49	Sammy Sosa	2.50
HR50	Greg Vaughn	.50
HR51	Sammy Sosa	2.50
HR52	Mark McGwire	4.00
HR53	Sammy Sosa	2.50
HR54	Mark McGwire	4.00
HR55	Sammy Sosa	2.50
HR56	Ken Griffey Jr.	2.50
HR57	Sammy Sosa	2.50
HR58	Mark McGwire	4.00
HR59	Sammy Sosa	2.50
HR60	Mark McGwire	4.00
HR61	Mark McGwire	6.00
HR62	Mark McGwire	6.00
HR63	Mark McGwire	4.00
HR64	Mark McGwire	4.00
HR65	Mark McGwire	4.00
HR66	Sammy Sosa	6.00
HR67	Mark McGwire	4.00
HR68	Mark McGwire	4.00
HR69	Mark McGwire	4.00
HR70	Mark McGwire	10.00

1999 SP Authentic Reflections

Dot Matrix technology is utilized to provide a unique look at 30 of the best players in the game. Card fronts are horizontal with two small and one large photo. These are seeded 1:23 packs.

		MT
Complete Set (30):		175.00
Common Player:		2.50
Inserted 1:23		
R01	Mo Vaughn	3.50
R02	Travis Lee	3.00
R03	Andres Galarraga	2.50
R04	Andruw Jones	6.00
R05	Chipper Jones	12.50
R06	Greg Maddux	8.00
R07	Cal Ripken Jr.	17.50
R08	Nomar Garciaparra	10.00
R09	Sammy Sosa	10.00
R10	Frank Thomas	10.00
R11	Kerry Wood	3.50
R12	Kenny Lofton	2.50
R13	Manny Ramirez	6.00
R14	Larry Walker	3.00
R15	Jeff Bagwell	6.00
R16	Paul Molitor	3.50
R17	Vladimir Guerrero	6.00
R18	Derek Jeter	12.50
R19	Tino Martinez	2.50
R20	Mike Piazza	12.50
R21	Ben Grieve	3.00
R22	Scott Rolen	5.00
R23	Mark McGwire	17.50
R24	Tony Gwynn	8.00
R25	Barry Bonds	10.00
R26	Ken Griffey Jr.	15.00
R27	Alex Rodriguez	15.00
R28	J.D. Drew	3.50
R29	Juan Gonzalez	5.00
R30	Roger Clemens	8.00

1999 SP Authentic SP Authentics

These 1:864 pack inserts are redemption cards that could be redeemed for special pieces of memorabilia from either Ken Griffey Jr. or Mark McGwire. The redemption period ended March 1, 2000. Because of rarity any surviving unredeemed McGwire home run-game autographed tickets cannot be valued.

		MT
Common Card:		9.00
(1)	Ken Griffey Jr. (autographed baseball) (75)	30.00
(2)	Ken Griffey Jr. (glove) (200)	12.50
(3)	Ken Griffey Jr. (home run cel card) (346)	9.00
(4)	Ken Griffey Jr. (autographed jersey) (25)	75.00
(5)	Ken Griffey Jr. (autographed mini-helmet) (75)	30.00
(6)	Ken Griffey Jr. (Sports Illustrated Cover) (200)	12.50
(7)	Ken Griffey Jr. (autographed SI cover) (75)	30.00
(8)	Ken Griffey Jr. (standee) (300)	11.00
(9)	Mark McGwire (autographed 62HR ticket) (1)	
(10)	Mark McGwire (autographed 70HR ticket) (3)	

1999 SP Authentic 500 Club Piece of History

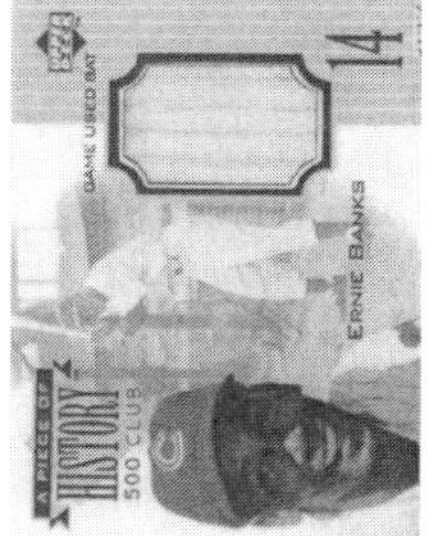

These cards feature a piece of game-used bat once swung by Ernie Banks. Approximately 350 cards exist. An autographed version of this card also exists, only 14 were produced.

		MT
EB	Ernie Banks	120.00
EB	Ernie Banks Auto./14	325.00

1999 SP Signature Edition

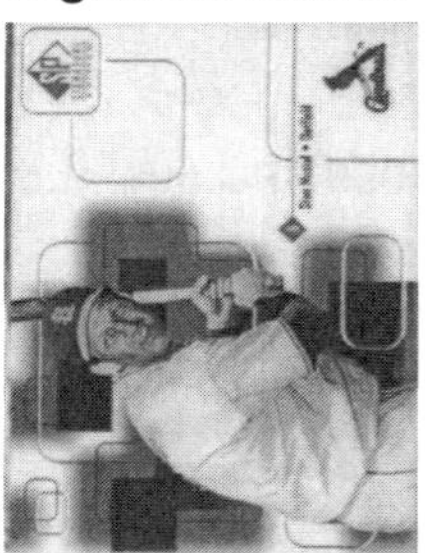

Even with one autograph per three-card pack, this single-series issue's price of $19.99 per pack shocked the hobby when it was introduced. Horizontal cards have color or black-and-white photos at the right end with foil highlights and airbrushed geometric designs on a white background. Backs repeat the portrait portion of the front photo and add player data and some stats.

		MT
Complete Set (180):		110.00
Common Player:		.50
Pack (3):		24.00
Wax Box (12):		280.00
1	Nomar Garciaparra	2.25
2	Ken Griffey Jr.	3.00
3	J.D. Drew	1.50
4	Alex Rodriguez	3.00
5	Juan Gonzalez	1.50
6	Mo Vaughn	1.00
7	Greg Maddux	2.00
8	Chipper Jones	2.50
9	Frank Thomas	2.25
10	Vladimir Guerrero	1.50
11	Mike Piazza	2.50
12	Eric Chavez	.75
13	Tony Gwynn	2.00
14	Orlando Hernandez	1.00
15	*Pat Burrell*	8.00
16	Darin Erstad	1.25
17	Greg Vaughn	.50
18	Russ Branyan	.50
19	Gabe Kapler	.75
20	Craig Biggio	.50
21	Troy Glaus	1.50
22	Pedro J. Martinez	1.00
23	Carlos Beltran	.75
24	Derrek Lee	.50
25	Manny Ramirez	1.50
26	*Shea Hillenbrand*	12.00
27	Carlos Lee	.50
28	Angel Pena	.50
29	Rafael Roque	.50
30	Octavio Dotel	.50
31	Jeromy Burnitz	.50
32	Jeremy Giambi	.50
33	Andruw Jones	1.50
34	Todd Helton	1.25
35	Scott Rolen	1.25
36	Jason Kendall	.50
37	Trevor Hoffman	.50
38	Barry Bonds	2.25
39	Ivan Rodriguez	1.25
40	Roy Halladay	.50
41	Rickey Henderson	1.00
42	Ryan Minor	.50
43	Brian Jordan	.50
44	Alex Gonzalez	.50
45	Raul Mondesi	.50
46	Corey Koskie	.50
47	Paul O'Neill	.50
48	Todd Walker	.50
49	Carlos Febles	.50
50	Travis Fryman	.50
51	Albert Belle	1.00
52	Travis Lee	.65
53	Bruce Chen	.50
54	Reggie Taylor	.50
55	Jerry Hairston Jr.	.50
56	Carlos Guillen	.50
57	Michael Barrett	.50
58	Jason Conti	.50
59	Joe Lawrence	.50
60	Jeff Cirillo	.50
61	Juan Melo	.50
62	Chad Hermansen	.50
63	Ruben Mateo	.50
64	Ben Davis	.50
65	Mike Caruso	.50
66	Jason Giambi	1.00
67	Jose Canseco	1.00
68	*Chad Hutchinson*	1.50
69	Mitch Meluskey	.50
70	Adrian Beltre	1.00
71	Mark Kotsay	.50
72	Juan Encarnacion	.50
73	Dermal Brown	.50
74	Kevin Witt	.50
75	Vinny Castilla	.50
76	Aramis Ramirez	.50
77	Marlon Anderson	.50
78	Mike Kinkade	.50
79	Kevin Barker	.50
80	Ron Belliard	.50
81	Chris Haas	.50
82	Bob Henley	.50
83	Fernando Seguignol	.50
84	Damon Minor	.50
85	*A.J. Burnett*	2.00
86	Calvin Pickering	.50
87	Mike Darr	.50
88	Cesar King	.50
89	Rob Bell	.50
90	Derrick Gibson	.50
91	*Ober Moreno*	.50
92	Robert Fick	.50
93	*Doug Mientkiewicz*	.75
94	A.J. Pierzynski	.50
95	Orlando Palmeiro	.50
96	Sidney Ponson	.50
97	*Ivanon Coffie*	.50
98	*Juan Pena*	1.00
99	Mark Karchner	.50
100	Carlos Castillo	.50
101	Bryan Ward	.50
102	Mario Valdez	.50
103	Billy Wagner	.50
104	Miguel Tejada	.75
105	Jose Cruz Jr.	.75
106	George Lombard	.50
107	Geoff Jenkins	.50
108	Ray Lankford	.50
109	Todd Stottlemyre	.50
110	Mike Lowell	.50
111	Matt Clement	.50
112	Scott Brosius	.50
113	Preston Wilson	.50
114	Bartolo Colon	.50
115	Rolando Arrojo	.50
116	Jose Guillen	.50
117	Ron Gant	.50
118	Ricky Ledee	.50
119	Carlos Delgado	.75
120	Abraham Nunez	.50
121	John Olerud	.50
122	Chan Ho Park	.75
123	Brad Radke	.50
124	Al Leiter	.50
125	Gary Matthews Jr.	.50
126	F.P. Santangelo	.50
127	Brad Fullmer	.50
128	Matt Anderson	.50
129	A.J. Hinch	.50
130	Sterling Hitchcock	.50
131	Edgar Martinez	.50
132	Fernando Tatis	.50
133	Bobby Smith	.50
134	Paul Konerko	.50
135	Sean Casey	.75
136	Donnie Sadler	.50
137	Denny Neagle	.50
138	Sandy Alomar	.50
139	Mariano Rivera	.75
140	Emil Brown	.50
141	J.T. Snow	.50
142	Eli Marrero	.50
143	Rusty Greer	.50
144	Johnny Damon	.50
145	Damion Easley	.50
146	Eric Milton	.50
147	Rico Brogna	.50
148	Ray Durham	.50
149	Wally Joyner	.50
150	Royce Clayton	.50
151	David Ortiz	.50
152	Wade Boggs	1.25
153	Ugueth Urbina	.50
154	Richard Hidalgo	.50
155	Bobby Abreu	.50
156	Robb Nen	.50
157	David Segui	.50
158	Sean Berry	.50
159	Kevin Tapani	.50
160	Jason Varitek	.50
161	Fernando Vina	.50
162	Jim Leyritz	.50
163	Enrique Wilson	.50
164	Jim Parque	.50
165	Doug Glanville	.50
166	Jesus Sanchez	.50
167	Nolan Ryan	4.00
168	Robin Yount	.75
169	Stan Musial	2.00
170	Tom Seaver	1.00
171	Mike Schmidt	1.00
172	Willie Stargell	.50
173	Rollie Fingers	.50
174	Willie McCovey	.75
175	Harmon Killebrew	.75
176	Eddie Mathews	.75
177	Reggie Jackson	1.00
178	Frank Robinson	.75
179	Ken Griffey Sr.	.50
180	Eddie Murray	1.00

1999 SP Signature Edition Autographs

Authentically autographed cards of nearly 100 current stars, top prospects and Hall of Famers were featured as one-per-pack inserts in SP Signature Edition. Some players did not return their signed cards in time for pack inclusion and had to be obtained by returning an exchange card prior to the May 12, 2000, deadline.

		MT
Common Player:		4.00
Inserted 1:1		
BA	Bobby Abreu	7.50
SA	Sandy Alomar	5.00
MA	Marlon Anderson	4.00
KB	Kevin Barker	4.00
MB	Michael Barrett	4.00
RoB	Rob Bell	4.00
AB	Albert Belle	15.00
RBe	Ron Belliard	4.00
CBe	Carlos Beltran	5.00
ABe	Adrian Beltre	7.50
BB	Barry Bonds	45.00
RB	Russ Branyan	4.00
SB	Scott Brosius	4.00
DB	Dermal Brown	4.00
EB	Emil Brown	4.00
AJB	A.J. Burnett (exchange card)	4.00
AJB	A.J. Burnett (autographed)	10.00
PB	Pat Burrell	20.00
JoC	Jose Canseco	45.00
MC	Mike Caruso	4.00
SC	Sean Casey (exchange card)	4.00
SC	Sean Casey (autographed)	15.00
VC	Vinny Castilla (exchange card)	4.00
VC	Vinny Castilla (autographed)	6.00
CC	Carlos Castillo	4.00
EC	Eric Chavez	12.50
BC	Bruce Chen	4.00
JCi	Jeff Cirillo	4.00
RC	Royce Clayton	4.00
MCl	Matt Clement	4.00
IC	Ivanon Coffie	4.00
BCo	Bartolo Colon (exchange card)	4.00
BCo	Bartolo Colon (autographed)	7.50
JC	Jason Conti	4.00
JDa	Johnny Damon	6.00
BD	Ben Davis	4.00
CD	Carlos Delgado	15.00
OD	Octavio Dotel	6.00
JD	J.D. Drew	12.50
RD	Ray Durham	4.00
DEa	Damion Easley	4.00
JE	Juan Encarnacion	6.00
DE	Darin Erstad	12.50
CF	Carlos Febles	5.00
Rob	Robert Fick	4.00
Rol	Rollie Fingers	10.00
BF	Brad Fullmer	7.50
RGa	Ron Gant	7.50
NG	Nomar Garciaparra	100.00
JaG	Jason Giambi	17.50
DG	Derrick Gibson	4.00
DGl	Doug Glanville	4.00
TGl	Troy Glaus	15.00
AG	Alex Gonzalez	4.00
RGr	Rusty Greer	4.00
Jr.	Ken Griffey Jr.	75.00
Sr.	Ken Griffey Sr.	10.00
VG	Vladimir Guerrero	25.00
JG	Jose Guillen	6.00
TG	Tony Gwynn	40.00
CHa	Chris Haas	4.00
JHj	Jerry Hairston Jr.	4.00
RH	Roy Halladay	6.00
THe	Todd Helton	15.00
BH	Bob Henley	4.00
ED	Orlando Hernandez	20.00
CH	Chad Hermansen	7.50
ShH	Shea Hillenbrand	4.00
StH	Sterling Hitchcock	4.00
THo	Trevor Hoffman	6.00
CHu	Chad Hutchinson	15.00
RJ	Reggie Jackson	50.00
GJ	Geoff Jenkins	7.50
AJ	Andruw Jones	17.50
CJ	Chipper Jones	40.00
WJ	Wally Joyner	7.50
GK	Gabe Kapler	7.50
MKa	Mark Karchner	4.00
JK	Jason Kendall	7.50
HK	Harmon Killebrew	20.00
CKi	Cesar King	4.00
MKi	Mike Kinkade	4.00
PK	Paul Konerko	6.00
CK	Corey Koskie	6.00
MK	Mark Kotsay	6.00
RL	Ray Lankford	7.50
JLa	Joe Lawrence	4.00
CL	Carlos Lee	10.00
DL	Derrek Lee	4.00

AL	Al Leiter	6.00
JLe	Jim Leyritz	4.00
GL	George Lombard	4.00
GM	Greg Maddux	60.00
Eli	Eli Marrero	4.00
EM	Edgar Martinez	10.00
PM	Pedro J. Martinez (exchange card)	4.00
PM	Pedro J. Martinez (autographed)	70.00
RMa	Ruben Mateo (exchange card)	4.00
RMa	Ruben Mateo (autographed)	10.00
EMa	Eddie Mathews	20.00
GMj	Gary Matthews Jr.	6.00
WMc	Willie McCovey	20.00
JM	Juan Melo	4.00
MMe	Mitch Meluskey	4.00
DoM	Doug Mientkiewicz	4.00
EMi	Eric Milton	4.00
DaM	Damon Minor	4.00
RM	Ryan Minor	4.00
EMu	Eddie Murray	20.00
SM	Stan Musial	55.00
RN	Robb Nen	4.00
AN	Abraham Nunez	4.00
JO	John Olerud	10.00
PO	Paul O'Neill	10.00
DO	David Ortiz	4.00
OP	Orlando Palmeiro	4.00
JP	Jim Parque	4.00
AP	Angel Pena	4.00
MP	Mike Piazza (exchange card)	6.00
MP	Mike Piazza (autographed)	200.00
CP	Calvin Pickering	6.00
AJP	A.J. Pierzynski	4.00
SP	Sidney Ponson	4.00
BR	Brad Radke	4.00
ARa	Aramis Ramirez	4.00
MR	Manny Ramirez	20.00
MRi	Mariano Rivera	10.00
FR	Frank Robinson	15.00
AR	Alex Rodriguez	75.00
PG	Ivan Rodriguez	30.00
SR	Scott Rolen (exchange card)	4.00
SR	Scott Rolen (autographed)	15.00
RR	Rafael Roque	4.00
NR	Nolan Ryan	100.00
DS	Donnie Sadler	4.00
JS	Jesus Sanchez	4.00
MS	Mike Schmidt	35.00
TSe	Tom Seaver	35.00
DSe	David Segui	4.00
FS	Fernando Seguignol	4.00
BS	Bobby Smith	4.00
JT	J.T. Snow (exchange card)	4.00
JT	J.T. Snow (autographed)	6.00
POP	Willie Stargell (exchange card)	4.00
POP	Willie Stargell (autographed)	20.00
TSt	Todd Stottlemyre	6.00
FTa	Fernando Tatis	5.00
RT	Reggie Taylor	4.00
MT	Miguel Tejada	10.00
FT	Frank Thomas	40.00
MV	Mario Valdez	4.00
JV	Jason Varitek	4.00
GV	Greg Vaughn	7.50
MO	Mo Vaughn	15.00
FV	Fernando Vina	6.00
BWa	Billy Wagner	6.00
TW	Todd Walker	4.00
BW	Bryan Ward	4.00
EW	Enrique Wilson	4.00
KW	Kevin Witt	4.00
RY	Robin Yount	30.00

1999 SP Signature Edition Autographs Gold

This parallel edition of the Signature Series Autographs features special gold graphic highlights on front and cards serially numbered within an edition of 50 each (except A.J. Burnett). Cards of 11 players were never signed, while cards of several others had to be obtained by sending in an exchange card, valid through May 12, 2000.

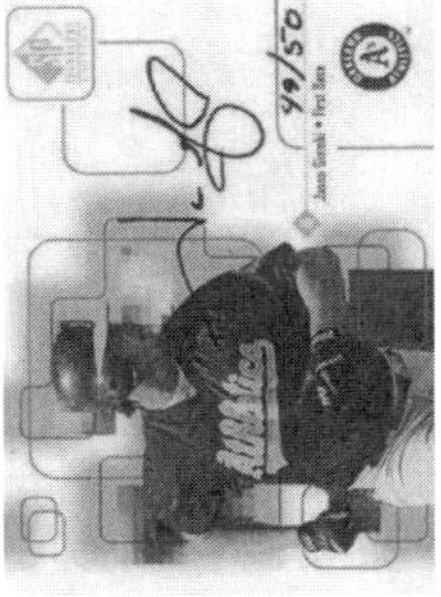

		MT
Common Player:		10.00
BA	Bobby Abreu	15.00
SA	Sandy Alomar	12.50
MA	Marlon Anderson	10.00
KB	Kevin Barker	10.00
MB	Michael Barrett	12.50
RoB	Rob Bell	10.00
AB	Albert Belle	20.00
RBe	Ron Belliard	10.00
CBe	Carlos Beltran	15.00
ABe	Adrian Beltre	15.00
CB	Craig Biggio (unsigned)	10.00
BB	Barry Bonds	95.00
RB	Russ Branyan	10.00
SB	Scott Brosius	10.00
DB	Dermal Brown	10.00
EB	Emil Brown	10.00
AJB	A.J. Burnett (exchange card)	10.00
AJB	A.J. Burnett (autographed edition of 20)	30.00
JB	Jeromy Burnitz (unsigned)	10.00
PB	Pat Burrell	75.00
JoC	Jose Canseco	40.00
MC	Mike Caruso	10.00
SC	Sean Casey	30.00
VC	Vinny Castilla (exchange card)	10.00
VC	Vinny Castilla (autographed)	15.00
CC	Carlos Castillo	10.00
EC	Eric Chavez	20.00
BC	Bruce Chen	10.00
JCi	Jeff Cirillo	10.00
RC	Royce Clayton	10.00
MCl	Matt Clement	10.00
IC	Ivanon Coffie	10.00
BCo	Bartolo Colon	10.00
JC	Jason Conti	10.00
JDa	Johnny Damon	12.50
MD	Mike Darr (unsigned)	10.00
BD	Ben Davis	10.00
CD	Carlos Delgado	15.00
OD	Octavio Dotel	10.00
JD	J.D. Drew	35.00
RD	Ray Durham	10.00
DEa	Damion Easley	10.00
JE	Juan Encarnacion	10.00
DE	Darin Erstad	30.00
CF	Carlos Febles	15.00
Rob	Robert Fick	10.00
Rol	Rollie Fingers	20.00
TF	Travis Fryman (unsigned)	10.00
BF	Brad Fullmer	15.00
RGa	Ron Gant	15.00
NG	Nomar Garciaparra	200.00
JaG	Jason Giambi	45.00
JeG	Jeremy Giambi (unsigned)	10.00
DG	Derrick Gibson	10.00
DGl	Doug Glanville	10.00
TGl	Troy Glaus	40.00
AG	Alex Gonzalez	10.00
JG	Juan Gonzalez (unsigned)	35.00
RGr	Rusty Greer	10.00
Jr.	Ken Griffey Jr.	150.00
Sr.	Ken Griffey Sr.	10.00
VG	Vladimir Guerrero	45.00
JG	Jose Guillen (unsigned)	10.00
TG	Tony Gwynn	60.00
CHa	Chris Haas	10.00
JHj	Jerry Hairston Jr.	10.00
RH	Roy Halladay	10.00
THe	Todd Helton	25.00
RH	Rickey Henderson (unsigned)	15.00
BH	Bob Henley	10.00
ED	Orlando Hernandez	40.00
CH	Chad Hermansen	10.00
ShH	Shea Hillenbrand	10.00
StH	Sterling Hitchcock	10.00
THo	Trevor Hoffman	10.00
CHu	Chad Hutchinson	25.00
RJ	Reggie Jackson	90.00
GJ	Geoff Jenkins	10.00
AJ	Andruw Jones	35.00
CJ	Chipper Jones	100.00
BJ	Brian Jordan (unsigned)	10.00
WJ	Wally Joyner	15.00
GK	Gabe Kapler	25.00
MKa	Mark Karchner	10.00
JK	Jason Kendall	15.00
HK	Harmon Killebrew	40.00
CKi	Cesar King	10.00
MKi	Mike Kinkade	10.00
PK	Paul Konerko	12.00
CK	Corey Koskie	12.00
MK	Mark Kotsay	12.00
RL	Ray Lankford	10.00
JLa	Joe Lawrence	10.00
CL	Carlos Lee	12.00
DL	Derrek Lee	10.00
TL	Travis Lee (unsigned)	10.00
AL	Al Leiter	10.00
JLe	Jim Leyritz	10.00
GL	George Lombard	10.00
GM	Greg Maddux	65.00
Eli	Eli Marrero	10.00
EM	Edgar Martinez	10.00
PM	Pedro Martinez (exchange card)	12.00
PM	Pedro Martinez (autographed)	90.00
RMa	Ruben Mateo (exchange card)	10.00
RMa	Ruben Mateo (autographed)	15.00
EMa	Eddie Mathews	50.00
GMj	Gary Matthews Jr.	10.00
WMc	Willie McCovey	35.00
JM	Juan Melo	10.00
MMe	Mitch Meluskey	10.00
DoM	Doug Mientkiewicz	10.00
EMi	Eric Milton	10.00
DaM	Damon Minor	10.00
RM	Ryan Minor	10.00
EMu	Eddie Murray	60.00
SM	Stan Musial	120.00
RN	Robb Nen	10.00
AN	Abraham Nunez	10.00
JO	John Olerud	20.00
PO	Paul O'Neill	20.00
DO	David Ortiz	10.00
OP	Orlando Palmeiro	10.00
JP	Jim Parque	10.00
AP	Angel Pena	10.00
MP	Mike Piazza (exchange card)	30.00
MP	Mike Piazza (autographed)	250.00
CP	Calvin Pickering	10.00
AJP	A.J. Pierzynski	10.00
SP	Sidney Ponson	10.00
BR	Brad Radke	10.00
ARa	Aramis Ramirez	10.00
MR	Manny Ramirez	40.00
MRi	Mariano Rivera	20.00
FR	Frank Robinson	40.00
AR	Alex Rodriguez	150.00
PG	Ivan Rodriguez	40.00
SR	Scott Rolen (exchange card)	15.00
SR	Scott Rolen (autographed)	35.00
RR	Rafael Roque	10.00
NR	Nolan Ryan	200.00
DS	Donnie Sadler	10.00
JS	Jesus Sanchez	10.00
MS	Mike Schmidt	100.00
TSe	Tom Seaver	90.00
DSe	David Segui	10.00
FS	Fernando Seguignol	10.00
BS	Bobby Smith	10.00
JT	J.T. Snow	10.00
POP	Willie Stargell	50.00
TSt	Todd Stottlemyre	10.00
FTa	Fernando Tatis	10.00
RT	Reggie Taylor	10.00
MT	Miguel Tejada	25.00
FT	Frank Thomas	60.00
MV	Mario Valdez	10.00
JV	Jason Varitek	10.00
GV	Greg Vaughn	10.00
MO	Mo Vaughn	25.00
FV	Fernando Vina	10.00
BWa	Billy Wagner	12.00
TW	Todd Walker	12.00
BW	Bryan Ward	10.00
EW	Enrique Wilson	10.00
KW	Kevin Witt	10.00
RY	Robin Yount	45.00

1999 SP Signature Edition Legendary Cuts

Each of the cards in this one-of-one insert series is unique, thus catalog values are impossible to assign.

		MT
Roy	Roy Campanella	
RC	Roy Campanella	
XX	Jimmie Foxx	
LG	Lefty Grove	
W	Walter Johnson	
MO	Mel Ott	
Mel1	Mel Ott	
Mel2	Mel Ott	
BR	Babe Ruth	
CY	Cy Young	

1999 SP Signature Edition 500 Club Piece of History

		MT
MO	Mel Ott (350)	100.00

1999 SPx

Formerly SPx Finite, this super-premium product showcases 80 of baseball's veteran players on regular cards and a 40-card rookie subset, which are serially numbered to 1,999. Two top rookies, J.D. Drew and Gabe Kapler autographed all 1,999 of their rookie subset cards. There are two parallels, SPx Radiance and SPx Spectrum. Radiance are serially numbered to 100 with Drew and Kapler signing all 100 of their cards. They are exclusive to Finite Radiance Hot Packs. Spectrums are limited to only one set and available only in Finite Spectrum Hot Packs. Packs consist of three cards with a S.R.P. of $5.99.

		MT
Complete Set (120):		190.00
Common Player:		.50
Common SPx Rookie (81-120):		1.00
Production 1,999 sets		
Radiance (1-80):		4X
Radiance SP (81-120):		1.5X
Spectrum (1-of-1):		
VALUE UNDETERMINED		
Pack (3):		3.00
Wax Box (18):		50.00
1	Mark McGwire #61	1.00
2	Mark McGwire #62	1.50
3	Mark McGwire #63	1.00
4	Mark McGwire #64	1.00
5	Mark McGwire #65	1.00
6	Mark McGwire #66	1.00
7	Mark McGwire #67	1.00
8	Mark McGwire #68	1.00
9	Mark McGwire #69	1.00
10	Mark McGwire #70	3.00
11	Mo Vaughn	1.50
12	Darin Erstad	2.00
13	Travis Lee	.75
14	Randy Johnson	2.00
15	Matt Williams	1.25
16	Chipper Jones	5.00
17	Greg Maddux	4.00
18	Andruw Jones	2.50
19	Andres Galarraga	.50
20	Cal Ripken Jr.	7.50
21	Albert Belle	1.50
22	Mike Mussina	2.00
23	Nomar Garciaparra	4.50
24	Pedro Martinez	2.00
25	John Valentin	.50
26	Kerry Wood	2.00
27	Sammy Sosa	4.50
28	Mark Grace	1.25
29	Frank Thomas	4.50
30	Mike Caruso	.50
31	Barry Larkin	.50
32	Sean Casey	.75
33	Jim Thome	.50
34	Kenny Lofton	.50
35	Manny Ramirez	2.50
36	Larry Walker	1.00
37	Todd Helton	2.00
38	Vinny Castilla	.50
39	Tony Clark	.50
40	Derrek Lee	.50
41	Mark Kotsay	.50
42	Jeff Bagwell	2.50
43	Craig Biggio	.50
44	Moises Alou	.65
45	Larry Sutton	.50
46	Johnny Damon	.50
47	Gary Sheffield	1.00
48	Raul Mondesi	.75
49	Jeromy Burnitz	.50
50	Todd Walker	.50
51	David Ortiz	.50
52	Vladimir Guerrero	2.50
53	Rondell White	.75
54	Mike Piazza	5.00
55	Derek Jeter	5.00
56	Tino Martinez	.50
57	David Wells	.50
58	Ben Grieve	.75
59	A.J. Hinch	.50
60	Scott Rolen	1.50
61	Doug Glanville	.50
62	Aramis Ramirez	.50
63	Jose Guillen	.50
64	Tony Gwynn	4.00
65	Greg Vaughn	.50
66	Ruben Rivera	.50
67	Barry Bonds	4.50
68	J.T. Snow	.50
69	Alex Rodriguez	6.00
70	Ken Griffey Jr.	6.00
71	Jay Buhner	.50
72	Mark McGwire	7.50
73	Fernando Tatis	.50
74	Quinton McCracken	.50
75	Wade Boggs	1.50
76	Ivan Rodriguez	2.00
77	Juan Gonzalez	2.50
78	Rafael Palmeiro	1.00
79	Jose Cruz Jr.	.75
80	Carlos Delgado	1.00
81	Troy Glaus	7.50
82	Vladimir Nunez	1.00
83	George Lombard	1.00
84	Bruce Chen	1.00
85	Ryan Minor	1.00
86	Calvin Pickering	1.00
87	Jin Ho Cho	2.00
88	Russ Branyon	2.00
89	Derrick Gibson	2.00
90	Gabe Kapler (autographed)	15.00
91	Matt Anderson	2.00
92	Robert Fick	1.00
93	Juan Encarnacion	2.00
94	Preston Wilson	2.00
95	Alex Gonzalez	2.00
96	Carlos Beltran	2.50
97	Jeremy Giambi	1.50
98	Dee Brown	1.00
99	Adrian Beltre	2.50
100	Alex Cora	1.00
101	Angel Pena	1.00
102	Geoff Jenkins	1.00
103	Ronnie Belliard	1.00
104	Corey Koskie	2.00
105	A.J. Pierzynski	1.00
106	Michael Barrett	2.00
107	Fernando Seguignol	1.00
108	Mike Kinkade	1.00
109	Mike Lowell	1.00
110	Ricky Ledee	1.00
111	Eric Chavez	4.00
112	Abraham Nunez	1.00
113	Matt Clement	1.00
114	Ben Davis	1.00
115	Mike Darr	1.00
116	Ramon Martinez	1.00
117	Carlos Guillen	1.50
118	Shane Monahan	1.00
119	J.D. Drew (autographed)	35.00
120	Kevin Witt	1.00

1999 SPx Dominance

This 20-card set showcases the most dominant MLB superstars, including Derek Jeter and Alex Rodriguez. These are seeded 1:17 packs and numbered with a FB prefix.

		MT
Complete Set (20):		60.00
Common Player:		1.00
Inserted 1:17		
1	Chipper Jones	5.00
2	Greg Maddux	4.00
3	Cal Ripken Jr.	6.00
4	Nomar Garciaparra	4.50
5	Mo Vaughn	2.00
6	Sammy Sosa	4.50
7	Albert Belle	1.50
8	Frank Thomas	4.50
9	Jim Thome	1.00
10	Jeff Bagwell	3.00
11	Vladimir Guerrero	3.00
12	Mike Piazza	5.00
13	Derek Jeter	5.00
14	Tony Gwynn	4.00
15	Barry Bonds	4.50
16	Ken Griffey Jr.	5.50
17	Alex Rodriguez	5.50
18	Mark McGwire	6.00
19	J.D. Drew	2.00
20	Juan Gonzalez	3.00

1999 SPx Power Explosion

This 30-card set salutes the top power hitters in the game today, including Mark McGwire and Sammy Sosa. These are seeded 1:3 packs, and numbered with a PE prefix.

		MT
Complete Set (30):		35.00
Common Player:		.40
Inserted 1:3		
1	Troy Glaus	1.25
2	Mo Vaughn	.75
3	Travis Lee	.75
4	Chipper Jones	3.00
5	Andres Galarraga	.40
6	Brady Anderson	.40
7	Albert Belle	1.00
8	Nomar Garciaparra	2.50
9	Sammy Sosa	2.50
10	Frank Thomas	2.50
11	Jim Thome	.40
12	Manny Ramirez	1.50
13	Larry Walker	.75
14	Tony Clark	.40
15	Jeff Bagwell	1.50
16	Moises Alou	.40
17	Ken Caminiti	.40
18	Vladimir Guerrero	1.50
19	Mike Piazza	3.00
20	Tino Martinez	.40
21	Ben Grieve	.75
22	Scott Rolen	1.25
23	Greg Vaughn	.40
24	Barry Bonds	2.50
25	Ken Griffey Jr.	3.50
26	Alex Rodriguez	3.50
27	Mark McGwire	4.00
28	J.D. Drew	1.00
29	Juan Gonzalez	1.50
30	Ivan Rodriguez	1.00

1999 SPx Premier Stars

This 30-card set captures baseball's most dominant players, including Randy Johnson and Ken Griffey Jr. Featured on a rainbow-foil design, these are seeded 1:17 packs and numbered with a PS prefix.

		MT
Complete Set (30):		60.00
Common Player:		.50
Inserted 1:17		
1	Mark McGwire	6.00
2	Sammy Sosa	3.50
3	Frank Thomas	3.50
4	J.D. Drew	.75
5	Kerry Wood	1.50
6	Moises Alou	.50
7	Kenny Lofton	.50
8	Jeff Bagwell	2.50
9	Tony Clark	.50
10	Roberto Alomar	1.00
11	Cal Ripken Jr.	6.00
12	Derek Jeter	4.00
13	Mike Piazza	4.00
14	Jose Cruz Jr.	.65
15	Chipper Jones	4.00
16	Nomar Garciaparra	3.50
17	Greg Maddux	3.00
18	Scott Rolen	2.00
19	Vladimir Guerrero	2.50
20	Albert Belle	1.00
21	Ken Griffey Jr.	5.00
22	Alex Rodriguez	5.00
23	Ben Grieve	.75
24	Juan Gonzalez	2.50
25	Barry Bonds	3.50
26	Larry Walker	.75
27	Tony Gwynn	3.00
28	Randy Johnson	1.50
29	Travis Lee	.75
30	Mo Vaughn	1.00

1999 SPx Star Focus

This 30-card set focuses on the 30 brightest stars in the game. These are seeded 1:8 packs and numbered with a SF prefix.

	MT
Complete Set (30):	60.00
Common Player:	.75

Inserted 1:8

1	Chipper Jones	4.00
2	Greg Maddux	3.00
3	Cal Ripken Jr.	6.00
4	Nomar Garciaparra	3.50
5	Mo Vaughn	1.00
6	Sammy Sosa	3.50
7	Albert Belle	1.50
8	Frank Thomas	3.50
9	Jim Thome	.75
10	Kenny Lofton	.75
11	Manny Ramirez	2.50
12	Larry Walker	1.25
13	Jeff Bagwell	2.50
14	Craig Biggio	.75
15	Randy Johnson	1.50
16	Vladimir Guerrero	2.50
17	Mike Piazza	4.00
18	Derek Jeter	4.00
19	Tino Martinez	.75
20	Bernie Williams	1.00
21	Curt Schilling	1.25
22	Tony Gwynn	3.00
23	Barry Bonds	3.50
24	Ken Griffey Jr.	5.00
25	Alex Rodriguez	5.00
26	Mark McGwire	6.00
27	J.D. Drew	1.50
28	Juan Gonzalez	2.50
29	Ivan Rodriguez	1.50
30	Ben Grieve	1.00

1999 SPx Winning Materials

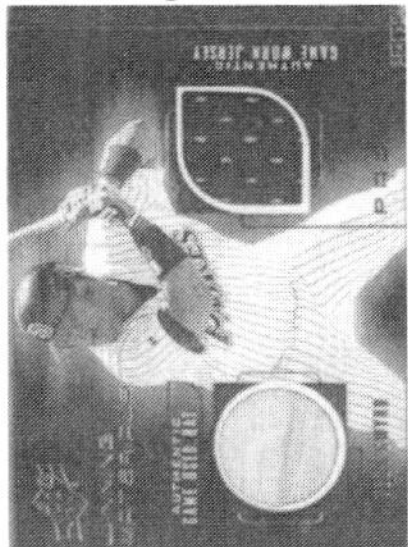

This eight-card set includes a piece of the featured player's game-worn jersey and game-used bat on each card. These are seeded 1:251 packs.

		MT
Complete Set (8):		250.00
Common Player:		20.00
Inserted 1:251		
VC	Vinny Castilla	20.00
JD	J.D. Drew	40.00
JR	Ken Griffey Jr.	100.00
VG	Vladimir Guerrero	25.00
TG	Tony Gwynn	40.00
TH	Todd Helton	25.00
TL	Travis Lee	20.00
IR	Ivan Rodriguez	35.00

1999 SPx 500 Club Piece of History

Each of these approximately 350 cards include a piece of game-used Louisville Slugger once swung by Wilie Mays. Mays also signed 24 of his Piece of History cards.

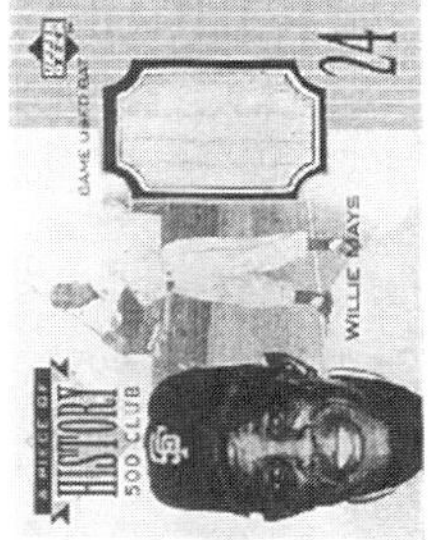

		MT
WM	Willie Mays (350)	180.00
WM	Willie Mays Auto./24	350.00

2000 SP Authentic

The 135-card base set is composed of 90 regular cards, 30 Future Watch subset cards (serial numbered to 2,500) and 15 SP Superstars (serial numbered to 2,500). The regular cards have a gold foiled stamped line around the player image with a matte finished white border around the player image. The player name is stamped in gold foil in the top portion and the SP Authentic logo is stamped in silver foil. Card backs have a small photo, a brief career note and up to the past five seasons of complete statistics. Five-card packs carried a $4.99 SRP.

		MT
Complete Set (135):		400.00
Common Player:		.20
Common (91-105):		4.00
Production 2,500 sets		
Common (106-135):		8.00
Production 2,500 sets		
Pack (5):		5.00
Box (24):		110.00
1	Mo Vaughn	.75
2	Troy Glaus	1.00
3	Jason Giambi	.30
4	Tim Hudson	.40
5	Eric Chavez	.30
6	Shannon Stewart	.20
7	Raul Mondesi	.30
8	Carlos Delgado	1.00
9	Jose Canseco	.60
10	Vinny Castilla	.20
11	Greg Vaughn	.30
12	Manny Ramirez	1.00
13	Roberto Alomar	.75
14	Jim Thome	.50
15	Richie Sexson	.20
16	Alex Rodriguez	3.00
17	Fred Garcia	.20
18	John Olerud	.40
19	Albert Belle	.60
20	Cal Ripken Jr.	3.00
21	Mike Mussina	.50
22	Ivan Rodriguez	1.00
23	Gabe Kapler	.40
24	Rafael Palmeiro	.50
25	Nomar Garciaparra	2.50
26	Pedro Martinez	1.00
27	Carl Everett	.20
28	Carlos Beltran	.20
29	Jermaine Dye	.20
30	Juan Gonzalez	1.00
31	Dean Palmer	.20
32	Corey Koskie	.20
33	Jacque Jones	.20
34	Frank Thomas	1.50
35	Paul Konerko	.20
36	Magglio Ordonez	.40
37	Bernie Williams	.75
38	Derek Jeter	2.50
39	Roger Clemens	1.50
40	Mariano Rivera	.40
41	Jeff Bagwell	1.00
42	Craig Biggio	.50
43	Jose Lima	.20
44	Moises Alou	.20
45	Chipper Jones	2.00
46	Greg Maddux	2.00
47	Andruw Jones	.75
48	Kevin Millwood	.20
49	Jeromy Burnitz	.20
50	Geoff Jenkins	.40
51	Mark McGwire	4.00
52	Fernando Tatis	.40
53	J.D. Drew	.40
54	Sammy Sosa	2.50
55	Kerry Wood	.50
56	Mark Grace	.40
57	Matt Williams	.50
58	Randy Johnson	1.00
59	Erubiel Durazo	.20
60	Gary Sheffield	.50
61	Kevin Brown	.40
62	Shawn Green	.50
63	Vladimir Guerrero	1.50
64	Michael Barrett	.20
65	Barry Bonds	1.50
66	Jeff Kent	.20
67	Russ Ortiz	.20
68	Preston Wilson	.20
69	Mike Lowell	.20
70	Mike Piazza	2.50
71	Mike Hampton	.20
72	Robin Ventura	.40
73	Edgardo Alfonzo	.40
74	Tony Gwynn	1.50
75	Ryan Klesko	.20
76	Trevor Hoffman	.20
77	Scott Rolen	.75
78	Bob Abreu	.30
79	Mike Lieberthal	.20
80	Curt Schilling	.30
81	Jason Kendall	.30
82	Brian Giles	.20
83	Kris Benson	.20
84	Ken Griffey Jr.	3.00
85	Sean Casey	.40
86	Pokey Reese	.20
87	Barry Larkin	.75
88	Larry Walker	.50
89	Todd Helton	1.00
90	Jeff Cirillo	.20
91	Ken Griffey Jr. SP Superstars)	15.00
92	Mark McGwire (SP Superstars)	20.00
93	Chipper Jones (SP Superstars)	10.00
94	Derek Jeter (SP Superstars)	12.00
95	Shawn Green (SP Superstars)	4.00
96	Pedro Martinez (SP Superstars)	5.00
97	Mike Piazza (SP Superstars)	12.00
98	Alex Rodriguez (SP Superstars)	15.00
99	Jeff Bagwell (SP Superstars)	5.00
100	Cal Ripken Jr. (SP Superstars)	15.00
101	Sammy Sosa (SP Superstars)	12.00
102	Barry Bonds (SP Superstars)	6.00
103	Jose Canseco (SP Superstars)	4.00
104	Nomar Garciaparra (SP Superstars)	12.00
105	Ivan Rodriguez (SP Superstars)	5.00
106	Rick Ankiel (Future Watch)	12.00
107	Pat Burrell (Future Watch)	30.00
108	Vernon Wells (Future Watch)	8.00
109	Nick Johnson Future Watch)	12.00
110	Kip Wells (Future Watch)	8.00
111	Matt Riley (Future Watch)	8.00
112	Alfonso Soriano (Future Watch)	12.00
113	Josh Beckett (Future Watch)	15.00
114	*Danys Baez* (Future Watch)	10.00
115	Travis Dawkins (Future Watch)	10.00
116	Eric Gagne (Future Watch)	8.00
117	*Mike Lamb* (Future Watch)	20.00
118	Eric Munson (Future Watch)	12.00
119	*Wilfredo Rodriguez* (Future Watch)	8.00
120	*Kazuhiro Sasaki* (Future Watch)	25.00
121	Chad Hutchinson (Future Watch)	8.00
122	Peter Bergeron (Future Watch)	10.00
123	*Wascar Serrano* (Future Watch)	10.00
124	Tony Armas Jr. (Future Watch)	12.00
125	Ramon Ortiz (Future Watch)	8.00
126	Adam Kennedy (Future Watch)	10.00
127	Joe Crede (Future Watch)	12.00
128	Roosevelt Brown (Future Watch)	8.00
129	Mark Mulder (Future Watch)	8.00
130	Brad Penny (Future Watch)	8.00
131	Terrence Long (Future Watch)	10.00
132	Ruben Mateo (Future Watch)	10.00
133	Wily Mo Pena (Future Watch)	15.00
134	Rafael Furcal (Future Watch)	10.00
135	Mario Encarnacion (Future Watch)	8.00

2000 SP Authentic Limited

A parallel to the 135-card base set these have "SP Limited" printed down the right side of the front and are serial numbered on the card front in an edition of 100 sets.

	MT
Cards (1-90):	15-25X
Cards (91-105):	3-5X
Cards (106-135):	1-2X
Production 100 sets	

2000 SP Authentic Chirography

This autographed insert set has a horizontal format with two player images on the card front. The player signature appears in the top right portion over a silver, checkered background. The insert name and logo have a silver tint. Card backs are numbered with the featured players first and last initial. Chirographies are seeded 1:23 packs.

		MT
Common Player:		10.00
Inserted 1:23		
RA	Rick Ankiel	15.00
CBe	Carlos Beltran	10.00
BB	Barry Bonds	60.00
PB	Pat Burrell	35.00
JC	Jose Canseco	50.00
SC	Sean Casey	15.00
RC	Roger Clemens	75.00
ED	Erubiel Durazo	10.00
TGl	Troy Glaus	35.00
VG	Vladimir Guerrero	60.00
TG	Tony Gwynn	60.00
DJ	Derek Jeter	150.00
NJ	Nick Johnson	20.00
CJ	Chipper Jones	75.00
AJ	Andruw Jones	35.00
SK	Sandy Koufax	200.00
BP	Ben Petrick	10.00
MQ	Mark Quinn	15.00
MR	Manny Ramirez	50.00
CR	Cal Ripken Jr.	175.00
AR	Alex Rodriguez	150.00
IR	Ivan Rodriguez	50.00
SR	Scott Rolen	25.00
AS	Alfonso Soriano	30.00
MV	Mo Vaughn	30.00
EY	Ed Yarnall	10.00

2000 SP Authentic Chirography Gold

Golds use the same photos as the regular Chirography inserts and can be differentiated by the gold checkered background of the player signature in the upper right portion as well as the gold tint in the insert name and logo. Golds are also hand-numbered to the player's jersey number on the card front and are numbered with a "G" prefix on the card back before the players initials.

		MT
Common Player:		
RA	Rick Ankiel/66 EXCH	80.00
JB	Jeff Bagwell/5 EXCH	
JOB	John Bale/49	
CBe	Carlos Beltran/15	75.00
BB	Barry Bonds/25	275.00
PB	Pat Burrell/33 EXCH	150.00
JC	Jose Canseco/33	150.00
SC	Sean Casey/21	75.00
EC	Eric Chavez/3	
RC	Roger Clemens /22	325.00
JD	J.D. Drew	
ED	Erubiel Durazo/44	40.00
RF	Rafael Furcal/1	
JG	Jason Giambi/16	
TGl	Troy Glaus/14	
VG	Vladimir Guerrero /27	125.00
WG	Wilton Guerrero/4	
TG	Tony Gwynn/19	325.00
DJ	Derek Jeter/2	
NJ	Nick Johnson/63	40.00
AJ	Andruw Jones/25 EXCH	
CJ	Chipper Jones/10 EXCH	
JK	Josh Kalinowski/62	
SK	Sandy Koufax/32	
JL	Jose Lima/42 EXCH	
KL	Kenny Lofton/7	
JMA	Joe Mays/53	
JMO	Jim Morris/63	
EM	Eric Munson/17	
RP	Robert Person/31	
BP	Ben Petrick/15	40.00
MQ	Mark Quinn/14	
MR	Manny Ramirez/24 EXCH	175.00
MRI	Matt Riley/25	
CR	Cal Ripken Jr./8	
AR	Alex Rodriguez/3 EXCH	
IR	Ivan Rodriguez/7	
SR	Scott Rolen/17 EXCH	
AS	Alfonso Soriano /53	60.00
MV	Mo Vaughn/42	50.00
VW	Vernon Wells/3	
EY	Ed Yarnall/41	30.00

2000 SP Authentic Joe DiMaggio Game Jersey

This is DiMaggio's first Game Jersey insert and has three different versions. The first is limited to 500 total cards, the second version is Gold and numbered to 56. The rarest version has a DiMaggio cut signature along with a piece of his game-used jersey and is limited to only five total cards.

		MT
DiMaggio Jersey card		
JD	Joe DiMaggio jersey /500	600.00
JD	Joe DiMaggio jersey gold/56	1200.
JD	Joe DiMaggio jersey/auto/5	

2000 SP Authentic Midsummer Classics

This 10-card set spotlights perennial All-Stars and has a silver holo-foiled front with gold foil etching and stamping. These are found 1:12 packs and are numbered on the card back with an "MC" prefix.

		MT
Complete Set (10):		
Common Player:		1.50
Inserted 1:12		
1	Cal Ripken Jr.	6.00
2	Roger Clemens	3.00
3	Jeff Bagwell	2.00
4	Barry Bonds	2.00
5	Jose Canseco	1.50
6	Frank Thomas	3.00
7	Mike Piazza	5.00
8	Tony Gwynn	3.00
9	Juan Gonzalez	2.00
10	Greg Maddux	4.00

2000 SP Authentic Premier Performers

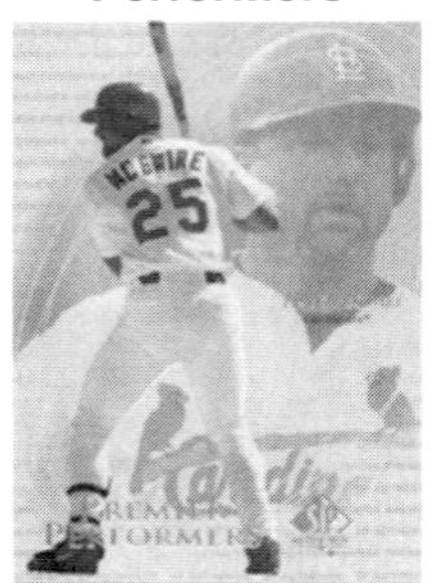

This 10-card set spotlight baseball's best on a silver holo- foiled card front with the player name, insert name and logo stamped in gold foil. Card backs are numbered with an "PP" prefix and are found 1:12 packs.

		MT
Complete Set (10):		40.00
Common Player:		2.00
Inserted 1:12		
1	Mark McGwire	8.00
2	Alex Rodriguez	6.00
3	Cal Ripken Jr.	6.00
4	Nomar Garciaparra	5.00
5	Ken Griffey Jr.	6.00
6	Chipper Jones	4.00
7	Derek Jeter	5.00
8	Ivan Rodriguez	2.00
9	Vladimir Guerrero	3.00
10	Sammy Sosa	5.00

2000 SP Authentic SP Supremacy

This seven-card set has a silver foiled card front with the insert name and logo stamped in gold foil. The inserts are found on the average of 1:23 packs and are numbered with a "S" prefix.

		MT
Complete Set (7):		20.00
Common Player:		2.00
Inserted 1:23		
1	Alex Rodriguez	8.00
2	Shawn Green	2.00
3	Pedro Martinez	2.50
4	Chipper Jones	5.00
5	Tony Gwynn	4.00
6	Ivan Rodriguez	2.50
7	Jeff Bagwell	2.50

2000 SP Authentic SP Cornerstones

Printed on a silver holo-foiled card front a close-up image of the player appears in a baseball diamond shaped enclosed by gold foil etching. Another shadow image of the featured player appears in the background.

The player name, insert name and logo are stamped in gold foil. These are seeded 1:23 packs and are numbered with a "C" prefix on the card back.

		MT
Complete Set (7):		40.00
Common Player:		2.00
Inserted 1:23		
1	Ken Griffey Jr.	8.00
2	Cal Ripken Jr.	8.00
3	Mike Piazza	6.00
4	Derek Jeter	6.00
5	Mark McGwire	10.00
6	Nomar Garciaparra	6.00
7	Sammy Sosa	6.00

2000 SP Authentic SP Buyback

This autographed set features previously issued SP cards that were re-purchased by Upper Deck. The cards are autographed by the featured player and hand-numbered on the card front. The number autographed and released by Upper Deck is listed after the player name. Buybacks are found 1:95 packs.

		MT
Complete Set (140):		
Common Player:		
1	Jeff Bagwell Exch.	50.00
2	Craig Biggio '93/59	50.00
3	Craig Biggio '94/69	50.00
4	Craig Biggio '95/171	90.00
5	Craig Biggio '96/71	50.00
6	Craig Biggio '97/46	70.00
7	Craig Biggio '98/40	75.00
8	Craig Biggio '99/125	40.00
9	Barry Bonds '93/12	
10	Barry Bonds '94/12	
11	Barry Bonds '95/21	
12	Barry Bonds '96	
13	Barry Bonds '97	
14	Barry Bonds '98/22	
15	Barry Bonds '99/520	75.00
16	Jose Canseco '93/29	200.00
17	Jose Canseco '94/20	250.00
18	Jose Canseco '95	
19	Jose Canseco '96/23	250.00
20	Jose Canseco '97/23	250.00
21	Jose Canseco '98/24	250.00
22	Jose Canseco '99/502	50.00
23	Sean Casey '98	
24	Sean Casey '99/139	25.00
25	Roger Clemens '93/68	25.00
26	Roger Clemens '94/60	25.00
27	Roger Clemens '95/68	25.00
28	Roger Clemens '96/68	
29	Roger Clemens '97/7	
30	Roger Clemens '98/25	300.00
31	Roger Clemens '99/134	100.00
32	Jason Giambi '97/34	60.00
33	Jason Giambi '98/25	90.00
34	Tom Glavine '93/99	50.00
35	Tom Glavine '94/107	40.00
36	Tom Glavine '95/97	50.00
37	Tom Glavine '96/42	75.00
38	Tom Glavine '98/40	75.00
39	Tom Glavine '99/138	40.00
40	Shawn Green '96/55	60.00
41	Shawn Green '99/530	30.00
42	Ken Griffey Jr. '96/12	300.00
43	Tony Gwynn '93	
44	Tony Gwynn '94	
45	Tony Gwynn '95	
46	Tony Gwynn '96	
47	Tony Gwynn '97/24	300.00
48	Tony Gwynn '98	
49	Tony Gwynn '99/129	80.00
50	Tony Gwynn '99/369	60.00
51	Derek Jeter '93	
52	Derek Jeter '95/17	
53	Derek Jeter '96	
54	Derek Jeter '97	
55	Derek Jeter '98/11	
56	Derek Jeter '99/119	200.00
57	Randy Johnson '93/60	100.00
58	Randy Johnson '94/45	120.00
59	Randy Johnson '95/70	100.00
60	Randy Johnson '96/60	100.00
61	Randy Johnson '97	
62	Randy Johnson '98	
63	Randy Johnson '99/113	75.00
64	Andruw Jones Exch.	60.00
65	Chipper Jones Exch.	100.00
66	Kenny Lofton '94/100	30.00
67	Kenny Lofton '95/84	30.00
68	Kenny Lofton '96/34	60.00
69	Kenny Lofton '97/82	30.00
70	Kenny Lofton '98/21	100.00
71	Kenny Lofton '99/99	30.00
72	Javy Lopez '93/106	20.00
73	Javy Lopez '94/160	25.00
74	Javy Lopez '96/99	20.00
75	Javy Lopez '97/61	20.00
76	Javy Lopez '98	
77	Greg Maddux '93/22	375.00
78	Greg Maddux '94/19	375.00
79	Greg Maddux '95	
80	Greg Maddux '96	
81	Greg Maddux '97/8	
82	Greg Maddux '98/11	
83	Greg Maddux '99/504	75.00
84	Paul O'Neill '93/110	25.00
85	Paul O'Neill '94/97	30.00
86	Paul O'Neill '95/142	25.00
87	Paul O'Neill '96/70	30.00
88	Paul O'Neill '98/23	75.00
89	Mario Ramirez Exch.	50.00
90	Cal Ripken Jr. '93/7	
91	Cal Ripken Jr. '94/22	600.00
92	Cal Ripken Jr. '95/10	
93	Cal Ripken Jr. '96/12	
94	Cal Ripken Jr. '97/12	
95	Cal Ripken Jr. '98/13	
96	Cal Ripken Jr. '99/510	125.00
97	Alex Rodriguez Exch.	200.00
98	Ivan Rodriguez '93/29	150.00
99	Ivan Rodriguez '94	
100	Ivan Rodriguez '95/18	200.00
101	Ivan Rodriguez '96/22	200.00
102	Ivan Rodriguez '97/14	
103	Ivan Rodriguez '98/27	150.00
104	Ivan Rodriguez '99/2	
105	Frank Thomas '93	
106	Frank Thomas '94	
107	Frank Thomas '95/5	
108	Frank Thomas '96/10	
109	Frank Thomas '97/20	300.00
110	Frank Thomas '98	
111	Frank Thomas '99/100	120.00
112	Greg Vaughn '93/79	30.00
113	Greg Vaughn '94/75	30.00
114	Greg Vaughn '95/155	25.00
115	Greg Vaughn '96/113	25.00
116	Greg Vaughn '97	
117	Greg Vaughn '99/527	15.00
118	Mo Vaughn '93/119	30.00
119	Mo Vaughn '94/96	40.00
120	Mo Vaughn '95/121	30.00
121	Mo Vaughn '96/114	30.00
122	Mo Vaughn '97/61	40.00
123	Mo Vaughn '98	
124	Mo Vaughn '99/537	20.00
125	Robin Ventura '93/59	30.00
126	Robin Ventura '94/49	40.00
127	Robin Ventura '95/125	25.00
128	Robin Ventura '96/55	30.00
129	Robin Ventura '97/44	50.00
130	Robin Ventura '98/28	60.00
131	Robin Ventura '99/370	20.00
132	Matt Williams '93	
133	Matt Williams '94/50	60.00
134	Matt Williams '95/137	40.00
135	Matt Williams '96/77	50.00
136	Matt Williams '97/54	50.00
137	Matt Williams '98/29	100.00
138	Matt Williams '99/529	25.00
139	Preston Wilson '94/249	20.00
140	Preston Wilson '99/195	20.00

2000 SP Authentic United Nations

Done on a horizontal format this 10-card set salutes the top international stars of the game. The featured player's country of origin flag is in the background of the player image. The card design features silver holofoil and silver foil etching and stamping. These are seeded 1:4 packs and are numbered with an "UN" prefix on the card back.

		MT
Complete Set (10):		10.00
Common Player:		.75
Inserted 1:4		
1	Sammy Sosa (Dominican Rep.)	2.50
2	Ken Griffey Jr. (USA)	3.00
3	Orlando Hernandez (Cuba)	.75
4	Andres Galarraga (Venezuela)	1.00
5	Kazuhiro Sasaki (Japan)	2.00
6	Larry Walker (Canada)	.75
7	Vinny Castilla (Mexico)	.75
8	Andruw Jones (Neth. Antilles)	1.00
9	Ivan Rodriguez (Puerto Rico)	1.00
10	Chan Ho Park (So. Korea)	.75

2000 SP Authentic 3,000 Hit Club

A continuation of Upper Deck's cross brand salute to players who have reached the magical 3,000 hit milestone. 350 game- used bat cards and five bat/cut signature combos were issued for each player.

		MT
PW	Paul Waner bat/350	250.00
TS	Tris Speaker bat/350	250.00
PW	Paul Waner bat/auto/5	
TS	Tris Speaker bat/auto/5	

2000 SPx

The base set consists of 120-cards including 30 Rookie/ Young Star subset cards which has three tiers. The first five are numbered to 1,000, the next 22 autographed and numbered to 1,500 and the final three are autographed and numbered to 500. Each base card has a holo-foiled front with the SPx logo, player name, team name stamped in gold foil.

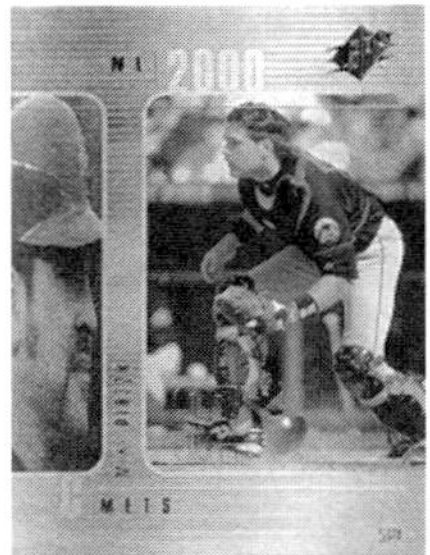

		MT
Complete Set (120):		800.00
Common Player:		.25
Common Rookie (91-120):		15.00
Pack (4):		7.00
Wax Box (18):		120.00
1	Troy Glaus	1.50
2	Mo Vaughn	.75
3	Ramon Ortiz	.25
4	Jeff Bagwell	1.25
5	Moises Alou	.40
6	Craig Biggio	.75
7	Jose Lima	.25
8	Jason Giambi	.50
9	John Jaha	.25
10	Matt Stairs	.25
11	Chipper Jones	2.50
12	Greg Maddux	2.50
13	Andres Galarraga	1.00
14	Andruw Jones	.75
15	Jeromy Burnitz	.40
16	Ron Belliard	.25
17	Carlos Delgado	1.00
18	David Wells	.25
19	Tony Batista	.25
20	Shannon Stewart	.25
21	Sammy Sosa	3.00
22	Mark Grace	.50
23	Henry Rodriguez	.25
24	Mark McGwire	5.00
25	J.D. Drew	.40
26	Luis Gonzalez	.25
27	Randy Johnson	1.00
28	Matt Williams	.75
29	Steve Finley	.25
30	Shawn Green	1.00
31	Kevin Brown	.50
32	Gary Sheffield	.50
33	Jose Canseco	1.25
34	Greg Vaughn	.50
35	Vladimir Guerrero	2.00
36	Michael Barrett	.25
37	Russ Ortiz	.25
38	Barry Bonds	1.50
39	Jeff Kent	.25
40	Richie Sexson	.25
41	Manny Ramirez	1.25
42	Jim Thome	.75
43	Roberto Alomar	1.00
44	Edgar Martinez	.40
45	Alex Rodriguez	4.00
46	John Olerud	.50
47	Alex Gonzalez	.25
48	Cliff Floyd	.25
49	Mike Piazza	3.00
50	Al Leiter	.40
51	Robin Ventura	.50
52	Edgardo Alfonzo	.50
53	Albert Belle	.75
54	Cal Ripken Jr.	4.00
55	B.J. Surhoff	.25
56	Tony Gwynn	2.50
57	Trevor Hoffman	.25
58	Brian Giles	.40
59	Jason Kendall	.40
60	Kris Benson	.25
61	Bob Abreu	.40
62	Scott Rolen	1.25
63	Curt Schilling	.40
64	Mike Lieberthal	.25
65	Sean Casey	.50
66	Dante Bichette	.50
67	Ken Griffey Jr.	4.00
68	Pokey Reese	.25
69	Mike Sweeney	.25
70	Carlos Febles	.25
71	Ivan Rodriguez	1.25
72	Ruben Mateo	.50
73	Rafael Palmeiro	1.00
74	Larry Walker	1.00
75	Todd Helton	1.00
76	Nomar Garciaparra	3.00
77	Pedro Martinez	1.25
78	Troy O'Leary	.25
79	Jacque Jones	.25
80	Corey Koskie	.25
81	Juan Gonzalez	1.25
82	Dean Palmer	.25
83	Juan Encarnacion	.25
84	Frank Thomas	1.50
85	Magglio Ordonez	.50
86	Paul Konerko	.50
87	Bernie Williams	1.00
88	Derek Jeter	3.00
89	Roger Clemens	2.00
90	Orlando Hernandez	.75
91	Vernon Wells AU-1,000	20.00
92	Rick Ankiel AU-1,000	40.00
93	Eric Chavez AU-1,000	20.00
94	Alfonso Soriano AU-1,000	40.00
95	Eric Gagne AU-1,000	25.00
96	Rob Bell AU-1,500	20.00
97	Matt Riley AU-1,500	20.00
98	Josh Beckett AU-1,500	40.00
99	Ben Petrick AU-1,500	20.00
100	*Rob Ramsay AU-1,500*	20.00
101	Scott Williamson AU-1,500	20.00
102	Doug Davis AU-1,500	20.00
103	Eric Munson AU-1,500	40.00
104	Pat Burrell AU-500	125.00
105	Jim Morris AU-1,500	20.00
106	Gabe Kapler AU-500	40.00
107	Lance Berkman 1,500	15.00
108	Erubiel Durazo AU-1,500	30.00
109	Tim Hudson AU-1,500	25.00
110	Ben Davis AU-1,500	20.00
111	Nick Johnson AU-1,500	40.00
112	Octavio Dotel AU-1,500	20.00
113	Jerry Hairston Jr. 1,500	15.00
114	Ruben Mateo 1,500	20.00
115	Chris Singleton 1,500	20.00
116	Bruce Chen AU-1,500	20.00
117	Derrick Gibson AU-1,500	20.00
118	Carlos Beltran AU-500	50.00
119	Fred Garcia AU-500	20.00
120	Preston Wilson AU-500	20.00

2000 SPx Radiance

A parallel to the 120-card base set these are serially numbered to 100. A one-of-one Spectrum parallel of each base card is also randomly seeded.

	MT
Stars (1-90):	10-20X
Common Yng Star (91-120):	10.00
Production 100 sets	

2000 SPx Foundations

This 10-card set features a holo-foiled front with gold foil stamping. Three miniature action shots appear to the right of a close-up shot of the featured player. Card backs are numbered with an "F" prefix and inserted 1:32 packs.

		MT
Complete Set (10):		80.00
Common Player:		4.00
Inserted 1:32		
1	Ken Griffey Jr.	15.00
2	Nomar Garciaparra	12.00
3	Cal Ripken Jr.	15.00
4	Chipper Jones	10.00
5	Mike Piazza	12.00
6	Derek Jeter	12.00
7	Manny Ramirez	5.00
8	Jeff Bagwell	5.00
9	Tony Gwynn	10.00
10	Larry Walker	4.00

2000 SPx Highlight Heroes

This 10-card set has a horizontal format on a holo-foiled front with gold foil stamping. Card backs are numbered with an "HH" prefix and inserted 1:16 packs.

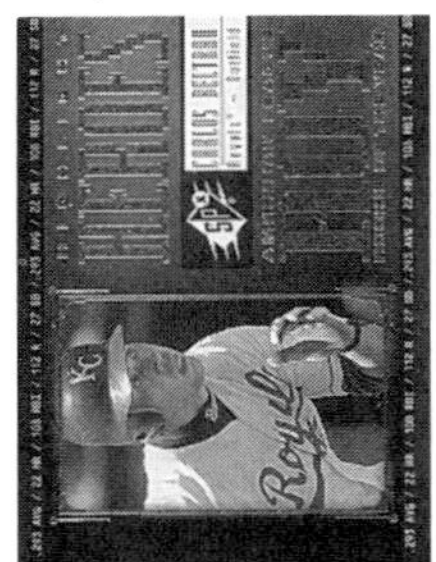

		MT
Complete Set (10):		35.00
Common Player:		1.50
Inserted 1:16		
1	Pedro Martinez	2.50
2	Ivan Rodriguez	2.50
3	Carlos Beltran	1.50
4	Nomar Garciaparra	6.00
5	Ken Griffey Jr.	8.00
6	Randy Johnson	2.00
7	Chipper Jones	5.00
8	Scott Williamson	1.50
9	Larry Walker	2.00
10	Mark McGwire	10.00

2000 SPx Power Brokers

This 20-card set has a horizontal format with the background of the player photo having a kaleidoscope effect. The SPx logo is stamped in gold foil. Card backs are numbered with an "PB" prefix and are inserted 1:8 packs.

		MT
Complete Set (20):		60.00
Common Player:		1.50
Inserted 1:8		
1	Rafael Palmeiro	2.00
2	Carlos Delgado	2.00
3	Ken Griffey Jr.	8.00
4	Matt Stairs	1.50
5	Mike Piazza	6.00
6	Vladimir Guerrero	4.00
7	Chipper Jones	5.00
8	Mark McGwire	10.00
9	Matt Williams	2.00
10	Juan Gonzalez	2.50
11	Shawn Green	2.00
12	Sammy Sosa	6.00
13	Brian Giles	1.50
14	Jeff Bagwell	2.50
15	Alex Rodriguez	8.00
16	Frank Thomas	3.00
17	Larry Walker	2.00
18	Albert Belle	2.00
19	Dean Palmer	1.50
20	Mo Vaughn	2.00

2000 SPx SPxcitement

This 20-card set features a holo-foiled front with gold foil stamping. Card backs are numbered with an "XC" prefix and are inserted 1:4 packs.

		MT
Complete Set (20):		35.00
Common Player:		1.00
Inserted 1:4		
1	Nomar Garciaparra	3.00
2	Mark McGwire	5.00
3	Derek Jeter	3.00
4	Cal Ripken Jr.	4.00
5	Barry Bonds	1.50
6	Alex Rodriguez	4.00
7	Scott Rolen	1.25
8	Pedro Martinez	1.25
9	Sean Casey	1.00
10	Sammy Sosa	3.00
11	Randy Johnson	1.00
12	Ivan Rodriguez	1.25
13	Frank Thomas	1.50
14	Greg Maddux	2.50
15	Tony Gwynn	2.50
16	Ken Griffey Jr.	4.00
17	Carlos Beltran	1.00
18	Mike Piazza	3.00
19	Chipper Jones	2.50
20	Craig Biggio	1.00

2000 SPx SPx Signatures

These autographed inserts are seeded 1:112 packs.

		MT
Common Player:		15.00
Inserted 1:179		
JB	Jeff Bagwell	50.00
JC	Jose Canseco	40.00
SC	Sean Casey	25.00
RC	Roger Clemens	100.00
KG	Ken Griffey Jr.	150.00
VG	Vladimir Guerrero	50.00
TG	Tony Gwynn	50.00
OH	Orlando Hernandez	40.00
DJ	Derek Jeter	200.00
CJ	Chipper Jones	50.00
MR	Manny Ramirez	50.00
CR	Cal Ripken Jr.	150.00
IR	Ivan Rodriguez	50.00
SR	Scott Rolen	35.00

2000 SPx The Heart of the Order

This 20-card set features a top hitter with his teams batting order to the left of his photo. The SPx logo and insert name are stamped in gold foil. Card backs are numbered with an "H" prefix and seeded 1:8 packs.

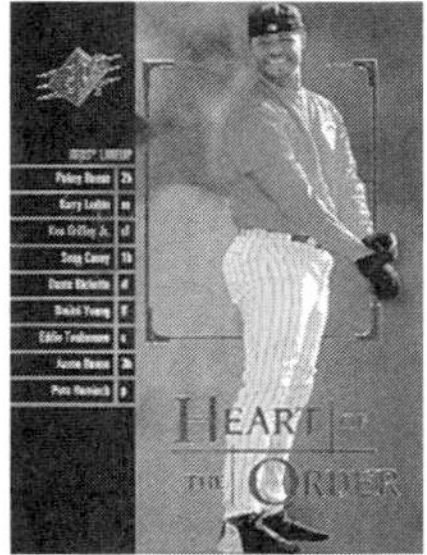

		MT
Complete Set (20):		60.00
Common Player:		1.50
Inserted 1:8		
1	Bernie Williams	2.00
2	Mike Piazza	6.00
3	Ivan Rodriguez	2.50
4	Mark McGwire	10.00
5	Manny Ramirez	2.50
6	Ken Griffey Jr.	8.00
7	Matt Williams	2.00
8	Sammy Sosa	6.00
9	Mo Vaughn	2.00
10	Carlos Delgado	2.00
11	Brian Giles	1.50
12	Chipper Jones	5.00
13	Sean Casey	1.50
14	Tony Gwynn	5.00
15	Barry Bonds	3.00
16	Carlos Beltran	1.50
17	Scott Rolen	2.50
18	Juan Gonzalez	2.50
19	Larry Walker	2.00
20	Vladimir Guerrero	4.00

2000 SPx Untouchable Talents

These inserts have a holo-foiled front and are numbered with an "UT" prefix. They are found on the average of 1:96 packs.

		MT
Complete Set (10):		220.00
Common Player:		10.00
Inserted 1:96		
1	Mark McGwire	50.00
2	Ken Griffey Jr.	40.00
3	Shawn Green	10.00
4	Ivan Rodriguez	15.00
5	Sammy Sosa	30.00
6	Derek Jeter	30.00
7	Sean Casey	10.00
8	Chipper Jones	25.00
9	Pedro Martinez	15.00
10	Vladimir Guerrero	20.00

2000 SPx Winning Materials

Five different tiers make up this memorabilia insert set with players having varying levels of their inserts in the set. Each insert has two pieces of memorabilia, combinations include Jersey/Bat, Jersey/Bat numbered to player's jersey number, Jersey/Cap, Jersey/Ball and Ball/Bat.

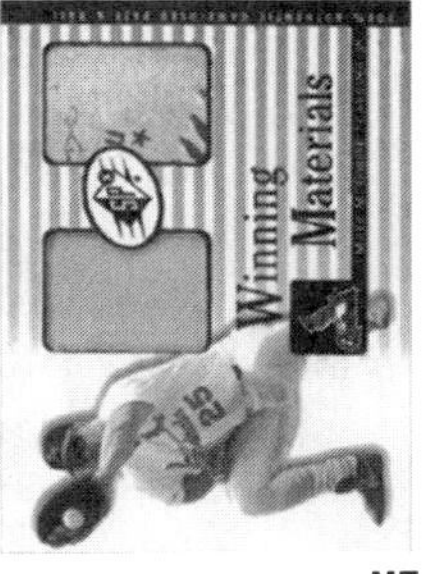

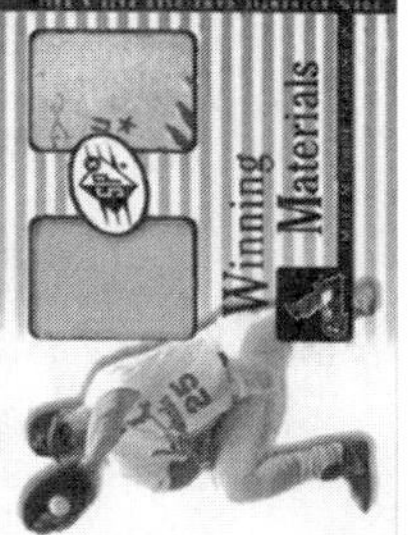

		MT
Common Player:		
AR	Alex Rodriguez bat/jersey	100.00
AR	Alex Rodriguez cap/jersey/100	250.00
AR	Alex Rodriguez ball/jersey/50	375.00
DJ	Derek Jeter bat/jersey	200.00
DJ	Derek Jeter ball/jersey/50	450.00
DJ	Derek Jeter bat/jersey/auto/2	
BB	Barry Bonds bat/jersey	80.00
BB	Barry Bonds cap/jersey/100	150.00
BB	Barry Bonds ball/jersey/auto/25	450.00
JB	Jeff Bagwell bat/jersey	80.00
JB	Jeff Bagwell cap/jersey/100	125.00
JB	Jeff Bagwell ball/jersey/50	200.00
KG	Ken Griffey Jr. bat/jersey	200.00
KG	Ken Griffey Jr. ball/jersey/50	350.00
KG	Ken Griffey Jr. jersey/bat/auto/24	750.00
TG	Tony Gwynn bat/jersey	75.00
TG	Tony Gwynn ball/jersey/50	200.00
TG	Tony Gwynn Cap/Jersey/100	150.00
BW	Bernie Williams bat/jersey	60.00
EC	Eric Chavez bat/jersey	40.00
EC	Eric Chavez cap/jersey/100	75.00
GM	Greg Maddux bat/jersey	125.00
IR	Ivan Rodriguez bat/jersey	75.00
JC	Jose Canseco bat/jersey	80.00
JL	Javy Lopez bat/jersey	50.00
JL	Javy Lopez cap/jersey/100	80.00
MM	Mark McGwire base/ball/500	200.00
MR	Manny Ramirez bat/jersey	75.00
MR	Manny Ramirez bat/jersey/auto./24	
MW	Matt Williams bat/jersey	50.00
PM	Pedro Martinez cap/jersey/100	200.00
PO	Paul O'Neill bat/jersey	50.00
VG	Vladimir Guerrero bat/jersey	75.00
VG	Vladimir Guerrero cap/jersey/100	125.00
VG	Vladimir Guerrero ball/jersey/50	200.00
TG	Troy Glaus bat/jersey	70.00

2000 SPx 3,000 Hit Club

A continuation of Upper Deck's cross brand insert program. This sets pays tribute to Ty Cobb with three variations. The collection includes 350 bat cards, three cut signatures and one bat/cut signature card.

		MT
TC-B	Ty Cobb bat/350	700.00
TC	Ty Cobb bat/cut/3	

2001 SP Authentic Sample

Base cards in the forthcoming SP Authentic issue were previewed with this card. In a format identical to the regularly issued version, the promo card has a large black "SAMPLE" overprinted diagonally on back.

		MT
90	Ken Griffey Jr.	3.00

2001 SP Authentic

		MT
Common Player:		.25
Common SP (91-135):		10.00
Production 1,250		
Common SP (136-180):		2.00
Production 1,250		
Pack (5):		3.75
Box (24):		85.00
1	Troy Glaus	1.25
2	Darin Erstad	.75

No.	Player	Price
3	Jason Giambi	.75
4	Tim Hudson	.50
5	Eric Chavez	.40
6	Miguel Tejada	.50
7	Jose Ortiz	.25
8	Carlos Delgado	1.00
9	Tony Batista	.25
10	Raul Mondesi	.25
11	Aubrey Huff	.25
12	Greg Vaughn	.25
13	Roberto Alomar	1.00
14	Juan Gonzalez	1.25
15	Jim Thome	.75
16	Omar Vizquel	.40
17	Edgar Martinez	.40
18	Fred Garcia	.25
19	Cal Ripken Jr.	4.00
20	Ivan Rodriguez	1.25
21	Rafael Palmeiro	.75
22	Alex Rodriguez	3.00
23	Manny Ramirez	1.25
24	Pedro Martinez	1.50
25	Nomar Garciaparra	3.00
26	Mike Sweeney	.25
27	Jermaine Dye	.25
28	Bobby Higginson	.25
29	Dean Palmer	.25
30	Matt Lawton	.25
31	Eric Milton	.25
32	Frank Thomas	1.25
33	Magglio Ordonez	.40
34	David Wells	.25
35	Paul Konerko	.25
36	Derek Jeter	4.00
37	Bernie Williams	1.00
38	Roger Clemens	1.50
39	Mike Mussina	.75
40	Jorge Posada	.50
41	Jeff Bagwell	1.25
42	Richard Hidalgo	.25
43	Craig Biggio	.50
44	Greg Maddux	2.50
45	Chipper Jones	2.50
46	Andruw Jones	.75
47	Rafael Furcal	.40
48	Tom Glavine	.50
49	Jeromy Burnitz	.25
50	Jeffrey Hammonds	.25
51	Mark McGwire	4.00
52	Jim Edmonds	.40
53	Rick Ankiel	.40
54	J.D. Drew	.50
55	Sammy Sosa	2.50
56	Corey Patterson	.50
57	Kerry Wood	.50
58	Randy Johnson	1.25
59	Luis Gonzalez	1.00
60	Curt Schilling	.40
61	Gary Sheffield	.40
62	Shawn Green	.40
63	Kevin Brown	.25
64	Vladimir Guerrero	1.25
65	Jose Vidro	.25
66	Barry Bonds	2.00
67	Jeff Kent	.40
68	Livan Hernandez	.25
69	Preston Wilson	.25
70	Charles Johnson	.25
71	Ryan Dempster	.25
72	Mike Piazza	3.00
73	Al Leiter	.40
74	Edgardo Alfonzo	.40
75	Robin Ventura	.25
76	Tony Gwynn	1.50
77	Phil Nevin	.25
78	Trevor Hoffman	.25
79	Scott Rolen	.50
80	Pat Burrell	.50
81	Bob Abreu	.25
82	Jason Kendall	.25
83	Brian Giles	.50
84	Kris Benson	.25
85	Ken Griffey Jr.	3.00
86	Barry Larkin	.50
87	Sean Casey	.50
88	Todd Helton	1.25
89	Mike Hampton	.25
90	Larry Walker	.75
91	*Ichiro Suzuki* (Future Watch)	100.00
92	*Wilson Betemit* (Future Watch)	30.00
93	*Adrian Hernandez* (Future Watch)	10.00
94	*Juan Uribe* (Future Watch)	15.00
95	*Travis Hafner* (Future Watch)	12.00
96	*Morgan Ensberg* (Future Watch)	15.00
97	*Sean Douglass* (Future Watch)	15.00
98	*Juan Diaz* (Future Watch)	10.00
99	*Erick Almonte* (Future Watch)	10.00
100	*Ryan Freel* (Future Watch)	10.00
101	*Elpidio Guzman* (Future Watch)	10.00
102	*Christian Parker* (Future Watch)	10.00
103	*Josh Fogg* (Future Watch)	15.00
104	*Bert Snow* (Future Watch)	10.00
105	*Horacio Ramirez* (Future Watch)	10.00
106	*Ricardo Rodriguez* (Future Watch)	10.00
107	*Tyler Walker* (Future Watch)	10.00
108	*Jose Mieses* (Future Watch)	10.00
109	*Billy Sylvester* (Future Watch)	10.00
110	*Martin Vargas* (Future Watch)	10.00
111	*Andres Torres* (Future Watch)	10.00
112	*Greg Miller* (Future Watch)	10.00
113	*Alexis Gomez* (Future Watch)	10.00
114	*Grant Balfour* (Future Watch)	10.00
115	*Henry Mateo* (Future Watch)	10.00
116	*Esix Snead* (Future Watch)	15.00
117	*Jackson Melian* (Future Watch)	15.00
118	*Nate Teut* (Future Watch)	10.00
119	*Tsuyoshi Shinjo* (Future Watch)	30.00
120	*Carlos Valderrama* (Future Watch)	10.00
121	*Johnny Estrada* (Future Watch)	10.00
122	*Jason Michaels* (Future Watch)	10.00
123	*William Ortega* (Future Watch)	10.00
124	*Jason Smith* (Future Watch)	10.00
125	*Brian Lawrence* (Future Watch)	12.00
126	*Albert Pujols* (Future Watch)	100.00
127	*Wilken Ruan* (Future Watch)	10.00
128	*Josh Towers* (Future Watch)	15.00
129	*Kris Keller* (Future Watch)	10.00
130	*Nick Maness* (Future Watch)	10.00
131	*Jack Wilson* (Future Watch)	10.00
132	*Brandon Duckworth* (Future Watch)	25.00
133	*Mike Penney* (Future Watch)	10.00
134	*Jay Gibbons* (Future Watch)	25.00
135	*Cesar Crespo* (Future Watch)	10.00
136	Ken Griffey Jr. (SP Superstars)	12.00
137	Mark McGwire (SP Superstars)	15.00
138	Derek Jeter (SP Superstars)	15.00
139	Alex Rodriguez (SP Superstars)	12.00
140	Sammy Sosa (SP Superstars)	10.00
141	Carlos Delgado (SP Superstars)	4.00
142	Cal Ripken Jr. (SP Superstars)	15.00
143	Pedro Martinez (SP Superstars)	6.00
144	Frank Thomas (SP Superstars)	5.00
145	Juan Gonzalez (SP Superstars)	5.00
146	Troy Glaus (SP Superstars)	5.00
147	Jason Giambi (SP Superstars)	4.00
148	Ivan Rodriguez (SP Superstars)	5.00
149	Chipper Jones (SP Superstars)	10.00
150	Vladimir Guerrero (SP Superstars)	5.00
151	Mike Piazza (SP Superstars)	12.00
152	Jeff Bagwell (SP Superstars)	5.00
153	Randy Johnson (SP Superstars)	5.00
154	Todd Helton (SP Superstars)	5.00
155	Gary Sheffield (SP Superstars)	3.00
156	Tony Gwynn (SP Superstars)	6.00
157	Barry Bonds (SP Superstars)	10.00
158	Nomar Garciaparra (SP Superstars)	12.00
159	Bernie Williams (SP Superstars)	4.00
160	Greg Vaughn (SP Superstars)	2.00
161	David Wells (SP Superstars)	2.00
162	Roberto Alomar (SP Superstars)	4.00
163	Jermaine Dye (SP Superstars)	2.00
164	Rafael Palmeiro (SP Superstars)	4.00
165	Andruw Jones (SP Superstars)	4.00
166	Preston Wilson (SP Superstars)	2.00
167	Edgardo Alfonzo (SP Superstars)	2.00
168	Pat Burrell (SP Superstars)	3.00
169	Jim Edmonds (SP Superstars)	3.00
170	Mike Hampton (SP Superstars)	2.50
171	Jeff Kent (SP Superstars)	3.00
172	Kevin Brown (SP Superstars)	2.50
173	Manny Ramirez (SP Superstars)	5.00
174	Magglio Ordonez (SP Superstars)	3.00
175	Roger Clemens (SP Superstars)	8.00
176	Jim Thome (SP Superstars)	3.00
177	Barry Zito (SP Superstars)	3.00
178	Brian Giles (SP Superstars)	3.00
179	Rick Ankiel (SP Superstars)	3.00
180	Corey Patterson (SP Superstars)	3.00

2001 SP Authentic Limited

	MT
Stars (1-90):	15-25X
SP (91-135):	1-2X
SP (136-180):	2-4X
Production 50 sets	

2001 SP Authentic SP Chirography

		MT
Common Player:		8.00
Inserted 1:72		
EA	Edgardo Alfonzo	10.00
AB	Albert Belle	15.00
CB	Carlos Beltran	10.00
MB	Milton Bradley	8.00
PB	Pat Burrell	20.00
JC	Jose Canseco	35.00
CD	Carlos Delgado	20.00
DD	Darren Dreifort/206	12.00
JD	J.D. Drew	25.00
JE	Jim Edmonds	20.00
DEr	Darin Erstad	15.00
DEs	David Espinosa	8.00
CF	Cliff Floyd	10.00
RF	Rafael Furcal/222	15.00
JG	Jason Giambi	25.00
TrG	Troy Glaus	20.00
LG	Luis Gonzalez /271	45.00
SG	Shawn Green/82	20.00
KG	Ken Griffey Jr/126	150.00
ToG	Tony Gwynn/76	
RH	Rick Helling/211	8.00
ToH	Todd Helton/152	40.00
TiH	Tim Hudson	20.00
RJ	Randy Johnson/143	50.00
AJ	Andruw Jones	25.00
CJ	Chipper Jones/184	50.00
DJ	David Justice	20.00
MK	Mark Kotsay/228	8.00
TL	Travis Lee/226	25.00
AlP	Albert Pujols	120.00
CR	Cal Ripken/109	
AR	Alex Rodriguez/229	75.00
DS	Dane Sardinha	8.00
BS	Ben Sheets	15.00
SS	Sammy Sosa/76	160.00
MS	Mike Sweeney	15.00
MV	Mo Vaughn/103	12.00
RV	Robin Ventura/92	15.00
DW	David Wells	20.00
RW	Rondell White	10.00
MW	Matt Williams	15.00

2001 SP Authentic Chirography Gold

		MT
Common Player:		
G-EA	Edgardo Alfonzo/13	
G-AB	Albert Belle/88	25.00
G-CB	Carlos Beltran/15	
G-MB	Milton Bradley/24	
G-PB	Pat Burrell/5	
G-CD	Carlos Delgado/25	75.00
G-DD	Darren Dreifort/37	25.00
G-JD	J.D. Drew/7	
G-JE	Jim Edmonds/15	
G-DER	Darin Erstad/17	
G-DES	David Espinosa/79	25.00
G-CF	Cliff Floyd/30	
G-RF	Rafael Furcal/1	
G-JG	Jason Giambi/16	

G-TRGTroy Glaus/25
G-LGLuis Gonzalez/20
G-SGShawn Green/15
G-KGKen Griffey Jr./30 275.00
G-TOGTony Gwynn/21
G-RHRick Helling/32 25.00
G-TOHTodd Helton/17
G-TIHTim Hudson/15
G-RJ Randy Johnson/51 80.00
G-AJ Andruw Jones/25
G-CJ Chipper Jones/10
G-DJ David Justice/28 40.00
G-MKMark Kotsay/4
G-TL Travis Lee/16
G-ALPAlbert Pujols/5
G-CRCal Ripken Jr./8
G-ARAlex Rodriguez/3
G-DSDane Sardinha/50 25.00
G-BSBen Sheets/15
G-SSSammy Sosa/21
G-MSMike Sweeney/29 35.00
G-MVMo Vaughn/42 25.00
G-RVRobin Ventura/4
G-DWDavid Wells/33 40.00
G-RWRondell White/22
G-MWMatt Williams/9

2001 SP Authentic Buyback Autographs

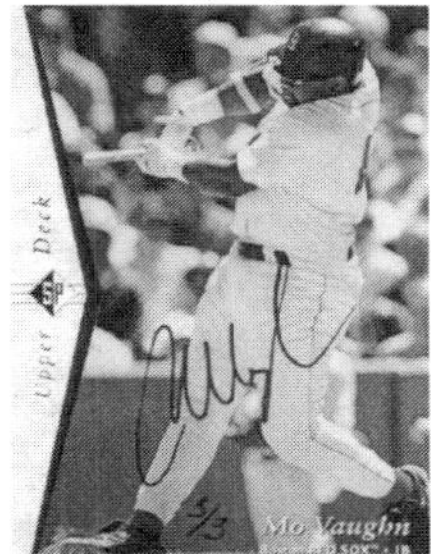

MT

Inserted 1:144

VALUES UNDETERMINED
4 Ken Griffey '93 SP/34
105 Ken Griffey '94 SP/187
190 Ken Griffey '94 SP Silver/2
190 Ken Griffey '95 SP/119
170 Ken Griffey '96 SP/54
165 Ken Griffey '97 SP/7
180 Ken Griffey '98 SP/8
84 Ken Griffey '00 SP/338
188 Alex Rodriguez '95 SP/2
188 Alex Rodriguez '95 SP Red/117
171 Alex Rodriguez '96 SP/74
166 Alex Rodriguez '97 SP/15
179 Alex Rodriguez '98 SP/11
16 Alex Rodriguez '00 SP/341
260 Frank Thomas '93 SP/81
193 Frank Thomas '94 SP/168
140 Frank Thomas '95 SP/3
50 Frank Thomas '97 SP/34
69 Frank Thomas '98 SP/10
34 Frank Thomas '00 SP/218
280 Chipper Jones '93 SP/14
34 Chipper Jones '95 SP/121
26 Chipper Jones '96 SP/74
25 Chipper Jones '97 SP/16
47 Chipper Jones '98 SP/11
45 Chipper Jones '00 SP/312
132 Randy Johnson '93 SP/99
106 Randy Johnson '94 SP/150
189 Randy Johnson '95 SP/6
189 Randy Johnson '95 SP/125
169 Randy Johnson '96 SP/80
167 Randy Johnson '97 SP/8
176 Randy Johnson '98 SP/12
58 Randy Johnson '00 SP/220
275 Carlos Delgado '93 SP/25
41 Carlos Delgado '94 SP/279
181 Carlos Delgado '96 SP/83
179 Carlos Delgado '97 SP/8
194 Carlos Delgado '98 SP/30
8 Carlos Delgado '00 SP/174
50 Jim Edmonds '96 SP/74
19 Jim Edmonds '97 SP/39
32 Jim Edmonds '98 SP/24
167 Tony Gwynn '93 SP/104
130 Tony Gwynn '94 SP/90
105 Tony Gwynn '95 SP/183
160 Tony Gwynn '96 SP/94
155 Tony Gwynn '97 SP/9
170 Tony Gwynn '98 SP/17
74 Tony Gwynn '00 SP/98
133 Jason Giambi '97 SP/15
148 Jason Giambi '98 SP/6
3 Jason Giambi '00 SP/298
9 Ivan Rodriguez '93 SP/90
198 Ivan Rodriguez '95 SP/16
180 Ivan Rodriguez '96 SP/65
170 Ivan Rodriguez '97 SP/8
192 Ivan Rodriguez '98 SP/13
22 Ivan Rodriguez '00 SP/168
206 Mo Vaughn '93 SP/97
157 Mo Vaughn '94 SP/105
125 Mo Vaughn '95 SP/3
125 Mo Vaughn '95 SP/131
40 Mo Vaughn '96 SP/83
35 Mo Vaughn '97 SP/37
57 Mo Vaughn '98 SP/24
1 Mo Vaughn '00 SP/318
1 Andruw Jones '97 SP/21
46 Andruw Jones '98 SP/13
47 Andruw Jones '00 SP/345
22 Edgardo Alfonzo '95 SP/79
136 Edgardo Alfonzo '98 SP/16
73 Edgardo Alfonzo '00 SP/289
10 Barry Bonds '93 SP/77
90 Barry Bonds '94 SP/105
115 Barry Bonds '95 SP/2
115 Barry Bonds '95 SP/31
166 Barry Bonds '96 SP/50
160 Barry Bonds '97 SP/16
175 Barry Bonds '98 SP/16
65 Barry Bonds '00 SP/149
18 Gary Sheffield '93 SP/83
114 Gary Sheffield '94 SP/2
114 Gary Sheffield '94 SP/70
86 Gary Sheffield '96 SP/69
75 Gary Sheffield '97 SP/44
110 Gary Sheffield '98 SP/28
60 Gary Sheffield '00 SP/133
89 Sammy Sosa '93 SP/74
72 Sammy Sosa '94 SP/20
35 Sammy Sosa '95 SP/31
51 Sammy Sosa '96 SP/9
40 Sammy Sosa '97 SP/15
8 Cal Ripken '93 SP/102
126 Cal Ripken '94 SP/38
1 Cal Ripken '95 SP/17
30 Cal Ripken '96 SP/10
187 Cal Ripken '96 SP/24
34 Cal Ripken '97 SP/12
55 Cal Ripken '98 SP/74
20 Cal Ripken '00 SP/300
89 Todd Helton '00 SP/200
4 Tim Hudson '00 SP/300
62 Shawn Green '00 SP/350
52 Fernando Tatis '00 SP/275
57 Matt Williams '00 SP/350
72 Robin Ventura '00 SP/349
2 Troy Glaus '00 SP/350
39 Roger Clemens '00 SP

2001 SP Authentic Cooperstown Calling Game Jersey

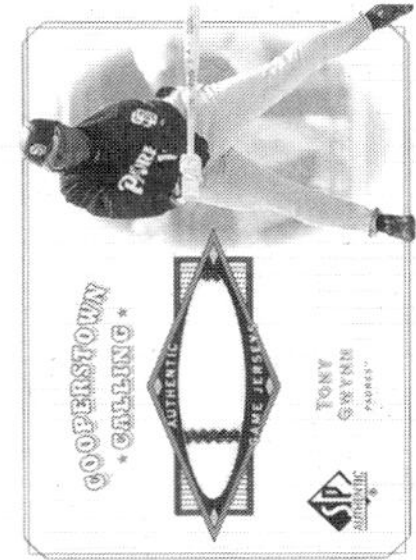

		MT
Common Player:		15.00
Overall jersey odds 1:24		
JB	Jeff Bagwell	25.00
WB	Wade Boggs	20.00
GC	Gary Carter	20.00
RC	Roger Clemens	30.00
AD	Andre Dawson	15.00
SG	Steve Garvey	15.00
GG	Goose Gossage	15.00
TG	Tony Gwynn	20.00
RM	Roger Maris/243	90.00
PM	Pedro Martinez/SP	25.00
DM	Don Mattingly	50.00
BM	Bill Mazeroski	20.00
PM	Paul Molitor	20.00
EM	Eddie Murray	15.00
MP	Mike Piazza/SP	40.00
KP	Kirby Puckett	50.00
MR	Manny Ramirez/SP	25.00
CR	Cal Ripken Jr.	40.00
RS	Ryne Sandberg	40.00
OS	Ozzie Smith	20.00
DW	Dave Winfield	15.00

2001 SP Authentic Combo Game Jersey

		MT
Common Player:		20.00
Overall jersey odds 1:24		
SD	Sammy Sosa, Andre Dawson	50.00
GD	Alex Rodriguez, Ozzie Smith	50.00
RS	Ken Griffey Jr., Joe DiMaggio/98	300.00
SW	Gary Sheffield, Dave Winfield	20.00
MD	Mickey Mantle, Joe DiMaggio/98	400.00
MG	Mickey Mantle, Ken Griffey /98	400.00

A card number in parentheses ( ) indicates the set is unnumbered.

2001 SP Authentic Game Jersey

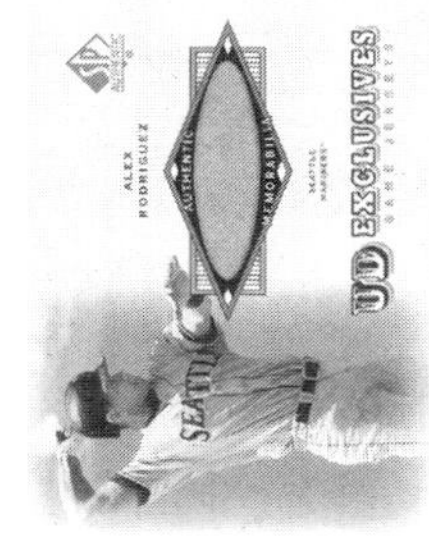

	MT
Common Player:	10.00
Overall jersey odds 1:24	
UD-JDJoe DiMaggio/243	150.00
UD-KGKen Griffey Jr.	30.00
UD-MMMickey Mantle/243	200.00
UD-ARAlex Rodriguez	25.00
UD-GSGary Sheffield	10.00
UD-SSSammy Sosa	30.00

2001 SP Authentic Stars of Japan

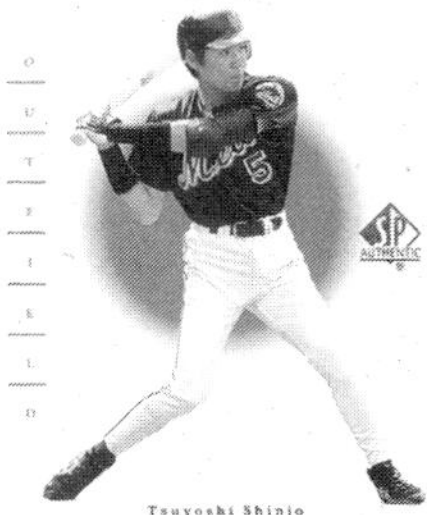

		MT
Complete Set (30):		50.00
Common Player:		1.00
One pack/hobby box		
RS1	Ichiro Suzuki, Tsuyoshi Shinjo	6.00
RS2	Shigetosi Hasegawa, Hideki Irabu	1.00
RS3	Tomokazu Ohka, Mac Suzuki	1.00
RS4	Tsuyoshi Shinjo, Hideki Irabu	2.00
RS5	Ichiro Suzuki, Hideo Nomo	6.00
RS6	Tsuyoshi Shinjo, Mac Suzuki	2.00
RS7	Tsuyoshi Shinjo, Kazuhiro Sasaki	2.00
RS8	Hideo Nomo, Tomokazu Ohka	1.50
RS9	Ichiro Suzuki, Mac Suzuki	6.00
RS10	Hideo Nomo, Shigetosi Hasegawa	1.50
RS11	Hideo Nomo, Masato Yoshii	1.50
RS12	Hideo Nomo, Hideki Irabu	1.50
RS13	Shigetosi Hasegawa, Kazuhiro Sasaki	1.00
RS14	Shigetosi Hasegawa, Mac Suzuki	1.00
RS15	Tsuyoshi Shinjo, Hideo Nomo	2.00
RS16	Tsuyoshi Shinjo, Tomokazu Ohka	2.00
RS17	Ichiro Suzuki, Kazuhiro Sasaki	6.00

RS18 Masato Yoshii, Hideki Irabu 1.00
RS19 Ichiro Suzuki, Tomokazu Ohka 6.00
RS20 Hideki Irabu, Kazuhiro Sasaki 1.00
RS21 Tsuyoshi Shinjo, Masato Yoshii 2.00
RS22 Ichiro Suzuki, Shigetosi Hasegawa 6.00
RS23 Mac Suzuki, Kazuhiro Sasaki 1.00
RS24 Ichiro Suzuki, Hideki Irabu 6.00
RS25 Tomokazu Ohka, Kazuhiro Sasaki 1.00
RS26 Tsuyoshi Shinjo, Shigetosi Hasegawa 2.00
RS27 Masato Yoshii, Kazuhiro Sasaki 1.00
RS28 Hideo Nomo, Kazuhiro Sasaki 1.50
RS29 Ichiro Suzuki, Masato Yoshii 6.00
RS30 Hideo Nomo, Ichiro Suzuki 6.00

2001 SP Authentic Stars of Japan Game Ball

MT
Common Player: 10.00
BB-SH Shigetosi Hasegawa SP/30 30.00
BB-HI Hideki Irabu 10.00
BB-KS Kazuhiro Sasaki 20.00
BB-TS Tsuyoshi Shinjo SP/50 75.00
BB-IS Ichiro Suzuki 150.00
BB-MY Masato Yoshii 15.00

2001 SP Authentic Stars of Japan Game Ball Gold

MT
Common Player: 50.00
Production 25 sets
BB-SH Shigetosi Hasegawa 70.00
BB-HI Hideki Irabu 50.00
BB-KS Kazuhiro Sasaki 100.00
BB-TS Tsuyoshi Shinjo 150.00
BB-IS Ichiro Suzuki 400.00
BB-MY Masato Yoshii 65.00

2001 SP Authentic Stars of Japan Game Ball-Base Combos

MT
Common Card: 25.00
Inserted 1:576
HI-KS Hideki Irabu, Kazuhiro Sasaki SP/30 40.00
HN-KS Hideo Nomo, Kazuhiro Sasaki SP/50 100.00
HN-SH Hideo Nomo, Shigetosi Hasegawa 40.00
IS-KS Ichiro Suzuki, Kazuhiro Sasaki SP/30 225.00
IS-MY Ichiro Suzuki, Masato Yoshii 75.00
IS-SH Ichiro Suzuki, Shigetosi Hasegawa SP/72 150.00
IS-TS Ichiro Suzuki, Tsuyoshi Shinjo SP/40 275.00
MS-KS Mac Suzuki, Kazuhiro Sasaki SP/30 40.00
MY-KS Masato Yoshii, Kazuhiro Sasaki SP/30 40.00
SH-KS Shigetosi Hasegawa, Kazuhiro Sasaki SP/30 40.00
TO-KS Tomokazu Ohka, Kazuhiro Sasaki 25.00
TS-HI Tsuyoshi Shinjo, Hideki Irabu SP/30 75.00
TS-KS Tsuyoshi Shinjo, Kazuhiro Sasaki SP/30 90.00
TS-SH Tsuyoshi Shinjo, Shigetosi Hasegawa SP/30 75.00

2001 SP Auth. Stars of Japan Game Ball-Base Combos Gold

MT
Common Card: 60.00
Production 25 sets
HI-KS Hideki Irabu, Kazuhiro Sasaki 60.00
HN-KS Hideo Nomo, Kazuhiro Sasaki 150.00
HN-SH Hideo Nomo, Shigetosi Hasegawa 150.00
IS-KS Ichiro Suzuki, Kazuhiro Sasaki 400.00
IS-MY Ichiro Suzuki, Masato Yoshii 300.00
IS-SH Ichiro Suzuki, Shigetosi Hasegawa 350.00
IS-TS Ichiro Suzuki, Tsuyoshi Shinjo 500.00
MS-KS Mac Suzuki, Kazuhiro Sasaki 75.00
MY-KS Masato Yoshii, Kazuhiro Sasaki 75.00
SH-KS Shigetosi Hasegawa, Kazuhiro Sasaki 75.00
TO-KS Tomokazu Ohka, Kazuhiro Sasaki 75.00
TS-HI Tsuyoshi Shinjo, Hideki Irabu 100.00
TS-KS Tsuyoshi Shinjo, Kazuhiro Sasaki 125.00
TS-SH Tsuyoshi Shinjo, Shigetosi Hasegawa 100.00

2001 SP Authentic Stars of Japan Game Ball-Base Trio

MT
Complete Set (1):
BBB-RS Kazuhiro Sasaki, Ichiro Suzuki, Hideo Nomo 400.00

2001 SP Auth. Stars of Japan Game Ball-Base Trio Gold

MT
Production 25
BBB-RS Kazuhiro Sasaki, Ichiro Suzuki, Hideo Nomo 700.00

2001 SP Authentic Stars of Japan Game Base

MT
Common Player: 30.00
SH Shigetosi Hasegawa SP/33 40.00
HI Hideki Irabu SP/33 30.00
TO Tomokazu Ohka SP/33 40.00
KS Kazuhiro Sasaki SP/33 75.00
TS Tsuyoshi Shinjo SP/33 100.00
IS Ichiro Suzuki SP/23 200.00
MS Mac Suzuki SP/23 30.00
MY Masato Yoshii SP/33 30.00

2001 SP Authentic Stars of Japan Game Base Gold

MT
Common Player: 50.00
Production 25 sets
SH Shigetosi Hasegawa 50.00
HI Hideki Irabu 50.00
TO Tomokazu Ohka 50.00
KS Kazuhiro Sasaki 80.00
TS Tsuyoshi Shinjo 150.00
IS Ichiro Suzuki 400.00
MS Mac Suzuki 50.00
MY Masato Yoshii 50.00

2001 SP Authentic Stars of Japan Game Bat

MT
Common Player: 10.00
Inserted 1:12
B-HN Hideo Nomo SP/30 100.00
B-TS Tsuyoshi Shinjo SP/30 100.00
B-MY Masato Yoshii 10.00

2001 SP Authentic Stars of Japan Game Bat Gold

MT
Common Player: 40.00
Production 25 sets
B-HN Hideo Nomo 150.00
B-TS Tsuyoshi Shinjo 150.00
B-MY Masato Yoshii 40.00

2001 SP Authentic Stars of Japan Game Jersey-Bat Combos

MT
Common Player: 25.00
BB-HS Shigetosi Hasegawa, Tsuyoshi Shinjo 40.00
JB-NN Hideo Nomo 125.00
JB-SN Kazuhiro Sasaki, Hideo Nomo 75.00
JJ-SH Kazuhiro Sasaki, Shigetosi Hasegawa 25.00

2001 SP Auth. Stars of Japan Game Bat-Jersey Combo Gold

MT
Common Player: 75.00
Production 25 sets
BB-HS Shigetosi Hasegawa, Tsuyoshi Shinjo 100.00
JB-NN Hideo Nomo 225.00
JB-SN Kazuhiro Sasaki, Hideo Nomo 150.00
JJ-SH Kazuhiro Sasaki, Shigetosi Hasegawa 75.00

2001 SP Authentic Stars of Japan Game Jersey

MT
Common Player: 10.00
Inserted 1:12
J-SH Shigetosi Hasegawa 15.00
J-HN Hideo Nomo 50.00
J-KS Kazuhiro Sasaki 20.00
J-TS Tsuyoshi Shinjo 50.00
J-IS Ichiro Suzuki SP/260 EXCH 200.00
J-MY Masato Yoshii 10.00

2001 SP Authentic Stars of Japan Game Jersey Gold

MT
Common Player: 40.00
Production 25 sets
J-SH Shigetosi Hasegawa 40.00
J-HN Hideo Nomo 150.00
J-KS Kazuhiro Sasaki 75.00
J-TS Tsuyoshi Shinjo 150.00
J-MY Masato Yoshii 40.00

2001 SP Authentic Sultan of Swatch Jersey or Pants

MT
Common Card:
Quantity produced listed
SOS1 Babe Ruth/14
SOS2 Babe Ruth/29 650.00
SOS3 Babe Ruth/94 400.00
SOS4 Babe Ruth/54 500.00
SOS5 Babe Ruth/59 500.00
SOS6 Babe Ruth/26 650.00
SOS7 Babe Ruth/27 650.00
SOS8 Babe Ruth/32 650.00
SOS9 Babe Ruth/20 700.00
SOS10 Babe Ruth/21 700.00
SOS11 Babe Ruth/23 700.00
SOS12 Babe Ruth/24 700.00
SOS13 Babe Ruth/26 650.00
SOS14 Babe Ruth/27 650.00
SOS15 Babe Ruth/28 650.00
SOS16 Babe Ruth/29 650.00
SOS17 Babe Ruth/30 650.00
SOS18 Babe Ruth/31 650.00
SOS19 Babe Ruth/33 650.00
SOS20 Babe Ruth/36 650.00
SOS21 Babe Ruth/48 500.00

2001 SP Authentic Sultan of Swatch Jersey/Cut

	MT
Complete Set (3):	
Common Player:	
SOS-JC1Babe Ruth	
SOS-JC2Babe Ruth	
SOS-JC3Babe Ruth	

2001 SP Game Bat

		MT
Complete Set (90):		80.00
Common Player:		.50
Pack (4):		14.00
Box (16):		200.00
1	Troy Glaus	2.00
2	Darin Erstad	1.00
3	Mo Vaughn	.75
4	Jason Giambi	1.00
5	Ben Grieve	1.00
6	Eric Chavez	1.00
7	Carlos Delgado	1.50
8	Tony Batista	.50
9	Shannon Stewart	.50
10	Jose Cruz Jr.	.50
11	Fred McGriff	.75
12	Greg Vaughn	.50
13	Roberto Alomar	1.50
14	Manny Ramirez	2.00
15	Jim Thome	1.00
16	Russ Branyan	.50
17	Alex Rodriguez	5.00
18	John Olerud	.75
19	Edgar Martinez	.50
20	Cal Ripken Jr.	6.00
21	Albert Belle	.75
22	Ivan Rodriguez	2.00
23	Rafael Palmeiro	1.00
24	Nomar Garciaparra	5.00
25	Carl Everett	.50
26	Dante Bichette	.50
27	Mike Sweeney	.50
28	Jermaine Dye	.50
29	Carlos Beltran	.50
30	Juan Gonzalez	2.00
31	Dean Palmer	.50
32	Bobby Higginson	.50
33	Matt Lawton	.50
34	Jacque Jones	.50
35	Frank Thomas	2.50
36	Magglio Ordonez	.75
37	Paul Konerko	.50
38	Carlos Lee	.50
39	Bernie Williams	1.50
40	Derek Jeter	6.00
41	Paul O'Neill	.75
42	Jose Canseco	1.00
43	Ken Caminiti	.50
44	Jeff Bagwell	2.00
45	Craig Biggio	.75
46	Richard Hidalgo	.75
47	Andruw Jones	1.50
48	Chipper Jones	4.00
49	Andres Galarraga	.75
50	B.J. Surhoff	.50
51	Jeromy Burnitz	.50
52	Geoff Jenkins	.50
53	Richie Sexson	.50
54	Mark McGwire	6.00
55	Jim Edmonds	1.00
56	J.D. Drew	.75
57	Fernando Tatis	.50
58	Sammy Sosa	4.00
59	Mark Grace	1.00
60	Eric Young	.50
61	Matt Williams	.75
62	Luis Gonzalez	.75
63	Steve Finley	.50
64	Shawn Green	.75
65	Gary Sheffield	1.00
66	Eric Karros	.75
67	Vladimir Guerrero	2.50
68	Jose Vidro	.50
69	Barry Bonds	2.00
70	Jeff Kent	.75
71	Preston Wilson	.50
72	Mike Lowell	.50
73	Luis Castillo	.50
74	Mike Piazza	5.00
75	Robin Ventura	.75
76	Edgardo Alfonzo	.75
77	Tony Gwynn	4.00
78	Eric Owens	.50
79	Ryan Klesko	.75
80	Scott Rolen	1.50
81	Bobby Abreu	.50
82	Pat Burrell	1.00
83	Brian Giles	.75
84	Jason Kendall	.50
85	Aaron Boone	.50
86	Ken Griffey Jr.	5.00
87	Barry Larkin	1.00
88	Todd Helton	2.00
89	Larry Walker	.75
90	Jeffrey Hammonds	.50

2001 SP Game Bat Big League Hit Parade

		MT
Complete Set (6):		35.00
Common Player:		2.50
Inserted 1:15		
1	Nomar Garciaparra	6.00
2	Ken Griffey Jr.	6.00
3	Sammy Sosa	5.00
4	Alex Rodriguez	8.00
5	Mark McGwire	10.00
6	Ivan Rodriguez	2.50

2001 SP Game Bat In the Swing

		MT
Complete Set (15):		50.00
Common Player:		1.00
Inserted 1:7		
1	Ken Griffey Jr.	6.00
2	Jim Edmonds	1.00
3	Carlos Delgado	2.00
4	Frank Thomas	3.00
5	Barry Bonds	3.00
6	Nomar Garciaparra	6.00
7	Gary Sheffield	1.50
8	Vladimir Guerrero	3.00
9	Alex Rodriguez	8.00
10	Todd Helton	2.50
11	Darin Erstad	1.50
12	Derek Jeter	8.00
13	Sammy Sosa	5.00
14	Mark McGwire	10.00
15	Jason Giambi	1.50

2001 SP Game Bat Lineup Time

		MT
Complete Set (11):		50.00
Common Player:		2.00
Inserted 1:8		
1	Mark McGwire	10.00
2	Roberto Alomar	2.00
3	Alex Rodriguez	8.00
4	Chipper Jones	5.00
5	Ivan Rodriguez	2.50
6	Ken Griffey Jr.	6.00
7	Sammy Sosa	5.00
8	Barry Bonds	3.00
9	Frank Thomas	3.00
10	Pedro Martinez	2.50
11	Derek Jeter	8.00

2001 SP Game Bat Piece of the Game

		MT
Common Player:		8.00
Inserted 1:1		
SP production 1,500 or fewer		
Golds:		3-6X
Production 25 sets		
EA	Edgardo Alfonzo SP	20.00
RA	Roberto Alomar	12.00
SA	Sandy Alomar	8.00
RA	Rick Ankiel	10.00
JB	Jeff Bagwell SP	30.00
TB	Tony Batista	10.00
CB	Carlos Beltran	10.00
JB	Johnny Bench SP	40.00
BB	Barry Bonds	25.00
KB	Kevin Brown SP	20.00
PB	Pat Burrell	20.00
JC	Jose Canseco	15.00
WC	Will Clark	15.00
CD	Carlos Delgado	15.00
JoD	Joe DiMaggio SP	180.00
JD	J.D. Drew	10.00
JE	Jim Edmonds	8.00
DE	Darin Erstad SP	50.00
RF	Rafael Furcal	15.00
BG	Bob Gibson SP	40.00
TGl	Tom Glavine SP	30.00
MG	Mark Grace	25.00
SG	Shawn Green	10.00
KG	Ken Griffey Jr.	65.00
TGw	Tony Gwynn	20.00
TH	Todd Helton	10.00
TH	Todd Hundley SP	20.00
RJ	Reggie Jackson SP	40.00
RJ	Randy Johnson	20.00
AJ	Andruw Jones	10.00
CJ	Chipper Jones	30.00
DJ	David Justice	8.00
KL	Kenny Lofton	8.00
GM	Greg Maddux	25.00
EM	Edgar Martinez	10.00
TM	Tino Martinez	10.00
FM	Fred McGriff SP	30.00
PN	Phil Nevin SP	25.00
JO	John Olerud	12.00
PO	Paul O'Neill	15.00
MO	Magglio Ordonez SP	25.00
MQ	Mark Quinn SP	20.00
MR	Manny Ramirez	15.00
CR	Cal Ripken Jr. SP	50.00
AR	Alex Rodriguez	20.00
IR	Ivan Rodriguez	15.00
SR	Scott Rolen	15.00
NR	Nolan Ryan SP	90.00
TS	Tim Salmon SP	25.00
GS	Gary Sheffield	10.00
SS	Sammy Sosa SP	50.00
SS	Shannon Stewart	8.00
FT	Frank Thomas	10.00
GV	Greg Vaughn	8.00
MV	Mo Vaughn	10.00
RV	Robin Ventura	10.00
BW	Bernie Williams	10.00
MW	Matt Williams	10.00
PW	Preston Wilson	8.00

2001 SP Game Bat Piece of the Game Autograph

		MT
Common Autograph:		50.00
Inserted 1:96		
BB	Barry Bonds	120.00
JC	Jose Canseco	65.00
KG	Ken Griffey Jr.	125.00
TGw	Tony Gwynn	90.00
AJ	Andruw Jones	50.00
AR	Alex Rodriguez	125.00
NR	Nolan Ryan	200.00
FT	Frank Thomas	50.00

2001 SP Game Bat The Lumber Yard

		MT
Complete Set (10):		30.00
Common Player:		1.00
Inserted 1:10		
1	Jason Giambi	1.50
2	Chipper Jones	5.00
3	Carl Everett	1.00
4	Alex Rodriguez	8.00
5	Frank Thomas	3.00
6	Barry Bonds	3.00
7	Jeff Bagwell	2.50
8	Sammy Sosa	5.00
9	Carlos Delgado	2.00
10	Mike Piazza	6.00

2001 SP Game Bat - Milestone

		MT
Complete Set (96):		
Common Player:		.40
Common Rookie (91-96):		15.00
Production 500		
Pack (4):		15.00
Box (10):		125.00
1	Troy Glaus	1.50
2	Darin Erstad	1.00
3	Jason Giambi	1.50
4	Jermaine Dye	.40
5	Eric Chavez	.40
6	Carlos Delgado	1.00
7	Raul Mondesi	.40
8	Shannon Stewart	.40
9	Greg Vaughn	.40
10	Aubrey Huff	.40
11	Juan Gonzalez	2.00
12	Roberto Alomar	1.50
13	Jim Thome	1.00
14	Omar Vizquel	.75
15	Mike Cameron	.40
16	Edgar Martinez	.40
17	John Olerud	.75
18	Bret Boone	.40
19	Cal Ripken Jr.	6.00
20	Tony Batista	.40
21	Alex Rodriguez	5.00
22	Ivan Rodriguez	2.00
23	Rafael Palmeiro	1.50
24	Manny Ramirez	2.00
25	Pedro Martinez	2.50
26	Nomar Garciaparra	5.00
27	Carl Everett	.40
28	Mike Sweeney	.40
29	Neifi Perez	.40

30	Mark Quinn	.40
31	Bobby Higginson	.40
32	Tony Clark	.40
33	Doug Mientkiewicz	.40
34	Cristian Guzman	.40
35	Joe Mays	.40
36	David Ortiz	.40
37	Frank Thomas	2.00
38	Magglio Ordonez	.75
39	Carlos Lee	.40
40	Alfonso Soriano	.75
41	Bernie Williams	1.50
42	Derek Jeter	6.00
43	Roger Clemens	3.00
44	Jeff Bagwell	2.00
45	Richard Hidalgo	.75
46	Moises Alou	.75
47	Chipper Jones	4.00
48	Greg Maddux	4.00
49	Rafael Furcal	.75
50	Andruw Jones	1.00
51	Jeromy Burnitz	.40
52	Geoff Jenkins	.75
53	Richie Sexson	.40
54	Edgar Renteria	.40
55	Mark McGwire	6.00
56	Jim Edmonds	.75
57	J.D. Drew	1.00
58	Sammy Sosa	4.00
59	Bill Mueller	.40
60	Luis Gonzalez	1.50
61	Randy Johnson	2.50
62	Gary Sheffield	.75
63	Shawn Green	.50
64	Kevin Brown	.40
65	Vladimir Guerrero	2.00
66	Jose Vidro	.40
67	Fernando Tatis	.40
68	Barry Bonds	4.00
69	Jeff Kent	.50
70	Rich Aurilia	.40
71	Preston Wilson	.40
72	Charles Johnson	.40
73	Cliff Floyd	.40
74	Mike Piazza	5.00
75	Matt Lawton	.40
76	Edgardo Alfonzo	.40
77	Tony Gwynn	2.50
78	Phil Nevin	.40
79	Scott Rolen	1.50
80	Pat Burrell	1.00
81	Bobby Abreu	.40
82	Brian Giles	1.00
83	Jason Kendall	.40
84	Aramis Ramirez	.40
85	Sean Casey	.75
86	Ken Griffey Jr.	5.00
87	Barry Larkin	1.00
88	Todd Helton	2.00
89	Mike Hampton	.40
90	Larry Walker	1.00
91	*Ichiro Suzuki*	150.00
92	*Albert Pujols*	120.00
93	*Tsuyoshi Shinjo*	35.00
94	*Jack Wilson*	15.00
95	*Donaldo Mendez*	15.00
96	*Junior Spivey*	25.00

2001 SP Game Bat-Milestone P.O.A. Int. Conn. Bat

	MT
Common Player:	5.00
Golds:	3-5X

Production 35 sets

RA	Roberto Alomar	12.00
AB	Adrian Beltre	8.00
RF	Rafael Furcal	10.00
JG	Juan Gonzalez	12.00
AJ	Andruw Jones	10.00
PM	Pedro Martinez	15.00
HN	Hideo Nomo	60.00
MO	Magglio Ordonez	10.00
CP	Chan Ho Park	15.00
JP	Jorge Posada	10.00
AP	Albert Pujols	50.00
MR	Manny Ramirez	15.00
TS	Tsuyoshi Shinjo	40.00
IS	Ichiro Suzuki	175.00
MT	Miguel Tejada	5.00
OV	Omar Vizquel	8.00

2001 SP Game Bat-Milestone P.O.A. Milestone Bat

	MT
Common Player:	5.00
Golds:	3-5X

Production 35 sets

JB	Jeff Bagwell	20.00
BB	Barry Bonds	25.00
RB	Russell Branyan	5.00
JB	Jeromy Burnitz	5.00
RC	Roger Clemens	25.00
DE	Darin Erstad	10.00
LG	Luis Gonzalez	15.00
KG	Ken Griffey Jr.	25.00
TH	Todd Helton	10.00
Chj	Chipper Jones	20.00
MP	Mike Piazza	25.00
CR	Cal Ripken Jr.	50.00
AR	Alex Rodriguez	20.00
GS	Gary Sheffield	5.00
SS	Sammy Sosa	15.00
IS	Ichiro Suzuki	200.00
FT	Frank Thomas	15.00
JT	Jim Thome	8.00

2001 SP Game Bat - Milestone P.O.A. BFH Bat

	MT
Common Player:	8.00
Golds:	3-5X

Production 35 sets

BB	Barry Bonds	25.00
RC	Roger Clemens	25.00
CD	Carlos Delgado	10.00
JG	Jason Giambi	15.00
KG	Ken Griffey Jr.	25.00
TGw	Tony Gwynn	15.00
GM	Greg Maddux	15.00
EM	Edgar Martinez	8.00
FM	Fred McGriff	8.00
RP	Rafael Palmeiro	10.00
MP	Mike Piazza	25.00
CR	Cal Ripken Jr.	50.00
AR	Alex Rodriguez	20.00
IR	Ivan Rodriguez	15.00
SS	Sammy Sosa	20.00

2001 SP Game Bat-Milestone P.O.A. Autograph Bat

	MT
Common Player:	20.00

Inserted 1:100

RB	Russell Branyan	20.00
CD	Carlos Delgado/97	40.00
JDr	J.D. Drew	50.00
JDy	Jermaine Dye	25.00
LG	Luis Gonzalez	50.00
JK	Jason Kendall	25.00
JK	Jeff Kent/194	35.00
AR	Alex Rodriguez/97	100.00
GS	Gary Sheffield/194	25.00
IS	Ichiro Suzuki/53	800.00
MT	Miguel Tejada	40.00
JV	Jose Vidro	20.00
PW	Preston Wilson	20.00

2001 SP Game Bat - Milestone P.O.A. Triple Bat

	MT
Common Card:	15.00

Inserted 1:50

GRS	Ken Griffey Jr., Alex Rodriguez, Sammy Sosa	65.00
JJF	Chipper Jones, Andruw Jones, Rafael Furcal	50.00
RRP	Alex Rodriguez, Ivan Rodriguez, Rafael Palmeiro	50.00
SGB	Gary Sheffield, Shawn Green, Adrian Beltre	20.00
TVA	Jim Thome, Omar Vizquel, Roberto Alomar	50.00
KGR	Jason Kendall, Brian Giles, Aramis Ramirez	20.00
OJC	Paul O'Neill, David Justice, Roger Clemens	50.00
CMG	Roger Clemens, Greg Maddux, Tom Glavine	50.00
VSA	Robin Ventura, Tsuyoshi Shinjo, Edgardo Alfonzo	50.00
OTA	Magglio Ordonez, Frank Thomas, Sandy Alomar	30.00
PWS	Kirby Puckett, Dave Winfield, Ozzie Smith	60.00
GRB	Tony Gwynn, Cal Ripken Jr., Barry Bonds	100.00
GBM	Ken Griffey Jr., Barry Bonds, Fred McGriff	50.00
SFR	Alfonso Soriano, Rafael Furcal, Alex Ramirez	25.00

2001 SP Game Bat - Milestone P.O.A. Quad Bat

	MT
Common Card:	25.00

Inserted 1:50

TVAL	Jim Thome, Omar Vizquel, Roberto Alomar, Kenny Lofton	60.00
RRPM	Alex Rodriguez, Ivan Rodriguez, Rafael Palmeiro, Ruben Mateo	60.00
OJCP	Paul O'Neill, David Justice, Roger Clemens, Jorge Posada	60.00
JJFM	Chipper Jones, Andruw Jones, Rafael Furcal, Greg Maddux	60.00
PWSG	Kirby Puckett, Dave Winfield, Ozzie Smith, Steve Garvey	75.00
GRSB	Ken Griffey Jr., Alex Rodriguez, Sammy Sosa, Barry Bonds	200.00
SGBP	Gary Sheffield, Shawn Green, Adrian Beltre, Chan Ho Park	25.00
GGRR	Ken Griffey Jr., Ken Griffey Jr., Alex Rodriguez, Alex Rodriguez	150.00
GRBM	Tony Gwynn, Cal Ripken Jr., Barry Bonds, Fred McGriff	100.00
TDTA	Frank Thomas, Jermaine Dye, Jim Thome, Roberto Alomar	40.00
GHSK	Luis Gonzalez, Todd Helton, Gary Sheffield, Jeff Kent	30.00
GDBS	Ken Griffey Jr., J.D. Drew, Jeromy Burnitz, Sammy Sosa	60.00
JVBW	Chipper Jones, Robin Ventura, Pat Burrell, Preston Wilson	40.00
RGGM	Alex Rodriguez, Troy Glaus, Jason Giambi, Edgar Martinez	50.00
ONRD	Paul O'Neill, Hideo Nomo, Cal Ripken Jr., Carlos Delgado	90.00

2001 SP Game Bat-Milestone Slugging Sensations

	MT
Complete Set (12):	40.00
Common Player:	1.50

Inserted 1:5
SS1 Troy Glaus 1.50
SS2 Mark McGwire 8.00
SS3 Sammy Sosa 5.00
SS4 Juan Gonzalez 2.50
SS5 Barry Bonds 5.00
SS6 Jeff Bagwell 2.50
SS7 Jason Giambi 2.00
SS8 Ivan Rodriguez 2.50
SS9 Mike Piazza 6.00
SS10 Chipper Jones 5.00
SS11 Ken Griffey Jr. 6.00
SS12 Gary Sheffield 1.50

2001 SP Game Bat - Milestone The Art of Hitting

MT
Complete Set (12): 30.00
Common Player: 1.50
Inserted 1:5
AH1 Tony Gwynn 3.00
AH2 Manny Ramirez 2.50
AH3 Todd Helton 2.50
AH4 Nomar Garciaparra 6.00
AH5 Vladimir Guerrero 2.50
AH6 Ichiro Suzuki 8.00
AH7 Darin Erstad 2.00
AH8 Alex Rodriguez 6.00
AH9 Carlos Delgado 2.00
AH10 Edgar Martinez 1.50
AH11 Luis Gonzalez 2.00
AH12 Barry Bonds 5.00

2001 SP Game Bat - Milestone The Trophy Room

MT
Complete Set (6): 25.00
Common Player: 1.50
Inserted 1:10
TR1 Sammy Sosa 5.00
TR2 Jason Giambi 2.00
TR3 Todd Helton 2.50
TR4 Alex Rodriguez 6.00
TR5 Mark McGwire 8.00
TR6 Ken Griffey Jr. 6.00

2001 SP Game-Used Edition

MT
Common Player: .75
Common SP (61-90): 15.00
Production 500
Pack (3): 18.00
Box (6): 90.00
1 Garrett Anderson .75
2 Troy Glaus 2.00
3 Darin Erstad 1.25
4 Jason Giambi 1.50
5 Tim Hudson 1.00
6 Johnny Damon .75
7 Carlos Delgado 1.50
8 Greg Vaughn .75
9 Juan Gonzalez 2.00
10 Roberto Alomar 1.50
11 Jim Thome 1.00
12 Edgar Martinez .75
13 Cal Ripken Jr. 6.00
14 Andres Galarraga 1.00
15 Alex Rodriguez 5.00
16 Rafael Palmeiro 1.50
17 Ivan Rodriguez 2.00
18 Manny Ramirez 3.00
19 Nomar Garciaparra 5.00
20 Pedro Martinez 3.00
21 Jermaine Dye .75
22 Dean Palmer .75
23 Matt Lawton .75
24 Frank Thomas 2.50
25 David Wells .75
26 Magglio Ordonez 1.00
27 Derek Jeter 6.00
28 Bernie Williams 1.50
29 Roger Clemens 3.00
30 Jeff Bagwell 2.00
31 Richard Hidalgo 1.00
32 Chipper Jones 4.00
33 Andruw Jones 1.50
34 Greg Maddux 4.00
35 Jeffrey Hammonds .75
36 Mark McGwire 6.00
37 Jim Edmonds 1.00
38 Sammy Sosa 4.00
39 Corey Patterson 1.00
40 Randy Johnson 2.00
41 Luis Gonzalez 1.50
42 Gary Sheffield 1.25
43 Shawn Green 1.00
44 Kevin Brown 1.00
45 Vladimir Guerrero 3.00
46 Barry Bonds 3.00
47 Jeff Kent 1.00
48 Preston Wilson .75
49 Charles Johnson .75
50 Mike Piazza 5.00
51 Edgardo Alfonzo .75
52 Tony Gwynn 3.00
53 Scott Rolen 1.50
54 Pat Burrell 1.50
55 Brian Giles 1.25
56 Jason Kendall 1.00
57 Ken Griffey Jr. 5.00
58 Mike Hampton 1.00
59 Todd Helton 2.00
60 Larry Walker 1.50
61 *Wilson Betemit* 25.00
62 *Travis Hafner* 15.00
63 *Ichiro Suzuki* 100.00
64 *Juan Diaz* 25.00
65 *Morgan Ensberg* 30.00
66 *Horacio Ramirez* 20.00
67 *Ricardo Rodriguez* 15.00
68 *Sean Douglass* 15.00
69 *Brandon Duckworth* 18.00
70 *Jackson Melian* 15.00
71 *Adrian Hernandez* 15.00
72 *Kyle Kessel* 15.00
73 *Jason Michaels* 15.00
74 *Esix Snead* 15.00
75 *Jason Smith* 15.00
76 *Tyler Walker* 15.00
77 *Juan Uribe* 20.00
78 *Adam Pettyjohn* 15.00
79 *Tsuyoshi Shinjo* 35.00
80 *Mike Penney* 15.00
81 *Josh Towers* 20.00
82 *Erick Almonte* 15.00
83 *Ryan Freel* 15.00
84 Juan Pena 20.00
85 *Albert Pujols* 80.00
86 *Henry Mateo* 20.00
87 *Greg Miller* 15.00
88 *Jose Mieses* 15.00
89 *Jack Wilson* 20.00
90 *Carlos Valderrama* 15.00

2001 SP Game-Used Edition Authentic Fabric Jersey Auto.

MT
Common Player: 60.00
S-EA Edgardo Alfonzo 60.00
S-RA Rick Ankiel 60.00
S-BB Barry Bonds /50 225.00
S-JC Jose Canseco 125.00
S-CD Carlos Delgado/ 50 90.00
S-JDr J.D. Drew /50 125.00
S-JG Jason Giambi /50 90.00
S-TGl Troy Glaus /50 125.00
S-KG Ken Griffey Jr. 350.00
S-TH Tim Hudson /50 90.00
S-RJ Randy Johnson 150.00
S-AJ Andruw Jones
S-CJ Chipper Jones
S-CR Cal Ripken /50 325.00
S-AR Alex Rodriguez 250.00
S-IR Ivan Rodriguez 125.00
S-NR Nolan Ryan /50 325.00
S-TS Tom Seaver /50 175.00
S-SS Sammy Sosa /50 225.00
S-FTh Frank Thomas
S-DW David Wells /50 65.00

2001 SP Game-Used Edition Authentic Fabric Jersey

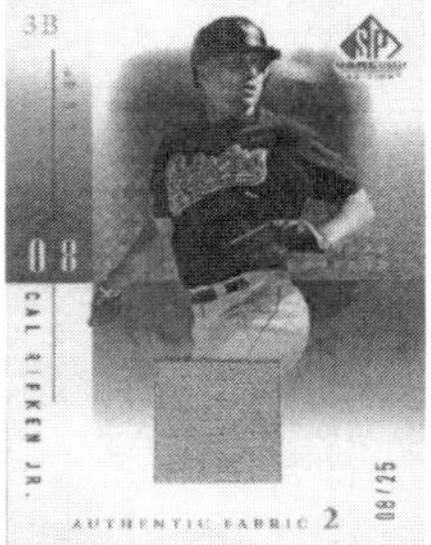

MT
Common Player: 10.00
Inserted 1:1
EA Edgardo Alfonzo 10.00
RA Roberto Alomar 25.00
RA Rick Ankiel 15.00
TB Tony Batista SP 20.00
BB Barry Bonds 30.00
KB Kevin Brown 10.00
JB Jeromy Burnitz 10.00
PB Pat Burrell 10.00
JC (B) Jose Canseco BLC 20.00
JC (H) Jose Canseco Yanks 25.00
EC Eric Chavez 10.00
JCi Jeff Cirillo 10.00
RC Roger Clemens 35.00
CD Carlos Delgado SP 25.00
JDi Joe DiMaggio SP/50 400.00
JDr J.D. Drew 15.00
JDy Jermaine Dye SP 20.00
JE Jim Edmonds 15.00
DE Darin Erstad 15.00
JG Jason Giambi 20.00
BG Brian Giles SP 25.00
TGl Troy Glaus 15.00
ToG Tom Glavine 15.00
LG Luis Gonzalez 20.00
MG Mark Grace 25.00
SG Shawn Green 12.00
KG (H) Ken Griffey Reds 25.00
KG (M) Ken Griffey M's 25.00
KG (R) Ken Griffey Reds 25.00
TGw Tony Gwynn 20.00
MH Mike Hampton 10.00
THe Todd Helton 20.00
TrH Trevor Hoffman 15.00
TH Tim Hudson 15.00
AH Aubrey Huff 15.00
JI J. Isringhausen SP 25.00
CJo Charles Johnson 15.00
RJ Randy Johnson 20.00
AJ Andruw Jones 20.00
CJ Chipper Jones 25.00
JK Jason Kendall 10.00
JK Jeff Kent 15.00
BL Barry Larkin 15.00
AL Al Leiter 12.00
KL Kenny Lofton 10.00
TL Terrence Long 10.00
GM Greg Maddux 25.00
MM Mickey Mantle SP/50 400.00
RM Roger Maris SP 120.00
EM Edgar Martinez 15.00
TM Tino Martinez 25.00
FM Fred McGriff 15.00
KM Kevin Millwood 10.00
PN Phil Nevin 10.00
JO John Olerud 15.00
MO Magglio Ordonez 12.00
AP Adam Piatt 10.00
CR Cal Ripken Jr. 50.00
MR Mariano Rivera 20.00
AR (H) Alex Rodriguez Rangers 25.00
AR (M) Alex Rodriguez M's 25.00
IR Ivan Rodriguez 20.00
SR Scott Rolen 15.00
NR Nolan Ryan SP/50 225.00
TS Tom Seaver SP/50 125.00
GS Gary Sheffield 12.00
SS (H) Sammy Sosa 25.00
SS (R) Sammy Sosa 25.00
FTa Fernando Tatis 10.00
MT Miguel Tejada 15.00
FTh Frank Thomas 20.00
JT Jim Thome 30.00
GV Greg Vaughn 10.00
RV Robin Ventura 10.00
JV Jose Vidro 10.00
DW David Wells SP 25.00
MW Matt Williams 15.00
PW Preston Wilson 10.00
DY Dmitri Young 10.00
TZ Todd Zeile 10.00

2001 SP Game-Used Edition 2-Player Auth. Fabric Jersey

MT
Common Card: 75.00
Production 50 sets
R-R Alex Rodriguez, Ivan Rodriguez 120.00
M-D Mickey Mantle, Joe DiMaggio 900.00
M-M Mickey Mantle, Roger Maris 650.00
R-S Nolan Ryan, Tom Seaver 475.00
B-C Barry Bonds, Jose Canseco 200.00
S-G Gary Sheffield, Shawn Green 80.00
J-J Chipper Jones, Andruw Jones 90.00
C-W Roger Clemens, Bernie Williams 100.00
J-R Randy Johnson, Nolan Ryan 300.00
S-T Sammy Sosa, Frank Thomas 90.00
G-S Ken Griffey Jr., Sammy Sosa 150.00
G-R Ken Griffey Jr., Alex Rodriguez 200.00
S-R Sammy Sosa, Alex Rodriguez 150.00
H-G Tim Hudson, Jason Giambi 80.00

2001 SP Game-Used Edition 3-Player Auth. Fabric Jersey

MT
Common Card: 200.00
Production 25 sets
G-R-S Ken Griffey Jr., Alex Rodriguez, Sammy Sosa 300.00

M-J-J	Greg Maddux, Chipper Jones, Andruw Jones	250.00
D-M-M	Joe DiMaggio, Mickey Mantle, Roger Maris	1500.
J-B-S	Andruw Jones, Barry Bonds, Sammy Sosa	250.00
J-S-M	Randy Johnson, Tom Seaver, Greg Maddux	325.00
D-G-S	Joe DiMaggio, Ken Griffey Jr., Sammy Sosa	675.00

2001 SP Legendary Cuts

		MT
Complete Set (90):		30.00
Common Player:		.40
Pack (4):		9.00
Box (18):		150.00
1	Al Simmons	.40
2	Jimmie Foxx (Height, weight and birthplace incorrect)	.75
3	Mickey Cochrane	.40
4	Phil Niekro	.40
5	Eddie Mathews	.75
6	Gary Matthews	.40
7	Hank Aaron	2.50
8	Joe Adcock	.40
9	Warren Spahn	.75
10	George Sisler	.40
11	Stan Musial	1.00
12	Dizzy Dean	.40
13	Frankie Frisch	.40
14	Harvey Haddix	.40
15	Johnny Mize	.40
16	Ken Boyer	.40
17	Rogers Hornsby	1.00
18	Cap Anson	.40
19	Andre Dawson	.40
20	Billy Williams	.40
21	Billy Herman	.40
22	Hack Wilson	.40
23	Ron Santo	.40
24	Ryne Sandberg	1.00
25	Ernie Banks	1.00
26	Burleigh Grimes	.40
27	Don Drysdale	.75
28	Gil Hodges	.40
29	Jackie Robinson	2.50
30	Tommy Lasorda	.40
31	Pee Wee Reese	.40
32	Roy Campanella	.75
33	Tommy Davis	.40
34	Branch Rickey	.40
35	Leo Durocher	.75
36	Walt Alston	.40
37	Bill Terry	.40
38	Carl Hubbell	.40
39	Eddie Stanky	.40
40	George Kelly	.40
41	Mel Ott	.75
42	Juan Marichal	.40
43	Rube Marquard	.40
44	Travis Jackson	.40
45	Bob Feller	.40
46	Earl Averill	.40
47	Elmer Flick	.40
48	Ken Keltner	.40
49	Lou Boudreau	.40
50	Early Wynn	.40
51	Satchel Paige	1.50
52	Ron Hunt	.40
53	Tom Seaver	1.00
54	Richie Ashburn	.40
55	Mike Schmidt	1.00
56	Honus Wagner	1.00
57	Lloyd Waner	.40
58	Max Carey	.40
59	Paul Waner	.40
60	Roberto Clemente	2.50
61	Nolan Ryan	3.00
62	Bobby Doerr	.40
63	Carlton Fisk	.75
64	Joe Cronin	.40
65	Smokey Joe Wood	.40
66	Tony Conigliaro	.40
67	Edd Roush	.40
68	Johnny Vander Meer	.40
69	Walter Johnson	1.00
70	Charlie Gehringer	.40
71	Al Kaline	.75
72	Ty Cobb	2.00
73	Tony Oliva	.40
74	Luke Appling	.40
75	Minnie Minoso	.40
76	Nellie Fox	.40
77	Shoeless Joe Jackson	2.50
78	Babe Ruth	3.00
79	Bill Dickey	.40
80	Elston Howard	.40
81	Joe DiMaggio	3.00
82	Lefty Gomez	.40
83	Lou Gehrig	2.50
84	Mickey Mantle	3.00
85	Reggie Jackson	.75
86	Roger Maris	1.00
87	Whitey Ford	.40
88	Waite Hoyt	.40
89	Yogi Berra	.75
90	Casey Stengel	.40

2001 SP Legendary Cuts Legendary Bat

		MT
Common Player:		10.00
Inserted 1:18		
HA	Hank Aaron	40.00
YB	Yogi Berra	30.00
WB	Wade Boggs	20.00
GB	George Brett	20.00
RCa	Roy Campanella	50.00
RC	Rico Carty	15.00
RCl	Roberto Clemente	80.00
TC	Ty Cobb	175.00
KC	Kiki Cuyler	20.00
TD	Tommy Davis	30.00
AD	Andre Dawson	15.00
JD	Joe DiMaggio	125.00
DD	Don Drysdale	30.00
CF	Carlton Fisk	20.00
NF	Nellie Fox	20.00
JF	Jimmie Foxx	50.00
GH	Gil Hodges	25.00
THo	Tommy Holmes (photo on front is Eddie Mathews)	15.00
RJ	Reggie Jackson	25.00
DJ	Davey Johnson	10.00
MM	Mickey Mantle	125.00
RM	Roger Maris	75.00
EM	Eddie Mathews	30.00
WMc	Willie McCovey	15.00
PM	Paul Molitor	20.00
MM	Manny Mota	15.00
MO	Mel Ott	50.00
VP	Vada Pinson	15.00
JR	Jackie Robinson	80.00
BR	Babe Ruth	225.00
NR	Nolan Ryan	50.00
RS	Ryne Sandberg	25.00
AS	Al Simmons	40.00
BT	Bill Terry	20.00
MW	Maury Wills	15.00
RY	Robin Yount	20.00

2001 SP Legendary Cuts Legendary Combo Bat

		MT
Complete Set (23):		
Common Player:		
JD-MM	Joe DiMaggio, Mickey Mantle	750.00
HW-BH	Hack Wilson, Billy Herman	200.00
JR-RC	Jackie Robinson, Roy Campanella	300.00
MM-NF	Minnie Minoso, Nellie Fox	180.00
JC-BD	Joe Cronin, Bobby Doerr	150.00
RM-MM	Roger Maris, Mickey Mantle	600.00
LB-BF	Lou Boudreau, Bob Feller	180.00
RS-AD	Ryne Sandberg, Andre Dawson	200.00
YB-EH	Yogi Berra, Elston Howard	250.00
MO-BT	Mel Ott, Bill Terry	200.00
TD-DD	Tommy Davis, Don Drysdale	150.00
JF-AS	Jimmie Foxx, Al Simmons	200.00
TC-CG	Ty Cobb, Charlie Gehringer	375.00
RJ-MM	Reggie Jackson, Mickey Mantle	475.00
TO-RC	Tony Oliva, Roberto Clemente	300.00
TC-BR	Ty Cobb, Babe Ruth	750.00
MO-JD	Mel Ott, Joe DiMaggio	500.00
BR-MM	Babe Ruth, Mickey Mantle	850.00
JF-BR	Jimmie Foxx, Babe Ruth	600.00
NR-BF	Nolan Ryan, Bob Feller	300.00
GS-BT	George Sisler, Bill Terry	180.00
SJ-PW	Shoeless Joe Jackson, Paul Waner	400.00
HA-BR	Hank Aaron, Babe Ruth	750.00

2001 SP Legendary Cuts Legendary Cuts

		MT
Inserted 1:252		
GA	Grover Cleveland Alexander/1	
WA	Walt Alston/34	175.00
CA	Cap Anson/2	
LA	Luke Appling/45	200.00
EA	Earl Averill/189	90.00
EB	E.G. Barrow/16	400.00
MC	Max Carey/73	150.00
TC	Ty Cobb/24	1525.
JC	Jocko Conlan/12	
SC	Stanley Coveleski/42	400.00
JC	Joe Cronin/12	
KC	Kiki Cuyler/6	
DDe	Dizzy Dean/56	415.00
BD	Bill Dickey/28	275.00
JD	Joe DiMaggio/25	650.00
JD	Joe DiMaggio/50	430.00
JD	Joe DiMaggio/150	400.00
JD	Joe DiMaggio/275	315.00
DDr	Don Drysdale/12	
LD	Leo Durocher/45	375.00
RF	Rick Ferrell/8	
EF	Elmer Flick/22	340.00
NF	Nellie Fox/9	
JF	Jimmie Foxx/16	
FF	Ford Frick/21	535.00
FF	Frankie Frisch/3	
LGe	Lou Gehrig/7	6000.
WG	Warren Giles/10	1000.
LGo	Lefty Gomez/85	235.00
BG	Burleigh Grimes/18	
LG	Lefty Grove/34	600.00
HH	Harvey Haddix/4	3000.
BH	Bucky Harris/10	750.00
BH	Billy Herman/88	105.00
GH	Gil Hodges/6	
HH	Harry Hooper/14	600.00
RH	Rogers Hornsby/4	
WH	Waite Hoyt/38	260.00
CH	Carl Hubbell/30	375.00
TJ	Travis Jackson/35	250.00
JJ	Judy Johnson/9	1200.
WJ	Walter Johnson/113	300.00
CK	Charlie Keller/16	515.00
GK	George Kelly/52	140.00
KK	Ken Keltner/11	500.00
MK	Mark Koenig/30	275.00
KL	Kenesaw M. Landis/4	
BL	Bob Lemon/23	255.00
FL	Freddie Lindstrom/2	
EL	Eddie Lopat/22	275.00
TL	Ted Lyons/59	185.00
SM	Sal Maglie/19	550.00
MM	Mickey Mantle/8	5000.
HM	Heinie Manush/50	240.00
RoM	Roger Maris/73	350.00
RuM	Rube Marquard/23	460.00
JMc	Joe McCarthy/40	245.00
JM	Joe Medwick/18	
BM	Bob Meusel/23	475.00
JMi	Johnny Mize/84	180.00
MO	Mel Ott/8	

SP	Satchel Paige/36	1000.
RP	Roger Peckinpaugh/ 45	200.00
VR	Vic Raschi/26	250.00
BRi	Branch Rickey/16	
JR	Jackie Robinson/ 147	550.00
ER	Edd Roush/83	115.00
RR	Red Ruffing/5	
BRu	Babe Ruth/7	8000.
GS	George Selkirk/15	1125.
JS	Joe Sewell/55	150.00
RS	Rip Sewell/39	170.00
BS	Bob Shawkey/39	215.00
GS	George Sisler/1	
CS	Casey Stengel/10	
BT	Bill Terry/184	100.00
VM	Johnny Vander Meer/ 65	135.00
HW	Honus Wagner/24	2850.
BW	Bucky Walters/ 13	825.00
LW	Lloyd Waner/217	90.00
PW	Paul Waner/4	
HW	Hack Wilson/4	7000.
JW	Smokey Joe Wood/ 43	275.00

2001 SP Legendary Cuts Legendary Debut Bat

		MT
Common Player:		15.00
Inserted 1:18		
JA	Joe Adcock	25.00
LA	Luke Appling	30.00
RA	Richie Ashburn	40.00
BB	Bobby Bonds	15.00
LB	Lou Boudreau	20.00
KB	Ken Boyer	40.00
BB	Bill Buckner	15.00
MC	Mickey Cochrane	40.00
TC	Tony Conigliaro	40.00
JC	Joe Cronin	25.00
BD	Bobby Doerr	25.00
BF	Bob Feller	35.00
BF	Bill Freehan	15.00
FF	Frankie Frisch	50.00
CG	Charlie Gehringer	40.00
BH	Billy Herman	25.00
WH	Willie Horton	15.00
EH	Elston Howard	20.00
RH	Ron Hunt	15.00
JJ	Joe Jackson	180.00
GL	Greg Luzinski	15.00
GM	Gary Matthews	15.00
MM	Minnie Minoso	25.00
TO	Tony Oliva	15.00
WP	Wes Parker	15.00
BR	Bobby Richardson	30.00
SS	Steve Sax	15.00
GS	George Sisler	40.00
ES	Eddie Stanky	15.00
AT	Alan Trammell	15.00
PW	Paul Waner	60.00
HW	Hack Wilson	50.00
SY	Steve Yeager	15.00

2001 SP Legendary Cuts Legendary Game Jersey

		MT
Common Player:		10.00
Inserted 1:18		
YB	Yogi Berra	40.00
WB	Wade Boggs	15.00
RC	Roberto Clemente	100.00
TC	Ty Cobb	600.00
TC	Tony Conigliaro	40.00
BD	Bill Dickey	40.00
JD	Joe DiMaggio	375.00
LD	Leo Durocher	20.00
WF	Whitey Ford	40.00
NF	Nellie Fox	20.00
JF	Jim Fregosi	10.00
GH	Gil Hodges	20.00
THo	Tommy Holmes	10.00
RJ	Reggie Jackson	25.00
TK	Ted Kluszewski	15.00
BL	Bob Lemon	15.00
VL	Vic Lombardi	10.00
MM	Mickey Mantle	475.00
JM	Juan Marichal	15.00
RM	Roger Maris	120.00
WM	Willie McCovey	15.00
JN	Joe Nuxhall	25.00
GP	Gaylord Perry	15.00
BR	Bobby Richardson	15.00
BRo	Brooks Robinson	20.00
BR	Babe Ruth	600.00
NR	Nolan Ryan	50.00
TS	Tom Seaver	250.00
CS	Casey Stengel	30.00
BT	Bobby Thomson	20.00
HW	Honus Wagner	750.00
BW	Billy Williams	25.00
MW	Maury Wills	15.00
RY	Robin Yount	20.00

2001 SPx Sample

To introduce the annual SPx brand, Upper Deck issued this sample card of spokesman Ken Griffey, Jr. The card is in the sam format as the later-issued version, but has a large red "SAMPLE" overprinted diagonally on back.

		MT
001	Ken Griffey Jr.	5.00

2001 SPx

		MT
Complete Set (150):		1350.
Common Player:		.25
Common Young Star (91-120):		8.00
Production 2,000		
Common Prospect Jersey (121-135):		12.00
Common Prosp. Auto. Jersey (136-150):		15.00
Pack (4):		8.00
Box (18):		135.00
1	Darin Erstad	.75
2	Troy Glaus	1.25
3	Mo Vaughn	.25
4	Johnny Damon	.25
5	Jason Giambi	.75
6	Tim Hudson	.40
7	Miguel Tejada	.40
8	Carlos Delgado	1.00
9	Raul Mondesi	.25
10	Tony Batista	.25
11	Ben Grieve	.40
12	Greg Vaughn	.25
13	Juan Gonzalez	1.25
14	Jim Thome	.50
15	Roberto Alomar	1.00
16	John Olerud	.40
17	Edgar Martinez	.25
18	Albert Belle	.25
19	Cal Ripken Jr.	4.00
20	Ivan Rodriguez	1.25
21	Rafael Palmeiro	.75
22	Alex Rodriguez	4.00
23	Nomar Garciaparra	4.00
24	Pedro J. Martinez	1.50
25	Manny Ramirez	1.50
26	Jermaine Dye	.25
27	Mark Quinn	.25
28	Carlos Beltran	.25
29	Tony Clark	.25
30	Bobby Higginson	.25
31	Eric Milton	.25
32	Matt Lawton	.25
33	Frank Thomas	1.50
34	Magglio Ordonez	.40
35	Ray Durham	.25
36	David Wells	.25
37	Derek Jeter	4.00
38	Bernie Williams	1.00
39	Roger Clemens	1.50
40	David Justice	.75
41	Jeff Bagwell	1.25
42	Richard Hidalgo	.40
43	Moises Alou	.40
44	Chipper Jones	2.50
45	Andruw Jones	1.00
46	Greg Maddux	2.50
47	Rafael Furcal	.50
48	Jeromy Burnitz	.25
49	Geoff Jenkins	.40
50	Mark McGwire	4.00
51	Jim Edmonds	.40
52	Rick Ankiel	.25
53	Edgar Renteria	.25
54	Sammy Sosa	3.00
55	Kerry Wood	.50
56	Rondell White	.25
57	Randy Johnson	1.25
58	Steve Finley	.25
59	Matt Williams	.40
60	Luis Gonzalez	.40
61	Kevin Brown	.25
62	Gary Sheffield	.40
63	Shawn Green	.25
64	Vladimir Guerrero	1.50
65	Jose Vidro	.25
66	Barry Bonds	1.50
67	Jeff Kent	.25
68	Livan Hernandez	.25
69	Preston Wilson	.25
70	Charles Johnson	.25
71	Cliff Floyd	.25
72	Mike Piazza	3.00
73	Edgardo Alfonzo	.25
74	Jay Payton	.25
75	Robin Ventura	.25
76	Tony Gwynn	1.50
77	Phil Nevin	.25
78	Ryan Klesko	.25
79	Scott Rolen	.75
80	Pat Burrell	.75
81	Bob Abreu	.25
82	Brian Giles	.40
83	Kris Benson	.25
84	Jason Kendall	.25
85	Ken Griffey Jr.	3.00
86	Barry Larkin	.40
87	Sean Casey	.40
88	Todd Helton	1.25
89	Larry Walker	.40
90	Mike Hampton	.25
91	*Billy Sylvester* (Rookies/Young Stars)	8.00
92	*Josh Towers* (Rookies/Young Stars)	8.00
93	*Zach Day* (Rookies/Young Stars)	15.00
94	*Martin Vargas* (Rookies/Young Stars)	8.00
95	*Adam Pettyjohn* (Rookies/Young Stars)	8.00
96	*Andres Torres* (Rookies/Young Stars)	12.00
97	*Kris Keller* (Rookies/Young Stars)	8.00
98	*Blaine Neal* (Rookies/Young Stars)	8.00
99	*Kyle Kessel* (Rookies/Young Stars)	8.00
100	*Greg Miller* (Rookies/Young Stars)	12.00
101	Shawn Sonnier (Rookies/Young Stars)	8.00
102	*Alexis Gomez* (Rookies/Young Stars)	10.00
103	*Grant Balfour* (Rookies/Young Stars)	8.00
104	*Henry Mateo* (Rookies/Young Stars)	8.00
105	*Wilkin Ruan* (Rookies/Young Stars)	12.00
106	*Nick Maness* (Rookies/Young Stars)	8.00
107	*Jason Michaels* (Rookies/Young Stars)	8.00
108	*Esix Snead* (Rookies/Young Stars)	8.00
109	*William Ortega* (Rookies/Young Stars)	15.00
110	*David Elder* (Rookies/Young Stars)	8.00
111	*Jackson Melian* (Rookies/Young Stars)	20.00
112	*Nate Teut* (Rookies/Young Stars)	8.00
113	*Jason Smith* (Rookies/Young Stars)	8.00
114	*Mike Penney* (Rookies/Young Stars)	8.00
115	*Jose Mieses* (Rookies/Young Stars)	8.00
116	Juan Pena (Rookies/Young Stars)	8.00
117	*Brian Lawrence* (Rookies/Young Stars)	10.00
118	*Jeremy Owens* (Rookies/Young Stars)	8.00
119	*Carlos Valderrama* (Rookies/Young Stars)	8.00
120	*Rafael Soriano* (Rookies/Young Stars)	8.00
121	*Horacio Ramirez*	12.00
122	*Ricardo Rodriguez*	15.00
123	*Juan Diaz*	12.00
124	Donnie Bridges	12.00
125	*Tyler Walker*	12.00
126	*Erick Almonte*	12.00
127	Jesus Colome	12.00
128	*Ryan Freel*	12.00
129	*Elpidio Guzman*	12.00

130 Jack Cust 12.00
131 *Eric Hinske* 30.00
132 *Josh Fogg* 20.00
133 *Juan Uribe* 12.00
134 *Bert Snow* 15.00
135 Pedro Feliz 12.00
136 *Wilson Betemit* 35.00
137 *Sean Douglass* 15.00
138 Dernell Stenson 15.00
139 Brandon Inge 20.00
140 *Morgan Ensberg* 25.00
141 Brian Cole 15.00
142 *Adrian Hernandez* 30.00
143 *Brandon Duckworth* 15.00
144 *Jack Wilson* 15.00
145 *Travis Hafner* 15.00
146 Carlos Pena 15.00
147 Corey Patterson 40.00
148 Xavier Nady 30.00
149 Jason Hart 25.00
150 *Ichiro Suzuki* 700.00

2001 SPx Spectrum

MT
Stars (1-90): 15-25X
SP's (91-120): 1-2X
Production 50 sets

2001 SPx Foundations

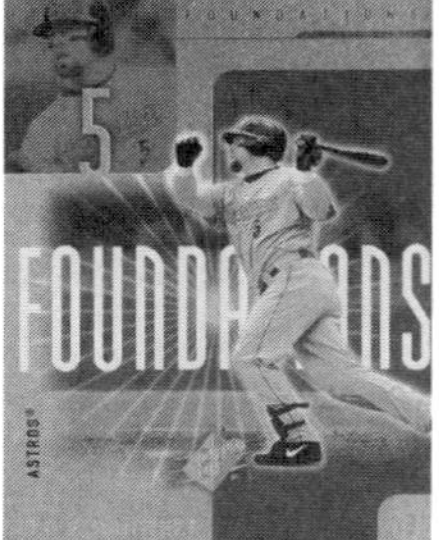

MT
Complete Set (12): 50.00
Common Player: 2.00
Inserted 1:8
F1 Mark McGwire 8.00
F2 Jeff Bagwell 2.50
F3 Alex Rodriguez 6.00
F4 Ken Griffey Jr. 6.00
F5 Andruw Jones 2.00
F6 Cal Ripken Jr. 8.00
F7 Barry Bonds 2.50
F8 Derek Jeter 8.00
F9 Frank Thomas 3.00
F10 Sammy Sosa 5.00
F11 Tony Gwynn 3.00
F12 Vladimir Guerrero 3.00

2001 SPx SPXcitement

MT
Complete Set (12): 45.00
Common Player: 2.00
Inserted 1:8
X1 Alex Rodriguez 6.00
X2 Jason Giambi 2.00
X3 Ken Griffey Jr. 6.00
X4 Sammy Sosa 5.00
X5 Frank Thomas 3.00
X6 Todd Helton 2.50
X7 Mark McGwire 8.00
X8 Mike Piazza 6.00
X9 Derek Jeter 8.00
X10 Vladimir Guerrero 3.00
X11 Carlos Delgado 2.00
X12 Chipper Jones 5.00

2001 SPx Untouchable Talents

MT
Complete Set (6): 30.00
Common Player: 2.00
Inserted 1:15
UT1 Ken Griffey Jr. 6.00
UT2 Mike Piazza 6.00
UT3 Mark McGwire 8.00
UT4 Alex Rodriguez 6.00
UT5 Sammy Sosa 5.00
UT6 Derek Jeter 8.00

2001 SPx Winning Materials Jersey/Bat

MT
Common Player: 20.00
Inserted 1:18
RA Rick Ankiel 20.00
BB1 Barry Bonds 30.00
BB2 Barry Bonds 30.00
CD Carlos Delgado 30.00
JD Joe DiMaggio 250.00
JE Jim Edmonds 20.00
KG1 Ken Griffey Jr. 50.00
KG2 Ken Griffey Jr. 50.00
RJ1 Randy Johnson 25.00
RJ2 Randy Johnson 25.00
AJ1 Andruw Jones 25.00
AJ2 Andruw Jones 25.00
CJ1 Chipper Jones 30.00
CJ2 Chipper Jones 30.00
CR Cal Ripken Jr. 75.00
AR1 Alex Rodriguez 40.00
AR2 Alex Rodriguez 40.00
IR1 Ivan Rodriguez 25.00
IR2 Ivan Rodriguez 25.00
SS Sammy Sosa 35.00
FT Frank Thomas 25.00

Figure values of lower-grade cards from 1981-date as: Near Mint (NM) 75% Excellent (EX) 40% of the listed Mint price

For cards through 1980, values should be figured as: Excellent (EX) 50% Very Good (VG) 30% of the listed Near Mint price

2001 SPx Winning Materials Jersey Combo

MT
Common Duo: 75.00
Production 50
Common Trio:
Production 25
KG-AR Ken Griffey Jr., Alex Rodriguez 325.00
KG-BB Ken Griffey Jr., Barry Bonds 250.00
KG-RJ Ken Griffey Jr., Randy Johnson 225.00
CJ-DW Chipper Jones, David Wells 75.00
BB-SS Barry Bonds, Sammy Sosa 125.00
KG-JD Ken Griffey Jr., Joe DiMaggio 600.00
KG-SS Ken Griffey Jr., Sammy Sosa 250.00
SS-CD Sammy Sosa, Carlos Delgado 90.00
SS-FT Sammy Sosa, Frank Thomas 90.00
IR-AR Ivan Rodriguez, Alex Rodriguez 125.00
AR-CR Alex Rodriguez, Cal Ripken Jr. 225.00
AJ-CJ Andruw Jones, Chipper Jones 120.00
KG-KG Ken Griffey Jr., Ken Griffey Jr.
G-R-B Ken Griffey Jr., Alex Rodriguez, Barry Bonds 400.00
S-G-C Sammy Sosa, Ken Griffey Jr., Chipper Jones 350.00
B-G-J Barry Bonds, Ken Griffey Jr., Andruw Jones 350.00
R-R-D Alex Rodriguez, Ivan Rodriguez, Carlos Delgado 225.00
D-G-J Joe DiMaggio, Ken Griffey Jr., Andruw Jones 750.00
D-B-S Carlos Delgado, Barry Bonds, Sammy Sosa 175.00
R-J-D Cal Ripken Jr., Chipper Jones, Carlos Delgado 375.00

2001 SPx Winning Materials Base/Ball

MT
Common Player: 30.00
Production 250 sets
B-BB Barry Bonds 60.00
B-NG Nomar Garciaparra 75.00
B-KG Ken Griffey Jr. 90.00
B-VG Vladimir Guerrero 30.00
B-DJ Derek Jeter 125.00
B-AJ Andruw Jones 35.00
B-CJ Chipper Jones 50.00
B-PM Pedro Martinez 75.00
B-MM Mark McGwire 125.00
B-MP Mike Piazza 85.00
B-AR Alex Rodriguez 75.00
B-SS Sammy Sosa 60.00
B-FT Frank Thomas 40.00

2001 SPx Winning Materials Base

MT
Common Duo: 80.00
Production 50
Common Trio: 300.00
Production 25
B2-MG Mark McGwire, Ken Griffey Jr. 300.00
B2-MS Mark McGwire, Sammy Sosa 180.00
B2-MR Mark McGwire, Alex Rodriguez 200.00
B2-GJ Nomar Garciaparra, Derek Jeter 200.00
B2-TR Frank Thomas, Alex Rodriguez 80.00
B2-JG Derek Jeter, Jason Giambi 125.00
B2-PB Mike Piazza, Barry Bonds 125.00
B2-RJ Alex Rodriguez, Derek Jeter 250.00
B2-PM Mike Piazza, Mark McGwire 200.00
B2-JP Derek Jeter, Mike Piazza 180.00
B3-MGS Mark McGwire, Ken Griffey Jr., Sammy Sosa 600.00
B3-JRG Derek Jeter, Alex Rodriguez, Nomar Garciaparra 375.00
B3-PJW Mike Piazza, Derek Jeter, Bernie Williams 400.00
B3-BMS Barry Bonds, Mark McGwire, Sammy Sosa 325.00
B3-GJR Ken Griffey Jr., Derek Jeter, Alex Rodriguez 450.00

2002 SP Authentic

MT
Complete Set (170): NA
Common Player: .25
Common SP (91-135): 5.00
Production 1,999
Common SP Auto (136-170): 10.00
Production 999
Pack (5): 5.00
Box (24): 90.00
1 Troy Glaus .50
2 Darin Erstad .50
3 Barry Zito .50
4 Eric Chavez .50
5 Tim Hudson .50
6 Miguel Tejada .75
7 Carlos Delgado .50
8 Shannon Stewart .25
9 Ben Grieve .25
10 Jim Thome .75
11 C.C. Sabathia .25
12 Ichiro Suzuki 2.00
13 Freddy Garcia .25
14 Edgar Martinez .25

15 Bret Boone .25
16 Jeff Conine .25
17 Alex Rodriguez 2.50
18 Juan Gonzalez .75
19 Ivan Rodriguez .50
20 Rafael Palmeiro .50
21 Hank Blalock .25
22 Pedro J. Martinez 1.00
23 Manny Ramirez .75
24 Nomar Garciaparra 2.50
25 Carlos Beltran .25
26 Mike Sweeney .25
27 Randall Simon .25
28 Dmitri Young .25
29 Bobby Higginson .25
30 Corey Koskie .25
31 Eric Milton .25
32 Torii Hunter .25
33 Joe Mays .25
34 Frank Thomas .75
35 Mark Buehrle .25
36 Magglio Ordonez .50
37 Kenny Lofton .25
38 Roger Clemens 1.50
39 Derek Jeter 3.00
40 Jason Giambi 1.50
41 Bernie Williams .50
42 Alfonso Soriano 2.50
43 Lance Berkman .75
44 Roy Oswalt .50
45 Jeff Bagwell .75
46 Craig Biggio .50
47 Chipper Jones 1.50
48 Greg Maddux 1.50
49 Gary Sheffield .50
50 Andruw Jones .50
51 Ben Sheets .25
52 Richie Sexson .50
53 Albert Pujols 1.50
54 Matt Morris .25
55 J.D. Drew .50
56 Sammy Sosa 1.50
57 Kerry Wood .50
58 Corey Patterson .25
59 Mark Prior .75
60 Randy Johnson .75
61 Luis Gonzalez .50
62 Curt Schilling .75
63 Shawn Green .50
64 Kevin Brown .25
65 Hideo Nomo .50
66 Vladimir Guerrero 1.00
67 Jose Vidro .25
68 Barry Bonds 2.50
69 Jeff Kent .50
70 Rich Aurilia .25
71 Preston Wilson .25
72 Josh Beckett .25
73 Mike Lowell .25
74 Roberto Alomar .50
75 Mo Vaughn .40
76 Jeromy Burnitz .25
77 Mike Piazza 2.00
78 Sean Burroughs .25
79 Phil Nevin .25
80 Bobby Abreu .40
81 Pat Burrell .50
82 Scott Rolen .50
83 Jason Kendall .25
84 Brian Giles .50
85 Ken Griffey Jr. 2.00
86 Adam Dunn .75
87 Sean Casey .25
88 Todd Helton .50
89 Larry Walker .50
90 Mike Hampton .25
91 *Brandon Puffer* 5.00
92 *Tom Shearn* 5.00
93 *Chris Baker* 5.00
94 *Gustavo Chacin* 5.00
95 *Joe Orloski* 5.00
96 Mike Smith 5.00
97 *John Ennis* 5.00
98 *John Foster* 5.00
99 *Kevin Gryboski* 5.00
100 *Brian Mallette* 5.00
101 *Takahito Nomura* 5.00
102 *So Taguchi* 10.00
103 *Jeremy Lambert* 5.00
104 *Jason Simontacchi* 15.00
105 *Jorge Sosa* 5.00
106 *Brandon Backe* 8.00
107 *P.J. Bevis* 5.00
108 *Jeremy Ward* 5.00
109 *Doug Devore* 5.00
110 Ron Chiavacci 5.00
111 *Ron Calloway* 5.00
112 *Nelson Castro* 5.00
113 Deivis Santos 5.00
114 *Earl Snyder* 5.00
115 *Julio Mateo* 5.00
116 *J.J. Putz* 5.00
117 *Allan Simpson* 5.00
118 *Satoru Komiyama* 5.00
119 *Adam Walker* 5.00
120 *Oliver Perez* 20.00
121 *Clifford Bartosh* 5.00
122 *Todd Donovan* 5.00
123 *Elio Serrano* 5.00
124 *Peter Zamora* 5.00
125 *Mike Gonzalez* 5.00
126 *Travis Hughes* 5.00
127 Jorge de la Rosa 5.00
128 *Anastacio Martinez* 5.00
129 *Colin Young* 5.00
130 *Nate Field* 5.00
131 *Tim Kalita* 5.00
132 *Julius Matos* 5.00
133 *Terry Pearson* 5.00
134 *Kyle Kane* 5.00
135 *Mitch Wylie* 5.00
136 *Rodrigo Rosario* 10.00
137 *Franklyn German* 10.00
138 *Reed Johnson* 10.00
139 *Luis Martinez* 12.00
140 *Michael Crudale* 12.00
141 *Francis Beltran* 10.00
142 *Steve Kent* 10.00
143 *Felix Escalona* 10.00
144 *Jose Valverde* 10.00
145 *Victor Alvarez* 10.00
146 *Kazuhisa Ishii/249* 75.00
147 *Jorge Nunez* 10.00
148 *Eric Good* 10.00
149 *Luis Ugueto* 10.00
150 Matt Thornton 10.00
151 *Wilson Valdez* 10.00
152 *Hansel Izquierdo/249* 20.00
153 *Jamie Cerda* 10.00
154 *Mark Corey* 10.00
155 *Tyler Yates* 10.00
156 *Steve Bechler* 10.00
157 *Ben Howard/249* 20.00
158 *Anderson Machado* 15.00
159 *Jorge Padilla* 15.00
160 *Eric Junge* 10.00
161 *Adrian Burnside* 10.00
162 *Josh Hancock* 12.00
163 *Chris Booker* 10.00
164 *Cam Esslinger* 10.00
165 *Rene Reyes* 10.00
166 *Aaron Cook* 10.00
167 *Juan Brito* 10.00
168 *Miguel Ascencio* 10.00
169 *Kevin Frederick* 10.00
170 *Edwin Almonte* 10.00

2002 SP Authentic Limited

MT
Stars (1-90): 5-10X
Cards (91-135): .5-1X
Cards (136-170): .5-1X
Production 125 sets
Golds (1-90): 10-20X
Golds (91-135): .75-1.5X
Golds (136-170): .75-1.5X
Production 50 sets

2002 SP Authentic SP Chirography

MT
Common Autograph: 10.00
Inserted 1:72
HB Hank Blalock/282 20.00
BB Barry Bonds/112 110.00
MB Milton Bradley/470 10.00
JB John Buck/427 10.00
MB Mark Buehrle/438 15.00
SB Sean Burroughs/275 10.00
AD Adam Dunn/348 30.00
DE Darin Erstad/80 35.00
CF Cliff Floyd/313 10.00
FG Freddy Garcia/456 15.00
JG Jason Giambi/244 55.00
TG Tom Glavine/376 25.00
AG Alex Graman/418 10.00
KG Ken Griffey Jr/238 110.00
JL Jon Lieber/462 15.00
JM Joe Mays/469 15.00
MM Mark McGwire/50 500.00
DM Doug Mientkiewicz/478 15.00
AR Alex Rodriguez/391 90.00
CS C.C. Sabathia/442 15.00
RS Richie Sexson/483 15.00
SS Sammy Sosa/247 160.00
IS Ichiro Suzuki/78 500.00
MS Mike Sweeney/265 15.00
BZ Barry Zito/419 30.00

2002 SP Authentic Authentic Excellence

MT
AuE Ken Griffey Jr., Sammy Sosa, Cal Ripken Jr., Jason Giambi, Mark McGwire

2002 SP Authentic Future USA Watch

MT
Complete Set (22): 100.00
Common Player: 6.00
Production 1,999 sets
USA1 Chad Cordero 6.00
USA2 Philip Humber 6.00
USA3 Grant Johnson 8.00
USA4 Wes Littleton 6.00
USA5 Kyle Sleeth 15.00
USA6 Huston Street 6.00
USA7 Brad Sullivan 6.00
USA8 Bob Zimmermann 6.00
USA9 Abe Alvarez 6.00
USA10 Kyle Bakker 6.00
USA11 Landon Powell 8.00
USA12 Clint Sammons 6.00
USA13 Michael Aubrey 10.00
USA14 Aaron Hill 6.00
USA15 Conor Jackson 6.00
USA16 Eric Patterson 6.00
USA17 Dustin Pedroia 6.00
USA18 Rickie Weeks 10.00
USA19 Shane Costa 6.00
USA20 Mark Jurich 6.00
USA21 Sam Fuld 6.00
USA22 Carlos Quentin 8.00

2002 SP Authentic SP Game Jerseys

MT
Common Player: 6.00
Inserted 1:24
RA Roberto Alomar 8.00
JB Jeff Bagwell 10.00
JB Jeromy Burnitz/SP 6.00
RC Roger Clemens 12.00
CD Carlos Delgado 6.00
JE Jim Edmonds 8.00
DE Darin Erstad 8.00
JGi Jason Giambi 12.00
JGo Juan Gonzalez 8.00
SG Shawn Green 8.00
KG Ken Griffey Jr/95 40.00
TH Todd Helton 8.00
KI Kazuhisa Ishii 15.00
RJ Randy Johnson 10.00
AJ Andruw Jones 8.00
CJ Chipper Jones 10.00
JK Jason Kendall 6.00
GM Greg Maddux 12.00
MM Mark McGwire/SP 100.00
MO Magglio Ordonez 8.00
AP Andy Pettitte 10.00
MP Mike Piazza 15.00
MR Manny Ramirez 10.00
AR Alex Rodriguez 15.00
IR Ivan Rodriguez 8.00
SR Scott Rolen 8.00
CC C.C. Sabathia 6.00
CS Curt Schilling 10.00
GS Gary Sheffield 6.00
TS Tsuyoshi Shinjo 10.00
SS Sammy Sosa 15.00
IS Ichiro Suzuki/SP 50.00
JT Jim Thome 10.00
RV Robin Ventura 6.00
OV Omar Vizquel 6.00
BW Bernie Williams 8.00
PW Preston Wilson 6.00
BZ Barry Zito 8.00

2002 SP Authentic Game Jersey Gold

MT
Complete Set (38):
Common Player:
J-RA Roberto Alomar/12
J-JBA Jeff Bagwell/5
J-JBU Jeromy Burnitz/20
J-RC Roger Clemens/22
J-CD Carlos Delgado/25
J-JE Jim Edmonds/15
J-DE Darin Erstad/17
J-JGR Jason Giambi/25
J-JGO Juan Gonzalez/19
J-SG Shawn Green/15
J-KG Ken Griffey Jr./30
J-TH Todd Helton/17
J-KI Kazuhisa Ishii/17
J-RJ Randy Johnson/51
J-AJ Andruw Jones/25
J-CJ Chipper Jones/10
J-JK Jason Kendall/18
J-GM Greg Maddux/31
J-MM Mark McGwire/25
J-MO Magglio Ordonez/30
J-AP Andy Pettitte/46
J-MP Mike Piazza/31
J-MR Manny Ramirez/24
J-AR Alex Rodriguez/3
J-IR Ivan Rodriguez/7
J-SR Scott Rolen/27
J-CC C.C. Sabathia/52
J-CS Curt Schilling/38
J-GS Gary Sheffield/11
J-TS Tsuyoshi Shinjo/5
J-SS Sammy Sosa/21
J-IS Ichiro Suzuki/51
J-JT Jim Thome/25
J-RV Robin Ventura/19
J-OV Omar Vizquel/13
J-BW Bernie Williams/51
J-PW Preston Wilson/44
J-BZ Barry Zito/75

2002 SP Authentic SP Authentic Prospect Signatures

MT
Common Autograph: 6.00
Inserted 1:36
JC Jose Cueto 8.00
JDe Jeff Deardorff 8.00
JDi Jose Diaz 6.00
AG Alex Graman 10.00
MG Matt Guerrier 8.00
BH Bill Hall 6.00
KH Ken Huckaby 8.00
DM Dustan Mohr 8.00
XN Xavier Nady 12.00
MS Marcos Scutaro 8.00
ST Steve Torrealba 6.00
DW Danny Wright 10.00

A player's name in *italic* type indicates a rookie card.

2002 SP Authentic Signed SP Big Mac

	MT
Quantity signed listed	
MM1 Mark McGwire/1	
MM2 Mark McGwire/25	
MM3 Mark McGwire/5	
MM4 Mark McGwire/4	
MM5 Mark McGwire/12	
MM6 Mark McGwire/70	
MM7 Mark McGwire/4	
MM8 Mark McGwire/7	
MM9 Mark McGwire/5	
MM10Mark McGwire/16	

2002 SPx

		MT
Common Player:		.25
Common SP (91-120):		4.00
Production 1,800		
Common SP Auto. (121-150):		10.00
Common Star Swatch (151-190):		8.00
Production 800		
Pack (4):		5.00
Box (18):		80.00
1	Troy Glaus	.75
2	Darin Erstad	.50
3	David Justice	.50
4	Tim Hudson	.50
5	Miguel Tejada	.40
6	Barry Zito	.40
7	Carlos Delgado	.50
8	Shannon Stewart	.25
9	Greg Vaughn	.25
10	Toby Hall	.25
11	Jim Thome	.60
12	C.C. Sabathia	.25
13	Ichiro Suzuki	4.00
14	Edgar Martinez	.25
15	Freddy Garcia	.40
16	Mike Cameron	.25
17	Jeff Conine	.25
18	Tony Batista	.25
19	Alex Rodriguez	2.50
20	Rafael Palmeiro	.75
21	Ivan Rodriguez	.75
22	Carl Everett	.25
23	Pedro J. Martinez	1.00
24	Manny Ramirez	1.00
25	Nomar Garciaparra	2.50
26	Johnny Damon	.25
27	Mike Sweeney	.25
28	Carlos Beltran	.25
29	Dmitri Young	.25
30	Joe Mays	.25
31	Doug Mientkiewicz	.25
32	Cristian Guzman	.25
33	Corey Koskie	.25
34	Frank Thomas	1.25
35	Magglio Ordonez	.40
36	Mark Buehrle	.25
37	Bernie Williams	.75
38	Roger Clemens	1.50
39	Derek Jeter	4.00
40	Jason Giambi	1.00
41	Mike Mussina	.75
42	Lance Berkman	.50
43	Jeff Bagwell	1.00
44	Roy Oswalt	.50
45	Greg Maddux	2.00
46	Chipper Jones	2.00
47	Andruw Jones	.75
48	Gary Sheffield	.40
49	Geoff Jenkins	.40
50	Richie Sexson	.50
51	Ben Sheets	.40
52	Albert Pujols	2.00
53	J.D. Drew	.50
54	Jim Edmonds	.50
55	Sammy Sosa	2.00
56	Moises Alou	.25
57	Kerry Wood	.50
58	Jon Lieber	.25
59	Fred McGriff	.40
60	Randy Johnson	1.00
61	Luis Gonzalez	.75
62	Curt Schilling	.75
63	Kevin Brown	.25
64	Hideo Nomo	.50
65	Shawn Green	.50
66	Vladimir Guerrero	1.00
67	Jose Vidro	.25
68	Barry Bonds	2.00
69	Jeff Kent	.25
70	Rich Aurilia	.25
71	Cliff Floyd	.25
72	Josh Beckett	.25
73	Preston Wilson	.25
74	Mike Piazza	2.50
75	Mo Vaughn	.50
76	Jeromy Burnitz	.25
77	Roberto Alomar	.75
78	Phil Nevin	.25
79	Ryan Klesko	.25
80	Scott Rolen	.60
81	Bobby Abreu	.25
82	Jimmy Rollins	.25
83	Brian Giles	.50
84	Aramis Ramirez	.25
85	Ken Griffey Jr.	3.00
86	Sean Casey	.50
87	Barry Larkin	.50
88	Mike Hampton	.25
89	Larry Walker	.50
90	Todd Helton	1.00
91	*Ron Calloway*	4.00
92	*Joe Orloski*	4.00
93	*Anderson Machado*	8.00
94	*Eric Good*	8.00
95	*Reed Johnson*	4.00
96	*Brendan Donnelly*	4.00
97	*Chris Baker*	4.00
98	*Wilson Valdez*	4.00
99	*Scotty Layfield*	8.00
100	*P.J. Bevis*	4.00
101	*Edwin Almonte*	4.00
102	*Francis Beltran*	4.00
103	Valentino Pasucci	4.00
104	*Nelson Castro*	4.00
105	*Michael Crudale*	4.00
106	*Colin Young*	8.00
107	*Todd Donovan*	8.00
108	*Felix Escalona*	4.00
109	*Brandon Backe*	4.00
110	*Corey Thurman*	4.00
111	*Kyle Kane*	4.00
112	*Allan Simpson*	4.00
113	*Jose Valverde*	4.00
114	*Chris Booker*	4.00
115	*Brandon Puffer*	8.00
116	*John Foster*	8.00
117	*Clifford Bartosh*	4.00
118	*Gustavo Chacin*	4.00
119	*Steve Kent*	4.00
120	*Nate Field*	4.00
121	*Victor Alvarez*	10.00
122	*Steve Bechler*	10.00
123	*Adrian Burnside*	12.00
124	Marlon Byrd	25.00
125	*Jaime Cerda*	12.00
126	Brandon Claussen	20.00
127	*Mark Corey*	12.00
128	*Doug Devore*	15.00
129	*Kazuhisa Ishii*	220.00
130	*John Ennis*	12.00
131	*Kevin Frederick*	10.00
132	*Josh Hancock*	15.00
133	*Ben Howard*	25.00
134	Orlando Hudson	15.00
135	*Hansel Izquierdo*	20.00
136	*Eric Junge*	10.00
137	Austin Kearns	60.00
138	Victor Martinez	15.00
139	*Luis Martinez*	10.00
140	*Danny Mota*	10.00
141	*Jorge Padilla*	20.00
142	*Andy Pratt*	10.00
143	*Rene Reyes*	10.00
144	*Rodrigo Rosario*	15.00
145	*Tom Shearn*	10.00
146	*So Taguchi*	50.00
147	Dennis Tankersley	25.00
148	Matt Thornton	15.00
149	*Jeremy Ward*	10.00
150	*Mitch Wylie*	10.00
151	Pedro Martinez	15.00
152	Cal Ripken Jr.	40.00
153	Roger Clemens	20.00
154	Bernie Williams	8.00
155	Jason Giambi	15.00
156	Robin Ventura	15.00
157	Carlos Delgado	8.00
158	Frank Thomas	15.00
159	Magglio Ordonez	15.00
160	Jim Thome	10.00
161	Darin Erstad	8.00
162	Tim Salmon	8.00
163	Tim Hudson	10.00
164	Barry Zito	8.00
165	Ichiro Suzuki	50.00
166	Edgar Martinez	8.00
167	Alex Rodriguez	20.00
168	Ivan Rodriguez	12.00
169	Juan Gonzalez	15.00
170	Greg Maddux	20.00
171	Chipper Jones	20.00
172	Andruw Jones	10.00
173	Tom Glavine	8.00
174	Mike Piazza	20.00
175	Roberto Alomar	10.00
176	Scott Rolen	10.00
177	Sammy Sosa	20.00
178	Moises Alou	8.00
179	Ken Griffey Jr.	30.00
180	Jeff Bagwell	15.00
181	Jim Edmonds	8.00
182	J.D. Drew	12.00
183	Brian Giles	8.00
184	Randy Johnson	20.00
185	Curt Schilling	15.00
186	Luis Gonzalez	10.00
187	Todd Helton	12.00
188	Shawn Green	8.00
189	David Wells	8.00
190	Jeff Kent	8.00

2002 SPx Sweet Spot Bat Barrel

	MT
Complete Set (29):	
Common Player:	
BB-RARoberto Alomar	
BB-CBCarlos Beltran	
BB-ECEric Chavez	
BB-RCRoger Clemens	
BB-CDCarlos Delgado	
BB-JDJ.D. Drew	
BB-JEJim Edmonds	
BB-JGJason Giambi	
BB-TGTom Glavine	
BB-SGShawn Green	
BB-KGKen Griffey Jr.	
BB-THTodd Helton	
BB-AJAndruw Jones	
BB-CJChipper Jones	
BB-GMGreg Maddux	
BB-EMEdgar Martinez	
BB-RPRafael Palmeiro	
BB-MPMike Piazza	
BB-MRManny Ramirez	
BB-ARAlex Rodriguez	
BB-IRIvan Rodriguez	
BB-GSGary Sheffield	
BB-SSSammy Sosa	
BB-ISIchiro Suzuki	
BB-FTFrank Thomas	
BB-JTJim Thome	
BB-WMMatt Williams	
BB-PWPreston Wilson	
BB-KWKerry Wood	

2002 SPx Winning Materials Jersey Combo

		MT
Common Card:		10.00
Inserted 1:18		
AR	Alex Rodriguez, Ivan Rodriguez	20.00
GC	Ken Griffey Jr., Sean Casey/SP	25.00
BR	Jeff Bagwell, Alex Rodriguez	20.00
WG	Bernie Williams, Jason Giambi	18.00
JS	Randy Johnson, Curt Schilling	20.00
MJ	Greg Maddux, Chipper Jones	20.00
MC	Edgar Martinez, Mike Cameron	15.00
SP	Sammy Sosa, Corey Patterson	30.00
ED	Jim Edmonds, J.D. Drew	15.00
PA	Mike Piazza, Roberto Alomar	20.00
DH	Jermaine Dye, Tim Hudson	10.00
RA	Scott Rolen, Bobby Abreu	10.00
TO	Frank Thomas, Magglio Ordonez	15.00
HW	Mike Hampton, Larry Walker	10.00
TS	Jim Thome, C.C. Sabathia	15.00
GK	Shawn Green, Eric Karros	10.00
KG	Jason Kendall, Brian Giles	12.00
WP	David Wells, Jorge Posada	12.00
NM	Hideo Nomo, Pedro Martinez/ SP	30.00
RP	Ivan Rodriguez, Chan Ho Park	15.00
LH	Al Leiter, Mike Hampton	10.00
BA	Jeromy Burnitz, Edgardo Alfonzo	10.00
DS	Carlos Delgado, Shannon Stewart	10.00
BG	Jeff Bagwell, Juan Gonzalez	15.00
GR	Juan Gonzalez, Ivan Rodriguez	15.00
VR	Omar Vizquel, Alex Rodriguez	15.00
SE	Aaron Sele, Darin Erstad	10.00
JJ	Chipper Jones, Andruw Jones	20.00
SH	Kazuhiro Sasaki, Shigetoshi Hasegawa	20.00

2002 SPx Winning Materials USA Jersey Combo

		MT
Common Card:		
Production 150		
AH	Brent Abernathy, Orlando Hudson	8.00
BE	Lance Berkman, Adam Everett	
BK	Lance Berkman, Austin Kearns	
BT	Sean Burroughs, Mark Teixeira	40.00
EH	Adam Everett, Bill Hall	
GB	Jason Giambi, Sean Burroughs	25.00
HD	Orlando Hudson, Jeff Deardorff	15.00
GT	Jason Giambi, Mark Teixeira	
HOU	Roy Oswalt, Adam Everett	25.00
HP	Dustin Hermanson, Mark Prior	50.00
JC	Jacques Jones, Michael Cuddyer	35.00
KB	Austin Kearns, Sean Burroughs	50.00
KB	Mark Kotsay, Lance Berkman	
KC	Austin Kearns, Michael Cuddyer	50.00
MG	Doug Mientkiewicz, Jason Giambi	25.00
MIL	Jeff Deardorff, Bill Hall	
MIN	Doug Mientkiewicz, Michael Cuddyer	25.00
MO	Matt Morris, Roy Oswalt	30.00
MP	Matt Morris, Mark Prior	70.00
AW	Matt Anderson, Jeff Weaver	35.00
MW	Matt Morris, Jeff Weaver	25.00
OB	Roy Oswalt, Lance Berkman	
PB	Mark Prior, Dewon Brazelton	40.00
PM	Mark Prior, Eric Milton	
RE	Brian Roberts, Adam Everett	15.00
SD	Mark Kotsay, Sean Burroughs	40.00
TB	Brent Abernathy, Dewon Brazelton	15.00
TP	Mark Teixeira, Mark Prior	75.00
WB	Jeff Weaver, Dewon Brazelton	20.00
WH	Jeff Weaver, Dustin Hermanson	20.00

2002 SPx Winning Materials Base Combo

		MT
Common Card:		15.00
Production 200		
PE	Mike Piazza, Jim Edmonds	25.00
RJ	Alex Rodriguez, Derek Jeter	40.00
BG	Barry Bonds, Shawn Green	20.00
IM	Ichiro Suzuki, Edgar Martinez	50.00
SG	Sammy Sosa, Luis Gonzalez	25.00
GR	Troy Glaus, Alex Rodriguez	20.00
WJ	Bernie Williams, Derek Jeter	30.00
GS	Ken Griffey Jr., Sammy Sosa	30.00
PI	Albert Pujols, Ichiro Suzuki	60.00
SR	Kazuhiro Sasaki, Mariano Rivera	20.00

2002 SPx Winning Materials Base/Patch Combo

	MT
Complete Set (8):	
Common Player:	
BP-JGJason Giambi	
BP-LGLuis Gonzalez	
BP-KGKen Griffey Jr.	
BP-MPMike Piazza	
BP-ARAlex Rodriguez	
BP-SSSammy Sosa	
BP-ISIchiro Suzuki	
BP-BWBernie Williams	

2002 SPx Winning Materials Ball/Patch Combo

	MT
Complete Set (9):	
Common Player:	
PC-RCRoger Clemens	
PC-SGShawn Green	
PC-KGKen Griffey Jr.	
PC-THTodd Helton	
PC-CJChipper Jones	
PC-MPMike Piazza	
PC-ARAlex Rodriguez	
PC-SSSammy Sosa	
PC-ISIchiro Suzuki	

2002 SP Legendary Cuts

		MT
Complete Set (90):		30.00
Common Player:		.40
Pack (4):		9.00
Box (12):		95.00
1	Al Kaline	.75
2	Alvin Dark	.40
3	Andre Dawson	.40
4	Babe Ruth	3.00
5	Ernie Banks	1.00
6	Bob Lemon	.40
7	Bobby Bonds	.40
8	Carl Erskine	.40
9	Carl Hubbell	.40
10	Casey Stengel	.40
11	Charlie Gehringer	.40
12	Christy Mathewson	.60
13	Dale Murphy	.40
14	Dave Concepcion	.40
15	Dave Parker	.40
16	Dazzy Vance	.40
17	Dizzy Dean	.40
18	Don Baylor	.40
19	Don Drysdale	.75
20	Duke Snider	1.00
21	Earl Averill	.40
22	Early Wynn	.40
23	Edd Roush	.40
24	Elston Howard	.40
25	Ferguson Jenkins	.40
26	Frank Crosetti	.40
27	Frankie Frisch	.40
28	Gaylord Perry	.40
29	George Foster	.40
30	George Kell	.40
31	Gil Hodges	.40
32	Hank Greenberg	.40
33	Phil Niekro	.40
34	Harvey Haddix	.40
35	Harvey Kuenn	.40
36	Honus Wagner	1.50
37	Jackie Robinson	2.00
38	Orlando Cepeda	.40
39	Joe Adcock	.40
40	Joe Cronin	.40
41	Joe DiMaggio	2.50
42	Joe Morgan	.40
43	Johnny Mize	.40
44	Lefty Gomez	.40
45	Lefty Grove	.40
46	Jim Palmer	.40
47	Lou Boudreau	.40
48	Lou Gehrig	2.50
49	Luke Appling	.40
50	Mark McGwire	2.50
51	Mel Ott	.75
52	Mickey Cochrane	.40
53	Mickey Mantle	3.00
54	Minnie Minoso	.40
55	Brooks Robinson	.75
56	Nellie Fox	.40
57	Nolan Ryan	3.00
58	Rollie Fingers	.40
59	Pee Wee Reese	.40
60	Phil Rizzuto	.75
61	Ralph Kiner	.40
62	Ray Dandridge	.40
63	Richie Ashburn	.40
64	Robin Yount	.75
65	Rocky Colavito	.40
66	Roger Maris	2.00
67	Rogers Hornsby	.75
68	Ron Santo	.40
69	Ryne Sandberg	1.00
70	Stan Musial	1.50
71	Sam McDowell	.40
72	Satchel Paige	.75
73	Willie McCovey	.40
74	Steve Garvey	.40
75	Ted Kluszewski	.40
76	Catfish Hunter	.40
77	Terry Moore	.40
78	Thurman Munson	1.00
79	Tom Seaver	.75
80	Tommy John	.40
81	Tony Gwynn	.75
82	Tony Kubek	.40
83	Tony Lazzeri	.40
84	Ty Cobb	1.50
85	Wade Boggs	.40
86	Waite Hoyt	.40
87	Walter Johnson	1.00
88	Willie Stargell	.40
89	Yogi Berra	1.00
90	Zack Wheat	.40

2002 SP Legendary Cuts Bat Barrel

	MT
Not priced due to scarcity	
BB-DBaDon Baylor/5	
BB-BBoBobby Bonds/3	
BB-RCoRocky Colavito/2	
BB-ADaAlvin Dark/4	
BB-AnDAndre Dawson/4	
BB-GFoGeorge Foster/5	
BB-HGrHank Greenberg/1	
BB-LGrLefty Grove/1	
BB-TGwTony Gwynn/11	
BB-TLaTony Lazzeri/1	
BB-MMaMickey Mantle/7	
BB-RMaRoger Maris/1	
BB-MMcMark McGwire/4	
BB-JMiJohnny Mize/2	
BB-TMuThurman Munson/4	
BB-DMuDale Murphy/3	
BB-DPaDave Parker/6	
BB-PWePee Wee Reese/4	
BB-JaRJackie Robinson/1	
BB-BRuBabe Ruth/3	
BB-NRyNolan Ryan/9	
BB-RSaRyne Sandberg/3	
BB-DSnDuke Snider/2	
BB-WStWillie Stargell/5	
BB-EWyEarly Wynn/1	
BB-RYoRobin Yount/8	

2002 SP Legendary Cuts Legendary Bat

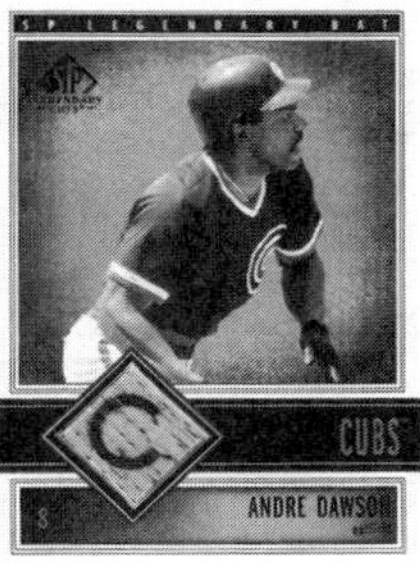

		MT
Common Player:		6.00
Inserted 1:8		
DBa	Don Baylor	6.00
YBe	Yogi Berra/SP	20.00
BBo	Bobby Bonds	6.00
RCo	Rocky Colavito	12.00
ADa	Alvin Dark	6.00
AnD	Andre Dawson	8.00
GFo	George Foster	6.00
NFo	Nellie Fox	15.00
SGa	Steve Garvey	6.00
HGr	Hank Greenberg/SP	35.00
LGr	Lefty Grove	15.00
TGw	Tony Gwynn	12.00
EHo	Elston Howard	10.00
GKe	George Kell	8.00
RKi	Ralph Kiner	10.00
TKu	Tonk (Tony) Kubek	8.00
TLa	Tony Lazzeri	10.00
MMa	Mickey Mantle/SP	110.00
RMa	Roger Maris	50.00
MMc	Mark McGwire	65.00
JMi	Johnny Mize	12.00
TMu	Thurman Munson	25.00
DMu	Dale Murphy	10.00
DPa	Dave Parker	6.00
GPe	Gaylord Perry	8.00
PWe	Pee Wee Reese	10.00
CRi	Cal Ripken Jr.	25.00
JaR	Jackie Robinson	40.00
BRu	Babe Ruth/SP	150.00
NRy	Nolan Ryan	25.00
RSa	Ryne Sandberg	12.00
TSe	Tom Seaver/SP	15.00
DSn	Duke Snider	12.00
WSt	Willie Stargell	8.00
RYo	Robin Yount	8.00
EWy	Early Wynn	8.00

2002 SP Legendary Cuts Legendary Jersey

		MT
Common Player:		6.00
Inserted 1:24		
DBa	Don Baylor	6.00
YBe	Yogi Berra	20.00
BBo	Bobby Bonds	6.00

FCr Frank Crosetti 10.00
AnD Andre Dawson 8.00
GFo George Foster 6.00
SGa Steve Garvey 8.00
MMa Mickey Mantle 100.00
RMa Roger Maris 50.00
DPa Dave Parker 6.00
PWe Pee Wee Reese 12.00
JRo Jackie Robinson 45.00
NRy Nolan Ryan 30.00
RSa Ryne Sandberg 25.00
TSe Tom Seaver 15.00

2002 SP Legendary Legendary Cuts Signature

MT

Quantity signed listed, some not priced
due to scarcity

JAd Joe Adcock/48 145.00
LAp Luke Appling/53 125.00
RAs Richie Ashburn/10
EAv Earl Averill/22 175.00
JBe Johnny Berardino/12
LBo Lou Boudreau/85 100.00
GBu Guy Bush/38 125.00
GCa George Case/36 180.00
HCh Happy Chandler/96 95.00
SCh Spud Chandler/17
TyC Ty Cobb/2
MCo Mickey Cochrane/2
JCo Johnny Cooney/64 75.00
SCo Stan Coveleski/85 100.00
JCr Joe Cronin/185 120.00
BDa Babe Dahlgren/51 180.00
RDa Ray Dandridge/179 85.00
DDe Dizzy Dean/4
JDi Joe DiMaggio/103
DDo Dick Donovan/23
TDo Taylor Douthit/60 165.00
DDr Don Drysdale/14
JDu Joe Dugan/39 140.00
BFa Bibb Falk/44 150.00
RFe Rick Ferrell/19
NFo Nellie Fox/1
FoF Ford Frick/1
FFr Frankie Frisch/35
LGe Lou Gehrig/3
CGe Charlie Gehringer/3
LGo Lefty Gomez/3
BGo Billy Goodman/53 140.00
HGr Hank Greenberg/94 425.00
LGr Lefty Grove/190 200.00
SHa Stan Hack/36 170.00
HHa Harvey Haddix/37
BHa Buddy Hassett/56 200.00
GHo Gil Hodges/1
RHo Rogers Hornsby/1
WHo Waite Hoyt/62
CHu Carl Hubbell/17 425.00
LJa Larry Jackson/37 125.00
NJa Newton "Bucky" Jacobs/44
EJo Earl Johnson/31
JJo Judy Johnson/86 150.00
WJo Walter Johnson/20
BKa Bob Kahle/53 150.00
WKa Willie Kamm/57 110.00
CKe Charlie Keller/29 280.00
KKe Ken Keltner/11
TKl Ted Kluszewski/23
MKo Mark Koenig/22 260.00
HKu Harvey Kuenn/23 230.00
CLa Cookie Lavagetto/22 200.00
BiL Billy Lee/40 150.00
BoL Bob Lemon/91 110.00
ELo Ed Lopat/58 150.00
SMa Sal Maglie/29 200.00
HMa Hank Majeski/21
MMa Mickey Mantle/2
RMa Roger Maris/1
ChrM Christy Mathewson/2
RMc Roy McMillan/18 190.00
JMi Johnny Mize/3
JMo Johnny Moore/22
TMo Terry Moore/86 95.00
ChM Chet Morgan/27 185.00
HNe Hal Newhouser/81 135.00
GPi George Pipgras/34
VRa Vic Raschi/98 110.00
PWe Pee Wee Reese/23
PRe Pete Reiser/73 140.00
RRe Rip Repulski/19
LRi Lance Richbourg/3
ORo Oscar Roettger/9
ERo Edd Roush/101 100.00
ERo2 Edd Roush/99 100.00
BRu Babe Ruth/3
BSc Bob Scheffing/19 100.00
WSc Willard Schmidt/10 350.00
HSc Hal Schumacher/17 280.00
BSe Bill Serena/16 295.00
JSe Joe Sewell/136 125.00
LSe Luke Sewell/2
BSh Bob Shawkey/10 120.00
BSh Bill Sherdel/10
BSz Bill Shantz/17 190.00
WSt Willie Stargell/153 95.00
CSt Casey Stengel/8
DVa Dazzy Vance/5
BVe Bill Veeck/11 450.00
HWa Honus Wagner/6
BWa Bucky Walters/31 165.00
VWe Vic Wertz/17
ZWh Zack Wheat/127 150.00
PWi Pete Whisenant/13
EWy Early Wynn/4

2002 SP Legendary Cuts Legendary Swatches

MT

Common Player: 6.00
Inserted 1:24

DBa Don Baylor 6.00
WBo Wade Boggs 8.00
FCr Frank Crosetti 10.00
DDr Don Drysdale 20.00
CEr Carl Erskine 8.00
TGw Tony Gwynn 12.00
FJe Ferguson Jenkins 8.00
TJo Tommy John 6.00
SMc Sam McDowell 6.00
MMi Minnie Minoso 8.00
JMo Joe Morgan 8.00
MOt Mel Ott 25.00
DPa Dave Parker 6.00
CRj Cal Ripken Jr. 25.00
RSa Ron Santo 10.00

1986 Sportflics

The premiere issue from Sportflics was distributed nationally by Amurol Division of Wrigley Gum Co. The three-phase "Magic Motion" cards depict three different photos per card, with each visible separately as the card is tilted. The 1986 issue features 200 full-color baseball cards plus 133 trivia cards. The cards are in the standard 2-1/2" x 3-1/2" size with the backs containing player stats and personal information. There are three different types of picture cards: 1) Tri-Star cards - 50 cards feature three players on one card; 2) Big Six cards - 10 cards which have six players in special categories; and 3) the Big Twelve card of 12 World Series players from the Kansas City Royals. The trivia cards are 1-3/4" x 2" and do not have player photos.

MT

Factory Set (200+133): 12.50
Complete Set (200): 10.00
Common Player: .10
Foil Pack (3+2): .75
Foil Box (36): 20.00

1 George Brett 2.00
2 Don Mattingly 2.50
3 Wade Boggs 1.50
4 Eddie Murray 1.00
5 Dale Murphy .65
6 Rickey Henderson .65
7 Harold Baines .10
8 Cal Ripken, Jr. 4.00
9 Orel Hershiser .10
10 Bret Saberhagen .10
11 Tim Raines .10
12 Fernando Valenzuela .10
13 Tony Gwynn 2.00
14 Pedro Guerrero .10
15 Keith Hernandez .10
16 Ernest Riles .10
17 Jim Rice .15
18 Ron Guidry .10
19 Willie McGee .10
20 Ryne Sandberg 1.50
21 Kirk Gibson .10
22 Ozzie Guillen .10
23 Dave Parker .10
24 Vince Coleman .10
25 Tom Seaver .75
26 Brett Butler .10
27 Steve Carlton .75
28 Gary Carter .60
29 Cecil Cooper .10
30 Jose Cruz .10
31 Alvin Davis .10
32 Dwight Evans .10
33 Julio Franco .10
34 Damaso Garcia .10
35 Steve Garvey .50
36 Kent Hrbek .10
37 Reggie Jackson .75
38 Fred Lynn .10
39 Paul Molitor .75
40 Jim Presley .10
41 Dave Righetti .10
42a Robin Yount (Yankees logo on back) 80.00
42b Robin Yount (Brewers logo) 1.25
43 Nolan Ryan 4.00
44 Mike Schmidt 1.50
45 Lee Smith .10
46 Rick Sutcliffe .10
47 Bruce Sutter .10
48 Lou Whitaker .10
49 Dave Winfield 1.50
50 Pete Rose 2.50
51 N.L. MVPs (Steve Garvey, Pete Rose, Ryne Sandberg) .75
52 Slugging Stars (Harold Baines, George Brett, Jim Rice) .35
53 No-Hitters (Phil Niekro, Jerry Reuss, Mike Witt) .25
54 Big Hitters (Don Mattingly, Cal Ripken, Jr., Robin Yount) 2.00
55 Bullpen Aces (Goose Gossage, Dan Quisenberry, Lee Smith) .10
56 Rookies of the Year (Pete Rose, Steve Sax, Darryl Strawberry) 1.00
57 A.L. MVPs (Don Baylor, Reggie Jackson, Cal Ripken, Jr.) .50
58 Repeat Batting Champs (Bill Madlock, Dave Parker, Pete Rose) .45
59 Cy Young Winners (Mike Flanagan, Ron Guidry, LaMarr Hoyt) .10
60 Double Award Winners (Tom Seaver, Rick Sutcliffe, Fernando Valenzuela) .20
61 Home Run Champs (Tony Armas, Reggie Jackson, Jim Rice) .25
62 N.L. MVPs (Keith Hernandez, Dale Murphy, Mike Schmidt) .40
63 A.L. MVPs (George Brett, Fred Lynn, Robin Yount) .30
64 Comeback Players (Bert Blyleven, John Denny, Jerry Koosman) .10
65 Cy Young Relievers (Rollie Fingers, Willie Hernandez, Bruce Sutter) .10
66 Rookies of the Year (Andre Dawson, Bob Horner, Gary Matthews) .20
67 Rookies of the Year (Carlton Fisk, Ron Kittle, Tom Seaver) .25
68 Home Run Champs (George Foster, Dave Kingman, Mike Schmidt) .25
69 Double Award Winners (Rod Carew, Cal Ripken, Jr., Pete Rose) 2.00
70 Cy Young Winners (Steve Carlton, Tom Seaver, Rick Sutcliffe) .25
71 Top Sluggers (Reggie Jackson, Fred Lynn, Robin Yount) .30
72 Rookies of the Year (Dave Righetti, Rick Sutcliffe, Fernando Valenzuela) .10
73 Rookies of the Year (Fred Lynn, Eddie Murray, Cal Ripken, Jr.) .50
74 Rookies of the Year (Rod Carew, Alvin Davis, Lou Whitaker) .20

75 Batting Champs (Wade Boggs, Carney Lansford, Don Mattingly) 1.00
76 Jesse Barfield .10
77 Phil Bradley .10
78 Chris Brown .10
79 Tom Browning .10
80 Tom Brunansky .10
81 Bill Buckner .10
82 Chili Davis .10
83 Mike Davis .10
84 Rich Gedman .10
85 Willie Hernandez .10
86 Ron Kittle .10
87 Lee Lacy .10
88 Bill Madlock .10
89 Mike Marshall .10
90 Keith Moreland .10
91 Graig Nettles .10
92 Lance Parrish .10
93 Kirby Puckett 2.00
94 Juan Samuel .10
95 Steve Sax .10
96 Dave Stieb .10
97 Darryl Strawberry .10
98 Willie Upshaw .10
99 Frank Viola .10
100 Dwight Gooden .10
101 Joaquin Andujar .10
102 George Bell .10
103 Bert Blyleven .10
104 Mike Boddicker .10
105 Britt Burns .10
106 Rod Carew .75
107 Jack Clark .10
108 Danny Cox .10
109 Ron Darling .10
110 Andre Dawson .35
111 Leon Durham .10
112 Tony Fernandez .10
113 Tom Herr .10
114 Teddy Higuera .10
115 Bob Horner .10
116 Dave Kingman .10
117 Jack Morris .10
118 Dan Quisenberry .10
119 Jeff Reardon .10
120 Bryn Smith .10
121 Ozzie Smith 1.50
122 John Tudor .10
123 Tim Wallach .10
124 Willie Wilson .10
125 Carlton Fisk .65
126 RBI Sluggers (Gary Carter, George Foster, Al Oliver) .10
127 Run Scorers (Keith Hernandez, Tim Raines, Ryne Sandberg) .25
128 Run Scorers (Paul Molitor, Cal Ripken, Jr., Willie Wilson) .50
129 No-Hitters (John Candelaria, Dennis Eckersley, Bob Forsch) .10
130 World Series MVPs (Ron Cey, Rollie Fingers, Pete Rose) .35
131 All-Star Game MVPs (Dave Concepcion, George Foster, Bill Madlock) .10
132 Cy Young Winners (Vida Blue, John Denny, Fernando Valenzuela) .10
133 Comeback Players (Doyle Alexander, Joaquin Andujar, Richard Dotson) .10
134 Big Winners (John Denny, Tom Seaver, Rick Sutcliffe) .10
135 Veteran Pitchers (Phil Niekro, Tom Seaver, Don Sutton) .25
136 Rookies of the Year (Vince Coleman, Dwight Gooden, Alfredo Griffin) .20
137 All-Star Game MVPs (Gary Carter, Steve Garvey, Fred Lynn) .20
138 Veteran Hitters (Tony Perez, Pete Rose, Rusty Staub) .50
139 Power Hitters (George Foster, Jim Rice, Mike Schmidt) .30
140 Batting Champs (Bill Buckner, Tony Gwynn, Al Oliver) .25
141 No-Hitters (Jack Morris, Dave Righetti, Nolan Ryan) .50
142 No-Hitters (Vida Blue, Bert Blyleven, Tom Seaver) .10
143 Strikeout Kings (Dwight Gooden, Nolan Ryan, Fernando Valenzuela) 1.25
144 Base Stealers (Dave Lopes, Tim Raines, Willie Wilson) .10
145 RBI Sluggers (Tony Armas, Cecil Cooper, Eddie Murray) .15
146 A.L. MVPs (Rod Carew, Rollie Fingers, Jim Rice) .15
147 World Series MVPs (Rick Dempsey, Reggie Jackson, Alan Trammell) .25
148 World Series MVPs (Pedro Guerrero, Darrell Porter, Mike Schmidt) .20
149 ERA Leaders (Mike Boddicker, Ron Guidry, Rick Sutcliffe) .10
150 Comeback Players (Reggie Jackson, Dave Kingman, Fred Lynn) .20
151 Buddy Bell .10
152 Dennis Boyd .10
153 Dave Concepcion .10
154 Brian Downing .10
155 Shawon Dunston .10
156 John Franco .10
157 Scott Garrelts .10
158 Bob James .10
159 Charlie Leibrandt .10
160 Oddibe McDowell .10
161 Roger McDowell .10
162 Mike Moore .10
163 Phil Niekro .65
164 Al Oliver .10
165 Tony Pena .10
166 Ted Power .10
167 Mike Scioscia .10
168 Mario Soto .10
169 Bob Stanley .10
170 Garry Templeton .10
171 Andre Thornton .10
172 Alan Trammell .10
173 Doug DeCinces .10
174 Greg Walker .10
175 Don Sutton .65
176 1985 Award Winners (Vince Coleman, Dwight Gooden, Ozzie Guillen, Don Mattingly, Willie McGee, Bret Saberhagen) .50
177 1985 Hot Rookies (Stewart Cliburn, Brian Fisher, Joe Hesketh, Joe Orsulak, Mark Salas, Larry Sheets) .10
178a Future Stars (Jose Canseco, Mark Funderburk, Mike Greenwell, Steve Lombardozzi, Billy Joe Robidoux, Danny Tartabull) 3.00
178b Future Stars (Jose Canseco, Mike Greenwell, Steve Lombardozzi, Billy Jo Robidoux, Danny Tartabull, Jim Wilson) 30.00
179 Gold Glove (George Brett, Ron Guidry, Keith Hernandez, Don Mattingly, Willie McGee, Dale Murphy) 1.00
180 .300 (Wade Boggs, George Brett, Rod Carew, Cecil Cooper, Don Mattingly, Willie Wilson) 1.00
181 .300 (Pedro Guerrero, Tony Gwynn, Keith Hernandez, Bill Madlock, Dave Parker, Pete Rose) .50
182 1985 Milestones (Rod Carew, Phil Niekro, Pete Rose, Nolan Ryan, Tom Seaver, Matt Tallman) 1.50
183 1985 Triple Crown (Wade Boggs, Darrell Evans, Don Mattingly, Willie McGee, Dale Murphy, Dave Parker) 1.00
184 1985 HL (Wade Boggs, Dwight Gooden, Rickey Henderson, Don Mattingly, Willie McGee, John Tudor) 1.00
185 1985 20-Game Winners (Joaquin Andujar, Tom Browning, Dwight Gooden, Ron Guidry, Bret Saberhagen, John Tudor) .10
186 World Series Champs (Steve Balboni, George Brett, Dane Iorg, Danny Jackson, Charlie Leibrandt, Darryl Motley, Dan Quisenberry, Bret Saberhagen, Lonnie Smith, Jim Sundberg, Frank White, Willie Wilson) .40
187 Hubie Brooks .10
188 Glenn Davis .10
189 Darrell Evans .10
190 Rich Gossage .10
191 Andy Hawkins .10
192 Jay Howell .10
193 LaMarr Hoyt .10
194 Davey Lopes .10
195 Mike Scott .10
196 Ted Simmons .10
197 Gary Ward .10
198 Bob Welch .10
199 Mike Young .10
200 Buddy Biancalana .10

1986 Sportflics Rookies

The 1986 Rookies set offers 50 cards and features 47 individual rookie players. In addition, there are two Tri-Star cards; one highlights former Rookies of the Year and the other features three prominent players. There is one "Big Six" card featuring six superstars. The full-color photos on the 2-1/2" x 3-1/2" cards use Sportflics three-phase "Magic Motion" animation. The set was packaged in a collector box which also contained 34 trivia cards that measure 1-3/4" x 2". The set was distributed only by hobby dealers.

		MT
Complete Set (50):		15.00
Common Player:		.10
1	John Kruk	.10
2	Edwin Correa	.10
3	Pete Incaviglia	.10
4	Dale Sveum	.10
5	Juan Nieves	.10
6	Will Clark	1.00
7	Wally Joyner	.75
8	Lance McCullers	.10
9	Scott Bailes	.10
10	Dan Plesac	.10
11	Jose Canseco	1.50
12	Bobby Witt	.10
13	Barry Bonds	12.00
14	Andres Thomas	.10
15	Jim Deshaies	.10
16	Ruben Sierra	.10
17	Steve Lombardozzi	.10
18	Cory Snyder	.10
19	Reggie Williams	.10
20	Mitch Williams	.10
21	Glenn Braggs	.10
22	Danny Tartabull	.10
23	Charlie Kerfeld	.10
24	Paul Assenmacher	.10
25	Robby Thompson	.10
26	Bobby Bonilla	.20
27	Andres Galarraga	.20
28	Billy Jo Robidoux	.10
29	Bruce Ruffin	.10
30	Greg Swindell	.10
31	John Cangelosi	.10
32	Jim Traber	.10
33	Russ Morman	.10
34	Barry Larkin	.25
35	Todd Worrell	.10
36	John Cerutti	.10
37	Mike Kingery	.10
38	Mark Eichhorn	.10
39	Scott Bankhead	.10
40	Bo Jackson	.25
41	Greg Mathews	.10
42	Eric King	.10
43	Kal Daniels	.10
44	Calvin Schiraldi	.10
45	Mickey Brantley	.10
46	Outstanding Rookie Seasons (Fred Lynn, Willie Mays, Pete Rose)	.60
47	Outstanding Rookie Seasons (Dwight Gooden, Tom Seaver, Fernando Valenzuela)	.25
48	Outstanding Rookie Seasons (Eddie Murray, Dave Righetti, Cal Ripken, Jr., Steve Sax, Darryl Strawberry, Lou Whitaker)	.50
49	Kevin Mitchell	.10
50	Mike Diaz	.10

1987 Sportflics

In its second year in the national market, Sportflics' basic issue was again a 200-card set of 2-1/2" x 3-1/2" "Magic Motion" cards, which offer three different photos on the same card, each visible in turn as the card is moved from top to bottom or side to side. Besides single-player cards, the '87 Sportflics set includes several three-

and six-player cards, though not as many as in the 1986 set. The card backs feature a small player portrait photo on the single-player cards, an innovation for 1987. The cards were issued with a series of 136 team logo trivia cards. Most cards exist in two variations, carrying 1986 or 1987 copyright dates on back.

		MT
Factory Set (200+136):		12.50
Complete Set (200):		10.00
Common Player:		.10
Foil Pack (3+2):		.75
Foil Box (36):		20.00
1	Don Mattingly	1.50
2	Wade Boggs	1.00
3	Dale Murphy	.50
4	Rickey Henderson	.75
5	George Brett	1.00
6	Eddie Murray	.75
7	Kirby Puckett	1.00
8	Ryne Sandberg	1.00
9	Cal Ripken, Jr.	3.00
10	Roger Clemens	.75
11	Ted Higuera	.10
12	Steve Sax	.10
13	Chris Brown	.10
14	Jesse Barfield	.10
15	Kent Hrbek	.10
16	Robin Yount	.65
17	Glenn Davis	.10
18	Hubie Brooks	.10
19	Mike Scott	.10
20	Darryl Strawberry	.10
21	Alvin Davis	.10
22	Eric Davis	.10
23	Danny Tartabull	.10
24a	Cory Snyder (Pat Tabler photo on back)	1.50
24b	Cory Snyder (Pat Tabler photo on back) (facing front, 1/4 swing on front)	1.50
24c	Cory Snyder (Snyder photo on back) (facing to side)	.50
25	Pete Rose	1.50
26	Wally Joyner	.10
27	Pedro Guerrero	.10
28	Tom Seaver	.75
29	Bob Knepper	.10
30	Mike Schmidt	1.00
31	Tony Gwynn	1.00
32	Don Slaught	.10
33	Todd Worrell	.10
34	Tim Raines	.10
35	Dave Parker	.10
36	Bob Ojeda	.10
37	Pete Incaviglia	.10
38	Bruce Hurst	.10
39	Bobby Witt	.10
40	Steve Garvey	.35
41	Dave Winfield	1.00
42	Jose Cruz	.10
43	Orel Hershiser	.10
44	Reggie Jackson	1.00
45	Chili Davis	.10
46	Robby Thompson	.10
47	Dennis Boyd	.10
48	Kirk Gibson	.10
49	Fred Lynn	.10
50	Gary Carter	.35
51	George Bell	.10
52	Pete O'Brien	.10
53	Ron Darling	.10
54	Paul Molitor	.75
55	Mike Pagliarulo	.10
56	Mike Boddicker	.10
57	Dave Righetti	.10
58	Len Dykstra	.10
59	Mike Witt	.10
60	Tony Bernazard	.10
61	John Kruk	.10
62	Mike Krukow	.10
63	Sid Fernandez	.10
64	Gary Gaetti	.10
65	Vince Coleman	.10
66	Pat Tabler	.10
67	Mike Scioscia	.10
68	Scott Garrelts	.10
69	Brett Butler	.10
70	Bill Buckner	.10
71a	Dennis Rasmussen (John Montefusco photo on back; mustache)	.25
71b	Dennis Rasmussen (correct photo on back, no mustache)	.10
72	Tim Wallach	.10
73	Bob Horner	.10
74	Willie McGee	.10
75	A.L. First Basemen (Wally Joyner, Don Mattingly, Eddie Murray)	.50
76	Jesse Orosco	.10
77	N.L. Relief Pitchers (Jeff Reardon, Dave Smith, Todd Worrell)	.10
78	Candy Maldonado	.10
79	N.L. Shortstops (Hubie Brooks, Shawon Dunston, Ozzie Smith)	.10
80	A.L. Left Fielders (George Bell, Jose Canseco, Jim Rice)	.25
81	Bert Blyleven	.10
82	Mike Marshall	.10
83	Ron Guidry	.10
84	Julio Franco	.10
85	Willie Wilson	.10
86	Lee Lacy	.10
87	Jack Morris	.10
88	Ray Knight	.10
89	Phil Bradley	.10
90	Jose Canseco	.75
91	Gary Ward	.10
92	Mike Easler	.10
93	Tony Pena	.10
94	Dave Smith	.10
95	Will Clark	.30
96	Lloyd Moseby	.10
97	Jim Rice	.15
98	Shawon Dunston	.10
99	Don Sutton	.50
100	Dwight Gooden	.10
101	Lance Parrish	.10
102	Mark Langston	.10
103	Floyd Youmans	.10
104	Lee Smith	.10
105	Willie Hernandez	.10
106	Doug DeCinces	.10
107	Ken Schrom	.10
108	Don Carman	.10
109	Brook Jacoby	.10
110	Steve Bedrosian	.10
111	A.L. Pitchers (Roger Clemens, Teddy Higuera, Jack Morris)	.25
112	A.L. Second Basemen (Marty Barrett, Tony Bernazard, Lou Whitaker)	.10
113	A.L. Shortstops (Tony Fernandez, Scott Fletcher, Cal Ripken, Jr.)	.25
114	A.L. Third Basemen (Wade Boggs, George Brett, Gary Gaetti)	.25
115	N.L. Third Basemen (Chris Brown, Mike Schmidt, Tim Wallach)	.20
116	N.L. Second Basemen (Bill Doran, Johnny Ray, Ryne Sandberg)	.10
117	N.L. Right Fielders (Kevin Bass, Tony Gwynn, Dave Parker)	.10
118	Hot Rookie Prospects (David Clark, Pat Dodson, Ty Gainey, Phil Lombardi, Benito Santiago), *(Terry Steinbach)*	.25
119	1986 Season Highlights (Dave Righetti, Mike Scott, Fernando Valenzuela)	.10
120	N.L. Pitchers (Dwight Gooden, Mike Scott, Fernando Valenzuela)	.10
121	Johnny Ray	.10
122	Keith Moreland	.10
123	Juan Samuel	.10
124	Wally Backman	.10
125	Nolan Ryan	3.00
126	Greg Harris	.10
127	Kirk McCaskill	.10
128	Dwight Evans	.10
129	Rick Rhoden	.10
130	Bill Madlock	.10
131	Oddibe McDowell	.10
132	Darrell Evans	.10
133	Keith Hernandez	.10
134	Tom Brunansky	.10
135	Kevin McReynolds	.10
136	Scott Fletcher	.10
137	Lou Whitaker	.10
138	Carney Lansford	.10
139	Andre Dawson	.35
140	Carlton Fisk	.75
141	Buddy Bell	.10
142	Ozzie Smith	1.00
143	Dan Pasqua	.10
144	Kevin Mitchell	.10
145	Bret Saberhagen	.10
146	Charlie Kerfeld	.10
147	Phil Niekro	.50
148	John Candelaria	.10
149	Rich Gedman	.10
150	Fernando Valenzuela	.10
151	N.L. Catchers (Gary Carter, Tony Pena, Mike Scioscia)	.10
152	N.L. Left Fielders (Vince Coleman, Jose Cruz, Tim Raines)	.10
153	A.L. Right Fielders (Harold Baines, Jesse Barfield, Dave Winfield)	.10
154	A.L. Catchers (Rich Gedman, Lance Parrish, Don Slaught)	.10
155	N.L. Center Fielders (Kevin McReynolds, Dale Murphy, Eric Davis)	.10
156	'86 Highlights (Jim Deshaies, Mike Schmidt, Don Sutton)	.10
157	A.L. Speedburners (John Cangelosi, Rickey Henderson, Gary Pettis)	.10
158	Hot Rookie Prospects (Randy Asadoor, Casey Candaele, Dave Cochrane, Rafael Palmeiro, Tim Pyznarski, Kevin Seitzer)	.50
159	The Best of the Best (Roger Clemens, Dwight Gooden, Rickey Henderson, Don Mattingly, Dale Murphy, Eddie Murray)	.75
160	Roger McDowell	.10
161	Brian Downing	.10
162	Bill Doran	.10
163	Don Baylor	.10
164	Alfredo Griffin	.10
165	Don Aase	.10
166	Glenn Wilson	.10
167	Dan Quisenberry	.10
168	Frank White	.10
169	Cecil Cooper	.10
170	Jody Davis	.10
171	Harold Baines	.10
172	Rob Deer	.10
173	John Tudor	.10
174	Larry Parrish	.10
175	Kevin Bass	.10
176	Joe Carter	.10
177	Mitch Webster	.10
178	Dave Kingman	.10
179	Jim Presley	.10
180	Mel Hall	.10
181	Shane Rawley	.10
182	Marty Barrett	.10
183	Damaso Garcia	.10
184	Bobby Grich	.10
185	Leon Durham	.10
186	Ozzie Guillen	.10
187	Tony Fernandez	.10
188	Alan Trammell	.10
189	Jim Clancy	.10
190	Bo Jackson	.15
191	Bob Forsch	.10
192	John Franco	.10
193	Von Hayes	.10
194	A.L. Relief Pitchers (Don Aase, Mark Eichhorn, Dave Righetti)	.10
195	N.L. First Basemen (Will Clark, Glenn Davis, Keith Hernandez)	.10
196	'86 Highlights (Roger Clemens, Joe Cowley, Bob Horner)	.10
197	The Best of the Best (Wade Boggs, George Brett, Hubie Brooks, Tony Gwynn, Tim Raines, Ryne Sandberg)	.80
198	A.L. Center Fielders (Rickey Henderson, Fred Lynn, Kirby Puckett)	.50
199	N.L. Speedburners (Vince Coleman, Tim Raines, Eric Davis)	.10
200	Steve Carlton	.75

1987 Sportflics Rookie Prospects

The Rookie Prospects set consists of 10 cards in standard 2-1/2" x 3-1/2" size. The card fronts feature Sportflics' "Magic Motion" process. Card backs contain a player photo plus a short biography and player personal and statistical information. The set was offered in two separately wrapped mylar packs of five cards to hobby dealers purchasing cases of Sportflics' Team Preview set. Twenty-four packs of "Rookie Prospects" cards were included with each case.

		MT
Complete Set (10):		5.00
Common Player:		.50
1	Terry Steinbach	.50
2	Rafael Palmeiro	2.00
3	Dave Magadan	.50
4	Marvin Freeman	.50
5	Brick Smith	.50
6	B.J. Surhoff	.50
7	John Smiley	.50
8	Alonzo Powell	.50
9	Benny Santiago	.50
10	Devon White	.50

1987 Sportflics Rookies

The Rookies set was issued in two boxed series of 25 cards. The first was released in July with the second series following in October. The cards, which are the standard 2-1/2" x 3-1/2", feature Sportflics' special "Magic Motion" process. The card fronts contain a full-color photo and present three different pictures, depending on how the card is held. The backs also contain a full-color photo along with player statistics and a biography.

		MT
Complete Set One (1-25):		6.00
Complete Set Two (26-50):		3.00
Common Player:		.10
	SET ONE	
1	Eric Bell	.10
2	Chris Bosio	.10
3	Bob Brower	.10
4	Jerry Browne	.10
5	Ellis Burks	.10
6	Casey Candaele	.10
7	Ken Gerhart	.10
8	Mike Greenwell	.10
9	Stan Jefferson	.10
10	Dave Magadan	.10
11	Joe Magrane	.10
12	Fred McGriff	.25
13	Mark McGwire	4.00
14	Mark McLemore	.10
15	Jeff Musselman	.10
16	Matt Nokes	.10
17	Paul O'Neill	.25
18	Luis Polonia	.10
19	Benny Santiago	.10
20	Kevin Seitzer	.10
21	John Smiley	.10
22	Terry Steinbach	.10
23	B.J. Surhoff	.15
24	Devon White	.25
25	Matt Williams	1.00
	SET TWO	
26	DeWayne Buice	.10
27	Willie Fraser	.10
28	Bill Ripken	.10
29	Mike Henneman	.10
30	Shawn Hillegas	.10
31	Shane Mack	.10
32	Rafael Palmeiro	1.50
33	Mike Jackson	.10
34	Gene Larkin	.10
35	Jimmy Jones	.10
36	Gerald Young	.10
37	Ken Caminiti	.25
38	Sam Horn	.10
39	David Cone	.25
40	Mike Dunne	.10
41	Ken Williams	.10
42	John Morris	.10
43	Jim Lindeman	.10
44	Mike Stanley	.10
45	Les Straker	.10
46	Jeff Robinson	.10
47	Todd Benzinger	.10
48	Jeff Blauser	.10
49	John Marzano	.10
50	Keith Miller	.10

1988 Sportflics

The design of the 1988 Sportflics set differs greatly from the previous two years. Besides increasing the number of cards in the set to 225, Sportflics included the player name, team and uniform number on the card front. The triple-action color photos are surrounded by a red border. The backs are re-designed, also. Full-color action photos, plus extensive statistics and informative biographies are utilized. Three highlights cards and three rookie prospects card are included in the set. The cards are the standard 2-1/2" x 3-1/2".

		MT
Factory Set (225+136):		15.00
Complete Set (225):		12.50
Common Player:		.10
Foil Pack (3+2):		.75
Foil Box (36):		20.00
1	Don Mattingly	1.50
2	Tim Raines	.10
3	Andre Dawson	.25
4	George Bell	.10
5	Joe Carter	.10
6	Matt Nokes	.10
7	Dave Winfield	1.00
8	Kirby Puckett	1.00
9	Will Clark	.30
10	Eric Davis	.10
11	Rickey Henderson	.75
12	Ryne Sandberg	1.00
13	Jesse Barfield	.10
14	Ozzie Guillen	.10
15	Bret Saberhagen	.10
16	Tony Gwynn	1.00
17	Kevin Seitzer	.10
18	Jack Clark	.10
19	Danny Tartabull	.10
20	Ted Higuera	.10
21	Charlie Leibrandt, Jr.	.10
22	Benny Santiago	.10
23	Fred Lynn	.10
24	Rob Thompson	.10
25	Alan Trammell	.10
26	Tony Fernandez	.10
27	Rick Sutcliffe	.10
28	Gary Carter	.35
29	Cory Snyder	.10
30	Lou Whitaker	.10
31	Keith Hernandez	.10
32	Mike Witt	.10
33	Harold Baines	.10
34	Robin Yount	.75
35	Mike Schmidt	1.00
36	Dion James	.10
37	Tom Candiotti	.10
38	Tracy Jones	.10
39	Nolan Ryan	2.50
40	Fernando Valenzuela	.10
41	Vance Law	.10
42	Roger McDowell	.10
43	Carlton Fisk	.65
44	Scott Garrelts	.10
45	Lee Guetterman	.10
46	Mark Langston	.10
47	Willie Randolph	.10
48	Bill Doran	.10
49	Larry Parrish	.10
50	Wade Boggs	.75
51	Shane Rawley	.10
52	Alvin Davis	.10
53	Jeff Reardon	.10
54	Jim Presley	.10
55	Kevin Bass	.10
56	Kevin McReynolds	.10
57	B.J. Surhoff	.10
58	Julio Franco	.10
59	Eddie Murray	.60
60	Jody Davis	.10
61	Todd Worrell	.10
62	Von Hayes	.10
63	Billy Hatcher	.10
64	John Kruk	.10
65	Tom Henke	.10
66	Mike Scott	.10
67	Vince Coleman	.10
68	Ozzie Smith	1.00
69	Ken Williams	.10
70	Steve Bedrosian	.10
71	Luis Polonia	.10
72	Brook Jacoby	.10
73	Ron Darling	.10
74	Lloyd Moseby	.10
75	Wally Joyner	.10
76	Dan Quisenberry	.10
77	Scott Fletcher	.10
78	Kirk McCaskill	.10
79	Paul Molitor	.75
80	Mike Aldrete	.10
81	Neal Heaton	.10
82	Jeffrey Leonard	.10
83	Dave Magadan	.10
84	Danny Cox	.10
85	Lance McCullers	.10
86	Jay Howell	.10
87	Charlie Hough	.10
88	Gene Garber	.10
89	Jesse Orosco	.10
90	Don Robinson	.10
91	Willie McGee	.10
92	Bert Blyleven	.10
93	Phil Bradley	.10
94	Terry Kennedy	.10
95	Kent Hrbek	.10
96	Juan Samuel	.10
97	Pedro Guerrero	.10
98	Sid Bream	.10
99	Devon White	.10
100	Mark McGwire	2.50
101	Dave Parker	.10
102	Glenn Davis	.10
103	Greg Walker	.10
104	Rick Rhoden	.10
105	Mitch Webster	.10
106	Lenny Dykstra	.10
107	Gene Larkin	.10
108	Floyd Youmans	.10
109	Andy Van Slyke	.10
110	Mike Scioscia	.10
111	Kirk Gibson	.10
112	Kal Daniels	.10
113	Ruben Sierra	.10
114	Sam Horn	.10
115	Ray Knight	.10
116	Jimmy Key	.10
117	Bo Diaz	.10
118	Mike Greenwell	.10
119	Barry Bonds	2.00
120	Reggie Jackson	1.00
121	Mike Pagliarulo	.10
122	Tommy John	.10
123	Bill Madlock	.10
124	Ken Caminiti	.10
125	Gary Ward	.10
126	Candy Maldonado	.10
127	Harold Reynolds	.10
128	Joe Magrane	.10
129	Mike Henneman	.10
130	Jim Gantner	.10
131	Bobby Bonilla	.10
132	John Farrell	.10
133	Frank Tanana	.10
134	Zane Smith	.10
135	Dave Righetti	.10
136	Rick Reuschel	.10
137	Dwight Evans	.10
138	Howard Johnson	.10
139	Terry Leach	.10
140	Casey Candaele	.10
141	Tom Herr	.10
142	Tony Pena	.10
143	Lance Parrish	.10
144	Ellis Burks	.10
145	Pete O'Brien	.10
146	Mike Boddicker	.10
147	Buddy Bell	.10
148	Bo Jackson	.15
149	Frank White	.10
150	George Brett	1.00
151	Tim Wallach	.10
152	Cal Ripken, Jr.	2.50
153	Brett Butler	.10
154	Gary Gaetti	.10
155	Darryl Strawberry	.10
156	Alfredo Griffin	.10
157	Marty Barrett	.10
158	Jim Rice	.15
159	Terry Pendleton	.10
160	Orel Hershiser	.10
161	Larry Sheets	.10
162	Dave Stewart	.10
163	Shawon Dunston	.10
164	Keith Moreland	.10
165	Ken Oberkfell	.10
166	Ivan Calderon	.10
167	Bob Welch	.10
168	Fred McGriff	.10
169	Pete Incaviglia	.10
170	Dale Murphy	.25
171	Mike Dunne	.10
172	Chili Davis	.10
173	Milt Thompson	.10
174	Terry Steinbach	.10
175	Oddibe McDowell	.10
176	Jack Morris	.10
177	Sid Fernandez	.10
178	Ken Griffey	.10
179	Lee Smith	.10
180	1987 Highlights (Juan Nieves, Kirby Puckett, Mike Schmidt)	.25
181	Brian Downing	.10
182	Andres Galarraga	.10
183	Rob Deer	.10
184	Greg Brock	.10
185	Doug DeCinces	.10
186	Johnny Ray	.10
187	Hubie Brooks	.10
188	Darrell Evans	.10
189	Mel Hall	.10
190	Jim Deshaies	.10
191	Dan Plesac	.10
192	Willie Wilson	.10
193	Mike LaValliere	.10
194	Tom Brunansky	.10
195	John Franco	.10
196	Frank Viola	.10
197	Bruce Hurst	.10
198	John Tudor	.10
199	Bob Forsch	.10
200	Dwight Gooden	.10
201	Jose Canseco	.75
202	Carney Lansford	.10
203	Kelly Downs	.10
204	Glenn Wilson	.10
205	Pat Tabler	.10
206	Mike Davis	.10
207	Roger Clemens	.75
208	Dave Smith	.10
209	Curt Young	.10
210	Mark Eichhorn	.10
211	Juan Nieves	.10

212	Bob Boone	.10
213	Don Sutton	.45
214	Willie Upshaw	.10
215	Jim Clancy	.10
216	Bill Ripken	.10
217	Ozzie Virgil	.10
218	Dave Concepcion	.10
219	Alan Ashby	.10
220	Mike Marshall	.10
221	'87 Highlights (Vince Coleman, Mark McGwire, Paul Molitor)	1.00
222	'87 Highlights (Steve Bedrosian, Don Mattingly, Benito Santiago)	.40
223	Hot Rookie Prospects (Shawn Abner), *(Jay Buhner,* Gary Thurman)	.25
224	Hot Rookie Prospects (Tim Crews, John Davis, Vincente Palacios)	.10
225	Hot Rookie Prospects (Keith Miller, Jody Reed, Jeff Treadway)	.10

1989 Sportflics

This basic issue includes 225 standard-size player cards (2-1/2" x 3-1/2") and 153 trivia cards, all featuring the patented Magic Motion design. A 5-card sub-set of "Tri-Star" cards features a mix of veterans and rookies. The card fronts feature a white outer border and double color inner border in one of six color schemes. The inner border color changes when the card is tilted and the bottom border carries a double stripe of colors. The player name appears in the top border, player postition and uniform number appear, alternately, in the bottom border. The card backs contain crisp 1-7/8" by 1-3/4" player action shots, along with personal information, stats and career highlights. "The Unforgettables" trivia cards in this set salute members of the Hall of Fame.

		MT
Factory Set (225+153):		15.00
Complete Set (225):		13.50
Common Player:		.10
Foil Pack (3+2):		.75
Foil Box (36):		20.00
1	Jose Canseco	.60
2	Wally Joyner	.10
3	Roger Clemens	.75
4	Greg Swindell	.10
5	Jack Morris	.10
6	Mickey Brantley	.10
7	Jim Presley	.10
8	Pete O'Brien	.10
9	Jesse Barfield	.10
10	Frank Viola	.10
11	Kevin Bass	.10
12	Glenn Wilson	.10
13	Chris Sabo	.10
14	Fred McGriff	.10
15	Mark Grace	.25
16	Devon White	.10
17	Juan Samuel	.10
18	Lou Whitaker	.10
19	Greg Walker	.10
20	Roberto Alomar	.50
21	Mike Schmidt	.75
22	Benny Santiago	.10
23	Dave Stewart	.10
24	Dave Winfield	.65
25	George Bell	.10
26	Jack Clark	.10
27	Doug Drabek	.10
28	Ron Gant	.10
29	Glenn Braggs	.10
30	Rafael Palmeiro	.25
31	Brett Butler	.10
32	Ron Darling	.10
33	Alvin Davis	.10
34	Bob Walk	.10
35	Dave Stieb	.10
36	Orel Hershiser	.10
37	John Farrell	.10
38	Doug Jones	.10
39	Kelly Downs	.10
40	Bob Boone	.10
41	Gary Sheffield	.40
42	Doug Dascenzo	.10
43	Chad Krueter	.10
44	Ricky Jordan	.10
45	Dave West	.10
46	Danny Tartabull	.10
47	Teddy Higuera	.10
48	Gary Gaetti	.10
49	Dave Parker	.10
50	Don Mattingly	1.00
51	David Cone	.10
52	Kal Daniels	.10
53	Carney Lansford	.10
54	Mike Marshall	.10
55	Kevin Seitzer	.10
56	Mike Henneman	.10
57	Bill Doran	.10
58	Steve Sax	.10
59	Lance Parrish	.10
60	Keith Hernandez	.10
61	Jose Uribe	.10
62	Jose Lind	.10
63	Steve Bedrosian	.10
64	George Brett	.75
65	Kirk Gibson	.10
66	Cal Ripken, Jr.	2.00
67	Mitch Webster	.10
68	Fred Lynn	.10
69	Eric Davis	.10
70	Bo Jackson	.15
71	Kevin Elster	.10
72	Rick Reuschel	.10
73	Tim Burke	.10
74	Mark Davis	.10
75	Claudell Washington	.10
76	Lance McCullers	.10
77	Mike Moore	.10
78	Robby Thompson	.10
79	Roger McDowell	.10
80	Danny Jackson	.10
81	Tim Leary	.10
82	Bobby Witt	.10
83	Jim Gott	.10
84	Andy Hawkins	.10
85	Ozzie Guillen	.10
86	John Tudor	.10
87	Todd Burns	.10
88	Dave Gallagher	.10
89	Jay Buhner	.10
90	Gregg Jefferies	.10
91	Bob Welch	.10
92	Charlie Hough	.10
93	Tony Fernandez	.10
94	Ozzie Virgil	.10
95	Andre Dawson	.35
96	Hubie Brooks	.10
97	Kevin McReynolds	.10
98	Mike LaValliere	.10
99	Terry Pendleton	.10
100	Wade Boggs	.75
101	Dennis Eckersley	.10
102	Mark Gubicza	.10
103	Frank Tanana	.10
104	Joe Carter	.10
105	Ozzie Smith	.75
106	Dennis Martinez	.10
107	Jeff Treadway	.10
108	Greg Maddux	.75
109	Bret Saberhagen	.10
110	Dale Murphy	.25
111	Rob Deer	.10
112	Pete Incaviglia	.10
113	Vince Coleman	.10
114	Tim Wallach	.10
115	Nolan Ryan	2.00
116	Walt Weiss	.10
117	Brian Downing	.10
118	Melido Perez	.10
119	Terry Steinbach	.10
120	Mike Scott	.10
121	Tim Belcher	.10
122	Mike Boddicker	.10
123	Len Dykstra	.10
124	Fernando Valenzuela	.10
125	Gerald Young	.10
126	Tom Henke	.10
127	Dave Henderson	.10
128	Dan Plesac	.10
129	Chili Davis	.10
130	Bryan Harvey	.10
131	Don August	.10
132	Mike Harkey	.10
133	Luis Polonia	.10
134	Craig Worthington	.10
135	Joey Meyer	.10
136	Barry Larkin	.10
137	Glenn Davis	.10
138	Mike Scioscia	.10
139	Andres Galarraga	.10
140	Doc Gooden	.10
141	Keith Moreland	.10
142	Kevin Mitchell	.10
143	Mike Greenwell	.10
144	Mel Hall	.10
145	Rickey Henderson	.75
146	Barry Bonds	1.00
147	Eddie Murray	.60
148	Lee Smith	.10
149	Julio Franco	.10
150	Tim Raines	.10
151	Mitch Williams	.10
152	Tim Laudner	.10
153	Mike Pagliarulo	.10
154	Floyd Bannister	.10
155	Gary Carter	.35
156	Kirby Puckett	.75
157	Harold Baines	.10
158	Dave Righetti	.10
159	Mark Langston	.10
160	Tony Gwynn	.75
161	Tom Brunansky	.10
162	Vance Law	.10
163	Kelly Gruber	.10
164	Gerald Perry	.10
165	Harold Reynolds	.10
166	Andy Van Slyke	.10
167	Jimmy Key	.10
168	Jeff Reardon	.10
169	Milt Thompson	.10
170	Will Clark	.30
171	Chet Lemon	.10
172	Pat Tabler	.10
173	Jim Rice	.15
174	Billy Hatcher	.10
175	Bruce Hurst	.10
176	John Franco	.10
177	Van Snider	.10
178	Ron Jones	.10
179	Jerald Clark	.10
180	Tom Browning	.10
181	Von Hayes	.10
182	Bobby Bonilla	.10
183	Todd Worrell	.10
184	John Kruk	.10
185	Scott Fletcher	.10
186	Willie Wilson	.10
187	Jody Davis	.10
188	Kent Hrbek	.10
189	Ruben Sierra	.10
190	Shawon Dunston	.10
191	Ellis Burks	.10
192	Brook Jacoby	.10
193	Jeff Robinson	.10
194	Rich Dotson	.10
195	Johnny Ray	.10
196	Cory Snyder	.10
197	Mike Witt	.10
198	Marty Barrett	.10
199	Robin Yount	.60
200	Mark McGwire	2.00
201	Ryne Sandberg	.75
202	John Candelaria	.10
203	Matt Nokes	.10
204	Dwight Evans	.10
205	Darryl Strawberry	.10
206	Willie McGee	.10
207	Bobby Thigpen	.10
208	B.J. Surhoff	.10
209	Paul Molitor	.60
210	Jody Reed	.10
211	Doyle Alexander	.10
212	Dennis Rasmussen	.10
213	Kevin Gross	.10
214	Kirk McCaskill	.10
215	Alan Trammell	.10
216	Damon Berryhill	.10
217	Rick Sutcliffe	.10
218	Don Slaught	.10
219	Carlton Fisk	.65
220	Allan Anderson	.10
221	'88 Highlights (Wade Boggs, Jose Canseco, Mike Greenwell)	.25
222	'88 Highlights (Tom Browning, Dennis Eckersley, Orel Hershiser)	.10
223	Hot Rookie Prospects (Sandy Alomar, Gregg Jefferies, Gary Sheffield)	.75
224	Hot Rookie Prospects (Randy Johnson, Ramon Martinez, Bob Milacki)	.75
225	Hot Rookie Prospects (Geronimo Berroa, Cameron Drew, Ron Jones)	.10

1990 Sportflics

ROBIN VENTURA
CHICAGO WHITE SOX

The Sportflics set for 1990 again contains 225 cards. The cards feature the unique "Magic Motion" effect which displays either of two different photos depending on how the card is tilted. (Previous years' sets had used three photos per card.) The two-photo "Magic Motion" sequence is designed to depict sequential game-action, showing a batter following through on his swing, a pitcher completing his motion, etc. Sportflics also added a moving red and yellow "marquee" border on the cards to complement the animation effect. The player's name, which appears below the animation, remains stationary. The set includes 19 special rookie cards. The backs contain a color player photo, team logo, player information and stats. The cards were distributed in non-transparent mylar packs with small MVP trivia cards.

		MT
Factory Set (225+153):		20.00
Complete Set (225):		18.00
Common Player:		.10
Foil Pack (3+2):		.75
Foil Box (36):		20.00
1	Kevin Mitchell	.10
2	Wade Boggs	.75
3	Cory Snyder	.10
4	Paul O'Neill	.10
5	Will Clark	.30
6	Tony Fernandez	.10
7	Ken Griffey, Jr.	2.00
8	Nolan Ryan	2.50
9	Rafael Palmeiro	.25
10	Jesse Barfield	.10
11	Kirby Puckett	1.00
12	Steve Sax	.10
13	Fred McGriff	.10
14	Gregg Jefferies	.10
15	Mark Grace	.25
16	Devon White	.10
17	Juan Samuel	.10
18	Robin Yount	.65
19	Glenn Davis	.10
20	Jeffrey Leonard	.10
21	Chili Davis	.10
22	Craig Biggio	.10
23	Jose Canseco	.60
24	Derek Lilliquist	.10
25	Chris Bosio	.10
26	Dave Steib	.10
27	Bobby Thigpen	.10
28	Jack Clark	.10
29	Kevin Ritz	.10
30	Tom Gordon	.10
31	Bryan Harvey	.10
32	Jim Deshaies	.10
33	Terry Steinbach	.10
34	Tom Glavine	.15
35	Bob Welch	.10
36	Charlie Hayes	.10
37	Jeff Reardon	.10
38	Joe Orsulak	.10
39	Scott Garrelts	.10
40	Bob Boone	.10
41	Scott Bankhead	.10
42	Tom Henke	.10
43	Greg Briley	.10
44	Teddy Higuera	.10
45	Pat Borders	.10
46	Kevin Seitzer	.10
47	Bruce Hurst	.10
48	Ozzie Guillen	.10
49	Wally Joyner	.10
50	Mike Greenwell	.10
51	Gary Gaetti	.10
52	Gary Sheffield	.35
53	Dennis Martinez	.10
54	Ryne Sandberg	.75
55	Mike Scott	.10
56	Todd Benzinger	.10
57	Kelly Gruber	.10
58	Jose Lind	.10
59	Allan Anderson	.10
60	Robby Thompson	.10
61	John Smoltz	.15
62	Mark Davis	.10
63	Tom Herr	.10
64	Randy Johnson	.45
65	Lonnie Smith	.10
66	Pedro Guerrero	.10
67	Jerome Walton	.10
68	Ramon Martinez	.10
69	Tim Raines	.10
70	Matt Williams	.30
71	Joe Oliver	.10
72	Nick Esasky	.10
73	Kevin Brown	.15
74	Walt Weiss	.10
75	Roger McDowell	.10
76	Jose DeLeon	.10
77	Brian Downing	.10
78	Jay Howell	.10
79	Jose Uribe	.10
80	Ellis Burks	.10
81	Sammy Sosa	1.50
82	Johnny Ray	.10
83	Danny Darwin	.10
84	Carney Lansford	.10
85	Jose Oquendo	.10
86	John Cerutti	.10
87	Dave Winfield	.75
88	Dave Righetti	.10
89	Danny Jackson	.10
90	Andy Benes	.10
91	Tom Browning	.10
92	Pete O'Brien	.10
93	Roberto Alomar	.50
94	Bret Saberhagen	.10
95	Phil Bradley	.10
96	Doug Jones	.10
97	Eric Davis	.10
98	Tony Gwynn	1.00
99	Jim Abbott	.10
100	Cal Ripken, Jr.	2.50
101	Andy Van Slyke	.10
102	Dan Plesac	.10
103	Lou Whitaker	.10
104	Steve Bedrosian	.10
105	Dave Gallagher	.10
106	Keith Hernandez	.10
107	Duane Ward	.10
108	Andre Dawson	.30
109	Howard Johnson	.10
110	Mark Langston	.10
111	Jerry Browne	.10
112	Alvin Davis	.10
113	Sid Fernandez	.10
114	Mike Devereaux	.10
115	Benny Santiago	.10
116	Bip Roberts	.10
117	Craig Worthington	.10
118	Kevin Elster	.10
119	Harold Reynolds	.10
120	Joe Carter	.10
121	Brian Harper	.10
122	Frank Viola	.10
123	Jeff Ballard	.10
124	John Kruk	.10
125	Harold Baines	.10
126	Tom Candiotti	.10
127	Kevin McReynolds	.10
128	Mookie Wilson	.10
129	Danny Tartabull	.10
130	Craig Lefferts	.10
131	Jose DeJesus	.10
132	John Orton	.10
133	Curt Schilling	.25
134	Marquis Grissom	.10
135	Greg Vaughn	.10
136	Brett Butler	.10
137	Rob Deer	.10
138	John Franco	.10
139	Keith Moreland	.10
140	Dave Smith	.10
141	Mark McGwire	2.50
142	Vince Coleman	.10
143	Barry Bonds	1.50
144	Mike Henneman	.10
145	Doc Gooden	.10
146	Darryl Strawberry	.10
147	Von Hayes	.10
148	Andres Galarraga	.10
149	Roger Clemens	1.00
150	Don Mattingly	1.50
151	Joe Magrane	.10
152	Dwight Smith	.10
153	Ricky Jordan	.10
154	Alan Trammell	.10
155	Brook Jacoby	.10
156	Lenny Dykstra	.10
157	Mike LaValliere	.10
158	Julio Franco	.10
159	Joey Belle	.50
160	Barry Larkin	.10
161	Rick Reuschel	.10
162	Nelson Santovenia	.10
163	Mike Scioscia	.10
164	Damon Berryhill	.10
165	Todd Worrell	.10
166	Jim Eisenreich	.10
167	Ivan Calderon	.10
168	Goose Gozzo	.10
169	Kirk McCaskill	.10
170	Dennis Eckersley	.10
171	Mickey Tettleton	.10
172	Chuck Finley	.10
173	Dave Magadan	.10
174	Terry Pendleton	.10
175	Willie Randolph	.10
176	Jeff Huson	.10
177	Todd Zeile	.10
178	Steve Olin	.10
179	Eric Anthony	.10
180	Scott Coolbaugh	.10
181	Rick Sutcliffe	.10
182	Tim Wallach	.10
183	Paul Molitor	.75
184	Roberto Kelly	.10
185	Mike Moore	.10
186	Junior Felix	.10
187	Mike Schooler	.10
188	Ruben Sierra	.10
189	Dale Murphy	.30
190	Dan Gladden	.10
191	John Smiley	.10
192	Jeff Russell	.10
193	Bert Blyleven	.10
194	Dave Stewart	.10
195	Bobby Bonilla	.10
196	Mitch Williams	.10
197	Orel Hershiser	.10
198	Kevin Bass	.10
199	Tim Burke	.10
200	Bo Jackson	.15
201	David Cone	.10
202	Gary Pettis	.10
203	Kent Hrbek	.10
204	Carlton Fisk	.65
205	Bob Geren	.10
206	Bill Spiers	.10
207	Oddibe McDowell	.10
208	Rickey Henderson	.65
209	Ken Caminiti	.10
210	Devon White	.10
211	Greg Maddux	1.00
212	Ed Whitson	.10
213	Carlos Martinez	.10
214	George Brett	1.00
215	Gregg Olson	.10
216	Kenny Rogers	.10
217	Dwight Evans	.10
218	Pat Tabler	.10
219	Jeff Treadway	.10
220	Scott Fletcher	.10
221	Deion Sanders	.15
222	Robin Ventura	.10
223	Chip Hale	.10
224	Tommy Greene	.10
225	Dean Palmer	.10

1994 Sportflics 2000 Promos

To reintroduce its "Magic Motion" baseball cards to the hobby (last produced by Score in 1990), Pinnacle Brands produced a three-card promo set which it sent to dealers along with a header card explaining the issue. In the same format as the regular issue, though some different photos were used, the promos feature on front what Sportflics calls "state-of-the-art lenticular technology" to create an action effect when the card is moved. Backs are produced by standard printing techniques and are gold-foil highlighted and UV-coated. Each of the promo cards has a large black "SAMPLE" overprinted diagonally across front and back.

		MT
Complete Set (4):		8.00
Common Player:		1.00
1	Lenny Dykstra	1.00
7	Javy Lopez (Shakers)	2.00
193	Greg Maddux (Starflics)	6.00
	Header card	.25
7	Javy Lopez (Shakers)	16.00
----	Header card	.40

1994 Sportflics 2000

The concept of "Magic Motion" baseball cards returned to the hobby in 1994 after a three-year hiatus. Pinnacle Brands refined its "state-of-the-art lenticular technology" to produce cards which show alternating pictures when viewed from different angles on the basic cards, and to create a striking 3-D effect on its "Starflics" A.L. and N.L. all-star team subset. Backs use conventional printing techniques and are UV-coated and gold-foil highlighted, featuring a player photo and recent stats. Cards were sold in eight-card foil packs with a suggested retail price of $2.49.

		MT
Complete Set (193):		20.00
Common Player:		.10
Pack (8):		1.00
Wax Box (24):		20.00
1	Len Dykstra	.10
2	Mike Stanley	.10
3	Alex Fernandez	.10
4	Mark McGuire (McGwire)	2.50
5	Eric Karros	.10
6	Dave Justice	.35
7	Jeff Bagwell	.75
8	Darren Lewis	.10
9	David McCarty	.10
10	Albert Belle	.45
11	Ben McDonald	.10
12	Joe Carter	.10
13	Benito Santiago	.10
14	Rob Dibble	.10
15	Roger Clemens	1.50
16	Travis Fryman	.10
17	Doug Drabek	.10
18	Jay Buhner	.10
19	Orlando Merced	.10

20 Ryan Klesko .10
21 Chuck Finley .10
22 Dante Bichette .10
23 Wally Joyner .10
24 Robin Yount 1.00
25 Tony Gwynn 1.50
26 Allen Watson .10
27 Rick Wilkins .10
28 Gary Sheffield .40
29 John Burkett .10
30 Randy Johnson .65
31 Roberto Alomar .60
32 Fred McGriff .10
33 Ozzie Guillen .10
34 Jimmy Key .10
35 Juan Gonzalez .75
36 Wil Cordero .10
37 Aaron Sele .10
38 Mark Langston .10
39 David Cone .10
40 John Jaha .10
41 Ozzie Smith 1.50
42 Kirby Puckett 1.50
43 Kenny Lofton .10
44 Mike Mussina .65
45 Ryne Sandberg .75
46 Robby Thompson .10
47 Bryan Harvey .10
48 Marquis Grissom .10
49 Bobby Bonilla .10
50 Dennis Eckersley .10
51 Curt Schilling .25
52 Andy Benes .10
53 Greg Maddux 1.50
54 Bill Swift .10
55 Andres Galarraga .10
56 Tony Phillips .10
57 Darryl Hamilton .10
58 Duane Ward .10
59 Bernie Williams .30
60 Steve Avery .10
61 Eduardo Perez .10
62 Jeff Conine .10
63 Dave Winfield 1.00
64 Phil Plantier .10
65 Ray Lankford .10
66 Robin Ventura .10
67 Mike Piazza 2.00
68 Jason Bere .10
69 Cal Ripken, Jr. 2.50
70 Frank Thomas 1.00
71 Carlos Baerga .10
72 Darryl Kile .10
73 Ruben Sierra .10
74 Gregg Jefferies .10
75 John Olerud .10
76 Andy Van Slyke .10
77 Larry Walker .30
78 Cecil Fielder .10
79 Andre Dawson .25
80 Tom Glavine .15
81 Sammy Sosa 1.75
82 Charlie Hayes .10
83 Chuck Knoblauch .10
84 Kevin Appier .10
85 Dean Palmer .10
86 Royce Clayton .10
87 Moises Alou .20
88 Ivan Rodriguez .60
89 Tim Salmon .20
90 Ron Gant .10
91 Barry Bonds 1.75
92 Jack McDowell .10
93 Alan Trammell .10
94 Dwight Gooden .10
95 Jay Bell .10
96 Devon White .10
97 Wilson Alvarez .10
98 Jim Thome .10
99 Ramon Martinez .10
100 Kent Hrbek .10
101 John Kruk .10
102 Wade Boggs .75
103 Greg Vaughn .10
104 Tom Henke .10
105 Brian Jordan .10
106 Paul Molitor .60
107 Cal Eldred .10
108 Deion Sanders .15
109 Barry Larkin .10
110 Mike Greenwell .10
111 Jeff Blauser .10
112 Jose Rijo .10
113 Pete Harnisch .10
114 Chris Hoiles .10
115 Edgar Martinez .10
116 Juan Guzman .10
117 Todd Zeile .10
118 Danny Tartabull .10
119 Chad Curtis .10
120 Mark Grace .30
121 J.T. Snow .10
122 Mo Vaughn .45
123 Lance Johnson .10
124 Eric Davis .10
125 Orel Hershiser .10
126 Kevin Mitchell .10
127 Don Mattingly 1.75
128 Darren Daulton .10
129 Rod Beck .10
130 Charles Nagy .10
131 Mickey Tettleton .10
132 Kevin Brown .15
133 Pat Hentgen .10
134 Terry Mulholland .10
135 Steve Finley .10
136 John Smoltz .15
137 Frank Viola .10
138 Jim Abbott .10
139 Matt Williams .30
140 Bernard Gilkey .10
141 Jose Canseco .50
142 Mark Whiten .10
143 Ken Griffey, Jr. 2.25
144 Rafael Palmeiro .30
145 Dave Hollins .10
146 Will Clark .30
147 Paul O'Neill .10
148 Bobby Jones .10
149 Butch Huskey .10
150 Jeffrey Hammonds .10
151 Manny Ramirez .75
152 Bob Hamelin .10
153 Kurt Abbott .10
154 Scott Stahoviak .10
155 Steve Hosey .10
156 Salomon Torres .10
157 Sterling Hitchcock .10
158 Nigel Wilson .10
159 Luis Lopez .10
160 Chipper Jones 2.00
161 Norberto Martin .10
162 Raul Mondesi .30
163 Steve Karsay .10
164 J.R. Phillips .10
165 Marc Newfield .10
166 Mark Hutton .10
167 Curtis Pride .10
168 Carl Everett .15
169 Scott Ruffcorn .10
170 Turk Wendell .10
171 Jeff McNeely .10
172 Javier Lopez .10
173 Cliff Floyd .10
174 Rondell White .25
175 Scott Lydy .10
176 Frank Thomas 1.00
177 Roberto Alomar .25
178 Travis Fryman .10
179 Cal Ripken, Jr. 1.25
180 Chris Hoiles .10
181 Ken Griffey, Jr. 1.00
182 Juan Gonzalez .75
183 Joe Carter .10
184 Jack McDowell .10
185 Fred McGriff .10
186 Robby Thompson .10
187 Matt Williams .15
188 Jay Bell .10
189 Mike Piazza 1.00
190 Barry Bonds 1.00
191 Len Dykstra .10
192 Dave Justice .15
193 Greg Maddux .75

1994 Sportflics 2000 Commemoratives

A pair of extra-rare commemorative chase cards was produced for the Sportflics 2000 set honoring Canada's veteran superstar Paul Molitor and its hottest rookie, Cliff Floyd. Cards, utilizing Magic Motion technology to alternate card-front pictures when the viewing angle changes, were inserted on average once in every 360 packs.

		MT
Complete Set (2):		7.00
1	Paul Molitor	6.00
2	Cliff Floyd	1.50

1994 Sportflics 2000 Movers

A dozen top veteran ballplayers were featured in the "Movers" insert set produced for inclusion in retail packaging of Sportflics 2000. The inserts feature the same Magic Motion features as the regular cards, showing different images on the card front when the card is viewed from different angles. The UV-coated, gold-foil highlighted backs are printed conventionally. A special "Movers" logo is found on both front and back. Stated odds of finding a Movers card are one in 24 packs.

		MT
Complete Set (12):		16.00
Common Player:		.75
1	Gregg Jefferies	.75
2	Ryne Sandberg	2.00
3	Cecil Fielder	.75
4	Kirby Puckett	2.50
5	Tony Gwynn	2.50
6	Andres Galarraga	.75
7	Sammy Sosa	4.00
8	Rickey Henderson	1.00
9	Don Mattingly	4.00
10	Joe Carter	.75
11	Carlos Baerga	.75
12	Len Dykstra	.75

1994 Sportflics 2000 Shakers

Hobby packs are the exclusive source for this 12-card insert set of top rookies, found on average once every 24 packs. The chase cards utilize the Sportflics Magic Motion technology to create two different images on the card front when the card is viewed from different angles. Backs are printed conventionally but feature UV-coating and gold-foil highlights. The "Shakers" logo appears on both front and back.

		MT
Complete Set (12):		15.00
Common Player:		.75
1	Kenny Lofton	.75
2	Tim Salmon	1.00
3	Jeff Bagwell	3.00
4	Jason Bere	.75
5	Salomon Torres	.75
6	Rondell White	1.00
7	Javier Lopez	.75
8	Dean Palmer	.75
9	Jim Thome	.75
10	J.T. Snow	.75
11	Mike Piazza	5.00
12	Manny Ramirez	3.00

1994 Sportflics 2000 Rookie/Traded Promos

This nine-card set was issued to promote the Sportflics Rookie/Traded update set which was released as a hobby-only product. Cards are virtually identical to the corresponding cards in the R/T set except for the overprinted "SAMPLE" in white on front and back.

		MT
Complete Set (9):		8.00
Common Player:		1.00
1	Will Clark	2.00
14	Bret Boone	1.50
20	Ellis Burks	1.00
25	Deion Sanders	1.50
62	Chris Turner	1.00
82	Tony Tarasco	1.00
102	Rich Becker	1.00
GG1	Gary Sheffield (Going, Going, Gone)	2.00
---	Header card	.25

1994 Sportflics 2000 Rookie/Traded

Each of the 150 regular cards in the Sportflics 2000 Rookie & Traded issue was also produced in a parallel chase card set designated on front with a black and gold "Artist's Proof" logo. Stated odds of finding an AP cards were one per 24 packs. Fewer than 1,000 or each AP card were reportedly produced.

		MT
Complete Set (150):		20.00
Common Player:		.15
Pack (5):		3.00
Wax Box (24):		90.00
1	Will Clark	.45
2	Sid Fernandez	.15
3	Joe Magrane	.15
4	Pete Smith	.15
5	Roberto Kelly	.15
6	Delino DeShields	.15
7	Brian Harper	.15
8	Darrin Jackson	.15
9	Omar Vizquel	.15
10	Luis Polonia	.15
11	Reggie Jefferson	.15
12	Geronimo Berroa	.15
13	Mike Harkey	.15
14	Bret Boone	.25
15	Dave Henderson	.15
16	Pedro Martinez	.75
17	Jose Vizcaino	.15
18	Xavier Hernandez	.15
19	Eddie Taubensee	.15
20	Ellis Burks	.15
21	Turner Ward	.15
22	Terry Mulholland	.15
23	Howard Johnson	.15
24	Vince Coleman	.15
25	Deion Sanders	.25
26	Rafael Palmeiro	.45
27	Dave Weathers	.15
28	Kent Mercker	.15
29	Gregg Olson	.15
30	Cory Bailey	.15
31	Brian Hunter	.15
32	Garey Ingram	.15
33	Daniel Smith	.15
34	Denny Hocking	.15
35	Charles Johnson	.15
36	Otis Nixon	.15
37	Hector Fajardo	.15
38	Lee Smith	.15
39	Phil Stidham	.15
40	Melvin Nieves	.15
41	Julio Franco	.15
42	Greg Gohr	.15
43	Steve Dunn	.15
44	Tony Fernandez	.15
45	Toby Borland	.15
46	Paul Shuey	.15
47	Shawn Hare	.15
48	Shawn Green	.50
49	*Julian Tavarez*	.15
50	Ernie Young	.15
51	Chris Sabo	.15
52	Greg O'Halloran	.15
53	Donnie Elliott	.15
54	Jim Converse	.15
55	Ray Holbert	.15
56	Keith Lockhart	.15
57	Tony Longmire	.15
58	Jorge Fabregas	.15
59	Ravelo Manzanillo	.15
60	Marcus Moore	.15
61	Carlos Rodriguez	.15
62	Mark Portugal	.15
63	Yorkis Perez	.15
64	Dan Miceli	.15
65	Chris Turner	.15
66	Mike Oquist	.15
67	Tom Quinlan	.15
68	Matt Walbeck	.15
69	Dave Staton	.15
70	*Bill Van Landingham*	.15
71	Dave Stevens	.15
72	Domingo Cedeno	.15
73	Alex Diaz	.15
74	Darren Bragg	.15
75	James Hurst	.15
76	Alex Gonzalez	.30
77	Steve Dreyer	.15
78	Robert Eenhoorn	.15
79	Derek Parks	.15
80	Jose Valentin	.15
81	Wes Chamberlain	.15
82	Tony Tarasco	.15
83	Steve Trachsel	.15
84	Willie Banks	.15
85	Rob Butler	.15
86	Miguel Jimenez	.15
87	Gerald Williams	.15
88	Aaron Small	.15
89	Matt Mieske	.15
90	Tim Hyers	.15
91	Eddie Murray	.75
92	Dennis Martinez	.15
93	Tony Eusebio	.15
94	*Brian Anderson*	.50
95	Blaise Ilsley	.15
96	Johnny Ruffin	.15
97	Carlos Reyes	.15
98	Greg Pirkl	.15
99	Jack Morris	.15
100	John Mabry	.15
101	Mike Kelly	.15
102	Rich Becker	.15
103	Chris Gomez	.15
104	Jim Edmonds	.25
105	Rich Rowland	.15
106	Damon Buford	.15
107	Mark Kiefer	.15
108	Matias Carrillo	.15
109	James Mouton	.15
110	Kelly Stinnett	.15
111	Billy Ashley	.15
112	*Fausto Cruz*	.25
113	Roberto Petagine	.15
114	Joe Hall	.15
115	*Brian Johnson*	.15
116	Kevin Jarvis	.15
117	Tim Davis	.15
118	John Patterson	.15
119	Stan Royer	.15
120	Jeff Juden	.15
121	Bryan Eversgerd	.15
122	*Chan Ho Park*	2.00
123	Shane Reynolds	.15
124	Danny Bautista	.15
125	Rikkert Faneyte	.15
126	Carlos Pulido	.15
127	Mike Matheny	.15
128	Hector Carrasco	.15
129	Eddie Zambrano	.15
130	Lee Tinsley	.15
131	Roger Salkeld	.15
132	Carlos Delgado	.50
133	Troy O'Leary	.15
134	Keith Mitchell	.15
135	Lance Painter	.15
136	Nate Minchey	.15
137	Eric Anthony	.15
138	Rafael Bournigal	.15
139	Joey Hamilton	.15
140	Bobby Munoz	.15
141	Rex Hudler	.15
142	Alex Cole	.15
143	Stan Javier	.15
144	Jose Oliva	.15
145	Tom Brunansky	.15
146	Greg Colbrunn	.15
147	Luis Lopez	.15
148	*Alex Rodriguez*	15.00
149	Darryl Strawberry	.15
150	Bo Jackson	.25

1994 Sportflics 2000 Rookie/Traded Artist's Proof

Each of the 150 regular cards in the Sportflics 2000 Rookie & Traded issue was also produced in a parallel chase set designated on front with a black and gold "Artist's Proof" logo. Stated odds of finding an AP card were one per 24 packs. Fewer than 1,000 of each AP card were reportedly produced.

	MT
Complete Set (150):	300.00
Common Player:	1.00
Stars:	15X

(See 1994 Sportflics 2000 Rookie/Traded for checklist and base card values.)

1994 Sportflics 2000 Rookie/Traded Going, Going, Gone

A dozen of the game's top home run hitters are featured in this insert set. On front, simulated 3-D action photos depict the player's swing for the fences. Backs have a portrait photo and information about the player's home run prowess. A crossed bats and "Going, Going Gone" logo appear on both front and back. Cards are numbered with a "GG" prefix. Stated odds of finding one of these inserts were once in 18 packs.

		MT
Complete Set (12):		12.00
Common Player:		.50
1	Gary Sheffield	.75
2	Matt Williams	.60
3	Juan Gonzalez	1.25
4	Ken Griffey Jr.	3.00
5	Mike Piazza	2.50
6	Frank Thomas	2.00
7	Tim Salmon	.65
8	Barry Bonds	2.00
9	Fred McGriff	.50
10	Cecil Fielder	.50
11	Albert Belle	1.00
12	Joe Carter	.50

1994 Sportflics 2000 Rookie/Traded Rookies of the Year

Sportflics' choices for Rookies of the Year were featured on this one-card insert set. Ryan Klesko (National League) and Manny Ramirez (American League) are shown on the card when viewed from different angles. Sportflics batted .000 in their guesses, however, as Raul Mondesi and Bob Hamelin were the actual R.O.Y. selections. This card was inserted at the average rate of once per 360 packs.

		MT
Complete Set (1):		
RO1	Ryan Klesko, Manny Ramirez	3.00

1994 Sportflics 2000 Rookie/Traded 3-D Rookies

Eighteen of 1994's premier rookies are featured in this insert set. Combining a 3-D look and Sportflics' "Magic Motion" technology, the horizontal-format Starflics rookie cards present a striking appearance. Backs feature a full-bleed color photo overprinted with gold foil. A notice on back gives the production run of the chase cards as "No more than 5,000 sets." Stated odds of finding a Starflics Rookie card were given as one per 36 packs. Cards are numbered with a "TR" prefix.

		MT
Complete Set (18):		80.00
Common Player:		2.00
1	John Hudek	2.00
2	Manny Ramirez	15.00
3	Jeffrey Hammonds	2.00
4	Carlos Delgado	5.00
5	Javier Lopez	2.00
6	Alex Gonzalez	2.50
7	Raul Mondesi	3.00
8	Bob Hamelin	2.00
9	Ryan Klesko	2.00
10	Brian Anderson	2.00
11	Alex Rodriguez	45.00
12	Cliff Floyd	2.00
13	Chan Ho Park	7.50
14	Steve Karsay	2.00
15	Rondell White	3.00
16	Shawn Green	6.00
17	Rich Becker	2.00
18	Charles Johnson	2.00

1995 Sportflix Samples

This nine-card promo pack was sent to Pinnacle's dealer network to introduce its revamped (new logo, spelling) magic-motion card set for 1995. The sample cards are identical in format to the regular-issue Sportflix cards except that a large white "SAMPLE" is printed diagonally on front and back of the promos.

		MT
Complete Set (9):		22.50
Common Player:		2.00
3	Fred McGriff	2.00
20	Frank Thomas	4.50
105	Manny Ramirez	3.50
122	Cal Ripken Jr.	6.50
128	Roberto Alomar	2.25
152	Russ Davis (Rookie)	2.00
162	Chipper Jones (Rookie)	5.50
DE2	Matt Williams (Detonators)	2.25
----	Advertising Card	.10

1995 Sportflix

With only 170 cards in the set, only the biggest stars and hottest rookies (25 of them in a specially designed subset) are included in this simulated 3-D issue. Fronts feature two borderless action photos which are alternately visible as the card's viewing angle is changed. Backs are conventionally printed and have a portrait photo, a few career stats and a couple of sentences about the player. The basic packaging options for '95 Sportflix were five- and eight card foils at $1.89 and $2.99, respectively.

		MT
Complete Set (170):		20.00
Common Player:		.15
Artist's Proofs:		12X
Pack (5):		2.00
Wax Box (36):		50.00
1	Ken Griffey Jr.	2.00
2	Jeffrey Hammonds	.15
3	Fred McGriff	.15
4	Rickey Henderson	.75
5	Derrick May	.15
6	Robin Ventura	.15
7	Royce Clayton	.15
8	Paul Molitor	.50
9	Charlie Hayes	.15
10	David Nied	.15
11	Ellis Burks	.15
12	Bernard Gilkey	.15
13	Don Mattingly	1.25
14	Albert Belle	.35
15	Doug Drabek	.15
16	Tony Gwynn	1.00
17	Delino DeShields	.15
18	Bobby Bonilla	.15
19	Cliff Floyd	.15
20	Frank Thomas	1.25
21	Raul Mondesi	.40
22	Dave Nilsson	.15
23	Todd Zeile	.15
24	Bernie Williams	.40
25	Kirby Puckett	1.00
26	David Cone	.15
27	Darren Daulton	.15
28	Marquis Grissom	.15
29	Randy Johnson	.65
30	Jeff Kent	.15
31	Orlando Merced	.15
32	Dave Justice	.35
33	Ivan Rodriguez	.60
34	Kirk Gibson	.15
35	Alex Fernandez	.15
36	Rick Wilkins	.15
37	Andy Benes	.15
38	Bret Saberhagen	.15
39	Billy Ashley	.15
40	Jose Rijo	.15
41	Matt Williams	.40
42	Lenny Dykstra	.15
43	Jay Bell	.15
44	Reggie Jefferson	.15
45	Greg Maddux	1.00
46	Gary Sheffield	.40
47	Bret Boone	.20
48	Jeff Bagwell	.75
49	Ben McDonald	.15
50	Eric Karros	.15
51	Roger Clemens	1.00
52	Sammy Sosa	1.25
53	Barry Bonds	1.25
54	Joey Hamilton	.15
55	Brian Jordan	.15
56	Wil Cordero	.15
57	Aaron Sele	.15
58	Paul O'Neill	.15
59	Carlos Garcia	.15
60	Mike Mussina	.40
61	John Olerud	.15
62	Kevin Appier	.15
63	Matt Mieske	.15
64	Carlos Baerga	.15
65	Ryan Klesko	.15
66	Jimmy Key	.15
67	James Mouton	.15
68	Tim Salmon	.25
69	Hal Morris	.15
70	Albie Lopez	.15
71	Dave Hollins	.15
72	Greg Colbrunn	.15
73	Juan Gonzalez	.75
74	Wally Joyner	.15
75	Bob Hamelin	.15
76	Brady Anderson	.15
77	Deion Sanders	.20
78	Javier Lopez	.15
79	Brian McRae	.15
80	Craig Biggio	.15
81	Kenny Lofton	.15
82	Cecil Fielder	.15
83	Mike Piazza	1.50
84	Rafael Palmeiro	.30
85	Jim Thome	.15
86	Ruben Sierra	.15
87	Mark Langston	.15
88	John Valentin	.15
89	Shawon Dunston	.15
90	Travis Fryman	.15
91	Chuck Knoblauch	.15
92	Dean Palmer	.15
93	Robby Thompson	.15
94	Barry Larkin	.15
95	Darren Lewis	.15
96	Andres Galarraga	.15
97	Tony Phillips	.15
98	Mo Vaughn	.40
99	Pedro Martinez	.50
100	Chad Curtis	.15
101	Brent Gates	.15
102	Pat Hentgen	.15
103	Rico Brogna	.15
104	Carlos Delgado	.40
105	Manny Ramirez	.75
106	Mike Greenwell	.15
107	Wade Boggs	.65
108	Ozzie Smith	1.00
109	Rusty Greer	.15
110	Willie Greene	.15
111	Chili Davis	.15
112	Reggie Sanders	.15
113	Roberto Kelly	.15
114	Tom Glavine	.20
115	Moises Alou	.25
116	Dennis Eckersley	.15
117	Danny Tartabull	.15
118	Jeff Conine	.15
119	Will Clark	.40
120	Joe Carter	.15
121	Mark McGwire	2.50
122	Cal Ripken Jr.	2.50
123	Danny Jackson	.15
124	Phil Plantier	.15
125	Dante Bichette	.15
126	Jack McDowell	.15
127	Jose Canseco	.45
128	Roberto Alomar	.45
129	Rondell White	.25
130	Ray Lankford	.15
131	Ryan Thompson	.15
132	Ken Caminiti	.15
133	Gregg Jefferies	.15
134	Omar Vizquel	.15
135	Mark Grace	.25
136	Derek Bell	.15
137	Mickey Tettleton	.15
138	Wilson Alvarez	.15
139	Larry Walker	.25
140	Bo Jackson	.20
141	Alex Rodriguez	2.00
142	Orlando Miller	.15
143	Shawn Green	.30
144	Steve Dunn	.15
145	Midre Cummings	.15
146	Chan Ho Park	.35
147	Jose Oliva	.15
148	Armando Benitez	.15
149	J.R. Phillips	.15
150	Charles Johnson	.15
151	Garret Anderson	.15
152	Russ Davis	.15
153	Brian Hunter	.15
154	Ernie Young	.15
155	Marc Newfield	.15
156	Greg Pirkl	.15
157	Scott Ruffcorn	.15
158	Rikkert Faneyte	.15
159	Duane Singleton	.15
160	Gabe White	.15
161	Alex Gonzalez	.15
162	Chipper Jones	1.50
163	Mike Kelly	.15
164	Kurt Miller	.15
165	Roberto Petagine	.15
166	Checklist (Jeff Bagwell)	.25
167	Checklist (Mike Piazza)	.65
168	Checklist (Ken Griffey Jr.)	1.00
169	Checklist (Frank Thomas)	.65
170	Checklist (Barry Bonds, Cal Ripken Jr.)	1.00

1995 Sportflix Artist's Proofs

Each of the 170 cards in the regular Sportflix set can be found with a special tombstone shaped black-and-gold "Artist's Proof" seal designating it as one of a parallel edition of 700 cards each. Cards are otherwise identical to the regular-issue version. AP cards were inserted at an average rate of one per 36 packs.

	MT
Complete Set (170):	300.00
Common Player:	1.00
Stars:	12X

(See 1995 Sportflix for checklist and base card values.)

1995 Sportflix 3D Hammer Team

Sledge hammers flying in formation through a cloud-studded sky are the background for this insert set featuring the game's heavy hitters. Backs have a portrait photo and a few words about the player's power hitting prowess. Hammer Team cards are picked on an average of once per four packs.

		MT
Complete Set (18):		6.50
Common Player:		.20
1	Ken Griffey Jr.	1.00
2	Frank Thomas	.60
3	Jeff Bagwell	.45
4	Mike Piazza	.75
5	Cal Ripken Jr.	1.00
6	Albert Belle	.35
7	Barry Bonds	.60
8	Don Mattingly	.60
9	Will Clark	.35
10	Tony Gwynn	.50
11	Matt Williams	.35
12	Kirby Puckett	.50
13	Manny Ramirez	.45
14	Fred McGriff	.20
15	Juan Gonzalez	.45
16	Kenny Lofton	.20
17	Raul Mondesi	.25
18	Tim Salmon	.25

1995 Sportflix 3D Detonators

With the players up ona pedestal and fireworks in the background. this chase set lives up to its name, "Detonators." The cards feature a deep 3-D look on front. Backs have a close-up photo of the plauer in the pedestal's column. Detonator cards are pulled at an average rate of one per 16 packs.

		MT
Complete Set (9):		7.00
Common Player:		.40
1	Jeff Bagwell	1.00
2	Matt Williams	.50
3	Ken Griffey Jr.	2.00
4	Frank Thomas	1.25
5	Mike Piazza	1.50
6	Barry Bonds	1.25
7	Albert Belle	.60
8	Cliff Floyd	.40
9	Juan Gonzalez	1.00

1995 Sportflix Double Take

A see-through plastic background and A.L. and N.L. stars at the same position sharing the card with their shadows marks this chase set as the top of the line for '95 Sportflix. Found at an average rate of one per 48packs, the Double Take inserts represent a new level in "magic motion" card technology.

		MT
Complete Set (12):		30.00
Common Player:		1.50
1	Frank Thomas, Jeff Bagwell	3.00
2	Will Clark, Fred McGriff	1.50
3	Roberto Alomar, Jeff Kent	1.50
4	Wade Boggs, Matt Williams	1.50
5	Cal Ripken Jr., Ozzie Smith	6.00
6	Alex Rodriguez, Wil Cordero	4.00
7	Carlos Delgado, Mike Piazza	3.50
8	Kenny Lofton, Dave Justice	1.50
9	Ken Griffey Jr., Barry Bonds	6.00
10	Albert Belle, Raul Mondesi	1.50
11	Kirby Puckett, Tony Gwynn	3.00
12	Jimmy Key, Greg Maddux	2.00

1995 Sportflix ProMotion

Twelve of baseball's biggest stars morph into team logos on a bright team-color background in this chase series. Backs have a portrait photo and a few words about the players. The ProMotion inserts are a one per 18 pack pick in jumbo packs only.

		MT
Complete Set (12):		32.50
Common Player:		1.50
1	Ken Griffey Jr.	6.00
2	Frank Thomas	3.50
3	Cal Ripken Jr.	7.00
4	Jeff Bagwell	2.50
5	Mike Piazza	4.50
6	Matt Williams	1.50
7	Albert Belle	1.50
8	Jose Canseco	2.00
9	Don Mattingly	3.50
10	Barry Bonds	3.50
11	Will Clark	1.50
12	Kirby Puckett	3.00

1995 Sportflix/UC3 Samples

To introduce the new technology it was bringing to the insert cards in the Sportflix UC3 issue, the company sent a sample of the Clear Shots insert, along with a header card describing the entire UC3 issue, to card dealers and the media in June, 1995. A large, black, "SAMPLE" is overprinted diagonally on the front. A similarly marked Fred McGriff previewed the set's regular cards.

		MT
Complete Set (3):		6.00
3	Fred McGriff	2.00
CS8	Cliff Floyd	2.50
CS10	Alex Gonzalez	2.50
--	Header card	.05

1995 Sportflix/UC3

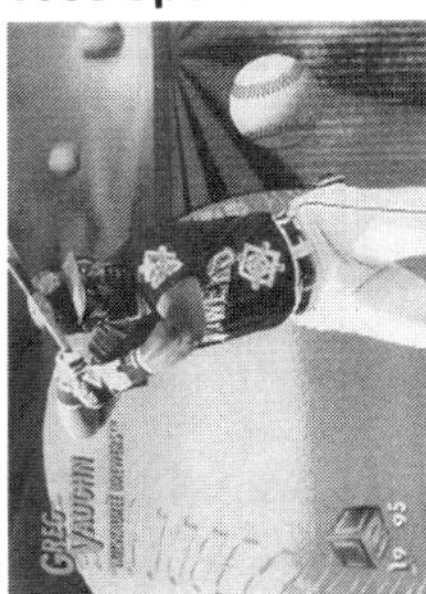

Using advanced technology to create a premium 3-D card brand and inserts, UC3 offers three distinctly different card formats in the base 147-card set, plus a parallel set and three insert sets. All cards have borderless fronts and feature a heavy ribbed plastic top layer. The first 95 cards are veteran players in a horizontal format. A central action photo is flanked at left by a large gold glove (National Leaguers) or baseball (A.L.), and at right by a blue and green vista from which flies one (N.L.) or three (A.L.) baseballs. Player identification is in red at upper-left, the UC3 logo at lower-left. Backs have another color photo and a few stats set against a background of the team logo. Cards #96-122 are a vertical-format Rookie subset. Player photos are set against a purple and green vista with a large bat, ball and glove behind the player. His name is at upper-right; team logo at lower-right. Horizontal backs are similar to the other cards. The final 25 cards of the set are a subset titled, "In-Depth." These vertically formatted cards feature eye-popping graphics on front in which the main player photo almost jumps from the background. The only graphics are the player's name at left and the UC3 logo at upper-left. Backs have a portrait photo at top, bathed in golden rays. A team logo is at center and an outer space design at bottom. There is a short paragraph describing the player at right.

		MT
Complete Set (147):		20.00
Common Player:		.10
Artist's Proofs:		12X
Pack (5):		1.50
Wax Box (36):		35.00
1	Frank Thomas	1.25
2	Wil Cordero	.10
3	John Olerud	.10
4	Deion Sanders	.15
5	Mike Mussina	.50
6	Mo Vaughn	.40
7	Will Clark	.30
8	Chili Davis	.10
9	Jimmy Key	.10
10	John Valentin	.10
11	Tony Tarasco	.10
12	Alan Trammell	.10
13	David Cone	.10
14	Tim Salmon	.25
15	Danny Tartabull	.10
16	Aaron Sele	.10
17	Alex Fernandez	.10
18	Barry Bonds	1.25
19	Andres Galarraga	.10
20	Don Mattingly	1.25
21	Kevin Appier	.10
22	Paul Molitor	.40
23	Omar Vizquel	.10
24	Andy Benes	.10
25	Rafael Palmeiro	.30
26	Barry Larkin	.10
27	Bernie Williams	.30
28	Gary Sheffield	.30
29	Wally Joyner	.10

30	Wade Boggs	.75
31	Rico Brogna	.10
32	Ken Caminiti	.10
33	Kirby Puckett	1.00
34	Bobby Bonilla	.10
35	Hal Morris	.10
36	Moises Alou	.15
37	Jim Thome	.10
38	Chuck Knoblauch	.10
39	Mike Piazza	1.50
40	Travis Fryman	.10
41	Rickey Henderson	.60
42	Jack McDowell	.10
43	Carlos Baerga	.10
44	Gregg Jeffries	.10
45	Kirk Gibson	.10
46	Bret Saberhagen	.10
47	Cecil Fielder	.10
48	Manny Ramirez	.75
49	Marquis Grissom	.10
50	Dave Winfield	.75
51	Mark McGwire	2.50
52	Dennis Eckersley	.10
53	Robin Ventura	.10
54	Ryan Klesko	.10
55	Jeff Bagwell	.75
56	Ozzie Smith	1.00
57	Brian McRae	.10
58	Albert Belle	.40
59	Darren Daulton	.10
60	Jose Canseco	.35
61	Greg Maddux	1.00
62	Ben McDonald	.10
63	Lenny Dykstra	.10
64	Randy Johnson	.50
65	Fred McGriff	.10
66	Ray Lankford	.10
67	Dave Justice	.30
68	Paul O'Neill	.10
69	Tony Gwynn	1.00
70	Matt Williams	.30
71	Dante Bichette	.10
72	Craig Biggio	.10
73	Ken Griffey Jr.	2.00
74	Juan Gonzalez	.75
75	Cal Ripken Jr.	2.50
76	Jay Bell	.10
77	Joe Carter	.10
78	Roberto Alomar	.60
79	Mark Langston	.10
80	Dave Hollins	.10
81	Tom Glavine	.15
82	Ivan Rodriguez	.45
83	Mark Whiten	.10
84	Raul Mondesi	.30
85	Kenny Lofton	.10
86	Ruben Sierra	.10
87	Mark Grace	.30
88	Royce Clayton	.10
89	Billy Ashley	.10
90	Larry Walker	.30
91	Sammy Sosa	1.25
92	Jason Bere	.10
93	Bob Hamelin	.10
94	Greg Vaughn	.10
95	Roger Clemens	1.00
96	Scott Ruffcorn	.10
97	*Hideo Nomo*	1.50
98	Michael Tucker	.10
99	J.R. Phillips	.10
100	Roberto Petagine	.10
101	Chipper Jones	1.50
102	Armando Benitez	.10
103	Orlando Miller	.10
104	Carlos Delgado	.40
105	Jeff Cirillo	.10
106	Shawn Green	.25
107	Joe Rando	.10
108	Vaughn Eshelman	.10
109	Frank Rodriguez	.10
110	Russ Davis	.10
111	Todd Hollandsworth	.10
112	Mark Grudzielanek	.10
113	Jose Oliva	.10
114	Ray Durham	.10
115	Alex Rodriguez	2.00
116	Alex Gonzalez	.15
117	Midre Cummings	.10
118	Marty Cordova	.10
119	John Mabry	.10
120	Jason Jacome	.10
121	Joe Vitiello	.10
122	Charles Johnson	.10
123	Cal Ripken Jr. (In Depth)	1.00
124	Ken Griffey Jr. (In Depth)	1.00
125	Frank Thomas (In Depth)	.75
126	Mike Piazza (In Depth)	.75
127	Matt Williams (In Depth)	.15
128	Barry Bonds (In Depth)	.75
129	Greg Maddux (In Depth)	.50
130	Randy Johnson (In Depth)	.25
131	Albert Belle (In Depth)	.20
132	Will Clark (In Depth)	.15
133	Tony Gwynn (In Depth)	.50
134	Manny Ramirez (In Depth)	.40
135	Raul Mondesi (In Depth)	.15
136	Mo Vaughn (In Depth)	.15
137	Mark McGwire (In Depth)	1.00
138	Kirby Puckett (In Depth)	.50
139	Don Mattingly (In Depth)	.75
140	Carlos Baerga (In Depth)	.10
141	Roger Clemens (In Depth)	.50
142	Fred McGriff (In Depth)	.10
143	Kenny Lofton (In Depth)	.10
144	Jeff Bagwell (In Depth)	.40
145	Larry Walker (In Depth)	.15
146	Joe Carter (In Depth)	.10
147	Rafael Palmeiro (In Depth)	.15

1995 Sportflix/UC3 Artist's Proof

This chase set parallels the 147 regular cards in the UC3 set with a version on which a round, gold "ARTIST'S PROOF" seal is printed on the front of the card. The AP cards are found on the average of one per box (36 packs).

	MT
Complete Set (147):	300.00
Common Player:	1.00
Stars:	12X

(See 1995 Sportflix UC3 for checklist and base card values.)

1995 Sportflix/UC3 Clear Shots

Seeded at the rate of about one per 24 packs, the 12 cards in this chase set feature top rookies in a technologically advanced format. The left two-thirds of the card are clear plastic, the right third is blue (American League) or red-purple (N.L.). At center is a circle which features the player photos, portrait and action, depending on the viewing angle. Also changing with the viewpoint are the words "CLEAR" and "SHOT" at top-right, and team and UC3 logos at bottom-right. The player's last name is in black at lower-left and appears to change size as the card is moved. Backs have a gray strip vertically at left with the card number, manufacturer and licensor logos and copyright information. Card numbers have a "CS" prefix.

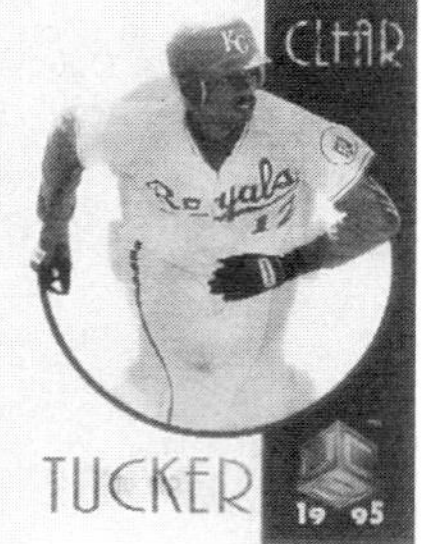

		MT
Complete Set (12):		12.00
Common Player:		.25
1	Alex Rodriguez	5.00
2	Shawn Green	1.00
3	Hideo Nomo	1.50
4	Charles Johnson	.25
5	Orlando Miller	.25
6	Billy Ashley	.25
7	Carlos Delgado	1.00
8	Cliff Floyd	.25
9	Chipper Jones	3.50
10	Alex Gonzalez	.25
11	J.R. Phillips	.25
12	Michael Tucker	.25

1995 Sportflix/UC3 Cyclone Squad

The most commonly encountered (one per four packs, on average) of the UC3 chase cards are the 20-card Cyclone Squad, featuring the game's top batsmen. Cards have a player in a batting pose set against a dark copper background with two golden pinwheels behind him which appear to spin when the card is moved. Horizontal backs have a green toned photo of the player in his follow-through swing, with shock waves radiating from the lower-left corner. Cards have a CS prefix.

		MT
Complete Set (20):		10.00
Common Player:		.25
1	Frank Thomas	1.00
2	Ken Griffey Jr.	1.50
3	Jeff Bagwell	.60
4	Cal Ripken Jr.	2.00
5	Barry Bonds	1.00
6	Mike Piazza	1.25
7	Matt Williams	.30
8	Kirby Puckett	.90
9	Jose Canseco	.45
10	Will Clark	.30
11	Don Mattingly	1.00
12	Albert Belle	.40
13	Tony Gwynn	.75
14	Raul Mondesi	.30
15	Bobby Bonilla	.25
16	Rafael Palmeiro	.30
17	Fred McGriff	.25
18	Tim Salmon	.30
19	Kenny Lofton	.25
20	Joe Carter	.25

1995 Sportflix/UC3 In Motion

Found on an average of once per 18 packs, the cards in this chase set feature maximim motion. When the card is held almost vertically a small eight-piece jigsaw puzzle photo of the player is visible against a light blue background. As the card is moved toward a horizontal postion, the pieces appear to become large and move together until the picture fills most of the card. The player's name is in orange at lower-left, with manufacturer's logos at top. Horizontal backs have a green background, two color player photos and a few words of career highlights. The In Motion card numbers are preceded by an "IM" prefix.

	MT
Complete Set (10):	7.50
Common Player:	.25

1	Cal Ripken Jr.	1.75
2	Ken Griffey Jr.	1.50
3	Frank Thomas	1.00
4	Mike Piazza	1.25
5	Barry Bonds	1.00
6	Matt Williams	.25
7	Kirby Puckett	.75
8	Greg Maddux	.75
9	Don Mattingly	1.00
10	Will Clark	.25

1996 Sportflix

Distributed in only retail locations, this 1996 Sportflix set has 144 cards, including 24-card UC3 and 21-card Rookies subsets. The set also has a parallel set, Artist's Proof; these cards are seeded one per every 48 packs. Four insert sets were also produced: Double Take, Hit Parade, Power Surge and ProMotion.

		MT
Complete Set (144):		25.00
Common Player:		.10
Common Artist's Proof:		1.50
AP Stars:		10X
Pack (5):		1.50
Wax Box (36):		40.00
1	Wade Boggs	.65
2	Tim Salmon	.20
3	Will Clark	.30
4	Dante Bichette	.10
5	Barry Bonds	1.25
6	Kirby Puckett	1.00
7	Albert Belle	.40
8	Greg Maddux	1.00
9	Tony Gwynn	1.00
10	Mike Piazza	1.50
11	Ivan Rodriguez	.30
12	Marty Cordova	.10
13	Frank Thomas	1.25
14	Raul Mondesi	.30
15	Johnny Damon	.15
16	Mark McGwire	2.50
17	Lenny Dykstra	.10
18	Ken Griffey Jr.	2.00
19	Chipper Jones	1.50
20	Alex Rodriguez	2.00
21	Jeff Bagwell	.75
22	Jim Edmonds	.10
23	Edgar Martinez	.10
24	David Cone	.10
25	Tom Glavine	.15
26	Eddie Murray	.50
27	Paul Molitor	.45
28	Ryan Klesko	.10
29	Rafael Palmeiro	.25
30	Manny Ramirez	.75
31	Mo Vaughn	.45
32	Rico Brogna	.10
33	Marc Newfield	.10
34	J.T. Snow	.10
35	Reggie Sanders	.10
36	Fred McGriff	.10
37	Craig Biggio	.10
38	Jeff King	.10
39	Kenny Lofton	.10
40	Gary Gaetti	.10
41	Eric Karros	.10
42	Jason Isringhausen	.10
43	B.J. Surhoff	.10
44	Michael Tucker	.10
45	Gary Sheffield	.30
46	Chili Davis	.10
47	Bobby Bonilla	.10
48	Hideo Nomo	.65
49	Ray Durham	.10
50	Phil Nevin	.10
51	Randy Johnson	.50
52	Bill Pulsipher	.10
53	Ozzie Smith	1.00
54	Cal Ripken Jr.	2.50
55	Cecil Fielder	.10
56	Matt Williams	.30
57	Sammy Sosa	1.25
58	Roger Clemens	1.00
59	Brian Hunter	.10
60	Barry Larkin	.10
61	Charles Johnson	.10
62	Dave Justice	.30
63	Garret Anderson	.10
64	Rondell White	.15
65	Derek Bell	.10
66	Andres Galarraga	.10
67	Moises Alou	.15
68	Travis Fryman	.10
69	Pedro Martinez	.50
70	Carlos Baerga	.10
71	John Valentin	.10
72	Larry Walker	.20
73	Roberto Alomar	.60
74	Mike Mussina	.60
75	Kevin Appier	.10
76	Bernie Williams	.20
77	Ray Lankford	.10
78	Gregg Jefferies	.10
79	Robin Ventura	.10
80	Kenny Rogers	.10
81	Paul O'Neill	.10
82	Mark Grace	.25
83	Deion Sanders	.15
84	Tino Martinez	.10
85	Joe Carter	.10
86	Pete Schourek	.10
87	Jack McDowell	.10
88	John Mabry	.10
89	Darren Daulton	.10
90	Jim Thome	.10
91	Jay Buhner	.10
92	Jay Bell	.10
93	Kevin Seitzer	.10
94	Jose Canseco	.50
95	Juan Gonzalez	.75
96	Jeff Conine	.10
97	Chipper Jones (UC3)	.75
98	Ken Griffey Jr. (UC3)	1.00
99	Frank Thomas (UC3)	.65
100	Cal Ripken Jr. (UC3)	1.25
101	Albert Belle (UC3)	.20
102	Mike Piazza (UC3)	.75
103	Dante Bichette (UC3)	.10
104	Sammy Sosa (UC3)	.65
105	Mo Vaughn (UC3)	.30
106	Tim Salmon (UC3)	.15
107	Reggie Sanders (UC3)	.10
108	Gary Sheffield (UC3)	.20
109	Ruben Rivera (UC3)	.10
110	Rafael Palmeiro (UC3)	.15
111	Edgar Martinez (UC3)	.10
112	Barry Bonds (UC3)	.65
113	Manny Ramirez (UC3)	.40
114	Larry Walker (UC3)	.15
115	Jeff Bagwell (UC3)	.40
116	Matt Williams (UC3)	.15
117	Mark McGwir (UC3)	1.50
118	Johnny Damon (UC3)	.10
119	Eddie Murray (UC3)	.30
120	Jay Buhner (UC3)	.10
121	Tim Unroe (Rookie)	.10
122	Todd Hollandsworth (Rookie)	.10
123	Tony Clark (Rookie)	.10
124	Roger Cedeno (Rookie)	.15
125	Jim Pittsley (Rookie)	.10
126	Ruben Rivera (Rookie)	.10
127	Bob Wolcott (Rookie)	.10
128	Chan Ho Park (Rookie)	.25
129	Chris Snopek (Rookie)	.10
130	Alex Ochoa (Rookie)	.10
131	Yamil Benitez (Rookie)	.10
132	Jimmy Haynes (Rookie)	.10
133	Dustin Hermanson (Rookie)	.15
134	Shawn Estes (Rookie)	.10
135	Howard Battle (Rookie)	.10
136	*Matt Lawton* (Rookie)	.50
137	Terrell Wade (Rookie)	.10
138	Jason Schmidt (Rookie)	.10
139	Derek Jeter (Rookie)	1.50
140	Shannon Stewart (Rookie)	.15
141	Chris Stynes (Rookie)	.10
142	Ken Griffey Jr. (Checklist)	.75
143	Greg Maddux (Checklist)	.50
144	Cal Ripken Jr. (Checklist)	1.25

1996 Sportflix Artist's Proofs

Artist's Proof parallels to 1996 Sportflix are a 1:48 find and are distinctively marked with an AP seal on front.

	MT
Complete Set (144):	250.00
Common Player:	1.50
AP Stars:	10X

(See 1996 Sportflix for checklist and base card values.)

1996 Sportflix Double Take

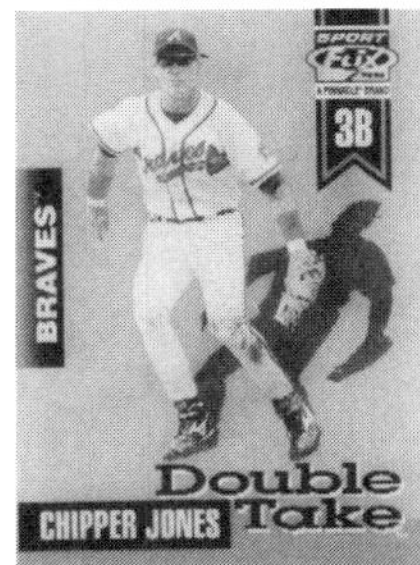

These 1996 Sportflix insert cards each feature two players who are tops at a particular position. Tilting the card to change the angle of view brings each player into focus. The cards were seeded one per 22 packs.

		MT
Complete Set (12):		55.00
Common Player:		2.50
1	Barry Larkin, Cal Ripken Jr.	9.00
2	Roberto Alomar, Craig Biggio	2.50
3	Chipper Jones, Matt Williams	5.00
4	Ken Griffey Jr., Ruben Rivera	9.00
5	Greg Maddux, Hideo Nomo	6.00
6	Frank Thomas, Mo Vaughn	4.50
7	Mike Piazza, Ivan Rodriguez	8.00
8	Albert Belle, Barry Bonds	3.00
9	Alex Rodriguez, Derek Jeter	10.00
10	Kirby Puckett, Tony Gwynn	4.50
11	Manny Ramirez, Sammy Sosa	7.00
12	Jeff Bagwell, Rico Brogna	2.50

1996 Sportflix Hit Parade

Sixteen of baseball's most productive hitters are featured on these inserts. Horizontal fronts have a player portrait at right. In the background is a lenticular-motion scene of a generic player swinging the bat. Backs have an action photo and a few career highlights. The cards were seeded one per every 35 packs.

		MT
Complete Set (16):		26.00
Common Player:		.50
1	Ken Griffey Jr.	3.50
2	Cal Ripken Jr.	4.00
3	Frank Thomas	2.50
4	Mike Piazza	3.00
5	Mo Vaughn	1.00
6	Albert Belle	1.00
7	Jeff Bagwell	1.75
8	Matt Williams	.60
9	Sammy Sosa	2.50
9p	Sammy Sosa (overprint-ed "SAMPLE")	3.00
10	Kirby Puckett	2.00
11	Dante Bichette	.50
12	Gary Sheffield	.75
13	Tony Gwynn	2.00
14	Wade Boggs	1.50
15	Chipper Jones	3.00
16	Barry Bonds	2.50

1996 Sportflix Power Surge

This 1996 Sportflix insert set showcases 24 sluggers on a clear 3-D parallel rendition of the UC3 subset in the main issue. These cards are seeded one per every 35 packs.

		MT
Complete Set (24):		75.00
Common Player:		1.00
1	Chipper Jones	8.00
2	Ken Griffey Jr.	10.00
3	Frank Thomas	6.50
4	Cal Ripken Jr.	12.50
5	Albert Belle	3.00
6	Mike Piazza	8.00
7	Dante Bichette	1.00
8	Sammy Sosa	6.50
9	Mo Vaughn	1.50
10	Tim Salmon	1.50
11	Reggie Sanders	1.00
12	Gary Sheffield	1.50
13	Ruben Rivera	1.00
14	Rafael Palmeiro	2.00
15	Edgar Martinez	1.00
16	Barry Bonds	6.50
17	Manny Ramirez	5.00
18	Larry Walker	1.25
19	Jeff Bagwell	5.00
20	Matt Williams	1.25
21	Mark McGwire	12.50
22	Johnny Damon	1.25
23	Eddie Murray	4.00
24	Jay Buhner	1.00

1996 Sportflix ProMotion

These 1996 Sportflix inserts were seeded one per every 17 packs. The cards' "morphing" technology turns baseball equipment, such as bats, balls and gloves, into 20 of the top veteran superstars using multiphase animation.

		MT
Complete Set (20):		25.00
Common Player:		.25
1	Cal Ripken Jr.	4.00
2	Greg Maddux	2.00
3	Mo Vaughn	.75
4	Albert Belle	1.00
5	Mike Piazza	3.00
6	Ken Griffey Jr.	3.50
7	Frank Thomas	2.50
8	Jeff Bagwell	1.50
9	Hideo Nomo	1.00
10	Chipper Jones	3.00
11	Tony Gwynn	2.00
12	Don Mattingly	2.50
13	Dante Bichette	.25
14	Matt Williams	.50
15	Manny Ramirez	1.50
16	Barry Bonds	2.50
17	Reggie Sanders	.25
18	Tim Salmon	.50
19	Ruben Rivera	.25
20	Garret Anderson	.25

1996 Sportflix Rookie Supers

Eight of the young players included in the Sportflix Rookies subset are featured in an enlarged version which was issued one per retail box. The cards measure 3" x 5" and are numbered "X of 8," on back, but are otherwise identical to the smaller version.

		MT
Complete Set (8):		17.50
Common player:		2.00
1	Jason Schmidt	2.00
2	Chris Snopek	2.00
3	Tony Clark	2.00
4	Todd Hollandsworth	2.00
5	Alex Ochoa	2.00
6	Derek Jeter	10.00
7	Howard Battle	2.00
8	Bob Wolcott	2.00

1997 Sports Illustrated

Fleer teamed up with Sports Illustrated to produce a 180-card World Series Fever set. The regular set is divided into six different subsets: 96 Player Cards, 27 Fresh Faces, 18 Inside Baseball, 18 SIber Vision, 12 covers and 9 Newsmakers. Inserts included the Extra Edition parallel set, Great Shots, Cooperstown Collection and Autographed Mini-Cover Redemption Cards. Cards were sold in six-card packs for $1.99 each.

		MT
Complete Set (180):		20.00
Common Player:		.10
Pack (6):		1.50
Wax Box (24):		25.00
1	Bob Abreu (Fresh Faces)	.20
2	Jaime Bluma (Fresh Faces)	.10
3	Emil Brown (Fresh Faces)	.10
4	Jose Cruz, Jr. (Fresh Faces)	.30
5	Jason Dickson (Fresh Faces)	.10
6	Nomar Garciaparra (Fresh Faces)	2.25
7	Todd Greene (Fresh Faces)	.10
8	Vladimir Guerrero (Fresh Faces)	1.50
9	Wilton Guerrero (Fresh Faces)	.10
10	Jose Guillen (Fresh Faces)	.10
11	Hideki Irabu (Fresh Faces)	.10
12	Russ Johnson (Fresh Faces)	.10
13	Andruw Jones (Fresh Faces)	1.50
14	Damon Mashore (Fresh Faces)	.10
15	Jason McDonald (Fresh Faces)	.10
16	Ryan McGuire (Fresh Faces)	.10
17	Matt Morris (Fresh Faces)	.10
18	Kevin Orie (Fresh Faces)	.10
19	Dante Powell (Fresh Faces)	.10
20	Pokey Reese (Fresh Faces)	.10
21	Joe Roa (Fresh Faces)	.10
22	Scott Rolen (Fresh Faces)	1.25
23	Glendon Rusch (Fresh Faces)	.10
24	Scott Spiezio (Fresh Faces)	.10
25	Bubba Trammell (Fresh Faces)	.25
26	Todd Walker "(Fresh Faces)	.30
27	Jamey Wright (Fresh Faces)	.10
28	Ken Griffey Jr. (Season Highlights)	1.00
29	Tino Martinez (Season Highlights)	.10
30	Roger Clemens (Season Highlights)	.50
31	Hideki Irabu (Season Highlights)	.10
32	Kevin Brown (Season Highlights)	.10
33	Chipper Jones, Cal Ripken Jr. (Season Highlights)	.50
34	Sandy Alomar (Season Highlights)	.10
35	Ken Caminiti (Season Highlights)	.10
36	Randy Johnson (Season Highlights)	.30
37	Andy Ashby (Inside Baseball)	.10
38	Jay Buhner (Inside Baseball)	.10
39	Joe Carter (Inside Baseball)	.10
40	Darren Daulton (Inside Baseball)	.10
41	Jeff Fassero (Inside Baseball)	.10
42	Andres Galarraga (Inside Baseball)	.10
43	Rusty Greer (Inside Baseball)	.10
44	Marquis Grissom (Inside Baseball)	.10
45	Joey Hamilton (Inside Baseball)	.10
46	Jimmy Key (Inside Baseball)	.10
47	Ryan Klesko (Inside Baseball)	.10
48	Eddie Murray (Inside Baseball)	.20
49	Charles Nagy (Inside Baseball)	.10
50	Dave Nilsson (Inside Baseball)	.10
51	Ricardo Rincon (Inside Baseball)	.10
52	Billy Wagner (Inside Baseball)	.10
53	Dan Wilson (Inside Baseball)	.10
54	Dmitri Young (Inside Baseball)	.10
55	Roberto Alomar (S.I.BER Vision)	.40
56	Sandy Alomar Jr. (S.I.BER Vision)	.10
57	Scott Brosius (S.I.BER Vision)	.10
58	Tony Clark (S.I.BER Vision)	.10
59	Carlos Delgado (S.I.BER Vision)	.25
60	Jermaine Dye (S.I.BER Vision)	.10
61	Darin Erstad (S.I.BER Vision)	.50
62	Derek Jeter (S.I.BER Vision)	1.25
63	Jason Kendall (S.I.BER Vision)	.10
64	Hideo Nomo (S.I.BER Vision)	.25
65	Rey Ordonez (S.I.BER Vision)	.10
66	Andy Pettitte (S.I.BER Vision)	.20
67	Manny Ramirez (S.I.BER Vision)	.60
68	Edgar Renteria (S.I.BER Vision)	.10
69	Shane Reynolds (S.I.BER Vision)	.10
70	Alex Rodriguez (S.I.BER Vision)	1.50
71	Ivan Rodriguez (S.I.BER Vision)	.40
72	Jose Rosado (S.I.BER Vision)	.10
73	John Smoltz	.15
74	Tom Glavine	.15
75	Greg Maddux	2.00
76	Chipper Jones	2.50
77	Kenny Lofton	.10
78	Fred McGriff	.10
79	Kevin Brown	.15
80	Alex Fernandez	.10
81	Al Leiter	.10
82	Bobby Bonilla	.10
83	Gary Sheffield	.30
84	Moises Alou	.20
85	Henry Rodriguez	.10
86	Mark Grudzielanek	.10
87	Pedro Martinez	.50
88	Todd Hundley	.10
89	Bernard Gilkey	.10
90	Bobby Jones	.10
91	Curt Schilling	.25
92	Ricky Bottalico	.10
93	Mike Lieberthal	.10
94	Sammy Sosa	2.25
95	Ryne Sandberg	1.50
96	Mark Grace	.35
97	Deion Sanders	.15

98 Reggie Sanders .10
99 Barry Larkin .15
100 Craig Biggio .15
101 Jeff Bagwell 1.50
102 Derek Bell .10
103 Brian Jordan .10
104 Ray Lankford .10
105 Ron Gant .10
106 Al Martin .10
107 Kevin Elster .10
108 Jermaine Allensworth .10
109 Vinny Castilla .10
110 Dante Bichette .10
111 Larry Walker .30
112 Mike Piazza 2.50
113 Eric Karros .10
114 Todd Hollandsworth .10
115 Raul Mondesi .25
116 Hideo Nomo .65
117 Ramon Martinez .10
118 Ken Caminiti .10
119 Tony Gwynn 2.00
120 Steve Finley .10
121 Barry Bonds 2.25
122 J.T. Snow .10
123 Rod Beck .10
124 Cal Ripken Jr. 3.00
125 Mike Mussina .75
126 Brady Anderson .10
127 Bernie Williams .40
128 Derek Jeter 2.50
129 Tino Martinez .10
130 Andy Pettitte .35
131 David Cone .10
132 Mariano Rivera .25
133 Roger Clemens 2.00
134 Pat Hentgen .10
135 Juan Guzman .10
136 Bob Higginson .15
137 Tony Clark .10
138 Travis Fryman .10
139 Mo Vaughn .60
140 Tim Naehring .10
141 John Valentin .10
142 Matt Williams .25
143 David Justice .30
144 Jim Thome .10
145 Chuck Knoblauch .10
146 Paul Molitor .50
147 Marty Cordova .10
148 Frank Thomas 2.25
149 Albert Belle .40
150 Robin Ventura .10
151 John Jaha .10
152 Jeff Cirillo .10
153 Jose Valentin .10
154 Jay Bell .10
155 Jeff King .10
156 Kevin Appier .10
157 Ken Griffey Jr. 2.75
158 Alex Rodriguez 2.75
158p Alex Rodriguez (overprinted "PROMOTIONAL SAMPLE") 2.00
159 Randy Johnson .75
160 Juan Gonzalez 1.50
161 Will Clark .30
162 Dean Palmer .10
163 Tim Salmon .25
164 Jim Edmonds .10
165 Jim Leyritz .10
166 Jose Canseco .45
167 Jason Giambi .30
168 Mark McGwire 3.00
169 Barry Bonds (Classic Covers) 1.00
170 Alex Rodriguez (Classic Covers) 1.50
171 Roger Clemens (Classic Covers) .75
172 Ken Griffey Jr. (Classic Covers) 1.00
173 Greg Maddux (Classic Covers) .75
174 Mike Piazza (Classic Covers) 1.25
175 Will Clark, Mark McGwire (Classic Covers) 1.00
176 Hideo Nomo (Classic Covers) .75
177 Cal Ripken Jr. (Classic Covers) 1.50
178 Ken Griffey Jr., Frank Thomas (Classic Covers) .50
179 Alex Rodriguez, Derek Jeter (Classic Covers) 1.00
180 John Wetteland (Classic Covers) .10
--- checklist (Jose Cruz Jr.) .15

1997 Sports Illustrated Extra Edition

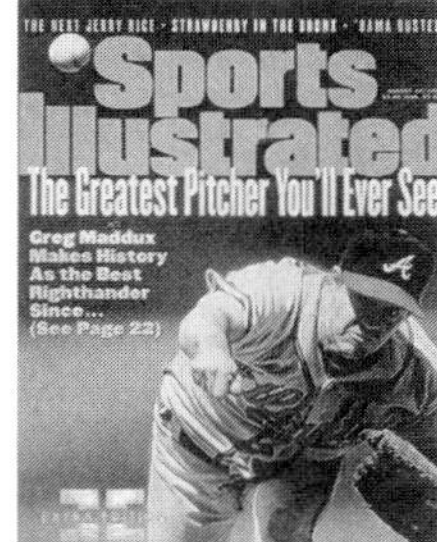

Each of the regular cards in the premiere Fleer SI issue is also found in a parallel set designated on front in gold holographic foil as "Extra Edition". Backs of the cards carry a serial number from within a production of 500 of each card.

	MT
Complete Set (180):	300.00
Common Player:	2.00
Extra Edition Stars:	8X

(See 1997 Sports Illustrated for checklist and base card values.)

1997 Sports Illustrated Autographed Mini-Covers

Six different players autographed 250 magazine mini-covers that were available through randomly seeded redemption cards. The players who autographed cards were Hank Aaron, Willie Mays, Frank Robinson, Kirby Puckett, Cal Ripken Jr., and Alex Rodriguez.

	MT
Complete Set (6):	400.00
Common Player:	30.00
Alex Rodriguez	100.00
Cal Ripken Jr.	125.00
Kirby Puckett	60.00
Willie Mays	75.00
Frank Robinson	30.00
Hank Aaron	75.00

1997 Sports Illustrated Box Topper

This special version of A-Rod's card was packaged one per box of foil packs. It was intended to be inserted into die-cuts on the box to create a sample display for the new issue. The card measures 2-1/2" x 4-1/16". The back is in black-and-white with instructions on how to insert the card into the box.

	MT
Alex Rodriguez	6.00

1997 Sports Illustrated Cooperstown Collection

This 12-card insert (found 1:12 packs) lets collectors relive classic SI baseball covers with a description of each issue on the back.

		MT
Complete Set (12):		27.50
Common Player:		2.00
1	Hank Aaron	6.00
2	Yogi Berra	3.00
3	Lou Brock	2.00
4	Rod Carew	2.00
5	Juan Marichal	2.00
6	Al Kaline	2.50
7	Joe Morgan	2.00
8	Brooks Robinson	3.00
9	Willie Stargell	2.00
10	Kirby Puckett	4.50
11	Willie Mays	6.00
12	Frank Robinson	3.00

1997 Sports Illustrated Great Shots

A 25-card insert, found one per pack, designed to highlight Sports Illustrated's classic photography. Each card in the set folds out to a 5" x 7" format to showcase a larger photo.

		MT
Complete Set (25):		6.00
Common Player:		.10
(1)	Roberto Alomar	.35
(2)	Andy Ashby	.10
(3)	Albert Belle	.25
(4)	Barry Bonds	.50
(5)	Jay Buhner	.10
(6)	Vinny Castilla, Andres Galarraga	.10
(7)	Darren Daulton	.10
(8)	Juan Gonzalez	.35
(9)	Ken Griffey Jr.	.75
(10)	Derek Jeter	.60
(11)	Randy Johnson	.40
(12)	Chipper Jones	.60
(13)	Eric Karros	.10
(14)	Ryan Klesko	.10
(15)	Kenny Lofton	.10
(16)	Greg Maddux	.45
(17)	Mark McGwire	1.00
(18)	Mike Piazza	.60
(19)	Cal Ripken Jr.	1.00
(20)	Alex Rodriguez	.75
(21)	Ryne Sandberg	.40
(22)	Deion Sanders	.15
(23)	John Smoltz	.15
(24)	Frank Thomas	.50
(25)	Mo Vaughn	.30

1998 Sports Illustrated Promo

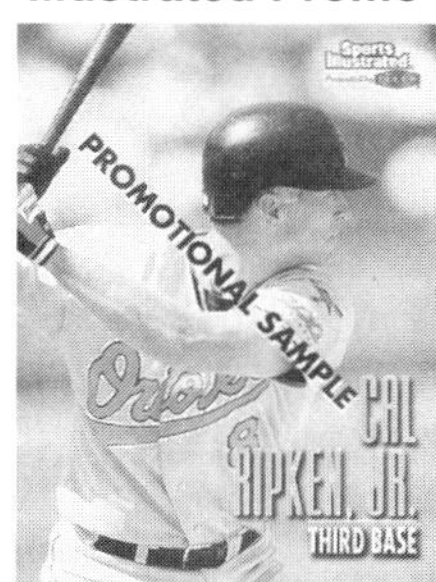

This sample card was issued to preview the 1998 Sports Illustrated set presented by Fleer. The card is in the same format as the regular issue, but has a different card number and is overprinted "PROMOTIONAL SAMPLE" on front and back.

		MT
8	Cal Ripken Jr.	4.00

1998 Sports Illustrated

The second of three Sports Illustrated releases of 1998 from Fleer contained 200 cards and featured exclusive Sports Illustrated photography and commentary. Cards arrived in six-card packs and carried a Sports Illustrated logo in a top corner. The set included a Travis Lee One to Watch cards (#201) that was inserted just before going to press. Subsets included: Baseball's Best (129-148), One to Watch (149-176), and '97 in Review (177-200). Inserts sets include: Extra Edition and First Edition parallels, Autographs, Covers, Editor's Choice and Opening Day Mini Posters.

		MT
Complete Set (201):		30.00
Common Player:		.10
Pack (6):		1.50
Wax Box (24):		35.00
1	Edgardo Alfonzo	.10
2	Roberto Alomar	.50
3	Sandy Alomar	.10
4	Moises Alou	.15
5	Brady Anderson	.10
6	Garret Anderson	.10
7	Kevin Appier	.10
8	Jeff Bagwell	1.00
9	Jay Bell	.10
10	Albert Belle	.40
11	Dante Bichette	.10
12	Craig Biggio	.15
13	Barry Bonds	1.50
14	Bobby Bonilla	.10
15	Kevin Brown	.15
16	Jay Buhner	.10
17	Ellis Burks	.10
18	Mike Cameron	.10
19	Ken Caminiti	.10
20	Jose Canseco	.45
21	Joe Carter	.10
22	Vinny Castilla	.10
23	Jeff Cirillo	.10
24	Tony Clark	.10
25	Will Clark	.25
26	Roger Clemens	1.25
27	David Cone	.10
28	Jose Cruz Jr.	.20
29	Carlos Delgado	.25
30	Jason Dickson	.10
31	Dennis Eckersley	.10
32	Jim Edmonds	.10
33	Scott Erickson	.10
34	Darin Erstad	.75
35	Shawn Estes	.10
36	Jeff Fassero	.10
37	Alex Fernandez	.10
38	Chuck Finley	.10
39	Steve Finley	.10
40	Travis Fryman	.10
41	Andres Galarraga	.10
42	Ron Gant	.10
43	Nomar Garciaparra	1.50
44	Jason Giambi	.30
45	Tom Glavine	.15
46	Juan Gonzalez	1.00
47	Mark Grace	.25
48	Willie Green	.10
49	Rusty Greer	.10
50	Ben Grieve	.25
51	Ken Griffey Jr.	2.25
52	Mark Grudzielanek	.10
53	Vladimir Guerrero	1.00
54	Juan Guzman	.10
55	Tony Gwynn	1.25
56	Joey Hamilton	.10
57	Rickey Henderson	.75
58	Pat Hentgen	.10
59	Livan Hernandez	.10
60	Bobby Higginson	.15
61	Todd Hundley	.10
62	Hideki Irabu	.10
63	John Jaha	.10
64	Derek Jeter	2.00
65	Charles Johnson	.10
66	Randy Johnson	.60
67	Andruw Jones	1.00
68	Bobby Jones	.10
69	Chipper Jones	2.00
70	Brian Jordan	.10
71	David Justice	.30
72	Eric Karros	.10
73	Jeff Kent	.10
74	Jimmy Key	.10
75	Darryl Kile	.10
76	Jeff King	.10
77	Ryan Klesko	.10
78	Chuck Knoblauch	.10
79	Ray Lankford	.10
80	Barry Larkin	.15
81	Kenny Lofton	.10
82	Greg Maddux	1.25
83	Al Martin	.10
84	Edgar Martinez	.10
85	Pedro Martinez	.45
86	Tino Martinez	.10
87	Mark McGwire	2.50
88	Paul Molitor	.60
89	Raul Mondesi	.25
90	Jamie Moyer	.10
91	Mike Mussina	.65
92	Tim Naehring	.10
93	Charles Nagy	.10
94	Denny Neagle	.10
95	Dave Nilsson	.10
96	Hideo Nomo	.65
97	Rey Ordonez	.10
98	Dean Palmer	.10
99	Rafael Palmeiro	.20
100	Andy Pettitte	.40
101	Mike Piazza	2.00
102	Brad Radke	.10
103	Manny Ramirez	1.00
104	Edgar Renteria	.10
105	Cal Ripken Jr.	2.50
106	Alex Rodriguez	2.25
106p	Alex Rodriguez ("PROMOTIONAL SAMPLE")	2.00
107	Henry Rodriguez	.10
108	Ivan Rodriguez	.60
109	Scott Rolen	.75
110	Tim Salmon	.25
111	Curt Schilling	.25
112	Gary Sheffield	.30
113	John Smoltz	.15
114	J.T. Snow	.10
115	Sammy Sosa	1.50
116	Matt Stairs	.10
117	Shannon Stewart	.10
118	Frank Thomas	1.50
119	Jim Thome	.10
120	Justin Thompson	.10
121	Mo Vaughn	.45
122	Robin Ventura	.10
123	Larry Walker	.30
124	Rondell White	.20
125	Bernie Williams	.45
126	Matt Williams	.25
127	Tony Womack	.10
128	Jaret Wright	.10
129	Edgar Renteria (Baseball's Best)	.10
130	Kenny Lofton (Baseball's Best)	.10
131	Tony Gwynn (Baseball's Best)	.65
132	Mark McGwire (Baseball's Best)	1.50
133	Craig Biggio (Baseball's Best)	.10
134	Charles Johnson (Baseball's Best)	.10
135	J.T. Snow (Baseball's Best)	.10
136	Ken Caminiti (Baseball's Best)	.10
137	Vladimir Guerrero (Baseball's Best)	.50
138	Jim Edmonds (Baseball's Best)	.10
139	Randy Johnson (Baseball's Best)	.25
140	Darryl Kile (Baseball's Best)	.10
141	John Smoltz (Baseball's Best)	.10
142	Greg Maddux (Baseball's Best)	.65
143	Andy Pettitte (Baseball's Best)	.25
144	Ken Griffey Jr. (Baseball's Best)	1.25
145	Mike Piazza (Baseball's Best)	1.00
146	Todd Greene (Baseball's Best)	.10
147	Vinny Castilla (Baseball's Best)	.10
148	Derek Jeter (Baseball's Best)	1.00
149	Robert Machado (One to Watch)	.10
150	Mike Gulan (One to Watch)	.10
151	Randall Simon (One to Watch)	.10
152	Michael Coleman (One to Watch)	.10
153	Brian Rose (One to Watch)	.10
154	*Scott Eyre* (One to Watch)	.10
155	*Magglio Ordonez* (One to Watch)	1.50
156	Todd Helton (One to Watch)	.65
157	Juan Encarnacion (One to Watch)	.10
158	Mark Kotsay (One to Watch)	.10
159	Josh Booty (One to Watch)	.15
160	*Melvin Rosario* (One to Watch)	.15
161	Shane Halter (One to Watch)	.10
162	Paul Konerko (One to Watch)	.15
163	*Henry Blanco* (One to Watch)	.10
164	Antone Williamson (One to Watch)	.10
165	Brad Fullmer (One to Watch)	.20
166	Ricky Ledee (One to Watch)	.10
167	Ben Grieve (One to Watch)	.15
168	*Frank Catalanotto* (One to Watch)	.25
169	Bobby Estalella (One to Watch)	.10
170	Dennis Reyes (One to Watch)	.10
171	Kevin Polcovich (One to Watch)	.10
172	Jacob Cruz (One to Watch)	.10
173	Ken Cloude (One to Watch)	.10
174	Eli Marrero (One to Watch)	.10
175	Fernando Tatis (One to Watch)	.10
176	Tom Evans (One to Watch)	.10
177	Carl Everett, Nomar Garciaparra (97 in Review)	.35
178	Eric Davis (97 in Review)	.10
179	Roger Clemens (97 in Review)	.50
180	Brett Butler, Eddie Murray (97 in Review)	.15
181	Frank Thomas (97 in Review)	.75
182	Curt Schilling (97 in Review)	.15
183	Jeff Bagwell (97 in Review)	.50
184	Mark McGwire, Ken Griffey, Jr. (97 in Review)	1.00
185	Kevin Brown (97 in Review)	.10
186	Marty Cordova, Ricardo Rincon (97 in Review)	.10
187	Charles Johnson (97 in Review)	.10
188	Hideki Irabu (97 in Review)	.10
189	Tony Gwynn (97 in Review)	.60
190	Sandy Alomar (97 in Review)	.10
191	Ken Griffey Jr. (97 in Review)	1.00
192	Larry Walker (97 in Review)	.10
193	Roger Clemens (97 in Review)	.50
194	Pedro Martinez (97 in Review)	.25
195	Nomar Garciaparra (97 in Review)	.75
196	Scott Rolen (97 in Review)	.40
197	Brian Anderson (97 in Review)	.10
198	Tony Saunders (97 in Review)	.10
199	Florida Celebration (97 in Review)	.10
200	Livan Hernandez (97 in Review)	.10
201	Travis Lee (One to Watch) (SP)	1.50

1998 Sports Illustrated Extra Edition

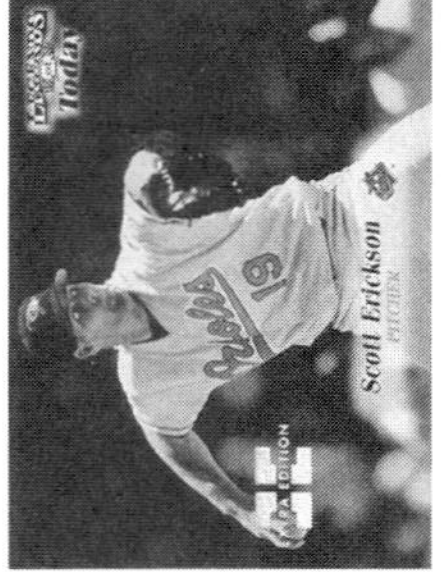

Extra Edition is a 201-card parallel set that includes a holofoil stamp on the front and sequential numbering to 250 on the back. There is also a First Edition version of these that was identical on the front, but contains the text

"The Only 1 of 1 First Edition" in purple lettering on the card back.

	MT
Common Player:	2.00
Extra Edition Stars:	12X

(See 1998 Sports Illustrated for checklist and base card values.)

1998 Sports Illustrated Autographs

This six-card insert featured autographs of players with the following production: Brock 500, Cruz Jr. 250, Fingers 500, Grieve 250, Konerko 250 and Robinson 500. The Konerko and Greive cards were available through redemptions until Nov. 1, 1999.

	MT
Common Player:	20.00
Lou Brock (500)	40.00
Jose Cruz Jr. (250)	20.00
Rollie Fingers (500)	20.00
Ben Grieve (exchange card) (250)	10.00
Ben Grieve (signed card)	20.00
Paul Konerko (exchange card) (250)	10.00
Paul Konerko (signed card)	20.00
Brooks Robinson (250)	50.00

1998 Sports Illustrated Covers

This 10-card insert set pictures actual Sports Illustrated covers on trading cards. The cards are numbered with a "C" prefix and inserted one per nine packs.

		MT
Complete Set (10):		15.00
Common Player:		1.00
Inserted 1:9		
1	Ken Griffey, Jr., Mike Piazza	2.00
2	Derek Jeter	2.50
3	Ken Griffey Jr.	2.75
4	Cal Ripken Jr.	3.00
5	Manny Ramirez	1.75
6	Jay Buhner	1.00
7	Matt Williams	1.00
8	Randy Johnson	1.50
9	Deion Sanders	1.00
10	Jose Canseco	1.50

1998 Sports Illustrated Editor's Choice

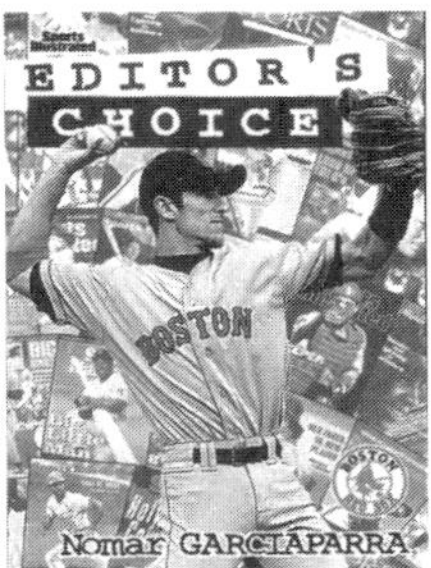

Editor's Choice includes 10 top players in 1998 as profiled by the editors of Sports Illustrated. Cards are numbered with an "EC" prefix and seeded one per 24 packs.

		MT
Complete Set (10):		21.00
Common Player:		1.00
Inserted 1:24		
1	Ken Griffey Jr.	3.50
2	Alex Rodriguez	3.50
3	Frank Thomas	2.50
4	Mark McGwire	4.00
5	Greg Maddux	2.00
6	Derek Jeter	3.00
7	Cal Ripken Jr.	4.00
8	Nomar Garciaparra	2.50
9	Jeff Bagwell	1.50
10	Jose Cruz Jr.	1.00

1998 Sports Illustrated Mini-Posters

Thirty 5" x 7" mini-posters were available at a rate of one per pack. The posters took the top player or two from each team and added their 1998 schedule. Backs were blank so the cards are numbered on the front with an "OD" prefix.

		MT
Complete Set (30):		8.00
Common Player:		.10
Inserted 1:1		
1	Tim Salmon	.15
2	Travis Lee	.15
3	John Smoltz, Greg Maddux	.50
4	Cal Ripken Jr.	1.00
5	Nomar Garciaparra	.50
6	Sammy Sosa	.50
7	Frank Thomas	.50
8	Barry Larkin	.15
9	David Justice	.20
10	Larry Walker	.15
11	Tony Clark	.10
12	Livan Hernandez	.10
13	Jeff Bagwell	.35
14	Kevin Appier	.10
15	Mike Piazza	.75
16	Fernando Vina	.10
17	Chuck Knoblauch	.10
18	Vladimir Guerrero	.35
19	Rey Ordonez	.10
20	Bernie Williams	.20
21	Matt Stairs	.10
22	Curt Schilling	.20
23	Tony Womack	.10
24	Mark McGwire	1.00
25	Tony Gwynn	.40
26	Barry Bonds	.50
27	Ken Griffey Jr.	1.00
28	Fred McGriff	.10
29	Juan Gonzalez, Alex Rodriguez	.50
30	Roger Clemens	.40

1998 Sports Illustrated Then & Now

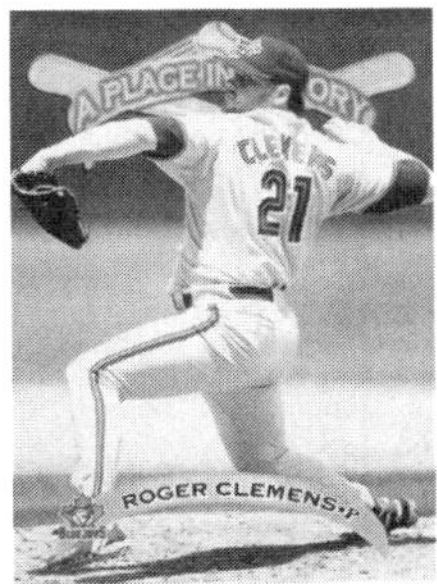

Then and Now was the first of three Sports Illustrated baseball releases in 1998. It contained 150 cards and sold in six-card packs, with five cards and a mini-poster. Fronts carried photos of active and retired players, as well as rookies. There was only one subset - A Place in History (#37-53) - which compares statistics between current players and retired greats. The product arrived with an Extra Edition parallel set, Art of the Game, Autograph Redemptions, Covers and Great Shots inserts. There was also an Alex Rodriguez checklist/ mini-poster seeded every 12th pack.

		MT
Complete Set (150):		25.00
Common Player:		.10
Pack (5):		2.00
Wax Box (24):		38.00
1	Luis Aparicio (Legends of the Game)	.10
2	Richie Ashburn (Legends of the Game)	.10
3	Ernie Banks (Legends of the Game)	.75
4	Yogi Berra (Legends of the Game)	.75
5	Lou Boudreau (Legends of the Game)	.10
6	Lou Brock (Legends of the Game)	.25
7	Jim Bunning (Legends of the Game)	.10
8	Rod Carew (Legends of the Game)	.25
9	Bob Feller (Legends of the Game)	.25
10	Rollie Fingers (Legends of the Game)	.10
11	Bob Gibson (Legends of the Game)	.50
12	Fergie Jenkins (Legends of the Game)	.10
13	Al Kaline (Legends of the Game)	.25
14	George Kell (Legends of the Game)	.10
15	Harmon Killebrew (Legends of the Game)	.50
16	Ralph Kiner (Legends of the Game)	.10
17	Tommy Lasorda (Legends of the Game)	.10
18	Juan Marichal (Legends of the Game)	.10
19	Eddie Mathews (Legends of the Game)	.40
20	Willie Mays (Legends of the Game)	1.50
21	Willie McCovey (Legends of the Game)	.10
22	Joe Morgan (Legends of the Game)	.15
23	Gaylord Perry (Legends of the Game)	.10
24	Kirby Puckett (Legends of the Game)	1.00
25	Pee Wee Reese (Legends of the Game)	.20
26	Phil Rizzuto (Legends of the Game)	.25
27	Robin Roberts (Legends of the Game)	.10
28	Brooks Robinson (Legends of the Game)	.60
29	Frank Robinson (Legends of the Game)	.50
30	Red Schoendienst (Legends of the Game)	.10
31	Enos Slaughter (Legends of the Game)	.10
32	Warren Spahn (Legends of the Game)	.50
33	Willie Stargell (Legends of the Game)	.20
34	Earl Weaver (Legends of the Game)	.10
35	Billy Williams (Legends of the Game)	.20
36	Early Wynn (Legends of the Game)	.10
37	Rickey Henderson (A Place in History)	.60
38	Greg Maddux (A Place in History)	1.00
39	Mike Mussina (A Place in History)	.65
40	Cal Ripken Jr. (A Place in History)	2.00
41	Albert Belle (A Place in History)	.40
42	Frank Thomas (A Place in History)	1.25
43	Jeff Bagwell (A Place in History)	.75
44	Paul Molitor (A Place in History)	.50
45	Chuck Knoblauch (A Place in History)	.10
46	Todd Hundley (A Place in History)	.10
47	Bernie Williams (A Place in History)	.40
48	Tony Gwynn (A Place in History)	1.00
49	Barry Bonds (A Place in History)	1.25
50	Ken Griffey Jr. (A Place in History)	1.75
51	Randy Johnson (A Place in History)	.65
52	Mark McGwire (A Place in History)	2.00

53 Roger Clemens (A Place in History) 1.00
54 Jose Cruz Jr. (A Place in History) .25
55 Roberto Alomar (Legends of Today) .50
56 Sandy Alomar (Legends of Today) .10
57 Brady Anderson (Legends of Today) .10
58 Kevin Appier (Legends of Today) .10
59 Jeff Bagwell (Legends of Today) .75
60 Albert Belle (Legends of Today) .40
61 Dante Bichette (Legends of Today) .10
62 Craig Biggio (Legends of Today) .15
63 Barry Bonds (Legends of Today) 1.25
64 Kevin Brown (Legends of Today) .10
65 Jay Buhner (Legends of Today) .10
66 Ellis Burks (Legends of Today) .10
67 Ken Caminiti (Legends of Today) .10
68 Jose Canseco (Legends of Today) .50
69 Joe Carter (Legends of Today) .10
70 Vinny Castilla (Legends of Today) .10
71 Tony Clark (Legends of Today) .10
72 Roger Clemens (Legends of Today) 1.00
73 David Cone (Legends of Today) .10
74 Jose Cruz Jr. (Legends of Today) .25
75 Jason Dickson (Legends of Today) .10
76 Jim Edmonds (Legends of Today) .10
77 Scott Erickson (Legends of Today) .10
78 Darin Erstad (Legends of Today) .60
79 Alex Fernandez (Legends of Today) .10
80 Steve Finley (Legends of Today) .10
81 Travis Fryman (Legends of Today) .10
82 Andres Galarraga (Legends of Today) .10
83 Nomar Garciaparra (Legends of Today) 12.50
84 Tom Glavine (Legends of Today) .15
85 Juan Gonzalez (Legends of Today) .75
86 Mark Grace (Legends of Today) .25
87 Willie Greene (Legends of Today) .10
88 Ken Griffey Jr. (Legends of Today) 1.75
89 Vladimir Guerrero (Legends of Today) .75
90 Tony Gwynn (Legends of Today) 1.00
91 Livan Hernandez (Legends of Today) .10
92 Bobby Higginson (Legends of Today) .15
93 Derek Jeter (Legends of Today) 1.50
94 Charles Johnson (Legends of Today) .10
95 Randy Johnson (Legends of Today) .65
96 Andruw Jones (Legends of Today) .75
97 Chipper Jones (Legends of Today) 1.50
98 David Justice (Legends of Today) .35
99 Eric Karros (Legends of Today) .10
100 Jason Kendall (Legends of Today) .10
101 Jimmy Key (Legends of Today) .10
102 Darryl Kile (Legends of Today) .10
103 Chuck Knoblauch (Legends of Today) .10
104 Ray Lankford (Legends of Today) .10
105 Barry Larkin (Legends of Today) .15
106 Kenny Lofton (Legends of Today) .10
107 Greg Maddux (Legends of Today) 12.50
108 Al Martin (Legends of Today) .10
109 Edgar Martinez (Legends of Today) .10
110 Pedro Martinez (Legends of Today) .50
111 Ramon Martinez (Legends of Today) .10
112 Tino Martinez (Legends of Today) .10
113 Mark McGwire (Legends of Today) 2.00
114 Raul Mondesi (Legends of Today) .25
115 Matt Morris (Legends of Today) .10
116 Charles Nagy (Legends of Today) .10
117 Denny Neagle (Legends of Today) .10
118 Hideo Nomo (Legends of Today) .60
119 Dean Palmer (Legends of Today) .10
120 Andy Pettitte (Legends of Today) .35
121 Mike Piazza (Legends of Today) 1.50
122 Manny Ramirez (Legends of Today) .75
123 Edgar Renteria (Legends of Today) .10
124 Cal Ripken Jr. (Legends of Today) 2.00
125 Alex Rodriguez (Legends of Today) 1.75
126 Henry Rodriguez (Legends of Today) .10
127 Ivan Rodriguez (Legends of Today) .60
128 Scott Rolen (Legends of Today) .65
129 Tim Salmon (Legends of Today) .15
130 Curt Schilling (Legends of Today) .20
131 Gary Sheffield (Legends of Today) .25
132 John Smoltz (Legends of Today) .15
133 Sammy Sosa (Legends of Today) 1.25
134 Frank Thomas (Legends of Today) 1.25
135 Jim Thome (Legends of Today) .10
136 Mo Vaughn (Legends of Today) .45
137 Robin Ventura (Legends of Today) .10
138 Larry Walker (Legends of Today) .25
139 Bernie Williams (Legends of Today) .40
140 Matt Williams (Legends of Today) .25
141 Jaret Wright (Legends of Today) .15
142 Michael Coleman (Legends of the Future) .10
143 Juan Encarnacion (Legends of the Future) .10
144 Brad Fullmer (Legends of the Future) .15
145 Ben Grieve (Legends of the Future) .25
146 Todd Helton (Legends of the Future) .65
147 Paul Konerko (Legends of the Future) .15
148 Derrek Lee (Legends of the Future) .10
149 *Magglio Ordonez* (Legends of the Future) 1.50
150 Enrique Wilson (Legends of the Future) .10
--- Alex Rodriguez (checklist) 1.50

1998 Sports Illustrated Then & Now Extra Edition

This 150-card set paralleled the base set and was distinguished by an "Extra Edition" foil stamp on the front. There were 500 sets of Extra Edition and the cards were individually numbered on the back.

	MT
Common Extra Edition:	2.00
Extra Edition Stars:	8X

Production 500 sets
(See 1998 Sports Illustrated Then & Now for checklist and base card values.)

1998 Sports Illustrated Then & Now Art of the Game

Art of the Game was an eight-card insert featuring reproductions of original artwork of current and retired baseball stars done by eight popular sports artists. Cards are numbered with a "AG" prefix and inserted one per nine packs.

	MT
Complete Set (8):	18.00
Common Player:	1.50

Inserted 1:9

1 It's Gone (Ken Griffey Jr.) 4.00
2 Alex Rodriguez 4.00
3 Mike Piazza 3.00
4 Brooks Robinson 2.00
5 David Justice (All-Star) 1.50
6 Cal Ripken Jr. 5.00
7 The Prospect and the Prospector 1.50
8 Barry Bonds 2.50

1998 Sports Illustrated Then & Now Autographs

Six autograph redemption cards were randomly inserted into packs of Then & Now and could be exchanged prior to Nov. 1, 1999. The signed cards were produced in the following quantities: Clemens 250, Gibson 500, Gwynn 250, Killebrew 500, Mays 250 and Rolen 250. Four of the six cards use the same fronts as the Covers insert; Gibson and Rolen cards each feature unique card fronts.

	MT
Common Autograph:	35.00

Redemption Cards: 10%

Bob Gibson (500) 50.00
Tony Gwynn (250) 80.00
Roger Clemens (250) 100.00
Scott Rolen (250) 40.00
Willie Mays (250) 125.00
Harmon Killebrew (500) 35.00

1998 Sports Illustrated Then & Now Covers

This 12-card insert features color shots of six actual Sports Illustrated covers, including six current players and six retired players. The cards are numbered with a "C" prefix and were seeded one per 18 packs.

		MT
Complete Set (12):		24.00
Common Player:		1.25
Inserted 1:18		
1	Lou Brock (10/16/67)	1.25
2	Kirby Puckett (4/6/92)	3.00
3	Harmon Killebrew (4/8/63 - inside)	1.25
4	Eddie Mathews (8/16/54)	3.00
5	Willie Mays (5/22/72)	3.00
6	Frank Robinson (10/6/69)	1.75
7	Cal Ripken Jr. (9/11/95)	4.00
8	Roger Clemens (5/12/86)	2.50
9	Ken Griffey Jr. (10/16/95)	3.50
10	Mark McGwire (6/1/92)	4.00
11	Tony Gwynn (7/28/97)	2.50
12	Ivan Rodriguez (8/11/97)	1.50

1998 Sports Illustrated Then & Now Great Shots!

This 25-card set featured 5" x 7" fold-out mini-posters using Sports Illustrated photos. Great Shots were inserted one per pack and contained a mix of retired and current players.

		MT
Complete Set (25):		7.50
Common Player:		.10
Inserted 1:1		
1	Ken Griffey Jr.	.75
2	Frank Thomas	.50
3	Alex Rodriguez	.75
4	Andruw Jones	.35
5	Chipper Jones	.60
6	Cal Ripken Jr.	1.00
7	Mark McGwire	1.00
8	Derek Jeter	.60
9	Greg Maddux	.45
10	Jeff Bagwell	.35
11	Mike Piazza	.60
12	Scott Rolen	.30
13	Nomar Garciaparra	.50
14	Jose Cruz Jr.	.15
15	Charles Johnson	.10
16	Fergie Jenkins	.10
17	Lou Brock	.10
18	Bob Gibson	.10
19	Harmon Killebrew	.10
20	Juan Marichal	.10
21	Brooks Robinson	.25
22	Rod Carew	.15
23	Yogi Berra	.25
24	Willie Mays	.50
25	Kirby Puckett	.45

1998 Sports Illustrated Then & Now Road to Cooperstown

Road to Cooperstown features 10 current players who are having Hall of Fame careers. The insert name is printed across the back in bold, gold letters. Cards are numbered with a "RC" prefix and were inserted one per 24 packs.

		MT
Complete Set (10):		15.00
Common Player:		.75
Inserted 1:24		
1	Barry Bonds	2.00
2	Roger Clemens	2.00
3	Ken Griffey Jr.	3.00
4	Tony Gwynn	1.50
5	Rickey Henderson	1.00
6	Greg Maddux	2.00
7	Paul Molitor	.75
8	Mike Piazza	3.00
9	Cal Ripken Jr.	4.00
10	Frank Thomas	1.50

1998 Sports Illustrated World Series Fever

The third and final Sports Illustrated release of 1998 contained 150 cards and focused on the World Series while recapping memorable moments from the season. The set also included many stars of tomorrow, like Kerry Wood, Orlando Hernandez, Ben Grieve and Travis Lee. Once again, all the photos were taken from Sports Illustrated archives. The set has two subsets - 10 Magnificent Moments and 20 Cover Collection. The set is paralleled twice in Extra and First Edition parallel sets, and has three insert sets - MVP Collection, Reggie Jackson's Picks and Autumn Excellence.

		MT
Complete Set (150):		30.00
Common Player:		.10
Pack (6):		2.00
Wax Box (24):		35.00
1	Mickey Mantle (Covers)	3.00
2	1957 World Series Preview (Covers)	.25
3	1958 World Series Preview (Covers)	.25
4	1959 World Series Preview (Covers)	.25
5	1962 World Series (Covers)	.20
6	Lou Brock (Covers)	.25
7	Brooks Robinson (Covers)	.75
8	Frank Robinson (Covers)	.50
9	1974 World Series (Covers)	.20
10	Reggie Jackson (Covers)	.50
11	1985 World Series (Covers)	.20
12	1987 World Series (Covers)	.20
13	Orel Hershiser (Covers)	.10
14	Rickey Henderson (Covers)	.25
15	1991 World Series (Covers)	.20
16	1992 World Series (Covers)	.10
17	Joe Carter (Covers)	.10
18	1995 World Series (Covers)	.20
19	1996 World Series (Covers)	.25
20	Edgar Renteria (Covers)	.10
21	Bill Mazeroski (Magnificent Moments)	.15
22	Joe Carter (Magnificent Moments)	.10
23	Carlton Fisk (Magnificent Moments)	.25
24	Bucky Dent (Magnificent Moments)	.25
25	Mookie Wilson (Magnificent Moments)	.10
26	Enos Slaughter (Magnificent Moments)	.10
27	Mickey Lolich (Magnificent Moments)	.10
28	Bobby Richardson (Magnificent Moments)	.10
29	Kirk Gibson (Magnificent Moments)	.10
30	Edgar Renteria (Magnificent Moments)	.10
31	Albert Belle	.40
32	Kevin Brown	.15
33	Brian Rose	.10
34	Ron Gant	.10
35	Jeromy Burnitz	.10
36	Andres Galarraga	.10
37	Jim Edmonds	.10
38	Jose Cruz Jr.	.25
39	Mark Grudzielanek	.10
40	Shawn Estes	.10
41	Mark Grace	.25
42	Nomar Garciaparra	1.75
43	Juan Gonzalez	1.25
44	Tom Glavine	.15
45	Brady Anderson	.10
46	Tony Clark	.10
47	Jeff Cirillo	.10
48	Dante Bichette	.10
49	Ben Grieve	.20
50	Ken Griffey Jr.	2.25
51	Edgardo Alfonzo	.10
52	Roger Clemens	1.50
53	Pat Hentgen	.10
54	Todd Helton	.75
55	Andy Benes	.10
56	Tony Gwynn	1.50
57	Andruw Jones	1.25
58	Bobby Higginson	.15
59	Bobby Jones	.10
60	Darryl Kile	.10
61	Chan Ho Park	.35
62	Charles Johnson	.10
63	Rusty Greer	.10
64	Travis Fryman	.10
65	Derek Jeter	2.00
66	Jay Buhner	.10
67	Chuck Knoblauch	.10
68	David Justice	.40
69	Brian Hunter	.10
70	Eric Karros	.10
71	Edgar Martinez	.10
72	Chipper Jones	2.00
73	Barry Larkin	.15
74	Mike Lansing	.10
75	Craig Biggio	.15
76	Al Martin	.10
77	Barry Bonds	1.75
78	Randy Johnson	.65
79	Ryan Klesko	.10
80	Mark McGwire	2.50
81	Fred McGriff	.10
82	Javy Lopez	.10
83	Kenny Lofton	.10
84	Sandy Alomar Jr.	.10
85	Matt Morris	.10
86	Paul Konerko	.15
87	Ray Lankford	.10
88	Kerry Wood	.75
89	Roberto Alomar	.50
90	Greg Maddux	1.50
91	Travis Lee	.15
92	Moises Alou	.25
93	Dean Palmer	.10
94	Hideo Nomo	.60
95	Ken Caminiti	.10
96	Pedro Martinez	.75
97	Raul Mondesi	.20
98	Denny Neagle	.10
99	Tino Martinez	.10
100	Mike Mussina	.65
101	Kevin Appier	.10
102	Vinny Castilla	.10
103	Jeff Bagwell	1.25
104	Paul O'Neill	.10
105	Rey Ordonez	.10
106	Vladimir Guerrero	1.25
107	Rafael Palmeiro	.25
108	Alex Rodriguez	2.25
109	Andy Pettitte	.35
110	Carl Pavano	.10
111	Henry Rodriguez	.10
112	Gary Sheffield	.25
113	Curt Schilling	.25
114	John Smoltz	.15
115	Reggie Sanders	.10
116	Scott Rolen	1.00
117	Mike Piazza	2.00
118	Manny Ramirez	1.25
119	Cal Ripken Jr.	2.50
120	Brad Radke	.10
121	Tim Salmon	.30
122	Brett Tomko	.10
123	Robin Ventura	.10
124	Mo Vaughn	.50
125	A.J. Hinch	.10
126	Derrek Lee	.10
127	*Orlando Hernandez*	1.50
128	Aramis Ramirez	.10
129	Frank Thomas	1.75
130	J.T. Snow	.10
131	*Magglio Ordonez*	1.50
132	Bobby Bonilla	.10
133	Marquis Grissom	.10

#	Player	MT
134	Jim Thome	.10
135	Justin Thompson	.10
136	Matt Williams	.30
137	Matt Stairs	.10
138	Wade Boggs	.60
139	Chuck Finley	.10
140	Jaret Wright	.10
141	Ivan Rodriguez	.75
142	Brad Fullmer	.15
143	Bernie Williams	.40
144	Jason Giambi	.25
145	Larry Walker	.30
146	Tony Womack	.10
147	Sammy Sosa	1.75
148	Rondell White	.20
149	Todd Stottlemyre	.10
150	Shane Reynolds	.10

1998 Sports Illustrated WS Fever Extra Edition

Extra Edition parallels the entire 150-card base set and is identified by a gold foil stamp on the card front and sequential numbering to 98 sets on the back. World Series Fever also includes one-of-one parallel versions called First Edition. These have the same fronts, but are numbered 1 of 1 on back.

	MT
Common Player:	3.00
Stars:	30X
Production 98 sets	

(See 1998 Sports Illustrated World Series Fever for checklist and base values.)

1998 Sports Illustrated WS Fever Autumn Excellence

Autumn Excellence honors players with the most select World Series records. The 10-card set was seeded one per 24 packs, while rarer Gold versions were seeded one per 240 packs.

		MT
Complete Set (10):		25.00
Common Player:		.75
Inserted 1:24		
Golds:		3X
Inserted 1:240		
AE1	Willie Mays	3.00
AE2	Kirby Puckett	3.00
AE3	Babe Ruth	6.00
AE4	Reggie Jackson	2.00
AE5	Whitey Ford	.75
AE6	Lou Brock	.75
AE7	Mickey Mantle	6.00
AE8	Yogi Berra	2.00
AE9	Bob Gibson	1.50
AE10	Don Larsen	1.50

1998 Sports Illustrated WS Fever MVP Collection

This 10-card insert set features select MVPs from the World Series. Card fronts contain a shot of the player over a white border with the year in black letters and the insert and player's name in blue foil. MVP Collection inserts were seeded one per four packs and numbered with a "MC" prefix.

		MT
Complete Set (10):		6.00
Common Player:		.50
Inserted 1:4		
1	Frank Robinson	1.00
2	Brooks Robinson	1.25
3	Willie Stargell	.50
4	Bret Saberhagen	.50
5	Rollie Fingers	.50
6	Orel Hershiser	.50
7	Paul Molitor	1.50
8	Tom Glavine	.50
9	John Wetteland	.50
10	Livan Hernandez	.50

1998 Sports Illustrated WS Fever Reggie Jackson Picks

Reggie Jackson's Picks contains top players that Jackson believes have what it takes to perform on center stage in the World Series. Fronts have a shot of the player with his name in the background, and a head shot of Reggie Jackson in the bottom right corner. These were numbered with a "RP" prefix and inserted one per 12 packs.

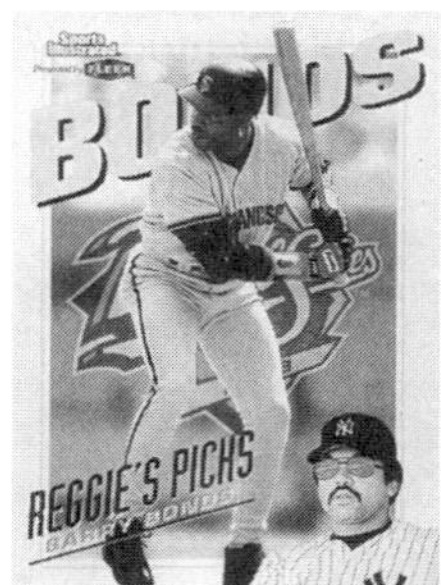

		MT
Complete Set (15):		40.00
Common Player:		.75
Inserted 1:12		
1	Paul O'Neill	.75
2	Barry Bonds	3.50
3	Ken Griffey Jr.	5.00
4	Juan Gonzalez	2.00
5	Greg Maddux	3.00
6	Mike Piazza	4.00
7	Larry Walker	1.00
8	Mo Vaughn	1.00
9	Roger Clemens	3.00
10	John Smoltz	.75
11	Alex Rodriguez	5.00
12	Frank Thomas	2.00
13	Mark McGwire	6.00
14	Jeff Bagwell	2.00
15	Randy Johnson	1.50

1999 Sports Illustrated

The Sports Illustrated Baseball by Fleer set consists of a 180-card base set. The base set is composed of 107 player cards, and four subsets. They include Team 2000, Postseason Review, Award Winners, and Season Highlights. Cards come in six-card packs with an SRP of $1.99. The set also includes five insert sets, along with hobby exclusive autographed J.D. Drew cards numbered to 250. The insert sets include: Headliners (1:4), Ones to Watch (1:12), Fabulous 40's (1:20), Fabulous 40's Extra (hobby exclusive), and The Dominators (1:90 and 1:180).

		MT
Complete Set (180):		30.00
Common Player:		.10
Pack (6):		1.50
Wax Box (24):		30.00
1	Yankees (Postseason Review)	.25
2	Scott Brosius (Postseason Review)	.10
3	David Wells (Postseason Review)	.10
4	Sterling Hitchcock (Postseason Review)	.10
5	David Justice (Postseason Review)	.25
6	David Cone (Postseason Review)	.10
7	Greg Maddux (Postseason Review)	.50
8	Jim Leyritz (Postseason Review)	.10
9	Gary Gaetti (Postseason Review)	.10
10	Mark McGwire (Award Winners)	1.25
11	Sammy Sosa (Award Winners)	.65
12	Larry Walker (Award Winners)	.15
13	Tony Womack (Award Winners)	.10
14	Tom Glavine (Award Winners)	.10
15	Curt Schilling (Award Winners)	.10
16	Greg Maddux (Award Winners)	.50
17	Trevor Hoffman (Award Winners)	.10
18	Kerry Wood (Award Winners)	.40
19	Tom Glavine (Award Winners)	.10
20	Sammy Sosa (Award Winners)	.65
21	Travis Lee (Season Highlights)	.10
22	Roberto Alomar (Season Highlights)	.15
23	Roger Clemens (Season Highlights)	.50
24	Barry Bonds (Season Highlights)	.65
25	Paul Molitor (Season Highlights)	.50
26	Todd Stottlemyre (Season Highlights)	.10
27	Chris Hoiles (Season Highlights)	.10
28	Albert Belle (Season Highlights)	.20
29	Tony Clark (Season Highlights)	.10
30	Kerry Wood (Season Highlights)	.40
31	David Wells (Season Highlights)	.10
32	Dennis Eckersley (Season Highlights)	.10
33	Mark McGwire (Season Highlights)	1.25
34	Cal Ripken Jr. (Season Highlights)	1.25
35	Ken Griffey Jr. (Season Highlights)	1.00
36	Alex Rodriguez (Season Highlights)	1.00
37	Craig Biggio (Season Highlights)	.10
38	Sammy Sosa (Season Highlights)	.65
39	Dennis Martinez (Season Highlights)	.10
40	Curt Schilling (Season Highlights)	.10
41	Orlando Hernandez (Season Highlights)	.50
42	Troy Glaus, *Ben Molina*, Todd Greene ("Team" 2000)	.50
43	Mitch Meluskey, Daryle Ward,	

Mike Grzanich ("Team" 2000) .10
44 Eric Chavez, Mike Neill,*Steve Connelly* ("Team" 2000) .50
45 Roy Halladay, Tom Evans, Kevin Witt ("Team" 2000) .10
46 George Lombard, Adam Butler, Bruce Chen ("Team" 2000) .10
47 Ronnie Belliard, Valerio de los Santos,*Rafael Roque* ("Team" 2000) .10
48 J.D. Drew, Placido Polanco, *Mark Little* ("Team" 2000) .20
49 Jason Maxwell,*Jose Nieves*, Jeremi Gonzalez ("Team" 2000) .20
50 Scott McClain, Kerry Robinson,*Mike Duvall* ("Team" 2000) .10
51 Ben Ford,*Bryan Corey*, Danny Klassen ("Team" 2000) .10
52 Angel Pena, Jeff Kubenka, Paul LoDuca ("Team" 2000) .10
53 Kirk Bullinger, Fernando Seguignol, Tim Young ("Team" 2000) .10
54 Ramon Martinez, Wilson Delgado, Armando Rios ("Team" 2000) .10
55 Russ Branyon, *Jolbert Cabrera*, Jason Rakers ("Team" 2000) .20
56 *Carlos Guillen*, *David Holdridge*, *Giomar Guevara* ("Team" 2000) .15
57 Alex Gonzalez, Joe Fontenot, Preston Wilson ("Team" 2000) .15
58 Mike Kinkade, Jay Payton, Masato Yoshii ("Team" 2000) .10
59 Willis Otanez, Ryan Minor, Calvin Pickering ("Team" 2000) .15
60 Ben Davis, Matt Clement, Stan Spencer ("Team" 2000) .10
61 Marlon Anderson, Mike Welch,*Gary Bennett* ("Team" 2000) .15
62 Abraham Nunez, *Sean Lawrence*, Aramis Ramirez ("Team" 2000) .10
63 Jonathan Johnson, *Rob Sasser*,*Scott Sheldon* ("Team" 2000) .10
64 *Keith Glauber*,*Guillermo Garcia*, Eddie Priest ("Team" 2000) .10
65 Brian Barkley, Jin Ho Cho, Donnie Sadler ("Team" 2000) .15
66 Derrick Gibson, Mark Strittmatter,*Edgard Clemente* ("Team" 2000) .15
67 Jeremy Giambi, Dermal Brown,*Chris Hatcher* ("Team" 2000) .15
68 *Rob Fick*, Gabe Kapler, Marino Santana ("Team" 2000) .50
69 Corey Koskie, A.J. Pierzynski, Benj Sampson ("Team" 2000) .15
70 Brian Simmons, Mark Johnson, Craig Wilson ("Team" 2000) .10
71 Ryan Bradley, Mike Lowell, Jay Tessmer ("Team" 2000) .10
72 Ben Grieve .25
73 Shawn Green .25
74 Rafael Palmeiro .25
75 Juan Gonzalez .75
76 Mike Piazza 1.50
77 Devon White .10
78 Jim Thome .10
79 Barry Larkin .15
80 Scott Rolen .65
81 Raul Mondesi .20
82 Jason Giambi .25
83 Jose Canseco .45
84 Tony Gwynn 1.00
85 Cal Ripken Jr. 2.50
86 Andy Pettitte .30
87 Carlos Delgado .25
88 Jeff Cirillo .10
89 Bret Saberhagen .10
90 John Olerud .10
91 Ron Coomer .10
92 Todd Helton .65
93 Ray Lankford .10
94 Tim Salmon .25
95 Fred McGriff .10
96 Matt Stairs .10
97 Ken Griffey Jr. 2.00
98 Chipper Jones 1.50
99 Mark Grace .20
100 Ivan Rodriguez .65
101 Jeromy Burnitz .10
102 Kenny Rogers .10
103 Kevin Millwood .20
104 Vinny Castilla .10
105 Jim Edmonds .10
106 Craig Biggio .15
107 Andres Galarraga .10
108 Sammy Sosa 1.25
109 Juan Encarnacion .10
110 Larry Walker .35
111 John Smoltz .15
112 Randy Johnson .50
113 Bobby Higginson .15
114 Albert Belle .40
115 Jaret Wright .10
116 Edgar Renteria .10
117 Andruw Jones .75
118 Barry Bonds 1.25
119 Rondell White .20
120 Jamie Moyer .10
121 Darin Erstad .65
122 Al Leiter .10
123 Mark McGwire 2.50
124 Mo Vaughn .50
125 Livan Hernandez .10
126 Jason Kendall .10
127 Frank Thomas 1.25
128 Denny Neagle .10
129 Johnny Damon .15
130 Derek Bell .10
131 Jeff Kent .10
132 Tony Womack .10
133 Trevor Hoffman .10
134 Gary Sheffield .30
135 Tino Martinez .10
136 Travis Fryman .10
137 Rolando Arrojo .10
138 Dante Bichette .10
139 Nomar Garciaparra 1.25
140 Moises Alou .20
141 Chuck Knoblauch .10
142 Robin Ventura .10
143 Scott Erickson .10
144 David Cone .10
145 Greg Vaughn .10
146 Wade Boggs .65
147 Mike Mussina .50
148 Tony Clark .10
149 Alex Rodriguez 2.00
150 Javy Lopez .10
151 Bartolo Colon .10
152 Derek Jeter 1.50
153 Greg Maddux 1.00
154 Kevin Brown .15
155 Curt Schilling .25
156 Jeff King .10
157 Bernie Williams .35
158 Roberto Alomar .45
159 Travis Lee .15
160 Kerry Wood .75
160p Kerry Wood ("PROMOTIONAL SAMPLE") 1.00
161 Jeff Bagwell .75
162 Roger Clemens 1.00
163 Matt Williams .30
164 Chan Ho Park .25
165 Damion Easley .10
166 Manny Ramirez .75
167 Quinton McCracken .10
168 Todd Walker .15
169 Eric Karros .10
170 Will Clark .30
171 Edgar Martinez .10
172 Cliff Floyd .10
173 Vladimir Guerrero .75
174 Tom Glavine .15
175 Pedro Martinez .45
176 Chuck Finley .10
177 Dean Palmer .10
178 Omar Vizquel .10
179 Checklist .10
180 Checklist .10

1999 Sports Illustrated Diamond Dominators

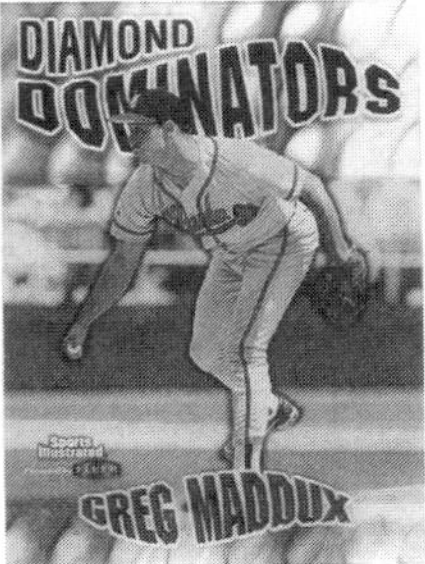

This 10-card insert set features five hitters and five pitchers on embossed cards. The hitters are seeded 1 in every 180 packs, while the pitchers are seeded 1 in every 90 packs.

	MT
Complete Set (10):	70.00
Common Player:	3.00
Pitchers inserted 1:90	
Hitters inserted 1:180	
1DD Kerry Wood	3.00
2DD Roger Clemens	7.50
3DD Randy Johnson	3.00
4DD Greg Maddux	7.50
5DD Pedro Martinez	3.00
6DD Ken Griffey Jr.	15.00
7DD Sammy Sosa	10.00
8DD Nomar Garciaparra	9.00
9DD Mark McGwire	17.50
10DD Alex Rodriguez	15.00

1999 Sports Illustrated Fabulous 40s

This 13-card insert set consists of the players that hit 40 or more homers during the 1998 season. The cards are sculpture embossed and foil-stamped, with the player's home run total also on the card. One card comes with every 20 packs.

	MT
Complete Set (13):	17.50
Common Player:	.60
Inserted 1:20	
1FF Mark McGwire	4.50
2FF Sammy Sosa	2.75
3FF Ken Griffey Jr.	3.50
4FF Greg Vaughn	.60
5FF Albert Belle	.75
6FF Jose Canseco	1.25
7FF Vinny Castilla	.60
8FF Juan Gonzalez	1.75
9FF Manny Ramirez	1.75
10FF Andres Galarraga	.60
11FF Rafael Palmeiro	.75
12FF Alex Rodriguez	3.50
13FF Mo Vaughn	1.00

1999 Sports Illustrated Fabulous 40s Extra

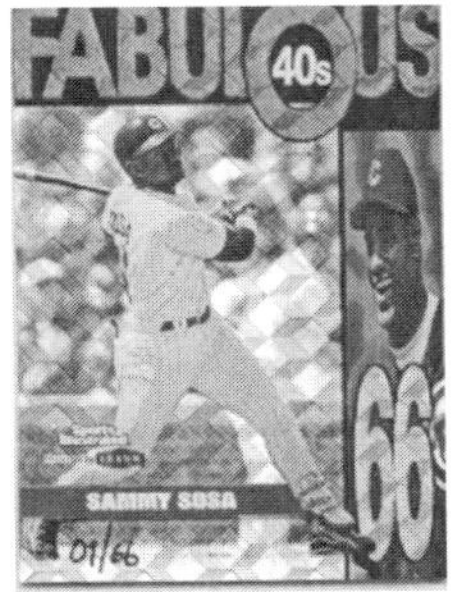

The insert set parallels the 13 cards in the Fabulous 40s set. The cards are hobby exclusive, highlgihted with silver patterned holofoil. Each player's cards are hand-numbered to the total number of home runs he hit in 1998.

	MT
Common Player:	12.00
Numbered to amount of HRs	
1FF Mark McGwire (70)	60.00
2FF Sammy Sosa (66)	50.00
3FF Ken Griffey Jr. (56)	35.00
4FF Greg Vaughn (50)	12.00
5FF Albert Belle (49)	15.00
6FF Jose Canseco (46)	25.00
7FF Vinny Castilla (46)	12.00
8FF Juan Gonzalez (45)	30.00
9FF Manny Ramirez (45)	30.00
10FF Andres Galarraga (44)	12.00
11FF Rafael Palmeiro (43)	15.00
12FF Alex Rodriguez (42)	45.00
13FF Mo Vaughn (40)	15.00

1999 Sports Illustrated Headliners

Headliners is a 25-card insert set that features silver foil stamped, team-color coded cards. One card comes with every four packs.

		MT
Complete Set (25):		18.00
Common Player:		.35
Inserted 1:4		
1H	Vladimir Guerrero	.75
2H	Randy Johnson	.60
3H	Mo Vaughn	.40
4H	Chipper Jones	1.25
5H	Jeff Bagwell	.75
6H	Juan Gonzalez	.75
7H	Mark McGwire	1.75
8H	Cal Ripken Jr.	1.75
9H	Frank Thomas	1.25
10H	Manny Ramirez	.75
11H	Ken Griffey Jr.	1.50
12H	Scott Rolen	.65
13H	Alex Rodriguez	1.50
14H	Barry Bonds	1.25
15H	Roger Clemens	1.00
16H	Darin Erstad	.50
17H	Nomar Garciaparra	1.00
18H	Mike Piazza	1.25
19H	Greg Maddux	1.00
20H	Ivan Rodriguez	.50
21H	Derek Jeter	1.25
22H	Sammy Sosa	1.00
23H	Andruw Jones	.75
24H	Pedro Martinez	.50
25H	Kerry Wood	.35

1999 Sports Illustrated Ones To Watch

This 15-card insert set features the game's top rookies and young stars. The cards have 100%-foil background, and are team-color coded. One card was inserted in every 12 packs.

		MT
Complete Set (15):		11.00
Common Player:		.40
Inserted 1:12		
1OW	J.D. Drew	.75
2OW	Marlon Anderson	.40
3OW	Roy Halladay	.75
4OW	Ben Grieve	.75
5OW	Todd Helton	.75
6OW	Gabe Kapler	1.25
7OW	Troy Glaus	1.50
8OW	Ben Davis	.40
9OW	Eric Chavez	1.25
10OW	Richie Sexson	.40
11OW	Fernando Seguignol	.40
12OW	Kerry Wood	1.00
13OW	Bobby Smith	.40
14OW	Ryan Minor	.40
15OW	Jeremy Giambi	.40
	J.D. Drew autograph (250)	20.00

1999 Sports Illustrated Greats of the Game

The 90-card base set includes many legendary major-leaguers including Babe Ruth and Cy Young. Card fronts feature a full bleed photo with the player name across the bottom and Greats of the Game printed on the bottom left portion of the card. Card backs have the player's vital information, along with career statistics and a few career highlights. Seven-card packs were issued with a SRP of $15.

		MT
Complete Set (90):		35.00
Common Player:		.15
Pack (7):		15.00
Wax Box (12):		150.00
1	Jimmie Foxx	.50
2	Red Schoendienst	.25
3	Babe Ruth	4.00
4	Lou Gehrig	3.00
5	Mel Ott	.25
6	Stan Musial	1.00
7	Mickey Mantle	4.00
8	Carl Yastrzemski	.50
9	Enos Slaughter	.25
10	Andre Dawson	.15
11	Luis Aparicio	.25
12	Ferguson Jenkins	.25
13	Christy Mathewson	.50
14	Ernie Banks	.50
15	Johnny Podres	.15
16	George Foster	.15
17	Jerry Koosman	.15
18	Curt Simmons	.15
19	Bob Feller	.25
20	Frank Robinson	.25
21	Gary Carter	.25
22	Frank Thomas	.15
23	Bill Lee	.15
24	Willie Mays	2.00
25	Tommie Agee	.15
26	Boog Powell	.15
27	Jimmy Wynn	.15
28	Sparky Lyle	.15
29	Bo Belinsky	.15
30	Maury Wills	.15
31	Bill Buckner	.15
32	Steve Carlton	.25
33	Harmon Killebrew	.25
34	Nolan Ryan	3.00
35	Randy Jones	.15
36	Robin Roberts	.25
37	Al Oliver	.15
38	Rico Petrocelli	.15
39	Dave Parker	.15
40	Eddie Mathews	.25
41	Earl Weaver	.25
42	Jackie Robinson	2.50
43	Lou Brock	.25
44	Reggie Jackson	.50
45	Bob Gibson	.25
46	Jeff Burroughs	.15
47	Jim Bouton	.15
48	Bob Forsch	.15
49	Ron Guidry	.15
50	Ty Cobb	2.00
51	Roy White	.15
52	Joe Rudi	.15
53	Moose Skowron	.15
54	Goose Gossage	.15
55	Ed Kranepool	.15
56	Paul Blair	.15
57	Kent Hrbek	.15
58	Orlando Cepeda	.25
59	Buck O'Neil	.25
60	Al Kaline	.25
61	Vida Blue	.15
62	Sam McDowell	.15
63	Jesse Barfield	.15
64	Dave Kingman	.15
65	Ron Santo	.25
66	Steve Garvey	.25
67	Gaylord Perry	.25
68	Darrell Evans	.15
69	Rollie Fingers	.25
70	Walter Johnson	.50
71	Al Hrabosky	.15
72	Mickey Rivers	.15
73	Mike Torrez	.15
74	Hank Bauer	.15
75	Tug McGraw	.15
76	David Clyde	.15
77	Jim Lonborg	.15
78	Clete Boyer	.15
79	Harry Walker	.15
80	Cy Young	.50
81	Bud Harrelson	.15
82	Paul Splittorff	.15
83	Bert Campaneris	.15
84	Joe Niekro	.15
85	Bob Horner	.15
86	Jerry Royster	.15
87	Tommy John	.15
88	Mark Fidrych	.15
89	Dick Williams	.15
90	Graig Nettles	.15

1999 Sports Illustrated Greats/Game Autographs

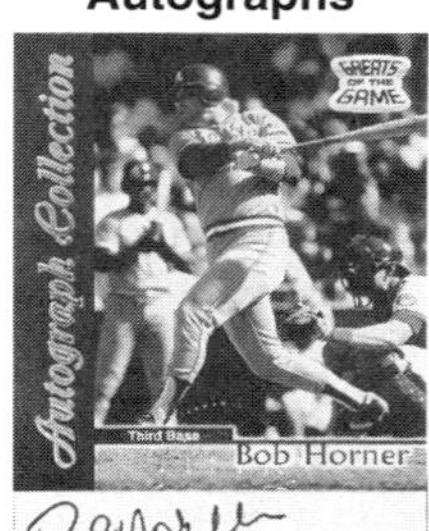

Each Greats of the Game pack has one autograph from the 80 card autograph checklist. Each card is autographed on the white portion on the bottom of the card, and is stamped "seal of authenticity". Card backs certify the autograph is authentic and "has been embossed with the Fleer Mark of Authenticity." The unnumbered cards are checklisted here in alphabetical order.

		MT
Common Player:		5.00
Inserted 1:1		
(1)	Tommie Agee	5.00
(2)	Luis Aparicio	15.00
(3)	Ernie Banks	25.00
(4)	Jesse Barfield	5.00
(5)	Hank Bauer	7.50
(6)	Bo Belinsky	6.50
(7)	Paul Blair	5.00
(8)	Vida Blue	7.50
(9)	Jim Bouton	10.00
(10)	Clete Boyer	10.00
(11)	Lou Brock	12.00
(12)	Bill Buckner	8.00
(13)	Jeff Burroughs	5.00
(14)	Bert Campaneris	7.50
(15)	Steve Carlton	20.00
(16)	Gary Carter	12.00
(17)	Orlando Cepeda	17.50
(18)	David Clyde	5.00
(19)	Andre Dawson	15.00
(20)	Darrell Evans	6.00
(21)	Bob Feller	12.50
(22)	Mark Fidrych	8.00
(23)	Rollie Fingers	9.00
(24)	Bob Forsch	5.00
(25)	George Foster	6.00
(26)	Steve Garvey	9.00
(27)	Bob Gibson	10.00
(28)	Goose Gossage	8.00
(29)	Ron Guidry	8.00
(30)	Bud Harrelson	5.00
(31)	Bob Horner	5.00
(32)	Al Hrabosky	5.00
(33)	Kent Hrbek	10.00
(34a)	Reggie Jackson	150.00
(34b)	Reggie Jackson ("Mr. October")	200.00
(34c)	Reggie Jackson ("HoF 93")	200.00
(35)	Ferguson Jenkins	15.00
(36)	Tommy John	7.50
(37)	Randy Jones	5.00
(38)	Al Kaline	12.50
(39)	Harmon Killebrew	20.00
(40)	Dave Kingman	7.50
(41)	Jerry Koosman	5.00
(42)	Ed Kranepool	5.00
(43)	Bill Lee	6.00
(44)	Jim Lonborg	5.00
(45)	Sparky Lyle	5.00
(46)	Eddie Mathews	40.00
(47)	Willie Mays	95.00
(48)	Sam McDowell	6.00
(49)	Tug McGraw	8.00
(50)	Stan Musial	150.00
(51)	Graig Nettles	10.00
(52)	Joe Niekro	5.00
(53)	Buck O'Neil	8.00
(54)	Al Oliver	8.00
(55)	Dave Parker	6.50
(56)	Gaylord Perry	7.50
(57)	Rico Petrocelli	5.00
(58)	Johnny Podres	10.00
(59)	Boog Powell	8.00
(60)	Mickey Rivers	5.00
(61)	Robin Roberts	12.00
(62)	Frank Robinson	25.00
(63)	Jerry Royster	5.00
(64)	Joe Rudi	5.00
(65)	Nolan Ryan	200.00
(66)	Ron Santo	9.00
(67)	Red Schoendienst	12.00
(68)	Curt Simmons	5.00
(69)	Moose Skowron	8.00
(70)	Enos Slaughter	17.50
(71)	Paul Splittorff	5.00
(72)	Frank Thomas	5.00
(73)	Mike Torrez	5.00
(74)	Harry Walker	5.00
(75)	Earl Weaver	8.00
(76)	Roy White	5.00
(77)	Dick Williams	5.00
(78)	Maury Wills	8.00
(79)	Jimmy Wynn	5.00
(80)	Carl Yastrzemski	60.00

1999 Sports Illustrated Greats/Game Cover Collection

Each pack features one of the 50 chosen baseball covers from the Sports Illustrated archives. Card fronts are a reprint of the actual cover, while the backs give a brief description of the cover article and date of the magazine cover. Each card is numbered with a "C" suffix.

		MT
Complete Set (50):		30.00
Common Player:		.25
Inserted 1:1		
1	Johnny Podres	.25
2	Mickey Mantle	4.00
3	Stan Musial	1.00
4	Eddie Mathews	.50
5	Frank Thomas	.25
6	Willie Mays	2.00
7	Red Schoendienst	.25
8	Luis Aparicio	.25
9	Mickey Mantle	4.00
10	Al Kaline	.50
11	Maury Wills	.25
12	Sam McDowell	.25
13	Harry Walker	.25
14	Carl Yastrzemski	.50
15	Carl Yastrzemski	.50
16	Lou Brock	.25
17	Ron Santo	.25
18	Reggie Jackson	1.00
19	Frank Robinson	.50
20	Jerry Koosman	.25
21	Bud Harrelson	.25
22	Vida Blue	.25
23	Ferguson Jenkins	.25
24	Sparky Lyle	.25
25	Steve Carlton	.50
26	Bert Campaneris	.25
27	Jimmy Wynn	.25
28	Steve Garvey	.25
29	Nolan Ryan	2.00
30	Randy Jones	.25
31	Reggie Jackson	1.00
32	Joe Rudi	.25
33	Reggie Jackson	1.00
34	Dave Parker	.25
35	Mark Fidrych	.25
36	Earl Weaver	.25
37	Nolan Ryan	2.00
38	Steve Carlton	.50
39	Reggie Jackson	1.00
40	Rollie Fingers	.25
41	Gary Carter	.25
42	Graig Nettles	.25
43	Gaylord Perry	.25
44	Kent Hrbek	.25
45	Gary Carter	.25
46	Steve Garvey	.25
47	Steve Carlton	.50
48	Nolan Ryan	2.00
49	Nolan Ryan	4.00
50	Mickey Mantle	4.00

1999 Sports Illustrated Greats/Game Record Breakers

This 10-card set spotlights the top record breakers in the past century from Christy Mathewson to Nolan Ryan. Card fronts are full foiled with a oblong stamp on the bottom portion detailing the player's respective record. Card backs are numbered with a "RB" suffix and gives more detail on the featured player's record. These are seeded 1:12 packs. A Gold parallel is also randomly seeded 1:120 packs and have gold holo-foil.

		MT
Complete Set (10):		40.00
Common Player:		1.75
Inserted 1:12		
Golds:		3X
Inserted 1:120		
1	Mickey Mantle	8.00
2	Stan Musial	3.25
3	Babe Ruth	8.00
4	Christy Mathewson	1.75
5	Cy Young	1.75
6	Nolan Ryan	6.50
7	Jackie Robinson	6.50
8	Lou Gehrig	6.50
9	Ty Cobb	3.25
10	Walter Johnson	1.75

1991 Stadium Club

One of the most popular sets of 1991, this 600-card issue was released in two 300-card series. The cards were available in foil packs only. No factory sets were available. The cards feature borderless high gloss photos on the front and a player evaluation and card photo on the back. Stadium Club cards were considered scarce in many areas, this driving up the price per pack. A special Stadium Club membership package was made available for $29.95 with 10 proof of purchase seals from wrappers.

		MT
Complete Set (600):		40.00
Complete Series 1 (300):		25.00
Complete Series 2 (300):		15.00
Common Player:		.20
Series 1 Pack (13):		2.00
Series 1 Wax Box (36):		50.00
Series 2 Pack (13):		1.50
Series 2 Wax Box (36):		25.00
1	Dave Stewart	.20
2	Wally Joyner	.20
3	Shawon Dunston	.20
4	Darren Daulton	.20
5	Will Clark	.60
6	Sammy Sosa	5.00
7	Dan Plesac	.20
8	Marquis Grissom	.20
9	Erik Hanson	.20
10	Geno Petralli	.20
11	Jose Rijo	.20
12	Carlos Quintana	.20
13	Junior Ortiz	.20
14	Bob Walk	.20
15	Mike Macfarlane	.20
16	Eric Yelding	.20
17	Bryn Smith	.20
18	Bip Roberts	.20
19	Mike Scioscia	.20
20	Mark Williamson	.20
21	Don Mattingly	5.00
22	John Franco	.20
23	Chet Lemon	.20
24	Tom Henke	.20
25	Jerry Browne	.20
26	Dave Justice	.75
27	Mark Langston	.20
28	Damon Berryhill	.20
29	Kevin Bass	.20
30	Scott Fletcher	.20
31	Moises Alou	.40
32	Dave Valle	.20
33	Jody Reed	.20
34	Dave West	.20
35	Kevin McReynolds	.20
36	Pat Combs	.20
37	Eric Davis	.20
38	Bret Saberhagen	.20
39	Stan Javier	.20
40	Chuck Cary	.20
41	Tony Phillips	.20
42	Lee Smith	.20
43	Tim Teufel	.20
44	Lance Dickson	.20
45	Greg Litton	.20
46	Teddy Higuera	.20
47	Edgar Martinez	.20
48	Steve Avery	.20
49	Walt Weiss	.20
50	David Segui	.20
51	Andy Benes	.20
52	Karl Rhodes	.20
53	Neal Heaton	.20
54	Dan Gladden	.20
55	Luis Rivera	.20
56	Kevin Brown	.40
57	Frank Thomas	5.00
58	Terry Mulholland	.20
59	Dick Schofield	.20
60	Ron Darling	.20
61	Sandy Alomar, Jr.	.20
62	Dave Stieb	.20
63	Alan Trammell	.20
64	Matt Nokes	.20
65	Lenny Harris	.20
66	Milt Thompson	.20
67	Storm Davis	.20
68	Joe Oliver	.20
69	Andres Galarraga	.20
70	Ozzie Guillen	.20
71	Ken Howell	.20
72	Garry Templeton	.20
73	Derrick May	.20
74	Xavier Hernandez	.20
75	Dave Parker	.20
76	Rick Aguilera	.20
77	Robby Thompson	.20
78	Pete Incaviglia	.20
79	Bob Welch	.20
80	Randy Milligan	.20
81	Chuck Finley	.20
82	Alvin Davis	.20
83	Tim Naehring	.20
84	Jay Bell	.20
85	Joe Magrane	.20
86	Howard Johnson	.20
87	Jack McDowell	.20
88	Kevin Seitzer	.20
89	Bruce Ruffin	.20
90	Fernando Valenzuela	.20
91	Terry Kennedy	.20
92	Barry Larkin	.30
93	Larry Walker	.75
94	Luis Salazar	.20
95	Gary Sheffield	.75
96	Bobby Witt	.20
97	Lonnie Smith	.20
98	Bryan Harvey	.20
99	Mookie Wilson	.20
100	Dwight Gooden	.20
101	Lou Whitaker	.20
102	Ron Karkovice	.20
103	Jesse Barfield	.20
104	Jose DeJesus	.20
105	Benito Santiago	.20
106	Brian Holman	.20
107	Rafael Ramirez	.20
108	Ellis Burks	.20
109	Mike Bielecki	.20
110	Kirby Puckett	4.00
111	Terry Shumpert	.20
112	Chuck Crim	.20
113	Todd Benzinger	.20
114	Brian Barnes	.20
115	Carlos Baerga	.20
116	Kal Daniels	.20
117	Dave Johnson	.20
118	Andy Van Slyke	.20
119	John Burkett	.20
120	Rickey Henderson	1.25
121	Tim Jones	.20
122	Daryl Irvine	.20
123	Ruben Sierra	.20
124	Jim Abbott	.20
125	Daryl Boston	.20
126	Greg Maddux	4.00
127	Von Hayes	.20
128	Mike Fitzgerald	.20
129	Wayne Edwards	.20
130	Greg Briley	.20
131	Rob Dibble	.20
132	Gene Larkin	.20
133	David Wells	.20
134	Steve Balboni	.20
135	Greg Vaughn	.20
136	Mark Davis	.20
137	Dave Rohde	.20
138	Eric Show	.20
139	Bobby Bonilla	.20
140	Dana Kiecker	.20
141	Gary Pettis	.20
142	Dennis Boyd	.20
143	Mike Benjamin	.20
144	Luis Polonia	.20
145	Doug Jones	.20
146	Al Newman	.20
147	Alex Fernandez	.20
148	Bill Doran	.20
149	Kevin Elster	.20
150	Len Dykstra	.20
151	Mike Gallego	.20
152	Tim Belcher	.20
153	Jay Buhner	.20
154	Ozzie Smith	4.00
155	Jose Canseco	1.50
156	Gregg Olson	.20
157	Charlie O'Brien	.20
158	Frank Tanana	.20
159	George Brett	4.00
160	Jeff Huson	.20
161	Kevin Tapani	.20
162	Jerome Walton	.20
163	Charlie Hayes	.20
164	Chris Bosio	.20
165	Chris Sabo	.20
166	Lance Parrish	.20

167 Don Robinson .20
168 Manuel Lee .20
169 Dennis Rasmussen .20
170 Wade Boggs 2.50
171 Bob Geren .20
172 Mackey Sasser .20
173 Julio Franco .20
174 Otis Nixon .20
175 Bert Blyleven .20
176 Craig Biggio .30
177 Eddie Murray 1.00
178 Randy Tomlin .20
179 Tino Martinez .20
180 Carlton Fisk 1.50
181 Dwight Smith .20
182 Scott Garrelts .20
183 Jim Gantner .20
184 Dickie Thon .20
185 John Farrell .20
186 Cecil Fielder .20
187 Glenn Braggs .20
188 Allan Anderson .20
189 Kurt Stillwell .20
190 Jose Oquendo .20
191 Joe Orsulak .20
192 Ricky Jordan .20
193 Kelly Downs .20
194 Delino DeShields .20
195 Omar Vizquel .20
196 Mark Carreon .20
197 Mike Harkey .20
198 Jack Howell .20
199 Lance Johnson .20
200 Nolan Ryan 6.00
201 John Marzano .20
202 Doug Drabek .20
203 Mark Lemke .20
204 Steve Sax .20
205 Greg Harris .20
206 B.J. Surhoff .20
207 Todd Burns .20
208 Jose Gonzalez .20
209 Mike Scott .20
210 Dave Magadan .20
211 Dante Bichette .20
212 Trevor Wilson .20
213 Hector Villanueva .20
214 Dan Pasqua .20
215 Greg Colbrunn .20
216 Mike Jeffcoat .20
217 Harold Reynolds .20
218 Paul O'Neill .20
219 Mark Guthrie .20
220 Barry Bonds 5.00
221 Jimmy Key .20
222 Billy Ripken .20
223 Tom Pagnozzi .20
224 Bo Jackson .30
225 Sid Fernandez .20
226 Mike Marshall .20
227 John Kruk .20
228 Mike Fetters .20
229 Eric Anthony .20
230 Ryne Sandberg 2.50
231 Carney Lansford .20
232 Melido Perez .20
233 Jose Lind .20
234 Darryl Hamilton .20
235 Tom Browning .20
236 Spike Owen .20
237 Juan Gonzalez 3.00
238 Felix Fermin .20
239 Keith Miller .20
240 Mark Gubicza .20
241 Kent Anderson .20
242 Alvaro Espinoza .20
243 Dale Murphy .50
244 Orel Hershiser .20
245 Paul Molitor 1.50
246 Eddie Whitson .20
247 Joe Girardi .20
248 Kent Hrbek .20
249 Bill Sampen .20
250 Kevin Mitchell .20
251 Mariano Duncan .20
252 Scott Bradley .20
253 Mike Greenwell .20
254 Tom Gordon .20
255 Todd Zeile .20
256 Bobby Thigpen .20
257 Gregg Jefferies .20
258 Kenny Rogers .20
259 Shane Mack .20
260 Zane Smith .20
261 Mitch Williams .20
262 Jim DeShaies .20
263 Dave Winfield 2.50
264 Ben McDonald .20
265 Randy Ready .20
266 Pat Borders .20
267 Jose Uribe .20
268 Derek Lilliquist .20
269 Greg Brock .20
270 Ken Griffey, Jr. 5.50
271 Jeff Gray .20
272 Danny Tartabull .20
273 Dennis Martinez .20
274 Robin Ventura .20
275 Randy Myers .20
276 Jack Daugherty .20
277 Greg Gagne .20
278 Jay Howell .20
279 Mike LaValliere .20
280 Rex Hudler .20
281 Mike Simms .20
282 Kevin Maas .20
283 Jeff Ballard .20
284 Dave Henderson .20
285 Pete O'Brien .20
286 Brook Jacoby .20
287 Mike Henneman .20
288 Greg Olson .20
289 Greg Myers .20
290 Mark Grace .75
291 Shawn Abner .20
292 Frank Viola .20
293 Lee Stevens .20
294 Jason Grimsley .20
295 Matt Williams .60
296 Ron Robinson .20
297 Tom Brunansky .20
298 Checklist .20
299 Checklist .20
300 Checklist .20
301 Darryl Strawberry .20
302 Bud Black .20
303 Harold Baines .20
304 Roberto Alomar 1.50
305 Norm Charlton .20
306 Gary Thurman .20
307 Mike Felder .20
308 Tony Gwynn 4.00
309 Roger Clemens 4.00
310 Andre Dawson .45
311 Scott Radinsky .20
312 Bob Melvin .20
313 Kirk McCaskill .20
314 Pedro Guerrero .20
315 Walt Terrell .20
316 Sam Horn .20
317 *Wes Chamberlain* .20
318 *Pedro Munoz* .20
319 Roberto Kelly .20
320 Mark Portugal .20
321 Tim McIntosh .20
322 Jesse Orosco .20
323 Gary Green .20
324 Greg Harris .20
325 Hubie Brooks .20
326 Chris Nabholz .20
327 Terry Pendleton .20
328 Eric King .20
329 Chili Davis .20
330 Anthony Telford .20
331 Kelly Gruber .20
332 Dennis Eckersley .20
333 Mel Hall .20
334 Bob Kipper .20
335 Willie McGee .20
336 Steve Olin .20
337 Steve Buechele .20
338 Scott Leius .20
339 Hal Morris .20
340 Jose Offerman .20
341 Kent Mercker .20
342 Ken Griffey .20
343 Pete Harnisch .20
344 Kirk Gibson .20
345 Dave Smith .20
346 Dave Martinez .20
347 Atlee Hammaker .20
348 Brian Downing .20
349 Todd Hundley .20
350 Candy Maldonado .20
351 Dwight Evans .20
352 Steve Searcy .20
353 Gary Gaetti .20
354 Jeff Reardon .20
355 Travis Fryman .20
356 Dave Righetti .20
357 Fred McGriff .20
358 Don Slaught .20
359 Gene Nelson .20
360 Billy Spiers .20
361 Lee Guetterman .20
362 Darren Lewis .20
363 Duane Ward .20
364 Lloyd Moseby .20
365 John Smoltz .30
366 Felix Jose .20
367 David Cone .20
368 Wally Backman .20
369 Jeff Montgomery .20
370 Rich Garces .20
371 Billy Hatcher .20
372 Bill Swift .20
373 Jim Eisenreich .20
374 Rob Ducey .20
375 Tim Crews .20
376 Steve Finley .20
377 Jeff Blauser .20
378 Willie Wilson .20
379 Gerald Perry .20
380 Jose Mesa .20
381 Pat Kelly .20
382 Matt Merullo .20
383 Ivan Calderon .20
384 Scott Chiamparino .20
385 Lloyd McClendon .20
386 Dave Bergman .20
387 Ed Sprague .20
388 *Jeff Bagwell* 8.00
389 Brett Butler .20
390 Larry Andersen .20
391 Glenn Davis .20
392 Alex Cole (photo is Otis Nixon) .20
393 Mike Heath .20
394 Danny Darwin .20
395 Steve Lake .20
396 Tim Layana .20
397 Terry Leach .20
398 Bill Wegman .20
399 Mark McGwire 6.00
400 Mike Boddicker .20
401 Steve Howe .20
402 Bernard Gilkey .20
403 Thomas Howard .20
404 Rafael Belliard .20
405 Tom Candiotti .20
406 Rene Gonzalez .20
407 Chuck McElroy .20
408 Paul Sorrento .20
409 Randy Johnson 1.50
410 Brady Anderson .20
411 Dennis Cook .20
412 Mickey Tettleton .20
413 Mike Stanton .20
414 Ken Oberkfell .20
415 Rick Honeycutt .20
416 Nelson Santovenia .20
417 Bob Tewksbury .20
418 Brent Mayne .20
419 Steve Farr .20
420 Phil Stephenson .20
421 Jeff Russell .20
422 Chris James .20
423 Tim Leary .20
424 Gary Carter .50
425 Glenallen Hill .20
426 Matt Young .20
427 Sid Bream .20
428 Greg Swindell .20
429 Scott Aldred .20
430 Cal Ripken, Jr. 6.00
431 Bill Landrum .20
432 Ernie Riles .20
433 Danny Jackson .20
434 Casey Candaele .20
435 Ken Hill .20
436 Jaime Navarro .20
437 Lance Blankenship .20
438 Randy Velarde .20
439 Frank DiPino .20
440 Carl Nichols .20
441 Jeff Robinson .20
442 Deion Sanders .30
443 Vincente Palacios .20
444 Devon White .20
445 John Cerutti .20
446 Tracy Jones .20
447 Jack Morris .20
448 Mitch Webster .20
449 Bob Ojeda .20
450 Oscar Azocar .20
451 Luis Aquino .20
452 Mark Whiten .20
453 Stan Belinda .20
454 Ron Gant .20
455 Jose DeLeon .20
456 Mark Salas .20
457 Junior Felix .20
458 Wally Whitehurst .20
459 *Phil Plantier* .20
460 Juan Berenguer .20
461 Franklin Stubbs .20
462 Joe Boever .20
463 Tim Wallach .20
464 Mike Moore .20
465 Albert Belle 1.00
466 Mike Witt .20
467 Craig Worthington .20
468 Jerald Clark .20
469 Scott Terry .20
470 Milt Cuyler .20
471 John Smiley .20
472 Charles Nagy .20
473 Alan Mills .20
474 John Russell .20
475 Bruce Hurst .20
476 Andujar Cedeno .20
477 Dave Eiland .20
478 *Brian McRae* .50
479 Mike LaCoss .20
480 Chris Gwynn .20
481 Jamie Moyer .20
482 John Olerud .20
483 Efrain Valdez .20
484 Sil Campusano .20
485 Pascual Perez .20
486 Gary Redus .20
487 Andy Hawkins .20
488 Cory Snyder .20
489 Chris Hoiles .20
490 Ron Hassey .20
491 Gary Wayne .20
492 Mark Lewis .20
493 Scott Coolbaugh .20
494 Gerald Young .20
495 Juan Samuel .20
496 Willie Fraser .20
497 Jeff Treadway .20
498 Vince Coleman .20
499 Cris Carpenter .20
500 Jack Clark .20
501 Kevin Appier .20
502 Rafael Palmeiro .50
503 Hensley Meulens .20
504 George Bell .20
505 Tony Pena .20
506 Roger McDowell .20
507 Luis Sojo .20
508 Mike Schooler .20
509 Robin Yount 1.50
510 Jack Armstrong .20
511 Rick Cerone .20
512 Curt Wilkerson .20
513 Joe Carter .20
514 Tim Burke .20
515 Tony Fernandez .20
516 Ramon Martinez .20
517 Tim Hulett .20
518 Terry Steinbach .20
519 Pete Smith .20
520 Ken Caminiti .20
521 Shawn Boskie .20
522 Mike Pagliarulo .20
523 Tim Raines .20
524 Alfredo Griffin .20
525 Henry Cotto .20
526 Mike Stanley .20
527 Charlie Leibrandt .20
528 Jeff King .20
529 Eric Plunk .20
530 Tom Lampkin .20
531 Steve Bedrosian .20
532 Tom Herr .20
533 Craig Lefferts .20
534 Jeff Reed .20
535 Mickey Morandini .20
536 Greg Cadaret .20
537 Ray Lankford .20
538 John Candelaria .20
539 Rob Deer .20
540 Brad Arnsberg .20
541 Mike Sharperson .20
542 Jeff Robinson .20
543 Mo Vaughn 1.50
544 Jeff Parrett .20
545 Willie Randolph .20
546 Herm Winningham .20
547 Jeff Innis .20
548 Chuck Knoblauch .20
549 Tommy Greene .20

550	Jeff Hamilton	.20
551	Barry Jones	.20
552	Ken Dayley	.20
553	Rick Dempsey	.20
554	Greg Smith	.20
555	Mike Devereaux	.20
556	Keith Comstock	.20
557	Paul Faries	.20
558	Tom Glavine	.30
559	Craig Grebeck	.20
560	Scott Erickson	.20
561	Joel Skinner	.20
562	Mike Morgan	.20
563	Dave Gallagher	.20
564	Todd Stottlemyre	.20
565	Rich Rodriguez	.20
566	*Craig Wilson*	.20
567	Jeff Brantley	.20
568	Scott Kamieniecki	.20
569	Steve Decker	.20
570	Juan Agosto	.20
571	Tommy Gregg	.20
572	Kevin Wickander	.20
573	Jamie Quirk	.20
574	Jerry Don Gleaton	.20
575	Chris Hammond	.20
576	*Luis Gonzalez*	8.00
577	Russ Swan	.20
578	*Jeff Conine*	2.00
579	Charlie Hough	.20
580	Jeff Kunkel	.20
581	Darrel Akerfelds	.20
582	Jeff Manto	.20
583	Alejandro Pena	.20
584	Mark Davidson	.20
585	Bob MacDonald	.20
586	Paul Assenmacher	.20
587	Dan Wilson	.20
588	Tom Bolton	.20
589	Brian Harper	.20
590	John Habyan	.20
591	John Orton	.20
592	Mark Gardner	.20
593	Turner Ward	.20
594	Bob Patterson	.20
595	Edwin Nunez	.20
596	Gary Scott	.20
597	Scott Bankhead	.20
598	Checklist	.20
599	Checklist	.20
600	Checklist	.20

1992 Stadium Club

This 900-card set was released in three 100-card series. Like the 1991 issue, the cards feature borderless high-gloss photos on the front. The flip sides feature the player's first Topps card and a player evaluation. Topps released updated cards in the third series for traded player and free agents. Several players appear on two cards. Special Members Choice cards are included in the set. Series III features special inserts of the last three number one draft picks: Phil Nevin, Brien Taylor and Chipper Jones.

	MT
Complete Set (900):	35.00
Common Player:	.10
Series 1, 2, 3 Pack (15):	.50
Series 1, 2, 3 Wax Box (36):	12.00

1	Cal Ripken, Jr.	1.50
2	Eric Yelding	.10
3	Geno Petralli	.10
4	Wally Backman	.10
5	Milt Cuyler	.10
6	Kevin Bass	.10
7	Dante Bichette	.10
8	Ray Lankford	.10
9	Mel Hall	.10
10	Joe Carter	.10
11	Juan Samuel	.10
12	Jeff Montgomery	.10
13	Glenn Braggs	.10
14	Henry Cotto	.10
15	Deion Sanders	.15
16	Dick Schofield	.10
17	David Cone	.10
18	Chili Davis	.10
19	Tom Foley	.10
20	Ozzie Guillen	.10
21	Luis Salazar	.10
22	Terry Steinbach	.10
23	Chris James	.10
24	Jeff King	.10
25	Carlos Quintana	.10
26	Mike Maddux	.10
27	Tommy Greene	.10
28	Jeff Russell	.10
29	Steve Finley	.10
30	Mike Flanagan	.10
31	Darren Lewis	.10
32	Mark Lee	.10
33	Willie Fraser	.10
34	Mike Henneman	.10
35	Kevin Maas	.10
36	Dave Hansen	.10
37	Erik Hanson	.10
38	Bill Doran	.10
39	Mike Boddicker	.10
40	Vince Coleman	.10
41	Devon White	.10
42	Mark Gardner	.10
43	Scott Lewis	.10
44	Juan Berenguer	.10
45	Carney Lansford	.10
46	Curt Wilkerson	.10
47	Shane Mack	.10
48	Bip Roberts	.10
49	Greg Harris	.10
50	Ryne Sandberg	.60
51	Mark Whiten	.10
52	Jack McDowell	.10
53	Jimmy Jones	.10
54	Steve Lake	.10
55	Bud Black	.10
56	Dave Valle	.10
57	Kevin Reimer	.10
58	Rich Gedman	.10
59	Travis Fryman	.10
60	Steve Avery	.10
61	Francisco de la Rosa	.10
62	Scott Hemond	.10
63	Hal Morris	.10
64	Hensley Meulens	.10
65	Frank Castillo	.10
66	Gene Larkin	.10
67	Jose DeLeon	.10
68	Al Osuna	.10
69	Dave Cochrane	.10
70	Robin Ventura	.10
71	John Cerutti	.10
72	Kevin Gross	.10
73	Ivan Calderon	.10
74	Mike Macfarlane	.10
75	Stan Belinda	.10
76	Shawn Hillegas	.10
77	Pat Borders	.10
78	Jim Vatcher	.10
79	Bobby Rose	.10
80	Roger Clemens	.75
81	Craig Worthington	.10
82	Jeff Treadway	.10
83	Jamie Quirk	.10
84	Randy Bush	.10
85	Anthony Young	.10
86	Trevor Wilson	.10
87	Jaime Navarro	.10
88	Les Lancaster	.10
89	Pat Kelly	.10
90	Alvin Davis	.10
91	Larry Andersen	.10
92	Rob Deer	.10
93	Mike Sharperson	.10
94	Lance Parrish	.10
95	Cecil Espy	.10
96	Tim Spehr	.10
97	Dave Stieb	.10
98	Terry Mulholland	.10
99	Dennis Boyd	.10
100	Barry Larkin	.15
101	Ryan Bowen	.10
102	Felix Fermin	.10
103	Luis Alicea	.10
104	Tim Hulett	.10
105	Rafael Belliard	.10
106	Mike Gallego	.10
107	Dave Righetti	.10
108	Jeff Schaefer	.10
109	Ricky Bones	.10
110	Scott Erickson	.10
111	Matt Nokes	.10
112	Bob Scanlan	.10
113	Tom Candiotti	.10
114	Sean Berry	.10
115	Kevin Morton	.10
116	Scott Fletcher	.10
117	B.J. Surhoff	.10
118	Dave Magadan	.10
119	Bill Gullickson	.10
120	Marquis Grissom	.10
121	Lenny Harris	.10
122	Wally Joyner	.10
123	Kevin Brown	.20
124	Braulio Castillo	.10
125	Eric King	.10
126	Mark Portugal	.10
127	Calvin Jones	.10
128	Mike Heath	.10
129	Todd Van Poppel	.10
130	Benny Santiago	.10
131	Gary Thurman	.10
132	Joe Girardi	.10
133	Dave Eiland	.10
134	Orlando Merced	.10
135	Joe Orsulak	.10
136	John Burkett	.10
137	Ken Dayley	.10
138	Ken Hill	.10
139	Walt Terrell	.10
140	Mike Scioscia	.10
141	Junior Felix	.10
142	Ken Caminiti	.10
143	Carlos Baerga	.10
144	Tony Fossas	.10
145	Craig Grebeck	.10
146	Scott Bradley	.10
147	Kent Mercker	.10
148	Derrick May	.10
149	Jerald Clark	.10
150	George Brett	.75
151	Luis Quinones	.10
152	Mike Pagliarulo	.10
153	Jose Guzman	.10
154	Charlie O'Brien	.10
155	Darren Holmes	.10
156	Joe Boever	.10
157	Rich Monteleone	.10
158	Reggie Harris	.10
159	Roberto Alomar	.50
160	Robby Thompson	.10
161	Chris Hoiles	.10
162	Tom Pagnozzi	.10
163	Omar Vizquel	.10
164	John Candelaria	.10
165	Terry Shumpert	.10
166	Andy Mota	.10
167	Scott Bailes	.10
168	Jeff Blauser	.10
169	Steve Olin	.10
170	Doug Drabek	.10
171	Dave Bergman	.10
172	Eddie Whitson	.10
173	Gilberto Reyes	.10
174	Mark Grace	.25
175	Paul O'Neill	.10
176	Greg Cadaret	.10
177	Mark Williamson	.10
178	Casey Candaele	.10
179	Candy Maldonado	.10
180	Lee Smith	.10
181	Harold Reynolds	.10
182	Dave Justice	.25
183	Lenny Webster	.10
184	Donn Pall	.10
185	Gerald Alexander	.10
186	Jack Clark	.10
187	Stan Javier	.10
188	Ricky Jordan	.10
189	Franklin Stubbs	.10
190	Dennis Eckersley	.10
191	Danny Tartabull	.10
192	Pete O'Brien	.10
193	Mark Lewis	.10
194	Mike Felder	.10
195	Mickey Tettleton	.10
196	Dwight Smith	.10
197	Shawn Abner	.10
198	Jim Leyritz	.10
199	Mike Devereaux	.10
200	Craig Biggio	.15
201	Kevin Elster	.10
202	Rance Mulliniks	.10
203	Tony Fernandez	.10
204	Allan Anderson	.10
205	Herm Winningham	.10
206	Tim Jones	.10
207	Ramon Martinez	.10
208	Teddy Higuera	.10
209	John Kruk	.10
210	Jim Abbott	.10
211	Dean Palmer	.10
212	Mark Davis	.10
213	Jay Buhner	.10
214	Jesse Barfield	.10
215	Kevin Mitchell	.10
216	Mike LaValliere	.10
217	Mark Wohlers	.10
218	Dave Henderson	.10
219	Dave Smith	.10
220	Albert Belle	.30
221	Spike Owen	.10
222	Jeff Gray	.10
223	Paul Gibson	.10
224	Bobby Thigpen	.10
225	Mike Mussina	.50
226	Darrin Jackson	.10
227	Luis Gonzalez	.25
228	Greg Briley	.10
229	Brent Mayne	.10
230	Paul Molitor	.50
231	Al Leiter	.10
232	Andy Van Slyke	.10
233	Ron Tingley	.10
234	Bernard Gilkey	.10
235	Kent Hrbek	.10
236	Eric Karros	.10
237	Randy Velarde	.10
238	Andy Allanson	.10
239	Willie McGee	.10
240	Juan Gonzalez	.60
241	Karl Rhodes	.10
242	Luis Mercedes	.10
243	Billy Swift	.10
244	Tommy Gregg	.10
245	David Howard	.10
246	Dave Hollins	.10
247	Kip Gross	.10
248	Walt Weiss	.10
249	Mackey Sasser	.10
250	Cecil Fielder	.10
251	Jerry Browne	.10
252	Doug Dascenzo	.10
253	Darryl Hamilton	.10
254	Dann Bilardello	.10
255	Luis Rivera	.10
256	Larry Walker	.25
257	Ron Karkovice	.10
258	Bob Tewksbury	.10
259	Jimmy Key	.10
260	Bernie Williams	.30
261	Gary Wayne	.10
262	Mike Simms	.10
263	John Orton	.10
264	Marvin Freeman	.10
265	Mike Jeffcoat	.10
266	Roger Mason	.10
267	Edgar Martinez	.10
268	Henry Rodriguez	.10
269	Sam Horn	.10
270	Brian McRae	.10
271	Kirt Manwaring	.10
272	Mike Bordick	.10
273	Chris Sabo	.10
274	Jim Olander	.10
275	Greg Harris	.10
276	Dan Gakeler	.10
277	Bill Sampen	.10
278	Joel Skinner	.10

No.	Player	Value
279	Curt Schilling	.20
280	Dale Murphy	.25
281	Lee Stevens	.10
282	Lonnie Smith	.10
283	Manuel Lee	.10
284	Shawn Boskie	.10
285	Kevin Seitzer	.10
286	Stan Royer	.10
287	John Dopson	.10
288	Scott Bullett	.10
289	Ken Patterson	.10
290	Todd Hundley	.10
291	Tim Leary	.10
292	Brett Butler	.10
293	Gregg Olson	.10
294	Jeff Brantley	.10
295	Brian Holman	.10
296	Brian Harper	.10
297	Brian Bohanon	.10
298	Checklist 1-100	.10
299	Checklist 101-200	.10
300	Checklist 201-300	.10
301	Frank Thomas	1.00
302	Lloyd McClendon	.10
303	Brady Anderson	.10
304	Julio Valera	.10
305	Mike Aldrete	.10
306	Joe Oliver	.10
307	Todd Stottlemyre	.10
308	Rey Sanchez	.10
309	Gary Sheffield	.35
310	Andujar Cedeno	.10
311	Kenny Rogers	.10
312	Bruce Hurst	.10
313	Mike Schooler	.10
314	Mike Benjamin	.10
315	Chuck Finley	.10
316	Mark Lemke	.10
317	Scott Livingstone	.10
318	Chris Nabholz	.10
319	Mike Humphreys	.10
320	Pedro Guerrero	.10
321	Willie Banks	.10
322	Tom Goodwin	.10
323	Hector Wagner	.10
324	Wally Ritchie	.10
325	Mo Vaughn	.50
326	Joe Klink	.10
327	Cal Eldred	.10
328	Daryl Boston	.10
329	Mike Huff	.10
330	Jeff Bagwell	1.00
331	Bob Milacki	.10
332	Tom Prince	.10
333	Pat Tabler	.10
334	Ced Landrum	.10
335	Reggie Jefferson	.10
336	Mo Sanford	.10
337	Kevin Ritz	.10
338	Gerald Perry	.10
339	Jeff Hamilton	.10
340	Tim Wallach	.10
341	Jeff Huson	.10
342	Jose Melendez	.10
343	Willie Wilson	.10
344	Mike Stanton	.10
345	Joel Johnston	.10
346	Lee Guetterman	.10
347	Francisco Olivares	.10
348	Dave Burba	.10
349	Tim Crews	.10
350	Scott Leius	.10
351	Danny Cox	.10
352	Wayne Housie	.10
353	Chris Donnels	.10
354	Chris George	.10
355	Gerald Young	.10
356	Roberto Hernandez	.10
357	Neal Heaton	.10
358	Todd Frohwirth	.10
359	Jose Vizcaino	.10
360	Jim Thome	.10
361	Craig Wilson	.10
362	Dave Haas	.10
363	Billy Hatcher	.10
364	John Barfield	.10
365	Luis Aquino	.10
366	Charlie Leibrandt	.10
367	Howard Farmer	.10
368	Bryn Smith	.10
369	Mickey Morandini	.10
370	Jose Canseco Members Choice, should have been #597)	.25
371	Jose Uribe	.10
372	Bob MacDonald	.10
373	Luis Sojo	.10
374	Craig Shipley	.10
375	Scott Bankhead	.10
376	Greg Gagne	.10
377	Scott Cooper	.10
378	Jose Offerman	.10
379	Billy Spiers	.10
380	John Smiley	.10
381	Jeff Carter	.10
382	Heathcliff Slocumb	.10
383	Jeff Tackett	.10
384	John Kiely	.10
385	John Vander Wal	.10
386	Omar Olivares	.10
387	Ruben Sierra	.10
388	Tom Gordon	.10
389	Charles Nagy	.10
390	Dave Stewart	.10
391	Pete Harnisch	.10
392	Tim Burke	.10
393	Roberto Kelly	.10
394	Freddie Benavides	.10
395	Tom Glavine	.15
396	Wes Chamberlain	.10
397	Eric Gunderson	.10
398	Dave West	.10
399	Ellis Burks	.10
400	Ken Griffey, Jr.	1.25
401	Thomas Howard	.10
402	Juan Guzman	.10
403	Mitch Webster	.10
404	Matt Merullo	.10
405	Steve Buechele	.10
406	Danny Jackson	.10
407	Felix Jose	.10
408	Doug Piatt	.10
409	Jim Eisenreich	.10
410	Bryan Harvey	.10
411	Jim Austin	.10
412	Jim Poole	.10
413	Glenallen Hill	.10
414	Gene Nelson	.10
415	Ivan Rodriguez	.60
416	Frank Tanana	.10
417	Steve Decker	.10
418	Jason Grimsley	.10
419	Tim Layana	.10
420	Don Mattingly	1.00
421	Jerome Walton	.10
422	Rob Ducey	.10
423	Andy Benes	.10
424	John Marzano	.10
425	Gene Harris	.10
426	Tim Raines	.10
427	Bret Barberie	.10
428	Harvey Pulliam	.10
429	Cris Carpenter	.10
430	Howard Johnson	.10
431	Orel Hershiser	.10
432	Brian Hunter	.10
433	Kevin Tapani	.10
434	Rick Reed	.10
435	Ron Witmeyer	.10
436	Gary Gaetti	.10
437	Alex Cole	.10
438	Chito Martinez	.10
439	Greg Litton	.10
440	Julio Franco	.10
441	Mike Munoz	.10
442	Erik Pappas	.10
443	Pat Combs	.10
444	Lance Johnson	.10
445	Ed Sprague	.10
446	Mike Greenwell	.10
447	Milt Thompson	.10
448	Mike Magnante	.10
449	Chris Haney	.10
450	Robin Yount	.50
451	Rafael Ramirez	.10
452	Gino Minutelli	.10
453	Tom Lampkin	.10
454	Tony Perezchica	.10
455	Dwight Gooden	.10
456	Mark Guthrie	.10
457	Jay Howell	.10
458	Gary DiSarcina	.10
459	John Smoltz	.15
460	Will Clark	.15
461	Dave Otto	.10
462	Rob Maurer	.10
463	Dwight Evans	.10
464	Tom Brunansky	.10
465	*Shawn Hare*	.10
466	Geronimo Pena	.10
467	Alex Fernandez	.10
468	Greg Myers	.10
469	Jeff Fassero	.10
470	Len Dykstra	.10
471	Jeff Johnson	.10
472	Russ Swan	.10
473	Archie Corbin	.10
474	Chuck McElroy	.10
475	Mark McGwire	1.50
476	Wally Whitehurst	.10
477	Tim McIntosh	.10
478	Sid Bream	.10
479	Jeff Juden	.10
480	Carlton Fisk	.50
481	Jeff Plympton	.10
482	Carlos Martinez	.10
483	Jim Gott	.10
484	Bob McClure	.10
485	Tim Teufel	.10
486	Vicente Palacios	.10
487	Jeff Reed	.10
488	Tony Phillips	.10
489	Mel Rojas	.10
490	Ben McDonald	.10
491	Andres Santana	.10
492	Chris Beasley	.10
493	Mike Timlin	.10
494	Brian Downing	.10
495	Kirk Gibson	.10
496	Scott Sanderson	.10
497	Nick Esasky	.10
498	*Johnny Guzman*	.10
499	Mitch Williams	.10
500	Kirby Puckett	.75
501	Mike Harkey	.10
502	Jim Gantner	.10
503	Bruce Egloff	.10
504	Josias Manzanillo	.10
505	Delino DeShields	.10
506	Rheal Cormier	.10
507	Jay Bell	.10
508	Rich Rowland	.10
509	Scott Servais	.10
510	Terry Pendleton	.10
511	Rich DeLucia	.10
512	Warren Newson	.10
513	Paul Faries	.10
514	Kal Daniels	.10
515	Jarvis Brown	.10
516	Rafael Palmeiro	.25
517	Kelly Downs	.10
518	Steve Chitren	.10
519	Moises Alou	.20
520	Wade Boggs	.65
521	Pete Schourek	.10
522	Scott Terry	.10
523	Kevin Appier	.10
524	Gary Redus	.10
525	George Bell	.10
526	Jeff Kaiser	.10
527	Alvaro Espinoza	.10
528	Luis Polonia	.10
529	Darren Daulton	.10
530	Norm Charlton	.10
531	John Olerud	.10
532	Dan Plesac	.10
533	Billy Ripken	.10
534	Rod Nichols	.10
535	Joey Cora	.10
536	Harold Baines	.10
537	Bob Ojeda	.10
538	Mark Leonard	.10
539	Danny Darwin	.10
540	Shawon Dunston	.10
541	Pedro Munoz	.10
542	Mark Gubicza	.10
543	Kevin Baez	.10
544	Todd Zeile	.10
545	Don Slaught	.10
546	Tony Eusebio	.10
547	Alonzo Powell	.10
548	Gary Pettis	.10
549	Brian Barnes	.10
550	Lou Whitaker	.10
551	Keith Mitchell	.10
552	Oscar Azocar	.10
553	Stu Cole	.10
554	Steve Wapnick	.10
555	Derek Bell	.10
556	Luis Lopez	.10
557	Anthony Telford	.10
558	Tim Mauser	.10
559	Glenn Sutko	.10
560	Darryl Strawberry	.10
561	Tom Bolton	.10
562	Cliff Young	.10
563	Bruce Walton	.10
564	Chico Walker	.10
565	John Franco	.10
566	Paul McClellan	.10
567	Paul Abbott	.10
568	Gary Varsho	.10
569	Carlos Maldonado	.10
570	Kelly Gruber	.10
571	Jose Oquendo	.10
572	Steve Frey	.10
573	Tino Martinez	.10
574	Bill Haselman	.10
575	Eric Anthony	.10
576	John Habyan	.10
577	Jeffrey McNeely	.10
578	Chris Bosio	.10
579	Joe Grahe	.10
580	Fred McGriff	.10
581	Rick Honeycutt	.10
582	Matt Williams	.15
583	Cliff Brantley	.10
584	Rob Dibble	.10
585	Skeeter Barnes	.10
586	Greg Hibbard	.10
587	Randy Milligan	.10
588	Checklist 301-400	.10
589	Checklist 401-500	.10
590	Checklist 501-600	.10
591	Frank Thomas (Members Choice)	.50
592	Dave Justice (Members Choice)	.15
593	Roger Clemens (Members Choice)	.40
594	Steve Avery (Members Choice)	.10
595	Cal Ripken, Jr. (Members Choice)	.75
596	Barry Larkin (Members Choice)	.15
597	Not issued (See #370)	
598	Will Clark (Members Choice)	.10
599	Cecil Fielder (Members Choice)	.10
600	Ryne Sandberg (Members Choice)	.35
601	Chuck Knoblauch (Members Choice)	.10
602	Dwight Gooden (Members Choice)	.10
603	Ken Griffey, Jr. (Members Choice)	.65
604	Barry Bonds (Members Choice)	.50
605	Nolan Ryan (Members Choice)	.75
606	Jeff Bagwell (Members Choice)	.50
607	Robin Yount (Members Choice)	.25
608	Bobby Bonilla (Members Choice)	.10
609	George Brett (Members Choice)	.40
610	Howard Johnson (Members Choice)	.10
611	Esteban Beltre	.10
612	Mike Christopher	.10
613	Troy Afenir	.10
614	Mariano Duncan	.10
615	Doug Henry	.10
616	Doug Jones	.10
617	Alvin Davis	.10
618	Craig Lefferts	.10
619	Kevin McReynolds	.10
620	Barry Bonds	1.00
621	Turner Ward	.10
622	Joe Magrane	.10
623	Mark Parent	.10
624	Tom Browning	.10
625	John Smiley	.10
626	Steve Wilson	.10
627	Mike Gallego	.10
628	Sammy Sosa	1.00
629	Rico Rossy	.10
630	Royce Clayton	.10
631	Clay Parker	.10
632	Pete Smith	.10
633	Jeff McKnight	.10
634	Jack Daugherty	.10
635	Steve Sax	.10
636	Joe Hesketh	.10
637	Vince Horsman	.10
638	Eric King	.10
639	Joe Boever	.10
640	Jack Morris	.10
641	Arthur Rhodes	.10

642	Bob Melvin	.10
643	Rick Wilkins	.10
644	Scott Scudder	.10
645	Bip Roberts	.10
646	Julio Valera	.10
647	Kevin Campbell	.10
648	Steve Searcy	.10
649	Scott Kamieniecki	.10
650	Kurt Stillwell	.10
651	Bob Welch	.10
652	Andres Galarraga	.10
653	Mike Jackson	.10
654	Bo Jackson	.15
655	Sid Fernandez	.10
656	Mike Bielecki	.10
657	Jeff Reardon	.10
658	Wayne Rosenthal	.10
659	Eric Bullock	.10
660	Eric Davis	.10
661	Randy Tomlin	.10
662	Tom Edens	.10
663	Rob Murphy	.10
664	Leo Gomez	.10
665	Greg Maddux	.75
666	Greg Vaughn	.10
667	Wade Taylor	.10
668	Brad Arnsberg	.10
669	Mike Moore	.10
670	Mark Langston	.10
671	Barry Jones	.10
672	Bill Landrum	.10
673	Greg Swindell	.10
674	Wayne Edwards	.10
675	Greg Olson	.10
676	*Bill Pulsipher*	.25
677	Bobby Witt	.10
678	Mark Carreon	.10
679	Patrick Lennon	.10
680	Ozzie Smith	.75
681	John Briscoe	.10
682	Matt Young	.10
683	Jeff Conine	.10
684	Phil Stephenson	.10
685	Ron Darling	.10
686	Bryan Hickerson	.10
687	Dale Sveum	.10
688	Kirk McCaskill	.10
689	Rich Amaral	.10
690	Danny Tartabull	.10
691	Donald Harris	.10
692	Doug Davis	.10
693	John Farrell	.10
694	Paul Gibson	.10
695	Kenny Lofton	.10
696	Mike Fetters	.10
697	Rosario Rodriguez	.10
698	Chris Jones	.10
699	Jeff Manto	.10
700	Rick Sutcliffe	.10
701	Scott Bankhead	.10
702	Donnie Hill	.10
703	Todd Worrell	.10
704	Rene Gonzales	.10
705	Rick Cerone	.10
706	Tony Pena	.10
707	Paul Sorrento	.10
708	Gary Scott	.10
709	Junior Noboa	.10
710	Wally Joyner	.10
711	Charlie Hayes	.10
712	Rich Rodriguez	.10
713	Rudy Seanez	.10
714	Jim Bullinger	.10
715	Jeff Robinson	.10
716	Jeff Branson	.10
717	Andy Ashby	.10
718	Dave Burba	.10
719	Rich Gossage	.10
720	Randy Johnson	.60
721	David Wells	.10
722	Paul Kilgus	.10
723	Dave Martinez	.10
724	Denny Neagle	.10
725	Andy Stankiewicz	.10
726	Rick Aguilera	.10
727	Junior Ortiz	.10
728	Storm Davis	.10
729	Don Robinson	.10
730	Ron Gant	.10
731	Paul Assenmacher	.10
732	Mark Gardiner	.10
733	Milt Hill	.10
734	Jeremy Hernandez	.10
735	Ken Hill	.10
736	Xavier Hernandez	.10
737	Gregg Jefferies	.10
738	Dick Schofield	.10
739	Ron Robinson	.10
740	Sandy Alomar	.10
741	Mike Stanley	.10
742	Butch Henry	.10
743	Floyd Bannister	.10
744	Brian Drahman	.10
745	Dave Winfield	.75
746	Bob Walk	.10
747	Chris James	.10
748	Don Prybylinski	.10
749	Dennis Rasmussen	.10
750	Rickey Henderson	.60
751	Chris Hammond	.10
752	Bob Kipper	.10
753	Dave Rohde	.10
754	Hubie Brooks	.10
755	Bret Saberhagen	.10
756	Jeff Robinson	.10
757	*Pat Listach*	.10
758	Bill Wegman	.10
759	John Wetteland	.10
760	Phil Plantier	.10
761	Wilson Alvarez	.10
762	Scott Aldred	.10
763	*Armando Reynoso*	.15
764	Todd Benzinger	.10
765	Kevin Mitchell	.10
766	Gary Sheffield	.35
767	Allan Anderson	.10
768	Rusty Meacham	.10
769	Rick Parker	.10
770	Nolan Ryan	1.50
771	Jeff Ballard	.10
772	Cory Snyder	.10
773	Denis Boucher	.10
774	Jose Gonzales	.10
775	Juan Guerrero	.10
776	Ed Nunez	.10
777	Scott Ruskin	.10
778	Terry Leach	.10
779	Carl Willis	.10
780	Bobby Bonilla	.10
781	Duane Ward	.10
782	Joe Slusarski	.10
783	David Segui	.10
784	Kirk Gibson	.10
785	Frank Viola	.10
786	Keith Miller	.10
787	Mike Morgan	.10
788	Kim Batiste	.10
789	Sergio Valdez	.10
790	Eddie Taubensee	.10
791	Jack Armstrong	.10
792	Scott Fletcher	.10
793	Steve Farr	.10
794	Dan Pasqua	.10
795	Eddie Murray	.50
796	John Morris	.10
797	Francisco Cabrera	.10
798	Mike Perez	.10
799	Ted Wood	.10
800	Jose Rijo	.10
801	Danny Gladden	.10
802	Arci Cianfrocco	.10
803	Monty Fariss	.10
804	Roger McDowell	.10
805	Randy Myers	.10
806	Kirk Dressendorfer	.10
807	Zane Smith	.10
808	Glenn Davis	.10
809	Torey Lovullo	.10
810	Andre Dawson	.20
811	Bill Pecota	.10
812	Ted Power	.10
813	Willie Blair	.10
814	Dave Fleming	.10
815	Chris Gwynn	.10
816	Jody Reed	.10
817	Mark Dewey	.10
818	Kyle Abbott	.10
819	Tom Henke	.10
820	Kevin Seitzer	.10
821	Al Newman	.10
822	Tim Sherrill	.10
823	Chuck Crim	.10
824	Darren Reed	.10
825	Tony Gwynn	.75
826	Steve Foster	.10
827	Steve Howe	.10
828	Brook Jacoby	.10
829	Rodney McCray	.10
830	Chuck Knoblauch	.10
831	John Wehner	.10
832	Scott Garrelts	.10
833	Alejandro Pena	.10
834	Jeff Parrett	.10
835	Juan Bell	.10
836	Lance Dickson	.10
837	Darryl Kile	.10
838	Efrain Valdez	.10
839	*Bob Zupcic*	.10
840	George Bell	.10
841	Dave Gallagher	.10
842	Tim Belcher	.10
843	Jeff Shaw	.10
844	Mike Fitzgerald	.10
845	Gary Carter	.25
846	John Russell	.10
847	*Eric Hillman*	.10
848	Mike Witt	.10
849	Curt Wilkerson	.10
850	Alan Trammell	.10
851	Rex Hudler	.10
852	*Michael Walkden*	.10
853	Kevin Ward	.10
854	Tim Naehring	.10
855	Bill Swift	.10
856	Damon Berryhill	.10
857	Mark Eichhorn	.10
858	Hector Villanueva	.10
859	Jose Lind	.10
860	Denny Martinez	.10
861	Bill Krueger	.10
862	Mike Kingery	.10
863	Jeff Innis	.10
864	Derek Lilliquist	.10
865	Reggie Sanders	.10
866	Ramon Garcia	.10
867	Bruce Ruffin	.10
868	Dickie Thon	.10
869	Melido Perez	.10
870	Ruben Amaro	.10
871	Alan Mills	.10
872	Matt Sinatro	.10
873	Eddie Zosky	.10
874	Pete Incaviglia	.10
875	Tom Candiotti	.10
876	Bob Patterson	.10
877	Neal Heaton	.10
878	*Terrel Hansen*	.10
879	Dave Eiland	.10
880	Von Hayes	.10
881	Tim Scott	.10
882	Otis Nixon	.10
883	Herm Winningham	.10
884	Dion James	.10
885	Dave Wainhouse	.10
886	Frank DiPino	.10
887	Dennis Cook	.10
888	Jose Mesa	.10
889	Mark Leiter	.10
890	Willie Randolph	.10
891	Craig Colbert	.10
892	Dwayne Henry	.10
893	Jim Lindeman	.10
894	Charlie Hough	.10
895	Gil Heredia	.10
896	Scott Chiamparino	.10
897	Lance Blankenship	.10
898	Checklist 601-700	.10
899	Checklist 701-800	.10
900	Checklist 801-900	.10

1992 Stadium Club Master Photos

Uncropped versions of the photos which appear on regular Stadium Club cards are featured on these large-format (5" x 7") cards. The photos are set against a white background and trimmed with holographic foil. Backs are blank and the cards are unnumbered. Members of Topps' Stadium Club received a Master Photo in their members' packs for 1992. The cards were also available as inserts in special boxes of Stadium Club cards sold at Wal-Mart stores.

		MT
Complete Set (15):		18.00
Common Player:		.50
(1)	Wade Boggs	1.50
(2)	Barry Bonds	2.50
(3)	Jose Canseco	1.50
(4)	Will Clark	.50
(5)	Cecil Fielder	.50
(6)	Dwight Gooden	.50
(7)	Ken Griffey, Jr.	3.00
(8)	Rickey Henderson	1.00
(9)	Lance Johnson	.50
(10)	Cal Ripken, Jr.	4.00
(11)	Nolan Ryan	4.00
(12)	Deion Sanders	.75
(13)	Darryl Strawberry	.50
(14)	Danny Tartabull	.50
(15)	Frank Thomas	2.50

1992 Stadium Club First Draft Picks

Issued as inserts with Stadium Club Series III, this three-card set features the No. 1 draft picks of 1990-92. Fronts have a full-bleed photo with S.C. logo and player name in the lower-right corner. At bottom-lerft in a red strip is a gold-foil stamping, "#1 Draft Pick of the '90's". An orage circle at upper-right has the year the player was the No. 1 choice. The basic red-and-black back has a color photo, a few biographical and draft details and a gold facsimile autograph among other gold-foil highlights.

		MT
Complete Set (3):		8.00
Common Player:		1.00
1	Chipper Jones	7.50
2	Brien Taylor	.50
3	Phil Nevin	.50

1992 Stadium Club Special Edition (SkyDome)

This 200-card special Stadium Club set from Topps was uniquely packaged in a plastic replica of the Toronto SkyDome, the home of the 1991 All-Star Game. Featured in the set are members of Team USA, All-Stars, draft picks, top prospects and hight cards from the World Series between the Twins and Braves. The cards are styled much like the regular Stadium Club cards. Some cards have been found with incorrect gold-foil identifiers as well as the correct version.

		MT
Complete Set (200):		25.00
Common Player:		.10
1	*Terry Adams*	.10
2	Tommy Adams	.10
3	Rick Aguilera	.10
4	Ron Allen	.10
5	Roberto Alomar (All-Star)	.50
6	Sandy Alomar	.10
7	Greg Anthony	.10
8	James Austin	.10
9	Steve Avery	.10
10	Harold Baines	.10
11	*Brian Barber*	.10
12	Jon Barnes	.10
13	George Bell	.10
14	Doug Bennett	.10
15	Sean Bergman	.10
16	Craig Biggio	.15
17	Bill Bliss	.10
18	Wade Boggs (AS)	.50
19	Bobby Bonilla (AS)	.10
20	Russell Brock	.10
21	Tarrik Brock	.10
22	Tom Browning	.10
23	Brett Butler	.10
24	Ivan Calderon	.10
25	Joe Carter	.10
26	Joe Caruso	.10
27	Dan Cholowsky	.10
28	Will Clark (AS)	.15
29	Roger Clemens (AS)	.75
30	Shawn Curran	.10
31	Chris Curtis	.10
32	Chili Davis	.10
33	Andre Dawson	.20
34	Joe DeBerry	.10
35	John Dettmer	.10
36	Rob Dibble	.10
37	*John Donati*	.10
38	Dave Doorneweerd	.10
39	Darren Dreifort	.10
40	Mike Durant	.10
41	Chris Durkin	.10
42	Dennis Eckersley	.10
43	*Brian Edmondson*	.10
44	*Vaughn Eshelman*	.10
45	*Shawn Estes*	.75
46	*Jorge Fabregas*	.15
47	Jon Farrell	.10
48	Cecil Fielder (AS)	.10
49	Carlton Fisk	.50
50	Tim Flannelly	.10
51	*Cliff Floyd*	4.00
52	Julio Franco	.10
53	Greg Gagne	.10
54	*Chris Gambs*	.10
55	Ron Gant	.10
56	Brent Gates	.10
57	Dwayne Gerald	.10
58	Jason Giambi	5.00
59	*Benji Gil*	.20
60	Mark Gipner	.10
61	Danny Gladden	.10
62	Tom Glavine	.15
63	Jimmy Gonzalez	.10
64	Jeff Granger	.10
65	Dan Grapenthien	.10
66	Dennis Gray	.10
67	*Shawn Green*	6.00
68	Tyler Green	.10
69	Todd Greene	.25
70	Ken Griffey, Jr. (AS)	1.00
71	Kelly Gruber	.10
72	Ozzie Guillen	.10
73	Tony Gwynn (AS)	.75
74	Shane Halter	.10
75	Jeffrey Hammonds	.10
76	Larry Hanlon	.10
77	Pete Harnisch	.10
78	Mike Harrison	.10
79	Bryan Harvey	.10
80	Scott Hatteberg	.10
81	Rick Helling	.10
82	Dave Henderson	.10
83	Rickey Henderson (AS)	.50
84	Tyrone Hill	.10
85	*Todd Hollandsworth*	.50
86	Brian Holliday	.10
87	Terry Horn	.10
88	Jeff Hostetler	.10
89	Kent Hrbek	.10
90	Mark Hubbard	.10
91	Charles Johnson	.15
92	Howard Johnson	.10
93	Todd Johnson	.10
94	*Bobby Jones*	.75
95	Dan Jones	.10
96	Felix Jose	.10
97	Dave Justice	.30
98	Jimmy Key	.10
99	*Marc Kroom*	.10
100	John Kruk	.10
101	Mark Langston	.10
102	Barry Larkin	.15
103	Mike LaValliere	.10
104a	Scott Leius (1991 N.L. All-Star - error)	.10
104b	Scott Leius (1991 World Series - correct)	.10
105	Mark Lemke	.10
106	Donnie Leshnock	.10
107	Jimmy Lewis	.10
108	Shawn Livesy	.10
109	Ryan Long	.10
110	Trevor Mallory	.10
111	Denny Martinez	.10
112	Justin Mashore	.10
113	Jason McDonald	.10
114	Jack McDowell	.10
115	Tom McKinnon	.10
116	Billy McKinnon	.10
117	*Buck McNabb*	.10
118	Jim Mecir	.10
119	Dan Melendez	.10
120	*Shawn Miller*	.10
121	Trever Miller	.10
122	Paul Molitor	.45
123	Vincent Moore	.10
124	Mike Morgan	.10
125	Jack Morris (World Series)	.10
126	Jack Morris (All-Star)	.10
127	Sean Mulligan	.10
128	Eddie Murray	.50
129	Mike Neill	.10
130	Phil Nevin	.50
131	Mark O'Brien	.10
132	*Alex Ochoa*	.25
133	*Chad Ogea*	.20
134	Greg Olson	.10
135	Paul O'Neill	.10
136	Jared Osentowski	.10
137	Mike Pagliarulo	.10
138	Rafael Palmeiro	.20
139	Rodney Pedraza	.10
140	Tony Phillips	.10
141	*Scott Pisciotta*	.10
142	Chris Pritchett	.10
143	Jason Pruitt	.10
144a	Kirby Puckett (1991 N.L. All-Star - error)	.75
144b	Kirby Puckett (1991 World Series - correct)	.75
145	Kirby Puckett (AS)	.75
146	*Manny Ramirez*	10.00
147	Eddie Ramos	.10
148	Mark Ratekin	.10
149	Jeff Reardon	.10
150	Sean Rees	.10
151	*Calvin Reese*	.75
152	*Desmond Relaford*	.20
153	Eric Richardson	.10
154	Cal Ripken, Jr. (AS)	1.50
155	Chris Roberts	.10
156	Mike Robertson	.10
157	Steve Rodriguez	.10
158	Mike Rossiter	.10
159	Scott Ruffcorn	.10
160a	Chris Sabo (1991 World Series - error)	.10
160b	Chris Sabo (1991 N.L. All-Star - correct)	.10
161	Juan Samuel	.10
162	Ryne Sandberg (AS)	.50
163	Scott Sanderson	.10
164	Benito Santiago	.10
165	*Gene Schall*	.10
166	Chad Schoenvogel	.10
167	*Chris Seelbach*	.10
168	*Aaron Sele*	.75
169	Basil Shabazz	.10
170	*Al Shirley*	.10
171	Paul Shuey	.10
172	Ruben Sierra	.10
173	John Smiley	.10
174	Lee Smith	.10
175	Ozzie Smith	.75
176	Tim Smith	.10
177	Zane Smith	.10
178	John Smoltz	.15
179	Scott Stahoviak	.10
180	Kennie Steenstra	.10
181	Kevin Stocker	.10
182	*Chris Stynes*	.10
183	Danny Tartabull	.10
184	Brien Taylor	.10
185	Todd Taylor	.10
186	Larry Thomas	.10
187a	*Ozzie Timmons*	.10
187b	David Tuttle (should be #188)	.10
188	Not issued	
189	Andy Van Slyke	.10
190a	Frank Viola (1991 World Series - error)	.10
190b	Frank Viola (1991 N.L. All-Star - correct)	.10
191	Michael Walkden	.10
192	Jeff Ware	.10
193	*Allen Watson*	.10
194	Steve Whitaker	.10
195a	Jerry Willard (1991 Draft Pick - error)	.10
195b	Jerry Willard (1991 World Series - correct)	.10
196	Craig Wilson	.10
197	Chris Wimmer	.10
198	*Steve Wojciechowski*	.10
199	Joel Wolfe	.10
200	Ivan Zweig	.10

1993 Stadium Club

Topps' premium set for 1993 was issued in three series, two 300-card series and a final series of 150. Boxes contained 24 packs this year, compared to 36 in the past. Packs had 14 cards and an insert card. Each box had a 5" x 7" Master Photo card.

		MT
Complete Set (750):		30.00
Complete Series 1 (300):		10.00
Complete Series 2 (300):		20.00
Complete Series 3 (150):		5.00
Common Player:		.10
First Day Production:		10X
Wax Pack (15):		1.50
Wax Box (24):		20.00
1	Pat Borders	.10
2	Greg Maddux	1.50
3	Daryl Boston	.10
4	Bob Ayrault	.10
5	Tony Phillips	.10
6	Damion Easley	.10
7	Kip Gross	.10
8	Jim Thome	.10
9	Tim Belcher	.10
10	Gary Wayne	.10
11	Sam Militello	.10
12	Mike Magnante	.10
13	Tim Wakefield	.10
14	Tim Hulett	.10
15	Rheal Cormier	.10
16	Juan Guerrero	.10
17	Rich Gossage	.10
18	Tim Laker	.10
19	Darrin Jackson	.10
20	Jack Clark	.10
21	Roberto Hernandez	.10
22	Dean Palmer	.10
23	Harold Reynolds	.10
24	Dan Plesac	.10
25	Brent Mayne	.10
26	Pat Hentgen	.10
27	Luis Sojo	.10
28	Ron Gant	.10
29	Paul Gibson	.10
30	Bip Roberts	.10
31	Mickey Tettleton	.10
32	Randy Velarde	.10
33	Brian McRae	.10
34	Wes Chamberlain	.10
35	Wayne Kirby	.10
36	Rey Sanchez	.10
37	Jesse Orosco	.10
38	Mike Stanton	.10
39	Royce Clayton	.10
40	Cal Ripken, Jr.	2.50
41	John Dopson	.10
42	Gene Larkin	.10
43	Tim Raines	.10
44	Randy Myers	.10
45	Clay Parker	.10
46	Mike Scioscia	.10
47	Pete Incaviglia	.10
48	Todd Van Poppel	.10
49	Ray Lankford	.10
50	Eddie Murray	.75
51	Barry Bonds	1.75
52	Gary Thurman	.10
53	Bob Wickman	.10
54	Joey Cora	.10
55	Kenny Rogers	.10
56	Mike Devereaux	.10
57	Kevin Seitzer	.10
58	Rafael Belliard	.10
59	David Wells	.10
60	Mark Clark	.10
61	Carlos Baerga	.10
62	Scott Brosius	.10
63	Jeff Grotewold	.10
64	Rick Wrona	.10
65	Kurt Knudsen	.10
66	Lloyd McClendon	.10
67	Omar Vizquel	.10
68	Jose Vizcaino	.10
69	Rob Ducey	.10
70	Casey Candaele	.10
71	Ramon Martinez	.10
72	Todd Hundley	.10
73	John Marzano	.10
74	Derek Parks	.10
75	Jack McDowell	.10
76	Tim Scott	.10
77	Mike Mussina	.60

No.	Player	Price
78	Delino DeShields	.10
79	Chris Bosio	.10
80	Mike Bordick	.10
81	Rod Beck	.10
82	Ted Power	.10
83	John Kruk	.10
84	Steve Shifflett	.10
85	Danny Tartabull	.10
86	Mike Greenwell	.10
87	Jose Melendez	.10
88	Craig Wilson	.10
89	Melvin Nieves	.10
90	Ed Sprague	.10
91	Willie McGee	.10
92	Joe Orsulak	.10
93	Jeff King	.10
94	Dan Pasqua	.10
95	Brian Harper	.10
96	Joe Oliver	.10
97	Shane Turner	.10
98	Lenny Harris	.10
99	Jeff Parrett	.10
100	Luis Polonia	.10
101	Kent Bottenfield	.10
102	Albert Belle	.35
103	Mike Maddux	.10
104	Randy Tomlin	.10
105	Andy Stankiewicz	.10
106	Rico Rossy	.10
107	Joe Hesketh	.10
108	Dennis Powell	.10
109	Derrick May	.10
110	Pete Harnisch	.10
111	Kent Mercker	.10
112	Scott Fletcher	.10
113	Rex Hudler	.10
114	Chico Walker	.10
115	Rafael Palmeiro	.20
116	Mark Leiter	.10
117	Pedro Munoz	.10
118	Jim Bullinger	.10
119	Ivan Calderon	.10
120	Mike Timlin	.10
121	Rene Gonzales	.10
122	Greg Vaughn	.10
123	Mike Flanagan	.10
124	Mike Hartley	.10
125	Jeff Montgomery	.10
126	Mike Gallego	.10
127	Don Slaught	.10
128	Charlie O'Brien	.10
129	Jose Offerman	.10
130	Mark Wohlers	.10
131	Eric Fox	.10
132	Doug Strange	.10
133	Jeff Frye	.10
134	Wade Boggs	.75
135	Lou Whitaker	.10
136	Craig Grebeck	.10
137	Rich Rodriguez	.10
138	Jay Bell	.10
139	Felix Fermin	.10
140	Denny Martinez	.10
141	Eric Anthony	.10
142	Roberto Alomar	.60
143	Darren Lewis	.10
144	Mike Blowers	.10
145	Scott Bankhead	.10
146	Jeff Reboulet	.10
147	Frank Viola	.10
148	Bill Pecota	.10
149	Carlos Hernandez	.10
150	Bobby Witt	.10
151	Sid Bream	.10
152	Todd Zeile	.10
153	Dennis Cook	.10
154	Brian Bohanon	.10
155	Pat Kelly	.10
156	Milt Cuyler	.10
157	Juan Bell	.10
158	Randy Milligan	.10
159	Mark Gardner	.10
160	Pat Tabler	.10
161	Jeff Reardon	.10
162	Ken Patterson	.10
163	Bobby Bonilla	.10
164	Tony Pena	.10
165	Greg Swindell	.10
166	Kirk McCaskill	.10
167	Doug Drabek	.10
168	Franklin Stubbs	.10
169	Ron Tingley	.10
170	Willie Banks	.10
171	Sergio Valdez	.10
172	Mark Lemke	.10
173	Robin Yount	1.00
174	Storm Davis	.10
175	Dan Walters	.10
176	Steve Farr	.10
177	Curt Wilkerson	.10
178	Luis Alicea	.10
179	Russ Swan	.10
180	Mitch Williams	.10
181	Wilson Alvarez	.10
182	Carl Willis	.10
183	Craig Biggio	.15
184	Sean Berry	.10
185	Trevor Wilson	.10
186	Jeff Tackett	.10
187	Ellis Burks	.10
188	Jeff Branson	.10
189	Matt Nokes	.10
190	John Smiley	.10
191	Danny Gladden	.10
192	Mike Boddicker	.10
193	Roger Pavlik	.10
194	Paul Sorrento	.10
195	Vince Coleman	.10
196	Gary DiSarcina	.10
197	Rafael Bournigal	.10
198	Mike Schooler	.10
199	Scott Ruskin	.10
200	Frank Thomas	1.75
201	Kyle Abbott	.10
202	Mike Perez	.10
203	Andre Dawson	.25
204	Bill Swift	.10
205	Alejandro Pena	.10
206	Dave Winfield	1.00
207	Andujar Cedeno	.10
208	Terry Steinbach	.10
209	Chris Hammond	.10
210	Todd Burns	.10
211	Hipolito Pichardo	.10
212	John Kiely	.10
213	Tim Teufel	.10
214	Lee Guetterman	.10
215	Geronimo Pena	.10
216	Brett Butler	.10
217	Bryan Hickerson	.10
218	Rick Trlicek	.10
219	Lee Stevens	.10
220	Roger Clemens	1.50
221	Carlton Fisk	1.00
222	Chili Davis	.10
223	Walt Terrell	.10
224	Jim Eisenreich	.10
225	Ricky Bones	.10
226	Henry Rodriguez	.10
227	Ken Hill	.10
228	Rick Wilkins	.10
229	Ricky Jordan	.10
230	Bernard Gilkey	.10
231	Tim Fortugno	.10
232	Geno Petralli	.10
233	Jose Rijo	.10
234	Jim Leyritz	.10
235	Kevin Campbell	.10
236	Al Osuna	.10
237	Pete Smith	.10
238	Pete Schourek	.10
239	Moises Alou	.20
240	Donn Pall	.10
241	Denny Neagle	.10
242	Dan Peltier	.10
243	Scott Scudder	.10
244	Juan Guzman	.10
245	Dave Burba	.10
246	Rick Sutcliffe	.10
247	Tony Fossas	.10
248	Mike Munoz	.10
249	Tim Salmon	.25
250	Rob Murphy	.10
251	Roger McDowell	.10
252	Lance Parrish	.10
253	Cliff Brantley	.10
254	Scott Leius	.10
255	Carlos Martinez	.10
256	Vince Horsman	.10
257	Oscar Azocar	.10
258	Craig Shipley	.10
259	Ben McDonald	.10
260	Jeff Brantley	.10
261	Damon Berryhill	.10
262	Joe Grahe	.10
263	Dave Hansen	.10
264	Rich Amaral	.10
265	*Tim Pugh*	.10
266	Dion James	.10
267	Frank Tanana	.10
268	Stan Belinda	.10
269	Jeff Kent	.10
270	Bruce Ruffin	.10
271	Xavier Hernandez	.10
272	Darrin Fletcher	.10
273	Tino Martinez	.10
274	Benny Santiago	.10
275	Scott Radinsky	.10
276	Mariano Duncan	.10
277	Kenny Lofton	.10
278	Dwight Smith	.10
279	Joe Carter	.10
280	Tim Jones	.10
281	Jeff Huson	.10
282	Phil Plantier	.10
283	Kirby Puckett	1.50
284	Johnny Guzman	.10
285	Mike Morgan	.10
286	Chris Sabo	.10
287	Matt Williams	.30
288	Checklist 1-100	.10
289	Checklist 101-200	.10
290	Checklist 201-300	.10
291	Dennis Eckersley (Members Choice)	.10
292	Eric Karros (Members Choice)	.10
293	Pat Listach (Members Choice)	.10
294	Andy Van Slyke (Members Choice)	.10
295	Robin Ventura (Members Choice)	.10
296	Tom Glavine (Members Choice)	.10
297	Juan Gonzalez (Members Choice)	.50
298	Travis Fryman (Members Choice)	.10
299	Larry Walker (Members Choice)	.15
300	Gary Sheffield (Members Choice)	.15
301	Chuck Finley	.10
302	Luis Gonzalez	.35
303	Darryl Hamilton	.10
304	Bien Figueroa	.10
305	Ron Darling	.10
306	Jonathan Hurst	.10
307	Mike Sharperson	.10
308	Mike Christopher	.10
309	Marvin Freeman	.10
310	Jay Buhner	.10
311	Butch Henry	.10
312	Greg Harris	.10
313	Darren Daulton	.10
314	Chuck Knoblauch	.10
315	Greg Harris	.10
316	John Franco	.10
317	John Wehner	.10
318	Donald Harris	.10
319	Benny Santiago	.10
320	Larry Walker	.30
321	Randy Knorr	.10
322	*Ramon D. Martinez*	.10
323	Mike Stanley	.10
324	Bill Wegman	.10
325	Tom Candiotti	.10
326	Glenn Davis	.10
327	Chuck Crim	.10
328	Scott Livingstone	.10
329	Eddie Taubensee	.10
330	George Bell	.10
331	Edgar Martinez	.10
332	Paul Assenmacher	.10
333	Steve Hosey	.10
334	Mo Vaughn	.40
335	Bret Saberhagen	.10
336	Mike Trombley	.10
337	Mark Lewis	.10
338	Terry Pendleton	.10
339	Dave Hollins	.10
340	Jeff Conine	.10
341	Bob Tewksbury	.10
342	Billy Ashley	.10
343	Zane Smith	.10
344	John Wetteland	.10
345	Chris Hoiles	.10
346	Frank Castillo	.10
347	Bruce Hurst	.10
348	Kevin McReynolds	.10
349	Dave Henderson	.10
350	Ryan Bowen	.10
351	Sid Fernandez	.10
352	Mark Whiten	.10
353	Nolan Ryan	2.50
354	Rick Aguilera	.10
355	Mark Langston	.10
356	Jack Morris	.10
357	Rob Deer	.10
358	Dave Fleming	.10
359	Lance Johnson	.10
360	Joe Millette	.10
361	Wil Cordero	.10
362	Chito Martinez	.10
363	Scott Servais	.10
364	Bernie Williams	.40
365	Pedro Martinez	.75
366	Ryne Sandberg	.75
367	Brad Ausmus	.10
368	Scott Cooper	.10
369	Rob Dibble	.10
370	Walt Weiss	.10
371	Mark Davis	.10
372	Orlando Merced	.10
373	Mike Jackson	.10
374	Kevin Appier	.10
375	Esteban Beltre	.10
376	Joe Slusarski	.10
377	William Suero	.10
378	Pete O'Brien	.10
379	Alan Embree	.10
380	Lenny Webster	.10
381	Eric Davis	.10
382	Duane Ward	.10
383	John Habyan	.10
384	Jeff Bagwell	1.00
385	Ruben Amaro	.10
386	Julio Valera	.10
387	Robin Ventura	.10
388	Archi Cianfrocco	.10
389	Skeeter Barnes	.10
390	Tim Costo	.10
391	Luis Mercedes	.10
392	Jeremy Hernandez	.10
393	Shawon Dunston	.10
394	Andy Van Slyke	.10
395	Kevin Maas	.10
396	Kevin Brown	.20
397	J.T. Bruett	.10
398	Darryl Strawberry	.10
399	Tom Pagnozzi	.10
400	Sandy Alomar	.10
401	Keith Miller	.10
402	Rich DeLucia	.10
403	Shawn Abner	.10
404	Howard Johnson	.10
405	Mike Benjamin	.10
406	*Roberto Mejia*	.10
407	Mike Butcher	.10
408	Deion Sanders	.15
409	Todd Stottlemyre	.10
410	Scott Kamieniecki	.10
411	Doug Jones	.10
412	John Burkett	.10
413	Lance Blankenship	.10
414	Jeff Parrett	.10
415	Barry Larkin	.15
416	Alan Trammell	.10
417	Mark Kiefer	.10
418	Gregg Olson	.10
419	Mark Grace	.25
420	Shane Mack	.10
421	Bob Walk	.10
422	Curt Schilling	.20
423	Erik Hanson	.10
424	George Brett	1.50
425	Reggie Jefferson	.10
426	Mark Portugal	.10
427	Ron Karkovice	.10
428	Matt Young	.10
429	Troy Neel	.10
430	Hector Fajardo	.10
431	Dave Righetti	.10
432	Pat Listach	.10
433	Jeff Innis	.10
434	Bob MacDonald	.10
435	Brian Jordan	.10
436	Jeff Blauser	.10
437	*Mike Myers*	.15
438	Frank Seminara	.10
439	Rusty Meacham	.10
440	Greg Briley	.10
441	Derek Lilliquist	.10
442	John Vander Wal	.10
443	Scott Erickson	.10
444	Bob Scanlan	.10
445	Todd Frohwirth	.10
446	Tom Goodwin	.10
447	William Pennyfeather	.10
448	Travis Fryman	.10
449	Mickey Morandini	.10
450	Greg Olson	.10

No.	Player	Value
451	Trevor Hoffman	.10
452	Dave Magadan	.10
453	Shawn Jeter	.10
454	Andres Galarraga	.10
455	Ted Wood	.10
456	Freddie Benavides	.10
457	Junior Felix	.10
458	Alex Cole	.10
459	John Orton	.10
460	Eddie Zosky	.10
461	Dennis Eckersley	.10
462	Lee Smith	.10
463	John Smoltz	.15
464	Ken Caminiti	.10
465	Melido Perez	.10
466	Tom Marsh	.10
467	Jeff Nelson	.10
468	Jesse Levis	.10
469	Chris Nabholz	.10
470	Mike Mcfarlane	.10
471	Reggie Sanders	.10
472	Chuck McElroy	.10
473	Kevin Gross	.10
474	*Matt Whiteside*	.15
475	Cal Eldred	.10
476	Dave Gallagher	.10
477	Len Dykstra	.10
478	Mark McGwire	2.50
479	David Segui	.10
480	Mike Henneman	.10
481	Bret Barberie	.10
482	Steve Sax	.10
483	Dave Valle	.10
484	Danny Darwin	.10
485	Devon White	.10
486	Eric Plunk	.10
487	Jim Gott	.10
488	Scooter Tucker	.10
489	Omar Oliveres	.10
490	Greg Myers	.10
491	Brian Hunter	.10
492	Kevin Tapani	.10
493	Rich Monteleone	.10
494	Steve Buechele	.10
495	Bo Jackson	.15
496	Mike LaValliere	.10
497	Mark Leonard	.10
498	Daryl Boston	.10
499	Jose Canseco	.50
500	Brian Barnes	.10
501	Randy Johnson	.75
502	Tim McIntosh	.10
503	Cecil Fielder	.10
504	Derek Bell	.10
505	Kevin Koslofski	.10
506	Darren Holmes	.10
507	Brady Anderson	.10
508	John Valentin	.10
509	Jerry Browne	.10
510	Fred McGriff	.10
511	Pedro Astacio	.10
512	Gary Gaetti	.10
513	*John Burke*	.10
514	Dwight Gooden	.10
515	Thomas Howard	.10
516	*Darrell Whitmore*	.10
517	Ozzie Guillen	.10
518	Darryl Kile	.10
519	Rich Rowland	.10
520	Carlos Delgado	.45
521	Doug Henry	.10
522	Greg Colbrunn	.10
523	Tom Gordon	.10
524	Ivan Rodriguez	.75
525	Kent Hrbek	.10
526	Eric Young	.10
527	Rod Brewer	.10
528	Eric Karros	.10
529	Marquis Grissom	.10
530	Rico Brogna	.10
531	Sammy Sosa	1.75
532	Bret Boone	.15
533	Luis Rivera	.10
534	Hal Morris	.10
535	Monty Fariss	.10
536	Leo Gomez	.10
537	Wally Joyner	.10
538	Tony Gwynn	1.50
539	Mike Williams	.10
540	Juan Gonzalez	1.00
541	Ryan Klesko	.10
542	Ryan Thompson	.10
543	Chad Curtis	.10
544	Orel Hershiser	.10
545	Carlos Garcia	.10
546	Bob Welch	.10
547	Vinny Castilla	.10
548	Ozzie Smith	1.50
549	Luis Salazar	.10
550	Mark Guthrie	.10
551	Charles Nagy	.10
552	Alex Fernandez	.10
553	Mel Rojas	.10
554	Orestes Destrade	.10
555	Mark Gubicza	.10
556	Steve Finley	.10
557	Don Mattingly	1.75
558	Rickey Henderson	.75
559	Tommy Greene	.10
560	Arthur Rhodes	.10
561	Alfredo Griffin	.10
562	Will Clark	.30
563	Bob Zupcic	.10
564	Chuck Carr	.10
565	Henry Cotto	.10
566	Billy Spiers	.10
567	Jack Armstrong	.10
568	Kurt Stillwell	.10
569	David McCarty	.10
570	Joe Vitiello	.10
571	Gerald Williams	.10
572	Dale Murphy	.25
573	Scott Aldred	.10
574	Bill Gullickson	.10
575	Bobby Thigpen	.10
576	Glenallen Hill	.10
577	Dwayne Henry	.10
578	Calvin Jones	.10
579	Al Martin	.10
580	Ruben Sierra	.10
581	Andy Benes	.10
582	Anthony Young	.10
583	Shawn Boskie	.10
584	*Scott Pose*	.10
585	Mike Piazza	2.00
586	Donovan Osborne	.10
587	James Austin	.10
588	Checklist 301-400	.10
589	Checklist 401-500	.10
590	Checklist 501-600	.10
591	Ken Griffey, Jr. (Members Choice)	1.00
592	Ivan Rodriguez (Members Choice)	.35
593	Carlos Baerga (Members Choice)	.10
594	Fred McGriff (Members Choice)	.10
595	Mark McGwire (Members Choice)	1.25
596	Roberto Alomar (Members Choice)	.25
597	Kirby Puckett (Members Choice)	.75
598	Marquis Grissom (Members Choice)	.10
599	John Smoltz (Members Choice)	.10
600	Ryne Sandberg (Members Choice)	.40
601	Wade Boggs	.75
602	Jeff Reardon	.10
603	Billy Ripken	.10
604	Bryan Harvey	.10
605	Carlos Quintana	.10
606	Greg Hibbard	.10
607	Ellis Burks	.10
608	Greg Swindell	.10
609	Dave Winfield	1.00
610	Charlie Hough	.10
611	Chili Davis	.10
612	Jody Reed	.10
613	Mark Williamson	.10
614	Phil Plantier	.10
615	Jim Abbott	.10
616	Dante Bichette	.10
617	Mark Eichhorn	.10
618	Gary Sheffield	.35
619	*Richie Lewis*	.10
620	Joe Girardi	.10
621	Jaime Navarro	.10
622	Willie Wilson	.10
623	Scott Fletcher	.10
624	Bud Black	.10
625	Tom Brunansky	.10
626	Steve Avery	.10
627	Paul Molitor	.75
628	Gregg Jefferies	.10
629	Dave Stewart	.10
630	Javier Lopez	.10
631	Greg Gagne	.10
632	Bobby Kelly	.10
633	Mike Fetters	.10
634	Ozzie Canseco	.10
635	Jeff Russell	.10
636	Pete Incaviglia	.10
637	Tom Henke	.10
638	Chipper Jones	2.00
639	Jimmy Key	.10
640	Dave Martinez	.10
641	Dave Stieb	.10
642	Milt Thompson	.10
643	Alan Mills	.10
644	Tony Fernandez	.10
645	Randy Bush	.10
646	Joe Magrane	.10
647	Ivan Calderon	.10
648	Jose Guzman	.10
649	John Olerud	.10
650	Tom Glavine	.15
651	Julio Franco	.10
652	Armando Reynoso	.10
653	Felix Jose	.10
654	Ben Rivera	.10
655	Andre Dawson	.25
656	Mike Harkey	.10
657	Kevin Seitzer	.10
658	Lonnie Smith	.10
659	Norm Charlton	.10
660	Dave Justice	.30
661	Fernando Valenzuela	.10
662	Dan Wilson	.10
663	Mark Gardner	.10
664	Doug Dascenzo	.10
665	Greg Maddux	1.50
666	Harold Baines	.10
667	Randy Myers	.10
668	Harold Reynolds	.10
669	Candy Maldonado	.10
670	Al Leiter	.10
671	Jerald Clark	.10
672	Doug Drabek	.10
673	Kirk Gibson	.10
674	*Steve Reed*	.10
675	Mike Felder	.10
676	Ricky Gutierrez	.10
677	Spike Owen	.10
678	Otis Nixon	.10
679	Scott Sanderson	.10
680	Mark Carreon	.10
681	Troy Percival	.10
682	Kevin Stocker	.10
683	*Jim Converse*	.10
684	Barry Bonds	1.75
685	Greg Gohr	.10
686	Tim Wallach	.10
687	Matt Mieske	.10
688	Robby Thompson	.10
689	Brien Taylor	.10
690	Kirt Manwaring	.10
691	*Mike Lansing*	.25
692	Steve Decker	.10
693	Mike Moore	.10
694	Kevin Mitchell	.10
695	Phil Hiatt	.10
696	*Tony Tarasco*	.10
697	Benji Gil	.10
698	Jeff Juden	.10
699	Kevin Reimer	.10
700	Andy Ashby	.10
701	John Jaha	.10
702	*Tim Bogar*	.10
703	David Cone	.10
704	Willie Greene	.10
705	*David Hulse*	.10
706	Cris Carpenter	.10
707	Ken Griffey, Jr.	2.25
708	Steve Bedrosian	.10
709	Dave Nilsson	.10
710	Paul Wagner	.10
711	B.J. Surhoff	.10
712	*Rene Arocha*	.10
713	Manny Lee	.10
714	Brian Williams	.10
715	*Sherman Obando*	.10
716	Terry Mulholland	.10
717	Paul O'Neill	.10
718	David Nied	.10
719	*J.T. Snow*	.75
720	Nigel Wilson	.10
721	Mike Bielecki	.10
722	Kevin Young	.10
723	Charlie Leibrandt	.10
724	Frank Bolick	.10
725	*Jon Shave*	.10
726	Steve Cooke	.10
727	*Domingo Martinez*	.10
728	Todd Worrell	.10
729	Jose Lind	.10
730	*Jim Tatum*	.10
731	Mike Hampton	.10
732	Mike Draper	.10
733	Henry Mercedes	.10
734	*John Johnstone*	.10
735	Mitch Webster	.10
736	Russ Springer	.10
737	Rob Natal	.10
738	Steve Howe	.10
739	*Darrell Sherman*	.10
740	Pat Mahomes	.10
741	Alex Arias	.10
742	Damon Buford	.10
743	Charlie Hayes	.10
744	Guillermo Velasquez	.10
745	Checklist 601-750	.10
746	Frank Thomas (Members Choice)	.75
747	Barry Bonds (Members Choice)	1.00
748	Roger Clemens (Members Choice)	.75
749	Joe Carter (Members Choice)	.10
750	Greg Maddux (Members Choice)	.75

1993 Stadium Club Series 1 Inserts

Four bonus cards were produced as special inserts in Series I Stadium Club packs. Two of the full-bleed, gold-foil enhanced cards honor Robin Yount and George Brett for achieving the 3,000-hit mark, while the other two commemorate the first picks in the 1993 expansion draft by the Colorado Rockies (David Nied) and Marlins (Nigel Wilson).

		MT
Complete Set (4):		4.00
Common Player:		.25
1	Robin Yount (3,000 hits)	1.50
2	George Brett (3,000 hits)	2.50
3	David Nied (#1 pick)	.25
4	Nigel Wilson (#1 pick)	.25

1993 Stadium Club Series 2 Inserts

Cross-town and regional rivals were featured in this four-card insert set found, on average, one per 24 packs of Series II Stadium Club. Each of the two-faced cards is typical S.C. quality with gold-foil stamping and UV coating front and back.

	MT
Complete Set (4):	10.00
Common Card:	3.00
1 Pacific Terrific (Will Clark, Mark McGwire)	3.00
2 Broadway Stars (Dwight Gooden, Don Mattingly)	3.00
3 Second City Sluggers (Ryne Sandberg, Frank Thomas)	3.00
4 Pacific Terrific (Ken Griffey, Jr., Darryl Strawberry)	3.00

1993 Stadium Club Series 3 Inserts

Team "firsts" - first game, first pitch, first batter, etc. - for the 1993 expansion Florida Marlins and Colorado Rockies are featured on this pair of inserts found in Series III Stadium Club packs. Fronts featured game-action photos with the player's name in gold foil. On back is a stadium scene with the team first overprinted in black. At top the team name and Stadium Club logo are in gold foil.

	MT
Complete Set (2):	.50
Common Player:	.25
1 David Nied	.25
2 Charlie Hough	.25

1993 Stadium Club Master Photos

Each box of 1993 Stadium Club packs included one Master Photo premium insert. Prize cards good for three Master Photos in a mail-in offer were also included in each of the three series. The 5" x 7" Master Photos feature wide white borders and a large Stadium Club logo at top, highlighted by prismatic foil. The same foil is used as a border for a larger-format version of the player's regular S.C. card at the center of the Master Photo. A "Members Only" version of each of the 1993 Master Photos was available as a premium with the purchase of a Members Only Stadium Club set. the Members Only Master Photos have a gold-foil seal in the upper-right corner.

	MT
Complete Set (30):	16.00
Common Player:	.25
Series 1	
(1) Carlos Baerga	.25
(2) Delino DeShields	.25
(3) Brian McRae	.25
(4) Sam Militello	.25
(5) Joe Oliver	.25
(6) Kirby Puckett	2.00
(7) Cal Ripken Jr.	4.00
(8) Bip Roberts	.25
(9) Mike Scioscia	.25
(10) Rick Sutcliffe	.25
(11) Danny Tartabull	.25
(12) Tim Wakefield	.25
Series 2	
(13) George Brett	2.00
(14) Jose Canseco	.75
(15) Will Clark	.50
(16) Travis Fryman	.25
(17) Dwight Gooden	.25
(18) Mark Grace	.75
Series 3	
(25) Barry Bonds	2.00
(26) Ken Griffey, Jr.	3.00
(27) Greg Maddux	1.50
(28) David Nied	.25
(29) J.T. Snow	.50
(30) Brien Taylor	.25

1993 Stadium Club Special (Murphy)

Though the packaging and the cards themselves identify this 200-card set as a 1992 issue, it was not released until 1993 and is thought of by the hobby at large as a 1993 set. The set is sold in a plastic replica of Jack Murphy Stadium in San Diego, venue for the 1993 All-Star Game. Fifty-six of the cards feature players from that contest and are so identified by a line of gold-foil on the card front and an All-Star logo on back. Twenty-five members of the 1992 Team U.S.A. Olympic baseball squad are also included in the set, with appropriate logos and notations front and back. There are 19 cards depicting action and stars of the the 1992 League Championships and World Series. The other 100 cards in the set are 1992 draft picks. All cards have the same basic format as the regular-issue 1992 Topps Stadium Club cards, full-bleed photos on front and back, UV coating on both sides and gold-foil highlights on front. Besides the 200 standard-size cards, the Special Edition set included a dozen "Master Photos," 5" x 7" white-bordered premium cards.

	MT
Complete Set (200):	60.00
Common Player:	.10
1 Dave Winfield	1.50
2 Juan Guzman	.10
3 Tony Gwynn	1.50
4 Chris Roberts	.10
5 Benny Santiago	.10
6 Sherard Clinkscales	.10
7 *Jonathan Nunnally*	.25
8 Chuck Knoblauch	.10
9 *Bob Wolcott*	.10
10 Steve Rodriguez	.10
11 *Mark Williams*	.10
12 *Danny Clyburn*	.10
13 Darren Dreifort	.10
14 Andy Van Slyke	.10
15 Wade Boggs	.75
16 Scott Patton	.10
17 Gary Sheffield	.25
18 Ron Villone	.10
19 Roberto Alomar	.65
20 Marc Valdes	.10
21 Daron Kirkreit	.10
22 Jeff Granger	.10
23 Levon Largusa	.10
24 Jimmy Key	.10
25 Kevin Pearson	.10
26 Michael Moore	.10
27 *Preston Wilson*	4.00
28 Kirby Puckett	1.50
29 *Tim Crabtree*	.15
30 Bip Roberts	.10
31 Kelly Gruber	.10
32 Tony Fernandez	.10
33 Jason Angel	.10
34 Calvin Murray	.10
35 Chad McConnell	.10
36 Jason Moler	.10
37 Mark Lemke	.10
38 Tom Knauss	.10
39 Larry Mitchell	.10
40 Doug Mirabelli	.10
41 Everett Stull II	.10
42 Chris Wimmer	.10
43 *Dan Serafini*	.10
44 Ryne Sandberg	1.00
45 Steve Lyons	.10
46 Ryan Freeburg	.10
47 Ruben Sierra	.10
48 David Mysel	.10
49 Joe Hamilton	.10
50 Steve Rodriguez	.10
51 Tim Wakefield	.10
52 Scott Gentile	.10
53 Doug Jones	.10
54 Willie Brown	.10
55 *Chad Mottola*	.15
56 Ken Griffey, Jr.	2.00
57 *Jon Lieber*	3.00
58 Denny Martinez	.10
59 Joe Petcka	.10
60 Benji Simonton	.10
61 Brett Backlund	.10
62 Damon Berryhill	.10
63 Juan Guzman	.10
64 Doug Hecker	.10
65 Jamie Arnold	.10
66 Bob Tewksbury	.10
67 Tim Leger	.10
68 Todd Etler	.10
69 Lloyd McClendon	.10
70 Kurt Ehmann	.10
71 Rick Magdaleno	.10
72 Tom Pagnozzi	.10
73 Jeffrey Hammonds	.10
74 Joe Carter	.10
75 Chris Holt	.10
76 Charles Johnson	.10
77 Bob Walk	.10
78 Fred McGriff	.10
79 Tom Evans	.10
80 Scott Klingenbeck	.10
81 Chad McConnell	.10
82 Chris Eddy	.10
83 Phil Nevin	.10
84 John Kruk	.10
85 Tony Sheffield	.10
86 John Smoltz	.15
87 Trevor Humphry	.10
88 Charles Nagy	.10
89 Sean Runyan	.10
90 Mike Gulan	.10
91 Darren Daulton	.10
92 Otis Nixon	.10
93 Nomar Garciaparra	18.00
94 Larry Walker	.35
95 Hut Smith	.10
96 Rick Helling	.10
97 Roger Clemens	1.50
98 Ron Gant	.10
99 Kenny Felder	.10
100 Steve Murphy	.10
101 Mike Smith	.10
102 Terry Pendleton	.10
103 Tim Davis	.10
104 Jeff Patzke	.10
105 Craig Wilson	.10
106 Tom Glavine	.15
107 Mark Langston	.10
108 Mark Thompson	.10
109 *Eric Owens*	.50
110 Keith Johnson	.10
111 Robin Ventura	.10
112 Ed Sprague	.10
113 *Jeff Schmidt*	.10
114 Don Wengert	.10
115 Craig Biggio	.15
116 Kenny Carlyle	.10
117 *Derek Jeter*	30.00
118 Manuel Lee	.10
119 Jeff Haas	.10
120 Roger Bailey	.10
121 Sean Lowe	.10
122 Rick Aguilera	.10
123 Sandy Alomar	.10
124 Derek Wallace	.10
125 B.J. Wallace	.10
126 Greg Maddux	1.50
127 Tim Moore	.10
128 Lee Smith	.10
129 Todd Steverson	.10
130 Chris Widger	.10
131 Paul Molitor	.75
132 Chris Smith	.10
133 *Chris Gomez*	.25
134 Jimmy Baron	.10
135 John Smoltz	.15
136 Pat Borders	.10
137 Donnie Leshnock	.10
138 Gus Gandarillos	.10
139 Will Clark	.25

140	*Ryan Luzinski*	.10
141	Cal Ripken, Jr.	2.50
142	B.J. Wallace	.10
143	*Trey Beamon*	.15
144	Norm Charlton	.10
145	Mike Mussina	.45
146	Billy Owens	.10
147	Ozzie Smith	1.50
148	*Jason Kendall*	4.00
149	*Mike Matthews*	.10
150	David Spykstra	.10
151	Benji Grigsby	.10
152	Sean Smith	.10
153	Mark McGwire	2.50
154	David Cone	.10
155	*Shon Walker*	.10
156	Jason Giambi	.50
157	Jack McDowell	.10
158	Paxton Briley	.10
159	Edgar Martinez	.10
160	Brian Sackinsky	.10
161	Barry Bonds	1.75
162	Roberto Kelly	.10
163	Jeff Alkire	.10
164	Mike Sharperson	.10
165	Jamie Taylor	.10
166	John Saffer	.10
167	Jerry Browne	.10
168	Travis Fryman	.10
169	Brady Anderson	.10
170	Chris Roberts	.10
171	Lloyd Peever	.10
172	Francisco Cabrera	.10
173	Ramiro Martinez	.10
174	Jeff Alkire	.10
175	Ivan Rodriguez	.60
176	Kevin Brown	.15
177	Chad Roper	.10
178	Rod Henderson	.10
179	Dennis Eckersley	.10
180	*Shannon Stewart*	6.00
181	DeShawn Warren	.10
182	Lonnie Smith	.10
183	Willie Adams	.10
184	Jeff Montgomery	.10
185	Damon Hollins	.10
186	Byron Matthews	.10
187	Harold Baines	.10
188	Rick Greene	.10
189	Carlos Baerga	.10
190	Brandon Cromer	.10
191	Roberto Alomar	.65
192	Rich Ireland	.10
193	Steve Montgomery	.10
194	Brant Brown	.10
195	Ritchie Moody	.10
196	Michael Tucker	.10
197	*Jason Varitek*	.75
198	David Manning	.10
199	Marquis Riley	.10
200	Jason Giambi	.50

1993 Stadium Club Special Master Photos

Each 1993 Stadium Club Special (Jack Murphy Stadium) set included 12 Master Photos replicating cards from the set. there were nine All-Stars, two '92 rookies and a Team USA player among the Master Photos. Gold-tone prismatic foil highlights the 5" x 7" cards, decorating the large logo at top and separating the card photo from the wide white border. Backs have Stadium Club and MLB logos and copyright information printed in black. The unnumbered cards are checklisted here in alphabetical order.

		MT
Complete Set (12):		7.00
Common Player:		.25
(1)	Sandy Alomar	.25
(2)	Tom Glavine	.25
(3)	Ken Griffey, Jr.	2.50
(4)	Tony Gwynn	1.50
(5)	Chuck Knoblauch	.25
(6)	Chad Mottola	.25
(7)	Kirby Puckett	1.50
(8)	Chris Roberts	.25
(9)	Ryne Sandberg	1.00
(10)	Gary Sheffield	.50
(11)	Larry Walker	.75
(12)	Preston Wilson	.75

1994 Stadium Club Pre-production

These sample cards introducing the 1994 Stadium Club set differ from their regular-issue counterparts only in the inclusion of a line of type vertically on the back-right, "Pre-Production Sample."

		MT
Complete Set (9):		6.50
Common Player:		.50
6	Al Martin	.50
15	Junior Ortiz	.50
36	Tim Salmon	.75
56	Jerry Spradlin	.50
122	Tom Pagnozzi	.50
123	Ron Gant	.50
125	Dennis Eckersley	.75
135	Jose Lind	.50
238	Barry Bonds	4.00

1994 Stadium Club

Issued in three series to a total of 720 cards, Topps' mid-price brand features a hip look and a wide range of insert specials. The regular cards feature a borderless photo with the player's name presented in a unique typewriter/label maker style at bottom. The player's last name and Topps Stadium Club logo at top are in red foil. Backs feature another player photo, some personal data and a headlined career summary. Various stats and skills rankings complete the data. Subsets within the issue include cards annotated with Major League debut dates, 1993 awards won, home run club cards, cards featuring two or three players, and Final Tribute cards for George Brett and Nolan Ryan.

		MT
Complete Set (720):		40.00
Common Player:		.10
1st Day Production:		10X
Golden Rainbow:		3X
Series 1, 2, 3 Pack (12):		1.00
Series 1, 2, 3 Wax Box (24):		20.00
1	Robin Yount	.75
2	Rick Wilkins	.10
3	Steve Scarsone	.10
4	Gary Sheffield	.40
5	George Brett	1.50
6	Al Martin	.10
7	Joe Oliver	.10
8	Stan Belinda	.10
9	Denny Hocking	.10
10	Roberto Alomar	.65
11	Luis Polonia	.10
12	Scott Hemond	.10
13	Joey Reed	.10
14	Mel Rojas	.10
15	Junior Ortiz	.10
16	Harold Baines	.10
17	Brad Pennington	.10
18	Jay Bell	.10
19	Tom Henke	.10
20	Jeff Branson	.10
21	Roberto Mejia	.10
22	Pedro Munoz	.10
23	Matt Nokes	.10
24	Jack McDowell	.10
25	Cecil Fielder	.10
26	Tony Fossas	.10
27	Jim Eisenreich	.10
28	Anthony Young	.10
29	Chuck Carr	.10
30	Jeff Treadway	.10
31	Chris Nabholz	.10
32	Tom Candiotti	.10
33	Mike Maddux	.10
34	Nolan Ryan	2.50
35	Luis Gonzalez	.40
36	Tim Salmon	.25
37	Mark Whiten	.10
38	Roger McDowell	.10
39	Royce Clayton	.10
40	Troy Neel	.10
41	Mike Harkey	.10
42	Darrin Fletcher	.10
43	Wayne Kirby	.10
44	Rich Amaral	.10
45	Robb Nen	.10
46	Tim Teufel	.10
47	Steve Cooke	.10
48	Jeff McNeely	.10
49	Jeff Montgomery	.10
50	Skeeter Barnes	.10
51	Scott Stahoviak	.10
52	Pat Kelly	.10
53	Brady Anderson	.10
54	Mariano Duncan	.10
55	Brian Bohanon	.10
56	Jerry Spradlin	.10
57	Ron Karkovice	.10
58	Jeff Gardner	.10
59	Bobby Bonilla	.10
60	Tino Martinez	.10
61	Todd Benzinger	.10
62	*Steve Trachsel*	.35
63	Brian Jordan	.10
64	Steve Bedrosian	.10
65	Brent Gates	.10
66	Shawn Green	.50
67	Sean Berry	.10
68	Joe Klink	.10
69	Fernando Valenzuela	.10
70	Andy Tomberlin	.10
71	Tony Pena	.10
72	Eric Young	.10
73	Chris Gomez	.10
74	Paul O'Neill	.10
75	Ricky Gutierrez	.10
76	Brad Holman	.10
77	Lance Painter	.10
78	Mike Butcher	.10
79	Sid Bream	.10
80	Sammy Sosa	1.75
81	Felix Fermin	.10
82	Todd Hundley	.10
83	Kevin Higgins	.10
84	Todd Pratt	.10
85	Ken Griffey, Jr.	2.25
86	John O'Donoghue	.10
87	Rick Renteria	.10
88	John Burkett	.10
89	Jose Vizcaino	.10
90	Kevin Seitzer	.10
91	Bobby Witt	.10
92	Chris Turner	.10
93	Omar Vizquel	.10
94	Dave Justice	.30
95	David Segui	.10
96	Dave Hollins	.10
97	Doug Strange	.10
98	Jerald Clark	.10
99	Mike Moore	.10
100	Joey Cora	.10
101	Scott Kamieniecki	.10
102	Andy Benes	.10
103	Chris Bosio	.10
104	Rey Sanchez	.10
105	John Jaha	.10
106	Otis Nixon	.10
107	Rickey Henderson	.75
108	Jeff Bagwell	1.00
109	Gregg Jefferies	.10
110	Topps Trios (Roberto Alomar, Paul Molitor, John Olerud)	.25
111	Topps Trios (Ron Gant, David Justice, Fred McGriff)	.15
112	Topps Trios (Juan Gonzalez, Rafael Palmeiro, Dean Palmer)	.20
113	Greg Swindell	.10
114	Bill Hasleman	.10
115	Phil Plantier	.10
116	Ivan Rodriguez	.75
117	Kevin Tapani	.10
118	Mike LaValliere	.10
119	Tim Costo	.10
120	Mickey Morandini	.10
121	Brett Butler	.10
122	Tom Pagnozzi	.10
123	Ron Gant	.10
124	Damion Easley	.10
125	Dennis Eckersley	.10
126	Matt Mieske	.10
127	Cliff Floyd	.10
128	*Julian Tavarez*	.10
129	Arthur Rhodes	.10
130	Dave West	.10
131	Tim Naehring	.10
132	Freddie Benavides	.10
133	Paul Assenmacher	.10
134	David McCarty	.10
135	Jose Lind	.10
136	Reggie Sanders	.10
137	Don Slaught	.10
138	Andujar Cedeno	.10

No.	Player	Value
139	Rob Deer	.10
140	Mike Piazza	2.00
141	Moises Alou	.20
142	Tom Foley	.10
143	Benny Santiago	.10
144	Sandy Alomar	.10
145	Carlos Hernandez	.10
146	Luis Alicea	.10
147	Tom Lampkin	.10
148	Ryan Klesko	.10
149	Juan Guzman	.10
150	Scott Servais	.10
151	Tony Gwynn	1.50
152	Tim Wakefield	.10
153	David Nied	.10
154	Chris Haney	.10
155	Danny Bautista	.10
156	Randy Velarde	.10
157	Darrin Jackson	.10
158	*J.R. Phillips*	.10
159	Greg Gagne	.10
160	Luis Aquino	.10
161	John Vander Wal	.10
162	Randy Myers	.10
163	Ted Power	.10
164	Scott Brosius	.10
165	Len Dykstra	.10
166	Jacob Brumfield	.10
167	Bo Jackson	.15
168	Eddie Taubensee	.10
169	Carlos Baerga	.10
170	Tim Bogar	.10
171	Jose Canseco	.65
172	Greg Blosser	.10
173	Chili Davis	.10
174	Randy Knorr	.10
175	Mike Perez	.10
176	Henry Rodriguez	.10
177	*Brian Turang*	.10
178	Roger Pavlik	.10
179	Aaron Sele	.10
180	Tale of 2 Players (Fred McGriff, Gary Sheffield)	.10
181	Tale of 2 Players (J.T. Snow, Tim Salmon)	.10
182	Roberto Hernandez	.10
183	Jeff Reboulet	.10
184	John Doherty	.10
185	Danny Sheaffer	.10
186	Bip Roberts	.10
187	Denny Martinez	.10
188	Darryl Hamilton	.10
189	Eduardo Perez	.10
190	Pete Harnisch	.10
191	Rick Gossage	.10
192	Mickey Tettleton	.10
193	Lenny Webster	.10
194	Lance Johnson	.10
195	Don Mattingly	1.75
196	Gregg Olson	.10
197	Mark Gubicza	.10
198	Scott Fletcher	.10
199	Jon Shave	.10
200	Tim Mauser	.10
201	Jeromy Burnitz	.10
202	Rob Dibble	.10
203	Will Clark	.30
204	Steve Buechele	.10
205	Brian Williams	.10
206	Carlos Garcia	.10
207	Mark Clark	.10
208	Rafael Palmeiro	.30
209	Eric Davis	.10
210	Pat Meares	.10
211	Chuck Finley	.10
212	Jason Bere	.10
213	Gary DiSarcina	.10
214	Tony Fernandez	.10
215	B.J. Surhoff	.10
216	Lee Guetterman	.10
217	Tim Wallach	.10
218	Kirt Manwaring	.10
219	Albert Belle	.40
220	Dwight Gooden	.10
221	Archi Cianfrocco	.10
222	Terry Mulholland	.10
223	Hipolito Pichardo	.10
224	Kent Hrbek	.10
225	Criag Grebeck	.10
226	Todd Jones	.10
227	Mike Bordick	.10
228	John Olerud	.10
229	Jeff Blauser	.10
230	Alex Arias	.10
231	Bernard Gilkey	.10
232	Denny Neagle	.10
233	*Pedro Borbon*	.10
234	Dick Schofield	.10
235	Matias Carrillo	.10
236	Juan Bell	.10
237	Mike Hampton	.10
238	Barry Bonds	1.75
239	Cris Carpenter	.10
240	Eric Karros	.10
241	Greg McMichael	.10
242	Pat Hentgen	.10
243	Tim Pugh	.10
244	Vinny Castilla	.10
245	Charlie Hough	.10
246	Bobby Munoz	.10
247	Kevin Baez	.10
248	Todd Frohwirth	.10
249	Charlie Hayes	.10
250	Mike Macfarlane	.10
251	Danny Darwin	.10
252	Ben Rivera	.10
253	Dave Henderson	.10
254	Steve Avery	.10
255	Tim Belcher	.10
256	Dan Plesac	.10
257	Jim Thome	.10
258	Albert Belle (35+ HR Hitter)	.20
259	Barry Bonds (35+ HR Hitter)	.90
260	Ron Gant (35+ HR Hitter)	.10
261	Juan Gonzalez (35+ HR Hitter)	.50
262	Ken Griffey, Jr. (35+ HR Hitter)	1.25
263	Dave Justice (35+ HR Hitter)	.20
264	Fred McGriff (35+ HR Hitter)	.10
265	Rafael Palmeiro (35+ HR Hitter)	.10
266	Mike Piazza (35+ HR Hitter)	1.00
267	Frank Thomas (35+ HR Hitter)	.90
268	Matt Williams (35+ HR Hitter)	.15
269a	Checklist 1-135	.10
269b	Checklist 271-408	.10
270a	Checklist 136-270	.10
270b	Checklist 409-540	.10
271	Mike Stanley	.10
272	Tony Tarasco	.10
273	Teddy Higuera	.10
274	Ryan Thompson	.10
275	Rick Aguilera	.10
276	Ramon Martinez	.10
277	Orlando Merced	.10
278	Guillermo Velasquez	.10
279	Mark Hutton	.10
280	Larry Walker	.40
281	Kevin Gross	.10
282	Jose Offerman	.10
283	Jim Leyritz	.10
284	Jamie Moyer	.10
285	Frank Thomas	1.75
286	Derek Bell	.10
287	Derrick May	.10
288	Dave Winfield	1.00
289	Curt Schilling	.25
290	Carlos Quintana	.10
291	Bob Natal	.10
292	David Cone	.10
293	Al Osuna	.10
294	Bob Hamelin	.10
295	Chad Curtis	.10
296	Danny Jackson	.10
297	Bob Welch	.10
298	Felix Jose	.10
299	Jay Buhner	.10
300	Joe Carter	.10
301	Kenny Lofton	.10
302	*Kirk Rueter*	.15
303	Kim Batiste	.10
304	Mike Morgan	.10
305	Pat Borders	.10
306	Rene Arocha	.10
307	Ruben Sierra	.10
308	Steve Finley	.10
309	Travis Fryman	.10
310	Zane Smith	.10
311	Willie Wilson	.10
312	Trevor Hoffman	.10
313	Terry Pendleton	.10
314	Salomon Torres	.10
315	Robin Ventura	.10
316	Randy Tomlin	.10
317	Dave Stewart	.10
318	Mike Benjamin	.10
319	Matt Turner	.10
320	Manny Ramirez	1.00
321	Kevin Young	.10
322	Ken Caminiti	.10
323	Joe Girardi	.10
324	Jeff McKnight	.10
325	Gene Harris	.10
326	Devon White	.10
327	Darryl Kile	.10
328	Craig Paquette	.10
329	Cal Eldred	.10
330	Bill Swift	.10
331	Alan Trammell	.10
332	Armando Reynoso	.10
333	Brent Mayne	.10
334	Chris Donnels	.10
335	Darryl Strawberry	.10
336	Dean Palmer	.10
337	Frank Castillo	.10
338	Jeff King	.10
339	John Franco	.10
340	Kevin Appier	.10
341	Lance Blankenship	.10
342	Mark McLemore	.10
343	Pedro Astacio	.10
344	Rich Batchelor	.10
345	Ryan Bowen	.10
346	Terry Steinbach	.10
347	Troy O'Leary	.10
348	Willie Blair	.10
349	Wade Boggs	.75
350	Tim Raines	.10
351	Scott Livingstone	.10
352	Rod Carreia	.10
353	Ray Lankford	.10
354	Pat Listach	.10
355	Milt Thompson	.10
356	Miguel Jimenez	.10
357	Marc Newfield	.10
358	Mark McGwire	2.50
359	Kirby Puckett	1.50
360	Kent Mercker	.10
361	John Kruk	.10
362	Jeff Kent	.10
363	Hal Morris	.10
364	Edgar Martinez	.10
365	Dave Magadan	.10
366	Dante Bichette	.10
367	Chris Hammond	.10
368	Bret Saberhagen	.10
369	Billy Ripken	.10
370	Bill Gullickson	.10
371	Andre Dawson	.25
372	Bobby Kelly	.10
373	Cal Ripken, Jr.	2.50
374	Craig Biggio	.15
375	Dan Pasqua	.10
376	Dave Nilsson	.10
377	Duane Ward	.10
378	Greg Vaughn	.10
379	Jeff Fassero	.10
380	Jerry Dipoto	.10
381	John Patterson	.10
382	Kevin Brown	.25
383	Kevin Roberson	.10
384	Joe Orsulak	.10
385	Hilly Hathaway	.10
386	Mike Greenwell	.10
387	Orestes Destrade	.10
388	Mike Gallego	.10
389	Ozzie Guillen	.10
390	Raul Mondesi	.30
391	Scott Lydy	.10
392	Tom Urbani	.10
393	Wil Cordero	.10
394	Tony Longmire	.10
395	Todd Zeile	.10
396	Scott Cooper	.10
397	Ryne Sandberg	.75
398	Ricky Bones	.10
399	Phil Clark	.10
400	Orel Hershiser	.10
401	Mike Henneman	.10
402	Mark Lemke	.10
403	Mark Grace	.30
404	Ken Ryan	.10
405	John Smoltz	.15
406	Jeff Conine	.10
407	Greg Harris	.10
408	Doug Drabek	.10
409	Dave Fleming	.10
410	Danny Tartabull	.10
411	Chad Kreuter	.10
412	Brad Ausmus	.10
413	Ben McDonald	.10
414	Barry Larkin	.15
415	Bret Barberie	.10
416	Chuck Knoblauch	.10
417	Ozzie Smith	1.50
418	Ed Sprague	.10
419	Matt Williams	.30
420	Jeremy Hernandez	.10
421	Jose Bautista	.10
422	Kevin Mitchell	.10
423	Manuel Lee	.10
424	Mike Devereaux	.10
425	Omar Olivares	.10
426	Rafael Belliard	.10
427	Richie Lewis	.10
428	Ron Darling	.10
429	Shane Mack	.10
430	Tim Hulett	.10
431	Wally Joyner	.10
432	Wes Chamberlain	.10
433	Tom Browning	.10
434	Scott Radinsky	.10
435	Rondell White	.30
436	Rod Beck	.10
437	Rheal Cormier	.10
438	Randy Johnson	.75
439	Pete Schourek	.10
440	Mo Vaughn	.40
441	Mike Timlin	.10
442	Mark Langston	.10
443	Lou Whitaker	.10
444	Kevin Stocker	.10
445	Ken Hill	.10
446	John Wetteland	.10
447	J.T. Snow	.10
448	Erik Pappas	.10
449	David Hulse	.10
450	Darren Daulton	.10
451	Chris Hoiles	.10
452	Bryan Harvey	.10
453	Darren Lewis	.10
454	Andres Galarraga	.10
455	Joe Hesketh	.10
456	Jose Valentin	.10
457	Dan Peltier	.10
458	Joe Boever	.10
459	Kevin Rogers	.10
460	Craig Shipley	.10
461	Alvaro Espinoza	.10
462	Wilson Alvarez	.10
463	Cory Snyder	.10
464	Candy Maldonado	.10
465	Blas Minor	.10
466	Rod Bolton	.10
467	Kenny Rogers	.10
468	Greg Myers	.10
469	Jimmy Key	.10
470	Tony Castillo	.10
471	Mike Stanton	.10
472	Deion Sanders	.15
473	Tito Navarro	.10
474	Mike Gardiner	.10
475	Steve Reed	.10
476	John Roper	.10
477	Mike Trombley	.10
478	Charles Nagy	.10
479	Larry Casian	.10
480	Eric Hillman	.10
481	Bill Wertz	.10
482	Jeff Schwarz	.10
483	John Valentin	.10
484	Carl Willis	.10
485	Gary Gaetti	.10
486	Bill Pecota	.10
487	John Smiley	.10
488	Mike Mussina	.60
489	*Mike Ignasiak*	.10
490	Billy Brewer	.10
491	Jack Voigt	.10
492	Mike Munoz	.10
493	Lee Tinsley	.10
494	Bob Wickman	.10
495	Roger Salkeld	.10
496	Thomas Howard	.10
497	Mark Davis	.10
498	Dave Clark	.10
499	Turk Wendell	.10
500	Rafael Bournigal	.10
501	Chip Hale	.10
502	Matt Whiteside	.10
503	Brian Koelling	.10
504	Jeff Reed	.10
505	Paul Wagner	.10

No.	Player	MT
506	Torey Lovullo	.10
507	Curtis Leskanic	.10
508	Derek Lilliquist	.10
509	Joe Magrane	.10
510	Mackey Sasser	.10
511	Lloyd McClendon	.10
512	*Jayhawk Owens*	.10
513	*Woody Williams*	.10
514	Gary Redus	.10
515	Tim Spehr	.10
516	Jim Abbott	.10
517	Lou Frazier	.10
518	Erik Plantenberg	.10
519	Tim Worrell	.10
520	Brian McRae	.10
521	*Chan Ho Park*	1.50
522	Mark Wohlers	.10
523	Geronimo Pena	.10
524	Andy Ashby	.10
525	Tale of 2 Players (Tim Raines, Andre Dawson)	.10
526	Tale of 2 Players (Paul Molitor, Dave Winfield)	.35
527	Joe Carter (RBI Leader)	.10
528	Frank Thomas (HR Leader)	.90
529	Ken Griffey, Jr. (TB Leader)	1.25
530	Dave Justice (HR Leader)	.10
531	Gregg Jefferies (AVG Leader)	.10
532	Barry Bonds (HR Leader)	.90
533	John Kruk (Quick Start)	.10
534	Roger Clemens (Quick Start)	.75
535	Cecil Fielder (Quick Start)	.10
536	Ruben Sierra (Quick Start)	.10
537	Tony Gwynn (Quick Start)	.75
538	Tom Glavine (Quick Start)	.10
539	Not issued, see #269	
540	Not issued, see #270	
541	Ozzie Smith (Career Leader)	.75
542	Eddie Murray (Career Leader)	.40
543a	Lee Smith (Career Leader)	.10
543b	Lonnie Smith (should be #643)	.10
544	Greg Maddux	1.50
545	Denis Boucher	.10
546	Mark Gardner	.10
547	Bo Jackson	.15
548	Eric Anthony	.10
549	Delino DeShields	.10
550	Turner Ward	.10
551	Scott Sanderson	.10
552	Hector Carrasco	.10
553	Tony Phillips	.10
554	Melido Perez	.10
555	Mike Felder	.10
556	Jack Morris	.10
557	Rafael Palmeiro	.40
558	Shane Reynolds	.10
559	Pete Incaviglia	.10
560	Greg Harris	.10
561	Matt Walbeck	.10
562	Todd Van Poppel	.10
563	Todd Stottlemyre	.10
564	Ricky Bones	.10
565	Mike Jackson	.10
566	Kevin McReynolds	.10
567	Melvin Nieves	.10
568	Juan Gonzalez	.75
569	Frank Viola	.10
570	Vince Coleman	.10
571	*Brian Anderson*	.45
572	Omar Vizquel	.10
573	Bernie Williams	.40
574	Tom Glavine	.15
575	Mitch Williams	.10
576	Shawon Dunston	.10
577	Mike Lansing	.10
578	Greg Pirkl	.10
579	Sid Fernandez	.10
580	Doug Jones	.10
581	Walt Weiss	.10
582	Tim Belcher	.10
583	Alex Fernandez	.10
584	Alex Cole	.10
585	Greg Cadaret	.10
586	Bob Tewksbury	.10
587	Dave Hansen	.10
588	*Kurt Abbott*	.25
589	*Rick White*	.15
590	Kevin Bass	.10
591	Geronimo Berroa	.10
592	Jaime Navarro	.10
593	Steve Farr	.10
594	Jack Armstrong	.10
595	Steve Howe	.10
596	Jose Rijo	.10
597	Otis Nixon	.10
598	Robby Thompson	.10
599	Kelly Stinnett	.10
600	Carlos Delgado	.40
601	*Brian Johnson*	.10
602	Gregg Olson	.10
603	Jim Edmonds	.10
604	Mike Blowers	.10
605	Lee Smith	.10
606	Pat Rapp	.10
607	Mike Magnante	.10
608	Karl Rhodes	.10
609	Jeff Juden	.10
610	Rusty Meacham	.10
611	Pedro Martinez	.75
612	Todd Worrell	.10
613	Stan Javier	.10
614	Mike Hampton	.10
615	Jose Guzman	.10
616	Xavier Hernandez	.10
617	David Wells	.10
618	John Habyan	.10
619	Chris Nabholz	.10
620	Bobby Jones	.10
621	Chris James	.10
622	Ellis Burks	.10
623	Erik Hanson	.10
624	Pat Meares	.10
625	Harold Reynolds	.10
626	Bob Hamelin (Rookie Rocker)	.10
627	Manny Ramirez (Rookie Rocker)	.40
628	Ryan Klesko (Rookie Rocker)	.10
629	Carlos Delgado (Rookie Rocker)	.25
630	Javier Lopez (Rookie Rocker)	.10
631	Steve Karsay (Rookie Rocket)	.10
632	Rick Helling (Rookie Rocket)	.10
633	Steve Trachsel (Rookie Rocket)	.10
634	Hector Carrasco (Rookie Rocket)	.10
635	Andy Stankiewicz	.10
636	Paul Sorrento	.10
637	Scott Erickson	.10
638	Chipper Jones	2.00
639	Luis Polonia	.10
640	Howard Johnson	.10
641	John Dopson	.10
642	Jody Reed	.10
643	Not issued, see #543	
644	Mark Portugal	.10
645	Paul Molitor	.75
646	Paul Assenmacher	.10
647	Hubie Brooks	.10
648	Gary Wayne	.10
649	Sean Berry	.10
650	Roger Clemens	1.50
651	Brian Hunter	.10
652	Wally Whitehurst	.10
653	Allen Watson	.10
654	Rickey Henderson	.75
655	Sid Bream	.10
656	Dan Wilson	.10
657	Ricky Jordan	.10
658	Sterling Hitchcock	.10
659	Darrin Jackson	.10
660	Junior Felix	.10
661	Tom Brunansky	.10
662	Jose Vizcaino	.10
663	Mark Leiter	.10
664	Gil Heredia	.10
665	Fred McGriff	.10
666	Will Clark	.30
667	Al Leiter	.10
668	James Mouton	.10
669	Billy Bean	.10
670	Scott Leius	.10
671	Bret Boone	.15
672	Darren Holmes	.10
673	Dave Weathers	.10
674	Eddie Murray	.65
675	Felix Fermin	.10
676	Chris Sabo	.10
677	Billy Spiers	.10
678	Aaron Sele	.10
679	Juan Samuel	.10
680	Julio Franco	.10
681	Heathcliff Slocumb	.10
682	Denny Martinez	.10
683	Jerry Browne	.10
684	*Pedro A. Martinez*	.10
685	Rex Hudler	.10
686	Willie McGee	.10
687	Andy Van Slyke	.10
688	Pat Mahomes	.10
689	Dave Henderson	.10
690	Tony Eusebio	.10
691	Rick Sutcliffe	.10
692	Willie Banks	.10
693	Alan Mills	.10
694	Jeff Treadway	.10
695	Alex Gonzalez	.15
696	David Segui	.10
697	Rick Helling	.10
698	Bip Roberts	.10
699	*Jeff Cirillo*	.25
700	Terry Mulholland	.10
701	Marvin Freeman	.10
702	Jason Bere	.10
703	Javier Lopez	.10
704	Greg Hibbard	.10
705	Tommy Greene	.10
706	Marquis Grissom	.10
707	Brian Harper	.10
708	Steve Karsay	.10
709	Jeff Brantley	.10
710	Jeff Russell	.10
711	Bryan Hickerson	.10
712	*Jim Pittsley*	.10
713	Bobby Ayala	.10
714	John Smoltz (Fantastic Finisher)	.10
715	Jose Rijo (Fantastic Finisher)	.10
716	Greg Maddux (Fantastic Finisher)	.75
717	Matt Williams (Fantastic Finisher)	.15
718	Frank Thomas (Fantastic Finisher)	.90
719	Ryne Sandberg (Fantastic Finisher)	.40
720	Checklist	.10

1994 Stadium Club 1st Day Issue

A special silver-foil embossment designating "1st Day Issue" was placed on fewer than 2,000 of each of the 720 regular cards in the '94 Stadium Club set. Inserted at the rate of one per 24 foil packs and one per 15 jumbo packs, the cards are otherwise identical to the regular TSC cards.

	MT
Common Player:	1.50
Stars:	10x

(See 1994 Stadium Club for checklist and base card values.)

1994 Stadium Club Golden Rainbow

Found at the rate of one per pack, Stadium Club "Golden Rainbow" cards were issued for each of the 720 cards in the regular set. These inserts are distinguished by the use of gold prismatic foil highlights for the S.C. logo and box with the player's last name, instead of the red foil found on regular S.C. cards.

	MT
Complete Set (720):	125.00
Common Player:	.50
Stars:	3X

(See 1994 Stadium Club for checklist and base card values.)

1994 Stadium Club Dugout Dirt

Cartoons of some of baseball's top stars are featured on the backs of this 12-card insert set. Fronts are virtually identical in format to regular S.C. cards, except the logo and box with the player's last name are in gold-foil, rather than red. Stated odds of finding a Dugout Dirt insert card were one per six packs, on average. Cards can also be found with a gold "Members Only" seal on front.

#	Player	MT
	Complete Set (12):	10.00
	Common Player:	.25
1	Mike Piazza (Catch of the Day)	2.00
2	Dave Winfield (The Road to 3,000)	1.00
3	John Kruk (From Coal Mine to Gold Mine)	.25
4	Cal Ripken, Jr. (On Track)	3.00
5	Jack McDowell (Chin Music)	.25
6	Barry Bonds (The Bonds Market)	1.50
7	Ken Griffey, Jr. (Gold Gloves/All-Star)	2.50
8	Tim Salmon (The Salmon Run)	.35
9	Frank Thomas (Big Hurt)	1.50
10	Jeff Kent (Super Kent)	.25
11	Randy Johnson (High Heat)	.50
12	Darren Daulton (Daulton's Gym)	.25

1994 Stadium Club Finest

This insert set was included only in Series III packs of Topps Stadium Club, at the rate of one card per six packs, on average. Cards utilize Topps Finest technology and feature a player action photo on front, set against a red-and-gold sunburst background. Backs have a player portrait photo, a few stats and appropriate logos. Cards can also be found with a "Members Only" logo on front.

#	Player	MT
	Complete Set (10):	12.00
	Common Player:	.50
1	Jeff Bagwell	1.25
2	Albert Belle	.75
3	Barry Bonds	2.00
4	Juan Gonzalez	1.25
5	Ken Griffey, Jr.	4.00
6	Marquis Grissom	.50
7	David Justice	.65
8	Mike Piazza	2.50
9	Tim Salmon	.75
10	Frank Thomas	2.00

1994 Stadium Club Finest Jumbo

Found only as a one per tub insert in special Wal-Mart repackaging of baseball packs, these 5" x 7" versions of the Series III Stadium Club inserts are identical to the smaller version. Cards utilize Topps Finest technology and feature a player action photo on front, set against a red-and-gold sunburst background. Backs have a player portrait photo, a few stats and appropriate logos.

#	Player	MT
	Complete Set (10):	60.00
	Common Player:	4.00
1	Jeff Bagwell	7.50
2	Albert Belle	6.00
3	Barry Bonds	9.00
4	Juan Gonzalez	7.50
5	Ken Griffey, Jr.	12.50
6	Marquis Grissom	4.00
7	David Justice	6.00
8	Mike Piazza	10.00
9	Tim Salmon	6.00
10	Frank Thomas	9.00

1994 Stadium Club Super Teams

With its football card issue the previous year, Topps Stadium Club debuted the idea of an insert card set whose value rose and fell with the on-field performance of each team. Super Team cards were issued for each of the 28 major league teams and inserted at the rate of one per 24 regular packs and one per 15 jumbo packs. At the end of the 1995 season (the promotion was carried over when the 1994 season was ended prematurely by the players' strike), persons holding Super Team cards of the division winners, league champions and World Champions could redeem the cards for prizes. Division winning team cards could be redeembed for a set of 10 S.C. cards of that team with a special division winner embossed logo. League champion cards could be redeemed for a set of 10 Master Photos of the team with a special league logo embossed. Persons with a Super Team card of the eventual World Series champion could trade the card in for a complete set of Stadium Club cards embossed with a World's Champion logo. Each of the Super Team cards features a small group of players on the front with the Super Team Card and S.C. logos in gold foil, and the team name in prismatic foil. Backs contain redemption rules. A version of the Super Team cards was distributed with "Members Only" sets containing such an indicia on front and team roster on back.

#	Team	MT
	Complete Set (28):	50.00
	Common Team:	1.50
	Expired Jan. 31, 1996	
1	Atlanta Braves	10.00
2	Chicago Cubs	1.50
3	Cincinnati Reds	2.50
4	Colorado Rockies	2.00
5	Florida Marlins	1.50
6	Houston Astros	2.00
7	Los Angeles Dodgers	3.00
8	Montreal Expos	2.00
9	New York Mets	1.50
10	Philadelphia Phillies	1.50
11	Pittsburgh Pirates	1.50
12	St. Louis Cardinals	1.50
13	San Diego Padres	1.50
14	San Francisco Giants	2.50
15	Baltimore Orioles	2.50
16	Boston Red Sox	2.00
17	California Angels	1.50
18	Chicago White Sox	3.00
19	Cleveland Indians	4.00
20	Detroit Tigers	1.50
21	Kansas City Royals	2.00
22	Milwaukee Brewers	1.50
23	Minnesota Twins	2.00
24	New York Yankees	3.00
25	Oakland Athletics	2.00
26	Seattle Mariners	4.00
27	Texas Rangers	2.00
28	Toronto Blue Jays	2.00

1994 Stadium Club Superstar Sampler

A small, round black-and-white "Topps Superstar Sampler" logo printed on the back is all that distinguishes these cards from regular-issue S.C. cards. This version of 45 of the top stars from the Stadium Club set was issued only in three-card cello packs inserted into 1994 Topps retail factory sets. The packs also contained the same player's cards from the Bowman and Finest sets, similarly marked.

#	Player	MT
	Complete Set (45):	160.00
	Common Player:	2.00
4	Gary Sheffield	2.50
10	Roberto Alomar	5.00
24	Jack McDowell	2.00
25	Cecil Fielder	2.00
36	Tim Salmon	2.50
59	Bobby Bonilla	2.00
85	Ken Griffey Jr.	20.00
94	Dave Justice	2.50
108	Jeff Bagwell	6.00
109	Gregg Jefferies	2.00
127	Cliff Floyd	2.00
140	Mike Piazza	18.00
151	Tony Gwynn	10.00
165	Len Dykstra	2.00
169	Carlos Baerga	2.00
171	Jose Canseco	4.00
195	Don Mattingly	16.00
203	Will Clark	2.00
208	Rafael Palmeiro	2.50
219	Albert Belle	2.50
228	John Olerud	2.00
238	Barry Bonds	16.00
280	Larry Walker	2.50
285	Frank Thomas	16.00
300	Joe Carter	2.00
320	Manny Ramirez	6.00
359	Kirby Puckett	10.00
373	Cal Ripken Jr.	24.00
390	Raul Mondesi	2.50
397	Ryne Sandberg	7.50
403	Mark Grace	3.50
414	Barry Larkin	2.00
419	Matt Williams	2.00
438	Randy Johnson	5.00
440	Mo Vaughn	3.00
450	Darren Daulton	2.00
454	Andres Galarraga	2.00
544	Greg Maddux	10.00
568	Juan Gonzalez	6.00
574	Tom Glavine	2.50
645	Paul Molitor	5.00
650	Roger Clemens	10.00
665	Fred McGriff	2.00
687	Andy Van Slyke	2.00
706	Marquis Grissom	2.00

1994 Stadium Club Draft Picks

Produced well after the end of the strike-truncated

1994 baseball season, this set was largely ignored by the hobby at the time of issue. The full-bleed card fronts feature up-close and personal poses of 1994's top draft picks in major league uniforms, giving the hobby a good first look at tomorrow's stars. A home plate design in an upper corner has "Draft '94 Pick" in gold-foil. The player's name is printed in gold foil down one of the sides. Backs are horizontally arranged and have a particolored background that includes standard scouting report phrases. There is another color portrait of the player at one end with his name and position printed above. At the opposite end are the team by which the player was drafted, a few biographical details, some amateur and pro career highlights and a box detailing how the team's other recent draft picks at that round have fared. A "Members Only" version of the set also produced, with each card bearing the round gold-foil MO seal. Though much scarcer than the regular cards, they have attained little or no premium value.

		MT
Complete Set (90):		17.50
Common Player:		.15
1	Jacob Shumate	.15
2	C.J. Nitkowski	.25
3	Doug Million	.15
4	Matt Smith	.15
5	Kevin Lovinger	.15
6	Alberto Castillo	.15
7	Mike Russell	.15
8	Dan Lock	.15
9	Tom Szimanski	.15
10	Aaron Boone	.45
11	Jayson Peterson	.15
12	Mark Johnson	.30
13	Cade Gaspar	.15
14	George Lombard	.50
15	Russ Johnson	.40
16	Travis Miller	.25
17	Jay Payton	1.00
18	Brian Buchanan	.25
19	Jacob Cruz	.25
20	Gary Rath	.15
21	Ramon Castro	.15
22	Tommy Davis	.15
23	Tony Terry	.15
24	Jerry Whittaker	.15
25	Mike Darr	.15
26	Doug Webb	.15
27	Jason Camilli	.15
28	Brad Rigby	.15
29	Ryan Nye	.15
30	Carl Dale	.15
31	Andy Taulbee	.15
32	Trey Moore	.15
33	John Crowther	.15
34	Joe Giuliano	.15
35	Brian Rose	.15
36	Paul Failla	.15
37	Brian Meadows	.15
38	Oscar Robles	.15
39	Mike Metcalff	.15
40	Larry Barnes	.15
41	Paul Ottavinia	.15
42	Chris McBride	.15
43	Ricky Stone	.15
44	Billy Blythe	.15
45	Eddie Priest	.15
46	Scott Forster	.15
47	Eric Pickett	.15
48	Matt Beaumont	.15
49	Darrell Nicolas	.15
50	Mike Hampton	.15
51	Paul O'Malley	.15
52	Steve Shoemaker	.15
53	Jason Sikes	.15
54	Bryan Farson	.15
55	Yates Hall	.15
56	Troy Brohawn	.15
57	Dan Hower	.15
58	Clay Caruthers	.15
59	Pepe McNeal	.15
60	Ray Ricken	.15
61	Scott Shores	.15
62	Eddie Brooks	.15
63	Dave Kauflin	.15
64	David Meyer	.15
65	Geoff Blum	.15
66	Roy Marsh	.15
67	Ryan Beeney	.15
68	Derek Dukart	.15
69	Nomar Garciaparra	5.00
70	Jason Kelley	.15
71	Jesse Ibarra	.15
72	Bucky Buckles	.15
73	Mark Little	.15
74	Heath Murray	.15
75	Greg Morris	.15
76	Mike Halperin	.15
77	Wes Helms	.25
78	Ray Brown	.15
79	Kevin Brown	.15
80	Paul Konerko	.50
81	Mike Thurman	.15
82	Paul Wilson	.50
83	Terrence Long	.50
84	Ben Grieve	1.50
85	Mark Farris	.50
86	Bret Wagner	.15
87	Dustin Hermanson	.75
88	Kevin Witt	.15
89	Corey Pointer	.15
90	Tim Grieve	.15

1994 Stadium Club Draft Picks First Day Issue

Identical to the regular-issue S.C. Draft Picks cards except for a silver-foil First Day Issue logo on front, this parallel set was found on the average of one card per six packs of S.C. Draft Picks.

	MT
Complete Set (90):	150.00
Common Player:	1.00
Stars:	6X

(See 1994 Stadium Club Draft Picks for checklist and base card values.)

1995 Stadium Club

Topps' upscale brand was issued for 1995 in three series of, respectively, 270, 225 and 135 cards. Fronts have borderless color photos with a gold-foil device at bottom holding the team logo. Also in gold are the player's name at bottom and the Stadium Club logo at top. Backs have another player photo at left with a pair of computer-enhanced close-ups above it. At right are bar graphs detailing the player's '94 stats and his skills rankings. A number of specially designed subsets - "Best Seat in the House, Cover Story, MLB Debut," etc., are spread throughout the issue, which also includes a full slate of chase cards depending on the series and packaging.

		MT
Complete Set (630):		45.00
Complete Series 1 (270):		17.50
Complete Series 2 (225):		17.50
Complete High Series (135):		12.50
Common Player:		.10
Series 1 or 2 Pack (14):		1.50
Series 1 or 2 Wax Box (24):		25.00
Series 3 Pack (13):		2.00
Series 3 Wax Box (24):		30.00
1	Cal Ripken Jr.	2.50
2	Bo Jackson	.15
3	Bryan Harvey	.10
4	Curt Schilling	.25
5	Bruce Ruffin	.10
6	Travis Fryman	.10
7	Jim Abbott	.10
8	David McCarty	.10
9	Gary Gaetti	.10
10	Roger Clemens	1.00
11	Carlos Garcia	.10
12	Lee Smith	.10
13	Bobby Ayala	.10
14	Charles Nagy	.10
15	Lou Frazier	.10
16	Rene Arocha	.10
17	Carlos Delgado	.30
18	Steve Finley	.10
19	Ryan Klesko	.10
20	Cal Eldred	.10
21	Rey Sanchez	.10
22	Ken Hill	.10
23	Benny Santiago	.10
24	Julian Tavarez	.10
25	Jose Vizcaino	.10
26	Andy Benes	.10
27	Mariano Duncan	.10
28	Checklist A	.10
29	Shawon Dunston	.10
30	Rafael Palmeiro	.35
31	Dean Palmer	.10
32	Andres Galarraga	.10
33	Joey Cora	.10
34	Mickey Tettleton	.10
35	Barry Larkin	.15
36	Carlos Baerga	.10
37	Orel Hershiser	.10
38	Jody Reed	.10
39	Paul Molitor	.60
40	Jim Edmonds	.10
41	Bob Tewksbury	.10
42	John Patterson	.10
43	Ray McDavid	.10
44	Zane Smith	.10
45	Bret Saberhagen	.10
46	Greg Maddux	1.00
47	Frank Thomas	1.00
48	Carlos Baerga	.10
49	Billy Spiers	.10
50	Stan Javier	.10
51	Rex Hudler	.10
52	Denny Hocking	.10
53	Todd Worrell	.10
54	Mark Clark	.10
55	Hipilito Pichardo	.10
56	Bob Wickman	.10
57	Raul Mondesi	.30
58	Steve Cooke	.10
59	Rod Beck	.10
60	Tim Davis	.10
61	Jeff Kent	.10
62	John Valentin	.10
63	Alex Arias	.10
64	Steve Reed	.10
65	Ozzie Smith	1.00
66	Terry Pendleton	.10
67	Kenny Rogers	.10
68	Vince Coleman	.10
69	Tom Pagnozzi	.10
70	Roberto Alomar	.60
71	Darrin Jackson	.10
72	Dennis Eckersley	.10
73	Jay Buhner	.10
74	Darren Lewis	.10
75	Dave Weathers	.10
76	Matt Walbeck	.10
77	Brad Ausmus	.10
78	Danny Bautista	.10
79	Bob Hamelin	.10
80	Steve Traschel	.10
81	Ken Ryan	.10
82	Chris Turner	.10
83	David Segui	.10
84	Ben McDonald	.10
85	Wade Boggs	.50
86	John Vander Wal	.10
87	Sandy Alomar	.10
88	Ron Karkovice	.10
89	Doug Jones	.10
90	Gary Sheffield	.30
91	Ken Caminiti	.10
92	Chris Bosio	.10
93	Kevin Tapani	.10
94	Walt Weiss	.10
95	Erik Hanson	.10
96	Ruben Sierra	.10
97	Nomar Garciaparra	1.50
98	Terrence Long	.10
99	Jacob Shumate	.10
100	Paul Wilson	.10
101	Kevin Witt	.10
102	Paul Konerko	.20
103	Ben Grieve	.50
104	*Mark Johnson*	.10
105	*Cade Gaspar*	.10
106	Mark Farris	.10
107	Dustin Hermanson	.15
108	*Scott Elarton*	.75
109	Doug Million	.10
110	Matt Smith	.10
111	*Brian Buchanan*	.20
112	*Jayson Peterson*	.20
113	Bret Wagner	.10
114	C.J. Nitkowski	.10
115	*Ramon Castro*	.10
116	Rafael Bournigal	.10
117	Jeff Fassero	.10
118	Bobby Bonilla	.10
119	Ricky Gutierrez	.10
120	Roger Pavlik	.10
121	Mike Greenwell	.10
122	Deion Sanders	.15
123	Charlie Hayes	.10
124	Paul O'Neill	.10
125	Jay Bell	.10
126	Royce Clayton	.10
127	Willie Banks	.10
128	Mark Wohlers	.10
129	Todd Jones	.10
130	Todd Stottlemyre	.10

131 Will Clark .30
132 Wilson Alvarez .10
133 Chili Davis .10
134 Dave Burba .10
135 Chris Hoiles .10
136 Jeff Blauser .10
137 Jeff Reboulet .10
138 Bret Saberhagen .10
139 Kirk Rueter .10
140 Dave Nilsson .10
141 Pat Borders .10
142 Ron Darling .10
143 Derek Bell .10
144 Dave Hollins .10
145 Juan Gonzalez .75
146 Andre Dawson .10
147 Jim Thome .10
148 Larry Walker .30
149 Mike Piazza 1.75
150 Mike Perez .10
151 Steve Avery .10
152 Dan Wilson .10
153 Andy Van Slyke .10
154 Junior Felix .10
155 Jack McDowell .10
156 Danny Tartabull .10
157 Willie Blair .10
158 William Van Landingham .10
159 Robb Nen .10
160 Lee Tinsley .10
161 Ismael Valdes .10
162 Juan Guzman .10
163 Scott Servais .10
164 Cliff Floyd .10
165 Allen Watson .10
166 Eddie Taubensee .10
167 Scott Hemond .10
168 Jeff Tackett .10
169 Chad Curtis .10
170 Rico Brogna .10
171 Luis Polonia .10
172 Checklist B .10
173 Lance Johnson .10
174 Sammy Sosa 1.50
175 Mike MacFarlane .10
176 Darryl Hamilton .10
177 Rick Aguilera .10
178 Dave West .10
179 Mike Gallego .10
180 Marc Newfield .10
181 Steve Buechele .10
182 David Wells .10
183 Tom Glavine .15
184 Joe Girardi .10
185 Craig Biggio .15
186 Eddie Murray .60
187 Kevin Gross .10
188 Sid Fernandez .10
189 John Franco .10
190 Bernard Gilkey .10
191 Matt Williams .30
192 Darrin Fletcher .10
193 Jeff Conine .10
194 Ed Sprague .10
195 Eduardo Perez .10
196 Scott Livingstone .10
197 Ivan Rodriguez .75
198 Orlando Merced .10
199 Ricky Bones .10
200 Javier Lopez .10
201 Miguel Jimenez .10
202 Terry McGriff .10
203 Mike Lieberthal .10
204 David Cone .10
205 Todd Hundley .10
206 Ozzie Guillen .10
207 Alex Cole .10
208 Tony Phillips .10
209 Jim Eisenreich .10
210 Greg Vaughn .10
211 Barry Larkin .15
212 Don Mattingly 1.50
213 Mark Grace .35
214 Jose Canseco .60
215 Joe Carter .10
216 David Cone .10
217 Sandy Alomar .10
218 Al Martin .10
219 Roberto Kelly .10
220 Paul Sorrento .10
221 Tony Fernandez .10
222 Stan Belinda .10
223 Mike Stanley .10
224 Doug Drabek .10
225 Todd Van Poppel .10
226 Matt Mieske .10
227 Tino Martinez .10
228 Andy Ashby .10
229 Midre Cummings .10
230 Jeff Frye .10
231 Hal Morris .10
232 Jose Lind .10
233 Shawn Green .30
234 Rafael Belliard .10
235 Randy Myers .10
236 Frank Thomas 1.00
237 Darren Daulton .10
238 Sammy Sosa 1.50
239 Cal Ripken Jr. 1.25
240 Jeff Bagwell 1.00
241 Ken Griffey Jr. 2.00
242 Brett Butler .10
243 Derrick May .10
244 Pat Listach .10
245 Mike Bordick .10
246 Mark Langston .10
247 Randy Velarde .10
248 Julio Franco .10
249 Chuck Knoblauch .10
250 Bill Gullickson .10
251 Dave Henderson .10
252 Bret Boone .15
253 Al Martin .10
254 Armando Benitez .10
255 Wil Cordero .10
256 Al Leiter .10
257 Luis Gonzalez .35
258 Charlie O'Brien .10
259 Tim Wallach .10
260 Scott Sanders .10
261 Tom Henke .10
262 Otis Nixon .10
263 Darren Daulton .10
264 Manny Ramirez .75
265 Bret Barberie .10
266 Mel Rojas .10
267 John Burkett .10
268 Brady Anderson .10
269 John Roper .10
270 Shane Reynolds .10
271 Barry Bonds 1.50
272 Alex Fernandez .10
273 Brian McRae .10
274 Todd Zeile .10
275 Greg Swindell .10
276 Johnny Ruffin .10
277 Troy Neel .10
278 Eric Karros .10
279 John Hudek .10
280 Thomas Howard .10
281 Joe Carter .10
282 Mike Devereaux .10
283 Butch Henry .10
284 Reggie Jefferson .10
285 Mark Lemke .10
286 Jeff Montgomery .10
287 Ryan Thompson .10
288 Paul Shuey .10
289 Mark McGwire 2.50
290 Bernie Williams .40
291 Mickey Morandini .10
292 Scott Leius .10
293 David Hulse .10
294 Greg Gagne .10
295 Moises Alou .15
296 Geronimo Berroa .10
297 Eddie Zambrano .10
298 Alan Trammell .10
299 Don Slaught .10
300 Jose Rijo .10
301 Joe Ausanio .10
302 Tim Raines .10
303 Melido Perez .10
304 Kent Mercker .10
305 James Mouton .10
306 Luis Lopez .10
307 Mike Kingery .10
308 Willie Greene .10
309 Cecil Fielder .10
310 Scott Kamieniecki .10
311 Mike Greenwell (Best Seat in the House) .10
312 Bobby Bonilla (Best Seat in the House) .10
313 Andres Galarraga (Best Seat in the House) .10
314 Cal Ripken Jr. (Best Seat in the House) 1.25
315 Matt Williams (Best Seat in the House) .15
316 Tom Pagnozzi (Best Seat in the House) .10
317 Len Dykstra (Best Seat in the House) .10
318 Frank Thomas (Best Seat in the House) .50
319 Kirby Puckett (Best Seat in the House) .50
320 Mike Piazza (Best Seat in the House) .75
321 Jason Jacome .10
322 Brian Hunter .10
323 Brent Gates .10
324 Jim Converse .10
325 Damion Easley .10
326 Dante Bichette .10
327 Kurt Abbott .10
328 Scott Cooper .10
329 Mike Henneman .10
330 Orlando Miller .10
331 John Kruk .10
332 Jose Oliva .10
333 Reggie Sanders .10
334 Omar Vizquel .10
335 Devon White .10
336 Mike Morgan .10
337 J.R. Phillips .10
338 Gary DiSarcina .10
339 Joey Hamilton .10
340 Randy Johnson .65
341 Jim Leyritz .10
342 Bobby Jones .10
343 Jaime Navarro .10
344 Bip Roberts .10
345 Steve Karsay .10
346 Kevin Stocker .10
347 Jose Canseco .50
348 Bill Wegman .10
349 Rondell White .30
350 Mo Vaughn .40
351 Joe Orsulak .10
352 Pat Meares .10
353 Albie Lopez .10
354 Edgar Martinez .10
355 Brian Jordan .10
356 Tommy Greene .10
357 Chuck Carr .10
358 Pedro Astacio .10
359 Russ Davis .10
360 Chris Hammond .10
361 Gregg Jefferies .10
362 Shane Mack .10
363 Fred McGriff .10
364 Pat Rapp .10
365 Bill Swift .10
366 Checklist .10
367 Robin Ventura .10
368 Bobby Witt .10
369 Karl Rhodes .10
370 Eddie Williams .10
371 John Jaha .10
372 Steve Howe .10
373 Leo Gomez .10
374 Hector Fajardo .10
375 Jeff Bagwell .75
376 Mark Acre .10
377 Wayne Kirby .10
378 Mark Portugal .10
379 Jesus Tavarez .10
380 Jim Lindeman .10
381 Don Mattingly 1.50
382 Trevor Hoffman .10
383 Chris Gomez .10
384 Garret Anderson .10
385 Bobby Munoz .10
386 Jon Lieber .10
387 Rick Helling .10
388 Marvin Freeman .10
389 Juan Castillo .10
390 Jeff Cirillo .10
391 Sean Berry .10
392 Hector Carrasco .10
393 Mark Grace .35
394 Pat Kelly .10
395 Tim Naehring .10
396 Greg Pirkl .10
397 John Smoltz .15
398 Robby Thompson .10
399 Rick White .10
400 Frank Thomas 1.00
401 Jeff Conine (Cover Story) .10
402 Jose Valentin (Cover Story) .10
403 Carlos Baerga (Cover Story) .10
404 Rick Aguilera (Cover Story) .10
405 Wilson Alvarez (Cover Story) .10
406 Juan Gonzalez (Cover Story) .40
407 Barry Larkin (Cover Story) .10
408 Ken Hill (Cover Story) .10
409 Chuck Carr (Cover Story) .10
410 Tim Raines (Cover Story) .10
411 Bryan Eversgerd .10
412 Phil Plantier .10
413 Josias Manzanillo .10
414 Roberto Kelly .10
415 Rickey Henderson .65
416 John Smiley .10
417 Kevin Brown .25
418 Jimmy Key .10
419 Wally Joyner .10
420 Roberto Hernandez .10
421 Felix Fermin .10
422 Checklist .10
423 Greg Vaughn .10
424 Ray Lankford .10
425 Greg Maddux 1.00
426 Mike Mussina .55
427 Geronimo Pena .10
428 David Nied .10
429 Scott Erickson .10
430 Kevin Mitchell .10
431 Mike Lansing .10
432 Brian Anderson .10
433 Jeff King .10
434 Ramon Martinez .10
435 Kevin Seitzer .10
436 Salomon Torres .10
437 Brian Hunter .10
438 Melvin Nieves .10
439 Mike Kelly .10
440 Marquis Grissom .10
441 Chuck Finley .10
442 Len Dykstra .10
443 Ellis Burks .10
444 Harold Baines .10
445 Kevin Appier .10
446 Dave Justice .30
447 Darryl Kile .10
448 John Olerud .10
449 Greg McMichael .10
450 Kirby Puckett 1.00
451 Jose Valentin .10
452 Rick Wilkins .10
453 Arthur Rhodes .10
454 Pat Hentgen .10
455 Tom Gordon .10
456 Tom Candiotti .10
457 Jason Bere .10
458 Wes Chamberlain .10
459 Greg Colbrunn .10
460 John Doherty .10
461 Kevin Foster .10
462 Mark Whiten .10
463 Terry Steinbach .10
464 Aaron Sele .10
465 Kirt Manwaring .10
466 Darren Hall .10
467 Delino DeShields .10
468 Andujar Cedeno .10
469 Billy Ashley .10
470 Kenny Lofton .10
471 Pedro Munoz .10
472 John Wetteland .10
473 Tim Salmon .25
474 Denny Neagle .10
475 Tony Gwynn 1.00
476 Vinny Castilla .10
477 Steve Dreyer .10
478 Jeff Shaw .10
479 Chad Ogea .10
480 Scott Ruffcorn .10
481 Lou Whitaker .10
482 J.T. Snow .10
483 Rich Rowland .10
484 Dennis Martinez .10

#	Player	Value
485	Pedro Martinez	.60
486	Rusty Greer	.10
487	Dave Fleming	.10
488	John Dettmer	.10
489	Albert Belle	.35
490	Ravelo Manzanillo	.10
491	Henry Rodriguez	.10
492	Andrew Lorraine	.10
493	Dwayne Hosey	.10
494	Mike Blowers	.10
495	Turner Ward	.10
496	Fred McGriff (Extreme Corps)	.10
497	Sammy Sosa (Extreme Corps)	.75
498	Barry Larkin (Extreme Corps)	.10
499	Andres Galarraga (Extreme Corps)	.10
500	Gary Sheffield (Extreme Corps)	.20
501	Jeff Bagwell (Extreme Corps)	.40
502	Mike Piazza (Extreme Corps)	.75
503	Moises Alou (Extreme Corps)	.15
504	Bobby Bonilla (Extreme Corps)	.10
505	Darren Daulton (Extreme Corps)	.10
506	Jeff King (Extreme Corps)	.10
507	Ray Lankford (Extreme Corps)	.10
508	Tony Gwynn (Extreme Corps)	.50
509	Barry Bonds (Extreme Corps)	.75
510	Cal Ripken Jr. (Extreme Corps)	1.25
511	Mo Vaughn (Extreme Corps)	.20
512	Tim Salmon (Extreme Corps)	.15
513	Frank Thomas (Extreme Corps)	.75
514	Albert Belle (Extreme Corps)	.20
515	Cecil Fielder (Extreme Corps)	.10
516	Kevin Appier (Extreme Corps)	.10
517	Greg Vaughn (Extreme Corps)	.10
518	Kirby Puckett (Extreme Corps)	.50
519	Paul O'Neill (Extreme Corps)	.10
520	Ruben Sierra (Extreme Corps)	.10
521	Ken Griffey Jr. (Extreme Corps)	1.00
522	Will Clark (Extreme Corps)	.15
523	Joe Carter (Extreme Corps)	.10
524	Antonio Osuna	.10
525	Glenallen Hill	.10
526	Alex Gonzalez	.15
527	Dave Stewart	.10
528	Ron Gant	.10
529	Jason Bates	.10
530	Mike Macfarlane	.10
531	Esteban Loaiza	.10
532	Joe Randa	.10
533	Dave Winfield	1.00
534	Danny Darwin	.10
535	Pete Harnisch	.10
536	Joey Cora	.10
537	Jaime Navarro	.10
538	Marty Cordova	.10
539	Andujar Cedeno	.10
540	Mickey Tettleton	.10
541	Andy Van Slyke	.10
542	*Carlos Perez*	.10
543	Chipper Jones	1.75
544	Tony Fernandez	.10
545	Tom Henke	.10
546	Pat Borders	.10
547	Chad Curtis	.10
548	Ray Durham	.10
549	Joe Oliver	.10
550	Jose Mesa	.10
551	Steve Finley	.10
552	Otis Nixon	.10
553	Jacob Brumfield	.10
554	Bill Swift	.10
555	Quilvio Veras	.10
556	*Hideo Nomo*	2.00
557	Joe Vitiello	.10
558	Mike Perez	.10
559	Charlie Hayes	.10
560	*Brad Radke*	.20
561	Darren Bragg	.10
562	Orel Hershiser	.10
563	Edgardo Alfonzo	.10
564	Doug Jones	.10
565	Andy Pettitte	.30
566	Benito Santiago	.10
567	John Burkett	.10
568	Brad Clontz	.10
569	Jim Abbott	.10
570	Joe Rosselli	.10
571	*Mark Grudzielanek*	.50
572	Dustin Hermanson	.10
573	Benji Gil	.10
574	Mark Whiten	.10
575	Mike Ignasiak	.10
576	Kevin Ritz	.10
577	Paul Quantrill	.10
578	Andre Dawson	.20
579	Jerald Clark	.10
580	Frank Rodriguez	.10
581	Mark Kiefer	.10
582	Trevor Wilson	.10
583	*Gary Wilson*	.10
584	Andy Stankiewicz	.10
585	Felipe Lira	.10
586	*Mike Mimbs*	.10
587	Jon Nunnally	.10
588	*Tomas Perez*	.10
589	Checklist	.10
590	Todd Hollandsworth	.10
591	Roberto Petagine	.10
592	Mariano Rivera	.30
593	Mark McLemore	.10
594	Bobby Witt	.10
595	Jose Offerman	.10
596	Jason Christiansen	.10
597	Jeff Manto	.10
598	Jim Dougherty	.10
599	Juan Acevedo	.10
600	Troy O'Leary	.10
601	Ron Villone	.10
602	Tripp Cromer	.10
603	Steve Scarsone	.10
604	Lance Parrish	.10
605	Ozzie Timmons	.10
606	Ray Holbert	.10
607	Tony Phillips	.10
608	Phil Plantier	.10
609	Shane Andrews	.10
610	Heathcliff Slocumb	.10
611	*Bobby Higginson*	1.00
612	Bob Tewksbury	.10
613	Terry Pendleton	.10
614	Scott Cooper (Trans-Action)	.10
615	John Wetteland (Trans-Action)	.10
616	Ken Hill (Trans-Action)	.10
617	Marquis Grissom (Trans-Action)	.10
618	Larry Walker (Trans-Action)	.15
619	Derek Bell (Trans-Action)	.10
620	David Cone (Trans-Action)	.10
621	Ken Caminiti (Trans-Action)	.10
622	Jack McDowell (Trans-Action)	.10
623	Vaughn Eshelman (Trans-Action)	.10
624	Brian McRae (Trans-Action)	.10
625	Gregg Jefferies (Trans-Action)	.10
626	Kevin Brown (Trans-Action)	.15
627	Lee Smith (Trans-Action)	.10
628	Tony Tarasco (Trans-Action)	.10
629	Brett Butler (Trans-Action)	.10
630	Jose Canseco (Trans-Action)	.35

1995 Stadium Club 1st Day Pre-production

Stadium Club 1st Day Preproduction cards were randomly packed into one every 36 packs of Topps Series I baseball. The set of nine cards is only found in hobby packs.

		MT
Complete Set (9):		15.00
Common Player:		1.00
29	Shawon Dunston	1.00
39	Paul Molitor	3.00
79	Bob Hamelin	1.00
96	Ruben Sierra	1.00
131	Will Clark	2.00
149	Mike Piazza	6.00
153	Andy Van Slyke	1.00
166	Jeff Tackett	1.00
197	Ivan Rodriguez	3.00

1995 Stadium Club 1st Day Issue

Series II hobby packs of Topps baseball featured a chase set of Stadium Club 1st Day Issue cards, #1-270. The FDI cards have a small gold embossed seal on front. Cards were seeded on an average of one per six packs. Ten FDI cards were also randomly inserted in each Factory set.

	MT
Common Player:	.50
Stars:	10X

(See 1995 Stadium Club #1-270 for checklist and base card values.)

1995 Stadium Club Clear Cut

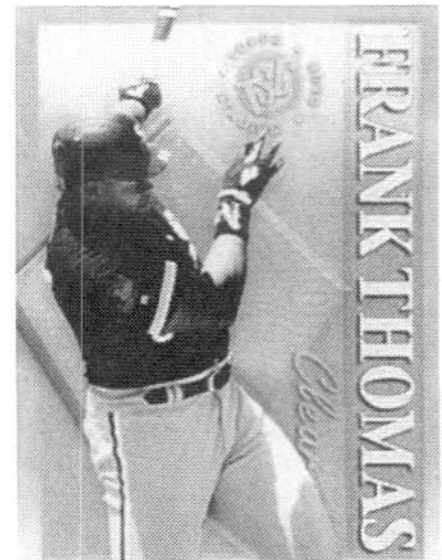

Among the most technically advanced of 1995's insert cards is the Clear Cut chase set found in Series I and II packs. Cards feature a color player action photo printed on see-through plastic. There is a rainbow-hued trapezoid behind the player with an overall background tinted in blue, green and gold. The player's name is in white in a vertical blue bar at right. Backs have a few stats and data in a blue bar vertically at left. Each of the cards can also be found in a version with the round Members Only seal embossed into the plastic at lower-left.

		MT
Complete Set (28):		30.00
Common Player:		.50
1	Mike Piazza	4.00
2	Ruben Sierra	.50
3	Tony Gwynn	2.50
4	Frank Thomas	2.00
5	Fred McGriff	.50
6	Rafael Palmeiro	.75
7	Bobby Bonilla	.50
8	Chili Davis	.50
9	Hal Morris	.50
10	Jose Canseco	1.50
11	Jay Bell	.50
12	Kirby Puckett	2.50
13	Gary Sheffield	.50
14	Bob Hamelin	.50
15	Jeff Bagwell	2.00
16	Albert Belle	.75
17	Sammy Sosa	3.00
18	Ken Griffey Jr.	5.00
19	Todd Zeile	.50
20	Mo Vaughn	1.00
21	Moises Alou	.50
22	Paul O'Neill	.50
23	Andres Galarraga	.50
24	Greg Vaughn	.50
25	Len Dykstra	.50
26	Joe Carter	.50
27	Barry Bonds	3.00
28	Cecil Fielder	.50

1995 Stadium Club Crunch Time

Series I rack packs were the exclusive provenance of these cards featuring baseball's top run creators. Fronts are printed on rainbow prismatic foil. The central color action photo is repeated as an enlarged background photo, along with a team logo. At bottom in gold foil are the player name and Crunch Time logo. Backs have a positive and a negative image of the same photo as background to a pie chart and stats relative to the player's runs-created stats.

		MT
Complete Set (20):		25.00
Common Player:		.75
1	Jeff Bagwell	2.00
2	Kirby Puckett	2.50
3	Frank Thomas	2.00
4	Albert Belle	1.00
5	Julio Franco	.75
6	Jose Canseco	1.50
7	Paul Molitor	1.50
8	Joe Carter	.75
9	Ken Griffey Jr.	4.00
10	Larry Walker	1.00
11	Dante Bichette	.75
12	Carlos Baerga	.75
13	Fred McGriff	.75
14	Ruben Sierra	.75
15	Will Clark	.75
16	Moises Alou	1.00
17	Rafael Palmeiro	1.00
18	Travis Fryman	.75
19	Barry Bonds	3.00
20	Cal Ripken Jr.	4.50

1995 Stadium Club Crystal Ball

Multi-colored swirls around a clear central circle with the player's photo, all printed on foil, are the front design for this Series III insert. Backs have a portrait photo in a floating crystal ball image at one side. At the other end are year-by-year minor league stats and a few words about each of the player's seasons. This insert was also produced in an edition of 4,000 bearing a gold-foil "Members Only" seal, sold in complete Stadium Club Members Only factory sets.

		MT
Complete Set (15):		30.00
Common Player:		1.25
1	Chipper Jones	10.00
2	Dustin Hermanson	1.50
3	Ray Durham	1.50
4	Phil Nevin	1.25
5	Billy Ashley	1.25
6	Shawn Green	4.00
7	Jason Bates	1.25
8	Benji Gil	1.25
9	Marty Cordova	1.25
10	Quilvio Veras	1.25
11	Mark Grudzielanek	1.50
12	Ruben Rivera	1.25
13	Bill Pulsipher	1.25
14	Derek Jeter	15.00
15	LaTroy Hawkins	1.25

1995 Stadium Club Power Zone

The performance in several parks around the league is chronicled on the back of these Series III inserts. Fronts are printed on foil and feature a player swinging into an exploding asteroid. His name is printed vertically down one side in prismatic glitter foil. Backs also have a portrait photo and a baseball with a weird red and green vapor trail. A special edition of 4,000 each of these inserts was included with the purchase of Stadium Club Members Only factory sets; those cards have an embossed gold-foil seal on front.

		MT
Complete Set (12):		25.00
Common Player:		1.00
1	Jeff Bagwell	4.00
2	Albert Belle	1.50
3	Barry Bonds	6.00
4	Joe Carter	1.00
5	Cecil Fielder	1.00
6	Andres Galarraga	1.00
7	Ken Griffey Jr.	8.00
8	Paul Molitor	2.50
9	Fred McGriff	1.00
10	Rafael Palmeiro	1.50
11	Frank Thomas	4.00
12	Matt Williams	1.00

1995 Stadium Club Ring Leaders

With a background that looks like an explosion at a jewelry factory, these cards feature players who have won championship, All-Star or other award rings. Fronts are foil-printed with a player action photo on a background of flying rings and stars, and, - for some reason - an attacking eagle. Backs repeat the background motif, have a player portrait in an oval frame at top-left, photos of some of his rings and a list of rings won. Cards were random inserts in both Series I and II; complete sets could also be won in Stadium Clug's phone card insert contest. A version with the Members Only gold seal was also issued for each.

		MT
Complete Set (40):		60.00
Common Player:		.50
1	Jeff Bagwell	3.00
2	Mark McGwire	8.00
3	Ozzie Smith	3.00
4	Paul Molitor	2.00
5	Darryl Strawberry	.50
6	Eddie Murray	1.50
7	Tony Gwynn	3.00
8	Jose Canseco	1.50
9	Howard Johnson	.50
10	Andre Dawson	1.00
11	Matt Williams	.75
12	Tim Raines	.50
13	Fred McGriff	.50
14	Ken Griffey Jr.	6.00
15	Gary Sheffield	.75
16	Dennis Eckersley	.50
17	Kevin Mitchell	.50
18	Will Clark	.75
19	Darren Daulton	.50
20	Paul O'Neill	.50
21	Julio Franco	.50
22	Albert Belle	1.00
23	Juan Gonzalez	3.00
24	Kirby Puckett	3.00
25	Joe Carter	.50
26	Frank Thomas	3.00
27	Cal Ripken Jr.	8.00
28	John Olerud	.50
29	Ruben Sierra	.50
30	Barry Bonds	4.00
31	Cecil Fielder	.50
32	Roger Clemens	3.00
33	Don Mattingly	5.00
34	Terry Pendleton	.50
35	Rickey Henderson	1.50
36	Dave Winfield	2.00
37	Edgar Martinez	.50
38	Wade Boggs	2.00
39	Willie McGee	.50
40	Andres Galarraga	.50

1995 Stadium Club Super Skills

These random hobby pack inserts in both Series I and II are printed on rainbow prismatic foil which features as a background an enlarged version of the front photo. The S.C. and Super Skills logos are printed in gold foil in opposite corners, while the player's name is in blue at bottom-right. Backs repeat the enlarged background image of a close-up foreground photo, while a few choice words about the player's particular specialties are in white at left. Each card can also be found in a version featuring the Members Only gold-foil seal on front.

		MT
Complete Set (20):		30.00
Complete Series 1 (9):		15.00
Complete Series 2 (11):		15.00
Common Player:		.75
1	Roberto Alomar	2.50
2	Barry Bonds	5.00
3	Jay Buhner	.75
4	Chuck Carr	.75
5	Don Mattingly	5.00
6	Raul Mondesi	1.00
7	Tim Salmon	1.00
8	Deion Sanders	.75
9	Devon White	.75
10	Mark Whiten	.75
11	Ken Griffey Jr.	10.00
12	Marquis Grissom	.75
13	Paul O'Neill	.75
14	Kenny Lofton	.75
15	Larry Walker	1.00
16	Scott Cooper	.75
17	Barry Larkin	.75
18	Matt Williams	1.00
19	John Wetteland	.75
20	Randy Johnson	2.50

1995 Stadium Club Virtual Reality

A partial parallel set found one per foil pack, two per rack pack, these cards share the basic front and back with the corresponding card in the regular S.C. issue. On front, however, is a "Virtual Reality" seal around the team logo at bottom (gold foil in Series I, silver-foil in Series II). Backs differ in that instead of actual 1994 season stats, they present a bar graph of computer projected stats representing full 162-game season instead of the strike-shortened reality. Each of these inserts can also be found in a version bearing the round gold- (Series 1) or silver-foil (Series 2) Members Only seal on the front.

		MT
Complete Set (270):		80.00
Complete Series 1 (135):		40.00
Complete Series 2 (135):		40.00
Common Player:		.15
1	Cal Ripken Jr.	7.50
2	Travis Fryman	.15
3	Jim Abbott	.15
4	Gary Gaetti	.15
5	Roger Clemens	3.50
6	Carlos Garcia	.15
7	Lee Smith	.15
8	Bobby Ayala	.15
9	Charles Nagy	.15
10	Rene Arocha	.15
11	Carlos Delgado	.45
12	Steve Finley	.15
13	Ryan Klesko	.15
14	Cal Eldred	.15
15	Rey Sanchez	.15
16	Ken Hill	.15
17	Jose Vizcaino	.15
18	Andy Benes	.15
19	Shawon Dunston	.15
20	Rafael Palmeiro	.50
21	Dean Palmer	.15
22	Joey Cora	.15
23	Mickey Tettleton	.15
24	Barry Larkin	.25
25	Carlos Baerga	.15
26	Orel Hershiser	.15
27	Jody Reed	.15
28	Paul Molitor	1.50
29	Jim Edmonds	.15
30	Bob Tewksbury	.15
31	Ray McDavid	.15
32	Stan Javier	.15
33	Todd Worrell	.15
34	Bob Wickman	.15
35	Raul Mondesi	.25
36	Rod Beck	.15
37	Jeff Kent	.15
38	John Valentin	.15
39	Ozzie Smith	3.50
40	Terry Pendleton	.15
41	Kenny Rogers	.15
42	Vince Coleman	.15
43	Roberto Alomar	1.50
44	Darrin Jackson	.15
45	Dennis Eckersley	.15
46	Jay Buhner	.15
47	Dave Weathers	.15
48	Danny Bautista	.15
49	Bob Hamelin	.15
50	Steve Trachsel	.15
51	Ben McDonald	.15
52	Wade Boggs	1.25
53	Sandy Alomar	.30
54	Ron Karkovice	.15
55	Doug Jones	.15
56	Gary Sheffield	.50
57	Ken Caminiti	.15
58	Kevin Tapani	.15
59	Ruben Sierra	.15
60	Bobby Bonilla	.15
61	Deion Sanders	.25
62	Charlie Hayes	.15
63	Paul O'Neill	.30
64	Jay Bell	.15
65	Todd Jones	.15
66	Todd Stottlemyre	.15
67	Will Clark	.45
68	Wilson Alvarez	.15
69	Chili Davis	.15
70	Chris Hoiles	.15
71	Bret Saberhagen	.15
72	Dave Nilsson	.15
73	Derek Bell	.15
74	Juan Gonzalez	2.50
75	Andre Dawson	.35
76	Jim Thome	.15
77	Larry Walker	.50
78	Mike Piazza	5.00
79	Dan Wilson	.15
80	Junior Felix	.15
81	Jack McDowell	.15
82	Danny Tartabull	.15
83	William Van Landingham	.15
84	Robb Nen	.15
85	Ismael Valdes	.15
86	Juan Guzman	.15
87	Cliff Floyd	.15
88	Rico Brogna	.15
89	Luis Polonia	.15
90	Lance Johnson	.15
91	Sammy Sosa	4.50
92	Dave West	.15
93	Tom Glavine	.25
94	Joe Girardi	.15
95	Craig Biggio	.25
96	Eddie Murray	1.50
97	Kevin Gross	.15
98	John Franco	.15
99	Matt Williams	.45
100	Darrin Fletcher	.15
101	Jeff Conine	.15
102	Ed Sprague	.15
103	Ivan Rodriguez	1.50
104	Orlando Merced	.15
105	Ricky Bones	.15
106	David Cone	.15
107	Todd Hundley	.15
108	Alex Cole	.15
109	Tony Phillips	.15
110	Jim Eisenreich	.15
111	Paul Sorrento	.15
112	Mike Stanley	.15
113	Doug Drabek	.15
114	Matt Mieske	.15
115	Tino Martinez	.30
116	Midre Cummings	.15
117	Hal Morris	.15
118	Shawn Green	.50
119	Randy Myers	.15
120	Ken Griffey Jr.	6.00
121	Brett Butler	.15
122	Julio Franco	.15
123	Chuck Knoblauch	.15
124	Bret Boone	.25
125	Wil Cordero	.15
126	Luis Gonzalez	.65
127	Tim Wallach	.15
128	Scott Sanders	.15
129	Tom Henke	.15
130	Otis Nixon	.15
131	Darren Daulton	.15
132	Manny Ramirez	2.50
133	Bret Barberie	.15
134	Brady Anderson	.15
135	Shane Reynolds	.15
136	Barry Bonds	4.50
137	Alex Fernandez	.15
138	Brian McRae	.15
139	Todd Zeile	.15
140	Greg Swindell	.15
141	Troy Neel	.15
142	Eric Karros	.15
143	John Hudek	.15
144	Joe Carter	.15
145	Mike Devereaux	.15
146	Butch Henry	.15
147	Mark Lemke	.15
148	Jeff Montgomery	.15
149	Ryan Thompson	.15
150	Bernie Williams	.60
151	Scott Leius	.15
152	Greg Gagne	.15
153	Moises Alou	.25
154	Geronimo Berroa	.15
155	Alan Trammell	.15
156	Don Slaught	.15
157	Jose Rijo	.15
158	Tim Raines	.15
159	Melido Perez	.15
160	Kent Mercker	.15
161	James Mouton	.15
162	Luis Lopez	.15
163	Mike Kingery	.15
164	Cecil Fielder	.15
165	Scott Kamieniecki	.15
166	Brent Gates	.15
167	Jason Jacome	.15
168	Dante Bichette	.15
169	Kurt Abbott	.15
170	Mike Henneman	.15
171	John Kruk	.15
172	Jose Oliva	.15
173	Reggie Sanders	.15
174	Omar Vizquel	.15
175	Devon White	.15
176	Mark McGwire	7.50
177	Gary DiSarcina	.15
178	Joey Hamilton	.15
179	Randy Johnson	1.50
180	Jim Leyritz	.15
181	Bobby Jones	.15
182	Bip Roberts	.15
183	Jose Canseco	1.25
184	Mo Vaughn	1.00
185	Edgar Martinez	.15
186	Tommy Greene	.15
187	Chuck Carr	.15
188	Pedro Astacio	.15
189	Shane Mack	.15
190	Fred McGriff	.15
191	Pat Rapp	.15
192	Bill Swift	.15
193	Robin Ventura	.35
194	Bobby Witt	.15
195	Steve Howe	.15
196	Leo Gomez	.15
197	Hector Fajardo	.15
198	Jeff Bagwell	2.50
199	Rondell White	.35
200	Don Mattingly	4.50
201	Trevor Hoffman	.15
202	Chris Gomez	.15
203	Bobby Munoz	.15
204	Marvin Freeman	.15
205	Sean Berry	.15
206	Mark Grace	.40
207	Pat Kelly	.15
208	Eddie Williams	.15
209	Frank Thomas	4.50
210	Bryan Eversgerd	.15
211	Phil Plantier	.15
212	Roberto Kelly	.15
213	Rickey Henderson	1.50
214	John Smiley	.15
215	Kevin Brown	.30
216	Jimmy Key	.15
217	Wally Joyner	.15
218	Roberto Hernandez	.15
219	Felix Fermin	.15
220	Greg Vaughn	.15
221	Ray Lankford	.30
222	Greg Maddux	3.50
223	Mike Mussina	1.50
224	David Nied	.15
225	Scott Erickson	.15
226	Kevin Mitchell	.15
227	Brian Anderson	.15
228	Jeff King	.15
229	Ramon Martinez	.15
230	Kevin Seitzer	.15
231	Marquis Grissom	.15
232	Chuck Finley	.15
233	Len Dykstra	.15
234	Ellis Burks	.15
235	Harold Baines	.15
236	Kevin Appier	.15
237	Dave Justice	.40
238	Darryl Kile	.15
239	John Olerud	.35
240	Greg McMichael	.15
241	Kirby Puckett	3.50
242	Jose Valentin	.15
243	Rick Wilkins	.15
244	Pat Hentgen	.15
245	Tom Gordon	.15
246	Tom Candiotti	.15
247	Jason Bere	.15
248	Wes Chamberlain	.15
249	Jeff Cirillo	.15
250	Kevin Foster	.15
251	Mark Whiten	.15
252	Terry Steinbach	.15
253	Aaron Sele	.15
254	Kirt Manwaring	.15
255	Delino DeShields	.15
256	Andujar Cedeno	.15
257	Kenny Lofton	.15
258	John Wetteland	.15
259	Tim Salmon	.40
260	Denny Neagle	.15
261	Tony Gwynn	3.50
262	Lou Whitaker	.15
263	J.T. Snow	.15
264	Dennis Martinez	.15
265	Pedro Martinez	.75
266	Rusty Greer	.15
267	Dave Fleming	.15
268	John Dettmer	.15
269	Albert Belle	.50
270	Henry Rodriguez	.15

1995 Stadium Club VR Extremist

A huge silver-blue metallic baseball separates the player from the background of the photo in this Series II insert found only in rack packs. A blue sky and clouds provides the front border. The player rises out of the clouds in a back photo in the foreground of which are some pie-in-the-sky stats. The metallic baseball is also repeated on the back, with the player's name in orange script on the sweet spot. Each card was also issued in the Members Only boxed set in a version with a round silver-foil Members Only seal on front. Cards are numbered with a "VRE" prefix.

		MT
Complete Set (10):		24.00
Common Player:		1.00
1	Barry Bonds	5.00
2	Ken Griffey Jr.	8.00
3	Jeff Bagwell	3.00
4	Albert Belle	2.00
5	Frank Thomas	5.00
6	Tony Gwynn	4.00
7	Kenny Lofton	1.00
8	Deion Sanders	1.00
9	Ken Hill	1.00
10	Jimmy Key	1.00

1996 Stadium Club

Consisting of 450 cards in a pair of 225-card series, Stadium Club continued Topps' 1996 tribute to Mickey Mantle with 19 Retrospective inserts. Cards feature full-bleed photos with gold-foil graphic highlights. Backs offer a TSC Skills Matrix along with another player photo, some biographical data and stats. Team TSC is the only subset with 45 cards each in Series 1 and 2. Stadium Club was issued in retail and hobby packs, with inserts found at differing ratios in each type of packaging.

	MT
Complete Set (450):	40.00
Common Player:	.10
Series 1 or 2 Pack (10):	1.50
Series 1 or 2 Wax Box (24):	30.00

1 Hideo Nomo (Extreme Player) .75
2 Paul Molitor .50
3 Garret Anderson (Extreme Player) .10
4 Jose Mesa (Extreme Player) .10
5 Vinny Castilla (Extreme Player) .10
6 Mike Mussina (Extreme Player) .65
7 Ray Durham (Extreme Player) .10
8 Jack McDowell (Extreme Player) .10
9 Juan Gonzalez (Extreme Player) 1.00
10 Chipper Jones (Extreme Player) 2.00
11 Deion Sanders (Extreme Player) .15
12 Rondell White (Extreme Player) .25
13 Tom Henke (Extreme Player) .10
14 Derek Bell (Extreme Player) .10
15 Randy Myers (Extreme Player) .10
16 Randy Johnson (Extreme Player) .75
17 Len Dykstra (Extreme Player) .10
18 Bill Pulsipher (Extreme Player) .10
19 Greg Colbrunn .10
20 David Wells .10
21 Chad Curtis (Extreme Player) .10
22 Roberto Hernandez (Extreme Player) .10
23 Kirby Puckett (Extreme Player) 1.50
24 Joe Vitiello .10
25 Roger Clemens (Extreme Player) 1.50
26 Al Martin .10
27 Chad Ogea .10
28 David Segui .10
29 Joey Hamilton .10
30 Dan Wilson .10
31 Chad Fonville (Extreme Player) .10
32 Bernard Gilkey (Extreme Player) .10
33 Kevin Seitzer .10
34 Shawn Green (Extreme Player) .25
35 Rick Aguilera (Extreme Player) .10
36 Gary DiSarcina .10
37 Jaime Navarro .10
38 Doug Jones .10
39 Brent Gates .10
40 Dean Palmer (Extreme Player) .10
41 Pat Rapp .10
42 Tony Clark .10
43 Bill Swift .10
44 Randy Velarde .10
45 Matt Williams (Extreme Player) .30
46 John Mabry .10
47 Mike Fetters .10
48 Orlando Miller .10
49 Tom Glavine (Extreme Player) .15
50 Delino DeShields (Extreme Player) .10
51 Scott Erickson .10
52 Andy Van Slyke .10
53 Jim Bullinger .10
54 Lyle Mouton .10
55 Bret Saberhagen .10
56 Benito Santiago (Extreme Player) .10
57 Dan Miceli .10
58 Carl Everett .15
59 Rod Beck (Extreme Player) .10
60 Phil Nevin .10
61 Jason Giambi .40
62 Paul Menhart .10
63 Eric Karros (Extreme Player) .10
64 Allen Watson .10
65 Jeff Cirillo .10
66 Lee Smith (Extreme Player) .10
67 Sean Berry .10
68 Luis Sojo .10
69 Jeff Montgomery (Extreme Player) .10
70 Todd Hundley (Extreme Player) .10
71 John Burkett .10
72 Mark Gubicza .10
73 Don Mattingly (Extreme Player) 1.75
74 Jeff Brantley .10
75 Matt Walbeck .10
76 Steve Parris .10
77 Ken Caminiti (Extreme Player) .10
78 Kirt Manwaring .10
79 Greg Vaughn .10
80 Pedro Martinez (Extreme Player) .75
81 Benji Gil .10
82 Heathcliff Slocumb (Extreme Player) .10
83 Joe Girardi (Extreme Player) .10
84 Sean Bergman .10
85 Matt Karchner .10
86 Butch Huskey .10
87 Mike Morgan .10
88 Todd Worrell (Extreme Player) .10
89 Mike Bordick .10
90 Bip Roberts (Extreme Player) .10
91 Mike Hampton .10
92 Troy O'Leary .10
93 Wally Joyner .10
94 Dave Stevens .10
95 Cecil Fielder (Extreme Player) .10
96 Wade Boggs (Extreme Player) .65
97 Hal Morris .10
98 Mickey Tettleton (Extreme Player) .10
99 Jeff Kent (Extreme Player) .10
100 Denny Martinez .10
101 Luis Gonzalez (Extreme Player) .25
102 John Jaha .10
103 Javy Lopez (Extreme Player) .10
104 Mark McGwire (Extreme Player) 3.00
105 Ken Griffey Jr. (Extreme Player) 2.50
106 Darren Daulton (Extreme Player) .10
107 Bryan Rekar .10
108 Mike Màcfarlane (Extreme Player) .10
109 Gary Gaetti (Extreme Player) .10
110 Shane Reynolds (Extreme Player) .10
111 Pat Meares .10
112 Jason Schmidt .10
113 Otis Nixon .10
114 John Franco (Extreme Player) .10
115 Marc Newfield .10
116 Andy Benes (Extreme Player) .10
117 Ozzie Guillen .10
118 Brian Jordan (Extreme Player) .10
119 Terry Pendleton (Extreme Player) .10
120 Chuck Finley (Extreme Player) .10
121 Scott Stahoviak .10
122 Sid Fernandez .10
123 Derek Jeter (Extreme Player) 2.00
124 John Smiley (Extreme Player) .10
125 David Bell .10
126 Brett Butler (Extreme Player) .10
127 Doug Drabek (Extreme Player) .10
128 J.T. Snow (Extreme Player) .10
129 Joe Carter (Extreme Player) .10
130 Dennis Eckersley (Extreme Player) .10
131 Marty Cordova (Extreme Player) .10
132 Greg Maddux (Extreme Player) 1.50
133 Tom Goodwin .10
134 Andy Ashby .10
135 Paul Sorrento (Extreme Player) .10
136 Ricky Bones .10
137 Shawon Dunston (Extreme Player) .10
138 Moises Alou (Extreme Player) .15
139 Mickey Morandini .10
140 Ramon Martinez (Extreme Player) .10
141 Royce Clayton (Extreme Player) .10
142 Brad Ausmus .10
143 Kenny Rogers (Extreme Player) .10
144 Tim Naehring (Extreme Player) .10
145 Chris Gomez (Extreme Player) .10
146 Bobby Bonilla (Extreme Player) .10
147 Wilson Alvarez .10
148 Johnny Damon (Extreme Player) .15
149 Pat Hentgen .10
150 Andres Galarraga (Extreme Player) .10
151 David Cone (Extreme Player) .10
152 Lance Johnson (Extreme Player) .10
153 Carlos Garcia .10
154 Doug Johns .10
155 Midre Cummings .10
156 Steve Sparks .10
157 *Sandy Martinez* .10
158 William Van Landingham .10
159 Dave Justice (Extreme Player) .40
160 Mark Grace (Extreme Player) .25
161 Robb Nen (Extreme Player) .10
162 Mike Greenwell (Extreme Player) .10
163 Brad Radke .10
164 Edgardo Alfonzo .10
165 Mark Leiter .10
166 Walt Weiss .10
167 Mel Rojas (Extreme Player) .10
168 Bret Boone (Extreme Player) .15
169 Ricky Bottalico .10
170 Bobby Higginson .15
171 Trevor Hoffman .10
172 Jay Bell (Extreme Player) .10
173 Gabe White .10
174 Curtis Goodwin .10
175 Tyler Green .10
176 Roberto Alomar (Extreme Player) .75
177 Sterling Hitchcock .10
178 Ryan Klesko (Extreme Player) .10
179 *Donne Wall* .10
180 Brian McRae .10
181 Will Clark (Team TSC) .15
182 Frank Thomas (Team TSC) .90
183 Jeff Bagwell (Team TSC) .50
184 Mo Vaughn (Team TSC) .25
185 Tino Martinez (Team TSC) .10
186 Craig Biggio (Team TSC) .10
187 Chuck Knoblauch (Team TSC) .10
188 Carlos Baerga (Team TSC) .10
189 Quilvio Veras (Team TSC) .10
190 Luis Alicea (Team TSC) .10
191 Jim Thome (Team TSC) .10
192 Mike Blowers (Team TSC) .10
193 Robin Ventura (Team TSC) .10
194 Jeff King (Team TSC) .10
195 Tony Phillips (Team TSC) .10
196 John Valentin (Team TSC) .10
197 Barry Larkin (Team TSC) .10
198 Cal Ripken Jr. (Team TSC) 1.50
199 Omar Vizquel (Team TSC) .10
200 Kurt Abbott (Team TSC) .10
201 Albert Belle (Team TSC) .20
202 Barry Bonds (Team TSC) .90
203 Ron Gant (Team TSC) .10
204 Dante Bichette (Team TSC) .10
205 Jeff Conine (Team TSC) .10
206 Jim Edmonds (Team TSC) .10
207 Stan Javier (Team TSC) .10
208 Kenny Lofton (Team TSC) .10
209 Ray Lankford (Team TSC) .10
210 Bernie Williams (Team TSC) .20
211 Jay Buhner (Team TSC) .10
212 Paul O'Neill (Team TSC) .10
213 Tim Salmon (Team TSC) .15
214 Reggie Sanders (Team TSC) .10
215 Manny Ramirez (Team TSC) .40
216 Mike Piazza (Team TSC) 1.25
217 Mike Stanley (Team TSC) .10
218 Tony Eusebio (Team TSC) .10
219 Chris Hoiles (Team TSC) .10
220 Ron Karkovice (Team TSC) .10
221 Edgar Martinez (Team TSC) .10
222 Chili Davis (Team TSC) .10
223 Jose Canseco (Team TSC) .25
224 Eddie Murray (Team TSC) .30
225 Geronimo Berroa (Team TSC) .10
226 Chipper Jones (Team TSC) 1.00
227 Garret Anderson (Team TSC) .10
228 Marty Cordova (Team TSC) .10
229 Jon Nunnally (Team TSC) .10
230 Brian Hunter (Team TSC) .10
231 Shawn Green (Team TSC) .15

232 Ray Durham (Team TSC) .10
233 Alex Gonzalez (Team TSC) .15
234 Bobby Higginson (Team TSC) .15
235 Randy Johnson (Team TSC) .40
236 Al Leiter (Team TSC) .10
237 Tom Glavine (Team TSC) .10
238 Kenny Rogers (Team TSC) .10
239 Mike Hampton (Team TSC) .10
240 David Wells (Team TSC) .10
241 Jim Abbott (Team TSC) .10
242 Denny Neagle (Team TSC) .10
243 Wilson Alvarez (Team TSC) .10
244 John Smiley (Team TSC) .10
245 Greg Maddux (Team TSC) .75
246 Andy Ashby (Team TSC) .10
247 Hideo Nomo (Team TSC) .40
248 Pat Rapp (Team TSC) .10
249 Tim Wakefield (Team TSC) .10
250 John Smoltz (Team TSC) .10
251 Joey Hamilton (Team TSC) .10
252 Frank Castillo (Team TSC) .10
253 Denny Martinez (Team TSC) .10
254 Jaime Navarro (Team TSC) .10
255 Karim Garcia (Team TSC) .10
256 Bob Abreu (Team TSC) .10
257 Butch Huskey (Team TSC) .10
258 Ruben Rivera (Team TSC) .10
259 Johnny Damon (Team TSC) .15
260 Derek Jeter (Team TSC) 1.25
261 Dennis Eckersley (Team TSC) .10
262 Jose Mesa (Team TSC) .10
263 Tom Henke (Team TSC) .10
264 Rick Aguilera (Team TSC) .10
265 Randy Myers (Team TSC) .10
266 John Franco (Team TSC) .10
267 Jeff Brantley (Team TSC) .10
268 John Wetteland (Team TSC) .10
269 Mark Wohlers (Team TSC) .10
270 Rod Beck (Team TSC) .10
271 Barry Larkin .15
272 Paul O'Neill .10
273 Bobby Jones .10
274 Will Clark .30
275 Steve Avery .10
276 Jim Edmonds .10
277 John Olerud .10
278 Carlos Perez .10
279 Chris Hoiles .10
280 Jeff Conine .10
281 Jim Eisenreich .10
282 Jason Jacome .10
283 Ray Lankford .10
284 John Wasdin .10
285 Frank Thomas 1.75
286 Jason Isringhausen .10
287 Glenallen Hill .10
288 Esteban Loaiza .10
289 Bernie Williams .40
290 Curtis Leskanic .10
291 Scott Cooper .10
292 Curt Schilling .25
293 Eddie Murray .60
294 Rick Krivda .10
295 Domingo Cedeno .10
296 Jeff Fassero .10
297 Albert Belle .40
298 Craig Biggio .15
299 Fernando Vina .10
300 Edgar Martinez .10
301 Tony Gwynn 1.50
302 Felipe Lira .10
303 Mo Vaughn .50
304 Alex Fernandez .10
305 Keith Lockhart .10
306 Roger Pavlik .10
307 Lee Tinsley .10
308 Omar Vizquel .10
309 Scott Servais .10
310 Danny Tartabull .10
311 Chili Davis .10
312 Cal Eldred .10
313 Roger Cedeno .10
314 Chris Hammond .10
315 Rusty Greer .10
316 Brady Anderson .10
317 Ron Villone .10
318 Mark Carreon .10
319 Larry Walker .30
320 Pete Harnisch .10
321 Robin Ventura .10
322 Tim Belcher .10
323 Tony Tarasco .10
324 Juan Guzman .10
325 Kenny Lofton .10
326 Kevin Foster .10
327 Wil Cordero .10
328 Troy Percival .10
329 Turk Wendell .10
330 Thomas Howard .10
331 Carlos Baerga .10
332 B.J. Surhoff .10
333 Jay Buhner .10
334 Andujar Cedeno .10
335 Jeff King .10
336 Dante Bichette .10
337 Alan Trammell .10
338 Scott Leius .10
339 Chris Snopek .10
340 Roger Bailey .10
341 Jacob Brumfield .10
342 Jose Canseco .50
343 Rafael Palmeiro .40
344 Quilvio Veras .10
345 Darrin Fletcher .10
346 Carlos Delgado .40
347 Tony Eusebio .10
348 Ismael Valdes .10
349 Terry Steinbach .10
350 Orel Hershiser .10
351 Kurt Abbott .10
352 Jody Reed .10
353 David Howard .10
354 Ruben Sierra .10
355 John Ericks .10
356 Buck Showalter .10
357 Jim Thome .10
358 Geronimo Berroa .10
359 Robby Thompson .10
360 Jose Vizcaino .10
361 Jeff Frye .10
362 Kevin Appier .10
363 Pat Kelly .10
364 Ron Gant .10
365 Luis Alicea .10
366 Armando Benitez .10
367 Rico Brogna .10
368 Manny Ramirez 1.00
369 Mike Lansing .10
370 Sammy Sosa 1.75
371 Don Wengert .10
372 Dave Nilsson .10
373 Sandy Alomar .10
374 Joey Cora .10
375 Larry Thomas .10
376 John Valentin .10
377 Kevin Ritz .10
378 Steve Finley .10
379 Frank Rodriguez .10
380 Ivan Rodriguez .75
381 Alex Ochoa .10
382 Mark Lemke .10
383 Scott Brosius .10
384 James Mouton .10
385 Mark Langston .10
386 Ed Sprague .10
387 Joe Oliver .10
388 Steve Ontiveros .10
389 Rey Sanchez .10
390 Mike Henneman .10
391 *Jose Valentin* .10
392 Tom Candiotti .10
393 Damon Buford .10
394 Erik Hanson .10
395 Mark Smith .10
396 Pete Schourek .10
397 John Flaherty .10
398 Dave Martinez .10
399 Tommy Greene .10
400 Gary Sheffield .40
401 Glenn Dishman .10
402 Barry Bonds 1.75
403 Tom Pagnozzi .10
404 Todd Stottlemyre .10
405 Tim Salmon .25
406 John Hudek .10
407 Fred McGriff .10
408 Orlando Merced .10
409 Brian Barber .10
410 Ryan Thompson .10
411 Mariano Rivera .25
412 Eric Young .10
413 Chris Bosio .10
414 Chuck Knoblauch .10
415 Jamie Moyer .10
416 Chan Ho Park .20
417 Mark Portugal .10
418 Tim Raines .10
419 Antonio Osuna .10
420 Todd Zeile .10
421 Steve Wojciechowski .10
422 Marquis Grissom .10
423 Norm Charlton .10
424 Cal Ripken Jr. 3.00
425 Gregg Jefferies .10
426 Mike Stanton .10
427 Tony Fernandez .10
428 Jose Rijo .10
429 Jeff Bagwell 1.00
430 Raul Mondesi .25
431 Travis Fryman .10
432 Ron Karkovice .10
433 Alan Benes .10
434 Tony Phillips .10
435 Reggie Sanders .10
436 Andy Pettitte .40
437 *Matt Lawton* .50
438 Jeff Blauser .10
439 Michael Tucker .10
440 Mark Loretta .10
441 Charlie Hayes .10
442 Mike Piazza 2.00
443 Shane Andrews .10
444 Jeff Suppan .10
445 Steve Rodriguez .10
446 Mike Matheny .10
447 Trenidad Hubbard .10
448 Denny Hocking .10
449 Mark Grudzielanek .10
450 Joe Randa .10

1996 Stadium Club Bash & Burn

Inserted in one per 24 retail packs and one per 48 hobby packs of Series II, Bash & Burn includes 10 players on double-fronted cards. Both sides are foil-etched with the Bash side highlighting home runs and runs batted in for 1995 and career, and the Burn side featured stolen base and runs scored leaders for 1995 and career. Cards are numbered with a "B&B" prefix.

		MT
Complete Set (10):		18.00
Common Player:		1.00
1	Sammy Sosa	9.00
2	Barry Bonds	9.00
3	Reggie Sanders	1.00
4	Craig Biggio	1.00
5	Raul Mondesi	1.00
6	Ron Gant	1.00
7	Ray Lankford	1.00
8	Glenallen Hill	1.00
9	Chad Curtis	1.00
10	John Valentin	1.00

1996 Stadium Club Extreme Player

A special interactive version of 179 players' cards in 1996 Stadium Club was issued as an insert set across Series 1 and 2. Specially stamped with an "Extreme Player" logo in bronze (1 per 12 packs average), silver (1:24) or gold (1:48), the cards have backs which detail a contest by which the player's on-field performance was used to rank each by position. At season's end, cards of the winning players at each position could be redeemed for special prizes. The contest cards do not have card numbers on back and are numbered here based on the regular version.

		MT
Complete Bronze Set (179):		100.00
Common Bronze:		.25
Silvers:		1.5X
Golds:		2.5X
1	(Hideo Nomo)	3.00
3	Garret Anderson	.25
4	Jose Mesa	.25
5	Vinny Castilla	.25
6	Mike Mussina	2.50
7	Ray Durham	.25
8	Jack McDowell	.25
9	Juan Gonzalez	4.50
10	Chipper Jones	7.50
11	Deion Sanders	.35
12	Rondell White	.35
13	Tom Henke	.25
14	Derek Bell	.25
15	Randy Myers	.25

16	Randy Johnson	3.00
17	Len Dykstra	.25
18	Bill Pulsipher	.25
21	Chad Curtis	.25
22	Roberto Hernandez	.25
23	Kirby Puckett	6.00
25	Roger Clemens	6.00
31	Chad Fonville	.25
32	Bernard Gilkey	.25
34	Shawn Green	.50
35	Rick Aguilera	.25
40	Dean Palmer	.25
45	Matt Williams	.75
49	Tom Glavine	.35
50	Delino DeShields	.25
56	Benito Santiago	.25
59	Rod Beck	.25
63	Eric Karros	.25
66	Lee Smith	.25
69	Jeff Montgomery	.25
70	Todd Hundley	.25
73	Don Mattingly	7.00
77	Ken Caminiti	.25
80	Pedro Martinez	1.50
82	Heathcliff Slocumb	.25
83	Joe Girardi	.25
88	Todd Worrell	.25
90	Bip Roberts	.25
95	Cecil Fielder	.25
96	Wade Boggs	2.50
98	Mickey Tettleton	.25
99	Jeff Kent	.25
101	Luis Gonzalez	.50
103	Javier Lopez	.25
104	Mark McGwire	10.00
105	Ken Griffey Jr.	9.00
106	Darren Daulton	.25
108	Mike Macfarlane	.25
109	Gary Gaetti	.25
110	Shane Reynolds	.25
114	John Franco	.25
116	Andy Benes	.25
118	Brian Jordan	.25
119	Terry Pendleton	.25
120	Chuck Finley	.25
123	Derek Jeter	7.50
124	John Smiley	.25
126	Brett Butler	.25
127	Doug Drabek	.25
128	J.T. Snow	.25
129	Joe Carter	.25
130	Dennis Eckersley	.25
131	Marty Cordova	.25
132	Greg Maddux	6.00
135	Paul Sorrento	.25
137	Shawon Dunston	.25
138	Moises Alou	.25
140	Ramon Martinez	.25
141	Royce Clayton	.25
143	Kenny Rogers	.25
144	Tim Naehring	.25
145	Chris Gomez	.25
146	Bobby Bonilla	.25
148	Johnny Damon	.35
150	Andres Galarraga	.25
151	David Cone	.25
152	Lance Johnson	.25
159	Dave Justice	.75
160	Mark Grace	1.25
161	Robb Nen	.25
162	Mike Greenwell	.25
167	Mel Rojas	.25
168	Bret Boone	.25
172	Jay Bell	.25
176	Roberto Alomar	3.00
178	Ryan Klesko	.25
271	Barry Larkin	.35
272	Paul O'Neill	.25
274	Will Clark	.75
275	Steve Avery	.25
276	Jim Edmonds	.25
277	John Olerud	.25
279	Chris Hoiles	.25
280	Jeff Conine	.25
283	Ray Lankford	.25
285	Frank Thomas	7.00
286	Jason Isringhausen	.25
287	Glenallen Hill	.25
289	Bernie Williams	.50
290	Eddie Murray	1.00
296	Jeff Fassero	.25
297	Albert Belle	1.00
298	Craig Biggio	.35
300	Edgar Martinez	.25
301	Tony Gwynn	6.00
303	Mo Vaughn	1.25
304	Alex Fernandez	.25
308	Omar Vizquel	.25
310	Danny Tartabull	.25
316	Brady Anderson	.25
319	Larry Walker	.75
321	Robin Ventura	.25
325	Kenny Lofton	.25
327	Wil Cordero	.25
328	Troy Percival	.25
331	Carlos Baerga	.25
333	Jay Buhner	.25
335	Jeff King	.25
336	Dante Bichette	.25
337	Alan Trammell	.25
342	Jose Canseco	1.25
343	Rafael Palmeiro	.35
344	Quilvio Veras	.25
345	Darrin Fletcher	.25
347	Tony Eusebio	.25
348	Ismael Valdes	.25
349	Terry Steinbach	.25
350	Orel Hershiser	.25
351	Kurt Abbott	.25
354	Ruben Sierra	.25
357	Jim Thome	.25
358	Geronimo Berroa	.25
359	Robby Thompson	.25
360	Jose Vizcaino	.25
362	Kevin Appier	.25
364	Ron Gant	.25
367	Rico Brogna	.25
368	Manny Ramirez	4.50
370	Sammy Sosa	7.00
373	Sandy Alomar	.25
378	Steve Finley	.25
380	Ivan Rodriguez	1.50
382	Mark Lemke	.25
385	Mark Langston	.25
386	Ed Sprague	.25
388	Steve Ontiveros	.25
392	Tom Candiotti	.25
394	Erik Hanson	.25
396	Pete Schourek	.25
400	Gary Sheffield	.75
402	Barry Bonds	7.00
403	Tom Pagnozzi	.25
404	Todd Stottlemyre	.25
405	Tim Salmon	.35
407	Fred McGriff	.25
408	Orlando Merced	.25
412	Eric Young	.25
414	Chuck Knoblauch	.25
417	Mark Portugal	.25
418	Tim Raines	.25
420	Todd Zeile	.25
422	Marquis Grissom	.25
423	Norm Charlton	.25
424	Cal Ripken Jr.	10.00
425	Gregg Jefferies	.25
428	Jose Rijo	.25
429	Jeff Bagwell	4.50
430	Raul Mondesi	.25
431	Travis Fryman	.25
434	Tony Phillips	.25
435	Reggie Sanders	.25
436	Andy Pettitte	.75
438	Jeff Blauser	.25
441	Charlie Hayes	.25
442	Mike Piazza	7.50

1996 Stadium Club Mega Heroes

Ten herois players are matched with a comic book-style illustration depicting their nickname in the Mega Heroes insert set. Printed on foil-board in a defraction technology, the cards are found, on average, once per 48 Series I hobby packs and twice as often in retail packs.

		MT
Complete Set (10):		28.00
Common Player:		1.50
1	Frank Thomas	6.00
2	Ken Griffey Jr.	9.00
3	Hideo Nomo	3.50
4	Ozzie Smith	4.50
5	Will Clark	2.00
6	Jack McDowell	1.50
7	Andres Galarraga	1.50
8	Roger Clemens	4.50
9	Deion Sanders	1.75
10	Mo Vaughn	3.00

1996 Stadium Club Metalists

Eight players who have won two or more major awards in their careers are featured in this Series II insert. Cards are printed on foilboard and feature intricate laser-cut designs that depict the player's face. Metalist inserts are found one per 96 retail and one per 48 hobby packs, on average. Cards are numbered with a "M" prefix.

		MT
Complete Set (8):		23.00
Common Player:		.75
1	Jeff Bagwell	3.00
2	Barry Bonds	5.00
3	Jose Canseco	1.50
4	Roger Clemens	4.00
5	Dennis Eckersley	.75
6	Greg Maddux	4.00
7	Cal Ripken Jr.	7.50
8	Frank Thomas	5.00

1996 Stadium Club Mickey Mantle Retrospective

Following the success of the Mantle reprints in Topps baseball, Stadium Club produced a series of 19 Mickey Mantle Retrospective inserts; nine black-and-white cards in Series 1 and 10 color cards in Series 2. The cards chronicle Mantle's career and provide insights from baseball contemporaries. Throughout both series, the Mantle cards are found on an average of once per 24 Series 1 packs and once per 12 Series 2 packs. Cards are numbered with an "MM" prefix.

		MT
Complete Set (19):		100.00
Complete Series 1 (9):		65.00
Complete Series 2 (10):		35.00
Common Series 1:		8.00
Common Series 2:		5.00
1	Mickey Mantle (1950, minor league)	8.00
2	Mickey Mantle (1951)	8.00
3	Mickey Mantle (1951)	8.00
4	Mickey Mantle (1953)	8.00
5	Mickey Mantle (1954 (w/ Yogi Berra)	8.00
6	Mickey Mantle (1956)	8.00
7	Mickey Mantle (1957)	8.00
8	Mickey Mantle (1958) (w/ Casey Stengel)	8.00
9	Mickey Mantle (1959)	8.00
10	Mickey Mantle (1960) (w/ Elston Howard)	5.00
11	Mickey Mantle (1961)	5.00
12	Mickey Mantle (1961) (w/ Roger Maris)	8.00
13	Mickey Mantle (1962)	5.00
14	Mickey Mantle (1963)	5.00
15	Mickey Mantle (1964)	5.00
16	Mickey Mantle	5.00
17	Mickey Mantle (1968)	5.00
18	Mickey Mantle (1969)	5.00
19	Mickey Mantle (In Memoriam)	5.00

1996 Stadium Club Midsummer Matchups

These inserts salute 1995 National League and

American League All-Stars on back-to-back etched-foil cards. Players are matched by position in the 10-card set. Average insertion rate is one per 48 hobby packs and one per 24 retail packs in Series I. Cards are numbered with a "M" prefix.

		MT
Complete Set (10):		37.50
Common Player:		2.00
1	Hideo Nomo, Randy Johnson	5.00
2	Mike Piazza, Ivan Rodriguez	9.00
3	Fred McGriff, Frank Thomas	6.00
4	Craig Biggio, Carlos Baerga	2.00
5	Vinny Castilla, Wade Boggs	2.25
6	Barry Larkin, Cal Ripken Jr.	11.00
7	Barry Bonds, Albert Belle	6.00
8	Len Dykstra, Kenny Lofton	2.00
9	Tony Gwynn, Kirby Puckett	5.50
10	Ron Gant, Edgar Martinez	2.00

1996 Stadium Club Power Packed

Topps' Power Matrix technology is used to showcase 15 of the biggest, strongest players in this Series II insert set. Card backs feature a diagram of the player's home park with baseball graphics measuring this home runs during the 1995 season. The inserts are a one in 48 packs pick, on average, both hobby and retail. Cards are numbered with a "PP" prefix.

		MT
Complete Set (15):		28.00
Common Player:		1.00
1	Albert Belle	1.50
2	Mark McGwire	7.50
3	Jose Canseco	1.75
4	Mike Piazza	5.00
5	Ron Gant	1.00
6	Ken Griffey Jr.	6.00
7	Mo Vaughn	1.50
8	Cecil Fielder	1.00
9	Tim Salmon	1.25
10	Frank Thomas	4.00
11	Juan Gonzalez	2.50
12	Andres Galarraga	1.00
13	Fred McGriff	1.00
14	Jay Buhner	1.00
15	Dante Bichette	1.00

1996 Stadium Club Power Streak

The best power hitters in baseball are featured in Power Matrix technology on these Series I inserts. Average insertion rate is one per 24 hobby and 48 retail packs. Cards are numbered with a "PS" prefix.

		MT
Complete Set (15):		35.00
Common Player:		1.50
1	Randy Johnson	3.00
2	Hideo Nomo	3.00
3	Albert Belle	2.00
4	Dante Bichette	1.50
5	Jay Buhner	1.50
6	Frank Thomas	5.00
7	Mark McGwire	10.00
8	Rafael Palmeiro	2.00
9	Mo Vaughn	2.50
10	Sammy Sosa	5.00
11	Larry Walker	2.00
12	Gary Gaetti	1.50
13	Tim Salmon	2.00
14	Barry Bonds	5.00
15	Jim Edmonds	1.50

1996 Stadium Club Prime Cuts

The purest swings in baseball are the focus on these laser-cut, defraction-foil inserts found in Series 1 packs at an average rate of one per 36 hobby and 72 retail packs. Cards are numbered with a "PC" prefix.

		MT
Complete Set (8):		25.00
Common Player:		1.50
1	Albert Belle	2.00
2	Barry Bonds	5.00
3	Ken Griffey Jr.	8.00
4	Tony Gwynn	4.00
5	Edgar Martinez	1.50
6	Rafael Palmeiro	2.00
7	Mike Piazza	6.00
8	Frank Thomas	5.00

1996 Stadium Club TSC Awards

TSC Awards insert cards allowed Topps' experts to honor best performances, newcomer, comeback, etc. The cards are found in Series II packs at an average rate of one per 24 retail and 48 hobby packs.

		MT
Complete Set (10):		25.00
Common Player:		.50
1	Cal Ripken Jr.	7.50
2	Albert Belle	2.00
3	Tom Glavine	1.00
4	Jeff Conine	.50
5	Ken Griffey Jr.	6.00
6	Hideo Nomo	3.00
7	Greg Maddux	4.00
8	Chipper Jones	5.00
9	Randy Johnson	3.00
10	Jose Mesa	.50

1997 Stadium Club

Stadium Club totalled 390 cards in 1997, issued in two Series of 195 cards each. In Series 1 (Feb.), cards #181-195 are a rookie subset called TSC 2000. In Series 2 (April), cards #376-390 form a subset called Stadium Slugger. Each of these subsets was short-printed and inserted about one per two packs. TSC is printed on an improved 20-point stock with Topps' Super Color process.

		MT
Complete Set (390):		60.00
Common Player:		.10
Series 1 or 2 Pack (9):		2.00
Series 1 or 2 Wax Box (24):		35.00
1	Chipper Jones	2.50
2	Gary Sheffield	.40
3	Kenny Lofton	.10
4	Brian Jordan	.10
5	Mark McGwire	3.00
6	Charles Nagy	.10
7	Tim Salmon	.25
8	Cal Ripken Jr.	3.00
9	Jeff Conine	.10
10	Paul Molitor	.50
11	Mariano Rivera	.25
12	Pedro Martinez	.75
13	Jeff Bagwell	1.00
14	Bobby Bonilla	.10
15	Barry Bonds	2.00
16	Ryan Klesko	.10
17	Barry Larkin	.15
18	Jim Thome	.10
19	Jay Buhner	.10
20	Juan Gonzalez	1.00
21	Mike Mussina	.60
22	Kevin Appier	.10
23	Eric Karros	.10
24	Steve Finley	.10
25	Ed Sprague	.10
26	Bernard Gilkey	.10
27	Tony Phillips	.10
28	Henry Rodriguez	.10
29	John Smoltz	.15
30	Dante Bichette	.10
31	Mike Piazza	2.50
32	Paul O'Neill	.10
33	Billy Wagner	.10
34	Reggie Sanders	.10
35	John Jaha	.10
36	Eddie Murray	.65
37	Eric Young	.10
38	Roberto Hernandez	.10
39	Pat Hentgen	.10
40	Sammy Sosa	2.00
41	Todd Hundley	.10
42	Mo Vaughn	.60
43	Robin Ventura	.10
44	Mark Grudzielanek	.10
45	Shane Reynolds	.10
46	Andy Pettitte	.40
47	Fred McGriff	.10
48	Rey Ordonez	.10
49	Will Clark	.30
50	Ken Griffey Jr.	2.75
51	Todd Worrell	.10
52	Rusty Greer	.10
53	Mark Grace	.25
54	Tom Glavine	.15
55	Derek Jeter	2.50
56	Rafael Palmeiro	.40
57	Bernie Williams	.40
58	Marty Cordova	.10
59	Andres Galarraga	.10
60	Ken Caminiti	.10
61	Garret Anderson	.10
62	Denny Martinez	.10
63	Mike Greenwell	.10
64	David Segui	.10
65	Julio Franco	.10
66	Rickey Henderson	.65
67	Ozzie Guillen	.10
68	Pete Harnisch	.10
69	Chan Ho Park	.30
70	Harold Baines	.10
71	Mark Clark	.10
72	Steve Avery	.10
73	Brian Hunter	.10
74	Pedro Astacio	.10
75	Jack McDowell	.10
76	Gregg Jefferies	.10
77	Jason Kendall	.10
78	Todd Walker	.10
79	B.J. Surhoff	.10
80	Moises Alou	.15
81	Fernando Vina	.10
82	Darryl Strawberry	.10
83	Jose Rosado	.10
84	Chris Gomez	.10
85	Chili Davis	.10
86	Alan Benes	.10
87	Todd Hollandsworth	.10
88	Jose Vizcaino	.10
89	Edgardo Alfonzo	.10
90	Ruben Rivera	.10
91	Donovan Osborne	.10
92	Doug Glanville	.10
93	Gary DiSarcina	.10
94	Brooks Kieschnick	.10
95	Bobby Jones	.10
96	Raul Casanova	.10
97	Jermaine Allensworth	.10

98 Kenny Rogers .10
99 Mark McLemore .10
100 Jeff Fassero .10
101 Sandy Alomar .10
102 Chuck Finley .10
103 Eric Owens .10
104 Billy McMillon .10
105 Dwight Gooden .10
106 Sterling Hitchcock .10
107 Doug Drabek .10
108 Paul Wilson .10
109 Chris Snopek .10
110 Al Leiter .10
111 Bob Tewksbury .10
112 Todd Greene .10
113 Jose Valentin .10
114 Delino DeShields .10
115 Mike Bordick .10
116 Pat Meares .10
117 Mariano Duncan .10
118 Steve Trachsel .10
119 Luis Castillo .10
120 Andy Benes .10
121 Donne Wall .10
122 Alex Gonzalez .15
123 Dan Wilson .10
124 Omar Vizquel .10
125 Devon White .10
126 Darryl Hamilton .10
127 Orlando Merced .10
128 Royce Clayton .10
129 William VanLandingham .10
130 Terry Steinbach .10
131 Jeff Blauser .10
132 Jeff Cirillo .10
133 Roger Pavlik .10
134 Danny Tartabull .10
135 Jeff Montgomery .10
136 Bobby Higginson .15
137 Mike Grace .10
138 Kevin Elster .10
139 *Brian Giles* 1.50
140 Rod Beck .10
141 Ismael Valdes .10
142 Scott Brosius .10
143 Mike Fetters .10
144 Gary Gaetti .10
145 Mike Lansing .10
146 Glenallen Hill .10
147 Shawn Green .40
148 Mel Rojas .10
149 Joey Cora .10
150 John Smiley .10
151 Marvin Benard .10
152 Curt Schilling .25
153 Dave Nilsson .10
154 Edgar Renteria .10
155 Joey Hamilton .10
156 Carlos Garcia .10
157 Nomar Garciaparra 2.00
158 Kevin Ritz .10
159 Keith Lockhart .10
160 Justin Thompson .10
161 Terry Adams .10
162 Jamey Wright .10
163 Otis Nixon .10
164 Michael Tucker .10
165 Mike Stanley .10
166 Ben McDonald .10
167 John Mabry .10
168 Troy O'Leary .10
169 Mel Nieves .10
170 Bret Boone .15
171 Mike Timlin .10
172 Scott Rolen 1.00
173 Reggie Jefferson .10
174 Neifi Perez .10
175 Brian McRae .10
176 Tom Goodwin .10
177 Aaron Sele .10
178 Benny Santiago .10
179 Frank Rodriguez .10
180 Eric Davis .10
181 Andruw Jones (TSC 2000) .50
182 Todd Walker (TSC 2000) .15
183 Wes Helms (TSC 2000) .10
184 *Nelson Figueroa* (TSC 2000) .10
185 Vladimir Guerrero (TSC 2000) .50
186 Billy McMillon (TSC 2000) .10
187 Todd Helton (TSC 2000) .50
188 Nomar Garciaparra (TSC 2000) 1.00
189 Katsuhiro Maeda (TSC 2000) .10
190 Russell Branyan (TSC 2000) .10
191 Glendon Rusch (TSC 2000) .10
192 Bartolo Colon (TSC 2000) .10
193 Scott Rolen (TSC 2000) .50
194 Angel Echevarria (TSC 2000) .10
195 Bob Abreu (TSC 2000) .15
196 Greg Maddux 1.50
197 Joe Carter .10
198 Alex Ochoa .10
199 Ellis Burks .10
200 Ivan Rodriguez .75
201 Marquis Grissom .10
202 Trevor Hoffman .10
203 Matt Williams .30
204 Carlos Delgado .30
205 Ramon Martinez .10
206 Chuck Knoblauch .10
207 Juan Guzman .10
208 Derek Bell .10
209 Roger Clemens 1.50
210 Vladimir Guerrero 1.00
211 Cecil Fielder .10
212 Hideo Nomo .65
213 Frank Thomas 2.00
214 Greg Vaughn .10
215 Javy Lopez .10
216 Raul Mondesi .25
217 Wade Boggs .65
218 Carlos Baerga .10
219 Tony Gwynn 1.50
220 Tino Martinez .10
221 Vinny Castilla .10
222 Lance Johnson .10
223 David Justice .40
224 Rondell White .25
225 Dean Palmer .10
226 Jim Edmonds .10
227 Albert Belle .50
228 Alex Fernandez .10
229 Ryne Sandberg .75
230 Jose Mesa .10
231 David Cone .10
232 Troy Percival .10
233 Edgar Martinez .10
234 Jose Canseco .65
235 Kevin Brown .20
236 Ray Lankford .10
237 Karim Garcia .15
238 J.T. Snow .10
239 Dennis Eckersley .10
240 Roberto Alomar .75
241 John Valentin .10
242 Ron Gant .10
243 Geronimo Berroa .10
244 Manny Ramirez 1.00
245 Travis Fryman .10
246 Denny Neagle .10
247 Randy Johnson .75
248 Darin Erstad .75
249 Mark Wohlers .10
250 Ken Hill .10
251 Larry Walker .30
252 Craig Biggio .10
253 Brady Anderson .10
254 John Wetteland .10
255 Andruw Jones 1.00
256 Turk Wendell .10
257 Jason Isringhausen .10
258 Jaime Navarro .10
259 Sean Berry .10
260 Albie Lopez .10
261 Jay Bell .10
262 Bobby Witt .10
263 Tony Clark .10
264 Tim Wakefield .10
265 Brad Radke .10
266 Tim Belcher .10
267 Mark Lewis .10
268 Roger Cedeno .10
269 Tim Naehring .10
270 Kevin Tapani .10
271 Joe Randa .10
272 Randy Myers .10
273 Dave Burba .10
274a Mike Sweeney .10
274b Tom Pagnozzi (should be #374) .10
275 Danny Graves .10
276 Chad Mottola .10
277 Ruben Sierra .10
278 Norm Charlton .10
279 Scott Servais .10
280 Jacob Cruz .10
281 Mike Macfarlane .10
282 Rich Becker .10
283 Shannon Stewart .15
284 Gerald Williams .10
285 Jody Reed .10
286 Jeff D'Amico .10
287 Walt Weiss .10
288 Jim Leyritz .10
289 Francisco Cordova .10
290 F.P. Santangelo .10
291 Scott Erickson .10
292 Hal Morris .10
293 Ray Durham .10
294 Andy Ashby .10
295 Darryl Kile .10
296 Jose Paniagua .10
297 Mickey Tettleton .10
298 Joe Girardi .10
299 Rocky Coppinger .10
300 Bob Abreu .10
301 John Olerud .10
302 Paul Shuey .10
303 Jeff Brantley .10
304 Bob Wells .10
305 Kevin Seitzer .10
306 Shawon Dunston .10
307 Jose Herrera .10
308 Butch Huskey .10
309 Jose Offerman .10
310 Rick Aguilera .10
311 Greg Gagne .10
312 John Burkett .10
313 Mark Thompson .10
314 Alvaro Espinoza .10
315 Todd Stottlemyre .10
316 Al Martin .10
317 James Baldwin .10
318 Cal Eldred .10
319 Sid Fernandez .10
320 Mickey Morandini .10
321 Robb Nen .10
322 Mark Lemke .10
323 Pete Schourek .10
324 Marcus Jensen .10
325 Rich Aurilia .10
326 Jeff King .10
327 Scott Stahoviak .10
328 Ricky Otero .10
329 Antonio Osuna .10
330 Chris Hoiles .10
331 Luis Gonzalez .40
332 Wil Cordero .10
333 Johnny Damon .15
334 Mark Langston .10
335 Orlando Miller .10
336 Jason Giambi .40
337 Damian Jackson .10
338 David Wells .10
339 Bip Roberts .10
340 Matt Ruebel .10
341 Tom Candiotti .10
342 Wally Joyner .10
343 Jimmy Key .10
344 Tony Batista .10
345 Paul Sorrento .10
346 Ron Karkovice .10
347 Wilson Alvarez .10
348 John Flaherty .10
349 Rey Sanchez .10
350 John Vander Wal .10
351a Jermaine Dye .10
351b Brant Brown (should be #361) .10
352 Mike Hampton .10
353 Greg Colbrunn .10
354 Heathcliff Slocumb .10
355 Ricky Bottalico .10
356 Marty Janzen .10
357 Orel Hershiser .10
358 Rex Hudler .10
359 Amaury Telemaco .10
360 Darrin Fletcher .10
361 Not issued - see #351
362 Russ Davis .10
363 Allen Watson .10
364 Mike Lieberthal .10
365 Dave Stevens .10
366 Jay Powell .10
367 Tony Fossas .10
368 Bob Wolcott .10
369 Mark Loretta .10
370 Shawn Estes .10
371 Sandy Martinez .10
372 Wendell Magee Jr. .10
373 John Franco .10
374 Not issued - see #274
375 Willie Adams .10
376 Chipper Jones (Stadium Sluggers) 5.00
377 Mo Vaughn (Stadium Sluggers) 1.25
378 Frank Thomas (Stadium Sluggers) 4.50
379 Albert Belle (Stadium Sluggers) 1.00
380 Andres Galarraga (Stadium Sluggers) .25
381 Gary Sheffield (Stadium Sluggers) .80
382 Jeff Bagwell (Stadium Sluggers) 2.00
383 Mike Piazza (Stadium Sluggers) 5.00
384 Mark McGwire (Stadium Sluggers) 6.00
385 Ken Griffey Jr. (Stadium Sluggers) 5.50
386 Barry Bonds (Stadium Sluggers) 4.50
387 Juan Gonzalez (Stadium Sluggers) 2.00
388 Brady Anderson (Stadium Sluggers) .25
389 Ken Caminiti (Stadium Sluggers) .25
390 Jay Buhner (Stadium Sluggers) .25

1997 Stadium Club Co-Signers

Each Series of Stadium Club included five different Co-Signers, with an insertion ratio of one per 168 hobby packs. These double-sided cards featured authentic autographs from each star, one per side.

		MT
Complete Set (10):		250.00
Common Card:		5.00
CO1	Andy Pettitte, Derek Jeter	100.00
CO2	Paul Wilson, Todd Hundley	5.00
CO3	Jermaine Dye, Mark Wohlers	10.00
CO4	Scott Rolen, Gregg Jefferies	20.00
CO5	Todd Hollandsworth, Jason Kendall	8.00
CO6	Alan Benes, Robin Ventura	15.00
CO7	Eric Karros, Raul Mondesi	15.00
CO8	Rey Ordonez, Nomar Garciaparra	75.00
CO9	Rondell White, Marty Cordova	8.00
CO10	Tony Gwynn, Karim Garcia	35.00

1997 Stadium Club Firebrand

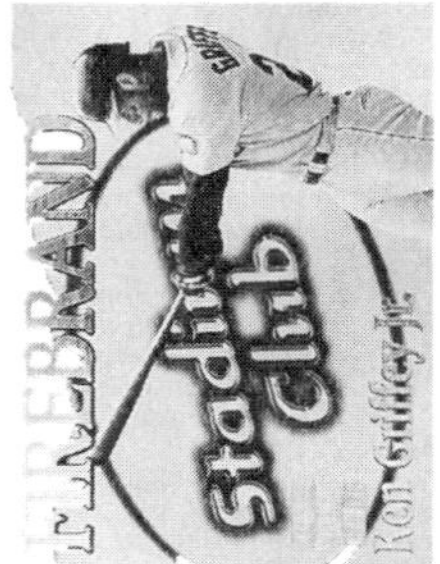

This 12-card insert was found only in packs sold at retail chains. Cards were inserted 1:36 packs. The hortizontal format cards are printed on thin wood stock, die-cut at top. Fronts are trimmed in gold foil. Cards are numbered with a "F" prefix.

		MT
Complete Set (12):		65.00
Common Player:		2.00
1	Jeff Bagwell	5.00
2	Albert Belle	2.50
3	Barry Bonds	7.50
4	Andres Galarraga	2.00
5	Ken Griffey Jr.	12.50
6	Brady Anderson	2.00
7	Mark McGwire	15.00
8	Chipper Jones	10.00
9	Frank Thomas	7.50
10	Mike Piazza	10.00
11	Mo Vaughn	3.00
12	Juan Gonzalez	5.00

1997 Stadium Club Firebrand Redemption

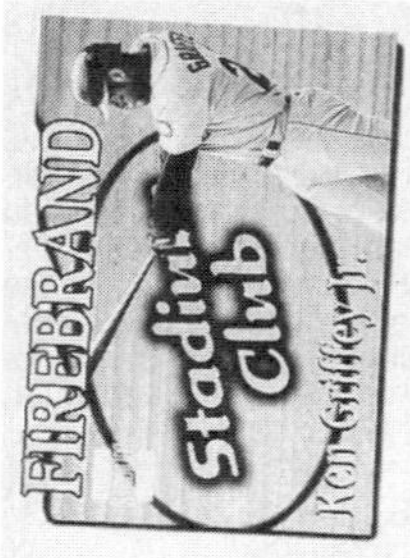

Because of production problems with its "Laser-Etched Wood" technology, Stadium Club was unable to package the Firebrand insert cards with the rest of the issue. Instead, a redemption card was substituted. The redemption card pictures the Firebrand card on its horizontal front; the back has details for exchanging the redemption card for the actual wood-printed, die-cut version. The exchange offer ended Sept. 30, 1997.

		MT
Complete Set (12):		40.00
Common Player:		1.25
F1	Jeff Bagwell	3.25
F2	Albert Belle	1.75
F3	Barry Bonds	5.00
F4	Andres Galarraga	1.25
F5	Ken Griffey Jr.	8.50
F6	Brady Anderson	1.25
F7	Mark McGwire	10.00
F8	Chipper Jones	6.50
F9	Frank Thomas	5.00
F10	Mike Piazza	6.50
F11	Mo Vaughn	2.00
F12	Juan Gonzalez	3.25

1997 Stadium Club Instavision

Instavision features holographic cards with exciting moments from the 1996 playoffs and World Series. Inserted one per 24 hobby packs and one per 36 retail packs, these cards are printed on a horizontal, plastic card. Cards carry an "I" prefix, with the first 10 found in Series I and the final 12 in Series II.

		MT
Complete Set (22):		30.00
Complete Series 1 Set (10):		12.50
Complete Series 2 Set (12):		17.50
Common Player:		.75
11	Eddie Murray	1.50
12	Paul Molitor	2.00
13	Todd Hundley	.75
14	Roger Clemens	3.00
15	Barry Bonds	4.00
16	Mark McGwire	5.00
17	Brady Anderson	.75
18	Barry Larkin	.75
19	Ken Caminiti	.75
110	Hideo Nomo	2.00
111	Bernie Williams	1.25
112	Juan Gonzalez	2.50
113	Andy Pettitte	1.50
114	Albert Belle	1.50
115	John Smoltz	1.00
116	Brian Jordan	.75
117	Derek Jeter	6.00
118	Ken Caminiti	.75
119	John Wetteland	.75
120	Brady Anderson	.75
121	Andruw Jones	2.50
122	Jim Leyritz	.75

1997 Stadium Club Millenium

Millennium was a 40-card insert that was released with 20 cards in Series I and Series II. The set featured 40 top prospects and rookies on a silver foil, holographic front, with a Future Forecast section on the back. Cards carried an "M" prefix and were numbered consecutively M1-M40. Millennium inserts were found every 24 hobby packs and every 36 retail packs.

		MT
Complete Set (40):		40.00
Complete Series 1 Set (20):		18.00
Complete Series 2 Set (20):		22.00
Common Player:		.50
1	Derek Jeter	8.00
2	Mark Grudzielanek	.50
3	Jacob Cruz	.50
4	Ray Durham	.50
5	Tony Clark	.50
6	Chipper Jones	6.50
7	Luis Castillo	.50
8	Carlos Delgado	1.50
9	Brant Brown	.50
10	Jason Kendall	.75
11	Alan Benes	.50
12	Rey Ordonez	.50
13	Justin Thompson	.50
14	Jermaine Allensworth	.50
15	Brian Hunter	.50
16	Marty Cordova	.50
17	Edgar Renteria	.50
18	Karim Garcia	.75
19	Todd Greene	.50
20	Paul Wilson	.50
21	Andruw Jones	5.00
22	Todd Walker	.50
23	Alex Ochoa	.50
24	Bartolo Colon	.50
25	Wendell Magee Jr.	.50
26	Jose Rosado	.50
27	Katsuhiro Maeda	.50
28	Bob Abreu	.75
29	Brooks Kieschnick	.50
30	Derrick Gibson	.50
31	Mike Sweeney	.50
32	Jeff D'Amico	.50
33	Chad Mottola	.50
34	Chris Snopek	.50
35	Jaime Bluma	.50
36	Vladimir Guerrero	5.00
37	Nomar Garciaparra	6.00
38	Scott Rolen	3.50
39	Dmitri Young	.50
40	Neifi Perez	.50

1997 Stadium Club Patent Leather

Patent Leather featured 13 of the top gloves in baseball on a leather, die-cut card. The cards carry a "PL" prefix and are inerted one per 36 retail packs.

		MT
Complete Set (13):		40.00
Common Player:		1.50
1	Ivan Rodriguez	4.00
2	Ken Caminiti	1.50
3	Barry Bonds	6.00
4	Ken Griffey Jr.	8.00
5	Greg Maddux	6.00
6	Craig Biggio	1.50
7	Andres Galarraga	1.50
8	Kenny Lofton	1.50
9	Barry Larkin	1.50
10	Mark Grace	2.50
11	Rey Ordonez	1.50
12	Roberto Alomar	4.00
13	Derek Jeter	10.00

1997 Stadium Club Pure Gold

Pure Gold featured 20 of the top players in baseball on gold, embossed foil cards. Cards carry a "PG" prefix and were inserted every 72 hobby packs and every 108 retail packs. The first 10 cards were in Series I packs, while the final 10 cards are exclusive to Series II.

		MT
Complete Set (20):		140.00
Complete Series 1 Set (10):		60.00
Complete Series 2 Set (10):		80.00
Common Player:		2.50
1	Brady Anderson	2.50
2	Albert Belle	3.00
3	Dante Bichette	2.50
4	Barry Bonds	12.00
5	Jay Buhner	2.50
6	Tony Gwynn	8.00
7	Chipper Jones	15.00
8	Mark McGwire	18.00
9	Gary Sheffield	3.00
10	Frank Thomas	6.00
11	Juan Gonzalez	6.00
12	Ken Caminiti	2.50
13	Kenny Lofton	2.50
14	Jeff Bagwell	6.00
15	Ken Griffey Jr.	18.00
16	Cal Ripken Jr.	20.00
17	Mo Vaughn	4.00

18	Mike Piazza	16.00
19	Derek Jeter	20.00
20	Andres Galarraga	2.50

1997 Stadium Club TSC Matrix

TSC Matrix consists of 120 cards from Series I and II reprinted with Power Matrix technology. In each Series, 60 of the 190 cards were selected for inclusion in TSC Matrix and inserted every 12 hobby packs and every 18 retail packs. Each insert carries the TSC Matrix logo in a top corner of the card.

		MT
Complete Set (120):		170.00
Common Player:		.50
1	Chipper Jones	8.00
2	Gary Sheffield	1.50
3	Kenny Lofton	.50
4	Brian Jordan	.50
5	Mark McGwire	12.50
6	Charles Nagy	.50
7	Tim Salmon	.75
8	Cal Ripken Jr.	12.50
9	Jeff Conine	.50
10	Paul Molitor	3.00
11	Mariano Rivera	1.50
12	Pedro Martinez	4.50
13	Jeff Bagwell	5.00
14	Bobby Bonilla	.50
15	Barry Bonds	7.00
16	Ryan Klesko	.50
17	Barry Larkin	.65
18	Jim Thome	.50
19	Jay Buhner	.50
20	Juan Gonzalez	5.00
21	Mike Mussina	3.00
22	Kevin Appier	.50
23	Eric Karros	.50
24	Steve Finley	.50
25	Ed Sprague	.50
26	Bernard Gilkey	.50
27	Tony Phillips	.50
28	Henry Rodriguez	.50
29	John Smoltz	.50
30	Dante Bichette	.50
31	Mike Piazza	8.00
32	Paul O'Neill	.50
33	Billy Wagner	.50
34	Reggie Sanders	.50
35	John Jaha	.50
36	Eddie Murray	2.00
37	Eric Young	.50
38	Roberto Hernandez	.50
39	Pat Hentgen	.50
40	Sammy Sosa	7.00
41	Todd Hundley	.50
42	Mo Vaughn	2.50
43	Robin Ventura	.50
44	Mark Grudzielanek	.50
45	Shane Reynolds	.50
46	Andy Pettitte	1.25
47	Fred McGriff	.50
48	Rey Ordonez	.50
49	Will Clark	1.25
50	Ken Griffey Jr.	10.00
51	Todd Worrell	.50
52	Rusty Greer	.50
53	Mark Grace	1.50
54	Tom Glavine	.50
55	Derek Jeter	8.00
56	Rafael Palmeiro	1.50
57	Bernie Williams	3.00
58	Marty Cordova	.50
59	Andres Galarraga	.50
60	Ken Caminiti	.50
196	Greg Maddux	6.00
197	Joe Carter	.50
198	Alex Ochoa	.50
199	Ellis Burks	.50
200	Ivan Rodriguez	4.00
201	Marquis Grissom	.50
202	Trevor Hoffman	.50
203	Matt Williams	1.25
204	Carlos Delgado	1.50
205	Ramon Martinez	.50
206	Chuck Knoblauch	.50
207	Juan Guzman	.50
208	Derek Bell	.50
209	Roger Clemens	6.00
210	Vladimir Guerrero	5.00
211	Cecil Fielder	.50
212	Hideo Nomo	2.50
213	Frank Thomas	7.00
214	Greg Vaughn	.50
215	Javy Lopez	.50
216	Raul Mondesi	1.00
217	Wade Boggs	2.50
218	Carlos Baerga	.50
219	Tony Gwynn	6.00
220	Tino Martinez	.50
221	Vinny Castilla	.50
222	Lance Johnson	.50
223	David Justice	1.25
224	Rondell White	.75
225	Dean Palmer	.50
226	Jim Edmonds	.50
227	Albert Belle	1.25
228	Alex Fernandez	.50
229	Ryne Sandberg	5.00
230	Jose Mesa	.50
231	David Cone	.50
232	Troy Percival	.50
233	Edgar Martinez	.50
234	Jose Canseco	2.50
235	Kevin Brown	.65
236	Ray Lankford	.50
237	Karim Garcia	.50
238	J.T. Snow	.50
239	Dennis Eckersley	.50
240	Roberto Alomar	4.50
241	John Valentin	.50
242	Ron Gant	.50
243	Geronimo Berroa	.50
244	Manny Ramirez	5.00
245	Travis Fryman	.50
246	Denny Neagle	.50
247	Randy Johnson	4.50
248	Darin Erstad	4.00
249	Mark Wohlers	.50
250	Ken Hill	.50
251	Larry Walker	1.25
252	Craig Biggio	.50
253	Brady Anderson	.50
254	John Wetteland	.50
255	Andruw Jones	5.00

1998 Stadium Club

Stadium Club was issued in two separate series for 1998, with 200 odd-numbered cards in Series I and 200 even- numbered cards in Series II. Retail packs contained six cards and an SRP of $2, hobby packs contained nine cards and an SRP of $3 and HTA packs contained 15 cards and an SRP of $5. Three subets were included in the set, with Future Stars (361-379) and Draft Picks (381-399) both being odd-numbered and Traded (356-400) being even- numbered. Inserts in Series I include: First Day Issue parallels (retail), One of a Kind parallels (hobby), Printing Plates parallels (HTA), Bowman Previews, Co-Signers (hobby), In the Wings, Never Comprimise, and Triumvirates (retail). Inserts in Series II include: First Day Issue parallels (retail), One of a Kind parallels (hobby), Printing Plates parallels (HTA), Bowman Prospect Previews, Co-Signers (hobby), Playing with Passion, Royal Court and Triumvirates (retail).

		MT
Complete Set (400):		55.00
Complete Series 1 (200):		30.00
Complete Series 2 (200):		25.00
Common Player:		.10
Hobby Pack (10):		3.00
Retail Pack (7):		2.00
Home Team Adv. Pack (16):		5.00
Wax Box (24):		45.00
1	Chipper Jones	2.00
2	Frank Thomas	1.75
3	Vladimir Guerrero	1.00
4	Ellis Burks	.10
5	John Franco	.10
6	Paul Molitor	.65
7	Rusty Greer	.10
8	Todd Hundley	.10
9	Brett Tomko	.10
10	Eric Karros	.10
11	Mike Cameron	.10
12	Jim Edmonds	.10
13	Bernie Williams	.40
14	Denny Neagle	.10
15	Jason Dickson	.10
16	Sammy Sosa	1.75
17	Brian Jordan	.10
18	Jose Vidro	.10
19	Scott Spiezio	.10
20	Jay Buhner	.10
21	Jim Thome	.10
22	Sandy Alomar	.10
23	Devon White	.10
24	Roberto Alomar	.65
25	John Flaherty	.10
26	John Wetteland	.10
27	Willie Greene	.10
28	Gregg Jefferies	.10
29	Johnny Damon	.15
30	Barry Larkin	.15
31	Chuck Knoblauch	.10
32	Mo Vaughn	.50
33	Tony Clark	.10
34	Marty Cordova	.10
35	Vinny Castilla	.10
36	Jeff King	.10
37	Reggie Jefferson	.10
38	Mariano Rivera	.25
39	Jermaine Allensworth	.10
40	Livan Hernandez	.10
41	Heathcliff Slocumb	.10
42	Jacob Cruz	.10
43	Barry Bonds	1.75
44	Dave Magadan	.10
45	Chan Ho Park	.20
46	Jeremi Gonzalez	.10
47	Jeff Cirillo	.10
48	Delino DeShields	.10
49	Craig Biggio	.15
50	Benito Santiago	.10
51	Mark Clark	.10
52	Fernando Vina	.10
53	F.P. Santangelo	.10
54	*Pep Harris*	.10
55	Edgar Renteria	.10
56	Jeff Bagwell	1.00
57	Jimmy Key	.10
58	Bartolo Colon	.10
59	Curt Schilling	.25
60	Steve Finley	.10
61	Andy Ashby	.10
62	John Burkett	.10
63	Orel Hershiser	.10
64	Pokey Reese	.10
65	Scott Servais	.10
66	Todd Jones	.10
67	Javy Lopez	.10
68	Robin Ventura	.10
69	Miguel Tejada	.25
70	Raul Casanova	.10
71	Reggie Sanders	.10
72	Edgardo Alfonzo	.10
73	Dean Palmer	.10
74	Todd Stottlemyre	.10
75	David Wells	.10
76	Troy Percival	.10
77	Albert Belle	.40
78	Pat Hentgen	.10
79	Brian Hunter	.10
80	Richard Hidalgo	.10
81	Darren Oliver	.10
82	Mark Wohlers	.10
83	Cal Ripken Jr.	2.50
84	Hideo Nomo	.65
85	Derrek Lee	.10
86	Stan Javier	.10
87	Rey Ordonez	.10
88	Randy Johnson	.75
89	Jeff Kent	.10
90	Brian McRae	.10
91	Manny Ramirez	1.00
92	Trevor Hoffman	.10
93	Doug Glanville	.10
94	Todd Walker	.10
95	Andy Benes	.10
96	Jason Schmidt	.10
97	Mike Matheny	.10
98	Tim Naehring	.10
99	Jeff Blauser	.10
100	Jose Rosado	.10
101	Roger Clemens	1.50
102	Pedro Astacio	.10
103	Mark Bellhorn	.10
104	Paul O'Neill	.10
105	Darin Erstad	.75
106	Mike Lieberthal	.10
107	Wilson Alvarez	.10
108	Mike Mussina	.65
109	George Williams	.10
110	Cliff Floyd	.10
111	Shawn Estes	.10
112	Mark Grudzielanek	.10
113	Tony Gwynn	1.50
114	Alan Benes	.10
115	Terry Steinbach	.10
116	Greg Maddux	1.50
117	Andy Pettitte	.25
118	Dave Nilsson	.10
119	Deivi Cruz	.10
120	Carlos Delgado	.40
121	Scott Hatteberg	.10
122	John Olerud	.10
123	Moises Alou	.20
124	Garret Anderson	.10
125	Royce Clayton	.10
126	Dante Powell	.10
127	Tom Glavine	.15
128	Gary DiSarcina	.10
129	Terry Adams	.10
130	Raul Mondesi	.25
131	Dan Wilson	.10
132	Al Martin	.10
133	Mickey Morandini	.10
134	Rafael Palmeiro	.30
135	Juan Encarnacion	.10
136	Jim Pittsley	.10
137	*Magglio Ordonez*	2.50
138	Will Clark	.30
139	Todd Helton	.75
140	Kelvim Escobar	.10
141	Esteban Loaiza	.10
142	John Jaha	.10
143	Jeff Fassero	.10
144	Harold Baines	.10

145 Butch Huskey .10
146 Pat Meares .10
147 Brian Giles .10
148 Ramiro Mendoza .10
149 John Smoltz .15
150 Felix Martinez .10
151 Jose Valentin .10
152 Brad Rigby .10
153 Ed Sprague .10
154 Mike Hampton .10
155 Mike Lansing .10
156 Ray Lankford .10
157 Bobby Bonilla .10
158 Bill Mueller .10
159 Jeffrey Hammonds .10
160 Charles Nagy .10
161 Rich Loiselle .10
162 Al Leiter .10
163 Larry Walker .30
164 Chris Hoiles .10
165 Jeff Montgomery .10
166 Francisco Cordova .10
167 James Baldwin .10
168 Mark McLemore .10
169 Kevin Appier .10
170 Jamey Wright .10
171 Nomar Garciaparra 1.75
172 Matt Franco .10
173 Armando Benitez .10
174 Jeromy Burnitz .10
175 Ismael Valdes .10
176 Lance Johnson .10
177 Paul Sorrento .10
178 Rondell White .20
179 Kevin Elster .10
180 Jason Giambi .40
181 Carlos Baerga .10
182 Russ Davis .10
183 Ryan McGuire .10
184 Eric Young .10
185 Ron Gant .10
186 Manny Alexander .10
187 Scott Karl .10
188 Brady Anderson .10
189 Randall Simon .10
190 Tim Belcher .10
191 Jaret Wright .10
192 Dante Bichette .10
193 John Valentin .10
194 Darren Bragg .10
195 Mike Sweeney .10
196 Craig Counsell .10
197 Jaime Navarro .10
198 Todd Dunn .10
199 Ken Griffey Jr. 2.25
200 Juan Gonzalez 1.00
201 Billy Wagner .10
202 Tino Martinez .10
203 Mark McGwire 2.50
204 Jeff D'Amico .10
205 Rico Brogna .10
206 Todd Hollandsworth .10
207 Chad Curtis .10
208 Tom Goodwin .10
209 Neifi Perez .10
210 Derek Bell .10
211 Quilvio Veras .10
212 Greg Vaughn .10
213 Roberto Hernandez .10
214 Arthur Rhodes .10
215 Cal Eldred .10
216 Bill Taylor .10
217 Todd Greene .10
218 Mario Valdez .10
219 Ricky Bottalico .10
220 Frank Rodriguez .10
221 Rich Becker .10
222 Roberto Duran .10
223 Ivan Rodriguez .75
224 Mike Jackson .10
225 Deion Sanders .15
226 Tony Womack .10
227 Mark Kotsay .10
228 Steve Trachsel .10
229 Ryan Klesko .10
230 Ken Cloude .10
231 Luis Gonzalez .35
232 Gary Gaetti .10
233 Michael Tucker .10
234 Shawn Green .30
235 Ariel Prieto .10
236 Kirt Manwaring .10
237 Omar Vizquel .10
238 Matt Beech .10
239 Justin Thompson .10
240 Bret Boone .15
241 Derek Jeter 2.00
242 Ken Caminiti .10
243 Jay Bell .10
244 Kevin Tapani .10
245 Jason Kendall .10
246 Jose Guillen .10
247 Mike Bordick .10
248 Dustin Hermanson .10
249 Darrin Fletcher .10
250 Dave Hollins .10
251 Ramon Martinez .10
252 Hideki Irabu .10
253 Mark Grace .30
254 Jason Isringhausen .10
255 Jose Cruz Jr. .15
256 Brian Johnson .10
257 Brad Ausmus .10
258 Andruw Jones 1.00
259 Doug Jones .10
260 Jeff Shaw .10
261 Chuck Finley .10
262 Gary Sheffield .40
263 David Segui .10
264 John Smiley .10
265 Tim Salmon .25
266 J.T. Snow Jr. .10
267 Alex Fernandez .10
268 Matt Stairs .10
269 B.J. Surhoff .10
270 Keith Foulke .10
271 Edgar Martinez .10
272 Shannon Stewart .15
273 Eduardo Perez .10
274 Wally Joyner .10
275 Kevin Young .10
276 Eli Marrero .10
277 Brad Radke .10
278 Jamie Moyer .10
279 Joe Girardi .10
280 Troy O'Leary .10
281 Aaron Sele .10
282 Jose Offerman .10
283 Scott Erickson .10
284 Sean Berry .10
285 Shigetosi Hasegawa .10
286 Felix Heredia .10
287 Willie McGee .10
288 Alex Rodriguez 2.25
289 Ugueth Urbina .10
290 Jon Lieber .10
291 Fernando Tatis .10
292 Chris Stynes .10
293 Bernard Gilkey .10
294 Joey Hamilton .10
295 Matt Karchner .10
296 Paul Wilson .10
297 Mel Nieves .10
298 *Kevin Millwood* 1.50
299 Quinton McCracken .10
300 Jerry DiPoto .10
301 Jermaine Dye .10
302 Travis Lee .10
303 Ron Coomer .10
304 Matt Williams .30
305 Bobby Higginson .15
306 Jorge Fabregas .10
307 Hal Morris .10
308 Jay Bell .10
309 Joe Randa .10
310 Andy Benes .10
311 Sterling Hitchcock .10
312 Jeff Suppan .10
313 Shane Reynolds .10
314 Willie Blair .10
315 Scott Rolen .75
316 Wilson Alvarez .10
317 David Justice .40
318 Fred McGriff .10
319 Bobby Jones .10
320 Wade Boggs .60
321 Tim Wakefield .10
322 Tony Saunders .10
323 David Cone .10
324 Roberto Hernandez .10
325 Jose Canseco .50
326 Kevin Stocker .10
327 Gerald Williams .10
328 Quinton McCracken .10
329 Mark Gardner .10
330 Ben Griev (Prime Rookie) .25
331 Kevin Brown .15
332 *Mike Lowell* (Prime Rookie) .75
333 Jed Hansen .10
334 Abraham Nunez (Prime Rookie) .15
335 John Thomson .10
336 Derrek Lee (Prime Rookie) .10
337 Mike Piazza 2.00
338 Brad Fullmer (Prime Rookie) .10
339 Ray Durham .10
340 Kerry Wood (Prime Rookie) .25
341 *Kevin Polcovich* .10
342 Russ Johnson (Prime Rookie) .10
343 Darryl Hamilton .10
344 David Ortiz (Prime Rookie) .15
345 Kevin Orie .10
346 Sean Casey (Prime Rookie) .25
347 Juan Guzman .10
348 Ruben Rivera (Prime Rookie) .10
349 Rick Aguilera .10
350 Bobby Estalella (Prime Rookie) .10
351 Bobby Witt .10
352 Paul Konerko (Prime Rookie) .15
353 Matt Morris .10
354 Carl Pavano (Prime Rookie) .10
355 Todd Zeile .10
356 Kevin Brown (Transaction) .10
357 Alex Gonzalez .15
358 Chuck Knoblauch (Transaction) .10
359 Joey Cora .10
360 Mike Lansing (Transaction) .10
361 Adrian Beltre (Future Stars) .25
362 Dennis Eckersley (Transaction) .10
363 A.J. Hinch (Future Stars) .15
364 Kenny Lofton (Transaction) .10
365 Alex Gonzalez (Future Stars) .10
366 Henry Rodriguez (Transaction) .10
367 *Mike Stoner* (Future Stars) .50
368 Darryl Kile (Transaction) .10
369 Carl Pavano (Future Stars) .10
370 Walt Weiss (Transaction) .10
371 Kris Benson (Future Stars) .10
372 Cecil Fielder (Transaction) .10
373 Dermal Brown (Future Stars) .15
374 Rod Beck (Transaction) .10
375 Eric Milton (Future Stars) .15
376 Travis Fryman (Transaction) .10
377 Preston Wilson (Future Stars) .10
378 Chili Davis (Transaction) .10
379 Travis Lee (Future Stars) .15
380 Jim Leyritz (Transaction) .10
381 Vernon Wells (Draft Picks) .15
382 Joe Carter (Transaction) .10
383 J.J. Davis (Draft Picks) .15
384 Marquis Grissom (Transaction) .10
385 *Mike Cuddyer* (Draft Picks) 1.50
386 Rickey Henderson (Transaction) .65
387 *Chris Enochs* (Draft Picks) .25
388 Andres Galarraga (Transaction) .10
389 Jason Dellaero (Draft Picks) .10
390 Robb Nen (Transaction) .10
391 Mark Mangum (Draft Picks) .10
392 Jeff Blauser (Transaction) .10
393 Adam Kennedy (Draft Picks) .15
394 Bob Abreu (Transaction) .10
395 *Jack Cust* (Draft Picks) 1.50
396 Jose Vizcaino (Transaction) .10
397 Jon Garland (Draft Picks) .15
398 Pedro Martinez (Transaction) .50
399 Aaron Akin (Draft Picks) .10
400 Jeff Conine (Transaction) .10

1998 Stadium Club First Day Issue

	MT
Common Player:	2.00
Stars:	45X

Production 200 sets

(See 1998 Stadium Club for checklist and base card values.)

1998 Stadium Club One of a Kind

This hobby-only parallel set includes all 400 cards from Series 1 and 2 printed on a silver mirror-board stock. Cards are sequentially numbered to 150 and inserted one per 21 Series 1 packs and one per 24 Series 2 packs.

	MT
Common Player:	2.00
Stars:	25X

Production 150 sets

(See 1998 Stadium Club for checklist and base card values.)

1998 Stadium Club Printing Plates

Inserted only in Home Team Advantage boxes at a rate of approximately one per 90 packs were the actual aluminum plates used to print the fronts of the base cards. Unlike some printing plate issues, the plates used for the card backs were not inserted. Each card's plate can be found in four different colors: Cyan, magenta, yellow and black. Because of their unique nature, pricing of individual player's plates cannot be provided.

	MT
Common Player:	25.00

(See 1998 Stadium Club for checklist.)

1998 Stadium Club Bowman Preview

This Series I insert gave collectors a sneak peak at Bowman's 50th anniversary set, with 10 top veterans displayed on the 1998 Bowman design. The cards were inserted one per 12 packs and numbered with a "BP" prefix.

	MT
Complete Set (10):	20.00
Common Player:	.50
Inserted 1:12	
BP1 Nomar Garciaparra	3.00
BP2 Scott Rolen	2.00
BP3 Ken Griffey Jr.	4.00
BP4 Frank Thomas	3.00
BP5 Larry Walker	.50
BP6 Mike Piazza	3.50
BP7 Chipper Jones	3.50
BP8 Tino Martinez	.50
BP9 Mark McGwire	5.00
BP10 Barry Bonds	3.00

1998 Stadium Club Bowman Prospect Preview

Bowman Prospect Previews were inserted into Series II retail and hobby packs at a rate of one per 12 and HTA packs at one per four. The 10-card insert previews the upcoming 1998 Bowman set and includes top prospects that are expected to make an impact in 1998.

	MT
Complete Set (10):	7.00
Common Player:	.50
Inserted 1:12	
BP1 Ben Grieve	2.00
BP2 Brad Fullmer	.50
BP3 Ryan Anderson	1.00
BP4 Mark Kotsay	.50
BP5 Bobby Estalella	.50
BP6 Juan Encarnacion	.75
BP7 Todd Helton	2.00
BP8 Mike Lowell	.50
BP9 A.J. Hinch	.50
BP10 Richard Hidalgo	.50

1998 Stadium Club Co-Signers

Co-Signers were inserted into both Series 1 and 2 hobby and HTA packs. The complete set is 36 cards and contains two top players on one side along with both autographs. They were available in three levels of scarcity: Series 1 Group A 1:4,372 hobby and 1:2,623 HTA; Series 1 Group B 1:1,457 hobby and HTA 1:874; Series 1 Group C 1:121 hobby and 1:73 HTA; Series 2 Group A 1:4,702 hobby and 1:2,821 HTA; Series 2 Group B 1:1,567 hobby and 1:940 HTA, Series 2 Group C 1:1,131 hobby and 1:78 HTA.

	MT
Common Player:	10.00
Group A 1:4,372	
Group B 1:1,457	
Group C 1:121	
CS1 Nomar Garciaparra, Scott Rolen (A)	400.00
CS2 Nomar Garciaparra, Derek Jeter (B)	300.00
CS3 Nomar Garciaparra, Eric Karros (C)	60.00
CS4 Scott Rolen, Derek Jeter (C)	100.00
CS5 Scott Rolen, Eric Karros (B)	50.00
CS6 Derek Jeter, Eric Karros (A)	300.00
CS7 Travis Lee, Jose Cruz Jr. (B)	15.00
CS8 Travis Lee, Mark Kotsay (C)	10.00
CS9 Travis Lee, Paul Konerko (A)	25.00
CS10 Jose Cruz Jr., Mark Kotsay (A)	20.00
CS11 Jose Cruz Jr., Paul Konerko (C)	15.00
CS12 Mark Kotsay, Paul Konerko (B)	20.00
CS13 Tony Gwynn, Larry Walker (A)	200.00
CS14 Tony Gwynn, Mark Grudzielanek (C)	35.00
CS15 Tony Gwynn, Andres Galarraga (B)	65.00
CS16 Larry Walker, Mark Grudzielanek (B)	25.00
CS17 Larry Walker, Andres Galarraga (C)	30.00
CS18 Mark Grudzielanek, Andres Galarraga (A)	30.00
CS19 Sandy Alomar, Roberto Alomar (A)	180.00
CS20 Sandy Alomar, Andy Pettitte (C)	15.00
CS21 Sandy Alomar, Tino Martinez (B)	30.00
CS22 Roberto Alomar, Andy Pettitte (B)	60.00
CS23 Roberto Alomar, Tino Martinez (C)	25.00
CS24 Andy Pettitte, Tino Martinez (A)	65.00
CS25 Tony Clark, Todd Hundley (A)	35.00
CS26 Tony Clark, Tim Salmon (B)	25.00
CS27 Tony Clark, Robin Ventura (C)	20.00
CS28 Todd Hundley, Tim Salmon (C)	15.00
CS29 Todd Hundley, Robin Ventura (B)	20.00
CS30 Tim Salmon, Robin Ventura (A)	40.00
CS31 Roger Clemens, Randy Johnson (B)	100.00
CS32 Roger Clemens, Jaret Wright (A)	150.00
CS33 Roger Clemens, Matt Morris (C)	40.00
CS34 Randy Johnson, Jaret Wright (C)	30.00
CS35 Randy Johnson, Matt Morris (A)	80.00
CS36 Jaret Wright, Matt Morris (B)	30.00

1998 Stadium Club In the Wings

In the Wings was a Series I insert found every 36 packs. It included 15 future stars on uniluster technology.

	MT
Complete Set (15):	20.00
Common Player:	1.00
Inserted 1:36	
W1 Juan Encarnacion	1.50
W2 Brad Fullmer	2.00
W3 Ben Grieve	3.00
W4 Todd Helton	4.00
W5 Richard Hidalgo	2.00
W6 Russ Johnson	1.00
W7 Paul Konerko	2.00
W8 Mark Kotsay	1.50
W9 Derrek Lee	1.00
W10 Travis Lee	1.50
W11 Eli Marrero	1.00
W12 David Ortiz	1.00
W13 Randall Simon	1.00
W14 Shannon Stewart	1.50
W15 Fernando Tatis	1.00

1998 Stadium Club Never Compromise

Never Compromise was a 20-card insert found in packs of Series I. Cards were inserted one per 12 packs and numbered with a "NC" prefix.

	MT
Complete Set (20):	25.00
Common Player:	.30
Inserted 1:12	
NC1 Cal Ripken Jr.	3.00
NC2 Ivan Rodriguez	.65
NC3 Ken Griffey Jr.	2.50
NC4 Frank Thomas	1.00
NC5 Tony Gwynn	1.50
NC6 Mike Piazza	2.00
NC7 Randy Johnson	.75
NC8 Greg Maddux	1.50
NC9 Roger Clemens	1.50
NC10 Derek Jeter	3.00
NC11 Chipper Jones	2.00
NC12 Barry Bonds	1.50
NC13 Larry Walker	.45
NC14 Jeff Bagwell	1.00
NC15 Barry Larkin	.30
NC16 Ken Caminiti	.30
NC17 Mark McGwire	3.00
NC18 Manny Ramirez	1.00
NC19 Tim Salmon	.30
NC20 Paul Molitor	.65

1998 Stadium Club Playing with Passion

This Series II insert displayed 10 players with a strong desire to win. The cards were inserted one per 12 packs and numbered with a "P" prefix.

	MT
Complete Set (10):	10.00

Common Player:		.50
Inserted 1:12		
P1	Bernie Williams	.75
P2	Jim Edmonds	.50
P3	Chipper Jones	1.50
P4	Cal Ripken Jr.	2.50
P5	Craig Biggio	.50
P6	Juan Gonzalez	1.00
P7	Alex Rodriguez	2.00
P8	Tino Martinez	.50
P9	Mike Piazza	2.00
P10	Ken Griffey Jr.	2.00

1998 Stadium Club Royal Court

Fifteen players were showcased on uniluster technology for this Series II insert. The set is broken up into 10 Kings (veterans) and five Princes (rookies) and inserted one per 36 packs.

		MT
Complete Set (15):		60.00
Common Player:		1.00
Inserted 1:36		
RC1	Ken Griffey Jr.	8.00
RC2	Frank Thomas	3.00
RC3	Mike Piazza	8.00
RC4	Chipper Jones	6.50
RC5	Mark McGwire	8.00
RC6	Cal Ripken Jr.	10.00
RC7	Jeff Bagwell	3.00
RC8	Barry Bonds	5.00
RC9	Juan Gonzalez	3.00
RC10	Alex Rodriguez	8.00
RC11	Travis Lee	1.00
RC12	Paul Konerko	1.00
RC13	Todd Helton	3.00
RC14	Ben Grieve	2.00
RC15	Mark Kotsay	1.00

1998 Stadium Club Triumvirate

Triumvirates were included in both series of Stadium Club and were available only in retail packs. Series 1 has 24 players, with three players from eight different teams, while Series 2 has 30 players, with three players from 10 different positions. The cards are all die-cut and fit together to form three-card panels. Three different versions of each card were available - Luminous (regular) versions were seeded one per 48 packs, Luminescent versions were seeded one per 192 packs and Illuminator versions were seeded one per 384 packs.

		MT
Complete Set (54):		275.00
Complete Series 1 (24):		125.00
Complete Series 2 (30):		150.00
Common Player:		2.00
Luminous 1:48		
Luminescents 1:192:		1.5X
Illuminators 1:384:		2.5X
T1a	Chipper Jones	12.00
T1b	Andruw Jones	5.00
T1c	Kenny Lofton	2.00
T2a	Derek Jeter	20.00
T2b	Bernie Williams	4.00
T2c	Tino Martinez	2.00
T3a	Jay Buhner	2.00
T3b	Edgar Martinez	2.00
T3c	Ken Griffey Jr.	18.00
T4a	Albert Belle	2.50
T4b	Robin Ventura	2.00
T4c	Frank Thomas	6.00
T5a	Brady Anderson	2.00
T5b	Cal Ripken Jr.	20.00
T5c	Rafael Palmeiro	3.00
T6a	Mike Piazza	15.00
T6b	Raul Mondesi	2.00
T6c	Eric Karros	2.00
T7a	Vinny Castilla	2.00
T7b	Andres Galarraga	2.00
T7c	Larry Walker	2.50
T8a	Jim Thome	2.50
T8b	Manny Ramirez	6.00
T8c	David Justice	2.50
T9a	Mike Mussina	4.00
T9b	Greg Maddux	8.00
T9c	Randy Johnson	5.00
T10a	Mike Piazza	15.00
T10b	Sandy Alomar	2.00
T10c	Ivan Rodriguez	5.00
T11a	Mark McGwire	20.00
T11b	Tino Martinez	2.00
T11c	Frank Thomas	6.00
T12a	Roberto Alomar	4.00
T12b	Chuck Knoblauch	2.00
T12c	Craig Biggio	2.00
T13a	Cal Ripken Jr.	20.00
T13b	Chipper Jones	12.00
T13c	Ken Caminiti	2.00
T14a	Derek Jeter	20.00
T14b	Nomar Garciaparra	12.00
T14c	Alex Rodriguez	18.00
T15a	Barry Bonds	10.00
T15b	David Justice	2.50
T15c	Albert Belle	2.50
T16a	Bernie Williams	3.00
T16b	Ken Griffey Jr.	18.00
T16c	Ray Lankford	2.00
T17a	Tim Salmon	2.50
T17b	Larry Walker	2.50
T17c	Tony Gwynn	8.00
T18a	Paul Molitor	4.00
T18b	Edgar Martinez	2.00
T18c	Juan Gonzalez	6.00

1999 Stadium Club

Released in two series with Series 1 170-cards and Series 2 185-cards. Base cards feature a full bleed design on 20-pt. stock with an embossed holographic logo. Draft Pick and Prospect subset cards are short-printed, seeded in every three packs. Card backs have 1998 statistics and personal information. Hobby packs consist of six cards with a S.R.P. of $2.

		MT
Complete Set (355):		90.00
Complete Series 1 Set (170):		50.00
Complete Series 2 Set (185):		40.00
Common Player:		.10
Common Prospect (141-148):		.75
Inserted 1:3		
Common Draft Pick (149-160):		.75
Inserted 1:3		
Common SP (311-335, 346-355):		.75
Common SP (336-345):		.75
Pack (6):		1.50
Wax Box (24):		35.00
1	Alex Rodriguez	2.25
2	Chipper Jones	2.00
3	Rusty Greer	.10
4	Jim Edmonds	.10
5	Ron Gant	.10
6	Kevin Polcovich	.10
7	Darryl Strawberry	.10
8	Bill Mueller	.10
9	Vinny Castilla	.10
10	Wade Boggs	.60
11	Jose Lima	.10
12	Darren Dreifort	.10
13	Jay Bell	.10
14	Ben Grieve	.25
15	Shawn Green	.25
16	Andres Galarraga	.10
17	Bartolo Colon	.10
18	Francisco Cordova	.10
19	Paul O'Neill	.10
20	Trevor Hoffman	.10
21	Darren Oliver	.10
22	John Franco	.10
23	Eli Marrero	.10
24	Roberto Hernandez	.10
25	Craig Biggio	.15
26	Brad Fullmer	.10
27	Scott Erickson	.10
28	Tom Gordon	.10
29	Brian Hunter	.10
30	Raul Mondesi	.20
31	Rick Reed	.10
32	Jose Canseco	.60
33	Robb Nen	.10
34	Turner Ward	.10
35	Bret Boone	.15
36	Jose Offerman	.10
37	Matt Lawton	.10
38	David Wells	.10
39	Bob Abreu	.15
40	Jeromy Burnitz	.10
41	Deivi Cruz	.10
42	Mike Cameron	.10
43	Rico Brogna	.10
44	Dmitri Young	.10
45	Chuck Knoblauch	.10
46	Johnny Damon	.15
47	Brian Meadows	.10
48	Jeremi Gonzalez	.10
49	Gary DiSarcina	.10
50	Frank Thomas	1.75
51	F.P. Santangelo	.10
52	Tom Candiotti	.10
53	Shane Reynolds	.10
54	Rod Beck	.10
55	Rey Ordonez	.10
56	Todd Helton	.75
57	Mickey Morandini	.10
58	Jorge Posada	.10
59	Mike Mussina	.65
60	Bobby Bonilla	.10
61	David Segui	.10
62	Brian McRae	.10
63	Fred McGriff	.10
64	Brett Tomko	.10
65	Derek Jeter	2.00
66	Sammy Sosa	1.75
67	Kenny Rogers	.10
68	Dave Nilsson	.10
69	Eric Young	.10
70	Mark McGwire	2.50
71	Kenny Lofton	.10
72	Tom Glavine	.15
73	Joey Hamilton	.10
74	John Valentin	.10
75	Mariano Rivera	.25
76	Ray Durham	.10
77	Tony Clark	.10
78	Livan Hernandez	.10
79	Rickey Henderson	.75
80	Vladimir Guerrero	1.00
81	J.T. Snow Jr.	.10
82	Juan Guzman	.10
83	Darryl Hamilton	.10
84	Matt Anderson	.10
85	Travis Lee	.25
86	Joe Randa	.10
87	Dave Dellucci	.10
88	Moises Alou	.20
89	Alex Gonzalez	.15
90	Tony Womack	.10
91	Neifi Perez	.10
92	Travis Fryman	.10
93	Masato Yoshii	.10
94	Woody Williams	.10
95	Ray Lankford	.10
96	Roger Clemens	1.50
97	Dustin Hermanson	.10
98	Joe Carter	.10
99	Jason Schmidt	.10
100	Greg Maddux	1.50
101	Kevin Tapani	.10
102	Charles Johnson	.10
103	Derrek Lee	.10
104	Pete Harnisch	.10
105	Dante Bichette	.10
106	Scott Brosius	.10
107	Mike Caruso	.10
108	Eddie Taubensee	.10
109	Jeff Fassero	.10
110	Marquis Grissom	.10
111	Jose Hernandez	.10
112	Chan Ho Park	.25
113	Wally Joyner	.10
114	Bobby Estalella	.10
115	Pedro Martinez	.65
116	Shawn Estes	.10
117	Walt Weiss	.10
118	John Mabry	.10
119	Brian Johnson	.10
120	Jim Thome	.10
121	Bill Spiers	.10
122	John Olerud	.10
123	Jeff King	.10
124	Tim Belcher	.10
125	John Wetteland	.10
126	Tony Gwynn	1.50
127	Brady Anderson	.10
128	Randy Winn	.10
129	Devon White	.10
130	Eric Karros	.10
131	Kevin Millwood	.25
132	Andy Benes	.10
133	Andy Ashby	.10
134	Ron Comer	.10
135	Juan Gonzalez	1.00
136	Randy Johnson	.75
137	Aaron Sele	.10
138	Edgardo Alfonzo	.10
139	B.J. Surhoff	.10
140	Jose Vizcaino	.10
141	*Chad Moeller* (Prospect)	1.00
142	*Mike Zwicka* (Prospect)	.75
143	Angel Pena (Prospect)	.75

144 *Nick Johnson* (Prospect) 8.00
145 *Giuseppe Chiaramonte* (Prospect) 1.00
146 *Kit Pellow* (Prospect) 1.00
147 *Clayton Andrews* (Prospect) .75
148 *Jerry Hairston Jr.* (Prospect) 1.50
149 *Jason Tyner* (Draft Pick) 1.00
150 *Chip Ambres* (Draft Pick) 1.00
151 *Pat Burrell* (Draft Pick) 8.00
152 *Josh McKinley* (Draft Pick) .75
153 *Choo Freeman* (Draft Pick) .75
154 *Rick Elder* (Draft Pick) .75
155 *Eric Valent* (Draft Pick) 1.00
156 *Jeff Winchester* (Draft Pick) .75
157 *Mike Nannini* (Draft Pick) 1.00
158 *Mamon Tucker* (Draft Pick) .75
159 *Nate Bump* (Draft Pick) 1.00
160 *Andy Brown* (Draft Pick) 1.00
161 Troy Glaus (Future Star) .25
162 Adrian Beltre (Future Star) .25
163 Mitch Meluskey (Future Star) .10
164 Alex Gonzalez (Future Star) .15
165 George Lombard (Future Star) .10
166 Eric Chavez (Future Star) .25
167 Ruben Mateo (Future Star) .15
168 Calvin Pickering (Future Star) .10
169 Gabe Kapler (Future Star) .25
170 Bruce Chen (Future Star) .10
171 Darin Erstad .75
172 Sandy Alomar .10
173 Miguel Cairo .10
174 Jason Kendall .10
175 Cal Ripken Jr. 2.50
176 Darryl Kile .10
177 David Cone .10
178 Mike Sweeney .10
179 Royce Clayton .10
180 Curt Schilling .30
181 Barry Larkin .15
182 Eric Milton .10
183 Ellis Burks .10
184 A.J. Hinch .10
185 Garret Anderson .10
186 Sean Bergman .10
187 Shannon Stewart .15
188 Bernard Gilkey .10
189 Jeff Blauser .10
190 Andruw Jones 1.00
191 Omar Daal .10
192 Jeff Kent .10
193 Mark Kotsay .10
194 Dave Burba .10
195 Bobby Higginson .15
196 Hideki Irabu .10
197 Jamie Moyer .10
198 Doug Glanville .10
199 Quinton McCracken .10
200 Ken Griffey Jr. 2.25
201 Mike Lieberthal .10
202 Carl Everett .15
203 Omar Vizquel .10
204 Mike Lansing .10
205 Manny Ramirez 1.00
206 Ryan Klesko .10
207 Jeff Montgomery .10
208 Chad Curtis .10
209 Rick Helling .10
210 Justin Thompson .10
211 Tom Goodwin .10
212 Todd Dunwoody .10
213 Kevin Young .10
214 Tony Saunders .10
215 Gary Sheffield .35
216 Jaret Wright .10
217 Quilvio Veras .10
218 Marty Cordova .10
219 Tino Martinez .10
220 Scott Rolen .75
221 Fernando Tatis .10
222 Damion Easley .10
223 Aramis Ramirez .10
224 Brad Radke .10
225 Nomar Garciaparra 1.75
226 Magglio Ordonez .15
227 Andy Pettitte .40
228 David Ortiz .10
229 Todd Jones .10
230 Larry Walker .40
231 Tim Wakefield .10
232 Jose Guillen .10
233 Gregg Olson .10
234 Ricky Gutierrez .10
235 Todd Walker .15
236 Abraham Nunez .10
237 Sean Casey .25
238 Greg Norton .10
239 Bret Saberhagen .10
240 Bernie Williams .40
241 Tim Salmon .25
242 Jason Giambi .35
243 Fernando Vina .10
244 Darrin Fletcher .10
245 Greg Vaughn .10
246 Dennis Reyes .10
247 Hideo Nomo .75
248 Reggie Sanders .10
249 Mike Hampton .10
250 Kerry Wood .65
251 Ismael Valdes .10
252 Pat Hentgen .10
253 Scott Spiezio .10
254 Chuck Finley .10
255 Troy Glaus .50
256 Bobby Jones .10
257 Wayne Gomes .10
258 Rondell White .25
259 Todd Zeile .10
260 Matt Williams .30
261 Henry Rodriguez .10
262 Matt Stairs .10
263 Jose Valentin .10
264 David Justice .40
265 Javy Lopez .10
266 Matt Morris .10
267 Steve Trachsel .10
268 Edgar Martinez .10
269 Al Martin .10
270 Ivan Rodriguez .65
271 Carlos Delgado .40
272 Mark Grace .35
273 Ugueth Urbina .10
274 Jay Buhner .10
275 Mike Piazza 2.25
276 Rick Aguilera .10
277 Javier Valentin .10
278 Brian Anderson .10
279 Cliff Floyd .10
280 Barry Bonds 1.75
281 Troy O'Leary .10
282 Seth Greisinger .10
283 Mark Grudzielanek .10
284 Jose Cruz Jr. .25
285 Jeff Bagwell 1.00
286 John Smoltz .15
287 Jeff Cirillo .10
288 Richie Sexson .10
289 Charles Nagy .10
290 Pedro Martinez .60
291 Juan Encarnacion .15
292 Phil Nevin .10
293 Terry Steinbach .10
294 Miguel Tejada .25
295 Dan Wilson .10
296 Chris Peters .10
297 Brian Moehler .10
298 Jason Christiansen .10
299 Kelly Stinnett .10
300 Dwight Gooden .10
301 Randy Velarde .10
302 Kirt Manwaring .10
303 Jeff Abbott .10
304 Dave Hollins .10
305 Kerry Ligtenberg .10
306 Aaron Boone .10
307 Carlos Hernandez .10
308 Mike DiFelice .10
309 Brian Meadows .10
310 Tim Bogar .10
311 Greg Vaughn (Transaction) .75
312 Brant Brown (Transaction) .75
313 Steve Finley (Transaction) .75
314 Bret Boone (Transaction) 1.00
315 Albert Belle (Transaction) .75
316 Robin Ventura (Transaction) .75
317 Eric Davis (Transaction) .75
318 Todd Hundley (Transaction) .75
319 Jose Offerman (Transaction) .75
320 Kevin Brown (Transaction) .75
321 Denny Neagle (Transaction) .75
322 Brian Jordan (Transaction) .75
323 Brian Giles (Transaction) .75
324 Bobby Bonilla (Transaction) .75
325 Roberto Alomar (Transaction) 1.00
326 Ken Caminiti (Transaction) .75
327 Todd Stottlemyre (Transaction) .75
328 Randy Johnson (Transaction) 1.50
329 Luis Gonzalez (Transaction) 1.25
330 Rafael Palmeiro (Transaction) 1.00
331 Devon White (Transaction) .75
332 Will Clark (Transaction) 1.00
333 Dean Palmer (Transaction) .75
334 Gregg Jefferies (Transaction) .75
335 Mo Vaughn (Transaction) 1.25
336 *Brad Lidge* (Draft Pick) .75
337 *Chris George* (Draft Pick) 1.00
338 *Austin Kearns* (Draft Pick) 5.00
339 *Matt Belisle* (Draft Pick) .75
340 *Nate Cornejo* (Draft Pick) 1.00
341 *Matt Holiday* (Draft Pick) 1.00
342 *J.M. Gold* (Draft Pick) 1.00
343 *Matt Roney* (Draft Pick) .75
344 *Seth Etherton* (Draft Pick) 1.00
345 *Adam Everett* (Draft Pick) 1.00
346 Marlon Anderson (Future Star) 1.00
347 Ron Belliard (Future Star) .75
348 Fernando Seguignol (Future Star) .75
349 Michael Barrett (Future Star) 1.00
350 Dernell Stenson (Future Star) .75
351 Ryan Anderson (Future Star) 1.00
352 Ramon Hernandez (Future Star) 1.00
353 Jeremy Giambi (Future Star) .75
354 Ricky Ledee (Future Star) .75
355 Carlos Lee (Future Star) 1.00

1999 Stadium Club First Day Issue

A parallel of the 355-card set inserted exclusively in retail packs, Series I (1-170) are serially numbered to 170 at a rate of 1:75 packs. Series 2 (171-355) are serially numbered to 200 and inserted at a rate of 1:60 packs.

	MT
Common Player:	2.00
Stars:	12X
SP Stars:	4X

(See 1999 Stadium Club for checklist and base card values.)

1999 Stadium Club One of a Kind

This insert set parallels the 355-card base set. Cards feature a mirror-board look and are serially numbered to 150. Inserted exclusively in hobby packs, insertion rate for Series 1 is 1:53 and Series 2 is 1:48 packs.

	MT
Common Player:	2.00
Stars:	12X
SP Stars:	4X

(See 1999 Stadium Club for checklist and base card values.)

1999 Stadium Club Printing Plates

Inserted only in Home Team Advantage boxes at a rate of approximately one per 175 packs were the actual aluminum plates used to print the fronts of the base cards. Unlike some printing plate issues, the plates used for the card backs were not inserted. Each card's plate can be found in four different colors: Cyan, magenta, yellow and black. Because of their unique nature, pricing of individual player's plates cannot be provided.

	MT
Common Player:	25.00

(See 1999 Stadium Club for checklist.)

1999 Stadium Club Autographs

This 10-card autographed set was issued in Series 1 and 2 with five players signing in each series. Available exclusively in retail chains, Series 1 autographs were seeded 1:1,107 packs, while series 2 were inserted in every 877 packs. Each autograph is marked with the Topps Certified Autograph Issue stamp. Card numbers have an "SCA" prefix.

		MT
Complete Set (10):		225.00
Complete Series 1 (5):		160.00
Complete Series 2 (5):		75.00
Common Player:		10.00
Inserted 1:1,107		
1	Alex Rodriguez	75.00
2	Chipper Jones	40.00
3	Barry Bonds	80.00
4	Tino Martinez	15.00
5	Ben Grieve	10.00
6	Juan Gonzalez	20.00
7	Vladimir Guerrero	20.00
8	Albert Belle	15.00
9	Kerry Wood	15.00
10	Todd Helton	20.00

1999 Stadium Club Chrome

This 40-card set was inserted in series 1 and 2 packs, with 1-20 in first series packs and 21-40 in Series 2. Chrome appropriately utilizes chromium technology. The insertion rate is 1:24 packs with Refractor parallel versions also seeded 1:96 packs. Card numbers have an "SCC" prefix.

		MT
Complete Set (40):		65.00
Common Player:		.75
Inserted 1:24		
Refractors:		2X
Inserted 1:96		
1	Nomar Garciaparra	3.50
2	Kerry Wood	1.50
3	Jeff Bagwell	2.00
4	Ivan Rodriguez	1.50
5	Albert Belle	1.00
6	Gary Sheffield	1.25
7	Andruw Jones	1.75
8	Kevin Brown	.75
9	David Cone	.75
10	Darin Erstad	1.50
11	Manny Ramirez	2.00
12	Larry Walker	1.25
13	Mike Piazza	4.00
14	Cal Ripken Jr.	6.00
15	Pedro Martinez	1.50
16	Greg Vaughn	.75
17	Barry Bonds	3.50
18	Mo Vaughn	1.25
19	Bernie Williams	1.25
20	Ken Griffey Jr.	5.00
21	Alex Rodriguez	5.00
22	Chipper Jones	4.00
23	Ben Grieve	1.25
24	Frank Thomas	3.50
25	Derek Jeter	4.00
26	Sammy Sosa	3.50
27	Mark McGwire	6.00
28	Vladimir Guerrero	1.75
29	Greg Maddux	3.00
30	Juan Gonzalez	2.00
31	Troy Glaus	1.75
32	Adrian Beltre	1.25
33	Mitch Meluskey	.75
34	Alex Gonzalez	.75
35	George Lombard	.75
36	Eric Chavez	1.25
37	Ruben Mateo	.75
38	Calvin Pickering	.75
39	Gabe Kapler	1.25
40	Bruce Chen	.75

1999 Stadium Club Co-Signers

Co-Signers feature two autographs on each card and also for the first time includes one level of four autographs per card. Co-Signers are grouped into categories A, B, C and D. Group A Co-Signers are autographed by four players, while B-D are signed by two players. Insertion odds are as follows: Group D, 1:254; C, 1:3,014; B, 1:9,043; A, 1:45,213. Each card features the Topps Certified Autograph Issue stamp.

		MT
Common Group A:		90.00
Inserted 1:18,085		
Common Group B:		20.00
Inserted 1:9043		
Common Group C:		9.00
Inserted 1:3014		
Common Group D:		6.00
Inserted 1:254		
CS1	Ben Grieve, Richie Sexson (D)	20.00
CS2	Todd Helton, Troy Glaus (D)	50.00
CS3	Alex Rodriguez, Scott Rolen (D)	75.00
CS4	Derek Jeter, Chipper Jones (D)	150.00
CS5	Cliff Floyd, Eli Marrero (D)	6.00
CS6	Jay Buhner, Kevin Young (D)	6.00
CS7	Ben Grieve, Troy Glaus (C)	50.00
CS8	Todd Helton, Richie Sexson (C)	40.00
CS9	Alex Rodriguez, Chipper Jones (C)	180.00
CS10	Derek Jeter, Scott Rolen (C)	125.00
CS11	Cliff Floyd, Kevin Young (C)	10.00
CS12	Jay Buhner, Eli Marrero (B)	20.00
CS13	Ben Grieve, Todd Helton (B)	75.00
CS14	Richie Sexson, Troy Glaus (B)	60.00
CS15	Alex Rodriguez, Derek Jeter (B)	250.00
CS16	Chipper Jones, Scott Rolen (B)	150.00
CS17	Cliff Floyd, Jay Buhner (B)	20.00
CS18	Eli Marrero, Kevin Young (B)	20.00
CS19	Ben Grieve, Todd Helton, Richie Sexson, Troy Glaus (A)	180.00
CS20	Alex Rodriguez, Derek Jeter, Chipper Jones, Scott Rolen (A)	2500.
CS21	Cliff Floyd, Jay Buhner, Eli Marrero, Kevin Young (A)	100.00
CS22	Edgardo Alfonzo, Jose Guillen (D)	15.00
CS23	Mike Lowell, Ricardo Rincon (D)	8.00
CS24	Juan Gonzalez, Vinny Castilla (D)	20.00
CS25	Moises Alou, Roger Clemens (D)	40.00
CS26	Scott Spezio, Tony Womack (D)	8.00
CS27	Fernando Vina, Quilvio Veras (D)	6.00
CS28	Edgardo Alfonzo, Ricardo Rincon (C)	17.50
CS29	Jose Guillen, Mike Lowell (C)	15.00
CS30	Juan Gonzalez, Moises Alou (C)	55.00
CS31	Roger Clemens, Vinny Castilla (C)	60.00
CS32	Scott Spezio, Fernando Vina (C)	12.00
CS33	Tony Womack, Quilvio Veras (B)	20.00
CS34	Edgardo Alfonzo, Mike Lowell (B)	30.00
CS35	Jose Guillen, Ricardo Rincon (B)	30.00
CS36	Juan Gonzalez, Roger Clemens (B)	135.00
CS37	Moises Alou, Vinny Castilla (B)	30.00
CS38	Scott Spezio, Quilvio Veras (B)	20.00
CS39	Tony Womack, Fernando Vina (B)	20.00
CS40	Edgardo Alfonzo, Jose Guillen, Mike Lowell, Ricardo Rincon (A)	90.00
CS41	Juan Gonzalez, Moises Alou, Roger Clemens, Vinny Castilla (A)	900.00
CS42	Scott Spezio, Tony Womack, Fernando Vina, Quilvio Veras (A)	90.00

1999 Stadium Club Never Compromise

Topps selected players who bring hard work and devotion to the field every game are highlighted, including Cal Ripken Jr. The first 10 cards in the set are inserted in series I packs while the remaining 10 are seeded in series II at a rate of 1:12 packs.

		MT
Complete Set (20):		18.00
Common Player:		.45
Inserted 1:12		
NC1	Mark McGwire	2.50
NC2	Sammy Sosa	1.25
NC3	Ken Griffey Jr.	1.75
NC4	Greg Maddux	1.00
NC5	Barry Bonds	1.25
NC6	Alex Rodriguez	1.75
NC7	Darin Erstad	.60
NC8	Roger Clemens	1.00
NC9	Nomar Garciaparra	1.25
NC10	Derek Jeter	1.50
NC11	Cal Ripken Jr.	2.50
NC12	Mike Piazza	1.50
NC13	Greg Vaughn	.45
NC14	Andres Galarraga	.45
NC15	Vinny Castilla	.45
NC16	Jeff Bagwell	.75
NC17	Chipper Jones	1.50
NC18	Eric Chavez	.60
NC19	Orlando Hernandez	.60
NC20	Troy Glaus	.75

1999 Stadium Club Photography

The photos used on some of Stadium's Club Series 1 cards was available as a special issue in the format of a framed 11" x 14" color photo. The borderless action photos could be ordered from a form found in TSC packs. With a $4 shipping charge, the initial cost per picture was $23.99. The numbers here are as given on the order form.

		MT
Complete Set (10):		200.00
Common Player:		20.00
1	Alex Rodriguez	20.00
65	Derek Jeter	20.00
66	Sammy Sosa	20.00
135	Juan Gonzalez	20.00
NC1	Mark McGwire	20.00
NC3	Ken Griffey Jr.	20.00
SCA5	Ben Grieve	20.00
SCC1	Nomar Garciaparra	20.00
SCC2	Kerry Wood	20.00
SCC13	Mike Piazza	20.00

1999 Stadium Club Triumvirate

Three of these inserts "fuse" together to form a set of three cards, forming a Triumvirate. 48 players, 24 from each series, are available in three different technologies, Luminous, Luminescent and Illuminator. The insert ratio is as follows: Luminous (1:36), Luminescent (1:144) and Illuminator (1:288).

		MT
Complete Set (48):		90.00
Common Player:		.75
Inserted 1:36		
Luminescents:		1.5X
Inserted 1:144		
Illuminators:		2.5X
Inserted 1:288		
T1A	Greg Vaughn	.75
T1B	Ken Caminiti	.75
T1C	Tony Gwynn	3.25
T2A	Andruw Jones	2.50
T2B	Chipper Jones	4.00
T2C	Andres Galarraga	.75
T3A	Jay Buhner	.75
T3B	Ken Griffey Jr.	5.00
T3C	Alex Rodriguez	5.00
T4A	Derek Jeter	4.00
T4B	Tino Martinez	.75
T4C	Bernie Williams	1.25
T5A	Brian Jordan	.75
T5B	Ray Lankford	.75
T5C	Mark McGwire	6.00
T6A	Jeff Bagwell	3.00
T6B	Craig Biggio	1.00
T6C	Randy Johnson	2.00
T7A	Nomar Garciaparra	3.50
T7B	Pedro Martinez	1.25
T7C	Mo Vaughn	1.50
T8A	Mark Grace	1.25
T8B	Sammy Sosa	3.50
T8C	Kerry Wood	1.25
T9A	Alex Rodriguez	5.00
T9B	Nomar Garciaparra	3.50
T9C	Derek Jeter	4.00
T10A	Todd Helton	2.00
T10B	Travis Lee	1.00
T10C	Pat Burrell	3.25
T11A	Greg Maddux	3.25
T11B	Kerry Wood	1.25
T11C	Tom Glavine	.75
T12A	Chipper Jones	4.00
T12B	Vinny Castilla	.75
T12C	Scott Rolen	2.00
T13A	Juan Gonzalez	3.00
T13B	Ken Griffey Jr.	5.00
T13C	Ben Grieve	2.00
T14A	Sammy Sosa	3.50
T14B	Vladimir Guerrero	3.00
T14C	Barry Bonds	3.50
T15A	Frank Thomas	3.50
T15B	Jim Thome	.75
T15C	Tino Martinez	.75
T16A	Mark McGwire	6.00
T16B	Andres Galarraga	.75
T16C	Jeff Bagwell	3.00

1999 Stadium Club Video Replay

Utilizing lenticular technology, these inserts capture highlights, such as McGwire's 70th home run, from the '98 season. By tilting the card, successive images show the selected highlight almost come to life. Video Replays are in inserted in series II packs at a rate of 1:12.

		MT
Complete Set (5):		9.00
Common Player:		1.50
Inserted 1:12		
VR1	Mark McGwire	3.00
VR2	Sammy Sosa	2.00
VR3	Ken Griffey Jr.	2.50
VR4	Kerry Wood	1.50
VR5	Alex Rodriguez	2.50

2000 Stadium Club

Released in one series, the base set consists of 250 cards, embossed and printed on 20-pt. stock with silver holo foil stamping. Card backs have a small photo, with the player's vital information and 1999 season statistical breakdown. The 20-card Draft Pick subset (#231-250) are short-printed, seeded 1:5 packs.

		MT
Complete Set (250):		200.00
Common Player:		.15
Common SP (201-250):		2.00
Inserted 1:5		
Pack (6):		2.00
Wax Box (24):		45.00
1	Nomar Garciaparra	2.00
2	Brian Jordan	.15
3	Mark Grace	.25
4	Jeromy Burnitz	.25
5	Shane Reynolds	.25
6	Alex Gonzalez	.15
7	Jose Offerman	.15
8	Orlando Hernandez	.25
9	Mike Caruso	.15
10	Tony Clark	.30
11	Sean Casey	.50
12	Johnny Damon	.15
13	Dante Bichette	.25
14	Kevin Young	.15
15	Juan Gonzalez	.75
16	Chipper Jones	1.50
17	Quilvio Veras	.15
18	Trevor Hoffman	.15
19	Roger Cedeno	.15
20	Ellis Burks	.15
21	Richie Sexson	.15
22	Gary Sheffield	.40
23	Delino DeShields	.15
24	Wade Boggs	.50
25	Ray Lankford	.15
26	Kevin Appier	.15
27	Roy Halladay	.15
28	Harold Baines	.15
29	Todd Zeile	.15
30	Barry Larkin	.40
31	Ron Coomer	.15
32	Jorge Posada	.25
33	Magglio Ordonez	.25
34	Brian Giles	.15
35	Jeff Kent	.15
36	Henry Rodriguez	.15
37	Fred McGriff	.25
38	Shawn Green	.50
39	Derek Bell	.15
40	Ben Grieve	.30
41	Dave Nilsson	.15
42	Mo Vaughn	.50
43	Rondell White	.25
44	Doug Glanville	.15
45	Paul O'Neill	.25
46	Carlos Lee	.15
47	Vinny Castilla	.20
48	Mike Sweeney	.15
49	Rico Brogna	.15
50	Alex Rodriguez	2.50
51	Luis Castillo	.15
52	Kevin Brown	.25
53	Jose Vidro	.15
54	John Smoltz	.15
55	Garret Anderson	.15
56	Matt Stairs	.15
57	Omar Vizquel	.15
58	Tom Goodwin	.15
59	Scott Brosius	.15
60	Robin Ventura	.25
61	B.J. Surhoff	.15
62	Andy Ashby	.15
63	Chris Widger	.15
64	Tim Hudson	.40
65	Javy Lopez	.15
66	Tim Salmon	.25
67	Warren Morris	.15
68	John Wetteland	.15
69	Gabe Kapler	.25
70	Bernie Williams	.50
71	Rickey Henderson	.40
72	Andruw Jones	.50
73	Eric Young	.15
74	Bob Abreu	.15
75	David Cone	.25
76	Rusty Greer	.15
77	Ron Belliard	.15
78	Troy Glaus	.75
79	Mike Hampton	.15
80	Miguel Tejada	.15
81	Jeff Cirillo	.15
82	Todd Hundley	.15
83	Roberto Alomar	.50
84	Charles Johnson	.15
85	Rafael Palmeiro	.40
86	Doug Mientkiewicz	.15
87	Mariano Rivera	.25
88	Neifi Perez	.15
89	Jermaine Dye	.15
90	Ivan Rodriguez	.75
91	Jay Buhner	.15
92	Pokey Reese	.15
93	John Olerud	.25
94	Brady Anderson	.20
95	Manny Ramirez	.75
96	Keith Osik	.15
97	Mickey Morandini	.15
98	Matt Williams	.40
99	Eric Karros	.25
100	Ken Griffey Jr.	2.00
101	Bret Boone	.15
102	Ryan Klesko	.15
103	Craig Biggio	.40
104	John Jaha	.15
105	Vladimir Guerrero	1.25
106	Devon White	.15
107	Tony Womack	.15
108	Marvin Benard	.15
109	Kenny Lofton	.40
110	Preston Wilson	.15
111	Al Leiter	.25
112	Reggie Sanders	.15
113	Scott Williamson	.15
114	Deivi Cruz	.15
115	Carlos Beltran	.15
116	Ray Durham	.15
117	Ricky Ledee	.15
118	Torii Hunter	.15
119	John Valentin	.15
120	Scott Rolen	.75
121	Jason Kendall	.25
122	Dave Martinez	.15
123	Jim Thome	.40
124	David Bell	.15
125	Jose Canseco	.75
126	Jose Lima	.15
127	Carl Everett	.15
128	Kevin Millwood	.25
129	Bill Spiers	.15
130	Omar Daal	.15
131	Miguel Cairo	.15
132	Mark Grudzielanek	.15
133	David Justice	.25
134	Russ Ortiz	.15
135	Mike Piazza	2.00
136	Brian Meadows	.15
137	Tony Gwynn	1.50
138	Cal Ripken Jr.	2.00
139	Kris Benson	.15
140	Larry Walker	.50
141	Cristian Guzman	.15
142	Tino Martinez	.25
143	Chris Singleton	.15
144	Lee Stevens	.15
145	Rey Ordonez	.15
146	Russ Davis	.15
147	J.T. Snow Jr.	.15
148	Luis Gonzalez	.15
149	Marquis Grissom	.15
150	Greg Maddux	1.50
151	Fernando Tatis	.25
152	Jason Giambi	.15
153	Carlos Delgado	.50
154	Joe McEwing	.15
155	Raul Mondesi	.25
156	Rich Aurilia	.15
157	Alex Fernandez	.15
158	Albert Belle	.60
159	Pat Meares	.15
160	Mike Lieberthal	.15
161	Mike Cameron	.15
162	Juan Encarnacion	.15
163	Chuck Knoblauch	.30
164	Pedro Martinez	.75
165	Randy Johnson	.50
166	Shannon Stewart	.15
167	Jeff Bagwell	.75
168	Edgar Renteria	.15
169	Barry Bonds	.75
170	Steve Finley	.15
171	Brian Hunter	.15
172	Tom Glavine	.25
173	Mark Kotsay	.15
174	Tony Fernandez	.15

175 Sammy Sosa 2.00
176 Geoff Jenkins .15
177 Adrian Beltre .15
178 Jay Bell .15
179 Mike Bordick .15
180 Ed Sprague .15
181 Dave Roberts .15
182 Greg Vaughn .25
183 Brian Daubach .15
184 Damion Easley .15
185 Carlos Febles .15
186 Kevin Tapani .15
187 Frank Thomas .75
188 Roger Clemens 1.00
189 Mike Benjamin .15
190 Curt Schilling .25
191 Edgardo Alfonzo .25
192 Mike Mussina .50
193 Todd Helton .75
194 Todd Jones .15
195 Dean Palmer .15
196 John Flaherty .15
197 Derek Jeter 2.00
198 Todd Walker .15
199 Brad Ausmus .15
200 Mark McGwire 3.00
201 Erubiel Durazo (Future Stars) 2.00
202 Nick Johnson (Future Stars) 2.50
203 Ruben Mateo (Future Stars) 1.50
204 Lance Berkman (Future Stars) 2.00
205 Pat Burrell (Future Stars) 8.00
206 Pablo Ozuna (Future Stars) 2.00
207 Roosevelt Brown (Future Stars) 2.00
208 Alfonso Soriano (Future Stars) 2.50
209 A.J. Burnett (Future Stars) 2.50
210 Rafael Furcal (Future Stars) 2.00
211 Scott Morgan (Future Stars) 2.00
212 Adam Piatt (Future Stars) 4.00
213 Dee Brown (Future Stars) 2.00
214 Corey Patterson (Future Stars) 3.00
215 Mickey Lopez (Future Stars) 2.00
216 Rob Ryan (Future Stars) 2.00
217 Sean Burroughs (Future Stars) 2.50
218 Jack Cust (Future Stars) 3.00
219 John Patterson (Future Stars) 2.00
220 Kit Pellow (Future Stars) 2.00
221 Chad Hermansen (Future Stars) 2.00
222 Daryle Ward (Future Stars) 2.00
223 Jayson Werth (Future Stars) 2.00
224 Jason Standridge (Future Stars) 2.00
225 Mark Mulder (Future Stars) 2.00
226 Peter Bergeron (Future Stars) 2.00
227 Willi Mo Pena (Future Stars) 2.50
228 Aramis Ramirez (Future Stars) 2.00
229 *John Sneed* (Future Stars) 3.00
230 Wilton Veras (Future Stars) 2.00
231 Josh Hamilton (Draft Picks) 8.00
232 Eric Munson (Draft Picks) 3.00
233 *Bobby Bradley* (Draft Picks) 6.00
234 *Larry Bigbie* (Draft Picks) 3.00
235 *B.J. Garbe* (Draft Picks) 6.00
236 *Brett Myers* (Draft Picks) 8.00
237 *Jason Stumm* (Draft Picks) 4.00
238 *Corey Myers* (Draft Picks) 3.00
239 *Ryan Christianson* (Draft Picks) 4.00
240 David Walling (Draft Picks) 2.00
241 Josh Girdley (Draft Picks) 2.00
242 Omar Ortiz (Draft Picks) 2.00
243 Jason Jennings (Draft Picks) 2.00
244 *Kyle Snyder* (Draft Picks) 2.00
245 Jay Gehrke (Draft Picks) 2.00
246 *Mike Paradis* (Draft Picks) 2.00
247 *Chance Caple* (Draft Picks) 3.00
248 *Ben Christiansen* (Draft Picks) 5.00
249 *Brad Baker* (Draft Picks) 5.00
250 *Rick Asadoorian* (Draft Picks) 5.00
--- Checklist (Nomar Garciaparra) .25

2000 Stadium Club One of a Kind

This 250-card set is a parallel to the base set, is hobby exclusive and limited to 150 serially numbered sets.

	MT
Stars:	20x-30x
Short-prints:	3x-5x
Production 150 sets H	

(See 2000 Stadium Club for checklist and base card values.)

2000 Stadium Club First Day Issue

Identifiable by the "First Day Issue" stamp, this retail exclusive parallel set is limited to 150 sequentially numbered sets.

	MT
Stars:	20x-30x
Short-prints:	3x-5x
Production 150 sets R	

(See 2000 Stadium Club for checklist and base card values.)

2000 Stadium Club Printing Plates

Inserted only in Home Team boxes at a rate of approximately one per 100 packs were the actual aluminum plates used to print the fronts of the base cards. Unlike some printing plate issues, the plates used for the card backs were not inserted. Each card's plate can be found in four different colors: Cyan, magenta, yellow and black. Because of their unique nature, pricing of individual player's plates cannot be provided.

	MT
Common Player:	60.00

(See 2000 Stadium Club for checklist.)

2000 Stadium Club Bats of Brilliance

This insert set focused on 10 of baseball's top hitters. Card fronts have a silver foil border over a black backdrop. Backs highlight the player's statistics from 1999 and his career statistics. They are numbered with a "BB" prefix and are seeded 1:12 packs. A die-cut parallel is also randomly seeded 1:60 packs.

		MT
Complete Set (10):		30.00
Common Player:		1.50
Inserted 1:12		
1	Mark McGwire	6.00
2	Sammy Sosa	4.00
3	Jose Canseco	1.50
4	Jeff Bagwell	1.50
5	Ken Griffey Jr.	4.00
6	Nomar Garciaparra	4.00
7	Mike Piazza	4.00
8	Alex Rodriguez	5.00
9	Vladimir Guerrero	2.50
10	Chipper Jones	3.00

2000 Stadium Club Capture The Action

This 20-card set is divided into 3 categories: Rookies, Stars and Legends. These were seeded 1:12 packs and have the insert head, player name and logo stamped in silver foil. They are numbered with a "CA" prefix on the backs. A hobby exclusive parallel version is also available. They are serially numbered to 100 and features a replica of the actual photo slide used to create the card and is viewable from both sides.

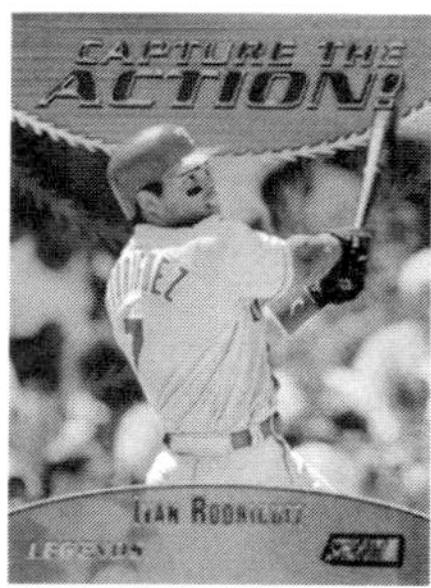

		MT
Complete Set (20):		75.00
Common Player:		1.50
Inserted 1:12		
Game View Stars:		8x-15x
Yng stars:		3x-6x
Production 100 sets H		
1	Josh Hamilton	8.00
2	Pat Burrell	5.00
3	Erubiel Durazo	1.50
4	Alfonso Soriano	2.00
5	A.J. Burnett	1.50
6	Alex Rodriguez	8.00
7	Sean Casey	1.50
8	Derek Jeter	6.00
9	Vladimir Guerrero	3.00
10	Nomar Garciaparra	6.00
11	Mike Piazza	6.00
12	Ken Griffey Jr.	6.00
13	Sammy Sosa	6.00
14	Juan Gonzalez	2.50
15	Mark McGwire	10.00
16	Ivan Rodriguez	2.50
17	Barry Bonds	2.50
18	Wade Boggs	1.50
19	Tony Gwynn	3.00
20	Cal Ripken Jr.	8.00

2000 Stadium Club Chrome Preview

This 20-card set features Topps Chromium technology, previewing the debut of Stadium Club Chrome, a later release. The insertion odds are 1:24 packs. A Refractor parallel version is also available seeded 1:120 packs.

		MT
Complete Set (20):		100.00
Common Player:		2.00
Inserted 1:24		
Refractors:		2x-3x
Inserted 1:120		
1	Nomar Garciaparra	10.00
2	Juan Gonzalez	4.00
3	Chipper Jones	8.00
4	Alex Rodriguez	12.00
5	Ivan Rodriguez	4.00
6	Manny Ramirez	4.00
7	Ken Griffey Jr.	12.00
8	Vladimir Guerrero	6.00
9	Mike Piazza	10.00
10	Pedro Martinez	4.00
11	Jeff Bagwell	4.00
12	Barry Bonds	4.00
13	Sammy Sosa	10.00
14	Derek Jeter	10.00
15	Mark McGwire	15.00
16	Erubiel Durazo	2.00
17	Nick Johnson	4.00
18	Pat Burrell	5.00
19	Alfonso Soriano	5.00
20	Adam Piatt	3.00

2000 Stadium Club Co-Signers

This 15-card hobby exclusive set features two signatures on the card front, with the Topps "Certified Autograph Issue" stamp as well as the Topps 3M sticker to ensure its authenticity. The cards are divided into three groupings with the following odds: Group A - 1:10,184; Group B - 1:5,092; and Group C - 1:508.

		MT
Common Player:		40.00
Group A 1:10,184		
Group B 1:5,092		
Group C 1:508		
1	Alex Rodriguez, Derek Jeter	800.00
2	Derek Jeter, Omar Vizquel	250.00
3	Alex Rodriguez, Rey Ordonez	250.00
4	Derek Jeter, Rey Ordonez	250.00
5	Omar Vizquel, Alex Rodriguez	250.00
6	Rey Ordonez, Omar Vizquel	50.00
7	Wade Boggs, Robin Ventura	80.00
8	Randy Johnson, Mike Mussina	120.00
9	Pat Burrell, Magglio Ordonez	60.00
10	Chad Hermansen, Pat Burrell	60.00
11	Magglio Ordonez, Chad Hermansen	40.00
12	Josh Hamilton, Corey Myers	60.00
13	B.J. Garbe, Josh Hamilton	80.00
14	Corey Myers, B.J. Garbe	60.00
15	Tino Martinez, Fred McGriff	50.00

2000 Stadium Club Lone Star Signatures

This 16-card autographed set features the Topps "Certified Autograph Issue" stamp to verify its authenticity. The cards are divided into four groupings with the following odds: Group 1, 1:1,979 hobby; Group 2, 1:2,374 hobby; Group 3, 1:1,979; and Group 4, 1:424 hobby.

		MT
Common Player:		20.00
Group 1 1:1,979		
Group 2 1:2,374		
Group 3 1:1,979		
Group 4 1:424		
1	Derek Jeter	250.00
2	Alex Rodriguez	250.00
3	Wade Boggs	75.00
4	Robin Ventura	40.00
5	Randy Johnson	60.00
6	Mike Mussina	60.00
7	Tino Martinez	40.00
8	Fred McGriff	30.00
9	Omar Vizquel	30.00
10	Rey Ordonez	30.00
11	Pat Burrell	40.00
12	Chad Hermansen	20.00
13	Magglio Ordonez	20.00
14	Josh Hamilton	60.00
15	Corey Myers	30.00
16	B.J. Garbe	50.00

2000 Stadium Club Onyx Extreme

This 10-card set features black styrene technology with silver foil stamping and are seeded 1:12 packs. A die-cut parallel is also randomly inserted 1:60 hobby packs.

		MT
Complete Set (10):		20.00
Common Player:		1.00
Inserted 1:12		
Die-cuts:		2x-3x
Inserted 1:60		
1	Ken Griffey Jr.	5.00
2	Derek Jeter	4.00
3	Vladimir Guerrero	2.50
4	Nomar Garciaparra	4.00
5	Barry Bonds	1.50
6	Alex Rodriguez	5.00
7	Sammy Sosa	4.00
8	Ivan Rodriguez	1.50
9	Larry Walker	1.00
10	Andruw Jones	1.00

2000 Stadium Club Scenes

Available only in hobby and Home Team Advantage boxes, these broaden the view of the featured player and have a format sized 2 1/2" x 4 11/16". These are boxtoppers, seeded one per box.

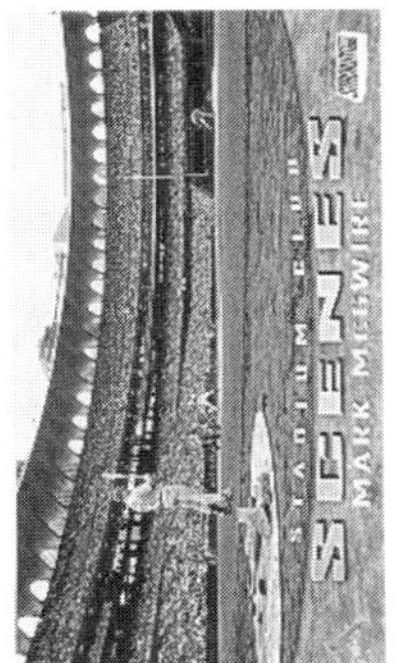

		MT
Complete Set (9):		30.00
Common Player:		1.00
Inserted 1:box		
1	Mark McGwire	6.00
2	Alex Rodriguez	5.00
3	Cal Ripken Jr.	5.00
4	Sammy Sosa	4.00
5	Derek Jeter	4.00
6	Ken Griffey Jr.	5.00
7	Raul Mondesi	1.00
8	Chipper Jones	3.00
9	Nomar Garciaparra	4.00

2000 Stadium Club Souvenirs

These memorabilia inserts feature die-cut technology that incorporates an actual piece of a game-used uniform. Each card back contains the Topps 3M sticker to ensure its authenticity. The insert rate is 2:339 hobby packs and 2:136 HTA packs.

		MT
Complete Set (3):		160.00
Common Player:		40.00
Inserted 2:339		
1	Wade Boggs	100.00
2	Randy Johnson	50.00
3	Robin Ventura	40.00

2000 Stadium Club 3 X 3

Ten groups of three top-notch players are arranged by position on three different laser-cut technologies. The three players can be "fused" together to form one oversize card. The three versions are luminous (1:18), luminescent (1:72) and illuminator (1:144).

		MT
Complete Set (30):		120.00
Common Player:		1.50
Inserted 1:18		
Luminescent:		2x
Inserted 1:72		
Illuminator:		3x-4x
Inserted 1:144		
1A	Randy Johnson	3.00
1B	Pedro Martinez	4.00
1C	Greg Maddux	8.00
2A	Mike Piazza	10.00
2B	Ivan Rodriguez	4.00
2C	Mike Lieberthal	1.50
3A	Mark McGwire	15.00
3B	Jeff Bagwell	4.00
3C	Sean Casey	2.00
4A	Craig Biggio	2.00
4B	Roberto Alomar	2.50
4C	Jay Bell	1.50
5A	Chipper Jones	8.00
5B	Matt Williams	2.00
5C	Robin Ventura	2.00
6A	Alex Rodriguez	12.00
6B	Derek Jeter	10.00
6C	Nomar Garciaparra	10.00
7A	Barry Bonds	4.00
7B	Luis Gonzalez	1.50
7C	Dante Bichette	1.50
8A	Ken Griffey Jr.	12.00
8B	Bernie Williams	3.00
8C	Andruw Jones	3.00
9A	Manny Ramirez	4.00
9B	Sammy Sosa	10.00
9C	Juan Gonzalez	4.00
10A	Jose Canseco	4.00
10B	Frank Thomas	4.00
10C	Rafael Palmeiro	2.50

2000 Stadium Club Chrome

The 250-card base set uses the same photography and is identical to 2000 Stadium Club besides the utilization of Chromium technology. Five-card packs had a $4 SRP.

		MT
Complete Set (250):		120.00
Common Player:		.25
Pack (11):		3.00
Wax Box (36):		65.00
1	Nomar Garciaparra	3.00
2	Brian Jordan	.25
3	Mark Grace	.40
4	Jeromy Burnitz	.40
5	Shane Reynolds	.25
6	Alex Gonzalez	.25
7	Jose Offerman	.25
8	Orlando Hernandez	.40
9	Mike Caruso	.25
10	Tony Clark	.50
11	Sean Casey	.50
12	Johnny Damon	.25

13 Dante Bichette .40
14 Kevin Young .25
15 Juan Gonzalez 1.00
16 Chipper Jones 2.50
17 Quilvio Veras .25
18 Trevor Hoffman .25
19 Roger Cedeno .25
20 Ellis Burks .25
21 Richie Sexson .25
22 Gary Sheffield .50
23 Delino DeShields .25
24 Wade Boggs .75
25 Ray Lankford .25
26 Kevin Appier .25
27 Roy Halladay .25
28 Harold Baines .25
29 Todd Zeile .25
30 Barry Larkin .50
31 Ron Coomer .25
32 Jorge Posada .40
33 Magglio Ordonez .40
34 Brian Giles .25
35 Jeff Kent .25
36 Henry Rodriguez .25
37 Fred McGriff .40
38 Shawn Green .75
39 Derek Bell .25
40 Ben Grieve .50
41 Dave Nilsson .25
42 Mo Vaughn .75
43 Rondell White .40
44 Doug Glanville .25
45 Paul O'Neill .40
46 Carlos Lee .25
47 Vinny Castilla .40
48 Mike Sweeney .25
49 Rico Brogna .25
50 Alex Rodriguez 4.00
51 Luis Castillo .25
52 Kevin Brown .40
53 Jose Vidro .25
54 John Smoltz .25
55 Garret Anderson .25
56 Matt Stairs .25
57 Omar Vizquel .25
58 Tom Goodwin .25
59 Scott Brosius .25
60 Robin Ventura .40
61 B.J. Surhoff .25
62 Andy Ashby .25
63 Chris Widger .25
64 Tim Hudson .40
65 Javy Lopez .40
66 Tim Salmon .40
67 Warren Morris .25
68 John Wetteland .25
69 Gabe Kapler .40
70 Bernie Williams .75
71 Rickey Henderson .50
72 Andruw Jones .50
73 Eric Young .25
74 Bobby Abreu .25
75 David Cone .25
76 Rusty Greer .25
77 Ron Belliard .25
78 Troy Glaus 1.00
79 Mike Hampton .25
80 Miguel Tejada .25
81 Jeff Cirillo .25
82 Todd Hundley .25
83 Roberto Alomar .75
84 Charles Johnson .25
85 Rafael Palmeiro .75
86 Doug Mientkiewicz .25
87 Mariano Rivera .40
88 Neifi Perez .25
89 Jermaine Dye .25
90 Ivan Rodriguez 1.00
91 Jay Buhner .25
92 Pokey Reese .25
93 John Olerud .40
94 Brady Anderson .40
95 Manny Ramirez 1.00
96 Keith Osik .25
97 Mickey Morandini .25
98 Matt Williams .50
99 Eric Karros .25
100 Ken Griffey Jr. 3.00
101 Bret Boone .25
102 Ryan Klesko .25
103 Craig Biggio .50
104 John Jaha .25
105 Vladimir Guerrero 1.50
106 Devon White .25
107 Tony Womack .25
108 Marvin Benard .25
109 Kenny Lofton .75
110 Preston Wilson .25
111 Al Leiter .40
112 Reggie Sanders .25
113 Scott Williamson .25
114 Deivi Cruz .25
115 Carlos Beltran .25
116 Ray Durham .25
117 Ricky Ledee .25
118 Torii Hunter .25
119 John Valentin .25
120 Scott Rolen 1.00
121 Jason Kendall .40
122 Dave Martinez .25
123 Jim Thome .75
124 David Bell .25
125 Jose Canseco 1.00
126 Jose Lima .25
127 Carl Everett .40
128 Kevin Millwood .40
129 Bill Spiers .25
130 Omar Daal .25
131 Miguel Cairo .25
132 Mark Grudzielanek .25
133 David Justice .40
134 Russ Ortiz .25
135 Mike Piazza 3.00
136 Brian Meadows .25
137 Tony Gwynn 2.00
138 Cal Ripken Jr. 4.00
139 Kris Benson .25
140 Larry Walker .75
141 Cristian Guzman .25
142 Tino Martinez .50
143 Chris Singleton .25
144 Lee Stevens .25
145 Rey Ordonez .25
146 Russ Davis .25
147 J.T. Snow Jr. .25
148 Luis Gonzalez .40
149 Marquis Grissom .25
150 Greg Maddux 2.00
151 Fernando Tatis .40
152 Jason Giambi .40
153 Carlos Delgado 1.00
154 Joe McEwing .25
155 Raul Mondesi .40
156 Rich Aurilia .25
157 Alex Fernandez .25
158 Albert Belle .75
159 Pat Meares .25
160 Mike Lieberthal .25
161 Mike Cameron .25
162 Juan Encarnacion .25
163 Chuck Knoblauch .40
164 Pedro Martinez 1.00
165 Randy Johnson 1.00
166 Shannon Stewart .25
167 Jeff Bagwell 1.00
168 Edgar Renteria .25
169 Barry Bonds 1.00
170 Steve Finley .25
171 Brian Hunter .25
172 Tom Glavine .50
173 Mark Kotsay .25
174 Tony Fernandez .25
175 Sammy Sosa 2.50
176 Geoff Jenkins .40
177 Adrian Beltre .40
178 Jay Bell .25
179 Mike Bordick .25
180 Ed Sprague .25
181 Dave Roberts .25
182 Greg Vaughn .50
183 Brian Daubach .25
184 Damion Easley .25
185 Carlos Febles .25
186 Kevin Tapani .25
187 Frank Thomas 1.50
188 Roger Clemens 1.50
189 Mike Benjamin .25
190 Curt Schilling .40
191 Edgardo Alfonzo .40
192 Mike Mussina .75
193 Todd Helton 1.00
194 Todd Jones .25
195 Dean Palmer .25
196 John Flaherty .25
197 Derek Jeter 4.00
198 Todd Walker .25
199 Brad Ausmus .25
200 Mark McGwire 5.00
201 Erubiel Durazo (Future Stars) 1.00
202 Nick Johnson (Future Stars) 3.00
203 Ruben Mateo (Future Stars) 1.00
204 Lance Berkman (Future Stars) 1.50
205 Pat Burrell (Future Stars) 3.00
206 Pablo Ozuna (Future Stars) 1.00
207 Roosevelt Brown (Future Stars) 1.00
208 Alfonso Soriano (Future Stars) 2.00
209 A.J. Burnett (Future Stars) 1.50
210 Rafael Furcal (Future Stars) .50
211 Scott Morgan (Future Stars) 1.00
212 Adam Piatt (Future Stars) 1.50
213 Dee Brown (Future Stars) 1.00
214 Corey Patterson (Future Stars) .75
215 Mickey Lopez (Future Stars) 1.00
216 Rob Ryan (Future Stars) 1.00
217 Sean Burroughs (Future Stars) 3.00
218 Jack Cust (Future Stars) 1.00
219 John Patterson (Future Stars) 1.50
220 Kit Pellow (Future Stars) 1.00
221 Chad Hermansen (Future Stars) 1.00
222 Daryle Ward (Future Stars) 1.50
223 Jayson Werth (Future Stars) 1.00
224 Jason Standridge (Future Stars) 1.00
225 Mark Mulder (Future Stars) 1.00
226 Peter Bergeron (Future Stars) 1.50
227 Willi Mo Pena (Future Stars) 4.00
228 Aramis Ramirez (Future Stars) 1.00
229 John Sneed (Future Stars) 2.50
230 Wilton Veras (Future Stars) 1.50
231 Josh Hamilton (Draft Picks) 5.00
232 Eric Munson (Draft Picks) 4.00
233 *Bobby Bradley* (Draft Picks) 6.00
234 *Larry Bigbie* (Draft Picks) 2.00
235 *B.J. Garbe* (Draft Picks) 4.00
236 *Brett Myers* (Draft Picks) 4.00
237 *Jason Stumm* (Draft Picks) 2.00
238 *Corey Myers* (Draft Picks) 3.00
239 *Ryan Christianson* (Draft Picks) 2.00
240 David Walling (Draft Picks) 1.00
241 Josh Girdley (Draft Picks) 1.00
242 Omar Ortiz (Draft Picks) 1.00
243 Jason Jennings (Draft Picks) 1.00
244 Kyle Snyder (Draft Picks) 1.00
245 Jay Gehrke (Draft Picks) 1.00
246 Mike Paradis (Draft Picks) 1.00
247 *Chance Caple* (Draft Picks) 2.00
248 *Ben Christensen* (Draft Picks) 2.00
249 *Brad Baker* (Draft Picks) 2.00
250 *Rick Asadoorian* (Draft Picks) 3.00

2000 Stadium Club Chrome First Day Issue

A parallel to the 250-card base set. Card fronts are identical besides "First Day Issue" printed three times over the player name and Stadium Club Chrome logo. Card backs are serial numbered in an edition of 100. A Refractor First Day Issue parallel is also randomly inserted, limited to 25 serial numbered sets.

	MT
Stars:	15-25X
Rookies:	5-10X
Production 100 sets	
Refractor:	40-75X
Rookies:	20-30X
Production 25 sets	

2000 Stadium Club Chrome Refractor

A parallel to the 250-card base set these utilize Refractor technology and have a mirror sheen to them when held up to a light source. "Refractor" is also written under the card number on the card back. Refractors are seeded 1:12 packs.

	MT
Stars:	5-10X
Rookies:	2-5X
Inserted 1:12	

2000 Stadium Club Chrome Capture The Action

This 20-card set is divided into three groups:

Rookies, Stars and Legends. Card backs are numbered with a "CA" prefix. These are found 1:18 packs. A Refractor parallel version is also randomly seeded 1:90 packs and also have "Refractor" written under the card number on the back.

		MT
Complete Set (20):		140.00
Common Player:		3.00
Inserted 1:18		
Refractors:		2-3X
Inserted 1:90		
1	Josh Hamilton	8.00
2	Pat Burrell	8.00
3	Erubiel Durazo	3.00
4	Alfonso Soriano	4.00
5	A.J. Burnett	3.00
6	Alex Rodriguez	15.00
7	Sean Casey	3.00
8	Derek Jeter	12.00
9	Vladimir Guerrero	6.00
10	Nomar Garciaparra	12.00
11	Mike Piazza	12.00
12	Ken Griffey Jr.	12.00
13	Sammy Sosa	12.00
14	Juan Gonzalez	5.00
15	Mark McGwire	20.00
16	Ivan Rodriguez	5.00
17	Barry Bonds	5.00
18	Wade Boggs	3.00
19	Tony Gwynn	6.00
20	Cal Ripken Jr.	15.00

2000 Stadium Club Chrome Clear Shots

Printed on a clear, acetate stock this 10-card insert set will depict the front of the player on the card front and the back on the card back. Card backs are numbered with a "CS" prefix. Clear Shots are inserted 1:24 packs. A die-cut Refractor parallel version is also randomly seeded 1:120 packs.

		MT
Complete Set (10):		45.00
Common Player:		2.50
Inserted 1:24		
Refractor:		2-3X
Inserted 1:120		
1	Derek Jeter	8.00
2	Bernie Williams	2.50
3	Roger Clemens	5.00
4	Chipper Jones	6.00
5	Greg Maddux	6.00
6	Andruw Jones	2.50
7	Juan Gonzalez	3.00
8	Manny Ramirez	3.00
9	Ken Griffey Jr.	10.00
10	Josh Hamilton	6.00

2000 Stadium Club Chrome Eyes of the Game

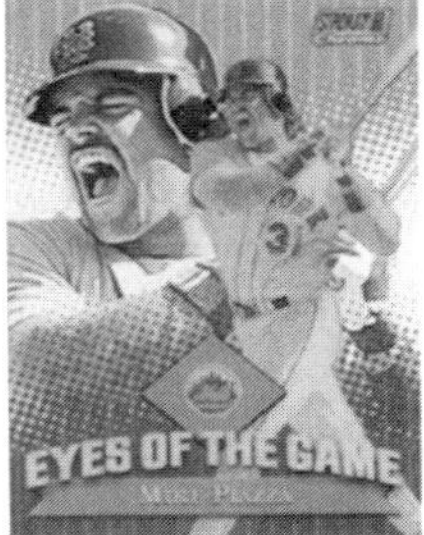

Printed on a clear, acetate stock this 10-card set focuses on the facial expression of the featured player. Two images are on the front with the background image a close-up shot of the player's facial expression. These were seeded 1:16. Card backs are numbered with an "EG" prefix. A Refractor parallel is randomly inserted in 1:80 packs and has "Refractor" written under the card number on the back.

		MT
Complete Set (10):		50.00
Common Player:		2.00
Inserted 1:16		
Refractors:		2-3X
Inserted 1:80		
1	Randy Johnson	2.50
2	Mike Piazza	6.00
3	Nomar Garciaparra	6.00
4	Mark McGwire	10.00
5	Alex Rodriguez	8.00
6	Derek Jeter	6.00
7	Tony Gwynn	5.00
8	Sammy Sosa	6.00
9	Larry Walker	2.00
10	Ken Griffey Jr.	8.00

2000 Stadium Club Chrome True Colors

This 10-card set focuses on players Topps deemed that performed best when the game's on the line. These were inserted 1:32 and are numbered with an "TC" prefix on the card back. A Refractor parallel is randomly inserted 1:160 packs.

		MT
Complete Set (10):		80.00
Common Player:		3.00
Inserted 1:32		
Refractors:		2-3X
Inserted 1:160		
1	Sammy Sosa	10.00
2	Nomar Garciaparra	10.00
3	Alex Rodriguez	12.00
4	Derek Jeter	10.00
5	Mark McGwire	15.00
6	Chipper Jones	8.00
7	Mike Piazza	10.00
8	Ken Griffey Jr.	10.00
9	Manny Ramirez	4.00
10	Vladimir Guerrero	6.00

2000 Stadium Club Chrome Visionaries

This 20-card set spotlights young prospects who are deemed destined for stardom. Card backs are numbered with a "V" prefix. These are found 1:18 packs. A Refractor parallel version is also seeded 1:90 packs. "Refractor" is written under the card number on the back.

		MT
Complete Set (20):		100.00
Common Player:		3.00
Inserted 1:18		
Refractors:		2X
Inserted 1:90		
1	Alfonso Soriano	6.00
2	Josh Hamilton	12.00
3	A.J. Burnett	3.00
4	Pat Burrell	10.00
5	Ruben Salazar	3.00
6	Aaron Rowand	3.00
7	Adam Piatt	5.00
8	Nick Johnson	8.00
9	Rafael Furcal	3.00
10	Jack Cust	3.00
11	Corey Patterson	4.00
12	Sean Burroughs	8.00
13	Pablo Ozuna	3.00
14	Dee Brown	3.00
15	John Patterson	3.00
16	Willi Mo Pena	8.00
17	Mark Mulder	4.00
18	Eric Munson	8.00
19	Alex Escobar	3.00
20	Rob Ryan	3.00

2001 Stadium Club

		MT
Complete Set (200):		100.00
Common Player:		.15
Common SP:		3.00
Inserted 1:6		
Pack (7):		2.50
Box (24):		55.00
1	Nomar Garciaparra	2.00
2	Chipper Jones	1.50
3	Jeff Bagwell	.75
4	Chad Kreuter	.15
5	Randy Johnson	.75
6	Mike Hampton	.25
7	Barry Larkin	.40
8	Bernie Williams	.60
9	Chris Singleton	.15
10	Larry Walker	.30
11	Brad Ausmus	.15
12	Ron Coomer	.15
13	Edgardo Alfonzo	.25
14	Delino DeShields	.15
15	Tony Gwynn	1.00
16	Andruw Jones	.50
17	Raul Mondesi	.25
18	Troy Glaus	.75
19	Ben Grieve	.25
20	Sammy Sosa	1.50
21	Fernando Vina	.15
22	Jeromy Burnitz	.15
23	Jay Bell	.15
24	Pete Harnisch	.15
25	Barry Bonds	.75
26	Eric Karros	.25
27	Alex Gonzalez	.15
28	Mike Lieberthal	.15
29	Juan Encarnacion	.15
30	Derek Jeter	2.50
31	Bruce Aven	.15
32	Eric Milton	.15
33	Aaron Boone	.15
34	Roberto Alomar	.60
35	John Olerud	.25
36	Orlando Cabrera	.15
37	Shawn Green	.40
38	Roger Cedeno	.15
39	Garret Anderson	.15
40	Jim Thome	.40
41	Gabe Kapler	.25
42	Mo Vaughn	.40
43	Sean Casey	.25
44	Preston Wilson	.15
45	Javy Lopez	.25
46	Ryan Klesko	.15
47	Ray Durham	.15
48	Dean Palmer	.15
49	Jorge Posada	.25
50	Alex Rodriguez	2.50
51	Tom Glavine	.25
52	Ray Lankford	.15
53	Jose Canseco	.40
54	Tim Salmon	.25
55	Cal Ripken Jr.	2.50
56	Bob Abreu	.15
57	Robin Ventura	.25
58	Damion Easley	.15
59	Paul O'Neill	.25
60	Ivan Rodriguez	.75
61	Carl Everett	.15

62 Doug Glanville .15
63 Jeff Kent .15
64 Jay Buhner .15
65 Cliff Floyd .15
66 Rick Ankiel .40
67 Mark Grace .25
68 Brian Jordan .15
69 Craig Biggio .25
70 Carlos Delgado .75
71 Brad Radke .15
72 Greg Maddux 1.50
73 Al Leiter .25
74 Pokey Reese .15
75 Todd Helton .75
76 Mariano Rivera .25
77 Shane Spencer .15
78 Jason Kendall .15
79 Chuck Knoblauch .25
80 Scott Rolen .50
81 Jose Offerman .15
82 J.T. Snow Jr. .15
83 Pat Meares .15
84 Quilvio Veras .15
85 Edgar Renteria .15
86 Luis Matos .15
87 Adrian Beltre .25
88 Luis Gonzalez .25
89 Rickey Henderson .40
90 Brian Giles .25
91 Carlos Febles .15
92 Tino Martinez .25
93 Magglio Ordonez .25
94 Rafael Furcal .25
95 Mike Mussina .40
96 Gary Sheffield .30
97 Kenny Lofton .30
98 Fred McGriff .25
99 Ken Caminiti .25
100 Mark McGwire 3.00
101 Tom Goodwin .15
102 Mark Grudzielanek .15
103 Derek Bell .15
104 Mike Lowell .15
105 Jeff Cirillo .15
106 Orlando Hernandez .25
107 Jose Valentin .15
108 Warren Morris .15
109 Mike Williams .15
110 Greg Zaun .15
111 Jose Vidro .15
112 Omar Vizquel .25
113 Vinny Castilla .15
114 Gregg Jefferies .15
115 Kevin Brown .25
116 Shannon Stewart .15
117 Marquis Grissom .15
118 Manny Ramirez .75
119 Albert Belle .40
120 Bret Boone .15
121 Johnny Damon .15
122 Juan Gonzalez .75
123 David Justice .50
124 Jeffrey Hammonds .15
125 Ken Griffey Jr. 2.00
126 Mike Sweeney .15
127 Tony Clark .25
128 Todd Zeile .15
129 Mark Johnson .15
130 Matt Williams .25
131 Geoff Jenkins .25
132 Jason Giambi .40
133 Steve Finley .15
134 Derrek Lee .15
135 Royce Clayton .15
136 Joe Randa .15
137 Rafael Palmeiro .40
138 Kevin Young .15
139 Curt Schilling .25
140 Vladimir Guerrero 1.00
141 Greg Vaughn .15
142 Jermaine Dye .15
143 Roger Clemens 1.00
144 Denny Hocking .15
145 Frank Thomas 1.00
146 Carlos Beltran .15
147 Eric Young .15
148 Pat Burrell .50
149 Pedro Martinez .75
150 Mike Piazza 2.00
151 Adrian Gonzalez .50
152 Adam Johnson .15
153 *Luis Montanez* 8.00
154 Mike Stodolka .15
155 Phil Dumatrait .15
156 Sean Burnett 3.00
157 *Dominic Rich* 3.00
158 Adam Wainwright .75
159 Scott Thorman .15
160 Scott Heard .25
161 *Chad Petty* 3.00
162 Matt Wheatland 5.00
163 Brad Digby .15
164 Rocco Baldelli .75
165 Grady Sizemore .15
166 *Brian Sellier* 3.00
167 *Rick Brosseau* 3.00
168 *Shawn Fagan* 4.00
169 Sean Smith 3.00
170 *Chris Bass* 10.00
171 Corey Patterson (Future Stars) .40
172 Sean Burroughs (Future Stars) .50
173 Ben Petrick (Future Stars) .15
174 Mike Glendenning (Future Stars) .15
175 Barry Zito (Future Stars) 2.00
176 Milton Bradley (Future Stars) .15
177 Bobby Bradley (Future Stars) .75
178 Jason Hart (Future Stars) .15
179 Ryan Anderson (Future Stars) .15
180 Ben Sheets (Future Stars) 2.00
181 Adam Everett (Future Stars) .15
182 Alfonso Soriano (Future Stars) .25
183 Josh Hamilton (Future Stars) 1.00
184 Eric Munson (Future Stars) .15
185 Chin-Feng Chen (Future Stars) 1.50
186 *Tim Christman* 4.00
187 J.R. House 5.00
188 *Brandon Parker* 3.00
189 *Sean Fesh* 3.00
190 *Joel Pieniero* 4.00
191 *Oscar Ramirez* 4.00
192 *Alex Santos* 3.00
193 *Eddy Reyes* 4.00
194 *Mike Jacobs* 3.00
195 *Erick Almonte* 3.00
196 *Brandon Claussen* 3.00
197 *Kris Keller* 3.00
198 *Wilson Betemit* 10.00
199 *Andy Phillips* 4.00
200 *Adam Pettyjohn* 4.00
--- Derek Jeter (Checklist) .25

2001 Stadium Club Beam Team

MT
Complete Set (30): 375.00
Common Player: 5.00
Production 500 sets
1 Sammy Sosa 15.00
2 Mark McGwire 30.00
3 Vladimir Guerrero 10.00
4 Chipper Jones 15.00
5 Manny Ramirez 8.00
6 Derek Jeter 30.00
7 Alex Rodriguez 30.00
8 Cal Ripken Jr. 30.00
9 Ken Griffey Jr. 25.00
10 Greg Maddux 15.00
11 Barry Bonds 10.00
12 Pedro Martinez 10.00
13 Nomar Garciaparra 20.00
14 Randy Johnson 8.00
15 Frank Thomas 10.00
16 Ivan Rodriguez 8.00
17 Jeff Bagwell 10.00
18 Mike Piazza 20.00
19 Todd Helton 10.00
20 Shawn Green 5.00
21 Juan Gonzalez 10.00
22 Larry Walker 6.00
23 Tony Gwynn 10.00
24 Pat Burrell 8.00
25 Rafael Furcal 5.00
26 Corey Patterson 6.00
27 Chin-Feng Chen 20.00
28 Sean Burroughs 5.00
29 Ryan Anderson 6.00
30 Josh Hamilton 15.00

2001 Stadium Club Capture The Action

MT
Complete Set (15): 30.00
Common Player: 1.00
Inserted 1:8
1 Cal Ripken Jr. 4.00
2 Alex Rodriguez 4.00
3 Mike Piazza 3.00
4 Mark McGwire 5.00
5 Greg Maddux 2.50
6 Derek Jeter 4.00
7 Chipper Jones 2.50
8 Pedro Martinez 1.25
9 Ken Griffey Jr. 3.00
10 Nomar Garciaparra 3.00
11 Randy Johnson 1.25
12 Sammy Sosa 2.50
13 Vladimir Guerrero 1.50
14 Barry Bonds 1.25
15 Ivan Rodriguez 1.25

2001 Stadium Club Capture The Action Game View

MT
Complete Set (15): 550.00
Common Player: 15.00
Production 100 sets
1 Cal Ripken Jr. 60.00
2 Alex Rodriguez 60.00
3 Mike Piazza 50.00
4 Mark McGwire 75.00
5 Greg Maddux 35.00
6 Derek Jeter 60.00
7 Chipper Jones 35.00
8 Pedro Martinez 20.00
9 Ken Griffey Jr. 50.00
10 Nomar Garciaparra 50.00
11 Randy Johnson 20.00
12 Sammy Sosa 35.00
13 Vladimir Guerrero 25.00
14 Barry Bonds 20.00
15 Ivan Rodriguez 20.00

2001 Stadium Club Co-Signers

MT
Common Duo: 30.00
Inserted 1:1,117
1 Nomar Garciaparra, Derek Jeter 500.00
2 Roberto Alomar, Edgardo Alfonzo 80.00
3 Rick Ankiel, Kevin Millwood 50.00
4 Chipper Jones, Troy Glaus 120.00
5 Magglio Ordonez, Bobby Abreu 40.00
6 Adam Piatt, Sean Burroughs 40.00
7 Corey Patterson, Nick Johnson 60.00
8 Adrian Gonzalez, Rocco Baldelli 75.00
9 Adam Johnson, Mike Stodolka 30.00

2001 Stadium Club Diamond Pearls

MT
Complete Set (20): 40.00
Common Player: 1.00
Inserted 1:8
1 Ken Griffey Jr. 4.00
2 Alex Rodriguez 5.00
3 Derek Jeter 5.00
4 Chipper Jones 3.00
5 Nomar Garciaparra 4.00
6 Vladimir Guerrero 2.00
7 Jeff Bagwell 1.50
8 Cal Ripken Jr. 5.00
9 Sammy Sosa 3.00
10 Mark McGwire 6.00
11 Frank Thomas 2.00
12 Pedro Martinez 1.50
13 Manny Ramirez 1.50
14 Randy Johnson 1.50
15 Barry Bonds 1.50
16 Ivan Rodriguez 1.50
17 Greg Maddux 3.00
18 Mike Piazza 4.00
19 Todd Helton 1.50
20 Shawn Green 1.00

2001 Stadium Club Game-Used Cards

MT
Common Player: 15.00
Inserted 1:285
1 Chin-Feng Chen 75.00
2 Bobby Bradley 30.00
3 Tomokazu Ohka 90.00
4 Kurt Ainsworth 30.00
5 Craig Anderson 20.00
6 Josh Hamilton 40.00
7 Felipe Lopez 20.00
8 Ryan Anderson 40.00
9 Alex Escobar 20.00
10 Ben Sheets 60.00
11 Ntema Ndungidi 20.00
12 Eric Munson 20.00
13 Aaron Myette 15.00
14 Jack Cust 25.00
15 Julio Zuleta 20.00
16 Corey Patterson 40.00
17 Carlos Pena 25.00
18 Marcus Giles 25.00
19 Travis Wilson 15.00
20 Barry Zito 60.00

2001 Stadium Club King of the Hill

MT
Complete Set (5): 60.00
Common Player: 8.00
Inserted 1:21
1 Pedro Martinez 20.00
2 Randy Johnson 15.00
3 Greg Maddux 20.00
4 Rick Ankiel 10.00
5 Kevin Brown 8.00

2001 Stadium Club Lone Star Signatures

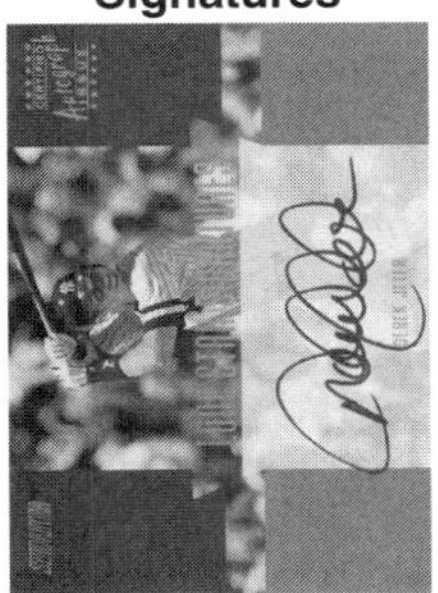

		MT
Common Player:		15.00
Inserted 1:196		
1	Nomar Garciaparra	150.00
2	Derek Jeter	200.00
3	Edgardo Alfonzo	40.00
4	Roberto Alomar	70.00
5	Magglio Ordonez	40.00
6	Bobby Abreu	30.00
7	Chipper Jones	90.00
8	Troy Glaus	50.00
9	Nick Johnson	20.00
10	Adam Piatt	25.00
11	Sean Burroughs	25.00
12	Corey Patterson	30.00
13	Rick Ankiel	35.00
14	Kevin Millwood	15.00
15	Adrian Gonzalez	25.00
16	Adam Johnson	15.00
17	Rocco Baldelli	25.00
18	Mike Stodolka	15.00

2001 Stadium Club Play at the Plate

		MT
Complete Set (10):		200.00
Common Player:		10.00
Inserted 1:11		
1	Mark McGwire	50.00
2	Sammy Sosa	25.00
3	Vladimir Guerrero	12.00
4	Ken Griffey Jr.	30.00
5	Mike Piazza	25.00
6	Chipper Jones	15.00
7	Barry Bonds	15.00
8	Alex Rodriguez	40.00
9	Jeff Bagwell	10.00
10	Nomar Garciaparra	25.00

2001 Stadium Club Souvenirs

		MT
Common Player:		15.00
1	Scott Rolen bat	40.00
2	Larry Walker bat	30.00
3	Rafael Furcal bat	35.00
4	Darin Erstad bat	30.00
5	Mike Sweeney jersey	15.00
6	Matt Lawton jersey	15.00
7	Jose Vidro jersey	15.00
8	Pat Burrell jersey	40.00

A card number in parentheses ( ) indicates the set is unnumbered.

2002 Stadium Club Relic Edition

		MT
Complete Set (125):		NA
Common Player:		.15
Common SP (101-125):		8.00
Production 2,999		
Pack (6):		3.00
Box (24):		60.00
1	Pedro Martinez	.75
2	Derek Jeter	3.00
3	Chipper Jones	1.50
4	Roberto Alomar	.50
5	Albert Pujols	1.00
6	Bret Boone	.15
7	Alex Rodriguez	2.00
8	Jose Cruz	.15
9	Mike Hampton	.15
10	Vladimir Guerrero	.75
11	Jim Edmonds	.25
12	Luis Gonzalez	.50
13	Jeff Kent	.15
14	Mike Piazza	2.00
15	Ben Sheets	.25
16	Tsuyoshi Shinjo	.25
17	Pat Burrell	.40
18	Jermaine Dye	.15
19	Rafael Furcal	.25
20	Randy Johnson	.75
21	Carlos Delgado	.40
22	Roger Clemens	1.00
23	Eric Chavez	.25
24	Nomar Garciaparra	2.00
25	Ivan Rodriguez	.75
26	Juan Gonzalez	.75
27	Reggie Sanders	.15
28	Jeff Bagwell	.75
29	Kazuhiro Sasaki	.15
30	Larry Walker	.40
31	Ben Grieve	.15
32	David Justice	.25
33	David Wells	.15
34	Kevin Brown	.25
35	Miguel Tejada	.25
36	Jorge Posada	.25
37	Javy Lopez	.15
38	Cliff Floyd	.15
39	Carlos Lee	.15
40	Manny Ramirez	.75
41	Jim Thome	.40
42	Pokey Reese	.15
43	Scott Rolen	.25
44	Richie Sexson	.25
45	Dean Palmer	.15
46	Rafael Palmeiro	.40
47	Alfonso Soriano	.40
48	Craig Biggio	.25
49	Troy Glaus	.50
50	Andruw Jones	.40
51	Ichiro Suzuki	3.00
52	Kenny Lofton	.25
53	Hideo Nomo	.40
54	Magglio Ordonez	.25
55	Brad Penny	.15
56	Omar Vizquel	.25
57	Mike Sweeney	.15
58	Gary Sheffield	.25
59	Ken Griffey Jr.	2.00
60	Curt Schilling	.25
61	Bobby Higginson	.15
62	Terrence Long	.15
63	Moises Alou	.25
64	Sandy Alomar	.15
65	Cristian Guzman	.15
66	Sammy Sosa	1.50
67	Jose Vidro	.15
68	Edgar Martinez	.15
69	Jason Giambi	.50
70	Mark McGwire	2.50
71	Barry Bonds	1.50
72	Greg Vaughn	.15
73	Phil Nevin	.15
74	Jason Kendall	.15
75	Greg Maddux	1.50
76	Jeromy Burnitz	.15
77	Mike Mussina	.50
78	Johnny Damon	.15
79	Shawn Green	.40
80	Jimmy Rollins	.15
81	Edgardo Alfonzo	.15
82	Barry Larkin	.25
83	Raul Mondesi	.15
84	Preston Wilson	.15
85	Mike Lieberthal	.15
86	J.D. Drew	.40
87	Ryan Klesko	.15
88	David Segui	.15
89	Derek Bell	.15
90	Bernie Williams	.50
91	Doug Mientkiewicz	.15
92	Rich Aurilia	.15
93	Ellis Burks	.15
94	Placido Polanco	.15
95	Darin Erstad	.40
96	Brian Giles	.25
97	Geoff Jenkins	.25
98	Kerry Wood	.40
99	Mariano Rivera	.40
100	Todd Helton	.75
101	Adam Dunn	15.00
102	Grant Balfour	8.00
103	Jae Weong Seo	8.00
104	Hank Blalock	10.00
105	Chris George	8.00
106	Jack Cust	8.00
107	Juan Cruz	8.00
108	Adrian Gonzalez	8.00
109	Nick Johnson	10.00
110	*Jeff Devanon*	10.00
111	Juan Diaz	8.00
112	Brandon Duckworth	10.00
113	Jason Lane	8.00
114	Seung Jun Song	8.00
115	Morgan Ensberg	8.00
116	*Marlyn Tisdale*	10.00
117	*Jason Botts*	8.00
118	*Henry Pichardo*	8.00
119	*John Rodriguez*	8.00
120	*Mike Peeples*	10.00
121	*Rob Bowen*	10.00
122	Jeremy Affeldt	8.00
123	*Jorge Buret*	10.00
124	*Manny Ravelo*	8.00
125	*Eudy Lajara*	8.00

2002 Stadium Club Relic Edition All-Star Relics

		MT
Common Player:		10.00
RA	Roberto Alomar	15.00
MA	Moises Alou	10.00
BB	Barry Bonds	25.00
BRB	Bret Boone	15.00
MC	Mike Cameron	10.00
SC	Sean Casey	15.00
CF	Cliff Floyd	10.00
BG	Brian Giles	15.00
JG	Juan Gonzalez	25.00
LG3	Luis Gonzalez	20.00
CG	Cristian Guzman	10.00
TG	Tony Gwynn	20.00
MH	Mike Hampton	10.00
TH	Todd Helton	20.00
RJ	Randy Johnson	20.00
CJ	Chipper Jones	25.00
JK	Jeff Kent	15.00
RK	Ryan Klesko	10.00
EM	Edgar Martinez	10.00
ERM	Eric Milton	10.00
JO	John Olerud	10.00
MO	Magglio Ordonez	20.00
MP	Mike Piazza	40.00
JP	Jorge Posada	15.00
AP	Albert Pujols	40.00
MR	Manny Ramirez	15.00
CR	Cal Ripken Jr.	10.00
IR	Ivan Rodriguez	15.00
KS	Kazuhiro Sasaki	20.00
MS	Mike Sweeney	10.00
LW	Larry Walker	10.00

2002 Stadium Club Relic Edition Chasing 500-500

		MT
Common Player:		
BB1	Barry Bonds dual	50.00
BB2	Barry Bonds jsy/600	50.00
BB3	Barry Bonds mult/200	90.00

2002 Stadium Club Relic Edition Passport to the Majors

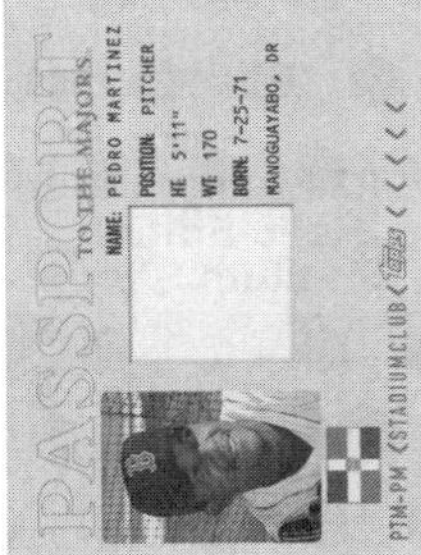

		MT
Common Player:		8.00
Jsy 1:84		
Bat 1:795		
BA	Bobby Abreu/400	15.00
EA	Edgardo Alfonzo	10.00
RA	Roberto Alomar	15.00
WB	Wilson Betemit /325	10.00
BC	Bartolo Colon	8.00
RF	Rafael Furcal	12.00
AG	Andres Galarraga	10.00
JG	Juan Gonzalez	15.00
SH	Shigetoshi Hasegawa	10.00
AJ	Andruw Jones	15.00
CL	Carlos Lee	8.00
JL	Javy Lopez	10.00
PM	Pedro Martinez	15.00
RM	Raul Mondesi	10.00
MO	Magglio Ordonez	15.00
RP	Rafael Palmeiro	15.00
CP	Chan Ho Park	15.00
AP	Albert Pujols/450	40.00
MR	Manny Ramirez	15.00
IR	Ivan Rodriguez	12.00
KS	Kazuhiro Sasaki	15.00
TS	Tsuyoshi Shinjo /400	35.00
AS	Alfonso Soriano /400	20.00
MT	Miguel Tejada/375	15.00
LW	Larry Walker	12.00

2002 Stadium Club Relic Edition Reel Time

	MT
Complete Set (20):	45.00
Common Player:	1.50

Inserted 1:8

RT1	Luis Gonzalez	2.00
RT2	Derek Jeter	6.00
RT3	Ken Griffey Jr.	4.00
RT4	Alex Rodriguez	4.00
RT5	Barry Bonds	3.00
RT6	Ichiro Suzuki	6.00
RT7	Carlos Delgado	1.50
RT8	Manny Ramirez	2.00
RT9	Mike Piazza	4.00
RT10	Mark McGwire	5.00
RT11	Todd Helton	2.00
RT12	Vladimir Guerrero	2.00
RT13	Jim Thome	1.50
RT14	Rich Aurilia	1.50
RT15	Bret Boone	1.50
RT16	Roberto Alomar	2.00
RT17	Jason Giambi	2.00
RT18	Chipper Jones	3.00
RT19	Albert Pujols	3.00
RT20	Sammy Sosa	3.00

2002 Stadium Club Relic Edition Stadium Shots

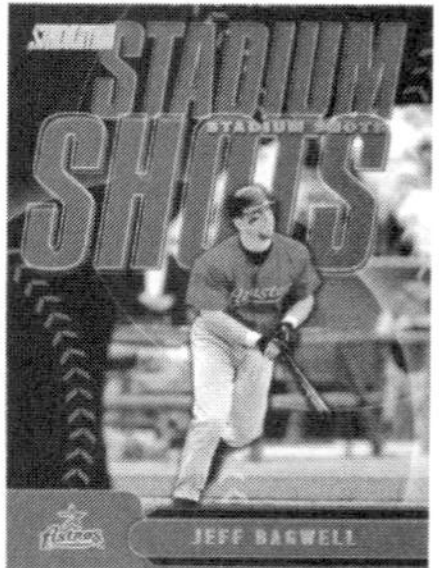

		MT
Complete Set (10):		20.00
Common Player:		1.50
Inserted 1:12		
SS1	Sammy Sosa	3.00
SS2	Manny Ramirez	2.00
SS3	Jason Giambi	2.00
SS4	Mike Piazza	4.00
SS5	Barry Bonds	3.00
SS6	Ken Griffey Jr.	4.00
SS7	Juan Gonzalez	2.00
SS8	Jeff Bagwell	2.00
SS9	Jim Thome	1.50
SS10	Mark McGwire	5.00

2002 Stadium Club Relic Edition Stadium Slices

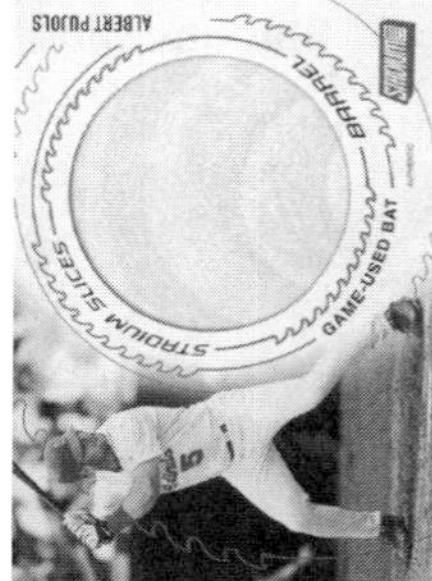

		MT
Common Player:		15.00
BB	Barry Bonds	50.00
LG	Luis Gonzalez	25.00
AP	Albert Pujols	50.00
IR	Ivan Rodriguez	20.00
BW	Bernie Williams	20.00

2002 Stadium Club Relic Edition World Champions Relics

		MT
Common Player:		8.00
Jersey 1:106		
Bat 1:94		
Pants 1:795		
Spikes 1:38,400		
RA	Roberto Alomar	20.00
MA	Moises Alou	8.00
DB	Don Baylor	8.00
JB	Johnny Bench	35.00
BB	Bert Blyleven	12.00
WB	Wade Boggs	30.00
BRB	Bob Boone	10.00
GB	George Brett	50.00
SB	Scott Brosius	10.00
AB	Al Bumbry	8.00
JC1	Jose Canseco	20.00
JC2	Jose Canseco	20.00
GC1	Gary Carter	20.00
GC2	Gary Carter	20.00
JC	Joe Carter	10.00
RC	Ron Cey	10.00
CC	Chris Chambliss	8.00
DC	Dave Concepcion	12.00
ED	Eric Davis	15.00
BD	Bucky Dent	8.00
GF	George Foster	12.00
PG	Phil Garner	10.00
KG1	Kirk Gibson	15.00
KG2	Kirk Gibson	15.00
TG	Tom Glavine	15.00
KG	Ken Griffey Sr.	10.00
RH	Rickey Henderson /50	200.00
GH	George Hendrick	8.00
KH	Keith Hernandez	25.00
WH	Willie Hernandez	8.00
OH	Orel Hershiser	15.00
RJ	Reggie Jackson	35.00
CJ	Charles Johnson	8.00
CWJ	Chipper Jones	25.00
DJ	David Justice	12.00
CK	Chuck Knoblauch	15.00
AL	Al Leiter	10.00
DL	Davey Lopes	10.00
JL	Javy Lopez	10.00
GL	Greg Luzinski	12.00
GM	Greg Maddux	35.00
BM	Bill Madlock	10.00
TLM	Tino Martinez	15.00
HM	Hal McCrae	8.00
FM	Fred McGriff	12.00
PM	Paul Molitor	40.00
TM	Thurman Munson	50.00
EM1	Eddie Murray	20.00
EM2	Eddie Murray	20.00
JO	John Olerud	12.00
PO	Paul O'Neill	20.00
DP	Dave Parker	10.00
TP	Tony Perez	15.00
LVP	Lou Pinella	12.00
JP	Jorge Posada	15.00
KP	Kirby Puckett	60.00
WR	Willie Randolph	12.00
MJS	Mike Schmidt	50.00
MS	Mike Scoscia	10.00
OS	Ozzie Smith	35.00
JS	John Smoltz	12.00
ES	Ed Sprague	8.00
WS	Willie Stargell	20.00
AT	Alan Trammell	30.00
LW	Lou Whitaker	15.00
BW	Bernie Williams	15.00
MW	Mookie Wilson	10.00
DW	Dave Winfield	15.00
FV	Fernando Valenzuela	10.00
JV	Jose Vizcaino	8.00

A player's name in *italic* type indicates a rookie card.

2003 Stadium Club

		MT
Complete Set (125):		30.00
Common Player:		.15
Hobby pack (6):		3.00
Hobby box (24):		55.00
1	Rafael Furcal	.15
2	Randy Winn	.15
3	Eric Chavez	.25
4	Fernando Vina	.15
5	Pat Burrell	.40
6	Derek Jeter	2.50
7	Ivan Rodriguez	.50
8	Eric Hinske	.15
9	Roberto Alomar	.50
10	Tony Batista	.15
11	Jacque Jones	.15
12	Alfonso Soriano	1.50
13	Omar Vizquel	.15
14	Paul Konerko	.25
15	Shawn Green	.25
16	Garret Anderson	.25
17	Darin Erstad	.25
18	Johnny Damon	.15
19	Juan Gonzalez	.50
20	Luis Gonzalez	.25
21	Sean Burroughs	.15
22	Mark Prior	.40
23	Javier Vazquez	.15
24	Shannon Stewart	.15
25	Jay Gibbons	.15
26	A.J. Pierzynski	.15
27	Vladimir Guerrero	.75
28	Austin Kearns	.25
29	Shea Hillenbrand	.15
30	Magglio Ordonez	.25
31	Mike Cameron	.15
32	Tim Salmon	.25
33	Brian Jordan	.15
34	Moises Alou	.15
35	Rich Aurilia	.15
36	Nick Johnson	.15
37	Junior Spivey	.15
38	Curt Schilling	.40
39	Jose Vidro	.15
40	Orlando Cabrera	.15
41	Jeff Bagwell	.60
42	Mo Vaughn	.25
43	Luis Castillo	.15
44	Vicente Padilla	.15
45	Pedro J. Martinez	.75
46	John Olerud	.25
47	Tom Glavine	.40
48	Torii Hunter	.25
49	J.D. Drew	.25
50	Alex Rodriguez	2.00
51	Randy Johnson	.75
52	Richie Sexson	.25
53	Jimmy Rollins	.15
54	Cristian Guzman	.15
55	Tim Hudson	.25
56	Mark Buehrle	.15
57	Paul LoDuca	.15
58	Aramis Ramirez	.15
59	Todd Helton	.50
60	Lance Berkman	.50
61	Josh Beckett	.15
62	Bret Boone	.15
63	Miguel Tejada	.50
64	Nomar Garciaparra	2.00
65	Albert Pujols	.75
66	Chipper Jones	1.25
67	Scott Rolen	.25
68	Kerry Wood	.25
69	Jorge Posada	.25
70	Ichiro Suzuki	2.00
71	Jeff Kent	.25
72	David Eckstein	.15
73	Phil Nevin	.15
74	Brian Giles	.25
75	Barry Zito	.25
76	Andruw Jones	.50
77	Jim Thome	.60
78	Robert Fick	.15
79	Rafael Palmeiro	.50
80	Barry Bonds	2.00
81	Gary Sheffield	.25
82	Jim Edmonds	.25
83	Kazuhisa Ishii	.15
84	Jose Hernandez	.15
85	Jason Giambi	1.25
86	Mark Mulder	.25
87	Roger Clemens	1.00
88	Troy Glaus	.60
89	Carlos Delgado	.25
90	Mike Sweeney	.15
91	Ken Griffey Jr.	1.50
92	Manny Ramirez	.60
93	Ryan Klesko	.15
94	Larry Walker	.25
95	Adam Dunn	.60
96	Raul Ibanez	.15
97	Preston Wilson	.15
98	Roy Oswalt	.25
99	Sammy Sosa	1.25
100	Mike Piazza	1.50
101	Jose Reyes	.15
102	Ed Rogers	.15
103	Hank Blalock	.15
104	Mark Teixeira	.15
105	Orlando Hudson	.15
106	Drew Henson	.15
107	Joe Mauer	.50
108	Carl Crawford	.15
109	Marlon Byrd	.15
110	Jason Stokes	.15
111	Miguel Cabrera	.15
112	Wilson Betemit	.15
113	Jerome Williams	.15
114	Walter Young	3.00
115	*Juan Camacho*	3.00
116	Chris Duncan	.15
117	*Franklin Gutierrez*	1.00
118	Adam LaRoche	1.50
119	*Manuel Ramirez*	.75
120	*Il Kim*	.75
121	*Wayne Lydon*	.75
122	Daryl Clark	.15
123	Sean Pierce	.15
124	Andy Marte	.15
125	*Matthew Peterson*	.75

2003 Stadium Club Photographer's Proof

	MT
Stars (1-100):	4-8X
Cards (101-125):	2-4X
Production 299 sets	
Royal Golds:	1-3X
Inserted 1:1	

2003 Stadium Club Beam Team

		MT
Complete Set (20):		50.00
Common Player:		1.00
Inserted 1:12		
BT1	Larry Walker	1.00
BT2	Miguel Tejada	1.50
BT3	Ichiro Suzuki	5.00
BT4	Sammy Sosa	4.00
BT5	Ivan Rodriguez	1.50

BT6	Alex Rodriguez	6.00
BT7	Mike Piazza	5.00
BT8	Jeff Kent	1.00
BT9	Chipper Jones	4.00
BT10	Derek Jeter	8.00
BT11	Todd Helton	1.50
BT12	Vladimir Guerrero	3.00
BT13	Shawn Green	1.00
BT14	Brian Giles	1.00
BT15	Jason Giambi	4.00
BT16	Nomar Garciaparra	5.00
BT17	Adam Dunn	2.00
BT18	Carlos Delgado	1.00
BT19	Barry Bonds	6.00
BT20	Lance Berkman	1.50

2003 Stadium Club Born In The USA

		MT
Common Player:		5.00
Jerseys inserted 1:52		
Bats inserted 1:76		
RA	Rich Aurilia/jsy	5.00
JB	Jeff Bagwell/jsy	12.00
CB	Craig Biggio/jsy	6.00
BB	Bret Boone/jsy	5.00
AB	A.J. Burnett/jsy	5.00
JNB	Jeromy Burnitz/bat	6.00
PB	Pat Burrell/bat	15.00
SB	Sean Burroughs/ bat	6.00
EC	Eric Chavez/jsy	6.00
TC	Tony Clark/bat	5.00
JD	Johnny Damon/bat	6.00
JDD	J.D. Drew/bat	6.00
AD	Adam Dunn/bat	12.00
JE	Jim Edmonds/jsy	6.00
CF	Cliff Floyd/bat	5.00
BF	Brad Fullmer/bat	5.00
NG	Nomar Garciaparra/ bat	20.00
LG	Luis Gonzalez/bat	6.00
MG	Mark Grace/jsy	12.00
SG	Shawn Green/bat	6.00
TJH	Toby Hall	5.00
JH	Josh Hamilton/bat	5.00
TH	Todd Helton/bat	8.00
RH	Rickey Henderson/ bat	35.00
RJ	Randy Johnson/ bat	12.00
CJ	Chipper Jones/jsy	12.00
RK	Ryan Klesko/bat	5.00
PK	Paul Konerko/bat	8.00
BL	Barry Larkin/jsy	8.00
TRL	Travis Lee/bat	5.00
TL	Terrence Long/jsy	5.00
GM	Greg Maddux/jsy	15.00
TM	Tino Martinez/bat	10.00
WM	Willie Mays/bat	40.00
EM	Eric Milton/jsy	6.00
JO	John Olerud/jsy	6.00
CP	Corey Patterson/ bat	5.00
MP	Mike Piazza/jsy	15.00
AR	Alex Rodriguez/ bat	15.00
SR	Scott Rolen/bat	15.00
RS	Richie Sexson/bat	6.00
GS	Gary Sheffield/bat	6.00
JS	John Smoltz/jsy	6.00
FT	Frank Thomas/bat	8.00
JT	Jim Thome/jsy	15.00
MV	Mo Vaughn/bat	6.00
RV	Robin Ventura/bat	8.00
MW	Matt Williams/bat	12.00
PW	Preston Wilson/jsy	5.00
KW	Kerry Wood/bat	6.00

2003 Stadium Club Clubhouse Exclusive

		MT
Jersey inserted 1:488		
Jersey & Bat 1:2,073		
Jersey, Bat & Spikes 1:2,750		
CE1	Albert Pujols/jsy	12.00
CE2	Albert Pujols/ bat/jsy	35.00
CE3	Albert Pujols/ jsy/bat/spike	

2003 Stadium Club Co-Signers

		MT
HTA Exclusive		
MI	Masanori Murakami, Kazuhisa Ishii	180.00
AM	Hank Aaron, Willie Mays	340.00

2003 Stadium Club License To Drive

		MT
Common Player:		5.00
Inserted 1:98		
RA	Roberto Alomar	15.00
MA	Moises Alou	6.00
AB	Adrian Beltre	6.00
LB	Lance Berkman	8.00
EC	Eric Chavez	10.00
AD	Adam Dunn	12.00
NG	Nomar Garciaparra	20.00
JG	Juan Gonzalez	8.00
LG	Luis Gonzalez	6.00
SG	Shawn Green	8.00
TH	Todd Helton	8.00
AJ	Andruw Jones	8.00
CJ	Chipper Jones	15.00
TM	Tino Martinez	8.00
RP	Rafael Palmeiro	10.00
MP	Mike Piazza	15.00
AP	Albert Pujols	20.00
ANR	Aramis Ramirez	5.00
AR	Alex Rodriguez	15.00
IR	Ivan Rodriguez	6.00
SR	Scott Rolen	15.00
GS	Gary Sheffield	8.00
FT	Frank Thomas	8.00
LW	Larry Walker	6.00
BW	Bernie Williams	15.00

2003 Stadium Club MLB Matchups

		MT
Inserted 1:485		
BB	Bret Boone	
TH	Todd Helton	15.00
AJ	Andruw Jones	12.00
GM	Greg Maddux	40.00
AP	Albert Pujols	30.00

2003 Stadium Club Stadium Shots

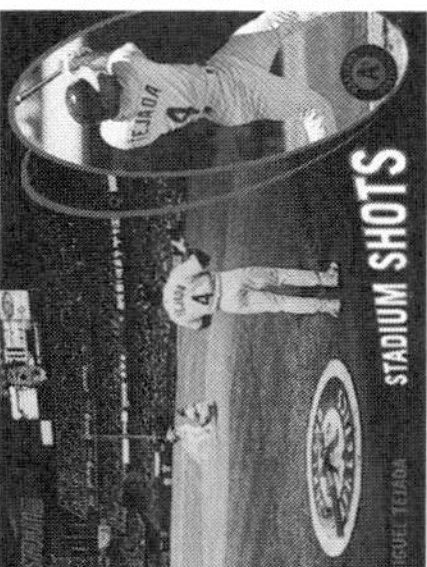

	MT
Complete Set (10):	25.00
Common Player:	1.00
Inserted 1:24	

SS1	Lance Berkman	1.50
SS2	Barry Bonds	6.00
SS3	Jason Giambi	4.00
SS4	Shawn Green	1.00
SS5	Vladimir Guerrero	3.00
SS6	Paul Konerko	1.00
SS7	Mike Piazza	5.00
SS8	Alex Rodriguez	6.00
SS9	Sammy Sosa	4.00
SS10	Jim Thome	2.00

2003 Stadium Club Stadium Slices Handle

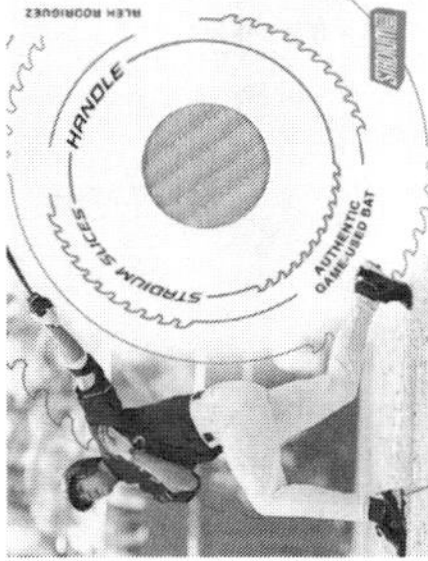

		MT
Common Player:		6.00
Inserted 1:237		
Trademarks:		1-1.5X
Inserted 1:415		
Barrels: 1.5-2X		
Inserted 1:550		
RA	Roberto Alomar	15.00
CD	Carlos Delgado	8.00
NG	Nomar Garciaparra	20.00
TH	Todd Helton	8.00
AJ	Andruw Jones	8.00
RP	Rafael Palmeiro	10.00
MP	Mike Piazza	15.00
AP	Albert Pujols	20.00
AR	Alex Rodriguez	15.00
GS	Gary Sheffield	6.00

2003 Stadium Club World Stage

		MT
Common Player:		5.00
Jerseys inserted 1:118		
Bats inserted 1:809		
AB	Adrian Beltre/jsy	5.00
KI	Kazuhisa Ishii/jsy	8.00
BK	Byung-Hyun Kim/ jsy	6.00
HN	Hideo Nomo/bat	30.00
AP	Albert Pujols/jsy	12.00
IR	Ivan Rodriguez/jsy	6.00
KS	Kazuhiro Sasaki/jsy	6.00
TS	Tsuyoshi Shinjo/bat	6.00
AS	Alfonso Soriano/ bat	20.00
MT	Miguel Tejada/jsy	8.00

1991 Studio Preview

Each 1991 Donruss set packaged for the retail trade included a pack of four cards previewing the debut Studio set. The cards are in the same format as the regular set, 2-1/2" x 3-1/2" with evocative black-and-white photos bordered in maroon on front, and a biographical write-up on the back.

		MT
Complete Set (18):		20.00
Common Player:		1.00
1	Juan Bell	1.00
2	Roger Clemens	6.00
3	Dave Parker	1.00
4	Tim Raines	1.00
5	Kevin Seitzer	1.00
6	Teddy Higuera	1.00
7	Bernie Williams	2.50
8	Harold Baines	1.00
9	Gary Pettis	1.00
10	Dave Justice	1.50
11	Eric Davis	1.00
12	Andujar Cedeno	1.00
13	Tom Foley	1.00
14	Dwight Gooden	1.00
15	Doug Drabek	1.00
16	Steve Decker	1.00
17	Joe Torre	1.50
18	Header card	.15

1991 Studio

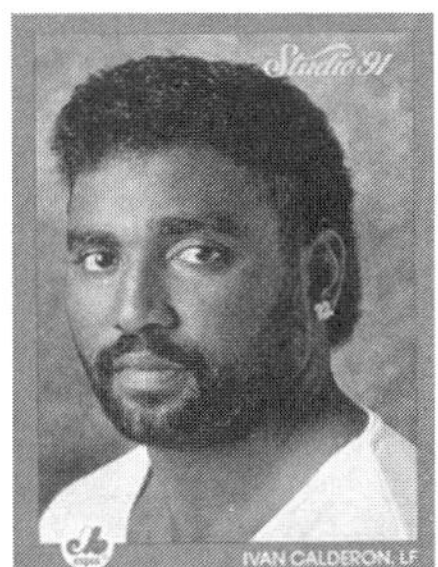

Donruss introduced this 264-card set in 1991. The cards feature maroon borders surrounding black and white posed player photos. The card backs are printed in black and white and feature personal data, career highlights, hobbies and interests and the player's hero. The cards were released in foil packs only and feature a special Rod Carew puzzle.

		MT
Complete Set (264):		15.00
Common Player:		.10
Pack (10):		1.00
Wax Box (48):		20.00
1	Glenn Davis	.10
2	Dwight Evans	.10
3	Leo Gomez	.10
4	Chris Hoiles	.10
5	Sam Horn	.10
6	Ben McDonald	.10
7	Randy Milligan	.10
8	Gregg Olson	.10
9	Cal Ripken, Jr.	2.00
10	David Segui	.10
11	Wade Boggs	.50

12	Ellis Burks	.10
13	Jack Clark	.10
14	Roger Clemens	.75
15	Mike Greenwell	.10
16	Tim Naehring	.10
17	Tony Pena	.10
18	*Phil Plantier*	.10
19	Jeff Reardon	.10
20	Mo Vaughn	.45
21	Jimmy Reese	.10
22	Jim Abbott	.10
23	Bert Blyleven	.10
24	Chuck Finley	.10
25	Gary Gaetti	.10
26	Wally Joyner	.10
27	Mark Langston	.10
28	Kirk McCaskill	.10
29	Lance Parrish	.10
30	Dave Winfield	.60
31	Alex Fernandez	.10
32	Carlton Fisk	.50
33	Scott Fletcher	.10
34	Greg Hibbard	.10
35	Charlie Hough	.10
36	Jack McDowell	.10
37	Tim Raines	.10
38	Sammy Sosa	1.00
39	Bobby Thigpen	.10
40	Frank Thomas	1.00
41	Sandy Alomar	.10
42	John Farrell	.10
43	Glenallen Hill	.10
44	Brook Jacoby	.10
45	Chris James	.10
46	Doug Jones	.10
47	Eric King	.10
48	Mark Lewis	.10
49	Greg Swindell	.10
50	Mark Whiten	.10
51	Milt Cuyler	.10
52	Rob Deer	.10
53	Cecil Fielder	.10
54	Travis Fryman	.10
55	Bill Gullickson	.10
56	Lloyd Moseby	.10
57	Frank Tanana	.10
58	Mickey Tettleton	.10
59	Alan Trammell	.10
60	Lou Whitaker	.10
61	Mike Boddicker	.10
62	George Brett	.75
63	Jeff Conine	.10
64	Warren Cromartie	.10
65	Storm Davis	.10
66	Kirk Gibson	.10
67	Mark Gubicza	.10
68	*Brian McRae*	.10
69	Bret Saberhagen	.10
70	Kurt Stillwell	.10
71	Tim McIntosh	.10
72	Candy Maldonado	.10
73	Paul Molitor	.50
74	Willie Randolph	.10
75	Ron Robinson	.10
76	Gary Sheffield	.25
77	Franklin Stubbs	.10
78	B.J. Surhoff	.10
79	Greg Vaughn	.10
80	Robin Yount	.50
81	Rick Aguilera	.10
82	Steve Bedrosian	.10
83	Scott Erickson	.10
84	Greg Gagne	.10
85	Dan Gladden	.10
86	Brian Harper	.10
87	Kent Hrbek	.10
88	Shane Mack	.10
89	Jack Morris	.10
90	Kirby Puckett	.75
91	Jesse Barfield	.10
92	Steve Farr	.10
93	Steve Howe	.10
94	Roberto Kelly	.10
95	Tim Leary	.10
96	Kevin Maas	.10
97	Don Mattingly	1.00
98	Hensley Meulens	.10
99	Scott Sanderson	.10
100	Steve Sax	.10
101	Jose Canseco	.40
102	Dennis Eckersley	.10
103	Dave Henderson	.10
104	Rickey Henderson	.65
105	Rick Honeycutt	.10
106	Mark McGwire	2.00
107	Dave Stewart	.10
108	Eric Show	.10
109	*Todd Van Poppel*	.10
110	Bob Welch	.10
111	Alvin Davis	.10
112	Ken Griffey, Jr.	1.50
113	Ken Griffey, Sr.	.10
114	Erik Hanson	.10
115	Brian Holman	.10
116	Randy Johnson	.50
117	Edgar Martinez	.10
118	Tino Martinez	.10
119	Harold Reynolds	.10
120	David Valle	.10
121	Kevin Belcher	.10
122	Scott Chiamparino	.10
123	Julio Franco	.10
124	Juan Gonzalez	.60
125	Rich Gossage	.10
126	Jeff Kunkel	.10
127	Rafael Palmeiro	.25
128	Nolan Ryan	2.00
129	Ruben Sierra	.10
130	Bobby Witt	.10
131	Roberto Alomar	.50
132	Tom Candiotti	.10
133	Joe Carter	.10
134	Ken Dayley	.10
135	Kelly Gruber	.10
136	John Olerud	.10
137	Dave Stieb	.10
138	Turner Ward	.10
139	Devon White	.10
140	Mookie Wilson	.10
141	Steve Avery	.10
142	Sid Bream	.10
143	Nick Esasky	.10
144	Ron Gant	.10
145	Tom Glavine	.15
146	Dave Justice	.25
147	Kelly Mann	.10
148	Terry Pendleton	.10
149	John Smoltz	.15
150	Jeff Treadway	.10
151	George Bell	.10
152	Shawn Boskie	.10
153	Andre Dawson	.35
154	Lance Dickson	.10
155	Shawon Dunston	.10
156	Joe Girardi	.10
157	Mark Grace	.25
158	Ryne Sandberg	.65
159	Gary Scott	.10
160	Dave Smith	.10
161	Tom Browning	.10
162	Eric Davis	.10
163	Rob Dibble	.10
164	Mariano Duncan	.10
165	Chris Hammond	.10
166	Billy Hatcher	.10
167	Barry Larkin	.15
168	Hal Morris	.10
169	Paul O'Neill	.10
170	Chris Sabo	.10
171	Eric Anthony	.10
172	*Jeff Bagwell*	3.00
173	Craig Biggio	.15
174	Ken Caminitti	.10
175	Jim Deshaies	.10
176	Steve Finley	.10
177	Pete Harnisch	.10
178	Darryl Kile	.10
179	Curt Schilling	.20
180	Mike Scott	.10
181	Brett Butler	.10
182	Gary Carter	.35
183	Orel Hershiser	.10
184	Ramon Martinez	.10
185	Eddie Murray	.55
186	Jose Offerman	.10
187	Bob Ojeda	.10
188	Juan Samuel	.10
189	Mike Scioscia	.10
190	Darryl Strawberry	.10
191	Moises Alou	.15
192	Brian Barnes	.10
193	Oil Can Boyd	.10
194	Ivan Calderon	.10
195	Delino DeShields	.10
196	Mike Fitzgerald	.10
197	Andres Galarraga	.10
198	Marquis Grissom	.10
199	Bill Sampen	.10
200	Tim Wallach	.10
201	Daryl Boston	.10
202	Vince Coleman	.10
203	John Franco	.10
204	Dwight Gooden	.10
205	Tom Herr	.10
206	Gregg Jefferies	.10
207	Howard Johnson	.10
208	Dave Magadan	.10
209	Kevin McReynolds	.10
210	Frank Viola	.10
211	Wes Chamberlain	.10
212	Darren Daulton	.10
213	Len Dykstra	.10
214	Charlie Hayes	.10
215	Ricky Jordan	.10
216	Steve Lake	.10
217	Roger McDowell	.10
218	Mickey Morandini	.10
219	Terry Mulholland	.10
220	Dale Murphy	.35
221	Jay Bell	.10
222	Barry Bonds	1.00
223	Bobby Bonilla	.10
224	Doug Drabek	.10
225	Bill Landrum	.10
226	Mike LaValliere	.10
227	Jose Lind	.10
228	Don Slaught	.10
229	John Smiley	.10
230	Andy Van Slyke	.10
231	Bernard Gilkey	.10
232	Pedro Guerrero	.10
233	Rex Hudler	.10
234	Ray Lankford	.10
235	Joe Magrane	.10
236	Jose Oquendo	.10
237	Lee Smith	.10
238	Ozzie Smith	.75
239	Milt Thompson	.10
240	Todd Zeile	.10
241	Larry Andersen	.10
242	Andy Benes	.10
243	Paul Faries	.10
244	Tony Fernandez	.10
245	Tony Gwynn	.75
246	Atlee Hammaker	.10
247	Fred McGriff	.10
248	Bip Roberts	.10
249	Benito Santiago	.10
250	Ed Whitson	.10
251	Dave Anderson	.10
252	Mike Benjamin	.10
253	John Burkett	.10
254	Will Clark	.30
255	Scott Garrelts	.10
256	Willie McGee	.10
257	Kevin Mitchell	.10
258	Dave Righetti	.10
259	Matt Williams	.30
260	Black & Decker (Bud Black, Steve Decker)	.20
261	Checklist	.05
262	Checklist	.05
263	Checklist	.05
---	Header card	.05

1992 Studio Preview

To introduce its 1992 Studio brand, Leaf produced 22 preview cards in format virtually identical to the issued versions of the same cards. The only differences are the appearance of the word "PREVIEW" in the lower-right corner of the card front, in place of the player's position, and the number "X of 22 / Preview Card" on the back where regular cards have the card number in the upper-right corner. The cards were distributed on a very limited basis to members of the Donruss dealers' network.

		MT
Complete Set (22):		250.00
Common Player:		6.00
1	Ruben Sierra	6.00
2	Kirby Puckett	20.00
3	Ryne Sandberg	15.00
4	John Kruk	6.00
5	Cal Ripken, Jr.	30.00
6	Robin Yount	15.00
7	Dwight Gooden	6.00
8	David Justice	12.00
9	Don Mattingly	25.00
10	Wally Joyner	6.00
11	Will Clark	10.00
12	Rob Dibble	6.00
13	Roberto Alomar	12.50
14	Wade Boggs	15.00
15	Barry Bonds	25.00
16	Jeff Bagwell	15.00
17	Mark McGwire	30.00
18	Frank Thomas	25.00
19	Brett Butler	6.00
20	Ozzie Smith	20.00
21	Jim Abbott	6.00
22	Tony Gwynn	20.00

1992 Studio

Donruss introduced the Studio line in 1991 and released another 264-card set entitled Leaf Studio for 1992. The cards feature a color player closeup with a large, rough-textured black-and-white photo of the player in the background. Tan borders surround the photos. The cards were only released in foil packs. Special Heritage insert cards featuring top players in vintage uniforms could be found in foil and jumbo packs.

		MT
Complete Set (264):		15.00
Common Player:		.05
Pack (12):		.50
Wax Box (36):		15.00
1	Steve Avery	.05
2	Sid Bream	.05
3	Ron Gant	.05
4	Tom Glavine	.10
5	Dave Justice	.25
6	Mark Lemke	.05
7	Greg Olson	.05
8	Terry Pendleton	.05

#	Player	MT
9	Deion Sanders	.10
10	John Smoltz	.10
11	Doug Dascenzo	.05
12	Andre Dawson	.25
13	Joe Girardi	.05
14	Mark Grace	.25
15	Greg Maddux	.75
16	Chuck McElroy	.05
17	Mike Morgan	.05
18	Ryne Sandberg	.65
19	Gary Scott	.05
20	Sammy Sosa	1.00
21	Norm Charlton	.05
22	Rob Dibble	.05
23	Barry Larkin	.10
24	Hal Morris	.05
25	Paul O'Neill	.05
26	Jose Rijo	.05
27	Bip Roberts	.05
28	Chris Sabo	.05
29	Reggie Sanders	.05
30	Greg Swindell	.05
31	Jeff Bagwell	.65
32	Craig Biggio	.10
33	Ken Caminiti	.05
34	Andujar Cedeno	.05
35	Steve Finley	.05
36	Pete Harnisch	.05
37	Butch Henry	.05
38	Doug Jones	.05
39	Darryl Kile	.05
40	Eddie Taubensee	.05
41	Brett Butler	.05
42	Tom Candiotti	.05
43	Eric Davis	.05
44	Orel Hershiser	.05
45	Eric Karros	.05
46	Ramon Martinez	.05
47	Jose Offerman	.05
48	Mike Scioscia	.05
49	Mike Sharperson	.05
50	Darryl Strawberry	.05
51	Bret Barbarie	.05
52	Ivan Calderon	.05
53	Gary Carter	.25
54	Delino DeShields	.05
55	Marquis Grissom	.05
56	Ken Hill	.05
57	Dennis Martinez	.05
58	Spike Owen	.05
59	Larry Walker	.25
60	Tim Wallach	.05
61	Bobby Bonilla	.05
62	Tim Burke	.05
63	Vince Coleman	.05
64	John Franco	.05
65	Dwight Gooden	.05
66	Todd Hundley	.05
67	Howard Johnson	.05
68	Eddie Murray	.40
69	Bret Saberhagen	.05
70	Anthony Young	.05
71	Kim Batiste	.05
72	Wes Chamberlain	.05
73	Darren Daulton	.05
74	Mariano Duncan	.05
75	Len Dykstra	.05
76	John Kruk	.05
77	Mickey Morandini	.05
78	Terry Mulholland	.05
79	Dale Murphy	.25
80	Mitch Williams	.05
81	Jay Bell	.05
82	Barry Bonds	1.00
83	Steve Buechele	.05
84	Doug Drabek	.05
85	Mike LaValliere	.05
86	Jose Lind	.05
87	Denny Neagle	.05
88	Randy Tomlin	.05
89	Andy Van Slyke	.05
90	Gary Varsho	.05
91	Pedro Guerrero	.05
92	Rex Hudler	.05
93	Brian Jordan	.05
94	Felix Jose	.05
95	Donovan Osborne	.05
96	Tom Pagnozzi	.05
97	Lee Smith	.05
98	Ozzie Smith	.75
99	Todd Worrell	.05
100	Todd Zeile	.05
101	Andy Benes	.05
102	Jerald Clark	.05
103	Tony Fernandez	.05
104	Tony Gwynn	.75
105	Greg Harris	.05
106	Fred McGriff	.05
107	Benito Santiago	.05
108	Gary Sheffield	.25
109	Kurt Stillwell	.05
110	Tim Teufel	.05
111	Kevin Bass	.05
112	Jeff Brantley	.05
113	John Burkett	.05
114	Will Clark	.15
115	Royce Clayton	.05
116	Mike Jackson	.05
117	Darren Lewis	.05
118	Bill Swift	.05
119	Robby Thompson	.05
120	Matt Williams	.15
121	Brady Anderson	.05
122	Glenn Davis	.05
123	Mike Devereaux	.05
124	Chris Hoiles	.05
125	Sam Horn	.05
126	Ben McDonald	.05
127	Mike Mussina	.45
128	Gregg Olson	.05
129	Cal Ripken, Jr.	2.00
130	Rick Sutcliffe	.05
131	Wade Boggs	.65
132	Roger Clemens	.75
133	Greg Harris	.05
134	Tim Naehring	.05
135	Tony Pena	.05
136	Phil Plantier	.05
137	Jeff Reardon	.05
138	Jody Reed	.05
139	Mo Vaughn	.40
140	Frank Viola	.05
141	Jim Abbott	.05
142	Hubie Brooks	.05
143	*Chad Curtis*	.10
144	Gary DiSarcina	.05
145	Chuck Finley	.05
146	Bryan Harvey	.05
147	Von Hayes	.05
148	Mark Langston	.05
149	Lance Parrish	.05
150	Lee Stevens	.05
151	George Bell	.05
152	Alex Fernandez	.05
153	Greg Hibbard	.05
154	Lance Johnson	.05
155	Kirk McCaskill	.05
156	Tim Raines	.05
157	Steve Sax	.05
158	Bobby Thigpen	.05
159	Frank Thomas	1.00
160	Robin Ventura	.05
161	Sandy Alomar, Jr.	.05
162	Jack Armstrong	.05
163	Carlos Baerga	.05
164	Albert Belle	.25
165	Alex Cole	.05
166	Glenallen Hill	.05
167	Mark Lewis	.05
168	Kenny Lofton	.05
169	Paul Sorrento	.05
170	Mark Whiten	.05
171	Milt Cuyler (color photo is Lou Whitaker)	.05
172	Rob Deer	.05
173	Cecil Fielder	.05
174	Travis Fryman	.05
175	Mike Henneman	.05
176	Tony Phillips	.05
177	Frank Tanana	.05
178	Mickey Tettleton	.05
179	Alan Trammell	.05
180	Lou Whitaker	.05
181	George Brett	.75
182	Tom Gordon	.05
183	Mark Gubicza	.05
184	Gregg Jefferies	.05
185	Wally Joyner	.05
186	Brent Mayne	.05
187	Brian McRae	.05
188	Kevin McReynolds	.05
189	Keith Miller	.05
190	Jeff Montgomery	.05
191	Dante Bichette	.05
192	Ricky Bones	.05
193	Scott Fletcher	.05
194	Paul Molitor	.60
195	Jaime Navarro	.05
196	Franklin Stubbs	.05
197	B.J. Surhoff	.05
198	Greg Vaughn	.05
199	Bill Wegman	.05
200	Robin Yount	.60
201	Rick Aguilera	.05
202	Scott Erickson	.05
203	Greg Gagne	.05
204	Brian Harper	.05
205	Kent Hrbek	.05
206	Scott Leius	.05
207	Shane Mack	.05
208	Pat Mahomes	.05
209	Kirby Puckett	.75
210	John Smiley	.05
211	Mike Gallego	.05
212	Charlie Hayes	.05
213	Pat Kelly	.05
214	Roberto Kelly	.05
215	Kevin Maas	.05
216	Don Mattingly	1.00
217	Matt Nokes	.05
218	Melido Perez	.05
219	Scott Sanderson	.05
220	Danny Tartabull	.05
221	Harold Baines	.05
222	Jose Canseco	.45
223	Dennis Eckersley	.05
224	Dave Henderson	.05
225	Carney Lansford	.05
226	Mark McGwire	2.00
227	Mike Moore	.05
228	Randy Ready	.05
229	Terry Steinbach	.05
230	Dave Stewart	.05
231	Jay Buhner	.05
232	Ken Griffey, Jr.	1.50
233	Erik Hanson	.05
234	Randy Johnson	.45
235	Edgar Martinez	.05
236	Tino Martinez	.05
237	Kevin Mitchell	.05
238	Pete O'Brien	.05
239	Harold Reynolds	.05
240	David Valle	.05
241	Julio Franco	.05
242	Juan Gonzalez	.65
243	Jose Guzman	.05
244	Rafael Palmeiro	.25
245	Dean Palmer	.05
246	Ivan Rodriguez	.65
247	Jeff Russell	.05
248	Nolan Ryan	2.00
249	Ruben Sierra	.05
250	Dickie Thon	.05
251	Roberto Alomar	.50
252	Derek Bell	.05
253	Pat Borders	.05
254	Joe Carter	.05
255	Kelly Gruber	.05
256	Juan Guzman	.05
257	Jack Morris	.05
258	John Olerud	.05
259	Devon White	.05
260	Dave Winfield	.65
261	Checklist	.05
262	Checklist	.05
263	Checklist	.05
264	History card	.05

1992 Studio Heritage

Superstars of 1992 were photographed in vintage-style uniforms in this 14-card insert set found in packages of Studio's 1992 issue. Cards #1-8 could be found in standard foil packs while #9-14 were inserted in Studio jumbos. Cards featured a sepia-tone photo bordered in turquoise and highlighted with copper foil. Cards carry a "BC" prefix to the card number on back.

		MT
Complete Set (14):		10.00
Common Player:		.50
1	Ryne Sandberg	.75
2	Carlton Fisk	.75
3	Wade Boggs	.75
4	Jose Canseco	.75
5	Don Mattingly	1.50
6	Darryl Strawberry	.50
7	Cal Ripken, Jr.	2.50
8	Will Clark	.50
9	Andre Dawson	.50
10	Andy Van Slyke	.50
11	Paul Molitor	.75
12	Jeff Bagwell	.75
13	Darren Daulton	.50
14	Kirby Puckett	1.00

1993 Studio

This 220-card set features full-bleed photos. The player's portrait appears against one of several backgrounds featuring his team's uniform. His signature and the Studio logo are printed in gold foil. Backs have an extreme closeup partial portrait of the player and insights into his personality.

		MT
Complete Set (220):		16.00
Common Player:		.10
Pack (12):		1.00
Wax Box (36):		20.00
1	Dennis Eckersley	.10
2	Chad Curtis	.10
3	Eric Anthony	.10
4	Roberto Alomar	.60
5	Steve Avery	.10
6	Cal Eldred	.10
7	Bernard Gilkey	.10
8	Steve Buechele	.10
9	Brett Butler	.10
10	Terry Mulholland	.10
11	Moises Alou	.15
12	Barry Bonds	1.50
13	Sandy Alomar Jr.	.10
14	Chris Bosio	.10
15	Scott Sanderson	.10
16	Bobby Bonilla	.10
17	Brady Anderson	.10
18	Derek Bell	.10
19	Wes Chamberlain	.10
20	Jay Bell	.10
21	Kevin Brown	.15
22	Roger Clemens	1.00
23	Roberto Kelly	.10
24	Dante Bichette	.10
25	George Brett	1.00
26	Rob Deer	.10

27	Brian Harper	.10
28	George Bell	.10
29	Jim Abbott	.10
30	Dave Henderson	.10
31	Wade Boggs	.60
32	Chili Davis	.10
33	Ellis Burks	.10
34	Jeff Bagwell	.75
35	Kent Hrbek	.10
36	Pat Borders	.10
37	Cecil Fielder	.10
38	Sid Bream	.10
39	Greg Gagne	.10
40	Darryl Hamilton	.10
41	Jerald Clark	.10
42	Mark Grace	.25
43	Barry Larkin	.15
44	John Burkett	.10
45	Scott Cooper	.10
46	*Mike Lansing*	.25
47	Jose Canseco	.45
48	Will Clark	.30
49	Carlos Garcia	.10
50	Carlos Baerga	.10
51	Darren Daulton	.10
52	Jay Buhner	.10
53	Andy Benes	.10
54	Jeff Conine	.10
55	Mike Devereaux	.10
56	Vince Coleman	.10
57	Terry Steinbach	.10
58	*J.T. Snow*	.75
59	Greg Swindell	.10
60	Devon White	.10
61	John Smoltz	.15
62	Todd Zeile	.10
63	Rick Wilkins	.10
64	Tim Wallach	.10
65	John Wetteland	.10
66	Matt Williams	.30
67	Paul Sorrento	.10
68	David Valle	.10
69	Walt Weiss	.10
70	John Franco	.10
71	Nolan Ryan	2.50
72	Frank Viola	.10
73	Chris Sabo	.10
74	David Nied	.10
75	Kevin McReynolds	.10
76	Lou Whitaker	.10
77	Dave Winfield	.75
78	Robin Ventura	.10
79	Spike Owen	.10
80	Cal Ripken, Jr.	2.50
81	Dan Walter	.10
82	Mitch Williams	.10
83	Tim Wakefield	.10
84	Rickey Henderson	.65
85	Gary DiSarcina	.10
86	Craig Biggio	.15
87	Joe Carter	.10
88	Ron Gant	.10
89	John Jaha	.10
90	Gregg Jefferies	.10
91	Jose Guzman	.10
92	Eric Karros	.10
93	Wil Cordero	.10
94	Royce Clayton	.10
95	Albert Belle	.40
96	Ken Griffey, Jr.	2.00
97	Orestes Destrade	.10
98	Tony Fernandez	.10
99	Leo Gomez	.10
100	Tony Gwynn	1.00
101	Len Dykstra	.10
102	Jeff King	.10
103	Julio Franco	.10
104	Andre Dawson	.25
105	Randy Milligan	.10
106	Alex Cole	.10
107	Phil Hiatt	.10
108	Travis Fryman	.10
109	Chuck Knoblauch	.10
110	Bo Jackson	.15
111	Pat Kelly	.10
112	Bret Saberhagen	.10
113	Ruben Sierra	.10
114	Tim Salmon	.30
115	Doug Jones	.10
116	Ed Sprague	.10
117	Terry Pendleton	.10
118	Robin Yount	.65
119	Mark Whiten	.10
120	Checklist	.10
121	Sammy Sosa	1.50
122	Darryl Strawberry	.10
123	Larry Walker	.25
124	Robby Thompson	.10
125	Carlos Martinez	.10
126	Edgar Martinez	.10
127	Benito Santiago	.10
128	Howard Johnson	.10
129	Harold Reynolds	.10
130	Craig Shipley	.10
131	Curt Schilling	.20
132	Andy Van Slyke	.10
133	Ivan Rodriguez	.60
134	Mo Vaughn	.50
135	Bip Roberts	.10
136	Charlie Hayes	.10
137	Brian McRae	.10
138	Mickey Tettleton	.10
139	Frank Thomas	1.50
140	Paul O'Neill	.10
141	Mark McGwire	2.50
142	Damion Easley	.10
143	Ken Caminiti	.10
144	Juan Guzman	.10
145	Tom Glavine	.15
146	Pat Listach	.10
147	Lee Smith	.10
148	Derrick May	.10
149	Ramon Martinez	.10
150	Delino DeShields	.10
151	Kirt Manwaring	.10
152	Reggie Jefferson	.10
153	Randy Johnson	.50
154	Dave Magadan	.10
155	Dwight Gooden	.10
156	Chris Hoiles	.10
157	Fred McGriff	.10
158	Dave Hollins	.10
159	Al Martin	.10
160	Juan Gonzalez	.75
161	Mike Greenwell	.10
162	Kevin Mitchell	.10
163	Andres Galarraga	.10
164	Wally Joyner	.10
165	Kirk Gibson	.10
166	Pedro Munoz	.10
167	Ozzie Guillen	.10
168	Jimmy Key	.10
169	Kevin Seitzer	.10
170	Luis Polonia	.10
171	Luis Gonzalez	.30
172	Paul Molitor	.65
173	Dave Justice	.25
174	B.J. Surhoff	.10
175	Ray Lankford	.10
176	Ryne Sandberg	.75
177	Jody Reed	.10
178	Marquis Grissom	.10
179	Willie McGee	.10
180	Kenny Lofton	.10
181	Junior Felix	.10
182	Jose Offerman	.10
183	John Kruk	.10
184	Orlando Merced	.10
185	Rafael Palmeiro	.25
186	Billy Hatcher	.10
187	Joe Oliver	.10
188	Joe Girardi	.10
189	Jose Lind	.10
190	Harold Baines	.10
191	Mike Pagliarulo	.10
192	Lance Johnson	.10
193	Don Mattingly	1.50
194	Doug Drabek	.10
195	John Olerud	.10
196	Greg Maddux	1.00
197	Greg Vaughn	.10
198	Tom Pagnozzi	.10
199	Willie Wilson	.10
200	Jack McDowell	.10
201	Mike Piazza	1.75
202	Mike Mussina	.50
203	Charles Nagy	.10
204	Tino Martinez	.10
205	Charlie Hough	.10
206	Todd Hundley	.10
207	Gary Sheffield	.25
208	Mickey Morandini	.10
209	Don Slaught	.10
210	Dean Palmer	.10
211	Jose Rijo	.10
212	Vinny Castilla	.10
213	Tony Phillips	.10
214	Kirby Puckett	1.00
215	Tim Raines	.10
216	Otis Nixon	.10
217	Ozzie Smith	1.00
218	Jose Vizcaino	.10
220	Checklist	.10

1993 Studio Heritage

All types of 1993 Leaf Studio packs were candidates for having one of 12 Heritage cards inserted in them. The fronts feature the player posing in an old-time uniform, framed in turquiose with copper highlights. The backs have a mug shot surrounded by an ornate frame and describe the uniform on the front. Team trivia is also included.

		MT
Complete Set (12):		18.00
Common Player:		.75
1	George Brett	2.50
2	Juan Gonzalez	1.50
3	Roger Clemens	2.50
4	Mark McGwire	6.00
5	Mark Grace	1.25
6	Ozzie Smith	2.50
7	Barry Larkin	.75
8	Frank Thomas	3.50
9	Carlos Baerga	.75
10	Eric Karros	.75
11	J.T. Snow	.75
12	John Kruk	.75

1993 Studio Frank Thomas

This five-card set is devoted to Frank Thomas. Cards were randomly included in all types of 1993 Leaf Studio packs. Topics covered on the cards include Thomas' childhood, his baseball memories, his family, his performance and being a role model.

		MT
Complete Set (5):		10.00
Common Player:		2.00
1	Childhood	2.00
2	Baseball Memories	2.00
3	Importance of Family	2.00
4	Performance	2.00
5	On Being a Role Model	2.00

1993 Studio Silhouettes

These insert cards were randomly included in jumbo packs only. The card fronts feature a ghosted image of the player against an action silhouette on a gray background. The player's name is in bronze foil at bottom. Backs have a player action photo and description of career highlights.

		MT
Complete Set (10):		8.00
Common Player:		.30
1	Frank Thomas	1.50
2	Barry Bonds	1.50
3	Jeff Bagwell	1.00
4	Juan Gonzalez	1.00
5	Travis Fryman	.30
6	J.T. Snow	.30
7	John Kruk	.30
8	Jeff Blauser	.30
9	Mike Piazza	2.00
10	Nolan Ryan	2.50

1993 Studio Superstars on Canvas

Ten players are featured on these insert cards, which were available in hobby and retail packs. The cards show player portraits which mix photography and artwork.

		MT
Complete Set (10):		20.00
Common Player:		.70
1	Ken Griffey, Jr.	6.00
2	Jose Canseco	1.50

3	Mark McGwire	7.50
4	Mike Mussina	1.50
5	Joe Carter	.75
6	Frank Thomas	4.50
7	Darren Daulton	.75
8	Mark Grace	1.25
9	Andres Galarraga	.75
10	Barry Bonds	4.50

1994 Studio Samples

To introduce its "locker-room look" issue for 1994 Leaf's Studio brand produced this three-star sample set and distributed it to its hobby dealer network. The cards are basically the same as the regular-issue cards of those players except for the addition of a "Promotional Sample" overprinted diagonally on front and back. The "Up Close" biographies on the cards' backs are different between the promos and the regular cards and there is a slight difference in front photo cropping on the Gonzalez card.

		MT
Complete Set (3):		7.50
Common Player:		2.00
83	Barry Bonds	2.50
154	Juan Gonzalez	2.00
209	Frank Thomas	2.50

1994 Studio

Studio baseball from Donruss returned in mid-August, 1994, with a three-time MVP spokesman, several jazzy and short-printed inserts subsets and a reduced overall production figure that represents a sharp drop from 1993. Barry Bonds is the MVP whose mug adorns Studio counter boxes and advertisements. According to Donruss officials, production was limited to 8,000 cases of 20 boxes each, which represents a 35 percent decrease from 1993 and works out to about 315,000 of each card. Only 2,000 cases were earmarked for retail distribution and no jumbo packs were produced. Studio 1994 features 220 cards issued in one series, once again with close-up personal portraits of the top stars in the game. Each card is foil-stamped with a borderless design and UV coating front and back. The front of the card features the player in the foreground with his locker in the background. As in the previous three Studio offerings, the backs of the cards contain personal information about the players.

		MT
Complete Set (220):		15.00
Common Player:		.10
Pack (12):		1.00
Wax Box (36):		25.00
1	Dennis Eckersley	.10
2	Brent Gates	.10
3	Rickey Henderson	.55
4	Mark McGwire	2.50
5	Troy Neel	.10
6	Ruben Sierra	.10
7	Terry Steinbach	.10
8	Chad Curtis	.10
9	Chili Davis	.10
10	Gary DiSarcina	.10
11	Damion Easley	.10
12	Bo Jackson	.15
13	Mark Langston	.10
14	Eduardo Perez	.10
15	Tim Salmon	.20
16	Jeff Bagwell	.75
17	Craig Biggio	.15
18	Ken Caminiti	.10
19	Andujar Cedeno	.10
20	Doug Drabek	.10
21	Steve Finley	.10
22	Luis Gonzalez	.30
23	Darryl Kile	.10
24	Roberto Alomar	.50
25	Pat Borders	.10
26	Joe Carter	.10
27	Carlos Delgado	.35
28	Pat Hentgen	.10
29	Paul Molitor	.60
30	John Olerud	.10
31	Ed Sprague	.10
32	Devon White	.10
33	Steve Avery	.10
34	Tom Glavine	.15
35	David Justice	.25
36	Roberto Kelly	.10
37	Ryan Klesko	.10
38	Javier Lopez	.10
39	Greg Maddux	1.00
40	Fred McGriff	.10
41	Terry Pendleton	.10
42	Ricky Bones	.10
43	Darryl Hamilton	.10
44	Brian Harper	.10
45	John Jaha	.10
46	Dave Nilsson	.10
47	Kevin Seitzer	.10
48	Greg Vaughn	.10
49	Turner Ward	.10
50	Bernard Gilkey	.10
51	Gregg Jefferies	.10
52	Ray Lankford	.10
53	Tom Pagnozzi	.10
54	Ozzie Smith	1.00
55	Bob Tewksbury	.10
56	Mark Whiten	.10
57	Todd Zeile	.10
58	Steve Buechele	.10
59	Shawon Dunston	.10
60	Mark Grace	.25
61	Derrick May	.10
62	Tuffy Rhodes	.10
63	Ryne Sandberg	.75
64	Sammy Sosa	1.50
65	Rick Wilkins	.10
66	Brett Butler	.10
67	Delino DeShields	.10
68	Orel Hershiser	.10
69	Eric Karros	.10
70	Raul Mondesi	.20
71	Jose Offerman	.10
72	Mike Piazza	2.00
73	Tim Wallach	.10
74	Moises Alou	.15
75	Sean Berry	.10
76	Wil Cordero	.10
77	Cliff Floyd	.10
78	Marquis Grissom	.10
79	Ken Hill	.10
80	Larry Walker	.25
81	John Wetteland	.10
82	Rod Beck	.10
83	Barry Bonds	1.50
84	Royce Clayton	.10
85	Darren Lewis	.10
86	Willie McGee	.10
87	Bill Swift	.10
88	Robby Thompson	.10
89	Matt Williams	.30
90	Sandy Alomar Jr.	.10
91	Carlos Baerga	.10
92	Albert Belle	.35
93	Kenny Lofton	.10
94	Eddie Murray	.50
95	Manny Ramirez	.75
96	Paul Sorrento	.10
97	Jim Thome	.10
98	Rich Amaral	.10
99	Eric Anthony	.10
100	Jay Buhner	.10
101	Ken Griffey, Jr.	2.25
102	Randy Johnson	.65
103	Edgar Martinez	.10
104	Tino Martinez	.10
105	*Kurt Abbott*	.15
106	Bret Barberie	.10
107	Chuck Carr	.10
108	Jeff Conine	.10
109	Chris Hammond	.10
110	Bryan Harvey	.10
111	Benito Santiago	.10
112	Gary Sheffield	.30
113	Bobby Bonilla	.10
114	Dwight Gooden	.10
115	Todd Hundley	.10
116	Bobby Jones	.10
117	Jeff Kent	.10
118	Kevin McReynolds	.10
119	Bret Saberhagen	.10
120	Ryan Thompson	.10
121	Harold Baines	.10
122	Mike Devereaux	.10
123	Jeffrey Hammonds	.10
124	Ben McDonald	.10
125	Mike Mussina	.45
126	Rafael Palmeiro	.30
127	Cal Ripken, Jr.	2.50
128	Lee Smith	.10
129	Brad Ausmus	.10
130	Derek Bell	.10
131	Andy Benes	.10
132	Tony Gwynn	1.00
133	Trevor Hoffman	.10
134	Scott Livingstone	.10
135	Phil Plantier	.10
136	Darren Daulton	.10
137	Mariano Duncan	.10
138	Len Dykstra	.10
139	Dave Hollins	.10
140	Pete Incaviglia	.10
141	Danny Jackson	.10
142	John Kruk	.10
143	Kevin Stocker	.10
144	Jay Bell	.10
145	Carlos Garcia	.10
146	Jeff King	.10
147	Al Martin	.10
148	Orlando Merced	.10
149	Don Slaught	.10
150	Andy Van Slyke	.10
151	Kevin Brown	.15
152	Jose Canseco	.45
153	Will Clark	.30
154	Juan Gonzalez	.75
155	David Hulse	.10
156	Dean Palmer	.10
157	Ivan Rodriguez	.65
158	Kenny Rogers	.10
159	Roger Clemens	1.00
160	Scott Cooper	.10
161	Andre Dawson	.25
162	Mike Greenwell	.10
163	Otis Nixon	.10
164	Aaron Sele	.10
165	John Valentin	.10
166	Mo Vaughn	.40
167	Bret Boone	.15
168	Barry Larkin	.15
169	Kevin Mitchell	.10
170	Hal Morris	.10
171	Jose Rijo	.10
172	Deion Sanders	.15
173	Reggie Sanders	.10
174	John Smiley	.10
175	Dante Bichette	.10
176	Ellis Burks	.10
177	Andres Galarraga	.10
178	Joe Girardi	.10
179	Charlie Hayes	.10
180	Roberto Mejia	.10
181	Walt Weiss	.10
182	David Cone	.10
183	Gary Gaetti	.10
184	Greg Gagne	.10
185	Felix Jose	.10
186	Wally Joyner	.10
187	Mike Macfarlane	.10
188	Brian McRae	.10
189	Eric Davis	.10
190	Cecil Fielder	.10
191	Travis Fryman	.10
192	Tony Phillips	.10
193	Mickey Tettleton	.10
194	Alan Trammell	.10
195	Lou Whitaker	.10
196	Kent Hrbek	.10
197	Chuck Knoblauch	.10
198	Shane Mack	.10
199	Pat Meares	.10
200	Kirby Puckett	1.00
201	Matt Walbeck	.10
202	Dave Winfield	.65
203	Wilson Alvarez	.10
204	Alex Fernandez	.10
205	Julio Franco	.10
206	Ozzie Guillen	.10
207	Jack McDowell	.10
208	Tim Raines	.10
209	Frank Thomas	1.50
210	Robin Ventura	.10
211	Jim Abbott	.10
212	Wade Boggs	.60
213	Pat Kelly	.10
214	Jimmy Key	.10
215	Don Mattingly	1.50
216	Paul O'Neill	.10
217	Mike Stanley	.10
218	Danny Tartabull	.10
219	Checklist	.10
220	Checklist	.10

1994 Studio Editor's Choice

Printed in similitude to a strip of color slide film, each of the cards in this insert set feature a complete player photo at center,

with partial "frames" at top and bottom. Printed on acetate, the back of the card shows a reversed image of the front. Stated odds of finding an Editor's Choice insert card are about one per box of 36 packs.

		MT
Complete Set (8):		17.50
Common Player:		.50
1	Barry Bonds	3.00
2	Frank Thomas	3.00
3	Ken Griffey, Jr.	6.00
4	Andres Galarraga	.50
5	Juan Gonzalez	2.00
6	Tim Salmon	1.00
7	Paul O'Neill	.50
8	Mike Piazza	4.00

1994 Studio Gold Stars

The scarcest of the 1994 Studio chase cards, only 5,000 cards of each of the 10 players were produced. Printed on acetate, fronts feature an action photo set against a clear plastic background. At bottom is a large gold-foil seal. Backs have another player photo, within the silhouette of the front photo, and a black-and-white version of the seal, including the card's unique serial number. According to the series wrapper, odds of finding a Gold Series Star card are one in 120 packs.

		MT
Complete Set (10):		110.00
Common Player:		6.00
1	Tony Gwynn	12.00
2	Barry Bonds	13.50
3	Frank Thomas	13.50
4	Ken Griffey, Jr.	20.00
5	Joe Carter	6.00
6	Mike Piazza	15.00
7	Cal Ripken, Jr.	25.00
8	Greg Maddux	12.00
9	Juan Gonzalez	10.00
10	Don Mattingly	13.50

1994 Studio Silver Stars

Each of the 10 players in this insert set was produced in an edition of 10,000 cards. Printed on acetate, fronts feature action photos set against a clear plastic background with a silver-foil seal at bottom. Within the player silhouette on back, a second photo is printed. The back also features a black-and-white version of the seal, including the card's unique serial number. Stated odds of picking a Silver Series Star are one per 60 packs, on average.

		MT
Complete Set (10):		35.00
Common Player:		1.50
1	Tony Gwynn	3.00
2	Barry Bonds	4.00
3	Frank Thomas	4.00
4	Ken Griffey, Jr.	7.00
5	Joe Carter	1.50
6	Mike Piazza	6.00
7	Cal Ripken, Jr.	8.00
8	Greg Maddux	3.00
9	Juan Gonzalez	2.50
10	Don Mattingly	4.00

1994 Studio Heritage

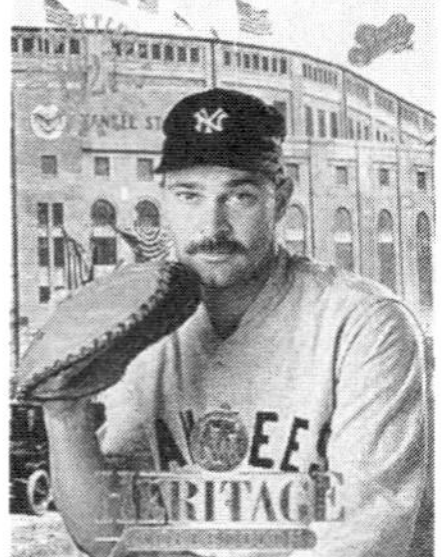

Besides picturing today's players in vintage uniforms, the 1994 Studio Heritage inserts have the player portraits set against sepia-toned photos of old ballparks. Fronts are enhanced by copper-foil logos and by a round device at upper-left containing the player's name, team and year represented. Backs have a second color player photo and a short write-up about the team represented. Unlike the other cards in the set, the Heritage cards are printed on a porous cardboard stock to enhance the image of antiquity. Stated odds of finding a Heritage Collection insert card are one in nine packs.

		MT
Complete Set (8):		15.00
Common Player:		1.00
1	Barry Bonds	3.00
2	Frank Thomas	4.00
3	Joe Carter	1.00
4	Don Mattingly	3.00
5	Ryne Sandberg	2.50
6	Javier Lopez	1.50
7	Gregg Jefferies	1.00
8	Mike Mussina	1.50

1995 Studio

Known since its inception as a brand name for its innovative design, Studio did not disappoint in 1995, unveiling a baseball card with a credit card look. In horizontal format the cards feature embossed stats and data on front, plus a team logo hologram. Backs have a color player photo, facsimile autograph and simulated magnetic data strip to carry through the credit card impression.

		MT
Complete Set (200):		25.00
Common Player:		.10
Pack (5):		1.50
Wax Box (36):		40.00
1	Frank Thomas	1.25
2	Jeff Bagwell	.75
3	Don Mattingly	1.25
4	Mike Piazza	1.50
5	Ken Griffey Jr.	2.00
6	Greg Maddux	1.00
7	Barry Bonds	1.25
8	Cal Ripken Jr.	2.50
9	Jose Canseco	.45
10	Paul Molitor	.60
11	Kenny Lofton	.10
12	Will Clark	.30
13	Tim Salmon	.25
14	Joe Carter	.10
15	Albert Belle	.35
'6	Roger Clemens	1.00
17	Roberto Alomar	.60
18	Alex Rodriguez	2.00
19	Raul Mondesi	.25
20	Deion Sanders	.15
21	Juan Gonzalez	.75
22	Kirby Puckett	1.00
23	Fred McGriff	.10
24	Matt Williams	.30
25	Tony Gwynn	1.00
26	Cliff Floyd	.10
27	Travis Fryman	.10
28	Shawn Green	.15
29	Mike Mussina	.45
30	Bob Hamelin	.10
31	Dave Justice	.25
32	Manny Ramirez	.75
33	David Cone	.10
34	Marquis Grissom	.10
35	Moises Alou	.15
36	Carlos Baerga	.10
37	Barry Larkin	.15
38	Robin Ventura	.10
39	Mo Vaughn	.45
40	Jeffrey Hammonds	.10
41	Ozzie Smith	1.00
42	Andres Galarraga	.10
43	Carlos Delgado	.35
44	Lenny Dykstra	.10
45	Cecil Fielder	.10
46	Wade Boggs	.50
47	Gregg Jefferies	.10
48	Randy Johnson	.45
49	Rafael Palmeiro	.20
50	Craig Biggio	.15
51	Steve Avery	.10
52	Ricky Bottalico	.10
53	Chris Gomez	.10
54	Carlos Garcia	.10
55	Brian Anderson	.10
56	Wilson Alvarez	.10
57	Roberto Kelly	.10
58	Larry Walker	.25
59	Dean Palmer	.10
60	Rick Aguilera	.10
61	Javy Lopez	.10
62	Shawon Dunston	.10
63	William Van Landingham	.10
64	Jeff Kent	.10
65	David McCarty	.10
66	Armando Benitez	.10
67	Brett Butler	.10
68	Bernard Gilkey	.10
69	Joey Hamilton	.10
70	Chad Curtis	.10
71	Dante Bichette	.10
72	Chuck Carr	.10
73	Pedro Martinez	.30
74	Ramon Martinez	.10
75	Rondell White	.15
76	Alex Fernandez	.10
77	Dennis Martinez	.10
78	Sammy Sosa	1.25
79	Bernie Williams	.35
80	Lou Whitaker	.10
81	Kurt Abbott	.10
82	Tino Martinez	.10
83	Willie Greene	.10
84	Garret Anderson	.10
85	Jose Rijo	.10
86	Jeff Montgomery	.10
87	Mark Langston	.10
88	Reggie Sanders	.10
89	Rusty Greer	.10
90	Delino DeShields	.10
91	Jason Bere	.10
92	Lee Smith	.10
93	Devon White	.10
94	John Wetteland	.10
95	Luis Gonzalez	.35
96	Greg Vaughn	.10
97	Lance Johnson	.10
98	Alan Trammell	.10
99	Bret Saberhagen	.10
100	Jack McDowell	.10
101	Trevor Hoffman	.10
102	Dave Nilsson	.10
103	Bryan Harvey	.10
104	Chuck Knoblauch	.10
105	Bobby Bonilla	.10
106	Hal Morris	.10
107	Mark Whiten	.10
108	Phil Plantier	.10
109	Ryan Klesko	.10
110	Greg Gagne	.10
111	Ruben Sierra	.10
112	J.R. Phillips	.10
113	Terry Steinbach	.10
114	Jay Buhner	.10
115	Ken Caminiti	.10
116	Gary DiSarcina	.10
117	Ivan Rodriguez	.50
118	Bip Roberts	.10
119	Jay Bell	.10
120	Ken Hill	.10
121	Mike Greenwell	.10
122	Rick Wilkins	.10
123	Rickey Henderson	.50
124	Dave Hollins	.10
125	Terry Pendleton	.10
126	Rich Becker	.10
127	Billy Ashley	.10
128	Derek Bell	.10
129	Dennis Eckersley	.10
130	Andujar Cedeno	.10
131	John Jaha	.10
132	Chuck Finley	.10
133	Steve Finley	.10

134	Danny Tartabull	.10
135	Jeff Conine	.10
136	Jon Lieber	.10
137	Jim Abbott	.10
138	Steve Traschel	.10
139	Bret Boone	.15
140	Charles Johnson	.10
141	Mark McGwire	2.50
142	Eddie Murray	.50
143	Doug Drabek	.10
144	Steve Cooke	.10
145	Kevin Seitzer	.10
146	Rod Beck	.10
147	Eric Karros	.10
148	Tim Raines	.10
149	Joe Girardi	.10
150	Aaron Sele	.10
151	Robby Thompson	.10
152	Chan Ho Park	.20
153	Ellis Burks	.10
154	Brian McRae	.10
155	Jimmy Key	.10
156	Rico Brogna	.10
157	Ozzie Guillen	.10
158	Chili Davis	.10
159	Darren Daulton	.10
160	Chipper Jones	1.50
161	Walt Weiss	.10
162	Paul O'Neill	.10
163	Al Martin	.10
164	John Valentin	.10
165	Tim Wallach	.10
166	Scott Erickson	.10
167	Ryan Thompson	.10
168	Todd Zeile	.10
169	Scott Cooper	.10
170	Matt Mieske	.10
171	Allen Watson	.10
172	Brian Hunter	.10
173	Kevin Stocker	.10
174	Cal Eldred	.10
175	Tony Phillips	.10
176	Ben McDonald	.10
177	Mark Grace	.25
178	Midre Cummings	.10
179	Orlando Merced	.10
180	Jeff King	.10
181	Gary Sheffield	.30
182	Tom Glavine	.15
183	Edgar Martinez	.10
184	Steve Karsay	.10
185	Pat Listach	.10
186	Wil Cordero	.10
187	Brady Anderson	.10
188	Bobby Jones	.10
189	Andy Benes	.10
190	Ray Lankford	.10
191	John Doherty	.10
192	Wally Joyner	.10
193	Jim Thome	.10
194	Royce Clayton	.10
195	John Olerud	.10
196	Steve Buechele	.10
197	Harold Baines	.10
198	Geronimo Berroa	.10
199	Checklist	.10
200	Checklist	.10

1995 Studio Gold

The chase cards in 1995 Studio are plastic versions of some of the regular cards. The round-cornered plastic format of the inserts gives them an even greater similitude to credit cards. The first 50 numbers in the regular set are reproduced in a parallel Studio Gold plastic version, found one per pack, except for those packs which have a platinum card.

		MT
Complete Set (50):		25.00
Common Player:		.25
1	Frank Thomas	1.50
2	Jeff Bagwell	.75
3	Don Mattingly	1.50
4	Mike Piazza	2.00
5	Ken Griffey Jr.	2.50
6	Greg Maddux	1.00
7	Barry Bonds	1.50
8	Cal Ripken Jr.	3.00
9	Jose Canseco	.65
10	Paul Molitor	.65
11	Kenny Lofton	.25
12	Will Clark	.50
13	Tim Salmon	.35
14	Joe Carter	.25
15	Albert Belle	.50
16	Roger Clemens	1.00
17	Roberto Alomar	.65
18	Alex Rodriguez	2.50
19	Raul Mondesi	.35
20	Deion Sanders	.35
21	Juan Gonzalez	.75
22	Kirby Puckett	1.00
23	Fred McGriff	.25
24	Matt Williams	.35
25	Tony Gwynn	1.00
26	Cliff Floyd	.25
27	Travis Fryman	.25
28	Shawn Green	.35
29	Mike Mussina	.65
30	Bob Hamelin	.25
31	Dave Justice	.50
32	Manny Ramirez	.75
33	David Cone	.25
34	Marquis Grissom	.25
35	Moises Alou	.35
36	Carlos Baerga	.25
37	Barry Larkin	.25
38	Robin Ventura	.25
39	Mo Vaughn	.60
40	Jeffrey Hammonds	.25
41	Ozzie Smith	1.00
42	Andres Galarraga	.25
43	Carlos Delgado	.50
44	Lenny Dykstra	.25
45	Cecil Fielder	.25
46	Wade Boggs	.65
47	Gregg Jefferies	.25
48	Randy Johnson	.65
49	Rafael Palmeiro	.40
50	Craig Biggio	.25

1995 Studio Platinum

Found at the rate of one per 10 packs, Studio Platinum cards are silver-toned plastic versions of the first 25 cards from the regular set.

		MT
Complete Set (25):		70.00
Common Player:		1.25
1	Frank Thomas	5.00
2	Jeff Bagwell	3.00
3	Don Mattingly	5.00
4	Mike Piazza	6.50
5	Ken Griffey Jr.	8.00
6	Greg Maddux	4.00
7	Barry Bonds	5.00
8	Cal Ripken Jr.	10.00
9	Jose Canseco	2.00
10	Paul Molitor	3.00
11	Kenny Lofton	1.25
12	Will Clark	1.25
13	Tim Salmon	1.50
14	Joe Carter	1.25
15	Albert Belle	1.50
16	Roger Clemens	4.00
17	Roberto Alomar	2.00
18	Alex Rodriguez	8.00
19	Raul Mondesi	1.25
20	Deion Sanders	1.25
21	Juan Gonzalez	3.00
22	Kirby Puckett	4.00
23	Fred McGriff	1.25
24	Matt Williams	1.25
25	Tony Gwynn	4.00

1996 Studio

The 1996 Studio set is the first Donruss product to be released under the Pinnacle Brands flagship. The 150-card set has three parallel sets - Bronze Press Proofs (2,000 sets), Silver Press Proofs (found only in magazine packs, 100 sets), and Gold Press Proofs (500 sets). Three insert sets were also made - Hit Parade, Masterstrokes and Stained Glass Stars.

		MT
Complete Set (150):		15.00
Common Player:		.10
Pack (7):		2.00
Wax Box (24):		30.00
1	Cal Ripken Jr.	2.50
2	Alex Gonzalez	.15
3	Roger Cedeno	.10
4	Todd Hollandsworth	.10
5	Gregg Jefferies	.10
6	Ryne Sandberg	.75
7	Eric Karros	.10
8	Jeff Conine	.10
9	Rafael Palmeiro	.25
10	Bip Roberts	.10
11	Roger Clemens	1.00
12	Tom Glavine	.15
13	Jason Giambi	.30
14	Rey Ordonez	.10
15	Chan Ho Park	.25
16	Vinny Castilla	.10
17	Butch Huskey	.10
18	Greg Maddux	1.00
19	Bernard Gilkey	.10
20	Marquis Grissom	.10
21	Chuck Knoblauch	.10
22	Ozzie Smith	1.00
23	Garret Anderson	.10
24	J.T. Snow	.10
25	John Valentin	.10
26	Barry Larkin	.15
27	Bobby Bonilla	.10
28	Todd Zeile	.10
29	Roberto Alomar	.65
30	Ramon Martinez	.10
31	Jeff King	.10
32	Dennis Eckersley	.10
33	Derek Jeter	2.00
34	Edgar Martinez	.10
35	Geronimo Berroa	.10
36	Hal Morris	.10
37	Troy Percival	.10
38	Jason Isringhausen	.10
39	Greg Vaughn	.10
40	Robin Ventura	.10
41	Craig Biggio	.15
42	Will Clark	.30
43	Sammy Sosa	1.50
44	Bernie Williams	.30
45	Kenny Lofton	.10
46	Wade Boggs	.50
47	Javy Lopez	.10
48	Reggie Sanders	.10
49	Jeff Bagwell	.75
50	Fred McGriff	.10
51	Charles Johnson	.10
52	Darren Daulton	.10
53	Jose Canseco	.50
54	Cecil Fielder	.10
55	Hideo Nomo	.65
56	Tim Salmon	.25
57	Carlos Delgado	.35
58	David Cone	.10
59	Tim Raines	.10
60	Lyle Mouton	.10
61	Wally Joyner	.10
62	Bret Boone	.15
63	Raul Mondesi	.30
64	Gary Sheffield	.30
65	Alex Rodriguez	2.25
66	Russ Davis	.10
67	Checklist	.10
68	Marty Cordova	.10
69	Ruben Sierra	.10
70	Jose Mesa	.10
71	Matt Williams	.30
72	Chipper Jones	2.00
73	Randy Johnson	.65
74	Kirby Puckett	1.00
75	Jim Edmonds	.10
76	Barry Bonds	1.50
77	David Segui	.10
78	Larry Walker	.30
79	Jason Kendall	.10
80	Mike Piazza	2.00
81	Brian Hunter	.10
82	Julio Franco	.10
83	Jay Bell	.10
84	Kevin Seitzer	.10
85	John Smoltz	.15
86	Joe Carter	.10
87	Ray Durham	.10
88	Carlos Baerga	.10
89	Ron Gant	.10
90	Orlando Merced	.10
91	Lee Smith	.10
92	Pedro Martinez	.30
93	Frank Thomas	1.50
94	Al Martin	.10
95	Chad Curtis	.10
96	Eddie Murray	.60
97	Rusty Greer	.10
98	Jay Buhner	.10
99	Rico Brogna	.10
100	Todd Hundley	.10
101	Moises Alou	.15
102	Chili Davis	.10
103	Ismael Valdes	.10
104	Mo Vaughn	.45
105	Juan Gonzalez	.75
106	Mark Grudzielanek	.10
107	Derek Bell	.10
108	Shawn Green	.15
109	David Justice	.25
110	Paul O'Neill	.10
111	Kevin Appier	.10
112	Ray Lankford	.10
113	Travis Fryman	.10
114	Manny Ramirez	.75
115	Brooks Kieschnick	.10
116	Ken Griffey Jr.	2.25
117	Jeffrey Hammonds	.10
118	Mark McGwire	2.50
119	Denny Neagle	.10

120	Quilvio Veras	.10
121	Alan Benes	.10
122	Rondell White	.20
123	*Osvaldo Fernandez*	.20
124	Andres Galarraga	.10
125	Johnny Damon	.15
126	Lenny Dykstra	.10
127	Jason Schmidt	.10
128	Mike Mussina	.65
129	Ken Caminiti	.10
130	Michael Tucker	.10
131	LaTroy Hawkins	.10
132	Checklist	.10
133	Delino DeShields	.10
134	Dave Nilsson	.10
135	Jack McDowell	.10
136	Joey Hamilton	.10
137	Dante Bichette	.10
138	Paul Molitor	.60
139	Ivan Rodriguez	.65
140	Mark Grace	.25
141	Paul Wilson	.10
142	Orel Hershiser	.10
143	Albert Belle	.40
144	Tino Martinez	.10
145	Tony Gwynn	1.00
146	George Arias	.10
147	Brian Jordan	.10
148	Brian McRae	.10
149	Rickey Henderson	.60
150	Ryan Klesko	.10

1996 Studio Press Proofs

The basic 150-card 1996 Studio set was also produced in three parallel press proof versions. Each is basically identical to the regular-issue cards except for appropriately colored foil highlights on front and a notation of edition size in the circle around the portrait photo on back. Bronze press proofs were issued in an edition of 2,000 each and were inserted at an average rate of one per six packs. Gold press proofs were an edition of 500 with an average insertion rate of one per 24 packs. The silver press proofs were inserted only into magazine packs and limited to just 100 cards of each.

	MT
Common Player, Bronze:	.75
Bronze Stars:	6X
Common Player, Gold:	2.00
Gold Stars:	15X
Common Player, Silver:	7.50
Silver Stars:	60X

(See 1996 Studio for checklist, base card values)

1996 Studio Hit Parade

These die-cut inserts resemble an album with half of the record pulled out of the sleeve. Hit Parade cards, which feature top long ball hitters, were seeded one per every 36 packs. The cards were individually numbered up to 7,500. Each card can also be found in a sample version which has a "XXXX/5000" serial number on back.

		MT
Complete Set (10):		16.00
Common Player:		1.00
1	Tony Gwynn	2.00
2	Ken Griffey Jr.	4.00
3	Frank Thomas	2.50
4	Jeff Bagwell	1.50
5	Kirby Puckett	2.00
6	Mike Piazza	3.00
7	Barry Bonds	2.50
8	Albert Belle	1.00
9	Tim Salmon	1.00
10	Mo Vaughn	1.00

1996 Studio Masterstrokes

Only 5,000 each of these 1996 Studio insert cards were made. The cards simulate oil painting detail on an embossed canvas-feel front. Backs are glossy and individually serial numbered. They are found on average of once per 70 packs. Sample versions of each card overprinted as such on the back and numbered "PROMO/5000" were also issued.

		MT
Complete Set (8):		25.00
Common Player:		2.50
Samples:		1X
1	Tony Gwynn	3.00
2	Mike Piazza	4.50
3	Jeff Bagwell	2.50
4	Manny Ramirez	2.50
5	Cal Ripken Jr.	6.00
6	Frank Thomas	3.50
7	Ken Griffey Jr.	5.00
8	Greg Maddux	3.00

1996 Studio Stained Glass Stars

Twelve superstars are featured on these clear, die-cut plastic cards which resemble stained glass windows. These 1996 Studio inserts were seeded one per every 30 packs.

		MT
Complete Set (12):		40.00
Common Player:		1.50
1	Cal Ripken Jr.	9.00
2	Ken Griffey Jr.	7.00
3	Frank Thomas	5.00
4	Greg Maddux	4.00
5	Chipper Jones	6.00
6	Mike Piazza	6.00
7	Albert Belle	1.50
8	Jeff Bagwell	3.00
9	Hideo Nomo	2.00
10	Barry Bonds	5.00
11	Manny Ramirez	3.00
12	Kenny Lofton	1.50

1997 Studio

Innovations in both product and packaging marked the seventh annual issue of Donruss' Studio brand. As in the past, the 165 cards in the base set rely on high-quality front photos to bring out the players' personalities. For '97, the photos are set against a background of variously shaded gray horizontal stripes. Backs have a second player photo, often an action shot, along with a short career summary. The "pack" for '97 Studio is something totally new to the hobby. An 8-1/2" x 12" cardboard envelope, complete with a zip strip opener in the style of an express-mail envelope, contains a cello pack of five standard-size cards plus either an 8" x 10" Studio Portrait card or an 8" x 10" version of the Master Strokes insert. Suggested retail price at issue was $2.49 per pack. Regular-size Master Strokes cards are one of several insert series which includes silver and gold press proofs and die-cut plastic Hard Hats.

		MT
Complete Set (165):		30.00
Common Player:		.10
Pack (5):		3.00
Wax Box (18):		40.00
1	Frank Thomas	1.75
2	Gary Sheffield	.25
3	Jason Isringhausen	.10
4	Ron Gant	.10
5	Andy Pettitte	.50
6	Todd Hollandsworth	.10
7	Troy Percival	.10
8	Mark McGwire	3.00
9	Barry Larkin	.15
10	Ken Caminiti	.10
11	Paul Molitor	.50
12	Travis Fryman	.10
13	Kevin Brown	.15
14	Robin Ventura	.10
15	Andres Galarraga	.10
16	Ken Griffey Jr.	2.50
17	Roger Clemens	1.50
18	Alan Benes	.10
19	David Justice	.25
20	Damon Buford	.10
21	Mike Piazza	2.00
22	Ray Durham	.10
23	Billy Wagner	.10
24	Dean Palmer	.10
25	David Cone	.10
26	Ruben Sierra	.10
27	Henry Rodriguez	.10
28	Ray Lankford	.10
29	Jamey Wright	.10
30	Brady Anderson	.10
31	Tino Martinez	.10
32	Manny Ramirez	1.00
33	Jeff Conine	.10
34	Dante Bichette	.10
35	Jose Canseco	.50
36	Mo Vaughn	.45
37	Sammy Sosa	1.75
38	Mark Grudzielanek	.10
39	Mike Mussina	.65
40	Bill Pulsipher	.10
41	Ryne Sandberg	.75
42	Rickey Henderson	.60
43	Alex Rodriguez	2.50
44	Eddie Murray	.40
45	Ernie Young	.10
46	Joey Hamilton	.10
47	Wade Boggs	.50
48	Rusty Greer	.10
49	Carlos Delgado	.30
50	Ellis Burks	.10
51	Cal Ripken Jr.	3.00
52	Alex Fernandez	.10
53	Wally Joyner	.10
54	James Baldwin	.10
55	Juan Gonzalez	1.00
56	John Smoltz	.15
57	Omar Vizquel	.10
58	Shane Reynolds	.10
59	Barry Bonds	1.75
60	Jason Kendall	.10
61	Marty Cordova	.10
62	Charles Johnson	.10
63	John Jaha	.10

64 Chan Ho Park .20
65 Jermaine Allensworth .10
66 Mark Grace .25
67 Tim Salmon .15
68 Edgar Martinez .10
69 Marquis Grissom .10
70 Craig Biggio .15
71 Bobby Higginson .15
72 Kevin Seitzer .10
73 Hideo Nomo .60
74 Dennis Eckersley .10
75 Bobby Bonilla .10
76 Dwight Gooden .10
77 Jeff Cirillo .10
78 Brian McRae .10
79 Chipper Jones 2.00
80 Jeff Fassero .10
81 Fred McGriff .10
82 Garret Anderson .10
83 Eric Karros .10
84 Derek Bell .10
85 Kenny Lofton .10
86 John Mabry .10
87 Pat Hentgen .10
88 Greg Maddux 1.50
89 Jason Giambi .35
90 Al Martin .10
91 Derek Jeter 2.00
92 Rey Ordonez .10
93 Will Clark .25
94 Kevin Appier .10
95 Roberto Alomar .50
96 Joe Carter .10
97 Bernie Williams .35
98 Albert Belle .40
99 Greg Vaughn .10
100 Tony Clark .10
101 Matt Williams .25
102 Jeff Bagwell 1.00
103 Reggie Sanders .10
104 Mariano Rivera .25
105 Larry Walker .35
106 Shawn Green .15
107 Alex Ochoa .10
108 Ivan Rodriguez .60
109 Eric Young .10
110 Javier Lopez .10
111 Brian Hunter .10
112 Raul Mondesi .25
113 Randy Johnson .60
114 Tony Phillips .10
115 Carlos Garcia .10
116 Moises Alou .15
117 Paul O'Neill .10
118 Jim Thome .10
119 Jermaine Dye .10
120 Wilson Alvarez .10
121 Rondell White .25
122 Michael Tucker .10
123 Mike Lansing .10
124 Tony Gwynn 1.50
125 Ryan Klesko .10
126 Jim Edmonds .10
127 Chuck Knoblauch .10
128 Rafael Palmeiro .20
129 Jay Buhner .10
130 Tom Glavine .15
131 Julio Franco .10
132 Cecil Fielder .10
133 Paul Wilson .10
134 Deion Sanders .15
135 Alex Gonzalez .15
136 Charles Nagy .10
137 Andy Ashby .10
138 Edgar Renteria .10
139 Pedro Martinez .35
140 Brian Jordan .10
141 Todd Hundley .10
142 Marc Newfield .10
143 Darryl Strawberry .10
144 Dan Wilson .10
145 *Brian Giles* 2.00
146 Bartolo Colon .10
147 Shannon Stewart .15
148 Scott Spiezio .10
149 Andruw Jones 1.00
150 Karim Garcia .15
151 Vladimir Guerrero 1.00
152 George Arias .10
153 Brooks Kieschnick .10
154 Todd Walker .10
155 Scott Rolen 1.00
156 Todd Greene .10
157 Dmitri Young .10
158 Ruben Rivera .10
159 Trey Beamon .10
160 Nomar Garciaparra 1.75
161 Bob Abreu .15
162 Darin Erstad 1.00
163 Ken Griffey Jr. (checklist) .75
164 Frank Thomas (checklist) .50
165 Alex Rodriguez (checklist) .75

1997 Studio Press Proofs

Each of the 165 cards in the base set of '97 Studio was also produced in a pair of Press Proof versions as random pack inserts. Fronts of the Press Proofs have either silver or gold holographic foil replacing the silver foil graphics found on regular cards, as well as foil strips down each side. Backs are identical to the regular issue. The silver Press Proofs were issued in an edition of 1,500 of each player; the golds are limited to 500 of each.

	MT
Common Player, Silver:	.75
Silver Stars:	7X
Common Player, Gold:	2.00
Gold Stars:	15X

(See 1997 Studio for checklist and base card values.)

1997 Studio Hard Hats

Die-cut plastic is used to represent a player's batting helmet in this set of '97 Studio inserts. A player action photo appears in the foreground with his name and other graphic elements in silver foil. Backs feature a small portrait photo, short career summary and a serial number from within the edition of 5,000 of each card.

		MT
Complete Set (24):		50.00
Common Player:		1.00
1	Ivan Rodriguez	2.50
2	Albert Belle	1.00
3	Ken Griffey Jr.	6.00
4	Chuck Knoblauch	1.00
5	Frank Thomas	4.00
6	Cal Ripken Jr.	8.00
7	Todd Walker	1.00
8	Alex Rodriguez	6.00
9	Jim Thome	1.00
10	Mike Piazza	4.50
11	Barry Larkin	1.00
12	Chipper Jones	4.50
13	Derek Jeter	4.50
14	Jermaine Dye	1.00
15	Jason Giambi	2.00
16	Tim Salmon	1.00
17	Brady Anderson	1.00
18	Rondell White	1.00
19	Bernie Williams	1.50
20	Juan Gonzalez	3.00
21	Karim Garcia	1.00
22	Scott Rolen	2.25
23	Darin Erstad	2.50
24	Brian Jordan	1.00

1997 Studio Master Strokes

The look and feel of a painting on canvas is the effect presented by '97 Studio's Master Strokes inserts. Card fronts feature unique player action art and are highlighted by gold-foil graphics. Each card has a facsimile autograph on front. UV-coated backs are team-color coordinated and have a few sentences about the player. Gold-foil serial numbering identifies the card from an edition of 2,000 of each player.

		MT
Complete Set (24):		135.00
Common Player:		2.00
1	Derek Jeter	9.00
2	Jeff Bagwell	6.00
3	Ken Griffey Jr.	10.00
4	Barry Bonds	8.00
5	Frank Thomas	8.00
6	Andy Pettitte	2.00
7	Mo Vaughn	2.50
8	Alex Rodriguez	10.00
9	Andruw Jones	6.00
10	Kenny Lofton	2.00
11	Cal Ripken Jr.	12.50
12	Greg Maddux	7.00
13	Manny Ramirez	6.00
14	Mike Piazza	9.00
14p	Mike Piazza (promo)	2.00
15	Vladimir Guerrero	6.00
16	Albert Belle	2.00
17	Chipper Jones	9.00
18	Hideo Nomo	4.00
19	Sammy Sosa	8.00
20	Tony Gwynn	7.00
21	Gary Sheffield	2.00
22	Mark McGwire	12.50
23	Juan Gonzalez	6.00
24	Paul Molitor	5.00

1997 Studio Master Strokes 8x10

The look and feel of a painting on canvas is the effect presented by the 8" x 10" version of '97 Studio's Master Strokes inserts. Card fronts feature unique player action art and are highlighted by gold-foil graphics. Each card has a facsimile autograph on front. UV-coated backs are team-color coordinated and have a few sentences about the player. Gold-foil serial numbering identifies the card from an edition of 5,000 of each player - making the super-size version more than twice as common as the 2-1/2" x 3-1/2" version.

		MT
Complete Set (24):		65.00
Common Player:		1.00
1	Derek Jeter	4.00
2	Jeff Bagwell	2.50
3	Ken Griffey Jr.	6.00
4	Barry Bonds	3.50
5	Frank Thomas	3.50
6	Andy Pettitte	1.50
7	Mo Vaughn	1.50
8	Alex Rodriguez	6.00
9	Andruw Jones	2.50
10	Kenny Lofton	1.00
11	Cal Ripken Jr.	8.00
12	Greg Maddux	3.00
13	Manny Ramirez	2.50
14	Mike Piazza	4.00
15	Vladimir Guerrero	2.50
16	Albert Belle	1.00
17	Chipper Jones	4.00
18	Hideo Nomo	2.00
19	Sammy Sosa	3.50
20	Tony Gwynn	3.00
21	Gary Sheffield	1.50
22	Mark McGwire	8.00
23	Juan Gonzalez	2.50
24	Paul Molitor	2.00

1997 Studio Portraits

Perhaps the most innovative feature of '97 Studio is the 8" x 10" Portrait cards which come one per pack (except when a pack contains a Master Strokes 8x10). Virtually identical to the player's regular-size Studio card, the jumbo version has the word "PORTRAIT" in black beneath the team name on front. Backs have different card numbers than the same player's card in the regular set. The Portrait cards are produced with a special UV coating on front to facilitate autographing. Preautographed cards of three youngsters in the series were included as random pack inserts.

		MT
Complete Set (24):		12.50
Common Player:		.25
1	Ken Griffey Jr.	1.25
1s	Frank Thomas (overprinted "SAMPLE")	.50
2	Frank Thomas	.75
3	Alex Rodriguez	1.25
4	Andruw Jones	.50
5	Cal Ripken Jr.	1.50
6	Greg Maddux	.65
7	Mike Piazza	1.00
8	Chipper Jones	1.00
9	Albert Belle	.35
10	Derek Jeter	1.00
11	Juan Gonzalez	.50
12	Todd Walker	.25
12a	Todd Walker (autographed edition of 1,250)	10.00
13	Mark McGwire	1.50
14	Barry Bonds	.75
15	Jeff Bagwell	.50
16	Manny Ramirez	.50
17	Kenny Lofton	.25
18	Mo Vaughn	.35
19	Hideo Nomo	.50
20	Tony Gwynn	.65
21	Vladimir Guerrero	.50
21a	Vladimir Guerrero (autographed edition of 500)	30.00
22	Gary Sheffield	.25
23	Ryne Sandberg	.50
24	Scott Rolen	.45
24a	Scott Rolen (autographed edition of 1,000)	20.00

1997 Studio Portrait Collection

In a departure from traditional sportscard marketing, the 1997 Studio program offered a pair of specially framed editions directly to consumers. The offer was made in a color brochure found in about half the packs advertising the "Portrait Collection." The offer includes one standard-size card and an 8" x 10" Portrait or Master card similar to those in the regular issue. These cards differ from the regular issue in that they are trimmed in platinum holographic foil, individually hand-numbered and signed by the photographer. The cards were sold framed with a metal plaque, also numbered, attesting to the limited-edition status. The framed Studio Portrait piece was produced in an edition of 500 of each player; the Master Strokes piece was limited to 100 for each player on the checklist. The former was issued at $159; the latter at $299.

		MT
Complete Set, Studio Portrait (24):		2850.
Complete Set, Master Strokes (24):		5250.
Common Plaque, Studio Portrait:		125.00
Common Plaque, Master Strokes:		225.00
P1	Ken Griffey Jr.	125.00
P2	Frank Thomas	125.00
P3	Alex Rodriquez	125.00
P4	Andruw Jones	125.00
P5	Cal Ripken Jr.	125.00
P6	Greg Maddux	125.00
P7	Mike Piazza	125.00
P8	Chipper Jones	125.00
P9	Albert Belle	125.00
P10	Derek Jeter	125.00
P11	Juan Gonzalez	125.00
P12	Todd Walker	125.00
P13	Mark McGwire	125.00
P14	Barry Bonds	125.00
P15	Jeff Bagwell	125.00
P16	Manny	125.00
P17	Kenny Lofton	125.00
P18	Mo Vaughn	125.00
P19	Hideo Nomo	125.00
P20	Tony Gwynn	125.00
P21	Vladimir Guerrero	125.00
P22	Gary Sheffield	125.00
P23	Ryne Sandberg	125.00
P24	Scott Rolen	125.00
M1	Derek Jeter	225.00
M2	Jeff Bagwell	225.00
M3	Ken Griffey Jr.	225.00
M4	Barry Bonds	225.00
M5	Frank Thomas	225.00
M6	Andy Pettitte	225.00
M7	Mo Vaughn	225.00
M8	Alex Rodriguez	225.00
M9	Andruw Jones	225.00
M10	Kenny Lofton	225.00
M11	Cal Ripken Jr.	225.00
M12	Greg Maddux	225.00
M13	Manny Ramirez	225.00
M14	Mike Piazza	225.00
M15	Vladimir Guerrero	225.00
M16	Albert Belle	225.00
M17	Chipper Jones	225.00
M18	Hideo Nomo	225.00
M19	Sammy Sosa	225.00
M20	Tony Gwynn	225.00
M21	Gary Sheffield	225.00
M22	Mark McGwire	225.00
M23	Juan Gonzalez	225.00
M24	Paul Molitor	225.00

1998 Studio

The Donruss Studio base set consists of 220 regular-sized cards and 36 8-x-10 portraits. The base cards feature a posed photo with an action shot in the background, surrounded by a white border. Silver Studio Proofs (numbered to 1,000) and Gold Studio Proofs (300) parallel the regular-size base set. Inserts included Freeze Frame, Hit Parade and Masterstrokes.

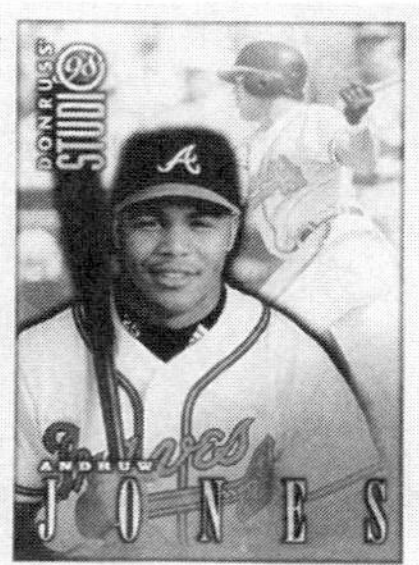

		MT
Complete Set (220):		35.00
Common Player:		.10
Pack (7 cards+8x10):		3.00
Wax Box (18):		40.00
1	Tony Clark	.10
2	Jose Cruz Jr.	.20
3	Ivan Rodriguez	.75
4	Mo Vaughn	.50
5	Kenny Lofton	.10
6	Will Clark	.30
7	Barry Larkin	.15
8	Jay Bell	.10
9	Kevin Young	.10
10	Francisco Cordova	.10
11	Justin Thompson	.10
12	Paul Molitor	.60
13	Jeff Bagwell	1.25
14	Jose Canseco	.50
15	Scott Rolen	1.00
16	Wilton Guerrero	.10
17	Shannon Stewart	.15
18	Hideki Irabu	.15
19	Michael Tucker	.10
20	Joe Carter	.10
21	Gabe Alvarez	.10
22	Ricky Ledee	.10
23	Karim Garcia	.20
24	Eli Marrero	.10
25	Scott Elarton	.10
26	Mario Valdez	.10
27	Ben Grieve	.75
28	Paul Konerko	.10
29	*Esteban Yan*	.15
30	Esteban Loaiza	.10
31	Delino DeShields	.10
32	Bernie Williams	.40
33	Joe Randa	.10
34	Randy Johnson	.65
35	Brett Tomko	.10
36	*Todd Erdos*	.20
37	Bobby Higginson	.15
38	Jason Kendall	.10
39	Ray Lankford	.10
40	Mark Grace	.30
41	Andy Pettitte	.40
42	Alex Rodriguez	2.25
43	Hideo Nomo	.60
44	Sammy Sosa	1.75
45	J.T. Snow	.10
46	Jason Varitek	.10
47	Vinny Castilla	.10
48	Neifi Perez	.10
49	Todd Walker	.10
50	Mike Cameron	.10
51	Jeffrey Hammonds	.10
52	Deivi Cruz	.10
53	Brian Hunter	.10
54	Al Martin	.10
55	Ron Coomer	.10
56	Chan Ho Park	.25
57	Pedro Martinez	.60
58	Darin Erstad	.75
59	Albert Belle	.40
60	Nomar Garciaparra	1.75
61	Tony Gwynn	1.50
62	Mike Piazza	2.00
63	Todd Helton	.75
64	David Ortiz	.10
65	Todd Dunwoody	.10
66	Orlando Cabrera	.10
67	Ken Cloude	.10
68	Andy Benes	.10
69	Mariano Rivera	.25
70	Cecil Fielder	.10
71	Brian Jordan	.10
72	Darryl Kile	.10
73	Reggie Jefferson	.10
74	Shawn Estes	.10
75	Bobby Bonilla	.10
76	Denny Neagle	.10
77	Robin Ventura	.10
78	Omar Vizquel	.10
79	Craig Biggio	.15
80	Moises Alou	.25
81	Garret Anderson	.10
82	Eric Karros	.10
83	Dante Bichette	.10
84	Charles Johnson	.10
85	Rusty Greer	.10
86	Travis Fryman	.10
87	Fernando Tatis	.10
88	Wilson Alvarez	.10
89	Carl Pavano	.10
90	Brian Rose	.10
91	Geoff Jenkins	.10
92	*Magglio Ordonez*	1.50
93	David Segui	.10
94	David Cone	.10
95	John Smoltz	.15
96	Jim Thome	.10
97	Gary Sheffield	.40
98	Barry Bonds	1.75
99	Andres Galarraga	.10
100	Brad Fullmer	.10
101	Bobby Estalella	.10
102	Enrique Wilson	.10
103	*Frank Catalanotto*	.20
104	*Mike Lowell*	.75
105	Kevin Orie	.10
106	Matt Morris	.10
107	Pokey Reese	.10
108	Shawn Green	.20
109	Tony Womack	.10
110	Ken Caminiti	.10
111	Roberto Alomar	.65
112	Ken Griffey Jr.	2.25
113	Cal Ripken Jr.	2.50
114	Lou Collier	.10
115	Larry Walker	.40
116	Fred McGriff	.10
117	Jim Edmonds	.10
118	Edgar Martinez	.10
119	Matt Williams	.30
120	Ismael Valdes	.10
121	Bartolo Colon	.10
122	Jeff Cirillo	.10
123	*Steve Woodard*	.25
124	*Kevin Millwood*	3.00
125	Derrick Gibson	.10
126	Jacob Cruz	.10
127	Russell Branyan	.10
128	Sean Casey	.40
129	Derrek Lee	.10
130	Paul O'Neill	.10
131	Brad Radke	.10
132	Kevin Appier	.10
133	John Olerud	.10
134	Alan Benes	.10
135	Todd Greene	.10
136	*Carlos Mendoza*	.10
137	Wade Boggs	.50
138	Jose Guillen	.10
139	Tino Martinez	.10
140	Aaron Boone	.10
141	Abraham Nunez	.10
142	Preston Wilson	.10
143	Randall Simon	.10
144	Dennis Reyes	.10
145	Mark Kotsay	.10
146	Richard Hidalgo	.15
147	Travis Lee	.30
148	*Hanley Frias*	.10

149	Ruben Rivera	.10
150	Rafael Medina	.10
151	Dave Nilsson	.10
152	Curt Schilling	.25
153	Brady Anderson	.10
154	Carlos Delgado	.35
155	Jason Giambi	.35
156	Pat Hentgen	.10
157	Tom Glavine	.15
158	Ryan Klesko	.10
159	Chipper Jones	2.00
160	Juan Gonzalez	.75
161	Mark McGwire	2.50
162	Vladimir Guerrero	1.25
163	Derek Jeter	2.00
164	Manny Ramirez	1.25
165	Mike Mussina	.65
166	Rafael Palmeiro	.30
167	Henry Rodriguez	.10
168	Jeff Suppan	.10
169	Eric Milton	.10
170	Scott Spiezio	.10
171	Wilson Delgado	.10
172	Bubba Trammell	.10
173	Ellis Burks	.10
174	Jason Dickson	.10
175	Butch Huskey	.10
176	Edgardo Alfonzo	.10
177	Eric Young	.10
178	Marquis Grissom	.10
179	Lance Johnson	.10
180	Kevin Brown	.15
181	Sandy Alomar Jr.	.10
182	Todd Hundley	.10
183	Rondell White	.25
184	Javier Lopez	.10
185	Damian Jackson	.10
186	Raul Mondesi	.30
187	Rickey Henderson	.60
188	David Justice	.40
189	Jay Buhner	.10
190	Jaret Wright	.25
191	Miguel Tejada	.40
192	Ron Wright	.10
193	Livan Hernandez	.10
194	A.J. Hinch	.25
195	Richie Sexson	.10
196	Bob Abreu	.15
197	Luis Castillo	.10
198	Michael Coleman	.10
199	Greg Maddux	1.50
200	Frank Thomas	1.75
201	Andruw Jones	.75
202	Roger Clemens	1.50
203	Tim Salmon	.30
204	Chuck Knoblauch	.10
205	Wes Helms	.10
206	Juan Encarnacion	.10
207	Russ Davis	.10
208	John Valentin	.10
209	Tony Saunders	.10
210	Mike Sweeney	.10
211	Steve Finley	.10
212	*David Dellucci*	.50
213	Edgar Renteria	.10
214	Jeremi Gonzalez	.10
215	Checklist (Jeff Bagwell)	.60
216	Checklist (Mike Piazza)	1.00
217	Checklist (Greg Maddux)	.75
218	Checklist (Cal Ripken Jr.)	1.25
219	Checklist (Frank Thomas)	1.00
220	Checklist (Ken Griffey Jr.)	1.00

1998 Studio Silver Proofs

This parallel set includes all 220 cards in Studio baseball. Cards are identified by a silver holographic strip around the borders. Silver versions are limited to 1,000 sets.

	MT
Common Player:	1.00
Silver Stars:	4X

(See 1998 Studio for checklist, base card values.)

1998 Studio Gold Proofs

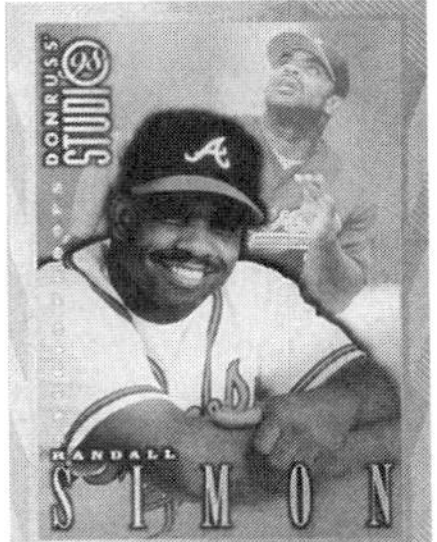

Gold proofs is a parallel of the 220-card base set. Card fronts feature gold holo-foil highlights. Backs are sequentially numbered to 300 each.

	MT
Common Player:	2.00
Stars:	20X

(See 1998 Studio for checklist and base card values.)

1998 Studio Autographs

Three top rookies signed a number of 8x10s for this product. Lee signed 500 while the other two autographed 1,000 each.

		MT
1	Travis Lee (500)	15.00
2	Todd Helton (1000)	40.00
3	Ben Grieve (1000)	25.00

1998 Studio Freeze Frame

Freeze Frame is a 30-card insert sequentially numbered to 5,000. The cards are designed to look like a piece of film with a color action photo. The first 500 of each card are die-cut.

		MT
Complete Set (30):		80.00
Common Player:		1.25
Production 4,500 sets		
Die-Cuts:		3X
Production 500 sets		
1	Ken Griffey Jr.	7.00
2	Derek Jeter	6.00
3	Ben Grieve	2.00
4	Cal Ripken Jr.	8.00
5	Alex Rodriguez	7.00
6	Greg Maddux	4.00
7	David Justice	2.00
8	Mike Piazza	6.00
9	Chipper Jones	6.00
10	Randy Johnson	2.50
11	Jeff Bagwell	3.00
12	Nomar Garciaparra	5.00
13	Andruw Jones	3.00
14	Frank Thomas	5.00
15	Scott Rolen	2.50
16	Barry Bonds	5.00
17	Kenny Lofton	1.25
18	Ivan Rodriguez	3.00
19	Chuck Knoblauch	1.25
20	Jose Cruz Jr.	1.75
21	Bernie Williams	1.75
22	Tony Gwynn	4.00
23	Juan Gonzalez	3.00
24	Gary Sheffield	1.50
25	Roger Clemens	4.00
26	Travis Lee	2.00
27	Brad Fullmer	2.00
28	Tim Salmon	1.25
29	Raul Mondesi	1.25
30	Roberto Alomar	2.50

1998 Studio Hit Parade

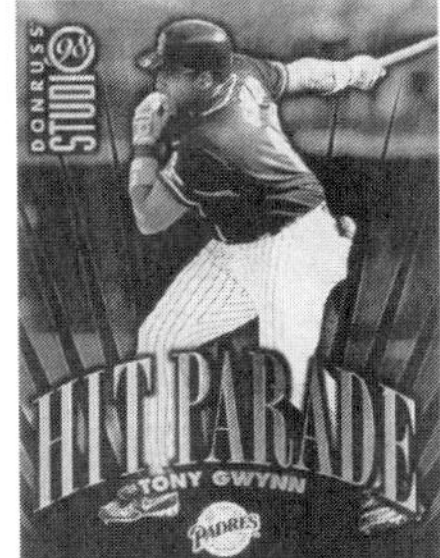

These 20 cards are printed on micro-etched foil board. This set honors baseball's top hitters and is sequentially numbered to 5,000.

		MT
Complete Set (20):		45.00
Common Player:		1.25
Production 5,000 sets		
1	Tony Gwynn	3.00
2	Larry Walker	1.50
3	Mike Piazza	5.00
4	Frank Thomas	4.00
5	Manny Ramirez	2.50
6	Ken Griffey Jr.	6.00
7	Todd Helton	1.75
8	Vladimir Guerrero	2.50
9	Albert Belle	1.25
10	Jeff Bagwell	2.50
11	Juan Gonzalez	2.50
12	Jim Thome	1.25
13	Scott Rolen	2.00
14	Tino Martinez	1.25
15	Mark McGwire	7.00
16	Barry Bonds	4.00
17	Tony Clark	1.25
18	Mo Vaughn	1.75
19	Darin Erstad	1.75
20	Paul Konerko	1.25

1998 Studio Masterstrokes

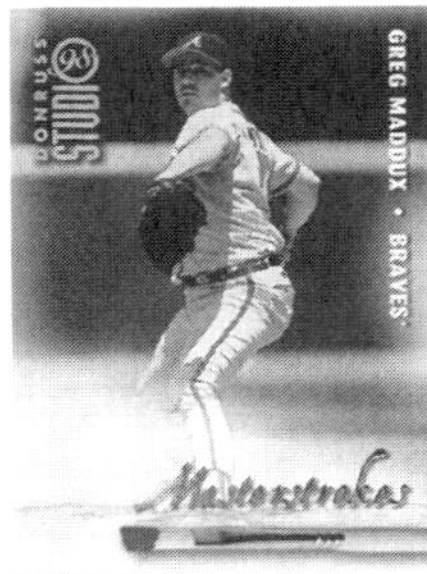

Printed on a canvas-like material, these 20 cards are numbered to 1,000.

		MT
Complete Set (20):		140.00
Common Player:		2.50
Production 1,000 sets		
1	Travis Lee	2.50
2	Kenny Lofton	2.50
3	Mo Vaughn	3.00
4	Ivan Rodriguez	5.00
5	Roger Clemens	8.00
6	Mark McGwire	17.50
7	Hideo Nomo	4.00
8	Andruw Jones	6.50
9	Nomar Garciaparra	10.00
10	Juan Gonzalez	6.50
11	Jeff Bagwell	6.50
12	Derek Jeter	12.50
13	Tony Gwynn	8.00
14	Chipper Jones	12.50
15	Mike Piazza	12.50
16	Greg Maddux	8.00
17	Alex Rodriguez	15.00
18	Cal Ripken Jr.	17.50
19	Frank Thomas	10.00
20	Ken Griffey Jr.	15.00

1998 Studio Sony MLB 99

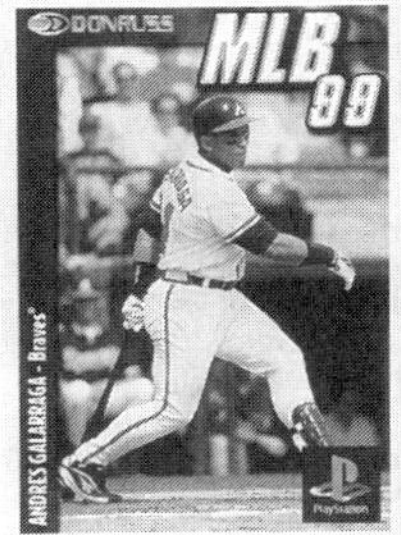

Twenty Sony MLB '99 sweepstakes cards were inserted one per two Studio packs. The fronts feature a color action shot and the backs have sweepstakes rules and a MLB '99 tip.

		MT
Complete Set (20):		10.00
Common Player:		.25
1	Cal Ripken Jr.	2.00
2	Nomar Garciaparra	1.25
3	Barry Bonds	1.25
4	Mike Mussina	.75
5	Pedro Martinez	.50
6	Derek Jeter	1.50
7	Andruw Jones	1.00
8	Kenny Lofton	.25
9	Gary Sheffield	.25
10	Raul Mondesi	.25
11	Jeff Bagwell	1.00
12	Tim Salmon	.25
13	Tom Glavine	.25
14	Ben Grieve	.50
15	Matt Williams	.25
16	Juan Gonzalez	1.00
17	Mark McGwire	2.00
18	Bernie Williams	.25
19	Andres Galarraga	.25
20	Jose Cruz Jr.	.25

1998 Studio 8x10 Portraits Samples

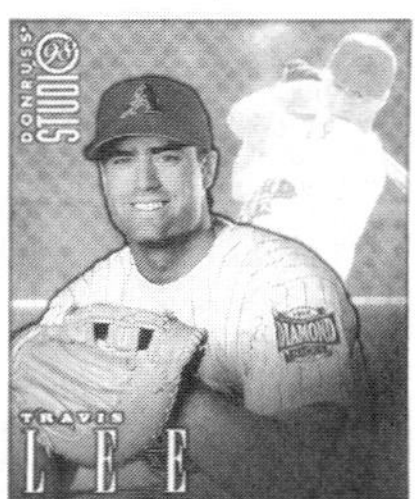

Sample versions of the 8x10 cards which would be found in '98 Studio packs were also issued. They are identical in format to the issued cards, with UV coating and silver-foil graphics on fronts. Backs have a large black "SAMPLE" overprinted diagonally.

		MT
001	Travis Lee	2.00
002	Todd Helton	3.00

1998 Studio 8x10 Portraits

One Studio 8-x-10 was included in each pack. The cards were blown-up versions of the regular-size base cards, which were inserted seven per pack. The large portraits are paralleled in the Gold Proofs set, which adds gold holo-foil to the cards. Gold Proofs are numbered to 300.

		MT
Complete Set (36):		95.00
Common Player:		1.00
Inserted 1:1		
1	Travis Lee	1.50
2	Todd Helton	2.50
3	Ben Grieve	2.50
4	Paul Konerko	1.00
5	Jeff Bagwell	3.50
6	Derek Jeter	5.50
7	Ivan Rodriguez	3.00
8	Cal Ripken Jr.	8.00
9	Mike Piazza	5.50
10	Chipper Jones	5.50
11	Frank Thomas	5.00
12	Tony Gwynn	4.50
13	Nomar Garciaparra	5.00
14	Juan Gonzalez	3.50
15	Greg Maddux	4.50
16	Hideo Nomo	2.50
17	Scott Rolen	2.50
18	Barry Bonds	5.00
19	Ken Griffey Jr.	7.00
20	Alex Rodriguez	7.00
21	Roger Clemens	4.50
22	Mark McGwire	8.00
23	Jose Cruz Jr.	1.00
24	Andruw Jones	3.50
25	Tino Martinez	1.00
26	Mo Vaughn	2.50
27	Vladimir Guerrero	3.50
28	Tony Clark	1.00
29	Andy Pettitte	2.00
30	Jaret Wright	1.00
31	Paul Molitor	2.00
32	Darin Erstad	3.00
33	Larry Walker	1.00
34	Chuck Knoblauch	1.00
35	Barry Larkin	1.00
36	Kenny Lofton	1.00

1998 Studio 8x10 Portraits Gold Proofs

This parallel of the 8x10 base set adds gold holo-foil treatments to the 36 cards, which are sequentially numbered to 300 and randomly inserted in packs.

	MT
Common Player:	10.00
Stars:	15X

(See 1998 Studio 8X10 Portraits for checklist and base card values.)

1995 Summit Samples

Nine-card cello packs of Summit cards, including "Big Bang" inserts, were released to dealers to debut the new Score brand. Cards are specially marked as promotional samples.

		MT
Complete Set (9):		10.00
Common Player:		1.00
10	Barry Larkin	1.00
11	Albert Belle	1.00
79	Cal Ripken Jr.	3.50
80	David Cone	1.00
125	Alex Gonzalez (Rookie)	1.00
130	Charles Johnson (Rookie)	1.00
BB12	Jose Canseco (Big Bang)	2.00
BB17	Fred McGriff (Big Bang)	1.00
---	Information card	.10

1995 Summit

A late-season release, Summit introduced the Score label to a premium brand card. Printed on extra heavy cardboard stock and UV coated on both sides the veteran player cards (#1-111) feature horizontal or vertical action photos with the player's name and team logo printed in gold-foil on front. Backs have a player portrait photo along with his 1994 stats in monthly charted form. The rookie cards subset (#112-173) have a large black "ROOKIE" on top-front while the back has a short career summary instead of stats. Other subsets include "BAT SPEED" (#174-188), honoring top hitters, and "SPECIAL DELIVERY" (#189-193), featuring top pitchers. Each are designated on front with special gold-foil logos. Seven checklists close out the regular 200-card set. The Summit issued featured a four-tiered chase card program, including a parallel "Nth Degree" set. Summit was a hobby-only issue sold in 7-card foil packs.

		MT
Complete Set (200):		15.00
Common Player:		.10
Pack (7):		1.50
Wax Box (24):		25.00
1	Ken Griffey Jr.	2.00
2	Alex Fernandez	.10
3	Fred McGriff	.10
4	Ben McDonald	.10
5	Rafael Palmeiro	.20
6	Tony Gwynn	1.00
7	Jim Thome	.10
8	Ken Hill	.10
9	Barry Bonds	1.25
10	Barry Larkin	.15
11	Albert Belle	.35
12	Billy Ashley	.10
13	Matt Williams	.30
14	Andy Benes	.10
15	Midre Cummings	.10
16	J.R. Phillips	.10
17	Edgar Martinez	.10
18	Manny Ramirez	.75
19	Jose Canseco	.50
20	Chili Davis	.10
21	Don Mattingly	1.25
22	Bernie Williams	.40
23	Tom Glavine	.15
24	Robin Ventura	.10
25	Jeff Conine	.10
26	Mark Grace	.25
27	Mark McGwire	2.50
28	Carlos Delgado	.40
29	Greg Colbrunn	.10
30	Greg Maddux	1.00
31	Craig Biggio	.15
32	Kirby Puckett	1.00
33	Derek Bell	.10
34	Lenny Dykstra	.10
35	Tim Salmon	.20
36	Deion Sanders	.15
37	Moises Alou	.15
38	Ray Lankford	.10
39	Willie Greene	.10
40	Ozzie Smith	1.00
41	Roger Clemens	1.00
42	Andres Galarraga	.10
43	Gary Sheffield	.30
44	Sammy Sosa	1.25
45	Larry Walker	.30
46	Kevin Appier	.10
47	Raul Mondesi	.25
48	Kenny Lofton	.10
49	Darryl Hamilton	.10
50	Roberto Alomar	.60
51	Hal Morris	.10
52	Cliff Floyd	.10
53	Brent Gates	.10
54	Rickey Henderson	.60
55	John Olerud	.10
56	Gregg Jefferies	.10
57	Cecil Fielder	.10
58	Paul Molitor	.50
59	Bret Boone	.15
60	Greg Vaughn	.10
61	Wally Joyner	.10
62	Jeffrey Hammonds	.10
63	James Mouton	.10
64	Omar Vizquel	.10
65	Wade Boggs	.60
66	Terry Steinbach	.10
67	Wil Cordero	.10
68	Joey Hamilton	.10
69	Rico Brogna	.10
70	Darren Daulton	.10
71	Chuck Knoblauch	.10
72	Bob Hamelin	.10
73	Carl Everett	.15
74	Joe Carter	.10
75	Dave Winfield	.75
76	Bobby Bonilla	.10
77	Paul O'Neill	.10
78	Javier Lopez	.10
79	Cal Ripken Jr.	2.50
80	David Cone	.10
81	Bernard Gilkey	.10
82	Ivan Rodriguez	.50
83	Dean Palmer	.10
84	Jason Bere	.10
85	Will Clark	.30
86	Scott Cooper	.10
87	Royce Clayton	.10
88	Mike Piazza	1.50
89	Ryan Klesko	.10
90	Juan Gonzalez	.75
91	Travis Fryman	.10
92	Frank Thomas	1.25
93	Eduardo Perez	.10
94	Mo Vaughn	.40
95	Jay Bell	.10
96	Jeff Bagwell	.75
97	Randy Johnson	.50
98	Jimmy Key	.10
99	Dennis Eckersley	.10
100	Carlos Baerga	.10
101	Eddie Murray	.50
102	Mike Mussina	.50
103	Brian Anderson	.10
104	Jeff Cirillo	.10
105	Dante Bichette	.10
106	Bret Saberhagen	.10
107	Jeff Kent	.10
108	Ruben Sierra	.10
109	Kirk Gibson	.10
110	Reggie Sanders	.10
111	Dave Justice	.25
112	Benji Gil	.10

113 Vaughn Eshelman .10
114 *Carlos Perez* .10
115 Chipper Jones 1.50
116 Shane Andrews .10
117 Orlando Miller .10
118 Scott Ruffcorn .10
119 Jose Oliva .10
120 Joe Vitiello .10
121 Jon Nunnally .10
122 Garret Anderson .10
123 Curtis Goodwin .10
124 *Mark Grudzielanek* .35
125 Alex Gonzalez .15
126 David Bell .10
127 Dustin Hermanson .10
128 Dave Nilsson .10
129 Wilson Heredia .10
130 Charles Johnson .10
131 Frank Rodriguez .10
132 Alex Ochoa .10
133 Alex Rodriguez 2.00
134 *Bobby Higginson* 1.50
135 Edgardo Alfonzo .10
136 Armando Benitez .10
137 Rich Aude .10
138 Tim Naehring .10
139 Joe Randa .10
140 Quilvio Veras .10
141 *Hideo Nomo* 2.00
142 Ray Holbert .10
143 Michael Tucker .10
144 Chad Mottola .10
145 John Valentin .10
146 James Baldwin .10
147 Esteban Loaiza .10
148 Marty Cordova .10
149 *Juan Acevedo* .10
150 *Tim Unroe* .10
151 Brad Clontz .10
152 Steve Rodriguez .10
153 Rudy Pemberton .10
154 Ozzie Timmons .10
155 Ricky Otero .10
156 Allen Battle .10
157 Joe Roselli .10
158 Roberto Petagine .10
159 Todd Hollandsworth .10
160 Shannon Penn .10
161 Antonio Osuna .10
162 Russ Davis .10
163 Jason Giambi .35
164 Terry Bradshaw .10
165 Ray Durham .10
166 Todd Steverson .10
167 Tim Belk .10
168 Andy Pettitte .40
169 Roger Cedeno .10
170 Jose Parra .10
171 Scott Sullivan .10
172 LaTroy Hawkins .10
173 Jeff McCurry .10
174 Ken Griffey Jr. (Bat Speed) 1.00
175 Frank Thomas (Bat Speed) .65
176 Cal Ripken Jr. (Bat Speed) 1.25
177 Jeff Bagwell (Bat Speed) .40
178 Mike Piazza (Bat Speed) .75
179 Barry Bonds (Bat Speed) .65
180 Matt Williams (Bat Speed) .10
181 Don Mattingly (Bat Speed) .65
182 Will Clark (Bat Speed) .10
183 Tony Gwynn (Bat Speed) .50
184 Kirby Puckett (Bat Speed) .50
185 Jose Canseco (Bat Speed) .25
186 Paul Molitor (Bat Speed) .25
187 Albert Belle (Bat Speed) .15
188 Joe Carter (Bat Speed) .10
189 Greg Maddux (Special Delivery) .50
190 Roger Clemens (Special Delivery) .50
191 David Cone (Special Delivery) .10
192 Mike Mussina (Special Delivery) .30
193 Randy Johnson (Special Delivery) .30
194 Checklist (Frank Thomas) .60
195 Checklist (Ken Griffey Jr.) 1.00
196 Checklist (Cal Ripken Jr.) 1.25
197 Checklist (Jeff Bagwell) .40
198 Checklist (Mike Piazza) .75
199 Checklist (Barry Bonds) .60
200 Checklist (Mo Vaughn, Matt Williams) .10

1995 Summit Nth Degree

A prismatic foil background differentiates the Nth Degree parallel inserts from the Summit base cards. Nth Degree inserts are found on a 1:4 pack ratio.

	MT
Complete Set (200):	100.00
Common Player:	.50
Stars:	4X

(See 1995 Summit for checklist, base card values.)

1995 Summit Big Bang

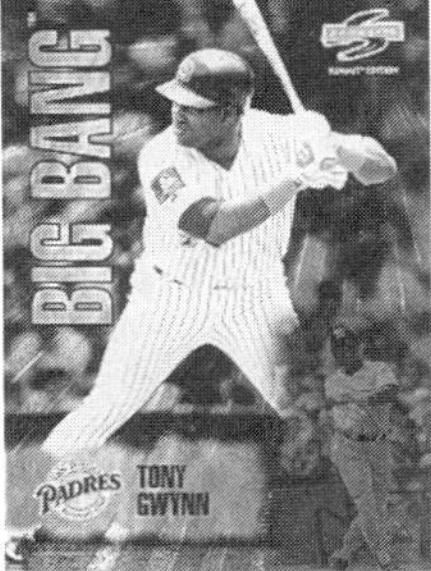

The game's top sluggers are featured in this insert set. The front is printed on prismatic metallic foil, a process which Score calls "Spectroetch," with large and small action photos. Backs are conventionally printed and have a large photo with a career highlight printed beneath. The toughest of the Summit chase cards, these are found on the average of once every two boxes (72 packs). Cards are numbered with a "BB" prefix.

		MT
Complete Set (20):		60.00
Common Player:		1.00
1	Ken Griffey Jr.	10.00
2	Frank Thomas	6.00
3	Cal Ripken Jr.	12.50
4	Jeff Bagwell	4.00
5	Mike Piazza	8.00
6	Barry Bonds	6.00
7	Matt Williams	1.00
8	Don Mattingly	6.00
9	Will Clark	1.00
10	Tony Gwynn	5.00
11	Kirby Puckett	5.00
12	Jose Canseco	3.00
13	Paul Molitor	3.00
14	Albert Belle	1.00
15	Joe Carter	1.00
16	Rafael Palmeiro	1.00
17	Fred McGriff	1.00
18	Dave Justice	1.25
19	Tim Salmon	1.00
20	Mo Vaughn	1.50

1995 Summit New Age

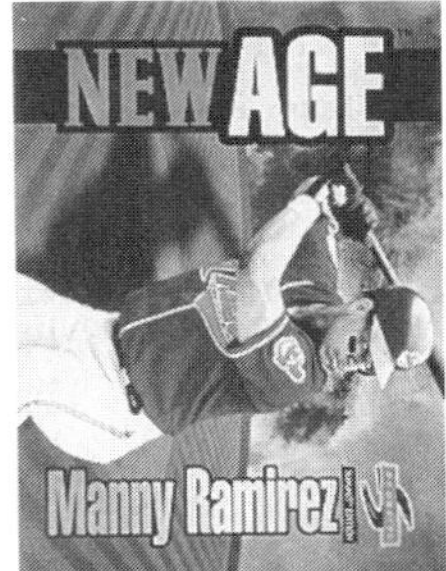

Printed on metallic foil in a horizontal format, the New Age inserts were seeded at a rate of about one per 18 packs. Red and silver colors predominate on front, while the backs are printed in standard technology and feature a second photo and a short career summary of the players who were generally in their second or third Major League season in 1995.

		MT
Complete Set (15):		16.00
Common Player:		.25
1	Cliff Floyd	.25
2	Manny Ramirez	2.00
3	Raul Mondesi	.35
4	Alex Rodriguez	5.00
5	Billy Ashley	.25
6	Alex Gonzalez	.35
7	Michael Tucker	.25
8	Charles Johnson	.25
9	Carlos Delgado	.75
10	Benji Gil	.25
11	Chipper Jones	4.00
12	Todd Hollandsworth	.25
13	Frank Rodriguez	.25
14	Shawn Green	.75
15	Ray Durham	.35

1995 Summit 21 Club

Metallic foil printing on front and back distinguishes this set of chase cards. A large red-foil "21 / CLUB" logo on each side identifies the theme of this set as players who professed to be that age during the 1955 baseball season. The players are pictured in action pose on front and a portrait on back. On average the 21 Club cards are seeded one per box (36 packs). Cards are numbered with a "TC" prefix.

		MT
Complete Set (9):		7.50
Common Player:		.75
1	Bob Abreu	1.50
2	Pokey Reese	1.00
3	Edgardo Alfonzo	1.50
4	Jim Pittsley	.75
5	Ruben Rivera	.75
6	Chan Ho Park	2.00
7	Julian Tavarez	.75
8	Ismael Valdes	.75
9	Dmitri Young	1.00

1996 Summit

Pinnacle's 1996 Summit baseball has 200 cards, including 35 rookies, four checklists and 10 Deja Vu subset cards. Each card is also reprinted in three parallel versions - Above and Beyond (one per seven packs), Artist's Proofs (one in 36) and a retail-only silver foil-bordered version. Above and Beyond cards use an all-prismatic foil design; Artist's Proof cards have holographic foil stamping. Five insert sets were produced: Big Bang; Mirage (a parallel set to Big Bang); Hitters, Inc.; Ballparks; and Positions (found one per every 50 magazine packs).

		MT
Complete Set (200):		16.00
Common Player:		.10
Pack (7):		2.00
Wax Box (18):		25.00
1	Mike Piazza	2.00
2	Matt Williams	.20
3	Tino Martinez	.10
4	Reggie Sanders	.10
5	Ray Durham	.10
6	Brad Radke	.10
7	Jeff Bagwell	.75
8	Ron Gant	.10
9	Lance Johnson	.10
10	Kevin Seitzer	.10
11	Dante Bichette	.10
12	Ivan Rodriguez	.60
13	Jim Abbott	.10
14	Greg Colbrunn	.10
15	Rondell White	.20
16	Shawn Green	.20
17	Gregg Jefferies	.10
18	Omar Vizquel	.10
19	Cal Ripken Jr.	3.00
20	Mark McGwire	3.00
21	Wally Joyner	.10
22	Chili Davis	.10
23	Jose Canseco	.50
24	Royce Clayton	.10
25	Jay Bell	.10
26	Travis Fryman	.10
27	Jeff King	.10
28	Todd Hundley	.10
29	Joe Vitiello	.10
30	Russ Davis	.10
31	Mo Vaughn	.40
32	Raul Mondesi	.30
33	Ray Lankford	.10
34	Mike Stanley	.10
35	B.J. Surhoff	.10
36	Greg Vaughn	.10
37	Todd Stottlemyre	.10
38	Carlos Delgado	.30
39	Kenny Lofton	.10
40	Hideo Nomo	.60
41	Sterling Hitchcock	.10
42	Pete Schourek	.10
43	Edgardo Alfonzo	.10
44	Ken Hill	.10
45	Ken Caminiti	.10
46	Bobby Higginson	.15
47	Michael Tucker	.10
48	David Cone	.10
49	Cecil Fielder	.10
50	Brian Hunter	.10
51	Charles Johnson	.10
52	Bobby Bonilla	.10
53	Eddie Murray	.40
54	Kenny Rogers	.10
55	Jim Edmonds	.10
56	Trevor Hoffman	.10
57	Kevin Mitchell	.10
58	Ruben Sierra	.10
59	Benji Gil	.10
60	Juan Gonzalez	.75
61	Larry Walker	.30
62	Jack McDowell	.10
63	Shawon Dunston	.10
64	Andy Benes	.10
65	Jay Buhner	.10
66	Rickey Henderson	.60
67	Alex Gonzalez	.15
68	Mike Kelly	.10
69	Fred McGriff	.10
70	Ryne Sandberg	.75
71	Ernie Young	.10
72	Kevin Appier	.10
73	Moises Alou	.15
74	John Jaha	.10
75	J.T. Snow	.10
76	Jim Thome	.10
77	Kirby Puckett	1.00
78	Hal Morris	.10
79	Robin Ventura	.10
80	Ben McDonald	.10
81	Tim Salmon	.20
82	Albert Belle	.35
83	Marquis Grissom	.10
84	Alex Rodriguez	2.50
85	Manny Ramirez	.75
86	Ken Griffey Jr.	2.50
87	Sammy Sosa	1.50
88	Frank Thomas	1.50
89	Lee Smith	.10
90	Marty Cordova	.10
91	Greg Maddux	1.00
92	Lenny Dykstra	.10
93	Butch Huskey	.10
94	Garret Anderson	.10
95	Mike Bordick	.10
96	Dave Justice	.25
97	Chad Curtis	.10
98	Carlos Baerga	.10
99	Jason Isringhausen	.10
100	Gary Sheffield	.30
101	Roger Clemens	1.00
102	Ozzie Smith	1.00
103	Ramon Martinez	.10
104	Paul O'Neill	.10
105	Will Clark	.20
106	Tom Glavine	.15
107	Barry Bonds	1.50
108	Barry Larkin	.15
109	Derek Bell	.10
110	Randy Johnson	.60
111	Jeff Conine	.10
112	John Mabry	.10
113	Julian Tavarez	.10
114	Gary DiSarcina	.10
115	Andres Galarraga	.10
116	Marc Newfield	.10
117	Frank Rodriguez	.10
118	Brady Anderson	.10
119	Mike Mussina	.60
120	Orlando Merced	.10
121	Melvin Nieves	.10
122	Brian Jordan	.10
123	Rafael Palmeiro	.20
124	Johnny Damon	.15
125	Wil Cordero	.10
126	Chipper Jones	2.00
127	Eric Karros	.10
128	Darren Daulton	.10
129	Vinny Castilla	.10
130	Joe Carter	.10
131	Bernie Williams	.35
132	Bernard Gilkey	.10
133	Bret Boone	.15
134	Tony Gwynn	1.00
135	Dave Nilsson	.10
136	Ryan Klesko	.10
137	Paul Molitor	.60
138	John Olerud	.10
139	Craig Biggio	.15
140	John Valentin	.10
141	Chuck Knoblauch	.10
142	Edgar Martinez	.10
143	Rico Brogna	.10
144	Dean Palmer	.10
145	Mark Grace	.25
146	Roberto Alomar	.65
147	Alex Fernandez	.10
148	Andre Dawson	.25
149	Wade Boggs	.50
150	Mark Lewis	.10
151	Gary Gaetti	.10
152	Paul Wilson, Roger Clemens (Deja Vu)	.40
153	Rey Ordonez, Ozzie Smith (Deja Vu)	.50
154	Derek Jeter, Cal Ripken Jr. (Deja Vu)	1.00
155	Alan Benes, Andy Benes (Deja Vu)	.10
156	Jason Kendall, Mike Piazza (Deja Vu)	.50
157	Ryan Klesko, Frank Thomas (Deja Vu)	.50
158	Johnny Damon, Ken Griffey Jr. (Deja Vu)	.50
159	Karim Garcia, Sammy Sosa (Deja Vu)	.50
160	Raul Mondesi, Tim Salmon (Deja Vu)	.10
161	Chipper Jones, Matt Williams (Deja Vu)	.50
162	Rey Ordonez	.10
163	Bob Wolcott	.10
164	Brooks Kieschnick	.10
165	Steve Gibralter	.10
166	Bob Abreu	.10
167	Greg Zaun	.10
168	Tavo Alvarez	.10
169	Sal Fasano	.10
170	George Arias	.10
171	Derek Jeter	2.00
172	*Livan Hernandez*	.50
173	Alan Benes	.10
174	George Williams	.10
175	John Wasdin	.10
176	Chan Ho Park	.25
177	Paul Wilson	.10
178	Jeff Suppan	.10
179	Quinton McCracken	.10
180	*Wilton Guerrero*	.25
181	Eric Owens	.10
182	Felipe Crespo	.10
183	LaTroy Hawkins	.10
184	Jason Schmidt	.10
185	Terrell Wade	.10
186	*Mike Grace*	.10
187	Chris Snopek	.10
188	Jason Kendall	.10
189	Todd Hollandsworth	.10
190	Jim Pittsley	.10
191	Jermaine Dye	.10
192	*Mike Busby*	.10
193	Richard Hidalgo	.15
194	Tyler Houston	.10
195	Jimmy Haynes	.10
196	Karim Garcia	.10
197	Ken Griffey Jr. (Checklist)	1.25
198	Frank Thomas (Checklist)	.65
199	Greg Maddux (Checklist)	.50
200	Cal Ripken Jr. (Checklist)	1.50

1996 Summit Above & Beyond

These 200 insert cards parallel Pinnacle's 1996 Summit set, using all-prismatic foil for each card. The cards were seeded one per every four packs.

	MT
Complete Set (200):	145.00
Common Player:	.50
Stars:	6X

(See 1996 Summit for checklist, base card values.)

1996 Summit Artist's Proof

Holographic-foil highlights and an "ARTIST'S PROOF" notation on the front photo distinguish the cards in this parallel edition. The AP cards are found once per 36 packs.

	MT
Complete Set (200):	350.00
Common Player:	1.00
Stars:	10X

(See 1996 Summit for checklist, base card values.)

1996 Summit Foil

This parallel issue was an exclusive in Summit seven-card magazine retail packaging. The black borders of the regular Summit versions have been replaced on these cards by silver foil.

	MT
Complete Set (200):	50.00
Common Player:	.25
Stars:	2X

(See 1996 Summit for checklist and base card values.)

1996 Summit Ballparks

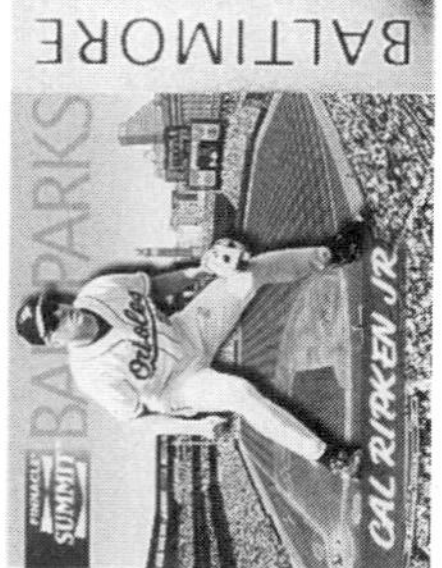

These 18 cards feature images of players superimposed over their respective teams' ballparks. The cards were seeded one per every 18 packs of 1996 Pinnacle Summit baseball and are serially within an edition of 8,000 each.

		MT
Complete Set (18):		65.00
Common Player:		1.50
1	Cal Ripken Jr.	9.00
2	Albert Belle	1.50
3	Dante Bichette	1.50
4	Mo Vaughn	2.50
5	Ken Griffey Jr.	8.00
6	Derek Jeter	7.00

7	Juan Gonzalez	4.00
8	Greg Maddux	5.00
9	Frank Thomas	6.00
10	Ryne Sandberg	4.00
11	Mike Piazza	7.00
12	Johnny Damon	2.50
13	Barry Bonds	6.00
14	Jeff Bagwell	4.00
15	Paul Wilson	1.50
16	Tim Salmon	1.50
17	Kirby Puckett	5.00
18	Tony Gwynn	5.00

1996 Summit Big Bang

Sixteen of the biggest hitters are featured on these 1996 Pinnacle Summit insert cards. The cards, seeded one per every 72 packs, use Spectroetched backgrounds with foil highlights.

		MT
Complete Set (16):		140.00
Common Player:		3.00
Mirages:		1X
1	Frank Thomas	17.50
2	Ken Griffey Jr.	22.50
3	Albert Belle	4.00
4	Mo Vaughn	5.00
5	Barry Bonds	17.50
6	Cal Ripken Jr.	25.00
7	Jeff Bagwell	10.00
8	Mike Piazza	20.00
9	Ryan Klesko	3.00
10	Manny Ramirez	10.00
11	Tim Salmon	3.00
12	Dante Bichette	3.00
13	Sammy Sosa	17.50
14	Raul Mondesi	3.00
15	Chipper Jones	20.00
16	Garret Anderson	3.00

1996 Summit Big Bang Mirage

These 18 cards form a parallel version to Pinnacle's Big Bang inserts. The cards, found one per every 72 packs, use an all-new technology that creates a floating background behind the player's image. By holding the card in direct sunlight or an incandescent bulb, a collector can see three dimensions and a floating baseball that seems to levitate in the background. Mirage cards are serially numbered in an edition of 600 each.

		MT
Complete Set (16):		140.00
Common Player:		3.00
1	Frank Thomas	17.50
2	Ken Griffey Jr.	22.50
3	Albert Belle	4.00
4	Mo Vaughn	5.00
5	Barry Bonds	17.50
6	Cal Ripken Jr.	25.00
7	Jeff Bagwell	10.00
8	Mike Piazza	20.00
9	Ryan Klesko	3.00
10	Manny Ramirez	10.00
11	Tim Salmon	3.00
12	Dante Bichette	3.00
13	Sammy Sosa	17.50
14	Raul Mondesi	3.00
15	Chipper Jones	20.00
16	Garret Anderson	3.00

1996 Summit Hitters, Inc.

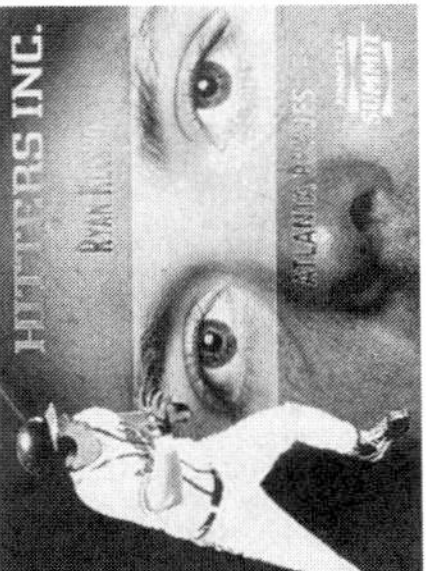

This 1996 Pinnacle Summit set honors 16 top hitters. The cards, seeded one per 36 packs, put an embossed highlight on an enlarged photo of the player's eyes. Backs are serially numbered within an edition of 4,000 each.

		MT
Complete Set (16):		32.50
Common Player:		.75
1	Tony Gwynn	2.50
2	Mo Vaughn	1.00
3	Tim Salmon	.75
4	Ken Griffey Jr.	4.50
5	Sammy Sosa	3.50
6	Frank Thomas	3.50
7	Wade Boggs	2.00
8	Albert Belle	1.00
9	Cal Ripken Jr.	5.00
10	Manny Ramirez	2.50
11	Ryan Klesko	.75
11p	Ryan Klesko (overprinted "SAMPLE")	.75
12	Dante Bichette	.75
13	Mike Piazza	4.00
14	Chipper Jones	4.00
15	Ryne Sandberg	2.50
16	Matt Williams	.75

1996 Summit Positions

This insert issue features top players at each position. It is an exclusive magazine pack find, seeded about one per 50 packs. Fronts have action photos of three top players at the position on a baseball infield background at top. Close-ups of those photo appear at bottom, separated by a gold-foil strip. Backs have narrow action photos of each player, a few stats and a serial number from within an edition of 1,500 each.

		MT
Complete Set (9):		115.00
Common Card:		7.50
1	Jeff Bagwell, Mo Vaughn, Frank Thomas (First Base)	12.50
2	Roberto Alomar, Craig Biggio, Chuck Knoblauch (Second Base)	7.50
3	Matt Williams, Jim Thome, Chipper Jones (Third Base)	12.50
4	Barry Larkin, Cal Ripken Jr., Alex Rodriguez (Short Stop)	25.00
5	Mike Piazza, Ivan Rodriguez, Charles Johnson (Catcher)	20.00
6	Hideo Nomo, Greg Maddux, Randy Johnson (Pitcher)	15.00
7	Barry Bonds, Albert Belle, Ryan Klesko (Left Field)	12.50
8	Johnny Damon, Jim Edmonds, Ken Griffey Jr. (Center Field)	20.00
9	Manny Ramirez, Gary Sheffield, Sammy Sosa (Right Field))	17.50

1981 Topps

This is another 726-card set of 2-1/2" x 3-1/2" cards from Topps. The cards have the usual color photo with all cards from the same team sharing the same color borders. Player names appear under the photo with team and position on a baseball cap at lower-left. The Topps logo returned in a small baseball in the lower-right. Card backs include the usual stats along with a headline and a cartoon if there was room. Specialty cards include previous season record-breakers, highlights of the playoffs and World Series, along with the final appearance of team cards. Eleven cards on each of the six press sheets were double-printed.

		MT
Complete Set (726):		45.00
Common Player:		.10
Wax Pack (15):		3.00
Wax Box (36):		70.00
Cello Pack (28):		6.00
Cello Box (24):		80.00
Grocery Rack (36):		10.00
Rack Pack (48):		4.00
Rack Box (24):		65.00
Vending Box (500):		45.00
1	Batting Leaders (George Brett, Bill Buckner)	.75
2	Home Run Leaders (Reggie Jackson, Ben Oglivie, Mike Schmidt)	.75
3	RBI Leaders (Cecil Cooper, Mike Schmidt)	.25
4	Stolen Base Leaders (Rickey Henderson, Ron LeFlore)	.50
5	Victory Leaders (Steve Carlton, Steve Stone)	.15
6	Strikeout Leaders (Len Barker, Steve Carlton)	.15
7	ERA Leaders (Rudy May, Don Sutton)	.10
8	Leading Firemen (Rollie Fingers, Tom Hume, Dan Quisenberry)	.10
9	Pete LaCock (DP)	.10
10	Mike Flanagan	.10
11	Jim Wohlford (DP)	.10
12	Mark Clear	.10
13	*Joe Charboneau*	.50
14	*John Tudor*	.20
15	Larry Parrish	.10
16	Ron Davis	.10
17	Cliff Johnson	.10
18	Glenn Adams	.10
19	Jim Clancy	.10
20	Jeff Burroughs	.10
21	Ron Oester	.10
22	Danny Darwin	.10
23	Alex Trevino	.10
24	Don Stanhouse	.10
25	Sixto Lezcano	.10
26	U.L. Washington	.10
27	Champ Summers (DP)	.10
28	Enrique Romo	.10
29	Gene Tenace	.10
30	Jack Clark	.10
31	Checklist 1-121 (DP)	.10
32	Ken Oberkfell	.10
33	Rick Honeycutt	.10
34	Aurelio Rodriguez	.10
35	Mitchell Page	.10
36	Ed Farmer	.10
37	Gary Roenicke	.10
38	Win Remmerswaal	.10
39	Tom Veryzer	.10
40	Tug McGraw	.10
41	Rangers Future Stars (Bob Babcock, John Butcher, Jerry Don Gleaton)	.10
42	Jerry White (DP)	.10

43 Jose Morales .10
44 Larry McWilliams .10
45 Enos Cabell .10
46 Rick Bosetti .10
47 Ken Brett .10
48 Dave Skaggs .10
49 Bob Shirley .10
50 Dave Lopes .10
51 Bill Robinson (DP) .10
52 Hector Cruz .10
53 Kevin Saucier .10
54 Ivan DeJesus .10
55 Mike Norris .10
56 Buck Martinez .10
57 Dave Roberts .10
58 Joel Youngblood .10
59 Dan Petry .10
60 Willie Randolph .10
61 Butch Wynegar .10
62 Joe Pettini .10
63 Steve Renko (DP) .10
64 Brian Asselstine .10
65 Scott McGregor .10
66 Royals Future Stars (Manny Castillo, Tim Ireland, Mike Jones) .10
67 Ken Kravec .10
68 Matt Alexander (DP) .10
69 Ed Halicki .10
70 Al Oliver (DP) .10
71 Hal Dues .10
72 Barry Evans (DP) .10
73 Doug Bair .10
74 Mike Hargrove .10
75 Reggie Smith .10
76 Mario Mendoza .10
77 Mike Barlow .10
78 Steve Dillard .10
79 Bruce Robbins .10
80 Rusty Staub .15
81 Dave Stapleton .10
82 Astros Future Stars (Danny Heep, Alan Knicely, Bobby Sprowl) (DP) .10
83 Mike Proly .10
84 Johnnie LeMaster .10
85 Mike Caldwell .10
86 Wayne Gross .10
87 Rick Camp .10
88 Joe Lefebvre .10
89 Darrell Jackson .10
90 Bake McBride .10
91 Tim Stoddard (DP) .10
92 Mike Easler .10
93 Ed Glynn (DP) .10
94 Harry Spilman (DP) .10
95 Jim Sundberg .10
96 A's Future Stars (Dave Beard), *(Ernie Camacho*, Pat Dempsey) .10
97 Chris Speier .10
98 Clint Hurdle .10
99 Eric Wilkins .10
100 Rod Carew 2.00
101 Benny Ayala .10
102 Dave Tobik .10
103 Jerry Martin .10
104 Terry Forster .10
105 Jose Cruz .10
106 Don Money .10
107 Rich Wortham .10
108 Bruce Benedict .10
109 Mike Scott .10
110 Carl Yastrzemski 2.00
111 Greg Minton .10
112 White Sox Future Stars (Rusty Kuntz, Fran Mullins, Leo Sutherland) .10
113 Mike Phillips .10
114 Tom Underwood .10
115 Roy Smalley .10
116 Joe Simpson .10
117 Pete Falcone .10
118 Kurt Bevacqua .10
119 Tippy Martinez .10
120 Larry Bowa .10
121 Larry Harlow .10
122 John Denny .10
123 Al Cowens .10
124 Jerry Garvin .10
125 Andre Dawson 1.00
126 *Charlie Leibrandt* .40
127 Rudy Law .10
128 Gary Allenson (DP) .10
129 Art Howe .10
130 Larry Gura .10
131 *Keith Moreland* .20
132 Tommy Boggs .10
133 Jeff Cox .10
134 Steve Mura .10
135 Gorman Thomas .10
136 Doug Capilla .10
137 Hosken Powell .10
138 *Rich Dotson* (DP) .20
139 Oscar Gamble .10
140 Bob Forsch .10
141 Miguel Dilone .10
142 Jackson Todd .10
143 Dan Meyer .10
144 Allen Ripley .10
145 Mickey Rivers .10
146 Bobby Castillo .10
147 Dale Berra .10
148 Randy Niemann .10
149 Joe Nolan .10
150 Mark Fidrych .15
151 Claudell Washington (DP) .10
152 John Urrea .10
153 Tom Poquette .10
154 Rick Langford .10
155 Chris Chambliss .10
156 Bob McClure .10
157 John Wathan .10
158 Fergie Jenkins .90
159 Brian Doyle .10
160 Garry Maddox .10
161 Dan Graham .10
162 Doug Corbett .10
163 Billy Almon .10
164 *Lamarr Hoyt (LaMarr)* .15
165 Tony Scott .10
166 Floyd Bannister .10
167 Terry Whitfield .10
168 Don Robinson (DP) .10
169 John Mayberry .10
170 Ross Grimsley .10
171 Gene Richards .10
172 Gary Woods .10
173 Bump Wills .10
174 Doug Rau .10
175 Dave Collins .10
176 Mike Krukow .10
177 Rick Peters .10
178 Jim Essian (DP) .10
179 Rudy May .10
180 Pete Rose 6.00
181 Elias Sosa .10
182 Bob Grich .10
183 Dick Davis (DP) .10
184 Jim Dwyer .10
185 Dennis Leonard .10
186 Wayne Nordhagen .10
187 Mike Parrott .10
188 Doug DeCinces .10
189 Craig Swan .10
190 Cesar Cedeno .10
191 Rick Sutcliffe .10
192 Braves Future Stars *(Terry Harper*, Ed Miller), *(Rafael Ramirez)* .10
193 Pete Vuckovich .10
194 *Rod Scurry* .10
195 Rich Murray .10
196 Duffy Dyer .10
197 Jim Kern .10
198 Jerry Dybzinski .10
199 Chuck Rainey .10
200 George Foster .15
201 Johnny Bench (Record Breaker) .45
202 Steve Carlton (Record Breaker) .25
203 Bill Gullickson (Record Breaker) .10
204 Ron LeFlore, Rodney Scott (Record Breaker) .10
205 Pete Rose (Record Breaker) 1.50
206 Mike Schmidt (Record Breaker) 1.00
207 Ozzie Smith (Record Breaker) 1.00
208 Willie Wilson (Record Breaker) .10
209 Dickie Thon (DP) .10
210 Jim Palmer 1.50
211 Derrel Thomas .10
212 Steve Nicosia .10
213 *Al Holland* .10
214 Angels Future Stars (Ralph Botting, Jim Dorsey, John Harris) .10
215 Larry Hisle .10
216 John Henry Johnson .10
217 Rich Hebner .10
218 Paul Splittorff .10
219 Ken Landreaux .10
220 Tom Seaver 2.00
221 Bob Davis .10
222 Jorge Orta .10
223 Roy Lee Jackson .10
224 Pat Zachry .10
225 Ruppert Jones .10
226 Manny Sanguillen (DP) .10
227 Fred Martinez .10
228 Tom Paciorek .10
229 Rollie Fingers .90
230 George Hendrick .10
231 Joe Beckwith .10
232 Mickey Klutts .10
233 Skip Lockwood .10
234 Lou Whitaker .10
235 Scott Sanderson .10
236 Mike Ivie .10
237 Charlie Moore .10
238 Willie Hernandez .10
239 Rick Miller (DP) .10
240 Nolan Ryan 10.00
241 Checklist 122-242 (DP) .10
242 Chet Lemon .10
243 Sal Butera .10
244 Cardinals Future Stars *(Tito Landrum*, Al Olmsted, Andy Rincon) .10
245 Ed Figueroa .10
246 Ed Ott (DP) .10
247 Glenn Hubbard (DP) .10
248 Joey McLaughlin .10
249 Larry Cox .10
250 Ron Guidry .20
251 Tom Brookens .10
252 Victor Cruz .10
253 Dave Bergman .10
254 Ozzie Smith 6.00
255 Mark Littell .10
256 Bombo Rivera .10
257 Rennie Stennett .10
258 *Joe Price* .10
259 Mets Future Stars (Juan Berenguer), *(Hubie Brooks)*, *(Mookie Wilson)* .75
260 Ron Cey .10
261 Rickey Henderson 9.00
262 Sammy Stewart .10
263 Brian Downing .10
264 Jim Norris .10
265 John Candelaria .10
266 Tom Herr .10
267 Stan Bahnsen .10
268 Jerry Royster .10
269 Ken Forsch .10
270 Greg Luzinski .10
271 Bill Castro .10
272 Bruce Kimm .10
273 Stan Papi .10
274 Craig Chamberlain .10
275 Dwight Evans .10
276 Dan Spillner .10
277 Alfredo Griffin .10
278 Rick Sofield .10
279 Bob Knepper .10
280 Ken Griffey .10
281 Fred Stanley .10
282 Mariners Future Stars (Rick Anderson, Greg Biercevicz, Rodney Craig) .10
283 Billy Sample .10
284 Brian Kingman .10
285 Jerry Turner .10
286 Dave Frost .10
287 Lenn Sakata .10
288 Bob Clark .10
289 Mickey Hatcher .10
290 Bob Boone (DP) .10
291 Aurelio Lopez .10
292 Mike Squires .10
293 *Charlie Lea* .15
294 Mike Tyson (DP) .10
295 Hal McRae .10
296 Bill Nahorodny (DP) .10
297 Bob Bailor .10
298 Buddy Solomon .10
299 Elliott Maddox .10
300 Paul Molitor 5.00
301 Matt Keough .10
302 Dodgers Future Stars *(Jack Perconte)*, *(Mike Scioscia)*, *(Fernando Valenzuela)* 2.00
303 Johnny Oates .10
304 John Castino .10
305 Ken Clay .10
306 Juan Beniquez (DP) .10
307 Gene Garber .10
308 Rick Manning .10
309 *Luis Salazar* .10
310 Vida Blue (DP) .10
311 Freddie Patek .10
312 Rick Rhoden .10
313 Luis Pujols .10
314 Rich Dauer .10
315 *Kirk Gibson* 3.00
316 Craig Minetto .10
317 Lonnie Smith .10
318 Steve Yeager .10
319 Rowland Office .10
320 Tom Burgmeier .10
321 *Leon Durham* .15
322 Neil Allen .10
323 Jim Morrison (DP) .10
324 Mike Willis .10
325 Ray Knight .10
326 Biff Pocoroba .10
327 Moose Haas .10
328 Twins Future Stars *(Dave Engle*, Greg Johnston, Gary Ward) .15
329 Joaquin Andujar .10
330 Frank White .10
331 Dennis Lamp .10
332 Lee Lacy (DP) .10
333 Sid Monge .10
334 Dane Iorg .10
335 Rick Cerone .10
336 Eddie Whitson .10
337 Lynn Jones .10
338 Checklist 243-363 .10
339 John Ellis .10
340 Bruce Kison .10
341 Dwayne Murphy .10
342 Eric Rasmussen (DP).10
343 Frank Taveras .10
344 Byron McLaughlin .10
345 Warren Cromartie .10
346 Larry Christenson (DP) .10
347 *Harold Baines* 7.00
348 Bob Sykes .10
349 Glenn Hoffman .10
350 J.R. Richard .15
351 Otto Velez .10
352 Dick Tidrow (DP) .10
353 Terry Kennedy .10
354 Mario Soto .10
355 Bob Horner .10
356 Padres Future Stars (George Stablein, Craig Stimac, Tom Tellmann) .10
357 Jim Slaton .10
358 Mark Wagner .10
359 Tom Hausman .10
360 Willie Wilson .10
361 Joe Strain .10
362 Bo Diaz .10
363 Geoff Zahn .10
364 *Mike Davis* .10
365 Graig Nettles (DP) .15
366 Mike Ramsey .10
367 Denny Martinez .10
368 Leon Roberts .10
369 Frank Tanana .10
370 Dave Winfield 4.00
371 Charlie Hough .10
372 Jay Johnstone .10
373 Pat Underwood .10
374 Tom Hutton .10
375 Dave Concepcion .10
376 Ron Reed .10
377 Jerry Morales .10
378 Dave Rader .10
379 Lary Sorensen .10
380 Willie Stargell 1.00
381 Cubs Future Stars (Carlos Lezcano, Steve Macko, Randy Martz) .10

382 *Paul Mirabella* .10
383 Eric Soderholm (DP) .10
384 Mike Sadek .10
385 Joe Sambito .10
386 Dave Edwards .10
387 Phil Niekro .90
388 Andre Thornton .10
389 Marty Pattin .10
390 Cesar Geronimo .10
391 Dave Lemanczyk (DP) .10
392 Lance Parrish .10
393 Broderick Perkins .10
394 Woodie Fryman .10
395 Scot Thompson .10
396 Bill Campbell .10
397 Julio Cruz .10
398 Ross Baumgarten .10
399 Orioles Future Stars (*Mike Boddicker*, Mark Corey), (*Floyd Rayford*) .20
400 Reggie Jackson 2.00
401 A.L. Championships (Royals Sweep Yankees) .75
402 N.L. Championships (Phillies Squeak Past Astros) .25
403 World Series (Phillies Beat Royals In 6) .25
404 World Series Summary (Phillies Win First World Series) .25
405 Nino Espinosa .10
406 Dickie Noles .10
407 Ernie Whitt .10
408 Fernando Arroyo .10
409 Larry Herndon .10
410 Bert Campaneris .10
411 Terry Puhl .10
412 *Britt Burns* .10
413 Tony Bernazard .10
414 John Pacella (DP) .10
415 Ben Oglivie .10
416 Gary Alexander .10
417 Dan Schatzeder .10
418 Bobby Brown .10
419 Tom Hume .10
420 Keith Hernandez .10
421 Bob Stanley .10
422 Dan Ford .10
423 Shane Rawley .10
424 Yankees Future Stars (Tim Lollar, Bruce Robinson, Dennis Werth) .10
425 Al Bumbry .10
426 Warren Brusstar .10
427 John D'Acquisto .10
428 John Stearns .10
429 Mick Kelleher .10
430 Jim Bibby .10
431 Dave Roberts .10
432 Len Barker .10
433 Rance Mulliniks .10
434 Roger Erickson .10
435 Jim Spencer .10
436 Gary Lucas .10
437 Mike Heath (DP) .10
438 John Montefusco .10
439 Denny Walling .10
440 Jerry Reuss .10
441 Ken Reitz .10
442 Ron Pruitt .10
443 Jim Beattie (DP) .10
444 Garth Iorg .10
445 Ellis Valentine .10
446 Checklist 364-484 .10
447 Junior Kennedy (DP) .10
448 Tim Corcoran .10
449 Paul Mitchell .10
450 Dave Kingman (DP) .10
451 Indians Future Stars (Chris Bando, Tom Brennan, Sandy Wihtol) .10
452 Renie Martin .10
453 Rob Wilfong (DP) .10
454 Andy Hassler .10
455 Rick Burleson .10
456 *Jeff Reardon* 1.50
457 Mike Lum .10
458 Randy Jones .10
459 Greg Gross .10
460 Rich Gossage .10
461 Dave McKay .10
462 Jack Brohamer .10
463 Milt May .10
464 Adrian Devine .10
465 Bill Russell .10
466 Bob Molinaro .10
467 Dave Stieb .10
468 Johnny Wockenfuss .10
469 Jeff Leonard .10
470 Manny Trillo .10
471 Mike Vail .10
472 Dyar Miller (DP) .10
473 Jose Cardenal .10
474 Mike LaCoss .10
475 Buddy Bell .10
476 Jerry Koosman .10
477 Luis Gomez .10
478 Juan Eichelberger .10
479 Expos Future Stars (*Bobby Pate*), (*Tim Raines*), (*Roberto Ramos*) 4.00
480 Carlton Fisk 2.00
481 Bob Lacey (DP) .10
482 Jim Gantner .10
483 Mike Griffin .10
484 Max Venable (DP) .10
485 Garry Templeton .10
486 Marc Hill .10
487 Dewey Robinson .10
488 *Damaso Garcia* .10
489 John Littlefield (photo actually Mark Riggins) .10
490 Eddie Murray 5.00
491 Gordy Pladson .10
492 Barry Foote .10
493 Dan Quisenberry .10
494 *Bob Walk* .20
495 Dusty Baker .15
496 Paul Dade .10
497 Fred Norman .10
498 Pat Putnam .10
499 Frank Pastore .10
500 Jim Rice .25
501 Tim Foli (DP) .10
502 Giants Future Stars (Chris Bourjos, Al Hargesheimer, Mike Rowland) .10
503 Steve McCatty .10
504 Dale Murphy 1.00
505 Jason Thompson .10
506 Phil Huffman .10
507 Jamie Quirk .10
508 Rob Dressler .10
509 Pete Mackanin .10
510 Lee Mazzilli .10
511 Wayne Garland .10
512 Gary Thomasson .10
513 Frank LaCorte .10
514 George Riley .10
515 Robin Yount 4.00
516 Doug Bird .10
517 Richie Zisk .10
518 Grant Jackson .10
519 John Tamargo (DP) .10
520 Steve Stone .10
521 Sam Mejias .10
522 Mike Colbern .10
523 John Fulgham .10
524 Willie Aikens .10
525 Mike Torrez .10
526 Phillies Future Stars (Marty Bystrom, Jay Loviglio, Jim Wright) .10
527 Danny Goodwin .10
528 Gary Matthews .10
529 Dave LaRoche .10
530 Steve Garvey .75
531 John Curtis .10
532 Bill Stein .10
533 Jesus Figueroa .10
534 *Dave Smith* .10
535 Omar Moreno .10
536 Bob Owchinko (DP) .10
537 Ron Hodges .10
538 Tom Griffin .10
539 Rodney Scott .10
540 Mike Schmidt (DP) 4.00
541 Steve Swisher .10
542 Larry Bradford (DP) .10
543 Terry Crowley .10
544 Rich Gale .10
545 Johnny Grubb .10
546 Paul Moskau .10
547 Mario Guerrero .10
548 Dave Goltz .10
549 Jerry Remy .10
550 Tommy John .20
551 Pirates Future Stars (*Vance Law*), (*Tony Pena*), (*Pascual Perez*) .75
552 Steve Trout .10
553 Tim Blackwell .10
554 Bert Blyleven .10
555 Cecil Cooper .10
556 Jerry Mumphrey .10
557 Chris Knapp .10
558 Barry Bonnell .10
559 Willie Montanez .10
560 Joe Morgan 2.00
561 Dennis Littlejohn .10
562 Checklist 485-605 .10
563 Jim Kaat .25
564 Ron Hassey (DP) .10
565 Burt Hooton .10
566 Del Unser .10
567 Mark Bomback .10
568 Dave Revering .10
569 Al Williams (DP) .10
570 Ken Singleton .10
571 Todd Cruz .10
572 Jack Morris .25
573 Phil Garner .10
574 Bill Caudill .10
575 Tony Perez 1.00
576 Reggie Cleveland .10
577 Blue Jays Future Stars (Luis Leal, Brian Milner), (*Ken Schrom*) .10
578 *Bill Gullickson* .20
579 Tim Flannery .10
580 Don Baylor .15
581 Roy Howell .10
582 Gaylord Perry .90
583 Larry Milbourne .10
584 Randy Lerch .10
585 Amos Otis .10
586 Silvio Martinez .10
587 Jeff Newman .10
588 Gary Lavelle .10
589 Lamar Johnson .10
590 Bruce Sutter .10
591 John Lowenstein .10
592 Steve Comer .10
593 Steve Kemp .10
594 Preston Hanna (DP) .10
595 Butch Hobson .10
596 Jerry Augustine .10
597 Rafael Landestoy .10
598 George Vukovich (DP) .10
599 Dennis Kinney .10
600 Johnny Bench 3.00
601 Don Aase .10
602 Bobby Murcer .10
603 John Verhoeven .10
604 Rob Picciolo .10
605 Don Sutton .90
606 Reds Future Stars (Bruce Berenyi, Geoff Combe, Paul Householder) (DP) .10
607 Dave Palmer .10
608 Greg Pryor .10
609 Lynn McGlothen .10
610 Darrell Porter .10
611 Rick Matula (DP) .10
612 Duane Kuiper .10
613 Jim Anderson .10
614 Dave Rozema .10
615 Rick Dempsey .10
616 Rick Wise .10
617 Craig Reynolds .10
618 John Milner .10
619 Steve Henderson .10
620 Dennis Eckersley .50
621 Tom Donohue .10
622 Randy Moffitt .10
623 Sal Bando .10
624 Bob Welch .10
625 Bill Buckner .15
626 Tigers Future Stars (Dave Steffen, Jerry Ujdur, Roger Weaver) .10
627 Luis Tiant .10
628 Vic Correll .10
629 Tony Armas .10
630 Steve Carlton 2.00
631 Ron Jackson .10
632 Alan Bannister .10
633 Bill Lee .10
634 Doug Flynn .10
635 Bobby Bonds .10
636 Al Hrabosky .10
637 Jerry Narron .10
638 Checklist 606 .10
639 Carney Lansford .10
640 Dave Parker .25
641 Mark Belanger .10
642 Vern Ruhle .10
643 *Lloyd Moseby* .20
644 Ramon Aviles (DP) .10
645 Rick Reuschel .10
646 Marvis Foley .10
647 Dick Drago .10
648 Darrell Evans .10
649 Manny Sarmiento .10
650 Bucky Dent .10
651 Pedro Guerrero .10
652 John Montague .10
653 Bill Fahey .10
654 Ray Burris .10
655 Dan Driessen .10
656 Jon Matlack .10
657 Mike Cubbage (DP) .10
658 Milt Wilcox .10
659 Brewers Future Stars (John Flinn, Ed Romero, Ned Yost) .10
660 Gary Carter 1.00
661 Orioles Team (Earl Weaver) .25
662 Red Sox Team (Ralph Houk) .20
663 Angels Team (Jim Fregosi) .10
664 White Sox Team (Tony LaRussa) .25
665 Indians Team (Dave Garcia) .10
666 Tigers Team (Sparky Anderson) .45
667 Royals Team (Jim Frey) .10
668 Brewers Team (Bob Rodgers) .10
669 Twins Team (John Goryl) .10
670 Yankees Team (Gene Michael) .25
671 A's Team (Billy Martin) .25
672 Mariners Team (Maury Wills) .20
673 Rangers Team (Don Zimmer) .20
674 Blue Jays Team (Bobby Mattick) .10
675 Braves Team (Bobby Cox) .25
676 Cubs Team (Joe Amalfitano) .10
677 Reds Team (John McNamara) .10
678 Astros Team (Bill Virdon) .10
679 Dodgers Team (Tom Lasorda) .40
680 Expos Team (Dick Williams) .20
681 Mets Team (Joe Torre) .35
682 Phillies Team (Dallas Green) .25
683 Pirates Team (Chuck Tanner) .10
684 Cardinals Team (Whitey Herzog) .25
685 Padres Team (Frank Howard) .20
686 Giants Team (Dave Bristol) .10
687 Jeff Jones .10
688 Kiko Garcia .10
689 Red Sox Future Stars (*Bruce Hurst*, Keith MacWhorter), (*Reid Nichols*) .60
690 Bob Watson .10
691 Dick Ruthven .10
692 Lenny Randle .10
693 *Steve Howe* .20
694 Bud Harrelson (DP) .10
695 Kent Tekulve .10
696 Alan Ashby .10
697 Rick Waits .10

No.	Player	Price
698	Mike Jorgensen	.10
699	Glenn Abbott	.10
700	George Brett	6.00
701	Joe Rudi	.10
702	George Medich	.10
703	Alvis Woods	.10
704	Bill Travers (DP)	.10
705	Ted Simmons	.10
706	Dave Ford	.10
707	Dave Cash	.10
708	Doyle Alexander	.10
709	Alan Trammell (DP)	.25
710	Ron LeFlore (DP)	.10
711	Joe Ferguson	.10
712	Bill Bonham	.10
713	Bill North	.10
714	Pete Redfern	.10
715	Bill Madlock	.10
716	Glenn Borgmann	.10
717	Jim Barr (DP)	.10
718	Larry Biittner	.10
719	Sparky Lyle	.10
720	Fred Lynn	.10
721	Toby Harrah	.10
722	Joe Niekro	.10
723	Bruce Bochte	.10
724	Lou Piniella	.15
725	Steve Rogers	.10
726	Rick Monday	.10

1981 Topps Stickers

The 262 stickers in this full-color set measure 1-15/16" x 2-9/16" and are numbered on both the front and back. They were produced for Topps by the Panini Company of Italy. The set includes a series of "All-Star" stickers printed on silver or gold "foil". An album to house the stickers was also available.

	MT
Complete Set (262):	15.00
Common Player:	.05
Sticker Album:	2.00
Wax Pack (5):	.25
Wax Box (100):	10.00

No.	Player	Price
1	Steve Stone	.05
2	Tommy John, Mike Norris	.05
3	Rudy May	.05
4	Mike Norris	.05
5	Len Barker	.05
6	Mike Norris	.05
7	Dan Quisenberry	.05
8	Rich Gossage	.05
9	George Brett	.30
10	Cecil Cooper	.05
11	Reggie Jackson, Ben Oglivie	.05
12	Gorman Thomas	.05
13	Cecil Cooper	.05
14	George Brett, Ben Oglivie	.05
15	Rickey Henderson	.25
16	Willie Wilson	.05
17	Bill Buckner	.05
18	Keith Hernandez	.05
19	Mike Schmidt	.30
20	Bob Horner	.05
21	Mike Schmidt	.30
22	George Hendrick	.05
23	Ron LeFlore	.05
24	Omar Moreno	.05
25	Steve Carlton	.20
26	Joe Niekro	.05
27	Don Sutton	.20
28	Steve Carlton	.20
29	Steve Carlton	.20
30	Nolan Ryan	.50
31	Rollie Fingers, Tom Hume	.05
32	Bruce Sutter	.05
33	Ken Singleton	.05
34	Eddie Murray	.25
35	Al Bumbry	.05
36	Rich Dauer	.05
37	Scott McGregor	.05
38	Rick Dempsey	.05
39	Jim Palmer	.20
40	Steve Stone	.05
41	Jim Rice	.15
42	Fred Lynn	.05
43	Carney Lansford	.05
44	Tony Perez	.25
45	Carl Yastrzemski	.30
46	Carlton Fisk	.25
47	Dave Stapleton	.05
48	Dennis Eckersley	.10
49	Rod Carew	.25
50	Brian Downing	.05
51	Don Baylor	.05
52	Rick Burleson	.05
53	Bobby Grich	.05
54	Butch Hobson	.05
55	Andy Hassler	.05
56	Frank Tanana	.05
57	Chet Lemon	.05
58	Lamar Johnson	.05
59	Wayne Nordhagen	.05
60	Jim Morrison	.05
61	Bob Molinaro	.05
62	Rich Dotson	.05
63	Britt Burns	.05
64	Ed Farmer	.05
65	Toby Harrah	.05
66	Joe Charboneau	.25
67	Miguel Dilone	.05
68	Mike Hargrove	.05
69	Rick Manning	.05
70	Andre Thornton	.05
71	Ron Hassey	.05
72	Len Barker	.05
73	Lance Parrish	.05
74	Steve Kemp	.05
75	Alan Trammell	.05
76	Champ Summers	.05
77	Rick Peters	.05
78	Kirk Gibson	.05
79	Johnny Wockenfuss	.05
80	Jack Morris	.05
81	Willie Wilson	.05
82	George Brett	.30
83	Frank White	.05
84	Willie Aikens	.05
85	Clint Hurdle	.05
86	Hal McRae	.05
87	Dennis Leonard	.05
88	Larry Gura	.05
89	American League Pennant Winner (Kansas City Royals Team)	.05
90	American League Pennant Winner (Kansas City Royals Team)	.05
91	Paul Molitor	.25
92	Ben Oglivie	.05
93	Cecil Cooper	.05
94	Ted Simmons	.05
95	Robin Yount	.25
96	Gorman Thomas	.05
97	Mike Caldwell	.05
98	Moose Haas	.05
99	John Castino	.05
100	Roy Smalley	.05
101	Ken Landreaux	.05
102	Butch Wynegar	.05
103	Ron Jackson	.05
104	Jerry Koosman	.05
105	Roger Erickson	.05
106	Doug Corbett	.05
107	Reggie Jackson	.30
108	Willie Randolph	.05
109	Rick Cerone	.05
110	Bucky Dent	.05
111	Dave Winfield	.25
112	Ron Guidry	.10
113	Rich Gossage	.05
114	Tommy John	.10
115	Rickey Henderson	.25
116	Tony Armas	.05
117	Dave Revering	.05
118	Wayne Gross	.05
119	Dwayne Murphy	.05
120	Jeff Newman	.05
121	Rick Langford	.05
122	Mike Norris	.05
123	Bruce Bochte	.05
124	Tom Paciorek	.05
125	Dan Meyer	.05
126	Julio Cruz	.05
127	Richie Zisk	.05
128	Floyd Bannister	.05
129	Shane Rawley	.05
130	Buddy Bell	.05
131	Al Oliver	.05
132	Mickey Rivers	.05
133	Jim Sundberg	.05
134	Bump Wills	.05
135	Jon Matlack	.05
136	Danny Darwin	.05
137	Damaso Garcia	.05
138	Otto Velez	.05
139	John Mayberry	.05
140	Alfredo Griffin	.05
141	Alvis Woods	.05
142	Dave Stieb	.05
143	Jim Clancy	.05
144	Gary Matthews	.05
145	Bob Horner	.05
146	Dale Murphy	.25
147	Chris Chambliss	.05
148	Phil Niekro	.20
149	Glenn Hubbard	.05
150	Rick Camp	.05
151	Dave Kingman	.05
152	Bill Caudill	.05
153	Bill Buckner	.05
154	Barry Foote	.05
155	Mike Tyson	.05
156	Ivan DeJesus	.05
157	Rick Reuschel	.05
158	Ken Reitz	.05
159	George Foster	.05
160	Johnny Bench	.30
161	Dave Concepcion	.05
162	Dave Collins	.05
163	Ken Griffey	.05
164	Dan Driessen	.05
165	Tom Seaver	.25
166	Tom Hume	.05
167	Cesar Cedeno	.05
168	Rafael Landestoy	.05
169	Jose Cruz	.05
170	Art Howe	.05
171	Terry Puhl	.05
172	Joe Sambito	.05
173	Nolan Ryan	.50
174	Joe Niekro	.05
175	Dave Lopes	.05
176	Steve Garvey	.15
177	Ron Cey	.05
178	Reggie Smith	.05
179	Bill Russell	.05
180	Burt Hooton	.05
181	Jerry Reuss	.05
182	Dusty Baker	.05
183	Larry Parrish	.05
184	Gary Carter	.20
185	Rodney Scott	.05
186	Ellis Valentine	.05
187	Andre Dawson	.20
188	Warren Cromartie	.05
189	Chris Speier	.05
190	Steve Rogers	.05
191	Lee Mazzilli	.05
192	Doug Flynn	.05
193	Steve Henderson	.05
194	John Stearns	.05
195	Joel Youngblood	.05
196	Frank Taveras	.05
197	Pat Zachry	.05
198	Neil Allen	.05
199	Mike Schmidt	.30
200	Pete Rose	.50
201	Larry Bowa	.05
202	Bake McBride	.05
203	Bob Boone	.05
204	Garry Maddox	.05
205	Tug McGraw	.05
206	Steve Carlton	.20
207	National League Pennant Winner (Philadelphia Phillies Team)	.05
208	National League Pennant Winner (Philadelphia Phillies Team)	.05
209	Phil Garner	.05
210	Dave Parker	.05
211	Omar Moreno	.05
212	Mike Easler	.05
213	Bill Madlock	.05
214	Ed Ott	.05
215	Willie Stargell	.25
216	Jim Bibby	.05
217	Garry Templeton	.05
218	Sixto Lezcano	.05
219	Keith Hernandez	.05
220	George Hendrick	.05
221	Bruce Sutter	.05
222	Ken Oberkfell	.05
223	Tony Scott	.05
224	Darrell Porter	.05
225	Gene Richards	.05
226	Broderick Perkins	.05
227	Jerry Mumphrey	.05
228	Luis Salazar	.05
229	Jerry Turner	.05
230	Ozzie Smith	.30
231	John Curtis	.05
232	Rick Wise	.05
233	Terry Whitfield	.05
234	Jack Clark	.05
235	Darrell Evans	.05
236	Larry Herndon	.05
237	Milt May	.05
238	Greg Minton	.05
239	Vida Blue	.05
240	Eddie Whitson	.05
241	Cecil Cooper	.05
242	Willie Randolph	.05
243	George Brett	.30
244	Robin Yount	.25
245	Reggie Jackson	.30
246	Al Oliver	.05
247	Willie Wilson	.05
248	Rick Cerone	.05
249	Steve Stone	.05
250	Tommy John	.10
251	Rich Gossage	.05
252	Steve Garvey	.15
253	Phil Garner	.05
254	Mike Schmidt	.30
255	Garry Templeton	.05
256	George Hendrick	.05
257	Dave Parker	.05
258	Cesar Cedeno	.05
259	Gary Carter	.20
260	Jim Bibby	.05
261	Steve Carlton	.20
262	Tug McGraw	.05

1981 Topps Traded

The 132 cards in this extension set are numbered from 727 to 858, technically making them a high-numbered series of the regular Topps set. The set was not packaged in gum packs, but rather placed in a specially designed red box and sold through baseball card dealers only. While many complained about the method, the fact remains, even at higher prices, the set has done well for its owners as it features not only mid-season trades, but also single-player rookie cards of some of the hottest prospects. The cards measure 2-1/2" x 3-1/2".

MT
Complete Set (132): 20.00
Common Player: .15
727 Danny Ainge 3.00
728 Doyle Alexander .15
729 Gary Alexander .15
730 Billy Almon .15
731 Joaquin Andujar .15
732 Bob Bailor .15
733 Juan Beniquez .15
734 Dave Bergman .15
735 Tony Bernazard .15
736 Larry Biittner .15
737 Doug Bird .15
738 Bert Blyleven .30
739 Mark Bomback .15
740 Bobby Bonds .30
741 Rick Bosetti .15
742 Hubie Brooks .15
743 Rick Burleson .15
744 Ray Burris .15
745 Jeff Burroughs .15
746 Enos Cabell .15
747 Ken Clay .15
748 Mark Clear .15
749 Larry Cox .15
750 Hector Cruz .15
751 Victor Cruz .15
752 Mike Cubbage .15
753 Dick Davis .15
754 Brian Doyle .15
755 Dick Drago .15
756 Leon Durham .15
757 Jim Dwyer .15
758 Dave Edwards .15
759 Jim Essian .15
760 Bill Fahey .15
761 Rollie Fingers 2.00
762 Carlton Fisk 3.00
763 Barry Foote .15
764 Ken Forsch .15
765 Kiko Garcia .15
766 Cesar Geronimo .15
767 Gary Gray .15
768 Mickey Hatcher .15
769 Steve Henderson .15
770 Marc Hill .15
771 Butch Hobson .15
772 Rick Honeycutt .15
773 Roy Howell .15
774 Mike Ivie .15
775 Roy Lee Jackson .15
776 Cliff Johnson .15
777 Randy Jones .15
778 Ruppert Jones .15
779 Mick Kelleher .15
780 Terry Kennedy .15
781 Dave Kingman .15
782 Bob Knepper .15
783 Ken Kravec .15
784 Bob Lacey .15
785 Dennis Lamp .15
786 Rafael Landestoy .15
787 Ken Landreaux .15
788 Carney Lansford .15
789 Dave LaRoche .15
790 Joe Lefebvre .15
791 Ron LeFlore .15
792 Randy Lerch .15
793 Sixto Lezcano .15
794 John Littlefield .15
795 Mike Lum .15
796 Greg Luzinski .15
797 Fred Lynn .15
798 Jerry Martin .15
799 Buck Martinez .15
800 Gary Matthews .15
801 Mario Mendoza .15
802 Larry Milbourne .15
803 Rick Miller .15
804 John Montefusco .15
805 Jerry Morales .15
806 Jose Morales .15
807 Joe Morgan 2.00
808 Jerry Mumphrey .15
809 *Gene Nelson* .15
810 Ed Ott .15
811 Bob Owchinko .15
812 Gaylord Perry 2.00
813 Mike Phillips .15
814 Darrell Porter .15
815 Mike Proly .15
816 Tim Raines 4.00
817 Lenny Randle .15
818 Doug Rau .15
819 Jeff Reardon .15
820 Ken Reitz .15
821 Steve Renko .15
822 Rick Reuschel .15
823 Dave Revering .15
824 Dave Roberts .15
825 Leon Roberts .15
826 Joe Rudi .15
827 Kevin Saucier .15
828 Tony Scott .15
829 Bob Shirley .15
830 Ted Simmons .15
831 Lary Sorensen .15
832 Jim Spencer .15
833 Harry Spilman .15
834 Fred Stanley .15
835 Rusty Staub .30
836 Bill Stein .15
837 Joe Strain .15
838 Bruce Sutter .15
839 Don Sutton 2.00
840 Steve Swisher .15
841 Frank Tanana .15
842 Gene Tenace .15
843 Jason Thompson .15
844 Dickie Thon .15
845 Bill Travers .15
846 Tom Underwood .15
847 John Urrea .15
848 Mike Vail .15
849 Ellis Valentine .15
850 Fernando Valenzuela 1.50
851 Pete Vuckovich .15
852 Mark Wagner .15
853 Bob Walk .15
854 Claudell Washington .15
855 Dave Winfield 4.00
856 Geoff Zahn .15
857 Richie Zisk .15
858 Checklist 727-858 .05

1982 Topps

At 792 cards, this was the largest issue produced up to that time, eliminating the need for double-printed cards. The 2-1/2" x 3-1/2" cards feature a front color photo with a pair of stripes down the left side. Under the player's photo are found his name, team and position. A facsimile autograph runs across the front of the picture. Specialty cards include great performances of the previous season, All-Stars, statistical leaders and "In Action" cards (indicated by "IA" in listings below). Managers and hitting/pitching leaders have cards, while rookies are shown as "Future Stars" on group cards.

MT
Complete Set (792): 80.00
Common Player: .10
Wax Pack (15): 6.00
Wax Box (36): 170.00
Cello Pack (28): 6.00
Cello Box (24): 180.00
Grocery Rack (36): 12.00
Rack Pack (51): 15.00
Rack Box (24): 350.00
Vending Box (500): 95.00
1 Steve Carlton (1981 Highlight) .25
2 Ron Davis (1981 Highlight) .10
3 Tim Raines (1981 Highlight) .10
4 Pete Rose (1981 Highlight) .75
5 Nolan Ryan (1981 Highlight) 3.00
6 Fernando Valenzuela (1981 Highlight) .10
7 Scott Sanderson .10
8 Rich Dauer .10
9 Ron Guidry .15
10 Ron Guidry (In Action) .10
11 Gary Alexander .10
12 Moose Haas .10
13 Lamar Johnson .10
14 Steve Howe .10
15 Ellis Valentine .10
16 Steve Comer .10
17 Darrell Evans .10
18 Fernando Arroyo .10
19 Ernie Whitt .10
20 Garry Maddox .10
21 Orioles Future Stars *(Bob Bonner)*, *(Cal Ripken, Jr.)*, *(Jeff Schneider)* 45.00
22 Jim Beattie .10
23 Willie Hernandez .10
24 Dave Frost .10
25 Jerry Remy .10
26 Jorge Orta .10
27 Tom Herr .10
28 John Urrea .10
29 Dwayne Murphy .10
30 Tom Seaver 1.50
31 Tom Seaver (In Action) 1.00
32 Gene Garber .10
33 Jerry Morales .10
34 Joe Sambito .10
35 Willie Aikens .10
36 Rangers Batting/Pitching Leaders (George Medich, Al Oliver) .10
37 Dan Graham .10
38 Charlie Lea .10
39 Lou Whitaker .10
40 Dave Parker .10
41 Dave Parker (In Action) .10
42 Rick Sofield .10
43 Mike Cubbage .10
44 Britt Burns .10
45 Rick Cerone .10
46 Jerry Augustine .10
47 Jeff Leonard .10
48 Bobby Castillo .10
49 Alvis Woods .10
50 Buddy Bell .10
51 Chicago Cubs Future Stars *(Jay Howell)*, *(Carlos Lezcano)*, *(Ty Waller)* .40
52 Larry Andersen .10
53 Greg Gross .10
54 Ron Hassey .10
55 Rick Burleson .10
56 Mark Littell .10
57 Craig Reynolds .10
58 John D'Acquisto .10
59 *Rich Gedman* .10
60 Tony Armas .10
61 Tommy Boggs .10
62 Mike Tyson .10
63 Mario Soto .10
64 Lynn Jones .10
65 Terry Kennedy .10
66 Astros Batting/Pitching Leaders (Art Howe, Nolan Ryan) .75
67 Rich Gale .10
68 Roy Howell .10
69 Al Williams .10
70 Tim Raines .50
71 Roy Lee Jackson .10
72 Rick Auerbach .10
73 Buddy Solomon .10
74 Bob Clark .10
75 Tommy John .20
76 Greg Pryor .10
77 Miguel Dilone .10
78 George Medich .10
79 Bob Bailor .10
80 Jim Palmer 1.00
81 Jim Palmer (In Action) .30
82 Bob Welch .10
83 Yankees Future Stars *(Steve Balboni)*, *(Andy McGaffigan)*, *(Andre Robertson)* .15
84 Rennie Stennett .10
85 Lynn McGlothen .10
86 Dane Iorg .10
87 Matt Keough .10
88 Biff Pocoroba .10
89 Steve Henderson .10
90 Nolan Ryan 10.00
91 Carney Lansford .10
92 Brad Havens .10
93 Larry Hisle .10
94 Andy Hassler .10
95 Ozzie Smith 3.00
96 Royals Batting/Pitching Leaders (George Brett, Larry Gura) .35
97 Paul Moskau .10
98 Terry Bulling .10
99 Barry Bonnell .10
100 Mike Schmidt 3.00
101 Mike Schmidt (In Action) 1.50
102 Dan Briggs .10
103 Bob Lacey .10
104 Rance Mulliniks .10
105 Kirk Gibson .10
106 Enrique Romo .10
107 Wayne Krenchicki .10
108 Bob Sykes .10
109 Dave Revering .10
110 Carlton Fisk 1.00
111 Carlton Fisk (In Action) .65
112 Billy Sample .10
113 Steve McCatty .10
114 Ken Landreaux .10
115 Gaylord Perry .75
116 Jim Wohlford .10
117 Rawly Eastwick .10
118 Expos Future Stars *(Terry Francona)*, *(Brad Mills)*, *(Bryn Smith)* .20
119 Joe Pittman .10
120 Gary Lucas .10
121 Ed Lynch .10
122 Jamie Easterly .10
123 Danny Goodwin .10
124 Reid Nichols .10
125 Danny Ainge 1.00
126 Braves Batting/Pitching Leaders (Rick Mahler, Claudell Washington) .10
127 Lonnie Smith .10
128 Frank Pastore .10
129 Checklist 1-132 .10
130 Julio Cruz .10
131 Stan Bahnsen .10
132 Lee May .10
133 Pat Underwood .10
134 Dan Ford .10
135 Andy Rincon .10
136 Lenn Sakata .10
137 George Cappuzzello .10
138 Tony Pena .10
139 Jeff Jones .10
140 Ron LeFlore .10
141 Indians Future Stars (Chris Bando, Tom Brennan), *(Von Hayes)* .20
142 Dave LaRoche .10

143 Mookie Wilson .10
144 Fred Breining .10
145 Bob Horner .10
146 Mike Griffin .10
147 Denny Walling .10
148 Mickey Klutts .10
149 Pat Putnam .10
150 Ted Simmons .10
151 Dave Edwards .10
152 Ramon Aviles .10
153 Roger Erickson .10
154 Dennis Werth .10
155 Otto Velez .10
156 A's Batting/Pitching Leaders (Rickey Henderson, Steve McCatty) .10
157 Steve Crawford .10
158 Brian Downing .10
159 Larry Biittner .10
160 Luis Tiant .10
161 Batting Leaders (Carney Lansford, Bill Madlock) .10
162 Home Run Leaders (Tony Armas, Dwight Evans, Bobby Grich, Eddie Murray, Mike Schmidt) .25
163 RBI Leaders (Eddie Murray, Mike Schmidt) .40
164 Stolen Base Leaders (Rickey Henderson, Tim Raines) .35
165 Victory Leaders (Denny Martinez, Steve McCatty, Jack Morris, Tom Seaver, Pete Vuckovich) .10
166 Strikeout Leaders (Len Barker, Fernando Valenzuela) .10
167 ERA Leaders (Steve McCatty, Nolan Ryan) 1.50
168 Leading Relievers (Rollie Fingers, Bruce Sutter) .10
169 Charlie Leibrandt .10
170 Jim Bibby .10
171 Giants Future Stars *(Bob Brenly)*, *(Chili Davis)*, *(Bob Tufts)* 3.00
172 Bill Gullickson .10
173 Jamie Quirk .10
174 Dave Ford .10
175 Jerry Mumphrey .10
176 Dewey Robinson .10
177 John Ellis .10
178 Dyar Miller .10
179 Steve Garvey .75
180 Steve Garvey (In Action) .30
181 Silvio Martinez .10
182 Larry Herndon .10
183 Mike Proly .10
184 Mick Kelleher .10
185 Phil Niekro 1.00
186 Cardinals Batting/Pitching Leaders (Bob Forsch, Keith Hernandez) .10
187 Jeff Newman .10
188 Randy Martz .10
189 Glenn Hoffman .10
190 J.R. Richard .15
191 *Tim Wallach* 2.50
192 Broderick Perkins .10
193 Darrell Jackson .10
194 Mike Vail .10
195 Paul Molitor 2.50
196 Willie Upshaw .10
197 Shane Rawley .10
198 Chris Speier .10
199 Don Aase .10
200 George Brett 4.00
201 George Brett (In Action) 3.00
202 Rick Manning .10
203 Blue Jays Future Stars *(Jesse Barfield*, Brian Milner, Boomer Wells) .50
204 Gary Roenicke .10
205 Neil Allen .10
206 Tony Bernazard .10
207 Rod Scurry .10
208 Bobby Murcer .10
209 Gary Lavelle .10
210 Keith Hernandez .10
211 Dan Petry .10
212 Mario Mendoza .10
213 *Dave Stewart* 4.00
214 Brian Asselstine .10
215 Mike Krukow .10
216 White Sox Batting/Pitching Leaders (Dennis Lamp, Chet Lemon) .10
217 Bo McLaughlin .10
218 Dave Roberts .10
219 John Curtis .10
220 Manny Trillo .10
221 Jim Slaton .10
222 Butch Wynegar .10
223 Lloyd Moseby .10
224 Bruce Bochte .10
225 Mike Torrez .10
226 Checklist 133-264 .10
227 Ray Burris .10
228 Sam Mejias .10
229 Geoff Zahn .10
230 Willie Wilson .10
231 Phillies Future Stars *(Mark Davis)*, *(Bob Dernier)*, *(Ozzie Virgil)* .20
232 Terry Crowley .10
233 Duane Kuiper .10
234 Ron Hodges .10
235 Mike Easler .10
236 John Martin .10
237 Rusty Kuntz .10
238 Kevin Saucier .10
239 Jon Matlack .10
240 Bucky Dent .10
241 Bucky Dent (In Action) .10
242 Milt May .10
243 Bob Owchinko .10
244 Rufino Linares .10
245 Ken Reitz .10
246 Mets Batting/Pitching Leaders (Hubie Brooks, Mike Scott) .10
247 Pedro Guerrero .10
248 Frank LaCorte .10
249 Tim Flannery .10
250 Tug McGraw .10
251 Fred Lynn .10
252 Fred Lynn (In Action) .10
253 Chuck Baker .10
254 *George Bell* 1.00
255 Tony Perez .75
256 Tony Perez (In Action) .10
257 Larry Harlow .10
258 Bo Diaz .10
259 Rodney Scott .10
260 Bruce Sutter .10
261 Tigers Future Stars (Howard Bailey, Marty Castillo, Dave Rucker) .10
262 Doug Bair .10
263 Victor Cruz .10
264 Dan Quisenberry .10
265 Al Bumbry .10
266 Rick Leach .10
267 Kurt Bevacqua .10
268 Rickey Keeton .10
269 Jim Essian .10
270 Rusty Staub .15
271 Larry Bradford .10
272 Bump Wills .10
273 Doug Bird .10
274 *Bob Ojeda* .50
275 Bob Watson .10
276 Angels Batting/Pitching Leaders (Rod Carew, Ken Forsch) .25
277 Terry Puhl .10
278 John Littlefield .10
279 Bill Russell .10
280 Ben Oglivie .10
281 John Verhoeven .10
282 Ken Macha .10
283 Brian Allard .10
284 Bob Grich .10
285 Sparky Lyle .10
286 Bill Fahey .10
287 Alan Bannister .10
288 Garry Templeton .10
289 Bob Stanley .10
290 Ken Singleton .10
291 Pirates Future Stars (Vance Law, Bob Long), *(Johnny Ray)* .15
292 Dave Palmer .10
293 Rob Picciolo .10
294 Mike LaCoss .10
295 Jason Thompson .10
296 Bob Walk .10
297 Clint Hurdle .10
298 Danny Darwin .10
299 Steve Trout .10
300 Reggie Jackson 3.00
301 Reggie Jackson (In Action) 1.50
302 Doug Flynn .10
303 Bill Caudill .10
304 Johnnie LeMaster .10
305 Don Sutton .75
306 Don Sutton (In Action) .20
307 Randy Bass .10
308 Charlie Moore .10
309 Pete Redfern .10
310 Mike Hargrove .10
311 Dodgers Batting/Pitching Leaders (Dusty Baker, Burt Hooton) .10
312 Lenny Randle .10
313 John Harris .10
314 Buck Martinez .10
315 Burt Hooton .10
316 Steve Braun .10
317 Dick Ruthven .10
318 Mike Heath .10
319 Dave Rozema .10
320 Chris Chambliss .10
321 Chris Chambliss (In Action) .10
322 Garry Hancock .10
323 Bill Lee .10
324 Steve Dillard .10
325 Jose Cruz .10
326 Pete Falcone .10
327 Joe Nolan .10
328 Ed Farmer .10
329 U.L. Washington .10
330 Rick Wise .10
331 Benny Ayala .10
332 Don Robinson .10
333 Brewers Future Stars *(Frank DiPino*, Marshall Edwards, Chuck Porter) .10
334 Aurelio Rodriguez .10
335 Jim Sundberg .10
336 Mariners Batting/Pitching Leaders (Glenn Abbott, Tom Paciorek) .10
337 Pete Rose (All-Star) 1.50
338 Dave Lopes (All-Star) .10
339 Mike Schmidt (All-Star) 1.00
340 Dave Concepcion (All-Star) .10
341 Andre Dawson (All-Star) .25
342a George Foster (All-Star no autograph) 2.00
342b George Foster (All-Star autograph on front) .10
343 Dave Parker (All-Star) .10
344 Gary Carter (All-Star) .15
345 Fernando Valenzuela (All-Star) .10
346 Tom Seaver (All-Star) .75
347 Bruce Sutter (All-Star) .10
348 Derrel Thomas .10
349 George Frazier .10
350 Thad Bosley .10
351 Reds Future Stars (Scott Brown, Geoff Combe, Paul Householder) .10
352 Dick Davis .10
353 Jack O'Connor .10
354 Roberto Ramos .10
355 Dwight Evans .10
356 Denny Lewallyn .10
357 Butch Hobson .10
358 Mike Parrott .10
359 Jim Dwyer .10
360 Len Barker .10
361 Rafael Landestoy .10
362 Jim Wright .10
363 Bob Molinaro .10
364 Doyle Alexander .10
365 Bill Madlock .10
366 Padres Batting/Pitching Leaders (Juan Eichelberger, Luis Salazar) .10
367 Jim Kaat .20
368 Alex Trevino .10
369 Champ Summers .10
370 Mike Norris .10
371 Jerry Don Gleaton .10
372 Luis Gomez .10
373 *Gene Nelson* .10
374 Tim Blackwell .10
375 Dusty Baker .15
376 Chris Welsh .10
377 Kiko Garcia .10
378 Mike Caldwell .10
379 Rob Wilfong .10
380 Dave Stieb .10
381 Red Sox Future Stars (Bruce Hurst, Dave Schmidt, Julio Valdez) .25
382 Joe Simpson .10
383a Pascual Perez (no position on front) 6.00
383b Pascual Perez ("Pitcher" on front) .10
384 Keith Moreland .10
385 Ken Forsch .10
386 Jerry White .10
387 Tom Veryzer .10
388 Joe Rudi .10
389 George Vukovich .10
390 Eddie Murray 2.50
391 Dave Tobik .10
392 Rick Bosetti .10
393 Al Hrabosky .10
394 Checklist 265-396 .10
395 Omar Moreno .10
396 Twins Batting/Pitching Leaders (Fernando Arroyo, John Castino) .10
397 Ken Brett .10
398 Mike Squires .10
399 Pat Zachry .10
400 Johnny Bench 1.50
401 Johnny Bench (In Action) .45
402 Bill Stein .10
403 Jim Tracy .10
404 Dickie Thon .10
405 Rick Reuschel .10
406 Al Holland .10
407 Danny Boone .10
408 Ed Romero .10
409 Don Cooper .10
410 Ron Cey .10
411 Ron Cey (In Action) .10
412 Luis Leal .10
413 Dan Meyer .10
414 Elias Sosa .10
415 Don Baylor .15
416 Marty Bystrom .10
417 Pat Kelly .10
418 Rangers Future Stars (John Butcher, Bobby Johnson), *(Dave Schmidt)* .10
419 Steve Stone .10
420 George Hendrick .10
421 Mark Clear .10
422 Cliff Johnson .10
423 Stan Papi .10
424 Bruce Benedict .10
425 John Candelaria .10
426 Orioles Batting/Pitching Leaders (Eddie Murray, Sammy Stewart) .25
427 Ron Oester .10
428 Lamarr Hoyt (LaMarr) .10
429 John Wathan .10
430 Vida Blue .10
431 Vida Blue (In Action) .10
432 Mike Scott .10
433 Alan Ashby .10
434 Joe Lefebvre .10
435 Robin Yount 2.50
436 Joe Strain .10
437 Juan Berenguer .10
438 Pete Mackanin .10

439 *Dave Righetti* .75
440 Jeff Burroughs .10
441 Astros Future Stars (Danny Heep, Billy Smith, Bobby Sprowl) .10
442 Bruce Kison .10
443 Mark Wagner .10
444 Terry Forster .10
445 Larry Parrish .10
446 Wayne Garland .10
447 Darrell Porter .10
448 Darrell Porter (In Action) .10
449 *Luis Aguayo* .10
450 Jack Morris .10
451 Ed Miller .10
452 *Lee Smith* 6.00
453 Art Howe .10
454 Rick Langford .10
455 Tom Burgmeier .10
456 Cubs Batting & Pitching Ldrs. (Bill Buckner, Randy Martz) .10
457 Tim Stoddard .10
458 Willie Montanez .10
459 Bruce Berenyi .10
460 Jack Clark .10
461 Rich Dotson .10
462 Dave Chalk .10
463 Jim Kern .10
464 Juan Bonilla .10
465 Lee Mazzilli .10
466 Randy Lerch .10
467 Mickey Hatcher .10
468 Floyd Bannister .10
469 Ed Ott .10
470 John Mayberry .10
471 Royals Future Stars (*Atlee Hammaker*, Mike Jones, Darryl Motley) .15
472 Oscar Gamble .10
473 Mike Stanton .10
474 Ken Oberkfell .10
475 Alan Trammell .10
476 Brian Kingman .10
477 Steve Yeager .10
478 Ray Searage .10
479 Rowland Office .10
480 Steve Carlton 1.00
481 Steve Carlton (In Action) .40
482 Glenn Hubbard .10
483 Gary Woods .10
484 Ivan DeJesus .10
485 Kent Tekulve .10
486 Yankees Batting & Pitching Ldrs. (Tommy John, Jerry Mumphrey) .10
487 Bob McClure .10
488 Ron Jackson .10
489 Rick Dempsey .10
490 Dennis Eckersley .20
491 Checklist 397-528 .10
492 Joe Price .10
493 Chet Lemon .10
494 Hubie Brooks .10
495 Dennis Leonard .10
496 Johnny Grubb .10
497 Jim Anderson .10
498 Dave Bergman .10
499 Paul Mirabella .10
500 Rod Carew 1.00
501 Rod Carew (In Action) .40
502 Braves Future Stars (*Steve Bedrosian*), (*Brett Butler*, Larry Owen) 2.00
503 Julio Gonzalez .10
504 Rick Peters .10
505 Graig Nettles .10
506 Graig Nettles (In Action) .10
507 Terry Harper .10
508 *Jody Davis* .15
509 Harry Spilman .10
510 Fernando Valenzuela .10
511 Ruppert Jones .10
512 Jerry Dybzinski .10
513 Rick Rhoden .10
514 Joe Ferguson .10
515 Larry Bowa .10
516 Larry Bowa (In Action) .10
517 Mark Brouhard .10
518 Garth Iorg .10
519 Glenn Adams .10
520 Mike Flanagan .10
521 Billy Almon .10
522 Chuck Rainey .10
523 Gary Gray .10
524 Tom Hausman .10
525 Ray Knight .10
526 Expos Batting & Pitching Ldrs. (Warren Cromartie, Bill Gullickson) .10
527 John Henry Johnson .10
528 Matt Alexander .10
529 Allen Ripley .10
530 Dickie Noles .10
531 A's Future Stars (Rich Bordi, Mark Budaska, Kelvin Moore) .10
532 Toby Harrah .10
533 Joaquin Andujar .10
534 Dave McKay .10
535 Lance Parrish .10
536 Rafael Ramirez .10
537 Doug Capilla .10
538 Lou Piniella .10
539 Vern Ruhle .10
540 Andre Dawson 1.00
541 Barry Evans .10
542 Ned Yost .10
543 Bill Robinson .10
544 Larry Christenson .10
545 Reggie Smith .10
546 Reggie Smith (In Action) .10
547 Rod Carew (All-Star) .25
548 Willie Randolph (All-Star) .10
549 George Brett (All-Star) 1.50
550 Bucky Dent (All-Star) .10
551 Reggie Jackson (All-Star) .75
552 Ken Singleton (All-Star) .10
553 Dave Winfield (All-Star) .60
554 Carlton Fisk (All-Star) .25
555 Scott McGregor (All-Star) .10
556 Jack Morris (All-Star) .10
557 Rich Gossage (All-Star) .10
558 John Tudor .10
559 Indians Batting & Pitching Ldrs. (Bert Blyleven, Mike Hargrove) .10
560 Doug Corbett .10
561 Cardinals Future Stars (Glenn Brummer, Luis DeLeon, Gene Roof) .10
562 Mike O'Berry .10
563 Ross Baumgarten .10
564 Doug DeCinces .10
565 Jackson Todd .10
566 Mike Jorgensen .10
567 Bob Babcock .10
568 Joe Pettini .10
569 Willie Randolph .10
570 Willie Randolph (In Action) .10
571 Glenn Abbott .10
572 Juan Beniquez .10
573 Rick Waits .10
574 Mike Ramsey .10
575 Al Cowens .10
576 Giants Batting & Pitching Ldrs. (Vida Blue, Milt May) .10
577 Rick Monday .10
578 Shooty Babitt .10
579 *Rick Mahler* .10
580 Bobby Bonds .10
581 Ron Reed .10
582 Luis Pujols .10
583 Tippy Martinez .10
584 Hosken Powell .10
585 Rollie Fingers .75
586 Rollie Fingers (In Action) .15
587 Tim Lollar .10
588 Dale Berra .10
589 Dave Stapleton .10
590 Al Oliver .10
591 Al Oliver (In Action) .10
592 Craig Swan .10
593 Billy Smith .10
594 Renie Martin .10
595 Dave Collins .10
596 Damaso Garcia .10
597 Wayne Nordhagen .10
598 Bob Galasso .10
599 White Sox Future Stars (Jay Loviglio, Reggie Patterson, Leo Sutherland) .10
600 Dave Winfield 2.50
601 Sid Monge .10
602 Freddie Patek .10
603 Rich Hebner .10
604 Orlando Sanchez .10
605 Steve Rogers .10
606 Blue Jays Batting & Pitching Ldrs. (John Mayberry, Dave Stieb) .10
607 Leon Durham .10
608 Jerry Royster .10
609 Rick Sutcliffe .10
610 Rickey Henderson 2.50
611 Joe Niekro .10
612 Gary Ward .10
613 Jim Gantner .10
614 Juan Eichelberger .10
615 Bob Boone .10
616 Bob Boone (In Action) .10
617 Scott McGregor .10
618 Tim Foli .10
619 Bill Campbell .10
620 Ken Griffey .10
621 Ken Griffey (In Action) .10
622 Dennis Lamp .10
623 Mets Future Stars (Ron Gardenhire), (*Terry Leach*), (*Tim Leary*) .20
624 Fergie Jenkins .75
625 Hal McRae .10
626 Randy Jones .10
627 Enos Cabell .10
628 Bill Travers .10
629 Johnny Wockenfuss .10
630 Joe Charboneau .10
631 Gene Tenace .10
632 Bryan Clark .10
633 Mitchell Page .10
634 Checklist 529-660 .10
635 Ron Davis .10
636 Phillies Batting & Pitching Ldrs. (Steve Carlton, Pete Rose) .50
637 Rick Camp .10
638 John Milner .10
639 Ken Kravec .10
640 Cesar Cedeno .10
641 Steve Mura .10
642 Mike Scioscia .10
643 Pete Vuckovich .10
644 John Castino .10
645 Frank White .10
646 Frank White (In Action) .10
647 Warren Brusstar .10
648 Jose Morales .10
649 Ken Clay .10
650 Carl Yastrzemski 1.50
651 Carl Yastrzemski (In Action) .65
652 Steve Nicosia .10
653 Angels Future Stars (*Tom Brunansky*), (*Luis Sanchez*), (*Daryl Sconiers*) .40
654 Jim Morrison .10
655 Joel Youngblood .10
656 Eddie Whitson .10
657 Tom Poquette .10
658 Tito Landrum .10
659 Fred Martinez .10
660 Dave Concepcion .10
661 Dave Concepcion (In Action) .10
662 Luis Salazar .10
663 Hector Cruz .10
664 Dan Spillner .10
665 Jim Clancy .10
666 Tigers Batting & Pitching Ldrs. (Steve Kemp, Dan Petry) .10
667 Jeff Reardon .25
668 Dale Murphy 1.00
669 Larry Milbourne .10
670 Steve Kemp .10
671 Mike Davis .10
672 Bob Knepper .10
673 Keith Drumright .10
674 Dave Goltz .10
675 Cecil Cooper .10
676 Sal Butera .10
677 Alfredo Griffin .10
678 Tom Paciorek .10
679 Sammy Stewart .10
680 Gary Matthews .10
681 Dodgers Future Stars (*Mike Marshall*), (*Ron Roenicke*), (*Steve Sax*) .75
682 Jesse Jefferson .10
683 Phil Garner .10
684 Harold Baines .15
685 Bert Blyleven .10
686 Gary Allenson .10
687 Greg Minton .10
688 Leon Roberts .10
689 Lary Sorensen .10
690 Dave Kingman .10
691 Dan Schatzeder .10
692 Wayne Gross .10
693 Cesar Geronimo .10
694 Dave Wehrmeister .10
695 Warren Cromartie .10
696 Pirates Batting & Pitching Ldrs. (Bill Madlock, Buddy Solomon) .10
697 John Montefusco .10
698 Tony Scott .10
699 Dick Tidrow .10
700 George Foster .10
701 George Foster (In Action) .10
702 Steve Renko .10
703 Brewers Batting & Pitching Ldrs. (Cecil Cooper, Pete Vuckovich) .10
704 Mickey Rivers .10
705 Mickey Rivers (In Action) .10
706 Barry Foote .10
707 Mark Bomback .10
708 Gene Richards .10
709 Don Money .10
710 Jerry Reuss .10
711 Mariners Future Stars (*Dave Edler*), (*Dave Henderson*), (*Reggie Walton*) .25
712 Denny Martinez .10
713 Del Unser .10
714 Jerry Koosman .10
715 Willie Stargell 1.00
716 Willie Stargell (In Action) .30
717 Rick Miller .10
718 Charlie Hough .10
719 Jerry Narron .10
720 Greg Luzinski .10
721 Greg Luzinski (In Action) .10
722 Jerry Martin .10
723 Junior Kennedy .10
724 Dave Rosello .10
725 Amos Otis .10
726 Amos Otis (In Action) .10
727 Sixto Lezcano .10
728 Aurelio Lopez .10
729 Jim Spencer .10
730 Gary Carter .75
731 Padres Future Stars (Mike Armstrong, Doug Gwosdz, Fred Kuhaulua) .10
732 Mike Lum .10
733 Larry McWilliams .10
734 Mike Ivie .10
735 Rudy May .10
736 Jerry Turner .10
737 Reggie Cleveland .10
738 Dave Engle .10
739 Joey McLaughlin .10
740 Dave Lopes .10
741 Dave Lopes (In Action) .10
742 Dick Drago .10
743 John Stearns .10
744 *Mike Witt* .25
745 Bake McBride .10
746 Andre Thornton .10
747 John Lowenstein .10
748 Marc Hill .10
749 Bob Shirley .10

750 Jim Rice .20
751 Rick Honeycutt .10
752 Lee Lacy .10
753 Tom Brookens .10
754 Joe Morgan 1.00
755 Joe Morgan (In Action) .25
756 Reds Batting & Pitching Ldrs. (Ken Griffey, Tom Seaver) .25
757 Tom Underwood .10
758 Claudell Washington .10
759 Paul Splittorff .10
760 Bill Buckner .10
761 Dave Smith .10
762 Mike Phillips .10
763 Tom Hume .10
764 Steve Swisher .10
765 Gorman Thomas .10
766 Twins Future Stars (*Lenny Faedo*), (*Kent Hrbek*), (*Tim Laudner*) 2.00
767 Roy Smalley .10
768 Jerry Garvin .10
769 Richie Zisk .10
770 Rich Gossage .10
771 Rich Gossage (In Action) .10
772 Bert Campaneris .10
773 John Denny .10
774 Jay Johnstone .10
775 Bob Forsch .10
776 Mark Belanger .10
777 Tom Griffin .10
778 Kevin Hickey .10
779 Grant Jackson .10
780 Pete Rose 4.00
781 Pete Rose (In Action) 2.00
782 Frank Taveras .10
783 *Greg Harris* .10
784 Milt Wilcox .10
785 Dan Driessen .10
786 Red Sox Batting & Pitching Ldrs. (Carney Lansford, Mike Torrez) .10
787 Fred Stanley .10
788 Woodie Fryman .10
789 Checklist 661-792 .10
790 Larry Gura .10
791 Bobby Brown .10
792 Frank Tanana .10

1982 Topps Insert Stickers

This 48-player set is actually an abbreviated version of the regular 1982 Topps sticker set with different backs. Used to promote the 1982 sticker set, Topps inserted these stickers in its baseball card wax packs. They are identical to the regular 1982 stickers, except for the backs, which advertise that the Topps sticker album will be "Coming Soon." The 48 stickers retain the same numbers used in the regular sticker set, resulting in the smaller set being skip-numbered.

MT
Complete Set (48): 3.00
Common Player: .05
17 Chris Chambliss .05
21 Bruce Benedict .05
25 Leon Durham .05
29 Bill Buckner .05
33 Dave Collins .05
37 Dave Concepcion .05
41 Nolan Ryan 1.00
45 Bob Knepper .05
49 Ken Landreaux .05
53 Burt Hooton .05
57 Andre Dawson .15
61 Gary Carter .15
65 Joel Youngblood .05
69 Ellis Valentine .05
73 Garry Maddox .05
77 Bob Boone .05
81 Omar Moreno .05
85 Willie Stargell .20
89 Ken Oberkfell .05
93 Darrell Porter .05
97 Juan Eichelberger .05
101 Luis Salazar .05
105 Enos Cabell .05
109 Larry Herndon .05
143 Scott McGregor .05
148 Mike Flanagan .05
151 Mike Torrez .05
156 Carney Lansford .05
161 Fred Lynn .05
166 Rich Dotson .05
171 Tony Bernazard .05
176 Bo Diaz .05
181 Alan Trammell .05
186 Milt Wilcox .05
191 Dennis Leonard .05
196 Willie Aikens .05
201 Ted Simmons .05
206 Hosken Powell .05
211 Roger Erickson .05
215 Graig Nettles .05
216 Reggie Jackson .25
221 Rickey Henderson .25
226 Cliff Johnson .05
231 Jeff Burroughs .05
236 Tom Paciorek .05
241 Pat Putnam .05
246 Lloyd Moseby .05
251 Barry Bonnell .05

1982 Topps Stickers

The 1982 Topps sticker set is complete at 260 stickers and includes another series of "foil" All-Stars. The stickers measure 1-15/16" x 2-9/16" and feature full-color photos surrounded by a red border for American League players or a blue border for National League players. They are numbered on both the front and back and were designed to be mounted in a special album.

MT
Complete Set (260): 12.00
Common Player: .05
Sticker Album: 2.00
Wax Pack (5): .25
Wax Box (100): 8.00
1 Bill Madlock .05
2 Carney Lansford .05
3 Mike Schmidt .30
4 Tony Armas, Dwight Evans, Bobby Grich, Eddie Murray .05
5 Mike Schmidt .30
6 Eddie Murray .20
7 Tim Raines .05
8 Rickey Henderson .25
9 Tom Seaver .20
10 Denny Martinez, Steve McCatty, Jack Morris, Pete Vuckovich .05
11 Fernando Valenzuela .05
12 Len Barker .05
13 Nolan Ryan .50
14 Steve McCatty .05
15 Bruce Sutter .05
16 Rollie Fingers .20
17 Chris Chambliss .05
18 Bob Horner .05
19 Dale Murphy .15
20 Phil Niekro .20
21 Bruce Benedict .05
22 Claudell Washington .05
23 Glenn Hubbard .05
24 Rick Camp .05
25 Leon Durham .05
26 Ken Reitz .05
27 Dick Tidrow .05
28 Tim Blackwell .05
29 Bill Buckner .05
30 Steve Henderson .05
31 Mike Krukow .05
32 Ivan DeJesus .05
33 Dave Collins .05
34 Ron Oester .05
35 Johnny Bench .25
36 Tom Seaver .20
37 Dave Concepcion .05
38 Ken Griffey .05
39 Ray Knight .05
40 George Foster .05
41 Nolan Ryan .50
42 Terry Puhl .05
43 Art Howe .05
44 Jose Cruz .05
45 Bob Knepper .05
46 Craig Reynolds .05
47 Cesar Cedeno .05
48 Alan Ashby .05
49 Ken Landreaux .05
50 Fernando Valenzuela .05
51 Ron Cey .05
52 Dusty Baker .05
53 Burt Hooton .05
54 Steve Garvey .15
55 Pedro Guerrero .05
56 Jerry Reuss .05
57 Andre Dawson .20
58 Chris Speier .05
59 Steve Rogers .05
60 Warren Cromartie .05
61 Gary Carter .20
62 Tim Raines .05
63 Scott Sanderson .05
64 Larry Parrish .05
65 Joel Youngblood .05
66 Neil Allen .05
67 Lee Mazzilli .05
68 Hubie Brooks .05
69 Ellis Valentine .05
70 Doug Flynn .05
71 Pat Zachry .05
72 Dave Kingman .05
73 Garry Maddox .05
74 Mike Schmidt .30
75 Steve Carlton .20
76 Manny Trillo .05
77 Bob Boone .05
78 Pete Rose .40
79 Gary Matthews .05
80 Larry Bowa .05
81 Omar Moreno .05
82 Rick Rhoden .05
83 Bill Madlock .05
84 Mike Easler .05
85 Willie Stargell .20
86 Jim Bibby .05
87 Dave Parker .05
88 Tim Foli .05
89 Ken Oberkfell .05
90 Bob Forsch .05
91 George Hendrick .05
92 Keith Hernandez .05
93 Darrell Porter .05
94 Bruce Sutter .05
95 Sixto Lezcano .05
96 Garry Templeton .05
97 Juan Eichelberger .05
98 Broderick Perkins .05
99 Ruppert Jones .05
100 Terry Kennedy .05
101 Luis Salazar .05
102 Gary Lucas .05
103 Gene Richards .05
104 Ozzie Smith .30
105 Enos Cabell .05
106 Jack Clark .05
107 Greg Minton .05
108 Johnnie LeMaster .05
109 Larry Herndon .05
110 Milt May .05
111 Vida Blue .05
112 Darrell Evans .05
113 Len Barker .05
114 Julio Cruz .05
115 Billy Martin .05
116 Tim Raines .05
117 Pete Rose .40
118 Bill Stein .05
119 Fernando Valenzuela .05
120 Carl Yastrzemski .25
121 Pete Rose .40
122 Manny Trillo .05
123 Mike Schmidt .30
124 Dave Concepcion .05
125 Andre Dawson .20
126 George Foster .05
127 Dave Parker .05
128 Gary Carter .20
129 Steve Carlton .20
130 Bruce Sutter .05
131 Rod Carew .20
132 Jerry Remy .05
133 George Brett .30
134 Rick Burleson .05
135 Dwight Evans .05
136 Ken Singleton .05
137 Dave Winfield .25
138 Carlton Fisk .20
139 Jack Morris .05
140 Rich Gossage .05
141 Al Bumbry .05
142 Doug DeCinces .05
143 Scott McGregor .05
144 Ken Singleton .05
145 Eddie Murray .20
146 Jim Palmer .20
147 Rich Dauer .05
148 Mike Flanagan .05
149 Jerry Remy .05
150 Jim Rice .15
151 Mike Torrez .05
152 Tony Perez .20
153 Dwight Evans .05
154 Mark Clear .05
155 Carl Yastrzemski .25
156 Carney Lansford .05
157 Rick Burleson .05
158 Don Baylor .10
159 Ken Forsch .05
160 Rod Carew .20
161 Fred Lynn .05
162 Bob Grich .05
163 Dan Ford .05
164 Butch Hobson .05
165 Greg Luzinski .05
166 Rich Dotson .05
167 Billy Almon .05
168 Chet Lemon .05
169 Steve Trout .05
170 Carlton Fisk .20
171 Tony Bernazard .05
172 Ron LeFlore .05
173 Bert Blyleven .05
174 Andre Thornton .05
175 Jorge Orta .05
176 Bo Diaz .05
177 Toby Harrah .05
178 Len Barker .05
179 Rick Manning .05
180 Mike Hargrove .05
181 Alan Trammell .05
182 Al Cowens .05
183 Jack Morris .05
184 Kirk Gibson .05
185 Steve Kemp .05
186 Milt Wilcox .05
187 Lou Whitaker .05
188 Lance Parrish .05
189 Willie Wilson .05
190 George Brett .30
191 Dennis Leonard .05
192 John Wathan .05
193 Frank White .05
194 Amos Otis .05
195 Larry Gura .05
196 Willie Aikens .05
197 Ben Oglivie .05
198 Rollie Fingers .20
199 Cecil Cooper .05
200 Paul Molitor .20
201 Ted Simmons .05
202 Pete Vuckovich .05
203 Robin Yount .20

204 Gorman Thomas .05
205 Rob Wilfong .05
206 Hosken Powell .05
207 Roy Smalley .05
208 Butch Wynegar .05
209 John Castino .05
210 Doug Corbett .05
211 Roger Erickson .05
212 Mickey Hatcher .05
213 Dave Winfield .25
214 Tommy John .10
215 Graig Nettles .05
216 Reggie Jackson .25
217 Rich Gossage .05
218 Rick Cerone .05
219 Willie Randolph .05
220 Jerry Mumphrey .05
221 Rickey Henderson .25
222 Mike Norris .05
223 Jim Spencer .05
224 Tony Armas .05
225 Matt Keough .05
226 Cliff Johnson .05
227 Dwayne Murphy .05
228 Steve McCatty .05
229 Richie Zisk .05
230 Lenny Randle .05
231 Jeff Burroughs .05
232 Bruce Bochte .05
233 Gary Gray .05
234 Floyd Bannister .05
235 Julio Cruz .05
236 Tom Paciorek .05
237 Danny Darwin .05
238 Buddy Bell .05
239 Al Oliver .05
240 Jim Sundberg .05
241 Pat Putnam .05
242 Steve Comer .05
243 Mickey Rivers .05
244 Bump Wills .05
245 Damaso Garcia .05
246 Lloyd Moseby .05
247 Ernie Whitt .05
248 John Mayberry .05
249 Otto Velez .05
250 Dave Stieb .05
251 Barry Bonnell .05
252 Alfredo Griffin .05
253 1981 N.L. Championship (Gary Carter) .10
254 1981 A.L. Championship (Mike Heath, Larry Milbourne) .05
255 1981 World Champions (Los Angeles Dodgers Team) .05
256 1981 World Champions (Los Angeles Dodgers Team) .05
257 1981 World Series - Game 3 (Fernando Valenzuela) .05
258 1981 World Series - Game 4 (Steve Garvey) .10
259 1981 World Series - Game 5 (Jerry Reuss, Steve Yeager) .05
260 1981 World Series - Game 6 (Pedro Guerrero) .05

1982 Topps Traded

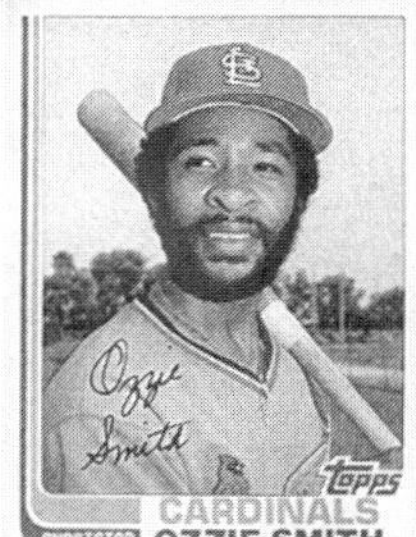

Topps released its second straight 132-card Traded set in September of 1982. Again, the 2-1/2" x 3-1/2" cards feature not only players who had been traded during the season, but also promising rookies who were given their first individual cards. The cards follow the basic design of the regular issues, but have their backs printed in red rather than the regular-issue green. As in 1981, the cards were not available in normal retail outlets and could only be purchased through regular baseball card dealers. Unlike the previous year, the cards are numbered 1-132 with the letter "T" following the number.

MT
Complete Set (132): 175.00
Common Player: .15
1T Doyle Alexander .15
2T Jesse Barfield .15
3T Ross Baumgarten .15
4T Steve Bedrosian .15
5T Mark Belanger .15
6T Kurt Bevacqua .15
7T Tim Blackwell .15
8T Vida Blue .15
9T Bob Boone .30
10T Larry Bowa .15
11T Dan Briggs .15
12T Bobby Brown .15
13T Tom Brunansky .15
14T Jeff Burroughs .15
15T Enos Cabell .15
16T Bill Campbell .15
17T Bobby Castillo .15
18T Bill Caudill .15
19T Cesar Cedeno .15
20T Dave Collins .15
21T Doug Corbett .15
22T Al Cowens .15
23T Chili Davis .50
24T Dick Davis .15
25T Ron Davis .15
26T Doug DeCinces .15
27T Ivan DeJesus .15
28T Bob Dernier .15
29T Bo Diaz .15
30T Roger Erickson .15
31T Jim Essian .15
32T Ed Farmer .15
33T Doug Flynn .15
34T Tim Foli .15
35T Dan Ford .15
36T George Foster .15
37T Dave Frost .15
38T Rich Gale .15
39T Ron Gardenhire .15
40T Ken Griffey .15
41T Greg Harris .15
42T Von Hayes .15
43T Larry Herndon .15
44T Kent Hrbek 2.00
45T Mike Ivie .15
46T Grant Jackson .15
47T Reggie Jackson 10.00
48T Ron Jackson .15
49T Fergie Jenkins 2.00
50T Lamar Johnson .15
51T Randy Johnson .15
52T Jay Johnstone .15
53T Mick Kelleher .15
54T Steve Kemp .15
55T Junior Kennedy .15
56T Jim Kern .15
57T Ray Knight .15
58T Wayne Krenchicki .15
59T Mike Krukow .15
60T Duane Kuiper .15
61T Mike LaCoss .15
62T Chet Lemon .15
63T Sixto Lezcano .15
64T Dave Lopes .15
65T Jerry Martin .15
66T Renie Martin .15
67T John Mayberry .15
68T Lee Mazzilli .15
69T Bake McBride .15
70T Dan Meyer .15
71T Larry Milbourne .15
72T Eddie Milner .15
73T Sid Monge .15
74T John Montefusco .15
75T Jose Morales .15
76T Keith Moreland .15
77T Jim Morrison .15
78T Rance Mulliniks .15
79T Steve Mura .15
80T Gene Nelson .15
81T Joe Nolan .15
82T Dickie Noles .15
83T Al Oliver .15
84T Jorge Orta .15
85T Tom Paciorek .15
86T Larry Parrish .15
87T Jack Perconte .15
88T Gaylord Perry 2.00
89T Rob Picciolo .15
90T Joe Pittman .15
91T Hosken Powell .15
92T Mike Proly .15
93T Greg Pryor .15
94T Charlie Puleo .15
95T Shane Rawley .15
96T Johnny Ray .15
97T Dave Revering .15
98T Cal Ripken, Jr. 150.00
99T Allen Ripley .15
100T Bill Robinson .15
101T Aurelio Rodriguez .15
102T Joe Rudi .15
103T Steve Sax .50
104T Dan Schatzeder .15
105T Bob Shirley .15
106T Eric Show .15
107T Roy Smalley .15
108T Lonnie Smith .15
109T Ozzie Smith 25.00
110T Reggie Smith .15
111T Lary Sorensen .15
112T Elias Sosa .15
113T Mike Stanton .15
114T Steve Stroughter .15
115T Champ Summers .15
116T Rick Sutcliffe .15
117T Frank Tanana .15
118T Frank Taveras .15
119T Garry Templeton .15
120T Alex Trevino .15
121T Jerry Turner .15
122T Ed Vande Berg .15
123T Tom Veryzer .15
124T Ron Washington .15
125T Bob Watson .15
126T Dennis Werth .15
127T Eddie Whitson .15
128T Rob Wilfong .15
129T Bump Wills .15
130T Gary Woods .15
131T Butch Wynegar .15
132T Checklist 1-132 .15

1983 Topps

topps
WADE
BOGGS
1st BASE-3rd BASE
RED SOX

The 1983 Topps set totals 792 cards. Missing among the regular 2-1/2" x 3-1/2" cards are some form of future stars cards, as Topps was saving them for the now-established late season "Traded" set. The 1983 cards carry a large color photo as well as a smaller color photo on the front, quite similar in design to the 1963 set. Team colors frame the card, which, at the bottom, have the player's name, position and team. At the upper right-hand corner is a Topps Logo. The backs are horizontal and include statistics, personal information and 1982 highlights. Specialty cards include record-breaking perfor- mances, league leaders, All-Stars, numbered check-lists "Team Leaders" and "Super Veteran" cards which are horizontal with a current and first-season picture of the honored player.

MT
Complete Set (792): 75.00
Common Player: .05
Pack (15): 6.00
Wax Box (36): 150.00
Crimp-end Test Pack (15): 6.00
Crimp-end Test Wax Box (36): 175.00
Cello Pack (28): 7.50
Cello Box (24): 150.00
Grocery Rack (36): 10.00
Rack Pack (51): 10.00
Rack Box (24): 180.00
Vending Box (500): 75.00
1 Tony Armas (Record Breaker) .05
2 Rickey Henderson (Record Breaker) .75
3 Greg Minton (Record Breaker) .05
4 Lance Parrish (Record Breaker) .05
5 Manny Trillo (Record Breaker) .05
6 John Wathan (Record Breaker) .05
7 Gene Richards .05
8 Steve Balboni .05
9 Joey McLaughlin .05
10 Gorman Thomas .05
11 Billy Gardner .05
12 Paul Mirabella .05
13 Larry Herndon .05
14 Frank LaCorte .05
15 Ron Cey .05
16 George Vukovich .05
17 Kent Tekulve .05
18 Kent Tekulve (Super Veteran) .05
19 Oscar Gamble .05
20 Carlton Fisk 1.50
21 Orioles Batting & Pitching Ldrs. (Eddie Murray, Jim Palmer) .25
22 Randy Martz .05
23 Mike Heath .05
24 Steve Mura .05
25 Hal McRae .05
26 Jerry Royster .05
27 Doug Corbett .05
28 Bruce Bochte .05
29 Randy Jones .05
30 Jim Rice .15
31 Bill Gullickson .05
32 Dave Bergman .05
33 Jack O'Connor .05
34 Paul Householder .05
35 Rollie Fingers .75
36 Rollie Fingers (Super Veteran) .15
37 Darrell Johnson .05
38 Tim Flannery .05
39 Terry Puhl .05
40 Fernando Valenzuela .05

41 Jerry Turner .05
42 Dale Murray .05
43 Bob Dernier .05
44 Don Robinson .05
45 John Mayberry .05
46 Richard Dotson .05
47 Dave McKay .05
48 Lary Sorensen .05
49 *Willie McGee* 1.50
50 Bob Horner .05
51 Cubs Batting & Pitching Ldrs. (Leon Durham, Fergie Jenkins) .05
52 *Onix Concepcion* .05
53 Mike Witt .05
54 Jim Maler .05
55 Mookie Wilson .05
56 Chuck Rainey .05
57 Tim Blackwell .05
58 Al Holland .05
59 Benny Ayala .05
60 Johnny Bench 2.00
61 Johnny Bench (Super Veteran) .75
62 Bob McClure .05
63 Rick Monday .05
64 Bill Stein .05
65 Jack Morris .05
66 Bob Lillis .05
67 Sal Butera .05
68 *Eric Show* .15
69 Lee Lacy .05
70 Steve Carlton 1.50
71 Steve Carlton (Super Veteran) .30
72 Tom Paciorek .05
73 Allen Ripley .05
74 Julio Gonzalez .05
75 Amos Otis .05
76 Rick Mahler .05
77 Hosken Powell .05
78 Bill Caudill .05
79 Mick Kelleher .05
80 George Foster .05
81 Yankees Batting & Pitching Ldrs. (Jerry Mumphrey, Dave Righetti) .05
82 Bruce Hurst .05
83 *Ryne Sandberg* 15.00
84 Milt May .05
85 Ken Singleton .05
86 Tom Hume .05
87 Joe Rudi .05
88 Jim Gantner .05
89 Leon Roberts .05
90 Jerry Reuss .05
91 Larry Milbourne .05
92 Mike LaCoss .05
93 John Castino .05
94 Dave Edwards .05
95 Alan Trammell .05
96 Dick Howser .05
97 Ross Baumgarten .05
98 Vance Law .05
99 Dickie Noles .05
100 Pete Rose 4.00
101 Pete Rose (Super Veteran) 2.00
102 Dave Beard .05
103 Darrell Porter .05
104 Bob Walk .05
105 Don Baylor .15
106 Gene Nelson .05
107 Mike Jorgensen .05
108 Glenn Hoffman .05
109 Luis Leal .05
110 Ken Griffey .05
111 Expos Batting & Pitching Ldrs. (Al Oliver, Steve Rogers) .05
112 Bob Shirley .05
113 Ron Roenicke .05
114 Jim Slaton .05
115 Chili Davis .05
116 Dave Schmidt .05
117 Alan Knicely .05
118 Chris Welsh .05
119 Tom Brookens .05
120 Len Barker .05
121 Mickey Hatcher .05
122 Jimmy Smith .05
123 George Frazier .05
124 Marc Hill .05
125 Leon Durham .05
126 Joe Torre .15
127 Preston Hanna .05
128 Mike Ramsey .05
129 Checklist 1-132 .05
130 Dave Stieb .05
131 Ed Ott .05
132 Todd Cruz .05
133 Jim Barr .05
134 Hubie Brooks .05
135 Dwight Evans .05
136 Willie Aikens .05
137 Woodie Fryman .05
138 Rick Dempsey .05
139 Bruce Berenyi .05
140 Willie Randolph .05
141 Indians Batting & Pitching Ldrs. (Toby Harrah, Rick Sutcliffe) .05
142 Mike Caldwell .05
143 Joe Pettini .05
144 Mark Wagner .05
145 Don Sutton .75
146 Don Sutton (Super Veteran) .20
147 Rick Leach .05
148 Dave Roberts .05
149 Johnny Ray .05
150 Bruce Sutter .05
151 Bruce Sutter (Super Veteran) .05
152 Jay Johnstone .05
153 Jerry Koosman .05
154 Johnnie LeMaster .05
155 Dan Quisenberry .05
156 Billy Martin .15
157 Steve Bedrosian .05
158 Rob Wilfong .05
159 Mike Stanton .05
160 Dave Kingman .05
161 Dave Kingman (Super Veteran) .05
162 Mark Clear .05
163 Cal Ripken, Jr. 12.00
164 Dave Palmer .05
165 Dan Driessen .05
166 John Pacella .05
167 Mark Brouhard .05
168 Juan Eichelberger .05
169 Doug Flynn .05
170 Steve Howe .05
171 Giants Batting & Pitching Ldrs. (Bill Laskey, Joe Morgan) .05
172 Vern Ruhle .05
173 Jim Morrison .05
174 Jerry Ujdur .05
175 Bo Diaz .05
176 Dave Righetti .05
177 Harold Baines .05
178 Luis Tiant .05
179 Luis Tiant (Super Veteran) .05
180 Rickey Henderson 2.00
181 Terry Felton .05
182 Mike Fischlin .05
183 *Ed Vande Berg* .05
184 Bob Clark .05
185 Tim Lollar .05
186 Whitey Herzog .05
187 Terry Leach .05
188 Rick Miller .05
189 Dan Schatzeder .05
190 Cecil Cooper .05
191 Joe Price .05
192 Floyd Rayford .05
193 Harry Spilman .05
194 Cesar Geronimo .05
195 Bob Stoddard .05
196 Bill Fahey .05
197 *Jim Eisenreich* .50
198 Kiko Garcia .05
199 Marty Bystrom .05
200 Rod Carew 1.50
201 Rod Carew (Super Veteran) .35
202 Blue Jays Batting & Pitching Ldrs. (Damaso Garcia, Dave Stieb) .05
203 Mike Morgan .05
204 Junior Kennedy .05
205 Dave Parker .05
206 Ken Oberkfell .05
207 Rick Camp .05
208 Dan Meyer .05
209 *Mike Moore* .15
210 Jack Clark .05
211 John Denny .05
212 John Stearns .05
213 Tom Burgmeier .05
214 Jerry White .05
215 Mario Soto .05
216 Tony LaRussa .05
217 Tim Stoddard .05
218 Roy Howell .05
219 Mike Armstrong .05
220 Dusty Baker .05
221 Joe Niekro .05
222 Damaso Garcia .05
223 John Montefusco .05
224 Mickey Rivers .05
225 Enos Cabell .05
226 Enrique Romo .05
227 Chris Bando .05
228 Joaquin Andujar .05
229 Phillies Batting/Pitching Leaders (Steve Carlton, Bo Diaz) .15
230 Fergie Jenkins .75
231 Fergie Jenkins (Super Veteran) .20
232 Tom Brunansky .05
233 Wayne Gross .05
234 Larry Andersen .05
235 Claudell Washington .05
236 Steve Renko .05
237 Dan Norman .05
238 *Bud Black* .25
239 Dave Stapleton .05
240 Rich Gossage .05
241 Rich Gossage (Super Veteran) .05
242 Joe Nolan .05
243 Duane Walker .05
244 Dwight Bernard .05
245 Steve Sax .05
246 George Bamberger .05
247 Dave Smith .05
248 Bake McBride .05
249 Checklist 133-264 .05
250 Bill Buckner .05
251 *Alan Wiggins* .05
252 Luis Aguayo .05
253 Larry McWilliams .05
254 Rick Cerone .05
255 Gene Garber .05
256 Gene Garber (Super Veteran) .05
257 Jesse Barfield .05
258 Manny Castillo .05
259 Jeff Jones .05
260 Steve Kemp .05
261 Tigers Batting & Pitching Ldrs. (Larry Herndon, Dan Petry) .05
262 Ron Jackson .05
263 Renie Martin .05
264 Jamie Quirk .05
265 Joel Youngblood .05
266 Paul Boris .05
267 Terry Francona .05
268 *Storm Davis* .05
269 Ron Oester .05
270 Dennis Eckersley .25
271 Ed Romero .05
272 Frank Tanana .05
273 Mark Belanger .05
274 Terry Kennedy .05
275 Ray Knight .05
276 Gene Mauch .05
277 Rance Mulliniks .05
278 Kevin Hickey .05
279 Greg Gross .05
280 Bert Blyleven .05
281 Andre Robertson .05
282 Reggie Smith .05
283 Reggie Smith (Super Veteran) .05
284 Jeff Lahti .05
285 Lance Parrish .05
286 Rick Langford .05
287 Bobby Brown .05
288 *Joe Cowley* .05
289 Jerry Dybzinski .05
290 Jeff Reardon .05
291 Pirates Batting & Pitching Ldrs. (John Candelaria, Bill Madlock) .05
292 Craig Swan .05
293 Glenn Gulliver .05
294 Dave Engle .05
295 Jerry Remy .05
296 Greg Harris .05
297 Ned Yost .05
298 Floyd Chiffer .05
299 George Wright .05
300 Mike Schmidt 3.50
301 Mike Schmidt (Super Veteran) 1.50
302 Ernie Whitt .05
303 Miguel Dilone .05
304 Dave Rucker .05
305 Larry Bowa .05
306 Tom Lasorda .25
307 Lou Piniella .05
308 Jesus Vega .05
309 Jeff Leonard .05
310 Greg Luzinski .05
311 Glenn Brummer .05
312 Brian Kingman .05
313 Gary Gray .05
314 Ken Dayley .05
315 Rick Burleson .05
316 Paul Splittorff .05
317 Gary Rajsich .05
318 John Tudor .05
319 Lenn Sakata .05
320 Steve Rogers .05
321 Brewers Batting & Pitching Ldrs. (Pete Vuckovich, Robin Yount) .10
322 Dave Van Gorder .05
323 Luis DeLeon .05
324 Mike Marshall .05
325 Von Hayes .05
326 Garth Iorg .05
327 Bobby Castillo .05
328 Craig Reynolds .05
329 Randy Niemann .05
330 Buddy Bell .05
331 Mike Krukow .05
332 *Glenn Wilson* .05
333 Dave LaRoche .05
334 Dave LaRoche (Super Veteran) .05
335 Steve Henderson .05
336 Rene Lachemann .05
337 Tito Landrum .05
338 Bob Owchinko .05
339 Terry Harper .05
340 Larry Gura .05
341 Doug DeCinces .05
342 Atlee Hammaker .05
343 Bob Bailor .05
344 Roger LaFrancois .05
345 Jim Clancy .05
346 Joe Pittman .05
347 Sammy Stewart .05
348 Alan Bannister .05
349 Checklist 265-396 .05
350 Robin Yount 2.00
351 Reds Batting & Pitching Ldrs. (Cesar Cedeno, Mario Soto) .05
352 Mike Scioscia .05
353 Steve Comer .05
354 Randy S. Johnson .05
355 Jim Bibby .05
356 Gary Woods .05
357 *Len Matuszek* .05
358 Jerry Garvin .05
359 Dave Collins .05
360 Nolan Ryan 8.00
361 Nolan Ryan (Super Veteran) 4.00
362 Bill Almon .05
363 *John Stuper* .05
364 Brett Butler .05
365 Dave Lopes .05
366 Dick Williams .05
367 Bud Anderson .05
368 Richie Zisk .05
369 Jesse Orosco .05
370 Gary Carter .30
371 Mike Richardt .05
372 Terry Crowley .05
373 Kevin Saucier .05
374 Wayne Krenchicki .05
375 Pete Vuckovich .05
376 Ken Landreaux .05
377 Lee May .05
378 Lee May (Super Veteran) .05
379 Guy Sularz .05
380 Ron Davis .05
381 Red Sox Batting & Pitching Ldrs. (Jim Rice, Bob Stanley) .05
382 Bob Knepper .05

383 Ozzie Virgil .05
384 *Dave Dravecky* .50
385 Mike Easler .05
386 Rod Carew (All-Star) .35
387 Bob Grich (All-Star) .05
388 George Brett (All-Star) 1.50
389 Robin Yount (All-Star) .60
390 Reggie Jackson (All-Star) 1.00
391 Rickey Henderson (All-Star) .50
392 Fred Lynn (All-Star) .05
393 Carlton Fisk (All-Star) .25
394 Pete Vuckovich (All-Star) .05
395 Larry Gura (All-Star) .05
396 Dan Quisenberry (All-Star) .05
397 Pete Rose (All-Star) 2.00
398 Manny Trillo (All-Star) .05
399 Mike Schmidt (All-Star) 1.50
400 Dave Concepcion (All-Star) .05
401 Dale Murphy (All-Star) .20
402 Andre Dawson (All-Star) .35
403 Tim Raines (All-Star) .05
404 Gary Carter (All-Star) .20
405 Steve Rogers (All-Star) .05
406 Steve Carlton (All-Star) .30
407 Bruce Sutter (All-Star) .05
408 Rudy May .05
409 Marvis Foley .05
410 Phil Niekro .75
411 Phil Niekro (Super Veteran) .25
412 Rangers Batting & Pitching Ldrs. (Buddy Bell, Charlie Hough) .05
413 Matt Keough .05
414 Julio Cruz .05
415 Bob Forsch .05
416 Joe Ferguson .05
417 Tom Hausman .05
418 Greg Pryor .05
419 Steve Crawford .05
420 Al Oliver .05
421 Al Oliver (Super Veteran) .05
422 George Cappuzzello .05
423 *Tom Lawless* .05
424 Jerry Augustine .05
425 Pedro Guerrero .05
426 Earl Weaver .25
427 Roy Lee Jackson .05
428 Champ Summers .05
429 Eddie Whitson .05
430 Kirk Gibson .05
431 *Gary Gaetti* .75
432 Porfirio Altamirano .05
433 Dale Berra .05
434 Dennis Lamp .05
435 Tony Armas .05
436 Bill Campbell .05
437 Rick Sweet .05
438 *Dave LaPoint* .05
439 Rafael Ramirez .05
440 Ron Guidry .20
441 Astros Batting & Pitching Ldrs. (Ray Knight, Joe Niekro) .05
442 Brian Downing .05
443 Don Hood .05
444 Wally Backman .05
445 Mike Flanagan .05
446 Reid Nichols .05
447 Bryn Smith .05
448 Darrell Evans .05
449 *Eddie Milner* .05
450 Ted Simmons .05
451 Ted Simmons (Super Veteran) .05
452 Lloyd Moseby .05
453 Lamar Johnson .05
454 Bob Welch .05
455 Sixto Lezcano .05
456 Lee Elia .05
457 Milt Wilcox .05
458 Ron Washington .05
459 Ed Farmer .05
460 Roy Smalley .05
461 Steve Trout .05
462 Steve Nicosia .05
463 Gaylord Perry .75
464 Gaylord Perry (Super Veteran) .20
465 Lonnie Smith .05
466 Tom Underwood .05
467 Rufino Linares .05
468 Dave Goltz .05
469 Ron Gardenhire .05
470 Greg Minton .05
471 Royals Batting & Pitching Ldrs. (Vida Blue, Willie Wilson) .05
472 Gary Allenson .05
473 John Lowenstein .05
474 Ray Burris .05
475 Cesar Cedeno .05
476 Rob Picciolo .05
477 Tom Niedenfuer .05
478 Phil Garner .05
479 Charlie Hough .05
480 Toby Harrah .05
481 Scot Thompson .05
482 *Tony Gwynn* 30.00
483 Lynn Jones .05
484 Dick Ruthven .05
485 Omar Moreno .05
486 Clyde King .05
487 Jerry Hairston Sr. .05
488 Alfredo Griffin .05
489 Tom Herr .05
490 Jim Palmer 1.00
491 Jim Palmer (Super Veteran) .20
492 Paul Serna .05
493 Steve McCatty .05
494 Bob Brenly .05
495 Warren Cromartie .05
496 Tom Veryzer .05
497 Rick Sutcliffe .05
498 *Wade Boggs* 12.00
499 Jeff Little .05
500 Reggie Jackson 2.50
501 Reggie Jackson (Super Veteran) .75
502 Braves Batting & Pitching Ldrs. (Dale Murphy, Phil Niekro) .20
503 Moose Haas .05
504 Don Werner .05
505 Garry Templeton .05
506 *Jim Gott* .25
507 Tony Scott .05
508 Tom Filer .05
509 Lou Whitaker .05
510 Tug McGraw .05
511 Tug McGraw (Super Veteran) .05
512 Doyle Alexander .05
513 Fred Stanley .05
514 Rudy Law .05
515 Gene Tenace .05
516 Bill Virdon .05
517 Gary Ward .05
518 Bill Laskey .05
519 Terry Bulling .05
520 Fred Lynn .05
521 Bruce Benedict .05
522 Pat Zachry .05
523 Carney Lansford .05
524 Tom Brennan .05
525 Frank White .05
526 Checklist 397-528 .05
527 Larry Biittner .05
528 Jamie Easterly .05
529 Tim Laudner .05
530 Eddie Murray 2.00
531 Athletics Batting & Pitching Ldrs. (Rickey Henderson, Rick Langford) .15
532 Dave Stewart .05
533 Luis Salazar .05
534 John Butcher .05
535 Manny Trillo .05
536 Johnny Wockenfuss .05
537 Rod Scurry .05
538 Danny Heep .05
539 Roger Erickson .05
540 Ozzie Smith 2.50
541 Britt Burns .05
542 Jody Davis .05
543 Alan Fowlkes .05
544 Larry Whisenton .05
545 Floyd Bannister .05
546 Dave Garcia .05
547 Geoff Zahn .05
548 Brian Giles .05
549 *Charlie Puleo* .05
550 Carl Yastrzemski 1.50
551 Carl Yastrzemski (Super Veteran) .50
552 Tim Wallach .05
553 Denny Martinez .05
554 Mike Vail .05
555 Steve Yeager .05
556 Willie Upshaw .05
557 Rick Honeycutt .05
558 Dickie Thon .05
559 Pete Redfern .05
560 Ron LeFlore .05
561 Cardinals Batting & Pitching Ldrs. (Joaquin Andujar, Lonnie Smith) .05
562 Dave Rozema .05
563 Juan Bonilla .05
564 Sid Monge .05
565 Bucky Dent .05
566 Manny Sarmiento .05
567 Joe Simpson .05
568 Willie Hernandez .05
569 Jack Perconte .05
570 Vida Blue .05
571 Mickey Klutts .05
572 Bob Watson .05
573 Andy Hassler .05
574 Glenn Adams .05
575 Neil Allen .05
576 Frank Robinson .25
577 Luis Aponte .05
578 David Green .05
579 Rich Dauer .05
580 Tom Seaver 2.00
581 Tom Seaver (Super Veteran) .50
582 Marshall Edwards .05
583 Terry Forster .05
584 Dave Hostetler .05
585 Jose Cruz .05
586 *Frank Viola* 1.50
587 Ivan DeJesus .05
588 Pat Underwood .05
589 Alvis Woods .05
590 Tony Pena .05
591 White Sox Batting & Pitching Ldrs. (LaMarr Hoyt, Greg Luzinski) .05
592 Shane Rawley .05
593 Broderick Perkins .05
594 Eric Rasmussen .05
595 Tim Raines .05
596 Randy S. Johnson .05
597 Mike Proly .05
598 Dwayne Murphy .05
599 Don Aase .05
600 George Brett 3.50
601 Ed Lynch .05
602 Rich Gedman .05
603 Joe Morgan 1.00
604 Joe Morgan (Super Veteran) .25
605 Gary Roenicke .05
606 Bobby Cox .05
607 Charlie Leibrandt .05
608 Don Money .05
609 Danny Darwin .05
610 Steve Garvey .75
611 Bert Roberge .05
612 Steve Swisher .05
613 Mike Ivie .05
614 Ed Glynn .05
615 Garry Maddox .05
616 Bill Nahorodny .05
617 Butch Wynegar .05
618 LaMarr Hoyt .05
619 Keith Moreland .05
620 Mike Norris .05
621 Mets Batting & Pitching Ldrs. (Craig Swan, Mookie Wilson) .05
622 Dave Edler .05
623 Luis Sanchez .05
624 Glenn Hubbard .05
625 Ken Forsch .05
626 Jerry Martin .05
627 Doug Bair .05
628 Julio Valdez .05
629 Charlie Lea .05
630 Paul Molitor 2.00
631 Tippy Martinez .05
632 Alex Trevino .05
633 Vicente Romo .05
634 Max Venable .05
635 Graig Nettles .05
636 Graig Nettles (Super Veteran) .05
637 Pat Corrales .05
638 Dan Petry .05
639 Art Howe .05
640 Andre Thornton .05
641 Billy Sample .05
642 Checklist 529-660 .05
643 Bump Wills .05
644 Joe Lefebvre .05
645 Bill Madlock .05
646 Jim Essian .05
647 Bobby Mitchell .05
648 Jeff Burroughs .05
649 Tommy Boggs .05
650 George Hendrick .05
651 Angels Batting & Pitching Ldrs. (Rod Carew, Mike Witt) .05
652 Butch Hobson .05
653 Ellis Valentine .05
654 Bob Ojeda .05
655 Al Bumbry .05
656 Dave Frost .05
657 Mike Gates .05
658 Frank Pastore .05
659 Charlie Moore .05
660 Mike Hargrove .05
661 Bill Russell .05
662 Joe Sambito .05
663 Tom O'Malley .05
664 Bob Molinaro .05
665 Jim Sundberg .05
666 Sparky Anderson .25
667 Dick Davis .05
668 Larry Christenson .05
669 Mike Squires .05
670 Jerry Mumphrey .05
671 Lenny Faedo .05
672 Jim Kaat .10
673 Jim Kaat (Super Veteran) .05
674 Kurt Bevacqua .05
675 Jim Beattie .05
676 Biff Pocoroba .05
677 Dave Revering .05
678 Juan Beniquez .05
679 Mike Scott .05
680 Andre Dawson .75
681 Dodgers Batting & Pitching Ldrs. (Pedro Guerrero, Fernando Valenzuela) .05
682 Bob Stanley .05
683 Dan Ford .05
684 Rafael Landestoy .05
685 Lee Mazzilli .05
686 Randy Lerch .05
687 U.L. Washington .05
688 Jim Wohlford .05
689 Ron Hassey .05
690 Kent Hrbek .15
691 Dave Tobik .05
692 Denny Walling .05
693 Sparky Lyle .05
694 Sparky Lyle (Super Veteran) .05
695 Ruppert Jones .05
696 Chuck Tanner .05
697 Barry Foote .05
698 Tony Bernazard .05
699 Lee Smith .15
700 Keith Hernandez .05
701 Batting Leaders (Al Oliver, Willie Wilson) .05
702 Home Run Leaders (Reggie Jackson, Dave Kingman, Gorman Thomas) .15
703 Runs Batted In Leaders (Hal McRae, Dale Murphy, Al Oliver) .05
704 Stolen Base Leaders (Rickey Henderson, Tim Raines) .10
705 Victory Leaders (Steve Carlton, LaMarr Hoyt) .05

706 Strikeout Leaders (Floyd Bannister, Steve Carlton) .05
707 Earned Run Average Leaders (Steve Rogers, Rick Sutcliffe) .05
708 Leading Firemen (Dan Quisenberry, Bruce Sutter) .05
709 Jimmy Sexton .05
710 Willie Wilson .05
711 Mariners Batting & Pitching Ldrs. (Jim Beattie, Bruce Bochte) .05
712 Bruce Kison .05
713 Ron Hodges .05
714 Wayne Nordhagen .05
715 Tony Perez .75
716 Tony Perez (Super Veteran) .05
717 Scott Sanderson .05
718 Jim Dwyer .05
719 Rich Gale .05
720 Dave Concepcion .05
721 John Martin .05
722 Jorge Orta .05
723 Randy Moffitt .05
724 Johnny Grubb .05
725 Dan Spillner .05
726 Harvey Kuenn .05
727 Chet Lemon .05
728 Ron Reed .05
729 Jerry Morales .05
730 Jason Thompson .05
731 Al Williams .05
732 Dave Henderson .05
733 Buck Martinez .05
734 Steve Braun .05
735 Tommy John .20
736 Tommy John (Super Veteran) .05
737 Mitchell Page .05
738 Tim Foli .05
739 Rick Ownbey .05
740 Rusty Staub .05
741 Rusty Staub (Super Veteran) .05
742 Padres Batting & Pitching Ldrs. (Terry Kennedy, Tim Lollar) .05
743 Mike Torrez .05
744 Brad Mills .05
745 Scott McGregor .05
746 John Wathan .05
747 Fred Breining .05
748 Derrel Thomas .05
749 Jon Matlack .05
750 Ben Oglivie .05
751 Brad Havens .05
752 Luis Pujols .05
753 Elias Sosa .05
754 Bill Robinson .05
755 John Candelaria .05
756 Russ Nixon .05
757 Rick Manning .05
758 Aurelio Rodriguez .05
759 Doug Bird .05
760 Dale Murphy .75
761 Gary Lucas .05
762 Cliff Johnson .05
763 Al Cowens .05
764 Pete Falcone .05
765 Bob Boone .05
766 Barry Bonnell .05
767 Duane Kuiper .05
768 Chris Speier .05
769 Checklist 661-792 .05
770 Dave Winfield 2.00
771 Twins Batting & Pitching Ldrs. (Bobby Castillo, Kent Hrbek) .05
772 Jim Kern .05
773 Larry Hisle .05
774 Alan Ashby .05
775 Burt Hooton .05
776 Larry Parrish .05
777 John Curtis .05
778 Rich Hebner .05
779 Rick Waits .05
780 Gary Matthews .05
781 Rick Rhoden .05
782 Bobby Murcer .05
783 Bobby Murcer (Super Veteran) .05
784 Jeff Newman .05
785 Dennis Leonard .05
786 Ralph Houk .05
787 Dick Tidrow .05
788 Dane Iorg .05
789 Bryan Clark .05
790 Bob Grich .05
791 Gary Lavelle .05
792 Chris Chambliss .05

1983 Topps All-Star Glossy Set of 40

This set was a "consolation prize" in a scratch-off contest in regular packs of 1983 cards. The 2-1/2" x 3-1/2" cards have a large color photo surrounded by a yellow frame on the front. In very small type on a white border is printed the player's name. Backs carry the player's name, team, position and the card number along with a Topps identification. A major feature is that the surface of the front is glossy, which most collectors find very attractive. With many top stars, the set is a popular one, but the price has not moved too far above the issue price.

		MT
Complete Set (40):		6.00
Common Player:		.10
1	Carl Yastrzemski	.40
2	Mookie Wilson	.10
3	Andre Thornton	.10
4	Keith Hernandez	.10
5	Robin Yount	.30
6	Terry Kennedy	.10
7	Dave Winfield	.40
8	Mike Schmidt	.50
9	Buddy Bell	.10
10	Fernando Valenzuela	.10
11	Rich Gossage	.10
12	Bob Horner	.10
13	Toby Harrah	.10
14	Pete Rose	1.00
15	Cecil Cooper	.10
16	Dale Murphy	.30
17	Carlton Fisk	.30
18	Ray Knight	.10
19	Jim Palmer	.30
20	Gary Carter	.30
21	Richard Zisk	.10
22	Dusty Baker	.10
23	Willie Wilson	.10
24	Bill Buckner	.10
25	Dave Stieb	.10
26	Bill Madlock	.10
27	Lance Parrish	.10
28	Nolan Ryan	1.00
29	Rod Carew	.30
30	Al Oliver	.10
31	George Brett	.50
32	Jack Clark	.10
33	Rickey Henderson	.30
34	Dave Concepcion	.10
35	Kent Hrbek	.10
36	Steve Carlton	.30
37	Eddie Murray	.30
38	Ruppert Jones	.10
39	Reggie Jackson	.40
40	Bruce Sutter	.10

1983 Topps Stickers

Topps increased the number of stickers in its set to 330 in 1983, but retained the same 1-15/16" x 2-9/16" size. The stickers are again numbered on both the front and back. Similar in style to previous sticker issues, the set includes 28 "foil" stickers, and various special stickers highlighting the 1982 season, playoffs and World Series. An album was also available.

		MT
Complete Set (330):		30.00
Common Player:		.05
Sticker Album:		2.00
Wax Pack (5):		.25
Wax Box (100):		8.00
1	Hank Aaron	1.00
2	Babe Ruth	2.00
3	Willie Mays	1.00
4	Frank Robinson	.25
5	Reggie Jackson	.50
6	Carl Yastrzemski	.50
7	Johnny Bench	.20
8	Tony Perez	.15
9	Lee May	.05
10	Mike Schmidt	.60
11	Dave Kingman	.05
12	Reggie Smith	.05
13	Graig Nettles	.05
14	Rusty Staub	.05
15	Willie Wilson	.05
16	LaMarr Hoyt	.05
17	Reggie Jackson, Gorman Thomas	.10
18	Floyd Bannister	.05
19	Hal McRae	.05
20	Rick Sutcliffe	.05
21	Rickey Henderson	.15
22	Dan Quisenberry	.05
23	Jim Palmer	.20
24	John Lowenstein	.05
25	Mike Flanagan	.05
26	Cal Ripken, Jr.	1.00
27	Rich Dauer	.05
28	Ken Singleton	.05
29	Eddie Murray	.20
30	Rick Dempsey	.05
31	Carl Yastrzemski	.25
32	Carney Lansford	.05
33	Jerry Remy	.05
34	Dennis Eckersley	.05
35	Dave Stapleton	.05
36	Mark Clear	.05
37	Jim Rice	.15
38	Dwight Evans	.05
39	Rod Carew	.20
40	Don Baylor	.10
41	Reggie Jackson	.25
42	Geoff Zahn	.05
43	Bobby Grich	.05
44	Fred Lynn	.05
45	Bob Boone	.05
46	Doug DeCinces	.05
47	Tom Paciorek	.05
48	Britt Burns	.05
49	Tony Bernazard	.05
50	Steve Kemp	.05
51	Greg Luzinski	.05
52	Harold Baines	.05
53	LaMarr Hoyt	.05
54	Carlton Fisk	.20
55	Andre Thornton	.05
56	Mike Hargrove	.05
57	Len Barker	.05
58	Toby Harrah	.05
59	Dan Spillner	.05
60	Rick Manning	.05
61	Rick Sutcliffe	.05
62	Ron Hassey	.05
63	Lance Parrish	.05
64	John Wockenfuss	.05
65	Lou Whitaker	.05
66	Alan Trammell	.05
67	Kirk Gibson	.05
68	Larry Herndon	.05
69	Jack Morris	.05
70	Dan Petry	.05
71	Frank White	.05
72	Amos Otis	.05
73	Willie Wilson	.05
74	Dan Quisenberry	.05
75	Hal McRae	.05
76	George Brett	.60
77	Larry Gura	.05
78	John Wathan	.05
79	Rollie Fingers	.15
80	Cecil Cooper	.05
81	Robin Yount	.20
82	Ben Oglivie	.05
83	Paul Molitor	.20
84	Gorman Thomas	.05
85	Ted Simmons	.05
86	Pete Vuckovich	.05
87	Gary Gaetti	.05
88	Kent Hrbek	.05
89	John Castino	.05
90	Tom Brunansky	.05
91	Bobby Mitchell	.05
92	Gary Ward	.05
93	Tim Laudner	.05
94	Ron Davis	.05
95	Willie Randolph	.05
96	Roy Smalley	.05
97	Jerry Mumphrey	.05
98	Ken Griffey	.05
99	Dave Winfield	.20
100	Rich Gossage	.05
101	Butch Wynegar	.05
102	Ron Guidry	.05
103	Rickey Henderson	.15
104	Mike Heath	.05
105	Dave Lopes	.05
106	Rick Langford	.05
107	Dwayne Murphy	.05
108	Tony Armas	.05
109	Matt Keough	.05
110	Dan Meyer	.05
111	Bruce Bochte	.05
112	Julio Cruz	.05
113	Floyd Bannister	.05
114	Gaylord Perry	.15
115	Al Cowens	.05
116	Richie Zisk	.05
117	Jim Essian	.05
118	Bill Caudill	.05
119	Buddy Bell	.05
120	Larry Parrish	.05
121	Danny Darwin	.05
122	Bucky Dent	.05
123	Johnny Grubb	.05
124	George Wright	.05
125	Charlie Hough	.05
126	Jim Sundberg	.05
127	Dave Stieb	.05
128	Willie Upshaw	.05
129	Alfredo Griffin	.05
130	Lloyd Moseby	.05
131	Ernie Whitt	.05
132	Jim Clancy	.05
133	Barry Bonnell	.05
134	Damaso Garcia	.05
135	Jim Kaat	.05
136	Jim Kaat	.05
137	Greg Minton	.05

138	Greg Minton	.05
139	Paul Molitor	.20
140	Paul Molitor	.20
141	Manny Trillo	.05
142	Manny Trillo	.05
143	Joel Youngblood	.05
144	Joel Youngblood	.05
145	Robin Yount	.20
146	Robin Yount	.20
147	Willie McGee	.05
148	Darrell Porter	.05
149	Darrell Porter	.05
150	Robin Yount	.20
151	Bruce Benedict	.05
152	Bruce Benedict	.05
153	George Hendrick	.05
154	Bruce Benedict	.05
155	Doug DeCinces	.05
156	Paul Molitor	.20
157	Charlie Moore	.05
158	Fred Lynn	.05
159	Rickey Henderson	.15
160	Dale Murphy	.15
161	Willie Wilson	.05
162	Jack Clark	.05
163	Reggie Jackson	.25
164	Andre Dawson	.15
165	Dan Quisenberry	.05
166	Bruce Sutter	.05
167	Robin Yount	.20
168	Ozzie Smith	.25
169	Frank White	.05
170	Phil Garner	.05
171	Doug DeCinces	.05
172	Mike Schmidt	.60
173	Cecil Cooper	.05
174	Al Oliver	.05
175	Jim Palmer	.20
176	Steve Carlton	.15
177	Carlton Fisk	.20
178	Gary Carter	.15
179	Joaquin Andujar	.05
180	Ozzie Smith	.25
181	Cecil Cooper	.05
182	Darrell Porter	.05
183	Darrell Porter	.05
184	Mike Caldwell	.05
185	Mike Caldwell	.05
186	Ozzie Smith	.25
187	Bruce Sutter	.05
188	Keith Hernandez	.05
189	Dane Iorg	.05
190	Dane Iorg	.05
191	Tony Armas	.05
192	Tony Armas	.05
193	Lance Parrish	.05
194	Lance Parrish	.05
195	John Wathan	.05
196	John Wathan	.05
197	Rickey Henderson	.15
198	Rickey Henderson	.15
199	Rickey Henderson	.15
200	Rickey Henderson	.15
201	Rickey Henderson	.15
202	Rickey Henderson	.15
203	Steve Carlton	.15
204	Steve Carlton	.15
205	Al Oliver	.05
206	Dale Murphy, Al Oliver	.05
207	Dave Kingman	.05
208	Steve Rogers	.05
209	Bruce Sutter	.05
210	Tim Raines	.05
211	Dale Murphy	.15
212	Chris Chambliss	.05
213	Gene Garber	.05
214	Bob Horner	.05
215	Glenn Hubbard	.05
216	Claudell Washington	.05
217	Bruce Benedict	.05
218	Phil Niekro	.15
219	Leon Durham	.05
220	Jay Johnstone	.05
221	Larry Bowa	.05
222	Keith Moreland	.05
223	Bill Buckner	.05
224	Fergie Jenkins	.15
225	Dick Tidrow	.05
226	Jody Davis	.05
227	Dave Concepcion	.05
228	Dan Driessen	.05
229	Johnny Bench	.20
230	Ron Oester	.05
231	Cesar Cedeno	.05
232	Alex Trevino	.05
233	Tom Seaver	.20
234	Mario Soto	.05
235	Nolan Ryan	1.00
236	Art Howe	.05
237	Phil Garner	.05
238	Ray Knight	.05
239	Terry Puhl	.05
240	Joe Niekro	.05
241	Alan Ashby	.05
242	Jose Cruz	.05
243	Steve Garvey	.15
244	Ron Cey	.05
245	Dusty Baker	.05
246	Ken Landreaux	.05
247	Jerry Reuss	.05
248	Pedro Guerrero	.05
249	Bill Russell	.05
250	Fernando Valenzuela	.05
251	Al Oliver	.05
252	Andre Dawson	.15
253	Tim Raines	.05
254	Jeff Reardon	.05
255	Gary Carter	.15
256	Steve Rogers	.05
257	Tim Wallach	.05
258	Chris Speier	.05
259	Dave Kingman	.05
260	Bob Bailor	.05
261	Hubie Brooks	.05
262	Craig Swan	.05
263	George Foster	.05
264	John Stearns	.05
265	Neil Allen	.05
266	Mookie Wilson	.05
267	Steve Carlton	.20
268	Manny Trillo	.05
269	Gary Matthews	.05
270	Mike Schmidt	.60
271	Ivan DeJesus	.05
272	Pete Rose	1.00
273	Bo Diaz	.05
274	Sid Monge	.05
275	Bill Madlock	.05
276	Jason Thompson	.05
277	Don Robinson	.05
278	Omar Moreno	.05
279	Dale Berra	.05
280	Dave Parker	.05
281	Tony Pena	.05
282	John Candelaria	.05
283	Lonnie Smith	.05
284	Bruce Sutter	.05
285	George Hendrick	.05
286	Tom Herr	.05
287	Ken Oberkfell	.05
288	Ozzie Smith	.25
289	Bob Forsch	.05
290	Keith Hernandez	.05
291	Garry Templeton	.05
292	Broderick Perkins	.05
293	Terry Kennedy	.05
294	Gene Richards	.05
295	Ruppert Jones	.05
296	Tim Lollar	.05
297	John Montefusco	.05
298	Sixto Lezcano	.05
299	Greg Minton	.05
300	Jack Clark	.05
301	Milt May	.05
302	Reggie Smith	.05
303	Joe Morgan	.20
304	John LeMaster	.05
305	Darrell Evans	.05
306	Al Holland	.05
307	Jesse Barfield	.05
308	Wade Boggs	.50
309	Tom Brunansky	.05
310	Storm Davis	.05
311	Von Hayes	.05
312	Dave Hostetler	.05
313	Kent Hrbek	.05
314	Tim Laudner	.05
315	Cal Ripken, Jr.	1.00
316	Andre Robertson	.05
317	Ed Vande Berg	.05
318	Glenn Wilson	.05
319	Chili Davis	.05
320	Bob Dernier	.05
321	Terry Francona	.05
322	Brian Giles	.05
323	David Green	.05
324	Atlee Hammaker	.05
325	Bill Laskey	.05
326	Willie McGee	.05
327	Johnny Ray	.05
328	Ryne Sandberg	.75
329	Steve Sax	.05
330	Eric Show	.05

1983 Topps 1952 Reprint Set

The first of several reprint/retro sets in different sports issued by Topps, the 402-card reprinting of its classic 1952 baseball card set was controversial at the time of issue, but has since gained hobby acceptance and market value. To avoid possible confusion of the reprints for originals, the reprints were done in the now-standard 2-1/2" x 3-1/2" format instead of the original 2-5/8" x 3-3/4". Backs, printed in red, carry a line "Topps 1952 Reprint Series" at bottom, though there is no indication of the year of reprinting. Fronts have a semi-gloss finish, which also differs from the originals. Because of inability to come to terms with five of the players from the original 1952 Topps set, they were not included in the reprint series. Those cards which weren't issued are: #20 Billy Loes, #22 Dom DiMaggio, #159 Saul Rogovin, #196 Solly Hemus, and #289 Tommy Holmes. The '52 reprints were available only as a complete boxed set with a retail price of about $40 at issue.

		MT
	Complete Sealed Boxed Set:	250.00
	Complete Set (402):	190.00
	Common Player:	.25
	Minor Stars:	.35
	Typical Hall of Famers:	2.00
	Superstar Hall of Famers:	8.00
311	Mickey Mantle	40.00
407	Eddie Mathews (sample card)	8.00

(See 1952 Topps for checklist)

1983 Topps Traded

These 2-1/2" x 3-1/2" cards mark a continuation of the traded set introduced in 1981. The 132 cards retain the basic design of the year's regular issue, with their numbering being 1-132 with the "T" suffix. Cards in the set include traded players, new managers and promising rookies. Sold only through dealers, the set was in heavy demand as it contained the first cards of Darryl Strawberry, Ron Kittle, Julio Franco and Mel Hall. While some of those cards were very hot in 1983, it seems likely that some of the rookies may not live up to their initial promise.

		MT
	Complete Set (132):	20.00
	Common Player:	.10
1T	Neil Allen	.10
2T	Bill Almon	.10
3T	Joe Altobelli	.10
4T	Tony Armas	.10
5T	Doug Bair	.10
6T	Steve Baker	.10
7T	Floyd Bannister	.10
8T	Don Baylor	.25
9T	Tony Bernazard	.10
10T	Larry Biittner	.10
11T	Dann Bilardello	.10
12T	Doug Bird	.10
13T	Steve Boros	.10
14T	Greg Brock	.10
15T	Mike Brown	.10
16T	Tom Burgmeier	.10
17T	Randy Bush	.10
18T	Bert Campaneris	.10
19T	Ron Cey	.10
20T	Chris Codiroli	.10
21T	Dave Collins	.10
22T	Terry Crowley	.10
23T	Julio Cruz	.10
24T	Mike Davis	.10
25T	Frank DiPino	.10
26T	Bill Doran	.10
27T	Jerry Dybzinski	.10
28T	Jamie Easterly	.10
29T	Juan Eichelberger	.10
30T	Jim Essian	.10
31T	Pete Falcone	.10
32T	Mike Ferraro	.10
33T	Terry Forster	.10
34T	*Julio Franco*	1.00
35T	Rich Gale	.10
36T	Kiko Garcia	.10
37T	Steve Garvey	2.00
38T	Johnny Grubb	.10
39T	Mel Hall	.10
40T	Von Hayes	.10
41T	Danny Heep	.10
42T	Steve Henderson	.10
43T	Keith Hernandez	.15
44T	Leo Hernandez	.10
45T	Willie Hernandez	.10
46T	Al Holland	.10
47T	Frank Howard	.15
48T	Bobby Johnson	.10
49T	Cliff Johnson	.10
50T	Odell Jones	.10
51T	Mike Jorgensen	.10
52T	Bob Kearney	.10
53T	Steve Kemp	.10
54T	Matt Keough	.10

55T Ron Kittle .10
56T Mickey Klutts .10
57T Alan Knicely .10
58T Mike Krukow .10
59T Rafael Landestoy .10
60T Carney Lansford .10
61T Joe Lefebvre .10
62T Bryan Little .10
63T Aurelio Lopez .10
64T Mike Madden .10
65T Rick Manning .10
66T Billy Martin .25
67T Lee Mazzilli .10
68T Andy McGaffigan .10
69T Craig McMurtry .10
70T John McNamara .10
71T Orlando Mercado .10
72T Larry Milbourne .10
73T Randy Moffitt .10
74T Sid Monge .10
75T Jose Morales .10
76T Omar Moreno .10
77T Joe Morgan 4.00
78T Mike Morgan .10
79T Dale Murray .10
80T Jeff Newman .10
81T Pete O'Brien .10
82T Jorge Orta .10
83T Alejandro Pena .10
84T Pascual Perez .10
85T Tony Perez 1.00
86T Broderick Perkins .10
87T *Tony Phillips* 1.00
88T Charlie Puleo .10
89T Pat Putnam .10
90T Jamie Quirk .10
91T Doug Rader .10
92T Chuck Rainey .10
93T Bobby Ramos .10
94T Gary Redus .10
95T Steve Renko .10
96T Leon Roberts .10
97T Aurelio Rodriguez .10
98T Dick Ruthven .10
99T Daryl Sconiers .10
100T Mike Scott .10
101T Tom Seaver 7.50
102T John Shelby .10
103T Bob Shirley .10
104T Joe Simpson .10
105T Doug Sisk .10
106T Mike Smithson .10
107T Elias Sosa .10
108T *Darryl Strawberry* 6.00
109T Tom Tellmann .10
110T Gene Tenace .10
111T Gorman Thomas .10
112T Dick Tidrow .10
113T Dave Tobik .10
114T Wayne Tolleson .10
115T Mike Torrez .10
116T Manny Trillo .10
117T Steve Trout .10
118T Lee Tunnell .10
119T Mike Vail .10
120T Ellis Valentine .10
121T Tom Veryzer .10
122T George Vukovich .10
123T Rick Waits .10
124T Greg Walker .10
125T Chris Welsh .10
126T Len Whitehouse .10
127T Eddie Whitson .10
128T Jim Wohlford .10
129T Matt Young .10
130T Joel Youngblood .10
131T Pat Zachry .10
132T Checklist 1-132 .10

1984 Topps

Another 792-card regular set from Topps. For the second straight year, the 2-1/2" x 3-1/2" cards featured a color action photo on the front along with a small portrait photo in the lower-left. The team name runs in big letters down the left side, while the player's name and position appear under the action photo. Backs have a team logo in the upper-right, along with statistics, personal information and a few highlights, all in a hard-to-read red and purple coloring. Specialty cards include past season highlights, team leaders, statistical leaders, All-Stars, active career leaders and numbered checklists. Again, promising rookies were saved for the traded set.

	MT
Complete Set (792):	40.00
Common Player:	.05
Pack (15):	2.00
Wax Box (36):	45.00
Cello Pack (28):	3.00
Cello Box (24):	50.00
Rack Pack (51):	4.00
Rack Box (24):	50.00
Vending Box (500):	20.00

1 Steve Carlton (1983 Highlight) .25
2 Rickey Henderson (1983 Highlight) .25
3 Dan Quisenberry (1983 Highlight) .05
4 Steve Carlton, Gaylord Perry, Nolan Ryan (1983 Highlight) .50
5 Bob Forsch, Dave Righetti, Mike Warren (1983 Highlight) .05
6 Johnny Bench, Gaylord Perry, Carl Yastrzemski (1983 Highlight) .25
7 Gary Lucas .05
8 *Don Mattingly* 11.00
9 Jim Gott .05
10 Robin Yount 1.00
11 Twins Batting & Pitching Leaders (Kent Hrbek, Ken Schrom) .05
12 Billy Sample .05
13 Scott Holman .05
14 Tom Brookens .05
15 Burt Hooton .05
16 Omar Moreno .05
17 John Denny .05
18 Dale Berra .05
19 *Ray Fontenot* .05
20 Greg Luzinski .05
21 Joe Altobelli .05
22 Bryan Clark .05
23 Keith Moreland .05
24 John Martin .05
25 Glenn Hubbard .05
26 Bud Black .05
27 Daryl Sconiers .05
28 Frank Viola .05
29 Danny Heep .05
30 Wade Boggs 3.00
31 Andy McGaffigan .05
32 Bobby Ramos .05
33 Tom Burgmeier .05
34 Eddie Milner .05
35 Don Sutton .65
36 Denny Walling .05
37 Rangers Batting & Pitching Leaders (Buddy Bell, Rick Honeycutt) .05
38 Luis DeLeon .05
39 Garth Iorg .05
40 Dusty Baker .05
41 Tony Bernazard .05
42 Johnny Grubb .05
43 Ron Reed .05
44 Jim Morrison .05
45 Jerry Mumphrey .05
46 Ray Smith .05
47 Rudy Law .05
48 Julio Franco .05
49 John Stuper .05
50 Chris Chambliss .05
51 Jim Frey .05
52 Paul Splittorff .05
53 Juan Beniquez .05
54 Jesse Orosco .05
55 Dave Concepcion .05
56 Gary Allenson .05
57 Dan Schatzeder .05
58 Max Venable .05
59 Sammy Stewart .05
60 Paul Molitor 1.00
61 *Chris Codiroli* .05
62 Dave Hostetler .05
63 Ed Vande Berg .05
64 Mike Scioscia .05
65 Kirk Gibson .05
66 Astros Batting & Pitching Leaders (Jose Cruz, Nolan Ryan) .25
67 Gary Ward .05
68 Luis Salazar .05
69 Rod Scurry .05
70 Gary Matthews .05
71 Leo Hernandez .05
72 Mike Squires .05
73 Jody Davis .05
74 Jerry Martin .05
75 Bob Forsch .05
76 Alfredo Griffin .05
77 Brett Butler .05
78 Mike Torrez .05
79 Rob Wilfong .05
80 Steve Rogers .05
81 Billy Martin .15
82 Doug Bird .05
83 Richie Zisk .05
84 Lenny Faedo .05
85 Atlee Hammaker .05
86 *John Shelby* .05
87 Frank Pastore .05
88 Rob Picciolo .05
89 *Mike Smithson* .05
90 Pedro Guerrero .05
91 Dan Spillner .05
92 Lloyd Moseby .05
93 Bob Knepper .05
94 Mario Ramirez .05
95 Aurelio Lopez .05
96 Royals Batting & Pitching Leaders (Larry Gura, Hal McRae) .05
97 LaMarr Hoyt .05
98 Steve Nicosia .05
99 *Craig Lefferts* .25
100 Reggie Jackson 1.50
101 Porfirio Altamirano .05
102 Ken Oberkfell .05
103 Dwayne Murphy .05
104 Ken Dayley .05
105 Tony Armas .05
106 Tim Stoddard .05
107 Ned Yost .05
108 Randy Moffitt .05
109 Brad Wellman .05
110 Ron Guidry .05
111 Bill Virdon .05
112 Tom Niedenfuer .05
113 Kelly Paris .05
114 Checklist 1-132 .05
115 Andre Thornton .05
116 George Bjorkman .05
117 Tom Veryzer .05
118 Charlie Hough .05
119 Johnny Wockenfuss .05
120 Keith Hernandez .05
121 *Pat Sheridan* .05
122 Cecilio Guante .05
123 Butch Wynegar .05
124 Damaso Garcia .05
125 Britt Burns .05
126 Braves Batting & Pitching Leaders (Craig McMurtry, Dale Murphy) .05
127 Mike Madden .05
128 Rick Manning .05
129 Bill Laskey .05
130 Ozzie Smith 1.50
131 Batting Leaders (Wade Boggs, Bill Madlock) .25
132 Home Run Leaders (Jim Rice, Mike Schmidt) .25
133 RBI Leaders (Cecil Cooper, Dale Murphy, Jim Rice) .10
134 Stolen Base Leaders (Rickey Henderson, Tim Raines) .25
135 Victory Leaders (John Denny, LaMarr Hoyt) .05
136 Strikeout Leaders (Steve Carlton, Jack Morris) .05
137 Earned Run Average Leaders (Atlee Hammaker, Rick Honeycutt) .05
138 Leading Firemen (Al Holland, Dan Quisenberry) .05
139 Bert Campaneris .05
140 Storm Davis .05
141 Pat Corrales .05
142 Rich Gale .05
143 Jose Morales .05
144 *Brian Harper* .20
145 Gary Lavelle .05
146 Ed Romero .05
147 Dan Petry .05
148 Joe Lefebvre .05
149 Jon Matlack .05
150 Dale Murphy .50
151 Steve Trout .05
152 Glenn Brummer .05
153 Dick Tidrow .05
154 Dave Henderson .05
155 Frank White .05
156 Athletics Batting & Pitching Leaders (Tim Conroy, Rickey Henderson) .15
157 Gary Gaetti .05
158 John Curtis .05
159 Darryl Cias .05
160 Mario Soto .05
161 *Junior Ortiz* .05
162 Bob Ojeda .05
163 Lorenzo Gray .05
164 Scott Sanderson .05
165 Ken Singleton .05
166 Jamie Nelson .05
167 Marshall Edwards .05
168 Juan Bonilla .05
169 Larry Parrish .05
170 Jerry Reuss .05
171 Frank Robinson .25
172 Frank DiPino .05
173 *Marvell Wynne* .05
174 Juan Berenguer .05
175 Graig Nettles .05
176 Lee Smith .05
177 Jerry Hairston Sr. .05
178 Bill Krueger .05
179 Buck Martinez .05
180 Manny Trillo .05
181 Roy Thomas .05
182 Darryl Strawberry .25
183 Al Williams .05
184 Mike O'Berry .05
185 Sixto Lezcano .05
186 Cardinals Batting & Pitching Leaders (Lonnie Smith, John Stuper) .05
187 Luis Aponte .05
188 Bryan Little .05
189 *Tim Conroy* .05
190 Ben Oglivie .05
191 Mike Boddicker .05
192 *Nick Esasky* .05
193 Darrell Brown .05
194 Domingo Ramos .05
195 Jack Morris .05
196 Don Slaught .05
197 Garry Hancock .05
198 *Bill Doran* .05
199 Willie Hernandez .05
200 Andre Dawson .60
201 Bruce Kison .05
202 Bobby Cox .05
203 Matt Keough .05
204 *Bobby Meacham* .05
205 Greg Minton .05
206 *Andy Van Slyke* .75

207 Donnie Moore .05
208 *Jose Oquendo* .05
209 Manny Sarmiento .05
210 Joe Morgan .75
211 Rick Sweet .05
212 Broderick Perkins .05
213 Bruce Hurst .05
214 Paul Householder .05
215 Tippy Martinez .05
216 White Sox Batting & Pitching Leaders (Richard Dotson, Carlton Fisk) .05
217 Alan Ashby .05
218 Rick Waits .05
219 Joe Simpson .05
220 Fernando Valenzuela .05
221 Cliff Johnson .05
222 Rick Honeycutt .05
223 Wayne Krenchicki .05
224 Sid Monge .05
225 Lee Mazzilli .05
226 Juan Eichelberger .05
227 Steve Braun .05
228 John Rabb .05
229 Paul Owens .05
230 Rickey Henderson 1.00
231 Gary Woods .05
232 Tim Wallach .05
233 Checklist 133-264 .05
234 Rafael Ramirez .05
235 *Matt Young* .05
236 Ellis Valentine .05
237 John Castino .05
238 Reid Nichols .05
239 Jay Howell .05
240 Eddie Murray 1.00
241 Billy Almon .05
242 Alex Trevino .05
243 Pete Ladd .05
244 Candy Maldonado .05
245 Rick Sutcliffe .05
246 Mets Batting & Pitching Leaders (Tom Seaver, Mookie Wilson) .25
247 Onix Concepcion .05
248 *Bill Dawley* .05
249 Jay Johnstone .05
250 Bill Madlock .05
251 Tony Gwynn 4.00
252 Larry Christenson .05
253 Jim Wohlford .05
254 Shane Rawley .05
255 Bruce Benedict .05
256 Dave Geisel .05
257 Julio Cruz .05
258 Luis Sanchez .05
259 Sparky Anderson .25
260 Scott McGregor .05
261 Bobby Brown .05
262 *Tom Candiotti* .25
263 Jack Fimple .05
264 Doug Frobel .05
265 *Donnie Hill* .05
266 Steve Lubratich .05
267 *Carmelo Martinez* .05
268 Jack O'Connor .05
269 Aurelio Rodriguez .05
270 *Jeff Russell* .05
271 Moose Haas .05
272 Rick Dempsey .05
273 Charlie Puleo .05
274 Rick Monday .05
275 Len Matuszek .05
276 Angels Batting & Pitching Leaders (Rod Carew, Geoff Zahn) .10
277 Eddie Whitson .05
278 Jorge Bell .05
279 Ivan DeJesus .05
280 Floyd Bannister .05
281 Larry Milbourne .05
282 Jim Barr .05
283 Larry Biittner .05
284 Howard Bailey .05
285 Darrell Porter .05
286 Lary Sorensen .05
287 Warren Cromartie .05
288 Jim Beattie .05
289 Randy S. Johnson .05
290 Dave Dravecky .05
291 Chuck Tanner .05
292 Tony Scott .05
293 Ed Lynch .05
294 U.L. Washington .05
295 Mike Flanagan .05
296 Jeff Newman .05
297 Bruce Berenyi .05
298 Jim Gantner .05
299 John Butcher .05
300 Pete Rose 3.00
301 Frank LaCorte .05
302 Barry Bonnell .05
303 Marty Castillo .05
304 Warren Brusstar .05
305 Roy Smalley .05
306 Dodgers Batting & Pitching Leaders (Pedro Guerrero, Bob Welch) .05
307 Bobby Mitchell .05
308 Ron Hassey .05
309 Tony Phillips .05
310 Willie McGee .05
311 Jerry Koosman .05
312 Jorge Orta .05
313 Mike Jorgensen .05
314 Orlando Mercado .05
315 Bob Grich .05
316 Mark Bradley .05
317 Greg Pryor .05
318 Bill Gullickson .05
319 Al Bumbry .05
320 Bob Stanley .05
321 Harvey Kuenn .05
322 Ken Schrom .05
323 Alan Knicely .05
324 *Alejandro Pena* .05
325 Darrell Evans .05
326 Bob Kearney .05
327 Ruppert Jones .05
328 Vern Ruhle .05
329 Pat Tabler .05
330 John Candelaria .05
331 Bucky Dent .05
332 *Kevin Gross* .05
333 Larry Herndon .05
334 Chuck Rainey .05
335 Don Baylor .15
336 Mariners Batting & Pitching Leaders (Pat Putnam, Matt Young) .05
337 Kevin Hagen .05
338 Mike Warren .05
339 Roy Lee Jackson .05
340 Hal McRae .05
341 Dave Tobik .05
342 Tim Foli .05
343 Mark Davis .05
344 Rick Miller .05
345 Kent Hrbek .05
346 Kurt Bevacqua .05
347 Allan Ramirez .05
348 Toby Harrah .05
349 Bob L. Gibson .05
350 George Foster .05
351 Russ Nixon .05
352 Dave Stewart .05
353 Jim Anderson .05
354 Jeff Burroughs .05
355 Jason Thompson .05
356 Glenn Abbott .05
357 Ron Cey .05
358 Bob Dernier .05
359 *Jim Acker* .05
360 Willie Randolph .05
361 Dave Smith .05
362 David Green .05
363 Tim Laudner .05
364 Scott Fletcher .05
365 Steve Bedrosian .05
366 Padres Batting & Pitching Leaders (Dave Dravecky, Terry Kennedy) .05
367 Jamie Easterly .05
368 Hubie Brooks .05
369 Steve McCatty .05
370 Tim Raines .05
371 Dave Gumpert .05
372 Gary Roenicke .05
373 Bill Scherrer .05
374 Don Money .05
375 Dennis Leonard .05
376 *Dave Anderson* .05
377 Danny Darwin .05
378 Bob Brenly .05
379 Checklist 265-396 .05
380 Steve Garvey .45
381 Ralph Houk .05
382 Chris Nyman .05
383 Terry Puhl .05
384 *Lee Tunnell* .05
385 Tony Perez .75
386 George Hendrick (All-Star) .05
387 Johnny Ray (All-Star) .05
388 Mike Schmidt (All-Star) .75
389 Ozzie Smith (All-Star) .50
390 Tim Raines (All-Star) .05
391 Dale Murphy (All-Star) .20
392 Andre Dawson (All-Star) .25
393 Gary Carter (All-Star) .20
394 Steve Rogers (All-Star) .05
395 Steve Carlton (All-Star) .25
396 Jesse Orosco (All-Star) .05
397 Eddie Murray (All-Star) .40
398 Lou Whitaker (All-Star) .05
399 George Brett (All-Star) .75
400 Cal Ripken, Jr. (All-Star) 4.00
401 Jim Rice (All-Star) .05
402 Dave Winfield (All-Star) .30
403 Lloyd Moseby (All-Star) .05
404 Ted Simmons (All-Star) .05
405 LaMarr Hoyt (All-Star) .05
406 Ron Guidry (All-Star) .05
407 Dan Quisenberry (All-Star) .05
408 Lou Piniella .05
409 *Juan Agosto* .05
410 Claudell Washington .05
411 Houston Jimenez .05
412 Doug Rader .05
413 *Spike Owen* .05
414 Mitchell Page .05
415 Tommy John .15
416 Dane Iorg .05
417 Mike Armstrong .05
418 Ron Hodges .05
419 John Henry Johnson .05
420 Cecil Cooper .05
421 Charlie Lea .05
422 Jose Cruz .05
423 Mike Morgan .05
424 Dann Bilardello .05
425 Steve Howe .05
426 Orioles Batting & Pitching Leaders (Mike Boddicker, Cal Ripken, Jr.) .50
427 Rick Leach .05
428 Fred Breining .05
429 *Randy Bush* .05
430 Rusty Staub .05
431 Chris Bando .05
432 *Charlie Hudson* .05
433 Rich Hebner .05
434 Harold Baines .05
435 Neil Allen .05
436 Rick Peters .05
437 Mike Proly .05
438 Biff Pocoroba .05
439 Bob Stoddard .05
440 Steve Kemp .05
441 Bob Lillis .05
442 Byron McLaughlin .05
443 Benny Ayala .05
444 Steve Renko .05
445 Jerry Remy .05
446 Luis Pujols .05
447 Tom Brunansky .05
448 Ben Hayes .05
449 Joe Pettini .05
450 Gary Carter .45
451 Bob Jones .05
452 Chuck Porter .05
453 Willie Upshaw .05
454 Joe Beckwith .05
455 Terry Kennedy .05
456 Cubs Batting & Pitching Leaders (Fergie Jenkins, Keith Moreland) .05
457 Dave Rozema .05
458 Kiko Garcia .05
459 Kevin Hickey .05
460 Dave Winfield 1.00
461 Jim Maler .05
462 Lee Lacy .05
463 Dave Engle .05
464 Jeff Jones .05
465 Mookie Wilson .05
466 Gene Garber .05
467 Mike Ramsey .05
468 Geoff Zahn .05
469 Tom O'Malley .05
470 Nolan Ryan 6.00
471 Dick Howser .05
472 Mike Brown .05
473 Jim Dwyer .05
474 Greg Bargar .05
475 *Gary Redus* .05
476 Tom Tellmann .05
477 Rafael Landestoy .05
478 Alan Bannister .05
479 Frank Tanana .05
480 Ron Kittle .05
481 *Mark Thurmond* .05
482 Enos Cabell .05
483 Fergie Jenkins .65
484 Ozzie Virgil .05
485 Rick Rhoden .05
486 Yankees Batting & Pitching Leaders (Don Baylor, Ron Guidry) .05
487 Ricky Adams .05
488 Jesse Barfield .05
489 Dave Von Ohlen .05
490 Cal Ripken, Jr. 6.00
491 Bobby Castillo .05
492 Tucker Ashford .05
493 Mike Norris .05
494 Chili Davis .05
495 Rollie Fingers .65
496 Terry Francona .05
497 Bud Anderson .05
498 Rich Gedman .05
499 Mike Witt .05
500 George Brett 2.00
501 Steve Henderson .05
502 Joe Torre .05
503 Elias Sosa .05
504 Mickey Rivers .05
505 Pete Vuckovich .05
506 Ernie Whitt .05
507 Mike LaCoss .05
508 Mel Hall .05
509 Brad Havens .05
510 Alan Trammell .05
511 Marty Bystrom .05
512 Oscar Gamble .05
513 Dave Beard .05
514 Floyd Rayford .05
515 Gorman Thomas .05
516 Expos Batting & Pitching Leaders (Charlie Lea, Al Oliver) .05
517 John Moses .05
518 *Greg Walker* .05
519 Ron Davis .05
520 Bob Boone .05
521 Pete Falcone .05
522 Dave Bergman .05
523 Glenn Hoffman .05
524 Carlos Diaz .05
525 Willie Wilson .05
526 Ron Oester .05
527 Checklist 397-528 .05
528 Mark Brouhard .05
529 *Keith Atherton* .05
530 Dan Ford .05
531 Steve Boros .05
532 Eric Show .05
533 Ken Landreaux .05
534 Pete O'Brien .05
535 Bo Diaz .05
536 Doug Bair .05
537 Johnny Ray .05
538 Kevin Bass .05
539 George Frazier .05
540 George Hendrick .05
541 Dennis Lamp .05
542 Duane Kuiper .05
543 *Craig McMurtry* .05
544 Cesar Geronimo .05
545 Bill Buckner .05
546 Indians Batting & Pitching Leaders (Mike Hargrove, Lary Sorensen) .05
547 Mike Moore .05
548 Ron Jackson .05
549 *Walt Terrell* .05
550 Jim Rice .15
551 Scott Ullger .05

552 Ray Burris .05
553 Joe Nolan .05
554 Ted Power .05
555 Greg Brock .05
556 Joey McLaughlin .05
557 Wayne Tolleson .05
558 Mike Davis .05
559 Mike Scott .05
560 Carlton Fisk .75
561 Whitey Herzog .05
562 Manny Castillo .05
563 Glenn Wilson .05
564 Al Holland .05
565 Leon Durham .05
566 Jim Bibby .05
567 Mike Heath .05
568 Pete Filson .05
569 Bake McBride .05
570 Dan Quisenberry .05
571 Bruce Bochy .05
572 Jerry Royster .05
573 Dave Kingman .05
574 Brian Downing .05
575 Jim Clancy .05
576 Giants Batting & Pitching Leaders (Atlee Hammaker, Jeff Leonard) .05
577 Mark Clear .05
578 Lenn Sakata .05
579 Bob James .05
580 Lonnie Smith .05
581 *Jose DeLeon* .05
582 Bob McClure .05
583 Derrel Thomas .05
584 Dave Schmidt .05
585 Dan Driessen .05
586 Joe Niekro .05
587 Von Hayes .05
588 Milt Wilcox .05
589 Mike Easler .05
590 Dave Stieb .05
591 Tony LaRussa .05
592 Andre Robertson .05
593 Jeff Lahti .05
594 Gene Richards .05
595 Jeff Reardon .05
596 Ryne Sandberg 3.00
597 Rick Camp .05
598 Rusty Kuntz .05
599 *Doug Sisk* .05
600 Rod Carew 1.00
601 John Tudor .05
602 John Wathan .05
603 Renie Martin .05
604 John Lowenstein .05
605 Mike Caldwell .05
606 Blue Jays Batting & Pitching Leaders (Lloyd Moseby, Dave Stieb) .05
607 Tom Hume .05
608 Bobby Johnson .05
609 Dan Meyer .05
610 Steve Sax .05
611 Chet Lemon .05
612 Harry Spilman .05
613 Greg Gross .05
614 Len Barker .05
615 Garry Templeton .05
616 Don Robinson .05
617 Rick Cerone .05
618 Dickie Noles .05
619 Jerry Dybzinski .05
620 Al Oliver .05
621 Frank Howard .05
622 Al Cowens .05
623 Ron Washington .05
624 Terry Harper .05
625 Larry Gura .05
626 Bob Clark .05
627 Dave LaPoint .05
628 Ed Jurak .05
629 Rick Langford .05
630 Ted Simmons .05
631 Denny Martinez .05
632 Tom Foley .05
633 Mike Krukow .05
634 Mike Marshall .05
635 Dave Righetti .05
636 Pat Putnam .05
637 Phillies Batting & Pitching Leaders (John Denny, Gary Matthews) .05
638 George Vukovich .05
639 Rick Lysander .05
640 Lance Parrish .05
641 Mike Richardt .05
642 Tom Underwood .05
643 Mike Brown .05
644 Tim Lollar .05
645 Tony Pena .05
646 Checklist 529-660 .05
647 Ron Roenicke .05
648 Len Whitehouse .05
649 Tom Herr .05
650 Phil Niekro .65
651 John McNamara .05
652 Rudy May .05
653 Dave Stapleton .05
654 Bob Bailor .05
655 Amos Otis .05
656 Bryn Smith .05
657 Thad Bosley .05
658 Jerry Augustine .05
659 Duane Walker .05
660 Ray Knight .05
661 Steve Yeager .05
662 Tom Brennan .05
663 Johnnie LeMaster .05
664 Dave Stegman .05
665 Buddy Bell .05
666 Tigers Batting & Pitching Leaders (Jack Morris, Lou Whitaker) .05
667 Vance Law .05
668 Larry McWilliams .05
669 Dave Lopes .05
670 Rich Gossage .05
671 Jamie Quirk .05
672 Ricky Nelson .05
673 Mike Walters .05
674 Tim Flannery .05
675 Pascual Perez .05
676 Brian Giles .05
677 Doyle Alexander .05
678 Chris Speier .05
679 Art Howe .05
680 Fred Lynn .05
681 Tom Lasorda .35
682 Dan Morogiello .05
683 *Marty Barrett* .05
684 Bob Shirley .05
685 Willie Aikens .05
686 Joe Price .05
687 Roy Howell .05
688 George Wright .05
689 Mike Fischlin .05
690 Jack Clark .05
691 *Steve Lake* .05
692 Dickie Thon .05
693 Alan Wiggins .05
694 Mike Stanton .05
695 Lou Whitaker .05
696 Pirates Batting & Pitching Leaders (Bill Madlock, Rick Rhoden) .05
697 Dale Murray .05
698 Marc Hill .05
699 Dave Rucker .05
700 Mike Schmidt 2.00
701 NL Active Career Batting Leaders (Bill Madlock, Dave Parker, Pete Rose) .25
702 NL Active Career Hit Leaders (Tony Perez, Pete Rose, Rusty Staub) .25
703 NL Active Career Home Run Leaders (Dave Kingman, Tony Perez, Mike Schmidt) .15
704 NL Active Career RBI Leaders (Al Oliver, Tony Perez, Rusty Staub) .05
705 NL Active Career Stolen Bases Leaders (Larry Bowa, Cesar Cedeno, Joe Morgan) .05
706 NL Active Career Victory Leaders (Steve Carlton, Fergie Jenkins, Tom Seaver) .05
707 NL Active Career Strike-out Leaders (Steve Carlton, Nolan Ryan, Tom Seaver) .35
708 NL Active Career ERA Leaders (Steve Carlton, Steve Rogers, Tom Seaver) .05
709 NL Active Career Save Leaders (Gene Garber, Tug McGraw, Bruce Sutter) .05
710 AL Active Career Batting Leaders (George Brett, Rod Carew, Cecil Cooper) .25
711 AL Active Career Hit Leaders (Bert Campaneris, Rod Carew, Reggie Jackson) .15
712 AL Active Career Home Run Leaders (Reggie Jackson, Greg Luzinski, Graig Nettles) .15
713 AL Active Career RBI Leaders (Reggie Jackson, Graig Nettles, Ted Simmons) .15
714 AL Active Career Stolen Bases Leaders (Bert Campaneris, Dave Lopes, Omar Moreno) .05
715 AL Active Career Victory Leaders (Tommy John, Jim Palmer, Don Sutton) .05
716 AL Active Strikeout Leaders (Bert Blyleven, Jerry Koosman, Don Sutton) .05
717 AL Active Career ERA Leaders (Rollie Fingers, Ron Guidry, Jim Palmer) .05
718 AL Active Career Save Leaders (Rollie Fingers, Rich Gossage, Dan Quisenberry) .05
719 Andy Hassler .05
720 Dwight Evans .05
721 Del Crandall .05
722 Bob Welch .05
723 Rich Dauer .05
724 Eric Rasmussen .05
725 Cesar Cedeno .05
726 Brewers Batting & Pitching Leaders (Moose Haas, Ted Simmons) .05
727 Joel Youngblood .05
728 Tug McGraw .05
729 Gene Tenace .05
730 Bruce Sutter .05
731 Lynn Jones .05
732 Terry Crowley .05
733 Dave Collins .05
734 Odell Jones .05
735 Rick Burleson .05
736 Dick Ruthven .05
737 Jim Essian .05
738 *Bill Schroeder* .05
739 Bob Watson .05
740 Tom Seaver 1.00
741 Wayne Gross .05
742 Dick Williams .05
743 Don Hood .05
744 Jamie Allen .05
745 Dennis Eckersley .05
746 Mickey Hatcher .05
747 Pat Zachry .05
748 Jeff Leonard .05
749 Doug Flynn .05
750 Jim Palmer 1.00
751 Charlie Moore .05
752 Phil Garner .05
753 Doug Gwosdz .05
754 Kent Tekulve .05
755 Garry Maddox .05
756 Reds Batting & Pitching Leaders (Ron Oester, Mario Soto) .05
757 Larry Bowa .05
758 Bill Stein .05
759 Richard Dotson .05
760 Bob Horner .05
761 John Montefusco .05
762 Rance Mulliniks .05
763 Craig Swan .05
764 Mike Hargrove .05
765 Ken Forsch .05
766 Mike Vail .05
767 Carney Lansford .05
768 Champ Summers .05
769 Bill Caudill .05
770 Ken Griffey .05
771 Billy Gardner .05
772 Jim Slaton .05
773 Todd Cruz .05
774 Tom Gorman .05
775 Dave Parker .05
776 Craig Reynolds .05
777 Tom Paciorek .05
778 *Andy Hawkins* .05
779 Jim Sundberg .05
780 Steve Carlton 1.00
781 Checklist 661-792 .05
782 Steve Balboni .05
783 Luis Leal .05
784 Leon Roberts .05
785 Joaquin Andujar .05
786 Red Sox Batting & Pitching Leaders (Wade Boggs, Bob Ojeda) .25
787 Bill Campbell .05
788 Milt May .05
789 Bert Blyleven .05
790 Doug DeCinces .05
791 Terry Forster .05
792 Bill Russell .05

1984 Topps Tiffany

In 1984 Topps introduced a specially boxed, limited edition version of its baseball card set. Sold only through hobby dealers, the cards differed from regular-issue 1984 Topps cards in their use of white cardboard stock and the application of a high-gloss finish to the front of the card. Production was limited to a reported 10,000 sets. The nickname "Tiffany" was coined by collectors to identify the glossy collectors edition.

	MT
Complete Set (792):	200.00
Common Player:	.15
Stars:	6X

(See 1984 Topps for checklist and base card values.)

1984 Topps All-Star Glossy Set of 22

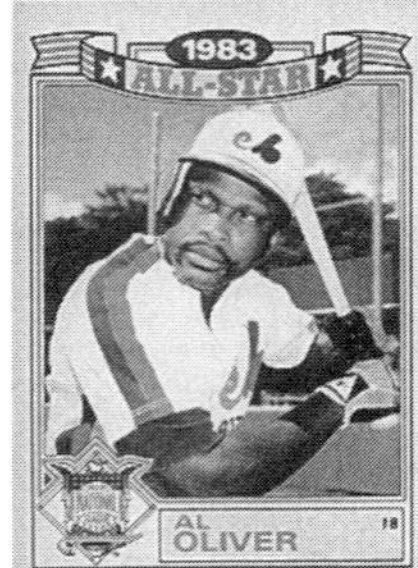

These 2-1/2" x 3-1/2" cards were a result of the success of Topps' efforts the previous year with glossy cards on a mail-in basis. The set is divided evenly between the two leagues. Each All-Star Game starter for both leagues, the managers and the honorary team captains have an All-Star Glossy card. Cards feature a large color photo on the front with an All-Star banner across the top and the league emblem in the lower-left. Player identification appears below the photo. Backs have a name, team, position and card number along with the phrase "1983 All-Star Game Commemorative Set". The '84 Glossy All-Stars were distributed one card per rack pack.

		MT
Complete Set (22):		4.00
Common Player:		.10
1	Harvey Kuenn	.10
2	Rod Carew	.50
3	Manny Trillo	.10
4	George Brett	.75
5	Robin Yount	.60
6	Jim Rice	.20
7	Fred Lynn	.10
8	Dave Winfield	.60
9	Ted Simmons	.10
10	Dave Stieb	.10
11	Carl Yastrzemski	.60
12	Whitey Herzog	.10
13	Al Oliver	.10
14	Steve Sax	.10
15	Mike Schmidt	.75
16	Ozzie Smith	.50
17	Tim Raines	.10
18	Andre Dawson	.15
19	Dale Murphy	.35
20	Gary Carter	.25
21	Mario Soto	.10
22	Johnny Bench	.60

1984 Topps All-Star Glossy Set of 40

For the second straight year in 1984, Topps produced a 40-card All-Star "Collector's Edition" set as a "consolation prize" for its sweepstakes game. By collecting game cards and sending them in with a bit of cash, the collector could receive one of eight different five-card series. As the previous year, the 2-1/2" x 3-1/2" cards feature a nearly full-frame color photo on its glossy finish front. Backs are printed in red and blue.

		MT
Complete Set (40):		8.00
Common Player:		.15
1	Pete Rose	2.00
2	Lance Parrish	.15
3	Steve Rogers	.15
4	Eddie Murray	.45
5	Johnny Ray	.15
6	Rickey Henderson	.40
7	Atlee Hammaker	.15
8	Wade Boggs	.45
9	Gary Carter	.20
10	Jack Morris	.15
11	Darrell Evans	.15
12	George Brett	.75
13	Bob Horner	.15
14	Ron Guidry	.15
15	Nolan Ryan	2.00
16	Dave Winfield	.35
17	Ozzie Smith	.40
18	Ted Simmons	.15
19	Bill Madlock	.15
20	Tony Armas	.15
21	Al Oliver	.15
22	Jim Rice	.20
23	George Hendrick	.15
24	Dave Stieb	.15
25	Pedro Guerrero	.15
26	Rod Carew	.30
27	Steve Carlton	.25
28	Dave Righetti	.15
29	Darryl Strawberry	.15
30	Lou Whitaker	.15
31	Dale Murphy	.20
32	LaMarr Hoyt	.15
33	Jesse Orosco	.15
34	Cecil Cooper	.15
35	Andre Dawson	.20
36	Robin Yount	.50
37	Tim Raines	.15
38	Dan Quisenberry	.15
39	Mike Schmidt	.75
40	Carlton Fisk	.25

1984 Topps Stickers

The largest sticker set issued by Topps, the 1984 set consists of 386 stickers, each measuring 1-15/16" x 2-9/16". The full color photos have stars in each of the corners and are numbered on both the front and the back. The back includes information about the sticker album and a promotion to order stickers through the mail. The back of the album is a tribute to Carl Yastrzemski, including a large photo and reproductions of his 1960-1983 cards in miniature.

		MT
Complete Set (386):		12.00
Common Player:		.05
Sticker Album:		2.00
Box (35):		3.00
1	Steve Carlton	.15
2	Steve Carlton	.15
3	Rickey Henderson	.25
4	Rickey Henderson	.25
5	Fred Lynn	.05
6	Fred Lynn	.05
7	Greg Luzinski	.05
8	Greg Luzinski	.05
9	Dan Quisenberry	.05
10	Dan Quisenberry	.05
11	1983 Championship (LaMarr Hoyt)	.05
12	1983 Championship (Mike Flanagan)	.05
13	1983 Championship (Mike Boddicker)	.05
14	1983 Championship (Tito Landrum)	.05
15	1983 Championship (Steve Carlton)	.10
16	1983 Championship (Fernando Valenzuela)	.05
17	1983 Championship (Charlie Hudson)	.05
18	1983 Championship (Gary Matthews)	.05
19	1983 World Series (John Denny)	.05
20	1983 World Series (John Lowenstein)	.05
21	1983 World Series (Jim Palmer)	.10
22	1983 World Series (Benny Ayala)	.05
23	1983 World Series (Rick Dempsey)	.05
24	1983 World Series (Cal Ripken)	.50
25	1983 World Series (Sammy Stewart)	.05
26	1983 World Series (Eddie Murray)	.10
27	Dale Murphy	.15
28	Chris Chambliss	.05
29	Glenn Hubbard	.05
30	Bob Horner	.05
31	Phil Niekro	.15
32	Claudell Washington	.05
33	Rafael Ramirez	.05
34	Bruce Benedict	.05
35	Gene Garber	.05
36	Pascual Perez	.05
37	Jerry Royster	.05
38	Steve Bedrosian	.05
39	Keith Moreland	.05
40	Leon Durham	.05
41	Ron Cey	.05
42	Bill Buckner	.05
43	Jody Davis	.05
44	Lee Smith	.05
45	Ryne Sandberg	.30
46	Larry Bowa	.05
47	Chuck Rainey	.05
48	Fergie Jenkins	.15
49	Dick Ruthven	.05
50	Jay Johnstone	.05
51	Mario Soto	.05
52	Gary Redus	.05
53	Ron Oester	.05
54	Cesar Cedeno	.05
55	Dan Driessen	.05
56	Dave Concepcion	.05
57	Dann Bilardello	.05
58	Joe Price	.05
59	Tom Hume	.05
60	Eddie Milner	.05
61	Paul Householder	.05
62	Bill Scherrer	.05
63	Phil Garner	.05
64	Dickie Thon	.05
65	Jose Cruz	.05
66	Nolan Ryan	.60
67	Terry Puhl	.05
68	Ray Knight	.05
69	Joe Niekro	.05
70	Jerry Mumphrey	.05
71	Bill Dawley	.05
72	Alan Ashby	.05
73	Denny Walling	.05
74	Frank DiPino	.05
75	Pedro Guerrero	.05
76	Ken Landreaux	.05
77	Bill Russell	.05
78	Steve Sax	.05
79	Fernando Valenzuela	.05
80	Dusty Baker	.05
81	Jerry Reuss	.05
82	Alejandro Pena	.05
83	Rick Monday	.05
84	Rick Honeycutt	.05
85	Mike Marshall	.05
86	Steve Yeager	.05
87	Al Oliver	.05
88	Steve Rogers	.05
89	Jeff Reardon	.05
90	Gary Carter	.15
91	Tim Raines	.05
92	Andre Dawson	.15
93	Manny Trillo	.05
94	Tim Wallach	.05
95	Chris Speier	.05
96	Bill Gullickson	.05
97	Doug Flynn	.05
98	Charlie Lea	.05
99	Bill Madlock	.05
100	Wade Boggs	.30
101	Mike Schmidt	.35
102a	Jim Rice	.15
102b	Reggie Jackson	.25
103	Hubie Brooks	.05
104	Jesse Orosco	.05
105	George Foster	.05
106	Tom Seaver	.25
107	Keith Hernandez	.05
108	Mookie Wilson	.05
109	Bob Bailor	.05
110	Walt Terrell	.05
111	Brian Giles	.05
112	Jose Oquendo	.05
113	Mike Torrez	.05
114	Junior Ortiz	.05
115	Pete Rose	.50
116	Joe Morgan	.15
117	Mike Schmidt	.35
118	Gary Matthews	.05
119	Steve Carlton	.15
120	Bo Diaz	.05
121	Ivan DeJesus	.05
122	John Denny	.05
123	Garry Maddox	.05
124	Von Hayes	.05
125	Al Holland	.05
126	Tony Perez	.15
127	John Candelaria	.05
128	Jason Thompson	.05
129	Tony Pena	.05
130	Dave Parker	.05
131	Bill Madlock	.05
132	Kent Tekulve	.05
133	Larry McWilliams	.05
134	Johnny Ray	.05
135	Marvell Wynne	.05
136	Dale Berra	.05
137	Mike Easler	.05
138	Lee Lacy	.05
139	George Hendrick	.05
140	Lonnie Smith	.05
141	Willie McGee	.05
142	Tom Herr	.05
143	Darrell Porter	.05
144	Ozzie Smith	.35
145	Bruce Sutter	.05
146	Dave LaPoint	.05
147	Neil Allen	.05
148	Ken Oberkfell	.05
149	David Green	.05
150	Andy Van Slyke	.05
151	Garry Templeton	.05
152	Juan Bonilla	.05
153	Alan Wiggins	.05
154	Terry Kennedy	.05
155	Dave Dravecky	.05
156	Steve Garvey	.10
157	Bobby Brown	.05
158	Ruppert Jones	.05
159	Luis Salazar	.05
160	Tony Gwynn	.35
161	Gary Lucas	.05
162	Eric Show	.05
163	Darrell Evans	.05
164	Gary Lavelle	.05
165	Atlee Hammaker	.05
166	Jeff Leonard	.05
167	Jack Clark	.05
168	Johnny LeMaster	.05
169	Duane Kuiper	.05
170	Tom O'Malley	.05
171	Chili Davis	.05
172	Bill Laskey	.05
173	Joel Youngblood	.05
174	Bob Brenly	.05
175	Atlee Hammaker	.05
176	Rick Honeycutt	.05
177	John Denny	.05
178	LaMarr Hoyt	.05
179	Tim Raines	.05
180	Dale Murphy	.15
181	Andre Dawson	.15
182	Steve Rogers	.05
183	Gary Carter	.15
184	Steve Carlton	.25
185	George Hendrick	.05
186	Johnny Ray	.05
187	Ozzie Smith	.35

No.	Player	Price
188	Mike Schmidt	.35
189	Jim Rice	.10
190	Dave Winfield	.25
191	Lloyd Moseby	.05
192	LaMarr Hoyt	.05
193	Ted Simmons	.05
194	Ron Guidry	.05
195	Eddie Murray	.25
196	Lou Whitaker	.05
197	Cal Ripken, Jr.	.60
198	George Brett	.40
199	Dale Murphy	.15
200a	Cecil Cooper	.05
200b	Jim Rice	.10
201	Tim Raines	.05
202	Rickey Henderson	.25
203	Eddie Murray	.25
204	Cal Ripken	.60
205	Gary Roenicke	.05
206	Ken Singleton	.05
207	Scott McGregor	.05
208	Tippy Martinez	.05
209	John Lowenstein	.05
210	Mike Flanagan	.05
211	Jim Palmer	.15
212	Dan Ford	.05
213	Rick Dempsey	.05
214	Rich Dauer	.05
215	Jerry Remy	.05
216	Wade Boggs	.30
217	Jim Rice	.10
218	Tony Armas	.05
219	Dwight Evans	.05
220	Bob Stanley	.05
221	Dave Stapleton	.05
222	Rich Gedman	.05
223	Glenn Hoffman	.05
224	Dennis Eckersley	.05
225	John Tudor	.05
226	Bruce Hurst	.05
227	Rod Carew	.25
228	Bobby Grich	.05
229	Doug DeCinces	.05
230	Fred Lynn	.05
231	Reggie Jackson	.25
232	Tommy John	.05
233	Luis Sanchez	.05
234	Bob Boone	.05
235	Bruce Kison	.05
236	Brian Downing	.05
237	Ken Forsch	.05
238	Rick Burleson	.05
239	Dennis Lamp	.05
240	LaMarr Hoyt	.05
241	Richard Dotson	.05
242	Harold Baines	.05
243	Carlton Fisk	.15
244	Greg Luzinski	.05
245	Rudy Law	.05
246	Tom Paciorek	.05
247	Floyd Bannister	.05
248	Julio Cruz	.05
249	Vance Law	.05
250	Scott Fletcher	.05
251	Toby Harrah	.05
252	Pat Tabler	.05
253	Gorman Thomas	.05
254	Rick Sutcliffe	.05
255	Andre Thornton	.05
256	Bake McBride	.05
257	Alan Bannister	.05
258	Jamie Easterly	.05
259	Lary Sorenson	.05
260	Mike Hargrove	.05
261	Bert Blyleven	.05
262	Ron Hassey	.05
263	Jack Morris	.05
264	Larry Herndon	.05
265	Lance Parrish	.05
266	Alan Trammell	.05
267	Lou Whitaker	.05
268	Aurelio Lopez	.05
269	Dan Petry	.05
270	Glenn Wilson	.05
271	Chet Lemon	.05
272	Kirk Gibson	.05
273	Enos Cabell	.05
274	Johnny Wockenfuss	.05
275	George Brett	.40
276	Willie Aikens	.05
277	Frank White	.05
278	Hal McRae	.05
279	Dan Quisenberry	.05
280	Willie Wilson	.05
281	Paul Splitorff	.05
282	U.L. Washington	.05
283	Bud Black	.05
284	John Wathan	.05
285	Larry Gura	.05
286	Pat Sheridan	.05
287a	Rusty Staub	.05
287b	Dave Righetti	.05
288a	Bob Forsch	.05
288b	Mike Warren	.05
289	Al Holland	.05
290	Dan Quisenberry	.05
291	Cecil Cooper	.05
292	Moose Haas	.05
293	Ted Simmons	.05
294	Paul Molitor	.25
295	Robin Yount	.25
296	Ben Oglivie	.05
297	Tom Tellmann	.05
298	Jim Gantner	.05
299	Rick Manning	.05
300	Don Sutton	.15
301	Charlie Moore	.05
302	Jim Slaton	.05
303	Gary Ward	.05
304	Tom Brunansky	.05
305	Kent Hrbek	.05
306	Gary Gaetti	.05
307	John Castino	.05
308	Ken Schrom	.05
309	Ron Davis	.05
310	Lenny Faedo	.05
311	Darrell Brown	.05
312	Frank Viola	.05
313	Dave Engle	.05
314	Randy Bush	.05
315	Dave Righetti	.05
316	Rich Gossage	.05
317	Ken Griffey	.05
318	Ron Guidry	.05
319	Dave Winfield	.25
320	Don Baylor	.10
321	Butch Wynegar	.05
322	Omar Moreno	.05
323	Andre Robertson	.05
324	Willie Randolph	.05
325	Don Mattingly	.45
326	Graig Nettles	.05
327	Rickey Henderson	.25
328	Carney Lansford	.05
329	Jeff Burroughs	.05
330	Chris Codiroli	.05
331	Dave Lopes	.05
332	Dwayne Murphy	.05
333	Wayne Gross	.05
334	Bill Almon	.05
335	Tom Underwood	.05
336	Dave Beard	.05
337	Mike Heath	.05
338	Mike Davis	.05
339	Pat Putnam	.05
340	Tony Bernazard	.05
341	Steve Henderson	.05
342	Richie Zisk	.05
343	Dave Henderson	.05
344	Al Cowens	.05
345	Bill Caudill	.05
346	Jim Beattie	.05
347	Ricky Nelson	.05
348	Roy Thomas	.05
349	Spike Owen	.05
350	Jamie Allen	.05
351	Buddy Bell	.05
352	Billy Sample	.05
353	George Wright	.05
354	Larry Parrish	.05
355	Jim Sundberg	.05
356	Charlie Hough	.05
357	Pete O'Brien	.05
358	Wayne Tolleson	.05
359	Danny Darwin	.05
360	Dave Stewart	.05
361	Mickey Rivers	.05
362	Bucky Dent	.05
363	Willie Upshaw	.05
364	Damaso Garcia	.05
365	Lloyd Moseby	.05
366	Cliff Johnson	.05
367	Jim Clancy	.05
368	Dave Stieb	.05
369	Alfredo Griffin	.05
370	Barry Bonnell	.05
371	Luis Leal	.05
372	Jesse Barfield	.05
373	Ernie Whitt	.05
374	Rance Mulliniks	.05
375	Mike Boddicker	.05
376	Greg Brock	.05
377	Bill Doran	.05
378	Nick Esasky	.05
379	Julio Franco	.05
380	Mel Hall	.05
381	Bob Kearney	.05
382	Ron Kittle	.05
383	Carmelo Martinez	.05
384	Craig McMurtry	.05
385	Darryl Strawberry	.05
386	Matt Young	.05

1984 Topps Traded

The popular Topps Traded set returned for its fourth year in 1984 with another 132-card set. The 2-1/2" x 3-1/2" cards have an identical design to the regular Topps cards except that the back cardboard is white and card numbers carry a "T" suffix. As before, the set was sold only through hobby dealers. Also as before, players who changed teams, new managers and promising rookies are included in the set. A glossy-finish "Tiffany" version of the set was also issued.

		MT
Complete Set (132):		25.00
Common Player:		.15
1T	Willie Aikens	.15
2T	Luis Aponte	.15
3T	Mike Armstrong	.15
4T	Bob Bailor	.15
5T	Dusty Baker	.25
6T	Steve Balboni	.15
7T	Alan Bannister	.15
8T	Dave Beard	.15
9T	Joe Beckwith	.15
10T	Bruce Berenyi	.15
11T	Dave Bergman	.15
12T	Tony Bernazard	.15
13T	Yogi Berra	.50
14T	Barry Bonnell	.15
15T	Phil Bradley	.15
16T	Fred Breining	.15
17T	Bill Buckner	.15
18T	Ray Burris	.15
19T	John Butcher	.15
20T	Brett Butler	.15
21T	Enos Cabell	.15
22T	Bill Campbell	.15
23T	Bill Caudill	.15
24T	Bob Clark	.15
25T	Bryan Clark	.15
26T	Jaime Cocanower	.15
27T	*Ron Darling*	1.00
28T	*Alvin Davis*	.15
29T	Ken Dayley	.15
30T	Jeff Dedmon	.15
31T	Bob Dernier	.15
32T	Carlos Diaz	.15
33T	Mike Easler	.15
34T	Dennis Eckersley	2.00
35T	Jim Essian	.15
36T	Darrell Evans	.15
37T	Mike Fitzgerald	.15
38T	Tim Foli	.15
39T	George Frazier	.15
40T	Rich Gale	.15
41T	Barbaro Garbey	.15
42T	*Dwight Gooden*	4.00
43T	Rich Gossage	.15
44T	Wayne Gross	.15
45T	*Mark Gubicza*	.25
46T	Jackie Gutierrez	.15
47T	Mel Hall	.15
48T	Toby Harrah	.15
49T	Ron Hassey	.15
50T	Rich Hebner	.15
51T	Willie Hernandez	.15
52T	Ricky Horton	.15
53T	Art Howe	.15
54T	Dane Iorg	.15
55T	Brook Jacoby	.15
56T	Mike Jeffcoat	.15
57T	Dave Johnson	.15
58T	Lynn Jones	.15
59T	Ruppert Jones	.15
60T	Mike Jorgensen	.15
61T	Bob Kearney	.15
62T	*Jimmy Key*	1.00
63T	Dave Kingman	.15
64T	Jerry Koosman	.15
65T	Wayne Krenchicki	.15
66T	Rusty Kuntz	.15
67T	Rene Lachemann	.15
68T	Frank LaCorte	.15
69T	Dennis Lamp	.15
70T	*Mark Langston*	1.00
71T	Rick Leach	.15
72T	Craig Lefferts	.15
73T	Gary Lucas	.15
74T	Jerry Martin	.15
75T	Carmelo Martinez	.15
76T	Mike Mason	.15
77T	Gary Matthews	.15
78T	Andy McGaffigan	.15
79T	Larry Milbourne	.15
80T	Sid Monge	.15
81T	Jackie Moore	.15
82T	Joe Morgan	3.00
83T	Graig Nettles	.15
84T	Phil Niekro	2.00
85T	Ken Oberkfell	.15
86T	Mike O'Berry	.15
87T	Al Oliver	.15
88T	Jorge Orta	.15
89T	Amos Otis	.15
90T	Dave Parker	.25
91T	Tony Perez	1.00
92T	Gerald Perry	.15
93T	Gary Pettis	.15
94T	Rob Picciolo	.15
95T	Vern Rapp	.15
96T	Floyd Rayford	.15
97T	Randy Ready	.15
98T	Ron Reed	.15
99T	Gene Richards	.15
100T	*Jose Rijo*	1.00
101T	Jeff Robinson	.15
102T	Ron Romanick	.15
103T	Pete Rose	8.00
104T	*Bret Saberhagen*	5.00
105T	Juan Samuel	.15
106T	Scott Sanderson	.15
107T	Dick Schofield	.15
108T	Tom Seaver	6.00
109T	Jim Slaton	.15
110T	Mike Smithson	.15
111T	Lary Sorensen	.15
112T	Tim Stoddard	.15
113T	Champ Summers	.15
114T	Jim Sundberg	.15
115T	Rick Sutcliffe	.15
116T	Craig Swan	.15
117T	Tim Teufel	.15
118T	Derrel Thomas	.15
119T	Gorman Thomas	.15
120T	Alex Trevino	.15
121T	Manny Trillo	.15
122T	John Tudor	.15
123T	Tom Underwood	.15
124T	Mike Vail	.15
125T	Tom Waddell	.15
126T	Gary Ward	.15
127T	Curt Wilkerson	.15
128T	Frank Williams	.15
129T	Glenn Wilson	.15
130T	Johnny Wockenfuss	.15
131T	Ned Yost	.15
132T	Checklist 1-132	.15

1984 Topps Traded Tiffany

Following up on its inaugural Tiffany collectors edition, Topps produced a special glossy version of its Traded set for 1984, as well. Cards in this special boxed set differ from regular Traded cards only in the use of white cardboard stock with a high-gloss finish coat on front.

	MT
Complete Set (132):	35.00
Common Player:	.25
Stars:	2X

(See 1984 Topps Traded for checklist and base card values.)

1985 Topps

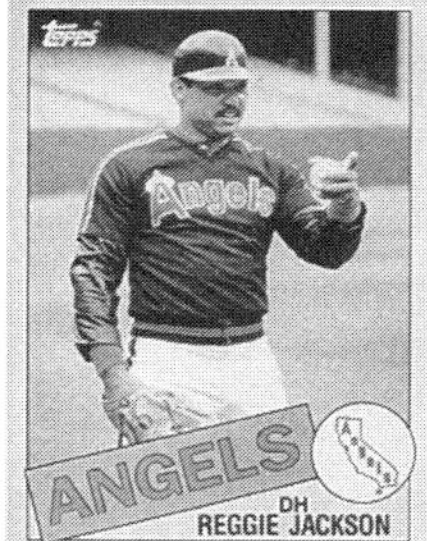

Holding the line at 792 cards, Topps initiated major design changes in its 2-1/2" x 3-1/2" cards in 1985. The use of two photos on the front was discontinued in favor of one large photo. The Topps logo appears in the upper-left corner. At bottom is a diagonal box with the team name. It joins a team logo, and below that point runs the player's position and name. The backs feature statistics, biographical information and a trivia question. Some interesting specialty sets were introduced in 1985, including the revival of the father/son theme from 1976, a subset of the 1984 U.S. Olympic Baseball Team members and a set featuring #1 draft choices since the inception of the baseball draft in 1965. Large numbers of uncut sheets were made available within the hobby, originally selling around $60 for a set of six.

	MT
Unopened Factory Set (792):	175.00
Complete Set (792):	100.00
Complete Set, Uncut Sheets (6):	250.00
Common Player:	.05
Wax Pack (15):	7.50
Wax Box (36):	200.00
Cello Pack (28):	10.00
Cello Box (24):	200.00
Rack Pack (51):	12.00
Rack Box (24):	260.00
Vending Box (500):	100.00

No.	Player	MT
1	Carlton Fisk (Record Breaker)	.25
2	Steve Garvey (Record Breaker)	.05
3	Dwight Gooden (Record Breaker)	.05
4	Cliff Johnson (Record Breaker)	.05
5	Joe Morgan (Record Breaker)	.10
6	Pete Rose (Record Breaker)	.50
7	Nolan Ryan (Record Breaker)	1.50
8	Juan Samuel (Record Breaker)	.05
9	Bruce Sutter (Record Breaker)	.05
10	Don Sutton (Record Breaker)	.05
11	Ralph Houk	.05
12	Dave Lopes	.05
13	Tim Lollar	.05
14	Chris Bando	.05
15	Jerry Koosman	.05
16	Bobby Meacham	.05
17	Mike Scott	.05
18	Mickey Hatcher	.05
19	George Frazier	.05
20	Chet Lemon	.05
21	Lee Tunnell	.05
22	Duane Kuiper	.05
23	Bret Saberhagen	.15
24	Jesse Barfield	.05
25	Steve Bedrosian	.05
26	Roy Smalley	.05
27	Bruce Berenyi	.05
28	Dann Bilardello	.05
29	Odell Jones	.05
30	Cal Ripken, Jr.	4.00
31	Terry Whitfield	.05
32	Chuck Porter	.05
33	Tito Landrum	.05
34	Ed Nunez	.05
35	Graig Nettles	.05
36	Fred Breining	.05
37	Reid Nichols	.05
38	Jackie Moore	.05
39	Johnny Wockenfuss	.05
40	Phil Niekro	.60
41	Mike Fischlin	.05
42	Luis Sanchez	.05
43	Andre David	.05
44	Dickie Thon	.05
45	Greg Minton	.05
46	Gary Woods	.05
47	Dave Rozema	.05
48	Tony Fernandez	.05
49	Butch Davis	.05
50	John Candelaria	.05
51	Bob Watson	.05
52	Jerry Dybzinski	.05
53	Tom Gorman	.05
54	Cesar Cedeno	.05
55	Frank Tanana	.05
56	Jim Dwyer	.05
57	Pat Zachry	.05
58	Orlando Mercado	.05
59	Rick Waits	.05
60	George Hendrick	.05
61	Curt Kaufman	.05
62	Mike Ramsey	.05
63	Steve McCatty	.05
64	*Mark Bailey*	.05
65	Bill Buckner	.05
66	Dick Williams	.05
67	*Rafael Santana*	.05
68	Von Hayes	.05
69	*Jim Winn*	.05
70	Don Baylor	.10
71	Tim Laudner	.05
72	Rick Sutcliffe	.05
73	Rusty Kuntz	.05
74	Mike Krukow	.05
75	Willie Upshaw	.05
76	Alan Bannister	.05
77	Joe Beckwith	.05
78	Scott Fletcher	.05
79	Rick Mahler	.05
80	Keith Hernandez	.05
81	Lenn Sakata	.05
82	Joe Price	.05
83	Charlie Moore	.05
84	Spike Owen	.05
85	Mike Marshall	.05
86	Don Aase	.05
87	David Green	.05
88	Bryn Smith	.05
89	Jackie Gutierrez	.05
90	Rich Gossage	.05
91	Jeff Burroughs	.05
92	Paul Owens	.05
93	*Don Schulze*	.05
94	Toby Harrah	.05
95	Jose Cruz	.05
96	Johnny Ray	.05
97	Pete Filson	.05
98	Steve Lake	.05
99	Milt Wilcox	.05
100	George Brett	2.00
101	Jim Acker	.05
102	Tommy Dunbar	.05
103	Randy Lerch	.05
104	Mike Fitzgerald	.05
105	Ron Kittle	.05
106	Pascual Perez	.05
107	Tom Foley	.05
108	Darnell Coles	.05
109	Gary Roenicke	.05
110	Alejandro Pena	.05
111	Doug DeCinces	.05
112	Tom Tellmann	.05
113	Tom Herr	.05
114	Bob James	.05
115	Rickey Henderson	1.00
116	Dennis Boyd	.05
117	Greg Gross	.05
118	Eric Show	.05
119	Pat Corrales	.05
120	Steve Kemp	.05
121	Checklist 1-132	.05
122	Tom Brunansky	.05
123	Dave Smith	.05
124	Rich Hebner	.05
125	Kent Tekulve	.05
126	Ruppert Jones	.05
127	Mark Gubicza	.05
128	Ernie Whitt	.05
129	Gene Garber	.05
130	Al Oliver	.05
131	Father - Son (Buddy Bell, Gus Bell)	.10
132	Father - Son (Dale Berra, Yogi Berra)	.20
133	Father - Son (Bob Boone, Ray Boone)	.10
134	Father - Son (Terry Francona, Tito Francona)	.05
135	Father - Son (Bob Kennedy, Terry Kennedy)	.05
136	Father - Son (Bill Kunkel, Jeff Kunkel)	.05
137	Father - Son (Vance Law, Vern Law)	.10
138	Father - Son (Dick Schofield, Dick Schofield, Jr.)	.05
139	Father - Son (Bob Skinner, Joel Skinner)	.05
140	Father - Son (Roy Smalley, Jr., Roy Smalley III)	.05
141	Father - Son (Dave Stenhouse, Mike Stenhouse)	.05
142	Father - Son (Dizzy Trout, Steve Trout)	.05
143	Father - Son (Ozzie Virgil, Ozzie Virgil)	.05
144	Ron Gardenhire	.05
145	Alvin Davis	.05
146	Gary Redus	.05
147	Bill Swaggerty	.05
148	Steve Yeager	.05
149	Dickie Noles	.05
150	Jim Rice	.10
151	Moose Haas	.05
152	Steve Braun	.05
153	Frank LaCorte	.05
154	Argenis Salazar	.05
155	Yogi Berra	.10
156	Craig Reynolds	.05
157	Tug McGraw	.05
158	Pat Tabler	.05
159	Carlos Diaz	.05
160	Lance Parrish	.05
161	Ken Schrom	.05
162	*Benny Distefano*	.05
163	Dennis Eckersley	.10
164	Jorge Orta	.05
165	Dusty Baker	.05
166	Keith Atherton	.05
167	Rufino Linares	.05
168	Garth Iorg	.05
169	Dan Spillner	.05
170	George Foster	.05
171	Bill Stein	.05
172	Jack Perconte	.05
173	Mike Young	.05
174	Rick Honeycutt	.05
175	Dave Parker	.05
176	Bill Schroeder	.05
177	Dave Von Ohlen	.05
178	Miguel Dilone	.05
179	Tommy John	.10
180	Dave Winfield	1.00
181	Roger Clemens	20.00
182	Tim Flannery	.05
183	Larry McWilliams	.05
184	Carmen Castillo	.05
185	Al Holland	.05
186	Bob Lillis	.05
187	Mike Walters	.05
188	Greg Pryor	.05
189	Warren Brusstar	.05
190	Rusty Staub	.05
191	Steve Nicosia	.05
192	Howard Johnson	.05
193	Jimmy Key	.05
194	Dave Stegman	.05
195	Glenn Hubbard	.05
196	Pete O'Brien	.05
197	Mike Warren	.05
198	Eddie Milner	.05
199	Denny Martinez	.05
200	Reggie Jackson	1.00
201	Burt Hooton	.05
202	Gorman Thomas	.05
203	Bob McClure	.05
204	Art Howe	.05
205	Steve Rogers	.05
206	Phil Garner	.05
207	Mark Clear	.05
208	Champ Summers	.05
209	Bill Campbell	.05
210	Gary Matthews	.05
211	Clay Christiansen	.05
212	George Vukovich	.05
213	Billy Gardner	.05
214	John Tudor	.05
215	Bob Brenly	.05
216	Jerry Don Gleaton	.05
217	Leon Roberts	.05
218	Doyle Alexander	.05
219	Gerald Perry	.05
220	Fred Lynn	.05
221	Ron Reed	.05
222	Hubie Brooks	.05
223	Tom Hume	.05
224	Al Cowens	.05
225	Mike Boddicker	.05
226	Juan Beniquez	.05
227	Danny Darwin	.05
228	Dion James	.05
229	Dave LaPoint	.05
230	Gary Carter	.40
231	Dwayne Murphy	.05
232	Dave Beard	.05
233	Ed Jurak	.05
234	Jerry Narron	.05
235	Garry Maddox	.05
236	Mark Thurmond	.05
237	Julio Franco	.05
238	Jose Rijo	.05
239	Tim Teufel	.05
240	Dave Stieb	.05
241	Jim Frey	.05
242	Greg Harris	.05
243	Barbaro Garbey	.05
244	Mike Jones	.05
245	Chili Davis	.05
246	Mike Norris	.05
247	Wayne Tolleson	.05
248	Terry Forster	.05
249	Harold Baines	.05
250	Jesse Orosco	.05
251	Brad Gulden	.05
252	Dan Ford	.05
253	*Sid Bream*	.10
254	Pete Vuckovich	.05
255	Lonnie Smith	.05
256	Mike Stanton	.05

No.	Player	Price
257	Brian Little (Bryan)	.05
258	Mike Brown	.05
259	Gary Allenson	.05
260	Dave Righetti	.05
261	Checklist 133-264	.05
262	*Greg Booker*	.05
263	Mel Hall	.05
264	Joe Sambito	.05
265	Juan Samuel	.05
266	Frank Viola	.05
267	*Henry Cotto*	.05
268	Chuck Tanner	.05
269	*Doug Baker*	.05
270	Dan Quisenberry	.05
271	Tim Foli (#1 Draft Pick)	.05
272	Jeff Burroughs (#1 Draft Pick)	.05
273	Bill Almon (#1 Draft Pick)	.05
274	Floyd Bannister (#1 Draft Pick)	.05
275	Harold Baines (#1 Draft Pick)	.10
276	Bob Horner (#1 Draft Pick)	.10
277	Al Chambers (#1 Draft Pick)	.05
278	Darryl Strawberry (#1 Draft Pick)	.30
279	Mike Moore (#1 Draft Pick)	.10
280	*Shawon Dunston* (#1 Draft Pick)	.40
281	*Tim Belcher* (#1 Draft Pick)	.30
282	*Shawn Abner* (#1 Draft Pick)	.05
283	Fran Mullins	.05
284	Marty Bystrom	.05
285	Dan Driessen	.05
286	Rudy Law	.05
287	Walt Terrell	.05
288	*Jeff Kunkel*	.05
289	Tom Underwood	.05
290	Cecil Cooper	.05
291	Bob Welch	.05
292	Brad Komminsk	.05
293	*Curt Young*	.05
294	*Tom Nieto*	.05
295	Joe Niekro	.05
296	Ricky Nelson	.05
297	Gary Lucas	.05
298	Marty Barrett	.05
299	Andy Hawkins	.05
300	Rod Carew	.75
301	John Montefusco	.05
302	Tim Corcoran	.05
303	*Mike Jeffcoat*	.05
304	Gary Gaetti	.05
305	Dale Berra	.05
306	Rick Reuschel	.05
307	Sparky Anderson	.20
308	John Wathan	.05
309	Mike Witt	.05
310	Manny Trillo	.05
311	Jim Gott	.05
312	Marc Hill	.05
313	Dave Schmidt	.05
314	Ron Oester	.05
315	Doug Sisk	.05
316	John Lowenstein	.05
317	*Jack Lazorko*	.05
318	Ted Simmons	.05
319	Jeff Jones	.05
320	Dale Murphy	.35
321	*Ricky Horton*	.05
322	Dave Stapleton	.05
323	Andy McGaffigan	.05
324	Bruce Bochy	.05
325	John Denny	.05
326	Kevin Bass	.05
327	Brook Jacoby	.05
328	Bob Shirley	.05
329	Ron Washington	.05
330	Leon Durham	.05
331	Bill Laskey	.05
332	Brian Harper	.05
333	Willie Hernandez	.05
334	Dick Howser	.05
335	Bruce Benedict	.05
336	Rance Mulliniks	.05
337	Billy Sample	.05
338	Britt Burns	.05
339	Danny Heep	.05
340	Robin Yount	.75
341	Floyd Rayford	.05
342	Ted Power	.05
343	Bill Russell	.05
344	Dave Henderson	.05
345	Charlie Lea	.05
346	*Terry Pendleton*	.75
347	Rick Langford	.05
348	Bob Boone	.05
349	Domingo Ramos	.05
350	Wade Boggs	1.50
351	Juan Agosto	.05
352	Joe Morgan	.60
353	Julio Solano	.05
354	Andre Robertson	.05
355	Bert Blyleven	.05
356	Dave Meier	.05
357	Rich Bordi	.05
358	Tony Pena	.05
359	Pat Sheridan	.05
360	Steve Carlton	.75
361	Alfredo Griffin	.05
362	Craig McMurtry	.05
363	Ron Hodges	.05
364	Richard Dotson	.05
365	Danny Ozark	.05
366	Todd Cruz	.05
367	Keefe Cato	.05
368	Dave Bergman	.05
369	*R.J. Reynolds*	.05
370	Bruce Sutter	.05
371	Mickey Rivers	.05
372	Roy Howell	.05
373	Mike Moore	.05
374	Brian Downing	.05
375	Jeff Reardon	.05
376	Jeff Newman	.05
377	Checklist 265-396	.05
378	Alan Wiggins	.05
379	Charles Hudson	.05
380	Ken Griffey	.05
381	Roy Smith	.05
382	Denny Walling	.05
383	Rick Lysander	.05
384	Jody Davis	.05
385	Jose DeLeon	.05
386	*Dan Gladden*	.30
387	*Buddy Biancalana*	.05
388	Bert Roberge	.05
389	Rod Dedeaux (Team USA)	.05
390	Sid Akins (Team USA)	.05
391	Flavio Alfaro (Team USA)	.05
392	Don August (Team USA)	.10
393	*Scott Bankhead* (Team USA)	.10
394	Bob Caffrey (Team USA)	.05
395	Mike Dunne (Team USA)	.10
396	Gary Green (Team USA)	.10
397	John Hoover (Team USA)	.05
398	*Shane Mack* (Team USA)	.10
399	John Marzano (Team USA)	.10
400	Oddibe McDowell (Team USA)	.10
401	*Mark McGwire* (Team USA)	60.00
402	Pat Pacillo (Team USA)	.05
403	*Cory Snyder* (Team USA)	.30
404	*Billy Swift* (Team USA)	.40
405	Tom Veryzer	.05
406	Len Whitehouse	.05
407	Bobby Ramos	.05
408	Sid Monge	.05
409	Brad Wellman	.05
410	Bob Horner	.05
411	Bobby Cox	.05
412	Bud Black	.05
413	Vance Law	.05
414	Gary Ward	.05
415	Ron Darling	.05
416	Wayne Gross	.05
417	*John Franco*	.45
418	Ken Landreaux	.05
419	Mike Caldwell	.05
420	Andre Dawson	.40
421	Dave Rucker	.05
422	Carney Lansford	.05
423	Barry Bonnell	.05
424	*Al Nipper*	.05
425	Mike Hargrove	.05
426	Verne Ruhle	.05
427	Mario Ramirez	.05
428	Larry Andersen	.05
429	Rick Cerone	.05
430	Ron Davis	.05
431	U.L. Washington	.05
432	Thad Bosley	.05
433	Jim Morrison	.05
434	Gene Richards	.05
435	Dan Petry	.05
436	Willie Aikens	.05
437	Al Jones	.05
438	Joe Torre	.15
439	Junior Ortiz	.05
440	Fernando Valenzuela	.05
441	Duane Walker	.05
442	Ken Forsch	.05
443	George Wright	.05
444	Tony Phillips	.05
445	Tippy Martinez	.05
446	Jim Sundberg	.05
447	Jeff Lahti	.05
448	Derrel Thomas	.05
449	*Phil Bradley*	.10
450	Steve Garvey	.25
451	Bruce Hurst	.05
452	John Castino	.05
453	Tom Waddell	.05
454	Glenn Wilson	.05
455	Bob Knepper	.05
456	Tim Foli	.05
457	Cecilio Guante	.05
458	Randy S. Johnson	.05
459	Charlie Leibrandt	.05
460	Ryne Sandberg	1.50
461	Marty Castillo	.05
462	Gary Lavelle	.05
463	Dave Collins	.05
464	*Mike Mason*	.05
465	Bob Grich	.05
466	Tony LaRussa	.10
467	Ed Lynch	.05
468	Wayne Krenchicki	.05
469	Sammy Stewart	.05
470	Steve Sax	.05
471	Pete Ladd	.05
472	Jim Essian	.05
473	Tim Wallach	.05
474	Kurt Kepshire	.05
475	Andre Thornton	.05
476	*Jeff Stone*	.05
477	Bob Ojeda	.05
478	Kurt Bevacqua	.05
479	Mike Madden	.05
480	Lou Whitaker	.05
481	Dale Murray	.05
482	Harry Spilman	.05
483	Mike Smithson	.05
484	Larry Bowa	.05
485	Matt Young	.05
486	Steve Balboni	.05
487	*Frank Williams*	.05
488	Joel Skinner	.05
489	Bryan Clark	.05
490	Jason Thompson	.05
491	Rick Camp	.05
492	Dave Johnson	.05
493	*Orel Hershiser*	1.50
494	Rich Dauer	.05
495	Mario Soto	.05
496	Donnie Scott	.05
497	Gary Pettis	.05
498	Ed Romero	.05
499	Danny Cox	.05
500	Mike Schmidt	2.00
501	Dan Schatzeder	.05
502	Rick Miller	.05
503	Tim Conroy	.05
504	Jerry Willard	.05
505	Jim Beattie	.05
506	*Franklin Stubbs*	.05
507	Ray Fontenot	.05
508	John Shelby	.05
509	Milt May	.05
510	Kent Hrbek	.05
511	Lee Smith	.05
512	Tom Brookens	.05
513	Lynn Jones	.05
514	Jeff Cornell	.05
515	Dave Concepcion	.05
516	Roy Lee Jackson	.05
517	Jerry Martin	.05
518	Chris Chambliss	.05
519	Doug Rader	.05
520	LaMarr Hoyt	.05
521	Rick Dempsey	.05
522	Paul Molitor	.75
523	Candy Maldonado	.05
524	Rob Wilfong	.05
525	Darrell Porter	.05
526	Dave Palmer	.05
527	Checklist 397-528	.05
528	Bill Krueger	.05
529	Rich Gedman	.05
530	Dave Dravecky	.05
531	Joe Lefebvre	.05
532	Frank DiPino	.05
533	Tony Bernazard	.05
534	Brian Dayett	.05
535	Pat Putnam	.05
536	Kirby Puckett	10.00
537	Don Robinson	.05
538	Keith Moreland	.05
539	Aurelio Lopez	.05
540	Claudell Washington	.05
541	Mark Davis	.05
542	Don Slaught	.05
543	Mike Squires	.05
544	Bruce Kison	.05
545	Lloyd Moseby	.05
546	Brent Gaff	.05
547	Pete Rose	1.00
548	Larry Parrish	.05
549	Mike Scioscia	.05
550	Scott McGregor	.05
551	Andy Van Slyke	.05
552	Chris Codiroli	.05
553	Bob Clark	.05
554	Doug Flynn	.05
555	Bob Stanley	.05
556	Sixto Lezcano	.05
557	Len Barker	.05
558	Carmelo Martinez	.05
559	Jay Howell	.05
560	Bill Madlock	.05
561	Darryl Motley	.05
562	Houston Jimenez	.05
563	Dick Ruthven	.05
564	Alan Ashby	.05
565	Kirk Gibson	.05
566	Ed Vande Berg	.05
567	Joel Youngblood	.05
568	Cliff Johnson	.05
569	Ken Oberkfell	.05
570	Darryl Strawberry	.10
571	Charlie Hough	.05
572	Tom Paciorek	.05
573	*Jay Tibbs*	.05
574	Joe Altobelli	.05
575	Pedro Guerrero	.05
576	Jaime Cocanower	.05
577	Chris Speier	.05
578	Terry Francona	.05
579	*Ron Romanick*	.05
580	Dwight Evans	.05
581	Mark Wagner	.05
582	Ken Phelps	.05
583	Bobby Brown	.05
584	Kevin Gross	.05
585	Butch Wynegar	.05
586	Bill Scherrer	.05
587	Doug Frobel	.05
588	Bobby Castillo	.05
589	Bob Dernier	.05
590	Ray Knight	.05
591	Larry Herndon	.05
592	*Jeff Robinson*	.05
593	Rick Leach	.05
594	Curt Wilkerson	.05
595	Larry Gura	.05
596	Jerry Hairston Sr.	.05
597	Brad Lesley	.05
598	Jose Oquendo	.05
599	Storm Davis	.05
600	Pete Rose	2.00
601	Tom Lasorda	.20
602	*Jeff Dedmon*	.05
603	Rick Manning	.05
604	Daryl Sconiers	.05
605	Ozzie Smith	1.50
606	Rich Gale	.05
607	Bill Almon	.05
608	Craig Lefferts	.05
609	Broderick Perkins	.05
610	Jack Morris	.05
611	Ozzie Virgil	.05

No.	Player	MT
612	Mike Armstrong	.05
613	Terry Puhl	.05
614	Al Williams	.05
615	Marvell Wynne	.05
616	Scott Sanderson	.05
617	Willie Wilson	.05
618	Pete Falcone	.05
619	Jeff Leonard	.05
620	Dwight Gooden	.50
621	Marvis Foley	.05
622	Luis Leal	.05
623	Greg Walker	.05
624	Benny Ayala	.05
625	Mark Langston	.25
626	German Rivera	.05
627	*Eric Davis*	.45
628	Rene Lachemann	.05
629	Dick Schofield	.05
630	Tim Raines	.05
631	Bob Forsch	.05
632	Bruce Bochte	.05
633	Glenn Hoffman	.05
634	Bill Dawley	.05
635	Terry Kennedy	.05
636	Shane Rawley	.05
637	Brett Butler	.05
638	*Mike Pagliarulo*	.10
639	Ed Hodge	.05
640	Steve Henderson	.05
641	Rod Scurry	.05
642	Dave Owen	.05
643	Johnny Grubb	.05
644	Mark Huismann	.05
645	Damaso Garcia	.05
646	Scot Thompson	.05
647	Rafael Ramirez	.05
648	Bob Jones	.05
649	Sid Fernandez	.05
650	Greg Luzinski	.05
651	Jeff Russell	.05
652	Joe Nolan	.05
653	Mark Brouhard	.05
654	Dave Anderson	.05
655	Joaquin Andujar	.05
656	Chuck Cottier	.05
657	Jim Slaton	.05
658	Mike Stenhouse	.05
659	Checklist 529-660	.05
660	Tony Gwynn	1.50
661	Steve Crawford	.05
662	Mike Heath	.05
663	Luis Aguayo	.05
664	*Steve Farr*	.05
665	Don Mattingly	3.00
666	Mike LaCoss	.05
667	Dave Engle	.05
668	Steve Trout	.05
669	Lee Lacy	.05
670	Tom Seaver	.75
671	Dane Iorg	.05
672	Juan Berenguer	.05
673	Buck Martinez	.05
674	Atlee Hammaker	.05
675	Tony Perez	.60
676	*Albert Hall*	.05
677	Wally Backman	.05
678	Joey McLaughlin	.05
679	Bob Kearney	.05
680	Jerry Reuss	.05
681	Ben Oglivie	.05
682	Doug Corbett	.05
683	Whitey Herzog	.05
684	Bill Doran	.05
685	Bill Caudill	.05
686	Mike Easler	.05
687	Bill Gullickson	.05
688	Len Matuszek	.05
689	Luis DeLeon	.05
690	Alan Trammell	.05
691	Dennis Rasmussen	.05
692	Randy Bush	.05
693	Tim Stoddard	.05
694	Joe Carter	.25
695	Rick Rhoden	.05
696	John Rabb	.05
697	Onix Concepcion	.05
698	Jorge Bell	.05
699	Donnie Moore	.05
700	Eddie Murray	1.00
701	Eddie Murray (All-Star)	.40
702	Damaso Garcia (All-Star)	.05
703	George Brett (All-Star)	.50
704	Cal Ripken, Jr. (All-Star)	1.50
705	Dave Winfield (All-Star)	.50
706	Rickey Henderson (All-Star)	.25
707	Tony Armas (All-Star)	.05
708	Lance Parrish (All-Star)	.05
709	Mike Boddicker (All-Star)	.05
710	Frank Viola (All-Star)	.05
711	Dan Quisenberry (All-Star)	.05
712	Keith Hernandez (All-Star)	.05
713	Ryne Sandberg (All-Star)	.40
714	Mike Schmidt (All-Star)	.75
715	Ozzie Smith (All-Star)	.50
716	Dale Murphy (All-Star)	.15
717	Tony Gwynn (All-Star)	.75
718	Jeff Leonard (All-Star)	.05
719	Gary Carter (All-Star)	.15
720	Rick Sutcliffe (All-Star)	.05
721	Bob Knepper (All-Star)	.05
722	Bruce Sutter (All-Star)	.05
723	Dave Stewart	.05
724	Oscar Gamble	.05
725	Floyd Bannister	.05
726	Al Bumbry	.05
727	Frank Pastore	.05
728	Bob Bailor	.05
729	Don Sutton	.60
730	Dave Kingman	.05
731	Neil Allen	.05
732	John McNamara	.05
733	Tony Scott	.05
734	John Henry Johnson	.05
735	Garry Templeton	.05
736	Jerry Mumphrey	.05
737	Bo Diaz	.05
738	Omar Moreno	.05
739	Ernie Camacho	.05
740	Jack Clark	.05
741	John Butcher	.05
742	Ron Hassey	.05
743	Frank White	.05
744	Doug Bair	.05
745	Buddy Bell	.05
746	Jim Clancy	.05
747	Alex Trevino	.05
748	Lee Mazzilli	.05
749	Julio Cruz	.05
750	Rollie Fingers	.60
751	Kelvin Chapman	.05
752	Bob Owchinko	.05
753	Greg Brock	.05
754	Larry Milbourne	.05
755	Ken Singleton	.05
756	Rob Picciolo	.05
757	Willie McGee	.05
758	Ray Burris	.05
759	Jim Fanning	.05
760	Nolan Ryan	4.00
761	Jerry Remy	.05
762	Eddie Whitson	.05
763	Kiko Garcia	.05
764	Jamie Easterly	.05
765	Willie Randolph	.05
766	Paul Mirabella	.05
767	Darrell Brown	.05
768	Ron Cey	.05
769	Joe Cowley	.05
770	Carlton Fisk	.75
771	Geoff Zahn	.05
772	Johnnie LeMaster	.05
773	Hal McRae	.05
774	Dennis Lamp	.05
775	Mookie Wilson	.05
776	Jerry Royster	.05
777	Ned Yost	.05
778	Mike Davis	.05
779	Nick Esasky	.05
780	Mike Flanagan	.05
781	Jim Gantner	.05
782	Tom Niedenfuer	.05
783	Mike Jorgensen	.05
784	Checklist 661-792	.05
785	Tony Armas	.05
786	Enos Cabell	.05
787	Jim Wohlford	.05
788	Steve Comer	.05
789	Luis Salazar	.05
790	Ron Guidry	.10
791	Ivan DeJesus	.05
792	Darrell Evans	.05

1985 Topps Tiffany

In its second year of producing a high-gloss collectors edition of its regular baseball card set, Topps cut production to a reported 5,000 sets. Other than the use of white cardboard stock and the glossy front coating, the cards in this specially boxed set are identical to regular 1985 Topps cards.

	MT
Complete Unopened Set (792):	600.00
Complete Set, Opened (792):	300.00
Common Player:	.25
Stars:	4X
401 Mark McGwire	200.00

(See 1985 Topps for checklist and base card values.)

1985 Topps All-Star Glossy Set of 22

This was the second straight year for this set of 22 cards featuring the starting players, honorary captains and managers in the All-Star Game. The set is virtually identical to that of the previous year in design with a color photo, All-Star banner, league emblem, and player ID on the front. Fronts have a high-gloss finish. The cards were available as inserts in Topps rack packs.

		MT
Complete Set (22):		2.50
Common Player:		.10
1	Paul Owens	.10
2	Steve Garvey	.30
3	Ryne Sandberg	.60
4	Mike Schmidt	.75
5	Ozzie Smith	.60
6	Tony Gwynn	.60
7	Dale Murphy	.30
8	Darryl Strawberry	.10
9	Gary Carter	.25
10	Charlie Lea	.10
11	Willie McCovey	.35
12	Joe Altobelli	.10
13	Rod Carew	.40
14	Lou Whitaker	.10
15	George Brett	.75
16	Cal Ripken, Jr.	1.00
17	Dave Winfield	.45
18	Chet Lemon	.10
19	Reggie Jackson	.45
20	Lance Parrish	.10
21	Dave Stieb	.10
22	Hank Greenberg	.25

1985 Topps All-Star Glossy Set of 40

Similar to previous years' glossy sets, the 1985 All-Star "Collector's Edition" set of 40 could be obtained through the mail in eight five-card subsets. To obtain the 2-1/2" x 3-1/2" cards, collectors had to accumulate sweepstakes insert cards from Topps packs, and pay 75Û postage and handling. Under the circumstances, the complete set of 40 cards was not inexpensive.

		MT
Complete Set (40):		6.00
Common Player:		.10
1	Dale Murphy	.30
2	Jesse Orosco	.10
3	Bob Brenly	.10
4	Mike Boddicker	.10
5	Dave Kingman	.10
6	Jim Rice	.20
7	Frank Viola	.10
8	Alvin Davis	.10
9	Rick Sutcliffe	.10
10	Pete Rose	2.00
11	Leon Durham	.10
12	Joaquin Andujar	.10
13	Keith Hernandez	.10
14	Dave Winfield	.50
15	Reggie Jackson	.75
16	Alan Trammell	.10
17	Bert Blyleven	.10
18	Tony Armas	.10
19	Rich Gossage	.10
20	Jose Cruz	.10
21	Ryne Sandberg	.75
22	Bruce Sutter	.10
23	Mike Schmidt	1.00
24	Cal Ripken, Jr.	2.00
25	Dan Petry	.10
26	Jack Morris	.10
27	Don Mattingly	1.00
28	Eddie Murray	.50
29	Tony Gwynn	.75
30	Charlie Lea	.10
31	Juan Samuel	.10
32	Phil Niekro	.25
33	Alejandro Pena	.10
34	Harold Baines	.10
35	Dan Quisenberry	.10
36	Gary Carter	.25
37	Mario Soto	.10
38	Dwight Gooden	.10
39	Tom Brunansky	.10
40	Dave Stieb	.10

1985 Topps Stickers

Topps went to a larger size for its stickers in 1985. Produced by Panini, each of the 376 stickers measures 2-1/8" x 3" and is numbered on both the front and the back. The backs contain either an offer to obtain an autographed team ball or a poster. An album was also available.

		MT
Complete Set (376):		16.00
Common Player:		.05
Sticker Album:		2.00
1	Steve Garvey	.15
2	Steve Garvey	.15
3	Dwight Gooden	.05
4	Dwight Gooden	.05
5	Joe Morgan	.30
6	Joe Morgan	.30
7	Don Sutton	.30
8	Don Sutton	.30
9	1984 A.L. Championships (Jack Morris)	.05
10	1984 A.L. Championships (Milt Wilcox)	.05
11	1984 A.L. Championships (Kirk Gibson)	.05
12	1984 N.L. Championships (Gary Matthews)	.05
13	1984 N.L. Championships (Steve Garvey)	.05
14	1984 N.L. Championships (Steve Garvey)	.05
15	1984 World Series (Jack Morris)	.05
16	1984 World Series (Kurt Bevacqua)	.05
17	1984 World Series (Milt Wilcox)	.05
18	1984 World Series (Alan Trammell)	.05
19	1984 World Series (Kirk Gibson)	.05
20	1984 World Series (Alan Trammell)	.05
21	1984 World Series (Chet Lemon)	.05
22	Dale Murphy	.25
23	Steve Bedrosian	.05
24	Bob Horner	.05
25	Claudell Washington	.05
26	Rick Mahler	.05
27	Rafael Ramirez	.05
28	Craig McMurtry	.05
29	Chris Chambliss	.05
30	Alex Trevino	.05
31	Bruce Benedict	.05
32	Ken Oberkfell	.05
33	Glenn Hubbard	.05
34	Ryne Sandberg	.40
35	Rick Sutcliffe	.05
36	Leon Durham	.05
37	Jody Davis	.05
38	Bob Dernier	.05
39	Keith Moreland	.05
40	Scott Sanderson	.05
41	Lee Smith	.05
42	Ron Cey	.05
43	Steve Trout	.05
44	Gary Matthews	.05
45	Larry Bowa	.05
46	Mario Soto	.05
47	Dave Parker	.05
48	Dave Concepcion	.05
49	Gary Redus	.05
50	Ted Power	.05
51	Nick Esasky	.05
52	Duane Walker	.05
53	Eddie Milner	.05
54	Ron Oester	.05
55	Cesar Cedeno	.05
56	Joe Price	.05
57	Pete Rose	.75
58	Nolan Ryan	.75
59	Jose Cruz	.05
60	Jerry Mumphrey	.05
61	Enos Cabell	.05
62	Bob Knepper	.05
63	Dickie Thon	.05
64	Phil Garner	.05
65	Craig Reynolds	.05
66	Frank DiPino	.05
67	Terry Puhl	.05
68	Bill Doran	.05
69	Joe Niekro	.05
70	Pedro Guerrero	.05
71	Fernando Valenzuela	.05
72	Mike Marshall	.05
73	Alejandro Pena	.05
74	Orel Hershiser	.10
75	Ken Landreaux	.05
76	Bill Russell	.05
77	Steve Sax	.05
78	Rick Honeycutt	.05
79	Mike Scioscia	.05
80	Tom Niedenfuer	.05
81	Candy Maldonado	.05
82	Tim Raines	.05
83	Gary Carter	.15
84	Charlie Lea	.05
85	Jeff Reardon	.05
86	Andre Dawson	.15
87	Tim Wallach	.05
88	Terry Francona	.05
89	Steve Rogers	.05
90	Bryn Smith	.05
91	Bill Gullickson	.05
92	Dan Driessen	.05
93	Doug Flynn	.05
94	Mike Schmidt	.50
95	Tony Armas	.05
96	Dale Murphy	.15
97	Rick Sutcliffe	.05
98	Keith Hernandez	.05
99	George Foster	.05
100	Darryl Strawberry	.05
101	Jesse Orosco	.05
102	Mookie Wilson	.05
103	Doug Sisk	.05
104	Hubie Brooks	.05
105	Ron Darling	.05
106	Wally Backman	.05
107	Dwight Gooden	.05
108	Mike Fitzgerald	.05
109	Walt Terrell	.05
110	Ozzie Virgil	.05
111	Mike Schmidt	.50
112	Steve Carlton	.30
113	Al Holland	.05
114	Juan Samuel	.05
115	Von Hayes	.05
116	Jeff Stone	.05
117	Jerry Koosman	.05
118	Al Oliver	.05
119	John Denny	.05
120	Charles Hudson	.05
121	Garry Maddox	.05
122	Bill Madlock	.05
123	John Candelaria	.05
124	Tony Pena	.05
125	Jason Thompson	.05
126	Lee Lacy	.05
127	Rick Rhoden	.05
128	Doug Frobel	.05
129	Kent Tekulve	.05
130	Johnny Ray	.05
131	Marvell Wynne	.05
132	Larry McWilliams	.05
133	Dale Berra	.05
134	George Hendrick	.05
135	Bruce Sutter	.05
136	Joaquin Andujar	.05
137	Ozzie Smith	.50
138	Andy Van Slyke	.05
139	Lonnie Smith	.05
140	Darrell Porter	.05
141	Willie McGee	.05
142	Tom Herr	.05
143	Dave LaPoint	.05
144	Neil Allen	.05
145	David Green	.05
146	Tony Gwynn	.50
147	Rich Gossage	.05
148	Terry Kennedy	.05
149	Steve Garvey	.15
150	Alan Wiggins	.05
151	Garry Templeton	.05
152	Ed Whitson	.05
153	Tim Lollar	.05
154	Dave Dravecky	.05
155	Graig Nettles	.05
156	Eric Show	.05
157	Carmelo Martinez	.05
158	Bob Brenly	.05
159	Gary Lavelle	.05
160	Jack Clark	.05
161	Jeff Leonard	.05
162	Chili Davis	.05
163	Mike Krukow	.05
164	Johnnie LeMaster	.05
165	Atlee Hammaker	.05
166	Dan Gladden	.05
167	Greg Minton	.05
168	Joel Youngblood	.05
169	Frank Williams	.05
170	Tony Gwynn	.50
171	Don Mattingly	.60
172	Bruce Sutter	.05
173	Dan Quisenberry	.05
174	Tony Gwynn	.50
175	Ryne Sandberg	.40
176	Steve Garvey	.15
177	Dale Murphy	.15
178	Mike Schmidt	.50
179	Darryl Strawberry	.05
180	Gary Carter	.15
181	Ozzie Smith	.50
182	Charlie Lea	.05
183	Lou Whitaker	.05
184	Rod Carew	.30
185	Cal Ripken, Jr.	.75
186	Dave Winfield	.40
187	Reggie Jackson	.40
188	George Brett	.50
189	Lance Parrish	.05
190	Chet Lemon	.05
191	Dave Stieb	.05
192	Gary Carter	.15
193	Mike Schmidt	.50
194	Tony Armas	.05
195	Mike Witt	.05
196	Eddie Murray	.25
197	Cal Ripken, Jr.	.75
198	Scott McGregor	.05
199	Rick Dempsey	.05
200	Tippy Martinez	.05
201	Ken Singleton	.05
202	Mike Boddicker	.05
203	Rich Dauer	.05
204	John Shelby	.05
205	Al Bumbry	.05
206	John Lowenstein	.05
207	Mike Flanagan	.05
208	Jim Rice	.10
209	Tony Armas	.05
210	Wade Boggs	.40
211	Bruce Hurst	.05
212	Dwight Evans	.05
213	Mike Easler	.05
214	Bill Buckner	.05
215	Bob Stanley	.05
216	Jackie Gutierrez	.05
217	Rich Gedman	.05
218	Jerry Remy	.05
219	Marty Barrett	.05
220	Reggie Jackson	.40
221	Geoff Zahn	.05
222	Doug DeCinces	.05
223	Rod Carew	.30
224	Brian Downing	.05
225	Fred Lynn	.05
226	Gary Pettis	.05
227	Mike Witt	.05
228	Bob Boone	.05
229	Tommy John	.05
230	Bobby Grich	.05
231	Ron Romanick	.05
232	Ron Kittle	.05
233	Richard Dotson	.05
234	Harold Baines	.05
235	Tom Seaver	.40
236	Greg Walker	.05
237	Roy Smalley	.05
238	Greg Luzinski	.05
239	Julio Cruz	.05
240	Scott Fletcher	.05
241	Rudy Law	.05
242	Vance Law	.05
243	Carlton Fisk	.30
244	Andre Thornton	.05
245	Julio Franco	.05
246	Brett Butler	.05
247	Bert Blyleven	.05
248	Mike Hargrove	.05
249	George Vukovich	.05
250	Pat Tabler	.05
251	Brook Jacoby	.05
252	Tony Bernazard	.05
253	Ernie Camacho	.05
254	Mel Hall	.05
255	Carmen Castillo	.05
256	Jack Morris	.05
257	Willie Hernandez	.05
258	Alan Trammell	.05
259	Lance Parrish	.05
260	Chet Lemon	.05
261	Lou Whitaker	.05
262	Howard Johnson	.05
263	Barbaro Garbey	.05
264	Dan Petry	.05
265	Aurelio Lopez	.05
266	Larry Herndon	.05
267	Kirk Gibson	.05
268	George Brett	.50
269	Dan Quisenberry	.05
270	Hal McRae	.05
271	Steve Balboni	.05
272	Pat Sheridan	.05
273	Jorge Orta	.05
274	Frank White	.05
275	Bud Black	.05
276	Darryl Motley	.05
277	Willie Wilson	.05
278	Larry Gura	.05
279	Don Slaught	.05
280	Dwight Gooden	.05
281	Mark Langston	.05
282	Tim Raines	.05
283	Rickey Henderson	.30
284	Robin Yount	.30
285	Rollie Fingers	.30
286	Jim Sundberg	.05
287	Cecil Cooper	.05
288	Jaime Cocanower	.05
289	Mike Caldwell	.05
290	Don Sutton	.30
291	Rick Manning	.05
292	Ben Oglivie	.05
293	Moose Haas	.05
294	Ted Simmons	.05
295	Jim Gantner	.05
296	Kent Hrbek	.05
297	Ron Davis	.05
298	Dave Engle	.05
299	Tom Brunansky	.05
300	Frank Viola	.05
301	Mike Smithson	.05
302	Gary Gaetti	.05
303	Tim Teufel	.05
304	Mickey Hatcher	.05
305	John Butcher	.05
306	Darrell Brown	.05
307	Kirby Puckett	.50
308	Dave Winfield	.40
309	Phil Niekro	.30
310	Don Mattingly	.60
311	Don Baylor	.10
312	Willie Randolph	.05
313	Ron Guidry	.05
314	Dave Righetti	.05
315	Bobby Meacham	.05
316	Butch Wynegar	.05
317	Mike Pagliarulo	.05
318	Joe Cowley	.05
319	John Montefusco	.05
320	Dave Kingman	.05
321	Rickey Henderson	.30
322	Bill Caudill	.05
323	Dwayne Murphy	.05
324	Steve McCatty	.05
325	Joe Morgan	.30
326	Mike Heath	.05
327	Chris Codiroli	.05
328	Ray Burris	.05
329	Tony Phillips	.05

330 Carney Lansford .05
331 Bruce Bochte .05
332 Alvin Davis .05
333 Al Cowens .05
334 Jim Beattie .05
335 Bob Kearney .05
336 Ed Vande Berg .05
337 Mark Langston .05
338 Dave Henderson .05
339 Spike Owen .05
340 Matt Young .05
341 Jack Perconte .05
342 Barry Bonnell .05
343 Mike Stanton .05
344 Pete O'Brien .05
345 Charlie Hough .05
346 Larry Parrish .05
347 Buddy Bell .05
348 Frank Tanana .05
349 Curt Wilkerson .05
350 Jeff Kunkel .05
351 Billy Sample .05
352 Danny Darwin .05
353 Gary Ward .05
354 Mike Mason .05
355 Mickey Rivers .05
356 Dave Stieb .05
357 Damaso Garcia .05
358 Willie Upshaw .05
359 Lloyd Moseby .05
360 George Bell .05
361 Luis Leal .05
362 Jesse Barfield .05
363 Dave Collins .05
364 Roy Lee Jackson .05
365 Doyle Alexander .05
366 Alfredo Griffin .05
367 Cliff Johnson .05
368 Alvin Davis .05
369 Juan Samuel .05
370 Brook Jacoby .05
371 Dwight Gooden, Mark Langston .05
372 Mike Fitzgerald .05
373 Jackie Gutierrez .05
374 Dan Gladden .05
375 Carmelo Martinez .05
376 Kirby Puckett .50

1985 Topps Traded

Topps continued the annual Traded set tradition with another 132-card set. The 2-1/2" x 3-1/2" cards follow the pattern of being virtually identical in design to the regular cards of that year. Sold only through hobby dealers, the set features traded veterans and promising rookies. A glossy-finish "Tiffany" edition of the set was also issued. Cards are numbered with a "T" suffix.

	MT
Complete Set (132):	8.00
Common Player:	.10
Wax Test Pack (8):	15.00
Wax Test Wax Box (36):	225.00

1 Don Aase .10
2 Bill Almon .10
3 Benny Ayala .10
4 Dusty Baker .25
5 George Bamberger .10
6 Dale Berra .10
7 Rich Bordi .10
8 Daryl Boston .10
9 Hubie Brooks .10
10 Chris Brown .10
11 Tom Browning .10
12 Al Bumbry .10
13 Ray Burris .10
14 Jeff Burroughs .10
15 Bill Campbell .10
16 Don Carman .10
17 Gary Carter 1.00
18 Bobby Castillo .10
19 Bill Caudill .10
20 Rick Cerone .10
21 Bryan Clark .10
22 Jack Clark .10
23 Pat Clements .10
24 *Vince Coleman* 1.00
25 Dave Collins .10
26 Danny Darwin .10
27 Jim Davenport .10
28 Jerry Davis .10
29 Brian Dayett .10
30 Ivan DeJesus .10
31 Ken Dixon .10
32 Mariano Duncan .10
33 John Felske .10
34 Mike Fitzgerald .10
35 Ray Fontenot .10
36 Greg Gagne .10
37 Oscar Gamble .10
38 Scott Garrelts .10
39 Bob L. Gibson .10
40 Jim Gott .10
41 David Green .10
42 Alfredo Griffin .10
43 *Ozzie Guillen* 1.00
44 Eddie Haas .10
45 Terry Harper .10
46 Toby Harrah .10
47 Greg Harris .10
48 Ron Hassey .10
49 Rickey Henderson 3.00
50 Steve Henderson .10
51 George Hendrick .10
52 Joe Hesketh .10
53 Teddy Higuera .10
54 Donnie Hill .10
55 Al Holland .10
56 Burt Hooton .10
57 Jay Howell .10
58 Ken Howell .10
59 LaMarr Hoyt .10
60 Tim Hulett .10
61 Bob James .10
62 Steve Jeltz .10
63 Cliff Johnson .10
64 Howard Johnson .25
65 Ruppert Jones .10
66 Steve Kemp .10
67 Bruce Kison .10
68 Alan Knicely .10
69 Mike LaCoss .10
70 Lee Lacy .10
71 Dave LaPoint .10
72 Gary Lavelle .10
73 Vance Law .10
74 Johnnie LeMaster .10
75 Sixto Lezcano .10
76 Tim Lollar .10
77 Fred Lynn .10
78 Billy Martin .25
79 Ron Mathis .10
80 Len Matuszek .10
81 Gene Mauch .10
82 Oddibe McDowell .10
83 Roger McDowell .10
84 John McNamara .10
85 Donnie Moore .10
86 Gene Nelson .10
87 Steve Nicosia .10
88 Al Oliver .10
89 Joe Orsulak .10
90 Rob Picciolo .10
91 Chris Pittaro .10
92 Jim Presley .10
93 Rick Reuschel .10
94 Bert Roberge .10
95 Bob Rodgers .10
96 Jerry Royster .10
97 Dave Rozema .10
98 Dave Rucker .10
99 Vern Ruhle .10
100 Paul Runge .10
101 Mark Salas .10
102 Luis Salazar .10
103 Joe Sambito .10
104 Rick Schu .10
105 Donnie Scott .10
106 Larry Sheets .10
107 Don Slaught .10
108 Roy Smalley .10
109 Lonnie Smith .10
110 Nate Snell .10
111 Chris Speier .10
112 Mike Stenhouse .10
113 Tim Stoddard .10
114 Jim Sundberg .10
115 Bruce Sutter .10
116 Don Sutton 1.00
117 Kent Tekulve .10
118 Tom Tellmann .10
119 Walt Terrell .10
120 *Mickey Tettleton* 1.00
121 Derrel Thomas .10
122 Rich Thompson .10
123 Alex Trevino .10
124 John Tudor .10
125 Jose Uribe .10
126 Bobby Valentine .10
127 Dave Von Ohlen .10
128 U.L. Washington .10
129 Earl Weaver .50
130 Eddie Whitson .10
131 Herm Winningham .10
132 Checklist 1-132 .10

1985 Topps Traded Tiffany

This specially boxed collectors version of the Topps Traded sets features cards that differ only in the use of a high-gloss finish coat on the fronts.

	MT
Complete Set (132):	40.00
Common Player:	.25
Stars:	4X

(See 1985 Topps Traded for checklist and base card values.)

1986 Topps

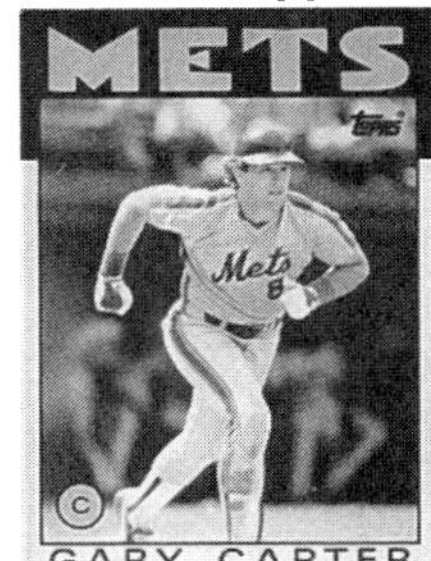

The 1986 Topps set consists of 792 cards. Fronts of the 2-1/2" x 3-1/2" cards feature color photos with the Topps logo in the upper right-hand corner while the player's position is in the lower left-hand corner. Above the picture is the team name, while below it is the player's name. The borders are a departure from previous practice, as the top 7/8" is black, while the remainder is white. Once again, a 5,000-set glossy-finish "Tiffany" edition was produced.

	MT
Unopened Factory Set (792):	30.00
Complete Set (792):	15.00
Common Player:	.05
Wax Pack (15):	.50
Wax Box (36):	25.00
Cello Pack (28):	2.00
Cello Box (24):	30.00
Rack Pack (49):	2.00
Rack Box (24):	25.00
Vending Box (500):	12.00

1 Pete Rose 1.00
2 Pete Rose (Special 1963-66) .50
3 Pete Rose (Special 1967-70) .50
4 Pete Rose (Special 1971-74) .50
5 Pete Rose (Special 1975-78) .50
6 Pete Rose (Special 1972-82) .50
7 Pete Rose (Special 1983-85) .50
8 Dwayne Murphy .05
9 Roy Smith .05
10 Tony Gwynn .75
11 Bob Ojeda .05
12 *Jose Uribe* .05
13 Bob Kearney .05
14 Julio Cruz .05
15 Eddie Whitson .05
16 Rick Schu .05
17 Mike Stenhouse .05
18 Brent Gaff .05
19 Rich Hebner .05
20 Lou Whitaker .05
21 George Bamberger .05
22 Duane Walker .05
23 *Manny Lee* .05
24 Len Barker .05
25 Willie Wilson .05
26 Frank DiPino .05
27 Ray Knight .05
28 Eric Davis .05
29 Tony Phillips .05
30 Eddie Murray .45
31 Jamie Easterly .05
32 Steve Yeager .05
33 Jeff Lahti .05
34 Ken Phelps .05
35 Jeff Reardon .05
36 Tigers Leaders (Lance Parrish) .05
37 Mark Thurmond .05
38 Glenn Hoffman .05
39 Dave Rucker .05
40 Ken Griffey .05
41 Brad Wellman .05
42 Geoff Zahn .05
43 Dave Engle .05
44 *Lance McCullers* .05
45 Damaso Garcia .05
46 Billy Hatcher .05
47 Juan Berenguer .05
48 Bill Almon .05
49 Rick Manning .05
50 Dan Quisenberry .05
51 Not issued, see #57
52 Chris Welsh .05
53 *Len Dykstra* .50
54 John Franco .05
55 Fred Lynn .05
56 Tom Niedenfuer .05
57a Bill Doran .05
57b Bobby Wine (supposed to be #51) .05
58 Bill Krueger .05
59 Andre Thornton .05
60 Dwight Evans .05
61 Karl Best .05
62 Bob Boone .05
63 Ron Roenicke .05
64 Floyd Bannister .05
65 Dan Driessen .05
66 Cardinals Leaders (Bob Forsch) .05
67 Carmelo Martinez .05
68 Ed Lynch .05
69 Luis Aguayo .05
70 Dave Winfield .60
71 Ken Schrom .05

72 Shawon Dunston .05
73 Randy O'Neal .05
74 Rance Mulliniks .05
75 Jose DeLeon .05
76 Dion James .05
77 Charlie Leibrandt .05
78 Bruce Benedict .05
79 Dave Schmidt .05
80 Darryl Strawberry .05
81 Gene Mauch .05
82 Tippy Martinez .05
83 Phil Garner .05
84 Curt Young .05
85 Tony Perez .50
86 Tom Waddell .05
87 Candy Maldonado .05
88 Tom Nieto .05
89 Randy St. Claire .05
90 Garry Templeton .05
91 Steve Crawford .05
92 Al Cowens .05
93 Scot Thompson .05
94 Rich Bordi .05
95 Ozzie Virgil .05
96 Blue Jay Leaders (Jim Clancy) .05
97 Gary Gaetti .05
98 Dick Ruthven .05
99 Buddy Biancalana .05
100 Nolan Ryan 2.00
101 Dave Bergman .05
102 *Joe Orsulak* .15
103 Luis Salazar .05
104 Sid Fernandez .05
105 Gary Ward .05
106 Ray Burris .05
107 Rafael Ramirez .05
108 Ted Power .05
109 Len Matuszek .05
110 Scott McGregor .05
111 Roger Craig .05
112 Bill Campbell .05
113 U.L. Washington .05
114 Mike Brown .05
115 Jay Howell .05
116 Brook Jacoby .05
117 Bruce Kison .05
118 Jerry Royster .05
119 Barry Bonnell .05
120 Steve Carlton .50
121 Nelson Simmons .05
122 Pete Filson .05
123 Greg Walker .05
124 Luis Sanchez .05
125 Dave Lopes .05
126 Mets Leaders (Mookie Wilson) .05
127 *Jack Howell* .05
128 John Wathan .05
129 Jeff Dedmon .05
130 Alan Trammell .05
131 Checklist 1-132 .05
132 Razor Shines .05
133 Andy McGaffigan .05
134 Carney Lansford .05
135 Joe Niekro .05
136 Mike Hargrove .05
137 Charlie Moore .05
138 Mark Davis .05
139 Daryl Boston .05
140 John Candelaria .05
141a Chuck Cottier .05
141b Bob Rodgers (supposed to be #171) .05
142 Bob Jones .05
143 Dave Van Gorder .05
144 Doug Sisk .05
145 Pedro Guerrero .05
146 Jack Perconte .05
147 Larry Sheets .05
148 Mike Heath .05
149 Brett Butler .05
150 Joaquin Andujar .05
151 Dave Stapleton .05
152 Mike Morgan .05
153 Ricky Adams .05
154 Bert Roberge .05
155 Bob Grich .05
156 White Sox Leaders (Richard Dotson) .05
157 Ron Hassey .05
158 Derrel Thomas .05
159 Orel Hershiser .10
160 Chet Lemon .05
161 Lee Tunnell .05
162 Greg Gagne .05
163 Pete Ladd .05
164 Steve Balboni .05
165 Mike Davis .05
166 Dickie Thon .05
167 Zane Smith .05
168 Jeff Burroughs .05
169 George Wright .05
170 Gary Carter .35
171 Not issued, see #141
172 Jerry Reed .05
173 Wayne Gross .05
174 Brian Snyder .05
175 Steve Sax .05
176 Jay Tibbs .05
177 Joel Youngblood .05
178 Ivan DeJesus .05
179 *Stu Cliburn* .05
180 Don Mattingly 1.00
181 Al Nipper .05
182 Bobby Brown .05
183 Larry Andersen .05
184 Tim Laudner .05
185 Rollie Fingers .45
186 Astros Leaders (Jose Cruz) .05
187 Scott Fletcher .05
188 Bob Dernier .05
189 Mike Mason .05
190 George Hendrick .05
191 Wally Backman .05
192 Milt Wilcox .05
193 Daryl Sconiers .05
194 Craig McMurtry .05
195 Dave Concepcion .05
196 Doyle Alexander .05
197 Enos Cabell .05
198 Ken Dixon .05
199 Dick Howser .05
200 Mike Schmidt .75
201 Vince Coleman (Record Breaker) .05
202 Dwight Gooden (Record Breaker) .05
203 Keith Hernandez (Record Breaker) .05
204 Phil Niekro (Record Breaker) .05
205 Tony Perez (Record Breaker) .05
206 Pete Rose (Record Breaker) .25
207 Fernando Valenzuela (Record Breaker) .05
208 Ramon Romero .05
209 Randy Ready .05
210 Calvin Schiraldi .05
211 Ed Wojna .05
212 Chris Speier .05
213 Bob Shirley .05
214 Randy Bush .05
215 Frank White .05
216 A's Leaders (Dwayne Murphy) .05
217 Bill Scherrer .05
218 Randy Hunt .05
219 Dennis Lamp .05
220 Bob Horner .05
221 Dave Henderson .05
222 Craig Gerber .05
223 Atlee Hammaker .05
224 Cesar Cedeno .05
225 Ron Darling .05
226 Lee Lacy .05
227 Al Jones .05
228 Tom Lawless .05
229 Bill Gullickson .05
230 Terry Kennedy .05
231 Jim Frey .05
232 Rick Rhoden .05
233 Steve Lyons .05
234 Doug Corbett .05
235 Butch Wynegar .05
236 Frank Eufemia .05
237 Ted Simmons .05
238 Larry Parrish .05
239 Joel Skinner .05
240 Tommy John .10
241 Tony Fernandez .05
242 Rich Thompson .05
243 Johnny Grubb .05
244 Craig Lefferts .05
245 Jim Sundberg .05
246 Phillies Leaders (Steve Carlton) .10
247 Terry Harper .05
248 Spike Owen .05
249 Rob Deer .05
250 Dwight Gooden .05
251 Rich Dauer .05
252 Bobby Castillo .05
253 Dann Bilardello .05
254 *Ozzie Guillen* .30
255 Tony Armas .05
256 Kurt Kepshire .05
257 Doug DeCinces .05
258 *Tim Burke* .05
259 Dan Pasqua .05
260 Tony Pena .05
261 Bobby Valentine .05
262 Mario Ramirez .05
263 Checklist 133-264 .05
264 Darren Daulton .05
265 Ron Davis .05
266 Keith Moreland .05
267 Paul Molitor .60
268 Mike Scott .05
269 Dane Iorg .05
270 Jack Morris .05
271 Dave Collins .05
272 Tim Tolman .05
273 Jerry Willard .05
274 Ron Gardenhire .05
275 Charlie Hough .05
276 Yankees Leaders (Willie Randolph) .05
277 Jaime Cocanower .05
278 Sixto Lezcano .05
279 Al Pardo .05
280 Tim Raines .05
281 Steve Mura .05
282 Jerry Mumphrey .05
283 Mike Fischlin .05
284 Brian Dayett .05
285 Buddy Bell .05
286 Luis DeLeon .05
287 *John Christensen* .05
288 Don Aase .05
289 Johnnie LeMaster .05
290 Carlton Fisk .50
291 Tom Lasorda .25
292 Chuck Porter .05
293 Chris Chambliss .05
294 Danny Cox .05
295 Kirk Gibson .05
296 Geno Petralli .05
297 Tim Lollar .05
298 Craig Reynolds .05
299 Bryn Smith .05
300 George Brett .75
301 Dennis Rasmussen .05
302 Greg Gross .05
303 Curt Wardle .05
304 *Mike Gallego* .10
305 Phil Bradley .05
306 Padres Leaders (Terry Kennedy) .05
307 Dave Sax .05
308 Ray Fontenot .05
309 John Shelby .05
310 Greg Minton .05
311 Dick Schofield .05
312 Tom Filer .05
313 Joe DeSa .05
314 Frank Pastore .05
315 Mookie Wilson .05
316 Sammy Khalifa .05
317 Ed Romero .05
318 Terry Whitfield .05
319 Rick Camp .05
320 Jim Rice .10
321 Earl Weaver .25
322 Bob Forsch .05
323 Jerry Davis .05
324 Dan Schatzeder .05
325 Juan Beniquez .05
326 Kent Tekulve .05
327 Mike Pagliarulo .05
328 Pete O'Brien .05
329 Kirby Puckett 2.00
330 Rick Sutcliffe .05
331 Alan Ashby .05
332 Darryl Motley .05
333 Tom Henke .05
334 Ken Oberkfell .05
335 Don Sutton .45
336 Indians Leaders (Andre Thornton) .05
337 Darnell Coles .05
338 Jorge Bell .05
339 Bruce Berenyi .05
340 Cal Ripken, Jr. 2.00
341 Frank Williams .05
342 Gary Redus .05
343 Carlos Diaz .05
344 Jim Wohlford .05
345 Donnie Moore .05
346 Bryan Little .05
347 *Teddy Higuera* .10
348 Cliff Johnson .05
349 Mark Clear .05
350 Jack Clark .05
351 Chuck Tanner .05
352 Harry Spilman .05
353 Keith Atherton .05
354 Tony Bernazard .05
355 Lee Smith .05
356 Mickey Hatcher .05
357 Ed Vande Berg .05
358 Rick Dempsey .05
359 Mike LaCoss .05
360 Lloyd Moseby .05
361 Shane Rawley .05
362 Tom Paciorek .05
363 Terry Forster .05
364 Reid Nichols .05
365 Mike Flanagan .05
366 Reds Leaders (Dave Concepcion) .05
367 Aurelio Lopez .05
368 Greg Brock .05
369 Al Holland .05
370 *Vince Coleman* .35
371 Bill Stein .05
372 Ben Oglivie .05
373 *Urbano Lugo* .05
374 Terry Francona .05
375 Rich Gedman .05
376 Bill Dawley .05
377 Joe Carter .05
378 Bruce Bochte .05
379 Bobby Meacham .05
380 LaMarr Hoyt .05
381 Ray Miller .05
382 *Ivan Calderon* .05
383 *Chris Brown* .05
384 Steve Trout .05
385 Cecil Cooper .05
386 *Cecil Fielder* .75
387 Steve Kemp .05
388 Dickie Noles .05
389 Glenn Davis .05
390 Tom Seaver .60
391 Julio Franco .05
392 John Russell .05
393 Chris Pittaro .05
394 Checklist 265-396 .05
395 Scott Garrelts .05
396 Red Sox Leaders (Dwight Evans) .05
397 *Steve Buechele* .20
398 *Earnie Riles* .05
399 Bill Swift .05
400 Rod Carew .50
401 Fernando Valenzuela (Turn Back the Clock) .05
402 Tom Seaver (Turn Back the Clock) .25
403 Willie Mays (Turn Back the Clock) .25
404 Frank Robinson (Turn Back the Clock) .15
405 Roger Maris (Turn Back the Clock) .25
406 Scott Sanderson .05
407 Sal Butera .05
408 Dave Smith .05
409 *Paul Runge* .05
410 Dave Kingman .05
411 Sparky Anderson .25
412 Jim Clancy .05
413 Tim Flannery .05
414 Tom Gorman .05
415 Hal McRae .05
416 Denny Martinez .05
417 R.J. Reynolds .05
418 Alan Knicely .05
419 Frank Wills .05
420 Von Hayes .05
421 Dave Palmer .05
422 Mike Jorgensen .05
423 Dan Spillner .05
424 Rick Miller .05
425 Larry McWilliams .05
426 Brewers Leaders (Charlie Moore) .05
427 Joe Cowley .05
428 Max Venable .05

No.	Card	Price
429	Greg Booker	.05
430	Kent Hrbek	.05
431	George Frazier	.05
432	Mark Bailey	.05
433	Chris Codiroli	.05
434	Curt Wilkerson	.05
435	Bill Caudill	.05
436	Doug Flynn	.05
437	Rick Mahler	.05
438	Clint Hurdle	.05
439	Rick Honeycutt	.05
440	Alvin Davis	.05
441	Whitey Herzog	.05
442	Ron Robinson	.05
443	Bill Buckner	.05
444	Alex Trevino	.05
445	Bert Blyleven	.05
446	Lenn Sakata	.05
447	Jerry Don Gleaton	.05
448	*Herm Winningham*	.05
449	Rod Scurry	.05
450	Graig Nettles	.05
451	Mark Brown	.05
452	Bob Clark	.05
453	Steve Jeltz	.05
454	Burt Hooton	.05
455	Willie Randolph	.05
456	Braves Leaders (Dale Murphy)	.10
457	Mickey Tettleton	.05
458	Kevin Bass	.05
459	Luis Leal	.05
460	Leon Durham	.05
461	Walt Terrell	.05
462	Domingo Ramos	.05
463	Jim Gott	.05
464	Ruppert Jones	.05
465	Jesse Orosco	.05
466	Tom Foley	.05
467	Bob James	.05
468	Mike Scioscia	.05
469	Storm Davis	.05
470	Bill Madlock	.05
471	Bobby Cox	.05
472	Joe Hesketh	.05
473	Mark Brouhard	.05
474	John Tudor	.05
475	Juan Samuel	.05
476	Ron Mathis	.05
477	Mike Easler	.05
478	Andy Hawkins	.05
479	*Bob Melvin*	.05
480	*Oddibe McDowell*	.05
481	Scott Bradley	.05
482	Rick Lysander	.05
483	George Vukovich	.05
484	Donnie Hill	.05
485	Gary Matthews	.05
486	Angels Leaders (Bob Grich)	.05
487	Bret Saberhagen	.05
488	Lou Thornton	.05
489	Jim Winn	.05
490	Jeff Leonard	.05
491	Pascual Perez	.05
492	Kelvin Chapman	.05
493	Gene Nelson	.05
494	Gary Roenicke	.05
495	Mark Langston	.05
496	Jay Johnstone	.05
497	John Stuper	.05
498	Tito Landrum	.05
499	Bob L. Gibson	.05
500	Rickey Henderson	.60
501	Dave Johnson	.05
502	Glen Cook	.05
503	Mike Fitzgerald	.05
504	Denny Walling	.05
505	Jerry Koosman	.05
506	Bill Russell	.05
507	*Steve Ontiveros*	.10
508	Alan Wiggins	.05
509	Ernie Camacho	.05
510	Wade Boggs	.65
511	Ed Nunez	.05
512	Thad Bosley	.05
513	Ron Washington	.05
514	Mike Jones	.05
515	Darrell Evans	.05
516	Giants Leaders (Greg Minton)	.05
517	*Milt Thompson*	.05
518	Buck Martinez	.05
519	Danny Darwin	.05
520	Keith Hernandez	.05
521	Nate Snell	.05
522	Bob Bailor	.05
523	Joe Price	.05
524	Darrell Miller	.05
525	Marvell Wynne	.05
526	Charlie Lea	.05
527	Checklist 397-528	.05
528	Terry Pendleton	.05
529	Marc Sullivan	.05
530	Rich Gossage	.05
531	Tony LaRussa	.05
532	*Don Carman*	.05
533	Billy Sample	.05
534	Jeff Calhoun	.05
535	Toby Harrah	.05
536	Jose Rijo	.05
537	Mark Salas	.05
538	Dennis Eckersley	.10
539	Glenn Hubbard	.05
540	Dan Petry	.05
541	Jorge Orta	.05
542	Don Schulze	.05
543	Jerry Narron	.05
544	Eddie Milner	.05
545	Jimmy Key	.05
546	Mariners Leaders (Dave Henderson)	.05
547	Roger McDowell	.05
548	Mike Young	.05
549	Bob Welch	.05
550	Tom Herr	.05
551	Dave LaPoint	.05
552	Marc Hill	.05
553	Jim Morrison	.05
554	Paul Householder	.05
555	Hubie Brooks	.05
556	John Denny	.05
557	Gerald Perry	.05
558	Tim Stoddard	.05
559	Tommy Dunbar	.05
560	Dave Righetti	.05
561	Bob Lillis	.05
562	Joe Beckwith	.05
563	Alejandro Sanchez	.05
564	Warren Brusstar	.05
565	Tom Brunansky	.05
566	Alfredo Griffin	.05
567	Jeff Barkley	.05
568	Donnie Scott	.05
569	Jim Acker	.05
570	Rusty Staub	.10
571	Mike Jeffcoat	.05
572	Paul Zuvella	.05
573	Tom Hume	.05
574	Ron Kittle	.05
575	Mike Boddicker	.05
576	Expos Leaders (Andre Dawson)	.05
577	Jerry Reuss	.05
578	Lee Mazzilli	.05
579	Jim Slaton	.05
580	Willie McGee	.05
581	Bruce Hurst	.05
582	Jim Gantner	.05
583	Al Bumbry	.05
584	*Brian Fisher*	.05
585	Garry Maddox	.05
586	Greg Harris	.05
587	Rafael Santana	.05
588	Steve Lake	.05
589	Sid Bream	.05
590	Bob Knepper	.05
591	Jackie Moore	.05
592	Frank Tanana	.05
593	Jesse Barfield	.05
594	Chris Bando	.05
595	Dave Parker	.05
596	Onix Concepcion	.05
597	Sammy Stewart	.05
598	Jim Presley	.05
599	*Rick Aguilera*	.25
600	Dale Murphy	.25
601	Gary Lucas	.05
602	Mariano Duncan	.05
603	Bill Laskey	.05
604	Gary Pettis	.05
605	Dennis Boyd	.05
606	Royals Leaders (Hal McRae)	.05
607	Ken Dayley	.05
608	Bruce Bochy	.05
609	Barbaro Garbey	.05
610	Ron Guidry	.05
611	Gary Woods	.05
612	Richard Dotson	.05
613	Roy Smalley	.05
614	Rick Waits	.05
615	Johnny Ray	.05
616	Glenn Brummer	.05
617	Lonnie Smith	.05
618	Jim Pankovits	.05
619	Danny Heep	.05
620	Bruce Sutter	.05
621	John Felske	.05
622	Gary Lavelle	.05
623	Floyd Rayford	.05
624	Steve McCatty	.05
625	Bob Brenly	.05
626	Roy Thomas	.05
627	Ron Oester	.05
628	*Kirk McCaskill*	.15
629	*Mitch Webster*	.05
630	Fernando Valenzuela	.05
631	Steve Braun	.05
632	Dave Von Ohlen	.05
633	Jackie Gutierrez	.05
634	Roy Lee Jackson	.05
635	Jason Thompson	.05
636	Cubs Leaders (Lee Smith)	.05
637	Rudy Law	.05
638	John Butcher	.05
639	Bo Diaz	.05
640	Jose Cruz	.05
641	Wayne Tolleson	.05
642	Ray Searage	.05
643	Tom Brookens	.05
644	Mark Gubicza	.05
645	Dusty Baker	.05
646	Mike Moore	.05
647	Mel Hall	.05
648	Steve Bedrosian	.05
649	Ronn Reynolds	.05
650	Dave Stieb	.05
651	Billy Martin	.10
652	Tom Browning	.05
653	Jim Dwyer	.05
654	Ken Howell	.05
655	Manny Trillo	.05
656	Brian Harper	.05
657	Juan Agosto	.05
658	Rob Wilfong	.05
659	Checklist 529-660	.05
660	Steve Garvey	.25
661	Roger Clemens	2.00
662	Bill Schroeder	.05
663	Neil Allen	.05
664	Tim Corcoran	.05
665	Alejandro Pena	.05
666	Rangers Leaders (Charlie Hough)	.05
667	Tim Teufel	.05
668	Cecilio Guante	.05
669	Ron Cey	.05
670	Willie Hernandez	.05
671	Lynn Jones	.05
672	Rob Picciolo	.05
673	Ernie Whitt	.05
674	Pat Tabler	.05
675	Claudell Washington	.05
676	Matt Young	.05
677	Nick Esasky	.05
678	Dan Gladden	.05
679	Britt Burns	.05
680	George Foster	.05
681	Dick Williams	.05
682	Junior Ortiz	.05
683	Andy Van Slyke	.05
684	Bob McClure	.05
685	Tim Wallach	.05
686	Jeff Stone	.05
687	Mike Trujillo	.05
688	Larry Herndon	.05
689	Dave Stewart	.05
690	Ryne Sandberg	.60
691	Mike Madden	.05
692	Dale Berra	.05
693	Tom Tellmann	.05
694	Garth Iorg	.05
695	Mike Smithson	.05
696	Dodgers Leaders (Bill Russell)	.05
697	Bud Black	.05
698	Brad Komminsk	.05
699	Pat Corrales	.05
700	Reggie Jackson	.60
701	Keith Hernandez (All-Star)	.05
702	Tom Herr (All-Star)	.05
703	Tim Wallach (All-Star)	.05
704	Ozzie Smith (All-Star)	.30
705	Dale Murphy (All-Star)	.10
706	Pedro Guerrero (All-Star)	.05
707	Willie McGee (All-Star)	.05
708	Gary Carter (All-Star)	.10
709	Dwight Gooden (All-Star)	.05
710	John Tudor (All-Star)	.05
711	Jeff Reardon (All-Star)	.05
712	Don Mattingly (All-Star)	.50
713	Damasco Garcia (All-Star)	.05
714	George Brett (All-Star)	.35
715	Cal Ripken, Jr. (All-Star)	1.00
716	Rickey Henderson (All-Star)	.25
717	Dave Winfield (All-Star)	.25
718	George Bell (All-Star)	.05
719	Carlton Fisk (All-Star)	.15
720	Bret Saberhagen (All-Star)	.05
721	Ron Guidry (All-Star)	.05
722	Dan Quisenberry (All-Star)	.05
723	Marty Bystrom	.05
724	Tim Hulett	.05
725	Mario Soto	.05
726	Orioles Leaders (Rick Dempsey)	.05
727	David Green	.05
728	Mike Marshall	.05
729	Jim Beattie	.05
730	Ozzie Smith	.75
731	Don Robinson	.05
732	*Floyd Youmans*	.05
733	Ron Romanick	.05
734	Marty Barrett	.05
735	Dave Dravecky	.05
736	Glenn Wilson	.05
737	Pete Vuckovich	.05
738	Andre Robertson	.05
739	Dave Rozema	.05
740	Lance Parrish	.05
741	Pete Rose	.50
742	Frank Viola	.05
743	Pat Sheridan	.05
744	Lary Sorensen	.05
745	Willie Upshaw	.05
746	Denny Gonzalez	.05
747	Rick Cerone	.05
748	Steve Henderson	.05
749	Ed Jurak	.05
750	Gorman Thomas	.05
751	Howard Johnson	.05
752	Mike Krukow	.05
753	Dan Ford	.05
754	*Pat Clements*	.05
755	Harold Baines	.05
756	Pirates Leaders (Rick Rhoden)	.05
757	Darrell Porter	.05
758	Dave Anderson	.05
759	Moose Haas	.05
760	Andre Dawson	.30
761	Don Slaught	.05
762	Eric Show	.05
763	Terry Puhl	.05
764	Kevin Gross	.05
765	Don Baylor	.10
766	Rick Langford	.05
767	Jody Davis	.05
768	Vern Ruhle	.05
769	*Harold Reynolds*	.25
770	Vida Blue	.05
771	John McNamara	.05
772	Brian Downing	.05
773	Greg Pryor	.05
774	Terry Leach	.05
775	Al Oliver	.05
776	Gene Garber	.05
777	Wayne Krenchicki	.05
778	Jerry Hairston Sr.	.05
779	Rick Reuschel	.05
780	Robin Yount	.50
781	Joe Nolan	.05
782	Ken Landreaux	.05
783	Ricky Horton	.05
784	Alan Bannister	.05
785	Bob Stanley	.05

786	Twins Leaders (Mickey Hatcher)	.05
787	Vance Law	.05
788	Marty Castillo	.05
789	Kurt Bevacqua	.05
790	Phil Niekro	.45
791	Checklist 661-792	.05
792	Charles Hudson	.05

1986 Topps Tiffany

A total of only 5,000 of these specially boxed collectors edition sets was reported produced. Sold only through hobby dealers the cards differ from the regular-issue 1986 Topps cards only in the use of white cardboard stock and the application of a high-gloss finish on the cards' fronts.

	MT
Unopened Set (792):	80.00
Complete Set (792):	65.00
Common Player:	.25

(Star cards valued at 4X corresponding cards in regular 1986 Topps issue)

1986 Topps All-Star Glossy Set of 22

As in previous years, Topps continued to make the popular glossy-surfaced cards as an insert in rack packs. The All-Star Glossy set of 2-1/2" x 3-1/2" cards shows little design change from previous years. Cards feature a front color photo and All-Star banner at the top. The bottom has the player's name and position. The set includes the All-Star starting teams as well as the managers and honorary captains.

		MT
Complete Set (22):		3.00
Common Player:		.20
1	Sparky Anderson	.20
2	Eddie Murray	.50
3	Lou Whitaker	.20
4	George Brett	.75
5	Cal Ripken, Jr.	1.00
6	Jim Rice	.25
7	Rickey Henderson	.50
8	Dave Winfield	.50
9	Carlton Fisk	.50
10	Jack Morris	.20
11	A.L. All-Star Team	.20
12	Dick Williams	.20
13	Steve Garvey	.30
14	Tom Herr	.20
15	Graig Nettles	.20
16	Ozzie Smith	.65
17	Tony Gwynn	.75
18	Dale Murphy	.40
19	Darryl Strawberry	.20
20	Terry Kennedy	.20
21	LaMarr Hoyt	.20
22	N.L. All-Star Team	.20

1986 Topps All-Star Glossy Set of 60

The Topps All-Star & Hot Prospects glossy set of 60 cards represents an expansion of a good idea. The 2-1/2" x 3-1/2" cards had a good following when they were limited to stars, but Topps realized that the addition of top young players would spice up the set even further, so in 1986 it was expanded from 40 to 60 cards. The cards themselves are basically all color glossy pictures with the player's name in very small print in the lower left-hand corner. To obtain the set, it was necessary to send $1 plus six special offer cards from wax packs to Topps for each series. At 60 cards, that meant the process had to be repeated six times as there were 10 cards in each series, making the set quite expensive from the outset.

		MT
Complete Set (60):		6.00
Common Player:		.15
1	Oddibe McDowell	.15
2	Reggie Jackson	.50
3	Fernando Valenzuela	.15
4	Jack Clark	.15
5	Rickey Henderson	.50
6	Steve Balboni	.15
7	Keith Hernandez	.15
8	Lance Parrish	.15
9	Willie McGee	.15
10	Chris Brown	.15
11	Darryl Strawberry	.15
12	Ron Guidry	.15
13	Dave Parker	.15
14	Cal Ripken	1.00
15	Tim Raines	.15
16	Rod Carew	.50
17	Mike Schmidt	.75
18	George Brett	.75
19	Joe Hesketh	.15
20	Dan Pasqua	.15
21	Vince Coleman	.15
22	Tom Seaver	.50
23	Gary Carter	.35
24	Orel Hershiser	.25
25	Pedro Guerrero	.15
26	Wade Boggs	.60
27	Bret Saberhagen	.15
28	Carlton Fisk	.50
29	Kirk Gibson	.15
30	Brian Fisher	.15
31	Don Mattingly	.90
32	Tom Herr	.15
33	Eddie Murray	.50
34	Ryne Sandberg	.60
35	Dan Quisenberry	.15
36	Jim Rice	.25
37	Dale Murphy	.35
38	Steve Garvey	.35
39	Roger McDowell	.15
40	Earnie Riles	.15
41	Dwight Gooden	.15
42	Dave Winfield	.50
43	Dave Stieb	.15
44	Bob Horner	.15
45	Nolan Ryan	1.00
46	Ozzie Smith	.65
47	Jorge Bell	.15
48	Gorman Thomas	.15
49	Tom Browning	.15
50	Larry Sheets	.15
51	Pete Rose	.90
52	Brett Butler	.15
53	John Tudor	.15
54	Phil Bradley	.15
55	Jeff Reardon	.15
56	Rich Gossage	.15
57	Tony Gwynn	.75
58	Ozzie Guillen	.15
59	Glenn Davis	.15
60	Darrell Evans	.15

1986 Topps Stickers

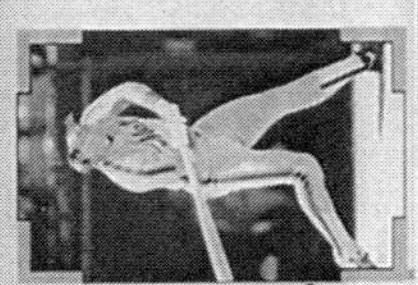

The 1986 Topps stickers are 2-1/8" x 3". The 200-piece set features 316 different subjects, with some stickers including two or three players. Numbers run only to 315, however. The set includes some specialty stickers such as League Championships and World Series themes. Stickers are numbered both front and back and included a chance to win a trip to spring training as well as an offer to buy a complete 1986 Topps regular set. An album for the stickers was available in stores. It feautres Pete Rose in action on the front cover and reproductions of his Topps cards on back.

		MT
Complete Set (315):		9.00
Common Player:		.05
Sticker Album:		1.50
Wax Pack (5):		.25
Wax Box (100):		12.00
1	Pete Rose	.60
2	Pete Rose	.60
3	George Brett	.50
4	Rod Carew	.20
5	Vince Coleman	.05
6	Dwight Gooden	.05
7	Phil Niekro	.15
8	Tony Perez	.20
9	Nolan Ryan	.75
10	Tom Seaver	.35
11	N.L. Championship Series (Ozzie Smith)	.10
12	N.L. Championship Series (Bill Madlock)	.05
13	N.L. Championship Series (Cardinals Celebrate)	.05
14	A.L. Championship Series (Al Oliver)	.05
15	A.L. Championship Series (Jim Sundberg)	.05
16	A.L. Championship Series (George Brett)	.10
17	World Series (Bret Saberhagen)	.05
18	World Series (Dane Iorg)	.05
19	World Series (Tito Landrum)	.05
20	World Series (John Tudor)	.05
21	World Series (Buddy Biancalana)	.05
22	World Series (Darryl Motley, Darrell Porter)	.05
23	World Series (George Brett, Frank White)	.05
24	Nolan Ryan	.75
25	Bill Doran	.05
26	Jose Cruz	.05
27	Mike Scott	.05
28	Kevin Bass	.05
29	Glenn Davis	.05
30	Mark Bailey	.05
31	Dave Smith	.05
32	Phil Garner	.05
33	Dickie Thon	.05
34	Bob Horner	.05
35	Dale Murphy	.15
36	Glenn Hubbard	.05
37	Bruce Sutter	.05
38	Ken Oberkfell	.05
39	Claudell Washington	.05
40	Steve Bedrosian	.05
41	Terry Harper	.05
42	Rafael Ramirez	.05
43	Rick Mahler	.05
44	Joaquin Andujar	.05
45	Willie McGee	.05
46	Ozzie Smith	.50
47	Vince Coleman	.05
48	Danny Cox	.05
49	Tom Herr	.05
50	Jack Clark	.05
51	Andy Van Slyke	.05
52	John Tudor	.05
53	Terry Pendleton	.05
54	Keith Moreland	.05
55	Ryne Sandberg	.35
56	Lee Smith	.05
57	Steve Trout	.05
58	Jody Davis	.05
59	Gary Matthews	.05
60	Leon Durham	.05
61	Rick Sutcliffe	.05
62	Dennis Eckersley	.05
63	Bob Dernier	.05
64	Fernando Valenzuela	.05
65	Pedro Guerrero	.05
66	Jerry Reuss	.05
67	Greg Brock	.05
68	Mike Scioscia	.05
69	Ken Howell	.05
70	Bill Madlock	.05
71	Mike Marshall	.05
72	Steve Sax	.05
73	Orel Hershiser	.10
74	Andre Dawson	.15
75	Tim Raines	.05
76	Jeff Reardon	.05
77	Hubie Brooks	.05
78	Bill Gullickson	.05
79	Bryn Smith	.05
80	Terry Francona	.05
81	Vance Law	.05
82	Tim Wallach	.05

83	Herm Winningham	.05
84	Jeff Leonard	.05
85	Chris Brown	.05
86	Scott Garrelts	.05
87	Jose Uribe	.05
88	Manny Trillo	.05
89	Dan Driessen	.05
90	Dan Gladden	.05
91	Mark Davis	.05
92	Bob Brenly	.05
93	Mike Krukow	.05
94	Dwight Gooden	.05
95	Darryl Strawberry	.05
96	Gary Carter	.15
97	Wally Backman	.05
98	Ron Darling	.05
99	Keith Hernandez	.05
100	George Foster	.05
101	Howard Johnson	.05
102	Rafael Santana	.05
103	Roger McDowell	.05
104	Steve Garvey	.15
105	Tony Gwynn	.50
106	Graig Nettles	.05
107	Rich Gossage	.05
108	Andy Hawkins	.05
109	Carmelo Martinez	.05
110	Garry Templeton	.05
111	Terry Kennedy	.05
112	Tim Flannery	.05
113	LaMarr Hoyt	.05
114	Mike Schmidt	.50
115	Ozzie Virgil	.05
116	Steve Carlton	.25
117	Garry Maddox	.05
118	Glenn Wilson	.05
119	Kevin Gross	.05
120	Von Hayes	.05
121	Juan Samuel	.05
122	Rick Schu	.05
123	Shane Rawley	.05
124	Johnny Ray	.05
125	Tony Pena	.05
126	Rick Reuschel	.05
127	Sammy Khalifa	.05
128	Marvell Wynne	.05
129	Jason Thompson	.05
130	Rick Rhoden	.05
131	Bill Almon	.05
132	Joe Orsulak	.05
133	Jim Morrison	.05
134	Pete Rose	.60
135	Dave Parker	.05
136	Mario Soto	.05
137	Dave Concepcion	.05
138	Ron Oester	.05
139	Buddy Bell	.05
140	Ted Power	.05
141	Tom Browning	.05
142	John Franco	.05
143	Tony Perez	.20
144	Willie McGee	.05
145	Dale Murphy	.15
146	Tony Gwynn	.50
147	Tom Herr	.05
148	Steve Garvey	.15
149	Dale Murphy	.25
150	Darryl Strawberry	.05
151	Graig Nettles	.05
152	Terry Kennedy	.05
153	Ozzie Smith	.50
154	LaMarr Hoyt	.05
155	Rickey Henderson	.40
156	Lou Whitaker	.05
157	George Brett	.50
158	Eddie Murray	.35
159	Cal Ripken, Jr.	.75
160	Dave Winfield	.45
161	Jim Rice	.10
162	Carlton Fisk	.20
163	Jack Morris	.05
164	Wade Boggs	.35
165	Darrell Evans	.05
166	Mike Davis	.05
167	Dave Kingman	.05
168	Alfredo Griffin	.05
169	Carney Lansford	.05
170	Bruce Bochte	.05
171	Dwayne Murphy	.05
172	Dave Collins	.05
173	Chris Codiroli	.05
174	Mike Heath	.05
175	Jay Howell	.05
176	Rod Carew	.25
177	Reggie Jackson	.40
178	Doug DeCinces	.05
179	Bob Boone	.05
180	Ron Romanick	.05
181	Bob Grich	.05
182	Donnie Moore	.05
183	Brian Downing	.05
184	Ruppert Jones	.05
185	Juan Beniquez	.05
186	Dave Stieb	.05
187	Jorge Bell	.05
188	Willie Upshaw	.05
189	Tom Henke	.05
190	Damaso Garcia	.05
191	Jimmy Key	.05
192	Jesse Barfield	.05
193	Dennis Lamp	.05
194	Tony Fernandez	.05
195	Lloyd Moseby	.05
196	Cecil Cooper	.05
197	Robin Yount	.35
198	Rollie Fingers	.20
199	Ted Simmons	.05
200	Ben Oglivie	.05
201	Moose Haas	.05
202	Jim Gantner	.05
203	Paul Molitor	.35
204	Charlie Moore	.05
205	Danny Darwin	.05
206	Brett Butler	.05
207	Brook Jacoby	.05
208	Andre Thornton	.05
209	Tom Waddell	.05
210	Tony Bernazard	.05
211	Julio Franco	.05
212	Pat Tabler	.05
213	Joe Carter	.05
214	George Vukovich	.05
215	Rich Thompson	.05
216	Gorman Thomas	.05
217	Phil Bradley	.05
218	Alvin Davis	.05
219	Jim Presley	.05
220	Matt Young	.05
221	Mike Moore	.05
222	Dave Henderson	.05
223	Ed Nunez	.05
224	Spike Owen	.05
225	Mark Langston	.05
226	Cal Ripken, Jr.	.75
227	Eddie Murray	.30
228	Fred Lynn	.05
229	Lee Lacy	.05
230	Scott McGregor	.05
231	Storm Davis	.05
232	Rick Dempsey	.05
233	Mike Boddicker	.05
234	Mike Young	.05
235	Sammy Stewart	.05
236	Pete O'Brien	.05
237	Oddibe McDowell	.05
238	Toby Harrah	.05
239	Gary Ward	.05
240	Larry Parrish	.05
241	Charlie Hough	.05
242	Burt Hooton	.05
243	Don Slaught	.05
244	Curt Wilkerson	.05
245	Greg Harris	.05
246	Jim Rice	.10
247	Wade Boggs	.40
248	Rich Gedman	.05
249	Dennis Boyd	.05
250	Marty Barrett	.05
251	Dwight Evans	.05
252	Bill Buckner	.05
253	Bob Stanley	.05
254	Tony Armas	.05
255	Mike Easler	.05
256	George Brett	.50
257	Dan Quisenberry	.05
258	Willie Wilson	.05
259	Jim Sundberg	.05
260	Bret Saberhagen	.05
261	Bud Black	.05
262	Charlie Leibrandt	.05
263	Frank White	.05
264	Lonnie Smith	.05
265	Steve Balboni	.05
266	Kirk Gibson	.05
267	Alan Trammell	.05
268	Jack Morris	.05
269	Darrell Evans	.05
270	Dan Petry	.05
271	Larry Herndon	.05
272	Lou Whitaker	.05
273	Lance Parrish	.05
274	Chet Lemon	.05
275	Willie Hernandez	.05
276	Tom Brunansky	.05
277	Kent Hrbek	.05
278	Mark Salas	.05
279	Bert Blyleven	.05
280	Tim Teufel	.05
281	Ron Davis	.05
282	Mike Smithson	.05
283	Gary Gaetti	.05
284	Frank Viola	.05
285	Kirby Puckett	.50
286	Carlton Fisk	.25
287	Tom Seaver	.35
288	Harold Baines	.05
289	Ron Kittle	.05
290	Bob James	.05
291	Rudy Law	.05
292	Britt Burns	.05
293	Greg Walker	.05
294	Ozzie Guillen	.05
295	Tim Hulett	.05
296	Don Mattingly	.60
297	Rickey Henderson	.20
298	Dave Winfield	.45
299	Butch Wynegar	.05
300	Don Baylor	.05
301	Eddie Whitson	.05
302	Ron Guidry	.05
303	Dave Righetti	.05
304	Bobby Meacham	.05
305	Willie Randolph	.05
306	Vince Coleman	.05
307	Oddibe McDowell	.05
308	Larry Sheets	.05
309	Ozzie Guillen	.05
310	Earnie Riles	.05
311	Chris Brown	.05
312	Brian Fisher, Roger McDowell	.05
313	Tom Browning	.05
314	Glenn Davis	.05
315	Mark Salas	.05

1986 Topps Traded

This 132-card set of 2-1/2" x 3-1/2" cards was, at issue, one of the most popular sets of recent times. As always, the set features traded veterans, and a better than usual crop of rookies. As in the previous two years, a glossy-finish "Tiffany" edition of 5,000 Traded sets was produced.

		MT
Unopened Set (132):		30.00
Complete Set (132):		20.00
Common Player:		.10
1T	Andy Allanson	.10
2T	Neil Allen	.10
3T	Joaquin Andujar	.10
4T	Paul Assenmacher	.10
5T	Scott Bailes	.10
6T	Don Baylor	.15
7T	Steve Bedrosian	.10
8T	Juan Beniquez	.10
9T	Juan Berenguer	.10
10T	Mike Bielecki	.10
11T	*Barry Bonds*	15.00
12T	*Bobby Bonilla*	.50
13T	Juan Bonilla	.10
14T	Rich Bordi	.10
15T	Steve Boros	.10
16T	Rick Burleson	.10
17T	Bill Campbell	.10
18T	Tom Candiotti	.10
19T	John Cangelosi	.10
20T	*Jose Canseco*	5.00
21T	Carmen Castillo	.10
22T	Rick Cerone	.10
23T	John Cerutti	.10
24T	*Will Clark*	1.50
25T	Mark Clear	.10
26T	Darnell Coles	.10
27T	Dave Collins	.10
28T	Tim Conroy	.10
29T	Joe Cowley	.10
30T	Joel Davis	.10
31T	Rob Deer	.10
32T	John Denny	.10
33T	Mike Easler	.10
34T	Mark Eichhorn	.10
35T	Steve Farr	.10
36T	Scott Fletcher	.10
37T	Terry Forster	.10
38T	Terry Francona	.10
39T	Jim Fregosi	.10
40T	Andres Galarraga	.50
41T	Ken Griffey	.10
42T	Bill Gullickson	.10
43T	Jose Guzman	.10
44T	Moose Haas	.10
45T	Billy Hatcher	.10
46T	Mike Heath	.10
47T	Tom Hume	.10
48T	*Pete Incaviglia*	.20
49T	Dane Iorg	.10
50T	*Bo Jackson*	1.00
51T	*Wally Joyner*	.40
52T	Charlie Kerfeld	.10
53T	Eric King	.10
54T	Bob Kipper	.10
55T	Wayne Krenchicki	.10
56T	*John Kruk*	.35
57T	Mike LaCoss	.10
58T	Pete Ladd	.10
59T	Mike Laga	.10
60T	Hal Lanier	.10
61T	Dave LaPoint	.10
62T	Rudy Law	.10
63T	Rick Leach	.10
64T	Tim Leary	.10
65T	Dennis Leonard	.10
66T	Jim Leyland	.10
67T	Steve Lyons	.10
68T	Mickey Mahler	.10
69T	Candy Maldonado	.10
70T	Roger Mason	.10
71T	Bob McClure	.10
72T	Andy McGaffigan	.10
73T	Gene Michael	.10
74T	*Kevin Mitchell*	.25
75T	Omar Moreno	.10
76T	Jerry Mumphrey	.10
77T	Phil Niekro	.25
78T	Randy Niemann	.10
79T	Juan Nieves	.10
80T	Otis Nixon	.10
81T	Bob Ojeda	.10
82T	Jose Oquendo	.10
83T	Tom Paciorek	.10
84T	Dave Palmer	.10
85T	Frank Pastore	.10
86T	Lou Piniella	.10
87T	Dan Plesac	.10
88T	Darrell Porter	.10
89T	Rey Quinones	.10
90T	Gary Redus	.10
91T	Bip Roberts	.10
92T	Billy Jo Robidoux	.10
93T	Jeff Robinson	.10
94T	Gary Roenicke	.10
95T	Ed Romero	.10
96T	Argenis Salazar	.10
97T	Joe Sambito	.10
98T	Billy Sample	.10
99T	Dave Schmidt	.10
100T	Ken Schrom	.10
101T	Tom Seaver	.50
102T	Ted Simmons	.10
103T	Sammy Stewart	.10
104T	Kurt Stillwell	.10
105T	Franklin Stubbs	.10
106T	Dale Sveum	.10
107T	Chuck Tanner	.10
108T	Danny Tartabull	.10
109T	Tim Teufel	.10

No.	Player	MT
110T	Bob Tewksbury	.15
111T	Andres Thomas	.10
112T	Milt Thompson	.10
113T	Robby Thompson	.10
114T	Jay Tibbs	.10
115T	Wayne Tolleson	.10
116T	Alex Trevino	.10
117T	Manny Trillo	.10
118T	Ed Vande Berg	.10
119T	Ozzie Virgil	.10
120T	Bob Walk	.10
121T	Gene Walter	.10
122T	Claudell Washington	.10
123T	Bill Wegman	.10
124T	Dick Williams	.10
125T	Mitch Williams	.15
126T	Bobby Witt	.15
127T	Todd Worrell	.10
128T	George Wright	.10
129T	Ricky Wright	.10
130T	Steve Yeager	.10
131T	Paul Zuvella	.10
132T	Checklist	.10

1986 Topps Traded Tiffany

This collectors edition differs from the regular 1986 Topps Traded set only in the use of a high-gloss front finish. The set was sold only through hobby channels in a specially design box.

	MT
Unopened Set (132):	600.00
Complete Set (132):	300.00
Common Player:	.25
11T Barry Bonds	250.00

(Star cards valued at 4X corresponding cards in regular Topps Traded)

1987 Topps

The design of Topps' set of 792 2-1/2" x 3-1/2" cards is closely akin to the 1962 set in that the player photo is set against a woodgrain border. Instead of a rolling corner, as in 1962, the player photos in '87 feature a couple of clipped corners at top left and bottom right, where the team logo and player name appear. The player's position is not given on the front of the card. For the first time in several years, the trophy which designates members of Topps All-Star Rookie Team returned to the card design. As in the previous three years, Topps issued a glossy-finish "Tiffany" edition of their 792-card set. However, it was speculated that as many as 30,000 sets were produced as opposed to the 5,000 sets printed in 1985 and 1986.

	MT
Unopened Factory Set (792):	15.00
Complete Set (792):	12.00
Factory Uncut Sheet Set (6):	35.00
Common Player:	.05
Pack (15):	.75
Wax Box (36):	20.00
Cello Pack (31):	1.00
Cello Box (24):	20.00
Rack Pack (49):	1.50
Rack Box (24):	24.00
Vending Box (500):	12.00

No.	Player	MT
1	Roger Clemens (Record Breaker)	.30
2	Jim Deshaies (Record Breaker)	.05
3	Dwight Evans (Record Breaker)	.05
4	Dave Lopes (Record Breaker)	.05
5	Dave Righetti (Record Breaker)	.05
6	Ruben Sierra (Record Breaker)	.05
7	Todd Worrell (Record Breaker)	.05
8	Terry Pendleton	.05
9	Jay Tibbs	.05
10	Cecil Cooper	.05
11	Indians Leaders (Jack Aker, Chris Bando, Phil Niekro)	.05
12	*Jeff Sellers*	.05
13	Nick Esasky	.05
14	Dave Stewart	.05
15	Claudell Washington	.05
16	Pat Clements	.05
17	Pete O'Brien	.05
18	Dick Howser	.05
19	Matt Young	.05
20	Gary Carter	.15
21	Mark Davis	.05
22	Doug DeCinces	.05
23	Lee Smith	.05
24	Tony Walker	.05
25	Bert Blyleven	.05
26	Greg Brock	.05
27	Joe Cowley	.05
28	Rick Dempsey	.05
29	Jimmy Key	.05
30	Tim Raines	.05
31	Braves Leaders (Glenn Hubbard, Rafael Ramirez)	.05
32	Tim Leary	.05
33	Andy Van Slyke	.05
34	Jose Rijo	.05
35	Sid Bream	.05
36	*Eric King*	.05
37	Marvell Wynne	.05
38	Dennis Leonard	.05
39	Marty Barrett	.05
40	Dave Righetti	.05
41	Bo Diaz	.05
42	Gary Redus	.05
43	Gene Michael	.05
44	Greg Harris	.05
45	Jim Presley	.05
46	Danny Gladden	.05
47	Dennis Powell	.05
48	Wally Backman	.05
49	Terry Harper	.05
50	Dave Smith	.05
51	Mel Hall	.05
52	Keith Atherton	.05
53	Ruppert Jones	.05
54	Bill Dawley	.05
55	Tim Wallach	.05
56	Brewers Leaders (Jamie Cocanower, Paul Molitor, Charlie Moore, Herm Starrette)	.10
57	*Scott Nielsen*	.05
58	Thad Bosley	.05
59	Ken Dayley	.05
60	Tony Pena	.05
61	*Bobby Thigpen*	.05
62	Bobby Meacham	.05
63	Fred Toliver	.05
64	Harry Spilman	.05
65	Tom Browning	.05
66	Marc Sullivan	.05
67	Bill Swift	.05
68	Tony LaRussa	.05
69	Lonnie Smith	.05
70	Charlie Hough	.05
71	*Mike Aldrete*	.05
72	Walt Terrell	.05
73	Dave Anderson	.05
74	Dan Pasqua	.05
75	Ron Darling	.05
76	Rafael Ramirez	.05
77	Bryan Oelkers	.05
78	Tom Foley	.05
79	Juan Nieves	.05
80	*Wally Joyner*	.35
81	Padres Leaders (Andy Hawkins, Terry Kennedy)	.05
82	*Rob Murphy*	.05
83	Mike Davis	.05
84	Steve Lake	.05
85	Kevin Bass	.05
86	Nate Snell	.05
87	Mark Salas	.05
88	Ed Wojna	.05
89	Ozzie Guillen	.05
90	Dave Stieb	.05
91	Harold Reynolds	.05
92a	Urbano Lugo (no trademark on front)	.10
92b	Urbano Lugo (trademark on front)	.05
93	Jim Leyland	.05
94	Calvin Schiraldi	.05
95	Oddibe McDowell	.05
96	Frank Williams	.05
97	Glenn Wilson	.05
98	Bill Scherrer	.05
99	Darryl Motley	.05
100	Steve Garvey	.15
101	*Carl Willis*	.05
102	Paul Zuvella	.05
103	Rick Aguilera	.05
104	Billy Sample	.05
105	Floyd Youmans	.05
106	Blue Jays Leaders (George Bell, Willie Upshaw)	.05
107	John Butcher	.05
108	Jim Gantner (photo reversed)	.05
109	R.J. Reynolds	.05
110	John Tudor	.05
111	Alfredo Griffin	.05
112	Alan Ashby	.05
113	Neil Allen	.05
114	Billy Beane	.05
115	Donnie Moore	.05
116	*Mike Stanley*	.05
117	Jim Beattie	.05
118	Bobby Valentine	.05
119	Ron Robinson	.05
120	Eddie Murray	.40
121	*Kevin Romine*	.05
122	Jim Clancy	.05
123	John Kruk	.05
124	Ray Fontenot	.05
125	Bob Brenly	.05
126	*Mike Loynd*	.05
127	Vance Law	.05
128	Checklist 1-132	.05
129	Rick Cerone	.05
130	Dwight Gooden	.05
131	Pirates Leaders (Sid Bream, Tony Pena)	.05
132	*Paul Assenmacher*	.05
133	Jose Oquendo	.05
134	*Rich Yett*	.05
135	Mike Easler	.05
136	Ron Romanick	.05
137	Jerry Willard	.05
138	Roy Lee Jackson	.05
139	*Devon White*	.40
140	Bret Saberhagen	.05
141	Herm Winningham	.05
142	Rick Sutcliffe	.05
143	Steve Boros	.05
144	Mike Scioscia	.05
145	Charlie Kerfeld	.05
146	*Tracy Jones*	.05
147	Randy Niemann	.05
148	Dave Collins	.05
149	Ray Searage	.05
150	Wade Boggs	.45
151	Mike LaCoss	.05
152	Toby Harrah	.05
153	*Duane Ward*	.05
154	Tom O'Malley	.05
155	Eddie Whitson	.05
156	Mariners Leaders (Bob Kearney, Phil Regan, Matt Young)	.05
157	Danny Darwin	.05
158	Tim Teufel	.05
159	Ed Olwine	.05
160	Julio Franco	.05
161	Steve Ontiveros	.05
162	*Mike LaValliere*	.10
163	Kevin Gross	.05
164	Sammy Khalifa	.05
165	Jeff Reardon	.05
166	Bob Boone	.05
167	*Jim Deshaies*	.10
168	Lou Piniella	.05
169	Ron Washington	.05
170	Bo Jackson (Future Stars)	.35
171	*Chuck Cary*	.05
172	Ron Oester	.05
173	Alex Trevino	.05
174	Henry Cotto	.05
175	Bob Stanley	.05
176	Steve Buechele	.05
177	Keith Moreland	.05
178	Cecil Fielder	.05
179	Bill Wegman	.05
180	Chris Brown	.05
181	Cardinals Leaders (Mike LaValliere, Ozzie Smith, Ray Soff)	.10
182	Lee Lacy	.05
183	Andy Hawkins	.05
184	Bobby Bonilla	.05
185	Roger McDowell	.05
186	Bruce Benedict	.05
187	Mark Huismann	.05
188	Tony Phillips	.05
189	Joe Hesketh	.05
190	Jim Sundberg	.05
191	Charles Hudson	.05
192	Cory Snyder	.05
193	Roger Craig	.05
194	Kirk McCaskill	.05
195	Mike Pagliarulo	.05
196	Randy O'Neal	.05
197	Mark Bailey	.05
198	Lee Mazzilli	.05
199	Mariano Duncan	.05
200	Pete Rose	.65
201	*John Cangelosi*	.05
202	Ricky Wright	.05
203	*Mike Kingery*	.05
204	Sammy Stewart	.05
205	Graig Nettles	.05
206	Twins Leaders (Tim Laudner, Frank Viola)	.05
207	George Frazier	.05
208	John Shelby	.05
209	Rick Schu	.05
210	Lloyd Moseby	.05
211	John Morris	.05
212	Mike Fitzgerald	.05
213	*Randy Myers*	.25
214	Omar Moreno	.05
215	Mark Langston	.05
216	*B.J. Surhoff* (Future Stars)	.20
217	Chris Codiroli	.05
218	Sparky Anderson	.20
219	Cecilio Guante	.05
220	Joe Carter	.05
221	Vern Ruhle	.05
222	Denny Walling	.05
223	Charlie Leibrandt	.05
224	Wayne Tolleson	.05
225	Mike Smithson	.05
226	Max Venable	.05
227	*Jamie Moyer*	.05
228	Curt Wilkerson	.05
229	*Mike Birkbeck*	.05
230	Don Baylor	.10
231	Giants Leaders (Bob Brenly, Mike Krukow)	.05
232	*Reggie Williams*	.05
233	*Russ Morman*	.05

234 Pat Sheridan .05
235 Alvin Davis .05
236 Tommy John .10
237 Jim Morrison .05
238 Bill Krueger .05
239 Juan Espino .05
240 Steve Balboni .05
241 Danny Heep .05
242 Rick Mahler .05
243 Whitey Herzog .05
244 Dickie Noles .05
245 Willie Upshaw .05
246 Jim Dwyer .05
247 Jeff Reed .05
248 Gene Walter .05
249 Jim Pankovits .05
250 Teddy Higuera .05
251 Rob Wilfong .05
252 Denny Martinez .05
253 Eddie Milner .05
254 *Bob Tewksbury* .20
255 Juan Samuel .05
256 Royals Leaders (George Brett, Frank White) .15
257 Bob Forsch .05
258 Steve Yeager .05
259 *Mike Greenwell* .25
260 Vida Blue .05
261 Ruben Sierra .05
262 Jim Winn .05
263 Stan Javier .05
264 Checklist 133-264 .05
265 Darrell Evans .05
266 *Jeff Hamilton* .05
267 Howard Johnson .05
268 Pat Corrales .05
269 Cliff Speck .05
270 Jody Davis .05
271 Mike Brown .05
272 Andres Galarraga .05
273 Gene Nelson .05
274 *Jeff Hearron* .05
275 LaMarr Hoyt .05
276 Jackie Gutierrez .05
277 Juan Agosto .05
278 Gary Pettis .05
279 *Dan Plesac* .05
280 Jeffrey Leonard .05
281 Reds Leaders (Bo Diaz, Bill Gullickson, Pete Rose) .10
282 Jeff Calhoun .05
283 *Doug Drabek* .25
284 John Moses .05
285 Dennis Boyd .05
286 Mike Woodard .05
287 Dave Von Ohlen .05
288 Tito Landrum .05
289 Bob Kipper .05
290 Leon Durham .05
291 Mitch Williams .05
292 Franklin Stubbs .05
293 Bob Rodgers .05
294 Steve Jeltz .05
295 Len Dykstra .05
296 *Andres Thomas* .05
297 Don Schulze .05
298 Larry Herndon .05
299 Joel Davis .05
300 Reggie Jackson .40
301 *Luis Aquino* .05
302 Bill Schroeder .05
303 Juan Berenguer .05
304 Phil Garner .05
305 John Franco .05
306 Red Sox Leaders (Rich Gedman, John McNamara, Tom Seaver) .10
307 *Lee Guetterman* .05
308 Don Slaught .05
309 Mike Young .05
310 Frank Viola .05
311 Rickey Henderson (Turn Back the Clock) .10
312 Reggie Jackson (Turn Back the Clock) .10
313 Roberto Clemente (Turn Back the Clock) .50
314 Carl Yastrzemski (Turn Back the Clock) .10
315 Maury Wills (Turn Back the Clock) .05
316 Brian Fisher .05
317 Clint Hurdle .05
318 Jim Fregosi .05
319 *Greg Swindell* .10
320 Barry Bonds 7.00
321 Mike Laga .05
322 Chris Bando .05
323 *Al Newman* .05
324 Dave Palmer .05
325 Garry Templeton .05
326 Mark Gubicza .05
327 *Dale Sveum* .05
328 Bob Welch .05
329 Ron Roenicke .05
330 Mike Scott .05
331 Mets Leaders (Gary Carter, Keith Hernandez, Dave Johnson, Darryl Strawberry) .10
332 Joe Price .05
333 Ken Phelps .05
334 *Ed Correa* .05
335 Candy Maldonado .05
336 *Allan Anderson* .05
337 Darrell Miller .05
338 Tim Conroy .05
339 Donnie Hill .05
340 Roger Clemens .60
341 Mike Brown .05
342 Bob James .05
343 Hal Lanier .05
344a Joe Niekro (copyright outside yellow on back) .25
344b Joe Niekro (copyright inside yellow on back) .05
345 Andre Dawson .15
346 Shawon Dunston .05
347 Mickey Brantley .05
348 Carmelo Martinez .05
349 Storm Davis .05
350 Keith Hernandez .05
351 Gene Garber .05
352 Mike Felder .05
353 Ernie Camacho .05
354 Jamie Quirk .05
355 Don Carman .05
356 White Sox Leaders (Ed Brinkman, Julio Cruz) .05
357 *Steve Fireovid* .05
358 Sal Butera .05
359 Doug Corbett .05
360 Pedro Guerrero .05
361 Mark Thurmond .05
362 *Luis Quinones* .05
363 Jose Guzman .05
364 Randy Bush .05
365 Rick Rhoden .05
366 Mark McGwire 4.00
367 Jeff Lahti .05
368 John McNamara .05
369 Brian Dayett .05
370 Fred Lynn .05
371 *Mark Eichhorn* .05
372 Jerry Mumphrey .05
373 Jeff Dedmon .05
374 Glenn Hoffman .05
375 Ron Guidry .10
376 Scott Bradley .05
377 John Henry Johnson .05
378 Rafael Santana .05
379 John Russell .05
380 Rich Gossage .05
381 Expos Leaders (Mike Fitzgerald, Bob Rodgers) .05
382 Rudy Law .05
383 Ron Davis .05
384 Johnny Grubb .05
385 Orel Hershiser .10
386 Dickie Thon .05
387 *T.R. Bryden* .05
388 Geno Petralli .05
389 Jeff Robinson .05
390 Gary Matthews .05
391 Jay Howell .05
392 Checklist 265-396 .05
393 Pete Rose .35
394 Mike Bielecki .05
395 Damaso Garcia .05
396 Tim Lollar .05
397 Greg Walker .05
398 Brad Havens .05
399 Curt Ford .05
400 George Brett .50
401 Billy Jo Robidoux .05
402 Mike Trujillo .05
403 Jerry Royster .05
404 Doug Sisk .05
405 Brook Jacoby .05
406 Yankees Leaders (Rickey Henderson, Don Mattingly) .25
407 Jim Acker .05
408 John Mizerock .05
409 Milt Thompson .05
410 Fernando Valenzuela .05
411 Darnell Coles .05
412 Eric Davis .05
413 Moose Haas .05
414 Joe Orsulak .05
415 *Bobby Witt* .05
416 Tom Nieto .05
417 Pat Perry .05
418 Dick Williams .05
419 *Mark Portugal* .10
420 Will Clark .40
421 Jose DeLeon .05
422 Jack Howell .05
423 Jaime Cocanower .05
424 Chris Speier .05
425 Tom Seaver .40
426 Floyd Rayford .05
427 Ed Nunez .05
428 Bruce Bochy .05
429 *Tim Pyznarski* (Future Stars) .05
430 Mike Schmidt .50
431 Dodgers Leaders (Tom Niedenfuer, Ron Perranoski, Alex Trevino) .05
432 Jim Slaton .05
433 *Ed Hearn* .05
434 Mike Fischlin .05
435 Bruce Sutter .05
436 *Andy Allanson* .05
437 Ted Power .05
438 *Kelly Downs* .05
439 Karl Best .05
440 Willie McGee .05
441 *Dave Leiper* .05
442 Mitch Webster .05
443 John Felske .05
444 Jeff Russell .05
445 Dave Lopes .05
446 *Chuck Finley* .25
447 Bill Almon .05
448 *Chris Bosio* .10
449 *Pat Dodson* (Future Stars) .05
450 Kirby Puckett .50
451 Joe Sambito .05
452 Dave Henderson .05
453 *Scott Terry* .05
454 Luis Salazar .05
455 Mike Boddicker .05
456 A's Leaders (Carney Lansford, Tony LaRussa, Mickey Tettleton, Dave Von Ohlen) .05
457 Len Matuszek .05
458 Kelly Gruber .05
459 Dennis Eckersley .10
460 Darryl Strawberry .05
461 Craig McMurtry .05
462 Scott Fletcher .05
463 Tom Candiotti .05
464 Butch Wynegar .05
465 Todd Worrell .05
466 Kal Daniels .05
467 Randy St. Claire .05
468 George Bamberger .05
469 *Mike Diaz* .05
470 Dave Dravecky .05
471 Ronn Reynolds .05
472 Bill Doran .05
473 Steve Farr .05
474 Jerry Narron .05
475 Scott Garrelts .05
476 Danny Tartabull .05
477 Ken Howell .05
478 Tim Laudner .05
479 *Bob Sebra* .05
480 Jim Rice .10
481 Phillies Leaders (Von Hayes, Juan Samuel, Glenn Wilson) .05
482 Daryl Boston .05
483 Dwight Lowry .05
484 Jim Traber .05
485 Tony Fernandez .05
486 Otis Nixon .05
487 Dave Gumpert .05
488 Ray Knight .05
489 Bill Gullickson .05
490 Dale Murphy .15
491 *Ron Karkovice* .05
492 Mike Heath .05
493 Tom Lasorda .15
494 *Barry Jones* .05
495 Gorman Thomas .05
496 Bruce Bochte .05
497 *Dale Mohorcic* .05
498 Bob Kearney .05
499 *Bruce Ruffin* .05
500 Don Mattingly .65
501 Craig Lefferts .05
502 Dick Schofield .05
503 Larry Andersen .05
504 Mickey Hatcher .05
505 Bryn Smith .05
506 Orioles Leaders (Rich Bordi, Rick Dempsey, Earl Weaver) .05
507 Dave Stapleton .05
508 *Scott Bankhead* .05
509 Enos Cabell .05
510 Tom Henke .05
511 Steve Lyons .05
512 *Dave Magadan* (Future Stars) .20
513 Carmen Castillo .05
514 Orlando Mercado .05
515 Willie Hernandez .05
516 Ted Simmons .05
517 Mario Soto .05
518 Gene Mauch .05
519 Curt Young .05
520 Jack Clark .05
521 Rick Reuschel .05
522 Checklist 397-528 .05
523 Earnie Riles .05
524 Bob Shirley .05
525 Phil Bradley .05
526 Roger Mason .05
527 Jim Wohlford .05
528 Ken Dixon .05
529 *Alvaro Espinoza* .05
530 Tony Gwynn .50
531 Astros Leaders (Yogi Berra, Hal Lanier, Denis Menke, Gene Tenace) .05
532 Jeff Stone .05
533 Argenis Salazar .05
534 Scott Sanderson .05
535 Tony Armas .05
536 *Terry Mulholland* .15
537 Rance Mulliniks .05
538 Tom Niedenfuer .05
539 Reid Nichols .05
540 Terry Kennedy .05
541 *Rafael Belliard* .05
542 Ricky Horton .05
543 Dave Johnson .05
544 Zane Smith .05
545 Buddy Bell .05
546 Mike Morgan .05
547 Rob Deer .05
548 *Bill Mooneyham* .05
549 Bob Melvin .05
550 Pete Incaviglia .05
551 Frank Wills .05
552 Larry Sheets .05
553 *Mike Maddux* .05
554 Buddy Biancalana .05
555 Dennis Rasmussen .05
556 Angels Leaders (Bob Boone, Marcel Lachemann, Mike Witt) .05
557 *John Cerutti* .05
558 Greg Gagne .05
559 Lance McCullers .05
560 Glenn Davis .05
561 *Rey Quinones* .05
562 *Bryan Clutterbuck* .05
563 John Stefero .05
564 Larry McWilliams .05
565 Dusty Baker .05
566 Tim Hulett .05
567 *Greg Mathews* .05
568 Earl Weaver .10
569 Wade Rowdon .05
570 Sid Fernandez .05
571 Ozzie Virgil .05
572 Pete Ladd .05
573 Hal McRae .05
574 Manny Lee .05

575 Pat Tabler .05
576 Frank Pastore .05
577 Dann Bilardello .05
578 Billy Hatcher .05
579 Rick Burleson .05
580 Mike Krukow .05
581 Cubs Leaders (Ron Cey, Steve Trout) .05
582 Bruce Berenyi .05
583 Junior Ortiz .05
584 Ron Kittle .05
585 *Scott Bailes* .05
586 Ben Oglivie .05
587 Eric Plunk .05
588 Wallace Johnson .05
589 Steve Crawford .05
590 Vince Coleman .05
591 Spike Owen .05
592 Chris Welsh .05
593 Chuck Tanner .05
594 Rick Anderson .05
595 Keith Hernandez (All-Star) .05
596 Steve Sax (All-Star) .05
597 Mike Schmidt (All-Star) .25
598 Ozzie Smith (All-Star) .20
599 Tony Gwynn (All-Star) .25
600 Dave Parker (All-Star) .05
601 Darryl Strawberry (All-Star) .05
602 Gary Carter (All-Star) .05
603a Dwight Gooden (All-Star, no trademark on front) .25
603b Dwight Gooden (All-Star, trademark on front) .05
604 Fernando Valenzuela (All-Star) .05
605 Todd Worrell (All-Star) .05
606a Don Mattingly (All-Star, no trademark on front) .75
606b Don Mattingly (All-Star, trademark on front) .25
607 Tony Bernazard (All-Star) .05
608 Wade Boggs (All-Star) .20
609 Cal Ripken, Jr. (All-Star) .40
610 Jim Rice (All-Star) .05
611 Kirby Puckett (All-Star) .35
612 George Bell (All-Star) .05
613 Lance Parrish (All-Star) .05
614 Roger Clemens (All-Star) .25
615 Teddy Higuera (All-Star) .05
616 Dave Righetti (All-Star) .05
617 Al Nipper .05
618 Tom Kelly .05
619 Jerry Reed .05
620 Jose Canseco .60
621 Danny Cox .05
622 *Glenn Braggs* .05
623 *Kurt Stillwell* .05
624 Tim Burke .05
625 Mookie Wilson .05
626 Joel Skinner .05
627 Ken Oberkfell .05
628 Bob Walk .05
629 Larry Parrish .05
630 John Candelaria .05
631 Tigers Leaders (Sparky Anderson, Mike Heath, Willie Hernandez) .05
632 Rob Woodward .05
633 Jose Uribe .05
634 *Rafael Palmeiro* 1.50
635 Ken Schrom .05
636 Darren Daulton .05
637 *Bip Roberts* .15
638 Rich Bordi .05
639 Gerald Perry .05
640 Mark Clear .05
641 Domingo Ramos .05
642 Al Pulido .05
643 Ron Shepherd .05
644 John Denny .05
645 Dwight Evans .05
646 Mike Mason .05
647 Tom Lawless .05
648 *Barry Larkin* .75
649 Mickey Tettleton .05
650 Hubie Brooks .05
651 Benny Distefano .05
652 Terry Forster .05
653 Kevin Mitchell .05
654 Checklist 529-660 .05
655 Jesse Barfield .05
656 Rangers Leaders (Bobby Valentine, Rickey Wright) .05
657 Tom Waddell .05
658 *Robby Thompson* .05
659 Aurelio Lopez .05
660 Bob Horner .05
661 Lou Whitaker .05
662 Frank DiPino .05
663 Cliff Johnson .05
664 Mike Marshall .05
665 Rod Scurry .05
666 Von Hayes .05
667 Ron Hassey .05
668 Juan Bonilla .05
669 Bud Black .05
670 Jose Cruz .05
671a Ray Soff (no "D*" before copyright line) .20
671b Ray Soff ("D*" before copyright line) .05
672 Chili Davis .05
673 Don Sutton .25
674 Bill Campbell .05
675 Ed Romero .05
676 Charlie Moore .05
677 Bob Grich .05
678 Carney Lansford .05
679 Kent Hrbek .05
680 Ryne Sandberg .45
681 George Bell .05
682 Jerry Reuss .05
683 Gary Roenicke .05
684 Kent Tekulve .05
685 Jerry Hairston Sr. .05
686 Doyle Alexander .05
687 Alan Trammell .05
688 Juan Beniquez .05
689 Darrell Porter .05
690 Dane Iorg .05
691 Dave Parker .05
692 Frank White .05
693 Terry Puhl .05
694 Phil Niekro .25
695 Chico Walker .05
696 Gary Lucas .05
697 Ed Lynch .05
698 Ernie Whitt .05
699 Ken Landreaux .05
700 Dave Bergman .05
701 Willie Randolph .05
702 Greg Gross .05
703 Dave Schmidt .05
704 Jesse Orosco .05
705 Bruce Hurst .05
706 Rick Manning .05
707 Bob McClure .05
708 Scott McGregor .05
709 Dave Kingman .05
710 Gary Gaetti .05
711 Ken Griffey .05
712 Don Robinson .05
713 Tom Brookens .05
714 Dan Quisenberry .05
715 Bob Dernier .05
716 Rick Leach .05
717 Ed Vande Berg .05
718 Steve Carlton .30
719 Tom Hume .05
720 Richard Dotson .05
721 Tom Herr .05
722 Bob Knepper .05
723 Brett Butler .05
724 Greg Minton .05
725 George Hendrick .05
726 Frank Tanana .05
727 Mike Moore .05
728 Tippy Martinez .05
729 Tom Paciorek .05
730 Eric Show .05
731 Dave Concepcion .05
732 Manny Trillo .05
733 Bill Caudill .05
734 Bill Madlock .05
735 Rickey Henderson .40
736 Steve Bedrosian .05
737 Floyd Bannister .05
738 Jorge Orta .05
739 Chet Lemon .05
740 Rich Gedman .05
741 Paul Molitor .30
742 Andy McGaffigan .05
743 Dwayne Murphy .05
744 Roy Smalley .05
745 Glenn Hubbard .05
746 Bob Ojeda .05
747 Johnny Ray .05
748 Mike Flanagan .05
749 Ozzie Smith .50
750 Steve Trout .05
751 Garth Iorg .05
752 Dan Petry .05
753 Rick Honeycutt .05
754 Dave LaPoint .05
755 Luis Aguayo .05
756 Carlton Fisk .40
757 Nolan Ryan .75
758 Tony Bernazard .05
759 Joel Youngblood .05
760 Mike Witt .05
761 Greg Pryor .05
762 Gary Ward .05
763 Tim Flannery .05
764 Bill Buckner .05
765 Kirk Gibson .05
766 Don Aase .05
767 Ron Cey .05
768 Dennis Lamp .05
769 Steve Sax .05
770 Dave Winfield .50
771 Shane Rawley .05
772 Harold Baines .05
773 Robin Yount .30
774 Wayne Krenchicki .05
775 Joaquin Andujar .05
776 Tom Brunansky .05
777 Chris Chambliss .05
778 Jack Morris .05
779 Craig Reynolds .05
780 Andre Thornton .05
781 Atlee Hammaker .05
782 Brian Downing .05
783 Willie Wilson .05
784 Cal Ripken, Jr. .75
785 Terry Francona .05
786 Jimy Williams .05
787 Alejandro Pena .05
788 Tim Stoddard .05
789 Dan Schatzeder .05
790 Julio Cruz .05
791 Lance Parrish .05
792 Checklist 661-792 .05

1987 Topps Tiffany

Produced in much greater quantity (reportedly 30,000 sets) than the previous years' sets, this specially boxed collectors edition differs from the regular 1987 Topps cards only in its use of white cardboard stock and a high-gloss finish on the cards' fronts.

	MT
Unopened Set (792):	100.00
Complete Set (792):	80.00
Common Player:	.15

(Star cards valued at 4X corresponding cards in regular 1987 Topps)

1987 Topps All-Star Glossy Set of 22

For the fourth consecutive year, Topps produced an All-Star Game commemorative set of 22 cards. The glossy cards, 2-1/2" x 3-1/2", were included in rack packs. Using the same basic design as in previous efforts with a few minor changes, the 1987 edition features American and National League logos on the card fronts. Cards #1-12 feature representatives from the American League, while #13-22 are National Leaguers.

		MT
Complete Set (22):		3.00
Common Player:		.10
1	Whitey Herzog	.10
2	Keith Hernandez	.10
3	Ryne Sandberg	.60
4	Mike Schmidt	.75
5	Ozzie Smith	.75
6	Tony Gwynn	.75
7	Dale Murphy	.25
8	Darryl Strawberry	.10
9	Gary Carter	.25
10	Dwight Gooden	.10
11	Fernando Valenzuela	.10
12	Dick Howser	.10
13	Wally Joyner	.10
14	Lou Whitaker	.10
15	Wade Boggs	.50
16	Cal Ripken, Jr.	1.00
17	Dave Winfield	.60
18	Rickey Henderson	.50
19	Kirby Puckett	.75
20	Lance Parrish	.10
21	Roger Clemens	.75
22	Teddy Higuera	.10

1987 Topps Glossy Rookies

The 1987 Topps Glossy Rookies set of 22 cards was introduced with Topps' new 100-card "Jumbo Packs". Intended for sale in supermarkets, the jumbo packs contained one glossy card. Measuring the standard 2-1/2" x 3-1/2" size, the special insert cards feature the top rookies from the previous season.

		MT
Complete Set (22):		3.00
Common Player:		.10
1	Andy Allanson	.10
2	John Cangelosi	.10
3	Jose Canseco	1.50
4	Will Clark	1.00
5	Mark Eichhorn	.10
6	Pete Incaviglia	.10
7	Wally Joyner	.10
8	Eric King	.10
9	Dave Magadan	.10
10	John Morris	.10
11	Juan Nieves	.10
12	Rafael Palmeiro	1.00
13	Billy Jo Robidoux	.10
14	Bruce Ruffin	.10
15	Ruben Sierra	.10
16	Cory Snyder	.10
17	Kurt Stillwell	.10
18	Dale Sveum	.10
19	Danny Tartabull	.10
20	Andres Thomas	.10
21	Robby Thompson	.10
22	Todd Worrell	.10

1987 Topps Mini League Leaders

Returning for 1987, the Topps "Major League Leaders" set was increased in size from 66 to 76 cards. The 2-1/8" x 3" cards feature woodgrain borders that encompass a white-bordered color photo. Backs are printed in yellow, orange and brown and list the player's official ranking based on his 1986 American or National League statistics. The players featured are those who finished the top five in their leagues' various batting and pitching categories. The cards were sold in plastic-wrapped packs, seven cards plus a game card per pack.

		MT
Complete Set (77):		4.00
Common Player:		.05
1	Bob Horner	.05
2	Dale Murphy	.15
3	Lee Smith	.05
4	Eric Davis	.05
5	John Franco	.05
6	Dave Parker	.05
7	Kevin Bass	.05
8	Glenn Davis	.05
9	Bill Doran	.05
10	Bob Knepper	.05
11	Mike Scott	.05
12	Dave Smith	.05
13	Mariano Duncan	.05
14	Orel Hershiser	.05
15	Steve Sax	.05
16	Fernando Valenzuela	.05
17	Tim Raines	.05
18	Jeff Reardon	.05
19	Floyd Youmans	.05
20	Gary Carter	.15
21	Ron Darling	.05
22	Sid Fernandez	.05
23	Dwight Gooden	.05
24	Keith Hernandez	.05
25	Bob Ojeda	.05
26	Darryl Strawberry	.05
27	Steve Bedrosian	.05
28	Von Hayes	.05
29	Juan Samuel	.05
30	Mike Schmidt	.50
31	Rick Rhoden	.05
32	Vince Coleman	.05
33	Danny Cox	.05
34	Todd Worrell	.05
35	Tony Gwynn	.50
36	Mike Krukow	.05
37	Candy Maldonado	.05
38	Don Aase	.05
39	Eddie Murray	.30
40	Cal Ripken, Jr.	.90
41	Wade Boggs	.30
42	Roger Clemens	.50
43	Bruce Hurst	.05
44	Jim Rice	.10
45	Wally Joyner	.05
46	Donnie Moore	.05
47	Gary Pettis	.05
48	Mike Witt	.05
49	John Cangelosi	.05
50	Tom Candiotti	.05
51	Joe Carter	.05
52	Pat Tabler	.05
53	Kirk Gibson	.05
54	Willie Hernandez	.05
55	Jack Morris	.05
56	Alan Trammell	.05
57	George Brett	.50
58	Willie Wilson	.05
59	Rob Deer	.05
60	Teddy Higuera	.05
61	Bert Blyleven	.05
62	Gary Gaetti	.05
63	Kirby Puckett	.50
64	Rickey Henderson	.40
65	Don Mattingly	.65
66	Dennis Rasmussen	.05
67	Dave Righetti	.05
68	Jose Canseco	.30
69	Dave Kingman	.05
70	Phil Bradley	.05
71	Mark Langston	.05
72	Pete O'Brien	.05
73	Jesse Barfield	.05
74	George Bell	.05
75	Tony Fernandez	.05
76	Tom Henke	.05
77	Checklist	.05

1987 Topps Traded

The Topps Traded set consists of 132 cards as did all Traded sets issued by Topps since 1981. Cards measure the standard 2-1/2" x 3-1/2" and are identical in design to the regular edition set. The purpose of the set is to update player trades and feature rookies not included in the regular issue. As they had done the previous three years, Topps produced a glossy-coated "Tiffany" edition of the Traded set. Cards are numbered with a "T" suffix.

		MT
Complete Set (132):		6.00
Common Player:		.05
1	Bill Almon	.05
2	Scott Bankhead	.05
3	Eric Bell	.05
4	Juan Beniquez	.05
5	Juan Berenguer	.05
6	Greg Booker	.05
7	Thad Bosley	.05
8	Larry Bowa	.05
9	Greg Brock	.05
10	Bob Brower	.05
11	Jerry Browne	.05
12	Ralph Bryant	.05
13	DeWayne Buice	.05
14	*Ellis Burks*	.50
15	Ivan Calderon	.05
16	Jeff Calhoun	.05
17	Casey Candaele	.05
18	John Cangelosi	.05
19	Steve Carlton	.30
20	Juan Castillo	.05
21	Rick Cerone	.05
22	Ron Cey	.05
23	John Christensen	.05
24	Dave Cone	.50
25	Chuck Crim	.05
26	Storm Davis	.05
27	Andre Dawson	.25
28	Rick Dempsey	.05
29	Doug Drabek	.05
30	Mike Dunne	.05
31	Dennis Eckersley	.25
32	Lee Elia	.05
33	Brian Fisher	.05
34	Terry Francona	.05
35	Willie Fraser	.05
36	Billy Gardner	.05
37	Ken Gerhart	.05
38	Danny Gladden	.05
39	Jim Gott	.05
40	Cecilio Guante	.05
41	Albert Hall	.05
42	Terry Harper	.05
43	Mickey Hatcher	.05
44	Brad Havens	.05
45	Neal Heaton	.05
46	*Mike Henneman*	.20
47	Donnie Hill	.05
48	Guy Hoffman	.05
49	Brian Holton	.05
50	Charles Hudson	.05
51	Danny Jackson	.05
52	Reggie Jackson	.25
53	Chris James	.05
54	Dion James	.05
55	Stan Jefferson	.05
56	Joe Johnson	.05
57	Terry Kennedy	.05
58	Mike Kingery	.05
59	Ray Knight	.05
60	Gene Larkin	.05
61	Mike LaValliere	.05
62	Jack Lazorko	.05
63	Terry Leach	.05
64	Tim Leary	.05
65	Jim Lindeman	.05
66	Steve Lombardozzi	.05
67	Bill Long	.05
68	Barry Lyons	.05
69	*Shane Mack*	.05
70	*Greg Maddux*	4.00
71	Bill Madlock	.05
72	Joe Magrane	.05
73	Dave Martinez	.05
74	Fred McGriff	.50
75	Mark McLemore	.15
76	Kevin McReynolds	.05
77	Dave Meads	.05
78	Eddie Milner	.05
79	Greg Minton	.05
80	John Mitchell	.05
81	Kevin Mitchell	.05
82	Charlie Moore	.05
83	Jeff Musselman	.05
84	Gene Nelson	.05
85	Graig Nettles	.05
86	Al Newman	.05
87	Reid Nichols	.05
88	Tom Niedenfuer	.05
89	Joe Niekro	.05
90	Tom Nieto	.05
91	*Matt Nokes*	.10
92	Dickie Noles	.05
93	Pat Pacillo	.05
94	Lance Parrish	.05
95	Tony Pena	.05
96	Luis Polonia	.05
97	Randy Ready	.05
98	Jeff Reardon	.05
99	Gary Redus	.05
100	Jeff Reed	.05
101	Rick Rhoden	.05
102	Cal Ripken, Sr.	.05
103	Wally Ritchie	.05
104	Jeff Robinson	.05
105	Gary Roenicke	.05
106	Jerry Royster	.05
107	Mark Salas	.05
108	Luis Salazar	.05
109	Benny Santiago	.25
110	Dave Schmidt	.05
111	Kevin Seitzer	.05
112	John Shelby	.05
113	Steve Shields	.05
114	*John Smiley*	.20
115	Chris Speier	.05
116	Mike Stanley	.05
117	Terry Steinbach	.25
118	Les Straker	.05
119	Jim Sundberg	.05
120	Danny Tartabull	.05
121	Tom Trebelhorn	.05
122	Dave Valle	.05
123	Ed Vande Berg	.05
124	Andy Van Slyke	.05
125	Gary Ward	.05
126	Alan Wiggins	.05
127	Bill Wilkinson	.05
128	Frank Williams	.05
129	*Matt Williams*	.75
130	Jim Winn	.05
131	Matt Young	.05
132	Checklist 1T-132T	.05

1987 Topps Traded Tiffany

The cards in this specially boxed limited edition version of the Traded set differ from the regular-issue cards only in the application of a high-gloss finish to the cards' fronts. Production was reported as 30,000 sets.

	MT
Complete Set (132):	35.00
Common Player:	.25

(Star cards valued at 2X corresponding cards in regular Topps Traded)

1988 Topps

The 1988 Topps set features a clean, attractive design of a player photo surrounded by a thin colored frame which is encompassed by a white border. The player's name appears in the lower-right corner in a diagonal colored strip. The team nickname is in large letters at the top of the card. Backs feature black print on orange and gray stock and include the usual player personal and career statistics. Many of the cards contain a new feature titled "This Way To The Clubhouse", which explains how the player joined his current team. The 792-card set includes a number of special subsets including "Future Stars," "Turn Back The Clock," All-Star teams, All-Star rookie selections, and Record Breakers.

	MT
Unopened Factory Set (792):	15.00
Complete Set (792):	10.00
Common Player:	.05
Wax Pack (15):	.50
Wax Box (36):	8.00
Cello Pack (28):	.75
Cello Box (24):	10.00
Rack Pack (43):	1.00
Rack Box (24):	12.00
Vending Box (500):	9.00

1 Vince Coleman (Record Breakers) .05
2 Don Mattingly (Record Breakers) .25
3a Mark McGwire (Record Breakers, white triangle by left foot) 1.00
3b Mark McGwire (Record Breakers, no white triangle) .40
4a Eddie Murray (Record Breakers, no mention of record on front) .25
4b Eddie Murray (Record Breakers, record in box on front) .20
5 Joe Niekro, Phil Niekro (Record Breakers) .10
6 Nolan Ryan (Record Breakers) .40
7 Benito Santiago (Record Breakers) .05
8 Kevin Elster (Future Stars) .05
9 Andy Hawkins .05
10 Ryne Sandberg .40
11 Mike Young .05
12 Bill Schroeder .05
13 Andres Thomas .05
14 Sparky Anderson .15
15 Chili Davis .05
16 Kirk McCaskill .05
17 Ron Oester .05
18a *Al Leiter* (Future Stars, no "NY" on shirt, photo actually Steve George) .40
18b *Al Leiter* (Future Stars, "NY" on shirt, correct photo) .20
19 *Mark Davidson* .05
20 Kevin Gross .05
21 Red Sox Leaders (Wade Boggs, Spike Owen) .10
22 Greg Swindell .05
23 Ken Landreaux .05
24 Jim Deshaies .05
25 Andres Galarraga .05
26 Mitch Williams .05
27 R.J. Reynolds .05
28 *Jose Nunez* .05
29 Argenis Salazar .05
30 Sid Fernandez .05
31 Bruce Bochy .05
32 Mike Morgan .05
33 Rob Deer .05
34 Ricky Horton .05
35 Harold Baines .05
36 Jamie Moyer .05
37 Ed Romero .05
38 Jeff Calhoun .05
39 Gerald Perry .05
40 Orel Hershiser .05
41 Bob Melvin .05
42 *Bill Landrum* .05
43 Dick Schofield .05
44 Lou Piniella .05
45 Kent Hrbek .05
46 Darnell Coles .05
47 Joaquin Andujar .05
48 Alan Ashby .05
49 Dave Clark .05
50 Hubie Brooks .05
51 Orioles Leaders (Eddie Murray, Cal Ripken, Jr.) .25
52 Don Robinson .05
53 Curt Wilkerson .05
54 Jim Clancy .05
55 Phil Bradley .05
56 Ed Hearn .05
57 *Tim Crews* .05
58 Dave Magadan .05
59 Danny Cox .05
60 Rickey Henderson .25
61 *Mark Knudson* .05
62 Jeff Hamilton .05
63 Jimmy Jones .05
64 *Ken Caminiti* .25
65 Leon Durham .05
66 Shane Rawley .05
67 Ken Oberkfell .05
68 Dave Dravecky .05
69 *Mike Hart* .05
70 Roger Clemens .50
71 Gary Pettis .05
72 Dennis Eckersley .05
73 Randy Bush .05
74 Tom Lasorda .15
75 Joe Carter .05
76 Denny Martinez .05
77 Tom O'Malley .05
78 Dan Petry .05
79 Ernie Whitt .05
80 Mark Langston .05
81 Reds Leaders (John Franco, Ron Robinson) .05
82 *Darrel Akerfelds* .05
83 Jose Oquendo .05
84 Cecilio Guante .05
85 Howard Johnson .05
86 Ron Karkovice .05
87 Mike Mason .05
88 Earnie Riles .05
89 *Gary Thurman* .05
90 Dale Murphy .15
91 *Joey Cora* .20
92 Len Matuszek .05
93 Bob Sebra .05
94 *Chuck Jackson* .05
95 Lance Parrish .05
96 *Todd Benzinger* .05
97 Scott Garrelts .05
98 *Rene Gonzales* .05
99 Chuck Finley .05
100 Jack Clark .05
101 Allan Anderson .05
102 Barry Larkin .10
103 Curt Young .05
104 Dick Williams .05
105 Jesse Orosco .05
106 *Jim Walewander* .05
107 Scott Bailes .05
108 Steve Lyons .05
109 Joel Skinner .05
110 Teddy Higuera .05
111 Expos Leaders (Hubie Brooks, Vance Law) .05
112 *Les Lancaster* .05
113 Kelly Gruber .05
114 Jeff Russell .05
115 Johnny Ray .05
116 Jerry Don Gleaton .05
117 *James Steels* .05
118 Bob Welch .05
119 *Robbie Wine* .05
120 Kirby Puckett .50
121 Checklist 1-132 .05
122 Tony Bernazard .05
123 Tom Candiotti .05
124 Ray Knight .05
125 Bruce Hurst .05
126 Steve Jeltz .05
127 Jim Gott .05
128 Johnny Grubb .05
129 Greg Minton .05
130 Buddy Bell .05
131 Don Schulze .05
132 Donnie Hill .05
133 Greg Mathews .05
134 Chuck Tanner .05
135 Dennis Rasmussen .05
136 Brian Dayett .05
137 Chris Bosio .05
138 Mitch Webster .05
139 Jerry Browne .05
140 Jesse Barfield .05
141 Royals Leaders (George Brett, Bret Saberhagen) .20
142 Andy Van Slyke .05
143 Mickey Tettleton .05
144 *Don Gordon* .05
145 Bill Madlock .05
146 *Donell Nixon* .05
147 Bill Buckner .05
148 Carmelo Martinez .05
149 Ken Howell .05
150 Eric Davis .05
151 Bob Knepper .05
152 *Jody Reed* .10
153 John Habyan .05
154 Jeff Stone .05
155 Bruce Sutter .05
156 Gary Matthews .05
157 Atlee Hammaker .05
158 Tim Hulett .05
159 *Brad Arnsberg* .05
160 Willie McGee .05
161 Bryn Smith .05
162 Mark McLemore .05
163 Dale Mohorcic .05
164 Dave Johnson .05
165 Robin Yount .25
166 *Rick Rodriguez* .05
167 Rance Mulliniks .05
168 Barry Jones .05
169 *Ross Jones* .05
170 Rich Gossage .05
171 Cubs Leaders (Shawon Dunston, Manny Trillo) .05
172 *Lloyd McClendon* .05
173 Eric Plunk .05
174 Phil Garner .05
175 Kevin Bass .05
176 Jeff Reed .05
177 Frank Tanana .05
178 Dwayne Henry .05
179 Charlie Puleo .05
180 Terry Kennedy .05
181 Dave Cone .05
182 Ken Phelps .05
183 Tom Lawless .05
184 Ivan Calderon .05
185 Rick Rhoden .05
186 Rafael Palmeiro .30
187 Steve Kiefer .05
188 John Russell .05
189 *Wes Gardner* .05
190 Candy Maldonado .05
191 John Cerutti .05
192 Devon White .05
193 Brian Fisher .05
194 Tom Kelly .05
195 Dan Quisenberry .05
196 Dave Engle .05
197 Lance McCullers .05
198 Franklin Stubbs .05
199 *Dave Meads* .05
200 Wade Boggs .35
201 Rangers Leaders (Steve Buechele, Pete Incaviglia, Pete O'Brien, Bobby Valentine) .05
202 Glenn Hoffman .05
203 Fred Toliver .05
204 Paul O'Neill .10
205 *Nelson Liriano* .05
206 Domingo Ramos .05
207 *John Mitchell* .05
208 Steve Lake .05
209 Richard Dotson .05
210 Willie Randolph .05
211 Frank DiPino .05
212 Greg Brock .05
213 Albert Hall .05
214 Dave Schmidt .05
215 Von Hayes .05
216 Jerry Reuss .05
217 Harry Spilman .05
218 Dan Schatzeder .05
219 Mike Stanley .05
220 Tom Henke .05
221 Rafael Belliard .05
222 Steve Farr .05
223 Stan Jefferson .05
224 Tom Trebelhorn .05
225 Mike Scioscia .05
226 Dave Lopes .05
227 Ed Correa .05
228 Wallace Johnson .05
229 Jeff Musselman .05
230 Pat Tabler .05
231 Pirates Leaders (Barry Bonds, Bobby Bonilla) .40
232 Bob James .05
233 Rafael Santana .05
234 Ken Dayley .05
235 Gary Ward .05
236 Ted Power .05
237 Mike Heath .05
238 *Luis Polonia* .10
239 Roy Smalley .05
240 Lee Smith .05
241 Damaso Garcia .05
242 Tom Niedenfuer .05
243 Mark Ryal .05
244 Jeff Robinson .05
245 Rich Gedman .05
246 *Mike Campbell* (Future Stars) .05
247 Thad Bosley .05
248 Storm Davis .05
249 Mike Marshall .05
250 Nolan Ryan .75
251 Tom Foley .05
252 Bob Brower .05
253 Checklist 133-264 .05
254 Lee Elia .05
255 Mookie Wilson .05
256 Ken Schrom .05
257 Jerry Royster .05
258 Ed Nunez .05
259 Ron Kittle .05
260 Vince Coleman .05
261 Giants Leaders (Will Clark, Candy Maldonado, Kevin Mitchell, Robby Thompson, Jose Uribe) .05
262 Drew Hall .05
263 Glenn Braggs .05
264 *Les Straker* .05
265 Bo Diaz .05
266 Paul Assenmacher .05
267 *Billy Bean* .05
268 Bruce Ruffin .05
269 Ellis Burks .10
270 Mike Witt .05
271 Ken Gerhart .05
272 Steve Ontiveros .05
273 Garth Iorg .05
274 Junior Ortiz .05
275 Kevin Seitzer .05
276 Luis Salazar .05
277 Alejandro Pena .05
278 Jose Cruz .05
279 Randy St. Claire .05
280 Pete Incaviglia .05
281 Jerry Hairston Sr. .05
282 Pat Perry .05
283 Phil Lombardi .05
284 Larry Bowa .05
285 Jim Presley .05
286 *Chuck Crim* .05
287 Manny Trillo .05
288 *Pat Pacillo* .05
289 Dave Bergman .05
290 Tony Fernandez .05
291 Astros Leaders (Kevin Bass, Billy Hatcher) .05
292 Carney Lansford .05
293 *Doug Jones* .05

294 *Al Pedrique* .05
295 Bert Blyleven .05
296 Floyd Rayford .05
297 Zane Smith .05
298 Milt Thompson .05
299 Steve Crawford .05
300 Don Mattingly .60
301 Bud Black .05
302 Jose Uribe .05
303 Eric Show .05
304 George Hendrick .05
305 Steve Sax .05
306 Billy Hatcher .05
307 Mike Trujillo .05
308 Lee Mazzilli .05
309 *Bill Long* .05
310 Tom Herr .05
311 Scott Sanderson .05
312 Joey Meyer (Future Stars) .05
313 Bob McClure .05
314 Jimy Williams .05
315 Dave Parker .05
316 Jose Rijo .05
317 Tom Nieto .05
318 Mel Hall .05
319 Mike Loynd .05
320 Alan Trammell .05
321 White Sox Leaders (Harold Baines, Carlton Fisk) .05
322 *Vicente Palacios* .05
323 Rick Leach .05
324 Danny Jackson .05
325 Glenn Hubbard .05
326 Al Nipper .05
327 Larry Sheets .05
328 *Greg Cadaret* .05
329 Chris Speier .05
330 Eddie Whitson .05
331 Brian Downing .05
332 Jerry Reed .05
333 Wally Backman .05
334 Dave LaPoint .05
335 Claudell Washington .05
336 Ed Lynch .05
337 Jim Gantner .05
338 Brian Holton .05
339 Kurt Stillwell .05
340 Jack Morris .05
341 Carmen Castillo .05
342 Larry Andersen .05
343 Greg Gagne .05
344 Tony LaRussa .05
345 Scott Fletcher .05
346 Vance Law .05
347 Joe Johnson .05
348 Jim Eisenreich .05
349 Bob Walk .05
350 Will Clark .15
351 Cardinals Leaders (Tony Pena, Red Schoendienst) .05
352 *Billy Ripken* .05
353 Ed Olwine .05
354 Marc Sullivan .05
355 Roger McDowell .05
356 Luis Aguayo .05
357 Floyd Bannister .05
358 Rey Quinones .05
359 Tim Stoddard .05
360 Tony Gwynn .50
361 Greg Maddux .75
362 Juan Castillo .05
363 Willie Fraser .05
364 Nick Esasky .05
365 Floyd Youmans .05
366 Chet Lemon .05
367 Tim Leary .05
368 *Gerald Young* .05
369 Greg Harris .05
370 Jose Canseco .40
371 Joe Hesketh .05
372 Matt Williams .75
373 Checklist 265-396 .05
374 Doc Edwards .05
375 Tom Brunansky .05
376 *Bill Wilkinson* .05
377 *Sam Horn* .05
378 *Todd Frohwirth* .05
379 Rafael Ramirez .05
380 *Joe Magrane* .05
381 Angels Leaders (Jack Howell, Wally Joyner) .05
382 *Keith Miller* .05
383 Eric Bell .05
384 Neil Allen .05
385 Carlton Fisk .25
386 Don Mattingly (All-Star) .30
387 Willie Randolph (All-Star) .05
388 Wade Boggs (All-Star) .15
389 Alan Trammell (All-Star) .05
390 George Bell (All-Star) .05
391 Kirby Puckett (All-Star) .25
392 Dave Winfield (All-Star) .20
393 Matt Nokes (All-Star) .05
394 Roger Clemens (All-Star) .25
395 Jimmy Key (All-Star) .05
396 Tom Henke (All-Star) .05
397 Jack Clark (All-Star) .05
398 Juan Samuel (All-Star) .05
399 Tim Wallach (All-Star) .05
400 Ozzie Smith (All-Star) .25
401 Andre Dawson (All-Star) .10
402 Tony Gwynn (All-Star) .25
403 Tim Raines (All-Star) .05
404 Benny Santiago (All-Star) .05
405 Dwight Gooden (All-Star) .05
406 Shane Rawley (All-Star) .05
407 Steve Bedrosian (All-Star) .05
408 Dion James .05
409 Joel McKeon .05
410 Tony Pena .05
411 Wayne Tolleson .05
412 Randy Myers .05
413 John Christensen .05
414 John McNamara .05
415 Don Carman .05
416 Keith Moreland .05
417 *Mark Ciardi* .05
418 Joel Youngblood .05
419 Scott McGregor .05
420 Wally Joyner .05
421 Ed Vande Berg .05
422 Dave Concepcion .05
423 John Smiley .10
424 Dwayne Murphy .05
425 Jeff Reardon .05
426 Randy Ready .05
427 *Paul Kilgus* .05
428 John Shelby .05
429 Tigers Leaders (Kirk Gibson, Alan Trammell) .05
430 Glenn Davis .05
431 Casey Candaele .05
432 Mike Moore .05
433 *Bill Pecota* .05
434 Rick Aguilera .05
435 Mike Pagliarulo .05
436 Mike Bielecki .05
437 *Fred Manrique* .05
438 *Rob Ducey* .05
439 Dave Martinez .05
440 Steve Bedrosian .05
441 Rick Manning .05
442 *Tom Bolton* .05
443 Ken Griffey .05
444 Cal Ripken, Sr. .05
445 Mike Krukow .05
446 Doug DeCinces .05
447 *Jeff Montgomery* .20
448 Mike Davis .05
449 *Jeff Robinson* .05
450 Barry Bonds .75
451 Keith Atherton .05
452 Willie Wilson .05
453 Dennis Powell .05
454 Marvell Wynne .05
455 *Shawn Hillegas* .05
456 Dave Anderson .05
457 Terry Leach .05
458 Ron Hassey .05
459 Yankees Leaders (Willie Randolph, Dave Winfield) .05
460 Ozzie Smith .50
461 Danny Darwin .05
462 Don Slaught .05
463 Fred McGriff .05
464 Jay Tibbs .05
465 Paul Molitor .25
466 Jerry Mumphrey .05
467 Don Aase .05
468 Darren Daulton .05
469 Jeff Dedmon .05
470 Dwight Evans .05
471 Donnie Moore .05
472 Robby Thompson .05
473 Joe Niekro .05
474 Tom Brookens .05
475 Pete Rose .60
476 Dave Stewart .05
477 Jamie Quirk .05
478 Sid Bream .05
479 Brett Butler .05
480 Dwight Gooden .05
481 Mariano Duncan .05
482 Mark Davis .05
483 *Rod Booker* .05
484 Pat Clements .05
485 Harold Reynolds .05
486 *Pat Keedy* .05
487 Jim Pankovits .05
488 Andy McGaffigan .05
489 Dodgers Leaders (Pedro Guerrero, Fernando Valenzuela) .05
490 Larry Parrish .05
491 B.J. Surhoff .05
492 Doyle Alexander .05
493 Mike Greenwell .05
494 *Wally Ritchie* .05
495 Eddie Murray .25
496 Guy Hoffman .05
497 Kevin Mitchell .05
498 Bob Boone .05
499 Eric King .05
500 Andre Dawson .15
501 Tim Birtsas .05
502 Danny Gladden .05
503 *Junior Noboa* .05
504 Bob Rodgers .05
505 Willie Upshaw .05
506 John Cangelosi .05
507 Mark Gubicza .05
508 Tim Teufel .05
509 Bill Dawley .05
510 Dave Winfield .25
511 Joel Davis .05
512 Alex Trevino .05
513 Tim Flannery .05
514 Pat Sheridan .05
515 Juan Nieves .05
516 Jim Sundberg .05
517 Ron Robinson .05
518 Greg Gross .05
519 Mariners Leaders (Phil Bradley, Harold Reynolds) .05
520 Dave Smith .05
521 Jim Dwyer .05
522 *Bob Patterson* .05
523 Gary Roenicke .05
524 Gary Lucas .05
525 Marty Barrett .05
526 Juan Berenguer .05
527 Steve Henderson .05
528a Checklist 397-528 (#455 is Steve Carlton) .05
528b Checklist 397-528 (#455 is Shawn Hillegas) .05
529 Tim Burke .05
530 Gary Carter .15
531 Rich Yett .05
532 Mike Kingery .05
533 *John Farrell* .05
534 John Wathan .05
535 Ron Guidry .05
536 John Morris .05
537 Steve Buechele .05
538 Bill Wegman .05
539 Mike LaValliere .05
540 Bret Saberhagen .05
541 Juan Beniquez .05
542 *Paul Noce* .05
543 Kent Tekulve .05
544 Jim Traber .05
545 Don Baylor .10
546 John Candelaria .05
547 *Felix Fermin* .05
548 Shane Mack .05
549 Braves Leaders (Ken Griffey, Dion James, Dale Murphy, Gerald Perry) .05
550 Pedro Guerrero .05
551 Terry Steinbach .05
552 Mark Thurmond .05
553 Tracy Jones .05
554 Mike Smithson .05
555 Brook Jacoby .05
556 *Stan Clarke* .05
557 Craig Reynolds .05
558 Bob Ojeda .05
559 *Ken Williams* .05
560 Tim Wallach .05
561 Rick Cerone .05
562 Jim Lindeman .05
563 Jose Guzman .05
564 Frank Lucchesi .05
565 Lloyd Moseby .05
566 *Charlie O'Brien* .05
567 Mike Diaz .05
568 Chris Brown .05
569 Charlie Leibrandt .05
570 Jeffrey Leonard .05
571 *Mark Williamson* .05
572 Chris James .05
573 Bob Stanley .05
574 Graig Nettles .05
575 Don Sutton .20
576 *Tommy Hinzo* .05
577 Tom Browning .05
578 Gary Gaetti .05
579 Mets Leaders (Gary Carter, Kevin McReynolds) .05
580 Mark McGwire .75
581 Tito Landrum .05
582 Mike Henneman .05
583 Dave Valle .05
584 Steve Trout .05
585 Ozzie Guillen .05
586 Bob Forsch .05
587 Terry Puhl .05
588 *Jeff Parrett* .05
589 Geno Petralli .05
590 George Bell .05
591 Doug Drabek .05
592 Dale Sveum .05
593 Bob Tewksbury .05
594 Bobby Valentine .05
595 Frank White .05
596 John Kruk .05
597 Gene Garber .05
598 Lee Lacy .05
599 Calvin Schiraldi .05
600 Mike Schmidt .50
601 Jack Lazorko .05
602 Mike Aldrete .05
603 Rob Murphy .05
604 Chris Bando .05
605 Kirk Gibson .05
606 Moose Haas .05
607 Mickey Hatcher .05
608 Charlie Kerfeld .05
609 Twins Leaders (Gary Gaetti, Kent Hrbek) .05
610 Keith Hernandez .05
611 Tommy John .05
612 Curt Ford .05
613 Bobby Thigpen .05
614 Herm Winningham .05
615 Jody Davis .05
616 *Jay Aldrich* .05
617 Oddibe McDowell .05
618 Cecil Fielder .05
619 *Mike Dunne* .05
620 Cory Snyder .05
621 Gene Nelson .05
622 Kal Daniels .05
623 Mike Flanagan .05
624 Jim Leyland .05
625 Frank Viola .05
626 Glenn Wilson .05
627 *Joe Boever* .05
628 Dave Henderson .05
629 Kelly Downs .05
630 Darrell Evans .05
631 Jack Howell .05
632 *Steve Shields* .05
633 *Barry Lyons* .05
634 Jose DeLeon .05
635 Terry Pendleton .05
636 Charles Hudson .05
637 *Jay Bell* .25

638	Steve Balboni	.05
639	Brewers Leaders (Glenn Braggs, Tony Muser)	.05
640	Garry Templeton	.05
641	Rick Honeycutt	.05
642	Bob Dernier	.05
643	*Rocky Childress*	.05
644	Terry McGriff	.05
645	Matt Nokes	.05
646	Checklist 529-660	.05
647	Pascual Perez	.05
648	Al Newman	.05
649	*DeWayne Buice*	.05
650	Cal Ripken, Jr.	.75
651	*Mike Jackson*	.10
652	Bruce Benedict	.05
653	Jeff Sellers	.05
654	Roger Craig	.05
655	Len Dykstra	.05
656	Lee Guetterman	.05
657	Gary Redus	.05
658	Tim Conroy	.05
659	Bobby Meacham	.05
660	Rick Reuschel	.05
661	Nolan Ryan (Turn Back the Clock)	.35
662	Jim Rice (Turn Back the Clock)	.05
663	Ron Blomberg (Turn Back the Clock)	.05
664	Bob Gibson (Turn Back the Clock)	.10
665	Stan Musial (Turn Back the Clock)	.15
666	Mario Soto	.05
667	Luis Quinones	.05
668	Walt Terrell	.05
669	Phillies Leaders (Lance Parrish, Mike Ryan)	.05
670	Dan Plesac	.05
671	Tim Laudner	.05
672	*John Davis*	.05
673	Tony Phillips	.05
674	Mike Fitzgerald	.05
675	Jim Rice	.10
676	Ken Dixon	.05
677	Eddie Milner	.05
678	Jim Acker	.05
679	Darrell Miller	.05
680	Charlie Hough	.05
681	Bobby Bonilla	.05
682	Jimmy Key	.05
683	Julio Franco	.05
684	Hal Lanier	.05
685	Ron Darling	.05
686	Terry Francona	.05
687	Mickey Brantley	.05
688	Jim Winn	.05
689	*Tom Pagnozzi*	.05
690	Jay Howell	.05
691	Dan Pasqua	.05
692	Mike Birkbeck	.05
693	Benny Santiago	.05
694	*Eric Nolte*	.05
695	Shawon Dunston	.05
696	Duane Ward	.05
697	Steve Lombardozzi	.05
698	Brad Havens	.05
699	Padres Leaders (Tony Gwynn, Benny Santiago)	.15
700	George Brett	.50
701	Sammy Stewart	.05
702	Mike Gallego	.05
703	Bob Brenly	.05
704	Dennis Boyd	.05
705	Juan Samuel	.05
706	Rick Mahler	.05
707	Fred Lynn	.05
708	Gus Polidor	.05
709	George Frazier	.05
710	Darryl Strawberry	.05
711	Bill Gullickson	.05
712	John Moses	.05
713	Willie Hernandez	.05
714	Jim Fregosi	.05
715	Todd Worrell	.05
716	Lenn Sakata	.05
717	Jay Baller	.05
718	Mike Felder	.05
719	Denny Walling	.05
720	Tim Raines	.05
721	Pete O'Brien	.05
722	Manny Lee	.05
723	Bob Kipper	.05
724	Danny Tartabull	.05
725	Mike Boddicker	.05
726	Alfredo Griffin	.05
727	Greg Booker	.05
728	Andy Allanson	.05
729	Blue Jays Leaders (George Bell, Fred McGriff)	.05
730	John Franco	.05
731	Rick Schu	.05
732	Dave Palmer	.05
733	Spike Owen	.05
734	Craig Lefferts	.05
735	Kevin McReynolds	.05
736	Matt Young	.05
737	Butch Wynegar	.05
738	Scott Bankhead	.05
739	Daryl Boston	.05
740	Rick Sutcliffe	.05
741	Mike Easler	.05
742	Mark Clear	.05
743	Larry Herndon	.05
744	Whitey Herzog	.05
745	Bill Doran	.05
746	*Gene Larkin*	.05
747	Bobby Witt	.05
748	Reid Nichols	.05
749	Mark Eichhorn	.05
750	Bo Jackson	.10
751	Jim Morrison	.05
752	Mark Grant	.05
753	Danny Heep	.05
754	Mike LaCoss	.05
755	Ozzie Virgil	.05
756	Mike Maddux	.05
757	*John Marzano*	.05
758	*Eddie Williams*	.05
759	A's Leaders (Jose Canseco, Mark McGwire)	.50
760	Mike Scott	.05
761	Tony Armas	.05
762	Scott Bradley	.05
763	Doug Sisk	.05
764	Greg Walker	.05
765	Neal Heaton	.05
766	Henry Cotto	.05
767	*Jose Lind* (Future Stars)	.15
768	Dickie Noles	.05
769	Cecil Cooper	.05
770	Lou Whitaker	.05
771	Ruben Sierra	.05
772	Sal Butera	.05
773	Frank Williams	.05
774	Gene Mauch	.05
775	Dave Stieb	.05
776	Checklist 661-792	.05
777	Lonnie Smith	.05
778a	*Keith Comstock* (white team letters)	.40
778b	*Keith Comstock* (blue team letters)	.10
779	*Tom Glavine*	.75
780	Fernando Valenzuela	.05
781	*Keith Hughes*	.05
782	*Jeff Ballard*	.05
783	Ron Roenicke	.05
784	Joe Sambito	.05
785	Alvin Davis	.05
786	Joe Price	.05
787	Bill Almon	.05
788	Ray Searage	.05
789	Indians Leaders (Joe Carter, Cory Snyder)	.05
790	Dave Righetti	.05
791	Ted Simmons	.05
792	John Tudor	.05

1988 Topps Tiffany

Sharing a checklist with the regular issue 1988 Topps baseball set, this specially boxed, limited-edition (25,000 sets) features cards printed on white cardboard stock with high-gloss front finish. Topps offered the sets directly to the public in ads in USA Today and Sporing News at a price of $99.

	MT
Complete Set (792):	40.00
Common Player:	.15

(Star cards valued at 3X corresponding cards in regular 1988 Topps issue)

1988 Topps All-Star Glossy Set of 22

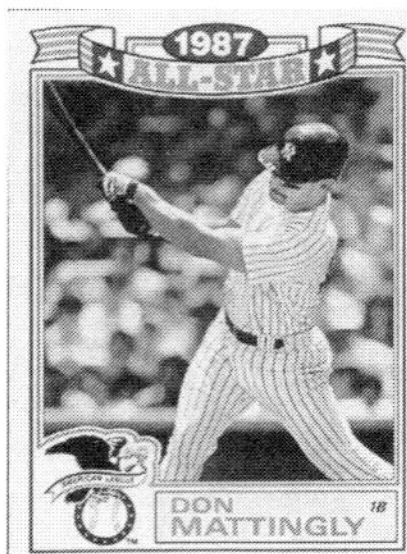

The fifth edition of Topps' special All-Star inserts was included in the company's 1988 rack packs. The 1987 American and National League All-Star lineup, plus honorary captains Jim Hunter and Billy Williams, are featured on the 2-1/2" x 3-1/2" cards. The glossy full-color fronts contain player photos centered between a red and yellow "1987 All-Star" logo at top and the player name (also red and yellow) which is printed in the bottom margin. A league logo is in the lower-left corner. Card backs are printed in red and blue on a white background, with the title and All-Star logo emblem printed above the player name and card number.

		MT
Complete Set (22):		2.50
Common Player:		.10
1	John McNamara	.10
2	Don Mattingly	.90
3	Willie Randolph	.10
4	Wade Boggs	.65
5	Cal Ripken, Jr.	1.00
6	George Bell	.10
7	Rickey Henderson	.50
8	Dave Winfield	.65
9	Terry Kennedy	.10
10	Bret Saberhagen	.10
11	Catfish Hunter	.10
12	Davey Johnson	.10
13	Jack Clark	.10
14	Ryne Sandberg	.65
15	Mike Schmidt	.75
16	Ozzie Smith	.65
17	Eric Davis	.10
18	Andre Dawson	.20
19	Darryl Strawberry	.10
20	Gary Carter	.20
21	Mike Scott	.10
22	Billy Williams	.10

1988 Topps Glossy Rookies

The Topps 1988 Rookies special insert cards follow the same basic design as the All-Star inserts. The set consists of 22 standard-size cards found one per pack in 100-card jumbo cellos. Large, glossy color player photos are printed on a white background below a red, yellow and blue "1987 Rookies" banner. A red and yellow player name appears beneath the photo. Red, white and blue card backs bear the title of the special insert set, the Rookies logo emblem, player name and card number.

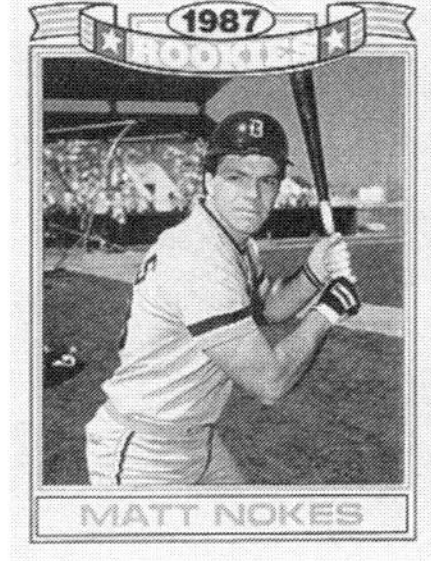

		MT
Complete Set (22):		4.00
Common Player:		.10
1	Billy Ripken	.10
2	Ellis Burks	.10
3	Mike Greenwell	.10
4	DeWayne Buice	.10
5	Devon White	.10
6	Fred Manrique	.10
7	Mike Henneman	.10
8	Matt Nokes	.10
9	Kevin Seitzer	.10
10	B.J. Surhoff	.10
11	Casey Candaele	.10
12	Randy Myers	.10
13	Mark McGwire	3.00
14	Luis Polonia	.10
15	Terry Steinbach	.10
16	Mike Dunne	.10
17	Al Pedrique	.10
18	Benny Santiago	.10
19	Kelly Downs	.10
20	Joe Magrane	.10
21	Jerry Browne	.10
22	Jeff Musselman	.10

1988 Topps Mini League Leaders

The third consecutive issue of Topps mini-cards (2-1/8" x 3") includes 77 cards spotlighting the top five ranked pitchers and batters. This set is unique in that it was the first time Topps included full-color player photos on both the front and back. Glossy action shots on the card fronts fade into a white border with a Topps logo in an upper corner. The player's name is printed in bold black letters beneath the photo. Horizontal reverses feature circular player photos on a blue and white background with the card number, player name, personal information, 1987 ranking and lifetime/1987 stats printed in red, black and yellow lettering.

		MT
Complete Set (77):		4.00
Common Player:		.10
Wax Pack (7):		.50
Wax Box (36):		15.00
1	Wade Boggs	.65
2	Roger Clemens	.75
3	Dwight Evans	.10
4	DeWayne Buice	.10
5	Brian Downing	.10
6	Wally Joyner	.10
7	Ivan Calderon	.10
8	Carlton Fisk	.50
9	Gary Redus	.10
10	Darrell Evans	.10
11	Jack Morris	.10
12	Alan Trammell	.10
13	Lou Whitaker	.10
14	Bret Saberhagen	.10
15	Kevin Seitzer	.10
16	Danny Tartabull	.10
17	Willie Wilson	.10
18	Teddy Higuera	.10
19	Paul Molitor	.50
20	Dan Plesac	.10
21	Robin Yount	.50
22	Kent Hrbek	.10
23	Kirby Puckett	.75
24	Jeff Reardon	.10
25	Frank Viola	.10
26	Rickey Henderson	.50
27	Don Mattingly	1.00
28	Willie Randolph	.10
29	Dave Righetti	.10
30	Jose Canseco	.50
31	Mark McGwire	1.50
32	Dave Stewart	.10
33	Phil Bradley	.10
34	Mark Langston	.10
35	Harold Reynolds	.10
36	Charlie Hough	.10
37	George Bell	.10
38	Tom Henke	.10
39	Jimmy Key	.10
40	Dion James	.10
41	Dale Murphy	.20
42	Zane Smith	.10
43	Andre Dawson	.20
44	Lee Smith	.10
45	Rick Sutcliffe	.10
46	Eric Davis	.10
47	John Franco	.10
48	Dave Parker	.10
49	Billy Hatcher	.10
50	Nolan Ryan	1.50
51	Mike Scott	.10
52	Pedro Guerrero	.10
53	Orel Hershiser	.10
54	Fernando Valenzuela	.10
55	Bob Welch	.10
56	Andres Galarraga	.10
57	Tim Raines	.10
58	Tim Wallach	.10
59	Len Dykstra	.10
60	Dwight Gooden	.10
61	Howard Johnson	.10
62	Roger McDowell	.10
63	Darryl Strawberry	.10
64	Steve Bedrosian	.10
65	Shane Rawley	.10
66	Juan Samuel	.10
67	Mike Schmidt	.75
68	Mike Dunne	.10
69	Jack Clark	.10
70	Vince Coleman	.10
71	Willie McGee	.10
72	Ozzie Smith	.75
73	Todd Worrell	.10
74	Tony Gwynn	.75
75	John Kruk	.10
76	Rick Rueschel	.10
77	Checklist	.10

1988 Topps Traded

In addition to new players and traded veterans, 21 members of the U.S.A. Olympic Baseball team are showcased in this 132-card set, numbered 1T-132T. The 2-1/2" x 3-1/2" cards follow the same design as the basic Topps issue - white borders, large full-color photos, team name (or U.S.A.) in large bold letters at the top of the card face, player name on a diagonal stripe across the lower-right corner. Topps had issued its traded series each year since 1981 in boxed complete sets available only through hobby dealers.

		MT
Complete Set (132):		8.00
Common Player:		.05
1	*Jim Abbott* (USA)	.25
2	Juan Agosto	.05
3	Luis Alicea	.05
4	*Roberto Alomar*	3.00
5	*Brady Anderson*	.50
6	Jack Armstrong	.05
7	Don August	.05
8	Floyd Bannister	.05
9	Bret Barberie (USA)	.10
10	Jose Bautista	.05
11	Don Baylor	.15
12	Tim Belcher	.05
13	Buddy Bell	.05
14	*Andy Benes* (USA)	.50
15	Damon Berryhill	.05
16	Bud Black	.05
17	Pat Borders	.05
18	Phil Bradley	.05
19	Jeff Branson (USA)	.05
20	Tom Brunansky	.05
21	*Jay Buhner*	.75
22	Brett Butler	.05
23	Jim Campanis (USA)	.10
24	Sil Campusano	.05
25	John Candelaria	.05
26	Jose Cecena	.05
27	Rick Cerone	.05
28	Jack Clark	.05
29	Kevin Coffman	.05
30	Pat Combs (USA)	.10
31	Henry Cotto	.05
32	Chili Davis	.05
33	Mike Davis	.05
34	Jose DeLeon	.05
35	Richard Dotson	.05
36	Cecil Espy	.05
37	Tom Filer	.05
38	Mike Fiore (USA)	.05
39	*Ron Gant*	.50
40	Kirk Gibson	.05
41	Rich Gossage	.05
42	*Mark Grace*	1.00
43	Alfredo Griffin	.05
44	Ty Griffin (USA)	.10
45	Bryan Harvey	.05
46	Ron Hassey	.05
47	Ray Hayward	.05
48	Dave Henderson	.05
49	Tom Herr	.05
50	Bob Horner	.05
51	Ricky Horton	.05
52	Jay Howell	.05
53	Glenn Hubbard	.05
54	Jeff Innis	.05
55	Danny Jackson	.05
56	Darrin Jackson	.05
57	Roberto Kelly	.05
58	Ron Kittle	.05
59	Ray Knight	.05
60	Vance Law	.05
61	Jeffrey Leonard	.05
62	*Mike Macfarlane*	.20
63	Scotti Madison	.05
64	Kirt Manwaring	.05
65	Mark Marquess (USA)	.05
66	*Tino Martinez* (USA)	2.00
67	Billy Masse (USA)	.05
68	*Jack McDowell*	.25
69	Jack McKeon	.05
70	Larry McWilliams	.05
71	Mickey Morandini (USA)	.10
72	Keith Moreland	.05
73	Mike Morgan	.05
74	Charles Nagy (USA)	.25
75	Al Nipper	.05
76	Russ Nixon	.05
77	Jesse Orosco	.05
78	Joe Orsulak	.05
79	Dave Palmer	.05
80	Mark Parent	.05
81	Dave Parker	.05
82	Dan Pasqua	.05
83	Melido Perez	.05
84	Steve Peters	.05
85	Dan Petry	.05
86	Gary Pettis	.05
87	Jeff Pico	.05
88	Jim Poole (USA)	.10
89	Ted Power	.05
90	Rafael Ramirez	.05
91	Dennis Rasmussen	.05
92	Jose Rijo	.05
93	Earnie Riles	.05
94	Luis Rivera	.05
95	Doug Robbins (USA)	.05
96	Frank Robinson	.15
97	Cookie Rojas	.05
98	*Chris Sabo*	.20
99	Mark Salas	.05
100	Luis Salazar	.05
101	Rafael Santana	.05
102	Nelson Santovenia	.05
103	Mackey Sasser	.05
104	Calvin Schiraldi	.05
105	Mike Schooler	.05
106	Scott Servais (USA)	.10
107	Dave Silvestri (USA)	.10
108	Don Slaught	.05
109	Joe Slusarski (USA)	.10
110	Lee Smith	.05
111	Pete Smith	.10
112	Jim Snyder	.05
113	Ed Sprague (USA)	.10
114	Pete Stanicek	.05
115	Kurt Stillwell	.05
116	Todd Stottlemyre	.05
117	Bill Swift	.05
118	Pat Tabler	.05
119	Scott Terry	.05
120	Mickey Tettleton	.05
121	Dickie Thon	.05
122	Jeff Treadway	.05
123	Willie Upshaw	.05
124	*Robin Ventura*	2.00
125	Ron Washington	.05
126	Walt Weiss	.10
127	Bob Welch	.05
128	David Wells	.25
129	Glenn Wilson	.05
130	Ted Wood (USA)	.05
131	Don Zimmer	.05
132	Checklist 1T-132T	.05

1988 Topps Traded Tiffany

The high-gloss front surface is all that distinguishes this limited-edition, hobby-only collectors version from the regular Topps Traded boxed set.

	MT
Complete Set (132):	40.00
Common Player:	.15

(Star cards valued at 3X corresponding cards in regular Topps Traded issue)

1988 Topps Big Baseball

Topps Big Baseball cards (2-5/8" x 3-3/4") were issued in three series, 88 cards per series (a total set of 264 cards) sold in seven-card packs. The glossy cards are similar in format, both front and back, to the 1956 Topps set. Each card features a portrait and a game-action photo on the front, framed by a wide white border. A white outline highlights the portrait. The player's name appears at bottom on a splash of color that fades from yellow to orange to red to pink. On the card back, the player's name is printed in large red letters across the top, followed by his team name and position in black. Personal info is printed in a red rectangle beside a Topps baseball logo bearing the card number. A triple cartoon strip, in full-color, illustrates career highlights, performance, personal background, etc. A red, white and blue statistics box (pitching, batting, fielding) is printed across the bottom.

	MT
Complete Set (264):	12.00
Common Player:	.05
Wax Pack (7):	.50

Wax Box, Series 1-3 (36): 10.00
1 Paul Molitor .50
2 Milt Thompson .05
3 Billy Hatcher .05
4 Mike Witt .05
5 Vince Coleman .05
6 Dwight Evans .05
7 Tim Wallach .05
8 Alan Trammell .05
9 Will Clark .15
10 Jeff Reardon .05
11 Dwight Gooden .05
12 Benny Santiago .05
13 Jose Canseco .60
14 Dale Murphy .15
15 George Bell .05
16 Ryne Sandberg .60
17 Brook Jacoby .05
18 Fernando Valenzuela .05
19 Scott Fletcher .05
20 Eric Davis .05
21 Willie Wilson .05
22 B.J. Surhoff .05
23 Steve Bedrosian .05
24 Dave Winfield .65
25 Bobby Bonilla .05
26 Larry Sheets .05
27 Ozzie Guillen .05
28 Checklist 1-88 .05
29 Nolan Ryan 2.00
30 Bob Boone .05
31 Tom Herr .05
32 Wade Boggs .60
33 Neal Heaton .05
34 Doyle Alexander .05
35 Candy Maldonado .05
36 Kirby Puckett .75
37 Gary Carter .15
38 Lance McCullers .05
39a Terry Steinbach (black Topps logo on front) .15
39b Terry Steinbach (white Topps logo on front) .15
40 Gerald Perry .05
41 Tom Henke .05
42 Leon Durham .05
43 Cory Snyder .05
44 Dale Sveum .05
45 Lance Parrish .05
46 Steve Sax .05
47 Charlie Hough .05
48 Kal Daniels .05
49 Bo Jackson .15
50 Ron Guidry .05
51 Bill Doran .05
52 Wally Joyner .05
53 Terry Pendleton .05
54 Marty Barrett .05
55 Andres Galarraga .05
56 Larry Herndon .05
57 Kevin Mitchell .05
58 Greg Gagne .05
59 Keith Hernandez .05
60 John Kruk .05
61 Mike LaValliere .05
62 Cal Ripken, Jr. 2.00
63 Ivan Calderon .05
64 Alvin Davis .05
65 Luis Polonia .05
66 Robin Yount .45
67 Juan Samuel .05
68 Andres Thomas .05
69 Jeff Musselman .05
70 Jerry Mumphrey .05
71 Joe Carter .05
72 Mike Scioscia .05
73 Pete Incaviglia .05
74 Barry Larkin .10
75 Frank White .05
76 Willie Randolph .05
77 Kevin Bass .05
78 Brian Downing .05
79 Willie McGee .05
80 Ellis Burks .05
81 Hubie Brooks .05
82 Darrell Evans .05
83 Robby Thompson .05
84 Kent Hrbek .05
85 Ron Darling .05
86 Stan Jefferson .05
87 Teddy Higuera .05
88 Mike Schmidt .75
89 Barry Bonds 1.00
90 Jim Presley .05
91 Orel Hershiser .05
92 Jesse Barfield .05
93 Tom Candiotti .05
94 Bret Saberhagen .05
95 Jose Uribe .05
96 Tom Browning .05
97 Johnny Ray .05
98 Mike Morgan .05
100 Jim Sundberg .05
101 Roger McDowell .05
102 Randy Ready .05
103 Mike Gallego .05
104 Steve Buechele .05
105 Greg Walker .05
106 Jose Lind .05
107 Steve Trout .05
108 Rick Rhoden .05
109 Jim Pankovits .05
110 Ken Griffey .05
111 Danny Cox .05
112 Franklin Stubbs .05
113 Lloyd Moseby .05
114 Mel Hall .05
115 Kevin Seitzer .05
116 Tim Raines .05
117 Juan Castillo .05
118 Roger Clemens .75
119 Mike Aldrete .05
120 Mario Soto .05
121 Jack Howell .05
122 Rick Schu .05
123 Jeff Robinson .05
124 Doug Drabek .05
125 Henry Cotto .05
126 Checklist 89-176 .05
127 Gary Gaetti .05
128 Rick Sutcliffe .05
129 Howard Johnson .05
130 Chris Brown .05
131 Dave Henderson .05
132 Curt Wilkerson .05
133 Mike Marshall .05
134 Kelly Gruber .05
135 Julio Franco .05
136 Kurt Stillwell .05
137 Donnie Hill .05
138 Mike Pagliarulo .05
139 Von Hayes .05
140 Mike Scott .05
141 Bob Kipper .05
142 Harold Reynolds .05
143 Bob Brenly .05
144 Dave Concepcion .05
145 Devon White .05
146 Jeff Stone .05
147 Chet Lemon .05
148 Ozzie Virgil .05
149 Todd Worrell .05
150 Mitch Webster .05
151 Rob Deer .05
152 Rich Gedman .05
153 Andre Dawson .15
154 Mike Davis .05
155 Nelson Liriano .05
156 Greg Swindell .05
157 George Brett .75
158 Kevin McReynolds .05
159 Brian Fisher .05
160 Mike Kingery .05
161 Tony Gwynn .75
162 Don Baylor .05
163 Jerry Browne .05
164 Dan Pasqua .05
165 Rickey Henderson .50
166 Brett Butler .05
167 Nick Esasky .05
168 Kirk McCaskill .05
169 Fred Lynn .05
170 Jack Morris .05
171 Pedro Guerrero .05
172 Dave Stieb .05
173 Pat Tabler .05
174 Floyd Bannister .05
175 Rafael Belliard .05
176 Mark Langston .05
177 Greg Mathews .05
178 Claudell Washington .05
179 Mark McGwire 2.00
180 Bert Blyleven .05
181 Jim Rice .10
182 Mookie Wilson .05
183 Willie Fraser .05
184 Andy Van Slyke .05
185 Matt Nokes .05
186 Eddie Whitson .05
187 Tony Fernandez .05
188 Rick Reuschel .05
189 Ken Phelps .05
190 Juan Nieves .05
191 Kirk Gibson .05
192 Glenn Davis .05
193 Zane Smith .05
194 Jose DeLeon .05
195 Gary Ward .05
196 Pascual Perez .05
197 Carlton Fisk .45
198 Oddibe McDowell .05
199 Mark Gubicza .05
200 Glenn Hubbard .05
201 Frank Viola .05
202 Jody Reed .05
203 Len Dykstra .05
204 Dick Schofield .05
205 Sid Bream .05
206 Guillermo Hernandez .05
207 Keith Moreland .05
208 Mark Eichhorn .05
209 Rene Gonzales .05
210 Dave Valle .05
211 Tom Brunansky .05
212 Charles Hudson .05
213 John Farrell .05
214 Jeff Treadway .05
215 Eddie Murray .45
216 Checklist 177-264 .05
217 Greg Brock .05
218 John Shelby .05
219 Craig Reynolds .05
220 Dion James .05
221 Carney Lansford .05
222 Juan Berenguer .05
223 Luis Rivera .05
224 Harold Baines .05
225 Shawon Dunston .05
226 Luis Aguayo .05
227 Pete O'Brien .05
228 Ozzie Smith .75
229 Don Mattingly 1.00
230 Danny Tartabull .05
231 Andy Allanson .05
232 John Franco .05
233 Mike Greenwell .05
234 Bob Ojeda .05
235 Chili Davis .05
236 Mike Dunne .05
237 Jim Morrison .05
238 Carmelo Martinez .05
239 Ernie Whitt .05
240 Scott Garrelts .05
241 Mike Moore .05
242 Dave Parker .05
243 Tim Laudner .05
244 Bill Wegman .05
245 Bob Horner .05
246 Rafael Santana .05
247 Alfredo Griffin .05
248 Mark Bailey .05
249 Ron Gant .05
250 Bryn Smith .05
251 Lance Johnson .05
252 Sam Horn .05
253 Darryl Strawberry .05
254 Chuck Finley .05
255 Darnell Coles .05
256 Mike Henneman .05
257 Andy Hawkins .05
258 Jim Clancy .05
259 Atlee Hammaker .05
260 Glenn Wilson .05
261 Larry McWilliams .05
262 Jack Clark .05
263 Walt Weiss .05
264 Gene Larkin .05

1989 Topps

Ten top young players from the June, 1988, draft are featured on "#1 Draft Pick" cards in this full-color basic set of 792 standard-size baseball cards. An additional five cards salute 1989 Future Stars, 22 cards highlight All-Stars, seven contain Record Breakers, five are designated Turn Back The Clock, and six contain checklists. This set features the familiar white borders, but upper-left and lower-right photo corners have been rounded off. A curved name banner in bright red or blue is beneath the team name in large script in the lower-right corner. The card backs are printed in black on a red background and include personal information and complete minor and major league stats. Another new addition in this set is the special Monthly Scoreboard chart that lists monthly stats (April through September) in two of several categories (hits, run, home runs, stolen bases, RBIs, wins, strikeouts, games or saves).

MT
Unopened Factory Set (792): 12.00
Complete Set (792): 8.00
Common Player: .05
Wax Pack (15): .50
Wax Box (36): 12.00
Cello Pack (29): .75
Cello Box (24): 8.00
Rack Pack (43): .75
Rack Box (24): 12.00
Vending Box (500): 7.00
1 George Bell (Record Breaker) .05
2 Wade Boggs (Record Breaker) .20
3 Gary Carter (Record Breaker) .05
4 Andre Dawson (Record Breaker) .05
5 Orel Hershiser (Record Breaker) .05
6 Doug Jones (Record Breaker) .05
7 Kevin McReynolds (Record Breaker) .05
8 *Dave Eiland* .05
9 Tim Teufel .05
10 Andre Dawson .15
11 Bruce Sutter .05
12 Dale Sveum .05
13 Doug Sisk .05
14 Tom Kelly .05
15 Robby Thompson .05
16 Ron Robinson .05
17 Brian Downing .05
18 Rick Rhoden .05
19 Greg Gagne .05
20 Steve Bedrosian .05
21 White Sox Leaders (Greg Walker) .05
22 Tim Crews .05
23 Mike Fitzgerald .05
24 Larry Andersen .05
25 Frank White .05
26 Dale Mohorcic .05
27 *Orestes Destrade* .05
28 Mike Moore .05
29 Kelly Gruber .05

30 Dwight Gooden .05
31 Terry Francona .05
32 Dennis Rasmussen .05
33 B.J. Surhoff .05
34 Ken Williams .05
35 John Tudor .05
36 Mitch Webster .05
37 Bob Stanley .05
38 Paul Runge .05
39 Mike Maddux .05
40 Steve Sax .05
41 Terry Mulholland .05
42 Jim Eppard .05
43 Guillermo Hernandez .05
44 Jim Snyder .05
45 Kal Daniels .05
46 Mark Portugal .05
47 Carney Lansford .05
48 Tim Burke .05
49 Craig Biggio .25
50 George Bell .05
51 Angels Leaders (Mark McLemore) .05
52 Bob Brenly .05
53 Ruben Sierra .05
54 Steve Trout .05
55 Julio Franco .05
56 Pat Tabler .05
57 Alejandro Pena .05
58 Lee Mazzilli .05
59 Mark Davis .05
60 Tom Brunansky .05
61 Neil Allen .05
62 Alfredo Griffin .05
63 Mark Clear .05
64 Alex Trevino .05
65 Rick Reuschel .05
66 Manny Trillo .05
67 Dave Palmer .05
68 Darrell Miller .05
69 Jeff Ballard .05
70 Mark McGwire .75
71 Mike Boddicker .05
72 John Moses .05
73 Pascual Perez .05
74 Nick Leyva .05
75 Tom Henke .05
76 *Terry Blocker* .05
77 Doyle Alexander .05
78 Jim Sundberg .05
79 Scott Bankhead .05
80 Cory Snyder .05
81 Expos Leaders (Tim Raines) .05
82 Dave Leiper .05
83 Jeff Blauser .05
84 *Bill Bene* (#1 Draft Pick) .05
85 Kevin McReynolds .05
86 Al Nipper .05
87 Larry Owen .05
88 *Darryl Hamilton* .10
89 Dave LaPoint .05
90 Vince Coleman .05
91 Floyd Youmans .05
92 Jeff Kunkel .05
93 Ken Howell .05
94 Chris Speier .05
95 Gerald Young .05
96 Rick Cerone .05
97 Greg Mathews .05
98 Larry Sheets .05
99 *Sherman Corbett* .05
100 Mike Schmidt .50
101 Les Straker .05
102 Mike Gallego .05
103 Tim Birtsas .05
104 Dallas Green .05
105 Ron Darling .05
106 Willie Upshaw .05
107 Jose DeLeon .05
108 Fred Manrique .05
109 *Hipolito Pena* .05
110 Paul Molitor .40
111 Reds Leaders (Eric Davis) .05
112 Jim Presley .05
113 Lloyd Moseby .05
114 Bob Kipper .05
115 Jody Davis .05
116 Jeff Montgomery .05
117 Dave Anderson .05
118 Checklist 1-132 .05
119 Terry Puhl .05
120 Frank Viola .05
121 Garry Templeton .05
122 Lance Johnson .05
123 Spike Owen .05
124 Jim Traber .05
125 Mike Krukow .05
126 Sid Bream .05
127 Walt Terrell .05
128 Milt Thompson .05
129 *Terry Clark* .05
130 Gerald Perry .05
131 Dave Otto .05
132 Curt Ford .05
133 Bill Long .05
134 Don Zimmer .05
135 Jose Rijo .05
136 Joey Meyer .05
137 Geno Petralli .05
138 Wallace Johnson .05
139 Mike Flanagan .05
140 Shawon Dunston .05
141 Indians Leaders (Brook Jacoby) .05
142 Mike Diaz .05
143 Mike Campbell .05
144 Jay Bell .05
145 Dave Stewart .05
146 Gary Pettis .05
147 DeWayne Buice .05
148 Bill Pecota .05
149 *Doug Dascenzo* .05
150 Fernando Valenzuela .05
151 Terry McGriff .05
152 Mark Thurmond .05
153 Jim Pankovits .05
154 Don Carman .05
155 Marty Barrett .05
156 *Dave Gallagher* .05
157 Tom Glavine .10
158 Mike Aldrete .05
159 Pat Clements .05
160 Jeffrey Leonard .05
161 *Gregg Olson* (#1 Draft Pick) .05
162 John Davis .05
163 Bob Forsch .05
164 Hal Lanier .05
165 Mike Dunne .05
166 *Doug Jennings* .05
167 *Steve Searcy* (Future Star) .05
168 Willie Wilson .05
169 Mike Jackson .05
170 Tony Fernandez .05
171 Braves Leaders (Andres Thomas) .05
172 Frank Williams .05
173 Mel Hall .05
174 *Todd Burns* .05
175 John Shelby .05
176 Jeff Parrett .05
177 *Monty Fariss* (#1 Draft Pick) .05
178 Mark Grant .05
179 Ozzie Virgil .05
180 Mike Scott .05
181 *Craig Worthington* .05
182 Bob McClure .05
183 Oddibe McDowell .05
184 *John Costello* .05
185 Claudell Washington .05
186 Pat Perry .05
187 Darren Daulton .05
188 Dennis Lamp .05
189 Kevin Mitchell .05
190 Mike Witt .05
191 *Sil Campusano* .05
192 Paul Mirabella .05
193 Sparky Anderson .15
194 *Greg Harris* .05
195 Ozzie Guillen .05
196 Denny Walling .05
197 Neal Heaton .05
198 Danny Heep .05
199 *Mike Schooler* .05
200 George Brett .50
201 Blue Jays Leaders (Kelly Gruber) .05
202 *Brad Moore* .05
203 Rob Ducey .05
204 Brad Havens .05
205 Dwight Evans .05
206 Roberto Alomar .50
207 Terry Leach .05
208 Tom Pagnozzi .05
209 *Jeff Bittiger* .05
210 Dale Murphy .15
211 Mike Pagliarulo .05
212 Scott Sanderson .05
213 Rene Gonzales .05
214 Charlie O'Brien .05
215 Kevin Gross .05
216 Jack Howell .05
217 Joe Price .05
218 Mike LaValliere .05
219 Jim Clancy .05
220 Gary Gaetti .05
221 Cecil Espy .05
222 *Mark Lewis* (#1 Draft Pick) .05
223 Jay Buhner .15
224 Tony LaRussa .05
225 *Ramon Martinez* .25
226 Bill Doran .05
227 John Farrell .05
228 *Nelson Santovenia* .05
229 Jimmy Key .05
230 Ozzie Smith .50
231 Padres Leaders (Roberto Alomar) .10
232 Ricky Horton .05
233 Gregg Jefferies (Future Star) .25
234 Tom Browning .05
235 John Kruk .05
236 Charles Hudson .05
237 Glenn Hubbard .05
238 Eric King .05
239 Tim Laudner .05
240 Greg Maddux .50
241 Brett Butler .05
242 Ed Vande Berg .05
243 Bob Boone .05
244 Jim Acker .05
245 Jim Rice .10
246 Rey Quinones .05
247 Shawn Hillegas .05
248 Tony Phillips .05
249 Tim Leary .05
250 Cal Ripken, Jr. .75
251 *John Dopson* .05
252 Billy Hatcher .05
253 *Jose Alvarez* .05
254 Tom LaSorda .15
255 Ron Guidry .10
256 Benny Santiago .05
257 Rick Aguilera .05
258 Checklist 133-264 .05
259 Larry McWilliams .05
260 Dave Winfield .40
261 Cardinals Leaders (Tom Brunansky) .05
262 *Jeff Pico* .05
263 Mike Felder .05
264 *Rob Dibble* .10
265 Kent Hrbek .05
266 Luis Aquino .05
267 Jeff Robinson .05
268 Keith Miller .05
269 Tom Bolton .05
270 Wally Joyner .05
271 Jay Tibbs .05
272 Ron Hassey .05
273 Jose Lind .05
274 Mark Eichhorn .05
275 Danny Tartabull .05
276 Paul Kilgus .05
277 Mike Davis .05
278 Andy McGaffigan .05
279 Scott Bradley .05
280 Bob Knepper .05
281 Gary Redus .05
282 *Cris Carpenter* .10
283 Andy Allanson .05
284 Jim Leyland .05
285 John Candelaria .05
286 Darrin Jackson .05
287 Juan Nieves .05
288 Pat Sheridan .05
289 Ernie Whitt .05
290 John Franco .05
291 Mets Leaders (Darryl Strawberry) .05
292 *Jim Corsi* .05
293 Glenn Wilson .05
294 Juan Berenguer .05
295 Scott Fletcher .05
296 Ron Gant .05
297 *Oswald Peraza* .05
298 Chris James .05
299 *Steve Ellsworth* .05
300 Darryl Strawberry .05
301 Charlie Leibrandt .05
302 Gary Ward .05
303 Felix Fermin .05
304 Joel Youngblood .05
305 Dave Smith .05
306 Tracy Woodson .05
307 Lance McCullers .05
308 Ron Karkovice .05
309 Mario Diaz .05
310 Rafael Palmeiro .25
311 Chris Bosio .05
312 Tom Lawless .05
313 Denny Martinez .05
314 Bobby Valentine .05
315 Greg Swindell .05
316 Walt Weiss .05
317 *Jack Armstrong* .05
318 Gene Larkin .05
319 Greg Booker .05
320 Lou Whitaker .05
321 Red Sox Leaders (Jody Reed) .05
322 John Smiley .05
323 Gary Thurman .05
324 *Bob Milacki* .05
325 Jesse Barfield .05
326 Dennis Boyd .05
327 *Mark Lemke* .05
328 Rick Honeycutt .05
329 Bob Melvin .05
330 Eric Davis .05
331 Curt Wilkerson .05
332 Tony Armas .05
333 Bob Ojeda .05
334 Steve Lyons .05
335 Dave Righetti .05
336 Steve Balboni .05
337 Calvin Schiraldi .05
338 Jim Adduci .05
339 Scott Bailes .05
340 Kirk Gibson .05
341 Jim Deshaies .05
342 Tom Brookens .05
343 *Gary Sheffield* (Future Star) 1.50
344 Tom Trebelhorn .05
345 Charlie Hough .05
346 Rex Hudler .05
347 John Cerutti .05
348 Ed Hearn .05
349 *Ron Jones* .05
350 Andy Van Slyke .05
351 Giants Leaders (Bob Melvin) .05
352 Rick Schu .05
353 Marvell Wynne .05
354 Larry Parrish .05
355 Mark Langston .05
356 Kevin Elster .05
357 Jerry Reuss .05
358 *Ricky Jordan* .05
359 Tommy John .10
360 Ryne Sandberg .40
361 Kelly Downs .05
362 Jack Lazorko .05
363 Rich Yett .05
364 Rob Deer .05
365 Mike Henneman .05
366 Herm Winningham .05
367 *Johnny Paredes* .05
368 Brian Holton .05
369 Ken Caminiti .05
370 Dennis Eckersley .10
371 Manny Lee .05
372 Craig Lefferts .05
373 Tracy Jones .05
374 John Wathan .05
375 Terry Pendleton .05
376 Steve Lombardozzi .05
377 Mike Smithson .05
378 Checklist 265-396 .05
379 Tim Flannery .05
380 Rickey Henderson .40
381 Orioles Leaders (Larry Sheets) .05
382 John Smoltz .50
383 Howard Johnson .05
384 Mark Salas .05
385 Von Hayes .05
386 Andres Galarraga (All-Star) .05
387 Ryne Sandberg (All-Star) .20
388 Bobby Bonilla (All-Star) .05
389 Ozzie Smith (All-Star) .25

390 Darryl Strawberry (All-Star) .05
391 Andre Dawson (All-Star) .05
392 Andy Van Slyke (All-Star) .05
393 Gary Carter (All-Star) .05
394 Orel Hershiser (All-Star) .05
395 Danny Jackson (All-Star) .05
396 Kirk Gibson (All-Star) .05
397 Don Mattingly (All-Star) .30
398 Julio Franco (All-Star) .05
399 Wade Boggs (All-Star) .20
400 Alan Trammell (All-Star) .05
401 Jose Canseco (All-Star) .20
402 Mike Greenwell (All-Star) .05
403 Kirby Puckett (All-Star) .25
404 Bob Boone (All-Star) .05
405 Roger Clemens (All-Star) .25
406 Frank Viola (All-Star) .05
407 Dave Winfield (All-Star) .20
408 Greg Walker .05
409 Ken Dayley .05
410 Jack Clark .05
411 Mitch Williams .05
412 Barry Lyons .05
413 Mike Kingery .05
414 Jim Fregosi .05
415 Rich Gossage .05
416 Fred Lynn .05
417 Mike LaCoss .05
418 Bob Dernier .05
419 Tom Filer .05
420 Joe Carter .05
421 Kirk McCaskill .05
422 Bo Diaz .05
423 Brian Fisher .05
424 Luis Polonia .05
425 Jay Howell .05
426 Danny Gladden .05
427 Eric Show .05
428 Craig Reynolds .05
429 Twins Leaders (Greg Gagne) .05
430 Mark Gubicza .05
431 Luis Rivera .05
432 *Chad Kreuter* .10
433 Albert Hall .05
434 *Ken Patterson* .05
435 Len Dykstra .05
436 Bobby Meacham .05
437 Andy Benes (#1 Draft Pick) .25
438 Greg Gross .05
439 Frank DiPino .05
440 Bobby Bonilla .05
441 Jerry Reed .05
442 Jose Oquendo .05
443 *Rod Nichols* .05
444 Moose Stubing .05
445 Matt Nokes .05
446 Rob Murphy .05
447 Donell Nixon .05
448 Eric Plunk .05
449 Carmelo Martinez .05
450 Roger Clemens .50
451 Mark Davidson .05
452 *Israel Sanchez* .05
453 Tom Prince .05
454 Paul Assenmacher .05
455 Johnny Ray .05
456 Tim Belcher .05
457 Mackey Sasser .05
458 *Donn Pall* .05
459 Mariners Leaders (Dave Valle) .05
460 Dave Stieb .05
461 Buddy Bell .05
462 Jose Guzman .05
463 Steve Lake .05
464 Bryn Smith .05
465 Mark Grace .25
466 Chuck Crim .05
467 Jim Walewander .05
468 Henry Cotto .05
469 *Jose Bautista* .05
470 Lance Parrish .05
471 *Steve Curry* .05
472 Brian Harper .05
473 Don Robinson .05
474 Bob Rodgers .05
475 Dave Parker .05
476 Jon Perlman .05
477 Dick Schofield .05
478 Doug Drabek .05
479 Mike Macfarlane .10
480 Keith Hernandez .05
481 Chris Brown .05
482 *Steve Peters* .05
483 Mickey Hatcher .05
484 Steve Shields .05
485 Hubie Brooks .05
486 Jack McDowell .05
487 Scott Lusader .05
488 Kevin Coffman .05
489 Phillies Leaders (Mike Schmidt) .15
490 Chris Sabo .10
491 Mike Birkbeck .05
492 Alan Ashby .05
493 Todd Benzinger .05
494 Shane Rawley .05
495 Candy Maldonado .05
496 Dwayne Henry .05
497 Pete Stanicek .05
498 Dave Valle .05
499 *Don Heinkel* .05
500 Jose Canseco .35
501 Vance Law .05
502 Duane Ward .05
503 Al Newman .05
504 Bob Walk .05
505 Pete Rose .60
506 Kirt Manwaring .05
507 Steve Farr .05
508 Wally Backman .05
509 Bud Black .05
510 Bob Horner .05
511 Richard Dotson .05
512 Donnie Hill .05
513 Jesse Orosco .05
514 Chet Lemon .05
515 Barry Larkin .10
516 Eddie Whitson .05
517 Greg Brock .05
518 Bruce Ruffin .05
519 Yankees Leaders (Willie Randolph) .05
520 Rick Sutcliffe .05
521 Mickey Tettleton .05
522 *Randy Kramer* .05
523 Andres Thomas .05
524 Checklist 397-528 .05
525 Chili Davis .05
526 Wes Gardner .05
527 Dave Henderson .05
528 *Luis Medina* .05
529 Tom Foley .05
530 Nolan Ryan .75
531 Dave Hengel .05
532 Jerry Browne .05
533 Andy Hawkins .05
534 Doc Edwards .05
535 Todd Worrell .05
536 Joel Skinner .05
537 Pete Smith .05
538 Juan Castillo .05
539 Barry Jones .05
540 Bo Jackson .10
541 Cecil Fielder .05
542 Todd Frohwirth .05
543 Damon Berryhill .05
544 Jeff Sellers .05
545 Mookie Wilson .05
546 Mark Williamson .05
547 Mark McLemore .05
548 Bobby Witt .05
549 Cubs Leaders (Jamie Moyer) .05
550 Orel Hershiser .05
551 Randy Ready .05
552 Greg Cadaret .05
553 Luis Salazar .05
554 Nick Esasky .05
555 Bert Blyleven .05
556 Bruce Fields .05
557 *Keith Miller* .05
558 Dan Pasqua .05
559 Juan Agosto .05
560 Tim Raines .05
561 Luis Aguayo .05
562 Danny Cox .05
563 Bill Schroeder .05
564 Russ Nixon .05
565 Jeff Russell .05
566 Al Pedrique .05
567 David Wells .10
568 Mickey Brantley .05
569 *German Jimenez* .05
570 Tony Gwynn .50
571 Billy Ripken .05
572 Atlee Hammaker .05
573 Jim Abbott (#1 Draft Pick) .15
574 Dave Clark .05
575 Juan Samuel .05
576 Greg Minton .05
577 Randy Bush .05
578 John Morris .05
579 Astros Leaders (Glenn Davis) .05
580 Harold Reynolds .05
581 Gene Nelson .05
582 Mike Marshall .05
583 *Paul Gibson* .05
584 Randy Velarde .05
585 Harold Baines .05
586 Joe Boever .05
587 Mike Stanley .05
588 *Luis Alicea* .10
589 Dave Meads .05
590 Andres Galarraga .05
591 Jeff Musselman .05
592 John Cangelosi .05
593 Drew Hall .05
594 Jimy Williams .05
595 Teddy Higuera .05
596 Kurt Stillwell .05
597 *Terry Taylor* .05
598 Ken Gerhart .05
599 Tom Candiotti .05
600 Wade Boggs .40
601 Dave Dravecky .05
602 Devon White .05
603 Frank Tanana .05
604 Paul O'Neill .05
605a Bob Welch (missing Complete Major League Pitching Record line) 1.00
605b Bob Welch (contains Complete Major League Pitching Record line) .05
606 Rick Dempsey .05
607 *Willie Ansley* (#1 Draft Pick) .05
608 Phil Bradley .05
609 Tigers Leaders (Frank Tanana) .05
610 Randy Myers .05
611 Don Slaught .05
612 Dan Quisenberry .05
613 *Gary Varsho* .05
614 Joe Hesketh .05
615 Robin Yount .40
616 *Steve Rosenberg* .05
617 *Mark Parent* .05
618 Rance Mulliniks .05
619 Checklist 529-660 .05
620 Barry Bonds .60
621 Rick Mahler .05
622 Stan Javier .05
623 Fred Toliver .05
624 Jack McKeon .05
625 Eddie Murray .35
626 Jeff Reed .05
627 Greg Harris .05
628 Matt Williams .15
629 Pete O'Brien .05
630 Mike Greenwell .05
631 Dave Bergman .05
632 *Bryan Harvey* .10
633 Daryl Boston .05
634 Marvin Freeman .05
635 Willie Randolph .05
636 Bill Wilkinson .05
637 Carmen Castillo .05
638 Floyd Bannister .05
639 Athletics Leaders (Walt Weiss) .05
640 Willie McGee .05
641 Curt Young .05
642 Argenis Salazar .05
643 *Louie Meadows* .05
644 Lloyd McClendon .05
645 Jack Morris .05
646 Kevin Bass .05
647 *Randy Johnson* 2.00
648 *Sandy Alomar* (Future Star) .25
649 Stewart Cliburn .05
650 Kirby Puckett .50
651 Tom Niedenfuer .05
652 Rich Gedman .05
653 *Tommy Barrett* .05
654 Whitey Herzog .05
655 Dave Magadan .05
656 Ivan Calderon .05
657 Joe Magrane .05
658 R.J. Reynolds .05
659 Al Leiter .05
660 Will Clark .15
661 Dwight Gooden (Turn Back the Clock) .05
662 Lou Brock (Turn Back the Clock) .05
663 Hank Aaron (Turn Back the Clock) .15
664 Gil Hodges (Turn Back the Clock) .05
665 Tony Oliva (Turn Back the Clock) .05
666 Randy St. Claire .05
667 Dwayne Murphy .05
668 Mike Bielecki .05
669 Dodgers Leaders (Orel Hershiser) .05
670 Kevin Seitzer .05
671 Jim Gantner .05
672 Allan Anderson .05
673 Don Baylor .10
674 Otis Nixon .05
675 Bruce Hurst .05
676 Ernie Riles .05
677 Dave Schmidt .05
678 Dion James .05
679 Willie Fraser .05
680 Gary Carter .15
681 Jeff Robinson .05
682 Rick Leach .05
683 *Jose Cecena* .05
684 Dave Johnson .05
685 Jeff Treadway .05
686 Scott Terry .05
687 Alvin Davis .05
688 Zane Smith .05
689 Stan Jefferson .05
690 Doug Jones .05
691 Roberto Kelly .05
692 Steve Ontiveros .05
693 *Pat Borders* .10
694 Les Lancaster .05
695 Carlton Fisk .40
696 Don August .05
697 Franklin Stubbs .05
698 Keith Atherton .05
699 Pirates Leaders (Al Pedrique) .05
700 Don Mattingly .60
701 Storm Davis .05
702 Jamie Quirk .05
703 Scott Garrelts .05
704 *Carlos Quintana* .05
705 Terry Kennedy .05
706 Pete Incaviglia .05
707 Steve Jeltz .05
708 Chuck Finley .05
709 Tom Herr .05
710 Dave Cone .05
711 *Candy Sierra* .05
712 Bill Swift .05
713 *Ty Griffin* (#1 Draft Pick) .05
714 Joe M. Morgan .05
715 Tony Pena .05
716 Wayne Tolleson .05
717 Jamie Moyer .05
718 Glenn Braggs .05
719 Danny Darwin .05
720 Tim Wallach .05
721 *Ron Tingley* .05
722 Todd Stottlemyre .05
723 Rafael Belliard .05
724 Jerry Don Gleaton .05
725 Terry Steinbach .05
726 Dickie Thon .05
727 Joe Orsulak .05
728 Charlie Puleo .05
729 Rangers Leaders (Steve Buechele) .05
730 Danny Jackson .05
731 Mike Young .05
732 Steve Buechele .05
733 *Randy Bockus* .05
734 Jody Reed .05
735 Roger McDowell .05
736 Jeff Hamilton .05

737	*Norm Charlton*	.10
738	Darnell Coles	.05
739	Brook Jacoby	.05
740	Dan Plesac	.05
741	Ken Phelps	.05
742	*Mike Harkey* (Future Star)	.05
743	Mike Heath	.05
744	Roger Craig	.05
745	Fred McGriff	.05
746	*German Gonzalez*	.05
747	Wil Tejada	.05
748	Jimmy Jones	.05
749	Rafael Ramirez	.05
750	Bret Saberhagen	.05
751	Ken Oberkfell	.05
752	Jim Gott	.05
753	Jose Uribe	.05
754	Bob Brower	.05
755	Mike Scioscia	.05
756	*Scott Medvin*	.05
757	Brady Anderson	.05
758	Gene Walter	.05
759	Brewers Leaders (Rob Deer)	.05
760	Lee Smith	.05
761	*Dante Bichette*	.25
762	Bobby Thigpen	.05
763	Dave Martinez	.05
764	Robin Ventura (#1 Draft Pick)	.75
765	Glenn Davis	.05
766	Cecilio Guante	.05
767	*Mike Capel*	.05
768	Bill Wegman	.05
769	Junior Ortiz	.05
770	Alan Trammell	.05
771	Ron Kittle	.05
772	Ron Oester	.05
773	Keith Moreland	.05
774	Frank Robinson	.15
775	Jeff Reardon	.05
776	Nelson Liriano	.05
777	Ted Power	.05
778	Bruce Benedict	.05
779	Craig McMurtry	.05
780	Pedro Guerrero	.05
781	*Greg Briley*	.05
782	Checklist 661-792	.05
783	*Trevor Wilson*	.10
784	*Steve Avery* (#1 Draft Pick)	.15
785	Ellis Burks	.05
786	Melido Perez	.05
787	*Dave West*	.05
788	Mike Morgan	.05
789	Royals Leaders (Bo Jackson)	.05
790	Sid Fernandez	.05
791	Jim Lindeman	.05
792	Rafael Santana	.05

1989 Topps Tiffany

This special hobby-only edition shares the checklist with the regular 1989 Topps set. Cards are identical except for the use of white cardboard stock and the high-gloss front coating. Production has been reported as 25,000 sets.

	MT
Complete Set (792):	60.00
Common Player:	.10

(Star cards valued at 3X corresponding cards in regular 1989 Topps issue)

1989 Topps All-Star Glossy Set of 22

The glossy All-Stars were included in the Topps 1989 rack packs. Format was very similar to the sets produced since 1984. Besides the starting lineups of the 1988 All-Star Game, the set included the managers and honorary team captains, Bobby Doerr and Willie Stargell.

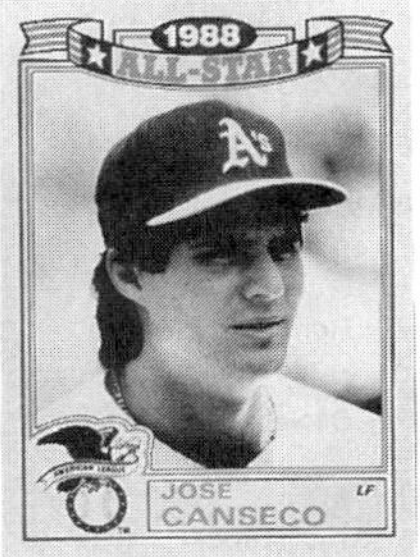

		MT
Complete Set (22):		3.00
Common Player:		.05
1	Tom Kelly	.05
2	Mark McGwire	1.00
3	Paul Molitor	.30
4	Wade Boggs	.40
5	Cal Ripken, Jr.	1.00
6	Jose Canseco	.30
7	Rickey Henderson	.40
8	Dave Winfield	.50
9	Terry Steinbach	.05
10	Frank Viola	.05
11	Bobby Doerr	.05
12	Whitey Herzog	.05
13	Will Clark	.15
14	Ryne Sandberg	.40
15	Bobby Bonilla	.05
16	Ozzie Smith	.50
17	Vince Coleman	.05
18	Andre Dawson	.20
19	Darryl Strawberry	.05
20	Gary Carter	.20
21	Dwight Gooden	.05
22	Willie Stargell	.15

1989 Topps Batting Leaders

The active career batting leaders are showcased in this 22-card set. The 2-1/2" x 3-1/2" cards are printed on super glossy stock with full-color photos and bright red borders. A "Top Active Career Batting Leaders" cup is displayed in a lower corner. The player's name appears above the photo. This set is specially numbered in accordance to career batting average. Wade Boggs is featured on card #1 as the top active career batting leader. The flip sides present batting statistics. One batting leader card was included in each K-Mart blister pack, which also includes 100 cards from the 1989 regular Topps set.

		MT
Complete Set (22):		30.00
Common Player:		.50
1	Wade Boggs	4.00
2	Tony Gwynn	5.00
3	Don Mattingly	6.00
4	Kirby Puckett	5.00
5	George Brett	5.00
6	Pedro Guerrero	.50
7	Tim Raines	.50
8	Keith Hernandez	.50
9	Jim Rice	1.50
10	Paul Molitor	3.00
11	Eddie Murray	3.00
12	Willie McGee	.50
13	Dave Parker	.50
14	Julio Franco	.50
15	Rickey Henderson	4.00
16	Kent Hrbek	.50
17	Willie Wilson	.50
18	Johnny Ray	.50
19	Pat Tabler	.50
20	Carney Lansford	.50
21	Robin Yount	3.00
22	Alan Trammell	.50

1989 Topps Double Headers All-Stars

This scarce test issue was produced in two versions, an All-Stars set and a set of exclusively Mets and Yankees players. The "cards" are two-sided miniature (1-5/8" x 2-1/4") reproductions of the player's 1989 Topps card and his Topps rookie card, encased in a clear plastic stand.

		MT
Complete Set (24):		25.00
Common Player:		.50
Wax Pack (1):		.50
Wax Box (24):		8.00
(1)	Alan Ashby	.50
(2)	Wade Boggs	2.50
(3)	Bobby Bonilla	.50
(4)	Jose Canseco	1.50
(5)	Will Clark	1.00
(6)	Roger Clemens	3.00
(7)	Andre Dawson	.50
(8)	Dennis Eckersley	.50
(9)	Carlton Fisk	2.00
(10)	John Franco	.50
(11)	Julio Franco	.50
(12)	Kirk Gibson	.50
(13)	Mike Greenwell	.50
(14)	Orel Hershiser	.50
(15)	Danny Jackson	.50
(16)	Don Mattingly	4.00
(17)	Mark McGwire	5.00
(18)	Kirby Puckett	3.00
(19)	Ryne Sandberg	2.00
(20)	Ozzie Smith	3.00
(21)	Darryl Strawberry	.50
(22)	Alan Trammell	.50
(23)	Andy Van Slyke	.50
(24)	Frank Viola	.50

1989 Topps Glossy Rookies Set of 22

Bearing the same design and style of the past two years, Topps featured the top first-year players from the 1988 season in this glossy set. The full-color player photo appears beneath the "1988 Rookies" banner. The player's name is displayed beneath the photo. The flip side features the "1988 Rookies Commemorative Set" logo followed by the player ID and card number. Glossy rookies were found only in 100-card jumbo cello packs.

		MT
Complete Set (22):		6.00
Common Player:		.10
1	Roberto Alomar	1.50
2	Brady Anderson	.25
3	Tim Belcher	.10
4	Damon Berryhill	.10
5	Jay Buhner	.25
6	Kevin Elster	.10
7	Cecil Espy	.10
8	Dave Gallagher	.10
9	Ron Gant	.50
10	Paul Gibson	.10
11	Mark Grace	1.50
12	Darrin Jackson	.10
13	Gregg Jefferies	.50
14	Ricky Jordan	.10
15	Al Leiter	.50
16	Melido Perez	.10
17	Chris Sabo	.25
18	Nelson Santovenia	.10
19	Mackey Sasser	.10
20	Gary Sheffield	1.00
21	Walt Weiss	.10
22	David Wells	.50

1989 Topps Mini League Leaders

This 77-card set features baseball's statistical leaders from the 1988 season. It is referred to as a "mini" set because of the cards' small (2-1/8" x 3") size. The glossy cards feature action photos that have a soft focus on all edges. The player's team and name appear along the bottom of the card. The back features a head- shot of the player along with his 1988 season ranking and stats.

		MT
Complete Set (77):		4.00
Common Player:		.05
Wax Pack (7):		.25
Wax Box (36):		6.00
1	Dale Murphy	.20
2	Gerald Perry	.05
3	Andre Dawson	.20
4	Greg Maddux	.75
5	Rafael Palmeiro	.25
6	Tom Browning	.05
7	Kal Daniels	.05
8	Eric Davis	.05
9	John Franco	.05
10	Danny Jackson	.05
11	Barry Larkin	.10
12	Jose Rijo	.05
13	Chris Sabo	.05
14	Nolan Ryan	1.00
15	Mike Scott	.05
16	Gerald Young	.05
17	Kirk Gibson	.05
18	Orel Hershiser	.05
19	Steve Sax	.05
20	John Tudor	.05
21	Hubie Brooks	.05
22	Andres Galarraga	.05
23	Otis Nixon	.05
24	Dave Cone	.05
25	Sid Fernandez	.05
26	Dwight Gooden	.05
27	Kevin McReynolds	.05
28	Darryl Strawberry	.05
29	Juan Samuel	.05
30	Bobby Bonilla	.05
31	Sid Bream	.05
32	Jim Gott	.05
33	Andy Van Slyke	.05
34	Vince Coleman	.05
35	Jose DeLeon	.05
36	Joe Magrane	.05
37	Ozzie Smith	.75
38	Todd Worrell	.05
39	Tony Gwynn	.75
40	Brett Butler	.05
41	Will Clark	.25
42	Rick Reuschel	.05
43	Checklist	.05
44	Eddie Murray	.50
45	Wade Boggs	.60
46	Roger Clemens	.75
47	Dwight Evans	.05
48	Mike Greenwell	.05
49	Bruce Hurst	.05
50	Johnny Ray	.05
51	Doug Jones	.05
52	Greg Swindell	.05
53	Gary Pettis	.05
54	George Brett	.75
55	Mark Gubicza	.05
56	Willie Wilson	.05
57	Teddy Higuera	.05
58	Paul Molitor	.50
59	Robin Yount	.50
60	Allan Anderson	.05
61	Gary Gaetti	.05
62	Kirby Puckett	.75
63	Jeff Reardon	.05
64	Frank Viola	.05
65	Jack Clark	.05
66	Rickey Henderson	.50
67	Dave Winfield	.60
68	Jose Canseco	.50
69	Dennis Eckersley	.05
70	Mark McGwire	1.00
71	Dave Stewart	.05
72	Alvin Davis	.05
73	Mark Langston	.05
74	Harold Reynolds	.05
75	George Bell	.05
76	Tony Fernandez	.05
77	Fred McGriff	.05

1989 Topps Traded

For the ninth straight year, Topps issued its annual 132-card "Traded" set at the end of the 1989 baseball season. The set, which was packaged in a special box and sold by hobby dealers, includes traded players and rookies who were not in the regular 1989 Topps set.

		MT
Unopened Retail Set (132):		20.00
Unopened Hobby Set (132):		15.00
Complete Set (132):		10.00
Common Player:		.05
1T	Don Aase	.05
2T	Jim Abbott	.05
3T	Kent Anderson	.05
4T	Keith Atherton	.05
5T	Wally Backman	.05
6T	Steve Balboni	.05
7T	Jesse Barfield	.05
8T	Steve Bedrosian	.05
9T	Todd Benzinger	.05
10T	Geronimo Berroa	.05
11T	Bert Blyleven	.05
12T	Bob Boone	.05
13T	Phil Bradley	.05
14T	*Jeff Brantley*	.05
15T	Kevin Brown	.05
16T	Jerry Browne	.05
17T	Chuck Cary	.05
18T	Carmen Castillo	.05
19T	Jim Clancy	.05
20T	Jack Clark	.05
21T	Bryan Clutterbuck	.05
22T	Jody Davis	.05
23T	Mike Devereaux	.05
24T	Frank DiPino	.05
25T	Benny Distefano	.05
26T	John Dopson	.05
27T	Len Dykstra	.05
28T	Jim Eisenreich	.05
29T	Nick Esasky	.05
30T	Alvaro Espinoza	.05
31T	Darrell Evans	.05
32T	Junior Felix	.05
33T	Felix Fermin	.05
34T	Julio Franco	.05
35T	Terry Francona	.05
36T	Cito Gaston	.05
37T	Bob Geren (photo actually Mike Fennell)	.05
38T	*Tom Gordon*	.10
39T	Tommy Gregg	.05
40T	Ken Griffey	.05
41T	*Ken Griffey, Jr.*	10.00
42T	Kevin Gross	.05
43T	Lee Guetterman	.05
44T	Mel Hall	.05
45T	Erik Hanson	.10
46T	Gene Harris	.05
47T	Andy Hawkins	.05
48T	Rickey Henderson	.50
49T	Tom Herr	.05
50T	*Ken Hill*	.10
51T	Brian Holman	.05
52T	Brian Holton	.05
53T	Art Howe	.05
54T	Ken Howell	.05
55T	Bruce Hurst	.05
56T	Chris James	.05
57T	Randy Johnson	1.50
58T	Jimmy Jones	.05
59T	Terry Kennedy	.05
60T	Paul Kilgus	.05
61T	Eric King	.05
62T	Ron Kittle	.05
63T	John Kruk	.05
64T	Randy Kutcher	.05
65T	Steve Lake	.05
66T	Mark Langston	.05
67T	Dave LaPoint	.05
68T	Rick Leach	.05
69T	Terry Leach	.05
70T	Jim Levebvre	.05
71T	Al Leiter	.05
72T	Jeffrey Leonard	.05
73T	Derek Lilliquist	.05
74T	Rick Mahler	.05
75T	Tom McCarthy	.05
76T	Lloyd McClendon	.05
77T	Lance McCullers	.05
78T	Oddibe McDowell	.05
79T	Roger McDowell	.05
80T	Larry McWilliams	.05
81T	Randy Milligan	.05
82T	Mike Moore	.05
83T	Keith Moreland	.05
84T	Mike Morgan	.05
85T	Jamie Moyer	.05
86T	Rob Murphy	.05
87T	Eddie Murray	.40
88T	Pete O'Brien	.05
89T	Gregg Olson	.05
90T	Steve Ontiveros	.05
91T	Jesse Orosco	.05
92T	Spike Owen	.05
93T	Rafael Palmeiro	.40
94T	Clay Parker	.05
95T	Jeff Parrett	.05
96T	Lance Parrish	.05
97T	Dennis Powell	.05
98T	Rey Quinones	.05
99T	Doug Rader	.05
100T	Willie Randolph	.05
101T	Shane Rawley	.05
102T	Randy Ready	.05
103T	Bip Roberts	.05
104T	*Kenny Rogers*	.10
105T	Ed Romero	.05
106T	Nolan Ryan	1.50
107T	Luis Salazar	.05
108T	Juan Samuel	.05
109T	Alex Sanchez	.05
110T	*Deion Sanders*	.50
111T	Steve Sax	.05
112T	Rick Schu	.05
113T	Dwight Smith	.05
114T	Lonnie Smith	.05
115T	Billy Spiers	.10
116T	Kent Tekulve	.05
117T	Walt Terrell	.05
118T	Milt Thompson	.05
119T	Dickie Thon	.05
120T	Jeff Torborg	.05
121T	Jeff Treadway	.05
122T	*Omar Vizquel*	.50
123T	Jerome Walton	.05
124T	Gary Ward	.05
125T	Claudell Washington	.05
126T	Curt Wilkerson	.05
127T	Eddie Williams	.05
128T	Frank Williams	.05
129T	Ken Williams	.05
130T	Mitch Williams	.05
131T	Steve Wilson	.05
---	Topps Magazine subscription offer card	.05

1989 Topps Traded Tiffany

The Topps Traded set was issued in a specially boxed, hobby-only editions. Cards are identical to the regular-issue Topps Traded cards except for the application of a high-gloss to the fronts. Production has been reported as 15,000 sets.

	MT
Unopened Set (132):	200.00
Complete Set (132):	150.00
Common Player:	.10

(Star cards valued at 3X corresponding cards in regular Topps Traded issue)

1989 Topps Big Baseball

Known by collectors as Topps "Big Baseball," the cards in this 330-card set measure 2-5/8" x 3-3/4" and are patterned after the 1956 Topps cards. The glossy card fronts are horizontally-designed and include two photos of each player, a portrait alongside an action photo. The backs include 1988 and career stats, but are dominated by a color cartoon featuring the player. Members of the 1988 Team U.S.A. Olympic baseball team are included in the set, which was issued in three series of 110 cards each.

		MT
Complete Set (330):		10.00
Common Player:		.05
Wax Pack:		.40
Wax Box (36):		7.00
1	Orel Hershiser	.05
2	Harold Reynolds	.05
3	Jody Davis	.05
4	Greg Walker	.05
5	Barry Bonds	.75
6	Bret Saberhagen	.05
7	Johnny Ray	.05
8	Mike Fiore	.05
9	Juan Castillo	.05
10	Todd Burns	.05
11	Carmelo Martinez	.05
12	Geno Petralli	.05
13	Mel Hall	.05
14	Tom Browning	.05
15	Fred McGriff	.05
16	Kevin Elster	.05
17	Tim Leary	.05
18	Jim Rice	.10
19	Bret Barberie	.05
20	Jay Buhner	.05
21	Atlee Hammaker	.05
22	Lou Whitaker	.05
23	Paul Runge	.05
24	Carlton Fisk	.40
25	Jose Lind	.05

26	Mark Gubicza	.05
27	Billy Ripken	.05
28	Mike Pagliarulo	.05
29	Jim Deshaies	.05
30	Mark McLemore	.05
31	Scott Terry	.05
32	Franklin Stubbs	.05
33	Don August	.05
34	Mark McGwire	1.00
35	Eric Show	.05
36	Cecil Espy	.05
37	Ron Tingley	.05
38	Mickey Brantley	.05
39	Paul O'Neill	.05
40	Ed Sprague	.05
41	Len Dykstra	.05
42	Roger Clemens	.65
43	Ron Gant	.05
44	Dan Pasqua	.05
45	Jeff Robinson	.05
46	George Brett	.65
47	Bryn Smith	.05
48	Mike Marshall	.05
49	Doug Robbins	.05
50	Don Mattingly	.75
51	Mike Scott	.05
52	Steve Jeltz	.05
53	Dick Schofield	.05
54	Tom Brunansky	.05
55	Gary Sheffield	.75
56	Dave Valle	.05
57	Carney Lansford	.05
58	Tony Gwynn	.65
59	Checklist	.05
60	Damon Berryhill	.05
61	Jack Morris	.05
62	Brett Butler	.05
63	Mickey Hatcher	.05
64	Bruce Sutter	.05
65	Robin Ventura	.50
66	Junior Oritiz	.05
67	Pat Tabler	.05
68	Greg Swindell	.05
69	Jeff Branson	.05
70	Manny Lee	.05
71	Dave Magadan	.05
72	Rich Gedman	.05
73	Tim Raines	.05
74	Mike Maddux	.05
75	Jim Presley	.05
76	Chuck Finley	.05
77	Jose Oquendo	.05
78	Rob Deer	.05
79	Jay Howell	.05
80	Terry Steinbach	.05
81	Eddie Whitson	.05
82	Ruben Sierra	.05
83	Bruce Benedict	.05
84	Fred Manrique	.05
85	John Smiley	.05
86	Mike Macfarlane	.05
87	Rene Gonzales	.05
88	Charles Hudson	.05
90	Les Straker	.05
91	Carmen Castillo	.05
92	Tracy Woodson	.05
93	Tino Martinez	.65
94	Herm Winningham	.05
95	Kelly Gruber	.05
96	Terry Leach	.05
97	Jody Reed	.05
98	Nelson Santovenia	.05
99	Tony Armas	.05
100	Greg Brock	.05
101	Dave Stewart	.05
102	Roberto Alomar	.35
103	Jim Sundberg	.05
104	Albert Hall	.05
105	Steve Lyons	.05
106	Sid Bream	.05
107	Danny Tartabull	.05
108	Rick Dempsey	.05
109	Rich Renteria	.05
110	Ozzie Smith	.65
111	Steve Sax	.05
112	Kelly Downs	.05
113	Larry Sheets	.05
114	Andy Benes	.25
115	Pete O'Brien	.05
116	Kevin McReynolds	.05
117	Juan Berenguer	.05
118	Billy Hatcher	.05
119	Rick Cerone	.05
120	Andre Dawson	.15
121	Storm Davis	.05
122	Devon White	.05
123	Alan Trammell	.05
124	Vince Coleman	.05
125	Al Leiter	.05
126	Dale Sveum	.05
127	Pete Incaviglia	.05
128	Dave Stieb	.05
129	Kevin Mitchell	.05
130	Dave Schmidt	.05
131	Gary Redus	.05
132	Ron Robinson	.05
133	Darnell Coles	.05
134	Benny Santiago	.05
135	John Farrell	.05
136	Willie Wilson	.05
137	Steve Bedrosian	.05
138	Don Slaught	.05
139	Darryl Strawberry	.05
140	Frank Viola	.05
141	Dave Silvestri	.05
142	Carlos Quintana	.05
143	Vance Law	.05
144	Dave Parker	.05
145	Tim Belcher	.05
146	Will Clark	.15
147	Mark Williamson	.05
148	Ozzie Guillen	.05
149	Kirk McCaskill	.05
150	Pat Sheridan	.05
151	Terry Pendleton	.05
152	Roberto Kelly	.05
153	Joey Meyer	.05
154	Mark Grant	.05
155	Joe Carter	.05
156	Steve Buechele	.05
157	Tony Fernandez	.05
158	Jeff Reed	.05
159	Bobby Bonilla	.05
160	Henry Cotto	.05
161	Kurt Stillwell	.05
162	Mickey Morandini	.10
163	Robby Thompson	.05
164	Rick Schu	.05
165	Stan Jefferson	.05
166	Ron Darling	.05
167	Kirby Puckett	.65
168	Bill Doran	.05
169	Dennis Lamp	.05
170	Ty Griffin	.05
171	Ron Hassey	.05
172	Dale Murphy	.15
173	Andres Galarraga	.05
174	Tim Flannery	.05
175	Cory Snyder	.05
176	Checklist	.05
177	Tommy Barrett	.05
178	Dan Petry	.05
179	Billy Masse	.05
180	Terry Kennedy	.05
181	Joe Orsulak	.05
182	Doyle Alexander	.05
183	Willie McGee	.05
184	Jim Gantner	.05
185	Keith Hernandez	.05
186	Greg Gagne	.05
187	Kevin Bass	.05
188	Mark Eichhorn	.05
189	Mark Grace	.30
190	Jose Canseco	.50
191	Bobby Witt	.05
192	Rafael Santana	.05
193	Dwight Evans	.05
194	Greg Booker	.05
195	Brook Jacoby	.05
196	Rafael Belliard	.05
197	Candy Maldonado	.05
198	Mickey Tettleton	.05
199	Barry Larkin	.10
200	Frank White	.05
201	Wally Joyner	.05
202	Chet Lemon	.05
203	Joe Magrane	.05
204	Glenn Braggs	.05
205	Scott Fletcher	.05
206	Gary Ward	.05
207	Nelson Liriano	.05
208	Howard Johnson	.05
209	Kent Hrbek	.05
210	Ken Caminiti	.05
211	Mike Greenwell	.05
212	Ryne Sandberg	.60
213	Joe Slusarski	.05
214	Donnell Nixon	.05
215	Tim Wallach	.05
216	John Kruk	.05
217	Charles Nagy	.25
218	Alvin Davis	.05
219	Oswald Peraza	.05
220	Mike Schmidt	.65
221	Spike Owen	.05
222	Mike Smithson	.05
223	Dion James	.05
224	Ernie Whitt	.05
225	Mike Davis	.05
226	Gene Larkin	.05
227	Pat Combs	.10
228	Jack Howell	.05
229	Ron Oester	.05
230	Paul Gibson	.05
231	Mookie Wilson	.05
232	Glenn Hubbard	.05
233	Shawon Dunston	.05
234	Otis Nixon	.05
235	Melido Perez	.05
236	Jerry Browne	.05
237	Rick Rhoden	.05
238	Bo Jackson	.10
239	Randy Velarde	.05
240	Jack Clark	.05
241	Wade Boggs	.60
242	Lonnie Smith	.05
243	Mike Flanagan	.05
244	Willie Randolph	.05
245	Oddibe McDowell	.05
246	Ricky Jordan	.05
247	Greg Briley	.05
248	Rex Hudler	.05
249	Robin Yount	.40
250	Lance Parrish	.05
251	Chris Sabo	.05
252	Mike Henneman	.05
253	Gregg Jefferies	.10
254	Curt Young	.05
255	Andy Van Slyke	.05
256	Rod Booker	.05
257	Rafael Palmeiro	.20
258	Jose Uribe	.05
259	Ellis Burks	.05
260	John Smoltz	.10
261	Tom Foley	.05
262	Lloyd Moseby	.05
263	Jim Poole	.05
264	Gary Gaetti	.05
265	Bob Dernier	.05
266	Harold Baines	.05
267	Tom Candiotti	.05
268	Rafael Ramirez	.05
269	Bob Boone	.05
270	Buddy Bell	.05
271	Rickey Henderson	.40
272	Willie Fraser	.05
273	Eric Davis	.05
274	Jeff Robinson	.05
275	Damaso Garcia	.05
276	Sid Fernandez	.05
277	Stan Javier	.05
278	Marty Barrett	.05
279	Gerald Perry	.05
280	Rob Ducey	.05
281	Mike Scioscia	.05
282	Randy Bush	.05
283	Tom Herr	.05
284	Glenn Wilson	.05
285	Pedro Guerrero	.05
286	Cal Ripken, Jr.	1.00
287	Randy Johnson	.25
288	Julio Franco	.05
289	Ivan Calderon	.05
290	Rich Yett	.05
291	Scott Servais	.05
292	Bill Pecota	.05
293	Ken Phelps	.05
294	Chili Davis	.05
295	Manny Trillo	.05
296	Mike Boddicker	.05
297	Geronimo Berroa	.05
298	Todd Stottlemyre	.05
299	Kirk Gibson	.05
300	Wally Backman	.05
301	Hubie Brooks	.05
302	Von Hayes	.05
303	Matt Nokes	.05
304	Dwight Gooden	.05
305	Walt Weiss	.05
306	Mike LaValliere	.05
307	Cris Carpenter	.05
308	Ted Wood	.05
309	Jeff Russell	.05
310	Dave Gallagher	.05
311	Andy Allanson	.05
312	Craig Reynolds	.05
313	Kevin Seitzer	.05
314	Dave Winfield	.50
315	Andy McGaffigan	.05
316	Nick Esasky	.05
317	Jeff Blauser	.05
318	George Bell	.05
319	Eddie Murray	.40
320	Mark Davidson	.05
321	Juan Samuel	.05
322	Jim Abbott	.10
323	Kal Daniels	.05
324	Mike Brumley	.05
325	Gary Carter	.15
326	Dave Henderson	.05
327	Checklist	.05
328	Garry Templeton	.05
329	Pat Perry	.05
330	Paul Molitor	.40

1990 Topps 1989 Major League Debut

This 150-card set chronicles the debut date of all 1989 Major League rookies. Two checklist cards are also included in this boxed set, listing the players in order of debut date, though the cards are numbered alphabetically. The card fronts resemble the 1990 Topps cards in style. A debut banner appears in an upper corner. The flip sides are horizontal and are printed in black on yellow stock, providing an overview of the player's first game. The set is packaged in a special collectors box and was only available through hobby dealers.

		MT
Complete Unopened Set (150):		20.00
Complete Set (150):		15.00
Common Player:		.05
1	Jim Abbott	.15
2	Beau Allred	.05
3	Wilson Alvarez	.05
4	Kent Anderson	.05
5	Eric Anthony	.05
6	Kevin Appier	.20
7	Larry Arndt	.05
8	John Barfield	.05
9	Billy Bates	.05
10	Kevin Batiste	.05
11	Blaine Beatty	.05
12	Stan Belinda	.05
13	Juan Bell	.05
14	Joey Belle	1.00
15	Andy Benes	.15
16	Mike Benjamin	.05
17	Geronimo Berroa	.05
18	Mike Blowers	.05
19	Brian Brady	.05
20	Francisco Cabrera	.05
21	George Canale	.05
22	Jose Cano	.05
23	Steve Carter	.05
24	Pat Combs	.05

25	Scott Coolbaugh	.05
26	Steve Cummings	.05
27	Pete Dalena	.05
28	Jeff Datz	.05
29	Bobby Davidson	.05
30	Drew Denson	.05
31	Gary DiSarcina	.05
32	Brian DuBois	.05
33	Mike Dyer	.05
34	Wayne Edwards	.05
35	Junior Felix	.05
36	Mike Fetters	.05
37	Steve Finley	.10
38	Darren Fletcher	.05
39	LaVel Freeman	.05
40	Steve Frey	.05
41	Mark Gardner	.05
42	Joe Girardi	.10
43	Juan Gonzalez	2.00
44	Goose Gozzo	.05
45	Tommy Greene	.05
46	Ken Griffey, Jr.	5.00
47	Jason Grimsley	.05
48	Marquis Grissom	.25
49	Mark Guthrie	.05
50	Chip Hale	.05
51	John Hardy	.05
52	Gene Harris	.05
53	Mike Hartley	.05
54	Scott Hemond	.05
55	Xavier Hernandez	.05
56	Eric Hetzel	.05
57	Greg Hibbard	.05
58	Mark Higgins	.05
59	Glenallen Hill	.10
60	Chris Hoiles	.05
61	Shawn Holman	.05
62	Dann Howitt	.05
63	Mike Huff	.05
64	Terry Jorgenson	.05
65	Dave Justice	1.50
66	Jeff King	.15
67	Matt Kinzer	.05
68	Joe Kraemer	.05
69	Marcus Lawton	.05
70	Derek Lilliquist	.05
71	Scott Little	.05
72	Greg Litton	.05
73	Rick Lueken	.05
74	Julio Machado	.05
75	Tom Magrann	.05
76	Kelly Mann	.05
77	Randy McCament	.05
78	Ben McDonald	.05
79	Chuck McElroy	.05
80	Jeff McKnight	.05
81	Kent Mercker	.05
82	Matt Merullo	.05
83	Hensley Meulens	.05
84	Kevin Mmahat	.05
85	Mike Munoz	.05
86	Dan Murphy	.05
87	Jaime Navarro	.05
88	Randy Nosek	.05
89	John Olerud	.25
90	Steve Olin	.05
91	Joe Oliver	.05
92	Francisco Oliveras	.05
93	Greg Olson	.05
94	John Orton	.05
95	Dean Palmer	.05
96	Ramon Pena	.05
97	Jeff Peterek	.05
98	Marty Pevey	.05
99	Rusty Richards	.05
100	Jeff Richardson	.05
101	Rob Richie	.05
102	Kevin Ritz	.05
103	Rosario Rodriguez	.05
104	Mike Roesler	.05
105	Kenny Rogers	.10
106	Bobby Rose	.05
107	Alex Sanchez	.05
108	Deion Sanders	.25
109	Jeff Schaefer	.05
110	Jeff Schulz	.05
111	Mike Schwabe	.05
112	Dick Scott	.05
113	Scott Scudder	.05
114	Rudy Seanez	.05
115	Joe Skalski	.05
116	Dwight Smith	.05
117	Greg Smith	.05
118	Mike Smith	.05
119	Paul Sorrento	.05
120	Sammy Sosa	8.00
121	Billy Spiers	.05
122	Mike Stanton	.05
123	Phil Stephenson	.05
124	Doug Strange	.05
125	Russ Swan	.05
126	Kevin Tapani	.10
127	Stu Tate	.05
128	Greg Vaughn	.20
129	Robin Ventura	.25
130	Randy Veres	.05
131	Jose Vizcaino	.05
132	Omar Vizquel	.15
133	Larry Walker	.50
134	Jerome Walton	.05
135	Gary Wayne	.05
136	Lenny Webster	.05
137	Mickey Weston	.05
138	Jeff Wetherby	.05
139	John Wetteland	.05
140	Ed Whited	.05
141	Wally Whitehurst	.05
142	Kevin Wickander	.05
143	Dean Wilkins	.05
144	Dana Williams	.05
145	Paul Wilmet	.05
146	Craig Wilson	.05
147	Matt Winters	.05
148	Eric Yelding	.05
149	Clint Zavaras	.05
150	Todd Zeile	.15
----	Checklist (1 of 2)	.05
----	Checklist (2 of 2)	.05

1990 Topps

The 1990 Topps set again included 792 cards, and sported a newly-designed front that featured six different color schemes. The set led off with a special four-card salute to Nolan Ryan, and features other specials including All-Stars, Number 1 Draft Picks, Record Breakers, managers, rookies, and "Turn Back the Clock" cards. The set also includes a special card commemorating A. Bartlett Giamatti, the late baseball commissioner. Backs are printed in black on a chartreuse background. The set features 725 different individual player cards, the most ever, including 138 players' first appearance in a regular Topps set.

	MT
Unopened Factory Set (792):	15.00
Complete Set (792):	9.00
Common Player:	.05
Wax Pack (16):	.75
Wax Box (36):	12.00
Cello Pack (31):	1.00
Cello Box (24):	20.00
Rack Pack (45):	1.00
Rack Box (24):	20.00
Vending Box (500):	10.00

1	Nolan Ryan	.75
2	Nolan Ryan (Mets)	.35
3	Nolan Ryan (Angels)	.25
4	Nolan Ryan (Astros)	.25
5	Nolan Ryan (Rangers)	.25
6	Vince Coleman (Record Breaker)	.05
7	Rickey Henderson (Record Breaker)	.20
8	Cal Ripken, Jr. (Record Breaker)	.40
9	Eric Plunk	.05
10	Barry Larkin	.10
11	Paul Gibson	.05
12	Joe Girardi	.05
13	Mark Williamson	.05
14	*Mike Fetters*	.05
15	Teddy Higuera	.05
16	*Kent Anderson*	.05
17	Kelly Downs	.05
18	Carlos Quintana	.05
19	Al Newman	.05
20	Mark Gubicza	.05
21	Jeff Torborg	.05
22	Bruce Ruffin	.05
23	Randy Velarde	.05
24	Joe Hesketh	.05
25	Willie Randolph	.05
26	Don Slaught	.05
27	Rick Leach	.05
28	Duane Ward	.05
29	John Cangelosi	.05
30	David Cone	.05
31	Henry Cotto	.05
32	John Farrell	.05
33	Greg Walker	.05
34	*Tony Fossas*	.05
35	Benito Santiago	.05
36	John Costello	.05
37	Domingo Ramos	.05
38	Wes Gardner	.05
39	Curt Ford	.05
40	Jay Howell	.05
41	Matt Williams	.15
42	Jeff Robinson	.05
43	Dante Bichette	.05
44	*Roger Salkeld* (#1 Draft Pick)	.15
45	Dave Parker	.05
46	Rob Dibble	.05
47	Brian Harper	.05
48	Zane Smith	.05
49	Tom Lawless	.05
50	Glenn Davis	.05
51	Doug Rader	.05
52	*Jack Daugherty*	.05
53	Mike LaCoss	.05
54	Joel Skinner	.05
55	Darrell Evans	.05
56	Franklin Stubbs	.05
57	Greg Vaughn	.05
58	Keith Miller	.05
59	Ted Power	.05
60	George Brett	.45
61	Deion Sanders	.10
62	Ramon Martinez	.05
63	Mike Pagliarulo	.05
64	Danny Darwin	.05
65	Devon White	.05
66	*Greg Litton*	.05
67	Scott Sanderson	.05
68	Dave Henderson	.05
69	Todd Frohwirth	.05
70	Mike Greenwell	.05
71	Allan Anderson	.05
72	*Jeff Huson*	.10
73	Bob Milacki	.05
74	*Jeff Jackson* (#1 Draft Pick)	.05
75	Doug Jones	.05
76	Dave Valle	.05
77	Dave Bergman	.05
78	Mike Flanagan	.05
79	Ron Kittle	.05
80	Jeff Russell	.05
81	Bob Rodgers	.05
82	Scott Terry	.05
83	Hensley Meulens	.05
84	Ray Searage	.05
85	Juan Samuel	.05
86	Paul Kilgus	.05
87	*Rick Luecken*	.05
88	Glenn Braggs	.05
89	*Clint Zavaras*	.05
90	Jack Clark	.05
91	*Steve Frey*	.05
92	Mike Stanley	.05
93	Shawn Hillegas	.05
94	Herm Winningham	.05
95	Todd Worrell	.05
96	Jody Reed	.05
97	Curt Schilling	.20
98	Jose Gonzalez	.05
99	*Rich Monteleone*	.05
100	Will Clark	.15
101	Shane Rawley	.05
102	Stan Javier	.05
103	Marvin Freeman	.05
104	Bob Knepper	.05
105	Randy Myers	.05
106	Charlie O'Brien	.05
107	Fred Lynn	.05
108	Rod Nichols	.05
109	Roberto Kelly	.05
110	Tommy Helms	.05
111	Ed Whited	.05
112	Glenn Wilson	.05
113	Manny Lee	.05
114	Mike Bielecki	.05
115	Tony Pena	.05
116	Floyd Bannister	.05
117	Mike Sharperson	.05
118	Erik Hanson	.05
119	Billy Hatcher	.05
120	John Franco	.05
121	Robin Ventura	.10
122	Shawn Abner	.05
123	Rich Gedman	.05
124	Dave Dravecky	.05
125	Kent Hrbek	.05
126	Randy Kramer	.05
127	Mike Devereaux	.05
128	Checklist 1-132	.05
129	Ron Jones	.05
130	Bert Blyleven	.05
131	Matt Nokes	.05
132	Lance Blankenship	.05
133	Ricky Horton	.05
134	*Earl Cunningham* (#1 Draft Pick)	.05
135	Dave Magadan	.05
136	Kevin Brown	.20
137	*Marty Pevey*	.05
138	Al Leiter	.05
139	Greg Brock	.05
140	Andre Dawson	.15
141	John Hart	.05
142	*Jeff Wetherby*	.05
143	Rafael Belliard	.05
144	Bud Black	.05
145	Terry Steinbach	.05
146	*Rob Richie*	.05
147	Chuck Finley	.05
148	Edgar Martinez	.10
149	Steve Farr	.05
150	Kirk Gibson	.05
151	Rick Mahler	.05
152	Lonnie Smith	.05
153	Randy Milligan	.05
154	Mike Maddux	.05
155	Ellis Burks	.05
156	Ken Patterson	.05
157	Craig Biggio	.10
158	Craig Lefferts	.05
159	Mike Felder	.05
160	Dave Righetti	.05
161	Harold Reynolds	.05
162	*Todd Zeile*	.20
163	Phil Bradley	.05
164	*Jeff Juden* (#1 Draft Pick)	.10
165	Walt Weiss	.05
166	Bobby Witt	.05
167	Kevin Appier	.10
168	Jose Lind	.05
169	Richard Dotson	.05
170	George Bell	.05
171	Russ Nixon	.05
172	Tom Lampkin	.05
173	Tim Belcher	.05
174	Jeff Kunkel	.05
175	Mike Moore	.05
176	Luis Quinones	.05
177	Mike Henneman	.05
178	Chris James	.05
179	Brian Holton	.05
180	Rock Raines	.05
181	Juan Agosto	.05
182	Mookie Wilson	.05

No.	Player	Price
183	Steve Lake	.05
184	Danny Cox	.05
185	Ruben Sierra	.05
186	Dave LaPoint	.05
187	*Rick Wrona*	.05
188	Mike Smithson	.05
189	Dick Schofield	.05
190	Rick Reuschel	.05
191	Pat Borders	.05
192	Don August	.05
193	Andy Benes	.05
194	Glenallen Hill	.10
195	Tim Burke	.05
196	Gerald Young	.05
197	Doug Drabek	.05
198	Mike Marshall	.05
199	*Sergio Valdez*	.05
200	Don Mattingly	.60
201	Cito Gaston	.05
202	Mike Macfarlane	.05
203	*Mike Roesler*	.05
204	Bob Dernier	.05
205	Mark Davis	.05
206	Nick Esasky	.05
207	Bob Ojeda	.05
208	Brook Jacoby	.05
209	Greg Mathews	.05
210	Ryne Sandberg	.30
211	John Cerutti	.05
212	Joe Orsulak	.05
213	Scott Bankhead	.05
214	Terry Francona	.05
215	Kirk McCaskill	.05
216	Ricky Jordan	.05
217	Don Robinson	.05
218	Wally Backman	.05
219	Donn Pall	.05
220	Barry Bonds	.60
221	*Gary Mielke*	.05
222	Kurt Stillwell	.05
223	Tommy Gregg	.05
224	*Delino DeShields*	.25
225	Jim Deshaies	.05
226	Mickey Hatcher	.05
227	*Kevin Tapani*	.25
228	Dave Martinez	.05
229	David Wells	.10
230	Keith Hernandez	.05
231	Jack McKeon	.05
232	Darnell Coles	.05
233	Ken Hill	.05
234	Mariano Duncan	.05
235	Jeff Reardon	.05
236	Hal Morris	.05
237	*Kevin Ritz*	.10
238	Felix Jose	.05
239	Eric Show	.05
240	Mark Grace	.20
241	Mike Krukow	.05
242	Fred Manrique	.05
243	Barry Jones	.05
244	Bill Schroeder	.05
245	Roger Clemens	.45
246	Jim Eisenreich	.05
247	Jerry Reed	.05
248	Dave Anderson	.05
249	*Mike Smith*	.05
250	Jose Canseco	.40
251	Jeff Blauser	.05
252	Otis Nixon	.05
253	Mark Portugal	.05
254	Francisco Cabrera	.05
255	Bobby Thigpen	.05
256	Marvell Wynne	.05
257	Jose DeLeon	.05
258	Barry Lyons	.05
259	Lance McCullers	.05
260	Eric Davis	.05
261	Whitey Herzog	.05
262	Checklist 133-264	.05
263	*Mel Stottlemyre, Jr.*	.10
264	Bryan Clutterbuck	.05
265	Pete O'Brien	.05
266	German Gonzalez	.05
267	Mark Davidson	.05
268	Rob Murphy	.05
269	Dickie Thon	.05
270	Dave Stewart	.05
271	Chet Lemon	.05
272	Bryan Harvey	.05
273	Bobby Bonilla	.05
274	*Goose Gozzo*	.05
275	Mickey Tettleton	.05
276	Gary Thurman	.05
277	Lenny Harris	.05
278	Pascual Perez	.05
279	Steve Buechele	.05
280	Lou Whitaker	.05
281	Kevin Bass	.05
282	Derek Lilliquist	.05
283	Albert Belle	.45
284	*Mark Gardner*	.05
285	Willie McGee	.05
286	Lee Guetterman	.05
287	Vance Law	.05
288	Greg Briley	.05
289	Norm Charlton	.05
290	Robin Yount	.30
291	Dave Johnson	.05
292	Jim Gott	.05
293	Mike Gallego	.05
294	Craig McMurtry	.05
295	Fred McGriff	.05
296	Jeff Ballard	.05
297	Tom Herr	.05
298	Danny Gladden	.05
299	Adam Peterson	.05
300	Bo Jackson	.10
301	Don Aase	.05
302	*Marcus Lawton*	.05
303	Rick Cerone	.05
304	Marty Clary	.05
305	Eddie Murray	.35
306	Tom Niedenfuer	.05
307	Bip Roberts	.05
308	Jose Guzman	.05
309	*Eric Yelding*	.15
310	Steve Bedrosian	.05
311	Dwight Smith	.05
312	Dan Quisenberry	.05
313	Gus Polidor	.05
314	*Donald Harris* (#1 Draft Pick)	.10
315	Bruce Hurst	.05
316	Carney Lansford	.05
317	*Mark Guthrie*	.05
318	Wallace Johnson	.05
319	Dion James	.05
320	Dave Steib	.05
321	Joe M. Morgan	.05
322	Junior Ortiz	.05
323	Willie Wilson	.05
324	Pete Harnisch	.05
325	Robby Thompson	.05
326	*Tom McCarthy*	.05
327	Ken Williams	.05
328	Curt Young	.05
329	Oddibe McDowell	.05
330	Ron Darling	.05
331	*Juan Gonzalez*	3.00
332	Paul O'Neill	.05
333	Bill Wegman	.05
334	Johnny Ray	.05
335	Andy Hawkins	.05
336	Ken Griffey, Jr.	1.50
337	Lloyd McClendon	.05
338	Dennis Lamp	.05
339	Dave Clark	.05
340	Fernando Valenzuela	.05
341	Tom Foley	.05
342	Alex Trevino	.05
343	Frank Tanana	.05
344	*George Canale*	.05
345	Harold Baines	.05
346	Jim Presley	.05
347	*Junior Felix*	.05
348	*Gary Wayne*	.05
349	*Steve Finley*	.15
350	Bret Saberhagen	.05
351	Roger Craig	.05
352	Bryn Smith	.05
353	Sandy Alomar	.05
354	*Stan Belinda*	.05
355	Marty Barrett	.05
356	Randy Ready	.05
357	Dave West	.05
358	Andres Thomas	.05
359	Jimmy Jones	.05
360	Paul Molitor	.35
361	*Randy McCament*	.05
362	Damon Berryhill	.05
363	Dan Petry	.05
364	Rolando Roomes	.05
365	Ozzie Guillen	.05
366	Mike Heath	.05
367	Mike Morgan	.05
368	Bill Doran	.05
369	Todd Burns	.05
370	Tim Wallach	.05
371	Jimmy Key	.05
372	Terry Kennedy	.05
373	Alvin Davis	.05
374	*Steve Cummings*	.05
375	Dwight Evans	.05
376	Checklist 265-396	.05
377	*Mickey Weston*	.05
378	Luis Salazar	.05
379	Steve Rosenberg	.05
380	Dave Winfield	.40
381	Frank Robinson	.10
382	Jeff Musselman	.05
383	John Morris	.05
384	*Pat Combs*	.05
385	Fred McGriff (All-Star)	.05
386	Julio Franco (All-Star)	.05
387	Wade Boggs (All-Star)	.20
388	Cal Ripken, Jr. (All-Star)	.40
389	Robin Yount (All-Star)	.15
390	Ruben Sierra (All-Star)	.05
391	Kirby Puckett (All-Star)	.25
392	Carlton Fisk (All-Star)	.15
393	Bret Saberhagen (All-Star)	.05
394	Jeff Ballard (All-Star)	.05
395	Jeff Russell (All-Star)	.05
396	A. Bartlett Giamatti	.20
397	Will Clark (All-Star)	.05
398	Ryne Sandberg (All-Star)	.20
399	Howard Johnson (All-Star)	.05
400	Ozzie Smith (All-Star)	.25
401	Kevin Mitchell (All-Star)	.05
402	Eric Davis (All-Star)	.05
403	Tony Gwynn (All-Star)	.25
404	Craig Biggio (All-Star)	.05
405	Mike Scott (All-Star)	.05
406	Joe Magrane (All-Star)	.05
407	Mark Davis (All-Star)	.05
408	Trevor Wilson	.05
409	Tom Brunansky	.05
410	Joe Boever	.05
411	Ken Phelps	.05
412	Jamie Moyer	.05
413	*Brian DuBois*	.05
414a	*Frank Thomas No Name* (#1 Draft Pick, no name on front)	500.00
414b	*Frank Thomas* (#1 Draft Pick, name on front)	3.00
415	Shawon Dunston	.05
416	*Dave Johnson*	.05
417	Jim Gantner	.05
418	Tom Browning	.05
419	*Beau Allred*	.05
420	Carlton Fisk	.35
421	Greg Minton	.05
422	Pat Sheridan	.05
423	Fred Toliver	.05
424	Jerry Reuss	.05
425	Bill Landrum	.05
426	Jeff Hamilton	.05
427	Carmem Castillo	.05
428	*Steve Davis*	.05
429	Tom Kelly	.05
430	Pete Incaviglia	.05
431	Randy Johnson	.30
432	Damaso Garcia	.05
433	*Steve Olin*	.05
434	Mark Carreon	.05
435	Kevin Seitzer	.05
436	Mel Hall	.05
437	Les Lancaster	.05
438	Greg Myers	.05
439	Jeff Parrett	.05
440	Alan Trammell	.05
441	Bob Kipper	.05
442	Jerry Browne	.05
443	Cris Carpenter	.05
444	*Kyle Abbott* (FDP)	.10
445	Danny Jackson	.05
446	Dan Pasqua	.05
447	Atlee Hammaker	.05
448	Greg Gagne	.05
449	Dennis Rasmussen	.05
450	Rickey Henderson	.35
451	Mark Lemke	.05
452	Luis de los Santos	.05
453	Jody Davis	.05
454	Jeff King	.10
455	Jeffrey Leonard	.05
456	Chris Gwynn	.05
457	Gregg Jefferies	.05
458	Bob McClure	.05
459	Jim Lefebvre	.05
460	Mike Scott	.05
461	*Carlos Martinez*	.05
462	Denny Walling	.05
463	Drew Hall	.05
464	*Jerome Walton*	.10
465	Kevin Gross	.05
466	Rance Mulliniks	.05
467	Juan Nieves	.05
468	Billy Ripken	.05
469	John Kruk	.05
470	Frank Viola	.05
471	Mike Brumley	.05
472	Jose Uribe	.05
473	Joe Price	.05
474	Rich Thompson	.05
475	Bob Welch	.05
476	Brad Komminsk	.05
477	Willie Fraser	.05
478	Mike LaValliere	.05
479	Frank White	.05
480	Sid Fernandez	.05
481	Garry Templeton	.05
482	*Steve Carter*	.05
483	Alejandro Pena	.05
484	Mike Fitzgerald	.05
485	John Candelaria	.05
486	Jeff Treadway	.05
487	Steve Searcy	.05
488	Ken Oberkfell	.05
489	Nick Leyva	.05
490	Dan Plesac	.05
491	*Dave Cochrane*	.05
492	Ron Oester	.05
493	*Jason Grimsley*	.05
494	Terry Puhl	.05
495	Lee Smith	.05
496	Cecil Espy	.05
497	Dave Schmidt	.05
498	Rick Schu	.05
499	Bill Long	.05
500	Kevin Mitchell	.05
501	Matt Young	.05
502	Mitch Webster	.05
503	Randy St. Claire	.05
504	Tom O'Malley	.05
505	Kelly Gruber	.05
506	Tom Glavine	.10
507	Gary Redus	.05
508	Terry Leach	.05
509	Tom Pagnozzi	.05
510	Dwight Gooden	.05
511	Clay Parker	.05
512	Gary Pettis	.05
513	Mark Eichhorn	.05
514	Andy Allanson	.05
515	Len Dykstra	.05
516	Tim Leary	.05
517	Roberto Alomar	.30
518	Bill Krueger	.05
519	Bucky Dent	.05
520	Mitch Williams	.05
521	Craig Worthington	.05
522	Mike Dunne	.05
523	Jay Bell	.05
524	Daryl Boston	.05
525	Wally Joyner	.05
526	Checklist 397-528	.05
527	Ron Hassey	.05
528	*Kevin Wickander*	.05
529	Greg Harris	.05
530	Mark Langston	.05
531	Ken Caminiti	.05
532	Cecilio Guante	.05
533	Tim Jones	.05
534	Louie Meadows	.05
535	John Smoltz	.15
536	*Bob Geren*	.05
537	Mark Grant	.05
538	*Billy Spiers*	.05
539	Neal Heaton	.05
540	Danny Tartabull	.05
541	Pat Perry	.05
542	Darren Daulton	.05
543	Nelson Liriano	.05
544	Dennis Boyd	.05
545	Kevin McReynolds	.05
546	Kevin Hickey	.05

#	Player	Price
547	Jack Howell	.05
548	Pat Clements	.05
549	Don Zimmer	.05
550	Julio Franco	.05
551	Tim Crews	.05
552	*Mike Smith*	.05
553	*Scott Scudder*	.05
554	Jay Buhner	.10
555	Jack Morris	.05
556	Gene Larkin	.05
557	*Jeff Innis*	.05
558	Rafael Ramirez	.05
559	Andy McGaffigan	.05
560	Steve Sax	.05
561	Ken Dayley	.05
562	Chad Kreuter	.05
563	Alex Sanchez	.05
564	*Tyler Houston* (#1 Draft Pick)	.10
565	Scott Fletcher	.05
566	Mark Knudson	.05
567	Ron Gant	.05
568	John Smiley	.05
569	Ivan Calderon	.05
570	Cal Ripken, Jr.	.75
571	Brett Butler	.05
572	Greg Harris	.05
573	Danny Heep	.05
574	Bill Swift	.05
575	Lance Parrish	.05
576	*Mike Dyer*	.05
577	Charlie Hayes	.05
578	Joe Magrane	.05
579	Art Howe	.05
580	Joe Carter	.05
581	Ken Griffey	.05
582	Rick Honeycutt	.05
583	Bruce Benedict	.05
584	*Phil Stephenson*	.05
585	Kal Daniels	.05
586	Ed Nunez	.05
587	Lance Johnson	.05
588	Rick Rhoden	.05
589	Mike Aldrete	.05
590	Ozzie Smith	.45
591	Todd Stottlemyre	.05
592	R.J. Reynolds	.05
593	Scott Bradley	.05
594	*Luis Sojo*	.05
595	Greg Swindell	.05
596	Jose DeJesus	.05
597	Chris Bosio	.05
598	Brady Anderson	.05
599	Frank Williams	.05
600	Darryl Strawberry	.05
601	Luis Rivera	.05
602	Scott Garrelts	.05
603	Tony Armas	.05
604	Ron Robinson	.05
605	Mike Scioscia	.05
606	Storm Davis	.05
607	Steve Jeltz	.05
608	*Eric Anthony*	.20
609	Sparky Anderson	.10
610	Pedro Guerrero	.05
611	Walt Terrell	.05
612	Dave Gallagher	.05
613	Jeff Pico	.05
614	Nelson Santovenia	.05
615	Rob Deer	.05
616	Brian Holman	.05
617	Geronimo Berroa	.05
618	Eddie Whitson	.05
619	Rob Ducey	.05
620	*Tony Castillo*	.05
621	Melido Perez	.05
622	Sid Bream	.05
623	Jim Corsi	.05
624	Darrin Jackson	.05
625	Roger McDowell	.05
626	Bob Melvin	.05
627	Jose Rijo	.05
628	Candy Maldonado	.05
629	Eric Hetzel	.05
630	Gary Gaetti	.05
631	*John Wetteland*	.25
632	Scott Lusader	.05
633	Dennis Cook	.05
634	Luis Polonia	.05
635	Brian Downing	.05
636	Jesse Orosco	.05
637	Craig Reynolds	.05
638	Jeff Montgomery	.05
639	Tony LaRussa	.05
640	Rick Sutcliffe	.05
641	*Doug Strange*	.05
642	Jack Armstrong	.05
643	Alfredo Griffin	.05
644	Paul Assenmacher	.05
645	Jose Oquendo	.05
646	Checklist 529-660	.05
647	Rex Hudler	.05
648	Jim Clancy	.05
649	*Dan Murphy*	.05
650	Mike Witt	.05
651	Rafael Santana	.05
652	Mike Boddicker	.05
653	John Moses	.05
654	*Paul Coleman* (#1 Draft Pick)	.05
655	Gregg Olson	.05
656	Mackey Sasser	.05
657	Terry Mulholland	.05
658	Donell Nixon	.05
659	Greg Cadaret	.05
660	Vince Coleman	.05
661	Dick Howser (Turn Back the Clock)	.05
662	Mike Schmidt (Turn Back the Clock)	.10
663	Fred Lynn (Turn Back the Clock)	.05
664	Johnny Bench (Turn Back the Clock)	.05
665	Sandy Koufax (Turn Back the Clock)	.15
666	Brian Fisher	.05
667	Curt Wilkerson	.05
668	*Joe Oliver*	.10
669	Tom Lasorda	.10
670	Dennis Eckersley	.05
671	Bob Boone	.05
672	Roy Smith	.05
673	Joey Meyer	.05
674	Spike Owen	.05
675	Jim Abbott	.05
676	Randy Kutcher	.05
677	Jay Tibbs	.05
678	Kirt Manwaring	.05
679	Gary Ward	.05
680	Howard Johnson	.05
681	Mike Schooler	.05
682	Dann Bilardello	.05
683	Kenny Rogers	.05
684	*Julio Machado*	.05
685	Tony Fernandez	.05
686	Carmelo Martinez	.05
687	Tim Birtsas	.05
688	Milt Thompson	.05
689	Rich Yett	.05
690	Mark McGwire	.75
691	Chuck Cary	.05
692	*Sammy Sosa*	5.00
693	Calvin Schiraldi	.05
694	*Mike Stanton*	.05
695	Tom Henke	.05
696	B.J. Surhoff	.05
697	Mike Davis	.05
698	Omar Vizquel	.10
699	Jim Leyland	.05
700	Kirby Puckett	.45
701	*Bernie Williams*	1.50
702	Tony Phillips	.05
703	Jeff Brantley	.05
704	*Chip Hale*	.05
705	Claudell Washington	.05
706	Geno Petralli	.05
707	Luis Aquino	.05
708	Larry Sheets	.05
709	Juan Berneguer	.05
710	Von Hayes	.05
711	Rick Aguilera	.05
712	Todd Benzinger	.05
713	*Tim Drummond*	.05
714	*Marquis Grissom*	.25
715	Greg Maddux	.45
716	Steve Balboni	.05
717	Ron Kakovice	.05
718	Gary Sheffield	.20
719	*Wally Whitehurst*	.05
720	Andres Galarraga	.05
721	Lee Mazzilli	.05
722	Felix Fermin	.05
723	Jeff Robinson	.05
724	Juan Bell	.10
725	Terry Pendleton	.05
726	Gene Nelson	.05
727	Pat Tabler	.05
728	Jim Acker	.05
729	Bobby Valentine	.05
730	Tony Gwynn	.45
731	Don Carman	.05
732	Ernie Riles	.05
733	John Dopson	.05
734	Kevin Elster	.05
735	Charlie Hough	.05
736	Rick Dempsey	.05
737	Chris Sabo	.05
738	*Gene Harris*	.05
739	Dale Sveum	.05
740	Jesse Barfield	.05
741	Steve Wilson	.05
742	Ernie Whitt	.05
743	Tom Candiotti	.05
744	*Kelly Mann*	.05
745	Hubie Brooks	.05
746	Dave Smith	.05
747	Randy Bush	.05
748	Doyle Alexander	.05
749	Mark Parent	.05
750	Dale Murphy	.15
751	Steve Lyons	.05
752	Tom Gordon	.05
753	Chris Speier	.05
754	Bob Walk	.05
755	Rafael Palmeiro	.20
756	Ken Howell	.05
757	*Larry Walker*	.75
758	Mark Thurmond	.05
759	Tom Trebelhorn	.05
760	Wade Boggs	.35
761	Mike Jackson	.05
762	Doug Dascenzo	.05
763	Denny Martinez	.05
764	Tim Teufel	.05
765	Chili Davis	.05
766	Brian Meyer	.05
767	Tracy Jones	.05
768	Chuck Crim	.05
769	*Greg Hibbard*	.10
770	Cory Snyder	.05
771	Pete Smith	.05
772	Jeff Reed	.05
773	Dave Leiper	.05
774	*Ben McDonald*	.20
775	Andy Van Slyke	.05
776	Charlie Leibrandt	.05
777	Tim Laudner	.05
778	Mike Jeffcoat	.05
779	Lloyd Moseby	.05
780	Orel Hershiser	.05
781	Mario Diaz	.05
782	Jose Alvarez	.05
783	Checklist 661-792	.05
784	Scott Bailes	.05
785	Jim Rice	.10
786	Eric King	.05
787	Rene Gonzales	.05
788	Frank DiPino	.05
789	John Wathan	.05
790	Gary Carter	.15
791	Alvaro Espinoza	.05
792	Gerald Perry	.05

1990 Topps Tiffany

This specially boxed version of Topps' 1990 baseball card set was sold through hobby channels only. The checklist is identical to the regular-issue Topps set and the cards are nearly so. The Tiffany version features white cardboard stock and a high-gloss finish on the fronts.

	MT
Complete Unopened Set (792):	200.00
Complete Set (792):	95.00
Common Player:	.10

(Star cards valued at 3X-4X corresponding cards in regular Topps issue)

1990 Topps All-Star Glossy Set of 22

One glossy All-Star card was included in each 1990 Topps rack pack. The cards measure 2-1/2" x 3-1/2" and feature a similar style to past glossy All-Star cards. Special cards of All-Star team captains Carl Yastrzemski and Don Drysdale are included in the set.

		MT
Complete Set (22):		4.00
Common Player:		.05
1	Tom Lasorda	.05
2	Will Clark	.15
3	Ryne Sandberg	.40
4	Howard Johnson	.05
5	Ozzie Smith	.60
6	Kevin Mitchell	.05
7	Eric Davis	.05
8	Tony Gwynn	.60
9	Benny Santiago	.05
10	Rick Rueschel	.05
11	Don Drysdale	.20
12	Tony LaRussa	.05
13	Mark McGwire	1.00
14	Julio Franco	.05
15	Wade Boggs	.40
16	Cal Ripken, Jr.	1.00
17	Bo Jackson	.10
18	Kirby Puckett	.60
19	Ruben Sierra	.05
20	Terry Steinbach	.05
21	Dave Stewart	.05
22	Carl Yastrzemski	.20

1990 Topps Batting Leaders

Once again produced as an exclusive insert in jumbo blister packs for K-Mart stores, the 1990 career batting leaders cards are similar in concept and design to the previous year's issue; in fact, some of the same player photos were used. The 22 cards in the set are arranged roughly in order of the players' standings in lifetime batting average. Cards fronts are bordered in bright green; backs are printed in red, white and dark green.

		MT
Complete Set (22):		36.00
Common Player:		.50
1	Wade Boggs	4.00
2	Tony Gwynn	5.00
3	Kirby Puckett	5.00
4	Don Mattingly	7.50
5	George Brett	5.00
6	Pedro Guerrero	.50
7	Tim Raines	.50
8	Paul Molitor	4.00
9	Jim Rice	1.00
10	Keith Hernandez	.50
11	Julio Franco	.50
12	Carney Lansford	.50
13	Dave Parker	.50
14	Willie McGee	.50
15	Robin Yount	3.00
16	Tony Fernandez	.50
17	Eddie Murray	3.00
18	Johnny Ray	.50
19	Lonnie Smith	.50
20	Phil Bradley	.50
21	Rickey Henderson	4.00
22	Kent Hrbek	.50

1990 Topps Double Headers

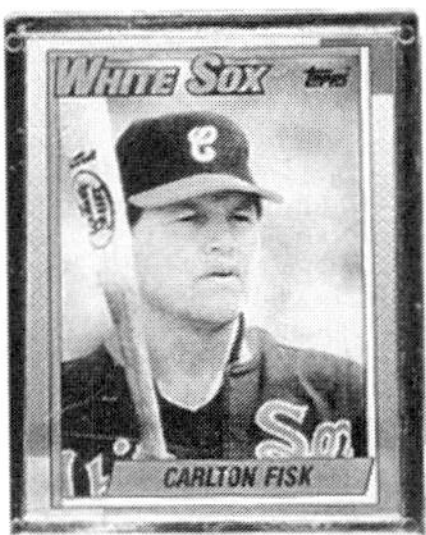

For a second (and final) year, Topps produced an issue of mini cards encased in plastic stands and marketed as Double Headers. Each piece features a 1-5/8" x 2-1/4" reproduction of the player's Topps rookie card, backed by a reproduction of his card from the regular 1990 Topps set. The size of the DH set was increased from 24 in 1989 to 72 for 1990. The novelties were sold for 50 cents apiece. The unnumbered cards are checklisted here alphabetically.

		MT
Complete Set (72):		32.50
Common Player:		.25
(1)	Jim Abbott	.25
(2)	Jeff Ballard	.25
(3)	George Bell	.25
(4)	Wade Boggs	1.25
(5)	Barry Bonds	2.00
(6)	Bobby Bonilla	.25
(7)	Ellis Burks	.25
(8)	Jose Canseco	.75
(9)	Joe Carter	.25
(10)	Will Clark	.50
(11)	Roger Clemens	1.50
(12)	Vince Coleman	.25
(13)	Alvin Davis	.25
(14)	Eric Davis	.25
(15)	Glenn Davis	.25
(16)	Mark Davis	.25
(17)	Andre Dawson	.35
(18)	Shawon Dunston	.25
(19)	Dennis Eckersley	.25
(20)	Sid Fernandez	.25
(21)	Tony Fernandez	.25
(22)	Chuck Finley	.25
(23)	Carlton Fisk	1.00
(24)	Julio Franco	.25
(25)	Gary Gaetti	.25
(26)	Dwight Gooden	.25
(27)	Mark Grace	.35
(28)	Mike Greenwell	.25
(29)	Ken Griffey, Jr.	2.50
(30)	Pedro Guerrero	.25
(31)	Tony Gwynn	1.50
(32)	Von Hayes	.25
(33)	Rickey Henderson	.75
(34)	Orel Hershiser	.25
(35)	Bo Jackson	.35
(36)	Gregg Jefferies	.25
(37)	Howard Johnson	.25
(38)	Ricky Jordan	.25
(39)	Carney Lansford	.25
(40)	Barry Larkin	.25
(41)	Greg Maddux	1.50
(42)	Joe Magrane	.25
(43)	Don Mattingly	2.00
(44)	Fred McGriff	.25
(45)	Mark McGwire	3.00
(46)	Kevin McReynolds	.25
(47)	Kevin Mitchell	.25
(48)	Gregg Olson	.25
(49)	Kirby Puckett	1.50
(50)	Tim Raines	.25
(51)	Harold Reynolds	.25
(52)	Cal Ripken, Jr.	3.00
(53)	Nolan Ryan	3.00
(54)	Bret Saberhagen	.25
(55)	Ryne Sandberg	1.25
(56)	Benito Santiago	.25
(57)	Steve Sax	.25
(58)	Mike Scioscia	.25
(59)	Mike Scott	.25
(60)	Ruben Sierra	.25
(61)	Lonnie Smith	.25
(62)	Ozzie Smith	1.50
(63)	Dave Stewart	.25
(64)	Darryl Strawberry	.25
(65)	Greg Swindell	.25
(66)	Alan Trammell	.25
(67)	Frank Viola	.25
(68)	Tim Wallach	.25
(69)	Jerome Walton	.25
(70)	Lou Whitaker	.25
(71)	Mitch Williams	.25
(72)	Robin Yount	1.00

1990 Topps Glossy Rookies

While the size of the annual glossy rookies set increased to 33 cards from previous years' issues of 22, the format remained identical in 1990. Above the player photo is a colored banner with "1989 Rookies." The player's name appears in red in a yellow bar beneath the photo. Backs are printed in red and blue and contain a shield design with the notation, "1989 Rookies Commemorative Set". The player's name, position and team are listed below, along with a card number. Cards are numbered alphabetically in the set. The glossy rookies were found one per pack in jumbo (100-card) cello packs.

		MT
Complete Set (33):		20.00
Common Player:		.50
1	Jim Abbott	.50
2	Joey Belle	2.00
3	Andy Benes	.50
4	Greg Briley	.50
5	Kevin Brown	1.00
6	Mark Carreon	.50
7	Mike Devereaux	.50
8	Junior Felix	.50
9	Bob Geren	.50
10	Tom Gordon	.60
11	Ken Griffey, Jr.	6.00
12	Pete Harnisch	.50
13	Greg W. Harris	.50
14	Greg Hibbard	.50
15	Ken Hill	.50
16	Gregg Jefferies	.60
17	Jeff King	.50
18	Derek Lilliquist	.50
19	Carlos Martinez	.50
20	Ramon Martinez	.60
21	Bob Milacki	.50
22	Gregg Olson	.50
23	Donn Pall	.50
24	Kenny Rogers	.50
25	Gary Sheffield	1.50
26	Dwight Smith	.50
27	Billy Spiers	.50
28	Omar Vizquel	.50
29	Jerome Walton	.50
30	Dave West	.50
31	John Wetteland	.50
32	Steve Wilson	.50
33	Craig Worthington	.50

1990 Topps Mini League Leaders

The last in a five-year string of mini cards, the 1990 league leaders' set offers players who were in the top five in major batting and pitching stats during the 1989 season. Fronts of the 2-1/8" x 3" cards mimic the regular Topps' design for 1990; featuring an action photo with multi-colored borders. Backs offer a round player portrait photo and information about the statistical achievement, all printed in full color. Cards are numbered alphabetically within teams. The 1990 minis are considerably scarcer than the previous years' offerings.

		MT
Complete Set (88):		9.00
Common Player:		.05
1	Jeff Ballard	.05
2	Phil Bradley	.05
3	Wade Boggs	.75
4	Roger Clemens	1.00
5	Nick Esasky	.05
6	Jody Reed	.05
7	Bert Blyleven	.05
8	Chuck Finley	.05
9	Kirk McCaskill	.05
10	Devon White	.05
11	Ivan Calderon	.05
12	Bobby Thigpen	.05
13	Joe Carter	.05
14	Gary Pettis	.05
15	Tom Gordon	.05
16	Bo Jackson	.10
17	Bret Saberhagen	.05
18	Kevin Seitzer	.05
19	Chris Bosio	.05
20	Paul Molitor	.50
21	Dan Plesac	.05
22	Robin Yount	.50
23	Kirby Puckett	1.00
24	Don Mattingly	1.50
25	Steve Sax	.05
26	Storm Davis	.05
27	Dennis Eckersley	.05
28	Rickey Henderson	.60
29	Carney Lansford	.05
30	Mark McGwire	2.00
31	Mike Moore	.05
32	Dave Stewart	.05
33	Alvin Davis	.05
34	Harold Reynolds	.05
35	Mike Schooler	.05
36	Cecil Espy	.05
37	Julio Franco	.05
38	Jeff Russell	.05
39	Nolan Ryan	2.00
40	Ruben Sierra	.05
41	George Bell	.05
42	Tony Fernandez	.05
43	Fred McGriff	.05
44	Dave Steib	.05
45	Checklist	.05
46	Lonnie Smith	.05
47	John Smoltz	.10
48	Mike Bielecki	.05
49	Mark Grace	.25
50	Greg Maddux	1.00
51	Ryne Sandberg	.75
52	Mitch Williams	.05
53	Eric Davis	.05
54	John Franco	.05
55	Glenn Davis	.05
56	Mike Scott	.05
57	Tim Belcher	.05
58	Orel Hershiser	.05
59	Jay Howell	.05
60	Eddie Murray	.50
61	Tim Burke	.05
62	Mark Langston	.05
63	Tim Raines	.05
64	Tim Wallach	.05
65	David Cone	.05
66	Sid Fernandez	.05
67	Howard Johnson	.05
68	Juan Samuel	.05
69	Von Hayes	.05
70	Barry Bonds	1.50
71	Bobby Bonilla	.05
72	Andy Van Slyke	.05
73	Vince Coleman	.05
74	Jose DeLeon	.05
75	Pedro Guerrero	.05
76	Joe Magrane	.05
77	Roberto Alomar	.40
78	Jack Clark	.05
79	Mark Davis	.05
80	Tony Gwynn	1.00
81	Bruce Hurst	.05
82	Eddie Whitson	.05
83	Brett Butler	.05
84	Will Clark	.15
85	Scott Garrelts	.05
86	Kevin Mitchell	.05
87	Rick Reuschel	.05
88	Robby Thompson	.05

1990 Topps Traded

For the first time, Topps "Traded" series cards were made available nationwide in retail wax packs. The 132-card set was also sold in complete boxed form as it has been in recent years. The wax pack traded cards feature gray backs, while the boxed set cards feature white backs. The cards are numbered 1T-132T and showcase rookies, players who changed teams and new managers.

		MT
Complete Set (132):		4.00
Common Player:		.05
1	Darrel Akerfelds	.05
2	Sandy Alomar, Jr.	.20
3	Brad Arnsberg	.05
4	Steve Avery	.10
5	Wally Backman	.05
6	*Carlos Baerga*	.10
7	Kevin Bass	.05
8	Willie Blair	.05
9	Mike Blowers	.05
10	Shawn Boskie	.10
11	Daryl Boston	.05
12	Dennis Boyd	.05
13	Glenn Braggs	.05
14	Hubie Brooks	.05
15	Tom Brunansky	.05
16	John Burkett	.15
17	Casey Candaele	.05
18	John Candelaria	.05
19	Gary Carter	.15
20	Joe Carter	.15
21	Rick Cerone	.05
22	Scott Coolbaugh	.05
23	Bobby Cox	.05
24	Mark Davis	.05
25	Storm Davis	.05
26	Edgar Diaz	.05
27	Wayne Edwards	.05
28	Mark Eichhorn	.05
29	Scott Erickson	.25
30	Nick Esasky	.05
31	Cecil Fielder	.15
32	John Franco	.05
33	*Travis Fryman*	.30
34	Bill Gullickson	.05
35	Darryl Hamilton	.05
36	Mike Harkey	.05
37	Bud Harrelson	.05
38	Billy Hatcher	.05
39	Keith Hernandez	.05
40	Joe Hesketh	.05
41	Dave Hollins	.15
42	Sam Horn	.05
43	Steve Howard	.05
44	*Todd Hundley*	.50
45	Jeff Huson	.05
46	Chris James	.05
47	Stan Javier	.05
48	*Dave Justice*	1.00
49	Jeff Kaiser	.05
50	Dana Kiecker	.05
51	Joe Klink	.05
52	Brent Knackert	.05
53	Brad Komminsk	.05
54	Mark Langston	.05
55	Tim Layana	.10
56	Rick Leach	.05
57	Terry Leach	.05
58	Tim Leary	.05
59	Craig Lefferts	.05
60	Charlie Leibrandt	.05
61	Jim Leyritz	.25
62	Fred Lynn	.05
63	Kevin Maas	.05
64	Shane Mack	.05
65	Candy Maldonado	.05
66	Fred Manrique	.05
67	Mike Marshall	.05
68	Carmelo Martinez	.05
69	John Marzano	.05
70	Ben McDonald	.05
71	Jack McDowell	.05
72	John McNamara	.05
73	Orlando Mercado	.05
74	Stump Merrill	.05
75	Alan Mills	.05
76	Hal Morris	.10
77	Lloyd Moseby	.05
78	Randy Myers	.10
79	Tim Naehring	.10
80	Junior Noboa	.05
81	Matt Nokes	.05
82	Pete O'Brien	.05
83	*John Olerud*	.75
84	Greg Olson	.05
85	Junior Ortiz	.05
86	Dave Parker	.10
87	Rick Parker	.10
88	Bob Patterson	.05
89	Alejandro Pena	.05
90	Tony Pena	.05
91	Pascual Perez	.05
92	Gerald Perry	.05
93	Dan Petry	.05
94	Gary Pettis	.05
95	Tony Phillips	.05
96	Lou Pinella	.05
97	Luis Polonia	.05
98	Jim Presley	.05
99	Scott Radinsky	.15
100	Willie Randolph	.05
101	Jeff Reardon	.05
102	Greg Riddoch	.05
103	Jeff Robinson	.05
104	Ron Robinson	.05
105	Kevin Romine	.05
106	Scott Ruskin	.05
107	John Russell	.05
108	Bill Sampen	.05
109	Juan Samuel	.05
110	Scott Sanderson	.05
111	Jack Savage	.05
112	Dave Schmidt	.05
113	Red Schoendienst	.10
114	Terry Shumpert	.05
115	Matt Sinatro	.05
116	Don Slaught	.05
117	Bryn Smith	.05
118	Lee Smith	.05
119	Paul Sorrento	.10
120	Franklin Stubbs	.05
121	Russ Swan	.05
122	Bob Tewksbury	.10
123	Wayne Tolleson	.05
124	John Tudor	.05
125	Randy Veres	.10
126	Hector Villanueva	.05
127	Mitch Webster	.05
128	Ernie Whitt	.05
129	Frank Wills	.05
130	Dave Winfield	.25
131	Matt Young	.05
132	Checklist	.05

1990 Topps Traded Tiffany

Identical to the regular Topps Traded issue except for the glossy front surface, this special hobby-only boxed set shares the same checklist.

	MT
Complete Set (132):	25.00
Common Player:	.15

(Star cards valued at 4X-6X corresponding cards in regular Topps Traded issue)

1990 Topps Big Baseball

For the third consecutive year, Topps issued a 330-card set of oversized cards (2-5/8" x 3-3/4") in three 110-card series. The cards are reminiscent of Topps cards from the mid-1950s, featuring players in portrait and action shots. As in previous years, the cards are printed on white stock with a glossy front finish. Backs include 1989 and career hitting, fielding and pitching stats and a player cartoon. Series 3 cards (#221-330) are believed to have been somewhat scarcer than the first two series.

		MT
Complete Set (330):		20.00
Common Player:		.05
Wax Pack (8):		.50
Wax Box, Series 1-2 (36):		9.00
Wax Box, Series 3 (36):		12.00
1	Dwight Evans	.05
2	Kirby Puckett	.75
3	Kevin Gross	.05
4	Ron Hassey	.05
5	Lloyd McClendon	.05
6	Bo Jackson	.10
7	Lonnie Smith	.05
8	Alvaro Espinoza	.05
9	Roberto Alomar	.25
10	Glenn Braggs	.05
11	David Cone	.05
12	Claudell Washington	.05
13	Pedro Guerrero	.05
14	Todd Benzinger	.05
15	Jeff Russell	.05
16	Terry Kennedy	.05
17	Kelly Gruber	.05
18	Alfredo Griffin	.05
19	Mark Grace	.20
20	Dave Winfield	.45
21	Bret Saberhagen	.05
22	Roger Clemens	.75
23	Bob Walk	.05
24	Dave Magadan	.05
25	Spike Owen	.05
26	Jody Davis	.05
27	Kent Hrbek	.05
28	Mark McGwire	2.00
29	Eddie Murray	.25
30	Paul O'Neill	.05
31	Jose DeLeon	.05
32	Steve Lyons	.05
33	Dan Plesac	.05
34	Jack Howell	.05
35	Greg Briley	.05
36	Andy Hawkins	.05
37	Cecil Espy	.05
38	Rick Sutcliffe	.05
39	Jack Clark	.05
40	Dale Murphy	.15
41	Mike Henneman	.05
42	Rick Honeycutt	.05
43	Willie Randolph	.05
44	Marty Barrett	.05
45	Willie Wilson	.05
46	Wallace Johnson	.05
47	Greg Brock	.05
48	Tom Browning	.05
49	Gerald Young	.05
50	Dennis Eckersley	.05
51	Scott Garrelts	.05
52	Gary Redus	.05
53	Al Newman	.05
54	Darryl Boston	.05
55	Ron Oester	.05
56	Danny Tartabull	.05
57	Gregg Jefferies	.05
58	Tom Foley	.05
59	Robin Yount	.40
60	Pat Borders	.05
61	Mike Greenwell	.05
62	Shawon Dunston	.05
63	Steve Buechele	.05
64	Dave Stewart	.05
65	Jose Oquendo	.05
66	Ron Gant	.05
67	Mike Scioscia	.05
68	Randy Velarde	.05
69	Charlie Hayes	.05
70	Tim Wallach	.05
71	Eric Show	.05
72	Eric Davis	.05
73	Mike Gallego	.05
74	Rob Deer	.05
75	Ryne Sandberg	.50
76	Kevin Seitzer	.05
77	Wade Boggs	.50
78	Greg Gagne	.05
79	John Smiley	.05
80	Ivan Calderon	.05
81	Pete Incaviglia	.05
82	Orel Hershiser	.05
83	Carney Lansford	.05
84	Mike Fitzgerald	.05
85	Don Mattingly	1.00
86	Chet Lemon	.05
87	Rolando Roomes	.05
88	Bill Spiers	.05
89	Pat Tabler	.05
90	Danny Heep	.05
91	Andre Dawson	.15
92	Randy Bush	.05
93	Tony Gwynn	.50
94	Tom Brunansky	.05
95	Johnny Ray	.05
96	Matt Williams	.15
97	Barry Lyons	.05
98	Jeff Hamilton	.05
99	Tom Glavine	.10
100	Ken Griffey, Sr.	.05
101	Tom Henke	.05
102	Dave Righetti	.05
103	Paul Molitor	.40
104	Mike LaValliere	.05
105	Frank White	.05
106	Bob Welch	.05
107	Ellis Burks	.05
108	Andres Galarraga	.05
109	Mitch Williams	.05
110	Checklist	.05
111	Craig Biggio	.10
112	Dave Steib	.05
113	Ron Darling	.05
114	Bert Blyleven	.05
115	Dickie Thon	.05
116	Carlos Martinez	.05
117	Jeff King	.05
118	Terry Steinbach	.05
119	Frank Tanana	.05
120	Mark Lemke	.05
121	Chris Sabo	.05
122	Glenn Davis	.05
123	Mel Hall	.05
124	Jim Gantner	.05
125	Benito Santiago	.05
126	Milt Thompson	.05
127	Rafael Palmeiro	.20
128	Barry Bonds	1.00
129	Mike Bielecki	.05
130	Lou Whitaker	.05
131	Bob Ojeda	.05
132	Dion James	.05
133	Denny Martinez	.05
134	Fred McGriff	.05
135	Terry Pendleton	.05
136	Pat Combs	.05
137	Kevin Mitchell	.05
138	Marquis Grissom	.05
139	Chris Bosio	.05

140 Omar Vizquel .05
141 Steve Sax .05
142 Nelson Liriano .05
143 Kevin Elster .05
144 Dan Pasqua .05
145 Dave Smith .05
146 Craig Worthington .05
147 Dan Gladden .05
148 Oddibe McDowell .05
149 Bip Roberts .05
150 Randy Ready .05
151 Dwight Smith .05
152 Ed Whitson .05
153 George Bell .05
154 Tim Raines .05
155 Sid Fernandez .05
156 Henry Cotto .05
157 Harold Baines .05
158 Willie McGee .05
159 Bill Doran .05
160 Steve Balboni .05
161 Pete Smith .05
162 Frank Viola .05
163 Gary Sheffield .20
164 Bill Landrum .05
165 Tony Fernandez .05
166 Mike Heath .05
167 Jody Reed .05
168 Wally Joyner .05
169 Robby Thompson .05
170 Ken Caminiti .05
171 Nolan Ryan 2.00
172 Ricky Jordan .05
173 Lance Blankenship .05
174 Dwight Gooden .05
175 Ruben Sierra .05
176 Carlton Fisk .40
177 Garry Templeton .05
178 Mike Devereaux .05
179 Mookie Wilson .05
180 Jeff Blauser .05
181 Scott Bradley .05
182 Luis Salazar .05
183 Rafael Ramirez .05
184 Vince Coleman .05
185 Doug Drabek .05
186 Darryl Strawberry .05
187 Tim Burke .05
188 Jesse Barfield .05
189 Barry Larkin .10
190 Alan Trammell .05
191 Steve Lake .05
192 Derek Lilliquist .05
193 Don Robinson .05
194 Kevin McReynolds .05
195 Melido Perez .05
196 Jose Lind .05
197 Eric Anthony .05
198 B.J. Surhoff .05
199 John Olerud .05
200 Mike Moore .05
201 Mark Gubicza .05
202 Phil Bradley .05
203 Ozzie Smith .50
204 Greg Maddux .75
205 Julio Franco .05
206 Tom Herr .05
207 Scott Fletcher .05
208 Bobby Bonilla .05
209 Bob Geren .05
210 Junior Felix .05
211 Dick Schofield .05
212 Jim Deshaies .05
213 Jose Uribe .05
214 John Kruk .05
215 Ozzie Guillen .05
216 Howard Johnson .05
217 Andy Van Slyke .05
218 Tim Laudner .05
219 Manny Lee .05
220 Checklist .05
221 Cory Snyder .05
222 Billy Hatcher .05
223 Bud Black .05
224 Will Clark .15
225 Kevin Tapani .05
226 Mike Pagliarulo .05
227 Dave Parker .05
228 Ben McDonald .05
229 Carlos Baerga .05
230 Roger McDowell .05
231 Delino DeShields .05
232 Mark Langston .05
233 Wally Backman .05
234 Jim Eisenreich .05
235 Mike Schooler .05
236 Kevin Bass .05
237 John Farrell .05
238 Kal Daniels .05
239 Tony Phillips .05
240 Todd Stottlemyre .05
241 Greg Olson .05
242 Charlie Hough .05
243 Mariano Duncan .05
244 Billy Ripken .05
245 Joe Carter .05
246 Tim Belcher .05
247 Roberto Kelly .05
248 Candy Maldonado .05
249 Mike Scott .05
250 Ken Griffey, Jr. 2.00
251 Nick Esasky .05
252 Tom Gordon .05
253 John Tudor .05
254 Gary Gaetti .05
255 Neal Heaton .05
256 Jerry Browne .05
257 Jose Rijo .05
258 Mike Boddicker .05
259 Brett Butler .05
260 Andy Benes .05
261 Kevin Brown .15
262 Hubie Brooks .05
263 Randy Milligan .05
264 John Franco .05
265 Sandy Alomar .05
266 Dave Valle .05
267 Jerome Walton .05
268 Bob Boone .05
269 Ken Howell .05
270 Jose Canseco .35
271 Joe Magrane .05
272 Brian DuBois .05
273 Carlos Quintana .05
274 Lance Johnson .05
275 Steve Bedrosian .05
276 Brook Jacoby .05
277 Fred Lynn .05
278 Jeff Ballard .05
279 Otis Nixon .05
280 Chili Davis .05
281 Joe Oliver .05
282 Brian Holman .05
283 Juan Samuel .05
284 Rick Aguilera .05
285 Jeff Reardon .05
286 Sammy Sosa 5.00
287 Carmelo Martinez .05
288 Greg Swindell .05
289 Erik Hanson .05
290 Tony Pena .05
291 Pascual Perez .05
292 Rickey Henderson .50
293 Kurt Stillwell .05
294 Todd Zeile .05
295 Bobby Thigpen .05
296 Larry Walker .25
297 Rob Murphy .05
298 Mitch Webster .05
299 Devon White .05
300 Len Dykstra .05
301 Keith Hernandez .05
302 Gene Larkin .05
303 Jeffrey Leonard .05
304 Jim Presley .05
305 Lloyd Moseby .05
306 John Smoltz .10
307 Sam Horn .05
308 Greg Litton .05
309 Dave Henderson .05
310 Mark McLemore .05
311 Gary Pettis .05
312 Mark Davis .05
313 Cecil Fielder .05
314 Jack Armstrong .05
315 Alvin Davis .05
316 Doug Jones .05
317 Eric Yelding .05
318 Joe Orsulak .05
319 Chuck Finley .05
320 Glenn Wilson .05
321 Harold Reynolds .05
322 Teddy Higuera .05
323 Lance Parrish .05
324 Bruce Hurst .05
325 Dave West .05
326 Kirk Gibson .05
327 Cal Ripken, Jr. 2.50
328 Rick Reuschel .05
329 Jim Abbott .05
330 Checklist .05

1991 Topps 1990 Major League Debut

This 171-card set features the players who made their Major League debut in 1990. The cards are styled like the 1991 Topps cards and are numbered in alphabetical order. The card backs are printed horizontally and feature information about the player's debut and statistics. The issue was sold only as a boxed set through hobby channels.

		MT
Complete Set (171):		12.00
Common Player:		.05
1	Paul Abbott	.05
2	Steve Adkins	.05
3	Scott Aldred	.05
4	Gerald Alexander	.05
5	Moises Alou	1.50
6	Steve Avery	.05
7	Oscar Azocar	.05
8	Carlos Baerga	.05
9	Kevin Baez	.05
10	Jeff Baldwin	.05
11	Brian Barnes	.05
12	Kevin Bearse	.05
13	Kevin Belcher	.05
14	Mike Bell	.05
15	Sean Berry	.10
16	Joe Bitker	.05
17	Willie Blair	.05
18	Brian Bohanon	.05
19	Mike Bordick	.05
20	Shawn Boskie	.05
21	Rod Brewer	.05
22	Kevin Brown	.15
23	Dave Burba	.05
24	Jim Campbell	.05
25	Ozzie Canseco	.10
26	Chuck Carr	.05
27	Larry Casian	.05
28	Andujar Cedeno	.05
29	Wes Chamberlain	.05
30	Scott Chiamparino	.05
31	Steve Chitren	.05
32	Pete Coachman	.05
33	Alex Cole	.05
34	Jeff Conine	.15
35	Scott Cooper	.05
36	Milt Cuyler	.05
37	Steve Decker	.05
38	Rich DeLucia	.05
39	Delino DeShields	.15
40	Mark Dewey	.05
41	Carlos Diaz	.05
42	Lance Dickson	.10
43	Narciso Elvira	.05
44	Luis Encarnacion	.05
45	Scott Erickson	.10
46	Paul Faries	.05
47	Howard Farmer	.05
48	Alex Fernandez	.10
49	Travis Fryman	.05
50	Rich Garces	.05
51	Carlos Garcia	.05
52	Mike Gardiner	.05
53	Bernard Gilkey	.15
54	Tom Gilles	.05
55	Jerry Goff	.05
56	Leo Gomez	.05
57	Luis Gonzalez	2.50
58	Joe Grahe	.05
59	Craig Grebeck	.05
60	Kip Gross	.05
61	Eric Gunderson	.05
62	Chris Hammond	.05
63	Dave Hansen	.05
64	Reggie Harris	.05
65	Bill Haselman	.05
66	Randy Hennis	.05
67	Carlos Hernandez	.10
68	Howard Hilton	.05
69	Dave Hollins	.10
70	Darren Holmes	.10
71	John Hoover	.05
72	Steve Howard	.05
73	Thomas Howard	.05
74	Todd Hundley	.25
75	Daryl Irvine	.05
76	Chris Jelic	.05
77	Dana Kiecker	.05
78	Brent Knackert	.05
79	Jimmy Kremers	.05
80	Jerry Kutzler	.05
81	Ray Lankford	.50
82	Tim Layana	.05
83	Terry Lee	.05
84	Mark Leiter	.05
85	Scott Leius	.05
86	Mark Leonard	.05
87	Darren Lewis	.25
88	Scott Lewis	.05
89	Jim Leyritz	.10
90	Dave Liddell	.05
91	Luis Lopez	.05
92	Kevin Maas	.05
93	Bob MacDonald	.05
94	Carlos Maldonado	.05
95	Chuck Malone	.05
96	Ramon Manon	.05
97	Jeff Manto	.05
98	Paul Marak	.05
99	Tino Martinez	.50
100	Derrick May	.05
101	Brent Mayne	.10
102	Paul McClellan	.05
103	Rodney McCray	.05
104	Tim McIntosh	.05
105	Brian McRae	.10
106	Jose Melendez	.05
107	Orlando Merced	.10
108	Alan Mills	.05
109	Gino Minutelli	.05
110	Mickey Morandini	.10
111	Pedro Munoz	.05
112	Chris Nabholz	.05
113	Tim Naehring	.05
114	Charles Nagy	.10
115	Jim Neidlinger	.05
116	Rafael Novoa	.05
117	Jose Offerman	.05
118	Omar Olivares	.05
119	Javier Ortiz	.05
120	Al Osuna	.05
121	Rick Parker	.05
122	Dave Pavlas	.05
123	Geronimo Pena	.05
124	Mike Perez	.05
125	Phil Plantier	.10
126	Jim Poole	.05
127	Tom Quinlan	.05
128	Scott Radinsky	.05
129	Darren Reed	.05
130	Karl Rhodes	.05
131	Jeff Richardson	.05
132	Rich Rodriguez	.15
133	Dave Rohde	.05
134	Mel Rojas	.10
135	Vic Rosario	.05
136	Rich Rowland	.05
137	Scott Ruskin	.05
138	Bill Sampen	.05
139	Andres Santana	.05
140	David Segui	.10
141	Jeff Shaw	.05
142	Tim Sherrill	.05
143	Terry Shumpert	.05
144	Mike Simms	.05
145	Daryl Smith	.05
146	Luis Sojo	.05
147	Steve Springer	.05
148	Ray Stephens	.05

149	Lee Stevens	.05
150	Mel Stottlemyre, Jr.	.05
151	Glenn Sutko	.05
152	Anthony Telford	.05
153	Frank Thomas	6.00
154	Randy Tomlin	.05
155	Brian Traxler	.05
156	Efrain Valdez	.05
157	Rafael Valdez	.05
158	Julio Valera	.05
159	Jim Vatcher	.05
160	Hector Villanueva	.05
161	Hector Wagner	.05
162	Dave Walsh	.05
163	Steve Wapnick	.05
164	Colby Ward	.05
165	Turner Ward	.05
166	Terry Wells	.05
167	Mark Whiten	.05
168	Mike York	.05
169	Cliff Young	.05
170	Checklist	.05
171	Checklist	.05

1991 Topps

Topps celebrated its 40th anniversary in 1991 with the biggest promotional campaign in baseball card history. More than 300,000 vintage Topps cards (or certificates redeemable for valuable older cards) produced from 1952 to 1990 were randomly inserted in packs. Also a grand prize winner received a complete set from each year, and others received a single set from 1952-1990. The 1991 Topps card fronts feature the "Topps 40 Years of Baseball" logo in the upper-left corner. Colored borders frame the player photos. All players of the same team have cards with the same frame/border colors. Both action and posed shots appear in full-color on the card fronts. The flip sides are printed horizontally and feature complete statistics. Record Breakers and other special cards were once again included in the set. The cards measure 2-1/2" x 3-1/2".

	MT
Unopened Factory Set (792):	16.00
Complete Set (792):	12.00
Common Player:	.05
Wax Pack (15):	.35
Wax Box (36):	9.00
Cello Pack (34):	.50
Cello Box (24):	15.00
Rack Pack (45):	.75
Rack Box (24):	16.00
Vending Box (500):	6.00

1	Nolan Ryan	.75
2	George Brett (Record Breaker)	.20
3	Carlton Fisk (Record Breaker)	.15
4	Kevin Maas (Record Breaker)	.05
5	Cal Ripken, Jr. (Record Breaker)	.40
6	Nolan Ryan (Record Breaker)	.40
7	Ryne Sandberg (Record Breaker)	.15
8	Bobby Thigpen (Record Breaker)	.05
9	Darrin Fletcher	.05
10	Gregg Olson	.05
11	Roberto Kelly	.05
12	Paul Assenmacher	.05
13	Mariano Duncan	.05
14	Dennis Lamp	.05
15	Von Hayes	.05
16	Mike Heath	.05
17	Jeff Brantley	.05
18	Nelson Liriano	.05
19	Jeff Robinson	.05
20	Pedro Guerrero	.05
21	Joe M. Morgan	.05
22	Storm Davis	.05
23	Jim Gantner	.05
24	Dave Martinez	.05
25	Tim Belcher	.05
26	Luis Sojo	.05
27	Bobby Witt	.05
28	Alvaro Espinoza	.05
29	Bob Walk	.05
30	Gregg Jefferies	.05
31	*Colby Ward*	.05
32	*Mike Simms*	.05
33	Barry Jones	.05
34	Atlee Hammaker	.05
35	Greg Maddux	.40
36	Donnie Hill	.05
37	Tom Bolton	.05
38	Scott Bradley	.05
39	*Jim Neidlinger*	.05
40	Kevin Mitchell	.05
41	Ken Dayley	.05
42a	*Chris Hoiles* (white inner photo frame)	.20
42b	*Chris Hoiles* (gray inner photo frame)	.10
43	Roger McDowell	.05
44	Mike Felder	.05
45	Chris Sabo	.05
46	Tim Drummond	.05
47	Brook Jacoby	.05
48	Dennis Boyd	.05
49a	Pat Borders (40 stolen bases in Kinston 1986)	.20
49b	Pat Borders (0 stolen bases in Kinston 1986)	.10
50	Bob Welch	.05
51	Art Howe	.05
52	*Francisco Oliveras*	.05
53	Mike Sharperson	.05
54	Gary Mielke	.05
55	Jeffrey Leonard	.05
56	Jeff Parrett	.05
57	Jack Howell	.05
58	Mel Stottlemyre	.05
59	Eric Yelding	.05
60	Frank Viola	.05
61	Stan Javier	.05
62	Lee Guetterman	.05
63	Milt Thompson	.05
64	Tom Herr	.05
65	Bruce Hurst	.05
66	Terry Kennedy	.05
67	Rick Honeycutt	.05
68	Gary Sheffield	.20
69	Steve Wilson	.05
70	Ellis Burks	.05
71	Jim Acker	.05
72	Junior Ortiz	.05
73	Craig Worthington	.05
74	*Shane Andrews* (#1 Draft Pick)	.10
75	Jack Morris	.05
76	Jerry Browne	.05
77	Drew Hall	.05
78	Geno Petralli	.05
79	Frank Thomas	.50
80a	Fernando Valenzuela (no diamond after 104 ER in 1990)	.25
80b	Fernando Valenzuela (diamond after 104 ER in 1990)	.05
81	Cito Gaston	.05
82	Tom Glavine	.10
83	Daryl Boston	.05
84	Bob McClure	.05
85	Jesse Barfield	.05
86	Les Lancaster	.05
87	Tracy Jones	.05
88	Bob Tewksbury	.05
89	Darren Daulton	.05
90	Danny Tartabull	.05
91	*Greg Colbrunn* (Future Star)	.10
92	Danny Jackson	.05
93	Ivan Calderon	.05
94	John Dopson	.05
95	Paul Molitor	.30
96	Trevor Wilson	.05
97a	Brady Anderson (3H, 2RBI in Sept. scoreboard)	.25
97b	Brady Anderson (14H, 3 RBI in Sept. scoreboard)	.05
98	Sergio Valdez	.05
99	Chris Gwynn	.05
100a	Don Mattingly (10 hits 1990)	.50
100b	Don Mattingly (101 hits in 1990)	.50
101	Rob Ducey	.05
102	Gene Larkin	.05
103	*Tim Costo* (#1 Draft Pick)	.05
104	Don Robinson	.05
105	Kevin McReynolds	.05
106	Ed Nunez	.05
107	Luis Polonia	.05
108	Matt Young	.05
109	Greg Riddoch	.05
110	Tom Henke	.05
111	Andres Thomas	.05
112	Frank DiPino	.05
113	*Carl Everett* (#1 Draft Pick)	.50
114	*Lance Dickson* (Future Star)	.10
115	Hubie Brooks	.05
116	Mark Davis	.05
117	Dion James	.05
118	*Tom Edens*	.05
119	Carl Nichols	.05
120	Joe Carter	.05
121	Eric King	.05
122	Paul O'Neill	.05
123	Greg Harris	.05
124	Randy Bush	.05
125	Steve Bedrosian	.05
126	*Bernard Gilkey*	.20
127	Joe Price	.05
128	Travis Fryman	.05
129	Mark Eichhorn	.05
130	Ozzie Smith	.40
131a	Checklist 1 (Phil Bradley #727)	.05
131b	Checklist 1 (Phil Bradley #717)	.05
132	Jamie Quirk	.05
133	Greg Briley	.05
134	Kevin Elster	.05
135	Jerome Walton	.05
136	Dave Schmidt	.05
137	Randy Ready	.05
138	Jamie Moyer	.05
139	Jeff Treadway	.05
140	Fred McGriff	.05
141	Nick Leyva	.05
142	Curtis Wilkerson	.05
143	John Smiley	.05
144	Dave Henderson	.05
145	Lou Whitaker	.05
146	Dan Plesac	.05
147	Carlos Baerga	.05
148	Rey Palacios	.05
149	*Al Osuna*	.05
150	Cal Ripken, Jr.	.75
151	Tom Browning	.05
152	Mickey Hatcher	.05
153	Bryan Harvey	.05
154	Jay Buhner	.05
155a	Dwight Evans (diamond after 162 G 1982)	.10
155b	Dwight Evans (no diamond after 162 G 1982)	.05
156	Carlos Martinez	.05
157	John Smoltz	.10
158	Jose Uribe	.05
159	Joe Boever	.05
160	Vince Coleman	.05
161	Tim Leary	.05
162	*Ozzie Canseco*	.10
163	Dave Johnson	.05
164	Edgar Diaz	.05
165	Sandy Alomar	.05
166	Harold Baines	.05
167a	*Randy Tomlin* ("Harriburg" 1989-90)	.10
167b	*Randy Tomlin* ("Harrisburg" 1989-90)	.05
168	John Olerud	.05
169	Luis Aquino	.05
170	Carlton Fisk	.30
171	Tony LaRussa	.05
172	Pete Incaviglia	.05
173	Jason Grimsley	.05
174	Ken Caminiti	.05
175	Jack Armstrong	.05
176	John Orton	.05
177	*Reggie Harris*	.05
178	Dave Valle	.05
179	Pete Harnisch	.05
180	Tony Gwynn	.40
181	Duane Ward	.05
182	Junior Noboa	.05
183	Clay Parker	.05
184	Gary Green	.05
185	Joe Magrane	.05
186	Rod Booker	.05
187	Greg Cadaret	.05
188	Damon Berryhill	.05
189	*Daryl Irvine*	.05
190	Matt Williams	.15
191	*Willie Blair*	.05
192	Rob Deer	.05
193	Felix Fermin	.05
194	Xavier Hernandez	.05
195	Wally Joyner	.05
196	*Jim Vatcher*	.05
197	*Chris Nabholz*	.10
198	R.J. Reynolds	.05
199	Mike Hartley	.05
200	Darryl Strawberry	.05
201	Tom Kelly	.05
202	*Jim Leyritz*	.20
203	Gene Harris	.05
204	Herm Winningham	.05
205	*Mike Perez*	.10
206	Carlos Quintana	.05
207	Gary Wayne	.05
208	Willie Wilson	.05
209	Ken Howell	.05
210	Lance Parrish	.05
211	*Brian Barnes* (Future Star)	.05
212	Steve Finley	.05
213	Frank Wills	.05
214	Joe Girardi	.05
215	Dave Smith	.05
216	Greg Gagne	.05
217	Chris Bosio	.05
218	*Rick Parker*	.05
219	Jack McDowell	.05
220	Tim Wallach	.05
221	Don Slaught	.05
222	*Brian McRae*	.10
223	Allan Anderson	.05
224	Juan Gonzalez	.30
225	Randy Johnson	.30
226	Alfredo Griffin	.05
227	Steve Avery	.05
228	Rex Hudler	.05
229	Rance Mulliniks	.05
230	Sid Fernandez	.05
231	Doug Rader	.05
232	Jose DeJesus	.05
233	Al Leiter	.05
234	*Scott Erickson*	.15
235	Dave Parker	.05
236a	Frank Tanana (no diamond after 269 SO 1975)	.10
236b	Frank Tanana (diamond after 269 SO 1975)	.05
237	Rick Cerone	.05

238 Mike Dunne .05
239 *Darren Lewis* .10
240 Mike Scott .05
241 Dave Clark .05
242 Mike LaCoss .05
243 Lance Johnson .05
244 Mike Jeffcoat .05
245 Kal Daniels .05
246 Kevin Wickander .05
247 Jody Reed .05
248 Tom Gordon .05
249 Bob Melvin .05
250 Dennis Eckersley .05
251 Mark Lemke .05
252 *Mel Rojas* .10
253 Garry Templeton .05
254 *Shawn Boskie* .10
255 Brian Downing .05
256 Greg Hibbard .05
257 Tom O'Malley .05
258 Chris Hammond .05
259 Hensley Meulens .05
260 Harold Reynolds .05
261 Bud Harrelson .05
262 Tim Jones .05
263 Checklist 2 .05
264 *Dave Hollins* .15
265 Mark Gubicza .05
266 Carmen Castillo .05
267 Mark Knudson .05
268 Tom Brookens .05
269 Joe Hesketh .05
270a Mark McGwire (1987 SLG .618) .75
270b Mark McGwire (1987 SLG 618) .75
271 *Omar Olivares* .15
272 Jeff King .05
273 Johnny Ray .05
274 Ken Williams .05
275 Alan Trammell .05
276 Bill Swift .05
277 Scott Coolbaugh .05
278 *Alex Fernandez* (#1 Draft Pick) .10
279a Jose Gonzalez (photo of Billy Bean, left-handed batter) .15
279b Jose Gonzalez (correct photo, right-handed batter) .05
280 Bret Saberhagen .05
281 Larry Sheets .05
282 Don Carman .05
283 Marquis Grissom .05
284 Bill Spiers .05
285 Jim Abbott .05
286 Ken Oberkfell .05
287 Mark Grant .05
288 Derrick May .05
289 Tim Birtsas .05
290 Steve Sax .05
291 John Wathan .05
292 Bud Black .05
293 Jay Bell .05
294 Mike Moore .05
295 Rafael Palmeiro .20
296 Mark Williamson .05
297 Manny Lee .05
298 Omar Vizquel .05
299 *Scott Radinsky* .15
300 Kirby Puckett .40
301 Steve Farr .05
302 Tim Teufel .05
303 Mike Boddicker .05
304 Kevin Reimer .05
305 Mike Scioscia .05
306a Lonnie Smith (136 G 1990) .10
306b Lonnie Smith (135 G 1990) .05
307 Andy Benes .05
308 Tom Pagnozzi .05
309 Norm Charlton .05
310 Gary Carter .15
311 Jeff Pico .05
312 Charlie Hayes .05
313 Ron Robinson .05
314 Gary Pettis .05
315 Roberto Alomar .30
316 Gene Nelson .05
317 Mike Fitzgerald .05
318 Rick Aguilera .05
319 Jeff McKnight .05
320 Tony Fernandez .05
321 Bob Rodgers .05
322 *Terry Shumpert* .05
323 Cory Snyder .05
324a Ron Kittle ("6 Home Runs" in career summary) .10
324b Ron Kittle ("7 Home Runs" in career summary) .05
325 Brett Butler .05
326 Ken Patterson .05
327 Ron Hassey .05
328 Walt Terrell .05
329 Dave Justice .25
330 Dwight Gooden .05
331 Eric Anthony .05
332 Kenny Rogers .05
333 *Chipper Jones* (#1 Draft Pick) 2.00
334 Todd Benzinger .05
335 Mitch Williams .05
336 Matt Nokes .05
337a Keith Comstock (Mariners logo) .05
337b Keith Comstock (Cubs logo) .10
338 Luis Rivera .05
339 Larry Walker .25
340 Ramon Martinez .05
341 John Moses .05
342 *Mickey Morandini* .10
343 Jose Oquendo .05
344 Jeff Russell .05
345 Len Dykstra .05
346 Jesse Orosco .05
347 Greg Vaughn .05
348 Todd Stottlemyre .05
349 Dave Gallagher .05
350 Glenn Davis .05
351 Joe Torre .05
352 Frank White .05
353 Tony Castillo .05
354 Sid Bream .05
355 Chili Davis .05
356 Mike Marshall .05
357 Jack Savage .05
358 Mark Parent .05
359 Chuck Cary .05
360 Tim Raines .05
361 Scott Garrelts .05
362 *Hector Villanueva* .05
363 Rick Mahler .05
364 Dan Pasqua .05
365 Mike Schooler .05
366a Checklist 3 (Carl Nichols #19) .05
366b Checklist 3 (Carl Nichols #119) .05
367 *Dave Walsh* .05
368 Felix Jose .05
369 Steve Searcy .05
370 Kelly Gruber .05
371 Jeff Montgomery .05
372 Spike Owen .05
373 Darrin Jackson .05
374 *Larry Casian* .05
375 Tony Pena .05
376 Mike Harkey .05
377 Rene Gonzales .05
378a *Wilson Alvarez* (no 1989 Port Charlotte stats) .30
378b *Wilson Alvarez* (1989 Port Charlotte stats) .20
379 Randy Velarde .05
380 Willie McGee .05
381 Jim Leyland .05
382 Mackey Sasser .05
383 Pete Smith .05
384 Gerald Perry .05
385 Mickey Tettleton .05
386 Cecil Fielder (All-Star) .05
387 Julio Franco (All-Star) .05
388 Kelly Gruber (All-Star) .05
389 Alan Trammell (All-Star) .05
390 Jose Canseco (All-Star) .15
391 Rickey Henderson (All-Star) .15
392 Ken Griffey, Jr. (All-Star) .30
393 Carlton Fisk (All-Star) .10
394 Bob Welch (All-Star) .05
395 Chuck Finley (All-Star) .05
396 Bobby Thigpen (All-Star) .05
397 Eddie Murray (All-Star) .10
398 Ryne Sandberg (All-Star) .15
399 Matt Williams (All-Star) .05
400 Barry Larkin (All-Star) .05
401 Barry Bonds (All-Star) .40
402 Darryl Strawberry (All-Star) .05
403 Bobby Bonilla (All-Star) .05
404 Mike Scoscia (All-Star) .05
405 Doug Drabek (All-Star) .05
406 Frank Viola (All-Star) .05
407 John Franco (All-Star) .05
408 Ernie Riles .05
409 Mike Stanley .05
410 Dave Righetti .05
411 Lance Blankenship .05
412 Dave Bergman .05
413 Terry Mulholland .05
414 Sammy Sosa .50
415 Rick Sutcliffe .05
416 Randy Milligan .05
417 Bill Krueger .05
418 Nick Esasky .05
419 Jeff Reed .05
420 Bobby Thigpen .05
421 Alex Cole .05
422 Rick Rueschel .05
423 Rafael Ramirez .05
424 Calvin Schiraldi .05
425 Andy Van Slyke .05
426 *Joe Grahe* .05
427 Rick Dempsey .05
428 *John Barfield* .05
429 Stump Merrill .05
430 Gary Gaetti .05
431 Paul Gibson .05
432 Delino DeShields .05
433 Pat Tabler .05
434 Julio Machado .05
435 Kevin Maas .05
436 Scott Bankhead .05
437 Doug Dascenzo .05
438 Vicente Palacios .05
439 Dickie Thon .05
440 George Bell .05
441 Zane Smith .05
442 Charlie O'Brien .05
443 Jeff Innis .05
444 Glenn Braggs .05
445 Greg Swindell .05
446 *Craig Grebeck* .05
447 John Burkett .05
448 Craig Lefferts .05
449 Juan Berenguer .05
450 Wade Boggs .30
451 Neal Heaton .05
452 Bill Schroeder .05
453 Lenny Harris .05
454a Kevin Appier (no 1990 Omaha stats) .15
454b Kevin Appier (1990 Omaha stats) .05
455 Walt Weiss .05
456 Charlie Leibrandt .05
457 Todd Hundley .05
458 Brian Holman .05
459 Tom Trebelhorn .05
460 Dave Steib .05
461a Robin Ventura (gray inner photo frame at left) .15
461b Robin Ventura (red inner photo frame at left) .05
462 Steve Frey .05
463 Dwight Smith .05
464 Steve Buechele .05
465 Ken Griffey .05
466 Charles Nagy .10
467 Dennis Cook .05
468 Tim Hulett .05
469 Chet Lemon .05
470 Howard Johnson .05
471 *Mike Lieberthal* (#1 Draft Pick) .50
472 Kirt Manwaring .05
473 Curt Young .05
474 *Phil Plantier* .10
475 Teddy Higuera .05
476 Glenn Wilson .05
477 Mike Fetters .05
478 Kurt Stillwell .05
479 Bob Patterson .05
480 Dave Magadan .05
481 Eddie Whitson .05
482 Tino Martinez .05
483 Mike Aldrete .05
484 Dave LaPoint .05
485 Terry Pendleton .05
486 Tommy Greene .05
487 Rafael Belliard .05
488 Jeff Manto .05
489 Bobby Valentine .05
490 Kirk Gibson .05
491 *Kurt Miller* (#1 Draft Pick) .05
492 Ernie Whitt .05
493 Jose Rijo .05
494 Chris James .05
495 Charlie Hough .05
496 Marty Barrett .05
497 Ben McDonald .05
498 Mark Salas .05
499 Melido Perez .05
500 Will Clark .15
501 Mike Bielecki .05
502 Carney Lansford .05
503 Roy Smith .05
504 *Julio Valera* .05
505 Chuck Finley .05
506 Darnell Coles .05
507 Steve Jeltz .05
508 *Mike York* .05
509 Glenallen Hill .05
510 John Franco .05
511 Steve Balboni .05
512 Jose Mesa .05
513 Jerald Clark .05
514 Mike Stanton .05
515 Alvin Davis .05
516 *Karl Rhodes* .10
517 Joe Oliver .05
518 Cris Carpenter .05
519 Sparky Anderson .10
520 Mark Grace .20
521 Joe Orsulak .05
522 Stan Belinda .05
523 *Rodney McCray* .05
524 Darrel Akerfelds .05
525 Willie Randolph .05
526a Moises Alou (37 R 1990 Pirates) .20
526b Moises Alou (0 R 1990 Pirates) .15
527a Checklist 4 (Kevin McReynolds #719) .05
527b Checklist 4 (Kevin McReynolds #105) .05
528 Denny Martinez .05
529 *Mark Newfield* (#1 Draft Pick) .05
530 Roger Clemens .40
531 *Dave Rhode* .05
532 Kirk McCaskill .05
533 Oddibe McDowell .05
534 Mike Jackson .05
535 Ruben Sierra .05
536 Mike Witt .05
537 Jose Lind .05
538 Bip Roberts .05
539 Scott Terry .05
540 George Brett .40
541 Domingo Ramos .05
542 Rob Murphy .05
543 Junior Felix .05
544 Alejandro Pena .05
545 Dale Murphy .15
546 Jeff Ballard .05
547 Mike Pagliarulo .05
548 Jaime Navarro .05
549 John McNamara .05
550 Eric Davis .05
551 Bob Kipper .05
552 Jeff Hamilton .05
553 *Joe Klink* .05
554 Brian Harper .05
555 *Turner Ward* .05
556 Gary Ward .05
557 Wally Whitehurst .05
558 Otis Nixon .05
559 Adam Peterson .05
560 Greg Smith .05
561 Tim McIntosh (Future Star) .05
562 Jeff Kunkel .05
563 *Brent Knackert* .05

564 Dante Bichette .05
565 Craig Biggio .10
566 *Craig Wilson* .10
567 Dwayne Henry .05
568 Ron Karkovice .05
569 Curt Schilling .05
570 Barry Bonds .50
571 Pat Combs .05
572 Dave Anderson .05
573 *Rich Rodriguez* .10
574 John Marzano .05
575 Robin Yount .30
576 Jeff Kaiser .05
577 Bill Doran .05
578 Dave West .05
579 Roger Craig .05
580 Dave Stewart .05
581 Luis Quinones .05
582 Marty Clary .05
583 Tony Phillips .05
584 Kevin Brown .05
585 Pete O'Brien .05
586 Fred Lynn .05
587 Jose Offerman (Future Star) .10
588a Mark Whiten (hand inside left border) .05
588b Mark Whiten (hand over left border) .20
589 *Scott Ruskin* .10
590 Eddie Murray .30
591 Ken Hill .05
592 B.J. Surhoff .05
593a *Mike Walker* (No 1990 Canton-Akron stats) .15
593b *Mike Walker* (1990 Canton-Akron stats) .05
594 *Rich Garces* (Future Star) .10
595 Bill Landrum .05
596 *Ronnie Walden* (#1 Draft Pick) .05
597 Jerry Don Gleaton .05
598 Sam Horn .05
599a Greg Myers (no 1990 Syracuse stats) .10
599b Greg Myers (1990 Syracuse stats) .05
600 Bo Jackson .10
601 Bob Ojeda .05
602 Casey Candaele .05
603a *Wes Chamberlain* (photo of Louie Meadows, no bat) .20
603b *Wes Chamberlain* (correct photo, holding bat) .05
604 Billy Hatcher .05
605 Jeff Reardon .05
606 Jim Gott .05
607 Edgar Martinez .05
608 Todd Burns .05
609 Jeff Torborg .05
610 Andres Galarraga .05
611 Dave Eiland .05
612 Steve Lyons .05
613 Eric Show .05
614 Luis Salazar .05
615 Bert Blyleven .05
616 Todd Zeile .05
617 Bill Wegman .05
618 Sil Campusano .05
619 David Wells .05
620 Ozzie Guillen .05
621 Ted Power .05
622 Jack Daugherty .05
623 Jeff Blauser .05
624 Tom Candiotti .05
625 Terry Steinbach .05
626 Gerald Young .05
627 *Tim Layana* .05
628 Greg Litton .05
629 Wes Gardner .05
630 Dave Winfield .30
631 Mike Morgan .05
632 Lloyd Moseby .05
633 Kevin Tapani .05
634 Henry Cotto .05
635 Andy Hawkins .05
636 Geronimo Pena .05
637 Bruce Ruffin .05
638 Mike Macfarlane .05
639 Frank Robinson .05
640 Andre Dawson .15
641 Mike Henneman .05
642 Hal Morris .05
643 Jim Presley .05
644 Chuck Crim .05
645 Juan Samuel .05
646 *Andujar Cedeno* .05
647 Mark Portugal .05
648 Lee Stevens .05
649 *Bill Sampen* .05
650 Jack Clark .05
651 *Alan Mills* .10
652 Kevin Romine .05
653 *Anthony Telford* .05
654 Paul Sorrento .05
655 Erik Hanson .05
656a Checklist 5 (Vincente Palacios #348) .05
656b Checklist 5 (Palacios #433) .05
656c Checklist 5 (Palacios #438) .05
657 Mike Kingery .05
658 *Scott Aldred* .05
659 *Oscar Azocar* .05
660 Lee Smith .05
661 Steve Lake .05
662 Rob Dibble .05
663 Greg Brock .05
664 John Farrell .05
665 Mike LaValliere .05
666 Danny Darwin .05
667 Kent Anderson .05
668 Bill Long .05
669 Lou Pinella .05
670 Rickey Henderson .35
671 Andy McGaffigan .05
672 Shane Mack .05
673 *Greg Olson* .05
674a Kevin Gross (no diamond after 89 BB 1988) .10
674b Kevin Gross (diamond after 89 BB 1988) .05
675 Tom Brunansky .05
676 *Scott Chiamparino* .05
677 Billy Ripken .05
678 Mark Davidson .05
679 Bill Bathe .05
680 David Cone .05
681 *Jeff Schaefer* .05
682 *Ray Lankford* .20
683 Derek Lilliquist .05
684 Milt Cuyler .05
685 Doug Drabek .05
686 Mike Gallego .05
687a John Cerutti (4.46 ERA 1990) .05
687b John Cerutti (4.76 ERA 1990) .05
688 *Rosario Rodriguez* .05
689 John Kruk .05
690 Orel Hershiser .05
691 Mike Blowers .05
692a *Efrain Valdez* (no text below stats) .15
692b *Efrain Valdez* (two lines of text below stats) .05
693 Francisco Cabrera .05
694 Randy Veres .05
695 Kevin Seitzer .05
696 Steve Olin .05
697 Shawn Abner .05
698 Mark Guthrie .05
699 Jim Lefebvre .05
700 Jose Canseco .30
701 Pascual Perez .05
702 *Tim Naehring* .05
703 Juan Agosto .05
704 Devon White .05
705 Robby Thompson .05
706a Brad Arnsberg (68.2 IP Rangers 1990) .05
706b Brad Arnsberg (62.2 IP Rangers 1990) .05
707 Jim Eisenreich .05
708 John Mitchell .05
709 Matt Sinatro .05
710 Kent Hrbek .05
711 Jose DeLeon .05
712 Ricky Jordan .05
713 Scott Scudder .05
714 Marvell Wynne .05
715 Tim Burke .05
716 Bob Geren .05
717 Phil Bradley .05
718 Steve Crawford .05
719 Keith Miller .05
720 Cecil Fielder .05
721 *Mark Lee* .05
722 Wally Backman .05
723 Candy Maldonado .05
724 *David Segui* .10
725 Ron Gant .05
726 Phil Stephenson .05
727 Mookie Wilson .05
728 Scott Sanderson .05
729 Don Zimmer .05
730 Barry Larkin .10
731 *Jeff Gray* .05
732 Franklin Stubbs .05
733 Kelly Downs .05
734 John Russell .05
735 Ron Darling .05
736 Dick Schofield .05
737 Tim Crews .05
738 Mel Hall .05
739 *Russ Swan* .05
740 Ryne Sandberg .30
741 Jimmy Key .05
742 Tommy Gregg .05
743 Bryn Smith .05
744 Nelson Santovenia .05
745 Doug Jones .05
746 John Shelby .05
747 Tony Fossas .05
748 Al Newman .05
749 Greg Harris .05
750 Bobby Bonilla .05
751 *Wayne Edwards* .05
752 Kevin Bass .05
753 *Paul Marak* .05
754 Bill Pecota .05
755 Mark Langston .05
756 Jeff Huson .05
757 Mark Gardner .05
758 Mike Devereaux .05
759 Bobby Cox .05
760 Benny Santiago .05
761 Larry Andersen .05
762 Mitch Webster .05
763 *Dana Kiecker* .05
764 Mark Carreon .05
765 Shawon Dunston .05
766 Jeff Robinson .05
767 *Dan Wilson* (#1 Draft Pick) .10
768 Donn Pall .05
769 *Tim Sherrill* .05
770 Jay Howell .05
771 Gary Redus .05
772 Kent Mercker .05
773 Tom Foley .05
774 Dennis Rasmussen .05
775 Julio Franco .05
776 Brent Mayne .05
777 John Candelaria .05
778 Danny Gladden .05
779 Carmelo Martinez .05
780a Randy Myers (Career losses 15) .10
780b Randy Myers (Career losses 19) .05
781 Darryl Hamilton .05
782 Jim Deshaies .05
783 Joel Skinner .05
784 Willie Fraser .05
785 Scott Fletcher .05
786 Eric Plunk .05
787 Checklist 6 .05
788 Bob Milacki .05
789 Tom Lasorda .10
790 Ken Griffey, Jr. .60
791 Mike Benjamin .05
792 Mike Greenwell .05

1991 Topps Tiffany

Topps ended its annual run of special collectors edition boxed sets in 1991, producing the glossy sets in considerably more limited quantity than in previous years. Cards are identical to the regular 1991 Topps set except for the use of white cardboard stock and a high-gloss front finish.

	MT
Unopened Set (792):	200.00
Complete Set (792):	125.00
Common Player:	.10

(Star cards valued at 3X corresponding regular issue Topps cards)

1991 Topps Desert Shield

As a special treat for U.S. armed services personnel serving in the Persian Gulf prior to and during the war with Iraq, Topps produced a special edition of its 1991 baseball card set featuring a gold-foil overprint honoring the military effort. Enough cards were produced to equal approximately 6,800 sets. While some cards actually reached the troops in the Middle East, many were shortstopped by military supply personnel stateside and sold into the hobby. Many of the cards sent to Saudi Arabia never returned to the U.S., however, making the supply of available cards somewhat scarce. At the peak of their popularity Desert Shield cards sold for price two to three times their current levels. The checklist cards in the set were not overprinted. At least two types of counterfeit overprint have been seen on genuine Topps cards in an attempt to cash in on the scarcity of these war "veterans."

	MT
Complete Set (792):	1000.
Common Player:	1.00
Wax Pack:	75.00

(Star cards valued at 80X-100X same cards in regular 1991 Topps issue.)

1991 Topps All-Star Glossy Set of 22

Continuing the same basic format used since 1984, these glossy-front rack-pak inserts honor the players, manager and honorary captains of the previous year's All-Star Game. Fronts have a league logo in the lower-left corner, a 1990 All-Star banner above the photo and a Topps 40th anniversary logo superimposed over the photo. Backs have a shield and star design and the legend "1990 All-Star Commemorative Set" above the player's name, position and card number. Backs are printed in red and blue.

		MT
Complete Set (22):		4.00
Common Player:		.05
1	Tony LaRussa	.05
2	Mark McGwire	1.00
3	Steve Sax	.05
4	Wade Boggs	.40
5	Cal Ripken, Jr.	1.00
6	Rickey Henderson	.40
7	Ken Griffey, Jr.	.75
8	Jose Canseco	.30
9	Sandy Alomar, Jr.	.05
10	Bob Welch	.05
11	Al Lopez	.05
12	Roger Craig	.05
13	Will Clark	.15
14	Ryne Sandberg	.45
15	Chris Sabo	.05
16	Ozzie Smith	.50
17	Kevin Mitchell	.05
18	Len Dykstra	.05
19	Andre Dawson	.15
20	Mike Scoscia	.05
21	Jack Armstrong	.05
22	Juan Marichal	.05

1991 Topps Glossy Rookies

Similar in format to previous years' glossy rookies sets, this 33-card issue was available one per pack in 100-card jumbo cello packs. Card fronts have a colored "1990 Rookies" banner above the player photo, with the player's name in red in a yellow bar beneath. The Topps 40th anniversary logo appears in one of the upper corners of the photo. Backs are printed in red and blue and feature a "1990 Rookies Commemorative Set" shield logo. The player's name, position, team and card number are printed beneath. Cards are numbered alphabetically.

		MT
Complete Set (33):		7.00
Common Player:		.10
1	Sandy Alomar, Jr.	.10
2	Kevin Appier	.10
3	Steve Avery	.10
4	Carlos Baerga	.10
5	John Burkett	.10
6	Alex Cole	.10
7	Pat Combs	.10
8	Delino DeShields	.10
9	Travis Fryman	.10
10	Marquis Grissom	.20
11	Mike Harkey	.10
12	Glenallen Hill	.10
13	Jeff Huson	.10
14	Felix Jose	.10
15	Dave Justice	.75
16	Jim Leyritz	.10
17	Kevin Maas	.10
18	Ben McDonald	.10
19	Kent Mercker	.10
20	Hal Morris	.10
21	Chris Nabholz	.10
22	Tim Naehring	.10
23	Jose Offerman	.10
24	John Olerud	.50
25	Scott Radinsky	.10
26	Scott Ruskin	.10
27	Kevin Tapani	.10
28	Frank Thomas	2.50
29	Randy Tomlin	.10
30	Greg Vaughn	.35
31	Robin Ventura	.50
32	Larry Walker	.50
33	Todd Zeile	.10

1991 Topps Traded

"Team USA" players are featured in the 1991 Topps Traded set. The cards feature the same style as the regular 1991 issue, including the 40th anniversary logo. The set includes 132 cards and showcases rookies and traded players along with "Team USA." The cards are numbered with a "T" designation in alphabetical order.

		MT
Unopened Retail Set (132):		40.00
Complete Hobby Set (132):		18.00
Common Player:		.05
1	Juan Agosto	.05
2	Roberto Alomar	.35
3	Wally Backman	.05
4	*Jeff Bagwell*	3.00
5	Skeeter Barnes	.05
6	Steve Bedrosian	.05
7	Derek Bell	.10
8	George Bell	.05
9	Rafael Belliard	.05
10	Dante Bichette	.05
11	Bud Black	.05
12	Mike Boddicker	.05
13	Sid Bream	.05
14	Hubie Brooks	.05
15	Brett Butler	.05
16	Ivan Calderon	.05
17	John Candelaria	.05
18	Tom Candiotti	.05
19	Gary Carter	.15
20	Joe Carter	.05
21	Rick Cerone	.05
22	Jack Clark	.05
23	Vince Coleman	.05
24	Scott Coolbaugh	.05
25	Danny Cox	.05
26	Danny Darwin	.05
27	Chili Davis	.05
28	Glenn Davis	.05
29	Steve Decker	.05
30	Rob Deer	.05
31	Rich DeLucia	.05
32	*John Dettmer* (USA)	.05
33	Brian Downing	.05
34	*Darren Dreifort* (USA)	.50
35	Kirk Dressendorfer	.05
36	Jim Essian	.05
37	Dwight Evans	.05
38	Steve Farr	.05
39	Jeff Fassero	.05
40	Junior Felix	.05
41	Tony Fernandez	.05
42	Steve Finley	.05
43	Jim Fregosi	.05
44	Gary Gaetti	.05
45	*Jason Giambi* (USA)	12.50
46	Kirk Gibson	.05
47	Leo Gomez	.05
48	*Luis Gonzalez*	2.50
49	*Jeff Granger* (USA)	.10
50	*Todd Greene* (USA)	.25
51	*Jeffrey Hammonds* (USA)	.25
52	Mike Hargrove	.05
53	Pete Harnisch	.05
54	*Rick Helling* (USA)	.35
55	Glenallen Hill	.05
56	Charlie Hough	.05
57	Pete Incaviglia	.05
58	Bo Jackson	.10
59	Danny Jackson	.05
60	Reggie Jefferson	.05
61	*Charles Johnson* (USA)	.75
62	Jeff Johnson	.05
63	*Todd Johnson* (USA)	.10
64	Barry Jones	.05
65	Chris Jones	.05
66	Scott Kamieniecki	.05
67	*Pat Kelly*	.05
68	Darryl Kile	.10
69	Chuck Knoblauch	.20
70	Bill Krueger	.05
71	Scott Leius	.05
72	*Donnie Leshnock* (USA)	.10
73	Mark Lewis	.05
74	Candy Maldonado	.05
75	*Jason McDonald* (USA)	.10
76	Willie McGee	.05
77	Fred McGriff	.05
78	*Billy McMillon* (USA)	.10
79	Hal McRae	.05
80	*Dan Melendez* (USA)	.10
81	Orlando Merced	.10
82	Jack Morris	.05
83	*Phil Nevin* (USA)	1.00
84	Otis Nixon	.05
85	Johnny Oates	.05
86	Bob Ojeda	.05
87	Mike Pagliarulo	.05
88	Dean Palmer	.05
89	Dave Parker	.05
90	Terry Pendleton	.05
91	*Tony Phillips* (USA)	.10
92	Doug Piatt	.05
93	Ron Polk (U.S.A.)	.05
94	Tim Raines	.05
95	Willie Randolph	.05
96	Dave Righetti	.05
97	Ernie Riles	.05
98	*Chris Roberts* (USA)	.10
99	Jeff Robinson (Angels)	.05
100	Jeff Robinson (Orioles)	.05
101	*Ivan Rodriguez*	2.00
102	*Steve Rodriguez* (USA)	.10
103	Tom Runnells	.05
104	Scott Sanderson	.05
105	Bob Scanlan	.05
106	*Pete Schourek*	.10
107	Gary Scott	.05
108	*Paul Shuey* (USA)	.10
109	*Doug Simons*	.05
110	Dave Smith	.05
111	Cory Snyder	.05
112	Luis Sojo	.05
113	*Kennie Steenstra* (USA)	.10
114	Darryl Strawberry	.05
115	Franklin Stubbs	.05
116	*Todd Taylor* (USA)	.10
117	Wade Taylor	.05
118	Garry Templeton	.05
119	Mickey Tettleton	.05
120	Tim Teufel	.05
121	Mike Timlin	.05
122	*David Tuttle* (USA)	.10
123	Mo Vaughn	.35
124	*Jeff Ware* (USA)	.10
125	Devon White	.05
126	Mark Whiten	.05
127	Mitch Williams	.05
128	*Craig Wilson* (USA)	.10
129	Willie Wilson	.05
130	*Chris Wimmer* (USA)	.10
131	*Ivan Zweig* (USA)	.10
132	Checklist	.05

1991 Topps Traded Tiffany

The final year of production for Topps "Tiffany" parallel boxed sets saw production levels slashed for the 132-card Traded version. Value of the sets has risen dramatically with the hobby's perception of the set's scarcity and the development of key rookies such as Bagwell, Giambi and I-Rod. Like the regular Traded set, cards are numbered in alphabetical order with a "T" suffix.

	MT
Complete Unopened Set (132):	300.00
Complete Set (132):	250.00
Common Player:	.50
Stars and Rookies:	8X

(See 1991 Topps Traded for checklist and base card values.)

1992 Topps 1991 Major League Debut

This 194-card set highlights the debut date of

1991 Major League rookies. Two checklist cards are also included in this boxed set. The card fronts resemble the 1992 Topps cards. A debut banner appears in the lower-right corner of the card front. The set is packaged in an attractive collector box and the cards are numbered alphabetically. This set was available only through hobby dealers.

		MT
Complete Set (194):		15.00
Common Player:		.05
1	Kyle Abbott	.05
2	Dana Allison	.05
3	Rich Amaral	.05
4	Ruben Amaro	.05
5	Andy Ashby	.10
6	Jim Austin	.05
7	Jeff Bagwell	2.50
8	Jeff Banister	.05
9	Willie Banks	.05
10	Bret Barberie	.05
11	Kim Batiste	.05
12	Chris Beasley	.05
13	Rod Beck	.05
14	Derek Bell	.05
15	Esteban Beltre	.05
16	Freddie Benavides	.05
17	Rickey Bones	.05
18	Denis Boucher	.05
19	Ryan Bowen	.05
20	Cliff Brantley	.05
21	John Briscoe	.05
22	Scott Brosius	.05
23	Terry Bross	.05
24	Jarvis Brown	.05
25	Scott Bullett	.05
26	Kevin Campbell	.05
27	Amalio Carreno	.05
28	Matias Carrillo	.05
29	Jeff Carter	.05
30	Vinny Castilla	.10
31	Braulio Castillo	.05
32	Frank Castillo	.05
33	Darrin Chapin	.05
34	Mike Christopher	.05
35	Mark Clark	.05
36	Royce Clayton	.05
37	Stu Cole	.05
38	Gary Cooper	.05
39	Archie Corbin	.05
40	Rheal Cormier	.05
41	Chris Cron	.05
42	Mike Dalton	.05
43	Mark Davis	.05
44	Francisco de la Rosa	.05
45	Chris Donnels	.05
46	Brian Drahman	.05
47	Tom Drees	.05
48	Kirk Dressendorfer	.05
49	Bruce Egloff	.05
50	Cal Eldred	.05
51	Jose Escobar	.05
52	Tony Eusebio	.05
53	Hector Fajardo	.05
54	Monty Farriss	.05
55	Jeff Fassero	.05
56	Dave Fleming	.05
57	Kevin Flora	.05
58	Steve Foster	.05
59	Dan Gakeler	.05
60	Ramon Garcia	.05
61	Chris Gardner	.05
62	Jeff Gardner	.05
63	Chris George	.05
64	Ray Giannelli	.05
65	Tom Goodwin	.05
66	Mark Grater	.05
67	Johnny Guzman	.05
68	Juan Guzman	.05
69	Dave Haas	.05
70	Chris Haney	.05
71	Shawn Hare	.05
72	Donald Harris	.05
73	Doug Henry	.05
74	Pat Hentgen	.05
75	Gil Heredia	.05
76	Jeremy Hernandez	.05
77	Jose Hernandez	.05
78	Roberto Hernandez	.10
79	Bryan Hickerson	.05
80	Milt Hill	.05
81	Vince Horsman	.05
82	Wayne Housie	.05
83	Chris Howard	.05
84	David Howard	.05
85	Mike Humphreys	.05
86	Brian Hunter	.05
87	Jim Hunter	.05
88	Mike Ignasiak	.05
89	Reggie Jefferson	.05
90	Jeff Johnson	.05
91	Joel Johnson	.05
92	Calvin Jones	.05
93	Chris Jones	.05
94	Stacy Jones	.05
95	Jeff Juden	.05
96	Scott Kamieniecki	.05
97	Eric Karros	.05
98	Pat Kelly	.05
99	John Kiely	.05
100	Darryl Kile	.10
101	Wayne Kirby	.05
102	Garland Kiser	.05
103	Chuck Knoblauch	.10
104	Randy Knorr	.05
105	Tom Kramer	.05
106	Ced Landrum	.05
107	Patrick Lennon	.05
108	Jim Lewis	.05
109	Mark Lewis	.05
110	Doug Lindsey	.05
111	Scott Livingstone	.05
112	Kenny Lofton	.10
113	Ever Magallanes	.05
114	Mike Magnante	.05
115	Barry Manuel	.05
116	Josias Manzanillo	.05
117	Chito Martinez	.05
118	Terry Mathews	.05
119	Rob Mauer	.05
120	Tim Mauser	.05
121	Terry McDaniel	.05
122	Rusty Meacham	.05
123	Luis Mercedes	.05
124	Paul Miller	.05
125	Keith Mitchell	.05
126	Bobby Moore	.05
127	Kevin Morton	.05
128	Andy Mota	.05
129	Jose Mota	.05
130	Mike Mussina	2.00
131	Jeff Mutis	.05
132	Denny Neagle	.05
133	Warren Newson	.05
134	Jim Olander	.05
135	Erik Pappas	.05
136	Jorge Pedre	.05
137	Yorkis Perez	.05
138	Mark Petkovsek	.05
139	Doug Piatt	.05
140	Jeff Plympton	.05
141	Harvey Pulliam	.05
142	John Ramos	.05
143	Mike Remlinger	.05
144	Laddie Renfroe	.05
145	Armando Reynoso	.05
146	Arthur Rhodes	.05
147	Pat Rice	.05
148	Nikco Riesgo	.05
149	Carlos Rodriguez	.05
150	Ivan Rodriguez	2.00
151	Wayne Rosenthal	.05
152	Rico Rossy	.05
153	Stan Royer	.05
154	Rey Sanchez	.05
155	Reggie Sanders	.05
156	Mo Sanford	.05
157	Bob Scanlan	.05
158	Pete Schourek	.05
159	Gary Scott	.05
160	Tim Scott	.05
161	Tony Scruggs	.05
162	Scott Servais	.05
163	Doug Simons	.05
164	Heathcliff Slocumb	.05
165	Joe Slusarski	.05
166	Tim Spehr	.05
167	Ed Sprague	.05
168	Jeff Tackett	.05
169	Eddie Taubensee	.05
170	Wade Taylor	.05
171	Jim Thome	.15
172	Mike Timlin	.05
173	Jose Tolentino	.05
174	John Vander Wal	.10
175	Todd Van Poppel	.10
176	Mo Vaughn	.75
177	Dave Wainhouse	.05
178	Don Wakamatsu	.05
179	Bruce Walton	.05
180	Kevin Ward	.05
181	Dave Weathers	.05
182	Eric Wedge	.05
183	John Wehner	.05
184	Rick Wilkins	.05
185	Bernie Williams	.50
186	Brian Williams	.05
187	Ron Witmeyer	.05
188	Mark Wohlers	.05
189	Ted Wood	.05
190	Anthony Young	.05
191	Eddie Zosky	.05
192	Bob Zupcic	.05
193	Checklist	.05
194	Checklist	.05

1992 Topps

This 792-card set features white stock much like the 1991 issue. The card fronts feature full-color action and posed photos with a gray inner frame and the player name and position at bottom. Backs feature biographical information, statistics and stadium photos on player cards where space is available. All-Star cards and #1 Draft Pick cards are once again included. Topps brought back four-player rookie cards in 1992. Nine Top Prospect cards of this nature can be found within the set. "Match the Stats" game cards were inserted into packs of 1992 Topps cards. Special bonus cards were given away to winners of this insert game. This was the first Topps regular-issue baseball card set since 1951 which was sold without bubblegum.

		MT
Unopened Factory Set (792):		15.00
Complete Set (792):		12.00
Common Player:		.05
Golds:		4X
Wax Pack (14):		.50
Wax Box (36):		14.00
Cello Pack (34):		.75
Cello Box (24):		16.00
Vending Box (500):		6.00
1	Nolan Ryan	1.00
2	Rickey Henderson (Record Breaker)	.10
3	Jeff Reardon (Record Breaker)	.05
4	Nolan Ryan (Record Breaker)	.40
5	Dave Winfield (Record Breaker)	.15
6	*Brien Taylor* (Draft Pick)	.10
7	*Jim Olander*	.05
8	*Bryan Hickerson*	.05
9	John Farrell (Draft Pick)	.05
10	Wade Boggs	.35
11	Jack McDowell	.05
12	Luis Gonzalez	.25
13	Mike Scioscia	.05
14	Wes Chamberlain	.05
15	Denny Martinez	.05
16	Jeff Montgomery	.05
17	Randy Milligan	.05
18	Greg Cadaret	.05
19	Jamie Quirk	.05
20	Bip Roberts	.05
21	Buck Rodgers	.05
22	Bill Wegman	.05
23	Chuck Knoblauch	.05
24	Randy Myers	.05
25	Ron Gant	.05
26	Mike Bielecki	.05
27	Juan Gonzalez	.40
28	Mike Schooler	.05
29	Mickey Tettleton	.05
30	John Kruk	.05
31	Bryn Smith	.05
32	Chris Nabholz	.05
33	Carlos Baerga	.05
34	Jeff Juden	.05
35	Dave Righetti	.05
36	*Scott Ruffcorn* (Draft Pick)	.05
37	Luis Polonia	.05
38	Tom Candiotti	.05
39	Greg Olson	.05
40	Cal Ripken, Jr.	1.00
41	Craig Lefferts	.05
42	Mike Macfarlane	.05
43	Jose Lind	.05
44	Rick Aguilera	.05
45	Gary Carter	.15
46	Steve Farr	.05
47	Rex Hudler	.05
48	Scott Scudder	.05
49	Damon Berryhill	.05
50	Ken Griffey, Jr.	.75
51	Tom Runnells	.05
52	Juan Bell	.05
53	Tommy Gregg	.05
54	David Wells	.05
55	Rafael Palmeiro	.20
56	Charlie O'Brien	.05
57	Donn Pall	.05
58	Top Prospects-Catchers (*Brad Ausmus*), (*Jim Campanis*), (*Dave Nilsson*), (*Doug Robbins*)	.15
59	Mo Vaughn	.30
60	Tony Fernandez	.05
61	Paul O'Neill	.05
62	Gene Nelson	.05
63	Randy Ready	.05
64	Bob Kipper	.05
65	Willie McGee	.05
66	*Scott Stahoviak* (Draft Pick)	.05
67	Luis Salazar	.05
68	Marvin Freeman	.05
69	Kenny Lofton	.05
70	Gary Gaetti	.05
71	Erik Hanson	.05
72	Eddie Zosky	.05
73	Brian Barnes	.05
74	Scott Leius	.05
75	Bret Saberhagen	.05
76	Mike Gallego	.05
77	Jack Armstrong	.05
78	Ivan Rodriguez	.30
79	Jesse Orosco	.05
80	Dave Justice	.20
81	*Ced Landrum*	.05
82	*Doug Simons*	.05
83	Tommy Greene	.05
84	Leo Gomez	.05
85	Jose DeLeon	.05
86	Steve Finley	.05
87	*Bob MacDonald*	.05
88	Darrin Jackson	.05
89	Neal Heaton	.05
90	Robin Yount	.30
91	Jeff Reed	.05

92 Lenny Harris .05
93 Reggie Jefferson .05
94 Sammy Sosa .65
95 Scott Bailes .05
96 *Tom McKinnon* (Draft Pick) .05
97 Luis Rivera .05
98 Mike Harkey .05
99 Jeff Treadway .05
100 Jose Canseco .35
101 Omar Vizquel .05
102 *Scott Kamieniecki* .10
103 Ricky Jordan .05
104 Jeff Ballard .05
105 Felix Jose .05
106 Mike Boddicker .05
107 Dan Pasqua .05
108 *Mike Timlin* .10
109 Roger Craig .05
110 Ryne Sandberg .40
111 Mark Carreon .05
112 Oscar Azocar .05
113 Mike Greenwell .05
114 Mark Portugal .05
115 Terry Pendleton .05
116 Willie Randolph .05
117 Scott Terry .05
118 Chili Davis .05
119 Mark Gardner .05
120 Alan Trammell .05
121 Derek Bell .05
122 Gary Varsho .05
123 Bob Ojeda .05
124 *Shawn Livsey* (Draft Pick) .10
125 Chris Hoiles .05
126 Top Prospects-1st Baseman (Rico Brogna, John Jaha, Ryan Klesko, Dave Staton) .10
127 Carlos Quintana .05
128 Kurt Stillwell .05
129 Melido Perez .05
130 Alvin Davis .05
131 Checklist 1 .05
132 Eric Show .05
133 Rance Mulliniks .05
134 Darryl Kile .05
135 Von Hayes .05
136 Bill Doran .05
137 Jeff Robinson .05
138 Monty Fariss .05
139 Jeff Innis .05
140 Mark Grace .20
141 Jim Leyland .05
142 Todd Van Poppel .05
143 Paul Gibson .05
144 Bill Swift .05
145 Danny Tartabull .05
146 Al Newman .05
147 Cris Carpenter .05
148 *Anthony Young* .05
149 *Brian Bohanon* .10
150 Roger Clemens .50
151 Jeff Hamilton .05
152 Charlie Leibrandt .05
153 Ron Karkovice .05
154 Hensley Meulens .05
155 Scott Bankhead .05
156 *Manny Ramirez* (Draft Pick) 2.00
157 Keith Miller .05
158 Todd Frohwirth .05
159 Darrin Fletcher .05
160 Bobby Bonilla .05
161 Casey Candaele .05
162 Paul Faries .05
163 Dana Kiecker .05
164 Shane Mack .05
165 Mark Langston .05
166 Geronimo Pena .05
167 Andy Allanson .05
168 Dwight Smith .05
169 Chuck Crim .05
170 Alex Cole .05
171 Bill Plummer .05
172 Juan Berenguer .05
173 Brian Downing .05
174 Steve Frey .05
175 Orel Hershiser .05
176 *Ramon Garcia* .05
177 Danny Gladden .05
178 Jim Acker .05
179 Top Prospects-2nd Baseman (*Cesar Bernhardt*), (*Bobby DeJardin*), (*Armando Moreno*), (*Andy Stankiewicz*) .10
180 Kevin Mitchell .05
181 Hector Villanueva .05
182 Jeff Reardon .05
183 Brent Mayne .05
184 Jimmy Jones .05
185 Benny Santiago .05
186 *Cliff Floyd* (Draft Pick) 1.50
187 Ernie Riles .05
188 Jose Guzman .05
189 Junior Felix .05
190 Glenn Davis .05
191 Charlie Hough .05
192 *Dave Fleming* .05
193 Omar Oliveras .05
194 Eric Karros .05
195 David Cone .05
196 *Frank Castillo* .05
197 Glenn Braggs .05
198 Scott Aldred .05
199 Jeff Blauser .05
200 Len Dykstra .05
201 Buck Showalter .05
202 Rick Honeycutt .05
203 Greg Myers .05
204 Trevor Wilson .05
205 Jay Howell .05
206 Luis Sojo .05
207 Jack Clark .05
208 Julio Machado .05
209 Lloyd McClendon .05
210 Ozzie Guillen .05
211 *Jeremy Hernandez* .05
212 Randy Velarde .05
213 Les Lancaster .05
214 *Andy Mota* .05
215 Rich Gossage .05
216 *Brent Gates* (Draft Pick) .05
217 Brian Harper .05
218 Mike Flanagan .05
219 Jerry Browne .05
220 Jose Rijo .05
221 Skeeter Barnes .05
222 Jaime Navarro .05
223 Mel Hall .05
224 *Brett Barberie* .05
225 Roberto Alomar .30
226 Pete Smith .05
227 Daryl Boston .05
228 Eddie Whitson .05
229 Shawn Boskie .05
230 Dick Schofield .05
231 *Brian Drahman* .05
232 John Smiley .05
233 Mitch Webster .05
234 Terry Steinbach .05
235 Jack Morris .05
236 Bill Pecota .05
237 *Jose Hernandez* .15
238 Greg Litton .05
239 Brian Holman .05
240 Andres Galarraga .05
241 Gerald Young .05
242 Mike Mussina .30
243 Alvaro Espinoza .05
244 Darren Daulton .05
245 John Smoltz .10
246 *Jason Pruitt* (Draft Pick) .10
247 Chuck Finley .05
248 Jim Gantner .05
249 Tony Fossas .05
250 Ken Griffey .05
251 Kevin Elster .05
252 Dennis Rasmussen .05
253 Terry Kennedy .05
254 *Ryan Bowen* .05
255 Robin Ventura .05
256 Mike Aldrete .05
257 Jeff Russell .05
258 Jim Lindeman .05
259 Ron Darling .05
260 Devon White .05
261 Tom Lasorda .10
262 Terry Lee .05
263 Bob Patterson .05
264 Checklist 2 .05
265 Teddy Higuera .05
266 Roberto Kelly .05
267 Steve Bedrosian .05
268 Brady Anderson .05
269 *Ruben Amaro* .10
270 Tony Gwynn .50
271 Tracy Jones .05
272 Jerry Don Gleaton .05
273 Craig Grebeck .05
274 *Bob Scanlan* .05
275 Todd Zeile .05
276 *Shawn Green* (Draft Pick) 1.50
277 Scott Chiamparino .05
278 Darryl Hamilton .05
279 Jim Clancy .05
280 Carlos Martinez .05
281 Kevin Appier .05
282 *John Wehner* .05
283 Reggie Sanders .05
284 Gene Larkin .05
285 Bob Welch .05
286 Gilberto Reyes .05
287 Pete Schourek .05
288 Andujar Cedeno .05
289 Mike Morgan .05
290 Bo Jackson .10
291 Phil Garner .05
292 Ray Lankford .05
293 Mike Henneman .05
294 Dave Valle .05
295 Alonzo Powell .05
296 Tom Brunansky .05
297 Kevin Brown .05
298 Kelly Gruber .05
299 Charles Nagy .05
300 Don Mattingly .65
301 Kirk McCaskill .05
302 Joey Cora .05
303 Dan Plesac .05
304 Joe Oliver .05
305 Tom Glavine .10
306 *Al Shirley* (Draft Pick) .05
307 Bruce Ruffin .05
308 *Craig Shipley* .05
309 Dave Martinez .05
310 Jose Mesa .05
311 Henry Cotto .05
312 Mike LaValliere .05
313 Kevin Tapani .05
314 Jeff Huson .05
315 Juan Samuel .05
316 Curt Schilling .20
317 Mike Bordick .05
318 Steve Howe .05
319 Tony Phillips .05
320 George Bell .05
321 Lou Pinella .05
322 Tim Burke .05
323 Milt Thompson .05
324 Danny Darwin .05
325 Joe Orsulak .05
326 Eric King .05
327 Jay Buhner .05
328 *Joel Johnston* .05
329 Franklin Stubbs .05
330 Will Clark .15
331 Steve Lake .05
332 *Chris Jones* .10
333 Pat Tabler .05
334 Kevin Gross .05
335 Dave Henderson .05
336 *Greg Anthony* (Draft Pick) .05
337 Alejandro Pena .05
338 Shawn Abner .05
339 Tom Browning .05
340 Otis Nixon .05
341 Bob Geren .05
342 *Tim Spehr* .10
343 *Jon Vander Wal* .20
344 Jack Daugherty .05
345 Zane Smith .05
346 *Rheal Cormier* .10
347 Kent Hrbek .05
348 *Rick Wilkins* .10
349 Steve Lyons .05
350 Gregg Olson .05
351 Greg Riddoch .05
352 Ed Nunez .05
353 *Braulio Castillo* .05
354 Dave Bergman .05
355 *Warren Newson* .10
356 Luis Quinones .05
357 Mike Witt .05
358 *Ted Wood* .05
359 Mike Moore .05
360 Lance Parrish .05
361 Barry Jones .05
362 *Javier Ortiz* .10
363 John Candelaria .05
364 Glenallen Hill .05
365 Duane Ward .05
366 Checklist 3 .05
367 Rafael Belliard .05
368 Bill Krueger .05
369 *Steve Whitaker* (Draft Pick) .05
370 Shawon Dunston .05
371 Dante Bichette .05
372 *Kip Gross* .05
373 Don Robinson .05
374 Bernie Williams .25
375 Bert Blyleven .05
376 *Chris Donnels* .10
377 *Bob Zupcic* .05
378 Joel Skinner .05
379 Steve Chitren .05
380 Barry Bonds .65
381 Sparky Anderson .10
382 Sid Fernandez .05
383 Dave Hollins .05
384 Mark Lee .05
385 Tim Wallach .05
386 Will Clark (All-Star) .05
387 Ryne Sandberg (All-Star) .15
388 Howard Johnson (All-Star) .05
389 Barry Larkin (All-Star) .05
390 Barry Bonds (All-Star) .30
391 Ron Gant (All-Star) .05
392 Bobby Bonilla (All-Star) .05
393 Craig Biggio (All-Star) .05
394 Denny Martinez (All-Star) .05
395 Tom Glavine (All-Star) .05
396 Lee Smith (All-Star) .05
397 Cecil Fielder (All-Star) .05
398 Julio Franco (All-Star) .05
399 Wade Boggs (All-Star) .15
400 Cal Ripken, Jr. (All-Star) .40
401 Jose Canseco (All-Star) .15
402 Joe Carter (All-Star) .05
403 Ruben Sierra (All-Star) .05
404 Matt Nokes (All-Star) .05
405 Roger Clemens (All-Star) .20
406 Jim Abbott (All-Star) .05
407 Bryan Harvey (All-Star) .05
408 Bob Milacki .05
409 Geno Petralli .05
410 Dave Stewart .05
411 Mike Jackson .05
412 Luis Aquino .05
413 Tim Teufel .05
414 Jeff Ware (Draft Pick) .05
415 Jim Deshaies .05
416 Ellis Burks .05
417 Allan Anderson .05
418 Alfredo Griffin .05
419 Wally Whitehurst .05
420 Sandy Alomar .05
421 Juan Agosto .05
422 Sam Horn .05
423 *Jeff Fassero* .10
424 *Paul McClellan* .05
425 Cecil Fielder .05
426 Tim Raines .05
427 *Eddie Taubensee* .10
428 Dennis Boyd .05
429 Tony LaRussa .05
430 Steve Sax .05
431 Tom Gordon .05
432 Billy Hatcher .05
433 Cal Eldred .05
434 Wally Backman .05
435 Mark Eichhorn .05
436 Mookie Wilson .05
437 *Scott Servais* .10
438 Mike Maddux .05
439 *Chico Walker* .05
440 Doug Drabek .05
441 Rob Deer .05
442 Dave West .05
443 Spike Owen .05
444 *Tyrone Hill* (Draft Pick) .05

445 Matt Williams .15
446 Mark Lewis .05
447 David Segui .05
448 Tom Pagnozzi .05
449 *Jeff Johnson* .05
450 Mark McGwire 1.00
451 Tom Henke .05
452 Wilson Alvarez .05
453 Gary Redus .05
454 Darren Holmes .05
455 Pete O'Brien .05
456 Pat Combs .05
457 Hubie Brooks .05
458 Frank Tanana .05
459 Tom Kelly .05
460 Andre Dawson .15
461 Doug Jones .05
462 Rich Rodriguez .05
463 *Mike Simms* .05
464 Mike Jeffcoat .05
465 Barry Larkin .10
466 Stan Belinda .05
467 Lonnie Smith .05
468 Greg Harris .05
469 Jim Eisenreich .05
470 Pedro Guerrero .05
471 Jose DeJesus .05
472 *Rich Rowland* .10
473 Top Prospects-3rd Baseman *(Frank Bolick)*, *(Craig Paquette)*, *(Tom Redington)*, *(Paul Russo)* .15
474 *Mike Rossiter* (Draft Pick) .05
475 Robby Thompson .05
476 Randy Bush .05
477 Greg Hibbard .05
478 Dale Sveum .05
479 *Chito Martinez* .05
480 Scott Sanderson .05
481 Tino Martinez .05
482 Jimmy Key .05
483 Terry Shumpert .05
484 Mike Hartley .05
485 Chris Sabo .05
486 Bob Walk .05
487 John Cerutti .05
488 Scott Cooper .05
489 Bobby Cox .05
490 Julio Franco .05
491 Jeff Brantley .05
492 Mike Devereaux .05
493 Jose Offerman .05
494 Gary Thurman .05
495 Carney Lansford .05
496 Joe Grahe .05
497 *Andy Ashby* .15
498 Gerald Perry .05
499 Dave Otto .05
500 Vince Coleman .05
501 *Rob Mallicoat* .05
502 Greg Briley .05
503 Pascual Perez .05
504 *Aaron Sele* (Draft Pick) .40
505 Bobby Thigpen .05
506 Todd Benzinger .05
507 Candy Maldonado .05
508 Bill Gullickson .05
509 Doug Dascenzo .05
510 Frank Viola .05
511 Kenny Rogers .05
512 Mike Heath .05
513 Kevin Bass .05
514 *Kim Batiste* .05
515 Delino DeShields .05
516 *Ed Sprague* .05
517 Jim Gott .05
518 *Jose Melendez* .05
519 Hal McRae .05
520 Jeff Bagwell .40
521 Joe Hesketh .05
522 Milt Cuyler .05
523 Shawn Hillegas .05
524 Don Slaught .05
525 Randy Johnson .30
526 *Doug Piatt* .05
527 Checklist 4 .05
528 *Steve Foster* .05
529 Joe Girardi .05
530 Jim Abbott .05
531 Larry Walker .25
532 Mike Huff .05
533 Mackey Sasser .05
534 *Benji Gil* (Draft Pick) .20
535 Dave Stieb .05
536 Willie Wilson .05
537 *Mark Leiter* .05
538 Jose Uribe .05
539 Thomas Howard .05
540 Ben McDonald .05
541 *Jose Tolentino* .05
542 *Keith Mitchell* .05
543 Jerome Walton .05
544 *Cliff Brantley* .05
545 Andy Van Slyke .05
546 Paul Sorrento .05
547 Herm Winningham .05
548 Mark Guthrie .05
549 Joe Torre .05
550 Darryl Strawberry .05
551 Top Prospects-Shortstops (Manny Alexander, Alex Arias, Wil Cordero, Chipper Jones) .50
552 Dave Gallagher .05
553 Edgar Martinez .05
554 Donald Harris .05
555 Frank Thomas .65
556 Storm Davis .05
557 Dickie Thon .05
558 Scott Garrelts .05
559 Steve Olin .05
560 Rickey Henderson .35
561 Jose Vizcaino .05
562 *Wade Taylor* .05
563 Pat Borders .05
564 *Jimmy Gonzalez* (Draft Pick) .10
565 Lee Smith .05
566 Bill Sampen .05
567 Dean Palmer .05
568 Bryan Harvey .05
569 Tony Pena .05
570 Lou Whitaker .05
571 Randy Tomlin .05
572 Greg Vaughn .05
573 Kelly Downs .05
574 Steve Avery .05
575 Kirby Puckett .50
576 *Heathcliff Slocumb* .05
577 Kevin Seitzer .05
578 Lee Guetterman .05
579 Johnny Oates .05
580 Greg Maddux .50
581 Stan Javier .05
582 Vicente Palacios .05
583 Mel Rojas .05
584 *Wayne Rosenthal* .05
585 Lenny Webster .05
586 Rod Nichols .05
587 Mickey Morandini .05
588 Russ Swan .05
589 Mariano Duncan .05
590 Howard Johnson .05
591 Top Prospects-Outfielders *(Jacob Brumfield)*, *(Jeremy Burnitz)*, *(Alan Cockrell*, D.J. Dozier) .25
592 *Denny Neagle* .10
593 Steve Decker .05
594 *Brian Barber* (Draft Pick) .10
595 Bruce Hurst .05
596 Kent Mercker .05
597 *Mike Magnante* .05
598 Jody Reed .05
599 Steve Searcy .05
600 Paul Molitor .30
601 Dave Smith .05
602 Mike Fetters .05
603 *Luis Mercedes* .10
604 Chris Gwynn .05
605 Scott Erickson .05
606 Brook Jacoby .05
607 Todd Stottlemyre .05
608 Scott Bradley .05
609 Mike Hargrove .05
610 Eric Davis .05
611 *Brian Hunter* .05
612 Pat Kelly .05
613 Pedro Munoz .05
614 Al Osuna .05
615 Matt Merullo .05
616 Larry Andersen .05
617 Junior Ortiz .05
618 Top Prospects-Outfielders *(Cesar Hernandez*, Steve Hosey, Dan Peltier), *(Jeff McNeely)* .10
619 Danny Jackson .05
620 George Brett .50
621 *Dan Gakeler* .05
622 Steve Buechele .05
623 Bob Tewksbury .05
624 *Shawn Estes* (Draft Pick) .25
625 Kevin McReynolds .05
626 *Chris Haney* .05
627 Mike Sharperson .05
628 Mark Williamson .05
629 Wally Joyner .05
630 Carlton Fisk .30
631 *Armando Reynoso* .10
632 Felix Fermin .05
633 Mitch Williams .05
634 Manuel Lee .05
635 Harold Baines .05
636 Greg Harris .05
637 Orlando Merced .05
638 Chris Bosio .05
639 *Wayne Housie* .05
640 Xavier Hernandez .05
641 *David Howard* .05
642 Tim Crews .05
643 Rick Cerone .05
644 Terry Leach .05
645 Deion Sanders .10
646 Craig Wilson .05
647 Marquis Grissom .05
648 Scott Fletcher .05
649 Norm Charlton .05
650 Jesse Barfield .05
651 *Joe Slusarski* .10
652 Bobby Rose .05
653 Dennis Lamp .05
654 *Allen Watson* (Draft Pick) .10
655 Brett Butler .05
656 Top Prospects-Outfielders *(Rudy Pemberton*, Henry Rodriguez), *(Lee Tinsley)*, *(Gerald Williams)* .25
657 Dave Johnson .05
658 Checklist 5 .05
659 Brian McRae .05
660 Fred McGriff .05
661 Bill Landrum .05
662 Juan Guzman .05
663 Greg Gagne .05
664 Ken Hill .05
665 *Dave Haas* .05
666 Tom Foley .05
667 *Roberto Hernandez* .10
668 Dwayne Henry .05
669 Jim Fregosi .05
670 Harold Reynolds .05
671 Mark Whiten .05
672 Eric Plunk .05
673 Todd Hundley .05
674 *Mo Sanford* .05
675 Bobby Witt .05
676 Top Prospects-Pitchers *(Pat Mahomes)*, *(Sam Militello*, Roger Salkeld), *(Turk Wendell)* .15
677 John Marzano .05
678 Joe Klink .05
679 Pete Incaviglia .05
680 Dale Murphy .15
681 Rene Gonzales .05
682 Andy Benes .05
683 Jim Poole .05
684 *Trever Miller* (Draft Pick) .10
685 *Scott Livingstone* .05
686 Rich DeLucia .05
687 *Harvey Pulliam* .05
688 Tim Belcher .05
689 Mark Lemke .05
690 John Franco .05
691 Walt Weiss .05
692 Scott Ruskin .05
693 Jeff King .05
694 Mike Gardiner .05
695 Gary Sheffield .20
696 Joe Boever .05
697 Mike Felder .05
698 John Habyan .05
699 Cito Gaston .05
700 Ruben Sierra .05
701 Scott Radinsky .05
702 Lee Stevens .05
703 *Mark Wohlers* .10
704 Curt Young .05
705 Dwight Evans .05
706 Rob Murphy .05
707 Gregg Jefferies .05
708 Tom Bolton .05
709 Chris James .05
710 Kevin Maas .05
711 *Ricky Bones* .10
712 Curt Wilkerson .05
713 Roger McDowell .05
714 *Calvin Reese* (Draft Pick) .20
715 Craig Biggio .10
716 *Kirk Dressendorfer* .10
717 Ken Dayley .05
718 B.J. Surhoff .05
719 Terry Mulholland .05
720 Kirk Gibson .05
721 Mike Pagliarulo .05
722 Walt Terrell .05
723 Jose Oquendo .05
724 Kevin Morton .05
725 Dwight Gooden .05
726 Kirt Manwaring .05
727 Chuck McElroy .05
728 Dave Burba .10
729 Art Howe .05
730 Ramon Martinez .05
731 Donnie Hill .05
732 Nelson Santovenia .05
733 Bob Melvin .05
734 *Scott Hatteberg* (Draft Pick) .10
735 Greg Swindell .05
736 Lance Johnson .05
737 Kevin Reimer .05
738 Dennis Eckersley .05
739 Rob Ducey .05
740 Ken Caminiti .05
741 Mark Gubicza .05
742 Billy Spiers .05
743 Darren Lewis .05
744 Chris Hammond .05
745 Dave Magadan .05
746 Bernard Gilkey .05
747 Willie Banks .05
748 Matt Nokes .05
749 Jerald Clark .05
750 Travis Fryman .05
751 Steve Wilson .05
752 Billy Ripken .05
753 Paul Assenmacher .05
754 Charlie Hayes .05
755 Alex Fernandez .05
756 Gary Pettis .05
757 Rob Dibble .05
758 Tim Naehring .05
759 Jeff Torborg .05
760 Ozzie Smith .50
761 Mike Fitzgerald .05
762 John Burkett .05
763 Kyle Abbott .05
764 *Tyler Green* (Draft Pick) .05
765 Pete Harnisch .05
766 Mark Davis .05
767 Kal Daniels .05
768 Jim Thome .05
769 Jack Howell .05
770 Sid Bream .05
771 *Arthur Rhodes* .10
772 Garry Templeton .05
773 Hal Morris .05
774 Bud Black .05
775 Ivan Calderon .05
776 *Doug Henry* .05
777 John Olerud .05
778 Tim Leary .05
779 Jay Bell .05
780 Eddie Murray .30
781 Paul Abbott .05
782 Phil Plantier .05
783 Joe Magrane .05
784 Ken Patterson .05
785 Albert Belle .20
786 Royce Clayton .05
787 Checklist 6 .05
788 Mike Stanton .05
789 Bobby Valentine .05
790 Joe Carter .05
791 Danny Cox .05
792 Dave Winfield .40

1992 Topps Gold

Topps Gold cards share a checklist and format with the regular-issue 1992 Topps baseball issue except the color bars with the player's name and team printed beneath the photo have been replaced with gold foil. On back the light blue Topps logo printed beneath the stats has been replaced with a gold "ToppsGold" logo. Topps Gold cards were random inserts in all forms of packs. Additionally, factory sets of Gold cards were sold which included an autographed card of Yankees #1 draft pick Brien Taylor, and which had the checklist cards replaced with player cards. Several errors connected with the gold name/team strips are noted; no corrected versions were issued.

		MT
Unopened Factory Set (793):		55.00
Complete Set (792):		50.00
Common Player:		.20
	(Star cards valued at 4X corresponding cards in regular-issue 1992 Topps)	
86	Steve Finley (incorrect name, Mark Davidson, on gold strip)	.20
131	Terry Mathews	.20
264	Rod Beck	1.00
288	Andujar Cedeno (incorrect team, Yankees, listed on gold strip)	.60
366	Tony Perezchica	.20
465	Barry Larkin (incorrect team, Astros, listed on gold strip)	2.50
527	Terry McDaniel	.20
532	Mike Huff (incorrect team, Red Sox, listed on gold strip)	.20
658	John Ramos	.20
787	Brian Williams	.20
793	Brien Taylor (autographed edition of 12,000; factory sets only)	10.00

1992 Topps Gold Winners

A second gold-foil enhanced parallel version of the regular 1992 Topps issue was the Gold Winner cards awarded as prizes in a scratch-off contest found in each pack. Winner cards are identical to the Topps Gold cards except for the addition of a gold-foil "Winner" and star added above the team name. Due to a flaw in the design of the scratch-off game cards, it was easy to win every time and the Winner cards had to be produced in quantities far greater than originally planned, making them rather common. Six checklist cards from the regular issue were replaced with player cards in the Winners edition. Cards were sent to winners in 10-card cello packs.

		MT
Complete Set (792):		20.00
Common Player:		.10
Cello Pack (10):		1.00
	(Star cards valued at 2X corresponding cards in regular 1992 Topps issue)	
131	Terry Mathews	.15
264	Rod Beck	.25
366	Tony Perezchica	.15
465a	Barry Larkin (team name incorrect, Astros)	2.00
465b	Barry Larkin (team name correct, Reds)	.75
527	Terry McDaniel	.15
658	John Ramos	.15
787	Brian Williams	.15

1992 Topps Traded

Members of the United States baseball team are featured in this 132-card boxed set released by Topps. The cards are styled after the regular 1992 Topps cards and are numbered alphabetically. Several United States baseball players featured in this set were also featured in the 1991 Topps Traded set.

		MT
Unopened Retail Set:		75.00
Complete Hobby Set (132):		65.00
Common Player:		.05
1	*Willie Adams* (USA)	.10
2	Jeff Alkire (USA)	.10
3	Felipe Alou	.05
4	Moises Alou	.50
5	Ruben Amaro	.05
6	Jack Armstrong	.05
7	Scott Bankhead	.05
8	Tim Belcher	.05
9	George Bell	.05
10	Freddie Benavides	.05
11	Todd Benzinger	.05
12	Joe Boever	.05
13	Ricky Bones	.05
14	Bobby Bonilla	.05
15	Hubie Brooks	.05
16	Jerry Browne	.05
17	Jim Bullinger	.05
18	Dave Burba	.05
19	Kevin Campbell	.05
20	Tom Candiotti	.05
21	Mark Carreon	.05
22	Gary Carter	.15
23	Archi Cianfrocco	.05
24	Phil Clark	.05
25	*Chad Curtis*	.50
26	Eric Davis	.05
27	Tim Davis (USA)	.10
28	Gary DiSarcina	.05
29	Darren Dreifort (USA)	.10
30	Mariano Duncan	.05
31	Mike Fitzgerald	.05
32	John Flaherty	.05
33	Darrin Fletcher	.05
34	Scott Fletcher	.05
35	Ron Fraser (USA)	.05
36	Andres Galarraga	.05
37	Dave Gallagher	.05
38	Mike Gallego	.05
39	*Nomar Garciaparra* (USA)	55.00
40	Jason Giambi (USA)	2.00
41	Danny Gladden	.05
42	Rene Gonzales	.05
43	Jeff Granger (USA)	.10
44	Rick Greene (USA)	.10
45	Jeffrey Hammonds (USA)	.10
46	Charlie Hayes	.05
47	Von Hayes	.05
48	Rick Helling (USA)	.10
49	Butch Henry	.05
50	Carlos Hernandez	.05
51	Ken Hill	.05
52	Butch Hobson	.05
53	Vince Horsman	.05
54	Pete Incaviglia	.05
55	Gregg Jefferies	.05
56	Charles Johnson (USA)	.25
57	Doug Jones	.05
58	*Brian Jordan*	3.00
59	Wally Joyner	.05
60	*Daron Kirkreit* (USA)	.20
61	Bill Krueger	.05
62	Gene Lamont	.05
63	Jim Lefebvre	.05
64	*Danny Leon*	.05
65	Pat Listach	.05
66	Kenny Lofton	.10
67	Dave Martinez	.05
68	Derrick May	.05
69	Kirk McCaskill	.05
70	*Chad McConnell* (USA)	.10
71	Kevin McReynolds	.05
72	Rusty Meacham	.05
73	Keith Miller	.05
74	Kevin Mitchell	.05
75	*Jason Moler* (USA)	.10
76	Mike Morgan	.05
77	Jack Morris	.05
78	*Calvin Murray* (USA)	.25
79	Eddie Murray	.75
80	Randy Myers	.05
81	Denny Neagle	.05
82	Phil Nevin (USA)	.25
83	Dave Nilsson	.05
84	Junior Ortiz	.05
85	Donovan Osborne	.05
86	Bill Pecota	.05
87	Melido Perez	.05
88	Mike Perez	.05
89	Hipolito Pena	.05
90	Willie Randolph	.05
91	Darren Reed	.05
92	Bip Roberts	.05
93	Chris Roberts (USA)	.10
94	Steve Rodriguez (USA)	.10
95	Bruce Ruffin	.05
96	Scott Ruskin	.05
97	Bret Saberhagen	.05
98	Rey Sanchez	.05
99	Steve Sax	.05
100	Curt Schilling	.20
101	Dick Schofield	.05
102	Gary Scott	.05
103	Kevin Seitzer	.05
104	Frank Seminara	.05
105	Gary Sheffield	.50
106	John Smiley	.05
107	Cory Snyder	.05
108	Paul Sorrento	.05
109	Sammy Sosa	1.50
110	*Matt Stairs*	.25
111	Andy Stankiewicz	.05
112	Kurt Stillwell	.05
113	Rick Sutcliffe	.05
114	Bill Swift	.05
115	Jeff Tackett	.05
116	Danny Tartabull	.05
117	Eddie Taubensee	.05
118	Dickie Thon	.05
119	*Michael Tucker* (USA)	.50
120	Scooter Tucker	.05
121	*Marc Valdes* (USA)	.10
122	Julio Valera	.05
123	*Jason Varitek* (USA)	2.00
124	*Ron Villone* (USA)	.10
125	Frank Viola	.05
126	*B.J. Wallace* (USA)	.05
127	Dan Walters	.05
128	Craig Wilson (USA)	.15
129	Chris Wimmer (USA)	.10
130	Dave Winfield	1.00
131	Herm Winningham	.05
132	Checklist	.05

1992 Topps Traded Gold

A reported 6,000 sets of 1992 Topps Traded were produced in a gold edition, with gold-foil strips on front bearing the player and team names. The cards are in all other respects identical to the regular boxed Traded issue.

	MT
Complete Unopened Set (132):	200.00
Complete Set (132):	180.00
Common Player:	.25
Stars/Rookies:	4X
(See 1992 Topps Traded for checklist and base card values.)	

1993 Topps

Topps issued in a two-series format in 1993. Series I includes cards #1-

396; Series II comprises #397-825. The card fronts feature full-color photos enclosed by a white border. The player's name and team appear at the bottom. The backs feature an additional player photo and biographical information at the top. The bottom box includes statistics and player information. The cards are numbered in red in a yellow flag on the back. The factory set includes the regular 825 cards plus 10 gold parallels, three Black Gold inserts and nine 1994 preview cards.

	MT
Unopened Factory Set (847):	40.00
Complete Set (825):	25.00
Common Player:	.05
Golds:	4X
Series 1 Wax Pack (15):	1.00
Series 1 Wax Box (36):	32.50
Series 2 Wax Pack (15):	.75
Series 2 Wax Box (36):	25.00
Series 1 Rack Pack (45):	1.50
Series 1 Rack Box (24):	60.00
Series 2 Rack Pack (45):	1.00
Series 2 Rack Box (24):	50.00
Series 1 Vending Box (500):	9.00
Series 2 Vending Box (500):	7.00

1	Robin Yount	.35
2	Barry Bonds	.65
3	Ryne Sandberg	.40
4	Roger Clemens	.50
5	Tony Gwynn	.50
6	*Jeff Tackett*	.05
7	Pete Incaviglia	.05
8	Mark Wohlers	.05
9	Kent Hrbek	.05
10	Will Clark	.15
11	Eric Karros	.05
12	Lee Smith	.05
13	Esteban Beltre	.05
14	Greg Briley	.05
15	Marquis Grissom	.05
16	Dan Plesac	.05
17	Dave Hollins	.05
18	Terry Steinbach	.05
19	Ed Nunez	.05
20	Tim Salmon	.25
21	Luis Salazar	.05
22	Jim Eisenreich	.05
23	Todd Stottlemyre	.05
24	Tim Naehring	.05
25	John Franco	.05
26	Skeeter Barnes	.05
27	*Carlos Garcia*	.05
28	Joe Orsulak	.05
29	Dwayne Henry	.05
30	Fred McGriff	.05
31	Derek Lilliquist	.05
32	Don Mattingly	.65
33	B.J. Wallace (1992 Draft Pick)	.05
34	Juan Gonzalez	.45
35	John Smoltz	.10
36	Scott Servais	.05
37	Lenny Webster	.05
38	Chris James	.05
39	Roger McDowell	.05
40	Ozzie Smith	.50
41	Alex Fernandez	.05
42	Spike Owen	.05
43	Ruben Amaro	.05
44	Kevin Seitzer	.05
45	Dave Fleming	.05
46	*Eric Fox*	.05
47	Bob Scanlan	.05
48	Bert Blyleven	.05
49	Brian McRae	.05
50	Roberto Alomar	.30
51	Mo Vaughn	.30
52	Bobby Bonilla	.05
53	Frank Tanana	.05
54	Mike LaValliere	.05
55	Mark McLemore	.05
56	*Chad Mottola* (1992 Draft Pick)	.15
57	Norm Charlton	.05
58	Jose Melendez	.05
59	Carlos Martinez	.05
60	Roberto Kelly	.05
61	Gene Larkin	.05
62	Rafael Belliard	.05
63	Al Osuna	.05
64	Scott Chiamparino	.05
65	Brett Butler	.05
66	John Burkett	.05
67	Felix Jose	.05
68	Omar Vizquel	.05
69	John Vander Wal	.05
70	Roberto Hernandez	.05
71	Ricky Bones	.05
72	*Jeff Grotewold*	.05
73	Mike Moore	.05
74	Steve Buechele	.05
75	Juan Guzman	.05
76	Kevin Appier	.05
77	Junior Felix	.05
78	Greg Harris	.05
79	Dick Schofield	.05
80	Cecil Fielder	.05
81	Lloyd McClendon	.05
82	David Segui	.05
83	Reggie Sanders	.05
84	Kurt Stillwell	.05
85	Sandy Alomar	.05
86	John Habyan	.05
87	Kevin Reimer	.05
88	Mike Stanton	.05
89	Eric Anthony	.05
90	Scott Erickson	.05
91	Craig Colbert	.05
92	Tom Pagnozzi	.05
93	*Pedro Astacio*	.25
94	Lance Johnson	.05
95	Larry Walker	.30
96	Russ Swan	.05
97	Scott Fletcher	.05
98	*Derek Jeter* (1992 Draft Pick)	10.00
99	*Mike Williams*	.05
100	Mark McGwire	1.50
101	*Jim Bullinger*	.05
102	Brian Hunter	.05
103	Jody Reed	.05
104	*Mike Butcher*	.05
105	Gregg Jefferies	.05
106	Howard Johnson	.05
107	*John Kiely*	.05
108	Jose Lind	.05
109	Sam Horn	.05
110	Barry Larkin	.10
111	Bruce Hurst	.05
112	Brian Barnes	.05
113	Thomas Howard	.05
114	Mel Hall	.05
115	Robby Thompson	.05
116	Mark Lemke	.05
117	Eddie Taubensee	.05
118	David Hulse	.05
119	Pedro Munoz	.05
120	Ramon Martinez	.05
121	Todd Worrell	.05
122	Joey Cora	.05
123	Moises Alou	.20
124	Franklin Stubbs	.05
125	Pete O'Brien	.05
126	*Bob Aryault*	.05
127	Carney Lansford	.05
128	Kal Daniels	.05
129	Joe Grahe	.05
130	Jeff Montgomery	.05
131	Dave Winfield	.35
132	*Preston Wilson* (1992 Draft Pick)	1.00
133	Steve Wilson	.05
134	Lee Guetterman	.05
135	Mickey Tettleton	.05
136	Jeff King	.05
137	Alan Mills	.05
138	Joe Oliver	.05
139	Gary Gaetti	.05
140	Gary Sheffield	.20
141	Dennis Cook	.05
142	Charlie Hayes	.05
143	Jeff Huson	.05
144	Kent Mercker	.05
145	*Eric Young*	.25
146	Scott Leius	.05
147	Bryan Hickerson	.05
148	Steve Finley	.05
149	Rheal Cormier	.05
150	Frank Thomas	.65
151	*Archi Cianfrocco*	.05
152	Rich DeLucia	.05
153	Greg Vaughn	.05
154	Wes Chamberlain	.05
155	Dennis Eckersley	.05
156	Sammy Sosa	.65
157	Gary DiSarcina	.05
158	*Kevin Koslofski*	.05
159	*Doug Linton*	.05
160	Lou Whitaker	.05
161	Chad McDonnell (1992 Draft Pick)	.05
162	Joe Hesketh	.05
163	*Tim Wakefield*	.10
164	Leo Gomez	.05
165	Jose Rijo	.05
166	*Tim Scott*	.05
167	Steve Olin	.05
168	Kevin Maas	.05
169	Kenny Rogers	.05
170	Dave Justice	.25
171	Doug Jones	.05
172	*Jeff Reboulet*	.10
173	Andres Galarraga	.05
174	Randy Velarde	.05
175	Kirk McCaskill	.05
176	Darren Lewis	.05
177	Lenny Harris	.05
178	Jeff Fassero	.05
179	Ken Griffey, Jr.	1.00
180	Darren Daulton	.05
181	John Jaha	.05
182	Ron Darling	.05
183	Greg Maddux	.50
184	*Damion Easley*	.10
185	Jack Morris	.05
186	Mike Magnante	.05
187	John Dopson	.05
188	Sid Fernandez	.05
189	Tony Phillips	.05
190	Doug Drabek	.05
191	*Sean Lowe* (1992 Draft Pick)	.10
192	Bob Milacki	.05
193	*Steve Foster*	.05
194	Jerald Clark	.05
195	Pete Harnisch	.05
196	Pat Kelly	.05
197	Jeff Frye	.05
198	Alejandro Pena	.05
199	Junior Ortiz	.05
200	Kirby Puckett	.50
201	Jose Uribe	.05
202	Mike Scioscia	.05
203	Bernard Gilkey	.05
204	Dan Pasqua	.05
205	Gary Carter	.15
206	Henry Cotto	.05
207	Paul Molitor	.40
208	Mike Hartley	.05
209	Jeff Parrett	.05
210	Mark Langston	.05
211	Doug Dascenzo	.05
212	Rick Reed	.05
213	Candy Maldonado	.05
214	Danny Darwin	.05
215	*Pat Howell*	.05
216	Mark Leiter	.05
217	Kevin Mitchell	.05
218	Ben McDonald	.05
219	Bip Roberts	.05
220	Benny Santiago	.05
221	Carlos Baerga	.05
222	Bernie Williams	.30
223	*Roger Pavlik*	.05
224	Sid Bream	.05
225	Matt Williams	.15
226	Willie Banks	.05
227	Jeff Bagwell	.45
228	Tom Goodwin	.05
229	Mike Perez	.05
230	Carlton Fisk	.30
231	John Wetteland	.05
232	Tino Martinez	.05
233	*Rick Greene* (1992 Draft Pick)	.05
234	Tim McIntosh	.05
235	Mitch Williams	.05
236	*Kevin Campbell*	.05
237	Jose Vizcaino	.05
238	Chris Donnels	.05
239	Mike Boddicker	.05
240	John Olerud	.05
241	Mike Gardiner	.05
242	Charlie O'Brien	.05
243	Rob Deer	.05
244	Denny Neagle	.05
245	Chris Sabo	.05
246	Gregg Olson	.05
247	Frank Seminara	.05
248	Scott Scudder	.05
249	Tim Burke	.05
250	Chuck Knoblauch	.05
251	Mike Bielecki	.05
252	Xavier Hernandez	.05
253	Jose Guzman	.05
254	Cory Snyder	.05
255	Orel Hershiser	.05
256	Wil Cordero	.05
257	Luis Alicea	.05
258	Mike Schooler	.05
259	Craig Grebeck	.05
260	Duane Ward	.05
261	Bill Wegman	.05
262	Mickey Morandini	.05
263	*Vince Horsman*	.05
264	Paul Sorrento	.05
265	Andre Dawson	.15
266	Rene Gonzales	.05
267	Keith Miller	.05
268	Derek Bell	.05
269	*Todd Steverson* (1992 Draft Pick)	.05
270	Frank Viola	.05
271	Wally Whitehurst	.05
272	*Kurt Knudsen*	.05
273	*Dan Walters*	.05
274	Rick Sutcliffe	.05
275	Andy Van Slyke	.05
276	Paul O'Neill	.05
277	Mark Whiten	.05
278	Chris Nabholz	.05
279	Todd Burns	.05
280	Tom Glavine	.10
281	*Butch Henry*	.05
282	Shane Mack	.05
283	Mike Jackson	.05
284	Henry Rodriguez	.05
285	Bob Tewksbury	.05
286	Ron Karkovice	.05
287	Mike Gallego	.05
288	Dave Cochrane	.05
289	Jesse Orosco	.05
290	Dave Stewart	.05
291	Tommy Greene	.05
292	Rey Sanchez	.05
293	Rob Ducey	.05
294	Brent Mayne	.05
295	Dave Stieb	.05
296	Luis Rivera	.05
297	Jeff Innis	.05
298	Scott Livingstone	.05
299	Bob Patterson	.05
300	Cal Ripken, Jr.	1.50
301	Cesar Hernandez	.05
302	Randy Myers	.05
303	Brook Jacoby	.05
304	Melido Perez	.05
305	Rafael Palmeiro	.20
306	Damon Berryhill	.05
307	*Dan Serafini* (1992 Draft Pick)	.10
308	Darryl Kile	.05
309	*J.T. Bruett*	.05
310	Dave Righetti	.05
311	Jay Howell	.05
312	Geronimo Pena	.05
313	Greg Hibbard	.05
314	Mark Gardner	.05
315	Edgar Martinez	.05
316	Dave Nilsson	.05
317	Kyle Abbott	.05
318	Willie Wilson	.05
319	Paul Assenmacher	.05
320	*Tim Fortugno*	.05
321	Rusty Meacham	.05
322	Pat Borders	.05
323	Mike Greenwell	.05
324	Willie Randolph	.05
325	Bill Gullickson	.05
326	Gary Varsho	.05
327	Tim Hulett	.05
328	Scott Ruskin	.05
329	Mike Maddux	.05
330	Danny Tartabull	.05
331	Kenny Lofton	.05
332	Geno Petralli	.05
333	Otis Nixon	.05

334 *Jason Kendall* (1992 Draft Pick) 1.50
335 Mark Portugal .05
336 Mike Pagliarulo .05
337 Kirt Manwaring .05
338 Bob Ojeda .05
339 *Mark Clark* .05
340 John Kruk .05
341 Mel Rojas .05
342 Erik Hanson .05
343 Doug Henry .05
344 Jack McDowell .05
345 Harold Baines .05
346 Chuck McElroy .05
347 Luis Sojo .05
348 Andy Stankiewicz .05
349 *Hipolito Pichardo* .10
350 Joe Carter .05
351 Ellis Burks .05
352 Pete Schourek .05
353 *Buddy Groom* .10
354 Jay Bell .05
355 Brady Anderson .05
356 Freddie Benavides .05
357 Phil Stephenson .05
358 Kevin Wickander .05
359 Mike Stanley .05
360 Ivan Rodriguez .35
361 Scott Bankhead .05
362 Luis Gonzalez .25
363 John Smiley .05
364 Trevor Wilson .05
365 Tom Candiotti .05
366 Craig Wilson .05
367 Steve Sax .05
368 Delino Deshields .05
369 Jaime Navarro .05
370 Dave Valle .05
371 Mariano Duncan .05
372 Rod Nichols .05
373 Mike Morgan .05
374 Julio Valera .05
375 Wally Joyner .05
376 Tom Henke .05
377 Herm Winningham .05
378 Orlando Merced .05
379 Mike Munoz .05
380 Todd Hundley .05
381 Mike Flanagan .05
382 Tim Belcher .05
383 Jerry Browne .05
384 Mike Benjamin .05
385 Jim Leyritz .05
386 Ray Lankford .05
387 Devon White .05
388 Jeremy Hernandez .05
389 Brian Harper .05
390 Wade Boggs .35
391 Derrick May .05
392 Travis Fryman .05
393 Ron Gant .05
394 Checklist 1-132 .05
395 Checklist 133-264 .05
396 Checklist 265-396 .05
397 George Brett .50
398 Bobby Witt .05
399 Daryl Boston .05
400 Bo Jackson .10
401 Fred McGriff, Frank Thomas (All-Star) .35
402 Ryne Sandberg, Carlos Baerga (All-Star) .20
403 Gary Sheffield, Edgar Martinez (All-Star) .05
404 Barry Larkin, Travis Fryman (All-Star) .05
405 Andy Van Slyke, Ken Griffey, Jr. (All-Star) .40
406 Larry Walker, Kirby Puckett (All-Star) .25
407 Barry Bonds, Joe Carter (All-Star) .35
408 Darren Daulton, Brian Harper (All-Star) .05
409 Greg Maddux, Roger Clemens (All-Star) .25
410 Tom Glavine, Dave Fleming (All-Star) .05
411 Lee Smith, Dennis Eckersley (All-Star) .05
412 Jamie McAndrew .05
413 Pete Smith .05
414 Juan Guerrero .05
415 Todd Frohwirth .05
416 Randy Tomlin .05
417 B.J. Surhoff .05
418 Jim Gott .05
419 Mark Thompson (1992 Draft Pick) .05
420 Kevin Tapani .05
421 Curt Schilling .20
422 *J.T. Snow* .50
423 Top Prospects 1B (Ryan Klesko, Ivan Cruz, Bubba Smith, Larry Sutton) .10
424 John Valentin .05
425 Joe Girardi .05
426 *Nigel Wilson* .10
427 Bob MacDonald .05
428 Todd Zeile .05
429 Milt Cuyler .05
430 Eddie Murray .30
431 Rich Amaral .05
432 Pete Young .05
433 Rockies Future Stars (Roger Bailey, Tom Schmidt) .05
434 Jack Armstrong .05
435 Willie McGee .05
436 Greg Harris .05
437 Chris Hammond .05
438 *Ritchie Moody* (1992 Draft Pick) .05
439 Bryan Harvey .05
440 Ruben Sierra .05
441 Marlins Future Stars (Don Lemon, Todd Pridy) .05
442 Kevin McReynolds .05
443 Terry Leach .05
444 David Nied .05
445 Dale Murphy .15
446 Luis Mercedes .05
447 *Keith Shepherd* .05
448 Ken Caminiti .05
449 James Austin .05
450 Darryl Strawberry .05
451 Top Prospects 2B (Ramon Caraballo, Jon Shave, Brent Gates), (*Quinton McCracken*) .10
452 Bob Wickman .05
453 Victor Cole .05
454 *John Johnstone* .05
455 Chili Davis .05
456 Scott Taylor .05
457 Tracy Woodson .05
458 David Wells .10
459 *Derek Wallace* (1992 Draft Pick) .05
460 Randy Johnson .35
461 *Steve Reed* .05
462 Felix Fermin .05
463 Scott Aldred .05
464 Greg Colbrunn .05
465 Tony Fernandez .05
466 Mike Felder .05
467 Lee Stevens .05
468 Matt Whiteside .05
469 Dave Hansen .05
470 Rob Dibble .05
471 Dave Gallagher .05
472 Chris Gwynn .05
473 Dave Henderson .05
474 Ozzie Guillen .05
475 Jeff Reardon .05
476 Rockies Future Stars (Mark Voisard, Will Scalzitti) .05
477 Jimmy Jones .05
478 Greg Cadaret .05
479 Todd Pratt .05
480 Pat Listach .05
481 *Ryan Luzinski* (1992 Draft Pick) .05
482 Darren Reed .05
483 *Brian Griffiths* .05
484 John Wehner .05
485 Glenn Davis .05
486 *Eric Wedge* .05
487 Jesse Hollins .05
488 Manuel Lee .05
489 *Scott Fredrickson* .05
490 Omar Olivares .05
491 Shawn Hare .05
492 Tom Lampkin .05
493 Jeff Nelson .05
494 Top Prospects 3B (Kevin Young, Adell Davenport, Eduardo Perez, Lou Lucca) .05
495 Ken Hill .05
496 Reggie Jefferson .05
497 Marlins Future Stars (Matt Petersen, Willie Brown) .05
498 Bud Black .05
499 Chuck Crim .05
500 Jose Canseco .40
501 Major League Managers (Johnny Oates, Bobby Cox) .05
502 Major League Managers (Butch Hobson, Jim Lefebvre) .05
503 Major League Managers (Buck Rodgers, Tony Perez) .10
504 Major League Managers (Gene Lamont, Don Baylor) .05
505 Major League Managers (Mike Hargrove, Rene Lachemann) .05
506 Major League Managers (Sparky Anderson, Art Howe) .10
507 Major League Managers (Hal McRae, Tommy Lasorda) .15
508 Major League Manager (Phil Garner, Felipe Alou) .05
509 Major League Managers (Tom Kelly, Jeff Torborg) .05
510 Major League Managers (Buck Showalter, Jim Fregosi) .05
511 Major League Managers (Tony LaRussa, Jim Leyland) .10
512 Major League Managers (Lou Piniella, Joe Torre) .10
513 Major League Managers (Toby Harrah, Jim Riggleman) .05
514 Major League Managers (Cito Gaston, Dusty Baker) .10
515 Greg Swindell .05
516 Alex Arias .05
517 Bill Pecota .05
518 *Benji Grigsby* (1992 Draft Pick) .05
519 David Howard .05
520 Charlie Hough .05
521 Kevin Flora .05
522 Shane Reynolds .05
523 *Doug Bochtler* .05
524 Chris Hoiles .05
525 Scott Sanderson .05
526 Mike Sharperson .05
527 Mike Fetters .05
528 Paul Quantrill .05
529 Top Propsects SS (Dave Silvestri, Chipper Jones, Benji Gil, Jeff Patzke) .75
530 Sterling Hitchcock .05
531 Joe Millette .05
532 Tom Brunansky .05
533 Frank Castillo .05
534 Randy Knorr .05
535 Jose Oquendo .05
536 Dave Haas .05
537 Rockies Future Stars (Jason Hutchins, Ryan Turner) .05
538 Jimmy Baron (1992 Draft Pick) .05
539 Kerry Woodson .05
540 Ivan Calderon .05
541 Denis Boucher .05
542 Royce Clayton .05
543 Reggie Williams .05
544 Steve Decker .05
545 Dean Palmer .05
546 Hal Morris .05
547 *Ryan Thompson* .10
548 Lance Blankenship .05
549 Hensley Meulens .05
550 Scott Radinsky .05
551 *Eric Young* .25
552 Jeff Blauser .05
553 Andujar Cedeno .05
554 Arthur Rhodes .05
555 Terry Mulholland .05
556 Darryl Hamilton .05
557 Pedro Martinez .40
558 Marlins Future Stars (Ryan Whitman, Mark Skeels) .05
559 *Jamie Arnold* (1992 Draft Pick) .10
560 Zane Smith .05
561 Matt Nokes .05
562 Bob Zupcic .05
563 Shawn Boskie .05
564 Mike Timlin .05
565 Jerald Clark .05
566 Rod Brewer .05
567 Mark Carreon .05
568 Andy Benes .05
569 Shawn Barton .05
570 Tim Wallach .05
571 Dave Mlicki .05
572 Trevor Hoffman .05
573 John Patterson .05
574 DeShawn Warren (1992 Draft Pick) .05
575 Monty Fariss .05
576 Top Prospects OF (Darrell Sherman, Damon Buford, Cliff Floyd, Michael Moore) .10
577 Tim Costo .05
578 Dave Magadan .05
579 Rockies Future Stars (Neil Garret, Jason Bates) .05
580 Walt Weiss .05
581 Chris Haney .05
582 Shawn Abner .05
583 Marvin Freeman .05
584 Casey Candaele .05
585 Ricky Jordan .05
586 Jeff Tabaka .05
587 Manny Alexander .05
588 Mike Trombley .05
589 Carlos Hernandez .05
590 Cal Eldred .05
591 Alex Cole .05
592 Phil Plantier .05
593 Brett Merriman .05
594 Jerry Nielsen .05
595 Shawon Dunston .05
596 Jimmy Key .05
597 Gerald Perry .05
598 Rico Brogna .05
599 Marlins Future Stars (Clemente Nunez, Dan Robinson) .05
600 Bret Saberhagen .05
601 Craig Shipley .05
602 Henry Mercedes .05
603 Jim Thome .05
604 Rod Beck .05
605 Chuck Finley .05
606 J. Owens .05
607 Dan Smith .05
608 Bill Doran .05
609 Lance Parrish .05
610 Denny Martinez .05
611 Tom Gordon .05
612 Byron Mathews (1992 Draft Pick) .05
613 Joel Adamson .05
614 Brian Williams .05
615 Steve Avery .05
616 Top Prospects OF (Matt Mieske, Tracy Sanders, Midre Cummings, Ryan Freeburg) .10
617 Craig Lefferts .05
618 Tony Pena .05
619 Billy Spiers .05
620 Todd Benzinger .05
621 Rockies Future Stars (Mike Kotarski, Greg Boyd) .05
622 Ben Rivera .05
623 Al Martin .05
624 Sam Militello .05
625 Rick Aguilera .05
626 Danny Gladden .05
627 Andres Berumen .05
628 Kelly Gruber .05
629 Cris Carpenter .05
630 Mark Grace .20
631 Jeff Brantley .05

632 Chris Widger (1992 Draft Pick) .05
633 Russian Angels (Rodolf Razjigaev, Evgenyi Puchkov, Ilya Bogatyrev) .10
634 Mo Sanford .05
635 Albert Belle .20
636 Tim Teufel .05
637 Greg Myers .05
638 Brian Bohanon .05
639 Mike Bordick .05
640 Dwight Gooden .05
641 Marlins Future Stars (Pat Leahy, Gavin Baugh) .05
642 Milt Hill .05
643 Luis Aquino .05
644 Dante Bichette .05
645 Bobby Thigpen .05
646 Rich Scheid .05
647 Brian Sackinsky (1992 Draft Pick) .05
648 Ryan Hawblitzel .05
649 Tom Marsh .05
650 Terry Pendleton .05
651 *Rafael Bournigal* .10
652 Dave West .05
653 Steve Hosey .05
654 Gerald Williams .05
655 Scott Cooper .05
656 Gary Scott .05
657 Mike Harkey .05
658 Top Prospects OF (Jeromy Burnitz, Melvin Nieves, Rich Becker, Shon Walker) .25
659 Ed Sprague .05
660 Alan Trammell .05
661 Rockies Future Stars (Garvin Alston, Mike Case) .05
662 Donovan Osborne .05
663 Jeff Gardner .05
664 Calvin Jones .05
665 Darrin Fletcher .05
666 Glenallen Hill .05
667 Jim Rosenbohm (1992 Draft Pick) .05
668 Scott Lewis .05
669 Kip Yaughn .05
670 Julio Franco .05
671 Dave Martinez .05
672 Kevin Bass .05
673 Todd Van Poppel .05
674 Mark Gubicza .05
675 Tim Raines .05
676 Rudy Seanez .05
677 Charlie Leibrandt .05
678 Randy Milligan .05
679 Kim Batiste .05
680 Craig Biggio .10
681 Darren Holmes .05
682 John Candelaria .05
683 Marlins Future Stars (Jerry Stafford, Eddie Christian) .05
684 Pat Mahomes .05
685 Bob Walk .05
686 Russ Springer .05
687 Tony Sheffield (1992 Draft Picks) .05
688 Dwight Smith .05
689 Eddie Zosky .05
690 Bien Figueroa .05
691 Jim Tatum .05
692 Chad Kreuter .05
693 Rich Rodriguez .05
694 Shane Turner .05
695 Kent Bottenfield .05
696 Jose Mesa .05
697 *Darrell Whitmore* .05
698 Ted Wood .05
699 Chad Curtis .05
700 Nolan Ryan 1.50
701 Top Prospects C (Mike Piazza, Carlos Delgado, Brook Fordyce, Donnie Leshnock) .75
702 *Tim Pugh* .05
703 Jeff Kent .05
704 Rockies Future Stars (Jon Goodrich, Danny Figueroa) .05
705 Bob Welch .05
706 Sherard Clinkscales (1992 Draft Pick) .05
707 Donn Pall .05
708 Greg Olson .05
709 Jeff Juden .05
710 Mike Mussina .35
711 Scott Chiamparino .05
712 Stan Javier .05
713 John Doherty .05
714 Kevin Gross .05
715 Greg Gagne .05
716 Steve Cooke .05
717 Steve Farr .05
718 Jay Buhner .05
719 Butch Henry .05
720 David Cone .05
721 Rick Wilkins .05
722 Chuck Carr .05
723 *Kenny Felder* (1992 Draft Pick) .05
724 Guillermo Velasquez .05
725 Billy Hatcher .05
726 Marlins Future Stars (Mike Veneziale, Ken Kendrena) .05
727 Jonathan Hurst .05
728 Steve Frey .05
729 Mark Leonard .05
730 Charles Nagy .05
731 Donald Harris .05
732 Travis Buckley .05
733 Tom Browning .05
734 Anthony Young .05
735 Steve Shifflett .05
736 Jeff Russell .05
737 Wilson Alvarez .05
738 Lance Painter .05
739 Dave Weathers .05
740 Len Dykstra .05
741 Mike Devereaux .05
742 Top Prospects SP (Rene Arocha, Alan Embree), *(Tim Crabtree*, Brien Taylor) .10
743 Dave Landaker (1992 Draft Pick) .05
744 Chris George .05
745 Eric Davis .05
746 Rockies Future Stars *(Mark Strittmatter*, LaMarr Rogers) .05
747 Carl Willis .05
748 Stan Belinda .05
749 Scott Kamieniecki .05
750 Rickey Henderson .35
751 Eric Hillman .05
752 Pat Hentgen .05
753 Jim Corsi .05
754 Brian Jordan .05
755 Bill Swift .05
756 Mike Henneman .05
757 Harold Reynolds .05
758 Sean Berry .05
759 Charlie Hayes .05
760 Luis Polonia .05
761 Darrin Jackson .05
762 Mark Lewis .05
763 Rob Maurer .05
764 Willie Greene .05
765 Vince Coleman .05
766 Todd Revenig .05
767 Rich Ireland (1992 Draft Pick) .05
768 Mike MacFarlane .05
769 Francisco Cabrera .05
770 Robin Ventura .05
771 Kevin Ritz .05
772 Chito Martinez .05
773 Cliff Brantley .05
774 Curtis Leskanic .05
775 Chris Bosio .05
776 Jose Offerman .05
777 Mark Guthrie .05
778 Don Slaught .05
779 Rich Monteleone .05
780 Jim Abbott .05
781 Jack Clark .05
782 Marlins Future Stars (Rafael Mendoza, Dan Roman) .05
783 Heathcliff Slocumb .05
784 Jeff Branson .05
785 Kevin Brown .05
786 Top Prospects RP (Mike Christopher, Ken Ryan, Aaron Taylor, Gus Gandarillas) .05
787 Mike Matthews (1992 Draft Pick) .05
788 Mackey Sasser .05
789 Jeff Conine .05
790 George Bell .05
791 Pat Rapp .05
792 Joe Boever .05
793 Jim Poole .05
794 Andy Ashby .05
795 Deion Sanders .10
796 Scott Brosius .05
797 Brad Pennington (Coming Attraction) .05
798 Greg Blosser (Coming Attraction) .05
799 *Jim Edmonds* (Coming Attraction) 1.50
800 Shawn Jeter (Coming Attraction) .05
801 Jesse Levis (Coming Attraction) .05
802 Phil Clark (Coming Attraction) .05
803 Ed Pierce (Coming Attraction) .05
804 *Jose Valentin* (Coming Attraction) .05
805 Terry Jorgensen (Coming Attraction) .05
806 Mark Hutton (Coming Attraction) .05
807 Troy Neel (Coming Attraction) .05
808 Bret Boone (Coming Attraction) .15
809 Chris Colon (Coming Attraction) .05
810 *Domingo Martinez* (Coming Attraction) .05
811 Javier Lopez (Coming Attraction) .05
812 Matt Walbeck (Coming Attraction) .05
813 Dan Wilson (Coming Attraction) .05
814 Scooter Tucker (Coming Attraction) .05
815 *Billy Ashley* (Coming Attraction) .05
816 *Tim Laker* (Coming Attraction) .10
817 Bobby Jones (Coming Attraction) .05
818 Brad Brink (Coming Attraction) .05
819 William Pennyfeather (Coming Attraction) .05
820 Stan Royer (Coming Attraction) .05
821 Doug Brocail (Coming Attraction) .05
822 Kevin Rogers (Coming Attraction) .05
823 Checklist 397-528 .05
824 Checklist 541-691 .05
825 Checklist 692-825 .05

1993 Topps Black Gold

Randomly inserted in regular 1993 Topps packs, as well as 10 per factory set, Black Gold cards are found in both single-player versions and "Winner" cards. The single-player cards feature an action photo set against a black background and highlighted at top and bottom with gold foil. Backs have another player photo at left, again on a black background. A career summary is printed in a blue box at right. A "Topps Black Gold" logo appears at top-left, and the player's name is printed in gold foil in an art deco device at top-right. The Winner cards picture tiny versions of the Black Gold player cards for which they could be redeemed by mail. Some, perhaps all, of the mail-in cards can also be found on which the miniature card pictures on front do not correspond to the players named on back. In addition, with each mail-in redemption set, a non-redeemable version of the Winner card was also sent.

		MT
Complete Set (44):		10.00
Common Player:		.25
Winner A (1-11):		.50
Winner B (12-22):		.50
Winner C (23-33):		.50
Winner D (34-44):		.50
Winner AB (1-22):		2.00
Winner CD (23-44):		2.00
Winner ABCD (1-44):		8.00
1	Barry Bonds	1.50
2	Will Clark	.25
3	Darren Daulton	.25
4	Andre Dawson	.25
5	Delino DeShields	.25
6	Tom Glavine	.25
7	Marquis Grissom	.25
8	Tony Gwynn	1.00
9	Eric Karros	.25
10	Ray Lankford	.25
11	Barry Larkin	.25
12	Greg Maddux	1.00
13	Fred McGriff	.25
14	Joe Oliver	.25
15	Terry Pendleton	.25
16	Bip Roberts	.25
17	Ryne Sandberg	.75
18	Gary Sheffield	.45
19	Lee Smith	.25
20	Ozzie Smith	1.00
21	Andy Van Slyke	.25
22	Larry Walker	.40
23	Roberto Alomar	.50
24	Brady Anderson	.25
25	Carlos Baerga	.25
26	Joe Carter	.25
27	Roger Clemens	1.00
28	Mike Devereaux	.25
29	Dennis Eckersley	.25
30	Cecil Fielder	.25
31	Travis Fryman	.25
32	Juan Gonzalez	.75
33	Ken Griffey Jr.	2.00
34	Brian Harper	.25
35	Pat Listach	.25
36	Kenny Lofton	.25
37	Edgar Martinez	.25
38	Jack McDowell	.25
39	Mark McGwire	2.50
40	Kirby Puckett	1.00
41	Mickey Tettleton	.25
42	Frank Thomas	1.50
43	Robin Ventura	.25
44	Dave Winfield	1.00

1993 Topps Traded

The 1993 Topps Traded baseball set features

many players in their new uniforms as a result of trades, free agent signings and rookie call-ups. The set also features 35 expansion players from the Colorado Rockies and Florida Marlins, as well as 22 Team USA members exclusive to Topps. The 132-card set is packed in a color deluxe printed box.

		MT
Complete Set (132):		35.00
Common Player:		.05
1	Barry Bonds	2.00
2	Rich Renteria	.05
3	Aaron Sele	.10
4	*Carlton Loewer* (USA)	.25
5	Erik Pappas	.05
6	*Greg McMichael*	.05
7	Freddie Benavides	.05
8	Kirk Gibson	.05
9	Tony Fernandez	.05
10	*Jay Gainer* (USA)	.10
11	Orestes Destrade	.05
12	*A.J. Hinch* (USA)	1.00
13	Bobby Munoz	.05
14	Tom Henke	.05
15	Rob Butler	.05
16	Gary Wayne	.05
17	David McCarty	.05
18	Walt Weiss	.05
19	*Todd Helton* (USA)	25.00
20	Mark Whiten	.05
21	Ricky Gutierrez	.05
22	*Dustin Hermanson* (USA)	1.00
23	*Sherman Obando*	.05
24	Mike Piazza	2.00
25	Jeff Russell	.05
26	Jason Bere	.05
27	*Jack Voight*	.05
28	Chris Bosio	.05
29	Phil Hiatt	.05
30	*Matt Beaumont* (USA)	.10
31	Andres Galarraga	.05
32	Greg Swindell	.05
33	Vinny Castilla	.05
34	*Pat Clougherty* (USA)	.10
35	Greg Briley	.05
36	Dallas Green, Davey Johnson	.05
37	Tyler Green	.05
38	Craig Paquette	.05
39	Danny Sheaffer	.05
40	Jim Converse	.05
41	Terry Harvey	.05
42	Phil Plantier	.05
43	*Doug Saunders*	.05
44	Benny Santiago	.05
45	*Dante Powell* (USA)	.25
46	Jeff Parrett	.05
47	Wade Boggs	.75
48	Paul Molitor	.75
49	Turk Wendell	.05
50	David Wells	.10
51	Gary Sheffield	.25
52	Kevin Young	.05
53	Nelson Liriano	.05
54	Greg Maddux	1.00
55	Derek Bell	.05
56	*Matt Turner*	.05
57	*Charlie Nelson* (USA)	.10
58	Mike Hampton	.05
59	*Troy O'Leary*	.25
60	Benji Gil	.05
61	*Mitch Lyden*	.05
62	J.T. Snow	.05
63	Damon Buford	.05
64	Gene Harris	.05
65	Randy Myers	.05
66	Felix Jose	.05
67	*Todd Dunn* (USA)	.10
68	Jimmy Key	.05
69	Pedro Castellano	.05
70	*Mark Merila* (USA)	.10
71	Rich Rodriguez	.05
72	Matt Mieske	.05
73	Pete Incaviglia	.05
74	Carl Everett	.25
75	Jim Abbott	.05
76	Luis Aquino	.05
77	*Rene Arocha*	.10
78	*Jon Shave*	.10
79	*Todd Walker* (USA)	1.00
80	Jack Armstrong	.05
81	Jeff Richardson	.05
82	Blas Minor	.05
83	Dave Winfield	.75
84	Paul O'Neill	.05
85	*Steve Reich* (USA)	.10
86	Chris Hammond	.05
87	*Hilly Hathaway*	.10
88	Fred McGriff	.05
89	*Dave Telgheder*	.10
90	*Richie Lewis*	.10
91	Brent Gates	.05
92	Andre Dawson	.15
93	*Andy Barkett* (USA)	.10
94	Doug Drabek	.05
95	Joe Klink	.05
96	Willie Blair	.05
97	*Danny Graves* (USA)	.25
98	Pat Meares	.05
99	Mike Lansing	.10
100	*Marcos Armas*	.05
101	*Darren Grass* (USA)	.10
102	Chris Jones	.05
103	*Ken Ryan*	.05
104	Ellis Burks	.05
105	Bobby Kelly	.05
106	Dave Magadan	.05
107	*Paul Wilson* (USA)	.25
108	Rob Natal	.05
109	Paul Wagner	.05
110	Jeromy Burnitz	.05
111	Monty Fariss	.05
112	Kevin Mitchell	.05
113	*Scott Pose*	.05
114	Dave Stewart	.05
115	*Russ Johnson* (USA)	.25
116	Armando Reynoso	.05
117	Geronimo Berroa	.05
118	*Woody Williams*	.25
119	*Tim Bogar*	.05
120	*Bob Scafa* (USA)	.10
121	Henry Cotto	.05
122	Gregg Jefferies	.05
123	Norm Charlton	.05
124	*Bret Wagner* (USA)	.10
125	David Cone	.05
126	Daryl Boston	.05
127	Tim Wallach	.05
128	*Mike Martin* (USA)	.10
129	*John Cummings*	.05
130	Ryan Bowen	.05
131	*John Powell* (USA)	.10
132	Checklist	.05

1994 Topps

Once again released in two series of 396 cards each, Topps' basic issue for 1994 offers a standard mix of regular player cards, Future Stars, multi-player rookie cards and double-header All-Star cards. On most cards the player photo on front is framed in a home-plate shaped design. The player's name appears in script beneath the photo and a team color-coded strip at bottom carries the team name and position designation. On back is a player photo, a red box at top with biographical details and a marbled panel which carries the stats and a career highlight. Cards are UV coated on each side. Inserts include a gold-foil enhanced parallel card in every pack, plus random Black Gold cards. Factory sets include the 792 base cards plus 10 gold parallels, three Black Gold inserts, three Superstar Sampler cards and nine 1995 preview cards.

		MT
Unopened Factory Set (817):		30.00
Complete Set (792):		20.00
Common Player:		.05
Golds:		2X
Series 1 or 2 Wax Pac (12):		.75
Series 1 Wax Box (36):		22.50
Series 2 Wax Box (36):		15.00
1	Mike Piazza (All-Star Rookie)	1.00
2	Bernie Williams	.30
3	Kevin Rogers	.05
4	Paul Carey (Future Star)	.05
5	Ozzie Guillen	.05
6	Derrick May	.05
7	Jose Mesa	.05
8	Todd Hundley	.05
9	Chris Haney	.05
10	John Olerud	.05
11	Andujar Cedeno	.05
12	John Smiley	.05
13	Phil Plantier	.05
14	Willie Banks	.05
15	Jay Bell	.05
16	Doug Henry	.05
17	Lance Blankenship	.05
18	Greg Harris	.05
19	Scott Livingstone	.05
20	Bryan Harvey	.05
21	Wil Cordero (All-Star Rookie)	.05
22	Roger Pavlik	.05
23	Mark Lemke	.05
24	Jeff Nelson	.05
25	Todd Zeile	.05
26	Billy Hatcher	.05
27	Joe Magrane	.05
28	Tony Longmire (Future Star)	.05
29	Omar Daal	.05
30	Kirt Manwaring	.05
31	Melido Perez	.05
32	Tim Hulett	.05
33	Jeff Schwarz	.05
34	Nolan Ryan	1.50
35	Jose Guzman	.05
36	Felix Fermin	.05
37	Jeff Innis	.05
38	Brent Mayne	.05
39	*Huck Flener*	.05
40	Jeff Bagwell	.50
41	Kevin Wickander	.05
42	Ricky Gutierrez	.05
43	Pat Mahomes	.05
44	Jeff King	.05
45	Cal Eldred	.05
46	Craig Paquette	.05
47	Richie Lewis	.05
48	Tony Phillips	.05
49	Armando Reynoso	.05
50	Moises Alou	.20
51	Manuel Lee	.05
52	Otis Nixon	.05
53	Billy Ashley (Future Star)	.05
54	Mark Whiten	.05
55	Jeff Russell	.05
56	Chad Curtis	.05
57	Kevin Stocker	.05
58	Mike Jackson	.05
59	Matt Nokes	.05
60	Chris Bosio	.05
61	Damon Buford	.05
62	Tim Belcher	.05
63	Glenallen Hill	.05
64	Bill Wertz	.05
65	Eddie Murray	.35
66	Tom Gordon	.05
67	Alex Gonzalez (Future Star)	.15
68	Eddie Taubensee	.05
69	Jacob Brumfield	.05
70	Andy Benes	.05
71	Rich Becker (Future Star)	.05
72	Steve Cooke (All-Star Rookie)	.05
73	Billy Spiers	.05
74	Scott Brosius	.05
75	Alan Trammell	.05
76	Luis Aquino	.05
77	Jerald Clark	.05
78	Mel Rojas	.05
79	OF Prospects (Billy Masse, Stanton Cameron, Tim Clark, Craig McClure)	.05
80	Jose Canseco	.40
81	Greg McMichael (All-Star Rookie)	.05
82	Brian Turang	.05
83	Tom Urban	.05
84	Garret Anderson (Future Star)	.10
85	Tony Pena	.05
86	Ricky Jordan	.05
87	Jim Gott	.05
88	Pat Kelly	.05
89	Bud Black	.05
90	Robin Ventura	.05
91	Rick Sutcliffe	.05
92	Jose Bautista	.05
93	Bob Ojeda	.05
94	Phil Hiatt	.05
95	Tim Pugh	.05
96	Randy Knorr	.05
97	Todd Jones (Future Star)	.05
98	Ryan Thompson	.05
99	Tim Mauser	.05
100	Kirby Puckett	.65
101	Mark Dewey	.05
102	B.J. Surhoff	.05
103	Sterling Hitchcock	.05
104	Alex Arias	.05
105	David Wells	.10
106	Daryl Boston	.05
107	Mike Stanton	.05
108	Gary Redus	.05
109a	Delino DeShields (red "Expos, 2B")	.15
109b	Delino DeShields (yellow "Expos, 2B")	.05
110	Lee Smith	.05
111	Greg Litton	.05
112	Frank Rodriguez (Future Star)	.05
113	Russ Springer	.05
114	Mitch Williams	.05
115	Eric Karros	.05
116	Jeff Brantley	.05
117	Jack Voight	.05
118	Jason Bere	.05
119	Kevin Roberson	.05
120	Jimmy Key	.05
121	Reggie Jefferson	.05

122 Jeremy Burnitz .05
123 Billy Brewer (Future Star) .05
124 Willie Canate .05
125 Greg Swindell .05
126 Hal Morris .05
127 Brad Ausmus .05
128 George Tsamis .05
129 Denny Neagle .05
130 Pat Listach .05
131 Steve Karsay .05
132 Bret Barberie .05
133 Mark Leiter .05
134 Greg Colbrunn .05
135 David Nied .05
136 Dean Palmer .05
137 Steve Avery .05
138 Bill Haselman .05
139 Tripp Cromer (Future Star) .05
140 Frank Viola .05
141 Rene Gonzales .05
142 Curt Schilling .20
143 Tim Wallach .05
144 Bobby Munoz .05
145 Brady Anderson .05
146 Rod Beck .05
147 Mike LaValliere .05
148 Greg Hibbard .05
149 Kenny Lofton .05
150 Dwight Gooden .05
151 Greg Gagne .05
152 Ray McDavid (Future Star) .05
153 Chris Donnels .05
154 Dan Wilson .05
155 Todd Stottlemyre .05
156 David McCarty .05
157 Paul Wagner .05
158 SS Prospects (Orlando Miller, Brandon Wilson, Derek Jeter, Mike Neal) 1.50
159 Mike Fetters .05
160 Scott Lydy .05
161 Darrell Whitmore .05
162 Bob MacDonald .05
163 Vinny Castilla .05
164 Denis Boucher .05
165 Ivan Rodriguez .40
166 Ron Gant .05
167 Tim Davis .05
168 Steve Dixon .05
169 Scott Fletcher .05
170 Terry Mulholland .05
171 Greg Myers .05
172 Brett Butler .05
173 Bob Wickman .05
174 Dave Martinez .05
175 Fernando Valenzuela .05
176 Craig Grebeck .05
177 Shawn Boskie .05
178 Albie Lopez .05
179 Butch Huskey (Future Star) .05
180 George Brett .65
181 Juan Guzman .05
182 Eric Anthony .05
183 Bob Dibble .05
184 Craig Shipley .05
185 Kevin Tapani .05
186 Marcus Moore .05
187 Graeme Lloyd .05
188 Mike Bordick .05
189 Chris Hammond .05
190 Cecil Fielder .05
191 Curtis Leskanic .05
192 Lou Frazier .05
193 Steve Dreyer .05
194 Javier Lopez (Future Star) .05
195 Edgar Martinez .05
196 Allen Watson .05
197 John Flaherty .05
198 Kurt Stillwell .05
199 Danny Jackson .05
200 Cal Ripken, Jr. 1.50
201 Mike Bell (Draft Pick) .05
202 *Alan Benes* (Draft Pick) .25
203 Matt Farner (Draft Pick) .05
204 *Jeff Granger* (Draft Pick) .05
205 *Brooks Kieschnick* (Draft Pick) .05
206 Jeremy Lee (Draft Pick) .05
207 *Charles Peterson* (Draft Pick) .05
208 Andy Rice (Draft Pick) .05
209 *Billy Wagner* (Draft Pick) .30
210 Kelly Wunsch (Draft Pick) .05
211 Tom Candiotti .05
212 Domingo Jean (Draft Pick) .05
213 John Burkett .05
214 George Bell .05
215 Dan Plesac .05
216 Manny Ramirez (Future Star) .75
217 Mike Maddux .05
218 Kevin McReynolds .05
219 Pat Borders .05
220 Doug Drabek .05
221 Larry Luebbers .05
222 Trevor Hoffman .05
223 Pat Meares .05
224 Danny Miceli (Future Star) .05
225 Greg Vaughn .05
226 Scott Hemond .05
227 Pat Rapp .05
228 Kirk Gibson .05
229 Lance Painter .05
230 Larry Walker .30
231 Benji Gil (Future Star) .05
232 Mark Wohlers .05
233 Rich Amaral .05
234 Erik Pappas .05
235 Scott Cooper .05
236 Mike Butcher .05
237 OF Prospects (*Curtis Pride*, Shawn Green, Mark Sweeney, Eddie Davis) .50
238 Kim Batiste .05
239 Paul Assenmacher .05
240 Will Clark .15
241 Jose Offerman .05
242 Todd Frohwirth .05
243 Tim Raines .05
244 Rick Wilkins .05
245 Bret Saberhagen .05
246 Thomas Howard .05
247 Stan Belinda .05
248 Rickey Henderson .50
249 Brian Williams .05
250 Barry Larkin .10
251 Jose Valentin (Future Star) .05
252 Lenny Webster .05
253 Blas Minor .05
254 Tim Teufel .05
255 Bobby Witt .05
256 Walt Weiss .05
257 Chad Kreuter .05
258 Roberto Mejia .05
259 Cliff Floyd (Future Star) .15
260 Julio Franco .05
261 Rafael Belliard .05
262 Marc Newfield .05
263 Gerald Perry .05
264 Ken Ryan .05
265 Chili Davis .05
266 Dave West .05
267 Royce Clayton .05
268 Pedro Martinez .40
269 Mark Hutton .05
270 Frank Thomas .75
271 Brad Pennington .05
272 Mike Harkey .05
273 Sandy Alomar .05
274 Dave Gallagher .05
275 Wally Joyner .05
276 Ricky Trlicek .05
277 Al Osuna .05
278 Calvin Reese (Future Star) .15
279 Kevin Higgins .05
280 Rick Aguilera .05
281 Orlando Merced .05
282 Mike Mohler .05
283 John Jaha .05
284 Robb Nen .05
285 Travis Fryman .05
286 Mark Thompson (Future Star) .05
287 Mike Lansing (All-Star Rookie) .05
288 Craig Lefferts .05
289 Damon Berryhill .05
290 Randy Johnson .40
291 Jeff Reed .05
292 Danny Darwin .05
293 J.T. Snow (All-Star Rookie) .10
294 Tyler Green .05
295 Chris Hoiles .05
296 Roger McDowell .05
297 Spike Owen .05
298 Salomon Torres (Future Star) .05
299 Wilson Alvarez .05
300 Ryne Sandberg .40
301 Derek Lilliquist .05
302 Howard Johnson .05
303 Greg Cadaret .05
304 Pat Hentgen .05
305 Craig Biggio .10
306 Scott Service .05
307 Melvin Nieves .05
308 Mike Trombley .05
309 Carlos Garcia (All-Star Rookie) .05
310 Robin Yount .35
311 Marcos Armas .05
312 Rich Rodriguez .05
313 Justin Thompson (Future Star) .05
314 Danny Sheaffer .05
315 Ken Hill .05
316 P Propsects(*Chad Ogea*), (*Duff Brumley*), (*Terrell Wade*), (*Chris Michalak*) .10
317 Cris Carpenter .05
318 Jeff Blauser .05
319 Ted Power .05
320 Ozzie Smith .65
321 John Dopson .05
322 Chris Turner .05
323 Pete Incaviglia .05
324 Alan Mills .05
325 Jody Reed .05
326 Rich Monteleone .05
327 Mark Carreon .05
328 Donn Pall .05
329 Matt Walbeck (Future Star) .05
330 Charles Nagy .05
331 Jeff McKnight .05
332 Jose Lind .05
333 Mike Timlin .05
334 Doug Jones .05
335 Kevin Mitchell .05
336 Luis Lopez .05
337 Shane Mack .05
338 Randy Tomlin .05
339 Matt Mieske .05
340 Mark McGwire 1.50
341 Nigel Wilson (Future Star) .05
342 Danny Gladden .05
343 Mo Sanford .05
344 Sean Berry .05
345 Kevin Brown .15
346 Greg Olson .05
347 Dave Magadan .05
348 Rene Arocha .05
349 Carlos Quintana .05
350 Jim Abbott .05
351 Gary DiSarcina .05
352 Ben Rivera .05
353 Carlos Hernandez .05
354 Darren Lewis .05
355 Harold Reynolds .05
356 Scott Ruffcorn (Future Star) .05
357 Mark Gubicza .05
358 Paul Sorrento .05
359 Anthony Young .05
360 Mark Grace .20
361 Rob Butler .05
362 Kevin Bass .05
363 Eric Helfand (Future Star) .05
364 Derek Bell .05
365 Scott Erickson .05
366 Al Martin .05
367 Ricky Bones .05
368 Jeff Branson .05
369 3B Prospects (Luis Ortiz, David Bell, Jason Giambi), (*George Arias*) .40
370a Benny Santiago .05
370b Mark McLemore (originally checklisted as #379) .05
371 John Doherty .05
372 Joe Girardi .05
373 Tim Scott .05
374 Marvin Freeman .05
375 Deion Sanders .10
376 Roger Salkeld .05
377 Bernard Gilkey .05
378 Tony Fossas .05
379 (Not issued, see #370)
380 Darren Daulton .05
381 Chuck Finley .05
382 Mitch Webster .05
383 Gerald Williams .05
384 Frank Thomas, Fred McGriff (All Star) .40
385 Roberto Alomar, Robby Thompson (All Star) .20
386 Wade Boggs, Matt Williams (All Star) .20
387 Cal Ripken, Jr., Jeff Blauser (All Star) .75
388 Ken Griffey, Jr., Len Dykstra (All Star) .50
389 Juan Gonzalez, Dave Justice (All Star) .30
390 Albert Belle, Barry Bonds (All Star) .40
391 Mike Stanley, Mike Piazza (All Star) .40
392 Jack McDowell, Greg Maddux (All Star) .35
393 Jimmy Key, Tom Glavine (All Star) .05
394 Jeff Montgomery, Randy Myers (All Star) .05
395 Checklist 1 .05
396 Checklist 2 .05
397 Tim Salmon (All-Star Rookie) .25
398 Todd Benzinger .05
399 Frank Castillo .05
400 Ken Griffey, Jr. 1.25
401 John Kruk .05
402 Dave Telgheder .05
403 Gary Gaetti .05
404 Jim Edmonds .05
405 Don Slaught .05
406 Jose Oquendo .05
407 Bruce Ruffin .05
408 Phil Clark .05
409 Joe Klink .05
410 Lou Whitaker .05
411 Kevin Seitzer .05
412 Darrin Fletcher .05
413 Kenny Rogers .05
414 Bill Pecota .05
415 Dave Fleming .05
416 Luis Alicea .05
417 Paul Quantrill .05
418 Damion Easley .05
419 Wes Chamberlain .05
420 Harold Baines .05
421 Scott Radinsky .05
422 Rey Sanchez .05
423 Junior Ortiz .05
424 Jeff Kent .05
425 Brian McRae .05
426 Ed Sprague .05
427 Tom Edens .05
428 Willie Greene .05
429 Bryan Hickerson .05
430 Dave Winfield .45
431 Pedro Astacio .05
432 Mike Gallego .05
433 Dave Burba .05
434 Bob Walk .05
435 Darryl Hamilton .05
436 Vince Horsman .05
437 Bob Natal .05
438 Mike Henneman .05
439 Willie Blair .05
440 Denny Martinez .05
441 Dan Peltier .05
442 Tony Tarasco .05
443 John Cummings .05
444 Geronimo Pena .05
445 Aaron Sele .05
446 Stan Javier .05
447 Mike Williams .05
448 1B Prospects (Greg Pirkl, Roberto Petagine, D.J. Boston, Shawn Wooten) .05

449 Jim Poole .05
450 Carlos Baerga .05
451 Bob Scanlan .05
452 Lance Johnson .05
453 Eric Hillman .05
454 Keith Miller .05
455 Dave Stewart .05
456 Pete Harnisch .05
457 Roberto Kelly .05
458 Tim Worrell .05
459 Pedro Munoz .05
460 Orel Hershiser .05
461 Randy Velarde .05
462 Trevor Wilson .05
463 Jerry Goff .05
464 Bill Wegman .05
465 Dennis Eckersley .05
466 Jeff Conine (All-Star Rookie) .10
467 Joe Boever .05
468 Dante Bichette .05
469 Jeff Shaw .05
470 Rafael Palmeiro .25
471 *Phil Leftwich* .05
472 Jay Buhner .05
473 Bob Tewksbury .05
474 Tim Naehring .05
475 Tom Glavine .10
476 Dave Hollins .05
477 Arthur Rhodes .05
478 Joey Cora .05
479 Mike Morgan .05
480 Albert Belle .30
481 John Franco .05
482 Hipolito Pichardo .05
483 Duane Ward .05
484 Luis Gonzalez .25
485 Joe Oliver .05
486 Wally Whitehurst .05
487 Mike Benjamin .05
488 Eric Davis .05
489 Scott Kamieniecki .05
490 Kent Hrbek .05
491 *John Hope* .05
492 Jesse Orosco .05
493 Troy Neel .05
494 Ryan Bowen .05
495 Mickey Tettleton .05
496 Chris Jones .05
497 John Wetteland .05
498 David Hulse .05
499 Greg Maddux .65
500 Bo Jackson .10
501 Donovan Osborne .05
502 Mike Greenwell .05
503 Steve Frey .05
504 Jim Eisenreich .05
505 Robby Thompson .05
506 Leo Gomez .05
507 Dave Staton .05
508 Wayne Kirby (All-Star Rookie) .05
509 Tim Bogar .05
510 David Cone .05
511 Devon White .05
512 Xavier Hernandez .05
513 Tim Costo .05
514 Gene Harris .05
515 Jack McDowell .05
516 Kevin Gross .05
517 Scott Leius .05
518 Lloyd McClendon .05
519 *Alex Diaz* .05
520 Wade Boggs .40
521 Bob Welch .05
522 Henry Cotto .05
523 Mike Moore .05
524 Tim Laker .05
525 Andres Galarraga .05
526 Jamie Moyer .05
527 2B Prospects (Norberto Martin, Ruben Santana, Jason Hardtke, Chris Sexton) .05
528 Sid Bream .05
529 Erik Hanson .05
530 Ray Lankford .05
531 Rob Deer .05
532 Rod Correia .05
533 Roger Mason .05
534 Mike Devereaux .05
535 Jeff Montgomery .05
536 Dwight Smith .05
537 Jeremy Hernandez .05
538 Ellis Burks .05
539 Bobby Jones .05
540 Paul Molitor .40
541 Jeff Juden .05
542 Chris Sabo .05
543 Larry Casian .05
544 Jeff Gardner .05
545 Ramon Martinez .05
546 Paul O'Neill .05
547 Steve Hosey .05
548 Dave Nilsson .05
549 Ron Darling .05
550 Matt Williams .15
551 Jack Armstrong .05
552 Bill Krueger .05
553 Freddie Benavides .05
554 Jeff Fassero .05
555 Chuck Knoblauch .05
556 Guillermo Velasquez .05
557 Joel Johnston .05
558 Tom Lampkin .05
559 Todd Van Poppel .05
560 Gary Sheffield .20
561 Skeeter Barnes .05
562 Darren Holmes .05
563 John Vander Wal .05
564 Mike Ignasiak .05
565 Fred McGriff .05
566 Luis Polonia .05
567 Mike Perez .05
568 John Valentin .05
569 Mike Felder .05
570 Tommy Greene .05
571 David Segui .05
572 Roberto Hernandez .05
573 Steve Wilson .05
574 Willie McGee .05
575 Randy Myers .05
576 Darrin Jackson .05
577 Eric Plunk .05
578 Mike MacFarlane .05
579 Doug Brocail .05
580 Steve Finley .05
581 John Roper .05
582 Danny Cox .05
583 Chip Hale .05
584 Scott Bullett .05
585 Kevin Reimer .05
586 Brent Gates .05
587 Matt Turner .05
588 Rich Rowland .05
589 Kent Bottenfield .05
590 Marquis Grissom .05
591 Doug Strange .05
592 Jay Howell .05
593 Omar Vizquel .05
594 Rheal Cormier .05
595 Andre Dawson .15
596 Hilly Hathaway .05
597 Todd Pratt .05
598 Mike Mussina .35
599 Alex Fernandez .05
600 Don Mattingly .75
601 Frank Thomas (Measures of Greatness) .40
602 Ryne Sandberg (Measures of Greatness) .20
603 Wade Boggs (Measures of Greatness) .20
604 Cal Ripken, Jr. (Measures of Greatness) .75
605 Barry Bonds (Measures of Greatness) .40
606 Ken Griffey, Jr. (Measures of Greatness) .50
607 Kirby Puckett (Measures of Greatness) .35
608 Darren Daulton (Measures of Greatness) .05
609 Paul Molitor (Measures of Greatness) .20
610 Terry Steinbach .05
611 Todd Worrell .05
612 Jim Thome .05
613 Chuck McElroy .05
614 John Habyan .05
615 Sid Fernandez .05
616 OF Prospects (Eddie Zambrano, Glenn Murray, Chad Mottola), *(Jermaine Allensworth)* .10
617 Steve Bedrosian .05
618 Rob Ducey .05
619 Tom Browning .05
620 Tony Gwynn .65
621 Carl Willis .05
622 Kevin Young .05
623 Rafael Novoa .05
624 Jerry Browne .05
625 Charlie Hough .05
626 Chris Gomez .05
627 Steve Reed .05
628 Kirk Rueter .05
629 Matt Whiteside .05
630 Dave Justice .25
631 Brad Holman .05
632 Brian Jordan .05
633 Scott Bankhead .05
634 Torey Lovullo .05
635 Len Dykstra .05
636 Ben McDonald .05
637 Steve Howe .05
638 Jose Vizcaino .05
639 Bill Swift .05
640 Darryl Strawberry .05
641 Steve Farr .05
642 Tom Kramer .05
643 Joe Orsulak .05
644 Tom Henke .05
645 Joe Carter .05
646 Ken Caminiti .05
647 Reggie Sanders .05
648 Andy Ashby .05
649 Derek Parks .05
650 Andy Van Slyke .05
651 Juan Bell .05
652 Roger Smithberg .05
653 Chuck Carr .05
654 Bill Gullickson .05
655 Charlie Hayes .05
656 Chris Nabholz .05
657 Karl Rhodes .05
658 Pete Smith .05
659 Bret Boone .10
660 Gregg Jefferies .05
661 Bob Zupcic .05
662 Steve Sax .05
663 Mariano Duncan .05
664 Jeff Tackett .05
665 Mark Langston .05
666 Steve Buechele .05
667 Candy Maldonado .05
668 Woody Williams .05
669 Tim Wakefield .05
670 Danny Tartabull .05
671 Charlie O'Brien .05
672 Felix Jose .05
673 Bobby Ayala .05
674 Scott Servais .05
675 Roberto Alomar .40
676 Pedro Martinez .05
677 Eddie Guardado .05
678 Mark Lewis .05
679 Jaime Navarro .05
680 Ruben Sierra .05
681 Rick Renteria .05
682 Storm Davis .05
683 Cory Snyder .05
684 Ron Karkovice .05
685 Juan Gonzalez .50
686 C Prospects (Chris Howard, Carlos Delgado, Jason Kendall, Paul Bako) .50
687 John Smoltz .10
688 Brian Dorsett .05
689 Omar Olivares .05
690 Mo Vaughn .35
691 Joe Grahe .05
692 Mickey Morandini .05
693 Tino Martinez .05
694 Brian Barnes .05
695 Mike Stanley .05
696 Mark Clark .05
697 Dave Hansen .05
698 Willie Wilson .05
699 Pete Schourek .05
700 Barry Bonds .75
701 Kevin Appier .05
702 Tony Fernandez .05
703 Darryl Kile .05
704 Archi Cianfrocco .05
705 Jose Rijo .05
706 Brian Harper .05
707 Zane Smith .05
708 Dave Henderson .05
709 Angel Miranda .05
710 Orestes Destrade .05
711 Greg Gohr .05
712 Eric Young .05
713 P Prospects (Todd Williams, Ron Watson, Kirk Bullinger, Mike Welch) .05
714 Tim Spehr .05
715 Hank Aaron (20th Anniversary #715) .50
716 Nate Minchey .05
717 Mike Blowers .05
718 Kent Mercker .05
719 Tom Pagnozzi .05
720 Roger Clemens .65
721 Eduardo Perez .05
722 Milt Thompson .05
723 Gregg Olson .05
724 Kirk McCaskill .05
725 Sammy Sosa .75
726 Alvaro Espinoza .05
727 Henry Rodriguez .05
728 Jim Leyritz .05
729 Steve Scarsone .05
730 Bobby Bonilla .05
731 Chris Gwynn .05
732 Al Leiter .05
733 Bip Roberts .05
734 Mark Portugal .05
735 Terry Pendleton .05
736 Dave Valle .05
737 Paul Kilgus .05
738 Greg Harris .05
739 *Jon Ratliff* (Draft Pick) .10
740 *Kirk Presley* (Draft Pick) .05
741 *Josue Estrada* (Draft Pick) .05
742 *Wayne Gomes* (Draft Pick) .10
743 *Pat Watkins* (Draft Pick) .05
744 *Jamey Wright* (Draft Pick) .10
745 *Jay Powell* (Draft Pick) .15
746 *Ryan McGuire* (Draft Pick) .10
747 *Marc Barcelo* (Draft Pick) .05
748 *Sloan Smith* (Draft Pick) .05
749 *John Wasdin* (Draft Pick) .10
750 Marc Valdes (Draft Pick) .05
751 *Dan Ehler* (Draft Pick) .05
752 *Andre King* (Draft Pick) .05
753 *Greg Keagle* (Draft Pick) .05
754 *Jason Myers* (Draft Pick) .05
755 *Dax Winslett* (Draft Pick) .05
756 *Casey Whitten* (Draft Pick) .05
757 *Tony Fuduric* (Draft Pick) .05
758 *Greg Norton* (Draft Pick) .05
759 *Jeff D'Amico* (Draft Pick) .15
760 *Ryan Hancock* (Draft Pick) .05
761 *David Cooper* (Draft Pick) .05
762 *Kevin Orie* (Draft Pick) .10
763 John O'Donoghue, Mike Oquist (Coming Attractions) .05
764 Cory Bailey, Scott Hatteberg (ComingAttractions) .05
765 Mark Holzemer, Paul Swingle (Coming Attractions) .05
766 James Baldwin, Rod Bolton (Coming Attractions) .05
767 *Jerry DiPoto* *Julian Tavarez* (Coming Attractions) .10
768 Danny Bautista, Sean Bergman (Coming Attractions) .05
769 Bob Hamelin, Joe Vitiello (Coming Attractions) .05
770 Mark Kiefer, Troy O'Leary (Coming Attractions) .05
771 Denny Hocking, Oscar Munoz (Coming Attractions) .05

772	Russ Davis, Brien Taylor (Coming Attractions)	.05
773	Kurt Abbott, Miguel Jimenez (Coming Attractions)	.05
774	Kevin King, Eric Plantenberg (Coming Attractions)	.05
775	Jon Shave, Desi Wilson (Coming Attractions)	.05
776	Domingo Cedeno, Paul Spoljaric (Coming Attractions)	.05
777	Chipper Jones, Ryan Klesko (ComingAttractions)	1.00
778	Steve Trachsel, Turk Wendell (Coming Attractions)	.05
779	Johnny Ruffin, Jerry Spradlin (Coming Attractions)	.05
780	Jason Bates, John Burke (Coming Attractions)	.05
781	Carl Everett, Dave Weathers (Coming Attractions)	.35
782	Gary Mota, James Mouton (Coming Attractions)	.05
783	Raul Mondesi, Ben Van Ryn (Coming Attractions)	.20
784	Gabe White, Rondell White (Coming Attractions)	.25
785	Brook Fordyce, Bill Pulsipher (Coming Attractions)	.05
786	Kevin Foster, Gene Schall (Coming Attractions)	.05
787	Rich Aude, Midre Cummings (Coming Attractions)	.05
788	Brian Barber, Richard Batchelor (Coming Attractions)	.05
789	*Brian Johnson*, Scott Sanders (Coming Attractions)	.05
790	Rikkert Faneyte, J.R. Phillips (Coming Attractions)	.05
791	Checklist 3	.05
792	Checklist 4	.05

1994 Topps Gold

This premium parallel set was issued as inserts in virtually all forms of Topps packaging. Identical in all other ways to the regular Topps cards, the Gold version replaces the white or black Topps logo on front with a gold-foil "Topps Gold" logo, and prints either the player name or card title in gold foil. The four checklist cards from the regular issue are replaced with cards of players not found in the regular Topps set.

	MT
Complete Set (792):	50.00
Common Player:	.15

(Star cards valued at 2X corresponding cards in regular Topps issue)

1994 Topps Black Gold

Black Gold inserts returned for 1994 randomly included in all types of Topps packaging. Single cards, as well as cards redeemable by mail for 11, 22 or 44 Black Gold cards, were produced. The basic single-player card features an action photo, the background of which has been almost completely blacked out. At top is the team name in black letters against a gold prismatic foil background. The player name at bottom is in the same gold foil. On back, bordered in white, is a background which fades from black at top to gray at the bottom and is gridded with white lines. At left is another player action photo. The Topps Black Gold logo and player name appear in gold foil; the latter printed on a simulated wooden board "hanging" from the top of the card. A second hanging plank has player stats and rankings from the 1993 season. The multi-card redemption cards come in two versions. The type found in packs has all 11, 22 or 44 of the cards pictured on front in miniature and redemption details printed on back. A second version, returned with the single cards won, has on back a checklist and non-redemption notice. Stated odds of winning Black Gold cards were one in 72 packs for single cards; one in 180 packs for 11-card winners and one in 720 packs (one per foil-pack case) for a 22-card winner.

		MT
	Complete Set (44):	15.00
	Complete Series 1 (22):	9.00
	Complete Series 2 (22):	6.00
	Common Player:	.15
1	Roberto Alomar	.40
2	Carlos Baerga	.15
3	Albert Belle	.30
4	Joe Carter	.15
5	Cecil Fielder	.15
6	Travis Fryman	.15
7	Juan Gonzalez	.60
8	Ken Griffey, Jr.	1.50
9	Chris Hoiles	.15
10	Randy Johnson	.35
11	Kenny Lofton	.15
12	Jack McDowell	.15
13	Paul Molitor	.45
14	Jeff Montgomery	.15
15	John Olerud	.15
16	Rafael Palmeiro	.25
17	Kirby Puckett	.75
18	Cal Ripken, Jr.	2.00
19	Tim Salmon	.20
20	Mike Stanley	.15
21	Frank Thomas	.75
22	Robin Ventura	.15
23	Jeff Bagwell	.60
24	Jay Bell	.15
25	Craig Biggio	.15
26	Jeff Blauser	.15
27	Barry Bonds	.75
28	Darren Daulton	.15
29	Len Dykstra	.15
30	Andres Galarraga	.15
31	Ron Gant	.15
32	Tom Glavine	.15
33	Mark Grace	.25
34	Marquis Grissom	.15
35	Gregg Jefferies	.15
36	Dave Justice	.20
37	John Kruk	.15
38	Greg Maddux	.75
39	Fred McGriff	.15
40	Randy Myers	.15
41	Mike Piazza	1.25
42	Sammy Sosa	1.00
43	Robby Thompson	.15
44	Matt Williams	.15
---	Winner A	.50
---	Winner B	.50
---	Winner C	.50
---	Winner D	.50
---	Winner A/B	.65
---	Winner C/D	.65
---	Winner A/B/C/D	.65

1994 Topps Traded

Topps Traded features top prospects and rookies as well as traded veterans. Also included in the boxed set is an eight-card Topps Finest subset of six MVPs and two Rookie of the Year cards. Regular cards have the same design as the previously released '94 Topps set. "Anatomy of a Trade" is a two-card subset that includes Roberto Kelly/Deion Sanders and Pedro Martinez/Delino DeShields on a split, puzzle-like front. There is also a Prospect card, showcasing a top prospect from AAA, AA and A, as well as a top-rated draft pick. In addition, there are 12 Draft Pick cards included in the Traded set. Finally, two cards pay tribute to Ryne Sandberg, one in a Phillies uniform, one with the Cubs.

		MT
	Unopened Factory Set (140):	50.00
	Complete Set (132):	30.00
	Common Player:	.05
1	Paul Wilson (Draft Pick)	.10
2	Bill Taylor	.05
3	Dan Wilson	.05
4	Mark Smith	.05
5	Toby Borland	.05
6	Dave Clark	.05
7	Denny Martinez	.05
8	Dave Gallagher	.05
9	Josias Manzanillo	.05
10	Brian Anderson	.05
11	Damon Berryhill	.05
12	Alex Cole	.05
13	Jacob Shumate (Draft Pick)	.15
14	Oddibe McDowell	.05
15	Willie Banks	.05
16	Jerry Browne	.05
17	Donnie Elliott	.05
18	Ellis Burks	.05
19	Chuck McElroy	.05
20	Luis Polonia	.05
21	Brian Harper	.05
22	Mark Portugal	.05
23	Dave Henderson	.05
24	Mark Acre	.15
25	Julio Franco	.05
26	Darren Hall	.05
27	Eric Anthony	.05
28	Sid Fernandez	.05
29	*Rusty Greer*	1.50
30	Riccardo Ingram	.15
31	Gabe White	.05
32	Tim Belcher	.05
33	*Terrence Long* (Draft Pick)	2.00
34	*Mark Dalesandro*	.05
35	Mike Kelly	.05
36	Jack Morris	.05
37	Jeff Brantley	.05
38	*Larry Barnes* (Draft Pick)	.15
39	Brian Hunter	.05
40	Otis Nixon	.05
41	Bret Wagner (Draft pick)	.05
42	Anatomy of a Trade (Pedro Martinez, Delino DeShields)	.50
43	Heathcliff Slocumb	.05
44	*Ben Grieve* (Draft Pick)	3.00
45	John Hudek	.15
46	Shawon Dunston	.05
47	Greg Colbrunn	.05
48	Joey Hamilton	.05
49	Marvin Freeman	.05
50	Terry Mulholland	.05
51	Keith Mitchell	.05
52	Dwight Smith	.05
53	Shawn Boskie	.05
54	*Kevin Witt* (Draft Pick)	.15
55	Ron Gant	.15
56	1994 Prospects (Trenidad Hubbard, Jason Schmidt, Larry Sutton, Stephen Larkin)	.10
57	Jody Reed	.05
58	Rick Helling	.05
59	John Powell (Draft Pick)	.05
60	Eddie Murray	.50
61	Joe Hall	.05
62	Jorge Fabregas	.05
63	Mike Mordecai	.05
64	Ed Vosberg	.05

65	Rickey Henderson	.60
66	Tim Grieve (Draft pick)	.15
67	Jon Lieber	.10
68	Chris Howard	.05
69	Matt Walbeck	.05
70	Chan Ho Park	2.00
71	Bryan Eversgerd	.05
72	John Dettmer	.05
73	Erik Hanson	.05
74	Mike Thurman (Draft pick)	.15
75	Bobby Ayala	.05
76	Rafael Palmeiro	.40
77	Bret Boone	.15
78	Paul Shuey (Future Star)	.05
79	Kevin Foster	.05
80	Dave Magadan	.05
81	Bip Roberts	.05
82	Howard Johnson	.05
83	Xavier Hernandez	.05
84	Ross Powell	.05
85	*Doug Million* (Draft Pick)	.05
86	Geronimo Berroa	.05
87	*Mark Farris* (Draft Pick)	.25
88	Butch Henry	.05
89	Junior Felix	.05
90	Bo Jackson	.10
91	Hector Carrasco	.05
92	Charlie O'Brien	.05
93	Omar Vizquel	.05
94	David Segui	.05
95	Dustin Hermanson (Draft Pick)	.20
96	Gar Finnvold	.05
97	Dave Stevens	.05
98	Corey Pointer (Draft Pick)	.15
99	Felix Fermin	.05
100	Lee Smith	.05
101	Reid Ryan (Draft Pick)	.15
102	Bobby Munoz	.05
103	Anatomy of a Trade (Deion Sanders, Roberto Kelly)	.10
104	Turner Ward	.05
105	William Van Landingham	.05
106	Vince Coleman	.05
107	Stan Javier	.05
108	Darrin Jackson	.05
109	C.J. Nitkowski (Draft Pick)	.10
110	Anthony Young	.05
111	Kurt Miller	.05
112	*Paul Konerko* (Draft Pick)	12.00
113	Walt Weiss	.05
114	Daryl Boston	.05
115	Will Clark	.20
116	*Matt Smith* (Draft Pick)	.05
117	Mark Leiter	.05
118	Gregg Olson	.05
119	Tony Pena	.05
120	Jose Vizcaino	.05
121	Rick White	.05
122	Rich Rowland	.05
123	Jeff Reboulet	.05
124	Greg Hibbard	.05
125	Chris Sabo	.05
126	Doug Jones	.05
127	Tony Fernandez	.05
128	Carlos Reyes	.05
129	Kevin Brown (Draft Pick)	.15
130	Commemorative (Ryne Sandberg)	1.00
131	Commemorative (Ryne Sandberg)	1.00
132	Checklist 1-132	.05

1994 Topps Traded Finest Inserts

Eight Finest cards were included in the 1994 Topps Traded set. Cards picture the player on a blue and gold background. Either Rookie of the Year or MVP is printed across the bottom opposite the player's name, indicating the player's candidacy for such an award in 1994. Backs offer a portrait photo, stats through the All-Star break and comments on the player's season to that point.

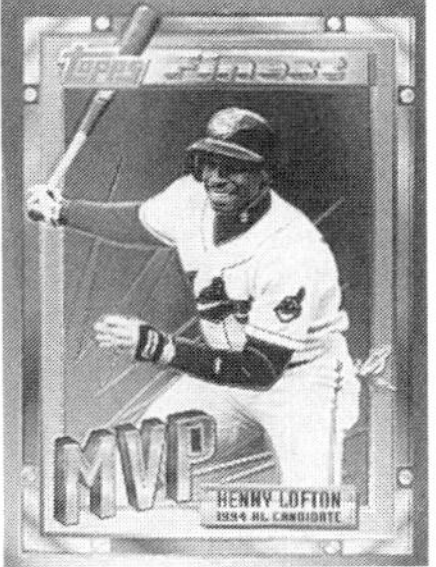

		MT
Complete Set (8):		7.50
Common Player:		.25
1	Greg Maddux	1.50
2	Mike Piazza	2.00
3	Matt Williams	.25
4	Raul Mondesi	.50
5	Ken Griffey Jr.	2.50
6	Kenny Lofton	.25
7	Frank Thomas	2.00
8	Manny Ramirez	1.00

1995 Topps

Topps 1995 baseball arrived offering Cyberstats, which projected full-season statistics for the strike shortened year, as well as League Leaders and Stadium Club First Day Issue pre-production inserts. Series 1 comprises 396 cards, including subsets of Draft Picks, Star Tracks, a Babe Ruth commemorative card and the Topps All-Stars, featuring two players per card at each position. Regular cards have a ragged white border around the player photo, with his name in gold foil under the picture. Series 2 concluded the Cyberstats inserts and added 264 cards to the regular set. Subsets in Series 2 include a continuation of the Draft Picks as well as two-player On Deck cards and four-player Prospects cards, arranged by position. Besides the 660 base cards, hobby-version factory sets include 10 Stadium Club 1st Day previews and seven Cyberstat Season in Review cards. Two versions of the retail factory sets were made. One has 660 regular cards, 20 Cyberstats parallels and four League Leader inserts. The other has the base set of 660 plus 10 Opening Day cards and seven Cyberstat Season in Review.

		MT
Unopened Hobby Factory Set (677):		75.00
Unopened Retail Factory Set (684):		70.00
Unopened Retail Factory Set (677):		65.00
Complete Set (660):		45.00
Common Player:		.05
Series 1 or 2 Pack (15):		1.25
Series 1 or 2 Wax Box (36):		30.00
1	Frank Thomas	1.25
2	Mickey Morandini	.05
3a	Babe Ruth (100th Birthday, no gold "Topps" logo)	2.00
3b	Babe Ruth (100th Birthday, gold "Topps" logo)	2.00
4	Scott Cooper	.05
5	David Cone	.05
6	Jacob Shumate (Draft Pick)	.05
7	Trevor Hoffman	.05
8	Shane Mack	.05
9	Delino DeShields	.05
10	Matt Williams	.15
11	Sammy Sosa	1.25
12	Gary DiSarcina	.05
13	Kenny Rogers	.05
14	Jose Vizcaino	.05
15	Lou Whitaker	.05
16	Ron Darling	.05
17	Dave Nilsson	.05
18	Chris Hammond	.05
19	Sid Bream	.05
20	Denny Martinez	.05
21	Orlando Merced	.05
22	John Wetteland	.05
23	Mike Devereaux	.05
24	Rene Arocha	.05
25	Jay Buhner	.05
26	Darren Holmes	.05
27	Hal Morris	.05
28	*Brian Buchanan* (Draft Pick)	.15
29	Keith Miller	.05
30	Paul Molitor	.50
31	Dave West	.05
32	Tony Tarasco	.05
33	Scott Sanders	.05
34	Eddie Zambrano	.05
35	Ricky Bones	.05
36	John Valentin	.05
37	Kevin Tapani	.05
38	Tim Wallach	.05
39	Darren Lewis	.05
40	Travis Fryman	.05
41	Mark Leiter	.05
42	Jose Bautista	.05
43	Pete Smith	.05
44	Bret Barberie	.05
45	Dennis Eckersley	.05
46	Ken Hill	.05
47	Chad Ogea (Star Track)	.05
48	Pete Harnisch	.05
49	James Baldwin (Future Star)	.05
50	Mike Mussina	.50
51	Al Martin	.05
52	Mark Thompson (Star Track)	.05
53	Matt Smith (Draft Pick)	.05
54	Joey Hamilton (All Star Rookie)	.10
55	Edgar Martinez	.05
56	John Smiley	.05
57	Rey Sanchez	.05
58	Mike Timlin	.05
59	Ricky Bottalico (Star Track)	.10
60	Jim Abbott	.05
61	Mike Kelly	.05
62	Brian Jordan	.05
63	Ken Ryan	.05
64	Matt Mieske	.05
65	Rick Aguilera	.05
66	Ismael Valdes	.05
67	Royce Clayton	.05
68	Junior Felix	.05
69	Harold Reynolds	.05
70	Juan Gonzalez	.75
71	Kelly Stinnett	.05
72	Carlos Reyes	.05
73	Dave Weathers	.05
74	Mel Rojas	.05
75	Doug Drabek	.05
76	Charles Nagy	.05
77	Tim Raines	.05
78	Midre Cummings	.05
79	1B Prospects (Gene Schall), (*Scott Talanoa*), (*Harold Williams*), (*Ray Brown*)	.10
80	Rafael Palmeiro	.25
81	Charlie Hayes	.05
82	Ray Lankford	.05
83	Tim Davis	.05
84	*C.J. Nitkowski* (Draft Pick)	.05
85	Andy Ashby	.05
86	Gerald Williams	.05
87	Terry Shumpert	.05
88	Heathcliff Slocumb	.05
89	Domingo Cedeno	.05
90	Mark Grace	.20
91	*Brad Woodall* (Star Track)	.10
92	Gar Finnvold	.05
93	Jaime Navarro	.05
94	Carlos Hernandez	.05
95	Mark Langston	.05
96	Chuck Carr	.05
97	Mike Gardiner	.05
98	David McCarty	.05
99	Cris Carpenter	.05
100	Barry Bonds	1.25
101	David Segui	.05
102	Scott Brosius	.05
103	Mariano Duncan	.05
104	Kenny Lofton	.05
105	Ken Caminiti	.05
106	Darrin Jackson	.05
107	Jim Poole	.05
108	Wil Cordero	.05
109	Danny Miceli	.05
110	Walt Weiss	.05
111	Tom Pagnozzi	.05
112	Terrence Long (Draft Pick)	.15
113	Bret Boone	.10
114	Daryl Boston	.05
115	Wally Joyner	.05
116	Rob Butler	.05
117	Rafael Belliard	.05
118	Luis Lopez	.05
119	Tony Fossas	.05
120	Len Dykstra	.05
121	Mike Morgan	.05
122	Denny Hocking	.05
123	Kevin Gross	.05
124	Todd Benzinger	.05
125	John Doherty	.05
126	Eduardo Perez	.05
127	Dan Smith	.05
128	Joe Orsulak	.05
129	Brent Gates	.05
130	Jeff Conine	.05
131	Doug Henry	.05
132	Paul Sorrento	.05
133	Mike Hampton	.05
134	Tim Spehr	.05
135	Julio Franco	.05
136	Mike Dyer	.05
137	Chris Sabo	.05
138	Rheal Cormier	.05
139	Paul Konerko (Draft Pick)	.50

No.	Card	Value
140	Dante Bichette	.05
141	Chuck McElroy	.05
142	Mike Stanley	.05
143	Bob Hamelin (All Star Rookie)	.05
144	Tommy Greene	.05
145	John Smoltz	.10
146	Ed Sprague	.05
147	Ray McDavid (Star Track)	.05
148	Otis Nixon	.05
149	Turk Wendell	.05
150	Chris James	.05
151	Derek Parks	.05
152	Jose Offerman	.05
153	Tony Clark (Future Star)	.25
154	Chad Curtis	.05
155	Mark Portugal	.05
156	Bill Pulsipher (Future Star)	.05
157	Troy Neel	.05
158	Dave Winfield	.75
159	Bill Wegman	.05
160	Benny Santiago	.05
161	Jose Mesa	.05
162	Luis Gonzalez	.25
163	Alex Fernandez	.05
164	Freddie Benavides	.05
165	Ben McDonald	.05
166	Blas Minor	.05
167	Bret Wagner (Draft Pick)	.05
168	Mac Suzuki (Future Star)	.05
169	Roberto Mejia	.05
170	Wade Boggs	.50
171	Calvin Reese (Future Star)	.10
172	Hipolito Pichardo	.05
173	Kim Batiste	.05
174	Darren Hall	.05
175	Tom Glavine	.10
176	Phil Plantier	.05
177	Chris Howard	.05
178	Karl Rhodes	.05
179	LaTroy Hawkins (Future Star)	.05
180	Raul Mondesi (All Star Rookie)	.30
181	Jeff Reed	.05
182	Milt Cuyler	.05
183	Jim Edmonds	.05
184	Hector Fajardo	.05
185	Jeff Kent	.05
186	Wilson Alvarez	.05
187	Geronimo Berroa	.05
188	Billy Spiers	.05
189	Derek Lilliquist	.05
190	Craig Biggio	.10
191	Roberto Hernandez	.05
192	Bob Natal	.05
193	Bobby Ayala	.05
194	*Travis Miller* (Draft Pick)	.10
195	Bob Tewksbury	.05
196	Rondell White	.15
197	Steve Cooke	.05
198	Jeff Branson	.05
199	Derek Jeter (Future Star)	2.00
200	Tim Salmon	.25
201	Steve Frey	.05
202	Kent Mercker	.05
203	Randy Johnson	.50
204	Todd Worrell	.05
205	Mo Vaughn	.35
206	Howard Johnson	.05
207	John Wasdin (Future Star)	.05
208	Eddie Williams	.05
209	Tim Belcher	.05
210	Jeff Montgomery	.05
211	Kirt Manwaring	.05
212	Ben Grieve (Draft Pick)	1.50
213	Pat Hentgen	.05
214	Shawon Dunston	.05
215	Mike Greenwell	.05
216	Alex Diaz	.05
217	Pat Mahomes	.05
218	Dave Hanson	.05
219	Kevin Rogers	.05
220	Cecil Fielder	.05
221	Andrew Lorraine (Star Track)	.05
222	Jack Armstrong	.05
223	Todd Hundley	.05
224	Mark Acre	.05
225	Darrell Whitmore	.05
226	Randy Milligan	.05
227	Wayne Kirby	.05
228	Darryl Kile	.05
229	Bob Zupcic	.05
230	Jay Bell	.05
231	Dustin Hermanson (Draft Pick)	.10
232	Harold Baines	.05
233	Alan Benes (Future Star)	.10
234	Felix Fermin	.05
235	Ellis Burks	.05
236	Jeff Brantley	.05
237	OF Prospects (Brian Hunter, Jose Malave, Shane Pullen), (*Karim Garcia*)	.40
238	Matt Nokes	.05
239	Ben Rivera	.05
240	Joe Carter	.05
241	Jeff Granger (Star Track)	.05
242	Terry Pendleton	.05
243	Melvin Nieves	.05
244	Frank Rodriguez (Future Star)	.05
245	Darryl Hamilton	.05
246	Brooks Kieschnick (Future Star)	.05
247	Todd Hollandsworth (Future Star)	.10
248	Joe Rosselli (Future Star)	.05
249	Bill Gullickson	.05
250	Chuck Knoblauch	.05
251	Kurt Miller (Star Track)	.05
252	Bobby Jones	.05
253	Lance Blankenship	.05
254	Matt Whiteside	.05
255	Darrin Fletcher	.05
256	Eric Plunk	.05
257	Shane Reynolds	.05
258	Norberto Martin	.05
259	Mike Thurman (Draft Pick)	.05
260	Andy Van Slyke	.05
261	Dwight Smith	.05
262	Allen Watson	.05
263	Dan Wilson	.05
264	Brent Mayne	.05
265	Bip Roberts	.05
266	Sterling Hitchcock	.05
267	Alex Gonzalez (Star Track)	.10
268	Greg Harris	.05
269	Ricky Jordan	.05
270	Johnny Ruffin	.05
271	Mike Stanton	.05
272	Rich Rowland	.05
273	Steve Trachsel	.05
274	Pedro Munoz	.05
275	Ramon Martinez	.05
276	Dave Henderson	.05
277	Chris Gomez (All Star Rookie)	.05
278	Joe Grahe	.05
279	Rusty Greer	.05
280	John Franco	.05
281	Mike Bordick	.05
282	Jeff D'Amico (Future Star)	.10
283	Dave Magadan	.05
284	Tony Pena	.05
285	Greg Swindell	.05
286	Doug Million (Draft Pick)	.05
287	Gabe White (Star Track)	.05
288	Trey Beamon (Future Star)	.05
289	Arthur Rhodes	.05
290	Juan Guzman	.05
291	Jose Oquendo	.05
292	Willie Blair	.05
293	Eddie Taubensee	.05
294	Steve Howe	.05
295	Greg Maddux	1.00
296	Mike MacFarlane	.05
297	Curt Schilling	.20
298	Phil Clark	.05
299	Woody Williams	.05
300	Jose Canseco	.50
301	Aaron Sele	.05
302	Carl Willis	.05
303	Steve Buechele	.05
304	Dave Burba	.05
305	Orel Hershiser	.05
306	Damion Easley	.05
307	Mike Henneman	.05
308	Josias Manzanillo	.05
309	Kevin Seitzer	.05
310	Ruben Sierra	.05
311	Bryan Harvey	.05
312	Jim Thome	.05
313	*Ramon Castro* (Draft Pick)	.10
314	Lance Johnson	.05
315	Marquis Grissom	.05
316	SP Prospects (Terrell Wade, Juan Acevedo, Matt Arrandale), (*Eddie Priest*)	.10
317	Paul Wagner	.05
318	Jamie Moyer	.05
319	Todd Zeile	.05
320	Chris Bosio	.05
321	Steve Reed	.05
322	Erik Hanson	.05
323	Luis Polonia	.05
324	Ryan Klesko	.05
325	Kevin Appier	.05
326	Jim Eisenreich	.05
327	Randy Knorr	.05
328	Craig Shipley	.05
329	Tim Naehring	.05
330	Randy Myers	.05
331	Alex Cole	.05
332	Jim Gott	.05
333	Mike Jackson	.05
334	John Flaherty	.05
335	Chili Davis	.05
336	Benji Gil (Star Track)	.05
337a	Jason Jacome (No Diamond Vision logo on back photo)	.15
337b	Jason Jacome (Diamond Vision logo on back photo)	.05
338	Stan Javier	.05
339	Mike Fetters	.05
340	Rick Renteria	.05
341	Kevin Witt (Draft Pick)	.05
342	Scott Servais	.05
343	Craig Grebeck	.05
344	Kirk Rueter	.05
345	Don Slaught	.05
346	*Armando Benitez* (Star Track)	.15
347	Ozzie Smith	1.00
348	Mike Blowers	.05
349	Armando Reynoso	.05
350	Barry Larkin	.10
351	Mike Williams	.05
352	Scott Kamieniecki	.05
353	Gary Gaetti	.05
354	Todd Stottlemyre	.05
355	Fred McGriff	.05
356	Tim Mauser	.05
357	Chris Gwynn	.05
358	Frank Castillo	.05
359	Jeff Reboulet	.05
360	Roger Clemens	1.00
361	Mark Carreon	.05
362	Chad Kreuter	.05
363	Mark Farris (Draft Pick)	.10
364	Bob Welch	.05
365	Dean Palmer	.05
366	Jeromy Burnitz	.05
367	B.J. Surhoff	.05
368	Mike Butcher	.05
369	RP Prospects (Brad Clontz, Steve Phoenix, Scott Gentile, Bucky Buckles)	.10
370	Eddie Murray	.40
371	Orlando Miller (Star Track)	.05
372	Ron Karkovice	.05
373	Richie Lewis	.05
374	Lenny Webster	.05
375	Jeff Tackett	.05
376	Tom Urbani	.05
377	Tino Martinez	.05
378	Mark Dewey	.05
379	Charlie O'Brien	.05
380	Terry Mulholland	.05
381	Thomas Howard	.05
382	Chris Haney	.05
383	Billy Hatcher	.05
384	Jeff Bagwell, Frank Thomas (All Stars)	.60
385	Bret Boone, Carlos Baerga (All Stars)	.05
386	Matt Williams, Wade Boggs (All Stars)	.15
387	Wil Cordero, Cal Ripken Jr. (All Stars)	.75
388	Barry Bonds, Ken Griffey Jr. (All Stars)	1.00
389	Tony Gwynn, Albert Belle (All Stars)	.50
390	Dante Bichette, Kirby Puckett (All Stars)	.50
391	Mike Piazza, Mike Stanley (All Stars)	.60
392	Greg Maddux, David Cone (All Stars)	.50
393	Danny Jackson, Jimmy Key (All Stars)	.05
394	John Franco, Lee Smith (All Stars)	.05
395	Checklist 1-198	.05
396	Checklist 199-396	.05
397	Ken Griffey Jr.	2.00
398	*Rick Heiserman* (Draft Pick)	.05
399	Don Mattingly	1.25
400	Henry Rodriguez	.05
401	Lenny Harris	.05
402	Ryan Thompson	.05
403	Darren Oliver	.05
404	Omar Vizquel	.05
405	Jeff Bagwell	.75
406	*Doug Webb* (Draft Pick)	.05
407	Todd Van Poppel	.05
408	Leo Gomez	.05
409	Mark Whiten	.05
410	Pedro Martinez	.05
411	Reggie Sanders	.05
412	Kevin Foster	.05
413	Danny Tartabull	.05
414	Jeff Blauser	.05
415	Mike Magnante	.05
416	Tom Candiotti	.05
417	Rod Beck	.05
418	Jody Reed	.05
419	Vince Coleman	.05
420	Danny Jackson	.05
421	*Ryan Nye* (Draft Pick)	.05
422	Larry Walker	.30
423	Russ Johnson (Draft Pick)	.05
424	Pat Borders	.05
425	Lee Smith	.05
426	Paul O'Neill	.05
427	Devon White	.05
428	Jim Bullinger	.05
429	SP Prospects (Greg Hansell, Brian Sackinsky, Carey Paige, Rob Welch)	.10
430	Steve Avery	.05
431	Tony Gwynn	1.00
432	Pat Meares	.05
433	Bill Swift	.05
434	David Wells	.10
435	John Briscoe	.05
436	Roger Pavlik	.05
437	*Jayson Peterson* (Draft Pick)	.05
438	Roberto Alomar	.50
439	Billy Brewer	.05
440	Gary Sheffield	.25
441	Lou Frazier	.05
442	Terry Steinbach	.05
443	*Jay Payton* (Draft Pick)	.25
444	Jason Bere	.05
445	Denny Neagle	.05
446	Andres Galarraga	.05
447	Hector Carrasco	.05
448	Bill Risley	.05
449	Andy Benes	.05
450	Jim Leyritz	.05
451	Jose Oliva	.05
452	Greg Vaughn	.05
453	Rich Monteleone	.05
454	Tony Eusebio	.05
455	Chuck Finley	.05
456	Kevin Brown	.15

457 Joe Boever .05
458 Bobby Munoz .05
459 Bret Saberhagen .05
460 Kurt Abbott .05
461 Bobby Witt .05
462 Cliff Floyd .10
463 Mark Clark .05
464 Andujar Cedeno .05
465 Marvin Freeman .05
466 Mike Piazza 1.50
467 Willie Greene .05
468 Pat Kelly .05
469 Carlos Delgado .50
470 Willie Banks .05
471 Matt Walbeck .05
472 Mark McGwire 2.50
473 McKay Christensen (Draft Pick) .05
474 Alan Trammell .05
475 Tom Gordon .05
476 Greg Colbrunn .05
477 Darren Daulton .05
478 Albie Lopez .05
479 Robin Ventura .05
480 C Prospects (*Eddie Perez*, Jason Kendall), (*Einar Diaz*, Bret Hemphill) .20
481 Bryan Eversgerd .05
482 Dave Fleming .05
483 Scott Livingstone .05
484 Pete Schourek .05
485 Bernie Williams .30
486 Mark Lemke .05
487 Eric Karros .05
488 Scott Ruffcorn .05
489 Billy Ashley .05
490 Rico Brogna .05
491 John Burkett .05
492 *Cade Gaspar* (Draft Pick) .05
493 Jorge Fabregas .05
494 Greg Gagne .05
495 Doug Jones .05
496 Troy O'Leary .05
497 Pat Rapp .05
498 Butch Henry .05
499 John Olerud .05
500 John Hudek .05
501 Jeff King .05
502 Bobby Bonilla .05
503 Albert Belle .25
504 Rick Wilkins .05
505 John Jaha .05
506 Nigel Wilson .05
507 Sid Fernandez .05
508 Deion Sanders .10
509 Gil Heredia .05
510 *Scott Elarton* (Draft Pick) .50
511 Melido Perez .05
512 Greg McMichael .05
513 Rusty Meacham .05
514 Shawn Green .40
515 Carlos Garcia .05
516 Dave Stevens .05
517 Eric Young .05
518 Omar Daal .05
519 Kirk Gibson .05
520 Spike Owen .05
521 *Jacob Cruz* (Draft Pick) .25
522 Sandy Alomar .05
523 Steve Bedrosian .05
524 Ricky Gutierrez .05
525 Dave Veres .05
526 Gregg Jefferies .05
527 Jose Valentin .05
528 Robb Nen .05
529 Jose Rijo .05
530 Sean Berry .05
531 Mike Gallego .05
532 Roberto Kelly .05
533 Kevin Stocker .05
534 Kirby Puckett 1.00
535 Chipper Jones 1.50
536 Russ Davis .05
537 Jon Lieber .05
538 *Trey Moore* (Draft Pick) .05
539 Joe Girardi .05
540 2B Prospects (Quilvio Veras, Arquimedez Pozo, Miguel Cairo, Jason Camilli) .10
541 Tony Phillips .05
542 Brian Anderson .05
543 Ivan Rodriguez .65
544 Jeff Cirillo .05
545 Joey Cora .05
546 Chris Hoiles .05
547 Bernard Gilkey .05
548 Mike Lansing .05
549 Jimmy Key .05
550 Mark Wohlers .05
551 *Chris Clemons* (Draft Pick) .05
552 Vinny Castilla .05
553 Mark Guthrie .05
554 Mike Lieberthal .05
555 *Tommy Davis* (Draft Pick) .05
556 Robby Thompson .05
557 Danny Bautista .05
558 Will Clark .15
559 Rickey Henderson .50
560 Todd Jones .05
561 Jack McDowell .05
562 Carlos Rodriguez .05
563 Mark Eichhorn .05
564 Jeff Nelson .05
565 Eric Anthony .05
566 Randy Velarde .05
567 Javy Lopez .05
568 Kevin Mitchell .05
569 Steve Karsay .05
570 *Brian Meadows* (Draft Pick) .10
571 SS Projects (*Rey Ordonez*, Mike Metcalfe, Ray Holbert, Kevin Orie) 1.00
572 John Kruk .05
573 Scott Leius .05
574 John Patterson .05
575 Kevin Brown .15
576 Mike Moore .05
577 Manny Ramirez .75
578 Jose Lind .05
579 Derrick May .05
580 Cal Eldred .05
581 3B Prospects (David Bell, Joel Chelmis, Lino Diaz), (*Aaron Boone*) .15
582 J.T. Snow .05
583 Luis Sojo .05
584 Moises Alou .20
585 Dave Clark .05
586 Dave Hollins .05
587 Nomar Garciaparra (Draft Pick) 4.00
588 Cal Ripken Jr. 2.50
589 Pedro Astacio .05
590 J.R. Phillips .05
591 Jeff Frye .05
592 Bo Jackson .10
593 Steve Ontiveros .05
594 David Nied .05
595 Brad Ausmus .05
596 Carlos Baerga .05
597 James Mouton .05
598 Ozzie Guillen .05
599 OF Prospects (Ozzie Timmons, Curtis Goodwin, Johnny Damon), (*Jeff Abbott*) .20
600 Yorkis Perez .05
601 Rich Rodriguez .05
602 Mark McLemore .05
603 Jeff Fassero .05
604 John Roper .05
605 *Mark Johnson* (Draft Pick) .15
606 Wes Chamberlain .05
607 Felix Jose .05
608 Tony Longmire .05
609 Duane Ward .05
610 Brett Butler .05
611 William Van Landingham .05
612 Mickey Tettleton .05
613 Brady Anderson .05
614 Reggie Jefferson .05
615 Mike Kingery .05
616 Derek Bell .05
617 Scott Erickson .05
618 Bob Wickman .05
619 Phil Leftwich .05
620 Dave Justice .20
621 Paul Wilson (Draft Pick) .05
622 Pedro Martinez .65
623 Terry Mathews .05
624 Brian McRae .05
625 Bruce Ruffin .05
626 Steve Finley .05
627 Ron Gant .05
628 Rafael Bournigal .05
629 Darryl Strawberry .05
630 Luis Alicea .05
631 Mark Smith, Scott Klingenbeck (On Deck) .05
632 Cory Bailey, Scott Hatteberg (On Deck) .05
633 Todd Greene, Troy Percival (On Deck) .05
634 Rod Bolton, Olmedo Saenz (On Deck) .05
635 Herb Perry, Steve Kline (On Deck) .05
636 Sean Bergman, Shannon Penn (On Deck) .05
637 Joe Vitiello, Joe Randa (On Deck) .10
638 Jose Mercedes, Duane Singleton (On Deck) .05
639 Marty Cordova, Marc Barcelo (On Deck) .10
640 Ruben Rivera, Andy Pettitte (On Deck) .50
641 Willie Adams, Scott Spiezio (On Deck) .05
642 Eddie Diaz, Desi Relaford (On Deck) .10
643 Jon Shave, Terrell Lowery (On Deck) .05
644 Paul Spoljaric, Angel Martinez (On Deck) .05
645 Damon Hollins, Tony Graffanino (On Deck) .05
646 Darron Cox, Doug Glanville (On Deck) .10
647 Tim Belk, Pat Watkins (On Deck) .05
648 Rod Pedraza, Phil Schneider (On Deck) .05
649 Marc Valdes, Vic Darensbourg (On Deck) .05
650 Rick Huisman, Roberto Petagine (On Deck) .05
651 Ron Coomer, Roger Cedeno (On Deck) .10
652 *Carlos Perez*, Shane Andrews (On Deck) .10
653 Jason Isringhausen, Chris Roberts (On Deck) .10
654 Kevin Jordan, Wayne Gomes (On Deck) .10
655 Esteban Loaiza, Steve Pegues (On Deck) .05
656 John Frascatore, Terry Bradshaw (On Deck) .05
657 Bryce Florie, Andres Berumen (On Deck) .05
658 Keith Williams, Dan Carlson (On Deck) .05
659 Checklist .05
660 Checklist .05

1995 Topps Cyberstats

Inserted into all types of Topps packaging at the rate of about one per 15 cards, this special series attempted to "complete" the statistics from the strike-shortened 1994 baseball season for nearly 400 players. Topps used computer modeling to predict how each player would have ended the season. Fronts of the cards are the same as found in the regular Topps set, except they have been printed on metallic foil. Backs have a black background.

		MT
Complete Set (396):		25.00
Common Player:		.10
1	Frank Thomas	2.25
2	Mickey Morandini	.10
3	Todd Worrell	.10
4	David Cone	.10
5	Trevor Hoffman	.10
6	Shane Mack	.10
7	Delino DeShields	.10
8	Matt Williams	.30
9	Sammy Sosa	2.25
10	Gary DiSarcina	.10
11	Kenny Rogers	.10
12	Jose Vizcaino	.10
13	Lou Whitaker	.10
14	Ron Darling	.10
15	Dave Nilsson	.10
16	Dennis Martinez	.10
17	Orlando Merced	.10
18	John Wetteland	.10
19	Mike Devereaux	.10
20	Rene Arocha	.10
21	Jay Buhner	.10
22	Hal Morris	.10
23	Paul Molitor	1.00
24	Dave West	.10
25	Scott Sanders	.10
26	Eddie Zambrano	.10
27	Ricky Bones	.10
28	John Valentin	.10
29	Kevin Tapani	.10
30	Tim Wallach	.10
31	Darren Lewis	.10
32	Travis Fryman	.10
33	Bret Barberie	.10
34	Dennis Eckersley	.10
35	Ken Hill	.10
36	Pete Harnisch	.10
37	Mike Mussina	.85
38	Dave Winfield	1.50
39	Joey Hamilton	.10
40	Edgar Martinez	.10
41	John Smiley	.10
42	Jim Abbott	.10
43	Mike Kelly	.10
44	Brian Jordan	.10
45	Ken Ryan	.10
46	Matt Mieske	.10
47	Rick Aguilera	.10
48	Ismael Valdes	.10
49	Royce Clayton	.10
50	Juan Gonzalez	1.50
51	Mel Rojas	.10
52	Doug Drabek	.10
53	Charles Nagy	.10
54	Tim Raines	.10
55	Midre Cummings	.10
56	Rafael Palmeiro	.30
57	Charlie Hayes	.10
58	Ray Lankford	.10
59	Tim Davis	.10
60	Andy Ashby	.10
61	Mark Grace	.30
62	Mark Langston	.10
63	Chuck Carr	.10
64	Barry Bonds	2.25
65	David Segui	.10
66	Mariano Duncan	.10
67	Kenny Lofton	.10
68	Ken Caminiti	.10
69	Darrin Jackson	.10
70	Wil Cordero	.10
71	Walt Weiss	.10
72	Tom Pagnozzi	.10

#	Player	MT
73	Bret Boone	.15
74	Wally Joyner	.10
75	Luis Lopez	.10
76	Len Dykstra	.10
77	Pedro Munoz	.10
78	Kevin Gross	.10
79	Eduardo Perez	.10
80	Brent Gates	.10
81	Jeff Conine	.10
82	Paul Sorrento	.10
83	Julio Franco	.10
84	Chris Sabo	.10
85	Dante Bichette	.10
86	Mike Stanley	.10
87	Bob Hamelin	.10
88	Tommy Greene	.10
89	Jeff Brantley	.10
90	Ed Sprague	.10
91	Otis Nixon	.10
92	Chad Curtis	.10
93	Chuck McElroy	.10
94	Troy Neel	.10
95	Benito Santiago	.10
96	Jose Mesa	.10
97	Luis Gonzalez	.40
98	Alex Fernandez	.10
99	Ben McDonald	.10
100	Wade Boggs	1.00
101	Tom Glavine	.15
102	Phil Plantier	.10
103	Raul Mondesi	.30
104	Jim Edmonds	.10
105	Jeff Kent	.10
106	Wilson Alvarez	.10
107	Geronimo Berroa	.10
108	Craig Biggio	.10
109	Roberto Hernandez	.10
110	Bobby Ayala	.10
111	Bob Tewksbury	.10
112	Rondell White	.20
113	Steve Cooke	.10
114	Tim Salmon	.30
115	Kent Mercker	.10
116	Randy Johnson	1.00
117	Mo Vaughn	.75
118	Eddie Williams	.10
119	Jeff Montgomery	.10
120	Kirt Manwaring	.10
121	Pat Hentgen	.10
122	Shawon Dunston	.10
123	Tim Belcher	.10
124	Cecil Fielder	.10
125	Todd Hundley	.10
126	Mark Acre	.10
127	Darrell Whitmore	.10
128	Darryl Kile	.10
129	Jay Bell	.10
130	Harold Baines	.10
131	Felix Fermin	.10
132	Ellis Burks	.10
133	Joe Carter	.10
134	Terry Pendleton	.10
135	Junior Felix	.10
136	Bill Gullickson	.10
137	Melvin Nieves	.10
138	Chuck Knoblauch	.10
139	Bobby Jones	.10
140	Darrin Fletcher	.10
141	Andy Van Slyke	.10
142	Allen Watson	.10
143	Dan Wilson	.10
144	Bip Roberts	.10
145	Sterling Hitchcock	.10
146	Johnny Ruffin	.10
147	Steve Trachsel	.10
148	Ramon Martinez	.10
149	Dave Henderson	.10
150	Chris Gomez	.10
151	Rusty Greer	.10
152	John Franco	.10
153	Mike Bordick	.10
154	Dave Magadan	.10
155	Greg Swindell	.10
156	Arthur Rhodes	.10
157	Juan Guzman	.10
158	Greg Maddux	2.00
159	Mike Macfarlane	.10
160	Curt Schilling	.30
161	Jose Canseco	.75
162	Aaron Sele	.10
163	Steve Buechele	.10
164	Orel Hershiser	.10
165	Mike Henneman	.10
166	Kevin Seitzer	.10
167	Ruben Sierra	.10
168	Alex Cole	.10
169	Jim Thome	.10
170	Lance Johnson	.10
171	Marquis Grissom	.10
172	Jamie Moyer	.10
173	Todd Zeile	.10
174	Chris Bosio	.10
175	Steve Howe	.10
176	Luis Polonia	.10
177	Ryan Klesko	.10
178	Kevin Appier	.10
179	Tim Naehring	.10
180	Randy Myers	.10
181	Mike Jackson	.10
182	Chili Davis	.10
183	Jason Jacome	.10
184	Stan Javier	.10
185	Scott Servais	.10
186	Kirk Rueter	.10
187	Don Slaught	.10
188	Ozzie Smith	2.00
189	Barry Larkin	.15
190	Gary Gaetti	.10
191	Fred McGriff	.10
192	Roger Clemens	2.00
193	Dean Palmer	.10
194	Jeromy Burnitz	.10
195	Scott Kamieniecki	.10
196	Eddie Murray	1.00
197	Ron Karkovice	.10
198	Tino Martinez	.10
199	Ken Griffey Jr.	2.75
200	Don Mattingly	2.25
201	Henry Rodriguez	.10
202	Lenny Harris	.10
203	Ryan Thompson	.10
204	Darren Oliver	.10
205	Omar Vizquel	.10
206	Jeff Bagwell	1.50
207	Todd Van Poppel	.10
208	Leo Gomez	.10
209	Mark Whiten	.10
210	Pedro Martinez	.10
211	Reggie Sanders	.10
212	Kevin Foster	.10
213	Danny Tartabull	.10
214	Jeff Blauser	.10
215	Mike Magnante	.10
216	Tom Candiotti	.10
217	Rod Beck	.10
218	Jody Reed	.10
219	Vince Coleman	.10
220	Danny Jackson	.10
221	Larry Walker	.30
222	Pat Borders	.10
223	Lee Smith	.10
224	Paul O'Neill	.10
225	Devon White	.10
226	Jim Bullinger	.10
227	Steve Avery	.10
228	Tony Gwynn	2.00
229	Pat Meares	.10
230	Bill Swift	.10
231	David Wells	.15
232	John Briscoe	.10
233	Roger Pavlik	.10
234	Roberto Alomar	.75
235	Billy Brewer	.10
236	Gary Sheffield	.25
237	Lou Frazier	.10
238	Terry Steinbach	.10
239	Omar Daal	.10
240	Jason Bere	.10
241	Denny Neagle	.10
242	Danny Bautista	.10
243	Hector Carrasco	.10
244	Bill Risley	.10
245	Andy Benes	.10
246	Jim Leyritz	.10
247	Jose Oliva	.10
248	Greg Vaughn	.10
249	Rich Monteleone	.10
250	Tony Eusebio	.10
251	Chuck Finley	.10
252	Joe Boever	.10
253	Bobby Munoz	.10
254	Bret Saberhagen	.10
255	Kurt Abbott	.10
256	Bobby Witt	.10
257	Cliff Floyd	.10
258	Mark Clark	.10
259	Andujar Cedeno	.10
260	Marvin Freeman	.10
261	Mike Piazza	2.50
262	Pat Kelly	.10
263	Carlos Delgado	.25
264	Willie Banks	.10
265	Matt Walbeck	.10
266	Mark McGwire	3.00
267	Alan Trammell	.10
268	Tom Gordon	.10
269	Greg Colbrunn	.10
270	Darren Daulton	.10
271	Albie Lopez	.10
272	Robin Ventura	.10
273	Bryan Eversgerd	.10
274	Dave Fleming	.10
275	Scott Livingstone	.10
276	Pete Schourek	.10
277	Bernie Williams	.35
278	Mark Lemke	.10
279	Eric Karros	.10
280	Billy Ashley	.10
281	Rico Brogna	.10
282	John Burkett	.10
283	Jorge Fabregas	.10
284	Greg Gagne	.10
285	Doug Jones	.10
286	Troy O'Leary	.10
287	Pat Rapp	.10
288	Butch Henry	.10
289	John Olerud	.10
290	John Hudek	.10
291	Jeff King	.10
292	Bobby Bonilla	.10
293	Albert Belle	.30
294	Rick Wilkins	.10
295	John Jaha	.10
296	Sid Fernandez	.10
297	Deion Sanders	.15
298	Gil Heredia	.10
299	Melido Perez	.10
300	Greg McMichael	.10
301	Rusty Meacham	.10
302	Shawn Green	.30
303	Carlos Garcia	.10
304	Dave Stevens	.10
305	Eric Young	.10
306	Kirk Gibson	.10
307	Spike Owen	.10
308	Sandy Alomar	.10
309	Ricky Gutierrez	.10
310	Dave Veres	.10
311	Gregg Jefferies	.10
312	Jose Valentin	.10
313	Robb Nen	.10
314	Jose Rijo	.10
315	Sean Berry	.10
316	Mike Gallego	.10
317	Roberto Kelly	.10
318	Kevin Stocker	.10
319	Kirby Puckett	2.00
320	Jon Lieber	.10
321	Joe Girardi	.10
322	Tony Phillips	.10
323	Brian Anderson	.10
324	Ivan Rodriguez	.50
325	Jeff Cirillo	.10
326	Joey Cora	.10
327	Chris Hoiles	.10
328	Bernard Gilkey	.10
329	Mike Lansing	.10
330	Jimmy Key	.10
331	Vinny Castilla	.10
332	Mark Guthrie	.10
333	Mike Lieberthal	.10
334	Will Clark	.30
335	Rickey Henderson	1.00
336	Todd Jones	.10
337	Jack McDowell	.10
338	Carlos Rodriguez	.10
339	Mark Eichhorn	.10
340	Jeff Nelson	.10
341	Eric Anthony	.10
342	Randy Velarde	.10
343	Javier Lopez	.10
344	Kevin Mitchell	.10
345	Steve Bedrosian	.10
346	John Kruk	.10
347	Scott Leius	.10
348	John Patterson	.10
349	Kevin Brown	.25
350	Mike Moore	.10
351	Manny Ramirez	1.50
352	Jose Lind	.10
353	Derrick May	.10
354	Cal Eldred	.10
355	J.T. Snow	.10
356	Luis Sojo	.10
357	Moises Alou	.25
358	Dave Clark	.10
359	Dave Hollins	.10
360	Cal Ripken Jr.	3.00
361	Pedro Astacio	.10
362	Tony Longmire	.10
363	Jeff Frye	.10
364	Bo Jackson	.15
365	Steve Ontiveros	.10
366	David Nied	.10
367	Brad Ausmus	.10
368	Carlos Baerga	.10
369	James Mouton	.10
370	Ozzie Guillen	.10
371	Yorkis Perez	.10
372	Rich Rodriguez	.10
373	Mark McLemore	.10
374	Jeff Fassero	.10
375	John Roper	.10
376	Wes Chamberlain	.10
377	Felix Jose	.10
378	Brett Butler	.10
379	William Van Landingham	.10
380	Mickey Tettleton	.10
381	Brady Anderson	.10
382	Reggie Jefferson	.10
383	Mike Kingery	.10
384	Derek Bell	.10
385	Scott Erickson	.10
386	Bob Wickman	.10
387	Phil Leftwich	.10
388	Dave Justice	.25
389	Pedro Martinez	.10
390	Terry Mathews	.10
391	Brian McRae	.10
392	Bruce Ruffin	.10
393	Steve Finley	.10
394	Rafael Bournigal	.10
395	Darryl Strawberry	.10
396	Luis Alicea	.10

1995 Topps Cyberstat Season in Review

This special edition of Cyberstat cards was available only in Topps factory sets. Carrying forward the idea of computerized projections to complete the strike-shortened 1994 season, the Season in Review cards speculate on career milestones and the playoffs that never happened. The Season in Review cards have player action photos printed on a foil background resembling the U.S. flag. Names are in gold foil. Backs have a black background and a recap of the computer simulation.

#		MT
	Complete Set (7):	10.00
	Common Player:	1.00
1	Barry Bonds (61 Home Runs)	5.00
2	Jose Canseco (AL West One-Game Playoff)	2.00
3	Juan Gonzalez (AL Divisional Playoffs)	3.00
4	Fred McGriff (NL Divisional Playoffs)	1.00
5	Carlos Baerga (ALCS MVP)	1.00

6 Ryan Klesko (NLCS MVP) 1.00
7 Kenny Lofton (World Series MVP) 1.00

1995 Topps League Leaders

League Leaders is a 50-card insert set found in one of every six retail packs only of both Series I and II. The set includes the top five players in each league across 10 statistical categories. Cards featured the statistical category running up the right side, with the player's name across the bottom. Photo backgrounds have been darkened and posterized to make the player action stand out. Backs have the player's stat rankings within his division and league, and a bar graph at bottom gives his performance in that statistical category for the previous five seasons.

		MT
Complete Set (50):		20.00
Common Player:		.15
1	Albert Belle	.40
2	Kevin Mitchell	.15
3	Wade Boggs	.60
4	Tony Gwynn	1.00
5	Moises Alou	.35
6	Andres Galarraga	.15
7	Matt Williams	.40
8	Barry Bonds	1.50
9	Frank Thomas	1.25
10	Jose Canseco	.60
11	Jeff Bagwell	.65
12	Kirby Puckett	1.00
13	Julio Franco	.15
14	Albert Belle	.40
15	Fred McGriff	.15
16	Kenny Lofton	.15
17	Otis Nixon	.15
18	Brady Anderson	.15
19	Deion Sanders	.25
20	Chuck Carr	.15
21	Pat Hentgen	.15
22	Andy Benes	.15
23	Roger Clemens	1.00
24	Greg Maddux	1.00
25	Pedro Martinez	.75
26	Paul O'Neill	.15
27	Jeff Bagwell	.65
28	Frank Thomas	1.25
29	Hal Morris	.15
30	Kenny Lofton	.15
31	Ken Griffey Jr.	3.00
32	Jeff Bagwell	.65
33	Albert Belle	.40
34	Fred McGriff	.15
35	Cecil Fielder	.15
36	Matt Williams	.40
37	Joe Carter	.15
38	Dante Bichette	.15
39	Frank Thomas	1.25
40	Mike Piazza	2.00
41	Craig Biggio	.15
42	Vince Coleman	.15
43	Marquis Grissom	.15
44	Chuck Knoblauch	.15
45	Darren Lewis	.15
46	Randy Johnson	.75
47	Jose Rijo	.15
48	Chuck Finley	.15
49	Bret Saberhagen	.15
50	Kevin Appier	.15

1995 Topps Total Bases Finest

Printed in Topps Finest technology, including a peel-off plastic protector coating on the front, these cards honor the 1994 statistical leaders in total bases. The cards have a silver waffle-texture background on front as a background to the color action photo. At bottom is a team logo and team-color bar with the player's name. Backs feature a portrait photo and the player's total base stats. These inserts are found in Series II Topps packs at an average rate of one per 36 packs (one box).

		MT
Complete Set (15):		12.50
Common Player:		.50
1	Jeff Bagwell	1.00
2	Albert Belle	.65
3	Ken Griffey Jr.	3.00
4	Frank Thomas	2.00
5	Matt Williams	.50
6	Dante Bichette	.50
7	Barry Bonds	2.00
8	Moises Alou	.75
9	Andres Galarraga	.50
10	Kenny Lofton	.50
11	Rafael Palmeiro	.65
12	Tony Gwynn	1.50
13	Kirby Puckett	1.50
14	Jose Canseco	.75
15	Jeff Conine	.50

1995 Topps Traded and Rookies

Traded players, free agents signed by new teams and all the up-and-coming rookies are the meat of the 1995 Topps Traded and Rookies set, sold for the first time exclusively in foil-pack form. Maintaining the same format used in Series 1 and 2 Topps, the updates also reused the Future Star, Draft Pick and Star Track subsets, along with four-player Prospects cards. New subsets included Rookie of the Year Candidates, All-Stars, On Deck and "At the Break," 10 cards chronicling star players' performances through the first half of the 1995 season. A double-thick, foil-printed version of the "At the Break" cards called "Power Boosters" were the only inserts in the Traded/Rookies set.

		MT
Complete Set (165):		40.00
Common Player:		.05
Pack (11):		1.50
Wax Box (36):		45.00
1	Frank Thomas (At The Break)	.65
2	Ken Griffey Jr. (At The Break)	.75
3	Barry Bonds (At The Break)	.65
4	Albert Belle (At The Break)	.20
5	Cal Ripken Jr. (At The Break)	1.00
6	Mike Piazza (At The Break)	.75
7	Tony Gwynn (At The Break)	.50
8	Jeff Bagwell (At The Break)	.45
9	Mo Vaughn (At The Break)	.35
10	Matt Williams (At The Break)	.15
11	Ray Durham	.10
12	*Juan LeBron* (Draft Pick)	.25
13	Shawn Green (Rookie of the Year Candidate)	.50
14	Kevin Gross	.05
15	Jon Nunnally	.05
16	*Brian Maxcy*	.05
17	Mark Kiefer	.05
18	*Carlos Beltran* (Draft Pick) (photo actually Juan Beltran)	4.00
19	*Mike Mimbs*	.05
20	Larry Walker	.30
21	Chad Curtis	.05
22	Jeff Barry	.05
23	Joe Oliver	.05
24	*Tomas Perez*	.15
25	*Michael Barrett* (Draft Pick)	.50
26	Brian McRae	.05
27	Derek Bell	.05
28	Ray Durham (Rookie of the Year Candidate)	.10
29	Todd Williams	.05
30	*Ryan Jaroncyk* (Draft Pick)	.05
31	Todd Steverson	.05
32	Mike Devereaux	.05
33	Rheal Cormier	.05
34	Benny Santiago	.05
35	*Bobby Higginson*	1.50
36	Jack McDowell	.05
37	Mike Macfarlane	.05
38	*Tony McKnight* (Draft Pick)	.05
39	Brian Hunter (Rookie of the Year Candidate)	.05
40	*Hideo Nomo* (Star Track)	3.00
41	Brett Butler	.05
42	Donovan Osborne	.05
43	Scott Karl	.05
44	Tony Phillips	.05
45	Marty Cordova (Rookie of the Year Candidate)	.20
46	Dave Mlicki	.05
47	*Bronson Arroyo* (Draft Pick)	.25
48	John Burkett	.05
49	*J.D. Smart* (Draft Pick)	.05
50	Mickey Tettleton	.05
51	Todd Stottlemyre	.05
52	Mike Perez	.05
53	Terry Mulholland	.05
54	Edgardo Alfonzo	.10
55	Zane Smith	.05
56	Jacob Brumfield	.05
57	Andujar Cedeno	.05
58	Jose Parra	.05
59	Manny Alexander	.05
60	Tony Tarasco	.05
61	Orel Hershiser	.05
62	Tim Scott	.05
63	*Felix Rodriguez*	.05
64	Ken Hill	.05
65	Marquis Grissom	.05
66	Lee Smith	.05
67	Jason Bates (Rookie of the Year Candidate)	.05
68	Felipe Lira	.05
69	*Alex Hernandez* (Draft Pick)	.50
70	Tony Fernandez	.05
71	Scott Radinsky	.05
72	Jose Canseco	.50
73	*Mark Grudzielanek*	.50
74	*Ben Davis* (Draft Pick)	1.00
75	Jim Abbott	.05
76	Roger Bailey	.05
77	Gregg Jefferies	.05
78	Erik Hanson	.05
79	*Brad Radke*	3.00
80	Jaime Navarro	.05
81	John Wetteland	.05
82	*Chad Fonville*	.10
83	John Mabry	.05
84	Glenallen Hill	.05
85	Ken Caminiti	.05
86	Tom Goodwin	.05
87	Darren Bragg	.05
88	1995 Prospects (Pitchers) (*Pat Ahearne*), (*Gary Rath*), (*Larry Wimberly*), (*Robbie Bell*)	.50
89	Jeff Russell	.05
90	Dave Gallagher	.05
91	Steve Finley	.05
92	Vaughn Eshelman	.05
93	Kevin Jarvis	.05
94	Mark Gubicza	.05
95	Tim Wakefield	.05
96	Bob Tewksbury	.05
97	*Sid Roberson*	.05
98	Tom Henke	.05
99	Michael Tucker (Future Star)	.05
100	Jason Bates	.05
101	Otis Nixon	.05
102	Mark Whiten	.05
103	Dilson Torres	.05
104	*Melvin Bunch*	.05
105	Terry Pendleton	.05
106	*Corey Jenkins* (Draft Pick)	.05
107	On Deck (*Glenn Dishman*), (*Rob Grable*)	.10
108	*Reggie Taylor* (Draft Pick)	.15
109	Curtis Goodwin (Rookie of the Year Candidate)	.05
110	David Cone	.05
111	Antonio Osuna	.05
112	Paul Shuey	.05
113	Doug Jones	.05
114	Mark McLemore	.05
115	Kevin Ritz	.05
116	John Kruk	.05
117	Trevor Wilson	.05
118	Jerald Clark	.05
119	Julian Tavarez	.05
120	Tim Pugh	.05
121	Todd Zeile	.05
122	1995 Prospects (Fielders) (*Mark Sweeney*, George Arias), (*Richie Sexson*), (*Brian Schneider*)	5.00
123	Bobby Witt	.05
124	Hideo Nomo (Rookie of the Year Candidate)	1.50

125	Joey Cora	.05
126	*Jim Scharrer* (Draft Pick)	.05
127	Paul Quantrill	.05
128	Chipper Jones (Rookie of the Year Candidate)	.75
129	*Kenny James* (Draft Pick)	.05
130	On Deck (Lyle Mouton, Mariano Rivera)	.25
131	Tyler Green (Rookie of the Year Candidate)	.05
132	Brad Clontz	.05
133	Jon Nunnally (Rookie of the Year Candidate)	.05
134	Dave Magadan	.05
135	Al Leiter	.05
136	Bret Barberie	.05
137	Bill Swift	.05
138	Scott Cooper	.05
139	Roberto Kelly	.05
140	Charlie Hayes	.05
141	Pete Harnisch	.05
142	Rich Amaral	.05
143	Rudy Seanez	.05
144	Pat Listach	.05
145	Quilvio Veras (Rookie of the Year Candidate)	.05
146	*Jose Olmeda* (Draft Pick)	.05
147	Roberto Petagine	.05
148	Kevin Brown	.20
149	Phil Plantier	.05
150	*Carlos Perez* (Rookie of the Year Candidate)	.10
151	Pat Borders	.05
152	Tyler Green	.05
153	Stan Belinda	.05
154	Dave Stewart	.05
155	Andre Dawson	.15
156	Frank Thomas, Fred McGriff (All-Star)	.30
157	Carlos Baerga, Craig Biggio (All-Star)	.10
158	Wade Boggs, Matt Williams (All-Star)	.10
159	Cal Ripken Jr., Ozzie Smith (All-Star)	.75
160	Ken Griffey Jr., Tony Gwynn (All-Star)	.40
161	Albert Belle, Barry Bonds (All-Star)	.35
162	Kirby Puckett, Len Dykstra (All-Star)	.25
163	Ivan Rodriguez, Mike Piazza (All-Star)	.35
164	Randy Johnson, Hideo Nomo (All-Star)	.35
165	Checklist	.05

1995 Topps Traded and Rookies Power Boosters

Virtually identical to the first 10 cards of the 1995 Topps Traded and Rookies issue, the "At the Break" subset is the only insert found in Traded packs. Cards are printed on double-thick cardboard stock on metallized foil. The chase cards are found at an average rate of one per 36 packs.

		MT
Complete Set (10):		13.00
Common Player:		.50
1	Frank Thomas	2.00
2	Ken Griffey Jr.	3.00
3	Barry Bonds	2.00
4	Albert Belle	.50
5	Cal Ripken Jr.	3.50
6	Mike Piazza	2.50
7	Tony Gwynn	1.50
8	Jeff Bagwell	1.00
9	Mo Vaughn	.75
10	Matt Williams	.50

1995 Topps/DIII

Describing its cards as featuring "infinite depth perspectives" with game-action photos, Topps entered the 3-D card market with its Dimension III product. Utilizing "super thick laminated construction" to provide the illusion of depth, the cards feature borderless action photos on front. Backs are conventionally printed with a color portrait photo and several sets of stats that go beyond the usual to the provide a more in-depth look at the player's performance.

		MT
Complete Set (59):		10.00
Common Player:		.15
Retail Pack (3):		.50
Retail Wax Box (24):		8.00
Hobby Pack (5):		.60
Hobby Wax Box (24):		10.00
1	Dave Justice	.25
2	Cal Ripken Jr.	2.50
3	Ruben Sierra	.15
4	Roberto Alomar	.75
5	Dennis Martinez	.15
6	Todd Zeile	.15
7	Albert Belle	.25
8	Chuck Knoblauch	.15
9	Roger Clemens	1.00
10	Cal Eldred	.15
11	Dennis Eckersley	.15
12	Andy Benes	.15
13	Moises Alou	.25
14	Andres Galarraga	.15
15	Jim Thome	.15
16	Tim Salmon	.25
17	Carlos Garcia	.15
18	Scott Leius	.15
19	Jeff Montgomery	.15
20	Brian Anderson	.15
21	Will Clark	.25
22	Bobby Bonilla	.15
23	Mike Stanley	.15
24	Barry Bonds	1.25
25	Jeff Conine	.15
26	Paul O'Neill	.15
27	Mike Piazza	1.50
28	Tom Glavine	.15
29	Jim Edmonds	.15
30	Lou Whitaker	.15
31	Jeff Frye	.15
32	Ivan Rodriguez	.60
33	Bret Boone	.15
34	Mike Greenwell	.15
35	Mark Grace	.45
36	Darren Lewis	.15
37	Don Mattingly	1.25
38	Jose Rijo	.15
39	Robin Ventura	.15
40	Bob Hamelin	.15
41	Tim Wallach	.15
42	Tony Gwynn	1.00
43	Ken Griffey Jr.	2.00
44	Doug Drabek	.15
45	Rafael Palmeiro	.25
46	Dean Palmer	.15
47	Bip Roberts	.15
48	Barry Larkin	.15
49	Dave Nilsson	.15
50	Wil Cordero	.15
51	Travis Fryman	.15
52	Chuck Carr	.15
53	Rey Sanchez	.15
54	Walt Weiss	.15
55	Joe Carter	.15
56	Len Dykstra	.15
57	Orlando Merced	.15
58	Ozzie Smith	1.00
59	Chris Gomez	.15

1995 Topps/DIII Zone

A barrage of baseballs in the background, behind a player action photo, are featured on the front of this DIII chase set.Backs have a blazing baseball across the top and a description and stats of the pictured player's hot streaks of the previous season -- those times when athletes are said to be "in the zone." The inserts are found on average of one per six packs.

		MT
Complete Set (6):		4.00
Common Player:		.50
1	Frank Thomas	2.00
2	Kirby Puckett	1.50
3	Jeff Bagwell	1.00
4	Fred McGriff	.50
5	Raul Mondesi	.50
6	Kenny Lofton	.50

1995 Topps/ Embossed

Taking the embossed sportscard idea which Action Packed developed years earlier to a new level, Topps Embossed baseball features the tactile image on both sides of the card. Fronts have a lightly textured border while the central player photo is deeply embossed. The player name is embossed in gold-foil letters at bottom. Backs have another embossed player photo and various levels of embossing around the borders and boxes which contain stats and trivia.

		MT
Complete Set (140):		10.00
Common Player:		.10
Embossed Golds:		2X
Wax Pack (6+1):		1.00
Wax Box (24):		15.00
1	Kenny Lofton	.10
2	Gary Sheffield	.25
3	Hal Morris	.10
4	Cliff Floyd	.10
5	Pat Hentgen	.10
6	Tony Gwynn	.65
7	Jose Valentin	.10
8	Jason Bere	.10
9	Jeff Kent	.10
10	John Valentin	.10
11	Brian Anderson	.10
12	Deion Sanders	.15
13	Ryan Thompson	.10
14	Ruben Sierra	.10
15	Jay Bell	.10
16	Chuck Carr	.10
17	Brent Gates	.10
18	Bret Boone	.15
19	Paul Molitor	.45
20	Chili Davis	.10
21	Ryan Klesko	.10
22	Will Clark	.25
23	Greg Vaughn	.10
24	Moises Alou	.15
25	Ray Lankford	.10
26	Jose Rijo	.10
27	Bobby Jones	.10
28	Rick Wilkins	.10
29	Cal Eldred	.10
30	Juan Gonzalez	.50
31	Royce Clayton	.10
32	Bryan Harvey	.10
33	Dave Nilsson	.10
34	Chris Hoiles	.10
35	David Nied	.10
36	Javy Lopez	.10
37	Tim Wallach	.10
38	Bobby Bonilla	.10
39	Danny Tartabull	.10
40	Andy Benes	.10
41	Dean Palmer	.10
42	Chris Gomez	.10
43	Kevin Appier	.10
44	Brady Anderson	.10
45	Alex Fernandez	.10
46	Roberto Kelly	.10
47	Dave Hollins	.10
48	Chuck Finley	.10
49	Wade Boggs	.50
50	Travis Fryman	.10
51	Ken Griffey Jr.	1.25
52	John Olerud	.10
53	Delino DeShields	.10
54	Ivan Rodriguez	.40
55	Tommy Greene	.10

56 Tom Pagnozzi .10
57 Bip Roberts .10
58 Luis Gonzalez .30
59 Rey Sanchez .10
60 Ken Ryan .10
61 Darren Daulton .10
62 Rick Aguilera .10
63 Wally Joyner .10
64 Mike Greenwell .10
65 Jay Buhner .10
66 Craig Biggio .10
67 Charles Nagy .10
68 Devon White .10
69 Randy Johnson .50
70 Shawon Dunston .10
71 Kirby Puckett .65
72 Paul O'Neill .10
73 Tino Martinez .10
74 Carlos Garcia .10
75 Ozzie Smith .65
76 Cecil Fielder .10
77 Mike Stanley .10
78 Lance Johnson .10
79 Tony Phillips .10
80 Bobby Munoz .10
81 Kevin Tapani .10
82 William Van Landingham .10
83 Dante Bichette .10
84 Tom Candiotti .10
85 Wil Cordero .10
86 Jeff Conine .10
87 Joey Hamilton .10
88 Mark Whiten .10
89 Jeff Montgomery .10
90 Andres Galarraga .10
91 Roberto Alomar .45
92 Orlando Merced .10
93 Mike Mussina .50
94 Pedro Martinez .40
95 Carlos Baerga .10
96 Steve Trachsel .10
97 Lou Whitaker .10
98 David Cone .10
99 Chuck Knoblauch .10
100 Frank Thomas .75
101 Dave Justice .25
102 Raul Mondesi .25
103 Rickey Henderson .50
104 Doug Drabek .10
105 Sandy Alomar .10
106 Roger Clemens .65
107 Mark McGwire 1.50
108 Tim Salmon .25
109 Greg Maddux .65
110 Mike Piazza 1.00
111 Tom Glavine .15
112 Walt Weiss .10
113 Cal Ripken Jr. 1.50
114 Eddie Murray .50
115 Don Mattingly .75
116 Ozzie Guillen .10
117 Bob Hamelin .10
118 Jeff Bagwell .50
119 Eric Karros .10
120 Barry Bonds .75
121 Mickey Tettleton .10
122 Mark Langston .10
123 Robin Ventura .10
124 Bret Saberhagen .10
125 Albert Belle .25
126 Rafael Palmeiro .10
127 Fred McGriff .10
128 Jimmy Key .10
129 Barry Larkin .15
130 Tim Raines .10
131 Len Dykstra .10
132 Todd Zeile .10
133 Joe Carter .10
134 Matt Williams .25
135 Terry Steinbach .10
136 Manny Ramirez .50
137 John Wetteland .10
138 Rod Beck .10
139 Mo Vaughn .40
140 Darren Lewis .10

1995 Topps/ Embossed Golden Idols

The only insert in the Topps Embossed baseball set was a parallel set of the 140 cards rendered in gold tones on front and inserted at the rate of one per pack. Backs are identical to the regular version.

	MT
Complete Set (140):	25.00
Common Player:	.25
(Star cards valued at 2X corresponding regular Embossed cards)	

1995 Topps Opening Day

This 10-card set featuring top performers on the belated opening day of the 1995 season was available exclusively in retail factory sets. Card fronts feature color action photos printed on textured foil in a U.S. flag-like design. A large colorful Opening Day logo appears in an upper corner while the player's key stats from that game appear in a foil box at lower-right. Backs have a portrait photo along with complete details and a stats line of the opening day performance.

	MT
Complete Set (10):	10.00
Common Player:	1.00
1 Kevin Appier	1.00
2 Dante Bichette	1.00
3 Ken Griffey Jr.	5.00
4 Todd Hundley	1.00
5 John Jaha	1.00
6 Fred McGriff	1.00
7 Raul Mondesi	1.00
8 Manny Ramirez	3.00
9 Danny Tartabull	1.00
10 Devon White	1.00

1996 Topps

At 440 cards, the basic Topps set for 1996 was the smallest regular-issue from the company since it adopted the 2-1/2" x 3-1/2" format in 1957. Honoring the late Mickey Mantle on card No. 7, Topps announced it would hereafter retire that card number. Subsets in the 220-card Series 1 are Star Power, Commemoratives, Draft Picks, Tribute, AAA Stars and Future Stars. Series 2 subsets repeat Star Power and Draft Picks and add Prospects, Now Appearing and Rookie All-Stars. Three different factory sets were available with each including the 440-card base set and various inserts. The "Cereal Box" set, so named because of the resemblance of its four component boxes to single-serving cereal boxes, has four of the Mantle inserts. The Retail and Hobby sets each include seven randomly packed chase cards, a plastic-cased #7 Mantle card labeled "Last Day Production" and a Mantle Foundation card. In addition the Retail version has one of the 19 Mantle reprints.

	MT
Unopened Hobby Factory Set (449):	40.00
Unopened Retail Factory Set (450):	40.00
Unopened Cereal Box Set (444):	35.00
Complete Set (440):	25.00
Common Player:	.05
Series 1 Pack (12):	2.00
Series 1 Wax Box (36):	60.00
Series 2 Pack (12):	1.25
Series 2 Wax Box (36):	35.00

1 Tony Gwynn (Star Power) .50
2 Mike Piazza (Star Power) .60
3 Greg Maddux (Star Power) .50
4 Jeff Bagwell (Star Power) .40
5 Larry Walker (Star Power) .20
6 Barry Larkin (Star Power) .05
7 Mickey Mantle (Commemorative) 3.00
8 Tom Glavine (Star Power) .05
9 Craig Biggio (Star Power) .05
10 Barry Bonds (Star Power) .65
11 Heathcliff Slocumb (Star Power) .05
12 Matt Williams (Star Power) .05
13 Todd Helton (Draft Pick) 1.00
14 Mark Redman (Draft Pick) .10
15 Michael Barrett (Draft Pick) .25
16 Ben Davis (Draft Pick) .25
17 Juan LeBron (Draft Pick) .05
18 Tony McKnight (Draft Pick) .05
19 Ryan Jaroncyk (Draft Pick) .05
20 Corey Jenkins (Draft Pick) .05
21 Jim Scharrer (Draft Pick) .05
22 *Mark Bellhorn* (Draft Pick) .20
23 *Jarrod Washburn* (Draft Pick) 1.00
24 *Geoff Jenkins* (Draft Pick) 2.50
25 *Sean Casey* (Draft Pick) 3.00
26 *Brett Tomko* (Draft Pick) .10
27 Tony Fernandez .05
28 Rich Becker .05
29 Andujar Cedeno .05
30 Paul Molitor .50
31 Brent Gates .05
32 Glenallen Hill .05
33 Mike MacFarlane .05
34 Manny Alexander .05
35 Todd Zeile .05
36 Joe Girardi .05
37 Tony Tarasco .05
38 Tim Belcher .05
39 Tom Goodwin .05
40 Orel Hershiser .05
41 Tripp Cromer .05
42 Sean Bergman .05
43 Troy Percival .05
44 Kevin Stocker .05
45 Albert Belle .40
46 Tony Eusebio .05
47 Sid Roberson .05
48 Todd Hollandsworth .05
49 Mark Wohlers .05
50 Kirby Puckett 1.00
51 Darren Holmes .05
52 Ron Karkovice .05
53 Al Martin .05
54 Pat Rapp .05
55 Mark Grace .20
56 Greg Gagne .05
57 Stan Javier .05
58 Scott Sanders .05
59 J.T. Snow .05
60 David Justice .20
61 Royce Clayton .05
62 Kevin Foster .05
63 Tim Naehring .05
64 Orlando Miller .05
65 Mike Mussina .45
66 Jim Eisenreich .05
67 Felix Fermin .05
68 Bernie Williams .30
69 Robb Nen .05
70 Ron Gant .05
71 Felipe Lira .05
72 Jacob Brumfield .05
73 John Mabry .05
74 Mark Carreon .05
75 Carlos Baerga .05
76 Jim Dougherty .05
77 Ryan Thompson .05
78 Scott Leius .05
79 Roger Pavlik .05
80 Gary Sheffield .35
81 Julian Tavarez .05
82 Andy Ashby .05
83 Mark Lemke .05
84 Omar Vizquel .05
85 Darren Daulton .05
86 Mike Lansing .05
87 Rusty Greer .05
88 Dave Stevens .05
89 Jose Offerman .05
90 Tom Henke .05

91 Troy O'Leary .05
92 Michael Tucker .05
93 Marvin Freeman .05
94 Alex Diaz .05
95 John Wetteland .05
96 Cal Ripken Jr. (Tribute Card) 1.50
97 Mike Mimbs .05
98 Bobby Higginson .15
99 Edgardo Alfonzo .05
100 Frank Thomas 1.25
101 Steve Gibralter, Bob Abreu (AAA Stars) .15
102 Brian Givens, T.J. Mathews (AAA Stars) .05
103 Chris Pritchett, Trenidad Hubbard (AAA Stars) .05
104 Eric Owens, Butch Huskey (AAA Stars) .10
105 Doug Drabek .05
106 Tomas Perez .05
107 Mark Leiter .05
108 Joe Oliver .05
109 Tony Castillo .05
110 Checklist .05
111 Kevin Seitzer .05
112 Pete Schourek .05
113 Sean Berry .05
114 Todd Stottlemyre .05
115 Joe Carter .05
116 Jeff King .05
117 Dan Wilson .05
118 Kurt Abbott .05
119 Lyle Mouton .05
120 Jose Rijo .05
121 Curtis Goodwin .05
122 *Jose Valentin* .05
123 Ellis Burks .05
124 David Cone .05
125 Eddie Murray .50
126 Brian Jordan .05
127 Darrin Fletcher .05
128 Curt Schilling .15
129 Ozzie Guillen .05
130 Kenny Rogers .05
131 Tom Pagnozzi .05
132 Garret Anderson .05
133 Bobby Jones .05
134 Chris Gomez .05
135 Mike Stanley .05
136 Hideo Nomo .75
137 Jon Nunnally .05
138 Tim Wakefield .05
139 Steve Finley .05
140 Ivan Rodriguez .50
141 Quilvio Veras .05
142 Mike Fetters .05
143 Mike Greenwell .05
144 Bill Pulsipher .05
145 Mark McGwire 2.00
146 Frank Castillo .05
147 Greg Vaughn .05
148 Pat Hentgen .05
149 Walt Weiss .05
150 Randy Johnson .50
151 David Segui .05
152 Benji Gil .05
153 Tom Candiotti .05
154 Geronimo Berroa .05
155 John Franco .05
156 Jay Bell .05
157 Mark Gubicza .05
158 Hal Morris .05
159 Wilson Alvarez .05
160 Derek Bell .05
161 Ricky Bottalico .05
162 Bret Boone .10
163 Brad Radke .05
164 John Valentin .05
165 Steve Avery .05
166 Mark McLemore .05
167 Danny Jackson .05
168 Tino Martinez .05
169 Shane Reynolds .05
170 Terry Pendleton .05
171 Jim Edmonds .05
172 Esteban Loaiza .05
173 Ray Durham .05
174 Carlos Perez .05
175 Raul Mondesi .25
176 Steve Ontiveros .05
177 Chipper Jones 1.50
178 Otis Nixon .05
179 John Burkett .05
180 Gregg Jefferies .05
181 Denny Martinez .05
182 Ken Caminiti .05
183 Doug Jones .05
184 Brian McRae .05
185 Don Mattingly 1.25
186 Mel Rojas .05
187 Marty Cordova .05
188 Vinny Castilla .05
189 John Smoltz .10
190 Travis Fryman .05
191 Chris Hoiles .05
192 Chuck Finley .05
193 Ryan Klesko .05
194 Alex Fernandez .05
195 Dante Bichette .05
196 Eric Karros .05
197 Roger Clemens 1.00
198 Randy Myers .05
199 Tony Phillips .05
200 Cal Ripken Jr. 2.00
201 Rod Beck .05
202 Chad Curtis .05
203 Jack McDowell .05
204 Gary Gaetti .05
205 Ken Griffey Jr. 1.75
206 Ramon Martinez .05
207 Jeff Kent .05
208 Brad Ausmus .05
209 Devon White .05
210 Jason Giambi (Future Star) .35
211 Nomar Garciaparra (Future Star) 1.00
212 Billy Wagner (Future Star) .10
213 Todd Greene (Future Star) .05
214 Paul Wilson (Future Star) .05
215 Johnny Damon (Future Star) .10
216 Alan Benes (Future Star) .05
217 Karim Garcia (Future Star) .10
218 Dustin Hermanson (Future Star) .10
219 Derek Jeter (Future Star) 1.50
220 Checklist .05
221 Kirby Puckett (Star Power) .50
222 Cal Ripken Jr. (Star Power) 1.00
223 Albert Belle (Star Power) .20
224 Randy Johnson (Star Power) .25
225 Wade Boggs (Star Power) .25
226 Carlos Baerga (Star Power) .05
227 Ivan Rodriguez (Star Power) .25
228 Mike Mussina (Star Power) .20
229 Frank Thomas (Star Power) .65
230 Ken Griffey Jr. (Star Power) .85
231 Jose Mesa (Star Power) .05
232 *Matt Morris* (Draft Pick) 1.50
233 Craig Wilson (Draft Pick) .05
234 *Alvie Shepherd* (Draft Pick) .05
235 *Randy Winn* (Draft Pick) .05
236 *David Yocum* (Draft Pick) .05
237 *Jason Brester* (Draft Pick) .05
238 *Shane Monahan* (Draft Pick) .05
239 *Brian McNichol* (Draft Pick) .05
240 Reggie Taylor (Draft Pick) .05
241 Garrett Long (Draft Pick) .05
242 *Jonathan Johnson* (Draft Pick) .10
243 *Jeff Liefer* (Draft Pick) .10
244 *Brian Powell* (Draft Pick) .05
245 Brian Buchanan (Draft Pick) .05
246 Mike Piazza 1.50
247 Edgar Martinez .05
248 Chuck Knoblauch .05
249 Andres Galarraga .05
250 Tony Gwynn 1.00
251 Lee Smith .05
252 Sammy Sosa 1.25
253 Jim Thome .05
254 Frank Rodriguez .05
255 Charlie Hayes .05
256 Bernard Gilkey .05
257 John Smiley .05
258 Brady Anderson .05
259 Rico Brogna .05
260 Kirt Manwaring .05
261 Len Dykstra .05
262 Tom Glavine .10
263 Vince Coleman .05
264 John Olerud .05
265 Orlando Merced .05
266 Kent Mercker .05
267 Terry Steinbach .05
268 Brian Hunter .05
269 Jeff Fassero .05
270 Jay Buhner .05
271 Jeff Brantley .05
272 Tim Raines .05
273 Jimmy Key .05
274 Mo Vaughn .35
275 Andre Dawson .15
276 Jose Mesa .05
277 Brett Butler .05
278 Luis Gonzalez .30
279 Steve Sparks .05
280 Chili Davis .05
281 Carl Everett .10
282 Jeff Cirillo .05
283 Thomas Howard .05
284 Paul O'Neill .05
285 Pat Meares .05
286 Mickey Tettleton .05
287 Rey Sanchez .05
288 Bip Roberts .05
289 Roberto Alomar .50
290 Ruben Sierra .05
291 John Flaherty .05
292 Bret Saberhagen .05
293 Barry Larkin .10
294 Sandy Alomar .05
295 Ed Sprague .05
296 Gary DiSarcina .05
297 Marquis Grissom .05
298 John Frascatore .05
299 Will Clark .15
300 Barry Bonds 1.25
301 Ozzie Smith 1.00
302 Dave Nilsson .05
303 Pedro Martinez .50
304 Joey Cora .05
305 Rick Aguilera .05
306 Craig Biggio .10
307 Jose Vizcaino .05
308 Jeff Montgomery .05
309 Moises Alou .15
310 Robin Ventura .05
311 David Wells .10
312 Delino DeShields .05
313 Trevor Hoffman .05
314 Andy Benes .05
315 Deion Sanders .10
316 Jim Bullinger .05
317 John Jaha .05
318 Greg Maddux 1.00
319 Tim Salmon .20
320 Ben McDonald .05
321 *Sandy Martinez* .05
322 Dan Miceli .05
323 Wade Boggs .50
324 Ismael Valdes .05
325 Juan Gonzalez .75
326 Charles Nagy .05
327 Ray Lankford .05
328 Mark Portugal .05
329 Bobby Bonilla .05
330 Reggie Sanders .05
331 Jamie Brewington .05
332 Aaron Sele .05
333 Pete Harnisch .05
334 Cliff Floyd .05
335 Cal Eldred .05
336 Jason Bates (Now Appearing) .05
337 Tony Clark (Now Appearing) .05
338 Jose Herrera (Now Appearing) .05
339 Alex Ochoa (Now Appearing) .05
340 Mark Loretta (Now Appearing) .05
341 *Donne Wall* (Now Appearing) .05
342 Jason Kendall (Now Appearing) .10
343 Shannon Stewart (Now Appearing) .10
344 Brooks Kieschnick (Now Appearing) .05
345 Chris Snopek (Now Appearing) .05
346 Ruben Rivera (Now Appearing) .05
347 Jeff Suppan (Now Appearing) .05
348 Phil Nevin (Now Appearing) .10
349 John Wasdin (Now Appearing) .05
350 Jay Payton (Now Appearing) .05
351 Tim Crabtree (Now Appearing) .05
352 Rick Krivda (Now Appearing) .05
353 Bob Wolcott (Now Appearing) .05
354 Jimmy Haynes (Now Appearing) .05
355 Herb Perry .05
356 Ryne Sandberg .75
357 Harold Baines .05
358 Chad Ogea .05
359 Lee Tinsley .05
360 Matt Williams .15
361 Randy Velarde .05
362 Jose Canseco .50
363 Larry Walker .35
364 Kevin Appier .05
365 Darryl Hamilton .05
366 Jose Lima .05
367 Javy Lopez .05
368 Dennis Eckersley .05
369 Jason Isringhausen .10
370 Mickey Morandini .05
371 Scott Cooper .05
372 Jim Abbott .05
373 Paul Sorrento .05
374 Chris Hammond .05
375 Lance Johnson .05
376 Kevin Brown .10
377 Luis Alicea .05
378 Andy Pettitte .25
379 Dean Palmer .05
380 Jeff Bagwell .75
381 Jaime Navarro .05
382 Rondell White .10
383 Erik Hanson .05
384 Pedro Munoz .05
385 Heathcliff Slocumb .05
386 Wally Joyner .05
387 Bob Tewksbury .05
388 David Bell .05
389 Fred McGriff .05
390 Mike Henneman .05
391 Robby Thompson .05
392 Norm Charlton .05
393 Cecil Fielder .05
394 Benito Santiago .05
395 Rafael Palmeiro .20
396 Ricky Bones .05
397 Rickey Henderson .50
398 C.J. Nitkowski .05
399 Shawon Dunston .05
400 Manny Ramirez .75
401 Bill Swift .05
402 Chad Fonville .05
403 Joey Hamilton .05
404 Alex Gonzalez .10
405 Roberto Hernandez .05
406 Jeff Blauser .05
407 LaTroy Hawkins .05
408 Greg Colbrunn .05
409 Todd Hundley .05
410 Glenn Dishman .05
411 Joe Vitiello .05
412 Todd Worrell .05
413 Wil Cordero .05
414 Ken Hill .05
415 Carlos Garcia .05
416 Bryan Rekar .05

417	Shawn Green (Topps Rookie All-Star)	.40
418	Tyler Green	.05
419	Mike Blowers	.05
420	Kenny Lofton	.05
421	Denny Neagle	.05
422	Jeff Conine	.05
423	Mark Langston	.05
424	Steve Cox,*Jesse Ibarra*, Derrek Lee,*Ron Wright* (Prospects)	.25
425	*Jim Bonnici*, Billy Owens, Richie Sexson,*Daryle Ward* (Prospects)	2.00
426	Kevin Jordan, *Bobby Morris*, Desi Relaford,*Adam Riggs* (Prospects)	.10
427	Tim Harkrider, Rey Ordonez, Neifi Perez, Enrique Wilson (Prospects)	.25
428	Bartolo Colon, Doug Million, Rafael Orellano,*Ray Ricken* (Prospects)	.10
429	Jeff D'Amico, *Marty Janzen*, Gary Rath, Clint Sodowsky (Prospects)	.10
430	Matt Drews,*Rich Hunter*,*Matt Ruebel*, Bret Wagner (Prospects)	.10
431	Jaime Bluma, *Dave Coggin*, Steve Montgomery, Brandon Reed (Prospects)	.10
432	Mike Figga,*Raul Ibanez*, Paul Konerko, Julio Mosquera (Prospects)	.20
433	Brian Barber, Marc Kroon, Marc Valdes, Don Wengert (Prospects)	.05
434	George Arias,*Chris Haas*, Scott Rolen, Scott Spiezio (Prospects)	.50
435	*Brian Banks*, Vladimir Guerrero, Andruw Jones, Billy McMillon (Prospects)	2.00
436	Roger Cedeno, Derrick Gibson, Ben Grieve,*Shane Spencer* (Prospects)	1.50
437	Anton French (Prospects)	.10
438	*Michael Coleman*, Jacob Cruz, Richard Hidalgo, Charles Peterson (Prospects)	.40
439	Trey Beamon, Yamil Benitez, Jermaine Dye, Angel Echevarria (Prospects)	.15
440	Checklist	.05

1996 Topps Classic Confrontations

Head-to-head stats among baseball's top pitchers and hitters are featured in this insert set. The cards were seeded one per pack in the special 50-cent packs sold exclusively at Wal-Mart during the T206 Honus Wagner card giveaway promotion. Fronts have player action poses against a granite background and are highlighted in gold foil. Backs have a portrait photo and stats.

		MT
Complete Set (15):		3.00
Common Player:		.12
1	Ken Griffey Jr.	.60
2	Cal Ripken Jr.	.75
3	Edgar Martinez	.10
4	Kirby Puckett	.40
5	Frank Thomas	.45
6	Barry Bonds	.45
7	Reggie Sanders	.10
8	Andres Galarraga	.10
9	Tony Gwynn	.40
10	Mike Piazza	.50
11	Randy Johnson	.30
12	Mike Mussina	.25
13	Roger Clemens	.40
14	Tom Glavine	.10
15	Greg Maddux	.40

1996 Topps Masters of the Game

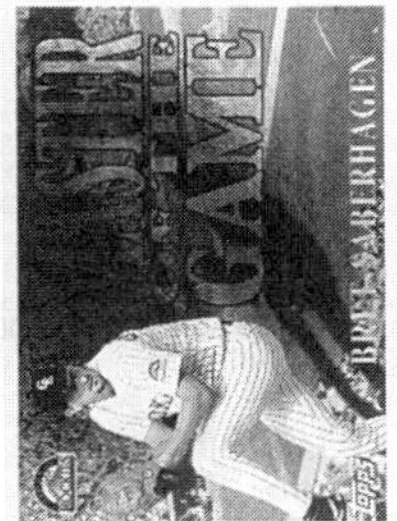

Appearing at a one per 18 pack rate, these inserts are exclusive to Series 1 hobby packs.

		MT
Complete Set (20):		25.00
Common Player:		.50
1	Dennis Eckersley	.50
2	Denny Martinez	.50
3	Eddie Murray	1.00
4	Paul Molitor	1.50
5	Ozzie Smith	1.50
6	Rickey Henderson	1.00
7	Tim Raines	.50
8	Lee Smith	.50
9	Cal Ripken Jr.	8.00
10	Chili Davis	.50
11	Wade Boggs	1.00
12	Tony Gwynn	4.00
13	Don Mattingly	2.00
14	Bret Saberhagen	.50
15	Kirby Puckett	1.50
16	Joe Carter	.50
17	Roger Clemens	3.00
18	Barry Bonds	3.00
19	Greg Maddux	5.00
20	Frank Thomas	2.00

1996 Topps Mickey Mantle Reprint Cards

One of Mickey Mantle's regular-issue Bowman or Topps cards from each year 1951-1969 was reproduced in 2-1/2" x 3-1/2" format as a Series 1 insert. Each card carries a gold-foil commemorative seal in one corner of the front. The reprints are found one per six retail packs and, in hobby, once per nine packs. The 1965-69 reprints were somewhat shortprinted (four 1965-69 cards for each five 1951-1964) and are 20% scarcer.

		MT
Complete Set (19):		60.00
Common Mantle:		3.00
Common SP Mantle (15-19):		4.00
1	1951 Bowman #253	8.00
2	1952 Topps #311	12.00
3	1953 Topps #82	4.00
4	1954 Bowman #65	3.00
5	1955 Bowman #202	3.00
6	1956 Topps #135	3.00
7	1957 Topps #95	3.00
8	1958 Topps #150	3.00
9	1959 Topps #10	3.00
10	1960 Topps #350	3.00
11	1961 Topps #300	3.00
12	1962 Topps #200	3.00
13	1963 Topps #200	3.00
14	1964 Topps #50	3.00
15	1965 Topps #350	4.00
16	1966 Topps #50	4.00
17	1967 Topps #150	4.00
18	1968 Topps #280	4.00
19	1969 Topps #500	4.00

1996 Topps/Finest Mickey Mantle

Nineteen of Mickey Mantle's regular-issue Bowman and Topps cards from 1951-1969 were printed in Finest technology for this Series 2 insert set. Each card's chrome front is protected with a peel-off plastic layer. Average insertion rate for the Mantle Finest reprints is one per 18 packs. The 1965-69 reprints were printed in a ratio of four for every five 1951-64 reprints, making them 20% scarcer.

		MT
Complete Set (19):		75.00
Common Card (1-14):		4.00
Common Shortprint (15-19):		6.00
1	1951 Bowman #253	10.00
2	1952 Topps #311	15.00
3	1953 Topps #82	6.00
4	1954 Bowman #65	4.00
5	1955 Bowman #202	4.00
6	1956 Topps #135	4.00
7	1957 Topps #95	4.00
8	1958 Topps #150	4.00
9	1959 Topps #10	4.00
10	1960 Topps #350	4.00
11	1961 Topps #300	4.00
12	1962 Topps #200	4.00
13	1963 Topps #200	4.00
14	1964 Topps #50	4.00
15	1965 Topps #350	6.00
16	1966 Topps #50	6.00
17	1967 Topps #150	6.00
18	1968 Topps #280	6.00
19	1969 Topps #500	6.00

1996 Topps/Finest Mickey Mantle Refractors

Each of the 19 Mickey Mantle Finest reprints in Series 2 can also be found in an unmarked Refractor version. Average insertion rate of these superscarce inserts is one per 144 packs.

		MT
Common Mantle:		15.00
Common SP Mantle (15-19):		20.00
1	1951 Bowman #253	50.00
2	1952 Topps #311	75.00
3	1953 Topps #82	25.00
4	1954 Bowman #65	15.00
5	1955 Bowman #202	15.00
6	1956 Topps #135	15.00
7	1957 Topps #95	15.00
8	1958 Topps #150	15.00
9	1959 Topps #10	15.00
10	1960 Topps #350	15.00
11	1961 Topps #300	15.00
12	1962 Topps #200	15.00
13	1963 Topps #200	15.00
14	1964 Topps #50	15.00
15	1965 Topps #350	20.00
16	1966 Topps #50	20.00
17	1967 Topps #150	20.00
18	1968 Topps #280	20.00
19	1969 Topps #500	20.00

1996 Topps Mickey Mantle Redemption

Each of the 19 Mantle reprint cards, minus the commemorative gold-foil stamp on front, was also issued in a sweepstakes set. Seeded one per 108 packs, these cards could be sent in for a chance to win the authentic Mantle card pictured on front. Between one and 10 genuine Mantles were awarded for each of the 19 years. Cards entered in the sweepstakes were not returned when the contest ended Oct. 15, 1996. The sweepstakes cards are a Series 2 exclusive insert.

		MT
Complete Set (19):		200.00
Common Mantle:		10.00
1	1951 Bowman #253	25.00
2	1952 Topps #311	35.00
3	1953 Topps #82	15.00
4	1954 Bowman #65	10.00
5	1955 Bowman #202	10.00
6	1956 Topps #135	10.00
7	1957 Topps #95	10.00
8	1958 Topps #150	10.00
9	1959 Topps #10	10.00
10	1960 Topps #350	10.00
11	1961 Topps #300	10.00
12	1962 Topps #200	10.00
13	1963 Topps #200	10.00
14	1964 Topps #50	10.00
15	1965 Topps #350	10.00
16	1966 Topps #50	10.00
17	1967 Topps #150	10.00
18	1968 Topps #280	10.00
19	1969 Topps #500	10.00

1996 Topps Mickey Mantle Case Inserts

Inserted one per case of Series 2 Topps, these special versions of the 19 Mickey Mantle reprint cards come sealed in a soft plastic holder. The plastic sleeve has a gold-foil stamp at bottom-back which reads "FACTRORY TOPPS SEAL 1996". Like the other Mantle reprints, the 1965-69 cards are somewhat scarcer due to short-printing.

		MT
Complete Set (19):		425.00
Common Mantle:		25.00
Common SP Mantle (15-19):		30.00
1	1951 Bowman #253	40.00
2	1952 Topps #311	50.00
3	1953 Topps #82	30.00
4	1954 Bowman #65	25.00
5	1955 Bowman #202	25.00
6	1956 Topps #135	25.00
7	1957 Topps #95	25.00
8	1958 Topps #150	25.00
9	1959 Topps #10	25.00
10	1960 Topps #350	25.00
11	1961 Topps #300	25.00
12	1962 Topps #200	25.00
13	1963 Topps #200	25.00
14	1964 Topps #50	25.00
15	1965 Topps #350	30.00
16	1966 Topps #50	30.00
17	1967 Topps #150	30.00
18	1968 Topps #280	30.00
19	1969 Topps #500	30.00

1996 Topps Mickey Mantle Foundation Card

This black-and-white card was an insert exclusive to specially marked 1996 Topps factory sets. In standard 2-1/2" x 3-1/2" format, the card offers on its back information about the foundation and it work in health care and organ donation causes.

	MT
Mickey Mantle	4.00

1996 Topps Mystery Finest

Each Mystery Finest insert has an opaque black film over the card front, concealing the identity of the player until removed. The inserts are seeded at the rate of one per 36 packs.

		MT
Complete Set (21)		25.00
Common Player:		.50
Refractors:		3X
M1	Hideo Nomo	1.00
M2	Greg Maddux	2.00
M3	Randy Johnson	1.50
M4	Chipper Jones	2.00
M5	Marty Cordova	.50
M6	Garret Anderson	.50
M7	Cal Ripken Jr.	4.00
M8	Kirby Puckett	1.50
M9	Tony Gwynn	1.50
M10	Manny Ramirez	1.50
M11	Jim Edmonds	.50
M12	Mike Piazza	2.00
M13	Barry Bonds	1.75
M14	Raul Mondesi	.50
M15	Sammy Sosa	2.00
M16	Ken Griffey Jr.	3.00
M17	Albert Belle	.50
M18	Dante Bichette	.50
M19	Mo Vaughn	.75
M20	Jeff Bagwell	1.50
M21	Frank Thomas	1.50

1996 Topps 5-Star Mystery Finest

The 5-Star Mystery Finest inserts have an opaque black film over the card front, like the regular Mystery Finest, but has the words "5-Star" in large letters across the background. They are inserted at the average rate of one per 36 packs.

		MT
Complete Set (5):		20.00
Common Player:		2.00
Refractors:		3X
M22	Hideo Nomo	2.00
M23	Cal Ripken Jr.	6.00
M24	Mike Piazza	4.00
M25	Ken Griffey Jr.	5.00
M26	Frank Thomas	3.00

1996 Topps Power Boosters

This insert set is printed in Topps' "Power Matrix" technology, replacing two regular cards when found on the average of once per 36 packs. The Power Boosters reproduce the Star Power and Draft Picks subsets on a double-thick card.

		MT
Complete Set (26):		70.00
Common Player:		1.00
1	Tony Gwynn (Star Power)	2.00
2	Mike Piazza (Star Power)	4.00
3	Greg Maddux (Star Power)	2.00
4	Jeff Bagwell (Star Power)	1.50
5	Larry Walker (Star Power)	1.00
6	Barry Larkin (Star Power)	1.00
8	Tom Glavine (Star Power)	1.00
9	Craig Biggio (Star Power)	1.00
10	Barry Bonds (Star Power)	2.50
11	Heathcliff Slocumb (Star Power)	1.00
12	Matt Williams (Star Power)	1.00
13	Todd Helton (Draft Pick)	8.00
14	Mark Redman (Draft Pick)	1.00
15	Michael Barrett (Draft Pick)	1.00
16	Ben Davis (Draft Pick)	1.25
17	Juan LeBron (Draft Pick)	1.00
18	Tony McKnight (Draft Pick)	1.00
19	Ryan Jaroncyk (Draft Pick)	1.00
20	Corey Jenkins (Draft Pick)	1.00
21	Jim Scharrer (Draft Pick)	1.00
22	Mark Bellhorn (Draft Pick)	1.00
23	Jarrod Washburn (Draft Pick)	5.00
24	Geoff Jenkins (Draft Pick)	30.00
25	Sean Casey (Draft Pick)	30.00
26	Brett Tomko (Draft Pick)	1.00

1996 Topps Profiles-AL

Ten cards from this insert issue can be found in each of Topps Series 1 and 2. Analyzing an up-and-coming star, the cards are found every 12th pack, on average.

		MT
Complete Set (20):		8.00
Common Player:		.25
1	Roberto Alomar	.50
2	Carlos Baerga	.25
3	Albert Belle	.35
4	Cecil Fielder	.25
5	Ken Griffey Jr.	1.00
6	Randy Johnson	.50
7	Paul O'Neill	.25
8	Cal Ripken Jr.	1.50
9	Frank Thomas	.75
10	Mo Vaughn	.40
11	Jay Buhner	.25
12	Marty Cordova	.25
13	Jim Edmonds	.25
14	Juan Gonzalez	.50
15	Kenny Lofton	.25
16	Edgar Martinez	.25

17	Don Mattingly	.75
18	Mark McGwire	1.50
19	Rafael Palmeiro	.35
20	Tim Salmon	.40

1996 Topps Profiles-NL

Projected future stars of the National League are featured in this insert set. Ten players each are found in Series 1 and 2 packs at the rate of one per 12, on average.

		MT
Complete Set (20):		7.00
Common Player:		.25
1	Jeff Bagwell	.50
2	Derek Bell	.25
3	Barry Bonds	.75
4	Greg Maddux	.65
5	Fred McGriff	.25
6	Raul Mondesi	.25
7	Mike Piazza	1.00
8	Reggie Sanders	.25
9	Sammy Sosa	.75
10	Larry Walker	.40
11	Dante Bichette	.25
12	Andres Galarraga	.25
13	Ron Gant	.25
14	Tom Glavine	.25
15	Chipper Jones	1.00
16	David Justice	.25
17	Barry Larkin	.25
18	Hideo Nomo	.50
19	Gary Sheffield	.35
20	Matt Williams	.35

1996 Topps Wrecking Crew

Printed on foilboard stock, cards of 15 players known for their hitting prowess are featured in this insert set. Found only in Series 2 hobby packs, the inserts are a one per 72 packs find, on average. Cards are numbered with a "WC" prefix.

		MT
Complete Set (15):		20.00
Common Player:		.50
1	Jeff Bagwell	1.50
2	Albert Belle	1.00
3	Barry Bonds	2.00
4	Jose Canseco	1.25
5	Joe Carter	.50
6	Cecil Fielder	.50
7	Ron Gant	.50
8	Juan Gonzalez	1.50
9	Ken Griffey Jr.	4.00
10	Fred McGriff	.50
11	Mark McGwire	5.00
12	Mike Piazza	4.00
13	Frank Thomas	1.50
14	Mo Vaughn	1.00
15	Matt Williams	.50

1996 Topps/Chrome

In conjunction with baseball's postseason, Topps introduced the premiere edition of Chrome Baseball. The set has 165 of the elite players from 1996 Topps Series 1 and 2. Card #7 is a Mickey Mantle tribute card. There are two insert sets: Masters of the Game and Wrecking Crew, and scarcer Refractor versions for each.

		MT
Complete Set (165):		65.00
Common Player:		.15
Common Refractor:		2.00
Refractors:		4X
Pack (4):		2.00
Wax Box (24):		40.00
1	Tony Gwynn (Star Power)	3.00
2	Mike Piazza (Star Power)	2.50
3	Greg Maddux (Star Power)	1.50
4	Jeff Bagwell (Star Power)	1.00
5	Larry Walker (Star Power)	.60
6	Barry Larkin (Star Power)	.15
7	Mickey Mantle (Commemorative)	6.00
8	Tom Glavine (Star Power)	.15
9	Craig Biggio (Star Power)	.15
10	Barry Bonds (Star Power)	2.00
11	Heathcliff Slocumb (Star Power)	.15
12	Matt Williams (Star Power)	.15
13	Todd Helton (Draft Pick)	5.00
14	Paul Molitor	1.50
15	Glenallen Hill	.15
16	Troy Percival	.15
17	Albert Belle	.50
18	Mark Wohlers	.15
19	Kirby Puckett	3.00
20	Mark Grace	.50
21	J.T. Snow	.15
22	David Justice	.50
23	Mike Mussina	1.50
24	Bernie Williams	.50
25	Ron Gant	.15
26	Carlos Baerga	.15
27	Gary Sheffield	.50
28	Cal Ripken Jr. (Tribute Card)	5.00
29	Frank Thomas	4.00
30	Kevin Seitzer	.15
31	Joe Carter	.15
32	Jeff King	.15
33	David Cone	.15
34	Eddie Murray	1.25
35	Brian Jordan	.15
36	Garret Anderson	.15
37	Hideo Nomo	1.25
38	Steve Finley	.15
39	Ivan Rodriguez	1.50
40	Quilvio Veras	.15
41	Mark McGwire	6.00
42	Greg Vaughn	.15
43	Randy Johnson	1.50
44	David Segui	.15
45	Derek Bell	.15
46	John Valentin	.15
47	Steve Avery	.15
48	Tino Martinez	.15
49	Shane Reynolds	.15
50	Jim Edmonds	.15
51	Raul Mondesi	.40
52	Chipper Jones	5.00
53	Gregg Jefferies	.15
54	Ken Caminiti	.15
55	Brian McRae	.15
56	Don Mattingly	4.00
57	Marty Cordova	.15
58	Vinny Castilla	.15
59	John Smoltz	.25
60	Travis Fryman	.15
61	Ryan Klesko	.15
62	Alex Fernandez	.15
63	Dante Bichette	.15
64	Eric Karros	.15
65	Roger Clemens	3.00
66	Randy Myers	.15
67	Cal Ripken Jr.	6.00
68	Rod Beck	.15
69	Jack McDowell	.15
70	Ken Griffey Jr.	6.00
71	Ramon Martinez	.15
72	Jason Giambi (Future Star)	1.00
73	Nomar Garciaparra (Future Star)	2.50
74	Billy Wagner (Future Star)	.50
75	Todd Greene (Future Star)	.15
76	Paul Wilson (Future Star)	.15
77	Johnny Damon (Future Star)	.25
78	Alan Benes (Future Star)	.15
79	Karim Garcia (Future Star)	.25
80	Derek Jeter (Future Star)	5.00
81	Kirby Puckett (Star Power)	1.50
82	Cal Ripken Jr. (Star Power)	3.00
83	Albert Belle (Star Power)	.25
84	Randy Johnson (Star Power)	.50
85	Wade Boggs (Star Power)	.75
86	Carlos Baerga (Star Power)	.15
87	Ivan Rodriguez (Star Power)	.50
88	Mike Mussina (Star Power)	.75
89	Frank Thomas (Star Power)	2.00
90	Ken Griffey Jr. (Star Power)	3.00
91	Jose Mesa (Star Power)	.15
92	*Matt Morris* (Draft Pick)	6.00
93	Mike Piazza	5.00
94	Edgar Martinez	.15
95	Chuck Knoblauch	.15
96	Andres Galarraga	.15
97	Tony Gwynn	3.00
98	Lee Smith	.15
99	Sammy Sosa	4.00
100	Jim Thome	.15
101	Bernard Gilkey	.15
102	Brady Anderson	.15
103	Rico Brogna	.15
104	Lenny Dykstra	.15
105	Tom Glavine	.25
106	John Olerud	.15
107	Terry Steinbach	.15
108	Brian Hunter	.15
109	Jay Buhner	.15
110	Mo Vaughn	1.25
111	Jose Mesa	.15
112	Brett Butler	.15
113	Chili Davis	.15
114	Paul O'Neill	.15
115	Roberto Alomar	1.50
116	Barry Larkin	.25
117	Marquis Grissom	.15
118	Will Clark	.25
119	Barry Bonds	4.00
120	Ozzie Smith	3.00
121	Pedro Martinez	2.50
122	Craig Biggio	.25
123	Moises Alou	.30
124	Robin Ventura	.15
125	Greg Maddux	3.00
126	Tim Salmon	.30
127	Wade Boggs	1.50
128	Ismael Valdes	.15
129	Juan Gonzalez	2.00
130	Ray Lankford	.15
131	Bobby Bonilla	.15
132	Reggie Sanders	.15
133	Alex Ochoa (Now Appearing)	.15
134	Mark Loretta (Now Appearing)	.15
135	Jason Kendall (Now Appearing)	.15
136	Brooks Kieschnick (Now Appearing)	.15
137	Chris Snopek (Now Appearing)	.15
138	Ruben Rivera (Now Appearing)	.15
139	Jeff Suppan (Now Appearing)	.15
140	John Wasdin (Now Appearing)	.15
141	Jay Payton (Now Appearing)	.15
142	Rick Krivda (Now Appearing)	.15
143	Jimmy Haynes (Now Appearing)	.15
144	Ryne Sandberg	2.00
145	Matt Williams	.50
146	Jose Canseco	1.25
147	Larry Walker	1.25
148	Kevin Appier	.15
149	Javy Lopez	.15
150	Dennis Eckersley	.15
151	Jason Isringhausen	.15
152	Dean Palmer	.15
153	Jeff Bagwell	2.00
154	Rondell White	.30
155	Wally Joyner	.15
156	Fred McGriff	.15
157	Cecil Fielder	.15
158	Rafael Palmeiro	.50
159	Rickey Henderson	1.50
160	Shawon Dunston	.15
161	Manny Ramirez	2.00
162	Alex Gonzalez	.15
163	Shawn Green	.50
164	Kenny Lofton	.15
165	Jeff Conine	.15

1996 Topps/Chrome Masters of the Game

These 1996 Topps Chrome inserts were seeded one per every 12 packs. Each of the cards is also reprinted in a Refractor version; these cards are seeded one per every 36 packs.

		MT
Complete Set (20):		35.00
Common Player:		.75
Refractors:		1.5X
1	Dennis Eckersley	.75
2	Denny Martinez	.75
3	Eddie Murray	1.50
4	Paul Molitor	2.00
5	Ozzie Smith	3.00
6	Rickey Henderson	1.50
7	Tim Raines	.75
8	Lee Smith	.75
9	Cal Ripken Jr.	5.00
10	Chili Davis	.75
11	Wade Boggs	1.50
12	Tony Gwynn	3.00
13	Don Mattingly	4.00
14	Bret Saberhagen	.75
15	Kirby Puckett	3.00
16	Joe Carter	.75
17	Roger Clemens	3.00
18	Barry Bonds	4.00
19	Greg Maddux	3.00
20	Frank Thomas	4.00

1996 Topps/Chrome Wrecking Crew

Wrecking Crew insert cards were inserted one per every 24 packs of 1996 Topps Chrome Baseball. Refractor versions were also made for these cards; they are seeded one per every 72 packs. Cards are numbered with a "WC" prefix.

		MT
Complete Set (15):		30.00
Common Player:		1.00
Refractors:		1.5X
1	Jeff Bagwell	2.50
2	Albert Belle	1.50
3	Barry Bonds	3.00
4	Jose Canseco	2.00
5	Joe Carter	1.00
6	Cecil Fielder	1.00
7	Ron Gant	1.00
8	Juan Gonzalez	2.50
9	Ken Griffey Jr.	5.00
10	Fred McGriff	1.00
11	Mark McGwire	6.00
12	Mike Piazza	4.00
13	Frank Thomas	3.00
14	Mo Vaughn	1.50
15	Matt Williams	1.00

1996 Topps/Gallery

This 180-card set is printed on 24-point stock utilizing metallic inks and a high-definition printing process. Then a high-gloss film is applied to each card, followed by foil stamping. The regular set is broken down into five subsets - The Classics, The Modernists, The Futurists, The Masters and New Editions. Each theme has a different design. Gallery also has four insert sets. Player's Private Issue cards are a parallel set to the main issue; these cards are seeded one per every 12 packs. The backs are sequentially numbered from 0-999, with the first 100 cards sent to the players; the rest are inserted into packs. The backs are UV coated on the photo only, to allow for autographing. The other insert sets are Expressionists, Photo Gallery and a Mickey Mantle Masterpiece card.

		MT
Complete Set (180):		30.00
Common Player:		.15
Private Issue:		8X
Pack (8):		2.00
Wax Box (24):		40.00
1	Tom Glavine	.25
2	Carlos Baerga	.15
3	Dante Bichette	.15
4	Mark Langston	.15
5	Ray Lankford	.15
6	Moises Alou	.30
7	Marquis Grissom	.15
8	Ramon Martinez	.15
8p	Ramon Martinez (unmarked promo, "Pitcher" spelled out under photo on back)	3.00
9	Steve Finley	.15
10	Todd Hundley	.15
11	Brady Anderson	.15
12	John Valentin	.15
13	Heathcliff Slocumb	.15
14	Ruben Sierra	.15
15	Jeff Conine	.15
16	Jay Buhner	.15
16p	Jay Buhner (unmarked promo; height, weight and "Bats" on same line)	3.00
17	Sammy Sosa	1.75
18	Doug Drabek	.15
19	Jose Mesa	.15
20	Jeff King	.15
21	Mickey Tettleton	.15
22	Jeff Montgomery	.15
23	Alex Fernandez	.15
24	Greg Vaughn	.15
25	Chuck Finley	.15
26	Terry Steinbach	.15
27	Rod Beck	.15
28	Jack McDowell	.15
29	Mark Wohlers	.15
30	Lenny Dykstra	.15
31	Bernie Williams	.45
32	Travis Fryman	.15
33	Jose Canseco	1.00
34	Ken Caminiti	.15
35	Devon White	.15
36	Bobby Bonilla	.15
37	Paul Sorrento	.15
38	Ryne Sandberg	1.25
39	Derek Bell	.15
40	Bobby Jones	.15
41	J.T. Snow	.15
42	Denny Neagle	.15
43	Tim Wakefield	.15
44	Andres Galarraga	.15
45	David Segui	.15
46	Lee Smith	.15
47	Mel Rojas	.15
48	John Franco	.15
49	Pete Schourek	.15
50	John Wetteland	.15
51	Paul Molitor	1.00
52	Ivan Rodriguez	1.00
53	Chris Hoiles	.15
54	Mike Greenwell	.15
55	Orel Hershiser	.15
56	Brian McRae	.15
57	Geronimo Berroa	.15
58	Craig Biggio	.25
59	David Justice	.30
59p	David Justice (unmarked promo; height, weight and "Bats" on same line)	3.00
60	Lance Johnson	.15
61	Andy Ashby	.15
62	Randy Myers	.15
63	Gregg Jefferies	.15
64	Kevin Appier	.15
65	Rick Aguilera	.15
66	Shane Reynolds	.15
67	John Smoltz	.25
68	Ron Gant	.15
69	Eric Karros	.15
70	Jim Thome	.15
71	Terry Pendleton	.15
72	Kenny Rogers	.15
73	Robin Ventura	.15
74	Dave Nilsson	.15
75	Brian Jordan	.15
76	Glenallen Hill	.15
77	Greg Colbrunn	.15
78	Roberto Alomar	1.00
79	Rickey Henderson	1.25
80	Carlos Garcia	.15
81	Dean Palmer	.15
82	Mike Stanley	.15
83	Hal Morris	.15
84	Wade Boggs	1.25
85	Chad Curtis	.15
86	Roberto Hernandez	.15
87	John Olerud	.15
88	Frank Castillo	.15
89	Rafael Palmeiro	.35
90	Trevor Hoffman	.15
91	Marty Cordova	.15
92	Hideo Nomo	1.00
93	Johnny Damon	.25
94	Bill Pulsipher	.15
95	Garret Anderson	.15
96	Ray Durham	.15
97	Ricky Bottalico	.15
98	Carlos Perez	.15
99	Troy Percival	.15
100	Chipper Jones	2.00
101	Esteban Loaiza	.15
102	John Mabry	.15
103	Jon Nunnally	.15
104	Andy Pettitte	.60
105	Lyle Mouton	.15
106	Jason Isringhausen	.15
107	Brian Hunter	.15
108	Quilvio Veras	.15
109	Jim Edmonds	.15
110	Ryan Klesko	.15
111	Pedro Martinez	.75
112	Joey Hamilton	.15
113	Vinny Castilla	.15
114	Alex Gonzalez	.15
115	Raul Mondesi	.40
116	Rondell White	.40
117	Dan Miceli	.15
118	Tom Goodwin	.15
119	Bret Boone	.25
120	Shawn Green	.75
121	Jeff Cirillo	.15
122	Rico Brogna	.15
123	Chris Gomez	.15
124	Ismael Valdes	.15
125	Javy Lopez	.15
126	Manny Ramirez	1.25
127	Paul Wilson	.15
128	Billy Wagner	.15
129	Eric Owens	.15
130	Todd Greene	.15
131	Karim Garcia	.15
132	Jimmy Haynes	.15
133	Michael Tucker	.15
134	John Wasdin	.15
135	Brooks Kieschnick	.15
136	Alex Ochoa	.15
137	Ariel Prieto	.15
138	Tony Clark	.15
139	Mark Loretta	.15
140	Rey Ordonez	.15
141	Chris Snopek	.15
142	Roger Cedeno	.15
143	Derek Jeter	3.00
144	Jeff Suppan	.15
145	Greg Maddux	1.50
146	Ken Griffey Jr.	2.50
147	Tony Gwynn	1.50
148	Darren Daulton	.15
149	Will Clark	.30
150	Mo Vaughn	.75
151	Reggie Sanders	.15
152	Kirby Puckett	1.50
153	Paul O'Neill	.15
154	Tim Salmon	.25
155	Mark McGwire	3.00
156	Barry Bonds	1.75
157	Albert Belle	.35
158	Edgar Martinez	.15
159	Mike Mussina	.75
160	Cecil Fielder	.15
161	Kenny Lofton	.15
162	Randy Johnson	1.00
163	Juan Gonzalez	1.25
164	Jeff Bagwell	1.25
165	Joe Carter	.15
166	Mike Piazza	2.00
167	Eddie Murray	1.00
168	Cal Ripken Jr.	3.00
169	Barry Larkin	.25
170	Chuck Knoblauch	.15
171	Chili Davis	.15
172	Fred McGriff	.15
173	Matt Williams	.35
174	Roger Clemens	1.50
175	Frank Thomas	1.00
176	Dennis Eckersley	.15
177	Gary Sheffield	.40
178	David Cone	.15
179	Larry Walker	.75
180	Mark Grace	.40

1996 Topps/Gallery Players Private Issue

The first 999 examples of each of the base cards in the Gallery issue are designated on the front with a gold-foil stamp as "Players Private Issue." The first 100 of those cards were given to the depicted player, the others are randomly packed. Besides the logo on front, the PPI cards are identified on back with an individual serial number.

	MT
Complete Set (180):	300.00
Common Player:	1.00
Stars:	8X

(See 1996 Topps Gallery for checklist and base card values.)

1996 Topps/Gallery Expressionists

These 1996 Topps Gallery inserts feature 20 team leaders printed on triple foil-stamped and texture-embossed cards. Cards are seeded one per every 24 packs.

		MT
Complete Set (20):		30.00
Common Player:		.50
1	Mike Piazza	4.00
2	J.T. Snow	.50
3	Ken Griffey Jr.	5.00
4	Kirby Puckett	3.00
5	Carlos Baerga	.50
6	Chipper Jones	4.00
7	Hideo Nomo	1.50
8	Mark McGwire	6.00
9	Gary Sheffield	.75
10	Randy Johnson	1.50
11	Ray Lankford	.50
12	Sammy Sosa	3.50
13	Denny Martinez	.50
14	Jose Canseco	1.25
15	Tony Gwynn	3.00
16	Edgar Martinez	.50
17	Reggie Sanders	.50
18	Andres Galarraga	.50
19	Albert Belle	.75
20	Barry Larkin	.50

1996 Topps/Gallery Masterpiece

Topps continues its tribute to Mickey Mantle with this 1996 Topps Gallery insert card. The card, seeded one per every 48 packs, has three photos of Mantle on the front, with his comprehensive career statistics on the back.

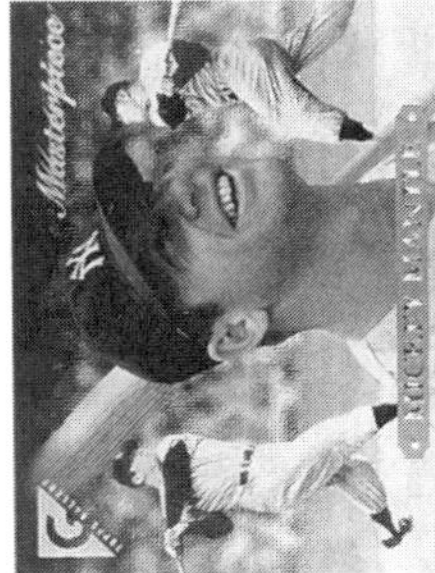

	MT
MP1 Mickey Mantle	5.00

1996 Topps/Gallery Photo Gallery

Photo Gallery is a collection of 15 cards featuring photography of baseball's biggest stars and greatest moments from the last season. The text on the card includes details of the card's front and back photos. The cards are seeded one per every 30 packs. Cards are numbered with a "PG" prefix.

		MT
Complete Set (15):		15.00
Common Player:		.50
1	Eddie Murray	.75
2	Randy Johnson	1.00
3	Cal Ripken Jr.	4.00
4	Bret Boone	.50
5	Frank Thomas	2.50
6	Jeff Conine	.50
7	Johnny Damon	.50
8	Roger Clemens	2.00
9	Albert Belle	.75
10	Ken Griffey Jr.	3.00
11	Kirby Puckett	2.00
12	David Justice	.75
13	Bobby Bonilla	.50
14	Larry Walker, Andres Galarraga, Vinny Castilla, Dante Bichette	.75
15	Mark Wohlers, Javier Lopez	.50

1996 Topps/Laser

Topps' 1996 Laser Baseball was the first set to use laser-cut technology on every card, creating surgically-precise laticework across the entire card. Every card in the 128-card regular issue set features one of four designs laser-cut into 20-point stock. One card from each of the four different designs is found in each four-card pack. Three different laser-cut insert sets were also produced: Bright Spots, Power Cuts and Stadium Stars. Cards 1-8 from each insert set were in Series 1 packs; cards 9-16 were seeded in Series 2 packs. A slightly oversize (1-5/8" x 3-5/8") checklist card in each pack helped protect the delicate die-cut details from damage.

		MT
Complete Set (128):		60.00
Common Player:		.15
Series 1 or 2 Pack (4):		2.00
Series 1 or 2 Wax Box (24):		40.00
1	Moises Alou	.35
2	Derek Bell	.15
3	Joe Carter	.15
4	Jeff Conine	.15
5	Darren Daulton	.15
6	Jim Edmonds	.15
7	Ron Gant	.15
8	Juan Gonzalez	2.00
9	Brian Jordan	.15
10	Ryan Klesko	.15
11	Paul Molitor	1.50
12	Tony Phillips	.15
13	Manny Ramirez	2.00
14	Sammy Sosa	3.50
15	Devon White	.15
16	Bernie Williams	.45
17	Garret Anderson	.15
18	Jay Bell	.15
19	Craig Biggio	.25
20	Bobby Bonilla	.15
21	Ken Caminiti	.15
22	Shawon Dunston	.15
23	Mark Grace	.45
23p	Mark Grace (unmarked promo, plain, rather than brushed, gold foil)	3.00
24	Gregg Jefferies	.15
25	Jeff King	.15
26	Javy Lopez	.15
27	Edgar Martinez	.15
28	Dean Palmer	.15
29	J.T. Snow	.15
30	Mike Stanley	.15
30p	Mike Stanley (unmarked promo; plain, rather than brushed, gold foil)	2.00
31	Terry Steinbach	.15
32	Robin Ventura	.15
33	Roberto Alomar	1.50
34	Jeff Bagwell	2.00
35	Dante Bichette	.15
36	Wade Boggs	1.50
37	Barry Bonds	3.50
38	Jose Canseco	1.50
39	Vinny Castilla	.15
40	Will Clark	.25
41	Marty Cordova	.15
42	Ken Griffey Jr.	5.00
43	Tony Gwynn	3.00
44	Rickey Henderson	1.50
45	Chipper Jones	4.00
46	Mark McGwire	6.00
47	Brian McRae	.15
48	Ryne Sandberg	2.00
49	Andy Ashby	.15
50	Alan Benes	.15
51	Andy Benes	.15
52	Roger Clemens	3.00
53	Doug Drabek	.15
54	Dennis Eckersley	.15
55	Tom Glavine	.25
56	Randy Johnson	1.50
57	Mark Langston	.15
58	Denny Martinez	.15
59	Jack McDowell	.15
60	Hideo Nomo	1.50
61	Shane Reynolds	.15
62	John Smoltz	.25
63	Paul Wilson	.15
64	Mark Wohlers	.15
65	Shawn Green	.45
66	Marquis Grissom	.15
67	Dave Hollins	.15
68	Todd Hundley	.15
69	David Justice	.45
70	Eric Karros	.15
71	Ray Lankford	.15
72	Fred McGriff	.15
73	Hal Morris	.15
74	Eddie Murray	1.00
75	Paul O'Neill	.15
76	Rey Ordonez	.15
77	Reggie Sanders	.15
78	Gary Sheffield	.35
79	Jim Thome	.15
80	Rondell White	.35
81	Travis Fryman	.15
82	Derek Jeter	5.00
83	Chuck Knoblauch	.15
84	Barry Larkin	.25
85	Tino Martinez	.15
86	Raul Mondesi	.30
87	John Olerud	.15
88	Rafael Palmeiro	.45
89	Mike Piazza	4.00
90	Cal Ripken Jr.	6.00
91	Ivan Rodriguez	1.00
92	Frank Thomas	3.50
93	John Valentin	.15
94	Mo Vaughn	1.00
95	Quilvio Veras	.15
96	Matt Williams	.25
97	Brady Anderson	.15
98	Carlos Baerga	.15
99	Albert Belle	.60
100	Jay Buhner	.15
101	Johnny Damon	.25
102	Chili Davis	.15
103	Ray Durham	.15
104	Lenny Dykstra	.15
105	Cecil Fielder	.15
106	Andres Galarraga	.15
107	Brian Hunter	.15
108	Kenny Lofton	.15
109	Kirby Puckett	3.00
110	Tim Salmon	.25
111	Greg Vaughn	.15
112	Larry Walker	.75
113	Rick Aguilera	.15
114	Kevin Appier	.15
115	Kevin Brown	.35
116	David Cone	.15
117	Alex Fernandez	.15
118	Chuck Finley	.15
119	Joey Hamilton	.15
120	Jason Isringhausen	.15
121	Greg Maddux	3.00
122	Pedro Martinez	1.25
123	Jose Mesa	.15
124	Jeff Montgomery	.15
125	Mike Mussina	1.50
126	Randy Myers	.15
127	Kenny Rogers	.15
128	Ismael Valdes	.15
	Series 1 checklist	.05
	Series 2 Checklist	.05

1996 Topps/Laser Bright Spots

Top young stars are featured on these 1996 Topps Laser cards, which use etched silver and gold diffraction foil. The cards are seeded one per every 20 packs. Numbers 1-8 are in Series I packs; cards 9-16 are in Series II packs.

		MT
Complete Set (16):		27.50
Common Player:		1.00
1	Brian Hunter	1.00
2	Derek Jeter	6.00
3	Jason Kendall	1.50
4	Brooks Kieschnick	1.00
5	Rey Ordonez	1.50
6	Jason Schmidt	1.00
7	Chris Snopek	1.00
8	Bob Wolcott	1.00
9	Alan Benes	1.00
10	Marty Cordova	1.00
11	Jimmy Haynes	1.00
12	Todd Hollandsworth	1.00
13	Derek Jeter	6.00
14	Chipper Jones	6.00
15	Hideo Nomo	3.00
16	Paul Wilson	1.00

1996 Topps/Laser Power Cuts

This 1996 Topps Laser insert set spotlights 16 of the game's top power hitters on etched foil and gold diffraction foil cards. These cards were seeded one per every 40 packs; numbers 1-8 were in Series I packs; cards 9-16 were in Series II packs.

		MT
Complete Set (16):		50.00
Common Player:		1.00
1	Albert Belle	2.00
2	Jay Buhner	1.00
3	Fred McGriff	1.00
4	Mike Piazza	8.00
5	Tim Salmon	2.00
6	Frank Thomas	6.00
7	Mo Vaughn	3.00
8	Matt Williams	1.00
9	Jeff Bagwell	4.00
10	Barry Bonds	6.00
11	Jose Canseco	3.00
12	Cecil Fielder	1.00
13	Juan Gonzalez	4.00
14	Ken Griffey Jr.	10.00
15	Sammy Sosa	6.00
16	Larry Walker	2.00

1996 Topps/Laser Stadium Stars

These 1996 Topps Laser cards are the most difficult to find; they are seeded one per every 60 packs. The 16 cards feature a laser-sculpted cover that folds back to reveal striated silver and gold etched diffraction foil on each card front. Cards 1-8 were in Series I packs; numbers 9-16 were Series II inserts.

		MT
Complete Set (16):		60.00
Common Player:		2.00
1	Carlos Baerga	2.00
2	Barry Bonds	6.00
3	Andres Galarraga	2.00
4	Ken Griffey Jr.	7.50
5	Barry Larkin	2.00
6	Raul Mondesi	2.00
7	Kirby Puckett	5.00
8	Cal Ripken Jr.	10.00
9	Will Clark	2.00
10	Roger Clemens	5.00
11	Tony Gwynn	5.00
12	Randy Johnson	4.00
13	Kenny Lofton	2.00
14	Edgar Martinez	2.00
15	Ryne Sandberg	4.00
16	Frank Thomas	6.00

1997 Topps

Topps' 1997 set includes the first-ever player cards of the expansion Diamondbacks and Devil Rays; 16 Mickey Mantle reprints; a special Jackie Robinson tribute card; 27 Willie Mays Topps and Bowman reprints; randomly-inserted Willie Mays autographed reprint cards; and Inter-League Finest and Finest Refractors cards. The base set has 275 cards in Series 1 and 220 cards in Series 2. Each card front has a glossy coating on the photo and a spot matte finish on the border, with gold-foil graphics. Card backs have informative text, complete player stats and biographies, and a second photo. Mantle reprints, seeded one per 12 packs, feature the 16 remaining Mantle cards which were not reprinted in 1996, stamped with a gold foil logo, and numbered from #21 to #36. Willie Mays has 27 of his cards reprinted and seeded one per eight packs. Each card also has a gold foil stamp. As a special hobby-exclusive bonus, 1,000 Mays reprints were autographed and randomly inserted in packs. Five other insert sets were made: All-Stars, Inter-League Finest and Inter-League Finest Refractors, Sweet Strokes and Hobby Masters. Two factory sets, comprising the 495 base cards and either seven or eight random inserts were produced and currently enjoy a significant premium over hand-collated sets.

		MT
Unopened Factory Set (504):		145.00
Unopened Factory Set (503):		135.00
Complete Set (495):		60.00
Common Player:		.05
Ser. 1 or 2 Pack (11):		1.50
Ser. 1 or 2 Wax Box (36):		35.00
1	Barry Bonds	1.25
2	Tom Pagnozzi	.05
3	Terrell Wade	.05
4	Jose Valentin	.05
5	Mark Clark	.05
6	Brady Anderson	.05
7	Not issued	
8	Wade Boggs	.75
9	Scott Stahoviak	.05
10	Andres Galarraga	.05
11	Steve Avery	.05
12	Rusty Greer	.05
13	Derek Jeter	1.50
14	Ricky Bottalico	.05
15	Andy Ashby	.05
16	Paul Shuey	.05
17	F.P. Santangelo	.05
18	Royce Clayton	.05
19	Mike Mohler	.05
20	Mike Piazza	1.50
21	Jaime Navarro	.05
22	Billy Wagner	.05
23	Mike Timlin	.05
24	Garret Anderson	.05
25	Ben McDonald	.05
26	Mel Rojas	.05
27	John Burkett	.05
28	Jeff King	.05
29	Reggie Jefferson	.05
30	Kevin Appier	.05
31	Felipe Lira	.05
32	Kevin Tapani	.05
33	Mark Portugal	.05
34	Carlos Garcia	.05
35	Joey Cora	.05
36	David Segui	.05
37	Mark Grace	.25
38	Erik Hanson	.05
39	Jeff D'Amico	.05
40	Jay Buhner	.05
41	B.J. Surhoff	.05
42	Jackie Robinson	2.00
43	Roger Pavlik	.05
44	Hal Morris	.05
45	Mariano Duncan	.05
46	Harold Baines	.05
47	Jorge Fabregas	.05
48	Jose Herrera	.05
49	Jeff Cirillo	.05
50	Tom Glavine	.10
51	Pedro Astacio	.05
52	Mark Gardner	.05
53	Arthur Rhodes	.05
54	Troy O'Leary	.05
55	Bip Roberts	.05
56	Mike Lieberthal	.05
57	Shane Andrews	.05
58	Scott Karl	.05
59	Gary DiSarcina	.05
60	Andy Pettitte	.25
61a	Kevin Elster	.05
61b	Mike Fetters (should be #84)	.05
62	Mark McGwire	2.00
63	Dan Wilson	.05
64	Mickey Morandini	.05
65	Chuck Knoblauch	.05
66	Tim Wakefield	.05
67	Raul Mondesi	.25
68	Todd Jones	.05
69	Albert Belle	.30
70	Trevor Hoffman	.05
71	Eric Young	.05
72	Robert Perez	.05
73	Butch Huskey	.05
74	Brian McRae	.05
75	Jim Edmonds	.05
76	Mike Henneman	.05
77	Frank Rodriguez	.05
78	Danny Tartabull	.05
79	Robby Nen	.05
80	Reggie Sanders	.05
81	Ron Karkovice	.05
82	Benny Santiago	.05
83	Mike Lansing	.05
84	Not issued - see #61b	
85	Craig Biggio	.10
86	Mike Bordick	.05
87	Ray Lankford	.05
88	Charles Nagy	.05
89	Paul Wilson	.05
90	John Wetteland	.05
91	Tom Candiotti	.05
92	Carlos Delgado	.30
93	Derek Bell	.05
94	Mark Lemke	.05
95	Edgar Martinez	.05
96	Rickey Henderson	.60
97	Greg Myers	.05
98	Jim Leyritz	.05
99	Mark Johnson	.05
100	Dwight Gooden (Season Highlights)	.05
101	Al Leiter (Season Highlights)	.05
102a	John Mabry (Season Highlights) (last line on back ends "... Mabry"))	.05
102b	John Mabry (Season Highlights) (last line on back ends "...walked.")	.05
103	Alex Ochoa (Season Highlights)	.05
104	Mike Piazza (Season Highlights)	.75
105	Jim Thome	.05
106	Ricky Otero	.05
107	Jamey Wright	.05
108	Frank Thomas	1.25
109	Jody Reed	.05
110	Orel Hershiser	.05
111	Terry Steinbach	.05
112	Mark Loretta	.05
113	Turk Wendell	.05

114 Marvin Benard .05
115 Kevin Brown .15
116 Robert Person .05
117 Joey Hamilton .05
118 Francisco Cordova .05
119 John Smiley .05
120 Travis Fryman .05
121 Jimmy Key .05
122 Tom Goodwin .05
123 Mike Greenwell .05
124 Juan Gonzalez .75
125 Pete Harnisch .05
126 Roger Cedeno .05
127 Ron Gant .05
128 Mark Langston .05
129 Tim Crabtree .05
130 Greg Maddux 1.00
131 William VanLandingham .05
132 Wally Joyner .05
133 Randy Myers .05
134 John Valentin .05
135 Bret Boone .10
136 Bruce Ruffin .05
137 Chris Snopek .05
138 Paul Molitor .50
139 Mark McLemore .05
140 Rafael Palmeiro .25
141 Herb Perry .05
142 Luis Gonzalez .30
143 Doug Drabek .05
144 Ken Ryan .05
145 Todd Hundley .05
146 Ellis Burks .05
147 Ozzie Guillen .05
148 Rich Becker .05
149 Sterling Hitchcock .05
150 Bernie Williams .40
151 Mike Stanley .05
152 Roberto Alomar .50
153 Jose Mesa .05
154 Steve Trachsel .05
155 Alex Gonzalez .10
156 Troy Percival .05
157 John Smoltz .10
158 Pedro Martinez .50
159 Jeff Conine .05
160 Bernard Gilkey .05
161 Jim Eisenreich .05
162 Mickey Tettleton .05
163 Justin Thompson .05
164 Jose Offerman .05
165 Tony Phillips .05
166 Ismael Valdes .05
167 Ryne Sandberg .65
168 Matt Mieske .05
169 Geronimo Berroa .05
170 Otis Nixon .05
171 John Mabry .05
172 Shawon Dunston .05
173 Omar Vizquel .05
174 Chris Holles .05
175 Doc Gooden .05
176 Wilson Alvarez .05
177 Todd Hollandsworth .05
178 Roger Salkeld .05
179 Rey Sanchez .05
180 Rey Ordonez .05
181 Denny Martinez .05
182 Ramon Martinez .05
183 Dave Nilsson .05
184 Marquis Grissom .05
185 Randy Velarde .05
186 Ron Coomer .05
187 Tino Martinez .05
188 Jeff Brantley .05
189 Steve Finley .05
190 Andy Benes .05
191 Terry Adams .05
192 Mike Blowers .05
193 Russ Davis .05
194 Darryl Hamilton .05
195 Jason Kendall .05
196 Johnny Damon .10
197 Dave Martinez .05
198 Mike Macfarlane .05
199 Norm Charlton .05
200 Doug Million, Damian Moss, Bobby Rodgers (Prospect) .10
201 Geoff Jenkins, Raul Ibanez, Mike Cameron (Prospect) .25
202 Sean Casey, Jim Bonnici, Dmitri Young (Prospect) 1.00
203 Jed Hansen, Homer Bush, Felipe Crespo (Prospect) .10
204 Kevin Orie, Gabe Alvarez, Aaron Boone (Prospect) .25
205 Ben Davis, Kevin Brown, Bobby Estalella (Prospect) .10
206 Billy McMillon, *Bubba Trammell*, Dante Powell (Prospect) .25
207 Jarrod Washburn, *Marc Wilkins*, Glendon Rusch (Prospect) .15
208 Brian Hunter .05
209 Jason Giambi .30
210 Henry Rodriguez .05
211 Edgar Renteria .05
212 Edgardo Alfonzo .05
213 Fernando Vina .05
214 Shawn Green .30
215 Ray Durham .05
216 Joe Randa .05
217 Armando Reynoso .05
218 Eric Davis .05
219 Bob Tewksbury .05
220 Jacob Cruz .05
221 Glenallen Hill .05
222 Gary Gaetti .05
223 Donne Wall .05
224 Brad Clontz .05
225 Marty Janzen .05
226 Todd Worrell .05
227 John Franco .05
228 David Wells .10
229 Gregg Jefferies .05
230 Tim Naehring .05
231 Thomas Howard .05
232 Roberto Hernandez .05
233 Kevin Ritz .05
234 Julian Tavarez .05
235 Ken Hill .05
236 Greg Gagne .05
237 Bobby Chouinard .05
238 Joe Carter .05
239 Jermaine Dye .05
240 Antonio Osuna .05
241 Julio Franco .05
242 Mike Grace .05
243 Aaron Sele .05
244 David Justice .25
245 Sandy Alomar .05
246 Jose Canseco .50
247 Paul O'Neill .05
248 Sean Berry .05
249 *Nick Bierbrodt, Kevin Sweeney* (Diamond Backs) .25
250 *Larry Rodriguez, Vladimir Nunez* (Diamond Backs) .10
251 Ron Hartman, David Hayman (Diamond Backs) .05
252 Alex Sanchez, Matt Quatraro (Devil Rays) .05
253 Ronni Seberino, *Pablo Ortega* (Devil Rays) .10
254 Rex Hudler .05
255 Orlando Miller .05
256 Mariano Rivera .25
257 Brad Radke .05
258 Bobby Higginson .10
259 Jay Bell .05
260 Mark Grudzielanek .05
261 Lance Johnson .05
262 Ken Caminiti .05
263 J.T. Snow .05
264 Gary Sheffield .25
265 Darrin Fletcher .05
266 Eric Owens .05
267 Luis Castillo .05
268 Scott Rolen .75
269 *Todd Noel*, John Oliver (Draft Pick) .10
270 *Robert Stratton, Corey Lee* (Draft Pick) .25
271 *Gil Meche, Matt Halloran* (Draft Pick) 1.00
272 *Eric Milton*, Dermal Brown (Draft Pick) .75
273 *Josh Garrett, Chris Reitsma* (Draft Pick) .10
274 *A.J. Zapp, Jason Marquis* (Draft Pick) .50
275 Checklist .05
276a Checklist .05
276b Chipper Jones (should be #277) 1.50
277 Not issued
278 Orlando Merced .05
279 Ariel Prieto .05
280 Al Leiter .05
281 Pat Meares .05
282 Darryl Strawberry .05
283 Jamie Moyer .05
284 Scott Servais .05
285 Delino DeShields .05
286 Danny Graves .05
287 Gerald Williams .05
288 Todd Greene .05
289 Rico Brogna .05
290 Derrick Gibson .05
291 Joe Girardi .05
292 Darren Lewis .05
293 Nomar Garciaparra 1.25
294 Greg Colbrunn .05
295 Jeff Bagwell .75
296 Brent Gates .05
297 Jose Vizcaino .05
298 Alex Ochoa .05
299 Sid Fernandez .05
300 Ken Griffey Jr. 1.75
301 Chris Gomez .05
302 Wendell Magee .05
303 Darren Oliver .05
304 Mel Nieves .05
305 Sammy Sosa 1.25
306 George Arias .05
307 Jack McDowell .05
308 Stan Javier .05
309 Kimera Bartee .05
310 James Baldwin .05
311 Rocky Coppinger .05
312 Keith Lockhart .05
313 C.J. Nitkowski .05
314 Allen Watson .05
315 Darryl Kile .05
316 Amaury Telemaco .05
317 Jason Isringhausen .05
318 Manny Ramirez .75
319 Terry Pendleton .05
320 Tim Salmon .20
321 Eric Karros .05
322 Mark Whiten .05
323 Rick Krivda .05
324 Brett Butler .05
325 Randy Johnson .50
326 Eddie Taubensee .05
327 Mark Leiter .05
328 Kevin Gross .05
329 Ernie Young .05
330 Pat Hentgen .05
331 Rondell White .20
332 Bobby Witt .05
333 Eddie Murray .50
334 Tim Raines .05
335 Jeff Fassero .05
336 Chuck Finley .05
337 Willie Adams .05
338 Chan Ho Park .20
339 Jay Powell .05
340 Ivan Rodriguez .50
341 Jermaine Allensworth .05
342 Jay Payton .05
343 T.J. Mathews .05
344 Tony Batista .05
345 Ed Sprague .05
346 Jeff Kent .05
347 Scott Erickson .05
348 Jeff Suppan .05
349 Pete Schourek .05
350 Kenny Lofton .05
351 Alan Benes .05
352 Fred McGriff .05
353 Charlie O'Brien .05
354 Darren Bragg .05
355 Alex Fernandez .05
356 Al Martin .05
357 Bob Wells .05
358 Chad Mottola .05
359 Devon White .05
360 David Cone .05
361 Bobby Jones .05
362 Scott Sanders .05
363 Karim Garcia .10
364 Kirt Manwaring .05
365 Chili Davis .05
366 Mike Hampton .05
367 Chad Ogea .05
368 Curt Schilling .20
369 Phil Nevin .10
370 Roger Clemens 1.00
371 Willie Greene .05
372 Kenny Rogers .05
373 Jose Rijo .05
374 Bobby Bonilla .05
375 Mike Mussina .50
376 Curtis Pride .05
377 Todd Walker .05
378 Jason Bere .05
379 Heathcliff Slocumb .05
380 Dante Bichette .05
381 Carlos Baerga .05
382 Livan Hernandez .05
383 Jason Schmidt .05
384 Kevin Stocker .05
385 Matt Williams .15
386 Bartolo Colon .05
387 Will Clark .15
388 Dennis Eckersley .05
389 Brooks Kieschnick .05
390 Ryan Klesko .05
391 Mark Carreon .05
392 Tim Worrell .05
393 Dean Palmer .05
394 Wil Cordero .05
395 Javy Lopez .05
396 Rich Aurilla .05
397 Greg Vaughn .05
398 Vinny Castilla .05
399 Jeff Montgomery .05
400 Cal Ripken Jr. 2.00
401 Walt Weiss .05
402 Brad Ausmus .05
403 Ruben Rivera .05
404 Mark Wohlers .05
405 Rick Aguilera .05
406 Tony Clark .05
407 Lyle Mouton .05
408 Bill Pulsipher .05
409 Jose Rosado .05
410 Tony Gwynn 1.00
411 Cecil Fielder .05
412 John Flaherty .05
413 Lenny Dykstra .05
414 Ugueth Urbina .05
415 Brian Jordan .05
416 Bob Abreu .10
417 Craig Paquette .05
418 Sandy Martinez .05
419 Jeff Blauser .05
420 Barry Larkin .10
421 Kevin Seitzer .05
422 Tim Belcher .05
423 Paul Sorrento .05
424 Cal Eldred .05
425 Robin Ventura .05
426 John Olerud .05
427 Bob Wolcott .05
428 Matt Lawton .05
429 Rod Beck .05
430 Shane Reynolds .05
431 Mike James .05
432 Steve Wojciechowski .05
433 Vladimir Guerrero 1.00
434 Dustin Hermanson .05
435 Marty Cordova .05
436 Marc Newfield .05
437 Todd Stottlemyre .05
438 Jeffrey Hammonds .05
439 Dave Stevens .05
440 Hideo Nomo .75
441 Mark Thompson .05
442 Mark Lewis .05
443 Quinton McCracken .05
444 Cliff Floyd .05
445 Denny Neagle .05
446 John Jaha .05
447 Mike Sweeney .05
448 John Wasdin .05
449 Chad Curtis .05
450 Mo Vaughn .40
451 Donovan Osborne .05
452 Ruben Sierra .05
453 Michael Tucker .05
454 Kurt Abbott .05
455 Andruw Jones .75
456 Shannon Stewart .10
457 Scott Brosius .05
458 Juan Guzman .05
459 Ron Villone .05
460 Moises Alou .20
461 Larry Walker .40
462 Eddie Murray (Season Highlights) .25

463 Paul Molitor (Season Highlights) .25
464 Hideo Nomo (Season Highlights) .50
465 Barry Bonds (Season Highlights) .65
466 Todd Hundley (Season Highlights) .05
467 Rheal Cormier .05
468 *Jason Conti* .25
469 *Rod Barajas* .05
470 Jared Sandberg, *Cedric Bowers* .25
471 Paul Wilders, *Chie Gunner* .05
472 Mike Decelle, *Marcus McCain* .05
473 Todd Zeile .05
474 Neifi Perez .05
475 Jeromy Burnitz .05
476 Trey Beamon .05
477 John Patterson,*Braden Looper* (Draft Picks) .25
478 *Danny Peoples ,Jake Westbrook* (Draft Picks) .25
479 *Eric Chavez*, Adam Eaton (Draft Picks) 1.50
480 *Joe Lawrence*, Pete Tucci (Draft Picks) .15
481 Kris Benson,*Billy Koch* (Draft Picks) .25
482 John Nicholson, Andy Prater (Draft Picks) .05
483 *Mark Kotsay*, Mark Johnson (Draft Picks).50
484 Armando Benitez .05
485 Mike Matheny .05
486 Jeff Reed .05
487 Mark Bellhorn, Russ Johnson, Enrique Wilson (Prospects) .05
488 Ben Grieve, Richard Hidalgo,*Scott Morgan* (Prospects) .75
489 Paul Konerko, Derrek Lee, Ron Wright (Prospects) .25
490 Wes Helms,*Bill Mueller*, Brad Seitzer (Prospects) .50
491 Jeff Abbott, Shane Monahan, Edgard Velazquez (Prospects) .10
492 *Jimmy Anderson*, Ron Blazier, Gerald Witasick, Jr. (Prospects) .25
493 Darin Blood, Heath Murray, Carl Pavano (Prospects) .10
494 Mark Redman, *Mike Villano*, Nelson Figueroa (Prospects) .20
495 Checklist .05
496 Checklist .05
NNO Derek Jeter (Auto) 100.00

1997 Topps All-Stars

Topps' 1997 All-Stars insert cards, printed on a dazzling rainbow foilboard, feature the top players from each position. There are 22 cards, 11 from each league, which showcase the top three players from each position as voted by Topps' sports department. On the front of each card is a photo of a "first team" all-star player; the back has a different photo of that player, who appears alongside the "second team" and "third team" selections. These cards are seeded one per every 18 1997 Topps Series I packs. Cards are numbered with an "AS" prefix.

		MT
Complete Set (22):		25.00
Common Player:		.50
1	Ivan Rodriguez	1.50
2	Todd Hundley	.50
3	Frank Thomas	2.50
4	Andres Galarraga	.50
5	Chuck Knoblauch	.50
6	Eric Young	.50
7	Jim Thome	.50
8	Chipper Jones	3.00
9	Cal Ripken Jr.	4.00
10	Barry Larkin	.50
11	Albert Belle	1.00
12	Barry Bonds	2.50
13	Ken Griffey Jr.	3.50
14	Ellis Burks	.50
15	Juan Gonzalez	2.00
16	Gary Sheffield	.75
17	Andy Pettitte	.75
18	Tom Glavine	.50
19	Pat Hentgen	.50
20	John Smoltz	.50
21	Roberto Hernandez	.50
22	Mark Wohlers	.50

1997 Topps Awesome Impact

This flashy insert exclusive to Series 2 retail packaging features young players who have quickly made their mark in the big leagues. Fronts have player action photos against a background of silver primatic geometric shapes. Backs are horizontal with a player portrait photo, recent stats and a few words about the player's current and projected impact. Stated odds of finding this insert are one per 18 packs. Cards are numbered with an "AI" prefix.

		MT
Complete Set (20):		25.00
Common Player:		.50
1	Jaime Bluma	.50
2	Tony Clark	.50
3	Jermaine Dye	.50
4	Nomar Garciaparra	5.00
5	Vladimir Guerrero	3.00
6	Todd Hollandsworth	.50
7	Derek Jeter	8.00
8	Andruw Jones	3.00
9	Chipper Jones	6.00
10	Jason Kendall	.75
11	Brooks Kieschnick	.50
12	Alex Ochoa	.50
13	Rey Ordonez	.75
14	Neifi Perez	.50
15	Edgar Renteria	.75
16	Mariano Rivera	.75
17	Ruben Rivera	.50
18	Scott Rolen	2.50
19	Billy Wagner	.50
20	Todd Walker	.50

1997 Topps Hobby Masters

These 10 cards lead the way as dealers' top selections. The cards, printed on 28-point diffraction foilboard, replace two regular cards in every 36th pack of 1997 Topps Series I product. Cards are numbered with a "HM" prefix.

		MT
Complete Set (20):		25.00
Common Player:		.50
1	Ken Griffey Jr.	2.75
2	Cal Ripken Jr.	3.00
3	Greg Maddux	2.00
4	Albert Belle	.75
5	Tony Gwynn	2.00
6	Jeff Bagwell	1.50
7	Randy Johnson	1.00
8	Raul Mondesi	.50
9	Juan Gonzalez	1.50
10	Kenny Lofton	.50
11	Frank Thomas	2.25
12	Mike Piazza	2.50
13	Chipper Jones	2.50
14	Brady Anderson	.50
15	Ken Caminiti	.50
16	Barry Bonds	2.25
17	Mo Vaughn	1.00
18	Derek Jeter	2.50
19	Sammy Sosa	2.25
20	Andres Galarraga	.50

1997 Topps Inter-League Match Ups

The double-sided Inter-League Finest and Inter-League Finest Refracators (seeded one in 36 and one in 216 Topps Series 1 packs respectively) feature top individual matchups from inter-league rivalries. One player from each major league team is represented, for a total of 28 players on 14 different cards. Each card is covered with a Finest clear protector. Cards are numbered with an "ILM" prefix.

		MT
Complete Set (14):		18.00
Common Player:		.50
Refractors:		2X
1	Mark McGwire, Barry Bonds	3.50
2	Tim Salmon, Mike Piazza	2.50
3	Ken Griffey Jr., Dante Bichette	2.00
4	Juan Gonzalez, Tony Gwynn	2.00
5	Frank Thomas, Sammy Sosa	2.50
6	Albert Belle, Barry Larkin	1.00
7	Johnny Damon, Brian Jordan	.50
8	Paul Molitor, Jeff King	.75
9	John Jaha, Jeff Bagwell	1.50
10	Bernie Williams, Todd Hundley	.50
11	Joe Carter, Henry Rodriguez	.50
12	Cal Ripken Jr., Gregg Jefferies	3.00
13	Mo Vaughn, Chipper Jones	2.00
14	Travis Fryman, Gary Sheffield	.50

1997 Topps Mickey Mantle Reprints

All 16 remaining Mickey Mantle cards that were not reprinted in 1996 Topps Baseball are found in this insert, seeded every 12 packs of Series I Topps. The set starts off with No. 21 and runs through No. 36 since the '96 reprints were numbered 1-20.

		MT
Complete Set (16):		35.00
Common Card:		3.00
21	1953 Bowman #44	3.00
22	1953 Bowman #59	4.00
23	1957 Topps #407	3.00
24	1958 Topps #418	3.00
25	1958 Topps #487	3.00
26	1959 Topps #461	3.00
27	1959 Topps #564	3.00
28	1960 Topps #160	3.00
29	1960 Topps #563	3.00
30	1961 Topps #406	3.00
31	1961 Topps #475	3.00
32	1961 Topps #578	3.00
33	1962 Topps #18	3.00
34	1962 Topps #318	3.00
35	1962 Topps #471	3.00
36	1964 Topps #331	3.00

1997 Topps Mickey Mantle Finest

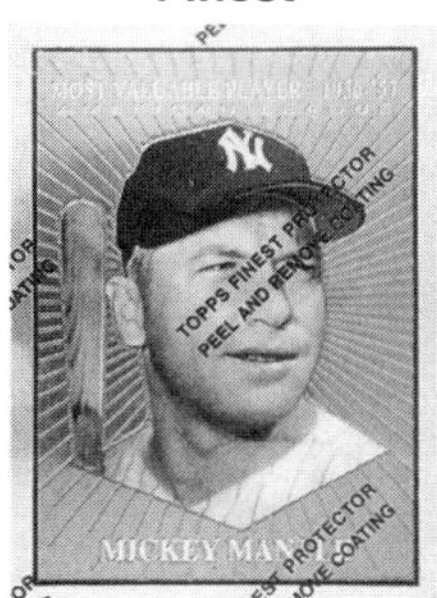

The 16-card Mickey Mantle reprints insert that was found in Series I was re-issued in Series II in the Topps Finest technology. The Finest versions are found on average of every 24 packs.

		MT
Complete Set (16):		60.00
Common Card:		4.00
21	1953 Bowman #44	4.00
22	1953 Bowman #59	5.00
23	1957 Topps #407	4.00
24	1958 Topps #418	4.00
25	1958 Topps #487	4.00
26	1959 Topps #461	4.00
27	1959 Topps #564	4.00
28	1960 Topps #160	4.00
29	1960 Topps #563	4.00
30	1961 Topps #406	4.00
31	1961 Topps #475	4.00
32	1961 Topps #578	4.00
33	1962 Topps #18	4.00
34	1962 Topps #318	4.00
35	1962 Topps #471	4.00
36	1964 Topps #331	4.00

1997 Topps Mickey Mantle Finest Refractors

Each of the 16 Mantle Finest reprints from Series II can also be found in a Refractor version. Refractors are found every 216 packs, on average.

		MT
Complete Set (16):		250.00
Common Card:		15.00
21	1953 Bowman #44	15.00
22	1953 Bowman #59	25.00
23	1957 Topps #407	15.00
24	1958 Topps #418	15.00
25	1958 Topps #487	15.00
26	1959 Topps #461	15.00
27	1959 Topps #564	15.00
28	1960 Topps #160	15.00
29	1960 Topps #563	15.00
30	1961 Topps #406	15.00
31	1961 Topps #475	15.00
32	1961 Topps #578	15.00
33	1962 Topps #18	15.00
34	1962 Topps #318	15.00
35	1962 Topps #471	15.00
36	1964 Topps #331	15.00

1997 Topps Mickey Mantle Case Inserts

WORLD SERIES BATTING FOES
MICKEY MANTLE • HANK AARON

Inserted one per case of Series 1 Topps, these reprints of 16 Mickey Mantle special cards of the 1950s-1960s come sealed in a soft plastic holder. The plastic sleeve has a gold-foil stamp at bottom-back which reads "FACTORY TOPPS SEAL 1997".

		MT
Complete Set (16):		250.00
Common Card:		20.00
21	1953 Bowman #44	20.00
22	1953 Bowman #59	24.00
23	1957 Topps #407	20.00
24	1958 Topps #418	20.00
25	1958 Topps #487	20.00
26	1959 Topps #461	20.00
27	1959 Topps #564	20.00
28	1960 Topps #160	20.00
29	1960 Topps #563	20.00
30	1961 Topps #406	20.00
31	1961 Topps #475	20.00
32	1961 Topps #578	20.00
33	1962 Topps #18	20.00
34	1962 Topps #318	20.00
35	1962 Topps #471	20.00
36	1964 Topps #331	20.00

1997 Topps Season's Best

Season's Best features 25 players on prismatic illusion foilboard, and can be found every six packs. The set has the top five players from five statistical categories: home runs, RBIs, batting average, steals, and wins. Season's Best were found in packs of Topps Series II, and later reprinted on chromium stock as part of Topps Chrome.

		MT
Complete Set (25):		12.00
Common Player:		.25
1	Tony Gwynn	1.50
2	Frank Thomas	2.00
3	Ellis Burks	.25
4	Paul Molitor	.75
5	Chuck Knoblauch	.25
6	Mark McGwire	3.00
7	Brady Anderson	.25
8	Ken Griffey Jr.	2.50
9	Albert Belle	.45
10	Andres Galarraga	.25
11	Andres Galarraga	.25
12	Albert Belle	.45
13	Juan Gonzalez	1.00
14	Mo Vaughn	.75
15	Rafael Palmeiro	.45
16	John Smoltz	.25
17	Andy Pettitte	.35
18	Pat Hentgen	.25
19	Mike Mussina	.75
20	Andy Benes	.25
21	Kenny Lofton	.25
22	Tom Goodwin	.25
23	Otis Nixon	.25
24	Eric Young	.25
25	Lance Johnson	.25

1997 Topps Sweet Strokes

These retail-exclusive Sweet Strokes insert cards consist of 15 Power Matrix foil cards of the top hitters in the game. These players have the swings to produce game winning-hits. The cards were seeded one per every 12 1997 Topps Series I retail packs. Cards are numbered with a "SS" prefix.

		MT
Complete Set (15):		30.00
Common Player:		.75
1	Roberto Alomar	1.50
2	Jeff Bagwell	2.25
3	Albert Belle	1.50
4	Barry Bonds	3.50
5	Mark Grace	1.25
6	Ken Griffey Jr.	5.00
7	Tony Gwynn	3.00
8	Chipper Jones	4.00
9	Edgar Martinez	.75
10	Mark McGwire	6.00
11	Rafael Palmeiro	1.25
12	Mike Piazza	4.00
13	Gary Sheffield	1.25
14	Frank Thomas	3.50
15	Mo Vaughn	1.25

1997 Topps Team Timber

Team Timber was a 16-card insert that was exclusive to retail packs and inserted one per 36. The set displays the game's top sluggers on laminated litho wood cards. Cards are numbered with a "TT" prefix.

		MT
Complete Set (16):		22.50
Common Player:		.50
1	Ken Griffey Jr.	4.00
2	Ken Caminiti	.50
3	Bernie Williams	1.00
4	Jeff Bagwell	1.50
5	Frank Thomas	2.00
6	Andres Galarraga	.50
7	Barry Bonds	2.00
8	Rafael Palmeiro	.75
9	Brady Anderson	.50
10	Juan Gonzalez	1.50
11	Mo Vaughn	1.00
12	Mark McGwire	5.00
13	Gary Sheffield	.75
14	Albert Belle	.75
15	Chipper Jones	3.00
16	Mike Piazza	3.00

1997 Topps Willie Mays Reprints

There are 27 different Willie Mays cards reprinted in Topps Series I and seeded every eight packs. The inserts form a collection of Topps and Bowman cards from throughout Mays' career and each is highlighted by a special commemorative gold foil stamp. Each of the Mays reprints can also be found in an autographed edition, bearing a special "Certified Autograph Issue" gold-foil logo.

		MT
Complete Set (27):		45.00
Common Card:		1.50
Autographed Card:		75.00
1	1951 Bowman #305	3.00
2	1952 Topps #261	2.00
3	1953 Topps #244	2.00
4	1954 Bowman #89	1.50
5	1954 Topps #90	1.50
6	1955 Bowman #184	1.50
7	1955 Topps #194	1.50
8	1956 Topps #130	1.50
9	1957 Topps #10	1.50
10	1958 Topps #5	1.50
11	1959 Topps #50	1.50
12	1960 Topps #200	1.50
13	1961 Topps #150	1.50
14	1961 Topps #579	1.50
15	1962 Topps #300	1.50
16	1963 Topps #300	1.50
17	1964 Topps #150	1.50
18	1965 Topps #250	1.50
19	1966 Topps #1	1.50
20	1967 Topps #200	1.50
21	1968 Topps #50	1.50
22	1969 Topps #190	1.50
23	1970 Topps #600	1.50
24	1971 Topps #600	1.50
25	1971 Topps #600	1.50
26	1972 Topps #49	1.50
27	1973 Topps #305	1.50

1997 Topps Willie Mays Finest

The introduction of Series II Topps offered collectors a chance to find Finest technology versions of each of the 27 commemorative reprint Topps and Bowman cards from throughout Mays' career. The Finest Mays reprints are found one in every 30 packs, on average.

		MT
Complete Set (27):		55.00
Common Card:		3.00
1	1951 Bowman #305	6.00
2	1952 Topps #261	4.50
3	1953 Topps #244	4.50
4	1954 Bowman #89	3.00
5	1954 Topps #90	3.00
6	1955 Bowman #184	3.00
7	1955 Topps #194	3.00
8	1956 Topps #130	3.00
9	1957 Topps #10	3.00
10	1958 Topps #5	3.00
11	1959 Topps #50	3.00
12	1960 Topps #200	3.00
13	1961 Topps #150	3.00
14	1961 Topps #579	3.00
15	1962 Topps #300	3.00
16	1963 Topps #300	3.00
17	1964 Topps #150	3.00
18	1965 Topps #250	3.00
19	1966 Topps #1	3.00
20	1967 Topps #200	3.00
21	1968 Topps #50	3.00
22	1969 Topps #190	3.00
23	1970 Topps #600	3.00
24	1971 Topps #600	3.00
25	1971 Topps #600	3.00
26	1972 Topps #49	3.00
27	1973 Topps #305	3.00

1997 Topps Willie Mays Finest Refractors

A high-end parallel set to the Willie Mays 27-card commemorative reprint issue is the Finest Refractor version issued in Series II. Refractors are found on average of once per 180 packs.

		MT
Complete Set (27):		125.00
Common Card:		7.50
1	1951 Bowman #305	12.50
2	1952 Topps #261	10.00
3	1953 Topps #244	10.00
4	1954 Bowman #89	7.50
5	1954 Topps #90	7.50
6	1955 Bowman #184	7.50
7	1955 Topps #194	7.50
8	1956 Topps #130	7.50
9	1957 Topps #10	7.50
10	1958 Topps #5	7.50
11	1959 Topps #50	7.50
12	1960 Topps #200	7.50
13	1961 Topps #150	7.50
14	1961 Topps #579	7.50
15	1962 Topps #300	7.50
16	1963 Topps #300	7.50
17	1964 Topps #150	7.50
18	1965 Topps #250	7.50
19	1966 Topps #1	7.50
20	1967 Topps #200	7.50
21	1968 Topps #50	7.50
22	1969 Topps #190	7.50
23	1970 Topps #600	7.50
24	1971 Topps #600	7.50
25	1971 Topps #600	7.50
26	1972 Topps #49	7.50
27	1973 Topps #305	7.50

1997 Topps/Chrome

Chrome Baseball reprinted the top 165 cards from Topps Series I and II baseball on a chromium, metallized stock. Chrome sold in four-card packs and included three insert sets: Diamond Duos, which was created exclusively for this product, Season's Best and Topps All-Stars, which were both reprinted from Topps products. Refractor versions of each card were found every 12 packs.

		MT
Complete Set (165):		50.00
Common Player:		.15
Common Refractors:		2.00
Star Refractors:		3X
Pack (4):		2.00
Wax Box (24):		40.00
1	Barry Bonds	3.00
2	Jose Valentin	.15
3	Brady Anderson	.15
4	Wade Boggs	1.25
5	Andres Galarraga	.15
6	Rusty Greer	.15
7	Derek Jeter	6.00
8	Ricky Bottalico	.15
9	Mike Piazza	4.00
10	Garret Anderson	.15
11	Jeff King	.15
12	Kevin Appier	.15
13	Mark Grace	.40
14	Jeff D'Amico	.15
15	Jay Buhner	.15
16	Hal Morris	.15
17	Harold Baines	.15
18	Jeff Cirillo	.15
19	Tom Glavine	.25
20	Andy Pettitte	.40
21	Mark McGwire	5.00
22	Chuck Knoblauch	.15
23	Raul Mondesi	.35
24	Albert Belle	.50
25	Trevor Hoffman	.15
26	Eric Young	.15
27	Brian McRae	.15
28	Jim Edmonds	.15
29	Robb Nen	.15
30	Reggie Sanders	.15
31	Mike Lansing	.15
32	Craig Biggio	.25
33	Ray Lankford	.15
34	Charles Nagy	.15
35	Paul Wilson	.15
36	John Wetteland	.15
37	Derek Bell	.15
38	Edgar Martinez	.15
39	Rickey Henderson	1.25
40	Jim Thome	.15
41	Frank Thomas	2.00
42	Jackie Robinson (Tribute)	5.00
43	Terry Steinbach	.15
44	Kevin Brown	.25
45	Joey Hamilton	.15
46	Travis Fryman	.15
47	Juan Gonzalez	1.50
48	Ron Gant	.15
49	Greg Maddux	3.00
50	Wally Joyner	.15
51	John Valentin	.15
42	Bret Boone	.25
53	Paul Molitor	1.25
54	Rafael Palmeiro	.40
55	Todd Hundley	.15
56	Ellis Burks	.15
57	Bernie Williams	.50
58	Roberto Alomar	1.00
59	Jose Mesa	.15
60	Troy Percival	.15
61	John Smoltz	.25
62	Jeff Conine	.15
63	Bernard Gilkey	.15
64	Mickey Tettleton	.15
65	Justin Thompson	.15
66	Tony Phillips	.15
67	Ryne Sandberg	1.50
68	Geronimo Berroa	.15
69	Todd Hollandsworth	.15
70	Rey Ordonez	.15
71	Marquis Grissom	.15
72	Tino Martinez	.15
73	Steve Finley	.15
74	Andy Benes	.15
75	Jason Kendall	.15
76	Johnny Damon	.25
77	Jason Giambi	.60
78	Henry Rodriguez	.15
79	Edgar Renteria	.15
80	Ray Durham	.15
81	Gregg Jefferies	.15
82	Roberto Hernandez	.15
83	Joe Carter	.15
84	Jermaine Dye	.15
85	Julio Franco	.15
86	David Justice	.35
87	Jose Canseco	1.00
88	Paul O'Neill	.15
89	Mariano Rivera	.40
90	Bobby Higginson	.25
91	Mark Grudzielanek	.15
92	Lance Johnson	.15
93	Ken Caminiti	.15
94	Gary Sheffield	.40
95	Luis Castillo	.15
96	Scott Rolen	1.00
97	Chipper Jones	4.00
98	Darryl Strawberry	.15
99	Nomar Garciaparra	3.00
100	Jeff Bagwell	1.50
101	Ken Griffey Jr.	5.00
102	Sammy Sosa	3.00
103	Jack McDowell	.15
104	James Baldwin	.15
105	Rocky Coppinger	.15
106	Manny Ramirez	1.50
107	Tim Salmon	.40
108	Eric Karros	.15
109	Brett Butler	.15
110	Randy Johnson	1.50
111	Pat Hentgen	.15
112	Rondell White	.35
113	Eddie Murray	1.00
114	Ivan Rodriguez	1.25
115	Jermaine Allensworth	.15
116	Ed Sprague	.15
117	Kenny Lofton	.15
118	Alan Benes	.15
119	Fred McGriff	.15
120	Alex Fernandez	.15
121	Al Martin	.15
122	Devon White	.15
123	David Cone	.15
124	Karim Garcia	.15
125	Chili Davis	.15
126	Roger Clemens	2.00
127	Bobby Bonilla	.15
128	Mike Mussina	1.00
129	Todd Walker	.15
130	Dante Bichette	.15
131	Carlos Baerga	.15
132	Matt Williams	.40
133	Will Clark	.40
134	Dennis Eckersley	.15
135	Ryan Klesko	.15
136	Dean Palmer	.15
137	Javy Lopez	.15
138	Greg Vaughn	.15
139	Vinny Castilla	.15
140	Cal Ripken Jr.	6.00
141	Ruben Rivera	.15
142	Mark Wohlers	.15
143	Tony Clark	.15
144	Jose Rosado	.15
145	Tony Gwynn	2.00
146	Cecil Fielder	.15
147	Brian Jordan	.15
148	Bob Abreu	.25
149	Barry Larkin	.25
150	Robin Ventura	.15
151	John Olerud	.15
152	Rod Beck	.15
153	Vladimir Guerrero	2.00
154	Marty Cordova	.15
155	Todd Stottlemyre	.15
156	Hideo Nomo	.75
157	Denny Neagle	.15
158	John Jaha	.15
159	Mo Vaughn	.60
160	Andruw Jones	1.50
161	Moises Alou	.30
162	Larry Walker	.50
163	Eddie Murray (Season Highlights)	.50
164	Paul Molitor (Season Highlights)	.50
165	Checklist	.15

1997 Topps/Chrome All-Stars

Topps Chrome All-Stars display the same 22 cards found in Topps Series I, however these are reprinted on a Chrome stock. Regular versions are seeded every 24 packs, while Refractor versions arrive every 72 packs. Cards are numbered with an "AS" prefix.

		MT
Complete Set (22):		40.00
Common Player:		1.00
Refractors:		2X
1	Ivan Rodriguez	2.00
2	Todd Hundley	1.00
3	Frank Thomas	3.00
4	Andres Galarraga	1.00
5	Chuck Knoblauch	1.00
6	Eric Young	1.00
7	Jim Thome	1.00
8	Chipper Jones	4.00
9	Cal Ripken Jr.	8.00
10	Barry Larkin	1.00
11	Albert Belle	1.25
12	Barry Bonds	3.00
13	Ken Griffey Jr.	6.00
14	Ellis Burks	1.00
15	Juan Gonzalez	2.50
16	Gary Sheffield	1.50
17	Andy Pettitte	1.50
18	Tom Glavine	1.25
19	Pat Hentgen	1.00
20	John Smoltz	1.25
21	Roberto Hernandez	1.00
22	Mark Wohlers	1.00

1997 Topps/Chrome Diamond Duos

Diamond Duos is the only one of the three insert sets in Chrome Baseball that was developed exclusively for this product. The set has 10 cards featuring two superstar teammates on double-sided chromium cards. Diamond Duos are found every 36 packs, while Refractor versions are found every 108 packs. Cards are numbered with a "DD" prefix.

		MT
Complete Set (10):		35.00
Common Player:		1.00
Refractors:		2X
1	Chipper Jones, Andruw Jones	4.00
2	Derek Jeter, Bernie Williams	8.00
3	Ken Griffey Jr., Jay Buhner	6.00
4	Kenny Lofton, Manny Ramirez	2.00
5	Jeff Bagwell, Craig Biggio	2.00
6	Juan Gonzalez, Ivan Rodriguez	3.00
7	Cal Ripken Jr., Brady Anderson	8.00
8	Mike Piazza, Hideo Nomo	5.00
9	Andres Galarraga, Dante Bichette	1.00
10	Frank Thomas, Albert Belle	2.00

1997 Topps/Chrome Season's Best

Season's Best includes the 25 players found in Topps Series II, but in a chromium version. The top five players from five statistical categories, including Leading Looters, Bleacher Reachers and Kings of Swing. Regular versions are seeded every 18 packs, with Refractors every 54 packs.

		MT
Complete Set (25):		35.00
Common Player:		1.00
Refractors:		2X
1	Tony Gwynn	2.00
2	Frank Thomas	2.00
3	Ellis Burks	1.00
4	Paul Molitor	1.50
5	Chuck Knoblauch	1.00
6	Mark McGwire	6.00
7	Brady Anderson	1.00
8	Ken Griffey Jr.	5.00
9	Albert Belle	1.00
10	Andres Galarraga	1.00
11	Andres Galarraga	1.00
12	Albert Belle	1.00
13	Juan Gonzalez	1.50
14	Mo Vaughn	1.50
15	Rafael Palmeiro	1.00
16	John Smoltz	1.00
17	Andy Pettitte	1.50
18	Pat Hentgen	1.00
19	Mike Mussina	1.50
20	Andy Benes	1.00
21	Kenny Lofton	1.00
22	Tom Goodwin	1.00
23	Otis Nixon	1.00
24	Eric Young	1.00
25	Lance Johnson	1.00

1997 Topps/Gallery

The second year of Gallery features 180 cards printed on extra-thick 24-point stock. Card fronts feature a player photo surrounded by an embossed foil "frame" to give each card the look of a piece of artwork. Backs contain career stats and biographical information on each player. Inserts include Peter Max Serigraphs, Signature Series Serigraphs, Player's Private Issue (parallel set), Photo Gallery and Gallery of Heroes. Cards were sold exclusively in hobby shops in eight-card packs for $4 each.

		MT
Complete Set (180):		30.00
Common Player:		.15
Pack (8):		2.00
Wax Box (24):		35.00
1	Paul Molitor	.75
2	Devon White	.15
3	Andres Galarraga	.15
4	Cal Ripken Jr.	5.00
5	Tony Gwynn	1.50
6	Mike Stanley	.15
7	Orel Hershiser	.15
8	Jose Canseco	.75
9	Chili Davis	.15
10	Harold Baines	.15
11	Rickey Henderson	1.00
12	Darryl Strawberry	.15
13	Todd Worrell	.15
14	Cecil Fielder	.15
15	Gary Gaetti	.15
16	Bobby Bonilla	.15
17	Will Clark	.40
18	Kevin Brown	.25
19	Tom Glavine	.25
20	Wade Boggs	.75
21	Edgar Martinez	.15
22	Lance Johnson	.15
23	Gregg Jefferies	.15
24	Bip Roberts	.15
25	Tony Phillips	.15
26	Greg Maddux	1.50
27	Mickey Tettleton	.15
28	Terry Steinbach	.15
29	Ryne Sandberg	.75
30	Wally Joyner	.15
31	Joe Carter	.15
32	Ellis Burks	.15
33	Fred McGriff	.15
34	Barry Larkin	.25
35	John Franco	.15
36	Rafael Palmeiro	.40
37	Mark McGwire	5.00
38	Ken Caminiti	.15
39	David Cone	.15
40	Julio Franco	.15
41	Roger Clemens	1.50
42	Barry Bonds	2.00
43	Dennis Eckersley	.15
44	Eddie Murray	.75
45	Paul O'Neill	.15
46	Craig Biggio	.15
47	Roberto Alomar	.65
48	Mark Grace	.40
49	Matt Williams	.40
50	Jay Buhner	.15
51	John Smoltz	.25
52	Randy Johnson	.75
53	Ramon Martinez	.15
54	Curt Schilling	.35
55	Gary Sheffield	.40
56	Jack McDowell	.15
57	Brady Anderson	.15
58	Dante Bichette	.15
59	Ron Gant	.15
60	Alex Fernandez	.15
61	Moises Alou	.30
62	Travis Fryman	.15
63	Dean Palmer	.15
64	Todd Hundley	.15
65	Jeff Brantley	.15
66	Bernard Gilkey	.15
67	Geronimo Berroa	.15
68	John Wetteland	.15
69	Robin Ventura	.15
70	Ray Lankford	.15
71	Kevin Appier	.15
72	Larry Walker	.50
73	Juan Gonzalez	1.00
74	Jeff King	.15
75	Greg Vaughn	.15
76	Steve Finley	.15
77	Brian McRae	.15
78	Paul Sorrento	.15
79	Ken Griffey Jr.	4.00
80	Omar Vizquel	.15
81	Jose Mesa	.15
82	Albert Belle	.50
83	Glenallen Hill	.15
84	Sammy Sosa	2.00
85	Andy Benes	.15
86	David Justice	.40
87	Marquis Grissom	.15
88	John Olerud	.15
89	Tino Martinez	.15
90	Frank Thomas	1.50
91	Raul Mondesi	.35
92	Steve Trachsel	.15
93	Jim Edmonds	.15
94	Rusty Greer	.15
95	Joey Hamilton	.15
96	Ismael Valdes	.15
97	Dave Nilsson	.15
98	John Jaha	.15
99	Alex Gonzalez	.15
100	Javy Lopez	.15
101	Ryan Klesko	.15
102	Tim Salmon	.25
103	Bernie Williams	.40
104	Roberto Hernandez	.15
105	Chuck Knoblauch	.15
106	Mike Lansing	.15
107	Vinny Castilla	.15
108	Reggie Sanders	.15
109	Mo Vaughn	.60
110	Rondell White	.25
111	Ivan Rodriguez	.75
112	Mike Mussina	.75
113	Carlos Baerga	.15
114	Jeff Conine	.15
115	Jim Thome	.15
116	Manny Ramirez	1.00
117	Kenny Lofton	.15
118	Wilson Alvarez	.15
119	Eric Karros	.15
120	Robb Nen	.15
121	Mark Wohlers	.15
122	Ed Sprague	.15
123	Pat Hentgen	.15
124	Juan Guzman	.15
125	Derek Bell	.15
126	Jeff Bagwell	1.00
127	Eric Young	.15
128	John Valentin	.15
129	Al Martin (photo actually Javy Lopez)	.15
130	Trevor Hoffman	.15
131	Henry Rodriguez	.15
132	Pedro Martinez	.75
133	Mike Piazza	3.00
134	Brian Jordan	.15
135	Jose Valentin	.15
136	Jeff Cirillo	.15
137	Chipper Jones	3.00
138	Ricky Bottalico	.15
139	Hideo Nomo	.75
140	Troy Percival	.15
141	Rey Ordonez	.15
142	Edgar Renteria	.15
143	Luis Castillo	.15
144	Vladimir Guerrero	1.00
145	Jeff D'Amico	.15
146	Andruw Jones	.75
147	Darin Erstad	.50
148	Bob Abreu	.25
149	Carlos Delgado	.35
150	Jamey Wright	.15

151 Nomar Garciaparra 2.00
152 Jason Kendall .15
153 Jermaine Allensworth .15
154 Scott Rolen .75
155 Rocky Coppinger .15
156 Paul Wilson .15
157 Garret Anderson .15
158 Mariano Rivera .40
159 Ruben Rivera .15
160 Andy Pettitte .35
161 Derek Jeter 4.00
162 Neifi Perez .15
163 Ray Durham .15
164 James Baldwin .15
165 Marty Cordova .15
166 Tony Clark .15
167 Michael Tucker .15
168 Mike Sweeney .15
169 Johnny Damon .25
170 Jermaine Dye .15
171 Alex Ochoa .15
172 Jason Isringhausen .15
173 Mark Grudzielanek .15
174 Jose Rosado .15
175 Todd Hollandsworth .15
176 Alan Benes .15
177 Jason Giambi .50
178 Billy Wagner .15
179 Justin Thompson .15
180 Todd Walker .15

1997 Topps/Gallery Players Private Issue

A parallel version of the Gallery issue called Players Private Issue was produced as a 1:12 pack insert. The PPI cards differ from the regular version in the use of a "PPI-" prefix to the card number on front and the application of a small silver PPI seal in a lower corner. On back, the line "One of 250 Issued" has been added.

	MT
Common Player:	2.00
Stars:	3X

(See 1997 Topps/Gallery for checklist and base card values.)

1997 Topps/Gallery of Heroes

This 10-card die-cut insert features a design resembling stained glass. Cards were inserted 1:36 packs. Cards are numbered with a "GH" prefix.

		MT
Complete Set (10):		70.00
Common Player:		3.00
1	Derek Jeter	15.00
2	Chipper Jones	10.00
3	Frank Thomas	6.00
4	Ken Griffey Jr.	12.00
5	Cal Ripken Jr.	15.00
6	Mark McGwire	12.00
7	Mike Piazza	10.00
8	Jeff Bagwell	5.00
9	Tony Gwynn	6.00
10	Mo Vaughn	3.00

1997 Topps/Gallery Peter Max

Noted artist Peter Max has painted renditions of 10 superstar players and offered his commentary about those players on the backs. Cards were inserted 1:24 packs. In addition, Max-autographed cards signed and numbered from an edition of 40 are inserted 1:1,200 packs.

		MT
Complete Set (10):		50.00
Common Player:		2.00
Complete Autographed Set (10):		1500.
Common Autographed Player:		20.00
1	Ken Griffey Jr.	6.00
1	Ken Griffey Jr. (autographed)	275.00
2	Frank Thomas	4.00
2	Frank Thomas (autographed)	100.00
3	Albert Belle	3.00
3	Albert Belle (autographed)	75.00
4	Barry Bonds	4.00
4	Barry Bonds (autographed)	300.00
5	Derek Jeter	8.00
5	Derek Jeter (autographed)	200.00
6	Ken Caminiti	2.00
6	Ken Caminiti (autographed)	20.00
7	Mike Piazza	5.00
7	Mike Piazza (autographed)	200.00
8	Cal Ripken Jr.	8.00
8	Cal Ripken Jr. (autographed)	225.00
9	Mark McGwire	7.50
9	Mark McGwire (autographed)	300.00
10	Chipper Jones	5.00
10	Chipper Jones (autographed)	150.00

1997 Topps/Gallery Photo Gallery

This 21-card set features full-bleed, high-gloss action photos of some of the game's top stars. Cards were inserted 1:24 packs. They are numbered with a "PG" prefix.

		MT
Complete Set (16):		50.00
Common Player:		1.50
1	World Series	2.00
2	Paul Molitor	2.50
3	Eddie Murray	2.00
4	Ken Griffey Jr.	8.00
5	Chipper Jones	6.00
6	Derek Jeter	10.00
7	Frank Thomas	3.00
8	Mark McGwire	8.00
9	Kenny Lofton	1.50
10	Gary Sheffield	2.00
11	Mike Piazza	6.00
12	Vinny Castilla	1.50
13	Andres Galarraga	1.50
14	Andy Pettitte	2.00
15	Robin Ventura	1.50
16	Barry Larkin	1.50

1997 Topps Stars

The premiere version of this product was sold only to hobby shops that were members of the Topps Home Team Advantage program. Each of the 125 regular cards in the set is printed on 20-point stock. Card fronts feature spot UV coating with a textured star pattern running down one side of the card. Inserts include the parallel Always Mint set, as well al '97 All-Stars, Future All-Stars, All-Star memories, and Autographed Rookie Reprints. Cards were sold in seven-card packs for $3 each.

		MT
Complete Set (125):		45.00
Common Player:		.15
Always Mint Stars, RCs:		6X
Pack (7):		3.00
Wax Box (24):		65.00
1	Larry Walker	.50
2	Tino Martinez	.15
3	Cal Ripken Jr.	3.00
4	Ken Griffey Jr.	2.50
5	Chipper Jones	2.00
6	David Justice	.35
7	Mike Piazza	2.00
8	Jeff Bagwell	1.00
9	Ron Gant	.15
10	Sammy Sosa	1.75
11	Tony Gwynn	1.50
12	Carlos Baerga	.15
13	Frank Thomas	1.00
14	Moises Alou	.30
15	Barry Larkin	.25
16	Ivan Rodriguez	.75
17	Greg Maddux	1.50
18	Jim Edmonds	.15
19	Jose Canseco	.75
20	Rafael Palmeiro	.40
21	Paul Molitor	.75
22	Kevin Appier	.15
23	Raul Mondesi	.25
24	Lance Johnson	.15
25	Edgar Martinez	.15
26	Andres Galarraga	.15
27	Mo Vaughn	.65
28	Ken Caminiti	.15
29	Cecil Fielder	.15
30	Harold Baines	.15
31	Roberto Alomar	.75
32	Shawn Estes	.15
33	Tom Glavine	.25
34	Dennis Eckersley	.15
35	Manny Ramirez	1.00
36	John Olerud	.15
37	Juan Gonzalez	1.00
38	Chuck Knoblauch	.15
39	Albert Belle	.45
40	Vinny Castilla	.15
41	John Smoltz	.25
42	Barry Bonds	1.75
43	Randy Johnson	.75
44	Brady Anderson	.15
45	Jeff Blauser	.15
46	Craig Biggio	.25
47	Jeff Conine	.15
48	Marquis Grissom	.15
49	Mark Grace	.40
50	Roger Clemens	1.50
51	Mark McGwire	3.00
52	Fred McGriff	.15
53	Gary Sheffield	.40
54	Bobby Jones	.15
55	Eric Young	.15
56	Robin Ventura	.15
57	Wade Boggs	.65
58	Joe Carter	.15
59	Ryne Sandberg	1.00
60	Matt Williams	.30
61	Todd Hundley	.15
62	Dante Bichette	.15
63	Chili Davis	.15
64	Kenny Lofton	.15
65	Jay Buhner	.15
66	Will Clark	.30
67	Travis Fryman	.15
68	Pat Hentgen	.15
69	Ellis Burks	.15
70	Mike Mussina	.75
71	Hideo Nomo	.65
72	Sandy Alomar	.15
73	Bobby Bonilla	.15
74	Rickey Henderson	.75
75	David Cone	.15

76	Terry Steinbach	.15
77	Pedro Martinez	.75
78	Jim Thome	.15
79	Rod Beck	.15
80	Randy Myers	.15
81	Charles Nagy	.15
82	Mark Wohlers	.15
83	Paul O'Neill	.15
84	Curt Schilling	.25
85	Joey Cora	.15
86	John Franco	.15
87	Kevin Brown	.25
88	Benito Santiago	.15
89	Ray Lankford	.15
90	Bernie Williams	.45
91	Jason Dickson	.15
92	Jeff Cirillo	.15
93	Nomar Garciaparra	2.00
94	Mariano Rivera	.30
95	Javy Lopez	.15
96	*Tony Womack*	1.00
97	Jose Rosado	.15
98	Denny Neagle	.15
99	Darryl Kile	.15
100	Justin Thompson	.15
101	Juan Encarnacion	.15
102	Brad Fullmer	.15
103	*Kris Benson*	1.50
104	Todd Helton	1.00
105	Paul Konerko	.15
106	*Travis Lee*	1.50
107	Todd Greene	.15
108	*Mark Kotsay*	2.00
109	Carl Pavano	.15
110	*Kerry Wood*	4.00
111	*Jason Romano*	1.00
112	*Geoff Goetz*	.50
113	*Scott Hodges*	.50
114	*Aaron Akin*	.15
115	*Vernon Wells*	2.00
116	*Chris Stowe*	.15
117	*Brett Caradonna*	.50
118	*Adam Kennedy*	3.00
119	*Jayson Werth*	1.00
120	*Glenn Davis*	.50
121	*Troy Cameron*	.50
122	*J.J. Davis*	.50
123	*Jason Dellaero*	.50
124	*Jason Standridge*	.50
125	*Lance Berkman*	30.00

1997 Topps Stars Always Mint

This set parallels the regular Topps Stars issue and was inserted at the announced rate of one card per 12 packs. Identical in design to the regular version, the Always Mint cards have metallic foil background on the player portion of the front photos. Backs of the Always Mint parallels have a shiny metallic silver background.

	MT
Complete Set (125):	300.00
Common Player:	.50
Stars/Rookies:	6X

(See 1997 Topps Stars for checklist and base card values.)

1997 Topps Stars All-Star Memories

This 10-card insert features stars who have had memorable performances in previous All-Star Games. Cards feature a laser-cut cascade of stars on a foilboard stock. Backs have another photo and a description of the All-Star memory. The cards were inserted 1:24 packs. Cards are numbered with an "ASM" prefix.

		MT
Complete Set (10):		25.00
Common Player:		1.00
1	Cal Ripken Jr.	7.50
2	Jeff Conine	1.00
3	Mike Piazza	6.00
4	Randy Johnson	2.00
5	Ken Griffey Jr.	6.00
6	Fred McGriff	1.00
7	Moises Alou	1.25
8	Hideo Nomo	2.00
9	Larry Walker	1.50
10	Sandy Alomar	1.00

1997 Topps Stars Autographed Rookie Reprints

Fourteen different Hall of Famers autographed reprinted versions of their Topps rookie cards as a one-per-30-pack insert. Each card features a special certified stamp. Richie Ashburn was to have been card #2, but he died before he could autograph them.

		MT
Complete Set (14):		210.00
Common Player:		12.00
(1)	Luis Aparicio	35.00
(3)	Jim Bunning	25.00
(4)	Bob Feller	35.00
(5)	Rollie Fingers	20.00
(6)	Monte Irvin	20.00
(7)	Al Kaline	40.00
(8)	Ralph Kiner	25.00
(9)	Eddie Mathews	50.00
(10)	Hal Newhouser	20.00
(11)	Gaylord Perry	20.00
(12)	Robin Roberts	20.00
(13)	Brooks Robinson	40.00
(14)	Enos Slaughter	20.00
(15)	Earl Weaver	25.00

1997 Topps Stars Future All-Stars

This 15-card set showcases the top candidates to make their All-Star Game debut in 1998. Cards feature a prismatic rainbow foil background and were inserted 1:12 packs. Cards are numbered with a "FAS" prefix.

		MT
Complete Set (15):		25.00
Common Player:		1.00
1	Derek Jeter	6.00
2	Andruw Jones	4.00
3	Vladimir Guerrero	4.00
4	Scott Rolen	3.00
5	Jose Guillen	1.00
6	Jose Cruz, Jr.	1.25
7	Darin Erstad	4.00
8	Tony Clark	1.50
9	Scott Spiezio	1.00
10	Kevin Orie	1.00
11	Calvin Reese	1.00
12	Billy Wagner	1.00
13	Matt Morris	1.50
14	Jeremi Gonzalez	1.00
15	Hideki Irabu	1.00

1997 Topps Stars Rookie Reprints

Fifteen Topps rookie cards of Hall of Famers were reprinted as a one-per-six-packs insert. Regardless of original size, all reprints are 2-1/2" x 3-1/2" with a reprint notice on back.

		MT
Complete Set (15):		30.00
Common Player:		2.00
(1)	Luis Aparicio	2.50
(2)	Richie Ashburn	2.50
(3)	Jim Bunning	2.00
(4)	Bob Feller	2.00
(5)	Rollie Fingers	2.00
(6)	Monte Irvin	2.00
(7)	Al Kaline	3.50
(8)	Ralph Kiner	2.00
(9)	Eddie Mathews	3.50
(10)	Hal Newhouser	2.00
(11)	Gaylord Perry	2.00
(12)	Robin Roberts	2.00
(13)	Brooks Robinson	3.50
(14)	Enos Slaughter	2.00
(15)	Earl Weaver	2.00

1997 Topps Stars 1997 All-Stars

This 20-card insert honors participants of the 1997 All-Star Game in Cleveland. Cards were inserted 1:24 packs. Fronts are printed on prismatic foil with hundreds of stars in the background. On back is another player photo and his All-Star Game 1997 and career stats. Cards are numbered with an "AS" prefix.

		MT
Complete Set (20):		150.00
Common Player:		3.00
1	Greg Maddux	15.00
2	Randy Johnson	8.00
3	Tino Martinez	3.00
4	Jeff Bagwell	8.00
5	Ivan Rodriguez	8.00
6	Mike Piazza	25.00
7	Cal Ripken Jr.	30.00
8	Ken Caminiti	3.00
9	Tony Gwynn	10.00
10	Edgar Martinez	3.00
11	Craig Biggio	3.00
12	Roberto Alomar	6.00
13	Larry Walker	4.00
14	Brady Anderson	3.00
15	Barry Bonds	15.00
16	Ken Griffey Jr.	25.00
17	Ray Lankford	3.00
18	Paul O'Neill	4.00
19	Jeff Blauser	3.00
20	Sandy Alomar	3.00

1997 Topps Screenplays

Twenty of the game's top stars were featured in this multi-part collectible. The packaging is a 5-1/8" diameter lithographed steel can. The can was shrink-wrapped at the factory with a round checklist disc covering the color player photo on top of the can. The top has a woodgrain border around the photo and a gold facsimile autograph. The back of the topper disc has a career summary of the player. Inside the tin is a 2-1/2" x 3-1/2" plastic motion card with several seconds of game action shown as the angle of view changes. The cards is covered by a peel-off protective layer on front and back. Foam pieces in the package allow both the can and card to be displayed upright. Issue price was about $10 per can. The unnumbered cans are checklisted here alphabetically. Values shown are for can/card combinations.

		MT
Complete Set (20):		35.00
Common Player:		.75
Pack (1):		2.00
Wax Box (21):		35.00
(1)	Jeff Bagwell	2.00
(2)	Albert Belle	1.00
(3)	Barry Bonds	3.25
(4)	Andres Galarraga	.75
(5)	Nomar Garciaparra	3.00
(6)	Juan Gonzalez	2.00
(7)	Ken Griffey Jr.	3.75
(8)	Tony Gwynn	2.50
(9)	Derek Jeter	3.50
(10)	Randy Johnson	1.25
(11)	Andruw Jones	1.50
(12)	Chipper Jones	3.50
(13)	Kenny Lofton	.75
(14)	Mark McGwire	4.00
(15)	Paul Molitor	1.25
(16)	Hideo Nomo	1.25
(17)	Cal Ripken Jr.	4.00
(18)	Sammy Sosa	3.25
(19)	Frank Thomas	3.25
(20)	Jim Thome	.75

1997 Topps Screenplays Inserts

		MT
Complete Set (6):		35.00
Common Player:		2.50
1	Larry Walker	2.50
2	Cal Ripken Jr.	12.00
3	Chipper Jones	7.50
4	Frank Thomas	5.00
5	Mike Piazza	7.50
6	Ken Griffey Jr.	10.00

1998 Topps

Topps issued two series in 1998, a total of 503 base cards; 282 in Series 1 and 221 in Series 2. Cards feature a gold border instead of the traditional white of past years. The product features Roberto Clemente inserts and a tribute card No. 21 in the base set. Series 1 subsets Series Highlights, Expansion Team Prospects, Interleague Highlights, Season Highlights, Prospects and Draft Picks. Subsets in Series II included: Expansion Teams, Inter-League Preview, Season Highlights, Prospects and Draft Picks. Every card in the set is paralleled in a Minted in Cooperstown insert that was stamped onsite at the Baseball Hall of Fame in Cooperstown. Inserts in Series 1 include: Roberto Clemente Reprints, Clemente Finest, Clemente Tribute, Memorabilila Madness, Etch a Sketch, Mystery Finest, Flashback and Baby Boomers. Inserts in Series 2 included: Clemente Reprints, Clemente Finest, 1998 Rookie Class, Mystery Finest, Milestones, Focal Points, and Clout 9. A factory set includes the 503 base cards, eight randomly selected inserts and one Clemente card sealed in a gold-foil stamped soft plastic case.

		MT
Unopened Factory Set (511):		70.00
Complete Set (503):		50.00
Common Player:		.05
Minted:		6X
Inserted 1:8		
Series 1 or 2 Pack (11):		1.00
Series 1 or 2 Wax Box (36):		30.00
1	Tony Gwynn	1.00
2	Larry Walker	.30
3	Billy Wagner	.05
4	Denny Neagle	.05
5	Vladimir Guerrero	.75
6	Kevin Brown	.15
7	NOT ISSUED	
8	Mariano Rivera	.25
9	Tony Clark	.05
10	Deion Sanders	.10
11	Francisco Cordova	.05
12	Matt Williams	.15
13	Carlos Baerga	.05
14	Mo Vaughn	.50
15	Bobby Witt	.05
16	Matt Stairs	.05
17	Chan Ho Park	.20
18	Mike Bordick	.05
19	Michael Tucker	.05
20	Frank Thomas	1.25
21	Roberto Clemente	1.50
22	Dmitri Young	.05
23	Steve Trachsel	.05
24	Jeff Kent	.05
25	Scott Rolen	.65
26	John Thomson	.05
27	Joe Vitiello	.05
28	Eddie Guardado	.05
29	Charlie Hayes	.05
30	Juan Gonzalez	.75
31	Garret Anderson	.05
32	John Jaha	.05
33	Omar Vizquel	.05
34	Brian Hunter	.05
35	Jeff Bagwell	.75
36	Mark Lemke	.05
37	Doug Glanville	.05
38	Dan Wilson	.05
39	Steve Cooke	.05
40	Chili Davis	.05
41	Mike Cameron	.05
42	F.P. Santangelo	.05
43	Brad Ausmus	.05
44	Gary DiSarcina	.05
45	Pat Hentgen	.05
46	Wilton Guerrero	.05
47	Devon White	.05
48	Danny Patterson	.05
49	Pat Meares	.05
50	Rafael Palmeiro	.25
51	Mark Gardner	.05
52	Jeff Blauser	.05
53	Dave Hollins	.05
54	Carlos Garcia	.05
55	Ben McDonald	.05
56	John Mabry	.05
57	Trevor Hoffman	.05
58	Tony Fernandez	.05
59	Rich Loiselle	.05
60	Mark Leiter	.05
61	Pat Kelly	.05
62	John Flaherty	.05
63	Roger Bailey	.05
64	Tom Gordon	.05
65	Ryan Klesko	.05
66	Darryl Hamilton	.05
67	Jim Eisenreich	.05
68	Butch Huskey	.05
69	Mark Grudzielanek	.05
70	Marquis Grissom	.05
71	Mark McLemore	.05
72	Gary Gaetti	.05
73	Greg Gagne	.05
74	Lyle Mouton	.05
75	Jim Edmonds	.05
76	Shawn Green	.30
77	Greg Vaughn	.05
78	Terry Adams	.05
79	*Kevin Polcovich*	.10
80	Troy O'Leary	.05
81	Jeff Shaw	.05
82	Rich Becker	.05
83	David Wells	.10
84	Steve Karsay	.05
85	Charles Nagy	.05
86	B.J. Surhoff	.05
87	Jamey Wright	.05
88	James Baldwin	.05
89	Edgardo Alfonzo	.05
90	Jay Buhner	.05
91	Brady Anderson	.05
92	Scott Servais	.05
93	Edgar Renteria	.05
94	Mike Lieberthal	.05
95	Rick Aguilera	.05
96	Walt Weiss	.05
97	Deivi Cruz	.05
98	Kurt Abbott	.05
99	Henry Rodriguez	.05
100	Mike Piazza	1.50
101	Bill Taylor	.05
102	Todd Zeile	.05
103	Rey Ordonez	.05
104	Willie Greene	.05
105	Tony Womack	.05
106	Mike Sweeney	.05
107	Jeffrey Hammonds	.05
108	Kevin Orie	.05
109	Alex Gonzalez	.10
110	Jose Canseco	.50
111	Paul Sorrento	.05
112	Joey Hamilton	.05
113	Brad Radke	.05
114	Steve Avery	.05
115	Esteban Loaiza	.05
116	Stan Javier	.05
117	Chris Gomez	.05
118	Royce Clayton	.05
119	Orlando Merced	.05
120	Kevin Appier	.05
121	Mel Nieves	.05
122	Joe Girardi	.05
123	Rico Brogna	.05
124	Kent Mercker	.05
125	Manny Ramirez	.75
126	Jeromy Burnitz	.05
127	Kevin Foster	.05
128	Matt Morris	.05
129	Jason Dickson	.05
130	Tom Glavine	.10
131	Wally Joyner	.05
132	Rick Reed	.05
133	Todd Jones	.05
134	Dave Martinez	.05
135	Sandy Alomar	.05
136	Mike Lansing	.05
137	Sean Berry	.05
138	Doug Jones	.05
139	Todd Stottlemyre	.05
140	Jay Bell	.05
141	Jaime Navarro	.05
142	Chris Hoiles	.05
143	Joey Cora	.05
144	Scott Spiezio	.05
145	Joe Carter	.05
146	Jose Guillen	.05
147	Damion Easley	.05
148	Lee Stevens	.05
149	Alex Fernandez	.05
150	Randy Johnson	.65
151	J.T. Snow	.05
152	Chuck Finley	.05
153	Bernard Gilkey	.05
154	David Segui	.05
155	Dante Bichette	.05
156	Kevin Stocker	.05
157	Carl Everett	.10
158	Jose Valentin	.05
159	Pokey Reese	.05
160	Derek Jeter	1.50
161	Roger Pavlik	.05
162	Mark Wohlers	.05
163	Ricky Bottalico	.05
164	Ozzie Guillen	.05
165	Mike Mussina	.65
166	Gary Sheffield	.25
167	Hideo Nomo	.65
168	Mark Grace	.25
169	Aaron Sele	.05
170	Darryl Kile	.05
171	Shawn Estes	.05
172	Vinny Castilla	.05
173	Ron Coomer	.05
174	Jose Rosado	.05
175	Kenny Lofton	.05
176	Jason Giambi	.25
177	Hal Morris	.05
178	Darren Bragg	.05
179	Orel Hershiser	.05
180	Ray Lankford	.05
181	Hideki Irabu	.05
182	Kevin Young	.05
183	Javy Lopez	.05
184	Jeff Montgomery	.05
185	Mike Holtz	.05
186	George Williams	.05
187	Cal Eldred	.05
188	Tom Candiotti	.05
189	Glenallen Hill	.05
190	Brian Giles	.05
191	Dave Mlicki	.05
192	Garrett Stephenson	.05
193	Jeff Frye	.05
194	Joe Oliver	.05
195	Bob Hamelin	.05
196	Luis Sojo	.05
197	LaTroy Hawkins	.05
198	Kevin Elster	.05
199	Jeff Reed	.05
200	Dennis Eckersley	.05
201	Bill Mueller	.05
202	Russ Davis	.05
203	Armando Benitez	.05
204	Quilvio Veras	.05

205 Tim Naehring .05
206 Quinton McCracken .05
207 Raul Casanova .05
208 Matt Lawton .05
209 Luis Alicea .05
210 Luis Gonzalez .30
211 Allen Watson .05
212 Gerald Williams .05
213 David Bell .05
214 Todd Hollandsworth .05
215 Wade Boggs .60
216 Jose Mesa .05
217 Jamie Moyer .05
218 Darren Daulton .05
219 Mickey Morandini .05
220 Rusty Greer .05
221 Jim Bullinger .05
222 Jose Offerman .05
223 Matt Karchner .05
224 Woody Williams .05
225 Mark Loretta .05
226 Mike Hampton .05
227 Willie Adams .05
228 Scott Hatteberg .05
229 Rich Amaral .05
230 Terry Steinbach .05
231 Glendon Rusch .05
232 Bret Boone .10
233 Robert Person .05
234 Jose Hernandez .05
235 Doug Drabek .05
236 Jason McDonald .05
237 Chris Widger .05
238 *Tom Martin* .05
239 Dave Burba .05
240 Pete Rose II .05
241 Bobby Ayala .05
242 Tim Wakefield .05
243 Dennis Springer .05
244 Tim Belcher .05
245 Jon Garland, Geoff Goetz (Draft Pick) .15
246 Glenn Davis, Lance Berkman (Draft Pick) .50
247 Vernon Wells, Aaron Akin (Draft Pick) .25
248 Adam Kennedy, Jason Romano (Draft Pick) .10
249 Jason Dellaero, Troy Cameron (Draft Pick) .10
250 Alex Sanchez, *Jared Sandberg* (Expansion Team Prospects) .10
251 Pablo Ortega, Jim Manias (Expansion Team Prospects) .10
252 Jason Conti, *Mike Stoner* (Expansion Team Prospects) .40
253 John Patterson, Larry Rodriguez (Expansion Team Prospects) .10
254 Adrian Beltre, *Ryan Minor*, Aaron Boone (Prospect) .75
255 Ben Grieve, Brian Buchanan, Dermal Brown (Prospect) .50
256 Carl Pavano, Kerry Wood, Gil Meche (Prospect) .50
257 David Ortiz, Daryle Ward, Richie Sexson (Prospect) .25
258 Randy Winn, Juan Encarnacion, Andrew Vessel (Prospect) .15
259 Kris Benson, Travis Smith, Courtney Duncan (Prospect) .15
260 Chad Hermansen, Brent Butler, *Warren Morris* (Prospect) .25
261 Ben Davis, Elieser Marrero, Ramon Hernandez (Prospect) .10
262 Eric Chavez, Russell Branyan, Russ Johnson (Prospect) .25
263 Todd Dunwoody, John Barnes, *Ryan Jackson* (Prospect) .25
264 Matt Clement, Roy Halladay, *Brian Fuentes* (Prospect) .25
265 Randy Johnson (Season Highlight) .10
266 Kevin Brown (Season Highlight) .05
267 Ricardo Rincon, Francisco Cordova (Season Highlight) .05
268 Nomar Garciaparra (Season Highlight) .65
269 Tino Martinez (Season Highlight) .05
270 Chuck Knoblauch (Interleague) .05
271 Pedro Martinez (Interleague) .35
272 Denny Neagle (Interleague) .05
273 Juan Gonzalez (Interleague) .40
274 Andres Galarraga (Interleague) .05
275 Checklist .05
276 Checklist .05
277 Moises Alou (World Series) .05
278 Sandy Alomar (World Series) .05
279 Gary Sheffield (World Series) .05
280 Matt Williams (World Series) .05
281 Livan Hernandez (World Series) .05
282 Chad Ogea (World Series) .05
283 Marlins Win (World Series) .05
284 Tino Martinez .05
285 Roberto Alomar .65
286 Jeff King .05
287 Brian Jordan .05
288 Darin Erstad .40
289 Ken Caminiti .05
290 Jim Thome .05
291 Paul Molitor .65
292 Ivan Rodriguez .65
293 Bernie Williams .30
294 Todd Hundley .05
295 Andres Galarraga .05
296 Greg Maddux 1.00
297 Edgar Martinez .05
298 Ron Gant .05
299 Derek Bell .05
300 Roger Clemens 1.00
301 Rondell White .15
302 Barry Larkin .10
303 Robin Ventura .05
304 Jason Kendall .05
305 Chipper Jones 1.50
306 John Franco .05
307 Sammy Sosa 1.25
308 Troy Percival .05
309 Chuck Knoblauch .05
310 Ellis Burks .05
311 Al Martin .05
312 Tim Salmon .20
313 Moises Alou .15
314 Lance Johnson .05
315 Justin Thompson .05
316 Will Clark .15
317 Barry Bonds 1.25
318 Craig Biggio .10
319 John Smoltz .10
320 Cal Ripken Jr. 2.00
321 Ken Griffey Jr. 1.75
322 Paul O'Neill .05
323 Todd Helton .60
324 John Olerud .05
325 Mark McGwire 2.50
326 Jose Cruz Jr. .10
327 Jeff Cirillo .05
328 Dean Palmer .05
329 John Wetteland .05
330 Steve Finley .05
331 Albert Belle .30
332 Curt Schilling .20
333 Raul Mondesi .20
334 Andruw Jones .40
335 Nomar Garciaparra 1.25
336 David Justice .20
337 Andy Pettitte .20
338 Pedro Martinez .65
339 Travis Miller .05
340 Chris Stynes .05
341 Gregg Jefferies .05
342 Jeff Fassero .05
343 Craig Counsell .05
344 Wilson Alvarez .05
345 Bip Roberts .05
346 Kelvim Escobar .05
347 Mark Bellhorn .05
348 *Cory Lidle* .25
349 Fred McGriff .05
350 Chuck Carr .05
351 Bob Abreu .05
352 Juan Guzman .05
353 Fernando Vina .05
354 Andy Benes .05
355 Dave Nilsson .05
356 Bobby Bonilla .05
357 Ismael Valdes .05
358 Carlos Perez .05
359 Kirk Rueter .05
360 Bartolo Colon .05
361 Mel Rojas .05
362 Johnny Damon .10
363 Geronimo Berroa .05
364 Reggie Sanders .05
365 Jermaine Allensworth .05
366 Orlando Cabrera .05
367 Jorge Fabregas .05
368 Scott Stahoviak .05
369 Ken Cloude .05
370 Donovan Osborne .05
371 Roger Cedeno .05
372 Neifi Perez .05
373 Chris Holt .05
374 Cecil Fielder .05
375 Marty Cordova .05
376 Tom Goodwin .05
377 Jeff Suppan .05
378 Jeff Brantley .05
379 Mark Langston .05
380 Shane Reynolds .05
381 Mike Fetters .05
382 Todd Greene .05
383 Ray Durham .05
384 Carlos Delgado .20
385 Jeff D'Amico .05
386 Brian McRae .05
387 Alan Benes .05
388 Heathcliff Slocumb .05
389 Eric Young .05
390 Travis Fryman .05
391 David Cone .05
392 Otis Nixon .05
393 Jeremi Gonzalez .05
394 Jeff Juden .05
395 Jose Vizcaino .05
396 Ugueth Urbina .05
397 Ramon Martinez .05
398 Robb Nen .05
399 Harold Baines .05
400 Delino DeShields .05
401 John Burkett .05
402 Sterling Hitchcock .05
403 Mark Clark .05
404 Terrell Wade .05
405 Scott Brosius .05
406 Chad Curtis .05
407 Brian Johnson .05
408 Roberto Kelly .05
409 *Dave Dellucci* .25
410 Michael Tucker .05
411 Mark Kotsay .05
412 Mark Lewis .05
413 Ryan McGuire .05
414 Shawon Dunston .05
415 Brad Rigby .05
416 Scott Erickson .05
417 Bobby Jones .05
418 Darren Oliver .05
419 John Smiley .05
420 T.J. Mathews .05
421 Dustin Hermanson .05
422 Mike Timlin .05
423 Willie Blair .05
424 Manny Alexander .05
425 Bob Tewksbury .05
426 Pete Schourek .05
427 Reggie Jefferson .05
428 Ed Sprague .05
429 Jeff Conine .05
430 Roberto Hernandez .05
431 Tom Pagnozzi .05
432 Jaret Wright .05
433 Livan Hernandez .05
434 Andy Ashby .05
435 Todd Dunn .05
436 Bobby Higginson .10
437 Rod Beck .05
438 Jim Leyritz .05
439 Matt Williams .15
440 Brett Tomko .05
441 Joe Randa .05
442 Chris Carpenter .05
443 Dennis Reyes .05
444 Al Leiter .05
445 Jason Schmidt .05
446 Ken Hill .05
447 Shannon Stewart .10
448 Enrique Wilson .05
449 Fernando Tatis .05
450 Jimmy Key .05
451 Darrin Fletcher .05
452 John Valentin .05
453 Kevin Tapani .05
454 Eric Karros .05
455 Jay Bell .05
456 Walt Weiss .05
457 Devon White .05
458 Carl Pavano .05
459 Mike Lansing .05
460 John Flaherty .05
461 Richard Hidalgo .05
462 Quinton McCracken .05
463 Karim Garcia .10
464 Miguel Cairo .05
465 Edwin Diaz .05
466 Bobby Smith .05
467 Yamil Benitez .05
468 *Rich Butler* .05
469 *Ben Ford* .05
470 Bubba Trammell .05
471 Brent Brede .05
472 Brooks Kieschnick .05
473 Carlos Castillo .05
474 Brad Radke (Season Highlight) .05
475 Roger Clemens (Season Highlight) .50
476 Curt Schilling (Season Highlight) .05
477 John Olerud (Season Highlight) .05
478 Mark McGwire (Season Highlight) 1.00
479 Mike Piazza, Ken Griffey Jr. (Interleague) .75
480 Jeff Bagwell, Frank Thomas (Interleague) .65
481 Chipper Jones, Nomar Garciaparra (Interleague) .75
482 Larry Walker, Juan Gonzalez (Interleague) .40
483 Gary Sheffield, Tino Martinez (Interleague) .05
484 Derrick Gibson, Michael Coleman, Norm Hutchins (Prospect) .10
485 Braden Looper, Cliff Politte, Brian Rose (Prospect) .10
486 Eric Milton, Jason Marquis, Corey Lee (Prospect) .25
487 A.J. Hinch, Mark Osborne, *Robert Fick* (Prospect) .50
488 Aramis Ramirez, Alex Gonzalez, Sean Casey (Prospect) .60
489 *Donnie Bridges*, *Tim Drew* (Draft Pick) .10
490 *Ntema Ndungidi*, *Darnell McDonald* (Draft Pick) .50
491 *Ryan Anderson*, Mark Mangum (Draft Pick) .50
492 J.J. Davis, *Troy Glaus* (Draft Pick) 2.00
493 Jayson Werth, *Dan Reichert* (Draft Pick) .10
494 *John Curtice*, *Mike Cuddyer* (Draft Pick) .75
495 *Jack Cust*, Jason Standridge (Draft Pick) .50
496 Brian Anderson (Expansion Team Prospect) .05
497 Tony Saunders (Expansion Team Prospect) .05
498 Vladimir Nunez, *Jhensy Sandoval* (Expansion Team Prospect) .10

499	Brad Penny, Nick Bierbrodt (Expansion Team Prospect)	.10
500	*Dustin Carr,Luis Cruz* (Expansion Team Prospect)	.10
501	*Marcus McCain,Cedrick Bowers* (Expansion Team Prospect)	.10
502	Checklist	.05
503	Checklist	.05
504	Alex Rodriguez	2.00

1998 Topps Baby Boomers

This 15-card retail exclusive insert was seeded one per 36 packs of Series I. It featured some of the top young players in the game and was numbered with a "BB" prefix.

		MT
Complete Set (15):		55.00
Common Player:		2.00
Inserted 1:36 retail		
1	Derek Jeter	10.00
2	Scott Rolen	5.00
3	Nomar Garciaparra	7.50
4	Jose Cruz Jr.	2.00
5	Darin Erstad	7.50
6	Todd Helton	7.50
7	Tony Clark	2.00
8	Jose Guillen	2.00
9	Andruw Jones	4.00
10	Vladimir Guerrero	7.50
11	Mark Kotsay	2.00
12	Todd Greene	2.00
13	Andy Pettitte	3.00
14	Justin Thompson	2.00
15	Alan Benes	2.00

1998 Topps Clout 9

Clout 9 captured nine players known for their statistical supremacy. Cards were numbered with a "C" prefix and inserted one per 72 packs of Series II.

		MT
Complete Set (9):		16.00
Common Player:		1.00
Inserted 1:72		
1	Edgar Martinez	1.00
2	Mike Piazza	4.00
3	Frank Thomas	2.00
4	Craig Biggio	1.00
5	Vinny Castilla	1.00
6	Jeff Blauser	1.00
7	Barry Bonds	2.50
8	Ken Griffey Jr.	5.00
9	Larry Walker	1.25

1998 Topps Etch-A-Sketch

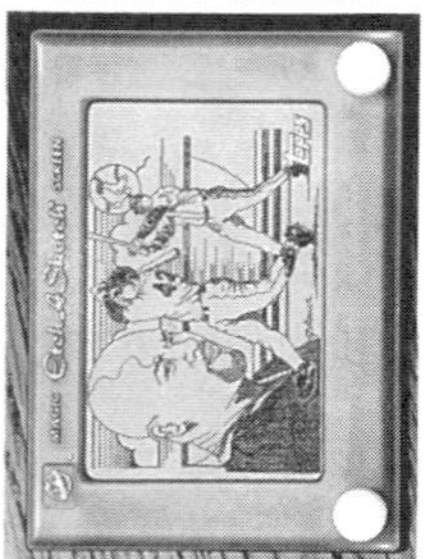

Etch a Sketch featured nine different players depicted by nationally acclaimed artist George Vlosich III. Known as "The Etch a Sketch Kid," Vlosich created each one of these Series I inserts, which were inserted at a rate of one per 36 packs. Cards are numbered with an "ES" prefix.

		MT
Complete Set (9):		20.00
Common Player:		1.00
Inserted 1:36		
1	Albert Belle	1.00
2	Barry Bonds	2.50
3	Ken Griffey Jr.	4.00
4	Greg Maddux	2.50
5	Hideo Nomo	1.50
6	Mike Piazza	4.00
7	Cal Ripken Jr.	5.00
8	Frank Thomas	1.50
9	Mo Vaughn	1.00

1998 Topps Flashback

This double-sided insert showed "then and now" photos of 10 top major leaguers. One side contained a shot of the player in 1998, while the other side showed him at the beginning of his major league career. Flashback inserts were seeded one per 72 packs and numbered with a "FB" prefix.

		MT
Complete Set (10):		25.00
Common Player:		1.50
Inserted 1:72		
1	Barry Bonds	4.00
2	Ken Griffey Jr.	5.00
3	Paul Molitor	2.00
4	Randy Johnson	2.00
5	Cal Ripken Jr.	6.00
6	Tony Gwynn	3.00
7	Kenny Lofton	1.50
8	Gary Sheffield	1.50
9	Deion Sanders	1.50
10	Brady Anderson	1.50

1998 Topps Focal Point

This hobby exclusive insert contained 15 top players and focused on the skills that have made that player great. Focal Point inserts were available in Series II packs and seeded one per 36 packs, and were numbered with a "FP" prefix.

		MT
Complete Set (15):		60.00
Common Player:		1.00
Inserted 1:36		
1	Juan Gonzalez	2.50
2	Nomar Garciaparra	4.00
3	Jose Cruz Jr.	1.00
4	Cal Ripken Jr.	8.00
5	Ken Griffey Jr.	6.00
6	Ivan Rodriguez	2.00
7	Larry Walker	2.00
8	Barry Bonds	4.00
9	Roger Clemens	3.00
10	Frank Thomas	2.50
11	Chuck Knoblauch	1.00
12	Mike Piazza	5.00
13	Greg Maddux	3.00
14	Vladimir Guerrero	2.50
15	Andruw Jones	2.00

1998 Topps Hallbound

Hall Bound featured 15 top players who are considered locks to be inducted into the Hall of Fame when there career is over. This insert was exclusive to Series I hobby packs and seeded one per 36 packs. Cards are numbered with a "HB" prefix.

		MT
Complete Set (15):		40.00
Common Player:		.75
1	Paul Molitor	1.50
2	Tony Gwynn	3.00
3	Wade Boggs	1.50
4	Roger Clemens	3.00
5	Dennis Eckersley	.75
6	Cal Ripken Jr.	8.00
7	Greg Maddux	3.00
8	Rickey Henderson	1.50
9	Ken Griffey Jr.	6.00
10	Frank Thomas	2.50
11	Mark McGwire	6.00
12	Barry Bonds	3.50
13	Mike Piazza	5.00
14	Juan Gonzalez	2.00
15	Randy Johnson	1.50

1998 Topps Inter-League Mystery Finest

Five of the 1997 season's most intriguing interleague matchups are showcased with four cards each in Inter-League Mystery Finest. Regular versions of this Series 1 insert are seeded one per 36 packs, while Refractor versions are seeded one per 144 packs. Cards are numbered with an "ILM" prefix.

		MT
Complete Set (20):		40.00
Common Player:		.75
Inserted 1:36		
Refractors:		1.5X
Inserted 1:144		
1	Chipper Jones	5.00
2	Cal Ripken Jr.	8.00
3	Greg Maddux	3.00
4	Rafael Palmeiro	1.00
5	Todd Hundley	.75
6	Derek Jeter	8.00
7	John Olerud	.75
8	Tino Martinez	.75
9	Larry Walker	1.00
10	Ken Griffey Jr.	6.00
11	Andres Galarraga	.75
12	Randy Johnson	2.00

13	Mike Piazza	6.00
14	Jim Edmonds	.75
15	Eric Karros	.75
16	Tim Salmon	1.50
17	Sammy Sosa	4.00
18	Frank Thomas	2.50
19	Mark Grace	1.50
20	Albert Belle	1.00

1998 Topps Milestones

Milestones features 10 records that could be broken in during the 1998 season and the player's who have the best shot at breaking them. This retail exclusive insert is seeded one per 36 packs and is numbered with a "MS" prefix.

		MT
Complete Set (10):		20.00
Common Player:		.50
MS1	Barry Bonds	3.00
MS2	Roger Clemens	2.00
MS3	Dennis Eckersley	.50
MS4	Juan Gonzalez	1.00
MS5	Ken Griffey Jr.	5.00
MS6	Tony Gwynn	2.00
MS7	Greg Maddux	2.00
MS8	Mark McGwire	5.00
MS9	Cal Ripken Jr.	6.00
MS10	Frank Thomas	1.50

1998 Topps Mystery Finest

This 20-card insert set features top players on bordered and borderless designs, with Refractor versions of each. Exclusive to Series 2 packs, bordered cards are seeded 1:36 packs, borderless are seeded 1:72 packs, bordered Refractors are 1:108 and borderless Refractors are seeded 1:288 packs. Mystery Finest inserts are numbered with a "M" prefix.

		MT
Complete Set (20):		60.00
Common Player:		1.50
Inserted 1:36		
Borderless 1:72:		1.5X
Bordered Refractors 1:108:		1.5X
Borderless Refractors 1:288:		2X
1	Nomar Garciaparra	4.00
2	Chipper Jones	5.00
3	Scott Rolen	2.00
4	Albert Belle	1.50
5	Mo Vaughn	1.50
6	Jose Cruz Jr.	1.50
7	Mark McGwire	6.00
8	Derek Jeter	8.00
9	Tony Gwynn	3.00
10	Frank Thomas	3.00
11	Tino Martinez	1.50
12	Greg Maddux	4.00
13	Juan Gonzalez	2.50
14	Larry Walker	1.50
15	Mike Piazza	5.00
16	Cal Ripken Jr.	8.00
17	Jeff Bagwell	2.50
18	Andruw Jones	2.00
19	Barry Bonds	4.00
20	Ken Griffey Jr.	6.00

1998 Topps Roberto Clemente Finest

Clemente Finest inserts were included in both Series I and II at a rate of one per 72 packs. There were a total of 19 different, with odd numbers in Series I and even numbers in Series II. The insert helped honor the memory of the 25th anniversary of his death.

		MT
Complete Set (19):		75.00
Common Card:		5.00
Inserted 1:72		
Refractors:		1.5X
Inserted 1:288		
1	1955	7.50
2	1956	5.00
3	1957	5.00
4	1958	5.00
5	1959	5.00
6	1960	5.00
7	1961	5.00
8	1962	5.00
9	1963	5.00
10	1964	5.00
11	1965	5.00
12	1966	5.00
13	1967	5.00
14	1968	5.00
15	1969	5.00
16	1970	5.00
17	1971	5.00
18	1972	5.00
19	1973	5.00

1998 Topps Roberto Clemente Reprints

Nineteen different Topps Clemente cards were reprinted with a gold foil stamp and included 1998 Topps. Odd numbers were included in Series I, while even numbers were inserted into Series II, both at a rate of one per 18 packs. The insert was created to honor the memory of the 25th anniversary of Clemente's death.

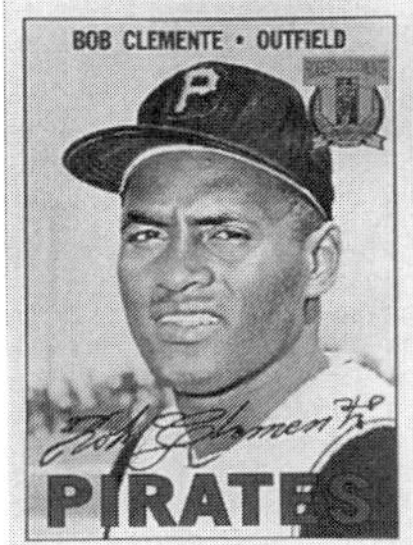

		MT
Complete Set (19):		35.00
Common Card:		2.00
Inserted 1:18		
1	1955	4.00
2	1956	2.00
3	1957	2.00
4	1958	2.00
5	1959	2.00
6	1960	2.00
7	1961	2.00
8	1962	2.00
9	1963	2.00
10	1964	2.00
11	1965	2.00
12	1966	2.00
13	1967	2.00
14	1968	2.00
15	1969	2.00
16	1970	2.00
17	1971	2.00
18	1972	2.00
19	1973	2.00

1998 Topps Roberto Clemente Tribute

Five Clemente Tribute cards were produced for Series I and inserted in one per 12 packs. The set features some classic photos of Clemente and honor his memory in the 25th anniversary of his death. Clemente Tribute cards are numbered with a "RC" prefix.

		MT
Complete Set (5):		6.00
Common Clemente:		1.50
Inserted 1:12		
1	Roberto Clemente	1.50
2	Roberto Clemente	1.50
3	Roberto Clemente	1.50
4	Roberto Clemente	1.50
5	Roberto Clemente	1.50

1998 Topps Rookie Class

Rookie Class features 10 young stars from 1998 and was exclusive to Series II packs. The cards were inserted one per 12 packs and numbered with a "R" prefix.

		MT
Complete Set (10):		5.50
Common Player:		.25
Inserted 1:12		
1	Travis Lee	.75
2	Richard Hidalgo	.40
3	Todd Helton	2.00
4	Paul Konerko	.60
5	Mark Kotsay	.50
6	Derrek Lee	.25
7	Eli Marrero	.25
8	Fernando Tatis	.50
9	Juan Encarnacion	.30
10	Ben Grieve	1.00

1998 Topps Chrome

All 502 1998 Topps cards were reprinted in chromium versions for Topps Chrome. Chrome was released in two series; Series 1 containing 282 cards and Series 2 including 220 cards. Four-card packs had a suggested retail price of $3. Card fronts include a Topps Chrome logo. The issue offers a sampling of the inserts from Topps, along with Refractor versions of every card and insert. Series 1 inserts included: Flashbacks, Baby Boomers and Hall Bound. Series 2 inserts included: Milestones, '98 Rookie Class and Clout 9.

		MT
	Complete Set (502):	200.00
	Common Player:	.15
	Refractors: 3X	
	Inserted 1:12	
	Foil Pack (4):	2.50
	Foil Box (24):	45.00
1	Tony Gwynn	4.00
2	Larry Walker	1.25
3	Billy Wagner	.15
4	Denny Neagle	.15
5	Vladimir Guerrero	2.00
6	Kevin Brown	.30
7	Not Issued	
8	Mariano Rivera	.75
9	Tony Clark	.15
10	Deion Sanders	.25
11	Francisco Cordova	.15
12	Matt Williams	.45
13	Carlos Baerga	.15
14	Mo Vaughn	1.25
15	Bobby Witt	.15
16	Matt Stairs	.15
17	Chan Ho Park	.50
18	Mike Bordick	.15
19	Michael Tucker	.15
20	Frank Thomas	4.50
21	Roberto Clemente (Tribute)	5.00
22	Dmitri Young	.15
23	Steve Trachsel	.15
24	Jeff Kent	.15
25	Scott Rolen	2.00
26	John Thomson	.15
27	Joe Vitiello	.15
28	Eddie Guardado	.15
29	Charlie Hayes	.15
30	Juan Gonzalez	2.00
31	Garret Anderson	.15
32	John Jaha	.15
33	Omar Vizquel	.15
34	Brian Hunter	.15
35	Jeff Bagwell	2.00
36	Mark Lemke	.15
37	Doug Glanville	.15
38	Dan Wilson	.15
39	Steve Cooke	.15
40	Chili Davis	.15
41	Mike Cameron	.15
42	F.P. Santangelo	.15
43	Brad Ausmus	.15
44	Gary DiSarcina	.15
45	Pat Hentgen	.15
46	Wilton Guerrero	.15
47	Devon White	.15
48	Danny Patterson	.15
49	Pat Meares	.15
50	Rafael Palmeiro	.45
51	Mark Gardner	.15
52	Jeff Blauser	.15
53	Dave Hollins	.15
54	Carlos Garcia	.15
55	Ben McDonald	.15
56	John Mabry	.15
57	Trevor Hoffman	.15
58	Tony Fernandez	.15
59	Rich Loiselle	.15
60	Mark Leiter	.15
61	Pat Kelly	.15
62	John Flaherty	.15
63	Roger Bailey	.15
64	Tom Gordon	.15
65	Ryan Klesko	.15
66	Darryl Hamilton	.15
67	Jim Eisenreich	.15
68	Butch Huskey	.15
69	Mark Grudzielanek	.15
70	Marquis Grissom	.15
71	Mark McLemore	.15
72	Gary Gaetti	.15
73	Greg Gagne	.15
74	Lyle Mouton	.15
75	Jim Edmonds	.15
76	Shawn Green	.45
77	Terry Vaughn	.15
78	Terry Adams	.15
79	*Kevin Polcovich*	.50
80	Troy O'Leary	.15
81	Jeff Shaw	.15
82	Rich Becker	.15
83	David Wells	.25
84	Steve Karsay	.15
85	Charles Nagy	.15
86	B.J. Surhoff	.15
87	Jamey Wright	.15
88	James Baldwin	.15
89	Edgardo Alfonzo	.15
90	Jay Buhner	.15
91	Brady Anderson	.15
92	Scott Servais	.15
93	Edgar Renteria	.15
94	Mike Lieberthal	.15
95	Rick Aguilera	.15
96	Walt Weiss	.15
97	Deivi Cruz	.15
98	Kurt Abbott	.15
99	Henry Rodriguez	.15
100	Mike Piazza	5.00
101	Bill Taylor	.15
102	Todd Zeile	.15
103	Rey Ordonez	.15
104	Willie Greene	.15
105	Tony Womack	.15
106	Mike Sweeney	.15
107	Jeffrey Hammonds	.15
108	Kevin Orie	.15
109	Alex Gonzalez	.15
110	Jose Canseco	1.50
111	Paul Sorrento	.15
112	Joey Hamilton	.15
113	Brad Radke	.15
114	Steve Avery	.15
115	Esteban Loaiza	.15
116	Stan Javier	.15
117	Chris Gomez	.15
118	Royce Clayton	.15
119	Orlando Merced	.15
120	Kevin Appier	.15
121	Mel Nieves	.15
122	Joe Girardi	.15
123	Rico Brogna	.15
124	Kent Mercker	.15
125	Manny Ramirez	2.00
126	Jeromy Burnitz	.15
127	Kevin Foster	.15
128	Matt Morris	.15
129	Jason Dickson	.15
130	Tom Glavine	.25
131	Wally Joyner	.15
132	Rick Reed	.15
133	Todd Jones	.15
134	Dave Martinez	.15
135	Sandy Alomar	.15
136	Mike Lansing	.15
137	Sean Berry	.15
138	Doug Jones	.15
139	Todd Stottlemyre	.15
140	Jay Bell	.15
141	Jaime Navarro	.15
142	Chris Hoiles	.15
143	Joey Cora	.15
144	Scott Spiezio	.15
145	Joe Carter	.15
146	Jose Guillen	.15
147	Damion Easley	.15
148	Lee Stevens	.15
149	Alex Fernandez	.15
150	Randy Johnson	1.50
151	J.T. Snow	.15
152	Chuck Finley	.15
153	Bernard Gilkey	.15
154	David Segui	.15
155	Dante Bichette	.15
156	Kevin Stocker	.15
157	Carl Everett	.25
158	Jose Valentin	.15
159	Pokey Reese	.15
160	Derek Jeter	5.00
161	Roger Pavlik	.15
162	Mark Wohlers	.15
163	Ricky Bottalico	.15
164	Ozzie Guillen	.15
165	Mike Mussina	1.50
166	Gary Sheffield	.60
167	Hideo Nomo	1.25
168	Mark Grace	.75
169	Aaron Sele	.15
170	Darryl Kile	.15
171	Shawn Estes	.15
172	Vinny Castilla	.15
173	Ron Coomer	.15
174	Jose Rosado	.15
175	Kenny Lofton	.15
176	Jason Giambi	.75
177	Hal Morris	.15
178	Darren Bragg	.15
179	Orel Hershiser	.15
180	Ray Lankford	.15
181	Hideki Irabu	.15
182	Kevin Young	.15
183	Javy Lopez	.15
184	Jeff Montgomery	.15
185	Mike Holtz	.15
186	George Williams	.15
187	Cal Eldred	.15
188	Tom Candiotti	.15
189	Glenallen Hill	.15
190	Brian Giles	.15
191	Dave Mlicki	.15
192	Garrett Stephenson	.15
193	Jeff Frye	.15
194	Joe Oliver	.15
195	Bob Hamelin	.15
196	Luis Sojo	.15
197	LaTroy Hawkins	.15
198	Kevin Elster	.15
199	Jeff Reed	.15
200	Dennis Eckersley	.15
201	Bill Mueller	.15
202	Russ Davis	.15
203	Armando Benitez	.15
204	Quilvio Veras	.15
205	Tim Naehring	.15
206	Quinton McCracken	.15
207	Raul Casanova	.15
208	Matt Lawton	.15
209	Luis Alicea	.15
210	Luis Gonzalez	.75
211	Allen Watson	.15
212	Gerald Williams	.15
213	David Bell	.15
214	Todd Hollandsworth	.15
215	Wade Boggs	1.50
216	Jose Mesa	.15
217	Jamie Moyer	.15
218	Darren Daulton	.15
219	Mickey Morandini	.15
220	Rusty Greer	.15
221	Jim Bullinger	.15
222	Jose Offerman	.15
223	Matt Karchner	.15
224	Woody Williams	.15
225	Mark Loretta	.15
226	Mike Hampton	.15
227	Willie Adams	.15
228	Scott Hatteberg	.15
229	Rich Amaral	.15
230	Terry Steinbach	.15
231	Glendon Rusch	.15
232	Bret Boone	.25
233	Robert Person	.15
234	Jose Hernandez	.15
235	Doug Drabek	.15
236	Jason McDonald	.15
237	Chris Widger	.15
238	*Tom Martin*	.15
239	Dave Burba	.15
240	Pete Rose	.15
241	Bobby Ayala	.15
242	Tim Wakefield	.15
243	Dennis Springer	.15
244	Tim Belcher	.15
245	Jon Garland, Geoff Goetz (Draft Pick)	.75
246	Glenn Davis, Lance Berkman (Draft Pick)	3.00
247	Vernon Wells, Aaron Akin (Draft Pick)	2.00
248	Adam Kennedy, Jason Romano (Draft Pick)	1.50
249	Jason Dellaero, Troy Cameron (Draft Pick)	.50
250	Alex Sanchez, *Jared Sandberg* (Expansion)	.75
251	Pablo Ortega, *James Manias* (Expansion)	.50
252	Jason Conti, *Mike Stoner* (Expansion)	2.00
253	John Patterson, Larry Rodriguez (Expansion)	.50
254	Adrian Beltre, *Ryan Minor*, Aaron Boone (Prospect)	4.00
255	Ben Grieve, Brian Buchanan, Dermal Brown (Prospect)	1.00
256	Carl Pavano, Kerry Wood, Gil Meche (Prospect)	3.00
257	David Ortiz, Daryle Ward, Richie Sexson (Prospect)	1.50
258	Randy Winn, Juan Encarnacion, Andrew Vessel (Prospect)	1.00
259	Kris Benson, Travis Smith, Courtney Duncan (Prospect)	1.00
260	Chad Hermansen, Brent Butler, *Warren Morris* (Prospect)	1.00
261	Ben Davis, Elieser Marrero, Ramon Hernandez (Prospect)	1.00
262	Eric Chavez, Russell Branyan, Russ Johnson (Prospect)	1.00
263	Todd Dunwoody, John Barnes, *Ryan Jackson* (Prospect)	.75
264	Matt Clement, Roy Halladay, Brian Fuentes (Prospect)	1.00
265	Randy Johnson (Season Highlight)	.60
266	Kevin Brown (Season Highlight)	.15
267	Francisco Cordova, Ricardo Rincon (Season Highlight)	.15
268	Nomar Garciaparra (Season Highlight)	2.00
269	Tino Martinez (Season Highlight)	.15
270	Chuck Knoblauch (Inter-League)	.15
271	Pedro Martinez (Inter-League)	.40
272	Denny Neagle (Inter-League)	.15
273	Juan Gonzalez (Inter-League)	1.00
274	Andres Galarraga (Inter-League)	.15
275	Checklist	.15
276	Checklist	.15
277	Moises Alou (World Series)	.15
278	Sandy Alomar (World Series)	.15
279	Gary Sheffield (World Series)	.15
280	Matt Williams (World Series)	.15
281	Livan Hernandez (World Series)	.15
282	Chad Ogea (World Series)	.15
283	Marlins Win (World Series)	.50
284	Tino Martinez	.15
285	Roberto Alomar	1.50
286	Jeff King	.15
287	Brian Jordan	.15
288	Darin Erstad	1.25
289	Ken Caminiti	.15
290	Jim Thome	.15
291	Paul Molitor	1.50
292	Ivan Rodriguez	1.50
293	Bernie Williams	.60
294	Todd Hundley	.15
295	Andres Galarraga	.15
296	Greg Maddux	4.00
297	Edgar Martinez	.15
298	Ron Gant	.15
299	Derek Bell	.15
300	Roger Clemens	4.00
301	Rondell White	.25
302	Barry Larkin	.25
303	Robin Ventura	.15
304	Jason Kendall	.15
305	Chipper Jones	5.00
306	John Franco	.15
307	Sammy Sosa	4.50
308	Troy Percival	.15
309	Chuck Knoblauch	.15
310	Ellis Burks	.15
311	Al Martin	.15
312	Tim Salmon	.45
313	Moises Alou	.30
314	Lance Johnson	.15
315	Justin Thompson	.15
316	Will Clark	.45
317	Barry Bonds	4.50
318	Craig Biggio	.25
319	John Smoltz	.25
320	Cal Ripken Jr.	6.00
321	Ken Griffey Jr.	5.50
322	Paul O'Neill	.15
323	Todd Helton	2.00
324	John Olerud	.15
325	Mark McGwire	6.00
326	Jose Cruz Jr.	.25

327	Jeff Cirillo	.15
328	Dean Palmer	.15
329	John Wetteland	.15
330	Steve Finley	.15
331	Albert Belle	.60
332	Curt Schilling	.25
333	Raul Mondesi	.25
334	Andruw Jones	1.50
335	Nomar Garciaparra	4.50
336	David Justice	.45
337	Andy Pettitte	.60
338	Pedro Martinez	2.00
339	Travis Miller	.15
340	Chris Stynes	.15
341	Gregg Jefferies	.15
342	Jeff Fassero	.15
343	Craig Counsell	.15
344	Wilson Alvarez	.15
345	Bip Roberts	.15
346	Kelvim Escobar	.15
347	Mark Bellhorn	.15
348	Cory Lidle	.15
349	Fred McGriff	.15
350	Chuck Carr	.15
351	Bob Abreu	.25
352	Juan Guzman	.15
353	Fernando Vina	.15
354	Andy Benes	.15
355	Dave Nilsson	.15
356	Bobby Bonilla	.15
357	Ismael Valdes	.15
358	Carlos Perez	.15
359	Kirk Rueter	.15
360	Bartolo Colon	.15
361	Mel Rojas	.15
362	Johnny Damon	.25
363	Geronimo Berroa	.15
364	Reggie Sanders	.15
365	Jermaine Allensworth	.15
366	Orlando Cabrera	.15
367	Jorge Fabregas	.15
368	Scott Stahoviak	.15
369	Ken Cloude	.15
370	Donovan Osborne	.15
371	Roger Cedeno	.15
372	Neifi Perez	.15
373	Chris Holt	.15
374	Cecil Fielder	.15
375	Marty Cordova	.15
376	Tom Goodwin	.15
377	Jeff Suppan	.15
378	Jeff Brantley	.15
379	Mark Langston	.15
380	Shane Reynolds	.15
381	Mike Fetters	.15
382	Todd Greene	.15
383	Ray Durham	.15
384	Carlos Delgado	.45
385	Jeff D'Amico	.15
386	Brian McRae	.15
387	Alan Benes	.15
388	Heathcliff Slocumb	.15
389	Eric Young	.15
390	Travis Fryman	.15
391	David Cone	.15
392	Otis Nixon	.15
393	Jeremi Gonzalez	.15
394	Jeff Juden	.15
395	Jose Vizcaino	.15
396	Ugueth Urbina	.15
397	Ramon Martinez	.15
398	Robb Nen	.15
399	Harold Baines	.15
400	Delino DeShields	.15
401	John Burkett	.15
402	Sterling Hitchcock	.15
403	Mark Clark	.15
404	Terrell Wade	.15
405	Scott Brosius	.15
406	Chad Curtis	.15
407	Brian Johnson	.15
408	Roberto Kelly	.15
409	*Dave Dellucci*	1.00
410	Michael Tucker	.15
411	Mark Kotsay	.15
412	Mark Lewis	.15
413	Ryan McGuire	.15
414	Shawon Dunston	.15
415	Brad Rigby	.15
416	Scott Erickson	.15
417	Bobby Jones	.15
418	Darren Oliver	.15
419	John Smiley	.15
420	T.J. Mathews	.15
421	Dustin Hermanson	.15
422	Mike Timlin	.15
423	Willie Blair	.15
424	Manny Alexander	.15
425	Bob Tewksbury	.15
426	Pete Schourek	.15
427	Reggie Jefferson	.15
428	Ed Sprague	.15
429	Jeff Conine	.15
430	Roberto Hernandez	.15
431	Tom Pagnozzi	.15
432	Jaret Wright	.15
433	Livan Hernandez	.15
434	Andy Ashby	.15
435	Todd Dunn	.15
436	Bobby Higginson	.25
437	Rod Beck	.15
438	Jim Leyritz	.15
439	Matt Williams	.45
440	Brett Tomko	.15
441	Joe Randa	.15
442	Chris Carpenter	.15
443	Dennis Reyes	.15
444	Al Leiter	.15
445	Jason Schmidt	.15
446	Ken Hill	.15
447	Shannon Stewart	.15
448	Enrique Wilson	.15
449	Fernando Tatis	.15
450	Jimmy Key	.15
451	Darrin Fletcher	.15
452	John Valentin	.15
453	Kevin Tapani	.15
454	Eric Karros	.15
455	Jay Bell	.15
456	Walt Weiss	.15
457	Devon White	.15
458	Carl Pavano	.15
459	Mike Lansing	.15
460	John Flaherty	.15
461	Richard Hidalgo	.15
462	Quinton McCracken	.15
463	Karim Garcia	.25
464	Miguel Cairo	.15
465	Edwin Diaz	.15
466	Bobby Smith	.15
467	Yamil Benitez	.15
468	*Rich Butler*	.15
469	*Ben Ford*	.25
470	Bubba Trammell	.15
471	Brent Brede	.15
472	Brooks Kieschnick	.15
473	Carlos Castillo	.15
474	Brad Radke (Season Highlight)	.15
475	Roger Clemens (Season Highlight)	1.50
476	Curt Schilling (Season Highlight)	.25
477	John Olerud (Season Highlight)	.15
478	Mark McGwire (Season Highlight)	3.00
479	Mike Piazza, Ken Griffey Jr. (Interleague)	3.00
480	Jeff Bagwell, Frank Thomas (Interleague)	1.50
481	Chipper Jones, Nomar Garciaparra (Interleague)	2.50
482	Larry Walker, Juan Gonzalez (Interleague)	1.00
483	Gary Sheffield, Tino Martinez (Interleague)	.15
484	Derrick Gibson, Michael Coleman, Norm Hutchins (Prospect)	.50
485	Braden Looper, Cliff Politte, Brian Rose (Prospect)	.50
486	Eric Milton, Jason Marquis, Corey Lee (Prospect)	1.00
487	A.J. Hinch, Mark Osborne, *Robert Fick* (Prospect)	1.50
488	Aramis Ramirez, Alex Gonzalez, Sean Casey (Prospect)	4.00
489	*Donnie Bridges, Tim Drew* (Draft Pick)	.60
490	*Ntema Ndungidi, Darnell McDonald* (Draft Pick)	1.00
491	*Ryan Anderson*, Mark Mangum (Draft Pick)	3.00
492	J.J. Davis, *Troy Glaus* (Draft Pick)	12.00
493	Jayson Werth, Dan Reichert (Draft Pick)	.25
494	*John Curtice, Mike Cuddyer* (Draft Pick)	3.00
495	*Jack Cust*, Jason Standridge (Draft Pick)	4.00
496	Brian Anderson (Expansion Team Prospect)	.15
497	Tony Saunders (Expansion Team Prospect)	.25
498	Vladimir Nunez, *Jhensy Sandoval* (Expansion Team Prospect)	.50
499	Brad Penny, Nick Bierbrodt (Expansion Team Prospect)	.50
500	*Dustin Carr, Luis Cruz* (Expansion Team Prospect)	.50
501	*Marcus McCain, Cedrick Bowers* (Expansion Team Prospect)	.15
502	Checklist	.15
503	Checklist	.15
504	Alex Rodriguez	6.00
		.15

1998 Topps Chrome Refractors

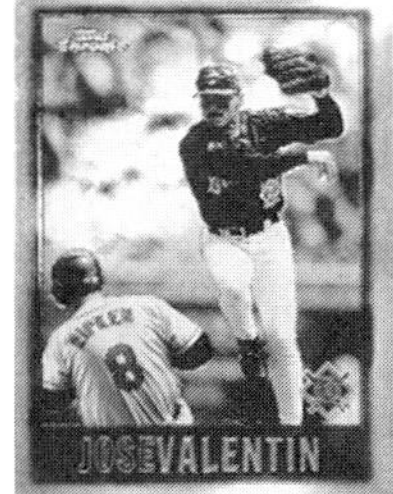

Each card in the regular Topps Series 1 and Series 2 Chrome issue could also be found in a refractor version seeded approximately one per 12 packs. Refractor versions are so designated above the card number of back.

	MT
Common Player:	1.00
Stars/Rookies:	3X

(See 1998 Topps Chrome for checklist and base card values.)

1998 Topps Chrome Baby Boomers

This 15-card insert featured players with less than three years of experience. Cards were inserted one per 24 packs, with Refractor versions found every 72 packs of Series I. Cards were numbered with a "BB" prefix.

		MT
Complete Set (15):		30.00
Common Player:		1.00
Inserted 1:24		
Refractors:		1.5X
Inserted 1:72		
1	Derek Jeter	8.00
2	Scott Rolen	3.00
3	Nomar Garciaparra	6.00
4	Jose Cruz Jr.	1.25
5	Darin Erstad	3.00
6	Todd Helton	4.00
7	Tony Clark	1.00
8	Jose Guillen	1.00
9	Andruw Jones	2.00
10	Vladimir Guerrero	5.00
11	Mark Kotsay	1.00
12	Todd Greene	1.00
13	Andy Pettitte	1.50
14	Justin Thompson	1.00
15	Alan Benes	1.00

1998 Topps Chrome Clout 9

This nine-card insert included players for their statistical supremacy. Clout 9 cards were found in Series II packs at a rate of one per 24 packs, with Refractor versions every 72 packs. Cards are numbered with a "C" prefix.

		MT
Complete Set (9):		30.00
Common Player:		1.50
Inserted 1:24		
Refractors:		1.5X
Inserted 1:72		
1	Edgar Martinez	1.50
2	Mike Piazza	8.00
3	Frank Thomas	3.00
4	Craig Biggio	1.50
5	Vinny Castilla	1.50
6	Jeff Blauser	1.50
7	Barry Bonds	5.00
8	Ken Griffey Jr.	10.00
9	Larry Walker	2.00

1998 Topps Chrome Flashback

This 10-card double-sided insert features top

players as they looked in 1998 on one side, and how they looked when they first appeared in the majors on the other side. Flashback inserts were seeded one per 24 packs of Series I, with Refractors every 72 packs. This insert was numbered with a "FB" prefix.

		MT
Complete Set (10):		25.00
Common Player:		1.50
Inserted 1:24		
Refractors:		1.5X
Inserted 1:72		
1	Barry Bonds	5.00
2	Ken Griffey Jr.	6.00
3	Paul Molitor	2.00
4	Randy Johnson	2.00
5	Cal Ripken Jr.	8.00
6	Tony Gwynn	3.50
7	Kenny Lofton	1.50
8	Gary Sheffield	1.50
9	Deion Sanders	1.50
10	Brady Anderson	1.50

1998 Topps Chrome Hallbound

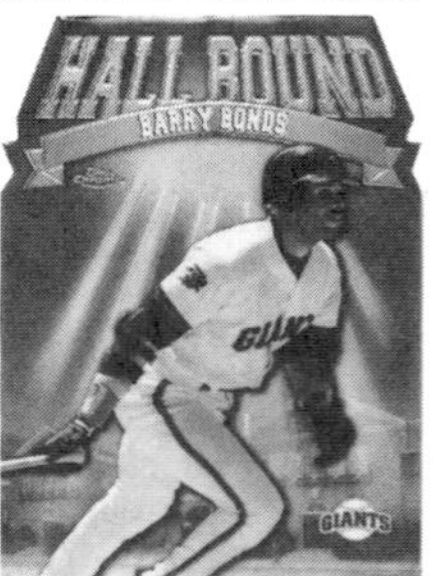

Hall Bound highlighted 15 players destined for the Hall of Fame on die-cut cards. Inserted at a rate of one per 24 packs of Series I, with Refractors every 72 packs, these were numbered with a "HB" prefix.

		MT
Complete Set (15):		60.00
Common Player:		1.00
Inserted 1:24		
Refractors:		1.5X
Inserted 1:72		
1	Paul Molitor	2.00
2	Tony Gwynn	3.00
3	Wade Boggs	2.00
4	Roger Clemens	5.00
5	Dennis Eckersley	1.00
6	Cal Ripken Jr.	12.00
7	Greg Maddux	6.00
8	Rickey Henderson	2.00
9	Ken Griffey Jr.	10.00
10	Frank Thomas	4.00
11	Mark McGwire	10.00
12	Barry Bonds	6.00
13	Mike Piazza	8.00
14	Juan Gonzalez	2.50
15	Randy Johnson	2.00

1998 Topps Chrome Milestones

Ten superstars who were within reach of major records for the 1998 season are featured in Milestones. This Series II insert was seeded one per 24 packs, with Refractor versions seeded one per 72 packs. Milestones were numbered with a "MS" prefix.

		MT
Complete Set (10):		45.00
Common Player:		1.00
Inserted 1:24		
Refractors:		1.5X
Inserted 1:72		
1	Barry Bonds	6.00
2	Roger Clemens	5.00
3	Dennis Eckersley	1.00
4	Juan Gonzalez	3.00
5	Ken Griffey Jr.	7.00
6	Tony Gwynn	5.00
7	Greg Maddux	5.00
8	Mark McGwire	8.00
9	Cal Ripken Jr.	8.00
10	Frank Thomas	4.00

1998 Topps Chrome Rookie Class

This insert featured 10 players with less than one year of major league experience. Inserted in Series II packs at a rate of one per 12 packs, with Refractors every 24 packs, '98 Rookie Class inserts were numbered with a "R" prefix.

		MT
Complete Set (10):		12.50
Common Player:		1.00
Inserted 1:12		
Refractors:		1.5X
Inserted 1:24		
1	Travis Lee	1.50
2	Richard Hidalgo	1.00
3	Todd Helton	4.00
4	Paul Konerko	1.50
5	Mark Kotsay	1.50
6	Derrek Lee	1.00
7	Eli Marrero	1.00
8	Fernando Tatis	1.00
9	Juan Encarnacion	1.00
10	Ben Grieve	2.50

1998 Topps Gallery

Gallery returned in 1998 with a 150-card set broken up into five different subsets - Exhibitions, Impressions, Expressionists, Portraits and Permanent Collection. The set was paralleled twice - first in a Player's Private Issue set and, second in Gallery Proofs. Gallery cards were made to look like works of art instead of simply a photo of the player on cardboard, and were sold in six-card packs. Inserts in this single-series product include: Photo Gallery, Gallery of Heroes and Awards Gallery.

		MT
Complete Set (150):		30.00
Common Player:		.15
Pack (6):		2.00
Wax Box (24):		40.00
1	Andruw Jones	1.00
2	Fred McGriff	.15
3	Wade Boggs	.75
4	Pedro Martinez	1.00
5	Matt Williams	.45
6	Wilson Alvarez	.15
7	Henry Rodriguez	.15
8	Jay Bell	.15
9	Marquis Grissom	.15
10	Darryl Kile	.15
11	Chuck Knoblauch	.15
12	Kenny Lofton	.15
13	Quinton McCracken	.15
14	Andres Galarraga	.15
15	Brian Jordan	.15
16	Mike Lansing	.15
17	Travis Fryman	.15
18	Tony Saunders	.15
19	Moises Alou	.35
20	Travis Lee	.25
21	Garret Anderson	.15
22	Ken Caminiti	.15
23	Pedro Astacio	.15
24	Ellis Burks	.15
25	Albert Belle	.45
26	Alan Benes	.15
27	Jay Buhner	.15
28	Derek Bell	.15
29	Jeromy Burnitz	.15
30	Kevin Appier	.15
31	Jeff Cirillo	.15
32	Bernard Gilkey	.15
33	David Cone	.15
34	Jason Dickson	.15
35	Jose Cruz Jr.	.25
36	Marty Cordova	.15
37	Ray Durham	.15
38	Jaret Wright	.15
39	Billy Wagner	.15
40	Roger Clemens	2.00
41	Juan Gonzalez	1.50
42	Jeremi Gonzalez	.15
43	Mark Grudzielanek	.15
44	Tom Glavine	.25
45	Barry Larkin	.25
46	Lance Johnson	.15
47	Bobby Higginson	.25
48	Mike Mussina	1.00
49	Al Martin	.15
50	Mark McGwire	4.00
51	Todd Hundley	.15
52	Ray Lankford	.15
53	Jason Kendall	.15
54	Javy Lopez	.15
55	Ben Grieve	.25
56	Randy Johnson	1.00
57	Jeff King	.15
58	Mark Grace	.40
59	Rusty Greer	.15
60	Greg Maddux	2.00
61	Jeff Kent	.15
62	Rey Ordonez	.15
63	Hideo Nomo	1.00
64	Charles Nagy	.15
65	Rondell White	.30
66	Todd Helton	1.25
67	Jim Thome	.15
68	Denny Neagle	.15
69	Ivan Rodriguez	1.25
70	Vladimir Guerrero	1.50
71	Jorge Posada	.15
72	J.T. Snow Jr.	.15
73	Reggie Sanders	.15
74	Scott Rolen	1.00
75	Robin Ventura	.15
76	Mariano Rivera	.40
77	Cal Ripken Jr.	4.00
78	Justin Thompson	.15
79	Mike Piazza	3.00
80	Kevin Brown	.25
81	Sandy Alomar	.15
82	Craig Biggio	.25
83	Vinny Castilla	.15
84	Eric Young	.15
85	Bernie Williams	.45
86	Brady Anderson	.15
87	Bobby Bonilla	.15
88	Tony Clark	.15
89	Dan Wilson	.15
90	John Wetteland	.15
91	Barry Bonds	2.50
92	Chan Ho Park	.25
93	Carlos Delgado	.30
94	David Justice	.40
95	Chipper Jones	3.00
96	Shawn Estes	.15
97	Jason Giambi	.75
98	Ron Gant	.15
99	John Olerud	.15
100	Frank Thomas	1.00
101	Jose Guillen	.15
102	Brad Radke	.15
103	Troy Percival	.15
104	John Smoltz	.25
105	Edgardo Alfonzo	.15
106	Dante Bichette	.15
107	Larry Walker	.60
108	John Valentin	.15
109	Roberto Alomar	.75
110	Mike Cameron	.15
111	Eric Davis	.15
112	Johnny Damon	.25
113	Darin Erstad	.60
114	Omar Vizquel	.15
115	Derek Jeter	4.00
116	Tony Womack	.15
117	Edgar Renteria	.15
118	Raul Mondesi	.25
119	Tony Gwynn	2.00
120	Ken Griffey Jr.	3.00
121	Jim Edmonds	.15
122	Brian Hunter	.15
123	Neifi Perez	.15
124	Dean Palmer	.15
125	Alex Rodriguez	3.00
126	Tim Salmon	.35
127	Curt Schilling	.25
128	Kevin Orie	.15
129	Andy Pettitte	.35
130	Gary Sheffield	.40
131	Jose Rosado	.15
132	Manny Ramirez	1.50
133	Rafael Palmeiro	.45
134	Sammy Sosa	2.00
135	Jeff Bagwell	1.50
136	Delino DeShields	.15
137	Ryan Klesko	.15
138	Mo Vaughn	.60
139	Steve Finley	.15
140	Nomar Garciaparra	2.50
141	Paul Molitor	.75
142	Pat Hentgen	.15
143	Eric Karros	.15
144	Bobby Jones	.15
145	Tino Martinez	.15
146	Matt Morris	.15
147	Livan Hernandez	.15
148	Edgar Martinez	.15
149	Paul O'Neill	.15
150	Checklist	.15

1998 Topps Gallery Player's Private Issue

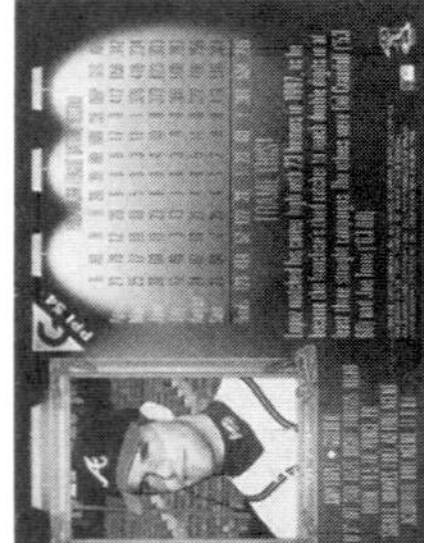

Players Private Issue inserts parallel the 150-card base set with a distinct design and embossing. The average insertion rate is one per 12 packs.

	MT
Common Player:	1.50
Stars/Rookies:	6X

Production 250 sets

(See 1998 Topps Gallery for checklist and base card values.)

#	Player	MT
1	Ken Griffey Jr.	6.00
2	Larry Walker	1.50
3	Roger Clemens	3.00
4	Pedro Martinez	2.50
5	Nomar Garciaparra	5.00
6	Scott Rolen	2.00
7	Frank Thomas	3.00
8	Tony Gwynn	3.00
9	Mark McGwire	8.00
10	Livan Hernandez	1.00

1998 Topps Gallery Printing Plates

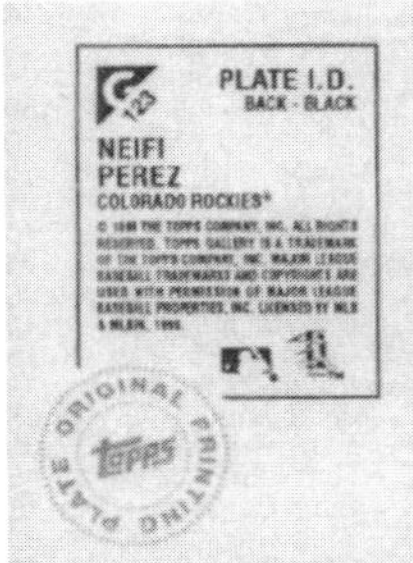

The aluminum press plates used to print the Gallery cards were issued as random pack inserts. Each card's front and back can be found in four different color variations. Because of the unique nature of each plate, assignment of catalog values is not feasible.

	MT
Common Player, Front:	75.00
Common Player, Back:	50.00

(See 1998 Topps Gallery for checklist.)

1998 Topps Gallery Awards Gallery

Awards Gallery featured 10 players who earned the highest honors in the game on a horizontal design. Fronts featured a shot of the player and the award he won on silver foilboard. These were inserted every 24 packs and numbered with an "AG" prefix.

	MT
Complete Set (10):	30.00
Common Player:	1.00

Inserted 1:24

1998 Topps Gallery Gallery Proofs

This hobby-only parallel set included all 150 cards in the base set. Gallery Proofs were sequentially numbered to 125 sets.

	MT
Common Player:	2.00
Stars/Rookies:	15X

Production 125 sets

(See 1998 Topps Gallery for checklist and base card values.)

1998 Topps Gallery of Heroes

Gallery of Heroes is a 15-card insert printed on colored, die-cut plastic that resembles a stained glass window. Cards were inserted one per 24 packs and numbered with a "GH" prefix. More is less in the case in the jumbo (3-1/4" x 4-1/2") version of the cards which were inserted one per hobby box. Cards are numbered with a "GH" prefix.

	MT
Complete Set (15):	80.00
Common Player:	1.25

Inserted 1:24
Jumbo Version (1:24): 75%

#	Player	MT
1	Ken Griffey Jr.	10.00
2	Derek Jeter	12.00
3	Barry Bonds	6.00
4	Alex Rodriguez	10.00
5	Frank Thomas	4.00
6	Nomar Garciaparra	6.00
7	Mark McGwire	10.00
8	Mike Piazza	8.00
9	Cal Ripken Jr.	12.00
10	Jose Cruz Jr.	1.25
11	Jeff Bagwell	4.00
12	Chipper Jones	8.00
13	Juan Gonzalez	4.00
14	Hideo Nomo	2.50
15	Greg Maddux	6.00

1998 Topps Gallery Photo Gallery

This 10-card insert captured unique shots of players on a silver foilboard design. Photo Gallery inserts were seeded one per 24 packs and numbered with a "PG" prefix.

	MT
Complete Set (10):	40.00
Common Player:	1.00

Inserted 1:24

#	Player	MT
1	Alex Rodriguez	6.00
2	Frank Thomas	3.00
3	Derek Jeter	8.00
4	Cal Ripken Jr.	8.00
5	Ken Griffey Jr.	6.00
6	Mike Piazza	5.00
7	Nomar Garciaparra	4.00
8	Tim Salmon	1.00
9	Jeff Bagwell	2.00
10	Barry Bonds	4.00

1998 Topps Gold Label Class 1 (Fielding, Follow-thru)

Topps debuted its Gold Label brand with 100 cards printed on 30-point "spectral-reflective stock" with gold foil stamping and two shots of the player on each card front. Cards arrived in Gold Label, Black Label and Red Label versions, each with varying levels of scarcity. The rarity of the cards was determined by the photo and foil stamping on the cards. In the foreground of each card front, the photograph is the same, but in the background one of three shots is featured. Class 1, fielding, are considered base cards; Class 2: running (inserted 1:4 packs) and Class 3, hitting (inserted 1:8 packs) are seeded levels. For pitching the levels are: Class 1, set position (base); Class 2, throwing (inserted 1:4 packs) and Class 3, follow-through (inserted 1:8 packs). Black Label cards are scarcer, while Red Label cards are scarcer yet. In addition, 1 of 1 cards exist for each Class and version. Class 1 cards have matte gold-foil graphic highlights on front. Black Label Class 1 cards were inserted one per eight packs. Red Label Class 1 cards are a 1:99 insert and are serially numbered to 100.

	MT
Complete Set (100):	30.00
Gold Label Common Player:	.15
Black Label Common Player:	.50
Black Label Stars/RCs:	5X
Red Label Common Player:	3.00
Red Label Stars/RCs:	12X
Pack (5):	3.00
Wax Box (24):	60.00

#	Player	MT
1	Kevin Brown	.30
2	Greg Maddux	1.50
3	Albert Belle	.45
4	Andres Galarraga	.15
5	Craig Biggio	.25
6	Matt Williams	.45
7	Derek Jeter	2.50
8	Randy Johnson	1.25
9	Jay Bell	.15
10	Jim Thome	.15
11	Roberto Alomar	.75
12	Tom Glavine	.25
13	Reggie Sanders	.15
14	Tony Gwynn	1.50
15	Mark McGwire	4.00
16	Jeromy Burnitz	.15
17	Andruw Jones	1.25
18	Jay Buhner	.15
19	Robin Ventura	.15
20	Jeff Bagwell	1.25
21	Roger Clemens	1.50
22	*Masato Yoshii*	.40
23	Travis Fryman	.15
24	Rafael Palmeiro	.45
25	Alex Rodriguez	3.00
26	Sandy Alomar	.15
27	Chipper Jones	2.50
28	Rusty Greer	.15
29	Cal Ripken Jr.	4.00
30	Tony Clark	.15
31	Derek Bell	.15
32	Fred McGriff	.15
33	Paul O'Neill	.15
34	Moises Alou	.30
35	Henry Rodriguez	.15
36	Steve Finley	.15
37	Marquis Grissom	.15
38	Jason Giambi	.65
39	Javy Lopez	.15
40	Damion Easley	.15
41	Mariano Rivera	.40
42	Mo Vaughn	.65
43	Mike Mussina	.75
44	Jason Kendall	.15
45	Pedro Martinez	1.00
46	Frank Thomas	2.00
47	Jim Edmonds	.15
48	Hideki Irabu	.15
49	Eric Karros	.15
50	Juan Gonzalez	1.25
51	Ellis Burks	.15
52	Dean Palmer	.15
53	Scott Rolen	1.00
54	Raul Mondesi	.30

55 Quinton McCraken .15
56 John Olerud .15
57 Ken Caminiti .15
58 Brian Jordan .15
59 Wade Boggs 1.25
60 Mike Piazza 2.50
61 Darin Erstad .75
62 Curt Schilling .30
63 David Justice .40
64 Kenny Lofton .15
65 Barry Bonds 2.00
66 Ray Lankford .15
67 Brian Hunter .15
68 Chuck Knoblauch .15
69 Vinny Castilla .15
70 Vladimir Guerrero 1.25
71 Tim Salmon .30
72 Larry Walker .60
73 Paul Molitor 1.25
74 Barry Larkin .25
75 Edgar Martinez .15
76 Bernie Williams .45
77 Dante Bichette .15
78 Nomar Garciaparra 2.00
79 Ben Grieve .35
80 Ivan Rodriguez 1.00
81 Todd Helton 1.00
82 Ryan Klesko .15
83 Sammy Sosa 2.00
84 Travis Lee .25
85 Jose Cruz .25
86 Mark Kotsay .15
87 Richard Hidalgo .15
88 Rondell White .25
89 Greg Vaughn .15
90 Gary Sheffield .40
91 Paul Konerko .25
92 Mark Grace .35
93 *Kevin Millwood* 3.00
94 Manny Ramirez 1.25
95 Tino Martinez .15
96 Brad Fullmer .15
97 Todd Walker .15
98 Carlos Delgado .30
99 Kerry Wood .50
100 Ken Griffey Jr. 3.00

1998 Topps Gold Label Class 2 (Running, Set Position)

Class 2 Gold Label and parallels feature background photos on front of position players running and pitchers in the set position. Class 2 cards have sparkling silver-foil graphic highlights on front and were inserted one per two packs. Black Label Class 2 cards were inserted one per 16 packs. Red Label Class 2 cards are a 1:198 insert and are serially numbered to 50.

	MT
Complete Set (100):	80.00
Gold Label Common Player:	.50
Gold Label Stars/RCs:	2.5X
Black Label Common Player:	1.00
Black Label Stars/RCs:	4X
Red Label Common Player:	5.00
Red Label Stars/RCs:	20X

1998 Topps Gold Label Class 3 (Hitting, Throwing)

Class 3 Gold Label and parallels feature background photos on front of position players hitting and pitchers throwing. Class 3 cards have sparkling gold-foil graphic highlights on front and were inserted one per four packs. Black Label Class 3 cards were inserted one per 32 packs. Red Label Class 2 cards are a 1:396 insert and are serially numbered to 25.

	MT
Complete Set (100):	150.00
Common Player:	1.00
Gold Label Stars/RCs:	3X
Black Label Common Player:	3.00
Black Label Stars/RCs	6X
Red Label Common Player:	10.00
Red Label Stars/RCs:	25X

1998 Topps Gold Label 1 of 1

Each of the Classes and color versions of Topps Gold Label cards was paralleled in a 1 of 1 insert which was to be found on average of one per 1,085 packs. Each player, thus, can be found on nine different 1 of 1 cards in the issue.

MT

(Due to scarcity and variance in demand, values cannot be quoted.)

1998 Topps Gold Label Home Run Race

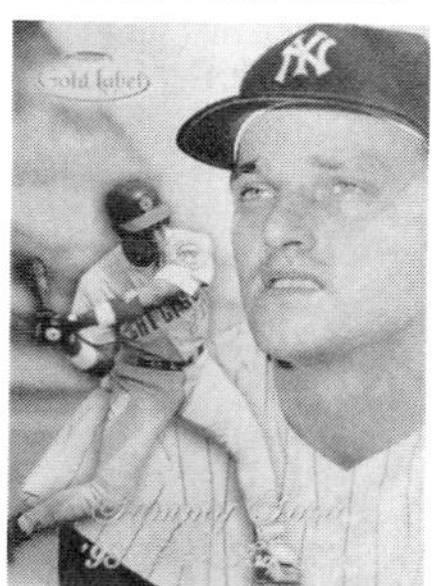

Home Run Race of '98 was a four-card insert set. Each of the current players' cards features a background photo of Roger Maris, while the fourth card features two shots of Maris. Gold, Black and Red Label versions are identified by the different foil-stamp logos. Gold cards were inserted 1:12 packs, Black Label cards were inserted 1:48 packs and Red Label cards were sequentially numbered to 61 and inserted 1:4,055 packs. The Home Run Race inserts are exclusive to Topps Home Team Advantage boxes.

	MT
Complete Set (4):	15.00
Common Player:	3.00
Black Label:	2X
Red Label:	8X
HR1 Roger Maris	3.00
HR2 Mark McGwire	8.00
HR3 Ken Griffey Jr.	5.00
HR4 Sammy Sosa	3.00

1998 Topps Opening Day

Topps Opening Day was a retail exclusive product comprising 165 cards, with 110 from Series 1 and 55 from Series 2. The cards from Series 2 were available in this product prior to the regular-issue cards being released. Opening Day cards feature a silver border vs. the gold border in the regular set, and include a silver-foil Opening Day stamp.

	MT
Complete Set (165):	15.00
Common Player:	.05

1 Tony Gwynn .65
2 Larry Walker .40
3 Billy Wagner .05
4 Denny Neagle .05
5 Vladimir Guerrero .50
6 Kevin Brown .10
7 Mariano Rivera .25
8 Tony Clark .05
9 Deion Sanders .10
10 Matt Williams .15
11 Carlos Baerga .05
12 Mo Vaughn .40
13 Chan Ho Park .15
14 Frank Thomas .75
15 John Jaha .05
16 Steve Trachsel .05
17 Jeff Kent .05
18 Scott Rolen .45
19 Juan Gonzalez .50
20 Garret Anderson .05
21 Roberto Clemente 1.00
22 Omar Vizquel .05
23 Brian Hunter .05
24 Jeff Bagwell .50
25 Chili Davis .05
26 Mike Cameron .05
27 Pat Hentgen .05
28 Wilton Guerrero .05
29 Devon White .05
30 Rafael Palmeiro .25
31 Jeff Blauser .05
32 Dave Hollins .05
33 Trevor Hoffman .05
34 Ryan Klesko .05
35 Butch Huskey .05
36 Mark Grudzielanek .05
37 Marquis Grissom .05
38 Jim Edmonds .05
39 Greg Vaughn .05
40 David Wells .10
41 Charles Nagy .05
42 B.J. Surhoff .05
43 Edgardo Alfonzo .05
44 Jay Buhner .05
45 Brady Anderson .05
46 Edgar Renteria .05
47 Rick Aguilera .05
48 Henry Rodriguez .05
49 Mike Piazza 1.00
50 Todd Zeile .05
51 Rey Ordonez .05
52 Tony Womack .05
53 Mike Sweeney .05
54 Jeffrey Hammonds .05
55 Kevin Orie .05
56 Alex Gonzalez .10
57 Jose Canseco .40
58 Joey Hamilton .05
59 Brad Radke .05
60 Kevin Appier .05
61 Manny Ramirez .50
62 Jeromy Burnitz .05
63 Matt Morris .05
64 Jason Dickson .05
65 Tom Glavine .10
66 Wally Joyner .05
67 Todd Jones .05
68 Sandy Alomar .05
69 Mike Lansing .05
70 Todd Stottlemyre .05
71 Jay Bell .05
72 Joey Cora .05
73 Scott Spiezio .05
74 Joe Carter .05
75 Jose Guillen .05
76 Damion Easley .05
77 Alex Fernandez .05
78 Randy Johnson .45
79 J.T. Snow .05

80 Bernard Gilkey .05
81 David Segui .05
82 Dante Bichette .05
83 Derek Jeter 1.00
84 Mark Wohlers .05
85 Ricky Bottalico .05
86 Mike Mussina .45
87 Gary Sheffield .20
88 Hideo Nomo .50
89 Mark Grace .20
90 Darryl Kile .05
91 Shawn Estes .05
92 Vinny Castilla .05
93 Jose Rosado .05
94 Kenny Lofton .05
95 Jason Giambi .35
96 Ray Lankford .05
97 Hideki Irabu .05
98 Javy Lopez .05
99 Jeff Montgomery .05
100 Dennis Eckersley .05
101 Armando Benitez .05
102 Tim Naehring .05
103 Luis Gonzalez .30
104 Todd Hollandsworth .05
105 Wade Boggs .40
106 Mickey Morandini .05
107 Rusty Greer .05
108 Terry Steinbach .05
109 Pete Rose II .05
110 Checklist .05
111 Tino Martinez .05
112 Roberto Alomar .45
113 Jeff King .05
114 Brian Jordan .05
115 Darin Erstad .45
116 Ken Caminiti .05
117 Jim Thome .05
118 Paul Molitor .45
119 Ivan Rodriguez .40
120 Bernie Williams .40
121 Todd Hundley .05
122 Andres Galarraga .05
123 Greg Maddux .65
124 Edgar Martinez .05
125 Ron Gant .05
126 Derek Bell .05
127 Roger Clemens .65
128 Rondell White .15
129 Barry Larkin .10
130 Robin Ventura .05
131 Jason Kendall .05
132 Chipper Jones 1.00
133 John Franco .05
134 Sammy Sosa .75
135 Chuck Knoblauch .05
136 Ellis Burks .05
137 Al Martin .05
138 Tim Salmon .20
139 Moises Alou .15
140 Lance Johnson .05
141 Justin Thompson .05
142 Will Clark .15
143 Barry Bonds .75
144 Craig Biggio .10
145 John Smoltz .10
146 Cal Ripken Jr. 1.50
147 Ken Griffey Jr. 1.25
148 Paul O'Neill .05
149 Todd Helton .45
150 John Olerud .05
151 Mark McGwire 1.50
152 Jose Cruz Jr. .10
153 Jeff Cirillo .05
154 Dean Palmer .05
155 John Wetteland .05
156 Eric Karros .05
157 Steve Finley .05
158 Albert Belle .20
159 Curt Schilling .15
160 Raul Mondesi .15
161 Andruw Jones .50
162 Nomar Garciaparra .75
163 David Justice .20
164 Andy Pettitte .15
165 Pedro Martinez .50

1998 Topps Stars

Topps Stars adopted an all-sequential numbering format in 1998 with a 150-card set. Every card was available in a bronze (numbered to 9,799), red (9,799), silver (4,399), gold (2,299) and gold rainbow format (99) with different color foil to distinguish the groups. Players were each judged in five categories: arm strength, hit for average, power, defense and speed. Inserts in the product include: Galaxy, Luminaries, Supernovas, Rookie Reprints and Rookie Reprint Autographs. All regular-issue cards and inserts were individually numbered except the Rookie Reprints.

	MT
Complete Set, Red or Bronze (150):	55.00
Common Player, Red or Bronze:	.15
Production 9,799 sets each	
Pack (6):	2.50
Wax Box (24):	50.00

1 Greg Maddux 3.00
2 Darryl Kile .15
3 Rod Beck .15
4 Ellis Burks .15
5 Gary Sheffield .50
6 David Ortiz .15
7 Marquis Grissom .15
8 Tony Womack .15
9 Mike Mussina 1.50
10 Bernie Williams .50
11 Andy Benes .15
12 Rusty Greer .15
13 Carlos Delgado .35
14 Jim Edmonds .15
15 Raul Mondesi .30
16 Andres Galarraga .15
17 Wade Boggs 1.50
18 Paul O'Neill .15
19 Edgar Renteria .15
20 Tony Clark .15
21 Vladimir Guerrero 2.50
22 Moises Alou .35
23 Bernard Gilkey .15
24 Lance Johnson .15
25 Ben Grieve .25
26 Sandy Alomar .15
27 Ray Durham .15
28 Shawn Estes .15
29 David Segui .15
30 Javy Lopez .15
31 Steve Finley .15
32 Rey Ordonez .15
33 Derek Jeter 6.00
34 Henry Rodriguez .15
35 Mo Vaughn 1.00
36 Richard Hidalgo .15
37 Omar Vizquel .15
38 Johnny Damon .25
39 Brian Hunter .15
40 Matt Williams .45
41 Chuck Finley .15
42 Jeromy Burnitz .15
43 Livan Hernandez .15
44 Delino DeShields .15
45 Charles Nagy .15
46 Scott Rolen 2.00
47 Neifi Perez .15
48 John Wetteland .15
49 Eric Milton .15
50 Mike Piazza 4.00
51 Cal Ripken Jr. 6.00
52 Mariano Rivera .45
53 Butch Huskey .15
54 Quinton McCracken .15
55 Jose Cruz Jr. .25
56 Brian Jordan .15
57 Hideo Nomo 1.00
58 Masato Yoshii .15
59 Cliff Floyd .15
60 Jose Guillen .15
61 Jeff Shaw .15
62 Edgar Martinez .15
63 Rondell White .25
64 Hal Morris .15
65 Barry Larkin .25
66 Eric Young .15
67 Ray Lankford .15
68 Derek Bell .15
69 Charles Johnson .15
70 Robin Ventura .15
71 Chuck Knoblauch .15
72 Kevin Brown .25
73 Jose Valentin .15
74 Jay Buhner .15
75 Tony Gwynn 2.50
76 Andy Pettitte .30
77 Edgardo Alfonzo .15
78 Kerry Wood .60
79 Darin Erstad .60
80 Paul Konerko .25
81 Jason Kendall .15
82 Tino Martinez .15
83 Brad Radke .15
84 Jeff King .15
85 Travis Lee .25
86 Jeff Kent .15
87 Trevor Hoffman .15
88 David Cone .15
89 Jose Canseco 2.00
90 Juan Gonzalez 2.50
91 Todd Hundley .15
92 John Valentin .15
93 Sammy Sosa 3.00
94 Jason Giambi .60
95 Chipper Jones 4.00
96 Jeff Blauser .15
97 Brad Fullmer .15
98 Derrek Lee .15
99 Denny Neagle .15
100 Ken Griffey Jr. 5.00
101 David Justice .50
102 Tim Salmon .35
103 J.T. Snow .15
104 Fred McGriff .15
105 Brady Anderson .15
106 Larry Walker 1.00
107 Jeff Cirillo .15
108 Andruw Jones 1.50
109 Manny Ramirez 2.50
110 Justin Thompson .15
111 Vinny Castilla .15
112 Chan Ho Park .25
113 Mark Grudzielanek .15
114 Mark Grace .45
115 Ken Caminiti .15
116 Ryan Klesko .15
117 Rafael Palmeiro .35
118 Pat Hentgen .15
119 Eric Karros .15
120 Randy Johnson 1.50
121 Roberto Alomar 1.50
122 John Olerud .15
123 Paul Molitor 1.50
124 Dean Palmer .15
125 Nomar Garciaparra 3.00
126 Curt Schilling .30
127 Jay Bell .15
128 Craig Biggio .25
129 Marty Cordova .15
130 Ivan Rodriguez 2.00
131 Todd Helton 1.00
132 Jim Thome .15
133 Albert Belle .45
134 Mike Lansing .15
135 Mark McGwire 5.00
136 Roger Clemens 3.00
137 Tom Glavine .25
138 Ron Gant .15
139 Alex Rodriguez 5.00
140 Jeff Bagwell 2.50
141 John Smoltz .25
142 Kenny Lofton .15
143 Dante Bichette .15
144 Pedro Martinez 2.00
145 Barry Bonds 3.00
146 Travis Fryman .15
147 Bobby Jones .15
148 Bobby Higginson .25
149 Reggie Sanders .15
150 Frank Thomas 2.00
Checklist .10

1998 Topps Stars Silver

	MT
Common Silver:	.50
Silver Stars:	1.5X
Production 4,399 sets	

(See 1998 Topps Stars for checklist and base card values.)

1998 Topps Stars Gold

	MT
Common Gold:	1.00
Gold Stars:	2X
Production 2,299 sets	

(See 1998 Topps Stars for checklist and base card values.)

1998 Topps Stars Gold Rainbow

Each card in Topps Stars was available in a Gold Rainbow version. This was the most limited of the five parallels and was numbered to 99. Cards featured gold prismatic foil on the front and were seeded every 46 packs.

	MT
Common Gold Rainbow:	4.00
Gold Rainbow Stars:	8X
Production 99 sets	

(See 1998 Topps Stars for checklist and base card values.)

1998 Topps Stars Supernovas

Supernovas was a 10-card insert in Topps Stars and included rookies and prospects who either have all five tools focused on in the product, or excel dramatically in one of the five. Four sequentially numbered levels were available, with insert rates as follows: bronze (numbered to 100, inserted 1:682), silver (numbered to 75, inserted 1:910), gold (numbered to 50, inserted 1:1,364) and gold rainbow (numbered to 5, inserted 1:13,643).

		MT
Complete Set (10):		55.00
Common Player:		3.00
Production 100 sets		
Silver:		1.5X
Production 75 sets		
Gold:		1.5X
Production 50 sets		
Gold Rainbow: VALUES UNDETERMINED		
Production 5 sets		
S1	Ben Grieve	12.00
S2	Travis Lee	6.00
S3	Todd Helton	20.00
S4	Adrian Beltre	6.00
S5	Derrek Lee	3.00
S6	David Ortiz	3.00
S7	Brad Fullmer	4.50
S8	Mark Kotsay	4.50
S9	Paul Konerko	4.50
S10	Kerry Wood	15.00

1998 Topps Stars Galaxy

Galaxy featured 10 players who possess all five skills featured in Topps Stars Baseball. Four versions were available and sequentially numbered, including: Bronze (numbered to 100, inserted 1:682 packs), Silver (numbered to 75, inserted 1:910), Gold (numbered to 50, inserted 1:1,364) and Gold Rainbow (numbered to 5, inserted 1:13,643).

		MT
Complete Set (10):		400.00
Common Player:		7.50
Production 100 sets		
Silvers:		1.5X
Production 75 sets		
Golds:		2X
Production 50 sets		
G1	Barry Bonds	60.00
G2	Jeff Bagwell	30.00
G3	Nomar Garciaparra	60.00
G4	Chipper Jones	75.00
G5	Ken Griffey Jr.	100.00
G6	Sammy Sosa	60.00
G7	Larry Walker	15.00
G8	Alex Rodriguez	100.00
G9	Craig Biggio	7.50
G10	Raul Mondesi	7.50

1998 Topps Stars Luminaries

Luminaries feature three top players in each "tool" group. The 15-card insert has four parallel sequentially numbered versions inserted as follows: bronze (numbered to 100, inserted 1:455), silver (numbered to 75, inserted 1:606), gold (numbered to 50, inserted 1:910) and gold rainbow (numbered to 5, inserted 1:9,095).

		MT
Complete Set (15):		200.00
Common Player:		4.00
Production 100 sets		
Silver (75 sets):		1.5X
Gold (50 sets):		1.5X
Gold Rainbow: VALUES UNDETERMINED (5 sets)		
L1	Ken Griffey Jr.	40.00
L2	Mark McGwire	50.00
L3	Juan Gonzalez	8.00
L4	Tony Gwynn	10.00
L5	Frank Thomas	15.00
L6	Mike Piazza	30.00
L7	Chuck Knoblauch	4.00
L8	Kenny Lofton	4.00
L9	Barry Bonds	20.00
L10	Matt Williams	4.00
L11	Raul Mondesi	5.00
L12	Ivan Rodriguez	8.00
L13	Alex Rodriguez	40.00
L14	Nomar Garciaparra	20.00
L15	Ken Caminiti	4.00

1998 Topps Stars Rookie Reprints

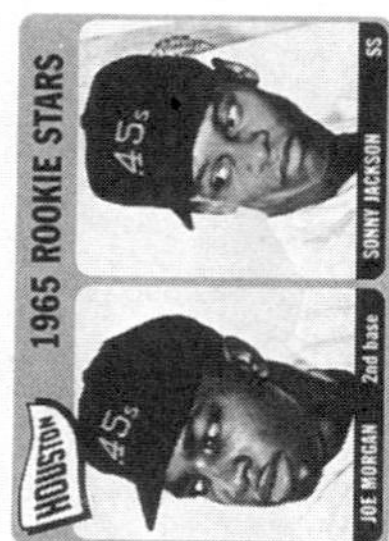

Topps reprinted the rookie cards of five Hall of Famers in Rookie Reprints. The cards are inserted one per 24 packs and have UV coating.

	MT
Complete Set (5):	15.00
Common Player:	2.00
Johnny Bench	4.00
Whitey Ford	2.00
Joe Morgan	2.00
Mike Schmidt	5.00
Carl Yastrzemski	4.00

1998 Topps Stars Rookie Reprints Autographs

Autographed versions of all five Rookie Reprint inserts were available and seeded one per 273 packs. Each card arrive with a Topps "Certified Autograph Issue" stamp to ensure its authenticity.

	MT
Complete Set (5):	175.00
Common Player:	25.00
Johnny Bench	75.00
Whitey Ford	40.00
Joe Morgan	40.00
Mike Schmidt	90.00
Carl Yastrzemski	75.00

1998 Topps Stars N' Steel

Stars 'N Steel was a 44-card set printed on four-colored textured film laminate bonded to a sheet of 25-gauge metal. Regular cards featured a silver colored border while gold versions were also available and seeded one per 12 packs. Stars 'N Steel was available only to Home Team Advantage members and was packaged in three-card packs that arrived in sturdy, trifold stand-up display unit. A second parallel version was also available featuring gold holographic technology and was seeded one per 40 packs.

		MT
Complete Set (44):		75.00
Common Player:		.50
Golds:		2X
Holographics:		7X
Pack (3):		5.00
Wax Box (12):		60.00
1	Roberto Alomar	2.00
2	Jeff Bagwell	2.50
3	Albert Belle	.75
4	Dante Bichette	.50
5	Barry Bonds	4.00
6	Jay Buhner	.50
7	Ken Caminiti	.50
8	Vinny Castilla	.50
9	Roger Clemens	3.00
10	Jose Cruz Jr.	.50
11	Andres Galarraga	.50
12	Nomar Garciaparra	5.00
13	Juan Gonzalez	2.50
14	Mark Grace	1.00
15	Ken Griffey Jr.	6.00
16	Tony Gwynn	3.00
17	Todd Hundley	.50
18	Derek Jeter	8.00
19	Randy Johnson	2.00
20	Andruw Jones	1.50
21	Chipper Jones	4.00
22	David Justice	.50
23	Ray Lankford	.50
24	Barry Larkin	.50
25	Kenny Lofton	.50
26	Greg Maddux	4.00
27	Edgar Martinez	.50
28	Tino Martinez	.50
29	Mark McGwire	8.00
30	Paul Molitor	2.00
31	Rafael Palmeiro	.75
32	Mike Piazza	5.00
33	Manny Ramirez	2.50
34	Cal Ripken Jr.	8.00
35	Ivan Rodriguez	1.50
36	Scott Rolen	1.50
37	Tim Salmon	.75
38	Gary Sheffield	.75
39	Sammy Sosa	4.00
40	Frank Thomas	3.00
41	Jim Thome	.50
42	Mo Vaughn	1.50
43	Larry Walker	1.00
44	Bernie Williams	.75

1998 Topps Super Chrome

This 36-card oversized set featured some of the top players from Chrome on 4-1/8" x 5-3/4" cards. The product sold in three-card packs and featured the same photography as Topps and Topps Chrome before it, but added a Super Chrome logo. Refractor versions of each card were also available, inserted one per 12 packs.

		MT
Complete Set (36):		30.00
Common Player:		.25
Refractors:		1.5X
Inserted 1:12		
Pack (3):		2.50
Wax Box (12):		20.00
1	Tony Gwynn	1.00
2	Larry Walker	.50
3	Vladimir Guerrero	.75
4	Mo Vaughn	.40
5	Frank Thomas	1.50
6	Barry Larkin	.25
7	Scott Rolen	.50
8	Juan Gonzalez	.75
9	Jeff Bagwell	.75
10	Ryan Klesko	.25
11	Mike Piazza	2.00
12	Randy Johnson	.75
13	Derek Jeter	2.00
14	Gary Sheffield	.35
15	Hideo Nomo	.60
16	Tino Martinez	.25
17	Ivan Rodriguez	.65
18	Bernie Williams	.45
19	Greg Maddux	1.00
20	Roger Clemens	1.00
21	Roberto Clemente	1.00
22	Chipper Jones	2.00

23	Sammy Sosa	1.50
24	Tony Clark	.25
25	Barry Bonds	1.50
26	Craig Biggio	.25
27	Cal Ripken Jr.	3.00
28	Ken Griffey Jr.	2.50
29	Todd Helton	.65
30	Mark McGwire	3.00
31	Jose Cruz	.25
32	Albert Belle	.45
33	Andruw Jones	.65
34	Nomar Garciaparra	1.50
35	Andy Pettitte	.35
36	Alex Rodriguez	2.50

1998 Topps TEK

A myriad of collecting methods was created with this innovative product which features 90 different players each printed on an acetate stock with 90 different background patterns. A parallel series utilizing Diffraction technology was inserted at the rate of one per six packs. Each of the 8,100 different cards was created in the same quantity, so there is no differentiation in value among patterns.

		MT
Complete Set (90):		90.00
Common Player:		.25
Pack (4):		4.00
Wax Box (20):		80.00
1	Ben Grieve	.75
2	Kerry Wood	.75
3	Barry Bonds	4.00
4	John Olerud	.50
5	Ivan Rodriguez	1.75
6	Frank Thomas	2.50
7	Bernie Williams	.75
8	Dante Bichette	.50
9	Alex Rodriguez	6.00
10	Tom Glavine	.50
11	Eric Karros	.50
12	Craig Biggio	.50
13	Mark McGwire	6.00
14	Derek Jeter	8.00
15	Nomar Garciaparra	5.00
16	Brady Anderson	.50
17	Vladimir Guerrero	2.50
18	David Justice	.75
19	Chipper Jones	4.00
20	Jim Edmonds	.50
21	Roger Clemens	3.00
22	Mark Kotsay	.50
23	Tony Gwynn	3.00
24	Todd Walker	.50
25	Tino Martinez	.50
26	Andruw Jones	1.50
27	Sandy Alomar	.50
28	Sammy Sosa	4.00
29	Gary Sheffield	.75
30	Ken Griffey Jr.	6.00
31	Aramis Ramirez	.50
32	Curt Schilling	.50
33	Robin Ventura	.50
34	Larry Walker	.75
35	Darin Erstad	1.00
36	Todd Dunwoody	.50
37	Paul O'Neill	.50
38	Vinny Castilla	.50
39	Randy Johnson	1.25
40	Rafael Palmeiro	.75
41	Pedro Martinez	1.75
42	Derek Bell	.50
43	Carlos Delgado	.50
44	Matt Williams	.50
45	Kenny Lofton	.50
46	Edgar Renteria	.50
47	Albert Belle	.75
48	Jeromy Burnitz	.50
49	Adrian Beltre	.75
50	Greg Maddux	4.00
51	Cal Ripken Jr.	8.00
52	Jason Kendall	.50
53	Ellis Burks	.50
54	Paul Molitor	1.00
55	Moises Alou	.50
56	Raul Mondesi	.50
57	Barry Larkin	.50
58	Tony Clark	.50
59	Travis Lee	.75
60	Juan Gonzalez	2.50
61	*Troy Glaus*	3.50
62	Jose Cruz Jr.	.50
63	Paul Konerko	.50
64	Edgar Martinez	.50
65	Javy Lopez	.50
66	Manny Ramirez	2.50
67	Roberto Alomar	1.00
68	Ken Caminiti	.50
69	Todd Helton	1.25
70	Chuck Knoblauch	.50
71	Kevin Brown	.50
72	Tim Salmon	.50
73	*Orlando Hernandez*	1.00
74	Jeff Bagwell	2.50
75	Brian Jordan	.50
76	Derrek Lee	.50
77	Brad Fullmer	.50
78	Mark Grace	.75
79	Jeff King	.50
80	Mike Mussina	1.00
81	Jay Buhner	.50
82	Quinton McCracken	.50
83	A.J. Hinch	.50
84	Richard Hidalgo	.50
85	Andres Galarraga	.50
86	Mike Piazza	4.00
87	Mo Vaughn	.75
88	Scott Rolen	1.50
89	Jim Thome	.50
90	Ray Lankford	.50

1998 Topps TEK Diffraction

Not only can each of the 90 cards in Topps TEK be found in 90 different background patterns, but each can be found in a parallel edition printed with diffraction foil. The parallels are inserted on an average of one per six packs. Like the regular issue TEKs, all patterns were produced equally and there is no value differentiation among them.

	MT
Complete Set (90):	450.00
Common Player:	3.00
Stars/RCs:	6X

(See 1998 Topps TEK for checklist and base card values.)

1999 Topps

Released in two series, the 462-card set includes two home run record subsets, featuring McGwire and Sosa. McGwire's subset card #220 has 70 different versions, commemorating each of his home runs, including where it was hit, the pitcher, date and estimated distance. Sosa's subset card #461 has 66 different versions. Other subsets include World Series Highlights, Prospects, Draft Picks and Season Highlights. Each pack contains 11 cards with an SRP of $1.29. MVPs are the only parallel. They feature a special Topps MVP logo; 100 cards of each player exist. If the player on the card was named a weekly Topps MVP, collectors won a special set of redemption cards.

		MT
Complete Set (462):		50.00
Complete Series 1 (241):		25.00
Complete Series 2 (221):		25.00
Common Player:		.05
Complete Hobby Set (462):		65.00
Complete X-Mas Set (463):		60.00
MVP Stars/Rookies:		20X
Series 1 Hobby Pack (11):		2.00
Series 2 Hobby Pack (11):		1.50
Series 1 Hobby Wax Box (36):		60.00
Series 2 Hobby Wax Box (36):		40.00
Retail Wax Box (22):		60.00
Wax Box (24):		30.00
1	Roger Clemens	1.00
2	Andres Galarraga	.05
3	Scott Brosius	.05
4	John Flaherty	.05
5	Jim Leyritz	.05
6	Ray Durham	.05
7	NOT ISSUED	
8	Joe Vizcaino	.05
9	Will Clark	.15
10	David Wells	.10
11	Jose Guillen	.05
12	Scott Hatteberg	.05
13	Edgardo Alfonzo	.05
14	Mike Bordick	.05
15	Manny Ramirez	.75
16	Greg Maddux	1.00
17	David Segui	.05
18	Darryl Strawberry	.05
19	Brad Radke	.05
20	Kerry Wood	.40
21	Matt Anderson	.05
22	Derrek Lee	.05
23	Mickey Morandini	.05
24	Paul Konerko	.10
25	Travis Lee	.10
26	Ken Hill	.05
27	Kenny Rogers	.05
28	Paul Sorrento	.05
29	Quilvio Veras	.05
30	Todd Walker	.05
31	Ryan Jackson	.05
32	John Olerud	.05
33	Doug Glanville	.05
34	Nolan Ryan	2.00
35	Ray Lankford	.05
36	Mark Loretta	.05
37	Jason Dickson	.05
38	Sean Bergman	.05
39	Quinton McCracken	.05
40	Bartolo Colon	.05
41	Brady Anderson	.05
42	Chris Stynes	.05
43	Jorge Posada	.05
44	Justin Thompson	.05
45	Johnny Damon	.10
46	Armando Benitez	.05
47	Brant Brown	.05
48	Charlie Hayes	.05
49	Darren Dreifort	.05
50	Juan Gonzalez	.75
51	Chuck Knoblauch	.05
52	Todd Helton (Rookie All-Star)	.60
53	Rick Reed	.05
54	Chris Gomez	.05
55	Gary Sheffield	.25
56	Rod Beck	.05
57	Rey Sanchez	.05
58	Garret Anderson	.05
59	Jimmy Haynes	.05
60	Steve Woodard	.05
61	Rondell White	.15
62	Vladimir Guerrero	.75
63	Eric Karros	.05
64	Russ Davis	.05
65	Mo Vaughn	.50
66	Sammy Sosa	1.25
67	Troy Percival	.05
68	Kenny Lofton	.05
69	Bill Taylor	.05
70	Mark McGwire	2.00
71	Roger Cedeno	.05
72	Javy Lopez	.05
73	Damion Easley	.05
74	Andy Pettitte	.25
75	Tony Gwynn	1.00
76	Ricardo Rincon	.05
77	F.P. Santangelo	.05
78	Jay Bell	.05
79	Scott Servais	.05
80	Jose Canseco	.40
81	Roberto Hernandez	.05
82	Todd Dunwoody	.05
83	John Wetteland	.05
84	Mike Caruso (Rookie All-Star)	.05
85	Derek Jeter	1.50
86	Aaron Sele	.05
87	Jose Lima	.05
88	Ryan Christenson	.05
89	Jeff Cirillo	.05
90	Jose Hernandez	.05
91	Mark Kotsay (Rookie All-Star)	.10
92	Darren Bragg	.05
93	Albert Belle	.25
94	Matt Lawton	.05
95	Pedro Martinez	.60
96	Greg Vaughn	.05
97	Neifi Perez	.05
98	Gerald Williams	.05
99	Derek Bell	.05
100	Ken Griffey Jr.	1.75
101	David Cone	.05
102	Brian Johnson	.05
103	Dean Palmer	.05
104	Javier Valentin	.05
105	Trevor Hoffman	.05

106 Butch Huskey .05
107 Dave Martinez .05
108 Billy Wagner .05
109 Shawn Green .20
110 Ben Grieve (Rookie All-Star) .25
111 Tom Goodwin .05
112 Jaret Wright .05
113 Aramis Ramirez .05
114 Dmitri Young .05
115 Hideki Irabu .05
116 Roberto Kelly .05
117 Jeff Fassero .05
118 Mark Clark .05
119 Jason McDonald .05
120 Matt Williams .15
121 Dave Burba .05
122 Bret Saberhagen .05
123 Deivi Cruz .05
124 Chad Curtis .05
125 Scott Rolen .60
126 Lee Stevens .05
127 J.T. Snow Jr. .05
128 Rusty Greer .05
129 Brian Meadows .05
130 Jim Edmonds .05
131 Ron Gant .05
132 A.J. Hinch (Rookie All-Star) .10
133 Shannon Stewart .10
134 Brad Fullmer .05
135 Cal Eldred .05
136 Matt Walbeck .05
137 Carl Everett .10
138 Walt Weiss .05
139 Fred McGriff .05
140 Darin Erstad .25
141 Dave Nilsson .05
142 Eric Young .05
143 Dan Wilson .05
144 Jeff Reed .05
145 Brett Tomko .05
146 Terry Steinbach .05
147 Seth Greisinger .05
148 Pat Meares .05
149 Livan Hernandez .05
150 Jeff Bagwell .75
151 Bob Wickman .05
152 Omar Vizquel .05
153 Eric Davis .05
154 Larry Sutton .05
155 Magglio Ordonez (Rookie All-Star) .15
156 Eric Milton .05
157 Darren Lewis .05
158 Rick Aguilera .05
159 Mike Lieberthal .05
160 Robb Nen .05
161 Brian Giles .05
162 Jeff Brantley .05
163 Gary DiSarcina .05
164 John Valentin .05
165 David Dellucci .05
166 Chan Ho Park .20
167 Masato Yoshii .05
168 Jason Schmidt .05
169 LaTroy Hawkins .05
170 Bret Boone .10
171 Jerry DiPoto .05
172 Mariano Rivera .25
173 Mike Cameron .05
174 Scott Erickson .05
175 Charles Johnson .05
176 Bobby Jones .05
177 Francisco Cordova .05
178 Todd Jones .05
179 Jeff Montgomery .05
180 Mike Mussina .60
181 Bob Abreu .15
182 Ismael Valdes .05
183 Andy Fox .05
184 Woody Williams .05
185 Denny Neagle .05
186 Jose Valentin .05
187 Darrin Fletcher .05
188 Gabe Alvarez .05
189 Eddie Taubensee .05
190 Edgar Martinez .05
191 Jason Kendall .05
192 Darryl Kile .05
193 Jeff King .05
194 Rey Ordonez .05
195 Andruw Jones .65
196 Tony Fernandez .05
197 Jamey Wright .05
198 B.J. Surhoff .05
199 Vinny Castilla .05
200 David Wells (Season Highlight) .05
201 Mark McGwire (Season Highlight) 1.00
202 Sammy Sosa (Season Highlight) .65
203 Roger Clemens (Season Highlight) .50
204 Kerry Wood (Season Highlight) .20
205 Lance Berkman, Mike Frank, Gabe Kapler (Prospects) .25
206 *Alex Escobar*, Ricky Ledee, Mike Stoner (Prospects) .50
207 *Peter Bergeron*, Jeremy Giambi, George Lombard (Prospects) .40
208 Michael Barrett, Ben Davis, Robert Fick (Prospects) .15
209 Pat Cline, Ramon Hernandez, Jayson Werth (Prospects) .10
210 Bruce Chen, Chris Enochs, Ryan Anderson (Prospects) .10
211 Mike Lincoln, Octavio Dotel, Brad Penny (Prospects) .15
212 Chuck Abbott, Brent Butler, Danny Klassen (Prospects) .05
213 Chris Jones, *Jeff Urban* (Draft Pick) .10
214 *Arturo McDowell, Tony Torcato* (Draft Pick) .25
215 *Josh McKinley, Jason Tyner* (Draft Pick) .25
216 *Matt Burch, Seth Etherton* (Draft Pick) .25
217 *Mamon Tucker, Rick Elder* (Draft Pick) .25
218 *J.M. Gold, Ryan Mills* (Draft Pick) .25
219 *Adam Brown, Choo Freeman* (Draft Pick) .25
220 Home Run Record #1 (M. McGwire) 20.00
220 HR Record #2-60 (M. McGwire) 8.00
220 HR Record #61-62 (M. McGwire) 20.00
220 HR Record #63-69 (M. McGwire) 8.00
220 HR Record #70 (Mark McGwire) 50.00
221 Larry Walker (League Leader) .10
222 Bernie Williams (League Leader) .15
223 Mark McGwire (League Leader) 1.00
224 Ken Griffey Jr. (League Leader) .90
225 Sammy Sosa (League Leader) .65
226 Juan Gonzalez (League Leader) .40
227 Dante Bichette (League Leader) .05
228 Alex Rodriguez (League Leader) .90
229 Sammy Sosa (League Leader) .65
230 Derek Jeter (League Leader) .75
231 Greg Maddux (League Leader) .50
232 Roger Clemens (League Leader) .50
233 Ricky Ledee (World Series) .05
234 Chuck Knoblauch (World Series) .05
235 Bernie Williams (World Series) .10
236 Tino Martinez (World Series) .05
237 Orlando Hernandez (World Series) .10
238 Scott Brosius (World Series) .05
239 Andy Pettitte (World Series) .10
240 Mariano Rivera (World Series) .10
241 Checklist .05
242 Checklist .05
243 Tom Glavine .10
244 Andy Benes .05
245 Sandy Alomar .05
246 Wilton Guerrero .05
247 Alex Gonzalez .10
248 Roberto Alomar .50
249 Ruben Rivera .05
250 Eric Chavez .15
251 Ellis Burks .05
252 Richie Sexson .05
253 Steve Finley .05
254 Dwight Gooden .05
255 Dustin Hermanson .05
256 Kirk Rueter .05
257 Steve Trachsel .05
258 Gregg Jefferies .05
259 Matt Stairs .05
260 Shane Reynolds .05
261 Gregg Olson .05
262 Kevin Tapani .05
263 Matt Morris .05
264 Carl Pavano .05
265 Nomar Garciaparra 1.25
266 Kevin Young .05
267 Rick Helling .05
268 Mark Leiter .05
269 Brian McRae .05
270 Cal Ripken Jr. 2.00
271 Jeff Abbott .05
272 Tony Batista .05
273 Bill Simas .05
274 Brian Hunter .05
275 John Franco .05
276 Devon White .05
277 Rickey Henderson .60
278 Chuck Finley .05
279 Mike Blowers .05
280 Mark Grace .25
281 Randy Winn .05
282 Bobby Bonilla .05
283 David Justice .25
284 Shane Monahan .05
285 Kevin Brown .10
286 Todd Zeile .05
287 Al Martin .05
288 Troy O'Leary .05
289 Darryl Hamilton .05
290 Tino Martinez .05
291 David Ortiz .05
292 Tony Clark .05
293 Ryan Minor .05
294 Reggie Sanders .05
295 Wally Joyner .05
296 Cliff Floyd .05
297 Shawn Estes .05
298 Pat Hentgen .05
299 Scott Elarton .05
300 Alex Rodriguez 1.75
301 Ozzie Guillen .05
302 Manny Martinez .05
303 Ryan McGuire .05
304 Brad Ausmus .05
305 Alex Gonzalez .10
306 Brian Jordan .05
307 John Jaha .05
308 Mark Grudzielanek .05
309 Juan Guzman .05
310 Tony Womack .05
311 Dennis Reyes .05
312 Marty Cordova .05
313 Ramiro Mendoza .05
314 Robin Ventura .05
315 Rafael Palmeiro .25
316 Ramon Martinez .05
317 John Mabry .05
318 Dave Hollins .05
319 Tom Candiotti .05
320 Al Leiter .05
321 Rico Brogna .05
322 Jimmy Key .05
323 Bernard Gilkey .05
324 Jason Giambi .30
325 Craig Biggio .10
326 Troy Glaus .25
327 Delino DeShields .05
328 Fernando Vina .05
329 John Smoltz .10
330 Jeff Kent .05
331 Roy Halladay .05
332 Andy Ashby .05
333 Tim Wakefield .05
334 Tim Belcher .05
335 Bernie Williams .25
336 Desi Relaford .05
337 John Burkett .05
338 Mike Hampton .05
339 Royce Clayton .05
340 Mike Piazza 1.50
341 Jeremi Gonzalez .05
342 Mike Lansing .05
343 Jamie Moyer .05
344 Ron Coomer .05
345 Barry Larkin .10
346 Fernando Tatis .05
347 Chili Davis .05
348 Bobby Higginson .10
349 Hal Morris .05
350 Larry Walker .35
351 Carlos Guillen .05
352 Miguel Tejada .05
353 Travis Fryman .05
354 Jarrod Washburn .05
355 Chipper Jones 1.50
356 Todd Stottlemyre .05
357 Henry Rodriguez .05
358 Eli Marrero .05
359 Alan Benes .05
360 Tim Salmon .25
361 Luis Gonzalez .30
362 Scott Spiezio .05
363 Chris Carpenter .05
364 Bobby Howry .05
365 Raul Mondesi .05
366 Ugueth Urbina .05
367 Tom Evans .05
368 *Kerry Ligtenberg* .25
369 Adrian Beltre .25
370 Ryan Klesko .05
371 Wilson Alvarez .05
372 John Thomson .05
373 Tony Saunders .05
374 Mike Stanley .05
375 Ken Caminiti .05
376 Jay Buhner .05
377 Bill Mueller .05
378 Jeff Blauser .05
379 Edgar Renteria .05
380 Jim Thome .05
381 Joey Hamilton .05
382 Calvin Pickering .05
383 Marquis Grissom .05
384 Omar Daal .05
385 Curt Schilling .20
386 Jose Cruz Jr. .10
387 Chris Widger .05
388 Pete Harnisch .05
389 Charles Nagy .05
390 Tom Gordon .05
391 Bobby Smith .05
392 Derrick Gibson .05
393 Jeff Conine .05
394 Carlos Perez .05
395 Barry Bonds 1.25
396 Mark McLemore .05
397 Juan Encarnacion .05
398 Wade Boggs .65
399 Ivan Rodriguez .50
400 Moises Alou .20
401 Jeromy Burnitz .05
402 Sean Casey .25
403 Jose Offerman .05
404 Joe Fontenot .05
405 Kevin Millwood .10
406 Lance Johnson .05
407 Richard Hidalgo .05
408 Mike Jackson .05
409 Brian Anderson .05
410 Jeff Shaw .05
411 Preston Wilson .05
412 Todd Hundley .05
413 Jim Parque .05
414 Justin Baughman .05
415 Dante Bichette .05
416 Paul O'Neill .05
417 Miguel Cairo .05
418 Randy Johnson .60
419 Jesus Sanchez .05
420 Carlos Delgado .20
421 Ricky Ledee .05
422 Orlando Hernandez .15
423 Frank Thomas 1.25
424 Pokey Reese .05
425 Carlos Lee, Mike Lowell, *Kit Pellow* (Prospect) .25
426 Michael Cuddyer, Mark DeRosa, Jerry Hairston Jr. (Prospect) .10

427 Marlon Anderson, Ron Belliard, Orlando Cabrera (Prospect) .10
428 *Micah Bowie*,*Phil Norton*, Randy Wolf (Prospect) .25
429 Jack Cressend, Jason Rakers, John Rocker (Prospect) .10
430 Ruben Mateo, Scott Morgan,*Mike Zywica* (Prospect) .15
431 Jason LaRue,*Matt LeCroy*, Mitch Meluskey (Prospect) .15
432 Gabe Kapler, Armando Rios, Fernando Seguignol (Prospect) .20
433 Adam Kennedy,*Mickey Lopez*, Jackie Rexrode (Prospect) .15
434 *Jose Fernandez*, Jeff Liefer, Chris Truby (Prospect) .10
435 Corey Koskie, Doug Mientkiewicz, Damon Minor (Prospect) .10
436 *Roosevelt Brown*, Dernell Stenson, Vernon Wells (Prospect) .20
437 *A.J. Burnett*, John Nicholson, Billy Koch (Prospect) .25
438 *Matt Belisle*,*Matt Roney* (Draft Pick) .10
439 *Austin Kearns*,*Chris George* (Draft Pick) 2.00
440 *Nate Bump*,*Nate Cornejo* (Draft Pick) .40
441 *Brad Lidge*,*Mike Nannini* (Draft Pick) .10
442 *Matt Holiday Jeff Winchester* (Draft Pick) .25
443 *Adam Everett*,*Chip Ambres* (Draft Pick) .50
444 *Pat Burrell*,*Eric Valent* (Draft Pick) 2.00
445 Roger Clemens (Strikeout Kings) .50
446 Kerry Wood (Strikeout Kings) .20
447 Curt Schilling (Strikeout Kings) .05
448 Randy Johnson (Strikeout Kings) .20
449 Pedro Martinez (Strikeout Kings) .20
450 Jeff Bagwell, Andres Galarraga, Mark McGwire (All-Topps) .50
451 John Olerud, Jim Thome, Tino Martinez (All-Topps) .05
452 Alex Rodriguez, Nomar Garciaparra, Derek Jeter (All-Topps) .50
453 Vinny Castilla, Chipper Jones, Scott Rolen (All-Topps) .40
454 Sammy Sosa, Ken Griffey Jr., Juan Gonzalez (All-Topps) .50
455 Barry Bonds, Manny Ramirez, Larry Walker (All-Topps) .50
456 Frank Thomas, Tim Salmon, David Justice (All-Topps) .40
457 Travis Lee, Todd Helton, Ben Grieve (All-Topps) .30
458 Vladimir Guerrero, Greg Vaughn, Bernie Williams (All-Topps) .25
459 Mike Piazza, Ivan Rodriguez, Jason Kendall (All-Topps) .50
460 Roger Clemens, Kerry Wood, Greg Maddux (All-Topps) .40
461 Home Run Parade #1 (Sammy Sosa) 8.00
461 HR Parade #2-60 (Sammy Sosa) 4.00
461 HR Parade #61-62 (Sammy Sosa) 12.00
461 HR Parade #63-65 (Sammy Sosa) 5.00
461 HR Parade #66 (Sammy Sosa) 15.00
462 Checklist .05
463 Checklist .05

1999 Topps MVP Redemption

Person redeeming winning MVP contest cards prior to Dec. 31, 1999, received this set of 25 cards corresponding to the weekly winners. Cards have an MVP prefix.

		MT
Complete Set (25):		18.00
Common Player:		.30
1	Raul Mondesi	.30
2	Tim Salmon	.40
3	Fernando Tatis	.30
4	Larry Walker	.40
5	Fred McGriff	.30
6	Nomar Garciaparra	1.50
7	Rafael Palmeiro	.50
8	Randy Johnson	.75
9	Mike Lieberthal	.30
10	B.J. Surhoff	.30
11	Todd Helton	.50
12	Tino Martinez	.30
13	Scott Rolen	.75
14	Mike Piazza	2.00
15	David Cone	.30
16	Tony Clark	.30
17	Roberto Alomar	.75
18	Miguel Tejada	.50
19	Alex Rodriguez	3.00
20	J.T. Snow	.30
21	Ray Lankford	.30
22	Mo Vaughn	.50
23	Paul O'Neill	.30
24	Chipper Jones	2.00
25	Mark McGwire	4.00

1999 Topps MVP Promotion

Each of the 198 regular-issue players' cards in Series 1 and cards #243-444 in Series 2 were issued in a parallel version of 100 each for use in an MVP of the Week sweepstakes. Overprinted with a large gold-foil seal on front, the MVP cards have contest rules on back. The MVP cards were inserted at ratios of between 1:142 (HTA) and 1:515 (Hobby) packs. Cards of players who won MVP of the Week during the 1999 season could be redeemed for a special set of MVP cards prior to the Dec. 31, 1999 deadline. Winning players' cards are checklisted here according to their regular-issue card number. Because they were not returned when redeemed, they are in shorter supply than non-winning cards, though market value is not significantly affected.

		MT
Common Player:		1.00
Stars/Rookies:		20X
(See 1999 Topps for checklist and base card values.)		
35	Ray Lankford	
52	Todd Helton	
70	Mark McGwire	
96	Greg Vaughn	
101	David Cone	
125	Scott Rolen	
127	J.T. Snow	
139	Fred McGriff	
159	Mike Lieberthal	
198	B.J. Surhoff	
248	Roberto Alomar	
265	Nomar Garciaparra	
290	Tino Martinez	
292	Tony Clark	
300	Alex Rodriguez	
315	Rafael Palmeiro	
340	Mike Piazza	
346	Fernando Tatis	
350	Larry Walker	
352	Miguel Tejada	
355	Chipper Jones	
360	Tim Salmon	
365	Raul Mondesi	
416	Paul O'Neill	
418	Randy Johnson	

1999 Topps All-Topps Mystery Finest

This 33-card set features a black opaque covering that collectors peel off to reveal the player. Each card is numbered with a "M" prefix and inserted 1:36 packs. A parallel Refractor version is also randomly seeded and inserted 1:144 packs.

		MT
Complete Set (33):		90.00
Common Player:		.75
Inserted 1:36		
Refractors:		1.5X
Inserted 1:144		
M1	Jeff Bagwell	3.00
M2	Andres Galarraga	.75
M3	Mark McGwire	10.00
M4	John Olerud	.75
M5	Jim Thome	.75
M6	Tino Martinez	.75
M7	Alex Rodriguez	10.00
M8	Nomar Garciaparra	8.00
M9	Derek Jeter	12.00
M10	Vinny Castilla	.75
M11	Chipper Jones	6.00
M12	Scott Rolen	2.00
M13	Sammy Sosa	6.00
M14	Ken Griffey Jr.	10.00
M15	Juan Gonzalez	3.00
M16	Barry Bonds	6.00
M17	Manny Ramirez	3.00
M18	Larry Walker	1.50
M19	Frank Thomas	3.00
M20	Tim Salmon	1.00
M21	David Justice	1.50
M22	Travis Lee	1.00
M23	Todd Helton	3.00
M24	Ben Grieve	1.00
M25	Bernie Williams	1.00
M26	Greg Vaughn	.75
M27	Vladimir Guerrero	3.00
M28	Mike Piazza	8.00
M29	Ivan Rodriguez	2.50
M30	Jason Kendall	.75
M31	Roger Clemens	4.00
M32	Kerry Wood	2.00
M33	Greg Maddux	5.00

1999 Topps Autographs

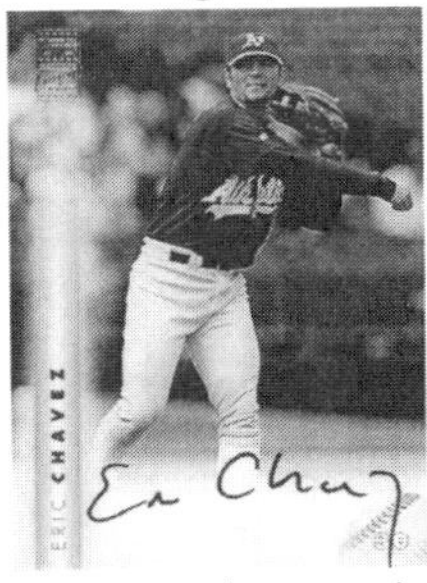

Autographs were inserted exclusively in hobby packs in both Topps series I and II. Each series had eight cards with each one carrying the Topps Certified Autograph Issue stamp. Series I Autographs were seeded 1:532 packs while Series II were found 1:501 packs.

		MT
Complete Set (16):		300.00
Common Player:		10.00
Series 1 Inserted 1:532 H		
Series 2 Inserted 1:501 H		
A1	Roger Clemens	50.00
A2	Chipper Jones	30.00
A3	Scott Rolen	15.00
A4	Alex Rodriguez	50.00
A5	Andres Galarraga	10.00
A6	Rondell White	15.00
A7	Ben Grieve	10.00
A8	Troy Glaus	20.00
A9	Moises Alou	15.00
A10	Barry Bonds	60.00
A11	Vladimir Guerrero	20.00
A12	Andruw Jones	15.00
A13	Darin Erstad	15.00
A14	Shawn Green	15.00
A15	Eric Chavez	10.00
A16	Pat Burrell	25.00

1999 Topps All-Matrix

This 30-card set features holo-foil card fronts and features the top stars in the game. Each card is numbered with a "AM" prefix on card backs and are seeded 1:18 packs.

	MT
Complete Set (30):	30.00
Common Player:	.50
Inserted 1:18	
AM1 Mark McGwire	5.00
AM2 Sammy Sosa	3.00
AM3 Ken Griffey Jr.	4.00
AM4 Greg Vaughn	.50
AM5 Albert Belle	.75
AM6 Vinny Castilla	.50
AM7 Jose Canseco	1.25
AM8 Juan Gonzalez	1.50
AM9 Manny Ramirez	1.50
AM10Andres Galarraga	.50
AM11Rafael Palmeiro	.75
AM12Alex Rodriguez	4.00
AM13Mo Vaughn	.75
AM14Eric Chavez	.75
AM15Gabe Kapler	.75
AM16Calvin Pickering	.50
AM17Ruben Mateo	.50
AM18Roy Halladay	.50
AM19Jeremy Giambi	.50
AM20Alex Gonzalez	.50
AM21Ron Belliard	.50
AM22Marlon Anderson	.50
AM23Carlos Lee	.50
AM24Kerry Wood	.75
AM25Roger Clemens	2.00
AM26Curt Schilling	.65
AM27Kevin Brown	.50
AM28Randy Johnson	1.00
AM29Pedro Martinez	1.25
AM30Orlando Hernandez	.65

1999 Topps Hall of Fame

Found exclusively in hobby packs, Hall of Fame Collection is a ten-card set featured on cards that silhouette their images against their respective Hall of Fame plaques. Featured players include Yogi Berra, Reggie Jackson and Ernie Banks among others. These were seeded 1:12 packs.

	MT
Complete Set (10):	7.50
Common Player:	.50
Inserted 1:12 H	
HOF1Mike Schmidt	2.00
HOF2Brooks Robinson	1.00
HOF3Stan Musial	1.50
HOF4Willie McCovey	.50
HOF5Eddie Mathews	.75
HOF6Reggie Jackson	2.00
HOF7Ernie Banks	1.25
HOF8Whitey Ford	.75
HOF9Bob Feller	.50
HOF10Yogi Berra	1.25

1999 Topps Lords of the Diamond

Inserted in every 18 packs this 15-card set features the top players in the game including Barry Bonds and Ken Griffey Jr. Card fronts include a holographic look with die-cutting across the top of the card on a silver background.

	MT
Complete Set (15):	20.00
Common Player:	.25
Inserted 1:18	
LD1 Ken Griffey Jr.	2.50
LD2 Chipper Jones	2.00
LD3 Sammy Sosa	2.00
LD4 Frank Thomas	2.00
LD5 Mark McGwire	3.00
LD6 Jeff Bagwell	.75
LD7 Alex Rodriguez	2.50
LD8 Juan Gonzalez	.75
LD9 Barry Bonds	2.00
LD10Nomar Garciaparra	2.00
LD11Darin Erstad	.50
LD12Tony Gwynn	1.50
LD13Andres Galarraga	.25
LD14Mike Piazza	2.00
LD15Greg Maddux	1.50

1999 Topps New Breed

The next generation of stars are featured in this 15-card set that showcases the young talent on a silver foil card. These are seeded 1:18 packs.

	MT
Complete Set (15):	10.00
Common Player:	.25
Inserted 1:18	
NB1 Darin Erstad	.35
NB2 Brad Fullmer	.25
NB3 Kerry Wood	.50
NB4 Nomar Garciaparra	1.50
NB5 Travis Lee	.35
NB6 Scott Rolen	.75
NB7 Todd Helton	.50
NB8 Vladimir Guerrero	1.00
NB9 Derek Jeter	3.00
NB10Alex Rodriguez	2.50
NB11Ben Grieve	.50
NB12Andruw Jones	.50
NB13Paul Konerko	.25
NB14Aramis Ramirez	.25
NB15Adrian Beltre	.25

1999 Topps Nolan Ryan Reprints

Topps reprinted all 27 of Nolan Ryan's basic Topps cards, with 14 odd numbers appearing in Series I and the remaining 13 even cards inserted into Series II packs. Each card is stamped with a gold Topps commemorative stamp on the front for identification. Reprints were seeded in every 18 packs. Nolan Ryan also autographed a number of the reprints for both series. Series I Ryan autographs are seeded 1:4,260 with Series II autographs found 1:5,007 packs. Ryan autographs were inserted exclusively in hobby packs.

	MT
Complete Set (27):	75.00
Common Ryan:	4.00
Inserted 1:18	
Nolan Ryan Autograph:	200.00
1 Nolan Ryan (1968)	10.00
2 Nolan Ryan (1969)	6.00
3 Nolan Ryan (1970)	4.00
4 Nolan Ryan (1971)	4.00
5 Nolan Ryan (1972)	4.00
6 Nolan Ryan (1973)	4.00
7 Nolan Ryan (1974)	4.00
8 Nolan Ryan (1975)	4.00
9 Nolan Ryan (1976)	4.00
10 Nolan Ryan (1977)	4.00
11 Nolan Ryan (1978)	4.00
12 Nolan Ryan (1979)	4.00
13 Nolan Ryan (1980)	4.00
14 Nolan Ryan (1981)	4.00
15 Nolan Ryan (1982)	4.00
16 Nolan Ryan (1983)	4.00
17 Nolan Ryan (1984)	4.00
18 Nolan Ryan (1985)	4.00
19 Nolan Ryan (1986)	4.00
20 Nolan Ryan (1987)	4.00
21 Nolan Ryan (1988)	4.00
22 Nolan Ryan (1989)	4.00
23 Nolan Ryan (1990)	4.00
24 Nolan Ryan (1991)	4.00
25 Nolan Ryan (1992)	4.00
26 Nolan Ryan (1993)	4.00
27 Nolan Ryan (1994)	4.00

1999 Topps Nolan Ryan Finest Reprints

This 27-card set reprinted all 27 of Ryan's basic Topps cards. Odd numbers were distributed in Series I packs, with even numbers distributed in Series II packs. These are seeded 1:72 packs in both series I and II packs. A Refractor parallel version is inserted 1:288 packs.

	MT
Complete Set (27):	140.00
Common Card:	6.00
Inserted 1:72	
Refractors:	2X
Inserted 1:288	
1 1968	15.00
2 1969	8.00
3 1970	6.00
4 1971	6.00
5 1972	6.00
6 1973	6.00
7 1974	6.00
8 1975	6.00
9 1976	6.00
10 1977	6.00
11 1978	6.00
12 1979	6.00
13 1980	6.00
14 1981	6.00
15 1982	6.00
16 1983	6.00
17 1984	6.00
18 1985	6.00
19 1986	6.00
20 1987	6.00
21 1988	6.00
22 1989	6.00
23 1990	6.00
24 1991	6.00
25 1992	6.00
26 1992	6.00
27 1992	6.00

1999 Topps Picture Perfect

This 10-card set features a full bleed photo of baseball's biggest stars, including Derek Jeter and Ken Griffey Jr. These are found one per eight packs.

		MT
Complete Set (10):		6.00
Common Player:		.25
Inserted 1:8		
P1	Ken Griffey Jr.	2.00
P2	Kerry Wood	.50
P3	Pedro Martinez	.65
P4	Mark McGwire	2.50
P5	Greg Maddux	1.00
P6	Sammy Sosa	1.25
P7	Greg Vaughn	.25
P8	Juan Gonzalez	.75
P9	Jeff Bagwell	.75
P10	Derek Jeter	1.50

1999 Topps Power Brokers

This 20-card set features baseball's biggest superstars including McGwire, Sosa and Chipper Jones. The cards are die-cut at the top and printed on Finest technology. Power Brokers are inserted in every 36 packs. A Refractor parallel version also exists, which are seeded 1:144 packs.

		MT
Complete Set (20):		20.00
Common Player:		.30
Inserted 1:36		
Refractors:		1.5X
Inserted 1:144		
PB1	Mark McGwire	4.00
PB2	Andres Galarraga	.30
PB3	Ken Griffey Jr.	4.00
PB4	Sammy Sosa	2.00
PB5	Juan Gonzalez	1.00
PB6	Alex Rodriguez	3.00
PB7	Frank Thomas	1.50
PB8	Jeff Bagwell	1.00
PB9	Vinny Castilla	.30
PB10	Mike Piazza	3.00
PB11	Greg Vaughn	.30
PB12	Barry Bonds	1.50
PB13	Mo Vaughn	.60
PB14	Jim Thome	.30
PB15	Larry Walker	.50
PB16	Chipper Jones	2.00
PB17	Nomar Garciaparra	2.00
PB18	Manny Ramirez	1.00
PB19	Roger Clemens	1.50
PB20	Kerry Wood	.75

1999 Topps Record Numbers

This 10-card set highlights achievements from the game's current stars, including Nomar Garciaparra's 30 game hitting streak, the longest by a rookie in major league history. These inserts are randomly seeded 1:8 packs, each card is numbered on the back with a "RN" prefix.

		MT
Complete Set (10):		12.00
Common Player:		.25
Inserted 1:8		
RN1	Mark McGwire	2.50
RN2	Mike Piazza	1.50
RN3	Curt Schilling	.25
RN4	Ken Griffey Jr.	2.00
RN5	Sammy Sosa	1.50
RN6	Nomar Garciaparra	1.50
RN7	Kerry Wood	.50
RN8	Roger Clemens	.75
RN9	Cal Ripken Jr.	2.00
RN10	Mark McGwire	2.50

1999 Topps Record Numbers Gold

This is a parallel of the Record Numbers insert set, each card features the appropriate sequential numbering based on the featured players' highlighted record. Each card is numbered with a "RN" prefix on the back.

		MT
Complete Set (10):		600.00
Common Player:		5.00
RN1	Mark McGwire (70)	125.00
RN2	Mike Piazza (362)	20.00
RN3	Curt Schilling (319)	5.00
RN4	Ken Griffey Jr. (350)	25.00
RN5	Sammy Sosa (20)	175.00
RN6	Nomar Garciaparra (30)	150.00
RN7	Kerry Wood (20)	50.00
RN8	Roger Clemens (20)	125.00
RN9	Cal Ripken Jr. (2,632)	12.50
RN10	Mark McGwire (162)	60.00

1999 Topps Traded and Rookies

Identical in design to the base 1999 Topps cards the 121- card set includes players involved in pre and mid-season transactions as well as top prospects and 1999 Draft Picks. Released in a boxed set, each set also includes one autographed card from the 75 rookie/draft pick cards in the set.

		MT
Unopened Set (122):		35.00
Complete Set, No Autograph (121):		15.00
Common Player:		.10
1	Seth Etherton	.10
2	*Mark Harriger*	.25
3	*Matt Wise*	.15
4	*Carlos Hernandez*	.25
5	*Julio Lugo*	1.00
6	Mike Nannini	.10
7	*Justin Bowles*	.10
8	*Mark Mulder*	1.50
9	*Roberto Vaz*	.15
10	*Felipe Lopez*	1.00
11	Matt Belisle	.10
12	Micah Bowie	.10
13	*Ruben Quevedo*	.25
14	*Jose Garcia*	.15
15	*David Kelton*	.50
16	Phillip Norton	.10
17	*Corey Patterson*	2.00
18	*Ron Walker*	.10
19	*Paul Hoover*	.15
20	*Ryan Rupe*	.25
21	*J.D. Closser*	.25
22	*Rob Ryan*	.15
23	*Steve Colyer*	.15
24	*Bubba Crosby*	.25
25	*Luke Prokopec*	.40
26	*Matt Blank*	.25
27	Josh McKinley	.10
28	Nate Bump	.10
29	*Giuseppe Chiaramonte*	.25
30	Arturo McDowell	.10
31	Tony Torcato	.10
32	Dave Roberts	.10
33	*C.C. Sabathia*	1.50
34	*Sean Spencer*	.25
35	Chip Ambres	.10
36	A.J. Burnett	.15
37	*Mo Bruce*	.25
38	Jason Tyner	.10
39	Mamon Tucker	.10
40	*Sean Burroughs*	2.50
41	*Kevin Eberwein*	.25
42	*Junior Herndon*	.25
43	*Bryan Wolff*	.15
44	Pat Burrell	1.00
45	Eric Valent	.15
46	*Carlos Pena*	2.00
47	Mike Zywica	.10
48	Adam Everett	.10
49	*Juan Pena*	.50
50	*Adam Dunn*	8.00
51	Austin Kearns	2.00
52	*Jacobo Sequea*	.15
53	Choo Freeman	.10
54	Jeff Winchester	.10
55	Matt Burch	.10
56	Chris George	.10
57	*Scott Mullen*	.25
58	Kit Pellow	.15
59	*Mark Quinn*	.50
60	Nate Cornejo	.25
61	*Ryan Mills*	.15
62	*Kevin Beirne*	.15
63	*Kip Wells*	.50
64	*Juan Rivera*	1.00
65	*Alfonso Soriano*	6.00
66	*Josh Hamilton*	1.50
67	*Josh Girdley*	.25
68	*Kyle Snyder*	.15
69	*Mike Paradis*	.15
70	*Jason Jennings*	.50
71	*David Walling*	.30
72	*Omar Ortiz*	.15
73	*Jay Gehrke*	.15
74	*Casey Burns*	.15
75	*Carl Crawford*	1.00
76	Reggie Sanders	.10
77	Will Clark	.25
78	David Wells	.15
79	Paul Konerko	.15
80	Armando Benitez	.10
81	Brant Brown	.10
82	Mo Vaughn	.35
83	Jose Canseco	.50
84	Albert Belle	.25
85	Dean Palmer	.10
86	Greg Vaughn	.10
87	Mark Clark	.10
88	Pat Meares	.10
89	Eric Davis	.10
90	Brian Giles	.10
91	Jeff Brantley	.10
92	Bret Boone	.15
93	Ron Gant	.10
94	Mike Cameron	.10
95	Charles Johnson	.10
96	Denny Neagle	.10
97	Brian Hunter	.10
98	Jose Hernandez	.10
99	Rick Aguilera	.10
100	Tony Batista	.10
101	Roger Cedeno	.10
102	Creighton Gubanich	.10
103	Tim Belcher	.10
104	Bruce Aven	.10
105	*Brian Daubach*	.50
106	Ed Sprague	.10
107	Michael Tucker	.10
108	Homer Bush	.10
109	Armando Reynoso	.10
110	Brook Fordyce	.10
111	Matt Mantei	.10
112	Jose Guillen	.10
113	Kenny Rogers	.10
114	Livan Hernandez	.10
115	Butch Huskey	.10
116	David Segui	.10
117	Darryl Hamilton	.10
118	Jim Leyritz	.10
119	Randy Velarde	.10
120	Bill Taylor	.10
121	Kevin Appier	.10

1999 Topps Traded and Rookies Autographs

These autographs have identical photos and design from the Traded and Rookies set. Seeded one per boxed set, each card has a "Topps Certified

Autograph Issue" stamp ensuring its authenticity. 75 of the rookie/draft picks included in the 121-card boxed set signed.

		MT
Common Player:		5.00
Inserted 1:set		
1	Seth Etherton	5.00
2	Mark Harriger	5.00
3	Matt Wise	5.00
4	Carlos Hernandez	5.00
5	Julio Lugo	5.00
6	Mike Nannini	5.00
7	Justin Bowles	5.00
8	Mark Mulder	30.00
9	Roberto Vaz	5.00
10	Felipe Lopez	25.00
11	Matt Belisle	8.00
12	Micah Bowie	5.00
13	Ruben Quevedo	5.00
14	Jose Garcia	5.00
15	David Kelton	15.00
16	Phillip Norton	5.00
17	Corey Patterson	50.00
18	Ron Walker	5.00
19	Paul Hoover	5.00
20	Ryan Rupe	5.00
21	J.D. Closser	8.00
22	Rob Ryan	5.00
23	Steve Colyer	5.00
24	Bubba Crosby	5.00
25	Luke Prokopec	10.00
26	Matt Blank	5.00
27	Josh McKinley	5.00
28	Nate Bump	8.00
29	Giuseppe Chiaramonte	5.00
30	Arturo McDowell	5.00
31	Tony Torcato	8.00
32	Dave Roberts	5.00
33	C.C. Sabathia	30.00
34	Sean Spencer	5.00
35	Chip Ambres	10.00
36	A.J. Burnett	10.00
37	Mo Bruce	5.00
38	Jason Tyner	8.00
39	Mamon Tucker	5.00
40	Sean Burroughs	50.00
41	Kevin Eberwein	5.00
42	Junior Herndon	5.00
43	Bryan Wolff	5.00
44	Pat Burrell	60.00
45	Eric Valent	12.00
46	Carlos Pena	45.00
47	Mike Zywica	5.00
48	Adam Everett	10.00
49	Juan Pena	8.00
50	Adam Dunn	125.00
51	Austin Kearns	70.00
52	Jacobo Sequea	5.00
53	Choo Freeman	8.00
54	Jeff Winchester	10.00
55	Matt Burch	5.00
56	Chris George	8.00
57	Scott Mullen	5.00
58	Kit Pellow	5.00
59	Mark Quinn	15.00
60	Nate Cornejo	10.00
61	Ryan Mills	5.00
62	Kevin Beirne	5.00
63	Kip Wells	15.00
64	Juan Rivera	30.00
65	Alfonso Soriano	220.00
66	Josh Hamilton	50.00
67	Josh Girdley	10.00
68	Kyle Snyder	8.00
69	Mike Paradis	5.00
70	Jason Jennings	12.00
71	David Walling	10.00
72	Omar Ortiz	5.00
73	Jay Gehrke	5.00
74	Casey Burns	5.00
75	Carl Crawford	30.00

1999 Topps Chrome

The 462-card base set is a chromium parallel version of Topps baseball. Included are the Mark McGwire #220 and Sammy Sosa #461 home run subset cards, which commemorate each of his home runs. Each pack contains four cards with a S.R.P. of $3.00 per pack.

		MT
Complete Set (461):		150.00
Series 1 Set (242):		75.00
Series 2 Set (221):		75.00
Common Player:		.25
Refractors:		6X
Inserted 1:12		
Series 1 Pack (4):		3.00
Series 1 Hobby Wax Box (24):		60.00
Series 2 Pack (4):		2.00
Series 2 Hobby Wax Box (24):		40.00
1	Roger Clemens	3.00
2	Andres Galarraga	.25
3	Scott Brosius	.25
4	John Flaherty	.25
5	Jim Leyritz	.25
6	Ray Durham	.25
7	not issued	.25
8	Joe Vizcaino	.25
9	Will Clark	.75
10	David Wells	.35
11	Jose Guillen	.25
12	Scott Hatteberg	.25
13	Edgardo Alfonzo	.25
14	Mike Bordick	.25
15	Manny Ramirez	2.50
16	Greg Maddux	3.00
17	David Segui	.25
18	Darryl Strawberry	.25
19	Brad Radke	.25
20	Kerry Wood	.75
21	Matt Anderson	.25
22	Derrek Lee	.25
23	Mickey Morandini	.25
24	Paul Konerko	.35
25	Travis Lee	.25
26	Ken Hill	.25
27	Kenny Rogers	.25
28	Paul Sorrento	.25
29	Quilvio Veras	.25
30	Todd Walker	.25
31	Ryan Jackson	.25
32	John Olerud	.25
33	Doug Glanville	.25
34	Nolan Ryan	6.00
35	Ray Lankford	.25
36	Mark Loretta	.25
37	Jason Dickson	.25
38	Sean Bergman	.25
39	Quinton McCracken	.25
40	Bartolo Colon	.25
41	Brady Anderson	.25
42	Chris Stynes	.25
43	Jorge Posada	.25
44	Justin Thompson	.25
45	Johnny Damon	.35
46	Armando Benitez	.25
47	Brant Brown	.25
48	Charlie Hayes	.25
49	Darren Dreifort	.25
50	Juan Gonzalez	2.50
51	Chuck Knoblauch	.25
52	Todd Helton (Rookie All-Star)	2.00
53	Rick Reed	.25
54	Chris Gomez	.25
55	Gary Sheffield	.75
56	Rod Beck	.25
57	Rey Sanchez	.25
58	Garret Anderson	.25
59	Jimmy Haynes	.25
60	Steve Woodard	.25
61	Rondell White	.35
62	Vladimir Guerrero	2.50
63	Eric Karros	.25
64	Russ Davis	.25
65	Mo Vaughn	1.00
66	Sammy Sosa	3.50
67	Troy Percival	.25
68	Kenny Lofton	.25
69	Bill Taylor	.25
70	Mark McGwire	6.00
71	Roger Cedeno	.25
72	Javy Lopez	.25
73	Damion Easley	.25
74	Andy Pettitte	.60
75	Tony Gwynn	3.00
76	Ricardo Rincon	.25
77	F.P. Santangelo	.25
78	Jay Bell	.25
79	Scott Servais	.25
80	Jose Canseco	1.25
81	Roberto Hernandez	.25
82	Todd Dunwoody	.25
83	John Wetteland	.25
84	Mike Caruso (Rookie All-Star)	.25
85	Derek Jeter	6.00
86	Aaron Sele	.25
87	Jose Lima	.25
88	Ryan Christenson	.25
89	Jeff Cirillo	.25
90	Jose Hernandez	.25
91	Mark Kotsay (Rookie All-Star)	.35
92	Darren Bragg	.25
93	Albert Belle	.75
94	Matt Lawton	.25
95	Pedro Martinez	2.00
96	Greg Vaughn	.25
97	Neifi Perez	.25
98	Gerald Williams	.25
99	Derek Bell	.25
100	Ken Griffey Jr.	5.00
101	David Cone	.25
102	Brian Johnson	.25
103	Dean Palmer	.25
104	Javier Valentin	.25
105	Trevor Hoffman	.25
106	Butch Huskey	.25
107	Dave Martinez	.25
108	Billy Wagner	.25
109	Shawn Green	.45
110	Ben Grieve (Rookie All-Star)	.75
111	Tom Goodwin	.25
112	Jaret Wright	.25
113	Aramis Ramirez	.25
114	Dmitri Young	.25
115	Hideki Irabu	.25
116	Roberto Kelly	.25
117	Jeff Fassero	.25
118	Mark Clark	.25
119	Jason McDonald	.25
120	Matt Williams	.75
121	Dave Burba	.25
122	Bret Saberhagen	.25
123	Deivi Cruz	.25
124	Chad Curtis	.25
125	Scott Rolen	1.50
126	Lee Stevens	.25
127	J.T. Snow Jr.	.25
128	Rusty Greer	.25
129	Brian Meadows	.25
130	Jim Edmonds	.25
131	Ron Gant	.25
132	A.J. Hinch (Rookie All-Star)	.35
133	Shannon Stewart	.25
134	Brad Fullmer	.25
135	Cal Eldred	.25
136	Matt Walbeck	.25
137	Carl Everett	.35
138	Walt Weiss	.25
139	Fred McGriff	.25
140	Darin Erstad	1.00
141	Dave Nilsson	.25
142	Eric Young	.25
143	Dan Wilson	.25
144	Jeff Reed	.25
145	Brett Tomko	.25
146	Terry Steinbach	.25
147	Seth Greisinger	.25
148	Pat Meares	.25
149	Livan Hernandez	.25
150	Jeff Bagwell	2.50
151	Bob Wickman	.25
152	Omar Vizquel	.25
153	Eric Davis	.25
154	Larry Sutton	.25
155	Magglio Ordonez (Rookie All-Star)	.75
156	Eric Milton	.25
157	Darren Lewis	.25
158	Rick Aguilera	.25
159	Mike Lieberthal	.25
160	Robb Nen	.25
161	Brian Giles	.25
162	Jeff Brantley	.25
163	Gary DiSarcina	.25
164	John Valentin	.25
165	David Dellucci	.25
166	Chan Ho Park	.60
167	Masato Yoshii	.25
168	Jason Schmidt	.25
169	LaTroy Hawkins	.25
170	Bret Boone	.35
171	Jerry DiPoto	.25
172	Mariano Rivera	.60
173	Mike Cameron	.25
174	Scott Erickson	.25
175	Charles Johnson	.25
176	Bobby Jones	.25
177	Francisco Cordova	.25
178	Todd Jones	.25
179	Jeff Montgomery	.25
180	Mike Mussina	1.50
181	Bob Abreu	.25
182	Ismael Valdes	.25
183	Andy Fox	.25
184	Woody Williams	.25
185	Denny Neagle	.25
186	Jose Valentin	.25
187	Darrin Fletcher	.25
188	Gabe Alvarez	.25
189	Eddie Taubensee	.25
190	Edgar Martinez	.25
191	Jason Kendall	.25
192	Darryl Kile	.25
193	Jeff King	.25
194	Rey Ordonez	.25
195	Andruw Jones	1.50
196	Tony Fernandez	.25
197	Jamey Wright	.25
198	B.J. Surhoff	.25
199	Vinny Castilla	.25
200	David Wells (Season Highlight)	.25
201	Mark McGwire (Season Highlight)	3.00
202	Sammy Sosa (Season Highlight)	1.75
203	Roger Clemens (Season Highlight)	1.50
204	Kerry Wood (Season Highlight)	.40
205	Lance Berkman, Mike Frank, Gabe Kapler (Prospects)	1.00
206	*Alex Escobar*, Ricky Ledee, Mike Stoner (Prospects)	2.00
207	*Peter Bergeron*, Jeremy Giambi, George Lombard (Prospects)	1.50
208	Michael Barrett, Ben Davis, Robert Fick (Prospects)	.75
209	Pat Cline, Ramon Hernandez, Jayson Werth (Prospects)	.50
210	Bruce Chen, Chris Enochs, Ryan Anderson (Prospects)	.50
211	Mike Lincoln, Octavio Dotel, Brad Penny (Prospects)	.25
212	Chuck Abbott, Brent Butler, Danny Klassen (Prospects)	.25
213	Chris Jones, *Jeff Urban* (Draft Pick)	.50
214	*Arturo McDowell, Tony Torcato* (Draft Pick)	.50
215	*Josh McKinley, Jason Tyner* (Draft Pick)	.50
216	*Matt Burch, Seth Etherton* (Draft Pick)	.25
217	*Mamon Tucker, Rick Elder* (Draft Pick)	.35

218 *J.M. Gold,Ryan Mills* (Draft Pick) .25
219 *Adam Brown,Choo Freeman* (Draft Pick) .35
220 Mark McGwire HR #1 (Record Breaker) 40.00
220 Mark McGwire HR #2-60 20.00
220 McGwire HR #61-62 40.00
220 McGwire HR #63-69 30.00
220 McGwire HR #70 100.00
221 Larry Walker (League Leader) .25
222 Bernie Williams (League Leader) .25
223 Mark McGwire (League Leader) 3.00
224 Ken Griffey Jr. (League Leader) 3.00
225 Sammy Sosa (League Leader) 1.75
226 Juan Gonzalez (League Leader) .75
227 Dante Bichette (League Leader) .25
228 Alex Rodriguez (League Leader) 2.50
229 Sammy Sosa (League Leader) 1.75
230 Derek Jeter (League Leader) 2.00
231 Greg Maddux (League Leader) 1.50
232 Roger Clemens (League Leader) 1.50
233 Ricky Ledee (World Series) .25
234 Chuck Knoblauch (World Series) .25
235 Bernie Williams (World Series) .25
236 Tino Martinez (World Series) .25
237 Orlando Hernandez (World Series) .25
238 Scott Brosius (World Series) .25
239 Andy Pettitte (World Series) .25
240 Mariano Rivera (World Series) .25
241 Checklist .25
242 Checklist .25
243 Tom Glavine .35
244 Andy Benes .25
245 Sandy Alomar .25
246 Wilton Guerrero .25
247 Alex Gonzalez .25
248 Roberto Alomar 1.50
249 Ruben Rivera .25
250 Eric Chavez .25
251 Ellis Burks .25
252 Richie Sexson .25
253 Steve Finley .25
254 Dwight Gooden .25
255 Dustin Hermanson .25
256 Kirk Rueter .25
257 Steve Trachsel .25
258 Gregg Jefferies .25
259 Matt Stairs .25
260 Shane Reynolds .25
261 Gregg Olson .25
262 Kevin Tapani .25
263 Matt Morris .25
264 Carl Pavano .25
265 Nomar Garciaparra 3.50
266 Kevin Young .25
267 Rick Helling .25
268 Matt Franco .25
269 Brian McRae .25
270 Cal Ripken Jr. 6.00
271 Jeff Abbott .25
272 Tony Batista .25
273 Bill Simas .25
274 Brian Hunter .25
275 John Franco .25
276 Devon White .25
277 Rickey Henderson 1.50
278 Chuck Finley .25
279 Mike Blowers .25
280 Mark Grace .75
281 Randy Winn .25
282 Bobby Bonilla .25
283 David Justice .65
284 Shane Monahan .25
285 Kevin Brown .35
286 Todd Zeile .25
287 Al Martin .25
288 Troy O'Leary .25
289 Darryl Hamilton .25
290 Tino Martinez .25
291 David Ortiz .25
292 Tony Clark .25
293 Ryan Minor .25
294 Reggie Sanders .25
295 Wally Joyner .25
296 Cliff Floyd .25
297 Shawn Estes .25
298 Pat Hentgen .25
299 Scott Elarton .25
300 Alex Rodriguez 5.00
301 Ozzie Guillen .25
302 Hideo Martinez .25
303 Ryan McGuire .25
304 Brad Ausmus .25
305 Alex Gonzalez .25
306 Brian Jordan .25
307 John Jaha .25
308 Mark Grudzielanek .25
309 Juan Guzman .25
310 Tony Womack .25
311 Dennis Reyes .25
312 Marty Cordova .25
313 Ramiro Mendoza .25
314 Robin Ventura .25
315 Rafael Palmeiro .65
316 Ramon Martinez .25
317 Pedro Astacio .25
318 Dave Hollins .25
319 Tom Candiotti .25
320 Al Leiter .25
321 Rico Brogna .25
322 Reggie Jefferson .25
323 Bernard Gilkey .25
324 Jason Giambi 1.00
325 Craig Biggio .35
326 Troy Glaus 2.00
327 Delino DeShields .25
328 Fernando Vina .25
329 John Smoltz .35
330 Jeff Kent .25
331 Roy Halladay .25
332 Andy Ashby .25
333 Tim Wakefield .25
334 Roger Clemens 3.00
335 Bernie Williams .65
336 Desi Relaford .25
337 John Burkett .25
338 Mike Hampton .25
339 Royce Clayton .25
340 Mike Piazza 4.00
341 Jeremi Gonzalez .25
342 Mike Lansing .25
343 Jamie Moyer .25
344 Ron Coomer .25
345 Barry Larkin .35
346 Fernando Tatis .25
347 Chili Davis .25
348 Bobby Higginson .35
349 Hal Morris .25
350 Larry Walker .65
351 Carlos Guillen .25
352 Miguel Tejada .50
353 Travis Fryman .25
354 Jarrod Washburn .25
355 Chipper Jones 4.00
356 Todd Stottlemyre .25
357 Henry Rodriguez .25
358 Eli Marrero .25
359 Alan Benes .25
360 Tim Salmon .65
361 Luis Gonzalez .60
362 Scott Spiezio .25
363 Chris Carpenter .25
364 Bobby Howry .25
365 Raul Mondesi .35
366 Ugueth Urbina .25
367 Tom Evans .25
368 *Kerry Ligtenberg* .75
369 Adrian Beltre .75
370 Ryan Klesko .25
371 Wilson Alvarez .25
372 John Thomson .25
373 Tony Saunders .25
374 Mike Stanley .25
375 Ken Caminiti .25
376 Jay Buhner .25
377 Bill Mueller .25
378 Jeff Blauser .25
379 Edgar Renteria .25
380 Jim Thome .25
381 Joey Hamilton .25
382 Calvin Pickering .25
383 Marquis Grissom .25
384 Omar Daal .25
385 Curt Schilling .50
386 Jose Cruz Jr. .50
387 Chris Widger .25
388 Pete Harnisch .25
389 Charles Nagy .25
390 Tom Gordon .25
391 Bobby Smith .25
392 Derrick Gibson .25
393 Jeff Conine .25
394 Carlos Perez .25
395 Barry Bonds 3.00
396 Mark McLemore .25
397 Juan Encarnacion .25
398 Wade Boggs 1.50
399 Ivan Rodriguez 2.00
400 Moises Alou .50
401 Jeromy Burnitz .25
402 Sean Casey .45
403 Jose Offerman .25
404 Joe Fontenot .25
405 Kevin Millwood .50
406 Lance Johnson .25
407 Richard Hidalgo .25
408 Mike Jackson .25
409 Brian Anderson .25
410 Jeff Shaw .25
411 Preston Wilson .25
412 Todd Hundley .25
413 Jim Parque .25
414 Justin Baughman .25
415 Dante Bichette .25
416 Paul O'Neill .25
417 Miguel Cairo .25
418 Randy Johnson 2.00
419 Jesus Sanchez .25
420 Carlos Delgado .35
421 Ricky Ledee .25
422 Orlando Hernandez .35
423 Frank Thomas 2.50
424 Pokey Reese .25
425 Carlos Lee, Mike Lowell,*Kit Pellow* (Prospect) .50
426 Michael Cuddyer, Mark DeRosa,*Jerry Hairston Jr.* (Prospect) 1.00
427 Marlon Anderson, Ron Belliard, Orlando Cabrera (Prospect) 1.00
428 *Micah Bowie,Phil Norton,* Randy Wolf (Prospect) 1.00
429 Jack Cressend, Jason Rakers, John Rocker (Prospect) .45
430 Ruben Mateo, Scott Morgan,*Mike Zywica* (Prospect) .75
431 Jason LaRue,*Matt LeCroy,Mitch Meluskey* (Prospect) 1.00
432 Gabe Kapler, *Armando Rios,* Fernando Seguignol (Prospect) 1.00
433 Adam Kennedy,*Mickey Lopez*, Jackie Rexrode (Prospect) .75
434 *Jose Fernandez,* Jeff Liefer, Chris Truby (Prospect) .75
435 Corey Koskie,*Doug Mientkiewicz*, Damon Minor (Prospect) 1.00
436 *Roosevelt Brown*, Dernell Stenson, Vernon Wells (Prospect) 1.00
437 *A.J. Burnett*, John Nicholson, Billy Koch (Prospect) 1.50
438 *Matt Belisle,Matt Roney* (Draft Pick) .50
439 *Austin Kearns,Chris George* (Draft Pick) 8.00
440 *Nate Bump,Nate Cornejo* (Draft Pick) .50
441 *Brad Lidge,Mike Nannini* (Draft Pick) .50
442 *Matt Holliday, Jeff Winchester* (Draft Pick) .50
443 *Adam Everett,Chip Ambres* (Draft Pick) .50
444 *Pat Burrell,Eric Valent* (Draft Pick) 12.00
445 Roger Clemens (Strikeout Kings) 1.50
446 Kerry Wood (Strikeout Kings) .50
447 Curt Schilling (Strikeout Kings) .25
448 Randy Johnson (Strikeout Kings) .75
449 Pedro Martinez (Strikeout Kings) .75
450 Jeff Bagwell, Andres Galarraga, Mark McGwire (All-Topps) 3.00
451 John Olerud, Jim Thome, Tino Martinez (All-Topps) .25
452 Alex Rodriguez, Nomar Garciaparra, Derek Jeter (All-Topps) 3.00
453 Vinny Castilla, Chipper Jones, Scott Rolen (All-Topps) 2.00
454 Sammy Sosa, Ken Griffey Jr., Juan Gonzalez (All-Topps) 2.50
455 Barry Bonds, Manny Ramirez, Larry Walker (All-Topps) 1.50
456 Frank Thomas, Tim Salmon, David Justice (All-Topps) 1.25
457 Travis Lee, Todd Helton, Ben Grieve (All-Topps) 1.25
458 Vladimir Guerrero, Greg Vaughn, Bernie Williams (All-Topps) 1.25
459 Mike Piazza, Ivan Rodriguez, Jason Kendall (All-Topps) 2.00
460 Roger Clemens, Kerry Wood, Greg Maddux (All-Topps) 1.50
461 Sammy Sosa #1 (Home Run Parade) 15.00
461 Sammy Sosa HR #2-60 8.00
461 S. Sosa HR #61-62 20.00
461 S. Sosa HR #63-65 10.00
461 S. Sosa HR #66 40.00
--- Checklist 1-100 .25
--- Checklist - inserts .25

1999 Topps Chrome All-Etch

Inserted in Series II packs, All-Etch has three different levels of inserts, all printed on All-Etch technology. The three levels include '99 Rookie Rush which features rookies who have the best shot of winning '99 Rookie of the Year. Club 40 features

13 players who hit 40 homers or more from the '98 season and Club K features seven pitchers who are known for their strikeout abilities including Roger Clemens and Pedro Martinez. Each of these three levels are inserted 1:6 packs while the Refractor versions are all seeded 1:24 packs.

		MT
Complete Set (30):		30.00
Common Player:		.50
Inserted 1:6		
Refractors:		1.5X
Inserted 1:24		
1	Mark McGwire	5.00
2	Sammy Sosa	3.00
3	Ken Griffey Jr.	4.00
4	Greg Vaughn	.50
5	Albert Belle	.75
6	Vinny Castilla	.50
7	Jose Canseco	1.00
8	Juan Gonzalez	1.25
9	Manny Ramirez	1.50
10	Andres Galarraga	.50
11	Rafael Palmeiro	.50
12	Alex Rodriguez	4.00
13	Mo Vaughn	.75
14	Eric Chavez	1.00
15	Gabe Kapler	1.00
16	Calvin Pickering	.50
17	Ruben Mateo	.50
18	Roy Halladay	.50
19	Jeremy Giambi	.75
20	Alex Gonzalez	.50
21	Ron Belliard	.50
22	Marlon Anderson	.50
23	Carlos Lee	.50
24	Kerry Wood	1.00
25	Roger Clemens	2.00
26	Curt Schilling	.65
27	Kevin Brown	.50
28	Randy Johnson	1.00
29	Pedro Martinez	1.00
30	Orlando Hernandez	1.00

1999 Topps Chrome Early Road to the Hall

This insert set spotlights 10 players with less than 10 years in the Majors but are gunning towards their respective spots in Cooperstown. Utilizing Chromium technology featured players include Alex Rodriguez and Derek Jeter, with an insert rate of 1:12 packs. A Refractor parallel edition, numbered to 100 each, was a 1:944 hobby-pack insert.

		MT
Complete Set (10):		35.00
Common Player:		2.00
Inserted 1:12		
Refractors (#d to 100):		6X
ER1	Nomar Garciaparra	4.00
ER2	Derek Jeter	8.00
ER3	Alex Rodriguez	6.00
ER4	Juan Gonzalez	2.50
ER5	Ken Griffey Jr.	6.00
ER6	Chipper Jones	5.00
ER7	Vladimir Guerrero	2.50
ER8	Jeff Bagwell	2.50
ER9	Ivan Rodriguez	2.00
ER10	Frank Thomas	3.00

1999 Topps Chrome Fortune 15

Fortune 15 showcases the baseball's best players and hot rookies. They are inserted in Series 2 packs at a rate of 1:12. A Refractor version also exists found exclusively in hobby packs at a rate of 1:627 packs. Refractors are sequentially numbered to 100.

		MT
Complete Set (15):		50.00
Common Player:		2.00
Inserted 1:12		
Refractors (# to 100):		4X
1	Alex Rodriguez	6.00
2	Nomar Garciaparra	4.00
3	Derek Jeter	8.00
4	Troy Glaus	2.50
5	Ken Griffey Jr.	6.00
6	Vladimir Guerrero	2.50
7	Kerry Wood	2.00
8	Eric Chavez	2.00
9	Greg Maddux	5.00
10	Mike Piazza	5.00
11	Sammy Sosa	4.00
12	Mark McGwire	6.00
13	Ben Grieve	2.00
14	Chipper Jones	5.00
15	Manny Ramirez	2.50

1999 Topps Chrome Lords of the Diamond

Parallel to the Topps version, the 15-card set features die-cutting across the card top and are seeded 1:8 in Series 1 packs. Refractor versions can be found 1:24 packs.

		MT
Complete Set (15):		25.00
Common Player:		.50
Inserted 1:8		
Refractors:		2X
Inserted 1:24		
LD1	Ken Griffey Jr.	4.00
LD2	Chipper Jones	2.50
LD3	Sammy Sosa	2.50
LD4	Frank Thomas	1.50
LD5	Mark McGwire	5.00
LD6	Jeff Bagwell	1.00
LD7	Alex Rodriguez	4.00
LD8	Juan Gonzalez	1.00
LD9	Barry Bonds	2.00
LD10	Nomar Garciaparra	2.50
LD11	Darin Erstad	1.00
LD12	Tony Gwynn	1.50
LD13	Andres Galarraga	.50
LD14	Mike Piazza	3.00
LD15	Greg Maddux	1.50

1999 Topps Chrome New Breed

A parallel version of Topps New Breed utilizing Chromium technology. The 15-card set features the top young stars in the game and are seeded 1:24 packs. A Refractor version also exists which are found 1:72 packs.

		MT
Complete Set (15):		18.00
Common Player:		.50
Inserted 1:24		
Refractors:		1.5X
Inserted 1:72		
NB1	Darin Erstad	1.25
NB2	Brad Fullmer	.50
NB3	Kerry Wood	1.25
NB4	Nomar Garciaparra	3.00
NB5	Travis Lee	1.00
NB6	Scott Rolen	1.25
NB7	Todd Helton	1.00
NB8	Vladimir Guerrero	2.00
NB9	Derek Jeter	4.00
NB10	Alex Rodriguez	4.00
NB11	Ben Grieve	1.25
NB12	Andruw Jones	1.50
NB13	Paul Konerko	.50
NB14	Aramis Ramirez	.50
NB15	Adrian Beltre	.50

1999 Topps Chrome Record Numbers

This 10-card insert set salutes 10 record-setters who have earned a mark of distinction, including Cal Ripken Jr. for his record setting consecutive game streak. Inserted randomly in series II packs at a rate of 1:36 packs. Refractor parallel versions are seeded 1:144 packs.

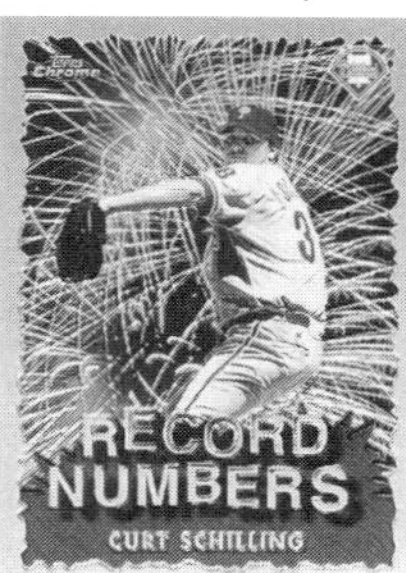

		MT
Complete Set (10):		45.00
Common Player:		1.00
Inserted 1:36		
Refractors:		1.5X
Inserted 1:144		
1	Mark McGwire	8.00
2	Craig Biggio	1.00
3	Barry Bonds	5.00
4	Ken Griffey Jr.	8.00
5	Sammy Sosa	5.00
6	Alex Rodriguez	8.00
7	Kerry Wood	1.50
8	Roger Clemens	4.00
9	Cal Ripken Jr.	10.00
10	Mark McGwire	8.00

1999 Topps Chrome Traded and Rookies

Actually issued in 2000, this parallel of the Topps Traded set utilizing Chromium technology was issued only in complete set form.

		MT
Complete Set (121):		135.00
Common Player:		.25
1	Seth Etherton	.25
2	*Mark Harriger*	.75
3	*Matt Wise*	.50
4	*Carlos Hernandez*	.75
5	*Julio Lugo*	2.50
6	Mike Nannini	.50
7	*Justin Bowles*	.25
8	*Mark Mulder*	6.00
9	*Roberto Vaz*	.50
10	*Felipe Lopez*	5.00
11	Matt Belisle	.25
12	Micah Bowie	.25
13	*Ruben Quevedo*	1.50
14	*Jose Garcia*	.50

15 *David Kelton* 3.00
16 Phillip Norton .25
17 *Corey Patterson* 10.00
18 *Ron Walker* .25
19 *Paul Hoover* .50
20 *Ryan Rupe* .75
21 *J.D. Closser* 1.00
22 *Rob Ryan* .50
23 *Steve Colyer* .50
24 *Bubba Crosby* .75
25 *Luke Prokopec* 1.25
26 *Matt Blank* .75
27 Josh McKinley .25
28 Nate Bump .25
29 *Giuseppe Chiaramonte* .75
30 Arturo McDowell .25
31 Tony Torcato .50
32 Dave Roberts .25
33 *C.C. Sabathia* 8.00
34 *Sean Spencer* .75
35 Chip Ambres .25
36 A.J. Burnett 4.00
37 *Mo Bruce* .75
38 Jason Tyner .50
39 Mamon Tucker .25
40 *Sean Burroughs* 12.00
41 *Kevin Eberwein* .75
42 *Junior Herndon* .75
43 *Bryan Wolff* .50
44 Pat Burrell 10.00
45 Eric Valent 1.00
46 *Carlos Pena* 10.00
47 Mike Zywica .25
48 Adam Everett .25
49 *Juan Pena* 1.50
50 *Adam Dunn* 25.00
51 Austin Kearns 8.00
52 *Jacobo Sequea* .50
53 Choo Freeman .25
54 Jeff Winchester .25
55 Matt Burch .25
56 Chris George 1.50
57 *Scott Mullen* .75
58 Kit Pellow .25
59 *Mark Quinn* 2.00
60 Nate Cornejo 1.50
61 *Ryan Mills* .50
62 *Kevin Beirne* .50
63 *Kip Wells* 1.50
64 *Juan Rivera* 5.00
65 *Alfonso Soriano* 30.00
66 *Josh Hamilton* 10.00
67 *Josh Girdley* 1.00
68 *Kyle Snyder* .50
69 *Mike Paradis* .50
70 *Jason Jennings* 3.00
71 *David Walling* 1.00
72 *Omar Ortiz* .50
73 *Jay Gehrke* .50
74 *Casey Burns* .50
75 *Carl Crawford* 7.00
76 Reggie Sanders .25
77 Will Clark .75
78 David Wells .50
79 Paul Konerko .50
80 Armando Benitez .25
81 Brant Brown .25
82 Mo Vaughn 1.00
83 Jose Canseco 1.50
84 Albert Belle .75
85 Dean Palmer .25
86 Greg Vaughn .25
87 Mark Clark .25
88 Pat Meares .25
89 Eric Davis .25
90 Brian Giles .25
91 Jeff Brantley .25
92 Bret Boone .50
93 Ron Gant .25
94 Mike Cameron .25
95 Charles Johnson .25
96 Denny Neagle .25
97 Brian Hunter .25
98 Jose Hernandez .25
99 Rick Aguilera .25
100 Tony Batista .25
101 Roger Cedeno .25
102 Creighton Gubanich .25
103 Tim Belcher .25
104 Bruce Aven .25
105 *Brian Daubach* 1.50
106 Ed Sprague .25
107 Michael Tucker .25
108 Homer Bush .25
109 Armando Reynoso .25
110 Brook Fordyce .25
111 Matt Mantei .25
112 Jose Guillen .25
113 Kenny Rogers .25
114 Livan Hernandez .25
115 Butch Huskey .25
116 David Segui .25
117 Darryl Hamilton .25
118 Jim Leyritz .25
119 Randy Velarde .25
120 Bill Taylor .25
121 Kevin Appier .25

1999 Topps Gallery

This 150-card base set features a white textured border surrounding the player image with the player's name, team name and Topps Gallery logo stamped in gold foil. The first 100 cards in the set portray veteran players while the final 50 cards are short-printed in three subsets: Masters, Artisans and Apprentices. Card backs have a monthly batting or pitching record from the '98 season, a player photo and vital information.

	MT
Complete Set (150):	100.00
Common Player (1-100):	.15
Common Player (101-150):	.50
Player's Private Issue:	5X
PPI SPs:	3X
Production 250 sets	
Pack (6):	3.00
Wax Box (24):	60.00

1 Mark McGwire 2.50
2 Jim Thome .15
3 Bernie Williams .45
4 Larry Walker .60
5 Juan Gonzalez 1.00
6 Ken Griffey Jr. 2.00
7 Raul Mondesi .35
8 Sammy Sosa 1.50
9 Greg Maddux 1.25
10 Jeff Bagwell 1.00
11 Vladimir Guerrero 1.00
12 Scott Rolen 1.00
13 Nomar Garciaparra 1.50
14 Mike Piazza 2.00
15 Travis Lee .45
16 Carlos Delgado .40
17 Darin Erstad .50
18 David Justice .40
19 Cal Ripken Jr. 2.50
20 Derek Jeter 2.50
21 Tony Clark .15
22 Barry Larkin .25
23 Greg Vaughn .15
24 Jeff Kent .15
25 Wade Boggs .75
26 Andres Galarraga .15
27 Ken Caminiti .15
28 Jason Kendall .15
29 Todd Helton 1.00
30 Chuck Knoblauch .15
31 Roger Clemens 1.25
32 Jeromy Burnitz .15
33 Javy Lopez .15
34 Roberto Alomar .75
35 Eric Karros .15
36 Ben Grieve .50
37 Eric Davis .15
38 Rondell White .25
39 Dmitri Young .15
40 Ivan Rodriguez .75
41 Paul O'Neill .15
42 Jeff Cirillo .15
43 Kerry Wood .50
44 Albert Belle .45
45 Frank Thomas 1.00
46 Manny Ramirez 1.00
47 Tom Glavine .25
48 Mo Vaughn .75
49 Jose Cruz Jr. .25
50 Sandy Alomar .15
51 Edgar Martinez .15
52 John Olerud .15
53 Todd Walker .15
54 Tim Salmon .40
55 Derek Bell .15
56 Matt Williams .45
57 Alex Rodriguez 2.00
58 Rusty Greer .15
59 Vinny Castilla .15
60 Jason Giambi .50
61 Mark Grace .40
62 Jose Canseco .75
63 Gary Sheffield .40
64 Brad Fullmer .15
65 Trevor Hoffman .15
66 Mark Kotsay .15
67 Mike Mussina .75
68 Johnny Damon .25
69 Tino Martinez .15
70 Curt Schilling .35
71 Jay Buhner .15
72 Kenny Lofton .15
73 Randy Johnson .75
74 Kevin Brown .35
75 Brian Jordan .15
76 Craig Biggio .25
77 Barry Bonds 1.50
78 Tony Gwynn 1.25
79 Jim Edmonds .15
80 Shawn Green .45
81 Todd Hundley .15
82 Cliff Floyd .15
83 Jose Guillen .15
84 Dante Bichette .15
85 Moises Alou .40
86 Chipper Jones 1.75
87 Ray Lankford .15
88 Fred McGriff .15
89 Rod Beck .15
90 Dean Palmer .15
91 Pedro Martinez .75
92 Andruw Jones 1.00
93 Robin Ventura .15
94 Ugueth Urbina .15
95 Orlando Hernandez .45
96 Sean Casey .60
97 Denny Neagle .15
98 Troy Glaus 1.00
99 John Smoltz .25
100 Al Leiter .15
101 Ken Griffey Jr. 5.00
102 Frank Thomas 3.50
103 Mark McGwire 6.00
104 Sammy Sosa 3.50
105 Chipper Jones 4.00
106 Alex Rodriguez 5.00
107 Nomar Garciaparra 3.50
108 Juan Gonzalez 2.50
109 Derek Jeter 4.00
110 Mike Piazza 4.00
111 Barry Bonds 3.50
112 Tony Gwynn 3.00
113 Cal Ripken Jr. 6.00
114 Greg Maddux 3.00
115 Roger Clemens 3.00
116 Brad Fullmer .50
117 Kerry Wood 1.50
118 Ben Grieve 1.00
119 Todd Helton 1.00
120 Kevin Millwood .75
121 Sean Casey 1.25
122 Vladimir Guerrero 2.50
123 Travis Lee .75
124 Troy Glaus 2.50
125 Bartolo Colon .50
126 Andruw Jones 2.00
127 Scott Rolen 2.00
128 *Alfonso Soriano* 8.00
129 *Nick Johnson* 8.00
130 *Matt Belisle* 1.00
131 *Jorge Toca* 1.00
132 *Masao Kida* .50
133 *Carlos Pena* 6.00
134 Adrian Beltre .75
135 Eric Chavez .75
136 Carlos Beltran .75
137 Alex Gonzalez .50
138 Ryan Anderson .75
139 Ruben Mateo .50
140 Bruce Chen .50
141 *Pat Burrell* 8.00
142 Michael Barrett .50
143 Carlos Lee .50
144 *Mark Mulder* 3.00
145 *Choo Freeman* .50
146 Gabe Kapler .75
147 Juan Encarnacion .50
148 Jeremy Giambi .50
149 *Jason Tyner* 1.50
150 George Lombard .50
Checklist folder 1 (1:3 packs) .10
Checklist folder 2 (1:3) .10
Checklist folder 3 (1:3) .10
Checklist folder 4 (1:12) .25
Checklist folder 5 (1:240) 3.00
Checklist folder 6 (1:640) 6.00

1999 Topps Gallery Player's Private Issue

This parallel to the 150 regular cards in 1999 Gallery is limited to 250 serially numbered cards of each. Stated odds of insertion were one per 17 packs.

	MT
Common Player:	1.00
Stars:	5X
SPs (101-127):	3X
Production 250 sets	

(See 1999 Topps Gallery for checklist and base card values.)

1999 Topps Gallery Press Plates

The aluminum press plates used to print the Gallery cards were inserted at a rate of one per 985 packs. Each card's front and back can be found in four different color variations. Because of the unique nature of each plate, assignment of catalog values in not feasible.

	MT
Common Player:	50.00

(See 1999 Topps Gallery for checklist.)

1999 Topps Gallery Autograph Cards

Three of baseball's top young third baseman are featured in this autographed set, Eric Chavez, Troy Glaus and Adrian Beltre. The insertion odds are 1:209.

	MT
Complete Set (3):	35.00
Common Player:	10.00
Inserted 1:209	
GA1 Troy Glaus	20.00
GA2 Adrian Beltre	10.00
GA3 Eric Chavez	10.00

1999 Topps Gallery Awards Gallery

This 10-card set features players who have earned the highest honors in baseball. Each insert commemorates the player's award by stamping his achievement on the bottom of the card front. Card fronts have silver borders surrounding the player's image. These are seeded 1:12 and card numbers have a "AG" prefix.

	MT
Complete Set (10):	15.00
Common Player:	.50
Inserted 1:12	
AG1 Kerry Wood	1.00
AG2 Ben Grieve	.75
AG3 Roger Clemens	2.00
AG4 Tom Glavine	.50
AG5 Juan Gonzalez	1.50
AG6 Sammy Sosa	2.50
AG7 Ken Griffey Jr.	4.00
AG8 Mark McGwire	4.00
AG9 Bernie Williams	.50
AG10Larry Walker	.60

1999 Topps Gallery Exhibitions

This 20-card set is done on textured 24-point stock and features baseball's top stars. Exhibitions are seeded 1:48 packs.

	MT
Complete Set (20):	100.00
Common Player:	2.00
Inserted 1:48	
E1 Sammy Sosa	8.00
E2 Mark McGwire	12.00
E3 Greg Maddux	8.00
E4 Roger Clemens	5.00
E5 Ben Grieve	2.50
E6 Kerry Wood	2.50
E7 Ken Griffey Jr.	12.00
E8 Tony Gwynn	4.00
E9 Cal Ripken Jr.	15.00
E10 Frank Thomas	5.00
E11 Jeff Bagwell	4.00
E12 Derek Jeter	15.00
E13 Alex Rodriguez	10.00
E14 Nomar Garciaparra	8.00
E15 Manny Ramirez	4.00
E16 Vladimir Guerrero	4.00
E17 Darin Erstad	2.50
E18 Scott Rolen	3.00
E19 Mike Piazza	10.00
E20 Andres Galarraga	2.00

1999 Topps Gallery Gallery of Heroes

This 10-card set is done on card stock that simulates medieval stained glass. Gallery of Heroes are found 1:24 packs.

	MT
Complete Set (10):	45.00
Common Player:	1.50
Inserted 1:24	
GH1 Mark McGwire	8.00
GH2 Sammy Sosa	5.00
GH3 Ken Griffey Jr.	8.00
GH4 Mike Piazza	8.00
GH5 Derek Jeter	10.00
GH6 Nomar Garciaparra	5.00
GH7 Kerry Wood	2.50
GH8 Ben Grieve	1.50
GH9 Chipper Jones	5.00
GH10Alex Rodriguez	8.00

1999 Topps Gallery Heritage

Nineteen contemporary legends and Hall-of-Famer Hank Aaron are artistically depicted using the 1953 Topps design as a template. For a chance to bid on the original art used in the development of this insert set, collectors were able to enter the Topps Gallery Auction. Collectors could accumulate auction points found in Topps Gallery packs. Heritages are seeded 1:12 packs. A parallel called Heritage Proofs are also randomly inserted 1:48 packs and have a chrome styrene finish.

	MT
Complete Set (20):	300.00
Common Player:	7.50
Inserted 1:12	
Heritage Proofs:	1.5X
Inserted 1:48	
TH1 Hank Aaron	30.00
TH2 Ben Grieve	8.00
TH3 Nomar Garciaparra	20.00
TH4 Roger Clemens	15.00
TH5 Travis Lee	8.00
TH6 Tony Gwynn	15.00
TH7 Alex Rodriguez	25.00
TH8 Ken Griffey Jr.	25.00
TH9 Derek Jeter	40.00
TH10Sammy Sosa	20.00
TH11Scott Rolen	7.50
TH12Chipper Jones	20.00
TH13Cal Ripken Jr.	40.00
TH14Kerry Wood	7.50
TH15Barry Bonds	15.00
TH16Juan Gonzalez	10.00
TH17Mike Piazza	20.00
TH18Greg Maddux	15.00
TH19Frank Thomas	15.00
TH20Mark McGwire	30.00

1999 Topps Gallery Heritage Lithographs

Eight of the paintings used to create the Heritage inserts for 1999 Topps Gallery were reproduced as enlarged limited-edition offset lithographs. The paintings of Bill Purdom and James Fiorentino were reproduced in an 18" x 25" serially-numbered, artist-signed edition of 600 pieces each. The lithos were offered through Bill Goff Inc / Good Sports at $60 each unframed.

	MT
Complete Set (8):	480.00
Single Player:	60.00
(1) Roger Clemens	60.00
(2) Nomar Garciaparra	60.00
(3) Ken Griffey Jr.	60.00
(4) Derek Jeter	60.00
(5) Mark McGwire	60.00
(6) Mike Piazza	60.00
(7) Cal Ripken Jr.	60.00
(8) Sammy Sosa	60.00

1999 Topps Gallery Heritage Proofs

Heritage Proofs are a parallel to the 1953-style inserts. Printed on chrome styrene, the proofs have a silver metallic background on front and the notation on bottom-back, "1953 TOPPS HERITAGE PROOF". The proof versions are found on average of one per 48 packs.

	MT
Complete Set (20):	400.00
Common Player:	10.00
TH1 Hank Aaron	50.00
TH2 Ben Grieve	10.00
TH3 Nomar Garciaparra	25.00
TH4 Roger Clemens	20.00
TH5 Travis Lee	10.00
TH6 Tony Gwynn	20.00
TH7 Alex Rodriguez	40.00
TH8 Ken Griffey Jr.	40.00
TH9 Derek Jeter	30.00
TH10Sammy Sosa	25.00
TH11Scott Rolen	10.00
TH12Chipper Jones	30.00
TH13Cal Ripken Jr.	50.00
TH14Kerry Wood	10.00
TH15Barry Bonds	25.00
TH16Juan Gonzalez	15.00
TH17Mike Piazza	30.00
TH18Greg Maddux	20.00
TH19Frank Thomas	25.00
TH20Mark McGwire	50.00

1999 Topps Gold Label Class 1

This set consists of 100 cards on 35-point

spectral-reflective rainbow stock with gold foil stamping. All cards are available in three versions each with the same foreground photo, but with different background photos that vary by category: Class 1 (fielding), Class 2 (running, 1:2), Class 3 (hitting, 1:4), In addition each variation has a different version of the player's team logo in the background. Variations for pitchers are Class 1, set position; Class 2, wind-up, and Class 3, throwing. Black Label parallels were inserted at the rate of between 1:8 and 1:12, depending on packaging. Red Label parallels, serially numbered to 100 each were inserted at rates from 1:118 to 1:148. A One to One parallel version also exists and is limited to one numbered card for each variation and color (Gold, Black and Red), for a total of 900 cards inserted about one per 1,500 packs.

		MT
Complete Set (100):		45.00
Common Gold Label:		.15
Common Black Label:		.50
Black Label Stars:		4X
Common Red Label:		4.00
Red Label Stars:		12X
Pack (5):		3.00
Wax Box (24):		60.00
1	Mike Piazza	2.00
2	Andres Galarraga	.15
3	Mark Grace	.45
4	Tony Clark	.15
5	Jim Thome	.15
6	Tony Gwynn	1.50
7	*Kelly Dransfeldt*	.50
8	Eric Chavez	.50
9	Brian Jordan	.15
10	Todd Hundley	.15
11	Rondell White	.25
12	Dmitri Young	.15
13	Jeff Kent	.15
14	Derek Bell	.15
15	Todd Helton	1.25
16	Chipper Jones	2.00
17	Albert Belle	.50
18	Barry Larkin	.25
19	Dante Bichette	.15
20	Gary Sheffield	.45
21	Cliff Floyd	.15
22	Derek Jeter	3.00
23	Jason Giambi	.60
24	Ray Lankford	.15
25	Alex Rodriguez	2.50
26	Ruben Mateo	.15
27	Wade Boggs	.75
28	Carlos Delgado	.50
29	Tim Salmon	.35
30	*Alfonso Soriano*	6.00
31	Javy Lopez	.15
32	Jason Kendall	.15
33	*Nick Johnson*	4.00
34	*A.J. Burnett*	2.00
35	Troy Glaus	1.00
36	*Pat Burrell*	6.00
37	Jeff Cirillo	.15
38	David Justice	.40
39	Ivan Rodriguez	1.00
40	Bernie Williams	.50
41	Jay Buhner	.15
42	Mo Vaughn	.75
43	Randy Johnson	1.25
44	Pedro Martinez	1.00
45	Larry Walker	.50
46	Todd Walker	.15
47	Roberto Alomar	1.00
48	Kevin Brown	.30
49	Mike Mussina	1.00
50	Tom Glavine	.25
51	Curt Schilling	.25
52	Ken Caminiti	.15
53	Brad Fullmer	.15
54	*Bobby Seay*	.50
55	Orlando Hernandez	.50
56	Sean Casey	.50
57	Al Leiter	.15
58	Sandy Alomar	.15
59	Mark Kotsay	.15
60	Matt Williams	.45
61	Raul Mondesi	.35
62	*Joe Crede*	3.00
63	Jim Edmonds	.15
64	Jose Cruz Jr.	.25
65	Juan Gonzalez	1.25
66	Sammy Sosa	1.50
67	Cal Ripken Jr.	3.00
68	Vinny Castilla	.15
69	Craig Biggio	.25
70	Mark McGwire	3.00
71	Greg Vaughn	.15
72	Greg Maddux	1.50
73	Paul O'Neill	.15
74	Scott Rolen	1.00
75	Ben Grieve	.50
76	Vladimir Guerrero	1.25
77	John Olerud	.15
78	Eric Karros	.15
79	Jeromy Burnitz	.15
80	Jeff Bagwell	1.25
81	Kenny Lofton	.15
82	Manny Ramirez	1.25
83	Andruw Jones	1.25
84	Travis Lee	.25
85	Darin Erstad	.40
86	Nomar Garciaparra	1.75
87	Frank Thomas	1.25
88	Moises Alou	.35
89	Tino Martinez	.15
90	*Carlos Pena*	5.00
91	Shawn Green	.50
92	Rusty Greer	.15
93	*Matt Belisle*	.50
94	Adrian Beltre	.40
95	Roger Clemens	1.50
96	John Smoltz	.25
97	*Mark Mulder*	4.00
98	Kerry Wood	.75
99	Barry Bonds	1.75
100	Ken Griffey Jr.	2.50
	Checklist folder	.05

1999 Topps Gold Label Class 2

Background photos for Class 2 Gold Label and color parallels show position players running and pitchers in their windup. Class 2 Gold Label cards are inserted at the rate of one in two Home Team Advantage packs, and one in four retail packs. Black Label versions are inserted 1:16 HTA and 1:24 R. Red Labels, numbered to 50 each, are found in HTA at a 1:237 rate, and in retail at 1:296.

	MT
Complete Set (100):	120.00
Common Gold Label:	.30
Gold Label Stars:	2X
Common Black Label:	2.00
Black Label Stars:	4X
Common Red Label:	6.00
Red Label Stars:	24X

(See 1999 Topps Gold Label Class 1 for checklist and base card values.)

1999 Topps Gold Label Class 3

Background photos for Class 3 Gold Label and color parallels show position players hitting and pitchers pitching. Class 3 Gold Label cards are inserted at the rate of one in four Home Team Advantage packs, and one in eight retail packs. Black Label versions are inserted 1:32 HTA and 1:48 R. Red Labels, numbered to 25 each, are found in HTA at a 1:473 rate, and in retail at 1:591.

	MT
Complete Set (100):	200.00
Common Gold Label:	.50
Gold Label Stars:	3X
Common Black Label:	3.00
Black Label Stars:	8X
Common Red Label:	12.00
Red Label Stars:	35X

(See 1999 Topps Gold Label Class 1 for checklist and base card values.)

1999 Topps Gold Label One to One

Depending on type of packaging, these rare parallels are found at the rate of only one per approximately 1,200-1,600 packs. Each of the three Classes in Gold, Red and Black versions can be found as a One to One insert, for a total of nine "unique" cards for each player in the base set and three in the Race to Aaron insert series. Backs of the One to One cards are printed in silver foil with a "1/1" foil serial number.

	MT
Common Player, Base Set:	50.00
Common Player, Race to Aaron:	150.00

(Star/rookie card values cannot be determined due to scarcity.)

1999 Topps Gold Label Race to Aaron

This 10-card set features the best current players who are chasing Hank Aaron's career home run and career RBI records. Each player is pictured in the foreground with Aaron silhouetted in the background on the card front. These are seeded 1:12 packs. Two parallel versions also exist: Black and Red. Blacks have black foil stamping and are seeded 1:48 packs. Reds have red foil stamping and are limited to 44 sequentially numbered sets.

		MT
Complete Set (10):		60.00
Common Player:		2.00
Blacks:		2X
Reds:		20X
1	Mark McGwire	12.00
2	Ken Griffey Jr.	10.00
3	Alex Rodriguez	10.00
4	Vladimir Guerrero	2.50
5	Albert Belle	2.00
6	Nomar Garciaparra	8.00
7	Ken Griffey Jr.	10.00
8	Alex Rodriguez	10.00
9	Juan Gonzalez	2.50
10	Barry Bonds	6.00

1999 Topps Stars

Topps Stars consists of 180 cards on 20-point stock with foil stamping and metallic inks. The set is comprised of 150 base cards and 30 subset cards: Luminaries and Supernovas. Packs contain six cards; three base cards, two One-Star cards and one Two-Star card on the average.

		MT
Complete Set (180):		75.00
Common Player:		.15
Pack (6):		3.00
Wax Box (24):		65.00
1	Ken Griffey Jr.	3.50
2	Chipper Jones	3.00
3	Mike Piazza	3.00
4	Nomar Garciaparra	2.50
5	Derek Jeter	4.00
6	Frank Thomas	1.50
7	Ben Grieve	.60
8	Mark McGwire	4.00
9	Sammy Sosa	2.50
10	Alex Rodriguez	3.50
11	Troy Glaus	1.25
12	Eric Chavez	.50
13	Kerry Wood	.50
14	Barry Bonds	2.50
15	Vladimir Guerrero	1.25
16	Albert Belle	.45
17	Juan Gonzalez	1.25
18	Roger Clemens	2.00
19	Ruben Mateo	.15
20	Cal Ripken Jr.	4.00
21	Darin Erstad	.40
22	Jeff Bagwell	1.25
23	Roy Halladay	.15
24	Todd Helton	.75
25	Michael Barrett	.15
26	Manny Ramirez	1.25
27	Fernando Seguignol	.15
28	*Pat Burrell*	4.00
29	Andruw Jones	1.25
30	Randy Johnson	1.00
31	Jose Canseco	.75
32	Brad Fullmer	.15
33	*Alex Escobar*	1.00
34	*Alfonso Soriano*	5.00
35	Larry Walker	.60
36	Matt Clement	.15
37	Mo Vaughn	.50
38	Bruce Chen	.15
39	Travis Lee	.40
40	Adrian Beltre	.40
41	Alex Gonzalez	.15
42	*Jason Tyner*	.50
43	George Lombard	.15
44	Scott Rolen	1.00
45	*Mark Mulder*	3.00
46	Gabe Kapler	.50
47	*Choo Freeman*	.25
48	Tony Gwynn	1.50
49	*A.J. Burnett*	1.00
50	*Matt Belisle*	.40
51	Greg Maddux	2.00
52	John Smoltz	.25
53	Mark Grace	.40
54	Wade Boggs	.65
55	Bernie Williams	.40
56	Pedro Martinez	1.00
57	Barry Larkin	.25
58	Orlando Hernandez	.25
59	Jason Kendall	.15
60	Mark Kotsay	.15
61	Jim Thome	.15
62	Gary Sheffield	.40
63	Preston Wilson	.15
64	Rafael Palmeiro	.35
65	David Wells	.15
66	Shawn Green	.45
67	Tom Glavine	.25
68	Jeromy Burnitz	.15
69	Kevin Brown	.25
70	Rondell White	.25
71	Roberto Alomar	.75
72	Cliff Floyd	.15
73	Craig Biggio	.25
74	Greg Vaughn	.15
75	Ivan Rodriguez	1.00
76	Vinny Castilla	.15
77	Todd Walker	.15
78	Paul Konerko	.25
79	*Andy Brown*	.25
80	Todd Hundley	.15
81	Dmitri Young	.15
82	Tony Clark	.15
83	*Nick Johnson*	2.50
84	Mike Caruso	.15
85	David Ortiz	.15
86	Matt Williams	.45
87	Raul Mondesi	.25
88	Kenny Lofton	.15
89	Miguel Tejada	.35
90	Dante Bichette	.15
91	Jorge Posada	.15
92	Carlos Beltran	.25
93	Carlos Delgado	.35
94	Javy Lopez	.15
95	Aramis Ramirez	.15
96	Neifi Perez	.15
97	Marlon Anderson	.15
98	David Cone	.15
99	Moises Alou	.25
100	John Olerud	.15
101	Tim Salmon	.30
102	Jason Giambi	.60
103	Sandy Alomar	.15
104	Curt Schilling	.25
105	Andres Galarraga	.15
106	Rusty Greer	.15
107	*Bobby Seay*	.25
108	Eric Young	.15
109	Brian Jordan	.15
110	Eric Davis	.15
111	Will Clark	.45
112	Andy Ashby	.15
113	Edgardo Alfonzo	.15
114	Paul O'Neill	.15
115	Denny Neagle	.15
116	Eric Karros	.15
117	Ken Caminiti	.15
118	Garret Anderson	.15
119	Todd Stottlemyre	.15
120	David Justice	.35
121	Francisco Cordova	.15
122	Robin Ventura	.15
123	Mike Mussina	.75
124	Hideki Irabu	.15
125	Justin Thompson	.15
126	Mariano Rivera	.35
127	Delino DeShields	.15
128	Steve Finley	.15
129	Jose Cruz Jr.	.25
130	Ray Lankford	.15
131	Jim Edmonds	.15
132	Charles Johnson	.15
133	Al Leiter	.15
134	Jose Offerman	.15
135	Eric Milton	.15
136	Dean Palmer	.15
137	Johnny Damon	.25
138	Andy Pettitte	.25
139	Ray Durham	.15
140	Ugueth Urbina	.15
141	Marquis Grissom	.15
142	Ryan Klesko	.15
143	Brady Anderson	.15
144	Bobby Higginson	.25
145	Chuck Knoblauch	.15
146	Rickey Henderson	1.00
147	Kevin Millwood	.50
148	Fred McGriff	.15
149	Damion Easley	.15
150	Tino Martinez	.15
151	Greg Maddux (Luminaries)	1.00
152	Scott Rolen (Luminaries)	.50
153	Pat Burrell (Luminaries)	2.00
154	Roger Clemens (Luminaries)	1.00
155	Albert Belle (Luminaries)	.25
156	Troy Glaus (Luminaries)	.65
157	Cal Ripken Jr. (Luminaries)	2.00
158	Alfonso Soriano (Luminaries)	1.00
159	Manny Ramirez (Luminaries)	.65
160	Eric Chavez (Luminaries)	.25
161	Kerry Wood (Luminaries)	.25
162	Tony Gwynn (Luminaries)	1.00
163	Barry Bonds (Luminaries)	1.75
164	Ruben Mateo (Luminaries)	.15
165	Todd Helton (Luminaries)	.25
166	Darin Erstad (Luminaries)	.25
167	Jeff Bagwell (Luminaries)	.65
168	Juan Gonzalez (Luminaries)	.65
169	Mo Vaughn (Luminaries)	.25
170	Vladimir Guerrero (Luminaries)	.65
171	Nomar Garciaparra (Supernovas)	1.25
172	Derek Jeter (Supernovas)	2.00
173	Alex Rodriguez (Supernovas)	1.75
174	Ben Grieve (Supernovas)	.25
175	Mike Piazza (Supernovas)	1.50
176	Chipper Jones (Supernovas)	1.50
177	Frank Thomas (Supernovas)	1.00
178	Ken Griffey Jr. (Supernovas)	1.75
179	Sammy Sosa (Supernovas)	1.25
180	Mark McGwire (Supernovas)	2.00
	Checklist 1 (1-45)	.05
	Checklist 2 (46-136)	.05
	Checklist 3 (137-150, inserts)	.05

1999 Topps Stars One-Star

One-Star inserts include card numbers 1-100 from the base set and have silver foil stamping with one star on the bottom left portion of the card front. These are seeded two per pack. A foil One-Star parallel also is randomly seeded and sequentially numbered to 249 sets. These are a 1:33 pack insert.

		MT
Complete Set (100):		60.00
Common Player:		.25
Foils (249 each):		2X
1	Ken Griffey Jr.	5.00
2	Chipper Jones	4.00
3	Mike Piazza	4.00
4	Nomar Garciaparra	3.50
5	Derek Jeter	6.00
6	Frank Thomas	2.50
7	Ben Grieve	1.00
8	Mark McGwire	5.00
9	Sammy Sosa	3.50
10	Alex Rodriguez	5.00
11	Troy Glaus	2.00
12	Eric Chavez	.75
13	Kerry Wood	.75
14	Barry Bonds	3.50
15	Vladimir Guerrero	2.00
16	Albert Belle	.65
17	Juan Gonzalez	2.00
18	Roger Clemens	3.00
19	Ruben Mateo	.25
20	Cal Ripken Jr.	6.00
21	Darin Erstad	.75
22	Jeff Bagwell	2.00
23	Roy Halladay	.25
24	Todd Helton	1.25
25	Michael Barrett	.25
26	Manny Ramirez	2.00
27	Fernando Seguignol	.25
28	Pat Burrell	5.00
29	Andruw Jones	2.00
30	Randy Johnson	1.50
31	Jose Canseco	1.25
32	Brad Fullmer	.25
33	Alex Escobar	1.25
34	Alfonso Soriano	3.00
35	Larry Walker	1.00
36	Matt Clement	.25
37	Mo Vaughn	.75
38	Bruce Chen	.25
39	Travis Lee	.60
40	Adrian Beltre	.60
41	Alex Gonzalez	.25
42	Jason Tyner	.50
43	George Lombard	.25
44	Scott Rolen	1.50
45	Mark Mulder	3.00
46	Gabe Kapler	.75
47	Choo Freeman	.35
48	Tony Gwynn	3.00
49	A.J. Burnett	1.25
50	Matt Belisle	.50
51	Greg Maddux	3.00
52	John Smoltz	.35
53	Mark Grace	.50
54	Wade Boggs	1.50
55	Bernie Williams	.60
56	Pedro Martinez	1.50
57	Barry Larkin	.35
58	Orlando Hernandez	.40
59	Jason Kendall	.25
60	Mark Kotsay	.25
61	Jim Thome	.25
62	Gary Sheffield	.60
63	Preston Wilson	.25
64	Rafael Palmeiro	.60
65	David Wells	.25
66	Shawn Green	.60
67	Tom Glavine	.35
68	Jeromy Burnitz	.25
69	Kevin Brown	.40
70	Rondell White	.40
71	Roberto Alomar	1.25
72	Cliff Floyd	.25
73	Craig Biggio	.35
74	Greg Vaughn	.25
75	Ivan Rodriguez	1.50
76	Vinny Castilla	.25
77	Todd Walker	.25
78	Paul Konerko	.35
79	Andy Brown	.45
80	Todd Hundley	.25
81	Dmitri Young	.25
82	Tony Clark	.25
83	Nick Johnson	3.00
84	Mike Caruso	.25
85	David Ortiz	.25
86	Matt Williams	.60
87	Raul Mondesi	.40
88	Kenny Lofton	.25
89	Miguel Tejada	.75
90	Dante Bichette	.25
91	Jorge Posada	.25
92	Carlos Beltran	.60
93	Carlos Delgado	.45
94	Javy Lopez	.25
95	Aramis Ramirez	.25
96	Neifi Perez	.25
97	Marlon Anderson	.25
98	David Cone	.25
99	Moises Alou	.35
100	John Olerud	.25

1999 Topps Stars Two-Star

Two-Stars are inserted one per pack and feature light gold metallic inks and foil stamping. Two-Stars include card numbers 1-50 from the base set. A Two-Star foil parallel is also randomly seeded and limited to 199 sequentially numbered sets.

		MT
Complete Set (50):		70.00
Common Player:		.50
Foils:		8X
1	Ken Griffey Jr.	7.50
2	Chipper Jones	6.00
3	Mike Piazza	6.00
4	Nomar Garciaparra	5.00
5	Derek Jeter	8.00
6	Frank Thomas	3.00
7	Ben Grieve	1.50
8	Mark McGwire	6.00

9	Sammy Sosa	5.00
10	Alex Rodriguez	7.50
11	Troy Glaus	3.00
12	Eric Chavez	1.25
13	Kerry Wood	1.50
14	Barry Bonds	5.00
15	Vladimir Guerrero	3.00
16	Albert Belle	.75
17	Juan Gonzalez	3.00
18	Roger Clemens	4.00
19	Ruben Mateo	.50
20	Cal Ripken Jr.	8.00
21	Darin Erstad	1.25
22	Jeff Bagwell	3.00
23	Roy Halladay	.50
24	Todd Helton	2.00
25	Michael Barrett	.50
26	Manny Ramirez	3.00
27	Fernando Seguignol	.50
28	Pat Burrell	7.50
29	Andruw Jones	3.00
30	Randy Johnson	2.50
31	Jose Canseco	2.00
32	Brad Fullmer	.50
33	Alex Escobar	2.00
34	Alfonso Soriano	4.00
35	Larry Walker	2.00
36	Matt Clement	.50
37	Mo Vaughn	2.00
38	Bruce Chen	.50
39	Travis Lee	.50
40	Adrian Beltre	.75
41	Alex Gonzalez	.50
42	Jason Tyner	.50
43	George Lombard	.50
44	Scott Rolen	2.00
45	Mark Mulder	4.00
46	Gabe Kapler	1.50
47	Choo Freeman	.50
48	Tony Gwynn	4.00
49	A.J. Burnett	2.00
50	Matt Belisle	2.00

1999 Topps Stars Three-Star

Three-Star inserts are a partial parallel from the base set including cards 1-20. Inserted 1:5 packs, these cards feature refractive silver foil stamping along with gold metallic inks. A Three-Star parallel also is randomly inserted featuring gold stamping and limited to 99 serial numbered sets, inserted one per 410 packs.

		MT
Complete Set (20):		65.00
Common Player:		1.00
Foils:		12X
1	Ken Griffey Jr.	8.00
2	Chipper Jones	6.50
3	Mike Piazza	6.50
4	Nomar Garciaparra	5.00
5	Derek Jeter	10.00
6	Frank Thomas	4.00
7	Ben Grieve	1.00
8	Mark McGwire	8.00
9	Sammy Sosa	5.00
10	Alex Rodriguez	8.00
11	Troy Glaus	3.00
12	Eric Chavez	1.00
13	Kerry Wood	1.00
14	Barry Bonds	5.00
15	Vladimir Guerrero	3.00
16	Albert Belle	1.00
17	Juan Gonzalez	3.00
18	Roger Clemens	4.00
19	Ruben Mateo	1.00
20	Cal Ripken Jr.	10.00

1999 Topps Stars Four-Star

Four-Star inserts include cards numbered 1-10 from the base set and are seeded 1:10 packs. The cards feature dark metallic inks and refractive foil stamping on front. A Four-Star parallel is also randomly seeded and has gold metallic inks. Sequentially numbered to 49, it is inserted at the rate of one per 650 packs.

		MT
Complete Set (10):		60.00
Common Player:		3.00
Foils:		20X
1	Ken Griffey Jr.	10.00
2	Chipper Jones	7.50
3	Mike Piazza	7.50
4	Nomar Garciaparra	6.00
5	Derek Jeter	12.00
6	Frank Thomas	5.00
7	Ben Grieve	3.00
8	Mark McGwire	10.00
9	Sammy Sosa	6.00
10	Alex Rodriguez	10.00

1999 Topps Stars Foil

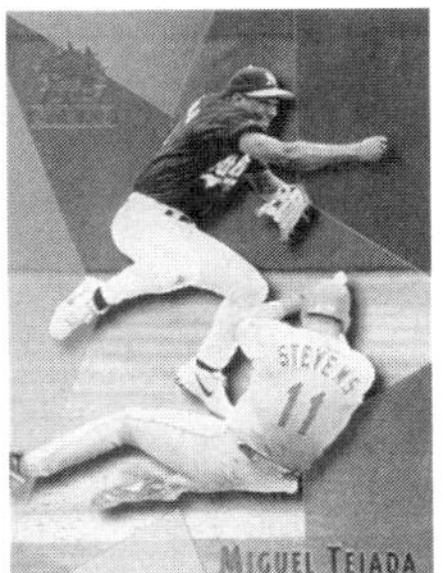

Metallic foil in the background and a serial number on back from within a specific edition identifies this parallel. Stated odds of insertion were one in 15 packs for parallels of the 180 base cards, numbered to 299 each. One-Star foil parallels are numbered to 249 and inserted 1:33. The Two-Star Foils are numbered to 199 each and found on average of one per 82 packs. With insertion odds of 1:410, the Three-Star Foil parallels are numbered within an edition of 99. At the top of the scarcity scale, the Foil Four-Star parallels are sequentially numbered to 49 and are a one per 650-pack find.

	MT
Complete Base Set (180):	125.00
Common Foil Player:	.25
Foil Stars:	4X

(See 1999 Topps Stars for checklist and base card values.)

1999 Topps Stars Bright Futures

This 10-card set features top prospects with a brilliant future ahead of them. Each card features foil stamping and is sequentially numbered to 1,999. Cards have a "BF" prefix to the number. A metallized foil parallel version is also randomly seeded (1:2702) and limited to 30 numbered sets.

		MT
Complete Set (10):		25.00
Common Player:		1.00
Production 1,999 sets		
Foil (30 each):		8X
1	Troy Glaus	4.00
2	Eric Chavez	2.00
3	Adrian Beltre	2.00
4	Michael Barrett	1.00
5	Fernando Seguignol	1.00
6	Alex Gonzalez	1.00
7	Matt Clement	1.00
8	Pat Burrell	7.50
9	Ruben Mateo	1.00
10	Alfonso Soriano	5.00

1999 Topps Stars Galaxy

This 10-card set highlights the top players in baseball with foil stamping and limited to 1,999 numbered sets, inserted at the rate of one per 41 packs. Each card is numbered on the back with a "G" prefix. A Galaxy foil parallel version is randomly seeded (1:2,702) and sequentially numbered to 30 sets.

		MT
Complete Set (10):		60.00
Common Player:		2.00
Production 1,999 sets		
Foil (30 each):		8X
1	Mark McGwire	12.00
2	Roger Clemens	5.00
3	Nomar Garciaparra	6.00
4	Alex Rodriguez	10.00
5	Kerry Wood	2.00
6	Ben Grieve	2.00
7	Derek Jeter	15.00
8	Vladimir Guerrero	4.00
9	Ken Griffey Jr.	10.00
10	Sammy Sosa	8.00

1999 Topps Stars Rookie Reprints

Topps reprinted five Hall of Famers' rookie cards. The rookie reprints are inserted 1:65 packs and limited to 2,500 numbered sets.

		MT
Complete Set (5):		15.00
Common Player:		3.00
Production 2,500 sets		
1	Frank Robinson	3.00
2	Ernie Banks	4.00
3	Yogi Berra	4.00
4	Bob Gibson	3.00
5	Tom Seaver	4.00

1999 Topps Stars Rookie Reprints Autographs

These foil stamped inserts feature the "Topps Certified Autograph Issue" stamp and are inserted 1:406 packs. The Ernie Banks autograph is inserted 1:812 packs.

		MT
Complete Set (5):		250.00
Common Player:		20.00
Inserted 1:406		
Banks inserted 1:812		
1	Frank Robinson	40.00
2	Ernie Banks	50.00
3	Yogi Berra	60.00
4	Bob Gibson	50.00
5	Tom Seaver	75.00

1999 Topps Stars 'N Steel

Using Serilusion technology, each borderless card features a four-colored textured film laminate bonded to a sheet of strong 25-gauge metal. Each pack contains three cards, packaged in a stand-up tri-fold display unit, at an S.R.P. of $9.99. There are two parallels to the 44-card set, Gold and Domed Holographics. Golds are seeded 1:12 packs, Holographics are found every 24 packs.

	MT
Complete Set (44):	50.00
Common Player:	.75
Gold:	2X
Inserted 1:12	
Holographic Dome:	4X
Inserted 1:24	
Pack (3):	5.00
Wax Box (12):	45.00

1	Kerry Wood	1.50
2	Ben Grieve	1.25
3	Chipper Jones	4.50
4	Alex Rodriguez	5.00
5	Mo Vaughn	1.50
6	Bernie Williams	1.25
7	Juan Gonzalez	2.50
8	Vinny Castilla	.75
9	Tony Gwynn	3.00
10	Manny Ramirez	2.50
11	Raul Mondesi	1.00
12	Roger Clemens	3.50
13	Darin Erstad	1.00
14	Barry Bonds	4.00
15	Cal Ripken Jr.	8.00
16	Barry Larkin	.75
17	Scott Rolen	2.00
18	Albert Belle	1.00
19	Craig Biggio	1.00
20	Tony Clark	.75
21	Mark McGwire	6.00
22	Andres Galarraga	.75
23	Kenny Lofton	.75
24	Pedro Martinez	2.00
25	Paul O'Neill	.75
26	Ken Griffey Jr.	6.00
27	Travis Lee	1.00
28	Tim Salmon	1.00
29	Frank Thomas	3.00
30	Larry Walker	1.25
31	Moises Alou	1.00
32	Vladimir Guerrero	2.50
33	Ivan Rodriguez	2.00
34	Derek Jeter	8.00
35	Greg Vaughn	.75
36	Gary Sheffield	1.00
37	Carlos Delgado	1.00
38	Greg Maddux	4.00
39	Sammy Sosa	4.00
40	Mike Piazza	5.00
41	Nomar Garciaparra	4.00
42	Dante Bichette	.75
43	Jeff Bagwell	2.50
44	Jim Thome	.75

1999 Topps Stars 'N Steel Gold Domed Holographics

This parallel edition was inserted at a rate of one per box. Cards are basically the same as the regular-issue, except for the use of holographic foil highlights on front and the presence of a thick plastic dome which covers the front.

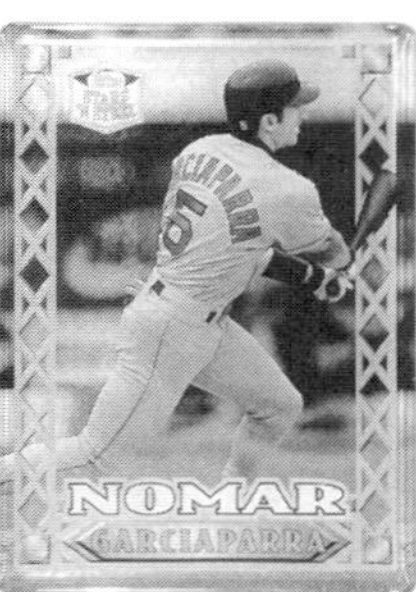

	MT
Complete Set (44):	1500.
Common Player:	6.00
Stars:	4X

(See 1999 Topps Stars 'N Steel for checklist and base card values.)

1999 Topps Super Chrome

Using identical photos from Topps Chrome Baseball, Topps super-sized 36 players to 4-1/8" x 5-3/4" card size. The cards are done on standard chromium technology. Each pack contains three oversized cards and sells for S.R.P. of $4.99. There also is a Refractor parallel set, which are seeded 1:12 packs.

	MT
Complete Set (36):	55.00
Common Player:	.25
Refractors:	2X
Inserted 1:12	
Pack (3):	2.50
Wax Box (12):	25.00

1	Roger Clemens	1.50
2	Andres Galarraga	.25
3	Manny Ramirez	1.25
4	Greg Maddux	1.50
5	Kerry Wood	1.00
6	Travis Lee	.60
7	Nolan Ryan	4.00
8	Juan Gonzalez	1.00
9	Vladimir Guerrero	1.25
10	Sammy Sosa	2.00
11	Mark McGwire	4.00
12	Javy Lopez	.25
13	Tony Gwynn	1.50
14	Derek Jeter	4.00
15	Albert Belle	.50
16	Pedro Martinez	.75
17	Greg Vaughn	.25
18	Ken Griffey Jr.	3.00
19	Ben Grieve	.75
20	Vinny Castilla	.25
21	Moises Alou	.25
22	Barry Bonds	2.50
23	Nomar Garciaparra	2.00
24	Chipper Jones	2.50
25	Mike Piazza	3.00
26	Alex Rodriguez	3.00
27	Ivan Rodriguez	1.00
28	Frank Thomas	1.50
29	Larry Walker	.60
30	Troy Glaus	1.00
31	David Wells (Season Highlight)	.25
32	Roger Clemens (Season Highlight)	.75
33	Kerry Wood (Season Highlight)	.25
34	Mark McGwire (Home Run Record)	2.00
35	Sammy Sosa (Home Run Parade)	1.50
36	World Series	.25

1999 Topps TEK

Topps TEK baseball contains 45 players, with all cards printed on a transparent, 27-point stock. Each player is featured in two different versions (A & B), which are noted on the card back. The versions are differentiated by type of player uniform (home is version A and away uniforms are version B). Each version also has 30 different baseball focused background patterns; as a result every player in the 45-card set has 60 total cards. There also is a Gold parallel set that has a gold design and all versions are paralleled. Each gold card is numbered to 10, with an insertion rate of 1:15 packs.

	MT
Complete Set (45):	50.00
Common Player:	.25
Gold (10 each variation):	7X
Pack (4):	3.00
Wax Box (20):	50.00

1	Ben Grieve	.50
2	Andres Galarraga	.25
3	Travis Lee	.35
4	Larry Walker	.45
5	Ken Griffey Jr.	4.00
6	Sammy Sosa	2.50
7	Mark McGwire	4.00
8	Roberto Alomar	1.00
9	Wade Boggs	.75
10	Troy Glaus	1.00
11	Craig Biggio	.25
12	Kerry Wood	.45
13	Vladimir Guerrero	1.00
14	Albert Belle	.35
15	Mike Piazza	3.00
16	Chipper Jones	2.00
17	Randy Johnson	1.00
18	Adrian Beltre	.35
19	Barry Bonds	2.00
20	Jim Thome	.25
21	Greg Vaughn	.25
22	Scott Rolen	.50
23	Ivan Rodriguez	.75
24	Derek Jeter	5.00
25	Cal Ripken Jr.	5.00
26	Mark Grace	.45
27	Bernie Williams	.45
28	Darin Erstad	.35
29	Eric Chavez	.35
30	Tom Glavine	.35
31	Jeff Bagwell	1.00
32	Manny Ramirez	1.00
33	Tino Martinez	.25
34	Todd Helton	.45
35	Jason Kendall	.25
36	*Pat Burrell*	2.50
37	Tony Gwynn	1.50
38	Nomar Garciaparra	2.50
39	Frank Thomas	1.50
40	Orlando Hernandez	.35
41	Juan Gonzalez	1.00
42	Alex Rodriguez	3.00
43	Greg Maddux	2.00
44	Mo Vaughn	.50
45	Roger Clemens	2.00
	Version A checklist folder (orange)	.05
	Version B checklist folder (green)	.05

1999 Topps TEK Gold

Each of the two player versions on each of the 30 background patterns was paralleled in a gold insert version. Cards share the same front and back designs and photos but feature gold graphics. Each card is serially numbered within an edition of just 10. Insertion rate is one per 15 packs.

	MT
Gold Parallels:	7X

(See 1999 Topps TEK for checklist, base card values.)

1999 Topps TEK Teknicians

This 10-card set focuses on baseball's top stars on a clear, plastic stock utilizing metallic blue, silver and red inks. These are inserted 1:18 packs.

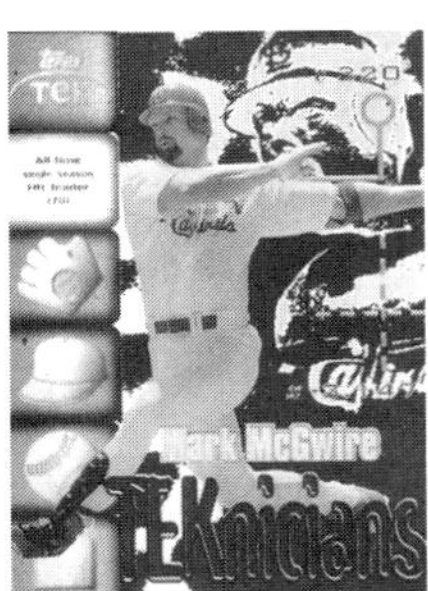

		MT
Complete Set (10):		25.00
Common Player:		1.00
Inserted 1:18		
T1	Ken Griffey Jr.	4.00
T2	Mark McGwire	5.00
T3	Kerry Wood	1.00
T4	Ben Grieve	1.00
T5	Sammy Sosa	3.00
T6	Derek Jeter	6.00
T7	Alex Rodriguez	4.00
T8	Roger Clemens	2.00
T9	Nomar Garciaparra	2.50
T10	Vladimir Guerrero	1.50

1999 Topps TEK Fantastek Phenoms

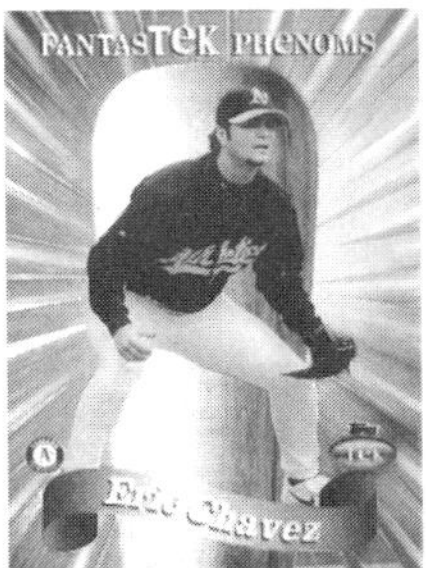

This 10-card set highlights top young prospects on a transparent plastic stock with silver and blue highlighting. These are inserted 1:18 packs.

		MT
Complete Set (10):		22.50
Common Player:		1.00
Inserted 1:18		
F1	Eric Chavez	3.00
F2	Troy Glaus	6.00
F3	Pat Burrell	7.50
F4	Alex Gonzalez	1.00
F5	Carlos Lee	1.00
F6	Ruben Mateo	1.00
F7	Carlos Beltran	1.50
F8	Adrian Beltre	3.00
F9	Bruce Chen	1.00
F10	Ryan Anderson	2.00

2000 Topps

Released in two series the card fronts have a silver border with the Topps logo, player name and position stamped with gold foil. Card backs have complete year-by-year statistics along with a small photo in the upper right portion and the player's vital information. Subsets within the first series 239-card set include Draft Picks, Prospects, Magic Moments, Season Highlights and 20th Century's Best. The Topps MVP promotion is a parallel of 200 of the base cards, excluding subsets, with a special Topps MVP logo. 100 cards of each player was produced and if the featured player is named MVP for a week, collectors win a prize.

		MT
Complete Set (478):		50.00
Complete Series I set (239):		25.00
Complete Series II set (239):		25.00
Common Player:		.10
MVP Stars:		30x to 60x
Yng Stars & RCs:		20x to 40x
Production 100 sets		
5 Versions for 236-240, 475-479		
Pack (11):		1.50
Wax Box (36):		45.00
1	Mark McGwire	2.50
2	Tony Gwynn	1.25
3	Wade Boggs	.25
4	Cal Ripken Jr.	2.00
5	Matt Williams	.25
6	Jay Buhner	.20
7	Not Issued	.10
8	Jeff Conine	.10
9	Todd Greene	.10
10	Mike Lieberthal	.10
11	Steve Avery	.10
12	Bret Saberhagen	.10
13	Magglio Ordonez	.20
14	Brad Radke	.10
15	Derek Jeter	1.25
16	Javy Lopez	.25
17	Russ David	.10
18	Armando Benitez	.10
19	B.J. Surhoff	.10
20	Darryl Kile	.10
21	Mark Lewis	.10
22	Mike Williams	.10
23	Mark McLemore	.10
24	Sterling Hitchcock	.10
25	Darin Erstad	.25
26	Ricky Gutierrez	.10
27	John Jaha	.10
28	Homer Bush	.10
29	Darrin Fletcher	.10
30	Mark Grace	.25
31	Fred McGriff	.25
32	Omar Daal	.10
33	Eric Karros	.20
34	Orlando Cabrera	.10
35	J.T. Snow Jr.	.10
36	Luis Castillo	.10
37	Rey Ordonez	.10
38	Bob Abreu	.10
39	Warren Morris	.10
40	Juan Gonzalez	.60
41	Mike Lansing	.10
42	Chili Davis	.10
43	Dean Palmer	.10
44	Hank Aaron	2.00
45	Jeff Bagwell	.50
46	Jose Valentin	.10
47	Shannon Stewart	.10
48	Kent Bottenfield	.10
49	Jeff Shaw	.10
50	Sammy Sosa	1.25
51	Randy Johnson	.40
52	Benny Agbayani	.10
53	Dante Bichette	.25
54	Pete Harnisch	.10
55	Frank Thomas	.60
56	Jorge Posada	.10
57	Todd Walker	.10
58	Juan Encarnacion	.10
59	Mike Sweeney	.10
60	Pedro Martinez	.60
61	Lee Stevens	.10
62	Brian Giles	.10
63	Chad Ogea	.10
64	Ivan Rodriguez	.50
65	Roger Cedeno	.10
66	David Justice	.20
67	Steve Trachsel	.10
68	Eli Marrero	.10
69	Dave Nilsson	.10
70	Ken Caminiti	.20
71	Tim Raines	.10
72	Brian Jordan	.10
73	Jeff Blauser	.10
74	Bernard Gilkey	.10
75	John Flaherty	.10
76	Brent Mayne	.10
77	Jose Vidro	.10
78	Jeff Fassero	.10
79	Bruce Aven	.10
80	John Olerud	.25
81	Pokey Reese	.10
82	Woody Williams	.10
83	Ed Sprague	.10
84	Joe Girardi	.10
85	Barry Larkin	.40
86	Mike Caruso	.10
87	Bobby Higginson	.10
88	Roberto Kelly	.10
89	Edgar Martinez	.20
90	Mark Kotsay	.10
91	Paul Sorrento	.10
92	Eric Young	.10
93	Carlos Delgado	.40
94	Troy Glaus	.60
95	Ben Grieve	.25
96	Jose Lima	.10
97	Garret Anderson	.10
98	Luis Gonzalez	.10
99	Carl Pavano	.10
100	Alex Rodriguez	1.25
101	Preston Wilson	.10
102	Ron Gant	.10
103	Harold Baines	.10
104	Rickey Henderson	.25
105	Gary Sheffield	.25
106	Mickey Morandini	.10
107	Jim Edmonds	.10
108	Kris Benson	.10
109	Adrian Beltre	.25
110	Alex Fernandez	.10
111	Dan Wilson	.10
112	Mark Clark	.10
113	Greg Vaughn	.25
114	Neifi Perez	.10
115	Paul O'Neill	.25
116	Jermaine Dye	.10
117	Todd Jones	.10
118	Terry Steinbach	.10
119	Greg Norton	.10
120	Curt Schilling	.20
121	Todd Zeile	.10
122	Edgardo Alfonzo	.25
123	Ryan McGuire	.10
124	Stan Javier	.10
125	John Smoltz	.20
126	Bob Wickman	.10
127	Richard Hidalgo	.10
128	Chuck Finley	.10
129	Billy Wagner	.10
130	Todd Hundley	.10
131	Dwight Gooden	.10
132	Russ Ortiz	.10
133	Mike Lowell	.10
134	Reggie Sanders	.10
135	John Valentin	.10
136	Brad Ausmus	.10
137	Chad Kreuter	.10
138	David Cone	.25
139	Brook Fordyce	.10
140	Roberto Alomar	.40
141	Charles Nagy	.10
142	Brian Hunter	.10
143	Mike Mussina	.40
144	Robin Ventura	.25
145	Kevin Brown	.25
146	Pat Hentgen	.10
147	Ryan Klesko	.20
148	Derek Bell	.10
149	Andy Sheets	.10
150	Larry Walker	.40
151	Scott Williamson	.10
152	Jose Offerman	.10
153	Doug Mientkiewicz	.10
154	*John Snyder*	.10
155	Sandy Alomar	.25
156	Joe Nathan	.10
157	Lance Johnson	.10
158	Odalis Perez	.10
159	Hideo Nomo	.25
160	Steve Finley	.10
161	Dave Martinez	.10
162	Matt Walbeck	.10
163	Bill Spiers	.10
164	Fernando Tatis	.25
165	Kenny Lofton	.50
166	Paul Byrd	.10
167	Aaron Sele	.10
168	Eddie Taubensee	.10
169	Reggie Jefferson	.10
170	Roger Clemens	1.00
171	Francisco Cordova	.10
172	Mike Bordick	.10
173	Wally Joyner	.10
174	Marvin Benard	.10
175	Jason Kendall	.10
176	Mike Stanley	.10
177	Chad Allen	.10
178	Carlos Beltran	.15
179	Deivi Cruz	.10
180	Chipper Jones	1.25
181	Vladimir Guerrero	.75
182	Dave Burba	.10
183	Tom Goodwin	.10
184	Brian Daubach	.10
185	Jay Bell	.10
186	Roy Halladay	.10
187	Miguel Tejada	.10
188	Armando Rios	.10
189	Fernando Vina	.10
190	Eric Davis	.10
191	Henry Rodriguez	.10
192	Joe McEwing	.10
193	Jeff Kent	.10
194	Mike Jackson	.10
195	Mike Morgan	.10
196	Jeff Montgomery	.10
197	Jeff Zimmerman	.10
198	Tony Fernandez	.10
199	Jason Giambi	.10
200	Jose Canseco	.50
201	Alex Gonzalez	.10
202	Jack Cust, Mike Colangelo, Dee Brown	.20
203	Felipe Lopez, Alfonso Soriano, Pablo Ozuna	.40
204	Erubiel Durazo, Pat Burrell, Nick Johnson	.50
205	*John Sneed*, Kip Wells, Matt Blank	.40
206	*Josh Kalinowski*,*Michael Tejera*, Chris Mears	.25
207	Roosevelt Brown, Corey Patterson, Lance Berkman	.25
208	Kit Pellow, Kevin Barker, Russ Branyan	.25
209	*B.J. Garbe*, *Larry Bigbie*	1.00
210	Eric Munson ,*Bobby Bradley*	1.00
211	Josh Girdley, Kyle Snyder	.40
212	*Chance Caple*, Jason Jennings	.40
213	*Ryan Christiansen*, *Brett Myers*	1.50
214	*Jason Stumm*, *Rob Purvis*	.50
215	David Walling, Mike Paradis	.40
216	Omar Ortiz, Jay Gehrke	.20
217	David Cone (Season Highlights)	.10
218	Jose Jimenez (Season Highlights)	.10
219	Chris Singleton (Season Highlights)	.10

220	Fernando Tatis (Season Highlights)	.10
221	Todd Helton (Season Highlights)	.20
222	Kevin Millwood (Post-Season Highlights)	.20
223	Todd Pratt (Post-Season Highlights)	.10
224	Orlando Hernandez (Post-Season Highlights)	.20
225	(Post-Season Highlights)	.10
226	(Post-Season Highlights)	.10
227	Bernie Williams (Post-Season Highlights)	.40
228	Mariano Rivera (Post-Season Highlights)	.20
229	Tony Gwynn (20th Century's Best)	.50
230	Wade Boggs (20th Century's Best)	.25
231	Tim Raines (20th Century's Best)	.10
232	Mark McGwire (20th Century's Best)	2.00
233	Rickey Henderson (20th Century's Best)	.25
234	Rickey Henderson (20th Century's Best)	.25
235	Roger Clemens (20th Century's Best)	.50
236	Mark McGwire (Magic Moments)	4.00
237	Hank Aaron (Magic Moments)	3.00
238	Cal Ripken Jr. (Magic Moments)	3.00
239	Wade Boggs (Magic Moments)	.75
240	Tony Gwynn (Magic Moments)	2.00
	Series 1 checklist (1-201)	.05
	Series 1 checklist (202-240, inserts)	.05
241	Tom Glavine	.25
242	David Wells	.10
243	Kevin Appier	.10
244	Troy Percival	.10
245	Ray Lankford	.10
246	Marquis Grissom	.10
247	Randy Winn	.10
248	Miguel Batista	.10
249	Darren Dreifort	.10
250	Barry Bonds	.75
251	Harold Baines	.10
252	Cliff Floyd	.10
253	Freddy Garcia	.20
254	Kenny Rogers	.10
255	Ben Davis	.10
256	Charles Johnson	.10
257	John Burkett	.10
258	Desi Relaford	.10
259	Al Martin	.10
260	Andy Pettitte	.20
261	Carlos Lee	.10
262	Matt Lawton	.10
263	Andy Fox	.10
264	Chan Ho Park	.10
265	Billy Koch	.10
266	Dave Roberts	.10
267	Carl Everett	.20
268	Orel Hershiser	.10
269	Trot Nixon	.10
270	Rusty Greer	.10
271	Will Clark	.25
272	Quilvio Veras	.10
273	Rico Brogna	.10
274	Devon White	.10
275	Tim Hudson	.25
276	Mike Hampton	.10
277	Miguel Cairo	.10
278	Darren Oliver	.10
279	Jeff Cirillo	.10
280	Al Leiter	.20
281	Brant Brown	.10
282	Carlos Febles	.10
283	Pedro Astacio	.10
284	Juan Guzman	.10
285	Orlando Hernandez	.25
286	Paul Konerko	.20
287	Tony Clark	.20
288	Aaron Boone	.10
289	Ismael Valdes	.10
290	Moises Alou	.20
291	Kevin Tapani	.10
292	John Franco	.10
293	Todd Zeile	.20
294	Jason Schmidt	.10
295	Johnny Damon	.10
296	Scott Brosius	.10
297	Travis Fryman	.20
298	Jose Vizcaino	.10
299	Eric Chavez	.20
300	Mike Piazza	1.50
301	Matt Clement	.10
302	Cristian Guzman	.10
303	Darryl Strawberry	.20
304	Jeff Abbott	.10
305	Brett Tomko	.10
306	Mike Lansing	.10
307	Eric Owens	.10
308	Livan Hernandez	.10
309	Rondell White	.20
310	Todd Stottlemyre	.20
311	Chris Carpenter	.10
312	Ken Hill	.10
313	Mark Loretta	.10
314	John Rocker	.10
315	Richie Sexson	.10
316	Ruben Mateo	.25
317	Joe Randa	.10
318	Mike Sirotka	.10
319	Jose Rosado	.10
320	Matt Mantei	.10
321	Kevin Millwood	.20
322	Gary DiSarcina	.10
323	Dustin Hermanson	.10
324	Mike Stanton	.10
325	Kirk Rueter	.10
326	Damian Miller	.10
327	Doug Glanville	.10
328	Scott Rolen	.60
329	Ray Durham	.10
330	Butch Huskey	.10
331	Mariano Rivera	.20
332	Darren Lewis	.10
333	Ramiro Mendoza	.10
334	Mark Grudzielanek	.10
335	Mike Cameron	.10
336	Kelvim Escobar	.10
337	Bret Boone	.10
338	Mo Vaughn	.40
339	Craig Biggio	.40
340	Michael Barrett	.10
341	Marlon Anderson	.10
342	Bobby Jones	.10
343	John Halama	.10
344	Todd Ritchie	.10
345	Chuck Knoblauch	.20
346	Rick Reed	.10
347	Kelly Stinnett	.10
348	Tim Salmon	.20
349	A.J. Hinch	.10
350	Jose Cruz Jr.	.10
351	Roberto Hernandez	.10
352	Edgar Renteria	.10
353	Jose Hernandez	.10
354	Brad Fullmer	.20
355	Trevor Hoffman	.10
356	Troy O'Leary	.10
357	Justin Thompson	.10
358	Kevin Young	.10
359	Hideki Irabu	.10
360	Jim Thome	.25
361	Todd Dunwoody	.10
362	Octavio Dotel	.10
363	Omar Vizquel	.20
364	Raul Mondesi	.20
365	Shane Reynolds	.10
366	Bartolo Colon	.20
367	Chris Widger	.10
368	Gabe Kapler	.20
369	Bill Simas	.10
370	Tino Martinez	.25
371	John Thomson	.10
372	Delino DeShields	.10
373	Carlos Perez	.10
374	Eddie Perez	.10
375	Jeromy Burnitz	.20
376	Jimmy Haynes	.10
377	Travis Lee	.20
378	Darryl Hamilton	.10
379	Jamie Moyer	.10
380	Alex Gonzalez	.10
381	John Wetteland	.10
382	Vinny Castilla	.20
383	Jeff Suppan	.10
384	Chad Curtis	.10
385	Robb Nen	.10
386	Wilson Alvarez	.10
387	Andres Galarraga	.25
388	Mike Remlinger	.10
389	Geoff Jenkins	.20
390	Matt Stairs	.10
391	Bill Mueller	.10
392	Mike Lowell	.10
393	Andy Ashby	.10
394	Ruben Rivera	.10
395	Todd Helton	.25
396	Bernie Williams	.50
397	Royce Clayton	.10
398	Manny Ramirez	.60
399	Kerry Wood	.25
400	Ken Griffey Jr.	2.00
401	Enrique Wilson	.10
402	Joey Hamilton	.10
403	Shawn Estes	.10
404	Ugueth Urbina	.10
405	Albert Belle	.40
406	Rick Helling	.10
407	Steve Parris	.10
408	Eric Milton	.10
409	Dave Mlicki	.10
410	Shawn Green	.50
411	Jaret Wright	.10
412	Tony Womack	.10
413	Vernon Wells	.10
414	Ron Belliard	.10
415	Ellis Burks	.10
416	Scott Erickson	.10
417	Rafael Palmeiro	.30
418	Damion Easley	.10
419	Jamey Wright	.10
420	Corey Koskie	.10
421	Bobby Howry	.10
422	Ricky Ledee	.10
423	Dmitri Young	.10
424	Sidney Ponson	.10
425	Greg Maddux	1.25
426	Jose Guillen	.10
427	Jon Lieber	.10
428	Andy Benes	.20
429	Randy Velarde	.10
430	Sean Casey	.25
431	Torii Hunter	.10
432	Ryan Rupe	.10
433	David Segui	.10
434	Rich Aurilia	.10
435	Nomar Garciaparra	1.50
436	Denny Neagle	.10
437	Ron Coomer	.10
438	Chris Singleton	.10
439	Tony Batista	.10
440	Andruw Jones	.40
441	Adam Piatt, Aubrey Huff, Sean Burroughs (Prospects)	.40
442	Rafael Furcal, Jason Dallero, Travis Dawkins (Prospects)	.25
443	Wilton Veras, Joe Crede, *Mike Lamb* (Prospects)	.10
444	*Julio Zuleta*, Dernell Stenson, Jorge Toca (Prospects)	.10
445	Tim Raines Jr., Gary Mathews Jr., *Garry Maddox Jr.* (Prospects)	.10
446	Matt Riley, Mark Mulder, C.C. Sabathia (Prospects)	.10
447	*Scott Downs*, Chris George, Matt Belisle (Prospects)	.10
448	Doug Mirabelli, Ben Petrick, Jayson Werth (Prospects)	.10
449	Josh Hamilton, *Corey Myers* (Draft Picks)	1.00
450	*Ben Christensen*, Brett Myers (Draft Picks)	.40
451	*Barry Zito*, *Ben Sheets* (Draft Picks)	2.00
452	*Ty Howington*, *Kurt Ainsworth* (Draft Picks)	.25
453	*Rick Asadoorian*, *Vince Faison* (Draft Picks)	.50
454	*Keith Reed*, *Jeff Heaverlo* (Draft Picks)	.25
455	*Mike MacDougal*, Jay Gehrke (Draft Picks)	.25
456	Mark McGwire (Season Highlights)	1.50
457	Cal Ripken Jr. (Season Highlights)	1.00
458	Wade Boggs (Season Highlights)	.25
459	Tony Gwynn (Season Highlights)	.75
460	Jesse Orosco (Season Highlights)	.10
461	Nomar Garciaparra, Larry Walker (League Leaders)	.50
462	Mark McGwire, Ken Griffey Jr. (League Leaders)	.75
463	Mark McGwire, Manny Ramirez (League Leaders)	.75
464	Randy Johnson, Pedro Martinez (League Leaders)	.25
465	Randy Johnson, Pedro Martinez (League Leaders)	.25
466	Luis Gonzalez, Derek Jeter (League Leaders)	.50
467	Manny Ramirez, Larry Walker (League Leaders)	.25
468	Tony Gwynn (20th Century's Best)	1.00
469	Mark McGwire (20th Century's Best)	2.00
470	Frank Thomas (20th Century's Best)	.75
471	Harold Baines (20th Century's Best)	.10
472	Roger Clemens (20th Century's Best)	.75
473	John Franco (20th Century's Best)	.10
474	John Franco (20th Century's Best)	.10
475	Ken Griffey Jr. (Magic Moments)	3.00
476	Barry Bonds (Magic Moments)	1.00
477	Sammy Sosa (Magic Moments)	2.50
478	Derek Jeter (Magic Moments)	2.50
479	Alex Rodriguez (Magic Moments)	2.50

2000 Topps All-Topps Team

This insert set spotlights 10 National League (Series 1) and 10 A.L. (Series 2) players who are deemed the best at their respective position. On front, a Hall of Fame style plaque design features gold-foil highlights. Backs offer stat comparisons to contemporary players and Hall of Fame greats at their position. These were seeded 1:12 packs. Cards are numbered with an "AT" prefix.

		MT
Complete Set (20):		25.00
Common Player:		.50
Inserted 1:12		
1	Greg Maddux	2.00
2	Mike Piazza	2.50
3	Mark McGwire	4.00

4	Craig Biggio	.50
5	Chipper Jones	2.00
6	Barry Larkin	.50
7	Barry Bonds	1.00
8	Andruw Jones	.75
9	Sammy Sosa	2.50
10	Larry Walker	.75
11	Pedro Martinez	1.00
12	Ivan Rodriguez	1.00
13	Rafael Palmeiro	.75
14	Roberto Alomar	.75
15	Cal Ripken Jr.	3.00
16	Derek Jeter	2.50
17	Albert Belle	.75
18	Ken Griffey Jr.	3.00
19	Manny Ramirez	1.00
20	Jose Canseco	1.00

2000 Topps All-Star Rookie Team

		MT
Complete Set (10):		35.00
Common Player:		.50
Inserted 1:36		
1	Mark McGwire	8.00
2	Chuck Knoblauch	1.00
3	Chipper Jones	4.00
4	Cal Ripken Jr.	6.00
5	Manny Ramirez	2.00
6	Jose Canseco	2.00
7	Ken Griffey Jr.	6.00
8	Mike Piazza	5.00
9	Dwight Gooden	.50
10	Billy Wagner	.50

2000 Topps Autographs

Inserted exclusively in Series 1 and 2 hobby packs, each card features the "Topps Certified Autograph Issue" stamp and is autographed on the card front.

		MT
Common Player:		15.00
Group A 1:7,589		
Group B 1:4,553		
Group C 1:518		
Group D 1:911		
Group E 1:1,138		
1	Alex Rodriguez (A)	275.00
2	Tony Gwynn (A)	175.00
3	Vinny Castilla (B)	50.00
4	Sean Casey (B)	20.00
5	Shawn Green (C)	50.00
6	Rey Ordonez (C)	20.00
7	Matt Lawton (C)	15.00
8	Tony Womack (C)	15.00
9	Gabe Kapler (D)	20.00
10	Pat Burrell (D)	50.00
11	Preston Wilson (D)	25.00
12	Troy Glaus (D)	30.00
13	Carlos Beltran (D)	15.00
14	Josh Girdley (E)	15.00
15	B.J. Garbe (E)	25.00
16	Derek Jeter (A)	200.00
17	Cal Ripken Jr. (A)	250.00
18	Ivan Rodriguez (B)	75.00
19	Rafael Palmeiro (B)	50.00
20	Vladimir Guerrero (E)	80.00
21	Raul Mondesi (C)	20.00
22	Scott Rolen (C)	40.00
23	Billy Wagner (C)	15.00
24	Fernando Tatis (C)	15.00
25	Ruben Mateo (D)	15.00
26	Carlos Febles (D)	15.00
27	Mike Sweeney (E)	20.00
28	Alex Gonzalez (D)	15.00
29	Miguel Tejada (D)	20.00
30	Josh Hamilton (E)	40.00

2000 Topps Century Best

		MT
Common Player:		15.00
Ser. 1 1:869 H		
Ser. 2 1:362		
CB1	Tony Gwynn (339)	80.00
CB2	Wade Boggs (578)	35.00
CB3	Lance Johnson (117)	20.00
CB4	Mark McGwire (522)	90.00
CB5	Rickey Henderson (1,334)	20.00
CB6	Rickey Henderson (2,103)	15.00
CB7	Roger Clemens (247)	80.00
CB8	Tony Gwynn (3,067)	25.00
CB9	Mark McGwire (587)	90.00
CB10	Frank Thomas (440)	40.00
CB11	Harold Baines (1,583)	15.00
CB12	Roger Clemens (3,316)	25.00
CB13	John Franco (264)	25.00
CB14	John Franco (416)	20.00

2000 Topps Combos

		MT
Complete Set (10):		40.00
Common Player:		1.00
Inserted 1:18		
1	Roberto Alomar, Manny Ramirez, Kenny Lofton, Jim Thome	2.00
2	Tom Glavine, Greg Maddux, John Smoltz	4.00
3	Derek Jeter, Bernie Williams, Tino Martinez	5.00
4	Ivan Rodriguez, Mike Piazza	5.00
5	Nomar Garciaparra, Alex Rodriguez, Derek Jeter	6.00
6	Sammy Sosa, Mark McGwire	8.00
7	Pedro Martinez, Randy Johnson	2.00
8	Barry Bonds, Ken Griffey Jr.	6.00
9	Chipper Jones, Ivan Rodriguez	4.00
10	Cal Ripken Jr., Tony Gwynn, Wade Boggs	6.00

2000 Topps Hands of Gold

This seven-card insert set highlights players who have won at least five gold gloves. Each card is foil stamped and die-cut and is seeded 1:18 packs.

		MT
Complete Set (7):		10.00
Common Player:		.50
Inserted 1:18		
1	Barry Bonds	1.00
2	Ivan Rodriguez	1.00
3	Ken Griffey Jr.	3.00
4	Roberto Alomar	.75
5	Tony Gwynn	2.00
6	Omar Vizquel	.50
7	Greg Maddux	2.00

2000 Topps Hank Aaron Reprints

This 23-card set reprints all of Aaron's 23-regular issued Topps cards and are seeded 1:18 packs.

		MT
Complete Set (23):		120.00
Common Aaron:		6.00
Inserted 1:18		
Autographed:		150.00
1	Hank Aaron - 1954	10.00
2	Hank Aaron - 1955	6.00
3	Hank Aaron - 1956	6.00
4	Hank Aaron - 1957	6.00
5	Hank Aaron - 1958	6.00
6	Hank Aaron - 1959	6.00
7	Hank Aaron - 1960	6.00
8	Hank Aaron - 1961	6.00
9	Hank Aaron - 1962	6.00
10	Hank Aaron - 1963	6.00
11	Hank Aaron - 1964	6.00
12	Hank Aaron - 1965	6.00
13	Hank Aaron - 1966	6.00
14	Hank Aaron - 1967	6.00
15	Hank Aaron - 1968	6.00
16	Hank Aaron - 1969	6.00
17	Hank Aaron - 1970	6.00
18	Hank Aaron - 1971	6.00
19	Hank Aaron - 1972	6.00
20	Hank Aaron - 1973	6.00
21	Hank Aaron - 1974	6.00
22	Hank Aaron - 1975	6.00
23	Hank Aaron - 1976	6.00

2000 Topps Hank Aaron Chrome Reprints

This 23-card set reprints Aaron's regular issued Topps cards utilizing Chromium technology. Each card has a commemorative logo and are seeded 1:72 packs. A Refractor parallel version is also randomly inserted 1:288 packs and have Refractor printed underneathe the number on the card back.

		MT
Complete Set (23):		200.00
Common Aaron:		10.00
Inserted 1:72		
Refractors:		2x to 3x
Inserted 1:288		
1	Hank Aaron - 1954	20.00
2	Hank Aaron - 1955	10.00
3	Hank Aaron - 1956	10.00
4	Hank Aaron - 1957	10.00
5	Hank Aaron - 1958	10.00
6	Hank Aaron - 1959	10.00
7	Hank Aaron - 1960	10.00
8	Hank Aaron - 1961	10.00
9	Hank Aaron - 1962	10.00
10	Hank Aaron - 1963	10.00
11	Hank Aaron - 1964	10.00
12	Hank Aaron - 1965	10.00
13	Hank Aaron - 1966	10.00
14	Hank Aaron - 1967	10.00
15	Hank Aaron - 1968	10.00
16	Hank Aaron -1969	10.00
17	Hank Aaron - 1970	10.00

18	Hank Aaron -1971	10.00
19	Hank Aaron - 1972	10.00
20	Hank Aaron - 1973	10.00
21	Hank Aaron - 1974	10.00
22	Hank Aaron - 1975	10.00
23	Hank Aaron - 1976	10.00

2000 Topps Mark McGwire 1985 Rookie Reprint

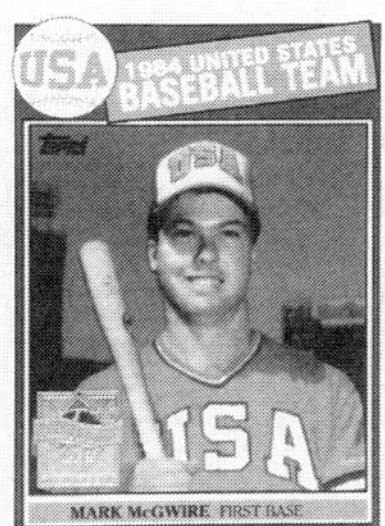

This insert pays tribute to baseball reigning single season home run record holder by reprinting his '85 Topps Rookie card. Card fronts have a commemorative gold stamp and is seeded 1:36 packs.

		MT
Complete Set (1):		8.00
	Mark McGwire	6.00

2000 Topps Own the Game

		MT
Complete Set (30):		75.00
Common Player:		.75
Inserted 1:12		
1	Derek Jeter	5.00
2	B.J. Surhoff	.75
3	Luis Gonzalez	.75
4	Manny Ramirez	2.00
5	Rafael Palmeiro	1.25
6	Mark McGwire	8.00
7	Mark McGwire	8.00
8	Sammy Sosa	5.00
9	Ken Griffey Jr.	6.00
10	Larry Walker	1.50
11	Nomar Garciaparra	5.00
12	Derek Jeter	5.00
13	Larry Walker	1.50
14	Mark McGwire	8.00
15	Manny Ramirez	2.00
16	Pedro Martinez	2.00
17	Randy Johnson	1.50
18	Kevin Millwood	1.00
19	Pedro Martinez	2.00
20	Randy Johnson	1.50
21	Kevin Brown	1.00
22	Chipper Jones	4.00
23	Ivan Rodriguez	2.00
24	Mariano Rivera	1.00
25	Scott Williamson	.75
26	Carlos Beltran	.75
27	Randy Johnson	1.50
28	Pedro Martinez	2.00
29	Sammy Sosa	5.00
30	Manny Ramirez	2.00

2000 Topps Perennial All-Stars

This 10-card set highlights 10 superstars who have consistently achieved All-Star recognition. Card fronts feature a silver holographic foil throughout, while card backs have the featured player's career All-Star statistics. These were seeded 1:18 packs. Cards are numbered with a "PA" prefix.

		MT
Complete Set (10):		20.00
Common Player:		.50
Inserted 1:18		
1	Ken Griffey Jr.	3.00
2	Derek Jeter	2.50
3	Sammy Sosa	2.50
4	Cal Ripken Jr.	3.00
5	Mike Piazza	2.50
6	Nomar Garciaparra	2.50
7	Jeff Bagwell	1.00
8	Barry Bonds	1.00
9	Alex Rodriguez	3.00
10	Mark McGwire	4.00

2000 Topps Power Players

This 20-card set highlights the top power hitters in the game and are printed on a holographic silver foil front. They are numbered with a "P' prefix and are seeded 1:8 packs.

		MT
Complete Set (20):		25.00
Common Player:		.50
Inserted 1:8		
1	Juan Gonzalez	1.00
2	Ken Griffey Jr.	3.00
3	Mark McGwire	4.00
4	Nomar Garciaparra	2.50
5	Barry Bonds	1.00
6	Mo Vaughn	.75
7	Larry Walker	.75
8	Alex Rodriguez	3.00
9	Jose Canseco	1.00
10	Jeff Bagwell	1.00
11	Manny Ramirez	1.00
12	Albert Belle	.75
13	Frank Thomas	1.50
14	Mike Piazza	2.50
15	Chipper Jones	2.00
16	Sammy Sosa	2.50
17	Vladimir Guerrero	2.00
18	Scott Rolen	1.00
19	Raul Mondesi	.50
20	Derek Jeter	2.50

2000 Topps Stadium Relics

Inserted exclusively in Home-Team Advantage packs, this five-card set features historical baseball stadiums and the autograph of the players who made them sacred. Besides the player autograph, the cards also have a piece of base from the featured stadium embedded into each card. These were seeded 1:165 HTA packs and are numbered with a "SR" prefix.

		MT
Common Player:		75.00
Inserted 1:165 HTA		
1	Don Mattingly	175.00
2	Carl Yastrzemski	100.00
3	Ernie Banks	75.00
4	Johnny Bench	100.00
5	Willie Mays	200.00
6	Mike Schmidt	125.00
7	Lou Brock	75.00
8	Al Kaline	100.00
9	Paul Molitor	75.00
10	Eddie Matthews	90.00

2000 Topps Supers

Each box of Topps foil packs includes one upwrapped box-topper card in an oversize (3-1/2" x 5") format. Except for its size, the super version differs from the same players' issued cards only in the numbering on back which designates each card "x of 8".

		MT
Complete Set (16):		35.00
Common Player:		1.00
Inserted 1:box		
	SERIES 1	
1	Mark McGwire	5.00
2	Hank Aaron	5.00
3	Derek Jeter	3.00
4	Sammy Sosa	3.00
5	Alex Rodriguez	3.00
6	Chipper Jones	4.00
7	Cal Ripken Jr.	4.00
8	Pedro Martinez	2.00
	SERIES 2	
1	Barry Bonds	1.50
2	Orlando Hernandez	1.00
3	Mike Piazza	3.00
4	Manny Ramirez	1.50
5	Ken Griffey Jr.	4.00
6	Rafael Palmeiro	1.00
7	Greg Maddux	2.50
8	Nomar Garciaparra	3.00

2000 Topps 21st Century Topps

Printed on a silver holographic foil front, this 10-card set highlights young players who are poised to thrive into the next millenium. These are seeded 1:18 packs are numbered on the card backs with a "C" prefix.

		MT
Complete Set (10):		10.00
Common Player:		.50
Inserted 1:18		
1	Ben Grieve	.75
2	Alex Gonzalez	.50
3	Derek Jeter	3.00
4	Sean Casey	.75
5	Nomar Garciaparra	3.00
6	Alex Rodriguez	3.00
7	Scott Rolen	1.25
8	Andruw Jones	1.00
9	Vladimir Guerrero	2.00
10	Todd Helton	1.00

2000 Topps Traded and Rookies

		MT
Complete Set (135):		25.00
Common Player:		.10
Unopened Set (136):		30.00
1	Mike MacDougal	.10
2	Andy Tracy	.20
3	Brandon Phillips	.20
4	Brandon Inge	.40
5	Robbie Morrison	.25
6	Josh Pressley	.10
7	Todd Moser	.25
8	Rob Purvis	.50
9	Chance Caple	.10
10	Ben Sheets	1.00
11	Russ Jacobson	.10
12	Brian Cole	.10
13	Brad Baker	.25
14	Alex Cintron	.40
15	Lyle Overbay	.75
16	Mike Edwards	.10
17	Sean McGowan	.25
18	Jose Molina	.25
19	Marcos Castillo	.10
20	Josue Espada	.10
21	Alex Gordon	.10
22	Rob Pugmire	.10
23	Jason Stumm	.40
24	Ty Howington	.40
25	Brett Myers	.40
26	Maicer Izturis	.10
27	John McDonald	.10
28	Wilfredo Rodriguez	.50
29	Carlos Zambrano	.50
30	Alejandro Diaz	.20
31	Geraldo Guzman	.20
32	J.R. House	2.50
33	Elvin Nina	.10
34	Juan Pierre	.50
35	Ben Johnson	.20
36	Jeff Bailey	.20
37	Miguel Olivo	.10
38	Francisco Rodriguez	2.50
39	Tony Pena Jr.	.25
40	Miguel Cabrera	1.25
41	Asdrubal Oropeza	.10
42	Junior Zamora	.10
43	Jovanny Cedeno	.50
44	John Sneed	.10
45	Josh Kalinowski	.10
46	Mike Young	.40
47	Rico Washington	.10
48	Chad Durbin	.40
49	Junior Brignac	.25
50	Carlos Hernandez	.75
51	Cesar Izturis	.75
52	Oscar Salazar	.25
53	Pat Strange	.25
54	Rick Asadoorian	.50
55	Keith Reed	.25
56	Leo Estrella	.10
57	Wascar Serrano	.10
58	Richard Gomez	.25
59	Ramon Santiago	.25
60	Jovanny Sosa	.25
61	Aaron Rowand	.50
62	Junior Guerrero	.25
63	Luis Terrero	.75
64	Brian Sanches	.10
65	Scott Sobkowiak	.25
66	Gary Majewski	.10
67	Barry Zito	1.00
68	Ryan Christianson	.40
69	Cristian Guerrero	1.50
70	Tomas de la Rosa	.10
71	Andrew Beinbrink	.25
72	Ryan Knox	.10
73	Alex Graman	.40
74	Juan Guzman	.10
75	Ruben Salazar	.50
76	Luis Matos	.25
77	Tony Mota	.10
78	Doug Davis	.25
79	Ben Christensen	.25
80	Mike Lamb	.10
81	Adrian Gonzalez (Draft Picks)	1.50
82	Mike Stodolka (Draft Picks)	.25
83	Adam Johnson (Draft Picks)	.25
84	Matt Wheatland (Draft Picks)	.40
85	Corey Smith (Draft Picks)	.50
86	Rocco Baldelli (Draft Picks)	2.00
87	Keith Bucktrot (Draft Picks)	.25
88	Adam Wainwright (Draft Picks)	.50
89	Scott Thorman (Draft Picks)	.50
90	Tripper Johnson (Draft Picks)	.50
91	Jim Edmonds	.25
92	Masato Yoshii	.10
93	Adam Kennedy	.10
94	Darryl Kile	.10
95	Mark McLemore	.10
96	Ricky Gutierrez	.10
97	Juan Gonzalez	.40
98	Melvin Mora	.10
99	Dante Bichette	.25
100	Lee Stevens	.10
101	Roger Cedeno	.10
102	John Olerud	.25
103	Eric Young	.10
104	Mickey Morandini	.10
105	Travis Lee	.10
106	Greg Vaughn	.10
107	Todd Zeile	.10
108	Chuck Finley	.10
109	Ismael Valdes	.10
110	Ron Henika	.10
111	Pat Hentgen	.10
112	Ryan Klesko	.10
113	Derek Bell	.10
114	Hideo Nomo	.40
115	Aaron Sele	.10
116	Fernando Vina	.10
117	Wally Joyner	.10
118	Brian Hunter	.10
119	Joe Girardi	.10
120	Omar Daal	.10
121	Brook Fordyce	.10
122	Jose Valentin	.10
123	Curt Schilling	.10
124	B.J. Surhoff	.10
125	Henry Rodriguez	.10
126	Mike Bordick	.10
127	David Justice	.50
128	Charles Johnson	.10
129	Will Clark	.25
130	Dwight Gooden	.10
131	David Segui	.10
132	Denny Neagle	.10
133	Andy Ashby	.10
134	Bruce Chen	.10
135	Jason Bere	.10

2000 Topps Traded and Rookies Autographs

		MT
Common Player:		5.00
Inserted 1:set		
1	Mike MacDougal	5.00
2	Andy Tracy	5.00
3	Brandon Phillips	5.00
4	Brandon Inge	10.00
5	Robbie Morrison	5.00
6	Josh Pressley	5.00
7	Todd Moser	5.00
8	Rob Purvis	10.00
9	Chance Caple	5.00
10	Ben Sheets	30.00
11	Russ Jacobson	5.00
12	Brian Cole	10.00
13	Brad Baker	10.00
14	Alex Cintron	10.00
15	Lyle Overbay	15.00
16	Mike Edwards	5.00
17	Sean McGowan	8.00
18	Jose Molina	5.00
19	Marcos Castillo	5.00
20	Josue Espada	5.00
21	Alex Gordon	10.00
22	Rob Pugmire	5.00
23	Jason Stumm	10.00
24	Ty Howington	8.00
25	Brett Myers	8.00
26	Maicer Izturis	5.00
27	John McDonald	5.00
28	Wilfredo Rodriguez	12.00
29	Carlos Zambrano	10.00
30	Alejandro Diaz	5.00
31	Geraldo Guzman	5.00
32	J.R. House	50.00
33	Elvin Nina	5.00
34	Juan Pierre	15.00
35	Ben Johnson	10.00
36	Jeff Bailey	5.00
37	Miguel Olivo	5.00
38	Francisco Rodriguez	60.00
39	Tony Pena Jr.	8.00
40	Miguel Cabrera	20.00
41	Asdrubal Oropeza	5.00
42	Junior Zamora	5.00
43	Jovanny Cedeno	20.00
44	John Sneed	5.00
45	Josh Kalinowski	5.00
46	Mike Young	5.00
47	Rico Washington	10.00
48	Chad Durbin	10.00
49	Junior Brignac	5.00
50	Carlos Hernandez	5.00
51	Cesar Izturis	5.00
52	Oscar Salazar	5.00
53	Pat Strange	15.00
54	Rick Asadoorian	25.00
55	Keith Reed	10.00
56	Leo Estrella	5.00
57	Wascar Serrano	10.00
58	Richard Gomez	10.00
59	Ramon Santiago	10.00
60	Jovanny Sosa	8.00
61	Aaron Rowand	15.00
62	Junior Guerrero	5.00
63	Luis Terrero	5.00
64	Brian Sanches	5.00
65	Scott Sobkowiak	5.00
66	Gary Majewski	5.00
67	Barry Zito	50.00
68	Ryan Christianson	8.00
69	Cristian Guerrero	50.00
70	Tomas de la Rosa	5.00
71	Andrew Beinbrink	5.00
72	Ryan Knox	5.00
73	Alex Graman	10.00
74	Juan Guzman	5.00
75	Ruben Salazar	15.00
76	Luis Matos	10.00
77	Tony Mota	5.00
78	Doug Davis	5.00
79	Ben Christensen	15.00
80	Mike Lamb	10.00

2000 Topps Chrome

The base set consists of 478 cards utilizing Topps Chromium technology and features the same photos and basic design as the 2000 Topps base set. Subsets include Prospects, Draft Picks, 20th Century's Best, Magic Moments and Post Season Highlights. A parallel Refractor version is also available 1:12 packs.

		MT
Complete Set (478):		300.00
Complete Series I Set (239):		150.00
Complete Series II Set (239):		160.00
Common Player:		.40
5 versions for #236-240, 475-479		
Pack (4):		3.00
Wax Box (24):		65.00
1	Mark McGwire	8.00
2	Tony Gwynn	4.00
3	Wade Boggs	1.00
4	Cal Ripken Jr.	6.00
5	Matt Williams	1.00
6	Jay Buhner	.50
7	Not Issued	
8	Jeff Conine	.40
9	Todd Greene	.40
10	Mike Lieberthal	.40
11	Steve Avery	.40
12	Bret Saberhagen	.40
13	Magglio Ordonez	.40
14	Brad Radke	.40
15	Derek Jeter	5.00
16	Javy Lopez	.50
17	Russ David	.40
18	Armando Benitez	.40
19	B.J. Surhoff	.40
20	Darryl Kile	.40
21	Mark Lewis	.40
22	Mike Williams	.40
23	Mark McLemore	.40
24	Sterling Hitchcock	.40
25	Darin Erstad	.60
26	Ricky Gutierrez	.40
27	John Jaha	.40
28	Homer Bush	.40
29	Darrin Fletcher	.40
30	Mark Grace	.75
31	Fred McGriff	.75
32	Omar Daal	.40
33	Eric Karros	.60
34	Orlando Cabrera	.40
35	J.T. Snow Jr.	.40
36	Luis Castillo	.40
37	Rey Ordonez	.40
38	Bob Abreu	.40
39	Warren Morris	.40
40	Juan Gonzalez	2.00
41	Mike Lansing	.40
42	Chili Davis	.40
43	Dean Palmer	.40
44	Hank Aaron	8.00
45	Jeff Bagwell	2.00
46	Jose Valentin	.40
47	Shannon Stewart	.40
48	Kent Bottenfield	.40
49	Jeff Shaw	.40
50	Sammy Sosa	5.00
51	Randy Johnson	1.50
52	Benny Agbayani	.40
53	Dante Bichette	.75
54	Pete Harnisch	.40
55	Frank Thomas	2.00
56	Jorge Posada	.75
57	Todd Walker	.40
58	Juan Encarnacion	.40

No.	Player	Price
59	Mike Sweeney	.40
60	Pedro Martinez	2.00
61	Lee Stevens	.40
62	Brian Giles	.40
63	Chad Ogea	.40
64	Ivan Rodriguez	2.00
65	Roger Cedeno	.40
66	David Justice	.75
67	Steve Trachsel	.40
68	Eli Marrero	.40
69	Dave Nilsson	.40
70	Ken Caminiti	.60
71	Tim Raines	.40
72	Brian Jordan	.40
73	Jeff Blauser	.40
74	Bernard Gilkey	.40
75	John Flaherty	.40
76	Brent Mayne	.40
77	Jose Vidro	.40
78	Jeff Fassero	.40
79	Bruce Aven	.40
80	John Olerud	.75
81	Juan Guzman	.40
82	Woody Williams	.40
83	Ed Sprague	.40
84	Joe Girardi	.40
85	Barry Larkin	1.00
86	Mike Caruso	.40
87	Bobby Higginson	.40
88	Roberto Kelly	.40
89	Edgar Martinez	.20
90	Mark Kotsay	.40
91	Paul Sorrento	.40
92	Eric Young	.40
93	Carlos Delgado	1.50
94	Troy Glaus	2.00
95	Ben Grieve	.75
96	Jose Lima	.40
97	Garret Anderson	.40
98	Luis Gonzalez	.40
99	Carl Pavano	.40
100	Alex Rodriguez	6.00
101	Preston Wilson	.40
102	Ron Gant	.60
103	Harold Baines	.40
104	Rickey Henderson	1.00
105	Gary Sheffield	.75
106	Mickey Morandini	.40
107	Jim Edmonds	.40
108	Kris Benson	.40
109	Adrian Beltre	.60
110	Alex Fernandez	.40
111	Dan Wilson	.40
112	Mark Clark	.40
113	Greg Vaughn	.75
114	Neifi Perez	.40
115	Paul O'Neill	.75
116	Jermaine Dye	.40
117	Todd Jones	.40
118	Terry Steinbach	.40
119	Greg Norton	.40
120	Curt Schilling	.60
121	Todd Zeile	.40
122	Edgardo Alfonzo	.75
123	Ryan McGuire	.40
124	Stan Javier	.40
125	John Smoltz	.60
126	Bob Wickman	.40
127	Richard Hidalgo	.40
128	Chuck Finley	.40
129	Billy Wagner	.40
130	Todd Hundley	.40
131	Dwight Gooden	.60
132	Russ Ortiz	.40
133	Mike Lowell	.40
134	Reggie Sanders	.40
135	John Valentin	.40
136	Brad Ausmus	.40
137	Chad Kreuter	.40
138	David Cone	.75
139	Brook Fordyce	.40
140	Roberto Alomar	1.50
141	Charles Nagy	.40
142	Brian Hunter	.40
143	Mike Mussina	1.50
144	Robin Ventura	.75
145	Kevin Brown	.60
146	Pat Hentgen	.40
147	Ryan Klesko	.60
148	Derek Bell	.40
149	Andy Sheets	.40
150	Larry Walker	1.50
151	Scott Williamson	.40
152	Jose Offerman	.40
153	Doug Mientkiewicz	.40
154	*John Snyder*	.40
155	Sandy Alomar	.25
156	Joe Nathan	.40
157	Lance Johnson	.40
158	Odalis Perez	.40
159	Hideo Nomo	.75
160	Steve Finley	.40
161	Dave Martinez	.40
162	Matt Walbeck	.40
163	Bill Spiers	.40
164	Fernando Tatis	.40
165	Kenny Lofton	1.25
166	Paul Byrd	.40
167	Aaron Sele	.40
168	Eddie Taubensee	.40
169	Reggie Jefferson	.40
170	Roger Clemens	3.00
171	Francisco Cordova	.40
172	Mike Bordick	.40
173	Wally Joyner	.40
174	Marvin Benard	.40
175	Jason Kendall	.60
176	Mike Stanley	.40
177	Chad Allen	.40
178	Carlos Beltran	.40
179	Deivi Cruz	.40
180	Chipper Jones	4.00
181	Vladimir Guerrero	3.00
182	Dave Burba	.40
183	Tom Goodwin	.40
184	Brian Daubach	.40
185	Jay Bell	.40
186	Roy Halladay	.40
187	Miguel Tejada	.40
188	Armando Rios	.40
189	Fernando Vina	.40
190	Eric Davis	.60
191	Henry Rodriguez	.40
192	Joe McEwing	.40
193	Jeff Kent	.40
194	Mike Jackson	.40
195	Mike Morgan	.40
196	Jeff Montgomery	.40
197	Jeff Zimmerman	.40
198	Tony Fernandez	.40
199	Jason Giambi	.40
200	Jose Canseco	2.00
201	Alex Gonzalez	.40
202	Jack Cust, Mike Colangelo, Dee Brown	1.50
203	Felipe Lopez, Alfonso Soriano, Pablo Ozuna	1.00
204	Erubiel Durazo, Pat Burrell, Nick Johnson	3.00
205	*John Sneed*, Kip Wells, Matt Blank	1.50
206	*Josh Kalinowski,Michael Tejera*, Chris Mears	1.00
207	Roosevelt Brown, Corey Patterson, Lance Berkman	.50
208	Kit Pellow, Kevin Barker, Russ Branyan	1.00
209	*B.J. Garbe, Larry Bigbie*	3.00
210	Eric Munson, *Bobby Bradley*	4.00
211	Josh Girdley, Kyle Snyder	1.50
212	*Chance Caple*, Jason Jennings	2.00
213	*Ryan Christiansen, Brett Myers*	6.00
214	*Jason Stumm, Rob Purvis*	8.00
215	David Walling, Mike Paradis	1.50
216	Omar Ortiz, Jay Gehrke	.75
217	David Cone (Season Highlights)	.75
218	Jose Jimenez (Season Highlights)	.40
219	Chris Singleton (Season Highlights)	.40
220	Fernando Tatis (Season Highlights)	.40
221	Todd Helton (Season Highlights)	1.00
222	Kevin Millwood (Post-Season Highlights)	.60
223	Todd Pratt (Post-Season Highlights)	.40
224	Orlando Hernandez (Post-Season Highlights)	.75
225	Post-Season Highlights	.40
226	Post-Season Highlights	.40
227	Bernie Williams (Post-Season Highlights)	1.00
228	Mariano Rivera (Post-Season Highlights)	.75
229	Tony Gwynn (20th Century's Best)	2.00
230	Wade Boggs (20th Century's Best)	1.00
231	Tim Raines (20th Century's Best)	.40
232	Mark McGwire (20th Century's Best)	8.00
233	Rickey Henderson (20th Century's Best)	.75
234	Rickey Henderson (20th Century's Best)	.75
235	Roger Clemens (20th Century's Best)	3.00
236	Mark McGwire (Magic Moments)	15.00
237	Hank Aaron (Magic Moments)	8.00
238	Cal Ripken Jr. (Magic Moments)	10.00
239	Wade Boggs (Magic Moments)	4.00
240	Tony Gwynn (Magic Moments)	8.00
	Series 1 checklist (1-201)	.05
	Series 1 checklist (202-240, inserts)	.05
241	Tom Glavine	.75
242	David Wells	.40
243	Kevin Appier	.40
244	Troy Percival	.40
245	Ray Lankford	.40
246	Marquis Grissom	.40
247	Randy Winn	.40
248	Miguel Batista	.40
249	Darren Dreifort	.40
250	Barry Bonds	2.00
251	Harold Baines	.40
252	Cliff Floyd	.40
253	Freddy Garcia	.75
254	Kenny Rogers	.40
255	Ben Davis	.40
256	Charles Johnson	.40
257	John Burkett	.40
258	Desi Relaford	.40
259	Al Martin	.40
260	Andy Pettitte	.75
261	Carlos Lee	.40
262	Matt Lawton	.40
263	Andy Fox	.40
264	Chan Ho Park	.40
265	Billy Koch	.40
266	Dave Roberts	.40
267	Carl Everett	.75
268	Orel Hershiser	.40
269	Trot Nixon	.40
270	Rusty Greer	.40
271	Will Clark	1.00
272	Quilvio Veras	.40
273	Rico Brogna	.40
274	Devon White	.40
275	Tim Hudson	.75
276	Mike Hampton	.40
277	Miguel Cairo	.40
278	Darren Oliver	.40
279	Jeff Cirillo	.75
280	Al Leiter	.60
281	Brant Brown	.40
282	Carlos Febles	.40
283	Pedro Astacio	.40
284	Juan Guzman	.40
285	Orlando Hernandez	.75
286	Paul Konerko	.75
287	Tony Clark	.60
288	Aaron Boone	.40
289	Ismael Valdes	.40
290	Moises Alou	.60
291	Kevin Tapani	.40
292	John Franco	.40
293	Todd Zeile	.40
294	Jason Schmidt	.40
295	Johnny Damon	.40
296	Scott Brosius	.40
297	Travis Fryman	.60
298	Jose Vizcaino	.40
299	Eric Chavez	.75
300	Mike Piazza	5.00
301	Matt Clement	.40
302	Cristian Guzman	.40
303	Darryl Strawberry	.75
304	Jeff Abbott	.40
305	Brett Tomko	.40
306	Mike Lansing	.40
307	Eric Owens	.40
308	Livan Hernandez	.40
309	Rondell White	.75
310	Todd Stottlemyre	.75
311	Chris Carpenter	.40
312	Ken Hill	.40
313	Mark Loretta	.40
314	John Rocker	.40
315	Richie Sexson	.40
316	Ruben Mateo	.75
317	Ramon Martinez	.40
318	Mike Sirotka	.40
319	Jose Rosado	.40
320	Matt Mantei	.40
321	Kevin Millwood	.75
322	Gary DiSarcina	.40
323	Dustin Hermanson	.40
324	Mike Stanton	.40
325	Kirk Rueter	.40
326	Damian Miller	.40
327	Doug Glanville	.40
328	Scott Rolen	2.00
329	Ray Durham	.40
330	Butch Huskey	.40
331	Mariano Rivera	.75
332	Darren Lewis	.40
333	Ramiro Mendoza	.40
334	Mark Grudzielanek	.40
335	Mike Cameron	.40
336	Kelvim Escobar	.40
337	Bret Boone	.40
338	Mo Vaughn	1.50
339	Craig Biggio	1.00
340	Michael Barrett	.40
341	Marlon Anderson	.40
342	Bobby Jones	.40
343	John Halama	.40
344	Todd Ritchie	.40
345	Chuck Knoblauch	.75
346	Rick Reed	.40
347	Kelly Stinnett	.40
348	Tim Salmon	.75
349	A.J. Hinch	.40
350	Jose Cruz Jr.	.40
351	Roberto Hernandez	.40
352	Edgar Renteria	.40
353	Jose Hernandez	.40
354	Brad Fullmer	.40
355	Trevor Hoffman	.40
356	Troy O'Leary	.40
357	Justin Thompson	.40
358	Kevin Young	.40
359	Hideki Irabu	.40
360	Jim Thome	1.00
361	Todd Dunwoody	.40
362	Octavio Dotel	.40
363	Omar Vizquel	.75
364	Raul Mondesi	.75
365	Shane Reynolds	.40
366	Bartolo Colon	.40
367	Chris Widger	.40
368	Gabe Kapler	.75
369	Bill Simas	.40
370	Tino Martinez	1.00
371	John Thomson	.40
372	Delino DeShields	.40
373	Carlos Perez	.40
374	Eddie Perez	.40
375	Jeromy Burnitz	.75
376	Jimmy Haynes	.40
377	Travis Lee	.75
378	Darryl Hamilton	.40
379	Jamie Moyer	.40
380	Alex Gonzalez	.40
381	John Wetteland	.40
382	Vinny Castilla	.60
383	Jeff Suppan	.40
384	Chad Curtis	.40
385	Robb Nen	.40
386	Wilson Alvarez	.40
387	Andres Galarraga	1.50
388	Mike Remlinger	.40
389	Geoff Jenkins	.75
390	Matt Stairs	.40
391	Bill Mueller	.40
392	Mike Lowell	.40
393	Andy Ashby	.40
394	Ruben Rivera	.40
395	Todd Helton	2.00
396	Bernie Williams	1.50

397 Royce Clayton .40
398 Manny Ramirez 2.00
399 Kerry Wood 1.00
400 Ken Griffey Jr. 6.00
401 Enrique Wilson .40
402 Joey Hamilton .40
403 Shawn Estes .40
404 Ugueth Urbina .40
405 Albert Belle 1.50
406 Rick Helling .40
407 Steve Parris .40
408 Eric Milton .40
409 Dave Mlicki .40
410 Shawn Green 2.00
411 Jaret Wright .40
412 Tony Womack .40
413 Vernon Wells .75
414 Ron Belliard .40
415 Ellis Burks .40
416 Scott Erickson .40
417 Rafael Palmeiro 1.50
418 Damion Easley .40
419 Jamey Wright .40
420 Corey Koskie .40
421 Bobby Howry .40
422 Ricky Ledee .40
423 Dmitri Young .40
424 Sidney Ponson .40
425 Greg Maddux 4.00
426 Jose Guillen .40
427 Jon Lieber .40
428 Andy Benes .40
429 Randy Velarde .40
430 Sean Casey 1.00
431 Torii Hunter .40
432 Ryan Rupe .40
433 David Segui .40
434 Rich Aurilia .40
435 Nomar Garciaparra 5.00
436 Denny Neagle .40
437 Ron Coomer .40
438 Chris Singleton .40
439 Tony Batista 1.00
440 Andruw Jones 1.50
441 Adam Piatt, Aubrey Huff, Sean Burroughs (Prospects) 3.00
442 Rafael Furcal, Jason Dallero, Travis Dawkins (Prospects) .75
443 Wilton Veras, Joe Crede,*Mike Lamb* (Prospects) .40
444 *Julio Zuleta*, Dernell Stenson, Jorge Toca (Prospects) .40
445 Tim Raines Jr., Gary Mathews Jr. ,*Garry Maddox Jr.* (Prospects) 2.00
446 Matt Riley, Mark Mulder, C.C. Sabathia (Prospects) .40
447 *Scott Downs*, Chris George, Matt Belisle (Prospects) 1.50
448 Doug Mirabelli, Ben Petrick, Jayson Werth (Prospects) .40
449 Josh Hamilton,*Corey Myers* (Draft Picks) 5.00
450 *Ben Christensen*, Brett Myers (Draft Picks) 3.00
451 *Barry Zito*,*Ben Sheets* (Draft Picks) 10.00
452 *Ty Howington*, *Kurt Ainsworth* (Draft Picks) 2.00
453 *Rick Asadoorian*,*Vince Faison* (Draft Picks) 2.50
454 *Keith Reed*,*Jeff Heaverlo* (Draft Picks) 2.00
455 *Mike MacDougal*, Jay Gehrke (Draft Picks) 1.50
456 Mark McGwire (Season Highlights) 4.00
457 Cal Ripken Jr. (Season Highlights) 3.00
458 Wade Boggs (Season Highlights) .75
459 Tony Gwynn (Season Highlights) 2.00
460 Jesse Orosco (Season Highlights) .40
461 Nomar Garciaparra, Larry Walker (League Leaders) 2.00
462 Mark McGwire, Ken Griffey Jr (League Leaders) 3.00
463 Mark McGwire, Manny Ramirez (League Leaders) 3.00
464 Randy Johnson, Pedro Martinez (League Leaders) 1.00
465 Randy Johnson, Pedro Martinez (League Leaders) 1.00
466 Luis Gonzalez, Derek Jeter (League Leaders) 2.00
467 Manny Ramirez, Larry Walker (League Leaders) .75
468 Tony Gwynn (20th Century's Best) .40
469 Mark McGwire (20th Century's Best) 4.00
470 Frank Thomas (20th Century's Best) 1.50
471 Harold Baines (20th Century's Best) .40
472 Roger Clemens (20th Century's Best) 1.50
473 John Franco (20th Century's Best) .40
474 John Franco (20th Century's Best) .40
475 Ken Griffey Jr. (Magic Moments) 12.00
476 Barry Bonds (Magic Moments) 4.00
477 Sammy Sosa (Magic Moments) 10.00
478 Derek Jeter (Magic Moments) 10.00
479 Alex Rodriguez (Magic Moments) 12.00

2000 Topps Chrome Refractors

A parallel to the base set, Refractors have a reflective sheen to them when held up to light. They are seeded 1:12 packs and have "Refractor" written underneath the card number on the back.

	MT
Stars:	5-10X
Young Stars/RCs:	2-4X
Inserted 1:12	

(See 2000 Topps Chrome for checklist and base card values.)

2000 Topps Chrome All-Topps Team

These feature top National League players and picks a top player for each position. They have a brown border utilizing Topps Chromium technology. Card backs have a small photo along with statistical comparisons made to current and former greats for their respective position. Backs are numbered with a "AT" prefix and are seeded 1:32 packs. A Refractor parallel is inserted 1:160 packs.

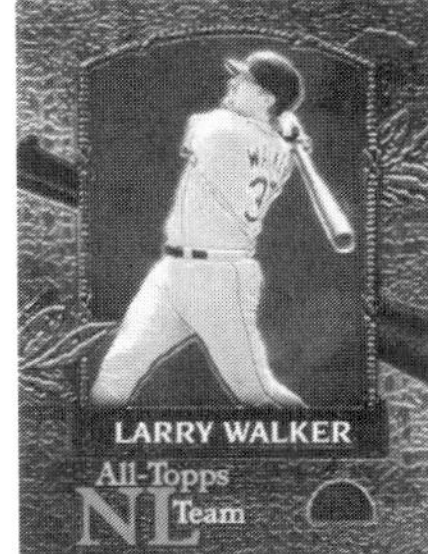

		MT
Complete Set (20):		120.00
Complete Series I Set (10):		60.00
Complete Series II Set (10):		60.00
Common Player:		3.00
Inserted 1:32		
Refractors:		2-3X
Inserted 1:160		
1	Greg Maddux	10.00
2	Mike Piazza	12.00
3	Mark McGwire	20.00
4	Craig Biggio	3.00
5	Chipper Jones	10.00
6	Barry Larkin	4.00
7	Barry Bonds	5.00
8	Andruw Jones	4.00
9	Sammy Sosa	12.00
10	Larry Walker	4.00
11	Pedro Martinez	5.00
12	Ivan Rodriguez	5.00
13	Rafael Palmeiro	4.00
14	Roberto Alomar	4.00
15	Cal Ripken Jr.	15.00
16	Derek Jeter	12.00
17	Albert Belle	3.00
18	Ken Griffey Jr.	15.00
19	Manny Ramirez	5.00
20	Jose Canseco	5.00

2000 Topps Chrome Allegiance

Allegiance features 20 stars who have spent their entire career with one team. They are seeded 1:16 and are numbered with a "TA" prefix. There is also a hobby-exclusive Refractor parallel version, sequentially numbered to 100 and inserted 1:424 packs.

		MT
Complete Set (20):		100.00
Common Player:		2.00
Inserted 1:16		
Refractors:		8X
Inserted 1:424		
1	Derek Jeter	12.00
2	Ivan Rodriguez	5.00
3	Alex Rodriguez	15.00
4	Cal Ripken Jr.	15.00
5	Mark Grace	2.00
6	Tony Gwynn	10.00
7	Juan Gonzalez	5.00
8	Frank Thomas	5.00
9	Manny Ramirez	5.00
10	Barry Larkin	4.00
11	Bernie Williams	4.00
12	Raul Mondesi	2.00
13	Vladimir Guerrero	8.00
14	Craig Biggio	3.00
15	Nomar Garciaparra	12.00
16	Andruw Jones	4.00
17	Jim Thome	3.00
18	Scott Rolen	5.00
19	Chipper Jones	10.00
20	Ken Griffey Jr.	15.00

2000 Topps Chrome All-Star Rookie Team

This 10-card set highlights players who lived up to the high expectations placed on them during their rookie season. These are seeded 1:16 packs and are numbered with an "RT" prefix on the card back. A Refractor parallel is also randomly inserted, seeded 1:80 packs. "Refractor" is printed under the card number on the back.

		MT
Complete Set (10):		40.00
Common Player:		1.00
Inserted 1:16		
Refractors:		2-3X
Inserted 1:80		
1	Mark McGwire	10.00
2	Chuck Knoblauch	1.50
3	Chipper Jones	5.00
4	Cal Ripken Jr.	8.00
5	Manny Ramirez	2.50
6	Jose Canseco	2.50
7	Ken Griffey Jr.	8.00
8	Mike Piazza	6.00
9	Dwight Gooden	1.50
10	Billy Wagner	1.00

2000 Topps Chrome Combos

Ten player combinations linked by a common

element are featured in this set. Combos are found 1:16 packs and are numbered with a "TC" prefix on the card back. A Refractor parallel is randomly seeded 1:80 packs and have "Refractor" printed under the card number on the back.

		MT
Complete Set (10):		80.00
Common Player:		3.00
Inserted 1:16		
Refractors:		2-3X
Inserted 1:80		
1	Roberto Alomar, Manny Ramirez, Kenny Lofton, Jim Thome	4.00
2	Tom Glavine, Greg Maddux, John Smoltz	8.00
3	Derek Jeter, Bernie Williams, Tino Martinez	10.00
4	Ivan Rodriguez, Mike Piazza	10.00
5	Nomar Garciaparra, Alex Rodriguez, Derek Jeter	12.00
6	Sammy Sosa, Mark McGwire	15.00
7	Pedro Martinez, Randy Johnson	4.00
8	Barry Bonds, Ken Griffey Jr.	12.00
9	Chipper Jones, Ivan Rodriguez	8.00
10	Cal Ripken Jr., Tony Gwynn, Wade Boggs	12.00

2000 Topps Chrome Kings

This 10-card set spotlights hitters who have average 30 or more homeruns per season for their career. Kings are seeded 1:32 packs and are numbered with an "CK" prefix on the card back. A Refractor parallel is also randomly inserted and are serially numbered to the featured player's career homerun total.

		MT
Complete Set (10):		90.00
Common Player:		4.00
Inserted 1:32		
1	Mark McGwire	20.00
2	Sammy Sosa	12.00
3	Ken Griffey Jr.	15.00
4	Mike Piazza	12.00
5	Alex Rodriguez	15.00
6	Manny Ramirez	5.00
7	Barry Bonds	6.00
8	Nomar Garciaparra	12.00
9	Chipper Jones	10.00
10	Vladimir Guerrero	8.00

2000 Topps Chrome Mark McGwire 1985 Rookie Reprint

This insert is a chromium reprinted version of McGwire's 1985 Topps rookie card. Each card features a commemorative gold-foil stamp. The insertion rate is 1:32 packs. A hobby-exclusive Refractor version is also inserted, limited to 70 sequentially numbered sets and seeded 1:12,116 packs.

	MT
Inserted 1:32	
Refractor:	150.00
Production 70 cards	
Mark McGwire	10.00

2000 Topps Chrome Millennium Stars

This 10-card set features stars who had less than three years major league experience in 2000. Millennium Stars are seeded 1:32 packs and are numbered with an "NMS" prefix. A Refractor parallel is randomly inserted in 1:160 packs and has "Refractor" printed under the card number on the back.

		MT
Complete Set (10):		50.00
Common Player:		4.00
Inserted 1:32		
Refractors:		2-3X
Inserted 1:160		
1	Nomar Garciaparra	12.00
2	Vladimir Guerrero	10.00
3	Sean Casey	4.00
4	Richie Sexson	3.00
5	Todd Helton	5.00
6	Carlos Beltran	3.00
7	Kevin Millwood	3.00
8	Ruben Mateo	2.00
9	Pat Burrell	8.00
10	Alfonso Soriano	8.00

2000 Topps Chrome Own the Game

This 30-card set spotlights statistical stars and 1999 Major League Baseball award winners. These were seeded 1:11 packs and are numbered with an "OTG" prefix on the card back. A Refractor parallel is randomly inserted 1:55 packs and has "Refractor" written under the card number on the back.

		MT
Complete Set (30):		160.00
Common Player:		2.00
Inserted 1:12		
Refractors:		2-3X
Inserted 1:55		
1	Derek Jeter	12.00
2	B.J. Surhoff	2.00
3	Luis Gonzalez	2.00
4	Manny Ramirez	5.00
5	Rafael Palmeiro	4.00
6	Mark McGwire	20.00
7	Mark McGwire	20.00
8	Sammy Sosa	12.00
9	Ken Griffey Jr.	15.00
10	Larry Walker	4.00
11	Nomar Garciaparra	12.00
12	Derek Jeter	12.00
13	Larry Walker	4.00
14	Mark McGwire	20.00
15	Manny Ramirez	5.00
16	Pedro Martinez	5.00
17	Randy Johnson	4.00
18	Kevin Millwood	3.00
19	Pedro Martinez	5.00
20	Randy Johnson	4.00
21	Kevin Brown	3.00
22	Chipper Jones	10.00
23	Ivan Rodriguez	5.00
24	Mariano Rivera	3.00
25	Scott Williamson	2.00
26	Carlos Beltran	2.00
27	Randy Johnson	4.00
28	Pedro Martinez	5.00
29	Sammy Sosa	12.00
30	Manny Ramirez	5.00

2000 Topps Chrome Power Players

Twenty of the leading power hitters are featured on a colorful design. They are seeded 1:8 packs and are numbered with a "P" prefix. A Refractor parallel is also randomly seeded 1:40 packs.

		MT
Complete Set (20):		75.00
Common Player:		1.00
Inserted 1:8		
Refractors:		2x-3x
Inserted 1:40		
1	Juan Gonzalez	3.00
2	Ken Griffey Jr.	10.00
3	Mark McGwire	12.00
4	Nomar Garciaparra	8.00
5	Barry Bonds	3.00
6	Mo Vaughn	2.00
7	Larry Walker	2.00
8	Alex Rodriguez	10.00
9	Jose Canseco	3.00
10	Jeff Bagwell	3.00
11	Manny Ramirez	3.00
12	Albert Belle	2.00
13	Frank Thomas	4.00
14	Mike Piazza	8.00
15	Chipper Jones	6.00
16	Sammy Sosa	8.00
17	Vladimir Guerrero	5.00
18	Scott Rolen	3.00
19	Raul Mondesi	1.00
20	Derek Jeter	8.00

2000 Topps Chrome 21st Century Topps

This 10-card set focuses on the top young stars in baseball heading into the next century. These were seeded 1:16 packs and are numbered with a "C" prefix on the card back. A Refractor parallel version is also seeded 1:80 packs.

	MT
Complete Set (10):	40.00
Common Player:	1.50
Inserted 1:16	
Refractors:	2x-3x
Inserted 1:80	

1	Ben Grieve	2.00
2	Alex Gonzalez	1.50
3	Derek Jeter	10.00
4	Sean Casey	2.50
5	Nomar Garciaparra	10.00
6	Alex Rodriguez	10.00
7	Scott Rolen	4.00
8	Andruw Jones	3.00
9	Vladimir Guerrero	4.00
10	Todd Helton	2.00

2000 Topps Chrome Traded and Rookies

		MT
Complete Set (135):		80.00
Common Player:		.25
1	*Mike MacDougal*	.75
2	*Andy Tracy*	.75
3	*Brandon Phillips*	1.50
4	*Brandon Inge*	2.00
5	*Robbie Morrison*	.75
6	*Josh Pressley*	.75
7	*Todd Moser*	.75
8	*Rob Purvis*	1.00
9	*Chance Caple*	1.00
10	Ben Sheets	4.00
11	*Russ Jacobson*	1.00
12	*Brian Cole*	.50
13	*Brad Baker*	2.00
14	*Alex Cintron*	1.00
15	*Lyle Overbay*	4.00
16	*Mike Edwards*	.75
17	*Sean McGowan*	.75
18	*Jose Molina*	.75
19	*Marcos Castillo*	.50
20	*Josue Espada*	.50
21	*Alex Gordon*	.50
22	*Rob Pugmire*	.50
23	*Jason Stumm*	.75
24	*Ty Howington*	2.00
25	Brett Myers	3.00
26	*Maicer Izturis*	1.00
27	*John McDonald*	.75
28	*Wilfredo Rodriguez*	1.00
29	*Carlos Zambrano*	2.00
30	*Alejandro Diaz*	.50
31	*Geraldo Guzman*	.75
32	*J.R. House*	5.00
33	*Elvin Nina*	.75
34	*Juan Pierre*	2.50
35	*Ben Johnson*	1.50
36	*Jeff Bailey*	.50
37	*Miguel Olivo*	.75
38	*Francisco Rodriguez*	6.00
39	*Tony Pena Jr.*	.75
40	*Miguel Cabrera*	6.00
41	*Asdrubal Oropeza*	.50
42	*Junior Zamora*	.50
43	*Jovanny Cedeno*	1.50
44	*John Sneed*	.50
45	*Josh Kalinowski*	.75
46	*Mike Young*	1.50
47	*Rico Washington*	.75
48	*Chad Durbin*	1.00
49	*Junior Brignac*	1.00
50	*Carlos Hernandez*	3.00
51	*Cesar Izturis*	3.00
52	*Oscar Salazar*	1.00
53	*Pat Strange*	2.00
54	Rick Asadoorian	1.50
55	*Keith Reed*	1.50
56	*Leo Estrella*	.75
57	*Wascar Serrano*	.75
58	*Richard Gomez*	1.50
59	*Ramon Santiago*	2.00
60	*Jovanny Sosa*	.75
61	*Aaron Rowand*	2.00
62	*Junior Guerrero*	1.00
63	*Luis Terrero*	2.50
64	*Brian Sanches*	.75
65	*Scott Sobkowiak*	.75
66	*Gary Majewski*	.50
67	Barry Zito	5.00
68	*Ryan Christianson*	2.50
69	*Cristian Guerrero*	6.00
70	*Tomas de la Rosa*	.75
71	*Andrew Beinbrink*	1.00
72	*Ryan Knox*	.75
73	*Alex Graman*	2.00
74	*Juan Guzman*	.75
75	*Ruben Salazar*	2.00
76	*Luis Matos*	.50
77	*Tony Mota*	.75
78	*Doug Davis*	1.00
79	*Ben Christensen*	.75
80	Mike Lamb	.50
81	*Adrian Gonzalez* (Draft Picks)	8.00
82	*Mike Stodolka* (Draft Picks)	1.50
83	*Adam Johnson* (Draft Picks)	2.00
84	*Matt Wheatland* (Draft Picks)	2.00
85	*Corey Smith* (Draft Picks)	2.00
86	*Rocco Baldelli* (Draft Picks)	8.00
87	*Keith Bucktrot* (Draft Picks)	1.00
88	*Adam Wainwright* (Draft Picks)	3.00
89	*Scott Thorman* (Draft Picks)	2.00
90	*Tripper Johnson* (Draft Picks)	3.00
91	Jim Edmonds	.50
92	Masato Yoshii	.25
93	Adam Kennedy	.25
94	Darryl Kile	.25
95	Mark McLemore	.25
96	Ricky Gutierrez	.25
97	Juan Gonzalez	1.00
98	Melvin Mora	.25
99	Dante Bichette	.50
100	Lee Stevens	.25
101	Roger Cedeno	.25
102	John Olerud	.40
103	Eric Young	.25
104	Mickey Morandini	.25
105	Travis Lee	.25
106	Greg Vaughn	.40
107	Todd Zeile	.25
108	Chuck Finley	.25
109	Ismael Valdes	.25
110	Ron Henika	.25
111	Pat Hentgen	.25
112	Ryan Klesko	.40
113	Derek Bell	.25
114	Hideo Nomo	1.00
115	Aaron Sele	.25
116	Fernando Vina	.25
117	Wally Joyner	.25
118	Brian Hunter	.25
119	Joe Girardi	.25
120	Omar Daal	.25
121	Brook Fordyce	.25
122	Jose Valentin	.25
123	Curt Schilling	.40
124	B.J. Surhoff	.25
125	Henry Rodriguez	.25
126	Mike Bordick	.25
127	David Justice	1.00
128	Charles Johnson	.25
129	Will Clark	.75
130	Dwight Gooden	.25
131	David Segui	.25
132	Denny Neagle	.25
133	Andy Ashby	.25
134	Bruce Chen	.25
135	Jason Bere	.25

2000 Topps Gallery

The base set consists of 150 cards. Cards 101-150 are broken down into two subsets Masters of the Game (20 cards) and Students of the Game (30 cards). The subset cards are found one per pack. Card fronts have a tan textured border around the player photo with the player name, team and Gallery logo stamped in gold foil. Card backs have a small photo, brief career note and the featured player's '99 statistics. Gallery was a hobby exclusive product. Five-card packs carried a $3 SRP.

		MT
Complete Set (150):		75.00
Common Player:		.15
Common (101-150):		.75
Inserted 1:1		
Pack (6):		3.00
Wax Box (24):		65.00
1	Nomar Garciaparra	2.00
2	Kevin Millwood	.25
3	Jay Bell	.15
4	Rusty Greer	.15
5	Bernie Williams	.60
6	Barry Larkin	.40
7	Carlos Beltran	.25
8	Damion Easley	.15
9	Magglio Ordonez	.25
10	Matt Williams	.40
11	Shannon Stewart	.15
12	Ray Lankford	.15
13	Vinny Castilla	.25
14	Miguel Tejada	.15
15	Craig Biggio	.40
16	Chipper Jones	1.50
17	Albert Belle	.50
18	Doug Glanville	.15
19	Brian Giles	.25
20	Shawn Green	.50
21	J.T. Snow Jr.	.15
22	Luis Gonzalez	.25
23	Carlos Delgado	.75
24	J.D. Drew	.25
25	Ivan Rodriguez	.75
26	Tino Martinez	.40
27	Erubiel Durazo	.25
28	Scott Rolen	.75
29	Gary Sheffield	.40
30	Manny Ramirez	.75
31	Luis Castillo	.15
32	Fernando Tatis	.25
33	Darin Erstad	.25
34	Tim Hudson	.25
35	Sammy Sosa	2.00
36	Jason Kendall	.25
37	Todd Walker	.15
38	Orlando Hernandez	.25
39	Pokey Reese	.15
40	Mike Piazza	2.00
41	B.J. Surhoff	.15
42	Tony Gwynn	1.50
43	Kevin Brown	.25
44	Preston Wilson	.15
45	Kenny Lofton	.40
46	Rondell White	.25
47	Frank Thomas	1.00
48	Neifi Perez	.15
49	Edgardo Alfonzo	.25
50	Ken Griffey Jr.	2.50
51	Barry Bonds	1.00
52	Brian Jordan	.15
53	Raul Mondesi	.25
54	Troy Glaus	.75
55	Curt Schilling	.25
56	Mike Mussina	.50
57	Brian Daubach	.15
58	Roger Clemens	1.00
59	Carlos Febles	.15
60	Todd Helton	.75
61	Mark Grace	.25
62	Randy Johnson	.75
63	Jeff Bagwell	.75
64	Tom Glavine	.40
65	Adrian Beltre	.25
66	Rafael Palmeiro	.50
67	Paul O'Neill	.25
68	Robin Ventura	.25
69	Ray Durham	.15
70	Mark McGwire	3.00
71	Greg Vaughn	.40
72	Javy Lopez	.25
73	Jeromy Burnitz	.25
74	Mike Lieberthal	.15
75	Cal Ripken Jr.	2.50
76	Juan Gonzalez	.75
77	Sean Casey	.25
78	Jermaine Dye	.15
79	John Olerud	.25
80	Jose Canseco	.75
81	Eric Karros	.25
82	Roberto Alomar	.50
83	Ben Grieve	.25
84	Greg Maddux	1.50
85	Pedro Martinez	.75
86	Tony Clark	.15
87	Richie Sexson	.15
88	Cliff Floyd	.15
89	Eric Chavez	.15
90	Andruw Jones	.50
91	Vladimir Guerrero	1.25
92	Alex Gonzalez	.15
93	Jim Thome	.40
94	Bob Abreu	.25
95	Derek Jeter	2.00
96	Larry Walker	.50
97	John Smoltz	.15
98	Mo Vaughn	.50
99	Jason Giambi	.25
100	Alex Rodriguez	2.50
101	Mark McGwire (Masters of the Game)	5.00
102	Sammy Sosa (Masters of the Game)	3.00
103	Alex Rodriguez (Masters of the Game)	4.00
104	Derek Jeter (Masters of the Game)	3.00
105	Greg Maddux (Masters of the Game)	2.50
106	Jeff Bagwell (Masters of the Game)	1.25
107	Nomar Garciaparra (Masters of the Game)	3.00
108	Mike Piazza (Masters of the Game)	3.00
109	Pedro Martinez (Masters of the Game)	1.25
110	Chipper Jones (Masters of the Game)	2.50
111	Randy Johnson (Masters of the Game)	1.25
112	Barry Bonds (Masters of the Game)	1.50
113	Ken Griffey Jr. (Masters of the Game)	4.00
114	Manny Ramirez (Masters of the Game)	1.25
115	Ivan Rodriguez (Masters of the Game)	1.25
116	Juan Gonzalez (Masters of the Game)	1.25
117	Vladimir Guerrero (Masters of the Game)	2.00
118	Tony Gwynn (Masters of the Game)	2.50
119	Larry Walker (Masters of the Game)	1.00
120	Cal Ripken Jr. (Masters of the Game)	4.00
121	Josh Hamilton (Students of the Game)	3.00
122	Corey Patterson (Students of the Game)	1.00
123	Pat Burrell (Students of the Game)	3.00
124	Nick Johnson (Students of the Game)	1.00
125	Adam Piatt (Students of the Game)	1.50
126	Rick Ankiel (Students of the Game)	1.00
127	A.J. Burnett (Students of the Game)	1.00
128	Ben Petrick (Students of the Game)	.75
129	Rafael Furcal (Students of the Game)	.75
130	Alfonso Soriano (Students of the Game)	1.00
131	Dee Brown (Students of the Game)	.75
132	Ruben Mateo (Students of the Game)	.75

133	Pablo Ozuna (Students of the Game)	.75
134	Sean Burroughs (Students of the Game)	1.50
135	Mark Mulder (Students of the Game)	.75
136	Jason Jennings (Students of the Game)	.75
137	Eric Munson (Students of the Game)	2.00
138	Vernon Wells (Students of the Game)	.75
139	*Brett Myers* (Students of the Game)	3.00
140	*Ben Christensen* (Students of the Game)	1.50
141	*Bobby Bradley* (Students of the Game)	3.00
142	*Ruben Salazar* (Students of the Game)	1.50
143	*Ryan Christianson* (Students of the Game)	1.50
144	*Corey Myers* (Students of the Game)	1.50
145	*Aaron Rowand* (Students of the Game)	2.00
146	*Julio Zuleta* (Students of the Game)	1.00
147	*Kurt Ainsworth* (Students of the Game)	1.00
148	*Scott Downs* (Students of the Game)	.75
149	*Larry Bigbie* (Students of the Game)	2.00
150	*Chance Caple* (Students of the Game)	1.00

2000 Topps Gallery Players Private Issue

A parallel to the 150-card base set, Players Private Issue differ from the base cards with silver foil stamping on the card front and "Players Private Issue" stamped in silver foil across the card bottom. Card backs are serial numbered in an edition of 250 sets.

	MT
Stars (1-100):	10-20X
SPs (101-150):	6-10X
Production 250 sets	

2000 Topps Gallery Press Plates

The aluminum press plates used to print the Gallery cards were inserted at a rate of one per 1,200 packs. Each card's front and back can be found in four different color variations. Because of the unique nature of each plate, assignment of catalog values in not feasible.

	MT
Common Player:	50.00
(See 2000 Topps Gallery for checklist.)	

2000 Topps Gallery Lithos

Eight cards from the Topps Gallery set were issued in the form of limited edition lithographs by Bill Goff Inc. Measuring 18" x 25", the lithographs were each produced in an edition of 600, with 60 artist's proofs. Issue price on the lithos was $80 for single-player pieces and $100 for the multi-player prints.

		MT
Complete Set (8):		675.00
Common Player:		80.00
(1)	Shawn Green (1954 Topps Style)	80.00
(2)	Ken Griffey Jr. (1954 Topps Style)	80.00
(3)	Chipper Jones (1954 Topps Style)	80.00
(4)	Pedro Martinez (1954 Topps Style)	80.00
(5)	Alex Rodriguez (1954 Topps Style)	80.00
(6)	Ivan Rodriguez (1954 Topps Style)	80.00
(7)	Three of a Kind (Nomar Garciaparra, Alex Rodriguez, Derek Jeter)	100.00
(8)	Torre's Terrors (Paul O'Neill, Derek Jeter, Bernie Williams, Tino Martinez)	100.00

2000 Topps Gallery Autographs

This five-card set features top prospects. Each card is stamped with the Topps Certified Autograph Issue logo and the Topps Authentication sticker. Autographs are seeded 1:153 packs.

		MT
Complete Set (5):		180.00
Common Player:		15.00
Inserted 1:153		
RA	Rick Ankiel	25.00
RM	Ruben Mateo	15.00
CP	Corey Patterson	30.00
BP	Ben Petrick	20.00
VW	Vernon Wells	20.00

2000 Topps Gallery Gallery Exhibits

This 30-card set traces the history of art from medieval to contemporary. Card fronts have gold foil stamping and the card backs are numbered with an "GE" prefix and are found 1:18 packs.

		MT
Complete Set (30):		300.00
Common Player:		3.00
Inserted 1:18		
1	Mark McGwire	30.00
2	Jeff Bagwell	8.00
3	Mike Piazza	20.00
4	Alex Rodriguez	25.00
5	Nomar Garciaparra	20.00
6	Ivan Rodriguez	8.00
7	Chipper Jones	15.00
8	Cal Ripken Jr.	25.00
9	Tony Gwynn	15.00
10	Jose Canseco	8.00
11	Albert Belle	6.00
12	Greg Maddux	15.00
13	Barry Bonds	8.00
14	Ken Griffey Jr.	25.00
15	Juan Gonzalez	8.00
16	Rickey Henderson	4.00
17	Craig Biggio	5.00
18	Vladimir Guerrero	12.00
19	Rey Ordonez	3.00
20	Roberto Alomar	6.00
21	Derek Jeter	20.00
22	Manny Ramirez	8.00
23	Shawn Green	6.00
24	Sammy Sosa	20.00
25	Larry Walker	6.00
26	Pedro Martinez	8.00
27	Randy Johnson	8.00
28	Pat Burrell	10.00
29	Josh Hamilton	12.00
30	Corey Patterson	4.00

2000 Topps Gallery of Heroes

This 10-card set is printed on an acetate stock that simulates stained glass. Gallery of Heroes are found on the average of 1:24 packs and are numbered with an "GH" prefix on the card back.

		MT
Complete Set (10):		100.00
Common Player:		4.00
Inserted 1:24		
1	Alex Rodriguez	15.00
2	Chipper Jones	10.00
3	Pedro Martinez	5.00
4	Sammy Sosa	12.00
5	Mark McGwire	18.00
6	Nomar Garciaparra	12.00
7	Vladimir Guerrero	8.00
8	Ken Griffey Jr.	15.00
9	Mike Piazza	12.00
10	Derek Jeter	12.00

2000 Topps Gallery Proof Positive

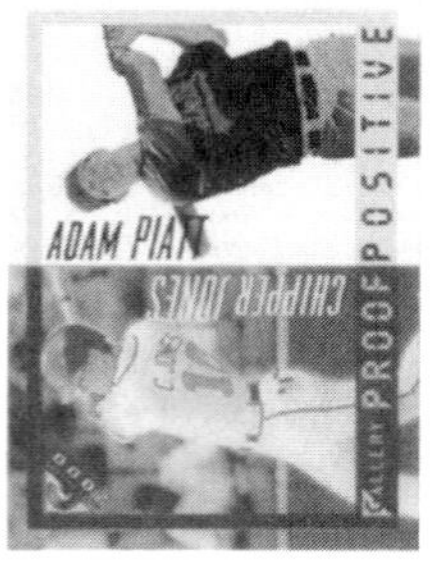

This 10-card set features both positive and negative photography. Done on a horizontal format the inserts pair a current star with a top prospect at the same position. Printed on a clear polycarbonate stock they were inserted 1:48 packs and are numbered with an "P" prefix.

		MT
Complete Set (10):		125.00
Common Player:		6.00
Inserted 1:48		
1	Ken Griffey Jr., Ruben Mateo	20.00
2	Derek Jeter, Alfonso Soriano	15.00
3	Mark McGwire, Pat Burrell	25.00
4	Pedro Martinez, A.J. Burnett	6.00
5	Alex Rodriguez, Rafael Furcal	15.00
6	Sammy Sosa, Corey Patterson	12.00
7	Randy Johnson, Rick Ankiel	8.00

8	Chipper Jones, Adam Piatt	12.00
9	Nomar Garciaparra, Pablo Ozuna	15.00
10	Mike Piazza, Eric Munson	15.00

2000 Topps Gallery Topps Heritage

Twenty current players are artistically depicted using the 1954 Topps card design as a template. They are seeded 1:12 packs and are numbered on the card back with an "TGH" prefix. As an added bonus the original artwork used in the development of the set is available through the Topps Gallery Auction. Auction points cards are found in every pack of Gallery.

		MT
Complete Set (20):		250.00
Common Player:		4.00
Inserted 1:12		
Proofs:		1-2X
Inserted 1:27		
1	Mark McGwire	30.00
2	Sammy Sosa	20.00
3	Greg Maddux	15.00
4	Mike Piazza	20.00
5	Ivan Rodriguez	8.00
6	Manny Ramirez	8.00
7	Jeff Bagwell	8.00
8	Sean Casey	4.00
9	Orlando Hernandez	4.00
10	Randy Johnson	8.00
11	Pedro Martinez	8.00
12	Vladimir Guerrero	12.00
13	Shawn Green	6.00
14	Ken Griffey Jr.	25.00
15	Alex Rodriguez	25.00
16	Nomar Garciaparra	20.00
17	Derek Jeter	20.00
18	Tony Gwynn	15.00
19	Chipper Jones	15.00
20	Cal Ripken Jr.	25.00

2000 Topps Gold Label Class 1

Each base card in the 100-card set has three different classes, each noted on the card back below the featured player's team logo. Each base card is also printed on 35-point rainbow styrene stock with gold foil stamping. Besides the notation on the card back, Class 1's can also be identified by the action in the background photo. Hitters are hitting and pitchers are at the start of their wind-up. A Gold die-cut parallel is also randomly seeded and are serially numbered to 100.

		MT
Complete Set (100):		90.00
Common Player:		.25
Gold parallel:		10-20X
Production 100 sets		
Pack (3):		3.00
Wax Box (24):		65.00
1	Sammy Sosa	3.00
2	Greg Maddux	2.50
3	Dee Brown	.25
4	Rondell White	.25
5	Fernando Tatis	.25
6	Troy Glaus	1.50
7	Nick Johnson	.50
8	Albert Belle	.75
9	Scott Rolen	1.00
10	Rafael Palmeiro	1.00
11	Tony Gwynn	2.00
12	Kevin Brown	.50
13	Roberto Alomar	1.00
14	John Olerud	.50
15	Rick Ankiel	.50
16	Chipper Jones	2.50
17	Craig Biggio	.50
18	Mark Mulder	.25
19	Carlos Delgado	1.00
20	Alex Gonzalez	.25
21	Gabe Kapler	.75
22	Derek Jeter	3.00
23	Carlos Beltran	.25
24	Todd Helton	1.25
25	Mark McGwire	5.00
26	Ben Grieve	.50
27	Rafael Furcal	.25
28	Vernon Wells	.25
29	Greg Vaughn	.50
30	Vladimir Guerrero	2.00
31	Mike Piazza	3.00
32	Roger Clemens	1.75
33	Barry Larkin	.75
34	Pedro Martinez	1.25
35	Matt Williams	.75
36	Mo Vaughn	.75
37	Tim Hudson	.50
38	Andruw Jones	.75
39	Vinny Castilla	.25
40	Frank Thomas	2.00
41	Pokey Reese	.25
42	Corey Patterson	.50
43	Jeromy Burnitz	.25
44	Preston Wilson	.25
45	Juan Gonzalez	1.25
46	Brian Giles	.25
47	Todd Walker	.25
48	Magglio Ordonez	.25
49	Alfonso Soriano	.50
50	Ken Griffey Jr.	4.00
51	Michael Barrett	.25
52	Shawn Green	.50
53	Erubiel Durazo	.25
54	Adam Piatt	.25
55	Pat Burrell	1.25
56	Mike Mussina	.75
57	Bernie Williams	1.00
58	Sean Casey	.50
59	Randy Johnson	1.25
60	Jeff Bagwell	1.25
61	Eric Chavez	.25
62	Josh Hamilton	1.50
63	A.J. Burnett	.25
64	Jim Thome	.75
65	Raul Mondesi	.50
66	Jason Kendall	.40
67	Mike Lieberthal	.25
68	Robin Ventura	.40
69	Ivan Rodriguez	1.25
70	Larry Walker	.75
71	Eric Munson	.50
72	Brian Jordan	.25
73	Edgardo Alfonzo	.50
74	Curt Schilling	.40
75	Nomar Garciaparra	3.00
76	Mark Grace	.50
77	Shannon Stewart	.25
78	J.D. Drew	.25
79	Jack Cust	.25
80	Cal Ripken Jr.	4.00
81	Bob Abreu	.25
82	Ruben Mateo	.25
83	Orlando Hernandez	.50
84	Kris Benson	.25
85	Barry Bonds	1.50
86	Manny Ramirez	1.25
87	Jose Canseco	.75
88	Sean Burroughs	.50
89	Kevin Millwood	.25
90	Alex Rodriguez	4.00
91	*Brett Myers*	3.00
92	*Rick Asadoorian*	1.50
93	*Ben Christensen*	1.50
94	*Bobby Bradley*	2.50
95	*Corey Myers*	1.00
96	*Brad Baisley*	.75
97	*Aaron McNeal*	1.00
98	*Aaron Rowand*	.50
99	*Scott Downs*	1.00
100	*Michael Tejera*	1.00

2000 Topps Gold Label Class 2

Each base card in the 100-card set has three different classes, each noted on the card back below the featured player's team logo. Each base card is also printed on 35-point rainbow styrene stock with gold foil stamping. Besides the notation on the card back, Class 2's can also be identified by the action in the background photo. Hitters are fielding and pitchers are in a throwing motion. A Gold die-cut parallel is also randomly seeded and are serially numbered to 100.

	MT
Same prices as Class 1	
Gold Parallel:	10-20X

2000 Topps Gold Label Class 3

Each base card in the 100-card set has three different classes, each noted on the card back below the featured player's team logo. Each base card is also printed on 35-point rainbow styrene stock with gold foil stamping. Besides the notation on the card back, Class 3's can also be identified by the action in the background photo. Hitters are running and pitchers are in their follow through. A Gold die-cut parallel is also randomly seeded and are serially numbered to 100.

	MT
Same prices as Class 1	
Gold parallel:	10-20X
Production 100 sets	

2000 Topps Gold Label Bullion

This 10-card set features three teammates superimposed over their team logo on a gold holo-foiled front with gold foil stamping. They are seeded 1:53 packs and are numbered on the card back with a "B" prefix.

		MT
Complete Set (10):		125.00
Common Player:		4.00
Inserted 1:53		
1	Jim Thome, Manny Ramirez, Roberto Alomar	6.00
2	Derek Jeter, Orlando Hernandez, Bernie Williams	15.00
3	Chipper Jones, Andruw Jones, Greg Maddux	12.00
4	Alex Rodriguez, Jay Buhner, John Olerud	20.00
5	Nomar Garciaparra, Pedro Martinez, Brian Daubach	15.00

6 Mark McGwire, J.D. Drew, Rick Ankiel 20.00
7 Sammy Sosa, Mark Grace, Kerry Wood 15.00
8 Ken Griffey Jr., Sean Casey, Barry Larkin 20.00
9 Mike Piazza, Edgardo Alfonzo, Robin Ventura 15.00
10 Randy Johnson, Matt Williams, Erubiel Durazo 6.00

2000 Topps Gold Label End of the Rainbow

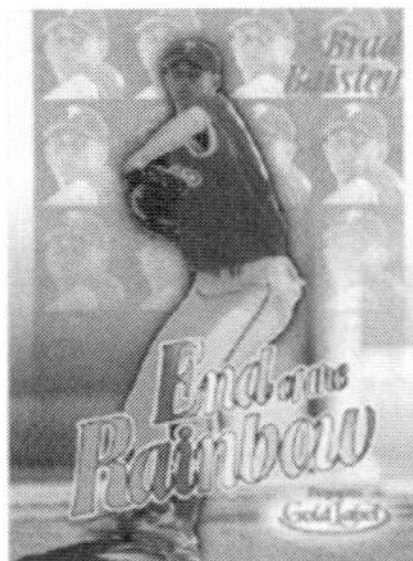

This 15-card set highlights some of baseball's top prospects on a silver holo foiled card front with gold foil stamping. Card backs are numbered with an "ER" prefix and are seeded 1:11 packs.

MT
Complete Set (15): 30.00
Common Player: 1.50
Inserted 1:11
1 Pat Burrell 5.00
2 Corey Patterson 2.00
3 Josh Hamilton 5.00
4 Eric Munson 2.50
5 Sean Burroughs 2.50
6 Jack Cust 2.00
7 Rafael Furcal 1.50
8 Ruben Salazar 1.50
9 Brett Myers 1.50
10 Wes Anderson 1.50
11 Nick Johnson 2.50
12 Scott Downs 1.50
13 Choo Freeman 1.50
14 Brad Baisley 1.50
15 A.J. Burnett 1.50

2000 Topps Gold Label Prospector's Dream

These inserts feature 10 players whose success was projected early in their careers. Card fronts feature gold holo foil with the player name, Gold Label logo and insert name stamped in gold foil. Card backs are numbered with an "PD" prefix. They are inserted 1:26 packs.

MT
Complete Set (10): 75.00
Common Player: 3.00
Inserted 1:26
1 Mark McGwire 20.00
2 Alex Rodriguez 15.00
3 Nomar Garciaparra 12.00
4 Pat Burrell 5.00
5 Todd Helton 5.00
6 Derek Jeter 12.00
7 Adam Piatt 4.00
8 Chipper Jones 10.00
9 Shawn Green 4.00
10 Josh Hamilton 5.00

2000 Topps Gold Label The Treasury

This 25-card set spotlights 15 veterans and 10 prospects on a silver holo foiled front with gold foil stamping. They have an insertion ratio of 1:21 packs and are numbered on the card back with an "T" prefix.

MT
Complete Set (25): 150.00
Common Player: 3.00
Inserted 1:21
1 Ken Griffey Jr. 15.00
2 Derek Jeter 12.00
3 Chipper Jones 10.00
4 Manny Ramirez 5.00
5 Nomar Garciaparra 12.00
6 Sammy Sosa 12.00
7 Cal Ripken Jr. 15.00
8 Alex Rodriguez 15.00
9 Mike Piazza 12.00
10 Pedro Martinez 5.00
11 Vladimir Guerrero 6.00
12 Jeff Bagwell 5.00
13 Shawn Green 4.00
14 Greg Maddux 10.00
15 Mark McGwire 20.00
16 Josh Hamilton 5.00
17 Corey Patterson 4.00
18 Dee Brown 3.00
19 Rafael Furcal 3.00
20 Pat Burrell 5.00
21 Alfonso Soriano 4.00
22 Adam Piatt 4.00
23 A.J. Burnett 3.00
24 Mark Mulder 3.00
25 Ruben Mateo 2.00

2000 Topps HD

This super-premium product consists of 100 regular base cards comprised of 88 veterans and 12 rookies. The base cards feature hyper-color technology and printed on a very thick 50-pt. card stock. Card backs have a small photo, career highlight and complete year-by-year statistics. A Platinum parallel to the base set is also randomly seeded and are sequentially numbered to 99 sets.

MT
Complete Set (100): 100.00
Common Player: .50
Platinums: 10x to 20x
Production 99 sets
Pack (4): 4.00
Wax Box (20): 70.00
1 Derek Jeter 5.00
2 Andruw Jones 1.25
3 Ben Grieve .75
4 Carlos Beltran .50
5 Randy Johnson 1.50
6 Javy Lopez .50
7 Gary Sheffield .75
8 John Olerud .75
9 Vinny Castilla .50
10 Barry Larkin 1.00
11 Tony Clark .50
12 Roberto Alomar 1.25
13 Brian Jordan .50
14 Wade Boggs 1.00
15 Carlos Febles .50
16 Alfonso Soriano .75
17 A.J. Burnett .50
18 Matt Williams .75
19 Alex Gonzalez .50
20 Larry Walker .75
21 Jeff Bagwell 1.50
22 Al Leiter .50
23 Ken Griffey Jr. 4.00
24 Ruben Mateo .50
25 Mark Grace .75
26 Carlos Delgado 1.25
27 Vladimir Guerrero 2.00
28 Kenny Lofton .75
29 Rusty Greer .50
30 Pedro Martinez 1.50
31 Todd Helton 1.50
32 Ray Lankford .50
33 Jose Canseco 1.00
34 Raul Mondesi .75
35 Mo Vaughn 1.00
36 Eric Chavez .75
37 Manny Ramirez 1.50
38 Jason Kendall .50
39 Mike Mussina 1.00
40 Dante Bichette .50
41 Troy Glaus 1.50
42 Rickey Henderson 1.00
43 Pablo Ozuna .50
44 Michael Barrett .50
45 Tony Gwynn 2.00
46 John Smoltz .50
47 Rafael Palmeiro 1.00
48 Curt Schilling .50
49 Todd Walker .50
50 Greg Vaughn .50
51 Orlando Hernandez .50
52 Jim Thome 1.00
53 Pat Burrell 1.00
54 Tim Salmon .75
55 Tom Glavine .75
56 Travis Lee .50
57 Gabe Kapler .50
58 Greg Maddux 3.00
59 Scott Rolen 1.00
60 Cal Ripken Jr. 5.00
61 Preston Wilson .50
62 Ivan Rodriguez 1.50
63 Johnny Damon .50
64 Bernie Williams 1.25
65 Barry Bonds 2.00
66 Sammy Sosa 3.00
67 Robin Ventura .50
68 Tony Fernandez .50
69 Jay Bell .50
70 Mark McGwire 6.00
71 Jeromy Burnitz .50
72 Chipper Jones 3.00
73 Josh Hamilton 1.00
74 Darin Erstad .50
75 Alex Rodriguez 5.00
76 Sean Casey .75
77 Tino Martinez .50
78 Juan Gonzalez 1.50
79 Cliff Floyd .50
80 Craig Biggio .75
81 Shawn Green 1.00
82 Adrian Beltre .50
83 Mike Piazza 4.00
84 Nomar Garciaparra 4.00
85 Kevin Brown .75
86 Roger Clemens 2.00
87 Frank Thomas 2.00
88 Albert Belle .75
89 Erubiel Durazo .50
90 David Walling .50
91 *John Sneed* 2.50
92 *Larry Bigbie* 2.00
93 *B.J. Garbe* 2.50
94 *Bobby Bradley* 4.00
95 *Ryan Christiansen* 1.50
96 *Jay Gerhke* 1.00
97 *Jason Stumm* 2.00
98 *Brett Myers* 3.00
99 *Chance Caple* 1.50
100 *Corey Myers* 2.00

2000 Topps HD Autographs

This two-card set features Cal Ripken Jr. and Derek Jeter. Card fronts include the Topps "Certified Autograph Issue" logo stamp as well as the Topps 3M authentication sticker to verify its authenticity. The insert rate for Jeter is 1:859 and Ripken Jr. 1:4,386.

MT
Complete Set (2): 600.00
Jeter 1:859
Ripken 1:4,386
1 Derek Jeter 250.00
2 Cal Ripken Jr. 400.00

2000 Topps HD Ballpark Figures

This 10-card set features a baseball field designed die-cut. These are seeded 1:11 packs and are numbered with a "BF" prefix on the card back.

		MT
Complete Set (10):		50.00
Common Player:		1.50
Inserted 1:11		
1	Mark McGwire	12.00
2	Ken Griffey Jr.	10.00
3	Nomar Garciaparra	8.00
4	Derek Jeter	8.00
5	Sammy Sosa	8.00
6	Mike Piazza	8.00
7	Juan Gonzalez	3.00
8	Larry Walker	2.50
9	Ben Grieve	1.50
10	Barry Bonds	3.00

2000 Topps HD Clearly Refined

This 10-card set focuses on baseball's top young stars heading into the 2000 season. They are printed on high definition card stock and are seeded 1:20 packs. These are numbered with a "CR" prefix on the card back.

		MT
Complete Set (10):		30.00
Common Player:		2.00
Inserted 1:20		
1	Alfonso Soriano	3.00
2	Ruben Mateo	1.50
3	Josh Hamilton	6.00
4	Chad Hermansen	2.00
5	Ryan Anderson	2.00
6	Nick Johnson	3.00
7	Octavio Dotel	2.00
8	Peter Bergeron	2.00
9	Adam Piatt	4.00
10	Pat Burrell	8.00

2000 Topps HD Image

This 10-card insert set highlights those batters with the best eyes at the plate. These were seeded 1:44 packs and are numbered with a "HD" prefix on the card back.

		MT
Complete Set (10):		150.00
Common Player:		5.00
Inserted 1:44		
1	Sammy Sosa	15.00
2	Mark McGwire	30.00
3	Derek Jeter	25.00
4	Albert Belle	5.00
5	Vladimir Guerrero	10.00
6	Ken Griffey Jr.	20.00
7	Mike Piazza	20.00
8	Alex Rodriguez	25.00
9	Barry Bonds	8.00
10	Nomar Garciaparra	20.00

2000 Topps HD On The Cutting Edge

This 10-card insert set is die-cut down the right hand side of the card highlighting the five-tool stars top five baseball attributes. These are inserted 1:22 packs and are numbered with a "CE" prefix on the card back.

		MT
Complete Set (10):		75.00
Common Player:		3.00
Inserted 1:22		
1	Andruw Jones	3.00
2	Nomar Garciaparra	12.00
3	Barry Bonds	5.00
4	Larry Walker	3.00
5	Vladimir Guerrero	8.00
6	Jeff Bagwell	5.00
7	Derek Jeter	12.00
8	Sammy Sosa	12.00
9	Alex Rodriguez	15.00
10	Ken Griffey Jr.	15.00

2000 Topps Opening Day

Essentially identical in design to 2000 Topps regular cards, Opening Day has a silver border with "2000 Opening Day" stamped in silver foil on the card front. The checklist is made up of cards from Series 1 and 2 from Topps base set with identical photos. The rookie reprint card of Hank Aaron was intended to carry card #110, but it does not appear, only the original '54 Topps card #128.

		MT
Complete Set (165):		40.00
Common Player:		.15
Pack (8):		1.00
Wax Box (36):		28.00
1	Mark McGwire	3.00
2	Tony Gwynn	1.50
3	Wade Boggs	.40
4	Cal Ripken Jr.	2.50
5	Matt Williams	.50
6	Jay Buhner	.15
7	Mike Lieberthal	.15
8	Magglio Ordonez	.25
9	Derek Jeter	2.00
10	Javy Lopez	.15
11	Armando Benitez	.15
12	Darin Erstad	.25
13	Mark Grace	.25
14	Eric Karros	.15
15	J.T. Snow Jr.	.15
16	Luis Castillo	.15
17	Rey Ordonez	.15
18	Bob Abreu	.15
19	Warren Morris	.15
20	Juan Gonzalez	1.00
21	Dean Palmer	.15
22	Hank Aaron	3.00
23	Jeff Bagwell	.75
24	Sammy Sosa	2.00
25	Randy Johnson	.50
26	Dante Bichette	.15
27	Frank Thomas	1.00
28	Pedro Martinez	.75
29	Brian Giles	.15
30	Ivan Rodriguez	.75
31	Roger Cedeno	.15
32	David Justice	.40
33	Ken Caminiti	.15
34	Brian Jordan	.15
35	John Olerud	.25
36	Pokey Reese	.15
37	Barry Larkin	.40
38	Edgar Martinez	.15
39	Carlos Delgado	.50
40	Troy Glaus	.40
41	Ben Grieve	.25
42	Jose Lima	.15
43	Luis Gonzalez	.15
44	Alex Rodriguez	2.00
45	Preston Wilson	.15
46	Rickey Henderson	.40
47	Gary Sheffield	.25
48	Jim Edmonds	.15
49	Greg Vaughn	.25
50	Neifi Perez	.15
51	Paul O'Neill	.25
52	Jermaine Dye	.15
53	Curt Schilling	.25
54	Edgardo Alfonzo	.15
55	John Smoltz	.15
56	Chuck Finley	.15
57	Billy Wagner	.15
58	David Cone	.25
59	Roberto Alomar	.50
60	Charles Nagy	.15
61	Mike Mussina	.50
62	Robin Ventura	.25
63	Kevin Brown	.15
64	Pat Hentgen	.15
65	Ryan Klesko	.15
66	Derek Bell	.15
67	Larry Walker	.50
68	Scott Williamson	.15
69	Jose Offerman	.15
70	Doug Mientkiewicz	.15
71	John Snyder	.15
72	Sandy Alomar	.15
73	Joe Nathan	.15
74	Steve Finley	.15
75	Dave Martinez	.15
76	Fernando Tatis	.15
77	Kenny Lofton	.40
78	Paul Byrd	.15
79	Aaron Sele	.15
80	Roger Clemens	1.00
81	Francisco Cordova	.15
82	Wally Joyner	.15
83	Jason Kendall	.25
84	Carlos Beltran	.15
85	Chipper Jones	1.50
86	Vladimir Guerrero	1.00
87	Tom Goodwin	.15
88	Brian Daubach	.15
89	Jay Bell	.15
90	Roy Halladay	.15
91	Miguel Tejada	.15
92	Eric Davis	.15
93	Henry Rodriguez	.15
94	Joe McEwing	.15
95	Jeff Kent	.15
96	Jeff Zimmerman	.15
97	Tony Fernandez	.15
98	Jason Giambi	.15
99	Jose Canseco	.75
100	Alex Gonzalez	.15
101	Erubiel Durazo, Pat Burrell, Nick Johnson (Prospects)	1.00
102	Corey Patterson, Roosevelt Brown, Lance Berkman (Prospects)	.25
103	Eric Munson, *Bobby Bradley* (Draft Picks)	1.00
104	Josh Hamilton, *Corey Myers* (Draft Picks)	1.00
105	Mark McGwire (Magic Moments)	3.00
106	Hank Aaron (Magic Moments)	3.00
107	Cal Ripken Jr. (Magic Moments)	2.50
108	Wade Boggs (Magic Moments)	.40
109	Tony Gwynn (Magic Moments)	1.50
(110)	Hank Aaron (Rookie Reprint)	3.00
111	Tom Glavine	.40
112	Mo Vaughn	.50
113	Tino Martinez	.25
114	Craig Biggio	.40
115	Tim Hudson	.25
116	John Wetteland	.15
117	Ellis Burks	.15
118	David Wells	.15
119	Rico Brogna	.15
120	Greg Maddux	1.50
121	Jeromy Burnitz	.15
122	Raul Mondesi	.25
123	Rondell White	.25
124	Barry Bonds	.75
125	Orlando Hernandez	.40
126	Bartolo Colon	.15
127	Tim Salmon	.25
128	Kevin Young	.15
129	Troy O'Leary	.15
130	Jim Thome	.40
131	Ray Durham	.15
132	Tony Clark	.40
133	Mariano Rivera	.25
134	Omar Vizquel	.15
135	Ken Griffey Jr.	2.50
136	Shawn Green	.50
137	Cliff Floyd	.15
138	Al Leiter	.15
139	Mike Hampton	.15
140	Mike Piazza	2.00
141	Andy Pettitte	.25
142	Albert Belle	.50
143	Scott Rolen	.75
144	Rusty Greer	.15
145	Kevin Millwood	.25
146	Ivan Rodriguez	.75
147	Nomar Garciaparra	2.00
148	Denny Neagle	.15
149	Manny Ramirez	.75
150	Vinny Castilla	.15
151	Andruw Jones	.50
152	Johnny Damon	.15
153	Eric Milton	.15
154	Todd Helton	.50
155	Rafael Palmeiro	.40
156	Damion Easley	.15
157	Carlos Febles	.15
158	Paul Konerko	.25

159	Bernie Williams	.50
160	Ken Griffey Jr. (Magic Moments)	2.50
161	Barry Bonds (Magic Moments)	.75
162	Sammy Sosa (Magic Moments)	2.00
163	Derek Jeter (Magic Moments)	2.00
164	Alex Rodriguez (Magic Moments)	2.00
165	Checklist (Magic Moments)	.15

2000 Topps Opening Day Autographs

		MT
Complete Set (5):		250.00
Common Player:		40.00
1	Edgardo Alfonzo	50.00
2	Wade Boggs	100.00
3	Robin Ventura	40.00
4	Josh Hamilton	50.00
5	Vernon Wells	40.00

2000 Topps Opening Day 2K

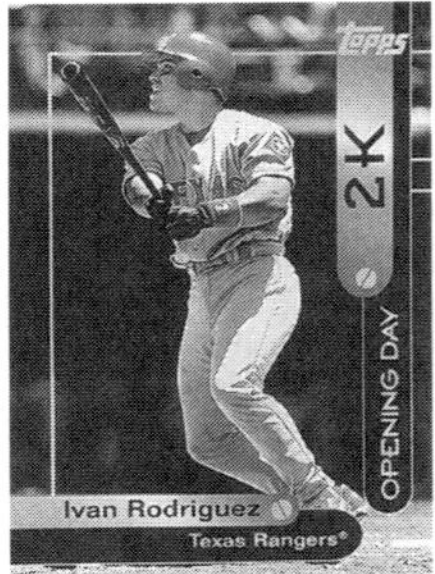

As part of a multi-manufacturer promotion, Topps issued eight cards of an "Opening Day 2K" set. Packages containing some of the 32 cards in the issue were distributed by MLB teams early in the season. The cards were also available exclusively as inserts in Topps Opening Day packs sold at KMart stores early in the season. The Topps OD2K cards have gold-foil graphic highlights on front. Backs have portrait photos, stats and are numbered with an "OD" prefix.

		MT
Complete Set (8):		6.00
Common Player:		.50
1	Mark McGwire	2.00
2	Barry Bonds	.75
3	Ivan Rodriguez	.75
4	Sean Casey	.65
5	Derek Jeter	1.00
6	Vladimir Guerrero	1.00
7	Preston Wilson	.65
8	Ben Grieve	.50

2000 Topps Stars

The base set consists of 200 cards, including a 50-card Spotlights subset (151-200). Card fronts have a shadow image of the featured player in the background of the player photo. The Topps Stars logo, player name, team logo and position are stamped in silver foil.

		MT
Complete Set (200):		35.00
Common Player:		.10
Pack (6):		2.75
Box (24):		60.00
1	Vladimir Guerrero	1.00
2	Eric Karros	.10
3	Omar Vizquel	.10
4	Ken Griffey Jr.	2.50
5	Preston Wilson	.10
6	Albert Belle	.50
7	Ryan Klesko	.10
8	Bob Abreu	.10
9	Warren Morris	.10
10	Rafael Palmeiro	.40
11	Nomar Garciaparra	2.00
12	Dante Bichette	.10
13	Jeff Cirillo	.10
14	Carlos Beltran	.10
15	Tony Clark	.10
16	Ray Durham	.10
17	Mark McGwire	3.00
18	Jim Thome	.40
19	Todd Walker	.10
20	Richie Sexson	.10
21	Adrian Beltre	.10
22	Jay Bell	.10
23	Craig Biggio	.25
24	Ben Grieve	.25
25	Greg Maddux	1.50
26	Fernando Tatis	.10
27	Jeromy Burnitz	.10
28	Vinny Castilla	.10
29	Mark Grace	.25
30	Derek Jeter	2.00
31	Larry Walker	.40
32	Ivan Rodriguez	.75
33	Curt Schilling	.20
34	*Mike Lamb*	.40
35	Kevin Brown	.20
36	Andruw Jones	.40
37	*Chris Mears*	.10
38	Bartolo Colon	.10
39	Edgardo Alfonzo	.25
40	Brady Anderson	.20
41	Andres Galarraga	.50
42	Scott Rolen	.50
43	Manny Ramirez	.75
44	Carlos Delgado	.75
45	David Cone	.10
46	Carl Everett	.10
47	Chipper Jones	1.50
48	Barry Bonds	1.00
49	Dean Palmer	.10
50	Frank Thomas	1.00
51	Paul O'Neill	.25
52	Mo Vaughn	.40
53	Todd Helton	.75
54	Jason Giambi	.20
55	Brian Jordan	.10
56	Luis Gonzalez	.10
57	Alex Rodriguez	2.50
58	J.D. Drew	.10
59	Javy Lopez	.10
60	Tony Gwynn	1.25
61	Jason Kendall	.20
62	Pedro Martinez	.75
63	Matt Williams	.40
64	Gary Sheffield	.40
65	Roberto Alomar	.50
66	*Lyle Overbay*	.10
67	Jeff Bagwell	.75
68	Tim Hudson	.20
69	Sammy Sosa	2.00
70	*Keith Reed*	.10
71	Robin Ventura	.20
72	Cal Ripken Jr.	2.50
73	Alex Gonzalez	.10
74	*Aaron McNeal*	.10
75	Mike Lieberthal	.10
76	Brian Giles	.25
77	Kevin Millwood	.10
78	Troy O'Leary	.10
79	Raul Mondesi	.20
80	John Olerud	.20
81	David Justice	.25
82	Erubiel Durazo	.10
83	Shawn Green	.40
84	Tino Martinez	.20
85	Greg Vaughn	.20
86	Tom Glavine	.20
87	Jose Canseco	.40
88	Kenny Lofton	.25
89	Brian Daubach	.10
90	Mike Piazza	2.00
91	Randy Johnson	.75
92	Pokey Reese	.10
93	Troy Glaus	.50
94	Kerry Wood	.25
95	Sean Casey	.20
96	Magglio Ordonez	.20
97	Bernie Williams	.50
98	Juan Gonzalez	.75
99	Barry Larkin	.30
100	Orlando Hernandez	.20
101	Roger Clemens	1.00
102	Bob Gibson (Retired Stars)	.40
103	Gary Carter (Retired Stars)	.10
104	Willie Stargell (Retired Stars)	.10
105	Joe Morgan (Retired Stars)	.40
106	Brooks Robinson (Retired Stars)	.50
107	Ozzie Smith (Retired Stars)	.50
108	Carl Yastrzemski (Retired Stars)	.25
109	Al Kaline (Retired Stars)	.40
110	Frank Robinson (Retired Stars)	.50
111	Lance Berkman (Shining Prospects)	.10
112	Adam Piatt (Shining Prospects)	.40
113	Vernon Wells (Shining Prospects)	.10
114	Rafael Furcal (Shining Prospects)	.25
115	Rick Ankiel (Shining Prospects)	.40
116	Corey Patterson (Shining Prospects)	.25
117	Josh Hamilton (Shining Prospects)	.75
118	Jack Cust (Shining Prospects)	.40
119	Josh Girdley (Shining Prospects)	.10
120	Pablo Ozuna (Shining Prospects)	.10
121	Sean Burroughs (Shining Prospects)	.40
122	Pat Burrell (Shining Prospects)	.75
123	Chad Hermansen (Shining Prospects)	.10
124	Ruben Mateo (Shining Prospects)	.10
125	Ben Petrick (Shining Prospects)	.10
126	Dee Brown (Shining Prospects)	.10
127	Eric Munson (Shining Prospects)	.10
128	Ruben Salazar (Shining Prospects)	.10
129	Kip Wells (Shining Prospects)	.10
130	Alfonso Soriano (Shining Prospects)	.50
131	Mark Mulder (Shining Prospects)	.10
132	Roosevelt Brown (Shining Prospects)	.10
133	Nick Johnson (Shining Prospects)	.40
134	Kyle Snyder (Shining Prospects)	.10
135	David Walling (Shining Prospects)	.10
136	*Geraldo Guzman*	.50
137	*John Sneed*	.50
138	*Ben Christensen*	.75
139	*Corey Myers*	1.00
140	*Jose Ortiz*	6.00
141	*Ryan Christianson*	1.00
142	*Brett Myers*	2.00
143	*Bobby Bradley*	1.50
144	*Rick Asadoorian*	1.00
145	*Julio Zuleta*	.40
146	*Ty Howington*	.50
147	*Josh Kalinowski*	.40
148	*B.J. Garbe*	1.50
149	*Scott Downs*	.40
150	*Dan Wright*	.50
151	Jeff Bagwell (Veterans)	.40
152	Vladimir Guerrero (Veterans)	.50
153	Mike Piazza (Veterans)	1.00
154	Juan Gonzalez (Veterans)	.40
155	Ivan Rodriguez (Veterans)	.40
156	Manny Ramirez (Veterans)	.40
157	Sammy Sosa (Veterans)	1.00
158	Chipper Jones (Veterans)	.75
159	Shawn Green (Veterans)	.20
160	Ken Griffey Jr. (Veterans)	1.25
161	Cal Ripken Jr. (Veterans)	1.25
162	Nomar Garciaparra (Veterans)	1.00
163	Derek Jeter (Veterans)	1.00
164	Barry Bonds (Veterans)	.50
165	Greg Maddux (Veterans)	.75
166	Mark McGwire (Veterans)	1.50
167	Roberto Alomar (Veterans)	.25
168	Alex Rodriguez (Veterans)	1.25
169	Randy Johnson (Veterans)	.40
170	Tony Gwynn (Veterans)	.60
171	Pedro Martinez (Veterans)	.40
172	Bob Gibson (Retired Stars)	.25
173	Gary Carter (Retired Stars)	.10
174	Willie Stargell (Retired Stars)	.25
175	Joe Morgan (Retired Stars)	.25
176	Brooks Robinson (Retired Stars)	.40
177	Ozzie Smith (Retired Stars)	.50

178	Carl Yastrzemski (Retired Stars)	.20
179	Al Kaline (Retired Stars)	.25
180	Frank Robinson (Retired Stars)	.40
181	Adam Piatt (Prospects)	.20
182	Alfonso Soriano (Prospects)	.40
183	Corey Patterson (Prospects)	.25
184	Vernon Wells (Prospects)	.10
185	Pat Burrell (Prospects)	.40
186	Mark Mulder (Prospects)	.10
187	Eric Munson (Prospects)	.10
188	Rafael Furcal (Prospects)	.15
189	Rick Ankiel (Prospects)	.20
190	Ruben Mateo (Prospects)	.10
191	Sean Burroughs (Prospects)	.20
192	Josh Hamilton (Prospects)	.40
193	Brett Myers	.50
194	Ben Christensen	.40
195	Ty Howington	.25
196	Rick Asadoorian	.40
197	Josh Kalinowski	.20
198	Corey Myers	.50
199	Ryan Christianson	.50
200	John Sneed	.25

2000 Topps Stars Blue

A parallel to the 200-card base set the player shadow has blue tint and the Topps Stars logo, player name, team logo and position are stamped in blue foil. Cards 1-150 are serially numbered on the card back to 299 and cards 151-200 are serially numbered to 99.

	MT
Stars (1-150):	5-10X
Production 299 sets	
Stars (151-180):	20-30X
Rookies (181-200):	8-15X
Production 99 sets	

2000 Topps Stars All-Star Authority

This 14-card set features a gold and silver holo foiled front with gold etching. Card backs are numbered with an "AS" prefix. They are found on the the average of 1:13 packs.

		MT
Complete Set (14):		50.00
Common Player:		1.50
Inserted 1:13		
1	Mark McGwire	8.00
2	Sammy Sosa	5.00
3	Ken Griffey Jr.	6.00
4	Cal Ripken Jr.	6.00
5	Tony Gwynn	3.00
6	Barry Bonds	2.00
7	Mike Piazza	5.00
8	Pedro Martinez	2.00
9	Chipper Jones	4.00
10	Manny Ramirez	2.00
11	Alex Rodriguez	6.00
12	Derek Jeter	5.00
13	Nomar Garciaparra	5.00
14	Roberto Alomar	1.50

2000 Topps Stars Autographs

A combination of retired and current players make up this 13-card set. The set is broken down into two levels: A and B. Level A autographs are seeded 1:382 packs and Level B autographs are found 1:1,636 packs. Each card features the Topps "Certified Autograph Issue" stamp and the Topps "Genuine Issue" sticker on the card back. Card backs are numbered with the featured player's initials.

		MT
Common Player:		15.00
Group A 1:382		
Group B 1:1,636		
RA	Rick Ankiel A	25.00
GC	Gary Carter B	60.00
RF	Rafael Furcal A	40.00
BG	Bob Gibson A	60.00
DJ	Derek Jeter A	180.00
AK	Al Kaline B	250.00
KM	Kevin Millwood A	15.00
JM	Joe Morgan B	90.00
BR	Brooks Robinson B	90.00
FR	Frank Robinson B	75.00
OS	Ozzie Smith B	100.00
WS	Willie Stargell B	50.00
CY	Carl Yastrzemski B	100.00

2000 Topps Stars Game Gear Bats

A piece of the featured player's game-used bat is embedded into the card front and are seeded 1:175 packs.

		MT
Common Player:		15.00
Group A 1:2,289		
Group B 1:1,153		
Group C 1:409		
1	Rafael Furcal C	20.00
2	Sean Burroughs B	20.00
3	Corey Patterson B	20.00
4	Chipper Jones B	45.00
5	Vernon Wells C	15.00
6	Alfonso Soriano B	30.00
7	Eric Munson C	15.00
8	Ben Petrick B	15.00
9	Dee Brown A	15.00
10	Lance Berkman C	20.00

2000 Topps Stars Game Gear Jersey

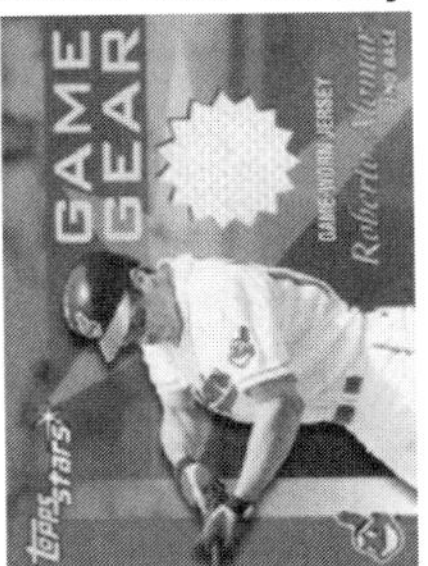

A piece of the featured player's game-used jersey is embedded into the card front and are seeded 1:382 packs.

		MT
Common Player:		20.00
Inserted 1:382		
1	Kevin Millwood	30.00
2	Brad Penny	20.00
3	J.D. Drew	40.00

2000 Topps Stars Progression

Each of the nine cards features three players on a horizontal format, progressing from past, present and future stars at each of the nine positions. They were seeded 1:13 packs and are numbered on the back with an "P" prefix.

		MT
Complete Set (9):		20.00
Common Player:		1.00
Inserted 1:13		
1	Bob Gibson, Pedro Martinez, Rick Ankiel	1.50
2	Gary Carter, Mike Piazza, Ben Petrick	4.00
3	Willie Stargell, Mark McGwire, Pat Burrell	6.00
4	Joe Morgan, Roberto Alomar, Ruben Salazar	1.00
5	Brooks Robinson, Chipper Jones, Sean Burroughs	3.00
6	Ozzie Smith, Derek Jeter, Rafael Furcal	3.00
7	Carl Yastrzemski, Barry Bonds, Josh Hamilton	1.50
8	Al Kaline, Ken Griffey Jr., Ruben Mateo	5.00
9	Frank Robinson, Manny Ramirez, Corey Patterson	1.50

2000 Topps Stars Walk of Fame

This 15-card set spotlights the top stars on a silver and gold holo foiled card front. Card backs feature comparative commentary with the all-time best at their respective positions and are numbered with an "WF" prefix. They are seeded 1:8 packs.

		MT
Complete Set (15):		40.00
Common Player:		1.00
Inserted 1:8		
1	Cal Ripken Jr.	5.00
2	Ken Griffey Jr.	4.00
3	Mark McGwire	6.00
4	Sammy Sosa	3.00
5	Alex Rodriguez	5.00
6	Derek Jeter	4.00
7	Nomar Garciaparra	4.00
8	Chipper Jones	3.00
9	Manny Ramirez	1.50
10	Mike Piazza	4.00
11	Vladimir Guerrero	2.00
12	Barry Bonds	1.50
13	Tony Gwynn	2.00
14	Roberto Alomar	1.00
15	Pedro Martinez	1.50

2000 Topps Subway Series

		MT
Complete Fact. Set (101):		70.00
Complete Set (100):		20.00
Common Player:		.20
1	Mike Piazza	3.00
2	Jay Payton	.20
3	Edgardo Alfonzo	.40
4	Todd Pratt	.20
5	Todd Zeile	.20
6	Mike Bordick	.20
7	Robin Ventura	.40
8	Benny Agbayani	.20
9	Timo Perez	.50
10	Kurt Abbott	.20
11	Matt Franco	.20
12	Bubba Trammell	.20
13	Darryl Hamilton	.20
14	Lenny Harris	.20
15	Joe McEwing	.20
16	Mike Hampton	.40
17	Al Leiter	.40
18	Rick Reed	.20
19	Bobby Jones	.20
20	Glendon Rusch	.20
21	Armando Benitez	.20
22	John Franco	.20
23	Rick White	.20
24	Dennis Cook	.20
25	Turk Wendell	.20
26	Bobby Valentine	.20
27	Derek Jeter	4.00
28	Chuck Knoblauch	.40
29	Tino Martinez	.30
30	Jorge Posada	.40
31	Luis Sojo	.20
32	Scott Brosius	.20
33	Chris Turner	.20
34	Bernie Williams	.75
35	David Justice	.75
36	Paul O'Neill	.40
37	Glenallen Hill	.20
38	Jose Vizcaino	.20
39	Luis Polonia	.20
40	Clay Bellinger	.20
41	Orlando Hernandez	.40
42	Roger Clemens	1.50
43	Andy Pettitte	.50
44	Denny Neagle	.20
45	Dwight Gooden	.30
46	David Cone	.20
47	Mariano Rivera	.50
48	Jeff Nelson	.20
49	Mike Stanton	.20
50	Jason Grimsley	.20
51	Jose Canseco	.75
52	Joe Torre	.50
53	Edgardo Alfonzo	.40
54	Darryl Hamilton	.20
55	John Franco	.20
56	Benny Agbayani	.20
57	Bobby Jones	.20
58	New York Mets	.20
59	Bobby Valentine	.20
60	Mike Piazza	3.00
61	Armando Benitez	.20
62	Mike Piazza	3.00
63	Mike Piazza	3.00
64	Todd Zeile	.20
65	Timo Perez	.50
66	Timo Perez	.50
67	Mike Hampton	.40
68	Andy Pettitte	.50
69	Tino Martinez	.30
70	Joe Torre	.50
71	New York Yankees	.40
72	Orlando Hernandez	.40
73	Bernie Williams	.75
74	Andy Pettitte	.50
75	Mariano Rivera	.50
76	New York Yankees	.40
77	Roger Clemens	1.50
78	Derek Jeter	4.00
79	David Justice	.75
80	Mariano Rivera	.50
81	Tino Martinez	.30
82	New York Yankees	.40
83	Jorge Posada	.40
84	Chuck Knoblauch	.40
85	Jose Vizcaino	.20
86	Roger Clemens	1.50
87	Mike Piazza	3.00
88	Clay Bellinger	.20
89	Robin Ventura	.40
90	Benny Agbayani	.20
91	Orlando Hernandez	.40
92	Derek Jeter	4.00
93	Mike Piazza	3.00
94	Mariano Rivera	.50
95	Derek Jeter	3.00
96	Luis Sojo	.20
97	New York Yankees	.40
98	Mike Hampton	.40
99	David Justice	.75
100	Derek Jeter	4.00

2000 Topps Subway Series Fan Fare

		MT
Common Player:		25.00
Inserted 1:set		
1	Timo Perez	35.00
2	Edgardo Alfonzo	40.00
3	Mike Piazza	150.00
4	Robin Ventura	35.00
5	Todd Zeile	25.00
6	Benny Agbayani	25.00
7	Jay Payton	25.00
8	Mike Bordick	25.00
9	Matt Franco	25.00
10	Mike Hampton	40.00
11	Al Leiter	40.00
12	Rick Reed	25.00
13	Bobby Jones	25.00
14	Glendon Rusch	25.00
15	Darryl Hamilton	25.00
16	Turk Wendell	25.00
17	John Franco	25.00
18	Armando Benitez	25.00
19	Chuck Knoblauch	35.00
20	Derek Jeter	250.00
21	David Justice	40.00
22	Bernie Williams	50.00
23	Jorge Posada	40.00
24	Paul O'Neill	50.00
25	Tino Martinez	35.00
26	Luis Sojo	25.00
27	Scott Brosius	25.00
28	Jose Canseco	80.00
29	Orlando Hernandez	35.00
30	Roger Clemens	100.00
31	Andy Pettitte	40.00
32	Denny Neagle	25.00
33	David Cone	25.00
34	Jeff Nelson	25.00
35	Mike Stanton	25.00
36	Mariano Rivera	60.00

2000 Topps TEK

Forty-five players make up this set including 5 rookies (41-45). Each card is printed on a transparent, polycarbonate stock with patterns 1-15 featuring silver foil metalization. All 45 players are featured on 20 different player focused background patterns. Card backs have two numbers, the first is the player's card number within the set and the second is the pattern number. Patterns 16-20 have color variations and have an insertion rate of 1:10 packs. Each pack contains 4 TEK cards with an SRP of $5.

		MT
Complete Set (45):		50.00
Common Player:		.40
Common Rookie (41-45):		1.00
2,000 serial numbered rookies		
Pack (4):		4.00
Box (20):		75.00
1	Mike Piazza	3.00
2	Chipper Jones	2.50
3	Juan Gonzalez	1.25
4	Ivan Rodriguez	1.25
5	Cal Ripken Jr.	4.00
6	A.J. Burnett	.40
7	Jim Thome	.75
8	Mo Vaughn	.75
9	Andruw Jones	.75
10	Mark McGwire	5.00
11	Jose Canseco	.75
12	Shawn Green	.75
13	Barry Bonds	1.50
14	Bernie Williams	1.00
15	Manny Ramirez	1.25
16	Greg Maddux	2.50
17	Carlos Beltran	.40
18	Pedro Martinez	1.25
19	Jeff Bagwell	1.25
20	Sammy Sosa	3.00
21	J.D. Drew	.40
22	Randy Johnson	1.25
23	Larry Walker	.75
24	Frank Thomas	2.00
25	Orlando Hernandez	.40
26	Scott Rolen	1.00
27	Tony Gwynn	2.00
28	Rick Ankiel	.50
29	Roberto Alomar	1.00
30	Ken Griffey Jr.	4.00
31	Vladimir Guerrero	1.50
32	Derek Jeter	3.00
33	Nomar Garciaparra	3.00
34	Alex Rodriguez	4.00
35	Sean Casey	.40
36	Adam Piatt (Prospects)	.40
37	Corey Patterson (Prospects)	.50
38	Josh Hamilton (Prospects)	1.25
39	Pat Burrell (Prospects)	1.25
40	Eric Munson (Prospects)	.40
41	*Ruben Salazar* (Rookies)	3.00
42	*John Sneed* (Rookies)	1.00
43	*Josh Girdley* (Rookies)	1.50
44	*Brett Myers* (Rookies)	4.00
45	*Rick Asadoorian* (Rookies)	2.50

2000 Topps TEK Color

Color variations make up patterns 16-20 of the base set and instead of metallic silver foil they have a different color background. They are seeded on the average of 1:10 packs.

	MT
Patterns 16-20:	1-2X
Inserted 1:10	

2000 Topps TEK Gold

This parallel to the base set has a rounded top corner and rounded bottom corner with a gold background. Each pattern is serially numbered on the card back in an edition of 10 sets.

	MT
Stars:	10-20X
Rookies:	5-10X
Production 10 sets	

2000 Topps TEK ArchiTEKs

Printed on a clear, polycarbonate card stock the TEK logo, and player name are stamped in gold foil. Card backs are numbered with an "A" prefix. They are found on the average of 1:5 packs.

		MT
Complete Set (18):		60.00
Common Player:		1.50
Inserted 1:5		
1	Nomar Garciaparra	5.00
2	Derek Jeter	5.00
3	Chipper Jones	4.00
4	Vladimir Guerrero	3.00
5	Mark McGwire	8.00
6	Ken Griffey Jr.	6.00
7	Mike Piazza	5.00
8	Jeff Bagwell	2.00
9	Larry Walker	1.50
10	Manny Ramirez	2.00
11	Alex Rodriguez	6.00
12	Sammy Sosa	5.00
13	Shawn Green	1.50
14	Juan Gonzalez	2.00
15	Barry Bonds	2.00
16	Pedro Martinez	2.00
17	Cal Ripken Jr.	6.00
18	Ivan Rodriguez	2.00

2000 Topps TEK DramaTEK Performers

Printed on a clear, polycarbonate stock, the insert name and TEK logo are stamped in blue foil. Card backs are numbered with an "DP" prefix and are seeded 1:10 packs.

		MT
Complete Set (9):		50.00
Common Player:		3.00
Inserted 1:10		
1	Mark McGwire	10.00
2	Sammy Sosa	6.00
3	Ken Griffey Jr.	8.00
4	Nomar Garciaparra	6.00
5	Chipper Jones	5.00
6	Mike Piazza	6.00
7	Alex Rodriguez	8.00
8	Derek Jeter	6.00
9	Vladimir Guerrero	3.00

2000 Topps TEK TEKtonics

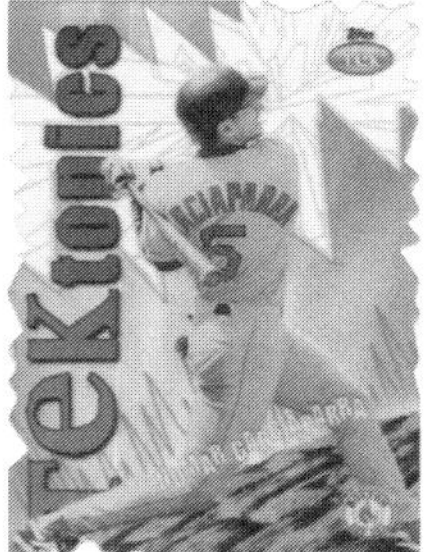

This nine-card set features baseball's top hitters on a die-cut design on a clear, polycarbonate stock. Card backs are numbered with an "TT" prefix and are inserted 1:30 packs.

		MT
Complete Set (9):		100.00
Common Player:		5.00
Inserted 1:30		
1	Derek Jeter	12.00
2	Mark McGwire	20.00
3	Ken Griffey Jr.	12.00
4	Mike Piazza	12.00
5	Alex Rodriguez	12.00
6	Chipper Jones	10.00
7	Nomar Garciaparra	12.00
8	Sammy Sosa	10.00
9	Cal Ripken Jr.	15.00

2001 Topps

		MT
Complete Set (790):		80.00
Complete Ser. 1 Set (405):		40.00
Complete Ser. 2 Set (385):		45.00
Complete Factory Set (795):		100.00
Common Player:		.10
Ser. 1 Pack (10):		2.00
Ser. 1 Box (36):		65.00
Ser. 2 Pack (10):		1.75
Ser. 2 Box (36):		60.00
1	Cal Ripken Jr.	1.50
2	Chipper Jones	1.00
3	Roger Cedeno	.10
4	Garret Anderson	.10
5	Robin Ventura	.20
6	Daryle Ward	.10
7	Not Issued	.10
8	Ron Gant	.20
9	Phil Nevin	.10
10	Jermaine Dye	.10
11	Chris Singleton	.10
12	Mike Stanton	.10
13	Brian Hunter	.10
14	Mike Redmond	.10
15	Jim Thome	.25
16	Brian Jordan	.10
17	Joe Girardi	.10
18	Steve Woodard	.10
19	Dustin Hermanson	.10
20	Shawn Green	.30
21	Todd Stottlemyre	.10
22	Dan Wilson	.10
23	Todd Pratt	.10
24	Derek Lowe	.10
25	Juan Gonzalez	.40
26	Clay Bellinger	.10
27	Jeff Fassero	.10
28	Pat Meares	.10
29	Eddie Taubensee	.10
30	Paul O'Neill	.25
31	Jeffrey Hammonds	.10
32	Pokey Reese	.10
33	Mike Mussina	.30
34	Rico Brogna	.10
35	Jay Buhner	.10
36	Steve Cox	.10
37	Quilvio Veras	.10
38	Marquis Grissom	.10
39	Shigetoshi Hasagawa	.10
40	Shane Reynolds	.10
41	Adam Piatt	.10
42	Luis Polonia	.10
43	Brook Fordyce	.10
44	Preston Wilson	.10
45	Ellis Burks	.10
46	Armando Rios	.10
47	Chuck Finley	.10
48	Dan Plesac	.10
49	Shannon Stewart	.10
50	Mark McGwire	1.50
51	Mark Loretta	.10
52	Gerald Williams	.10
53	Eric Young	.10
54	Peter Bergeron	.10
55	Dave Hansen	.10
56	Arthur Rhodes	.10
57	Bobby Jones	.10
58	Matt Clement	.10
59	Mike Benjamin	.10
60	Pedro Martinez	.50
61	Jose Canseco	.40
62	Matt Anderson	.10
63	Torii Hunter	.10
64	Carlos Lee	.10
65	David Cone	.10
66	Ray Sanchez	.10
67	Eric Chavez	.20
68	Rick Helling	.10
69	Manny Alexander	.10
70	John Franco	.10
71	Mike Bordick	.10
72	Andres Galarraga	.25
73	Jose Cruz Jr.	.10
74	Mike Matheny	.10
75	Randy Johnson	.50
76	Richie Sexson	.10
77	Vladimir Nunez	.10
78	Harold Baines	.10
79	Aaron Boone	.10
80	Darin Erstad	.40
81	Alex Gonzalez	.10
82	Gil Heredia	.10
83	Shane Andrews	.10
84	Todd Hundley	.10
85	Bill Mueller	.10
86	Mark McLemore	.10
87	Scott Spiezio	.10
88	Kevin McGlinchy	.10
89	Bubba Trammell	.10
90	Manny Ramirez	.50
91	Mike Lamb	.10
92	Scott Karl	.10
93	Brian Buchanan	.10
94	Chris Turner	.10
95	Mike Sweeney	.10
96	John Wetteland	.10
97	Rob Bell	.10
98	Pat Rapp	.10
99	John Burkett	.10
100	Derek Jeter	1.50
101	J.D. Drew	.25
102	Jose Offerman	.10
103	Rick Reed	.10
104	Will Clark	.30
105	Rickey Henderson	.25
106	Dave Berg	.10
107	Kirk Rueter	.10
108	Lee Stevens	.10
109	Jay Bell	.10
110	Fred McGriff	.20
111	Julio Zuleta	.10
112	Brian Anderson	.10
113	Orlando Cabrera	.10
114	Alex Fernandez	.10
115	Derek Bell	.10
116	Eric Owens	.10
117	Brian Bohannon	.10
118	Dennys Reyes	.10
119	Mike Stanley	.10
120	Jorge Posada	.20
121	Rich Becker	.10
122	Paul Konerko	.10
123	Mike Remlinger	.10
124	Travis Lee	.10
125	Ken Caminiti	.10
126	Kevin Barker	.10
127	Paul Quantrill	.10
128	Ozzie Guillen	.10
129	Kevin Tapani	.10
130	Mark Johnson	.10
131	Randy Wolf	.10
132	Michael Tucker	.10
133	Darren Lewis	.10
134	Joe Randa	.10
135	Jeff Cirillo	.10
136	David Ortiz	.10
137	Herb Perry	.10
138	Jeff Nelson	.10
139	Chris Stynes	.10
140	Johnny Damon	.10
141	Desi Relaford	.10
142	Jason Schmidt	.10
143	Charles Johnson	.10
144	Pat Burrell	.40
145	Gary Sheffield	.25
146	Tom Glavine	.25
147	Jason Isringhausen	.10
148	Chris Carpenter	.10
149	Jeff Suppan	.10
150	Ivan Rodriguez	.50
151	Luis Sojo	.10
152	Ron Villone	.10
153	Mike Sirotka	.10
154	Chuck Knoblauch	.20
155	Jason Kendall	.10
156	Dennis Cook	.10
157	Bobby Estalella	.10
158	Jose Guillen	.10
159	Thomas Howard	.10
160	Carlos Delgado	.50
161	Benji Gil	.10
162	Tim Bogar	.10
163	Kevin Elster	.10
164	Scott Downs	.10
165	Andy Benes	.10
166	Adrian Beltre	.10
167	David Bell	.10
168	Turk Wendell	.10
169	Pete Harnisch	.10
170	Roger Clemens	.75
171	Scott Williamson	.10
172	Kevin Jordan	.10
173	Brad Penny	.10
174	John Flaherty	.10
175	Troy Glaus	.50
176	Kevin Appier	.10
177	Walt Weiss	.10
178	Tyler Houston	.10
179	Michael Barrett	.10
180	Mike Hampton	.10
181	Francisco Cordova	.10
182	Mike Jackson	.10
183	David Segui	.10
184	Carlos Febles	.10
185	Roy Halladay	.10
186	Seth Etherton	.10
187	Charlie Hayes	.10
188	Fernando Tatis	.10
189	Steve Trachsel	.10
190	Livan Hernandez	.10
191	Joe Oliver	.10
192	Stan Javier	.10
193	B.J. Surhoff	.10
194	Rob Ducey	.10
195	Barry Larkin	.25
196	Danny Patterson	.10
197	Bobby Howry	.10
198	Dmitri Young	.10
199	Brian Hunter	.10
200	Alex Rodriguez	1.25
201	Hideo Nomo	.25
202	Luis Alicea	.10
203	Warren Morris	.10
204	Antonio Alfonseca	.10
205	Edgardo Alfonzo	.20
206	Mark Grudzielanek	.10
207	Fernando Vina	.10
208	Willie Greene	.10
209	Homer Bush	.10
210	Jason Giambi	.30

211 Mike Morgan .10
212 Steve Karsay .10
213 Matt Lawton .10
214 Wendell Magee Jr. .10
215 Rusty Greer .10
216 Keith Lockhart .10
217 Billy Koch .10
218 Todd Hollandsworth .10
219 Raul Ibanez .10
220 Tony Gwynn .75
221 Carl Everett .20
222 Hector Carrasco .10
223 Jose Valentin .10
224 Deivi Cruz .10
225 Bret Boone .10
226 Kurt Abbott .10
227 Melvin Mora .10
228 Danny Graves .10
229 Jose Jimenez .10
230 James Baldwin .10
231 C.J. Nitkowski .10
232 Jeff Zimmerman .10
233 Mike Lowell .10
234 Hideki Irabu .10
235 Greg Vaughn .20
236 Omar Daal .10
237 Darren Dreifort .10
238 Gil Meche .10
239 Damian Jackson .10
240 Frank Thomas .75
241 Travis Miller .10
242 Jeff Frye .10
243 Dave Magadan .10
244 Luis Castillo .10
245 Bartolo Colon .10
246 Steve Kline .10
247 Shawon Dunston .10
248 Rick Aguilera .10
249 Omar Olivares .10
250 Craig Biggio .20
251 Scott Schoeneweis .10
252 Dave Veres .10
253 Ramon Martinez .10
254 Jose Vidro .10
255 Todd Helton .50
256 Greg Norton .10
257 Jacque Jones .10
258 Jason Grimsley .10
259 Dan Reichert .10
260 Robb Nen .10
261 Mark Clark .10
262 Scott Hatteberg .10
263 Doug Brocail .10
264 Mark Johnson .10
265 Eric Davis .20
266 Terry Shumpert .10
267 Kevin Millar .10
268 Ismael Valdes .10
269 Richard Hidalgo .20
270 Randy Velarde .10
271 Bengie Molina .10
272 Tony Womack .10
273 Enrique Wilson .10
274 Jeff Brantley .10
275 Rick Ankiel .25
276 Terry Mulholland .10
277 Ron Belliard .10
278 Terrence Long .10
279 Alberto Castillo .10
280 Royce Clayton .10
281 Joe McEwing .10
282 Jason McDonald .10
283 Ricky Bottalico .10
284 Keith Foulke .10
285 Brad Radke .10
286 Gabe Kapler .10
287 Pedro Astacio .10
288 Armando Reynoso .10
289 Darryl Kile .10
290 Reggie Sanders .10
291 Esteban Yan .10
292 Joe Nathan .10
293 Jay Payton .10
294 Francisco Cordero .10
295 Gregg Jefferies .10
296 LaTroy Hawkins .10
297 Jeff Tam .10
298 Jacob Cruz .10
299 Chris Holt .10
300 Vladimir Guerrero .75
301 Marvin Benard .10
302 Matt Franco .10
303 Mike Williams .10
304 Sean Bergman .10
305 Juan Encarnacion .10
306 Russ Davis .10
307 Hanley Frias .10
308 Ramon Hernandez .10
309 Matt Walbeck .10
310 Bill Spiers .10
311 Bob Wickman .10
312 Sandy Alomar .10
313 Eddie Guardado .10
314 Shane Halter .10
315 Geoff Jenkins .20
316 Gerald Witasick .10
317 Damian Miller .10
318 Darrin Fletcher .10
319 Rafael Furcal .25
320 Mark Grace .25
321 Mark Mulder .10
322 Joe Torre (Managers) .10
323 Bobby Cox (Managers) .10
324 Mike Scioscia (Managers) .10
325 Mike Hargrove (Managers) .10
326 Jimy Williams (Managers) .10
327 Jerry Manuel (Managers) .10
328 Buck Showalter (Managers) .10
329 Charlie Manuel (Managers) .10
330 Don Baylor (Managers) .10
331 Phil Garner (Managers) .10
332 Jack McKeon (Managers) .10
333 Tony Muser (Managers) .10
334 Buddy Bell (Managers) .10
335 Tom Kelly (Managers) .10
336 John Boles (Managers) .10
337 Art Howe (Managers) .10
338 Larry Dierker (Managers) .10
339 Lou Pinella (Managers) .10
340 Davey Johnson (Managers) .10
341 Larry Rothschild (Managers) .10
342 Davey Lopes (Managers) .10
343 Johnny Oates (Managers) .10
344 Felipe Alou (Managers) .10
345 Jim Fregosi (Managers) .10
346 Bobby Valentine (Managers) .10
347 Terry Francona (Managers) .10
348 Gene Lamont (Managers) .10
349 Tony LaRussa (Managers) .10
350 Bruce Bochy (Managers) .10
351 Dusty Baker (Managers) .10
352 Adrian Gonzalez, Adam Johnson (Draft Picks) .75
353 Matt Wheatland, Brian Digby (Draft Picks) .40
354 Tripper Johnson, Scott Thorman (Draft Picks) .40
355 Phil Dumatrait, Adam Wainwright (Draft Picks) .40
356 Scott Heard, *David Parrish* (Draft Picks) .75
357 Rocco Baldelli, *Mark Folsom* (Draft Picks) .40
358 *Dominic Rich*, Aaron Herr (Draft Picks) .40
359 Mike Stodolka, Sean Burnett (Draft Picks) .25
360 Derek Thompson, Corey Smith (Draft Picks) .40
361 *Danny Borrell ,Jason Bourgeois* (Draft Picks) .40
362 Chin-Feng Chen, Corey Patterson, Josh Hamilton (Prospects) .25
363 Ryan Anderson, Barry Zito, C.C. Sabathia (Prospects) .75
364 Scott Sobkowiak, David Walling, Ben Sheets (Prospects) .50
365 Ty Howington, Josh Kalinowski, Josh Girdley (Prospects) .10
366 *Hee Seop Choi*, Aaron McNeal, Jason Hart (Prospects) 1.50
367 Bobby Bradley, Kurt Ainsworth, Chin-Hui Tsao (Prospects) .75
368 Mike Glendenning, Kenny Kelly, *Juan Silvestri* (Prospects) .25
369 J.R. House, Ramon Castro, Ben Davis (Prospects) .75
370 Chance Caple ,*Rafael Soriano*, Pasqual Coco (Prospects) .40
371 *Travis Hafner*, Eric Munson, Bucky Jacobsen (Prospects) .25
372 Jason Conti, Chris Wakeland, Brian Cole (Prospects) .20
373 Scott Seabol, Aubrey Huff, Joe Crede (Prospects) .40
374 Adam Everett, Jose Ortiz, Keith Ginter (Prospects) .75
375 Carlos Hernandez, Geraldo Guzman, Adam Eaton (Prospects) .25
376 Bobby Kielty, Milton Bradley, Juan Rivera (Prospects) .25
377 Mark McGwire (Golden Moments) .75
378 Don Larsen (Golden Moments) .20
379 Bobby Thomson (Golden Moments) .10
380 Bill Mazeroski (Golden Moments) .20
381 Reggie Jackson (Golden Moments) .40
382 Kirk Gibson (Golden Moments) .10
383 Roger Maris (Golden Moments) .40
384 Cal Ripken Jr. (Golden Moments) .75
385 Hank Aaron (Golden Moments) .75
386 Joe Carter (Golden Moments) .10
387 Cal Ripken Jr. (Season Highlights) .75
388 Randy Johnson (Season Highlights) .30
389 Ken Griffey Jr. (Season Highlights) .75
390 Troy Glaus (Season Highlights) .30
391 Kazuhiro Sasaki (Season Highlights) .40
392 Sammy Sosa, Troy Glaus (League Leaders) .50
393 Todd Helton, Edgar Martinez (League Leaders) .25
394 Nomar Garciaparra, Todd Helton (League Leaders) .50
395 Barry Bonds, Jason Giambi (League Leaders) .40
396 Todd Helton, Manny Ramirez (League Leaders) .25
397 Todd Helton, Darin Erstad (League Leaders) .25
398 Kevin Brown, Pedro Martinez (League Leaders) .25
399 Randy Johnson, Pedro Martinez (League Leaders) .25
400 Will Clark (Playoff Highlights) .20
401 NY Mets Divisional Highlight .10
402 NY Yankees Divisional Highlight .10
403 Seattle Mariners Divisional Highlight .10
404 Mike Hampton (Playoff Highlights) .10
405 NY Yankees ALCS Highlight .75
406 World Series Highlight 1.00
407 Jeff Bagwell .50
408 Brant Brown .10
409 Brad Fullmer .10
410 Dean Palmer .10
411 Greg Zaun .10
412 Jose Vizcaino .10
413 Jeff Abbott .10
414 Travis Fryman .15
415 Mike Cameron .10
416 Matt Mantei .10
417 Alan Benes .10
418 Mickey Morandini .10
419 Troy Percival .10
420 Eddie Perez .10
421 Vernon Wells .10
422 Ricky Gutierrez .10
423 Carlos Hernandez .10
424 Chan Ho Park .15
425 Armando Benitez .10
426 Sidney Ponson .10
427 Adrian Brown .10
428 Ruben Mateo .20
429 Alex Ochoa .10
430 Jose Rosado .10
431 Masato Yoshii .10
432 Corey Koskie .10
433 Andy Pettitte .20
434 Brian Daubach .10
435 Sterling Hitchcock .10
436 Timo Perez .10
437 Shawn Estes .10
438 Tony Armas Jr. .10
439 Danny Bautista .10
440 Randy Winn .10
441 Wilson Alvarez .10
442 Rondell White .15
443 Jeromy Burnitz .10
444 Kelvim Escobar .10
445 Paul Bako .10
446 Javier Vazquez .10
447 Eric Gagne .10
448 Kenny Lofton .20
449 Mark Kotsay .10
450 Jamie Moyer .10
451 Delino DeShields .10
452 Rey Ordonez .10
453 Russ Ortiz .10
454 Dave Burba .10
455 Eric Karros .15
456 Felix Martinez .10
457 Tony Batista .10
458 Bobby Higginson .10
459 Jeff D'Amico .10
460 Shane Spencer .10
461 Brent Mayne .10
462 Glendon Rusch .10
463 Chris Gomez .10
464 Jeff Shaw .10
465 Damon Buford .10
466 Mike DiFelice .10
467 Jimmy Haynes .10
468 Billy Wagner .10
469 A.J. Hinch .10
470 Gary DiSarcina .10
471 Tom Lampkin .10
472 Adam Eaton .10
473 Brian Giles .15
474 John Thomson .10
475 Cal Eldred .10
476 Ramiro Mendoza .10
477 Scott Sullivan .10
478 Scott Rolen .25
479 Todd Ritchie .10
480 Pablo Ozuna .10
481 Carl Pavano .10
482 Matt Morris .10
483 Matt Stairs .10
484 Tim Belcher .10
485 Lance Berkman .15
486 Brian Meadows .10
487 Bobby Abreu .10
488 John Vander Wal .10
489 Donnie Sadler .10
490 Damion Easley .10
491 David Justice .25
492 Ray Durham .10

493 Todd Zeile .10
494 Desi Relaford .10
495 Cliff Floyd .10
496 Scott Downs .10
497 Barry Bonds .75
498 Jeff D'Amico .10
499 Octavio Dotel .10
500 Kent Mercker .10
501 Craig Grebeck .10
502 Roberto Hernandez .10
503 Matt Williams .15
504 Bruce Aven .10
505 Brett Tomko .10
506 Kris Benson .10
507 Neifi Perez .10
508 Alfonso Soriano .40
509 Keith Osik .10
510 Matt Franco .10
511 Steve Finley .10
512 Olmedo Saenz .10
513 Esteban Loaiza .10
514 Adam Kennedy .10
515 Scott Elarton .10
516 Moises Alou .15
517 Bryan Rekar .10
518 Darryl Hamilton .10
519 Osvaldo Fernandez .10
520 Kip Wells .10
521 Bernie Williams .40
522 Mike Darr .10
523 Marlon Anderson .10
524 Derrek Lee .10
525 Ugueth Urbina .10
526 Vinny Castilla .10
527 David Wells .10
528 Jason Marquis .10
529 Orlando Palmeiro .10
530 Carlos Perez .10
531 J.T. Snow Jr. .10
532 Al Leiter .15
533 Jimmy Anderson .10
534 Brett Laxton .10
535 Butch Huskey .10
536 Orlando Hernandez .20
537 Magglio Ordonez .15
538 Willie Blair .10
539 Kevin Sefcik .10
540 Chad Curtis .10
541 John Halama .10
542 Andy Fox .10
543 Juan Guzman .10
544 Frank Menechino .10
545 Raul Mondesi .15
546 Tim Salmon .15
547 Ryan Rupe .10
548 Jeff Reed .10
549 Mike Mordecai .10
550 Jeff Kent .15
551 Wiki Gonzalez .10
552 Kenny Rogers .10
553 Kevin Young .10
554 Brian Johnson .10
555 Tom Goodwin .10
556 Tony Clark .10
557 Mac Suzuki .10
558 Brian Moehler .10
559 Jim Parque .10
560 Mariano Rivera .20
561 Trot Nixon .10
562 Mike Mussina .30
563 Nelson Figueroa .10
564 Alex Gonzalez .10
565 Benny Agbayani .10
566 Ed Sprague .10
567 Scott Erickson .10
568 Abraham Nunez .10
569 Jerry DiPoto .10
570 Sean Casey .10
571 Wilton Veras .10
572 Joe Mays .10
573 Bill Simas .10
574 Doug Glanville .10
575 Scott Sauerbeck .10
576 Ben Davis .10
577 Jesus Sanchez .10
578 Ricardo Rincon .10
579 John Olerud .15
580 Curt Schilling .15
581 Alex Cora .10
582 Pat Hentgen .10
583 Javy Lopez .15
584 Ben Grieve .15
585 Frank Castillo .10
586 Kevin Stocker .10
587 Mark Sweeney .10
588 Ray Lankford .10
589 Turner Ward .10
590 Felipe Crespo .10
591 Omar Vizquel .15
592 Mike Lieberthal .10
593 Ken Griffey Jr. 1.50
594 Troy O'Leary .10
595 Dave Mlicki (Front photo actually Brian Moehler.) .10
596 Manny Ramirez .50
597 Mike Lansing .10
598 Rich Aurilia .10
599 Russ Branyan .10
600 Russ Johnson .10
601 Gregg Colbrunn .10
602 Andruw Jones .40
603 Henry Blanco .10
604 Jarrod Washburn .10
605 Tony Eusebio .10
606 Aaron Sele .10
607 Charles Nagy .10
608 Ryan Klesko .10
609 Dante Bichette .10
610 Bill Haselman .10
611 Jerry Spradlin .10
612 Alex Rodriguez 1.25
613 Jose Silva .10
614 Darren Oliver .10
615 Pat Mahomes .10
616 Roberto Alomar .40
617 Edgar Renteria .10
618 Jon Lieber .10
619 John Rocker .10
620 Miguel Tejada .15
621 Mo Vaughn .15
622 Jose Lima .10
623 Kerry Wood .15
624 Mike Timlin .10
625 Wil Cordero .10
626 Albert Belle .15
627 Bobby Jones .10
628 Doug Mirabelli .10
629 Jason Tyner .10
630 Andy Ashby .10
631 Jose Hernandez .10
632 Devon White .10
633 Ruben Rivera .10
634 Steve Parris .10
635 David McCarty .10
636 Jose Canseco .25
637 Todd Walker .10
638 Stan Spencer .10
639 Wayne Gomes .10
640 Freddy Garcia .10
641 Jeremy Giambi .10
642 Luis Lopez .10
643 John Smoltz .10
644 Kelly Stinnett .10
645 Kevin Brown .10
646 Wilton Guerrero .10
647 Al Martin .10
648 Woody Williams .10
649 Brian Rose .10
650 Rafael Palmeiro .30
651 Pete Schourek .10
652 Kevin Jarvis .10
653 Mark Redman .10
654 Ricky Ledee .10
655 Larry Walker .20
656 Paul Byrd .10
657 Jason Bere .10
658 Rick White .10
659 Calvin Murray .10
660 Greg Maddux 1.00
661 Ron Gant .10
662 Eli Marrero .10
663 Graeme Lloyd .10
664 Trevor Hoffman .10
665 Nomar Garciaparra 1.25
666 Glenallen Hill .10
667 Matt LeCroy .10
668 Justin Thompson .10
669 Brady Anderson .10
670 Miguel Batista .10
671 Erubiel Durazo .10
672 Kevin Millwood .10
673 Mitch Meluskey .10
674 Luis Gonzalez .15
675 Edgar Martinez .10
676 Robert Person .10
677 Benito Santiago .10
678 Todd Jones .10
679 Tino Martinez .15
680 Carlos Beltran .10
681 Gabe White .10
682 Bret Saberhagen .10
683 Jeff Conine .10
684 Jaret Wright .10
685 Bernard Gilkey .10
686 Garrett Stephenson .10
687 Jamey Wright .10
688 Sammy Sosa 1.00
689 John Jaha .10
690 Ramon Martinez .10
691 Robert Fick .10
692 Eric Milton .10
693 Denny Neagle .10
694 Ron Coomer .10
695 John Valentin .10
696 Placido Polanco .10
697 Tim Hudson .15
698 Marty Cordova .10
699 Chad Kreuter .10
700 Frank Catalanotto .10
701 Tim Wakefield .10
702 Jim Edmonds .15
703 Michael Tucker .10
704 Cristian Guzman .10
705 Joey Hamilton .10
706 Mike Piazza 1.25
707 Dave Martinez .10
708 Mike Hampton .15
709 Bobby Bonilla .10
710 Juan Pierre .10
711 John Parrish .10
712 Kory DeHaan .10
713 Brian Tollberg .10
714 Chris Truby .10
715 Emil Brown .10
716 Ryan Dempster .10
717 Rich Garces .10
718 Mike Myers .10
719 Luis Ordaz .10
720 Kazuhiro Sasaki .10
721 Mark Quinn .10
722 Ramon Ortiz .10
723 Kerry Ligtenberg .10
724 Rolando Arrojo .10
725 *Tsuyoshi Shinjo* 1.50
726 *Ichiro Suzuki* 12.00
727 Roy Oswalt, Pat Strange, Jon Rauch (Prospects) .75
728 *Phil Wilson,Jake Peavy,Darwin Cubillan* (Prospects) .50
729 *Steve Smyth*, Mike Bynum, Nathan Haynes (Prospects) .40
730 Michael Cuddyer, Joe Lawrence, Choo Freeman (Prospects) .10
731 Carlos Pena, Larry Barnes, Dewayne Wise (Prospects) .10
732 Gookie Dawkins,*Erick Almonte*, Felipe Lopez (Prospects) .40
733 Alex Escobar, Eric Valent, Brad Wilkerson (Prospects) .10
734 Toby Hall, Rod Barajas,*Jeff Goldbach* (Prospects) .10
735 Jason Romano, Marcus Giles, Pablo Ozuna (Prospects) .10
736 Dee Brown, Jack Cust, Vernon Wells (Prospects) .10
737 David Espinosa, *Luis Montanez* (Draft Picks) 1.00
738 John Lackey,*Justin Wayne* (Draft Picks) .75
739 *Josh Axelson,Carmen Cali* (Draft Picks) .50
740 *Shaun Boyd,Chris Morris* (Draft Picks) .50
741 *Tommy Arko,Dan Moylan* (Draft Picks) .50
742 *Luis Cotto*, Luis Escobar (Draft Picks) .40
743 *Brandon Mims,Blake Williams* (Draft Picks) .75
744 *Chris Russ*, Bryan Edwards (Draft Picks) .40
745 Joe Torres, Ben Diggins (Draft Picks) .10
746 Mark Dalesandro, *Edwin Encarnacion* (Draft Picks) .40
747 *Brian Bass,Odannis Ayala* (Draft Picks) .40
748 *Jason Kaanoi,Michael Mathews* (Draft Picks) .10
749 *Stuart McFarland,Adam Sterrett* (Draft Picks) .40
750 David Krynzel, Grady Sizemore (Draft Picks) .50
751 Keith Bucktrot, Dane Sardinha (Draft Picks) .10
752 Anaheim Angels .10
753 Arizona Diamondbacks .10
754 Atlanta Braves .10
755 Baltimore Orioles .10
756 Boston Red Sox .10
757 Chicago Cubs .10
758 Chicago White Sox .10
759 Cincinnati Reds .10
760 Cleveland Indians .10
761 Colorado Rockies .10
762 Detroit Tigers .10
763 Florida Marlins .10
764 Houston Astros .10
765 Kansas City Royals .10
766 Los Angeles Dodgers .10
767 Milwaukee Brewers .10
768 Minnesota Twins .10
769 Montreal Expos .10
770 New York Mets .10
771 New York Yankees .75
772 Oakland Athletics .10
773 Philadelphia Phillies .10
774 Pittsburgh Pirates .10
775 San Diego Padres .10
776 San Francisco Giants .10
777 Seattle Mariners .10
778 St. Louis Cardinals .10
779 Tampa Bay Devil Rays .10
780 Texas Rangers .10
781 Toronto Blue Jays .10
782 Bucky Dent (Golden Moments) .10
783 Jackie Robinson (Golden Moments) 1.00
784 Roberto Clemente (Golden Moments) 1.00
785 Nolan Ryan (Golden Moments) 1.50
786 Kerry Wood (Golden Moments) .10
787 Rickey Henderson (Golden Moments) .20
788 Lou Brock (Golden Moments) .25
789 David Wells (Golden Moments) .10
790 Andruw Jones (Golden Moments) .25
791 Carlton Fisk (Golden Moments) .10

2001 Topps Golden Anniversary

		MT
Complete Set (50):		100.00
Common Player:		1.00
Inserted 1:10		
1	Hank Aaron	6.00
2	Ernie Banks	2.50
3	Mike Schmidt	4.00
4	Willie Mays	5.00
5	Johnny Bench	2.50
6	Tom Seaver	2.50
7	Frank Robinson	1.50
8	Sandy Koufax	6.00

9	Bob Gibson	2.00
10	Ted Williams	8.00
11	Cal Ripken Jr.	8.00
12	Tony Gwynn	3.00
13	Mark McGwire	8.00
14	Ken Griffey Jr.	6.00
15	Greg Maddux	5.00
16	Roger Clemens	3.00
17	Barry Bonds	3.00
18	Rickey Henderson	1.00
19	Mike Piazza	6.00
20	Jose Canseco	2.00
21	Derek Jeter	8.00
22	Nomar Garciaparra	6.00
23	Alex Rodriguez	6.00
24	Sammy Sosa	5.00
25	Ivan Rodriguez	2.50
26	Vladimir Guerrero	3.00
27	Chipper Jones	5.00
28	Jeff Bagwell	2.50
29	Pedro Martinez	3.00
30	Randy Johnson	2.50
31	Pat Burrell	2.00
32	Josh Hamilton	2.00
33	Nick Johnson	1.00
34	Corey Patterson	1.00
35	Eric Munson	1.00
36	Sean Burroughs	1.00
37	Alfonso Soriano	1.00
38	Chin-Feng Chen	2.00
39	Barry Zito	3.00
40	Adrian Gonzalez	3.00
41	Mark McGwire	8.00
42	Nomar Garciaparra	6.00
43	Todd Helton	2.50
44	Matt Williams	1.00
45	Troy Glaus	2.50
46	Geoff Jenkins	1.00
47	Frank Thomas	3.00
48	Mo Vaughn	1.00
49	Barry Larkin	1.50
50	J.D. Drew	1.00

2001 Topps Gold

	MT
Stars:	8-15X
Prospects and RCs:	6-12X
Inserted 1:17	

2001 Topps A Look Ahead

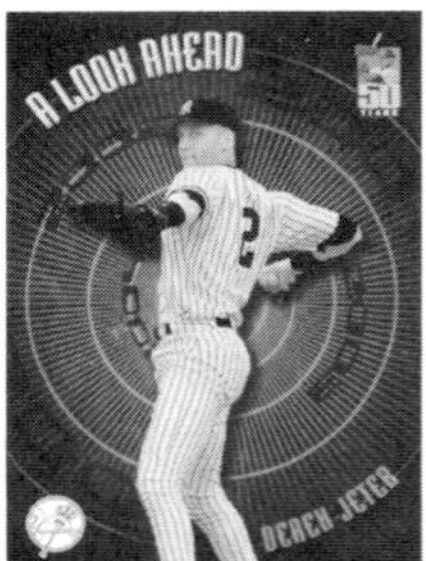

		MT
Complete Set (10):		40.00
Common Player:		2.00
Inserted 1:25		
1	Vladimir Guerrero	3.00
2	Derek Jeter	8.00
3	Todd Helton	2.50
4	Alex Rodriguez	8.00
5	Ken Griffey Jr.	6.00
6	Nomar Garciaparra	6.00
7	Chipper Jones	5.00
8	Ivan Rodriguez	2.50
9	Pedro Martinez	2.50
10	Rick Ankiel	1.50

2001 Topps A Tradition Continued

		MT
Complete Set (30):		100.00
Common Player:		1.00
Inserted 1:17		
1	Chipper Jones	6.00
2	Cal Ripken Jr.	10.00
3	Mike Piazza	8.00
4	Ken Griffey Jr.	8.00
5	Randy Johnson	3.00
6	Derek Jeter	10.00
7	Scott Rolen	1.50
8	Nomar Garciaparra	8.00
9	Roberto Alomar	2.50
10	Greg Maddux	6.00
11	Ivan Rodriguez	3.00
12	Jeff Bagwell	3.00
13	Ivan Rodriguez	3.00
14	Pedro Martinez	4.00
15	Sammy Sosa	6.00
16	Jim Edmonds	1.50
17	Mo Vaughn	1.00
18	Barry Bonds	3.00
19	Larry Walker	1.50
20	Mark McGwire	10.00
21	Vladimir Guerrero	4.00
22	Andruw Jones	2.50
23	Todd Helton	3.00
24	Kevin Brown	1.00
25	Tony Gwynn	4.00
26	Manny Ramirez	3.00
27	Roger Clemens	4.00
28	Frank Thomas	4.00
29	Shawn Green	1.50
30	Jim Thome	1.50

2001 Topps Autographs

		MT
Common Player:		
Group A 1:22,866		
Group B 1:3,054		
Group C 1:1,431		
Group D 1:18,339		
Group E 1:13,737		
Group F 1:11,015		
Group G 1:625		
HA	Hank Aaron	200.00
DA	Dick Allen	40.00
RA	Rick Ankiel	40.00
RB	Rocco Baldelli	25.00
EB	Ernie Banks	125.00
GB	George Bell	
JB	Johnny Bench	
YB	Yogi Berra	125.00
GB	George Brett	
LB	Lou Brock	75.00
PB	Pat Burrell	35.00
RC	Rod Carew	90.00
MC	Mike Cuellar	30.00
WD	Willie Davis	
CE	Carl Erskine	
WF	Whitey Ford	
RF	Rafael Furcal	40.00
BG	Bob Gibson	
AG	Adrian Gonzalez	35.00
DG	Dick Groat	
SH	Scott Heard	25.00
WH	Willie Hernandez	25.00
KH	Ken Holtzman	
RJ	Reggie Jackson	
AJ	Adam Johnson	20.00
CJ	Chipper Jones	90.00
SK	Sandy Koufax	400.00
ML	Mike Lamb	20.00
VL	Vernon Law	30.00
JM	Jason Marquis	20.00
GM	Gary Matthews	
WM	Willie Mays	300.00
SM	Stan Musial	
BO	Ben Oglivie	
MO	Magglio Ordonez	40.00
AP	Andy Pafko	75.00
BR	Brooks Robinson	100.00
JR	Joe Rudi	30.00
NR	Nolan Ryan	
MS	Mike Schmidt	160.00
TS	Tom Seaver	
MS	Mike Stodolka	15.00
RS	Ron Swoboda	30.00
KT	Kent Tekulve	
GT	Garry Templeton	30.00
JV	Jose Vidro	20.00
MW	Matt Wheatland	20.00
TW	Ted Williams	
WW	Wilbur Wood	
CY	Carl Yastrzemski	
TZ	Todd Zeile	20.00

2001 Topps Autographs Series 2

		MT
Common Player:		10.00
DA	Denny Abreu	15.00
TA	Tony Alvarez	15.00
RB	Rocco Baldelli	20.00
GB	George Bell	15.00
JB	Johnny Bench	150.00
BB	Barry Bonds	160.00
MB	Milton Bradley	25.00
GHB	George Brett	150.00
KB	Keith Bucktrot	
MAB	Mike Bynum	20.00
EB	Eric Byrnes	10.00
JC	Jorge Cantu	20.00
CC	Chris Clapinski	20.00
WD	Willie Davis	60.00
JDD	J.D. Drew	30.00
TDLR	Tomas de la Rosa	10.00
PD	Phil Dumatrait	
CD	Chad Durbin	10.00
CE	Carl Erskine	40.00
BE	Brian Esposito	15.00
WF	Whitey Ford	125.00
EF	Eddy Furniss	25.00
BG	Bob Gibson	125.00
MG	Mike Glendenning	30.00
AG	Adrian Gonzalez	40.00
NG	Nick Green	15.00
KG	Kevin Gregg	15.00
DG	Dick Groat	50.00
GG	Geraldo Guzman	15.00
YH	Yamid Haad	20.00
TH	Todd Helton	50.00
AH	Aaron Herr	25.00
KH	Ken Holtzman	40.00
RJ	Reggie Jackson	125.00
NJ	Neil Jenkins	25.00
AJ	Adam Johnson	15.00
TJ	Tripper Johnson	25.00
BK	Bobby Kielty	20.00
JL	John Lackey	10.00
YL	Yovanny Lara	
ML	Matt Lawton	20.00
CL	Colby Lewis	15.00
MFL	Mike Lockwood	15.00
GM	Gary Matthews	40.00
PM	Phil Merrell	
LM	Luis Montanez	25.00
EM	Eric Munson	30.00
SM	Stan Musial	125.00
BO	Ben Oglivie	25.00
AO	Augie Ojeda	15.00
ER	Erasmo Ramirez	20.00
CR	Chris Richard	25.00
JR	Juan Rincon	20.00
LR	Luis Rivas	35.00
SR	Scott Rolen	30.00
NR	Nolan Ryan	
JS	Juan Salas	10.00
TS	Tom Seaver	125.00
CS	Carlos Silva	10.00
GS	Grady Sizemore	35.00
CCS	Corey Smith	20.00
MS	Mike Stodolka	20.00
MS	Mike Sweeney	30.00
KT	Kent Tekulve	40.00
DT	Derek Thompson	15.00
ST	Scott Thorman	15.00
BT	Brian Tollberg	25.00
YT	Yorvit Torrealba	
JW	Justin Wayne	25.00
MW	Michael Wenner	25.00
MJW	Matt Wheatland	25.00
WW	Wilbur Wood	25.00
CY	Carl Yastrzemski	140.00

2001 Topps Base Hit

		MT
Complete Set (28):		450.00
Common Player:		25.00
BH1	Mike Scioscia	35.00
BH2	Larry Dierker	25.00
BH3	Art Howe	25.00
BH4	Jim Fregosi	25.00
BH5	Bobby Cox	35.00
BH6	Davey Lopes	25.00
BH7	Tony LaRussa	30.00
BH8	Don Baylor	35.00
BH9	Larry Rothschild	25.00
BH10	Buck Showalter	30.00
BH11	Davey Johnson	30.00
BH12	Felipe Alou	30.00
BH13	Charlie Manuel	25.00
BH14	Lou Piniella	30.00
BH15	John Boles	25.00
BH16	Bobby Valentine	30.00
BH17	Mike Hargrove	25.00
BH18	Bruce Bochy	25.00
BH19	Terry Francona	25.00
BH20	Gene Lamont	25.00
BH21	Johnny Oates	25.00
BH22	Jimy Williams	25.00
BH23	Jack McKeon	25.00
BH24	Buddy Bell	25.00
BH25	Tony Muser	25.00
BH26	Phil Garner	25.00
BH27	Tom Kelly	25.00
BH28	Jerry Manuel	25.00

2001 Topps Before There Was Topps

	MT
Complete Set (10):	25.00
Common Player:	1.50

Inserted 1:25

BT1	Lou Gehrig	6.00
BT2	Babe Ruth	6.00
BT3	Cy Young	2.00
BT4	Walter Johnson	2.00
BT5	Ty Cobb	4.00
BT6	Tris Speaker	1.50
BT7	Honus Wagner	2.00
BT8	Christy Mathewson	1.50

2001 Topps Combos

		MT
Complete Set (20):		60.00
Common Player:		2.00
Inserted 1:12		
1	Yogi Berra, Whitey Ford, Reggie Jackson, Don Mattingly, Derek Jeter	5.00
2	Brooks Robinson, Cal Ripken Jr.	5.00
3	Barry Bonds, Willie Mays	4.00
4	Bob Gibson, Pedro Martinez	2.00
5	Ivan Rodriguez, Johnny Bench	2.00
6	Ernie Banks, Alex Rodriguez	4.00
7	Sandy Koufax, Randy Johnson, Warren Spahn, Steve Carlton	4.00
8	Vladimir Guerrero, Roberto Clemente	4.00
9	Ted Williams, Carl Yastrzemski, Nomar Garciaparra	5.00
10	Joe Torre, Casey Stengel	2.00
11	Kevin Brown, Sandy Koufax, Don Drysdale	3.00
12	Mark McGwire, Sammy Sosa, Roger Maris, Babe Ruth	6.00
13	Ted Williams, Carl Yastrzemski, Nomar Garciaparra	4.00
14	Greg Maddux, Roger Clemens, Cy Young	3.00
15	Tony Gwynn, Ted Williams	4.00
16	Cal Ripken Jr., Lou Gehrig	5.00
17	Sandy Koufax, Randy Johnson, Warren Spahn, Steve Carlton	3.00
18	Mike Piazza, Josh Gibson	3.00
19	Barry Bonds, Willie Mays	3.00
20	Jackie Robinson, Larry Doby	4.00

A card number in parentheses ( ) indicates the set is unnumbered.

2001 Topps King of Kings

		MT
Common card:		75.00
Inserted 1:2,056		
1	Hank Aaron	125.00
2	Nolan Ryan	150.00
3	Rickey Henderson	50.00
4	Mark McGwire	250.00
5	Bob Gibson	75.00
6	Nolan Ryan	125.00

2001 Topps King of Kings Golden Edition

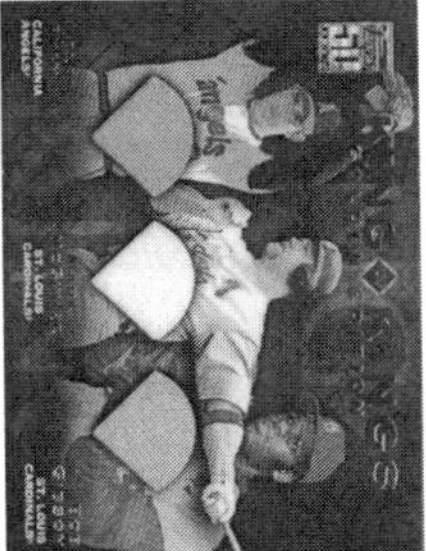

		MT
Production 50 cards		
KKGE	Hank Aaron, Nolan Ryan, Rickey Henderson	700.00
KKLE2	Mark McGwire, Bob Gibson, Nolan Ryan	900.00

2001 Topps Noteworthy

		MT
Complete Set (50):		160.00
Common Player:		1.00
Inserted 1:8		
TN1	Mark McGwire	8.00
TN2	Derek Jeter	8.00
TN3	Sammy Sosa	5.00
TN4	Todd Helton	2.50
TN5	Alex Rodriguez	6.00
TN6	Chipper Jones	5.00
TN7	Barry Bonds	2.50
TN8	Ken Griffey Jr.	6.00
TN9	Nomar Garciaparra	6.00
TN10	Frank Thomas	3.00
TN11	Randy Johnson	2.50
TN12	Cal Ripken Jr.	8.00
TN13	Mike Piazza	6.00
TN14	Ivan Rodriguez	2.50
TN15	Jeff Bagwell	2.50
TN16	Vladimir Guerrero	3.00
TN17	Greg Maddux	5.00
TN18	Tony Gwynn	3.00
TN19	Larry Walker	1.00
TN20	Juan Gonzalez	2.50
TN21	Scott Rolen	1.50
TN22	Jason Giambi	1.50
TN23	Jeff Kent	1.00
TN24	Pat Burrell	1.50
TN25	Pedro Martinez	3.00
TN26	Willie Mays	6.00
TN27	Whitey Ford	1.00
TN28	Jackie Robinson	6.00
TN29	Ted Williams	8.00
TN30	Babe Ruth	8.00
TN31	Warren Spahn	2.00
TN32	Nolan Ryan	8.00
TN33	Yogi Berra	4.00
TN34	Mike Schmidt	3.00
TN35	Steve Carlton	1.00
TN36	Brooks Robinson	2.00
TN37	Bob Gibson	1.50
TN38	Reggie Jackson	3.00
TN39	Johnny Bench	4.00
TN40	Ernie Banks	2.50
TN41	Eddie Mathews	1.50
TN42	Don Mattingly	4.00
TN43	Duke Snider	2.00
TN44	Hank Aaron	6.00
TN45	Roberto Clemente	6.00
TN46	Harmon Killebrew	1.50
TN47	Frank Robinson	1.50
TN48	Stan Musial	4.00
TN49	Lou Brock	1.50
TN50	Joe Morgan	1.50

2001 Topps Originals

		MT
Common Player:		25.00
Series 1 1:1,172		
Series 2 1:1,023		
1	Roberto Clemente 1955	250.00
2	Carl Yastrzemski 1960	100.00
3	Mike Schmidt 1974	80.00
4	Wade Boggs 1983	50.00
5	Chipper Jones 1991	60.00
6	Willie Mays	100.00
7	Lou Brock	60.00
8	Dave Parker	25.00
9	Barry Bonds	75.00
10	Alex Rodriguez	75.00

2001 Topps The Shot Heard Round The World Autograph

	MT
B. Thomson/R. Branca Ralph Branca, Bobby Thomson	100.00

2001 Topps Through the Years

		MT
Complete Set (50):		200.00
Common Player:		3.00
Inserted 1:8		
1	Yogi Berra	4.00
2	Roy Campanella	4.00
3	Willie Mays	6.00
4	Andy Pafko	3.00
5	Jackie Robinson	10.00
6	Stan Musial	5.00
7	Duke Snider	3.00
8	Warren Spahn	4.00
9	Ted Williams	10.00
10	Eddie Matthews	3.00
11	Willie McCovey	3.00
12	Frank Robinson	3.00
13	Ernie Banks	4.00
14	Hank Aaron	8.00
15	Sandy Koufax	8.00
16	Bob Gibson	4.00
17	Harmon Killebrew	3.00
18	Whitey Ford	3.00
19	Roberto Clemente	8.00
20	Juan Marichal	3.00
21	Johnny Bench	4.00
22	Willie Stargell	3.00
23	Joe Morgan	3.00
24	Carl Yastrzemski	4.00
25	Reggie Jackson	4.00
26	Tom Seaver	4.00
27	Steve Carlton	3.00
28	Jim Palmer	3.00
29	Rod Carew	3.00
30	George Brett	6.00
31	Roger Clemens	4.00
32	Don Mattingly	6.00
33	Ryne Sandberg	3.00
34	Mike Schmidt	4.00
35	Cal Ripken Jr.	8.00
36	Tony Gwynn	3.00
37	Ozzie Smith	4.00
38	Wade Boggs	3.00
39	Nolan Ryan	10.00
40	Robin Yount	3.00
41	Mark McGwire	10.00
42	Ken Griffey Jr.	6.00
43	Sammy Sosa	6.00
44	Alex Rodriguez	8.00
45	Barry Bonds	3.00
46	Mike Piazza	6.00
47	Chipper Jones	5.00
48	Greg Maddux	5.00
49	Nomar Garciaparra	6.00
50	Derek Jeter	8.00

2001 Topps Two of a Kind

		MT
Inserted 1:30,167		
TK	Bo Jackson, Deion Sanders	90.00

2001 Topps What Could've Been

	MT
Complete Set (10):	18.00
Common Player:	1.00
Inserted 1:25	

WCB1 Josh Gibson 4.00
WCB2 Leroy "Satchel" Paige 5.00
WCB3 Walter "Buck" Leonard 2.00
WCB4 James "Cool Papa" Bell 2.00
WCB5 Andrew "Rube" Foster 2.00
WCB6 Martin Dihigo 1.00
WCB7 William "Judy" Johnson 1.50
WCB8 Mule Suttles 1.00
WCB9 Ray Dandridge 1.00
WCB10 John Henry "Pop" Lloyd 2.00

2001 Topps American Pie

		MT
Complete Set (150):		30.00
Common Player:		.20
Pack (5):		2.75
Box (24):		55.00
1	Al Kaline	.40
2	Al Oliver	.20
3	Andre Dawson	.20
4	Bert Blyleven	.20
5	Bill Buckner	.20
6	Bill Mazeroski	.20
7	Bob Gibson	.50
8	Bill Freeman	.20
9	Bobby Grich	.20
10	Bobby Murcer	.20
11	Bobby Richardson	.20
12	Boog Powell	.20
13	Brooks Robinson	.50
14	Carl Yastrzemski	.75
15	Carlton Fisk	.40
16	Clete Boyer	.20
17	Curt Flood	.20
18	Dale Murphy	.30
19	Tony Conigliaro	.20
20	Dave Parker	.20
21	Dave Winfield	.50
22	Dick Allen	.20
23	Dick Groat	.20
24	Don Drysdale	.50
25	Don Sutton	.20
26	Dwight Evans	.20
27	Eddie Mathews	.75
28	Elston Howard	.20
29	Frank Howard	.20
30	Frank Robinson	.50
31	Fred Lynn	.20
32	Gary Carter	.20
33	Gaylord Perry	.20
34	Norm Cash	.20
35	George Brett	1.50
36	George Foster	.20
37	Goose Gossage	.20
38	Graig Nettles	.20
39	Greg Luzinski	.20
41	Harmon Killebrew	.75
42	Jack Clark	.20
43	Jack Morris	.20
44	Jim Wynn	.20
45	Jim Kaat	.20
46	Jim Palmer	.20
47	Joe Pepitone	.20
48	Joe Rudi	.20
49	Johnny Bench	1.00
50	Juan Marichal	.40
51	Keith Hernandez	.20
52	Bucky Dent	.20
53	Lou Brock	.40
54	Ron Cey	.20
55	Luis Aparicio	.20
56	Luis Tiant	.20
57	Mark Fidrych	.20
58	Maury Wills	.20
59	Mickey Lolich	.20
60	Mickey Rivers	.20
61	Mike Schmidt	1.00
62	Moose Skowron	.20
63	Nolan Ryan	3.00
64	Orlando Cepeda	.20
65	Ozzie Smith	.75
66	Phil Niekro	.20
67	Reggie Jackson	.75
68	Reggie Smith	.20
69	Rico Carty	.20
70	Roberto Clemente	2.00
71	Robin Yount	.75
72	Roger Maris	1.50
73	Rollie Fingers	.20
74	Ron Guidry	.20
75	Ron Santo	.20
76	Ron Swoboda	.20
77	Sal Bando	.20
78	Sam McDowell	.20
79	Steve Carlton	.40
80	Thurman Munson	1.00
81	Tim McCarver	.20
82	Tom Seaver	.75
83	Mike Cuellar	.20
84	Tony Kubek	.20
85	Tommy John	.20
86	Tony Perez	.20
87	Tug McGraw	.20
88	Vida Blue	.20
89	Warren Spahn	.75
90	Whitey Ford	.50
91	Willie Mays	2.00
92	Willie McCovey	.20
93	Willie Stargell	.50
94	Yogi Berra	1.00
95	Stan Musial	1.00
96	Jim Piersall	.20
97	Duke Snider	.50
98	Bruce Sutter	.20
99	Dave Concepcion	.20
100	Darrell Evans	.20
101	Dennis Eckersley	.20
102	Hoyt Wilhelm	.20
103	Minnie Minoso	.20
104	Don Newcombe	.20
105	Richie Ashburn	.20
106	Alan Trammell	.20
107	Jim "Catfish" Hunter	.20
108	Lou Whitaker	.20
109	Johnny Podres	.20
110	Denny Martinez	.20
111	Willie Horton	.20
112	Dean Chance	.20
113	Fergie Jenkins	.20
114	Cecil Cooper	.20
115	Rick Reuschel	.20
116	Space Race (Events)	.20
117	Man On The Moon (Events)	.50
118	Woodstock (Events)	.50
119	Peace Movement/Flower Power (Events)	.20
120	N.Y. Worlds Fair (Events)	.20
121	Vietnam War (Events)	.20
122	Vietnam Cease Fire (Events)	.20
123	Kennedy Elected President (Events)	.50
124	Kennedy Assassination (Events)	.20
125	(Malcom X) (Events)	.20
126	Nixon Elected President (Events)	.20
127	Watergate (Events)	.20
128	Nixon Resigns (Events)	.20
129	Cuban Missile Crisis (Events)	.20
130	Astrodome (Events)	.20
131	Secretariat (Events)	.20
132	Lyndon Johnson Signs Civil Rights Bill (Events)	.20
133	Atomic Bomb Test Ban Treaty (Events)	.20
134	Bi Centennial (Events)	.20
135	String Bikini (Events)	.20
136	Birth Control Pill (Events)	.20
137	Studio 54 (Events)	.20
138	Motown (Events)	.20
139	Microsoft Started (Events)	.20
140	Internet Developed (Events)	.20
141	John F. Kennedy (Personalities)	1.50
142	Marilyn Monroe (Personalities)	1.50
143	Elvis Presley (Personalities)	1.50
144	Jimi Hendrix (Personalities)	1.00
145	Arthur Ashe (Personalities)	.20
146	Richard Nixon (Personalities)	.20
147	James Dean (Personalities)	.20
148	Janis Joplin (Personalities)	.50
149	Frank Sinatra (Personalities)	1.00
150	Malcom X (Personalities)	.50

2001 Topps American Pie Decade Leaders

		MT
Complete Set (10):		20.00
Common Player:		1.00
Inserted 1:12		
DL1	Willie Stargell	1.50
DL2	Harmon Killebrew	2.00
DL3	Johnny Bench	2.50
DL4	Hank Aaron	4.00
DL5	Rod Carew	1.00
DL6	Roberto Clemente	4.00
DL7	Nolan Ryan	6.00
DL8	Bob Gibson	2.00
DL9	Jim Palmer	1.00
DL10	Juan Marichal	1.00

2001 Topps American Pie Entertainment Stars

		MT
Common Player:		40.00
Production 500 sets		
1	Lou Ferrigno (Incredible Hulk)	50.00
2	Adam West (Batman)	60.00
3	Danny Bonaduce (Partridge Family)	40.00

2001 Topps American Pie Legends Autographs

		MT
Common Player:		15.00
Inserted 1:211		
TT1R	Willie Mays	125.00
TT14R	Johnny Bench	65.00
TT48R	Bobby Richardson	30.00
TT8R	Carl Yastrzemski	100.00
TT13R	Warren Spahn	40.00
TT15R	Reggie Jackson	50.00
TT18R	Bob Gibson	40.00
TT25R	Luis Tiant	20.00
TT29R	Moose Skowron	15.00
TT31R	Clete Boyer	15.00
TT33R	Vida Blue	20.00
TT35R	Joe Pepitone	20.00
TT37R	Tug McGraw	25.00
TT47R	Frank Howard	25.00
TT49R	Tony Kubek	50.00
TT50R	Mickey Lolich	15.00

2001 Topps American Pie Piece of American Pie Relics

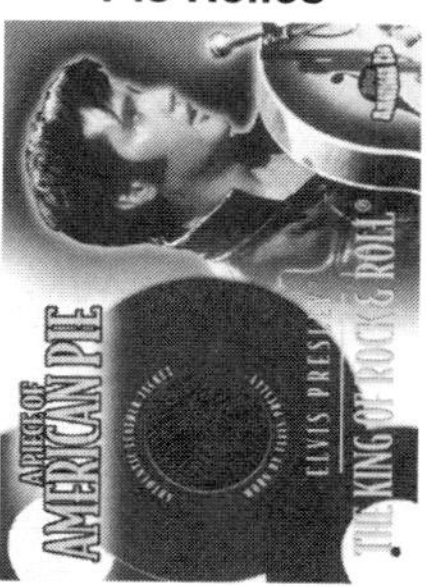

		MT
Common Card:		15.00
Inserted 1:29		
PAPM1	Frank Sinatra	60.00
PAPM2	JFK/Berlin Wall	15.00
PAPM3	Elvis Presley	120.00
PAPM4	Janis Joplin	60.00
PAPM5	Jimi Hendrix	

2001 Topps American Pie Profiles In Courage

		MT
Complete Set (20):		40.00
Common Player:		1.00
Inserted 1:8		
PIC1	Roger Maris	2.50
PIC2	Lou Brock	1.00
PIC3	Brooks Robinson	2.00
PIC4	Carl Yastrzemski	1.50
PIC5	Mike Schmidt	2.00
PIC6	Hank Aaron	4.00
PIC7	Tom Seaver	2.00
PIC8	Willie Mays	4.00
PIC9	Graig Nettles	1.00
PIC10	Frank Robinson	1.50
PIC11	Rollie Fingers	1.00
PIC12	Tony Perez	1.00
PIC13	George Brett	3.00
PIC14	Robin Yount	2.00
PIC15	Nolan Ryan	6.00
PIC16	Warren Spahn	2.00
PIC17	Johnny Bench	2.00
PIC18	Vida Blue	1.00
PIC19	Roberto Clemente	4.00
PIC20	Thurman Munson	2.00

A card number in parentheses ( ) indicates the set is unnumbered.

2001 Topps American Pie Rookie Reprint Relics

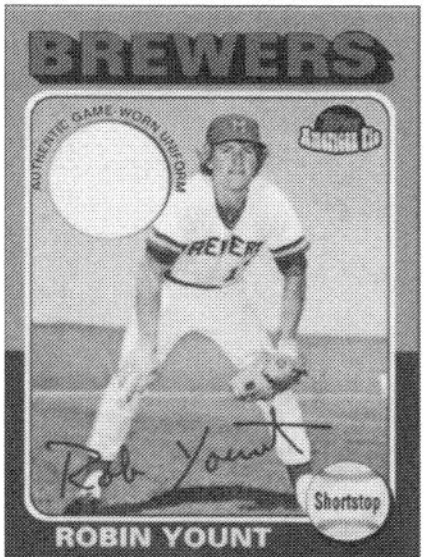

		MT
Common Player:		15.00
Inserted 1:116		
JB	Johnny Bench	40.00
GB	George Brett	50.00
SC	Steve Carlton	25.00
GC	Gary Carter	20.00
AD	Andre Dawson	20.00
DE	Dennis Eckersley	20.00
MF	Mark Fidrych	20.00
BG	Bobby Grich	15.00
RJ	Reggie Jackson	25.00
JK	Jim Kaat	15.00
TMC	Tim McCarver	15.00
TM	Thurman Munson	65.00
BM	Bobby Murcer	20.00
AO	Al Oliver	15.00
BP	Boog Powell	20.00
OS	Ozzie Smith	40.00
DS	Don Sutton	15.00
DW	Dave Winfield	15.00
RY	Robin Yount	40.00

2001 Topps American Pie Timeless Classics Relics

	MT
Common Player:	10.00
Inserted 1:80	
Sam McDowell	15.00
Frank Howard	20.00
Dick Groat	15.00
Roger Maris	75.00
Orlando Cepeda	20.00
Willie Mays	50.00
Carl Yastrzemski	60.00
Roberto Clemente	75.00
Harmon Killebrew	50.00
Brooks Robinson	40.00
Tony Conigliaro	40.00
Frank Robinson	25.00
Hank Aaron	50.00
Willie McCovey	25.00
Rico Carty	10.00
Johnny Bench	35.00
Willie Stargell	25.00
Steve Carlton	25.00
Norm Cash	25.00
Reggie Jackson	25.00
Mike Schmidt	40.00
Mickey Rivers	15.00
Tom Seaver	40.00
George Brett	50.00
George Foster	15.00
Graig Nettles	35.00
Nolan Ryan	60.00
Dave Parker	15.00
Dick Allen	20.00
Fred Lynn	15.00
Keith Hernandez	25.00
Dave Winfield	20.00

2001 Topps American Pie Woodstock Relics

		MT
Common Player:		15.00
Inserted 1:138		
GB	George Brett	60.00
BB	Bill Buckner	15.00
OC	Orlando Cepeda	20.00
DE	Dwight Evans	15.00
CF	Carlton Fisk	25.00
BF	Bill Freehan	20.00
DG	Dick Groat	15.00
RJ	Reggie Jackson	35.00
TK	Ted Kluszewski	20.00
FL	Fred Lynn	20.00
WM	Willie Mays	50.00
SM	Stan Musial	50.00
TP	Tony Perez	15.00
JP	Jimmy Piersall	20.00
BR	Brooks Robinson	40.00
FR	Frank Robinson	25.00
JR	Joe Rudi	15.00
DS	Duke Snider	25.00
WS	Willie Stargell	20.00
MW	Maury Wills	15.00
DW	Dave Winfield	15.00
WS	Woodstock	35.00
JW	Jim Wynn	15.00
CY	Carl Yastrzemski	50.00
RY	Robin Yount	60.00

2001 Topps Archives

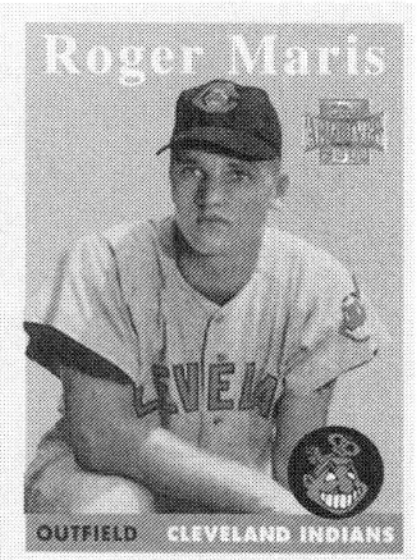

		MT
Complete Set (450):		200.00
Complete Series 1 (225):		100.00
Complete Series 2 (225):		100.00
Common Player:		.40
Pack (8):		4.00
Box (20):		75.00
1	Johnny Antonelli	.40
2	Yogi Berra	2.50
3	Dom DiMaggio	.40
4	Carl Erskine	.40
5	Joe Garagiola	.50
6	Monte Irvin	.40
7	Vernon Law	.40
8	Eddie Mathews	2.00
9	Willie Mays	5.00
10	Gil McDougald	.40
11	Andy Pafko	.40
12	Phil Rizzuto	.75
13	Preacher Roe	.40
14	Hank Sauer	.50
15	Bobby Shantz	.40
16	Enos Slaughter	.50
17	Warren Spahn	2.00
18	Mickey Vernon	.40
19	Early Wynn	.40
20	Whitey Ford	1.00
21	Johnny Podres	.40
22	Ernie Banks	2.00
23	Moose Skowron	.40
24	Harmon Killebrew	2.00
25	Ted Williams	6.00
26	Jimmy Piersall	.40
27	Frank Thomas	.40
28	Bill Mazeroski	.50
29	Bobby Richardson	.40
30	Frank Robinson	1.50
31	Stan Musial	3.00
32	Johnny Callison	.40
33	Bob Gibson	2.00
34	Frank Howard	.50
35	Willie McCovey	.40
36	Carl Yastrzemski	2.00
37	Jim Maloney	.40
38	Ron Santo	.40
39	Lou Brock	.75
40	Tim McCarver	.50
41	Joe Pepitone	.40
42	Boog Powell	.50
43	Bill Freehan	.40
44	Dick Allen	.40
45	Willie Horton	.40
46	Mickey Lolich	.40
47	Wilbur Wood	.40
48	Bert Campaneris	.40
49	Rod Carew	1.50
50	Tug McGraw	.40
51	Tony Perez	.75
52	Luis Tiant	.40
53	Bobby Murcer	.40
54	Don Sutton	.75
55	Ken Holtzman	.40
56	Reggie Smith	.40
57	Hal McRae	.40
58	Roy White	.40
59	Reggie Jackson	3.00
60	Graig Nettles	.40
61	Joe Rudi	.40
62	Vida Blue	.50
63	Darrell Evans	.40
64	David Concepcion	.40
65	Bobby Grich	.40
66	Greg Luzinski	.40
67	Cecil Cooper	.40
68	George Hendrick	.40
69	Dwight Evans	.40
70	Gary Matthews	.40
71	Mike Schmidt	3.00
72	Dave Parker	.40
73	Dave Winfield	1.00
74	Gary Carter	.40
75	Dennis Eckersley	.40
76	Kent Tekulve	.40
77	Andre Dawson	.75
78	Denny Martinez	.40
79	Bruce Sutter	.40
80	Jack Morris	.40
81	Ozzie Smith	1.50
82	Lee Smith	.40
83	Don Mattingly	4.00
84	Joe Carter	.40
85	Kirby Puckett	3.00
86	Joe Adcock	.40
87	Gus Bell	.40
88	Roy Campanella	2.00
89	Jackie Jensen	.40
90	Johnny Mize	.75
91	Allie Reynolds	.40
92	Al Rosen	.40
93	Hal Newhouser	.40
94	Harvey Kuenn	.40
95	Nellie Fox	.75
96	Elston Howard	.40
97	Sal Maglie	.40
98	Roger Maris	3.00
99	Norm Cash	.40
100	Thurman Munson	2.50
101	Roy Campanella	1.50
102	Joe Garagiola	.75
103	Dom DiMaggio	.40
104	Johnny Mize	.50
105	Allie Reynolds	.40
106	Preacher Roe	.40
107	Hal Newhouser	.40
108	Monte Irvin	.40
109	Carl Erskine	.40
110	Enos Slaughter	.40
111	Gil McDougald	.40
112	Andy Pafko	.40
113	Sal Maglie	.40
114	Johnny Antonelli	.40
115	Phil Rizzuto	.50
116	Yogi Berra	1.50
117	Early Wynn	.40
118	Mickey Vernon	.40
119	Gus Bell	.40
120	Ted Williams	4.00
121	Frank Thomas	.40
122	Bobby Richardson	.40
123	Whitey Ford	1.00
124	Vernon Law	.40
125	Jimmy Piersall	.40
126	Moose Skowron	.40
127	Joe Adcock	.40
128	Johnny Podres	.40
129	Ernie Banks	1.50
130	Jim Maloney	.40
131	Johnny Callison	.40
132	Eddie Mathews	1.50
133	Joe Pepitone	.40
134	Warren Spahn	1.50
135	Bill Mazeroski	.40
136	Norm Cash	.40
137	Bob Gibson	1.00
138	Harmon Killebrew	1.50
139	Frank Robinson	1.00
140	Ron Santo	.40
141	Hank Sauer	.40
142	Bobby Shantz	.40
143	Nellie Fox	.50
144	Elston Howard	.40
145	Jackie Jensen	.40
146	Al Rosen	.40
147	Dick Allen	.40
148	Bill Freehan	.40
149	Boog Powell	.40
150	Lou Brock	.75
151	Rod Carew	.75
152	Wilbur Wood	.40
153	Thurman Munson	1.50
154	Ken Holtzman	.40
155	Willie Horton	.40
156	Mickey Lolich	.40
157	Tim McCarver	.40
158	Willie McCovey	.40
159	Roy White	.40
160	Bobby Murcer	.40
161	Joe Rudi	.40
162	Reggie Smith	.40
163	Luis Tiant	.40
164	Bert Campaneris	.40
165	Frank Howard	.40
166	Harvey Kuenn	.50
167	Greg Luzinski	.40
168	Tug McGraw	.40
169	Willie Mays	3.00
170	Roger Maris	2.00
171	Vida Blue	.40
172	Bobby Grich	.40
173	Reggie Jackson	2.00
174	Hal McRae	.40
175	Carl Yastrzemski	1.00
176	David Concepcion	.40
177	Cecil Cooper	.40
178	George Hendrick	.40
179	Gary Matthews	.40
180	Stan Musial	2.00
181	Graig Nettles	.40
182	Don Sutton	.50
183	Kent Tekulve	.40
184	Bruce Sutter	.40
185	Darrell Evans	.40
186	Mike Schmidt	2.00
187	Dave Parker	.40
188	Dwight Evans	.40
189	Gary Carter	.40
190	Jack Morris	.40
191	Tony Perez	.50
192	Dave Winfield	.75
193	Andre Dawson	.50
194	Lee Smith	.40
195	Ozzie Smith	1.00
196	Denny Martinez	.40
197	Don Mattingly	2.50
198	Joe Carter	.40
199	Dennis Eckersley	.40
200	Kirby Puckett	2.00
201	Walter Alston	.40
202	Casey Stengel	.75
203	Sparky Anderson	.40
204	Tommy Lasorda	.75
205	Whitey Herzog	.40
206	Harmon Killebrew, Frank Howard, Reggie Jackson (League Leader)	.40

207 Hank Aaron, Early Wynn, Ron Santo, Willie McCovey (League Leader) 2.50
208 Frank Robinson, Harmon Killebrew, Boog Powell (League Leader) 1.50
209 Tony Oliva, Frank Robinson, Frank Howard (League Leader) .75
210 Hank Aaron, Willie McCovey, Willie Mays, Orlando Cepeda (League Leader) 2.50
211 Hank Aaron, Frank Robinson, Willie Mays, Ernie Banks (League Leaders) 2.50
212 Carl Yastrzemski, Harmon Killebrew, Frank Howard (League Leaders) 1.50
213 Ernie Banks (Highlight) 1.50
214 Hank Aaron (Highlight) 2.50
215 Willie Mays (Highlight) 2.50
216 Al Kaline (Highlight) .75
217 Stan Musial (Highlight) 2.00
218 Duke Snider (Highlight) .75
219 Frank Robinson, Hank Bauer, Frank Robinson (Highlight) .50
220 Willie Mays, Stan Musial (Highlight) 1.50
221 Whitey Ford (World Series Highlight) .75
222 Jerry Koosman (World Series Highlight) .40
223 Bob Gibson (World Series Highlight) .75
224 Gil Hodges (World Series Highlight) .40
225 Reggie Jackson (World Series Highlight) 1.50
226 Hank Bauer .40
227 Ralph Branca .40
228 Joe Garagiola .75
229 Bob Feller 2.00
230 Dick Groat .40
231 George Kell .40
232 Bob Boone .40
233 Minnie Minoso .40
234 Billy Pierce .40
235 Robin Roberts .50
236 Johnny Sain .40
237 Red Schoendienst .40
238 Curt Simmons .40
239 Duke Snider 2.00
240 Bobby Thomson .40
241 Hoyt Wilhelm .40
242 Elroy Face .40
243 Ralph Kiner .75
244 Hank Aaron 5.00
245 Al Kaline 2.00
246 Don Larsen 1.50
247 Tug McGraw .40
248 Don Newcombe .75
249 Herb Score .40
250 Clete Boyer .40
251 Lindy McDaniel .40
252 Brooks Robinson 2.50
253 Orlando Cepeda .60
254 Larry Bowa .40
255 Mike Cuellar .40
256 Jim Perry .40
257 Dave Parker .40
258 Maury Wills .40
259 Willie Davis .40
260 Juan Marichal .60
261 Jim Bouton .40
262 Dean Chance .40
263 Sam McDowell .40
264 Whitey Ford 3.00
265 Bob Uecker 2.00
266 Willie Stargell 2.00
267 Rico Carty .40
268 Tommy John .40
269 Phil Niekro .60
270 Paul Blair .40
271 Steve Carlton 3.00
272 Jim Lonborg .40
273 Tony Perez .60
274 Ron Swoboda .40
275 Fergie Jenkins .75
276 Jim Palmer 1.50
277 Sal Bando .40
278 Tom Seaver 4.00
279 Johnny Bench 4.00
280 Nolan Ryan 8.00
281 Rollie Fingers .50
282 Sparky Lyle .40
283 Al Oliver .40
284 Bob Watson .40
285 Bill Buckner .40
286 Bert Blyleven .40
287 George Foster .40
288 Al Hrabosky .40
289 Cecil Cooper .40
290 Carlton Fisk 1.00
291 Mickey Rivers .40
292 Goose Gossage .40
293 Rick Reuschel .40
294 Bucky Dent .40
295 Frank Tanana .40
296 George Brett 4.00
297 Keith Hernandez .40
298 Fred Lynn .40
299 Robin Yount 3.00
300 Ron Guidry .40
301 Jack Clark .40
302 Mark Fidrych .40
303 Dale Murphy 1.50
304 Willie Hernandez .40
305 Lou Whitaker .40
306 Kirk Gibson .75
307 Wade Boggs 3.00
308 Ryne Sandberg 4.00
309 Orel Hershiser .40
310 Jimmy Key .40
311 Richie Ashburn .40
312 Smokey Burgess .40
313 Gil Hodges 1.50
314 Ted Kluszewski .40
315 Pee Wee Reese 1.00
316 Jackie Robinson 5.00
317 Harvey Haddix .40
318 Satchel Paige 4.00
319 Roberto Clemente 5.00
320 Carl Furillo .40
321 Don Drysdale 2.00
322 Curt Flood .40
323 Bob Allison .40
324 Tony Conigliaro .40
325 Dan Quisenberry .40
326 Ralph Branca .40
327 Bob Feller 1.00
328 Satchel Paige 4.00
329 George Kell .40
330 Pee Wee Reese 1.00
331 Bobby Thomson .40
332 Carl Furillo .40
333 Hank Bauer .40
334 Herb Score .40
335 Richie Ashburn .40
336 Billy Pierce .40
337 Duke Snider 2.00
338 Harvey Haddix .40
339 Robin Roberts .40
340 Dick Groat .40
341 Curt Simmons .40
342 Bob Uecker 1.00
343 Smokey Burgess .40
344 Jim Bouton .40
345 Elroy Face .40
346 Don Drysdale 1.00
347 Bob Allison .40
348 Clete Boyer .40
349 Dean Chance .40
350 Tony Conigliaro .40
351 Curt Flood .40
352 Hoyt Wilhelm .40
353 Ron Swoboda .40
354 Roberto Clemente 3.00
355 Tug McGraw .40
356 Orlando Cepeda .40
357 Joe Garagiola .40
358 Juan Marichal .50
359 Sam McDowell .40
360 Johnny Sain .40
361 Ted Kluszewski .40
362 Al Kaline 2.00
363 Lindy McDaniel .40
364 Don Newcombe .40
365 Jim Perry .40
366 Hank Aaron 4.00
367 Don Larsen 1.00
368 Mike Cuellar .40
369 Willie Davis .40
370 Ralph Kiner .50
371 Minnie Minoso .40
372 Larry Bowa .40
373 Brooks Robinson 1.00
374 Bob Boone .40
375 Jim Lonborg .40
376 Paul Blair .40
377 Rico Carty .40
378 Sal Bando .40
379 Mark Fidrych .40
380 Al Hrabosky .40
381 Willie Stargell 1.00
382 Johnny Bench 2.50
383 Dave Parker .40
384 Sparky Lyle .40
385 Fergie Jenkins .50
386 Jim Palmer 1.00
387 Whitey Ford 2.00
388 Tony Perez .40
389 Mickey Rivers .40
390 Bob Watson .40
391 Rollie Fingers .40
392 George Foster .40
393 Al Oliver .40
394 Tom Seaver 3.00
395 Maury Wills .40
396 Steve Carlton 1.00
397 Cecil Cooper .40
398 Bill Buckner .40
399 Phil Niekro .40
400 Red Schoendienst .40
401 Ron Guidry .40
402 Willie Hernandez .40
403 Tommy John .40
404 Gil Hodges .40
405 Bucky Dent .40
406 Keith Hernandez .40
407 Dan Quisenberry .40
408 Fred Lynn .40
409 Rick Reuschel .40
410 Jackie Robinson 3.00
411 Goose Gossage .40
412 Bert Blyleven .40
413 Jack Clark .40
414 Carlton Fisk .50
415 Dale Murphy .75
416 Frank Tanana .40
417 George Brett 3.00
418 Robin Yount 2.50
419 Kirk Gibson .50
420 Lou Whitaker .40
421 Ryne Sandberg 2.50
422 Jimmy Key .40
423 Nolan Ryan 5.00
424 Wade Boggs .75
425 Orel Hershiser .40
426 Billy Martin (Managers) .40
427 Ralph Houk (Managers) .40
428 Chuck Tanner (Managers) .40
429 Earl Weaver (Managers) .40
430 Leo Durocher (Managers) .40
431 Tony Conigliaro, Norm Cash, Willie Horton (League Leaders) .40
432 Ernie Banks, Hank Aaron, Eddie Mathews, Clete Boyer (League Leaders) 1.50
433 Norm Cash, Frank Howard, Al Kaline, Jimmy Piersall (League Leaders) .40
434 Goose Gossage, Rollie Fingers (League Leaders) .40
435 Nolan Ryan, Tom Seaver (League Leaders) .40
436 Reggie Jackson, Willie Stargell (League Leaders) .75
437 Johnny Bench, Dick Allen (League Leaders) .75
438 Roger Maris (Decade Highlights) 3.00
439 Carl Yastrzemski (Decade Highlights) 2.00
440 Nolan Ryan (Decade Highlights) 4.00
441 Cincinnati Reds (Decade Highlights) .75
442 Tony Perez (Decade Highlights) .40
443 Steve Carlton (Decade Highlights) .75
444 Wade Boggs (Decade Highlights) .75
445 Andre Dawson (Decade Highlights) .40
446 Whitey Ford (World Series Highlights) 1.50
447 Hank Aaron (World Series Highlights) 4.00
448 Bob Gibson (World Series Highlights) .75
449 Roberto Clemente (World Series Highlights) 4.00
450 Orioles/Jackie Robinson (World Series Highlights) 1.50

2001 Topps Archives Autographs

	MT
Common Player:	20.00
Inserted 1:box	
TAA1 Johnny Antonelli	25.00
TAA2 Hank Bauer	25.00
TAA3 Yogi Berra/50	275.00
TAA4 Ralph Branca	25.00
TAA5 Dom DiMaggio	40.00
TAA6 Joe Garagiola	40.00
TAA7 Carl Erskine	30.00
TAA8 Bob Feller	40.00
TAA10 Dick Groat	25.00
TAA11 Monte Irvin	35.00
TAA12 George Kell	25.00
TAA13 Vernon Law	20.00
TAA14 Bob Boone	20.00
TAA16 Willie Mays/50	375.00
TAA17 Gil McDougald	30.00
TAA18 Minnie Minoso	30.00
TAA19 Andy Pafko	35.00
TAA20 Billy Pierce	20.00
TAA21 Phil Rizzuto/200	100.00
TAA22 Robin Roberts	50.00
TAA23 Preacher Roe	30.00
TAA24 Johnny Sain	25.00
TAA25 Hank Sauer	25.00
TAA26 Red Schoendienst	25.00
TAA27 Bobby Shantz	20.00
TAA28 Curt Simmons	20.00
TAA29 Enos Slaughter	25.00
TAA30 Duke Snider	80.00
TAA31 Warren Spahn	80.00
TAA32 Bobby Thomson	30.00
TAA33 Mickey Vernon	25.00
TAA34 Hoyt Wilhelm	30.00
TAA35 Jim Wynn	20.00
TAA36 Elroy Face	20.00
TAA37 Gaylord Perry	35.00
TAA38 Ralph Kiner	50.00
TAA39 Johnny Podres	20.00
TAA40 Hank Aaron/50	400.00
TAA41 Ernie Banks/50	325.00
TAA42 Al Kaline	125.00
TAA43 Moose Skowron	25.00
TAA44 Don Larsen	120.00
TAA45 Harmon Killebrew	80.00
TAA46 Tug McGraw	25.00
TAA48 Don Newcombe	25.00
TAA49 Jimmy Piersall	20.00
TAA50 Herb Score	20.00
TAA51 Frank Thomas	20.00
TAA52 Clete Boyer	25.00
TAA53 Bill Mazeroski	50.00
TAA54 Lindy McDaniel	20.00
TAA55 Bobby Richardson	25.00
TAA56 Brooks Robinson	150.00
TAA57 Frank Robinson	80.00
TAA58 Orlando Cepeda	60.00

TAA59Stan Musial	30.00
TAA60Larry Bowa	25.00
TAA61Johnny Callison	20.00
TAA62Mike Cuellar	25.00
TAA63Bob Gibson	120.00
TAA64Jim Perry	20.00
TAA65Frank Howard	25.00
TAA66David Palmer	25.00
TAA67Willie McCovey	80.00
TAA68Maury Wills	25.00
TAA69Carl Yastrzemski	160.00
TAA70Willie Davis	20.00
TAA71Jim Maloney	20.00
TAA72Juan Marichal	40.00
TAA73Ron Santo	25.00
TAA74Jim Bouton	30.00
TAA75Lou Brock/50	
TAA76Dean Chance	20.00
TAA77Tim McCarver/200	50.00
TAA78Sam McDowell	25.00
TAA79Joe Pepitone	25.00
TAA80Whitey Ford	80.00
TAA81Boog Powell	20.00
TAA82Bob Uecker	40.00
TAA83Bill Freehan	20.00
TAA85Dick Allen	25.00
TAA86Rico Carty	20.00
TAA87Willie Horton	20.00
TAA88Tommy John	25.00
TAA89Mickey Lolich	20.00
TAA90Phil Niekro	30.00
TAA91Wilbur Wood	20.00
TAA92Paul Blair	20.00
TAA93Bert Campaneris	20.00
TAA94Steve Carlton	40.00
TAA95Rod Carew	
TAA96Jim Lonborg	20.00
TAA97Luis Aparicio	50.00
TAA98Tony Perez	50.00
TAA99Joe Morgan/200	80.00
TAA100Ron Swoboda	30.00
TAA101Luis Tiant	30.00
TAA102Fergie Jenkins	30.00
TAA103Bobby Murcer	25.00
TAA104Jim Palmer	70.00
TAA105Don Sutton/200	40.00
TAA106Sal Bando	20.00
TAA107Ken Holtzman	40.00
TAA108Tom Seaver/50	
TAA109Reggie Smith	20.00
TAA110Johnny Bench	300.00
TAA111Hal McRae	20.00
TAA112Nolan Ryan	550.00
TAA113Roy White	20.00
TAA114Rollie Fingers	30.00
TAA115Reggie Jackson/50	
TAA116Sparky Lyle	25.00
TAA117Graig Nettles	25.00
TAA118Al Oliver	20.00
TAA119Joe Rudi	25.00
TAA120Bob Watson	20.00
TAA121Vida Blue	20.00
TAA122Bill Buckner	20.00
TAA123Darrell Evans	20.00
TAA124Bert Blyleven	25.00
TAA125David Concepcion	25.00
TAA126George Foster	20.00
TAA127Bobby Grich	20.00
TAA128Al Hrabosky	20.00
TAA129Greg Luzinski	25.00
TAA130Cecil Cooper	20.00
TAA131Ron Cey	20.00
TAA132Carlton Fisk	75.00
TAA133George Hendrick	20.00
TAA134Mickey Rivers	20.00
TAA135Dwight Evans	40.00
TAA136Goose Gossage	20.00
TAA137Gary Matthews	20.00
TAA138Rick Reuschel	20.00
TAA139Mike Schmidt	400.00
TAA140Bucky Dent	25.00
TAA141Jim Kaat	25.00
TAA142Frank Tanana	20.00
TAA143Dave Winfield/200	90.00
TAA144George Brett	300.00
TAA145Gary Carter/200	75.00
TAA146Keith Hernandez	40.00
TAA147Fred Lynn	30.00
TAA148Robin Yount SP/200	190.00
TAA149Dennis Eckersley	90.00
TAA150Ron Guidry	25.00
TAA151Kent Tekulve	25.00
TAA152Jack Clark	20.00
TAA153Andre Dawson SP/200	50.00
TAA154Mark Fidrych	25.00
TAA155Denny Martinez SP/200	35.00
TAA156Dale Murphy	50.00
TAA157Bruce Sutter	25.00
TAA158Willie Hernandez	20.00
TAA159Jack Morris	40.00
TAA160Lou Whitaker	30.00
TAA161Ozzie Smith	75.00
TAA162Kirk Gibson	30.00
TAA163Lee Smith	20.00
TAA164Wade Boggs	80.00
TAA165Ryne Sandberg SP/200	175.00
TAA166Don Mattingly	120.00
TAA167Joe Carter SP/200	50.00
TAA168Orel Hershiser	25.00
TAA169Kirby Puckett	250.00
TAA170Jimmy Key	30.00

2001 Topps Archives Game-Used Bat

		MT
Common Player:		40.00
1	Johnny Bench	100.00
2	George Brett	120.00
3	Fred Lynn	40.00
4	Reggie Jackson	75.00
5	Mike Schmidt	80.00
6	Willie Stargell	60.00

2001 Topps Archives Game-Used Bat Autograph

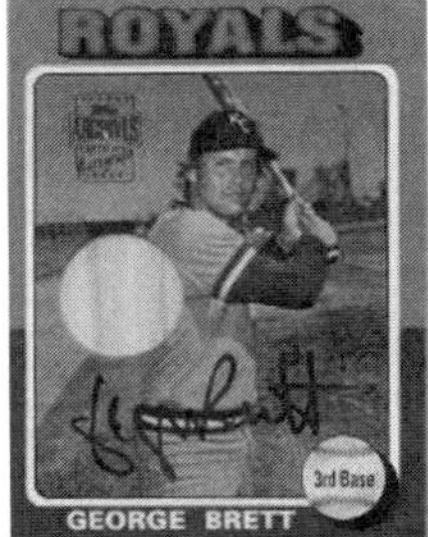

		MT
Common Player:		120.00
1	Johnny Bench	350.00
2	George Brett	375.00
3	Fred Lynn	100.00
4	Reggie Jackson	
5	Mike Schmidt	
6	Willie Stargell	

2001 Topps Archives Topps Final Autoproof

	MT
Complete Set (5):	
Common Player:	
Carlton Fisk	
Jim Palmer	
Robin Roberts	
Duke Snider	
Willie Stargell	

2001 Topps Archives Reserve

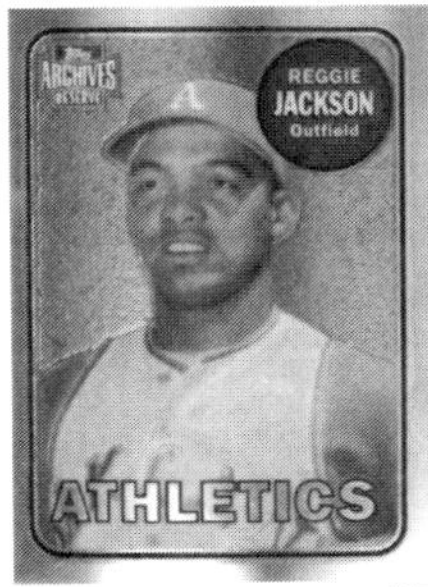

		MT
Complete Set (100):		125.00
Common Player:		.75
Hobby Pack (5):		8.00
Hobby Box:		130.00
1	Joe Adcock	.75
2	Brooks Robinson	3.00
3	Luis Aparicio	.75
4	Richie Ashburn	.75
5	Hank Bauer	.75
6	Johnny Bench	4.00
7	Wade Boggs	2.00
8	Moose Skowron	.75
9	George Brett	5.00
10	Lou Brock	2.00
11	Roy Campanella	4.00
12	Willie Hernandez	.75
13	Steve Carlton	2.00
14	Gary Carter	.75
15	Hoyt Wilhelm	.75
16	Orlando Cepeda	.75
17	Roberto Clemente	8.00
18	Dale Murphy	1.50
19	Dave Concepcion	.75
20	Dom DiMaggio	.75
21	Larry Doby	.75
22	Don Drysdale	4.00
23	Dennis Eckersley	.75
24	Bob Feller	2.00
25	Rollie Fingers	.75
26	Carlton Fisk	2.00
27	Nellie Fox	1.50
28	Mickey Rivers	.75
29	Tommy John	.75
30	Johnny Sain	.75
31	Keith Hernandez	.75
32	Gil Hodges	.75
33	Elston Howard	3.00
34	Frank Howard	.75
35	Bob Gibson	5.00
36	Fergie Jenkins	.75
37	Jackie Jensen	.75
38	Al Kaline	3.00
39	Harmon Killebrew	5.00
40	Ralph Kiner	.75
41	Dick Groat	.75
42	Don Larsen	.75
43	Ralph Branca	.75
44	Mickey Lolich	.75
45	Juan Marichal	3.00
46	Roger Maris	6.00
47	Bobby Thomson	.75
48	Eddie Mathews	4.00
49	Don Mattingly	8.00
50	Willie McCovey	2.00
51	Gil McDougald	.75
52	Tug McGraw	.75
53	Billy Pierce	.75
54	Minnie Minoso	.75
55	Johnny Mize	2.00
56	Elroy Face	.75
57	Joe Morgan	1.50
58	Thurman Munson	5.00
59	Stan Musial	5.00
60	Phil Niekro	.75
61	Paul Blair	.75
62	Andy Pafko	.75
63	Satchel Paige	5.00
64	Tony Perez	.75
65	Sal Bando	.75
66	Jimmy Piersall	.75
67	Kirby Puckett	5.00
68	Phil Rizzuto	3.00
69	Robin Roberts	.75
70	Jackie Robinson	8.00
71	Ryne Sandberg	3.00
72	Mike Schmidt	4.00
73	Red Schoendienst	.75
74	Herb Score	.75
75	Enos Slaughter	.75
76	Ozzie Smith	3.00
77	Warren Spahn	2.00
78	Don Sutton	.75
79	Luis Tiant	.75
80	Ted Kluszewski	.75
81	Whitey Ford	3.00
82	Maury Wills	.75
83	Dave Winfield	2.00
84	Early Wynn	.75
85	Carl Yastrzemski	3.00
86	Robin Yount	4.00
87	Bob Allison	.75
88	Clete Boyer	.75
89	Reggie Jackson	3.00
90	Yogi Berra	5.00
91	Willie Mays	8.00
92	Jim Palmer	.75
93	Pee Wee Reese	2.00
94	Frank Robinson	2.00
95	Boog Powell	.75
96	Willie Stargell	3.00
97	Nolan Ryan	10.00
98	Tom Seaver	4.00
99	Duke Snider	3.00
100	Bill Mazeroski	.75

2001 Topps Archives Reserve Autographed Baseball

		MT
Common Autograph:		15.00
Inserted 1:box		
1	Johnny Bench/100	80.00
2	Paul Blair/1,000	15.00
3	Clete Boyer/1,000	20.00
4	Ralph Branca/400	25.00
5	Elroy Face/1,000	20.00
6	Bob Feller/1,000	25.00
7	Whitey Ford/100	80.00
8	Bob Gibson/1,000	40.00
9	Dick Groat/1,000	20.00
10	Frank Howard/1,000	20.00
11	Reggie Jackson/100	75.00
12	Don Larsen/100	35.00
13	Mickey Lolich/500	20.00
14	Willie Mays/100	125.00
15	Gil McDougald/500	25.00
16	Tug McGraw/1,000	20.00
17	Minnie Minoso/1,000	20.00
18	Andy Pafko/500	25.00
19	Joe Pepitone/1,000	20.00
20	Robin Roberts/1,000	25.00
21	Frank Robinson/100	50.00

22 Nolan Ryan/100 150.00
23 Herb Score/500 20.00
24 Tom Seaver/100 100.00
25 Moose Skowron/1,000 20.00
26 Warren Spahn/100 50.00
27 Bobby Thomson/400 20.00
28 Luis Tiant/500 20.00
29 Carl Yastrzemski/100 100.00
30 Maury Wills/1,000 20.00

2001 Topps Archives Reserve Autographs

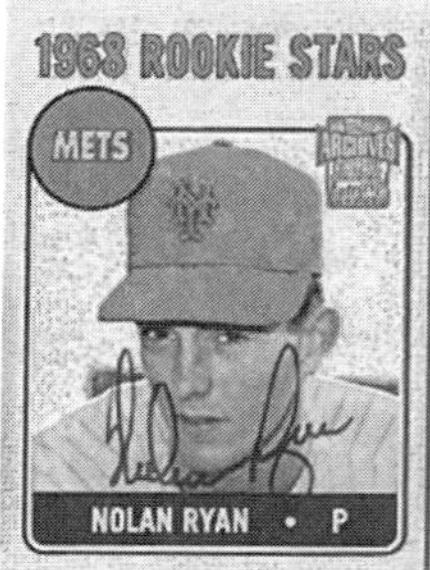

MT
Common Autograph: 15.00
Inserted 1:10
ARA1Willie Mays 150.00
ARA2Whitey Ford 60.00
ARA3Nolan Ryan 200.00
ARA4Carl Yastrzemski 100.00
ARA5Frank Robinson 40.00
ARA6Tom Seaver 80.00
ARA7Warren Spahn 70.00
ARA8Johnny Bench 100.00
ARA9Reggie Jackson 120.00
ARA10Bob Gibson 50.00
ARA11Bob Feller 25.00
ARA12Gil McDougald 25.00
ARA13Luis Tiant 15.00
ARA14Minnie Minoso 15.00
ARA16Herb Score 15.00
ARA17Moose Skowron 20.00
ARA18Maury Wills 15.00
ARA19Clete Boyer 20.00
ARA21Don Larsen 40.00
ARA23Tug McGraw 20.00
ARA25Robin Roberts 30.00
ARA26Frank Howard 30.00
ARA27Mickey Lolich 15.00
ARA29Tommy John 15.00
ARA32Dick Groat 20.00
ARA33Elroy Face 15.00
ARA34Paul Blair 15.00

2001 Topps Archives Reserve Bat Relics

MT
Common Player: 15.00
Overall Relic Odds 1:10
ARR21Al Kaline 40.00
ARR22Carl Yastrzemski 40.00
ARR23Carlton Fisk 20.00
ARR24Dale Murphy 60.00
ARR25Dave Winfield 20.00
ARR26Dick Groat 20.00
ARR27Dom DiMaggio 25.00
ARR28Don Mattingly 50.00
ARR29Gary Carter 20.00
ARR30George Kell 20.00
ARR31Harmon Killebrew 50.00
ARR32Jackie Jensen 20.00
ARR33Jackie Robinson 120.00
ARR34Jimmy Piersall 25.00
ARR35Joe Adcock 20.00
ARR36Joe Carter 20.00
ARR37Johnny Mize 30.00
ARR38Kirk Gibson 15.00
ARR39Mickey Vernon 15.00
ARR40Mike Schmidt 60.00
ARR41Ryne Sandberg 40.00
ARR42Ozzie Smith 40.00
ARR43Ted Kluszewski 30.00
ARR44Wade Boggs 20.00
ARR45Willie Mays 60.00
ARR46Duke Snider 40.00
ARR47Harvey Kuenn 15.00
ARR48Robin Yount 25.00
ARR49Red Schoendienst 15.00
ARR50Elston Howard 30.00
ARR51Bob Allison 15.00

2001 Topps Archives Reserve Jersey Relics

MT
Common Player: 15.00
Overall Relic Odds 1:10
ARR1Brooks Robinson 35.00
ARR2Tony Conigliaro 40.00
ARR3Frank Howard 20.00
ARR4Don Sutton 20.00
ARR5Ferguson Jenkins 15.00
ARR6Frank Robinson 25.00
ARR7Don Mattingly 60.00
ARR8Willie Stargell 25.00
ARR9Moose Skowron 25.00
ARR10Fred Lynn 20.00
ARR11George Brett 50.00
ARR12Nolan Ryan 75.00
ARR13Orlando Cepeda 20.00
ARR14Reggie Jackson 40.00
ARR15Steve Carlton 30.00
ARR16Tom Seaver 40.00
ARR17Thurman Munson 60.00
ARR18Yogi Berra 40.00
ARR19Willie McCovey 25.00
ARR20Robin Yount 30.00

A player's name in *italic* type indicates a rookie card.

2001 Topps Chrome

MT
Complete Set (660): 340.00
Complete Series 1 (330): 140.00
Complete Series 2 (330): 200.00
Common Player: .25
Pack (4): 3.00
Box (24): 60.00
1 Cal Ripken Jr. 5.00
2 Chipper Jones 3.00
3 Roger Cedeno .25
4 Garret Anderson .25
5 Robin Ventura .40
6 Daryle Ward .25
7 Not Issued (Retired) .25
8 Phil Nevin .25
9 Jermaine Dye .25
10 Chris Singleton .25
11 Mike Redmond .25
12 Jim Thome .75
13 Brian Jordan .25
14 Dustin Hermanson .25
15 Shawn Green .50
16 Todd Stottlemyre .25
17 Dan Wilson .25
18 Derek Lowe .25
19 Juan Gonzalez 1.50
20 Pat Meares .25
21 Paul O'Neill .75
22 Jeffrey Hammonds .25
23 Pokey Reese .25
24 Mike Mussina 1.25
25 Rico Brogna .25
26 Jay Buhner .25
27 Steve Cox .25
28 Quilvio Veras .25
29 Marquis Grissom .25
30 Shigetoshi Hasagawa .25
31 Shane Reynolds .25
32 Adam Piatt .40
33 Preston Wilson .25
34 Ellis Burks .25
35 Armando Rios .25
36 Chuck Finley .25
37 Shannon Stewart .25
38 Mark McGwire 5.00
39 Gerald Williams .25
40 Eric Young .25
41 Peter Bergeron .25
42 Arthur Rhodes .25
43 Bobby Jones .25
44 Matt Clement .25
45 Pedro Martinez 2.00
46 Jose Canseco 1.00
47 Matt Anderson .25
48 Torii Hunter .25
49 Carlos Lee .25
50 Eric Chavez .50
51 Rick Helling .25
52 John Franco .25
53 Mike Bordick .25
54 Andres Galarraga .50
55 Jose Cruz Jr. .25
56 Mike Matheny .25
57 Randy Johnson 1.50
58 Richie Sexson .25
59 Vladimir Nunez .25
60 Aaron Boone .25
61 Darin Erstad .75
62 Alex Gonzalez .25
63 Gil Heredia .25
64 Shane Andrews .25
65 Todd Hundley .25
66 Bill Mueller .25
67 Mark McLemore .25
68 Scott Spiezio .25
69 Kevin McGlinchy .25
70 Manny Ramirez 1.50
71 Mike Lamb .25
72 Brian Buchanan .25
73 Mike Sweeney .25
74 John Wetteland .25
75 Rob Bell .25
76 John Burkett .25
77 Derek Jeter 5.00
78 J.D. Drew .50
79 Jose Offerman .25
80 Rick Reed .25
81 Will Clark 1.00
82 Rickey Henderson .75
83 Kirk Rueter .25
84 Lee Stevens .25
85 Jay Bell .25
86 Fred McGriff 1.00
87 Julio Zuleta .25
88 Brian Anderson .25
89 Orlando Cabrera .25
90 Alex Fernandez .25
91 Derek Bell .25
92 Eric Owens .25
93 Dennys Reyes .25
94 Mike Stanley .25
95 Jorge Posada .40
96 Paul Konerko .25
97 Mike Remlinger .25
98 Travis Lee .25
99 Ken Caminiti .25
100 Kevin Barker .25
101 Ozzie Guillen .25
102 Randy Wolf .25
103 Michael Tucker .25
104 Darren Lewis .25
105 Joe Randa .25
106 Jeff Cirillo .25
107 David Ortiz .25
108 Herb Perry .25
109 Jeff Nelson .25
110 Chris Stynes .25
111 Johnny Damon .25
112 Jason Schmidt .25
113 Charles Johnson .25
114 Pat Burrell 1.50
115 Gary Sheffield .75
116 Tom Glavine 1.00
117 Jason Isringhausen .25
118 Chris Carpenter .25
119 Jeff Suppan .25
120 Ivan Rodriguez 1.50
121 Luis Sojo .25
122 Ron Villone .25
123 Mike Sirotka .25
124 Chuck Knoblauch .40
125 Jason Kendall .25
126 Bobby Estalella .25
127 Jose Guillen .25
128 Carlos Delgado 1.25
129 Benji Gil .25
130 Einar Diaz .25
131 Andy Benes .25
132 Adrian Beltre .50
133 Roger Clemens 2.00
134 Scott Williamson .25
135 Brad Penny .25
136 Troy Glaus 1.50
137 Kevin Appier .25
138 Walt Weiss .25
139 Michael Barrett .25
140 Mike Hampton .40
141 Francisco Cordova .25
142 David Segui .25
143 Carlos Febles .25
144 Roy Halladay .25
145 Seth Etherton .25
146 Fernando Tatis .25
147 Livan Hernandez .25
148 B.J. Surhoff .25
149 Barry Larkin 1.00
150 Bobby Howry .25
151 Dmitri Young .25
152 Brian Hunter .25
153 Alex Rodriguez 4.00
154 Hideo Nomo 1.00
155 Warren Morris .25
156 Antonio Alfonseca .25
157 Edgardo Alfonzo .50
158 Mark Grudzielanek .25
159 Fernando Vina .25

160 Homer Bush .25
161 Jason Giambi .75
162 Steve Karsay .25
163 Matt Lawton .25
164 Rusty Greer .25
165 Billy Koch .25
166 Todd Hollandsworth .25
167 Raul Ibanez .25
168 Tony Gwynn 2.00
169 Carl Everett .25
170 Hector Carrasco .25
171 Jose Valentin .25
172 Deivi Cruz .25
173 Bret Boone .25
174 Melvin Mora .25
175 Danny Graves .25
176 Jose Jimenez .25
177 James Baldwin .25
178 C.J. Nitkowski .25
179 Jeff Zimmerman .25
180 Mike Lowell .25
181 Hideki Irabu .25
182 Greg Vaughn .25
183 Omar Daal .25
184 Darren Dreifort .25
185 Gil Meche .25
186 Damian Jackson .25
187 Frank Thomas 2.00
188 Luis Castillo .25
189 Bartolo Colon .25
190 Craig Biggio .40
191 Scott Schoeneweis .25
192 Dave Veres .25
193 Ramon Martinez .25
194 Jose Vidro .25
195 Todd Helton 1.50
196 Greg Norton .25
197 Jacque Jones .25
198 Jason Grimsley .25
199 Dan Reichert .25
200 Robb Nen .25
201 Scott Hatteberg .25
202 Terry Shumpert .25
203 Kevin Millar .25
204 Ismael Valdes .25
205 Richard Hidalgo .50
206 Randy Velarde .25
207 Bengie Molina .25
208 Tony Womack .25
209 Enrique Wilson .25
210 Jeff Brantley .25
211 Rick Ankiel .50
212 Terry Mulholland .25
213 Ron Belliard .25
214 Terrence Long .25
215 Alberto Castillo .25
216 Royce Clayton .25
217 Joe McEwing .25
218 Jason McDonald .25
219 Ricky Bottalico .25
220 Keith Foulke .25
221 Brad Radke .25
222 Gabe Kapler .25
223 Pedro Astacio .25
224 Armando Reynoso .25
225 Darryl Kile .25
226 Reggie Sanders .25
227 Esteban Yan .25
228 Joe Nathan .25
229 Jay Payton .25
230 Francisco Cordero .25
231 Gregg Jefferies .25
232 LaTroy Hawkins .25
233 Jacob Cruz .25
234 Chris Holt .25
235 Vladimir Guerrero 2.00
236 Marvin Benard .25
237 Alex Ramirez .25
238 Mike Williams .25
239 Sean Bergman .25
240 Juan Encarnacion .25
241 Russ Davis .25
242 Ramon Hernandez .25
243 Sandy Alomar .25
244 Eddie Guardado .25
245 Shane Halter .25
246 Geoff Jenkins .25
247 Brian Meadows .25
248 Damian Miller .25
249 Darrin Fletcher .25
250 Rafael Furcal .50
251 Mark Grace .75
252 Mark Mulder .25
253 Joe Torre (Managers) .75
254 Bobby Cox (Managers) .25
255 Mike Scioscia (Managers) .25
256 Mike Hargrove (Managers) .25
257 Jimy Williams (Managers) .25
258 Jerry Manuel (Managers) .25
259 Charlie Manuel (Managers) .25
260 Don Baylor (Managers) .25
261 Phil Garner (Managers) .25
262 Tony Muser (Managers) .25
263 Buddy Bell (Managers) .25
264 Tom Kelly (Managers) .25
265 John Boles (Managers) .25
266 Art Howe (Managers) .25
267 Larry Dierker (Managers) .25
268 Lou Pinella (Managers) .25
269 Larry Rothschild (Managers) .25
270 Davey Lopes (Managers) .25
271 Johnny Oates (Managers) .25
272 Felipe Alou (Managers) .25
273 Bobby Valentine (Managers) .25
274 Tony LaRussa (Managers) .25
275 Bruce Bochy (Managers) .25
276 Dusty Baker (Managers) .25
277 Adrian Gonzalez, Adam Johnson (Draft Picks and Prospects) 4.00
278 Matt Wheatland, Brian Digby (Draft Picks and Prospects) 2.00
279 Tripper Johnson, Scott Thorman (Draft Picks and Prospects) 1.00
280 Phil Dumatrait, Adam Wainwright (Draft Picks and Prospects) 1.00
281 Scott Heard, *David Parrish* (Draft Picks and Prospects) 3.00
282 Rocco Baldelli, *Mark Folsom* (Draft Picks and Prospects) 1.50
283 *Dominic Rich*, Aaron Herr (Draft Picks and Prospects) 1.50
284 Mike Stodolka, Sean Burnett (Draft Picks and Prospects) 1.00
285 Derek Thompson, Corey Smith (Draft Picks and Prospects) 1.50
286 *Danny Borrell*, *Jason Bourgeois* (Draft Picks and Prospects) 4.00
287 Chin-Feng Chen, Corey Patterson, Josh Hamilton (Draft Picks and Prospects) 1.00
288 Ryan Anderson, Barry Zito, C.C. Sabathia (Draft Picks and Prospects) 2.00
289 Scott Sobkowiak, David Walling, Ben Sheets (Draft Picks and Prospects) 2.50
290 Ty Howington, Josh Kalinowski, Josh Girdley (Draft Picks and Prospects) .25
291 *Hee Seop Choi*, Aaron McNeal, Jason Hart (Draft Picks and Prospects) 10.00
292 Bobby Bradley, Kurt Ainsworth, Chin-Hui Tsao (Draft Picks and Prospects) 3.00
293 Mike Glendenning, Kenny Kelly, Juan Silvestri (Draft Picks and Prospects) .25
294 J.R. House, Ramon Castro, Ben Davis (Draft Picks and Prospects) 3.00
295 Chance Caple, *Rafael Soriano*, Pascual Coco (Draft Picks and Prospects) 3.00
296 *Travis Hafner*, Eric Munson, Bucky Jacobsen (Draft Picks and Prospects) 1.00
297 Jason Conti, Chris Wakeland, Brian Cole (Draft Picks and Prospects) .75
298 Scott Seabol, Aubrey Huff, Joe Crede (Draft Picks and Prospects) 2.00
299 Adam Everett, Jose Ortiz, Keith Ginter (Draft Picks and Prospects) 2.00
300 Carlos Hernandez, Geraldo Guzman, Adam Eaton (Draft Picks and Prospects) .75
301 Bobby Kielty, Milton Bradley, Juan Rivera (Draft Picks and Prospects) .75
302 Mark McGwire (Golden Moments) 3.00
303 Don Larsen (Golden Moments) 1.00
304 Bobby Thomson (Golden Moments) .25
305 Bill Mazeroski (Golden Moments) .35
306 Reggie Jackson (Golden Moments) 1.00
307 Kirk Gibson (Golden Moments) .25
308 Roger Maris (Golden Moments) 1.50
309 Cal Ripken Jr. (Golden Moments) 3.00
310 Hank Aaron (Golden Moments) 3.00
311 Joe Carter (Golden Moments) .25
312 Cal Ripken Jr. (Season Highlights) 3.00
313 Randy Johnson (Season Highlights) 1.00
314 Ken Griffey Jr. (Season Highlights) 2.50
315 Troy Glaus (Season Highlights) 1.00
316 Kazuhiro Sasaki (Season Highlights) .25
317 Sammy Sosa, Troy Glaus (League Leaders) 1.00
318 Todd Helton, Edgar Martinez (League Leaders) .50
319 Todd Helton, Nomar Garciaparra (League Leaders) 1.50
320 Barry Bonds, Jason Giambi (League Leaders) .75
321 Todd Helton, Manny Ramirez (League Leaders) .50
322 Todd Helton, Darin Erstad (League Leaders) .50
323 Kevin Brown, Pedro Martinez (League Leaders) .50
324 Randy Johnson, Pedro Martinez (League Leaders) .50
325 Will Clark (Post Season Highlights) .40
326 New York Mets (Post Season Highlights) .25
327 New York Yankees (Post Season Highlights) 1.00
328 Seattle Mariners (Post Season Highlights) .25
329 Mike Hampton (Post Season Highlights) .25
330 New York Yankees (Post Season Highlights) 1.00
331 World Series (Post Season Highlights) 4.00
332 Jeff Bagwell 1.50
333 Andy Pettite .50
334 Tony Armas Jr. .25
335 Jeromy Burnitz .25
336 Javier Vazquez .25
337 Eric Karros .25
338 Brian Giles .40
339 Scott Rolen .75
340 David Justice .75
341 Ray Durham .25
342 Todd Zeile .25
343 Cliff Floyd .25
344 Barry Bonds 2.00
345 Matt Williams .50
346 Steve Finley .25
347 Scott Elarton .25
348 Bernie Williams 1.25
349 David Wells .25
350 J.T. Snow .25
351 Al Leiter .40
352 Magglio Ordonez .40
353 Raul Mondesi .25
354 Tim Salmon .25
355 Jeff Kent .40
356 Mariano Rivera .40
357 John Olerud .40
358 Javy Lopez .40
359 Ben Grieve .40
360 Ray Lankford .25
361 Ken Griffey Jr. 4.00
362 Rich Aurilia .25
363 Andruw Jones 1.00
364 Ryan Klesko .25
365 Roberto Alomar 1.25
366 Miguel Tejada .50
367 Mo Vaughn .25
368 Albert Belle .25
369 Jose Canseco .75
370 Kevin Brown .40
371 Rafael Palmeiro .75
372 Mark Redman .25
373 Larry Walker .50
374 Greg Maddux 3.00
375 Nomar Garciaparra 4.00
376 Kevin Millwood .25
377 Edgar Martinez .25
378 Sammy Sosa 3.00
379 Tim Hudson .40
380 Jim Edmonds .40
381 Mike Piazza 4.00
382 Brant Brown .25
383 Brad Fullmer .25
384 Alan Benes .25
385 Mickey Morandini .25
386 Troy Percival .25
387 Eddie Perez .25
388 Vernon Wells .25
389 Ricky Gutierrez .25
390 Rondell White .25
391 Kevin Escobar .25
392 Tony Batista .25
393 Jimmy Haynes .25
394 Billy Wagner .25
395 A.J. Hinch .25
396 Matt Morris .25
397 Lance Berkman .25
398 Jeff D'Amico .25
399 Octavio Dotel .25
400 Olmedo Saenz .25
401 Esteban Loaiza .25
402 Adam Kennedy .25
403 Moises Alou .40
404 Orlando Palmeiro .25
405 Kevin Young .25
406 Tom Goodwin .25
407 Mac Suzuki .25
408 Pat Hentgen .25
409 Kevin Stocker .25
410 Mark Sweeney .25
411 Tony Eusebio .25
412 Edgar Renteria .25
413 John Rocker .25
414 Jose Lima .25
415 Kerry Wood .50
416 Mike Timlin .25
417 Jose Hernandez .25
418 Jeremy Giambi .25
419 Luis Lopez .25
420 Mitch Meluskey .25
421 Garrett Stephenson .25

422 Jamey Wright .25
423 John Jaha .25
424 Placido Polanco .25
425 Marty Cordova .25
426 Joey Hamilton .25
427 Travis Fryman .25
428 Mike Cameron .25
429 Matt Mantei .25
430 Chan Ho Park .40
431 Shawn Estes .25
432 Danny Bautista .25
433 Wilson Alvarez .25
434 Kenny Lofton .40
435 Russ Ortiz .25
436 Dave Burba .25
437 Felix Martinez .25
438 Jeff Shaw .25
439 Mike Difelice .25
440 Roberto Hernandez .25
441 Bryan Rekar .25
442 Ugueth Urbina .25
443 Vinny Castilla .25
444 Carlos Perez .25
445 Juan Guzman .25
446 Ryan Rupe .25
447 Mike Mordecai .25
448 Ricardo Rincon .25
449 Curt Schilling .40
450 Alex Cora .25
451 Turner Ward .25
452 Omar Vizquel .40
453 Russ Branyan .25
454 Russ Johnson .25
455 Gregg Colbrunn .25
456 Charles Nagy .25
457 Wil Cordero .25
458 Jason Tyner .25
459 Devon White .25
460 Kelly Stinnett .25
461 Wilton Guerrero .25
462 Jason Bere .25
463 Calvin Murray .25
464 Miguel Batista .25
465 Erubiel Durazo .25
466 Luis Gonzalez .50
467 Jaret Wright .25
468 Chad Kreuter .25
469 Armando Benitez .25
470 Sidney Ponson .25
471 Adrian Brown .25
472 Sterling Hitchcock .25
473 Timoniel Perez .25
474 Jamie Moyer .25
475 Delino DeShields .25
476 Glendon Rusch .25
477 Chris Gomez .25
478 Adam Eaton .25
479 Pablo Ozuna .25
480 Bob Abreu .25
481 Kris Benson .25
482 Keith Osik .25
483 Darryl Hamilton .25
484 Marlon Anderson .25
485 Jimmy Anderson .25
486 John Halama .25
487 Nelson Figueroa .25
488 Alex Gonzalez .25
489 Benny Agbayani .25
490 Ed Sprague .25
491 Scott Erickson .25
492 Doug Glanville .25
493 Jesus Sanchez .25
494 Mike Lieberthal .25
495 Aaron Sele .25
496 Pat Mahomes .25
497 Ruben Rivera .25
498 Wayne Gomes .25
499 Freddy Garcia .25
500 Al Martin .25
501 Woody Williams .25
502 Paul Byrd .25
503 Rick White .25
504 Trevor Hoffman .25
505 Brady Anderson .25
506 Robert Person .25
507 Jeff Conine .25
508 Chris Truby .25
509 Emil Brown .25
510 Ryan Dempster .25
511 Ruben Mateo .25
512 Alex Ochoa .25
513 Jose Rosado .25
514 Masato Yoshii .25
515 Brian Daubach .25
516 Jeff D'Amico .25
517 Brent Mayne .25
518 John Thomson .25
519 Todd Ritchie .25
520 John Vander Wal .25
521 Neifi Perez .25
522 Chad Curtis .25
523 Kenny Rogers .25
524 Trot Nixon .25
525 Sean Casey .25
526 Wilton Veras .25
527 Troy O'Leary .25
528 Dante Bichette .25
529 Jose Silva .25
530 Darren Oliver .25
531 Steve Parris .25
532 David McCarty .25
533 Todd Walker .25
534 Brian Rose .25
535 Pete Schourek .25
536 Ricky Ledee .25
537 Justin Thompson .25
538 Benito Santiago .25
539 Carlos Beltran .25
540 Gabe White .25
541 Bret Saberhagen .25
542 Ramon Martinez .25
543 John Valentin .25
544 Frank Catalanotto .25
545 Tim Wakefield .25
546 Michael Tucker .25
547 Juan Pierre .25
548 Rich Garces .25
549 Luis Ordaz .25
550 Jerry Spradlin .25
551 Corey Koskie .25
552 Cal Eldred .25
553 Alfonso Soriano .75
554 Kip Wells .25
555 Orlando Hernandez .40
556 Bill Simas .25
557 Jim Parque .25
558 Joe Mays .25
559 Tim Belcher .25
560 Shane Spencer .25
561 Glenallen Hill .25
562 Matt LeCroy .25
563 Tino Martinez .25
564 Eric Milton .25
565 Ron Coomer .25
566 Cristian Guzman .25
567 Kazuhiro Sasaki .25
568 Mark Quinn .25
569 Eric Gagne .25
570 Kerry Ligtenberg .25
571 Rolando Arrojo .25
572 Jon Lieber .25
573 Jose Vizcaino .25
574 Jeff Abbott .25
575 Carlos Hernandez .25
576 Scott Sullivan .25
577 Matt Stairs .25
578 Tom Lampkin .25
579 Donnie Sadler .25
580 Desi Relaford .25
581 Scott Downs .25
582 Mike Mussina .75
583 Ramon Ortiz .25
584 Mike Myers .25
585 Frank Castillo .25
586 Manny Ramirez 1.75
587 Alex Rodriguez 4.00
588 Andy Ashby .25
589 Felipe Crespo .25
590 Bobby Bonilla .25
591 Denny Neagle .25
592 Dave Martinez .25
593 Mike Hampton .25
594 Gary DiSarcina .25
595 *Tsuyoshi Shinjo* 5.00
596 *Albert Pujols* 35.00
597 Roy Oswalt, Pat Strange, Jon Rauch (Prospects) 2.50
598 *Phil Wilson,Jake Peavy,Darwin Cubillan* (Prospects) 2.00
599 Nathan Haynes,*Steve Smyth*, Mike Bynum (Prospects) 1.50
600 Joe Lawrence, Choo Freeman, Michael Cuddyer (Prospects) .25
601 Larry Barnes, Dewayne Wise, Carlos Pena (Prospects) .25
602 Felipe Lopez, Gookie Dawkins,*Erick Almonte* (Prospects) 1.50
603 Brad Wilkerson, Alex Escobar, Eric Valent (Prospects) .25
604 *Jeff Goldbach*, Toby Hall, Rod Barajas (Prospects) .25
605 Marcus Giles, Pablo Ozuna, Jason Romano (Prospects) .25
606 Vernon Wells, Jack Cust, Dee Brown (Prospects) .25
607 *Luis Montanez*, David Espinosa (Draft Picks) 4.00
608 John Lackey,*Justin Wayne* (Draft Picks) 3.00
609 *Josh Axelson,Carmen Cali* (Draft Picks) 2.00
610 *Shaun Boyd,Chris Morris* (Draft Picks) 2.00
611 *Dan Moylan,Tommy Arko* (Draft Picks) 2.00
612 *Luis Cotto*, Luis Escobar (Draft Picks) 1.50
613 *Blake Williams,Brandon Mims* (Draft Picks) 3.00
614 *Chris Russ*, Bryan Edwards (Draft Picks) 1.50
615 Joe Torres, Ben Diggins (Draft Picks) .25
616 Mark Dalesandro, *Edwin Encarnacion* (Draft Picks) 1.50
617 *Brian Bass,Odannis Ayala* (Draft Picks) 1.50
618 *Jason Kaanoi,Michael Mathews* (Draft Picks) .25
619 *Stuart McFarland,Adam Sterrett* (Draft Picks) 1.50
620 David Krynzel, Grady Sizemore (Draft Picks) 1.50
621 Keith Bucktrot, Dane Sardinha (Draft Picks) .25
622 Anaheim Angels .25
623 Arizona Diamondbacks .25
624 Atlanta Braves .25
625 Baltimore Orioles .25
626 Boston Red Sox .25
627 Chicago Cubs .25
628 Chicago White Sox .25
629 Cincinnati Reds .25
630 Cleveland Indians .25
631 Colorado Rockies .25
632 Detroit Tigers .25
633 Florida Marlins .25
634 Houston Astros .25
635 Kansas City Royals .25
636 Los Angeles Dodgers .25
637 Milwaukee Brewers .25
638 Minnesota Twins .25
639 Montreal Expos .25
640 New York Mets .25
641 New York Yankees 2.00
642 Oakland Athletics .25
643 Philadelphia Phillies .25
644 Pittsburgh Pirates .25
645 San Diego Padres .25
646 San Francisco Giants .25
647 Seattle Mariners .25
648 St. Louis Cardinals .25
649 Tampa Bay Devil Rays .25
650 Texas Rangers .25
651 Toronto Blue Jays .25
652 Bucky Dent (Golden Moments) .25
653 Jackie Robinson (Golden Moments) 1.50
654 Roberto Clemente (Golden Moments) 1.50
655 Nolan Ryan (Golden Moments) 2.50
656 Kerry Wood (Golden Moments) .75
657 Rickey Henderson (Golden Moments) .75
658 Lou Brock (Golden Moments) .50
659 David Wells (Golden Moments) .25
660 Andruw Jones (Golden Moments) .75
661 Carlton Fisk (Golden Moments) .25

2001 Topps Chrome Retrofractors

MT
Stars: 5-10X
Inserted 1:12

2001 Topps Chrome Before There Was Topps

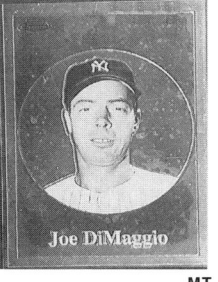

MT
Complete Set (10): 60.00
Common Player: 3.00
Inserted 1:20
Refractors: 2-4X
Inserted 1:200
BT1 Lou Gehrig 15.00
BT2 Babe Ruth 15.00
BT3 Cy Young 8.00
BT4 Walter Johnson 4.00
BT5 Ty Cobb 10.00
BT6 Rogers Hornsby 4.00
BT7 Honus Wagner 4.00
BT8 Christy Mathewson 3.00
BT9 Grover Alexander 3.00
BT10 Joe DiMaggio 15.00

2001 Topps Chrome Combos

MT
Complete Set (20): 120.00
Common Card: 3.00
Inserted 1:12
Refractors: 2-4X
Inserted 1:120
1 Derek Jeter, Yogi Berra, Whitey Ford, Don Mattingly, Reggie Jackson 10.00
2 Chipper Jones, Mike Schmidt 6.00
3 Brooks Robinson, Cal Ripken Jr. 10.00
4 Bob Gibson, Pedro Martinez 5.00
5 Ivan Rodriguez, Johnny Bench 4.00

6 Ernie Banks, Alex Rodriguez 8.00
7 Joe Morgan, Ken Griffey Jr., Barry Larkin 10.00
8 Vladimir Guerrero, Roberto Clemente 8.00
9 Ken Griffey Jr., Hank Aaron 10.00
10 Casey Stengel, Joe Torre 3.00
TC11 Kevin Brown, Sandy Koufax, Don Drysdale 6.00
TC12 Mark McGwire, Sammy Sosa, Roger Marris, Babe Ruth 12.00
TC13 Ted Williams, Carl Yastrzemski, Nomar Garciaparra 8.00
TC14 Greg Maddux, Roger Clemens, Cy Young 5.00
TC15 Tony Gwynn, Ted Williams 6.00
TC16 Cal Ripken Jr., Lou Gehrig 10.00
TC17 Sandy Koufax, Randy Johnson, Warren Spahn, Steve Carlton 5.00
TC18 Mike Piazza, Josh Gibson 8.00
TC19 Barry Bonds, Willie Mays 8.00
TC20 Jackie Robinson, Larry Doby 8.00

2001 Topps Chrome Golden Anniversary

MT
Complete Set (50): 200.00
Common Player: 2.00
Inserted 1:10
Refractors: 2-4X
Inserted 1:100
1 Hank Aaron 12.00
2 Ernie Banks 4.00
3 Mike Schmidt 4.00
4 Willie Mays 10.00
5 Johnny Bench 4.00
6 Tom Seaver 4.00
7 Frank Robinson 3.00
8 Sandy Koufax 12.00
9 Bob Gibson 4.00
10 Ted Williams 15.00
11 Cal Ripken Jr. 15.00
12 Tony Gwynn 6.00
13 Mark McGwire 15.00
14 Ken Griffey Jr. 12.00
15 Greg Maddux 10.00
16 Roger Clemens 8.00
17 Barry Bonds 5.00
18 Rickey Henderson 2.00
19 Mike Piazza 12.00
20 Jose Canseco 4.00
21 Derek Jeter 15.00
22 Nomar Garciaparra 12.00
23 Alex Rodriguez 12.00
24 Sammy Sosa 10.00
25 Ivan Rodriguez 5.00
26 Vladimir Guerrero 6.00
27 Chipper Jones 10.00
28 Jeff Bagwell 5.00
29 Pedro Martinez 6.00
30 Randy Johnson 5.00
31 Pat Burrell 5.00
32 Josh Hamilton 4.00
33 Ryan Anderson 2.00
34 Corey Patterson 2.00
35 Eric Munson 2.00
36 Sean Burroughs 2.00
37 C.C. Sabathia 2.00
38 Chin-Feng Chen 4.00
39 Barry Zito 4.00
40 Adrian Gonzalez 4.00
41 Mark McGwire 15.00
42 Nomar Garciaparra 12.00
43 Todd Helton 5.00
44 Matt Williams 3.00
45 Troy Glaus 5.00
46 Geoff Jenkins 2.00
47 Frank Thomas 6.00
48 Mo Vaughn 3.00
49 Barry Larkin 3.00
50 J.D. Drew 2.00

2001 Topps Chrome King of Kings

MT
Common Player: 125.00
Inserted 1:5,175 H
Inserted 1:5,209 R
KKR1 Hank Aaron 250.00
KKR2 Nolan Ryan 350.00
KKR3 Rickey Henderson 125.00
KKR5 Bob Gibson 140.00
KKR6 Nolan Ryan 250.00

2001 Topps Chrome King of Kings Golden Edition

MT
Complete Set (1):
Inserted 1:59,220 H
KKGE Hank Aaron, Nolan Ryan, Rickey Henderson
KKLE2 Mark McGwire, Bob Gibson, Nolan Ryan

2001 Topps Chrome Past To Present

MT
Complete Set (10): 40.00
Common Player: 3.00
Inserted 1:18
1 Phil Rizzuto, Derek Jeter 10.00
2 Warren Spahn, Greg Maddux 6.00
3 Yogi Berra, Jorge Posada 6.00
4 Willie Mays, Barry Bonds 6.00
5 Red Schoendienst, Fernando Vina 3.00
6 Duke Snider, Shawn Green 4.00
7 Bob Feller, Bartolo Colon 3.00
8 Johnny Mize, Tino Martinez 3.00
9 Larry Doby, Manny Ramirez 4.00
10 Eddie Mathews, Chipper Jones 6.00

2001 Topps Chrome Through The Years

MT
Complete Set (50): 400.00
Common Player: 5.00
Inserted 1:10
Refractors: 2-4X
Inserted 1:100
1 Yogi Berra 8.00
2 Roy Campanella 8.00
3 Willie Mays 12.00
4 Andy Pafko 5.00
5 Jackie Robinson 20.00
6 Stan Musial 10.00
7 Duke Snider 8.00
8 Warren Spahn 8.00
9 Ted Williams 20.00
10 Eddie Matthews 8.00
11 Willie McCovey 5.00
12 Frank Robinson 6.00
13 Ernie Banks 8.00
14 Hank Aaron 15.00
15 Sandy Koufax 15.00
16 Bob Gibson 8.00
17 Harmon Killebrew 5.00
18 Whitey Ford 5.00
19 Roberto Clemente 15.00
20 Juan Marichal 5.00
21 Johnny Bench 8.00
22 Willie Stargell 6.00
23 Joe Morgan 6.00
24 Carl Yastrzemski 8.00
25 Reggie Jackson 8.00
26 Tom Seaver 8.00
27 Steve Carlton 5.00
28 Jim Palmer 6.00
29 Rod Carew 6.00
30 George Brett 12.00
31 Roger Clemens 8.00
32 Don Mattingly 12.00
33 Ryne Sandberg 6.00
34 Mike Schmidt 8.00
35 Cal Ripken Jr. 20.00
36 Tony Gwynn 8.00
37 Ozzie Smith 8.00
38 Wade Boggs 5.00
39 Nolan Ryan 20.00
40 Robin Yount 6.00
41 Mark McGwire 20.00
42 Ken Griffey Jr. 15.00
43 Sammy Sosa 12.00
44 Alex Rodriguez 15.00
45 Barry Bonds 8.00
46 Mike Piazza 15.00
47 Chipper Jones 12.00
48 Greg Maddux 12.00
49 Nomar Garciaparra 15.00
50 Derek Jeter 20.00

2001 Topps Chrome Topps Originals

MT
Common Player: 100.00
Inserted 1:1,783 H
Inserted 1:1,788 R
Refractors 10 sets produced
1 Roberto Clemente 750.00
2 Carl Yastrzemski 300.00
3 Mike Schmidt 250.00
4 Wade Boggs 100.00
5 Chipper Jones 100.00
6 Willie Mays
7 Lou Brock 60.00
8 Dave Parker 40.00
9 Barry Bonds 150.00
10 Alex Rodriguez 150.00

2001 Topps Chrome What Could've Been

MT
Complete Set (10): 40.00
Common Player: 3.00
Inserted 1:30
Refractors: 2-4X
Inserted 1:300
WCB1 Josh Gibson 8.00
WCB2 Satchel Paige 10.00
WCB3 Buck Leonard 4.00
WCB4 James "Cool Pap Bell 6.00
WCB5 Andrew "Rube" Foster 4.00
WCB6 Martin Dihigo 3.00
WCB7 William "Judy" Johnson 3.00
WCB8 Mule Suttles 3.00
WCB9 Ray Dandridge 3.00
WCB10 John Henry Lloyd 3.00

2001 Topps & Topps Chrome Traded & Rookies

MT
Complete Topps Set (265): 45.00
Common Player: .10
Chrome cards: 2-4X
Pack (10): 4.00
Box (24): 85.00

T1 Sandy Alomar Jr. .10
T2 Kevin Appier .10
T3 Brad Ausmus .10
T4 Derek Bell .10
T5 Bret Boone .20
T6 Rico Brogna .10
T7 Ellis Burks .10
T8 Ken Caminiti .10
T9 Roger Cedeno .10
T10 Royce Clayton .10
T11 Enrique Wilson .10
T12 Rheal Cormier .10
T13 Eric Davis .10
T14 Shawon Duston .10
T15 Andres Galarraga .20
T16 Tom Gordon .10
T17 Mark Grace .50
T18 Jeffrey Hammonds .10
T19 Dustin Hermanson .10
T20 Quinton McCracken .10
T21 Todd Hundley .10
T22 Charles Johnson .10
T23 Marquis Grissom .10
T24 Jose Mesa .10
T25 Terry Mulholland .10
T26 John Rocker .10
T27 Jeff Frye .10
T28 Reggie Sanders .10
T29 David Segui .10
T30 Mike Sirotka .10
T31 Fernando Tatis .10
T32 Steve Trachsel .10
T33 Ismael Valdes .10
T34 Randy Velarde .10
T35 Brian Boehringer .10
T36 Mike Bordick .10
T37 Ken Bottenfield .10
T38 Pat Rapp .10
T39 Jeff Nelson .10
T40 Ricky Bottalico .10
T41 Deion Sanders .20
T42 Hideo Nomo .50
T43 Bill Mueller .10
T44 Roberto Kelly .10
T45 Chris Holt .10
T46 Mike Jackson .10
T47 Devon White .10
T48 Gerald Williams .10
T49 Eddie Taubensee .10
T50 Brian Hunter .10
T51 Nelson Cruz .10
T52 Jeff Fassero .10
T53 Bubba Trammell .10
T54 Bo Porter .10
T55 Greg Norton .10
T56 Benito Santiago .10
T57 Ruben Rivera .10
T58 Dee Brown .10
T59 Jose Canseco .40
T60 Chris Michalak .10
T61 Tim Worrell .10
T62 Matt Clement .10
T63 Bill Pulsipher .10
T64 Troy Brohawn .10
T65 Mark Kotsay .10
T66 Jose Lima .10
T67 Shea Hillenbrand .10
T68 Ted Lilly .10
T69 Jermaine Dye .10
T70 Jerry Hairston Jr. .10
T71 John Mabry .10
T72 Kurt Abbott .10
T73 Eric Owens .10
T74 Jeff Brantley .10
T75 Vinny Castilla .10
T76 Ron Villone .10
T77 Ricky Henderson .40
T78 Jason Grimsley .10
T79 *Christian Parker* .10
T80 Donnie Wall .10
T81 Alex Arias .10
T82 Willis Roberts .10
T83 Ryan Minor .10
T84 Jason LaRue .10
T85 Ruben Sierra .10
T86 Johnny Damon .10
T87 Juan Gonzalez .60
T88 Mac Suzuki .10
T89 Tony Batista .10
T90 Jay Witasick .10
T91 Brent Abernathy .10
T92 Paul LoDuca .10
T93 Wes Helms .10
T94 Milton Bradley .10
T95 Matt LeCroy .10
T96 A.J. Hinch .10
T97 *Bud Smith* .10
T98 Adam Dunn .75
T99 Albert Pujols, Ichiro Suzuki 10.00
T100 Carlton Fisk .25
T101 Tim Raines .10
T102 Juan Marichal .10
T103 Dave Winfield .25
T104 Reggie Jackson .50
T105 Cal Ripken Jr. 2.50
T106 Ozzie Smith .50
T107 Tom Seaver .50
T108 Lou Piniella .10
T109 Dwight Gooden .10
T110 Bret Saberhagen .10
T111 Gary Carter .10
T112 Jack Clark .10
T113 Rickey Henderson .50
T114 Barry Bonds 1.00
T115 Bobby Bonilla .10
T116 Jose Canseco .40
T117 Will Clark .25
T118 Andres Galarraga .10
T119 Bo Jackson .10
T120 Wally Joyner .10
T121 Ellis Burks .10
T122 David Cone .10
T123 Greg Maddux .50
T124 Willie Randolph .10
T125 Dennis Eckersley .10
T126 Matt Williams .20
T127 Joe Morgan .10
T128 Fred McGriff .10
T129 Roberto Alomar .25
T130 Lee Smith .10
T131 David Wells .10
T132 Ken Griffey Jr. 1.50
T133 Deion Sanders .10
T134 Nolan Ryan 2.00
T135 David Justice .25
T136 Joe Carter .10
T137 Jack Morris .10
T138 Mike Piazza 1.50
T139 Barry Bonds 1.00
T140 Terrence Long .10
T141 Ben Grieve .10
T142 Richie Sexson .10
T143 Sean Burroughs .10
T144 Alfonso Soriano .40
T145 Bob Boone .10
T146 Larry Bowa .10
T147 Bob Brenly .10
T148 Buck Martinez .10
T149 Lloyd McClendon .10
T150 Jim Tracy .10
T151 *Jared Abruzzo* .50
T152 Kurt Ainsworth .10
T153 Willie Bloomquist .10
T154 Ben Broussard .10
T155 Bobby Bradley .10
T156 Mike Bynum .10
T157 Ken Harvey .10
T158 Ryan Christianson .10
T159 Ryan Kohlmeier .10
T160 Joe Crede .10
T161 Jack Cust .10
T162 Ben Diggins .10
T163 Phil Dumatrait .10
T164 Alex Escobar .10
T165 Miguel Olivo .10
T166 Chris George .10
T167 Marcus Giles .10
T168 Keith Ginter .10
T169 Josh Girdley .10
T170 Tony Alvarez .10
T171 Scott Seabol .10
T172 Josh Hamilton .25
T173 Jason Hart .10
T174 Israel Alcantara .10
T175 Jake Peavy .10
T176 *Stubby Clapp* .40
T177 D'Angelo Jimenez .10
T178 Nick Johnson .10
T179 Ben Johnson .10
T180 Larry Bigbie .10
T181 Allen Levrault .10
T182 Felipe Lopez .10
T183 Sean Burnett .10
T184 Nick Neugebauer .10
T185 Austin Kearns .10
T186 Corey Patterson .25
T187 Carlos Pena .10
T188 *Ricardo Rodriguez* .50
T189 Juan Rivera .10
T190 Grant Roberts .10
T191 *Adam Pettyjohn* .10
T192 Jared Sandberg .10
T193 Xavier Nady .20
T194 Dane Sardinha .10
T195 Shawn Sonnier .10
T196 Rafael Soriano .10
T197 *Brian Specht* .25
T198 Aaron Myette .10
T199 *Juan Uribe* .40
T200 Jayson Werth .10
T201 Brad Wilkerson .10
T202 Horacio Estrada .10
T203 Joel Pineiro .10
T204 Matt LeCroy .10
T205 Michael Coleman .10
T206 Ben Sheets .25
T207 Eric Byrnes .10
T208 Sean Burroughs .10
T209 Ken Harvey .10
T210 Travis Hafner .10
T211 Erick Almonte .10
T212 *Jason Belcher* 1.00
T213 *Wilson Betemit* 2.00
T214 *Hank Blalock* 4.00
T215 Danny Borrell .10
T216 *John Buck* .40
T217 *Freddie Bynum* .50
T218 *Noel Devarez* .25
T219 *Juan Diaz* .25
T220 *Felix Diaz* .25
T221 *Josh Fogg* .50
T222 *Matt Ford* .25
T223 Scott Heard .10
T224 *Ben Hendrickson* .25
T225 *Cody Ross* .25
T226 *Adrian Hernandez* .75
T227 *Alfredo Amezaga* .75
T228 *Bob Keppel* .25
T229 *Ryan Madson* .50
T230 *Octavio Martinez* .25
T231 Hee Seop Choi .10
T232 Thomas Mitchell .10
T233 Luis Montanez .10
T234 *Andy Morales* .40
T235 *Justin Morneau* 1.50
T236 *Greg "Toe" Nash* 1.00
T237 *Valentino Pasucci* .10
T238 *Roy Smith* .40
T239 *Antonio Perez* .75
T240 *Chad Petty* .50
T241 Steve Smyth .10
T242 *Jose Reyes* 2.00
T243 *Eric Reynolds* .50
T244 Dominic Rich .10
T245 *Jason Richardson* .25
T246 *Ed Rogers* .40
T247 *Albert Pujols* 15.00
T248 *Esix Snead* .25
T249 *Luis Torres* .25
T250 *Matt White* .40
T251 Blake Williams .10
T252 Chris Russ .10
T253 *Joe Kennedy* .25
T254 *Jeff Randazzo* .25
T255 *Beau Hale* .50
256 *Brad Hennessey* .25
257 *Jake Gautreau* .10
258 *Jeff Mathis* .50
259 *Aaron Heilman* 1.00
260 *Bronson Sardinha* 1.50
261 *Irvin Guzman* 1.00
262 *Gabe Gross* 1.50
263 *J.D. Martin* 1.00
264 *Chris Smith* .25
265 *Kenny Baugh* .50
266 *Ichiro Suzuki (chrome)* 30.00

2001 Topps & Topps Chrome Traded & Rookies Autographs

MT
Common Autograph: 20.00
TTA-JDJohnny Damon 20.00
TTA-MMMike Mussina 40.00

2001 Topps & TC Traded & Rookies Legends Autographs

MT
Common Player:
TT51 Ralph Branca 15.00
TT6F Whitey Ford
TTF47 Frank Howard 25.00
TTF50 Mickey Lolich 15.00
TTF1 Willie Mays
TT37 Tug McGraw 15.00
TT35F Joe Pepitone
TT48F Bobby Richardson 25.00
TT36F Enos Slaughter 30.00
TT13 Warren Spahn 40.00
TT43 Bobby Thomson 25.00

2001 Topps & TC Traded & Rookies Dual-Traded Relics

MT
Complete Set (5):
Common Player:
TTR-DB Derek Bell
TTR-MG Mark Grace
TTR-BG Ben Grieve 20.00
TTR-DH Dustin Hermanson
TTR-MR Manny Ramirez 40.00

2001 Topps & TC Traded & Rookies Farewell Dual Relic

		MT
Inserted 1:4,693		
RG	Cal Ripken, Tony Gwynn	150.00

2001 Topps & TC Traded & Rookies Hall of Fame Relics

		MT
Complete Set (1):		
PW	Kirby Puckett, Dave Winfield	75.00

2001 Topps & Topps Chrome Traded & Rookies Relics

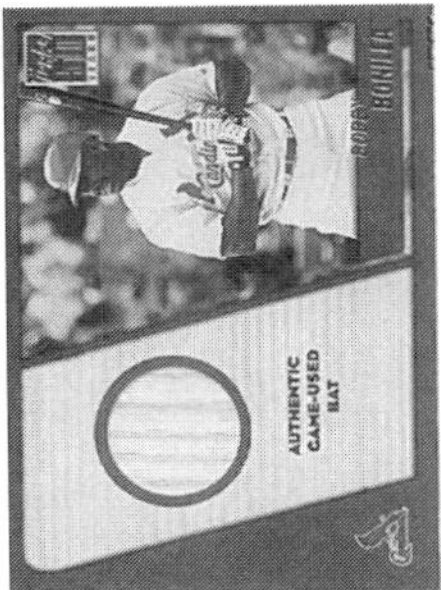

		MT
Common Player:		10.00
Inserted 1:29		
SA	Sandy Alomar Jr.	10.00
DB	Derek Bell	10.00
BB	Bobby Bonilla	10.00
BB	Bret Boone	20.00
RB	Rico Brogna	10.00
KC	Ken Caminiti	10.00
JC	Jose Canseco	15.00
ROC	Roger Cedeno	10.00
RSC	Royce Clayton	10.00
JD	Johnny Damon	15.00
ED	Eric Davis	15.00
JD	Jermaine Dye	15.00
AG	Andres Galarraga	20.00
RG	Ron Gant	10.00
JG	Juan Gonzalez	20.00
MG	Mark Grace	25.00
BG	Ben Grieve (dual)	20.00
MG	Marquis Grissom	10.00
JH	Jeffrey Hammonds	10.00
MH	Mike Hampton	10.00
DH	Dustin Hermanson	10.00
TH	Todd Hundley	10.00
CJ	Charles Johnson	10.00
FM	Fred McGriff	15.00
BM	Bill Mueller	10.00
DN	Denny Neagle	10.00
HR	Hideo Nomo	50.00
NP	Neifi Perez	10.00
TR	Tim Raines	15.00
RS	Ruben Sierra	10.00
MS	Matt Stairs	10.00
KS	Kelly Stinnett	10.00
FT	Fernando Tatis	10.00
DW	David Wells	15.00
GW	Gerald Williams	10.00
EW	Enrique Wilson	10.00

A card number in parentheses ( ) indicates the set is unnumbered.

2001 Topps & TC Traded & Rookies Rookie Relics

		MT
Common Player:		10.00
Inserted 1:91		
AP	Albert Pujols	60.00
TS	Tsuyoshi Shinjo	60.00
AB	*Angel Berroa*	10.00
BO	Bill Ortega	10.00
HC	Humberto Cota	10.00
JL	Jason Lane	25.00
JS	Jamal Strong	15.00
JV	Jose Valverde	15.00
JY	Jason Young	10.00
NC	Nate Cornejo	15.00
NN	Nick Neugebauer	15.00
PF	Pedro Feliz	10.00
RS	Richard Stahl	10.00
SB	Sean Burroughs	15.00
SS	Jae Weong Seo	15.00
WB	Wilson Betemit	20.00
WR	Wilken Ruan	10.00

2001 Topps & TC Traded & Rookies Who Would Have Thought

	MT
Complete Set (20):	20.00
Common Player:	.75
Inserted 1:8	
WWH1Nolan Ryan	5.00
WWH2Ozzie Smith	1.50
WWH3Tom Seaver	1.50
WWH4Steve Carlton	.75
WWH5Reggie Jackson	1.50
WWH6Frank Robinson	1.00
WWH7Keith Hernandez	.75
WWH8Andre Dawson	.75
WWH9Lou Brock	.75
WWH10Dennis Eckersley	.75
WWH11Dave Winfield	1.00
WWH12Rod Carew	1.00
WWH13Willie Randolph	.75
WWH14Doc Gooden	.75
WWH15Carlton Fisk	1.00
WWH16Dale Murphy	.75
WWH17Paul Molitor	1.50
WWH18Gary Carter	.75
WWH19Wade Boggs	1.00
WWH20Willie Mays	4.00

2001 Topps eTopps

Operating along the lines of a stock exchange, with collectors able to buy and sell the cards without ever taking physical possession, eTopps was launched in October and had about 10 "Initial Player Offerings" (new cards) issued per week to a total of 75. Issue price and quantity available were announced at the time of release. If a card was not sold out during its five-day order period, the unsold cards were destroyed. Fronts have portrait and action photos, player identification and an eTopps logo, printed on refractive metalic foil. Backs, labeled, "Inaugural Edition," have a portrait photo, personal data and stats, along with 2000 highlights and a projection for the 2001 season. A circular holographic seal at top-right has a serial number. Each card is issued in a thick plastic holder that is sealed with an eTopps holographic sticker. Cards are skip-numbered between 1-150, as it was originally intended that 150 cards would be issued the first year. Shown in parentheses for each player are the initial offering price and the quantity reported issued by Topps.

		MT
As of 11/19/02		
1	Nomar Garciaparra ($9.50/1,315)	22.35
2	Chipper Jones ($9.50/674)	25.05
3	Jeff Bagwell ($6.50/485)	52.50
4	Randy Johnson ($6.50/1,499)	19.79
7	Adam Dunn ($6.50/4,197)	8.10
8	J.D. Drew ($6.50/767)	14.80
9	Larry Walker ($6.50/420)	42.01
10	Edgardo Alfonzo ($6.50/338)	143.73
11	Lance Berkman ($6.50/595)	57.50
12	Tony Gwynn ($6.50/828)	30.50
13	Andruw Jones ($6.50/908)	25.19
15	Troy Glaus ($6.50/862)	25.88
17	Sammy Sosa ($9.50/2,487)	26.01
21	Darin Erstad ($3.50/664)	16.99
22	Barry Bonds ($9.50/1,567)	51.01
27	Derek Jeter ($9.50/1,041)	40.00
29	Curt Schilling ($6.50/2,125)	9.02
30	Roberto Alomar ($6.50/448)	44.69
31	Luis Gonzalez ($6.50/1,104)	9.31
32	Jimmy Rollins ($3.50/1,307)	9.60
34	Joe Crede ($3.50/1,050)	17.22
39	Sean Casey ($6.50/537)	19.99
46	Alex Rodriguez ($9.50/2,212)	39.00
47	Tom Glavine ($6.50/437)	56.00
50	Jose Ortiz ($3.50/738)	14.00
51	Cal Ripken Jr. ($6.50/2,201)	23.06
52	Bobby Abreu ($3.50/677)	16.01
55	Alex Escobar ($3.50/931)	11.01
56	Ivan Rodriguez ($6.50/698)	24.01
59	Jeff Kent ($6.50/452)	27.00
62	Rick Ankiel ($6.50/752)	12.51
65	Craig Biggio ($6.50/410)	50.75
66	Carlos Delgado ($6.50/398)	31.00
68	Greg Maddux ($6.50/1,031)	19.05
69	Kerry Wood ($3.50/1,056)	13.10
71	Todd Helton ($6.50/978)	21.29
72	Mariano Rivera ($6.50/824)	12.95
73	Jason Kendall ($3.50/672)	20.24
75	Scott Rolen ($6.50/498)	28.27
76	Kazuhiro Sasaki ($6.50/5,000)	5.50
77	Roy Oswalt ($6.50/915)	19.19
78	C.C. Sabathia ($6.50/1,974)	7.71
83	Brian Giles ($6.50/400)	51.01
87	Rafael Furcal ($3.50/646)	18.00
88	Mike Mussina ($6.50/793)	17.34
89	Gary Sheffield ($6.50/359)	51.63
92	Mark McGwire ($9.50/2,908)	12.00
94	Tsuyoshi Shinjo ($3.50/3,000)	4.23
99	Jose Vidro ($3.50/443)	30.55
100	Ichiro Suzuki ($6.50/10,000)	7.17
105	Manny Ramirez ($6.50/1,074)	17.40
109	Juan Gonzalez ($6.50/558)	15.00
112	Ken Griffey Jr. ($9.50/2,398)	18.51
114	Tim Hudson ($6.50/663)	22.50
115	Nick Johnson ($6.50/1,217)	11.00
118	Jason Giambi ($9.50/897)	26.26
122	Rafael Palmeiro ($6.50/464)	33.11
124	Vladimir Guerrero ($6.50/854)	39.54
125	Vernon Wells ($6.50/349)	86.05
127	Roger Clemens ($9.50/1,462)	17.20

128 Frank Thomas ($6.50/834) 16.70
129 Carlos Beltran ($3.50/489) 25.99
130 Pat Burrell ($3.50/1,253) 18.58
131 Pedro Martinez ($9.50/1,038) 17.69
132 Mike Piazza ($9.50/1,379) 17.06
135 Luis Montanez ($3.50/5,000) 3.28
140 Sean Burroughs ($3.50/5,000) 8.33
141 Barry Zito ($6.50/843) 44.99
142 Bobby Bradley ($3.50/5,000) 3.44
143 Albert Pujols ($6.50/5,000) 13.30
144 Ben Sheets ($3.50/1,713) 7.53
145 Alfonso Soriano ($6.50/1,699) 39.61
146 Josh Hamilton ($3.50/5,000) 4.01
147 Eric Munson ($3.50/5,000) 3.73
150 Mark Mulder ($3.50/4,335) 7.54

2001 Topps Fusion

		MT
Complete Set (250):		200.00
Common Player:		.25
Pack (5):		4.00
Box (24):		90.00
1	Albert Belle	.25
2	Albert Belle	.25
3	Albert Belle	.25
4	Nick Bierbrodt	.25
5	Alex Rodriguez	2.50
6	Alex Rodriguez	2.50
7	Alex Rodriguez	2.50
8	Alex Rodriguez	2.50
9	Eric Munson	.25
10	Barry Bonds	1.00
11	Andruw Jones	1.00
12	Antonio Alfonseca	.25
13	Andres Galarraga	.40
14	Joe Crede	.25
15	Barry Larkin	.40
16	Barry Bonds	1.00
17	Barry Bonds	1.00
18	Andruw Jones	1.00
19	C.C. Sabathia	.25
20	Bobby Higginson	.25
21	Barry Larkin	.40
22	Ben Grieve	.25
23	Barry Bonds	1.00
24	Corey Patterson	.25
25	Carlos Delgado	1.00
26	Bernie Williams	.75
27	Brian Giles	.30
28	Barry Larkin	.40
29	Gookie Dawkins	.25
30	Chipper Jones	2.00
31	Brian Giles	.30
32	Carlos Delgado	1.00
33	Ben Grieve	.25
34	Geoff Goetz	.25
35	Cristian Guzman	.25
36	Cal Ripken Jr.	3.00
37	Chipper Jones	2.00
38	Bernie Williams	.75
39	Pablo Ozuna	.25
40	Dante Bichette	.25
41	Carlos Delgado	1.00
42	Craig Biggio	.25
43	Cal Ripken Jr.	3.00
44	Tim Redding	.25
45	Darin Erstad	.50
46	Chipper Jones	2.00
47	Darin Erstad	.50
48	Carlos Delgado	1.00
49	Josh Hamilton	.50
50	Derek Jeter	3.00
51	Darin Erstad	.50
52	Dean Palmer	.25
53	Chipper Jones	2.00
54	Chin-Feng Chen	.25
55	Edgar Martinez	.25
56	Derek Jeter	3.00
57	Derek Jeter	3.00
58	Craig Biggio	.25
59	Keith Ginter	.25
60	Edgardo Alfonzo	.25
61	Edgar Martinez	.25
62	Edgardo Alfonzo	.25
63	David Justice	.50
64	Roy Oswalt	.25
65	Eric Karros	.25
66	Edgardo Alfonzo	.25
67	Frank Thomas	1.50
68	Dean Palmer	.25
69	Alfonso Soriano	.50
70	Fernando Vina	.25
71	Frank Thomas	1.50
72	Garret Anderson	.25
73	Derek Jeter	3.00
74	Bobby Bradley	.25
75	Frank Thomas	1.50
76	Gary Sheffield	.40
77	Geoff Jenkins	.25
78	Edgar Martinez	.25
79	Nick Johnson	.25
80	Fred McGriff	.30
81	Geoff Jenkins	.25
82	Greg Maddux	2.00
83	Edgardo Alfonzo	.25
84	*Hee Seop Choi*	8.00
85	Garret Anderson	.25
86	Greg Maddux	2.00
87	Ivan Rodriguez	1.00
88	Eric Karros	.25
89	Scott Seabol	.25
90	Ivan Rodriguez	1.00
91	Ivan Rodriguez	1.00
92	J.D. Drew	.25
93	Frank Thomas	1.50
94	Ryan Anderson	.25
95	Jason Giambi	.40
96	Jason Giambi	.40
97	Jason Kendall	.25
98	Gary Sheffield	.40
99	Milton Bradley	.25
100	Jason Kendall	.25
101	Jason Kendall	.25
102	Jeff Bagwell	1.00
103	Greg Maddux	2.00
104	Sean Burroughs	.25
105	Jay Bell	.25
106	Jeff Bagwell	1.00
107	Jeffrey Hammonds	.25
108	Ivan Rodriguez	1.00
109	Ben Petrick	.25
110	Jeff Bagwell	1.00
111	Jeff Cirillo	.25
112	Jermaine Dye	.25
113	J.T. Snow Jr.	.25
114	Ben Davis	.25
115	Jeff Cirillo	.25
116	Jeff Kent	.25
117	Jeromy Burnitz	.25
118	Jay Bell	.25
119	Jason Hart	.25
120	Jeff Kent	.25
121	Jermaine Dye	.25
122	John Olerud	.25
123	Jeff Bagwell	1.00
124	*Jeff Segar*	2.00
125	Jeromy Burnitz	.25
126	Jeromy Burnitz	.25
127	Johnny Damon	.25
128	Jim Edmonds	.40
129	*Tim Christman*	1.00
130	Jim Thome	.40
131	Jim Edmonds	.40
132	Jorge Posada	.40
133	Jim Thome	.40
134	*Danny Borrell*	.75
135	Johnny Damon	.25
136	Jim Thome	.40
137	Jose Vidro	.25
138	Ken Griffey Jr.	2.50
139	Sean Burnett	.25
140	Larry Walker	.40
141	Jose Vidro	.25
142	Ken Griffey Jr.	2.50
143	Larry Walker	.40
144	*Robert Keppell*	1.50
145	Luis Castillo	.25
146	Ken Griffey Jr.	2.50
147	Kevin Brown	.25
148	Manny Ramirez	1.00
149	*David Parrish*	.25
150	Manny Ramirez	1.00
151	Kevin Brown	.25
152	Luis Castillo	.25
153	Mark Grace	.40
154	*Mike Jacobs*	.50
155	Mark Grace	.40
156	Larry Walker	.40
157	Magglio Ordonez	.25
158	Mark McGwire	3.00
159	Adam Johnson	.25
160	Mark McGwire	3.00
161	Magglio Ordonez	.25
162	Mark McGwire	2.00
163	Matt Williams	.40
164	*Oscar Ramirez*	.50
165	Mike Piazza	2.50
166	Manny Ramirez	1.00
167	Mike Piazza	2.50
168	Mike Mussina	.50
169	*Odannis Ayala*	.25
170	Mike Sweeney	.25
171	Mark McGwire	3.00
172	Nomar Garciaparra	2.50
173	Mike Piazza	2.50
174	J.R. House	3.00
175	Neifi Perez	.25
176	Mike Piazza	2.50
177	Pedro Martinez	1.25
178	Mo Vaughn	.30
179	*Shawn Fagan*	2.00
180	Nomar Garciaparra	2.50
181	Mo Vaughn	.30
182	Rafael Palmeiro	.50
183	Nomar Garciaparra	2.50
184	*Chris Bass*	4.00
185	Raul Mondesi	.25
186	Nomar Garciaparra	2.50
187	Randy Johnson	1.00
188	Omar Vizquel	.25
189	*Erick Almonte*	2.00
190	Ray Durham	.25
191	Pedro Martinez	1.25
192	Robb Nen	.25
193	Pedro Martinez	1.25
194	*Luis Montanez*	4.00
195	Ray Lankford	.25
196	Rafael Palmeiro	.50
197	Roberto Alomar	.75
198	Rafael Palmeiro	.50
199	*Chad Petty*	1.50
200	Richard Hidalgo	.25
201	Randy Johnson	1.00
202	Robin Ventura	.25
203	Randy Johnson	1.00
204	Derek Thompson	.25
205	Sammy Sosa	2.00
206	Roberto Alomar	.75
207	Sammy Sosa	2.00
208	Raul Mondesi	.25
209	Scott Heard	.25
210	Scott Rolen	.50
211	Sammy Sosa	2.00
212	Scott Rolen	.50
213	Roberto Alomar	.75
214	*Dominic Rich*	.50
215	Sean Casey	.25
216	Scott Rolen	.50
217	Sean Casey	.25
218	Robin Ventura	.25
219	*William Smith*	2.00
220	Tim Salmon	.30
221	Sean Casey	.25
222	Shannon Stewart	.25
223	Sammy Sosa	2.00
224	*Joel Pieniero*	.50
225	Tino Martinez	.25
226	Shawn Green	.30
227	Shawn Green	.30
228	Scott Rolen	.50
229	*Greg Morrison*	1.00
230	Tony Gwynn	1.25
231	Todd Helton	1.00
232	Steve Finley	.25
233	Scott Williamson	.25
234	Talmadge Nunnari	.25
235	Tony Womack	.25
236	Tony Batista	.25
237	Tim Salmon	.30
238	Shawn Green	.30
239	*Carlos Villalobos*	.75
240	Troy Glaus	1.00
241	Troy Glaus	1.00
242	Todd Helton	1.00
243	Tim Salmon	.30
244	*Marcos Scutaro*	.75
245	Troy O'Leary	.25
246	Vladimir Guerrero	1.25
247	Vladimir Guerrero	1.25
248	Vladimir Guerrero	1.25
249	Horacio Estrada	.25
250	Vladimir Guerrero	1.25

2001 Topps Fusion Autographs

		MT
Common Player:		10.00
Inserted 1:23		
1	Rafael Furcal	25.00
2	Mike Lamb	15.00
3	Jason Marquis	10.00
4	Milton Bradley	10.00
5	Barry Zito	30.00
6	Derrek Lee	15.00
7	Corey Patterson	30.00
8	Josh Hamilton	30.00
9	Sean Burroughs	15.00
10	Jason Hart	20.00
11	Luis Montanez	25.00
12	Robert Keppell	15.00
13	Blake Williams	15.00
14	Phil Wilson	10.00
15	Jake Peavy	10.00
16	Alex Rodriguez	80.00
17	Ivan Rodriguez	40.00
18	Don Larsen	30.00
19	Todd Helton	40.00
20	Carlos Delgado	30.00
21	Geoff Jenkins	25.00
22	Willie Stargell	25.00
23	Frank Robinson	30.00
24	Warren Spahn	50.00
25	Harmon Killebrew	45.00
26	Chipper Jones	50.00
27	Chipper Jones	50.00
28	Chipper Jones	50.00
29	Chipper Jones	50.00
30	Chipper Jones	50.00
31	Rocco Baldelli	15.00
32	Keith Ginter	15.00
33	J.R. House	30.00
34	Alex Cabrera	10.00
35	Tony Alvarez	10.00
36	Pablo Ozuna	10.00
37	Juan Salas	10.00

2001 Topps Fusion Double Feature

		MT
Common Player:		25.00
1	Ivan Rodriguez, Rickey Henderson	60.00
2	John Smoltz, Tom Glavine	40.00
3	Willie Stargell, Frank Thomas	50.00

4	Carlos Delgado, Todd Helton	50.00
5	Adrian Gonzalez, Pat Burrell	50.00
6	Jose Vidro, Roberto Alomar	40.00
7	Chipper Jones, Robin Ventura	40.00
8	J.D. Drew, Matt Lawton	30.00
9	Josh Hamilton, Chin-Feng Chen	80.00
10	Rafael Furcal, Miguel Tejada	40.00
11	Josh Beckett, Ryan Anderson	60.00

2001 Topps Fusion Feature

		MT
Common Player:		10.00
Inserted 1:51		
1	Ivan Rodriguez	25.00
2	Rickey Henderson	30.00
3	John Smoltz	10.00
4	Tom Glavine	15.00
5	Willie Stargell	25.00
6	Frank Thomas	30.00
7	Carlos Delgado	25.00
8	Todd Helton	30.00
9	Adrian Gonzalez	20.00
10	Pat Burrell	30.00
11	Jose Vidro	10.00
12	Roberto Alomar	25.00
13	Chipper Jones	35.00
14	Robin Ventura	15.00
15	J.D. Drew	20.00
16	Matt Lawton	10.00
17	Josh Hamilton	35.00
18	Chin-Feng Chen	40.00
19	Rafael Furcal	25.00
20	Miguel Tejada	20.00
21	Josh Beckett	20.00
22	Ryan Anderson	20.00

2001 Topps Gallery

		MT
Complete Set (152):		150.00
Common Player:		.15
Common Rookie:		1.50
Inserted 1:3.5		
Common Prospect:		.50
Inserted 1:2.5		
Common Retired:		1.00
Inserted 1:5		
Pack (6):		5.50
Box (24):		120.00
set price includes one Suzuki rookie		
1	Darin Erstad	.50
2	Chipper Jones	2.00
3	Nomar Garciaparra	2.50
4	Fernando Vina	.15
5	Bartolo Colon	.15
6	Bobby Higginson	.15
7	Antonio Alfonseca	.15
8	Mike Sweeney	.15
9	Kevin Brown	.15
10	Jose Vidro	.15
11	Derek Jeter	3.00
12	Jason Giambi	.50
13	Pat Burrell	.50
14	Jeff Kent	.25
15	Alex Rodriguez	2.50
16	Rafael Palmeiro	.50
17	Garret Anderson	.15
18	Brad Fullmer	.15
19	Doug Glanville	.15
20	Mark Quinn	.15
21	Mo Vaughn	.25
22	Andruw Jones	.75
23	Pedro Martinez	1.25
24	Ken Griffey Jr.	2.50
25	Roberto Alomar	.75
26	Dean Palmer	.15
27	Jeff Bagwell	1.00
28	Jermaine Dye	.15
29	Chan Ho Park	.15
30	Vladimir Guerrero	1.25
31	Bernie Williams	.75
32	Ben Grieve	.25
33	Jason Kendall	.15
34	Barry Bonds	1.25
35	Jim Edmonds	.25
36	Ivan Rodriguez	1.00
37	Javy Lopez	.25
38	J.T. Snow	.15
39	Erubiel Durazo	.15
40	Terrence Long	.15
41	Tim Salmon	.15
42	Greg Maddux	2.00
43	Sammy Sosa	2.00
44	Sean Casey	.25
45	Jeff Cirillo	.15
46	Juan Gonzalez	1.00
47	Richard Hidalgo	.25
48	Shawn Green	.25
49	Jeremy Burnitz	.15
50	Willie Mays	15.00
51	David Justice	.40
52	Tim Hudson	.25
53	Brian Giles	.25
54	Robb Nen	.15
55	Fernando Tatis	.15
56	Tony Batista	.15
57	Pokey Reese	.15
58	Ray Durham	.15
59	Greg Vaughn	.15
60	Kazuhiro Sasaki	.15
61	Troy Glaus	1.00
62	Rafael Furcal	.40
63	Magglio Ordonez	.25
64	Jim Thome	.25
65	Todd Helton	1.00
66	Preston Wilson	.15
67	Moises Alou	.25
68	Gary Sheffield	.30
69	Geoff Jenkins	.25
70	Mike Piazza	2.50
71	Jorge Posada	.25
72	Bobby Abreu	.15
73	Phil Nevin	.15
74	John Olerud	.25
75	Mark McGwire	3.00
76	Jose Cruz Jr.	.15
77	David Segui	.15
78	Neifi Perez	.15
79	Omar Vizquel	.25
80	Rick Ankiel	.15
81	Randy Johnson	1.00
82	Albert Belle	.15
83	Frank Thomas	1.00
84	Manny Ramirez	1.25
85	Larry Walker	.40
86	Luis Castillo	.15
87	Johnny Damon	.15
88	Adrian Beltre	.25
89	Cristian Guzman	.15
90	Jay Payton	.15
91	Miguel Tejada	.25
92	Scott Rolen	.50
93	Ryan Klesko	.15
94	Edgar Martinez	.15
95	Fred McGriff	.15
96	Carlos Delgado	.75
97	Barry Zito	.25
98	Mike Lieberthal	.15
99	Trevor Hoffman	.15
100	Gabe Kapler	.25
101	Edgardo Alfonzo	.15
102	Corey Patterson	.50
103	Alfonso Soriano	1.50
104	Keith Ginter	.50
105	Keith Reed	.50
106	Nick Johnson	.75
107	Carlos Pena	.50
108	Vernon Wells	.50
109	Roy Oswalt	1.00
110	Alex Escobar	.50
111	Adam Everett	.50
112	Jimmy Rollins	.50
113	Marcus Giles	.50
114	Jack Cust	.50
115	Chin-Feng Chen	1.00
116	Pablo Ozuna	.50
117	Ben Sheets	1.00
118	Adrian Gonzalez	1.00
119	Ben Davis	.50
120	Eric Valent	.50
121	Scott Heard	.50
122	*David Parrish*	1.50
123	Sean Burnett	.50
124	Derek Thompson	.50
125	*Tim Christman*	1.50
126	*Mike Jacobs*	1.00
127	*Luis Montanez*	5.00
128	*Chris Bass*	5.00
129	*William Smith*	5.00
130	*Justin Wayne*	4.00
131	*Shawn Fagan*	3.00
132	*Chad Petty*	2.00
133	J.R. House	.50
134	Joel Pineiro	.50
135	*Albert Pujols*	20.00
136	*Carmen Cali*	3.00
137	*Steve Smyth*	2.00
138	John Lackey	.50
139	*Bob Keppel*	2.00
140	*Dominic Rich*	2.50
141	Josh Hamilton	1.00
142	Nolan Ryan	6.00
143	Tom Seaver	1.50
144	Reggie Jackson	1.50
145	Johnny Bench	1.50
146	Warren Spahn	1.50
147	Brooks Robinson	1.50
148	Carl Yastrzemski	1.00
149	Al Kaline	1.00
150	Bob Feller	1.00
151a	*Ichiro Suzuki english*	30.00
151b	*Ichiro Suzuki japanese*	25.00

2001 Topps Gallery Press Plates

The aluminum press plates used to print the Gallery cards were inserted at a rate of one per 1,200 packs. Each card's front and back can be found in four different color variations. Because of the unique nature of each plate, assignment of catalog values in not feasible.

	MT
Common Player:	50.00

(See 2001 Topps Gallery for checklist.)

2001 Topps Gallery Autographs

	MT
Common Autograph:	20.00
Inserted 1:232	
GA-RARick Ankiel	20.00
GA-BBBarry Bonds	140.00
GA-PBPat Burrell	35.00
GA-AGAdrian Gonzalez	20.00
GA-ARAlex Rodriguez	125.00
GA-IRIvan Rodriguez	60.00

2001 Topps Gallery Heritage

		MT
Complete Set (10):		60.00
Common Player:		3.00
Inserted 1:12		
GH1	Todd Helton	4.00
GH2	Greg Maddux	8.00
GH3	Pedro Martinez	5.00
GH4	Orlando Cepeda	3.00
GH5	Willie McCovey	3.00
GH6	Ken Griffey Jr.	10.00
GH7	Alex Rodriguez	10.00
GH8	Derek Jeter	12.00
GH9	Mark McGwire	12.00
GH10	Vladimir Guerrero	5.00

2001 Topps Gallery Heritage Relic

	MT
Common Player:	20.00
Inserted 1:133	
Orlando Cepeda	30.00
Vladimir Guerrero	
Greg Maddux	40.00
Pedro Martinez	40.00
Willie McCovey	30.00

2001 Topps Gallery Heritage Autographed Relic

	MT
Common Autograph:	150.00
Production 25 sets	
Orlando Cepeda	150.00
Willie McCovey	250.00

2001 Topps Gallery Originals Relics

	MT
Common Player:	10.00
Inserted 1:133	
GR-RARoberto Alomar	30.00
GR-JDJermaine Dye	10.00
GR-DEDarin Erstad	25.00
GR-JGJason Giambi	
GR-AGAdrian Gonzalez	30.00
GR-SGShawn Green	20.00
GR-AJAndruw Jones	25.00
GR-JKJason Kendall	20.00
GR-JFKJeff Kent	20.00
GR-RPRafael Palmeiro	30.00
GR-PRPokey Reese	20.00
GR-SSSammy Sosa	
GR-RVRobin Ventura	15.00
GR-BWBernie Williams	30.00
GR-PWPreston Wilson	10.00

2001 Topps Gallery Star Gallery

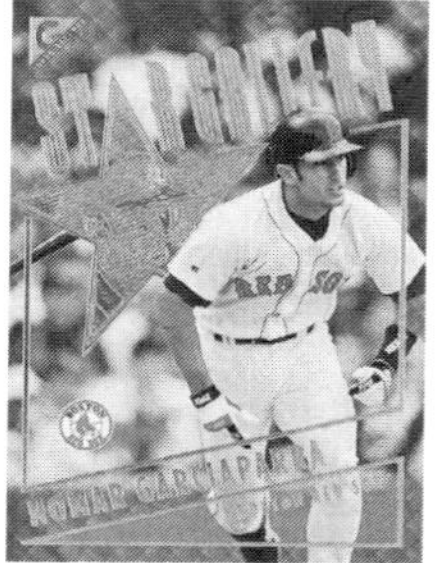

	MT
Complete Set (10):	35.00
Common Player:	1.50
Inserted 1:8	
SG1 Vladimir Guerrero	2.50
SG2 Alex Rodriguez	5.00
SG3 Derek Jeter	6.00
SG4 Nomar Garciaparra	5.00
SG5 Ken Griffey Jr.	5.00
SG6 Mark McGwire	6.00
SG7 Chipper Jones	4.00
SG8 Sammy Sosa	4.00
SG9 Barry Bonds	2.50
SG10Mike Piazza	5.00

2001 Topps Gallery Team Topps Legends Autographs

	MT
Common Autograph:	20.00
Inserted 1:286	
TT23RGil McDougald	20.00
TT27FAndy Pafko	30.00
TT10RFrank Robinson	40.00
TT28FHerb Score	20.00
TT25RLuis Tiant	25.00

2001 Topps Gold Label

		MT
Complete Set (115):		140.00
Common Player:		.25
Common Rookie:		8.00
Production 999		
Golds:		2-3X
Production 999		
Gold Rookies:		2-3X
Production 99		
Pack (5):		5.00
Box (24):		110.00
1	Adrian Beltre	.25
2	*Danny Borrell*	10.00
3	Albert Belle	.25
4	Alex Cabrera	.25
5	Alex Rodriguez	3.00
6	Andruw Jones	1.00
7	Antonio Alfonseca	.25
8	Barry Bonds	1.50
9	Barry Larkin	.50
10	Ben Grieve	.40
11	Ben Molina	.25
12	Bernie Williams	1.00
13	Bobby Abreu	.25
14	Bobby Higginson	.25
15	Brad Fullmer	.25
16	Brian Giles	.40
17	Cal Ripken Jr.	4.00
18	Carlos Delgado	1.00
19	*Chad Petty*	10.00
20	Charles Johnson	.25
21	Chipper Jones	2.50
22	Cristian Guzman	.25
23	Darin Erstad	.75
24	David Justice	.75
25	David Segui	.25
26	Derek Jeter	4.00
27	Edgar Martinez	.25
28	Edgardo Alfonzo	.25
29	Fernando Tatis	.25
30	Eric Karros	.25
31	Eric Munson	.25
32	Eric Young	.25
33	Frank Thomas	1.50
34	Fernando Vina	.25
35	Garret Anderson	.25
36	Gary Sheffield	.50
37	Geoff Jenkins	.40
38	Greg Maddux	2.50
39	Ivan Rodriguez	1.25
40	J.D. Drew	.50
41	J.R. House	.25
42	J.T. Snow Jr.	.25
43	Jason Giambi	.75
44	Jason Kendall	.25
45	Jay Payton	.25
46	Jeff Bagwell	1.25
47	Jeff Cirillo	.25
48	Jeff Kent	.25
49	Chan Ho Park	.40
50	Jermaine Dye	.25
51	Jeromy Burnitz	.25
52	Jim Edmonds	.50
53	Jim Thome	.50
54	John Olerud	.50
55	Johnny Damon	.25
56	Jorge Posada	.50
57	Jose Cruz Jr.	.25
58	Jose Vidro	.25
59	Josh Hamilton	.25
60	Juan Gonzalez	1.25
61	*Steve Smyth*	8.00
62	*Justin Wayne*	15.00
63	Kazuhiro Sasaki	.25
64	Ken Griffey Jr.	3.00
65	Kevin Brown	.25
66	Kevin Young	.25
67	Larry Walker	.50
68	Luis Castillo	.25
69	Steve Finley	.25
70	Magglio Ordonez	.40
71	Manny Ramirez	1.25
72	Mark McGwire	4.00
73	Mark Quinn	.25
74	Miguel Tejada	.50
75	Mike Piazza	3.00
76	Mike Sweeney	.25
77	Mo Vaughn	.25
78	Moises Alou	.25
79	Nomar Garciaparra	3.00
80	Pat Burrell	.50
81	Paul Konerko	.25
82	Pedro Martinez	1.50
83	Phil Nevin	.25
84	Preston Wilson	.25
85	Rafael Furcal	.25
86	Todd Zeile	.25
87	Randy Johnson	1.25
88	Travis Lee	.25
89	Carl Everett	.25
90	Quilvio Veras	.25
91	Rick Ankiel	.40
92	*Rick Brosseau*	8.00
93	*Robert Keppell*	10.00
94	Roberto Alomar	1.00
95	Ryan Klesko	.25
96	Sammy Sosa	2.50
97	Scott Heard	10.00
98	Scott Rolen	.50
99	Sean Casey	.50
100	Shawn Green	.40
101	Terrence Long	.25
102	Tim Salmon	.25
103	Todd Helton	1.25
104	Tom Glavine	.50
105	Tony Batista	.25
106	*Travis Baptist*	12.00
107	Troy Glaus	1.25
108	*Victor Hall*	15.00
109	Vladimir Guerrero	1.50
110	Tim Hudson	.40
111	*Brian Roberts*	8.00
112	*Virgil Chevalier*	10.00
113	*Fernando Rodney*	15.00
114	*Paul Phillips*	8.00
115	*Cesar Bolivar*	10.00

2001 Topps Gold Label Class 2

	MT
Stars:	1-2X
Inserted 1:4	
Rookies:	1-1.5X
Production 699	
Golds:	2-3X
Production 699	
Gold Rookies:	2-3X
Production 69	

(See 2001 Topps Gold Label for checklist and base card values.)

2001 Topps Gold Label Class 3

	MT
Stars:	2-3X
Inserted 1:12	
Rookies:	1.5-2X
Production 299	
Golds:	3-5X
Production 299	
Gold Rookies:	2-4X
Production 29	

(See 2001 Topps Gold Label for checklist and base card values.)

2001 Topps Gold Label Gold Fixtures

		MT
Complete Set (10):		225.00
Common Player:		10.00
Inserted 1:374		
1	Alex Rodriguez	30.00
2	Mark McGwire	40.00
3	Derek Jeter	40.00
4	Nomar Garciaparra	30.00
5	Chipper Jones	25.00
6	Sammy Sosa	25.00
7	Ken Griffey Jr.	30.00
8	Carlos Delgado	10.00
9	Frank Thomas	15.00
10	Barry Bonds	15.00

2001 Topps Gold Label MLB Awards Ceremony

		MT
Common Player:		10.00
Inserted 1:24		
SA	Sandy Alomar bat	10.00
JB	Jeff Bagwell bat	35.00
AB	Albert Belle bat	10.00
CB	Carlos Beltran bat	10.00
DB	Dante Bichette	10.00
BB	Barry Bonds jersey	40.00
BB	Barry Bonds bat	40.00
SB	Scott Brosius bat	25.00
JC	Jose Canseco jersey	25.00
JC	Jose Canseco bat	25.00
WC	Will Clark bat	40.00
RC	Roger Clemens jersey	40.00
MC	Marty Cordova bat	10.00
RF	Rafael Furcal bat	15.00
AG	Andres Galarraga bat	15.00
NG	Nomar Garciaparra jsy	75.00
NG	Nomar Garciaparra bat	75.00
JG	Jason Giambi bat	25.00
TG	Troy Glaus bat	25.00
TG	Tom Glavine jsy	20.00
JG	Juan Gonzalez jsy	25.00
JG	Juan Gonzalez bat	25.00
DG	Dwight Gooden jsy	20.00
BG	Ben Grieve jsy	15.00
KG	Ken Griffey Jr. jsy	50.00
KG	Ken Griffey Jr. bat	50.00
TG	Tony Gwynn bat	35.00
TH	Todd Helton bat	30.00
RH	Rickey Henderson jsy	30.00
TH	Todd Hollandsworth bat	10.00

DJ Derek Jeter bat 75.00
RJ Randy Johnson jsy 25.00
CJ Chipper Jones jsy 25.00
DJ David Justice jsy 15.00
JK Jeff Kent bat 20.00
CK Chuck Knoblauch bat 20.00
BL Barry Larkin bat 25.00
'M Greg Maddux jsy 30.00
EM Edgar Martinez bat 25.00
PM Pedro Martinez jsy 35.00
FM Fred McGriff bat 15.00
MM Mark McGwire bat 150.00
MM Mark McGwire jsy 150.00
RM Raul Mondesi bat 10.00
HN Hideo Nomo jsy 150.00
JO John Olerud bat 20.00
PO Paul O'Neill bat 30.00
MP Mike Piazza bat 60.00
CR Cal Ripken Jr. jsy 60.00
AR Alex Rodriguez bat 40.00
IR Ivan Rodriguez jsy 20.00
SR Scott Rolen jsy 15.00
TS Tim Salmon jsy 10.00
KS Kazuhiro Sasaki jsy 60.00
GS Gary Sheffield bat 15.00
JS John Smoltz jsy 10.00
SS Sammy Sosa bat 30.00
SS Sammy Sosa jsy 30.00
DS Darryl Strawberry jsy 20.00
DS Darryl Strawberry bat 20.00
FT Frank Thomas bat 25.00
FT Frank Thomas jsy 25.00
MV Mo Vaughn jsy 10.00
MV Mo Vaughn bat 10.00
LW Larry Walker bat 15.00
LW Larry Walker jsy 15.00
JW John Wetteland jsy 10.00
BW Bernie Williams bat 30.00
MW Matt Williams bat 15.00

2001 Topps Heritage

MT
Complete Set (407): 550.00
Common Player: .50
Common SP (311-407): 2.50
Inserted 1:2
Pack (8): 8.00
Box (24): 185.00
1 Kris Benson .50
2 Brian Jordan .50
3 Fernando Vina .50
4 Mike Sweeney .50
5 Rafael Palmeiro 2.00
6 Paul O'Neill 1.00
7 Todd Helton 2.50
8 Ramiro Mendoza .50
9 Kevin Millwood .50
10 Chuck Knoblauch .75
11 Derek Jeter 10.00
12 Alex Rodriguez 8.00
13 Geoff Jenkins .75
14 David Justice 2.00
15 David Cone .50
16 Andres Galarraga 1.00
17 Garret Anderson .50
18 Roger Cedeno .50
19 Randy Velarde .50
20 Carlos Delgado 2.00
21 Quilvio Veras .50
22 Jose Vidro .50
23 Corey Patterson .75
24 Jorge Posada .75
25 Eddie Perez .50
26 Jack Cust .50
27 Sean Burroughs .75
28 Randy Wolf .50
29 Mike Lamb .50
30 Rafael Furcal .75
31 Barry Bonds 3.00
32 Tim Hudson .50
33 Tom Glavine 1.50
34 Javy Lopez .75
35 Aubrey Huff .50
36 Wally Joyner .50
37 Magglio Ordonez .75
38 Matt Lawton .50
39 Mariano Rivera 1.00
40 Andy Ashby .50
41 *Mark Buerhle* 4.00
42 Esteban Loaiza .50
43 Mark Redman .50
44 Mark Quinn .50
45 Tino Martinez .75
46 Joe Mays .50
47 Walt Weiss .50
48 Roger Clemens 4.00
49 Greg Maddux 5.00
50 Richard Hidalgo .75
51 Orlando Hernandez .75
52 Chipper Jones 5.00
53 Ben Grieve 1.00
54 Jimmy Haynes .50
55 Ken Caminiti .50
56 Tim Salmon 1.00
57 Andy Pettitte .75
58 Darin Erstad 1.50
59 Marquis Grissom .50
60 Raul Mondesi .75
61 Bengie Molina .50
62 Miguel Tejada .50
63 Jose Cruz Jr. .50
64 Billy Koch .50
65 Troy Glaus 2.50
66 Cliff Floyd .50
67 Tony Batista .50
68 Jeff Bagwell 2.50
69 Billy Wagner .50
70 Eric Chavez .75
71 Troy Percival .50
72 Andruw Jones 2.50
73 Shane Reynolds .50
74 Barry Zito 2.50
75 Roy Halladay .50
76 David Wells .50
77 Jason Giambi 1.50
78 Scott Elarton .50
79 Moises Alou .75
80 Adam Piatt .75
81 Wilton Veras .50
82 Darryl Kile .50
83 Johnny Damon .50
84 Tony Armas Jr. .50
85 Ellis Burks .50
86 Jamey Wright .50
87 Jose Vizcaino .50
88 Bartolo Colon .50
89 *Carmen Cali* 2.00
90 Kevin Brown .75
91 Josh Hamilton .50
92 Jay Buhner .50
93 *Scott Pratt* 3.00
94 Alex Cora .50
95 *Luis Montanez* 2.50
96 Dmitri Young .50
97 J.T. Snow Jr. .50
98 Damion Easley .50
99 Greg Norton .50
100 Matt Wheatland .50
101 Chin-Feng Chen 1.00
102 Tony Womack .50
103 Adam Kennedy .50
104 J.D. Drew 1.00
105 Carlos Febles .50
106 Jim Thome 1.00
107 Danny Graves .50
108 Dave Mlicki .50
109 Ron Coomer .50
110 James Baldwin .50
111 *Shaun Boyd* 2.00
112 Brian Bohannon .50
113 Jacque Jones .50
114 Alfonso Soriano 1.00
115 Tony Clark .50
116 Terrence Long .50
117 Todd Hundley .50
118 Kazuhiro Sasaki 2.00
119 *Brian Sellier* 2.50
120 John Olerud .75
121 Javier Vazquez .50
122 Sean Burnett .50
123 Matt LeCroy .50
124 Erubiel Durazo .50
125 Juan Encarnacion .50
126 Pablo Ozuna .50
127 Russ Ortiz .50
128 David Segui .50
129 Mark McGwire 8.00
130 Mark Grace 1.00
131 Fred McGriff 1.00
132 Carl Pavano .50
133 Derek Thompson .50
134 Shawn Green 1.00
135 B.J. Surhoff .50
136 Michael Tucker .50
137 Jason Isringhausen .50
138 Eric Milton .50
139 Mike Stodolka .50
140 Milton Bradley .50
141 Curt Schilling .75
142 Sandy Alomar .50
143 Brent Mayne .50
144 Todd Jones .50
145 Charles Johnson .50
146 Dean Palmer .50
147 Masato Yoshii .50
148 Edgar Renteria .50
149 Joe Randa .50
150 Adam Johnson .50
151 Greg Vaughn .50
152 Adrian Beltre .75
153 Glenallen Hill .50
154 *David Parrish* 1.50
155 Neifi Perez .50
156 Pete Harnisch .50
157 Paul Konerko .50
158 Dennys Reyes .50
159 Jose Lima .50
160 Eddie Taubensee .50
161 Miguel Cairo .50
162 Jeff Kent .75
163 Dustin Hermanson .50
164 Alex Gonzalez .50
165 Hideo Nomo 1.00
166 Sammy Sosa 5.00
167 C.J. Nitkowski .50
168 Cal Eldred .50
169 Jeff Abbott .50
170 Jim Edmonds 1.00
171 Mark Mulder .50
172 *Dominic Rich* 2.50
173 Ray Lankford .50
174 *Danny Borrell* 2.00
175 Rick Aguilera .50
176 Shannon Stewart .50
177 Steve Finley .50
178 Jim Parque .50
179 Kevin Appier .50
180 Adrian Gonzalez 2.00
181 Tom Goodwin .50
182 Kevin Tapani .50
183 Fernando Tatis .50
184 Mark Grudzielanek .50
185 Ryan Anderson .50
186 Jeffrey Hammonds .50
187 Corey Koskie .50
188 Brad Fullmer .50
189 Rey Sanchez .50
190 Michael Barrett .50
191 Rickey Henderson 1.00
192 Jermaine Dye .50
193 Scott Brosius .50
194 Matt Anderson .50
195 Brian Buchanan .50
196 Derrek Lee .50
197 Larry Walker 1.00
198 David Krynzel .50
199 Vinny Castilla .50
200 Ken Griffey Jr. 6.00
201 Matt Stairs .50
202 Ty Howington .50
203 Andy Benes .50
204 Luis Gonzalez .75
205 Brian Moehler .50
206 Harold Baines .50
207 Pedro Astacio .50
208 Cristian Guzman .50
209 Kip Wells .50
210 Frank Thomas 3.00
211 Jose Rosado .50
212 Vernon Wells .50
213 Bobby Higginson .50
214 Juan Gonzalez 2.50
215 Omar Vizquel .75
216 Bernie Williams 2.00
217 Aaron Sele .50
218 Shawn Estes .50
219 Roberto Alomar 2.00
220 Rick Ankiel 1.00
221 Josh Kalinowski .50
222 David Bell .50
223 Keith Foulke .50
224 Craig Biggio .75
225 *Shawn Fagan* 1.50
226 Scott Williamson .50
227 Ron Belliard .50
228 Chris Singleton .50
229 Alex Serrano .50
230 Deivi Cruz .50
231 Eric Munson .75
232 Luis Castillo .50
233 Edgar Martinez .50
234 Jeff Shaw .50
235 Jeromy Burnitz .50
236 Richie Sexson .50
237 Will Clark 1.50
238 Ron Villone .50
239 Kerry Wood .75
240 Rich Aurilia .50
241 Mo Vaughn .75
242 Travis Fryman .75
243 Manny Ramirez 4.00
244 Chris Stynes .50
245 Ray Durham .50
246 *Juan Uribe* .50
247 Juan Guzman .50
248 Lee Stevens .50
249 Devon White .50
250 *Kyle Lohse* 2.00
251 Bryan Wolff .50
252 *Rick Brousseau* 2.00
253 Eric Young .50
254 Freddy Garcia .50
255 Jay Bell .50
256 Steve Cox .50
257 Torii Hunter .50
258 Jose Canseco 2.00
259 Brad Ausmus .50
260 Jeff Cirillo .50
261 Brad Penny .50
262 Antonio Alfonseca .50
263 Russ Branyan .50
264 Scott Heard .50
265 John Lackey .50
266 *Justin Wayne* 3.00
267 Brad Radke .50
268 Todd Stottlemyre .50
269 Mark Loretta .50
270 Matt Williams 1.00
271 Kenny Lofton 1.00
272 Jeff D'Amico .50
273 Jamie Moyer .50
274 Darren Dreifort .50
275 Denny Neagle .50
276 Orlando Cabrera .50
277 Chuck Finley .50
278 Miguel Batista .50
279 Carlos Beltran .50
280 Eric Karros .75
281 Mark Kotsay .50
282 Ryan Dempster .50
283 Barry Larkin 1.00
284 Jeff Suppan .50
285 Gary Sheffield 1.50
286 Jose Valentin .50
287 Robb Nen .50
288 Chan Ho Park .50
289 John Halama .50
290 *Steve Smyth* 1.50
291 Gerald Williams .50
292 Preston Wilson .50
293 *Victor Hall* 1.50
294 Ben Sheets 1.50
295 Eric Davis .50
296 Kirk Rueter .50
297 *Chad Petty* 1.00
298 Kevin Millar .50
299 Marvin Benard .50
300 Vladimir Guerrero 3.00
301 Livan Hernandez .50
302 *Travis Baptist* 1.00
303 Bill Mueller .50
304 Mike Cameron .50
305 Randy Johnson 2.50
306 *Alan Mahaffey* 2.00
307 *Wilson Betemit* 5.00
308 Pokey Reese .50
309 Ryan Rupe .50
310 Carlos Lee .50
311 Doug Glanville 2.50
312 Jay Payton 2.50
313 Troy O'Leary 2.50

314	Francisco Cordero	2.50
315	Rusty Greer	2.50
316	Cal Ripken Jr.	25.00
317	Ricky Ledee	2.50
318	Brian Daubach	2.50
319	Robin Ventura	3.00
320	Todd Zeile	3.00
321	Francisco Cordova	2.50
322	Henry Rodriguez	2.50
323	Pat Meares	2.50
324	Glendon Rusch	2.50
325	Keith Osik	2.50
326	*Robert Keppell*	15.00
327	Bobby Jones	2.50
328	Alex Ramirez	2.50
329	Robert Person	2.50
330	Ruben Mateo	2.50
331	Rob Bell	2.50
332	Carl Everett	2.50
333	Jason Schmidt	2.50
334	Scott Rolen	5.00
335	Jimmy Anderson	2.50
336	Bret Boone	2.50
337	Delino DeShields	2.50
338	Trevor Hoffman	2.50
339	Bob Abreu	2.50
341	Mike Hampton	3.00
342	John Wetteland	2.50
343	Scott Erickson	2.50
344	Enrique Wilson	2.50
345	Tim Wakefield	2.50
345	Mike Williams	2.50
346	Mike Lowell	2.50
347	Todd Pratt	2.50
348	Brook Fordyce	2.50
349	Benny Agbayani	2.50
350	Gabe Kapler	3.00
351	Sean Casey	4.00
352	Darren Oliver	2.50
353	Todd Ritchie	2.50
354	Kenny Rogers	2.50
355	Jason Kendall	3.00
356	John Vander Wal	2.50
357	Ramon Martinez	2.50
358	Edgardo Alfonzo	3.00
359	Phil Nevin	2.50
360	Albert Belle	3.00
361	Ruben Rivera	2.50
362	Pedro Martinez	10.00
363	Derek Lowe	2.50
364	Pat Burrell	5.00
365	Mike Mussina	5.00
366	Brady Anderson	3.00
367	Darren Lewis	2.50
368	Sidney Ponson	2.50
369	Adam Eaton	2.50
370	Eric Owens	2.50
371	Aaron Boone	2.50
372	Matt Clement	2.50
373	Derek Bell	2.50
374	Trot Nixon	2.50
375	Travis Lee	2.50
376	Mike Benjamin	2.50
377	Jeff Zimmerman	2.50
378	Mike Lieberthal	2.50
379	Rick Reed	2.50
380	Nomar Garciaparra	20.00
381	Omar Daal	2.50
382	Ryan Klesko	3.00
383	Rey Ordonez	2.50
384	Kevin Young	2.50
385	Rick Helling	2.50
386	Brian Giles	4.00
387	Tony Gwynn	8.00
388	Ed Sprague	2.50
389	J.R. House	15.00
390	Scott Hatteberg	2.50
391	John Valentin	2.50
392	Melvin Mora	2.50
393	Royce Clayton	2.50
394	Jeff Fassero	2.50
395	Manny Alexander	2.50
396	John Franco	2.50
397	Luis Alicea	2.50
398	Ivan Rodriguez	6.00
399	Kevin Jordan	2.50
400	Jose Offerman	2.50
401	Jeff Conine	2.50
402	Seth Etherton	2.50
403	Mike Bordick	2.50
404	Al Leiter	4.00
405	Mike Piazza	20.00
406	Armando Benitez	2.50
407	Warren Morris	2.50

2001 Topps Heritage Chrome

		MT
Common Player:		3.00
Production 552 sets		
1	Cal Ripken Jr.	50.00
2	Jim Thome	8.00
3	Derek Jeter	50.00
4	Andres Galarraga	6.00
5	Carlos Delgado	12.00
6	Roberto Alomar	12.00
7	Tom Glavine	10.00
8	Gary Sheffield	8.00
9	Mo Vaughn	6.00
10	Preston Wilson	3.00
11	Mike Mussina	10.00
12	Greg Maddux	30.00
13	Ivan Rodriguez	15.00
14	Al Leiter	5.00
15	Seth Etherton	3.00
16	Edgardo Alfonzo	4.00
17	Richie Sexson	3.00
18	Andruw Jones	12.00
19	Bartolo Colon	3.00
20	Darin Erstad	8.00
21	Kevin Brown	4.00
22	Mike Sweeney	3.00
23	Mike Piazza	35.00
24	Rafael Palmeiro	10.00
25	Terrence Long	3.00
26	Kazuhiro Sasaki	15.00
27	John Olerud	5.00
28	Mark McGwire	50.00
29	Fred McGriff	6.00
30	Todd Helton	15.00
31	Curt Schilling	5.00
32	Alex Rodriguez	35.00
33	Jeff Kent	5.00
34	Pat Burrell	10.00
35	Jim Edmonds	8.00
36	Mark Mulder	3.00
37	Troy Glaus	15.00
38	Jay Payton	3.00
39	Jermaine Dye	3.00
40	Larry Walker	8.00
41	Ken Griffey Jr.	40.00
42	Jeff Bagwell	15.00
43	Rick Ankiel	5.00
44	Mark Redman	3.00
45	Edgar Martinez	3.00
46	Mike Hampton	4.00
47	Manny Ramirez	15.00
48	Ray Durham	3.00
49	Rafael Furcal	3.00
50	Sean Casey	5.00
51	Jose Canseco	10.00
52	Barry Bonds	25.00
53	Tim Hudson	5.00
54	Barry Zito	25.00
55	Chuck Finley	3.00
56	Magglio Ordonez	4.00
57	David Wells	3.00
58	Jason Giambi	8.00
59	Tony Gwynn	25.00
60	Vladimir Guerrero	15.00
61	Randy Johnson	15.00
62	Bernie Williams	12.00
63	Craig Biggio	5.00
64	Jason Kendall	3.00
65	Pedro Martinez	20.00
66	Mark Quinn	3.00
67	Frank Thomas	20.00
68	Nomar Garciaparra	35.00
69	Brian Giles	5.00
70	Shawn Green	5.00
71	Roger Clemens	20.00
72	Sammy Sosa	30.00
73	Juan Gonzalez	15.00
74	Orlando Hernandez	5.00
75	Chipper Jones	30.00
76	Josh Hamilton	15.00
77	Adam Johnson	3.00
78	Shaun Boyd	10.00
79	Alfonso Soriano	5.00
80	Derek Thompson	3.00
81	Adrian Gonzalez	12.00
82	Ryan Anderson	5.00
83	Corey Patterson	5.00
84	J.R. House	30.00
85	Sean Burroughs	8.00
86	Scott Heard	3.00
87	John Lackey	3.00
88	Ben Sheets	20.00
89	Wilson Betemit	15.00
90	Robert Keppell	20.00
91	Luis Montanez	30.00
92	Sean Burnett	3.00
93	Justin Wayne	5.00
94	Eric Munson	5.00
95	Steve Smyth	6.00
96	Rick Brousseau	3.00
97	Carmen Cali	8.00
98	Brian Sellier	10.00
99	David Parrish	8.00
100	Danny Borrell	5.00
101	Chad Petty	10.00
102	Dominic Rich	10.00
103	Shawn Fagan	3.00
104	Alex Serrano	6.00
105	Juan Uribe	3.00
106	Travis Baptist	3.00
107	Alan Mahaffey	3.00
108	Kyle Lohse	8.00
109	Victor Hall	6.00
110	Scott Pratt	3.00

2001 Topps Heritage Classic Renditions

		MT
Complete Set (10):		20.00
Common Player:		1.00
Inserted 1:5		
1	Mark McGwire	4.00
2	Nomar Garciaparra	3.00
3	Barry Bonds	1.50
4	Sammy Sosa	2.50
5	Chipper Jones	2.50
6	Pat Burrell	1.00
7	Frank Thomas	1.50
8	Manny Ramirez	1.50
9	Derek Jeter	4.00
10	Ken Griffey Jr.	3.00

2001 Topps Heritage Clubhouse Collection Game-used

		MT
Common Player:		30.00
MM	Minnie Monoso	30.00
RS	Red Schoendienst	40.00
DS	Duke Snider	70.00
EM	Eddie Mathews	100.00
CJ	Chipper Jones	60.00
RA	Richie Ashburn	50.00
FT	Frank Thomas	50.00
FV	Fernando Vina	40.00
SG	Shawn Green	50.00
WM	Willie Mays	150.00
BB	Barry Bonds	80.00
SR	Scott Rolen	40.00

2001 Topps Heritage Clubhouse Collection Autographs

		MT
Common Player:		
MM	Minnie Monoso/25	120.00
RS	Red Schoendienst/25	150.00
DS	Duke Snider	

2001 Topps Heritage Clubhouse Collection Dual Game-used

		MT
Common Card:		80.00
Production 52 sets		
MMFT	Minnie Monoso, Frank Thomas	120.00
RSFV	Red Schoendienst, Fernando Vina	75.00
DSSG	Duke Snider, Shawn Green	180.00
RAPB	Richie Ashburn, Scott Rolen	90.00
EMCJ	Eddie Mathews, Chipper Jones	250.00
WMBB	Willie Mays, Barry Bonds	300.00

2001 Topps Heritage Grandstand Glory

		MT
Complete Set (7):		350.00
Common Player:		40.00
Inserted 1:211		
PR	Phil Rizzuto	40.00
YB	Yogi Berra	60.00

RA	Richie Ashburn	40.00
RR	Robin Roberts	40.00
WM	Willie Mays	100.00
NF	Nellie Fox	40.00
JR	Jackie Robinson	80.00

2001 Topps Heritage New Age Performers

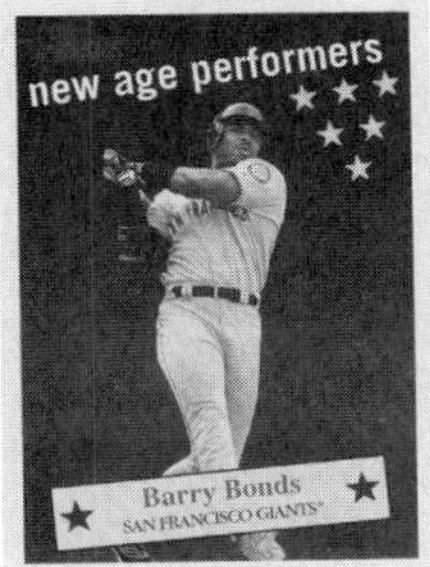

		MT
Complete Set (15):		40.00
Common Player:		1.50
Inserted 1:8		
1	Mike Piazza	5.00
2	Sammy Sosa	4.00
3	Alex Rodriguez	5.00
4	Barry Bonds	2.00
5	Ken Griffey Jr.	5.00
6	Chipper Jones	4.00
7	Randy Johnson	2.00
8	Derek Jeter	6.00
9	Nomar Garciaparra	5.00
10	Mark McGwire	6.00
11	Jeff Bagwell	2.00
12	Pedro Martinez	2.00
13	Todd Helton	2.00
14	Vladimir Guerrero	2.50
15	Greg Maddux	4.00

2001 Topps Heritage Real One Autographs

		MT
Common Player:		20.00
Current MLB Players		
200 Blue-inked produced		
52 Red-inked produced		
Prices listed for Blue sigs		
RH	Richard Hidalgo	50.00
TL	Terrence Long	30.00
CD	Carlos Delgado	60.00
CJ	Chipper Jones	150.00
TG	Tom Glavine	90.00
GJ	Geoff Jenkins	100.00
JM	Joe Mays	30.00
FV	Fernando Vina	40.00
CP	Corey Patterson	60.00
JV	Jose Vidro	25.00
BB	Barry Bonds	160.00
AR	Alex Rodriguez	200.00
AH	Aubrey Huff	25.00
SPB	Sean Burroughs	40.00
RW	Randy Wolf	40.00
KB	Kris Benson	40.00
ML	Mike Lamb	20.00
TH	Todd Helton	100.00
MQ	Mark Quinn	40.00
MS	Mike Sweeney	
ML	Matt Lawton	30.00
MO	Magglio Ordonez	50.00
MB	Mark Buerhle	25.00
MR	Mark Redman	40.00
CF	Cliff Floyd	25.00
NG	Nomar Garciaparra	200.00
1952 MLB Players		
MV	Mickey Vernon	50.00
HB	Hank Bauer	70.00
DD	Dom DiMaggio	90.00
LD	Larry Doby	75.00
JG	Joe Garagiola	75.00
DG	Dick Groat	75.00
MI	Monte Irvin	50.00
VL	Vernon Law	
EM	Eddie Matthews	200.00
WM	Willie Mays	400.00
GM	Gil McDougald	60.00
MM	Minnie Monoso	75.00
AP	Andy Pafko	50.00
PFR	Phil Rizzuto	100.00
PR	Preacher Roe	80.00
JS	Johnny Sain	60.00
HS	Hank Sauer	50.00
RS	Red Schoendienst	50.00
BS	Bobby Shantz	40.00
CS	Curt Simmons	50.00
ES	Enos Slaughter	75.00
DS	Duke Snider	150.00
WS	Warren Spahn	200.00
BT	Bobby Thompson	75.00
HW	Hoyt Wilhelm	75.00
RR	Robin Roberts	75.00

2001 Topps Heritage Then and Now

		MT
Complete Set (10):		30.00
Common Player:		1.50
Inserted 1:8		
1	Yogi Berra, Mike Piazza	4.00
2	Duke Snider, Sammy Sosa	3.00
3	Willie Mays, Ken Griffey Jr.	4.00
4	Phil Rizzuto, Derek Jeter	5.00
5	Pee Wee Reese, Nomar Garciaparra	4.00
6	Jackie Robinson, Alex Rodriguez	4.00
7	Johnny Mize, Mark McGwire	5.00
8	Bob Feller, Pedro Martinez	1.50
9	Robin Roberts, Greg Maddux	3.00
10	Warren Spahn, Randy Johnson	1.50

2001 Topps Heritage Time Capsule

		MT
Common Player:		25.00
Inserted 1:369		
WM	Willie Mays	100.00
TW	Ted Williams	120.00
DN	Don Newcombe	25.00
WF	Whitey Ford	50.00
WMTW	Ted Williams, Willie Mays/52	475.00

2001 Topps HD

		MT
Complete Set (120):		100.00
Common Player:		.25
Common (101-120):		1.00
Inserted 1:6		
Pack (4):		4.00
Box (20):		70.00
1	Derek Jeter	4.00
2	Magglio Ordonez	.40
3	Eric Munson	.25
4	Jermaine Dye	.25
5	Larry Walker	.50
6	Pokey Reese	.25
7	Pedro Martinez	1.25
8	Rafael Palmeiro	.75
9	Jason Kendall	.25
10	Mike Lieberthal	.25
11	Ryan Klesko	.25
12	Cal Ripken Jr.	4.00
13	Mike Piazza	3.00
14	*Adam Sterrett*	.75
15	John Olerud	.40
16	Manny Ramirez	1.25
17	*Chad Petty*	1.00
18	Vladimir Guerrero	1.50
19	Kevin Brown	.40
20	*Luis Cotto*	.50
21	Josh Hamilton	.75
22	Mark Grace	.50
23	Mark McGwire	5.00
24	Jeromy Burnitz	.25
25	Andruw Jones	1.00
26	Raul Mondesi	.40
27	*Stuart McFarland*	.75
28	Craig Biggio	.40
29	Troy Glaus	1.25
30	Carlos Delgado	1.00
31	Rafael Furcal	.25
32	J.D. Drew	.40
33	Corey Patterson	.40
34	Gary Sheffield	.40
35	Jeff Kent	.25
36	Alex Rodriguez	4.00
37	Edgardo Alfonzo	.40
38	*Jeff Segar*	1.50
39	Bobby Abreu	.25
40	Brian Giles	.40
41	*Jason Smith*	1.50
42	Mo Vaughn	.50
43	Pat Burrell	.50
44	Barry Larkin	.50
45	Carlos Beltran	.25
46	*Eric Mosley*	1.50
47	Alfonso Soriano	.40
48	Tim Salmon	.40
49	Jason Giambi	.50
50	Greg Maddux	2.50
51	Randy Johnson	1.25
52	Jose Vidro	.25
53	Edgar Martinez	.25
54	Albert Belle	.50
55	Ivan Rodriguez	1.25
56	Sean Casey	.25
57	Jorge Posada	.40
58	Preston Wilson	.25
59	Paul Konerko	.25
60	Todd Helton	1.25
61	*Dominic Rich*	.75
62	Tony Gwynn	1.50
63	Bernie Williams	1.00
64	*Anthony Brewer*	1.50
65	Shawn Green	.50
66	Jeff Bagwell	1.25
67	Jose Cruz Jr.	.25
68	Darin Erstad	.75
69	Jim Edmonds	.40
70	Frank Thomas	1.50
71	Ryan Anderson	.25
72	Scott Rolen	.75
73	Jeff Cirillo	.25
74	*Chris Bass*	3.00
75	*William Smith*	2.00
76	Trot Nixon	.25
77	Bobby Bradley	.25
78	*Odannis Ayala*	.75
79	Jim Thome	.50
80	Sammy Sosa	2.50
81	Geoff Jenkins	.40
82	Ben Grieve	.40
83	Andres Galarraga	.50
84	Rick Ankiel	.40
85	Barry Bonds	1.50
86	Alex Gonzalez	.25
87	Sean Burroughs	.25
88	Nomar Garciaparra	3.00
89	Ken Griffey Jr.	3.00
90	Tim Hudson	.40
91	Chipper Jones	2.50
92	Matt Williams	.40
93	Roberto Alomar	1.00
94	Adrian Gonzalez	.75
95	Juan Gonzalez	1.25
96	*Brian Bass*	1.00
97	*Rick Brosseau*	.75
98	Mariano Rivera	.40
99	James Baldwin	.25
100	Dean Palmer	.25
101	Pedro Martinez	2.00
102	Randy Johnson	2.00
103	Greg Maddux	4.00
104	Sammy Sosa	4.00
105	Mark McGwire	8.00
106	Ivan Rodriguez	2.00
107	Mike Piazza	5.00
108	Chipper Jones	4.00
109	Vladimir Guerrero	3.00
110	Alex Rodriguez	6.00
111	Ken Griffey Jr.	5.00
112	Cal Ripken Jr.	6.00
113	Derek Jeter	6.00
114	Barry Bonds	2.50
115	Nomar Garciaparra	5.00
116	Jeff Bagwell	2.00
117	Todd Helton	2.00
118	Darin Erstad	1.50
119	Shawn Green	1.00
120	Roberto Alomar	1.50

2001 Topps HD Platinum

	MT
Stars (1-100):	5-10X
Stars (101-120):	3-6X
Production 199 sets	

2001 Topps HD Autographed Cards

MT

Complete Set (4): 140.00
Common Player: 20.00
Inserted 1:431

1	Todd Helton	50.00
2	Rick Ankiel	30.00
3	Mark Quinn	20.00
4	Adrian Gonzalez	50.00

2001 Topps HD Game Defined

MT

Complete Set (10): 90.00
Common Player: 5.00
Inserted 1:24
Platinum: 1.5-2X
Inserted 1:72

1	Ken Griffey Jr.	12.00
2	Derek Jeter	15.00
3	Sammy Sosa	10.00
4	Mark McGwire	18.00
5	Todd Helton	5.00
6	Mike Piazza	12.00
7	Chipper Jones	10.00
8	Vladimir Guerrero	6.00
9	Alex Rodriguez	15.00
10	Nomar Garciaparra	12.00

2001 Topps HD Game-Worn Jersey

MT

Complete Set (8): 160.00
Common Card: 20.00
Inserted 1:108
Cards 5-8 are redemptions

1	Grant Roberts	25.00
2	Vernon Wells	25.00
3	Travis Dawkins	20.00
4	Ramon Ortiz	25.00
5	Steve Finley	25.00
6	Ramon Hernandez	20.00
7	Jay Payton	30.00
8	Jeromy Burnitz	25.00

2001 Topps HD Images of Excellence

MT

Complete Set (10): 30.00
Common Player: 2.00
Inserted 1:8
Platinum: 1.5-2X
Inserted 1:24

1	Willie Mays	5.00
2	Reggie Jackson	3.00
3	Ernie Banks	2.00
4	Hank Aaron	5.00
5	Ted Williams	5.00
6	Mike Schmidt	3.00
7	Tom Seaver	2.00
8	Johnny Bench	3.00
9	George Brett	4.00
10	Nolan Ryan	6.00

2001 Topps HD 20-20

MT

Complete Set (10): 40.00
Common Player: 1.50
Inserted 1:12
Platinum: 1.5-2X
Inserted 1:36

1	Barry Bonds	3.00
2	Chipper Jones	5.00
3	Ken Griffey Jr.	8.00
4	Alex Rodriguez	10.00
5	Ivan Rodriguez	2.50
6	Sammy Sosa	5.00
7	Roberto Alomar	2.00
8	Larry Walker	1.50
9	Shawn Green	1.50
10	Jeff Bagwell	2.50

2001 Topps Opening Day

MT

Complete Set (165): 35.00
Common Player: .15
Pack (7): 1.00
Box (24): 20.00

1	Cal Ripken Jr.	2.50
2	Chipper Jones	1.50
3	Garret Anderson	.15
4	Robin Ventura	.20
5	Jermaine Dye	.15
6	Jim Thome	.25
7	Brian Jordan	.15
8	Shawn Green	.25
9	Juan Gonzalez	.75
10	Paul O'Neill	.25
11	Pokey Reese	.15
12	Mike Mussina	.40
13	Jay Buhner	.15
14	Shane Reynolds	.15
15	Adam Piatt	.15
16	Preston Wilson	.15
17	Ellis Burks	.15
18	Chuck Finley	.15
19	Shannon Stewart	.15
20	Mark McGwire	2.50
21	Mark Loretta	.15
22	Bobby Jones	.15
23	Matt Clement	.15
24	Pedro J. Martinez	1.00
25	Carlos Lee	.15
26	John Franco	.15
27	Andres Galarraga	.25
28	Jose Cruz Jr.	.15
29	Randy Johnson	.75
30	Richie Sexson	.15
31	Darin Erstad	.30
32	Manny Ramirez	.75
33	Mike Sweeney	.15
34	John Wetteland	.15
35	Derek Jeter	2.50
36	J.D. Drew	.15
37	Rick Reed	.15
38	Jay Bell	.15
39	Fred McGriff	.25
40	Orlando Cabrera	.15
41	Eric Owens	.15
42	Jorge Posada	.25
43	Jeff Cirillo	.15
44	Johnny Damon	.15
45	Charles Johnson	.15
46	Pat Burrell	.40
47	Gary Sheffield	.25
48	Tom Glavine	.30
49	Ivan Rodriguez	.75
50	Chuck Knoblauch	.25
51	Jason Kendall	.15
52	Carlos Delgado	.60
53	Roger Clemens	1.00
54	Brad Penny	.15
55	Troy Glaus	.75
56	Mike Hampton	.15
57	Carlos Febles	.15
58	Seth Etherton	.15
59	Fernando Tatis	.15
60	Livan Hernandez	.15
61	Barry Larkin	.30
62	Alex Rodriguez	2.00
63	Warren Morris	.15
64	Antonio Alfonseca	.15
65	Edgardo Alfonzo	.15
66	Fernando Vina	.15
67	Jason Giambi	.30
68	Matt Lawton	.15
69	Rusty Greer	.15
70	Tony Gwynn	1.00
71	Carl Everett	.15
72	Bret Boone	.15
73	James Baldwin	.15
74	Greg Vaughn	.15
75	Darren Dreifort	.15
76	Frank Thomas	1.00
77	Luis Castillo	.15
78	Bartolo Colon	.15
79	Craig Biggio	.25
80	Jose Vidro	.15
81	Todd Helton	.75
82	Jacque Jones	.15
83	Robb Nen	.15
84	Richard Hidalgo	.25
85	Tony Womack	.15
86	Rick Ankiel	.25
87	Terrence Long	.15
88	Brad Radke	.15
89	Gabe Kapler	.15
90	Pedro Astacio	.15
91	Darryl Kile	.15
92	Jay Payton	.15
93	Vladimir Guerrero	1.00
94	Juan Encarnacion	.15
95	Ramon Hernandez	.15
96	Sandy Alomar	.15
97	Geoff Jenkins	.25
98	Rafael Furcal	.25
99	Mark Grace	.25
100	Mark Mulder	.15
101	Jim Edmonds	.25
102	Tim Salmon	.25
103	Jeff Bagwell	.75
104	Jose Canseco	.40
105	Ben Grieve	.25
106	Ryan Klesko	.15
107	Javy Lopez	.25
108	Greg Maddux	1.50
109	Andruw Jones	.50
110	Jeromy Burnitz	.15
111	Ray Lankford	.15
112	Sammy Sosa	1.50
113	Raul Mondesi	.25
114	Mike Piazza	2.00
115	Todd Zeile	.15
116	Eric Karros	.15
117	Barry Bonds	.75
118	J.T. Snow	.15
119	Jeff Kent	.15
120	David Justice	.25
121	Matt Williams	.25
122	Brian Giles	.25
123	Edgar Martinez	.15
124	Ken Griffey Jr.	2.50
125	Al Leiter	.25
126	Kevin Brown	.25
127	John Olerud	.25
128	Roberto Alomar	.50
129	Rafael Palmeiro	.40
130	Steve Finley	.15
131	Tim Hudson	.25
132	Scott Rolen	.50
133	Nomar Garciaparra	1.50
134	Mo Vaughn	.20
135	Larry Walker	.30
136	Albert Belle	.15
137	Ray Durham	.15
138	Andy Pettitte	.25
139	Mariano Rivera	.25
140	Bernie Williams	.50
141	David Wells	.15
142	Magglio Ordonez	.25
143	Kevin Millwood	.15
144	Cliff Floyd	.15
145	Rich Aurilia	.15
146	Eric Chavez	.15
147	Scott Elarton	.15
148	Tony Armas Jr.	.15
149	Mark Redman	.15
150	Javier Vazquez	.15
151	Adrian Gonzalez, Adam Johnson	1.00
152	Mike Stodolka, Sean Burnett	.15
153	David Walling, Ben Sheets	1.00
154	Chin-Feng Chen, Corey Patterson, Josh Hamilton	.25
155	Mark McGwire (Golden Moments)	1.00
156	Bobby Thomson (Golden Moments)	.15
157	Bill Mazeroski (Golden Moments)	.15
158	Cal Ripken Jr. (Golden Moments)	1.00
159	Hank Aaron (Golden Moments)	1.00
160	Bucky Dent (Golden Moments)	.15
161	Jackie Robinson (Golden Moments)	1.00
162	Roberto Clemente (Golden Moments)	1.00
163	Nolan Ryan (Golden Moments)	1.00
164	Kerry Wood (Golden Moments)	.15
165	Checklist	.15

2001 Topps Opening Day Autographs

MT

Common Autograph:

TH	Todd Helton	100.00
CJ	Chipper Jones	125.00
MO	Magglio Ordonez	
CP	Corey Patterson	

2001 Topps Opening Day Stickers

MT

Complete Set (30): 6.00
Sticker: .25
Each team represented

2001 Topps Reserve

		MT
Complete Set (151):		
Common Player:		.40
Common SP (101-150):		8.00
Production 1,500		
Sealed Hobby Box (10):		100.00
1	Darin Erstad	.50
2	Moises Alou	.40
3	Tony Batista	.40
4	Andruw Jones	.75
5	Edgar Renteria	.40
6	Eric Young	.40
7	Steve Finley	.40
8	Adrian Beltre	.40
9	Vladimir Guerrero	1.00
10	Barry Bonds	2.00
11	Juan Gonzalez	1.00
12	Jay Buhner	.40
13	Luis Castillo	.40
14	Cal Ripken Jr.	3.00
15	Bob Abreu	.40
16	Ivan Rodriguez	1.00
17	Nomar Garciaparra	2.50
18	Todd Helton	1.00
19	Bobby Higginson	.40
20	Jorge Posada	.40
21	Tim Salmon	.40
22	Jason Giambi	.75
23	Jose Cruz Jr.	.40
24	Chipper Jones	2.00
25	Jim Edmonds	.50
26	Gerald Williams	.40
27	Randy Johnson	1.00
28	Gary Sheffield	.40
29	Jeff Kent	.40
30	Jim Thome	.50
31	John Olerud	.50
32	Cliff Floyd	.40
33	Mike Lowell	.40
34	Phil Nevin	.40
35	Scott Rolen	.50
36	Alex Rodriguez	2.50
37	Ken Griffey Jr.	2.50
38	Neifi Perez	.40
39	Christian Guzman	.40
40	Mariano Rivera	.40
41	Troy Glaus	1.00
42	Johnny Damon	.40
43	Rafael Furcal	.40
44	Jeromy Burnitz	.40
45	Mark McGwire	3.00
46	Fred McGriff	.40
47	Matt Williams	.40
48	Kevin Brown	.40
49	J.T. Snow	.40
50	Kenny Lofton	.40
51	Al Martin	.40
52	Antonio Alfonseca	.40
53	Edgardo Alfonzo	.40
54	Ryan Klesko	.40
55	Pat Burrell	.50
56	Rafael Palmeiro	.75
57	Sean Casey	.40
58	Jeff Cirillo	.40
59	Ray Durham	.40
60	Derek Jeter	3.00
61	Jeff Bagwell	1.00
62	Carlos Delgado	.75
63	Tom Glavine	.50
64	Richie Sexson	.40
65	J.D. Drew	.40
66	Ben Grieve	.40
67	Mark Grace	.50
68	Shawn Green	.40
69	Robb Nen	.40
70	Omar Vizquel	.40
71	Edgar Martinez	.40
72	Preston Wilson	.40
73	Mike Piazza	2.50
74	Tony Gwynn	1.25
75	Jason Kendall	.40
76	Manny Ramirez	1.25
77	Pokey Reese	.40
78	Mike Sweeney	.40
79	Magglio Ordonez	.40
80	Bernie Williams	.75
81	Richard Hidalgo	.40
82	Brad Fullmer	.40
83	Greg Maddux	2.00
84	Geoff Jenkins	.40
85	Sammy Sosa	2.00
86	Luis Gonzalez	.75
87	Eric Karros	.40
88	Jose Vidro	.40
89	Rich Aurilia	.40
90	Roberto Alomar	.75
91	Mike Cameron	.40
92	Mike Mussina	.60
93	Albert Belle	.40
94	Mike Lieberthal	.40
95	Brian Giles	.40
96	Pedro Martinez	1.25
97	Barry Larkin	.50
98	Jermaine Dye	.40
99	Frank Thomas	1.25
100	David Justice	.50
101	*Gary Johnson*	8.00
102	*Matt Ford*	10.00
103	*Albert Pujols*	75.00
104	Brad Cresse	8.00
105	*Valentino Pascucci*	8.00
106	*Bob Keppel*	8.00
107	*Luis Torres*	10.00
108	*Tony Blanco*	25.00
109	*Ronnie Corona*	8.00
110	*Phil Wilson*	10.00
111	*John Buck*	8.00
112	*Jim Journell*	8.00
113	*Victor Hall*	10.00
114	*Jeff Andra*	8.00
115	*Greg Nash*	20.00
116	*Travis Hafner*	12.00
117	*Casey Fossum*	15.00
118	Miguel Olivo	8.00
119	*Elpidio Guzman*	8.00
120	*Jason Belcher*	10.00
121	*Esix Snead*	8.00
122	*Joe Thurston*	8.00
123	*Rafael Soriano*	10.00
124	*Ed Rogers*	12.00
125	*Omar Beltre*	15.00
126	*Brett Gray*	8.00
127	*Deivi Mendez*	15.00
128	*Freddie Bynum*	10.00
129	David Kryznel	8.00
130	*Blake Williams*	10.00
131	*Reggie Abercrombie*	12.00
132	*Miguel Villilo*	10.00
133	*Ryan Madson*	15.00
134	*Matt Thompson*	12.00
135	*Mark Burnett*	12.00
136	*Andy Beal*	12.00
137	*Ryan Ludwick*	20.00
138	*Roberto Miniel*	10.00
139	*Steve Smyth*	10.00
140	*Ben Washburn*	20.00
141	*Marvin Seale*	12.00
142	*Reggie Griggs*	15.00
143	*Seung Song*	20.00
144	*Chad Petty*	10.00
145	*Noel Devarez*	8.00
146	*Matt Butler*	10.00
147	*Brett Evert*	12.00
148	Cesar Izturis	8.00
149	*Troy Farnsworth*	8.00
150	*Brian Schmitt*	8.00
151	*Ichiro Suzuki*	90.00

A player's name in *italic* type indicates a rookie card.

2001 Topps Reserve Game-Used Bat

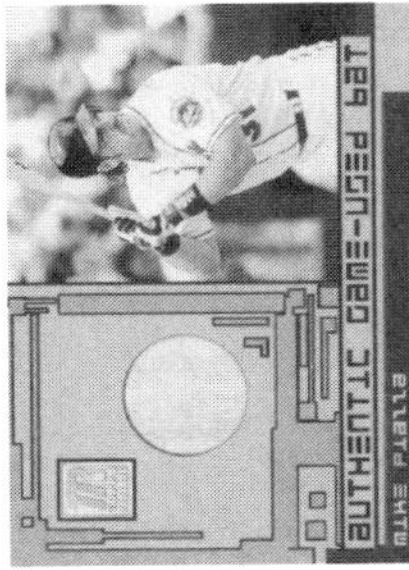

		MT
Common Player:		15.00
Inserted 1:box		
JB	Jeff Bagwell	25.00
BB	Barry Bonds	35.00
CD	Carlos Delgado	15.00
JE	Jim Edmonds	15.00
DE	Darin Erstad	15.00
RF	Rafael Furcal	15.00
NG	Nomar Garciaparra	50.00
VG	Vladimir Guerrero	18.00
TG	Tony Gwynn	20.00
CJ	Chipper Jones	20.00
MP	Mike Piazza	40.00
AR	Alex Rodriguez	25.00
IR	Ivan Rodriguez	20.00
BW	Bernie Williams	15.00

2001 Topps Reserve Game-Worn Uniform

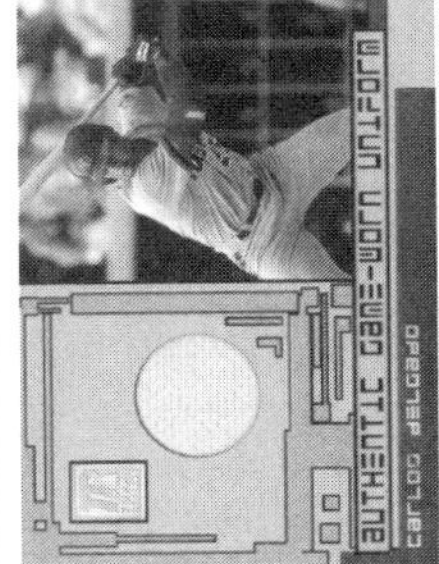

		MT
Common Player:		10.00
Inserted 1:box		
RA	Roberto Alomar	20.00
BB	Barry Bonds	30.00
CD	Carlos Delgado	15.00
JE	Jim Edmonds	10.00
NG	Nomar Garciaparra	40.00
JG	Juan Gonzalez	20.00
SG	Shawn Green	10.00
VG	Vladimir Guerrero	15.00
TG	Tony Gwynn	20.00
TH	Todd Helton	20.00
RJ	Randy Johnson	15.00
CJ	Chipper Jones	20.00
DJ	David Justice	15.00
GM	Greg Maddux	25.00
PM	Pedro Martinez	25.00
RP	Rafael Palmeiro	15.00
AR	Alex Rodriguez	25.00
IR	Ivan Rodriguez	15.00
SR	Scott Rolen	15.00
FT	Frank Thomas	20.00

2001 Topps Reserve Rookie Autographed Baseballs

	MT
Common Player:	15.00
Inserted 1:box w/holder	
Reggie Abercrombie	15.00
Jeff Andra	15.00
Andy Beal	20.00
Jason Belcher	25.00
Omar Beltre	15.00
Tony Blanco	35.00
John Buck	20.00
Mark Burnett	15.00
Freddie Bynum	20.00
Ronnie Corona	15.00
Noel Devarez	15.00
Matt Ford	15.00
Casey Fossum	30.00
Brett Gray	15.00
Reggie Griggs	20.00
Elpidio Guzman	20.00
Travis Hafner	25.00
Victor Hall	20.00
Gary Johnson	15.00
Jim Journell	
Bob Keppel	20.00
David Krynzel	20.00
Ryan Ludwick	30.00
Ryan Madson	20.00
Deivi Mendez	25.00
Roberto Miniel	20.00
Greg Nash	40.00
Miguel Olivo	
Valentino Pascucci	
Chad Petty	20.00
Albert Pujols	125.00
Ed Rogers	20.00
Marvin Seale	20.00
Steve Smyth	20.00
Esix Snead	20.00
Seung Song	25.00
Rafael Soriano	20.00
Matt Thompson	20.00
Joe Thurston	15.00
Luis Torres	15.00
Miguel Villilo	15.00
Ben Washburn	25.00
Blake Williams	
Phil Wilson	

2001 Topps Reserve Rookie Graded Autograph

	MT
Common Rookie:	15.00
Inserted 1:box	
Prices for PSA 8	
PSA 9s:	2X
Reggie Abercrombie	15.00
Jeff Andra	15.00
Andy Beal	20.00
Jason Belcher	20.00
Omar Beltre	15.00
Tony Blanco	35.00
John Buck	20.00
Mark Burnett	15.00

Freddie Bynum	20.00
Ronnie Corona	15.00
Noel Devarez	15.00
Matt Ford	15.00
Casey Fossum	30.00
Brett Gray	15.00
Reggie Griggs	20.00
Elpidio Guzman	15.00
Travis Hafner	25.00
Victor Hall	15.00
Gary Johnson	15.00
Jim Journell	15.00
Bob Keppel	
David Krynzel	20.00
Ryan Ludwick	30.00
Ryan Madson	20.00
Deivi Mendez	25.00
Roberto Miniel	20.00
Greg Nash	40.00
Miguel Olivo	15.00
Valentino Pascucci	20.00
Chad Petty	20.00
Albert Pujols	125.00
Ed Rogers	20.00
Marvin Seale	20.00
Steve Smyth	20.00
Esix Snead	20.00
Seung Song	25.00
Rafael Soriano	20.00
Matt Thompson	20.00
Joe Thurston	15.00
Luis Torres	15.00
Miguel Villilo	15.00
Ben Washburn	25.00
Blake Williams	15.00
Phil Wilson	15.00

2001 Topps Stars

		MT
Complete Set (200):		60.00
Common Player:		.15
Pack (6):		2.50
Box (24):		50.00
1	Darin Erstad	.40
2	Luis Gonzalez	.40
3	Rafael Furcal	.25
4	Dante Bichette	.15
5	Sammy Sosa	1.50
6	Ken Griffey Jr.	2.50
7	Jim Thome	.40
8	Bobby Higginson	.15
9	Cliff Floyd	.15
10	Lance Berkman	.25
11	Eric Karros	.25
12	Jeromy Burnitz	.15
13	Jose Vidro	.15
14	Benny Agbayani	.15
15	Jorge Posada	.25
16	Ramon Hernandez	.15
17	Jason Kendall	.15
18	Jeff Kent	.25
19	John Olerud	.25
20	Al Martin	.15
21	Gerald Williams	.15
22	Gabe Kapler	.25
23	Carlos Delgado	.60
24	Mariano Rivera	.25
25	Javy Lopez	.25
26	Paul Konerko	.25
27	Daryle Ward	.15
28	Mike Lieberthal	.15
29	Tom Goodwin	.15
30	Garret Anderson	.15
31	Steve Finley	.15
32	Brian Jordan	.15
33	Nomar Garciaparra	2.00
34	Ray Durham	.15
35	Sean Casey	.25
36	Kenny Lofton	.25
37	Dean Palmer	.15
38	Jeff Bagwell	.75
39	Mike Sweeney	.15
40	Adrian Beltre	.25
41	Richie Sexson	.15
42	Vladimir Guerrero	1.00
43	Derek Jeter	2.50
44	Miguel Tejada	.25
45	Doug Glanville	.15
46	Brian Giles	.25
47	Marvin Benard	.15
48	Edgar Martinez	.15
49	Edgar Renteria	.15
50	Fred McGriff	.25
51	Ivan Rodriguez	.75
52	Brad Fullmer	.15
53	Antonio Alfonseca	.15
54	Tom Glavine	.40
55	Warren Morris	.15
56	Johnny Damon	.15
57	Dmitri Young	.15
58	Mo Vaughn	.15
59	Randy Johnson	.75
60	Greg Maddux	1.50
61	Carl Everett	.15
62	Magglio Ordonez	.25
63	Pokey Reese	.15
64	Todd Helton	.75
65	Preston Wilson	.15
66	Richard Hidalgo	.25
67	Jermaine Dye	.15
68	Gary Sheffield	.25
69	Geoff Jenkins	.25
70	Edgardo Alfonzo	.15
71	Paul O'Neill	.25
72	Terrence Long	.15
73	Bob Abreu	.15
74	Kevin Young	.15
75	J.T. Snow	.15
76	Alex Rodriguez	2.00
77	Jim Edmonds	.25
78	Mark McGwire	2.50
79	Tony Batista	.15
80	Darrin Fletcher	.15
81	Robb Nen	.15
82	Jose Offerman	.15
83	Travis Fryman	.25
84	Joe Randa	.15
85	Omar Vizquel	.25
86	Tim Salmon	.15
87	Andruw Jones	.60
88	Albert Belle	.15
89	Manny Ramirez	1.00
90	Frank Thomas	1.00
91	Barry Larkin	.40
92	Neifi Perez	.15
93	Luis Castillo	.15
94	Moises Alou	.25
95	Mark Quinn	.15
96	Kevin Brown	.25
97	Cristian Guzman	.15
98	Mike Piazza	2.00
99	Bernie Williams	.60
100	Jason Giambi	.40
101	Scott Rolen	.40
102	Phil Nevin	.15
103	Rich Aurilia	.15
104	Mike Cameron	.15
105	Fernando Vina	.15
106	Greg Vaughn	.15
107	Jose Cruz	.15
108	Raul Mondesi	.15
109	Ben Molina	.15
110	Pedro Martinez	1.00
111	Todd Hollandsworth	.15
112	Jacque Jones	.15
113	Rickey Henderson	.25
114	Troy Glaus	.75
115	Chipper Jones	1.50
116	Delino DeShields	.15
117	Eric Young	.15
118	Jose Valentin	.15
119	Roberto Alomar	.60
120	Jeff Cirillo	.15
121	Mike Lowell	.15
122	Julio Lugo	.15
123	Shawn Green	.25
124	Marquis Grissom	.15
125	Matt Lawton	.15
126	Jay Payton	.15
127	David Justice	.40
128	Eric Chavez	.25
129	Pat Burrell	.50
130	Ryan Klesko	.15
131	Barry Bonds	1.00
132	Jay Buhner	.15
133	J.D. Drew	.25
134	Rafael Palmeiro	.40
135	Shannon Stewart	.15
136	Juan Gonzalez	.75
137	Tony Womack	.15
138	Carlos Lee	.15
139	Derrek Lee	.15
140	Ben Grieve	.25
141	Ron Belliard	.15
142	Stan Musial	1.50
143	Ernie Banks	1.00
144	Jim Palmer	.75
145	Tony Perez	.25
146	Duke Snider	.75
147	Rod Carew	.40
148	Warren Spahn	.75
149	Yogi Berra	1.50
150	Juan Marichal	.25
151	Eric Munson	.15
152	Carlos Pena	.15
153	Joe Crede	.15
154	Ryan Anderson	.15
155	Milton Bradley	.15
156	Sean Burroughs	.15
157	Corey Patterson	.20
158	C.C. Sabathia	.15
159	Ben Petrick	.15
160	Aubrey Huff	.15
161	Gookie Dawkins	.15
162	Ben Sheets	.50
163	Pablo Ozuna	.15
164	Eric Valent	.15
165	Rod Barajas	.15
166	Chin-Feng Chen	.40
167	Josh Hamilton	.75
168	Keith Ginter	.15
169	Vernon Wells	.15
170	Dernell Stenson	.15
171	Alfonso Soriano	.25
172	Jason Marquis	.15
173	Nick Johnson	.15
174	Adam Everett	.15
175	Jimmy Rollins	.15
176	Ben Diggins	.15
177	John Lackey	.15
178	Scott Heard	.15
179	*Brian Hitchcox*	.50
180	*Odannis Ayala*	.50
181	*Scott Pratt*	.75
182	*Greg Runser*	.75
183	*Chris Russ*	.50
184	Derek Thompson	.50
185	*Jason Jones*	.50
186	*Dominic Rich*	.50
187	*Chad Petty*	1.00
188	*Steve Smyth*	.50
189	*Bryan Hebson*	.50
190	*Danny Borrell*	.75
191	*Bob Keppel*	.75
192	*Justin Wayne*	1.50
193	*Reggie Abercrombie*	.50
194	*Travis Baptist*	.75
195	*Shawn Fagan*	.75
196	*Jose Reyes*	2.50
197	*Chris Bass*	1.50
198	*Albert Pujols*	12.00
199	*Luis Cotto*	.50
200	*Jake Peavy*	1.00

2001 Topps Stars Gold

	MT
Stars:	3-5X
Production 499 sets	

2001 Topps Stars Onyx

	MT
Stars:	10-20X
Rookies:	5-10X
Production 99 sets	

2001 Topps Stars Elimination

	MT
Stars:	8-15X
Production 100 sets	
Redemp. deadline 10/19/01	

2001 Topps Stars Autographs

	MT
Common Player:	15.00
Inserted 1:353	
TSA-EBErnie Banks	60.00
TSA-YBYogi Berra	50.00
TSA-RCRod Carew	50.00
TSA-CDCarlos Delgado	40.00
TSA-THTodd Helton	30.00
TSA-JMJuan Marichal	125.00
TSA-EMEric Munson	15.00
TSA-SMStan Musial	125.00
TSA-JPJim Palmer	50.00
TSA-TPTony Perez	25.00
TSA-IRIvan Rodriguez	40.00
TSA-DSDuke Snider	50.00
TSA-WSWarren Spahn	50.00

2001 Topps Stars Game Gear Bats

	MT
Common Player:	10.00
Inserted 1:187	
TSR-ABAdrian Beltre	15.00
TSR-LBLance Berkman	25.00
TSR-SBSean Burroughs	15.00
TSR-MCMichael Cuddyer	10.00
TSR-BDBen Davis	10.00
TSR-JDDJ.D. Drew	25.00
TSR-EDErubiel Durazo	10.00
TSR-JEJuan Encarnacion	10.00
TSR-RFRafael Furcal	20.00
TSR-AKAdam Kennedy	15.00
TSR-GLGeorge Lombard	10.00
TSR-TLTerrence Long	10.00
TSR-FLFelipe Lopez	10.00
TSR-GMGary Mathews	10.00
TSR-CPCorey Patterson	20.00
TSR-NPNeifi Perez	10.00
TSR-APAdam Piatt	10.00
TSR-SRScott Rolen	20.00
TSR-FSFernando Seguignol	10.00
TSR-RSRichie Sexson	15.00

2001 Topps Stars Game Gear Bats Autographs

	MT
Common Player:	
Inserted 1:12,240	
TSRA-RFRafael Furcal	
TSRA-TLTerrence Long	
TSRA-CPCorey Patterson	

2001 Topps Stars Game Gear Jerseys

	MT
Common Player:	10.00
Inserted 1:61	
TSR-EAEdgardo Alfonzo	15.00

TSR-RARoberto Alomar 25.00
TSR-BBBarry Bonds 40.00
TSR-LCLuis Castillo 10.00
TSR-TGTony Gwynn 25.00
TSR-THTodd Helton 20.00
TSR-AJAndruw Jones 20.00
TSR-CJChipper Jones 30.00
TSR-EMEdgar Martinez 15.00
TSR-MOMagglio Ordonez 15.00
TSR-MPMike Piazza 50.00
TSR-SSSammy Sosa 30.00
TSR-SHSShannon Stewart 15.00
TSR-FTFrank Thomas 25.00
TSR-JVJose Vidro 10.00

2001 Topps Stars Game Gear Jerseys Autographs

MT
Common Player:
Inserted 1:19,288
TSRA-BBBarry Bonds
TSRA-THTodd Helton

2001 Topps Stars Players Choice Award Nominees

		MT
Complete Set (10):		20.00
Common Player:		1.50
Inserted 1:12		
PCA1	Barry Bonds, Carlos Delgado, Todd Helton	2.00
PCA2	Gary Sheffield, Eric Davis, Turk Wendell	1.50
PCA3	Alex Rodriguez, Carlos Delgado, Frank Thomas	5.00
PCA4	David Wells, Pedro Martinez, Andy Pettitte	2.50
PCA5	Mark Quinn, Terrence Long, Kazuhiro Sasaki	2.00
PCA6	Jay Buhner, Frank Thomas, Bobby Higginson	2.50
PCA7	Barry Bonds, Todd Helton, Jeff Kent	2.50
PCA8	Tom Glavine, Randy Johnson, Greg Maddux	4.00
PCA9	Rick Ankiel, Rafael Furcal, Jay Payton	1.50
PCA10	Moises Alou, Andres Galarraga, Jeff D'Amico	1.50

2001 Topps Stars Player Choice Awards Relics

MT
Common Player: 15.00
Inserted 1:1,530

PCAR1Carlos Delgado 25.00
PCAR2Eric Davis 15.00
PCAR3Carlos Delgado 25.00
PCAR4Pedro Martinez 50.00
PCAR5Terrence Long 15.00
PCAR6Frank Thomas 50.00
PCAR7Todd Helton 40.00
PCAR8Randy Johnson 40.00
PCAR9Rafael Furcal 25.00
PCAR10Andres Galarraga 25.00

2001 Topps Stars Progression

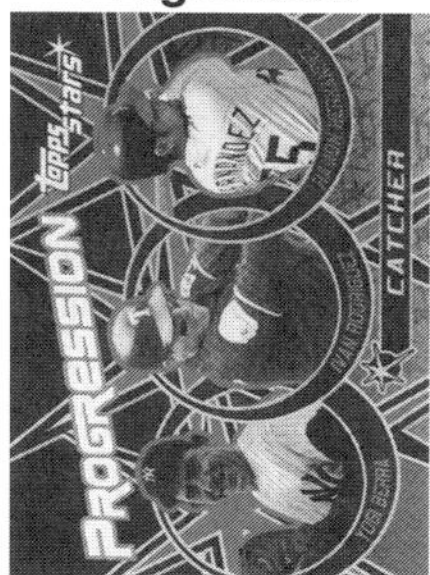

		MT
Complete Set (9):		12.00
Common Player:		1.00
Inserted 1:8		
P1	Ernie Banks, Alex Rodriguez, Felipe Lopez	4.00
P2	Yogi Berra, Ivan Rodriguez, Ramon Hernandez	2.00
P3	Tony Perez, Carlos Delgado, Eric Munson	1.00
P4	Rod Carew, Roberto Alomar, Jose Ortiz	1.00
P5	Stan Musial, Darin Erstad, Alex Escobar	2.00
P6	Jim Palmer, Kevin Brown, Kurt Ainsworth	1.00
P7	Duke Snider, Jim Edmonds, Vernon Wells	1.00
P8	Warren Spahn, Randy Johnson, Ryan Anderson	1.50
P9	Juan Marichal, Bartolo Colon, Bobby Bradley	1.00

2001 Topps Tribute

		MT
Complete Set (90):		375.00
Common Player:		2.00
Pack (3):		75.00
Box (6):		425.00
1	Pee Wee Reese	2.00
2	Babe Ruth	20.00
3	Ralph Kiner	2.00
4	Brooks Robinson	5.00
5	Don Sutton	2.00
6	Carl Yastrzemski	8.00
7	Roger Maris	12.00
8	Andre Dawson	2.00
9	Luis Aparicio	2.00
10	Wade Boggs	4.00
11	Johnny Bench	8.00
12	Ernie Banks	6.00
13	Thurman Munson	8.00
14	Harmon Killebrew	6.00
15	Ted Kluszewski	2.00
16	Bob Feller	3.00
17	Mike Schmidt	10.00
18	Warren Spahn	5.00
19	Jim Palmer	3.00
20	Don Mattingly	15.00
21	Willie Mays	10.00
22	Gil Hodges	2.00
23	Juan Marichal	2.00
24	Robin Yount	8.00
25	Nolan Ryan	15.00
26	Dave Winfield	3.00
27	Hank Greenberg	2.00
28	Honus Wagner	12.00
29	Nolan Ryan	15.00
30	Phil Niekro	2.00
31	Robin Roberts	2.00
32	Casey Stengel	3.00
33	Willie McCovey	2.00
34	Roy Campanella	6.00
35	Rollie Fingers	2.00
36	Tom Seaver	6.00
37	Jackie Robinson	15.00
38	Hank Aaron	10.00
39	Bob Gibson	6.00
40	Carlton Fisk	4.00
41	Hank Aaron	10.00
42	George Brett	10.00
43	Orlando Cepeda	2.00
44	Red Schoendienst	2.00
45	Don Drysdale	5.00
46	Mel Ott	4.00
47	Casey Stengel	3.00
48	Al Kaline	4.00
49	Reggie Jackson	8.00
50	Tony Perez	2.00
51	Ozzie Smith	8.00
52	Billy Martin	4.00
53	Bill Dickey	2.00
54	Catfish Hunter	2.00
55	Duke Snider	4.00
56	Dale Murphy	2.00
57	Bobby Doerr	2.00
58	Earl Averill	2.00
59	Carlton Fisk	4.00
60	Tom Lasorda	2.00
61	Lou Gehrig	15.00
62	Enos Slaughter	2.00
63	Jim Bunning	2.00
64	Rollie Fingers	2.00
65	Frank Robinson	4.00
66	Earl Weaver	2.00
67	Eddie Mathews	5.00
68	Kirby Puckett	10.00
69	Phil Rizzuto	4.00
70	Lou Brock	4.00
71	Walt Alston	2.00
72	Bill Pierce	2.00
73	Joe Morgan	2.00
74	Roberto Clemente	12.00
75	Whitey Ford	4.00
76	Richie Ashburn	2.00
77	Elston Howard	2.00
78	Gary Carter	2.00
79	Carl Hubbell	2.00
80	Yogi Berra	10.00
81	Ken Boyer	2.00
82	Nolan Ryan	15.00
83	Bill Mazeroski	2.00
84	Dizzy Dean	4.00
85	Nellie Fox	2.00
86	Stan Musial	10.00
87	Steve Carlton	4.00
88	Willie Stargell	4.00
89	Hal Newhouser	2.00
90	Frank Robinson	4.00

2001 Topps Tribute Casey Stengel Dual Relic

		MT
Complete Set (1):		
CS	Casey Stengel	200.00

2001 Topps Tribute Franchise Figures

		MT
Common Card:		40.00
Inserted 1:34		
AL	Walt Alston, Tommy Lasorda	50.00
AFF	Luis Aparicio, Nellie Fox, Carlton Fisk	150.00
BPKR	Johnny Bench, Tony Perez, Ted Kluszewski, Frank Robinson, Joe Morgan	250.00
CD	Gary Carter, Andre Dawson	40.00
HDB	Bill Dickey, Elston Howard, Yogi Berra	
FY	Carlton Fisk, Carl Yastrzemski	150.00
HSS	Gil Hodges, Casey Stengel, Tom Seaver	200.00
JM	Reggie Jackson, Billy Martin	125.00
KG	Al Kaline, Hank Greenberg	150.00
MMC	Willie Mays, Willie McCovey, Orlando Cepeda	250.00
MCS	Bill Mazeroski, Roberto Clemente, Willie Stargell	
MM	Thurman Munson, Don Mattingly	400.00
MMA	Dale Murphy, Ed Mathews, Hank Aaron	
PK	Kirby Puckett, Harmon Killebrew	100.00
RSC	Pee Wee Reese, Duke Snider, Roy Campanella	200.00
RR	Brooks Robinson, Frank Robinson	75.00
RG	Babe Ruth, Lou Gehrig	500.00
SAC	Mike Schmidt, Richie Ashburn, Steve Carlton	250.00
SBSM	Ozzie Smith, Lou Brock, Red Schoendienst, Stan Musial	275.00

A card number in parentheses ( ) indicates the set is unnumbered.

2001 Topps Tribute Game-Used Bat Relics

		MT
Common Player:		20.00
Inserted 1:2		
HA	Hank Aaron	50.00
LA	Luis Aparicio	25.00
RA	Richie Ashburn	30.00
KB	Ken Boyer	25.00
GB	George Brett	40.00
LB	Lou Brock	30.00
RC	Roy Campanella	50.00
RCL	Roberto Clemente	80.00
CF	Carlton Fisk	30.00
LG	Lou Gehrig	160.00
HG	Hank Greenberg	50.00
GH	Gil Hodges	30.00
RJ	Reggie Jackson	30.00
AK	Al Kaline	50.00
HK	Harmon Killebrew	40.00
RM	Roger Maris	100.00
BM	Billy Martin	30.00
DM	Don Mattingly	70.00
WM	Willie McCovey	25.00
TM	Thurman Munson	65.00
PWR	Pee Wee Reese	25.00
BRO	Brooks Robinson	30.00
FRR	Frank Robinson	30.00
JR	Jackie Robinson	
BR	Babe Ruth	200.00
OS	Ozzie Smith	40.00
CS	Casey Stengel	30.00
HW	Honus Wagner	200.00
CY	Carl Yastrzemski	40.00

2001 Topps Tribute Game-Worn Patch And Number Relics

		MT
Common Player:		60.00
Inserted 1:61		
WA	Walt Alston	60.00
JB	Johnny Bench	180.00
YB	Yogi Berra	150.00
WB	Wade Boggs	80.00
GB	George Brett	
LB	Lou Brock	60.00
BD	Bill Dickey	150.00
BDO	Bobby Doerr	100.00
HK	Harmon Killebrew	250.00
TL	Tom Lasorda	80.00
JM	Juan Marichal	75.00
EM	Eddie Mathews	150.00
DM	Don Mattingly	
JP	Jim Palmer	
KB	Kirby Puckett	250.00
NR	Nolan Ryan	300.00
MS	Mike Schmidt	250.00
RS	Red Schoendienst	80.00
DW	Dave Winfield	80.00
CY	Carl Yastrzemski	200.00
RY	Robin Yount	80.00

2001 Topps Tribute Retired Game-Worn Relics

		MT
Common Player:		20.00
Inserted 1:2		
WA	Walt Alston	20.00
EB	Ernie Banks	40.00
EBA	Ernie Banks	40.00
JB	Johnny Bench	40.00
YB	Yogi Berra	35.00
WB	Wade Boggs	25.00
GB	George Brett	50.00
LB	Lou Brock	40.00
SC	Steve Carlton	30.00
DD	Dizzy Dean	40.00
BD	Bill Dickey	20.00
BDO	Bobby Doerr	30.00
NF	Nellie Fox	35.00
HK	Harmon Killebrew	40.00
TL	Tom Lasorda	20.00
JMG	Juan Marichal	30.00
EM	Eddie Mathews	40.00
DM	Don Mattingly	65.00
WMF	Willie Mays	75.00
WMW	Willie Mays	75.00
SM	Stan Musial	75.00
JP	Jim Palmer	25.00
KP	Kirby Puckett	60.00
FR	Frank Robinson	30.00
NRA	Nolan Ryan	80.00
NRH	Nolan Ryan	80.00
NRR	Nolan Ryan	80.00
MSB	Mike Schmidt	50.00
MSW	Mike Schmidt	50.00
RS	Red Schoendienst	25.00
WST	Willie Stargell	25.00
CS	Casey Stengel	20.00
DW	Dave Winfield	25.00
CY	Carl Yastrzemski/ white	40.00
CYA	Carl Yastrzemski/ gray	40.00
RY	Robin Yount	35.00

2001 Topps Tribute Vintage Buy-Back Cards

	MT
Complete Set (3):	
Common Player:	
Mickey Mantle	
Jackie Robinson	
Ted Williams	

2002 Topps

		MT
Complete Set (719):		75.00
Complete Series I (365):		35.00
Complete Series II (354):		40.00
Common Player:		.10
Pack (10):		1.75
Box (36):		50.00
1	Pedro Martinez	.50
2	Mike Stanton	.10
3	Brad Penny	.10
4	Mike Matheny	.10
5	Johnny Damon	.10
6	Bret Boone	.10
7	not issued (retired)	.10
8	Chris Truby	.10
9	B.J. Surhoff	.10
10	Mike Hampton	.10
11	Juan Pierre	.10
12	Mark Buehrle	.10
13	Bob Abreu	.10
14	David Cone	.10
15	Aaron Sele	.10
16	Fernando Tatis	.10
17	Bobby Jones	.10
18	Rick Helling	.10
19	Dmitri Young	.10
20	Mike Mussina	.40
21	Mike Sweeney	.10
22	Cristian Guzman	.10
23	Ryan Kohlmeier	.10
24	Adam Kennedy	.10
25	Larry Walker	.40
26	Eric Davis	.10
27	Jason Tyner	.10
28	Eric Young	.10
29	Jason Marquis	.10
30	Luis Gonzalez	.40
31	Kevin Tapani	.10
32	Orlando Cabrera	.10
33	Marty Cordova	.10
34	Brad Ausmus	.10
35	Livan Hernandez	.10
36	Alex Gonzalez	.10
37	Edgar Renteria	.10
38	Bengie Molina	.10
39	Frank Menechino	.10
40	Rafael Palmeiro	.25
41	Brad Fullmer	.10
42	Julio Zuleta	.10
43	Darren Dreifort	.10
44	Trot Nixon	.10
45	Trevor Hoffman	.10
46	Vladimir Nunez	.10
47	Mark Kotsay	.10
48	Kenny Rogers	.10
49	Ben Petrick	.10
50	Jeff Bagwell	.50
51	Juan Encarnacion	.10
52	Ramiro Mendoza	.10
53	Brian Meadows	.10
54	Chad Curtis	.10
55	Aramis Ramirez	.10
56	Mark McLemore	.10
57	Dante Bichette	.10
58	Scott Schoeneweis	.10
59	Jose Cruz Jr.	.10
60	Roger Clemens	.75
61	Jose Guillen	.10
62	Darren Oliver	.10
63	Chris Reitsma	.10
64	Jeff Abbott	.10
65	Robin Ventura	.10
66	Denny Neagle	.10
67	Al Martin	.10
68	Benito Santiago	.10
69	Roy Oswalt	.20
70	Juan Gonzalez	.50
71	Garret Anderson	.10
72	Bobby Bonilla	.10
73	Danny Bautista	.10
74	J.T. Snow Jr.	.10
75	Derek Jeter	2.00
76	John Olerud	.25
77	Kevin Appier	.10
78	Phil Nevin	.20
79	Sean Casey	.20
80	Troy Glaus	.50
81	Joe Randa	.10
82	Jose Valentin	.10
83	Ricky Bottalico	.10
84	Todd Zeile	.10
85	Barry Larkin	.25
86	Bob Wickman	.10
87	Jeff Shaw	.10
88	Greg Vaughn	.10
89	Fernando Vina	.10
90	Mark Mulder	.10
91	Paul Bako	.10
92	Aaron Boone	.10
93	Esteban Loaiza	.10
94	Richie Sexson	.10
95	Alfonso Soriano	.25
96	Tony Womack	.10
97	Paul Shuey	.10
98	Melvin Mora	.10
99	Tony Gwynn	.60
100	Vladimir Guerrero	.50
101	Keith Osik	.10
102	Randy Velarde	.10
103	Scott Williamson	.10
104	Daryle Ward	.10
105	Doug Mientkiewicz	.10
106	Stan Javier	.10
107	Russ Ortiz	.10
108	Wade Miller	.10
109	Luke Prokopec	.10
110	Andruw Jones	.40
111	Ron Coomer	.10
112	Dan Wilson	.10
113	Luis Castillo	.10
114	Derek Bell	.10
115	Gary Sheffield	.20
116	Ruben Rivera	.10
117	Paul O'Neill	.20
118	Craig Paquette	.10
119	Chris Michalak	.10
120	Brad Radke	.10
121	Jorge Fabregas	.10
122	Randy Winn	.10
123	Tom Goodwin	.10
124	Jaret Wright	.10
125	Manny Ramirez	.50
126	Al Leiter	.20
127	Ben Davis	.10
128	Frank Catalanotto	.10
129	Jose Cabrera	.10
130	Magglio Ordonez	.20
131	Jose Macias	.10
132	Ted Lilly	.10
133	Chris Holt	.10
134	Eric Milton	.10
135	Shannon Stewart	.10
136	Omar Olivares	.10
137	David Segui	.10
138	Jeff Nelson	.10
139	Matt Williams	.25
140	Ellis Burks	.10
141	Jason Bere	.10
142	Jimmy Haynes	.10
143	Ramon Hernandez	.10
144	Craig Counsell (Front photo actually Greg Colbrunn)	.10
145	John Smoltz	.10
146	Homer Bush	.10
147	Quilvio Veras	.10
148	Esteban Yan	.10
149	Ramon Ortiz	.10
150	Carlos Delgado	.30
151	Lee Stevens	.10
152	Wil Cordero	.10
153	Mike Bordick	.10
154	John Flaherty	.10
155	Omar Daal	.10
156	Todd Ritchie	.10
157	Carl Everett	.10
158	Scott Sullivan	.10
159	Deivi Cruz	.10
160	Albert Pujols	1.00
161	Royce Clayton	.10

No.	Player	Price
162	Jeff Suppan	.10
163	C.C. Sabathia	.10
164	Jimmy Rollins	.10
165	Rickey Henderson	.25
166	Rey Ordonez	.10
167	Shawn Estes	.10
168	Reggie Sanders	.10
169	Jon Lieber	.10
170	Armando Benitez	.10
171	Mike Remlinger	.10
172	Billy Wagner	.10
173	Troy Percival	.10
174	Devon White	.10
175	Ivan Rodriguez	.50
176	Dustin Hermanson	.10
177	Brian Anderson	.10
178	Graeme Lloyd	.10
179	Russ Branyan	.10
180	Bobby Higginson	.10
181	Alex Gonzalez	.10
182	John Franco	.10
183	Sidney Ponson	.10
184	Jose Mesa	.10
185	Todd Hollandsworth	.10
186	Kevin Young	.10
187	Tim Wakefield	.10
188	Craig Biggio	.20
189	Jason Isringhausen	.10
190	Mark Quinn	.10
191	Glendon Rusch	.10
192	Damian Miller	.10
193	Sandy Alomar	.10
194	Scott Brosius	.10
195	Dave Martinez	.10
196	Danny Graves	.10
197	Shea Hillenbrand	.10
198	Jimmy Anderson	.10
199	Travis Lee	.10
200	Randy Johnson	.50
201	Carlos Beltran	.10
202	Jerry Hairston Jr.	.10
203	Jesus Sanchez	.10
204	Eddie Taubensee	.10
205	David Wells	.10
206	Russ Davis	.10
207	Michael Barrett	.10
208	Marquis Grissom	.10
209	Byung-Hyun Kim	.10
210	Hideo Nomo	.25
211	Ryan Rupe	.10
212	Ricky Gutierrez	.10
213	Darryl Kile	.10
214	Rico Brogna	.10
215	Terrence Long	.10
216	Mike Jackson	.10
217	Jamey Wright	.10
218	Adrian Beltre	.10
219	Benny Agbayani	.10
220	Chuck Knoblauch	.10
221	Randy Wolf	.10
222	Andy Ashby	.10
223	Corey Koskie	.10
224	Roger Cedeno	.10
225	Ichiro Suzuki	2.00
226	Keith Foulke	.10
227	Ryan Minor	.10
228	Shawon Dunston	.10
229	Alex Cora	.10
230	Jeromy Burnitz	.10
231	Mark Grace	.25
232	Aubrey Huff	.10
233	Jeffrey Hammonds	.10
234	Olmedo Saenz	.10
235	Brian Jordan	.10
236	Jeremy Giambi	.10
237	Joe Girardi	.10
238	Eric Gagne	.10
239	Masato Yoshii	.10
240	Greg Maddux	1.00
241	Bryan Rekar	.10
242	Ray Durham	.10
243	Torii Hunter	.10
244	Derrek Lee	.10
245	Jim Edmonds	.20
246	Einar Diaz	.10
247	Brian Bohanon	.10
248	Ron Belliard	.10
249	Mike Lowell	.10
250	Sammy Sosa	1.00
251	Richard Hidalgo	.10
252	Bartolo Colon	.10
253	Jorge Posada	.25
254	LaTroy Hawkins	.10
255	Paul LoDuca	.10
256	Carlos Febles	.10
257	Nelson Cruz	.10
258	Edgardo Alfonzo	.10
259	Joey Hamilton	.10
260	Cliff Floyd	.10
261	Wes Helms	.10
262	Jay Bell	.10
263	Mike Cameron	.10
264	Paul Konerko	.10
265	Jeff Kent	.10
266	Robert Fick	.10
267	Allen Levrault	.10
268	Placido Polanco	.10
269	Marlon Anderson	.10
270	Mariano Rivera	.20
271	Chan Ho Park	.10
272	Jose Vizcaino	.10
273	Jeff D'Amico	.10
274	Mark Gardner	.10
275	Travis Fryman	.10
276	Darren Lewis	.10
277	Bruce Bochy	.10
278	Jerry Manuel	.10
279	Bob Brenly	.10
280	Don Baylor	.10
281	Davey Lopes	.10
282	Jerry Narron	.10
283	Tony Muser	.10
284	Hal McRae	.10
285	Bobby Cox	.10
286	Larry Dierker	.10
287	Phil Garner	.10
288	Jimy Williams	.10
289	Bobby Valentine	.10
290	Dusty Baker	.10
291	Lloyd McClendon	.10
292	Mike Scioscia	.10
293	Buck Martinez	.10
294	Larry Bowa	.10
295	Tony LaRussa	.10
296	Jeff Torborg	.10
297	Tom Kelly	.10
298	Mike Hargrove	.10
299	Art Howe	.10
300	Lou Pinella	.10
301	Charlie Manuel	.10
302	Buddy Bell	.10
303	Tony Perez	.10
304	Bob Boone	.10
305	Joe Torre	.25
306	Jim Tracy	.10
307	Jason Lane	.10
308	Chris George	.10
309	Hank Blalock	.10
310	Joe Borchard	.10
311	Marlon Byrd	.10
312	*Raymond Cabrera*	.40
313	*Freddy Sanchez*	.40
314	*Scott Wiggins*	.40
315	*Jason Maule*	.30
316	*Dionys Cesar*	.40
317	Boof Bonser	.10
318	*Juan Tolentino*	.40
319	*Earl Snyder*	.30
320	*Travis Wade*	.30
321	*Napoleon Calzado*	.40
322	*Eric Glaser*	.40
323	*Craig Kuzmic*	.40
324	*Nic Jackson*	.50
325	Mike Rivera	.10
326	*Jason Bay*	.40
327	Chris Smith	.10
328	Jake Gautreau	.10
329	Gabe Gross	.10
330	Kenny Baugh	.10
331	J.D. Martin	.10
332	Barry Bonds	.75
333	Rickey Henderson	.25
334	Bud Smith	.25
335	Rickey Henderson	.25
336	Barry Bonds	.50
337	Ichiro Suzuki, Jason Giambi, Roberto Alomar	.50
338	Alex Rodriguez, Ichiro Suzuki, Bret Boone	.50
339	Alex Rodriguez, Jim Thome, Rafael Palmeiro	.40
340	Bret Boone, Juan Gonzalez, Alex Rodriguez	.40
341	Freddy Garcia, Mike Mussina, Joe Mays	.15
342	Hideo Nomo, Mike Mussina, Roger Clemens	.40
343	Larry Walker, Todd Helton, Moises Alou	.25
344	Sammy Sosa, Todd Helton, Barry Bonds	.40
345	Barry Bonds, Sammy Sosa, Luis Gonzalez	.40
346	Sammy Sosa, Todd Helton, Luis Gonzalez	.40
347	Curt Schilling, Randy Johnson, John Burkett	.20
348	Randy Johnson, Curt Schilling, Chan Ho Park	.20
349	Seattle Mariners	.25
350	Oakland A's	.10
351	New York Yankees	.50
352	Cleveland Indians	.10
353	Arizona Diamondbacks	.10
354	Atlanta Braves	.10
355	St. Louis Cardinals	.10
356	Houston Astros	.10
357	D'Backs vs Rockies	.10
358	Mets vs. Pirates	.10
359	Braves vs. Phillies	.10
360	D'Backs vs. Rockies	.10
361	Yankees vs. White Sox	.10
362	Cubs vs. Reds	.10
363	Angels vs. Mariners	.10
364	Astros vs. Giants	.10
365	Barry Bonds Race to 70 #1	15.00
365	Barry Bonds HR #2-69	8.00
365	Barry Bonds HR #70	12.00
365	Barry Bonds HR #71	15.00
365	Barry Bonds HR #72	12.00
365	Barry Bonds HR #73	60.00
366	Pat Meares	.10
367	Mike Lieberthal	.10
368	Scott Erickson	.10
369	Ron Gant	.10
370	Moises Alou	.15
371	Chad Kreuter	.10
372	Willis Roberts	.10
373	Toby Hall	.10
374	Miguel Batista	.10
375	John Burkett	.10
376	Cory Lidle	.10
377	Nick Neugebauer	.10
378	Jay Payton	.10
379	Steve Karsay	.10
380	Eric Chavez	.20
381	Kelly Stinnett	.10
382	Jarrod Washburn	.10
383	C.J. Nitkowski	.10
384	Jeff Conine	.10
385	Fred McGriff	.10
386	Marvin Benard	.10
387	Dave Burba	.10
388	Dennis Cook	.10
389	Rick Reed	.10
390	Tom Glavine	.25
391	Rondell White	.15
392	Matt Morris	.20
393	Pat Rapp	.10
394	Robert Person	.10
395	Omar Vizquel	.15
396	Jeff Cirillo	.10
397	Dave Mlicki	.10
398	Jose Ortiz	.10
399	Ryan Dempster	.10
400	Curt Schilling	.20
401	Peter Bergeron	.10
402	Kyle Lohse	.10
403	Craig Wilson	.10
404	David Justice	.20
405	Darin Erstad	.20
406	Jose Mercedes	.10
407	Carl Pavano	.10
408	Albie Lopez	.10
409	Alex Ochoa	.10
410	Chipper Jones	1.00
411	Tyler Houston	.10
412	Dean Palmer	.10
413	Damian Jackson	.10
414	Josh Towers	.10
415	Rafael Furcal	.10
416	Ken Caminiti	.10
417	Herb Perry	.10
418	Mike Sirotka	.10
419	Mark Wohlers	.10
420	Nomar Garciaparra	1.00
421	Felipe Lopez	.10
422	Joe McEwing	.10
423	Jacque Jones	.10
424	Julio Franco	.10
425	Frank Thomas	.60
426	*So Taguchi*	2.50
427	*Kazuhisa Ishii*	5.00
428	D'Angelo Jimenez	.10
429	Chris Stynes	.10
430	Kerry Wood	.25
431	Chris Singleton	.10
432	Erubiel Durazo	.10
433	Matt Lawton	.10
434	Bill Mueller	.10
435	Jose Canseco	.25
436	Ben Grieve	.15
437	Terry Mulholland	.10
438	David Bell	.10
439	A.J. Pierzynski	.10
440	Adam Dunn	.50
441	Jon Garland	.10
442	Jeff Fassero	.10
443	Julio Lugo	.10
444	Carlos Guillen	.10
445	Orlando Hernandez	.20
446	Mark Loretta	.10
447	Scott Spiezio	.10
448	Kevin Millwood	.10
449	Jamie Moyer	.10
450	Todd Helton	.50
451	Todd Walker	.10
452	Jose Lima	.10
453	Brook Fordyce	.10
454	Aaron Rowand	.10
455	Barry Zito	.15
456	Eric Owens	.10
457	Charles Nagy	.10
458	Raul Ibanez	.10
459	Joe Mays	.10
460	Jim Thome	.25
461	Adam Eaton	.10
462	Felix Martinez	.10
463	Vernon Wells	.10
464	Donnie Sadler	.10
465	Tony Clark	.10
466	Jose Hernandez	.10
467	Ramon Martinez	.10
468	Rusty Greer	.10
469	Rod Barajas	.10
470	Lance Berkman	.25
471	Brady Anderson	.10
472	Pedro Astacio	.10
473	Shane Halter	.10
474	Bret Prinz	.10
475	Edgar Martinez	.10
476	Steve Trachsel	.10
477	Gary Matthews Jr.	.10
478	Ismael Valdes	.10
479	Juan Uribe	.10
480	Shawn Green	.20
481	Kirk Rueter	.10
482	Damion Easley	.10
483	Chris Carpenter	.10
484	Kris Benson	.10
485	Antonio Alfonseca	.10
486	Kyle Farnsworth	.10
487	Brandon Lyon	.10
488	Hideki Irabu	.10
489	David Ortiz	.10
490	Mike Piazza	1.50
491	Derek Lowe	.10
492	Chris Gomez	.10
493	Mark Johnson	.10
494	John Rocker	.10
495	Eric Karros	.10
496	Bill Haselman	.10
497	Dave Veres	.10
498	Gil Heredia	.10
499	Tomokazu Ohka	.10
500	Barry Bonds	1.00
501	David Dellucci	.10
502	Ed Sprague	.10
503	Tom Gordon	.10
504	Javier Vazquez	.10
505	Ben Sheets	.20
506	Wilton Guerrero	.10
507	John Halama	.10
508	Mark Redman	.10
509	Jack Wilson	.10
510	Bernie Williams	.40
511	Miguel Cairo	.10
512	Denny Hocking	.10
513	Tony Batista	.10
514	Mark Grudzielanek	.10

No.	Player	Price
515	Jose Vidro	.10
516	Sterling Hitchcock	.10
517	Billy Koch	.10
518	Matt Clement	.10
519	Bruce Chen	.10
520	Roberto Alomar	.40
521	Orlando Palmeiro	.10
522	Steve Finley	.10
523	Danny Patterson	.10
524	Terry Adams	.10
525	Tino Martinez	.10
526	Tony Armas Jr.	.10
527	Geoff Jenkins	.15
528	Chris Michalak	.10
529	Corey Patterson	.20
530	Brian Giles	.15
531	Jose Jimenez	.10
532	Joe Kennedy	.10
533	Armando Rios	.10
534	Osvaldo Fernandez	.10
535	Ruben Sierra	.10
536	Octavio Dotel	.10
537	Luis Sojo	.10
538	Brent Butler	.10
539	Pablo Ozuna	.10
540	Freddy Garcia	.10
541	Chad Durbin	.10
542	Orlando Merced	.10
543	Michael Tucker	.10
544	Roberto Hernandez	.10
545	Pat Burrell	.20
546	A.J. Burnett	.10
547	Bubba Trammell	.10
548	Scott Elarton	.10
549	Mike Darr	.10
550	Ken Griffey Jr.	1.50
551	Ugueth Urbina	.10
552	Todd Jones	.10
553	Delino DeShields	.10
554	Adam Piatt	.10
555	Jason Kendall	.10
556	Hector Ortiz	.10
557	Turk Wendell	.10
558	Rob Bell	.10
559	Sun-Woo Kim	.10
560	Raul Mondesi	.15
561	Brent Abernathy	.10
562	Seth Etherton	.10
563	Shawn Wooten	.10
564	Jay Buhner	.10
565	Andres Galarraga	.10
566	Shane Reynolds	.10
567	Rod Beck	.10
568	Dee Brown	.10
569	Pedro Feliz	.10
570	Ryan Klesko	.10
571	John Vander Wal	.10
572	Nick Bierbrodt	.10
573	Joe Nathan	.10
574	James Baldwin	.10
575	J.D. Drew	.20
576	Greg Colbrunn	.10
577	Doug Glanville	.10
578	Rey Sanchez	.10
579	Todd Van Poppel	.10
580	Rich Aurilia	.10
581	Chuck Finley	.10
582	Abraham Nunez	.10
583	Kenny Lofton	.10
584	Brian Daubach	.10
585	Miguel Tejada	.15
586	Nate Cornejo	.10
587	Kazuhiro Sasaki	.10
588	Chris Richard	.10
589	Armando Reynoso	.10
590	Tim Hudson	.20
591	Neifi Perez	.10
592	Steve Cox	.10
593	Henry Blanco	.10
594	Ricky Ledee	.10
595	Tim Salmon	.15
596	Luis Rivas	.10
597	Jeff Zimmerman	.10
598	Matt Stairs	.10
599	Preston Wilson	.10
600	Mark McGwire	1.50
601	Timo Perez	.10
602	Matt Anderson	.10
603	Todd Hundley	.10
604	Rick Ankiel	.10
605	Tsuyoshi Shinjo	.10
606	Woody Williams	.10
607	Jason LaRue	.10
608	Carlos Lee	.10
609	Russ Johnson	.10
610	Scott Rolen	.25
611	Brent Mayne	.10
612	Darrin Fletcher	.10
613	Ray Lankford	.10
614	Troy O'Leary	.10
615	Javier Lopez	.10
616	Randy Velarde	.10
617	Vinny Castilla	.10
618	Milton Bradley	.10
619	Ruben Mateo	.10
620	Jason Giambi	.50
621	Andy Benes	.10
622	Tony Eusebio	.10
623	Andy Pettitte	.20
624	Jose Offerman	.10
625	Mo Vaughn	.20
626	Steve Sparks	.10
627	Mike Matthews	.10
628	Robb Nen	.10
629	Kip Wells	.10
630	Kevin Brown	.10
631	Arthur Rhodes	.10
632	Gabe Kapler	.10
633	Jermaine Dye	.10
634	Josh Beckett	.20
635	Pokey Reese	.10
636	Benji Gil	.10
637	Marcus Giles	.10
638	Julian Tavarez	.10
639	Jason Schmidt	.10
640	Alex Rodriguez	1.25
641	Anaheim Angels	.10
642	Arizona Diamondbacks	.10
643	Atlanta Braves	.10
644	Baltimore Orioles	.10
645	Boston Red Sox	.10
646	Chicago Cubs	.10
647	Chicago White Sox	.10
648	Cincinnati Reds	.10
649	Cleveland Indians	.10
650	Colorado Rockies	.10
651	Detroit Tigers	.10
652	Florida Marlins	.10
653	Houston Astros	.10
654	Kansas City Royals	.10
655	Los Angeles Dodgers	.10
656	Milwaukee Brewers	.10
657	Minnesota Twins	.10
658	Montreal Expos	.10
659	New York Mets	.10
660	New York Yankees	.10
661	Oakland Athletics	.10
662	Philadelphia Phillies	.10
663	Pittsburgh Pirates	.10
664	San Diego Padres	.10
665	San Francisco Giants	.10
666	Seattle Mariners	.10
667	St. Louis Cardinals	.10
668	Tampa Bay Devil Rays	.10
669	Texas Rangers	.10
670	Toronto Blue Jays	.10
671	Juan Cruz	.25
672	*Kevin Cash*	.75
673	*Jimmy Gobble*	2.00
674	*Mike Hill*	1.50
675	*Taylor Buchholz*	1.00
676	Bill Hall	.10
677	*Brett Roneberg*	1.00
678	*Royce Huffman*	.50
679	*Chris Tritle*	2.00
680	*Nate Espy*	1.00
681	*Nick Alvarez*	.50
682	*Jason Botts*	2.00
683	*Ryan Gripp*	1.00
684	*Dan Phillips*	.50
685	*Pablo Arias*	.50
686	*John Rodriguez*	1.50
687	*James Harden*	.50
688	*Neal Frendling*	.50
689	*Rich Thompson*	.75
690	*Greg Montalbano*	.50
691	*Leonard Dinardo*	.75
692	*Ryan Raburn*	.50
693	Josh Barfield	.25
694	*David Bacani*	1.00
695	*Dan Johnson*	.50
696	Mike Mussina (Gold Glove Award Winners)	.25
697	Ivan Rodriguez (Gold Glove Award Winners)	.25
698	Doug Mientkiewicz (Gold Glove Award Winners)	.10
699	Roberto Alomar (Gold Glove Award Winners)	.25
700	Eric Chavez (Gold Glove Award Winners)	.15
701	Omar Vizquel (Gold Glove Award Winners)	.10
702	Mike Cameron (Gold Glove Award Winners)	.10
703	Torii Hunter (Gold Glove Award Winners)	.10
704	Ichiro Suzuki (Gold Glove Award Winners)	1.00
705	Greg Maddux (Gold Glove Award Winners)	.50
706	Brad Ausmus (Gold Glove Award Winners)	.10
707	Todd Helton (Gold Glove Award Winners)	.25
708	Fernando Vina (Gold Glove Award Winners)	.10
709	Scott Rolen (Gold Glove Award Winners)	.20
710	Orlando Cabrera (Gold Glove Award Winners)	.10
711	Andruw Jones (Gold Glove Award Winners)	.15
712	Jim Edmonds (Gold Glove Award Winners)	.10
713	Larry Walker (Gold Glove Award Winners)	.15
714	Roger Clemens (Cy Young Award Winners)	.40
715	Randy Johnson (Cy Young Award Winners)	.25
716	Ichiro Suzuki (MVP Award Winners)	1.00
717	Barry Bonds (MVP Award Winners)	.50
718	Ichiro Suzuki (ROY Award Winners)	1.00
719	Albert Pujols (ROY Award Winners)	.50

2002 Topps Gold

	MT
Stars:	6-12X
Production 2,002 sets	

2002 Topps Aces

		MT
Common Player:		10.00
Inserted 1:1,180		
MH	Mike Hampton	10.00
RJ	Randy Johnson	30.00
GM	Greg Maddux	30.00
PM	Pedro Martinez	35.00
MM	Mark Mulder	25.00

2002 Topps All-World Team

		MT
Complete Set (25):		35.00
Common Player:		.50
AW-1	Ichiro Suzuki	6.00
AW-2	Barry Bonds	3.00
AW-3	Pedro Martinez	1.50
AW-4	Juan Gonzalez	1.50
AW-5	Larry Walker	.75
AW-6	Sammy Sosa	3.00
AW-7	Mariano Rivera	.75
AW-8	Vladimir Guerrero	1.50
AW-9	Alex Rodriguez	4.00
AW-10	Albert Pujols	3.00
AW-11	Luis Gonzalez	1.00
AW-12	Ken Griffey Jr.	4.00
AW-13	Kazuhiro Sasaki	.50
AW-14	Bob Abreu	.50
AW-15	Todd Helton	1.50
AW-16	Nomar Garciaparra	3.00
AW-17	Miguel Tejada	.75
AW-18	Roger Clemens	2.00
AW-19	Mike Piazza	4.00
AW-20	Carlos Delgado	1.00
AW-21	Derek Jeter	6.00
AW-22	Hideo Nomo	1.00
AW-23	Randy Johnson	1.50
AW-24	Ivan Rodriguez	1.00
AW-25	Chan Ho Park	.50

2002 Topps Autographs

		MT
Common Player:		10.00
TA1	Carlos Delgado	40.00
TA2	Ivan Rodriguez	50.00
TA3	Miguel Tejada	25.00
TA4	Geoff Jenkins	40.00
TA5	Johnny Damon	
TA6	Tim Hudson	30.00
TA7	Terrence Long	20.00
TA8	Gabe Kapler	15.00
TA9	Magglio Ordonez	20.00
TA10	Barry Bonds	
TA11	Pat Burrell	25.00
TA12	Mike Mussina	40.00
TA13	Eric Valent	10.00
TA14	Xavier Nady	15.00
TA15	Cristian Guerrero	10.00
TA16	Ben Sheets	20.00
TA17	Corey Patterson	
TA18	Carlos Pena	15.00
TA19	Alex Rodriguez	100.00
Series 2		
TA-AB	Adrian Beltre	25.00
TA-RC	Roger Clemens	
TA-JD	Jermaine Dye	30.00
TA-JE	Jim Edmonds	
TA-AE	Alex Escobar	15.00
TA-CF	Cliff Floyd	25.00
TA-RF	Rafael Furcal	25.00
TA-JG	Jason Giambi	
TA-BG	Brian Giles	30.00
TA-KG	Keith Ginter	15.00
TA-TG	Troy Glaus	40.00
TA-BGR	Ben Grieve	30.00
TA-CG	Cristian Guzman	15.00
TA-JH	Josh Hamilton	20.00
TA-NJ	Nick Johnson	30.00
TA-RK	Ryan Klesko	35.00
TA-JO	Jose Ortiz	25.00

TA-RORoy Oswalt 30.00
TA-RPRafael Palmeiro 80.00
TA-ARAlex Rodriguez 80.00
TA-JRJimmy Rollins 20.00
TA-RSRichie Sexson 30.00
TA-ASAlfonso Soriano
TA-MSMike Sweeney 30.00
TA-FTFernando Tatis
TA-JWJustin Wayne 35.00
TA-VWVernon Wells
TA-BWBrad Wilkerson 15.00
TA-BZBarry Zito

2002 Topps Battery Mates Relic

MT
Complete Set (2):
Common Card: 30.00
Inserted 1:4,401
ML Greg Maddux, Javy Lopez 30.00
LP Al Leiter, Mike Piazza 50.00

2002 Topps Dual Ebbets/Yankee Autographed Seat Relic

MT
Complete Set (1):
EFYSARPPhil Rizzuto, Andy Pafko

2002 Topps Dueces Are Wild

MT
Common Card:
Inserted 1:1,962
JG Randy Johnson, Luis Gonzalez 40.00
BK Barry Bonds, Jeff Kent 40.00
TA Jim Thome, Roberto Alomar 35.00
WH Larry Walker, Todd Helton 35.00
BG Bret Boone, Freddy Garcia 20.00

2002 Topps East Meets West

MT
Complete Set (8):
Common Player: 1.00
Inserted 1:24
EW-HNHideo Nomo, Masanori Murakami 3.00
EW-HIHideki Irabu, Masanori Murakami 1.00
EW-SHShigetoshi Hasegawa, Masanori Murakami 1.00
EW-MYMasato Yoshii, Masanori Murakami 1.00
EW-TSTsuyoshi Shinjo, Masanori Murakami 5.00
EW-KSKazuhiro Sasaki, Masanori Murakami 1.00
EW-MSMac Suzuki, Masanori Murakami 1.00
EW-TOTomo Ohka, Masanori Murakami 1.00

2002 Topps East Meets West Relics

MT
Complete Set (3):
Common Player: 20.00
Inserted 1:3,419
HN Hideo Nomo 40.00
KS Kazuhiro Sasaki 20.00
TS Tsuyoshi Shinjo 25.00

2002 Topps Ebbets Field Seat Relics

MT
Common Player: 25.00
Inserted 1:9,116
JB Joe Black 75.00
RC Roy Campanella
BC Billy Cox 30.00
CF Carl Furillo
GH Gil Hodges
AP Andy Pafko 80.00
PWR Pee Wee Reese 50.00
JR Jackie Robinson 150.00
DS Duke Snider 75.00

2002 Topps Hall of Fame Vintage BuyBacks AutoProofs

MT
Complete Set (19):
Common Player:
BR16Brooks Robinson 82 KM/200
EW10Earl Weaver 87/100
FJ33 Fergie Jenkins 84/100
GP26Gaylord Perry 82/100
GP29Gaylord Perry 83/100
GP30Gaylord Perry 83 SV/200
OC1 Orlando Cepeda 82 KM/200
RF15Rollie Fingers 81/300
RF16Rollie Fingers 81 LL/100
RF18Rollie Fingers 82/100
RF19Rollie Fingers 82 IA/200
RF21Rollie Fingers 82 KM/300
RF22Rollie Fingers 83/200
RF24Rollie Fingers 84/200
RF27Rollie Fingers 85/300
RF28Rollie Fingers 86/100
SC5 Steve Carlton 84 LL/100
SC6 Steve Carlton 85/200
SC8 Steve Carlton 87/200

2002 Topps Heart of the Order Relic

MT
Complete Set (4):
Common Card:
Inserted 1:4,247
KBA Jeff Kent, Barry Bonds, Rich Aurilia
TGA Jim Thome, Juan Gonzalez, Roberto Alomar 50.00
ARB Bob Abreu, Scott Rolen, Pat Burrell
OWMPaul O'Neill, Bernie Williams, Tino Martinez 50.00

2002 Topps Hit and Run Relic

MT
Complete Set (3):
Common Player: 15.00
Inserted 1:4,241
JD Johnny Damon
DE Darin Erstad 20.00
RF Rafael Furcal 15.00

2002 Topps Hobby Masters

MT
Complete Set (20): 60.00
Common Player: 1.50
Inserted 1:25
1 Mark McGwire 6.00
2 Derek Jeter 8.00
3 Chipper Jones 5.00
4 Roger Clemens 3.00
5 Vladimir Guerrero 2.50
6 Ichiro Suzuki 10.00
7 Todd Helton 2.50
8 Alex Rodriguez 6.00
9 Albert Pujols 4.00
10 Sammy Sosa 5.00
11 Ken Griffey Jr. 6.00
12 Randy Johnson 2.50
13 Nomar Garciaparra 6.00
14 Ivan Rodriguez 2.50
15 Manny Ramirez 2.50
16 Barry Bonds 4.00
17 Mike Piazza 6.00
18 Pedro Martinez 3.00
19 Jeff Bagwell 2.50
20 Luis Gonzalez 2.00

2002 Topps Jack of All Trades

MT
Inserted 1:1,350
RO Roberto Alomar/bat 30.00
BB Barry Bonds/jsy 35.00
AJ Andruw Jones/jsy 25.00
IR Ivan Rodriguez/jsy 15.00
BW Bernie Williams/jsy 20.00

2002 Topps Kings of the Clubhouse

MT
Common Player: 10.00
Inserted 1:1,449 Ser. 2
TG Tom Glavine/jsy 20.00
TH Todd Helton/jsy 15.00
RJ Randy Johnson/jsy 20.00
EM Edgar Martinez/jsy 10.00
PO Paul O'Neill/bat 35.00

2002 Topps Own The Game

MT
Complete Set (30): 40.00
Common Player: .75
Inserted 1:12
OG1 Moises Alou .75
OG2 Roberto Alomar 1.50
OG3 Luis Gonzalez 1.50
OG4 Bret Boone .75
OG5 Barry Bonds 4.00
OG6 Jim Thome 1.00
OG7 Jimmy Rollins .75
OG8 Cristian Guzman .75
OG9 Lance Berkman 1.00
OG10Mike Sweeney .75
OG11Rich Aurilia .75
OG12Ichiro Suzuki 8.00
OG13Luis Gonzalez 1.50
OG14Ichiro Suzuki 8.00
OG15Jimmy Rollins .75
OG16Roger Cedeno .75
OG17Barry Bonds 4.00
OG18Jim Thome 1.00
OG19Curt Schilling 1.00
OG20Roger Clemens 3.00
OG21Curt Schilling 1.00
OG22Brad Radke .75
OG23Greg Maddux 4.00
OG24Mark Mulder .75
OG25Jeff Shaw .75
OG26Mariano Rivera 1.00
OG27Randy Johnson 2.00
OG28Pedro Martinez 2.00
OG29John Burkett .75
OG30Tim Hudson 1.00

2002 Topps Pine Tar Series

MT
Common Player:
Inserted 1:4,420
BB Barry Bonds
LG Luis Gonzalez 50.00
TG Tony Gwynn
TH Todd Helton 25.00
AP Albert Pujols 40.00
Series 2
Inserted 1:1,043
Trademark Series: 1.5-2X
Inserted 1:2,087 Ser. 2
Prime Cuts: 2-4X
Inserted 1:7,824 Ser. 2
WB Wilson Betemit 30.00
SB Sean Burroughs 40.00
JC Joe Crede 20.00
AD Adam Dunn 50.00
AE Alex Escobar 20.00
MG Marcus Giles 35.00
AG Alexis Gomez
TH Toby Hall 25.00
JH Josh Hamilton 25.00
NJ Nick Johnson 45.00
XN Xavier Nady 30.00
CP Corey Patterson 40.00
CPE Carlos Pena 35.00
AR Aaron Rowand 25.00
RS Ruben Salazar 20.00

2002 Topps Prime Cuts Series

MT
Complete Set (8):
Common Player:
PCA-SBSean Burroughs
PCA-JCJoe Crede
PCA-ADAdam Dunn
PCA-MGMarcus Giles
PCA-AGAlexis Gomez
PCA-CPCorey Patterson
PCA-ARAaron Rowand
PCA-RSRuben Salazar

2002 Topps Prime Cuts Autograph Series

MT
Complete Set (7):
Common Player:
PCA-WBWilson Betemit
PCA-AEAlex Escobar
PCA-THToby Hall
PCA-JHJosh Hamilton
PCA-NJNick Johnson
PCA-XNXavier Nady
PCA-CPECarlos Pena

2002 Topps Prime Cuts Bat Relics Signature

MT
Complete Set (5):
Common Player:
PCA-BBBarry Bonds
PCA-LGLuis Gonzalez
PCA-TGTony Gwynn
PCA-THTodd Helton
PCA-APAlbert Pujols

2002 Topps Ring Masters

MT
Complete Set (10): 20.00
Common Player: 1.00
Inserted 1:25
1 Derek Jeter 6.00
2 Mark McGwire 5.00
3 Mariano Rivera 1.00
4 Gary Sheffield 1.00
5 Al Leiter 1.00
6 Chipper Jones 4.00
7 Roger Clemens 3.00
8 Greg Maddux 4.00
9 Roberto Alomar 1.50
10 Paul O'Neill 1.00

2002 Topps Team Topps Legends Autographs

MT
Common Player: 25.00
TT6RWhitey Ford 60.00

TT8R Bob Gibson 40.00
TT47R Frank Howard 25.00
TT48F Bobby Richardson
TT46F Robin Roberts 25.00
TT13F Warren Spahn 40.00

2002 Topps Three of a Kind

MT

Common Card:
Inserted 1:2,039

SPA Tsuyoshi Shinjo, Mike Piazza, Edgardo Alfonzo 50.00
LOC Carlos Lee, Magglio Ordonez, Jose Canseco 50.00
FBJ Rafael Furcal, Wilson Betemit, Andruw Jones 40.00
PSW Jorge Posada, Alfonso Soriano, Bernie Williams 70.00
BDB A.J. Burnett, Ryan Dempster, Josh Beckett 40.00

2002 Topps Turn Two Relic

MT

Complete Set (2):
Common Card: 40.00

TW Alan Trammell, Lou Whitaker 50.00
VA Omar Vizquel, Roberto Alomar 40.00

2002 Topps Yankee Stadium Seat Relics

MT

Complete Set (9):
Common Player:

YSR-HB Hank Bauer
YSR-YB Yogi Berra
YSR-JC Joe Collins
YSR-BM Billy Martin
YSR-GM Gil McDougald
YSR-JM Johnny Mize
YSR-AR Allie Reynolds
YSR-PR Phil Rizzuto
YSR-GW Gene Woodling

2002 Topps 1952 World Series Tribute

MT

Complete Set (21): 65.00
Common Player: 3.00
Inserted 1:25

1 Roy Campanella 6.00
2 Duke Snider 6.00
3 Carl Erskine 3.00
4 Andy Pafko 3.00
5 Joe Black 3.00
6 George Shuba 3.00
7 Johnny Mize 4.00
8 Billy Martin 5.00
9 Phil Rizzuto 5.00
10 Gil McDougal 3.00
11 Allie Reynolds 3.00
12 Ed Lopat 3.00

Series 2

52R-10 Jackie Robinson 8.00
52R-11 Pee Wee Reese 4.00
52R-12 Billy Loes 3.00
52R-13 Preacher Roe 3.00
52R-14 Gil Hodges 3.00
52R-15 Billy Cox 3.00
52R-16 Yogi Berra 5.00
52R-17 Gene Woodling 3.00
52R-18 Jerry Sain 3.00
52R-19 Ralph Houk 3.00
52R-20 Joe Collins 3.00
52R-21 Hank Bauer 3.00

2002 Topps 1952 Reprint Autographs

MT

Common Autograph: 25.00
Inserted 1:10,268

JBA Joe Black 90.00
CEA Carl Erskine 35.00
GMA Gil McDougal 30.00
APA Andy Pafko
PRA Phil Rizzuto
DSA Duke Snider 100.00

2002 Topps 1952 World Series Highlights

MT

Complete Set (7): 12.00
Common Player: 2.00
Inserted 1:25

52WS-1 Dodgers' Game 1 Starting Line Up 4.00
52WS-2 Dodgers Celebrate Game 3 Win! 3.00
52WS-3 Carl Erskine Wins Game 5 2.00

Series 2

52WS-2 Game 2 2.00
52WS-4 Game 4 2.00
52WS-6 Game 6 2.00
52WS-7 Game 7 2.00

2002 Topps 1952 Player Autographs

MT

Inserted 1:7,524

HBA Hank Bauer 75.00
YBA Yogi Berra 150.00
RHA Ralph Houk
BLA Billy Loes
PRA Preacher Roe 70.00
JSA Johnny Sain

2002 Topps 2 Bagger Relic

MT

Complete Set (4):
Common Player: 15.00
Inserted 1:3,733

TG Tony Gwynn 30.00
TH Todd Helton 20.00
CR Cal Ripken Jr.
SR Scott Rolen 15.00

2002 Topps American Pie Spirit of America

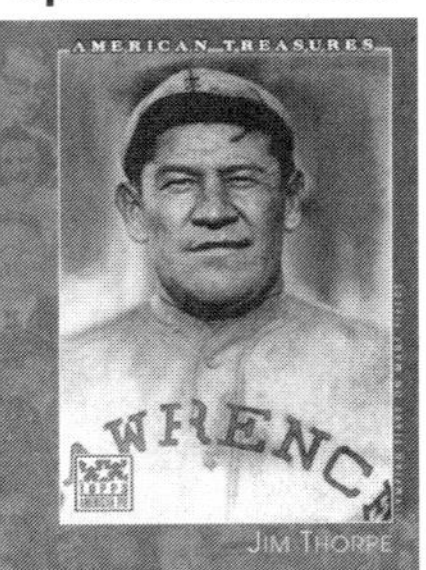

MT

Complete Set (150): 30.00
Common Player: .25
Pack (7): 3.00
Box (24): 65.00

1 Warren Spahn .75
2 Reggie Jackson .75
3 Bill Mazeroski .25
4 Carl Yastrzemski .75
5 Whitey Ford .75
6 Ralph Houk .25
7 Rod Carew .50
8 Kirk Gibson .25
9 Bobby Thomson .25
10 Don Newcombe .25
11 Gaylord Perry .25
12 Bruce Sutter .25
13 Bob Gibson .50
14 Brooks Robinson 1.00
15 Steve Carlton .50
16 Robin Yount 1.00
17 Ernie Banks .75
18 Lou Brock .25
19 Al Kaline .75
20 Carlton Fisk .75
21 Frank Robinson .75
22 Bobby Bonds .25
23 Andre Dawson .25
24 Rich "Goose" Gossage .25
25 Fred Lynn .25
26 Keith Hernandez .25
27 Rollie Fingers .25
28 Juan Marichal .25
29 Maury Wills .25
30 Dave Winfield .50
31 Frank Howard .25
32 Tony Gwynn 1.50
33 Jim Palmer .50
34 Mike Schmidt 1.50
35 Bo Jackson .75
36 Ferguson Jenkins .25
37 Bobby Richardson .25
38 Harmon Killebrew .75
39 Monte Irvin .25
40 Jim Abbott .50
41 Wade Boggs .75
42 Jackie Robinson 2.00
43 Ralph Branca .25
44 Minnie Minoso .25
45 Tug McGraw .25
46 Willie Mays 2.00
47 Nolan Ryan 3.00
48 Duke Snider 1.00
49 Tom Seaver 1.00
50 Casey Stengel .50
51 D-Day .75
52 Gulf War .25
53 Vietnam War .25
54 Korean War .25
55 Secret Service .25
56 Crayons .25
57 Hoover Dam .25
58 Penicillin .25
59 Polio Vaccine .25
60 Empire State Building .25
61 Television .25
62 Free Speech .25
63 Voyager Mission .25
64 Space Shuttle .25
65 Ellis Island .25
66 Statue of Liberty .25
67 Battle of the Bulge .25
68 Battle of Midway .25
69 Iwo Jima .25
70 Panama Canal .25
71 Spirit of St. Louis/ Lindbergh .25
72 Civil Rights/We Shall Overcome .25
73 Space Race .25
74 Alaska Pipeline .25
75 Teddy Bear .25
76 Sea Biscuit .25
77 Bazooka Joe .25
78 Mt. Rushmore .25
79 Yellowstone Park .25
80 Niagara Falls .25
81 Grand Canyon .25
82 Hoola Hoop .25
83 George Patton .50
84 Audie Murphy .25
85 Amelia Earhart .25
86 Glen Miller .25
87 Rick Monday .25
88 Buzz Aldrin .25
89 Rosa Parks .25
90 Edward R. Murrow .25
91 Susan B. Anthony .25
92 Bobby Kennedy .25
93 Gloria Steinem .25
94 Hank Greenberg .75
95 Jimmy Doolittle .25
96 Thurgood Marshall .25
97 Ernest Hemingway .75
98 Henry Ford .25
99 Wright Brothers .25
100 Thomas Edison .75
101 Albert Einstein .75
102 Will Rogers .25
103 George Gershwin .25
104 Irving Berlin .25
105 Frank Lloyd Wright .25
106 Howard Hughes .25
107 George M. Cohan .25
108 Jack Kerouac .25
109 Harry Houdini .25
110 Helen Keller .25
111 John McCain .25
112 Andrew Carnegie .25
113 Sandra Day O'Connor .25
114 Brooklyn Bridge .25
115 Douglas MacArthur .25
116 Elvis Presley 1.00
117 George Burns .25
118 Judy Garland .50
119 Buddy Holly .25
120 Don McLean .25
121 Marilyn Monroe 1.00
122 Humphrey Bogart .50
123 Gary Cooper .25
124 The Andrews Sisters .25
125 Jim Thorpe 1.00
126 Joe Louis .75
127 Jesse Owens .50
128 Kate Smith .25
129 W.C. Fields .25
130 Bette Davis .25
131 Jayne Mansfield .25
132 Teddy Roosevelt .50
133 Franklin D. Roosevelt .75
134 Harry Truman .25
135 Dwight Eisenhower .50
136 George H. W. Bush .50
137 George W. Bush .50
138 John F. Kennedy 1.00
139 Lyndon B. Johnson .25
140 William Taft .25
141 Horace Harding .25
142 Woodrow Wilson .25
143 Richard Nixon .25
144 Bill Clinton .25
145 Jimmy Carter .25
146 Herbert Hoover .25
147 Gerald Ford .25
148 Ronald Reagan .25
149 Calvin Coolidge .25
150 William McKinley .25

2002 Topps American Pie Piece of American Pie

		MT
Common Card:		25.00
Inserted 1:119		
HB	Humphrey Bogart	90.00
GB	George Burns	50.00
GC	Gary Cooper	50.00
JD	Judy Garland	65.00
MM	Marilyn Monroe	200.00
EP	Elvis Presley/ shirt	100.00
EP2	Elvis Presley/ coat	100.00
RR	Ronald Reagan/ Berlin Wall	25.00
JM	Jayne Mansfield	65.00
BD	Bette Davis	60.00

2002 Topps American Pie Pres. First Pitch Relics

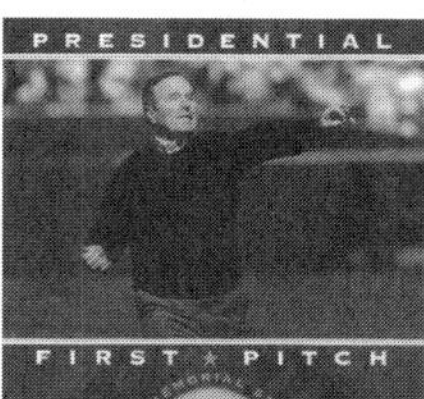

		MT
Common Player:		15.00
Inserted 1:32		
GHWB	George H. W. Bush	25.00
GWB	George W. Bush	25.00
BC	Bill Clinton	40.00
CC	Calvin Coolidge	15.00
DE	Dwight Eisenhower	25.00
GF	Gerald Ford	25.00
WH	Warren Harding	15.00
HH	Herbert Hoover	20.00
LBJ	Lyndon B. Johnson	15.00
JFK	John F. Kennedy	35.00
RN	Richard Nixon	30.00
RR	Ronald Reagan	30.00
FDR	Franklin D. Roosevelt	15.00
WT	William Taft	20.00
HT	Harry Truman	20.00
WW	Woodrow Wilson	15.00

2002 Topps American Pie Through the Years Relics

		MT
Common Player:		8.00
Inserted 1:11		
JA	Jim Abbott	15.00
DA	Dick Allen	10.00
JB	Johnny Bench	20.00
WB	Wade Boggs	10.00
BB	Bill Buckner	8.00
JC	Jack Clark	8.00
AD	Andre Dawson	12.00
KT	Jim Kaat	10.00
EM	Eddie Mathews	15.00
DM	Don Mattingly	40.00
WM	Willie Mays	40.00
MM	Minnie Minoso	15.00
RM	Rick Monday	12.00
JM	Joe Morgan	10.00
TM	Thurman Munson	40.00
AL	Al Oliver	8.00
DP	Dave Parker	10.00
GP	Gaylord Perry	10.00
FR	Frank Robinson	15.00
JR	Joe Rudi	10.00
NR	Nolan Ryan	40.00
TS	Tom Seaver	15.00
WS	Willie Stargell	15.00
DS	Darryl Strawberry	15.00
DW	Dave Winfield	12.00
CY	Carl Yastrzemski	20.00

2002 Topps Archives

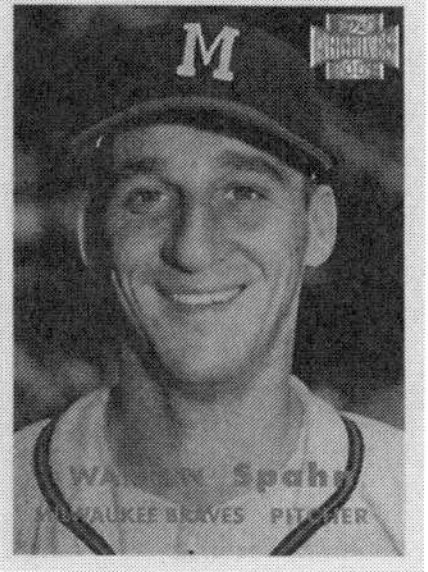

		MT
Complete Set (200):		70.00
Common Player:		.40
Pack (8):		5.00
Box (20):		80.00
1	Willie Mays	3.00
2	Dale Murphy	.40
3	Dave Winfield	.75
4	Roger Maris	2.00
5	Ron Cey	.40
6	Lee Smith	.40
7	Len Dykstra	.40
8	Ray Fosse	.40
9	Warren Spahn	1.00
10	Herb Score	.40
11	Jim Wynn	.40
12	Sam McDowell	.40
13	Fred Lynn	.40
14	Yogi Berra	1.50
15	Ron Santo	.40
16	Alvin Dark	.40
17	Bill Buckner	.40
18	Rollie Fingers	.60
19	Tony Gwynn	1.50
20	Red Schoendienst	.40
21	Gaylord Perry	.40
22	Jose Cruz	.40
23	Dennis Martinez	.40
24	Dave McNally	.40
25	Norm Cash	.40
26	Ted Kluszewski	.40
27	Rick Reuschel	.40
28	Bruce Sutter	.40
29	Don Larsen	.40
30	Claudell Washington	.40
31	Luis Aparicio	.40
32	Clete Boyer	.40
33	Rich "Goose" Gossage	.40
34	Ray Knight	.40
35	Roy Campanella	1.50
36	Tug McGraw	.40
37	Bob Lemon	.40
38	Willie Stargell	1.00
39	Roberto Clemente	3.00
40	Jim Fregosi	.40
41	Reggie Smith	.40
42	Dave Parker	.40
43	Darrell Evans	.40
44	Ryne Sandberg	2.00
45	Manny Mota	.40
46	Dennis Eckersley	.40
47	Nellie Fox	.40
48	Gil Hodges	.40
49	Reggie Jackson	1.50
50	Bobby Shantz	.40
51	Cecil Cooper	.40
52	Jim Kaat	.40
53	George Hendrick	.40
54	Johnny Podres	.40
55	Bob Gibson	1.00
56	Vern Law	.40
57	Joe Adcock	.40
58	Jack Clark	.40
59	Bill Mazeroski	.40
60	Carl Yastrzemski	1.50
61	Bobby Murcer	.40
62	Davey Johnson	.40
63	Jim Palmer	.75
64	Roy Face	.40
65	Dean Chance	.40
66	Bill "Moose" Skowron	.40
67	Dwight Evans	.40
68	Kirk Gibson	.40
69	Sal Bando	.40
70	Mike Schmidt	2.00
71	Bo Jackson	.75
72	Chris Chambliss	.40
73	Fergie Jenkins	.75
74	Brooks Robinson	1.50
75	Bobby Richardson	.40
76	Duke Snider	1.50
77	Allie Reynolds	.40
78	Harmon Killebrew	1.50
79	Steve Carlton	1.00
80	Bert Blyleven	.40
81	Phil Niekro	.40
82	Lew Burdette	.40
83	Hoyt Wilhelm	.40
84	Curt Flood	.40
85	Guillermo Hernandez	.40
86	Robin Yount	1.50
87	Robin Roberts	.40
88	Whitey Ford	1.00
89	Tony Oliva	.75
90	Don Newcombe	.40
91	Al Oliver	.40
92	Mike Cuellar	.40
93	Mike Scott	.40
94	Dick Allen	.40
95	Jimmy Piersall	.40
96	Bill Freehan	.40
97	Willie Horton	.40
98	Bob Friend	.40
99	Ken Holtzman	.40
100	Rico Carty	.40
101	Gil McDougald	.40
102	Lee May	.40
103	Joe Pepitone	.40
104	Gene Tenace	.40
105	Gary Carter	.40
106	Tim McCarver	.40
107	Ernie Banks	1.50
108	George Foster	.40
109	Lou Brock	1.00
110	Dick Groat	.40
111	Graig Nettles	.40
112	Boog Powell	.40
113	Joe Carter	.40
114	Juan Marichal	.75
115	Larry Doby	.40
116	Fernando Valenzuela	.40
117	Luis Tiant	.40
118	Early Wynn	.40
119	Bill Madlock	.40
120	Eddie Mathews	1.50
121	George Brett	3.00
122	Al Kaline	1.50
123	Frank Howard	.40
124	Mickey Lolich	.40
125	Kirby Puckett	3.00
126	Bob Cerv	.40
127	Will Clark	1.00
128	Vida Blue	.40
129	Kevin Mitchell	.40
130	Bucky Dent	.40
131	Tom Seaver	2.00
132	Jerry Koosman	.40
133	Orlando Cepeda	.40
134	Nolan Ryan	4.00
135	Tony Kubek	.40
136	Don Drysdale	1.00
137	Paul Blair	.40
138	Elston Howard	.40
139	Joe Rudi	.40
140	Tommie Agee	.40
141	Richie Ashburn	.40
142	Jim Bunning	.40
143	Hank Sauer	.40
144	Greg Luzinski	.40
145	Ron Guidry	.40
146	Rod Carew	1.00
147	Andre Dawson	.75
148	Keith Hernandez	.40
149	Carlton Fisk	1.00
150	Cleon Jones	.40
151	Don Mattingly	3.00
152	Vada Pinson	.40
153	Ozzie Smith	1.50
154	Dave Concepcion	.40
155	Al Rosen	.40
156	Tommy John	.40
157	Bob Ojeda	.40
158	Frank Robinson	1.50
159	Darryl Strawberry	.40
160	Bobby Bonds	.40
161	Bert Campaneris	.40
162	Jim "Catfish" Hunter	.40
163	Bud Harrelson	.40
164	Dwight Gooden	.40
165	Wade Boggs	1.00
166	Joe Morgan	1.00
167	Ron Swoboda	.40
168	Hank Aaron	4.00
169	Steve Garvey	.40
170	Mickey Rivers	.40
171	Johnny Bench	3.00
172	Ralph Terry	.40
173	Billy Pierce	.40
174	Thurman Munson	2.50
175	Don Sutton	.40
176	Sparky Anderson	.40
177	Gil Hodges	.40
178	Davey Johnson	.40
179	Frank Robinson	1.50
180	Red Schoendienst	.40
181	Roger Maris	2.00
182	Willie Mays	3.00
183	Luis Aparicio	.40
184	Nellie Fox	.40
185	Ernie Banks	1.50
186	Orlando Cepeda	.75
187	Whitey Ford	1.00
188	Bob Gibson	1.00
189	Bill Mazeroski	.40
190	Hank Aaron	3.00
191	League Leaders (Elston Howard, Harmon Killebrew, Carl Yastrzemski)	.75
192	League Leaders (Orlando Cepeda, Jackie Robinson, Willie Mays)	2.00
193	League Leaders (Hank Aaron, Roberto Clemente, Dick Allen)	2.00

194 League Leaders (Tom Seaver, Phil Niekro, Fergie Jenkins, Juan Marichal) 1.00
195 League Leaders (Jim Palmer, Jim Hunter, Dennis Eckersley) .40
196 Hank Aaron 3.00
197 Brooks Robinson 1.50
198 Tom Seaver 1.50
199 Jim Palmer .75
200 Lou Brock 1.00

2002 Topps Archives Autographs

MT
Common Autograph: 15.00
Inserted 1:22
HA Hank Aaron 350.00
DA Dick Allen 35.00
SB Sal Bando 20.00
EB Ernie Banks 130.00
BB Bobby Bonds 30.00
GB George Brett 375.00
JBU Jim Bunning 40.00
LB Lew Burdette 25.00
BC Bert Campaneris 20.00
GC Gary Carter 30.00
RCE Ron Cey 15.00
CC Chris Chambliss 30.00
JCR Jose Cruz 20.00
AD Alvin Dark 40.00
BD Bucky Dent 20.00
LD Len Dykstra 30.00
DEV Darrell Evans 15.00
GF George Foster 15.00
JF Jim Fregosi 20.00
SG Steve Garvey 25.00
DG Dwight Gooden 25.00
DGR Dick Groat 20.00
BH Bud Harrelson 20.00
WH Willie Hernandez 15.00
KH Keith Hernandez 40.00
BJ Bo Jackson 80.00
FJ Fergie Jenkins 40.00
TJ Tommy John 20.00
JK Jim Kaat 25.00
AK Al Kaline 125.00
HK Harmon Killebrew 110.00
JKO Jerry Koosman 65.00
GL Greg Luzinski 20.00
FL Fred Lynn 25.00
DM Dave McNally 30.00
KM Kevin Mitchell 35.00
DN Don Newcombe 25.00
TO Tony Oliva 30.00
JP Jim Palmer 50.00
DP Dave Parker 30.00
GP Gaylord Perry 20.00
BP Billy Pierce 15.00
JPI Jimmy Piersall 25.00
JPO Johnny Podres 25.00
BPO Boog Powell 25.00
KP Kirby Puckett 150.00
MR Mickey Rivers 20.00
FRO Frank Robinson 35.00
JR Joe Rudi 20.00
RS Ron Santo 35.00
MS Mike Schmidt 150.00
LS Lee Smith 20.00
RSM Reggie Smith 25.00
DS Duke Snider
BS Bruce Sutter 20.00
RT Ralph Terry 50.00
HW Hoyt Wilhelm 25.00
DW Dave Winfield 85.00
RY Robin Yount 240.00

2002 Topps Archives Game-Worn Uniform

MT
Common Player: 10.00
SA Sparky Anderson 15.00
WB Wade Boggs 20.00
BB Bobby Bonds 10.00
GB George Brett 40.00
OC Orlando Cepeda 15.00
WC Will Clark 25.00
DC Dave Concepcion 15.00
DE Dennis Eckersley 15.00
SG Steve Garvey 15.00
FL Fred Lynn 10.00
DM Dale Murphy 35.00
PN Phil Niekro 12.00
GP Gaylord Perry 15.00
KP Kirby Puckett 35.00
FR Frank Robinson 20.00
NR Nolan Ryan 50.00
RS Ryne Sandberg 40.00
OS Ozzie Smith 30.00
DS Don Sutton 12.00
DW Dave Winfield 15.00

2002 Topps Archives Game-Used Bat

MT
Common Player:
Group A 1:106
Group B 1:282
JB Johnny Bench 40.00
GB George Brett 40.00
GC Gary Carter 10.00
JC Joe Carter 10.00
NC Norm Cash 40.00
AD Andre Dawson 25.00
DE Dwight Evans 15.00
BF Bill Freehan 10.00
WH Willie Horton 15.00
RJ Reggie Jackson 25.00
DM Don Mattingly 50.00
RM Roger Maris 50.00
JM Joe Morgan 15.00
DP Dave Parker 15.00
BR Brooks Robinson 30.00
RS Ron Santo 35.00
WS Willie Stargell 25.00
CY Carl Yastrzemski 40.00
RY Robin Yount 25.00

2002 Topps Archives Stadium Seat

MT
Common Player: 8.00
RA Richie Ashburn 20.00
SA Sparky Anderson 20.00
EB Ernie Banks 25.00
YB Yogi Berra 20.00
JB Jim Bunning 12.00
RC Rod Carew 30.00
JC Joe Carter 10.00
NF Nellie Fox 25.00
RG Ron Guidry 25.00
TK Ted Kluszewski 25.00
BL Bob Lemon 12.00
ML Mickey Lolich 20.00
EM Eddie Mathews 20.00
SM Sam McDowell 8.00
JP Jim Palmer 10.00
DP Dave Parker 20.00
HS Herb Score 10.00
DS Duke Snider 25.00
WS Warren Spahn 15.00

2002 Topps Archives Reserve

MT
Complete Set (100): 100.00
Common Player: .75
Box (10 packs + Auto. Baseball): 135.00
1 Lee Smith .75
2 Gaylord Perry .75
3 Al Oliver .75
4 Rich "Goose" Gossage .75
5 Bill Madlock .75
6 Rod Carew 1.50
7 Fred Lynn .75
8 Frank Robinson 2.50
9 Al Kaline 2.50
10 Len Dykstra .75
11 Carlton Fisk 1.50
12 Nellie Fox 1.00
13 Reggie Jackson 3.00
14 Bob Gibson 2.00
15 Bill Buckner .75
16 Harmon Killebrew 2.00
17 Gary Carter .75
18 Dave Winfield 1.50
19 Ozzie Smith 2.50
20 Dwight Evans .75
21 Dave Concepcion .75
22 Joe Morgan 1.00
23 Clete Boyer .75
24 Will Clark 1.50
25 Lee May .75
26 Kevin Mitchell .75
27 Roger Maris 3.00
28 Mickey Lolich .75
29 Luis Aparicio .75
30 George Foster .75
31 Don Mattingly 8.00
32 Fernando Valenzuela .75
33 Bobby Bonds 1.00
34 Jim Palmer 1.50
35 Dennis Eckersley .75
36 Kirby Puckett 4.00
37 Jose Cruz .75
38 Richie Ashburn .75
39 Whitey Ford 2.00
40 Robin Roberts .75
41 Don Newcombe .75
42 Roy Campanella 2.50
43 Dennis Martinez .75
44 Larry Doby 1.00
45 Steve Garvey .75
46 Thurman Munson 3.00
47 Dale Murphy 1.50
48 Bill "Moose" Skowron .75
49 Tom Seaver 3.00
50 Orlando Cepeda .75
51 Graig Nettles .75
52 Willie Stargell 1.50
53 Yogi Berra 2.50
54 Steve Carlton 1.50
55 Don Sutton .75
56 Brooks Robinson 1.50
57 Vida Blue .75
58 Rollie Fingers 1.00
59 Jim Bunning .75
60 Nolan Ryan 8.00
61 Hank Aaron 6.00
62 Fergie Jenkins .75
63 Andre Dawson 1.00
64 Ernie Banks 2.50
65 Early Wynn .75
66 Duke Snider 1.50
67 Red Schoendienst .75
68 Don Drysdale 1.00
69 Jim "Catfish" Hunter 1.00
70 George Brett 6.00
71 Elston Howard 1.00
72 Wade Boggs 1.50
73 Keith Hernandez .75
74 Billy Pierce .75
75 Ted Kluszewski .75
76 Carl Yastrzemski 4.00
77 Bert Blyleven .75
78 Tony Oliva .75
79 Joe Carter .75
80 Johnny Bench 3.00
81 Tony Gwynn 3.00
82 Mike Schmidt 4.00
83 Phil Niekro .75
84 Juan Marichal .75
85 Eddie Mathews 2.50
86 Boog Powell .75
87 Dwight Gooden .75
88 Darryl Strawberry .75
89 Roberto Clemente 6.00
90 Ryne Sandberg 5.00
91 Jack Clark .75
92 Willie Mays 6.00
93 Ron Guidry .75
94 Kirk Gibson .75
95 Lou Brock 1.00
96 Robin Yount 2.50
97 Bill Mazeroski .75
98 Dave Parker .75
99 Hoyt Wilhelm .75
100 Warren Spahn 1.50

2002 Topps Archives Reserve Autographed Baseballs

MT
Common Auto. Ball: 15.00
Inserted 1:box
Luis Aparicio/1,600 35.00
Ernie Banks/50
Yogi Berra/100 85.00
Lou Brock/400 40.00
Jim Bunning/500 35.00
Gary Carter/500 30.00
Rich Gossage/500 20.00
Fergie Jenkins/1,000 15.00
Al Kaline/250 65.00
Harmon Killebrew/250 60.00
Willie Mays/50
Joe Morgan/250 40.00
Graig Nettles/1,600 15.00
Jim Palmer/400 35.00
Gaylord Perry/500 15.00
Brooks Robinson/500 35.00
Mike Schmidt/250 125.00
Duke Snider/100 65.00
Robin Yount/250 90.00

2002 Topps Archives Reserve Best Years Autographs

		MT
Common Autograph:		12.00
Inserted 1:15 Hobby		
LA	Luis Aparicio	15.00
EB	Ernie Banks	70.00
YB	Yogi Berra	60.00
LB	Lou Brock	25.00
GC	Gary Carter	20.00
FJ	Fergie Jenkins	12.00
AK	Al Kaline	40.00
HK	Harmon Killebrew	35.00
WM	Willie Mays	120.00
JM	Joe Morgan	25.00
GN	Graig Nettles	12.00
GP	Gaylord Perry	15.00
BR	Brooks Robinson	25.00
MS	Mike Schmidt	125.00
LS	Lee Smith	12.00
DS	Duke Snider	60.00
RY	Robin Yount	80.00

2002 Topps Archives Reserve Best Years Game-Worn Uni.

		MT
Common Player:		10.00
Inserted 1:7 Hobby		
EB	Ernie Banks	25.00
JBU	Johnny Bench	15.00
WBJ	Wade Boggs	10.00
GCJ	Gary Carter	12.00
WC	Will Clark	15.00
NF	Nellie Fox	25.00
TG	Tony Gwynn	15.00
JM	Juan Marichal	12.00
WM	Willie Mays	35.00
KPJ	Kirby Puckett	20.00
BR	Brooks Robinson	12.00
NR	Nolan Ryan	30.00
RSJ	Red Schoendienst	10.00
WS	Willie Stargell	15.00
RYU	Robin Yount	12.00

Figure values of lower-grade cards from 1981-date as: Near Mint (NM) 75% Excellent (EX) 40% of the listed Mint price

For cards through 1980, values should be figured as: Excellent (EX) 50% Very Good (VG) 30% of the listed Near Mint price

2002 Topps Archives Reserve Best Years Game-Used Bat

		MT
Common Player:		10.00
Inserted 1:22		
HAB	Hank Aaron	40.00
GBB	George Brett	35.00
OC	Orlando Cepeda	10.00
CF	Carlton Fisk	20.00
RM	Roger Maris	70.00
EMB	Eddie Mathews	20.00
DMB	Don Mattingly	25.00
TM	Thurman Munson	30.00
DW	Dave Winfield	10.00
CYB	Carl Yastrzemski	20.00

2002 Topps Chrome

		MT
Complete Set (685):		200.00
Common Player:		.25
Gold Chrome parallel:		3-5X
Inserted 1:4		
Pack (4):		2.75
Box (24):		55.00
1	Pedro Martinez	1.25
2	Mike Stanton	.25
3	Brad Penny	.25
4	Mike Matheny	.25
5	Johnny Damon	.25
6	Bret Boone	.25
7	Retired # not issued	.25
8	Chris Truby	.25
9	B.J. Surhoff	.25
10	Mike Hampton	.40
11	Juan Pierre	.25
12	Mark Buehrle	.25
13	Bob Abreu	.40
14	David Cone	.25
15	Aaron Sele	.25
16	Fernando Tatis	.25
17	Bobby Jones	.25
18	Rick Helling	.25
19	Dmitri Young	.25
20	Mike Mussina	1.00
21	Mike Sweeney	.25
22	Cristian Guzman	.25
23	Ryan Kohlmeier	.25
24	Adam Kennedy	.25
25	Larry Walker	.75
26	Eric Davis	.40
27	Jason Tyner	.25
28	Eric Young	.25
29	Jason Marquis	.25
30	Luis Gonzalez	.75
31	Kevin Tapani	.25
32	Orlando Cabrera	.25
33	Marty Cordova	.25
34	Brad Ausmus	.25
35	Livan Hernandez	.25
36	Alex Gonzalez	.25
37	Edgar Renteria	.25
38	Bengie Molina	.25
39	Frank Menechino	.25
40	Rafael Palmeiro	.75
41	Brad Fullmer	.25
42	Julio Zuleta	.25
43	Darren Dreifort	.25
44	Trot Nixon	.25
45	Trevor Hoffman	.25
46	Vladimir Nunez	.25
47	Mark Kotsay	.25
48	Kenny Rogers	.25
49	Ben Petrick	.25
50	Jeff Bagwell	1.25
51	Juan Encarnacion	.25
52	Ramiro Mendoza	.25
53	Brian Meadows	.25
54	Chad Curtis	.25
55	Aramis Ramirez	.25
56	Mark McLemore	.25
57	Dante Bichette	.25
58	Scott Schoeneweis	.25
59	Jose Cruz	.25
60	Roger Clemens	1.50
61	Jose Guillen	.25
62	Darren Oliver	.25
63	Chris Reitsma	.25
64	Jeff Abbott	.25
65	Robin Ventura	.25
66	Denny Neagle	.25
67	Al Martin	.25
68	Benito Santiago	.25
69	Roy Oswalt	.50
70	Juan Gonzalez	1.25
71	Garret Anderson	.25
72	Bobby Bonilla	.25
73	Danny Bautista	.25
74	J.T. Snow	.25
75	Derek Jeter	5.00
76	John Olerud	.50
77	Kevin Appier	.25
78	Phil Nevin	.25
79	Sean Casey	.50
80	Troy Glaus	1.25
81	Joe Randa	.25
82	Jose Valentin	.25
83	Ricky Bottalico	.25
84	Todd Zeile	.25
85	Barry Larkin	.60
86	Bob Wickman	.25
87	Jeff Shaw	.25
88	Greg Vaughn	.25
89	Fernando Vina	.25
90	Mark Mulder	.50
91	Paul Bako	.25
92	Aaron Boone	.25
93	Esteban Loaiza	.25
94	Richie Sexson	.25
95	Alfonso Soriano	.50
96	Tony Womack	.25
97	Paul Shuey	.25
98	Melvin Mora	.25
99	Tony Gwynn	1.25
100	Vladimir Guerrero	1.25
101	Keith Osik	.25
102	Randy Velarde	.25
103	Scott Williamson	.25
104	Daryle Ward	.25
105	Doug Mientkiewicz	.25
106	Stan Javier	.25
107	Russ Ortiz	.25
108	Wade Miller	.25
109	Luke Prokopec	.25
110	Andruw Jones	1.00
111	Ron Coomer	.25
112	Dan Wilson	.25
113	Luis Castillo	.25
114	Derek Bell	.25
115	Gary Sheffield	.60
116	Ruben Rivera	.25
117	Paul O'Neill	.60
118	Craig Paquette	.25
119	Kelvim Escobar	.25
120	Brad Radke	.25
121	Jorge Fabregas	.25
122	Randy Winn	.25
123	Tom Goodwin	.25
124	Jaret Wright	.25
125	Bonds-Race to 73	40.00
126	Al Leiter	.40
127	Ben Davis	.25
128	Frank Catalanotto	.25
129	Jose Cabrera	.25
130	Magglio Ordonez	.25
131	Jose Macias	.25
132	Ted Lilly	.25
133	Chris Holt	.25
134	Eric Milton	.25
135	Shannon Stewart	.25
136	Omar Olivares	.25
137	David Segui	.25
138	Jeff Nelson	.25
139	Matt Williams	.25
140	Ellis Burks	.25
141	Jason Bere	.25
142	Jimmy Haynes	.25
143	Ramon Hernandez	.25
144	Craig Counsell	.25
145	John Smoltz	.25
146	Homer Bush	.25
147	Quilvio Veras	.25
148	Esteban Yan	.25
149	Ramon Ortiz	.25
150	Carlos Delgado	.75
151	Lee Stevens	.25
152	Wil Cordero	.25
153	Mike Bordick	.25
154	John Flaherty	.25
155	Omar Daal	.25
156	Todd Ritchie	.25
157	Carl Everett	.25
158	Scott Sullivan	.25
159	Deivi Cruz	.25
160	Albert Pujols	2.50
161	Royce Clayton	.25
162	Jeff Suppan	.25
163	C.C. Sabathia	.25
164	Jimmy Rollins	.25
165	Rickey Henderson	.60
166	Rey Ordonez	.25
167	Shawn Estes	.25
168	Reggie Sanders	.25
169	Jon Lieber	.25
170	Armando Benitez	.25
171	Mike Remlinger	.25
172	Billy Wagner	.25
173	Troy Percival	.25
174	Devon White	.25
175	Ivan Rodriguez	1.25
176	Dustin Hermanson	.25
177	Brian Anderson	.25
178	Graeme Lloyd	.25
179	Russell Branyan	.25
180	Bobby Higginson	.25
181	Alex Gonzalez	.25
182	John Franco	.25
183	Sidney Ponson	.25
184	Jose Mesa	.25
185	Todd Hollandsworth	.25
186	Kevin Young	.25
187	Tim Wakefield	.25
188	Craig Biggio	.50
189	Jason Isringhausen	.25
190	Mark Quinn	.25
191	Glendon Rusch	.25
192	Damian Miller	.25
193	Sandy Alomar	.25
194	Scott Brosius	.25
195	Dave Martinez	.25
196	Danny Graves	.25
197	Shea Hillenbrand	.25
198	Jimmy Anderson	.25
199	Travis Lee	.25
200	Randy Johnson	1.25
201	Carlos Beltran	.25
202	Jerry Hairston Jr.	.25
203	Jesus Sanchez	.25
204	Eddie Taubensee	.25
205	David Wells	.25
206	Russ Davis	.25
207	Michael Barrett	.25
208	Marquis Grissom	.25
209	Byung-Hyun Kim	.25
210	Hideo Nomo	.75
211	Ryan Rupe	.25
212	Ricky Gutierrez	.25
213	Darryl Kile	.25
214	Rico Brogna	.25
215	Terrence Long	.25
216	Mike Jackson	.25
217	Jamey Wright	.25
218	Adrian Beltre	.25

219 Benny Agbayani .25
220 Chuck Knoblauch .40
221 Randy Wolf .25
222 Andy Ashby .25
223 Corey Koskie .25
224 Roger Cedeno .25
225 Ichiro Suzuki 5.00
226 Keith Foulke .25
227 Ryan Minor .25
228 Shawon Dunston .25
229 Alex Cora .25
230 Jeromy Burnitz .25
231 Mark Grace .75
232 Aubrey Huff .25
233 Jeffrey Hammonds .25
234 Olmedo Saenz .25
235 Brian Jordan .25
236 Jeremy Giambi .25
237 Joe Girardi .25
238 Eric Gagne .25
239 Masato Yoshii .25
240 Greg Maddux 2.50
241 Bryan Rekar .25
242 Ray Durham .25
243 Torii Hunter .25
244 Derrek Lee .25
245 Jim Edmonds .40
246 Einar Diaz .25
247 Brian Bohanon .25
248 Ron Belliard .25
249 Mike Lowell .25
250 Sammy Sosa 2.50
251 Richard Hidalgo .40
252 Bartolo Colon .25
253 Jorge Posada .50
254 LaTroy Hawkins .25
255 Paul LoDuca .25
256 Carlos Febles .25
257 Nelson Cruz .25
258 Edgardo Alfonzo .25
259 Joey Hamilton .25
260 Cliff Floyd .25
261 Wes Helms .25
262 Jay Bell .25
263 Mike Cameron .25
264 Paul Konerko .25
265 Jeff Kent .40
266 Robert Fick .25
267 Allen Levrault .25
268 Placido Polanco .25
269 Marlon Anderson .25
270 Mariano Rivera .50
271 Chan Ho Park .25
272 Jose Vizcaino .25
273 Jeff D'Amico .25
274 Mark Gardner .25
275 Travis Fryman .25
276 Darren Lewis .25
277 Bruce Bochy .25
278 Jerry Manuel .25
279 Bob Brenly .25
280 Don Baylor .25
281 Davey Lopes .25
282 Jerry Narron .25
283 Tony Muser .25
284 Hal McRae .25
285 Bobby Cox .25
286 Larry Dierker .25
287 Phil Garner .25
288 Jimy Williams .25
289 Bobby Valentine .25
290 Dusty Baker .25
291 Lloyd McLendon .25
292 Mike Scioscia .25
293 Buck Martinez .25
294 Larry Bowa .25
295 Tony LaRussa .25
296 Jeff Torborg .25
297 Tom Kelly .25
298 Mike Hargrove .25
299 Art Howe .25
300 Lou Piniella .25
301 Charlie Manuel .25
302 Buddy Bell .25
303 Tony Perez .25
304 Bob Boone .25
305 Joe Torre .25
306 Jim Tracy .25
307 Jason Lane 1.00
308 Chris George .25
309 Hank Blalock 2.00
310 Joe Borchard .25
311 Marlon Byrd .25
312 *Raymond Cabrera* 1.50
313 *Freddy Sanchez* 1.50
314 *Scott Wiggins* 1.50
315 *Jason Maule* 1.50
316 *Dionys Cesar* 1.50
317 Boof Bonser .25
318 *Juan Tolentino* 1.50
319 *Earl Snyder* 8.00
320 *Travis Wade* 3.00
321 *Napoleon Calzado* 1.50
322 *Eric Glaser* 1.50
323 *Craig Kuzmic* 3.00
324 *Nic Jackson* 4.00
325 Mike Rivera .25
326 *Jason Bay* 1.50
327 Chris Smith .25
328 Jake Gautreau .25
329 Gabe Gross .25
330 Kenny Baugh .25
331 J.D. Martin .25
366 Pat Meares .25
367 Mike Lieberthal .25
368 Scott Erickson .25
369 Ron Gant .25
370 Moises Alou .40
371 Chad Kreuter .25
372 Willis Roberts .25
373 Toby Hall .25
374 Miguel Batista .25
375 John Burkett .25
376 Cory Lidle .25
377 Nick Neugebauer .25
378 Jay Payton .25
379 Steve Karsay .25
380 Eric Chavez .50
381 Kelly Stinnett .25
382 Jarrod Washburn .25
383 C.J. Nitkowski .25
384 Jeff Conine .25
385 Fred McGriff .50
386 Marvin Benard .25
387 Dave Burba .25
388 Dennis Cook .25
389 Rick Reed .25
390 Tom Glavine .75
391 Rondell White .25
392 Matt Morris .25
393 Pat Rapp .25
394 Robert Person .25
395 Omar Vizquel .40
396 Jeff Cirillo .25
397 Dave Mlicki .25
398 Jose Ortiz .25
399 Ryan Dempster .25
400 Curt Schilling .75
401 Peter Bergeron .25
402 Kyle Lohse .25
403 Craig Wilson .25
404 David Justice .75
405 Darin Erstad .75
406 Jose Mercedes .25
407 Carl Pavano .25
408 Albie Lopez .25
409 Alex Ochoa .25
410 Chipper Jones 2.50
411 Tyler Houston .25
412 Dean Palmer .25
413 Damian Jackson .25
414 Josh Towers .25
415 Rafael Furcal .40
416 Mike Morgan .25
417 Herb Perry .25
418 Mike Sirotka .25
419 Mark Wohlers .25
420 Nomar Garciaparra 3.00
421 Felipe Lopez .25
422 Joe McEwing .25
423 Jacque Jones .25
424 Julio Franco .25
425 Frank Thomas 1.50
426 Kent Bottenfield .25
427 Mac Suzuki .25
428 D'Angelo Jimenez .25
429 Chris Stynes .25
430 Kerry Wood .75
431 Chris Singleton .25
432 Erubiel Durazo .25
433 Matt Lawton .25
434 Bill Mueller .25
435 Jose Canseco .50
436 Ben Grieve .25
437 Terry Mulholland .25
438 David Bell .25
439 A.J. Pierzynski .25
440 Adam Dunn 1.50
441 Jon Garland .25
442 Jeff Fassero .25
443 Julio Lugo .25
444 Carlos Guillen .25
445 Orlando Hernandez .25
446 Mark Loretta .25
447 Scott Spiezio .25
448 Kevin Millwood .25
449 Jamie Moyer .25
450 Todd Helton 1.25
451 Todd Walker .25
452 Jose Lima .25
453 Brook Fordyce .25
454 Aaron Rowand .25
455 Barry Zito .50
456 Eric Owens .25
457 Charles Nagy .25
458 Raul Ibanez .25
459 Joe Mays .25
460 Jim Thome .75
461 Adam Eaton .25
462 Felix Martinez .25
463 Vernon Wells .25
464 Donnie Sadler .25
465 Tony Clark .25
466 Jose Hernandez .25
467 Ramon Martinez .25
468 Rusty Greer .25
469 Rod Barajas .25
470 Lance Berkman .75
471 Brady Anderson .25
472 Pedro Astacio .25
473 Shane Halter .25
474 Bret Prinz .25
475 Edgar Martinez .25
476 Steve Trachsel .25
477 Gary Matthews Jr. .25
478 Ismael Valdes .25
479 Juan Uribe .25
480 Shawn Green .75
481 Kirk Rueter .25
482 Damion Easley .25
483 Chris Carpenter .25
484 Kris Benson .25
485 Antonio Alfonseca .25
486 Kyle Farnsworth .25
487 Brandon Lyon .25
488 Hideki Irabu .25
489 David Ortiz .25
490 Mike Piazza 3.00
491 Derek Lowe .25
492 Chris Gomez .25
493 Mark Johnson .25
494 John Rocker .25
495 Eric Karros .25
496 Bill Haselman .25
497 Dave Veres .25
498 Gil Heredia .25
499 Tomokazu Ohka .25
500 Barry Bonds 2.50
501 David Dellucci .25
502 Ed Sprague .25
503 Tom Gordon .25
504 Javier Vazquez .25
505 Ben Sheets .50
506 Wilton Guerrero .25
507 John Halama .25
508 Mark Redman .25
509 Jack Wilson .25
510 Bernie Williams .75
511 Miguel Cairo .25
512 Denny Hocking .25
513 Tony Batista .25
514 Mark Grudzielanek .25
515 Jose Vidro .25
516 Sterling Hitchcock .25
517 Billy Koch .25
518 Matt Clement .25
519 Bruce Chen .25
520 Roberto Alomar 1.00
521 Orlando Palmeiro .25
522 Steve Finley .25
523 Danny Patterson .25
524 Terry Adams .25
525 Tino Martinez .25
526 Tony Armas Jr. .25
527 Geoff Jenkins .50
528 Chris Michalak .25
529 Corey Patterson .25
530 Brian Giles .50
531 Jose Jimenez .25
532 Joe Kennedy .25
533 Armando Rios .25
534 Osvaldo Fernandez .25
535 Ruben Sierra .25
536 Octavio Dotel .25
537 Luis Sojo .25
538 Brent Butler .25
539 Pablo Ozuna .25
540 Freddy Garcia .25
541 Chad Durbin .25
542 Orlando Merced .25
543 Michael Tucker .25
544 Roberto Hernandez .25
545 Pat Burrell .50
546 A.J. Burnett .25
547 Bubba Trammell .25
548 Scott Elarton .25
549 Mike Darr .25
550 Ken Griffey Jr. 3.00
551 Ugueth Urbina .25
552 Todd Jones .25
553 Delino DeShields .25
554 Adam Piatt .25
555 Jason Kendall .25
556 Hector Ortiz .25
557 Turk Wendell .25
558 Rob Bell .25
559 Sun-Woo Kim .25
560 Raul Mondesi .25
561 Brent Abernathy .25
562 Seth Etherton .25
563 Shawn Wooten .25
564 Jay Buhner .25
565 Andres Galarraga .40
566 Shane Reynolds .25
567 Rod Beck .25
568 Dee Brown .25
569 Pedro Feliz .25
570 Ryan Klesko .25
571 John Vander Wal .25
572 Nick Bierbrodt .25
573 Joe Nathan .25
574 James Baldwin .25
575 J.D. Drew .75
576 Greg Colbrunn .25
577 Doug Glanville .25
578 Rey Sanchez .25
579 Todd Van Poppel .25
580 Rich Aurilia .25
581 Chuck Finley .25
582 Abraham Nunez .25
583 Kenny Lofton .25
584 Brian Daubach .25
585 Miguel Tejada .50
586 Nate Cornejo .25
587 Kazuhiro Sasaki .50
588 Chris Richard .25
589 Armando Reynoso .25
590 Tim Hudson .75
591 Neifi Perez .25
592 Steve Cox .25
593 Henry Blanco .25
594 Ricky Ledee .25
595 Tim Salmon .50
596 Luis Rivas .25
597 Jeff Zimmerman .25
598 Matt Stairs .25
599 Preston Wilson .25
600 Mark McGwire 4.00
601 Timo Perez .25
602 Matt Anderson .25
603 Todd Hundley .25
604 Rick Ankiel .50
605 Tsuyoshi Shinjo .25
606 Woody Williams .25
607 Jason LaRue .25
608 Carlos Lee .25
609 Russ Johnson .25
610 Scott Rolen .75
611 Brent Mayne .25
612 Darrin Fletcher .25
613 Ray Lankford .25
614 Troy O'Leary .25
615 Javier Lopez .25
616 Randy Velarde .25
617 Vinny Castilla .25
618 Milton Bradley .25
619 Ruben Mateo .25
620 Jason Giambi 1.50
621 Andy Benes .25
622 Tony Eusebio .25
623 Andy Pettitte .75
624 Jose Offerman .25
625 Mo Vaughn .50
626 Steve Sparks .25
627 Mike Matthews .25
628 Robb Nen .25
629 Kip Wells .25
630 Kevin Brown .50
631 Arthur Rhodes .25
632 Gabe Kapler .25
633 Jermaine Dye .25
634 Josh Beckett .25
635 Pokey Reese .25
636 Benji Gil .25

637	Marcus Giles	.25
638	Julian Tavarez	.25
639	Jason Schmidt	.25
640	Alex Rodriguez	3.00
641	Anaheim Angels	.25
642	Arizona Diamondbacks	.25
643	Atlanta Braves	.25
644	Baltimore Orioles	.25
645	Boston Red Sox	.25
646	Chicago Cubs	.25
647	Chicago White Sox	.25
648	Cincinnati Reds	.25
649	Cleveland Indians	.25
650	Colorado Rockies	.25
651	Detroit Tigers	.25
652	Florida Marlins	.25
653	Houston Astros	.25
654	Kansas City Royals	.25
655	Los Angeles Dodgers	.25
656	Milwaukee Brewers	.25
657	Minnesota Twins	.25
658	Montreal Expos	.25
659	New York Mets	.25
660	New York Yankees	1.00
661	Oakland Athletics	.25
662	Philadelphia Phillies	.25
663	Pittsburgh Pirates	.25
664	San Diego Padres	.25
665	San Francisco Giants	.25
666	Seattle Mariners	.25
667	St. Louis Cardinals	.25
668	Tampa Bay Devil Rays	.25
669	Texas Rangers	.25
670	Toronto Blue Jays	.25
671	Juan Cruz	.25
672	*Kevin Cash*	3.00
673	*Jimmy Gobble*	4.00
674	*Mike Hill*	.75
675	*Taylor Buchholz*	.75
676	Bill Hall	.75
677	*Brett Roneberg*	.75
678	*Royce Huffman*	.75
679	*Chris Tritle*	3.00
680	*Nate Espy*	.50
681	*Nick Alvarez*	1.00
682	*Jason Botts*	1.50
683	*Ryan Gripp*	.75
684	*Dan Phillips*	.50
685	*Pablo Arias*	.75
686	*John Rodriguez*	.75
687	*James Harden*	1.50
688	*Neal Frendling*	1.00
689	*Rich Thompson*	.50
690	*Greg Montalbano*	2.00
691	*Leonard Dinardo*	.75
692	*Ryan Raburn*	.50
693	Josh Barfield	1.00
694	*David Bacani*	.75
695	*Dan Johnson*	.75
696	Mike Mussina	.50
697	Ivan Rodriguez	.50
698	Doug Mientkiewicz	.25
699	Roberto Alomar	.50
700	Eric Chavez	.25
701	Omar Vizquel	.25
702	Mike Cameron	.25
703	Torii Hunter	.25
704	Ichiro Suzuki	2.00
705	Greg Maddux	1.00
706	Brad Ausmus	.25
707	Todd Helton	.75
708	Fernando Vina	.25
709	Scott Rolen	.50
710	Orlando Cabrera	.25
711	Andruw Jones	.40
712	Jim Edmonds	.25
713	Larry Walker	.25
714	Roger Clemens	.75
715	Randy Johnson	.50
716	Ichiro Suzuki	2.00
717	Barry Bonds	1.00
718	Ichiro Suzuki	2.00
719	Albert Pujols	.75

2002 Topps Chrome Aces

		MT
Common Player:		10.00
KB	Kevin Brown	10.00
TH	Tim Hudson	12.00
AL	Al Leiter	10.00
CS	Curt Schilling	15.00
BZ	Barry Zito	15.00

2002 Topps Chrome Batterymates

		MT
Inserted 1:349		
GL	Tom Glavine, Javy Lopez	25.00
HP	Mike Hampton, Ben Petrick	15.00

2002 Topps Chrome Deuces Are Wild

		MT
Common Card:		
CA	Andruw Jones, Chipper Jones	60.00
BT	Bernie Williams, Tino Martinez	35.00
RC	Ryan Dempster, Cliff Floyd	15.00

2002 Topps Chrome Jack of All Trades

		MT
Common Player:		15.00
CJ	Chipper Jones	20.00
MO	Magglio Ordonez	15.00
AR	Alex Rodriguez	25.00

2002 Topps Chrome Kings of the Clubhouse

		MT
Common Player:		15.00
JB	Jeff Bagwell	15.00
TG	Tony Gwynn	25.00
AR	Alex Rodriguez	25.00

2002 Topps Chrome Like Father, Like Son Relics

		MT
Inserted 1:790		
WI	Preston Wilson, Mookie Wilson	20.00

2002 Topps Chrome Three of a Kind

		MT
Common Card		
AIR	Alex Rodriguez, Ivan Rodriguez, Rafael Palmeiro	50.00
BEJ	Bret Boone, Edgar Martinez, John Olerud	25.00
JCL	Jeff Bagwell, Craig Biggio, Lance Berkman	55.00

2002 Topps Chrome Top Of The Order

		MT
Common Player:		10.00
Inserted 1:106		
BA	Benny Agbayani/jsy	15.00
PB	Peter Bergeron/jsy	15.00
CB	Craig Biggio/jsy	15.00
JD	Johnny Damon/bat	25.00
RF	Rafael Furcal/bat	20.00
RH	Rickey Henderson/bat	75.00
JK	Jason Kendall/bat	20.00
CK	Chuck Knoblauch/bat	15.00
PL	Paul LoDuca/bat	20.00
KL	Kenny Lofton/jsy	15.00
JP	Juan Pierre/bat	10.00
SS	Shannon Stewart/jsy	12.00

2002 Topps Chrome 1952 Player Reprints

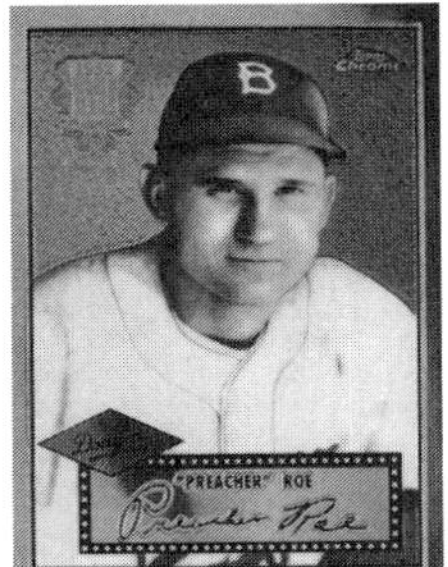

	MT
Complete Set (19):	50.00
Common Card:	3.00
Inserted 1:8	
Refractors:	2X
Inserted 1:24	
52R-1Roy Campanella	5.00
52R-2Duke Snider	4.00
52R-3Carl Erskine	3.00
52R-4Andy Pafko	3.00
52R-5Johnny Mize	3.00
52R-6Billy Martin	5.00
52R-7Phil Rizzuto	4.00
52R-8Gil McDougald	3.00
52R-9Allie Reynolds	3.00
52R-10Jackie Robinson	8.00
52R-11Preacher Roe	3.00
52R-12Gil Hodges	3.00
52R-13Billy Cox	3.00
52R-14Yogi Berra	6.00
52R-15Gene Woodling	3.00
52R-16Johnny Sain	3.00
52R-17Ralph Houk	3.00
52R-18Joe Collins	3.00
52R-19Hank Bauer	3.00

2002 Topps eTopps

Topps continued its on-line card program with a second annual eTopps edition in 2002. Initial Player Offerings were again made for only one week with allocations having to made for some cards in high demand. After the IPO, cards could be bought and sold within portfolios, or physically delivered (for a fee) for more traditional venues. The 2-1/2" x 3-1/2" cards are printed on metallic foil with vertical portrait and action photos on front. Horizontal backs have another portrait photo, a 2001 recap and 2002 "prospectus," and a few biographical bits and stats. The listings here include the initial offering price and the number of cards sold during the open ordering period.

		MT
As of 11/19/02		
1	Ichiro Suzuki ($9.50 / 9477)	5.00
2	Jason Giambi ($9.50 / 5,142)	3.92
3	Roberto Alomar ($6.50 / 2,711)	4.40
4	Bret Boone ($4 / 2,000)	25.00
5	Frank Catalanotto ($6.50 / 2,000)	10.71
6	Alex Rodriguez ($9.50 / 6,393)	7.38
7	Jim Thome ($6.50 / 2,927)	7.50
8	Toby Hall ($6.50 / 2,000)	5.50
9	Troy Glaus ($6.50 / 4,323)	5.55
10	Derek Jeter ($9.50 / 8,000)	6.51
11	Alfonso Soriano ($6.50 / 5,000)	9.05
12	Eric Chavez ($6.50 / 4,334)	6.11
13	Preston Wilson ($4 / 2,000)	7.60
14	Bernie Williams ($6.50 / 4,436)	4.31
15	Larry Walker ($6.50 / 2,546)	5.35
16	Todd Helton ($9.50 / 3,430)	4.60
17	Moises Alou ($6.50 / 2,856)	4.15
18	Lance Berkman ($6.50 / 5,000)	4.99
19	Chipper Jones ($6.50 / 4,734)	4.77
20	Andruw Jones ($6.50 / 4,849)	2.77
21	Barry Bonds ($9.50 / 6,658)	10.98
22	Sammy Sosa ($9.50 / 8,000)	5.00
23	Luis Gonzalez ($6.50 / 2,671)	2.89
24	Shawn Green ($6.50 / 4,438)	4.00
25	Jeff Bagwell ($9.50 / 3,359)	5.00
26	Albert Pujols ($6.50 / 5,531)	4.80
27	Rafael Palmeiro ($6.50 / 2,700)	6.00
28	Jimmy Rollins ($4 / 5,000)	3.26
29	Vladimir Guerrero ($6.50 / 6,000)	4.50
30	Jeff Kent ($6.50 / 3,000)	3.32
31	Ken Griffey Jr. ($9.50 / 4,569)	7.00
32	Magglio Ordonez ($6.50 / 4,000)	5.25
33	Mike Piazza ($9.50 / 4,202)	5.08
34	Pedro Martinez ($9.50 / 6,000)	5.50
35	Mark Mulder ($6.50 / 4,000)	5.29

36	Roger Clemens ($9.50 / 4,567)	7.00
37	Freddy Garcia ($6.50 / 4,986)	5.55
38	Tim Hudson ($6.50 / 2,000)	5.50
39	Mike Mussina ($6.50 / 3,708)	4.50
40	Joe Mays ($4 / 3,000)	4.26
41	Barry Zito ($6.50 / 3,590)	6.50
42	Jermaine Dye ($6.50 / 2,693)	4.48
43	Mariano Rivera ($6.50 / 3,709)	2.76
44	Randy Johnson ($9.50 / 6,211)	5.85
45	Curt Schilling ($6.50 / 5,190)	4.89
46	Greg Maddux ($9.50 / 4,008)	4.64
47	Javier Vazquez ($6.50 / 3,000)	5.37
48	Kerry Wood ($6.50 / 3,346)	4.65
49	Wilson Betemit ($6.50 / 2,377)	8.27
50	Adam Dunn ($6.50 / 6,000)	4.48
51	Josh Beckett ($6.50 / 5,000)	6.05
52	Paul LoDuca $4 / 3,998)	4.12
53	Ben Sheets ($4 / 3,842)	3.25
54	Eric Valent ($4 / 5,000)	3.00
55	Brian Giles ($6.50 / 2,000)	7.33
56	Mo Vaughn ($6.50 / 2,772)	3.27
57	C.C. Sabathia ($6.50 / 2,525)	3.87
58	Nick Johnson ($6.50 / 5,000)	3.16
59	Miguel Tejada ($6.50 / 4,000)	7.37
60	Carlos Delgado ($6.50 / 3,604)	3.84
61	Tsuyoshi Shinjo ($4 / 3,000)	2.17
62	Juan Gonzalez ($6.50 / 2,361)	4.33
63	Mike Sweeney ($6.50 / 3,175)	4.86
64	Ivan Rodriguez ($9.50 / 3,000)	5.06
65	Bud Smith ($4.00 / 3,000)	4.81
66	Brandon Duckworth ($6.50 / 2,000)	8.09
67	Xavier Nady ($4 / 4,000)	5.01
68	D'Angelo Jiminez ($6.50 / 1,725)	8.03
69	Roy Oswalt ($6.50 / 3,523)	4.83
70	J.D. Drew ($9.50 / 3,195)	5.01
71	Cliff Floyd ($6.50 / 3,575)	4.81
72	Kevin Brown ($6.50 / 3,000)	3.00
73	Gary Sheffield ($6.50 / 2,593)	4.33
74	Aramis Ramirez ($6.50 / 3,000)	4.30
75	Nomar Garciaparra ($9.50 / 5,090)	7.00
76	Phil Nevin ($6.50 / 2,348)	4.94
77	Juan Cruz ($4 / 4,000)	3.72
78	Hideo Nomo ($6.50 / 2,857)	3.75
79	Chris George ($4 / 3,000)	3.27
80	Matt Morris ($4 / 3,000)	4.76
81	Corey Patterson ($6.50 / 4,000)	6.41
82	Joel Piniero ($6.50 / 4,776)	6.05
83	Mark Buehrle ($4 / 3,000)	6.88
84	Shannon Stewart ($4 / 1,992)	4.27
85	Kazuhiro Sasaki ($6.50 / 4,000)	4.03
86	Carlos Pena ($4 / 4,000)	6.13
87	Brad Penny ($6.50 / 3,000)	3.96
88	Rich Aurilia ($6.50 / 2,795)	5.12
89	Wade Miller ($4 / 4,000)	4.50
90	Tim Raines Jr. ($4 / 5,000)	3.00
91	Kazuhisa Ishii ($6.50 / 6,000)	5.00
92	Hank Blalock ($6.50 / 5,000)	5.79
93	So Taguchi ($4 /5,000)	4.26
94	Mark Prior ($9.50 / 5,000)	15.86
95	Rickey Henderson ($9.50 / 4,013)	6.00
96	Austin Kearns ($6.50 / 6,000)	5.51
97	Tom Glavine ($9.50 / 3,000)	7.00
98	Manny Ramirez ($6.50 / 4,905)	4.02
99	Shea Hillenbrand ($6.50 / 4,000)	4.34
100	Junior Spivey ($6.50 / 5,000)	3.50
101	Derek Lowe ($6.50 / 4,911)	2.27
102	Torii Hunter ($6.50 / 4,000)	6.27
103	Juan Rivera ($6.50 / 4,000)	6.23
104	Eric Hinske ($6.50 / 5,000)	5.29
105	Bobby Hill ($6.50 / 3,000)	6.05
106	Rafael Soriano ($6.50 / 4,000)	5.11
107	Jim Edmonds ($6.50 / 3,851)	4.04

2002 Topps eTopps Events

Special events during the 2002 season were commemorated by Topps with the issue of special eTopps cards. Like the regular-issue eTopps, the cards were only available directly from Topps on-line. Five thousand of each card were issued with an initial order price of $8 each. Only the baseball related Events cards are listed here.

As of 11/19/02

		MT
1	Mike Cameron (Four HR in game)	2.40
2	Shawn Green (Four HR, 19 TB in game)	3.13
4	Oakland A's (20 Straight Wins)	2.65
5	Greg Maddux (15+ Wins, 15 Years Straight)	5.89

2002 Topps eTopps Classics

Topps expanded its eTopps line-up in 2002 with the issue of 20 cards of former greats. Like regular eTopps cards, they could only be ordered during a one-week Initial Player Offering period. Cards were issued in a quantity of 4,000 each at $12.50. Fronts have a color or colorized action photo, backs have a picture of one of that player's Topps cards, along with career notes, stats, etc. Values shown are for cards "in hand," that is, no longer part of a virtual portfolio.

As of 11/19/02
IPO for all cards is $12.50

		MT
1	Babe Ruth	38.52
2	Tom Seaver	8.05
3	Honus Wagner	10.11
4	Warren Spahn	8.16
5	Frank Robinson	7.45
6	Whitey Ford	8.72
7	Bob Gibson	8.00
8	Reggie Jackson	8.61
9	Joe Morgan	7.10
10	Harmon Killebrew	6.50
11	Eddie Mathews	6.55
12	Willie Mays	15.11
13	Brooks Robinson	8.00
14	Ty Cobb	15.66
15	Carl Yastrzemski	8.03
16	Jackie Robinson	10.00
17	Mike Schmidt	8.00
18	Nolan Ryan	15.63
19	Duke Snider	6.25
20	Stan Musial	10.75

2002 Topps Gallery

		MT
Complete Set (200):		65.00
Common Player:		.25
Common (151-200):		.75
Inserted 1:1		
Pack (6):		3.00
Box (24):		60.00
1	Jason Giambi	1.00
2	Mark Grace	.50
3	Bret Boone	.25
4	Antonio Alfonseca	.25
5	Kevin Brown	.40
6	Cristian Guzman	.25
7	Magglio Ordonez	.50
8	Luis Gonzalez	.50
9	Jorge Posada	.50
10	Roberto Alomar	.50
11	Mike Sweeney	.25
12	Jeff Kent	.40
13	Matt Morris	.25
14	Alfonso Soriano	1.50
15	Adam Dunn	.75
16	Neifi Perez	.25
17	Todd Walker	.25
18	J.D. Drew	.40
19	Eric Chavez	.40
20	Alex Rodriguez	2.50
21	Ray Lankford	.25
22	Roger Cedeno	.25
23	Chipper Jones	1.50
24	Jose Canseco	.50
25	Mike Piazza	2.50
26	Freddy Garcia	.25
27	Todd Helton	.75
28	Tino Martinez	.40
29	Kazuhiro Sasaki	.40
30	Curt Schilling	.75
31	Mark Buehrle	.25
32	John Olerud	.50
33	Brad Radke	.25
34	Steve Sparks	.25
35	Jason Tyner	.25
36	Jeff Shaw	.25
37	Mariano Rivera	.50
38	Russ Ortiz	.25
39	Richard Hidalgo	.25
40	Barry Bonds	1.50
41	John Burkett	.25
42	Tim Hudson	.50
43	Mike Hampton	.25
44	Orlando Cabrera	.25
45	Barry Zito	.25
46	C.C. Sabathia	.25
47	Chan Ho Park	.25
48	Tom Glavine	.50
49	Aramis Ramirez	.25
50	Lance Berkman	.75
51	Al Leiter	.25
52	Phil Nevin	.25
53	Javier Vazquez	.25
54	Troy Glaus	.50
55	Tsuyoshi Shinjo	.50
56	Albert Pujols	1.50
57	John Smoltz	.25
58	Derek Jeter	3.00
59	Robb Nen	.25
60	Jason Kendall	.25
61	Eric Gagne	.25
62	Vladimir Guerrero	.75
63	Corey Patterson	.25
64	Rickey Henderson	.50
65	Jack Wilson	.25
66	Jason LaRue	.25
67	Sammy Sosa	1.50
68	Ken Griffey Jr.	2.00
69	Randy Johnson	.75
70	Nomar Garciaparra	2.00
71	Ivan Rodriguez	.50
72	J.T. Snow	.25
73	Darryl Kile	.25
74	Andruw Jones	.50
75	Brian Giles	.50
76	Pedro Martinez	.75
77	Jeff Bagwell	.75
78	Rafael Palmeiro	.50
79	Ryan Dempster	.25
80	Jeff Cirillo	.25
81	Geoff Jenkins	.25
82	Brandon Duckworth	.25
83	Roger Clemens	1.00
84	Fred McGriff	.50
85	Hideo Nomo	.50
86	Larry Walker	.40
87	Sean Casey	.40
88	Trevor Hoffman	.25
89	Robert Fick	.25
90	Armando Benitez	.25
91	Jeromy Burnitz	.25
92	Bernie Williams	.50
93	Carlos Delgado	.50

94	Troy Percival	.25
95	Nate Cornejo	.25
96	Derrek Lee	.25
97	Jose Ortiz	.25
98	Brian Jordan	.25
99	Jose Cruz	.25
100	Ichiro Suzuki	2.50
101	Jose Mesa	.25
102	Tim Salmon	.25
103	Bud Smith	.25
104	Paul LoDuca	.25
105	Juan Pierre	.25
106	Ben Grieve	.25
107	Russell Branyan	.25
108	Bobby Abreu	.25
109	Moises Alou	.25
110	Richie Sexson	.50
111	Jerry Hairston Jr.	.25
112	Marlon Anderson	.25
113	Juan Gonzalez	.75
114	Craig Biggio	.50
115	Carlos Beltran	.25
116	Eric Milton	.25
117	Cliff Floyd	.25
118	Rich Aurilia	.25
119	Adrian Beltre	.40
120	Jason Bere	.25
121	Darin Erstad	.50
122	Ben Sheets	.50
123	Johnny Damon	.25
124	Jimmy Rollins	.50
125	Shawn Green	.50
126	Greg Maddux	1.50
127	Mark Mulder	.25
128	Bartolo Colon	.25
129	Shannon Stewart	.25
130	Ramon Ortiz	.25
131	Kerry Wood	.50
132	Ryan Klesko	.25
133	Preston Wilson	.25
134	Roy Oswalt	.50
135	Rafael Furcal	.25
136	Eric Karros	.25
137	Nick Neugebauer	.25
138	Doug Mientkiewicz	.25
139	Paul Konerko	.50
140	Bobby Higginson	.25
141	Garret Anderson	.25
142	Wes Helms	.25
143	Brent Abernathy	.25
144	Scott Rolen	.50
145	Dmitri Young	.25
146	Jim Thome	.75
147	Raul Mondesi	.25
148	Pat Burrell	.50
149	Gary Sheffield	.50
150	Miguel Tejada	.50
151	Brandon Inge	.75
152	Carlos Pena	.75
153	Jason Lane	.75
154	Nathan Haynes	.75
155	Hank Blalock	1.50
156	Juan Cruz	.75
157	Morgan Ensberg	.75
158	Sean Burroughs	1.50
159	Ed Rogers	.75
160	Nick Johnson	1.50
161	Orlando Hudson	.75
162	*Anastacio Martinez*	4.00
163	Jeremy Affeldt	.75
164	Brandon Claussen	.75
165	Deivis Santos	.75
166	Mike Rivera	.75
167	Carlos Silva	.75
168	Valentino Pascucci	.75
169	Xavier Nady	.75
170	David Espinosa	.75
171	*Dan Phillips*	1.50
172	*Tony Fontana*	2.00
173	Juan Silvestre	.75
174	*Henry Pichardo*	3.00
175	*Pablo Arias*	3.00
176	*Brett Roneberg*	2.00
177	*Chad Qualls*	1.00
178	*Greg Sain*	2.00
179	*Rene Reyes*	2.00
180	*So Taguchi*	3.00
181	*Dan Johnson*	1.00
182	*Justin Backsmeyer*	1.00
183	Juan Gonzalez	1.00
184	*Jason Ellison*	2.00
185	*Kazuhisa Ishii*	8.00
186	*Joe Mauer*	8.00
187	*James Shanks*	1.50
188	*Kevin Cash*	1.00
189	*J.J. Trujillo*	1.00
190	*Jorge Padilla*	3.00
191	Nolan Ryan	4.00
192	George Brett	3.00
193	Ryne Sandberg	2.00
194	Robin Yount	1.50
195	Tom Seaver	1.00
196	Mike Schmidt	2.00
197	Frank Robinson	1.00
198	Harmon Killebrew	1.00
199	Kirby Puckett	2.50
200	Don Mattingly	4.00

2002 Topps Gallery Press Plates

The aluminum press plates used to print the Gallery cards were inserted at a rate of one per 1,200 packs. Each card's front and back can be found in four different color variations. Because of the unique nature of each plate, assignment of catalog values in not feasible.

	MT
Common Player:	50.00

(See 2002 Topps Gallery for checklist.)

2002 Topps Gallery Autographs

		MT
Common Player:		10.00
Inserted 1:192		
LB	Lance Berkman	40.00
BBO	Bret Boone	20.00
JD	J.D. Drew	40.00
LG	Luis Gonzalez	25.00
SG	Shawn Green	25.00
JL	Jason Lane	10.00
MO	Magglio Ordonez	30.00
JP	Jorge Posada	45.00
JS	Juan Silvestre	10.00

2002 Topps Gallery Heritage

	MT
Complete Set (25):	140.00
Common Player:	3.00
Inserted 1:12	
GH-RARoberto Alomar	4.00
GH-BBOBret Boone	3.00
GH-RCRoger Clemens	8.00
GH-JGJason Giambi	5.00
GH-LGLuis Gonzalez	5.00
GH-SGShawn Green	4.00
GH-KGKen Griffey Jr.	10.00
GH-TGTony Gwynn	5.00
GH-RJReggie Jackson	6.00
GH-CJChipper Jones	6.00
GH-AKAl Kaline	8.00
GH-GMGreg Maddux	8.00
GH-PMPedro Martinez	6.00
GH-MMMark McGwire	12.00
GH-SMStan Musial	6.00
GH-MPMike Piazza	10.00
GH-BRBrooks Robinson	6.00
GH-ARAlex Rodriguez	10.00
GH-NRNolan Ryan	15.00
GH-MSMike Schmidt	7.00
GH-TSTom Seaver	5.00
GH-TSHTsuyoshi Shinjo	4.00
GH-SSSammy Sosa	8.00
GH-CYCarl Yastrzemski	8.00
GH-RYRobin Yount	8.00

2002 Topps Gallery Heritage Autographs

		MT
Inserted 1:240		
BBO	Bret Boone	20.00
LG	Luis Gonzalez	30.00
SG	Shawn Green	25.00

2002 Topps Gallery Heritage Relics

		MT
Common Player:		8.00
Inserted 1:85		
BBO	Bret Boone	8.00
LG	Luis Gonzalez	12.00
TG	Tony Gwynn	15.00
CJ	Chipper Jones	15.00
GM	Greg Maddux	15.00
PM	Pedro Martinez	15.00
MP	Mike Piazza	20.00
AR	Alex Rodriguez	15.00
TS	Tsuyoshi Shinjo	15.00

2002 Topps Gallery Originals Relics

		MT
Common Player:		8.00
Inserted 1:169		
BBO	Bret Boone	10.00
JC	Jose Canseco	30.00
CD	Carlos Delgado	8.00
JG	Juan Gonzalez	10.00
LG	Luis Gonzalez	10.00
TG	Tony Gwynn	20.00
TH	Todd Helton	12.00
AJ	Andruw Jones	10.00
CJ	Chipper Jones	15.00
TM	Tino Martinez	20.00
MP	Mike Piazza	20.00
AP	Albert Pujols	35.00
AR	Alex Rodriguez	15.00
AS	Alfonso Soriano	25.00
BW	Bernie Williams	15.00

2002 Topps Gallery Team Topps Legends Autographs

	MT
Common Player:	
Inserted 1:1,019	
Luis Aparicio	
Jim Bunning	
Fergie Jenkins	
Carl Yastrzemski	65.00

A card number in parentheses ( ) indicates the set is unnumbered.

2002 Topps Gold Label

		MT
Complete Set (200):		100.00
Common Player:		.25
Pack (4):		3.00
Box (18):		48.00
1	Alex Rodriguez	2.50
2	Derek Jeter	3.00
3	Luis Gonzalez	.50
4	Troy Glaus	.50
5	Albert Pujols	1.00
6	Lance Berkman	.75
7	J.D. Drew	.50
8	Chipper Jones	1.50
9	Miguel Tejada	.50
10	Randy Johnson	.75
11	Mike Cameron	.25
12	Brian Giles	.40
13	Roger Cedeno	.25
14	Kerry Wood	.50
15	Ken Griffey Jr.	2.00
16	Carlos Lee	.25
17	Todd Helton	.75
18	Gary Sheffield	.40
19	Richie Sexson	.40
20	Vladimir Guerrero	.75
21	Bobby Higginson	.25
22	Roger Clemens	1.00
23	Barry Zito	.40
24	Juan Pierre	.25
25	Pedro Martinez	.75
26	Sean Casey	.25
27	David Segui	.25
28	Jose Garcia	.25
29	Curt Schilling	.60
30	Bernie Williams	.50
31	Ben Grieve	.25
32	Hideo Nomo	.50
33	Aramis Ramirez	.25
34	Cristian Guzman	.25
35	Rich Aurilia	.25
36	Greg Maddux	1.50
37	Eric Chavez	.40
38	Shawn Green	.40
39	Luis Rivas	.25
40	Magglio Ordonez	.40
41	Jose Vidro	.25
42	Mariano Rivera	.40
43	*Chris Tritle*	2.50
44	C.C. Sabathia	.25
45	Larry Walker	.40
46	Raul Mondesi	.25
47	Kevin Brown	.25
48	Jeff Bagwell	.75
49	*Earl Snyder*	1.00
50	Jason Giambi	.75
51	Ichiro Suzuki	2.50
52	Andruw Jones	.50
53	Ivan Rodriguez	.60
54	Jim Edmonds	.50
55	Preston Wilson	.25
56	Greg Vaughn	.25
57	Jon Lieber	.25
58	*Justin Sherrod*	4.00
59	Marcus Giles	.25
60	Roberto Alomar	.60
61	Pat Burrell	.50
62	Doug Mientkiewicz	.25
63	Mark Mulder	.25
64	Mike Hampton	.25
65	Adam Dunn	1.00
66	Moises Alou	.25
67	Jose Cruz Jr.	.25
68	Derek Bell	.25

69	Sammy Sosa	2.00
70	Joe Mays	.25
71	Phil Nevin	.25
72	Edgardo Alfonzo	.25
73	Barry Bonds	1.50
74	Edgar Martinez	.25
75	Juan Encarnacion	.25
76	Jason Tyner	.25
77	Edgar Renteria	.25
78	Bret Boone	.25
79	Scott Rolen	.40
80	Nomar Garciaparra	2.00
81	Frank Thomas	.75
82	Roy Oswalt	.50
83	Tsuyoshi Shinjo	.25
84	Ben Sheets	.40
85	Hank Blalock	.25
86	Carlos Delgado	.50
87	Tim Hudson	.50
88	Alfonso Soriano	1.00
89	*Michael Hill*	.75
90	Jim Thome	.60
91	Craig Biggio	.25
92	Ryan Klesko	.25
93	Geoff Jenkins	.25
94	Matt Morris	.40
95	Jorge Posada	.50
96	Cliff Floyd	.40
97	Jimmy Rollins	.25
98	Mike Sweeney	.25
99	Frank Catalanotto	.25
100	Mike Piazza	2.00
101	Mark Quinn	.25
102	Torii Hunter	.25
103	Lee Stevens	.25
104	Byung-Hyug Kim	.25
105	*Freddy Sanchez*	2.00
106	David Cone	.25
107	Jerry Hairston Jr.	.25
108	Kyle Farnsworth	.25
109	Rafael Furcal	.25
110	Bartolo Colon	.25
111	Juan Rivera	.25
112	Kevin Young	.25
113	*Chris Narveson*	2.50
114	Richard Hidalgo	.25
115	Andy Pettitte	.50
116	Darin Erstad	.50
117	Corey Koskie	.25
118	Rickey Henderson	.50
119	Derrek Lee	.25
120	Sean Burroughs	.25
121	Paul Konerko	.25
122	*Ross Peeples*	2.00
123	Terrence Long	.25
124	John Smoltz	.25
125	Brandon Duckworth	.25
126	Luis Maza	.25
127	Morgan Ensberg	.25
128	Eric Valent	.25
129	Shannon Stewart	.25
130	D'Angelo Jimenez	.25
131	Jeff Cirillo	.25
132	Jack Cust	.25
133	Dmitri Young	.25
134	Darryl Kile	.25
135	Reggie Sanders	.25
136	Marlon Byrd	.50
137	*Napoleon Calzado*	1.00
138	Javy Lopez	.25
139	Orlando Cabrera	.25
140	Mike Mussina	.25
141	Josh Beckett	.25
142	Kazuhiro Sasaki	.25
143	Jermaine Dye	.25
144	Carlos Beltran	.25
145	Trevor Hoffman	.25
146	*Kazuhisa Ishii*	6.00
147	Alex Gonzalez	.25
148	Marty Cordova	.25
149	*Kevin Deaton*	.75
150	Toby Hall	.25
151	Rafael Palmeiro	.50
152	John Olerud	.40
153	David Eckstein	.25
154	Doug Glanville	.25
155	Johnny Damon	.25
156	Javier Vazquez	.25
157	*Jason Bay*	1.00
158	Robb Nen	.25
159	Rafael Soriano	.25
160	Placido Polanco	.25
161	Garret Anderson	.25
162	Aaron Boone	.25
163	Mike Lieberthal	.25
164	*Joe Mauer*	6.00
165	Matt Lawton	.25
166	*Juan Tolentino*	.75
167	Alex Gonzalez	.25
168	Steve Finley	.25
169	Troy Percival	.25
170	Bud Smith	.25
171	Freddie Garcia	.25
172	Ray Lankford	.25
173	Tim Redding	.25
174	Ryan Dempster	.25
175	Travis Lee	.25
176	Jeff Kent	.25
177	Ramon Hernandez	.25
178	Carl Everett	.25
179	Tom Glavine	.50
180	Juan Gonzalez	.75
181	Nick Johnson	.50
182	Mike Lowell	.25
183	Al Leiter	.25
184	*Jason Maule*	.75
185	Wilson Betemit	.25
186	Tino Martinez	.25
187	Jason Standridge	.25
188	*Mike Peeples*	.75
189	Jason Kendall	.40
190	Fred McGriff	.40
191	*John Rodriguez*	.75
192	*Brett Roneberg*	.75
193	*Marlyn Tisdale*	1.00
194	J.T. Snow	.25
195	*Craig Kuzmic*	1.00
196	Cory Lidle	.25
197	Alex Cintron	.25
198	Fernando Vina	.25
199	Austin Kearns	.75
200	Paul LoDuca	.25

2002 Topps Gold Label Class One Gold

	MT
Stars:	2-4X
Production 500 sets	

2002 Topps Gold Label Class Two Platinum

	MT
Stars:	3-8X
Production 250 sets	

2002 Topps Gold Label Class Three Titanium

	MT
Stars:	6-12X
Production 100 sets	

2002 Topps Gold Label All-Star MVP Winners

		MT
Common Player:		8.00
RA	Roberto Alomar	10.00
SA	Sandy Alomar	8.00
BLB	Bobby Bonds	8.00
DC	Dave Concepcion	8.00
SG2	Steve Garvey	10.00
KG	Ken Griffey Sr.	8.00
BM1	Bill Madlock	8.00
FM	Fred McGriff	10.00
DP3	Dave Parker	8.00
TP	Tony Perez	10.00
MP	Mike Piazza	20.00
KP2	Kirby Puckett	30.00
TR	Tim Raines	8.00

2002 Topps Gold Label Batting Average

		MT
Common Player:		8.00
WB	Wade Boggs	15.00
BB	Bill Buckner	8.00
RC2	Rod Carew	20.00
RAC	Rico Carty	8.00
NC	Norm Cash	15.00
TG1	Tony Gwynn	15.00
TG2	Tony Gwynn	15.00
BM2	Bill Madlock	8.00
DP4	Dave Parker	8.00
KP3	Kirby Puckett	30.00
LW	Larry Walker	10.00
CY2	Carl Yastrzemski	30.00

2002 Topps Gold Label Cy Young Winners

		MT
Common Player:		8.00
RWC	Roger Clemens	15.00
DE	Dennis Eckersley	8.00
RJ	Randy Johnson	12.00
BS	Bret Saberhagen	8.00
JS	John Smoltz	8.00

2002 Topps Gold Label Home Run Champions

		MT
Common Player:		8.00
BB2	Barry Bonds	20.00
GF	George Foster	8.00
TK2	Ted Kluszewski	20.00
KM2	Kevin Mitchell	8.00
DM2	Dale Murphy	40.00
AR	Alex Rodriguez	15.00
DS1	Darryl Strawberry	15.00

2002 Topps Gold Label League Championship MVP Winners

		MT
Common Player:		8.00
GB2	George Brett	40.00
WC	Will Clark	20.00
CC	Craig Counsell	20.00
RH	Rickey Henderson	15.00
JL	Javier Lopez	8.00
AEP	Andy Pettitte	12.00
KP1	Kirby Puckett	30.00
FW	Frank White	8.00
BFW	Bernie Williams	10.00

2002 Topps Gold Label MLB Moments in Time

		MT
Common Player:		8.00
BLB	Barry Bonds	20.00
BB1	Bret Boone	8.00
BB2	Bret Boone	8.00
CD	Carlos Delgado	8.00
TG	Tony Gwynn	15.00
TH	Toby Hall	8.00
CL	Carlos Lee	8.00
JL	Javy Lopez	8.00
MO	Magglio Ordonez	10.00
RP1	Rafael Palmeiro	10.00
RP2	Rafael Palmeiro	10.00
AR	Alex Rodriguez	15.00

2002 Topps Gold Label MVP Winners

		MT
Common Player:		8.00
EB	Ernie Banks	20.00
DB	Don Baylor	8.00
YB	Yogi Berra	20.00
BB1	Barry Bonds	20.00
GB1	George Brett	40.00
SG1	Steve Garvey	8.00
KHG	Kirk Gibson	8.00
KH	Keith Hernandez	12.00
RJ1	Reggie Jackson	15.00
DM	Don Mattingly	40.00
KM1	Kevin Mitchell	8.00
JM	Joe Morgan	8.00
DM1	Dale Murphy	40.00
DP1	Dave Parker	8.00
BR	Brooks Robinson	15.00
FR	Frank Robinson	12.00
RS	Ryne Sandberg	40.00
HS	Hank Sauer	8.00
WS	Willie Stargell	15.00
JT	Joe Torre	10.00
MW	Maury Wills	8.00
CY1	Carl Yastrzemski	30.00
RY	Robin Yount	18.00

2002 Topps Gold Label Rookie of the Year Winners

		MT
Common Player:		8.00
DA	Dick Allen	15.00
AB	Al Bumbry	8.00
RC1	Rod Carew	20.00
CF	Carlton Fisk	15.00
MH	Mike Hargrove	8.00
DJ	Dave Justice	10.00
EM2	Eddie Murray	12.00
LP	Lou Piniella	10.00
AP	Albert Pujols	20.00
DS2	Darryl Strawberry	15.00
FV	Fernando Valenzuela	8.00
BW	Billy Williams	10.00

2002 Topps Gold Label RBI Leaders

		MT
Common Player:		8.00
BRB	Bret Boone	8.00
BRB2	Bret Boone	8.00
GC	Gary Carter	8.00
GL	Greg Luzinski	8.00
EM1	Eddie Murray	12.00
AO	Al Oliver	8.00
DP2	Dave Parker	8.00
DW	Dave Winfield	12.00

2002 Topps Gold Label World Series MVP Winners

		MT
Common Player:		8.00
JB	Johnny Bench	20.00
RCC	Ron Cey	8.00
RJ2	Reggie Jackson	15.00
PM	Paul Molitor	15.00
MR	Mariano Rivera	10.00

2002 Topps Gold Label Platinum Memorabilia

MT
Platinum: .75-1.5X
Titanium Memorabilia: 1-2X

2002 Topps Heritage

MT
Complete Set (440): 375.00
Common Player: .40
Common (364-446): 3.00
Inserted 1:2
Pack (8): 5.00
Box (24): 110.00
1 Ichiro Suzuki SP 20.00
2 Darin Erstad .60
3 Rod Beck .40
4 Doug Mientkiewicz .40
5 Mike Sweeney .40
6 Roger Clemens 2.50
7 Jason Tyner .40
8 Alex Gonzalez .40
9 Eric Young .40
10 Randy Johnson 1.25
10 Randy Johnson SP 6.00
11 Aaron Sele .40
12 Tony Clark .40
13 C.C. Sabathia .40
14 Melvin Mora .40
15 Tim Hudson .75
16 Ben Petrick .40
17 Tom Glavine .75
18 Jason Lane .40
19 Larry Walker .75
20 Mark Mulder .40
21 Steve Finley .40
22 Bengie Molina .40
23 Rob Bell .40
24 Nathan Haynes .40
25 Rafael Furcal .60
25 Rafael Furcal SP 3.00
26 Mike Mussina 1.00
27 Paul LoDuca .40
28 Torii Hunter .40
29 Carlos Lee .40
30 Jimmy Rollins .40
31 Arthur Rhodes .40
32 Ivan Rodriguez 1.25
33 Wes Helms .40
34 Cliff Floyd .40
35 Julian Tavarez .40
36 Mark McGwire 4.00
37 Chipper Jones SP 8.00
38 Denny Neagle .40
39 Odalis Perez .40
40 Antonio Alfonseca .40
41 Edgar Renteria .40
42 Troy Glaus 1.00
43 Scott Brosius .40
44 Abraham Nunez .40
45 Jamey Wright .40
46 Bobby Bonilla .40
47 Ismael Valdes .40
48 Chris Reitsma .40
49 Neifi Perez .40
50 Juan Cruz .40
51 Kevin Brown .60
52 Ben Grieve .40
53 Alex Rodriguez SP 12.00
54 Charles Nagy .40
55 Reggie Sanders .40
56 Nelson Figueroa .40
57 Felipe Lopez .40
58 Bill Ortega .40
59 Mac Suzuki .40
60 Johnny Estrada .40
61 Bob Wickman .40
62 Doug Glanville .40
63 Jeff Cirillo .50
63 Jeff Cirillo SP 3.00
64 Corey Patterson .50
65 Aaron Myette .40
66 Magglio Ordonez .40
67 Ellis Burks .40
68 Miguel Tejada .40
69 John Olerud .75
69 John Olerud SP 4.00
70 Greg Vaughn .40
71 Andy Pettitte .75
72 Mike Matheny .40
73 Brandon Duckworth .40
74 Scott Schoeneweis .40
75 Mike Lowell .40
76 Einar Diaz .40
77 Tino Martinez .75
78 Matt Williams .60
79 *Jason Young* 1.50
80 Nate Cornejo .40
81 Andres Galarraga .60
82 Bernie Williams SP 8.00
83 Ryan Klesko .40
84 Dan Wilson .40
85 *Henry Pichardo* .40
86 Ray Durham .40
87 Omar Daal .40
88 Derrek Lee .40
89 Al Leiter .60
90 Darrin Fletcher .40
91 Josh Beckett .75
92 Johnny Damon .50
92 Johnny Damon SP 4.00
93 Abraham Nunez .40
94 Ricky Ledee .40
95 Richie Sexson .40
96 Adam Kennedy .40
97 Raul Mondesi .40
98 John Burkett .40
99 Ben Sheets .60
99 Ben Sheets SP 4.00
100 Preston Wilson .40
100 Preston Wilson SP 3.00
101 Boof Bonser .40
102 Shigetoshi Hasegawa .40
103 Carlos Febles .40
104 Jorge Posada SP 4.00
105 Michael Tucker .40
106 Roberto Hernandez .40
107 *John Rodriguez* .75
108 Danny Graves .40
109 Rich Aurilia .40
110 Jon Lieber .40
111 *Tim Hummel* .40
112 J.T. Snow .40
113 Kris Benson .40
114 Derek Jeter 5.00
115 John Franco .40
116 Matt Stairs .40
117 Ben Davis .40
118 Darryl Kile .40
119 *Mike Peeples* 1.00
120 Kevin Tapani .40
121 Armando Benitez .40
122 Damian Miller .40
123 Jose Jimenez .40
124 Pedro Astacio .40
125 *Marlyn Tisdale* .75
126 Deivi Cruz .40
127 Paul O'Neill .75
128 Jermaine Dye .40
129 Marcus Giles .40
130 Mark Loretta .40
131 Garret Anderson .40
132 Todd Ritchie .40
133 Joe Crede .40
134 Kevin Millwood .40
135 Shane Reynolds .40
136 Mark Grace .75
137 Shannon Stewart .40
138 Nick Neugebauer .40
139 *Nic Jackson* 1.00
140 Robb Nen .40
141 Dmitri Young .40
142 Kevin Appier .40
143 Jack Cust .40
144 Andres Torres .40
145 Frank Thomas 1.25
146 Jason Kendall .40
147 Greg Maddux 2.50
148 David Justice .75
149 Hideo Nomo .75
150 Bret Boone .40
151 Wade Miller .40
152 Jeff Kent .40
153 Scott Williamson .40
154 Julio Lugo .40
155 Bobby Higginson .40
156 Geoff Jenkins .60
157 Darren Dreifort .40
158 *Freddy Sanchez* .75
159 Bud Smith .75
160 Phil Nevin .40
161 Cesar Izturis .40
162 Sean Casey .75
163 Jose Ortiz .40
164 Brent Abernathy .40
165 Kevin Young .40
166 Daryle Ward .40
167 Trevor Hoffman .40
168 Rondell White .40
169 Kip Wells .40
170 John Vander Wal .40
171 Jose Lima .40
172 Wilton Guerrero .40
173 Aaron Dean .40
174 Rick Helling .40
175 Juan Pierre .40
176 Jay Bell .40
177 Craig House .40
178 David Bell .40
179 Pat Burrell .60
180 Eric Gagne .40
181 Adam Pettyjohn .40
182 Ugueth Urbina .40
183 Peter Bergeron .40
184 Adrian Gonzalez .40
184 Adrian Gonzalez SP 4.00
185 Damion Easley .40
186 Gookie Dawkins .40
187 Matt Lawton .40
188 Frank Catalanotto .40
189 David Wells .40
190 Roger Cedeno .40
191 Brian Giles .75
192 Julio Zuleta .40
193 Timo Perez .40
194 Billy Wagner .40
195 Craig Counsell .40
196 Bart Miadich .40
197 Gary Sheffield .75
198 Richard Hidalgo .60
199 Juan Uribe .40
200 Curt Schilling .75
201 Javy Lopez .40
202 Jimmy Haynes .40
203 Jim Edmonds .60
204 Pokey Reese .40
204 Pokey Reese SP 3.00
205 Matt Clement .40
206 Dean Palmer .40
207 Nick Johnson .40
208 *Nate Espy* .75
209 Pedro Feliz .40
210 Aaron Rowand .40
211 Masato Yoshii .40
212 Jose Cruz .40
213 Paul Byrd .40
214 *Mark Phillips* 1.00
215 Benny Agbayani .40
216 Frank Menechino .40
217 John Flaherty .40
218 Brian Boehringer .40
219 Todd Hollandsworth .40
220 Sammy Sosa SP 10.00
221 Steve Sparks .40
222 Homer Bush .40
223 Mike Hampton .50
224 Bobby Abreu .60
225 Barry Larkin .75
226 Ryan Rupe .40
227 Bubba Trammell .40
228 Todd Zeile .40
229 Jeff Shaw .40
230 Alex Ochoa .40
231 Orlando Cabrera .40
232 Jeremy Giambi .40
233 Tomo Ohka .40
234 Luis Castillo .40
235 Chris Holt .40
236 Shawn Green .75
237 Sidney Ponson .40
238 Lee Stevens .40
239 Hank Blalock .40
240 Randy Winn .40
241 Pedro Martinez 1.50
242 Vinny Castillo .40
243 Steve Karsay .40
244 Barry Bonds SP 12.00
245 Jason Bere .40
246 Scott Rolen .75
246 Scott Rolen SP 5.00
247 Ryan Kohlmeier .40
248 Kerry Wood .75
249 Aramis Ramirez .40
250 Lance Berkman .75
251 Omar Vizquel .60
252 Juan Encarnacion .40
254 David Segui .40
255 Brian Anderson .40
256 Jay Payton .40
257 Mark Grudzielanek .40
258 Jimmy Anderson .40
259 Eric Valent .40
260 Chad Durbin .40
262 Alex Gonzalez .40
263 Scott Dunn .40
264 Scott Elarton .40
265 Tom Gordon .40
266 Moises Alou .60
269 Mark Buehrle .40
270 Jerry Hairston Jr. .40
272 Luke Prokopec .40
273 Graeme Lloyd .40
274 Bret Prinz .40
276 Chris Carpenter .40
277 Ryan Minor .40
278 Jeff D'Amico .40
279 Raul Ibanez .40
280 Joe Mays .40
281 Livan Hernandez .40
282 Robin Ventura .60
283 Gabe Kapler .60
284 Tony Batista .40
285 Ramon Hernandez .40
286 Craig Paquette .40
287 Mark Kotsay .40
288 Mike Lieberthal .40
289 Joe Borchard .40
290 Cristian Guzman .40
291 Craig Biggio .60
292 Joaquin Benoit .40
293 Ken Caminiti .40
294 Sean Burroughs .40
295 Eric Karros .50
296 Eric Chavez .60
297 LaTroy Hawkins .40
298 Alfonso Soriano .75
299 John Smoltz .40
300 Adam Dunn 1.50
301 Ryan Dempster .40
302 Travis Hafner .40
303 Russell Branyan .40
304 Dustin Hermanson .40
305 Jim Thome 1.00
306 Carlos Beltran .40
307 *Jason Botts* .75
308 David Cone .40
309 Ivanon Coffie .40
310 Brian Jordan .40
311 Todd Walker .40
312 Jeromy Burnitz .40
313 Tony Armas .40
314 Jeff Conine .40
315 Todd Jones .40
316 Roy Oswalt .75
317 Aubrey Huff .40
318 Josh Fogg .40
319 Jose Vidro .40
320 Jace Brewer .40
321 Mike Redmond .40
322 *Noochie Varner* 1.00
323 Russ Ortiz .40
324 Edgardo Alfonzo .40
325 Ruben Sierra .40
326 Calvin Murray .40
327 Marlon Anderson .40
328 Albie Lopez .40
329 Chris Gomez .40
330 Fernando Tatis .40
331 Stubby Clapp .40
332 Rickey Henderson .75
333 Brad Radke .40
334 Brent Mayne .40
335 Cory Lidle .40
336 Edgar Martinez .50

337	Aaron Boone	.40
338	Jay Witasick	.40
339	Benito Santiago	.40
340	Jose Mercedes	.40
341	Fernando Vina	.40
342	A.J. Pierzynski	.40
343	Jeff Bagwell	1.25
344	Brian Bohanon	.40
345	Adrian Beltre	.40
346	Troy Percival	.40
347	*Napoleon Calzado*	.75
348	Ruben Rivera	.40
349	Rafael Soriano	.40
350	Damian Jackson	.40
351	Joe Randa	.40
352	Chan Ho Park	.60
353	Dante Bichette	.40
354	Bartolo Colon	.40
355	*Jason Bay*	1.00
356	Shea Hillenbrand	.40
357	Matt Morris	.40
358	Brad Penny	.40
359	Mark Quinn	.40
360	Marquis Grissom	.40
361	Henry Blanco	.40
362	Billy Koch	.40
363	Mike Cameron	.40
364	Albert Pujols	10.00
365	Paul Konerko	3.00
366	Eric Milton	3.00
367	Nick Bierbrodt	3.00
368	Rafael Palmeiro	5.00
369	*Jorge Padilla*	4.00
370	Jason Giambi	5.00
371	Mike Piazza	12.00
372	Alex Cora	3.00
373	Todd Helton	6.00
374	Juan Gonzalez	6.00
375	Mariano Rivera	4.00
376	Jason LaRue	3.00
377	Tony Gwynn	6.00
378	Wilson Betemit	4.00
379	*J.J. Trujillo*	4.00
380	Brad Ausmus	3.00
381	Chris George	3.00
382	Jose Canseco	5.00
383	Ramon Ortiz	3.00
384	John Rocker	3.00
385	Rey Ordonez	3.00
386	Ken Griffey Jr.	15.00
387	Juan Pena	3.00
388	Michael Barrett	3.00
389	J.D. Drew	5.00
390	Corey Koskie	3.00
391	Vernon Wells	3.00
392	*Juan Tolentino*	4.00
393	Luis Gonzalez	5.00
394	Terrance Long	3.00
395	Travis Lee	3.00
396	*Earl Snyder*	4.00
397	Nomar Garciaparra	15.00
398	Jason Schmidt	3.00
399	David Espinosa	3.00
400	Steve Green	3.00
401	Jack Wilson	3.00
402	*Chris Tritle*	6.00
403	Angel Berroa	3.00
404	Josh Towers	3.00
405	Andruw Jones	4.00
406	Brent Butler	3.00
407	*Craig Kuzmic*	5.00
408	Derek Bell	3.00
409	*Eric Glaser*	5.00
410	Joel Pineiro	3.00
411	Alexis Gomez	3.00
412	Mike Rivera	3.00
413	Shawn Estes	3.00
414	Milton Bradley	3.00
415	Carl Everett	3.00
416	Kazuhiro Sasaki	4.00
417	*Tony Fontana*	4.00
418	Josh Pearce	3.00
419	Gary Matthews Jr.	3.00
420	*Raymond Cabrera*	4.00
421	Joe Kennedy	3.00
422	*Jason Maule*	4.00
423	Casey Fossum	3.00
424	Christian Parker	3.00
425	*Laynce Nix*	5.00
426	Byung-Hyun Kim	3.00
427	Freddy Garcia	3.00
428	Herbert Perry	3.00
429	Jason Marquis	3.00
430	Sandy Alomar Jr.	3.00
431	Roberto Alomar	5.00
432	Tsuyoshi Shinjo	4.00
433	Tim Wakefield	3.00
434	Robert Fick	3.00
435	Vladimir Guerrero	6.00
436	Jose Mesa	3.00
437	Scott Spiezio	3.00
438	Jose Hernandez	3.00
439	Jose Acevedo	3.00
440	*Brian West*	4.00
441	Barry Zito	3.00
442	Luis Maza	3.00
443	Marlon Byrd	4.00
444	A.J. Burnett	3.00
445	Dee Brown	3.00
446	Carlos Delgado	5.00

2002 Topps Heritage Chrome

	MT
Stars (1-100):	6-12X
RC's:	4-8X
Production 553 sets	

2002 Topps Heritage Classic Renditions

		MT
Complete Set (10):		12.00
Common Player:		1.00
Inserted 1:12		
CR-1	Kerry Wood	2.00
CR-2	Brian Giles	1.50
CR-3	Roger Cedeno	1.00
CR-4	Jason Giambi	2.00
CR-5	Albert Pujols	5.00
CR-6	Mark Buehrle	1.00
CR-7	Cristian Guzman	1.00
CR-8	Jimmy Rollins	1.00
CR-9	Jim Thome	1.50
CR-10	Shawn Green	1.50

2002 Topps Heritage Classic Renditions Autographs

		MT
Production 25 sets		
BG	Brian Giles	
CG	Cristian Guzman	
JR	Jimmy Rollins	

2002 Topps Heritage Clubhouse Collection

		MT
Common Player:		15.00
Jersey 1:332		
Bat 1:498		
RA	Rich Aurilia/bat	15.00
YB	Yogi Berra/jsy	40.00
BB	Barry Bonds/bat	45.00
AD	Alvin Dark/bat	25.00
NG	Nomar Garciaparra/bat	50.00
GK	George Kell/jsy	20.00
GM	Greg Maddux/jsy	25.00
EM	Eddie Mathews/jsy	35.00
WM	Willie Mays/bat	75.00
CP	Corey Patterson/bat	20.00
JP	Jorge Posada/bat	20.00
HS	Hank Sauer/bat	20.00

2002 Topps Heritage Clubhouse Collection Auto. Relics

		MT
Complete Set (5):		
Common Player:		
CCA-YB	Yogi Berra	
CCA-AD	Alvin Dark	
CCA-GK	George Kell	
CCA-WM	Willie Mays	
CCA-HS	Hank Sauer	

2002 Topps Heritage Clubhouse Collection Dual Relics

		MT
CC2-SM	Eddie Mathews, Greg Maddux	
CC2-BP	Yogi Berra, Jorge Posada	
CC2-SP	Hank Sauer, Corey Patterson	
CC2-KR	George Kell, Nomar Garciaparra	
CC2-DA	Alvin Dark, Rich Aurilia	
CC2-MB	Willie Mays, Barry Bonds	

2002 Topps Heritage Grandstand Glory Stadium Seat

		MT
Common Player:		10.00
Inserted 1:133		
RC	Roy Campanella	25.00
BF	Bob Feller	20.00
WF	Whitey Ford	20.00
TK	Ted Kluszewski	20.00
BM	Billy Martin	25.00
HN	Hal Newhouser	15.00
SP	Satchel Paige	30.00
BP	Billy Pierce	15.00
HS	Hank Sauer	10.00
BS	Bobby Shantz	15.00
WS	Warren Spahn	20.00
EW	Early Wynn	15.00

2002 Topps Heritage New Age Performers

		MT
Complete Set (15):		30.00
Common Player:		1.00
Inserted 1:15		
NA-1	Luis Gonzalez	1.25
NA-2	Mark McGwire	5.00
NA-3	Barry Bonds	3.00
NA-4	Ken Griffey Jr.	4.00
NA-5	Ichiro Suzuki	6.00
NA-6	Sammy Sosa	3.00
NA-7	Andruw Jones	1.00
NA-8	Derek Jeter	6.00
NA-9	Todd Helton	1.50
NA-10	Alex Rodriguez	4.00
NA-11	Jason Giambi	1.50
NA-12	Bret Boone	1.00
NA-13	Roberto Alomar	1.25
NA-14	Albert Pujols	3.00
NA-15	Vladimir Guerrero	1.50

2002 Topps Heritage Real One Autographs

		MT
Common Player:		20.00
Inserted 1:180		
YB	Yogi Berra	120.00
JB	Joe Black	50.00
RB	Ray Boone	80.00
AC	Andy Carey	80.00
RCL	Roger Clemens	120.00
AD	Alvin Dark	80.00
DD	Dom DiMaggio	80.00
JE	Jim Edmonds	50.00
RF	Roy Face	80.00
BF	Bob Feller	60.00
WF	Whitey Ford	120.00
CG	Brian Giles	25.00
CG	Cristian Guzman	20.00
MI	Monte Irvin	80.00
GK	George Kell	100.00
WM	Willie Mays	240.00
GM	Gil McDougald	60.00
OM	Orestes Minoso	75.00
JP	John Podres	80.00
PR	Phil Rizzuto	120.00
ARO	Alex Rodriguez	140.00
PRO	Preacher Roe	60.00
AR	Al Rosen	90.00
HS	Hank Sauer	
ASC	Al Schoendienst	60.00
BS	Bobby Shantz	50.00
ES	Enos Slaughter	75.00
WS	Warren Spahn	100.00
HW	Hoyt Wilhelm	80.00

2002 Topps Heritage Team Topps Legends Autographs

	MT
Inserted 1:613	
Vida Blue	20.00
Frank Howard	30.00
Mickey Lolich	25.00
Frank Robinson	40.00
Bobby Thomson	30.00

2002 Topps Heritage Then and Now

	MT
Complete Set (10):	20.00
Common Player:	1.00

Inserted 1:15

TN-1	Ed Mathews, Barry Bonds	4.00
TN-2	Al Rosen, Alex Rodriguez	4.00
TN-3	Carl Furillo, Larry Walker	1.00
TN-4	Mickey Vernon, Ichiro Suzuki	6.00
TN-5	Roy Campanella, Sammy Sosa	4.00
TN-6	Al Rosen, Bret Boone	1.00
TN-7	Warren Spahn, Randy Johnson	2.00
TN-8	Ed Lopat, Freddy Garcia	1.00
TN-9	Robin Roberts, Randy Johnson	2.00
TN-10	Billy Pierce, Hideo Nomo	1.50

2002 Topps Opening Day

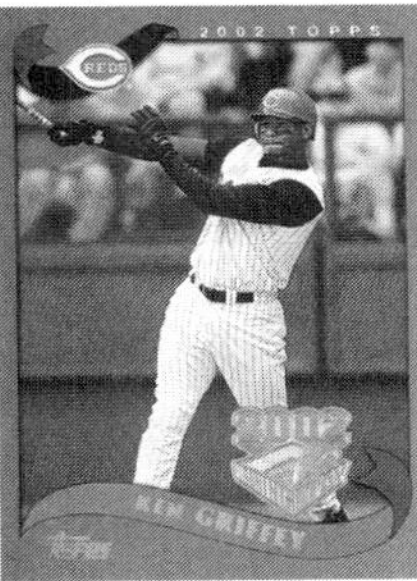

		MT
Complete Set (165):		40.00
Common Player:		.10
Pack (7):		1.25
Box (36):		38.00
1	Roy Oswalt	.25
2	Derek Jeter	2.50
3	Dmitri Young	.10
4	Ramon Hernandez	.10
5	Albert Pujols	1.25
6	Sean Casey	.25
7	Joe Randa	.10
8	Craig Counsell	.10
9	John Olerud	.25
10	Troy Glaus	.50
11	Adam Kennedy	.10
12	Carlos Delgado	.50
13	Bobby Abreu	.20
14	J.T. Snow Jr.	.10
15	Ivan Rodriguez	.50
16	Mike Lowell	.10
17	Juan Pierre	.10
18	Magglio Ordonez	.30
19	Greg Maddux	1.25
20	Jorge Posada	.25
21	Johnny Damon	.10
22	Mike Hampton	.10
23	Paul LoDuca	.10
24	Terrence Long	.10
25	Jeff Bagwell	.60
26	Shannon Stewart	.10
27	Brad Radke	.10
28	Brian Jordan	.10
29	Lee Stevens	.10
30	Cliff Floyd	.10
31	Roger Clemens	1.00
32	Mike Matheny	.10
33	Alfonso Soriano	.40
34	Randy Johnson	.60
35	Mike Sweeney	.10
36	Jose Cruz Jr.	.20
37	Fernando Tatis	.10
38	Eric Young	.10
39	Ruben Rivera	.10
40	Mike Mussina	.50
41	Alex Gonzalez	.10
42	Edgardo Alfonzo	.10
43	Torii Hunter	.10
44	Richie Sexson	.10
45	Bret Boone	.10
46	John Smoltz	.10
47	Bengie Molina	.10
48	Trot Nixon	.10
49	Mike Cameron	.10
50	Mariano Rivera	.20
51	Ichiro Suzuki	2.50
52	Cristian Guzman	.10
53	Andruw Jones	.40
54	Jerry Hairston Jr.	.10
55	Brad Fullmer	.10
56	Luis Gonzalez	.40
57	Placido Polanco	.10
58	Jason Tyner	.10
59	Dan Wilson	.10
60	Jim Edmonds	.10
61	Larry Walker	.40
62	Edgar Renteria	.10
63	Orlando Cabrera	.10
64	Sammy Sosa	1.50
65	Derrek Lee	.10
66	C.C. Sabathia	.10
67	Aaron Boone	.10
68	Royce Clayton	.10
69	Darryl Kile	.10
70	Vladimir Guerrero	.60
71	Bud Smith	.20
72	Adrian Beltre	.20
73	Barry Bonds	15.00
74	Ben Petrick	.10
75	Derek Bell	.10
76	Jeff Kent	.20
77	Ricky Gutierrez	.10
78	Rafael Palmeiro	.40
79	Doug Mientkiewicz	.10
80	Fernando Vina	.10
81	Mark Mulder	.20
82	Carlos Beltran	.10
83	Juan Encarnacion	.10
84	Jimmy Rollins	.10
85	Pedro J. Martinez	.60
86	Aramis Ramirez	.10
87	Reggie Sanders	.10
88	Gary Sheffield	.25
89	Bartolo Colon	.10
90	Jose Macias	.10
91	Bobby Higginson	.10
92	Craig Biggio	.20
93	Al Leiter	.20
94	Juan Gonzalez	.60
95	Jose Valentin	.10
96	Jon Lieber	.10
97	Alex Gonzalez	.10
98	Jose Mesa	.10
99	Sandy Alomar	.10
100	Barry Bonds	1.50
101	Todd Walker	.10
102	Kevin Young	.10
103	Ken Griffey Jr.	2.00
104	Mark McGwire	2.00
105	Jason Giambi	.60
106	Todd Helton	.60
107	Mike Piazza	2.00
108	Nomar Garciaparra	1.50
109	Bernie Williams	.40
110	Shawn Wooten	.10
111	Eric Chavez	.20
112	Curt Schilling	.20
113	Roberto Alomar	.50
114	Chipper Jones	1.25
115	Edgar Martinez	.10
116	Shawn Green	.20
117	Ben Grieve	.10
118	Jermaine Dye	.10
119	Steve Finley	.10
120	Adam Dunn	.25
121	Preston Wilson	.10
122	Lance Berkman	.20
123	Ben Sheets	.20
124	Ryan Klesko	.10
125	Brian Giles	.20
126	Marcus Giles	.10
127	Craig Wilson	.10
128	Miguel Tejada	.20
129	Andres Galarraga	.20
130	Alex Rodriguez	1.50
131	David Justice	.25
132	Barry Zito	.10
133	Scott Rolen	.30
134	Brent Abernathy	.10
135	Raul Mondesi	.20
136	Josh Towers	.10
137	Rafael Furcal	.10
138	Gabe Kapler	.10
139	Fred McGriff	.25
140	Jeff Conine	.10
141	Mike Lieberthal	.10
142	Frank Thomas	.60
143	Jason Kendall	.10
144	Toby Hall	.10
145	Pat Burrell	.30
146	J.D. Drew	.25
147	Javier Lopez	.10
148	Carlos Lee	.10
149	Doug Glanville	.10
150	Ruben Sierra	.10
151	Julio Franco	.10
152	Tim Hudson	.20
153	Rich Aurilia	.10
154	Geoff Jenkins	.10
155	Tsuyoshi Shinjo	.10
156	Moises Alou	.10
157	Jim Thome	.40
158	Steve Cox	.10
159	Kevin Brown	.20
160	Barry Bonds	.50
161	Rickey Henderson	.20
162	Bud Smith	.10
163	Rickey Henderson	.20
164	Barry Bonds	.50
165	Checklist	.10

2002 Topps Opening Day Autographs

		MT
Common Auto.:		15.00
GJ	Geoff Jenkins	15.00
NJ	Nick Johnson	30.00
BS	Ben Sheets	25.00

2002 Topps Pristine

		MT
Complete Set (210):		N/A
Common Player:		1.00
Common Uncommon RC:		5.00
Production 1,999		
Common Rare RC:		6.00
Production 799		
Pack (8):		30.00
Box (5):		140.00
1	Alex Rodriguez	8.00
2	Carlos Delgado	1.50
3	Jimmy Rollins	1.00
4	Jason Kendall	1.00
5	John Olerud	1.50
6	Albert Pujols	5.00
7	Curt Schilling	2.00
8	Gary Sheffield	1.50
9	Johnny Damon	1.00
10	Ichiro Suzuki	8.00
11	Pat Burrell	2.00
12	Garret Anderson	1.50
13	Andruw Jones	2.00
14	Kerry Wood	1.50
15	Kenny Lofton	1.00
16	Adam Dunn	2.50
17	Juan Pierre	1.00
18	Josh Beckett	1.00
19	Roy Oswalt	1.50
20	Derek Jeter	10.00
21	Jose Vidro	1.00
22	Richie Sexson	1.50
23	Mike Sweeney	1.00
24	Jeff Kent	1.50
25	Jason Giambi	5.00
26	Bret Boone	1.00
27	J.D. Drew	1.50
28	Shannon Stewart	1.00
29	Miguel Tejada	2.00
30	Barry Bonds	8.00
31	Randy Johnson	2.50
32	Pedro J. Martinez	3.00
33	Magglio Ordonez	1.50
34	Todd Helton	2.00
35	Craig Biggio	1.50
36	Shawn Green	1.50
37	Vladimir Guerrero	3.00
38	Mo Vaughn	1.50
39	Alfonso Soriano	8.00
40	Barry Zito	2.00
41	Aramis Ramirez	1.00
42	Ryan Klesko	1.00
43	Ruben Sierra	1.00
44	Tino Martinez	1.00
45	Toby Hall	1.00
46	Ivan Rodriguez	2.00
47	Raul Mondesi	1.00
48	Carlos Pena	1.00
49	Darin Erstad	1.50
50	Sammy Sosa	5.00
51	Bartolo Colon	1.50
52	Robert Fick	1.00
53	Cliff Floyd	1.00
54	Brian Jordan	1.00
55	Torii Hunter	1.50
56	Roberto Alomar	2.00
57	Roger Clemens	4.00
58	Mark Mulder	1.50
59	Brian Giles	1.50
60	Mike Piazza	6.00
61	Rich Aurilia	1.00
62	Freddy Garcia	1.00
63	Jim Edmonds	1.50
64	Eric Hinske	1.00
65	Jeremy Giambi	1.00
66	Javier Vazquez	1.00
67	Cristian Guzman	1.00
68	Paul LoDuca	1.00
69	Bobby Abreu	1.50
70	Nomar Garciaparra	6.00
71	Troy Glaus	2.00
72	Chipper Jones	5.00
73	Scott Rolen	2.00
74	Lance Berkman	2.00
75	C.C. Sabathia	1.00
76	Bernie Williams	2.00
77	Rafael Palmeiro	2.00
78	Phil Nevin	1.00
79	Kazuhiro Sasaki	1.00
80	Eric Chavez	1.50
81	Jorge Posada	2.00
82	Edgardo Alfonzo	1.00
83	Geoff Jenkins	1.00
84	Preston Wilson	1.00
85	Jim Thome	2.00
86	Frank Thomas	2.50
87	Jeff Bagwell	2.50
88	Greg Maddux	5.00
89	Mark Prior	2.00
90	Larry Walker	1.50
91	Luis Gonzalez	1.50
92	Tim Hudson	1.50
93	Tsuyoshi Shinjo	1.00
94	Juan Gonzalez	2.00
95	Shea Hillenbrand	1.00
96	Paul Konerko	1.00
97	Tom Glavine	2.00
98	Marty Cordova	1.00
99	Moises Alou	1.00
100	Ken Griffey Jr.	6.00
101	Hank Blalock	1.50
102	Matt Morris	1.50
103	Robb Nen	1.00
104	Mike Cameron	1.00
105	Mark Buehrle	1.00
106	Sean Burroughs	1.00
107	Orlando Cabrera	1.00
108	Jeromy Burnitz	1.00
109	Juan Uribe	1.00
110	Eric Milton	1.00
111	Carlos Lee	1.00
112	Jose Mesa	1.00
113	Morgan Ensberg	1.00
114	Mike Rivera	1.00
115	Juan Cruz	1.00
116	Mike Lieberthal	1.00
117	Armando Benitez	1.00
118	Vinny Castilla	1.00
119	Russ Ortiz	1.00
120	Mike Lowell	1.00
121	Corey Patterson	1.00
122	Mike Mussina	2.00
123	Rafael Furcal	1.00
124	Mark Grace	1.50

125	Ben Sheets	1.00
126	John Smoltz	1.00
127	Fred McGriff	1.50
128	Nick Johnson	1.50
129	J.T. Snow	1.00
130	Jeff Cirillo	1.00
131	Trevor Hoffman	1.00
132	Kevin Brown	1.00
133	Mariano Rivera	1.50
134	Marlon Anderson	1.00
135	Al Leiter	1.00
136	Doug Mientkiewicz	1.00
137	Eric Karros	1.00
138	Bobby Higginson	1.00
139	Sean Casey	1.00
140	Troy Percival	1.00
141	Willie Mays	6.00
142	Carl Yastrzemski	3.00
143	Stan Musial	5.00
144	Harmon Killebrew	3.00
145	Mike Schmidt	5.00
146	Duke Snider	3.00
147	Brooks Robinson	3.00
148	Frank Robinson	2.00
149	Nolan Ryan	12.00
150	Reggie Jackson	4.00
151	*Joe Mauer C*	12.00
152	*Joe Mauer U*	18.00
153	*Joe Mauer R*	25.00
154	Colt Griffin C	5.00
155	Colt Griffin U	8.00
156	Colt Griffin R	10.00
157	*Jason Simontacchi C*	10.00
158	*Jason Simontacchi U*	12.00
159	*Jason Simontacchi R*	20.00
160	Casey Kotchman C	8.00
161	Casey Kotchman U	12.00
162	Casey Kotchman R	25.00
163	*Greg Sain C*	4.00
164	*Greg Sain U*	5.00
165	*Greg Sain R*	6.00
166	David Wright C	5.00
167	David Wright U	8.00
168	David Wright R	10.00
169	Scott Hairston C	5.00
170	Scott Hairston U	8.00
171	Scott Hairston R	10.00
172	*Rolando Viera C*	4.00
173	*Rolando Viera U*	5.00
174	*Rolando Viera R*	6.00
175	Tyrell Godwin C	4.00
176	Tyrell Godwin U	6.00
177	Tyrell Godwin R	10.00
178	*Jesus Cota C*	8.00
179	*Jesus Cota U*	10.00
180	*Jesus Cota R*	15.00
181	*Dan Johnson C*	4.00
182	*Dan Johnson U*	5.00
183	*Dan Johnson R*	6.00
184	Mario Ramos C	4.00
185	Mario Ramos U	5.00
186	Mario Ramos R	6.00
187	*Jason Dubois C*	4.00
188	*Jason Dubois U*	6.00
189	*Jason Dubois R*	8.00
190	*Jonny Gomes C*	6.00
191	*Jonny Gomes U*	10.00
192	*Jonny Gomes R*	20.00
193	*Chris Snelling C*	8.00
194	*Chris Snelling U*	10.00
195	*Chris Snelling R*	15.00
196	*Hansel Izquierdo C*	4.00
197	*Hansel Izquierdo U*	5.00
198	*Hansel Izquierdo R*	6.00
199	*So Taguchi C*	6.00
200	*So Taguchi U*	8.00
201	*So Taguchi R*	10.00
202	*Kazuhisa Ishii C*	6.00
203	*Kazuhisa Ishii U*	8.00
204	*Kazuhisa Ishii R*	10.00
205	*Jorge Padilla C*	4.00
206	*Jorge Padilla U*	6.00
207	*Jorge Padilla R*	8.00
208	*Earl Snyder C*	4.00
209	*Earl Snyder U*	6.00
210	*Earl Snyder R*	8.00

2002 Topps Pristine Refractors

	MT
Stars (1-150):	3-5X
Production 149	
Common Rookies:	.75-1.5X
Production 1,999	
Uncommon Rookies:	1-2X
Production 799	
Rare Rookies:	2-4X
Production 149	
Gold Refractors (1-150):	5-10X
Gold Common RC's:	4-8X
Gold Uncommon RC's:	2-4X
Gold Rare RC's:	1-3X
Production 70 sets	
All Refractors are Uncirculated	

2002 Topps Pristine Fall Memories

		MT
Common Player:		6.00
Varying quantities produced		
JB	Johnny Bench	20.00
BB	Barry Bonds	25.00
GB	George Brett	30.00
TG	Tom Glavine	10.00
LG	Luis Gonzalez	6.00
MG	Mark Grace	12.00
SG	Shawn Green	6.00
TH	Todd Helton	6.00
RJ	Reggie Jackson	20.00
AJ	Andruw Jones	10.00
CP	Chipper Jones	15.00
TM	Tino Martinez	8.00
WM	Willie Mays	40.00
EM	Eddie Murray	15.00
JP	Jorge Posada	8.00
KP	Kirby Puckett	30.00
CS	Curt Schilling	8.00
GS	Gary Sheffield	6.00
AS	Alfonso Soriano	25.00
BW	Bernie Williams	10.00

2002 Topps Pristine In The Gap

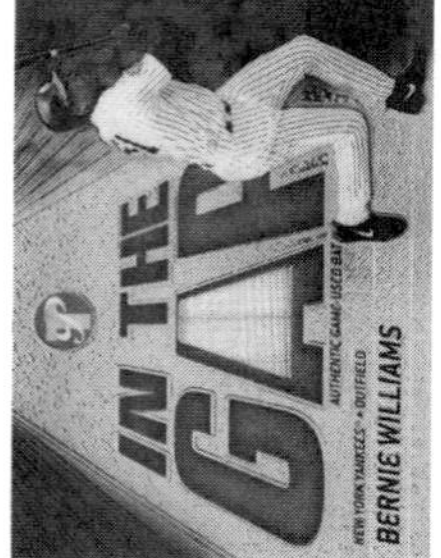

		MT
Common Player:		6.00
Varying quantities produced		
RA	Roberto Alomar	10.00
LB	Lance Berkman	10.00
WBE	Wilson Betemit	8.00
WB	Wade Boggs	8.00
BBO	Barry Bonds	25.00
BB	Bret Boone	6.00
EC	Eric Chavez	8.00
CD	Carlos Delgado	6.00
AD	Adam Dunn	15.00
JE	Jim Edmonds	6.00
DE	Darin Erstad	10.00
NG	Nomar Garciaparra	25.00
TG	Tony Gwynn	15.00
TH	Todd Helton	8.00
RH	Rickey Henderson	25.00
AJ	Andruw Jones	10.00
JK	Jeff Kent	6.00
RK	Ryan Klesko	10.00
PL	Paul LoDuca	10.00
RP	Rafael Palmeiro	6.00
MP	Mike Piazza	20.00
AP	Albert Pujols	15.00
ARA	Aramis Ramirez	6.00
AR	Alex Rodriguez	15.00
IR	Ivan Rodriguez	6.00
TS	Tsuyoshi Shinjo	10.00
AS	Alfonso Soriano	25.00
LW	Larry Walker	6.00
BW	Bernie Williams	15.00
PW	Preston Wilson	12.00

2002 Topps Pristine Patches

	MT
Common Player:	
Production 25 sets not priced	
PA-WBWade Boggs	
PA-BBOBarry Bonds	
PA-BBBret Boone	
PA-GBGeorge Brett	
PA-ECEric Chavez	
PA-CDCarlos Delgado	
PA-ADAdam Dunn	
PA-NGNomar Garciaparra	
PA-TGLTom Glavine	
PA-TGTony Gwynn	
PA-THTodd Helton	
PA-AJAndruw Jones	
PA-CJChipper Jones	
PA-GMGreg Maddux	
PA-PMPedro J. Martinez	
PA-DMDon Mattingly	
PA-RPRafael Palmeiro	
PA-MPMike Piazza	
PA-APAlbert Pujols	
PA-ARAlex Rodriguez	
PA-SRScott Rolen	
PA-KSKazuhiro Sasaki	
PA-CSCurt Schilling	
PA-FTFrank Thomas	
PA-LWLarry Walker	

2002 Topps Pristine Personal Endorsements

		MT
Common Autograph:		8.00
Inserted 1:box		
Some not priced yet		
RA	Roberto Alomar	30.00
KB	Kenny Baugh	10.00
LB	Lance Berkman	30.00
WB	Wilson Betemit	
HB	Hank Blalock	
BB	Barry Bonds	120.00
DB	Dewon Brazelton	15.00
EC	Eric Chavez	
BC	Ben Christensen	
JC	Jose Cruz Jr.	
JD	Johnny Damon	20.00
GF	Gavin Floyd	25.00
RF	Rafael Furcal	
CG	Cristian Guzman	15.00
IG	Irvin Guzman	15.00
DH	Drew Henson	
OH	Orlando Hudson	15.00
KI	Kazuhisa Ishii	
NJ	Nick Johnson	
CK	Casey Kotchman	30.00
JL	Jason Lane	12.00
PL	Paul LoDuca	
CW	Corwin Malone	10.00
JM	Joe Mauer	
NN	Nick Neugebauer	12.00
AP	Albert Pujols	75.00
JRI	Juan Rivera	
JR	Jimmy Rollins	15.00
BS	Ben Sheets	15.00
JS	Juan Silvestre	8.00
BSM	Bud Smith	
ST	So Taguchi	25.00
MT	Marcus Thames	18.00

2002 Topps Pristine Popular Demand

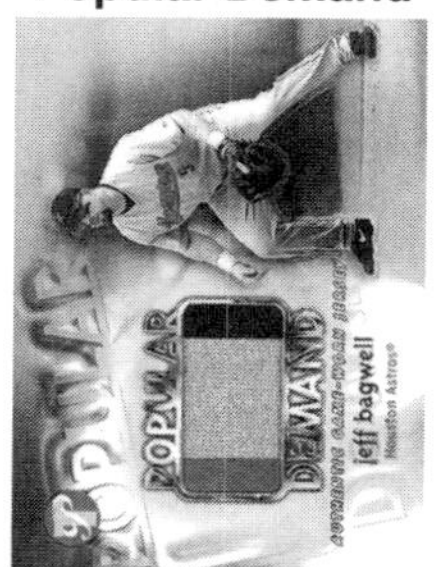

		MT
Common Player:		6.00
Varying quantities produced		
RA	Roberto Alomar	10.00
JB	Jeff Bagwell	12.00
WB	Wade Boggs	10.00
BBO	Barry Bonds	25.00
BB	Bret Boone	6.00
CD	Carlos Delgado	6.00
AD	Adam Dunn	15.00
NG	Nomar Garciaparra	15.00
SG	Shawn Green	6.00
TG	Tony Gwynn	12.00
TH	Todd Helton	6.00
CJ	Chipper Jones	12.00
DM	Don Mattingly	35.00
MP	Mike Piazza	15.00
AP	Albert Pujols	15.00
AR	Alex Rodriguez	15.00
IR	Ivan Rodriguez	6.00
CS	Curt Schilling	8.00
FT	Frank Thomas	10.00
LW	Larry Walker	6.00

2002 Topps Pristine Portions

		MT
Common Player:		6.00
Varying quantities produced		
RA	Roberto Alomar	10.00
JB	Jeff Bagwell	12.00
LB	Lance Berkman	10.00
CB	Craig Biggio	8.00
BBO	Barry Bonds	25.00
BB	Bret Boone	6.00
CD	Carlos Delgado	6.00
RD	Ryan Dempster	6.00
AD	Adam Dunn	15.00
CF	Cliff Floyd	6.00
RF	Rafael Furcal	8.00
NG	Nomar Garciaparra	15.00

CG	Cristian Guzman	10.00
TH	Todd Helton	6.00
NJ	Nick Johnson	8.00
LD	Paul LoDuca	6.00
GM	Greg Maddux	20.00
EM	Edgar Martinez	10.00
MM	Mike Mussina	10.00
MO	Magglio Ordonez	8.00
RP	Rafael Palmeiro	8.00
MP	Mike Piazza	20.00
JP	Jorge Posada	8.00
AP	Albert Pujols	15.00
AR	Alex Rodriguez	15.00
IR	Ivan Rodriguez	6.00
NR	Nolan Ryan	40.00
KS	Kazuhiro Sasaki	10.00

2002 Topps Reserve

	MT
Complete Set (150):	120.00
Common Player:	.40
Common (136-150):	5.00
Production 999	
Silver parallel (1-135):	4-8X
Silver (136-150):	.75-1.5X
Production 150	
Box (10 packs & 1 auto. helmet:	100.00

1	Alex Rodriguez	2.50
2	Tsuyoshi Shinjo	.40
3	Craig Biggio	.40
4	Troy Glaus	.50
5	Mike Rivera	.40
6	Curt Schilling	.75
7	Garret Anderson	.40
8	Ben Sheets	.40
9	Todd Helton	.75
10	Paul Konerko	.50
11	Sammy Sosa	2.00
12	Bud Smith	.40
13	Jeff Bagwell	.75
14	Albert Pujols	1.50
15	Jose Vidro	.40
16	Carlos Delgado	.50
17	Torii Hunter	.40
18	Jerry Hairston Jr.	.40
19	Troy Percival	.40
20	Vladimir Guerrero	1.00
21	Geoff Jenkins	.40
22	Carlos Pena	.40
23	Juan Gonzalez	.75
24	Raul Mondesi	.40
25	Jimmy Rollins	.40
26	Mariano Rivera	.50
27	Jorge Posada	.50
28	Magglio Ordonez	.50
29	Roberto Alomar	.50
30	Randy Johnson	.75
31	Xavier Nady	.40
32	Terrence Long	.40
33	Chipper Jones	1.50
34	Rich Aurilia	.40
35	Aramis Ramirez	.40
36	Jim Thome	.50
37	Bret Boone	.40
38	Angel Berroa	.40
39	Jeff Conine	.40
40	Cliff Floyd	.40
41	Pedro J. Martinez	1.00
42	J.D. Drew	.40
43	Kazuhiro Sasaki	.40
44	Jon Rauch	.40
45	Orlando Hudson	.40
46	Scott Rolen	.50
47	Rafael Furcal	.40
48	Brad Penny	.40
49	Miguel Tejada	.50
50	Orlando Cabrera	.40
51	Bobby Abreu	.40
52	Darin Erstad	.40
53	Edgar Martinez	.40
54	Ben Grieve	.40
55	Shawn Green	.50
56	Ivan Rodriguez	.50
57	Josh Beckett	.40
58	Ray Durham	.40
59	Jason Hart	.40
60	Nathan Haynes	.40
61	Jason Giambi	1.50
62	Eric Chavez	.40
63	Matt Morris	.40
64	Lance Berkman	.75
65	Jeff Kent	.40
66	Andruw Jones	.50
67	Brian Giles	.50
68	Morgan Ensberg	.40
69	Pat Burrell	.50
70	Ken Griffey Jr.	2.00
71	Carlos Beltran	.40
72	Ichiro Suzuki	2.50
73	Larry Walker	.50
74	*J.J. Putz*	.50
75	Mike Piazza	2.00
76	Rafael Palmeiro	.50
77	Mark Prior	2.00
78	Toby Hall	.40
79	Pokey Reese	.40
80	Mike Mussina	.50
81	Omar Vizquel	.40
82	Shannon Stewart	.40
83	Jeromy Burnitz	.40
84	Bernie Williams	.50
85	C.C. Sabathia	.40
86	Mike Hampton	.40
87	Kevin Brown	.40
88	Juan Cruz	.40
89	Jeff Weaver	.40
90	Jason Lane	.40
91	Adam Dunn	.75
92	Jose Cruz Jr.	.40
93	Marlon Anderson	.40
94	Jeff Cirillo	.40
95	Mark Buehrle	.40
96	Austin Kearns	.50
97	Tim Hudson	.50
98	Brian Jordan	.40
99	Phil Nevin	.40
100	Barry Bonds	2.00
101	Derek Jeter	3.00
102	Javier Vazquez	.40
103	Jason Kendall	.40
104	Jim Edmonds	.40
105	Kenny Kelly	.40
106	Juan Pena	.40
107	Mark Grace	.50
108	Roger Clemens	1.50
109	Barry Zito	.40
110	Greg Vaughn	.40
111	Greg Maddux	1.50
112	Richie Sexson	.50
113	Jermaine Dye	.40
114	Kerry Wood	.50
115	Matt Lawton	.40
116	Sean Casey	.40
117	Gary Sheffield	.40
118	Preston Wilson	.40
119	Cristian Guzman	.40
120	Mike Sweeney	.40
121	Neifi Perez	.40
122	Paul LoDuca	.40
123	Luis Gonzalez	.50
124	Ryan Klesko	.40
125	Alfonso Soriano	2.00
126	Bobby Higginson	.40
127	Juan Pierre	.40
128	Moises Alou	.40
129	Roy Oswalt	.50
130	Nomar Garciaparra	2.00
131	Fred McGriff	.40
132	Edgardo Alfonzo	.40
133	Johnny Damon	.40
134	Dewon Brazelton	.40
135	Mark Mulder	.50
136	*So Taguchi*	8.00
137	Mario Ramos	5.00
138	*Dan Johnson*	5.00
139	*Hansel Izquierdo*	5.00
140	*Kazuhisa Ishii*	15.00
141	Jon Switzer	8.00
142	*Chris Tritle*	10.00
143	*Chris Snelling*	15.00
144	*Chone Figgins*	5.00
145	*Dan Phillips*	5.00
146	*John Rodriguez*	5.00
147	Colt Griffin	15.00
148	*Jonny Gomes*	15.00
149	Josh Barfield	5.00
150	*Joe Mauer*	25.00

2002 Topps Reserve Autographed Mini-Helmets

	MT
Common Helmet:	25.00
1:box	
Roberto Alomar	45.00
Moises Alou	25.00
Lance Berkman	45.00
Bret Boone	35.00
Eric Chavez	35.00
Adam Dunn	50.00
Cliff Floyd	25.00
Troy Glaus	40.00
Luis Gonzalez	45.00
Todd Helton	60.00
Magglio Ordonez	25.00
Rafael Palmeiro	40.00
Albert Pujols	65.00
Alex Rodriguez	100.00
Scott Rolen	30.00
Jimmy Rollins	25.00
Alfonso Soriano	100.00
Miguel Tejada	

2002 Topps Reserve Game-Used Baseball

		MT
Inserted 1:1,761		
AR	Alex Rodriguez	
I	Ichiro Suzuki	65.00

2002 Topps Reserve Game-Used Bat

		MT
Common Player:		8.00
Inserted 1:12		
RA	Roberto Alomar	12.00
JB	Jeff Bagwell	10.00
BB	Barry Bonds	20.00
CD	Carlos Delgado	8.00
JG	Juan Gonzalez	8.00
LG	Luis Gonzalez	8.00
TG	Tony Gwynn	12.00
RH	Rickey Henderson	20.00
CJ	Chipper Jones	15.00
AJ	Andruw Jones	8.00
TM	Tino Martinez	8.00
RP	Rafael Palmeiro	8.00
MB	Mike Piazza	15.00
AP	Albert Pujols	15.00
AR	Alex Rodriguez	12.00
IR	Ivan Rodriguez	8.00
TS	Tsuyoshi Shinjo	8.00
AS	Alfonso Soriano	20.00
FT	Frank Thomas	8.00
BW	Bernie Williams	8.00

2002 Topps Reserve Game-Worn Uniform

		MT
Common Player:		5.00
Inserted 1:5		
BB	Barry Bonds	20.00
BBO	Bret Boone	5.00
DE	Darin Erstad	5.00
NG	Nomar Garciaparra	15.00
LG	Luis Gonzalez	5.00
TG	Tony Gwynn	10.00
TH	Todd Helton	8.00
RJ	Randy Johnson	10.00
AJ	Andruw Jones	6.00
CJ	Chipper Jones	12.00
GM	Greg Maddux	12.00
PM	Pedro Martinez	10.00
MM	Mark Mulder	5.00
MO	Magglio Ordonez	6.00
RP	Rafael Palmeiro	6.00
MP	Mike Piazza	12.00
AP	Albert Pujols	12.00
AR	Alex Rodriguez	12.00
IR	Ivan Rodriguez	6.00
SR	Scott Rolen	5.00
KS	Kazuhiro Sasaki	8.00
CS	Curt Schilling	8.00
FT	Frank Thomas	8.00
KW	Kerry Wood	10.00

2002 Topps Super Teams

	MT
Complete Set:	40.00
Common Player:	.25

Pack (7): 3.50
Box (20): 60.00
1 Leo Durocher .25
2 Whitey Lockman .25
3 Alvin Dark .25
4 Monte Irvin .50
5 Willie Mays 2.50
6 Wes Westrum .25
7 Johnny Antonelli .25
8 Sal Maglie .25
9 Dusty Rhodes .25
10 Davey Williams .25
11 Hoyt Wilhelm .25
12 Don Mueller .25
13 Dusty Rhodes .25
14 Willie Mays, Monte Irvin, Dusty Rhodes .75
15 Walt Alston .25
16 Gil Hodges .75
17 Jim Gilliam .25
18 Pee Wee Reese .50
19 Jackie Robinson 3.00
20 Duke Snider 1.00
21 Carl Furillo .25
22 Roy Campanella 1.00
23 Don Newcombe .25
24 Don Hoak .25
25 Johnny Podres .25
26 Clem Labine .25
27 Johnny Podres .25
28 Pee Wee Reese, Jackie Robinson, Duke Snider 1.00
29 Fred Haney .25
30 Joe Adcock .25
31 Frank Torre .25
32 Red Schoendienst .25
33 Johnny Logan .25
34 Eddie Mathews 1.00
35 Hank Aaron 3.00
36 Andy Pafko .25
37 Wes Covington .25
38 Lew Burdette .25
39 Warren Spahn 1.00
40 Del Crandall .25
41 Lew Burdette .25
42 Warren Spahn, Eddie Mathews, Hank Aaron 1.50
43 Danny Murtaugh .25
44 Dick Stuart .25
45 Bill Mazeroski .25
46 Dick Groat .25
47 Don Hoak .25
48 Gino Cimoli .25
49 Bill Virdon .25
50 Roberto Clemente 2.50
51 Smokey Burgess .25
52 Bob Friend .25
53 Vernon Law .25
55 Roy Face .25
56 Bill Mazeroski .25
57 Roberto Clemente, Bill Mazeroski, Dick Groat 1.00
58 Ralph Houk .25
59 Bill "Moose" Skowron .50
60 Bobby Richardson .25
61 Tony Kubek .25
62 Clete Boyer .25
63 Yogi Berra 1.50
64 Bob Cerv .25
65 Roger Maris 1.50
66 Elston Howard .25
67 Whitey Ford 1.00
68 Ralph Terry .25
69 Johnny Blanchard .25
70 Whitey Ford 1.00
71 Yogi Berra, Roger Maris, Elston Howard, Bill "Moose" Skowron 1.00
72 Red Schoendienst .25
73 Orlando Cepeda .40
74 Julian Javier .25
75 Dal Maxvill .25
76 Mike Shannon .25
77 Lou Brock .75
78 Roger Maris 1.50
79 Curt Flood .25
80 Tim McCarver .25
81 Steve Carlton .75
82 Bob Gibson 1.00
83 Nelson Briles .25
84 Bobby Tolan .25
85 Bob Gibson 1.00
86 Bob Gibson, Steve Carlton, Orlando Cepeda, Lou Brock .50
87 Gil Hodges .25
88 Ed Kranepool .25
89 Buddy Harrelson .25
90 Wayne Garrett .25
91 Cleon Jones .25
92 Tommie Agee .25
93 Ron Swoboda .25
94 Al Weis .25
95 Jerry Grote .25
96 Tom Seaver 1.00
97 Jerry Koosman .25
98 Tug McGraw .25
99 Nolan Ryan 3.00
100 Donn Clendenon .25
101 Tom Seaver, Jerry Koosman, Tug McGraw, Nolan Ryan 1.00
102 Earl Weaver .25
103 Boog Powell .25
104 Davey Johnson .25
105 Mark Belanger .25
106 Brooks Robinson 1.00
107 Don Buford .25
108 Paul Blair .25
109 Frank Robinson 1.00
110 Dick Hall .25
111 Jim Palmer .75
112 Mike Cuellar .25
113 Dave McNally .25
114 Andy Etchebarren .25
115 Brooks Robinson 1.00
116 Dick Hall, Jim Palmer, Mike Cuellar, Dave McNally .40
117 Alvin Dark .25
118 Gene Tenace .25
119 Dick Green .25
120 Bert Campaneris .25
121 Sal Bando .25
122 Reggie Jackson 1.00
123 Joe Rudi .25
124 Claudell Washington .25
125 Ray Fosse .25
126 Vida Blue .40
127 Rollie Fingers .25
128 Jim "Catfish" Hunter .50
129 Ken Holtzman .25
130 Rollie Fingers .25
131 Jim "Catfish" Hunter, Sal Bando, Reggie Jackson, Rollie Fingers .50
132 Davey Johnson .25
133 Keith Hernandez .25
134 Wally Backman .25
135 Rafael Santana .25
136 Ray Knight .25
137 Len Dykstra .25
138 Darryl Strawberry .25
139 Kevin Mitchell .25
140 Dwight Gooden .25
141 Bob Ojeda .25
142 Sid Fernandez .25
143 Ron Darling .25
144 Gary Carter .25
145 Ray Knight .25
146 Darryl Strawberry, Dwight Gooden, Keith Hernandez .25

2002 Topps Super Teams Retrofractor

MT
Cards (1-146): 2-4X
#'d to year team won World Series

2002 Topps Super Teams Autographs

MT
Common Autograph: 10.00
Inserted 1:19
SB Sal Bando
YB Yogi Berra
VB Vida Blue 15.00
CB Clete Boyer 15.00
LB Lou Brock
SC Steve Carlton 25.00
GC Gary Carter
OC Orlando Cepeda
MC Mike Cuellar
EF Elroy Face
WF Whitey Ford
BF Bob Friend
BG Bob Gibson
DG Dick Groat
KH Keith Hernandez
MI Monte Irvin 15.00
RJ Reggie Jackson 40.00
CJ Cleon Jones
RK Ray Knight
EK Ed Kranepool
TK Tony Kubek 30.00
VL Vern Law
WM Willie Mays
BM Bill Mazeroski
TM Tug McGraw 15.00
DN Don Newcombe
AP Andy Pafko 15.00
JP Jim Palmer 25.00
JPO Johnny Podres 15.00
BP Boog Powell
BR Bobby Richardson 15.00
BRO Brooks Robinson 30.00
FR Frank Robinson
JR Joe Rudi
NR Nolan Ryan 150.00
RS Red Schoendienst
TS Tom Seaver 60.00
MSH Mike Shannon
MS Bill "Moose" Skowron 20.00
DS Duke Snider
WS Warren Spahn
RSW Ron Swoboda
HW Hoyt Wilhelm 15.00

2002 Topps Super Teams A View To A Thrill Auto. Relics

MT
Produced listed
WFA Whitey Ford/61 100.00
BGA Bob Gibson/67 60.00
WMA Willie Mays/54 150.00
DSA Duke Snider/55 80.00
WSA Warren Spahn/57 60.00

2002 Topps Super Teams A View To a Thrill Seat Relics

MT
Common Player: 10.00
Inserted 1:30
HA Hank Aaron 20.00
YB Yogi Berra 25.00
LB Lew Burdette 10.00
RC Roberto Clemente 50.00
WF Whitey Ford 20.00
BG Bob Gibson 15.00
RMB Roger Maris/cardinals 20.00
RMY Roger Maris/yankees 40.00
EM Eddie Mathews 25.00
WM Willie Mays 30.00
BM Bill Mazeroski 25.00
JP Jim Palmer 15.00
BP Boog Powell 15.00
BR Brooks Robinson 15.00
FR Frank Robinson 15.00
RS Red Schoendienst 15.00
DS Duke Snider 20.00
WS Warren Spahn 15.00

2002 Topps Super Teams Classic Combos

MT
Common Card: 40.00
Inserted 1:865
AJ Tommie Agee, Cleon Jones 50.00
JR Reggie Jackson, Joe Rudi 40.00
RR Brooks Robinson, Frank Robinson 50.00
SK Tom Seaver, Jerry Koosman 60.00
SRBK "Moose" Skowron, Bobby Richardson, Clete Boyer, Tony Kubek 80.00

2002 Topps Super Teams Relics

MT
Common Player:
TA Tommie Agee/bat 20.00
SBB Sal Bando/bat 10.00
SBJ Sal Bando/jsy 10.00
MB Mark Belanger/bat 10.00
PB Paul Blair/bat 10.00
CB Clete Boyer/bat 10.00
LB Lew Burdette/jsy 15.00
SB Smokey Burgess/bat 40.00
BC Bert Campaneris/jsy 15.00
GC Gary Carter/jacket 20.00
GCB Gary Carter/bat 15.00
GCJ Gary Carter/jsy 15.00
OC Orlando Cepeda/bat 15.00
BCE Bob Cerv/bat 10.00
GCI Gino Cimoli/bat 10.00
DC Del Crandel/bat 10.00
MC Mike Cuellar/jsy 10.00
RD Ron Darling/jsy 10.00
LD Len Dykstra/bat 15.00
RF Ray Fosse/bat 10.00
BF Bob Friend/jsy 10.00
WG Wayne Garrett/bat 10.00
DG Dwight Gooden/jsy 15.00
DH Don Hoak/bat 10.00
RH Ralph Houk/jsy 10.00
RJ Reggie Jackson/bat 35.00
DJ Davey Johnson/bat 10.00
CJ Cleon Jones/bat 20.00
RK Ray Knight/bat 10.00
JK Jerry Koosman/jsy 10.00
EK Ed Kranepool/jsy 15.00
TK Tony Kubek/bat 25.00
TM Tug McGraw/jsy 15.00
DM Dave McNally/jsy 10.00
KM Kevin Mitchell/bat 10.00
AP Andy Pafko/bat 10.00
BR Bobby Richardson/bat 60.00
BRO Brooks Robinson/bat 25.00
FR Frank Robinson/bat 20.00
JR Joe Rudi/bat 10.00
NR Nolan Ryan/bat 90.00
RS Red Schoendienst/bat 10.00
TS Tom Seaver/bat 40.00
MS "Moose" Skowron/bat 20.00
DS Darryl Strawberry/bat 30.00
CW Claudell Washington/bat 10.00

2002 Topps Super Teams Super Teammates

MT
Complete Set (5): 10.00
Common Card: 2.00
Inserted 1:10
ST-BG Lou Brock, Bob Gibson 2.00
ST-FB Whitey Ford, Yogi Berra 4.00
ST-MI Willie Mays, Monte Irvin 4.00
ST-RR Brooks Robinson, Frank Robinson 3.00

ST-SRBK	Bill "Moose" Skowron, Bobby Richardson, Clete Boyer, Tony Kubek	2.00

2002 Topps Super Teams Super Teammates Autographs

		MT
Production 50 sets		
BGA	Lou Brock, Bob Gibson	100.00
FBA	Whitey Ford, Yogi Berra	150.00
MIA	Willie Mays, Monte Irvin	180.00
RRA	Brooks Robinson, Frank Robinson	100.00
SRBKA	Bill "Moose" Skowron, Bobby Richardson, Clete Boyer, Tony Kubek	260.00

2002 Topps Ten

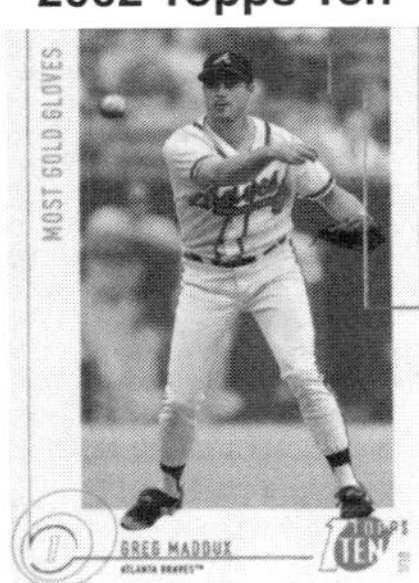

		MT
Complete Set (200):		40.00
Common Player:		.15
Pack (7):		2.50
Box (24):		55.00
1	Ichiro Suzuki	1.50
2	Rich Aurilia	.15
3	Bret Boone	.15
4	Juan Pierre	.15
5	Shannon Stewart	.15
6	Alex Rodriguez	1.00
7	Luis Gonzalez	.40
8	Todd Helton	.50
9	Garret Anderson	.15
10	Albert Pujols	1.00
11	Lance Berkman	.25
12	Todd Helton	.50
13	Jeff Kent	.15
14	Bob Abreu	.15
15	Jason Giambi	.40
16	Albert Pujols	1.00
17	Mike Sweeney	.15
18	Vladimir Guerrero	.50
19	Cliff Floyd	.15
20	Shannon Stewart	.15
21	Cristian Guzman	.15
22	Roberto Alomar	.40
23	Carlos Beltran	.15
24	Jimmy Rollins	.15
25	Roger Cedeno	.15
26	Juan Pierre	.15
27	Juan Uribe	.15
28	Luis Castillo	.15
29	Ray Durham	.15
30	Mark McLemore	.15
31	Barry Bonds	1.00
32	Sammy Sosa	1.00
33	Luis Gonzalez	.40
34	Alex Rodriguez	1.00
35	Shawn Green	.20
36	Todd Helton	.50
37	Jim Thome	.25
38	Rafael Palmeiro	.25
39	Richie Sexson	.15
40	Phil Nevin	.15
41	Troy Glaus	.50
42	Sammy Sosa	1.00
43	Todd Helton	.50
44	Luis Gonzalez	.40
45	Bret Boone	.15
46	Juan Gonzalez	.50
47	Barry Bonds	1.00
48	Alex Rodriguez	1.00
49	Jeff Bagwell	.50
50	Albert Pujols	1.00
51	Phil Nevin	.15
52	Ichiro Suzuki	1.50
53	Larry Walker	.25
54	Jason Giambi	.40
55	Roberto Alomar	.40
56	Todd Helton	.50
57	Moises Alou	.15
58	Lance Berkman	.25
59	Bret Boone	.15
60	Frank Catalanotto	.15
61	Chipper Jones	1.00
62	Barry Bonds	1.00
63	Sammy Sosa	1.00
64	Luis Gonzalez	.40
65	Todd Helton	.50
66	Larry Walker	.25
67	Jason Giambi	.40
68	Jim Thome	.25
69	Alex Rodriguez	1.00
70	Lance Berkman	.25
71	Albert Pujols	1.00
72	Ichiro Suzuki	1.50
73	Roger Cedeno	.15
74	Juan Pierre	.15
75	Jimmy Rollins	.15
76	Alfonso Soriano	.40
77	Mark McLemore	.15
78	Chuck Knoblauch	.15
79	Vladimir Guerrero	.50
80	Bob Abreu	.15
81	Mike Cameron	.15
82	Sammy Sosa	1.00
83	Alex Rodriguez	1.00
84	Todd Helton	.50
85	Barry Bonds	1.00
86	Luis Gonzalez	.40
87	Ichiro Suzuki	1.50
88	Jeff Bagwell	.50
89	Cliff Floyd	.15
90	Shawn Green	.20
91	Craig Biggio	.15
92	Juan Pierre	.15
93	Fernando Vina	.15
94	Paul LoDuca	.15
95	Mark Grace	.25
96	Eric Young	.15
97	Placido Polanco	.15
98	Jason Kendall	.15
99	Ichiro Suzuki	1.50
100	Orlando Cabrera	.15
101	Rey Sanchez	.15
102	Ichiro Suzuki	1.50
103	Edgar Martinez	.15
104	Bret Boone	.15
105	Barry Bonds	1.00
106	Ivan Rodriguez	.40
107	Mike Piazza	1.00
108	Sammy Sosa	1.00
109	John Olerud	.25
110	Roberto Alomar	.40
111	Roberto Alomar	.40
112	Mark McGwire	1.50
113	Barry Larkin	.15
114	Ken Griffey Jr.	1.00
115	Rickey Henderson	.25
116	Barry Bonds	1.00
117	Ivan Rodriguez	.40
118	Mike Piazza	1.00
119	Roger Clemens	.75
120	Randy Johnson	.50
121	Albert Pujols	1.00
122	Ichiro Suzuki	1.50
123	Roy Oswalt	.40
124	C.C. Sabathia	.15
125	Jimmy Rollins	.15
126	Alfonso Soriano	.40
127	David Eckstein	.15
128	Adam Dunn	.50
129	Bud Smith	.15
130	Tsuyoshi Shinjo	.15
131	Matt Morris	.15
132	Curt Schilling	.25
133	Randy Johnson	.50
134	Mark Mulder	.25
135	Roger Clemens	.75
136	Jon Lieber	.15
137	Jamie Moyer	.15
138	Freddy Garcia	.15
139	Tim Hudson	.15
140	C.C. Sabathia	.15
141	Randy Johnson	.50
142	Curt Schilling	.25
143	John Burkett	.15
144	Freddy Garcia	.15
145	Greg Maddux	1.00
146	Darryl Kile	.15
147	Mike Mussina	.40
148	Joe Mays	.15
149	Matt Morris	.15
150	Russ Ortiz	.15
151	Randy Johnson	.50
152	Curt Schilling	.25
153	Hideo Nomo	.15
154	Chan Ho Park	.15
155	Kerry Wood	.25
156	Mike Mussina	.40
157	Roger Clemens	.75
158	Javier Vazquez	.15
159	Barry Zito	.15
160	Bartolo Colon	.15
161	Mariano Rivera	.25
162	Robb Nen	.15
163	Kazuhiro Sasaki	.15
164	Armando Benitez	.15
165	Trevor Hoffman	.15
166	Jeff Shaw	.15
167	Keith Foulke	.15
168	Jose Mesa	.15
169	Troy Percival	.15
170	Billy Wagner	.15
171	Pat Burrell	.25
172	Raul Mondesi	.15
173	Gary Sheffield	.25
174	Carlos Beltran	.15
175	Vladimir Guerrero	.50
176	Torii Hunter	.15
177	Jeromy Burnitz	.15
178	Tim Salmon	.15
179	Jim Edmonds	.15
180	Tsuyoshi Shinjo	.15
181	Greg Maddux	1.00
182	Roberto Alomar	.40
183	Ken Griffey Jr.	1.00
184	Ivan Rodriguez	.40
185	Omar Vizquel	.15
186	Barry Bonds	1.00
187	Devon White	.15
188	J.T. Snow	.15
189	Larry Walker	.25
190	Robin Ventura	.15
191	*Mark Phillips*	6.00
192	*Clint Nageotte*	2.00
193	*Mauricio Lara*	2.00
194	*Nic Jackson*	2.00
195	*Chris Tritle*	6.00
196	*Ryan Gripp*	1.50
197	*Greg Montalbano*	2.00
198	*Noochie Varner*	2.00
199	*Nick Alvarez*	1.50
200	*Craig Kuzmic*	3.00

2002 Topps Ten Die-Cut

	MT
Stars (1-200):	2-5X
Inserted 1:4	

2002 Topps Ten Autographs

		MT
Common Autograph:		15.00
BB	Barry Bonds	120.00
BBO	Bret Boone	25.00
RCL	Roger Clemens	100.00
JE	Jim Edmonds	30.00
CF	Cliff Floyd	15.00
LG	Luis Gonzalez	35.00
CG	Cristian Guzman	15.00
RO	Roy Oswalt	40.00
JR	Jimmy Rollins	25.00
BZ	Barry Zito	25.00

A player's name in *italic* type indicates a rookie card.

2002 Topps Ten Relics

		MT
Common Player:		8.00
Bat Relic 1:27		
Jersey Relic 1:26		
BA	Bob Abreu/bat	12.00
RA	Roberto Alomar/bat	15.00
MA	Moises Alou/bat	8.00
GA	Garret Anderson/bat	10.00
JBA	Jeff Bagwell/jsy	15.00
CB	Carlos Beltran/bat	10.00
AB	Armando Benitez /jsy	10.00
LB	Lance Berkman/bat	15.00
CBI	Craig Biggio/jsy	15.00
BB	Barry Bonds/jsy	30.00
BBO	Bret Boone/bat	10.00
JBU	John Burkett/jsy	8.00
JB	Jeromy Burnitz/jsy	8.00
MC	Mike Cameron/bat	20.00
LC	Luis Castillo/bat	8.00
RC	Roger Cedeno/bat	8.00
BC	Bartolo Colon/jsy	15.00
RD	Ray Durham/bat	8.00
JE	Jim Edmonds/bat	15.00
CF	Cliff Floyd/bat	8.00
FG	Freddy Garcia/jsy	15.00
JGO	Juan Gonzalez/bat	15.00
LG	Luis Gonzalez/bat	12.00
MG	Mark Grace/bat	20.00
SG	Shawn Green/bat	12.00
CG	Cristian Guzman/bat	15.00
TH	Todd Helton/bat	15.00
THO	Trevor Hoffman/jsy	10.00
THU	Torii Hunter/bat	25.00
RJ	Randy Johnson/sy	20.00
CJ	Chipper Jones/bat	20.00
JK	Jason Kendall/jsy	10.00
JKE	Jeff Kent/jsy	10.00
CK	Chuck Knoblauch/bat	10.00
PL	Paul LoDuca/bat	10.00
GM	Greg Maddux/jsy	20.00
EM	Edgar Martinez/jsy	12.00
MM	Mark McLemore/bat	10.00
PM	Raul Mondesi/bat	8.00
PN	Phil Nevin/bat	10.00
JO	John Olerud/jsy	10.00
RP	Rafael Palmeiro/jsy	12.00
CP	Chan Ho Park/jsy	10.00
MP	Mike Piazza/jsy	30.00
JP	Juan Pierre/jsy	10.00
PP	Placido Polanco/bat	20.00
AP	Albert Pujols/bat	30.00
AR	Alex Rodriguez/jsy	20.00
TS	Tim Salmon/bat	15.00
CS	Curt Schilling/jsy	15.00
RS	Richie Sexson/bat	15.00
GS	Gary Sheffield/jsy	10.00
TSH	Tsuyoshi Shinjo/bat	20.00
JS	J.T. Snow/bat	8.00
AS	Alfonso Soriano/bat	20.00

SS Shannon Stewart/bat 8.00
MS Mike Sweeney/bat 15.00
JT Jim Thome/bat 20.00
RV Robin Ventura/bat 12.00
FV Fernando Vina/bat 25.00
OV Omar Vizquel/bat 15.00
BW Billy Wagner/jsy 10.00
LW Larry Walker/bat 10.00
DW Devon White/bat 8.00
BZ Barry Zito/jsy 15.00

2002 Topps Ten Team Topps Legends Autographs

MT

Whitey Ford
Bobby Richardson
Bobby Thomson
Carl Yastrzemski

2002 Topps Total

MT

Complete Set (990): 150.00
Common Player: .10
Pack (10): 1.00
Box (36): 32.00
1 *Joe Mauer* 5.00
2 Derek Jeter 2.00
3 Shawn Green .25
4 Vladimir Guerrero .50
5 Mike Piazza 1.50
6 Brandon Duckworth .10
7 Aramis Ramirez .10
8 Josh Barfield .50
9 Troy Glaus .40
10 Sammy Sosa 1.00
11 Rod Barajas .10
12 Tsuyoshi Shinjo .25
13 Larry Bigbie .10
14 Tino Martinez .10
15 Craig Biggio .25
16 *Anastacio Martinez* .40
17 John McDonald .10
18 *Kyle Kane* .30
19 Aubrey Huff .10
20 Juan Cruz .10
21 Doug Creek .10
22 Luther Hackman .10
23 Rafael Furcal .10
24 Andres Torres .10
25 Jason Giambi .75
26 Jose Paniagua .10
27 Jose Offerman .10
28 Alex Arias .10
29 J.M. Gold .10
30 Jeff Bagwell .50
31 *Brent Cookson* .20
32 Kelly Wunsch .10
33 Larry Walker .25
34 Luis Gonzalez .25
35 John Franco .10
36 Roy Oswalt .25
37 Tom Glavine .25
38 C.C. Sabathia .10
39 Jay Gibbons .10
40 Wilson Betemit .10
41 Tony Armas .10
42 Mo Vaughn .10
43 *Gerard Oakes* .40
44 Dmitri Young .10
45 Tim Salmon .10
46 Barry Zito .10
47 Adrian Gonzalez .10
48 Joe Davenport .10
49 Adrian Hernandez .10
50 Randy Johnson .50
51 Benito Baez .10
52 Adam Pettyjohn .10
53 Alex Escobar .10
54 *Stevenson Agosto* .25
55 Omar Daal .10
56 Mike Buddie .10
57 Dave Williams .10
58 Marquis Grissom .10
59 Pat Burrell .25
60 Mark Prior 2.50
61 Mike Bynum .10
62 *Mike Hill* .25
63 *Brandon Backe* .25
64 Dan Wilson .10
65 Nick Johnson .10
66 Jason Grimsley .10
67 Russ Johnson .10
68 Todd Walker .10
69 Kyle Farnsworth .10
70 Ben Broussard .10
71 *Garrett Guzman* .50
72 Terry Mulholland .10
73 Tyler Houston .10
74 Jace Brewer .10
75 *Chris Baker* .25
76 Frank Catalanotto .10
77 Mike Redmond .10
78 Matt Wise .10
79 Fernando Vina .10
80 Kevin Brown .10
81 Grant Balfour .10
82 *Clint Nageotte* .75
83 Jeff Tam .10
84 Steve Trachsel .10
85 Tomokazu Ohka .10
86 Keith McDonald .10
87 Jose Ortiz .10
88 Rusty Greer .10
89 Jeff Suppan .10
90 Moises Alou .10
91 Juan Encarnacion .10
92 *Tyler Yates* .40
93 Scott Strickland .10
94 Brent Butler .10
95 Jon Rauch .10
96 *Brian Mallette* .25
97 Joe Randa .10
98 Cesar Crespo .10
99 Felix Rodriguez .10
100 Chipper Jones 1.00
101 Victor Martinez .10
102 Danny Graves .10
103 *Brandon Berger* .10
104 Carlos Garcia .10
105 Alfonso Soriano .75
106 *Allan Simpson* .25
107 Brad Thomas .10
108 Devon White .10
109 Scott Chiasson .10
110 Cliff Floyd .10
111 Scott Williamson .10
112 Julio Zuleta .10
113 Terry Adams .10
114 Zach Day .10
115 Ben Grieve .10
116 Mark Ellis .10
117 *Bobby Jenks* .75
118 LaTroy Hawkins .10
119 Tim Raines Jr. .10
120 Juan Uribe .10
121 Bob Scanlan .10
122 *Brad Nelson* 1.50
123 Adam Johnson .10
124 Raul Casanova .10
125 Jeff D'Amico .10
126 *Aaron Cook* .50
127 Alan Benes .10
128 Mark Little .10
129 Randy Wolf .10
130 Phil Nevin .10
131 Guillermo Mota .10
132 Nick Neugebauer .10
133 Pedro Borbon .10
134 Doug Mientkiewicz .10
135 Edgardo Alfonzo .10
136 Dustan Mohr .10
137 Dan Reichert .10
138 Dewon Brazelton .10
139 Orlando Cabrera .10
140 Todd Hollandsworth .10
141 Darren Dreifort .10
142 Jose Valentin .10
143 Josh Kalinowski .10
144 Randy Keisler .10
145 Bret Boone .10
146 Roosevelt Brown .10
147 Brent Abernathy .10
148 Jorge Julio .10
149 Alex Gonzalez .10
150 Juan Pierre .10
151 Roger Cedeno .10
152 Javier Vazquez .10
153 Armando Benitez .10
154 Dave Burba .10
155 Brad Penny .10
156 Ryan Jensen .10
157 Jeromy Burnitz .10
158 *Matt Childers* .40
159 Wilmy Caceres .10
160 Roger Clemens .10
161 Michael Tejera .10
162 Jason Christiansen .10
163 Pokey Reese .10
164 Ivanon Coffie .10
165 Joaquin Benoit .10
166 Mike Matheny .10
167 Eric Cammack .10
168 Alex Graman .10
169 Brook Fordyce .10
170 Mike Lieberthal .10
171 Giovanni Carrara .10
172 Antonio Perez .10
173 Fernando Tatis .10
174 *Jason Bay* .50
175 *Jason Botts* .50
176 Danys Baez .10
177 Shea Hillenbrand .10
178 Jack Cust .10
179 Clay Bellinger .10
180 Roberto Alomar .10
181 Graeme Lloyd .10
182 *Clint Weibl* .40
183 Royce Clayton .10
184 Ben Davis .10
185 Brian Adams .25
186 Jack Wilson .10
187 David Coggin .10
188 Derrick Turnbow .10
189 Vladimir Nunez .10
190 Mariano Rivera .10
191 Wilson Guzman .10
192 Michael Barrett .10
193 Corey Patterson .10
194 Luis Sojo .10
195 Scott Elarton .10
196 Charles Thomas .25
197 Ricky Bottalico .10
198 Wilfredo Rodriguez .10
199 Ricardo Rincon .10
200 John Smoltz .10
201 Travis Miller .10
202 Ben Weber .10
203 T.J. Tucker .10
204 Terry Shumpert .10
205 Bernie Williams .10
206 Russ Ortiz .10
207 Nate Rolison .10
208 Jose Cruz Jr. .10
209 Bill Ortega .10
210 Carl Everett .10
211 Luis Lopez .10
212 *Brian Wolfe* .25
213 Doug Davis .10
214 Troy Mattes .10
215 Al Leiter .10
216 Joe Mays .10
217 Bobby Smith .10
218 *J.J. Trujillo* .25
219 Hideo Nomo .25
220 Jimmy Rollins .10
221 Bobby Seay .10
222 Mike Thurman .10
223 Bartolo Colon .10
224 Jesus Sanchez .10
225 Ray Durham .10
226 Juan Diaz .10
227 Lee Stevens .10
228 *Ben Howard* 1.00
229 James Moulton .10
230 Paul Quantrill .10
231 Randy Knorr .10
232 Abraham Nunez .10
233 Mike Fetters .10
234 Mario Encarnacion .10
235 Jeremy Fikac .10
236 Travis Lee .10
237 Bob File .10
238 Pete Harnisch .10
239 *Randy Galvez* .25
240 Geoff Goetz .10
241 Gary Glover .10
242 Troy Percival .10
243 *Lenny Dinardo* .40
244 *Jonny Gomes* 1.00
245 *Jesus Medrano* .25
246 Rey Ordonez .10
247 Juan Gonzalez .50
248 Jose Guillen .10
249 *Franklin German* .25
250 Mike Mussina .40
251 Ugueth Urbina .10
252 Melvin Mora .10
253 Gerald Williams .10
254 Jared Sandberg .10
255 Darrin Fletcher .10
256 A.J. Pierzynski .10
257 Lenny Harris .10
258 Blaine Neal .10
259 Denny Neagle .10
260 Jason Hart .10
261 Henry Mateo .10
262 Rheal Cormier .10
263 Luis Terrero .10
264 Shigetoshi Hasegawa .10
265 Bill Haselman .10
266 Scott Hatteberg .10
267 Adam Hyzdu .10
268 Mike Williams .10
269 Marlon Anderson .10
270 Bruce Chen .10
271 Eli Marrero .10
272 Jimmy Haynes .10
273 Bronson Arroyo .10
274 Kevin Jordan .10
275 Rick Helling .10
276 Mark Loretta .10
277 Dustin Hermanson .10
278 Pablo Ozuna .10
279 *Syketo Anderson* .25
280 Jermaine Dye .10
281 Will Smith .10
282 Brian Daubach .10
283 Eric Hinske .10
284 *Joe Jiannetti* .40
285 Chan Ho Park .10
286 *Curtis Legendre* .25
287 Jeff Reboulet .10
288 Scott Rolen .25
289 Chris Richard .10
290 Eric Chavez .25
291 Scott Shields .10
292 Donnie Sadler .10
293 Dave Veres .10
294 Craig Counsell .10
295 Armando Reynoso .10
296 Kyle Lohse .10
297 Arthur Rhodes .10
298 Sidney Ponson .10
299 Trevor Hoffman .10
300 Kerry Wood .25
301 Danny Bautista .10
302 Scott Sauerbeck .10
303 Johnny Estrada .10
304 Mike Timlin .10
305 Orlando Hernandez .25
306 Tony Clark .10
307 Tomas Perez .10
308 Marcus Giles .10
309 Mike Bordick .10
310 Jorge Posada .25
311 Jason Conti .10
312 Kevin Millar .10
313 Paul Shuey .10
314 *Jake Mauer* .75
315 Luke Hudson .10
316 Angel Berroa .10
317 *Fred Bastardo* .25
318 Shawn Estes .10
319 Andy Ashby .10
320 Ryan Klesko .10
321 Kevin Appier .10
322 Juan Pena .10
323 Alex Herrera .10
324 Robb Nen .10
325 Orlando Hudson .10
326 Lyle Overbay .10
327 Ben Sheets .25
328 Mike DiFelice .10
329 *Pablo Arias* .25
330 Mike Sweeney .10
331 Rick Ankiel .10
332 Tomas De La Rosa .25
333 *Kazuhisa Ishii* 4.00
334 Jose Reyes .10
335 Jeremy Giambi .10
336 Jose Mesa .10
337 *Ralph Roberts* .25
338 Jose Nunez .10

339 Curt Schilling .40
340 Sean Casey .20
341 Bob Wells .10
342 Carlos Beltran .10
343 Alexis Gomez .10
344 Brandon Claussen .25
345 Buddy Groom .10
346 *Mark Phillips* .75
347 Francisco Cordova .10
348 Joe Oliver .10
349 Danny Patterson .10
350 Joel Pineiro .10
351 J.R. House .10
352 Benny Agbayani .10
353 Jose Vidro .10
354 *Reed Johnson* .10
355 Mike Lowell .10
356 Scott Schoeneweis .10
357 Brian Jordan .10
358 Steve Finley .10
359 Randy Choate .10
360 Jose Lima .10
361 Miguel Olivo .10
362 Kenny Rogers .10
363 David Justice .20
364 Brandon Knight .10
365 Joe Kennedy .10
366 Eric Valent .10
367 Nelson Cruz .10
368 Brian Giles .25
369 Charles Gibson Jr. .10
370 Juan Pena .10
371 Mark Redman .10
372 Billy Koch .10
373 Ted Lilly .10
374 Craig Paquette .10
375 Kevin Jarvis .10
376 Scott Erickson .10
377 Josh Paul .10
378 Darwin Cubillan .10
379 Nelson Figueroa .10
380 Darin Erstad .20
381 *Jeremy Hill* .25
382 Elvin Nina .10
383 *Boomer Wells* .25
384 *Jay Caligiuri* .40
385 Freddy Garcia .10
386 Damian Miller .10
387 Bobby Higginson .10
388 *Alejandro Giron* .25
389 Ivan Rodriguez .40
390 Ed Rogers .10
391 Andy Benes .10
392 Matt Blank .10
393 Ryan Vogelsong .10
394 *Kelly Ramos* .25
395 Eric Karros .10
396 Bobby Jones .10
397 Omar Vizquel .25
398 Matt Perisho .10
399 Delino DeShields .10
400 Carlos Hernandez .10
401 Derrek Lee .10
402 Kirk Rueter .10
403 David Wright 1.50
404 Paul LoDuca .10
405 Brian Schneider .10
406 Milton Bradley .10
407 Daryle Ward .10
408 Cody Ransom .10
409 Fernando Rodney .10
410 *John Suomi* .20
411 Joe Girardi .10
412 *Demetrius Heath* .25
413 *John Foster* .25
414 Doug Glanville .10
415 Ryan Kohlmeier .10
416 Mike Matthews .10
417 Craig Wilson .10
418 Jay Witasick .10
419 Jay Payton .10
420 Andruw Jones .40
421 Benji Gil .10
422 Jeff Liefer .10
423 Kevin Young .10
424 Richie Sexson .25
425 Cory Lidle .10
426 Shane Halter .10
427 Jesse Foppert .75
428 Jose Molina .10
429 *Nick Alvarez* .40
430 Brian L. Hunter .10
431 *Clifford Bartosh* .25
432 Junior Spivey .10
433 *Eric Good* .25
434 Chin-Feng Chen .10
435 T.J. Mathews .10
436 Rich Rodriguez .10

437 Bobby Abreu .20
438 Joe McEwing .10
439 Michael Tucker .10
440 Preston Wilson .10
441 Mike MacDougal .10
442 Shannon Stewart .10
443 Bob Howry .10
444 Mike Benjamin .10
445 Erik Hiljus .10
446 *Ryan Gripp* .25
447 Jose Vizcaino .10
448 Shawn Wooten .10
449 *Steve Kent* .25
450 Ramiro Mendoza .10
451 Jake Westbrook .10
452 Joe Lawrence .10
453 Jae Weong Seo .10
454 *Ryan Fry* .20
455 Darren Lewis .10
456 Brad Wilkerson .10
457 *Gustavo Chacin* .25
458 Adrian Brown .10
459 Mike Cameron .10
460 Bud Smith .10
461 Derrick Lewis .10
462 Derek Lowe .10
463 Matt Williams .10
464 Jason Jennings .10
465 Albie Lopez .10
466 Felipe Lopez .10
467 Luke Allen .10
468 Brian Anderson .10
469 Matt Riley .10
470 Ryan Dempster .10
471 Matt Ginter .10
472 David Ortiz .10
473 Cole Barthel .10
474 Damian Jackson .10
475 Andy Van Hekken .10
476 Doug Brocail .10
477 Denny Hocking .10
478 Sean Douglass .10
479 Eric Owens .10
480 Ryan Ludwick .10
481 Todd Pratt .10
482 Aaron Sele .10
483 Edgar Renteria .10
484 *Raymond Cabrera* .25
485 Brandon Lyon .10
486 Chase Utley .10
487 Robert Fick .10
488 Wilfredo Cordero .10
489 Octavio Dotel .10
490 Paul Abbott .10
491 Jason Kendall .10
492 Jarrod Washburn .10
493 Dane Sardinha .10
494 Jung Bong .10
495 J.D. Drew .10
496 Jason Schmidt .10
497 Mike Magnante .10
498 *Jorge Padilla* .75
499 Eric Gagne .10
500 Todd Helton .50
501 Jeff Weaver .10
502 Alex Sanchez .10
503 Ken Griffey Jr. .10
504 Abraham Nunez .10
505 Reggie Sanders .10
506 Casey Kotchman 3.00
507 Jim Mann .10
508 Matt LeCroy .10
509 Frank Castillo .10
510 Geoff Jenkins .20
511 *Jayson Durocher* .20
512 Ellis Burks .10
513 Aaron Fultz .10
514 Hiram Bocachica .10
515 *Nate Espy* .10
516 Placido Polanco .10
517 Kerry Ligtenberg .10
518 Doug Nickle .10
519 Ramon Ortiz .10
520 Greg Swindell .10
521 J.J. Davis .10
522 Sandy Alomar .10
523 Chris Carpenter .10
524 Vance Wilson .10
525 Nomar Garciaparra 1.25
526 Jim Mecir .10
527 *Taylor Buchholz* .25
528 Brent Mayne .10
529 *John Rodriguez* .25
530 David Segui .10
531 Nate Cornejo .10
532 Gil Heredia .10
533 Esteban Loaiza .10
534 Pat Mahomes .10

535 Matt Morris .20
536 Todd Stottlemyre .10
537 Brian Lesher .10
538 Arturo McDowell .10
539 Felix Diaz .10
540 Mark Mulder .10
541 *Kevin Frederick* .25
542 Andy Fox .10
543 *Dionys Cesar* .10
544 Justin Miller .10
545 Keith Osik .10
546 Shane Reynolds .10
547 Mike Myers .10
548 *Raul Chavez* .25
549 Joe Nathan .10
550 Ryan Anderson .10
551 Jason Marquis .10
552 Marty Cordova .10
553 Kevin Tapani .10
554 Jimmy Anderson .10
555 Pedro Martinez .50
556 Rocky Biddle .10
557 Alex Ochoa .10
558 D'Angelo Jimenez .10
559 Wilkin Ruan .10
560 Terrence Long .10
561 Mark Lukasiewicz .10
562 Jose Santiago .10
563 Brad Fullmer .10
564 Corky Miller .10
565 Matt White .10
566 Mark Grace .30
567 Raul Ibanez .10
568 Josh Towers .10
569 Juan Gonzalez .40
570 Brian Buchanan .10
571 Ken Harvey .10
572 Jeffrey Hammonds .10
573 Wade Miller .10
574 Elpidio Guzman .10
575 Kevin Olsen .10
576 Austin Kearns .40
577 *Tim Kalita* .40
578 David Dellucci .10
579 Alex Gonzalez .10
580 *Joe Orloski* .20
581 Gary Matthews Jr. .10
582 Ryan Mills .10
583 Erick Almonte .10
584 Jeremy Affeldt .10
585 *Chris Tritle* 1.00
586 Michael Cuddyer .10
587 Kris Foster .10
588 Russell Branyan .10
589 Darren Oliver .10
590 *Freddie Money* .25
591 Carlos Lee .10
592 Tim Wakefield .10
593 Bubba Trammell .10
594 *John Koronka* .20
595 Geoff Blum .10
596 Darryl Kile .10
597 Neifi Perez .10
598 Torii Hunter .10
599 Luis Castillo .10
600 Mark Buehrle .10
601 Jeff Zimmerman .10
602 Mike DeJean .10
603 Julio Lugo .10
604 Chad Hermansen .10
605 Keith Foulke .10
606 Lance Davis .10
607 *Jeff Austin* .25
608 Brandon Inge .10
609 Orlando Merced .10
610 Johnny Damon .10
611 Doug Henry .10
612 Adam Kennedy .10
613 Wiki Gonzalez .10
614 *Brian West* .25
615 Andy Pettitte .25
616 *Chone Figgins* .25
617 Matt Lawton .10
618 Paul Rigdon .10
619 Keith Lockhart .10
620 Tim Redding .10
621 John Parrish .10
622 Chad Hutchinson .10
623 Todd Greene .10
624 David Eckstein .10
625 *Greg Montalbano* 1.00
626 Joe Beimel .10
627 Adrian Beltre .20
628 Charles Nagy .10
629 Cristian Guzman .10
630 Toby Hall .10
631 Jose Hernandez .10
632 Jose Macias .10

633 Jaret Wright .10
634 Steve Parris .10
635 Gene Kingsdale .10
636 Tim Worrell .10
637 Billy Martin .10
638 Jovanny Cedeno .10
639 Curt Leskanic .10
640 Tim Hudson .20
641 Juan Castro .10
642 Rafael Soriano .10
643 Juan Rincon .10
644 Mark DeRosa .10
645 Carlos Pena .10
646 Robin Ventura .20
647 Odalis Perez .10
648 Damion Easley .10
649 Benito Santiago .10
650 Alex Rodriguez 1.50
651 Aaron Rowand .10
652 Alex Cora .10
653 Bobby Kielty .10
654 Jose Rodriguez .10
655 Herbert Perry .10
656 Jeff Urban .10
657 Paul Bako .10
658 Shane Spencer .10
659 Pat Hentgen .10
660 Jeff Kent .20
661 Mark McLemore .10
662 Chuck Knoblauch .10
663 Blake Stein .10
664 *Brett Roneberg* .25
665 Josh Phelps .10
666 Byung-Hyun Kim .10
667 Dave Martinez .10
668 Mike Maroth .10
669 Shawn Chacon .10
670 Billy Wagner .10
671 Luis Alicea .10
672 Sterling Hitchcock .10
673 Adam Piatt .10
674 Ryan Franklin .10
675 Luke Prokopec .10
676 Alfredo Amezega .10
677 Gookie Dawkins .10
678 Eric Byrnes .10
679 Barry Larkin .25
680 Albert Pujols 1.00
681 Edwards Guzman .10
682 Jason Bere .10
683 Adam Everett .10
684 Greg Colbrunn .10
685 *Brandon Puffer* .40
686 Mark Kotsay .10
687 Willie Bloomquist .10
688 Hank Blalock .25
689 Travis Hafner .10
690 Lance Berkman .40
691 Joe Crede .10
692 Chuck Finley .10
693 John Grabow .10
694 Randy Winn .10
695 Mike James .10
696 Kris Benson .10
697 Bret Prinz .10
698 Jeff Williams .10
699 Eric Munson .10
700 Mike Hampton .10
701 Ramon E. Martinez .10
702 *Hansel Izquierdo* .25
703 Nathan Haynes .10
704 Eddie Taubensee .10
705 Esteban German .10
706 Ross Gload .10
707 *Matthew Merricks* .20
708 *Chris Piersoll* .25
709 Seth Greisinger .10
710 Ichiro Suzuki 1.50
711 Cesar Izturis .10
712 Brad Cresse .10
713 Carl Pavano .10
714 Steve Sparks .10
715 Dennis Tankersley .10
716 Kelvim Escobar .10
717 Jason LaRue .10
718 Corey Koskie .10
719 Vinny Castilla .10
720 Tim Drew .10
721 Chin-Hui Tsao .10
722 Paul Byrd .10
723 Alex Cintron .10
724 Orlando Palmeiro .10
725 Ramon Hernandez .10
726 Mark Johnson .10
727 B.J. Ryan .10
728 Wendell Magee .10
729 Michael Coleman .10
730 Mario Ramos .75

731 Mike Stanton .10
732 Dee Brown .10
733 Brad Ausmus .10
734 *Napoleon Calzado* .25
735 Woody Williams .10
736 Paxton Crawford .10
737 Jason Karnuth .10
738 Michael Restovich .10
739 Ramon Castro .10
740 Magglio Ordonez .25
741 Tom Gordon .10
742 Mark Grudzielanek .10
743 Jaime Moyer .10
744 *Marlyn Tisdale* .20
745 Steve Kline .10
746 Adam Eaton .10
747 *Eric Glaser* .25
748 Sean DePaula .10
749 Greg Norton .10
750 Steve Reed .10
751 Ricardo Aramboles .10
752 Matt Mantei .10
753 Gene Stechschulte .10
754 Chuck McElroy .10
755 Barry Bonds 1.00
756 Matt Anderson .10
757 Yorvit Torrealba .10
758 Jason Standridge .10
759 Desi Relaford .10
760 Jolbert Cabrera .10
761 Chris George .10
762 Erubiel Durazo .10
763 Paul Konerko .25
764 Tike Redman .10
765 *Chad Ricketts* .20
766 Roberto Hernandez .10
767 Mark Lewis .10
768 Livan Hernandez .10
769 *Carlos Brackley* .25
770 Kazuhiro Sasaki .10
771 Bill Hall .10
772 *Nelson Castro* .25
773 Eric Milton .10
774 Tom Davey .10
775 Todd Ritchie .10
776 Seth Etherton .10
777 Chris Singleton .10
778 *Robert Averette* .20
779 Robert Person .10
780 Fred McGriff .25
781 Richard Hidalgo .10
782 Kris Wilson .10
783 John Rocker .10
784 Justin Kaye .10
785 Glendon Rusch .10
786 Greg Vaughn .10
787 Mike Lamb .10
788 Greg Myers .10
789 *Nate Field* .25
790 Jim Edmonds .25
791 Olmedo Saenz .10
792 Jason Johnson .10
793 Mike Lincoln .10
794 Todd Coffey .10
795 Jesus Sanchez .10
796 Aaron Myette .10
797 Tony Womack .10
798 Chad Kreuter .10
799 Brady Clark .10
800 Adam Dunn .50
801 Jacque Jones .10
802 Kevin Millwood .10
803 Mike Rivera .10
804 Jim Thome .40
805 Jeff Conine .10
806 Elmer Dessens .10
807 Randy Velarde .10
808 Carlos Delgado .30
809 Steve Karsay .10
810 Casey Fossum .10
811 J.C. Romero .10
812 Chris Truby .10
813 Tony Graffanino .10
814 Wascar Serrano .10
815 Delvin James .10
816 Pedro Feliz .10
817 Damian Rolls .10
818 Scott Linebrink .10
819 Rafael Palmeiro .40
820 Javy Lopez .10
821 Larry Barnes .10
822 Brian Lawrence .10
823 *Scotty Layfield* .25
824 Jeff Cirillo .10
825 Willis Roberts .10
826 *James Harden* .25
827 *Chris Snelling* 1.00
828 Gary Sheffield .25
829 Jeff Heaverlo .10
830 Matt Clement .10
831 Rich Garces .10
832 Rondell White .10
833 *Henry Pichardo* .25
834 Aaron Boone .10
835 Ruben Sierra .10
836 Deivis Santos .10
837 Tony Batista .10
838 Rob Bell .10
839 Frank Thomas .50
840 Jose Silva .10
841 *Dan Johnson* .25
842 Steve Cox .10
843 Jose Acevedo .10
844 Jay Bell .10
845 Mike Sirotka .10
846 Garret Anderson .10
847 *James Shanks* .25
848 Trot Nixon .10
849 Keith Ginter .10
850 Tim Spooneybarger .10
851 Matt Stairs .10
852 Chris Stynes .10
853 Marvin Bernard .10
854 Raul Mondesi .20
855 Jeremy Owens .10
856 Jon Garland .10
857 Mitch Meluskey .10
858 Chad Durbin .10
859 John Burkett .10
860 Jon Switzer .10
861 Peter Bergeron .10
862 Jesus Colome .10
863 Todd Hundley .10
864 Ben Petrick .10
865 *So Taguchi* .75
866 Ryan Drese .10
867 Mike Trombley .10
868 Rick Reed .10
869 Mark Teixeira .20
870 *Corey Thurman* .10
871 Brian Roberts .10
872 Mike Timlin .10
873 Chris Reitsma .10
874 Jeff Fassero .10
875 Carlos Valderrama .10
876 John Lackey .10
877 Travis Fryman .10
878 Ismael Valdes .10
879 Rick White .10
880 Edgar Martinez .10
881 Dean Palmer .10
882 *Matt Allegra* .20
883 *Greg Sain* .25
884 Carlos Silva .10
885 *Jose Valverde* .25
886 Dernell Stenson .10
887 Todd Van Poppel .10
888 Wes Anderson .10
889 Bill Mueller .10
890 Morgan Ensberg .10
891 Marcus Thames .10
892 *Adam Walker* .10
893 John Halama .10
894 Frank Menechino .10
895 Greg Maddux 1.00
896 Gary Bennett .10
897 *Mauricio Lara* .25
898 Mike Young .10
899 Travis Phelps .10
900 Rich Aurilia .10
901 Henry Blanco .10
902 Carlos Febles .10
903 Scott MacRae .10
904 Lou Merloni .10
905 Dicky Gonzalez .10
906 Jeff DaVanon .10
907 A.J. Burnett .10
908 Einar Diaz .10
909 Julio Franco .10
910 John Olerud .25
911 *Mark Hamilton* .25
912 David Riske .10
913 Jason Tyner .10
914 Britt Reames .10
915 Vernon Wells .10
916 Eddie Perez .10
917 *Edwin Almonte* .25
918 Enrique Wilson .10
919 Chris Gomez .10
920 Jayson Werth .10
921 Jeff Nelson .10
922 *Freddy Sanchez* .75
923 John Vander Wal .10
924 *Chad Qualls* .25
925 Gabe White .10
926 Chad Harville .10
927 Ricky Gutierrez .10
928 Carlos Guillen .10
929 B.J. Surhoff .10
930 Chris Woodard .10
931 Ricardo Rodriguez .10
932 *Jimmy Gobble* 1.50
933 Jon Lieber .10
934 *Craig Kuzmic* .25
935 Eric Young .10
936 Greg Zaun .10
937 Miguel Batista .10
938 Danny Wright .10
939 Todd Zeile .10
940 Chad Zerbe .10
941 *Jason Young* .75
942 Ronnie Belliard .10
943 *John Ennis* .10
944 John Flaherty .10
945 Jerry Hairston Jr. .10
946 Al Levine .10
947 Antonio Alfonseca .10
948 Brian Moehler .10
949 Calvin Murray .10
950 Nick Bierbrodt .10
951 Sun-Woo Kim .10
952 *Noochie Varner* .75
953 Luis Rivas .10
954 Donnie Bridges .10
955 Ramon Vazquez .10
956 Luis Garcia .10
957 Mark Quinn .10
958 Armando Rios .10
959 Chad Fox .10
960 Hee Seop Choi .10
961 Turk Wendell .10
962 *Adam Roller* .20
963 Grant Roberts .10
964 Ben Molina .10
965 Juan Rivera .10
966 Matt Kinney .10
967 Rod Beck .10
968 Xavier Nady .10
969 Masato Yoshii .10
970 Miguel Tejada .25
971 Danny Kolb .10
972 Mike Remlinger .10
973 Ray Lankford .10
974 Ryan Minor .10
975 J.T. Snow .10
976 Brad Radke .10
977 Jason Lane .10
978 Jamey Wright .10
979 Tom Goodwin .10
980 Erik Bedard .10
981 Gabe Kapler .10
982 Brian Reith .10
983 *Nic Jackson* .75
984 Kurt Ainsworth .10
985 Jason Isringhausen .10
986 Willie Harris .10
987 David Cone .10
988 Bob Wickman .10
989 Wes Helms .10
990 Josh Beckett .25

2002 Topps Total Award Winners

MT

Complete Set (30): 35.00
Common Player: .75
Inserted 1:6

AW1 Ichiro Suzuki 4.00
AW2 Albert Pujols 2.00
AW3 Barry Bonds 2.00
AW4 Ichiro Suzuki 4.00
AW5 Randy Johnson 1.00
AW6 Roger Clemens 1.50
AW7 Jason Giambi 1.00
AW8 Bret Boone .75
AW9 Troy Glaus .75
AW10 Alex Rodriguez 3.00
AW11 Juan Gonzalez 1.00
AW12 Ichiro Suzuki 4.00
AW13 Jorge Posada .75
AW14 Edgar Martinez .75
AW15 Todd Helton .75
AW16 Jeff Kent .75
AW17 Albert Pujols 2.00
AW18 Rich Aurilia .75
AW19 Barry Bonds 2.00
AW20 Luis Gonzalez .75
AW21 Sammy Sosa 2.00
AW22 Mike Piazza 3.00
AW23 Mike Hampton .75
AW24 Ruben Sierra .75
AW25 Matt Morris .75
AW26 Curt Schilling .75
AW27 Alex Rodriguez 3.00
AW28 Barry Bonds 2.00
AW29 Jim Thome .75
AW30 Barry Bonds 2.00

2002 Topps Total Production

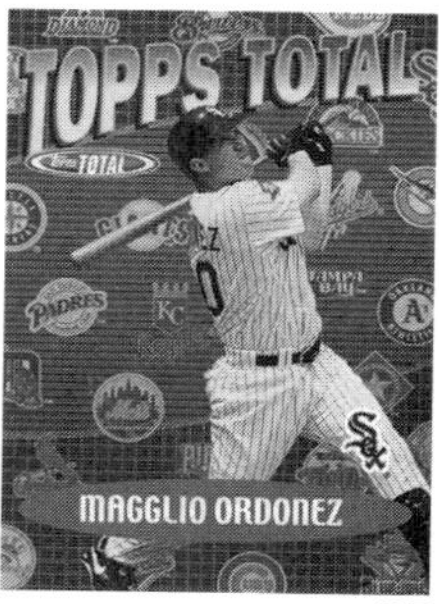

MT

Complete Set (10): 15.00
Common Player: .75
Inserted 1:12

TP1 Alex Rodriguez 3.00
TP2 Barry Bonds 2.00
TP3 Ichiro Suzuki 4.00
TP4 Edgar Martinez .75
TP5 Jason Giambi 1.00
TP6 Todd Helton 1.00
TP7 Nomar Garciaparra 2.50
TP8 Vladimir Guerrero 1.00
TP9 Sammy Sosa 2.00
TP10 Chipper Jones 2.00

2002 Topps Total Total Topps

MT

Complete Set (50): 35.00
Common Player: .50
Inserted 1:3

TT1 Roberto Alomar .75
TT2 Moises Alou .50
TT3 Jeff Bagwell 1.00
TT4 Lance Berkman .75
TT5 Barry Bonds 2.00
TT6 Bret Boone .50
TT7 Kevin Brown .50
TT8 Eric Chavez .50
TT9 Roger Clemens 1.50
TT10 Carlos Delgado .50
TT11 Cliff Floyd .50
TT12 Nomar Garciaparra 2.50
TT13 Jason Giambi 1.00
TT14 Brian Giles .75
TT15 Troy Glaus .75
TT16 Tom Glavine .50
TT17 Luis Gonzalez .50
TT18 Juan Gonzalez .75
TT19 Shawn Green .50
TT20 Ken Griffey Jr. 2.50
TT21 Vladimir Guerrero 1.00
TT22 Jorge Posada .50
TT23 Todd Helton .75
TT24 Tim Hudson .50

TT25	Derek Jeter	4.00
TT26	Randy Johnson	1.00
TT27	Andruw Jones	.75
TT28	Chipper Jones	2.00
TT29	Jeff Kent	.50
TT30	Greg Maddux	2.00
TT31	Edgar Martinez	.50
TT32	Pedro Martinez	1.00
TT33	Magglio Ordonez	.50
TT34	Rafael Palmeiro	.50
TT35	Mike Piazza	3.00
TT36	Albert Pujols	2.00
TT37	Aramis Ramirez	.50
TT38	Mariano Rivera	.50
TT39	Alex Rodriguez	3.00
TT40	Ivan Rodriguez	.75
TT41	Curt Schilling	.75
TT42	Gary Sheffield	.50
TT43	Sammy Sosa	2.00
TT44	Ichiro Suzuki	4.00
TT45	Miguel Tejada	.50
TT46	Frank Thomas	1.00
TT47	Jim Thome	.75
TT48	Larry Walker	.50
TT49	Bernie Williams	.50
TT50	Kerry Wood	.50

2002 Topps206

SCHMIDT, PHILADELPHIA

	MT
Complete Set (307):	100.00
Common Player:	.20
Common (141-155, 271-285):	1.00
Inserted 1:2	
Series I Pack (8):	7.00
Series I Box (20):	120.00
Series II Pack (8):	4.00
Series II Box (20):	70.00

1	Vladimir Guerrero	.75
2	Sammy Sosa	1.50
3	Garret Anderson	.20
4	Rafael Palmeiro	.50
5	Juan Gonzalez	.75
6	John Smoltz	.20
7	Mark Mulder	.30
8	Jon Lieber	.20
9	Greg Maddux	1.50
10	Moises Alou	.25
11	Joe Randa	.20
12	Bobby Abreu	.30
13	Ryan Kohlmeier	.20
14	Kerry Wood	.40
15	Craig Biggio	.30
16	Curt Schilling	.40
17	Brian Jordan	.20
18	Edgardo Alfonzo	.20
19	Darren Dreifort	.20
20	Todd Helton	.75
21	Ramon Ortiz	.20
22	Ichiro Suzuki	3.00
23	Jimmy Rollins	.20
24	Darin Erstad	.25
25	Shawn Green	.40
26	Tino Martinez	.30
27	Bret Boone	.20
28	Alfonso Soriano	.40
29	Chan Ho Park	.40
30	Roger Clemens	1.25
31	Cliff Floyd	.20
32	Johnny Damon	.20
33	Frank Thomas	.75
34	Barry Bonds	1.50
35	Luis Gonzalez	.50
36	Carlos Lee	.20
37	Roberto Alomar	.60
38	Carlos Delgado	.50
39	Nomar Garciaparra	2.00
40	Jason Kendall	.20
41	Scott Rolen	.40
42	Tom Glavine	.40
43	Ryan Klesko	.20
44	Brian Giles	.30
45	Bud Smith	.30
46	Charles Nagy	.20
47	Tony Gwynn	.75
48	C.C. Sabathia	.20
49	Manny Ramirez	.75
50	Jerry Hairston Jr.	.20
51	Jeromy Burnitz	.20
52	David Justice	.40
53	Bartolo Colon	.20
54	Andres Galarraga	.30
55	Jeff Weaver	.20
56	Terrance Long	.20
57	Tsuyoshi Shinjo	.20
58	Barry Zito	.20
59	Mariano Rivera	.30
60	John Olerud	.40
61	Randy Johnson	.75
62	Kenny Lofton	.30
63	Jermaine Dye	.20
64	Troy Glaus	.60
65	Larry Walker	.40
66	Hideo Nomo	.40
67	Mike Mussina	.60
68	Paul LoDuca	.20
69	Magglio Ordonez	.20
70	Paul O'Neill	.30
71	Sean Casey	.30
72	Lance Berkman	.30
73	Adam Dunn	.75
74	Aramis Ramirez	.20
75	Rafael Furcal	.20
76	Gary Sheffield	.30
77	Todd Hollandsworth	.20
78	Chipper Jones	1.50
79	Bernie Williams	.60
80	Richard Hidalgo	.25
81	Eric Chavez	.20
82	Mike Piazza	2.00
83	J.D. Drew	.40
84	Ken Griffey Jr.	2.50
85	Joe Kennedy	.20
86	Joel Pineiro	.20
87	Josh Towers	.20
88	Andruw Jones	.50
89	Carlos Beltran	.20
90	Mike Cameron	.20
91	Albert Pujols	1.50
92	Alex Rodriguez	2.00
93	Omar Vizquel	.30
94	Juan Encarnacion	.20
95	Jeff Bagwell	.75
96	Jose Canseco	.40
97	Ben Sheets	.20
98	Mark Grace	.40
99	Mike Sweeney	.20
100	Mark McGwire	2.50
101	Ivan Rodriguez	.75
102	Rich Aurilia	.20
103	Cristian Guzman	.20
104	Roy Oswalt	.40
105	Tim Hudson	.40
106	Brent Abernathy	.20
107	Mike Hampton	.30
108	Miguel Tejada	.30
109	Bobby Higginson	.20
110	Edgar Martinez	.25
111	Jorge Posada	.30
112	Jason Giambi	.75
113	Pedro Astacio	.20
114	Kazuhiro Sasaki	.20
115	Preston Wilson	.20
116	Jason Bere	.20
117	Mark Quinn	.20
118	Pokey Reese	.20
119	Derek Jeter	3.00
120	Shannon Stewart	.20
121	Jeff Kent	.25
122	Jeremy Giambi	.20
123	Pat Burrell	.30
124	Jim Edmonds	.30
125	Mark Buehrle	.20
126	Kevin Brown	.30
127	Raul Mondesi	.20
128	Pedro Martinez	.75
129	Jim Thome	.40
130	Russ Ortiz	.20
131	Brandon Duckworth	.20
132	*Ryan Jamison*	.50
133	Brandon Inge	.20
134	Felipe Lopez	.20
135	Jason Lane	.20
136	*Forrest Johnson*	1.50
137	Greg Nash	1.00
138	Covelli Crisp	.20
139	Nick Neugebauer	.20
140	Dustan Mohr	.20
141	*Freddy Sanchez*	2.00
142	*Justin Backsmeyer*	2.00
143	Jorge Julio	1.00
144	*Ryan Mottl*	2.00
145	*Chris Tritle*	3.00
146	*Noochie Varner*	3.00
147	Brian Rogers	1.00
148	*Michael Hill*	1.00
149	Luis Pineda	1.00
150	*Rich Thompson*	1.50
151	Bill Hall	1.00
152	*Jose Dominguez*	1.50
153	*Justin Woodrow*	2.00
154	*Nic Jackson*	3.00
155	*Laynce Nix*	1.50
156	Hank Aaron	2.50
157	Ernie Banks	1.00
158	Johnny Bench	1.00
159	George Brett	2.00
160	Carlton Fisk	.40
161	Bob Gibson	.50
162	Reggie Jackson	.75
163	Don Mattingly	2.50
164	Kirby Puckett	1.50
165	Frank Robinson	.75
166	Nolan Ryan	3.00
167	Tom Seaver	1.00
168	Mike Schmidt	1.00
169	Dave Winfield	.40
170	Carl Yastrzemski	.75
171	Frank Chance	.50
172	Ty Cobb	2.50
173	Sam Crawford	1.00
174	Johnny Evers	.75
175	John McGraw	1.00
176	Eddie Plank	.50
177	Tris Speaker	1.00
178	Joe Tinker	.50
179	Honus Wagner	5.00
180	Cy Young	2.50
181	Javier Vazquez	.20
182	Mark Mulder	.40
183	Roger Clemens	1.50
184	*Kazuhisa Ishii*	4.00
185	Roberto Alomar	.50
186	Lance Berkman	.75
187	Adam Dunn	.75
188	Aramis Ramirez	.20
189	Chuck Knoblauch	.20
190	Nomar Garciaparra	2.00
191	Brad Penny	.20
192	Gary Sheffield	.40
193	Alfonso Soriano	2.00
194	Andruw Jones	.50
195	Randy Johnson	.75
196	Corey Patterson	.20
197	Milton Bradley	.20
198	Johnny Damon	.20
199	Paul LoDuca	.20
200	Albert Pujols	1.50
201	Scott Rolen	.50
202	J.D. Drew	.40
203	Vladimir Guerrero	1.00
204	Jason Giambi	1.50
205	Moises Alou	.20
206	Magglio Ordonez	.40
207	Carlos Febles	.20
208	*So Taguchi*	1.50
209	Rafael Palmeiro	.50
210	*Boomer Wells*	.50
211	Orlando Cabrera	.20
212	Sammy Sosa	1.50
213	Armando Benitez	.20
214	Wes Helms	.20
215	Mariano Rivera	.40
216	Jimmy Rollins	.20
217	Matt Lawton	.20
218	Shawn Green	.40
219	Bernie Williams	.50
220	Bret Boone	.20
221	Alex Rodriguez	2.50
222	Roger Cedeno	.20
223	Marty Cordova	.20
224	Fred McGriff	.40
225	Chipper Jones	1.50
226	Kerry Wood	.50
227	Larry Walker	.40
228	Robin Ventura	.40
229	Robert Fick	.20
230	Tino Martinez	.40
231	Ben Petrick	.20
232	Neifi Perez	.20
233	Pedro Martinez	1.00
234	Brian Jordan	.20
235	Freddy Garcia	.20
236	Derek Jeter	3.00
237	Ben Grieve	.20
238	Barry Bonds	2.50
239	Luis Gonzalez	.50
240	Shane Halter	.20
241	Brian Giles	.50
242	Bud Smith	.20
243	Richie Sexson	.40
244	Barry Zito	.40
245	Eric Milton	.20
246	Ivan Rodriguez	.50
247	Toby Hall	.20
248	Mike Piazza	2.00
249	Ruben Sierra	.20
250	Tsuyoshi Shinjo	.20
251	Jermaine Dye	.20
252	Roy Oswalt	.50
253	Todd Helton	.75
254	Adrian Beltre	.40
255	Doug Mientkiewicz	.20
256	Ichiro Suzuki	2.50
257	C.C. Sabathia	.20
258	Paul Konerko	.20
259	Ken Griffey Jr.	2.00
260	Jeromy Burnitz	.20
261	Hank Blalock	.20
262	Mark Prior	1.00
263	Josh Beckett	.20
264	Carlos Pena	.20
265	Sean Burroughs	.20
266	Austin Kearns	.50
267	Chin-Hui Tsao	.20
268	Dewon Brazelton	.20
269	J.D. Martin	.20
270	Marlon Byrd	.20
271	*Joe Mauer*	5.00
272	*Jason Botts*	1.00
273	*Mauricio Lara*	1.00
274	*Jonny Gomes*	1.00
275	Gavin Floyd	1.00
276	*Alexander Requena*	1.00
277	*Jimmy Gobble*	3.00
278	*Chris Duffy*	1.50
279	Colt Griffin	1.00
280	*Ryan Church*	2.00
281	Beltran Perez	1.00
282	*Clint Nageotte*	2.00
283	*Justin Schuda*	1.00
284	Scott Hairston	1.00
285	Mario Ramos	1.00
286	Tom Seaver	2.00
287	Hank Aaron	3.00
288	Mike Schmidt	3.00
289	Robin Yount	1.50
290	Joe Morgan	1.00
291	Frank Robinson	1.00
292	Reggie Jackson	2.00
293	Nolan Ryan	4.00
294	Dave Winfield	1.00
295	Willie Mays	3.00
296	Brooks Robinson	1.50
297	Mark McGwire	3.00
298	Honus Wagner	3.00
299	Sherry Magee	1.00
300	Frank Chance	1.00
301	Larry Doyle	1.00
302	John McGraw	2.00
303	Jimmy Collins	1.00
304	Buck Herzog	1.00
305	Sam Crawford	1.00
306	Cy Young	3.00
307	Honus Wagner	3.00
308	Alex Rodriguez	
309	Vernon Wells	
310	Byung-Hyun Kim	
311	Vicente Padilla	
312	Alfonso Soriano	
313	Mike Piazza	
314	Jacque Jones	
315	Shawn Green	
316	Paul Byrd	
317	Lance Berkman	
318	Larry Walker	
319	Ken Griffey Jr.	
320	Shea Hillenbrand	
321	Jay Gibbons	
322	Andruw Jones	
323	Luis Gonzalez	
324	Garret Anderson	
325	Roy Halladay	

326 Randy Winn
327 Matt Morris
328 Robb Nen
329 Trevor Hoffman
330 Kip Wells
331 Orlando Hernandez
332 Rey Ordonez
333 Torii Hunter
334 Geoff Jenkins
335 Eric Karros
336 Mike Lowell
337 Nick Johnson
338 Randall Simon
339 Ellis Burks
340 Sammy Sosa
341 Pedro J. Martinez
342 Junior Spivey
343 Vinny Castilla
344 Randy Johnson
345 Chipper Jones
346 Orlando Hudson
347 Albert Pujols
348 Rondell White
349 Vladimir Guerrero
350 Mark Prior
351 Eric Gagne
352 Todd Zeile
353 Manny Ramirez
354 Kevin Millwood
355 Troy Percival
356 Jason Giambi
357 Bartolo Colon
358 Jeremy Giambi
359 Jose Cruz Jr.
360 Ichiro Suzuki
361 Eddie Guardado
362 Ivan Rodriguez
363 Carl Crawford
364 Jason Simontacchi
365 Kenny Lofton
366 Raul Mondesi
367 A.J. Pierzynski
368 Ugueth Urbina
369 Rodrigo Lopez
370 Nomar Garciaparra
371 Craig Counsell
372 Barry Larkin
373 Carlos Pena
374 Luis Castillo
375 Raul Ibanez
376 Kazuhisa Ishii
377 Derek Lowe
378 Curt Schilling
379 Jim Thome
380 Derek Jeter
381 Pat Burrell
382 Jamie Moyer
383 Eric Hinske
384 Scott Rolen
385 Miguel Tejada
386 Andy Pettitte
387 Mike Lieberthal
388 Al Leiter
389 Todd Helton
390 Adam Dunn
391 Cliff Floyd
392 Ron Gardenhire
393 Joe Torre
394 Bobby Cox
395 Tony LaRussa
396 Art Howe
397 Bob Brenly
398 Brandon Phillips
399 Mike Cuddyer
400 Joe Mauer
401 Mark Teixeira
402 Hee Seop Choi
403 Angel Berroa
404 Jesse Foppert
405 Bobby Crosby
406 Jose Reyes
407 Casey Kotchman
408 Aaron Heilman
409 Adrian Gonzalez
410 Cliff Lee
411 Brett Myers
412 Justin Huber
413 Drew Henson
414 Taggert Bozied
415 Dontrelle Willis
416 Rocco Baldelli
417 Jason Stokes
418 Ruddy Lugo
419 Daryl Clark
420 Jaime Bubela
421 Craig Brazell
422 Andy Marte
423 Walter Young
424 Adam LaRoche
425 Jason Perry
426 *Chris Duncan*
427 Darrell Rasner
428 Mitch Talbot
429 Brian Barden
430 Chris Snyder
431 B.J. Upton
432 Lou Brock
433 Ozzie Smith
434 Wade Boggs
435 Yogi Berra
436 Al Kaline
437 Robin Roberts
438 Roberto Clemente
439 Steve Carlton
440 Fergie Jenkins
441 Orlando Cepeda
442 Rod Carew
443 Harmon Killebrew
444 Duke Snider
445 Stan Musial
446 Hank Greenberg
447 Honus Wagner
448 Joe Tinker
449 John McGraw
450 Mordecai Brown
451 Christy Mathewson
452 Sam Crawford
453 Bill O'Hara
454 Ray Demmitt
455 Napoleon Lajoie
456 Kid Elberfeld

2002 Topps206 T206 mini parallel

	MT
Polar Bear:	2-3X
Tolstoi Black:	2-5X
Average 4:box	
Tolstoi Red:	4-8X
Average 2:box	
Cycle:	6-12X
Average 1:box	
Series 2	
Polar Bear:	2-3X
Piedmont Black:	3-5X
Piedmond Red:	4-8X
Carolina Brights:	6-12X

2002 Topps206 Autographs

		MT
Common Player:		15.00
Inserted 1:41		
BB	Barry Bonds	140.00
RC	Roger Clemens	150.00
JE	Jim Edmonds	30.00
BG	Brian Giles	25.00
CG	Cristian Guzman	20.00
BI	Brandon Inge	20.00
RJ	Ryan Jamison	20.00
FJ	Forrest Johnson	20.00
JJ	Jorge Julio	15.00
FL	Felipe Lopez	20.00
GN	Greg Nash	30.00
MO	Magglio Ordonez	25.00
AR	Alex Rodriguez	100.00
JR	Jimmy Rollins	25.00
BZ	Barry Zito	30.00

2002 Topps206 Autographs Series 2

		MT
Common Player:		10.00
Inserted 1:55		
MA	Moises Alou	30.00
LB	Lance Berkman	35.00
HB	Hank Blalock	20.00
DB	Dewon Brazelton	10.00
MB	Marlon Byrd	15.00
EC	Eric Chavez	30.00
JD	Johnny Damon	20.00
GF	Gavin Floyd	20.00
LG	Luis Gonzalez	25.00
KI	Kazuhisa Ishii	60.00
JDM	J.D. Martin	12.00
JM	Joe Mauer	40.00
AP	Albert Pujols	65.00
BS	Ben Sheets	15.00
BSM	Bud Smith	15.00
CT	Chris Tritle	12.00

2002 Topps206 Relics

		MT
Common Player:		8.00
Overall Relics 1:11		
RA	Roberto Alomar/jsy	15.00
JB	Jeff Bagwell/jsy	15.00
CB	Craig Biggio/jsy	12.00
BB	Barry Bonds/jsy	40.00
BBO	Bret Boone/jsy	15.00
MC	Mike Cameron/jsy	12.00
JC	Jose Canseco/bat	30.00
CD	Carlos Delgado/jsy	10.00
JED	Jim Edmonds/jsy	10.00
CF	Cliff Floyd/jsy	10.00
JGI	Jason Giambi/jsy	25.00
JG	Jeremy Giambi/jsy	10.00
TG	Tom Glavine/jsy	15.00
SG	Shawn Green/jsy	10.00
TGW	Tony Gwynn/jsy	20.00
TH	Todd Helton/jsy	20.00
RJ	Randy Johnson/jsy	20.00
AJ	Andruw Jones/jsy	20.00
CJ	Chipper Jones/jsy	20.00
CL	Carlos Lee/jsy	8.00
KL	Kenny Lofton/jsy	10.00
GM	Greg Maddux/jsy	20.00
EM	Edgar Martinez/jsy	12.00
TM	Tino Martinez/jsy	25.00
JO	John Olerud/jsy	10.00
PO	Paul O'Neill/jsy	20.00
MO	Magglio Ordonez/jsy	10.00
CP	Chan Ho Park/bat	25.00
MP	Mike Piazza/jsy	35.00
AP	Albert Pujols/bat	50.00
IR	Ivan Rodriguez/jsy	15.00
AS	Alfonso Soriano/bat	40.00
SS	Shannon Stewart/bat	15.00
FT	Frank Thomas/jsy	20.00
JT	Jim Thome/jsy	20.00
LW	Larry Walker/jsy	12.00
JW	Jeff Weaver/jsy	10.00
BW	Bernie Williams/sy	20.00
BZ	Barry Zito/jsy	12.00

2002 Topps206 Relics Series 2

		MT
Common Player:		6.00
Jerseys 1:18		
Bats 1:40		
RA	Roberto Alomar/bat	10.00
JB	Jeff Bagwell/jsy	10.00
BB	Barry Bonds/jsy	20.00
BBO	Bret Boone/jsy	6.00
KB	Kevin Brown/jsy	6.00
AB	A.J. Burnett/jsy	6.00
SB	Sean Burroughs/bat	8.00
EC	Eric Chavez/bat	8.00
TC	Ty Cobb/bat	400.00
JC	Jimmy Collins/bat	45.00
SCR	Sam Crawford/bat	80.00
JD	Johnny Damon/bat	12.00
RD	Ryan Dempster/jsy	6.00
BD	Brandon Duckworth/jsy	8.00
AD	Adam Dunn/bat	25.00
DE	Darin Erstad/jsy	8.00
JEV	Johnny Evers/bat	50.00
CF	Cliff Floyd/jsy	8.00
TGL	Tom Glavine/jsy	8.00
JG	Juan Gonzalez/bat	10.00
MG	Mark Grace/bat	12.00
SG	Shawn Green/jsy	6.00
CG	Cristian Guzman/jsy	8.00
TG	Tony Gwynn/jsy	15.00
TH	Toby Hall/jsy	6.00
JH	Josh Hamilton/bat	8.00
THE	Todd Helton/jsy	8.00
RH	Rickey Henderson/bat	25.00
BH	Buck Herzog/bat	30.00
JJ	Jason Jennings/jsy	6.00
RJ	Randy Johnson/jsy	10.00
AJ	Andruw Jones/jsy	8.00
CJO	Chipper Jones/jsy	12.00
JK	Jeff Kent/jsy	8.00
BL	Barry Larkin/jsy	8.00
TL	Travis Lee/bat	8.00
GM	Greg Maddux/jsy	12.00
EM	Edgar Martinez/jsy	8.00
TM	Tino Martinez/bat	15.00
JM	Joe Mays/jsy	6.00
JMC	John McGraw/bat	40.00
FM	Fred McGriff/bat	8.00
JO	John Olerud/jsy	6.00
RP	Rafael Palmeiro/jsy	8.00
BP	Brad Penny/jsy	6.00
MP	Mike Piazza/jsy	15.00
AP	Albert Pujols/jsy	15.00
ARA	Aramis Ramirez/bat	8.00
AR	Alex Rodriguez/bat	20.00
IR	Ivan Rodriguez/jsy	8.00
CS	Curt Schilling/bat	15.00
GS	Gary Sheffield/bat	8.00
TS	Tsuyoshi Shinjo/bat	10.00
AS	Alfonso Soriano/bat	25.00
MT	Miguel Tejada/bat	8.00
FT	Frank Thomas/jsy	8.00
JTH	Jim Thome/bat	10.00
JT	Joe Tinker/bat	40.00
MV	Mo Vaughn/bat	8.00
RV	Robin Ventura/bat	10.00
HWA	Honus Wagner/bat	400.00
LW	Larry Walker/jsy	6.00
BW	Bernie Williams/jsy	10.00
MW	Matt Williams/jsy	6.00
PW	Preston Wilson/jsy	6.00

2002 Topps206 Reprint Relics

		MT
Common Player:		75.00
SC	Sam Crawford	90.00
JE	Johnny Evers	90.00
JM	John McGraw	75.00
TS	Tris Speaker	140.00
HW	Honus Wagner	400.00

2002 Topps206 Team 206

		MT
Complete Set (20):		20.00
Common Player:		.40
Inserted 1:pack		
1	Barry Bonds	2.50
2	Ivan Rodriguez	.75
3	Luis Gonzalez	.75
4	Jason Giambi	1.00
5	Pedro Martinez	1.00
6	Larry Walker	.60
7	Bobby Abreu	.40
8	Derek Jeter	3.00
9	Bret Boone	.40
10	Mike Piazza	2.50
11	Alex Rodriguez	2.50
12	Roger Clemens	1.50
13	Albert Pujols	2.00
14	Randy Johnson	1.00
15	Sammy Sosa	2.00
16	Cristian Guzman	.40
17	Shawn Green	.50
18	Curt Schilling	.50
19	Ichiro Suzuki	2.50
20	Chipper Jones	2.00

2002 Topps206 Team 206 Series 2

		MT
Complete Set (25):		20.00
Common Player:		.40
Inserted 1:1		
1	Alex Rodriguez	2.50
2	Sammy Sosa	2.00
3	Jason Giambi	1.50
4	Nomar Garciaparra	2.00
5	Ichiro Suzuki	2.50
6	Chipper Jones	1.50
7	Derek Jeter	3.00
8	Barry Bonds	2.00
9	Mike Piazza	2.00
10	Randy Johnson	.75
11	Shawn Green	.40
12	Todd Helton	.50
13	Luis Gonzalez	.50
14	Albert Pujols	1.50
15	Curt Schilling	.75
16	Scott Rolen	.50
17	Ivan Rodriguez	.50
18	Roberto Alomar	.50
19	Cristian Guzman	.40
20	Bret Boone	.40
21	Barry Zito	.40
22	Larry Walker	.40
23	Eric Chavez	.40
24	Roger Clemens	1.50
25	Pedro Martinez	1.00

2002 Topps206 Team Topps Legends Autographs Series 2

	MT
Inserted 1:260	
Ralph Branca	25.00
Andy Pafko	20.00
Joe Pepitone	10.00
Herb Score	
Tom Seaver	60.00
Warren Spahn	25.00
Bobby Thomson	
Luis Tiant	10.00

Figure values of lower-grade cards from 1981-date as:
Near Mint (NM) 75%
Excellent (EX) 40%
of the listed Mint price

For cards through 1980, values should be figured as:
Excellent (EX) 50%
Very Good (VG) 30%
of the listed Near Mint price

2002 Topps Traded & Rookies

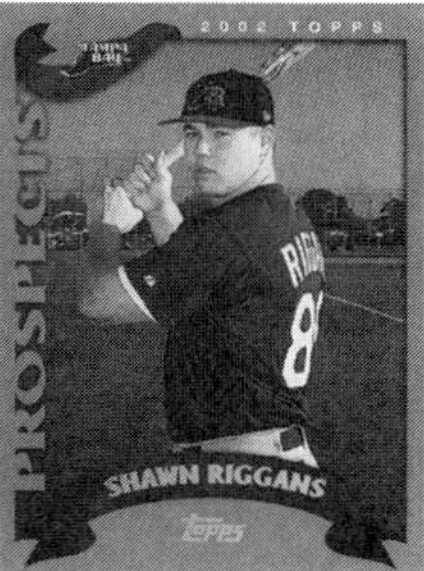

		MT
Complete Set (275):		110.00
Common Player:		.15
Common SP (1-110):		.75
Chrome cards:		2-4X
2:pack		
Pack (10):		3.00
Box (24):		60.00
T1	Jeff Weaver	.50
T2	Jay Powell	.50
T3	Alex Gonzalez	.50
T4	Jason Isringhausen	.50
T5	Darren Oliver	.50
T6	Hector Ortiz	.50
T7	Chuck Knoblauch	.50
T8	Brian L. Hunter	.50
T9	Dustan Mohr	.50
T10	Eric Hinske	1.00
T11	Roger Cedeno	.50
T12	Eddie Perez	.50
T13	Jeromy Burnitz	.50
T14	Bartolo Colon	.75
T15	Rick Helling	.50
T16	Dan Plesac	.50
T17	Scott Strickland	.50
T18	Antonio Alfonseca	.50
T19	Ricky Gutierrez	.50
T20	John Valentin	.50
T21	Raul Mondesi	.50
T22	Ben Davis	.50
T23	Nelson Figueroa	.50
T24	Earl Snyder	.50
T25	Robin Ventura	.75
T26	Jimmy Haynes	.50
T27	Kenny Kelly	.50
T28	Morgan Ensberg	.50
T29	Reggie Sanders	.50
T30	Shigetoshi Hasegawa	.50
T31	Allen Levrault	.50
T32	Russell Branyan	.50
T33	Jose Guillen	.50
T34	Jose Paniagua	.50
T35	Kent Mercker	.50
T36	Jesse Orosco	.50
T37	Gregg Zaun	.50
T38	Reggie Taylor	.50
T39	Andres Galarraga	.50
T40	Chris Truby	.50
T41	Bruce Chen	.50
T42	Darren Lewis	.50
T43	Ryan Kohlmeier	.50
T44	John McDonald	.50
T45	Omar Daal	.50
T46	Matt Clement	.50
T47	Glendon Rusch	.50
T48	Chan Ho Park	.50
T49	Benny Agbayani	.50
T50	Juan Gonzalez	1.50
T51	Carlos Baerga	.50
T52	Tim Raines	.50
T53	Kevin Appier	.50
T54	Marty Cordoua	.50
T55	Jeff D'Amico	.50
T56	Dmitri Young	.50
T57	Roosevelt Brown	.50
T58	Dustin Hermanson	.50
T59	Jose Rijo	.50
T60	Todd Ritchie	.50
T61	Lee Stevens	.50
T62	Shane Heams	.50
T63	Eric Young	.50
T64	Chuck Finley	.50
T65	Dicky Gonzalez	.50
T66	Jose Macias	.50
T67	Gabe Kapler	.50
T68	Sandy Alomar Jr.	.50
T69	Henry Blanco	.50
T70	Julian Tavarez	.50
T71	Paul Bako	.50
T72	Dave Burba	.50
T73	Brian Jordan	.50
T74	Rickey Henderson	1.00
T75	Kevin Mench	.50
T76	Hideo Nomo	1.00
T77	Mark Sweeney	.50
T78	Brad Fullmer	.50
T79	Carl Everett	.50
T80	Boomer Wells	.50
T81	Aaron Sele	.50
T82	Todd Hollandsworth	.50
T83	Vicente Padilla	.50
T84	Chris Latham	.50
T85	Corky Miller	.50
T86	Josh Fogg	.50
T87	Calvin Murray	.50
T88	Craig Paquette	.50
T89	Jay Payton	.50
T90	Carlos Pena	.50
T91	Juan Encarnacion	.50
T92	Rey Sanchez	.50
T93	Ryan Dempster	.50
T94	Mario Encarnacion	.50
T95	Jorge Julio	.50
T96	John Mabry	.50
T97	Todd Zeile	.50
T98	Johnny Damon	.50
T99	Deivi Cruz	.50
T100	Gary Sheffield	.75
T101	Ted Lilly	.50
T102	Todd Van Poppel	.50
T103	Shawn Estes	.50
T104	Cesar Izturis	.50
T105	Ron Coomer	.50
T106	Grady Little	.50
T107	Jimy Williams	.50
T108	Tony Pena	.50
T109	Frank Robinson	.50
T110	Ron Gardenhire	.50
T111	Dennis Tankersley	.15
T112	*Alejandro Cadena*	.25
T113	*Justin Reid*	.25
T114	*Nate Field*	.25
T115	*Rene Reyes*	.25
T116	*Nelson Castro*	.25
T117	Miguel Olivo	.15
T118	David Espinosa	.15
T119	*Chris Bootcheck*	.50
T120	*Rob Henkel*	.25
T121	*Steve Bechler*	.25
T122	*Mark Outlaw*	.25
T123	*Henry Pichardo*	.25
T124	*Michael Floyd*	.25
T125	*Richard Lane*	.25
T126	*Peter Zamora*	.25
T127	Javier Colina	.15
T128	*Greg Sain*	.25
T129	Ronnie Merrill	.25
T130	Gavin Floyd	1.50
T131	*Josh Bonifay*	.25
T132	*Tommy Marx*	.25
T133	*Gary Cates Jr.*	.25
T134	Neal Cotts	.25
T135	Angel Berroa	.25
T136	*Elio Serrano*	.25
T137	*J.J. Putz*	.25
T138	*Ruben Gotay*	.25
T139	*Eddie Rogers*	.25
T140	Wily Mo Pena	.15
T141	*Tyler Yates*	.25
T142	*Colin Young*	.25
T143	Chance Caple	.15
T144	*Ben Howard*	.25
T145	*Ryan Bukvich*	.25
T146	*Clifford Bartosh*	.25
T147	Brandon Claussen	.15
T148	Cristian Guerrero	.15
T149	Derrick Lewis	.15
T150	*Eric Miller*	.25
T151	*Justin Huber*	1.50
T152	Adrian Gonzalez	.15
T153	*Brian West*	.25
T154	*Chris Baker*	.25
T155	Drew Henson	.15
T156	Scott Hairston	.50
T157	*Jason Simontacchi*	.75
T158	Jason Arnold	.15
T159	Brandon Phillips	.15
T160	*Adam Roller*	.25
T161	*Scotty Layfield*	.25
T162	*Freddie Money*	.25
T163	*Noochie Varner*	.50
T164	*Terrance Hill*	.25
T165	*Jeremy Hill*	.25
T166	*Carlos Cabrera*	.25
T167	*Jose Morban*	.25
T168	*Kevin Frederick*	.25
T169	Mark Teixeira	.20
T170	Brian Rogers	.15
T171	*Anastacio Martinez*	.25
T172	*Bobby Jenks*	.50
T173	*David Gil*	.25
T174	Andres Torres	.15
T175	*James Barrett*	.25
T176	Jimmy Journell	.15
T177	*Brett Kay*	.25
T178	*Jason Young*	.25
T179	*Mark Hamilton*	.25
T180	*Jose Bautista*	.50
T181	*Blake McGinley*	.25
T182	*Ryan Mottl*	.25
T183	*Jeff Austin*	.25
T184	Xavier Nady	.15
T185	*Kyle Kane*	.25
T186	Travis Foley	.15
T187	*Nathan Kaup*	.25
T188	*Eric Cyr*	.25
T189	*Josh Cisneros*	.25
T190	*Brad Nelson*	.25
T191	*Clint Weibl*	.25
T192	*Ron Calloway*	.25
T193	Jung Bong	.15
T194	*Rolando Viera*	.25
T195	*Jason Bulger*	.25
T196	*Chone Figgins*	.25
T197	*Jimmy Alvarez*	.25
T198	*Joel Crump*	.25
T199	*Ryan Doumit*	.50
T200	*Demetrius Heath*	.25
T201	*John Ennis*	.25
T202	*Doug Sessions*	.25
T203	*Clinton Hosford*	.25
T204	*Chris Narveson*	.25
T205	*Ross Peeples*	.25
T206	*Alexander Requena*	.25
T207	*Matt Erickson*	.25
T208	*Brian Forystek*	.25
T209	Dewon Brazelton	.15
T210	Nathan Haynes	.15
T211	Jack Cust	.15
T212	Jesse Foppert	.50
T213	*Jesus Cota*	1.00
T214	Juan Gonzalez	.15
T215	*Tim Kalita*	.25
T216	*Manny Delcarmen*	.50
T217	Jim Kavourias	.15
T218	*C.J. Wilson*	.25
T219	*Edwin Yan*	.25
T220	Andy Van Hekken	.15
T221	Michael Cuddyer	.15
T222	*Jeff Verplancke*	.25
T223	*Mike Wilson*	.25
T224	Corwin Malone	.15
T225	*Chris Snelling*	.75
T226	*Joe Rogers*	.25
T227	Jason Bay	.15
T228	*Ezequiel Astacio*	.25
T229	*Joey Hammond*	.25
T230	*Chris Duffy*	.25
T231	Mark Prior	.50
T232	*Hansel Izquierdo*	.25
T233	*Franklyn German*	.25
T234	Alexis Gomez	.15
T235	*Jorge Padilla*	.40
T236	*Ryan Snare*	.25
T237	Deivis Santos	.15
T238	*Taggert Bozied*	1.50
T239	*Mike Peeples*	.25
T240	*Ronald Acuna*	.25
T241	Koyie Hill	.15
T242	*Garrett Guzman*	.25
T243	*Ryan Church*	.25
T244	*Tony Fontana*	.25
T245	*Keto Anderson*	.25
T246	*Brad Bouras*	.25
T247	*Jason Dubois*	.25
T248	*Angel Guzman*	.25
T249	*Joel Hanrahan*	.25
T250	*Joe Jiannetti*	.50
T251	*Sean Pierce*	.25
T252	*Jake Mauer*	.25
T253	*Marshall McDougall*	.50
T254	*Edwin Almonte*	.25
T255	*Shawn Riggans*	.25
T256	Steven Shell	.15

T257 *Kevin Hooper* 1.00
T258 *Michael Frick* .25
T259 *Travis Chapman* 1.00
T260 *Tim Hummel* .25
T261 *Adam Morrissey* .25
T262 *Dontrelle Willis* 1.00
T263 *Justin Sherrod* .25
T264 *Gerald Smiley* .25
T265 *Tony Miller* .25
T266 Nolan Ryan 1.50
T267 Reggie Jackson .50
T268 Steve Garvey .15
T269 Wade Boggs .25
T270 Sammy Sosa .75
T271 Curt Schilling .25
T272 Mark Grace .25
T273 Jason Giambi .75
T274 Ken Griffey Jr. .60
T275 Roberto Alomar .40

2002 Topps Traded & Rookies Gold

MT
Gold Stars: 2-5X
Production 2,002 sets
Chrome Refractors: 2-5X
Inserted 1:12

2002 Topps Traded & Rookies Farewell Relics

MT
Randomly inserted
JC Jose Canseco 12.00

2002 Topps Traded & Rookies Hall of Fame Relics

MT
Randomly inserted
HOF-OS Ozzie Smith 25.00

2002 Topps Traded & Rookies Tools of the Trade Relics

MT
Common Player: 5.00
Bat Relics 1:34
Jersey Relics 1:426
RAB Roberto Alomar/bat 8.00
MA Moises Alou/bat 5.00
DB David Bell/bat 5.00
JBU Jeromy Burnitz/bat 5.00
JC Jose Canseco/bat 10.00
VC Vinny Castilla/bat 5.00
JCI Jeff Cirillo/bat 5.00
TC Tony Clark/bat 5.00
JDB Johnny Damon/bat 6.00
CE Carl Everett/bat 5.00
BF Brad Fullmer/bat 5.00
AG Andres Galarraga/bat 6.00
JG Juan Gonzalez/jsy 8.00
RHB Rickey Henderson/bat 12.00
BJ Brian Jordan/bat 5.00
DJ David Justice/bat 6.00
CK Chuck Knoblauch/bat 5.00
MLB Matt Lawton/bat 5.00
KL Kenny Lofton/bat 5.00
TM Tino Martinez/bat 6.00
CP Carlos Pena/bat 10.00
JP Josh Phelps/jsy 8.00
TR Tim Raines/bat 5.00
RS Reggie Sanders/bat 5.00
GS Gary Sheffield/bat 5.00
TS Tsuyoshi Shinjo/bat 8.00
RSI Ruben Sierra/bat 5.00
MT Michael Tucker/bat 5.00
JV John Vander Wal
MV Mo Vaughn/jsy 6.00
MVB Mo Vaughn/bat 6.00
RV Robin Ventura/bat 6.00
RW Rondell White/bat 5.00
EY Eric Young/bat 5.00

2002 Topps T & R Topps of the Trade Dual Relics

MT
Common Card: 8.00
Inserted 1:539
MA Moises Alou 8.00
HN Hideo Nomo 35.00
CP Chan Ho Park 8.00

2002 Topps Traded & Rookies Signature Moves Autographs

MT
Common Autograph: 8.00
Inserted 1:91
RA Roberto Alomar 30.00
MA Moises Alou 10.00
TBL Tony Blanco 8.00
BB Boof Bonser 8.00
AC Antoine Cameron 12.00
BC Brandon Claussen 8.00
MC Matt Cooper 8.00
JD Johnny Damon 25.00
JDA Jeff DaVanon 8.00
VD Victor Diaz 12.00
MFO Mike Fontenot
RH Ryan Hannaman 8.00
KI Kazuhisa Ishii 60.00
FJ Forrest Johnson 8.00
TL Todd Linden 15.00
CM Corwin Malone 8.00
JM Jake Mauer 12.00
AM Andy Morales 10.00
RM Ramon Moreta 8.00
JMO Justin Morneau 15.00
JP Juan Pena 8.00
JS Juan Silvestre 8.00
CS Chris Smith 8.00
DT Dennis Tankersley 8.00
MT Marcus Thames 12.00
CU Chase Utley 15.00
JW Justin Wayne 8.00

2002 Topps T & R Team Topps Legends Autographs

MT
Common Autograph: 10.00
Inserted 1:1,097
Johnny Bench 40.00
Vida Blue 10.00
Clete Boyer 12.00
Whitey Ford 30.00
Bob Gibson 25.00
Joe Pepitone 10.00
Bobby Richardson 10.00
Bill "Moose" Skowron 10.00
Enos Slaughter 18.00
Carl Yastrzemski 50.00

2002 Topps Tribute

MT
Complete Set (90): 190.00
Common Player: 1.50
Pack (5): 50.00
Box (6): 270.00
1 Hank Aaron 6.00
2 Rogers Hornsby 2.50
3 Bobby Thomson 1.50
4 Eddie Collins 1.50
5 Joe Carter 1.50
6 Jim Palmer 1.50
7 Willie Mays 6.00
8 Willie Stargell 2.50
9 Vida Blue 1.50
10 Whitey Ford 3.00
11 Bob Gibson 3.00
12 Nellie Fox 2.00
13 Napoleon Lajoie 2.00
14 Frankie Frisch 1.50
15 Nolan Ryan 10.00
16 Brooks Robinson 2.50
17 Kirby Puckett 5.00
18 Fergie Jenkins 1.50
19 Edd Roush 1.50
20 Honus Wagner 6.00
21 Richie Ashburn 1.50
22 Bob Feller 1.50
23 Joe Morgan 1.50
24 Orlando Cepeda 1.50
25 Steve Garvey 1.50
26 Hank Greenberg 1.50
27 Stan Musial 5.00
28 Sam Crawford 1.50
29 Jim Rice 1.50
30 Hack Wilson 2.50
31 Lou Brock 1.50
32 Mickey Vernon 1.50
33 Chuck Klein 1.50
34 Joe Jackson 6.00
35 Duke Snider 3.00
36 Ryne Sandberg 5.00
37 Johnny Bench 5.00
38 Sam Rice 1.50
39 Lou Gehrig 8.00
40 Robin Yount 3.00
41 Don Sutton 1.50
42 Jim Bottomley 1.50
43 Billy Herman 1.50
44 Zach Wheat 1.50
45 Juan Marichal 1.50
46 Bert Blyleven 1.50
47 Jackie Robinson 6.00
48 Gil Hodges 1.50
49 Mike Schmidt 6.00
50 Dale Murphy 1.50
51 Phil Rizzuto 1.50
52 Ty Cobb 6.00
53 Andre Dawson 1.50
54 Fred Lindstrom 1.50
55 Roy Campanella 3.00
56 Don Larsen 2.00
57 Harry Heilmann 1.50
58 Jim "Catfish" Hunter 1.50
59 Frank Robinson 2.00
60 Bill Mazeroski 1.50
61 Roger Maris 6.00
62 Dave Winfield 2.50
63 Warren Spahn 2.50
64 Babe Ruth 10.00
65 Ernie Banks 4.00
66 Wade Boggs 2.00
67 Carl Yastrzemski 3.00
68 Ron Santo 1.50
69 Dennis Martinez 1.50
70 Yogi Berra 4.00
71 Paul Waner 1.50
72 George Brett 6.00
73 Eddie Mathews 3.00
74 Bill Dickey 1.50
75 Carlton Fisk 2.00
76 Thurman Munson 5.00
77 Reggie Jackson 4.00
78 Phil Niekro 1.50
79 Luis Aparicio 1.50
80 Steve Carlton 1.50
81 Tris Speaker 1.50
82 Johnny Mize 1.50
83 Tom Seaver 4.00
84 Heinie Manush 1.50
85 Tommy John 1.50
86 Joe Cronin 1.50
87 Don Mattingly 8.00
88 Kirk Gibson 1.50
89 Bo Jackson 3.00
90 Mel Ott 1.50

2002 Topps Tribute First Impressions

MT
Cards #'d 51-86: 3-5X
Cards #'d 26-50: 4-8X
#'d to last two digits of Rk year
Lasting Impressions
Cards #'d 51-96: 3-5X
Cards #'d 26-50: 4-8X
#'d to last two digits of final season
Production under 25 not priced

2002 Topps Tribute Marks of Excellence

MT
Inserted 1:61
LB Lou Brock 55.00
SC Steve Carlton 50.00
DL Don Larsen 55.00
SM Stan Musial 100.00
MS Mike Schmidt 85.00
WS Warren Spahn 60.00

2002 Topps Tribute Marks of Excellence Relics

MT
Inserted 1:61
FJ Fergie Jenkins 50.00
DM Don Mattingly 110.00
JP Jim Palmer 50.00
BR Brooks Robinson 100.00
DS Duke Snider 60.00
RY Robin Yount 70.00

2002 Topps Tribute Matching Marks Dual

MT
Common Card: 10.00
Inserted 1:11
SBA Ron Santo, Ernie Banks 45.00
YK Carl Yastrzemski, Chuck Klein 50.00
WY Dave Winfield, Carl Yastrzemski 25.00
WYO Dave Winfield, Robin Yount 20.00
SM Duke Snider, Willie Mays 85.00
RJ Frank Robinson, Reggie Jackson
BMA George Brett, Don Mattingly 90.00
GH Steve Garvey, Gil Hodges 20.00
AR Hank Aaron, Babe Ruth
GA Hank Greenberg, Richie Ashburn 75.00
PJ Jim Palmer, Tommy John 20.00
NS Phil Niekro, Tom Seaver 15.00
SR Willie Stargell, Jim Rice 15.00
BF Johnny Bench, Carlton Fisk
RS Nolan Ryan, Tom Seaver 160.00
JS Fergie Jenkins, Tom Seaver 25.00
YP Robin Yount, Kirby Puckett
SB Tris Speaker, George Brett 140.00
BM Vida Blue, Dennis Martinez 10.00
BB Wade Boggs, George Brett 45.00
MA Willie Mays, Hank Aaron
BS Bert Blyleven, DonSutton 15.00

2002 Topps Tribute Memorable Materials

MT
Common Player: 10.00
Season parallel: 1.5-3X
#'d to last two digits yr event occurred
Jsy Number para.#'d 40-75: 1.5-3X
Under 40 not priced
Numbered to jersey #

HA Hank Aaron 40.00
GB George Brett 35.00
RC Roy Campanella 25.00
JC Joe Carter 10.00
CF Carlton Fisk 15.00
LG Lou Gehrig
KG Kirk Gibson 15.00
BJ Bo Jackson 25.00
RJ Reggie Jackson 15.00
CK Chuck Klein 25.00
RM Roger Maris 75.00
DM Don Mattingly 40.00
BM Bill Mazeroski 15.00
JM Joe Morgan 15.00
TM Thurman Munson 60.00
KP Kirby Puckett 25.00
PR Phil Rizzuto 40.00
JR Jackie Robinson 50.00
NR Nolan Ryan 75.00
BT Bobby Thomson 15.00
HW Hack Wilson 40.00
CY Carl Yastrzemski 30.00

2002 Topps Tribute Milestone Materials

MT
Common Player: 10.00
Inserted 1:4
Season parallel #'d 51-95: 1.5-3X
#'d to last two digits milestone season
Jersey Number par.#'d 51-95: 1.5-3X
Numbered to Jersey Number
Under 50 not priced yet

LA Luis Aparicio 15.00
EB Ernie Banks 25.00
JB Johnny Bench 20.00
YB Yogi Berra 25.00
WB Wade Boggs 15.00
JBO Jim Bottomley 20.00
OC Orlando Cepeda 15.00
TC Ty Cobb 180.00
EC Eddie Collins 25.00
SC Sam Crawford 25.00
JC Joe Cronin 20.00
AD Andre Dawson 15.00
BD Bill Dickey 15.00
BF Bob Feller 15.00
WF Whitey Ford 25.00
NF Nellie Fox 30.00
FF Frankie Frisch 25.00
LG Lou Gehrig 150.00
BG Bob Gibson 15.00
HG Hank Greenberg
HH Harry Heilmann 20.00
BH Billy Herman 10.00
RH Rogers Hornsby 50.00
CH Jim "Catfish" Hunter 12.00
JJ Joe Jackson
RJ Reggie Jackson 20.00
NL Napoleon Lajoie 60.00
FL Fred Lindstrom 15.00
HM Heinie Manush 20.00
JMA Juan Marichal 15.00
EM Eddie Mathews 15.00
WH Willie Mays 40.00
JM Johnny Mize 15.00
DM Dale Murphy 15.00
MO Mel Ott 30.00
JP Jim Palmer 15.00
SR Sam Rice 20.00
BRO Brooks Robinson 20.00
FR Frank Robinson 15.00
ER Edd Roush 25.00
BR Babe Ruth 160.00
NR Nolan Ryan 50.00
RS Ryne Sandberg 25.00
TS Tom Seaver 15.00
DS Duke Snider 20.00
TSP Tris Speaker 65.00
WS Willie Stargell 15.00
MV Mickey Vernon 12.00
HW Honus Wagner 120.00
PW Paul Waner 25.00
ZW Zach Wheat 25.00
RY Robin Yount 15.00

2002 Topps Tribute Pasttime Patches

MT
Inserted 1:92

JB Johnny Bench 130.00
WB Wade Boggs 70.00
GB George Brett 240.00
BD Bill Dickey
JM Juan Marichal
EM Eddie Mathews 125.00
DM Don Mattingly 160.00
JP Jim Palmer 75.00
KP Kirby Puckett 170.00
NRA Nolan Ryan 250.00
NRR Nolan Ryan 250.00
DW Dave Winfield 85.00
CY Carl Yastrzemski 180.00
RY Robin Yount 90.00

2002 Topps Tribute "The Catch" Dual

MT
Inserted 1:1,023

MW Willie Mays, Vic Wertz 175.00
MW Willie Mays, Vic Wertz/54 250.00

2003 Topps

MT
Complete Set (367): 35.00
Common Player: .10
Pack (10): 1.75
Box (36): 55.00

1 Alex Rodriguez 1.50
2 Dan Wilson .10
3 Jimmy Rollins .10
4 Jermaine Dye .10
5 Steve Karsay .10
6 Timoniel Perez .10
7 Not Issued .10
8 Jose Vidro .10
9 Eddie Guardado .10
10 Mark Prior .25
11 Curt Schilling .40
12 Dennis Cook .10
13 Andruw Jones .40
14 David Segui .10
15 Trot Nixon .10
16 Antonio Alfonseca .10
17 Magglio Ordonez .20
18 Jason LaRue .10
19 Danys Baez .10
20 Todd Helton .25
21 Denny Neagle .10
22 Dave Mlicki .10
23 Roberto Hernandez .10
24 Odalis Perez .10
25 Nick Neugebauer .10
26 David Ortiz .10
27 Andres Galarraga .15
28 Edgardo Alfonzo .10
29 Chad Bradford .10
30 Jason Giambi 1.00
31 Brian Giles .25
32 Deivi Cruz .10
33 Robb Nen .10
34 Jeff Nelson .10
35 Edgar Renteria .10
36 Aubrey Huff .10
37 Brandon Duckworth .10
38 Juan Gonzalez .40
39 Sidney Ponson .10
40 Eric Hinske .10
41 Kevin Appier .10
42 Danny Bautista .10
43 Javier Lopez .10
44 Jeff Conine .10
45 Carlos Baerga .10
46 Ugueth Urbina .10
47 Mark Buehrle .10
48 Aaron Boone .10
49 Chuck Finley .10
50 Sammy Sosa 1.00
51 Jose Jimenez .10
52 Chris Truby .10
53 Luis Castillo .10
54 Orlando Merced .10
55 Brian Jordan .10
56 Eric Young .10
57 Bobby Kielty .10
58 Luis Rivas .10
59 Brad Wilkerson .10
60 Roberto Alomar .40
61 Roger Clemens 1.00
62 Scott Hatteberg .10
63 Andy Ashby .10
64 Mike Williams .10
65 Ron Gant .10
66 Benito Santiago .10
67 Bret Boone .10
68 Matt Morris .10
69 Troy Glaus .50
70 Austin Kearns .25
71 Jim Thome .40
72 Rickey Henderson .40
73 Luis Gonzalez .25
74 Brad Fullmer .10
75 Benny Agbayani .10
76 Randy Wolf .10
77 Miguel Tejada .25
78 Jimmy Anderson .10
79 Ramon Martinez .10
80 Ivan Rodriguez .40
81 John Flaherty .10
82 Shannon Stewart .10
83 Orlando Palmeiro .10
84 Rafael Furcal .10
85 Kenny Rogers .10
86 Bud Smith .10
87 Mo Vaughn .15
88 Jose Cruz Jr. .10
89 Mike Matheny .10
90 Alfonso Soriano 1.25
91 Orlando Cabrera .10
92 Jeffrey Hammonds .10
93 Hideo Nomo .25
94 Carlos Febles .10
95 Billy Wagner .10
96 Alex Gonzalez .10
97 Todd Zeile .10
98 Omar Vizquel .20
99 Jose Rijo .10
100 Ichiro Suzuki 1.50
101 Steve Cox .10
102 Hideki Irabu .10
103 Roy Halladay .10
104 David Eckstein .10
105 Greg Maddux 1.00
106 Chris Richard .10
107 Travis Driskill .10
108 Fred McGriff .15
109 Frank Thomas .50
110 Shawn Green .25
111 Ruben Quevedo .10
112 Jacque Jones .10
113 Tomokazu Ohka .10
114 Joe McEwing .10
115 Ramiro Mendoza .10
116 Mark Mulder .20
117 Mike Lieberthal .10
118 Jack Wilson .10
119 Randall Simon .10
120 Bernie Williams .40
121 Marvin Benard .10
122 Jamie Moyer .10
123 Andy Benes .10
124 Tino Martinez .10
125 Esteban Yan .10
126 Gabe Kapler .10
127 Jason Isringhausen .10
128 Chris Carpenter .10
129 Mike Cameron .10
130 Gary Sheffield .20
131 Geronimo Gil .10
132 Brian Daubach .10
133 Corey Patterson .10
134 Aaron Rowand .10
135 Chris Reitsma .10
136 Bob Wickman .10
137 Paul Shuey .10
138 Jason Jennings .10
139 Brandon Inge .10
140 Larry Walker .20
141 Ramon Santiago .10
142 Hansel Izquierdo .10
143 Jose Vizcaino .10
144 Mark Quinn .10
145 Michael Tucker .10
146 Darren Dreifort .10
147 Mark Loretta .10
148 Corey Koskie .10
149 Tony Armas Jr. .10
150 Kazuhisa Ishii .10
151 Al Leiter .10
152 Steve Trachsel .10
153 Mike Stanton .10
154 David Justice .15
155 Marlon Anderson .10
156 Jason Kendall .10
157 Brian Lawrence .10
158 J.T. Snow Jr. .10
159 Edgar Martinez .10
160 Pat Burrell .25
161 Kerry Robinson .10
162 Greg Vaughn .10
163 Carl Everett .10
164 Vernon Wells .10
165 Jose Mesa .10
166 Troy Percival .10
167 Erubiel Durazo .10
168 Jason Marquis .10
169 Jerry Hairston Jr. .10
170 Vladimir Guerrero .60
171 Byung-Hyun Kim .10
172 Marcus Giles .10
173 Johnny Damon .10
174 Jon Lieber .10
175 Ray Durham .10
176 Sean Casey .10
177 Adam Dunn .40
178 Juan Pierre .10
179 Damion Easley .10
180 Barry Zito .25
181 Abraham Nunez .10
182 Pokey Reese .10
183 Jeff Kent .20
184 Russ Ortiz .10
185 Ruben Sierra .10
186 Brent Abernathy .10
187 Ismael Valdes .10
188 Darrin Fletcher .10
189 Craig Counsell .10
190 Boomer Wells .10
191 Ramon Hernandez .10
192 Adam Kennedy .10
193 Tony Womack .10
194 Wes Helms .10
195 Tony Batista .10
196 Rolando Arrojo .10
197 Matt Clement .10
198 Sandy Alomar .10
199 Scott Sullivan .10
200 Albert Pujols .60
201 Kirk Rueter .10
202 Phil Nevin .10
203 Kip Wells .10
204 Ron Coomer .10
205 Jeromy Burnitz .10
206 Kyle Lohse .10
207 Paul Bako .10
208 Paul LoDuca .10
209 Carlos Beltran .10
210 Roy Oswalt .25
211 Mike Lowell .10
212 Robert Fick .10
213 Todd Jones .10
214 C.C. Sabathia .10
215 Danny Graves .10
216 Todd Hundley .10
217 Tim Wakefield .10

218 Dustin Hermanson .10
219 Kevin Millwood .10
220 Jorge Posada .25
221 Bobby Jones .10
222 Carlos Guillen .10
223 Fernando Vina .10
224 Ryan Rupe .10
225 Kelvim Escobar .10
226 Ramon Ortiz .10
227 Junior Spivey .10
228 Juan Cruz .10
229 Melvin Mora .10
230 Lance Berkman .40
231 Brent Butler .10
232 Matt Anderson .10
233 Derrek Lee .10
234 Matt Lawton .10
235 Chuck Knoblauch .10
236 Eric Gagne .10
237 Alex Sanchez .10
238 Denny Hocking .10
239 Rick Reed .10
240 Rey Ordonez .10
241 Orlando Hernandez .10
242 Robert Person .10
243 Sean Burroughs .10
244 Jeff Cirillo .10
245 Mike Lamb .10
246 Jose Valentin .10
247 Ellis Burks .10
248 Shawn Chacon .10
249 Josh Beckett .10
250 Nomar Garciaparra 1.25
251 Craig Biggio .20
252 Joe Randa .10
253 Mark Grudzielanek .10
254 Glendon Rusch .10
255 Michael Barrett .10
256 Tyler Houston .10
257 Ryan Dempster .10
258 Wade Miller .10
259 Adrian Beltre .20
260 Vicente Padilla .10
261 Kazuhiro Sasaki .10
262 Mike Scioscia .10
263 Bobby Cox .10
264 Mike Hargrove .10
265 Grady Little .10
266 Bruce Kimm .10
267 Jerry Manuel .10
268 Bob Boone .10
269 Joel Skinner .10
270 Clint Hurdle .10
271 Luis Pujols .10
272 Bob Brenly .10
273 Jeff Torborg .10
274 Jimy Williams .10
275 Tony Pena .10
276 Jim Tracy .10
277 Jerry Royster .10
278 Ron Gardenhire .10
279 Frank Robinson .10
280 Bobby Valentine .10
281 Joe Torre .10
282 Art Howe .10
283 Larry Bowa .10
284 Lloyd McClendon .10
285 Bruce Bochy .10
286 Dusty Baker .10
287 Lou Pinella .10
288 Tony LaRussa .10
289 Hal McRae .10
290 Jerry Narron .10
291 Carlos Tosca .10
292 Chris Duncan .10
293 *Franklin Gutierrez* .10
294 Adam LaRoche .10
295 *Manuel Ramirez* .10
296 *Il Kim* .10
297 *Wayne Lydon* .10
298 Daryl Clark .10
299 Sean Pierce .10
300 Andy Marte .10
301 *Matt Peterson* .25
302 Gonzalo Lopez .10
303 Bernie Castro .10
304 Cliff Lee .10
305 Jason Perry .10
306 Jaime Bubela .10
307 Alexis Rios .10
308 Brendan Harris .10
309 Ramon Martinez .10
310 Terry Tiffee .10
311 Kevin Youkilis .10
312 Ruddy Lugo .10
313 C.J. Wilson .10
314 Mike McNutt .10
315 Jeff Clark .10
316 Mark Malaska .10
317 Doug Waechter .10
318 Derell McCall .10
319 Scott Tyler .10
320 Craig Brazell .10
321 Walter Young .10
322 Marlon Byrd, Jorge Padilla .10
323 Chris Snelling, Shin-Soo Choo .10
324 Hank Blalock, Mark Teixeira .10
325 Josh Hamilton, Carl Crawford .10
326 Orlando Hudson, Josh Phelps .10
327 Jack Cust, Rene Reyes .10
328 Angel Berroa, Alexis Gomez .10
329 Michael Cuddyer, Michael Restovich .10
330 Juan Rivera, Marcus Thames .10
331 Brandon Puffer, Jung Bong .10
332 Mike Cameron .10
333 Shawn Green .25
334 Team Shot .10
335 Jason Giambi .50
336 Derek Lowe .10
337 Manny Ramirez, Mike Sweeney, Bernie Williams .25
338 Alfonso Soriano, Alex Rodriguez, Derek Jeter .50
339 Alex Rodriguez, Jim Thome, Rafael Palmeiro .40
340 Magglio Ordonez, Alex Rodriguez, Miguel Tejada .40
341 Pedro Martinez, Derek Lowe, Barry Zito .25
342 Pedro Martinez, Roger Clemens, Mike Mussina .25
343 Larry Walker, Vladimir Guerrero, Todd Helton .25
344 Sammy Sosa, Albert Pujols, Shawn Green .40
345 Sammy Sosa, Lance Berkman, Shawn Green .40
346 Lance Berkman, Albert Pujols, Pat Burrell .25
347 Randy Johnson, Greg Maddux, Tom Glavine .25
348 Randy Johnson, Curt Schilling, Kerry Wood .25
349 AL Divison Series .20
350 AL & NL Divison Series .20
351 AL & NL Divison Series .20
352 NL Divison Series .20
353 AL Championship Series .20
354 Postseason Highlight .20
355 NL Championship Series .10
356 Jason Giambi .50
357 Alfonso Soriano .50
358 Alex Rodriguez .75
359 Eric Chavez .10
360 Torii Hunter .10
361 Bernie Williams .20
362 Garret Anderson .10
363 Jorge Posada .20
364 Derek Lowe .10
365 Barry Zito .20
366 Manny Ramirez .25
367 Mike Scioscia .10

2003 Topps Autographs

MT

Common Autograph:
HB Hank Blalock
MB Mark Buehrle
EC Eric Chavez
DE Darin Erstad
OH Orlando Hudson
AJ Andruw Jones
AK Austin Kearns 25.00
JL Jason Lane
PL Paul LoDuca
JDM J.D. Martin 15.00
JM Joe Mauer 30.00
EM Eric Milton
NN Nick Neugebauer
MP Mark Prior
SR Scott Rolen
BS Ben Sheets
AS Alfonso Soriano
MTE Mark Teixeira
MT Miguel Tejada
MTH Marcus Thames

2003 Topps Blue Backs

MT

Complete Set (40): 75.00
Common Player: .75
Inserted 1:12
BB1 Albert Pujols 3.00
BB2 Barry Bonds 6.00
BB3 Ichiro Suzuki 5.00
BB4 Sammy Sosa 4.00
BB5 Kazuhisa Ishii 1.00
BB6 Alex Rodriguez 6.00
BB7 Derek Jeter 8.00
BB8 Vladimir Guerrero 2.50
BB9 Ken Griffey Jr. 4.00
BB10Jason Giambi 4.00
BB11Todd Helton 1.00
BB12Mike Piazza 5.00
BB13Nomar Garciaparra 5.00
BB14Chipper Jones 4.00
BB15Ivan Rodriguez 1.25
BB16Luis Gonzalez .75
BB17Pat Burrell 1.00
BB18Mark Prior 1.50
BB19Adam Dunn 2.00
BB20Jeff Bagwell 2.00
BB21Austin Kearns 1.00
BB22Alfonso Soriano 5.00
BB23Jim Thome 2.00
BB24Bernie Williams 1.50
BB25Pedro J. Martinez 2.50
BB26Lance Berkman 1.00
BB27Randy Johnson 2.50
BB28Rafael Palmeiro 1.00
BB29Richie Sexson .75
BB30Troy Glaus 1.50
BB31Shawn Green .75
BB32Larry Walker .75
BB33Eric Hinske .75
BB34Andruw Jones 1.50
BB35Carlos Delgado 1.00
BB36Curt Schilling 1.50
BB37Greg Maddux 4.00
BB38Jimmy Rollins .75
BB39Eric Chavez 1.00
BB40Scott Rolen 1.00

2003 Topps Flashback

MT

Complete Set (14): 50.00
Common Player: 2.00
HTA exclusive
GB George Brett 6.00
LD Lenny Dykstra 3.00
HK Harmon Killebrew 6.00
BM Bill Madlock 2.00
EM Eddie Mathews 4.00
DM Dale Murphy 5.00
JP Jim Palmer 3.00
MP Mike Piazza 6.00
RR Robin Roberts 3.00
AR Al Rosen 4.00
NR Nolan Ryan 10.00
TS Tom Seaver 5.00
WS Warren Spahn 4.00
CY Carl Yastrzemski 6.00

2003 Topps Hobby Masters

MT

Complete Set (20): 40.00
Common Player: 1.00
Inserted 1:18
HM1 Ichiro Suzuki 4.00
HM2 Kazuhisa Ishii 1.00
HM3 Derek Jeter 6.00
HM4 Barry Bonds 5.00
HM5 Sammy Sosa 3.00
HM6 Alex Rodriguez 5.00
HM7 Mike Piazza 4.00
HM8 Chipper Jones 3.00
HM9 Vladimir Guerrero 2.00
HM10Nomar Garciaparra 4.00
HM11Todd Helton 1.00
HM12Jason Giambi 3.00
HM13Ken Griffey Jr. 3.00
HM14Albert Pujols 2.00
HM15Ivan Rodriguez 1.00
HM16Mark Prior 1.00
HM17Adam Dunn 1.50
HM18Randy Johnson 2.00
HM19Pedro J. Martinez 2.00
HM20Alfonso Soriano 4.00

2003 Topps Own The Game

MT

Complete Set (30): 30.00
Common Player: .50
Inserted 1:12
OG1 Ichiro Suzuki 3.00
OG2 Barry Bonds 4.00
OG3 Todd Helton .75
OG4 Larry Walker .75
OG5 Mike Sweeney .50
OG6 Sammy Sosa 2.50
OG7 Lance Berkman .75
OG8 Alex Rodriguez 4.00
OG9 Jim Thome 1.25
OG10Shawn Green .75
OG11Troy Glaus 1.00

OG12 Richie Sexson .50
OG13 Paul Konerko .50
OG14 Jason Giambi 2.50
OG15 Chipper Jones 2.50
OG16 Torii Hunter .50
OG17 Albert Pujols 1.50
OG18 Jose Vidro .50
OG19 Alfonso Soriano 3.00
OG20 Luis Castillo .50
OG21 Mike Lowell .50
OG22 Garrett Anderson .50
OG23 Jimmy Rollins .50
OG24 Curt Schilling 1.00
OG25 Kazuhisa Ishii .50
OG26 Randy Johnson 1.50
OG27 Tom Glavine .75
OG28 Roger Clemens 2.50
OG29 Pedro J. Martinez 1.50
OG30 Derek Lowe .50

2003 Topps Prime Cuts Pine Tar Series

MT

Pine Tar Series
Production 200 sets
Trademark Series: 1-1.5X
Production 100 sets
Prime Cuts Series: 1.5-2X
Production 50 sets
RA Roberto Alomar
LB Lance Berkman
EC Eric Chavez
AD Adam Dunn
DE Darin Erstad
NG Nomar Garciaparra 65.00
JG Juan Gonzalez 15.00
TH Todd Helton 25.00
AJ Andruw Jones
CJ Chipper Jones
RP Rafael Palmeiro 20.00
MP Mike Piazza
AP Albert Pujols
AR Alex Rodriguez
IR Ivan Rodriguez 15.00
SR Scott Rolen
AS Alfonso Soriano 55.00
MT Miguel Tejada
FT Frank Thomas
MV Mo Vaughn
BW Bernie Williams

2003 Topps Prime Cuts Autograph

MT

Complete Set (8):
Common Player:
PCA-EC Eric Chavez
PCA-DE Darin Erstad
PCA-AJ Andruw Jones
PCA-CJ Chipper Jones
PCA-RP Rafael Palmeiro
PCA-SR Scott Rolen
PCA-AS Alfonso Soriano
PCA-MT Miguel Tejada

2003 Topps Record Breakers

MT

Complete Set (50): 40.00
Common Player: .50
Inserted 1:6
JB Jeff Bagwell 1.50
LBE Lance Berkman 1.00
BB Barry Bonds 5.00
GB George Brett 2.50
LB Lou Brock .50
RCA Rod Carew .50
LC Luis Castillo .50
RC Roger Clemens 2.50
CD Carlos Delgado .50
CF Cliff Floyd .50
GF George Foster .50
AG Andres Galarraga .50
JG Jason Giambi 2.50
BG Bob Gibson 1.00
TG Troy Glaus 1.00
JGO Juan Gonzalez 1.00
LGO Luis Gonzalez .50
SG Shawn Green .75
HG Hank Greenberg .50
KG Ken Griffey Jr. 3.00
VG Vladimir Guerrero 1.50
RG Ron Guidry .50
TH Todd Helton 1.00
RH Rickey Henderson .75
FJ Fergie Jenkins .50
RJ Randy Johnson 1.50
CJ Chipper Jones 3.00
HK Harmon Killebrew 1.00
CK Chuck Klein .50
JM Juan Marichal .50
PM Pedro J. Martinez 1.50
EM Eddie Mathews 1.00
DM Don Mattingly 4.00
FM Fred McGriff .50
JO John Olerud .50
RP Rafael Palmeiro 1.00
MP Mike Piazza 4.00
FR Frank Robinson 1.00
AR Alex Rodriguez 4.00
NR Nolan Ryan 6.00
MSC Mike Schmidt 3.00
CS Curt Schilling 1.00
TS Tom Seaver 1.00
RS Richie Sexson .50
GS Gary Sheffield .50
SS Sammy Sosa 3.00
MS Mike Sweeney .50
HW Hack Wilson .50
PW Preston Wilson .50
RY Robin Yount 1.00

2003 Topps Record Breakers Autographs

MT

Common Autograph:
CF Cliff Floyd
LG Luis Gonzalez
FJ Fergie Jenkins 25.00
CJ Chipper Jones
HK Harmon Killebrew
RP Rafael Palmeiro
MS Mike Schmidt
RS Richie Sexson
MSW Mike Sweeney
RY Robin Yount

2003 Topps Record Breakers Relics

MT

Common Player: 6.00
JB Jeff Bagwell/jsy 8.00
LB Lance Berkman/bat 12.00
GB George Brett/bat 25.00
LC Luis Castillo/bat 6.00
CD Carlos Delgado/jsy 8.00
LGO Luis Gonzalez/jsy 6.00
SG Shawn Green/jsy 8.00
HG Hank Greenberg/bat 30.00
TH Todd Helton/jsy 6.00
RH Rickey Henderson/bat 15.00
CJ Chipper Jones/jsy 12.00
PM Pedro Martinez/jsy 10.00
DM Don Mattingly/bat 35.00
MP Mike Piazza/bat 15.00
FR Frank Robinson/bat 12.00
AR Alex Rodriguez/jsy 15.00
NR Nolan Ryan/jsy 35.00
MS Mike Sweeney/bat 8.00
HW Hack Wilson/bat 50.00
RY Robin Yount/jsy 15.00

2003 Topps Turn Back The Clock Autographs

MT

Common Player:
LD Lenny Dykstra 15.00
HK Harmon Killebrew
BM Bill Madlock 10.00
DM Dale Murphy 40.00
JP Jim Palmer 25.00

1992 Triple Play

This set was released only in wax pack form. Cards feature red borders. Boyhood photos, mascots and ballparks are among the featured cards. This set was designed to give collectors an alternative product to the high-end card sets. The cards are standard size.

MT

Complete Set (264): 8.00
Common Player: .05
Wax Box (36): 9.00
1 SkyDome .05
2 Tom Foley .05
3 Scott Erickson .05
4 Matt Williams .15
5 Dave Valle .05
6 Andy Van Slyke (Little Hotshot) .05
7 Tom Glavine .10
8 Kevin Appier .05
9 Pedro Guerrero .05
10 Terry Steinbach .05
11 Terry Mulholland .05
12 Mike Boddicker .05
13 Gregg Olson .05
14 Tim Burke .05
15 Candy Maldonado .05
16 Orlando Merced .05
17 Robin Ventura .05
18 Eric Anthony .05
19 Greg Maddux .50
20 Erik Hanson .05
21 Bob Ojeda .05
22 Nolan Ryan 1.00
23 Dave Righetti .05
24 Reggie Jefferson .05
25 Jody Reed .05
26 Awesome Action (Steve Finley, Gary Carter) .05
27 Chili Davis .05
28 Hector Villanueva .05
29 Cecil Fielder .05
30 Hal Morris .05
31 Barry Larkin .10
32 Bobby Thigpen .05
33 Andy Benes .05
34 Harold Baines .05
35 David Cone .05
36 Mark Langston .05
37 Bryan Harvey .05
38 John Kruk .05
39 Scott Sanderson .05
40 Lonnie Smith .05
41 Awesome Action (Rex Hudler) .05
42 George Bell .05
43 Steve Finley .05
44 Mickey Tettleton .05
45 Robby Thompson .05
46 Pat Kelly .05
47 Marquis Grissom .05
48 Tony Pena .05
49 Alex Cole .05
50 Steve Buechele .05
51 Ivan Rodriguez .35
52 John Smiley .05
53 Gary Sheffield .20
54 Greg Olson .05
55 Ramon Martinez .05
56 B.J. Surhoff .05
57 Bruce Hurst .05
58 Todd Stottlemyre .05
59 Brett Butler .05
60 Glenn Davis .05
61 Awesome Action (Glenn Braggs, Kirt Manwaring) .05
62 Lee Smith .05
63 Rickey Henderson .35
64 Fun at the Ballpark (David Cone, Jeff Innis, John Franco) .05
65 Rick Aguilera .05
66 Kevin Elster .05
67 Dwight Evans .05
68 Andujar Cedeno .05
69 Brian McRae .05
70 Benito Santiago .05
71 Randy Johnson .35
72 Roberto Kelly .05
73 Awesome Action (Juan Samuel) .05
74 Alex Fernandez .05
75 Felix Jose .05
76 Brian Harper .05
77 Scott Sanderson (Little Hotshot) .05
78 Ken Caminiti .05
79 Mo Vaughn .20
80 Roger McDowell .05
81 Robin Yount .30
82 Dave Magadan .05
83 Julio Franco .05
84 Roberto Alomar .35
85 Steve Avery .05
86 Travis Fryman .05
87 Fred McGriff .05
88 Dave Stewart .05
89 Larry Walker .20
90 Chris Sabo .05
91 Chuck Finley .05
92 Dennis Martinez .05
93 Jeff Johnson .05
94 Len Dykstra .05
95 Mark Whiten .05
96 Wade Taylor .05
97 Lance Dickson .05
98 Kevin Tapani .05
99 Awesome Action (Luis Polonia, Tony Phillips) .05
100 Milt Cuyler .05
101 Willie McGee .05
102 Awesome Action (Tony Fernandez, Ryne Sandberg) .05
103 Albert Belle .15
104 Todd Hundley .05
105 Ben McDonald .05
106 Doug Drabek .05
107 Tim Raines .05
108 Joe Carter .05
109 Reggie Sanders .05
110 John Olerud .05
111 Darren Lewis .05
112 Juan Gonzalez .40
113 Awesome Action (Andre Dawson) .05
114 Mark Grace .20
115 George Brett .50
116 Barry Bonds .60
117 Lou Whitaker .05

118 Jose Oquendo .05
119 Lee Stevens .05
120 Phil Plantier .05
121 Awesome Action (Devon White, Matt Merullo) .05
122 Greg Vaughn .05
123 Royce Clayton .05
124 Bob Welch .05
125 Juan Samuel .05
126 Ron Gant .05
127 Edgar Martinez .05
128 Andy Ashby .05
129 Jack McDowell .05
130 Awesome Action (Dave Henderson, Jerry Browne) .05
131 Leo Gomez .05
132 Checklist 1-88 .05
133 Phillie Phanatic .05
134 Bret Barbarie .05
135 Kent Hrbek .05
136 Hall of Fame .05
137 Omar Vizquel .05
138 The Famous Chicken .05
139 Terry Pendleton .05
140 Jim Eisenreich .05
141 Todd Zeile .05
142 Todd Van Poppel .05
143 Darren Daulton .05
144 Mike Macfarlane .05
145 Luis Mercedes .05
146 Trevor Wilson .05
147 Dave Steib .05
148 Andy Van Slyke .05
149 Carlton Fisk .30
150 Craig Biggio .10
151 Joe Girardi .05
152 Ken Griffey, Jr. .75
153 Jose Offerman .05
154 Bobby Witt .05
155 Will Clark .15
156 Steve Olin .05
157 Greg Harris .05
158 Dale Murphy (Little Hotshot) .05
159 Don Mattingly .60
160 Shawon Dunston .05
161 Bill Gullickson .05
162 Paul O'Neill .05
163 Norm Charlton .05
164 Bo Jackson .10
165 Tony Fernandez .05
166 Dave Henderson .05
167 Dwight Gooden .05
168 Junior Felix .05
169 Lance Parrish .05
170 Pat Combs .05
171 Chuck Knoblauch .05
172 John Smoltz .10
173 Wrigley Field .05
174 Andre Dawson .15
175 Pete Harnisch .05
176 Alan Trammell .05
177 Kirk Dressendorfer .05
178 Matt Nokes .05
179 Wil Cordero .05
180 Scott Cooper .05
181 Glenallen Hill .05
182 John Franco .05
183 Rafael Palmeiro .10
184 Jay Bell .05
185 Bill Wegman .05
186 Deion Sanders .10
187 Darryl Strawberry .05
188 Jaime Navarro .05
189 Darren Jackson .05
190 Eddie Zosky .05
191 Mike Scioscia .05
192 Chito Martinez .05
193 Awesome Action (Pat Kelly, Ron Tingley) .05
194 Ray Lankford .05
195 Dennis Eckersley .05
196 Awesome Action (Ivan Calderon, Mike Maddux) .05
197 Shane Mack .05
198 Checklist 89-176 .05
199 Cal Ripken, Jr. 1.00
200 Jeff Bagwell .40
201 David Howard .05
202 Kirby Puckett .50
203 Harold Reynolds .05
204 Jim Abbott .05
205 Mark Lewis .05
206 Frank Thomas .60
207 Rex Hudler .05
208 Vince Coleman .05
209 Delino DeShields .05
210 Luis Gonzalez .20
211 Wade Boggs .40
212 Orel Hershiser .05
213 Cal Eldred .05
214 Jose Canseco .30
215 Jose Guzman .05
216 Roger Clemens .50
217 Dave Justice .20
218 Tony Phillips .05
219 Tony Gwynn .50
220 Mitch Williams .05
221 Bill Sampen .05
222 Billy Hatcher .05
223 Gary Gaetti .05
224 Tim Wallach .05
225 Kevin Maas .05
226 Kevin Brown .10
227 Sandy Alomar .10
228 John Habyan .05
229 Ryne Sandberg .40
230 Greg Gagne .05
231 Autographs (Mark McGwire) .50
232 Mike LaValliere .05
233 Mark Gubicza .05
234 Lance Parrish (Little Hotshot) .05
235 Carlos Baerga .05
236 Howard Johnson .05
237 Mike Mussina .35
238 Ruben Sierra .05
239 Lance Johnson .05
240 Devon White .05
241 Dan Wilson .05
242 Kelly Gruber .05
243 Brett Butler (Little Hotshot) .05
244 Ozzie Smith .50
245 Chuck McElroy .05
246 Shawn Boskie .05
247 Mark Davis .05
248 Bill Landrum .05
249 Frank Tanana .05
250 Darryl Hamilton .05
251 Gary DiSarcina .05
252 Mike Greenwell .05
253 Cal Ripken, Jr. (Little Hotshot) .25
254 Paul Molitor .30
255 Tim Teufel .05
256 Chris Hoiles .05
257 Rob Dibble .05
258 Sid Bream .05
259 Chito Martinez .05
260 Dale Murphy .15
261 Greg Hibbard .05
262 Mark McGwire 1.00
263 Oriole Park .05
264 Checklist 177-264 .05

1992 Triple Play Gallery of Stars

Two levels of scarcity are represented in this insert issue. Cards #1-6 (all cards have a GS prefix to the card number) feature in their new uniforms players who changed teams for 1993. Those inserts were found in the standard Triple Play foil packs and are somewhat more common than cards #7-12, which were found only in jumbo packs and which feature a better selection of established stars and rookies. All of the inserts feature the artwork of Dick Perez, with player portraits set against a colorful background. Silver-foil accents highlight the front design. Backs are red with a white "tombstone" containing a career summary.

		MT
Complete Set (12):		4.00
Common Player:		.15
1	Bobby Bonilla	.15
2	Wally Joyner	.15
3	Jack Morris	.15
4	Steve Sax	.15
5	Danny Tartabull	.15
6	Frank Viola	.15
7	Jeff Bagwell	.60
8	Ken Griffey, Jr.	1.00
9	David Justice	.25
10	Ryan Klesko	.15
11	Cal Ripken, Jr.	1.50
12	Frank Thomas	.75

1993 Triple Play

For the second year, Leaf-Donruss used the "Triple Play" brand name for its base-level card set aimed at the younger collector. The 264-card set was available in several types of retail packaging and included a number of special subsets, such as childhood photos (labeled LH - Little Hotshots - in the checklist) and insert sets. Checklist card #264 incorrectly shows card #129, Joe Robbie Stadium, as #259. There is a second card, "Equipment," which also bears #129. An "Action Baseball" scratch-off game card was included in each foil pack.

		MT
Complete Set (264):		6.00
Common Player:		.05
Wax Box (24):		7.50
1	Ken Griffey, Jr.	.50
2	Roberto Alomar	.25
3	Cal Ripken, Jr.	.65
4	Eric Karros	.05
5	Cecil Fielder	.05
6	Gary Sheffield	.20
7	Darren Daulton	.05
8	Andy Van Slyke	.05
9	Dennis Eckersley	.05
10	Ryne Sandberg	.30
11	Mark Grace (Little Hotshots)	.05
12	Awesome Action #1 (Luis Polonia, David Segui)	.05
13	Mike Mussina	.25
14	Vince Coleman	.05
15	Rafael Belliard	.05
16	Ivan Rodriguez	.25
17	Eddie Taubensee	.05
18	Cal Eldred	.05
19	Rick Wilkins	.05
20	Edgar Martinez	.05
21	Brian McRae	.05
22	Darren Holmes	.05
23	Mark Whiten	.05
24	Todd Zeile	.05
25	Scott Cooper	.05
26	Frank Thomas	.40
27	Wil Cordero	.05
28	Juan Guzman	.05
29	Pedro Astacio	.05
30	Steve Avery	.05
31	Barry Larkin	.10
32	President Clinton	1.00
33	Scott Erickson	.05
34	Mike Devereaux	.05
35	Tino Martinez	.05
36	Brent Mayne	.05
37	Tim Salmon	.15
38	Dave Hollins	.05
39	Royce Clayton	.05
40	Shawon Dunston	.05
41	Eddie Murray	.20
42	Larry Walker	.15
43	Jeff Bagwell	.30
44	Milt Cuyler	.05
45	Mike Bordick	.05
46	Mike Greenwell	.05
47	Steve Sax	.05
48	Chuck Knoblauch	.05
49	Charles Nagy	.05
50	Tim Wakefield	.05
51	Tony Gwynn	.35
52	Rob Dibble	.05
53	Mickey Morandini	.05
54	Steve Hosey	.05
55	Mike Piazza	.45
56	Bill Wegman	.05
57	Kevin Maas	.05
58	Gary DiSarcina	.05
59	Travis Fryman	.05
60	Ruben Sierra	.05
61	Awesome Action #2 (Ken Caminiti)	.05
62	Brian Jordan	.05
63	Scott Chiamparino	.05
64	Awesome Action #3 (Mike Bordick, George Brett)	.05
65	Carlos Garcia	.05
66	Checklist 1-66	.05
67	John Smoltz	.10
68	Awesome Action #4 (Mark McGwire, Brian Harper)	.20
69	Kurt Stillwell	.05
70	Chad Curtis	.05
71	Rafael Palmeiro	.10
72	Kevin Young	.05
73	Glenn Davis	.05
74	Dennis Martinez	.05
75	Sam Militello	.05
76	Mike Morgan	.05
77	Frank Thomas (Little Hotshots)	.20
78	Staying Fit (Bip Roberts, Mike Devereaux)	.05
79	Steve Buechele	.05
80	Carlos Baerga	.05
81	Robby Thompson	.05
82	Kirk McCaskill	.05
83	Lee Smith	.05
84	Gary Scott	.05
85	Tony Pena	.05
86	Howard Johnson	.05
87	Mark McGwire	.65
88	Bip Roberts	.05
89	Devon White	.05
90	John Franco	.05
91	Tom Browning	.05
92	Mickey Tettleton	.05

93 Jeff Conine .05
94 Albert Belle .15
95 Fred McGriff .05
96 Nolan Ryan .65
97 Paul Molitor (Little Hotshots) .10
98 Juan Bell .05
99 Dave Fleming .05
100 Craig Biggio .10
101a Andy Stankiewicz (white name on front) .05
101b Andy Stankiewicz (red name on front) .25
102 Delino DeShields .05
103 Damion Easley .05
104 Kevin McReynolds .05
105 David Nied .05
106 Rick Sutcliffe .05
107 Will Clark .15
108 Tim Raines .05
109 Eric Anthony .05
110 Mike LaValliere .05
111 Dean Palmer .05
112 Eric Davis .05
113 Damon Berryhill .05
114 Felix Jose .05
115 Ozzie Guillen .05
116 Pat Listach .05
117 Tom Glavine .10
118 Roger Clemens .35
119 Dave Henderson .05
120 Don Mattingly .40
121 Orel Hershiser .05
122 Ozzie Smith .35
123 Joe Carter .05
124 Bret Saberhagen .05
125 Mitch Williams .05
126 Jerald Clark .05
127 Mile High Stadium .05
128 Kent Hrbek .05
129a Equipment (Curt Schilling, Mark Whiten) .05
129b Joe Robbie Stadium .05
130 Gregg Jefferies .05
131 John Orton .05
132 Checklist 67-132 .05
133 Bret Boone .10
134 Pat Borders .05
135 Gregg Olson .05
136 Brett Butler .05
137 Rob Deer .05
138 Darrin Jackson .05
139 John Kruk .05
140 Jay Bell .05
141 Bobby Witt .05
142 New Cubs (Dan Plesac, Randy Myers, Jose Guzman) .05
143 Wade Boggs (Little Hotshots) .10
144 Awesome Action #5 (Kenny Lofton) .05
145 Ben McDonald .05
146 Dwight Gooden .05
147 Terry Pendleton .05
148 Julio Franco .05
149 Ken Caminiti .05
150 Greg Vaughn .05
151 Sammy Sosa .40
152 David Valle .05
153 Wally Joyner .05
154 Dante Bichette .05
155 Mark Lewis .05
156 Bob Tewksbury .05
157 Billy Hatcher .05
158 Jack McDowell .05
159 Marquis Grissom .05
160 Jack Morris .05
161 Ramon Martinez .05
162 Deion Sanders .10
163 Tim Belcher .05
164 Mascots .05
165 Scott Leius .05
166 Brady Anderson .05
167 Randy Johnson .25
168 Mark Gubicza .05
169 Chuck Finley .05
170 Terry Mulholland .05
171 Matt Williams .15
172 Dwight Smith .05
173 Bobby Bonilla .05
174 Ken Hill .05
175 Doug Jones .05
176 Tony Phillips .05
177 Terry Steinbach .05
178 Frank Viola .05
179 Robin Ventura .05
180 Shane Mack .05
181 Kenny Lofton .05
182 Jeff King .05
183 Tim Teufel .05
184 Chris Sabo .05
185 Lenny Dykstra .05
186 Trevor Wilson .05
187 Darryl Strawberry .05
188 Robin Yount .25
189 Bob Wickman .05
190 Luis Polonia .05
191 Alan Trammell .05
192 Bob Welch .05
193 Awesome Action #6 .05
194 Tom Pagnozzi .05
195 Bret Barberie .05
196 Awesome Action #7 (Mike Scioscia) .05
197 Randy Tomlin .05
198 Checklist 133-198 .05
199 Ron Gant .05
200 Awesome Action #8 (Roberto Alomar) .05
201 Andy Benes .05
202 Pepper .05
203 Steve Finley .05
204 Steve Olin .05
205 Chris Hoiles .05
206 John Wetteland .05
207 Danny Tartabull .05
208 Bernard Gilkey .05
209 Tom Glavine (Little Hotshots) .05
210 Benito Santiago .05
211 Mark Grace .20
212 Glenallen Hill .05
213 Jeff Brantley .05
214 George Brett .35
215 Mark Lemke .05
216 Ron Karkovice .05
217 Tom Brunansky .05
218 Todd Hundley .05
219 Rickey Henderson .30
220 Joe Oliver .05
221 Juan Gonzalez .30
222 John Olerud .05
223 Hal Morris .05
224 Lou Whitaker .05
225 Bryan Harvey .05
226 Mike Gallego .05
227 Willie McGee .05
228 Jose Oquendo .05
229 Darren Daulton (Little Hotshots) .05
230 Curt Schilling .10
231 Jay Buhner .05
232 New Astros (Doug Drabek, Greg Swindell) .05
233 Jaime Navarro .05
234 Kevin Appier .05
235 Mark Langston .05
236 Jeff Montgomery .05
237 Joe Girardi .05
238 Ed Sprague .05
239 Dan Walters .05
240 Kevin Tapani .05
241 Pete Harnisch .05
242 Al Martin .05
243 Jose Canseco .25
244 Moises Alou .10
245 Mark McGwire (Little Hotshots) .25
246 Luis Rivera .05
247 George Bell .05
248 B.J. Surhoff .05
249 Dave Justice .20
250 Brian Harper .05
251 Sandy Alomar, Jr. .05
252 Kevin Brown .10
253 New Dodgers (Tim Wallach, Jody Reed, Todd Worrell) .05
254 Ray Lankford .05
255 Derek Bell .05
256 Joe Grahe .05
257 Charlie Hayes .05
258 New Yankees (Wade Boggs, Jim Abbott) .15
259 Joe Robbie Stadium .05
260 Kirby Puckett .35
261 Fun at the Ballpark (Jay Bell, Vince Coleman) .05
262 Bill Swift .05
263 Fun at the Ballpark (Roger McDowell) .05
264 Checklist 199-264 .05

1993 Triple Play Action Baseball

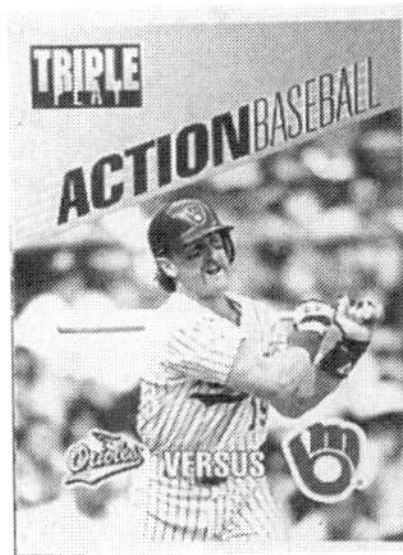

These game folders were inserted in each 1993 Triple Play foil pack. Because collation of the folders was very bad, few collectors bothered to save them. Measuring 2-1/2" x 5", fronts have an action photo of an unnamed player. Printed over the bottom of the photo are two full-color team logos, with a white "Versus" between. Inside the folder is a baseball diamond diagram, a three-inning scoreboard, rules for playing the game and 32 scratch-off squares for playing. Backs have a number designating the folder as "of 30."

		MT
Complete Set (30):		3.50
Common Player:		.10
1	Andy Van Slyke	.10
2	Bobby Bonilla	.10
3	Ozzie Smith	.30
4	Ryne Sandberg	.25
5	Darren Daulton	.10
6	Larry Walker	.15
7	Eric Karros	.10
8	Barry Larkin	.15
9	Deion Sanders	.15
10	Gary Sheffield	.20
11	Will Clark	.15
12	Jeff Bagwell	.25
13	Roberto Alomar	.25
14	Roger Clemens	.30
15	Cecil Fielder	.10
16	Robin Yount	.25
17	Cal Ripken, Jr.	.50
18	Carlos Baerga	.10
19	Don Mattingly	.35
20	Kirby Puckett	.30
21	Frank Thomas	.35
22	Juan Gonzalez	.25
23	Mark McGwire	.50
24	Ken Griffey, Jr.	.45
25	Wally Joyner	.10
26	Chad Curtis	.10
27	Batting glove	.10
28	Juan Guzman	.10
29	Dave Justice	.15
30	Joe Carter	.10

1993 Triple Play Gallery

The Gallery of Stars cards were found as random inserts in Triple Play jumbo packs. The cards feature Dick Perez painted representations of the players.

		MT
Complete Set (10):		5.00
Common Player:		.15
1	Barry Bonds	3.00
2	Andre Dawson	.25
3	Wade Boggs	.45
4	Greg Maddux	.60
5	Dave Winfield	.50
6	Paul Molitor	.45
7	Jim Abbott	.15
8	J.T. Snow	.15
9	Benito Santiago	.15
10	David Nied	.15

1993 Triple Play League Leaders

These "double-headed" cards feature one player on each side. The six cards were random inserts in Triple Play retail packs.

		MT
Complete Set (6):		7.00
Common Player:		.50
1	Barry Bonds, Dennis Eckersley	3.50
2	Greg Maddux, Dennis Eckersley	2.00
3	Eric Karros, Pat Listach	.50
4	Fred McGriff, Juan Gonzalez	1.50
5	Darren Daulton, Cecil Fielder	.50
6	Gary Sheffield, Edgar Martinez	.50

1993 Triple Play Nicknames

Popular nicknames of 10 of the game's top stars are featured in silver foil on this insert set found in Triple Play foil packs.

		MT
Complete Set (10):		18.00
Common Player:		1.00
1	Frank Thomas (Big Hurt)	2.00
2	Roger Clemens (Rocket)	1.50
3	Ryne Sandberg (Ryno)	1.25
4	Will Clark (Thrill)	1.00
5	Ken Griffey, Jr. (Junior)	4.00
6	Dwight Gooden (Doc)	1.00
7	Nolan Ryan (Express)	5.00
8	Deion Sanders (Prime Time)	1.00
9	Ozzie Smith (Wizard)	1.50
10	Fred McGriff (Crime Dog)	1.00

1994 Triple Play

Triple Play cards returned for a third year in 1994, this time with a borderless design. According to company officials, production was less than 1994 Donruss Series I baseball, which was roughly 17,500 20-box cases. In the regular-issue 300-card set, 10 players from each team were featured, along with a 17-card Rookie Review subset and several insert sets.

		MT
Complete Set (300):		7.50
Common Player:		.05
Wax Box (36):		9.00
1	Mike Bordick	.05
2	Dennis Eckersley	.05
3	Brent Gates	.05
4	Rickey Henderson	.35
5	Mark McGwire	.75
6	Troy Neel	.05
7	Craig Paquette	.05
8	Ruben Sierra	.05
9	Terry Steinbach	.05
10	Bobby Witt	.05
11	Chad Curtis	.05
12	Chili Davis	.05
13	Gary DiSarcina	.05
14	Damion Easley	.05
15	Chuck Finley	.05
16	Joe Grahe	.05
17	Mark Langston	.05
18	Eduardo Perez	.05
19	Tim Salmon	.15
20	J.T. Snow	.05
21	Jeff Bagwell	.40
22	Craig Biggio	.10
23	Ken Caminiti	.05
24	Andujar Cedeno	.05
25	Doug Drabek	.05
26	Steve Finley	.05
27	Luis Gonzalez	.20
28	Pete Harnisch	.05
29	Darryl Kile	.05
30	Mitch Williams	.05
31	Roberto Alomar	.30
32	Joe Carter	.05
33	Juan Guzman	.05
34	Pat Hentgen	.05
35	Paul Molitor	.35
36	John Olerud	.05
37	Ed Sprague	.05
38	Dave Stewart	.05
39	Duane Ward	.05
40	Devon White	.05
41	Steve Avery	.05
42	Jeff Blauser	.05
43	Ron Gant	.05
44	Tom Glavine	.10
45	Dave Justice	.20
46	Greg Maddux	.50
47	Fred McGriff	.05
48	Terry Pendleton	.05
49	Deion Sanders	.10
50	John Smoltz	.10
51	Ricky Bones	.05
52	Cal Eldred	.05
53	Darryl Hamilton	.05
54	John Jaha	.05
55	Pat Listach	.05
56	Jaime Navarro	.05
57	Dave Nilsson	.05
58	B.J. Surhoff	.05
59	Greg Vaughn	.05
60	Robin Yount	.25
61	Bernard Gilkey	.05
62	Gregg Jefferies	.05
63	Brian Jordan	.05
64	Ray Lankford	.05
65	Tom Pagnozzi	.05
66	Ozzie Smith	.50
67	Bob Tewksbury	.05
68	Allen Watson	.05
69	Mark Whiten	.05
70	Todd Zeile	.05
71	Steve Buechele	.05
72	Mark Grace	.20
73	Jose Guzman	.05
74	Derrick May	.05
75	Mike Morgan	.05
76	Randy Myers	.05
77	Ryne Sandberg	.40
78	Sammy Sosa	.55
79	Jose Vizcaino	.05
80	Rick Wilkins	.05
81	Pedro Astacio	.05
82	Brett Butler	.05
83	Delino DeShields	.05
84	Orel Hershiser	.05
85	Eric Karros	.05
86	Ramon Martinez	.05
87	Jose Offerman	.05
88	Mike Piazza	.60
89	Darryl Strawberry	.05
90	Tim Wallach	.05
91	Moises Alou	.10
92	Wil Cordero	.05
93	Jeff Fassero	.05
94	Darrin Fletcher	.05
95	Marquis Grissom	.05
96	Ken Hill	.05
97	Mike Lansing	.05
98	Kirk Rueter	.05
99	Larry Walker	.20
100	John Wetteland	.05
101	Rod Beck	.05
102	Barry Bonds	.55
103	John Burkett	.05
104	Royce Clayton	.05
105	Darren Lewis	.05
106	Kirt Manwaring	.05
107	Willie McGee	.05
108	Bill Swift	.05
109	Robby Thompson	.05
110	Matt Williams	.15
111	Sandy Alomar Jr.	.05
112	Carlos Baerga	.05
113	Albert Belle	.20
114	Wayne Kirby	.05
115	Kenny Lofton	.05
116	Jose Mesa	.05
117	Eddie Murray	.30
118	Charles Nagy	.05
119	Paul Sorrento	.05
120	Jim Thome	.05
121	Rich Amaral	.05
122	Eric Anthony	.05
123	Mike Blowers	.05
124	Chris Bosio	.05
125	Jay Buhner	.05
126	Dave Fleming	.05
127	Ken Griffey, Jr.	.70
128	Randy Johnson	.35
129	Edgar Martinez	.05
130	Tino Martinez	.05
131	Bret Barberie	.05
132	Ryan Bowen	.05
133	Chuck Carr	.05
134	Jeff Conine	.05
135	Orestes Destrade	.05
136	Chris Hammond	.05
137	Bryan Harvey	.05
138	Dave Magadan	.05
139	Benito Santiago	.05
140	Gary Sheffield	.20
141	Bobby Bonilla	.05
142	Jeromy Burnitz	.05
143	Dwight Gooden	.05
144	Todd Hundley	.05
145	Bobby Jones	.05
146	Jeff Kent	.05
147	Joe Orsulak	.05
148	Bret Saberhagen	.05
149	Pete Schourek	.05
150	Ryan Thompson	.05
151	Brady Anderson	.05
152	Harold Baines	.05
153	Mike Devereaux	.05
154	Chris Hoiles	.05
155	Ben McDonald	.05
156	Mark McLemore	.05
157	Mike Mussina	.30
158	Rafael Palmeiro	.15
159	Cal Ripken, Jr.	.75
160	Chris Sabo	.05
161	Brad Ausmus	.05
162	Derek Bell	.05
163	Andy Benes	.05
164	Doug Brocail	.05
165	Archi Cianfrocco	.05
166	Ricky Gutierrez	.05
167	Tony Gwynn	.50
168	Gene Harris	.05
169	Pedro Martinez	.35
170	Phil Plantier	.05
171	Darren Daulton	.05
172	Mariano Duncan	.05
173	Len Dykstra	.05
174	Tommy Greene	.05
175	Dave Hollins	.05
176	Danny Jackson	.05
177	John Kruk	.05
178	Terry Mulholland	.05
179	Curt Schilling	.10
180	Kevin Stocker	.05
181	Jay Bell	.05
182	Steve Cooke	.05
183	Carlos Garcia	.05
184	Joel Johnston	.05
185	Jeff King	.05
186	Al Martin	.05
187	Orlando Merced	.05
188	Don Slaught	.05
189	Andy Van Slyke	.05
190	Kevin Young	.05
191	Kevin Brown	.10
192	Jose Canseco	.30
193	Will Clark	.15
194	Juan Gonzalez	.40
195	Tom Henke	.05
196	David Hulse	.05
197	Dean Palmer	.05
198	Roger Pavlik	.05
199	Ivan Rodriguez	.35
200	Kenny Rogers	.05
201	Roger Clemens	.50
202	Scott Cooper	.05
203	Andre Dawson	.15
204	Mike Greenwell	.05
205	Billy Hatcher	.05
206	Jeff Russell	.05
207	Aaron Sele	.05
208	John Valentin	.05
209	Mo Vaughn	.25
210	Frank Viola	.05
211	Rob Dibble	.05
212	Willie Greene	.05
213	Roberto Kelly	.05
214	Barry Larkin	.10
215	Kevin Mitchell	.05
216	Hal Morris	.05
217	Joe Oliver	.05
218	Jose Rijo	.05
219	Reggie Sanders	.05
220	John Smiley	.05
221	Dante Bichette	.05
222	Ellis Burks	.05
223	Andres Galarraga	.05
224	Joe Girardi	.05
225	Charlie Hayes	.05
226	Darren Holmes	.05
227	Howard Johnson	.05
228	Roberto Mejia	.05
229	David Nied	.05
230	Armando Reynoso	.05
231	Kevin Appier	.05
232	David Cone	.05
233	Greg Gagne	.05
234	Tom Gordon	.05
235	Felix Jose	.05
236	Wally Joyner	.05
237	Jose Lind	.05
238	Brian McRae	.05
239	Mike MacFarlane	.05
240	Jeff Montgomery	.05
241	Eric Davis	.05
242	John Doherty	.05
243	Cecil Fielder	.05
244	Travis Fryman	.05
245	Bill Gullickson	.05
246	Mike Henneman	.05
247	Tony Phillips	.05
248	Mickey Tettleton	.05
249	Alan Trammell	.05
250	Lou Whitaker	.05
251	Rick Aguilera	.05
252	Scott Erickson	.05
253	Kent Hrbek	.05
254	Chuck Knoblauch	.05
255	Shane Mack	.05
256	Dave McCarty	.05
257	Pat Meares	.05
258	Kirby Puckett	.50
259	Kevin Tapani	.05
260	Dave Winfield	.40
261	Wilson Alvarez	.05
262	Jason Bere	.05
263	Alex Fernandez	.05
264	Ozzie Guillen	.05
265	Roberto Hernandez	.05
266	Lance Johnson	.05
267	Jack McDowell	.05
268	Tim Raines	.05
269	Frank Thomas	.55
270	Robin Ventura	.05
271	Jim Abbott	.05
272	Wade Boggs	.40
273	Mike Gallego	.05
274	Pat Kelly	.05
275	Jimmy Key	.05
276	Don Mattingly	.55
277	Paul O'Neill	.05
278	Mike Stanley	.05
279	Danny Tartabull	.05
280	Bernie Williams	.15
281	Chipper Jones	.60
282	Ryan Klesko	.05
283	Javier Lopez	.05
284	Jeffrey Hammonds	.05
285	Jeff McNeely	.05
286	Manny Ramirez	.40
287	Billy Ashley	.05
288	Raul Mondesi	.10
289	Cliff Floyd	.05
290	Rondell White	.10
291	Steve Karsay	.05
292	Midre Cummings	.05
293	Salomon Torres	.05
294	J.R. Phillips	.05
295	Marc Newfield	.05
296	Carlos Delgado	.20
297	Butch Huskey	.05

298 Checklist (Frank Thomas) .05
299 Checklist (Barry Bonds) .05
300 Checklist (Juan Gonzalez) .05

1994 Triple Play Bomb Squad

Ten of the top major league home run hitters are included in this insert set. Fronts feature sepia-toned player photos within a wide brown frame. Gold foil enhances the typography. Backs have a white background with representations of vintage airplanes. A bar chart at left gives the player's home run totals by year. A small color portrait photo is at upper-right. Below are a few words about his homer history.

		MT
Complete Set (10):		10.00
Common Player:		.35
1	Frank Thomas	1.50
2	Cecil Fielder	.35
3	Juan Gonzalez	1.00
4	Barry Bonds	2.00
5	Dave Justice	.50
6	Fred McGriff	.35
7	Ron Gant	.35
8	Ken Griffey, Jr.	3.00
9	Albert Belle	.50
10	Matt Williams	.35

1994 Triple Play Medalists

Statistical performance over the 1992-93 seasons was used to rank the players appearing in the Medalists insert set. Horizontal format cards have photos of the first, second and third place winners in appropriate boxes of gold, silver and bronze foil. "Medalists," the "medals" and "Triple Play 94" are embossed on the front. Backs have color action photos of each player along with team logos and a few stats.

		MT
Complete Set (15):		20.00
Common Player:		1.00
1	A.L. Catchers (Chris Hoiles, Mickey Tettleton, Brian Harper)	1.00
2	N.L. Catchers (Darren Daulton, Rick Wilkins, Kirt Manwaring)	1.00
3	A.L. First Basemen (Frank Thomas, Rafael Palmeiro, John Olerud)	2.00
4	N.L. First Basemen(Mark Grace, Fred McGriff, Jeff Bagwell)	2.50
5	A.L. Second Basemen (Roberto Alomar, Carlos Baerga, Lou Whitaker)	1.25
6	N.L. Second Basemen (Ryne Sandberg, Craig Biggio, Robby Thompson)	2.50
7	A.L. Shortstops (Tony Fernandez, Cal Ripken, Jr., Alan Trammell)	4.00
8	N.L. Shortstops (Barry Larkin, Jay Bell, Jeff Blauser)	1.00
9	A.L. Third Basemen (Robin Ventura, Travis Fryman, Wade Boggs)	1.25
10	N.L. Third Basemen (Terry Pendleton, Dave Hollins, Gary Sheffield)	1.00
11	A.L. Outfielders (Ken Griffey, Jr., Kirby Puckett, Albert Belle)	3.50
12	N.L. Outfielders (Barry Bonds, Andy Van Slyke, Len Dykstra)	2.50
13	A.L. Starters (Jack McDowell, Kevin Brown, Randy Johnson)	1.25
14	N.L. Starters (Greg Maddux, Jose Rijo, Billy Swift)	2.00
15	Designated Hitters (Paul Molitor, Dave Winfield, Harold Baines)	1.25

1994 Triple Play Nicknames

Eight of baseball's most colorful team nicknames are featured in this insert set. Fronts feature a background photo representative of the nickname, with a player photo is superimposed over that. Backs have another player photo and a history of the team's nickname.

		MT
Complete Set (8):		15.00
Common Player:		1.50
1	Cecil Fielder	1.00
2	Ryne Sandberg	2.00
3	Gary Sheffield	1.00
4	Joe Carter	1.00
5	John Olerud	1.00
6	Cal Ripken, Jr.	5.00
7	Mark McGwire	5.00
8	Gregg Jefferies	1.00

1991 Ultra

This 400-card set was originally going to be called the Elite set, but Fleer chose to use the Ultra label. The card fronts feature gray borders surrounding full-color action photos. The backs feature three player photos and statistics. Hot Prospects and Great Performers are among the special cards featured within the set.

		MT
Complete Set (400):		15.00
Common Player:		.05
Wax Pack (14):		.75
Wax Box (36):		12.50
1	Steve Avery	.05
2	Jeff Blauser	.05
3	Francisco Cabrera	.05
4	Ron Gant	.05
5	Tom Glavine	.10
6	Tommy Gregg	.05
7	Dave Justice	.25
8	Oddibe McDowell	.05
9	Greg Olson	.05
10	Terry Pendleton	.05
11	Lonnie Smith	.05
12	John Smoltz	.10
13	Jeff Treadway	.05
14	Glenn Davis	.05
15	Mike Devereaux	.05
16	Leo Gomez	.05
17	Chris Hoiles	.05
18	Dave Johnson	.05
19	Ben McDonald	.05
20	Randy Milligan	.05
21	Gregg Olson	.05
22	Joe Orsulak	.05
23	Bill Ripken	.05
24	Cal Ripken, Jr.	2.00
25	David Segui	.05
26	Craig Worthington	.05
27	Wade Boggs	.50
28	Tom Bolton	.05
29	Tom Brunansky	.05
30	Ellis Burks	.05
31	Roger Clemens	1.00
32	Mike Greenwell	.05
33	Greg Harris	.05
34	Daryl Irvine	.05
35	Mike Marshall	.05
36	Tim Naehring	.05
37	Tony Pena	.05
38	*Phil Plantier*	.05
39	Carlos Quintana	.05
40	Jeff Reardon	.05
41	Jody Reed	.05
42	Luis Rivera	.05
43	Jim Abbott	.05
44	Chuck Finley	.05
45	Bryan Harvey	.05
46	Donnie Hill	.05
47	Jack Howell	.05
48	Wally Joyner	.05
49	Mark Langston	.05
50	Kirk McCaskill	.05
51	Lance Parrish	.05
52	Dick Schofield	.05
53	Lee Stevens	.05
54	Dave Winfield	.50
55	George Bell	.05
56	Damon Berryhill	.05
57	Mike Bielecki	.05
58	Andre Dawson	.20
59	Shawon Dunston	.05
60	Joe Girardi	.05
61	Mark Grace	.20
62	Mike Harkey	.05
63	Les Lancaster	.05
64	Greg Maddux	1.00
65	Derrick May	.05
66	Ryne Sandberg	.60
67	Luis Salazar	.05
68	Dwight Smith	.05
69	Hector Villanueva	.05
70	Jerome Walton	.05
71	Mitch Williams	.05
72	Carlton Fisk	.50
73	Scott Fletcher	.05
74	Ozzie Guillen	.05
75	Greg Hibbard	.05
76	Lance Johnson	.05
77	Steve Lyons	.05
78	Jack McDowell	.05
79	Dan Pasqua	.05
80	Melido Perez	.05
81	Tim Raines	.05
82	Sammy Sosa	1.25
83	Cory Snyder	.05
84	Bobby Thigpen	.05
85	Frank Thomas	1.25
86	Robin Ventura	.05
87	Todd Benzinger	.05
88	Glenn Braggs	.05
89	Tom Browning	.05
90	Norm Charlton	.05
91	Eric Davis	.05
92	Rob Dibble	.05
93	Bill Doran	.05
94	Mariano Duncan	.05
95	Billy Hatcher	.05
96	Barry Larkin	.10
97	Randy Myers	.05
98	Hal Morris	.05
99	Joe Oliver	.05
100	Paul O'Neill	.05
101a	Jeff Reed	.05
101b	Beau Allred (Should be #104)	.05
102	Jose Rijo	.05
103a	Chris Sabo	.05
103b	Carlos Baerga (Should be #106)	.05
104	Not Issued (See #101b)	
105	Sandy Alomar,Jr.	.05
106	Not Issued (See #103b)	
107	Albert Belle	.25
108	Jerry Browne	.05
109	Tom Candiotti	.05
110	Alex Cole	.05
111a	John Farrell	.05
111b	Chris James (Should be #114)	.05
112	Felix Fermin	.05
113	Brook Jacoby	.05
114	Not Issued (See #111b)	

115	Doug Jones	.05
116a	Steve Olin	.05
116b	Mitch Webster (Should be #119)	.05
117	Greg Swindell	.05
118	Turner Ward	.05
119	Not Issued (See #116b)	
120	Dave Bergman	.05
121	Cecil Fielder	.05
122	Travis Fryman	.05
123	Mike Henneman	.05
124	Lloyd Moseby	.05
125	Dan Petry	.05
126	Tony Phillips	.05
127	Mark Salas	.05
128	Frank Tanana	.05
129	Alan Trammell	.05
130	Lou Whitaker	.05
131	Eric Anthony	.05
132	Craig Biggio	.10
133	Ken Caminiti	.05
134	Casey Candaele	.05
135	Andujar Cedeno	.05
136	Mark Davidson	.05
137	Jim Deshaies	.05
138	Mark Portugal	.05
139	Rafael Ramirez	.05
140	Mike Scott	.05
141	Eric Yelding	.05
142	Gerald Young	.05
143	Kevin Appier	.05
144	George Brett	1.00
145	*Jeff Conine*	.40
146	Jim Eisenreich	.05
147	Tom Gordon	.05
148	Mark Gubicza	.05
149	Bo Jackson	.10
150	Brent Mayne	.05
151	Mike Macfarlane	.05
152	*Brian McRae*	.25
153	Jeff Montgomery	.05
154	Bret Saberhagen	.05
155	Kevin Seitzer	.05
156	Terry Shumpert	.05
157	Kurt Stillwell	.05
158	Danny Tartabull	.05
159	Tim Belcher	.05
160	Kal Daniels	.05
161	Alfredo Griffin	.05
162	Lenny Harris	.05
163	Jay Howell	.05
164	Ramon Martinez	.05
165	Mike Morgan	.05
166	Eddie Murray	.40
167	Jose Offerman	.05
168	Juan Samuel	.05
169	Mike Scioscia	.05
170	Mike Sharperson	.05
171	Darryl Strawberry	.05
172	Greg Brock	.05
173	Chuck Crim	.05
174	Jim Gantner	.05
175	Ted Higuera	.05
176	Mark Knudson	.05
177	Tim McIntosh	.05
178	Paul Molitor	.40
179	Dan Plesac	.05
180	Gary Sheffield	.30
181	Bill Spiers	.05
182	B.J. Surhoff	.05
183	Greg Vaughn	.05
184	Robin Yount	.50
185	Rick Aguilera	.05
186	Greg Gagne	.05
187	Dan Gladden	.05
188	Brian Harper	.05
189	Kent Hrbek	.05
190	Gene Larkin	.05
191	Shane Mack	.05
192	Pedro Munoz	.05
193	Al Newman	.05
194	Junior Ortiz	.05
195	Kirby Puckett	1.00
196	Kevin Tapani	.05
197	Dennis Boyd	.05
198	Tim Burke	.05
199	Ivan Calderon	.05
200	Delino DeShields	.05
201	Mike Fitzgerald	.05
202	Steve Frey	.05
203	Andres Galarraga	.05
204	Marquis Grissom	.05
205	Dave Martinez	.05
206	Dennis Martinez	.05
207	Junior Noboa	.05
208	Spike Owen	.05
209	Scott Ruskin	.05
210	Tim Wallach	.05
211	Daryl Boston	.05
212	Vince Coleman	.05
213	David Cone	.05
214	Ron Darling	.05
215	Kevin Elster	.05
216	Sid Fernandez	.05
217	John Franco	.05
218	Dwight Gooden	.05
219	Tom Herr	.05
220	Todd Hundley	.05
221	Gregg Jefferies	.05
222	Howard Johnson	.05
223	Dave Magadan	.05
224	Kevin McReynolds	.05
225	Keith Miller	.05
226	Mackey Sasser	.05
227	Frank Viola	.05
228	Jesse Barfield	.05
229	Greg Cadaret	.05
230	Alvaro Espinoza	.05
231	Bob Geren	.05
232	Lee Guetterman	.05
233	Mel Hall	.05
234	Andy Hawkins	.05
235	Roberto Kelly	.05
236	Tim Leary	.05
237	Jim Leyritz	.05
238	Kevin Maas	.05
239	Don Mattingly	1.25
240	Hensley Meulens	.05
241	Eric Plunk	.05
242	Steve Sax	.05
243	Todd Burns	.05
244	Jose Canseco	.50
245	Dennis Eckersley	.05
246	Mike Gallego	.05
247	Dave Henderson	.05
248	Rickey Henderson	.50
249	Rick Honeycutt	.05
250	Carney Lansford	.05
251	Mark McGwire	2.00
252	Mike Moore	.05
253	Terry Steinbach	.05
254	Dave Stewart	.05
255	Walt Weiss	.05
256	Bob Welch	.05
257	Curt Young	.05
258	Wes Chamberlain	.05
259	Pat Combs	.05
260	Darren Daulton	.05
261	Jose DeJesus	.05
262	Len Dykstra	.05
263	Charlie Hayes	.05
264	Von Hayes	.05
265	Ken Howell	.05
266	John Kruk	.05
267	Roger McDowell	.05
268	Mickey Morandini	.05
269	Terry Mulholland	.05
270	Dale Murphy	.15
271	Randy Ready	.05
272	Dickie Thon	.05
273	Stan Belinda	.05
274	Jay Bell	.05
275	Barry Bonds	1.25
276	Bobby Bonilla	.05
277	Doug Drabek	.05
278	*Carlos Garcia*	.15
279	Neal Heaton	.05
280	Jeff King	.05
281	Bill Landrum	.05
282	Mike LaValliere	.05
283	Jose Lind	.05
284	*Orlando Merced*	.20
285	Gary Redus	.05
286	Don Slaught	.05
287	Andy Van Slyke	.05
288	Jose DeLeon	.05
289	Pedro Guerrero	.05
290	Ray Lankford	.05
291	Joe Magrane	.05
292	Jose Oquendo	.05
293	Tom Pagnozzi	.05
294	Bryn Smith	.05
295	Lee Smith	.05
296	Ozzie Smith	1.00
297	Milt Thompson	.05
298	*Craig Wilson*	.05
299	Todd Zeile	.05
300	Shawn Abner	.05
301	Andy Benes	.05
302	Paul Faries	.05
303	Tony Gwynn	1.00
304	Greg Harris	.05
305	Thomas Howard	.05
306	Bruce Hurst	.05
307	Craig Lefferts	.05
308	Fred McGriff	.05
309	Dennis Rasmussen	.05
310	Bip Roberts	.05
311	Benito Santiago	.05
312	Garry Templeton	.05
313	Ed Whitson	.05
314	Dave Anderson	.05
315	Kevin Bass	.05
316	Jeff Brantley	.05
317	John Burkett	.05
318	Will Clark	.15
319	Steve Decker	.05
320	Scott Garrelts	.05
321	Terry Kennedy	.05
322	Mark Leonard	.05
323	Darren Lewis	.05
324	Greg Litton	.05
325	Willie McGee	.05
326	Kevin Mitchell	.05
327	Don Robinson	.05
328	Andres Santana	.05
329	Robby Thompson	.05
330	Jose Uribe	.05
331	Matt Williams	.15
332	Scott Bradley	.05
333	Henry Cotto	.05
334	Alvin Davis	.05
335	Ken Griffey, Sr.	.05
336	Ken Griffey, Jr.	1.50
337	Erik Hanson	.05
338	Brian Holman	.05
339	Randy Johnson	.50
340	Edgar Martinez	.05
341	Tino Martinez	.05
342	Pete O'Brien	.05
343	Harold Reynolds	.05
344	David Valle	.05
345	Omar Vizquel	.05
346	Brad Arnsberg	.05
347	Kevin Brown	.15
348	Julio Franco	.05
349	Jeff Huson	.05
350	Rafael Palmeiro	.25
351	Geno Petralli	.05
352	Gary Pettis	.05
353	Kenny Rogers	.05
354	Jeff Russell	.05
355	Nolan Ryan	2.00
356	Ruben Sierra	.05
357	Bobby Witt	.05
358	Roberto Alomar	.50
359	Pat Borders	.05
360	Joe Carter	.05
361	Kelly Gruber	.05
362	Tom Henke	.05
363	Glenallen Hill	.05
364	Jimmy Key	.05
365	Manny Lee	.05
366	Rance Mulliniks	.05
367	John Olerud	.05
368	Dave Stieb	.05
369	Duane Ward	.05
370	David Wells	.10
371	Mark Whiten	.05
372	Mookie Wilson	.05
373	Willie Banks	.05
374	Steve Carter	.05
375	Scott Chiamparino	.05
376	Steve Chitren	.05
377	Darrin Fletcher	.05
378	Rich Garces	.05
379	Reggie Jefferson	.05
380	*Eric Karros*	.75
381	Pat Kelly	.05
382	Chuck Knoblauch	.05
383	Denny Neagle	.05
384	Dan Opperman	.05
385	John Ramos	.05
386	*Henry Rodriguez*	.50
387	Mo Vaughn	.50
388	Gerald Williams	.05
389	Mike York	.05
390	Eddie Zosky	.05
391	Barry Bonds (Great Performer)	.65
392	Cecil Fielder (Great Performer)	.05
393	Rickey Henderson (Great Performer)	.15
394	Dave Justice (Great Performer)	.15
395	Nolan Ryan (Great Performer)	1.00
396	Bobby Thigpen (Great Performer)	.05
397	Checklist	.05
398	Checklist	.05
399	Checklist	.05
400	Checklist	.05

1991 Ultra Gold

A pair of action photos flanking and below a portrait in a home plate frame at top-center are featured on these cards. Background is a graduated gold coloring. The Fleer Ultra Team logo is in the upper-left corner. Backs have narrative career information. The Puckett and Sandberg cards feature incorrect historical information on the backs.

		MT
Complete Set (10):		5.00
Common Player:		.15
1	Barry Bonds	1.75
2	Will Clark	.20
3	Doug Drabek	.15
4	Ken Griffey, Jr.	2.00
5	Rickey Henderson	.75
6	Bo Jackson	.25
7	Ramon Martinez	.15
8	Kirby Puckett	1.50
9	Chris Sabo	.15
10	Ryne Sandberg	1.00

1991 Ultra Update

This 120-card set was produced as a supplement to the premier Fleer Ultra set. Cards feature the same style as the regular Fleer Ultra cards. The cards were sold only as complete sets in full color, shrinkwrapped boxes.

		MT
Complete Set (120):		45.00
Common Player:		.05
1	Dwight Evans	.05
2	Chito Martinez	.05
3	Bob Melvin	.05
4	*Mike Mussina*	7.50
5	Jack Clark	.05
6	Dana Kiecker	.05
7	Steve Lyons	.05
8	Gary Gaetti	.05

9	Dave Gallagher	.05
10	Dave Parker	.05
11	Luis Polonia	.05
12	Luis Sojo	.05
13	Wilson Alvarez	.05
14	Alex Fernandez	.05
15	Craig Grebeck	.05
16	Ron Karkovice	.05
17	Warren Newson	.05
18	Scott Radinsky	.05
19	Glenallen Hill	.05
20	Charles Nagy	.10
21	Mark Whiten	.05
22	Milt Cuyler	.05
23	Paul Gibson	.05
24	Mickey Tettleton	.05
25	Todd Benzinger	.05
26	Storm Davis	.05
27	Kirk Gibson	.05
28	Bill Pecota	.05
29	Gary Thurman	.05
30	Darryl Hamilton	.05
31	Jaime Navarro	.05
32	Willie Randolph	.05
33	Bill Wegman	.05
34	Randy Bush	.05
35	Chili Davis	.05
36	Scott Erickson	.05
37	Chuck Knoblauch	.05
38	Scott Leius	.05
39	Jack Morris	.05
40	John Habyan	.05
41	Pat Kelly	.05
42	Matt Nokes	.05
43	Scott Sanderson	.05
44	Bernie Williams	3.00
45	Harold Baines	.05
46	Brook Jacoby	.05
47	Ernest Riles	.05
48	Willie Wilson	.05
49	Jay Buhner	.10
50	Rich DeLucia	.05
51	Mike Jackson	.05
52	Bill Krueger	.05
53	Bill Swift	.05
54	Brian Downing	.05
55	Juan Gonzalez	4.00
56	Dean Palmer	.05
57	Kevin Reimer	.05
58	*Ivan Rodriguez*	7.50
59	Tom Candiotti	.05
60	Juan Guzman	.05
61	Bob MacDonald	.05
62	Greg Myers	.05
63	Ed Sprague	.05
64	Devon White	.05
65	Rafael Belliard	.05
66	Juan Berenguer	.05
67	Brian Hunter	.05
68	Kent Mercker	.05
69	Otis Nixon	.05
70	Danny Jackson	.05
71	Chuck McElroy	.05
72	Gary Scott	.05
73	Heathcliff Slocumb	.05
74	Chico Walker	.05
75	Rick Wilkins	.05
76	Chris Hammond	.05
77	Luis Quinones	.05
78	Herm Winningham	.05
79	*Jeff Bagwell*	10.00
80	Jim Corsi	.05
81	Steve Finley	.05
82	*Luis Gonzalez*	6.00
83	Pete Harnisch	.05
84	Darryl Kile	.05
85	Brett Butler	.05
86	Gary Carter	.25
87	Tim Crews	.05
88	Orel Hershiser	.05
89	Bob Ojeda	.05
90	Bret Barberie	.05
91	Barry Jones	.05
92	Gilberto Reyes	.05
93	Larry Walker	1.00
94	Hubie Brooks	.05
95	Tim Burke	.05
96	Rick Cerone	.05
97	Jeff Innis	.05
98	Wally Backman	.05
99	Tommy Greene	.05
100	Ricky Jordan	.05
101	Mitch Williams	.05
102	John Smiley	.05
103	Randy Tomlin	.05
104	Gary Varsho	.05
105	Cris Carpenter	.05
106	Ken Hill	.05
107	Felix Jose	.05
108	*Omar Oliveras*	.25
109	Gerald Perry	.05
110	Jerald Clark	.05
111	Tony Fernandez	.05
112	Darrin Jackson	.05
113	Mike Maddux	.05
114	Tim Teufel	.05
115	Bud Black	.05
116	Kelly Downs	.05
117	Mike Felder	.05
118	Willie McGee	.05
119	Trevor Wilson	.05
120	Checklist	.05

1992 Ultra

Fleer released its second annual Ultra set in 1992. Card fronts feature full-color action photos with a marble accent at the card bottom. The flip sides are horizontal with two additional player photos. Many insert sets were randomly included in foil packs as premiums. These included rookie, All-Star and award winners, among others. A two-card Tony Gwynn send-away set was also available through an offer from Fleer. For $1 and 10 Ultra wrappers, collectors could receive the Gwynn cards. The set is numbered by team; cards #1-300 comprise Series I, cards #301-600 are Series II.

		MT
Complete Set (600):		15.00
Common Player:		.05
Series 1 Pack (14):		.75
Series 1 Wax Box (36):		10.00
Series 2 Pack (14):		.50
Series 2 Wax Box (36):		10.00
1	Glenn Davis	.05
2	Mike Devereaux	.05
3	Dwight Evans	.05
4	Leo Gomez	.05
5	Chris Hoiles	.05
6	Sam Horn	.05
7	Chito Martinez	.05
8	Randy Milligan	.05
9	Mike Mussina	.65
10	Billy Ripken	.05
11	Cal Ripken, Jr.	2.00
12	Tom Brunansky	.05
13	Ellis Burks	.05
14	Jack Clark	.05
15	Roger Clemens	1.00
16	Mike Greenwell	.05
17	Joe Hesketh	.05
18	Tony Pena	.05
19	Carlos Quintana	.05
20	Jeff Reardon	.05
21	Jody Reed	.05
22	Luis Rivera	.05
23	Mo Vaughn	.40
24	Gary DiSarcina	.05
25	Chuck Finley	.05
26	Gary Gaetti	.05
27	Bryan Harvey	.05
28	Lance Parrish	.05
29	Luis Polonia	.05
30	Dick Schofield	.05
31	Luis Sojo	.05
32	Wilson Alvarez	.05
33	Carlton Fisk	.75
34	Craig Grebeck	.05
35	Ozzie Guillen	.05
36	Greg Hibbard	.05
37	Charlie Hough	.05
38	Lance Johnson	.05
39	Ron Karkovice	.05
40	Jack McDowell	.05
41	Donn Pall	.05
42	Melido Perez	.05
43	Tim Raines	.05
44	Frank Thomas	1.25
45	Sandy Alomar, Jr.	.05
46	Carlos Baerga	.05
47	Albert Belle	.30
48	Jerry Browne	.05
49	Felix Fermin	.05
50	Reggie Jefferson	.05
51	Mark Lewis	.05
52	Carlos Martinez	.05
53	Steve Olin	.05
54	Jim Thome	.05
55	Mark Whiten	.05
56	Dave Bergman	.05
57	Milt Cuyler	.05
58	Rob Deer	.05
59	Cecil Fielder	.05
60	Travis Fryman	.05
61	Scott Livingstone	.05
62	Tony Phillips	.05
63	Mickey Tettleton	.05
64	Alan Trammell	.05
65	Lou Whitaker	.05
66	Kevin Appier	.05
67	Mike Boddicker	.05
68	George Brett	1.00
69	Jim Eisenreich	.05
70	Mark Gubicza	.05
71	David Howard	.05
72	Joel Johnston	.05
73	Mike Macfarlane	.05
74	Brent Mayne	.05
75	Brian McRae	.05
76	Jeff Montgomery	.05
77	Terry Shumpert	.05
78	Don August	.05
79	Dante Bichette	.05
80	Ted Higuera	.05
81	Paul Molitor	.75
82	Jamie Navarro	.05
83	Gary Sheffield	.25
84	Bill Spiers	.05
85	B.J. Surhoff	.05
86	Greg Vaughn	.05
87	Robin Yount	.65
88	Rick Aguilera	.05
89	Chili Davis	.05
90	Scott Erickson	.05
91	Brian Harper	.05
92	Kent Hrbek	.05
93	Chuck Knoblauch	.05
94	Scott Leius	.05
95	Shane Mack	.05
96	Mike Pagliarulo	.05
97	Kirby Puckett	1.00
98	Kevin Tapani	.05
99	Jesse Barfield	.05
100	Alvaro Espinoza	.05
101	Mel Hall	.05
102	Pat Kelly	.05
103	Roberto Kelly	.05
104	Kevin Maas	.05
105	Don Mattingly	1.25
106	Hensley Meulens	.05
107	Matt Nokes	.05
108	Steve Sax	.05
109	Harold Baines	.05
110	Jose Canseco	.50
111	Ron Darling	.05
112	Mike Gallego	.05
113	Dave Henderson	.05
114	Rickey Henderson	.60
115	Mark McGwire	2.00
116	Terry Steinbach	.05
117	Dave Stewart	.05
118	Todd Van Poppel	.05
119	Bob Welch	.05
120	Greg Briley	.05
121	Jay Buhner	.05
122	Rich DeLucia	.05
123	Ken Griffey, Jr.	1.50
124	Erik Hanson	.05
125	Randy Johnson	.75
126	Edgar Martinez	.05
127	Tino Martinez	.05
128	Pete O'Brien	.05
129	Harold Reynolds	.05
130	Dave Valle	.05
131	Julio Franco	.05
132	Juan Gonzalez	.75
133	Jeff Huson	.05
134	Mike Jeffcoat	.05
135	Terry Mathews	.05
136	Rafael Palmeiro	.30
137	Dean Palmer	.05
138	Geno Petralli	.05
139	Ivan Rodriguez	.75
140	Jeff Russell	.05
141	Nolan Ryan	2.00
142	Ruben Sierra	.05
143	Roberto Alomar	.65
144	Pat Borders	.05
145	Joe Carter	.05
146	Kelly Gruber	.05
147	Jimmy Key	.05
148	Manny Lee	.05
149	Rance Mulliniks	.05
150	Greg Myers	.05
151	John Olerud	.05
152	Dave Stieb	.05
153	Todd Stottlemyre	.05
154	Duane Ward	.05
155	Devon White	.05
156	Eddie Zosky	.05
157	Steve Avery	.05
158	Rafael Belliard	.05
159	Jeff Blauser	.05
160	Sid Bream	.05
161	Ron Gant	.05
162	Tom Glavine	.10
163	Brian Hunter	.05
164	Dave Justice	.25
165	Mark Lemke	.05
166	Greg Olson	.05
167	Terry Pendleton	.05
168	Lonnie Smith	.05
169	John Smoltz	.10
170	Mike Stanton	.05
171	Jeff Treadway	.05
172	Paul Assenmacher	.05
173	George Bell	.05
174	Shawon Dunston	.05
175	Mark Grace	.20
176	Danny Jackson	.05
177	Les Lancaster	.05
178	Greg Maddux	1.00
179	Luis Salazar	.05
180	Rey Sanchez	.05
181	Ryne Sandberg	.75
182	Jose Vizcaino	.05
183	Chico Walker	.05
184	Jerome Walton	.05
185	Glenn Braggs	.05
186	Tom Browning	.05
187	Rob Dibble	.05
188	Bill Doran	.05
189	Chris Hammond	.05
190	Billy Hatcher	.05
191	Barry Larkin	.10
192	Hal Morris	.05
193	Joe Oliver	.05
194	Paul O'Neill	.05
195	Jeff Reed	.05
196	Jose Rijo	.05
197	Chris Sabo	.05
198	Jeff Bagwell	.75
199	Craig Biggio	.10
200	Ken Caminiti	.05
201	Andujar Cedeno	.05
202	Steve Finley	.05
203	Luis Gonzalez	.20
204	Pete Harnisch	.05
205	Xavier Hernandez	.05
206	Darryl Kile	.05
207	Al Osuna	.05
208	Curt Schilling	.15
209	Brett Butler	.05
210	Kal Daniels	.05
211	Lenny Harris	.05
212	Stan Javier	.05
213	Ramon Martinez	.05

214 Roger McDowell .05
215 Jose Offerman .05
216 Juan Samuel .05
217 Mike Scioscia .05
218 Mike Sharperson .05
219 Darryl Strawberry .05
220 Delino DeShields .05
221 Tom Foley .05
222 Steve Frey .05
223 Dennis Martinez .05
224 Spike Owen .05
225 Gilberto Reyes .05
226 Tim Wallach .05
227 Daryl Boston .05
228 Tim Burke .05
229 Vince Coleman .05
230 David Cone .05
231 Kevin Elster .05
232 Dwight Gooden .05
233 Todd Hundley .05
234 Jeff Innis .05
235 Howard Johnson .05
236 Dave Magadan .05
237 Mackey Sasser .05
238 Anthony Young .05
239 Wes Chamberlain .05
240 Darren Daulton .05
241 Len Dykstra .05
242 Tommy Greene .05
243 Charlie Hayes .05
244 Dave Hollins .05
245 Ricky Jordan .05
246 John Kruk .05
247 Mickey Morandini .05
248 Terry Mulholland .05
249 Dale Murphy .20
250 Jay Bell .05
251 Barry Bonds 1.25
252 Steve Buechele .05
253 Doug Drabek .05
254 Mike LaValliere .05
255 Jose Lind .05
256 Lloyd McClendon .05
257 Orlando Merced .05
258 Don Slaught .05
259 John Smiley .05
260 Zane Smith .05
261 Randy Tomlin .05
262 Andy Van Slyke .05
263 Pedro Guerrero .05
264 Felix Jose .05
265 Ray Lankford .05
266 Omar Olivares .05
267 Jose Oquendo .05
268 Tom Pagnozzi .05
269 Bryn Smith .05
270 Lee Smith .05
271 Ozzie Smith 1.00
272 Milt Thompson .05
273 Todd Zeile .05
274 Andy Benes .05
275 Jerald Clark .05
276 Tony Fernandez .05
277 Tony Gwynn 1.00
278 Greg Harris .05
279 Thomas Howard .05
280 Bruce Hurst .05
281 Mike Maddux .05
282 Fred McGriff .05
283 Benito Santiago .05
284 Kevin Bass .05
285 Jeff Brantley .05
286 John Burkett .05
287 Will Clark .15
288 Royce Clayton .05
289 Steve Decker .05
290 Kelly Downs .05
291 Mike Felder .05
292 Darren Lewis .05
293 Kirt Manwaring .05
294 Willie McGee .05
295 Robby Thompson .05
296 Matt Williams .15
297 Trevor Wilson .05
298 Checklist 1-108 (Sandy Alomar, Jr.) .05
299 Checklist 109-208 (Rey Sanchez) .05
300 Checklist 209-300 (Nolan Ryan) .25
301 Brady Anderson .05
302 Todd Frohwirth .05
303 Ben McDonald .05
304 Mark McLemore .05
305 Jose Mesa .05
306 Bob Milacki .05
307 Gregg Olson .05
308 David Segui .05
309 Rick Sutcliffe .05
310 Jeff Tackett .05
311 Wade Boggs .60
312 Scott Cooper .05
313 John Flaherty .05
314 Wayne Housie .05
315 Peter Hoy .05
316 John Marzano .05
317 Tim Naehring .05
318 Phil Plantier .05
319 Frank Viola .05
320 Matt Young .05
321 Jim Abbott .05
322 Hubie Brooks .05
323 *Chad Curtis* .25
324 Alvin Davis .05
325 Junior Felix .05
326 Von Hayes .05
327 Mark Langston .05
328 Scott Lewis .05
329 Don Robinson .05
330 Bobby Rose .05
331 Lee Stevens .05
332 George Bell .05
333 Esteban Beltre .05
334 Joey Cora .05
335 Alex Fernandez .05
336 Roberto Hernandez .05
337 Mike Huff .05
338 Kirk McCaskill .05
339 Dan Pasqua .05
340 Scott Radinsky .05
341 Steve Sax .05
342 Bobby Thigpen .05
343 Robin Ventura .05
344 Jack Armstrong .05
345 Alex Cole .05
346 Dennis Cook .05
347 Glenallen Hill .05
348 Thomas Howard .05
349 Brook Jacoby .05
350 Kenny Lofton .05
351 Charles Nagy .05
352 Rod Nichols .05
353 Junior Ortiz .05
354 Dave Otto .05
355 Tony Perezchica .05
356 Scott Scudder .05
357 Paul Sorrento .05
358 Skeeter Barnes .05
359 Mark Carreon .05
360 John Doherty .05
361 Dan Gladden .05
362 Bill Gullickson .05
363 Shawn Hare .05
364 Mike Henneman .05
365 Chad Kreuter .05
366 Mark Leiter .05
367 Mike Munoz .05
368 Kevin Ritz .05
369 Mark Davis .05
370 Tom Gordon .05
371 Chris Gwynn .05
372 Gregg Jefferies .05
373 Wally Joyner .05
374 Kevin McReynolds .05
375 Keith Miller .05
376 Rico Rossy .05
377 Curtis Wilkerson .05
378 Ricky Bones .05
379 Chris Bosio .05
380 Cal Eldred .05
381 Scott Fletcher .05
382 Jim Gantner .05
383 Darryl Hamilton .05
384 Doug Henry .05
385 *Pat Listach* .05
386 Tim McIntosh .05
387 Edwin Nunez .05
388 Dan Plesac .05
389 Kevin Seitzer .05
390 Franklin Stubbs .05
391 William Suero .05
392 Bill Wegman .05
393 Willie Banks .05
394 Jarvis Brown .05
395 Greg Gagne .05
396 Mark Guthrie .05
397 Bill Krueger .05
398 *Pat Mahomes* .15
399 Pedro Munoz .05
400 John Smiley .05
401 Gary Wayne .05
402 Lenny Webster .05
403 Carl Willis .05
404 Greg Cadaret .05
405 Steve Farr .05
406 Mike Gallego .05
407 Charlie Hayes .05
408 Steve Howe .05
409 Dion James .05
410 Jeff Johnson .05
411 Tim Leary .05
412 Jim Leyritz .05
413 Melido Perez .05
414 Scott Sanderson .05
415 Andy Stankiewicz .05
416 Mike Stanley .05
417 Danny Tartabull .05
418 Lance Blankenship .05
419 Mike Bordick .05
420 *Scott Brosius* .05
421 Dennis Eckersley .05
422 Scott Hemond .05
423 Carney Lansford .05
424 Henry Mercedes .05
425 Mike Moore .05
426 Gene Nelson .05
427 Randy Ready .05
428 Bruce Walton .05
429 Willie Wilson .05
430 Rich Amaral .05
431 Dave Cochrane .05
432 Henry Cotto .05
433 Calvin Jones .05
434 Kevin Mitchell .05
435 Clay Parker .05
436 Omar Vizquel .05
437 Floyd Bannister .05
438 Kevin Brown .10
439 John Cangelosi .05
440 Brian Downing .05
441 Monty Fariss .05
442 Jose Guzman .05
443 Donald Harris .05
444 Kevin Reimer .05
445 Kenny Rogers .05
446 Wayne Rosenthal .05
447 Dickie Thon .05
448 Derek Bell .05
449 Juan Guzman .05
450 Tom Henke .05
451 Candy Maldonado .05
452 Jack Morris .05
453 David Wells .10
454 Dave Winfield .65
455 Juan Berenguer .05
456 Damon Berryhill .05
457 Mike Bielecki .05
458 Marvin Freeman .05
459 Charlie Leibrandt .05
460 Kent Mercker .05
461 Otis Nixon .05
462 Alejandro Pena .05
463 Ben Rivera .05
464 Deion Sanders .10
465 Mark Wohlers .05
466 Shawn Boskie .05
467 Frank Castillo .05
468 Andre Dawson .15
469 Joe Girardi .05
470 Chuck McElroy .05
471 Mike Morgan .05
472 Ken Patterson .05
473 Bob Scanlan .05
474 Gary Scott .05
475 Dave Smith .05
476 Sammy Sosa 1.25
477 Hector Villanueva .05
478 Scott Bankhead .05
479 Tim Belcher .05
480 Freddie Benavides .05
481 Jacob Brumfield .05
482 Norm Charlton .05
483 Dwayne Henry .05
484 Dave Martinez .05
485 Bip Roberts .05
486 Reggie Sanders .05
487 Greg Swindell .05
488 Ryan Bowen .05
489 Casey Candaele .05
490 Juan Guerrero .05
491 Pete Incaviglia .05
492 Jeff Juden .05
493 Rob Murphy .05
494 Mark Portugal .05
495 Rafael Ramirez .05
496 Scott Servais .05
497 Ed Taubensee .05
498 Brian Williams .05
499 Todd Benzinger .05
500 John Candelaria .05
501 Tom Candiotti .05
502 Tim Crews .05
503 Eric Davis .05
504 Jim Gott .05
505 Dave Hansen .05
506 Carlos Hernandez .05
507 Orel Hershiser .05
508 Eric Karros .05
509 Bob Ojeda .05
510 Steve Wilson .05
511 Moises Alou .20
512 Bret Barberie .05
513 Ivan Calderon .05
514 Gary Carter .20
515 Archi Cianfrocco .05
516 Jeff Fassero .05
517 Darrin Fletcher .05
518 Marquis Grissom .05
519 Chris Haney .05
520 Ken Hill .05
521 Chris Nabholz .05
522 Bill Sampen .05
523 John VanderWal .05
524 David Wainhouse .05
525 Larry Walker .20
526 John Wetteland .05
527 Bobby Bonilla .05
528 Sid Fernandez .05
529 John Franco .05
530 Dave Gallagher .05
531 Paul Gibson .05
532 Eddie Murray .50
533 Junior Noboa .05
534 Charlie O'Brien .05
535 Bill Pecota .05
536 Willie Randolph .05
537 Bret Saberhagen .05
538 Dick Schofield .05
539 Pete Schourek .05
540 Ruben Amaro .05
541 Andy Ashby .05
542 Kim Batiste .05
543 Cliff Brantley .05
544 Mariano Duncan .05
545 Jeff Grotewold .05
546 Barry Jones .05
547 Julio Peguero .05
548 Curt Schilling .15
549 Mitch Williams .05
550 Stan Belinda .05
551 Scott Bullett .05
552 Cecil Espy .05
553 Jeff King .05
554 Roger Mason .05
555 Paul Miller .05
556 Denny Neagle .05
557 Vocente Palacios .05
558 Bob Patterson .05
559 Tom Prince .05
560 Gary Redus .05
561 Gary Varsho .05
562 Juan Agosto .05
563 Cris Carpenter .05
564 *Mark Clark* .05
565 Jose DeLeon .05
566 Rich Gedman .05
567 Bernard Gilkey .05
568 Rex Hudler .05
569 Tim Jones .05
570 Donovan Osborne .05
571 Mike Perez .05
572 Gerald Perry .05
573 Bob Tewksbury .05
574 Todd Worrell .05
575 Dave Eiland .05
576 Jeremy Hernandez .05
577 Craig Lefferts .05
578 Jose Melendez .05
579 Randy Myers .05
580 Gary Pettis .05
581 Rich Rodriguez .05
582 Gary Sheffield .25
583 Craig Shipley .05
584 Kurt Stillwell .05
585 Tim Teufel .05
586 *Rod Beck* .05
587 Dave Burba .05
588 Craig Colbert .05
589 Bryan Hickerson .05
590 Mike Jackson .05
591 Mark Leonard .05
592 Jim McNamara .05
593 John Patterson .05
594 Dave Righetti .05

595	Cory Snyder	.05
596	Bill Swift	.05
597	Ted Wood	.05
598	Checklist 301-403 (Scott Sanderson)	.05
599	Checklist 404-498 (Junior Ortiz)	.05
600	Checklist 499-600 (Mike Morgan)	.05

1992 Ultra All-Rookies

The 10 promising rookies in this set could be found on special cards inserted in Ultra Series 2 foil packs.

		MT
Complete Set (10):		4.00
Common Player:		.25
1	Eric Karros	.50
2	Andy Stankiewicz	.25
3	Gary DiSarcina	.25
4	Archi Cianfrocco	.25
5	Jim McNamara	.25
6	Chad Curtis	.50
7	Kenny Lofton	.50
8	Reggie Sanders	.50
9	Pat Mahomes	.25
10	Donovan Osborne	.25

1992 Ultra All-Stars

An All-Star team from each league, with two pitchers, could be assembled by collecting these inserts from Ultra Series 2 foil packs.

		MT
Complete Set (20):		10.00
Common Player:		.20
1	Mark McGwire	1.50
2	Roberto Alomar	.50
3	Cal Ripken, Jr.	1.50
4	Wade Boggs	.60
5	Mickey Tettleton	.20
6	Ken Griffey, Jr.	1.25
7	Roberto Kelly	.20
8	Kirby Puckett	.75
9	Frank Thomas	1.00
10	Jack McDowell	.20
11	Will Clark	.35
12	Ryne Sandberg	.60
13	Barry Larkin	.25
14	Gary Sheffield	.45
15	Tom Pagnozzi	.20
16	Barry Bonds	1.00
17	Deion Sanders	.25
18	Darryl Strawberry	.20
19	David Cone	.20
20	Tom Glavine	.25

1992 Ultra Award Winners

The 25 cards in this insert issue were randomly packaged with Series 1 Ultra. One of the Cal Ripken cards (#21) can be found with a photo made from a reversed negative, as well as with the proper orientation. Neither version carries a premium.

		MT
Complete Set (26):		20.00
Common Player:		.30
1	Jack Morris	.30
2	Chuck Knoblauch	.30
3	Jeff Bagwell	1.25
4	Terry Pendleton	.30
5	Cal Ripken, Jr.	2.50
6	Roger Clemens	1.50
7	Tom Glavine	.40
8	Tom Pagnozzi	.30
9	Ozzie Smith	1.50
10	Andy Van Slyke	.30
11	Barry Bonds	2.00
12	Tony Gwynn	1.50
13	Matt Williams	.45
14	Will Clark	.45
15	Robin Ventura	.30
16	Mark Langston	.30
18	Devon White	.30
19	Don Mattingly	2.00
20	Roberto Alomar	.75
21a	Cal Ripken, Jr. (reversed negative)	2.50
21b	Cal Ripken, Jr. (correct)	2.50
22	Ken Griffey, Jr.	2.25
23	Kirby Puckett	1.50
24	Greg Maddux	1.50
25	Ryne Sandberg	1.00

1992 Ultra Tony Gwynn

This 12-card subset of Ultra's spokesman features 10 cards which were available as inserts in Series I foil packs, plus two cards labeled "Special No. 1" and "Special No. 2" which could only be obtained in a send-away offer. Some 2,000 of these cards carry a "certified" Gwynn autograph. Not part of the issue, but similar in format were a pair of extra Tony Gwynn cards. One pictures him with Fleer CEO Paul Mullan, the other shows him with the poster child for Casa de Amparo, a children's shelter in San Diego County.

		MT
Complete Set (12):		5.00
Common Card:		.50
Certified Autograph Card:		75.00
	INSERT CARDS	
1	Tony Gwynn (fielding)	.50
2	Tony Gwynn (batting)	.50
3	Tony Gwynn (fielding)	.50
4	Tony Gwynn (batting)	.50
5	Tony Gwynn (base-running)	.50
6	Tony Gwynn (awards)	.50
7	Tony Gwynn (bunting)	.50
8	Tony Gwynn (batting)	.50
9	Tony Gwynn (running)	.50
10	Tony Gwynn (batting)	.50
	SEND-AWAY CARDS	
1	Tony Gwynn (batting)	2.00
2	Tony Gwynn (fielding)	2.00
	SPECIAL CARDS	.50
---	Tony Gwynn, Paul Mullan	3.00
---	Tony Gwynn (Casa de Amparo)	7.50
1	Tony Gwynn (leaping at outfield wall)	.50
2	Tony Gwynn (batting in brown warm-up jersey)	.50
1	Tony Gwynn (batting)	.50
2	Tony Gwynn (fielding)	.50
---	Tony Gwynn, Paul Mullan	3.00
---	Casa de Amparo Salute (Tony Gwynn)	7.50

1993 Ultra

The first series of 300 cards retains Fleer's successful features from 1992, including additional gold foil stamping, UV coating, and team color-coded marbled bars on the fronts. The backs feature a stylized ballpark background, which creates a 3-D effect, stats and portrait and an action photo. Dennis Eckersley is featured in a limited-edition "Career Highlights" set and personally autographed more than 2,000 of his cards, to be randomly inserted into both series' packs. A 10-card Home Run Kings subset and 25-card Ultra Awards Winners subset were also randomly inserted in packs. Ultra Rookies cards are included in both series. Ultra's second series has three limited-edition subsets: Ultra All-Stars, Ultra All-Rookie Team, and Strikeout Kings, plus cards featuring Colorado Rockies and Florida Marlins players.

		MT
Complete Set (650):		15.00
Common Player:		.05
Series 1 or 2 Pack (14):		.75
Series 1 or 2 Wax Box (36):		10.00
1	Steve Avery	.05
2	Rafael Belliard	.05
3	Damon Berryhill	.05
4	Sid Bream	.05
5	Ron Gant	.05
6	Tom Glavine	.10
7	Ryan Klesko	.05
8	Mark Lemke	.05
9	Javier Lopez	.05
10	Greg Olson	.05
11	Terry Pendleton	.05
12	Deion Sanders	.10
13	Mike Stanton	.05
14	Paul Assenmacher	.05
15	Steve Buechele	.05
16	Frank Castillo	.05
17	Shawon Dunston	.05
18	Mark Grace	.20
19	Derrick May	.05
20	Chuck McElroy	.05
21	Mike Morgan	.05
22	Bob Scanlan	.05
23	Dwight Smith	.05
24	Sammy Sosa	1.50
25	Rick Wilkins	.05
26	Tim Belcher	.05
27	Jeff Branson	.05
28	Bill Doran	.05
29	Chris Hammond	.05
30	Barry Larkin	.10
31	Hal Morris	.05
32	Joe Oliver	.05
33	Jose Rijo	.05
34	Bip Roberts	.05
35	Chris Sabo	.05
36	Reggie Sanders	.05
37	Craig Biggio	.10
38	Ken Caminiti	.05
39	Steve Finley	.05
40	Luis Gonzalez	.20
41	Juan Guerrero	.05
42	Pete Harnisch	.05
43	Xavier Hernandez	.05
44	Doug Jones	.05
45	Al Osuna	.05
46	Eddie Taubensee	.05
47	Scooter Tucker	.05
48	Brian Williams	.05
49	Pedro Astacio	.05
50	Rafael Bournigal	.05
51	Brett Butler	.05
52	Tom Candiotti	.05

53 Eric Davis .05
54 Lenny Harris .05
55 Orel Hershiser .05
56 Eric Karros .05
57 Pedro Martinez 1.00
58 Roger McDowell .05
59 Jose Offerman .05
60 Mike Piazza 2.00
61 Moises Alou .15
62 Kent Bottenfield .05
63 Archi Cianfrocco .05
64 Greg Colbrunn .05
65 Wil Cordero .05
66 Delino DeShields .05
67 Darrin Fletcher .05
68 Ken Hill .05
69 Chris Nabholz .05
70 Mel Rojas .05
71 Larry Walker .30
72 Sid Fernandez .05
73 John Franco .05
74 Dave Gallagher .05
75 Todd Hundley .05
76 Howard Johnson .05
77 Jeff Kent .05
78 Eddie Murray .50
79 Bret Saberhagen .05
80 Chico Walker .05
81 Anthony Young .05
82 Kyle Abbott .05
83 Ruben Amaro Jr. .05
84 Juan Bell .05
85 Wes Chamberlain .05
86 Darren Daulton .05
87 Mariano Duncan .05
88 Dave Hollins .05
89 Ricky Jordan .05
90 John Kruk .05
91 Mickey Morandini .05
92 Terry Mulholland .05
93 Ben Rivera .05
94 Mike Williams .05
95 Stan Belinda .05
96 Jay Bell .05
97 Jeff King .05
98 Mike LaValliere .05
99 Lloyd McClendon .05
100 Orlando Merced .05
101 Zane Smith .05
102 Randy Tomlin .05
103 Andy Van Slyke .05
104 Tim Wakefield .05
105 John Wehner .05
106 Bernard Gilkey .05
107 Brian Jordan .05
108 Ray Lankford .05
109 Donovan Osborne .05
110 Tom Pagnozzi .05
111 Mike Perez .05
112 Lee Smith .05
113 Ozzie Smith 1.50
114 Bob Tewksbury .05
115 Todd Zeile .05
116 Andy Benes .05
117 Greg Harris .05
118 Darrin Jackson .05
119 Fred McGriff .05
120 Rich Rodriguez .05
121 Frank Seminara .05
122 Gary Sheffield .25
123 Craig Shipley .05
124 Kurt Stillwell .05
125 Dan Walters .05
126 Rod Beck .05
127 Mike Benjamin .05
128 Jeff Brantley .05
129 John Burkett .05
130 Will Clark .15
131 Royce Clayton .05
132 Steve Hosey .05
133 Mike Jackson .05
134 Darren Lewis .05
135 Kirt Manwaring .05
136 Bill Swift .05
137 Robby Thompson .05
138 Brady Anderson .05
139 Glenn Davis .05
140 Leo Gomez .05
141 Chito Martinez .05
142 Ben McDonald .05
143 Alan Mills .05
144 Mike Mussina .75
145 Gregg Olson .05
146 David Segui .05
147 Jeff Tackett .05
148 Jack Clark .05
149 Scott Cooper .05
150 Danny Darwin .05
151 John Dopson .05
152 Mike Greenwell .05
153 Tim Naehring .05
154 Tony Pena .05
155 Paul Quantrill .05
156 Mo Vaughn .40
157 Frank Viola .05
158 Bob Zupcic .05
159 Chad Curtis .05
160 Gary DiScarcina .05
161 Damion Easley .05
162 Chuck Finley .05
163 Tim Fortugno .05
164 Rene Gonzales .05
165 Joe Grahe .05
166 Mark Langston .05
167 John Orton .05
168 Luis Polonia .05
169 Julio Valera .05
170 Wilson Alvarez .05
171 George Bell .05
172 Joey Cora .05
173 Alex Fernandez .05
174 Lance Johnson .05
175 Ron Karkovice .05
176 Jack McDowell .05
177 Scott Radinsky .05
178 Tim Raines .05
179 Steve Sax .05
180 Bobby Thigpen .05
181 Frank Thomas 1.50
182 Sandy Alomar Jr. .05
183 Carlos Baerga .05
184 Felix Fermin .05
185 Thomas Howard .05
186 Mark Lewis .05
187 Derek Lilliquist .05
188 Carlos Martinez .05
189 Charles Nagy .05
190 Scott Scudder .05
191 Paul Sorrento .05
192 Jim Thome .05
193 Mark Whiten .05
194 Milt Cuyler .05
195 Rob Deer .05
196 John Doherty .05
197 Travis Fryman .05
198 Dan Gladden .05
199 Mike Henneman .05
200 John Kiely .05
201 Chad Kreuter .05
202 Scott Livingstone .05
203 Tony Phillips .05
204 Alan Trammell .05
205 Mike Boddicker .05
206 George Brett 1.50
207 Tom Gordon .05
208 Mark Gubicza .05
209 Gregg Jefferies .05
210 Wally Joyner .05
211 Kevin Koslofski .05
212 Brent Mayne .05
213 Brian McRae .05
214 Kevin McReynolds .05
215 Rusty Meacham .05
216 Steve Shifflett .05
217 James Austin .05
218 Cal Eldred .05
219 Darryl Hamilton .05
220 Doug Henry .05
221 John Jaha .05
222 Dave Nilsson .05
223 Jesse Orosco .05
224 B.J. Surhoff .05
225 Greg Vaughn .05
226 Bill Wegman .05
227 Robin Yount .75
228 Rick Aguilera .05
229 J.T. Bruett .05
230 Scott Erickson .05
231 Kent Hrbek .05
232 Terry Jorgensen .05
233 Scott Leius .05
234 Pat Mahomes .05
235 Pedro Munoz .05
236 Kirby Puckett 1.25
237 Kevin Tapani .05
238 Lenny Webster .05
239 Carl Willis .05
240 Mike Gallego .05
241 John Habyan .05
242 Pat Kelly .05
243 Kevin Maas .05
244 Don Mattingly 1.50
245 Hensley Meulens .05
246 Sam Militello .05
247 Matt Nokes .05
248 Melido Perez .05
249 Andy Stankiewicz .05
250 Randy Velarde .05
251 Bob Wickman .05
252 Bernie Williams .30
253 Lance Blankenship .05
254 Mike Bordick .05
255 Jerry Browne .05
256 Ron Darling .05
257a Dennis Eckersley .05
257b Dennis Eckersley (Wt. 195; no "MLBPA" on back - unmarked sample card) 2.00
257c Dennis Eckersley (Wt, 195; no "Printed in USA" on back - unmarked sample card) 2.00
258 Rickey Henderson .65
259 Vince Horsman .05
260 Troy Neel .05
261 Jeff Parrett .05
262 Terry Steinbach .05
263 Bob Welch .05
264 Bobby Witt .05
265 Rich Amaral .05
266 Bret Boone .10
267 Jay Buhner .05
268 Dave Fleming .05
269 Randy Johnson .75
270 Edgar Martinez .05
271 Mike Schooler .05
272 Russ Swan .05
273 Dave Valle .05
274 Omar Vizquel .05
275 Kerry Woodson .05
276 Kevin Brown .10
277 Julio Franco .05
278 Jeff Frye .05
279 Juan Gonzalez 1.00
280 Jeff Huson .05
281 Rafael Palmeiro .30
282 Dean Palmer .05
283 Roger Pavlik .05
284 Ivan Rodriguez .75
285 Kenny Rogers .05
286 Derek Bell .05
287 Pat Borders .05
288 Joe Carter .05
289 Bob MacDonald .05
290 Jack Morris .05
291 John Olerud .05
292 Ed Sprague .05
293 Todd Stottlemyre .05
294 Mike Timlin .05
295 Duane Ward .05
296 David Wells .10
297 Devon White .05
298 Checklist (Ray Lankford) .05
299 Checklist (Bobby Witt) .05
300 Checklist (Mike Piazza) .75
301 Steve Bedrosian .05
302 Jeff Blauser .05
303 Francisco Cabrera .05
304 Marvin Freeman .05
305 Brian Hunter .05
306 Dave Justice .25
307 Greg Maddux 1.25
308 *Greg McMichael* .05
309 Kent Mercker .05
310 Otis Nixon .05
311 Pete Smith .05
312 John Smoltz .10
313 Jose Guzman .05
314 Mike Harkey .05
315 Greg Hibbard .05
316 Candy Maldonado .05
317 Randy Myers .05
318 Dan Plesac .05
319 Rey Sanchez .05
320 Ryne Sandberg .75
321 *Tommy Shields* .05
322 Jose Vizcaino .05
323 *Matt Walbeck* .10
324 Willie Wilson .05
325 Tom Browning .05
326 Tim Costo .05
327 Rob Dibble .05
328 Steve Foster .05
329 Roberto Kelly .05
330 Randy Milligan .05
331 Kevin Mitchell .05
332 *Tim Pugh* .05
333 Jeff Reardon .05
334 *John Roper* .05
335 Juan Samuel .05
336 John Smiley .05
337 San Wilson .05
338 Scott Aldred .05
339 Andy Ashby .05
340 Freddie Benavides .05
341 Dante Bichette .05
342 Willie Blair .05
343 Daryl Boston .05
344 Vinny Castilla .05
345 Jerald Clark .05
346 Alex Cole .05
347 Andres Galarraga .05
348 Joe Girardi .05
349 *Ryan Hawblitzel* .05
350 Charlie Hayes .05
351 Butch Henry .05
352 Darren Holmes .05
353 Dale Murphy .20
354 David Nied .05
355 Jeff Parrett .05
356 *Steve Reed* .05
357 Bruce Ruffin .05
358 *Danny Sheaffer* .05
359 Bryn Smith .05
360 *Jim Tatum* .05
361 Eric Young .05
362 Gerald Young .05
363 Luis Aquino .05
364 *Alex Arias* .05
365 Jack Armstrong .05
366 Bret Barberie .05
367 Ryan Bowen .05
368 Greg Briley .05
369 Cris Carpenter .05
370 Chuck Carr .05
371 *Jeff Conine* .25
372 Steve Decker .05
373 Orestes Destrade .05
374 Monty Fariss .05
375 Junior Felix .05
376 Chris Hammond .05
377 Bryan Harvey .05
378 *Trevor Hoffman* .25
379 Charlie Hough .05
380 Joe Klink .05
381 *Richie Lewis* .05
382 Dave Magadan .05
383 Bob McCLure .05
384 *Scott Pose* .05
385 *Rich Renteria* .05
386 Benito Santiago .05
387 Walt Weiss .05
388 Nigel Wilson .05
389 Eric Anthony .05
390 Jeff Bagwell 1.00
391 Andujar Cedeno .05
392 Doug Drabek .05
393 Darryl Kile .05
394 Mark Portugal .05
395 Karl Rhodes .05
396 Scott Servais .05
397 Greg Swindell .05
398 Tom Goodwin .05
399 Kevin Gross .05
400 Carlos Hernandez .05
401 Ramon Martinez .05
402 Raul Mondesi .20
403 Jody Reed .05
404 Mike Sharperson .05
405 Cory Snyder .05
406 Darryl Strawberry .05
407 *Rick Trlicek* .05
408 Tim Wallach .05
409 Todd Worrell .05
410 Tavo Alvarez .05
411 *Sean Berry* .15
412 *Frank Bolick* .05
413 Cliff Floyd .05
414 Mike Gardiner .05
415 Marquis Grissom .05
416 *Tim Laker* .05
417 *Mike Lansing* .25
418 Dennis Martinez .05
419 John Vander Wal .05
420 John Wetteland .05
421 Rondell White .15
422 Bobby Bonilla .05
423 Jeromy Burnitz .05
424 *Vince Burnitz* .05
425 *Mike Draper* .05

426	Tony Fernandez	.05
427	Dwight Gooden	.05
428	Jeff Innis	.05
429	Bobby Jones	.05
430	Mike Maddux	.05
431	Charlie O'Brien	.05
432	Joe Orsulak	.05
433	Pete Schourek	.05
434	Frank Tanana	.05
435	*Ryan Thompson*	.05
436	Kim Batiste	.05
437	Mark Davis	.05
438	Jose DeLeon	.05
439	Len Dykstra	.05
440	Jim Eisenreich	.05
441	Tommy Greene	.05
442	Pete Incaviglia	.05
443	Danny Jackson	.05
444	*Todd Pratt*	.15
445	Curt Schilling	.15
446	Milt Thompson	.05
447	David West	.05
448	Mitch Williams	.05
449	Steve Cooke	.05
450	Carlos Garcia	.05
451	Al Martin	.05
452	*Blas Minor*	.05
453	Dennis Moeller	.05
454	Denny Neagle	.05
455	Don Slaught	.05
456	Lonnie Smith	.05
457	Paul Wagner	.05
458	Bob Walk	.05
459	Kevin Young	.05
460	*Rene Arocha*	.10
461	Brian Barber	.05
462	Rheal Cormier	.05
463	Gregg Jefferies	.05
464	Joe Magrane	.05
465	Omar Olivares	.05
466	Geronimo Pena	.05
467	Allen Watson	.05
468	Mark Whiten	.05
469	Derek Bell	.05
470	Phil Clark	.05
471	*Pat Gomez*	.05
472	Tony Gwynn	1.25
473	Jeremy Hernandez	.05
474	Bruce Hurst	.05
475	Phil Plantier	.05
476	*Scott Sanders*	.05
477	*Tim Scott*	.05
478	*Darrell Sherman*	.05
479	Guillermo Velasquez	.05
480	*Tim Worrell*	.05
481	Todd Benzinger	.05
482	Bud Black	.05
483	Barry Bonds	1.50
484	Dave Burba	.05
485	Bryan Hickerson	.05
486	Dave Martinez	.05
487	Willie McGee	.05
488	Jeff Reed	.05
489	Kevin Rogers	.05
490	Matt Williams	.15
491	Trevor Wilson	.05
492	Harold Baines	.05
493	Mike Devereaux	.05
494	Todd Frohwirth	.05
495	Chris Hoiles	.05
496	Luis Mercedes	.05
497	*Sherman Obando*	.05
498	*Brad Pennington*	.05
499	Harold Reynolds	.05
500	Arthur Rhodes	.05
501	Cal Ripken, Jr.	2.50
502	Rick Sutcliffe	.05
503	Fernando Valenzuela	.05
504	Mark Williamson	.05
505	Scott Bankhead	.05
506	Greg Blosser	.05
507	Ivan Calderon	.05
508	Roger Clemens	1.25
509	Andre Clemens	.05
510	Scott Fletcher	.05
511	Greg Harris	.05
512	Billy Hatcher	.05
513	Bob Melvin	.05
514	Carlos Quintana	.05
515	Luis Rivera	.05
516	Jeff Russell	.05
517	*Ken Ryan*	.05
518	Chili Davis	.05
519	*Jim Edmonds*	2.00
520	Gary Gaetti	.05
521	Torey Lovullo	.05
522	*Tony Percival*	.05
523	Tim Salmon	.15
524	Scott Sanderson	.05
525	*J.T. Snow*	.75
526	Jerome Walton	.05
527	Jason Bere	.05
528	*Rod Bolton*	.05
529	Ellis Burks	.05
530	Carlton Fisk	.75
531	Craig Grebeck	.05
532	Ozzie Guillen	.05
533	Roberto Hernandez	.05
534	Bo Jackson	.10
535	Kirk McCaskill	.05
536	Dave Stieb	.05
537	Robin Ventura	.05
538	Albert Belle	.30
539	Mike Bielecki	.05
540	Glenallen Hill	.05
541	Reggie Jefferson	.05
542	Kenny Lofton	.05
543	*Jeff Mutis*	.05
544	Junior Ortiz	.05
545	Manny Ramirez	1.00
546	Jeff Treadway	.05
547	Kevin Wickander	.05
548	Cecil Fielder	.05
549	Kirk Gibson	.05
550	*Greg Gohr*	.05
551	David Haas	.05
552	Bill Krueger	.05
553	Mike Moore	.05
554	Mickey Tettleton	.05
555	Lou Whitaker	.05
556	Kevin Appier	.05
557	*Billy Brewer*	.05
558	David Cone	.05
559	Greg Gagne	.05
560	Mark Gardner	.05
561	Phil Hiatt	.05
562	Felix Jose	.05
563	Jose Lind	.05
564	Mike Macfarlane	.05
565	Keith Miller	.05
566	Jeff Montgomery	.05
567	Hipolito Pechardo	.05
568	Ricky Bones	.05
569	Tom Brunansky	.05
570	*Joe Kmak*	.05
571	Pat Listach	.05
572	*Graeme Lloyd*	.10
573	*Carlos Maldonado*	.05
574	Josias Manzanillo	.05
575	Matt Mieske	.05
576	Kevin Reimer	.05
577	Bill Spiers	.05
578	Dickie Thon	.05
579	Willie Banks	.05
580	Jim Deshaies	.05
581	Mark Guthrie	.05
582	Brian Harper	.05
583	Chuck Knoblauch	.05
584	Gene Larkin	.05
585	Shane Mack	.05
586	David McCarty	.05
587	Mike Pagliarulo	.05
588	Mike Trombley	.05
589	Dave Winfield	1.00
590	Jim Abbott	.05
591	Wade Boggs	.60
592	*Russ Davis*	.20
593	Steve Farr	.05
594	Steve Howe	.05
595	*Mike Humphreys*	.05
596	Jimmy Key	.05
597	Jim Leyritz	.05
598	*Bobby Munoz*	.05
599	Paul O'Neill	.05
600	Spike Owen	.05
601	Mike Stanley	.05
602	Danny Tartabull	.05
603	Scott Brosius	.05
604	Storm Davis	.05
605	Eric Fox	.05
606	Goose Gossage	.05
607	Scott Hammond	.05
608	Dave Henderson	.05
609	Mark McGwire	2.50
610	*Mike Mohler*	.05
611	Edwin Nunez	.05
612	Kevin Seitzer	.05
613	Ruben Sierra	.05
614	Chris Bosio	.05
615	Norm Charlton	.05
616	*Jim Converse*	.05
617	*John Cummings*	.05
618	Mike Felder	.05
619	Ken Griffey, Jr.	2.25
620	Mike Hampton	.05
621	Erik Hanson	.05
622	Bill Haselman	.05
623	Tino Martinez	.05
624	Lee Tinsley	.05
625	*Fernando Vina*	.25
626	*David Wainhouse*	.05
627	Jose Canseco	.60
628	Benji Gil	.05
629	Tom Henke	.05
630	*David Hulse*	.05
631	Manuel Lee	.05
632	Craig Lefferts	.05
633	*Robb Nen*	.15
634	Gary Redus	.05
635	Bill Ripken	.05
636	Nolan Ryan	2.50
637	Dan Smith	.05
638	*Matt Whiteside*	.05
639	Roberto Alomar	.65
640	Juan Guzman	.05
641	Pat Hentgen	.05
642	Darrin Jackson	.05
643	Randy Knorr	.05
644	*Domingo Martinez*	.05
645	Paul Molitor	.60
646	Dick Schofield	.05
647	Dave Stewart	.05
648	Checklist (Rey Sanchez)	.05
649	Checklist (Jeremy Hernandez)	.05
650	Checklist (Junior Ortiz)	.05

1993 Ultra All-Rookies

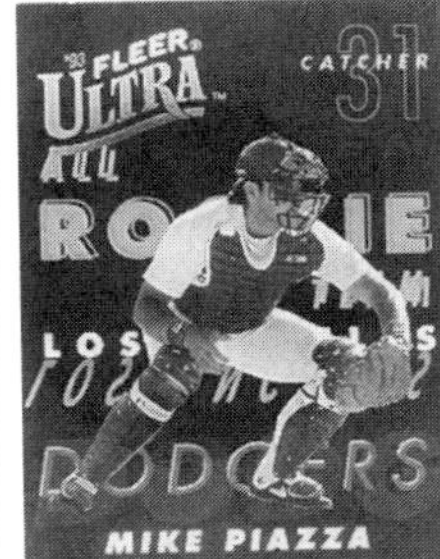

These insert cards are foil stamped on both sides and were randomly inserted into Series 2 packs. The cards have black fronts, with six different colors of type. The player's uniform number and position are located in the upper-right corner. The player's name and Ultra logo are gold-foil stamped. Backs have a black background with a player photo and career summary.

		MT
	Complete Set (10):	10.00
	Common Player:	.35
1	Rene Arocha	.35
2	Jeff Conine	.75
3	Phil Hiatt	.35
4	Mike Lansing	.50
5	Al Martin	.50
6	David Nied	.35
7	Mike Piazza	6.00
8	Tim Salmon	2.00
9	J.T. Snow	1.50
10	Kevin Young	.35

1993 Ultra All-Stars

This 20-card set features 10 of the top players from each league. Cards were randomly inserted into Series II packs and are foil stamped on both sides.

		MT
	Complete Set (20):	30.00
	Common Player:	.50
1	Darren Daulton	.50
2	Will Clark	.75
3	Ryne Sandberg	2.00
4	Barry Larkin	.50
5	Gary Sheffield	.75
6	Barry Bonds	4.00
7	Ray Lankford	.50
8	Larry Walker	1.00
9	Greg Maddux	3.00
10	Lee Smith	.50
11	Ivan Rodriguez	2.00
12	Mark McGwire	5.00
13	Carlos Baerga	.50
14	Cal Ripken, Jr.	5.00
15	Edgar Martinez	.50
16	Juan Gonzalez	2.00
17	Ken Griffey, Jr.	4.50
18	Kirby Puckett	3.00
19	Frank Thomas	4.00
20	Mike Mussina	2.00

1993 Ultra Award Winners

This insert set features 18 Top Glove players (nine from each league), two rookies of the year, three MVPs (both leagues and World Series), both Cy Young Award winners and one Player of the Year. All cards are UV coated and foil stamped on both sides and were found in Series I packs. Fronts have a black background with "Fleer Ultra Award Winners" splashed around in trendy colors. The Ultra logo, player's name and his award are spelled out in gold foil. The horizontally arranged backs have much the same elements, plus a summary of the season's performance which led to the award. There is a close-up player photo, as well.

		MT
Complete Set (25):		27.50
Common Player:		.50
1	Greg Maddux	2.00
2	Tom Pagnozzi	.50
3	Mark Grace	.75
4	Jose Lind	.50
5	Terry Pendleton	.50
6	Ozzie Smith	2.00
7	Barry Bonds	2.50
8	Andy Van Slyke	.50
9	Larry Walker	.75
10	Mark Langston	.50
11	Ivan Rodriguez	1.50
12	Don Mattingly	2.50
13	Roberto Alomar	1.50
14	Robin Ventura	.50
15	Cal Ripken, Jr.	4.00
16	Ken Griffey, Jr.	3.00
17	Kirby Puckett	2.00
18	Devon White	.50
19	Pat Listach	.50
20	Eric Karros	.50
21	Pat Borders	.50
22	Greg Maddux	2.00
23	Dennis Eckersley	.50
24	Barry Bonds	2.50
25	Gary Sheffield	.75

1993 Ultra Dennis Eckersley Career Highlights

This limited-edition subset chronicles Dennis Eckersley's illustrious career. Cards, which are UV coated and silver foil-stamped on both sides, were randomly inserted into both series' packs. Eckersley autographed more than 2,000 of the cards, which were also randomly inserted into packs. By sending in 10 Fleer Ultra wrappers plus $1, collectors could receive two additional Eckersley cards which were not available in regular packs. Card fronts have a color action photo, the background of which has been colorized into shades of purple. A black marble strip at bottom has the city name and years he was with the team in silver foil. A large black marble box in one corner has the "Dennis Eckersley Career Highlights" logo in silver foil. On back, a purple box is dropped out of a color photo, and silver-foil typography describes some phrase of Eck's career.

		MT
Complete Set (12):		2.50
Common Card:		.25
Autographed Card:		25.00
1	"Perfection" (A's 1987-92)	.25
2	"The Kid" (Indians 1975-77)	.25
3	"The Warrior" (Indians 1975-77)	.25
4	"Beantown Blazer" (Red Sox 1978-84)	.25
5	"Eckspeak" (Red Sox 1978-84)	.25
6	"Down to Earth" (Red Sox 1978-84)	.25
7	"Wrigley Bound" (Cubs 1984-86)	.25
8	"No Relief" (A's 1987-92)	.25
9	"In Control" (A's 1987-92)	.25
10	"Simply the Best" (A's 1987-92)	.25
11	"Reign of Perfection" (A's 1987-92)	.25
12	"Leaving His Mark" (A's 1987-92)	.25

1993 Ultra Home Run Kings

This insert set features top home run kings. Cards, which are UV coated and have gold foil stamping on both sides, were inserts in Series I packs.

		MT
Complete Set (10):		12.50
Common Player:		.75
1	Juan Gonzalez	2.00
2	Mark McGwire	5.00
3	Cecil Fielder	.75
4	Fred McGriff	.75
5	Albert Belle	1.00
6	Barry Bonds	3.00
7	Joe Carter	.75
8	Gary Sheffield	1.00
9	Darren Daulton	.75
10	Dave Hollins	.75

1993 Ultra Performers

An Ultra Performers set of Fleer Ultra baseball cards was offered directly to collectors in 1993. The set, available only by mail, was limited to 150,000 sets. The cards featured gold-foil stamping and UV coating on each side and a six-photo design, including five on the front of the card. Each card was identified on the back by set serial number jet-printed in black in a strip at bottom.

		MT
Complete Set (10):		6.00
Common Player:		.25
1	Barry Bonds	1.50
2	Juan Gonzalez	.75
3	Ken Griffey, Jr.	2.00
4	Eric Karros	.25
5	Pat Listach	.25
6	Greg Maddux	1.00
7	David Nied	.25
8	Gary Sheffield	.40
9	J.T. Snow	.50
10	Frank Thomas	1.50

1993 Ultra Strikeout Kings

Five of baseball's top strikeout pitchers are featured in this second-series Ultra insert set. Cards are UV coated and foil stamped on both sides. Each card front has a picture of a pitcher winding up to throw. A baseball is in the background, with the pitcher in the forefront.

		MT
Complete Set (5):		9.00
Common Player:		.50
1	Roger Clemens	2.50
2	Juan Guzman	.50
3	Randy Johnson	2.00
4	Nolan Ryan	5.00
5	John Smoltz	1.00

1994 Ultra

Issued in two series of 300 cards each, Ultra for 1994 represented a new highwater mark in production values for a mid-priced brand. Each side of the basic cards is UV coated and gold-foil embossed. Fronts feature full-bleed action photos. At bottom the player name, team, position and Fleer Ultra logo appear in gold foil above a gold-foil strip. Some rookie cards are specially designated with a large gold "ROOKIE" above the Ultra logo. Backs feature a basic background that is team color coordinated. Three more player action photos are featured on the back, along with a team logo and a modicum of stats and personal data. There is a gold stripe along the left edge and the player's name and card number appear in gold in the lower-left corner. The set features seven types of insert cards, packaged one per pack.

		MT
Complete Set (600):		20.00
Common Player:		.05
Series 1 or 2 Pack (14):		.75
Series 1 or 2 Wax Box (36):		15.00
1	Jeffrey Hammonds	.05
2	Chris Hoiles	.05
3	Ben McDonald	.05
4	Mark McLemore	.05
5	Alan Mills	.05
6	Jamie Moyer	.05
7	Brad Pennington	.05
8	Jim Poole	.05
9	Cal Ripken, Jr.	2.50
10	Jack Voigt	.05
11	Roger Clemens	1.00
12	Danny Darwin	.05
13	Andre Dawson	.20
14	Scott Fletcher	.05
15	Greg Harris	.05
16	Billy Hatcher	.05
17	Jeff Russell	.05
18	Aaron Sele	.05
19	Mo Vaughn	.40
20	Mike Butcher	.05
21	Rod Correia	.05
22	Steve Frey	.05
23	*Phil Leftwich*	.05
24	Torey Lovullo	.05
25	Ken Patterson	.05
26	Eduardo Perez	.05
27	Tim Salmon	.25
28	J.T. Snow	.10
29	Chris Turner	.05
30	Wilson Alvarez	.05
31	Jason Bere	.05
32	Joey Cora	.05
33	Alex Fernandez	.05
34	Roberto Hernandez	.05
35	Lance Johnson	.05
36	Ron Karkovice	.05
37	Kirk McCaskill	.05
38	Jeff Schwarz	.05
39	Frank Thomas	1.50
40	Sandy Alomar Jr.	.05
41	Albert Belle	.30
42	Felix Fermin	.05

43 Wayne Kirby .05
44 Tom Kramer .05
45 Kenny Lofton .05
46 Jose Mesa .05
47 Eric Plunk .05
48 Paul Sorrento .05
49 Jim Thome .05
50 Bill Wertz .05
51 John Doherty .05
52 Cecil Fielder .05
53 Travis Fryman .05
54 Chris Gomez .05
55 Mike Henneman .05
56 Chad Kreuter .05
57 Bob MacDonald .05
58 Mike Moore .05
59 Tony Phillips .05
60 Lou Whitaker .05
61 Kevin Appier .05
62 Greg Gagne .05
63 Chris Gwynn .05
64 Bob Hamelin .05
65 Chris Haney .05
66 Phil Hiatt .05
67 Felix Jose .05
68 Jose Lind .05
69 Mike Macfarlane .05
70 Jeff Montgomery .05
71 Hipolito Pichardo .05
72 Juan Bell .05
73 Cal Eldred .05
74 Darryl Hamilton .05
75 Doug Henry .05
76 Mike Ignasiak .05
77 John Jaha .05
78 Graeme Lloyd .05
79 Angel Miranda .05
80 Dave Nilsson .05
81 Troy O'Leary .05
82 Kevin Reimer .05
83 Willie Banks .05
84 Larry Casian .05
85 Scott Erickson .05
86 Eddie Guardado .05
87 Kent Hrbek .05
88 Terry Jorgensen .05
89 Chuck Knoblauch .05
90 Pat Meares .05
91 Mike Trombley .05
92 Dave Winfield 1.00
93 Wade Boggs .60
94 Scott Kamieniecki .05
95 Pat Kelly .05
96 Jimmy Key .05
97 Jim Leyritz .05
98 Bobby Munoz .05
99 Paul O'Neill .05
100 Melido Perez .05
101 Mike Stanley .05
102 Danny Tartabull .05
103 Bernie Williams .30
104 *Kurt Abbott* .25
105 Mike Bordick .05
106 Ron Darling .05
107 Brent Gates .05
108 Miguel Jimenez .05
109 Steve Karsay .05
110 Scott Lydy .05
111 Mark McGwire 2.50
112 Troy Neel .05
113 Craig Paquette .05
114 Bob Welch .05
115 Bobby Witt .05
116 Rich Amaral .05
117 Mike Blowers .05
118 Jay Buhner .05
119 Dave Fleming .05
120 Ken Griffey, Jr. 2.25
121 Tino Martinez .05
122 Marc Newfield .05
123 Ted Power .05
124 Mackey Sasser .05
125 Omar Vizquel .05
126 Kevin Brown .10
127 Juan Gonzalez .75
128 Tom Henke .05
129 David Hulse .05
130 Dean Palmer .05
131 Roger Pavlik .05
132 Ivan Rodriguez .65
133 Kenny Rogers .05
134 Doug Strange .05
135 Pat Borders .05
136 Joe Carter .05
137 Darnell Coles .05
138 Pat Hentgen .05
139 Al Leiter .05
140 Paul Molitor .60
141 John Olerud .05
142 Ed Sprague .05
143 Dave Stewart .05
144 Mike Timlin .05
145 Duane Ward .05
146 Devon White .05
147 Steve Avery .05
148 Steve Bedrosian .05
149 Damon Berryhill .05
150 Jeff Blauser .05
151 Tom Glavine .10
152 Chipper Jones 2.00
153 Mark Lemke .05
154 Fred McGriff .05
155 Greg McMichael .05
156 Deion Sanders .10
157 John Smoltz .10
158 Mark Wohlers .05
159 Jose Bautista .05
160 Steve Buechele .05
161 Mike Harkey .05
162 Greg Hibbard .05
163 Chuck McElroy .05
164 Mike Morgan .05
165 Kevin Roberson .05
166 Ryne Sandberg .75
167 Jose Vizcaino .05
168 Rick Wilkins .05
169 Willie Wilson .05
170 Willie Greene .05
171 Roberto Kelly .05
172 Larry Luebbers .05
173 Kevin Mitchell .05
174 Joe Oliver .05
175 John Roper .05
176 Johnny Ruffin .05
177 Reggie Sanders .05
178 John Smiley .05
179 Jerry Spradlin .05
180 Freddie Benavides .05
181 Dante Bichette .05
182 Willie Blair .05
183 Kent Bottenfield .05
184 Jerald Clark .05
185 Joe Girardi .05
186 Roberto Mejia .05
187 Steve Reed .05
188 Armando Reynoso .05
189 Bruce Ruffin .05
190 Eric Young .05
191 Luis Aquino .05
192 Bret Barberie .05
193 Ryan Bowen .05
194 Chuck Carr .05
195 Orestes Destrade .05
196 Richie Lewis .05
197 Dave Magadan .05
198 Bob Natal .05
199 Gary Sheffield .25
200 Matt Turner .05
201 Darrell Whitmore .05
202 Eric Anthony .05
203 Jeff Bagwell .75
204 Andujar Cedeno .05
205 Luis Gonzalez .20
206 Xavier Hernandez .05
207 Doug Jones .05
208 Darryl Kile .05
209 Scott Servais .05
210 Greg Swindell .05
211 Brian Williams .05
212 Pedro Astacio .05
213 Brett Butler .05
214 Omar Daal .05
215 Jim Gott .05
216 Raul Mondesi .25
217 Jose Offerman .05
218 Mike Piazza 2.00
219 Cory Snyder .05
220 Tim Wallach .05
221 Todd Worrell .05
222 Moises Alou .15
223 Sean Berry .05
224 Wil Cordero .05
225 Jeff Fassero .05
226 Darrin Fletcher .05
227 Cliff Floyd .05
228 Marquis Grissom .05
229 Ken Hill .05
230 Mike Lansing .05
231 Kirk Rueter .05
232 John Wetteland .05
233 Rondell White .15
234 Tim Bogar .05
235 Jeromy Burnitz .05
236 Dwight Gooden .05
237 Todd Hundley .05
238 Jeff Kent .05
239 Josias Manzanillo .05
240 Joe Orsulak .05
241 Ryan Thompson .05
242 Kim Batiste .05
243 Darren Daulton .05
243a Darren Daulton (promotional sample) 1.00
244 Tommy Greene .05
245 Dave Hollins .05
246 Pete Incaviglia .05
247 Danny Jackson .05
248 Ricky Jordan .05
249 John Kruk .05
249a John Kruk (promotional sample) 1.00
250 Mickey Morandini .05
251 Terry Mulholland .05
252 Ben Rivera .05
253 Kevin Stocker .05
254 Jay Bell .05
255 Steve Cooke .05
256 Jeff King .05
257 Al Martin .05
258 Danny Micelli .05
259 Blas Minor .05
260 Don Slaught .05
261 Paul Wagner .05
262 Tim Wakefield .05
263 Kevin Young .05
264 Rene Arocha .05
265 *Richard Batchelor* .05
266 Gregg Jefferies .05
267 Brian Jordan .05
268 Jose Oquendo .05
269 Donovan Osborne .05
270 Erik Pappas .05
271 Mike Perez .05
272 Bob Tewksbury .05
273 Mark Whiten .05
274 Todd Zeile .05
275 Andy Ashby .05
276 Brad Ausmus .05
277 Phil Clark .05
278 Jeff Gardner .05
279 Ricky Gutierrez .05
280 Tony Gwynn 1.00
281 Tim Mauser .05
282 Scott Sanders .05
283 Frank Seminara .05
284 Wally Whitehurst .05
285 Rod Beck .05
286 Barry Bonds 1.50
287 Dave Burba .05
288 Mark Carreon .05
289 Royce Clayton .05
290 Mike Jackson .05
291 Darren Lewis .05
292 Kirt Manwaring .05
293 Dave Martinez .05
294 Billy Swift .05
295 Salomon Torres .05
296 Matt Williams .15
297 Checklist 1-103 (Joe Orsulak) .05
298 Checklist 104-201 (Pete Incaviglia) .05
299 Checklist 202-300 (Todd Hundley) .05
300 Checklist - Inserts (John Doherty) .05
301 Brady Anderson .05
302 Harold Baines .05
303 Damon Buford .05
304 Mike Devereaux .05
305 Sid Fernandez .05
306 Rick Krivda .05
307 Mike Mussina .65
308 Rafael Palmeiro .30
309 Arthur Rhodes .05
310 Chris Sabo .05
311 Lee Smith .05
312 *Gregg Zaun* .15
313 Scott Cooper .05
314 Mike Greenwell .05
315 Tim Naehring .05
316 Otis Nixon .05
317 Paul Quantrill .05
318 John Valentin .05
319 Dave Valle .05
320 Frank Viola .05
321 *Brian Anderson* .15
322 Garret Anderson .05
323 Chad Curtis .05
324 Chili Davis .05
325 Gary DiSarcina .05
326 Damion Easley .05
327 Jim Edmonds .05
328 Chuck Finley .05
329 Joe Grahe .05
330 Bo Jackson .10
331 Mark Langston .05
332 Harold Reynolds .05
333 James Baldwin .05
334 *Ray Durham* .75
335 Julio Franco .05
336 Craig Grebeck .05
337 Ozzie Guillen .05
338 Joe Hall .05
339 Darrin Jackson .05
340 Jack McDowell .05
341 Tim Raines .05
342 Robin Ventura .05
343 Carlos Baerga .05
344 Derek Lilliquist .05
345 Dennis Martinez .05
346 Jack Morris .05
347 Eddie Murray .35
348 Chris Nabholz .05
349 Charles Nagy .05
350 Chad Ogea .05
351 Manny Ramirez .75
352 Omar Vizquel .05
353 Tim Belcher .05
354 Eric Davis .05
355 Kirk Gibson .05
356 Rick Greene .05
357 Mickey Tettleton .05
358 Alan Trammell .05
359 David Wells .10
360 Stan Belinda .05
361 Vince Coleman .05
362 David Cone .05
363 Gary Gaetti .05
364 Tom Gordon .05
365 Dave Henderson .05
366 Wally Joyner .05
367 Brent Mayne .05
368 Brian McRae .05
369 Michael Tucker .05
370 Ricky Bones .05
371 Brian Harper .05
372 Tyrone Hill .05
373 Mark Kiefer .05
374 Pat Listach .05
375 *Mike Matheny* .15
376 *Jose Mercedes* .05
377 Jody Reed .05
378 Kevin Seitzer .05
379 B.J. Surhoff .05
380 Greg Vaughn .05
381 Turner Ward .05
382 *Wes Weger* .05
383 Bill Wegman .05
384 Rick Aguilera .05
385 Rich Becker .05
386 Alex Cole .05
387 Steve Dunn .05
388 *Keith Garagozzo* .05
389 *LaTroy Hawkins* .10
390 Shane Mack .05
391 David McCarty .05
392 Pedro Munoz .05
393 *Derek Parks* .05
394 Kirby Puckett 1.00
395 Kevin Tapani .05
396 Matt Walbeck .05
397 Jim Abbott .05
398 Mike Gallego .05
399 Xavier Hernandez .05
400 Don Mattingly 1.50
401 Terry Mulholland .05
402 Matt Nokes .05
403 Luis Polonia .05
404 Bob Wickman .05
405 Mark Acre .05
406 *Fausto Cruz* .05
407 Dennis Eckersley .05
408 Rickey Henderson .60
409 Stan Javier .05
410 *Carlos Reyes* .05
411 Ruben Sierra .05
412 Terry Steinbach .05
413 Bill Taylor .05
414 Todd Van Poppel .05
415 Eric Anthony .05
416 Bobby Ayala .05
417 Chris Bosio .05
418 Tim Davis .05

419 Randy Johnson .75
420 Kevin King .05
421 *Anthony Manahan* .05
422 Edgar Martinez .05
423 Keith Mitchell .05
424 Roger Salkeld .05
425 *Mac Suzuki* .05
426 Dan Wilson .05
427 *Duff Brumley* .05
428 Jose Canseco .50
429 Will Clark .15
430 Steve Dreyer .05
431 Rick Helling .05
432 Chris James .05
433 Matt Whiteside .05
434 Roberto Alomar .60
435 Scott Brow .05
436 *Domingo Cedeno* .05
437 Carlos Delgado .35
438 Juan Guzman .05
439 Paul Spoljaric .05
440 Todd Stottlemyre .05
441 Woody Williams .05
442 Dave Justice .20
443 Mike Kelly .05
444 Ryan Klesko .05
445 Javier Lopez .05
446 Greg Maddux 1.00
447 Kent Mercker .05
448 Charlie O'Brien .05
449 Terry Pendleton .05
450 Mike Stanton .05
451 Tony Tarasco .05
452 *Terrell Wade* .05
453 Willie Banks .05
454 Shawon Dunston .05
455 Mark Grace .20
456 Jose Guzman .05
457 Jose Hernandez .05
458 Glenallen Hill .05
459 Blaise Ilsley .05
460 *Brooks Kieschnick* .05
461 Derrick May .05
462 Randy Myers .05
463 Karl Rhodes .05
464 Sammy Sosa 1.50
465 *Steve Trachsel* .25
466 Anthony Young .05
467 *Eddie Zambrano* .05
468 Bret Boone .10
469 Tom Browning .05
470 *Hector Carrasco* .05
471 Rob Dibble .05
472 Erik Hanson .05
473 Thomas Howard .05
474 Barry Larkin .10
475 Hal Morris .05
476 Jose Rijo .05
477 John Burke .05
478 Ellis Burks .05
479 Marvin Freeman .05
480 Andres Galarraga .05
481 Greg Harris .05
482 Charlie Hayes .05
483 Darren Holmes .05
484 Howard Johnson .05
485 *Marcus Moore* .05
486 David Nied .05
487 Mark Thompson .05
488 Walt Weiss .05
489 Kurt Abbott .05
490 Matias Carrillo .05
491 Jeff Conine .05
492 Chris Hammond .05
493 Bryan Harvey .05
494 Charlie Hough .05
495 *Yorkis Perez* .05
496 Pat Rapp .05
497 Benito Santiago .05
498 David Weathers .05
499 Craig Biggio .10
500 Ken Caminiti .05
501 Doug Drabek .05
502 *Tony Eusebio* .20
503 Steve Finley .05
504 Pete Harnisch .05
505 Brian Hunter .05
506 Domingo Jean .05
507 Todd Jones .05
508 Orlando Miller .05
509 James Mouton .05
510 Roberto Petagine .05
511 Shane Reynolds .05
512 Mitch Williams .05
513 Billy Ashley .05
514 Tom Candiotti .05
515 Delino DeShields .05
516 Kevin Gross .05
517 Orel Hershiser .05
518 Eric Karros .05
519 Ramon Martinez .05
520 *Chan Ho Park* .75
521 Henry Rodriguez .05
522 Joey Eischen .05
523 Rod Henderson .05
524 Pedro Martinez .75
525 Mel Rojas .05
526 Larry Walker .30
527 *Gabe White* .20
528 Bobby Bonilla .05
529 Jonathan Hurst .05
530 Bobby Jones .05
531 Kevin McReynolds .05
532 Bill Pulsipher .05
533 Bret Saberhagen .05
534 David Segui .05
535 Pete Smith .05
536 *Kelly Stinnett* .10
537 Dave Telgheder .05
538 *Quilvio Veras* .15
539 Jose Vizcaino .05
540 Pete Walker .05
541 Ricky Bottalico .05
542 Wes Chamberlain .05
543 Mariano Duncan .05
544 Len Dykstra .05
545 Jim Eisenreich .05
546 *Phil Geisler* .05
547 *Wayne Gomes* .15
548 Doug Jones .05
549 Jeff Juden .05
550 Mike Lieberthal .05
551 *Tony Longmire* .05
552 Tom Marsh .05
553 Bobby Munoz .05
554 Curt Schilling .15
555 Carlos Garcia .05
556 *Ravelo Manzanillo* .05
557 Orlando Merced .05
558 *Will Pennyfeather* .05
559 Zane Smith .05
560 Andy Van Slyke .05
561 Rick White .05
562 Luis Alicea .05
563 *Brian Barber* .05
564 *Clint Davis* .05
565 Bernard Gilkey .05
566 Ray Lankford .05
567 Tom Pagnozzi .05
568 Ozzie Smith 1.00
569 Rick Sutcliffe .05
570 Allen Watson .05
571 Dmitri Young .05
572 Derek Bell .05
573 Andy Benes .05
574 Archi Cianfrocco .05
575 Joey Hamilton .05
576 Gene Harris .05
577 Trevor Hoffman .05
578 *Tim Hyers* .05
579 *Brian Johnson* .05
580 *Keith Lockhart* .10
581 Pedro Martinez .05
582 Ray McDavid .05
583 Phil Plantier .05
584 Bip Roberts .05
585 Dave Staton .05
586 Todd Benzinger .05
587 John Burkett .05
588 Bryan Hickerson .05
589 Willie McGee .05
590 John Patterson .05
591 Mark Portugal .05
592 Kevin Rogers .05
593 *Joe Rosselli* .05
594 *Steve Soderstrom* .05
595 Robby Thompson .05
596 125th Anniversary card .05
597 Checklist .05
598 Checklist .05
599 Checklist .05
600 Checklist .05

1994 Ultra All-Rookie Team

A stylized sunrise landscape is the background for this insert set featuring top rookies and inserted into Ultra Series II packs at the rate of about one per 10. Backs repeat the motif with an action photo. Both sides are gold-foil enhanced and UV-coated.

		MT
Complete Set (10):		6.00
Common Player:		.50
1	Kurt Abbott	.50
2	Carlos Delgado	3.00
3	Cliff Floyd	1.00
4	Jeffrey Hammonds	.50
5	Ryan Klesko	1.00
6	Javier Lopez	1.00
7	Raul Mondesi	1.00
8	James Mouton	.50
9	Chan Ho Park	1.00
10	Dave Staton	.50

1994 Ultra All-Rookie Team Supers

This super-size (3-1/2" x 5-1/2") version of the Fleer Ultra II insert set featuring top rookies was included one per case of hobby packaging. Cards are identical to the smaller version. Both sides are gold-foil enhanced and UV-coated.

		MT
Complete Set (10):		12.50
Common Player:		.75
1	Kurt Abbott	.75
2	Carlos Delgado	3.00
3	Cliff Floyd	2.00
4	Jeffrey Hammonds	.75
5	Ryan Klesko	2.00
6	Javier Lopez	2.00
7	Raul Mondesi	2.00
8	James Mouton	.75
9	Chan Ho Park	2.00
10	Dave Staton	.75

1994 Ultra All-Stars

Fleer's opinion of the top 20 players in 1994 are featured in this most common of the Series II Ultra insert sets. Silver-foil highlights enhance the chase cards, found, according to stated odds, once per three packs, on average. National Leaguers have purple backgrounds front and back, American Leaguers have red.

		MT
Complete Set (20):		7.50
Common Player:		.25
1	Chris Hoiles	.25
2	Frank Thomas	.75
3	Roberto Alomar	.50
4	Cal Ripken, Jr.	1.50
5	Robin Ventura	.25
6	Albert Belle	.35
7	Juan Gonzalez	.50
8	Ken Griffey, Jr.	1.25
9	John Olerud	.25
10	Jack McDowell	.25
11	Mike Piazza	1.00
12	Fred McGriff	.25
13	Ryne Sandberg	.50
14	Jay Bell	.25
15	Matt Williams	.30
16	Barry Bonds	.75
17	Len Dykstra	.25
18	Dave Justice	.35
19	Tom Glavine	.30
20	Greg Maddux	.65

1994 Ultra Award Winners

The most common of the Fleer Ultra insert sets for 1994 is the 25-card "Award Winners." Horizontal format cards feature front and back background with a gold-embossed look. A player action photo appears on the front. A gold-foil seal on the front has a symbolic player representation flanked by the pictured player's name and award. A gold Fleer Ultra logo is at top. Backs have a player portrait photo and a write-up about the award. The name of the award and the player's name appear in gold foil at the top. Stated odds of finding an Award Winners card were one in three packs.

		MT
Complete Set (25):		10.00
Common Player:		.20
1	Ivan Rodriguez	.50
2	Don Mattingly	1.00
3	Roberto Alomar	.50
4	Robin Ventura	.20
5	Omar Vizquel	.20
6	Ken Griffey, Jr.	1.50
7	Kenny Lofton	.20
8	Devon White	.20
9	Mark Langston	.20
10	Kirt Manwaring	.20
11	Mark Grace	.30
12	Robby Thompson	.20
13	Matt Williams	.25
14	Jay Bell	.20
15	Barry Bonds	1.00
16	Marquis Grissom	.20
17	Larry Walker	.30
18	Greg Maddux	.75
19	Frank Thomas	1.00
20	Barry Bonds	1.00
21	Paul Molitor	.40
22	Jack McDowell	.20
23	Greg Maddux	.75
24	Tim Salmon	.25
25	Mike Piazza	1.25

1994 Ultra Career Achievement Awards

The outstanding careers of five of baseball's top veteran stars are recognized in this chase set, inserted on average once every 21 packs of Ultra Series II. The gold-highlighted horizontal fronts combine a current color photo with a background single-tint photo from the player's earlier days. Backs flip-flop the photo use, with the current photo in the background and the earlier photo in full color in the foreground. The gold Ultra Career Achievement Award seal is repeated on back, as well.

		MT
Complete Set (5):		4.00
Common Player:		.50
1	Joe Carter	.50
2	Paul Molitor	.75
3	Cal Ripken, Jr.	2.50
4	Ryne Sandberg	.75
5	Dave Winfield	1.00

1994 Ultra Firemen

Ten of the major leagues' leading relief pitchers are featured in this Ultra insert set. Cards have an action photo of the player superimposed over a background photo of a fire truck. A shield at top, in gold foil, has a smoke-eater's helmet, stylized flames and proclaims the player an "Ultra Fireman." Backs are horizontal in format and feature the pumper's control panel in the background photo. A color player portrait photo appears on one side, with a description of his relief role and successes in a whitened box. Fireman crads are found, on average, once per 11 packs, according to stated odds.

		MT
Complete Set (10):		2.50
Common Player:		.25
1	Jeff Montgomery	.25
2	Duane Ward	.25
3	Tom Henke	.25
4	Roberto Hernandez	.25
5	Dennis Eckersley	.50
6	Randy Myers	.25
7	Rod Beck	.25
8	Bryan Harvey	.25
9	John Wetteland	.25
10	Mitch Williams	.25

1994 Ultra Hitting Machines

A heavy metal background of gears and iron-letter logo is featured in this insert set honoring the game's top hitters. The cards turn up about once in every five packs of Ultra Series II. Both front and back are highlighted in silver foil.

		MT
Complete Set (10):		5.00
Common Player:		.25
1	Roberto Alomar	.50
2	Carlos Baerga	.25
3	Barry Bonds	.75
4	Andres Galarraga	.25
5	Juan Gonzalez	.50
6	Tony Gwynn	.65
7	Paul Molitor	.40
8	John Olerud	.25
9	Mike Piazza	1.25
10	Frank Thomas	.75

1994 Ultra Home Run Kings

One of two high-end insert sets in '94 Ultra is the 12-card "Home Run Kings" found exclusively in 14-card foil packs, on an average of once per 36-pack box. Featuring the technology Fleer calls "etched metallization," the cards have a black background with a red and blue foil representation of a batter. An action photo of a player taking a mighty cut or starting his home-run trot is featured. A large gold-foil "Home Run King" crown-and-shield device are in an upper corner, while the Ultra logo and player name are in gold foil at bottom. Backs have a white background with the red and blue batter symbol. The player's name appears in gold foil at the top, along with a portrait photo and a summary of his home run prowess.

		MT
Complete Set (12):		22.50
Common Player:		1.00
1	Juan Gonzalez	2.50
2	Ken Griffey, Jr.	6.00
3	Frank Thomas	4.00
4	Albert Belle	1.50
5	Rafael Palmeiro	1.50
6	Joe Carter	1.00
7	Barry Bonds	4.00
8	Dave Justice	1.50
9	Matt Williams	1.25
10	Fred McGriff	1.00
11	Ron Gant	1.00
12	Mike Piazza	5.00

1994 Ultra League Leaders

Arguably the least attractive of the '94 Ultra inserts are the "League Leaders." Fronts feature a full-bleed action photo on which the bottom has been re-colored to a team hue giving the effect of teal, purple and magenta miasmas rising from the turf. An Ultra logo appears in gold foil in an upper corner, with the player's name in gold foil at about the dividing line between the natural color and colorized portions of the photo. A large "League Leader" appears in the bottom half of the photo, with the category led printed in the lower-left. Backs repeat the team color at top, fading to white at the bottom. In gold foil are "League Leader" and the category. A portrait photo appears at bottom. Several paragraphs detail the league leading performance of the previous season.

		MT
Complete Set (10):		3.00
Common Player:		.25
1	John Olerud	.25
2	Rafael Palmeiro	.40
3	Kenny Lofton	.25
4	Jack McDowell	.25
5	Randy Johnson	1.00
6	Andres Galarraga	.25
7	Len Dykstra	.25
8	Chuck Carr	.25
9	Tom Glavine	.35
10	Jose Rijo	.25

1994 Ultra On-Base Leaders

One of the lesser-known, but most valuable, stats - on-base percentage - is featured in this subset found exclusively in 17-card packs, at the rate of about one per 37 packs. The fronts feature color photos against a stat-filled printed-foil background.

		MT
Complete Set (12):		35.00
Common Player:		2.00
1	Roberto Alomar	4.00
2	Barry Bonds	6.00
3	Len Dykstra	2.00
4	Andres Galarraga	2.00
5	Mark Grace	3.00
6	Ken Griffey, Jr.	7.50
7	Gregg Jefferies	2.00
8	Orlando Merced	2.00
9	Paul Molitor	4.00
10	John Olerud	2.00
11	Tony Phillips	2.00
12	Frank Thomas	6.00

1994 Ultra Phillies Finest

As a tribute to two of Fleer's home-team heroes, the Philadelphia-based card company created an Ultra insert set featuring 12 cards each of "Phillies Finest," John Kruk and Darren Daulton. Twenty of the cards were issued as Series 1 and 2 inserts, about one in every eight packs, while four were available only by a mail-in offer. Fronts feature action photos with large block letters popping out of the background. The Ultra logo and player name appear in gold foil. Backs have portrait photos and career summaries, with the player's name and card number in gold foil. Daulton and Kruk each autographed 1,000 of the inserts. Stated odds of finding the autographed cards were one in 11,000 packs. Values listed are per card.

		MT
Complete Set (24):		5.00
Common player:		.25
Autographed Daulton:		25.00
Autographed Kruk:		40.00
1-5	Darren Daulton	.25
6-10	John Kruk	.25
11-15	Darren Daulton	.25
16-20	John Kruk	.25
9a	John Kruk (PROMOTIONAL SAMPLE)	1.50
	MAIL-IN CARDS	
1M, 3M	Darren Daulton	.75
2M, 4M	John Kruk	.75

1	Darren Daulton (holding mask and glove)	.25
2	Darren Daulton (power swing, home uniform)	.25
3	Darren Daulton (blocking home plate)	.25
4	Darren Daulton (home run trot, home uniform)	.25
1M	Darren Daulton (standing, throwing)	.70
2M	John Kruk (ready to field)	.70
3M	Darren Daulton (awaiting pitch)	.70
4M	John Kruk (running)	.70

1994 Ultra Rising Stars

An outer space background printed on metallic foil sets this chase set apart from most of the rest of the Ultra Series II inserts. The silver-foil enhanced cards of projected superstars of tomorrow are found on average once every 37 packs.

		MT
Complete Set (12):		25.00
Common Player:		1.50
1	Carlos Baerga	1.50
2	Jeff Bagwell	5.00
3	Albert Belle	3.00
4	Cliff Floyd	1.50
5	Travis Fryman	1.50
6	Marquis Grissom	1.50
7	Kenny Lofton	1.50
8	John Olerud	1.50
9	Mike Piazza	8.00
10	Kirk Rueter	1.50
11	Tim Salmon	2.50
12	Aaron Sele	1.50

1994 Ultra RBI Kings

Exclusive to the 19-card jumbo packs of Fleer Ultra are a series of 12 "RBI Kings" insert cards, found, according to stated odds, one per 36 packs. The horizontal-format card front uses Fleer's "etched metallized" technology to produce a sepia-toned background action photo, in front of which is a color player photo. An Ultra logo appears in gold foil in an upper corner while a fancy shield-and-scroll "RBI King" logo and the player's name are in gold at the bottom. Backs repeat the basic front motif and include a color player portrait photo, his name in gold foil and a paragraph justifying his selection as an RBI King.

		MT
Complete Set (12):		32.50
Common Player:		2.00
1	Albert Belle	2.50
2	Frank Thomas	5.00
3	Joe Carter	2.00
4	Juan Gonzalez	4.00
5	Cecil Fielder	2.00
6	Carlos Baerga	2.00
7	Barry Bonds	5.00
8	David Justice	2.50
9	Ron Gant	2.00
10	Mike Piazza	7.50
11	Matt Williams	2.50
12	Darren Daulton	2.00

1994 Ultra Second Year Standouts

Approximately once every 11 packs, the Ultra insert find is a "Second Year Standout" card. Ten of the game's sophomore stars are featured. Fronts feature a pair of action photos against a team-color background. Gold-foil highlights are the Ultra logo, the player's name and a "Second Year Standout" shield. The shield and player name are repeated in gold foil on the back, as is the team color background. There is a player portrait photo at bottom and a summary of the player's 1993 season.

		MT
Complete Set (10):		6.00
Common Player:		.25
1	Jason Bere	.40
2	Brent Gates	.25
3	Jeffrey Hammonds	.25
4	Tim Salmon	1.00
5	Aaron Sele	.40
6	Chuck Carr	.25
7	Jeff Conine	.60
8	Greg McMichael	.25
9	Mike Piazza	4.00
10	Kevin Stocker	.25

1994 Ultra Strikeout Kings

A gold-foil "Strikeout Kings" crown-and-shield logo is featured on the front of this chase set. Cards are found on average once per seven packs. Each of the cards features the K-king in sequential action photos. Backs have a larger action photo with a large version of the Strikeout King shield in the background.

		MT
Complete Set (5):		2.50
Common Player:		.40
1	Randy Johnson	.75
2	Mark Langston	.40
3	Greg Maddux	1.00
4	Jose Rijo	.40
5	John Smoltz	.60

1995 Ultra

A clean design enhanced with three different colors of metallic foil graphics is featured on the basic cards of 1995 Fleer Ultra. Two series of 250 cards each were issued with cards arranged alphabetically within team, also sequenced alphabetically. Fronts have a gold-foil Ultra logo in an upper corner, with the player's name and team logo in a team-color coded foil at bottom. There are no other graphic elements on the borderless photos. Backs have a large photo rendered in a single color, again team-coded. A postage-stamp sized color photo in one corner is flanked by a few vital stats in silver foil. Career and '94 stats are printed at bottom, enhanced by the foil color from the front. Cards were issued in 12-card retail and hobby packs at $1.99 and jumbo prepriced ($2.69) magazine packs. Each pack contains one of the several insert series from the appropriate series.

		MT
Complete Set (450):		15.00
Common Player:		.05
Gold Medallion:		2X
Series 1 or 2 Pack (12):		1.00
Series 1 or 2 Wax Box (36):		25.00
1	Brady Anderson	.05
2	Sid Fernandez	.05
3	Jeffrey Hammonds	.05
4	Chris Hoiles	.05
5	Ben McDonald	.05
6	Mike Mussina	.65
7	Rafael Palmeiro	.30
8	Jack Voigt	.05
9	Wes Chamberlain	.05
10	Roger Clemens	1.00
11	Chris Howard	.05
12	Tim Naehring	.05
13	Otis Nixon	.05
14	Rich Rowland	.05
15	Ken Ryan	.05
16	John Valentin	.05
17	Mo Vaughn	.40
18	Brian Anderson	.05
19	Chili Davis	.05
20	Damion Easley	.05
21	Jim Edmonds	.05
22	Mark Langston	.05
23	Tim Salmon	.25
24	J.T. Snow	.05
25	Chris Turner	.05
26	Wilson Alvarez	.05
27	Joey Cora	.05
28	Alex Fernandez	.05
29	Roberto Hernandez	.05
30	Lance Johnson	.05
31	Ron Karkovice	.05
32	Kirk McCaskill	.05
33	Tim Raines	.05
34	Frank Thomas	1.25
35	Sandy Alomar	.05
36	Albert Belle	.30
37	Mark Clark	.05
38	Kenny Lofton	.05
39	Eddie Murray	.50
40	Eric Plunk	.05
41	Manny Ramirez	.75
42	Jim Thome	.05
43	Omar Vizquel	.05
44	Danny Bautista	.05
45	Junior Felix	.05
46	Cecil Fielder	.05
47	Chris Gomez	.05
48	Chad Kreuter	.05
49	Mike Moore	.05
50	Tony Phillips	.05
51	Alan Trammell	.05
52	David Wells	.10
53	Kevin Appier	.05
54	Billy Brewer	.05
55	David Cone	.05
56	Greg Gagne	.05
57	Bob Hamelin	.05
58	Jose Lind	.05
59	Brent Mayne	.05
60	Brian McRae	.05
61	Terry Shumpert	.05
62	Ricky Bones	.05
63	Mike Fetters	.05
64	Darryl Hamilton	.05
65	John Jaha	.05
66	Graeme Lloyd	.05
67	Matt Mieske	.05
68	Kevin Seitzer	.05
69	Jose Valentin	.05
70	Turner Ward	.05
71	Rick Aguilera	.05
72	Rich Becker	.05
73	Alex Cole	.05
74	Scott Leius	.05
75	Pat Meares	.05
76	Kirby Puckett	1.00
77	Dave Stevens	.05
78	Kevin Tapani	.05
79	Matt Walbeck	.05
80	Wade Boggs	.65
81	Scott Kamieniecki	.05
82	Pat Kelly	.05
83	Jimmy Key	.05
84	Paul O'Neill	.05
85	Luis Polonia	.05
86	Mike Stanley	.05
87	Danny Tartabull	.05
88	Bob Wickman	.05
89	Mark Acre	.05
90	Geronimo Berroa	.05
91	Mike Bordick	.05
92	Ron Darling	.05
93	Stan Javier	.05
94	Mark McGwire	2.00
95	Troy Neel	.05
96	Ruben Sierra	.05
97	Terry Steinbach	.05
98	Eric Anthony	.05
99	Chris Bosio	.05
100	Dave Fleming	.05
101	Ken Griffey Jr.	1.75
102	Reggie Jefferson	.05
103	Randy Johnson	.65
104	Edgar Martinez	.05
105	Bill Risley	.05
106	Dan Wilson	.05
107	Cris Carpenter	.05
108	Will Clark	.15
109	Juan Gonzalez	.75
110	Rusty Greer	.05
111	David Hulse	.05
112	Roger Pavlik	.05
113	Ivan Rodriguez	.65
114	Doug Strange	.05
115	Matt Whiteside	.05
116	Roberto Alomar	.60
117	Brad Cornett	.05
118	Carlos Delgado	.35
119	Alex Gonzalez	.10
120	Darren Hall	.05
121	Pat Hentgen	.05
122	Paul Molitor	.65
123	Ed Sprague	.05
124	Devon White	.05
125	Tom Glavine	.10
126	Dave Justice	.20
127	Roberto Kelly	.05
128	Mark Lemke	.05
129	Greg Maddux	1.00
130	Charles Johnson	.05
131	Kent Mercker	.05
132	Charlie O'Brien	.05
133	John Smoltz	.10
134	Willie Banks	.05
135	Steve Buechele	.05
136	Kevin Foster	.05
137	Glenallen Hill	.05
138	Ray Sanchez	.05
139	Sammy Sosa	1.25
140	Steve Trachsel	.05
141	Rick Wilkins	.05
142	Jeff Brantley	.05
143	Hector Carrasco	.05
144	Kevin Jarvis	.05
145	Barry Larkin	.10
146	Chuck McElroy	.05
147	Jose Rijo	.05
148	Johnny Ruffin	.05
149	Deion Sanders	.10
150	Eddie Taubensee	.05
151	Dante Bichette	.05
152	Ellis Burks	.05
153	Joe Girardi	.05
154	Charlie Hayes	.05
155	Mike Kingery	.05
156	Steve Reed	.05
157	Kevin Ritz	.05
158	Bruce Ruffin	.05
159	Eric Young	.05
160	Kurt Abbott	.05
161	Chuck Carr	.05
162	Chris Hammond	.05
163	Bryan Harvey	.05
164	Terry Mathews	.05
165	Yorkis Perez	.05
166	Pat Rapp	.05
167	Gary Sheffield	.25
168	Dave Weathers	.05
169	Jeff Bagwell	.75
170	Ken Caminiti	.05
171	Doug Drabek	.05
172	Steve Finley	.05
173	John Hudek	.05
174	Todd Jones	.05
175	James Mouton	.05
176	Shane Reynolds	.05
177	Scott Servais	.05
178	Tom Candiotti	.05
179	Omar Daal	.05
180	Darren Dreifort	.05
181	Eric Karros	.05
182	Ramon Martinez	.05
183	Raul Mondesi	.20
184	Henry Rodriguez	.05
185	Todd Worrell	.05
186	Moises Alou	.15
187	Sean Berry	.05
188	Wil Cordero	.05
189	Jeff Fassero	.05
190	Darrin Fletcher	.05
191	Butch Henry	.05
192	Ken Hill	.05
193	Mel Rojas	.05
194	John Wetteland	.05
195	Bobby Bonilla	.05
196	Rico Brogna	.05
197	Bobby Jones	.05
198	Jeff Kent	.05
199	Josias Manzanillo	.05
200	Kelly Stinnett	.05
201	Ryan Thompson	.05
202	Jose Vizcaino	.05
203	Lenny Dykstra	.05
204	Jim Eisenreich	.05
205	Dave Hollins	.05
206	Mike Lieberthal	.05
207	Mickey Morandini	.05
208	Bobby Munoz	.05
209	Curt Schilling	.15
210	Heathcliff Slocumb	.05
211	David West	.05
212	Dave Clark	.05
213	Steve Cooke	.05
214	Midre Cummings	.05
215	Carlos Garcia	.05
216	Jeff King	.05
217	Jon Lieber	.05
218	Orlando Merced	.05
219	Don Slaught	.05
220	Rick White	.05
221	Rene Arocha	.05
222	Bernard Gilkey	.05
223	Brian Jordan	.05
224	Tom Pagnozzi	.05
225	Vicente Palacios	.05
226	Geronimo Pena	.05
227	Ozzie Smith	1.00
228	Allen Watson	.05
229	Mark Whiten	.05
230	Brad Ausmus	.05
231	Derek Bell	.05
232	Andy Benes	.05
233	Tony Gwynn	1.00
234	Joey Hamilton	.05
235	Luis Lopez	.05
236	Pedro A. Martinez	.05
237	Scott Sanders	.05
238	Eddie Williams	.05
239	Rod Beck	.05
240	Dave Burba	.05
241	Darren Lewis	.05
242	Kirt Manwaring	.05
243	Mark Portugal	.05
244	Darryl Strawberry	.05
245	Robby Thompson	.05
246	William VanLandingham	.05
247	Matt Williams	.15
248	Checklist	.05
249	Checklist	.05
250	Checklist	.05
251	Harold Baines	.05
252	Bret Barberie	.05
253	Armando Benitez	.05
254	Mike Devereaux	.05
255	Leo Gomez	.05
256	Jamie Moyer	.05
257	Arthur Rhodes	.05
258	Cal Ripken Jr.	2.00
259	Luis Alicea	.05
260	Jose Canseco	.50
261	Scott Cooper	.05
262	Andre Dawson	.20
263	Mike Greenwell	.05
264	Aaron Sele	.05
265	Garret Anderson	.05
266	Chad Curtis	.05
267	Gary DiSarcina	.05
268	Chuck Finley	.05
269	Rex Hudler	.05
270	Andrew Lorraine	.05
271	Spike Owen	.05
272	Lee Smith	.05
273	Jason Bere	.05
274	Ozzie Guillen	.05
275	Norberto Martin	.05
276	Scott Ruffcorn	.05
277	Robin Ventura	.05
278	Carlos Baerga	.05
279	Jason Grimsley	.05
280	Dennis Martinez	.05
281	Charles Nagy	.05
282	Paul Sorrento	.05
283	Dave Winfield	1.00
284	John Doherty	.05
285	Travis Fryman	.05
286	Kirk Gibson	.05
287	Lou Whitaker	.05
288	Gary Gaetti	.05
289	Tom Gordon	.05
290	Mark Gubicza	.05
291	Wally Joyner	.05
292	Mike Macfarlane	.05
293	Jeff Montgomery	.05
294	Jeff Cirillo	.05
295	Cal Eldred	.05
296	Pat Listach	.05
297	Jose Mercedes	.05
298	Dave Nilsson	.05
299	Duane Singleton	.05
300	Greg Vaughn	.05
301	Scott Erickson	.05
302	Denny Hocking	.05
303	Chuck Knoblauch	.05
304	Pat Mahomes	.05
305	Pedro Munoz	.05
306	Erik Schullstrom	.05
307	Jim Abbott	.05
308	Tony Fernandez	.05
309	Sterling Hitchcock	.05
310	Jim Leyritz	.05
311	Don Mattingly	1.25
312	Jack McDowell	.05
313	Melido Perez	.05
314	Bernie Williams	.30
315	Scott Brosius	.05
316	Dennis Eckersley	.05
317	Brent Gates	.05
318	Rickey Henderson	.75
319	Steve Karsay	.05
320	Steve Ontiveros	.05
321	Bill Taylor	.05
322	Todd Van Poppel	.05
323	Bob Welch	.05
324	Bobby Ayala	.05
325	Mike Blowers	.05
326	Jay Buhner	.05
327	Felix Fermin	.05
328	Tino Martinez	.05
329	Marc Newfield	.05
330	Greg Pirkl	.05
331	Alex Rodriguez	2.00
332	Kevin Brown	.10
333	John Burkett	.05
334	Jeff Frye	.05
335	Kevin Gross	.05
336	Dean Palmer	.05
337	Joe Carter	.05
338	Shawn Green	.30
339	Juan Guzman	.05
340	Mike Huff	.05
341	Al Leiter	.05
342	John Olerud	.05
343	Dave Stewart	.05
344	Todd Stottlemyre	.05
345	Steve Avery	.05
346	Jeff Blauser	.05
347	Chipper Jones	1.50
348	Mike Kelly	.05
349	Ryan Klesko	.05
350	Javier Lopez	.05
351	Fred McGriff	.05
352	Jose Oliva	.05
353	Terry Pendleton	.05
354	Mike Stanton	.05
355	Tony Tarasco	.05

356	Mark Wohlers	.05
357	Jim Bullinger	.05
358	Shawon Dunston	.05
359	Mark Grace	.25
360	Derrick May	.05
361	Randy Myers	.05
362	Karl Rhodes	.05
363	Bret Boone	.10
364	Brian Dorsett	.05
365	Ron Gant	.05
366	Brian R. Hunter	.05
367	Hal Morris	.05
368	Jack Morris	.05
369	John Roper	.05
370	Reggie Sanders	.05
371	Pete Schourek	.05
372	John Smiley	.05
373	Marvin Freeman	.05
374	Andres Galarraga	.05
375	Mike Munoz	.05
376	David Nied	.05
377	Walt Weiss	.05
378	Greg Colbrunn	.05
379	Jeff Conine	.05
380	Charles Johnson	.05
381	Kurt Miller	.05
382	Robb Nen	.05
383	Benito Santiago	.05
384	Craig Biggio	.10
385	Tony Eusebio	.05
386	Luis Gonzalez	.20
387	Brian L. Hunter	.05
388	Darryl Kile	.05
389	Orlando Miller	.05
390	Phil Plantier	.05
391	Greg Swindell	.05
392	Billy Ashley	.05
393	Pedro Astacio	.05
394	Brett Butler	.05
395	Delino DeShields	.05
396	Orel Hershiser	.05
397	Garey Ingram	.05
398	Chan Ho Park	.15
399	Mike Piazza	1.50
400	Ismael Valdes	.05
401	Tim Wallach	.05
402	Cliff Floyd	.05
403	Marquis Grissom	.05
404	Mike Lansing	.05
405	Pedro Martinez	.65
406	Kirk Rueter	.05
407	Tim Scott	.05
408	Jeff Shaw	.05
409	Larry Walker	.30
410	Rondell White	.10
411	John Franco	.05
412	Todd Hundley	.05
413	Jason Jacome	.05
414	Joe Orsulak	.05
415	Bret Saberhagen	.05
416	David Segui	.05
417	Darren Daulton	.05
418	Mariano Duncan	.05
419	Tommy Greene	.05
420	Gregg Jefferies	.05
421	John Kruk	.05
422	Kevin Stocker	.05
423	Jay Bell	.05
424	Al Martin	.05
425	Denny Neagle	.05
426	Zane Smith	.05
427	Andy Van Slyke	.05
428	Paul Wagner	.05
429	Tom Henke	.05
430	Danny Jackson	.05
431	Ray Lankford	.05
432	John Mabry	.05
433	Bob Tewksbury	.05
434	Todd Zeile	.05
435	Andy Ashby	.05
436	Andujar Cedeno	.05
437	Donnie Elliott	.05
438	Bryce Florie	.05
439	Trevor Hoffman	.05
440	Melvin Nieves	.05
441	Bip Roberts	.05
442	Barry Bonds	1.25
443	Royce Clayton	.05
444	Mike Jackson	.05
445	John Patterson	.05
446	J.R. Phillips	.05
447	Bill Swift	.05
448	Checklist	.05
449	Checklist	.05
450	Checklist	.05

1995 Ultra Gold Medallion

Less than 10% of the production run of Fleer Ultra (regular and insert sets) was produced in a special parallel Gold Medallion edition. On these special cards an embossed round gold seal replaces the Fleer Ultra logo in the upper corner. One Gold Medallion card was inserted into each Ultra foil pack.

	MT
Complete Set (450):	80.00
Common Player:	.25

(See 1995 Ultra for checklist and base card values.)

1995 Ultra All-Rookies

Enlarged pieces of the central color action photo, set on a white background, make up the front design on these inserts. The player's name, card title and Ultra logo are printed in silver foil. Horizontal backs have another color photo, which is also repeated in single-color fashion. A career summary is printed over the larger photo. The All-Rookie inserts are found only in 12-card packs, at the rate of about one per four packs.

		MT
Complete Set (10):		4.50
Common Player:		.30
Gold Medallion:		2X
1	Cliff Floyd	.50
2	Chris Gomez	.30
3	Rusty Greer	.30
4	Bob Hamelin	.30
5	Joey Hamilton	.30
6	John Hudek	.30
7	Ryan Klesko	.50
8	Raul Mondesi	.75
9	Manny Ramirez	3.00
10	Steve Trachsel	.30

1995 Ultra All-Stars

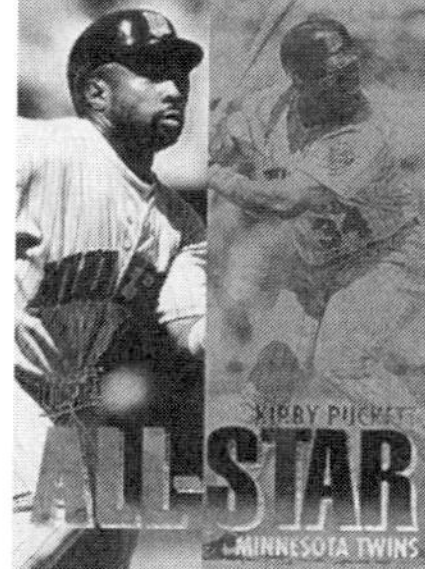

Twenty of the top players in the majors were chosen as Ultra All-Stars in this Series II chase set. Fronts have a color player photo at left. At right is a second photo, printed in only one color. A large "ALL-STAR" is at bottom, with the player's name above and team below in silver foil. An Ultra logo is at left. Backs have another color photo, with a '94 season summary printed in a black panel at right. These cards were found one per five packs, on average.

		MT
Complete Set (20):		12.50
Common Player:		.25
Gold Medallion:		2X
1	Moises Alou	.25
2	Albert Belle	.50
3	Craig Biggio	.35
4	Wade Boggs	.50
5	Barry Bonds	1.50
6	David Cone	.25
7	Ken Griffey Jr.	2.50
8	Tony Gwynn	1.00
9	Chuck Knoblauch	.25
10	Barry Larkin	.25
11	Kenny Lofton	.25
12	Greg Maddux	1.00
13	Fred McGriff	.25
14	Paul O'Neill	.25
15	Mike Piazza	2.00
16	Kirby Puckett	1.00
17	Cal Ripken Jr.	3.00
18	Ivan Rodriguez	.75
19	Frank Thomas	1.50
20	Matt Williams	.35

1995 Ultra Award Winners

Various official and unofficial award winners from the 1994 season are featured in this Series I insert set. Horizontal cards have a color player photo on the right side, with a single-color, vertically compressed action photo at left. The player's award is printed in a white strip at top, while his name and team logo, along with the Ultra logo, are at bottom. All front typography is in gold foil. Backs repeat the compressed photo at left, combined with another color photo at right. A season summary is printed over the photo at left. The Award Winners inserts were common to all types of packaging, found at the rate of about one per four packs.

		MT
Complete Set (25):		11.00
Common Player:		.15
Gold Medallion:		2x
1	Ivan Rodriguez	.60
2	Don Mattingly	1.50
3	Roberto Alomar	.60
4	Wade Boggs	.65
5	Omar Vizquel	.15
6	Ken Griffey Jr.	2.00
7	Kenny Lofton	.20
8	Devon White	.15
9	Mark Langston	.15
10	Tom Pagnozzi	.15
11	Jeff Bagwell	.75
12	Craig Biggio	.20
13	Matt Williams	.20
14	Barry Larkin	.20
15	Barry Bonds	1.50
16	Marquis Grissom	.15
17	Darren Lewis	.15
18	Greg Maddux	1.00
19	Frank Thomas	1.50
20	Jeff Bagwell	.75
21	David Cone	.15
22	Greg Maddux	1.00
23	Bob Hamelin	.15
24	Raul Mondesi	.20
25	Moises Alou	.20

1995 Ultra Golden Prospects

A hobby-pack exclusive, found at the rate of one per eight packs on average in Series I. Fronts feature a player photo at right, with three horizontally and vertically compressed versions of the same photo at right. The photo's background has been rendered in a single color. All typography - Ultra logo, card title, name and team - is in gold foil. Backs are also horizontal and have a color player photo and career summary.

		MT
Complete Set (10):		5.00
Common Player:		.20
Gold Medallion:		2X
1	James Baldwin	.20
2	Alan Benes	.20
3	Armando Benitez	.20
4	Ray Durham	.40
5	LaTroy Hawkins	.20
6	Brian Hunter	.20
7	Derek Jeter	2.00
8	Charles Johnson	.30
9	Alex Rodriguez	2.50
10	Michael Tucker	.20

1995 Ultra Hitting Machines

Various mechanical devices and dynamics make up the letters of "HITTING MACHINE" behind the color player action photo in this insert set. Both of those elements, along with the gold-foil player name, team and Ultra logo are in UV-coated contrast to the matte-finish gray background. Backs are also horizontal in format and feature a portrait photo at right, against a gray-streaked background. A career summary is printed at right. The Hitting Machines series is found only in Series II Ultra retail packs, at the rate of one card per eight packs, on average.

		MT
Complete Set (10):		8.00
Common Player:		.40
Gold Medallion:		2X
1	Jeff Bagwell	.75
2	Albert Belle	.50
3	Dante Bichette	.40
4	Barry Bonds	1.25
5	Jose Canseco	.60
6	Ken Griffey Jr.	2.00
7	Tony Gwynn	1.00
8	Fred McGriff	.40
9	Mike Piazza	1.50
10	Frank Thomas	1.25

1995 Ultra Home Run Kings

Retail packaging of Fleer Ultra Series I was the hiding place for this sluggers' chase set. An average of one out of eight packs yielded a Home Run King insert. Fronts have a photo of the player's home run cut, while large letters "H," "R" and "K" are stacked vertically down one side. All front typography is in gold foil. Backs have another batting photo and a couple of sentences of recent career slugging prowess.

		MT
Complete Set (10):		9.00
Common Player:		.30
Gold Medallion:		2X
1	Ken Griffey Jr.	3.00
2	Frank Thomas	2.00
3	Albert Belle	.60
4	Jose Canseco	1.00
5	Cecil Fielder	.30
6	Matt Williams	.45
7	Jeff Bagwell	1.50
8	Barry Bonds	2.00
9	Fred McGriff	.30
10	Andres Galarraga	.30

1995 Ultra League Leaders

Top performers in major statistical categories are featured in this Series I insert. Cards were seeded in all types of Ultra packaging at the rate of about one card per three packs. Cards have a horizontal orientation with a color player action photo printed over a black logo of the appropriate league. American Leaguers' cards have a light brown overall background color, National Leaguers have dark green. The player's name, team and Ultra logos, and box with his league-leading category are printed in silver foil. The background from the front is carried over to the back, where a color portrait photo is at left, and a '94 season summary printed at right.

		MT
Complete Set (10):		4.00
Common Player:		.25
Gold Medallion:		2X
1	Paul O'Neill	.25
2	Kenny Lofton	.25
3	Jimmy Key	.25
4	Randy Johnson	.75
5	Lee Smith	.25
6	Tony Gwynn	1.00
7	Craig Biggio	.35
8	Greg Maddux	1.00
9	Andy Benes	.25
10	John Franco	.25

1995 Ultra On-Base Leaders

Numerous smaller versions in several sizes of the central action photo against a graduated color background from the front design of this Series II insert set. The player name, card title and Ultra logo are printed in gold foil down one side. Backs have a horizontal player photo with a large team logo at top, a smaller version at bottom and a 1994 season summary. One out of eight (on average) pre-priced packs yielded an On-Base Leaders insert.

		MT
Complete Set (10):		15.00
Common Player:		1.00
Gold Medallion:		2X
1	Jeff Bagwell	2.00
2	Albert Belle	1.50
3	Craig Biggio	1.00
4	Wade Boggs	2.00
5	Barry Bonds	3.00
6	Will Clark	1.00
7	Tony Gwynn	2.50
8	Dave Justice	1.50
9	Paul O'Neill	1.00
10	Frank Thomas	3.00

1995 Ultra Power Plus

The scarcest of the Series I Ultra inserts are the Power Plus cards, printed on 100% etched foil and inserted at the rate of less than one per box. Fronts have a player action photo overprinted on a background of "POWER PLUS" logos in various metallic colors. A team logo and player name are at bottom in gold foil, as is the Ultra logo at top. Backs are conventionally printed and have a player photo on one side and season summary on the other.

		MT
Complete Set (6):		12.00
Common Player:		1.25
Gold Medallion:		2X
1	Albert Belle	1.50
2	Ken Griffey Jr.	4.00
3	Frank Thomas	2.50
4	Jeff Bagwell	2.00
5	Barry Bonds	2.50
6	Matt Williams	1.25

1995 Ultra Rising Stars

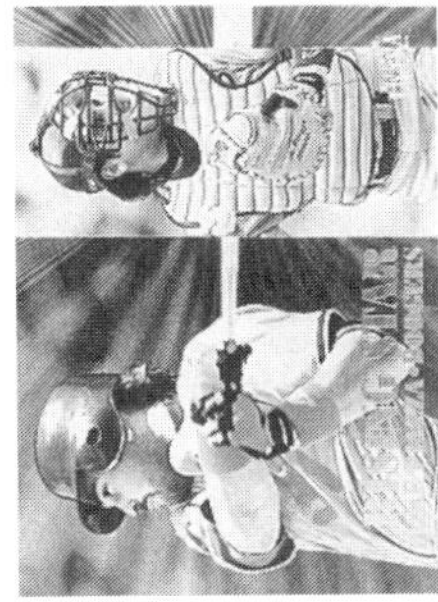

The top of the line among Series II chase cards is this set printed on 100% etched foil and seeded at the rate of less than one per box, on average. Horizontal-format cards have two player photos on a background of multi-colored rays. The Ultra logo, card title, player name and team are printed in gold foil. Backs repeat the colored rays, have another player photo and a career summary.

		MT
Complete Set (9):		18.00
Common Player:		1.00
Gold Medallion:		2X
1	Moises Alou	1.25
2	Jeff Bagwell	3.00
3	Albert Belle	1.25
4	Juan Gonzalez	3.00
5	Chuck Knoblauch	1.00
6	Kenny Lofton	1.00
7	Raul Mondesi	1.25
8	Mike Piazza	6.00
9	Frank Thomas	4.00

1995 Ultra RBI Kings

A bright aura surrounds the central player action photo on these cards, separating the player image from an indistinct colored background. At center is a large gold-foil "RBI KING" with the player's name above and team below. Backs have a similar design with a white box at bottom covering the player's RBI abilities. This set is found only in Series I jumbo packs, at an average rate of one per eight packs.

		MT
Complete Set (10):		20.00
Common Player:		1.00
Gold Medallion:		2X
1	Kirby Puckett	3.50
2	Joe Carter	1.00
3	Albert Belle	1.25
4	Frank Thomas	4.00
5	Julio Franco	1.00
6	Jeff Bagwell	2.50
7	Matt Williams	1.25
8	Dante Bichette	1.25
9	Fred McGriff	1.00
10	Mike Piazza	5.00

1995 Ultra Second Year Standouts

Fifteen of the game's sophomore stars are featured in this Series I insert set. Horizontal-format cards have player action photos front and back set against a background of orange and yellow rays. Besides the player name, card title and Ultra logo in gold-foil, the front features a pair of leafed branches flanking a team logo, all in embossed gold-foil. Backs have a career summary. The series was seeded at the average rate of one per six packs.

		MT
Complete Set (15):		5.00
Common Player:		.25
Gold Medallion:		2X
1	Cliff Floyd	.50
2	Chris Gomez	.25
3	Rusty Greer	.25
4	Darren Hall	.25
5	Bob Hamelin	.25
6	Joey Hamilton	.40
7	Jeffrey Hammonds	.25
8	John Hudek	.25
9	Ryan Klesko	.50
10	Raul Mondesi	.75
11	Manny Ramirez	3.50
12	Bill Risley	.25
13	Steve Trachsel	.25
14	William Van Landingham	.25
15	Rondell White	.75

1995 Ultra Strikeout Kings

A purple background with several types of concentric and overlapping circular designs in white are the background of this Series II chase set. An action color photo of the K-King is at center, while down one side are stacked photos of the grips used for various pitches. The player name, card title and Ultra logo are in silver foil. Backs have a portrait photo and career summary with purple circles behind and a black background. Stated odds of finding a Strikeout King card are one in five packs, on average.

		MT
Complete Set (6):		3.00
Common Player:		.25
Gold Medallion:		2X
1	Andy Benes	.25
2	Roger Clemens	1.00
3	Randy Johnson	.75
4	Greg Maddux	1.00
5	Pedro Martinez	.50
6	Jose Rijo	.25

1996 Ultra

A 40% thicker cardboard stock and silver-foil highlights are featured in this year's edition. Fronts are very basic with a borderless action photo and silver-foil graphics. Backs feature a three-photo montage along with 1995 and career stats. The set was released in two 300-card series; each card is also reprinted as part of a limited-edition Gold Medallion parallel set. One Gold Medallion card is found in every pack. Each series has eight insert sets. Series 1 inserts are RBI Kings, Home Run Kings, Fresh Foundations, Diamond Producers, Power Plus, Season Crowns, Golden Prospects and Prime Leather. Series 2 inserts are Call to the Hall, Golden Prospects, Hitting Machines, On-Base Leaders, RESPECT, Rawhide, Rising Stars and Thunderclap. Checklist cards were also randomly inserted into packs from both series.

		MT
Complete Set (600):		40.00
Common Player:		.10
Gold Medallions:		2X
Series 1 or 2 Pack (12):		1.50
Series 1 or 2 Wax Box (24):		35.00
1	Manny Alexander	.10
2	Brady Anderson	.10
3	Bobby Bonilla	.10
4	Scott Erickson	.10
5	Curtis Goodwin	.10
6	Chris Hoiles	.10
7	Doug Jones	.10
8	Jeff Manto	.10
9	Mike Mussina	.60
10	Rafael Palmeiro	.35
11	Cal Ripken Jr.	2.50
12	Rick Aguilera	.10
13	Luis Alicea	.10
14	Stan Belinda	.10
15	Jose Canseco	.50
16	Roger Clemens	1.50
17	Mike Greenwell	.10
18	Mike Macfarlane	.10
19	Tim Naehring	.10
20	Troy O'Leary	.10
21	John Valentin	.10
22	Mo Vaughn	.40
23	Tim Wakefield	.10
24	Brian Anderson	.10
25	Garret Anderson	.10
26	Chili Davis	.10
27	Gary DiSarcina	.10
28	Jim Edmonds	.10
29	Jorge Fabregas	.10
30	Chuck Finley	.10
31	Mark Langston	.10
32	Troy Percival	.10
33	Tim Salmon	.25
34	Lee Smith	.10
35	Wilson Alvarez	.10
36	Ray Durham	.10
37	Alex Fernandez	.10
38	Ozzie Guillen	.10
39	Roberto Hernandez	.10
40	Lance Johnson	.10
41	Ron Karkovice	.10
42	Lyle Mouton	.10
43	Tim Raines	.10
44	Frank Thomas	1.00
45	Carlos Baerga	.10
46	Albert Belle	.25
47	Orel Hershiser	.10
48	Kenny Lofton	.10
49	Dennis Martinez	.10
50	Jose Mesa	.10
51	Eddie Murray	.60
52	Chad Ogea	.10
53	Manny Ramirez	.75
54	Jim Thome	.10
55	Omar Vizquel	.10
56	Dave Winfield	1.00
57	Chad Curtis	.10
58	Cecil Fielder	.10
59	John Flaherty	.10
60	Travis Fryman	.10
61	Chris Gomez	.10
62	Bob Higginson	.15
63	Felipe Lira	.10
64	Brian Maxcy	.10
65	Alan Trammell	.10
66	Lou Whitaker	.10
67	Kevin Appier	.10
68	Gary Gaetti	.10
69	Tom Goodwin	.10
70	Tom Gordon	.10
71	Jason Jacome	.10
72	Wally Joyner	.10
73	Brent Mayne	.10
74	Jeff Montgomery	.10
75	Jon Nunnally	.10
76	Joe Vitiello	.10
77	Ricky Bones	.10
78	Jeff Cirillo	.10
79	Mike Fetters	.10
80	Darryl Hamilton	.10
81	David Hulse	.10
82	Dave Nilsson	.10
83	Kevin Seitzer	.10
84	Steve Sparks	.10
85	B.J. Surhoff	.10
86	Jose Valentin	.10
87	Greg Vaughn	.10
88	Marty Cordova	.10
89	Chuck Knoblauch	.10
90	Pat Meares	.10
91	Pedro Munoz	.10
92	Kirby Puckett	1.50
93	Brad Radke	.10
94	Scott Stahoviak	.10
95	Dave Stevens	.10
96	Mike Trombley	.10
97	Matt Walbeck	.10
98	Wade Boggs	.65
99	Russ Davis	.10
100	Jim Leyritz	.10
101	Don Mattingly	1.75
102	Jack McDowell	.10
103	Paul O'Neill	.10
104	Andy Pettitte	.30
105	Mariano Rivera	.25
106	Ruben Sierra	.10
107	Darryl Strawberry	.10
108	John Wetteland	.10
109	Bernie Williams	.40
110	Geronimo Berroa	.10
111	Scott Brosius	.10
112	Dennis Eckersley	.10

113 Brent Gates .10
114 Rickey Henderson .60
115 Mark McGwire 2.50
116 Ariel Prieto .10
117 Terry Steinbach .10
118 Todd Stottlemyre .10
119 Todd Van Poppel .10
120 Steve Wojciechowski .10
121 Rich Amaral .10
122 Bobby Ayala .10
123 Mike Blowers .10
124 Chris Bosio .10
125 Joey Cora .10
126 Ken Griffey Jr. 2.25
127 Randy Johnson .65
128 Edgar Martinez .10
129 Tino Martinez .10
130 Alex Rodriguez 2.25
131 Dan Wilson .10
132 Will Clark .30
133 Jeff Frye .10
134 Benji Gil .10
135 Juan Gonzalez .75
136 Rusty Greer .10
137 Mark McLemore .10
138 Roger Pavlik .10
139 Ivan Rodriguez .65
140 Kenny Rogers .10
141 Mickey Tettleton .10
142 Roberto Alomar .60
143 Joe Carter .10
144 Tony Castillo .10
145 Alex Gonzalez .15
146 Shawn Green .35
147 Pat Hentgen .10
148 *Sandy Martinez* .10
149 Paul Molitor .50
150 John Olerud .10
151 Ed Sprague .10
152 Jeff Blauser .10
153 Brad Clontz .10
154 Tom Glavine .15
155 Marquis Grissom .10
156 Chipper Jones 2.00
157 David Justice .25
158 Ryan Klesko .10
159 Javier Lopez .10
160 Greg Maddux 1.50
161 John Smoltz .15
162 Mark Wohlers .10
163 Jim Bullinger .10
164 Frank Castillo .10
165 Shawon Dunston .10
166 Kevin Foster .10
167 Luis Gonzalez .25
168 Mark Grace .25
169 Rey Sanchez .10
170 Scott Servais .10
171 Sammy Sosa 1.75
172 Ozzie Timmons .10
173 Steve Trachsel .10
174 Bret Boone .15
175 Jeff Branson .10
176 Jeff Brantley .10
177 Dave Burba .10
178 Ron Gant .10
179 Barry Larkin .15
180 Darren Lewis .10
181 Mark Portugal .10
182 Reggie Sanders .10
183 Pete Schourek .10
184 John Smiley .10
185 Jason Bates .10
186 Dante Bichette .10
187 Ellis Burks .10
188 Vinny Castilla .10
189 Andres Galarraga .10
190 Darren Holmes .10
191 Armando Reynoso .10
192 Kevin Ritz .10
193 Bill Swift .10
194 Larry Walker .40
195 Kurt Abbott .10
196 John Burkett .10
197 Greg Colbrunn .10
198 Jeff Conine .10
199 Andre Dawson .20
200 Chris Hammond .10
201 Charles Johnson .10
202 Robb Nen .10
203 Terry Pendleton .10
204 Quilvio Veras .10
205 Jeff Bagwell .75
206 Derek Bell .10
207 Doug Drabek .10
208 Tony Eusebio .10
209 Mike Hampton .10
210 Brian Hunter .10
211 Todd Jones .10
212 Orlando Miller .10
213 James Mouton .10
214 Shane Reynolds .10
215 Dave Veres .10
216 Billy Ashley .10
217 Brett Butler .10
218 Chad Fonville .10
219 Todd Hollandsworth .10
220 Eric Karros .10
221 Ramon Martinez .10
222 Raul Mondesi .20
223 Hideo Nomo .50
224 Mike Piazza 2.00
225 Kevin Tapani .10
226 Ismael Valdes .10
227 Todd Worrell .10
228 Moises Alou .20
229 Wil Cordero .10
230 Jeff Fassero .10
231 Darrin Fletcher .10
232 Mike Lansing .10
233 Pedro Martinez .65
234 Carlos Perez .10
235 Mel Rojas .10
236 David Segui .10
237 Tony Tarasco .10
238 Rondell White .20
239 Edgardo Alfonzo .10
240 Rico Brogna .10
241 Carl Everett .15
242 Todd Hundley .10
243 Butch Huskey .10
244 Jason Isringhausen .10
245 Bobby Jones .10
246 Jeff Kent .10
247 Bill Pulsipher .10
248 Jose Vizcaino .10
249 Ricky Bottalico .10
250 Darren Daulton .10
251 Jim Eisenreich .10
252 Tyler Green .10
253 Charlie Hayes .10
254 Gregg Jefferies .10
255 Tony Longmire .10
256 Michael Mimbs .10
257 Mickey Morandini .10
258 Paul Quantrill .10
259 Heathcliff Slocumb .10
260 Jay Bell .10
261 Jacob Brumfield .10
262 *Angelo Encarnacion* .10
263 John Ericks .10
264 Mark Johnson .10
265 Esteban Loaiza .10
266 Al Martin .10
267 Orlando Merced .10
268 Dan Miceli .10
269 Denny Neagle .10
270 Brian Barber .10
271 Scott Cooper .10
272 Tripp Cromer .10
273 Bernard Gilkey .10
274 Tom Henke .10
275 Brian Jordan .10
276 John Mabry .10
277 Tom Pagnozzi .10
278 *Mark Petkovsek* .15
279 Ozzie Smith 1.50
280 Andy Ashby .10
281 Brad Ausmus .10
282 Ken Caminiti .10
283 Glenn Dishman .10
284 Tony Gwynn 1.50
285 Joey Hamilton .10
286 Trevor Hoffman .10
287 Phil Plantier .10
288 Jody Reed .10
289 Eddie Williams .10
290 Barry Bonds 1.75
291 Jamie Brewington .10
292 Mark Carreon .10
293 Royce Clayton .10
294 Glenallen Hill .10
295 Mark Leiter .10
296 Kirt Manwaring .10
297 J.R. Phillips .10
298 Deion Sanders .15
299 William VanLandingham .10
300 Matt Williams .30
301 Roberto Alomar .60
302 Armando Benitez .10
303 Mike Devereaux .10
304 Jeffrey Hammonds .10
305 Jimmy Haynes .10
306 *Scott McClain* .10
307 Kent Mercker .10
308 Randy Myers .10
309 B.J. Surhoff .10
310 Tony Tarasco .10
311 David Wells .15
312 Wil Cordero .10
313 Alex Delgado .10
314 Tom Gordon .10
315 Dwayne Hosey .10
316 Jose Malave .10
317 Kevin Mitchell .10
318 Jamie Moyer .10
319 Aaron Sele .10
320 Heathcliff Slocumb .10
321 Mike Stanley .10
322 Jeff Suppan .10
323 Jim Abbott .10
324 George Arias .10
325 Todd Greene .10
326 Bryan Harvey .10
327 J.T. Snow .10
328 Randy Velarde .10
329 Tim Wallach .10
330 Harold Baines .10
331 Jason Bere .10
332 Darren Lewis .10
333 Norberto Martin .10
334 Tony Phillips .10
335 Bill Simas .10
336 Chris Snopek .10
337 Kevin Tapani .10
338 Danny Tartabull .10
339 Robin Ventura .10
340 Sandy Alomar .10
341 Julio Franco .10
342 Jack McDowell .10
343 Charles Nagy .10
344 Julian Tavarez .10
345 Kimera Bartee .10
346 Greg Keagle .10
347 Mark Lewis .10
348 Jose Lima .10
349 Melvin Nieves .10
350 Mark Parent .10
351 Eddie Williams .10
352 Johnny Damon .15
353 Sal Fasano .10
354 Mark Gubicza .10
355 Bob Hamelin .10
356 Chris Haney .10
357 Keith Lockhart .10
358 Mike Macfarlane .10
359 Jose Offerman .10
360 Bip Roberts .10
361 Michael Tucker .10
362 Chuck Carr .10
363 Bobby Hughes .10
364 John Jaha .10
365 Mark Loretta .10
366 Mike Matheny .10
367 Ben McDonald .10
368 Matt Mieske .10
369 Angel Miranda .10
370 Fernando Vina .10
371 Rick Aguilera .10
372 Rich Becker .10
373 LaTroy Hawkins .10
374 Dave Hollins .10
375 Roberto Kelly .10
376 *Matt Lawton* .75
377 Paul Molitor .50
378 *Dan Naulty* .10
379 Rich Robertson .10
380 Frank Rodriguez .10
381 David Cone .10
382 Mariano Duncan .10
383 *Andy Fox* .10
384 Joe Girardi .10
385 Dwight Gooden .10
386 Derek Jeter 2.00
387 Pat Kelly .10
388 Jimmy Key .10
389 *Matt Luke* .10
390 Tino Martinez .10
391 Jeff Nelson .10
392 Melido Perez .10
393 Tim Raines .10
394 Ruben Rivera .10
395 Kenny Rogers .10
396 *Tony Batista* .75
397 Allen Battle .10
398 Mike Bordick .10
399 Steve Cox .10
400 Jason Giambi .25
401 Doug Johns .10
402 Pedro Munoz .10
403 Phil Plantier .10
404 Scott Spiezio .10
405 George Williams .10
406 Ernie Young .10
407 Darren Bragg .10
408 Jay Buhner .10
409 Norm Charlton .10
410 Russ Davis .10
411 Sterling Hitchcock .10
412 Edwin Hurtado .10
413 *Raul Ibanez* .10
414 Mike Jackson .10
415 Luis Sojo .10
416 Paul Sorrento .10
417 Bob Wolcott .10
418 Damon Buford .10
419 Kevin Gross .10
420 Darryl Hamilton .10
421 Mike Henneman .10
422 Ken Hill .10
423 Dean Palmer .10
424 Bobby Witt .10
425 Tilson Brito .10
426 Giovanni Carrara .10
427 Domingo Cedeno .10
428 Felipe Crespo .10
429 Carlos Delgado .45
430 Juan Guzman .10
431 Erik Hanson .10
432 *Marty Janzen* .10
433 Otis Nixon .10
434 Robert Perez .10
435 Paul Quantrill .10
436 Bill Risley .10
437 Steve Avery .10
438 Jermaine Dye .10
439 Mark Lemke .10
440 *Marty Malloy* .10
441 Fred McGriff .10
442 Greg McMichael .10
443 Wonderful Monds .10
444 Eddie Perez .10
445 Jason Schmidt .10
446 Terrell Wade .10
447 Terry Adams .10
448 Scott Bullett .10
449 *Robin Jennings* .10
450 Doug Jones .10
451 Brooks Kieschnick .10
452 Dave Magadan .10
453 *Jason Maxwell* .10
454 Brian McRae .10
455 Rodney Myers .10
456 Jaime Navarro .10
457 Ryne Sandberg .75
458 Vince Coleman .10
459 Eric Davis .10
460 Steve Gibralter .10
461 Thomas Howard .10
462 Mike Kelly .10
463 Hal Morris .10
464 Eric Owens .10
465 Jose Rijo .10
466 Chris Sabo .10
467 Eddie Taubensee .10
468 Trenidad Hubbard .10
469 Curt Leskanic .10
470 Quinton McCracken .10
471 Jayhawk Owens .10
472 Steve Reed .10
473 Bryan Rekar .10
474 Bruce Ruffin .10
475 Bret Saberhagen .10
476 Walt Weiss .10
477 Eric Young .10
478 Kevin Brown .15
479 Al Leiter .10
480 Pat Rapp .10
481 Gary Sheffield .30
482 Devon White .10
483 Bob Abreu .15
484 Sean Berry .10
485 Craig Biggio .15
486 Jim Dougherty .10
487 Richard Hidalgo .15
488 Darryl Kile .10
489 Derrick May .10
490 Greg Swindell .10
491 Rick Wilkins .10
492 Mike Blowers .10
493 Tom Candiotti .10
494 Roger Cedeno .10

495	Delino DeShields	.10
496	Greg Gagne	.10
497	Karim Garcia	.15
498	*Wilton Guerrero*	.10
499	Chan Ho Park	.15
500	Israel Alcantara	.10
501	Shane Andrews	.10
502	Yamil Benitez	.10
503	Cliff Floyd	.10
504	Mark Grudzielanek	.10
505	Ryan McGuire	.10
506	Sherman Obando	.10
507	Jose Paniagua	.10
508	Henry Rodriguez	.10
509	Kirk Rueter	.10
510	Juan Acevedo	.10
511	John Franco	.10
512	Bernard Gilkey	.10
513	Lance Johnson	.10
514	Rey Ordonez	.10
515	Robert Person	.10
516	Paul Wilson	.10
517	Toby Borland	.10
518	*David Doster*	.10
519	Lenny Dykstra	.10
520	Sid Fernandez	.10
521	*Mike Grace*	.10
522	*Rich Hunter*	.10
523	Benito Santiago	.10
524	Gene Schall	.10
525	Curt Schilling	.15
526	*Kevin Sefcik*	.10
527	Lee Tinsley	.10
528	David West	.10
529	Mark Whiten	.10
530	Todd Zeile	.10
531	Carlos Garcia	.10
532	Charlie Hayes	.10
533	Jason Kendall	.15
534	Jeff King	.10
535	Mike Kingery	.10
536	Nelson Liriano	.10
537	Dan Plesac	.10
538	Paul Wagner	.10
539	Luis Alicea	.10
540	David Bell	.10
541	Alan Benes	.10
542	Andy Benes	.10
543	*Mike Busby*	.10
544	Royce Clayton	.10
545	Dennis Eckersley	.10
546	Gary Gaetti	.10
547	Ron Gant	.10
548	Aaron Holbert	.10
549	Ray Lankford	.10
550	T.J. Mathews	.10
551	Willie McGee	.10
552	*Miguel Mejia*	.10
553	Todd Stottlemyre	.10
554	Sean Bergman	.10
555	Willie Blair	.10
556	Andujar Cedeno	.10
557	Steve Finley	.10
558	Rickey Henderson	.60
559	Wally Joyner	.10
560	Scott Livingstone	.10
561	Marc Newfield	.10
562	Bob Tewksbury	.10
563	Fernando Valenzuela	.10
564	Rod Beck	.10
565	Doug Creek	.10
566	Shawon Dunston	.10
567	*Osvaldo Fernandez*	.20
568	Stan Javier	.10
569	Marcus Jensen	.10
570	Steve Scarsone	.10
571	Robby Thompson	.10
572	Allen Watson	.10
573	Roberto Alomar (Ultra Stars)	.30
574	Jeff Bagwell (Ultra Stars)	.40
575	Albert Belle (Ultra Stars)	.20
576	Wade Boggs (Ultra Stars)	.30
577	Barry Bonds (Ultra Stars)	.75
578	Juan Gonzalez (Ultra Stars)	.40
579	Ken Griffey Jr. (Ultra Stars)	1.00
580	Tony Gwynn (Ultra Stars)	.50
581	Randy Johnson (Ultra Stars)	.35
582	Chipper Jones (Ultra Stars)	.75
583	Barry Larkin (Ultra Stars)	.10
584	Kenny Lofton (Ultra Stars)	.10
585	Greg Maddux (Ultra Stars)	.60
586	Raul Mondesi (Ultra Stars)	.10
587	Mike Piazza (Ultra Stars)	1.00
588	Cal Ripken Jr. (Ultra Stars)	1.25
589	Tim Salmon (Ultra Stars)	.10
590	Frank Thomas (Ultra Stars)	.75
591	Mo Vaughn (Ultra Stars)	.20
592	Matt Williams (Ultra Stars)	.10
593	Marty Cordova (Raw Power)	.10
594	Jim Edmonds (Raw Power)	.10
595	Cliff Floyd (Raw Power)	.10
596	Chipper Jones (Raw Power)	.75
597	Ryan Klesko (Raw Power)	.10
598	Raul Mondesi (Raw Power)	.10
599	Manny Ramirez (Raw Power)	.40
600	Ruben Rivera (Raw Power)	.10

1996 Ultra Gold Medallion

Limited to less than 10% of the regular edition's production, the Gold Medallion parallel set replaces the front photo's background with gold foil featuring a large embossed Fleer Ultra Gold Medallion seal at center. One Gold Medallion card is found in each foil pack.

	MT
Complete Set (600):	100.00
Common Player:	.25
(Star cards valued at 2X regular edition Fleer Ultra.)	

1996 Ultra Call to the Hall

Ten probable future Hall of Famers are featured on these cards, which use classic style original illustrations of the players. The cards were seeded one per every 24 Series 2 packs.

		MT
Complete Set (10):		25.00
Common Player:		1.25
Gold Medallion Edition:		2X
1	Barry Bonds	3.00
2	Ken Griffey Jr.	5.00
3	Tony Gwynn	2.00
4	Rickey Henderson	1.50
5	Greg Maddux	2.00
6	Eddie Murray	1.25
7	Cal Ripken Jr.	6.00
8	Ryne Sandberg	2.00
9	Ozzie Smith	2.00
10	Frank Thomas	2.50

1996 Ultra Checklists

Fleer Ultra featured 10 checklist cards that were inserted every four packs. These cards featured a superstar player on the front and, throughout the set, a full checklist of all cards in the 1996 Ultra set on the back.

		MT
Complete Set (20):		10.00
Common Player:		.15
	SERIES 1	
1	Jeff Bagwell	.50
2	Barry Bonds	.75
3	Juan Gonzalez	.50
4	Ken Griffey Jr.	1.25
5	Chipper Jones	1.00
6	Mike Piazza	1.00
7	Manny Ramirez	.50
8	Cal Ripken Jr.	1.50
9	Frank Thomas	.75
10	Matt Williams	.15
	SERIES 2	
1	Albert Belle	.25
2	Cecil Fielder	.15
3	Ken Griffey Jr.	1.25
4	Tony Gwynn	.60
5	Derek Jeter	1.00
6	Jason Kendall	.15
7	Ryan Klesko	.15
8	Greg Maddux	.60
9	Cal Ripken Jr.	1.50
10	Frank Thomas	.75

1996 Ultra Diamond Producers

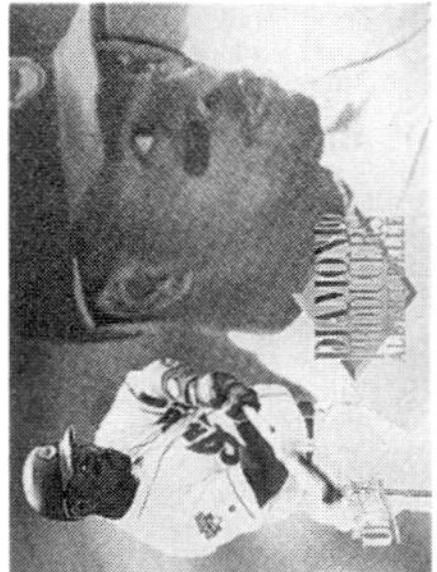

A horizontal layout and two versions of the same photo printed on holographic foil are featured in this insert set. Stated odds of finding a Diamond Producers card are one per every 20 Series I packs.

		MT
Complete Set (12):		25.00
Common Player:		.75
Gold Medallions:		2X
1	Albert Belle	.75
2	Barry Bonds	3.00
3	Ken Griffey Jr.	5.00
4	Tony Gwynn	1.50
5	Greg Maddux	1.50
6	Hideo Nomo	1.00
7	Mike Piazza	4.00
8	Kirby Puckett	1.50
9	Cal Ripken Jr.	6.00
10	Frank Thomas	2.00
11	Mo Vaughn	1.00
12	Matt Williams	.75

1996 Ultra Fresh Foundations

Rising stars who can carry their teams' fortunes into the next century are featured in this foil-printed insert set, found on average of one card per every three Series I foil packs.

		MT
Complete Set (10):		3.00
Common Player:		.30
Gold Medallions:		2X
1	Garret Anderson	.30
2	Marty Cordova	.30
3	Jim Edmonds	.30
4	Brian Hunter	.30
5	Chipper Jones	1.00
6	Ryan Klesko	.30
7	Raul Mondesi	.45
8	Hideo Nomo	.60
9	Manny Ramirez	.75
10	Rondell White	.30

1996 Ultra Golden Prospects, Series 1

A hobby-pack-only insert, these horizontal format cards have rainbow foil ballpark backgrounds and feature 1996's rookie crop. They are found on average of one per every five Series I packs.

		MT
Complete Set (10):		5.00
Common Player:		.25
Gold Medallions:		2X
1	Yamil Benitez	.25
2	Alberto Castillo	.25
3	Roger Cedeno	.50
4	Johnny Damon	.50
5	Micah Franklin	.25
6	Jason Giambi	1.50
7	Jose Herrera	.25
8	Derek Jeter	4.00
9	Kevin Jordan	.25
10	Ruben Rivera	.25

1996 Ultra Golden Prospects, Series 2

The Golden Prospects insert series continued with 15 more young stars found exclusively in Series 2 hobby packs, though in much lower numbers than the Series 1 inserts.

		MT
Complete Set (15):		35.00
Common Player:		2.00
Gold Medallions:		2X
1	Bob Abreu	8.00
2	Israel Alcantara	2.00
3	Tony Batista	3.00
4	Mike Cameron	4.00
5	Steve Cox	2.00
6	Jermaine Dye	4.00
7	Wilton Guerrero	2.00
8	Richard Hidalgo	5.00
9	Raul Ibanez	2.00
10	Marty Janzen	2.00
11	Robin Jennings	2.00
12	Jason Maxwell	2.00
13	Scott McClain	2.00
14	Wonderful Monds	2.00
15	Chris Singleton	4.00

1996 Ultra Hitting Machines

These die-cut 1996 Fleer Ultra Series II insert cards showcase the heaviest hitters on cards featuring a machine-gear design. The cards were seeded one per every 288 Series II packs.

		MT
Complete Set (10):		70.00
Common Player:		3.00
Gold Medallion:		2X
1	Albert Belle	4.00
2	Barry Bonds	10.00
3	Juan Gonzalez	8.00
4	Ken Griffey Jr.	20.00
5	Edgar Martinez	3.00
6	Rafael Palmeiro	5.00
7	Mike Piazza	15.00
8	Tim Salmon	3.00
9	Frank Thomas	8.00
10	Matt Williams	4.00

1996 Ultra Home Run Kings

Printed on a thin wood veneer, these superscarce inserts are seeded one per every 75 Series 1 packs. Because of quality control problems, the cards were initially released as exchange cards, with instructions on back for a mail-in redemption offer for the actual wooden card.

		MT
Complete Set (12):		35.00
Common Player:		2.00
Gold Medallions:		2X
1	Albert Belle	2.50
2	Dante Bichette	2.00
3	Barry Bonds	8.00
4	Jose Canseco	6.50
5	Juan Gonzalez	4.00
6	Ken Griffey Jr.	10.00
7	Mark McGwire	12.00
8	Manny Ramirez	4.00
9	Tim Salmon	2.00
10	Frank Thomas	8.00
11	Mo Vaughn	3.00
12	Matt Williams	3.00

1996 Ultra On-Base Leaders

These 1996 Fleer Ultra Series II inserts feature 10 of the game's top on-base leaders. The cards were seeded one per every four packs.

		MT
Complete Set (10):		6.00
Common Player:		.50
Gold Medallion:		2X
1	Wade Boggs	.75
2	Barry Bonds	1.50
3	Tony Gwynn	1.00
4	Rickey Henderson	.75
5	Chuck Knoblauch	.50
6	Edgar Martinez	.50
7	Mike Piazza	2.00
8	Tim Salmon	.50
9	Frank Thomas	1.50
10	Jim Thome	.50

1996 Ultra Power Plus

Etched-foil backgrounds, multiple player photos and a horizontal format are featured in this chase set. Stated odds of finding one of the dozen Power Plus cards are one per every 10 Series I packs.

		MT
Complete Set (12):		18.00
Common Player:		.50
Gold Medallions:		2X
1	Jeff Bagwell	1.50
2	Barry Bonds	3.00
3	Ken Griffey Jr.	6.00
4	Raul Mondesi	.50
5	Rafael Palmeiro	.75
6	Mike Piazza	4.50
7	Manny Ramirez	1.50
8	Tim Salmon	.50
9	Reggie Sanders	.50
10	Frank Thomas	3.00
11	Larry Walker	.75
12	Matt Williams	.50

1996 Ultra Prime Leather

An embossed leather-feel background is featured on these cards of top fielders, seeded one per every eight Series I packs, on average.

		MT
Complete Set (18):		25.00
Common Player:		.50
Gold Medallions:		2X
1	Ivan Rodriguez	1.50
2	Will Clark	.50
3	Roberto Alomar	1.00
4	Cal Ripken Jr.	5.00
5	Wade Boggs	1.50
6	Ken Griffey Jr.	4.00
7	Kenny Lofton	.50
8	Kirby Puckett	2.00
9	Tim Salmon	.50
10	Mike Piazza	4.00
11	Mark Grace	.75
12	Craig Biggio	.50
13	Barry Larkin	.50
14	Matt Williams	.50
15	Barry Bonds	2.50
16	Tony Gwynn	2.00
17	Brian McRae	.50
18	Raul Mondesi	.50

1996 Ultra R-E-S-P-E-C-T

These cards feature 10 players held in high esteem by their major league peers. The cards were seeded one per every 18 1996 Ultra Series II packs.

	MT
Complete Set (10):	25.00
Common Player:	.75

Gold Medallion:		2X
1	Joe Carter	.75
2	Ken Griffey Jr.	5.00
3	Tony Gwynn	3.00
4	Greg Maddux	3.00
5	Eddie Murray	1.50
6	Kirby Puckett	3.00
7	Cal Ripken Jr.	6.00
8	Ryne Sandberg	2.50
9	Frank Thomas	2.00
10	Mo Vaughn	1.50

1996 Ultra Rawhide

Ten top fielders are featured on these 1996 Fleer Ultra Series II inserts. The cards were seeded one per every eight packs.

		MT
Complete Set (10):		10.00
Common Player:		.50
Gold Medallion:		2X
1	Roberto Alomar	.75
2	Barry Bonds	1.50
3	Mark Grace	.75
4	Ken Griffey Jr.	2.00
5	Kenny Lofton	.50
6	Greg Maddux	1.00
7	Raul Mondesi	.50
8	Mike Piazza	1.75
9	Cal Ripken Jr.	2.50
10	Matt Williams	.50

1996 Ultra Rising Stars

Ten of baseball's best young players are spotlighted on these 1996 Fleer Ultra Series II inserts. Cards were seeded one per every four packs.

		MT
Complete Set (10):		3.50
Common Player:		.15
Gold Medallion:		2X
1	Garret Anderson	.15
2	Marty Cordova	.15
3	Jim Edmonds	.25
4	Cliff Floyd	.15
5	Brian Hunter	.15
6	Chipper Jones	1.50
7	Ryan Klesko	.15
8	Hideo Nomo	.75
9	Manny Ramirez	1.00
10	Rondell White	.25

1996 Ultra RBI Kings

Retail packs are the exclusive provenance of this 10-card set of top RBI men. Stated odds of finding an RBI King card are one per every five Series I packs.

		MT
Complete Set (10):		8.00
Common Player:		.20
Gold Medallions:		2X
1	Derek Bell	.20
2	Albert Belle	.40
3	Dante Bichette	.20
4	Barry Bonds	2.50
5	Jim Edmonds	.25
6	Manny Ramirez	1.50
7	Reggie Sanders	.20
8	Sammy Sosa	5.00
9	Frank Thomas	1.50
10	Mo Vaughn	.75

1996 Ultra Season Crowns

Large coats-of-arms printed on "Ultra Crystal" clear plastic are the background for player action photos in this insert set. Odds of one per every 10 Series II packs were stated.

		MT
Complete Set (10):		18.00
Common Player:		1.00
Gold Medallions:		2X
1	Barry Bonds	3.00
2	Tony Gwynn	2.50
3	Randy Johnson	2.00
4	Kenny Lofton	1.00
5	Greg Maddux	2.50
6	Edgar Martinez	1.00
7	Hideo Nomo	1.50
8	Cal Ripken Jr.	6.00
9	Frank Thomas	2.50
10	Tim Wakefield	1.00

1996 Ultra Thunderclap

The active career home run leaders are featured in this retail-exclusive Ultra insert set. Seeded only one per 72 packs, the Thunderclap cards have action photos on front with simulated lightning in the background and other graphic highlights rendered in holographic foil. Backs have a large portrait photo and career summary. Each of these scarce retail inserts can also be found in an even more elusive Gold Medallion version.

		MT
Complete Set (20):		200.00
Common Player:		4.00
Gold Medallion:		2X
1	Albert Belle	5.00
2	Barry Bonds	25.00
3	Bobby Bonilla	4.00
4	Jose Canseco	8.00
5	Joe Carter	4.00
6	Will Clark	6.00
7	Andre Dawson	5.00
8	Cecil Fielder	4.00
9	Andres Galarraga	5.00
10	Juan Gonzalez	15.00
11	Ken Griffey Jr.	40.00
12	Fred McGriff	5.00
13	Mark McGwire	40.00
14	Eddie Murray	6.00
15	Rafael Palmeiro	8.00
16	Kirby Puckett	15.00
17	Cal Ripken Jr.	45.00
18	Ryne Sandberg	15.00
19	Frank Thomas	15.00
20	Matt Williams	6.00

1996 Ultra Diamond Dust

This card commemorates Cal Ripken's history-making 1995 record of playing in 2,131 consecutive regular-season games. Horizontal in format, the front has a color action photo of Ripken on a simulated leather background. Back has a photo of Ripken on the night he set the new record. Sandwiched between front and back is a dime-sized plastic capsule of dirt certified, according to the facsimile autograph on back of the team's head groundskeeper, to have been used on the infield at Oriole Park in Camden Yards during the 1995 season. Two versions of the card were made. A hand-numbered version limited to 2,131 was offered direct to dealers for $39.99. An unnumbered version was available to collectors as a wrapper redemption for $24.99.

	MT
Cal Ripken Jr. (numbered)	150.00
Cal Ripken Jr. (unnumbered)	90.00

1997 Ultra

Ultra arrived in a 300-card Series I issue with two parallel sets, Gold and Platinum, which featured "G" and "P" prefixes on the card number, respectively. Cards were issued in 10-card packs. Player names and the Ultra logo are in silver holographic foil. Backs contains complete year-by-year statistics, plus two photos of the player. This also marked the first time that the Gold and Platinum parallel sets displayed a different photo than the base cards. Inserts in Ultra included: Rookie Reflections, Double Trouble, Checklists, Season Crowns, RBI Kings, Power Plus, Fielder's Choice, Diamond Producers, HR Kings and Baseball Rules.

	MT
Complete Set (553):	40.00
Common Player:	.10

Gold Medallion: 2X
Platinum Medallion: 15X
Series 1 or 2 Pack (10): 1.50
Series 1 or 2 Wax Box (24): 25.00

1 Roberto Alomar .65
2 Brady Anderson .10
3 Rocky Coppinger .10
4 Jeffrey Hammonds .10
5 Chris Hoiles .10
6 Eddie Murray .50
7 Mike Mussina .65
8 Jimmy Myers .10
9 Randy Myers .10
10 Arthur Rhodes .10
11 Cal Ripken Jr. 2.50
12 Jose Canseco .50
13 Roger Clemens 1.50
14 Tom Gordon .10
15 Jose Malave .10
16 Tim Naehring .10
17 Troy O'Leary .10
18 Bill Selby .10
19 Heathcliff Slocumb .10
20 Mike Stanley .10
21 Mo Vaughn .40
22 Garret Anderson .10
23 George Arias .10
24 Chili Davis .10
25 Jim Edmonds .10
26 Darin Erstad .50
27 Chuck Finley .10
28 Todd Greene .10
29 Troy Percival .10
30 Tim Salmon .20
31 Jeff Schmidt .10
32 Randy Velarde .10
33 Shad Williams .10
34 Wilson Alvarez .10
35 Harold Baines .10
36 James Baldwin .10
37 Mike Cameron .10
38 Ray Durham .10
39 Ozzie Guillen .10
40 Roberto Hernandez .10
41 Darren Lewis .10
42 Jose Munoz .10
43 Tony Phillips .10
44 Frank Thomas 1.00
45 Sandy Alomar Jr. .10
46 Albert Belle .30
47 Mark Carreon .10
48 Julio Franco .10
49 Orel Hershiser .10
50 Kenny Lofton .10
51 Jack McDowell .10
52 Jose Mesa .10
53 Charles Nagy .10
54 Manny Ramirez 1.00
55 Julian Tavarez .10
56 Omar Vizquel .10
57 Raul Casanova .10
58 Tony Clark .10
59 Travis Fryman .10
60 Bob Higginson .15
61 Melvin Nieves .10
62 Curtis Pride .10
63 Justin Thompson .10
64 Alan Trammell .10
65 Kevin Appier .10
66 Johnny Damon .20
67 Keith Lockhart .10
68 Jeff Montgomery .10
69 Jose Offerman .10
70 Bip Roberts .10
71 Jose Rosado .10
72 Chris Stynes .10
73 Mike Sweeney .10
74 Jeff Cirillo .10
75 Jeff D'Amico .10
76 John Jaha .10
77 Scott Karl .10
78 Mike Matheny .10
79 Ben McDonald .10
80 Matt Mieske .10
81 Marc Newfield .10
82 Dave Nilsson .10
83 Jose Valentin .10
84 Fernando Vina .10
85 Rick Aguilera .10
86 Marty Cordova .10
87 Chuck Knoblauch .10
88 Matt Lawton .10
89 Pat Meares .10
90 Paul Molitor .65
91 Greg Myers .10
92 Dan Naulty .10
93 Kirby Puckett 1.50
94 Frank Rodriguez .10
95 Wade Boggs .50
96 Cecil Fielder .10
97 Joe Girardi .10
98 Dwight Gooden .10
99 Derek Jeter 2.50
100 Tino Martinez .10
101 *Ramiro Mendoza* .50
102 Andy Pettitte .30
103 Mariano Rivera .20
104 Ruben Rivera .10
105 Kenny Rogers .10
106 Darryl Strawberry .10
107 Bernie Williams .30
108 Tony Batista .10
109 Geronimo Berroa .10
110 Bobby Chouinard .10
111 Brent Gates .10
112 Jason Giambi .30
113 *Damon Mashore* .10
114 Mark McGwire 2.50
115 Scott Spiezio .10
116 John Wasdin .10
117 Steve Wojciechowski .10
118 Ernie Young .10
119 Norm Charlton .10
120 Joey Cora .10
121 Ken Griffey Jr. 2.00
122 Sterling Hitchcock .10
123 Raul Ibanez .10
124 Randy Johnson .75
125 Edgar Martinez .10
126 Alex Rodriguez 2.00
127 Matt Wagner .10
128 Bob Wells .10
129 Dan Wilson .10
130 Will Clark .30
131 Kevin Elster .10
132 Juan Gonzalez 1.00
133 Rusty Greer .10
134 Darryl Hamilton .10
135 Mike Henneman .10
136 Ken Hill .10
137 Mark McLemore .10
138 Dean Palmer .10
139 Roger Pavlik .10
140 Ivan Rodriguez .65
141 Joe Carter .10
142 Carlos Delgado .30
143 Alex Gonzalez .15
144 Juan Guzman .10
145 Pat Hentgen .10
146 Marty Janzen .10
147 Otis Nixon .10
148 Charlie O'Brien .10
149 John Olerud .10
150 Robert Perez .10
151 Jermaine Dye .10
152 Tom Glavine .15
153 Andruw Jones 1.00
154 Chipper Jones 2.00
155 Ryan Klesko .10
156 Javier Lopez .10
157 Greg Maddux 1.50
158 Fred McGriff .10
159 Wonderful Monds .10
160 John Smoltz .15
161 Terrell Wade .10
162 Mark Wohlers .10
163 Brant Brown .10
164 Mark Grace .25
165 Tyler Houston .10
166 Robin Jennings .10
167 Jason Maxwell .10
168 Ryne Sandberg .75
169 Sammy Sosa 1.50
170 Amaury Telemaco .10
171 Steve Trachsel .10
172 *Pedro Valdes* .10
173 Tim Belk .10
174 Bret Boone .15
175 Jeff Brantley .10
176 Eric Davis .10
177 Barry Larkin .15
178 Chad Mottola .10
179 Mark Portugal .10
180 Reggie Sanders .10
181 John Smiley .10
182 Eddie Taubensee .10
183 Dante Bichette .10
184 Ellis Burks .10
185 Andres Galarraga .10
186 Curt Leskanic .10
187 Quinton McCracken .10
188 Jeff Reed .10
189 Kevin Ritz .10
190 Walt Weiss .10
191 Jamey Wright .10
192 Eric Young .10
193 Kevin Brown .15
194 Luis Castillo .10
195 Jeff Conine .10
196 Andre Dawson .15
197 Charles Johnson .10
198 Al Leiter .10
199 Ralph Milliard .10
200 Robb Nen .10
201 Edgar Renteria .20
202 Gary Sheffield .40
203 Bob Abreu .15
204 Jeff Bagwell 1.00
205 Derek Bell .10
206 Sean Berry .10
207 Richard Hidalgo .15
208 Todd Jones .10
209 Darryl Kile .10
210 Orlando Miller .10
211 Shane Reynolds .10
212 Billy Wagner .10
213 Donne Wall .10
214 Roger Cedeno .10
215 Greg Gagne .10
216 Karim Garcia .15
217 Wilton Guerrero .10
218 Todd Hollandsworth .10
219 Ramon Martinez .10
220 Raul Mondesi .20
221 Hideo Nomo .50
222 Chan Ho Park .15
223 Mike Piazza 2.00
224 Ismael Valdes .10
225 Moises Alou .15
226 Derek Aucoin .10
227 Yamil Benitez .10
228 Jeff Fassero .10
229 Darrin Fletcher .10
230 Mark Grudzielanek .10
231 Barry Manuel .10
232 Pedro Martinez .75
233 Henry Rodriguez .10
234 Ugueth Urbina .10
235 Rondell White .15
236 Carlos Baerga .10
237 John Franco .10
238 Bernard Gilkey .10
239 Todd Hundley .10
240 Butch Huskey .10
241 Jason Isringhausen .10
242 Lance Johnson .10
243 Bobby Jones .10
244 Alex Ochoa .10
245 Rey Ordonez .10
246 Paul Wilson .10
247 Ron Blazier .10
248 David Doster .10
249 Jim Eisenreich .10
250 Mike Grace .10
251 Mike Lieberthal .10
252 Wendell Magee .10
253 Mickey Morandini .10
254 Ricky Otero .10
255 Scott Rolen .65
256 Curt Schilling .15
257 Todd Zeile .10
258 Jermaine Allensworth .10
259 Trey Beamon .10
260 Carlos Garcia .10
261 Mark Johnson .10
262 Jason Kendall .10
263 Jeff King .10
264 Al Martin .10
265 Denny Neagle .10
266 Matt Ruebel .10
267 *Marc Wilkins* .10
268 Alan Benes .10
269 Dennis Eckersley .10
270 Ron Gant .10
271 Aaron Holbert .10
272 Brian Jordan .10
273 Ray Lankford .10
274 John Mabry .10
275 T.J. Mathews .10
276 Ozzie Smith 1.50
277 Todd Stottlemyre .10
278 Mark Sweeney .10
279 Andy Ashby .10
280 Steve Finley .10
281 John Flaherty .10
282 Chris Gomez .10
283 Tony Gwynn 1.00
284 Joey Hamilton .10
285 Rickey Henderson 65.00
286 Trevor Hoffman .10
287 Jason Thompson .10
288 Fernando Valenzuela .10
289 Greg Vaughn .10
290 Barry Bonds 1.50
291 Jay Canizaro .10
292 Jacob Cruz .10
293 Shawon Dunston .10
294 Shawn Estes .10
295 Mark Gardner .10
296 Marcus Jensen .10
297 *Bill Mueller* .40
298 Chris Singleton .10
299 Allen Watson .10
300 Matt Williams .30
301 Rod Beck .10
302 Jay Bell .10
303 Shawon Dunston .10
304 Reggie Jefferson .10
305 Darren Oliver .10
306 Benito Santiago .10
307 Gerald Williams .10
308 Damon Buford .10
309 Jeromy Burnitz .10
310 Sterling Hitchcock .10
311 Dave Hollins .10
312 Mel Rojas .10
313 Robin Ventura .10
314 David Wells .15
315 Cal Eldred .10
316 Gary Gaetti .10
317 John Hudek .10
318 Brian Johnson .10
319 Denny Neagle .10
320 Larry Walker .30
321 Russ Davis .10
322 Delino DeShields .10
323 Charlie Hayes .10
324 Jermaine Dye .10
325 John Ericks .10
326 Jeff Fassero .10
327 Nomar Garciaparra 1.75
328 Willie Greene .10
329 Greg McMichael .10
330 Damion Easley .10
331 Ricky Bones .10
332 John Burkett .10
333 Royce Clayton .10
334 Greg Colbrunn .10
335 Tony Eusebio .10
336 Gregg Jefferies .10
337 Wally Joyner .10
338 Jim Leyritz .10
339 Paul O'Neill .10
340 Bruce Ruffin .10
341 Michael Tucker .10
342 Andy Benes .10
343 Craig Biggio .15
344 Rex Hudler .10
345 Brad Radke .10
346 Deion Sanders .15
347 Moises Alou .15
348 Brad Ausmus .10
349 Armando Benitez .10
350 Mark Gubicza .10
351 Terry Steinbach .10
352 Mark Whiten .10
353 Ricky Bottalico .10
354 *Brian Giles* 2.00
355 Eric Karros .10
356 Jimmy Key .10
357 Carlos Perez .10
358 Alex Fernandez .10
359 J.T. Snow .10
360 Bobby Bonilla .10
361 Scott Brosius .10
362 Greg Swindell .10
363 Jose Vizcaino .10
364 Matt Williams .30
365 Darren Daulton .10
366 Shane Andrews .10
367 Jim Eisenreich .10
368 Ariel Prieto .10
369 Bob Tewksbury .10
370 Mike Bordick .10
371 Rheal Cormier .10
372 Cliff Floyd .10
373 David Justice .30
374 John Wetteland .10
375 Mike Blowers .10
376 Jose Canseco .50

377	Roger Clemens	1.50
378	Kevin Mitchell	.10
379	Todd Zeile	.10
380	Jim Thome	.10
381	Turk Wendell	.10
382	Rico Brogna	.10
383	Eric Davis	.10
384	Mike Lansing	.10
385	Devon White	.10
386	Marquis Grissom	.10
387	Todd Worrell	.10
388	Jeff Kent	.10
389	Mickey Tettleton	.10
390	Steve Avery	.10
391	David Cone	.10
392	Scott Cooper	.10
393	Lee Stevens	.10
394	Kevin Elster	.10
395	Tom Goodwin	.10
396	Shawn Green	.25
397	Pete Harnisch	.10
398	Eddie Murray	.50
399	Joe Randa	.10
400	Scott Sanders	.10
401	John Valentin	.10
402	Todd Jones	.10
403	Terry Adams	.10
404	Brian Hunter	.10
405	Pat Listach	.10
406	Kenny Lofton	.10
407	Hal Morris	.10
408	Ed Sprague	.10
409	Rich Becker	.10
410	Edgardo Alfonzo	.10
411	Albert Belle	.30
412	Jeff King	.10
413	Kirt Manwaring	.10
414	Jason Schmidt	.10
415	Allen Watson	.10
416	Lee Tinsley	.10
417	Brett Butler	.10
418	Carlos Garcia	.10
419	Mark Lemke	.10
420	Jaime Navarro	.10
421	David Segui	.10
422	Ruben Sierra	.10
423	B.J. Surhoff	.10
424	Julian Tavarez	.10
425	Billy Taylor	.10
426	Ken Caminiti	.10
427	Chuck Carr	.10
428	Benji Gil	.10
429	Terry Mulholland	.10
430	Mike Stanton	.10
431	Wil Cordero	.10
432	Chili Davis	.10
433	Mariano Duncan	.10
434	Orlando Merced	.10
435	Kent Mercker	.10
436	John Olerud	.10
437	Quilvio Veras	.10
438	Mike Fetters	.10
439	Glenallen Hill	.10
440	Bill Swift	.10
441	Tim Wakefield	.10
442	Pedro Astacio	.10
443	Vinny Castilla	.10
444	Doug Drabek	.10
445	Alan Embree	.10
446	Lee Smith	.10
447	Darryl Hamilton	.10
448	Brian McRae	.10
449	Mike Timlin	.10
450	Bob Wickman	.10
451	Jason Dickson	.10
452	Chad Curtis	.10
453	Mark Leiter	.10
454	Damon Berryhill	.10
455	Kevin Orie	.10
456	Dave Burba	.10
457	Chris Holt	.10
458	*Ricky Ledee*	.50
459	Mike Devereaux	.10
460	Pokey Reese	.10
461	Tim Raines	.10
462	Ryan Jones	.10
463	Shane Mack	.10
464	Darren Dreifort	.10
465	Mark Parent	.10
466	Mark Portugal	.10
467	Dante Powell	.10
468	Craig Grebeck	.10
469	Ron Villone	.10
470	Dmitri Young	.10
471	Shannon Stewart	.15
472	Rick Helling	.10
473	Bill Haselman	.10
474	Albie Lopez	.10
475	Glendon Rusch	.10
476	Derrick May	.10
477	Chad Ogea	.10
478	Kirk Reuter	.10
479	Chris Hammond	.10
480	Russ Johnson	.10
481	James Mouton	.10
482	Mike Macfarlane	.10
483	Scott Ruffcorn	.10
484	Jeff Frye	.10
485	Richie Sexson	.10
486	*Emil Brown*	.10
487	Desi Wilson	.10
488	Brent Gates	.10
489	Tony Graffanino	.10
490	Dan Miceli	.10
491	*Orlando Cabrera*	.65
492	*Tony Womack*	.50
493	Jerome Walton	.10
494	Mark Thompson	.10
495	Jose Guillen	.10
496	Willie Blair	.10
497	*T.J. Staton*	.10
498	Scott Kamieniecki	.10
499	Vince Coleman	.10
500	Jeff Abbott	.10
501	Chris Widger	.10
502	Kevin Tapani	.10
503	*Carlos Castillo*	.10
504	Luis Gonzalez	.25
505	Tim Belcher	.10
506	Armando Reynoso	.10
507	Jamie Moyer	.10
508	*Randall Simon*	.10
509	Vladimir Guerrero	1.00
510	*Wady Almonte*	.10
511	Dustin Hermanson	.10
512	*Deivi Cruz*	.50
513	Luis Alicea	.10
514	*Felix Heredia*	.25
515	Don Slaught	.10
516	Shigetosi Hasegawa	.10
517	Matt Walbeck	.10
518	*David Arias* (last name actually Ortiz)	.50
519	*Brady Raggio*	.10
520	Rudy Pemberton	.10
521	Wayne Kirby	.10
522	Calvin Maduro	.10
523	Mark Lewis	.10
524	Mike Jackson	.10
525	Sid Fernandez	.10
526	Mike Bielecki	.10
527	*Bubba Trammell*	.25
528	*Brent Brede*	.10
529	Matt Morris	.10
530	Joe Borowski	.10
531	Orlando Miller	.10
532	Jim Bullinger	.10
533	Robert Person	.10
534	Doug Glanville	.10
535	Terry Pendleton	.10
536	Jorge Posada	.10
537	*Marc Sagmoen*	.10
538	*Fernando Tatis*	.75
539	Aaron Sele	.10
540	Brian Banks	.10
541	Derrek Lee	.10
542	John Wasdin	.10
543	*Justin Towle*	.10
544	Pat Cline	.10
545	Dave Magadan	.10
546	Jeff Blauser	.10
547	Phil Nevin	.10
548	Todd Walker	.10
549	Elieser Marrero	.10
550	Bartolo Colon	.10
551	*Jose Cruz Jr.*	.75
552	Todd Dunwoody	.10
553	*Hideki Irabu*	.50

1997 Ultra Gold Medallion Edition

A new concept in parallel editions was debuted by Ultra in Series I. While sharing the card numbers with regular-issue Ultra cards, the Gold Medallion Edition features a "G" prefix to the card number and gold-foil highlights on front. Unlike past parallels, however, the '97 Ultra Gold Medallion and Platinum Medallion inserts share a photograph which is entirely different from the regular Ultra base cards. Gold Medallion Edition cards are identified as such in the lower-right corner and were inserted at a rate of one per pack.

	MT
Complete Set (553):	100.00
Common Player:	.25
Stars/Rookies:	2X

(See 1997 Ultra for checklist and base card values.)

1997 Ultra Platinum Medallion Edition

A new concept in parallel editions was debuted by Ultra in Series I. While sharing the card numbers with regular-issue Ultra cards, the Platinum Medallion Edition features a "P" prefix to the card number and holographic-foil highlights on front. Unlike past parallels, however, the '97 Ultra Gold Medallion and Platinum Medallion inserts share a photograph which is entirely different from the regular Ultra base cards are identified as such in the lower-right corner and were inserted at a rate of one per 100 packs.

	MT
Complete Set (553):	600.00
Common Player:	2.00
Stars/Rookies:	15X

(See 1997 Ultra for checklist and base card values.)

1997 Ultra Baseball "Rules"!

Baseball Rules was a 10-card insert that was found only in retail packs at a rate of one per 36 packs. The cards are die-cut with a player in front of a mound of baseballs with embossed seams on the front, while each card back explains a baseball term or rule.

		MT
Complete Set (10):		40.00
Common Player:		.75
1	Barry Bonds	3.00
2	Ken Griffey Jr.	6.00
3	Derek Jeter	8.00
4	Chipper Jones	4.00
5	Greg Maddux	3.00
6	Mark McGwire	6.00
7	Troy Percival	.75
8	Mike Piazza	5.00
9	Cal Ripken Jr.	8.00
10	Frank Thomas	2.50

1997 Ultra Checklists

There are 10 Checklist cards in each series of Ultra baseball covering all regular-issue cards and inserts. The front of the card features a superstar, while the back contains a portion of the set checklist. The cards have the player's name and "CHECKLIST" in bold, all caps across the bottom in silver foil.

		MT
Complete Set (20):		15.00
Common Player:		.25
	SERIES 1	
1	Dante Bichette	.25
2	Barry Bonds	1.00
3	Ken Griffey Jr.	1.75
4	Greg Maddux	.75
5	Mark McGwire	2.00
6	Mike Piazza	1.50
7	Cal Ripken Jr.	2.00
8	John Smoltz	.25
9	Sammy Sosa	1.00
10	Frank Thomas	1.00
	SERIES 2	
1	Andruw Jones	.50
2	Ken Griffey Jr.	1.75
3	Frank Thomas	1.00
4	Alex Rodriguez	1.75
5	Cal Ripken Jr.	2.00
6	Mike Piazza	1.50
7	Greg Maddux	.75
8	Chipper Jones	1.50
9	Derek Jeter	1.50
10	Juan Gonzalez	.50

1997 Ultra Diamond Producers

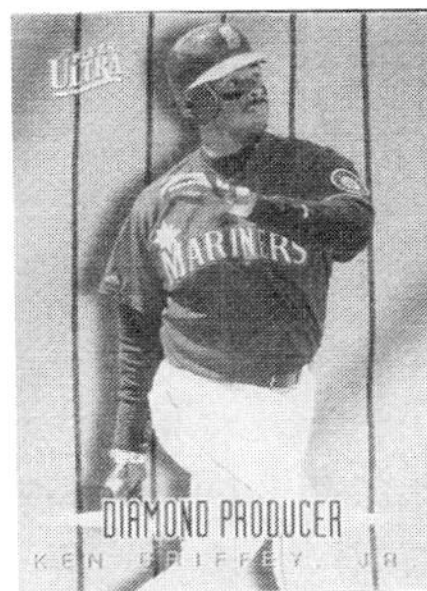

Printed on textured, uniform-like matterial, this 12-card insert contains some of the most consistent producers in baseball. Horizontal backs are conventionally printed with another color player photo on a pin-striped background and a few words about him. This was the most difficult insert Ultra foil-pack insert, with a ratio of one per 288.

		MT
Complete Set (12):		150.00
Common Player:		4.00
1	Jeff Bagwell	10.00
2	Barry Bonds	15.00
3	Ken Griffey Jr.	25.00
4	Chipper Jones	15.00
5	Kenny Lofton	4.00
6	Greg Maddux	15.00
7	Mark McGwire	25.00
8	Mike Piazza	25.00
9	Cal Ripken Jr.	30.00
10	Alex Rodriguez	20.00
11	Frank Thomas	10.00
12	Matt Williams	4.00

1997 Ultra Double Trouble

Double Trouble is a 20-card, team color coded set pairing two stars from the same team on a horizontal front. These inserts were found every four packs.

		MT
Complete Set (20):		8.00
Common Player:		.15
1	Roberto Alomar, Cal Ripken Jr.	1.25
2	Mo Vaughn, Jose Canseco	.60
3	Jim Edmonds, Tim Salmon	.25
4	Harold Baines, Frank Thomas	.75
5	Albert Belle, Kenny Lofton	.25
6	Chuck Knoblauch, Marty Cordova	.15
7	Andy Pettitte, Derek Jeter	1.00
8	Jason Giambi, Mark McGwire	1.50
9	Ken Griffey Jr., Alex Rodriguez	1.50
10	Juan Gonzalez, Will Clark	.60
11	Greg Maddux, Chipper Jones	1.00
12	Mark Grace, Sammy Sosa	1.00
13	Dante Bichette, Andres Galarraga	.15
14	Jeff Bagwell, Derek Bell	.45
15	Hideo Nomo, Mike Piazza	1.00
16	Henry Rodriguez, Moises Alou	.25
17	Rey Ordonez, Alex Ochoa	.15
18	Ray Lankford, Ron Gant	.15
19	Tony Gwynn, Rickey Henderson	.75
20	Barry Bonds, Matt Williams	1.00

1997 Ultra Fielder's Choice

Fielder's Choice highlights 18 of the top defensive players in baseball. Fronts of the horizontal cards have a leather look and feel and are highlighted in gold foil. Backs are conventionally printed with another player photo and some words about his fielding ability. Fielder's Choice inserts were found every 144 packs.

		MT
Complete Set (18):		120.00
Common Player:		1.50
1	Roberto Alomar	6.00
2	Jeff Bagwell	10.00
3	Wade Boggs	6.00
4	Barry Bonds	15.00
5	Mark Grace	4.00
6	Ken Griffey Jr.	25.00
7	Marquis Grissom	1.50
8	Charles Johnson	1.50
9	Chuck Knoblauch	1.50
10	Barry Larkin	3.00
11	Kenny Lofton	2.00
12	Greg Maddux	15.00
13	Raul Mondesi	1.50
14	Rey Ordonez	1.50
15	Cal Ripken Jr.	30.00
16	Alex Rodriguez	20.00
17	Ivan Rodriguez	8.00
18	Matt Williams	2.00

1997 Ultra Golden Prospects

This 10-card set was exclusive to hobby shop packs and highlighted the top young players in baseball. Action photos on front and portraits on back are set on a sepia background. Cards were inserted 1:4 packs.

		MT
Complete Set (10):		4.00
Common Player:		.25
1	Andruw Jones	1.50
2	Vladimir Guerrero	1.50
3	Todd Walker	.50
4	Karim Garcia	.25
5	Kevin Orie	.25
6	Brian Giles	.50
7	Jason Dickson	.25
8	Jose Guillen	.25
9	Ruben Rivera	.25
10	Derrek Lee	.25

1997 Ultra Hitting Machines

This 36-card insert was only found in hobby packs and showcases the game's top hitters. Cards were inserted at a ratio of 1:36 packs.

		MT
Complete Set (18):		75.00
Common Player:		1.50
1	Andruw Jones	3.00
2	Ken Griffey Jr.	10.00
3	Frank Thomas	4.00
4	Alex Rodriguez	9.00
5	Cal Ripken Jr.	12.00
6	Mike Piazza	8.00
7	Derek Jeter	12.00
8	Albert Belle	2.00
9	Tony Gwynn	4.00
10	Jeff Bagwell	3.00
11	Mark McGwire	10.00
12	Kenny Lofton	1.50
13	Manny Ramirez	3.00
14	Roberto Alomar	2.50
15	Ryne Sandberg	3.00
16	Eddie Murray	2.50
17	Sammy Sosa	6.00
18	Ken Caminiti	1.50

1997 Ultra HR Kings

HR Kings are printed on clear plastic with transparent refractive holofoil crowns and other objects in the plastic. Backs contain a white silhouette of the player with career summary and logos within the figure. Stated odds of finding an HR King card were one per 36 packs.

		MT
Complete Set (12):		30.00
Common Player:		1.00
1	Albert Belle	1.50
2	Barry Bonds	3.00
3	Juan Gonzalez	2.50
4	Ken Griffey Jr.	6.00
5	Todd Hundley	1.00
6	Ryan Klesko	1.00
7	Mark McGwire	10.00
8	Mike Piazza	4.50
9	Sammy Sosa	3.00
10	Frank Thomas	3.00
11	Mo Vaughn	1.50
12	Matt Williams	1.00

1997 Ultra Power Plus Series 2

Similar in design to the Power Plus insert in Series I, this 12-card insert salutes the game's top sluggers and was found only in hobby packs. Cards were inserted at a ratio of 1:8 packs. Front design features gold holographic foil graphics.

Backs have another photo and a description of the player's skills.

		MT
Complete Set (12):		24.00
Common Player:		.75
1	Ken Griffey Jr.	4.00
2	Frank Thomas	2.00
3	Alex Rodriguez	4.00
4	Cal Ripken Jr.	4.50
5	Mike Piazza	3.00
6	Chipper Jones	3.00
7	Albert Belle	.75
8	Juan Gonzalez	1.25
9	Jeff Bagwell	1.25
10	Mark McGwire	4.50
11	Mo Vaughn	.75
12	Barry Bonds	2.00

1997 Ultra Leather Shop

Baseball's best fielders are honored in this 12-card hobby-exclusive insert. Cards were inserted at a ratio of 1:6 packs and feature an embossed grain-like finish on the fronts.

		MT
Complete Set (12):		10.00
Common Player:		.25
1	Ken Griffey Jr.	2.25
2	Alex Rodriguez	2.25
3	Cal Ripken Jr.	2.50
4	Derek Jeter	2.00
5	Juan Gonzalez	.75
6	Tony Gwynn	1.00
7	Jeff Bagwell	.75
8	Roberto Alomar	.60
9	Ryne Sandberg	.75
10	Ken Caminiti	.25
11	Kenny Lofton	.25
12	John Smoltz	.25

1997 Ultra Power Plus Series 1

Series 1 Power Plus is a 12-card insert utilizing silver rainbow holofoil in the background, with the featured player in the foreground. Backs another action photo and the player's credentials. The insert captures power hitters that also excel in other areas of the game. Power Plus inserts can be found every 24 packs.

		MT
Complete Set (12):		30.00
Common Player:		1.00
1	Jeff Bagwell	1.25
2	Barry Bonds	2.50
3	Juan Gonzalez	1.25
4	Ken Griffey Jr.	5.00
5	Chipper Jones	3.00
6	Mark McGwire	5.00
7	Mike Piazza	4.00
8	Cal Ripken Jr.	6.00
9	Alex Rodriguez	4.00
10	Sammy Sosa	3.00
11	Frank Thomas	1.50
12	Matt Williams	1.00

1997 Ultra Rookie Reflections

Rookie Reflections features 10 of the 1996 season's top first-year stars. Cards are inserted every four packs. Front features an action photo on a black-and-silver starburst pattern. Horizontal backs have another photo and a career summary of the prospect.

		MT
Complete Set (10):		5.00
Common Player:		.25
1	James Baldwin	.25
2	Jermaine Dye	.25
3	Darin Erstad	.50
4	Todd Hollandsworth	.25
5	Derek Jeter	3.00
6	Jason Kendall	.40
7	Alex Ochoa	.25
8	Rey Ordonez	.40
9	Edgar Renteria	.25
10	Scott Rolen	1.00

1997 Ultra RBI Kings

Ten different players are featured in RBI Kings, which contain a metallic paisley background, with an English shield of armor and latin words in the background. RBI Kings were inserted every 18 packs of Series I.

		MT
Complete Set (10):		15.00
Common Player:		.75
1	Jeff Bagwell	1.50
2	Albert Belle	1.25
3	Dante Bichette	.75
4	Barry Bonds	2.00
5	Jay Buhner	.75
6	Juan Gonzalez	1.50
7	Ken Griffey Jr.	4.00
8	Sammy Sosa	2.00
9	Frank Thomas	2.00
10	Mo Vaughn	1.25

1997 Ultra Season Crowns

Season Crowns were found at a rate of one per eight packs of Ultra I Baseball. This etched, silver-foil insert contained 12 statistical leaders and award winners from the 1996 season.

		MT
Complete Set (12):		14.00
Common Player:		.50
1	Albert Belle	.50
2	Dante Bichette	.50
3	Barry Bonds	2.00
4	Kenny Lofton	.50
5	Edgar Martinez	.50
6	Mark McGwire	3.50
7	Andy Pettitte	.75
8	Mike Piazza	2.50
9	Alex Rodriguez	3.00
10	John Smoltz	.50
11	Sammy Sosa	2.00
12	Frank Thomas	1.00

1997 Ultra Starring Role

Another hobby-exclusive insert, these 12 cards salute baseball's clutch performers and were found 1:288 packs.

		MT
Complete Set (12):		200.00
Common Player:		8.00
1	Andruw Jones	10.00
2	Ken Griffey Jr.	30.00
3	Frank Thomas	12.00
4	Alex Rodriguez	30.00
5	Cal Ripken Jr.	35.00
6	Mike Piazza	25.00
7	Greg Maddux	15.00
8	Chipper Jones	25.00
9	Derek Jeter	35.00
10	Juan Gonzalez	12.00
11	Albert Belle	8.00
12	Tony Gwynn	15.00

1997 Ultra Fame Game

This eight-card hobby-exclusive insert showcases players who have displayed Hall of Fame potential. The player photo on front and Fame Game logo are embossed and highlighted in gold and silver foil. Backs have a color portrait photo and a few words about the player. Cards were inserted 1:8 packs.

		MT
Complete Set (18):		35.00
Common Player:		.50
1	Ken Griffey Jr.	5.00
2	Frank Thomas	2.50
3	Alex Rodriguez	4.00
4	Cal Ripken Jr.	6.00
5	Mike Piazza	4.00
6	Greg Maddux	2.50
7	Derek Jeter	6.00
8	Jeff Bagwell	1.50
9	Juan Gonzalez	1.50

10	Albert Belle	.60
11	Tony Gwynn	2.00
12	Mark McGwire	5.00
13	Andy Pettitte	.75
14	Kenny Lofton	.50
15	Roberto Alomar	1.25
16	Ryne Sandberg	1.25
17	Barry Bonds	3.00
18	Eddie Murray	.75

1997 Ultra Thunderclap

This 10-card hobby-exclusive insert showcases hitters who strike fear in opposing pitchers. Cards were inserted 1:18 packs. Fronts are highlighted by streaks of gold prismatic foil lightning in a story sky. Backs have another player photo and a few words about him.

		MT
Complete Set (10):		25.00
Common Player:		1.25
1	Barry Bonds	2.00
2	Mo Vaughn	1.25
3	Mark McGwire	6.00
4	Jeff Bagwell	1.50
5	Juan Gonzalez	1.50
6	Alex Rodriguez	5.00
7	Chipper Jones	4.00
8	Ken Griffey Jr.	5.00
9	Mike Piazza	4.00
10	Frank Thomas	2.00

1997 Ultra Top 30

This 30-card insert was found only in retail store packs and salutes the 30 most collectible players in the game. Cards were inserted one per pack. A Top 30 Gold Medallion parallel set, die-cut around the top, was also produced and inserted 1:18 packs.

		MT
Complete Set (30):		18.00
Common Player:		.20
Gold Medallions:		5X
1	Andruw Jones	.75
2	Ken Griffey Jr.	1.75
3	Frank Thomas	1.25
4	Alex Rodriguez	1.75
5	Cal Ripken Jr.	2.00
6	Mike Piazza	1.25
7	Greg Maddux	1.00
8	Chipper Jones	1.25
9	Derek Jeter	1.50
10	Juan Gonzalez	.75
11	Albert Belle	.40
12	Tony Gwynn	1.00
13	Jeff Bagwell	.75
14	Mark McGwire	2.00
15	Andy Pettitte	.40
16	Mo Vaughn	.40
17	Kenny Lofton	.20
18	Manny Ramirez	.75
19	Roberto Alomar	.60
20	Ryne Sandberg	.75
21	Hideo Nomo	.65
22	Barry Bonds	1.25
23	Eddie Murray	.50
24	Ken Caminiti	.20
25	John Smoltz	.25
26	Pat Hentgen	.20
27	Todd Hollandsworth	.20
28	Matt Williams	.25
29	Bernie Williams	.40
30	Brady Anderson	.20

1998 Ultra

Ultra was released in two series with a total of 501 cards; 250 in Series 1 and 251 in Series 2. The product sold in 10-card packs for an SRP of $2.59. There were three parallel sets: Gold Medallion, Platinum Medallion and Masterpieces. Series 1 has 210 regular cards, 25 Prospects (seeded 1:4 packs), 10 Season's Crowns (1:12) and five Checklists (1:8). Series 2 has 202 regular cards, 25 Pizzazz (1:4), 20 New Horizons and three checklists. Series 2 also added a Mike Piazza N.Y. Mets card as #501, inserted every 20 packs. Inserts in Series 1 include: Big Shots, Double Trouble, Kid Gloves, Back to the Future, Artistic Talents, Fall Classics, Power Plus, Prime Leather, Diamond Producers, Diamond Ink and Million Dollar Moments. Series 2 included: Notables, Rocket to Stardom, Millennium Men, Win Now, Ticket Studs, Diamond Immortals, Diamond Ink, Top 30 and 750 sequentially numbered Alex Rodriguez autographed promo cards.

		MT
Complete Set (501):		125.00
Common Player:		.10
Alex Rodriguez Autograph (750):		60.00
Pack (10):		1.50
Wax Box (24):		25.00
1	Ken Griffey Jr.	2.25
2	Matt Morris	.10
3	Roger Clemens	1.00
4	Matt Williams	.30
5	Roberto Hernandez	.10
6	Rondell White	.15
7	Tim Salmon	.25
8	Brad Radke	.10
9	Brett Butler	.10
10	Carl Everett	.15
11	Chili Davis	.10
12	Chuck Finley	.10
13	Darryl Kile	.10
14	Deivi Cruz	.10
15	Gary Gaetti	.10
16	Matt Stairs	.10
17	Pat Meares	.10
18	Will Cunnane	.10
19	*Steve Woodard*	.25
20	Andy Ashby	.10
21	Bobby Higginson	.15
22	Brian Jordan	.10
23	Craig Biggio	.15
24	Jim Edmonds	.10
25	Ryan McGuire	.10
26	Scott Hatteberg	.10
27	Willie Greene	.10
28	Albert Belle	.30
29	Ellis Burks	.10
30	Hideo Nomo	.65
31	Jeff Bagwell	.75
32	Kevin Brown	.15
33	Nomar Garciaparra	1.50
34	Pedro Martinez	.65
35	Raul Mondesi	.25
36	Ricky Bottalico	.10
37	Shawn Estes	.10
38	Shawon Dunston	.10
39	Terry Steinbach	.10
40	Tom Glavine	.15
41	Todd Dunwoody	.10
42	Deion Sanders	.15
43	Gary Sheffield	.35
44	Mike Lansing	.10
45	Mike Lieberthal	.10
46	Paul Sorrento	.10
47	Paul O'Neill	.10
48	Tom Goodwin	.10
49	Andruw Jones	.75
50	Barry Bonds	1.50
51	Bernie Williams	.30
52	Jeremi Gonzalez	.10
53	Mike Piazza	2.00
54	Russ Davis	.10
55	Vinny Castilla	.10
56	Rod Beck	.10
57	Andres Galarraga	.10
58	Ben McDonald	.10
59	Billy Wagner	.10
60	Charles Johnson	.10
61	Fred McGriff	.10
62	Dean Palmer	.10
63	Frank Thomas	1.00
64	Ismael Valdes	.10
65	Mark Bellhorn	.10
66	Jeff King	.10
67	John Wetteland	.10
68	Mark Grace	.30
69	Mark Kotsay	.10
70	Scott Rolen	.65
71	Todd Hundley	.10
72	Todd Worrell	.10
73	Wilson Alvarez	.10
74	Bobby Jones	.10
75	Jose Canseco	.40
76	Kevin Appier	.10
77	Neifi Perez	.10
78	Paul Molitor	.65
79	Quilvio Veras	.10
80	Randy Johnson	.75
81	Glendon Rusch	.10
82	Curt Schilling	.15
83	Alex Rodriguez	2.25
84	Rey Ordonez	.10
85	Jeff Juden	.10
86	Mike Cameron	.10
87	Ryan Klesko	.10
88	Trevor Hoffman	.10
89	Chuck Knoblauch	.10
90	Larry Walker	.30
91	Mark McLemore	.10
92	B.J. Surhoff	.10
93	Darren Daulton	.10
94	Ray Durham	.10
95	Sammy Sosa	1.50
96	Eric Young	.10
97	Gerald Williams	.10
98	Javy Lopez	.10
99	John Smiley	.10
100	Juan Gonzalez	.75
101	Shawn Green	.30
102	Charles Nagy	.10
103	David Justice	.25
104	Joey Hamilton	.10
105	Pat Hentgen	.10
106	Raul Casanova	.10
107	Tony Phillips	.10
108	Tony Gwynn	1.00
109	Will Clark	.30
110	Jason Giambi	.40
111	Jay Bell	.10
112	Johnny Damon	.15
113	Alan Benes	.10
114	Jeff Suppan	.10
115	*Kevin Polcovich*	.10
116	Shigetosi Hasegawa	.10
117	Steve Finley	.10
118	Tony Clark	.10
119	David Cone	.10
120	Jose Guillen	.10
121	*Kevin Millwood*	1.00
122	Greg Maddux	1.00
123	Dave Nilsson	.10
124	Hideki Irabu	.10
125	Jason Kendall	.10
126	Jim Thome	.10
127	Delino DeShields	.10
128	Edgar Renteria	.10
129	Edgardo Alfonzo	.10
130	J.T. Snow	.10
131	Jeff Abbott	.10
132	Jeffrey Hammonds	.10
133	Rich Loiselle	.10
134	Vladimir Guerrero	.75
135	Jay Buhner	.10
136	Jeff Cirillo	.10
137	Jeromy Burnitz	.10
138	Mickey Morandini	.10
139	Tino Martinez	.10
140	Jeff Shaw	.10
141	Rafael Palmeiro	.30
142	Bobby Bonilla	.10
143	Cal Ripken Jr.	2.50
144	*Chad Fox*	.15
145	Dante Bichette	.10
146	Dennis Eckersley	.10
147	Mariano Rivera	.20
148	Mo Vaughn	.40
149	Reggie Sanders	.10
150	Derek Jeter	2.50
151	Rusty Greer	.10
152	Brady Anderson	.10
153	Brett Tomko	.10
154	Jaime Navarro	.10
155	Kevin Orie	.10
156	Roberto Alomar	.60
157	Edgar Martinez	.10
158	John Olerud	.10
159	John Smoltz	.15
160	Ryne Sandberg	.75
161	Billy Taylor	.10
162	Chris Holt	.10
163	Damion Easley	.10
164	Darin Erstad	.75
165	Joe Carter	.10
166	Kelvim Escobar	.10
167	Ken Caminiti	.10
168	Pokey Reese	.10
169	Ray Lankford	.10
170	Livan Hernandez	.10
171	Steve Kline	.10
172	Tom Gordon	.10
173	Travis Fryman	.10
174	Al Martin	.10
175	Andy Pettitte	.30
176	Jeff Kent	.10
177	Jimmy Key	.10
178	Mark Grudzielanek	.10

179 Tony Saunders .10
180 Barry Larkin .15
181 Bubba Trammell .10
182 Carlos Delgado .40
183 Carlos Baerga .10
184 Derek Bell .10
185 Henry Rodriguez .10
186 Jason Dickson .10
187 Ron Gant .10
188 Tony Womack .10
189 Justin Thompson .10
190 Fernando Tatis .10
191 Mark Wohlers .10
192 Takashi Kashiwada .10
193 Garret Anderson .10
194 Jose Cruz, Jr. .25
195 Ricardo Rincon .10
196 Tim Naehring .10
197 Moises Alou .20
198 Eric Karros .10
199 John Jaha .10
200 Marty Cordova .10
201 Travis Lee .15
202 Mark Davis .10
203 Vladimir Nunez .10
204 Stanton Cameron .10
205 *Mike Stoner* .50
206 *Rolando Arrojo* .40
207 Rick White .10
208 Luis Polonia .10
209 Greg Blosser .10
210 Cesar Devarez .10
211 Jeff Bagwell (Season Crown) 1.25
212 Barry Bonds (Season Crown) 2.50
213 Roger Clemens (Season Crown) 2.00
214 Nomar Garciaparra (Season Crown) 2.50
215 Ken Griffey Jr. (Season Crown) 3.50
216 Tony Gwynn (Season Crown) 2.00
217 Randy Johnson (Season Crown) .75
218 Mark McGwire (Season Crown) 5.00
219 Scott Rolen (Season Crown) 1.00
220 Frank Thomas (Season Crown) 2.00
221 Matt Perisho (Prospect) .50
222 Wes Helms (Prospect) .75
223 *David Dellucci* (Prospect) 1.00
224 Todd Helton (Prospect) 2.00
225 Brian Rose (Prospect) .50
226 Aaron Boone (Prospect) .50
227 Keith Foulke (Prospect) .50
228 Homer Bush (Prospect) .50
229 Shannon Stewart (Prospect) .75
230 Richard Hidalgo (Prospect) .75
231 Russ Johnson (Prospect) .50
232 *Henry Blanco* (Prospect) .75
233 Paul Konerko (Prospect) .75
234 Antone Williamson (Prospect) .50
235 *Shane Bowers* (Prospect) .50
236 Jose Vidro (Prospect) .60
237 Derek Wallace (Prospect) .50
238 Ricky Ledee (Prospect) .75
239 Ben Grieve (Prospect) 1.50
240 Lou Collier (Prospect) .50
241 Derrek Lee (Prospect) .75
242 Ruben Rivera (Prospect) .50
243 Jorge Velandia (Prospect) .50
244 Andrew Vessel (Prospect) .50
245 Chris Carpenter (Prospect) .50
246 Checklist (Ken Griffey Jr.) .75
247 Checklist (Andruw Jones) .50
248 Checklist (Alex Rodriguez) .75
249 Checklist (Frank Thomas) .60
250 Checklist (Cal Ripken Jr.) 1.00
251 Carlos Perez .10
252 Larry Sutton .10
253 Brad Rigby .10
254 Wally Joyner .10
255 Todd Stottlemyre .10
256 Nerio Rodriguez .10
257 Jeff Frye .10
258 Pedro Astacio .10
259 Cal Eldred .10
260 Chili Davis .10
261 Freddy Garcia .10
262 Bobby Witt .10
263 Michael Coleman .10
264 Mike Caruso .10
265 Mike Lansing .10
266 Dennis Reyes .10
267 F.P. Santangelo .10
268 Darryl Hamilton .10
269 Mike Fetters .10
270 Charlie Hayes .10
271 Royce Clayton .10
272 Doug Drabek .10
273 James Baldwin .10
274 Brian Hunter .10
275 Chan Ho Park .20
276 John Franco .10
277 David Wells .15
278 Eli Marrero .10
279 Kerry Wood .40
280 Donnie Sadler .10
281 *Scott Winchester* .10
282 Hal Morris .10
283 Brad Fullmer .10
284 Bernard Gilkey .10
285 Ramiro Mendoza .10
286 Kevin Brown .15
287 David Segui .10
288 Willie McGee .10
289 Darren Oliver .10
290 Antonio Alfonseca .10
291 Eric Davis .10
292 Mickey Morandini .10
293 *Frank Catalanotto* .20
294 Derrek Lee .10
295 Todd Zeile .10
296 Chuck Knoblauch .10
297 Wilson Delgado .10
298 Raul Ibanez .10
299 Orel Hershiser .10
300 Ozzie Guillen .10
301 Aaron Sele .10
302 Joe Carter .10
303 Darryl Kile .10
304 Shane Reynolds .10
305 Todd Dunn .10
306 Bob Abreu .15
307 Doug Strange .10
308 Jose Canseco .40
309 Lance Johnson .10
310 Harold Baines .10
311 Todd Pratt .10
312 Greg Colbrunn .10
313 *Masato Yoshii* .40
314 Felix Heredia .10
315 Dennis Martinez .10
316 Geronimo Berroa .10
317 Darren Lewis .10
318 Billy Ripken .10
319 Enrique Wilson .10
320 Alex Ochoa .10
321 Doug Glanville .10
322 Mike Stanley .10
323 Gerald Williams .10
324 Pedro Martinez .65
325 Jaret Wright .10
326 Terry Pendleton .10
327 LaTroy Hawkins .10
328 Emil Brown .10
329 Walt Weiss .10
330 Omar Vizquel .10
331 Carl Everett .15
332 Fernando Vina .10
333 Mike Blowers .10
334 Dwight Gooden .10
335 Mark Lewis .10
336 Jim Leyritz .10
337 Kenny Lofton .10
338 *John Halama* .30
339 Jose Valentin .10
340 Desi Relaford .10
341 Dante Powell .10
342 Ed Sprague .10
343 Reggie Jefferson .10
344 Mike Hampton .10
345 Marquis Grissom .10
346 Heathcliff Slocumb .10
347 Francisco Cordova .10
348 Ken Cloude .10
349 Benito Santiago .10
350 Denny Neagle .10
351 Sean Casey .25
352 Robb Nen .10
353 Orlando Merced .10
354 Adrian Brown .10
355 Gregg Jefferies .10
356 Otis Nixon .10
357 Michael Tucker .10
358 Eric Milton .10
359 Travis Fryman .10
360 Gary DiSarcina .10
361 Mario Valdez .10
362 Craig Counsell .10
363 Jose Offerman .10
364 Tony Fernandez .10
365 Jason McDonald .10
366 Sterling Hitchcock .10
367 Donovan Osborne .10
368 Troy Percival .10
369 Henry Rodriguez .10
370 Dmitri Young .10
371 Jay Powell .10
372 Jeff Conine .10
373 Orlando Cabrera .15
374 Butch Huskey .10
375 *Mike Lowell* .75
376 Kevin Young .10
377 Jamie Moyer .10
378 Jeff D'Amico .10
379 Scott Erickson .10
380 *Magglio Ordonez* 2.00
381 Melvin Nieves .10
382 Ramon Martinez .10
383 A.J. Hinch .10
384 Jeff Brantley .10
385 Kevin Elster .10
386 Allen Watson .10
387 Moises Alou .20
388 Jeff Blauser .10
389 Pete Harnisch .10
390 Shane Andrews .10
391 Rico Brogna .10
392 Stan Javier .10
393 David Howard .10
394 Darryl Strawberry .10
395 Kent Mercker .10
396 Juan Encarnacion .10
397 Sandy Alomar .10
398 Al Leiter .10
399 Tony Graffanino .10
400 Terry Adams .10
401 Bruce Aven .10
402 Derrick Gibson .10
403 Jose Cabrera .10
404 Rich Becker .10
405 David Ortiz .10
406 Brian McRae .10
407 Bobby Estalella .10
408 Bill Mueller .10
409 Dennis Eckersley .10
410 Sandy Martinez .10
411 Jose Vizcaino .10
412 Jermaine Allensworth .10
413 Miguel Tejada .20
414 Turner Ward .10
415 Glenallen Hill .10
416 Lee Stevens .10
417 Cecil Fielder .10
418 Ruben Sierra .10
419 Jon Nunnally .10
420 Rod Myers .10
421 Dustin Hermanson .15
422 James Mouton .10
423 Dan Wilson .10
424 Roberto Kelly .10
425 Antonio Osuna .10
426 Jacob Cruz .10
427 Brent Mayne .10
428 Matt Karchner .10
429 Damian Jackson .10
430 Roger Cedeno .10
431 Rickey Henderson .65
432 Joe Randa .10
433 Greg Vaughn .10
434 Andres Galarraga .10
435 Rod Beck .10
436 Curtis Goodwin .10
437 Brad Ausmus .10
438 Bob Hamelin .10
439 Todd Walker .10
440 Scott Brosius .10
441 Lenny Dykstra .10
442 Abraham Nunez .10
443 Brian Johnson .10
444 Randy Myers .10
445 Bret Boone .15
446 Oscar Henriquez .10
447 Mike Sweeney .10
448 Kenny Rogers .10
449 Mark Langston .10
450 Luis Gonzalez .35
451 John Burkett .10
452 Bip Roberts .10
453 Travis Lee (New Horizons) .15
454 Felix Rodriguez (New Horizons) .10
455 Andy Benes (New Horizons) .10
456 Willie Blair (New Horizons) .10
457 Brian Anderson (New Horizons) .10
458 Jay Bell (New Horizons) .10
459 Matt Williams (New Horizons) .15
460 Devon White (New Horizons) .10
461 Karim Garcia (New Horizons) .15
462 Jorge Fabregas (New Horizons) .10
463 Wilson Alvarez (New Horizons) .10
464 Roberto Hernandez (New Horizons) .10
465 Tony Saunders (New Horizons) .10
466 *Rolando Arrojo* (New Horizons) .20
467 Wade Boggs (New Horizons) .65
468 Fred McGriff (New Horizons) .10
469 Paul Sorrento (New Horizons) .10
470 Kevin Stocker (New Horizons) .10
471 Bubba Trammell (New Horizons) .25
472 Quinton McCracken (New Horizons) .10
473 Checklist (Ken Griffey Jr.) .75
474 Checklist (Cal Ripken Jr.) 1.00
475 Checklist (Frank Thomas) .60
476 Ken Griffey Jr. (Pizzazz) 3.50
477 Cal Ripken Jr. (Pizzazz) 4.00
478 Frank Thomas (Pizzazz) 2.00
479 Alex Rodriguez (Pizzazz) 3.00
480 Nomar Garciaparra (Pizzazz) 2.00
481 Derek Jeter (Pizzazz) 4.00
482 Andruw Jones (Pizzazz) 1.00
483 Chipper Jones (Pizzazz) 2.50
484 Greg Maddux (Pizzazz) 1.50
485 Mike Piazza (Pizzazz) 2.50
486 Juan Gonzalez (Pizzazz) 1.00
487 Jose Cruz (Pizzazz) .75
488 Jaret Wright (Pizzazz) .75

489	Hideo Nomo (Pizzazz)	.75
490	Scott Rolen (Pizzazz)	1.00
491	Tony Gwynn (Pizzazz)	1.50
492	Roger Clemens (Pizzazz)	1.50
493	Darin Erstad (Pizzazz)	.75
494	Mark McGwire (Pizzazz)	4.00
495	Jeff Bagwell (Pizzazz)	1.00
496	Mo Vaughn (Pizzazz)	.75
497	Albert Belle (Pizzazz)	.75
498	Kenny Lofton (Pizzazz)	.75
499	Ben Grieve (Pizzazz)	1.00
500	Barry Bonds (Pizzazz)	2.50
501	Mike Piazza (Mets)	3.00

1998 Ultra Gold Medallion

This parallel to the Ultra set is found seeded on a one per pack ratio. Cards are similar to the regular-issue Ultra except for a gold presentation of the embossed player name on front and a shower of gold specks in the photo background. Backs have a "G" suffix to the card number and a "GOLD MEDALLION EDITION" notation at bottom. The short-printed subset cards from the regular Ultra edition are not short-printed in Gold Medallion.

	MT
Complete Set (501):	200.00
Common Player:	.25
Stars/RCs:	2X
Checklists:	3X
Season Crowns: 50%	
Prospects: 50%	
Pizzazz:	1X

(See 1998 Ultra for checklist and base card values.)

1998 Ultra Platinum Medallion

Insertion odds on this super-scarce insert set are not given but each card is produced and serially numbered in an edition of only 100 (Series 1) or 98 (Series 2). Fronts are similar to regular Ultra cards except the photo is black-and-white and the name is rendered in silver prismatic foil. Backs are in color with the serial number printed in silver foil at bottom. Series 2 checklist cards #473-475 were not printed in Platinum, and the short-prints from the regular issue are not short-printed in this parallel edition.

	MT
Common Player:	3.00
Stars/RCs:	30X
Checklists:	3X
Season Crowns:	6X
Prospects:	8X
Pizzazz:	8X

(See 1998 Ultra for checklist and base card values.)

1998 Ultra Masterpiece

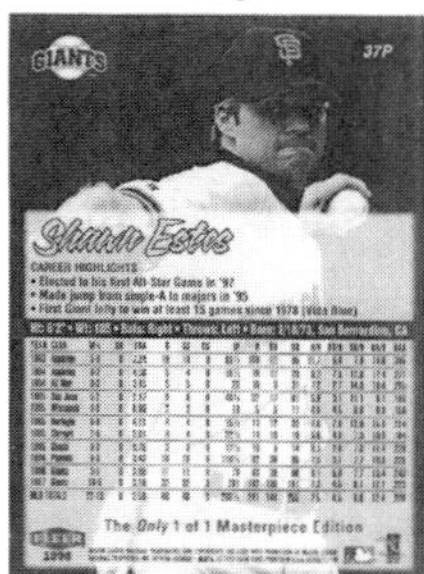

This top of the line parallel to '98 Ultra consists of a 1 of 1 version of each regular card.

	MT
Common Player:	50.00

(Individual players cannot be priced due to scarcity and fluctuating demand.)

1998 Ultra Artistic Talents

This 18-card insert featured top players in the game on a canvas-like surface with the insert name in silver holographic letters across the top. The backs are done in black and white and numbered with an "AT" suffix. Artistic Talents are inserted one per eight packs.

		MT
Complete Set (18):		40.00
Common Player:		1.00
Inserted 1:8		
1	Ken Griffey Jr.	3.50
2	Andruw Jones	2.00
3	Alex Rodriguez	3.50
4	Frank Thomas	2.75
5	Cal Ripken Jr.	4.00
6	Derek Jeter	4.00
7	Chipper Jones	3.00
8	Greg Maddux	2.50
9	Mike Piazza	3.00
10	Albert Belle	1.00
11	Darin Erstad	1.00
12	Juan Gonzalez	2.00
13	Jeff Bagwell	2.00
14	Tony Gwynn	2.50
15	Mark McGwire	4.00
16	Scott Rolen	1.50
17	Barry Bonds	2.75
18	Kenny Lofton	1.00

1998 Ultra Back to the Future

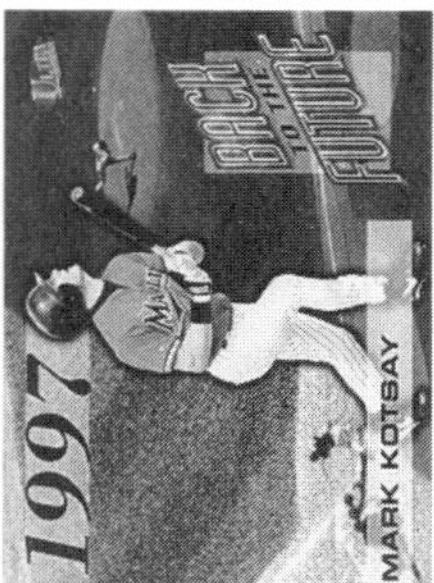

This 15-card insert was printed in a horizontal format with a baseball field background. Cards were numbered with a "BF" suffix and seeded one per six packs.

		MT
Complete Set (15):		10.00
Common Player:		.25
Inserted 1:6		
1	Andruw Jones	1.00
2	Alex Rodriguez	2.50
3	Derek Jeter	3.00
4	Darin Erstad	.50
5	Mike Cameron	.25
6	Scott Rolen	1.00
7	Nomar Garciaparra	1.50
8	Hideki Irabu	.25
9	Jose Cruz, Jr.	.25
10	Vladimir Guerrero	1.00
11	Mark Kotsay	.40
12	Tony Womack	.25
13	Jason Dickson	.25
14	Jose Guillen	.25
15	Tony Clark	.25

1998 Ultra Big Shots

Big Shots was a 15-card insert displaying some of the top home run hitters in baseball. A generic stadium is pictured across the bottom with the insert name running up the left side. Cards were numbered with a "BS" suffix and inserted one per four Series I packs.

		MT
Complete Set (15):		10.00
Common Player:		.25
Inserted 1:4		
1	Ken Griffey Jr.	2.00
2	Frank Thomas	1.00
3	Chipper Jones	1.50
4	Albert Belle	.35
5	Juan Gonzalez	.75
6	Jeff Bagwell	.75
7	Mark McGwire	2.50
8	Barry Bonds	1.00
9	Manny Ramirez	.75
10	Mo Vaughn	.50
11	Matt Williams	.35
12	Jim Thome	.25
13	Tino Martinez	.25
14	Mike Piazza	1.50
15	Tony Clark	.25

1998 Ultra Diamond Immortals

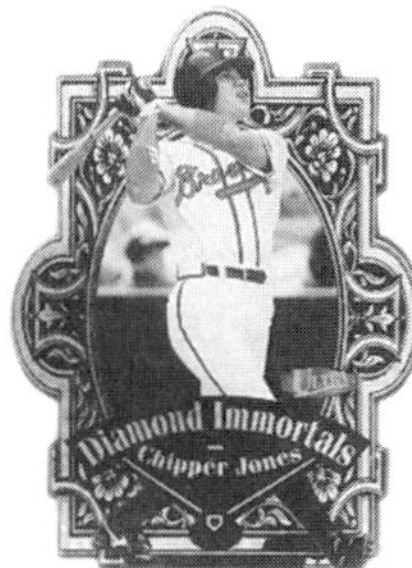

This Series II insert showcased 15 top player on an intricate silver holographic foil design that frames each player. Cards were numbered with a "DI" suffix and inserted one per 288 packs.

		MT
Complete Set (15):		375.00
Common Player:		7.50
Inserted 1:288		
1	Ken Griffey Jr.	40.00
2	Frank Thomas	20.00
3	Alex Rodriguez	40.00
4	Cal Ripken Jr.	50.00
5	Mike Piazza	40.00
6	Mark McGwire	40.00
7	Greg Maddux	20.00

8	Andruw Jones	15.00
9	Chipper Jones	40.00
10	Derek Jeter	50.00
11	Tony Gwynn	20.00
12	Juan Gonzalez	15.00
13	Jose Cruz	7.50
14	Roger Clemens	20.00
15	Barry Bonds	25.00

1998 Ultra Diamond Producers

This 15-card insert captured players on a prismatic silver design, with a wood backdrop and a black felt frame around the border. Cards were seeded one per 288 Series I packs and numbered with a "DP" suffix.

		MT
Complete Set (15):		200.00
Common Player:		4.00
Inserted 1:288		
1	Ken Griffey Jr.	25.00
2	Andruw Jones	8.00
3	Alex Rodriguez	25.00
4	Frank Thomas	12.00
5	Cal Ripken Jr.	30.00
6	Derek Jeter	30.00
7	Chipper Jones	20.00
8	Greg Maddux	15.00
9	Mike Piazza	20.00
10	Juan Gonzalez	10.00
11	Jeff Bagwell	10.00
12	Tony Gwynn	15.00
13	Mark McGwire	25.00
14	Barry Bonds	15.00
15	Jose Cruz, Jr.	4.00

1998 Ultra Double Trouble

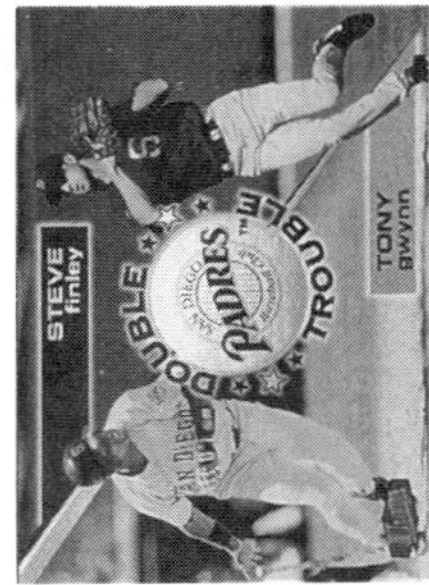

Double Trouble includes 20 cards and pairs two teammates on a horizontal format with the team's logo and the insert name featured in a silver holographic circle in the middle. These were numbered with a "DT" suffix and exclusive to Series I packs at a rate of one per four.

		MT
Complete Set (20):		12.00
Common Player:		.15
Inserted 1:4		
1	Ken Griffey Jr., Alex Rodriguez	1.50
2	Vladimir Guerrero, Pedro Martinez	.60
3	Andruw Jones, Kenny Lofton	.50
4	Chipper Jones, Greg Maddux	1.00
5	Derek Jeter, Tino Martinez	1.00
6	Frank Thomas, Albert Belle	.75
7	Cal Ripken Jr., Roberto Alomar	1.50
8	Mike Piazza, Hideo Nomo	1.00
9	Darin Erstad, Jason Dickson	.15
10	Juan Gonzalez, Ivan Rodriguez	.75
11	Jeff Bagwell, Darryl Kile	.60
12	Tony Gwynn, Steve Finley	.75
13	Mark McGwire, Ray Lankford	1.50
14	Barry Bonds, Jeff Kent	.65
15	Andy Pettitte, Bernie Williams	.25
16	Mo Vaughn, Nomar Garciaparra	1.00
17	Matt Williams, Jim Thome	.15
18	Hideki Irabu, Mariano Rivera	.25
19	Roger Clemens, Jose Cruz, Jr.	.75
20	Manny Ramirez, David Justice	.60

1998 Ultra Fall Classics

This Series I insert pictures 15 stars over a green holographic bacground that contains the insert name in script. Fall Classics were inserted one per 18 packs and numbered with a "FC" suffix.

		MT
Complete Set (15):		45.00
Common Player:		1.50
Inserted 1:18		
1	Ken Griffey Jr.	5.00
2	Andruw Jones	2.00
3	Alex Rodriguez	5.00
4	Frank Thomas	3.50
5	Cal Ripken Jr.	8.00
6	Derek Jeter	8.00
7	Chipper Jones	4.00
8	Greg Maddux	3.00
9	Mike Piazza	4.00
10	Albert Belle	1.50
11	Juan Gonzalez	2.00
12	Jeff Bagwell	2.00
13	Tony Gwynn	3.00
14	Mark McGwire	6.00
15	Barry Bonds	3.50

1998 Ultra Kid Gloves

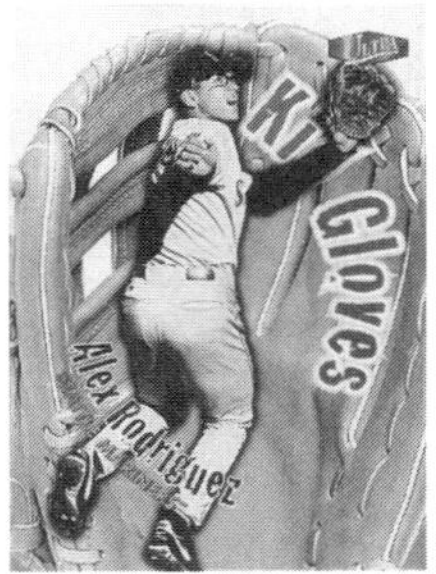

Kid Gloves featured top fielders in the game over an embossed glove background. Exclusive to Series I packs, they were inserted in one per eight packs and numbered with a "KG" suffix.

		MT
Complete Set (12):		15.00
Common Player:		.50
Inserted 1:8		
1	Andruw Jones	1.25
2	Alex Rodriguez	4.00
3	Derek Jeter	3.00
4	Chipper Jones	3.00
5	Darin Erstad	.75
6	Todd Walker	.50
7	Scott Rolen	1.00
8	Nomar Garciaparra	2.50
9	Jose Cruz, Jr.	.50
10	Charles Johnson	.50
11	Rey Ordonez	.50
12	Vladimir Guerrero	1.25

1998 Ultra Millennium Men

Millenium Men was a 15-card hobby-only insert exclusive to Series II packs. These tri-fold cards featured an embossed wax seal design and could be unfolded to reveal another shot of the player, team logo and statistics. They were numbered with a "MM" suffix and inserted every 35 packs.

		MT
Complete Set (15):		40.00
Common Player:		1.00
Inserted 1:35		
1	Jose Cruz	1.00
2	Ken Griffey Jr.	5.00
3	Cal Ripken Jr.	6.00
4	Derek Jeter	6.00
5	Andruw Jones	1.75
6	Alex Rodriguez	5.00
7	Chipper Jones	4.00
8	Scott Rolen	1.50
9	Nomar Garciaparra	3.50
10	Frank Thomas	3.00
11	Mike Piazza	4.00
12	Greg Maddux	2.50
13	Juan Gonzalez	2.00
14	Ben Grieve	1.25
15	Jaret Wright	1.00

1998 Ultra Power Plus

This 10-card insert was exclusive to Series I packs and seeded one per 36 packs. Cards pictured the player over an embossed blue background featuring plus signs. These were numbered with a "PP" suffix.

		MT
Complete Set (10):		25.00
Common Player:		1.00
Inserted 1:36		
1	Ken Griffey Jr.	8.00
2	Andruw Jones	2.00
3	Alex Rodriguez	8.00
4	Frank Thomas	3.00
5	Mike Piazza	6.00
6	Albert Belle	1.25
7	Juan Gonzalez	2.00
8	Jeff Bagwell	2.00
9	Barry Bonds	3.00
10	Jose Cruz, Jr.	1.00

1998 Ultra Prime Leather

This 18-card insert features top fielders on a leather-like card stock, with a large baseball in the background. Cards are seeded one per 144 Series I packs and numbered with a "PL" suffix.

		MT
Complete Set (18):		250.00
Common Player:		1.50
Inserted 1:144		
1	Ken Griffey Jr.	30.00
2	Andruw Jones	8.00
3	Alex Rodriguez	30.00
4	Frank Thomas	10.00
5	Cal Ripken Jr.	40.00
6	Derek Jeter	40.00
7	Chipper Jones	20.00
8	Greg Maddux	20.00
9	Mike Piazza	25.00
10	Albert Belle	4.00
11	Darin Erstad	4.00
12	Juan Gonzalez	10.00
13	Jeff Bagwell	10.00
14	Tony Gwynn	10.00
15	Roberto Alomar	8.00
16	Barry Bonds	20.00
17	Kenny Lofton	4.00
18	Jose Cruz, Jr.	3.00

1998 Ultra Notables

This 20-card insert pictured a player over a holographic background with either an American League or National League logo in the background. Notables were seeded one per four Series II packs and numbered with a "N" suffix.

		MT
Complete Set (20):		27.50
Common Player:		.50
Inserted 1:4		
1	Frank Thomas	2.00
2	Ken Griffey Jr.	3.50
3	Edgar Renteria	.50
4	Albert Belle	.75
5	Juan Gonzalez	1.00
6	Jeff Bagwell	1.00
7	Mark McGwire	4.00
8	Barry Bonds	2.00
9	Scott Rolen	1.00
10	Mo Vaughn	.75
11	Andruw Jones	1.00
12	Chipper Jones	2.50
13	Tino Martinez	.50
14	Mike Piazza	2.50
15	Tony Clark	.50
16	Jose Cruz	.50
17	Nomar Garciaparra	2.00
18	Cal Ripken Jr.	4.00
19	Alex Rodriguez	3.50
20	Derek Jeter	2.50

1998 Ultra Rocket to Stardom

This 15-card insert set was exclusive to Series II packs and inserted in one per 20 packs. Cards were in black-and- white and were die-cut and embossed. The insert contained a collection of top young stars and was numbered with a "RS" suffix.

		MT
Complete Set (15):		24.00
Common Player:		.75
Inserted 1:20		
1	Ben Grieve	2.50
2	Magglio Ordonez	8.00
3	Travis Lee	1.50
4	Carl Pavano	.75
5	Brian Rose	.75
6	Brad Fullmer	1.00
7	Michael Coleman	.75
8	Juan Encarnacion	1.00
9	Karim Garcia	1.00
10	Todd Helton	4.00
11	Richard Hildalgo	1.00
12	Paul Konerko	1.50
13	Rod Myers	.75
14	Jaret Wright	1.50
15	Miguel Tejada	2.50

1998 Ultra Ticket Studs

Fifteen players are featured on fold-out game ticket-like cards in Ticket Studs. The cards arrived folded across the middle and open to reveal a full-length shot of the player with prismatic team color stipes in over a white background that has section, seat and row numbers. Cards were inserted one per 144 Series II packs and are numbered with a "TS" suffix.

		MT
Complete Set (15):		200.00
Common Player:		3.00
Inserted 1:144		
1	Travis Lee	4.00
2	Tony Gwynn	12.00
3	Scott Rolen	7.50
4	Nomar Garciaparra	15.00
5	Mike Piazza	20.00
6	Mark McGwire	30.00
7	Ken Griffey Jr.	25.00
8	Juan Gonzalez	8.00
9	Jose Cruz	3.00
10	Frank Thomas	12.00
11	Derek Jeter	30.00
12	Chipper Jones	20.00
13	Cal Ripken Jr.	30.00
14	Andruw Jones	8.00
15	Alex Rodriguez	25.00

1998 Ultra Top 30

Top 30 was a retail-only insert found only in Series 2 at the rate of one per pack.

		MT
Complete Set (30):		30.00
Common Player:		.25
Inserted 1:1 R		
1	Barry Bonds	1.75
2	Ivan Rodriguez	1.00
3	Kenny Lofton	.25
4	Albert Belle	.50
5	Mo Vaughn	.75
6	Jeff Bagwell	1.25
7	Mark McGwire	3.00
8	Darin Erstad	.75
9	Roger Clemens	1.50
10	Tony Gwynn	1.50
11	Scott Rolen	1.00
12	Hideo Nomo	.65
13	Juan Gonzalez	1.25
14	Mike Piazza	2.00
15	Greg Maddux	1.50
16	Chipper Jones	2.00
17	Andruw Jones	1.25
18	Derek Jeter	2.00
19	Nomar Garciaparra	1.75
20	Alex Rodriguez	2.50
21	Frank Thomas	1.75
22	Cal Ripken Jr.	3.00
23	Ken Griffey Jr.	2.50
24	Jose Cruz Jr.	.25
25	Jaret Wright	.25
26	Travis Lee	.40
27	Wade Boggs	.75
28	Chuck Knoblauch	.25
29	Joe Carter	.25
30	Ben Grieve	.75

1998 Ultra Win Now

This Series II insert has 20 top players printed on plastic card stock, with a color shot of the player on the left side and a close-up shot on the right with black lines through it. Win Now cards were seeded one per 72 packs and numbered with a "WN" suffix.

		MT
Complete Set (20):		150.00
Common Player:		2.00
Inserted 1:72		
1	Alex Rodriguez	15.00
2	Andruw Jones	5.00
3	Cal Ripken Jr.	20.00
4	Chipper Jones	10.00
5	Darin Erstad	3.00
6	Derek Jeter	20.00
7	Frank Thomas	6.00
8	Greg Maddux	10.00
9	Hideo Nomo	3.00
10	Jeff Bagwell	5.00
11	Jose Cruz	2.00
12	Juan Gonzalez	5.00
13	Ken Griffey Jr.	15.00
14	Mark McGwire	20.00
15	Mike Piazza	15.00
16	Mo Vaughn	3.00
17	Nomar Garciaparra	12.00
18	Roger Clemens	8.00
19	Scott Rolen	4.00
20	Tony Gwynn	6.00

1999 Ultra

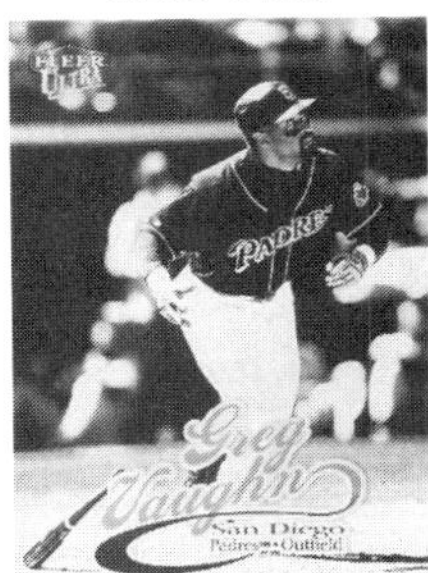

Base cards feature the full career stats by year in 15 categories and career highlights. There are short-printed subsets including Season Crowns (216-225) found 1:8 packs and Prospects (226-250) found 1:4 packs. Card fronts feature full bleed photography, and metallic foil stamping. There are three parallel versions Gold Medallion seeded 1 per pack with Prospects 1:40 and Season Crowns 1:80. Platinum Medallions are numbered to 99 with Prospects numbered to 65 and Season Crowns numbered to 50 sets. One of One Masterpiece parallels also exist. Packs consist of 10 cards with a S.R.P. of $2.69.

	MT
Complete Set (250):	60.00
Common Player:	.10
Common Season Crown:	.50
Inserted 1:8	
Common Prospect:	.25
Inserted 1:4	
Gold Medallion (1-215):	2X
Inserted 1:1	
Gold Medall. Prospect:	4X
Inserted 1:40	
Gold Medall. Season Crown:	3X
Inserted 1:80	
Platinums (1-215):	25X
Production 99 sets	
Platinum Prospects:	6X
Production 65 sets	
Platinum Season Crowns:	20X
Production 50 sets	
Pack (10):	1.50
Wax Box (24):	25.00

#	Player	MT
1	Greg Maddux	.75
2	Greg Vaughn	.10
3	John Wetteland	.10
4	Tino Martinez	.10
5	Todd Walker	.10
6	Troy O'Leary	.10
7	Barry Larkin	.15
8	Mike Lansing	.10
9	Delino DeShields	.10
10	Brett Tomko	.10
11	Carlos Perez	.10
12	Mark Langston	.10
13	Jamie Moyer	.10
14	Jose Guillen	.10
15	Bartolo Colon	.10
16	Brady Anderson	.10
17	Walt Weiss	.10
18	Shane Reynolds	.10
19	David Segui	.10
20	Vladimir Guerrero	.60
21	Freddy Garcia	.10
22	Carl Everett	.15
23	Jose Cruz Jr.	.20
24	David Ortiz	.10
25	Andruw Jones	.60
26	Darren Lewis	.10
27	Ray Lankford	.10
28	Wally Joyner	.10
29	Charles Johnson	.10
30	Derek Jeter	2.00
31	Sean Casey	.25
32	Bobby Bonilla	.10
33	Todd Zelle	.10
34	Todd Helton	.50
35	David Wells	.15
36	Darin Erstad	.50
37	Ivan Rodriguez	.50
38	Antonio Osuna	.10
39	Mickey Morandini	.10
40	Rusty Greer	.10
41	Rod Beck	.10
42	Larry Sutton	.10
43	Edgar Renteria	.10
44	Otis Nixon	.10
45	Eli Marrero	.10
46	Reggie Jefferson	.10
47	Trevor Hoffman	.10
48	Andres Galarraga	.10
49	Scott Brosius	.10
50	Vinny Castilla	.10
51	Bret Boone	.15
52	Masato Yoshii	.10
53	Matt Williams	.30
54	Robin Ventura	.10
55	Jay Powell	.10
56	Dean Palmer	.10
57	Eric Milton	.10
58	Willie McGee	.10
59	Tony Gwynn	.75
60	Tom Gordon	.10
61	Dante Bichette	.10
62	Jaret Wright	.10
63	Devon White	.10
64	Frank Thomas	.90
65	Mike Piazza	1.00
66	Jose Offerman	.10
67	Pat Meares	.10
68	Brian Meadows	.10
69	Nomar Garciaparra	.90
70	Mark McGwire	1.50
71	Tony Graffanino	.10
72	Ken Griffey Jr.	1.25
73	Ken Caminiti	.10
74	Todd Jones	.10
75	A.J. Hinch	.10
76	Marquis Grissom	.10
77	Jay Buhner	.10
78	Albert Belle	.30
79	Brian Anderson	.10
80	Quinton McCracken	.10
81	Omar Vizquel	.10
82	Todd Stottlemyre	.10
83	Cal Ripken Jr.	2.00
84	Magglio Ordonez	.25
85	John Olerud	.10
86	Hal Morris	.10
87	Derrek Lee	.10
88	Doug Glanville	.10
89	Marty Cordova	.10
90	Kevin Brown	.15
91	Kevin Young	.10
92	Rico Brogna	.10
93	Wilson Alvarez	.10
94	Bob Wickman	.10
95	Jim Thome	.10
96	Mike Mussina	.50
97	Al Leiter	.10
98	Travis Lee	.10
99	Jeff King	.10
100	Kerry Wood	.20
101	Cliff Floyd	.10
102	Jose Valentin	.10
103	Manny Ramirez	.60
104	Butch Huskey	.10
105	Scott Erickson	.10
106	Ray Durham	.10
107	Johnny Damon	.15
108	Craig Counsell	.10
109	Rolando Arrojo	.10
110	Bob Abreu	.15
111	Tony Womack	.10
112	Mike Stanley	.10
113	Kenny Lofton	.10
114	Eric Davis	.10
115	Jeff Conine	.10
116	Carlos Baerga	.10
117	Rondell White	.20
118	Billy Wagner	.10
119	Ed Sprague	.10
120	Jason Schmidt	.10
121	Edgar Martinez	.10
122	Travis Fryman	.10
123	Armando Benitez	.10
124	Matt Stairs	.10
125	Roberto Hernandez	.10
126	Jay Bell	.10
127	Justin Thompson	.10
128	John Jaha	.10
129	Mike Caruso	.10
130	Miguel Tejada	.20
131	Geoff Jenkins	.10
132	Wade Boggs	.60
133	Andy Benes	.10
134	Aaron Sele	.10
135	Bret Saberhagen	.10
136	Mariano Rivera	.20
137	Neifi Perez	.10
138	Paul Konerko	.15
139	Barry Bonds	.90
140	Garret Anderson	.10
141	Bernie Williams	.30
142	Gary Sheffield	.25
143	Rafael Palmeiro	.30
144	Orel Hershiser	.10
145	Craig Biggio	.15
146	Dmitri Young	.10
147	Damion Easley	.10
148	Henry Rodriguez	.10
149	Brad Radke	.10
150	Pedro Martinez	.50
151	Mike Lieberthal	.10
152	Jim Leyritz	.10
153	Chuck Knoblauch	.10
154	Darryl Kile	.10
155	Brian Jordan	.10
156	Chipper Jones	1.00
157	Pete Harnisch	.10
158	Moises Alou	.15
159	Ismael Valdes	.10
160	Stan Javier	.10
161	Mark Grace	.25
162	Jason Giambi	.35
163	Chuck Finley	.10
164	Juan Encarnacion	.10
165	Chan Ho Park	.15
166	Randy Johnson	.65
167	J.T. Snow	.10
168	Tim Salmon	.25
169	Brian Hunter	.10
170	Rickey Henderson	.60
171	Cal Eldred	.10
172	Curt Schilling	.15
173	Alex Rodriguez	1.25
174	Dustin Hermanson	.10
175	Mike Hampton	.10
176	Shawn Green	.30
177	Roberto Alomar	.50
178	Sandy Alomar Jr.	.10
179	Larry Walker	.30
180	Mo Vaughn	.40
181	Raul Mondesi	.25
182	Hideki Irabu	.10
183	Jim Edmonds	.10
184	Shawn Estes	.10
185	Tony Clark	.10
186	Dan Wilson	.10
187	Michael Tucker	.10
188	Jeff Shaw	.10
189	Mark Grudzielanek	.10
190	Roger Clemens	.75
191	Juan Gonzalez	.60
192	Sammy Sosa	.90
193	Troy Percival	.10
194	Robb Nen	.10
195	Bill Mueller	.10
196	Ben Grieve	.30
197	Luis Gonzalez	.35
198	Will Clark	.30
199	Jeff Cirillo	.10
200	Scott Rolen	.50
201	Reggie Sanders	.10
202	Fred McGriff	.10
203	Denny Neagle	.10
204	Brad Fullmer	.10
205	Royce Clayton	.10
206	Jose Canseco	.50
207	Jeff Bagwell	.60
208	Hideo Nomo	.50
209	Karim Garcia	.15
210	Kenny Rogers	.10
211	Checklist (Kerry Wood)	.25
212	Checklist (Alex Rodriguez)	.75
213	Checklist (Cal Ripken Jr.)	1.00
214	Checklist (Frank Thomas)	.60
215	Checklist (Ken Griffey Jr.)	.75
216	Alex Rodriguez (Season Crowns)	2.00
217	Greg Maddux (Season Crowns)	1.00
218	Juan Gonzalez (Season Crowns)	.75
219	Ken Griffey Jr. (Season Crowns)	2.50
220	Kerry Wood (Season Crowns)	.75
221	Mark McGwire (Season Crowns)	3.00
222	Mike Piazza (Season Crowns)	1.50
223	Rickey Henderson (Season Crowns)	.75
224	Sammy Sosa (Season Crowns)	1.50
225	Travis Lee (Season Crowns)	.50
226	Gabe Alvarez (Prospects)	.50
227	Matt Anderson (Prospects)	.50
228	Adrian Beltre (Prospects)	1.00
229	Orlando Cabrera (Prospects)	.50
230	Orlando Hernandez (Prospects)	1.00
231	Aramis Ramirez (Prospects)	.75
232	Troy Glaus (Prospects)	2.00
233	Gabe Kapler (Prospects)	1.50
234	Jeremy Giambi (Prospects)	.50
235	Derrick Gibson (Prospects)	.25
236	Carlton Loewer (Prospects)	.25
237	Mike Frank (Prospects)	.25
238	Carlos Guillen (Prospects)	.25
239	Alex Gonzalez (Prospects)	.25
240	Enrique Wilson (Prospects)	.25
241	J.D. Drew (Prospects)	1.00
242	Bruce Chen (Prospects)	.25
243	Ryan Minor (Prospects)	.25
244	Preston Wilson (Prospects)	.50
245	Josh Booty (Prospects)	.50
246	Luis Ordaz (Prospects)	.25
247	George Lombard (Prospects)	.25
248	Matt Clement (Prospects)	.25
249	Eric Chavez (Prospects)	1.00
250	Corey Koskie (Prospects)	.50

1999 Ultra Gold Medallion

The basic cards (#1-215) in this parallel set are found one per pack, while the short-printed versions are seen one per 40 packs (Prospects) or one per 80 packs (Season Crowns). Sharing the photos and format of the regular-issue cards, these inserts have a gold-foil background on front. On back, "GOLD MEDALLION EDITION" is printed in gold foil.

	MT
Common Player (1-215):	.25
Stars/RCs	2X
Season Crowns (216-225):	4X
Prospects (226-250):	3X

(See 1999 Ultra for checklist and base card values.)

1999 Ultra Platinum Medallion

The basic cards (#1-215) in this parallel set are

found in an individually serial numbered edition of 99. The short-printed cards were released in editions of 65 (Prospects) and 50 (Season Crowns). Sharing the photos and format of the regular-issue cards, these inserts have a silver-foil background on front. On back, "PLATINUM MEDALLION" is printed in silver foil along with the serial number.

	MT
Common Player (1-215):	3.00
Stars/RCs:	30X
Season Crowns (216-225):	30X
Prospects (226-250):	6X

(See 1999 Ultra for checklist and base card values.)

1999 Ultra Masterpiece

This top of the line parallel to '99 Ultra consists of a 1 of 1 version of each regular card.

	MT
Common Player:	50.00

(Individual player cards cannot be valued due to scarcity and fluctuating demand.)

1999 Ultra Book On

This 20-card set features insider scouting reports on the game's best players, utilizing embossing and gold foil stamping. These are found 1:6 packs.

		MT
Complete Set (20):		20.00
Common Player:		.25
Inserted 1:6		
1	Kerry Wood	.50
2	Ken Griffey Jr.	1.75
3	Frank Thomas	.75
4	Albert Belle	.30
5	Juan Gonzalez	.75
6	Jeff Bagwell	.75
7	Mark McGwire	2.00
8	Barry Bonds	1.25
9	Andruw Jones	.75
10	Mo Vaughn	.40
11	Scott Rolen	.60
12	Travis Lee	.25
13	Tony Gwynn	1.00
14	Greg Maddux	1.00
15	Mike Piazza	1.50
16	Chipper Jones	1.50
17	Nomar Garciaparra	1.25
18	Cal Ripken Jr.	2.00
19	Derek Jeter	2.00
20	Alex Rodriguez	1.75

1999 Ultra Damage Inc.

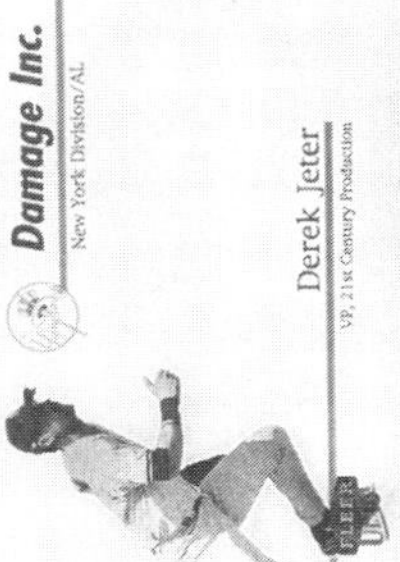

This 15-card insert set has a buisness card design, for players who mean business. These are seeded 1:72 packs.

		MT
Complete Set (15):		60.00
Common Player:		1.00
Inserted 1:72		
1	Alex Rodriguez	6.00
2	Greg Maddux	4.00
3	Cal Ripken Jr.	10.00
4	Chipper Jones	5.00
5	Derek Jeter	10.00
6	Frank Thomas	4.00
7	Juan Gonzalez	2.50
8	Ken Griffey Jr.	8.00
9	Kerry Wood	1.50
10	Mark McGwire	8.00
11	Mike Piazza	6.00
12	Nomar Garciaparra	5.00
13	Scott Rolen	1.50
14	Tony Gwynn	3.00
15	Travis Lee	1.00

1999 Ultra Diamond Producers

This die-cut set uses full-foil plastic with custom embossing. Baseball's biggest stars comprise this 10-card set, which are seeded 1:288 packs.

		MT
Complete Set (10):		175.00
Common Player:		7.50
Inserted 1:288		
1	Ken Griffey Jr.	25.00
2	Frank Thomas	12.00
3	Alex Rodriguez	25.00
4	Cal Ripken Jr.	30.00
5	Mike Piazza	20.00
6	Mark McGwire	25.00
7	Greg Maddux	15.00
8	Kerry Wood	7.50
9	Chipper Jones	20.00
10	Derek Jeter	30.00

1999 Ultra RBI Kings

Found exclusively in retail packs, this 30-card set showcases baseball's top run producers. These are seeded one per retail pack.

		MT
Complete Set (30):		18.00
Common Player:		.25
Inserted 1:1 R		
1	Rafael Palmeiro	.25
2	Mo Vaughn	.45
3	Ivan Rodriguez	.50
4	Barry Bonds	1.00
5	Albert Belle	.35
6	Jeff Bagwell	.65
7	Mark McGwire	2.00
8	Darin Erstad	.25
9	Manny Ramirez	.65
10	Chipper Jones	1.25
11	Jim Thome	.25
12	Scott Rolen	.60
13	Tony Gwynn	.75
14	Juan Gonzalez	.65
15	Mike Piazza	1.25
16	Sammy Sosa	1.00
17	Andruw Jones	.65
18	Derek Jeter	1.25
19	Nomar Garciaparra	1.00
20	Alex Rodriguez	1.50
21	Frank Thomas	1.00
22	Cal Ripken Jr.	2.00
23	Ken Griffey Jr.	1.50
24	Travis Lee	.35
25	Paul O'Neill	.25
26	Greg Vaughn	.25
27	Andres Galarraga	.25
28	Tino Martinez	.25
29	Jose Canseco	.50
30	Ben Grieve	.40

1999 Ultra Thunderclap

This set highlights the top hitters in the game, such as Nomar Garciaparra. Card fronts feature a lightning bolt in the background and are seeded 1:36 packs.

		MT
Complete Set (15):		65.00
Common Player:		1.00
Inserted 1:36		
1	Alex Rodriguez	8.00
2	Andruw Jones	2.50
3	Cal Ripken Jr.	10.00
4	Chipper Jones	5.00
5	Darin Erstad	1.50
6	Derek Jeter	10.00
7	Frank Thomas	4.00
8	Jeff Bagwell	3.00
9	Juan Gonzalez	3.00
10	Ken Griffey Jr.	8.00
11	Mark McGwire	8.00
12	Mike Piazza	6.00
13	Travis Lee	1.00
14	Nomar Garciaparra	5.00
15	Scott Rolen	2.00

1999 Ultra World Premiere

This 15-card set highlights rookies who made debuts in 1998, including J.D. Drew and Ben Grieve. These are seeded 1:18 packs.

		MT
Complete Set (15):		8.00
Common Player:		.50
Inserted 1:18		
1	Gabe Alvarez	.50
2	Kerry Wood	1.25
3	Orlando Hernandez	1.25
4	Mike Caruso	.50
5	Matt Anderson	.50
6	Randall Simon	.50
7	Adrian Beltre	1.00
8	Scott Elarton	.50
9	Karim Garcia	.60
10	Mike Frank	.50
11	Richard Hidalgo	.60
12	Paul Konerko	.60
13	Travis Lee	.60
14	J.D. Drew	1.50
15	Miguel Tejada	.75

2000 Ultra

The 300-card base set features a borderless design with silver holographic foil stamping on the card front. Card backs have an action image along with complete year-by-year statistics. The base set includes a 50-card short-printed Prospects (1:4) subset. A Masterpiece one-of-one parallel was produced.

	MT
Complete Set (300):	120.00
Common Player:	.10
Common Player (251-300):	.75
Inserted 1:4	
Pack (10):	3.00
Wax Box (24):	65.00

#	Player	MT
1	Alex Rodriguez	2.50
2	Shawn Green	.40
3	Magglio Ordonez	.40
4	Tony Gwynn	1.00
5	Joe McEwing	.10
6	Jose Rosado	.10
7	Sammy Sosa	1.50
8	Gary Sheffield	.30
9	Mickey Morandini	.10
10	Mo Vaughn	.40
11	Todd Hollandsworth	.10
12	Tom Gordon	.10
13	Charles Johnson	.10
14	Derek Bell	.10
15	Kevin Young	.10
16	Jay Buhner	.20
17	J.T. Snow	.10
18	Jay Bell	.10
19	John Rocker	.10
20	Ivan Rodriguez	.75
21	Pokey Reese	.10
22	Paul O'Neill	.20
23	Ronnie Belliard	.10
24	Ryan Rupe	.10
25	Travis Fryman	.20
26	Trot Nixon	.10
27	Wally Joyner	.10
28	Andy Pettitte	.25
29	Dan Wilson	.10
30	Orlando Hernandez	.25
31	Dmitri Young	.10
32	Edgar Renteria	.10
33	Eric Karros	.20
34	Fernando Seguignol	.10
35	Jason Kendall	.20
36	Jeff Shaw	.10
37	Matt Lawton	.10
38	Robin Ventura	.20
39	Scott Williamson	.10
40	Ben Grieve	.25
41	Billy Wagner	.10
42	Javy Lopez	.20
43	Joe Randa	.10
44	Neifi Perez	.10
45	David Justice	.40
46	Ray Durham	.10
47	Dustin Hermanson	.10
48	Andres Galarraga	.40
49	Brad Fullmer	.10
50	Nomar Garciaparra	2.00
51	David Cone	.20
52	David Nilsson	.10
53	David Wells	.10
54	Miguel Tejada	.10
55	Ismael Valdes	.10
56	Jose Lima	.10
57	Juan Encarnacion	.10
58	Fred McGriff	.25
59	Kenny Rogers	.10
60	Vladimir Guerrero	1.00
61	Benito Santiago	.10
62	Chris Singleton	.10
63	Carlos Lee	.10
64	Sean Casey	.20
65	Tom Goodwin	.10
66	Todd Hundley	.10
67	Ellis Burks	.10
68	Tim Hudson	.25
69	Matt Stairs	.10
70	Chipper Jones	1.50
71	Craig Biggio	.20
72	Brian Rose	.10
73	Carlos Delgado	.60
74	Eddie Taubensee	.10
75	John Smoltz	.20
76	Ken Caminiti	.20
77	Rafael Palmeiro	.50
78	Sidney Ponson	.10
79	Todd Helton	.75
80	Juan Gonzalez	.75
81	Bruce Aven	.10
82	Desi Relaford	.10
83	Johnny Damon	.10
84	Albert Belle	.50
85	Mark McGwire	3.00
86	Rico Brogna	.10
87	Tom Glavine	.25
88	Harold Baines	.10
89	Chad Allen	.10
90	Barry Bonds	1.00
91	Mark Grace	.25
92	Paul Byrd	.10
93	Roberto Alomar	.50
94	Roberto Hernandez	.10
95	Steve Finley	.10
96	Bret Boone	.10
97	Charles Nagy	.10
98	Eric Chavez	.10
99	Jamie Moyer	.10
100	Ken Griffey Jr.	2.00
101	J.D. Drew	.25
102	Todd Stottlemyre	.10
103	Tony Fernandez	.10
104	Jeromy Burnitz	.10
105	Jeremy Giambi	.10
106	Livan Hernandez	.10
107	Marlon Anderson	.10
108	Troy Glaus	1.00
109	Troy O'Leary	.10
110	Scott Rolen	.50
111	Bernard Gilkey	.10
112	Brady Anderson	.20
113	Chuck Knoblauch	.20
114	Jeff Weaver	.20
115	B.J. Surhoff	.10
116	Alex Gonzalez	.10
117	Vinny Castilla	.10
118	Tim Salmon	.25
119	Brian Jordan	.10
120	Corey Koskie	.10
121	Dean Palmer	.10
122	Gabe Kapler	.25
123	Jim Edmonds	.20
124	John Jaha	.10
125	Mark Grudzielanek	.10
126	Mike Bordick	.10
127	Mike Lieberthal	.10
128	Pete Harnisch	.10
129	Russ Ortiz	.10
130	Kevin Brown	.20
131	Troy Percival	.10
132	Alex Gonzalez	.10
133	Bartolo Colon	.10
134	John Valentin	.10
135	Jose Hernandez	.10
136	Marquis Grissom	.10
137	Wade Boggs	.40
138	Dante Bichette	.25
139	Bobby Higginson	.10
140	Frank Thomas	1.00
141	Geoff Jenkins	.20
142	Jason Giambi	.40
143	Jeff Cirillo	.10
144	Sandy Alomar Jr.	.20
145	Luis Gonzalez	.20
146	Preston Wilson	.10
147	Carlos Beltran	.10
148	Greg Vaughn	.20
149	Carlos Febles	.10
150	Jose Canseco	.50
151	Kris Benson	.10
152	Chuck Finley	.10
153	Michael Barrett	.10
154	Rey Ordonez	.10
155	Adrian Beltre	.25
156	Andruw Jones	.50
157	Barry Larkin	.40
158	Brian Giles	.20
159	Carl Everett	.10
160	Manny Ramirez	.75
161	Darryl Kile	.10
162	Edgar Martinez	.15
163	Jeff Kent	.10
164	Matt Williams	.25
165	Mike Piazza	2.00
166	Pedro J. Martinez	.75
167	Ray Lankford	.10
168	Roger Cedeno	.10
169	Ron Coomer	.10
170	Cal Ripken Jr.	2.50
171	Jose Offerman	.10
172	Kenny Lofton	.30
173	Kent Bottenfield	.10
174	Kevin Millwood	.20
175	Omar Daal	.10
176	Orlando Cabrera	.10
177	Pat Hentgen	.10
178	Tino Martinez	.25
179	Tony Clark	.20
180	Roger Clemens	1.00
181	Brad Radke	.10
182	Darin Erstad	.40
183	Jose Jimenez	.10
184	Jim Thome	.40
185	John Wetteland	.10
186	Justin Thompson	.10
187	John Hamala	.10
188	Lee Stevens	.10
189	Miguel Cairo	.10
190	Mike Mussina	.60
191	Raul Mondesi	.20
192	Armando Rios	.10
193	Trevor Hoffman	.10
194	Tony Batista	.10
195	Will Clark	.40
196	Brad Ausmus	.10
197	Chili Davis	.10
198	Cliff Floyd	.10
199	Curt Schilling	.20
200	Derek Jeter	2.00
201	Henry Rodriguez	.10
202	Jose Cruz Jr.	.10
203	Omar Vizquel	.20
204	Randy Johnson	.75
205	Reggie Sanders	.10
206	Al Leiter	.20
207	Damion Easley	.10
208	David Bell	.10
209	Fernando Tatis	.20
210	Kerry Wood	.25
211	Kevin Appier	.10
212	Mariano Rivera	.25
213	Mike Caruso	.10
214	Moises Alou	.20
215	Randy Winn	.10
216	Roy Halladay	.10
217	Shannon Stewart	.10
218	Todd Walker	.10
219	Jim Parque	.10
220	Travis Lee	.10
221	Andy Ashby	.10
222	Ed Sprague	.10
223	Larry Walker	.30
224	Rick Helling	.10
225	Rusty Greer	.10
226	Todd Zeile	.10
227	Freddy Garcia	.15
228	Hideo Nomo	.40
229	Marty Cordova	.10
230	Greg Maddux	1.50
231	Rondell White	.20
232	Paul Konerko	.20
233	Warren Morris	.10
234	Bernie Williams	.50
235	Bobby Abreu	.10
236	John Olerud	.25
237	Doug Glanville	.10
238	Eric Young	.10
239	Robb Nen	.10
240	Jeff Bagwell	.75
241	Sterling Hitchcock	.10
242	Todd Greene	.10
243	Bill Mueller	.10
244	Rickey Henderson	.25
245	Chan Ho Park	.20
246	Jason Schmidt	.10
247	Jeff Zimmerman	.10
248	Jermaine Dye	.10
249	Randall Simon	.10
250	Richie Sexson	.10
251	Micah Bowie	.75
252	Joe Nathan	.75
253	Chris Woodward	.75
254	Lance Berkman	.75
255	Ruben Mateo	.75
256	Russell Branyan	.75
257	Randy Wolf	.75
258	A.J. Burnett	1.50
259	Mark Quinn	2.00
260	Buddy Carlyle	.75
261	Ben Davis	.75
262	Yamid Haad	.75
263	Mike Colangelo	.75
264	Rick Ankiel	1.50
265	Jacque Jones	.75
266	Kelly Dransfeldt	.75
267	Matt Riley	.75
268	Adam Kennedy	.75
269	Octavio Dotel	.75
270	Francisco Cordero	.75
271	Wilton Veras	.75
272	Calvin Pickering	.75
273	Alex Sanchez	.75
274	Tony Armas Jr.	1.00
275	Pat Burrell	8.00
276	Chad Meyers	1.00
277	Ben Petrick	.75
278	Ramon Hernandez	.75
279	Ed Yarnall	1.00
280	Erubiel Durazo	.75
281	Vernon Wells	.75
282	Gary Matthews	.75
283	Kip Wells	.75
284	Peter Bergeron	1.00
285	Travis Dawkins	.75
286	Jorge Toca	.75
287	Cole Liniak	.75
288	Chad Hermansen	.75
289	Eric Gagne	.75
290	Chad Hutchinson	.75
291	Eric Munson	1.50
292	(Wiki Gonzalez)	.75
293	(Alfonso Soriano)	1.50
294	Trent Durrington	.75
295	(Ben Molina)	.75
296	Aaron Myette	.75
297	(Willi Mo Pena)	2.00
298	Kevin Barker	.75
299	(Geoff Blum)	.75
300	Josh Beckett	4.00

2000 Ultra Gold Medallion

A parallel to the 300-card base set these have gold foil stamping over a metallic gold background. Cards 1-250 are seeded one per pack, Prospects 251-300 are seeded 1:24 packs. Card backs are numbered with a "G" suffix.

	MT
Stars:	2x
Young Stars:	1.5x
Inserted 1:1	
Prospects (251-300):	2x to 4x
Inserted 1:24	

(See 2000 Ultra for checklist and base card values.)

2000 Ultra Platinum Medallion

Platinum Medallion are a parallel to the 300-card base set and are die-cut like the Gold Medallion parallel inserts. Card fronts are stamped with silver foil over a metallic silver background. Card backs are serially numbered with cards 1-250 limited to 50 sets and Prospects limited to 25 numbered sets. Card backs are numbered with a "P" suffix.

	MT
Stars:	50x to 75x
Young Stars:	30x to 50x
Production 50 sets	
Prospects (251-300):	6x to 12x
Production 25 sets	

(See 2000 Ultra for checklist and base card values.)

2000 Ultra Masterpiece Edition

Masterpiece Edition is a 1 of 1 parallel to the 300-card base set and are "tombstone" die-cut like the Gold and Platinum Medallion inserts. Card fronts are stamped with purple foil over a metallic purple background. Card backs are overprinted with "The only 1 of 1 Masterpiece."

MT

(Star card values undetermined because of unique status.)

2000 Ultra Club 3000

This three-card set is die-cut around the number 3,000 and commemorates 3,000 hit club members Wade Boggs, Tony Gwynn and Carl Yastrzemski. These were seeded 1:24 packs.

	MT
Complete Set (3):	10.00
Common Player:	3.00
Inserted 1:24	
Wade Boggs	4.00
Tony Gwynn	6.00
Carl Yastrzemski	3.00

2000 Ultra Club 3000 Memorabilia

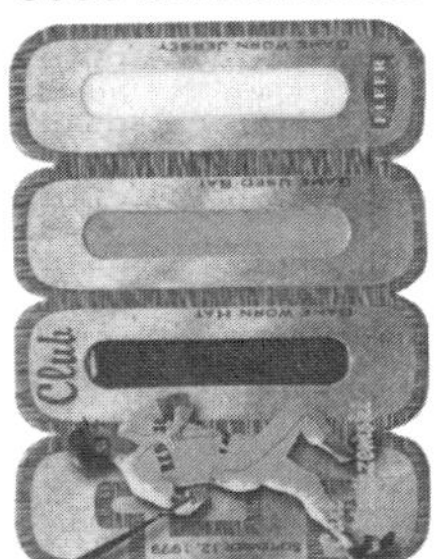

Each featured player has a total of four different memorabilia based inserts: hat, jersey, bat/jersey and bat/hat/jersey.

	MT
Wade Boggs - bat/250	75.00
Wade Boggs - hat/100	100.00
Wade Boggs - jersey/440	65.00
Wade Boggs - bat, jersey/100	150.00
Wade Boggs - bat, hat, jersey/25	400.00
Tony Gwynn - bat/260	150.00
Tony Gwynn - hat/115	60.00
Tony Gwynn - jersey/450	50.00
Tony Gwynn - bat, jersey/100	250.00
Tony Gwynn - bat, hat, jersey/25	700.00
Carl Yastrzemski - bat/250	90.00
Carl Yastrzemski - hat/100	200.00
Carl Yastrzemski - jersey/440	60.00
Carl Yastrzemski - bat, jersey/100	200.00
Carl Yastrzemski - bat, hat, jersey/25	500.00

2000 Ultra Crunch Time

This 15-card insert set is printed on suede stock with gold foil stamping. These were seeded 1:72 packs and numbered with a "CT" suffix on the card back.

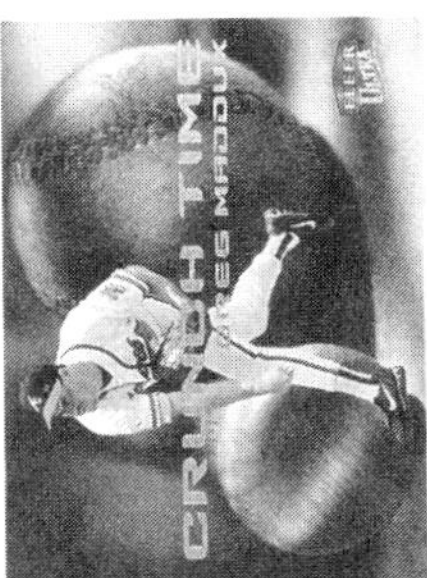

		MT
Complete Set (15):		160.00
Common Player:		4.00
Inserted 1:72		
1	Nomar Garciaparra	15.00
2	Ken Griffey Jr.	15.00
3	Mark McGwire	25.00
4	Alex Rodriguez	20.00
5	Derek Jeter	20.00
6	Sammy Sosa	12.00
7	Mike Piazza	15.00
8	Cal Ripken Jr.	20.00
9	Frank Thomas	8.00
10	Juan Gonzalez	6.00
11	J.D. Drew	4.00
12	Greg Maddux	12.00
13	Tony Gwynn	8.00
14	Vladimir Guerrero	8.00
15	Ben Grieve	4.00

2000 Ultra Diamond Mine

These were printed on a silver foil card front with Diamond Mine stamped in the background of the player image. These were inserted 1:6 packs and numbered with a "DM" suffix on the card back.

		MT
Complete Set (15):		25.00
Common Player:		1.00
Inserted 1:6		
1	Greg Maddux	2.00
2	Mark McGwire	4.00
3	Ken Griffey Jr.	2.50
4	Cal Ripken Jr.	3.00
5	Nomar Garciaparra	2.50
6	Mike Piazza	2.50
7	Alex Rodriguez	3.00
8	Frank Thomas	1.50
9	Juan Gonzalez	1.00
10	Derek Jeter	3.00
11	Tony Gwynn	1.50
12	Chipper Jones	2.00
13	Sammy Sosa	2.00
14	Roger Clemens	1.50
15	Vladimir Guerrero	1.50

2000 Ultra Feel the Game

These memorabilia based inserts have a piece of game worn jersey or batting glove embedded into the card front.

	MT
Common Player:	25.00
Roberto Alomar	100.00
J.D. Drew	50.00
Tony Gwynn	100.00
Randy Johnson	75.00
Greg Maddux	120.00
Edgar Martinez	30.00
Pedro Martinez	100.00
Kevin Millwood	25.00
Cal Ripken Jr.	150.00
Alex Rodriguez	150.00
Scott Rolen	50.00
Curt Schilling	30.00
Chipper Jones	75.00
Frank Thomas	150.00
Robin Ventura	30.00

2000 Ultra Fresh Ink

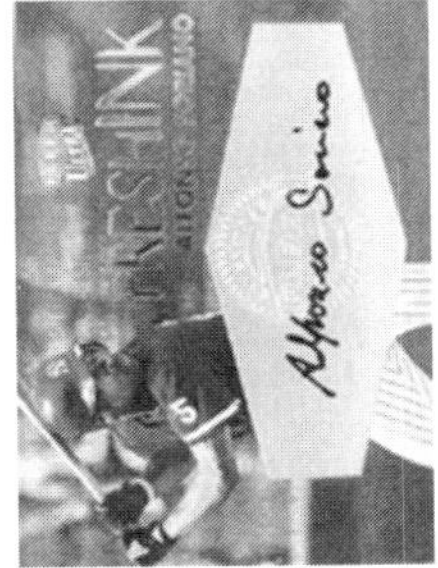

These autographed cards have the words "Fresh Ink" printed continually in the background image of the player. The signature is in a designated blank box intended for the autograph. Production numbers vary from player to player and are listed in parentheses after the player name.

		MT
Common Player:		10.00
1	Bobby Abreu (400)	20.00
2	Chad Allen (1,000)	10.00
3	Marlon Anderson (1,000)	10.00
4	Glen Barker (1,000)	10.00
5	Michael Barrett (1,000)	10.00

6	Carlos Beltran (1,000)	20.00
7	Adrian Beltre (1,000)	20.00
8	Wade Boggs (250)	50.00
9	Barry Bonds (250)	80.00
10	Peter Bergeron (1,000)	10.00
11	Pat Burrell (500)	40.00
12	Roger Cedeno (500)	10.00
13	Eric Chavez (750)	20.00
14	Bruce Chen (600)	15.00
15	Johnny Damon (750)	15.00
16	Ben Davis (1,000)	10.00
17	Carlos Delgado (300)	50.00
18	Einar Diaz (1,000)	10.00
19	Octavio Dotel (1,000)	10.00
20	J.D. Drew (600)	40.00
21	Scott Elarton (1,000)	10.00
22	Freddy Garcia (500)	20.00
23	Jeremy Giambi (1,000)	10.00
24	Troy Glaus (500)	40.00
25	Shawn Green (350)	30.00
26	Tony Gwynn (250)	100.00
27	Richard Hidalgo (500)	15.00
28	Bobby Higginson (1,000)	10.00
29	Tim Hudson (1,000)	20.00
30	Norm Hutchins (1,000)	10.00
31	Derek Jeter (95)	300.00
32	Randy Johnson (150)	60.00
33	Gabe Kapler (750)	25.00
34	Jason Kendall (400)	20.00
35	Paul Konerko (500)	15.00
36	Matt Lawton (1,000)	10.00
37	Carlos Lee (1,000)	15.00
38	Jose Macias (1,000)	10.00
39	Greg Maddux (250)	160.00
40	Ruben Mateo (250)	15.00
41	Kevin Millwood (500)	15.00
42	Warren Morris (1,000)	10.00
43	Eric Munson (1,000)	20.00
44	Heath Murray (1,000)	10.00
45	Joe Nathan (1,000)	10.00
46	Magglio Ordonez (350)	20.00
47	Angel Pena (1,000)	10.00
48	Cal Ripken Jr. (350)	200.00
49	Alex Rodriguez (350)	150.00
50	Scott Rolen (250)	50.00
51	Ryan Rupe (1,000)	10.00
52	Curt Schilling (375)	20.00
53	Randall Simon (1,000)	10.00
54	Alfonso Soriano (1,000)	25.00
55	Shannon Stewart (300)	10.00
56	Miguel Tejada (1,000)	10.00
57	Frank Thomas (150)	140.00
58	Jeff Weaver (1,000)	15.00
59	Randy Wolf (1,000)	10.00
60	Ed Yarnall (1,000)	20.00
61	Kevin Young (1,000)	10.00
62	Tony Gwynn, Wade Boggs, Nolan Ryan (100)	700.00
63	Rick Ankiel (500)	40.00

2000 Ultra Swing King

Printed on a clear, plastic stock this 10-card set features the top hitters in the game. Card fronts also utilize silver foil stamping. These were seeded 1:24 packs and are numbered on the card back with a "SK" suffix.

		MT
Complete Set (10):		50.00
Common Player:		3.00
Inserted 1:24		
1	Cal Ripken Jr.	8.00
2	Nomar Garciaparra	6.00
3	Frank Thomas	3.00
4	Tony Gwynn	3.00
5	Ken Griffey Jr.	6.00
6	Chipper Jones	5.00
7	Mark McGwire	10.00
8	Sammy Sosa	5.00
9	Derek Jeter	8.00
10	Alex Rodriguez	8.00

2000 Ultra Ultra Talented

Available exclusively in hobby packs these were printed on a holofoil background with gold foil stamping. Each card is serially numbered to 100 and are numbered on the card back with a "UT" suffix.

		MT
Complete Set (10):		675.00
Common Player:		15.00
Production 100 sets		
1	Sammy Sosa	60.00
2	Derek Jeter	100.00
3	Alex Rodriguez	100.00
4	Mike Piazza	75.00
5	Ken Griffey Jr.	75.00
6	Nomar Garciaparra	75.00
7	Mark McGwire	120.00
8	Cal Ripken Jr.	100.00
9	Frank Thomas	40.00
10	J.D. Drew	15.00

2000 Ultra World Premiere

This insert set highlights ten young potential stars on a die-cut, silver foil etched design. These were inserted 1:12 packs and are numbered with a "WP" suffix on the card back.

		MT
Complete Set (10):		15.00
Common Player:		.75
Inserted 1:12		
1	Ruben Mateo	1.00
2	Lance Berkman	1.00
3	Octavio Dotel	.75
4	Joe McEwing	.75
5	Ben Davis	.75
6	Warren Morris	.75
7	Carlos Lee	.75
8	Rick Ankiel	2.00
9	Adam Kennedy	.75
10	Tim Hudson	3.00

2001 Ultra

		MT
Complete Set (275):		100.00
Common Player:		.15
Common Prospect (251-275):		2.00
Inserted 1:4		
Pack (10):		4.00
Box (24):		80.00
1	Pedro Martinez	.75
2	Derek Jeter	2.50
3	Cal Ripken Jr.	2.50
4	Alex Rodriguez	2.50
5	Vladimir Guerrero	1.00
6	Troy Glaus	.75
7	Sammy Sosa	1.50
8	Mike Piazza	2.00
9	Tony Gwynn	1.00
10	Tim Hudson	.25
11	John Flaherty	.15
12	Jeff Cirillo	.15
13	Ellis Burks	.15
14	Carlos Lee	.15
15	Carlos Beltran	.15
16	Ruben Rivera	.15
17	Richard Hidalgo	.25
18	Omar Vizquel	.25
19	Michael Barrett	.15
20	Jose Canseco	.50
21	Jason Giambi	.40
22	Greg Maddux	1.50
23	Charles Johnson	.15
24	Sandy Alomar	.15
25	Rick Ankiel	.40
26	Richie Sexson	.15
27	Matt Williams	.30
28	Joe Girardi	.15
29	Jason Kendall	.15
30	Brad Fullmer	.15
31	Alex Gonzalez	.15
32	Rick Helling	.15
33	Mike Mussina	.50
34	Joe Randa	.15
35	J.T. Snow	.15
36	Edgardo Alfonzo	.25
37	Dante Bichette	.25
38	Brad Ausmus	.15
39	Bobby Abreu	.15
40	Warren Morris	.15
41	Tony Womack	.15
42	Russell Branyan	.15
43	Mike Lowell	.15
44	Mark Grace	.25
45	Jeromy Burnitz	.15
46	J.D. Drew	.25
47	David Justice	.40
48	Alex Gonzalez	.15
49	Tino Martinez	.25
50	Raul Mondesi	.25
51	Rafael Furcal	.25
52	Marquis Grissom	.15
53	Kevin Young	.15
54	Jon Lieber	.15
55	Henry Rodriguez	.15
56	Dave Burba	.15
57	Shannon Stewart	.15
58	Preston Wilson	.15
59	Paul O'Neill	.25
60	Jimmy Haynes	.15
61	Darryl Kile	.15
62	Bret Boone	.15
63	Bartolo Colon	.15
64	Andres Galarraga	.30
65	Trot Nixon	.15
66	Steve Finley	.15
67	Shawn Green	.30
68	Robert Person	.15
69	Kenny Rogers	.15
70	Bobby Higginson	.15
71	Barry Larkin	.30
72	Al Martin	.15
73	Tom Glavine	.30
74	Rondell White	.15
75	Ray Lankford	.15
76	Moises Alou	.15
77	Matt Clement	.15
78	Geoff Jenkins	.25
79	David Wells	.15
80	Chuck Finley	.15
81	Andy Pettitte	.25
82	Travis Fryman	.25
83	Ron Coomer	.15
84	Mark McGwire	3.00
85	Kerry Wood	.25
86	Jorge Posada	.25
87	Jeff Bagwell	.75
88	Andruw Jones	.50
89	Ryan Klesko	.15
90	Mariano Rivera	.25
91	Lance Berkman	.15
92	Kenny Lofton	.30
93	Jacque Jones	.15
94	Eric Young	.15
95	Edgar Renteria	.15
96	Chipper Jones	1.50
97	Todd Helton	.75
98	Shawn Estes	.15
99	Mark Mulder	.15
100	Lee Stevens	.15
101	Jermaine Dye	.15
102	Greg Vaughn	.15
103	Chris Singleton	.15
104	Brady Anderson	.20
105	Terrence Long	.15
106	Quilvio Veras	.15
107	Magglio Ordonez	.40
108	Johnny Damon	.15
109	Jeffrey Hammonds	.15
110	Fred McGriff	.25
111	Carl Pavano	.15
112	Bobby Estalella	.15
113	Todd Hundley	.15
114	Scott Rolen	.50
115	Robin Ventura	.20
116	Pokey Reese	.15
117	Luis Gonzalez	.25
118	Jose Offerman	.15
119	Edgar Martinez	.15
120	Dean Palmer	.15
121	David Segui	.15
122	Troy O'Leary	.15
123	Tony Batista	.25
124	Todd Zeile	.15
125	Randy Johnson	.75

126 Luis Castillo .15
127 Kris Benson .15
128 John Olerud .25
129 Eric Karros .25
130 Eddie Taubensee .15
131 Neifi Perez .15
132 Matt Stairs .15
133 Luis Alicea .15
134 Jeff Kent .25
135 Javier Vazquez .15
136 Garret Anderson .15
137 Frank Thomas 1.00
138 Carlos Febles .15
139 Albert Belle .40
140 Tony Clark .20
141 Pat Burrell .50
142 Mike Sweeney .15
143 Jay Buhner .15
144 Gabe Kapler .15
145 Derek Bell .15
146 B.J. Surhoff .15
147 Adam Kennedy .15
148 Aaron Boone .15
149 Todd Stottlemyre .15
150 Roberto Alomar .60
151 Orlando Hernandez .25
152 Jason Varitek .15
153 Gary Sheffield .30
154 Cliff Floyd .15
155 Chad Hermansen .15
156 Carlos Delgado .50
157 Aaron Sele .15
158 Sean Casey .15
159 Ruben Mateo .15
160 Mike Bordick .15
161 Mike Cameron .15
162 Doug Glanville .15
163 Damion Easley .15
164 Carl Everett .15
165 Bengie Molina .15
166 Adrian Beltre .25
167 Tom Goodwin .15
168 Rickey Henderson .30
169 Mo Vaughn .40
170 Mike Lieberthal .15
171 Ken Griffey Jr. 2.00
172 Juan Gonzalez .75
173 Ivan Rodriguez .75
174 Al Leiter .25
175 Vinny Castilla .15
176 Peter Bergeron .15
177 Pedro Astacio .15
178 Paul Konerko .15
179 Mitch Meluskey .15
180 Kevin Millwood .15
181 Ben Grieve .25
182 Barry Bonds 1.00
183 Rusty Greer .15
184 Miguel Tejada .15
185 Mark Quinn .15
186 Larry Walker .30
187 Jose Valentin .15
188 Jose Vidro .15
189 Delino DeShields .15
190 Darin Erstad .40
191 Bill Mueller .15
192 Ray Durham .15
193 Ken Caminiti .15
194 Jim Thome .40
195 Javy Lopez .15
196 Fernando Vina .15
197 Eric Chavez .25
198 Eric Owens .15
199 Brad Radke .15
200 Travis Lee .15
201 Tim Salmon .25
202 Rafael Palmeiro .40
203 Nomar Garciaparra 2.00
204 Mike Hampton .15
205 Kevin Brown .25
206 Juan Encarnacion .15
207 Danny Graves .15
208 Carlos Guillen .15
209 Phil Nevin .15
210 Matt Lawton .15
211 Manny Ramirez .75
212 James Baldwin .15
213 Fernando Tatis .15
214 Craig Biggio .25
215 Brian Jordan .15
216 Bernie Williams .60
217 Ryan Dempster .15
218 Roger Clemens 1.00
219 Jose Cruz Jr. .15
220 John Valentin .15
221 Dmitri Young .15
222 Curt Schilling .25
223 Jim Edmonds .30
224 Chan Ho Park .15
225 Brian Giles .25
226 Jimmy Anderson .15
227 Adam Piatt .75
228 Kenny Kelly .15
229 Randy Choate .15
230 Eric Cammack .15
231 Yovanny Lara .15
232 Wayne Franklin .15
233 Cameron Cairncross .15
234 J.C. Romero .15
235 Geraldo Guzman .15
236 Morgan Burkhart .15
237 Pascual Coco .15
238 John Parrish .15
239 Keith McDonald .15
240 Carlos Casimiro .15
241 Daniel Garibay .15
242 Sang-Hoon Lee .15
243 Hector Ortiz .15
244 Jeff Sparks .15
245 Jason Boyd .15
246 Mark Buehrle .15
247 Adam Melhuse .15
248 Kane Davis .15
249 Mike Darr .15
250 Vicente Padilla .15
251 Barry Zito (Prospects) 8.00
252 Tim Drew (Prospects) 2.00
253 Luis Matos (Prospects) 3.00
254 Alex Cabrera (Prospects) 3.00
255 Jon Garland (Prospects) 2.00
256 Milton Bradley (Prospects) 3.00
257 Juan Pierre (Prospects) 2.00
258 Ismael Villegas (Prospects) 4.00
259 Eric Munson (Prospects) 4.00
260 Tomas De La Rosa (Prospects) 3.00
261 Chris Richard (Prospects) 3.00
262 Jason Tyner (Prospects) 3.00
263 B.J. Waszgis (Prospects) 2.00
264 Jason Marquis (Prospects) 2.00
265 Dusty Allen (Prospects) 2.00
266 Corey Patterson (Prospects) 2.00
267 Eric Byrnes (Prospects) 5.00
268 Xavier Nady (Prospects) 10.00
269 George Lombard (Prospects) 2.00
270 Timoniel Perez (Prospects) 4.00
271 Gary Matthews Jr. (Prospects) 2.00
272 Chad Durbin (Prospects) 2.00
273 Tony Armas Jr. (Prospects) 3.00
274 Francisco Cordero (Prospects) 2.00
275 Alfonso Soriano (Prospects) 2.00

2001 Ultra Gold Medallion

MT
Stars (1-250): 2-3X
Inserted 1:1
Prospects (251-275): 1-2X
Inserted 1:24

2001 Ultra Platinum Medallion

MT
Stars (1-250): 30-60X
Production 50 sets
Prospects (251-275): 6-12X
Production 25 sets

2001 Ultra Autographics

MT
Common Player: 10.00
Inserted 1:48
Silvers: 1-2X
Production 250 sets
1 Roberto Alomar 50.00
2 Jimmy Anderson 10.00
3 Lance Berkman 10.00
4 Barry Bonds
5 Roosevelt Brown 10.00
6 Jeromy Burnitz 15.00
7 Pat Burrell 25.00
8 Alex Cabrera 10.00
9 Eric Chavez 15.00
10 Joe Crede 15.00
11 Johnny Damon 15.00
12 Carlos Delgado
13 Adam Dunn 15.00
14 Jim Edmonds 20.00
15 Chad Green 10.00
16 Dustin Hermanson 10.00
17 Randy Johnson
18 Corey Lee 10.00
19 Derrek Lee 10.00
20 Terrence Long 10.00
21 Julio Lugo 10.00
22 Edgar Martinez 20.00
23 Justin Miller 10.00
24 Russ Ortiz 10.00
25 Pablo Ozuna 10.00
26 Adam Piatt 20.00
27 Mark Redman 10.00
28 Richie Sexson
29 Gary Sheffield 30.00
30 Alfonso Soriano 25.00
31 Jose Vidro 15.00
32 Vernon Wells 10.00
33 Preston Wilson 15.00
34 Jamey Wright 10.00
35 Julio Zuleta 10.00

2001 Ultra Decade of Dominance

MT
Complete Set (15): 20.00
Common Player: .40
Inserted 1:8
1 Barry Bonds 1.25
2 Mark McGwire 5.00
3 Sammy Sosa 2.50
4 Ken Griffey Jr. 3.00
5 Cal Ripken Jr. 4.00
6 Tony Gwynn 1.50
7 Albert Belle .50
8 Frank Thomas 1.50
9 Randy Johnson 1.25
10 Juan Gonzalez 1.25
11 Greg Maddux 2.50
12 Craig Biggio .40
13 Edgar Martinez .40
14 Roger Clemens 1.50
15 Andres Galarraga .60

2001 Ultra Fall Classics

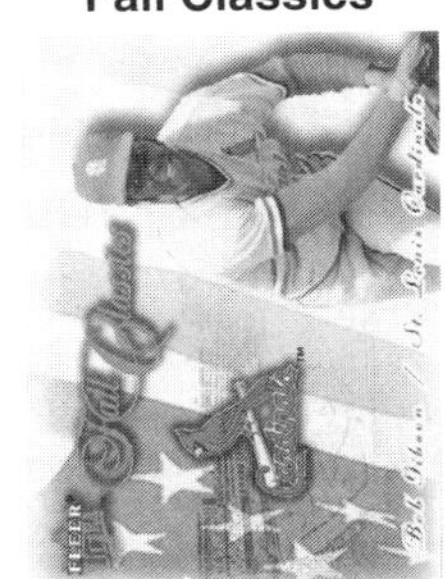

MT
Complete Set (37): 200.00
Common Player: 2.50
Inserted 1:20
1 Jackie Robinson 15.00
2 Enos Slaughter 2.50
3 Mariano Rivera 2.50
4 Hank Bauer 3.00
5 Cal Ripken Jr. 12.00
6 Babe Ruth 20.00
7 Thurman Munson 8.00
8 Tom Glavine 3.00
9 Fred Lynn 2.50
10 Johnny Bench 8.00
11 Tony Lazzeri 2.50
12 Al Kaline 5.00
13 Reggie Jackson 8.00
14 Derek Jeter 12.00
15 Willie Stargell 4.00
16 Roy Campanella 8.00
17 Phil Rizzuto 5.00
18 Roberto Clemente 15.00
19 Carlton Fisk 4.00
20 Duke Snider 6.00
21 Ted Williams 15.00
22 Bill Skowron 2.50
23 Bucky Dent 4.00
24 Mike Schmidt 8.00
25 Lou Brock 5.00
26 Whitey Ford 5.00
27 Brooks Robinson 6.00
28 Roberto Alomar 4.00
29 Yogi Berra 10.00
30 Joe Carter 2.50
31 Bill Mazeroski 4.00
32 Bob Gibson 8.00
33 Hank Greenberg 4.00
34 Andruw Jones 4.00
35 Bernie Williams 5.00
36 Don Larsen 6.00
37 Billy Martin 6.00

2001 Ultra Fall Classics Memorabilia

MT
Common Player: 30.00
Inserted 1:288
1 Jackie Robinson pants 325.00
2 Enos Slaughter bat 50.00
3 Mariano Rivera jersey 50.00
4 Hank Bauer bat 40.00
5 Cal Ripken Jr. jersey 150.00
6 Thurman Munson bat 125.00
7 Tom Glavine jersey 40.00
8 Fred Lynn bat 40.00
9 Babe Ruth bat 700.00
10 Tony Lazzeri bat 50.00
11 Al Kaline jersey 150.00
12 Reggie Jackson jersey 75.00
13 Derek Jeter jersey 160.00
14 Willie Stargell bat 50.00
15 Roy Campanella bat 150.00
16 Phil Rizzuto bat 75.00
17 Roberto Clemente bat 300.00
18 Carlton Fisk jersey 75.00
19 Duke Snider bat 150.00

20 Ted Williams bat 500.00
21 Bill Skowron bat 40.00
22 Bucky Dent bat 30.00
23 Mike Schmidt jersey 90.00
24 Lou Brock jersey 60.00
25 Brooks Robinson bat 100.00
26 Johnny Bench jersey 75.00

2001 Ultra Fall Classics Memorabilia Autographs

MT
Complete Set (6):
Common Player:
1 Enos Slaughter
2 Cal Ripken Jr.
3 Al Kaline
4 Reggie Jackson
5 Carlton Fisk
6 Mike Schmidt

2001 Ultra Feel the Game

MT
Common Player: 6.00
Inserted 1:48
Golds: 2X
Production 50 sets
1 Moises Alou 6.00
2 Brady Anderson 6.00
3 Adrian Beltre 8.00
4 Carlos Delgado 8.00
5 J.D. Drew 10.00
6 Jermaine Dye 6.00
7 Jason Giambi 15.00
8 Richard Hidalgo 6.00
9 Chipper Jones 15.00
10 Eric Karros 6.00
11 Raul Mondesi 6.00
12 Chan Ho Park 6.00
13 Ivan Rodriguez 10.00
14 Matt Stairs 6.00
15 Frank Thomas 15.00
16 Jose Vidro 6.00
17 Matt Williams 8.00
18 Preston Wilson 6.00

2001 Ultra Power Plus

MT
Complete Set (10): 40.00
Common Player: 1.50
Inserted 1:24
1 Vladimir Guerrero 3.00
2 Mark McGwire 8.00
3 Mike Piazza 5.00
4 Derek Jeter 6.00
5 Chipper Jones 4.00
6 Carlos Delgado 1.50
7 Sammy Sosa 4.00
8 Ken Griffey Jr. 5.00
9 Nomar Garciaparra 5.00
10 Alex Rodriguez 6.00

2001 Ultra The Greatest Hits of ...

MT
Complete Set (10): 20.00
Common Player: .50
Inserted 1:12
1 Mark McGwire 5.00
2 Alex Rodriguez 4.00
3 Ken Griffey Jr. 3.00
4 Ivan Rodriguez 1.25
5 Cal Ripken Jr. 4.00
6 Todd Helton 1.25
7 Derek Jeter 4.00
8 Pedro Martinez 1.25
9 Tony Gwynn 2.50
10 Jim Edmonds .50

2001 Ultra Tomorrow's Legends

MT
Complete Set (15): 10.00
Common Player: .25
Inserted 1:4
1 Rick Ankiel .50
2 J.D. Drew .40
3 Carlos Delgado .75
4 Todd Helton .75
5 Andruw Jones .75
6 Troy Glaus .75
7 Jermaine Dye .25
8 Vladimir Guerrero 1.00
9 Brian Giles .25
10 Scott Rolen .50
11 Darin Erstad .40
12 Derek Jeter 3.00
13 Alex Rodriguez 3.00
14 Pat Burrell .50
15 Nomar Garciaparra 2.00

2002 Ultra

MT
Complete Set (285): 100.00
Common Player: .15
Common SP (201-285): .50
Inserted 1:4
Pack (10): 3.00
Box (24): 60.00
1 Jeff Bagwell 1.00
2 Derek Jeter 2.50
3 Alex Rodriguez 2.00
4 Eric Chavez .25
5 Tsuyoshi Shinjo .40
6 Chris Stynes .15
7 Ivan Rodriguez .75
8 Cal Ripken Jr. 2.50
9 Freddy Garcia .15
10 Chipper Jones 1.50
11 Hideo Nomo .50
12 Rafael Furcal .25
13 Preston Wilson .15
14 Jimmy Rollins .15
15 Cristian Guzman .15
16 Garret Anderson .15
17 Todd Helton .75
18 Moises Alou .25
19 Tony Gwynn 1.00
20 Jorge Posada .25
21 Sean Casey .25
22 Kazuhiro Sasaki .25
23 Ray Lankford .15
24 Manny Ramirez .75
25 Barry Bonds 1.50
26 Fred McGriff .25
27 Vladimir Guerrero .75
28 Jermaine Dye .15
29 Adrian Beltre .15
30 Ken Griffey Jr. 2.00
31 Ramon Hernandez .15
32 Kerry Wood .25
33 Greg Maddux 1.50
34 Rondell White .15
35 Mike Mussina .50
36 Jim Edmonds .25
37 Scott Rolen .40
38 Mike Lowell .15
39 Al Leiter .25
40 Tony Clark .15
41 Joe Mays .15
42 Mo Vaughn .20
43 Geoff Jenkins .25
44 Curt Schilling .40
45 Pedro Martinez 1.00
46 Andy Pettitte .40
47 Tim Salmon .25
48 Carl Everett .15
49 Lance Berkman .25
50 Troy Glaus .50
51 Ichiro Suzuki 4.00
52 Alfonso Soriano .25
53 Tomo Ohka .15
54 Dean Palmer .15
55 Kevin Brown .15
56 Albert Pujols 1.50
57 Homer Bush .15
58 Tim Hudson .40
59 Frank Thomas .75
60 Joe Randa .15
61 Chan Ho Park .25
62 Bobby Higginson .15
63 Bartolo Colon .15
64 Aramis Ramirez .15
65 Jeff Cirillo .15
66 Roberto Alomar .50
67 Mark Kotsay .15
68 Mike Cameron .15
69 Mike Hampton .15
70 Trot Nixon .15
71 Juan Gonzalez .75
72 Damian Rolls .15
73 Brad Fullmer .15
74 David Ortiz .15
75 Brandon Inge .15
76 Orlando Hernandez .15
77 Matt Stairs .15
78 Jay Gibbons .15
79 Greg Vaughn .15
80 Brady Anderson .15
81 Jim Thome .40
82 Ben Sheets .25
83 Rafael Palmeiro .40
84 Edgar Renteria .15
85 Doug Mientkiewicz .15
86 Raul Mondesi .15
87 Shane Reynolds .15
88 Steve Finley .15
89 Jose Cruz Jr. .15
90 Edgardo Alfonzo .15
91 Jose Valentin .15
92 Mark McGwire 2.00
93 Mark Grace .40
94 Mike Lieberthal .15
95 Barry Larkin .25
96 Chuck Knoblauch .15
97 Deivi Cruz .15
98 Jeromy Burnitz .15
99 Shannon Stewart .15
100 David Wells .15
101 Brook Fordyce .15
102 Rusty Greer .15
103 Andruw Jones .50
104 Jason Kendall .15
105 Nomar Garciaparra 2.00
106 Shawn Green .25
107 Craig Biggio .25
108 Masato Yoshii .15
109 Ben Petrick .15
110 Gary Sheffield .25
111 Travis Lee .15
112 Matt Williams .25
113 Billy Wagner .15
114 Robin Ventura .15
115 Jerry Hairston Jr. .15
116 Paul LoDuca .15
117 Darin Erstad .25
118 Ruben Sierra .15
119 Ricky Gutierrez .15
120 Bret Boone .15
121 John Rocker .15
122 Roger Clemens 1.50
123 Eric Karros .15
124 J.D. Drew .25
125 Carlos Delgado .40
126 Jeffrey Hammonds .15
127 Jeff Kent .15
128 David Justice .25
129 Cliff Floyd .15
130 Omar Vizquel .25
131 Matt Morris .15
132 Rich Aurilia .15
133 Larry Walker .25
134 Miguel Tejada .25
135 Eric Young .15
136 Aaron Sele .15
137 Eric Milton .15
138 Travis Fryman .15
139 Magglio Ordonez .15
140 Sammy Sosa 1.50
141 Pokey Reese .15
142 Adam Eaton .15
143 Adam Kennedy .15
144 Mike Piazza 2.00
145 Larry Barnes .15
146 Darryl Kile .15
147 Tom Glavine .25
148 Ryan Klesko .15
149 Jose Vidro .15
150 Joe Kennedy .15
151 Bernie Williams .60
152 C.C. Sabathia .15
153 Alex Ochoa .15
154 A.J. Pierzynski .15
155 Johnny Damon .15
156 Omar Daal .15
157 A.J. Burnett .15
158 Eric Munson .15
159 Fernando Vina .15
160 Chris Singleton .15
161 Juan Pierre .15
162 John Olerud .25
163 Randy Johnson .75
164 Paul Konerko .15
165 Tino Martinez .25
166 Richard Hidalgo .15
167 Luis Gonzalez .50
168 Ben Grieve .15
169 Matt Lawton .15
170 Gabe Kapler .25
171 Mariano Rivera .25
172 Kenny Lofton .25
173 Brian Jordan .15
174 Brian Giles .25
175 Mark Quinn .15
176 Neifi Perez .15
177 Ellis Burks .15
178 Bobby Abreu .15
179 Jeff Weaver .15
180 Andres Galarraga .25
181 Javy Lopez .25
182 Todd Walker .15
183 Fernando Tatis .15
184 Charles Johnson .15
185 Pat Burrell .50
186 Jay Bell .15
187 Aaron Boone .15
188 Jason Giambi .50
189 Jay Payton .15
190 Carlos Lee .15
191 Phil Nevin .15
192 Mike Sweeney .15
193 J.T. Snow .15
194 Dmitri Young .15
195 Richie Sexson .15
196 Derrek Lee .15
197 Corey Koskie .15
198 Edgar Martinez .15
199 Wade Miller .15
200 Tony Batista .15
201 John Olerud .75
202 Bret Boone .50
203 Cal Ripken Jr. 3.00
204 Alex Rodriguez 2.50
205 Ichiro Suzuki 2.50
206 Manny Ramirez .75
207 Juan Gonzalez .75
208 Ivan Rodriguez .75
209 Roger Clemens 1.50
210 Edgar Martinez .50
211 Todd Helton .75
212 Jeff Kent .50
213 Chipper Jones 1.50
214 Rich Aurilia .50

215 Barry Bonds 2.50
216 Sammy Sosa 1.50
217 Luis Gonzalez .50
218 Mike Piazza 2.00
219 Randy Johnson .75
220 Larry Walker .50
221 Todd Helton, Juan Uribe .50
222 Pat Burrell, Eric Valent .50
223 Edgar Martinez, Ichiro Suzuki 2.00
224 Ben Grieve, Jason Tyner .50
225 Mark Quinn, Dee Brown .50
226 Cal Ripken Jr., Brian Roberts 3.00
227 Cliff Floyd, Abraham Nunez .50
228 Jeff Bagwell, Adam Everett .75
229 Mark McGwire, Albert Pujols 2.50
230 Doug Mientkiewicz, Luis Rivas .50
231 Juan Gonzalez, Danny Peoples .75
232 Kevin Brown, Luke Prokopec .50
233 Richie Sexson, Ben Sheets .50
234 Jason Giambi, Jason Hart 1.50
235 Barry Bonds, Carlos Valderrama 2.50
236 Tony Gwynn, Cesar Crespo 1.00
237 Ken Griffey Jr., Adam Dunn 2.00
238 Frank Thomas, Joe Crede .75
239 Derek Jeter, Drew Henson 3.00
240 Chipper Jones, Wilson Betemit 1.50
241 Luis Gonzalez, Junior Spivey .50
242 Bobby Higginson, Andres Torres .50
243 Carlos Delgado, Vernon Wells .50
244 Sammy Sosa, Corey Patterson 1.50
245 Nomar Garciaparra, Shea Hillenbrand 2.50
246 Alex Rodriguez, Jason Romano 2.50
247 Troy Glaus, David Eckstein .75
248 Mike Piazza, Alex Escobar 2.00
249 Brian Giles, Jack Wilson .50
250 Vladimir Guerrero, Scott Hodges .75
251 Bud Smith 5.00
252 Juan Diaz 1.00
253 Wilkin Ruan 1.00
254 *Chris Spurling* 1.00
255 Toby Hall 1.00
256 Jason Jennings 1.00
257 George Perez 1.00
258 D'Angelo Jimenez 3.00
259 Jose Acevedo 2.00
260 Josue Perez 1.00
261 Brian Rogers 1.00
262 Carlos Maldonado 1.00
263 Travis Phelps 5.00
264 Rob Mackowiak 5.00
265 Ryan Drese 4.00
266 Carlos Garcia 2.00
267 Alexis Gomez 6.00
268 Jeremy Affeldt 1.00
269 Scott Podsednik 1.00
270 Adam Johnson 5.00
271 Pedro Santana 1.00
272 Les Walrond 1.00
273 Jackson Melian 1.00
274 Carlos Hernandez 1.00
275 *Mark Nussbeck* 2.00
276 Cory Aldridge 1.00
277 Troy Mattes 1.00
278 Brent Abernathy 1.00
279 J.J. Davis 1.00
280 Brandon Duckworth 3.00
281 Kyle Lohse 4.00
282 Justin Kaye 1.00
283 Cody Ransom 1.00
284 Dave Williams 1.00
285 Luis Lopez 6.00

2002 Ultra Gold Medallion

MT
Stars (1-200): 2-3X
Inserted 1:1
Stars (201-250): 3-5X
Inserted 1:24
Prospects (251-285): 4-8X
Production 100

2002 Ultra Fall Classic

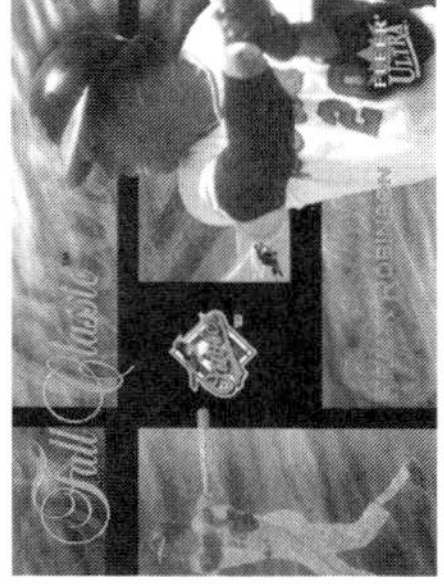

MT
Complete Set (39): 220.00
Common Player: 2.50
Inserted 1:20
1FC Ty Cobb 12.00
2FC Lou Gehrig 15.00
3FC Babe Ruth 20.00
4FC Stan Musial 10.00
5FC Ted Williams 15.00
6FC Dizzy Dean 20.00
7FC Mickey Cochrane 2.50
8FC Jimmie Foxx 8.00
9FC Mel Ott 5.00
10FC Rogers Hornsby 6.00
11FC Hank Aaron 10.00
12FC Clete Boyer 2.50
13FC George Brett 8.00
14FC Bob Gibson 5.00
15FC Carlton Fisk 4.00
16FC Johnny Bench 8.00
17FC Rusty Staub 2.50
18FC Willie McCovey 2.50
19FC Paul Molitor 5.00
20FC Jim Palmer 4.00
21FC Frank Robinson 5.00
22FC Derek Jeter 15.00
23FC Earl Weaver 2.50
24FC Lefty Grove 2.50
25FC Tony Perez 2.50
26FC Reggie Jackson 5.00
27FC Sparky Anderson 2.50
28FC Casey Stengel 2.50
29FC Roy Campanella 8.00
30FC Roberto Clemente 15.00
31FC Don Drysdale 6.00
32FC Joe Morgan 4.00
33FC Eddie Murray 5.00
34FC Nolan Ryan 15.00
35FC Tom Seaver 8.00
36FC Bill Mazeroski 2.50
37FC Jackie Robinson 15.00
38FC Kirk Gibson 2.50
39FC Robin Yount 8.00

2002 Ultra Fall Classic Autographs

MT
Inserted 1:240
1 Sparky Anderson 15.00
2 Johnny Bench SP
3 George Brett SP
4 Carlton Fisk 40.00
5 Bob Gibson 30.00
6 Kirk Gibson 10.00
7 Reggie Jackson SP
8 Derek Jeter SP
9 Bill Mazeroski 15.00
10 Willie McCovey SP
11 Joe Morgan 20.00
12 Eddie Murray SP
13 Stan Musial SP
14 Jim Palmer
15 Tony Perez 15.00
16 Frank Robinson
17 Nolan Ryan SP 175.00
18 Tom Seaver SP
19 Earl Weaver
20 Robin Yount SP

2002 Ultra Glove Works

MT
Complete Set (15): 35.00
Common Player: 1.00
Inserted 1:20
1GW Andruw Jones 1.50
2GW Derek Jeter 8.00
3GW Cal Ripken Jr. 8.00
4GW Larry Walker 1.50
5GW Chipper Jones 5.00
6GW Barry Bonds 5.00
7GW Scott Rolen 1.50
8GW Jim Edmonds 1.00
9GW Robin Ventura 1.00
10GW Darin Erstad 1.00
11GW Barry Larkin 1.00
12GW Raul Mondesi 1.00
13GW Mark Grace 1.50
14GW Bernie Williams 2.00
15GW Ivan Rodriguez 2.50

2002 Ultra Glove Works (game-worn)

MT
Common Player: 10.00
Production 450 sets
Platinum (25 sets) randomly inserted
1GWG Derek Jeter 60.00
2GWG Andruw Jones
3GWG Cal Ripken Jr. 60.00
5GWG Chipper Jones
6GWG Barry Bonds 40.00
7GWG Robin Ventura 10.00
8GWG Barry Larkin 20.00
9GWG Raul Mondesi 10.00
10GWG Ivan Rodriguez 15.00

2002 Ultra Hitting Machine

MT
Complete Set (25): 75.00
Common Player: 1.50
Inserted 1:20
1HM Frank Thomas 3.00
2HM Derek Jeter 12.00
3HM Vladimir Guerrero 4.00
4HM Jim Edmonds 1.50
5HM Mike Piazza 10.00
6HM Ivan Rodriguez 4.00
7HM Chipper Jones 8.00
8HM Tony Gwynn 4.00
9HM Manny Ramirez 4.00
10HM Andruw Jones 2.50
11HM Carlos Delgado 2.50
12HM Bernie Williams 3.00
13HM Larry Walker 2.00
14HM Juan Gonzalez 4.00
15HM Ichiro Suzuki 15.00
16HM Albert Pujols 5.00
17HM Barry Bonds 6.00
18HM Cal Ripken Jr. 12.00
19HM Edgar Martinez 1.50
20HM Luis Gonzalez 3.00
21HM Moises Alou 1.50
22HM Roberto Alomar 3.00
23HM Todd Helton 3.00
24HM Rafael Palmeiro 2.50
25HM Bobby Abreu 1.50

2002 Ultra Hitting Machine (game-worn)

MT
Common Player: 10.00
Inserted 1:81
Platinum (25 sets) randomly inserted
1HMG Frank Thomas 15.00
2HMG Derek Jeter 50.00
3HMG Jim Edmonds 10.00
4HMG Mike Piazza 25.00
5HMG Ivan Rodriguez 15.00
6HMG Chipper Jones 20.00
7HMG Tony Gwynn 20.00
8HMG Manny Ramirez 20.00
9HMG Andruw Jones 10.00
10HMG Carlos Delgado 10.00
11HMG Bernie Williams 15.00
12HMG Larry Walker 10.00
13HMG Juan Gonzalez 15.00
15HMG Albert Pujols 25.00
16HMG Barry Bonds 25.00
17HMG Cal Ripken Jr. 40.00
18HMG Edgar Martinez 10.00
19HMG Luis Gonzalez 15.00
20HMG Moises Alou 10.00
21HMG Roberto Alomar 15.00
22HMG Todd Helton 15.00
23HMG Rafael Palmeiro 10.00
24HMG Bobby Abreu 10.00

2002 Ultra On the Road (game-used)

		MT
Common Player:		10.00
Inserted 1:93		
Platinum (25 sets) randomly inserted		
1OTR	Derek Jeter	50.00
2OTR	Ivan Rodriguez	10.00
3OTR	Carlos Delgado	10.00
4OTR	Larry Walker	10.00
5OTR	Roberto Alomar	15.00
6OTR	Tony Gwynn	15.00
7OTR	Greg Maddux	20.00
8OTR	Barry Bonds	25.00
9OTR	Todd Helton	15.00
10OTR	Kazuhiro Sasaki	20.00
11OTR	Jeff Bagwell	25.00
12OTR	Omar Vizquel	10.00
13OTR	Chan Ho Park	15.00
14OTR	Tom Glavine	10.00

2002 Ultra Rising Stars

		MT
Complete Set (15):		25.00
Common Player:		1.00
Inserted 1:12		
1RS	Ichiro Suzuki	8.00
2RS	Derek Jeter	5.00
3RS	Albert Pujols	3.00
4RS	Jimmy Rollins	1.00
5RS	Adam Dunn	2.00
6RS	Sean Casey	1.00
7RS	Kerry Wood	1.00
8RS	Tsuyoshi Shinjo	1.50
9RS	Shea Hillenbrand	1.00
10RS	Pat Burrell	1.50
11RS	Ben Sheets	1.50
12RS	Alfonso Soriano	1.50
13RS	J.D. Drew	1.50
14RS	Kazuhiro Sasaki	1.00
15RS	Corey Patterson	1.00

2002 Ultra Rising Stars (game-worn)

		MT
Common Player:		20.00
Production 100 sets		
Platinum (25 sets) randomly seeded		
2RSG	Derek Jeter	75.00
3RSG	Albert Pujols	
4RSG	Tsuyoshi Shinjo	40.00
5RSG	Alfonso Soriano	25.00
6RSG	J.D. Drew	50.00
7RSG	Kazuhiro Sasaki	20.00

A card number in parentheses ( ) indicates the set is unnumbered.

2003 Ultra

		MT
Complete Set (250):		75.00
Common Player:		.15
Common SP (201-250):		.50
Inserted 1:4		
Hobby pack (10):		3.00
Hobby Box (24):		60.00
1	Barry Bonds	2.00
2	Derek Jeter	2.50
3	Ichiro Suzuki	1.50
4	Mike Lowell	.15
5	Hideo Nomo	.50
6	Javier Vazquez	.15
7	Jeremy Giambi	.15
8	Jamie Moyer	.15
9	Rafael Palmeiro	.40
10	Magglio Ordonez	.25
11	Trot Nixon	.15
12	Luis Castillo	.15
13	Paul Byrd	.15
14	Adam Kennedy	.15
15	Trevor Hoffman	.15
16	Matt Morris	.15
17	Nomar Garciaparra	1.50
18	Matt Lawton	.15
19	Carlos Beltran	.15
20	Jason Giambi	1.25
21	Brian Giles	.25
22	Jim Edmonds	.25
23	Garret Anderson	.25
24	Tony Batista	.15
25	Aaron Boone	.15
26	Mike Hampton	.15
27	Billy Wagner	.15
28	Kazuhisa Ishii	.15
29	Al Leiter	.25
30	Pat Burrell	.40
31	Jeff Kent	.25
32	Randy Johnson	.75
33	Ray Durham	.15
34	Josh Beckett	.15
35	Cristian Guzman	.15
36	Roger Clemens	1.25
37	Freddy Garcia	.15
38	Roy Halladay	.15
39	David Eckstein	.15
40	Jerry Hairston Jr.	.15
41	Barry Larkin	.25
42	Larry Walker	.25
43	Craig Biggio	.25
44	Edgardo Alfonzo	.15
45	Marlon Byrd	.15
46	J.T. Snow	.15
47	Juan Gonzalez	.50
48	Ramon Ortiz	.15
49	Jay Gibbons	.15
50	Adam Dunn	.60
51	Juan Pierre	.15
52	Jeff Bagwell	.60
53	Kevin Brown	.15
54	Pedro Astacio	.15
55	Mike Lieberthal	.15
56	Johnny Damon	.15
57	Tim Salmon	.25
58	Mike Bordick	.15
59	Ken Griffey Jr.	1.50
60	Jason Jennings	.15
61	Lance Berkman	.50
62	Jeromy Burnitz	.15
63	Jimmy Rollins	.15
64	Tsuyoshi Shinjo	.15
65	Alex Rodriguez	2.00
66	Greg Maddux	1.25
67	Mark Prior	.40
68	Mike Maroth	.15
69	Geoff Jenkins	.15
70	Tony Armas Jr.	.15
71	Jermaine Dye	.15
72	Albert Pujols	.75
73	Shannon Stewart	.15
74	Troy Glaus	.60
75	Brook Fordyce	.15
76	Juan Encarnacion	.15
77	Todd Hollandsworth	.15
78	Roy Oswalt	.25
79	Paul LoDuca	.15
80	Mike Piazza	1.50
81	Bobby Abreu	.15
82	Sean Burroughs	.15
83	Randy Winn	.15
84	Curt Schilling	.50
85	Chris Singleton	.15
86	Sean Casey	.25
87	Todd Zeile	.15
88	Richard Hidalgo	.15
89	Roberto Alomar	.50
90	Tim Hudson	.25
91	Ryan Klesko	.15
92	Greg Vaughn	.15
93	Tony Womack	.15
94	Fred McGriff	.25
95	Tom Glavine	.40
96	Todd Walker	.15
97	Travis Fryman	.15
98	Shane Reynolds	.15
99	Shawn Green	.25
100	Mo Vaughn	.25
101	Adam Piatt	.15
102	Deivi Cruz	.15
103	Steve Cox	.15
104	Luis Gonzalez	.25
105	Russell Branyan	.15
106	Daryle Ward	.15
107	Mariano Rivera	.25
108	Phil Nevin	.15
109	Ben Grieve	.15
110	Moises Alou	.15
111	Omar Vizquel	.25
112	Joe Randa	.15
113	Jorge Posada	.40
114	Mark Kotsay	.15
115	Ryan Rupe	.15
116	Javy Lopez	.15
117	Corey Patterson	.15
118	Bobby Higginson	.15
119	Jose Vidro	.15
120	Barry Zito	.25
121	Matt Morris	.15
122	Gary Sheffield	.25
123	Kerry Wood	.15
124	Brandon Inge	.15
125	Jose Hernandez	.15
126	Michael Barrett	.15
127	Miguel Tejada	.40
128	Edgar Renteria	.15
129	Junior Spivey	.15
130	Jose Valentin	.15
131	Derrek Lee	.15
132	A.J. Pierzynski	.15
133	Mike Mussina	.50
134	Bret Boone	.15
135	Chan Ho Park	.15
136	Steve Finley	.15
137	Mark Buehrle	.15
138	A.J. Burnett	.15
139	Ben Sheets	.15
140	David Ortiz	.15
141	Nick Johnson	.15
142	Randall Simon	.15
143	Carlos Delgado	.40
144	Darin Erstad	.25
145	Shea Hillenbrand	.15
146	Todd Helton	.40
147	Preston Wilson	.15
148	Eric Gagne	.15
149	Vladimir Guerrero	.75
150	Brandon Duckworth	.15
151	Rich Aurilia	.15
152	Ivan Rodriguez	.50
153	Andruw Jones	.50
154	Carlos Lee	.15
155	Robert Fick	.15
156	Jacque Jones	.15
157	Bernie Williams	.50
158	John Olerud	.25
159	Eric Hinske	.15
160	Matt Clement	.15
161	Dmitri Young	.15
162	Torii Hunter	.15
163	Carlos Pena	.15
164	Mike Cameron	.15
165	Raul Mondesi	.15
166	Pedro J. Martinez	.75
167	Bob Wickman	.15
168	Mike Sweeney	.15
169	David Wells	.15
170	Jason Kendall	.15
171	Tino Martinez	.15
172	Matt Williams	.15
173	Frank Thomas	.60
174	Cliff Floyd	.15
175	Corey Koskie	.15
176	Orlando Hernandez	.15
177	Edgar Martinez	.15
178	Richie Sexson	.25
179	Manny Ramirez	.60
180	Jim Thome	.50
181	Andy Pettitte	.40
182	Aramis Ramirez	.15
183	J.D. Drew	.25
184	Brian Jordan	.15
185	Sammy Sosa	1.25
186	Jeff Weaver	.15
187	Jeffrey Hammonds	.15
188	Eric Milton	.15
189	Eric Chavez	.25
190	Kazuhiro Sasaki	.15
191	Jose Cruz Jr.	.15
192	Derek Lowe	.15
193	C.C. Sabathia	.15
194	Adrian Beltre	.15
195	Alfonso Soriano	1.50
196	Jack Wilson	.15
197	Fernando Vina	.15
198	Chipper Jones	1.25
199	Paul Konerko	.15
200	Rusty Greer	.15
201	Jason Giambi	2.00
202	Alfonso Soriano	3.00
203	Shea Hillenbrand	.50
204	Alex Rodriguez	3.00
205	Jorge Posada	.60
206	Ichiro Suzuki	3.00
207	Manny Ramirez	1.00
208	Torii Hunter	.50
209	Todd Helton	.75
210	Roberto Alomar	.75
211	Scott Rolen	.75
212	Jimmy Rollins	.50
213	Mike Piazza	3.00
214	Barry Bonds	3.00
215	Sammy Sosa	2.00
216	Vladimir Guerrero	1.50
217	Lance Berkman	.75
218	Derek Jeter	4.00
219	Nomar Garciaparra	3.00
220	Luis Gonzalez	.75
221	Kazuhisa Ishii	1.00
222	Satoru Komiyama	.50
223	So Taguchi	.50
224	Jorge Padilla	.50
225	Ben Howard	.50
226	Jason Simontacchi	.50
227	Barry Wesson	.50
228	Howie Clark	.50
229	Aaron Guiel	.50
230	Oliver Perez	.75
231	David Ross	.50
232	Julius Matos	.50
233	Chris Snelling	.50
234	Rodrigo Lopez	.50
235	Wilbert Nieves	.50
236	Brendan Donnelly	.50
237	Aaron Cook	.50
238	Anderson Machado	.50
239	Corey Thurman	.50
240	Tyler Yates	.50
241	*Coco Crisp*	4.00
242	Andy Van Hekken	1.50
243	Jim Rushford	2.00
244	Jeriome Robertson	1.00
245	Shane Nance	1.00
246	Kevin Cash	.50
247	Kirk Saarloos	1.50
248	Josh Bard	2.00
249	*David Pember*	1.00
250	Freddy Sanchez	1.50

2003 Ultra Gold Medallion

	MT
Stars (1-200):	2-3X
Inserted 1:1	
Stars (201-220):	3-4X
Inserted 1:24	
Rookies (221-250):	1-3X
Inserted 1:24	

2003 Ultra Back 2 Back

	MT
Complete Set (17):	60.00
Common Player:	2.00
Production 1,000 sets	
1B2B Derek Jeter	10.00
2B2B Barry Bonds	8.00
3B2B Mike Piazza	6.00
4B2B Alex Rodriguez	8.00
5B2B Todd Helton	2.00
6B2B Edgar Martinez	2.00
7B2B Chipper Jones	5.00
8B2B Shawn Green	2.00
9B2B Chan Ho Park	2.00
10B2B Preston Wilson	2.00
11B2B Manny Ramirez	3.00
12B2B Aramis Ramirez	2.00
13B2B Pedro J. Martinez	4.00
14B2B Ivan Rodriguez	2.00
15B2B Ichiro Suzuki	6.00
16B2B Sammy Sosa	5.00
17B2B Jason Giambi	5.00

2003 Ultra Back 2 Back Memorabilia

	MT
Common Player:	5.00
Production 500 sets	
Golds:	1.5-3X
Production 50 sets	
Derek Jeter	
Barry Bonds/bat	20.00
Mike Piazza/jsy	12.00
Alex Rodriguez/jsy	12.00
Todd Helton/jsy	8.00
Edgar Martinez/jsy	6.00
Chipper Jones/jsy	15.00
Shawn Green/jsy	6.00
Chan Ho Park/bat	6.00
Preston Wilson/jsy	5.00
Manny Ramirez/jsy	8.00
Aramis Ramirez/jsy	5.00
Pedro Martinez/jsy	10.00
Ivan Rodriguez/jsy	8.00
Ichiro Suzuki/base	15.00
Sammy Sosa/base	10.00
Jason Giambi/base	8.00

A player's name in *italic* type indicates a rookie card.

2003 Ultra Double Up

	MT
Complete Set (16):	30.00
Common Card:	1.00
Inserted 1:8	
1DU Derek Jeter, Mike Piazza	4.00
2DU Alex Rodriguez, Rafael Palmeiro	3.00
3DU Chipper Jones, Andruw Jones	2.00
4DU Derek Jeter, Alex Rodriguez	4.00
5DU Nomar Garciaparra, Derek Jeter	4.00
6DU Barry Bonds, Jason Giambi	3.00
7DU Ichiro Suzuki, Hideo Nomo	3.00
8DU Randy Johnson, Curt Schilling	1.00
9DU Pedro J. Martinez, Nomar Garciaparra	2.50
10DU Roger Clemens, Kevin Brown	2.00
11DU Nomar Garciaparra, Manny Ramirez	2.50
12DU Kazuhiro Sasaki, Hideo Nomo	1.00
13DU Mike Piazza, Ivan Rodriguez	3.00
14DU Ichiro Suzuki, Ken Griffey Jr.	3.00
15DU Barry Bonds, Sammy Sosa	3.00
16DU Alfonso Soriano, Roberto Alomar	2.50

2003 Ultra Double Up Memorabilia

	MT
Common Card:	15.00
Production 100 sets	
Derek Jeter, Mike Piazza	50.00
Alex Rodriguez, Rafael Palmeiro	25.00
Chipper Jones, Andruw Jones	15.00
Derek Jeter, Alex Rodriguez	50.00
Nomar Garciaparra, Derek Jeter	50.00
Barry Bonds, Jason Giambi	30.00
Ichiro Suzuki, Hideo Nomo	80.00
Randy Johnson, Curt Schilling	20.00
Pedro J. Martinez, Nomar Garciaparra	30.00
Roger Clemens, Kevin Brown	25.00
Nomar Garciaparra, Manny Ramirez	25.00
Kazuhiro Sasaki, Hideo Nomo	50.00
Mike Piazza, Ivan Rodriguez	25.00
Ichiro Suzuki, Ken Griffey Jr.	50.00
Barry Bonds, Sammy Sosa	40.00
Alfonso Soriano, Roberto Alomar	30.00

2003 Ultra Moonshots

	MT
Complete Set (20):	30.00
Common Player:	.75
Inserted 1:12	
1M Mike Piazza	4.00
2M Alex Rodriguez	4.00
3M Manny Ramirez	1.50
4M Ivan Rodriguez	1.00
5M Luis Gonzalez	.75
6M Shawn Green	.75
7M Barry Bonds	5.00
8M Jason Giambi	3.00
9M Nomar Garciaparra	4.00
10M Edgar Martinez	.75
11M Mo Vaughn	.75
12M Chipper Jones	3.00
13M Todd Helton	1.00
14M Raul Mondesi	.75
15M Preston Wilson	.75
16M Rafael Palmeiro	1.00
17M Jim Edmonds	.75
18M Bernie Williams	1.00
19M Vladimir Guerrero	2.00
20M Alfonso Soriano	3.00

2003 Ultra Moonshots Memorabilia

	MT
Common Player:	4.00
Inserted 1:20	
Mike Piazza/jsy	12.00
Alex Rodriguez/jsy	12.00
Manny Ramirez/jsy	5.00
Ivan Rodriguez/jsy	5.00
Luis Gonzalez/jsy	4.00
Shawn Green/jsy	4.00
Barry Bonds/jsy	12.00
Jason Giambi/base	8.00
Nomar Garciaparra/jsy	12.00
Edgar Martinez/jsy	5.00
Mo Vaughn/jsy	4.00
Chipper Jones/jsy	8.00
Todd Helton/jsy	6.00
Raul Mondesi/jsy	5.00
Preston Wilson/jsy	4.00
Rafael Palmeiro/jsy	5.00
Jim Edmonds/jsy	5.00
Bernie Williams/jsy	6.00
Vladimir Guerrero/base	5.00
Alfonso Soriano/jsy	10.00

2003 Ultra Photo Effex

	MT
Complete Set (20):	45.00
Common Player:	1.00
Inserted 1:12	
Golds:	6-12X
Production 25 sets	
1PE Derek Jeter	6.00
2PE Barry Bonds	5.00
3PE Sammy Sosa	3.00
4PE Troy Glaus	1.50
5PE Albert Pujols	2.00
6PE Alex Rodriguez	5.00
7PE Ichiro Suzuki	4.00
8PE Greg Maddux	3.00
9PE Nomar Garciaparra	4.00
10PE Jeff Bagwell	1.50
11PE Chipper Jones	3.00
12PE Mike Piazza	4.00
13PE Randy Johnson	2.00
14PE Vladimir Guerrero	2.00
15PE Alfonso Soriano	4.00
16PE Lance Berkman	1.00
17PE Todd Helton	1.00
18PE Mike Lowell	1.00
19PE Carlos Delgado	1.00
20PE Jason Giambi	3.00

2003 Ultra When it was a Game

	MT
Complete Set (40):	125.00
Common Player:	2.00
Inserted 1:20	
1WG Derek Jeter	10.00
2WG Barry Bonds	8.00
3WG Luis Aparicio	2.00
4WG Richie Ashburn	2.00
5WG Ernie Banks	5.00
6WG Enos Slaughter	3.00
7WG Yogi Berra	5.00
8WG Lou Boudreau	2.00
9WG Lou Brock	4.00

10WGJim Bunning 2.00
11WGRod Carew 4.00
12WGOrlando Cepeda 2.00
13WGLarry Doby 4.00
14WGBobby Doerr 2.00
15WGBob Feller 3.00
16WGBrooks Robinson 5.00
17WGRollie Fingers 2.00
18WGWhitey Ford 3.00
19WGBob Gibson 4.00
20WGJim "Catfish" Hunter 3.00
21WGNolan Ryan 15.00
22WGReggie Jackson 5.00
23WGFergie Jenkins 3.00
24WGAl Kaline 6.00
25WGMike Schmidt 8.00
26WGHarmon Killebrew 8.00
27WGRalph Kiner 4.00
28WGWillie Stargell 4.00
29WGBilly Williams 2.00
30WGTom Seaver 5.00
31WGJuan Marichal 3.00
32WGEddie Mathews 6.00
33WGWillie McCovey 4.00
34WGJoe Morgan 4.00
35WGStan Musial 8.00
36WGRobin Roberts 4.00
37WGRobin Yount 8.00
38WGJim Palmer 3.00
39WGPhil Rizzuto 4.00
40WGPee Wee Reese 4.00

2003 Ultra When it was a Game Memorabilia

MT

Common Player:
Varying quantities produced
Derek Jeter/jsy/200 35.00
Barry Bonds/bat/200 25.00
Luis Aparicio
Richie Ashburn
Ernie Banks
Enos Slaughter
Yogi Berra
Lou Boudreau
Lou Brock
Jim Bunning
Rod Carew
Orlando Cepeda
Larry Doby/bat/150 20.00
Bobby Doerr
Bob Feller
Brooks Robinson
Rollie Fingers
Whitey Ford
Bob Gibson
Catfish Hunter/jsy 8.00
Nolan Ryan
Reggie Jackson/bat 12.00
Fergie Jenkins
Al Kaline
Mike Schmidt
Harmon Killebrew
Ralph Kiner
Willie Stargell
Billy Williams
Tom Seaver/jsy 12.00
Juan Marichal/jsy 8.00
Eddie Mathews/bat 30.00
Willie McCovey/jsy/150 15.00
Joe Morgan/jsy/200 10.00
Stan Musial
Robin Roberts
Robin Yount
Jim Palmer/jsy/300 10.00
Phil Rizzuto
Pee Wee Reese

1989 Upper Deck

This premiere "Collector's Choice" issue from Upper Deck contains 700 cards (2-1/2"x 3-1/2") with full-color photos on both sides. The first 26 cards feature Star Rookies. The set also includes 26 special portrait cards with team checklist backs and seven numberical checklist cards. Major 1988 award winners (Cy Young, Rookie of Year, MVP) are honored on 10 cards in the set, in addition to their individual player cards. There are also special cards for the Most Valuable Players in both League Championship series and the World Series. The card fronts feature player photos framed by a white border. A vertical brown and green artist's rendition of the runner's lane that leads from home plate to first base is found along the right margin. Backs carry full-color action poses that fill the card back, except for a compact (yet complete) stats chart. A high-number series, cards 701-800, featuring rookies and traded players, was released in mid-season in foil packs mixed within the complete set, in boxed complete sets and in high number set boxes.

MT

Complete Set (800): 125.00
Unopened Factory Set (800): 150.00
Complete Low Set (700): 115.00
Complete High Set (100): 10.00
Common Player: .10
Low Foil Pack (15): 10.00
Low Foil Wax Box (36): 300.00
High Foil Pack (15): 9.00
High Foil Wax Box (36): 250.00

1 *Ken Griffey, Jr.* 65.00
2 *Luis Medina* .10
3 *Tony Chance* .10
4 *Dave Otto* .10
5 *Sandy Alomar, Jr.* 1.50
6 *Rolando Roomes* .10
7 *David West* .10
8 *Cris Carpenter* .10
9 Gregg Jefferies .25
10 *Doug Dascenzo* .10
11 *Ron Jones* .10
12 *Luis de los Santos* .10
13a *Gary Sheffield* ("SS" upside-down) 6.00
13b *Gary Sheffield* ("SS" correct) 6.00
14 *Mike Harkey* .10
15 *Lance Blankenship* .10
16 *William Brennan* .10
17 John Smoltz .25
18 *Ramon Martinez* .65
19 *Mark Lemke* .10
20 *Juan Bell* .10
21 *Rey Palacios* .10
22 *Felix Jose* .10
23 *Van Snider* .10
24 *Dante Bichette* 1.00
25 *Randy Johnson* 18.00
26 *Carlos Quintana* .10
27 Star Rookie Checklist 1-26 .10
28 *Mike Schooler* .10
29 Randy St. Claire .10
30 *Jerald Clark* .10
31 Kevin Gross .10
32 *Dan Firova* .10
33 Jeff Calhoun .10
34 Tommy Hinzo .10
35 *Ricky Jordan* .10
36 Larry Parrish .10
37 Bret Saberhagen .10
38 Mike Smithson .10
39 Dave Dravecky .10
40 Ed Romero .10
41 Jeff Musselman .10
42 Ed Hearn .10
43 Rance Mulliniks .10
44 Jim Eisenreich .10
45 *Sil Campusano* .10
46 Mike Krukow .10
47 *Paul Gibson* .10
48 Mike LaCoss .10
49 Larry Herndon .10
50 Scott Garrelts .10
51 Dwayne Henry .10
52 Jim Acker .10
53 Steve Sax .10
54 Pete O'Brien .10
55 Paul Runge .10
56 Rick Rhoden .10
57 *John Dopson* .10
58 Casey Candaele .10
59 Dave Righetti .10
60 Joe Hesketh .10
61 Frank DiPino .10
62 Tim Laudner .10
63 Jamie Moyer .10
64 Fred Toliver .10
65 Mitch Webster .10
66 John Tudor .10
67 John Cangelosi .10
68 Mike Devereaux .10
69 Brian Fisher .10
70 Mike Marshall .10
71 Zane Smith .10
72a Brian Holton (ball not visible on card front,photo a ctually Shawn Hillegas) .75
72b Brian Holton (ball visible, correct photo) .10
73 Jose Guzman .10
74 Rick Mahler .10
75 John Shelby .10
76 Jim Deshaies .10
77 Bobby Meacham .10
78 Bryn Smith .10
79 Joaquin Andujar .10
80 Richard Dotson .10
81 Charlie Lea .10
82 Calvin Schiraldi .10
83 Les Straker .10
84 Les Lancaster .10
85 Allan Anderson .10
86 Junior Ortiz .10
87 Jesse Orosco .10
88 Felix Fermin .10
89 Dave Anderson .10
90 Rafael Belliard .10
91 Franklin Stubbs .10
92 Cecil Espy .10
93 Albert Hall .10
94 Tim Leary .10
95 Mitch Williams .10
96 Tracy Jones .10
97 Danny Darwin .10
98 Gary Ward .10
99 Neal Heaton .10
100 Jim Pankovits .10
101 Bill Doran .10
102 Tim Wallach .10
103 Joe Magrane .10
104 Ozzie Virgil .10
105 Alvin Davis .10
106 Tom Brookens .10
107 Shawon Dunston .10
108 Tracy Woodson .10
109 Nelson Liriano .10
110 Devon White .10
111 Steve Balboni .10
112 Buddy Bell .10
113 *German Jimenez* .10
114 Ken Dayley .10
115 Andres Galarraga .10
116 Mike Scioscia .10
117 Gary Pettis .10
118 Ernie Whitt .10
119 Bob Boone .15
120 Ryne Sandberg 1.25
121 Bruce Benedict .10
122 Hubie Brooks .10
123 Mike Moore .10
124 Wallace Johnson .10
125 Bob Horner .10
126 Chili Davis .10
127 Manny Trillo .10
128 Chet Lemon .10
129 John Cerutti .10
130 Orel Hershiser .10
131 Terry Pendleton .10
132 Jeff Blauser .10
133 Mike Fitzgerald .10
134 Henry Cotto .10
135 Gerald Young .10
136 Luis Salazar .10
137 Alejandro Pena .10
138 Jack Howell .10
139 Tony Fernandez .10
140 Mark Grace .30
141 Ken Caminiti .10
142 Mike Jackson .10
143 Larry McWilliams .10
144 Andres Thomas .10
145 Nolan Ryan 2.00
146 Mike Davis .10
147 DeWayne Buice .10
148 Jody Davis .10
149 Jesse Barfield .10
150 Matt Nokes .10
151 Jerry Reuss .10
152 Rick Cerone .10
153 Storm Davis .10
154 Marvell Wynne .10
155 Will Clark .30
156 Luis Aguayo .10
157 Willie Upshaw .10
158 Randy Bush .10
159 Ron Darling .10
160 Kal Daniels .10
161 Spike Owen .10
162 Luis Polonia .10
163 Kevin Mitchell .10
164 *Dave Gallagher* .10
165 Benito Santiago .10
166 Greg Gagne .10
167 Ken Phelps .10
168 Sid Fernandez .10
169 Bo Diaz .10
170 Cory Snyder .10
171 Eric Show .10
172 Robby Thompson .10
173 Marty Barrett .10
174 Dave Henderson .10
175 Ozzie Guillen .10
176 Barry Lyons .10
177 *Kelvin Torve* .10
178 Don Slaught .10
179 Steve Lombardozzi .10
180 *Chris Sabo* .10
181 Jose Uribe .10
182 Shane Mack .10
183 Ron Karkovice .10
184 Todd Benzinger .10
185 Dave Stewart .10
186 Julio Franco .10
187 Ron Robinson .10
188 Wally Backman .10
189 Randy Velarde .10
190 Joe Carter .10
191 Bob Welch .10
192 Kelly Paris .10
193 Chris Brown .10
194 Rick Reuschel .10
195 Roger Clemens 1.50
196 Dave Concepcion .10
197 Al Newman .10

No.	Player	Price
198	Brook Jacoby	.10
199	Mookie Wilson	.10
200	Don Mattingly	1.75
201	Dick Schofield	.10
202	Mark Gubicza	.10
203	Gary Gaetti	.10
204	Dan Pasqua	.10
205	Andre Dawson	.25
206	Chris Speier	.10
207	Kent Tekulve	.10
208	Rod Scurry	.10
209	Scott Bailes	.10
210	Rickey Henderson	.75
211	Harold Baines	.10
212	Tony Armas	.10
213	Kent Hrbek	.10
214	Darrin Jackson	.10
215	George Brett	1.50
216	Rafael Santana	.10
217	Andy Allanson	.10
218	Brett Butler	.10
219	Steve Jeltz	.10
220	Jay Buhner	.10
221	Bo Jackson	.15
222	Angel Salazar	.10
223	Kirk McCaskill	.10
224	Steve Lyons	.10
225	Bert Blyleven	.10
226	Scott Bradley	.10
227	Bob Melvin	.10
228	Ron Kittle	.10
229	Phil Bradley	.10
230	Tommy John	.15
231	Greg Walker	.10
232	Juan Berenguer	.10
233	Pat Tabler	.10
234	*Terry Clark*	.10
235	Rafael Palmeiro	.30
236	Paul Zuvella	.10
237	Willie Randolph	.10
238	Bruce Fields	.10
239	Mike Aldrete	.10
240	Lance Parrish	.10
241	Greg Maddux	1.50
242	John Moses	.10
243	Melido Perez	.10
244	Willie Wilson	.10
245	Mark McLemore	.10
246	Von Hayes	.10
247	Matt Williams	.30
248	John Candelaria	.10
249	Harold Reynolds	.10
250	Greg Swindell	.10
251	Juan Agosto	.10
252	Mike Felder	.10
253	Vince Coleman	.10
254	Larry Sheets	.10
255	George Bell	.10
256	Terry Steinbach	.10
257	*Jack Armstrong*	.10
258	Dickie Thon	.10
259	Ray Knight	.10
260	Darryl Strawberry	.10
261	Doug Sisk	.10
262	Alex Trevino	.10
263	Jeff Leonard	.10
264	Tom Henke	.10
265	Ozzie Smith	1.50
266	Dave Bergman	.10
267	Tony Phillips	.10
268	Mark Davis	.10
269	Kevin Elster	.10
270	Barry Larkin	.15
271	Manny Lee	.10
272	Tom Brunansky	.10
273	Craig Biggio	.15
274	Jim Gantner	.10
275	Eddie Murray	.60
276	Jeff Reed	.10
277	Tim Teufel	.10
278	Rick Honeycutt	.10
279	Guillermo Hernandez	.10
280	John Kruk	.10
281	*Luis Alicea*	.20
282	Jim Clancy	.10
283	Billy Ripken	.10
284	Craig Reynolds	.10
285	Robin Yount	1.00
286	Jimmy Jones	.10
287	Ron Oester	.10
288	Terry Leach	.10
289	Dennis Eckersley	.10
290	Alan Trammell	.10
291	Jimmy Key	.10
292	Chris Bosio	.10
293	Jose DeLeon	.10
294	Jim Traber	.10
295	Mike Scott	.10
296	Roger McDowell	.10
297	Garry Templeton	.10
298	Doyle Alexander	.10
299	Nick Esasky	.10
300	Mark McGwire	2.00
301	*Darryl Hamilton*	.20
302	Dave Smith	.10
303	Rick Sutcliffe	.10
304	Dave Stapleton	.10
305	Alan Ashby	.10
306	Pedro Guerrero	.10
307	Ron Guidry	.10
308	Steve Farr	.10
309	Curt Ford	.10
310	Claudell Washington	.10
311	Tom Prince	.10
312	*Chad Kreuter*	.15
313	Ken Oberkfell	.10
314	Jerry Browne	.10
315	R.J. Reynolds	.10
316	Scott Bankhead	.10
317	Milt Thompson	.10
318	Mario Diaz	.10
319	Bruce Ruffin	.10
320	Dave Valle	.10
321a	*Gary Varsho* (batting righty on card back, photo actually Mike Bielecki)	1.50
321b	*Gary Varsho* (batting lefty on card back, correct photo)	.10
322	Paul Mirabella	.10
323	Chuck Jackson	.10
324	Drew Hall	.10
325	Don August	.10
326	*Israel Sanchez*	.10
327	Denny Walling	.10
328	Joel Skinner	.10
329	Danny Tartabull	.10
330	Tony Pena	.10
331	Jim Sundberg	.10
332	Jeff Robinson	.10
333	Odibbe McDowell	.10
334	Jose Lind	.10
335	Paul Kilgus	.10
336	Juan Samuel	.10
337	Mike Campbell	.10
338	Mike Maddux	.10
339	Darnell Coles	.10
340	Bob Dernier	.10
341	Rafael Ramirez	.10
342	Scott Sanderson	.10
343	B.J. Surhoff	.10
344	Billy Hatcher	.10
345	Pat Perry	.10
346	Jack Clark	.10
347	Gary Thurman	.10
348	*Timmy Jones*	.10
349	Dave Winfield	1.00
350	Frank White	.10
351	Dave Collins	.10
352	Jack Morris	.10
353	Eric Plunk	.10
354	Leon Durham	.10
355	Ivan DeJesus	.10
356	*Brian Holman*	.10
357a	Dale Murphy (reversed negative)	30.00
357b	Dale Murphy (corrected)	.25
358	Mark Portugal	.10
359	Andy McGaffigan	.10
360	Tom Glavine	.15
361	Keith Moreland	.10
362	Todd Stottlemyre	.10
363	Dave Leiper	.10
364	Cecil Fielder	.10
365	Carmelo Martinez	.10
366	Dwight Evans	.10
367	Kevin McReynolds	.10
368	Rich Gedman	.10
369	Len Dykstra	.10
370	Jody Reed	.10
371	Jose Canseco	.60
372	Rob Murphy	.10
373	Mike Henneman	.10
374	Walt Weiss	.10
375	*Rob Dibble*	.10
376	Kirby Puckett	1.50
377	Denny Martinez	.10
378	Ron Gant	.10
379	Brian Harper	.10
380	*Nelson Santovenia*	.10
381	Lloyd Moseby	.10
382	Lance McCullers	.10
383	Dave Stieb	.10
384	Tony Gwynn	1.50
385	Mike Flanagan	.10
386	Bob Ojeda	.10
387	Bruce Hurst	.10
388	Dave Magadan	.10
389	Wade Boggs	.65
390	Gary Carter	.25
391	Frank Tanana	.10
392	Curt Young	.10
393	Jeff Treadway	.10
394	Darrell Evans	.10
395	Glenn Hubbard	.10
396	Chuck Cary	.10
397	Frank Viola	.10
398	Jeff Parrett	.10
399	*Terry Blocker*	.10
400	Dan Gladden	.10
401	*Louie Meadows*	.10
402	Tim Raines	.10
403	Joey Meyer	.10
404	Larry Andersen	.10
405	Rex Hudler	.10
406	Mike Schmidt	1.50
407	John Franco	.10
408	Brady Anderson	.10
409	Don Carman	.10
410	Eric Davis	.10
411	Bob Stanley	.10
412	Pete Smith	.10
413	Jim Rice	.15
414	Bruce Sutter	.10
415	Oil Can Boyd	.10
416	Ruben Sierra	.10
417	Mike LaValliere	.10
418	Steve Buechele	.10
419	Gary Redus	.10
420	Scott Fletcher	.10
421	Dale Sveum	.10
422	Bob Knepper	.10
423	Luis Rivera	.10
424	Ted Higuera	.10
425	Kevin Bass	.10
426	Ken Gerhart	.10
427	Shane Rawley	.10
428	Paul O'Neill	.10
429	Joe Orsulak	.10
430	Jackie Gutierrez	.10
431	Gerald Perry	.10
432	Mike Greenwell	.10
433	Jerry Royster	.10
434	Ellis Burks	.10
435	Ed Olwine	.10
436	Dave Rucker	.10
437	Charlie Hough	.10
438	Bob Walk	.10
439	Bob Brower	.10
440	Barry Bonds	1.75
441	Tom Foley	.10
442	Rob Deer	.10
443	Glenn Davis	.10
444	Dave Martinez	.10
445	Bill Wegman	.10
446	Lloyd McClendon	.10
447	Dave Schmidt	.10
448	Darren Daulton	.10
449	Frank Williams	.10
450	Don Aase	.10
451	Lou Whitaker	.10
452	Goose Gossage	.10
453	Ed Whitson	.10
454	Jim Walewander	.10
455	Damon Berryhill	.10
456	Tim Burke	.10
457	Barry Jones	.10
458	Joel Youngblood	.10
459	Floyd Youmans	.10
460	Mark Salas	.10
461	Jeff Russell	.10
462	Darrell Miller	.10
463	Jeff Kunkel	.10
464	*Sherman Corbett*	.10
465	Curtis Wilkerson	.10
466	Bud Black	.10
467	Cal Ripken, Jr.	2.00
468	John Farrell	.10
469	Terry Kennedy	.10
470	Tom Candiotti	.10
471	Roberto Alomar	1.00
472	Jeff Robinson	.10
473	Vance Law	.10
474	Randy Ready	.10
475	Walt Terrell	.10
476	Kelly Downs	.10
477	*Johnny Paredes*	.10
478	Shawn Hillegas	.10
479	Bob Brenly	.10
480	Otis Nixon	.10
481	Johnny Ray	.10
482	Geno Petralli	.10
483	Stu Cliburn	.10
484	Pete Incaviglia	.10
485	Brian Downing	.10
486	Jeff Stone	.10
487	Carmen Castillo	.10
488	Tom Niedenfuer	.10
489	Jay Bell	.10
490	Rick Schu	.10
491	*Jeff Pico*	.10
492	*Mark Parent*	.10
493	Eric King	.10
494	Al Nipper	.10
495	Andy Hawkins	.10
496	Daryl Boston	.10
497	Ernie Riles	.10
498	Pascual Perez	.10
499	Bill Long	.10
500	Kirt Manwaring	.10
501	Chuck Crim	.10
502	Candy Maldonado	.10
503	Dennis Lamp	.10
504	Glenn Braggs	.10
505	Joe Price	.10
506	Ken Williams	.10
507	Bill Pecota	.10
508	Rey Quinones	.10
509	*Jeff Bittiger*	.10
510	Kevin Seitzer	.10
511	Steve Bedrosian	.10
512	Todd Worrell	.10
513	Chris James	.10
514	Jose Oquendo	.10
515	David Palmer	.10
516	John Smiley	.10
517	Dave Clark	.10
518	Mike Dunne	.10
519	Ron Washington	.10
520	Bob Kipper	.10
521	Lee Smith	.10
522	Juan Castillo	.10
523	Don Robinson	.10
524	Kevin Romine	.10
525	Paul Molitor	.75
526	Mark Langston	.10
527	Donnie Hill	.10
528	Larry Owen	.10
529	Jerry Reed	.10
530	Jack McDowell	.10
531	Greg Mathews	.10
532	John Russell	.10
533	Dan Quisenberry	.10
534	Greg Gross	.10
535	Danny Cox	.10
536	Terry Francona	.10
537	Andy Van Slyke	.10
538	Mel Hall	.10
539	Jim Gott	.10
540	Doug Jones	.10
541	Criag Lefferts	.10
542	Mike Boddicker	.10
543	Greg Brock	.10
544	Atlee Hammaker	.10
545	Tom Bolton	.10
546	*Mike Macfarlane*	.25
547	*Rich Renteria*	.10
548	John Davis	.10
549	Floyd Bannister	.10
550	Mickey Brantley	.10
551	Duane Ward	.10
552	Dan Petry	.10
553	Mickey Tettleton	.10
554	Rick Leach	.10
555	Mike Witt	.10
556	Sid Bream	.10
557	Bobby Witt	.10
558	Tommy Herr	.10
559	Randy Milligan	.10
560	*Jose Cecena*	.10
561	Mackey Sasser	.10
562	Carney Lansford	.10
563	Rick Aguilera	.10
564	Ron Hassey	.10
565	Dwight Gooden	.10
566	Paul Assenmacher	.10
567	Neil Allen	.10
568	Jim Morrison	.10
569	Mike Pagliarulo	.10
570	Ted Simmons	.10
571	Mark Thurmond	.10

572 Fred McGriff .10
573 Wally Joyner .10
574 *Jose Bautista* .10
575 Kelly Gruber .10
576 Cecilio Guante .10
577 Mark Davidson .10
578 Bobby Bonilla .10
579 Mike Stanley .10
580 Gene Larkin .10
581 Stan Javier .10
582 Howard Johnson .10
583a Mike Gallego (photo on card back reversed) .75
583b Mike Gallego (correct photo) .10
584 David Cone .10
585 *Doug Jennings* .10
586 Charlie Hudson .10
587 Dion James .10
588 Al Leiter .10
589 Charlie Puleo .10
590 Roberto Kelly .10
591 Thad Bosley .10
592 Pete Stanicek .10
593 *Pat Borders* .25
594 *Bryan Harvey* .10
595 Jeff Ballard .10
596 Jeff Reardon .10
597 Doug Drabek .10
598 Edwin Correa .10
599 Keith Atherton .10
600 Dave LaPoint .10
601 Don Baylor .15
602 Tom Pagnozzi .10
603 Tim Flannery .10
604 Gene Walter .10
605 Dave Parker .10
606 Mike Diaz .10
607 Chris Gwynn .10
608 Odell Jones .10
609 Carlton Fisk 1.00
610 Jay Howell .10
611 Tim Crews .10
612 Keith Hernandez .10
613 Willie Fraser .10
614 Jim Eppard .10
615 Jeff Hamilton .10
616 Kurt Stillwell .10
617 Tom Browning .10
618 Jeff Montgomery .10
619 Jose Rijo .10
620 Jamie Quirk .10
621 Willie McGee .10
622 Mark Grant .10
623 Bill Swift .10
624 Orlando Mercado .10
625 *John Costello* .10
626 Jose Gonzalez .10
627a Bill Schroeder (putting on shin guards on card back, photo actually Ronn Reynolds) .75
627b Bill Schroeder (arms crossed on card back, correct photo) .10
628a Fred Manrique (throwing on card back, photo actually Ozzie Guillen) .75
628b Fred Manrique (batting on card back, correct photo) .10
629 Ricky Horton .10
630 Dan Plesac .10
631 Alfredo Griffin .10
632 Chuck Finley .10
633 Kirk Gibson .10
634 Randy Myers .10
635 Greg Minton .10
636 Herm Winningham .10
637 Charlie Leibrandt .10
638 Tim Birtsas .10
639 Bill Buckner .10
640 Danny Jackson .10
641 Greg Booker .10
642 Jim Presley .10
643 Gene Nelson .10
644 Rod Booker .10
645 Dennis Rasmussen .10
646 Juan Nieves .10
647 Bobby Thigpen .10
648 Tim Belcher .10
649 Mike Young .10
650 Ivan Calderon .10
651 *Oswaldo Peraza* .10
652a Pat Sheridan (no position on front) 10.00
652b Pat Sheridan (position on front) .10
653 Mike Morgan .10
654 Mike Heath .10
655 Jay Tibbs .10
656 Fernando Valenzuela .10
657 Lee Mazzilli .10
658 Frank Viola .10
659 Jose Canseco .60
660 Walt Weiss .10
661 Orel Hershiser .10
662 Kirk Gibson .10
663 Chris Sabo .10
664 Dennis Eckersley .10
665 Orel Hershiser .10
666 Kirk Gibson .10
667 Orel Hershiser .10
668 Wally Joyner (TC) .10
669 Nolan Ryan (TC) 1.00
670 Jose Canseco (TC) .30
671 Fred McGriff (TC) .10
672 Dale Murphy (TC) .15
673 Paul Molitor (TC) .35
674 Ozzie Smith (TC) .75
675 Ryne Sandberg (TC) .40
676 Kirk Gibson (TC) .10
677 Andres Galarraga (TC) .10
678 Will Clark (TC) .15
679 Cory Snyder (TC) .10
680 Alvin Davis (TC) .10
681 Darryl Strawberry (TC) .10
682 Cal Ripken, Jr. (TC) 1.00
683 Tony Gwynn (TC) .40
684 Mike Schmidt (TC) .75
685 Andy Van Slyke (TC) .10
686 Ruben Sierra (TC) .10
687 Wade Boggs (TC) .30
688 Eric Davis (TC) .10
689 George Brett (TC) .75
690 Alan Trammell (TC) .10
691 Frank Viola (TC) .10
692 Harold Baines (TC) .10
693 Don Mattingly (TC) .75
694 Checklist 1-100 .10
695 Checklist 101-200 .10
696 Checklist 201-300 .10
697 Checklist 301-400 .10
698 Checklist 401-500 .10
699 Checklist 501-600 .10
700 Checklist 601-700 .10
701 Checklist 701-800 .10
702 Jessie Barfield .10
703 Walt Terrell .10
704 Dickie Thon .10
705 Al Leiter .10
706 Dave LaPoint .10
707 *Charlie Hayes* .25
708 Andy Hawkins .10
709 Mickey Hatcher .10
710 Lance McCullers .10
711 Ron Kittle .10
712 Bert Blyleven .10
713 Rick Dempsey .10
714 Ken Williams .10
715 Steve Rosenberg .10
716 Joe Skalski .10
717 Spike Owen .10
718 Todd Burns .10
719 Kevin Gross .10
720 Tommy Herr .10
721 Rob Ducey .10
722 Gary Green .10
723 *Gregg Olson* .25
724 Greg Harris .10
725 Craig Worthington .10
726 Tom Howard .10
727 Dale Mohorcic .10
728 Rich Yett .10
729 Mel Hall .10
730 Floyd Youmans .10
731 Lonnie Smith .10
732 Wally Backman .10
733 Trevor Wilson .10
734 Jose Alvarez .10
735 Bob Milacki .10
736 *Tom Gordon* .50
737 Wally Whitehurst .10
738 Mike Aldrete .10
739 Keith Miller .10
740 Randy Milligan .10
741 Jeff Parrett .10
742 *Steve Finley* 1.00
743 *Junior Felix* .10
744 *Pete Harnisch* .25
745 Bill Spiers .10
746 Hensley Meulens .10
747 Juan Bell .10
748 Steve Sax .10
749 Phil Bradley .10
750 Rey Quinones .10
751 Tommy Gregg .10
752 Kevin Brown .25
753 Derek Lilliquist .10
754 *Todd Zeile* .75
755 Jim Abbott .15
756 *Ozzie Canseco* .10
757 Nick Esasky .10
758 Mike Moore .10
759 Rob Murphy .10
760 Rick Mahler .10
761 Fred Lynn .10
762 *Kevin Blankenship* .10
763 Eddie Murray .60
764 *Steve Searcy* .10
765 *Jerome Walton* .10
766 *Erik Hanson* .10
767 Bob Boone .15
768 Edgar Martinez .10
769 *Jose DeJesus* .10
770 *Greg Briley* .10
771 *Steve Peters* .10
772 Rafael Palmeiro .30
773 Jack Clark .10
774 Nolan Ryan 2.00
775 Lance Parrish .10
776 *Joe Girardi* .40
777 Willie Randolph .10
778 Mitch Williams .10
779 *Dennis Cook* .10
780 *Dwight Smith* .10
781 *Lenny Harris* .15
782 *Torey Lovullo* .10
783 *Norm Charlton* .15
784 Chris Brown .10
785 Todd Benzinger .10
786 Shane Rawley .10
787 *Omar Vizquel* 2.00
788 *LaVel Freeman* .10
789 Jeffrey Leonard .10
790 *Eddie Williams* .10
791 Jamie Moyer .10
792 Bruce Hurst .10
793 Julio Franco .10
794 Claudell Washington .10
795 Jody Davis .10
796 Oddibe McDowell .10
797 Paul Kilgus .10
798 Tracy Jones .10
799 Steve Wilson .10
800 Pete O'Brien .10

1990 Upper Deck

Tom Gordon

Following the success of its first issue, Upper Deck released another 800-card set in 1990. The cards feature full-color photos on both sides in the standard 2-1/2" x 3-1/2" format. The artwork of Vernon Wells Sr. is featured on the front of all team checklist cards. The 1990 set also introduces two new Wells illustrations - a tribute to Mike Schmidt upon his retirement and one commemorating Nolan Ryan's 5,000 career strikeouts. The cards are similar in design to the 1989 issue. The high-number series (701-800) was released as a boxed set, in factory sets and in foil packs at mid-season. Cards #101-199 can be found either with or without the copyright line on back; no premium attaches to either.

MT

Unopened Factory Set (800): 20.00
Complete Set (800): 15.00
Complete Low Set (700): 12.00
Complete High Set (100): 3.00
Common Player: .05
Low Foil Pack (15): 1.00
Low Foil Wax Box (36): 20.00
High Foil Pack (15): 1.00
High Foil Wax Box (36): 25.00
1 Star Rookie Checklist .05
2 *Randy Nosek* .05
3 *Tom Drees* .05
4 Curt Young .05
5 Angels checklist (Devon White) .05
6 Luis Salazar .05
7 Phillies checklist (Von Hayes) .05
8 Jose Bautista .05
9 *Marquis Grissom* .50
10 Dodgers checklist (Orel Hershiser) .05
11 Rick Aguilera .05
12 Padres checklist (Benito Santiago) .05
13 Deion Sanders .10
14 Marvell Wynne .05
15 David West .05
16 Pirates checklist (Bobby Bonilla) .05
17 *Sammy Sosa* 10.00
18 Yankees checklist (Steve Sax) .05
19 Jack Howell .05
20 Mike Schmidt Retires (Mike Schmidt) .75
21 Robin Ventura .05
22 Brian Meyer .05
23 *Blaine Beatty* .05
24 Mariners checklist (Ken Griffey, Jr.) 1.00
25 Greg Vaughn .05
26 *Xavier Hernandez* .05
27 *Jason Grimsley* .05
28 *Eric Anthony* .05
29 Expos checklist (Tim Raines) .05
30 David Wells .10
31 Hal Morris .05
32 Royals checklist (Bo Jackson) .10
33 *Kelly Mann* .05
34 Nolan Ryan 5000 Strikeouts (Nolan Ryan) 1.00
35 *Scott Service* .05
36 Athletics checklist (Mark McGwire) 1.00
37 Tino Martinez .05
38 Chili Davis .05
39 Scott Sanderson .05
40 Giants checklist (Kevin Mitchell) .05
41 Tigers checklist (Lou Whitaker) .05
42 *Scott Coolbaugh* .05
43 *Jose Cano* .05
44 *Jose Vizcaino* .10
45 *Bob Hamelin* .05
46 *Jose Offerman* .25
47 Kevin Blankenship .05
48 Twins checklist (Kirby Puckett) .40
49 *Tommy Greene* .05

No.	Player	Price
50	N.L. Top Vote Getter (Will Clark)	.10
51	Rob Nelson	.05
52	*Chris Hammond*	.15
53	Indians checklist (Joe Carter)	.05
54a	*Ben McDonald* (Orioles Logo)	1.00
54b	*Ben McDonald* (Star Rookie logo)	.25
55	Andy Benes	.05
56	*John Olerud*	1.00
57	Red Sox checklist (Roger Clemens)	.40
58	Tony Armas	.05
59	*George Canale*	.05
60a	Orioles checklist (Mickey Tettleton) (#683 Jamie Weston)	1.00
60b	Orioles checklis t(Mickey Tettleton) (#683 Mickey Weston)	.05
61	*Mike Stanton*	.05
62	Mets checklist (Dwight Gooden)	.05
63	*Kent Mercker*	.10
64	*Francisco Cabrera*	.05
65	Steve Avery	.05
66	Jose Canseco	.40
67	*Matt Merullo*	.05
68	Cardinals checklist (Vince Coleman)	.05
69	Ron Karkovice	.05
70	*Kevin Maas*	.05
71	Dennis Cook	.05
72	*Juan Gonzalez*	3.00
73	Cubs checklist (Andre Dawson)	.10
74	*Dean Palmer*	.50
75	A.L. Top Vote Getter (Bo Jackson)	.10
76	*Rob Richie*	.05
77	*Bobby Rose*	.05
78	*Brian DuBois*	.05
79	White Sox checklist (Ozzie Guillen)	.05
80	Gene Nelson	.05
81	Bob McClure	.05
82	Rangers checklist (Julio Franco)	.05
83	Greg Minton	.05
84	Braves checklist (John Smoltz)	.05
85	Willie Fraser	.05
86	Neal Heaton	.05
87	*Kevin Tapani*	.05
88	Astros checklist (Mike Scott)	.05
89a	Jim Gott (incorrect photo)	1.00
89b	Jim Gott (correct photo)	.05
90	Lance Johnson	.05
91	Brewers checklist (Robin Yount)	.35
92	Jeff Parrett	.05
93	*Julio Machado*	.05
94	Ron Jones	.05
95	Blue Jays checklist (George Bell)	.05
96	Jerry Reuss	.05
97	Brian Fisher	.05
98	*Kevin Ritz*	.05
99	Reds checklist (Barry Larkin)	.05
100	Checklist 1-100	.05
101	Gerald Perry	.05
102	Kevin Appier	.05
103	Julio Franco	.05
104	Craig Biggio	.10
105	Bo Jackson	.10
106	*Junior Felix*	.05
107	Mike Harkey	.05
108	Fred McGriff	.05
109	Rick Sutcliffe	.05
110	Pete O'Brien	.05
111	Kelly Gruber	.05
112	Pat Borders	.05
113	Dwight Evans	.05
114	Dwight Gooden	.05
115	*Kevin Batiste*	.05
116	Eric Davis	.05
117	Kevin Mitchell	.05
118	Ron Oester	.05
119	Brett Butler	.05
120	Danny Jackson	.05
121	Tommy Gregg	.05
122	Ken Caminiti	.05
123	Kevin Brown	.10
124	George Brett	.75
125	Mike Scott	.05
126	Cory Snyder	.05
127	George Bell	.05
128	Mark Grace	.30
129	Devon White	.05
130	Tony Fernandez	.05
131	Don Aase	.05
132	Rance Mulliniks	.05
133	Marty Barrett	.05
134	Nelson Liriano	.05
135	Mark Carreon	.05
136	Candy Maldonado	.05
137	Tim Birtsas	.05
138	Tom Brookens	.05
139	John Franco	.05
140	Mike LaCoss	.05
141	Jeff Treadway	.05
142	Pat Tabler	.05
143	Darrell Evans	.05
144	Rafael Ramirez	.05
145	Oddibe McDowell	.05
146	Brian Downing	.05
147	Curtis Wilkerson	.05
148	Ernie Whitt	.05
149	Bill Schroeder	.05
150	Domingo Ramos	.05
151	Rick Honeycutt	.05
152	Don Slaught	.05
153	Mitch Webster	.05
154	Tony Phillips	.05
155	Paul Kilgus	.05
156	Ken Griffey, Jr.	2.50
157	Gary Sheffield	.35
158	Wally Backman	.05
159	B.J. Surhoff	.05
160	Louie Meadows	.05
161	Paul O'Neill	.05
162	*Jeff McKnight*	.05
163	Alvaro Espinoza	.05
164	*Scott Scudder*	.05
165	Jeff Reed	.05
166	Gregg Jefferies	.05
167	Barry Larkin	.10
168	Gary Carter	.25
169	Robby Thompson	.05
170	Rolando Roomes	.05
171	Mark McGwire	2.00
172	Steve Sax	.05
173	Mark Williamson	.05
174	Mitch Williams	.05
175	Brian Holton	.05
176	Rob Deer	.05
177	Tim Raines	.05
178	Mike Felder	.05
179	Harold Reynolds	.05
180	Terry Francona	.05
181	Chris Sabo	.05
182	Darryl Strawberry	.05
183	Willie Randolph	.05
184	Billy Ripken	.05
185	Mackey Sasser	.05
186	Todd Benzinger	.05
187	Kevin Elster	.05
188	Jose Uribe	.05
189	Tom Browning	.05
190	Keith Miller	.05
191	Don Mattingly	.75
192	Dave Parker	.05
193	Roberto Kelly	.05
194	Phil Bradley	.05
195	Ron Hassey	.05
196	Gerald Young	.05
197	Hubie Brooks	.05
198	Bill Doran	.05
199	Al Newman	.05
200	Checklist 101-200	.05
201	Terry Puhl	.05
202	Frank DiPino	.05
203	Jim Clancy	.05
204	Bob Ojeda	.05
205	Alex Trevino	.05
206	Dave Henderson	.05
207	Henry Cotto	.05
208	Rafael Belliard	.05
209	Stan Javier	.05
210	Jerry Reed	.05
211	Doug Dascenzo	.05
212	Andres Thomas	.05
213	Greg Maddux	.75
214	Mike Schooler	.05
215	Lonnie Smith	.05
216	Jose Rijo	.05
217	Greg Gagne	.05
218	Jim Gantner	.05
219	Allan Anderson	.05
220	Rick Mahler	.05
221	Jim Deshaies	.05
222	Keith Hernandez	.05
223	Vince Coleman	.05
224	David Cone	.05
225	Ozzie Smith	.75
226	Matt Nokes	.05
227	Barry Bonds	1.00
228	Felix Jose	.05
229	Dennis Powell	.05
230	Mike Gallego	.05
231	Shawon Dunston	.05
232	Ron Gant	.05
233	Omar Vizquel	.05
234	Derek Lilliquist	.05
235	Erik Hanson	.05
236	Kirby Puckett	.75
237	Bill Spiers	.05
238	Dan Gladden	.05
239	Bryan Clutterbuck	.05
240	John Moses	.05
241	Ron Darling	.05
242	Joe Magrane	.05
243	Dave Magadan	.05
244	Pedro Guerrero	.05
245	Glenn Davis	.05
246	Terry Steinbach	.05
247	Fred Lynn	.05
248	Gary Redus	.05
249	Kenny Williams	.05
250	Sid Bream	.05
251	Bob Welch	.05
252	Bill Buckner	.05
253	Carney Lansford	.05
254	Paul Molitor	.50
255	Jose DeJesus	.05
256	Orel Hershiser	.05
257	Tom Brunansky	.05
258	Mike Davis	.05
259	Jeff Ballard	.05
260	Scott Terry	.05
261	Sid Fernandez	.05
262	Mike Marshall	.05
263	Howard Johnson	.05
264	Kirk Gibson	.05
265	Kevin McReynolds	.05
266	Cal Ripken, Jr.	2.00
267	Ozzie Guillen	.05
268	Jim Traber	.05
269	Bobby Thigpen	.05
270	Joe Orsulak	.05
271	Bob Boone	.10
272	Dave Stewart	.05
273	Tim Wallach	.05
274	Luis Aquino	.05
275	Mike Moore	.05
276	Tony Pena	.05
277	Eddie Murray	.45
278	Milt Thompson	.05
279	Alejandro Pena	.05
280	Ken Dayley	.05
281	Carmen Castillo	.05
282	Tom Henke	.05
283	Mickey Hatcher	.05
284	Roy Smith	.05
285	Manny Lee	.05
286	Dan Pasqua	.05
287	Larry Sheets	.05
288	Garry Templeton	.05
289	Eddie Williams	.05
290	Brady Anderson	.05
291	Spike Owen	.05
292	Storm Davis	.05
293	Chris Bosio	.05
294	Jim Eisenreich	.05
295	Don August	.05
296	Jeff Hamilton	.05
297	Mickey Tettleton	.05
298	Mike Scioscia	.05
299	Kevin Hickey	.05
300	Checklist 201-300	.05
301	Shawn Abner	.05
302	Kevin Bass	.05
303	Bip Roberts	.05
304	Joe Girardi	.05
305	Danny Darwin	.05
306	Mike Heath	.05
307	Mike Macfarlane	.05
308	Ed Whitson	.05
309	Tracy Jones	.05
310	Scott Fletcher	.05
311	Darnell Coles	.05
312	Mike Brumley	.05
313	Bill Swift	.05
314	Charlie Hough	.05
315	Jim Presley	.05
316	Luis Polonia	.05
317	Mike Morgan	.05
318	Lee Guetterman	.05
319	Jose Oquendo	.05
320	Wayne Tollenson	.05
321	Jody Reed	.05
322	Damon Berryhill	.05
323	Roger Clemens	.75
324	Ryne Sandberg	.60
325	Benito Santiago	.05
326	Bret Saberhagen	.05
327	Lou Whitaker	.05
328	Dave Gallagher	.05
329	Mike Pagliarulo	.05
330	Doyle Alexander	.05
331	Jeffrey Leonard	.05
332	Torey Lovullo	.05
333	Pete Incaviglia	.05
334	Rickey Henderson	.60
335	Rafael Palmeiro	.25
336	Ken Hill	.05
337	Dave Winfield	.60
338	Alfredo Griffin	.05
339	Andy Hawkins	.05
340	Ted Power	.05
341	Steve Wilson	.05
342	Jack Clark	.05
343	Ellis Burks	.05
344	Tony Gwynn	.75
345	Jerome Walton	.05
346	Roberto Alomar	.60
347	*Carlos Martinez*	.05
348	Chet Lemon	.05
349	Willie Wilson	.05
350	Greg Walker	.05
351	Tom Bolton	.05
352	German Gonzalez	.05
353	Harold Baines	.05
354	Mike Greenwell	.05
355	Ruben Sierra	.05
356	Andres Galarraga	.05
357	Andre Dawson	.20
358	*Jeff Brantley*	.05
359	Mike Bielecki	.05
360	Ken Oberkfell	.05
361	Kurt Stillwell	.05
362	Brian Holman	.05
363	Kevin Seitzer	.05
364	Alvin Davis	.05
365	Tom Gordon	.05
366	Bobby Bonilla	.05
367	Carlton Fisk	.60
368	*Steve Carter*	.05
369	Joel Skinner	.05
370	John Cangelosi	.05
371	Cecil Espy	.05
372	*Gary Wayne*	.05
373	Jim Rice	.10
374	*Mike Dyer*	.05
375	Joe Carter	.05
376	Dwight Smith	.05
377	*John Wetteland*	.15
378	Ernie Riles	.05
379	Otis Nixon	.05
380	Vance Law	.05
381	Dave Bergman	.05
382	Frank White	.05
383	Scott Bradley	.05
384	Israel Sanchez	.05
385	Gary Pettis	.05
386	Donn Pall	.05
387	John Smiley	.05
388	Tom Candiotti	.05
389	Junior Ortiz	.05
390	Steve Lyons	.05
391	Brian Harper	.05
392	Fred Manrique	.05
393	Lee Smith	.05
394	Jeff Kunkel	.05
395	Claudell Washington	.05
396	John Tudor	.05
397	Terry Kennedy	.05
398	Lloyd McClendon	.05
399	Craig Lefferts	.05
400	Checklist 301-400	.05
401	Keith Moreland	.05
402	Rich Gedman	.05
403	Jeff Robinson	.05
404	Randy Ready	.05
405	Rick Cerone	.05
406	Jeff Blauser	.05
407	Larry Andersen	.05
408	Joe Boever	.05

409 Felix Fermin .05
410 Glenn Wilson .05
411 Rex Hudler .05
412 Mark Grant .05
413 Dennis Martinez .05
414 Darrin Jackson .05
415 Mike Aldrete .05
416 Roger McDowell .05
417 Jeff Reardon .05
418 Darren Daulton .05
419 Tim Laudner .05
420 Don Carman .05
421 Lloyd Moseby .05
422 Doug Drabek .05
423 Lenny Harris .05
424 Jose Lind .05
425 *Dave Johnson* .05
426 Jerry Browne .05
427 *Eric Yelding* .05
428 Brad Komminsk .05
429 Jody Davis .05
430 Mariano Duncan .05
431 Mark Davis .05
432 Nelson Santovenia .05
433 Bruce Hurst .05
434 *Jeff Huson* .05
435 Chris James .05
436 *Mark Guthrie* .05
437 Charlie Hayes .05
438 Shane Rawley .05
439 Dickie Thon .05
440 Juan Berenguer .05
441 Kevin Romine .05
442 Bill Landrum .05
443 Todd Frohwirth .05
444 Craig Worthington .05
445 Fernando Valenzuela .05
446 Albert Belle .30
447 *Ed Whited* .05
448 Dave Smith .05
449 Dave Clark .05
450 Juan Agosto .05
451 Dave Valle .05
452 Kent Hrbek .05
453 Von Hayes .05
454 Gary Gaetti .05
455 Greg Briley .05
456 Glenn Braggs .05
457 Kirt Manwaring .05
458 Mel Hall .05
459 Brook Jacoby .05
460 Pat Sheridan .05
461 Rob Murphy .05
462 Jimmy Key .05
463 Nick Esasky .05
464 Rob Ducey .05
465 Carlos Quintana .05
466 *Larry Walker* 1.00
467 Todd Worrell .05
468 Kevin Gross .05
469 Terry Pendleton .05
470 Dave Martinez .05
471 Gene Larkin .05
472 Len Dykstra .05
473 Barry Lyons .05
474 Terry Mulholland .05
475 *Chip Hale* .05
476 Jesse Barfield .05
477 Dan Plesac .05
478a Scott Garrelts (Photo actually Bill Bathe) 1.00
478b Scott Garrelts (Correct photo) .05
479 Dave Righetti .05
480 Gus Polidor .05
481 Mookie Wilson .05
482 Luis Rivera .05
483 Mike Flanagan .05
484 Dennis "Oil Can" Boyd .05
485 John Cerutti .05
486 John Costello .05
487 Pascual Perez .05
488 Tommy Herr .05
489 Tom Foley .05
490 Curt Ford .05
491 Steve Lake .05
492 Tim Teufel .05
493 Randy Bush .05
494 Mike Jackson .05
495 Steve Jeltz .05
496 Paul Gibson .05
497 Steve Balboni .05
498 Bud Black .05
499 Dale Sveum .05
500 Checklist 401-500 .05
501 Timmy Jones .05
502 Mark Portugal .05
503 Ivan Calderon .05
504 Rick Rhoden .05
505 Willie McGee .05
506 Kirk McCaskill .05
507 Dave LaPoint .05
508 Jay Howell .05
509 Johnny Ray .05
510 Dave Anderson .05
511 Chuck Crim .05
512 Joe Hesketh .05
513 Dennis Eckersley .05
514 Greg Brock .05
515 Tim Burke .05
516 Frank Tanana .05
517 Jay Bell .05
518 Guillermo Hernandez .05
519 Randy Kramer .05
520 Charles Hudson .05
521 Jim Corsi .05
522 Steve Rosenberg .05
523 Cris Carpenter .05
524 *Matt Winters* .05
525 Melido Perez .05
526 Chris Gwynn .05
527 Bert Blyleven .05
528 Chuck Cary .05
529 Daryl Boston .05
530 Dale Mohorcic .05
531 Geronimo Berroa .05
532 Edgar Martinez .05
533 Dale Murphy .20
534 Jay Buhner .05
535 John Smoltz .10
536 Andy Van Slyke .05
537 Mike Henneman .05
538 Miguel Garcia .05
539 Frank Williams .05
540 R.J. Reynolds .05
541 Shawn Hillegas .05
542 Walt Weiss .05
543 *Greg Hibbard* .05
544 Nolan Ryan 2.00
545 Todd Zeile .05
546 Hensley Meulens .05
547 Tim Belcher .05
548 Mike Witt .05
549 Greg Cadaret .05
550 Franklin Stubbs .05
551 *Tony Castillo* .05
552 Jeff Robinson .05
553 *Steve Olin* .05
554 Alan Trammell .05
555 Wade Boggs .60
556 Will Clark .30
557 Jeff King .05
558 Mike Fitzgerald .05
559 Ken Howell .05
560 Bob Kipper .05
561 Scott Bankhead .05
562a *Jeff Innis* (Photo actually David West) 1.00
562b *Jeff Innis* (Correct photo) .05
563 Randy Johnson .65
564 *Wally Whitehurst* .05
565 *Gene Harris* .05
566 Norm Charlton .05
567 Robin Yount .60
568 *Joe Oliver* .05
569 Mark Parent .05
570 John Farrell .05
571 Tom Glavine .10
572 Rod Nichols .05
573 Jack Morris .05
574 Greg Swindell .05
575 Steve Searcy .05
576 Ricky Jordan .05
577 Matt Williams .30
578 Mike LaValliere .05
579 Bryn Smith .05
580 Bruce Ruffin .05
581 Randy Myers .05
582 *Rick Wrona* .05
583 Juan Samuel .05
584 Les Lancaster .05
585 Jeff Musselman .05
586 Rob Dibble .05
587 Eric Show .05
588 Jesse Orosco .05
589 Herm Winningham .05
590 Andy Allanson .05
591 Dion James .05
592 Carmelo Martinez .05
593 Luis Quinones .05
594 Dennis Rasmussen .05
595 Rich Yett .05
596 Bob Walk .05
597a Andy McGaffigan (player #48, photo actually Rich Thompson) .75
597b Andy McGaffigan (player #27, correct photo) .05
598 Billy Hatcher .05
599 Bob Knepper .05
600 Checklist 501-600 .05
601 Joey Cora .05
602 *Steve Finley* .20
603 Kal Daniels .05
604 Gregg Olson .05
605 Dave Steib .05
606 *Kenny Rogers* .05
607 Zane Smith .05
608 *Bob Geren* .05
609 Chad Kreuter .05
610 Mike Smithson .05
611 *Jeff Wetherby* .05
612 *Gary Mielke* .05
613 Pete Smith .05
614 *Jack Daugherty* .05
615 Lance McCullers .05
616 Don Robinson .05
617 Jose Guzman .05
618 Steve Bedrosian .05
619 Jamie Moyer .05
620 Atlee Hammaker .05
621 *Rick Luecken* .05
622 Greg W. Harris .05
623 Pete Harnisch .05
624 Jerald Clark .05
625 Jack McDowell .05
626 Frank Viola .05
627 Ted Higuera .05
628 *Marty Pevey* .05
629 Bill Wegman .05
630 Eric Plunk .05
631 Drew Hall .05
632 Doug Jones .05
633 Geno Petralli .05
634 Jose Alvarez .05
635 Bob Milacki .05
636 Bobby Witt .05
637 Trevor Wilson .05
638 Jeff Russell .05
639 Mike Krukow .05
640 Rick Leach .05
641 Dave Schmidt .05
642 Terry Leach .05
643 Calvin Schiraldi .05
644 Bob Melvin .05
645 Jim Abbott .05
646 *Jaime Navarro* .05
647 Mark Langston .05
648 Juan Nieves .05
649 Damaso Garcia .05
650 Charlie O'Brien .05
651 Eric King .05
652 Mike Boddicker .05
653 Duane Ward .05
654 Bob Stanley .05
655 Sandy Alomar, Jr. .05
656 Danny Tartabull .05
657 Randy McCament .05
658 Charlie Leibrandt .05
659 Dan Quisenberry .05
660 Paul Assenmacher .05
661 Walt Terrell .05
662 Tim Leary .05
663 Randy Milligan .05
664 Bo Diaz .05
665 Mark Lemke .05
666 Jose Gonzalez .05
667 Chuck Finley .05
668 John Kruk .05
669 Dick Schofield .05
670 Tim Crews .05
671 John Dopson .05
672 *John Orton* .05
673 Eric Hetzel .05
674 Lance Parrish .05
675 Ramon Martinez .05
676 Mark Gubicza .05
677 Greg Litton .05
678 Greg Mathews .05
679 Dave Dravecky .05
680 Steve Farr .05
681 Mike Devereaux .05
682 Ken Griffey, Sr. .05
683a *Jamie Weston* (first name incorrect) 1.00
683b *Mickey Weston* (corrected) .05
684 Jack Armstrong .05
685 Steve Buechele .05
686 Bryan Harvey .05
687 Lance Blankenship .05
688 Dante Bichette .05
689 Todd Burns .05
690 Dan Petry .05
691 *Kent Anderson* .05
692 Todd Stottlemyre .05
693 Wally Joyner .05
694 Mike Rochford .05
695 Floyd Bannister .05
696 Rick Reuschel .05
697 Jose DeLeon .05
698 Jeff Montgomery .05
699 Kelly Downs .05
700a Checklist 601-700 (#683 Jamie Weston) .05
700b Checklist 601-700 (# 683 Mickey Weston) .05
701 Jim Gott .05
702 "Rookie Threats" (Delino DeShields, Larry Walker, Marquis Grissom) .40
703 Alejandro Pena .05
704 Willie Randolph .05
705 Tim Leary .05
706 Chuck McElroy .05
707 Gerald Perry .05
708 Tom Brunansky .05
709 John Franco .05
710 Mark Davis .05
711 *Dave Justice* 1.50
712 Storm Davis .05
713 Scott Ruskin .05
714 Glenn Braggs .05
715 Kevin Bearse .05
716 Jose Nunez .05
717 Tim Layana .05
718 Greg Myers .05
719 Pete O'Brien .05
720 John Candelaria .05
721 Craig Grebeck .05
722 Shawn Boskie .05
723 Jim Leyritz .10
724 Bill Sampen .05
725 Scott Radinsky .05
726 *Todd Hundley* .40
727 Scott Hemond .05
728 Lenny Webster .05
729 Jeff Reardon .05
730 Mitch Webster .05
731 Brian Bohanon .05
732 Rick Parker .05
733 Terry Shumpert .05
734a Nolan Ryan (300-win stripe on front) 1.50
734b Nolan Ryan (no stripe) 4.00
735 John Burkett .05
736 *Derrick May* .05
737 *Carlos Baerga* .05
738 Greg Smith .05
739 Joe Kraemer .05
740 Scott Sanderson .05
741 Hector Villanueva .05
742 Mike Fetters .05
743 Mark Gardner .05
744 Matt Nokes .05
745 Dave Winfield .60
746 *Delino DeShields* .15
747 Dann Howitt .05
748 Tony Pena .05
749 Oil Can Boyd .05
750 Mike Benjamin .05
751 Alex Cole .05
752 Eric Gunderson .05
753 Howard Farmer .05
754 Joe Carter .05
755 *Ray Lankford* .50
756 Sandy Alomar,Jr. .05
757 Alex Sanchez .05
758 Nick Esasky .05
759 Stan Belinda .05
760 Jim Presley .05
761 Gary DiSarcina .05
762 Wayne Edwards .05
763 Pat Combs .05
764 Mickey Pina .05
765 *Wilson Alvarez* .25
766 Dave Parker .05
767 Mike Blowers .05
768 Tony Phillips .05

769	Pascual Perez	.05
770	Gary Pettis	.05
771	Fred Lynn	.05
772	*Mel Rojas*	.10
773	David Segui	.25
774	Gary Carter	.25
775	Rafael Valdez	.05
776	Glenallen Hill	.05
777	Keith Hernandez	.05
778	Billy Hatcher	.05
779	Marty Clary	.05
780	Candy Maldonado	.05
781	Mike Marshall	.05
782	Billy Jo Robidoux	.05
783	Mark Langston	.05
784	*Paul Sorrento*	.05
785	*Dave Hollins*	.10
786	Cecil Fielder	.05
787	Matt Young	.05
788	Jeff Huson	.05
789	Lloyd Moseby	.05
790	Ron Kittle	.05
791	Hubie Brooks	.05
792	Craig Lefferts	.05
793	Kevin Bass	.05
794	Bryn Smith	.05
795	Juan Samuel	.05
796	Sam Horn	.05
797	Randy Myers	.05
798	Chris James	.05
799	Bill Gullickson	.05
800	Checklist 701-800	.05

1990 Upper Deck Reggie Jackson Heroes

This Baseball Heroes set is devoted to Reggie Jackson. The cards, numbered 1-9, are the first in a continuing series of cards issued in subsequent years. An unnumbered cover card that says "Baseball Heroes" was also issued. The Jackson cards were randomly inserted in high number foil packs only. Jackson also autographed 2,500 numbered cards, which were randomly included in high number packs.

		MT
	Complete Set (10):	4.00
	Common Player:	.50
	Autographed Card:	75.00
1	1969 Emerging Superstar (Reggie Jackson)	.50
2	1973 An MVP Year (Reggie Jackson)	.50
3	1977 "Mr. October" (Reggie Jackson)	.50
4	1978 Jackson vs. Welch (Reggie Jackson)	.50
5	1982 Under the Halo (Reggie Jackson)	.50
6	1984 500! (Reggie Jackson)	.50
7	1986 Moving Up the List (Reggie Jackson)	.50
8	1987 A Great Career Ends (Reggie Jackson)	.50
9	Heroes Checklist 1-9 (Reggie Jackson)	.50
----	Header card	.50

1991 Upper Deck

More than 110 rookies are included among the first 700 cards in the 1991 Upper Deck set. A 100-card high-number series was released in late summer. Cards feature top quality white stock and color photos on front and back. A nine-card "Baseball Heroes" bonus set honoring Nolan Ryan, is among the many insert specials in the '91 UD set. Others include a card of Chicago Bulls superstar Michael Jordan. Along with the Ryan bonus cards, 2,500 cards personally autographed and numbered by Ryan were randomly inserted. Upper Deck cards are packaged in tamper-proof foil packs. Each pack contains 15 cards and cards and a 3-1/2" x 2-1/2" 3-D team logo hologram sticker.

		MT
	Unopened Factory Set (800):	15.00
	Complete Set (800):	10.00
	Complete Low Series (1-700):	12.00
	Complete High Series (701-800):	3.00
	Common Player:	.05
	Low or High Pack (15):	.75
	Low or High Wax Box (36):	18.00
1	Star Rookie Checklist	.05
2	*Phil Plantier*	.05
3	*D.J. Dozier*	.05
4	Dave Hansen	.05
5	Mo Vaughn	.40
6	*Leo Gomez*	.05
7	*Scott Aldred*	.05
8	*Scott Chiamparino*	.05
9	*Lance Dickson*	.05
10	*Sean Berry*	.15
11	Bernie Williams	.40
12	*Brian Barnes*	.05
13	*Narciso Elvira*	.05
14	*Mike Gardiner*	.05
15	*Greg Colbrunn*	.15
16	*Bernard Gilkey*	.15
17	Mark Lewis	.05
18	*Mickey Morandini*	.05
19	Charles Nagy	.05
20	*Geronimo Pena*	.05
21	*Henry Rodriguez*	.30
22	Scott Cooper	.05
23	*Andujar Cedeno*	.05
24	*Eric Karros*	.75
25	*Steve Decker*	.05
26	*Kevin Belcher*	.05
27	*Jeff Conine*	.25
28	Oakland Athletics checklist (Dave Stewart)	.05
29	Chicago White Sox checklist (Carlton Fisk)	.25
30	Texas Rangers checklist (Rafael Palmeiro)	.10
31	California Angels checklist (Chuck Finley)	.05
32	Seattle Mariners checklist (Harold Reynolds)	.05
33	Kansas City Royals checklist (Bret Saberhagen)	.05
34	Minnesota Twins checklist (Gary Gaetti)	.05
35	Scott Leius	.05
36	Neal Heaton	.05
37	*Terry Lee*	.05
38	Gary Redus	.05
39	Barry Jones	.05
40	Chuck Knoblauch	.05
41	Larry Andersen	.05
42	Darryl Hamilton	.05
43	Boston Red Sox checklist (Mike Greenwell)	.05
44	Toronto Blue Jays checklist (Kelly Gruber)	.05
45	Detroit Tigers checklist (Jack Morris)	.05
46	Cleveland Indians checklist (Sandy Alomar Jr.)	.05
47	Baltimore Orioles checklist (Gregg Olson)	.05
48	Milwaukee Brewers checklist (Dave Parker)	.05
49	New York Yankees checklist (Roberto Kelly)	.05
50	Top Prospect '91 checklist	.05
51	*Kyle Abbott* (Top Prospect)	.10
52	Jeff Juden (Top Prospect)	.05
53	*Todd Van Poppel* (Top Prospect)	.10
54	*Steve Karsay* (Top Prospect)	.15
55	*Chipper Jones* (Top Prospect)	4.00
56	*Chris Johnson* (Top Prospect)	.05
57	*John Ericks* (Top Prospect)	.05
58	*Gary Scott* (Top Prospect)	.05
59	Kiki Jones (Top Prospect)	.05
60	*Wil Cordero* (Top Prospect)	.15
61	*Royce Clayton* (Top Prospect)	.10
62	*Tim Costo* (Top Prospect)	.05
63	Roger Salkeld (Top Prospect)	.10
64	*Brook Fordyce* (Top Prospect)	.05
65	*Mike Mussina* (Top Prospect)	2.00
66	*Dave Staton* (Top Prospect)	.05
67	*Mike Lieberthal* (Top Prospect)	.75
68	*Kurt Miller* (Top Prospect)	.05
69	*Dan Peltier* (Top Prospect)	.05
70	Greg Blosser (Top Prospect)	.05
71	*Reggie Sanders* (Top Prospect)	.15
72	Brent Mayne (Top Prospect)	.10
73	*Rico Brogna* (Top Prospect)	.05
74	*Willie Banks* (Top Prospect)	.05
75	*Len Brutcher* (Top Prospect)	.05
76	*Pat Kelly* (Top Prospect)	.05
77	Cincinnati Reds checklist (Chris Sabo)	.05
78	Los Angeles Dodgers checklist (Ramon Martinez)	.05
79	San Francisco Giants checklist (Matt Williams)	.05
80	San Diego Padres checklist (Roberto Alomar)	.10
81	Houston Astros checklist (Glenn Davis)	.05
82	Atlanta Braves checklist (Ron Gant)	.05
83	"Fielder's Feat" (Cecil Fielder)	.05
84	*Orlando Merced*	.10
85	Domingo Ramos	.05
86	Tom Bolton	.05
87	*Andres Santana*	.05
88	John Dopson	.05
89	Kenny Williams	.05
90	Marty Barrett	.05
91	Tom Pagnozzi	.05
92	Carmelo Martinez	.05
93	"Save Master" (Bobby Thigpen)	.05
94	Pittsburgh Pirates checklist (Barry Bonds)	.40
95	New York Mets checklist (Gregg Jefferies)	.05
96	Montreal Expos checklist (Tim Wallach)	.05
97	Philadelphia Phillies checklist (Lenny Dykstra)	.05
98	St. Louis Cardinals checklist (Pedro Guerrero)	.05
99	Chicago Cubs checklist (Mark Grace)	.10
100	Checklist 1-100	.05
101	Kevin Elster	.05
102	Tom Brookens	.05
103	Mackey Sasser	.05
104	Felix Fermin	.05
105	Kevin McReynolds	.05
106	Dave Steib	.05
107	Jeffrey Leonard	.05
108	Dave Henderson	.05
109	Sid Bream	.05
110	Henry Cotto	.05
111	Shawon Dunston	.05
112	Mariano Duncan	.05
113	Joe Girardi	.05
114	Billy Hatcher	.05
115	Greg Maddux	.60
116	Jerry Browne	.05
117	Juan Samuel	.05
118	Steve Olin	.05
119	Alfredo Griffin	.05
120	Mitch Webster	.05
121	Joel Skinner	.05
122	Frank Viola	.05
123	Cory Snyder	.05
124	Howard Johnson	.05
125	Carlos Baerga	.05
126	Tony Fernandez	.05
127	Dave Stewart	.05
128	Jay Buhner	.05
129	Mike LaValliere	.05
130	Scott Bradley	.05
131	Tony Phillips	.05
132	Ryne Sandberg	.50
133	Paul O'Neill	.05
134	Mark Grace	.20
135	Chris Sabo	.05
136	Ramon Martinez	.05
137	Brook Jacoby	.05
138	Candy Maldonado	.05
139	Mike Scioscia	.05
140	Chris James	.05
141	Craig Worthington	.05
142	Manny Lee	.05
143	Tim Raines	.05
144	Sandy Alomar, Jr.	.05
145	John Olerud	.05

146 *Ozzie Canseco* .05
147 Pat Borders .05
148 Harold Reynolds .05
149 Tom Henke .05
150 R.J. Reynolds .05
151 Mike Gallego .05
152 Bobby Bonilla .05
153 Terry Steinbach .05
154 Barry Bonds .65
155 Jose Canseco .40
156 Gregg Jefferies .05
157 Matt Williams .15
158 Craig Biggio .05
159 Daryl Boston .05
160 Ricky Jordan .05
161 Stan Belinda .05
162 Ozzie Smith .60
163 Tom Brunansky .05
164 Todd Zeile .05
165 Mike Greenwell .05
166 Kal Daniels .05
167 Kent Hrbek .05
168 Franklin Stubbs .05
169 Dick Schofield .05
170 Junior Ortiz .05
171 *Hector Villanueva* .05
172 Dennis Eckersley .05
173 Mitch Williams .05
174 Mark McGwire 1.00
175 Fernando Valenzuela .05
176 Gary Carter .25
177 Dave Magadan .05
178 Robby Thompson .05
179 Bob Ojeda .05
180 Ken Caminiti .05
181 Don Slaught .05
182 Luis Rivera .05
183 Jay Bell .05
184 Jody Reed .05
185 Wally Backman .05
186 Dave Martinez .05
187 Luis Polonia .05
188 Shane Mack .05
189 Spike Owen .05
190 Scott Bailes .05
191 John Russell .05
192 Walt Weiss .05
193 Jose Oquendo .05
194 Carney Lansford .05
195 Jeff Huson .05
196 Keith Miller .05
197 Eric Yelding .05
198 Ron Darling .05
199 John Kruk .05
200 Checklist 101-200 .05
201 John Shelby .05
202 Bob Geren .05
203 Lance McCullers .05
204 Alvaro Espinoza .05
205 Mark Salas .05
206 Mike Pagliarulo .05
207 Jose Uribe .05
208 Jim Deshaies .05
209 Ron Karkovice .05
210 Rafael Ramirez .05
211 Donnie Hill .05
212 Brian Harper .05
213 Jack Howell .05
214 Wes Gardner .05
215 Tim Burke .05
216 Doug Jones .05
217 Hubie Brooks .05
218 Tom Candiotti .05
219 Gerald Perry .05
220 Jose DeLeon .05
221 Wally Whitehurst .05
222 *Alan Mills* .10
223 Alan Trammell .05
224 Dwight Gooden .05
225 Travis Fryman .05
226 Joe Carter .05
227 Julio Franco .05
228 Craig Lefferts .05
229 Gary Pettis .05
230 Dennis Rasmussen .05
231a Brian Downing (no position on front) .50
231b Brian Downing (DH on front) .05
232 Carlos Quintana .05
233 Gary Gaetti .05
234 Mark Langston .05
235 Tim Wallach .05
236 Greg Swindell .05
237 Eddie Murray .50
238 Jeff Manto .05
239 Lenny Harris .05
240 Jesse Orosco .05
241 Scott Lusader .05
242 Sid Fernandez .05
243 Jim Leyritz .05
244 Cecil Fielder .05
245 Darryl Strawberry .05
246 Frank Thomas .75
247 Kevin Mitchell .05
248 Lance Johnson .05
249 Rick Rueschel .05
250 Mark Portugal .05
251 Derek Lilliquist .05
252 Brian Holman .05
253 Rafael Valdez .05
254 B.J. Surhoff .05
255 Tony Gwynn .60
256 Andy Van Slyke .05
257 Todd Stottlemyre .05
258 Jose Lind .05
259 Greg Myers .05
260 Jeff Ballard .05
261 Bobby Thigpen .05
262 *Jimmy Kremers* .05
263 Robin Ventura .05
264 John Smoltz .10
265 Sammy Sosa .65
266 Gary Sheffield .20
267 Len Dykstra .05
268 Bill Spiers .05
269 Charlie Hayes .05
270 Brett Butler .05
271 Bip Roberts .05
272 Rob Deer .05
273 Fred Lynn .05
274 Dave Parker .05
275 Andy Benes .05
276 Glenallen Hill .05
277 *Steve Howard* .05
278 Doug Drabek .05
279 Joe Oliver .05
280 Todd Benzinger .05
281 Eric King .05
282 Jim Presley .05
283 Ken Patterson .05
284 Jack Daugherty .05
285 Ivan Calderon .05
286 *Edgar Diaz* .05
287 Kevin Bass .05
288 Don Carman .05
289 Greg Brock .05
290 John Franco .05
291 Joey Cora .05
292 Bill Wegman .05
293 Eric Show .05
294 Scott Bankhead .05
295 Garry Templeton .05
296 Mickey Tettleton .05
297 Luis Sojo .05
298 Jose Rijo .05
299 Dave Johnson .05
300 Checklist 201-300 .05
301 Mark Grant .05
302 Pete Harnisch .05
303 Greg Olson .05
304 *Anthony Telford* .05
305 Lonnie Smith .05
306 Chris Hoiles .05
307 Bryn Smith .05
308 Mike Devereaux .05
309a Milt Thompson ("86" in stats obscured by "bull's eye") .50
309b Milt Thompson ("86" visible) .05
310 Bob Melvin .05
311 Luis Salazar .05
312 Ed Whitson .05
313 Charlie Hough .05
314 Dave Clark .05
315 *Eric Gunderson* .05
316 Dan Petry .05
317 Dante Bichette .05
318 Mike Heath .05
319 Damon Berryhill .05
320 Walt Terrell .05
321 Scott Fletcher .05
322 Dan Plesac .05
323 Jack McDowell .05
324 Paul Molitor .60
325 Ozzie Guillen .05
326 Gregg Olson .05
327 Pedro Guerrero .05
328 Bob Milacki .05
329 John Tudor .05
330 Steve Finley .05
331 Jack Clark .05
332 Jerome Walton .05
333 Andy Hawkins .05
334 Derrick May .05
335 Roberto Alomar .50
336 Jack Morris .05
337 Dave Winfield .50
338 Steve Searcy .05
339 Chili Davis .05
340 Larry Sheets .05
341 Ted Higuera .05
342 *David Segui* .15
343 Greg Cadaret .05
344 Robin Yount .50
345 Nolan Ryan 1.00
346 Ray Lankford .05
347 Cal Ripken, Jr. 1.00
348 Lee Smith .05
349 Brady Anderson .05
350 Frank DiPino .05
351 Hal Morris .05
352 Deion Sanders .10
353 Barry Larkin .10
354 Don Mattingly .65
355 Eric Davis .05
356 Jose Offerman .05
357 Mel Rojas .05
358 Rudy Seanez .05
359 Oil Can Boyd .05
360 Nelson Liriano .05
361 Ron Gant .05
362 *Howard Farmer* .05
363 Dave Justice .20
364 Delino DeShields .05
365 Steve Avery .05
366 David Cone .05
367 Lou Whitaker .05
368 Von Hayes .05
369 Frank Tanana .05
370 Tim Teufel .05
371 Randy Myers .05
372 Roberto Kelly .05
373 Jack Armstrong .05
374 Kelly Gruber .05
375 Kevin Maas .05
376 Randy Johnson .50
377 David West .05
378 *Brent Knackert* .05
379 Rick Honeycutt .05
380 Kevin Gross .05
381 Tom Foley .05
382 Jeff Blauser .05
383 *Scott Ruskin* .05
384 Andres Thomas .05
385 Dennis Martinez .05
386 Mike Henneman .05
387 Felix Jose .05
388 Alejandro Pena .05
389 Chet Lemon .05
390 *Craig Wilson* .05
391 Chuck Crim .05
392 Mel Hall .05
393 Mark Knudson .05
394 Norm Charlton .05
395 Mike Felder .05
396 *Tim Layana* .05
397 Steve Frey .05
398 Bill Doran .05
399 Dion James .05
400 Checklist 301-400 .05
401 Ron Hassey .05
402 Don Robinson .05
403 Gene Nelson .05
404 Terry Kennedy .05
405 Todd Burns .05
406 Roger McDowell .05
407 Bob Kipper .05
408 Darren Daulton .05
409 Chuck Cary .05
410 Bruce Ruffin .05
411 Juan Berenguer .05
412 Gary Ward .05
413 Al Newman .05
414 Danny Jackson .05
415 Greg Gagne .05
416 Tom Herr .05
417 Jeff Parrett .05
418 Jeff Reardon .05
419 Mark Lemke .05
420 Charlie O'Brien .05
421 Willie Randolph .05
422 Steve Bedrosian .05
423 Mike Moore .05
424 Jeff Brantley .05
425 Bob Welch .05
426 Terry Mulholland .05
427 *Willie Blair* .05
428 Darrin Fletcher .10
429 Mike Witt .05
430 Joe Boever .05
431 Tom Gordon .05
432 *Pedro Munoz* .05
433 Kevin Seitzer .05
434 Kevin Tapani .05
435 Bret Saberhagen .05
436 Ellis Burks .05
437 Chuck Finley .05
438 Mike Boddicker .05
439 Francisco Cabrera .05
440 Todd Hundley .05
441 Kelly Downs .05
442 *Dann Howitt* .05
443 Scott Garrelts .05
444 Rickey Henderson .50
445 Will Clark .15
446 Ben McDonald .05
447 Dale Murphy .15
448 Dave Righetti .05
449 Dickie Thon .05
450 Ted Power .05
451 Scott Coolbaugh .05
452 Dwight Smith .05
453 Pete Incaviglia .05
454 Andre Dawson .20
455 Ruben Sierra .05
456 Andres Galarraga .05
457 Alvin Davis .05
458 Tony Castillo .05
459 Pete O'Brien .05
460 Charlie Leibrandt .05
461 Vince Coleman .05
462 Steve Sax .05
463 *Omar Oliveras* .05
464 *Oscar Azocar* .05
465 Joe Magrane .05
466 *Karl Rhodes* .10
467 Benito Santiago .05
468 *Joe Klink* .05
469 Sil Campusano .05
470 Mark Parent .05
471 *Shawn Boskie* .10
472 Kevin Brown .10
473 Rick Sutcliffe .05
474 Rafael Palmeiro .25
475 Mike Harkey .05
476 Jaime Navarro .05
477 Marquis Grissom .05
478 Marty Clary .05
479 Greg Briley .05
480 Tom Glavine .10
481 Lee Guetterman .05
482 Rex Hudler .05
483 Dave LaPoint .05
484 Terry Pendleton .05
485 Jesse Barfield .05
486 Jose DeJesus .05
487 *Paul Abbott* .05
488 Ken Howell .05
489 Greg W. Harris .05
490 Roy Smith .05
491 Paul Assenmacher .05
492 Geno Petralli .05
493 Steve Wilson .05
494 Kevin Reimer .05
495 Bill Long .05
496 Mike Jackson .05
497 Oddibe McDowell .05
498 Bill Swift .05
499 Jeff Treadway .05
500 Checklist 401-500 .05
501 Gene Larkin .05
502 Bob Boone .10
503 Allan Anderson .05
504 Luis Aquino .05
505 Mark Guthrie .05
506 Joe Orsulak .05
507 *Dana Kiecker* .05
508 Dave Gallagher .05
509 Greg A. Harris .05
510 Mark Williamson .05
511 Casey Candaele .05
512 Mookie Wilson .05
513 Dave Smith .05
514 *Chuck Carr* .05
515 Glenn Wilson .05
516 Mike Fitzgerald .05
517 Devon White .05
518 Dave Hollins .05
519 Mark Eichhorn .05
520 Otis Nixon .05
521 *Terry Shumpert* .05

522 *Scott Erickson* .15
523 Danny Tartabull .05
524 Orel Hershiser .05
525 George Brett .60
526 Greg Vaughn .05
527 Tim Naehring .05
528 Curt Schilling .15
529 Chris Bosio .05
530 Sam Horn .05
531 Mike Scott .05
532 George Bell .05
533 Eric Anthony .05
534 *Julio Valera* .05
535 Glenn Davis .05
536 Larry Walker .25
537 Pat Combs .05
538 *Chris Nabholz* .05
539 Kirk McCaskill .05
540 Randy Ready .05
541 Mark Gubicza .05
542 Rick Aguilera .05
543 *Brian McRae* .05
544 Kirby Puckett .60
545 Bo Jackson .10
546 Wade Boggs .50
547 Tim McIntosh .05
548 Randy Milligan .05
549 Dwight Evans .05
550 Billy Ripken .05
551 Erik Hanson .05
552 Lance Parrish .05
553 Tino Martinez .05
554 Jim Abbott .05
555 Ken Griffey, Jr. .75
556 Milt Cuyler .05
557 *Mark Leonard* .05
558 Jay Howell .05
559 Lloyd Moseby .05
560 Chris Gwynn .05
561 *Mark Whiten* .05
562 Harold Baines .05
563 Junior Felix .05
564 Darren Lewis .05
565 Fred McGriff .05
566 Kevin Appier .05
567 *Luis Gonzalez* 2.50
568 Frank White .05
569 Juan Agosto .05
570 Mike Macfarlane .05
571 Bert Blyleven .05
572 Ken Griffey, Sr. .05
573 Lee Stevens .05
574 Edgar Martinez .05
575 Wally Joyner .05
576 Tim Belcher .05
577 John Burkett .05
578 Mike Morgan .05
579 Paul Gibson .05
580 Jose Vizcaino .05
581 Duane Ward .05
582 Scott Sanderson .05
583 David Wells .10
584 Willie McGee .05
585 John Cerutti .05
586 Danny Darwin .05
587 Kurt Stillwell .05
588 Rich Gedman .05
589 Mark Davis .05
590 Bill Gullickson .05
591 Matt Young .05
592 Bryan Harvey .05
593 Omar Vizquel .05
594 *Scott Lewis* .05
595 Dave Valle .05
596 Tim Crews .05
597 Mike Bielecki .05
598 Mike Sharperson .05
599 Dave Bergman .05
600 Checklist 501-600 .05
601 Steve Lyons .05
602 Bruce Hurst .05
603 Donn Pall .05
604 *Jim Vatcher* .05
605 Dan Pasqua .05
606 Kenny Rogers .05
607 *Jeff Schulz* .05
608 Brad Arnsberg .05
609 Willie Wilson .05
610 Jamie Moyer .05
611 Ron Oester .05
612 Dennis Cook .05
613 Rick Mahler .05
614 Bill Landrum .05
615 Scott Scudder .05
616 *Tom Edens* .05
617 "1917 Revisited" (Chicago White Sox team photo) .05
618 Jim Gantner .05
619 Darrel Akerfelds .05
620 Ron Robinson .05
621 Scott Radinsky .05
622 Pete Smith .05
623 Melido Perez .05
624 Jerald Clark .05
625 Carlos Martinez .05
626 *Wes Chamberlain* .05
627 Bobby Witt .05
628 Ken Dayley .05
629 *John Barfield* .05
630 Bob Tewksbury .05
631 Glenn Braggs .05
632 *Jim Neidlinger* .05
633 Tom Browning .05
634 Kirk Gibson .05
635 Rob Dibble .05
636 "Stolen Base Leaders" (Lou Brock, Rickey Henderson) .15
637 Jeff Montgomery .05
638 Mike Schooler .05
639 Storm Davis .05
640 *Rich Rodriguez* .05
641 Phil Bradley .05
642 Kent Mercker .05
643 Carlton Fisk .50
644 Mike Bell .05
645 *Alex Fernandez* .05
646 Juan Gonzalez .50
647 Ken Hill .05
648 Jeff Russell .05
649 *Chuck Malone* .05
650 Steve Buechele .05
651 Mike Benjamin .05
652 Tony Pena .05
653 Trevor Wilson .05
654 Alex Cole .05
655 Roger Clemens .60
656 "The Bashing Years" (Mark McGwire) .50
657 *Joe Grahe* .05
658 Jim Eisenreich .05
659 Dan Gladden .05
660 Steve Farr .05
661 *Bill Sampen* .05
662 *Dave Rohde* .05
663 Mark Gardner .05
664 *Mike Simms* .05
665 Moises Alou .15
666 Mickey Hatcher .05
667 Jimmy Key .05
668 John Wetteland .05
669 John Smiley .05
670 Jim Acker .05
671 Pascual Perez .05
672 *Reggie Harris* .05
673 Matt Nokes .05
674 *Rafael Novoa* .05
675 Hensley Meulens .05
676 Jeff M. Robinson .05
677 "Ground Breaking" (New Comiskey Park) .15
678 Johnny Ray .05
679 Greg Hibbard .05
680 Paul Sorrento .05
681 Mike Marshall .05
682 Jim Clancy .05
683 Rob Murphy .05
684 Dave Schmidt .05
685 *Jeff Gray* .05
686 Mike Hartley .05
687 Jeff King .05
688 Stan Javier .05
689 Bob Walk .05
690 Jim Gott .05
691 Mike LaCoss .05
692 John Farrell .05
693 Tim Leary .05
694 *Mike Walker* .05
695 Eric Plunk .05
696 Mike Fetters .05
697 Wayne Edwards .05
698 Tim Drummond .05
699 Willie Fraser .05
700 Checklist 601-700 .05
701 Mike Heath .05
702 "Rookie Threats" (Luis Gonzalez, Karl Rhodes, Jeff Bagwell) .60
703 Jose Mesa .05
704 Dave Smith .05
705 Danny Darwin .05
706 Rafael Belliard .05
707 Rob Murphy .05
708 Terry Pendleton .05
709 Mike Pagliarulo .05
710 Sid Bream .05
711 Junior Felix .05
712 Dante Bichette .05
713 Kevin Gross .05
714 Luis Sojo .05
715 Bob Ojeda .05
716 Julio Machado .05
717 Steve Farr .05
718 Franklin Stubbs .05
719 Mike Boddicker .05
720 Willie Randolph .05
721 Willie McGee .05
722 Chili Davis .05
723 Danny Jackson .05
724 Cory Snyder .05
725 "MVP Lineup" (Andre Dawson, George Bell, Ryne Sandberg) .15
726 Rob Deer .05
727 Rich DeLucia .05
728 Mike Perez .05
729 Mickey Tettleton .05
730 Mike Blowers .05
731 Gary Gaetti .05
732 Brett Butler .05
733 Dave Parker .05
734 Eddie Zosky .05
735 Jack Clark .05
736 Jack Morris .05
737 Kirk Gibson .05
738 Steve Bedrosian .05
739 Candy Maldonado .05
740 Matt Young .05
741 Rich Garces .05
742 George Bell .05
743 Deion Sanders .10
744 Bo Jackson .10
745 Luis Mercedes .05
746 Reggie Jefferson .05
747 Pete Incaviglia .05
748 Chris Hammond .05
749 Mike Stanton .05
750 Scott Sanderson .05
751 Paul Faries .05
752 Al Osuna .05
753 Steve Chitren .05
754 Tony Fernandez .05
755 *Jeff Bagwell* 3.00
756 Kirk Dressendorfer .05
757 Glenn Davis .05
758 Gary Carter .25
759 Zane Smith .05
760 Vance Law .05
761 Denis Boucher .05
762 Turner Ward .05
763 Roberto Alomar .30
764 Albert Belle .30
765 Joe Carter .05
766 Pete Schourek .05
767 Heathcliff Slocumb .05
768 Vince Coleman .05
769 Mitch Williams .05
770 Brian Downing .05
771 Dana Allison .05
772 Pete Harnisch .05
773 Tim Raines .05
774 Darryl Kile .05
775 Fred McGriff .05
776 Dwight Evans .05
777 Joe Slusarski .05
778 Dave Righetti .05
779 Jeff Hamilton .05
780 Ernest Riles .05
781 Ken Dayley .05
782 Eric King .05
783 Devon White .05
784 Beau Allred .05
785 Mike Timlin .05
786 Ivan Calderon .05
787 Hubie Brooks .05
788 Juan Agosto .05
789 Barry Jones .05
790 Wally Backman .05
791 Jim Presley .05
792 Charlie Hough .05
793 Larry Andersen .05
794 Steve Finley .05
795 Shawn Abner .05
796 Jeff M. Robinson .05
797 Joe Bitker .05
798 Eric Show .05
799 Bud Black .05
800 Checklist 701-800 .05
SP1 Michael Jordan 6.00
SP2 "A Day to Remember" (Rickey Henderson, Nolan Ryan) .60
HH1 Hank Aaron (hologram) 1.50

1991 Upper Deck Final Edition

Upper Deck surprised the hobby with the late-season release of this 100-card boxed set. The cards are numbered with an "F" designation. A special "Minor League Diamond Skills" subset (cards #1-21) features several top prospects. An All-Star subset (cards #79-99) is also included in this set. The cards are styled like the regular 1991 Upper Deck issue Special team hologram cards are included with the set.

MT
Complete Set (100): 10.00
Common Player: .05
1 Ryan Klesko, Reggie Sanders (Minor League Diamond Skills Checklist) .25
2 *Pedro Martinez* 8.00
3 Lance Dickson .05
4 Royce Clayton .05
5 Scott Bryant .05
6 Dan Wilson .05
7 *Dmitri Young* .25
8 *Ryan Klesko* .40
9 Tom Goodwin .05
10 *Rondell White* .50
11 Reggie Sanders .05
12 Todd Van Poppel .05
13 Arthur Rhodes .05
14 Eddie Zosky .05
15 Gerald Williams .05
16 Robert Eenhoorn .05
17 *Jim Thome* 1.00
18 *Marc Newfield* .05
19 Kerwin Moore .05
20 Jeff McNeely .05
21 Frankie Rodriguez .05
22 Andy Mota .05
23 Chris Haney .05
24 *Kenny Lofton* .50
25 Dave Nilsson .05
26 Derek Bell .05
27 Frank Castillo .05
28 Candy Maldonado .05
29 Chuck McElroy .05
30 Chito Martinez .05
31 Steve Howe .05
32 Freddie Benavides .05
33 Scott Kamieniecki .05
34 Denny Neagle .05
35 Mike Humphreys .05
36 Mike Remlinger .05
37 Scott Coolbaugh .05
38 Darren Lewis .05
39 Thomas Howard .05
40 John Candelaria .05
41 Todd Benzinger .05

42 Wilson Alvarez .05
43 Patrick Lennon .05
44 Rusty Meacham .05
45 *Ryan Bowen* .05
46 *Rick Wilkins* .10
47 *Ed Sprague* .05
48 *Bob Scanlan* .05
49 Tom Candiotti .05
50 Dennis Martinez (Perfecto) .05
51 Oil Can Boyd .05
52 Glenallen Hill .05
53 *Scott Livingstone* .05
54 *Brian Hunter* .05
55 *Ivan Rodriguez* 1.50
56 *Keith Mitchell* .05
57 Roger McDowell .05
58 Otis Nixon .05
59 *Juan Bell* .05
60 Bill Krueger .05
61 *Chris Donnels* .05
62 Tommy Greene .05
63 Doug Simons .05
64 *Andy Ashby* .15
65 *Anthony Young* .05
66 *Kevin Morton* .05
67 *Bret Barberie* .05
68 *Scott Servais* .05
69 Ron Darling .05
70 Vicente Palacios .05
71 *Tim Burke* .05
72 *Gerald Alexander* .05
73 Reggie Jefferson .05
74 Dean Palmer .05
75 Mark Whiten .05
76 Randy Tomlin .05
77 *Mark Wohlers* .05
78 Brook Jacoby .05
79 Ken Griffey Jr., Ryne Sandberg (All-Star Checklist) .35
80 Jack Morris (AS) .05
81 Sandy Alomar, Jr. (AS) .05
82 Cecil Fielder (AS) .05
83 Roberto Alomar (AS) .20
84 Wade Boggs (AS) .25
85 Cal Ripken, Jr. (AS) .50
86 Rickey Henderson (AS) .15
87 Ken Griffey, Jr. (AS) .45
88 Dave Henderson (AS) .05
89 Danny Tartabull (AS) .05
90 Tom Glavine (AS) .10
91 Benito Santiago (AS) .05
92 Will Clark (AS) .15
93 Ryne Sandberg (AS) .35
94 Chris Sabo (AS) .05
95 Ozzie Smith (AS) .45
96 Ivan Calderon (AS) .05
97 Tony Gwynn (AS) .25
98 Andre Dawson (AS) .05
99 Bobby Bonilla (AS) .05
100 Checklist .05

1991 Upper Deck Hank Aaron Heroes

This set devoted to Hank Aaron is numbered 19-27 and includes an unnumbered "Baseball Heroes" cover card. The cards are found in foil and jumbo packs of Upper Deck high-number cards.

	MT
Complete Set (10):	4.50
Common Aaron:	.50
Autographed Card:	100.00
Aaron Header:	1.50
19 1954 Rookie Year	.50
20 1957 MVP	.50
21 1966 Move to Atlanta	.50
22 1970 3,000	.50
23 1974 715	.50
24 1975 Return to Milwaukee	.50
25 1976 755	.50
26 1982 Hall of Fame	.50
27 Checklist - Heroes 19-27	.50

1991 Upper Deck Heroes of Baseball

This four-card set features three members of Baseball's Hall of Fame: Harmon Killebrew, Gaylord Perry and Ferguson Jenkins. Each has a card for himself, plus there's a card which features all three players. The cards were found in specially-marked low number foil packs. The cards are numbered H1-H4. Upper Deck also produced 3,000 autographed and numbered cards for each player.

	MT
Complete Set (4):	9.00
Common Card:	3.00
1 Harmon Killebrew	3.00
1a Harmon Killebrew (autographed)	15.00
2 Gaylord Perry	3.00
2a Gaylord Perry (autographed)	15.00
3 Ferguson Jenkins	3.00
3a Ferguson Jenkins (autographed)	15.00
4 Gaylord Perry, Ferguson Jenkins, Harmon Killebrew	3.00

1991 Upper Deck Nolan Ryan Heroes

This set devoted to Nolan Ryan is numbered 10-18 and includes an unnumbered "Baseball Heroes" cover card. The cards are found in low-number foil and jumbo boxes.

	MT
Complete Set (10):	4.50
Common Player:	.50
Ryan header Card:	1.50
Autographed Card:	200.00
10 1968 Victory #1	.50
11 1973 A Career Year	.50
12 1975 Double Milestone	.50
13 1979 Back Home	.50
14 1981 All-Time Leader	.50
15 1989 5,000	.50
16 1990 The Sixth	.50
17 1990 ... and Still Counting	.50
18 Checklist - Heroes 10-18	.50

1991 Upper Deck Silver Sluggers

Each year the "Silver Slugger" award is presented to the player at each position with the highest batting average in each league. Upper Deck produced special cards in honor of the 1990 season award winners. The cards were randomly inserted in jumbo packs of Upper Deck cards. The cards feature a "SS" designation along with the card number. The cards are designed like the regular issue Upper Deck cards from 1991, but feature a Silver Slugger bat along the left border of the card.

	MT
Complete Set (18):	7.50
Common Player:	.25
1 Julio Franco	.25
2 Alan Trammell	.25
3 Rickey Henderson	.75
4 Jose Canseco	1.00
5 Barry Bonds	2.00
6 Eddie Murray	.60
7 Kelly Gruber	.25
8 Ryne Sandberg	1.50
9 Darryl Strawberry	.25
10 Ellis Burks	.25
11 Lance Parrish	.25
12 Cecil Fielder	.25
13 Matt Williams	.35
14 Dave Parker	.25
15 Bobby Bonilla	.25
16 Don Robinson	.25
17 Benito Santiago	.25
18 Barry Larkin	.35

1992 Upper Deck

Upper Deck introduced a new look in 1992. The baseline style was no longer used. The cards feature full-color action photos on white stock, with the player's name and the Upper Deck logo along the top border. The team name is in the photo's bottom-right corner. Once again a 100-card high number series was released in late summer. Ted Williams autographed 2,500 Baseball Heroes cards which were randomly inserted into packs. Subsets featured in the 1992 issue include Star Rookies and Top Prospects. Cards originating from factory sets have gold-foil holograms on back, rather than silver.

	MT
Unopened Factory Set (800):	12.00
Complete Set (800):	10.00
Complete Low Series (1-700):	8.00
Complete High Series (701-800):	2.00
Common Player:	.05
Low or Hi Pack (15):	.75
Low or Hi Wax Box (36):	15.00
1 Star Rookie Checklist (Ryan Klesko, Jim Thome)	.05
2 Royce Clayton (Star Rookie)	.05
3 *Brian Jordan* (Star Rookie)	.40
4 *Dave Fleming* (Star Rookie)	.05
5 Jim Thome (Star Rookie)	.05
6 Jeff Juden (Star Rookie)	.05
7 *Roberto Hernandez* (Star Rookie)	.15
8 Kyle Abbott (Star Rookie)	.05
9 *Chris George* (Star Rookie)	.05
10 *Rob Maurer* (Star Rookie)	.05

11 *Donald Harris* (Star Rookie) .05
12 *Ted Wood* (Star Rookie) .05
13 *Patrick Lennon* (Star Rookie) .05
14 Willie Banks (Star Rookie) .05
15 Roger Salkeld (Star Rookie) .05
16 Wil Cordero (Star Rookie) .05
17 *Arthur Rhodes* (Star Rookie) .05
18 Pedro Martinez (Star Rookie) .50
19 *Andy Ashby* (Star Rookie) .10
20 Tom Goodwin (Star Rookie) .05
21 *Braulio Castillo* (Star Rookie) .05
22 Todd Van Poppel (Star Rookie) .05
23 *Brian Williams* (Star Rookie) .05
24 Ryan Klesko (Star Rookie) .05
25 Kenny Lofton (Star Rookie) .05
26 Derek Bell (Star Rookie) .05
27 Reggie Sanders (Star Rookie) .05
28 Dave Winfield (Winfield's 400th) .25
29 Atlanta Braves Checklist (Dave Justice) .10
30 Cincinnati Reds Checklist (Rob Dibble) .05
31 Houston Astros Checklist (Craig Biggio) .05
32 Los Angeles Dodgers Checklist (Eddie Murray) .20
33 San Diego Padres Checklist (Fred McGriff) .05
34 San Francisco Giants Checklist (Willie McGee) .05
35 Chicago Cubs Checklist (Shawon Dunston) .05
36 Montreal Expos Checklist (Delino DeShields) .05
37 New York Mets Checklist (Howard Johnson) .05
38 Philadelphia Phillies Checklist (John Kruk) .05
39 Pittsburgh Pirates Checklist (Doug Drabek) .05
40 St. Louis Cardinals Checklist (Todd Zeile) .05
41 Steve Avery (Playoff Perfection) .05
42 *Jeremy Hernandez* .05
43 *Doug Henry* .05
44 *Chris Donnels* .05
45 *Mo Sanford* .05
46 *Scott Kamieniecki* .10
47 Mark Lemke .05
48 Steve Farr .05
49 Francisco Oliveras .05
50 *Ced Landrum* .05
51 Top Prospect Checklist (Rondell White, Marc Newfield) .05
52 *Eduardo Perez* (Top Prospect) .10
53 *Tom Nevers* (Top Prospect) .05
54 *David Zancanaro* (Top Prospect) .05
55 *Shawn Green* (Top Prospect) 2.00
56 *Mark Wohlers* (Top Prospect) .05
57 Dave Nilsson (Top Prospect) .05
58 Dmitri Young (Top Prospect) .05
59 *Ryan Hawblitzel* (Top Prospect) .05
60 Raul Mondesi (Top Prospect) .30
61 Rondell White (Top Prospect) .15
62 Steve Hosey (Top Prospect) .05
63 *Manny Ramirez* (Top Prospect) 3.00
64 Marc Newfield (TopProspect) .05
65 Jeromy Burnitz (Top Prospect) .05
66 *Mark Smith* (Top Prospect) .05
67 *Joey Hamilton* (Top Prospect) .25
68 *Tyler Green* (Top Prospect) .05
69 *John Farrell* (Top Prospect) .05
70 *Kurt Miller* (Top Prospect) .05
71 *Jeff Plympton* (Top Prospect) .05
72 Dan Wilson (Top Prospect) .05
73 *Joe Vitiello* (Top Prospect) .05
74 Rico Brogna (Top Prospect) .05
75 *David McCarty* (Top Prospect) .10
76 *Bob Wickman* (Top Prospect) .05
77 *Carlos Rodriguez* (Top Prospect) .05
78 Jim Abbott (Stay in School) .05
79 Bloodlines (Pedro Martinez, Ramon Martinez) .25
80 Bloodlines (Kevin Mitchell, Keith Mitchell) .05
81 Bloodlines (Sandy Jr. & Roberto Alomar, Sandy Jr. & Roberto Alomar) .15
82 Bloodlines (Cal Jr. & Billy Ripken, Cal Jr. & Billy Ripken) .40
83 Bloodlines (Tony & Chris Gwynn, Tony & Chris Gwynn) .20
84 Bloodlines (Dwight Gooden, Gary Sheffield) .15
85 Bloodlines (Ken, Sr.; Ken, Jr.; & Craig Griffey, Ken, Sr.; Ken, Jr.; & Craig Griffey, Ken, Sr.; Ken, Jr.; & Craig Griffey) .40
86 California Angels Checklist (Jim Abbott) .05
87 Chicago White Sox Checklist (Frank Thomas) .40
88 Kansas City Royals Checklist (Danny Tartabull) .05
89 Minnesota Twins Checklist (Scott Erickson) .05
90 Oakland Athletics Checklist (Rickey Henderson) .25
91 Seattle Mariners Checklist (Edgar Martinez) .05
92 Texas Rangers Checklist (Nolan Ryan) .50
93 Baltimore Orioles Checklist (Ben McDonald) .05
94 Boston Red Sox Checklist (Ellis Burks) .05
95 Cleveland Indians Checklist (Greg Swindell) .05
96 Detroit Tigers Checklist (Cecil Fielder) .05
97 Milwaukee Brewers Checklist (Greg Vaughn) .05
98 New York Yankees Checklist (Kevin Maas) .05
99 Toronto Blue Jays Checklist (Dave Steib) .05
100 Checklist 1-100 .05
101 Joe Oliver .05
102 Hector Villanueva .05
103 Ed Whitson .05
104 Danny Jackson .05
105 Chris Hammond .05
106 Ricky Jordan .05
107 Kevin Bass .05
108 Darrin Fletcher .05
109 Junior Ortiz .05
110 Tom Bolton .05
111 Jeff King .05
112 Dave Magadan .05
113 Mike LaValliere .05
114 Hubie Brooks .05
115 Jay Bell .05
116 David Wells .10
117 Jim Leyritz .05
118 Manuel Lee .05
119 Alvaro Espinoza .05
120 B.J. Surhoff .05
121 Hal Morris .05
122 Shawon Dunston .05
123 Chris Sabo .05
124 Andre Dawson .20
125 Eric Davis .05
126 Chili Davis .05
127 Dale Murphy .15
128 Kirk McCaskill .05
129 Terry Mulholland .05
130 Rick Aguilera .05
131 Vince Coleman .05
132 Andy Van Slyke .05
133 Gregg Jefferies .05
134 Barry Bonds .75
135 Dwight Gooden .05
136 Dave Stieb .05
137 Albert Belle .25
138 Teddy Higuera .05
139 Jesse Barfield .05
140 Pat Borders .05
141 Bip Roberts .05
142 Rob Dibble .05
143 Mark Grace .25
144 Barry Larkin .10
145 Ryne Sandberg .50
146 Scott Erickson .05
147 Luis Polonia .05
148 John Burkett .05
149 Luis Sojo .05
150 Dickie Thon .05
151 Walt Weiss .05
152 Mike Scioscia .05
153 Mark McGwire 1.00
154 Matt Williams .15
155 Rickey Henderson .50
156 Sandy Alomar, Jr. .05
157 Brian McRae .05
158 Harold Baines .05
159 Kevin Appier .05
160 Felix Fermin .05
161 Leo Gomez .05
162 Craig Biggio .10
163 Ben McDonald .05
164 Randy Johnson .45
165 Cal Ripken, Jr. 1.00
166 Frank Thomas .75
167 Delino DeShields .05
168 Greg Gagne .05
169 Ron Karkovice .05
170 Charlie Leibrandt .05
171 Dave Righetti .05
172 Dave Henderson .05
173 Steve Decker .05
174 Darryl Strawberry .05
175 Will Clark .15
176 Ruben Sierra .05
177 Ozzie Smith .65
178 Charles Nagy .05
179 Gary Pettis .05
180 Kirk Gibson .05
181 Randy Milligan .05
182 Dave Valle .05
183 Chris Hoiles .05
184 Tony Phillips .05
185 Brady Anderson .05
186 Scott Fletcher .05
187 Gene Larkin .05
188 Lance Johnson .05
189 Greg Olson .05
190 Melido Perez .05
191 Lenny Harris .05
192 Terry Kennedy .05
193 Mike Gallego .05
194 Willie McGee .05
195 Juan Samuel .05
196 Jeff Huson .05
197 Alex Cole .05
198 Ron Robinson .05
199 Joel Skinner .05
200 Checklist 101-200 .05
201 Kevin Reimer .05
202 Stan Belinda .05
203 Pat Tabler .05
204 Jose Guzman .05
205 Jose Lind .05
206 Spike Owen .05
207 Joe Orsulak .05
208 Charlie Hayes .05
209 Mike Devereaux .05
210 Mike Fitzgerald .05
211 Willie Randolph .05
212 Rod Nichols .05
213 Mike Boddicker .05
214 Bill Spiers .05
215 Steve Olin .05
216 *David Howard* .05
217 Gary Varsho .05
218 Mike Harkey .05
219 Luis Aquino .05
220 Chuck McElroy .05
221 Doug Drabek .05
222 Dave Winfield .50
223 Rafael Palmeiro .25
224 Joe Carter .05
225 Bobby Bonilla .05
226 Ivan Calderon .05
227 Gregg Olson .05
228 Tim Wallach .05
229 Terry Pendleton .05
230 Gilberto Reyes .05
231 Carlos Baerga .05
232 Greg Vaughn .05
233 Bret Saberhagen .05
234 Gary Sheffield .15
235 Mark Lewis .05
236 George Bell .05
237 Danny Tartabull .05
238 Willie Wilson .05
239 Doug Dascenzo .05
240 Bill Pecota .05
241 Julio Franco .05
242 Ed Sprague .05
243 Juan Gonzalez .50
244 Chuck Finley .05
245 Ivan Rodriguez .45
246 Len Dykstra .05
247 Deion Sanders .10
248 Dwight Evans .05
249 Larry Walker .25
250 Billy Ripken .05
251 Mickey Tettleton .05
252 Tony Pena .05
253 Benito Santiago .05
254 Kirby Puckett .65
255 Cecil Fielder .05
256 Howard Johnson .05
257 Andujar Cedeno .05
258 Jose Rijo .05
259 Al Osuna .05
260 Todd Hundley .05
261 Orel Hershiser .05
262 Ray Lankford .05
263 Robin Ventura .05
264 Felix Jose .05
265 Eddie Murray .45
266 Kevin Mitchell .05
267 Gary Carter .20
268 Mike Benjamin .05
269 Dick Schofield .05
270 Jose Uribe .05
271 Pete Incaviglia .05
272 Tony Fernandez .05
273 Alan Trammell .05
274 Tony Gwynn .65
275 Mike Greenwell .05
276 Jeff Bagwell .50
277 Frank Viola .05
278 Randy Myers .05
279 Ken Caminiti .05
280 Bill Doran .05
281 Dan Pasqua .05
282 Alfredo Griffin .05
283 Jose Oquendo .05
284 Kal Daniels .05
285 Bobby Thigpen .05

No.	Player	Price
286	Robby Thompson	.05
287	Mark Eichhorn	.05
288	Mike Felder	.05
289	Dave Gallagher	.05
290	Dave Anderson	.05
291	Mel Hall	.05
292	Jerald Clark	.05
293	Al Newman	.05
294	Rob Deer	.05
295	Matt Nokes	.05
296	Jack Armstrong	.05
297	Jim Deshaies	.05
298	Jeff Innis	.05
299	Jeff Reed	.05
300	Checklist 201-300	.05
301	Lonnie Smith	.05
302	Jimmy Key	.05
303	Junior Felix	.05
304	Mike Heath	.05
305	Mark Langston	.05
306	Greg W. Harris	.05
307	Brett Butler	.05
308	Luis Rivera	.05
309	Bruce Ruffin	.05
310	Paul Faries	.05
311	Terry Leach	.05
312	*Scott Brosius*	.10
313	Scott Leius	.05
314	Harold Reynolds	.05
315	Jack Morris	.05
316	David Segui	.05
317	Bill Gullickson	.05
318	Todd Frohwirth	.05
319	*Mark Leiter*	.05
320	Jeff M. Robinson	.05
321	Gary Gaetti	.05
322	John Smoltz	.10
323	Andy Benes	.05
324	Kelly Gruber	.05
325	Jim Abbott	.05
326	John Kruk	.05
327	Kevin Seitzer	.05
328	Darrin Jackson	.05
329	Kurt Stillwell	.05
330	Mike Maddux	.05
331	Dennis Eckersley	.05
332	Dan Gladden	.05
333	Jose Canseco	.40
334	Kent Hrbek	.05
335	Ken Griffey, Sr.	.05
336	Greg Swindell	.05
337	Trevor Wilson	.05
338	Sam Horn	.05
339	Mike Henneman	.05
340	Jerry Browne	.05
341	Glenn Braggs	.05
342	Tom Glavine	.10
343	Wally Joyner	.05
344	Fred McGriff	.05
345	Ron Gant	.05
346	Ramon Martinez	.05
347	Wes Chamberlain	.05
348	Terry Shumpert	.05
349	Tim Teufel	.05
350	Wally Backman	.05
351	Joe Girardi	.05
352	Devon White	.05
353	Greg Maddux	.65
354	*Ryan Bowen*	.05
355	Roberto Alomar	.40
356	Don Mattingly	.75
357	Pedro Guerrero	.05
358	Steve Sax	.05
359	Joey Cora	.05
360	Jim Gantner	.05
361	Brian Barnes	.05
362	Kevin McReynolds	.05
363	*Bret Barberie*	.05
364	David Cone	.05
365	Dennis Martinez	.05
366	*Brian Hunter*	.05
367	Edgar Martinez	.05
368	Steve Finley	.05
369	Greg Briley	.05
370	Jeff Blauser	.05
371	Todd Stottlemyre	.05
372	Luis Gonzalez	.20
373	Rick Wilkins	.05
374	*Darryl Kile*	.10
375	John Olerud	.05
376	Lee Smith	.05
377	Kevin Maas	.05
378	Dante Bichette	.05
379	Tom Pagnozzi	.05
380	Mike Flanagan	.05
381	Charlie O'Brien	.05
382	Dave Martinez	.05
383	Keith Miller	.05
384	Scott Ruskin	.05
385	Kevin Elster	.05
386	Alvin Davis	.05
387	Casey Candaele	.05
388	Pete O'Brien	.05
389	Jeff Treadway	.05
390	Scott Bradley	.05
391	Mookie Wilson	.05
392	Jimmy Jones	.05
393	Candy Maldonado	.05
394	Eric Yelding	.05
395	Tom Henke	.05
396	Franklin Stubbs	.05
397	Milt Thompson	.05
398	Mark Carreon	.05
399	Randy Velarde	.05
400	Checklist 301-400	.05
401	Omar Vizquel	.05
402	Joe Boever	.05
403	Bill Krueger	.05
404	Jody Reed	.05
405	Mike Schooler	.05
406	Jason Grimsley	.05
407	Greg Myers	.05
408	Randy Ready	.05
409	*Mike Timlin*	.15
410	Mitch Williams	.05
411	Garry Templeton	.05
412	Greg Cadaret	.05
413	Donnie Hill	.05
414	Wally Whitehurst	.05
415	Scott Sanderson	.05
416	Thomas Howard	.05
417	Neal Heaton	.05
418	Charlie Hough	.05
419	Jack Howell	.05
420	Greg Hibbard	.05
421	Carlos Quintana	.05
422	*Kim Batiste*	.05
423	Paul Molitor	.50
424	Ken Griffey, Jr.	.90
425	Phil Plantier	.05
426	Denny Neagle	.05
427	Von Hayes	.05
428	Shane Mack	.05
429	Darren Daulton	.05
430	Dwayne Henry	.05
431	Lance Parrish	.05
432	*Mike Humphreys*	.05
433	Tim Burke	.05
434	Bryan Harvey	.05
435	Pat Kelly	.05
436	Ozzie Guillen	.05
437	Bruce Hurst	.05
438	Sammy Sosa	.75
439	Dennis Rasmussen	.05
440	Ken Patterson	.05
441	Jay Buhner	.05
442	Pat Combs	.05
443	Wade Boggs	.50
444	George Brett	.65
445	Mo Vaughn	.35
446	Chuck Knoblauch	.05
447	Tom Candiotti	.05
448	Mark Portugal	.05
449	Mickey Morandini	.05
450	Duane Ward	.05
451	Otis Nixon	.05
452	Bob Welch	.05
453	Rusty Meacham	.05
454	Keith Mitchell	.05
455	Marquis Grissom	.05
456	Robin Yount	.50
457	*Harvey Pulliam*	.05
458	Jose DeLeon	.05
459	Mark Gubicza	.05
460	Darryl Hamilton	.05
461	Tom Browning	.05
462	Monty Fariss	.05
463	Jerome Walton	.05
464	Paul O'Neill	.05
465	Dean Palmer	.05
466	Travis Fryman	.05
467	John Smiley	.05
468	Lloyd Moseby	.05
469	*John Wehner*	.05
470	Skeeter Barnes	.05
471	Steve Chitren	.05
472	Kent Mercker	.05
473	Terry Steinbach	.05
474	Andres Galarraga	.05
475	Steve Avery	.05
476	Tom Gordon	.05
477	Cal Eldred	.05
478	Omar Olivares	.05
479	Julio Machado	.05
480	Bob Milacki	.05
481	Les Lancaster	.05
482	John Candelaria	.05
483	Brian Downing	.05
484	Roger McDowell	.05
485	Scott Scudder	.05
486	Zane Smith	.05
487	John Cerutti	.05
488	Steve Buechele	.05
489	Paul Gibson	.05
490	Curtis Wilkerson	.05
491	Marvin Freeman	.05
492	Tom Foley	.05
493	Juan Berenguer	.05
494	Ernest Riles	.05
495	Sid Bream	.05
496	Chuck Crim	.05
497	Mike Macfarlane	.05
498	Dale Sveum	.05
499	Storm Davis	.05
500	Checklist 401-500	.05
501	Jeff Reardon	.05
502	Shawn Abner	.05
503	Tony Fossas	.05
504	Cory Snyder	.05
505	Matt Young	.05
506	Allan Anderson	.05
507	Mark Lee	.05
508	Gene Nelson	.05
509	Mike Pagliarulo	.05
510	Rafael Belliard	.05
511	Jay Howell	.05
512	Bob Tewksbury	.05
513	Mike Morgan	.05
514	John Franco	.05
515	Kevin Gross	.05
516	Lou Whitaker	.05
517	Orlando Merced	.05
518	Todd Benzinger	.05
519	Gary Redus	.05
520	Walt Terrell	.05
521	Jack Clark	.05
522	Dave Parker	.05
523	Tim Naehring	.05
524	Mark Whiten	.05
525	Ellis Burks	.05
526	*Frank Castillo*	.10
527	Brian Harper	.05
528	Brook Jacoby	.05
529	Rick Sutcliffe	.05
530	Joe Klink	.05
531	Terry Bross	.05
532	Jose Offerman	.05
533	Todd Zeile	.05
534	Eric Karros	.05
535	*Anthony Young*	.05
536	Milt Cuyler	.05
537	Randy Tomlin	.05
538	*Scott Livingstone*	.05
539	Jim Eisenreich	.05
540	Don Slaught	.05
541	Scott Cooper	.05
542	Joe Grahe	.05
543	Tom Brunansky	.05
544	Eddie Zosky	.05
545	Roger Clemens	.65
546	Dave Justice	.20
547	Dave Stewart	.05
548	David West	.05
549	Dave Smith	.05
550	Dan Plesac	.05
551	Alex Fernandez	.05
552	Bernard Gilkey	.05
553	Jack McDowell	.05
554	Tino Martinez	.05
555	Bo Jackson	.10
556	Bernie Williams	.20
557	Mark Gardner	.05
558	Glenallen Hill	.05
559	Oil Can Boyd	.05
560	Chris James	.05
561	*Scott Servais*	.10
562	*Rey Sanchez*	.05
563	*Paul McClellan*	.05
564	*Andy Mota*	.05
565	Darren Lewis	.05
566	*Jose Melendez*	.05
567	Tommy Greene	.05
568	Rich Rodriguez	.05
569	*Heathcliff Slocumb*	.05
570	Joe Hesketh	.05
571	Carlton Fisk	.50
572	Erik Hanson	.05
573	Wilson Alvarez	.05
574	*Rheal Cormier*	.05
575	Tim Raines	.05
576	Bobby Witt	.05
577	Roberto Kelly	.05
578	Kevin Brown	.10
579	Chris Nabholz	.05
580	Jesse Orosco	.05
581	Jeff Brantley	.05
582	Rafael Ramirez	.05
583	Kelly Downs	.05
584	Mike Simms	.05
585	*Mike Remlinger*	.05
586	Dave Hollins	.05
587	Larry Andersen	.05
588	Mike Gardiner	.05
589	Craig Lefferts	.05
590	Paul Assenmacher	.05
591	Bryn Smith	.05
592	Donn Pall	.05
593	Mike Jackson	.05
594	Scott Radinsky	.05
595	Brian Holman	.05
596	Geronimo Pena	.05
597	Mike Jeffcoat	.05
598	Carlos Martinez	.05
599	Geno Petralli	.05
600	Checklist 501-600	.05
601	Jerry Don Gleaton	.05
602	Adam Peterson	.05
603	Craig Grebeck	.05
604	Mark Guthrie	.05
605	Frank Tanana	.05
606	Hensley Meulens	.05
607	Mark Davis	.05
608	Eric Plunk	.05
609	Mark Williamson	.05
610	Lee Guetterman	.05
611	Bobby Rose	.05
612	Bill Wegman	.05
613	Mike Hartley	.05
614	*Chris Beasley*	.05
615	Chris Bosio	.05
616	Henry Cotto	.05
617	*Chico Walker*	.05
618	Russ Swan	.05
619	Bob Walk	.05
620	Billy Swift	.05
621	*Warren Newson*	.05
622	Steve Bedrosian	.05
623	*Ricky Bones*	.05
624	Kevin Tapani	.05
625	*Juan Guzman*	.05
626	*Jeff Johnson*	.05
627	Jeff Montgomery	.05
628	Ken Hill	.05
629	Gary Thurman	.05
630	Steve Howe	.05
631	Jose DeJesus	.05
632	Bert Blyleven	.05
633	Jaime Navarro	.05
634	Lee Stevens	.05
635	Pete Harnisch	.05
636	Bill Landrum	.05
637	Rich DeLucia	.05
638	Luis Salazar	.05
639	Rob Murphy	.05
640	A.L. Diamond Skills Checklist (Rickey Henderson, Jose Canseco)	.05
641	Roger Clemens (Diamond Skills)	.35
642	Jim Abbott (Diamond Skills)	.05
643	Travis Fryman (Diamond Skills)	.05
644	Jesse Barfield (Diamond Skills)	.05
645	Cal Ripken, Jr. (Diamond Skills)	.50
646	Wade Boggs (Diamond Skills)	.25
647	Cecil Fielder (Diamond Skills)	.05
648	Rickey Henderson (Diamond Skills)	.25
649	Jose Canseco (Diamond Skills)	.20
650	Ken Griffey, Jr. (Diamond Skills)	.45
651	Kenny Rogers	.05
652	*Luis Mercedes*	.05
653	Mike Stanton	.05
654	Glenn Davis	.05
655	Nolan Ryan	1.00
656	Reggie Jefferson	.05

657 *Javier Ortiz* .05
658 Greg A. Harris .05
659 Mariano Duncan .05
660 Jeff Shaw .05
661 Mike Moore .05
662 *Chris Haney* .05
663 *Joe Slusarski* .05
664 *Wayne Housie* .05
665 Carlos Garcia .05
666 Bob Ojeda .05
667 *Bryan Hickerson* .05
668 Tim Belcher .05
669 Ron Darling .05
670 Rex Hudler .05
671 Sid Fernandez .05
672 *Chito Martinez* .05
673 *Pete Schourek* .05
674 *Armando Renoso* .05
675 Mike Mussina .40
676 Kevin Morton .05
677 Norm Charlton .05
678 Danny Darwin .05
679 Eric King .05
680 Ted Power .05
681 Barry Jones .05
682 Carney Lansford .05
683 Mel Rojas .05
684 Rick Honeycutt .05
685 *Jeff Fassero* .05
686 Cris Carpenter .05
687 Tim Crews .05
688 Scott Terry .05
689 Chris Gwynn .05
690 Gerald Perry .05
691 John Barfield .05
692 Bob Melvin .05
693 Juan Agosto .05
694 Alejandro Pena .05
695 Jeff Russell .05
696 Carmelo Martinez .05
697 Bud Black .05
698 Dave Otto .05
699 Billy Hatcher .05
700 Checklist 601-700 .05
701 Clemente Nunez .05
702 "Rookie Threats" (Donovan Osborne, Brian Jordan, Mark Clark) .05
703 Mike Morgan .05
704 Keith Miller .05
705 Kurt Stillwell .05
706 Damon Berryhill .05
707 Von Hayes .05
708 Rick Sutcliffe .05
709 Hubie Brooks .05
710 Ryan Turner .05
711 N.L. Diamond Skills Checklist (Barry Bonds, Andy Van Slyke) .25
712 Jose Rijo (Diamond Skills) .05
713 Tom Glavine (Diamond Skills) .05
714 Shawon Dunston (Diamond Skills) .05
715 Andy Van Slyke (Diamond Skills) .05
716 Ozzie Smith (Diamond Skills) .35
717 Tony Gwynn (Diamond Skills) .35
718 Will Clark (Diamond Skills) .05
719 Marquis Grissom (Diamond Skills) .05
720 Howard Johnson (Diamond Skills) .05
721 Barry Bonds (Diamond Skills) .40
722 Kirk McCaskill .05
723 Sammy Sosa .75
724 George Bell .05
725 Gregg Jefferies .05
726 Gary DiSarcina .05
727 Mike Bordick .05
728 Eddie Murray (400 Home Run Club) .15
729 Rene Gonzales .05
730 Mike Bielecki .05
731 Calvin Jones .05
732 Jack Morris .05
733 Frank Viola .05
734 Dave Winfield .50
735 Kevin Mitchell .05
736 Billy Swift .05
737 Dan Gladden .05
738 Mike Jackson .05
739 Mark Carreon .05
740 Kirt Manwaring .05
741 Randy Myers .05
742 Kevin McReynolds .05
743 Steve Sax .05
744 Wally Joyner .05
745 Gary Sheffield .20
746 Danny Tartabull .05
747 Julio Valera .05
748 Denny Neagle .05
749 Lance Blankenship .05
750 Mike Gallego .05
751 Bret Saberhagen .05
752 Ruben Amaro .05
753 Eddie Murray .40
754 Kyle Abbott .05
755 Bobby Bonilla .05
756 Eric Davis .05
757 Eddie Taubensee .05
758 Andres Galarraga .05
759 Pete Incaviglia .05
760 Tom Candiotti .05
761 Tim Belcher .05
762 Ricky Bones .05
763 Bip Roberts .05
764 Pedro Munoz .05
765 Greg Swindell .05
766 Kenny Lofton .05
767 Gary Carter .20
768 Charlie Hayes .05
769 Dickie Thon .05
770 Diamond Debuts Checklist (Donovan Osborne) .05
771 Bret Boone (Diamond Debuts) .15
772 *Archi Cianfrocco* (Diamond Debuts) .05
773 *Mark Clark* (Diamond Debuts) .05
774 *Chad Curtis* (Diamond Debuts) .20
775 *Pat Listach* (Diamond Debuts) .05
776 *Pat Mahomes* (Diamond Debuts) .05
777 *Donovan Osborne* (Diamond Debuts) .05
778 *John Patterson* (Diamond Debuts) .05
779 *Andy Stankiewicz* (Diamond Debuts) .05
780 *Turk Wendell* (Diamond Debuts) .10
781 Bill Krueger .05
782 Rickey Henderson (Grand Theft) .25
783 Kevin Seitzer .05
784 Dave Martinez .05
785 John Smiley .05
786 Matt Stairs .05
787 Scott Scudder .05
788 John Wetteland .05
789 Jack Armstrong .05
790 Ken Hill .05
791 Dick Schofield .05
792 Mariano Duncan .05
793 Bill Pecota .05
794 *Mike Kelly* .05
795 Willie Randolph .05
796 *Butch Henry* .05
797 *Carlos Hernandez* .05
798 Doug Jones .05
799 Melido Perez .05
800 Checklist .05
SP3 "Prime Time's Two" (Deion Sanders) .50
SP4 "Mr. Baseball" (Tom Selleck, Frank Thomas) 3.00
HH2 (Ted Williams) (hologram) 2.00

1992 Upper Deck Bench/Morgan Heroes

This set is devoted to two of the vital cogs in Cincinnati's Big Red Machine: Hall of Famers Johnny Bench and Joe Morgan. Cards, numbered 37-45, were included in high number packs. An unnumbered cover card was also produced. Both players autographed 2,500 of card #45, the painting of the Reds duo by sports artist Vernon Wells.

		MT
Complete Set (10):		5.00
Common Card:		.35
Autographed Card:		100.00
---	Header Card	.75
37	1968 Rookie of the Year (Johnny Bench)	.75
38	1968-77 Ten Straight Gold Gloves (Johnny Bench)	.75
39	1970 & 1972 MVP (Johnny Bench)	.75
40	1965 Rookie Year (Joe Morgan)	.50
41	1975-76 Back-to-Back MVP (Joe Morgan)	.50
42	1980-83 The Golden Years (Joe Morgan)	.50
43	1972-79 Big Red Machine (Johnny Bench, Joe Morgan)	.60
44	1989 & 1990 Hall of Fame (Johnny Bench, Joe Morgan)	.60
45	Checklist - Heroes 37-45 (Johnny Bench, Joe Morgan)	.60

1992 Upper Deck College POY Holograms

This three-card hologram set features the College Player of the Year winners from 1989-91. Cards were randomly inserted in high number foil packs and have a CP prefix for numbering.

		MT
Complete Set (3):		.75
Common Player:		.25
1	David McCarty	.25
2	Mike Kelly	.25
3	Ben McDonald	.25

1992 Upper Deck Hall of Fame Heroes

This set features three top players from the 1970s: Vida Blue, Lou Brock and Rollie Fingers. The cards continue from last year's set by using numbers H5-H8. The three players are each on one card; the fourth card features all three. They were found in low-number foil packs and specially-marked jumbo packs. Both types of packs could also contain autographed cards; each player signed 3,000 cards.

		MT
Complete Set (4):		2.00
Common Player:		.40
5	Vida Blue	.40
5a	Vida Blue (autographed)	15.00
6	Lou Brock	1.00
6a	Lou Brock (autographed)	24.00
7	Rollie Fingers	.50
7a	Rollie Fingers (autographed)	15.00
8	Vida Blue, Lou Brock, Rollie Fingers	1.00

1992 Upper Deck Heroes Highlights

Special packaging of 1992 Upper Deck high numbers produced for sales to dealers at its Heroes of Baseball show series included these cards of former players as inserts.

Cards have a Heroes Highlights banner including the player's name and the date of his career highlight beneath the photo. In a tombstone frame on back, the highlight is chronicled. Cards are numbered alphabetically by player name, with the card number carrying an HI prefix.

		MT
Complete Set (10):		7.00
Common Player:		.70
1	Bobby Bonds	.50
2	Lou Brock	.75
3	Rollie Fingers	.50
4	Bob Gibson	.75
5	Reggie Jackson	1.00
6	Gaylord Perry	.50
7	Robin Roberts	.75
8	Brooks Robinson	.75
9	Billy Williams	.75
10	Ted Williams	2.50

1992 Upper Deck Home Run Heroes

This 26-card set features a top home run hitter from each major league team. The cards, numbered HR1-HR26, were found in low-number jumbo packs, one per pack.

		MT
Complete Set (26):		5.00
Common Player:		.10
1	Jose Canseco	.30
2	Cecil Fielder	.10
3	Howard Johnson	.10
4	Cal Ripken, Jr.	1.00
5	Matt Williams	.25
6	Joe Carter	.10
7	Ron Gant	.10
8	Frank Thomas	.75
9	Andre Dawson	.25
10	Fred McGriff	.10
11	Danny Tartabull	.10
12	Chili Davis	.10
13	Albert Belle	.25
14	Jack Clark	.10
15	Paul O'Neill	.10
16	Darryl Strawberry	.10
17	Dave Winfield	.50
18	Jay Buhner	.10
19	Juan Gonzalez	.35
20	Greg Vaughn	.10
21	Barry Bonds	.75
22	Matt Nokes	.10
23	John Kruk	.10
24	Ivan Calderon	.10
25	Jeff Bagwell	.35
26	Todd Zeile	.10

1992 Upper Deck Scouting Report

These cards were randomly inserted in Upper Deck high-number jumbo packs. The set is numbered SR1-SR25 and features 25 top prospects, including 1992 Rookies of the Year Pat Listach and Eric Karros. "Scouting Report" is written down the side on the front in silver lettering. The back features a clipboard which shows a photo, a player profile and a major league scouting report.

		MT
Complete Set (25):		6.50
Common Player:		.25
1	Andy Ashby	.35
2	Willie Banks	.25
3	Kim Batiste	.25
4	Derek Bell	.50
5	Archi Cianfrocco	.25
6	Royce Clayton	.25
7	Gary DiSarcina	.25
8	Dave Fleming	.25
9	Butch Henry	.25
10	Todd Hundley	.50
11	Brian Jordan	.50
12	Eric Karros	.50
13	Pat Listach	.25
14	Scott Livingstone	.25
15	Kenny Lofton	.50
16	Pat Mahomes	.25
17	Denny Neagle	.25
18	Dave Nilsson	.25
19	Donovan Osborne	.25
20	Reggie Sanders	.35
21	Andy Stankiewicz	.25
22	Jim Thome	.50
23	Julio Valera	.25
24	Mark Wohlers	.25
25	Anthony Young	.25

1992 Upper Deck Ted Williams' Best Hitters/Future

Twenty of the best hitters in baseball according to legend Ted Williams are featured in this special insert set from Upper Deck. The cards are styled much like the 1992 FanFest cards and showcase each chosen player. Each card is numbered with a "T" designation.

		MT
Complete Set (20):		8.00
Common Player:		.25
1	Wade Boggs	.60
2	Barry Bonds	1.00
3	Jose Canseco	.50
4	Will Clark	.30
5	Cecil Fielder	.25
6	Tony Gwynn	.75
7	Rickey Henderson	.55
8	Fred McGriff	.25
9	Kirby Puckett	.75
10	Ruben Sierra	.25
11	Roberto Alomar	.45
12	Jeff Bagwell	.65
13	Albert Belle	.35
14	Juan Gonzalez	.65
15	Ken Griffey, Jr.	2.00
16	Chris Hoiles	.25
17	Dave Justice	.35
18	Phil Plantier	.25
19	Frank Thomas	1.00
20	Robin Ventura	.25

1992 Upper Deck Ted Williams Heroes

This Baseball Heroes set devoted to Ted Williams continues where previous efforts left off by numbering it from 28-36. An unnumbered "Baseball Heroes" cover card is also included. Cards were found in low-number foil and jumbo packs. Williams also autographed 2,500 cards, which were numbered and randomly inserted in low-number packs.

		MT
Complete Set (10):		8.00
Common Player:		.50
Autographed Card:		350.00
---	Header Card	.75
28	1939 Rookie Year (Ted Williams)	.50
29	1941 .406! (Ted Williams)	.50
30	1942 Triple Crown Year (Ted Williams)	.50
31	1946 & 1949 MVP (Ted Williams)	.50
32	1947 Second Triple Crown (Ted Williams)	.50
33	1950s Player of the Decade (Ted Williams)	.50
34	1960 500 Home Run Club (Ted Williams)	.50
35	1966 Hall of Fame (Ted Williams)	.50
36	Checklist - Heroes 28-36 (Ted Williams)	.50

1993 Upper Deck

Upper Deck introduced its 1993 set in a two-series format to adjust to expansion. Cards 1-420 make up the first series. Special subsets in Series 1 include rookies, teammates and community heroes. Fronts feature color player photos surrounded by a white border. Backs feature vertical photos, a change from the past, and more complete statistics than Upper Deck had in the past. The hologram appears in the lower-left corner on the card back. One out of 20 factory sets featured cards with gold, rather than silver, holograms.

		MT
Unopened Factory Set (840):		15.00
Complete Set (840):		12.00
Common Player:		.05
Gold Hologram:		3X
Distributed 1:20 in Factory Set form		
Series 1 or 2 Pack (15):		.75
Series 1 or 2 Wax Box (36):		15.00
1	Tim Salmon (Checklist)	.15
2	Mike Piazza (Star Rookie)	1.50
3	*Rene Arocha* (Star Rookie)	.15
4	*Willie Greene* (Star Rookie)	.05
5	*Manny Alexander* (Star Rookie)	.05
6	Dan Wilson (Star Rookie)	.05
7	*Dan Smith* (Star Rookie)	.05
8	*Kevin Rogers* (Star Rookie)	.05
9	*Nigel Wilson* (Star Rookie)	.05
10	*Joe Vitko* (Star Rookie)	.05
11	Tim Costo (Star Rookie)	.05
12	Alan Embree (Star Rookie)	.05
13	*Jim Tatum* (Star Rookie)	.05
14	*Cris Colon* (Star Rookie)	.05
15	Steve Hosey (Star Rookie)	.05
16	*Sterling Hitchcock* (Star Rookie)	.15
17	*Dave Mlicki* (Star Rookie)	.05
18	*Jessie Hollins* (Star Rookie)	.05

19 *Bobby J. Jones* (Star Rookie) .15
20 *Kurt Miller* (Star Rookie) .05
21 *Melvin Nieves* (Star Rookie) .05
22 *Billy Ashley* (Star Rookie) .05
23 *J.T. Snow* (Star Rookie) .50
24 Chipper Jones (Star Rookie) 1.50
25 Tim Salmon (Star Rookie) .25
26 *Tim Pugh* (Star Rookie) .05
27 David Nied (Star Rookie) .05
28 *Mike Trombley* (Star Rookie) .05
29 Javier Lopez (Star Rookie) .05
30 Community Heroes Checklist (Jim Abbott) .05
31 Jim Abbott (Community Heroes) .05
32 Dale Murphy (Community Heroes) .10
33 Tony Pena (Community Heroes) .05
34 Kirby Puckett (Community Heroes) .40
35 Harold Reynolds (Community Heroes) .05
36 Cal Ripken, Jr. (Community Heroes) .75
37 Nolan Ryan (Community Heroes) .75
38 Ryne Sandberg (Community Heroes) .25
39 Dave Stewart (Community Heroes) .05
40 Dave Winfield (Community Heroes) .25
41 Teammates Checklist (Joe Carter, Mark McGwire) .75
42 Blockbuster Trade (Joe Carter, Roberto Alomar) .15
43 Brew Crew (Pat Listach, Robin Yount, Paul Molitor) .15
44 Iron and Steal (Brady Anderson, Cal Ripken, Jr.) .45
45 Youthful Tribe (Albert Belle, Sandy Alomar Jr., Jim Thome, Carlos Baerga, Kenny Lofton) .15
46 Motown Mashers (Cecil Fielder, Mickey Tettleton) .05
47 Yankee Pride (Roberto Kelly, Don Mattingly) .40
48 Boston Cy Sox (Frank Viola, Roger Clemens) .30
49 Bash Brothers (Ruben Sierra, Mark McGwire) .75
50 Twin Titles (Kent Hrbek, Kirby Puckett) .35
51 Southside Sluggers (Robin Ventura, Frank Thomas) .35
52 Latin Stars (Jose Canseco, Ivan Rodriguez, Rafael Palmeiro, Juan Gonzalez) .35
53 Lethal Lefties (Mark Langston, Jim Abbott, Chuck Finley) .05
54 Royal Family (Gregg Jefferies, George Brett, Wally Joyner) .35
55 Pacific Sox Exchange (Kevin Mitchell, Jay Buhner, Ken Griffey, Jr.) .40
56 George Brett .75
57 Scott Cooper .05
58 Mike Maddux .05
59 *Rusty Meacham* .05
60 Wil Cordero .05
61 Tim Teufel .05
62 Jeff Montgomery .05
63 Scott Livingstone .05
64 Doug Dascenzo .05
65 Bret Boone .10
66 *Tim Wakefield* .10
67 Curt Schilling .15
68 Frank Tanana .05
69 Len Dykstra .05
70 Derek Lilliquist .05
71 Anthony Young .05
72 *Hipolito Pichardo* .05
73 Rod Beck .05
74 Kent Hrbek .05
75 Tom Glavine .10
76 Kevin Brown .10
77 Chuck Finley .05
78 Bob Walk .05
79 Rheal Cormier .05
80 Rick Sutcliffe .05
81 Harold Baines .05
82 Lee Smith .05
83 Geno Petralli .05
84 Jose Oquendo .05
85 Mark Gubicza .05
86 Mickey Tettleton .05
87 Bobby Witt .05
88 Mark Lewis .05
89 Kevin Appier .05
90 Mike Stanton .05
91 Rafael Belliard .05
92 Kenny Rogers .05
93 Randy Velarde .05
94 Luis Sojo .05
95 Mark Leiter .05
96 Jody Reed .05
97 Pete Harnisch .05
98 Tom Candiotti .05
99 Mark Portugal .05
100 Dave Valle .05
101 Shawon Dunston .05
102 B.J. Surhoff .05
103 Jay Bell .05
104 Sid Bream .05
105 Checklist 1-105 (Frank Thomas) .35
106 Mike Morgan .05
107 Bill Doran .05
108 Lance Blankenship .05
109 Mark Lemke .05
110 Brian Harper .05
111 Brady Anderson .05
112 Bip Roberts .05
113 Mitch Williams .05
114 Craig Biggio .10
115 Eddie Murray .40
116 Matt Nokes .05
117 Lance Parrish .05
118 Bill Swift .05
119 Jeff Innis .05
120 Mike LaValliere .05
121 Hal Morris .05
122 Walt Weiss .05
123 Ivan Rodriguez .60
124 Andy Van Slyke .05
125 Roberto Alomar .40
126 Robby Thompson .05
127 Sammy Sosa 1.00
128 Mark Langston .05
129 Jerry Browne .05
130 Chuck McElroy .05
131 Frank Viola .05
132 Leo Gomez .05
133 Ramon Martinez .05
134 Don Mattingly 1.00
135 Roger Clemens .75
136 Rickey Henderson .60
137 Darren Daulton .05
138 Ken Hill .05
139 Ozzie Guillen .05
140 Jerald Clark .05
141 Dave Fleming .05
142 Delino DeShields .05
143 Matt Williams .15
144 Larry Walker .25
145 Ruben Sierra .05
146 Ozzie Smith .75
147 Chris Sabo .05
148 *Carlos Hernandez* .05
149 Pat Borders .05
150 Orlando Merced .05
151 Royce Clayton .05
152 Kurt Stillwell .05
153 Dave Hollins .05
154 Mike Greenwell .05
155 Nolan Ryan 1.50
156 Felix Jose .05
157 Junior Felix .05
158 Derek Bell .05
159 Steve Buechele .05
160 John Burkett .05
161 *Pat Howell* .05
162 Milt Cuyler .05
163 Terry Pendleton .05
164 Jack Morris .05
165 Tony Gwynn .75
166 Deion Sanders .10
167 Mike Devereaux .05
168 Ron Darling .05
169 Orel Hershiser .05
170 Mike Jackson .05
171 Doug Jones .05
172 *Dan Walters* .05
173 Darren Lewis .05
174 Carlos Baerga .05
175 Ryne Sandberg .65
176 Gregg Jefferies .05
177 John Jaha .05
178 Luis Polonia .05
179 Kirt Manwaring .05
180 Mike Magnante .05
181 Billy Ripken .05
182 Mike Moore .05
183 Eric Anthony .05
184 Lenny Harris .05
185 Tony Pena .05
186 Mike Felder .05
187 Greg Olson .05
188 Rene Gonzales .05
189 Mike Bordick .05
190 Mel Rojas .05
191 Todd Frohwirth .05
192 Darryl Hamilton .05
193 Mike Fetters .05
194 Omar Olivares .05
195 Tony Phillips .05
196 Paul Sorrento .05
197 Trevor Wilson .05
198 Kevin Gross .05
199 Ron Karkovice .05
200 Brook Jacoby .05
201 Mariano Duncan .05
202 Dennis Cook .05
203 Daryl Boston .05
204 Mike Perez .05
205 Manuel Lee .05
206 Steve Olin .05
207 Charlie Hough .05
208 Scott Scudder .05
209 Charlie O'Brien .05
210 Checklist 106-210 (Barry Bonds) .50
211 Jose Vizcaino .05
212 Scott Leius .05
213 Kevin Mitchell .05
214 Brian Barnes .05
215 Pat Kelly .05
216 Chris Hammond .05
217 Rob Deer .05
218 Cory Snyder .05
219 Gary Carter .20
220 Danny Darwin .05
221 Tom Gordon .05
222 Gary Sheffield .20
223 Joe Carter .05
224 Jay Buhner .05
225 Jose Offerman .05
226 Jose Rijo .05
227 Mark Whiten .05
228 Randy Milligan .05
229 Bud Black .05
230 Gary DiSarcina .05
231 Steve Finley .05
232 Dennis Martinez .05
233 Mike Mussina .35
234 Joe Oliver .05
235 Chad Curtis .05
236 Shane Mack .05
237 Jaime Navarro .05
238 Brian McRae .05
239 Chili Davis .05
240 Jeff King .05
241 Dean Palmer .05
242 Danny Tartabull .05
243 Charles Nagy .05
244 Ray Lankford .05
245 Barry Larkin .10
246 Steve Avery .05
247 John Kruk .05
248 Derrick May .05
249 Stan Javier .05
250 Roger McDowell .05
251 Dan Gladden .05
252 Wally Joyner .05
253 Pat Listach .05
254 Chuck Knoblauch .05
255 Sandy Alomar Jr. .05
256 Jeff Bagwell .65
257 Andy Stankiewicz .05
258 Darrin Jackson .05
259 Brett Butler .05
260 Joe Orsulak .05
261 Andy Benes .05
262 Kenny Lofton .05
263 Robin Ventura .05
264 Ron Gant .05
265 Ellis Burks .05
266 Juan Guzman .05
267 Wes Chamberlain .05
268 John Smiley .05
269 Franklin Stubbs .05
270 Tom Browning .05
271 Dennis Eckersley .05
272 Carlton Fisk .50
273 Lou Whitaker .05
274 Phil Plantier .05
275 Bobby Bonilla .05
276 Ben McDonald .05
277 Bob Zupcic .05
278 Terry Steinbach .05
279 Terry Mulholland .05
280 Lance Johnson .05
281 Willie McGee .05
282 Bret Saberhagen .10
283 Randy Myers .05
284 Randy Tomlin .05
285 Mickey Morandini .05
286 Brian Williams .05
287 Tino Martinez .05
288 Jose Melendez .05
289 Jeff Huson .05
290 Joe Grahe .05
291 Mel Hall .05
292 Otis Nixon .05
293 Todd Hundley .05
294 Casey Candaele .05
295 Kevin Seitzer .05
296 Eddie Taubensee .05
297 Moises Alou .15
298 Scott Radinsky .05
299 Thomas Howard .05
300 Kyle Abbott .05
301 Omar Vizquel .05
302 Keith Miller .05
303 Rick Aguilera .05
304 Bruce Hurst .05
305 Ken Caminiti .05
306 Mike Pagiarulo .05
307 Frank Seminara .05
308 Andre Dawson .20
309 Jose Lind .05
310 Joe Boever .05
311 Jeff Parrett .05
312 Alan Mills .05
313 Kevin Tapani .05
314 Darryl Kile .05
315 Checklist 211-315 (Will Clark) .05
316 Mike Sharperson .05
317 John Orton .05
318 Bob Tewksbury .05
319 Xavier Hernandez .05
320 Paul Assenmacher .05
321 John Franco .05
322 Mike Timlin .05
323 Jose Guzman .05
324 Pedro Martinez .60
325 Bill Spiers .05
326 Melido Perez .05
327 Mike Macfarlane .05
328 Ricky Bones .05
329 Scott Bankhead .05
330 Rich Rodriguez .05
331 Geronimo Pena .05
332 Bernie Williams .30
333 Paul Molitor .50
334 Roger Mason .05
335 David Cone .05
336 Randy Johnson .50
337 Pat Mahomes .05
338 Erik Hanson .05
339 Duane Ward .05
340 Al Martin .05
341 Pedro Munoz .05
342 Greg Colbrunn .05

343 Julio Valera .05
344 John Olerud .05
345 George Bell .05
346 Devon White .05
347 Donovan Osborne .05
348 Mark Gardner .05
349 Zane Smith .05
350 Wilson Alvarez .05
351 *Kevin Koslofski* .05
352 Roberto Hernandez .05
353 Glenn Davis .05
354 Reggie Sanders .05
355 Ken Griffey, Jr. 1.25
355a Ken Griffey Jr. (promo, 1992-dated hologram on back) 3.00
355b Ken Griffey, Jr. (8-1/2" x 11" limited edition of 1,000) 15.00
356 Marquis Grissom .05
357 Jack McDowell .05
358 Jimmy Key .05
359 Stan Belinda .05
360 Gerald Williams .05
361 Sid Fernandez .05
362 Alex Fernandez .05
363 John Smoltz .10
364 Travis Fryman .05
365 Jose Canseco .50
366 Dave Justice .20
367 *Pedro Astacio* .15
368 Tim Belcher .05
369 Steve Sax .05
370 Gary Gaetti .05
371 Jeff Frye .05
372 Bob Wickman .05
373 *Ryan Thompson* .10
374 *David Hulse* .05
375 Cal Eldred .05
376 Ryan Klesko .05
377 *Damion Easley* .10
378 *John Kiely* .05
379 *Jim Bullinger* .05
380 Brian Bohanon .05
381 Rod Brewer .05
382 *Fernando Ramsey* .05
383 Sam Militello .05
384 Arthur Rhodes .05
385 Eric Karros .05
386 Rico Brogna .05
387 *John Valentin* .25
388 *Kerry Woodson* .05
389 *Ben Rivera* .05
390 *Matt Whiteside* .05
391 Henry Rodriguez .05
392 John Wetteland .05
393 Kent Mercker .05
394 Bernard Gilkey .05
395 Doug Henry .05
396 Mo Vaughn .40
397 Scott Erickson .05
398 Bill Gullickson .05
399 Mark Guthrie .05
400 Dave Martinez .05
401 *Jeff Kent* .50
402 Chris Hoiles .05
403 Mike Henneman .05
404 Chris Nabholz .05
405 Tom Pagnozzi .05
406 Kelly Gruber .05
407 Bob Welch .05
408 Frank Castillo .05
409 John Dopson .05
410 Steve Farr .05
411 Henry Cotto .05
412 Bob Patterson .05
413 Todd Stottlemyre .05
414 Greg A. Harris .05
415 Denny Neagle .05
416 Bill Wegman .05
417 Willie Wilson .05
418 Terry Leach .05
419 Willie Randolph .05
420 Checklist 316-420 (Mark McGwire) .75
421 Calvin Murray (Top Prospects Checklist) .05
422 *Pete Janicki* (Top Prospect) .05
423 Todd Jones (Top Prospect) .05
424 Mike Neill (Top Prospect) .05
425 Carlos Delgado (Top Prospect) .40
426 Jose Oliva (Top Prospect) .05
427 Tyrone Hill (Top Prospect) .05
428 Dmitri Young (Top Prospect) .05
429 *Derek Wallace* (Top Prospect) .05
430 *Michael Moore* (Top Prospect) .05
431 Cliff Floyd (Top Prospect) .05
432 Calvin Murray (Top Prospect) .05
433 Manny Ramirez (Top Prospect) .75
434 Marc Newfield (TopProspect) .05
435 Charles Johnson (Top Prospect) .10
436 Butch Huskey (Top Prospect) .05
437 Brad Pennington (Top Prospect) .05
438 *Ray McDavid* (Top Prospect) .05
439 Chad McConnell (Top Prospect) .05
440 *Midre Cummings* (Top Prospect) .05
441 Benji Gil (Top Prospect) .05
442 Frank Rodriguez (Top Prospect) .05
443 *Chad Mottola* (Top Prospect) .05
444 *John Burke* (Top Prospect) .05
445 Michael Tucker (Top Prospect) .05
446 Rick Greene (Top Prospect) .05
447 Rich Becker (Top Prospect) .05
448 Mike Robertson (Top Prospect) .05
449 *Derek Jeter* (Top Prospect) 10.00
450 Checklist 451-470 Inside the Numbers (David McCarty, Ivan Rodriguez) .05
451 Jim Abbott (Inside the Numbers) .05
452 Jeff Bagwell (Inside the Numbers) .40
453 Jason Bere (Inside the Numbers) .05
454 Delino DeShields (Inside the Numbers) .05
455 Travis Fryman (Inside the Numbers) .05
456 Alex Gonzalez (Inside the Numbers) .05
457 Phil Hiatt (Inside the Numbers) .05
458 Dave Hollins (Inside the Numbers) .05
459 Chipper Jones (Inside the Numbers) .75
460 Dave Justice (Inside the Numbers) .10
461 Ray Lankford (Inside the Numbers) .05
462 David McCarty (Inside the Numbers) .05
463 Mike Mussina (Inside the Numbers) .20
464 Jose Offerman (Inside the Numbers) .05
465 Dean Palmer (Inside the Numbers) .05
466 Geronimo Pena (Inside the Numbers) .05
467 Eduardo Perez (Inside the Numbers) .05
468 Ivan Rodriguez (Inside the Numbers) .20
469 Reggie Sanders (Inside the Numbers) .05
470 Bernie Williams (Inside the Numbers) .10
471 Checklist 472-485 Team Stars (Barry Bonds, Matt Williams, Will Clark) .40
472 Strike Force (John Smoltz, Steve Avery, Greg Maddux, Tom Glavine) .10
473 Red October (Jose Rijo, Rob Dibble, Roberto Kelly, Reggie Sanders, Barry Larkin) .10
474 Four Corners (Gary Sheffield, Phil Plantier, Tony Gwynn, Fred McGriff) .20
475 Shooting Stars (Doug Drabek, Craig Biggio, Jeff Bagwell) .15
476 Giant Sticks (Will Clark, Barry Bonds, Matt Williams) .40
477 Boyhood Friends (Darryl Strawberry, Eric Davis) .05
478 Rock Solid (Dante Bichette, David Nied, Andres Galarraga) .05
479 Inaugural Catch (Dave Magadan, Orestes Destrade, Bret Barbarie, Jeff Conine) .05
480 Steel City Champions (Tim Wakefield, Andy Van Slyke, Jay Bell) .05
481 "Les Grandes Etoiles" (Marquis Grissom, Delino DeShields, Dennis Martinez, Larry Walker) .05
482 Runnin' Redbirds (Geronimo Pena, Ray Lankford, Ozzie Smith, Bernard Gilkey) .10
483 Ivy Leaguers (Ryne Sandberg, Mark Grace, Randy Myers) .15
484 Big Apple Power Switch (Eddie Murray, Bobby Bonilla, Howard Johnson) .10
485 Hammers & Nails (John Kruk, Dave Hollins, Darren Daulton, Len Dykstra) .05
486 Barry Bonds (Award Winners) .50
487 Dennis Eckersley (Award Winners) .05
488 Greg Maddux (Award Winners) .40
489 Dennis Eckersley (Award Winners) .05
490 Eric Karros (Award Winners) .05
491 Pat Listach (Award Winners) .05
492 Gary Sheffield (Award Winners) .10
493 Mark McGwire (Award Winners) .75
494 Gary Sheffield (Award Winners) .10
495 Edgar Martinez (Award Winners) .05
496 Fred McGriff (Award Winners) .05
497 Juan Gonzalez (Award Winners) .35
498 Darren Daulton (Award Winners) .05
499 Cecil Fielder (Award Winners) .05
500 Checklist 501-510 Diamond Debuts (Brent Gates) .05
501 Tavo Alvarez (Diamond Debuts) .05
502 Rod Bolton (Diamond Debuts) .05
503 *John Cummings* (Diamond Debuts) .05
504 Brent Gates (Diamond Debuts) .05
505 Tyler Green (Diamond Debuts) .05
506 *Jose Martinez* (Diamond Debuts) .05
507 Troy Percival (Diamond Debuts) .05
508 Kevin Stocker (Diamond Debuts) .05
509 *Matt Walbeck* (Diamond Debuts) .10
510 Rondell White (Diamond Debuts) .20
511 Billy Ripken .05
512 Mike Moore .05
513 Jose Lind .05
514 Chito Martinez .05
515 Jose Guzman .05
516 Kim Batiste .05
517 Jeff Tackett .05
518 Charlie Hough .05
519 Marvin Freeman .05
520 Carlos Martinez .05
521 Eric Young .05
522 Pete Incaviglia .05
523 Scott Fletcher .05
524 Orestes Destrade .05
525 Checklist 421-525 (Ken Griffey, Jr.) .40
526 Ellis Burks .05
527 Juan Samuel .05
528 Dave Magadan .05
529 Jeff Parrett .05
530 Bill Krueger .05
531 Frank Bolick .05
532 Alan Trammell .05
533 Walt Weiss .05
534 David Cone .05
535 Greg Maddux .75
536 Kevin Young .05
537 Dave Hansen .05
538 Alex Cole .05
539 Greg Hibbard .05
540 Gene Larkin .05
541 Jeff Reardon .05
542 Felix Jose .05
543 Jimmy Key .05
544 Reggie Jefferson .05
545 Gregg Jefferies .05
546 Dave Stewart .05
547 Tim Wallach .05
548 Spike Owen .05
549 Tommy Greene .05
550 Fernando Valenzuela .05
551 Rich Amaral .05
552 Bret Barberie .05
553 Edgar Martinez .05
554 Jim Abbott .05
555 Frank Thomas 1.00
556 Wade Boggs .50
557 Tom Henke .05
558 Milt Thompson .05
559 Lloyd McClendon .05
560 Vinny Castilla .05
561 Ricky Jordan .05
562 Andujar Cedeno .05
563 Greg Vaughn .05
564 Cecil Fielder .05
565 Kirby Puckett .75
566 Mark McGwire 1.50
567 Barry Bonds 1.00
568 Jody Reed .05
569 Todd Zeile .05
570 Mark Carreon .05
571 Joe Girardi .05
572 Luis Gonzalez .20
573 Mark Grace .20
574 Rafael Palmeiro .20
575 Darryl Strawberry .05
576 Will Clark .15
577 Fred McGriff .05
578 Kevin Reimer .05
579 Dave Righetti .05
580 Juan Bell .05
581 Jeff Brantley .05
582 Brian Hunter .05
583 Tim Naehring .05
584 Glenallen Hill .05
585 Cal Ripken, Jr. 1.50
586 Albert Belle .30
587 Robin Yount .50
588 Chris Bosio .05
589 Pete Smith .05
590 Chuck Carr .05
591 Jeff Blauser .05
592 Kevin McReynolds .05
593 Andres Galarraga .05
594 Kevin Maas .05
595 Eric Davis .05
596 Brian Jordan .05
597 Tim Raines .05
598 Rick Wilkins .05
599 Steve Cooke .05
600 Mike Gallego .05

601 Mike Munoz .05
602 Luis Rivera .05
603 Junior Ortiz .05
604 Brent Mayne .05
605 Luis Alicea .05
606 Damon Berryhill .05
607 Dave Henderson .05
608 Kirk McCaskill .05
609 Jeff Fassero .05
610 Mike Harkey .05
611 Francisco Cabrera .05
612 Rey Sanchez .05
613 Scott Servais .05
614 Darrin Fletcher .05
615 Felix Fermin .05
616 Kevin Seitzer .05
617 Bob Scanlan .05
618 Billy Hatcher .05
619 John Vander Wal .05
620 Joe Hesketh .05
621 Hector Villanueva .05
622 Randy Milligan .05
623 *Tony Tarasco* .05
624 Russ Swan .05
625 Willie Wilson .05
626 Frank Tanana .05
627 Pete O'Brien .05
628 Lenny Webster .05
629 Mark Clark .05
630 Checklist 526-630 (Roger Clemens) .35
631 Alex Arias .05
632 Chris Gwynn .05
633 Tom Bolton .05
634 Greg Briley .05
635 Kent Bottenfield .05
636 Kelly Downs .05
637 Manuel Lee .05
638 Al Leiter .05
639 Jeff Gardner .05
640 Mike Gardiner .05
641 Mark Gardner .05
642 Jeff Branson .05
643 Paul Wagner .05
644 Sean Berry .05
645 Phil Hiatt .05
646 Kevin Mitchell .05
647 Charlie Hayes .05
648 Jim Deshaies .05
649 Dan Pasqua .05
650 Mike Maddux .05
651 *Domingo Martinez* .05
652 *Greg McMichael* .05
653 *Eric Wedge* .05
654 Mark Whiten .05
655 Bobby Kelly .05
656 Julio Franco .05
657 Gene Harris .05
658 Pete Schourek .05
659 Mike Bielecki .05
660 Ricky Gutierrez .05
661 Chris Hammond .05
662 Tim Scott .05
663 Norm Charlton .05
664 Doug Drabek .05
665 Dwight Gooden .05
666 Jim Gott .05
667 Randy Myers .05
668 Darren Holmes .05
669 Tim Spehr .05
670 Bruce Ruffin .05
671 Bobby Thigpen .05
672 Tony Fernandez .05
673 Darrin Jackson .05
674 Gregg Olson .05
675 Rob Dibble .05
676 Howard Johnson .05
677 *Mike Lansing* .15
678 Charlie Leibrandt .05
679 Kevin Bass .05
680 Hubie Brooks .05
681 Scott Brosius .05
682 Randy Knorr .05
683 Dante Bichette .05
684 Bryan Harvey .05
685 Greg Gohr .05
686 Willie Banks .05
687 Robb Nen .05
688 Mike Scioscia .05
689 John Farrell .05
690 John Candelaria .05
691 Damon Buford .05
692 Todd Worrell .05
693 Pat Hentgen .05
694 John Smiley .05
695 Greg Swindell .05
696 Derek Bell .05
697 Terry Jorgensen .05
698 Jimmy Jones .05
699 David Wells .10
700 Dave Martinez .05
701 Steve Bedrosian .05
702 Jeff Russell .05
703 Joe Magrane .05
704 Matt Mieske .05
705 Paul Molitor .50
706 Dale Murphy .15
707 Steve Howe .05
708 Greg Gagne .05
709 Dave Eiland .05
710 David West .05
711 Luis Aquino .05
712 Joe Orsulak .05
713 Eric Plunk .05
714 Mike Felder .05
715 Joe Klink .05
716 Lonnie Smith .05
717 Monty Fariss .05
718 Craig Lefferts .05
719 John Habyan .05
720 Willie Blair .05
721 Darnell Coles .05
722 Mark Williamson .05
723 Bryn Smith .05
724 Greg W. Harris .05
725 *Graeme Lloyd* .05
726 Cris Carpenter .05
727 Chico Walker .05
728 Tracy Woodson .05
729 Jose Uribe .05
730 Stan Javier .05
731 Jay Howell .05
732 Freddie Benavides .05
733 Jeff Reboulet .05
734 Scott Sanderson .05
735 Checklist 631-735 (Ryne Sandberg) .20
736 Archi Cianfrocco .05
737 Daryl Boston .05
738 Craig Grebeck .05
739 Doug Dascenzo .05
740 Gerald Young .05
741 Candy Maldonado .05
742 Joey Cora .05
743 Don Slaught .05
744 Steve Decker .05
745 Blas Minor .05
746 Storm Davis .05
747 Carlos Quintana .05
748 Vince Coleman .05
749 Todd Burns .05
750 Steve Frey .05
751 Ivan Calderon .05
752 *Steve Reed* .05
753 Danny Jackson .05
754 Jeff Conine .05
755 Juan Gonzalez .65
756 Mike Kelly .05
757 John Doherty .05
758 Jack Armstrong .05
759 John Wehner .05
760 Scott Bankhead .05
761 Jim Tatum .05
762 *Scott Pose* .05
763 Andy Ashby .05
764 Ed Sprague .05
765 Harold Baines .05
766 Kirk Gibson .05
767 Troy Neel .05
768 Dick Schofield .05
769 Dickie Thon .05
770 Butch Henry .05
771 Junior Felix .05
772 *Ken Ryan* .05
773 Trevor Hoffman .05
774 Phil Plantier .05
775 Bo Jackson .10
776 Benito Santiago .05
777 Andre Dawson .20
778 Bryan Hickerson .05
779 Dennis Moeller .05
780 Ryan Bowen .05
781 Eric Fox .05
782 Joe Kmak .05
783 Mike Hampton .05
784 *Darrell Sherman* .05
785 J.T. Snow .10
786 Dave Winfield .50
787 Jim Austin .05
788 Craig Shipley .05
789 Greg Myers .05
790 Todd Benzinger .05
791 Cory Snyder .05
792 David Segui .05
793 Armando Reynoso .05
794 Chili Davis .05
795 Dave Nilsson .05
796 Paul O'Neill .05
797 Jerald Clark .05
798 Jose Mesa .05
799 Brian Holman .05
800 Jim Eisenreich .05
801 Mark McLemore .05
802 Luis Sojo .05
803 Harold Reynolds .05
804 Dan Plesac .05
805 Dave Stieb .05
806 Tom Brunansky .05
807 Kelly Gruber .05
808 Bob Ojeda .05
809 Dave Burba .05
810 Joe Boever .05
811 Jeremy Hernandez .05
812 Angels Checklist (Tim Salmon) .10
813 Astros Checklist (Jeff Bagwell) .35
814 Athletics Checklist (Mark McGwire) .75
815 Blue Jays Checklist (Roberto Alomar) .15
816 Braves Checklist (Steve Avery) .05
817 Brewers Checklist (Pat Listach) .05
818 Cardinals Checklist (Gregg Jefferies) .05
819 Cubs Checklist (Sammy Sosa) .50
820 Dodgers Checklist (Darryl Strawberry) .05
821 Expos Checklist (Dennis Martinez) .05
822 Giants Checklist (Robby Thompson) .05
823 Indians Checklist (Albert Belle) .10
824 Mariners Checklist (Randy Johnson) .30
825 Marlins Checklist (Nigel Wilson) .05
826 Mets Checklist (Bobby Bonilla) .05
827 Orioles Checklist (Glenn Davis) .05
828 Padres Checklist (Gary Sheffield) .10
829 Phillies Checklist (Darren Daulton) .05
830 Pirates Checklist (Jay Bell) .05
831 Rangers Checklist (Juan Gonzalez) .35
832 Red Sox Checklist (Andre Dawson) .10
833 Reds Checklist (Hal Morris) .05
834 Rockies Checklist (David Nied) .05
835 Royals Checklist (Felix Jose) .05
836 Tigers Checklist (Travis Fryman) .05
837 Twins Checklist (Shane Mack) .05
838 White Sox Checklist (Robin Ventura) .05
839 Yankees Checklist (Danny Tartabull) .05
840 Checklist 736-840 (Roberto Alomar) .15
SP5 3,000 Hits (Robin Yount, George Brett) 1.00
SP6 Nolan Ryan 1.50

1993 Upper Deck Clutch Performers

Reggie Jackson has selected the players who perform the best under pressure for this 20-card insert set. Cards were available only in Series II retail packs and use the prefix R for numbering. Fronts have a black bottom panel with "Clutch Performers" printed in dark gray. Jackson's facsimile autograph is overprinted in gold foil. On back, under a second player photo, is Jackson's picture and his assessment of the player. There are a few lines of stats to support the player's selection to this exclusive company.

		MT
Complete Set (20):		7.50
Common Player:		.15
1	Roberto Alomar	.60
2	Wade Boggs	.65
3	Barry Bonds	1.50
4	Jose Canseco	.65
5	Joe Carter	.15
6	Will Clark	.45
7	Roger Clemens	1.00
8	Dennis Eckersley	.15
9	Cecil Fielder	.15
10	Juan Gonzalez	.75
11	Ken Griffey, Jr.	2.00
12	Rickey Henderson	.60
13	Barry Larkin	.25
14	Don Mattingly	1.50
15	Fred McGriff	.15
16	Terry Pendleton	.15
17	Kirby Puckett	1.00
18	Ryne Sandberg	.75
19	John Smoltz	.25
20	Frank Thomas	1.50

1993 Upper Deck Highlights

These 20 insert cards commemorate highlights from the 1992 season. Cards, which were randomly inserted in Series II packs, have a '92 Season Highlights logo on the bottom, with the player's name inside a banner trailing from the logo. The date of the significant event is under the player's name. Card backs have the logo at the top and are numbered with an HI prefix. A headline describes what highlight occurred, while the text describes the event.

		MT
Complete Set (20):		35.00
Common Player:		.50
1	Roberto Alomar	1.00
2	Steve Avery	.50
3	Harold Baines	.50
4	Damon Berryhill	.50
5	Barry Bonds	6.00
6	Bret Boone	.65
7	George Brett	4.00
8	Francisco Cabrera	.50
9	Ken Griffey, Jr.	7.50
10	Rickey Henderson	2.00
11	Kenny Lofton	.50
12	Mickey Morandini	.50
13	Eddie Murray	1.50
14	David Nied	.50
15	Jeff Reardon	.50
16	Bip Roberts	.50
17	Nolan Ryan	10.00
18	Ed Sprague	.50
19	Dave Winfield	2.50
20	Robin Yount	2.50

1993 Upper Deck Home Run Heroes

This 28-card insert set features the top home run hitters from each team for 1992. Cards, inserted in Series I jumbo packs, are numbered with an HR prefix. The card fronts have "Home Run Heroes" printed vertically at the left edge and an embossed bat with the player's name and Upper Deck trademark at bottom. Backs have a purple or pink posterized photo and a few words about the player.

		MT
Complete Set (28):		16.00
Common Player:		.25
1	Juan Gonzalez	1.50
2	Mark McGwire	3.50
3	Cecil Fielder	.25
4	Fred McGriff	.25
5	Albert Belle	.65
6	Barry Bonds	2.50
7	Joe Carter	.25
8	Darren Daulton	.25
9	Ken Griffey, Jr.	3.00
10	Dave Hollins	.25
11	Ryne Sandberg	1.50
12	George Bell	.25
13	Danny Tartabull	.25
14	Mike Devereaux	.25
15	Greg Vaughn	.25
16	Larry Walker	.75
17	Dave Justice	.75
18	Terry Pendleton	.25
19	Eric Karros	.25
20	Ray Lankford	.25
21	Matt Williams	.60
22	Eric Anthony	.25
23	Bobby Bonilla	.25
24	Kirby Puckett	2.00
25	Mike Macfarlane	.25
26	Tom Brunansky	.25
27	Paul O'Neill	.25
28	Gary Gaetti	.25

1993 Upper Deck Iooss Collection

Sports photographer Walter Iooss Jr. has captured 26 current players in this insert set featuring their candid portraits. Cards have full-bleed photos and gold foil stamping. Backs have biographical sketches and are numbered using a WI prefix. They are available in Series I retail packs.

		MT
Complete Set (27):		24.00
Common Player:		.50
Header Card:		.50
1	Tim Salmon	.75
2	Jeff Bagwell	1.50
3	Mark McGwire	4.00
4	Roberto Alomar	1.00
5	Steve Avery	.50
6	Paul Molitor	1.25
7	Ozzie Smith	2.00
8	Mark Grace	.75
9	Eric Karros	.50
10	Delino DeShields	.50
11	Will Clark	.75
12	Albert Belle	.75
13	Ken Griffey, Jr.	3.00
14	Howard Johnson	.50
15	Cal Ripken, Jr.	4.00
16	Fred McGriff	.50
17	Darren Daulton	.50
18	Andy Van Slyke	.50
19	Nolan Ryan	4.00
20	Wade Boggs	1.50
21	Barry Larkin	.50
22	George Brett	2.00
23	Cecil Fielder	.50
24	Kirby Puckett	2.00
25	Frank Thomas	2.50
26	Don Mattingly	2.50

1993 Upper Deck Iooss Collection Supers

Upper Deck issued a series of 27 individually numbered oversized cards identical to the Iooss Collection inserts from the regular 1993 Upper Deck set. The cards are 3-1/2" x 5" and each is numbered on back to a limit of 10,000. The cards were available in retail outlets such as Wal-Mart, packaged in blister packs with two foil packs of 1993 Upper Deck cards for around $5. Authetically autographed and numbered (on card fronts) of some players' cards were sold by Upper Deck Authenticated.

		MT
Complete Set (27):		45.00
Common Player:		1.50
Header Card:		1.00
1	Tim Salmon	1.75
2	Jeff Bagwell	2.00
3	Mark McGwire	5.00
4	Roberto Alomar	1.75
5	Steve Avery	1.50
6	Paul Molitor	1.75
7	Ozzie Smith	2.50
8	Mark Grace	1.75
9	Eric Karros	1.50
10	Delino DeShields	1.50
11	Will Clark	1.75
12	Albert Belle	1.50
13	Ken Griffey, Jr.	4.00
14	Howard Johnson	1.50
15	Cal Ripken, Jr.	5.00
16	Fred McGriff	1.50
17	Darren Daulton	1.50
18	Andy Van Slyke	1.50
19	Nolan Ryan	5.00
20	Wade Boggs	2.00
21	Barry Larkin	1.50
22	George Brett	2.50
23	Cecil Fielder	1.50
24	Kirby Puckett	2.50
25	Frank Thomas	3.00
26	Don Mattingly	3.00

1994 Upper Deck Next Generation

Next Generation linked 20 of the top current stars with all-time greats, using the HoloView card printing technology. Next Generation trade cards could be redeemed for a complete set matching the cards found in retail packs. This insert set was inserted at a rate of one per 20 packs, while the Trade Card was inserted one per case.

		MT
Complete Set (18):		45.00
Common Player:		.60
1	Roberto Alomar	2.00
2	Carlos Delgado	1.00
3	Cliff Floyd	.60
4	Alex Gonzalez	.60
5	Juan Gonzalez	3.00
6	Ken Griffey, Jr.	6.00
7	Jeffrey Hammonds	.60
8	Michael Jordan	12.50
9	Dave Justice	1.00
10	Ryan Klesko	.60
11	Javier Lopez	.60
12	Raul Mondesi	.75
13	Mike Piazza	5.00
14	Kirby Puckett	4.00
15	Manny Ramirez	3.00
16	Alex Rodriguez	12.50
17	Tim Salmon	.75
18	Gary Sheffield	1.50

1993 Upper Deck On Deck

These UV-coated cards feature 25 of the game's top players. Each card has a full-bleed photo on the front and questions and answers on the back. Available only in Series II jumbo packs, the cards have a D prefix for numbering.

		MT
Complete Set (25):		25.00
Common Player:		.25
1	Jim Abbott	.25
2	Roberto Alomar	1.25
3	Carlos Baerga	.25
4	Albert Belle	.75
5	Wade Boggs	1.25
6	George Brett	1.75
7	Jose Canseco	1.25
8	Will Clark	.50
9	Roger Clemens	1.75
10	Dennis Eckersley	.25
11	Cecil Fielder	.25
12	Juan Gonzalez	1.50
13	Ken Griffey, Jr.	3.50
14	Tony Gwynn	1.75
15	Bo Jackson	.35
16	Chipper Jones	3.00
17	Eric Karros	.25
18	Mark McGwire	4.00
19	Kirby Puckett	1.75
20	Nolan Ryan	4.00
21	Tim Salmon	.50
22	Ryne Sandberg	1.50
23	Darryl Strawberry	.25
24	Frank Thomas	2.00
25	Andy Van Slyke	.25

1993 Upper Deck Then And Now

This 18-card lithogram set features both Hall of Famers and current players. The cards feature a combination of four-color player photos and a holographic background. They were random inserts in both Series I and Series II packs. Numbering includes the prefix TN. A limited edition of 2,500 supersize 5" by 7" Mickey Mantle Then And Now cards was created for sale through Upper Deck Authenticated.

		MT
Complete Set (18):		27.50
Common Player:		.50
1	Wade Boggs	1.00
2	George Brett	2.00
3	Rickey Henderson	.75
4	Cal Ripken, Jr.	4.00
5	Nolan Ryan	4.00
6	Ryne Sandberg	1.50
7	Ozzie Smith	2.00
8	Darryl Strawberry	.50
9	Dave Winfield	1.00
10	Dennis Eckersley	.50
11	Tony Gwynn	2.00
12	Howard Johnson	.50
13	Don Mattingly	2.50
14	Eddie Murray	.75
15	Robin Yount	1.00
16	Reggie Jackson	.75
17	Mickey Mantle	5.00
17a	Mickey Mantle (5" x 7")	20.00
18	Willie Mays	3.00

1993 Upper Deck Triple Crown Contenders

These insert cards were available in 1993 Upper Deck Series I foil packs sold by hobby dealers. The set features 10 players who are candidates to win baseball's Triple Crown. Card fronts have a crown and the player's name at the bottom. Backs put that material at the top and explain why the player might lead the league in home runs, batting average and runs batted in.

		MT
Complete Set (10):		10.00
Common Player:		.50
1	Barry Bonds	1.50
2	Jose Canseco	1.00
3	Will Clark	.75
4	Ken Griffey, Jr.	2.00
5	Fred McGriff	.50
6	Kirby Puckett	1.25
7	Cal Ripken, Jr.	2.50
8	Gary Sheffield	.50
9	Frank Thomas	1.50
10	Larry Walker	.75

1993 Upper Deck Willie Mays Heroes

This 10-card insert set includes eight individually-titled cards, an illustrated checklist and one header card. The set is a continuation of Upper Deck's previous Heroes efforts, honoring greats such as Hank Aaron, Nolan Ryan and Reggie Jackson, and is numbered 46-54. Cards were randomly inserted into Series 1 foil packs.

		MT
Complete Set (10):		4.00
Common Card:		.50
Header Card:		1.50
46	1951 Rookie-of-the-Year	.50
47	1954 The Catch	.50
48	1956-57 30-30 Club	.50
49	1961 Four-Homer Game	.50
50	1965 Most Valuable Player	.50
51	1969 600-Home Run Club	.50
52	1972 New York Homecoming	.50
53	1979 Hall of Fame	.50
54	Checklist - Heroes 46-54	.50

1993 Upper Deck 5th Anniversary

This 15-card insert set replicates 15 of Upper Deck's most popular cards from its first five years. Foil stamping and a fifth-anniversary logo appear on the cards, which are otherwise reproductions of the originals. The prefix A appears before each card number. The cards were available in Series II hobby packs only.

		MT
Complete Set (15):		16.00
Common Player:		.50
1	Ken Griffey, Jr.	3.50
2	Gary Sheffield	.75
3	Roberto Alomar	1.00
4	Jim Abbott	.50
5	Nolan Ryan	4.00
6	Juan Gonzalez	1.50
7	Dave Justice	.75
8	Carlos Baerga	.50
9	Reggie Jackson	.75
10	Eric Karros	.50
11	Chipper Jones	2.50
12	Ivan Rodriguez	1.00
13	Pat Listach	.50
14	Frank Thomas	2.00
15	Tim Salmon	.75

1994 Upper Deck

Upper Deck's 1994 offering was a typical presentation for the company, combining high-quality regular-issue cards with innovative subsets and high-tech chase cards. Series 1, besides the standard player cards, features subsets including Star Rookies with metallic borders, "Fantasy Team" stars who excelled in Rotisserie League stats, Home Field Advantage cards showcasing National League stadiums and hometeam stars, and, stars under the age of 25 in a subset titled, "The Future is Now." Regular issue cards feature a color photo on front and a second, black-and-white version of the same photo at left in a vertically stretched format. The player's name, team and Upper Deck logo appear on front in copper foil. Backs have a color photo, recent and career major league stats and an infield-shaped hologram. Series 2 offered in addition to regular cards, subsets of American League Home Field Advantage cards, a group of "Classic Alumni" minor league players, a selection of "Diamond Debuts" cards and a group of "Top Prospects." Series 1 retail packaging contained a special Mickey Mantle/Ken Griffey, Jr. card which could be found bearing either one or both of the players' autographs in an edition of 1,000 each. Series 2 retail packs offered a chance to find an autographed version of Alex Rodriguez' Classic Alumni card.

		MT
Complete Set (550):		30.00
Complete Series 1 (280):		20.00
Complete Series 2 (270):		10.00
Common Player:		.05
Series 1 Hobby Pack (12):		1.50
Series 1 Hobby Box (36):		40.00
Series 1 Retail Pack (12):		2.50
Series 1 Retail Box (36):		60.00
Series 2 Hobby Pack (12):		1.00
Series 2 Hobby Box (36):		20.00
Series 2 Retail Pack (12):		1.50
Series 2 Retail Box (36):		40.00
1	*Brian Anderson* (Star Rookie)	.25
2	Shane Andrews (Star Rookie)	.10
3	James Baldwin (Star Rookie)	.05
4	Rich Becker (Star Rookie)	.05
5	Greg Blosser (Star Rookie)	.05
6	*Ricky Bottalico* (Star Rookie)	.10
7	Midre Cummings (Star Rookie)	.05
8	Carlos Delgado (Star Rookie)	.50
9	*Steve Dreyer* (Star Rookie)	.05
10	*Joey Eischen* (Star Rookie)	.05
11	Carl Everett (Star Rookie)	.15
12	Cliff Floyd (Star Rookie)	.05
13	Alex Gonzalez (Star Rookie)	.10
14	Jeff Granger (Star Rookie)	.05
15	Shawn Green (Star Rookie)	.35
16	Brian Hunter (Star Rookie)	.05
17	Butch Huskey (Star Rookie)	.05
18	Mark Hutton (Star Rookie)	.05
19	*Michael Jordan* (Star Rookie)	10.00
20	Steve Karsay (Star Rookie)	.05
21	Jeff McNeely (Star Rookie)	.05
22	Marc Newfield (Star Rookie)	.05
23	Manny Ramirez (Star Rookie)	.75
24	*Alex Rodriguez* (Star Rookie)	12.00
25	Scott Ruffcorn (Star Rookie)	.05
26	Paul Spoljaric (Star Rookie)	.05
27	*Salomon Torres* (Star Rookie)	.05
28	Steve Trachsel (Star Rookie)	.05
29	*Chris Turner* (Star Rookie)	.05
30	Gabe White (Star Rookie)	.05
31	Randy Johnson (Fantasy Team)	.40
32	John Wetteland (Fantasy Team)	.05
33	Mike Piazza (Fantasy Team)	.75
34	Rafael Palmeiro	

No.	Card	Value
	(Fantasy Team)	.15
35	Roberto Alomar (Fantasy Team)	.30
36	Matt Williams (Fantasy Team)	.10
37	Travis Fryman (Fantasy Team)	.05
38	Barry Bonds (Fantasy Team)	.75
39	Marquis Grissom (Fantasy Team)	.05
40	Albert Belle (Fantasy Team)	.15
41	Steve Avery (Future/Now)	.05
42	Jason Bere (Future/Now)	.05
43	Alex Fernandez (Future/Now)	.15
44	Mike Mussina (Future/Now)	.30
45	Aaron Sele (Future/Now)	.05
46	Rod Beck (Future/Now)	.05
47	Mike Piazza (Future/Now)	.75
48	John Olerud (Future/Now)	.05
49	Carlos Baerga (Future/Now)	.05
50	Gary Sheffield (Future/Now)	.15
51	Travis Fryman (Future/Now)	.05
52	Juan Gonzalez (Future/Now)	.40
53	Ken Griffey, Jr. (Future/Now)	.90
54	Tim Salmon (Future/Now)	.15
55	Frank Thomas (Future/Now)	.75
56	Tony Phillips	.05
57	Julio Franco	.05
58	Kevin Mitchell	.05
59	Raul Mondesi	.25
60	Rickey Henderson	.60
61	Jay Buhner	.05
62	Bill Swift	.05
63	Brady Anderson	.05
64	Ryan Klesko	.05
65	Darren Daulton	.05
66	Damion Easley	.05
67	Mark McGwire	2.00
68	John Roper	.05
69	Dave Telgheder	.05
70	Dave Nied	.05
71	Mo Vaughn	.50
72	Tyler Green	.05
73	Dave Magadan	.05
74	Chili Davis	.05
75	Archi Cianfrocco	.05
76	Joe Girardi	.05
77	Chris Hoiles	.05
78	Ryan Bowen	.05
79	Greg Gagne	.05
80	Aaron Sele	.05
81	Dave Winfield	.75
82	Chad Curtis	.05
83	Andy Van Slyke	.05
84	Kevin Stocker	.05
85	Deion Sanders	.10
86	Bernie Williams	.30
87	John Smoltz	.10
88	*Ruben Santana*	.05
89	Dave Stewart	.05
90	Don Mattingly	1.25
91	Joe Carter	.05
92	Ryne Sandberg	.75
93	Chris Gomez	.05
94	Tino Martinez	.05
95	Terry Pendleton	.05
96	Andre Dawson	.20
97	Wil Cordero	.05
98	Kent Hrbek	.05
99	John Olerud	.05
100	Kirt Manwaring	.05
101	Tim Bogar	.05
102	Mike Mussina	.60
103	Nigel Wilson	.05
104	Ricky Gutierrez	.05
105	Roberto Mejia	.05
106	Tom Pagnozzi	.05
107	Mike Macfarlane	.05
108	Jose Bautista	.05
109	Luis Ortiz	.05
110	Brent Gates	.05
111	Tim Salmon	.25
112	Wade Boggs	.50
113	*Tripp Cromer*	.05
114	Denny Hocking	.05
115	Carlos Baerga	.05
116	*J.R. Phillips*	.05
117	Bo Jackson	.10
118	Lance Johnson	.05
119	Bobby Jones	.05
120	Bobby Witt	.05
121	Ron Karkovice	.05
122	Jose Vizcaino	.05
123	Danny Darwin	.05
124	Eduardo Perez	.05
125	Brian Looney	.05
126	Pat Hentgen	.05
127	Frank Viola	.05
128	Darren Holmes	.05
129	Wally Whitehurst	.05
130	Matt Walbeck	.05
131	Albert Belle	.30
132	Steve Cooke	.05
133	Kevin Appier	.05
134	Joe Oliver	.05
135	Benji Gil	.05
136	Steve Buechele	.05
137	Devon White	.05
138	Sterling Hitchcock	.05
139	*Phil Leftwich*	.05
140	Jose Canseco	.50
141	Rick Aguilera	.05
142	Rod Beck	.05
143	Jose Rijo	.05
144	Tom Glavine	.10
145	Phil Plantier	.05
146	Jason Bere	.05
147	Jamie Moyer	.05
148	Wes Chamberlain	.05
149	Glenallen Hill	.05
150	Mark Whiten	.05
151	Bret Barberie	.05
152	Chuck Knoblauch	.05
153	Trevor Hoffman	.05
154	Rick Wilkins	.05
155	Juan Gonzalez	.75
156	Ozzie Guillen	.05
157	Jim Eisenreich	.05
158	Pedro Astacio	.05
159	Joe Magrane	.05
160	Ryan Thompson	.05
161	Jose Lind	.05
162	Jeff Conine	.05
163	Todd Benzinger	.05
164	Roger Salkeld	.05
165	Gary DiSarcina	.05
166	Kevin Gross	.05
167	Charlie Hayes	.05
168	Tim Costo	.05
169	Wally Joyner	.05
170	Johnny Ruffin	.05
171	*Kirk Rueter*	.10
172	Len Dykstra	.05
173	Ken Hill	.05
174	Mike Bordick	.05
175	Billy Hall	.05
176	Rob Butler	.05
177	Jay Bell	.05
178	Jeff Kent	.05
179	David Wells	.10
180	Dean Palmer	.05
181	Mariano Duncan	.05
182	Orlando Merced	.05
183	Brett Butler	.05
184	Milt Thompson	.05
185	Chipper Jones	1.50
186	Paul O'Neill	.05
187	Mike Greenwell	.05
188	Harold Baines	.05
189	Todd Stottlemyre	.05
190	Jeromy Burnitz	.05
191	Rene Arocha	.05
192	Jeff Fassero	.05
193	Robby Thompson	.05
194	Greg W. Harris	.05
195	Todd Van Poppel	.05
196	Jose Guzman	.05
197	Shane Mack	.05
198	Carlos Garcia	.05
199	Kevin Roberson	.05
200	David McCarty	.05
201	Alan Trammell	.05
202	Chuck Carr	.05
203	Tommy Greene	.05
204	Wilson Alvarez	.05
205	Dwight Gooden	.05
206	Tony Tarasco	.05
207	Darren Lewis	.05
208	Eric Karros	.05
209	Chris Hammond	.05
210	Jeffrey Hammonds	.05
211	Rich Amaral	.05
212	Danny Tartabull	.05
213	Jeff Russell	.05
214	Dave Staton	.05
215	Kenny Lofton	.05
216	Manuel Lee	.05
217	Brian Koelling	.05
218	Scott Lydy	.05
219	Tony Gwynn	1.00
220	Cecil Fielder	.05
221	Royce Clayton	.05
222	Reggie Sanders	.05
223	Brian Jordan	.05
224	Ken Griffey, Jr.	1.75
224a	Ken Griffey, Jr. (promo card)	3.00
225	Fred McGriff	.05
226	Felix Jose	.05
227	Brad Pennington	.05
228	Chris Bosio	.05
229	Mike Stanley	.05
230	Willie Greene	.05
231	Alex Fernandez	.05
232	Brad Ausmus	.05
233	Darrell Whitmore	.05
234	Marcus Moore	.05
235	Allen Watson	.05
236	Jose Offerman	.05
237	Rondell White	.10
238	Jeff King	.05
239	Luis Alicea	.05
240	Dan Wilson	.05
241	Ed Sprague	.05
242	Todd Hundley	.05
243	Al Martin	.05
244	Mike Lansing	.05
245	Ivan Rodriguez	.75
246	Dave Fleming	.05
247	John Doherty	.05
248	Mark McLemore	.05
249	Bob Hamelin	.05
250	*Curtis Pride*	.05
251	Zane Smith	.05
252	Eric Young	.05
253	Brian McRae	.05
254	Tim Raines	.05
255	Javier Lopez	.05
256	Melvin Nieves	.05
257	Randy Myers	.05
258	Willie McGee	.05
259	Jimmy Key	.05
260	Tom Candiotti	.05
261	Eric Davis	.05
262	Craig Paquette	.05
263	Robin Ventura	.05
264	Pat Kelly	.05
265	Gregg Jefferies	.05
266	Cory Snyder	.05
267	Dave Justice (Home Field Advantage)	.10
268	Sammy Sosa (Home Field Advantage)	.75
269	Barry Larkin (Home Field Advantage)	.05
270	Andres Galarraga (Home Field Advantage)	.05
271	Gary Sheffield (Home Field Advantage)	.15
272	Jeff Bagwell (Home Field Advantage)	.40
273	Mike Piazza (Home Field Advantage)	.75
274	Larry Walker (Home Field Advantage)	.20
275	Bobby Bonilla (Home Field Advantage)	.05
276	John Kruk (Home Field Advantage)	.05
277	Jay Bell (Home Field Advantage)	.05
278	Ozzie Smith (Home Field Advantage)	.50
279	Tony Gwynn (Home Field Advantage)	.50
280	Barry Bonds (Home Field Advantage)	.75
281	Cal Ripken, Jr. (Home Field Advantage)	1.00
282	Mo Vaughn (Home Field Advantage)	.25
283	Tim Salmon (Home Field Advantage)	.15
284	Frank Thomas (Home Field Advantage)	.75
285	Albert Belle (Home Field Advantage)	.15
286	Cecil Fielder (Home Field Advantage)	.05
287	Wally Joyner (Home Field Advantage)	.05
288	Greg Vaughn (Home Field Advantage)	.05
289	Kirby Puckett (Home Field Advantage)	.50
290	Don Mattingly (Home Field Advantage)	.75
291	Terry Steinbach (Home Field Advantage)	.05
292	Ken Griffey, Jr. (Home Field Advantage)	.90
293	Juan Gonzalez (Home Field Advantage)	.40
294	Paul Molitor (Home Field Advantage)	.25
295	Tavo Alvarez (Classic Alumni)	.05
296	Matt Brunson (Classic Alumni)	.05
297	Shawn Green (Classic Alumni)	.25
298	Alex Rodriguez (Classic Alumni)	1.50
299	Shannon Stewart (Classic Alumni)	.15
300	Frank Thomas	1.25
301	Mickey Tettleton	.05
302	Pedro Munoz	.05
303	Jose Valentin	.05
304	Orestes Destrade	.05
305	Pat Listach	.05
306	Scott Brosius	.05
307	*Kurt Miller*	.05
308	Rob Dibble	.05
309	Mike Blowers	.05
310	Jim Abbott	.05
311	Mike Jackson	.05
312	Craig Biggio	.10
313	*Kurt Abbott*	.20
314	Chuck Finley	.05
315	Andres Galarraga	.05
316	Mike Moore	.05
317	Doug Strange	.05
318	Pedro J. Martinez	.65
319	Kevin McReynolds	.05
320	Greg Maddux	1.00
321	Mike Henneman	.05
322	Scott Leius	.05
323	John Franco	.05
324	Jeff Blauser	.05
325	Kirby Puckett	1.00
326	Darryl Hamilton	.05
327	John Smiley	.05
328	Derrick May	.05
329	Jose Vizcaino	.05
330	Randy Johnson	.75
331	Jack Morris	.05
332	Graeme Lloyd	.05
333	Dave Valle	.05
334	Greg Myers	.05
335	John Wetteland	.05
336	Jim Gott	.05
337	Tim Naehring	.05
338	Mike Kelly	.05
339	Jeff Montgomery	.05
340	Rafael Palmeiro	.30
341	Eddie Murray	.45
342	Xavier Hernandez	.05
343	Bobby Munoz	.05
344	Bobby Bonilla	.05
345	Travis Fryman	.05
346	Steve Finley	.05
347	Chris Sabo	.05
348	Armando Reynoso	.05
349	Ramon Martinez	.05
350	Will Clark	.15
351	Moises Alou	.15
352	Jim Thome	.05
353	Bob Tewksbury	.05
354	Andujar Cedeno	.05
355	Orel Hershiser	.05
356	Mike Devereaux	.05
357	Mike Perez	.05
358	Dennis Martinez	.05
359	Dave Nilsson	.05
360	Ozzie Smith	1.00
361	Eric Anthony	.05

362 Scott Sanders .05
363 Paul Sorrento .05
364 Tim Belcher .05
365 Dennis Eckersley .05
366 Mel Rojas .05
367 Tom Henke .05
368 Randy Tomlin .05
369 B.J. Surhoff .05
370 Larry Walker .40
371 Joey Cora .05
372 Mike Harkey .05
373 John Valentin .05
374 Doug Jones .05
375 Dave Justice .25
376 Vince Coleman .05
377 David Hulse .05
378 Kevin Seitzer .05
379 Pete Harnisch .05
380 Ruben Sierra .05
381 Mark Lewis .05
382 Bip Roberts .05
383 Paul Wagner .05
384 Stan Javier .05
385 Barry Larkin .10
386 Mark Portugal .05
387 Roberto Kelly .05
388 Andy Benes .05
389 Felix Fermin .05
390 Marquis Grissom .05
391 Troy Neel .05
392 Chad Kreuter .05
393 Gregg Olson .05
394 Charles Nagy .05
395 Jack McDowell .05
396 Luis Gonzalez .25
397 Benito Santiago .05
398 Chris James .05
399 Terry Mulholland .05
400 Barry Bonds 1.25
401 Joe Grahe .05
402 Duane Ward .05
403 John Burkett .05
404 Scott Servais .05
405 Bryan Harvey .05
406 Bernard Gilkey .05
407 Greg McMichael .05
408 Tim Wallach .05
409 Ken Caminiti .05
410 John Kruk .05
411 Darrin Jackson .05
412 Mike Gallego .05
413 David Cone .05
414 Lou Whitaker .05
415 Sandy Alomar Jr. .05
416 Bill Wegman .05
417 Pat Borders .05
418 Roger Pavlik .05
419 Pete Smith .05
420 Steve Avery .05
421 David Segui .05
422 Rheal Cormier .05
423 Harold Reynolds .05
424 Edgar Martinez .05
425 Cal Ripken, Jr. 2.00
426 Jaime Navarro .05
427 Sean Berry .05
428 Bret Saberhagen .05
429 Bob Welch .05
430 Juan Guzman .05
431 Cal Eldred .05
432 Dave Hollins .05
433 Sid Fernandez .05
434 Willie Banks .05
435 Darryl Kile .05
436 Henry Rodriguez .05
437 Tony Fernandez .05
438 Walt Weiss .05
439 Kevin Tapani .05
440 Mark Grace .25
441 Brian Harper .05
442 Kent Mercker .05
443 Anthony Young .05
444 Todd Zeile .05
445 Greg Vaughn .05
446 Ray Lankford .05
447 David Weathers .05
448 Bret Boone .10
449 Charlie Hough .05
450 Roger Clemens 1.00
451 Mike Morgan .05
452 Doug Drabek .05
453 Danny Jackson .05
454 Dante Bichette .05
455 Roberto Alomar .65
456 Ben McDonald .05
457 Kenny Rogers .05
458 Bill Gullickson .05
459 Darrin Fletcher .05
460 Curt Schilling .15
461 Billy Hatcher .05
462 Howard Johnson .05
463 Mickey Morandini .05
464 Frank Castillo .05
465 Delino DeShields .05
466 Gary Gaetti .05
467 Steve Farr .05
468 Roberto Hernandez .05
469 Jack Armstrong .05
470 Paul Molitor .50
471 Melido Perez .05
472 Greg Hibbard .05
473 Jody Reed .05
474 Tom Gordon .05
475 Gary Sheffield .25
476 John Jaha .05
477 Shawon Dunston .05
478 Reggie Jefferson .05
479 Don Slaught .05
480 Jeff Bagwell .75
481 Tim Pugh .05
482 Kevin Young .05
483 Ellis Burks .05
484 Greg Swindell .05
485 Mark Langston .05
486 Omar Vizquel .05
487 Kevin Brown .10
488 Terry Steinbach .05
489 Mark Lemke .05
490 Matt Williams .15
491 Pete Incaviglia .05
492 Karl Rhodes .05
493 Shawn Green .50
494 Hal Morris .05
495 Derek Bell .05
496 Luis Polonia .05
497 Otis Nixon .05
498 Ron Darling .05
499 Mitch Williams .05
500 Mike Piazza 1.50
501 Pat Meares .05
502 Scott Cooper .05
503 Scott Erickson .05
504 Jeff Juden .05
505 Lee Smith .05
506 Bobby Ayala .05
507 Dave Henderson .05
508 Erik Hanson .05
509 Bob Wickman .05
510 Sammy Sosa 1.25
511 Hector Carrasco (Diamond Debuts) .05
512 Tim Davis (Diamond Debuts) .05
513 Joey Hamilton (Diamond Debuts) .05
514 Robert Eenhoorn (Diamond Debuts) .05
515 Jorge Fabregas (Diamond Debuts) .05
516 Tim Hyers (Diamond Debuts) .05
517 John Hudek (Diamond Debuts) .05
518 *James Mouton* (Diamond Debuts) .05
519 Herbert Perry (Diamond Debuts) .05
520 *Chan Ho Park* (Diamond Debuts) 1.00
521 Bill VanLandingham (Diamond Debuts) .05
522 Paul Shuey (Diamond Debuts) .05
523 *Ryan Hancock* (Top Prospects) .05
524 *Billy Wagner* (Top Prospects) .50
525 Jason Giambi (Top Prospects) .50
526 *Jose Silva* (Top Prospects) .05
527 *Terrell Wade* (Top Prospects) .05
528 Todd Dunn (Top Prospects) .05
529 *Alan Benes* (Top Prospects) .25
530 *Brooks Kieschnick* (Top Prospects) .05
531 Todd Hollandsworth (Top Prospects) .05
532 *Brad Fullmer* (Top Prospects) .75
533 *Steve Soderstrom* (Top Prospects) .05
534 Daron Kirkreit (Top Prospects) .05
535 *Arquimedez Pozo* (Top Prospects) .05
536 Charles Johnson (Top Prospects) .05
537 Preston Wilson (Top Prospects) .25
538 Alex Ochoa (Top Prospects) .05
539 *Derrek Lee* (Top Prospects) .50
540 *Wayne Gomes* (Top Prospects) .10
541 *Jermaine Allensworth* (Top Prospects) .15
542 *Mike Bel* (Top Prospects) .05
543 *Trot Nixon* (Top Prospects) 1.50
544 Pokey Reese (Top Prospects) .10
545 *Neifi Perez* (Top Prospects) .25
546 Johnny Damon (Top Prosepcts) .15
547 Matt Brunson (Top Prospects) .05
548 *LaTroy Hawkins* (Top Prospects) .10
549 *Eddie Pearson* (Top Prosepcts) .05
550 Derek Jeter (Top Prospects) 2.00

1994 Upper Deck Electric Diamond

Each of the regular-issue and subset cards from 1994 Upper Deck was also produced in a limited edition premium insert "Electric Diamond" version. Where the regular cards have the Upper Deck logo, player and team name in copper foil, the Electric Diamond version has those elements in a silver prismatic foil, along with an "Electric Diamond" identification line next to the UD logo. Backs are identical to the regular cards. (Forty-five of the first series cards can be found with player names on back in either silver or copper.) Electric Diamond cards are found, on average, about every other pack.

	MT
Complete Set (550):	75.00
Common Player:	.25
Stars:	1.5X

(See 1994 Upper Deck for checklist and base card values.)

1994 Upper Deck Alex Rodriguez Autograph

Available exclusively in Series 2 retail packaging was this special version of A-Rod's Classic Alumni card. The card is authentically signed in blue Sharpie and carries on its back an authentication hologram.

	MT
A298 Alex Rodriguez (Classic Alumni, autographed)	175.00

1994 Upper Deck Diamond Collection

The premium chase cards in 1994 Upper Deck are a series of Diamond Collection cards issued in regional subsets. Ten cards are found unique to each of three geographic areas of distribution. Western region cards carry a "W" prefix to the card number, Central cards have a "C" prefix and Eastern cards have an "E" prefix. The region is also indicated in silver-foil printing on the front of the card, with a large "W, C" or "E" in a compass design. The player's name and team are presented in a foil strip at bottom. A "Diamond Collection" logo is shown in embossed-look typography in the background. Diamond Collection cards are inserted only in hobby packs.

		MT
Complete Set (30):		75.00
Common Player:		.50
Complete Central (10):		30.00
1	Michael Jordan	15.00
2	Jeff Bagwell	4.00
3	Barry Larkin	.50
4	Kirby Puckett	5.00
5	Manny Ramirez	4.00
6	Ryne Sandberg	3.00
7	Ozzie Smith	4.00
8	Frank Thomas	5.00
9	Andy Van Slyke	.50
10	Robin Yount	3.00
Complete East (10):		17.50
1	Roberto Alomar	2.00
2	Roger Clemens	5.00
3	Len Dykstra	.50
4	Cecil Fielder	.50
5	Cliff Floyd	.50
6	Dwight Gooden	.50
7	Dave Justice	1.00
8	Don Mattingly	6.00
9	Cal Ripken, Jr.	12.00
10	Gary Sheffield	1.00
Complete West (10):		25.00
1	Barry Bonds	5.00
2	Andres Galarraga	.50
3	Juan Gonzalez	3.00
4	Ken Griffey, Jr.	6.00
5	Tony Gwynn	4.00
6	Rickey Henderson	2.50
7	Bo Jackson	1.00
8	Mark McGwire	8.00
9	Mike Piazza	6.00
10	Tim Salmon	1.00

1994 Upper Deck Mickey Mantle Heroes

Mickey Mantle Baseball Hero is a 10-card set that chronicles his career. The cards, which include an unnumbered header card, were randomly inserted into both hobby and retail packs of Series II Upper Deck Baseball. This set starts with his rookie season in 1951 and concludes with his induction into The Hall of Fame. It is numbered 64-72 and was the eighth in the continuing "Baseball Heroes" series, which began in 1990.

		MT
Complete Set (10):		60.00
Common Card:		8.00
64	1951 - The Early Years (Mickey Mantle)	3.00
65	1953 - Tape Measure Home Runs (Mickey Mantle)	3.00
66	1956 - Triple Crown Season (Mickey Mantle)	3.00
67	1957 - 2nd Consecutive MVP (Mickey Mantle)	3.00
68	1961 - Chases The Babe (Mickey Mantle)	3.00
69	1964 - Series Home Run Record (Mickey Mantle)	3.00
70	1967 - 500th Home Run (Mickey Mantle)	3.00
71	1974: Hall of Fame (Mickey Mantle)	3.00
72	(Mickey Mantle) (portrait)	3.00
----	Header card (Mickey Mantle)	3.00

1994 Upper Deck Mickey Mantle's Long Shots

Retail packaging was the exclusive venue for this insert set of contemporary long-ball sluggers. Horizontal fronts feature game-action photos with holographic foil rendering of the background. In one of the lower corners appears the logo "1994 Mickey Mantle's Long Shots". Backs have a color player photo at top, with a photo of Mantle beneath and a statement by him about the featured player. Previous season and career stats are included. Cards are numbered with an "MM" prefix. Besides the 20 current player cards there is a Mickey Mantle card and two trade cards which could be redeemed for complete insert card sets.

		MT
Complete Set (21):		30.00
Common Player:		.50
(1)	Mickey Mantle Trade Card (silver): (Redeemable for 21-card Mantle Long Shots set)	4.00
(2)	Mickey Mantle Trade Card (blue): (Redeemable for Electric Diamond version Mantle Long Shots set)	4.00
1	Jeff Bagwell	2.00
2	Albert Belle	.75
3	Barry Bonds	3.00
4	Jose Canseco	1.50
5	Joe Carter	.50
6	Carlos Delgado	.75
7	Cecil Fielder	.50
8	Cliff Floyd	.50
9	Juan Gonzalez	2.00
10	Ken Griffey Jr.	4.00
11	David Justice	.75
12	Fred McGriff	.50
13	Mark McGwire	5.00
14	Dean Palmer	.50
15	Mike Piazza	4.00
16	Manny Ramirez	2.00
17	Tim Salmon	.75
18	Frank Thomas	3.00
19	Mo Vaughn	1.00
20	Matt Williams	.75
21	Header (Mickey Mantle)	6.00

1994 Upper Deck Mantle-Griffey Autographed Inserts

First series retail packs of '94 UD were the exclusive venue for a special card featuring spokesmen Ken Griffey Jr. and Mickey Mantle. The front has a painting of the two stars. On back are career highlights and a comparison of the players' first five seasons. A large numbered elliptical hologram on back authenticates the autographs. One thousand cards were issued with either or both signatures.

		MT
KG1	Ken Griffey Jr., Mickey Mantle (Griffey autograph)	150.00
MM1	Ken Griffey Jr., Mickey Mantle (Mantle autograph)	500.00
GM1	Ken Griffey Jr., Mickey Mantle (both autographs)	1000.

1994 Upper Deck SP Insert

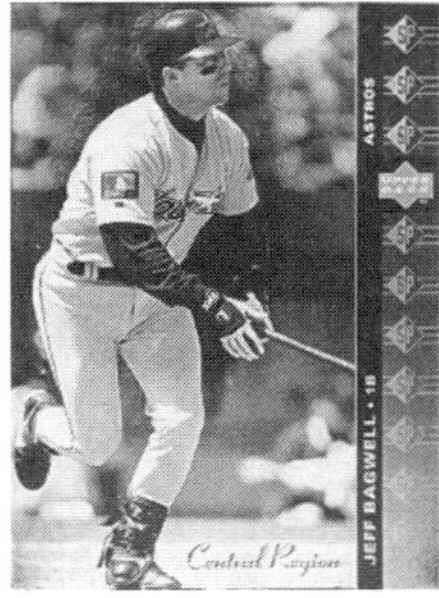

Fifteen SP Preview cards were inserted into Series II packs of Upper Deck baseball. The cards were inserted with regional distribution and gave collectors a chance to see what the SP super-premium cards would look like. There were five cards available in the East, Central and West and were inserted at a rate of about one per 36 packs. Most of the preview inserts have different front and back photos than the regularly issued SPs, along with other differences in typography and graphics elements.

		MT
Complete Set (15):		70.00
Common Player:		.50
EASTERN REGION		
1	Roberto Alomar	2.50
2	Cliff Floyd	.50
3	Javier Lopez	.50
4	Don Mattingly	6.00
5	Cal Ripken, Jr.	10.00
CENTRAL REGION		
1	Jeff Bagwell	3.00
2	Michael Jordan	15.00
3	Kirby Puckett	5.00
4	Manny Ramirez	3.00
5	Frank Thomas	6.00
WESTERN REGION		
1	Barry Bonds	6.00
2	Juan Gonzalez	3.00
3	Ken Griffey, Jr.	8.00
4	Mike Piazza	8.00
5	Tim Salmon	1.00

1995 Upper Deck

Issued in two series of 225 base cards each, with loads of subsets and inserts, the 1995 Upper Deck set was a strong collector favorite from the outset. Basic cards feature a borderless front photo with the player's name and UD logo in bronze foil. Backs have another large color photo, recent stats and career totals and appropriate logos, along with the infield-shaped hologram. Subsets in each series include Star Rookies and Top Prospects, each with special designs highlighting the game's young stars. Series I has a "'90s Midpoint Analysis" subset studying the decade's superstars, and Series II has another hot rookies' subset, Diamond Debuts. The set closes with a five-card "Final Tribute" subset summarizing the careers of five recently retired superstars. Retail and hobby versions were sold with each featuring some unique insert cards. Basic packaging of each type was the 12-card foil pack at $1.99, though several other configurations were also released.

	MT
Complete Set (450):	40.00
Common Player:	.05
Electric Diamond:	2X
Electric Diamond Golds:	8X
Series 1 or 2 Pack (12):	1.50
Series 1 or 2 Wax Box (36):	40.00

1 Ruben Rivera (Top Prospect) .05
2 Bill Pulsipher (Top Prospect) .05
3 Ben Grieve (Top Prospect) .75
4 Curtis Goodwin (Top Prospect) .05
5 Damon Hollins (Top Prospect) .05
6 Todd Greene (Top Prospect) .05
7 Glenn Williams (Top Prospect) .05
8 Bret Wagner (Top Prospect) .05
9 *Karim Garcia* (Top Prospect) .50
10 Nomar Garciaparra (Top Prospect) 3.00
11 *Raul Casanova* (Top Prospect) .10
12 Matt Smith (Top Prospect) .05
13 Paul Wilson (Top Prospect) .10
14 Jason Isringhausen (Top Prospect) .10
15 Reid Ryan (Top Prospect) .05
16 Lee Smith .05
17 Chili Davis .05
18 Brian Anderson .05
19 Gary DiSarcina .05
20 Bo Jackson .10
21 Chuck Finley .05
22 Darryl Kile .05
23 Shane Reynolds .05
24 Tony Eusebio .05
25 Craig Biggio .10
26 Doug Drabek .05
27 Brian L. Hunter .05
28 James Mouton .05
29 Geronimo Berroa .05
30 Rickey Henderson .65
31 Steve Karsay .05
32 Steve Ontiveros .05
33 Ernie Young .05
34 Dennis Eckersley .05
35 Mark McGwire 2.50
36 Dave Stewart .05
37 Pat Hentgen .05
38 Carlos Delgado .20
39 Joe Carter .05
40 Roberto Alomar .50
41 John Olerud .05
42 Devon White .05
43 Roberto Kelly .05
44 Jeff Blauser .05
45 Fred McGriff .05
46 Tom Glavine .10
47 Mike Kelly .05
48 Javy Lopez .05
49 Greg Maddux 1.50
50 Matt Mieske .05
51 Troy O'Leary .05
52 Jeff Cirillo .05
53 Cal Eldred .05
54 Pat Listach .05
55 Jose Valentin .05
56 John Mabry .05
57 Bob Tewksbury .05
58 Brian Jordan .05
59 Gregg Jefferies .05
60 Ozzie Smith 1.50
61 Geronimo Pena .05
62 Mark Whiten .05
63 Rey Sanchez .05
64 Willie Banks .05
65 Mark Grace .20
66 Randy Myers .05
67 Steve Trachsel .05
68 Derrick May .05
69 Brett Butler .05
70 Eric Karros .05
71 Tim Wallach .05
72 Delino DeShields .05
73 Darren Dreifort .05
74 Orel Hershiser .05
75 Billy Ashley .05
76 Sean Berry .05
77 Ken Hill .05
78 John Wetteland .05
79 Moises Alou .20
80 Cliff Floyd .05
81 Marquis Grissom .05
82 Larry Walker .20
83 Rondell White .20
84 William VanLandingham .05
85 Matt Williams .15
86 Rod Beck .05
87 Darren Lewis .05
88 Robby Thompson .05
89 Darryl Strawberry .05
90 Kenny Lofton .05
91 Charles Nagy .05
92 Sandy Alomar Jr. .05
93 Mark Clark .05
94 Dennis Martinez .05
95 Dave Winfield 1.00
96 Jim Thome .05
97 Manny Ramirez 1.00
98 Goose Gossage .05
99 Tino Martinez .05
100 Ken Griffey Jr. 2.50
100a Ken Griffey Jr. (overprinted "For Promotional Use Only") 2.50
101 Greg Maddux (Analysis: '90s Midpoint) .75
102 Randy Johnson (Analysis: '90s Midpoint) .25
103 Barry Bonds (Analysis: '90s Midpoint) .75
104 Juan Gonzalez (Analysis: '90s Midpoint) .40
105 Frank Thomas (Analysis: '90s Midpoint) .75
106 Matt Williams (Analysis: '90s Midpoint) .05
107 Paul Molitor (Analysis: '90s Midpoint) .25
108 Fred McGriff (Analysis: '90s Midpoint) .05
109 Carlos Baerga (Analysis: '90s Midpoint) .05
110 Ken Griffey Jr. (Analysis: '90s Midpoint) 1.25
111 Reggie Jefferson .05
112 Randy Johnson .50
113 Marc Newfield .05
114 Robb Nen .05
115 Jeff Conine .05
116 Kurt Abbott .05
117 Charlie Hough .05
118 Dave Weathers .05
119 Juan Castillo .05
120 Bret Saberhagen .05
121 Rico Brogna .05
122 John Franco .05
123 Todd Hundley .05
124 Jason Jacome .05
125 Bobby Jones .05
126 Bret Barberie .05
127 Ben McDonald .05
128 Harold Baines .05
129 Jeffrey Hammonds .05
130 Mike Mussina .40
131 Chris Hoiles .05
132 Brady Anderson .05
133 Eddie Williams .05
134 Andy Benes .05
135 Tony Gwynn 1.50
136 Bip Roberts .05
137 Joey Hamilton .05
138 Luis Lopez .05
139 Ray McDavid .05
140 Lenny Dykstra .05
141 Mariano Duncan .05
142 Fernando Valenzuela .05
143 Bobby Munoz .05
144 Kevin Stocker .05
145 John Kruk .05
146 Jon Lieber .05
147 Zane Smith .05
148 Steve Cooke .05
149 Andy Van Slyke .05
150 Jay Bell .05
151 Carlos Garcia .05
152 John Dettmer .05
153 Darren Oliver .05
154 Dean Palmer .05
155 Otis Nixon .05
156 Rusty Greer .05
157 Rick Helling .05
158 Jose Canseco .50
159 Roger Clemens 1.50
160 Andre Dawson .25
161 Mo Vaughn .50
162 Aaron Sele .05
163 John Valentin .05
164 Brian Hunter .05
165 Bret Boone .10
166 Hector Carrasco .05
167 Pete Schourek .05
168 Willie Greene .05
169 Kevin Mitchell .05
170 Deion Sanders .10
171 John Roper .05
172 Charlie Hayes .05
173 David Nied .05
174 Ellis Burks .05
175 Dante Bichette .05
176 Marvin Freeman .05
177 Eric Young .05
178 David Cone .05
179 Greg Gagne .05
180 Bob Hamelin .05
181 Wally Joyner .05
182 Jeff Montgomery .05
183 Jose Lind .05
184 Chris Gomez .05
185 Travis Fryman .05
186 Kirk Gibson .05
187 Mike Moore .05
188 Lou Whitaker .05
189 Sean Bergman .05
190 Shane Mack .05
191 Rick Aguilera .05
192 Denny Hocking .05
193 Chuck Knoblauch .05
194 Kevin Tapani .05
195 Kent Hrbek .05
196 Ozzie Guillen .05
197 Wilson Alvarez .05
198 Tim Raines .05
199 Scott Ruffcorn .05
200 Michael Jordan 3.00
201 Robin Ventura .05
202 Jason Bere .05
203 Darrin Jackson .05
204 Russ Davis .05
205 Jimmy Key .05
206 Jack McDowell .05
207 Jim Abbott .05
208 Paul O'Neill .05
209 Bernie Williams .25
210 Don Mattingly 1.75
211 Orlando Miller (Star Rookie) .05
212 Alex Gonzalez (Star Rookie) .10
213 Terrell Wade (Star Rookie) .05
214 Jose Oliva (Star Rookie) .05
215 Alex Rodriguez (Star Rookie) 2.50
216 Garret Anderson (Star Rookie) .05
217 Alan Benes (Star Rookie) .05
218 Armando Benitez (Star Rookie) .05
219 Dustin Hermanson (Star Rookie) .10
220 Charles Johnson (Star Rookie) .05
221 Julian Tavarez (Star Rookie) .05
222 Jason Giambi (Star Rookie) .50
223 LaTroy Hawkins (Star Rookie) .05
224 Todd Hollandsworth (Star Rookie) .05
225 Derek Jeter (Star Rookie) 2.00
226 *Hideo Nomo* (Star Rookie) 1.50
227 Tony Clark (Star Rookie) .05
228 Roger Cedeno (Star Rookie) .05
229 Scott Stahoviak (Star Rookie) .05
230 Michael Tucker (Star Rookie) .05
231 Joe Rosselli (Star Rookie) .05
232 Antonio Osuna (Star Rookie) .05
233 *Bobby Higginson* (Star Rookie) 1.00
234 *Mark Grudzielanek* (Star Rookie) .35
235 Ray Durham (Star Rookie) .10
236 Frank Rodriguez (Star Rookie) .05
237 Quilvio Veras (Star Rookie) .05
238 Darren Bragg (Star Rookie) .05
239 Ugueth Urbina (Star Rookie) .05
240 Jason Bates (Star Rookie) .05
241 David Bell (Diamond Debuts) .05
242 Ron Villone (Diamond Debuts) .05
243 Joe Randa (Diamond Debuts) .05
244 *Carlos Perez* (Diamond Debuts) .10
245 Brad Clontz (Diamond Debuts) .05
246 Steve Rodriguez Diamond Debuts) .05
247 Joe Vitiello (Diamond Debuts) .05
248 Ozzie Timmons (Diamond Debuts) .05
249 Rudy Pemberton (Diamond Debuts) .05
250 Marty Cordova (Diamond Debuts) .05
251 Tony Graffanino (Top Prospect) .05
252 *Mark Johnson* (Top Prospect) .05
253 *Tomas Perez* (Top Prospect) .05
254 Jimmy Hurst (Top Prospect) .05
255 Edgardo Alfonzo (Top Prospect) .05
256 Jose Malave (Top Prospect) .05
257 *Brad Radke* (Top Prospect) .30
258 Jon Nunnally (Top Prospect) .05
259 Dilson Torres (Top Prospect) .05
260 Esteban Loaiza (Top Prospect) .05
261 *Freddy Garcia* (Top Prospect) .05
262 Don Wengert (Top Prospect) .05
263 *Robert Person* (Top Prospect) .15
264 *Tim Unroe* (Top Prospect) .05
265 Juan Acevedo (Top Prospect) .05
266 Eduardo Perez .05
267 Tony Phillips .05
268 Jim Edmonds .05
269 Jorge Fabregas .05
270 Tim Salmon .10
271 Mark Langston .05
272 J.T. Snow .05
273 Phil Plantier .05
274 Derek Bell .05
275 Jeff Bagwell 1.00
276 Luis Gonzalez .25
277 John Hudek .05

278	Todd Stottlemyre	.05
279	Mark Acre	.05
280	Ruben Sierra	.05
281	Mike Bordick	.05
282	Ron Darling	.05
283	Brent Gates	.05
284	Todd Van Poppel	.05
285	Paul Molitor	.60
286	Ed Sprague	.05
287	Juan Guzman	.05
288	David Cone	.05
289	Shawn Green	.30
290	Marquis Grissom	.05
291	Kent Mercker	.05
292	Steve Avery	.05
293	Chipper Jones	2.00
294	John Smoltz	.10
295	Dave Justice	.20
296	Ryan Klesko	.05
297	Joe Oliver	.05
298	Ricky Bones	.05
299	John Jaha	.05
300	Greg Vaughn	.05
301	Dave Nilsson	.05
302	Kevin Seitzer	.05
303	Bernard Gilkey	.05
304	Allen Battle	.05
305	Ray Lankford	.05
306	Tom Pagnozzi	.05
307	Allen Watson	.05
308	Danny Jackson	.05
309	Ken Hill	.05
310	Todd Zeile	.05
311	Kevin Roberson	.05
312	Steve Buechele	.05
313	Rick Wilkins	.05
314	Kevin Foster	.05
315	Sammy Sosa	1.75
316	Howard Johnson	.05
317	Greg Hansell	.05
318	Pedro Astacio	.05
319	Rafael Bournigal	.05
320	Mike Piazza	2.00
321	Ramon Martinez	.05
322	Raul Mondesi	.20
323	Ismael Valdes	.05
324	Wil Cordero	.05
325	Tony Tarasco	.05
326	Roberto Kelly	.05
327	Jeff Fassero	.05
328	Mike Lansing	.05
329	Pedro J. Martinez	.75
330	Kirk Rueter	.05
331	Glenallen Hill	.05
332	Kirt Manwaring	.05
333	Royce Clayton	.05
334	J.R. Phillips	.05
335	Barry Bonds	1.75
336	Mark Portugal	.05
337	Terry Mulholland	.05
338	Omar Vizquel	.05
339	Carlos Baerga	.05
340	Albert Belle	.30
341	Eddie Murray	.50
342	Wayne Kirby	.05
343	Chad Ogea	.05
344	Tim Davis	.05
345	Jay Buhner	.05
346	Bobby Ayala	.05
347	Mike Blowers	.05
348	Dave Fleming	.05
349	Edgar Martinez	.05
350	Andre Dawson	.25
351	Darrell Whitmore	.05
352	Chuck Carr	.05
353	John Burkett	.05
354	Chris Hammond	.05
355	Gary Sheffield	.25
356	Pat Rapp	.05
357	Greg Colbrunn	.05
358	David Segui	.05
359	Jeff Kent	.05
360	Bobby Bonilla	.05
361	Pete Harnisch	.05
362	Ryan Thompson	.05
363	Jose Vizcaino	.05
364	Brett Butler	.05
365	Cal Ripken Jr.	2.50
366	Rafael Palmeiro	.20
367	Leo Gomez	.05
368	Andy Van Slyke	.05
369	Arthur Rhodes	.05
370	Ken Caminiti	.05
371	Steve Finley	.05
372	Melvin Nieves	.05
373	Andujar Cedeno	.05
374	Trevor Hoffman	.05
375	Fernando Valenzuela	.05
376	Ricky Bottalico	.05
377	Dave Hollins	.05
378	Charlie Hayes	.05
379	Tommy Greene	.05
380	Darren Daulton	.05
381	Curt Schilling	.15
382	Midre Cummings	.05
383	Al Martin	.05
384	Jeff King	.05
385	Orlando Merced	.05
386	Denny Neagle	.05
387	Don Slaught	.05
388	Dave Clark	.05
389	Kevin Gross	.05
390	Will Clark	.15
391	Ivan Rodriguez	.75
392	Benji Gil	.05
393	Jeff Frye	.05
394	Kenny Rogers	.05
395	Juan Gonzalez	1.00
396	Mike Macfarlane	.05
397	Lee Tinsley	.05
398	Tim Naehring	.05
399	Tim Vanegmond	.05
400	Mike Greenwell	.05
401	Ken Ryan	.05
402	John Smiley	.05
403	Tim Pugh	.05
404	Reggie Sanders	.05
405	Barry Larkin	.10
406	Hal Morris	.05
407	Jose Rijo	.05
408	Lance Painter	.05
409	Joe Girardi	.05
410	Andres Galarraga	.05
411	Mike Kingery	.05
412	Roberto Mejia	.05
413	Walt Weiss	.05
414	Bill Swift	.05
415	Larry Walker	.20
416	Billy Brewer	.05
417	Pat Borders	.05
418	Tom Gordon	.05
419	Kevin Appier	.05
420	Gary Gaetti	.05
421	Greg Gohr	.05
422	Felipe Lira	.05
423	John Doherty	.05
424	Chad Curtis	.05
425	Cecil Fielder	.05
426	Alan Trammell	.05
427	David McCarty	.05
428	Scott Erickson	.05
429	Pat Mahomes	.05
430	Kirby Puckett	1.50
431	Dave Stevens	.05
432	Pedro Munoz	.05
433	Chris Sabo	.05
434	Alex Fernandez	.05
435	Frank Thomas	1.75
436	Roberto Hernandez	.05
437	Lance Johnson	.05
438	Jim Abbott	.05
439	John Wetteland	.05
440	Melido Perez	.05
441	Tony Fernandez	.05
442	Pat Kelly	.05
443	Mike Stanley	.05
444	Danny Tartabull	.05
445	Wade Boggs	.50
446	Robin Yount (Final Tribute)	.60
447	Ryne Sandberg (Final Tribute)	.75
448	Nolan Ryan (Final Tribute)	2.00
449	George Brett (Final Tribute)	.75
450	Mike Schmidt (Final Tribute)	.75

1995 Upper Deck Electric Diamond

Included as an insert at the rate of one per retail foil pack and two per jumbo pack, this set parallels the regular issue. The only differences are that the Electric Diamond cards utilize silver-foil highlights on front, compared to the copper foil on the regular cards. The Electric Diamond cards also include a home-plate shaped logo printed in silver foil in one of the upper corners.

	MT
Complete Set (1-450):	85.00
Common Player:	.25
Stars/Rookies:	2X

(See 1995 Upper Deck for checklist and base card values.)

1995 Upper Deck Electric Diamond Gold

A parallel set of a parallet set, the Electric Diamond Gold cards were found at an average rate of one per 36 retail packs. They differ from the standard ED inserts in that the home plate-shaped Electric Diamond logo in the upper corner and the player's name at bottom are printed in gold foil, rather than the silver of the ED cards or the copper of the regular-issue UD cards.

	MT
Complete Set (450):	750.00
Common Player:	2.00
Stars/Rookies:	8X

(See 1995 Upper Deck for checklist and base card values.)

1995 Upper Deck Autograph Trade Cards

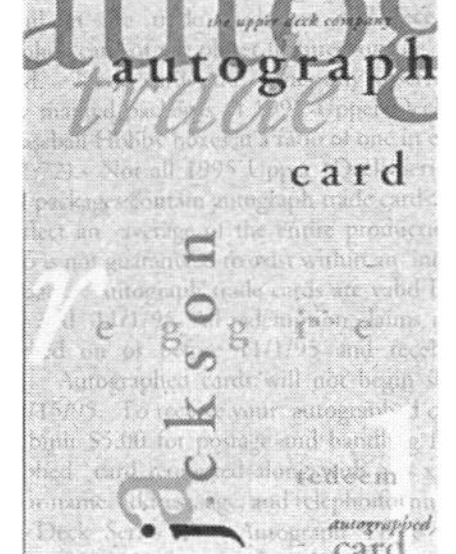

On the average of once every 72 packs (two boxes) of Series II hobby, a trade card good for an autographed player card could be found as an insert. The cards feature the player name, but no picture, on front, while the reverse has instructions for redeeming the card for a $5 fee. The autograph trade cards expired on Nov. 1, 1995.

		MT
Complete Set (5):		8.00
Common Player:		1.00
(1)	Roger Clemens	2.00
(2)	Reggie Jackson	1.50
(3)	Willie Mays	3.00
(4)	Raul Mondesi	1.00
(5)	Frank Robinson	1.50

1995 Upper Deck Autographed Jumbos

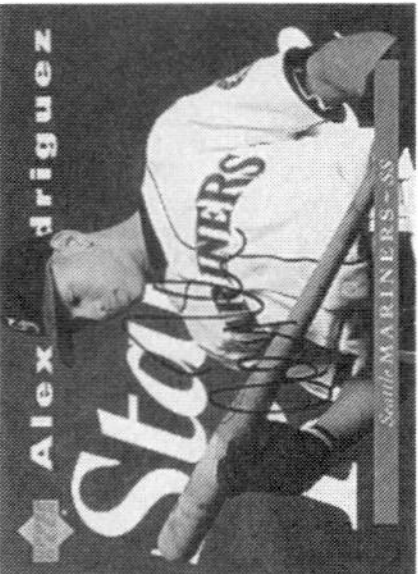

By sending in quantities of foil wrappers from Upper Deck baseball cards, collectors could receive a jumbo 5" x 7" blow-up of a player's card. The offer was limited to 8,000 Roger Clemens cards (Series I) and 6,000 Alex Rodriguez cards (Series II). Each card bears a serial number hologram on back and comes with a matching Upper Deck Authenticated auhtenticity guarantee card.

		MT
Complete Set (2):		100.00
Common Player:		35.00
(1)	Roger Clemens	35.00
(2)	Alex Rodriguez	75.00

1995 Upper Deck Autograph Redemption Cards

These cards were sent to collectors who redeemed Autograph Trade cards found in Series II Upper Deck baseball. A certificate of authenticity with a holographic serial number matching that on the card back was issued with each card.

		MT
Complete Set (5):		160.00
Common Player:		15.00
(1)	Roger Clemens	50.00
(2)	Reggie Jackson	25.00
(3)	Willie Mays	80.00
(4)	Raul Mondesi	15.00
(5)	Frank Robinson	25.00

1995 Upper Deck Award Winners Predictors (Hobby)

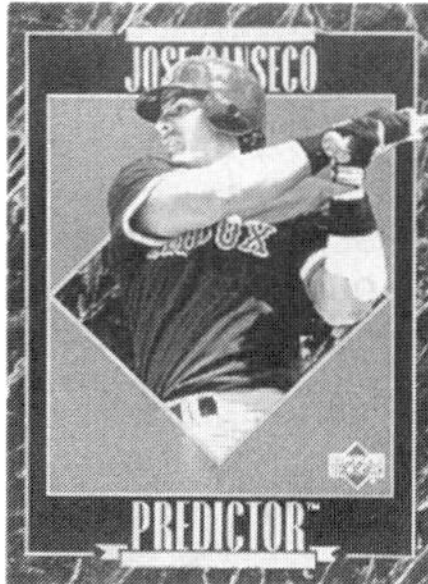

Candidates for 1995 MVP and Rookie of the Year in each league are featured in the interactive insert series called Predictors. Twenty potential award winners were released in each of Series I and II at the rate of one per 30 packs on average. Cards feature on front a player photo inside a diamond cutout on a rich looking black and marbled background. In gold foil are his name and team at top, and "PREDICTOR" and the category at bottom. Backs feature game rules and details for redeeming the card if the pictured player wins the specified award. Winners could trade in the card for a foil-enhanced set of Predictor cards. The trade-in offer expired at the end of 1995. Cards are numbered with a "H" prefix.

		MT
Complete Set (40):		45.00
Common Player:		.50
Winner Exchange Cards:		1X
1	Albert Belle	1.00
2	Juan Gonzalez	2.00
3	Ken Griffey Jr.	4.00
4	Kirby Puckett	2.50
5	Frank Thomas	3.00
6	Jeff Bagwell	2.00
7	Barry Bonds	3.00
8	Mike Piazza	3.50
9	Matt Williams	1.00
10	1995 MVP Long Shot (Winner)	.50
11	Armando Benitez	.50
12	Alex Gonzalez	.50
13	Shawn Green	1.50
14	Derek Jeter	3.50
15	Alex Rodriguez	4.00
16	Alan Benes	.50
17	Brian L. Hunter	.50
18	Charles Johnson	.50
19	Jose Oliva	.50
20	1995 ROY Long Shot	.50
21	Cal Ripken Jr.	5.00
22	Don Mattingly	3.00
23	Roberto Alomar	1.50
24	Kenny Lofton	.50
25	Will Clark	1.00
26	Mark McGwire	5.00
27	Greg Maddux	2.50
28	Fred McGriff	.50
29	Andres Galarraga	.50
30	Jose Canseco	1.50
31	Ray Durham	.50
32	Mark Grudzielanek	.50
33	Scott Ruffcorn	.50
34	Michael Tucker	.50
35	Garret Anderson	.50
36	Darren Bragg	.50
37	Quilvio Veras	.50
38	Hideo Nomo (Winner)	1.50
39	Chipper Jones	3.50
40	Marty Cordova (Winner)	.75

1995 Upper Deck Babe Ruth Baseball Heroes

In the 100th anniversary year of his birth, Babe Ruth was the featured star in Upper Deck continuing "Heroes" insert set. Ten cards, including an unnumbered header, were issued in Series II packs. The cards featured colorized photos printed on metallic foil on the front. Backs have stats and/or biographical data. On average, one Babe Ruth Heroes card is found per 34 packs.

		MT
Complete Set (10):		100.00
Common Player:		10.00
73	1914-18 Pitching Career (Babe Ruth)	10.00
74	1919 - Move to Outfield (Babe Ruth)	10.00
75	1920 - Renaissance Man (Babe Ruth)	10.00
76	1923 - House That Ruth Built (Babe Ruth)	10.00
77	1927 - 60-Homer Season (Babe Ruth)	10.00
78	1928 - Three-homer Game (Babe Ruth)	10.00
79	1932 - The Called Shot (Babe Ruth)	10.00
80	1930-35 - Milestones (Babe Ruth)	10.00
81	1935 - The Last Hurrah (Babe Ruth)	10.00
---	Header card	3.00

1995 Upper Deck Checklists

Upscale checklists for the 1995 UD set were part of the insert card program, seeded about one per 17 packs, on average. Horizontally formatted fronts are printed on metallic foil and include a career highlight of the pictured player. Backs have the checklist data. Five checklists were issued in each of Series I and Series II.

		MT
Complete Set (10):		15.00
Common Player:		
	Series I	
1	Checklist 1-75 (Montreal Expos)	1.00
2	Checklist 76-150 (Fred McGriff)	1.50
3	Checklist 151-225 (John Valentin) (unassisted triple play)	1.00
4	Special Edition Checklist (Greg Maddux)	3.00
5	Special Edition Checklist 69-135 (Kenny Rogers) (perfect game)	1.00
	Series II	
1	Checklist 226-300 (Cecil Fielder)	1.00
2	Checklist 301-375 (Tony Gwynn)	2.50
3	Checklist 376-450 (Greg Maddux)	3.00
4	Special Edition Checklist 136-203 (Randy Johnson)	1.50
5	Special Edition Checklist 204-270 (Mike Schmidt)	3.00

1995 Upper Deck League Leaders Predictors (Retail)

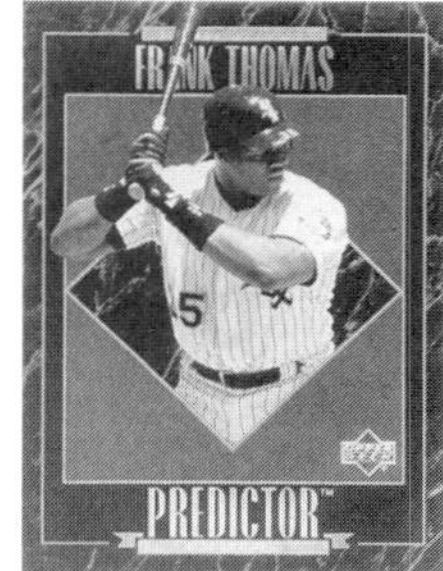

Candidates for the Triple Crown categories of league leaders in hits, home runs and RBIs are featured in this retail-only insert set, found at the average rate of one per 30 packs in both Series I and II. If the player pictured on the card front won the category specified on his card, it could be redeemed for a special foil-enhanced version of the subset prior to the Dec. 31, 1995, deadline. Cards are numbered with a "R" prefix.

		MT
Complete Set (60):		60.00
Common Player:		.50
Winner Exchange Cards:		1X
1	Albert Belle (Winner)	1.00
2	Jose Canseco	1.50
3	Juan Gonzalez	1.50
4	Ken Griffey Jr.	4.00
5	Frank Thomas	2.50
6	Jeff Bagwell	1.50
7	Barry Bonds	2.50
8	Fred McGriff	.50
9	Matt Williams	.75
10	1995 Home Run Long Shot (Winner)	.50
11	Albert Belle (Winner)	1.00
12	Joe Carter	.50
13	Cecil Fielder	.50
14	Kirby Puckett	2.00
15	Frank Thomas	2.50
16	Jeff Bagwell	1.50
17	Barry Bonds	2.50
18	Mike Piazza	4.00
19	Matt Williams	.75
20	1995 RBI Long Shot (Winner)	.50
21	Wade Boggs	1.50
22	Kenny Lofton	.50
23	Paul Molitor	1.50
24	Paul O'Neill	.50
25	Frank Thomas	2.50
26	Jeff Bagwell	1.50
27	Tony Gwynn (Winner)	3.00
28	Gregg Jefferies	.50

29	Hal Morris	.50
30	1995 Batting Long Shot (Winner)	.50
31	Joe Carter	.50
32	Cecil Fielder	.50
33	Rafael Palmeiro	.75
34	Larry Walker	.75
35	Manny Ramirez	1.50
36	Tim Salmon	.75
37	Mike Piazza	4.00
38	Andres Galarraga	.50
39	Dave Justice	.75
40	Gary Sheffield	.75
41	Juan Gonzalez	1.50
42	Jose Canseco	1.50
43	Will Clark	.75
44	Rafael Palmeiro	.75
45	Ken Griffey Jr.	4.00
46	Ruben Sierra	.50
47	Larry Walker	.75
48	Fred McGriff	.50
49	Dante Bichette (Winner)	1.00
50	Darren Daulton	.50
51	Will Clark	.75
52	Ken Griffey Jr.	4.00
53	Don Mattingly	2.50
54	John Olerud	.50
55	Kirby Puckett	2.00
56	Raul Mondesi	.65
57	Moises Alou	.65
58	Bret Boone	.65
59	Albert Belle	.65
60	Mike Piazza	4.00

1995 Upper Deck Special Edition

Printed on metallic foil on front, and inserted into hobby packs only at the rate of one per pack, this insert set is found in both Series 1 (#1-135) and Series 2 (#136-270). A silver stripe at top has the name of the issue and the issuer, while stacked black and silver bars at bottom have the player name, team and position. Backs are conventionally printed and have another color photo, career data and 1994 and lifetime stats.

		MT
Complete Set (270):		60.00
Common Player:		.10
Gold:		4X
1	Cliff Floyd	.10
2	Wil Cordero	.10
3	Pedro Martinez	1.50
4	Larry Walker	.30
5	Derek Jeter	4.00
6	Mike Stanley	.10
7	Melido Perez	.10
8	Jim Leyritz	.10
9	Danny Tartabull	.10
10	Wade Boggs	1.00
11	Ryan Klesko	.10
12	Steve Avery	.10
13	Damon Hollins	.10
14	Chipper Jones	3.00
15	Dave Justice	.25
16	Glenn Williams	.10
17	Jose Oliva	.10
18	Terrell Wade	.10
19	Alex Fernandez	.10
20	Frank Thomas	1.50
21	Ozzie Guillen	.10
22	Roberto Hernandez	.10
23	Albie Lopez	.10
24	Eddie Murray	1.00
25	Albert Belle	.30
26	Omar Vizquel	.10
27	Carlos Baerga	.10
28	Jose Rijo	.10
29	Hal Morris	.10
30	Reggie Sanders	.10
31	Jack Morris	.10
32	Raul Mondesi	.20
33	Karim Garcia	.15
34	Todd Hollandsworth	.10
35	Mike Piazza	3.00
36	Chan Ho Park	.25
37	Ramon Martinez	.10
38	Kenny Rogers	.10
39	Will Clark	.30
40	Juan Gonzalez	1.50
41	Ivan Rodriguez	1.25
42	Orlando Miller	.10
43	John Hudek	.10
44	Luis Gonzalez	.45
45	Jeff Bagwell	1.50
46	Cal Ripken Jr.	4.00
47	Mike Oquist	.10
48	Armando Benitez	.10
49	Ben McDonald	.10
50	Rafael Palmeiro	.30
51	Curtis Goodwin	.10
52	Vince Coleman	.10
53	Tom Gordon	.10
54	Mike Macfarlane	.10
55	Brian McRae	.10
56	Matt Smith	.10
57	David Segui	.10
58	Paul Wilson	.10
59	Bill Pulsipher	.10
60	Bobby Bonilla	.10
61	Jeff Kent	.10
62	Ryan Thompson	.10
63	Jason Isringhausen	.10
64	Ed Sprague	.10
65	Paul Molitor	1.00
66	Juan Guzman	.10
67	Alex Gonzalez	.15
68	Shawn Green	.40
69	Mark Portugal	.10
70	Barry Bonds	2.50
71	Robby Thompson	.10
72	Royce Clayton	.10
73	Ricky Bottalico	.10
74	Doug Jones	.10
75	Darren Daulton	.10
76	Gregg Jefferies	.10
77	Scott Cooper	.10
78	Nomar Garciaparra	2.50
79	Ken Ryan	.10
80	Mike Greenwell	.10
81	LaTroy Hawkins	.10
82	Rich Becker	.10
83	Scott Erickson	.10
84	Pedro Munoz	.10
85	Kirby Puckett	2.00
86	Orlando Merced	.10
87	Jeff King	.10
88	Midre Cummings	.10
89	Bernard Gilkey	.10
90	Ray Lankford	.10
91	Todd Zeile	.10
92	Alan Benes	.10
93	Bret Wagner	.10
94	Rene Arocha	.10
95	Cecil Fielder	.10
96	Alan Trammell	.10
97	Tony Phillips	.10
98	Junior Felix	.10
99	Brian Harper	.10
100	Greg Vaughn	.10
101	Ricky Bones	.10
102	Walt Weiss	.10
103	Lance Painter	.10
104	Roberto Mejia	.10
105	Andres Galarraga	.10
106	Todd Van Poppel	.10
107	Ben Grieve	.25
108	Brent Gates	.10
109	Jason Giambi	.35
110	Ruben Sierra	.10
111	Terry Steinbach	.10
112	Chris Hammond	.10
113	Charles Johnson	.10
114	Jesus Tavarez	.10
115	Gary Sheffield	.25
116	Chuck Carr	.10
117	Bobby Ayala	.10
118	Randy Johnson	1.50
119	Edgar Martinez	.10
120	Alex Rodriguez	3.50
121	Kevin Foster	.10
122	Kevin Roberson	.10
123	Sammy Sosa	2.50
124	Steve Trachsel	.10
125	Eduardo Perez	.10
126	Tim Salmon	.20
127	Todd Greene	.10
128	Jorge Fabregas	.10
129	Mark Langston	.10
130	Mitch Williams	.10
131	Raul Casanova	.10
132	Mel Nieves	.10
133	Andy Benes	.10
134	Dustin Hermanson	.10
135	Trevor Hoffman	.10
136	Mark Grudzielanek	.10
137	Ugueth Urbina	.10
138	Moises Alou	.20
139	Roberto Kelly	.10
140	Rondell White	.20
141	Paul O'Neill	.10
142	Jimmy Key	.10
143	Jack McDowell	.10
144	Ruben Rivera	.10
145	Don Mattingly	2.50
146	John Wetteland	.10
147	Tom Glavine	.15
148	Marquis Grissom	.10
149	Javy Lopez	.10
150	Fred McGriff	.10
151	Greg Maddux	2.00
152	Chris Sabo	.10
153	Ray Durham	.10
154	Robin Ventura	.10
155	Jim Abbott	.10
156	Jimmy Hurst	.10
157	Tim Raines	.10
158	Dennis Martinez	.10
159	Kenny Lofton	.10
160	Dave Winfield	1.00
161	Manny Ramirez	1.50
162	Jim Thome	.10
163	Barry Larkin	.15
164	Bret Boone	.15
165	Deion Sanders	.15
166	Ron Gant	.10
167	Benito Santiago	.10
168	Hideo Nomo	.50
169	Billy Ashley	.10
170	Roger Cedeno	.10
171	Ismael Valdes	.10
172	Eric Karros	.10
173	Rusty Greer	.10
174	Rick Helling	.10
175	Nolan Ryan	4.00
176	Dean Palmer	.10
177	Phil Plantier	.10
178	Darryl Kile	.10
179	Derek Bell	.10
180	Doug Drabek	.10
181	Craig Biggio	.15
182	Kevin Brown	.15
183	Harold Baines	.10
184	Jeffrey Hammonds	.10
185	Chris Hoiles	.10
186	Mike Mussina	1.00
187	Bob Hamelin	.10
188	Jeff Montgomery	.10
189	Michael Tucker	.10
190	George Brett	2.00
191	Edgardo Alfonzo	.10
192	Brett Butler	.10
193	Bobby Jones	.10
194	Todd Hundley	.10
195	Bret Saberhagen	.10
196	Pat Hentgen	.10
197	Roberto Alomar	1.00
198	David Cone	.10
199	Carlos Delgado	.30
200	Joe Carter	.10
201	William Van Landingham	.10
202	Rod Beck	.10
203	J.R. Phillips	.10
204	Darren Lewis	.10
205	Matt Williams	.30
206	Lenny Dykstra	.10
207	Dave Hollins	.10
208	Mike Schmidt	2.00
209	Charlie Hayes	.10
210	Mo Vaughn	1.00
211	Jose Malave	.10
212	Roger Clemens	2.00
213	Jose Canseco	1.00
214	Mark Whiten	.10
215	Marty Cordova	.10
216	Rick Aguilera	.10
217	Kevin Tapani	.10
218	Chuck Knoblauch	.10
219	Al Martin	.10
220	Jay Bell	.10
221	Carlos Garcia	.10
222	Freddy Garcia	.10
223	Jon Lieber	.10
224	Danny Jackson	.10
225	Ozzie Smith	1.50
226	Brian Jordan	.10
227	Ken Hill	.10
228	Scott Cooper	.10
229	Chad Curtis	.10
230	Lou Whitaker	.10
231	Kirk Gibson	.10
232	Travis Fryman	.10
233	Jose Valentin	.10
234	Dave Nilsson	.10
235	Cal Eldred	.10
236	Matt Mieske	.10
237	Bill Swift	.10
238	Marvin Freeman	.10
239	Jason Bates	.10
240	Larry Walker	.30
241	David Nied	.10
242	Dante Bichette	.10
243	Dennis Eckersley	.10
244	Todd Stottlemyre	.10
245	Rickey Henderson	1.00
246	Geronimo Berroa	.10
247	Mark McGwire	4.00
248	Quilvio Veras	.10
249	Terry Pendleton	.10
250	Andre Dawson	.25
251	Jeff Conine	.10
252	Kurt Abbott	.10
253	Jay Buhner	.10
254	Darren Bragg	.10
255	Ken Griffey Jr.	3.50
256	Tino Martinez	.10
257	Mark Grace	.25
258	Ryne Sandberg	1.50
259	Randy Myers	.10
260	Howard Johnson	.10
261	Lee Smith	.10
262	J.T. Snow	.10
263	Chili Davis	.10
264	Chuck Finley	.10
265	Eddie Williams	.10
266	Joey Hamilton	.10
267	Ken Caminiti	.10
268	Andujar Cedeno	.10
269	Steve Finley	.10
270	Tony Gwynn	2.00

1995 Upper Deck Special Edition Gold

An insert set within an insert set, gold-foil enhanced versions of the

Special Edition cards were seeded into hobby packs at the rate of about one per box. The substitution of gold ink for silver is also carried over onto the background of the card back.

	MT
Complete Set (270):	700.00
Common Player:	2.00
Stars/Rookies:	4X

(See 1995 Upper Deck Special Edition for checklist and base card values.)

1995 Upper Deck Steal of a Deal

A horizontal format with an action photo printed over a green foil background and a large bronze seal indicating how the player was acquired are featured in this 15-card insert set. The front has a terra-cotta border, which is carried over to the back. A large green box on back details the transaction and describes why it can be categorized as a "steal" for the player's new team. These top-of-the-line chase cards were seeded in both hobby and retail packs of Series I at the average rate of one per 34 packs. Cards are numbered with a "SD" prefix.

		MT
Complete Set (15):		40.00
Common Player:		1.00
1	Mike Piazza	8.00
2	Fred McGriff	1.00
3	Kenny Lofton	1.00
4	Jose Oliva	1.00
5	Jeff Bagwell	3.00
6	Roberto Alomar, Joe Carter	1.00
7	Steve Karsay	1.00
8	Ozzie Smith	3.00
9	Dennis Eckersley	1.00
10	Jose Canseco	2.00
11	Carlos Baerga	1.00
12	Cecil Fielder	1.00
13	Don Mattingly	6.00
14	Bret Boone	1.00
15	Michael Jordan	15.00

1995 Upper Deck Update

These 45 cards depicting traded and free agent players in the uniforms of their new 1995 teams were available only by redeeming trade-in cards found in Series II packs. Each trade-in card was good for one nine-card segment of the Update series when sent with $2 prior to the Feb. 1, 1996, deadline. Update cards share the same format as the regular 1995 Upper Deck set. The Updates are sequenced according to team nickname.

		MT
Complete Set (45):		9.00
Common Player:		.15
451	Jim Abbott	.15
452	Danny Tartabull	.15
453	Ariel Prieto	.15
454	Scott Cooper	.15
455	Tom Henke	.15
456	Todd Zeile	.15
457	Brian McRae	.15
458	Luis Gonzalez	1.50
459	Jaime Navarro	.15
460	Todd Worrell	.15
461	Roberto Kelly	.15
462	Chad Fonville	.15
463	Shane Andrews	.15
464	David Segui	.15
465	Deion Sanders	.25
466	Orel Hershiser	.15
467	Ken Hill	.15
468	Andy Benes	.15
469	Terry Pendleton	.15
470	Bobby Bonilla	.15
471	Scott Erickson	.15
472	Kevin Brown	.25
473	Glenn Dishman	.15
474	Phil Plantier	.15
475	Gregg Jefferies	.15
476	Tyler Green	.15
477	Heathcliff Slocumb	.15
478	Mark Whiten	.15
479	Mickey Tettleton	.15
480	Tim Wakefield	.15
481	Vaughn Eshelman	.15
482	Rick Aguilera	.15
483	Erik Hanson	.15
484	Willie McGee	.15
485	Troy O'Leary	.15
486	Benito Santiago	.15
487	Darren Lewis	.15
488	Dave Burba	.15
489	Ron Gant	.15
490	Bret Saberhagen	.15
491	Vinny Castilla	.15
492	Frank Rodriguez	.15
493	Andy Pettitte	3.00
494	Ruben Sierra	.15
495	David Cone	.15

1995 Upper Deck Update Trade Cards

Inserted into Series II at the rate of about one per 11 packs was this five-card series of trade cards. Each card could be mailed in with $2 to receive nine cards from a special UD Update set picturing traded or free agent players in the uniforms of their new teams. The front of each trade card pictures one of the traded players in his old uniform against a red and blue background. Backs have instructions for redeeming the trade cards. The mail-in offer expired Feb. 1, 1996. Cards are numbered with a "TC" prefix.

		MT
Complete Set (5):		6.00
Common Player:		1.00
1	Orel Hershiser	1.00
2	Terry Pendleton	1.00
3	Benito Santiago	1.00
4	Kevin Brown	1.00
5	Gregg Jefferies	1.00

1996 Upper Deck

Upper Deck Series 1 consists of 240 base cards. There are 187 regular player cards plus subsets of Star Rookies, Young at Heart, Beat the Odds, Milestones, Postseason, checklists and expansion logos. The issue was marketed in 10-card foil packs in hobby and retail versions. Series 1 insert sets are Blue Chip Prospects, Future Shock and Power Driven. Cal Ripken Jr. Collection cards are inserted in both series, as are Retail Predictor (home runs, batting average and RBIs) and Hobby Predictor (Player of the Month, Pitcher of the Month and rookie hits leaders) cards. Series 2 has 240 cards, including subsets for Star Rookies, Diamond Debuts, Strange But True, Managerial Salutes and Best of a Generation. Insert sets include Hot Commodities, Hideo Nomo Highlights, Run Producers and the Lovero Collection. Factory sets comprising both regular series and the Update series were issued in two serially numbered versions, a regular boxed set in an edition of 15,000 and a wooden boxed set numbered to 500.

		MT
Unopened Factory Set (510):		40.00
Complete Set (480):		30.00
Common Player:		.05
Wax Pack (10):		1.50
Wax Box (32):		40.00
1	Cal Ripken Jr. (Milestones)	1.50
2	Eddie Murray (Milestones)	.30
3	Mark Wohlers	.05
4	Dave Justice	.20
5	Chipper Jones	2.00
6	Javier Lopez	.05
7	Mark Lemke	.05
8	Marquis Grissom	.05
9	Tom Glavine	.10
10	Greg Maddux	1.50
11	Manny Alexander	.05
12	Curtis Goodwin	.05
13	Scott Erickson	.05
14	Chris Hoiles	.05
15	Rafael Palmeiro	.30
16	Rick Krivda	.05
17	Jeff Manto	.05
18	Mo Vaughn	.60
19	Tim Wakefield	.05
20	Roger Clemens	1.50
21	Tim Naehring	.05
22	Troy O'Leary	.05
23	Mike Greenwell	.05
24	Stan Belinda	.05
25	John Valentin	.05
26	J.T. Snow	.05
27	Gary DiSarcina	.05
28	Mark Langston	.05
29	Brian Anderson	.05
30	Jim Edmonds	.05
31	Garret Anderson	.05
32	Orlando Palmeiro	.05
33	Brian McRae	.05
34	Kevin Foster	.05
35	Sammy Sosa	1.75
36	Todd Zeile	.05
37	Jim Bullinger	.05
38	Luis Gonzalez	.30
39	Lyle Mouton	.05
40	Ray Durham	.05
41	Ozzie Guillen	.05
42	Alex Fernandez	.05
43	Brian Keyser	.05
44	Robin Ventura	.05
45	Reggie Sanders	.05
46	Pete Schourek	.05
47	John Smiley	.05
48	Jeff Brantley	.05
49	Thomas Howard	.05
50	Bret Boone	.10
51	Kevin Jarvis	.05
52	Jeff Branson	.05
53	Carlos Baerga	.05
54	Jim Thome	.05
55	Manny Ramirez	1.00
56	Omar Vizquel	.05
57	Jose Mesa	.05
58	Julian Tavarez	.05
59	Orel Hershiser	.05
60	Larry Walker	.30
61	Bret Saberhagen	.05
62	Vinny Castilla	.05
63	Eric Young	.05
64	Bryan Rekar	.05

65 Andres Galarraga .05
66 Steve Reed .05
67 Chad Curtis .05
68 Bobby Higginson .10
69 Phil Nevin .10
70 Cecil Fielder .05
71 Felipe Lira .05
72 Chris Gomez .05
73 Charles Johnson .05
74 Quilvio Veras .05
75 Jeff Conine .05
76 John Burkett .05
77 Greg Colbrunn .05
78 Terry Pendleton .05
79 Shane Reynolds .05
80 Jeff Bagwell 1.00
81 Orlando Miller .05
82 Mike Hampton .05
83 James Mouton .05
84 Brian L. Hunter .05
85 Derek Bell .05
86 Kevin Appier .05
87 Joe Vitiello .05
88 Wally Joyner .05
89 Michael Tucker .05
90 Johnny Damon .15
91 Jon Nunnally .05
92 Jason Jacome .05
93 Chad Fonville .05
94 Chan Ho Park .15
95 Hideo Nomo .50
96 Ismael Valdes .05
97 Greg Gagne .05
98 Diamondbacks-Devil Rays (Expansion Card) .25
99 Raul Mondesi .20
100 Dave Winfield (Young at Heart) .75
101 Dennis Eckersley (Young at Heart) .05
102 Andre Dawson (Young at Heart) .10
103 Dennis Martinez (Young at Heart) .05
104 Lance Parrish (Young at Heart) .05
105 Eddie Murray (Young at Heart) .25
106 Alan Trammell (Young at Heart) .05
107 Lou Whitaker (Young at Heart) .05
108 Ozzie Smith (Young at Heart) .75
109 Paul Molitor (Young at Heart) .25
110 Rickey Henderson (Young at Heart) .25
111 Tim Raines (Young at Heart) .05
112 Harold Baines (Young at Heart) .05
113 Lee Smith (Young at Heart) .05
114 Fernando Valenzuela (Young at Heart) .05
115 Cal Ripken Jr. (Young at Heart) 1.25
116 Tony Gwynn (Young at Heart) .75
117 Wade Boggs (Young at Heart) .40
118 Todd Hollandsworth .05
119 Dave Nilsson .05
120 *Jose Valentin* .05
121 Steve Sparks .05
122 Chuck Carr .05
123 John Jaha .05
124 Scott Karl .05
125 Chuck Knoblauch .05
126 Brad Radke .05
127 Pat Meares .05
128 Ron Coomer .05
129 Pedro Munoz .05
130 Kirby Puckett 1.50
131 David Segui .05
132 Mark Grudzielanek .05
133 Mike Lansing .05
134 Sean Berry .05
135 Rondell White .15
136 Pedro Martinez .75
137 Carl Everett .15
138 Dave Mlicki .05
139 Bill Pulsipher .05
140 Jason Isringhausen .05
141 Rico Brogna .05
142 Edgardo Alfonzo .05
143 Jeff Kent .05
144 Andy Pettitte .15
145 Mike Piazza (Beat the Odds) 1.00
146 Cliff Floyd (Beat the Odds) .05
147 Jason Isringhausen (Beat the Odds) .05
148 Tim Wakefield (Beat the Odds) .05
149 Chipper Jones (Beat the Odds) 1.00
150 Hideo Nomo (Beat the Odds) .25
151 Mark McGwire (Beat the Odds) 1.25
152 Ron Gant (Beat the Odds) .05
153 Gary Gaetti (Beat the Odds) .05
154 Don Mattingly 1.75
155 Paul O'Neill .05
156 Derek Jeter 2.50
157 Joe Girardi .05
158 Ruben Sierra .05
159 Jorge Posada .05
160 Geronimo Berroa .05
161 Steve Ontiveros .05
162 George Williams .05
163 Doug Johns .05
164 Ariel Prieto .05
165 Scott Brosius .05
166 Mike Bordick .05
167 Tyler Green .05
168 Mickey Morandini .05
169 Darren Daulton .05
170 Gregg Jefferies .05
171 Jim Eisenreich .05
172 Heathcliff Slocumb .05
173 Kevin Stocker .05
174 Esteban Loaiza .05
175 Jeff King .05
176 Mark Johnson .05
177 Denny Neagle .05
178 Orlando Merced .05
179 Carlos Garcia .05
180 Brian Jordan .05
181 Mike Morgan .05
182 Mark Petkovsek .05
183 Bernard Gilkey .05
184 John Mabry .05
185 Tom Henke .05
186 Glenn Dishman .05
187 Andy Ashby .05
188 Bip Roberts .05
189 Melvin Nieves .05
190 Ken Caminiti .05
191 Brad Ausmus .05
192 Deion Sanders .10
193 Jamie Brewington .05
194 Glenallen Hill .05
195 Barry Bonds 1.50
196 William VanLandingham .05
197 Mark Carreon .05
198 Royce Clayton .05
199 Joey Cora .05
200 Ken Griffey Jr. 2.25
201 Jay Buhner .05
202 Alex Rodriguez 2.25
203 Norm Charlton .05
204 Andy Benes .05
205 Edgar Martinez .05
206 Juan Gonzalez 1.00
207 Will Clark .15
208 Kevin Gross .05
209 Roger Pavlik .05
210 Ivan Rodriguez .75
211 Rusty Greer .05
212 Angel Martinez .05
213 Tomas Perez .05
214 Alex Gonzalez .10
215 Joe Carter .05
216 Shawn Green .30
217 Edwin Hurtado .05
218 (Edgar Martinez, Tony Pena) (Post Season Checklist) .05
219 Chipper Jones, Barry Larkin (Post Season Checklist) .05
220 Orel Hershiser (Post Season Checklist) .05
221 Mike Devereaux (Post Season Checklist) .05
222 Tom Glavine (Post Season Checklist) .05
223 Karim Garcia (Star Rookies) .15
224 Arquimedez Pozo (Star Rookies) .05
225 Billy Wagner (Star Rookies) .10
226 John Wasdin (Star Rookies) .05
227 Jeff Suppan (Star Rookies) .05
228 Steve Gibralter (Star Rookies) .05
229 Jimmy Haynes (Star Rookies) .05
230 Ruben Rivera (Star Rookies) .05
231 Chris Snopek (Star Rookies) .05
232 Alex Ochoa (Star Rookies) .05
233 Shannon Stewart (Star Rookies) .10
234 Quinton McCracken (Star Rookies) .05
235 Trey Beamon (Star Rookies) .05
236 Billy McMillon (Star Rookies) .05
237 Steve Cox (Star Rookies) .05
238 George Arias (Star Rookies) .05
239 Yamil Benitez (Star Rookies) .05
240 Todd Greene (Star Rookies) .05
241 Jason Kendall (Star Rookie) .10
242 Brooks Kieschnick (Star Rookie) .05
243 *Osvaldo Fernandez* (Star Rookie) .15
244 *Livan Hernandez* (Star Rookie) .50
245 Rey Ordonez (Star Rookie) .10
246 *Mike Grace* (Star Rookie) .05
247 Jay Canizaro (Star Rookie) .05
248 Bob Wolcott (Star Rookie) .05
249 Jermaine Dye (Star Rookie) .05
250 Jason Schmidt (Star Rookie) .05
251 *Mike Sweeney* (Star Rookie) 2.00
252 Marcus Jensen (Star Rookie) .05
253 Mendy Lopez (Star Rookie) .05
254 *Wilton Guerrero* (Star Rookie) .35
255 Paul Wilson (Star Rookie) .10
256 Edgar Renteria (Star Rookie) .10
257 Richard Hidalgo (Star Rookie) .10
258 Bob Abreu (Star Rookie) .25
259 *Robert Smith* (Diamond Debuts) .05
260 Sal Fasano (Diamond Debuts) .05
261 Enrique Wilson (Diamond Debuts) .05
262 *Rich Hunter* (Diamond Debuts) .05
263 Sergio Nunez (Diamond Debuts) .05
264 Dan Serafini (Diamond Debuts) .05
265 *David Doster* (Diamond Debuts) .05
266 Ryan McGuire (Diamond Debuts) .05
267 Scott Spiezio (Diamond Debuts) .05
268 Rafael Orellano (Diamond Debuts) .05
269 Steve Avery .05
270 Fred McGriff .05
271 John Smoltz .10
272 Ryan Klesko .05
273 Jeff Blauser .05
274 Brad Clontz .05
275 Roberto Alomar .65
276 B.J. Surhoff .05
277 Jeffrey Hammonds .05
278 Brady Anderson .05
279 Bobby Bonilla .05
280 Cal Ripken Jr. 2.50
281 Mike Mussina .60
282 Wil Cordero .05
283 Mike Stanley .05
284 Aaron Sele .05
285 Jose Canseco .50
286 Tom Gordon .05
287 Heathcliff Slocumb .05
288 Lee Smith .05
289 Troy Percival .05
290 Tim Salmon .25
291 Chuck Finley .05
292 Jim Abbott .05
293 Chili Davis .05
294 Steve Trachsel .05
295 Mark Grace .25
296 Rey Sanchez .05
297 Scott Servais .05
298 Jaime Navarro .05
299 Frank Castillo .05
300 Frank Thomas 1.00
301 Jason Bere .05
302 Danny Tartabull .05
303 Darren Lewis .05
304 Roberto Hernandez .05
305 Tony Phillips .05
306 Wilson Alvarez .05
307 Jose Rijo .05
308 Hal Morris .05
309 Mark Portugal .05
310 Barry Larkin .10
311 Dave Burba .05
312 Eddie Taubensee .05
313 Sandy Alomar Jr. .05
314 Dennis Martinez .05
315 Albert Belle .35
316 Eddie Murray .60
317 Charles Nagy .05
318 Chad Ogea .05
319 Kenny Lofton .05
320 Dante Bichette .05
321 Armando Reynoso .05
322 Walt Weiss .05
323 Ellis Burks .05
324 Kevin Ritz .05
325 Bill Swift .05
326 Jason Bates .05
327 Tony Clark .05
328 Travis Fryman .05
329 Mark Parent .05
330 Alan Trammell .05
331 C.J. Nitkowski .05
332 Jose Lima .05
333 Phil Plantier .05
334 Kurt Abbott .05
335 Andre Dawson .25
336 Chris Hammond .05
337 Robb Nen .05
338 Pat Rapp .05
339 Al Leiter .05
340 Gary Sheffield .20
341 Todd Jones .05
342 Doug Drabek .05
343 Greg Swindell .05
344 Tony Eusebio .05
345 Craig Biggio .10
346 Darryl Kile .05
347 Mike Macfarlane .05
348 Jeff Montgomery .05
349 Chris Haney .05
350 Bip Roberts .05
351 Tom Goodwin .05
352 Mark Gubicza .05
353 Joe Randa .05
354 Ramon Martinez .05
355 Eric Karros .05
356 Delino DeShields .05
357 Brett Butler .05
358 Todd Worrell .05
359 Mike Blowers .05
360 Mike Piazza 2.00
361 Ben McDonald .05
362 Ricky Bones .05
363 Greg Vaughn .05
364 Matt Mieske .05
365 Kevin Seitzer .05

366 Jeff Cirillo .05
367 LaTroy Hawkins .05
368 Frank Rodriguez .05
369 Rick Aguilera .05
370 Roberto Alomar (Best of a Generation) .30
371 Albert Belle (Best of a Generation) .20
372 Wade Boggs (Best of a Generation) .25
373 Barry Bonds (Best of a Generation) 1.00
374 Roger Clemens (Best of a Generation) .75
375 Dennis Eckersley (Best of a Generation) .05
376 Ken Griffey Jr. (Best of a Generation) 1.25
377 Tony Gwynn (Best of a Generation) .75
378 Rickey Henderson (Best of a Generation) .25
379 Greg Maddux (Best of a Generation) .75
380 Fred McGriff (Best of a Generation) .05
381 Paul Molitor (Best of a Generation) .25
382 Eddie Murray (Best of a Generation) .25
383 Mike Piazza (Best of a Generation) 1.00
384 Kirby Puckett (Best of a Generation) .75
385 Cal Ripken Jr. (Best of a Generation) 1.25
386 Ozzie Smith (Best of a Generation) .75
387 Frank Thomas (Best of a Generation) .50
388 Matt Walbeck .05
389 Dave Stevens .05
390 Marty Cordova .05
391 Darrin Fletcher .05
392 Cliff Floyd .05
393 Mel Rojas .05
394 Shane Andrews .05
395 Moises Alou .20
396 Carlos Perez .05
397 Jeff Fassero .05
398 Bobby Jones .05
399 Todd Hundley .05
400 John Franco .05
401 Jose Vizcaino .05
402 Bernard Gilkey .05
403 Pete Harnisch .05
404 Pat Kelly .05
405 David Cone .05
406 Bernie Williams .30
407 John Wetteland .05
408 Scott Kamieniecki .05
409 Tim Raines .05
410 Wade Boggs .75
411 Terry Steinbach .05
412 Jason Giambi .35
413 Todd Van Poppel .05
414 Pedro Munoz .05
415 Eddie Murray-1990 (Strange But True) .25
416 Dennis Eckersley-1990 (Strange But True) .05
417 Bip Roberts-1992 (Strange But True) .05
418 Glenallen Hill-1992 (Strange But True) .05
419 John Hudek-1994 (Strange But True) .05
420 Derek Bell-1995 (Strange But True) .05
421 Larry Walker-1995 (Strange But True) .10
422 Greg Maddux-1995 (Strange But True) .75
423 Ken Caminiti-1995 (Strange But True) .05
424 Brent Gates .05
425 Mark McGwire 2.50
426 Mark Whiten .05
427 Sid Fernandez .05
428 Ricky Bottalico .05
429 Mike Mimbs .05
430 Lenny Dykstra .05
431 Todd Zeile .05
432 Benito Santiago .05
433 Danny Miceli .05
434 Al Martin .05
435 Jay Bell .05
436 Charlie Hayes .05
437 Mike Kingery .05
438 Paul Wagner .05
439 Tom Pagnozzi .05
440 Ozzie Smith 1.50
441 Ray Lankford .05
442 Dennis Eckersley .05
443 Ron Gant .05
444 Alan Benes .05
445 Rickey Henderson .75
446 Jody Reed .05
447 Trevor Hoffman .05
448 Andujar Cedeno .05
449 Steve Finley .05
450 Tony Gwynn 1.50
451 Joey Hamilton .05
452 Mark Leiter .05
453 Rod Beck .05
454 Kirt Manwaring .05
455 Matt Williams .15
456 Robby Thompson .05
457 Shawon Dunston .05
458 Russ Davis .05
459 Paul Sorrento .05
460 Randy Johnson .65
461 Chris Bosio .05
462 Luis Sojo .05
463 Sterling Hitchcock .05
464 Benji Gil .05
465 Mickey Tettleton .05
466 Mark McLemore .05
467 Darryl Hamilton .05
468 Ken Hill .05
469 Dean Palmer .05
470 Carlos Delgado .30
471 Ed Sprague .05
472 Otis Nixon .05
473 Pat Hentgen .05
474 Juan Guzman .05
475 John Olerud .05
476 Checklist (Buck Showalter) .05
477 Checklist (Bobby Cox) .05
478 Checklist (Tommy Lasorda) .05
479 Checklist (Jim Leyland) .05
480 Checklist (Sparky Anderson) .05

1996 Upper Deck Blue Chip Prospects

Twenty top young stars who could make a major impact in the major leagues in upcoming seasons are featured in this insert set. Each card is highlighted with blue-foil printing and double die-cut technology, which includes a zig-zag pattern around the top and a die-cut around both bottom corners. The cards are found one per 20 packs in Series 1 foil packs. Cards are numbered with a "BC" prefix.

		MT
Complete Set (20):		70.00
Common Player:		1.50
1	Hideo Nomo	4.00
2	Johnny Damon	2.00
3	Jason Isringhausen	2.00
4	Bill Pulsipher	1.50
5	Marty Cordova	1.50
6	Michael Tucker	1.50
7	John Wasdin	1.50
8	Karim Garcia	2.00
9	Ruben Rivera	1.50
10	Chipper Jones	20.00
11	Billy Wagner	2.00
12	Brooks Kieschnick	1.50
13	Alex Ochoa	1.50
14	Roger Cedeno	2.00
15	Alex Rodriguez	20.00
16	Jason Schmidt	1.50
17	Derek Jeter	25.00
18	Brian L. Hunter	1.50
19	Garret Anderson	1.50
20	Manny Ramirez	8.00

1996 Upper Deck Cal Ripken Collection

Part of a cross-brand insert set, four cards are included as Series I inserts at the rate of one per 24 packs. Five cards are also included in Series II, one per every 23 packs. They chronicle Cal Ripken's career and highlights.

		MT
Complete Set (8):		25.00
Common Card:		4.00
Header:		4.00
5	Cal Ripken Jr.	4.00
6	Cal Ripken Jr.	4.00
7	Cal Ripken Jr.	4.00
8	Cal Ripken Jr.	4.00
13	Cal Ripken Jr.	4.00
14	Cal Ripken Jr.	4.00
15	Cal Ripken Jr.	4.00
16	Cal Ripken Jr.	4.00
17	Cal Ripken Jr.	4.00

1996 Upper Deck Diamond Destiny

This late-season release is found exclusively in retail foil packs labeled "Upper Deck Tech." They are inserted at a rate of one per pack, sold with eight regular 1996 Upper Deck cards at a suggested retail of around $3. The cards have three versions of the same action photo; in color and black-and-white on front, and in black-and-white on back. A large team logo also appears on front and back. In the upper half of the card is a 1-3/16" diameter round color transparency portrait of the player. The basic version of this chase set had bronze foil highlights. Parallel silver and gold versions are found on average of one per 35 and one per 143 packs, respectively. Cards are numbered with a "DD" prefix.

		MT
Complete Set (Bronze):		75.00
Common Player (Bronze):		.60
Silver:		5X
Gold:		15X
1	Chipper Jones	4.00
2	Fred McGriff	.60
3	Ryan Klesko	.60
4	John Smoltz	.75
5	Greg Maddux	3.00
6	Cal Ripken Jr.	6.00
7	Roberto Alomar	2.00
8	Eddie Murray	2.00
9	Brady Anderson	.60
10	Mo Vaughn	1.50
11	Roger Clemens	3.00
12	Darin Erstad	3.00
13	Sammy Sosa	3.50
14	Frank Thomas	3.50
15	Barry Larkin	.75
16	Albert Belle	.75
17	Manny Ramirez	2.50
18	Kenny Lofton	.60
19	Dante Bichette	.60
20	Gary Sheffield	1.00
21	Jeff Bagwell	2.50
22	Hideo Nomo	1.50
23	Mike Piazza	4.00
24	Kirby Puckett	3.00
25	Paul Molitor	2.00
26	Chuck Knoblauch	.60
27	Wade Boggs	2.50
28	Derek Jeter	4.00
29	Rey Ordonez	.60
30	Mark McGwire	6.00
31	Ozzie Smith	3.00
32	Tony Gwynn	3.00
33	Barry Bonds	3.50
34	Matt Williams	.75
35	Ken Griffey Jr.	5.00
36	Jay Buhner	.60
37	Randy Johnson	2.00
38	Alex Rodriguez	5.00
39	Juan Gonzalez	2.50
40	Joe Carter	.60

1996 Upper Deck Future Stock

Future Stock inserts are found on average of one per six packs of Series 1, highlighting 20 top young stars on a die-cut design. Each card has a blue border, vertical photo and silver-foil stamping on the front. Cards are numbered with a "FS" prefix.

		MT
Complete Set (20):		4.00
Common Player:		.25
1	George Arias	.25
2	Brian Barnes	.25
3	Trey Beamon	.25
4	Yamil Benitez	.25
5	Jamie Brewington	.25
6	Tony Clark	.50
7	Steve Cox	.25
8	Carlos Delgado	.50
9	Chad Fonville	.25
10	Steve Gibralter	.25
11	Curtis Goodwin	.25
12	Todd Greene	.25
13	Jimmy Haynes	.25
14	Quinton McCracken	.25
15	Billy McMillon	.25
16	Chan Ho Park	.75
17	Arquimedez Pozo	.25
18	Chris Snopek	.25
19	Shannon Stewart	.50
20	Jeff Suppan	.25

1996 Upper Deck Gameface

		MT
Complete Set (10):		6.00
Common Player:		.15
1	Ken Griffey Jr.	1.25
2	Frank Thomas	.75
3	Barry Bonds	.75
4	Albert Belle	.35
5	Cal Ripken Jr.	1.50
6	Mike Piazza	1.00
7	Chipper Jones	1.00
8	Matt Williams	.15
9	Hideo Nomo	.45
10	Greg Maddux	.60

1996 Upper Deck Hideo Nomo R.O.Y.

The Japanese pitcher's 1995 Rookie of the Year season was commemorated with this large-format (3-1/2" x 5"), die-cut card sold only via TV shopping programs. The card has an action photo of Nomo on front and is highlighted in gold foil, including a replica of his autograph. On back is an action photo, major league career summary and stats and a serial number from within an edition of 5,000 pieces.

	MT
Hideo Nomo	15.00

1996 Upper Deck Hobby Predictor

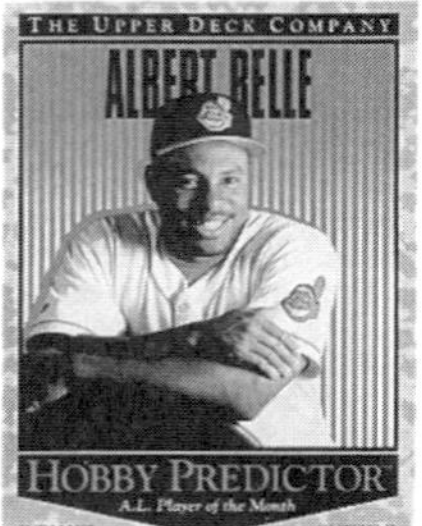

These inserts depict 60 top players as possible winners in the categories of Player of the Month, Pitcher of the Month and Rookie Hits Leader. If the pictured player won that category any month of the season the card was redeemable for a 10-card set with a different look, action photos and printed on silver-foil stock. Hobby Predictor inserts are found on average once per dozen packs in both series. Winning cards are indicated by (W). Cards are numbered with a "H" prefix.

		MT
Complete Set (60):		55.00
Common Player:		.50
1	Albert Belle	.75
2	Kenny Lofton	.50
3	Rafael Palmeiro	.75
4	Ken Griffey Jr.	3.50
5	Tim Salmon	.75
6	Cal Ripken Jr.	4.00
7	Mark McGwire (W)	5.00
8	Frank Thomas (W)	3.00
9	Mo Vaughn (W)	1.50
10	Player of the Month Long Shot (W)	.50
11	Roger Clemens	2.50
12	David Cone	.50
13	Jose Mesa	.50
14	Randy Johnson	1.00
15	Steve Finley	.50
16	Mike Mussina	1.00
17	Kevin Appier	.50
18	Kenny Rogers	.50
19	Lee Smith	.50
20	Pitcher of the Month Long Shot (W)	.50
21	George Arias	.50
22	Jose Herrera	.50
23	Tony Clark	.50
24	Todd Greene	.50
25	Derek Jeter (W)	4.00
26	Arquimedez Pozo	.50
27	Matt Lawton	.50
28	Shannon Stewart	.50
29	Chris Snopek	.50
30	Rookie Hits Long Shot	.50
31	Jeff Bagwell (W)	2.50
32	Dante Bichette	.50
33	Barry Bonds (W)	3.00
34	Tony Gwynn	2.50
35	Chipper Jones	3.00
36	Eric Karros	.50
37	Barry Larkin	.50
38	Mike Piazza	3.00
39	Matt Williams	.75
40	Player of the Month Long Shot (W)	.50
41	Osvaldo Fernandez	.50
42	Tom Glavine	.50
43	Jason Isringhausen	.50
44	Greg Maddux	2.50
45	Pedro Martinez	1.50
46	Hideo Nomo	1.00
47	Pete Schourek	.50
48	Paul Wilson	.50
49	Mark Wohlers	.50
50	Pitcher of the Month Long Shot	.50
51	Bob Abreu	.50
52	Trey Beamon	.50
53	Yamil Benitez	.50
54	Roger Cedeno (W)	.75
55	Todd Hollandsworth	.50
56	Marvin Benard	.50
57	Jason Kendall	.50
58	Brooks Kieschnick	.50
59	Rey Ordonez (W)	1.50
60	Rookie Hits Long Shot (W)	.50

1996 Upper Deck Hot Commodities

These 20 die-cut cards were seeded one per every 37 1996 Upper Deck Series II packs. Cards are numbered with a "HC" prefix.

		MT
Complete Set (20):		75.00
Common Player:		1.50
1	Ken Griffey Jr.	9.00
2	Hideo Nomo	2.25
3	Roberto Alomar	2.50
4	Paul Wilson	1.50
5	Albert Belle	2.00
6	Manny Ramirez	4.50
7	Kirby Puckett	6.00
8	Johnny Damon	1.50
9	Randy Johnson	2.50
10	Greg Maddux	6.00
11	Chipper Jones	7.50
12	Barry Bonds	6.50
13	Mo Vaughn	2.50
14	Mike Piazza	7.50
15	Cal Ripken Jr.	10.00
16	Tim Salmon	2.00
17	Sammy Sosa	6.50
18	Kenny Lofton	1.50
19	Tony Gwynn	6.00
20	Frank Thomas	6.50

1996 Upper Deck Lovero Collection

Every sixth pack of 1996 Upper Deck Series II has a V.J. Lovero insert card. This 20-card set features unique shots from Lovero, one of the most well-known photographers in the country. Some of the cards feature Randy Johnson wearing a conehead, Frank Thomas blowing a bubble while throwing the ball, and Jay Buhner and his child both chewing on a bat. Cards are numbered with a "VJ" prefix.

		MT
Complete Set (20):		26.00
Common Player:		.35
1	Rod Carew	.50
2	Hideo Nomo	.75
3	Derek Jeter	5.00
4	Barry Bonds	2.75
5	Greg Maddux	2.50
6	Mark McGwire	5.00
7	Jose Canseco	1.50
8	Ken Caminiti	.35
9	Raul Mondesi	.50
10	Ken Griffey Jr.	4.00
11	Jay Buhner	.35
12	Randy Johnson	.75
13	Roger Clemens	2.00
14	Brady Anderson	.35
15	Frank Thomas	1.50
16	Angels Outfielders	.35
17	Mike Piazza	3.50
18	Dante Bichette	.35
19	Tony Gwynn	2.00
20	Jim Abbott	.35

1996 Upper Deck Power Driven

Twenty of the game's top power hitters are analyzed in depth by baseball writer Peter Gammons on these Series 1 insert cards. Found once per 36 packs, on average, the cards are printed on an embossed light F/X design. Cards are numbered with a "PD" prefix.

		MT
Complete Set (20):		50.00
Common Player:		.50
1	Albert Belle	.75
2	Barry Bonds	5.00
3	Jay Buhner	.50
4	Jose Canseco	1.50
5	Cecil Fielder	.50
6	Juan Gonzalez	3.00
7	Ken Griffey Jr.	10.00
8	Eric Karros	.50
9	Fred McGriff	.50
10	Mark McGwire	10.00
11	Rafael Palmeiro	.75
12	Mike Piazza	8.00
13	Manny Ramirez	3.00
14	Tim Salmon	.75
15	Reggie Sanders	.50
16	Sammy Sosa	5.00
17	Frank Thomas	3.00
18	Mo Vaughn	1.00
19	Larry Walker	.75
20	Matt Williams	.75

1996 Upper Deck Retail Predictor

Retail Predictor inserts feature 60 possible winners in the categories of monthly leader in home runs, batting average and RBIs. If the pictured player led a category in any month, his card was redeemable for a 10-card set featuring action photos on silver foil. Retail Predictors are found on average once per 12 packs in each series. Winning cards are indicated by (W). Cards are numbered with a "R" prefix.

		MT
Complete Set (60):		60.00
Common Player:		.50
1	Albert Belle (W)	1.00
2	Jay Buhner (W)	.65
3	Juan Gonzalez	1.50
4	Ken Griffey Jr.	3.50
5	Mark McGwire (W)	5.00
6	Rafael Palmeiro	.75
7	Tim Salmon	.50
8	Frank Thomas	2.50
9	Mo Vaughn (W)	1.00
10	Home Run Long Shot (W)	.50
11	Albert Belle (W)	1.00
12	Jay Buhner	.50
13	Jim Edmonds	.50
14	Cecil Fielder	.50
15	Ken Griffey Jr.	3.50
16	Edgar Martinez	.50
17	Manny Ramirez	1.50
18	Frank Thomas	2.50
19	Mo Vaughn (W)	1.00
20	RBI Long Shot (W)	.50
21	Roberto Alomar (W)	1.00
22	Carlos Baerga	.50
23	Wade Boggs	1.00
24	Ken Griffey Jr.	3.50
25	Chuck Knoblauch	.50
26	Kenny Lofton	.50
27	Edgar Martinez	.50
28	Tim Salmon	.50
29	Frank Thomas	2.50
30	Batting Average Long Shot (W)	.50
31	Dante Bichette	.50
32	Barry Bonds (W)	3.50
33	Ron Gant	.50
34	Chipper Jones	3.25
35	Fred McGriff	.50
36	Mike Piazza	3.25
37	Sammy Sosa	3.00
38	Larry Walker	.75
39	Matt Williams	.75
40	Home Run Long Shot	.50
41	Jeff Bagwell (W)	2.50
42	Dante Bichette	.50
43	Barry Bonds (W)	3.50
44	Jeff Conine	.50
45	Andres Galarraga	.50
46	Mike Piazza	3.25
47	Reggie Sanders	.50
48	Sammy Sosa	3.00
49	Matt Williams	.75
50	RBI Long Shot	.50
51	Jeff Bagwell	1.50
52	Derek Bell	.50
53	Dante Bichette	.50
54	Craig Biggio	.50
55	Barry Bonds	3.00
56	Bret Boone	.50
57	Tony Gwynn	2.00
58	Barry Larkin	.50
59	Mike Piazza (W)	5.00
60	AVG Long Shot	.50

1996 Upper Deck Run Producers

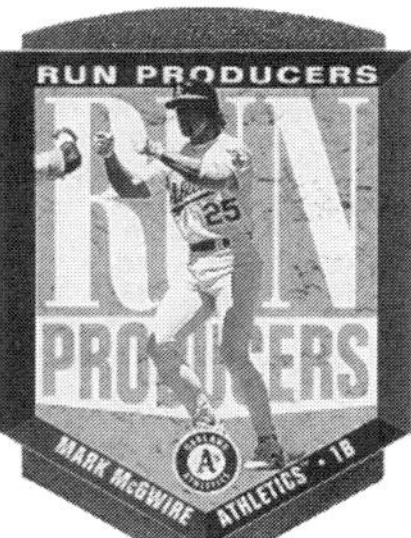

These double die-cut, embossed and color foil-stamped cards feature 20 of the game's top RBI men. The cards were seeded one per every 71 packs of 1996 Upper Deck Series II. Cards are numbered with a "RP" prefix.

		MT
Complete Set (20):		70.00
Common Player:		.75
1	Albert Belle	1.00
2	Dante Bichette	.75
3	Barry Bonds	8.00
4	Jay Buhner	.75
5	Jose Canseco	3.00
6	Juan Gonzalez	4.00
7	Ken Griffey Jr.	12.00
8	Tony Gwynn	4.00
9	Kenny Lofton	.75
10	Edgar Martinez	.75
11	Fred McGriff	.75
12	Mark McGwire	15.00
13	Rafael Palmeiro	2.00
14	Mike Piazza	12.00
15	Manny Ramirez	4.00
16	Tim Salmon	1.00
17	Sammy Sosa	8.00
18	Frank Thomas	5.00
19	Mo Vaughn	2.00
20	Matt Williams	1.50

1996 Upper Deck Update

Available on via a mail-in wrapper redemption or in factory sets, this update set offers cards of players who changed teams after the base card set was issued, as well as a few rookies and others. Cards share the earlier issue's format and are numbered with a "U" suffix.

		MT
Complete Set (30):		10.00
Common Player:		.25
481	Randy Myers	.25
482	Kent Mercker	.25
483	David Wells	.35
484	Kevin Mitchell	.25
485	Randy Velarde	.25
486	Ryne Sandberg	3.00
487	Doug Jones	.25
488	Terry Adams	.25
489	Kevin Tapani	.25
490	Harold Baines	.25
491	Eric Davis	.25
492	Julio Franco	.25
493	Jack McDowell	.25
494	Devon White	.25
495	Kevin Brown	.35
496	Rick Wilkins	.25
497	Sean Berry	.25
498	Keith Lockhart	.25
499	Mark Loretta	.25
500	Paul Molitor	2.50
501	Roberto Kelly	.25
502	Lance Johnson	.25
503	Tino Martinez	.25
504	Kenny Rogers	.25
505	Todd Stottlemyre	.25
506	Gary Gaetti	.25
507	Royce Clayton	.25
508	Andy Benes	.25
509	Wally Joyner	.25
510	Erik Hanson	.25

1997 Upper Deck

The 520-card, regular-sized set was available in 12-card packs. The base card fronts feature a full action shot with the player's name near the bottom edge above a bronze-foil, woodgrain stripe. The player's team logo is in the lower left corner in silver foil. Each card front has the date of the game pictured with a brief description. The card backs contain more detailed game highlight descriptions and statistics, along with a small action shot in the upper left quadrant. Subsets are: Jackie Robinson Tribute (1-9), Strike Force (65-72), Defensive Gems (136-153), Global Impact (181-207), Season Highlights Checklist (214-222) and Star Rookies (223-240). Inserts are: Game Jerseys, Ticket To Stardom, Power Package, Amazing Greats and Rock Solid Foundation. A 30-card update to Series I was released early in the season featuring 1996 post-season highlights and star rookies. The card faces had red or purple borders and were numbered 241 to 270. A second update set of 30 was released near the end of the 1997 season, numbered 521-550 and featuring traded players and rookies in a format identical to Series I and II UD. Both of the update sets were available only via a mail-in redemption offer.

		MT
Complete Set (550):		100.00
Complete Series 1 Set (240):		30.00
Complete Update Set (241-270):		20.00
Complete Series 2 Set (271-520):		40.00
Complete Update Set (521-550):		10.00
Common Player:		.05
Series 1 or 2 Pack (12):		2.00
Series 1 or 2 Wax Box (28):		45.00
1	Jackie Robinson	1.00
2	Jackie Robinson	1.00
3	Jackie Robinson	1.00
4	Jackie Robinson	1.00
5	Jackie Robinson	1.00
6	Jackie Robinson	1.00
7	Jackie Robinson	1.00
8	Jackie Robinson	1.00
9	Jackie Robinson	1.00
10	Chipper Jones	2.00
11	Marquis Grissom	.05
12	Jermaine Dye	.05
13	Mark Lemke	.05
14	Terrell Wade	.05
15	Fred McGriff	.05
16	Tom Glavine	.10
17	Mark Wohlers	.05
18	Randy Myers	.05
19	Roberto Alomar	.65
20	Cal Ripken Jr.	3.00
21	Rafael Palmeiro	.30
22	Mike Mussina	.60
23	Brady Anderson	.05
24	Jose Canseco	.50
25	Mo Vaughn	.60
26	Roger Clemens	1.50
27	Tim Naehring	.05
28	Jeff Suppan	.05
29	Troy Percival	.05
30	Sammy Sosa	1.75
31	Amaury Telemaco	.05

No.	Card	Value
32	Rey Sanchez	.05
33	Scott Servais	.05
34	Steve Trachsel	.05
35	Mark Grace	.20
36	Wilson Alvarez	.05
37	Harold Baines	.05
38	Tony Phillips	.05
39	James Baldwin	.05
40	Frank Thomas (wrong (Ken Griffey Jr.'s) vital data)	1.00
41	Lyle Mouton	.05
42	Chris Snopek	.05
43	Hal Morris	.05
44	Eric Davis	.05
45	Barry Larkin	.10
46	Reggie Sanders	.05
47	Pete Schourek	.05
48	Lee Smith	.05
49	Charles Nagy	.05
50	Albert Belle	.35
51	Julio Franco	.05
52	Kenny Lofton	.05
53	Orel Hershiser	.05
54	Omar Vizquel	.05
55	Eric Young	.05
56	Curtis Leskanic	.05
57	Quinton McCracken	.05
58	Kevin Ritz	.05
59	Walt Weiss	.05
60	Dante Bichette	.05
61	Marc Lewis	.05
62	Tony Clark	.05
63	Travis Fryman	.05
64	John Smoltz (Strike Force)	.05
65	Greg Maddux (Strike Force)	.75
66	Tom Glavine (Strike Force)	.05
67	Mike Mussina (Strike Force)	.30
68	Andy Pettitte (Strike Force)	.30
69	Mariano Rivera (Strike Force)	.10
70	Hideo Nomo (Strike Force)	.30
71	Kevin Brown (Strike Force)	.05
72	Randy Johnson (Strike Force)	.25
73	Felipe Lira	.05
74	Kimera Bartee	.05
75	Alan Trammell	.05
76	Kevin Brown	.10
77	Edgar Renteria	.05
78	Al Leiter	.05
79	Charles Johnson	.05
80	Andre Dawson	.20
81	Billy Wagner	.05
82	Donne Wall	.05
83	Jeff Bagwell	1.00
84	Keith Lockhart	.05
85	Jeff Montgomery	.05
86	Tom Goodwin	.05
87	Tim Belcher	.05
88	Mike Macfarlane	.05
89	Joe Randa	.05
90	Brett Butler	.05
91	Todd Worrell	.05
92	Todd Hollandsworth	.05
93	Ismael Valdes	.05
94	Hideo Nomo	.60
95	Mike Piazza	2.00
96	Jeff Cirillo	.05
97	Ricky Bones	.05
98	Fernando Vina	.05
99	Ben McDonald	.05
100	John Jaha	.05
101	Mark Loretta	.05
102	Paul Molitor	.60
103	Rick Aguilera	.05
104	Marty Cordova	.05
105	Kirby Puckett	1.50
106	Dan Naulty	.05
107	Frank Rodriguez	.05
108	Shane Andrews	.05
109	Henry Rodriguez	.05
110	Mark Grudzielanek	.05
111	Pedro Martinez	.75
112	Ugueth Urbina	.05
113	David Segui	.05
114	Rey Ordonez	.05
115	Bernard Gilkey	.05
116	Butch Huskey	.05
117	Paul Wilson	.05
118	Alex Ochoa	.05
119	John Franco	.05
120	Dwight Gooden	.05
121	Ruben Rivera	.05
122	Andy Pettitte	.65
123	Tino Martinez	.05
124	Bernie Williams	.30
125	Wade Boggs	.60
126	Paul O'Neill	.05
127	Scott Brosius	.05
128	Ernie Young	.05
129	Doug Johns	.05
130	Geronimo Berroa	.05
131	Jason Giambi	.30
132	John Wasdin	.05
133	Jim Eisenreich	.05
134	Ricky Otero	.05
135	Ricky Bottalico	.05
136	Mark Langston (Defensive Gems)	.05
137	Greg Maddux (Defensive Gems)	.75
138	Ivan Rodriguez (Defensive Gems)	.30
139	Charles Johnson (Defensive Gems)	.05
140	J.T. Snow (Defensive Gems)	.05
141	Mark Grace (Defensive Gems)	.10
142	Roberto Alomar (Defensive Gems)	.30
143	Craig Biggio (Defensive Gems)	.05
144	Ken Caminiti (Defensive Gems)	.05
145	Matt Williams (Defensive Gems)	.05
146	Omar Vizquel (Defensive Gems)	.05
147	Cal Ripken Jr. (Defensive Gems)	1.50
148	Ozzie Smith (Defensive Gems)	.75
149	Rey Ordonez (Defensive Gems)	.05
150	Ken Griffey Jr. (Defensive Gems)	1.25
151	Devon White (Defensive Gems)	.05
152	Barry Bonds (Defensive Gems)	.90
153	Kenny Lofton (Defensive Gems)	.05
154	Mickey Morandini	.05
155	Gregg Jefferies	.05
156	Curt Schilling	.15
157	Jason Kendall	.05
158	Francisco Cordova	.05
159	Dennis Eckersley	.05
160	Ron Gant	.05
161	Ozzie Smith	1.50
162	Brian Jordan	.05
163	John Mabry	.05
164	Andy Ashby	.05
165	Steve Finley	.05
166	Fernando Valenzuela	.05
167	Archi Cianfrocco	.05
168	Wally Joyner	.05
169	Greg Vaughn	.05
170	Barry Bonds	1.75
171	William VanLandingham	.05
172	Marvin Benard	.05
173	Rich Aurilla	.05
174	Jay Canizaro	.05
175	Ken Griffey Jr.	2.50
176	Bob Wells	.05
177	Jay Buhner	.05
178	Sterling Hitchcock	.05
179	Edgar Martinez	.05
180	Rusty Greer	.05
181	Dave Nilsson (Global Impact)	.05
182	Larry Walker (Global Impact)	.10
183	Edgar Renteria (Global Impact)	.05
184	Rey Ordonez (Global Impact)	.05
185	Rafael Palmeiro (Global Impact)	.10
186	Osvaldo Fernandez (Global Impact)	.05
187	Raul Mondesi (Global Impact)	.10
188	Manny Ramirez (Global Impact)	.50
189	Sammy Sosa (Global Impact)	.90
190	Robert Eenhoorn (Global Impact)	.05
191	Devon White (Global Impact)	.05
192	Hideo Nomo (Global Impact)	.30
193	Mac Suzuki (Global Impact)	.05
194	Chan Ho Park (Global Impact)	.10
195	Fernando Valenzuela (Global Impact)	.05
196	Andruw Jones (Global Impact)	.50
197	Vinny Castilla (Global Impact)	.05
198	Dennis Martinez (Global Impact)	.05
199	Ruben Rivera (Global Impact)	.05
200	Juan Gonzalez (Global Impact)	.50
201	Roberto Alomar (Global Impact)	.30
202	Edgar Martinez (Global Impact)	.05
203	Ivan Rodriguez (Global Impact)	.30
204	Carlos Delgado (Global Impact)	.50
205	Andres Galarraga (Global Impact)	.05
206	Ozzie Guillen (Global Impact)	.05
207	Midre Cummings (Global Impact)	.05
208	Roger Pavlik	.05
209	Darren Oliver	.05
210	Dean Palmer	.05
211	Ivan Rodriguez	.75
212	Otis Nixon	.05
213	Pat Hentgen	.05
214	Ozzie Smith, Andre Dawson, Kirby Puckett CL (Season Highlights)	.40
215	Barry Bonds, Gary Sheffield, Brady Anderson (Checklist/Season Highlights)	.50
216	Ken Caminiti (Checklist/ Season Highlights)	.05
217	John Smoltz (Checklist/ Season Highlights)	.05
218	Eric Young (Checklist/ Season Highlights)	.05
219	Juan Gonzalez (Checklist/ Season Highlights)	.50
220	Eddie Murray (Checklist/ Season Highlights)	.20
221	Tommy Lasorda (Checklist/Season Highlights)	.05
222	Paul Molitor (Checklist/ Season Highlights)	.20
223	Luis Castillo	.05
224	Justin Thompson	.05
225	Rocky Coppinger	.05
226	Jermaine Allensworth	.05
227	Jeff D'Amico	.05
228	Jamey Wright	.05
229	Scott Rolen	1.00
230	Darin Erstad	.50
231	Marty Janzen	.05
232	Jacob Cruz	.05
233	Raul Ibanez	.05
234	Nomar Garciaparra	1.75
235	Todd Walker	.05
236	*Brian Giles*	1.50
237	Matt Beech	.05
238	Mike Cameron	.05
239	Jose Paniagua	.05
240	Andruw Jones	1.00
241	Brant Brown (Star Rookies)	.25
242	Robin Jennings (Star Rookies)	.25
243	Willie Adams (Star Rookies)	.25
244	Ken Caminiti (Division Series)	.25
245	Brian Jordan (Division Series)	.25
246	Chipper Jones (Division Series)	3.00
247	Juan Gonzalez (Division Series)	1.25
248	Bernie Williams (Division Series)	.75
249	Roberto Alomar (Division Series)	1.00
250	Bernie Williams (Post-Season)	.75
251	David Wells (Post-Season)	.35
252	Cecil Fielder (Post-Season)	.25
253	Darryl Strawberry (Post-Season)	.25
254	Andy Pettitte (Post-Season)	.50
255	Javier Lopez (Post-Season)	.25
256	Gary Gaetti (Post-Season)	.25
257	Ron Gant (Post-Season)	.25
258	Brian Jordan (Post-Season)	.25
259	John Smoltz (Post-Season)	.25
260	Greg Maddux (Post-Season)	2.50
261	Tom Glavine (Post-Season)	.35
262	Chipper Jones (World Series)	3.00
263	Greg Maddux (World Series)	2.50
264	David Cone (World Series)	.25
265	Jim Leyritz (World Series)	.25
266	Andy Pettitte (World Series)	.50
267	John Wetteland (World Series)	.25
268	*Dario Veras* (Star Rookie)	.25
269	Neifi Perez (Star Rookie)	.25
270	Bill Mueller (Star Rookie)	.25
271	Vladimir Guerrero (Star Rookie)	1.00
272	Dmitri Young (Star Rookie)	.05
273	*Nerio Rodriguez* (Star Rookie)	.05
274	Kevin Orie (Star Rookie)	.05
275	Felipe Crespo (Star Rookie)	.05
276	Danny Graves (Star Rookie)	.05
277	Roderick Myers (Star Rookie)	.05
278	*Felix Heredia* (Star Rookie)	.25
279	Ralph Milliard (Star Rookie)	.05
280	Greg Norton (Star Rookie)	.05
281	Derek Wallace (Star Rookie)	.05
282	Trot Nixon (Star Rookie)	.10
283	Bobby Chouinard (Star Rookie)	.05
284	Jay Witasick (Star Rookie)	.05
285	Travis Miller (Star Rookie)	.05
286	Brian Bevil (Star Rookie)	.05
287	Bobby Estalella (Star Rookie)	.05
288	Steve Soderstrom (Star Rookie)	.05
289	Mark Langston	.05
290	Tim Salmon	.20
291	Jim Edmonds	.05
292	Garret Anderson	.05

293 George Arias .05
294 Gary DiSarcina .05
295 Chuck Finley .05
296 Todd Greene .05
297 Randy Velarde .05
298 David Justice .25
299 Ryan Klesko .05
300 John Smoltz .10
301 Javier Lopez .05
302 Greg Maddux 1.50
303 Denny Neagle .05
304 B.J. Surhoff .05
305 Chris Hoiles .05
306 Eric Davis .05
307 Scott Erickson .05
308 Mike Bordick .05
309 John Valentin .05
310 Heathcliff Slocumb .05
311 Tom Gordon .05
312 Mike Stanley .05
313 Reggie Jefferson .05
314 Darren Bragg .05
315 Troy O'Leary .05
316 John Mabry (Season Highlight) .05
317 Mark Whiten (Season Highlight) .05
318 Edgar Martinez (Season Highlight) .05
319 Alex Rodriguez (Season Highlight) 2.50
320 Mark McGwire (Season Highlight) 1.50
321 Hideo Nomo (Season Highlight) .30
322 Todd Hundley (Season Highlight) .05
323 Barry Bonds (Season Highlight) .90
324 Andruw Jones (Season Highlight) .50
325 Ryne Sandberg 1.00
326 Brian McRae .05
327 Frank Castillo .05
328 Shawon Dunston .05
329 Ray Durham .05
330 Robin Ventura .05
331 Ozzie Guillen .05
332 Roberto Hernandez .05
333 Albert Belle .35
334 Dave Martinez .05
335 Willie Greene .05
336 Jeff Brantley .05
337 Kevin Jarvis .05
338 John Smiley .05
339 Eddie Taubensee .05
340 Bret Boone .10
341 Kevin Seitzer .05
342 Jack McDowell .05
343 Sandy Alomar Jr. .05
344 Chad Curtis .05
345 Manny Ramirez 1.00
346 Chad Ogea .05
347 Jim Thome .05
348 Mark Thompson .05
349 Ellis Burks .05
350 Andres Galarraga .05
351 Vinny Castilla .05
352 Kirt Manwaring .05
353 Larry Walker .30
354 Omar Olivares .05
355 Bobby Higginson .10
356 Melvin Nieves .05
357 Brian Johnson .05
358 Devon White .05
359 Jeff Conine .05
360 Gary Sheffield .25
361 Robb Nen .05
362 Mike Hampton .05
363 Bob Abreu .10
364 Luis Gonzalez .30
365 Derek Bell .05
366 Sean Berry .05
367 Craig Biggio .10
368 Darryl Kile .05
369 Shane Reynolds .05
370 Jeff Bagwell (Capture the Flag) .50
371 Ron Gant (Capture the Flag) .05
372 Andy Benes (Capture the Flag) .05
373 Gary Gaetti (Capture the Flag) .05
374a Ramon Martinez (Capture the Flag) (gold back) .05
374b Ramon Martinez (Capture the Flag) (white back) .05
375 Raul Mondesi (Capture the Flag) .05
376a Steve Finley (Capture the Flag) (gold back) .05
376b Steve Finley (Capture the Flag) (white back) .05
377 Ken Caminiti (Capture the Flag) .05
378 Tony Gwynn (Capture the Flag) .75
379 Dario Veras (Capture the Flag) .05
380 Andy Pettitte (Capture the Flag) .30
381 Ruben Rivera (Capture the Flag) .05
382 David Cone (Capture the Flag) .05
383 Roberto Alomar (Capture the Flag) .30
384 Edgar Martinez (Capture the Flag) .05
385 Ken Griffey Jr. (Capture the Flag) 1.25
386 Mark McGwire (Capture the Flag) 1.50
387 Rusty Greer (Capture the Flag) .05
388 Jose Rosado .05
389 Kevin Appier .05
390 Johnny Damon .10
391 Jose Offerman .05
392 Michael Tucker .05
393 Craig Paquette .05
394 Bip Roberts .05
395 Ramon Martinez .05
396 Greg Gagne .05
397 Chan Ho Park .20
398 Karim Garcia .10
399 Wilton Guerrero .05
400 Eric Karros .05
401 Raul Mondesi .20
402 Matt Mieske .05
403 Mike Fetters .05
404 Dave Nilsson .05
405 Jose Valentin .05
406 Scott Karl .05
407 Marc Newfield .05
408 Cal Eldred .05
409 Rich Becker .05
410 Terry Steinbach .05
411 Chuck Knoblauch .05
412 Pat Meares .05
413 Brad Radke .05
414 Not Issued
415a Kirby Puckett (should be #414) 1.50
415b Andruw Jones (Griffey Hot List) 2.00
416 Chipper Jones (Griffey Hot List) 4.00
417 Mo Vaughn (Griffey Hot List) 1.00
418 Frank Thomas (Griffey Hot List) 2.00
419 Albert Belle (Griffey Hot List) 1.00
420 Mark McGwire (Griffey Hot List) 6.00
421 Derek Jeter (Griffey Hot List) 6.00
422 Alex Rodriguez (Griffey Hot List) 5.00
423 Juan Gonzalez (Griffey Hot List) 2.00
424 Ken Griffey Jr. (Griffey Hot List) 5.00
425 Rondell White .15
426 Darrin Fletcher .05
427 Cliff Floyd .05
428 Mike Lansing .05
429 F.P. Santangelo .05
430 Todd Hundley .05
431 Mark Clark .05
432 Pete Harnisch .05
433 Jason Isringhausen .05
434 Bobby Jones .05
435 Lance Johnson .05
436 Carlos Baerga .05
437 Mariano Duncan .05
438 David Cone .05
439 Mariano Rivera .20
440 Derek Jeter 3.00
441 Joe Girardi .05
442 Charlie Hayes .05
443 Tim Raines .05
444 Darryl Strawberry .05
445 Cecil Fielder .05
446 Ariel Prieto .05
447 Tony Batista .05
448 Brent Gates .05
449 Scott Spiezio .05
450 Mark McGwire 3.00
451 Don Wengert .05
452 Mike Lieberthal .05
453 Lenny Dykstra .05
454 Rex Hudler .05
455 Darren Daulton .05
456 Kevin Stocker .05
457 Trey Beamon .05
458 Midre Cummings .05
459 Mark Johnson .05
460 Al Martin .05
461 Kevin Elster .05
462 Jon Lieber .05
463 Jason Schmidt .05
464 Paul Wagner .05
465 Andy Benes .05
466 Alan Benes .05
467 Royce Clayton .05
468 Gary Gaetti .05
469 Curt Lyons (Diamond Debuts) .05
470 Eugene Kingsale (Diamond Debuts) .05
471 Damian Jackson (Diamond Debuts) .05
472 Wendell Magee (Diamond Dubuts) .05
473 Kevin L. Brown (Diamond Debuts) .05
474 Raul Casanova (Diamond Debuts) .05
475 *Ramiro Mendoza* (Diamond Debuts) .25
476 Todd Dunn (Diamond Debuts) .05
477 Chad Mottola (Diamond Debuts) .05
478 Andy Larkin (Diamond Debuts) .05
479 Jaime Bluma (Diamond Debuts) .05
480 Mac Suzuki (Diamond Debuts) .05
481 Brian Banks (Diamond Debuts) .05
482 Desi Wilson (Diamond Debuts) .05
483 Einar Diaz (Diamond Debuts) .05
484 Tom Pagnozzi .05
485 Ray Lankford .05
486 Todd Stottlemyre .05
487 Donovan Osborne .05
488 Trevor Hoffman .05
489 Chris Gomez .05
490 Ken Caminiti .05
491 John Flaherty .05
492 Tony Gwynn 1.50
493 Joey Hamilton .05
494 Rickey Henderson .60
495 Glenallen Hill .05
496 Rod Beck .05
497 Osvaldo Fernandez .05
498 Rick Wilkins .05
499 Joey Cora .05
500 Alex Rodriguez 2.50
501 Randy Johnson .60
502 Paul Sorrento .05
503 Dan Wilson .05
504 Jamie Moyer .05
505 Will Clark .15
506 Mickey Tettleton .05
507 John Burkett .05
508 Ken Hill .05
509 Mark McLemore .05
510 Juan Gonzalez 1.00
511 Bobby Witt .05
512 Carlos Delgado .30
513 Alex Gonzalez .10
514 Shawn Green .30
515 Joe Carter .05
516 Juan Guzman .05
517 Charlie O'Brien .05
518 Ed Sprague .05
519 Mike Timlin .05
520 Roger Clemens 1.50
521 Eddie Murray .40
522 Jason Dickson .05
523 Jim Leyritz .05
524 Michael Tucker .05
525 Kenny Lofton .05
526 Jimmy Key .05
527 Mel Rojas .05
528 Deion Sanders .10
529 Bartolo Colon .05
530 Matt Williams .15
531 Marquis Grissom .05
532 David Justice .25
533 *Bubba Trammell* .25
534 Moises Alou .15
535 Bobby Bonilla .05
536 Alex Fernandez .05
537 Jay Bell .05
538 Chili Davis .05
539 Jeff King .05
540 Todd Zeile .05
541 John Olerud .05
542 Jose Guillen .05
543 Derrek Lee .05
544 Dante Powell .05
545 J.T. Snow .05
546 Jeff Kent .05
547 *Jose Cruz Jr.* 1.00
548 John Wetteland .05
549 Orlando Merced .05
550 *Hideki Irabu* .50

1997 Upper Deck Amazing Greats

The 20-card, regular-sized insert set was included every 138 packs of 1997 Upper Deck baseball. The cards include real wood with two player shots imaged on the card front. The team logo appears in the upper right corner of the horizontal card. The cards are numbered with the "AG" prefix.

		MT
Complete Set (20):		140.00
Common Player:		2.00
1	Ken Griffey Jr.	15.00
2	Roberto Alomar	4.00
3	Alex Rodriguez	15.00
4	Paul Molitor	4.00
5	Chipper Jones	10.00
6	Tony Gwynn	6.00
7	Kenny Lofton	2.00
8	Albert Belle	2.00
9	Matt Williams	2.00
10	Frank Thomas	6.00
11	Greg Maddux	10.00
12	Sammy Sosa	10.00
13	Kirby Puckett	8.00
14	Jeff Bagwell	6.00
15	Cal Ripken Jr.	20.00
16	Manny Ramirez	5.00
17	Barry Bonds	8.00
18	Mo Vaughn	2.50
19	Eddie Murray	3.00
20	Mike Piazza	15.00

1997 Upper Deck Blue Chip Prospects

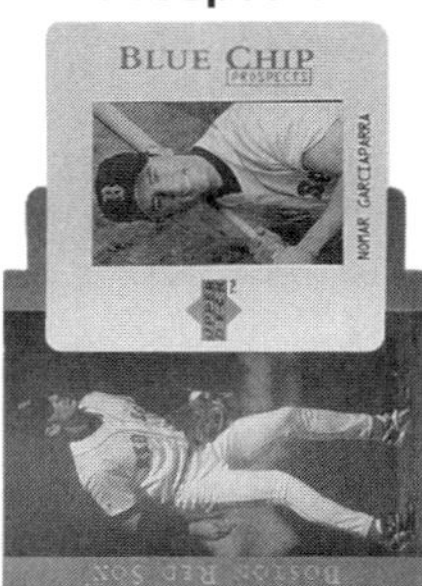

This 20-card insert was found in packs of Series II and features a die-cut design. Cards appear to have a photo slide attached to them featuring a portrait shot of the promising youngster depicted on the card. A total of 500 of each card were produced. Cards are numbered with a "BC" prefix.

		MT
Complete Set (20):		170.00
Common Player:		3.00
1	Andruw Jones	15.00
2	Derek Jeter	35.00
3	Scott Rolen	10.00
4	Manny Ramirez	15.00
5	Todd Walker	3.00
6	Rocky Coppinger	3.00
7	Nomar Garciaparra	25.00
8	Darin Erstad	10.00
9	Jermaine Dye	3.00
10	Vladimir Guerrero	15.00
11	Edgar Renteria	3.00
12	Bob Abreu	6.00
13	Karim Garcia	3.00
14	Jeff D'Amico	3.00
15	Chipper Jones	30.00
16	Todd Hollandsworth	3.00
17	Andy Pettitte	6.00
18	Ruben Rivera	3.00
19	Jason Kendall	3.00
20	Alex Rodriguez	35.00

1997 Upper Deck Game Jersey

The three-card, regular-sized set was inserted every 800 packs of Upper Deck Series I. The cards contained a square of the player's game-used jersey, and carried a "GJ" card number prefix.

		MT
Complete Set (3):		260.00
Common Player:		30.00
GJ1	Ken Griffey Jr.	150.00
GJ2	Tony Gwynn	50.00
GJ3	Rey Ordonez	30.00

1997 Upper Deck Home Team Heroes

These large-format cards were issued both as a 12-card boxed set (original price about $20) and as a blister-pack insert to enhance the sales of special Collector's Choice team sets at Wal-Mart. Each $4.99 pack contains a 14-card team set and a Home Team Heroes card of one of 12 teams, plus a random assortment of Collector's Choice cards. The Heroes cards are 5" x 3-1/2" with a die-cut pattern at top. Fronts are rendered in team colors with two player action photos superimposed on a background of the players' home ballpark. The ballpark scene is executed in etched silver foil and there are silver-foil graphics around the card front. Backs are conventionally printed with small photos and a few sentences about each player.

		MT
Complete Set (12):		13.50
Common Player:		1.00
1	Alex Rodriguez, Ken Griffey Jr.	2.00
2	Bernie Williams, Derek Jeter	1.75
3	Bernard Gilkey, Randy Hundley	1.00
4	Hideo Nomo, Mike Piazza	1.75
5	Andruw Jones, Chipper Jones	1.75
6	John Smoltz, Greg Maddux	1.50
7	Mike Mussina, Cal Ripken Jr.	1.75
8	Andres Galarraga, Dante Bichette	1.00
9	Juan Gonzalez, Ivan Rodriguez	1.25
10	Albert Belle, Frank Thomas	1.00
11	Jim Thome, Manny Ramirez	1.25
12	Ken Caminiti, Tony Gwynn	1.00

1997 Upper Deck Hot Commodities

This 20-card insert from Series II features a flame pattern behind the image of the player depicted on the front of the card. Odds of finding a card were 1:13 packs. Cards are numbered with a "HC" prefix.

		MT
Complete Set (20):		50.00
Common Player:		1.00
1	Alex Rodriguez	6.00
2	Andruw Jones	2.50
3	Derek Jeter	8.00
4	Frank Thomas	3.00
5	Ken Griffey Jr.	6.00
6	Chipper Jones	4.00
7	Juan Gonzalez	2.50
8	Cal Ripken Jr.	8.00
9	John Smoltz	1.00
10	Mark McGwire	6.00
11	Barry Bonds	4.00
12	Albert Belle	1.00
13	Mike Piazza	5.00
14	Manny Ramirez	2.50
15	Mo Vaughn	1.50
16	Tony Gwynn	3.00
17	Vladimir Guerrero	2.50
18	Hideo Nomo	2.00
19	Greg Maddux	4.00
20	Kirby Puckett	3.00

1997 Upper Deck Long Distance Connection

This 20-card insert from Series II features the top home run hitters in the game. Odds of finding a card were 1:35 packs. Cards are numbered with a "LD" prefix.

		MT
Complete Set (20):		40.00
Common Player:		.75
1	Mark McGwire	8.00
2	Brady Anderson	.75
3	Ken Griffey Jr.	6.00
4	Albert Belle	1.00
5	Juan Gonzalez	2.50
6	Andres Galarraga	.75
7	Jay Buhner	.75
8	Mo Vaughn	1.00
9	Barry Bonds	4.00
10	Gary Sheffield	1.00
11	Todd Hundley	.75
12	Frank Thomas	3.00
13	Sammy Sosa	4.00
14	Rafael Palmeiro	1.00
15	Alex Rodriguez	6.00
16	Mike Piazza	5.00
17	Ken Caminiti	.75
18	Chipper Jones	4.00
19	Manny Ramirez	2.50
20	Andruw Jones	2.50

1997 Upper Deck Memorable Moments

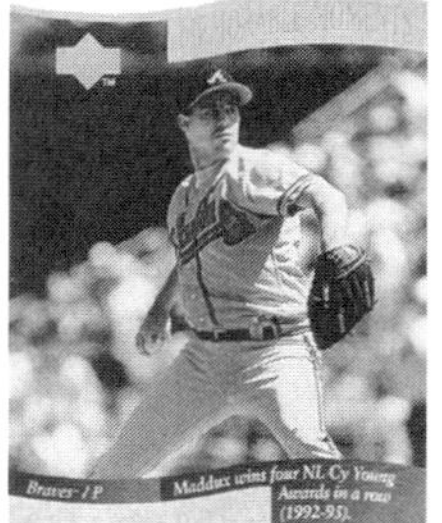

This issue was a one per pack insert in special Series 1 and 2 Collector's Choice six-card retail packs. In standard 2-1/2" x 3-1/2", the cards are die-cut at top and bottom in a wave pattern. Fronts, highlighted in matte bronze foil, have action photos and a career highlight. Backs have another photo and a more complete explanation of the Memorable Moment.

		MT
Complete Set (20):		20.00
Common Player:		.50
	SERIES 1	
1	Andruw Jones	.75
2	Chipper Jones	1.50
3	Cal Ripken Jr.	2.50
4	Frank Thomas	1.25
5	Manny Ramirez	.75
6	Mike Piazza	1.50
7	Mark McGwire	2.50
8	Barry Bonds	1.25
9	Ken Griffey Jr.	2.00
10	Alex Rodriguez	2.00
	SERIES 2	
1	Ken Griffey Jr.	2.00
2	Albert Belle	.60
3	Derek Jeter	1.50
4	Greg Maddux	1.00
5	Tony Gwynn	1.00
6	Ryne Sandberg	.75
7	Juan Gonzalez	.75
8	Roger Clemens	1.00
9	Jose Cruz Jr.	.50
10	Mo Vaughn	.75

1997 Upper Deck Power Package

The 20-card, regular-sized, die-cut set was inserted every 23 packs of 1997 Upper Deck baseball. The player's name is printed in gold foil along the top border of the card face, which also features Light F/X. The die-cut cards have a silver-foil border and team-color frame with a "Power Package" logo in gold foil centered on the bottom border. The card backs have a short highlight in a brown box bordered by team colors and are numbered with the "PP" prefix.

		MT
Complete Set (20):		55.00
Common Player:		2.00
1	Ken Griffey Jr.	7.50
2	Joe Carter	2.00
3	Rafael Palmeiro	2.50
4	Jay Buhner	2.00
5	Sammy Sosa	5.00
6	Fred McGriff	2.00
7	Jeff Bagwell	3.00
8	Albert Belle	2.00
9	Matt Williams	2.50
10	Mark McGwire	10.00
11	Gary Sheffield	2.50
12	Tim Salmon	2.50
13	Ryan Klesko	2.00
14	Manny Ramirez	3.00
15	Mike Piazza	6.00
16	Barry Bonds	4.50
17	Mo Vaughn	2.50
18	Jose Canseco	2.50
19	Juan Gonzalez	3.00
20	Frank Thomas	3.00

1997 Upper Deck Predictor

A new concept in interactive cards was UD's Series II Predictor inserts. Each player's card has four scratch-off baseball bats at the top-right. Under each bat is printed a specific accomplishment - hit for cycle, CG shutout, etc. - If the player attained that goal during the '97 season, and if the collector had scratched off the correct bat among the four, the Predictor card could be redeemed (with $2) for a premium TV cel card of the player. Thus if the player made one of his goals, the collector had a 25% chance of choosing the right bat. Two goals gave a 50% chance, etc. The Predictor cards have color action photos of the players at the left end of the horizontal format. The background at left and bottom is a red scorecard motif. Behind the bats is a black-and-white stadium scene. Backs repeat the red scorecard design with contest rules printed in white. A (W) in the checklist here indicates the player won one or more of his goals making his cards eligible for redemption. The redemption period ended Nov. 22, 1997. Values shown are for unscratched cards.

		MT
Complete Set (30):		25.00
Common Player:		.25
Values for Unscratched Cards		
1	Andruw Jones	.50
2	Chipper Jones	1.75
3	Greg Maddux (W)	1.50
4	Fred McGriff (W)	.50
5	John Smoltz (W)	.50
6	Brady Anderson (W)	.50
7	Cal Ripken Jr. (W)	2.50
8	Mo Vaughn (W)	.50
9	Sammy Sosa	1.50
10	Albert Belle (W)	.75
11	Frank Thomas	1.50
12	Kenny Lofton (W)	.50
13	Jim Thome	.25
14	Dante Bichette (W)	.50
15	Andres Galarraga	.25
16	Gary Sheffield	.35
17	Hideo Nomo (W)	1.00
18	Mike Piazza (W)	2.00
19	Derek Jeter (W)	2.00
20	Bernie Williams	.35
21	Mark McGwire (W)	2.50
22	Ken Caminiti (W)	.50
23	Tony Gwynn (W)	1.50
24	Barry Bonds (W)	1.75
25	Jay Buhner (W)	.50
26	Ken Griffey Jr. (W)	2.25
27	Alex Rodriguez (W)	2.25
28	Juan Gonzalez (W)	1.00
29	Dean Palmer (W)	.50
30	Roger Clemens (W)	1.50

1997 Upper Deck Rock Solid Foundation

The 20-card, regular-sized set was inserted every seven packs of 1997 Upper Deck baseball. The card fronts feature rainbow foil with the player's name in silver foil along the top border. The team logo appears in gold foil in the lower right corner with "Rock Solid Foundation" also printed in gold foil over a marbled background. The card backs have the same marbled background with a close-up shot on the upper half. A short text is also included and the cards are numbered with the "RS" prefix.

		MT
Complete Set (20):		15.00
Common Player:		.25
1	Alex Rodriguez	3.00
2	Rey Ordonez	.35
3	Derek Jeter	4.00
4	Darin Erstad	1.50
5	Chipper Jones	2.50
6	Johnny Damon	.50
7	Ryan Klesko	.25
8	Charles Johnson	.25
9	Andy Pettitte	1.00
10	Manny Ramirez	2.00
11	Ivan Rodriguez	1.50
12	Jason Kendall	.40
13	Rondell White	.75
14	Alex Ochoa	.25
15	Javy Lopez	.25
16	Pedro Martinez	1.50
17	Carlos Delgado	1.00
18	Paul Wilson	.25
19	Alan Benes	.25
20	Raul Mondesi	.40

1997 Upper Deck Run Producers

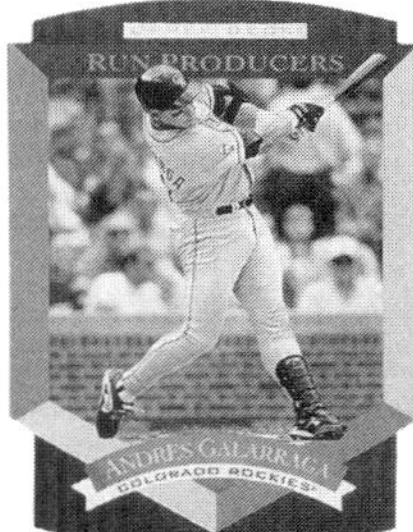

A 24-card insert found in Series II, Run Producers salutes the top offensive players in the game. Cards were inserted 1:69 packs. Die-cut into a shield shape, the cards have an action photo in a home-plate shaped center section and several colors of foil highlights. Backs have recent stats and career highlights. Cards are numbered with a "RP" prefix.

		MT
Complete Set (24):		100.00
Common Player:		2.00
1	Ken Griffey Jr.	15.00
2	Barry Bonds	6.00
3	Albert Belle	2.00
4	Mark McGwire	15.00
5	Frank Thomas	6.00
6	Juan Gonzalez	4.00
7	Brady Anderson	2.00
8	Andres Galarraga	2.00
9	Rafael Palmeiro	3.00
10	Alex Rodriguez	15.00
11	Jay Buhner	2.00
12	Gary Sheffield	2.50
13	Sammy Sosa	8.00
14	Dante Bichette	2.00
15	Mike Piazza	12.00
16	Manny Ramirez	4.00
17	Kenny Lofton	2.00
18	Mo Vaughn	2.50
19	Tim Salmon	2.50
20	Chipper Jones	8.00
21	Jim Thome	2.00
22	Ken Caminiti	2.00
23	Jeff Bagwell	4.00
24	Paul Molitor	4.00

1997 Upper Deck Star Attractions

These die-cut cards were inserted one per pack of retail "Memorabila Madness" Collector's Choice (#11-20) and Upper Deck (#1-10) cards. Fronts have action photos, backs have portrait photos. A gold version of the inserts is believed to have been an exclusive to retail packaging.

		MT
Complete Set (20):		35.00
Common Player:		.50
Gold:		1.5X
1	Ken Griffey Jr.	4.00
2	Barry Bonds	2.50
3	Jeff Bagwell	1.50
4	Nomar Garciaparra	2.50
5	Tony Gwynn	2.00
6	Roger Clemens	2.00
7	Chipper Jones	3.00
8	Tino Martinez	.50
9	Albert Belle	.75
10	Kenny Lofton	.50
11	Alex Rodriguez	4.00
12	Mark McGwire	5.00
13	Cal Ripken Jr.	5.00
14	Larry Walker	.75
15	Mike Piazza	3.00
16	Frank Thomas	2.50
17	Juan Gonzalez	1.50
18	Greg Maddux	2.00
19	Jose Cruz Jr.	.50
20	Mo Vaughn	.75

1997 Upper Deck Ticket to Stardom

The 20-card, regular-sized, die-cut set was inserted every 34 packs of 1997 Upper Deck baseball. Card fronts have a gold-foil border on three sides with a portrait and action photo. Half of the player's league emblem appears on either the left or right border of the horizontal cards, as two cards can be placed together to form a "ticket." The card backs feature an in-depth text with the same headshot as the card front and are numbered with the "TS" prefix.

		MT
Complete Set (20):		35.00
Common Player:		.75
1	Chipper Jones	7.50
2	Jermaine Dye	.75
3	Rey Ordonez	1.00
4	Alex Ochoa	.75
5	Derek Jeter	10.00
6	Ruben Rivera	.75
7	Billy Wagner	1.00
8	Jason Kendall	1.00
9	Darin Erstad	1.50
10	Alex Rodriguez	8.00
11	Bob Abreu	1.00
12	Richard Hidalgo	1.00
13	Karim Garcia	1.00
14	Andruw Jones	3.00
15	Carlos Delgado	2.00
16	Rocky Coppinger	.75
17	Jeff D'Amico	.75
18	Johnny Damon	1.00
19	John Wasdin	.75
20	Manny Ramirez	4.00

1997 Upper Deck Ticket to Stardom Retail

Double-size "full ticket" versions of Upper Deck's Series 1 Ticket to Stardom inserts were produced as an incentive for collectors to buy a boxed three-pack of Collector's Choice cards in a special retail-only packaging. Unlike the insert Ticket cards which feature only one player and measure 3-1/2" x 2-1/2", the retail version measures 5" x 2-1/2" and features two players. The basic format of the retail cards follows the inserts, with gold-foil background, a vignetted player portrait at one end with an action photo toward center and a league logo at center. Arrangement of graphics on the retail ticket prevent unscrupulous persons from cutting them in half and passing them off as the more valuable insert cards. Backs repeat the player portrait photo and present a career summary. Cards are numbered in the upper-left corner. Seven players were dropped from the original Ticket checklist and replaced in the retail issue with new faces. Cards are numbered with a "TS" prefix.

		MT
Complete Set (10):		40.00
Common Player:		3.00
1	Chipper Jones, Andruw Jones	8.00
2	Rey Ordonez, Kevin Orie	3.00
3	Derek Jeter, Nomar Garciaparra	8.00
4	Billy Wagner, Jason Kendall	3.00
5	Darin Erstad, Alex Rodriguez	10.00
6	Bob Abreu, Jose Guillen	3.00
7	Wilton Guerrero, Vladimir Guerrero	6.00
8	Carlos Delgado, Rocky Coppinger	3.00
9	Jason Dickson, Johnny Damon	3.00
10	Bartolo Colon, Manny Ramirez	6.00

1997 Upper Deck UD3

Released in April, this 60-card set is broken down into three different 20-card subsets, each utilizing a different print technology. There are 20 PROmotion cards (Light F/X cards featuring a special foil stock), 20 Future Impact cards (Cel-Chrome cards that feature a 3-D image on transparent chromium), and 20 Homerun Heroes (Electric Wood cards printed on an embossed wood/paper stock). Cards were sold in three-card packs (with one subset card per pack) for $3.99 each. Inserts include Superb Signatures, Generation Next and Marquee Attraction.

		MT
Complete Set (60):		40.00
Common Player:		.25
Pack (3):		2.00
Wax Box (24):		40.00
1	Mark McGwire	3.00
2	Brady Anderson	.25
3	Ken Griffey Jr.	3.00
4	Albert Belle	.50
5	Andres Galarraga	.25
6	Juan Gonzalez	1.50
7	Jay Buhner	.25
8	Mo Vaughn	.75
9	Barry Bonds	2.50
10	Gary Sheffield	.45
11	Todd Hundley	.25
12	Ellis Burks	.25
13	Ken Caminiti	.25
14	Vinny Castilla	.25
15	Sammy Sosa	2.50
16	Frank Thomas	1.50
17	Rafael Palmeiro	.45
18	Mike Piazza	3.00
19	Matt Williams	.50
20	Eddie Murray	.60
21	Roger Clemens	2.00
22	Tim Salmon	.35
23	Robin Ventura	.25
24	Ron Gant	.25
25	Cal Ripken Jr.	4.00
26	Bernie Williams	.50
27	Hideo Nomo	.80
28	Ivan Rodriguez	1.50
29	John Smoltz	.35
30	Paul Molitor	1.00
31	Greg Maddux	2.00
32	Raul Mondesi	.35
33	Roberto Alomar	.75
34	Barry Larkin	.35
35	Tony Gwynn	2.00
36	Jim Thome	.25
37	Kenny Lofton	.25
38	Jeff Bagwell	1.50
39	Ozzie Smith	2.00
40	Kirby Puckett	2.00
41	Andruw Jones	1.00
42	Vladimir Guerrero	1.50
43	Edgar Renteria	.25
44	Luis Castillo	.25
45	Darin Erstad	.60
46	Nomar Garciaparra	2.50
47	Todd Greene	.25
48	Jason Kendall	.25
49	Rey Ordonez	.25
50	Alex Rodriguez	3.25
51	Manny Ramirez	1.50
52	Todd Walker	.25
53	Ruben Rivera	.25
54	Andy Pettitte	.40
55	Derek Jeter	4.00
56	Todd Hollandsworth	.25
57	Rocky Coppinger	.25
58	Scott Rolen	1.00
59	Jermaine Dye	.25
60	Chipper Jones	3.00

1997 Upper Deck UD3 Generation Next

A 20-card insert saluting the game's up-and-coming stars with two different photos of the player on each card front. Odds of finding these cards were 1:11 packs. Cards are numbered with a "GN" prefix.

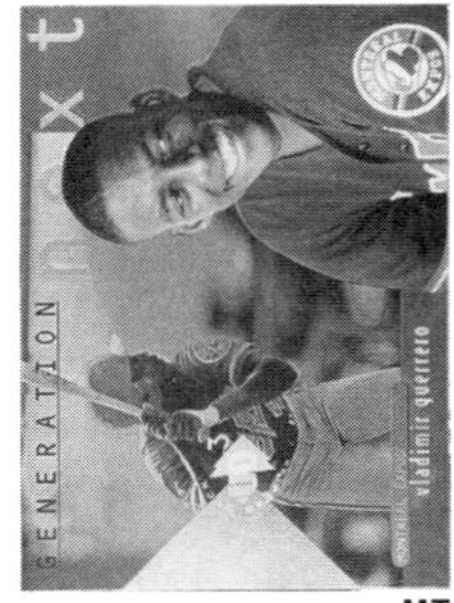

		MT
Complete Set (20):		70.00
Common Player:		2.00
1	Alex Rodriguez	10.00
2	Vladimir Guerrero	5.00
3	Luis Castillo	2.00
4	Rey Ordonez	2.00
5	Andruw Jones	5.00
6	Darin Erstad	3.50
7	Edgar Renteria	2.00
8	Jason Kendall	2.00
9	Jermaine Dye	2.00
10	Chipper Jones	8.00
11	Rocky Coppinger	2.00
12	Andy Pettitte	2.50
13	Todd Greene	2.00
14	Todd Hollandsworth	2.00
15	Derek Jeter	12.00
16	Ruben Rivera	2.00
17	Todd Walker	2.00
18	Nomar Garciaparra	7.50
19	Scott Rolen	5.00
20	Manny Ramirez	5.00

1997 Upper Deck UD3 Marquee Attraction

The game's top names are featured in this insert set, inserted 1:144 packs. Cards featured a peel-off protector that would expose a holographic image on the card fronts. Cards are numbered with a "MA" prefix.

		MT
Complete Set (10):		125.00
Common Player:		4.00
1	Ken Griffey Jr.	25.00
2	Mark McGwire	25.00
3	Juan Gonzalez	8.00
4	Barry Bonds	15.00
5	Frank Thomas	10.00
6	Albert Belle	4.00
7	Mike Piazza	20.00
8	Cal Ripken Jr.	30.00
9	Mo Vaughn	4.00
10	Alex Rodriguez	20.00

1997 Upper Deck UD3 Superb Signatures

Autographed cards of Ken Griffey Jr., Ken Caminiti, Vladimir Guerrero and Derek Jeter were inserted 1:1,500 packs.

		MT
Complete Set (4):		400.00
Common Autograph:		20.00
1	Ken Caminiti	20.00
2	Ken Griffey Jr.	175.00
3	Vladimir Guerrero	50.00
4	Derek Jeter	200.00

1998 Upper Deck

Upper Deck Baseball was released in three series. Series 1 consists of 270 base cards, with five subsets. Inserts included A Piece of the Action, Amazing Greats, National Pride, Ken Griffey Jr.'s Home Run Chronicles and 10th Anniversary Preview. The 270-card Series 2 also has five subsets. Inserts include Prime Nine, Ken Griffey Jr.'s Home Run Chronicles, Tape Measure Titans, Blue Chip Prospects, Clearly Dominant and A Piece of the Action. The third series, Upper Deck Rookie Edition, has a 210-card base set. Cards #601-630, the Eminent Prestige subset, are short-printed, about one per four packs. Mike Piazza's card in Series 3 can be found depicting him either as a Marlin or a Met. Insert sets were Ken Griffey Jr. Game Jersey, Game Jersey Rookie Cards, Unparalleled, Destination Stardom, All-Star Credentials and Retrospectives.

		MT
Complete Set (750):		140.00
Complete Series 1 Set (270):		30.00
Complete Series 2 Set (270):		30.00
Complete Series 3 Set (210):		80.00
Common Emminent Prestige (601-630):		.50
Common Player:		.05
Series 1 or 2 Pack (12):		1.25
Series 3 Pack (10):		1.50
Series 1 or 2 Wax Box (24):		25.00
Series 3 Wax Box (24):		35.00
1	Tino Martinez (History in the Making)	.05
2	Jimmy Key (History in the Making)	.05
3	Jay Buhner (History in the Making)	.05
4	Mark Gardner (History in the Making)	.05
5	Greg Maddux (History in the Making)	.30
6	Pedro Martinez (History in the Making)	.20
7	Hideo Nomo, Shigetosi Hasegawa (History in the Making)	.25
8	Sammy Sosa (History in the Making)	.40
9	Mark McGwire (Griffey Hot List)	.75
10	Ken Griffey Jr. (Griffey Hot List)	.65
11	Larry Walker (Griffey Hot List)	.10
12	Tino Martinez (Griffey Hot List)	.05
13	Mike Piazza (Griffey Hot List)	.50
14	Jose Cruz, Jr. (Griffey Hot List)	.10
15	Tony Gwynn (Griffey Hot List)	.30
16	Greg Maddux (Griffey Hot List)	.30
17	Roger Clemens (Griffey Hot List)	.30
18	Alex Rodriguez (Griffey Hot List)	.65
19	Shigetosi Hasegawa	.05
20	Eddie Murray	.35
21	Jason Dickson	.05
22	Darin Erstad	.35
23	Chuck Finley	.05
24	Dave Hollins	.05
25	Garret Anderson	.05
26	Michael Tucker	.05
27	Kenny Lofton	.05
28	Javier Lopez	.05
29	Fred McGriff	.05
30	Greg Maddux	.60
31	Jeff Blauser	.05
32	John Smoltz	.10
33	Mark Wohlers	.05
34	Scott Erickson	.05
35	Jimmy Key	.05
36	Harold Baines	.05
37	Randy Myers	.05
38	B.J. Surhoff	.05
39	Eric Davis	.05
40	Rafael Palmeiro	.20
41	Jeffrey Hammonds	.05
42	Mo Vaughn	.30
43	Tom Gordon	.05
44	Tim Naehring	.05
45	Darren Bragg	.05
46	Aaron Sele	.05
47	Troy O'Leary	.05
48	John Valentin	.05
49	Doug Glanville	.05
50	Ryne Sandberg	.50
51	Steve Trachsel	.05
52	Mark Grace	.20
53	Kevin Foster	.05
54	Kevin Tapani	.05
55	Kevin Orie	.05
56	Lyle Mouton	.05
57	Ray Durham	.05
58	Jaime Navarro	.05
59	Mike Cameron	.05
60	Albert Belle	.20
61	Doug Drabek	.05
62	Chris Snopek	.05
63	Eddie Taubensee	.05
64	Terry Pendleton	.05
65	Barry Larkin	.10
66	Willie Greene	.05
67	Deion Sanders	.10
68	Pokey Reese	.05
69	Jeff Shaw	.05
70	Jim Thome	.05
71	Orel Hershiser	.05
72	Omar Vizquel	.05
73	Brian Giles	.05
74	David Justice	.20
75	Bartolo Colon	.05
76	Sandy Alomar Jr.	.05
77	Neifi Perez	.05
78	Eric Young	.05
79	Vinny Castilla	.05
80	Dante Bichette	.05
81	Quinton McCracken	.05
82	Jamey Wright	.05
83	John Thomson	.05
84	Damion Easley	.05
85	Justin Thompson	.05
86	Willie Blair	.05
87	Raul Casanova	.05
88	Bobby Higginson	.10
89	Bubba Trammell	.05
90	Tony Clark	.05
91	Livan Hernandez	.05
92	Charles Johnson	.05
93	Edgar Renteria	.05
94	Alex Fernandez	.05
95	Gary Sheffield	.25
96	Moises Alou	.10
97	Tony Saunders	.05
98	Robb Nen	.05
99	Darryl Kile	.05
100	Craig Biggio	.10
101	Chris Holt	.05
102	Bob Abreu	.10
103	Luis Gonzalez	.35
104	Billy Wagner	.05
105	Brad Ausmus	.05
106	Chili Davis	.05
107	Tim Belcher	.05
108	Dean Palmer	.05
109	Jeff King	.05
110	Jose Rosado	.05
111	Mike Macfarlane	.05
112	Jay Bell	.05
113	Todd Worrell	.05
114	Chan Ho Park	.15
115	Raul Mondesi	.20
116	Brett Butler	.05
117	Greg Gagne	.05
118	Hideo Nomo	.40
119	Todd Zeile	.05
120	Eric Karros	.05
121	Cal Eldred	.05
122	Jeff D'Amico	.05
123	Antone Williamson	.05
124	Doug Jones	.05
125	Dave Nilsson	.05
126	Gerald Williams	.05
127	Fernando Vina	.05
128	Ron Coomer	.05
129	Matt Lawton	.05
130	Paul Molitor	.45
131	Todd Walker	.05
132	Rick Aguilera	.05
133	Brad Radke	.05
134	Bob Tewksbury	.05
135	Vladimir Guerrero	.50
136	Tony Gwynn (Define The Game)	.30
137	Roger Clemens (Define The Game)	.30
138	Dennis Eckersley (Define The Game)	.05
139	Brady Anderson (Define The Game)	.05
140	Ken Griffey Jr. (Define The Game)	.65
141	Derek Jeter (Define The Game)	.50
142	Ken Caminiti (Define The Game)	.05
143	Frank Thomas (Define The Game)	.40
144	Barry Bonds (Define The Game)	.40
145	Cal Ripken Jr. (Define The Game)	.75
146	Alex Rodriguez (Define The Game)	.65
147	Greg Maddux (Define The Game)	.30
148	Kenny Lofton (Define The Game)	.05
149	Mike Piazza (Define The Game)	.50
150	Mark McGwire (Define The Game)	.75
151	Andruw Jones (Define The Game)	.25
152	Rusty Greer (Define The Game)	.05
153	F.P. Santangel (Define The Game)	.05
154	Mike Lansing	.05
155	Lee Smith	.05
156	Carlos Perez	.05
157	Pedro Martinez	.40
158	Ryan McGuire	.05
159	F.P. Santangelo	.05
160	Rondell White	.15
161	*Takashi Kashiwada*	.05
162	Butch Huskey	.05
163	Edgardo Alfonzo	.05
164	John Franco	.05
165	Todd Hundley	.05
166	Rey Ordonez	.05
167	Armando Reynoso	.05
168	John Olerud	.05
169	Bernie Williams	.25
170	Andy Pettitte	.15
171	Wade Boggs	.40
172	Paul O'Neill	.05
173	Cecil Fielder	.05
174	Charlie Hayes	.05
175	David Cone	.05
176	Hideki Irabu	.05
177	Mark Bellhorn	.05
178	Steve Karsay	.05
179	Damon Mashore	.05
180	Jason McDonald	.05
181	Scott Spiezio	.05
182	Ariel Prieto	.05
183	Jason Giambi	.35
184	Wendell Magee	.05
185	Rico Brogna	.05
186	Garrett Stephenson	.05
187	Wayne Gomes	.05
188	Ricky Bottalico	.05
189	Mickey Morandini	.05
190	Mike Lieberthal	.05
191	*Kevin Polcovich*	.10
192	Francisco Cordova	.05
193	Kevin Young	.05
194	Jon Lieber	.05
195	Kevin Elster	.05
196	Tony Womack	.05
197	Lou Collier	.05
198	*Mike Defelice*	.10
199	Gary Gaetti	.05
200	Dennis Eckersley	.05
201	Alan Benes	.05
202	Willie McGee	.05
203	Ron Gant	.05
204	Fernando Valenzuela	.05
205	Mark McGwire	1.50
206	Archi Cianfrocco	.05
207	Andy Ashby	.05
208	Steve Finley	.05
209	Quilvio Veras	.05
210	Ken Caminiti	.05
211	Rickey Henderson	.50
212	Joey Hamilton	.05
213	Derrek Lee	.05
214	Bill Mueller	.05
215	Shawn Estes	.05
216	J.T. Snow	.05
217	Mark Gardner	.05
218	Terry Mulholland	.05
219	Dante Powell	.05
220	Jeff Kent	.05
221	Jamie Moyer	.05
222	Joey Cora	.05
223	Jeff Fassero	.05
224	Dennis Martinez	.05
225	Ken Griffey Jr.	1.25
226	Edgar Martinez	.05
227	Russ Davis	.05
228	Dan Wilson	.05

229 Will Clark .15
230 Ivan Rodriguez .40
231 Benji Gil .05
232 Lee Stevens .05
233 Mickey Tettleton .05
234 Julio Santana .05
235 Rusty Greer .05
236 Bobby Witt .05
237 Ed Sprague .05
238 Pat Hentgen .05
239 Kevin Escobar .05
240 Joe Carter .05
241 Carlos Delgado .20
242 Shannon Stewart .05
243 Benito Santiago .05
244 Tino Martinez (Season Highlights) .05
245 Ken Griffey Jr. (Season Highlights) .65
246 Kevin Brown (Season Highlights) .05
247 Ryne Sandberg (Season Highlights) .25
248 Mo Vaughn (Season Highlights) .20
249 Darryl Hamilton (Season Highlights) .05
250 Randy Johnson (Season Highlights) .20
251 Steve Finley (Season Highlights) .05
252 Bobby Higginson (Season Highlights) .05
253 Brett Tomko (Star Rookie) .05
254 Mark Kotsay (Star Rookie) .05
255 Jose Guillen (Star Rookie) .05
256 Elieser Marrero (Star Rookie) .05
257 Dennis Reyes (Star Rookie) .05
258 Richie Sexson (Star Rookie) .05
259 Pat Cline (Star Rookie) .05
260 Todd Helton (Star Rookie) .40
261 Juan Melo (Star Rookie) .05
262 Matt Morris (Star Rookie) .05
263 Jeremi Gonzalez (Star Rookie) .10
264 Jeff Abbott (Star Rookie) .05
265 Aaron Boone (Star Rookie) .05
266 Todd Dunwoody (Star Rookie) .05
267 Jaret Wright (Star Rookie) .05
268 Derrick Gibson (Star Rookie) .05
269 Mario Valdez (Star Rookie) .05
270 Fernando Tatis (Star Rookie) .05
271 Craig Counsell (Star Rookie) .05
272 Brad Rigby (Star Rookie) .05
273 Danny Clyburn (Star Rookie) .05
274 Brian Rose (Star Rookie) .05
275 Miguel Tejada (Star Rookie) .15
276 Jason Varitek (Star Rookie) .10
277 *David Dellucci* (Star Rookie) .25
278 Michael Coleman (Star Rookie) .05
279 Adam Riggs (Star Rookie) .05
280 Ben Grieve (Star Rookie) .15
281 Brad Fullmer (Star Rookie) .05
282 Ken Cloude (Star Rookie) .05
283 Tom Evans (Star Rookie) .05
284 *Kevin Millwood* (Star Rookie) .50
285 Paul Konerko (Star Rookie) .10
286 Juan Encarnacion (Star Rookie) .05
287 Chris Carpenter (Star Rookie) .05
288 Tom Fordham (Star Rookie) .05
289 Gary DiSarcina .05
290 Tim Salmon .10
291 Troy Percival .05
292 Todd Greene .05
293 Ken Hill .05
294 Dennis Springer .05
295 Jim Edmonds .05
296 Allen Watson .05
297 Brian Anderson .05
298 Keith Lockhart .05
299 Tom Glavine .10
300 Chipper Jones 1.00
301 Randall Simon .05
302 Mark Lemke .05
303 Ryan Klesko .05
304 Denny Neagle .05
305 Andruw Jones .50
306 Mike Mussina .40
307 Brady Anderson .05
308 Chris Hoiles .05
309 Mike Bordick .05
310 Cal Ripken Jr. 1.50
311 Geronimo Berroa .05
312 Armando Benitez .05
313 Roberto Alomar .40
314 Tim Wakefield .05
315 Reggie Jefferson .05
316 Jeff Frye .05
317 Scott Hatteberg .05
318 Steve Avery .05
319 Robinson Checo .05
320 Nomar Garciaparra .75
321 Lance Johnson .05
322 Tyler Houston .05
323 Mark Clark .05
324 Terry Adams .05
325 Sammy Sosa .75
326 Scott Servais .05
327 Manny Alexander .05
328 Norberto Martin .05
329 *Scott Eyre* .10
330 Frank Thomas .75
331 Robin Ventura .05
332 Matt Karchner .05
333 Keith Foulke .05
334 James Baldwin .05
335 Chris Stynes .05
336 Bret Boone .10
337 Jon Nunnally .05
338 Dave Burba .05
339 Eduardo Perez .05
340 Reggie Sanders .05
341 Mike Remlinger .05
342 Pat Watkins .05
343 Chad Ogea .05
344 John Smiley .05
345 Kenny Lofton .05
346 Jose Mesa .05
347 Charles Nagy .05
348 Bruce Aven .05
349 Enrique Wilson .05
350 Manny Ramirez .50
351 Jerry DiPoto .05
352 Ellis Burks .05
353 Kirt Manwaring .05
354 Vinny Castilla .05
355 Larry Walker .30
356 Kevin Ritz .05
357 Pedro Astacio .05
358 Scott Sanders .05
359 Deivi Cruz .05
360 Brian L. Hunter .05
361 Pedro Martinez (History in the Making) .20
362 Tom Glavine (History in the Making) .05
363 Willie McGee (History in the Making) .05
364 J.T. Snow (History in the Making) .05
365 Rusty Greer (History in the Making) .05
366 Mike Grace (History in the Making) .05
367 Tony Clark (History in the Making) .05
368 Ben Grieve (History in the Making) .05
369 Gary Sheffield (History in the Making) .10
370 Joe Oliver .05
371 Todd Jones .05
372 *Frank Catalanotto* .10
373 Brian Moehler .05
374 Cliff Floyd .05
375 Bobby Bonilla .05
376 Al Leiter .05
377 Josh Booty .05
378 Darren Daulton .05
379 Jay Powell .05
380 Felix Heredia .05
381 Jim Eisenreich .05
382 Richard Hidalgo .05
383 Mike Hampton .05
384 Shane Reynolds .05
385 Jeff Bagwell .50
386 Derek Bell .05
387 Ricky Gutierrez .05
388 Bill Spiers .05
389 Jose Offerman .05
390 Johnny Damon .10
391 Jermaine Dye .05
392 Jeff Montgomery .05
393 Glendon Rusch .05
394 Mike Sweeney .05
395 Kevin Appier .05
396 Joe Vitiello .05
397 Ramon Martinez .05
398 Darren Dreifort .05
399 Wilton Guerrero .05
400 Mike Piazza 1.00
401 Eddie Murray .40
402 Ismael Valdes .05
403 Todd Hollandsworth .05
404 Mark Loretta .05
405 Jeromy Burnitz .05
406 Jeff Cirillo .05
407 Scott Karl .05
408 Mike Matheny .05
409 Jose Valentin .05
410 John Jaha .05
411 Terry Steinbach .05
412 Torii Hunter .05
413 Pat Meares .05
414 Marty Cordova .05
415 Jaret Wright (Postseason Headliners) .05
416 Mike Mussina (Postseason Headliners) .20
417 John Smoltz (Postseason Headliners) .05
418 Devon White (Postseason Headliners) .05
419 Denny Neagle (Postseason Headliners) .05
420 Livan Hernandez (Postseason Headliners) .05
421 Kevin Brown (Postseason Headliners) .05
422 Marquis Grissom (Postseason Headliners) .05
423 Mike Mussina (Postseason Headliners) .20
424 Eric Davis (Postseason Headliners) .05
425 Tony Fernandez (Postseason Headliners) .05
426 Moises Alou (Postseason Headliners) .05
427 Sandy Alomar Jr. (Postseason Headliners) .05
428 Gary Sheffield (Postseason Headliners) .10
429 Jaret Wright (Postseason Headliners) .05
430 Livan Hernandez (Postseason Headliners) .05
431 Chad Ogea (Postseason Headliners) .05
432 Edgar Renteria (Postseason Headliners) .05
433 LaTroy Hawkins .05
434 Rich Robertson .05
435 Chuck Knoblauch .05
436 Jose Vidro .05
437 Dustin Hermanson .05
438 Jim Bullinger .05
439 Orlando Cabrera (Star Rookie) .10
440 Vladimir Guerrero .50
441 Ugueth Urbina .05
442 Brian McRae .05
443 Matt Franco .05
444 Bobby Jones .05
445 Bernard Gilkey .05
446 Dave Mlicki .05
447 Brian Bohanon .05
448 Mel Rojas .05
449 Tim Raines .05
450 Derek Jeter 1.00
451 Roger Clemens (Upper Echelon) .30
452 Nomar Garciaparra (Upper Echelon) .40
453 Mike Piazza (Upper Echelon) .50
454 Mark McGwire (Upper Echelon) .75
455 Ken Griffey Jr. (Upper Echelon) .65
456 Larry Walker (Upper Echelon) .10
457 Alex Rodriguez (Upper Echelon) .65
458 Tony Gwynn (Upper Echelon) .30
459 Frank Thomas (Upper Echelon) .40
460 Tino Martinez .05
461 Chad Curtis .05
462 Ramiro Mendoza .05
463 Joe Girardi .05
464 David Wells .10
465 Mariano Rivera .15
466 Willie Adams .05
467 George Williams .05
468 Dave Telgheder .05
469 Dave Magadan .05
470 Matt Stairs .05
471 Billy Taylor .05
472 Jimmy Haynes .05
473 Gregg Jefferies .05
474 Midre Cummings .05
475 Curt Schilling .15
476 Mike Grace .05
477 Mark Leiter .05
478 Matt Beech .05
479 Scott Rolen .35
480 Jason Kendall .05
481 Esteban Loaiza .05
482 Jermaine Allensworth .05
483 Mark Smith .05
484 Jason Schmidt .05
485 Jose Guillen .05
486 Al Martin .05
487 Delino DeShields .05
488 Todd Stottlemyre .05
489 Brian Jordan .05
490 Ray Lankford .05
491 Matt Morris .05
492 Royce Clayton .05
493 John Mabry .05
494 Wally Joyner .05
495 Trevor Hoffman .05
496 Chris Gomez .05
497 Sterling Hitchcock .05
498 Pete Smith .05
499 Greg Vaughn .05
500 Tony Gwynn .60
501 Will Cunnane .05
502 Darryl Hamilton .05
503 Brian Johnson .05
504 Kirk Rueter .05
505 Barry Bonds .75
506 Osvaldo Fernandez .05
507 Stan Javier .05
508 Julian Tavarez .05
509 Rich Aurilia .05
510 Alex Rodriguez 1.25
511 David Segui .05
512 Rich Amaral .05
513 Raul Ibanez .05
514 Jay Buhner .05

515 Randy Johnson .45
516 Heathcliff Slocumb .05
517 Tony Saunders .05
518 Kevin Elster .05
519 John Burkett .05
520 Juan Gonzalez .50
521 John Wetteland .05
522 Domingo Cedeno .05
523 Darren Oliver .05
524 Roger Pavlik .05
525 Jose Cruz Jr. .10
526 Woody Williams .05
527 Alex Gonzalez .10
528 Robert Person .05
529 Juan Guzman .05
530 Roger Clemens .60
531 Shawn Green .30
532 Cordova, Ricon, Smith (Season Highlights) .05
533 Nomar Garciaparra (Season Highlights) .40
534 Roger Clemens (Season Highlights) .30
535 Mark McGwire (Season Highlights) .75
536 Larry Walker (Season Highlights) .10
537 Mike Piazza (Season Highlights) .50
538 Curt Schilling (Season Highlights) .05
539 Tony Gwynn (Season Highlights) .30
540 Ken Griffey Jr. (Season Highlights) .65
541 Carl Pavano (Star Rookies) .05
542 Shane Monahan (Star Rookies) .05
543 *Gabe Kapler* (Star Rookies) .75
544 Eric Milton (Star Rookies) .05
545 *Gary Matthews Jr.* (Star Rookies) .15
546 *Mike Kinkade* (Star Rookies) .25
547 *Ryan Christenson* (Star Rookies) .10
548 *Corey Koskie* (Star Rookies) .25
549 Norm Hutchins (Star Rookies) .05
550 Russell Branyan (Star Rookies) .05
551 *Masato Yoshii* (Star Rookies) .25
552 *Jesus Sanchez* (Star Rookies) .10
553 Anthony Sanders (Star Rookies) .05
554 Edwin Diaz (Star Rookies) .05
555 Gabe Alvarez (Star Rookies) .05
556 *Carlos Lee* (Star Rookies) .50
557 Mike Darr (Star Rookies) .05
558 Kerry Wood (Star Rookies) .25
559 Carlos Guillen (Star Rookies) .05
560 Sean Casey (Star Rookies) .25
561 *Manny Aybar* (Star Rookies) .15
562 Octavio Dotel (Star Rookies) .05
563 Jarrod Washburn (Star Rookies) .05
564 Mark L. Johnson (Star Rookies) .05
565 Ramon Hernandez (Star Rookies) .05
566 *Rich Butler* (Star Rookies) .05
567 Mike Caruso (Star Rookies) .05
568 Cliff Politte (Star Rookies) .05
569 Scott Elarton (Star Rookies) .05
570 *Magglio Ordonez* (Star Rookies) 2.00
571 *Adam Butler* (Star Rookies) .05
572 Marlon Anderson (Star Rookies) .05
573 *Julio Ramirez* (Star Rookies) .15
574 *Darron Ingram* (Star Rookies) .10
575 Bruce Chen (Star Rookies) .05
576 *Steve Woodard* (Star Rookies) .10
577 Hiram Bocachica (Star Rookies) .05
578 Kevin Witt (Star Rookies) .05
579 Javier Vazquez (Star Rookies) .10
580 Alex Gonzalez (Star Rookies) .10
581 Brian Powell (Star Rookies) .05
582 Wes Helms (Star Rookies) .05
583 Ron Wright (Star Rookies) .05
584 Rafael Medina (Star Rookies) .05
585 Daryle Ward (Star Rookies) .05
586 Geoff Jenkins (Star Rookies) .05
587 Preston Wilson (Star Rookies) .10
588 *Jim Chamblee* (Star Rookies) .05
589 *Mike Lowell* (Star Rookies) .50
590 A.J. Hinch (Star Rookies) .05
591 *Francisco Cordero* (Star Rookies) .10
592 *Rolando Arrojo* (Star Rookies) .25
593 Braden Looper (Star Rookies) .05
594 Sidney Ponson (Star Rookies) .05
595 Matt Clement (Star Rookies) .05
596 Carlton Loewer (Star Rookies) .05
597 Brian Meadows (Star Rookies) .05
598 Danny Klassen (Star Rookies) .05
599 Larry Sutton (Star Rookies) .05
600 Travis Lee (Star Rookies) .10
601 Randy Johnson (Eminent Prestige) 1.25
602 Greg Maddux (Eminent Prestige) 2.00
603 Roger Clemens (Eminent Prestige) 2.00
604 Jaret Wright (Eminent Prestige) .50
605 Mike Piazza (Eminent Prestige) 3.00
606 Tino Martinez (Eminent Prestige) .50
607 Frank Thomas (Eminent Prestige) 3.00
608 Mo Vaughn (Eminent Prestige) .75
609 Todd Helton (Eminent Prestige) 1.25
610 Mark McGwire (Eminent Prestige) 4.00
611 Jeff Bagwell (Eminent Prestige) 1.50
612 Travis Lee (Eminent Prestige) .50
613 Scott Rolen (Eminent Prestige) 1.00
614 Cal Ripken Jr. (Eminent Prestige) 4.00
615 Chipper Jones (Eminent Prestige) 3.00
616 Nomar Garciaparra (Eminent Prestige) 2.50
617 Alex Rodriguez (Eminent Prestige) 3.50
618 Derek Jeter (Eminent Prestige) 3.00
619 Tony Gwynn (Eminent Prestige) 2.00
620 Ken Griffey Jr. (Eminent Prestige) 3.50
621 Kenny Lofton (Eminent Prestige) .50
622 Juan Gonzalez (Eminent Prestige) 1.50
623 Jose Cruz Jr. (Eminent Prestige) .75
624 Larry Walker (Eminent Prestige) .75
625 Barry Bonds (Eminent Prestige) 2.50
626 Ben Grieve (Eminent Prestige) .75
627 Andruw Jones (Eminent Prestige) 1.25
628 Vladimir Guerrero (Eminent Prestige) 1.50
629 Paul Konerko (Eminent Prestige) .50
630 Paul Molitor (Eminent Prestige) 1.25
631 Cecil Fielder .05
632 Jack McDowell .05
633 Mike James .05
634 Brian Anderson .05
635 Jay Bell .05
636 Devon White .05
637 Andy Stankiewicz .05
638 Tony Batista .05
639 Omar Daal .05
640 Matt Williams .15
641 Brent Brede .05
642 Jorge Fabregas .05
643 Karim Garcia .10
644 Felix Rodriguez .05
645 Andy Benes .05
646 Willie Blair .05
647 Jeff Suppan .05
648 Yamil Benitez .05
649 Walt Weiss .05
650 Andres Galarraga .05
651 Doug Drabek .05
652 Ozzie Guillen .05
653 Joe Carter .05
654 Dennis Eckersley .05
655 Pedro Martinez .40
656 Jim Leyritz .05
657 Henry Rodriguez .05
658 Rod Beck .05
659 Mickey Morandini .05
660 Jeff Blauser .05
661 Ruben Sierra .05
662 Mike Sirotka .05
663 Pete Harnisch .05
664 Damian Jackson .05
665 Dmitri Young .05
666 Steve Cooke .05
667 Geronimo Berroa .05
668 Shawon Dunston .05
669 Mike Jackson .05
670 Travis Fryman .05
671 Dwight Gooden .05
672 Paul Assenmacher .05
673 Eric Plunk .05
674 Mike Lansing .05
675 Darryl Kile .05
676 Luis Gonzalez .35
677 Frank Castillo .05
678 Joe Randa .05
679 Bip Roberts .05
680 Derrek Lee .05
681a Mike Piazza (Marlins) 1.00
681b Mike Piazza (Mets) 1.00
682 Sean Berry .05
683 Ramon Garcia .05
684 Carl Everett .10
685 Moises Alou .10
686 Hal Morris .05
687 Jeff Conine .05
688 Gary Sheffield .25
689 Jose Vizcaino .05
690 Charles Johnson .05
691 Bobby Bonilla .05
692 Marquis Grissom .05
693 Alex Ochoa .05
694 Mike Morgan .05
695 Orlando Merced .05
696 David Ortiz .05
697 Brent Gates .05
698 Otis Nixon .05
699 Trey Moore .05
700 Derrick May .05
701 Rich Becker .05
702 Al Leiter .05
703 Chili Davis .05
704 Scott Brosius .05
705 Chuck Knoblauch .05
706 Kenny Rogers .05
707 Mike Blowers .05
708 Mike Fetters .05
709 Tom Candiotti .05
710 Rickey Henderson .50
711 Bob Abreu .10
712 Mark Lewis .05
713 Doug Glanville .05
714 Desi Relaford .05
715 Kent Mercker .05
716 J. Kevin Brown .10
717 James Mouton .05
718 Mark Langston .05
719 Greg Myers .05
720 Orel Hershiser .05
721 Charlie Hayes .05
722 Robb Nen .05
723 Glenallen Hill .05
724 Tony Saunders .05
725 Wade Boggs .45
726 Kevin Stocker .05
727 Wilson Alvarez .05
728 Albie Lopez .05
729 Dave Martinez .05
730 Fred McGriff .05
731 Quinton McCracken .05
732 Bryan Rekar .05
733 Paul Sorrento .05
734 Roberto Hernandez .05
735 Bubba Trammell .05
736 Miguel Cairo .05
737 John Flaherty .05
738 Terrell Wade .05
739 Roberto Kelly .05
740 Mark Mclemore (McLemore) .05
741 Danny Patterson .05
742 Aaron Sele .05
743 Tony Fernandez .05
744 Randy Myers .05
745 Jose Canseco .45
746 Darrin Fletcher .05
747 Mike Stanley .05
748 Marquis Grissom (Season Highlights) .05
749 Fred McGriff (Season Highlights) .05
750 Travis Lee (Season Highlights) .05

1998 Upper Deck A Piece of the Action

A Piece of the Action was inserted in Series One, Two and Three packs. Series One featured 10 cards: five with a piece of game-used jersey and five with a piece of game-used bat. Series Two offered a piece of game-used bat and jersey on four cards. Series Three inserts featured a piece of jersey only. The cards were inserted one per 2,500 packs in Series 1 and 2; the insertion rate in Series 3 was not revealed.

		MT
Complete Set (18):		500.00
Common Player:		10.00
Inserted 1:2,500		
(1)	Tony Gwynn (Jersey)	50.00
(2)	Tony Gwynn (Bat)	40.00
(3)	Alex Rodriguez (Jersey)	75.00
(4)	Alex Rodriguez (Bat)	65.00
(5)	Gary Sheffield (Jersey)	15.00
(6)	Gary Sheffield (Bat)	15.00
(7)	Todd Hollandsworth (Jersey)	10.00
(8)	Todd Hollandsworth (Bat)	10.00
(9)	Greg Maddux (Jersey)	50.00
(10)	Jay Buhner (Bat)	10.00
RA	Roberto Alomar	90.00
JB	Jay Buhner	20.00
AJ	Andruw Jones	75.00
GS	Gary Sheffield	30.00

1998 Upper Deck Amazing Greats

The 30-card Amazing Greats insert is printed on acetate. The cards are labeled "One of 2,000". A die-cut parallel was sequentially numbered to 250. Amazing Greats was an insert in Upper Deck Series One packs. Cards carry an "AG" prefix.

		MT
Complete Set (30):		200.00
Common Player:		1.50
Die-Cuts (250):		4X
1	Ken Griffey Jr.	18.00
2	Derek Jeter	20.00
3	Alex Rodriguez	18.00
4	Paul Molitor	5.00
5	Jeff Bagwell	7.50
6	Larry Walker	3.00
7	Kenny Lofton	1.50
8	Cal Ripken Jr.	20.00
9	Juan Gonzalez	7.50
10	Chipper Jones	12.00
11	Greg Maddux	10.00
12	Roberto Alomar	5.00
13	Mike Piazza	15.00
14	Andres Galarraga	1.50
15	Barry Bonds	10.00
16	Andy Pettitte	3.00
17	Nomar Garciaparra	12.00
18	Hideki Irabu	1.50
19	Tony Gwynn	8.00
20	Frank Thomas	7.50
21	Roger Clemens	8.00
22	Sammy Sosa	12.00
23	Jose Cruz, Jr.	2.00
24	Manny Ramirez	7.50
25	Mark McGwire	20.00
26	Randy Johnson	7.50
27	Mo Vaughn	3.00
28	Gary Sheffield	2.00
29	Andruw Jones	6.00
30	Albert Belle	1.50

1998 Upper Deck Blue Chip Prospects

Inserted in Series Two packs, Blue Chip Prospects is printed on die-cut acetate. The cards are sequentially numbered to 2,000. They carry a "BC" prefix.

		MT
Complete Set (30):		120.00
Common Player:		2.00
1	Nomar Garciaparra	18.00
2	Scott Rolen	6.00
3	Jason Dickson	2.00
4	Darin Erstad	6.00
5	Brad Fullmer	2.00
6	Jaret Wright	2.00
7	Justin Thompson	2.00
8	Matt Morris	4.00
9	Fernando Tatis	2.00
10	Alex Rodriguez	20.00
11	Todd Helton	8.00
12	Andy Pettitte	4.00
13	Jose Cruz Jr.	3.00
14	Mark Kotsay	2.50
15	Derek Jeter	25.00
16	Paul Konerko	3.00
17	Todd Dunwoody	2.00
18	Vladimir Guerrero	8.00
19	Miguel Tejada	5.00
20	Chipper Jones	15.00
21	Kevin Orie	2.00
22	Juan Encarnacion	2.00
23	Brian Rose	2.00
24	Andruw Jones	8.00
25	Livan Hernandez	2.00
26	Brian Giles	3.00
27	Brett Tomko	2.00
28	Jose Guillen	2.00
29	Aaron Boone	2.00
30	Ben Grieve	4.00

1998 Upper Deck Clearly Dominant

Clearly Dominant was an insert in Series Two. Printed on Light F/X plastic stock, the 30-card set is sequentially numbered to 250. They carry a "CD" prefix.

		MT
Complete Set (30):		260.00
Common Player:		2.00
Production 250 sets		
1	Mark McGwire	25.00
2	Derek Jeter	30.00
3	Alex Rodriguez	25.00
4	Paul Molitor	7.00
5	Jeff Bagwell	8.00
6	Ivan Rodriguez	6.00
7	Kenny Lofton	2.00
8	Cal Ripken Jr.	30.00
9	Albert Belle	3.00
10	Chipper Jones	20.00
11	Gary Sheffield	3.00
12	Roberto Alomar	6.00
13	Mo Vaughn	4.00
14	Andres Galarraga	2.00
15	Nomar Garciaparra	15.00
16	Randy Johnson	7.00
17	Mike Mussina	6.00
18	Greg Maddux	12.00
19	Tony Gwynn	12.00
20	Frank Thomas	8.00
21	Roger Clemens	12.00
22	Dennis Eckersley	2.00
23	Juan Gonzalez	8.00
24	Tino Martinez	2.00
25	Andruw Jones	7.00
26	Larry Walker	3.00
27	Ken Caminiti	2.00
28	Mike Piazza	20.00
29	Barry Bonds	15.00
30	Ken Griffey Jr.	25.00

1998 Upper Deck Jumbos

For $3 and 10 foil-pack wrappers, collectors could receive this set of large-format (3-1/2" x 5") cards in a mail-in redemption. The cards are identical to the standard-size versions.

		MT
Complete Set (15):		9.00
Common Player:		.25
27	Kenny Lofton	.25
30	Greg Maddux	.75
40	Rafael Palmeiro	.35
50	Ryne Sandberg	.50
60	Albert Belle	.40
65	Barry Larkin	.25
67	Deion Sanders	.25
95	Gary Sheffield	.35
130	Paul Molitor	.60
135	Vladimir Guerrero	.50
176	Hideki Irabu	.25
205	Mark McGwire	3.00
211	Rickey Henderson	.60
225	Ken Griffey Jr.	2.50
230	Ivan Rodriguez	.45

1998 Upper Deck Ken Griffey Jr.'s HR Chronicles

Griffey's Home Run Chronicles was inserted in both Series 1 and 2 packs. Series 1 had cards spotlighting one of Junior's first 30 home runs of the 1997 season. Series 2 had 26 cards highlighting the rest of his 1997 home run output. In both series, the cards were inserted one per nine packs. Cards are numbered "XX of 56" and printed on silver-metallic foil on front.

		MT
Complete Set (56):		75.00
Common Card:		3.00
Inserted 1:9		
1	Ken Griffey Jr.	3.00
2	Ken Griffey Jr.	3.00
3	Ken Griffey Jr.	3.00
4	Ken Griffey Jr.	3.00
5	Ken Griffey Jr.	3.00
6	Ken Griffey Jr.	3.00
7	Ken Griffey Jr.	3.00
8	Ken Griffey Jr.	3.00
9	Ken Griffey Jr.	3.00
10	Ken Griffey Jr.	3.00
11	Ken Griffey Jr.	3.00
12	Ken Griffey Jr.	3.00
13	Ken Griffey Jr.	3.00
14	Ken Griffey Jr.	3.00
15	Ken Griffey Jr.	3.00
16	Ken Griffey Jr.	3.00
17	Ken Griffey Jr.	3.00
18	Ken Griffey Jr.	3.00
19	Ken Griffey Jr.	3.00
20	Ken Griffey Jr.	3.00
21	Ken Griffey Jr.	3.00
22	Ken Griffey Jr.	3.00
23	Ken Griffey Jr.	3.00
24	Ken Griffey Jr.	3.00
25	Ken Griffey Jr.	3.00
26	Ken Griffey Jr.	3.00
27	Ken Griffey Jr.	3.00
28	Ken Griffey Jr.	3.00
29	Ken Griffey Jr.	3.00
30	Ken Griffey Jr.	3.00

1998 Upper Deck National Pride

National Pride is a 42-card insert printed on die-cut rainbow foil. The set honors the nationality of the player with their country's flag in the background. The cards were inserted one per 24 packs. Cards are numbered with a "NP" prefix.

		MT
Complete Set (42):		120.00
Common Player:		1.50
1	Dave Nilsson	1.50
2	Larry Walker	2.00
3	Edgar Renteria	1.50
4	Jose Canseco	2.50
5	Rey Ordonez	1.50
6	Rafael Palmeiro	2.00
7	Livan Hernandez	1.50
8	Andruw Jones	5.00
9	Manny Ramirez	5.00
10	Sammy Sosa	8.00
11	Raul Mondesi	2.00
12	Moises Alou	2.00
13	Pedro Martinez	4.00
14	Vladimir Guerrero	5.00
15	Chili Davis	1.50
16	Hideo Nomo	3.00
17	Hideki Irabu	1.50
18	Shigetosi Hasegawa	1.50
19	Takashi Kashiwada	1.50
20	Chan Ho Park	2.00
21	Fernando Valenzuela	1.50
22	Vinny Castilla	1.50
23	Armando Reynoso	1.50
24	Karim Garcia	2.00
25	Marvin Benard	1.50
26	Mariano Rivera	2.50
27	Juan Gonzalez	5.00
28	Roberto Alomar	3.00
29	Ivan Rodriguez	4.00
30	Carlos Delgado	2.00
31	Bernie Williams	2.00
32	Edgar Martinez	1.50
33	Frank Thomas	8.00
34	Barry Bonds	8.00
35	Mike Piazza	10.00
36	Chipper Jones	10.00
37	Cal Ripken Jr.	15.00
38	Alex Rodriguez	12.00
39	Ken Griffey Jr.	12.00
40	Andres Galarraga	1.50
41	Omar Vizquel	1.50
42	Ozzie Guillen	1.50

1998 Upper Deck Prime Nine

Nine of the most popular players are featured in this insert set. The cards are printed on silver foil stock and inserted 1:5 in Series 2 packs.

	MT
Complete Set (60):	75.00
Common Griffey:	2.00
Common Piazza:	1.50
Common Thomas:	1.25
Common McGwire:	2.50
Common Ripken:	2.50
Common Gonzalez:	1.00
Common Gwynn:	1.00
Common Bonds:	1.25
Common Maddux:	1.00
Inserted 1:5	
PN1 Ken Griffey Jr. (1989-1992)	2.00
PN2 Ken Griffey Jr. (1993)	2.00
PN3 Ken Griffey Jr. (1994)	2.00
PN4 Ken Griffey Jr. (1995)	2.00
PN5 Ken Griffey Jr. (1996)	2.00
PN6 Ken Griffey Jr. (1997)	2.00
PN7 Ken Griffey Jr. (1997)	2.00
PN8 Mike Piazza (1991)	1.50
PN9 Mike Piazza (1992)	1.50
PN10 Mike Piazza (1993)	1.50
PN11 Mike Piazza (1994)	1.50
PN12 Mike Piazza (1995)	1.50
PN13 Mike Piazza (1996)	1.50
PN14 Mike Piazza (1997)	1.50
PN15 Frank Thomas (1991)	1.25
PN16 Frank Thomas (1992)	1.25
PN17 Frank Thomas (1993)	1.25
PN18 Frank Thomas (1994)	1.25
PN19 Frank Thomas (1995)	1.25
PN20 Frank Thomas (1996)	1.25
PN21 Frank Thomas (1997)	1.25
PN22 Mark McGwire (1987)	2.50
PN23 Mark McGwire (1988-1990)	2.50
PN24 Mark McGwire (1992)	2.50
PN25 Mark McGwire (1995-1996)	2.50
PN26 Mark McGwire (1997)	2.50
PN27 Mark McGwire (1997)	2.50
PN28 Mark McGwire (1997)	2.50
PN29 Cal Ripken Jr. (1982)	2.50
PN30 Cal Ripken Jr. (1983)	2.50
PN31 Cal Ripken Jr. (1989)	2.50
PN32 Cal Ripken Jr. (1991)	2.50
PN33 Cal Ripken Jr. (1995)	2.50
PN34 Cal Ripken Jr. (1996)	2.50
PN35 Cal Ripken Jr. (1997)	2.50
PN36 Juan Gonzalez (1992)	1.00
PN37 Juan Gonzalez (1993)	1.00
PN38 Juan Gonzalez (1994)	1.00
PN39 Juan Gonzalez (1995)	1.00
PN40 Juan Gonzalez (1996)	1.00
PN41 Juan Gonzalez (1996)	1.00
PN42 Juan Gonzalez (1997)	1.00
PN43 Tony Gwynn (1984)	1.00
PN44 Tony Gwynn (1987-1989)	1.00
PN45 Tony Gwynn (1990-1993)	1.00
PN46 Tony Gwynn (1994)	1.00
PN47 Tony Gwynn (1996)	1.00
PN48 Tony Gwynn (1997)	1.00
PN49 Tony Gwynn (1997)	1.00
PN50 Barry Bonds (1986-1992)	1.25
PN51 Barry Bonds (1990-1993)	1.25
PN52 Barry Bonds (1993)	1.25
PN53 Barry Bonds (1994)	1.25
PN54 Barry Bonds (1996)	1.25
PN55 Barry Bonds (1997)	1.25
PN56 Greg Maddux (1992)	1.00
PN57 Greg Maddux (1993-1994)	1.00
PN58 Greg Maddux (1995)	1.00
PN59 Greg Maddux (1996)	1.00
PN60 Greg Maddux (1997)	1.00

1998 Upper Deck Tape Measure Titans

Tape Measure Titans is a 30-card insert seeded 1:23 in Series 2. The set honors the game's top home run hitters. A parallel gold version was also created with each card serially numbered to 2,667 on front.

		MT
Complete Set (30):		90.00
Common Player:		.75
Inserted 1:23		
Gold:		1.5X
1	Mark McGwire	15.00
2	Andres Galarraga	.75
3	Jeff Bagwell	5.00
4	Larry Walker	1.00
5	Frank Thomas	5.00
6	Rafael Palmeiro	1.50
7	Nomar Garciaparra	8.00
8	Mo Vaughn	1.00
9	Albert Belle	1.00
10	Ken Griffey Jr.	10.00
11	Manny Ramirez	4.00
12	Jim Thome	.75
13	Tony Clark	.75
14	Juan Gonzalez	4.00
15	Mike Piazza	10.00
16	Jose Canseco	2.00
17	Jay Buhner	.75
18	Alex Rodriguez	10.00
19	Jose Cruz Jr.	1.00
20	Tino Martinez	.75
21	Carlos Delgado	1.00
22	Andruw Jones	2.50
23	Chipper Jones	10.00
24	Fred McGriff	.75
25	Matt Williams	1.00
26	Sammy Sosa	10.00
27	Vinny Castilla	.75
28	Tim Salmon	1.00
29	Ken Caminiti	.75
30	Barry Bonds	8.00

1998 Upper Deck 10th Anniversary Preview

10th Anniversary Preview is a 60-card set. The foil cards have the same design as the 1989 Upper Deck base cards. The set was inserted one per five packs.

		MT
Complete Set (60):		45.00
Common Player:		.25
1	Greg Maddux	2.25
2	Mike Mussina	1.00
3	Roger Clemens	2.25
4	Hideo Nomo	1.50
4	David Cone	.25
6	Tom Glavine	.35
7	Andy Pettitte	.75
8	Jimmy Key	.25
9	Randy Johnson	1.00
10	Dennis Eckersley	.25
11	Lee Smith	.25
12	John Franco	.25
13	Randy Myers	.25
14	Mike Piazza	2.75
15	Ivan Rodriguez	1.50
16	Todd Hundley	.25
17	Sandy Alomar Jr.	.25
18	Frank Thomas	2.50
19	Rafael Palmeiro	.35
20	Mark McGwire	3.50
21	Mo Vaughn	.75
22	Fred McGriff	.25
23	Andres Galarraga	.25
24	Mark Grace	.50
25	Jeff Bagwell	2.00
26	Roberto Alomar	1.00
27	Chuck Knoblauch	.25
28	Ryne Sandberg	2.00
29	Eric Young	.25
30	Craig Biggio	.35
31	Carlos Baerga	.25
32	Robin Ventura	.25
33	Matt Williams	.35
34	Wade Boggs	.75
35	Dean Palmer	.25
36	Chipper Jones	2.75
37	Vinny Castilla	.25
38	Ken Caminiti	.25
39	Omar Vizquel	.25
40	Cal Ripken Jr.	3.50
41	Derek Jeter	2.75
42	Alex Rodriguez	3.00
43	Barry Larkin	.35
44	Mark Grudzielanek	.25
45	Albert Belle	.75
46	Manny Ramirez	2.00
47	Jose Canseco	1.00
48	Ken Griffey Jr.	3.00
49	Juan Gonzalez	2.00
50	Kenny Lofton	.25
51	Sammy Sosa	2.50
52	Larry Walker	.35
53	Gary Sheffield	.40
54	Rickey Henderson	.75
55	Tony Gwynn	2.25
56	Barry Bonds	2.50
57	Paul Molitor	1.00
58	Edgar Martinez	.25
59	Chili Davis	.25
60	Eddie Murray	.60

1998 Upper Deck Rookie Edition A Piece of the Action

A Piece of the Action consists of five Game Jersey cards. Three rookie Game Jersey cards were sequentially numbered to 200, while a Ken Griffey Jr.

Game Jersey card was numbered to 300. Griffey also signed and hand-numbered 24 Game Jersey cards.

		MT
Common Card:		15.00
KG	Ken Griffey Jr. (300)	150.00
KGS	Ken Griffey Jr. (24) (Signed)	400.00
BG	Ben Grieve (200)	25.00
JC	Jose Cruz Jr. (200)	25.00
TL	Travis Lee (200)	25.00

1998 Upper Deck Rookie Edition All-Star Credentials

All-Star Credentials is a 30-card insert seeded 1:9. It features the game's top players.

		MT
Complete Set (30):		30.00
Common Player:		.25
Inserted 1:9		
AS1	Ken Griffey Jr.	3.00
AS2	Travis Lee	.35
AS3	Ben Grieve	.50
AS4	Jose Cruz Jr.	.35
AS5	Andruw Jones	.75
AS6	Craig Biggio	.35
AS7	Hideo Nomo	.65
AS8	Cal Ripken Jr.	4.00
AS9	Jaret Wright	.25
AS10	Mark McGwire	3.00
AS11	Derek Jeter	4.00
AS12	Scott Rolen	.65
AS13	Jeff Bagwell	.75
AS14	Manny Ramirez	.75
AS15	Alex Rodriguez	2.50
AS16	Chipper Jones	2.00
AS17	Larry Walker	.45
AS18	Barry Bonds	1.50
AS19	Tony Gwynn	1.00
AS20	Mike Piazza	2.50
AS21	Roger Clemens	1.00
AS22	Greg Maddux	1.00
AS23	Jim Thome	.25
AS24	Tino Martinez	.25
AS25	Nomar Garciaparra	2.00
AS26	Juan Gonzalez	.75
AS27	Kenny Lofton	.25
AS28	Randy Johnson	.65
AS29	Todd Helton	.65
AS30	Frank Thomas	1.25

1998 Upper Deck Rookie Edition Destination Stardom

This 60-card insert features top young players. Fronts are printed on a foil background. The insertion rate was one card per five packs. Cards have a "DS" prefix to the card number.

		MT
Complete Set (60):		55.00
Common Player:		.50
Inserted 1:5		
1	Travis Lee	1.00
2	Nomar Garciaparra	6.00
3	Alex Gonzalez	.50
4	Richard Hidalgo	.75
5	Jaret Wright	.50
6	Mike Kinkade	.50
7	Matt Morris	.75
8	Gary Mathews Jr.	.50
9	Brett Tomko	.50
10	Todd Helton	3.00
11	Scott Elarton	.50
12	Scott Rolen	3.00
13	Jose Cruz Jr.	1.00
14	Jarrod Washburn	.50
15	Sean Casey	2.50
16	Magglio Ordonez	2.50
17	Gabe Alvarez	.50
18	Todd Dunwoody	.50
19	Kevin Witt	.50
20	Ben Grieve	1.00
21	Daryle Ward	.50
22	Matt Clement	.50
23	Carlton Loewer	.50
24	Javier Vazquez	.75
25	Paul Konerko	1.00
26	Preston Wilson	1.00
27	Wes Helms	.50
28	Derek Jeter	8.00
29	Corey Koskie	.75
30	Russell Branyan	.75
31	Vladimir Guerrero	4.00
32	Ryan Christenson	.50
33	Carlos Lee	1.00
34	David Dellucci	.50
35	Bruce Chen	.50
36	Ricky Ledee	1.00
37	Ron Wright	.50
38	Derrek Lee	.50
39	Miguel Tejada	1.50
40	Brad Fullmer	1.00
41	Rich Butler	.50
42	Chris Carpenter	.50
43	Alex Rodriguez	10.00
44	Darron Ingram	.50
45	Kerry Wood	2.50
46	Jason Varitek	.50
47	Ramon Hernandez	.50
48	Aaron Boone	.50
49	Juan Encarnacion	.50
50	A.J. Hinch	.50
51	Mike Lowell	.50
52	Fernando Tatis	.50
53	Jose Guillen	.50
54	Mike Caruso	.50
55	Carl Pavano	.50
56	Chris Clemons	.50
57	Mark L. Johnson	.50
58	Ken Cloude	.50
59	Rolando Arrojo	.50
60	Mark Kotsay	.75

1998 Upper Deck Rookie Edition Eminent Prestige 5x7

This 4X super-size (5" x 7") version is a partial parallel of the Rookie Edition Eminent Prestige subset. It was available only in specially marked retail packaging.

		MT
Complete Set (10):		35.00
Common Player:		2.00
605	Mike Piazza	4.00
607	Frank Thomas	4.00
610	Mark McGwire	6.00
611	Jeff Bagwell	2.50
612	Travis Lee	2.00
614	Cal Ripken Jr.	6.00
616	Nomar Garciaparra	3.50
617	Alex Rodriguez	5.00
619	Tony Gwynn	3.00
620	Ken Griffey Jr.	5.00

1998 Upper Deck Rookie Edition Unparalleled

Unparalleled is a 20-card, hobby-only insert. The set consists of holo-pattern foil-stamped cards. They were inserted one per 72 packs.

		MT
Complete Set (20):		165.00
Common Player:		2.00
Inserted 1:72		
1	Ken Griffey Jr.	17.50
2	Travis Lee	2.50
3	Ben Grieve	3.50
4	Jose Cruz Jr.	2.50
5	Nomar Garciaparra	12.50
6	Hideo Nomo	6.00
7	Kenny Lofton	2.00
8	Cal Ripken Jr.	20.00
9	Roger Clemens	10.00
10	Mike Piazza	15.00
11	Jeff Bagwell	7.50
12	Chipper Jones	15.00
13	Greg Maddux	10.00
14	Randy Johnson	6.00
15	Alex Rodriguez	17.50
16	Barry Bonds	12.50
17	Frank Thomas	12.50
18	Juan Gonzalez	7.50
19	Tony Gwynn	10.00
20	Mark McGwire	20.00

1998 Upper Deck Rookie Edition Retrospectives

Retrospectives is a 30-card insert seeded 1:24. The cards offer a look back at the careers of baseball's top stars.

		MT
Complete Set (30):		75.00
Common Player:		.75
Inserted 1:24		
1	Dennis Eckersley	.75
2	Rickey Henderson	2.50
3	Harold Baines	.75
4	Cal Ripken Jr.	9.00
5	Tony Gwynn	4.00
6	Wade Boggs	2.50
7	Orel Hershiser	.75
8	Joe Carter	.75
9	Roger Clemens	4.00
10	Barry Bonds	5.00
11	Mark McGwire	9.00
12	Greg Maddux	4.00
13	Fred McGriff	.75
14	Rafael Palmeiro	1.25
15	Craig Biggio	1.00
16	Brady Anderson	.75
17	Randy Johnson	3.00
18	Gary Sheffield	1.25
19	Albert Belle	1.00
20	Ken Griffey Jr.	7.50
21	Juan Gonzalez	3.00
22	Larry Walker	1.00
23	Tino Martinez	.75
24	Frank Thomas	5.00
25	Jeff Bagwell	3.00
26	Kenny Lofton	.75
27	Mo Vaughn	1.25
28	Mike Piazza	6.00
29	Alex Rodriguez	7.50
30	Chipper Jones	6.00

1998 Upper Deck Special F/X

Special F/X is a retail-only product. The 150-card set consists of 125 regular cards, the 15-card Star Rookies subset and a 10-card subset called Ken Griffey Jr.'s Hot List. The base cards are printed on 20-point stock. The only insert is Power Zone which has four levels: Level One, Level Two - Octoberbest, Level Three - Power Driven and Level Four - Superstar Xcitement.

		MT
Complete Set (150):		32.50
Common Player:		.15
1	Ken Griffey Jr. (Griffey Hot List)	1.25
2	Mark McGwire (Griffey Hot List)	1.50
3	Alex Rodriguez (Griffey Hot List)	1.25
4	Larry Walker (Griffey Hot List)	.35
5	Tino Martinez (Griffey Hot List)	.15
6	Mike Piazza (Griffey Hot List)	2.00
7	Jose Cruz Jr. (Griffey Hot List)	.25
8	Greg Maddux (Griffey Hot List)	.75
9	Tony Gwynn (Griffey Hot List)	1.00
10	Roger Clemens (Griffey Hot List)	1.00
11	Jason Dickson	.15
12	Darin Erstad	.90
13	Chuck Finley	.15
14	Dave Hollins	.15
15	Garret Anderson	.15
16	Michael Tucker	.15
17	Javier Lopez	.15
18	John Smoltz	.25
19	Mark Wohlers	.15
20	Greg Maddux	1.50
21	Scott Erickson	.15
22	Jimmy Key	.15
23	B.J. Surhoff	.15
24	Eric Davis	.15
25	Rafael Palmeiro	.30
26	Tim Naehring	.15
27	Darren Bragg	.15
28	Troy O'Leary	.15
29	John Valentin	.15
30	Mo Vaughn	.50
31	Mark Grace	.45
32	Kevin Foster	.15
33	Kevin Tapani	.15
34	Kevin Orie	.15
35	Albert Belle	.45
36	Ray Durham	.15
37	Jaime Navarro	.15
38	Mike Cameron	.15
39	Eddie Taubensee	.15
40	Barry Larkin	.25
41	Willie Greene	.15
42	Jeff Shaw	.15
43	Omar Vizquel	.15
44	Brian Giles	.15
45	Jim Thome	.15
46	David Justice	.45
47	Sandy Alomar Jr.	.15
48	Neifi Perez	.15
49	Dante Bichette	.15
50	Vinny Castilla	.15
51	John Thomson	.15
52	Damion Easley	.15
53	Justin Thompson	.15
54	Bobby Higginson	.25
55	Tony Clark	.15
56	Charles Johnson	.15
57	Edgar Renteria	.15
58	Alex Fernandez	.15
59	Gary Sheffield	.35
60	Livan Hernandez	.15
61	Craig Biggio	.25
62	Chris Holt	.15
63	Billy Wagner	.15
64	Brad Ausmus	.15
65	Dean Palmer	.15
66	Tim Belcher	.15
67	Jeff King	.15
68	Jose Rosado	.15
69	Chan Ho Park	.45
70	Raul Mondesi	.25
71	Hideo Nomo	.50
72	Todd Zeile	.15
73	Eric Karros	.15
74	Cal Eldred	.15
75	Jeff D'Amico	.15
76	Doug Jones	.15
77	Dave Nilsson	.15
78	Todd Walker	.15
79	Rick Aguilera	.15
80	Paul Molitor	.60
81	Brad Radke	.15
82	Vladimir Guerrero	1.00
83	Carlos Perez	.15
84	F.P. Santangelo	.15
85	Rondell White	.25
86	Butch Huskey	.15
87	Edgardo Alfonzo	.15
88	John Franco	.15
89	John Olerud	.15
90	Todd Hundley	.15
91	Bernie Williams	.25
92	Andy Pettitte	.45
93	Paul O'Neill	.15
94	David Cone	.15
95	Jason Giambi	.50
96	Damon Mashore	.15
97	Scott Spiezio	.15
98	Ariel Prieto	.15
99	Rico Brogna	.15
100	Mike Lieberthal	.15
101	Garrett Stephenson	.15
102	Ricky Bottalico	.15
103	Kevin Polcovich	.15
104	Jon Lieber	.15
105	Kevin Young	.15
106	Tony Womack	.15
107	Gary Gaetti	.15
108	Alan Benes	.15
109	Willie McGee	.15
110	Mark McGwire	3.00
111	Ron Gant	.15
112	Andy Ashby	.15
113	Steve Finley	.15
114	Quilvio Veras	.15
115	Ken Caminiti	.15
116	Joey Hamilton	.15
117	Bill Mueller	.15
118	Mark Gardner	.15
119	Shawn Estes	.15
120	J.T. Snow	.15
121	Dante Powell	.15
122	Jeff Kent	.15
123	Jamie Moyer	.15
124	Joey Cora	.15
125	Ken Griffey Jr.	2.50
126	Jeff Fassero	.15
127	Edgar Martinez	.15
128	Will Clark	.45
129	Lee Stevens	.15
130	Ivan Rodriguez	.90
131	Rusty Greer	.15
132	Ed Sprague	.15
133	Pat Hentgen	.15
134	Shannon Stewart	.15
135	Carlos Delgado	.25
136	Brett Tomko (Star Rookie)	.15
137	Jose Guillen (Star Rookie)	.15
138	Elieser Marrero (Star Rookie)	.15
139	Dennis Reyes (Star Rookie)	.15
140	Mark Kotsay (Star Rookie)	.25
141	Richie Sexson (Star Rookie)	.15
142	Todd Helton (Star Rookie)	.90
143	Jeremi Gonzalez (Star Rookie)	.15
144	Jeff Abbott (Star Rookie)	.15
145	Matt Morris (Star Rookie)	.25
146	Aaron Boone (Star Rookie)	.15
147	Todd Dunwoody (Star Rookie)	.15
148	Mario Valdez (Star Rookie)	.15
149	Fernando Tatis (Star Rookie)	.15
150	Jaret Wright (Star Rookie)	.15

1998 Upper Deck Special F/X OctoberBest

OctoberBest is Level Two of the Power Zone insert. This 20-card insert is die-cut and printed on silver foil. Inserted one per 34 packs, the set features the postseason exploits of 20 players from Power Zone Level One.

		MT
Complete Set (15):		50.00
Common Player:		1.00
Inserted 1:34		
PZ1	Frank Thomas	5.00
PZ2	Juan Gonzalez	3.00
PZ3	Mike Piazza	6.50
PZ4	Mark McGwire	10.00
PZ5	Jeff Bagwell	3.00
PZ6	Barry Bonds	5.00
PZ7	Ken Griffey Jr.	8.00
PZ8	John Smoltz	1.00
PZ9	Andruw Jones	3.00
PZ10	Greg Maddux	4.00
PZ11	Sandy Alomar Jr.	1.00
PZ12	Roberto Alomar	2.00
PZ13	Chipper Jones	6.50
PZ14	Kenny Lofton	1.00
PZ15	Tom Glavine	1.00

1998 Upper Deck Special F/X Power Driven

Power Driven is Level Three of the Power Zone insert. Inserted 1:69, the set features the top 10 power hitters from Power Zone Level Two. The cards feature gold Light F/X technology.

		MT
Complete Set (10):		55.00
Common Player:		1.50
Inserted 1:69		
PZ1	Frank Thomas	7.50
PZ2	Juan Gonzalez	4.50
PZ3	Mike Piazza	10.00
PZ4	Larry Walker	2.00
PZ5	Mark McGwire	15.00
PZ6	Jeff Bagwell	4.50
PZ7	Mo Vaughn	3.00
PZ8	Barry Bonds	7.50
PZ9	Tino Martinez	1.50
PZ10	Ken Griffey Jr.	13.50

1998 Upper Deck Special F/X Power Zone

Power Zone Level One is a 30-card insert seeded one per seven packs. The cards are printed using silver Light F/X technology.

		MT
Complete Set (20):		40.00
Common Player:		.50
Inserted 1:7		
PZ1	Jose Cruz Jr.	.50
PZ2	Frank Thomas	3.50
PZ3	Juan Gonzalez	2.50
PZ4	Mike Piazza	4.00
PZ5	Mark McGwire	6.00
PZ6	Barry Bonds	3.50
PZ7	Greg Maddux	3.00
PZ8	Alex Rodriguez	5.00
PZ9	Nomar Garciaparra	3.50
PZ10	Ken Griffey Jr.	5.00
PZ11	John Smoltz	.50
PZ12	Andruw Jones	2.50
PZ13	Sandy Alomar Jr.	.50
PZ14	Roberto Alomar	1.50
PZ15	Chipper Jones	4.00
PZ16	Kenny Lofton	.50
PZ17	Larry Walker	.75
PZ18	Jeff Bagwell	2.50
PZ19	Mo Vaughn	1.25
PZ20	Tom Glavine	.50

1998 Upper Deck Special F/X Superstar Xcitement

Printed on Light F/X gold foil, this 10-card set features the same players as the Power Driven insert.

This set is Power Zone Level Four and is sequentially numbered to 250.

MT
Complete Set (10): 125.00
Common Player: 4.00
Production 250 sets
PZ1 Jose Cruz Jr. 4.00
PZ2 Frank Thomas 15.00
PZ3 Juan Gonzalez 10.00
PZ4 Mike Piazza 17.50
PZ5 Mark McGwire 25.00
PZ6 Barry Bonds 15.00
PZ7 Greg Maddux 12.50
PZ8 Alex Rodriguez 20.00
PZ9 Nomar Garciaparra 15.00
PZ10 Ken Griffey Jr. 20.00

1998 Upper Deck UD 3

The 270-card base set of UD 3 is actually three levels of the same 90 players. Light FX cards comprise #1-90. The first 30 cards are Future Impact players. Cards #31-60 are Power Corps and cards #61-90 are The Establishment. Cards #91-180 repeat the three subsets in Embossed technology while the final 90 cards repeat the basic sequence in Rainbow technology. Because each subset at each level is seeded at a different rate few collectors bother to try to understand the relative scarcities and the issue is largely ignored. The insertion ratio for each tier is shown in the checklist. UD 3 was offered in three-card packs at an SRP of $3.99.

MT
Complete Set (270): 700.00
Common Future Impact (1-30): 1.00
Inserted 1:12
Die-Cuts (2,000 sets): 1X
Common Power Corps (31-60): .25
Inserted 1:1
Die-Cuts (2,000 sets): 3X
Common Establishment (61-90): .50
Inserted 1:6
Die-Cuts (2,000 sets): 2X
Common Future Impact Embossed (91-120): .50
Inserted 1:6
Die-Cuts (1,000 sets): 3X
Common Power Corps Embossed (121-150): .50
Inserted 1:4
Die-Cuts (1,000 sets): 6X
Common Establishment Embossed (151-180): .25
Inserted 1:1
Die-Cuts (1,000 sets): 12X
Common Future Impact Rainbow (181-210): .25
Inserted 1:1
Die-Cuts (100 sets): 15X
Common Power Corps Rainbow (211-240): 1.00
Inserted 1:12
Die-Cuts (100 sets): 8X
Common Establishment Rainbow (241-270): 1.50
Inserted 1:24
Die-Cuts (100 sets): 5X
Pack (3): 2.00
Wax Box (24): 40.00

LIGHT FX FUTURE IMPACT (1:12)
1 Travis Lee 1.50
2 A.J. Hinch 1.00
3 Mike Caruso 1.00
4 Miguel Tejada 1.50
5 Brad Fullmer 1.00
6 Eric Milton 1.00
7 Mark Kotsay 1.50
8 Darin Erstad 4.00
9 Magglio Ordonez 2.00
10 Ben Grieve 1.50
11 Brett Tomko 1.00
12 *Mike Kinkade* 1.50
13 Rolando Arrojo 1.00
14 Todd Helton 3.00
15 Scott Rolen 4.00
16 Bruce Chen 1.00
17 Daryle Ward 1.00
18 Jaret Wright 1.00
19 Sean Casey 2.00
20 Paul Konerko 1.25
21 Kerry Wood 3.00
22 Russell Branyan 1.25
23 Gabe Alvarez 1.00
24 Juan Encarnacion 1.25
25 Andruw Jones 5.00
26 Vladimir Guerrero 5.00
27 Eli Marrero 1.00
28 Matt Clement 1.00
29 Gary Matthews Jr. 1.00
30 Derrek Lee 1.00

LIGHT FX POWER CORPS (1:1)
31 Ken Caminiti .25
32 Gary Sheffield .50
33 Jay Buhner .25
34 Ryan Klesko .25
35 Nomar Garciaparra 2.00
36 Vinny Castilla .25
37 Tony Clark .25
38 Sammy Sosa 2.00
39 Tino Martinez .25
40 Mike Piazza 3.00
41 Manny Ramirez 1.50
42 Larry Walker .50
43 Jose Cruz Jr. .50
44 Matt Williams .50
45 Frank Thomas 2.00
46 Jim Edmonds .25
47 Raul Mondesi .50
48 Alex Rodriguez 4.50
49 Albert Belle .50
50 Mark McGwire 6.00
51 Tim Salmon .50
52 Andres Galarraga .25
53 Jeff Bagwell 1.50
54 Jim Thome .25
55 Barry Bonds 2.00
56 Carlos Delgado .50
57 Mo Vaughn 1.00
58 Chipper Jones 3.00
59 Juan Gonzalez 1.50
60 Ken Griffey Jr. 4.50

LIGHT FX THE ESTABLISHMENT (1:6)
61 David Cone .50
62 Hideo Nomo 2.00
63 Edgar Martinez .50
64 Fred McGriff .50
65 Cal Ripken Jr. 8.00
66 Todd Hundley .50
67 Barry Larkin .50
68 Dennis Eckersley .50
69 Randy Johnson 3.00
70 Paul Molitor 3.00
71 Eric Karros .50
72 Rafael Palmeiro .50
73 Chuck Knoblauch .50
74 Ivan Rodriguez 3.00
75 Greg Maddux 5.00
76 Dante Bichette .50
77 Brady Anderson .50
78 Craig Biggio .75
79 Derek Jeter 7.00
80 Roger Clemens 5.00
81 Roberto Alomar 2.50
82 Wade Boggs 2.50
83 Charles Johnson .50
84 Mark Grace .75
85 Kenny Lofton .50
86 Mike Mussina 2.00
87 Pedro Martinez 2.00
88 Curt Schilling 1.00
89 Bernie Williams 1.00
90 Tony Gwynn 5.00

EMBOSSED FUTURE IMPACT (1:6)
91 Travis Lee .75
92 A.J. Hinch .50
93 Mike Caruso .50
94 Miguel Tejada .75
95 Brad Fullmer .50
96 Eric Milton .50
97 Mark Kotsay .75
98 Darin Erstad 2.00
99 Magglio Ordonez 1.00
100 Ben Grieve .75
101 Brett Tomko .50
102 *Mike Kinkade* .75
103 Rolando Arrojo .50
104 Todd Helton 1.50
105 Scott Rolen 2.00
106 Bruce Chen .50
107 Daryle Ward .50
108 Jaret Wright .50
109 Sean Casey 1.00
110 Paul Konerko .75
111 Kerry Wood 1.50
112 Russell Branyan .65
113 Gabe Alvarez .50
114 Juan Encarnacion .65
115 Andruw Jones 2.50
116 Vladimir Guerrero 2.50
117 Eli Marrero .50
118 Matt Clement .50
119 Gary Matthews Jr. .50
120 Derrek Lee .50

EMBOSSED POWER CORPS (1:4)
121 Ken Caminiti .50
122 Gary Sheffield 1.00
123 Jay Buhner .50
124 Ryan Klesko .50
125 Nomar Garciaparra 4.00
126 Vinny Castilla .50
127 Tony Clark .50
128 Sammy Sosa 4.00
129 Tino Martinez .50
130 Mike Piazza 6.00
131 Manny Ramirez 3.00
132 Larry Walker 1.00
133 Jose Cruz Jr. 1.00
134 Matt Williams 1.00
135 Frank Thomas 4.00
136 Jim Edmonds .50
137 Raul Mondesi 1.00
138 Alex Rodriguez 9.00
139 Albert Belle 1.00
140 Mark McGwire 12.00
141 Tim Salmon 1.00
142 Andres Galarraga .50
143 Jeff Bagwell 3.00
144 Jim Thome .50
145 Barry Bonds 4.00
146 Carlos Delgado 1.00
147 Mo Vaughn 2.00
148 Chipper Jones 6.00
149 Juan Gonzalez 3.00
150 Ken Griffey Jr. 9.00

EMBOSSED THE ESTABLISHMENT (1:1)
151 David Cone .25
152 Hideo Nomo 1.00
153 Edgar Martinez .25
154 Fred McGriff .25
155 Cal Ripken Jr. 4.00
156 Todd Hundley .25
157 Barry Larkin .25
158 Dennis Eckersley .25
159 Randy Johnson 1.50
160 Paul Molitor 1.50
161 Eric Karros .25
162 Rafael Palmeiro .35
163 Chuck Knoblauch .25
164 Ivan Rodriguez 1.50
165 Greg Maddux 2.50
166 Dante Bichette .25
167 Brady Anderson .25
168 Craig Biggio .35
169 Derek Jeter 3.50
170 Roger Clemens 2.50
171 Roberto Alomar 1.25
172 Wade Boggs 1.25
173 Charles Johnson .25
174 Mark Grace .45
175 Kenny Lofton .25
176 Mike Mussina 1.00
177 Pedro Martinez 1.00
178 Curt Schilling .50
179 Bernie Williams .50
180 Tony Gwynn 2.50

RAINBOW FUTURE IMPACT (1:1)
181 Travis Lee .50
182 A.J. Hinch .25
183 Mike Caruso .25
184 Miguel Tejada .50
185 Brad Fullmer .25
186 Eric Milton .25
187 Mark Kotsay .50
188 Darin Erstad 1.00
189 Magglio Ordonez 1.00
190 Ben Grieve .50
191 Brett Tomko .25
192 *Mike Kinkade* .50
193 Rolando Arrojo .25
194 Todd Helton 1.00
195 Scott Rolen 1.50
196 Bruce Chen .25
197 Daryle Ward .25
198 Jaret Wright .25
199 Sean Casey 1.00
200 Paul Konerko .40
201 Kerry Wood 1.50
202 Russell Branyan .40
203 Gabe Alvarez .25
204 Juan Encarnacion .35
205 Andruw Jones 1.50
206 Vladimir Guerrero 1.50
207 Eli Marrero .25
208 Matt Clement .25
209 Gary Matthews Jr. .25
210 Derrek Lee .25

RAINBOW POWER CORPS (1:12)
211 Ken Caminiti 1.00
212 Gary Sheffield 2.00
213 Jay Buhner 1.00
214 Ryan Klesko 1.00
215 Nomar Garciaparra 8.00
216 Vinny Castilla 1.00
217 Tony Clark 1.00
218 Sammy Sosa 8.00
219 Tino Martinez 1.00
220 Mike Piazza 12.00
221 Manny Ramirez 6.00
222 Larry Walker 2.00
223 Jose Cruz Jr. 2.00
224 Matt Williams 2.00
225 Frank Thomas 8.00
226 Jim Edmonds 1.00
227 Raul Mondesi 2.00
228 Alex Rodriguez 18.00
229 Albert Belle 2.00
230 Mark McGwire 24.00
231 Tim Salmon 2.00
232 Andres Galarraga 1.00
233 Jeff Bagwell 6.00
234 Jim Thome 1.00
235 Barry Bonds 8.00
236 Carlos Delgado 2.00
267 Mo Vaughn 4.00
238 Chipper Jones 12.00
239 Juan Gonzalez 6.00
240 Ken Griffey Jr. 18.00

RAINBOW THE ESTABLISHMENT (1:24)
241 David Cone 1.50
242 Hideo Nomo 6.00
243 Edgar Martinez 1.50
244 Fred McGriff 1.50
245 Cal Ripken Jr. 24.00
246 Todd Hundley 1.50
247 Barry Larkin 1.50
248 Dennis Eckersley 1.50
249 Randy Johnson 9.00
250 Paul Molitor 9.00
251 Eric Karros 1.50
252 Rafael Palmeiro 2.00
253 Chuck Knoblauch 1.50
254 Ivan Rodriguez 9.00
255 Greg Maddux 15.00
256 Dante Bichette 1.50
257 Brady Anderson 1.50
258 Craig Biggio 2.00
259 Derek Jeter 21.00
260 Roger Clemens 15.00
261 Roberto Alomar 7.50

262	Wade Boggs	7.50
263	Charles Johnson	1.50
264	Mark Grace	2.25
265	Kenny Lofton	1.50
266	Mike Mussina	6.00
267	Pedro Martinez	6.00
268	Curt Schilling	3.00
269	Bernie Williams	3.00
270	Tony Gwynn	15.00

1998 Upper Deck UD 3 Die-Cut

Die-cut versions of all 270 cards in UD 3 were available in three sequentially numbered tiers. Light FX were numbered to 2,000 sets; Embossed cards were numbered to 1,000 and Rainbow cards were numbered to 100.

	MT
Light FX Die-Cuts (2,000 each)	
Future Impact (1-30):	.75X
Power Corps (31-60):	3X
Establishment (61-90):	2X
Embossed Die-Cuts (1,000 each)	
Future Impact (91-120):	1X
Power Corps (121-150):	3X
Establishment (151-180):	6X
Rainbow Die-Cuts (100 each)	
Future Impact (181-210):	20X
Power Corps (211-240):	4X
Establishment (241-270):	12X

(See 1998 UD 3 for checklist and base card values.)

1998 Upper Deck UD 3 Power Corps Jumbos

Ten of the Power Corps cards from UD 3 were selected to be reproduced in jumbo 4X (5" x 7") format as box-toppers for special retail packaging of UD 3.

		MT
Complete Set (10):		100.00
Common Player:		5.00
35	Ken Griffey Jr.	20.00
38	Sammy Sosa	10.00
40	Mike Piazza	12.50
45	Frank Thomas	10.00
48	Alex Rodriguez	15.00
50	Mark McGwire	20.00
55	Barry Bonds	10.00
58	Chipper Jones	12.50
59	Juan Gonzalez	5.00
60	Ken Griffey Jr.	15.00

1998 UD Retro

The 129-card set is comprised of 99 regular player cards and 30 Futurama subset cards. Card fronts have a white border encasing the player photo. Retro is packaged in a lunchbox featuring one of six players. Each lunchbox contains 24 six-card packs.

		MT
Complete Set (129):		40.00
Common Player:		.10
Pack (6):		3.00
Wax Box (24):		60.00
1	Jim Edmonds	.10
2	Darin Erstad	.65
3	Tim Salmon	.25
4	Jay Bell	.10
5	Matt Williams	.30
6	Andres Galarraga	.10
7	Andruw Jones	1.00
8	Chipper Jones	2.00
9	Greg Maddux	1.50
10	Rafael Palmeiro	.25
11	Cal Ripken Jr.	3.00
12	Brooks Robinson	.25
13	Nomar Garciaparra	1.75
14	Pedro Martinez	1.00
15	Mo Vaughn	.60
16	Ernie Banks	.75
17	Mark Grace	.30
18	Gary Matthews	.10
19	Sammy Sosa	1.50
20	Albert Belle	.30
21	Carlton Fisk	.25
22	Frank Thomas	1.00
23	Ken Griffey Sr.	.10
24	Paul Konerko	.15
25	Barry Larkin	.15
26	Sean Casey	.60
27	Tony Perez	.10
28	Bob Feller	.25
29	Kenny Lofton	.10
30	Manny Ramirez	1.00
31	Jim Thome	.10
32	Omar Vizquel	.10
33	Dante Bichette	.10
34	Larry Walker	.30
35	Tony Clark	.10
36	Damion Easley	.10
37	Cliff Floyd	.10
38	Livan Hernandez	.10
39	Jeff Bagwell	1.00
40	Craig Biggio	.15
41	Al Kaline	.25
42	Johnny Damon	.15
43	Dean Palmer	.10
44	Charles Johnson	.10
45	Eric Karros	.10
46	Gaylord Perry	.10
47	Raul Mondesi	.20
48	Gary Sheffield	.25
49	Eddie Mathews	.25
50	Warren Spahn	.25
51	Jeromy Burnitz	.10
52	Jeff Cirillo	.10
53	Marquis Grissom	.10
54	Paul Molitor	.75
55	Kirby Puckett	1.50
56	Brad Radke	.10
57	Todd Walker	.10
58	Vladimir Guerrero	1.00
59	Brad Fullmer	.10
60	Rondell White	.20
61	Bobby Jones	.10
62	Hideo Nomo	.50
63	Mike Piazza	2.00
64	Tom Seaver	.25
65	Frank J. Thomas	.10
66	Yogi Berra	.75
67	Derek Jeter	3.00
68	Tino Martinez	.10
69	Paul O'Neill	.10
70	Andy Pettitte	.35
71	Rollie Fingers	.10
72	Rickey Henderson	.75
73	Matt Stairs	.10
74	Scott Rolen	.85
75	Curt Schilling	.25
76	Jose Guillen	.10
77	Jason Kendall	.10
78	Lou Brock	.25
79	Bob Gibson	.25
80	Ray Lankford	.10
81	Mark McGwire	3.00
83	Kevin Brown	.15
84	Ken Caminiti	.10
85	Tony Gwynn	1.50
86	Greg Vaughn	.10
87	Barry Bonds	1.75
88	Willie Stargell	.25
89	Willie McCovey	.25
90	Ken Griffey Jr.	2.50
91	Randy Johnson	.75
92	Alex Rodriguez	2.50
93	Quinton McCracken	.10
94	Fred McGriff	.10
95	Juan Gonzalez	1.00
96	Ivan Rodriguez	.85
97	Nolan Ryan	2.00
98	Jose Canseco	.75
99	Roger Clemens	1.50
100	Jose Cruz Jr.	.15
101	*Justin Baughman*	.10
102	*David Dellucci* (Futurama)	.50
103	Travis Lee (Futurama)	.15
104	*Troy Glaus* (Futurama)	4.00
105	Kerry Wood (Futurama)	.50
106	Mike Caruso (Futurama)	.10
107	*Jim Parque* (Futurama)	.25
108	Brett Tomko (Futurama)	.10
109	Russell Branyan (Futurama)	.10
110	Jaret Wright (Futurama)	.10
111	Todd Helton (Futurama)	1.00
112	Gabe Alvarez (Futurama)	.10
113	*Matt Anderson* (Futurama)	.50
114	Alex Gonzalez (Futurama)	.10
115	Mark Kotsay (Futurama)	.15
116	Derrek Lee (Futurama)	.10
117	Richard Hidalgo (Futurama)	.10
118	Adrian Beltre (Futurama)	.50
119	Geoff Jenkins (Futurama)	.10
120	Eric Milton (Futurama)	.10
121	Brad Fullmer (Futurama)	.10
122	Vladimir Guerrero (Futurama)	1.00
123	Carl Pavano (Futurama)	.10
124	*Orlando Hernandez* (Futurama)	1.00
125	Ben Grieve (Futurama)	.25
126	A.J. Hinch (Futurama)	.10
127	Matt Clement (Futurama)	.10
128	*Gary Matthews Jr.* (Futurama)	.15
129	Aramis Ramirez (Futurama)	.25
130	Rolando Arrojo (Futurama)	.25

1998 UD Retro Big Boppers

The game's heavy hitters are the focus of this insert set. Cards have a color action photo on a sepia background. Each card is individually serial numbered in red foil in the upper-right, within an edition of 500. Backs repeat part of the front photo, in sepia only, and have recent stats and hitting highlights. Cards are numbered with a "B" prefix.

		MT
Complete Set (30):		120.00
Common Player:		1.00
Production 500 sets		
B1	Darin Erstad	2.00
B2	Rafael Palmeiro	2.50
B3	Cal Ripken Jr.	20.00
B4	Nomar Garciaparra	10.00
B5	Mo Vaughn	2.00
B6	Frank Thomas	5.00
B7	Albert Belle	1.00
B8	Jim Thome	1.50
B9	Manny Ramirez	5.00
B10	Tony Clark	1.00
B11	Tino Martinez	1.00
B12	Ben Grieve	1.50
B13	Ken Griffey Jr.	15.00
B14	Alex Rodriguez	15.00
B15	Jay Buhner	1.00
B16	Juan Gonzalez	5.00
B17	Jose Cruz Jr.	1.00
B18	Jose Canseco	3.00
B19	Travis Lee	1.00
B20	Chipper Jones	10.00
B21	Andres Galarraga	1.00
B22	Andruw Jones	3.00
B23	Sammy Sosa	10.00
B24	Vinny Castilla	1.00
B25	Larry Walker	1.50
B26	Jeff Bagwell	5.00
B27	Gary Sheffield	1.50
B28	Mike Piazza	12.00
B29	Mark McGwire	15.00
B30	Barry Bonds	8.00

1998 UD Retro Groovy Kind of Glove

This 30-card set showcases baseball's top defensive players on a psychadelic, wavy and colorful background. They were inserted 1:7 packs.

		MT
Complete Set (30):		70.00
Common Player:		1.00
Inserted 1:7		
G1	Roberto Alomar	2.00
G2	Cal Ripken Jr.	8.00
G3	Nomar Garciaparra	5.00
G4	Frank Thomas	2.50
G5	Robin Ventura	1.00
G6	Omar Vizquel	1.00
G7	Kenny Lofton	1.00
G8	Ben Grieve	1.00
G9	Alex Rodriguez	7.00
G10	Ken Griffey Jr.	7.00
G11	Ivan Rodriguez	2.50
G12	Travis Lee	1.00
G13	Matt Williams	1.00
G14	Greg Maddux	4.00
G15	Andres Galarraga	1.00
G16	Andruw Jones	2.50
G17	Kerry Wood	2.50
G18	Mark Grace	1.50
G19	Craig Biggio	1.00
G20	Charles Johnson	1.00
G21	Raul Mondesi	1.00
G22	Mike Piazza	6.00
G23	Rey Ordonez	1.00
G24	Derek Jeter	8.00
G25	Scott Rolen	2.00
G26	Mark McGwire	8.00
G27	Ken Caminiti	1.00
G28	Tony Gwynn	4.00
G29	J.T. Snow	1.00
G30	Barry Bonds	4.00

1998 UD Retro Legendary Cut

This insert features an actual Babe Ruth cut signature and is limited to a total of three cards.

		MT
LC	Babe Ruth (Value Undetermined)	

1998 UD Retro Lunchbox

Lunchboxes were the form of packaging for UD Retro. Six different players are featured with each lunchbox containing 24 six-card packs, with a SRP of $4.99.

	MT
Complete Set (6):	45.00
Common Lunchbox:	4.00
Nomar Garciaparra	7.50
Ken Griffey Jr.	10.00
Chipper Jones	8.00
Travis Lee	4.00
Mark McGwire	12.00
Cal Ripken Jr.	12.00

1998 UD Retro New Frontier

This 30-card set spotlights 30 of baseball's top young prospects and is limited to 1,000 sequentially numbered sets.

		MT
Complete Set (30):		40.00
Common Player:		1.00
Production 1,000 sets		
NF1	Justin Baughman	1.00
NF2	David Dellucci	1.00
NF3	Travis Lee	1.00
NF4	Troy Glaus	7.50
NF5	Mike Caruso	1.00
NF6	Jim Parque	1.00
NF7	Kerry Wood	2.00
NF8	Brett Tomko	1.00
NF9	Russell Branyan	1.50
NF10	Jaret Wright	1.00
NF11	Todd Helton	4.00
NF12	Gabe Alvarez	1.00
NF13	Matt Anderson	1.00
NF14	Alex Gonzalez	1.00
NF15	Mark Kotsay	1.00
NF16	Derrek Lee	1.00
NF17	Richard Hidalgo	1.50
NF18	Adrian Beltre	2.00
NF19	Geoff Jenkins	1.00
NF20	Eric Milton	1.00
NF21	Brad Fullmer	1.00
NF22	Vladimir Guerrero	6.00
NF23	Carl Pavano	1.00
NF24	Orlando Hernandez	2.50
NF25	Ben Grieve	1.50
NF26	A.J. Hinch	1.00
NF27	Matt Clement	1.00
NF28	Gary Matthews	1.00
NF29	Aramis Ramirez	1.50
NF30	Rolando Arrojo	1.00

1998 UD Retro Quantum Leap

This 30-card insert set highlights the technology advancements of current Upper Deck products on a horizontal format. A total of 500 serially numbered sets were produced.

		MT
Common Player:		15.00
Production 50 sets		
Q1	Darin Erstad	35.00
Q2	Cal Ripken Jr.	125.00
Q3	Nomar Garciaparra	90.00
Q4	Frank Thomas	90.00
Q5	Kenny Lofton	15.00
Q6	Ben Grieve	15.00
Q7	Ken Griffey Jr.	110.00
Q8	Alex Rodriguez	110.00
Q9	Juan Gonzalez	60.00
Q10	Jose Cruz Jr.	15.00
Q11	Roger Clemens	75.00
Q12	Travis Lee	15.00
Q13	Chipper Jones	100.00
Q14	Greg Maddux	75.00
Q15	Kerry Wood	35.00
Q16	Jeff Bagwell	60.00
Q17	Mike Piazza	100.00
Q18	Scott Rolen	35.00
Q19	Mark McGwire	125.00
Q20	Tony Gwynn	75.00
Q21	Larry Walker	25.00
Q22	Derek Jeter	100.00
Q23	Sammy Sosa	90.00
Q24	Barry Bonds	90.00
Q25	Mo Vaughn	30.00
Q26	Roberto Alomar	35.00
Q27	Todd Helton	45.00
Q28	Ivan Rodriguez	40.00
Q29	Vladimir Guerrero	60.00
Q30	Albert Belle	20.00

1998 UD Retro Sign of the Times

This retro-style autographed set features both retired legends and current players. They were inserted 1:36 packs.

		MT
Common Autograph:		10.00
Inserted 1:36		
EB	Ernie Banks (300)	40.00
YB	Yogi Berra (150)	80.00
RB	Russell Branyan (750)	10.00
LB	Lou Brock (300)	25.00
JC	Jose Cruz Jr. (300)	15.00
RF	Rollie Fingers (600)	10.00
BF	Bob Feller (600)	25.00
CF	Carlton Fisk (600)	30.00
BGi	Bob Gibson (300)	30.00
BGr	Ben Grieve (300)	10.00
KGj	Ken Griffey Jr. (100)	300.00
KGs	Ken Griffey Sr. (600)	10.00
TG	Tony Gwynn (200)	60.00
AK	Al Kaline (600)	35.00
PK	Paul Konerko (750)	10.00
TLe	Travis Lee (300)	10.00
EM	Eddie Mathews (600)	40.00
GMj	Gary Matthews Jr. (750)	10.00
GMs	Gary Matthews (600)	10.00
WM	Willie McCovey (600)	25.00
TP	Tony Perez (600)	25.00
GP	Gaylord Perry (1,000)	15.00
KP	Kirby Puckett (450)	75.00
BR	Brooks Robinson (300)	30.00
SR	Scott Rolen (300)	25.00
NR	Nolan Ryan (500)	85.00
TS	Tom Seaver (300)	50.00
WS	Warren Spahn (600)	30.00
WiS	Willie Stargell (600)	40.00
FT	Frank Thomas (600)	10.00
KW	Kerry Wood (200)	40.00

1998 UD Retro Time Capsule

Another retro-styled card that featured current stars who were destined to earn a place in baseball history. They were inserted 1:2 packs.

		MT
Complete Set (50):		35.00
Common Player:		.25
Inserted 1:2		
TC1	Mike Mussina	.75
TC2	Rafael Palmeiro	.40
TC3	Cal Ripken Jr.	3.00
TC4	Nomar Garciaparra	1.75
TC5	Pedro Martinez	1.00
TC6	Mo Vaughn	.60
TC7	Albert Belle	.35
TC8	Frank Thomas	1.75
TC9	David Justice	.45
TC10	Kenny Lofton	.25
TC11	Manny Ramirez	1.00
TC12	Jim Thome	.25
TC13	Derek Jeter	3.00
TC14	Tino Martinez	.25
TC15	Ben Grieve	.40
TC16	Rickey Henderson	.75
TC17	Ken Griffey Jr.	2.50
TC18	Randy Johnson	.75
TC19	Alex Rodriguez	2.50
TC20	Wade Boggs	.75
TC21	Fred McGriff	.25
TC22	Juan Gonzalez	1.00
TC23	Ivan Rodriguez	.65
TC24	Nolan Ryan	2.50

TC25 Jose Canseco .75
TC26 Roger Clemens 1.50
TC27 Jose Cruz Jr. .35
TC28 Travis Lee .35
TC29 Matt Williams .40
TC30 Andres Galarraga .25
TC31 Andruw Jones 1.00
TC32 Chipper Jones 2.00
TC33 Greg Maddux 1.50
TC34 Kerry Wood .50
TC35 Barry Larkin .35
TC36 Dante Bichette .25
TC37 Larry Walker .40
TC38 Livan Hernandez .25
TC39 Jeff Bagwell 1.00
TC40 Craig Biggio .35
TC41 Charles Johnson .25
TC42 Gary Sheffield .40
TC43 Marquis Grissom .25
TC44 Mike Piazza 2.00
TC45 Scott Rolen .75
TC46 Curt Schilling .40
TC47 Mark McGwire 3.00
TC48 Ken Caminiti .25
TC49 Tony Gwynn 1.50
TC50 Barry Bonds 1.75

1999 Upper Deck

Released in two series, base card fronts feature a textured silver border along the left and right sides. The player name and Upper Deck logo also are stamped in silver foil. Backs have a small photo, with stats and career highlights. Randomly seeded in packs are 100 Ken Griffey Jr. rookie cards that were bought back by Upper Deck from the hobby and autographed. Upper Deck also re-inserted one pack of '89 Upper Deck inside every hobby box. Ten-card hobby packs carry a S.R.P. of $2.99. Cards #256-265 were never produced.

	MT
Complete Set (525):	60.00
Complete Series 1 (255):	35.00
Complete Series 2 (270):	25.00
Common Player:	.05
Common SR (1-18):	.25
Exclusive Stars/RCs:	20X
Production 100 each	
Pack (10):	1.50
Wax Box (24):	35.00

1 Troy Glaus (Star Rookies) 1.50
2 Adrian Beltre (Star Rookies) .50
3 Matt Anderson (Star Rookies) .35
4 Eric Chavez (Star Rookies) 1.50
5 Jin Cho (Star Rookies) .25
6 Robert Smith (Star Rookies) .25
7 George Lombard (Star Rookies) .25
8 Mike Kinkade (Star Rookies) .40
9 Seth Greisinger (Star Rookies) .25
10 J.D. Drew (Star Rookies) .50
11 Aramis Ramirez (Star Rookies) .50
12 Carlos Guillen (Star Rookies) .25
13 Justin Baughman (Star Rookies) .25
14 Jim Parque (Star Rookies) .25
15 Ryan Jackson (Star Rookies) .25
16 Ramon Martinez (Star Rookies) .25
17 Orlando Hernandez (Star Rookies) 1.50
18 Jeremy Giambi (Star Rookies) .35
19 Gary DiSarcina .05
20 Darin Erstad .40
21 Troy Glaus .75
22 Chuck Finley .05
23 Dave Hollins .05
24 Troy Percival .05
25 Tim Salmon .15
26 Brian Anderson .05
27 Jay Bell .05
28 Andy Benes .05
29 Brent Brede .05
30 David Dellucci .05
31 Karim Garcia .10
32 Travis Lee .15
33 Andres Galarraga .05
34 Ryan Klesko .05
35 Keith Lockhart .05
36 Kevin Millwood .05
37 Denny Neagle .05
38 John Smoltz .10
39 Michael Tucker .05
40 Walt Weiss .05
41 Dennis Martinez .05
42 Javy Lopez .05
43 Brady Anderson .05
44 Harold Baines .05
45 Mike Bordick .05
46 Roberto Alomar .50
47 Scott Erickson .05
48 Mike Mussina .50
49 Cal Ripken Jr. 2.00
50 Darren Bragg .05
51 Dennis Eckersley .05
52 Nomar Garciaparra 1.00
53 Scott Hatteberg .05
54 Troy O'Leary .05
55 Bret Saberhagen .05
56 John Valentin .05
57 Rod Beck .05
58 Jeff Blauser .05
59 Brant Brown .05
60 Mark Clark .05
61 Mark Grace .20
62 Kevin Tapani .05
63 Henry Rodriguez .05
64 Mike Cameron .05
65 Mike Caruso .05
66 Ray Durham .05
67 Jaime Navarro .05
68 Magglio Ordonez .10
69 Mike Sirotka .05
70 Sean Casey .10
71 Barry Larkin .10
72 Jon Nunnally .05
73 Paul Konerko .10
74 Chris Stynes .05
75 Brett Tomko .05
76 Dmitri Young .05
77 Sandy Alomar .05
78 Bartolo Colon .05
79 Travis Fryman .05
80 Brian Giles .05
81 David Justice .20
82 Omar Vizquel .05
83 Jaret Wright .05
84 Jim Thome .05
85 Charles Nagy .05
86 Pedro Astacio .05
87 Todd Helton .40
88 Darryl Kile .05
89 Mike Lansing .05
90 Neifi Perez .05
91 John Thomson .05
92 Larry Walker .20
93 Tony Clark .05
94 Deivi Cruz .05
95 Damion Easley .05
96 Brian L. Hunter .05
97 Todd Jones .05
98 Brian Moehler .05
99 Gabe Alvarez .05
100 Craig Counsell .05
101 Cliff Floyd .05
102 Livan Hernandez .05
103 Andy Larkin .05
104 Derrek Lee .05
105 Brian Meadows .05
106 Moises Alou .15
107 Sean Berry .05
108 Craig Biggio .10
109 Ricky Gutierrez .05
110 Mike Hampton .05
111 Jose Lima .05
112 Billy Wagner .05
113 Hal Morris .05
114 Johnny Damon .10
115 Jeff King .05
116 Jeff Montgomery .05
117 Glendon Rusch .05
118 Larry Sutton .05
119 Bobby Bonilla .05
120 Jim Eisenreich .05
121 Eric Karros .05
122 Matt Luke .05
123 Ramon Martinez .05
124 Gary Sheffield .25
125 Eric Young .05
126 Charles Johnson .05
127 Jeff Cirillo .05
128 Marquis Grissom .05
129 Jeremy Burnitz .05
130 Bob Wickman .05
131 Scott Karl .05
132 Mark Loretta .05
133 Fernando Vina .05
134 Matt Lawton .05
135 Pat Meares .05
136 Eric Milton .05
137 Paul Molitor .50
138 David Ortiz .05
139 Todd Walker .15
140 Shane Andrews .05
141 Brad Fullmer .05
142 Vladimir Guerrero .65
143 Dustin Hermanson .05
144 Ryan McGuire .05
145 Ugueth Urbina .05
146 John Franco .05
147 Butch Huskey .05
148 Bobby Jones .05
149 John Olerud .05
150 Rey Ordonez .05
151 Mike Piazza 1.25
152 Hideo Nomo .35
153 Masato Yoshii .05
154 Derek Jeter 2.00
155 Chuck Knoblauch .05
156 Paul O'Neill .05
157 Andy Pettitte .25
158 Mariano Rivera .15
159 Darryl Strawberry .05
160 David Wells .10
161 Jorge Posada .05
162 Ramiro Mendoza .05
163 Miguel Tejada .15
164 Ryan Christenson .05
165 Rickey Henderson .50
166 A.J. Hinch .05
167 Ben Grieve .25
168 Kenny Rogers .05
169 Matt Stairs .05
170 Bob Abreu .10
171 Rico Brogna .05
172 Doug Glanville .05
173 Mike Grace .05
174 Desi Relaford .05
175 Scott Rolen .50
176 Jose Guillen .05
177 Francisco Cordova .05
178 Al Martin .05
179 Jason Schmidt .05
180 Turner Ward .05
181 Kevin Young .05
182 Mark McGwire 1.50
183 Delino DeShields .05
184 Eli Marrero .05
185 Tom Lampkin .05
186 Ray Lankford .05
187 Willie McGee .05
188 Matt Morris .05
189 Andy Ashby .05
190 Kevin Brown .10
191 Ken Caminiti .05
192 Trevor Hoffman .05
193 Wally Joyner .05
194 Greg Vaughn .05
195 Danny Darwin .05
196 Shawn Estes .05
197 Orel Hershiser .05
198 Jeff Kent .05
199 Bill Mueller .05
200 Robb Nen .05
201 J.T. Snow .05
202 Ken Cloude .05
203 Russ Davis .05
204 Jeff Fassero .05
205 Ken Griffey Jr. 1.50
206 Shane Monahan .05
207 David Segui .05
208 Dan Wilson .05
209 Wilson Alvarez .05
210 Wade Boggs .50
211 Miguel Cairo .05
212 Bubba Trammell .05
213 Quinton McCracken .05
214 Paul Sorrento .05
215 Kevin Stocker .05
216 Will Clark .15
217 Rusty Greer .05
218 Rick Helling .05
219 Mike McLemore .05
220 Ivan Rodriguez .45
221 John Wetteland .05
222 Jose Canseco .40
223 Roger Clemens .75
224 Carlos Delgado .20
225 Darrin Fletcher .05
226 Alex Gonzalez .10
227 Jose Cruz Jr. .20
228 Shannon Stewart .10
229 Rolando Arrojo (Foreign Focus) .05
230 Livan Hernandez (Foreign Focus) .05
231 Orlando Hernandez (Foreign Focus) .75
232 Raul Mondesi (Foreign Focus) .05
233 Moises Alou (Foreign Focus) .10
234 Pedro Martinez (Foreign Focus) .20
235 Sammy Sosa (Foreign Focus) .45
236 Vladimir Guerrero (Foreign Focus) .40
237 Bartolo Colon (Foreign Focus) .05
238 Miguel Tejada (Foreign Focus) .05
239 Ismael Valdes (Foreign Focus) .05
240 Mariano Rivera (Foreign Focus) .05
241 Jose Cruz Jr. (Foreign Focus) .10
242 Juan Gonzalez (Foreign Focus) .35
243 Ivan Rodriguez (Foreign Focus) .20
244 Sandy Alomar (Foreign Focus) .05
245 Roberto Alomar (Foreign Focus) .25
246 Magglio Ordonez (Foreign Focus) .05
247 Kerry Wood (Highlights Checklist) .10
248 Mark McGwire (Highlights Checklist) .75
249 David Wells (Highlights Checklist) .05
250 Rolando Arrojo (Highlights Checklist) .05
251 Ken Griffey Jr. (Highlights Checklist) .65
252 Trevor Hoffman (Highlights Checklist) .05
253 Travis Lee (Highlights Checklist) .05
254 Roberto Alomar (Highlights Checklist) .25

255 Sammy Sosa (Highlights Checklist) .45
256
257
258
259
260
261
262
263
264
265
266 *Pat Burrell* (Star Rookie) 2.50
267 *Shea Hillenbrand* (Star Rookie) 3.00
268 Robert Fick (Star Rookie) .05
269 Roy Halladay (Star Rookie) .10
270 Ruben Mateo (Star Rookie) .05
271 Bruce Chen (Star Rookie) .05
272 Angel Pena (Star Rookie) .05
273 Michael Barrett (Star Rookie) .10
274 Kevin Witt (Star Rookie) .05
275 Damon Minor (Star Rookie) .05
276 Ryan Minor (Star Rookie) .05
277 A.J. Pierzynski (Star Rookie) .05
278 *A.J. Burnett* (Star Rookie) .75
279 Dermal Brown (Star Rookie) .05
280 Joe Lawrence (Star Rookie) .05
281 Derrick Gibson (Star Rookie) .10
282 Carlos Febles (Star Rookie) .40
283 Chris Haas (Star Rookie) .05
284 Cesar King (Star Rookie) .05
285 Calvin Pickering (Star Rookie) .05
286 Mitch Meluskey (Star Rookie) .05
287 Carlos Beltran (Star Rookie) .15
288 Ron Belliard (Star Rookie) .05
289 Jerry Hairston Jr. (Star Rookie) .05
290 Fernando Seguignol (Star Rookie) .05
291 Kris Benson (Star Rookie) .05
292 *Chad Hutchinson* (Star Rookie) .75
293 Jarrod Washburn .05
294 Jason Dickson .05
295 Mo Vaughn .45
296 Garrett Anderson .05
297 Jim Edmonds .05
298 Ken Hill .05
299 Shigetosi Hasegawa .05
300 Todd Stottlemyre .05
301 Randy Johnson .50
302 Omar Daal .05
303 Steve Finley .05
304 Matt Williams .15
305 Danny Klassen .05
306 Tony Batista .05
307 Brian Jordan .05
308 Greg Maddux .75
309 Chipper Jones 1.00
310 Bret Boone .10
311 Ozzie Guillen .05
312 John Rocker .05
313 Tom Glavine .10
314 Andruw Jones .65
315 Albert Belle .30
316 Charles Johnson .05
317 Will Clark .15
318 B.J. Surhoff .05
319 Delino DeShields .05
320 Heathcliff Slocumb .05
321 Sidney Ponson .05
322 Juan Guzman .05
323 Reggie Jefferson .05
324 Mark Portugal .05
325 Tim Wakefield .05
326 Jason Varitek .05
327 Jose Offerman .05
328 Pedro Martinez .50
329 Trot Nixon .05
330 Kerry Wood .25
331 Sammy Sosa 1.00
332 Glenallen Hill .05
333 Gary Gaetti .05
334 Mickey Morandini .05
335 Benito Santiago .05
336 Jeff Blauser .05
337 Frank Thomas .75
338 Paul Konerko .10
339 Jaime Navarro .05
340 Carlos Lee .05
341 Brian Simmons .05
342 Mark Johnson .05
343 Jeff Abbot .05
344 Steve Avery .05
345 Mike Cameron .05
346 Michael Tucker .05
347 Greg Vaughn .05
348 Hal Morris .05
349 Pete Harnisch .05
350 Denny Neagle .05
351 Manny Ramirez .65
352 Roberto Alomar .50
353 Dwight Gooden .05
354 Kenny Lofton .05
355 Mike Jackson .05
356 Charles Nagy .05
357 Enrique Wilson .05
358 Russ Branyan .05
359 Richie Sexson .05
360 Vinny Castilla .05
361 Dante Bichette .05
362 Kirt Manwaring .05
363 Darryl Hamilton .05
364 Jamey Wright .05
365 Curt Leskanic .05
366 Jeff Reed .05
367 Bobby Higginson .10
368 Justin Thompson .05
369 Brad Ausmus .05
370 Dean Palmer .05
371 Gabe Kapler .15
372 Juan Encarnacion .05
373 Karim Garcia .10
374 Alex Gonzalez .10
375 Braden Looper .05
376 Preston Wilson .05
377 Todd Dunwoody .05
378 Alex Fernandez .05
379 Mark Kotsay .05
380 Mark Mantei .05
381 Ken Caminiti .05
382 Scott Elarton .05
383 Jeff Bagwell .65
384 Derek Bell .05
385 Ricky Gutierrez .05
386 Richard Hildalgo .10
387 Shane Reynolds .05
388 Carl Everett .10
389 Scott Service .05
390 Jeff Suppan .05
391 Joe Randa .05
392 Kevin Appier .05
393 Shane Halter .05
394 Chad Kreuter .05
395 Mike Sweeney .05
396 Kevin Brown .15
397 Devon White .05
398 Todd Hollandsworth .05
399 Todd Hundley .05
400 Chan Ho Park .10
401 Mark Grudzielanek .05
402 Raul Mondesi .15
403 Ismael Valdes .05
404 Rafael Roque .05
405 Sean Berry .05
406 Kevin Barker .05
407 Dave Nilsson .05
408 Geoff Jenkins .05
409 Jim Abbott .05
410 Bobby Hughes .05
411 Corey Koskie .05
412 Rick Aguilera .05
413 LaTroy Hawkins .05
414 Ron Coomer .05
415 Denny Hocking .05
416 Marty Cordova .05
417 Terry Steinbach .05
418 Rondell White .10
419 Wilton Guerrero .05
420 Shane Andrews .05
421 Orlando Cabrera .10
422 Carl Pavano .05
423 Jeff Vasquez .05
424 Chris Widger .05
425 Robin Ventura .05
426 Rickey Henderson .50
427 Al Leiter .05
428 Bobby Jones .05
429 Brian McRae .05
430 Roger Cedeno .05
431 Bobby Bonilla .05
432 Edgardo Alfonzo .05
433 Bernie Williams .25
434 Ricky Ledee .05
435 Chili Davis .05
436 Tino Martinez .05
437 Scott Brosius .05
438 David Cone .05
439 Joe Girardi .05
440 Roger Clemens .75
441 Chad Curtis .05
442 Hideki Irabu .05
443 Jason Giambi .35
444 Scott Spezio .05
445 Tony Phillips .05
446 Ramon Hernandez .05
447 Mike Macfarlane .05
448 Tom Candiotti .05
449 Billy Taylor .05
450 Bobby Estella .05
451 Curt Schilling .15
452 Carlton Loewer .05
453 Marlon Anderson .05
454 Kevin Jordan .05
455 Ron Gant .05
456 Chad Ogea .05
457 Abraham Nunez .05
458 Jason Kendall .05
459 Pat Meares .05
460 Brant Brown .05
461 Brian Giles .05
462 Chad Hermansen .05
463 Freddy Garcia 1.50
464 Edgar Renteria .05
465 Fernando Tatis .05
466 Eric Davis .05
467 Darren Bragg .05
468 Donovan Osborne .05
469 Manny Aybar .05
470 Jose Jimenez .05
471 Kent Mercker .05
472 Reggie Sanders .05
473 Ruben Rivera .05
474 Tony Gwynn .75
475 Jim Leyritz .05
476 Chris Gomez .05
477 Matt Clement .05
478 Carlos Hernandez .05
479 Sterling Hitchcock .05
480 Ellis Burks .05
481 Barry Bonds 1.00
482 Marvin Bernard .05
483 Kirk Rueter .05
484 F.P. Santangelo .05
485 Stan Javier .05
486 Jeff Kent .05
487 Alex Rodriguez 1.50
488 Tom Lampkin .05
489 Jose Mesa .05
490 Jay Buhner .05
491 Edgar Martinez .05
492 Butch Huskey .05
493 John Mabry .05
494 Jamie Moyer .05
495 Roberto Hernandez .05
496 Tony Saunders .05
497 Fred McGriff .05
498 Dave Martinez .05
499 Jose Canseco .40
500 Rolando Arrojo .05
501 Esteban Yan .05
502 Juan Gonzalez .65
503 Rafael Palmeiro .20
504 Aaron Sele .05
505 Royce Clayton .05
506 Todd Zeile .05
507 Tom Goodwin .05
508 Lee Stevens .05
509 Esteban Loaiza .05
510 Joey Hamilton .05
511 Homer Bush .05
512 Willie Greene .05
513 Shawn Green .25
514 David Wells .10
515 Kelvim Escobar .05
516 Tony Fernandez .05
517 Pat Hentgen .05
518 Mark McGwire (Arms Race) 1.50
519 Ken Griffey Jr. (Arms Race) .65
520 Sammy Sosa (Arms Race) .45
521 Juan Gonzalez (Arms Race) .35
522 J.D. Drew (Arms Race) .10
523 Chipper Jones (Arms Race) .50
524 Alex Rodriguez (Arms Race) .65
525 Mike Piazza (Arms Race) .50
526 Nomar Garciaparra (Arms Race) .45
527 Season Highlights Checklist (Mark McGwire) .75
528 Season Highlights Checklist (Sammy Sosa) .45
529 Season Highlights Checklist (Scott Brosius) .05
530 Season Highlights Checklist (Cal Ripken Jr.) .75
531 Season Highlights Checklist (Barry Bonds) .50
532 Season Highlights Checklist (Roger Clemens) .40
533 Season Highlights Checklist (Ken Griffey Jr.) .65
534 Season Highlights Checklist (Alex Rodriguez) .65
535 Season Highlights Checklist (Curt Schilling) .05

1999 Upper Deck Exclusives

Randomly inserted into hobby packs, this parallel issue is individually serial numbered on back from within an edition of 100 of each card. Besides the serial number, the inserts are readily apparent by the use of copper metallic foil graphic highlights on front. Series 1 Exclusive cards have the serial number on back in gold foil; Series 2 Exclusives have the number ink-jetted in black. A green-foil parallel of the parallel was issued in quantities of just one card each for Series 1, and 10 cards each for Series 2.

	MT
Common Player:	2.00
Stars/Rookies:	15X
Greens (1-255): VALUES	

UNDERMINED
Greens (266-535): 100X
(See 1999 Upper Deck for checklist and base card values.)

1999 Upper Deck Babe Ruth Piece of History Bat

Limited to approximately 400, this card has an imbedded chip of a bat from an actual game-used Louisville Slugger swung by the Bambino himself. A "signed" version of this card also exists, which incorporates a cut signature of Ruth along with a piece of his game-used bat; only three exist.

		MT
PH	Babe Ruth (bat card)	900.00
PHLC	Babe Ruth (Legendary Cut autograph)	25000.

1999 Upper Deck Crowning Glory

These double-sided cards feature players who reached milestones during the '98 season. There are three cards in the set, with four different versions of each card. The regular version is seeded 1:23 packs. Doubles are numbered to 1,000, Triples numbered to 25 and Home Runs are limited to one each.

		MT
Complete Set (3):		30.00
Common Player:		5.00
Inserted 1:23		
Doubles (1,000 sets):		2X
Triples (25 sets):		8X
Home Runs (1 set): Values Undetermined		
CG1	Roger Clemens, Kerry Wood	5.00
CG2	Mark McGwire, Barry Bonds	10.00
CG3	Ken Griffey Jr., Mark McGwire	20.00

1999 Upper Deck Forte

This 30-card set features the top players in the game, highlighted by blue holofoil treatment. Numbers on card backs have a "F" prefix and are seeded 1:23 packs. There are also die-cut parallels to Forte: Double, Triple and Home Run. Doubles are sequentially numbered to 2,000 sets, Triples are limited to 100 numbered sets and Home Runs are limited to 10 numbered sets.

		MT
Complete Set (30):		32.50
Common Player:		.50
Inserted 1:23		
Doubles (2,000 sets):		1X
Triples (100):		3X
Quadruples (10):		20X
1	Darin Erstad	.75
2	Troy Glaus	1.00
3	Mo Vaughn	.75
4	Greg Maddux	2.50
5	Andres Galarraga	.50
6	Chipper Jones	2.50
7	Cal Ripken Jr.	5.00
8	Albert Belle	.65
9	Nomar Garciaparra	2.00
10	Sammy Sosa	2.50
11	Kerry Wood	.65
12	Frank Thomas	1.50
13	Jim Thome	.50
14	Jeff Bagwell	1.25
15	Vladimir Guerrero	1.25
16	Mike Piazza	3.00
17	Derek Jeter	5.00
18	Ben Grieve	.65
19	Eric Chavez	.75
20	Scott Rolen	.85
21	Mark McGwire	4.00
22	J.D. Drew	.75
23	Tony Gwynn	1.25
24	Barry Bonds	2.00
25	Alex Rodriguez	4.00
26	Ken Griffey Jr.	4.00
27	Ivan Rodriguez	1.00
28	Juan Gonzalez	1.25
29	Roger Clemens	1.50
30	Andruw Jones	1.00

1999 Upper Deck Game Jersey

A piece of game-worn jersey is framed by a baseball diamond schematic. A round portrait photo appears at top-right, along with the player's uniform number. A small action photo is at bottom center. Backs have another round portrait photo and a statement of authenticity. Game Jersey cards bearing an H1 or H2 designation were hobby-only inserts at a rate of one per 288 packs in the appropriate series. Cards with an HR1 or HR2 notation were found in both hobby and retail packs at a rate of 1:2,500. Autographed versions of some cards were produced, with the edition number noted.

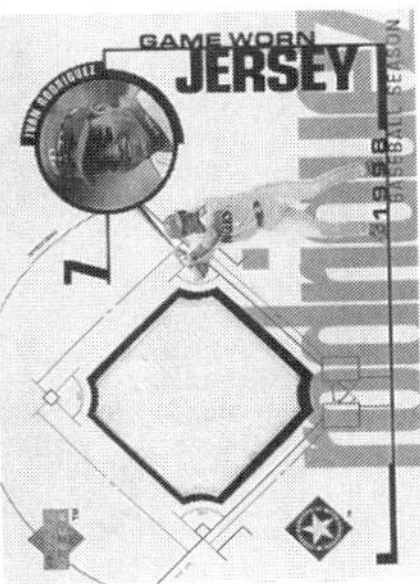

		MT
Common Player:		15.00
AB	Adrian Beltre (H1)	20.00
EC	Eric Chavez (H2)	20.00
JD	J.D. Drew (H2)	25.00
JDs	J.D. Drew (autographed/8) (H2)	200.00
DE	Darin Erstad (H1)	25.00
BF	Brad Fullmer (H2)	15.00
JG	Juan Gonzalez (HR1)	30.00
BG	Ben Grieve (H1)	15.00
KG	Ken Griffey Jr. (H1)	60.00
KGs	Ken Griffey Jr. (autographed/24) (H1)	400.00
JR	Ken Griffey Jr. (HR2)	65.00
JRs	Ken Griffey Jr. (autographed/24) (HR2)	400.00
TGw	Tony Gwynn (H2)	25.00
TH	Todd Helton (H2)	25.00
CJ	Charles Johnson (HR1)	25.00
CJ	Chipper Jones (H2)	30.00
TL	Travis Lee (H1)	15.00
GM	Greg Maddux (HR2)	40.00
MP	Mike Piazza (HR1)	50.00
MR	Manny Ramirez (H2)	25.00
AR	Alex Rodriguez (HR1)	50.00
IR	Ivan Rodriguez (H1)	25.00
NRa	Nolan Ryan (Astros) (H2)	60.00
NRas	Nolan Ryan (autographed/34) (H2)	575.00
NRb	Nolan Ryan (Rangers) (HR2)	60.00
SS	Sammy Sosa (H2)	45.00
BT	Bubba Trammell (H2)	15.00
FT	Frank Thomas (HR2)	40.00
KW	Kerry Wood (HR1)	25.00
KWs	Kerry Wood (autographed/34) (HR1)	200.00

1999 Upper Deck Immaculate Perception

Done in a horizontal format, this 27-card set features baseball's most celebrated players. Card fronts are enhanced with copper and silver foil stamping, encasing the player's image. The cards are numbered with an I prefix and are seeded 1:23 packs. There are also three parallel versions: Doubles numbered to 1,000, Triples numbered to 25 and Home Runs which are limited to one.

		MT
Complete Set (27):		60.00
Common Player:		.50
Inserted 1:23		
Doubles (1,000 sets):		1.5X
Triples (25):		8X
Home Runs (1): VALUES UNDETERMINED		
I1	Jeff Bagwell	2.00
I2	Craig Biggio	.50
I3	Barry Bonds	4.00
I4	Roger Clemens	3.00
I5	Jose Cruz Jr.	.50
I6	Nomar Garciaparra	4.00
I7	Tony Clark	.50
I8	Ben Grieve	.75
I9	Ken Griffey Jr.	6.00
I10	Tony Gwynn	3.00
I11	Randy Johnson	2.00
I12	Chipper Jones	5.00
I13	Travis Lee	.50
I14	Kenny Lofton	.50
I15	Greg Maddux	3.00
I16	Mark McGwire	6.00
I17	Hideo Nomo	1.00
I18	Mike Piazza	5.00
I19	Manny Ramirez	2.00
I20	Cal Ripken Jr.	8.00
I21	Alex Rodriguez	6.00
I22	Scott Rolen	1.50
I23	Frank Thomas	3.00
I24	Kerry Wood	1.00
I25	Larry Walker	.75
I26	Vinny Castilla	.50
I27	Derek Jeter	8.00

1999 Upper Deck Ken Griffey Jr. 1989 Buyback Autograph

One hundred authentically autographed 1989 Ken Griffey Jr. Upper Deck rookie cards were seeded into Series 1 packs. UD bought the cards on the open market, had them autographed by

Griffey and added a diamond-shaped authentication hologram on back

	MT
Ken Griffey Jr. (100)	1000.

1999 Upper Deck Piece of History 500 Club Babe Ruth

Limited to a reported 50 pieces and inserted into Series 2 Upper Deck packs, this card differs from the Piece of History Ruth bat cards on the photos used and the 500 Club notation.

		MT
BR	Babe Ruth	4000.

1999 Upper Deck Textbook Excellence

This 30-card set features the game's most fundamentally sound performers. Card fronts have a photo of the featured player on a silver-foil stamped grid background. Vertically at left is player identification on a brown background. These are seeded 1:23 packs. Three hobby-only parallels were also issued: Double, Triple and Home Run. Doubles are numbered to 2,000 sets, Triples are limited to 100 numbered sets and Home Runs are limited to 10 numbered sets. Cards are numbered with a "T" prefix.

		MT
Complete Set (30):		25.00
Common Player:		.40
Inserted 1:4		
Doubles (2,000 sets):		1X
Triples (100):		3X
Quadruples (10):		20X
T1	Mo Vaughn	.50
T2	Greg Maddux	1.00
T3	Chipper Jones	2.00
T4	Andruw Jones	.75
T5	Cal Ripken Jr.	3.00
T6	Albert Belle	.45
T7	Roberto Alomar	.65
T8	Nomar Garciaparra	1.50
T9	Kerry Wood	.50
T10	Sammy Sosa	1.50
T11	Greg Vaughn	.40
T12	Jeff Bagwell	.75
T13	Kevin Brown	.40
T14	Vladimir Guerrero	.75
T15	Mike Piazza	2.00
T16	Bernie Williams	.45
T17	Derek Jeter	3.00
T18	Ben Grieve	.50
T19	Eric Chavez	.50
T29	Scott Rolen	.50
T21	Mark McGwire	3.00
T22	David Wells	.40
T23	J.D. Drew	.50
T24	Tony Gwynn	1.00
T25	Barry Bonds	1.50
T26	Alex Rodriguez	2.50
T27	Ken Griffey Jr.	2.50
T28	Juan Gonzalez	.75
T29	Ivan Rodriguez	.65
T30	Roger Clemens	1.00

1999 Upper Deck View to a Thrill

This 30-card set focuses on baseball's best overall athletes. There are two photos of the featured player on the card front, highlighted by silver foil and some embossing. These are inserted 1:7 packs. Numbered parallel sets were produced of: Doubles (2,000), Triples (100) and Quadruples (10).

		MT
Complete Set (30):		40.00
Common Player:		.50
Inserted 1:7		
Doubles (2,000 sets):		1.5X
Triples (100):		4X
Quadruples (10):		30X
V1	Mo Vaughn	.75
V2	Darin Erstad	.75
V3	Travis Lee	.50
V4	Chipper Jones	3.00
V5	Greg Maddux	2.00
V6	Gabe Kapler	.50
V7	Cal Ripken Jr.	5.00
V8	Nomar Garciaparra	2.50
V9	Kerry Wood	.65
V10	Frank Thomas	1.50
V11	Manny Ramirez	1.50
V12	Larry Walker	.50
V13	Tony Clark	.50
V14	Jeff Bagwell	1.50
V15	Craig Biggio	.50
V16	Vladimir Guerrero	1.50
V17	Mike Piazza	3.00
V18	Bernie Williams	.60
V19	Derek Jeter	5.00
V20	Ben Grieve	.60
V21	Eric Chavez	.60
V22	Scott Rolen	1.00
V23	Mark McGwire	5.00
V24	Tony Gwynn	2.00
V25	Barry Bonds	2.50
V26	Ken Griffey Jr.	4.00
V27	Alex Rodriguez	4.00
V28	J.D. Drew	.75
V29	Juan Gonzalez	1.50
V30	Roger Clemens	2.00

1999 Upper Deck Wonder Years

These inserts look like a throwback to the groovin' '70s, with brightly striped green and pink borders. "Wonder Years" is across the top of the front in yellow. Backs have the player's three best seasons stats along with a mention of a milestone. The cards are numbered with a WY prefix and are seeded 1:7 packs. There are three parallel versions: Doubles which are numbered to 1,000, Triples numbered to 25 and Home Runs which are limited to one.

		MT
Complete Set (30):		50.00
Common Player:		.50
Inserted 1:7		
Doubles (2,000):		1.5X
Triples (50):		10X
Home Runs (1): VALUES UNDETERMINED		
WY1	Kerry Wood	1.00
WY2	Travis Lee	.50
WY3	Jeff Bagwell	1.50
WY4	Barry Bonds	2.00
WY5	Roger Clemens	2.50
WY6	Jose Cruz Jr.	.50
WY7	Andres Galarraga	.50
WY8	Nomar Garciaparra	3.00
WY9	Juan Gonzalez	1.50
WY10	Ken Griffey Jr.	4.00
WY11	Tony Gwynn	2.00
WY12	Derek Jeter	5.00
WY13	Randy Johnson	1.50
WY14	Andruw Jones	1.50
WY15	Chipper Jones	3.50
WY16	Kenny Lofton	.50
WY17	Greg Maddux	2.50
WY18	Tino Martinez	.50
WY19	Mark McGwire	4.00
WY20	Paul Molitor	1.00
WY21	Mike Piazza	3.50
WY22	Manny Ramirez	2.00
WY23	Cal Ripken Jr.	5.00
WY24	Alex Rodriguez	4.00
WY25	Sammy Sosa	3.00
WY26	Frank Thomas	1.50
WY27	Mo Vaughn	.75
WY28	Larry Walker	.50
WY29	Scott Rolen	1.25
WY30	Ben Grieve	.65

1999 Upper Deck 10th Anniversary Team

This 30-card set commemorates Upper Deck's 10th Anniversary, as collectors selected their favorite players for this set. Regular versions are seeded 1:4 packs, Doubles numbered to 4,000, Triples numbered to 100 and Home Runs which are limited to one set.

		MT
Complete Set (30):		25.00
Common Player:		.15
Inserted 1:4		
Doubles (4,000 sets):		1X
Triples (100):		6X
Home Runs (1): VALUES UNDETERMINED		
X1	Mike Piazza	2.00
X2	Mark McGwire	2.50
X3	Roberto Alomar	.50
X4	Chipper Jones	1.50
X5	Cal Ripken Jr.	3.00
X6	Ken Griffey Jr.	2.50
X7	Barry Bonds	1.50
X8	Tony Gwynn	1.00
X9	Nolan Ryan	3.00
X10	Randy Johnson	.75
X11	Dennis Eckersley	.15
X12	Ivan Rodriguez	.65
X13	Frank Thomas	1.00
X14	Craig Biggio	.25
X15	Wade Boggs	.65
X16	Alex Rodriguez	2.50
X17	Albert Belle	.25
X18	Juan Gonzalez	.75
X19	Rickey Henderson	.65
X20	Greg Maddux	1.00
X21	Tom Glavine	.25
X22	Randy Myers	.15
X23	Sandy Alomar	.15
X24	Jeff Bagwell	.75
X25	Derek Jeter	3.00
X26	Matt Williams	.25
X27	Kenny Lofton	.15
X28	Sammy Sosa	1.50
X29	Larry Walker	.25
X30	Roger Clemens	1.00

1999 Upper Deck Black Diamond

This 120-card base set features metallic foil fronts, while card backs have the featured player's vital information along with a close-up photo. The

Diamond Debut subset (91-120) are short-printed and seeded 1:4 packs.

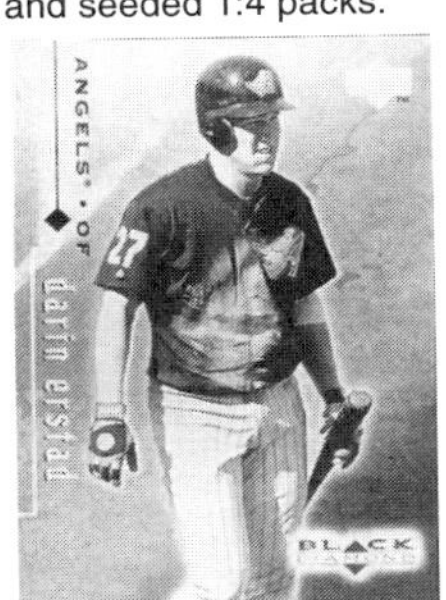

	MT
Complete Set (120):	75.00
Common Player:	.15
Common Diamond Debut (91-120):	1.00
Inserted 1:4	
Double Diamonds (3,000 each):	3X
Double Diamond Debuts (2,500):	2X
Triple Diamonds (1,500):	4X
Triple Diamond Debuts (1,000):	2X
Pack (6):	3.00
Wax Box (30):	70.00

1	Darin Erstad	.50
2	Tim Salmon	.30
3	Jim Edmonds	.15
4	Matt Williams	.35
5	David Dellucci	.15
6	Jay Bell	.15
7	Andres Galarraga	.15
8	Chipper Jones	1.50
9	Greg Maddux	1.25
10	Andruw Jones	.75
11	Cal Ripken Jr.	2.50
12	Rafael Palmeiro	.35
13	Brady Anderson	.15
14	Mike Mussina	.60
15	Nomar Garciaparra	1.25
16	Mo Vaughn	.50
17	Pedro Martinez	.65
18	Sammy Sosa	1.50
19	Henry Rodriguez	.15
20	Frank Thomas	1.00
21	Magglio Ordonez	.35
22	Albert Belle	.35
23	Paul Konerko	.20
24	Sean Casey	.35
25	Jim Thome	.15
26	Kenny Lofton	.15
27	Sandy Alomar Jr.	.15
28	Jaret Wright	.15
29	Larry Walker	.30
30	Todd Helton	.60
31	Vinny Castilla	.15
32	Tony Clark	.15
33	Damion Easley	.15
34	Mark Kotsay	.15
35	Derrek Lee	.15
36	Moises Alou	.20
37	Jeff Bagwell	.75
38	Craig Biggio	.25
39	Randy Johnson	.65
40	Dean Palmer	.15
41	Johnny Damon	.20
42	Chan Ho Park	.20
43	Raul Mondesi	.20
44	Gary Sheffield	.25
45	Jeromy Burnitz	.15
46	Marquis Grissom	.15
47	Jeff Cirillo	.15
48	Paul Molitor	.65
49	Todd Walker	.15
50	Vladimir Guerrero	.75
51	Brad Fullmer	.15
52	Mike Piazza	1.50
53	Hideo Nomo	.45
54	Carlos Baerga	.15
55	John Olerud	.15
56	Derek Jeter	2.50
57	Hideki Irabu	.15
58	Tino Martinez	.15
59	Bernie Williams	.30
60	Miguel Tejada	.35
61	Ben Grieve	.35
62	Jason Giambi	.40
63	Scott Rolen	.65
64	Doug Glanville	.15
65	Desi Relaford	.15
66	Tony Womack	.15
67	Jason Kendall	.15
68	Jose Guillen	.15
69	Tony Gwynn	1.00
70	Ken Caminiti	.15
71	Greg Vaughn	.15
72	Kevin Brown	.20
73	Barry Bonds	1.25
74	J.T. Snow	.15
75	Jeff Kent	.15
76	Ken Griffey Jr.	2.00
77	Alex Rodriguez	2.00
78	Edgar Martinez	.15
79	Jay Buhner	.15
80	Mark McGwire	2.50
81	Delino DeShields	.15
82	Brian Jordan	.15
83	Quinton McCracken	.15
84	Fred McGriff	.15
85	Juan Gonzalez	.75
86	Ivan Rodriguez	.65
87	Will Clark	.35
88	Roger Clemens	1.00
89	Jose Cruz Jr.	.20
90	Babe Ruth	3.00
91	Troy Glaus (Diamond Debut)	4.00
92	Jarrod Washburn (Diamond Debut)	.50
93	Travis Lee (Diamond Debut)	1.00
94	Bruce Chen (Diamond Debut)	.50
95	Mike Caruso (Diamond Debut)	.50
96	Jim Parque (Diamond Debut)	.50
97	Kerry Wood (Diamond Debut)	2.00
98	Jeremy Giambi (Diamond Debut)	1.00
99	Matt Anderson (Diamond Debut)	.50
100	Seth Greisinger (Diamond Debut)	.50
101	Gabe Alvarez (Diamond Debut)	.50
102	Rafael Medina (Diamond Debut)	.50
103	Daryle Ward (Diamond Debut)	.50
104	Alex Cora (Diamond Debut)	.50
105	Adrian Beltre (Diamond Debut)	1.00
106	Geoff Jenkins (Diamond Debut)	.50
107	Eric Milton (Diamond Debut)	.50
108	Carl Pavano (Diamond Debut)	.50
109	Eric Chavez (Diamond Debut)	.75
110	Orlando Hernandez (Diamond Debut)	1.50
111	A.J. Hinch (Diamond Debut)	.50
112	Carlton Loewer (Diamond Debut)	.50
113	Aramis Ramirez (Diamond Debut)	.65
114	Cliff Politte (Diamond Debut)	.50
115	Matt Clement (Diamond Debut)	.50
116	Alex Gonzalez (Diamond Debut)	.50
117	J.D. Drew (Diamond Debut)	1.50
118	Shane Monahan (Diamond Debut)	.50
119	Rolando Arrojo (Diamond Debut)	.50
120	George Lombard (Diamond Debut)	.50

1999 Upper Deck Black Diamond Double Diamond

Double Diamonds are the most common parallels to the Black Diamond base set. Cards feature a red metallic-foil background or highlights. Regular-player cards (#1-90) are serially numbered on back from within an edition of 3,000 each. Diamond Debut cards (#91-120) are individually numbered within an edition of 2,500 each.

	MT
Complete Set (120):	200.00
Common Player (1-90):	.25
Common Diamond Debut (91-120):	1.00
Stars (1-90):	3X
Diamond Debuts (91-120):	2X

(See 1999 Upper Deck Black Diamond for checklist and base card values.)

1999 Upper Deck Black Diamond Triple Diamond

Triple Diamonds are the mid-level of scarcity among the parallel inserts to the Black Diamond base cards. They feature yellow metallic-foil backgrounds (1-90) and highlights (91-120). Regular-player cards are serially numbered on back from within an edition of 1,500 each. Diamond Debut cards are individually numbered within an edition of 1,000 each.

	MT
Common Player (1-90):	1.00
Common Diamond Debut (91-120):	1.50
Stars (1-90):	4X
Diamond Debuts (91-120):	2X

(See 1999 Upper Deck Black Diamond for checklist and base card values.)

1999 Upper Deck Black Diamond Quadruple Diamond

Quadruple Diamonds are the scarcest of the parallel inserts to the Black Diamond base cards. The regular player cards (#1-90) feature a green metallic-foil background and are serially numbered on back from within an edition of 150 each. Diamond Debut cards (#91-120) also feature green foil highlights on front and are individually numbered within an edition of 100 each. Quad Diamond cards of Sosa, Griffey and McGwire were limited to the number of home runs each hit the previous season.

	MT
Common Player (1-90):	4.00
Production 150 each	
Common Diamond Debut (91-120):	6.00
Production 100 each	
Stars (1-90):	25X
Diamond Debuts (91-120):	5X

18	Sammy Sosa/66	50.00
76	Ken Griffey Jr. /56	60.00
80	Mark McGwire/70	75.00

(See 1999 Upper Deck Black Diamond for checklist and base card values.)

1999 Upper Deck Black Diamond A Piece of History

This six-card set features green metallic foil fronts with a diamond-shaped piece of game-used bat from the featured player embedded on the card front. No insertion ratio was released.

		MT
Common Player:		15.00
JG	Juan Gonzalez	30.00
TG	Tony Gwynn	30.00
BW	Bernie Williams	25.00
MM	Mark McGwire	400.00
MV	Mo Vaughn	15.00
SS	Sammy Sosa	80.00

1999 Upper Deck Black Diamond Diamond Dominance

This 30-card set features full-bleed metallic foil fronts and includes the top stars of the game along with Babe Ruth. Each card is numbered with a "D" prefix and is limited to 1,500 sequentially numbered sets.

		MT
Complete Set (30):		150.00
Common Player:		1.00
Production 1,500 sets		
D01	Kerry Wood	3.50
D02	Derek Jeter	15.00
D03	Alex Rodriguez	12.00
D04	Frank Thomas	5.00
D05	Jeff Bagwell	6.00
D06	Mo Vaughn	3.50
D07	Ivan Rodriguez	4.50
D08	Cal Ripken Jr.	15.00
D09	Rolando Arrojo	1.00
D10	Chipper Jones	10.00
D11	Kenny Lofton	1.00
D12	Paul Konerko	1.00
D13	Mike Piazza	10.00
D14	Ben Grieve	1.50
D15	Nomar Garciaparra	8.00
D16	Travis Lee	1.50
D17	Scott Rolen	4.50
D18	Juan Gonzalez	6.00
D19	Tony Gwynn	5.00
D20	Tony Clark	1.00
D21	Roger Clemens	7.50
D22	Sammy Sosa	8.00
D23	Larry Walker	1.50
D24	Ken Griffey Jr.	12.00
D25	Mark McGwire	15.00
D26	Barry Bonds	8.00
D27	Vladimir Guerrero	6.00
D28	Tino Martinez	1.00
D29	Greg Maddux	7.50
D30	Babe Ruth	20.00

1999 Upper Deck Black Diamond Mystery Numbers

The player's card number determines scarcity in this hobby-only insert set. The basic set has an action photo set against a silver-foil background of repated numerals. Backs have a portrait photo and significant stat numbers from the 1998 season. Each base Mystery Numbers card is individually numbered within an edition of 100 cards times the card number within the 30-card set (i.e., card #24 has an edition of 2,400) for a total of 46,500 cards. An emerald version of the Mystery Numbers cards has a total issue of 465 cards, with cards issued to a limit of the player's card number multiplied by 1.

		MT
Complete Set (30):		375.00
Common Player:		2.50
M1	Babe Ruth (100)	100.00
M2	Ken Griffey Jr. (200)	50.00
M3	Kerry Wood (300)	12.50
M4	Mark McGwire (400)	50.00
M5	Alex Rodriguez (500)	35.00
M6	Chipper Jones (600)	20.00
M7	Nomar Garciaparra (700)	20.00
M8	Derek Jeter (800)	25.00
M9	Mike Piazza (900)	20.00
M10	Roger Clemens (1,000)	15.00
M11	Greg Maddux (1,100)	15.00
M12	Scott Rolen (1,200)	8.00
M13	Cal Ripken Jr. (1,300)	20.00
M14	Ben Grieve (1,400)	5.00
M15	Troy Glaus (1,500)	8.00
M16	Sammy Sosa (1,600)	15.00
M17	Darin Erstad (1,700)	4.00
M18	Juan Gonzalez (1,800)	8.00
M19	Pedro Martinez (1,900)	5.00
M20	Larry Walker (2,000)	4.00
M21	Vladimir Guerrero (2,100)	8.00
M22	Jeff Bagwell (2,200)	5.00
M23	Jaret Wright (2,300)	2.50
M24	Travis Lee (2,400)	3.50
M25	Barry Bonds (2,500)	4.00
M26	Orlando Hernandez (2,600)	7.00
M27	Frank Thomas (2,700)	6.00
M28	Tony Gwynn (2,800)	7.00
M29	Andres Galarraga (2,900)	3.00
M30	Craig Biggio (3,000)	2.50

1999 Upper Deck Black Diamond Piece of History 500 Club

A veneer of lumber from one of Mr. October's war clubs is included in this special insert card. A facsimile autograph is also featured on front. A premium version with an authentic autographed serially numbered from within an edition of 44 (his uniform number) was also issued. Backs have a congratulatory authentication message from US CEO Richard McWilliam.

	MT
Reggie Jackson	100.00
Reggie Jackson Auto.	350.00

1999 Upper Deck Century Legends

The first 47 cards in the 131-card set are taken from the Sporting News' list of Baseball's 100 Greatest Players. Each card bears a Sporting News photo of the featured player and his ranking in silver and copper foil. The next 50 cards tout Upper Deck's rankings of the Top 50 contemporary players. Rounding out the base set are two Because of contrctual problems, cards #11, 25, 26 and 126 were never issued. A die-cut parallel version of each card, serially numbered to 100 each, was produced as the "Century Collection."

		MT
Complete Set (131):		25.00
Common Player:		.10
Century Collection:		15X
Production 100 sets		
Pack (5):		3.00
Wax Box (24):		60.00
1	Babe Ruth (Sporting News Top 50)	2.00
1	Babe Ruth (SAMPLE overprint on back)	2.00
2	Willie Mays (Sporting News Top 50)	1.00
3	Ty Cobb (Sporting News Top 50)	1.00
4	Walter Johnson (Sporting News Top 50)	.40
5	Hank Aaron (Sporting News Top 50)	1.00
6	Lou Gehrig (Sporting News Top 50)	1.50
7	Christy Mathewson (Sporting News Top 50)	.40
8	Ted Williams (Sporting News Top 50)	1.25
9	Rogers Hornsby (Sporting News Top 50)	.25
10	Stan Musial (Sporting News Top 50)	.65
12	Grover Alexander (Sporting News Top 50)	.25
13	Honus Wagner (Sporting News Top 50)	.40
14	Cy Young (Sporting News Top 50)	.40
15	Jimmie Foxx (Sporting News Top 50)	.25
16	Johnny Bench (Sporting News Top 50)	.50
17	Mickey Mantle (Sporting News Top 50)	2.00
18	Josh Gibson (Sporting News Top 50)	.25
19	Satchel Paige (Sporting News Top 50)	.50
20	Roberto Clemente (Sporting News Top 50)	1.50
21	Warren Spahn (Sporting News Top 50)	.20
22	Frank Robinson (Sporting News Top 50)	.20
23	Lefty Grove (Sporting News Top 50)	.20
24	Eddie Collins (Sporting News Top 50)	.10
27	Tris Speaker (Sporting News Top 50)	.25
28	Mike Schmidt (Sporting News Top 50)	.50
29	Napoleon LaJoie (Sporting News Top 50)	.20
30	Steve Carlton (Sporting News Top 50)	.25
31	Bob Gibson (Sporting News Top 50)	.25
32	Tom Seaver (Sporting News Top 50)	.25
33	George Sisler (Sporting News Top 50)	.10
34	Barry Bonds (Sporting News Top 50)	.75
35	Joe Jackson (Sporting News Top 50)	1.25
36	Bob Feller (Sporting News Top 50)	.25
37	Hank Greenberg (Sporting News Top 50)	.25
38	Ernie Banks (Sporting News Top 50)	.40
39	Greg Maddux (Sporting News Top 50)	.50
40	Yogi Berra (Sporting News Top 50)	.40
41	Nolan Ryan (Sporting News Top 50)	2.00
42	Mel Ott (Sporting News Top 50)	.25
43	Al Simmons (Sporting News Top 50)	.10
44	Jackie Robinson (Sporting News Top 50)	1.25

45 Carl Hubbell (Sporting News Top 50) .25
46 Charley Gehringer (Sporting News Top 50) .10
47 Buck Leonard (Sporting News Top 50) .10
48 Reggie Jackson (Sporting News Top 50) .40
49 Tony Gwynn (Sporting News Top 50) .50
50 Roy Campanella (Sporting News Top 50) .40
51 Ken Griffey Jr. (Contemporaries) 1.25
52 Barry Bonds (Contemporaries) .85
53 Roger Clemens (Contemporaries) .75
54 Tony Gwynn (Contemporaries) .75
55 Cal Ripken Jr. (Contemporaries) 1.50
56 Greg Maddux (Contemporaries) .75
57 Frank Thomas (Contemporaries) .85
58 Mark McGwire (Contemporaries) 1.50
59 Mike Piazza (Contemporaries) 1.00
60 Wade Boggs (Contemporaries) .50
61 Alex Rodriguez (Contemporaries) 1.25
62 Juan Gonzalez (Contemporaries) .60
63 Mo Vaughn (Contemporaries) .30
64 Albert Belle (Contemporaries) .30
65 Sammy Sosa (Contemporaries) .85
66 Nomar Garciaparra (Contemporaries) .85
67 Derek Jeter (Contemporaries) 1.50
68 Kevin Brown (Contemporaries) .15
69 Jose Canseco (Contemporaries) .35
70 Randy Johnson (Contemporaries) .50
71 Tom Glavine (Contemporaries) .15
72 Barry Larkin (Contemporaries) .15
73 Curt Schilling (Contemporaries) .15
74 Moises Alou (Contemporaries) .15
75 Fred McGriff (Contemporaries) .10
76 Pedro Martinez (Contemporaries) .45
77 Andres Galarraga (Contemporaries) .10
78 Will Clark (Contemporaries) .25
79 Larry Walker (Contemporaries) .30
80 Ivan Rodriguez (Contemporaries) .50
81 Chipper Jones (Contemporaries) 1.00
82 Jeff Bagwell (Contemporaries) .60
83 Craig Biggio (Contemporaries) .15
84 Kerry Wood (Contemporaries) .35
85 Roberto Alomar (Contemporaries) .45
86 Vinny Castilla (Contemporaries) .10
87 Kenny Lofton (Contemporaries) .10
88 Rafael Palmeiro (Contemporaries) .20
89 Manny Ramirez (Contemporaries) .60
90 David Wells (Contemporaries) .15
91 Mark Grace (Contemporaries) .25
92 Bernie Williams (Contemporaries) .25
93 David Cone (Contemporaries) .10
94 John Olerud (Contemporaries) .10
95 John Smoltz (Contemporaries) .15
96 Tino Martinez (Contemporaries) .10
97 Raul Mondesi (Contemporaries) .20
98 Gary Sheffield (Contemporaries) .20
99 Orel Hershiser (Contemporaries) .10
100 Rickey Henderson (Contemporaries) .50
101 J.D. Drew (21st Century Phenoms) .25
102 Troy Glaus (21st Century Phenoms) .60
103 Nomar Garciaparra (21st Century Phenoms) 1.00
104 Scott Rolen (21st Century Phenoms) .40
105 Ryan Minor (21st Century Phenoms) .10
106 Travis Lee (21st Century Phenoms) .25
107 Roy Halladay (21st Century Phenoms) .10
108 Carlos Beltran (21st Century Phenoms) .15
109 Alex Rodriguez (21st Century Phenoms) 1.50
110 Eric Chavez (21st Century Phenoms) .25
111 Vladimir Guerrero (21st Century Phenoms) .75
112 Ben Grieve (21st Century Phenoms) .25
113 Kerry Wood (21st Century Phenoms) .40
114 Alex Gonzalez (21st Century Phenoms) .10
115 Darin Erstad (21st Century Phenoms) .40
116 Derek Jeter (21st Century Phenoms) 1.50
117 Jaret Wright (21st Century Phenoms) .10
118 Jose Cruz Jr. (21st Century Phenoms) .20
119 Chipper Jones (21st Century Phenoms) 1.25
120 Gabe Kapler (21st Century Phenoms) .25
121 Satchel Paige (Century Memories) .50
122 Willie Mays (Century Memories) .75
123 Roberto Clemente (Century Memories) 1.50
124 Lou Gehrig (Century Memories) 1.50
125 Mark McGwire (Century Memories) 1.50
127 Bob Gibson (Century Memories) .25
128 Johnny Vander Meer (Century Memories) .10
129 Walter Johnson (Century Memories) .25
130 Ty Cobb (Century Memories) .75
131 Don Larsen (Century Memories) .20
132 Jackie Robinson (Century Memories) 1.00
133 Tom Seaver (Century Memories) .25
134 Johnny Bench (Century Memories) .35
135 Frank Robinson (Century Memories) .25

1999 Upper Deck Century Legends All-Century Team

This 10-card set highlights Upper Deck's all-time all-star team. These were seeded 1:23 packs.

		MT
Complete Set (10):		25.00
Common Player:		2.00
Inserted 1:23		
1	Babe Ruth	7.50
2	Ty Cobb	3.00
3	Willie Mays	3.00
4	Lou Gehrig	5.00
5	Jackie Robinson	4.00
6	Mike Schmidt	2.00
7	Ernie Banks	2.00
8	Johnny Bench	2.00
9	Cy Young	2.00
10	Lineup Sheet	.50

1999 Upper Deck Century Legends Century Artifacts

A total of nine cards were inserted, redeemable for memorabilia from some of the top players of the century. Due to the limited nature of these one-of-one inserts and the fact that most or all were redeemed, no pricing is assigned. Each cut signature was framed with the player's Century Legends card.

MT

1900s Framed Cut of Cobb
1910s Framed Cut of Ruth
1920s Framed Cut of Hornsby
1930s Framed Cut of Paige
1950s Auto. Balls: Aaron, Mays, Mantle
1960s Auto. Balls: Banks, Gibson, Bench
1970s Auto. Balls: Seaver, Schmidt, Carlton
1980s Auto. Balls: Ryan, Griffey Jr.
1990s Ken Griffey Autographed Jersey

1999 Upper Deck Century Legends Epic Signatures

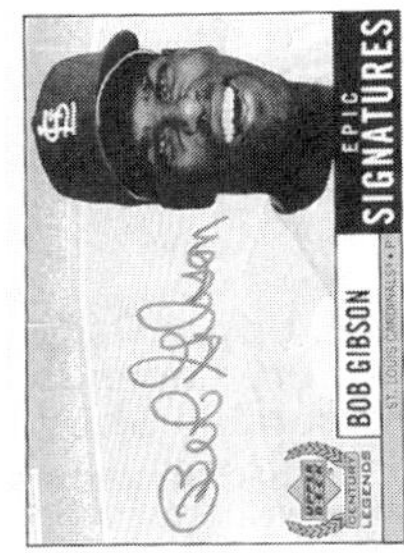

This 30-card set features autographs from retired and current stars on a horizonal format. A player portrait appears over a ballpark background on front. The portrait is repeated on back with a statement of authenticity. Cards are numbered with player initials. These autographed cards are seeded 1:24 packs. Exchange cards of Fisk, Bench, Berra and McCovey were originally inserted into packs and had to be mail in for the autographed card. They are valued about 10% of the corresponding signed card.

		MT
Common Player:		15.00
Inserted 1:24		
EB	Ernie Banks	30.00
JB	Johnny Bench	40.00
YB	Yogi Berra	35.00
BB	Barry Bonds	125.00
SC	Steve Carlton	20.00
BD	Bucky Dent	15.00
BF	Bob Feller	15.00
CF	Carlton Fisk	25.00
BG	Bob Gibson	25.00
JG	Juan Gonzalez	25.00
Jr.	Ken Griffey Jr.	100.00
Sr.	Ken Griffey Sr.	15.00
VG	Vladimir Guerrero	30.00
TG	Tony Gwynn	70.00
RJ	Reggie Jackson	45.00
HK	Harmon Killebrew	25.00
DL	Don Larsen	20.00
GM	Greg Maddux	100.00
EMa	Eddie Mathews	50.00
BM	Bill Mazeroski	20.00
WMc	Willie McCovey	25.00
SM	Stan Musial	50.00
FR	Frank Robinson	25.00
AR	Alex Rodriguez	90.00
NR	Nolan Ryan	200.00
MS	Mike Schmidt	50.00
TS	Tom Seaver	50.00
WS	Warren Spahn	30.00
FT	Frank Thomas	25.00
BT	Bobby Thomson	15.00

1999 Upper Deck Century Legends Century Epic Signatures

This 32-card autographed set features signatures from retired and current stars. The cards have a horizontal format and have gold foil stamping. Each card is hand numbered to 100.

		MT
Common Player:		25.00
Production 100 sets		
EB	Ernie Banks	65.00

JB	Johnny Bench	85.00
YB	Yogi Berra	80.00
BB	Barry Bonds	200.00
SC	Steve Carlton	40.00
BD	Bucky Dent	25.00
BF	Bob Feller	40.00
CF	Carlton Fisk	65.00
BG	Bob Gibson	60.00
JG	Juan Gonzalez	60.00
Jr.	Ken Griffey Jr.	175.00
Sr.	Ken Griffey Sr.	25.00
VG	Vladimir Guerrero	70.00
TG	Tony Gwynn	100.00
RJ	Reggie Jackson	65.00
HK	Harmon Killebrew	60.00
DL	Don Larsen	30.00
GM	Greg Maddux	125.00
EMa	Eddie Mathews	80.00
WM	Willie Mays	250.00
BM	Bill Mazeroski	30.00
WMc	Willie McCovey	40.00
SM	Stan Musial	100.00
FR	Frank Robinson	50.00
AR	Alex Rodriguez	160.00
NR	Nolan Ryan	300.00
MS	Mike Schmidt	100.00
TS	Tom Seaver	80.00
WS	Warren Spahn	75.00
FT	Frank Thomas	60.00
BT	Bobby Thomson	25.00
TW	Ted Williams	650.00

1999 Upper Deck Century Legends Epic Milestones

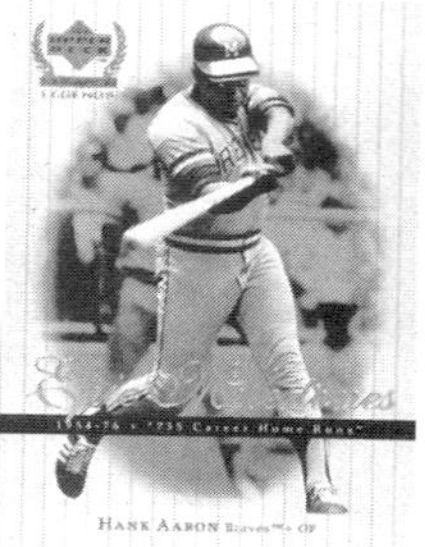

This nine-card set showcases nine of the most impressive milestones established in major league history. Each card is numbered with a "EM" prefix and are seeded 1:12 packs. Because of a contractual dispute, card #1 was never issued.

		MT
Complete Set (9):		20.00
Common Player:		1.00
Inserted 1:12		
2	Jackie Robinson	3.00
3	Nolan Ryan	5.00
4	Mark McGwire	4.00
5	Roger Clemens	1.00
6	Sammy Sosa	2.50
7	Cal Ripken Jr.	5.00
8	Rickey Henderson	1.00
9	Hank Aaron	3.00
10	Barry Bonds	2.00

1999 Upper Deck Century Legends Hank Aaron Blowup

This was a Shop at Home television exclusive. The card is an approximately 16" x 20" enlargement of the Hank Aaron card from The Sporting News Top 50 subset of 1999 UD Century Legends which was autographed by Aaron in an edition of 144 pieces. Original price was $229.95.

		MT
5	Hank Aaron	125.00

1999 Upper Deck Century Legends Jerseys of the Century

This eight-card set features a swatch of game-worn jersey from the featured player, which includes current and retired players. These are seeded 1:418 packs.

		MT
Common Player:		20.00
Inserted 1:418		
GB	George Brett	40.00
RC	Roger Clemens	40.00
TG	Tony Gwynn	30.00
GM	Greg Maddux	40.00
EM	Eddie Murray	20.00
NR	Nolan Ryan	120.00
MS	Mike Schmidt	45.00
OZ	Ozzie Smith	25.00
DW	Dave Winfield	20.00

1999 Upper Deck Century Legends Legendary Cuts

A total of nine of these one-fo-one inserts exist. These are actual "cut" signatures from some of baseball's all-time greats.

		MT
VALUES UNDETERMINED DUE TO RARITY		
RC	Roy Campanella	
TY	Ty Cobb	
XX	Jimmie Foxx	
LG	Lefty Grove	
WJ	Walter Johnson	
MO	Mel Ott	
SP	Satchel Paige	
BR	Babe Ruth	
CY	Cy Young (11/00 auction)	1850.

1999 Upper Deck Century Legends Memorable Shots

This 10-card insert set focuses on the most memorable home runs launched during this century. The player's image is framed in an embossed foil, frame-like design. These are seeded 1:12 packs, each card back is numbered with a "HR" prefix.

		MT
Complete Set (10):		16.00
Common Player:		.50
Inserted 1:12		
1	Babe Ruth	5.00
2	Bobby Thomson	1.00
3	Kirk Gibson	.50
4	Carlton Fisk	.50
5	Bill Mazeroski	1.00
6	Bucky Dent	.50
7	Mark McGwire	3.00
8	Mickey Mantle	5.00
9	Joe Carter	.50
10	Mark McGwire	3.00

1999 Upper Deck Century Legends 500 Club Piece History

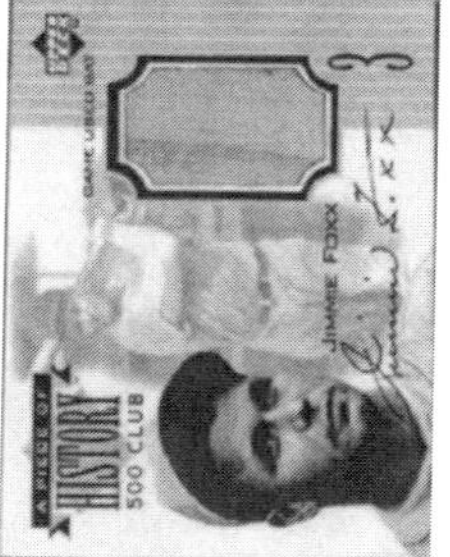

This Jimmie Foxx insert has a piece of of a game-used Louisville Slugger once swung by Foxx, embedded into the card front. An estimated 350 cards of this one exist.

		MT
JF	Jimmie Foxx	170.00

1999 Upper Deck Challengers for 70

Celebrating Mark McGwire's record-setting season of 1998, and featuring those who would chase his single-season home run crown in 1999, Upper Deck issued this specialty product. The base set of 90 cards is fractured into subsets of Power Elite (#1-10), Power Corps (#11-40), Rookie Power (#41-45), and Home Run Highlights (#46-90). Several styles of inserts and numbered parallels were included in the 5-card foil packs. A parallel set with each card serially numbered to 600 was also issued, titled "Challengers Edition".

		MT
Complete Set (90):		15.00
Common Player:		.10
Challenger's Edition (600 sets):		15X
Pack (5):		2.00
Wax Box (20):		30.00
1	Mark McGwire (Power Elite)	1.50
2	Sammy Sosa (Power Elite)	.85
3	Ken Griffey Jr. (Power Elite)	1.25
4	Alex Rodriguez (Power Elite)	1.25
5	Albert Belle (Power Elite)	.25
6	Mo Vaughn (Power Elite)	.35
7	Mike Piazz (Power Elite)	1.00
8	Frank Thomas (Power Elite)	.85
9	Juan Gonzalez (Power Elite)	.65
10	Barry Bonds (Power Elite)	.85
11	Rafael Palmeiro (Power Corps)	.20
12	Jose Canseco (Power Corps)	.50
13	Nomar Garciaparra (Power Corps)	.85
14	Carlos Delgado (Power Corps)	.20
15	Brian Jordan (Power Corps)	.10
16	Vladimir Guerrero (Power Corps)	.65
17	Vinny Castilla (Power Corps)	.10
18	Chipper Jones (Power Corps)	1.00
19	Jeff Bagwell (Power Corps)	.65
20	Moises Alou (Power Corps)	.15
21	Tony Clark (Power Corps)	.10
22	Jim Thome (Power Corps)	.10
23	Tino Martinez (Power Corps)	.10
24	Greg Vaughn (Power Corps)	.10
25	Javy Lopez (Power Corps)	.10
26	Jeromy Burnitz (Power Corps)	.10
27	Cal Ripken Jr. (Power Corps)	2.00
28	Manny Ramirez (Power Corps)	.65
29	Darin Erstad (Power Corps)	.25
30	Ken Caminiti (Power Corps)	.10
31	Edgar Martinez (Power Corps)	.10
32	Ivan Rodriguez (Power Corps)	.60
33	Larry Walker (Power Corps)	.20
34	Todd Helton (Power Corps)	.35
35	Andruw Jones (Power Corps)	.65
36	Ray Lankford (Power Corps)	.10
37	Travis Lee (Power Corps)	.15
38	Raul Mondesi (Power Corps)	.15

39	Scott Rolen (Power Corps)	.60
40	Ben Grieve (Power Corps)	.20
41	J.D. Drew (Rookie Power)	.50
42	Troy Glaus (Rookie Power)	.50
43	Eric Chavez (Rookie Power)	.15
44	Gabe Kapler (Rookie Power)	.10
45	Michael Barrett (Rookie Power)	.10
46	Mark McGwire (Home Run Highlights)	.75
47	Jose Canseco (Home Run Highlights)	.25
48	Greg Vaughn (Home Run Highlights)	.10
49	Albert Belle (Home Run Highlights)	.15
50	Mark McGwire (Home Run Highlights)	.75
51	Vinny Castilla (Home Run Highlights)	.10
52	Vladimir Guerrero (Home Run Highlights)	.35
53	Andres Galarraga (Home Run Highlights)	.10
54	Rafael Palmeiro (Home Run Highlights)	.10
55	Juan Gonzalez (Home Run Highlights)	.35
56	Ken Griffey Jr. (Home Run Highlights)	.65
57	Barry Bonds (Home Run Highlights)	.45
58	Mo Vaughn (Home Run Highlights)	.10
59	Nomar Garciaparra (Home Run Highlights)	.45
60	Tino Martinez (Home Run Highlights)	.10
61	Mark McGwire (Home Run Highlights)	.75
62	Mark McGwire (Home Run Highlights)	.75
63	Mark McGwire (Home Run Highlights)	.75
64	Mark McGwire (Home Run Highlights)	.75
65	Mark McGwire (Home Run Highlights)	.75
66	Sammy Sosa (Home Run Highlights)	.50
67	Mark McGwire (Home Run Highlights)	.75
68	Mark McGwire (Home Run Highlights)	.75
69	Mark McGwire (Home Run Highlights)	.75
70	Mark McGwire (Home Run Highlights)	.75
71	Mark McGwire (Home Run Highlights)	.75
72	Scott Brosius (Home Run Highlights)	.10
73	Tony Gwynn (Home Run Highlights)	.40
74	Chipper Jones (Home Run Highlights)	.50
75	Jeff Bagwell (Home Run Highlights)	.35
76	Moises Alou (Home Run Highlights)	.10
77	Manny Ramirez (Home Run Highlights)	.35
78	Carlos Delgado (Home Run Highlights)	.10
79	Kerry Wood (Home Run Highlights)	.10
80	Ken Griffey Jr. (Home Run Highlights)	.65
81	Cal Ripken Jr. (Home Run Highlights)	.75
82	Alex Rodriguez (Home Run Highlights)	.65
83	Barry Bonds (Home Run Highlights)	.45
84	Ken Griffey Jr. (Home Run Highlights)	.65
85	Travis Lee (Home Run Highlights)	.10
86	George Lombard (Home Run Highlights)	.10
87	Michael Barrett (Home Run Highlights)	.10
88	Jeremy Giambi (Home Run Highlights)	.10
89	Troy Glaus (Home Run Highlights)	.25
90	J.D. Drew (Home Run Highlights)	.25

1999 Upper Deck Challengers for 70 Edition of 70

In this parallel of the 90-card base set, each card is serially numbered within an edition of 70 each.

	MT
Commons:	2.50
Stars:	35X

(See 1999 Challengers for 70 Insert Set for base card values.)

1999 Upper Deck Challengers for 70 Insert Set

Found one per pack, this insert series identifies 30 of the top contenders for the 1999 home run crown. Action photos on front are highlighted by red graphics and silver-foil. Backs repeat a detail of the front photo and present a capsule of the player's 1998 season. Cards have a "C" prefix to the number. A parallel edition, utilizing refractive foil details on front, is serially numbered within an edition of 70 each.

		MT
	Complete Set (30):	15.00
	Common Player:	.25
	Parallel Edition (70 sets):	35X
1	Mark McGwire	2.00
2	Sammy Sosa	1.00
3	Ken Griffey Jr.	1.50
4	Alex Rodriguez	1.50
5	Albert Belle	.35
6	Mo Vaughn	.35
7	Mike Piazza	1.25
8	Frank Thomas	1.00
9	Juan Gonzalez	.65
10	Barry Bonds	1.00
11	Rafael Palmeiro	.25
12	Nomar Garciaparra	1.00
13	Vladimir Guerrero	.65
14	Vinny Castilla	.25
15	Chipper Jones	1.25
16	Jeff Bagwell	.65
17	Moises Alou	.25
18	Tony Clark	.25
19	Jim Thome	.25
20	Tino Martinez	.25
21	Greg Vaughn	.25
22	Manny Ramirez	.65
23	Darin Erstad	.45
24	Ken Caminiti	.25
25	Ivan Rodriguez	.45
26	Andruw Jones	.65
27	Travis Lee	.25
28	Scott Rolen	.45
29	Ben Grieve	.25
30	J.D. Drew	.45

1999 Upper Deck Challengers for 70 Longball Legends

Top home-run threats are featured in this insert series. The action photos on front are repeated in a diffused version on back, where they are joined by a second photo and a bar-graph of the player's home run production in recent seasons. Cards have an "L" prefix to the number. Stated odds of picking a Longball Legends card are one per 39 packs.

		MT
	Complete Set (30):	60.00
	Common Player:	1.00
1	Ken Griffey Jr.	5.00
2	Mark McGwire	6.00
3	Sammy Sosa	3.50
4	Cal Ripken Jr.	8.00
5	Barry Bonds	3.50
6	Larry Walker	1.25
7	Fred McGriff	1.00
8	Alex Rodriguez	5.00
9	Frank Thomas	2.50
10	Juan Gonzalez	2.00
11	Jeff Bagwell	2.00
12	Mo Vaughn	1.50
13	Albert Belle	1.25
14	Mike Piazza	4.00
15	Vladimir Guerrero	2.00
16	Chipper Jones	4.00
17	Ken Caminiti	1.00
18	Rafael Palmeiro	1.25
19	Nomar Garciaparra	3.50
20	Jim Thome	1.00
21	Edgar Martinez	1.00
22	Ivan Rodriguez	1.50
23	Andres Galarraga	1.00
24	Scott Rolen	1.50
25	Darin Erstad	2.00
26	Moises Alou	1.25
27	J.D. Drew	1.50
28	Andruw Jones	2.00
29	Manny Ramirez	2.00
30	Tino Martinez	1.00

1999 Upper Deck Challengers for 70 Mark on History

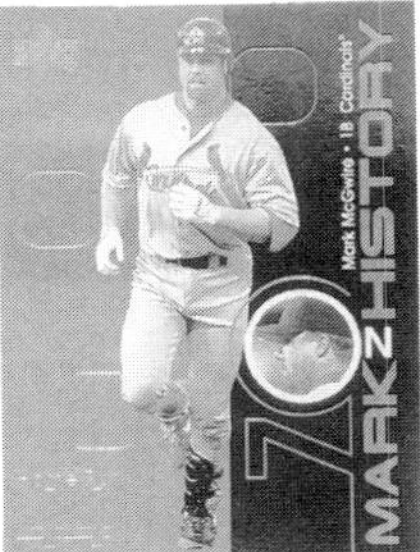

The details of Mark McGwire successful assault on the single-season home run record are captured in this 25-card insert set, found on average of one per five packs. Cards have action photos set against split red and black backgrounds and are highlighted in red metallic foil. Backs have details of the home run featured on front, a quote from McGwire and another photo. Cards have an "M" prefix to the number. A parallel edition number to 70 was also issued.

		MT
	Complete Set (25):	35.00
	Common McGwire:	2.00
	Parallel:	8X
01	Mark McGwire	2.00
02	Mark McGwire	2.00
03	Mark McGwire	2.00
04	Mark McGwire	2.00
05	Mark McGwire	2.00
06	Mark McGwire	2.00
07	Mark McGwire	2.00
08	Mark McGwire	2.00
09	Mark McGwire	2.00
10	Mark McGwire	2.00
11	Mark McGwire	2.00
12	Mark McGwire	2.00
13	Mark McGwire	2.00
14	Mark McGwire	2.00
15	Mark McGwire	2.00
16	Mark McGwire	2.00
17	Mark McGwire	2.00
18	Mark McGwire	2.00
19	Mark McGwire	2.00
20	Mark McGwire	2.00
21	Mark McGwire	2.00
22	Mark McGwire	2.00
23	Mark McGwire	2.00
24	Mark McGwire	2.00
25	Mark McGwire	2.00

1999 Upper Deck Challengers for 70 Piece of History 500

A piece of game-used bat from 500-HR club

member Harmon Killebrew is featured on these inserts. Only 350 cards were issued, along with three (his uniform number) authentically autographed versions. Backs have an action photo and a congratulatory authentication message from UD CEO Richard McWilliam.

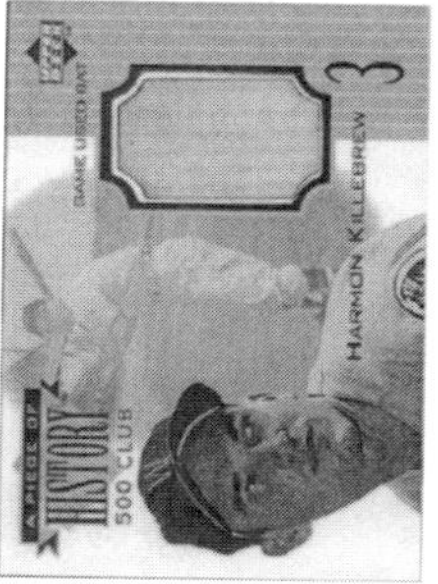

	MT
Harmon Killebrew	120.00
Harmon Killebrew (autographed)	450.00

1999 Upper Deck Challengers for 70 Swinging/Fences

Fifteen top sluggers are included in this insert set. The players' power swing is captured on a muted textured-look background. Back has a color portrait photo and an "S" prefix to the card number. Stated insertion rate is one per 19 packs.

		MT
Complete Set (15):		30.00
Common Player:		1.00
1	Ken Griffey Jr.	4.00
2	Mark McGwire	5.00
3	Sammy Sosa	2.50
4	Alex Rodriguez	4.00
5	Nomar Garciaparra	2.50
6	J.D. Drew	1.50
7	Vladimir Guerrero	2.00
8	Ben Grieve	1.00
9	Chipper Jones	3.00
10	Gabe Kapler	1.00
11	Travis Lee	1.00
12	Todd Helton	1.50
13	Juan Gonzalez	2.00
14	Mike Piazza	3.00
15	Mo Vaughn	1.25

1999 Upper Deck Challengers for 70 Autographed Swinging

A total of 2,700 autographed versions of Swinging for the Fences inserts were featured in the Challengers for 70 issue. Only six of the 15 players' cards were included in this premium version.

		MT
Complete Set (6):		200.00
Common Player:		10.00
JR	Ken Griffey Jr.	100.00
VG	Vladimir Guerrero	30.00
TH	Todd Helton	20.00
GK	Gabe Kapler	10.00
TL	Travis Lee	10.00
AR	Alex Rodriguez	90.00

1999 Upper Deck Encore

Encore is a 180-card partial parallel of Upper Deck Series 1, utilizing a special holo-foil treatment on each card. The Encore set consists of 90 base cards and three short-printed subsets: 45 Star Rookies (1:4), 30 Homer Odyssey (1:6) and 15 Stroke of Genius (1:8).

		MT
Complete Set (180):		150.00
Common Player (1-90):		.10
Common Player (91-135):		.50
Inserted 1:4		
Common Player (136-165):		.75
Inserted 1:6		
Common Player (166-180):		1.00
Inserted 1:8		
Gold (1-90):		10X
Gold (91-135):		1.5X
Gold (136-165):		3X
Gold (166-180):		4X
Production 125 sets		
Pack (4):		2.75
Wax Box (24):		55.00
1	Darin Erstad	.40
2	Mo Vaughn	.60
3	Travis Lee	.20
4	Randy Johnson	.75
5	Matt Williams	.30
6	John Smoltz	.15
7	Greg Maddux	1.50
8	Chipper Jones	2.50
9	Tom Glavine	.15
10	Andruw Jones	1.00
11	Cal Ripken Jr.	3.00
12	Mike Mussina	.75
13	Albert Belle	.35
14	Nomar Garciaparra	2.00
15	Jose Offerman	.10
16	Pedro Martinez	.75
17	Trot Nixon	.15
18	Kerry Wood	.50
19	Sammy Sosa	2.00
20	Frank Thomas	2.00
21	Paul Konerko	.15
22	Sean Casey	.25
23	Barry Larkin	.15
24	Greg Vaughn	.10
25	Travis Fryman	.10
26	Jaret Wright	.10
27	Jim Thome	.10
28	Manny Ramirez	1.00
29	Roberto Alomar	.75
30	Kenny Lofton	.10
31	Todd Helton	.75
32	Larry Walker	.35
33	Vinny Castilla	.10
34	Dante Bichette	.10
35	Tony Clark	.10
36	Dean Palmer	.10
37	Gabe Kapler	.15
38	Juan Encarnacion	.10
39	Alex Gonzalez	.10
40	Preston Wilson	.10
41	Mark Kotsay	.10
42	Moises Alou	.20
43	Craig Biggio	.15
44	Ken Caminiti	.10
45	Jeff Bagwell	1.00
46	Johnny Damon	.15
47	Gary Sheffield	.35
48	Kevin Brown	.15
49	Raul Mondesi	.20
50	Jeff Cirillo	.10
51	Jeromy Burnitz	.10
52	Todd Walker	.15
53	Corey Koskie	.10
54	Brad Fullmer	.10
55	Vladimir Guerrero	1.00
56	Mike Piazza	2.50
57	Robin Ventura	.10
58	Rickey Henderson	.60
59	Derek Jeter	2.50
60	Paul O'Neill	.10
61	Bernie Williams	.30
62	Tino Martinez	.10
63	Roger Clemens	1.50
64	Ben Grieve	.40
65	Jason Giambi	.40
66	Bob Abreu	.15
67	Scott Rolen	.60
68	Curt Schilling	.20
69	Marlon Anderson	.10
70	Kevin Young	.10
71	Jason Kendall	.10
72	Brian Giles	.10
73	Mark McGwire	3.00
74	Fernando Tatis	.10
75	Eric Davis	.10
76	Trevor Hoffman	.10
77	Tony Gwynn	1.50
78	Matt Clement	.10
79	Robb Nen	.10
80	Barry Bonds	2.00
81	Ken Griffey Jr.	2.75
82	Alex Rodriguez	2.75
83	Wade Boggs	.75
84	Fred McGriff	.10
85	Jose Canseco	.75
86	Ivan Rodriguez	.85
87	Juan Gonzalez	1.00
88	Rafael Palmeiro	.40
89	Carlos Delgado	.25
90	David Wells	.15
91	Troy Glaus (Star Rookies)	2.00
92	Adrian Beltre (Star Rookies)	.75
93	Matt Anderson (Star Rookies)	.50
94	Eric Chavez (StarRookies)	.75
95	*Jeff Weaver* (Star Rookies)	2.50
96	Warren Morris (Star Rookies)	.50
97	George Lombard (Star Rookies)	.50
98	Mike Kinkade (Star Rookies)	.65
99	*Kyle Farnsworth* (Star Rookies)	1.00
100	J.D. Drew (Star Rookies)	1.00
101	*Joe McEwing* (Star Rookies)	1.50
102	Carlos Guillen (Star Rookies)	.50
103	*Kelly Dransfeldt* (Star Rookies)	1.00
104	*Eric Munson* (Star Rookies)	4.00
105	Armando Rios (Star Rookies)	.50
106	Ramon Martinez (Star Rookies)	.50
107	Orlando Hernandez (Star Rookies)	1.00
108	Jeremy Giambi (Star Rookies)	1.00
109	*Pat Burrell* (Star Rookies)	10.00
110	*Shea Hillenbrand* (Star Rookies)	6.00
111	Billy Koch (Star Rookies)	.50
112	Roy Halladay (Star Rookies)	.50
113	Ruben Mateo (Star Rookies)	1.00
114	Bruce Chen (Star Rookies)	.50
115	Angel Pena (StarRookies)	.50
116	Michael Barrett (Star Rookies)	1.50
117	Kevin Witt (Star Rookies)	.50
118	Damon Minor (Star Rookies)	1.00
119	Ryan Minor (Star Rookies)	1.00
120	A.J. Pierzynski (Star Rookies)	.50
121	*A.J. Burnett* (Star Rookies)	2.00
122	Christian Guzman (Star Rookies)	.75
123	Joe Lawrence (Star Rookies)	.50
124	Derrick Gibson (Star Rookies)	.75
125	Carlos Febles (Star Rookies)	1.00
126	Chris Haas (Star Rookies)	.50
127	Cesar King (StarRookies)	.50
128	Calvin Pickering (Star Rookies)	.50
129	Mitch Meluskey (Star Rookies)	.50
130	Carlos Beltran (Star Rookies)	.75
131	Ron Belliard (Star Rookies)	.50
132	Jerry Hairston Jr. (Star Rookies)	.50
133	Fernando Seguignol (Star Rookies)	.50
134	Kris Benson (Star Rookies)	.50
135	*Chad Hutchinson* (Star Rookies)	2.00
136	Ken Griffey Jr. (Homer Odyssey)	4.00
137	Mark McGwir (Homer Odyssey)	5.00
138	Sammy Sosa (Homer Odyssey)	2.50
139	Albert Belle (Homer Odyssey)	1.00
140	Mo Vaughn (Homer Odyssey)	1.50

141 Alex Rodriguez (Homer Odyssey) 4.00
142 Manny Ramirez (Homer Odyssey) 1.50
143 J.D. Drew (Homer Odyssey) 1.25
144 Juan Gonzalez (Homer Odyssey) 1.50
145 Vladimir Guerrero (Homer Odyssey) 1.50
146 Fernando Tatis (Homer Odyssey) .50
147 Mike Piazza (Homer Odyssey) 3.00
148 Barry Bonds (Homer Odyssey) 2.50
149 Ivan Rodriguez (Homer Odyssey) 1.25
150 Jeff Bagwell (Homer Odyssey) 1.50
151 Raul Mondesi (Homer Odyssey) .75
152 Nomar Garciaparra (Homer Odyssey) 2.50
153 Jose Canseco (Homer Odyssey) 1.00
154 Greg Vaughn (Homer Odyssey) .50
155 Scott Rolen (Homer Odyssey) 1.00
156 Vinny Castilla (Homer Odyssey) .50
157 Troy Glaus (Homer Odyssey) 1.25
158 Craig Biggio (Homer Odyssey) .75
159 Tino Martinez (Homer Odyssey) .50
160 Jim Thome (Homer Odyssey) .50
161 Frank Thomas (Homer Odyssey) 2.50
162 Tony Clark (Homer Odyssey) .50
163 Ben Grieve (Homer Odyssey) .75
164 Matt Williams (Homer Odyssey) .75
165 Derek Jeter (Homer Odyssey) 5.00
166 Ken Griffey Jr. (Strokes of Genius) 6.00
167 Tony Gwynn (Strokes of Genius) 3.00
168 Mike Piazza (Strokes of Genius) 5.00
169 Mark McGwire (Strokes of Genius) 7.00
170 Sammy Sosa (Strokes of Genius) 4.00
171 Juan Gonzalez (Strokes of Genius) 2.00
172 Mo Vaughn (Strokes of Genius) 1.50
173 Derek Jeter (Strokes of Genius) 6.00
174 Bernie Williams (Strokes of Genius) 1.00
175 Ivan Rodriguez (Strokes of Genius) 1.75
176 Barry Bonds (Strokes of Genius) 4.00
177 Scott Rolen (Strokes of Genius) 1.75
178 Larry Walker (Strokes of Genius) 1.00
179 Chipper Jones (Strokes of Genius) 5.00
180 Alex Rodriguez (Strokes of Genius) 6.00

1999 Upper Deck Encore FX Gold

This is a 180-card parallel to the base set featuring gold holo-foil treatment and limited to 125 sequentially numbered sets.

	MT
Common Player:	1.00
Gold (1-90):	10X
Gold (91-135):	1.5X
Gold (136-165):	3X
Gold (166-180):	4X

(See 1999 Upper Deck Encore for checklist and base card values.)

1999 Upper Deck Encore Batting Practice Caps

This 15-card set features actual swatch pieces of the highlighted players' batting practice cap embedded into each card. These are seeded 1:750 packs.

		MT
Common Player:		10.00
Inserted 1:750		
CB	Carlos Beltran	15.00
BB	Barry Bonds	90.00
VC	Vinny Castilla	15.00
EC	Eric Chavez	30.00
TC	Tony Clark	10.00
JD	J.D. Drew	25.00
VG	Vladimir Guerrero	40.00
TG	Tony Gwynn	50.00
TH	Todd Helton	25.00
GK	Gabe Kapler	10.00
JK	Jason Kendall	15.00
DP	Dean Palmer	10.00
BH	Frank Thomas	25.00
GV	Greg Vaughn	10.00
TW	Todd Walker	10.00

1999 Upper Deck Encore Driving Forces

This 15-card set is highlighted by holo-foil treatment on the card fronts on a thick card stock. Baseball's top performers are featured in this set and are seeded 1:23 packs. A Gold parallel exists and is limited to 10 sets.

		MT
Complete Set (15):		35.00
Common Player:		1.00
Inserted 1:23		
Gold (10 sets):		30X
D1	Ken Griffey Jr.	5.00
D2	Mark McGwire	6.00
D3	Sammy Sosa	3.00
D4	Albert Belle	1.00
D5	Alex Rodriguez	5.00
D6	Mo Vaughn	1.00
D7	Juan Gonzalez	2.00
D8	Jeff Bagwell	2.00
D9	Mike Piazza	4.00
D10	Frank Thomas	3.00
D11	Barry Bonds	3.00
D12	Vladimir Guerrero	2.00
D13	Chipper Jones	4.00
D14	Tony Gwynn	2.50
D15	J.D. Drew	1.50

1999 Upper Deck Encore McGwired!

This 10-card set salutes baseball's reigning single season home run king. These are seeded 1:23 packs. A gold parallel also is randomly seeded and is limited to 500 sequentially numbered sets. A small photo of the pitcher McGwire hit the historic home run off of is pictured as well.

		MT
Complete Set (10):		30.00
Common Card:		2.50
Inserted 1:23		
Parallel:		2X
Production 500 sets		
1	Mark McGwire, Carl Pavano	2.50
2	Mark McGwire, Michael Morgan	2.50
3	Mark McGwire, Steve Trachsel	2.50
4	Mark McGwire	4.00
5	Mark McGwire	4.00
6	Mark McGwire, Scott Elarton	2.50
7	Mark McGwire, Jim Parque	2.50
8	Mark McGwire	4.00
9	Mark McGwire, Rafael Roque	2.50
10	Mark McGwire, Jaret Wright	2.50

1999 Upper Deck Encore Pure Excitement

This 30-card set features Light F/X technology and includes the top players in baseball. These are seeded 1:7 packs.

		MT
Complete Set (30):		40.00
Common Player:		.50
Inserted 1:7		
1	Mo Vaughn	1.00
2	Darin Erstad	.75
3	Travis Lee	.65
4	Chipper Jones	3.00
5	Greg Maddux	2.00
6	Gabe Kapler	.50
7	Cal Ripken Jr.	4.00
8	Nomar Garciaparra	2.50
9	Kerry Wood	1.00
10	Frank Thomas	1.50
11	Manny Ramirez	1.50
12	Larry Walker	.75
13	Tony Clark	.50
14	Jeff Bagwell	1.50
15	Craig Biggio	.75
16	Vladimir Guerrero	1.50
17	Mike Piazza	3.00
18	Bernie Williams	.65
19	Derek Jeter	4.00
20	Ben Grieve	.75
21	Eric Chavez	.75
22	Scott Rolen	1.25
23	Mark McGwire	3.00
24	Tony Gwynn	1.50
25	Barry Bonds	2.50
26	Ken Griffey Jr.	3.50
27	Alex Rodriguez	3.50
28	J.D. Drew	1.00
29	Juan Gonzalez	1.50
30	Roger Clemens	2.00

1999 Upper Deck Encore Rookie Encore

This 10-card set highlights the top rookie prospects in 1999, including J.D. Drew and Gabe Kapler. These are seeded 1:23 packs. A parallel version is also randomly seeded and limited to 500 sequentially numbered sets.

		MT
Complete Set (10):		17.50
Common Player:		1.00
Inserted 1:23		
FX Gold:		2X
Production 500 sets		
1	J.D. Drew	2.00
2	Eric Chavez	1.50
3	Gabe Kapler	1.00
4	Bruce Chen	1.00
5	Carlos Beltran	1.50
6	Troy Glaus	4.00
7	Roy Halladay	1.00
8	Adrian Beltre	1.50
9	Michael Barrett	2.00
10	Pat Burrell	6.00

1999 Upper Deck Encore Upper Realm

This 15-card set focuses on the top stars of the game. Card fronts utilize holo-foil treatment, with the initials UR lightly foiled. Card backs are numbered with an "U" prefix and are seeded 1:11 packs.

		MT
Complete Set (15):		25.00
Common Player:		.50
Inserted 1:11		
1	Ken Griffey Jr.	3.00
2	Mark McGwire	4.00
3	Sammy Sosa	2.00
4	Tony Gwynn	1.50
5	Alex Rodriguez	3.00
6	Juan Gonzalez	1.00
7	J.D. Drew	.50
8	Roger Clemens	1.50
9	Greg Maddux	1.50
10	Randy Johnson	1.00
11	Mo Vaughn	.50
12	Derek Jeter	4.00
13	Vladimir Guerrero	1.00
14	Cal Ripken Jr.	4.00
15	Nomar Garciaparra	2.00

1999 Upper Deck Encore UD Authentics

This six-card autographed set features signatures of Griffey Jr. and Nomar Garciaparra. These are seeded 1:288 packs.

		MT
Complete Set (6):		175.00
Common Player:		10.00
Inserted 1:288		
MB	Michael Barrett	10.00
PB	Pat Burrell	25.00
JD	J.D. Drew	20.00
NG	Nomar Garciaparra	75.00
TG	Troy Glaus	25.00
JR	Ken Griffey Jr.	75.00

1999 Upper Deck Encore 2K Countdown

This set recognizes the countdown to the next century with a salute to baseball's next century of superstars including Derek Jeter and Alex Rodriguez. These are done on a horizontal format and inserted 1:11 packs.

		MT
Complete Set (10):		15.00
Common Player:		.75
Inserted 1:11		
1	Ken Griffey Jr.	2.50
2	Derek Jeter	3.00
3	Mike Piazza	2.00
4	J.D. Drew	.75
5	Vladimir Guerrero	1.00
6	Chipper Jones	2.00
7	Alex Rodriguez	2.50
8	Nomar Garciaparra	1.50
9	Mark McGwire	3.00
10	Sammy Sosa	1.50

1999 Upper Deck HoloGrFX

HoloGrFX was distributed exclusively to retail and the base set is comprised of 60 base cards, each utilizing holographic technology.

		MT
Complete Set (60):		20.00
Common Player:		.15
AUsome:		1.5X
Inserted 1:8		
Pack (3):		1.25
Wax Box (36):		30.00
1	Mo Vaughn	.50
2	Troy Glaus	.75
3	Tim Salmon	.40
4	Randy Johnson	.65
5	Travis Lee	.25
6	Chipper Jones	2.00
7	Greg Maddux	1.50
8	Andruw Jones	.75
9	Tom Glavine	.25
10	Cal Ripken Jr.	2.50
11	Albert Belle	.45
12	Nomar Garciaparra	1.75
13	Pedro J. Martinez	.75
14	Sammy Sosa	1.75
15	Frank Thomas	1.00
16	Greg Vaughn	.15
17	Kenny Lofton	.15
18	Jim Thome	.15
19	Manny Ramirez	1.00
20	Todd Helton	.65
21	Larry Walker	.45
22	Tony Clark	.15
23	Juan Encarnacion	.15
24	Mark Kotsay	.15
25	Jeff Bagwell	1.00
26	Craig Biggio	.25
27	Ken Caminiti	.15
28	Carlos Beltran	.25
29	Jeremy Giambi	.15
30	Raul Mondesi	.30
31	Kevin Brown	.25
32	Jeromy Burnitz	.15
33	Corey Koskie	.15
34	Todd Walker	.15
35	Vladimir Guerrero	1.00
36	Mike Piazza	2.00
37	Robin Ventura	.15
38	Derek Jeter	2.50
39	Roger Clemens	1.50
40	Bernie Williams	.40
41	Orlando Hernandez	.25
42	Ben Grieve	.35
43	Eric Chavez	.35
44	Scott Rolen	.75
45	*Pat Burrell*	2.00
46	Warren Morris	.15
47	Jason Kendall	.15
48	Mark McGwire	2.50
49	J.D. Drew	.50
50	Tony Gwynn	1.50
51	Trevor Hoffman	.15
52	Barry Bonds	1.75
53	Ken Griffey Jr.	2.25
54	Alex Rodriguez	2.25
55	Jose Canseco	.65
56	Juan Gonzalez	1.00
57	Ivan Rodriguez	.65
58	Rafael Palmeiro	.40
59	David Wells	.15
60	Carlos Delgado	.30

1999 Upper Deck HoloGrFX Future Fame

This six-card set focuses on players who are destined for Hall of Fame greatness. Card fronts feature a horizontal format on a die-cut design. These are seeded 1:34 packs. A parallel Gold (AU) version is also randomly seeded in every 1:432 packs.

		MT
Complete Set (6):		30.00
Common Player:		5.00
Inserted 1:34		
Gold:		2X
Inserted 1:210		
1	Tony Gwynn	4.00
2	Cal Ripken Jr.	10.00
3	Mark McGwire	8.00
4	Ken Griffey Jr.	7.50
5	Greg Maddux	5.00
6	Roger Clemens	5.00

1999 Upper Deck HoloGrFX Launchers

This 15-card set highlights the top home run hitters on holographic patterned foil fronts, including McGwier and Sosa. These are seeded 1:3 packs. A Gold (AU) parallel version is also seeded 1:105 packs.

		MT
Complete Set (15):		20.00
Common Player:		.50
Inserted 1:3		
Gold:		2X
Inserted 1:105		
1	Mark McGwire	3.50
2	Ken Griffey Jr.	3.00
3	Sammy Sosa	2.00
4	J.D. Drew	.75
5	Mo Vaughn	.50
6	Juan Gonzalez	1.00
7	Mike Piazza	2.50
8	Alex Rodriguez	2.50
9	Chipper Jones	2.50
10	Nomar Garciaparra	2.00
11	Vladimir Guerrero	1.00
12	Albert Belle	.50

13	Barry Bonds	2.00
14	Frank Thomas	2.00
15	Jeff Bagwell	1.00

1999 Upper Deck HoloGrFX StarView

This nine-card set highlights the top players in the game on a rainbow foil, full bleed design. These are seeded 1:17 packs. A Gold parallel version is also randomly seeded 1:210 packs.

		MT
Complete Set (9):		30.00
Common Player:		3.00
Inserted 1:17		
Gold:		2X
Inserted 1:210		
1	Mark McGwire	6.00
2	Ken Griffey Jr.	5.00
3	Sammy Sosa	3.50
4	Nomar Garciaparra	3.50
5	Roger Clemens	3.00
6	Greg Maddux	3.00
7	Mike Piazza	4.00
8	Alex Rodriguez	5.00
9	Chipper Jones	4.00

1999 Upper Deck HoloGrFX UD Authentics

This 12-card autographed set is done on a horizontal format, with the player signature across the front of a shadow image, of the featured player in the background. These are inserted 1:431 packs.

		MT
Common Player:		8.00
Inserted 1:431		
CB	Carlos Beltran	10.00
BC	Bruce Chen	8.00
JD	J.D. Drew	20.00
AG	Alex Gonzalez	8.00
JR	Ken Griffey Jr.	100.00
CJ	Chipper Jones	60.00
GK	Gabe Kapler	10.00
MK	Mike Kinkade	8.00
CK	Corey Koskie	8.00
GL	George Lombard	8.00
RM	Ryan Minor	8.00
SM	Shane Monahan	8.00

1999 Upper Deck HoloGrFX 500 Club Piece of History

This two card collection features game-used bat chips from bats swung by Willie McCovey and Eddie Mathews embedded into each card. 350 cards of each player exist. Each player also autographed these inserts to their respective jersey numbers: McCovey (44) and Mathews (41).

	MT
	250.00
Eddie Mathews (350)	150.00
Eddie Mathews (autographed/41)	550.00
Willie McCovey (350)	120.00
Willie McCovey (autographed/44)	450.00

1999 Upper Deck MVP

Card fronts of the 220-card set feature silver foil stamping and a white border. Backs feature year-by-year statistics, a small photo of the featured player and a brief career note. MVP was distributed in 36-pack boxes, with a SRP of $1.59 for 10-card packs.

		MT
Complete Set (220):		15.00
Common Player:		.10
Silver Script:		2.5X
Inserted 1:2		
Gold Script:		25X
Production 100 sets		
Super Script:		75X
Production 25 sets		
Pack (10):		1.25
Wax Box (36):		30.00
1	Mo Vaughn	.40
2	Tim Belcher	.10
3	Jack McDowell	.10
4	Troy Glaus	.50
5	Darin Erstad	.50
6	Tim Salmon	.25
7	Jim Edmonds	.10
8	Randy Johnson	.60
9	Steve Finley	.10
10	Travis Lee	.15
11	Matt Williams	.25
12	Todd Stottlemyre	.10
13	Jay Bell	.10
14	David Dellucci	.10
15	Chipper Jones	1.50
16	Andruw Jones	.75
17	Greg Maddux	1.00
18	Tom Glavine	.15
19	Javy Lopez	.10
20	Brian Jordan	.10
21	George Lombard	.10
22	John Smoltz	.15
23	Cal Ripken Jr.	2.00
24	Charles Johnson	.10
25	Albert Belle	.30
26	Brady Anderson	.10
27	Mike Mussina	.50
28	Calvin Pickering	.10
29	Ryan Minor	.10
30	Jerry Hairston Jr.	.10
31	Nomar Garciaparra	1.25
32	Pedro Martinez	.40
33	Jason Varitek	.10
34	Troy O'Leary	.10
35	Donnie Sadler	.10
36	Mark Portugal	.10
37	John Valentin	.10
38	Kerry Wood	.35
39	Sammy Sosa	1.25
40	Mark Grace	.30
41	Henry Rodriguez	.10
42	Rod Beck	.10
43	Benito Santiago	.10
44	Kevin Tapani	.10
45	Frank Thomas	1.25
46	Mike Caruso	.10
47	Magglio Ordonez	.25
48	Paul Konerko	.10
49	Ray Durham	.10
50	Jim Parque	.10
51	Carlos Lee	.10
52	Denny Neagle	.10
53	Pete Harnisch	.10
54	Michael Tucker	.10
55	Sean Casey	.25
56	Eddie Taubensee	.10
57	Barry Larkin	.15
58	Pokey Reese	.10
59	Sandy Alomar	.10
60	Roberto Alomar	.40
61	Bartolo Colon	.10
62	Kenny Lofton	.10
63	Omar Vizquel	.10
64	Travis Fryman	.10
65	Jim Thome	.10
66	Manny Ramirez	.75
67	Jaret Wright	.10
68	Darryl Kile	.10
69	Kirt Manwaring	.10
70	Vinny Castilla	.10
71	Todd Helton	.50
72	Dante Bichette	.10
73	Larry Walker	.30
74	Derrick Gibson	.10
75	Gabe Kapler	.10
76	Dean Palmer	.10
77	Matt Anderson	.10
78	Bobby Higginson	.15
79	Damion Easley	.10
80	Tony Clark	.10
81	Juan Encarnacion	.10
82	Livan Hernandez	.10
83	Alex Gonzalez	.15
84	Preston Wilson	.10
85	Derrek Lee	.10
86	Mark Kotsay	.10
87	Todd Dunwoody	.10
88	Cliff Floyd	.10
89	Ken Caminiti	.10
90	Jeff Bagwell	.75
91	Moises Alou	.20
92	Craig Biggio	.15
93	Billy Wagner	.10
94	Richard Hidalgo	.10
95	Derek Bell	.10
96	Hipolito Pichardo	.10
97	Jeff King	.10
98	Carlos Beltran	.15
99	Jeremy Giambi	.10
100	Larry Sutton	.10
101	Johnny Damon	.15
102	Dee Brown	.10
103	Kevin Brown	.15
104	Chan Ho Park	.15
105	Raul Mondesi	.20
106	Eric Karros	.10
107	Adrian Beltre	.20
108	Devon White	.10
109	Gary Sheffield	.30
110	Sean Berry	.10
111	Alex Ochoa	.10
112	Marquis Grissom	.10
113	Fernando Vina	.10
114	Jeff Cirillo	.10
115	Geoff Jenkins	.10
116	Jeromy Burnitz	.10
117	Brad Radke	.10
118	Eric Milton	.10
119	A.J. Pierzynski	.10
120	Todd Walker	.15
121	David Ortiz	.10
122	Corey Koskie	.10
123	Vladimir Guerrero	.75
124	Rondell White	.15
125	Brad Fullmer	.10
126	Ugueth Urbina	.10
127	Dustin Hermanson	.10
128	Michael Barrett	.15
129	Fernando Seguignol	.10
130	Mike Piazza	1.50
131	Rickey Henderson	.50
132	Rey Ordonez	.10
133	John Olerud	.10
134	Robin Ventura	.10
135	Hideo Nomo	.40
136	Mike Kinkade	.10
137	Al Leiter	.10
138	Brian McRae	.10
139	Derek Jeter	1.50
140	Bernie Williams	.20
141	Paul O'Neill	.10
142	Scott Brosius	.10
143	Tino Martinez	.10
144	Roger Clemens	1.00
145	Orlando Hernandez	.40
146	Mariano Rivera	.20
147	Ricky Ledee	.10
148	A.J. Hinch	.10
149	Ben Grieve	.25
150	Eric Chavez	.25
151	Miguel Tejada	.25
152	Matt Stairs	.10
153	Ryan Christenson	.10
154	Jason Giambi	.35
155	Curt Schilling	.20
156	Scott Rolen	.50
157	*Pat Burrell*	2.00
158	Doug Glanville	.10
159	Bobby Abreu	.15
160	Rico Brogna	.10
161	Ron Gant	.10
162	Jason Kendall	.10
163	Aramis Ramirez	.10
164	Jose Guillen	.10
165	Emil Brown	.10
166	Pat Meares	.10
167	Kevin Young	.10
168	Brian Giles	.10
169	Mark McGwire	2.00
170	J.D. Drew	.40
171	Edgar Renteria	.10
172	Fernando Tatis	.10
173	Matt Morris	.10
174	Eli Marrero	.10
175	Ray Lankford	.10
176	Tony Gwynn	1.00
177	Sterling Hitchcock	.10
178	Ruben Rivera	.10
179	Wally Joyner	.10
180	Trevor Hoffman	.10
181	Jim Leyritz	.10

182	Carlos Hernandez	.10
183	Barry Bonds	1.25
184	Ellis Burks	.10
185	F.P. Santangelo	.10
186	J.T. Snow	.10
187	Ramon Martinez	.10
188	Jeff Kent	.10
189	Robb Nen	.10
190	Ken Griffey Jr.	1.75
191	Alex Rodriguez	1.75
192	Shane Monahan	.10
193	Carlos Guillen	.10
194	Edgar Martinez	.10
195	David Segui	.10
196	Jose Mesa	.10
197	Jose Canseco	.50
198	Rolando Arrojo	.10
199	Wade Boggs	.50
200	Fred McGriff	.10
201	Quinton McCracken	.10
202	Bobby Smith	.10
203	Bubba Trammell	.10
204	Juan Gonzalez	.75
205	Ivan Rodriguez	.60
206	Rafael Palmeiro	.30
207	Royce Clayton	.10
208	Rick Helling	.10
209	Todd Zeile	.10
210	Rusty Greer	.10
211	David Wells	.15
212	Roy Halladay	.10
213	Carlos Delgado	.25
214	Darrin Fletcher	.10
215	Shawn Green	.25
216	Kevin Witt	.10
217	Jose Cruz Jr.	.25
218	Checklist (Ken Griffey Jr.)	.90
219	Checklist (Sammy Sosa)	.65
220	Checklist (Mark McGwire)	1.00

1999 Upper Deck MVP Scripts/ Super Scripts

Three different parallels of the 220 base cards in MVP are inserted bearing a metallic-foil facsimile autograph on front. Silver Script cards are found about every other pack. Gold Script cards are hobby-only and serially numbered to 100 apiece. Also hobby-only are Super Script versions on which the autograph is in holographic foil and the cards are numbered on the back to 25 apiece.

	MT
Silver Script:	2.5X
Gold Script:	25X
Super Script:	75X

(See 1999 UD MVP for checklist and base card values.)

1999 Upper Deck MVP All-Star Game

In conjunction with FanFest held in Boston prior to the All-Star Game, UD issued a set of specially marked versions of its MVP issue. It was reported that 15,000 three-card packs were distributed at the show, with some cards are reportedly short-printed. The cards have a format virtually identical to the regular-issue MVP cards, except for the presence on front of a bright silver-foil All-Star logo and an AS prefix to the card number on back.

		MT
Complete Set (30):		12.50
Common Player:		.25
1	Mo Vaughn	.25
2	Randy Johnson	.40
3	Chipper Jones	1.25
4	Greg Maddux	.75
5	Cal Ripken Jr.	2.00
6	Albert Belle	.25
7	Nomar Garciaparra	1.00
8	Pedro Martinez	.40
9	Sammy Sosa	1.00
10	Frank Thomas	1.00
11	Sean Casey	.35
12	Roberto Alomar	.25
13	Manny Ramirez	.50
14	Larry Walker	.25
15	Jeff Bagwell	.50
16	Craig Biggio	.25
17	Raul Mondesi	.25
18	Vladimir Guerrero	.50
19	Mike Piazza	1.25
20	Derek Jeter	1.25
21	Roger Clemens	.75
22	Scott Rolen	.40
23	Mark McGwire	2.00
24	Tony Gwynn	.75
25	Barry Bonds	1.00
26	Ken Griffey Jr.	1.50
27	Alex Rodriguez	1.50
28	Jose Canseco	.40
29	Juan Gonzalez	.50
30	Ivan Rodriguez	.40

1999 Upper Deck MVP Dynamics

This 15-card set features holofoil treatment on the card fronts with silver foil stamping. Card backs are numbered with a "D" prefix and are inserted 1:28 packs.

		MT
Complete Set (15):		45.00
Common Player:		1.50
Inserted 1:28		
1	Ken Griffey Jr.	5.50
2	Alex Rodriguez	5.50
3	Nomar Garciaparra	4.00
4	Mike Piazza	4.50
5	Mark McGwire	7.00
6	Sammy Sosa	4.00
7	Chipper Jones	4.50
8	Mo Vaughn	1.50
9	Tony Gwynn	3.50
10	Vladimir Guerrero	2.50
11	Derek Jeter	4.50
12	Jeff Bagwell	2.50
13	Cal Ripken Jr.	7.00
14	Juan Gonzalez	2.50
15	J.D. Drew	1.50

1999 Upper Deck MVP Game Used Souvenirs

This 10-card set have a piece of game-used bat from the featured player embedded into each card. These are found exclusively in hobby packs at a rate of 1:144 packs.

		MT
Complete Set (9):		200.00
Common Player:		15.00
Inserted 1:144		
JB	Jeff Bagwell	15.00
BB	Barry Bonds	45.00
JD	J.D. Drew	25.00
KGj	Ken Griffey Jr.	45.00
CJ	Chipper Jones	25.00
MP	Mike Piazza	30.00
CR	Cal Ripken Jr.	45.00
SR	Scott Rolen	15.00
MV	Mo Vaughn	15.00

1999 Upper Deck MVP Signed Game Used Souvenirs

Ken Griffey Jr. and Chipper Jones both signed their Game Used Souvenir inserts to their jersey number, Griffey (24) and Jones (10). These were seeded exclusively in hobby packs.

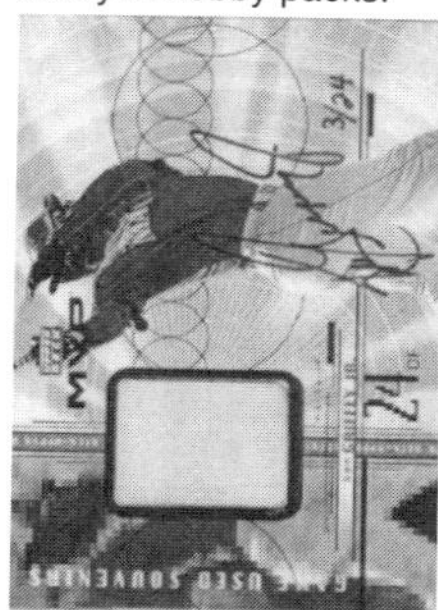

		MT
KGj	Ken Griffey Jr.	350.00
CJ	Chipper Jones	250.00

1999 Upper Deck MVP Power Surge

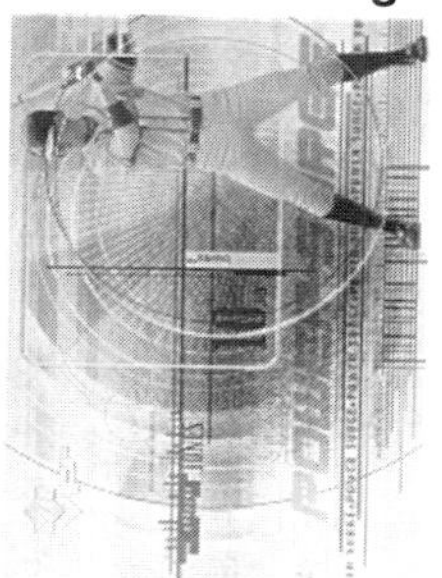

This 15-card set features baseball's top home run hitters, utilizing rainbow foil technology. Card backs are numbered with a "P" prefix and are seeded 1:9 packs.

		MT
Complete Set (15):		30.00
Common Player:		1.00
Inserted 1:9		
1	Mark McGwire	5.00
2	Sammy Sosa	2.50
3	Ken Griffey Jr.	4.00
4	Alex Rodriguez	4.00
5	Juan Gonzalez	1.50
6	Nomar Garciaparra	2.50
7	Vladimir Guerrero	1.50
8	Chipper Jones	3.00
9	Albert Belle	1.00
10	Frank Thomas	2.50
11	Mike Piazza	3.00
12	Jeff Bagwell	1.50
13	Manny Ramirez	1.50
14	Mo Vaughn	1.25
15	Barry Bonds	2.50

1999 Upper Deck MVP ProSign

This 30-card autographed set is randomly seeded exclusively in retail packs at a rate of 1:216 packs. Card backs are numbered with the featured player's initials.

		MT
Common Player:		3.00
Inserted 1:216 R		
MA	Matt Anderson	4.50
CB	Carlos Beltran	4.50
RB	Russ Branyan	6.00
EC	Eric Chavez	6.00
BC	Bruce Chen	3.00
BF	Brad Fuller	4.50
NG	Nomar Garciaparra	40.00
JG	Jeremy Giambi	4.50
DG	Derrick Gibson	4.50
CG	Chris Gomez	3.00
AG	Alex Gonzalez	4.50
BG	Ben Grieve	9.00
JR.	Ken Griffey Jr.	80.00
RH	Richard Hidalgo	4.50
SH	Shea Hillenbrand	15.00
CJ	Chipper Jones	35.00
GK	Gabe Kapler	6.00
SK	Scott Karl	3.00
CK	Corey Koskie	4.50
RL	Ricky Ledee	3.00
ML	Mike Lincoln	3.00
GL	George Lombard	3.00
MLo	Mike Lowell	6.00
RM	Ryan Minor	4.50
SM	Shane Monahan	3.00
AN	Abraham Nunez	6.00
JP	Jim Parque	3.00
CP	Calvin Pickering	3.00
JRa	Jason Rakers	3.00
RR	Ruben Rivera	3.00
IR	Ivan Rodriguez	25.00
KW	Kevin Witt	3.00

1999 Upper Deck MVP Scout's Choice

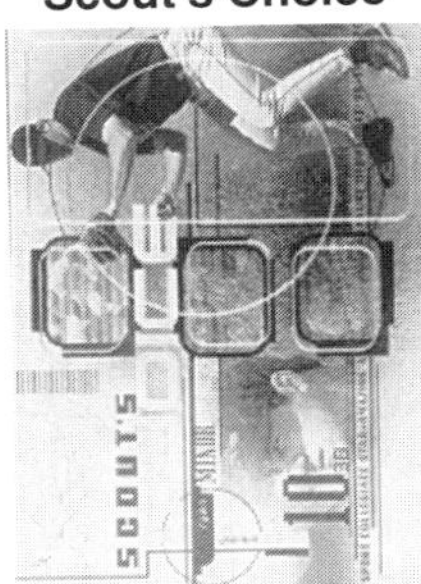

Utilizing Light F/X technology, this 15-card set highlights the top young prospects in the game. Card backs are numbered with a "SC" prefix and are seeded 1:9 packs.

		MT
Complete Set (15):		6.00
Common Player:		.25
Inserted 1:9		
1	J.D. Drew	.75
2	Ben Grieve	.50
3	Troy Glaus	1.00
4	Gabe Kapler	.25
5	Carlos Beltran	.25
6	Aramis Ramirez	.25
7	Pat Burrell	1.50
8	Kerry Wood	.75
9	Ryan Minor	.25
10	Todd Helton	.65
11	Eric Chavez	.50
12	Russ Branyon	.25
13	Travis Lee	.25
14	Ruben Mateo	.25
15	Roy Halladay	.25

1999 Upper Deck MVP Super Tools

This 15-card insert set focuses on baseball's top stars and utilizes holo foil technology on the card fronts. Card backs are numbered with a "T" prefix and are seeded 1:14 packs.

		MT
Complete Set (15):		30.00
Common Player:		.50
Inserted 1:14		
1	Ken Griffey Jr.	4.50
2	Alex Rodriguez	4.50
3	Sammy Sosa	3.00
4	Derek Jeter	3.50
5	Vladimir Guerrero	2.00
6	Ben Grieve	1.00
7	Mike Piazza	3.50
8	Kenny Lofton	.50
9	Barry Bonds	3.00
10	Darin Erstad	1.00
11	Nomar Garciaparra	3.00
12	Cal Ripken Jr.	5.00
13	J.D. Drew	1.50
14	Larry Walker	.75
15	Chipper Jones	3.50

1999 Upper Deck MVP Swing Time

This 12-card set focuses on top hitters in the game and points out three aspects why the featured player is such a successful hitter. Printed on a full foiled front these are seeded 1:6 packs. Card backs are numbered with a "S" prefix.

		MT
Complete Set (12):		22.50
Common Player:		1.00
Inserted 1:6		
1	Ken Griffey Jr.	3.00
2	Mark McGwire	3.50
3	Sammy Sosa	2.00
4	Tony Gwynn	1.50
5	Alex Rodriguez	3.00
6	Nomar Garciaparra	2.00
7	Barry Bonds	2.00
8	Frank Thomas	2.00
9	Chipper Jones	2.50
10	Ivan Rodriguez	1.00
11	Mike Piazza	2.50
12	Derek Jeter	2.50

1999 Upper Deck MVP 500 Club Piece of History

This insert has a piece of game-used bat once swung by Mike Schmidt embedded into each card. A total of 350 of this insert was produced. Schmidt also signed 20 of the inserts.

	MT
Mike Schmidt (350)	160.00
Mike Schmidt (autographed/20)	600.00

1999 Upper Deck Ovation

Cards 1-60 in the base set have the look and feel of an actual baseball. A player photo is in the foreground with a partial image of a baseball in the background on the card front. Cards 61-90 make up two subsets: World Premiere (61-80) is a 20-card collection consisting of 20 rookie prospects and Superstar Spotlight (81-90) is a 10-card lineup of baseball's biggest stars. Both subsets are short-printed, World Premiere are seeded 1:3.5 packs and Superstar Spotlight 1:6 packs. Five card packs carry a S.R.P. of $3.99 per pack.

		MT
Complete Set (90):		60.00
Common Player:		.20
Common World Premiere:		.50
Inserted 1:3.5		
Common Superstar Spotlight:		1.00
Inserted 1:6		
Pack (5):		2.50
Wax Box (20):		45.00
1	Ken Griffey Jr.	2.00
2	Rondell White	.25
3	Tony Clark	.20
4	Barry Bonds	1.25
5	Larry Walker	.40
6	Greg Vaughn	.20
7	Mark Grace	.30
8	John Olerud	.20
9	Matt Williams	.40
10	Craig Biggio	.25
11	Quinton McCracken	.20
12	Kerry Wood	.45
13	Derek Jeter	1.50
14	Frank Thomas	1.25
15	Tino Martinez	.20
16	Albert Belle	.35
17	Ben Grieve	.35
18	Cal Ripken Jr.	2.50
19	Johnny Damon	.25
20	Jose Cruz Jr.	.30
21	Barry Larkin	.25
22	Jason Giambi	.40
23	Sean Casey	.40
24	Scott Rolen	.60
25	Jim Thome	.20
26	Curt Schilling	.30
27	Moises Alou	.30
28	Alex Rodriguez	2.00
29	Mark Kotsay	.20
30	Darin Erstad	.40
31	Mike Mussina	.50
32	Todd Walker	.20
33	Nomar Garciaparra	1.25
34	Vladimir Guerrero	.75
35	Jeff Bagwell	.75
36	Mark McGwire	2.50
37	Travis Lee	.25
38	Dean Palmer	.20
39	Fred McGriff	.20
40	Sammy Sosa	1.25
41	Mike Piazza	1.50
42	Andres Galarraga	.20
43	Pedro Martinez	.60
44	Juan Gonzalez	.75
45	Greg Maddux	1.00
46	Jeromy Burnitz	.20
47	Roger Clemens	1.00
48	Vinny Castilla	.20
49	Kevin Brown	.25
50	Mo Vaughn	.45
51	Raul Mondesi	.25
52	Randy Johnson	.60
53	Ray Lankford	.20
54	Jaret Wright	.20
55	Tony Gwynn	1.00
56	Chipper Jones	1.50
57	Gary Sheffield	.35
58	Ivan Rodriguez	.60
59	Kenny Lofton	.20
60	Jason Kendall	.20
61	J.D. Drew (World Premiere)	1.00
62	Gabe Kapler (World Premiere)	.75
63	Adrian Beltre (World Premiere)	.75
64	Carlos Beltran (World Premiere)	.75
65	Eric Chavez (World Premiere)	.75
66	Mike Lowell (World Premiere)	.50

67	Troy Glaus (World Premiere)	2.00
68	George Lombard (World Premiere)	.50
69	Alex Gonzalez (World Premiere)	.50
70	Mike Kinkade (World Premiere)	.75
71	Jeremy Giambi (World Premiere)	.65
72	Bruce Chen (World Premiere)	.50
73	Preston Wilson (World Premiere)	.75
74	Kevin Witt (World Premiere)	.50
75	Carlos Guillen (World Premiere)	.50
76	Ryan Minor (World Premiere)	.75
77	Corey Koskie (World Premiere)	.50
78	Robert Fick (World Premiere)	.50
79	Michael Barrett (World Premiere)	1.00
80	Calvin Pickering (World Premiere)	.50
81	Ken Griffey Jr. (Superstar Spotlight)	2.50
82	Mark McGwire (Superstar Spotlight)	3.00
83	Cal Ripken Jr. (Superstar Spotlight)	3.00
84	Derek Jeter (Superstar Spotlight)	2.00
85	Chipper Jones (Superstar Spotlight)	2.00
86	Nomar Garciapparra (Garciaparra) (Superstar Spotlight)	1.50
87	Sammy Sosa (Superstar Spotlight)	1.50
88	Juan Gonzalez (Superstar Spotlight)	1.00
89	Mike Piazza (Superstar Spotlight)	2.00
90	Alex Rodriguez (Superstar Spotlight)	2.50

1999 Upper Deck Ovation Standing Ovation

	MT
Common Player:	1.50
Stars (1-60):	2X
World Premiere (61-80):	1.5X
Superstar Spotlight (81-90):	2X
Production 500 sets	

(See 1999 Upper Deck Ovation for checklist and base card values.)

1999 Upper Deck Ovation Curtain Calls

This 20-card set focuses on the most memorable accomplishments posted during the '98 season. Card fronts have two images of the player, one on the right half and a smaller image on the bottom left. Copper foil stamping is used to enhance the card front. These are numbered with a R-prefix and are seeded 1:8 packs.

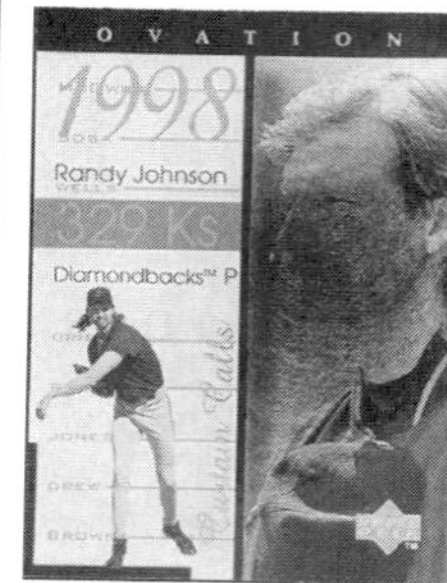

		MT
Complete Set (20):		30.00
Common Player:		.40
Inserted 1:8		
R1	Mark McGwire	4.00
R2	Sammy Sosa	2.50
R3	Ken Griffey Jr.	3.50
R4	Alex Rodriguez	3.50
R5	Roger Clemens	2.00
R6	Cal Ripken Jr.	4.00
R7	Barry Bonds	2.50
R8	Kerry Wood	.60
R9	Nomar Garciaparra	2.50
R10	Derek Jeter	3.00
R11	Juan Gonzalez	1.50
R12	Greg Maddux	2.00
R13	Pedro Martinez	1.00
R14	David Wells	.40
R15	Moises Alou	.40
R16	Tony Gwynn	2.00
R17	Albert Belle	.60
R18	Mike Piazza	3.00
R19	Ivan Rodriguez	1.00
R20	Randy Johnson	1.00

1999 Upper Deck Ovation Major Production

This 20-card set utilizes thermography technology to simulate the look and feel of home plate and highlights some of the game's most productive players. These are inserted 1:45 packs and are numbered with a S prefix.

		MT
Complete Set (20):		55.00
Common Player:		1.00
Inserted 1:45		
S1	Mike Piazza	5.00
S2	Mark McGwire	7.50
S3	Chipper Jones	5.00
S4	Cal Ripken Jr.	7.50
S5	Ken Griffey Jr.	6.00
S6	Barry Bonds	4.00
S7	Tony Gwynn	3.00
S8	Randy Johnson	1.50
S9	Ivan Rodriguez	1.50
S10	Frank Thomas	4.00
S11	Alex Rodriguez	6.00
S12	Albert Belle	1.25
S13	Juan Gonzalez	2.00
S14	Greg Maddux	3.00
S15	Jeff Bagwell	2.00
S16	Derek Jeter	5.00
S17	Matt Williams	1.00
S18	Kenny Lofton	1.00
S19	Sammy Sosa	4.00
S20	Roger Clemens	3.00

1999 Upper Deck Ovation Piece of History

This 14-card set has actual pieces of game-used bat, from the featured player, imbedded into the card. These are inserted 1:247 packs. Ben Grieve autographed 25 versions of his Piece of History insert cards. Although there is no regular Piece of History Kerry Wood card, Upper Deck inserted 25 autographed Piece of History game-used baseball cards. These have a piece of one of Wood's game-hurled baseballs from the 1998 season.

		MT
Common Player:		10.00
Inserted 1:247		
BB	Barry Bonds	35.00
CJ	Chipper Jones	25.00
BW	Bernie Williams	15.00
KGj	Ken Griffey Jr.	40.00
NG	Nomar Garciaparra	50.00
JG	Juan Gonzalez	15.00
DJ	Derek Jeter	50.00
SS	Sammy Sosa	40.00
TG	Tony Gwynn	20.00
AR	Alex Rodriguez	35.00
CR	Cal Ripken Jr.	50.00
BG	Ben Grieve	10.00
VG	Vladimir Guerrero	25.00
MP	Mike Piazza	40.00
BGAU	Ben Grieve (autographed/25)	75.00
KWAU	Kerry Wood (autographed/25)	100.00

1999 Upper Deck Ovation ReMarkable

This three-tiered 15-card insert showcases Mark McGwire's historic '98 season. Cards #1-5 are Bronze and inserted 1:9 packs; cards #6-10 are Silver and inserted 1:25 packs; and cards #11-15 are Gold and inserted 1:99 packs.

		MT
Complete Set (15):		50.00
Common #1-5:		2.00
Inserted 1:9		
Common #6-10:		4.00
Inserted 1:25		
Common # 11-15		8.00
Inserted 1:99		
MM1	Mark McGwire	2.00
MM2	Mark McGwire	2.00
MM3	Mark McGwire	2.00
MM4	Mark McGwire	2.00
MM5	Mark McGwire	2.00
MM6	Mark McGwire	4.00
MM7	Mark McGwire	4.00
MM8	Mark McGwire	4.00
MM9	Mark McGwire	4.00
MM10	Mark McGwire	4.00
MM11	Mark McGwire	8.00
MM12	Mark McGwire	8.00
MM13	Mark McGwire	8.00
MM14	Mark McGwire	8.00
MM15	Mark McGwire	8.00

1999 Upper Deck Ovation 500 Club Piece of History

Each of these cards actually has a piece of game-used Louisville Slugger, once swung by Mickey Mantle, embedded. Approximately 350 cards exist. There is also one card with a cut signature of Mantle and a piece of his game-used bat on it.

		MT
MIC-P	Mickey Mantle (350)	700.00
	Mickey Mantle (bat/autograph, 6/01 auction)	8000.

1999 Upper Deck PowerDeck

This 25-card set is comprised of 25 digital PowerDeck interactive trading cards, complete with video and audio content. There is also a parallel "paper" version of the base set called Auxiliary Power. Each digital card includes 32 megabytes of information and is compatible with almost any internet ready computer. One PowerDeck digital card comes in every three-card pack.

		MT
Complete Set (25):		60.00
Common Player:		1.50
Pack (3):		2.00
Wax Box (24):		40.00
1	Ken Griffey Jr.	5.50
2	Mark McGwire	7.00
3	Cal Ripken Jr.	7.00
4	Sammy Sosa	4.00
5	Derek Jeter	4.50
6	Mike Piazza	4.50
7	Nomar Garciaparra	4.00
8	Greg Maddux	3.50
9	Tony Gwynn	3.50
10	Roger Clemens	3.50
11	Scott Rolen	1.75
12	Alex Rodriguez	5.50
13	Manny Ramirez	2.25
14	Chipper Jones	4.50
15	Juan Gonzalez	2.25
16	Ivan Rodriguez	1.75
17	Frank Thomas	4.00
18	Mo Vaughn	1.50
19	Barry Bonds	4.00
20	Vladimir Guerrero	2.25
21	Jose Canseco	1.50
22	Jeff Bagwell	2.25
23	Pedro Martinez	1.75
24	Gabe Kapler	1.50
25	J.D. Drew	1.50
	Checklist card	.10

1999 Upper Deck PowerDeck Auxiliary Power

A "paper" parallel version of the 25-card digital set. These have a horizontal format with silver-foil graphics. Backs repeat the front portrait photo along with the player's past five years of statistics and a brief career highlight. Card numbers are prefixed with "AUX-"

		MT
Complete Set (25):		12.50
Common Player:		.25
1	Ken Griffey Jr.	1.25
2	Mark McGwire	1.50
3	Cal Ripken Jr.	1.50
4	Sammy Sosa	.75
5	Derek Jeter	1.00
6	Mike Piazza	1.00
7	Nomar Garciaparra	.75
8	Greg Maddux	.65
9	Tony Gwynn	.65
10	Roger Clemens	.65
11	Scott Rolen	.40
12	Alex Rodriguez	1.25
13	Manny Ramirez	.50
14	Chipper Jones	1.00
15	Juan Gonzalez	.50
16	Ivan Rodriguez	.40
17	Frank Thomas	.75
18	Mo Vaughn	.25
19	Barry Bonds	.75
20	Vladimir Guerrero	.50
21	Jose Canseco	.40
22	Jeff Bagwell	.50
23	Pedro Martinez	.40
24	Gabe Kapler	.25
25	J.D. Drew	.25

1999 Upper Deck PowerDeck A Season to Remember

This special box-topper CD insert presents audio-visual highlights of the 1999 season, featuring players like David Cone, Ken Griffey, Jr., Mark McGwire, Tony Gwynn, Wade Boggs, Sammy Sosa and Cal Ripken, Jr. McGwire is pictured on this CD hitting his 500th home run.

	MT
Mark McGwire	3.00

1999 Upper Deck PowerDeck Most Valuable Performances

This seven-card digital insert set consists of capturing true MVP performances from some of baseball's greatest players. These were seeded 1:287 packs.

		MT
Complete Set (7):		125.00
Common Player:		12.50
Inserted 1:287		
1	Sammy Sosa	25.00
2	Barry Bonds	20.00
3	Cal Ripken Jr.	30.00
4	Juan Gonzalez	12.50
5	Ken Griffey Jr.	25.00
6	Roger Clemens	17.50
7	Mark McGwire, Sammy Sosa	30.00

1999 Upper Deck PowerDeck MVP Auxiliary

A "paper" parallel version of the digital set, these also were inserted 1:287 packs. They have a horizontal format using silver holofoil and also have different photos from the digital version.

		MT
Complete Set (7):		80.00
Common Player:		7.50
Inserted 1:287		
1	Sammy Sosa	12.50
2	Barry Bonds	12.50
3	Cal Ripken Jr.	20.00
4	Juan Gonzalez	7.50
5	Ken Griffey Jr.	15.00
6	Roger Clemens	10.00
7	Mark McGwire, Sammy Sosa	20.00

1999 Upper Deck PowerDeck Powerful Moments

This six-card digital interactive set has game-action footage pinpointing specific milestones in each of the featured players' careers. These were inserted 1:7 packs.

		MT
Complete Set (6):		30.00
Common Player:		4.00
Inserted 1:7		
1	Mark McGwire	7.50
2	Sammy Sosa	4.00
3	Cal Ripken Jr.	7.50
4	Ken Griffey Jr.	6.00
5	Derek Jeter	5.00
6	Alex Rodriguez	6.00

1999 Upper Deck PowerDeck Powerful Moments Auxiliary

This "paper" parallel version of the digital set is also inserted 1:7 packs on a horizontal format. Different photos were used from the digital set.

		MT
Complete Set (6):		16.00
Common Player:		2.50
Inserted 1:7		
Gold (one each): VALUE UNDETERMINED		
1	Mark McGwire	4.00
2	Sammy Sosa	2.50
3	Cal Ripken Jr.	4.00
4	Ken Griffey Jr.	3.50
5	Derek Jeter	3.00
6	Alex Rodriguez	3.50

1999 Upper Deck PowerDeck Time Capsule

Five previous MLB Rookies of the Year are honored in this digital set with the digital content going back to the rookie seasons of the featured players. These were seeded 1:23 packs.

		MT
Complete Set (6):		30.00
Common Player:		3.00
Inserted 1:23		
1	Ken Griffey Jr.	7.50
2	Mike Piazza	6.00
3	Mark McGwire	9.00
4	Derek Jeter	6.00
5	Jose Canseco	3.00
6	Nomar Garciaparra	5.00

1999 Upper Deck PowerDeck Time Capsule-Auxiliary Power

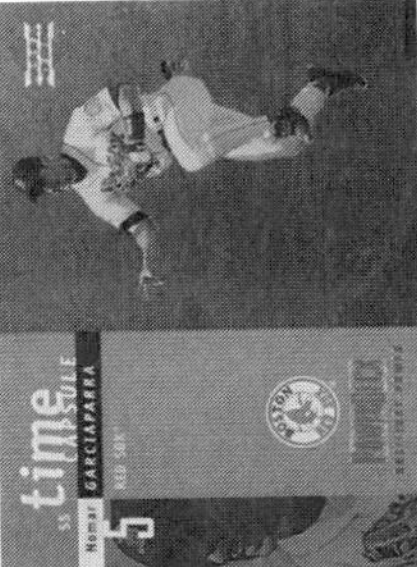

This "paper' parallel set of the digital version utilizes a similar design as the digital insert and uses different photos as well. Horizontal fronts have a thin vertical monochromatic portrait at left. At right is an action photos set on a metallized background. Backs repeat the front portrait and have a screen simulation along with stats and data. These were inserted 1:23 packs.

		MT
Complete Set (6):		22.50
Common Player:		2.50
Inserted 1:23		
Gold (one of each): VALUES UNDETERMINED		
1	Ken Griffey Jr.	6.00
2	Mike Piazza	4.00
3	Mark McGwire	7.50
4	Derek Jeter	4.00
5	Jose Canseco	2.50
6	Nomar Garciaparra	3.00

1999 Upper Deck Ultimate Victory

The 180-card base set includes two 30-card short-printed (1:4) subsets: McGwire Magic (151-180) and 1999 Rookie (121-150). The base cards have a silver foil border with the featured players' last five seasons of statistics along with a brief career highlight. There are two parallels randomly inserted: Victory Collection and Ultimate Collection. Victory Collection are seeded 1:12 packs with a holographic, prismatic look. Ultimate Collection have a gold holographic, prismatic look and are serially numbered "xxx/100" on the card front.

		MT
Complete Set (180):		200.00
Common Player:		.15
Common 99 Rookie (121-150):		1.00
Common McGwire Magic (151-180):		1.00
Victory (1-120):		3X
Victory SP (121-180):		2X
Inserted 1:12		
Ultimate (1-120):		12X
Ultimate SP (121-180):		4X
Production 100 sets		
Pack (5):		5.00
Wax Box (24):		150.00
1	Troy Glaus	1.00
2	Tim Salmon	.30
3	Mo Vaughn	.45
4	Garret Anderson	.15
5	Darin Erstad	.50
6	Randy Johnson	.75
7	Matt Williams	.30
8	Travis Lee	.25
9	Jay Bell	.15
10	Steve Finley	.15
11	Luis Gonzalez	.40
12	Greg Maddux	1.50
13	Chipper Jones	2.50
14	Javy Lopez	.15
15	Tom Glavine	.25
16	John Smoltz	.25
17	Cal Ripken Jr.	4.00
18	Charles Johnson	.15
19	Albert Belle	.35
20	Mike Mussina	.65
21	Pedro Martinez	1.00
22	Nomar Garciaparra	2.00
23	Jose Offerman	.15
24	Sammy Sosa	2.00
25	Mark Grace	.40
26	Kerry Wood	.45
27	Frank Thomas	2.00
28	Ray Durham	.15
29	Paul Konerko	.15
30	Pete Harnisch	.15
31	Greg Vaughn	.15
32	Sean Casey	.35
33	Manny Ramirez	1.25
34	Jim Thome	.15
35	Sandy Alomar	.15
36	Roberto Alomar	.75
37	Travis Fryman	.15
38	Kenny Lofton	.15
39	Omar Vizquel	.15
40	Larry Walker	.40
41	Todd Helton	.75
42	Vinny Castilla	.15
43	Tony Clark	.15
44	Juan Encarnacion	.15
45	Dean Palmer	.15
46	Damion Easley	.15
47	Mark Kotsay	.15
48	Cliff Floyd	.15
49	Jeff Bagwell	1.25
50	Ken Caminiti	.15
51	Craig Biggio	.25
52	Moises Alou	.30
53	Johnny Damon	.25
54	Larry Sutton	.15
55	Kevin Brown	.25
56	Adrian Beltre	.35
57	Raul Mondesi	.25
58	Gary Sheffield	.40
59	Jeromy Burnitz	.15
60	Sean Berry	.15
61	Jeff Cirillo	.15
62	Brad Radke	.15
63	Todd Walker	.15
64	Matt Lawton	.15
65	Vladimir Guerrero	1.25
66	Rondell White	.25
67	Dustin Hermanson	.15
68	Mike Piazza	2.50
69	Rickey Henderson	.65
70	Robin Ventura	.15
71	John Olerud	.15
72	Derek Jeter	2.50
73	Roger Clemens	1.50
74	Orlando Hernandez	.35
75	Paul O'Neill	.15
76	Bernie Williams	.30
77	Chuck Knoblauch	.15
78	Tino Martinez	.15
79	Jason Giambi	.40
80	Ben Grieve	.25
81	Matt Stairs	.15
82	Scott Rolen	.75
83	Ron Gant	.15
84	Bobby Abreu	.25
85	Curt Schilling	.25
86	Brian Giles	.15
87	Jason Kendall	.15
88	Kevin Young	.15
89	Mark McGwire	4.00
90	Fernando Tatis	.15
91	Ray Lankford	.15
92	Eric Davis	.15
93	Tony Gwynn	1.50
94	Reggie Sanders	.15
95	Wally Joyner	.15
96	Trevor Hoffman	.15
97	Robb Nen	.15
98	Barry Bonds	2.00
99	Jeff Kent	.15
100	J.T. Snow	.15
101	Ellis Burks	.15
102	Ken Griffey Jr.	3.00
103	Alex Rodriguez	3.00
104	Jay Buhner	.15
105	Edgar Martinez	.15
106	David Bell	.15
107	Bobby Smith	.15
108	Wade Boggs	.65
109	Fred McGriff	.15
110	Rolando Arrojo	.15
111	Jose Canseco	.75
112	Ivan Rodriguez	1.00
113	Juan Gonzalez	1.25
114	Rafael Palmeiro	.30
115	Rusty Greer	.15
116	Todd Zeile	.15
117	Jose Cruz Jr.	.25
118	Carlos Delgado	.25
119	Shawn Green	.30
120	David Wells	.25
121	*Eric Munson* (99 Rookie)	6.00
122	Lance Berkman (99 Rookie)	5.00
123	Ed Yarnall (99 Rookie)	1.00
124	Jacque Jones (99 Rookie)	2.00
125	Kyle Farnsworth (99 Rookie)	1.00
126	Ryan Rupe (99 Rookie)	1.00
127	*Jeff Weaver* (99 Rookie)	4.00
128	Gabe Kapler (99 Rookie)	2.00
129	Alex Gonzalez (99 Rookie)	1.00
130	Randy Wolf (99 Rookie)	1.00
131	Ben Davis (99 Rookie)	1.00
132	Carlos Beltran (99 Rookie)	1.00
133	Jim Morris (99 Rookie)	4.00
134	Jeff Zimmerman (99 Rookie)	1.00
135	Bruce Aven (99 Rookie)	1.00
136	*Alfonso Soriano* (99 Rookie)	95.00
137	*Tim Hudson* (99 Rookie)	20.00
138	*Josh Beckett* (99 Rookie)	40.00
139	Michael Barrett (99 Rookie)	2.00
140	Eric Chavez (99 Rookie)	2.00
141	*Pat Burrell* (99 Rookie)	30.00
142	Kris Benson (99 Rookie)	1.00
143	J.D. Drew (99 Rookie)	3.00
144	Matt Clement (99 Rookie)	1.00
145	*Rick Ankiel* (99 Rookie)	15.00
146	Vernon Wells (99 Rookie)	1.00
147	Ruben Mateo (99 Rookie)	1.00
148	Roy Halladay (99 Rookie)	1.00
149	Joe McEwing (99 Rookie)	1.00
150	*Freddy Garcia* (99 Rookie)	15.00
151	Mark McGwire (McGwire Magic)	1.00
152	Mark McGwire (McGwire Magic)	1.00
153	Mark McGwire (McGwire Magic)	1.00
154	Mark McGwire (McGwire Magic)	1.00
155	Mark McGwire (McGwire Magic)	1.00
156	Mark McGwire (McGwire Magic)	1.00
157	Mark McGwire (McGwire Magic)	1.00
158	Mark McGwire (McGwire Magic)	1.00
159	Mark McGwire (McGwire Magic)	1.00
160	Mark McGwire (McGwire Magic)	1.00
161	Mark McGwire (McGwire Magic)	1.00
162	Mark McGwire (McGwire Magic)	1.00
163	Mark McGwire (McGwire Magic)	1.00
164	Mark McGwire (McGwire Magic)	1.00
165	Mark McGwire (McGwire Magic)	1.00
166	Mark McGwire (McGwire Magic)	1.00
167	Mark McGwire (McGwire Magic)	1.00
168	Mark McGwire (McGwire Magic)	1.00
169	Mark McGwire (McGwire Magic)	1.00
170	Mark McGwire (McGwire Magic)	1.00
171	Mark McGwire (McGwire Magic)	1.00
172	Mark McGwire (McGwire Magic)	1.00
173	Mark McGwire (McGwire Magic)	1.00
174	Mark McGwire (McGwire Magic)	1.00
175	Mark McGwire (McGwire Magic)	1.00
176	Mark McGwire (McGwire Magic)	1.00
177	Mark McGwire (McGwire Magic)	1.00
178	Mark McGwire (McGwire Magic)	1.00
179	Mark McGwire (McGwire Magic)	1.00
180	Mark McGwire (McGwire Magic)	1.00

1999 Upper Deck Ultimate Victory Victory Collection

This parallel of the base set features a prismatic foil design on front. The cards are found on average of one per 12 packs. A 1-of-1 edition also exists, but is not priced here due to rarity and demand variability.

	MT
Common Player (1-120, 151-180):	1.00
Common Player (121-150):	6.00
Stars (1-120):	3X
Stars (121-150):	2X

(See 1999 Ultimate Victory for checklist and base card values.)

1999 Upper Deck Ultimate Victory Ultimate Collection

This parallel insert set is individually serial numbered on front from within an edition of 100 cards each. Card fronts have silver holographic prismatic foil background and a silver-foil serial number. Backs are identical to the regular-issue cards.

	MT
Common Player (1-120, 151-180):	3.00
Common Player (121-150):	15.00
Stars (1-120):	12X
Stars (121-150):	4X

(See 1999 Upper Deck Ultimate Victory for checklist and base card values.)

1999 Upper Deck Ultimate Victory Bleacher Reachers

This 11-card set focuses on the hitters who were vying for the 1999 home run title. They have a horizontal format with a holographic foil card front. Card backs have a small photo along with his 3-year statistical totals. They are numbered with a "BR" prefix and were inserted 1:23 packs.

		MT
Complete Set (11):		20.00
Common Player:		.75
Inserted 1:23		
1	Ken Griffey Jr.	4.00
2	Mark McGwire	5.00
3	Sammy Sosa	2.00
4	Barry Bonds	2.00
5	Nomar Garciaparra	2.00
6	Juan Gonzalez	.75
7	Jose Canseco	.75
8	Manny Ramirez	.75
9	Mike Piazza	3.00
10	Jeff Bagwell	.75
11	Alex Rodriguez	4.00

1999 Upper Deck Ultimate Victory Fame-Used Memorabilia

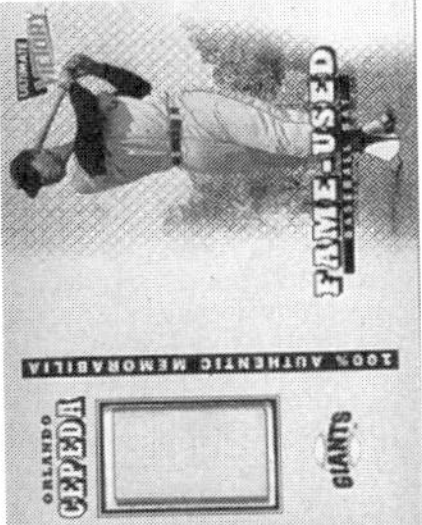

This four-card set has a piece of game-used bat embedded into each card, from either George Brett, Robin Yount, Nolan Ryan and Orlando Cepeda. A total of approximately 350 bat cards of each player was produced.

		MT
Complete Set (4):		100.00
Common Player:		12.50
Production 350 cards		
GB	George Brett	35.00
OC	Orlando Cepeda	12.50
NR	Nolan Ryan	65.00
RY	Robin Yount	20.00

1999 Upper Deck Ultimate Victory Fame-Used Combo

This insert has a piece of game-used bat from each of the 1999 Hall of Fame inductees and is limited to 99 sequentially numbered singles.

		MT
Edition of 99:		
HOF	Nolan Ryan, George Brett, Robin Yount, Orlando Cepeda	350.00

1999 Upper Deck Ultimate Victory Frozen Ropes

This 10-card set spotlights baseball's top hitters and are seeded 1:23 packs.

		MT
Complete Set (10):		22.50
Common Player:		.50
Inserted 1:23		
1	Ken Griffey Jr.	4.00
2	Mark McGwire	5.00
3	Sammy Sosa	2.50
4	Derek Jeter	3.00
5	Tony Gwynn	2.00
6	Nomar Garciaparra	2.50
7	Alex Rodriguez	4.00
8	Mike Piazza	3.00
9	Mo Vaughn	1.00
10	Craig Biggio	.50

1999 Upper Deck Ultimate Victory STATure

This 15-card set highlights players with outstanding statistical achievements. The featured stat for the player runs down the right side of the card. Fronts are printed on metallic foil with a textured pattern behind the player photo. Conventionally printed backs repeat the front design numbered with an "S" prefix. These were seeded 1:6 packs.

		MT
Complete Set (15):		8.00
Common Player:		.40
Inserted 1:6		
1	Ken Griffey Jr.	1.00
2	Mark McGwire	2.00
3	Sammy Sosa	.60
4	Nomar Garciaparra	.60
5	Roger Clemens	.50
6	Greg Maddux	.50
7	Alex Rodriguez	1.00
8	Derek Jeter	.75
9	Juan Gonzalez	.40
10	Manny Ramirez	.40
11	Mike Piazza	.75
12	Tony Gwynn	.50
13	Chipper Jones	.75
14	Pedro Martinez	.40
15	Frank Thomas	.60

1999 Upper Deck Ultimate Victory Tribute 1999

This four-card set is devoted to 1999's Hall of Fame inductees. Card fronts have a horizontal format over a holographic foil design. Card backs have the featured players' year-by-year statistics and are numbered with a "T" prefix.

		MT
Complete Set (4):		6.00
Common Player:		1.00
Inserted 1:11		
1	Nolan Ryan	3.00
2	Robin Yount	1.50
3	George Brett	2.00
4	Orlando Cepeda	1.00

1999 Upper Deck Ultimate Victory Ultimate Competitors

This 12-card set has a close-up photo, along with two miniature action photos in the foreground, all printed on silver foil. Backs repeat the front photos and have a few words about the player's competitive desire. These were seeded 1:23 packs and are numbered with a "U" prefix on the card back.

		MT
Complete Set (12):		22.50
Common Player:		.50
Inserted 1:23		
1	Ken Griffey Jr.	4.00
2	Roger Clemens	2.00
3	Scott Rolen	1.00
4	Greg Maddux	2.00
5	Mark McGwire	5.00
6	Derek Jeter	3.00
7	Randy Johnson	1.50
8	Cal Ripken Jr.	5.00
9	Craig Biggio	.50
10	Kevin Brown	.50
11	Chipper Jones	3.00
12	Vladimir Guerrero	1.50

1999 Upper Deck Ultimate Victory Ultimate Hit Men

This insert set spotlights the eight candidates who competed for the 1999 batting titles. Inserted on the average of 1:23 packs they were numbered with an "H" prefix on the card back.

		MT
Complete Set (8):		18.00
Common Player:		1.00
Inserted 1:23		
1	Tony Gwynn	2.00
2	Cal Ripken Jr.	5.00
3	Wade Boggs	1.50
4	Larry Walker	1.00
5	Alex Rodriguez	4.00
6	Derek Jeter	3.00
7	Ivan Rodriguez	1.50
8	Ken Griffey Jr.	5.00

1999 Upper Deck UD Choice

The 155-card base set consists of 110 regular player cards and two subsets, 27 Star Rookies and 18 Cover Glory subset cards. Card fronts have a white border, with the Upper Deck UD Choice logo on the bottom right of the front. Card backs have complete year-by-year stats along with some vital information. Each pack contains 12 cards. A parallel version also exists, called Prime Choice Reserve and are numbered to 100.

		MT
Complete Set (155):		15.00
Common Player:		.10
Prime Choice Reserve Stars:		60X
Production 100 sets		
Pack (12):		1.00
Wax Box (36):		30.00
1	Gabe Kapler (Rookie Class)	.25
2	Jin Ho Cho (Rookie Class)	.15
3	Matt Anderson (Rookie Class)	.10
4	Ricky Ledee (Rookie Class)	.10
5	Bruce Chen (Rookie Class)	.10
6	Alex Gonzalez (Rookie Class)	.10
7	Ryan Minor (Rookie Class)	.10
8	Michael Barrett (Rookie Class)	.15
9	Carlos Beltran (Rookie Class)	.15
10	Ramon Martinez (Rookie Class)	.10
11	Dermal Brown (Rookie Class)	.10
12	Robert Fick (Rookie Class)	.10
13	Preston Wilson (Rookie Class)	.15
14	Orlando Hernandez (Rookie Class)	.50
15	Troy Glaus (Rookie Class)	1.00
16	Calvin Pickering (Rookie Class)	.10
17	Corey Koskie (Rookie Class)	.10
18	Fernando Seguignol (Rookie Class)	.10
19	Carlos Guillen (Rookie Class)	.10
20	Kevin Witt (Rookie Class)	.10
21	Mike Kinkade (Rookie Class)	.10
22	Eric Chavez (Rookie Class)	.30
23	Mike Lowell (Rookie Class)	.10
24	Adrian Beltre (Rookie Class)	.25
25	George Lombard (Rookie Class)	.10
26	Jeremy Giambi (Rookie Class)	.10
27	J.D. Drew (Rookie Class)	.25
28	Mark McGwire (Cover Glory)	1.00
29	Kerry Wood (Cover Glory)	.40
30	David Wells (Cover Glory)	.10
31	Juan Gonzalez (Cover Glory)	.40
32	Randy Johnson (Cover Glory)	.25
33	Derek Jeter (Cover Glory)	.75
34	Tony Gwynn (Cover Glory)	.50
35	Greg Maddux (Cover Glory)	.50
36	Cal Ripken Jr. (Cover Glory)	1.00
37	Ken Griffey Jr. (Cover Glory)	.90
38	Bartolo Colon (Cover Glory)	.10
39	Troy Glaus (Cover Glory)	.25
40	Ben Grieve (Cover Glory)	.10
41	Roger Clemens (Cover Glory)	.50
42	Chipper Jones (Cover Glory)	.75
43	Scott Rolen (Cover Glory)	.20
44	Nomar Garciaparra (Cover Glory)	.65
45	Sammy Sosa (Cover Glory)	.65
46	Tim Salmon	.25
47	Darin Erstad	.50
48	Chuck Finley	.10
49	Garrett Anderson	.10
50	Matt Williams	.30
51	Jay Bell	.10
52	Travis Lee	.25
53	Andruw Jones	.75
54	Andres Galarraga	.10
55	Chipper Jones	1.50
56	Greg Maddux	1.00
57	Javy Lopez	.10
58	Cal Ripken Jr.	2.00
59	Brady Anderson	.10
60	Rafael Palmeiro	.25
61	B.J. Surhoff	.10
62	Nomar Garciaparra	1.25
63	Troy O'Leary	.10
64	Pedro Martinez	.65
65	Jason Varitek	.10
66	Kerry Wood	.50
67	Sammy Sosa	1.25
68	Mark Grace	.25
69	Mickey Morandini	.10
70	Albert Belle	.30
71	Mike Caruso	.10
72	Frank Thomas	1.25
73	Sean Casey	.25
74	Pete Harnisch	.10
75	Dmitri Young	.10
76	Manny Ramirez	.75
77	Omar Vizquel	.10
78	Travis Fryman	.10
79	Jim Thome	.10
80	Kenny Lofton	.10
81	Todd Helton	.50
82	Larry Walker	.30
83	Vinny Castilla	.10
84	Gabe Alvarez	.10
85	Tony Clark	.10
86	Damion Easley	.10
87	Livan Hernandez	.10
88	Mark Kotsay	.10
89	Cliff Floyd	.10
90	Jeff Bagwell	.75
91	Moises Alou	.20
92	Randy Johnson	.60
93	Craig Biggio	.15
94	Larry Sutton	.10
95	Dean Palmer	.10
96	Johnny Damon	.15
97	Charles Johnson	.10
98	Gary Sheffield	.20
99	Raul Mondesi	.20
100	Mark Grudzielanek	.10
101	Jeromy Burnitz	.10
102	Jeff Cirillo	.10
103	Jose Valentin	.10
104	Mark Loretta	.10
105	Todd Walker	.20
106	David Ortiz	.10
107	Brad Radke	.10
108	Brad Fullmer	.10
109	Rondell White	.20
110	Vladimir Guerrero	.75
111	Mike Piazza	1.50
112	Brian McRae	.10
113	John Olerud	.10
114	Rey Ordonez	.10
115	Derek Jeter	1.50
116	Bernie Williams	.30
117	David Wells	.15
118	Paul O'Neill	.10
119	Tino Martinez	.10
120	A.J. Hinch	.10
121	Jason Giambi	.35
122	Miguel Tejada	.15
123	Ben Grieve	.25
124	Scott Rolen	.50
125	Desi Relaford	.10
126	Bobby Abreu	.15
127	Jose Guillen	.10
128	Jason Kendall	.10
129	Aramis Ramirez	.20
130	Mark McGwire	2.00
131	Ray Lankford	.10
132	Eli Marrero	.10
133	Wally Joyner	.10
134	Greg Vaughn	.10
135	Trevor Hoffman	.10
136	Kevin Brown	.15
137	Tony Gwynn	1.00
138	Bill Mueller	.10
139	Ellis Burks	.10
140	Barry Bonds	1.50
141	Robb Nen	.10
142	Ken Griffey Jr.	1.75
143	Alex Rodriguez	1.75
144	Jay Buhner	.10
145	Edgar Martinez	.10
146	Rolando Arrojo	.10
147	Robert Smith	.10
148	Quinton McCracken	.10
149	Ivan Rodriguez	.65
150	Will Clark	.30
151	Mark McLemore	.10
152	Juan Gonzalez	.75
153	Jose Cruz Jr.	.15
154	Carlos Delgado	.25
155	Roger Clemens	1.00

1999 Upper Deck UD Choice All-Star Game '99

These super-size (3-1/2" x 5") versions of 1999 UD Choice cards were issued as a boxed set exclusively for retail outlet sales. The cards are in a format identical to the regular-issue UD Choice except for a large All-Star Game logo in one of the upper corners. Fronts have game-action photos; backs have a small portrait, major league stats and career highlights. The set was sold in a green-foil enhanced box with a special card commemorating the 1999 game July 13 in Boston.

		MT
Complete Set (21):		10.00
Common Player:		.25
1	Kenny Lofton	.25
2	Pedro Martinez	.60
3	Nomar Garciaparra	.85
4	Ken Griffey Jr.	1.25
5	Derek Jeter	1.00
6	Manny Ramirez	.65
7	Ivan Rodriguez	.60
8	Bernie Williams	.25
9	Cal Ripken Jr.	1.50
10	Jim Thome	.25
11	Mike Piazza	1.00
12	Jeff Bagwell	.65
13	Craig Biggio	.25
14	Mark McGwire	1.50
15	Matt Williams	.25
16	Chipper Jones	1.00
17	Tony Gwynn	.75
18	Sammy Sosa	.85
19	Raul Mondesi	.25
20	Larry Walker	.25
---	Header card	.05

1999 Upper Deck UD Choice Mini Bobbing Head

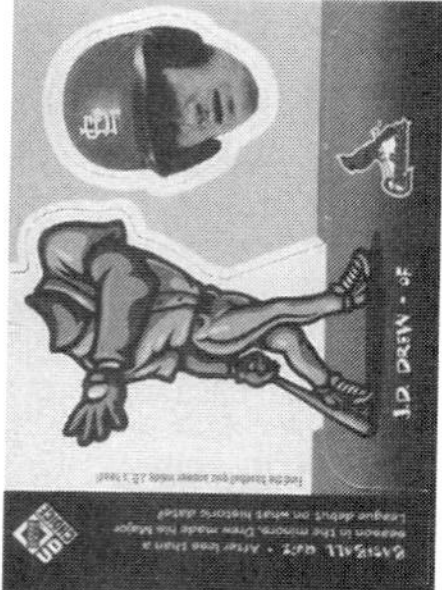

Inserted 1:5 packs, some of the game's best players can be assembled into a miniature bobbing head figure by following the instructions on the card backs.

		MT
Complete Set (30):		16.00
Common Player:		.25
Inserted 1:5		
B1	Randy Johnson	.50
B2	Troy Glaus	.50
B3	Chipper Jones	1.25
B4	Cal Ripken Jr.	2.00
B5	Nomar Garciaparra	1.00
B6	Pedro Martinez	.40
B7	Kerry Wood	.40

B8	Sammy Sosa	1.00
B9	Frank Thomas	1.00
B10	Paul Konerko	.25
B11	Omar Vizquel	.25
B12	Kenny Lofton	.25
B13	Gabe Kapler	.25
B14	Adrian Beltre	.25
B15	Orlando Hernandez	.35
B16	Derek Jeter	1.25
B17	Mike Piazza	1.25
B18	Tino Martinez	.25
B19	Ben Grieve	.35
B20	Rickey Henderson	.50
B21	Scott Rolen	.40
B22	Aramis Ramirez	.25
B23	Greg Vaughn	.25
B24	Tony Gwynn	.75
B25	Barry Bonds	1.00
B26	Alex Rodriguez	1.50
B27	Ken Griffey Jr.	1.50
B28	Mark McGwire	2.00
B29	J.D. Drew	.45
B30	Juan Gonzalez	.65

1999 Upper Deck UD Choice Piece of History 500 Club

A piece from a Eddie Murray game-used bat was incorporated into each of these cards, which are limited to 350.

		MT
EM	Eddie Murray (350)	100.00

1999 Upper Deck UD Choice Previews

A month prior to the release of its new UD Choice brand baseball series, Upper Deck issued this 55-card Preview version. Sold in five-card cello packs for about 75 cents only at retail outlets, the cards are identical to the issued versions of the same players except for the appearance at top front of a gold foil-stamped "PREVIEW".

		MT
Complete Set (55):		12.50
Common Player:		.10
46	Tim Salmon	.25
48	Chuck Finley	.10
50	Matt Williams	.30
52	Travis Lee	.25
54	Andres Galarraga	.10
56	Greg Maddux	.65
58	Cal Ripken Jr.	1.50
60	Rafael Palmeiro	.25
62	Nomar Garciaparra	.75
64	Pedro Martinez	.40
66	Kerry Wood	.25
67	Sammy Sosa	.75
70	Albert Belle	.30
72	Frank Thomas	.75
74	Pete Harnisch	.10
76	Manny Ramirez	.50
78	Travis Fryman	.10
80	Kenny Lofton	.10
82	Larry Walker	.30
84	Gabe Alvarez	.10
86	Damion Easley	.10
88	Mark Kotsay	.10
90	Jeff Bagwell	.50
93	Craig Biggio	.15
94	Larry Sutton	.10
96	Johnny Damon	.15
98	Gary Sheffield	.25
100	Mark Grudzielanek	.10
102	Jeff Cirillo	.10
104	Mark Loretta	.10
106	David Ortiz	.10
108	Brad Fullmer	.10
110	Vladimir Guerrero	.50
112	Brian McRae	.10
114	Rey Ordonez	.10
115	Derek Jeter	1.00
118	Paul O'Neill	.10
120	A.J. Hinch	.10
122	Miguel Tejada	.15
124	Scott Rolen	.45
126	Bobby Abreu	.15
128	Jason Kendall	.10
130	Mark McGwire	1.50
132	Eli Marrero	.10
136	Kevin Brown	.15
137	Tony Gwynn	.65
138	Bill Mueller	.10
140	Barry Bonds	.75
142	Ken Griffey Jr.	1.25
143	Alex Rodriguez	1.25
146	Rolando Arrojo	.10
148	Quinton McCracken	.10
150	Will Clark	.30
152	Juan Gonzalez	.50
154	Carlos Delgado	.15

1999 Upper Deck UD Choice Prime Choice Reserve

Each card in the UD Choice set is also found in a parallel version with the words "Prime Choice Reserve" repeated in the background of the photo in refractive foil. On back, the parallels are individually serial numbered within an edition of 100 each.

	MT
Common Player:	3.00
Stars:	60X

(See 1999 UD Choice for checklist and base card values.)

1999 Upper Deck UD Choice StarQuest

This four-tiered 30-card set features four different colors for each of the levels. Singles are seeded one per pack and have blue foil etching, Doubles (1:8) have green foil etching, Triples (1:23) have red foil etching and Home Runs are limited to 100 numbered sets with gold foil etching.

		MT
Complete Set (30):		20.00
Common Player:		.25
Inserted 1:1		
Green (1:8):		1.5X
Red (1:23):		3X
Gold (100 sets):		50X
SQ1	Ken Griffey Jr.	1.75
SQ2	Sammy Sosa	1.25
SQ3	Alex Rodriguez	1.75
SQ4	Derek Jeter	1.50
SQ5	Troy Glaus	.65
SQ6	Mike Piazza	1.50
SQ7	Barry Bonds	1.25
SQ8	Tony Gwynn	1.00
SQ9	Juan Gonzalez	.75
SQ10	Chipper Jones	1.50
SQ11	Greg Maddux	1.00
SQ12	Randy Johnson	.60
SQ13	Roger Clemens	1.00
SQ14	Ben Grieve	.50
SQ15	Nomar Garciaparra	1.25
SQ16	Travis Lee	.35
SQ17	Frank Thomas	1.25
SQ18	Vladimir Guerrero	.75
SQ19	Scott Rolen	.60
SQ20	Ivan Rodriguez	.60
SQ21	Cal Ripken Jr.	2.00
SQ22	Mark McGwire	2.00
SQ23	Jeff Bagwell	.75
SQ24	Tony Clark	.25
SQ25	Kerry Wood	.50
SQ26	Kenny Lofton	.25
SQ27	Adrian Beltre	.40
SQ28	Larry Walker	.35
SQ29	Curt Schilling	.35
SQ30	Jim Thome	.25

1999 Upper Deck UD Choice Yard Work

This 30-card set showcases the top power hitters in the game. The right side of the card is covered in bronze foil and stamped with Yard Work. They are numbered with a Y-prefix and seeded 1:13 packs.

		MT
Complete Set (30):		30.00
Common Player:		.50
Inserted 1:13		
Y1	Andres Galarraga	.50
Y2	Chipper Jones	2.50
Y3	Rafael Palmeiro	.75
Y4	Nomar Garciaparra	2.25
Y5	Sammy Sosa	2.25
Y6	Frank Thomas	2.25
Y7	J.D. Drew	1.00
Y8	Albert Belle	.65
Y9	Jim Thome	.50
Y10	Manny Ramirez	1.50
Y11	Larry Walker	.60
Y12	Vinny Castilla	.50
Y13	Tony Clark	.50
Y14	Jeff Bagwell	1.50
Y15	Moises Alou	.60
Y16	Dean Palmer	.50
Y17	Gary Sheffield	.75
Y18	Vladimir Guerrero	1.50
Y19	Mike Piazza	2.50
Y20	Tino Martinez	.50
Y21	Ben Grieve	.75
Y22	Greg Vaughn	.50
Y23	Ken Caminiti	.50
Y24	Barry Bonds	2.25
Y25	Ken Griffey Jr.	3.00
Y26	Alex Rodriguez	3.00
Y27	Mark McGwire	4.00
Y28	Juan Gonzalez	1.50
Y29	Jose Canseco	1.25
Y30	Jose Cruz Jr.	.60

1999 Upper Deck Victory

This 470-card base set is printed on 20-point stock and has a white border with UV coating. The set consists of a number of subsets including, 30-card Mark McGwire Magic, 30 team checklist cards, 50 '99 rookies, 15 Power Trip, 20 Rookie

Flashback, 15 Big Play Makers and 10 History in the Making. Twelve-card packs had an SRP of $.99.

	MT
Complete Set (470):	40.00
Common Player:	.05
Pack (12):	.75
Wax Box (36):	25.00

1	Anaheim Angels (Team Checklist)	.05
2	*Mark Harriger* (99 Rookie)	.15
3	Mo Vaughn (Power Trip)	.15
4	Darin Erstad (Big Play Makers)	.15
5	Troy Glaus	.40
6	Tim Salmon	.20
7	Mo Vaughn	.30
8	Darin Erstad	.35
9	Garret Anderson	.05
10	Todd Greene	.05
11	Troy Percival	.05
12	Chuck Finley	.05
13	Jason Dickson	.05
14	Jim Edmonds	.05
15	Arizona Diamondbacks (Team Checklist)	.05
16	Randy Johnson	.35
17	Matt Williams	.15
18	Travis Lee	.10
19	Jay Bell	.05
20	Tony Womack	.05
21	Steve Finley	.05
22	Bernard Gilkey	.05
23	Tony Batista	.05
24	Todd Stottlemyre	.05
25	Omar Daal	.05
26	Atlanta Braves (Team Checklist)	.05
27	Bruce Chen (99 Rookie)	.05
28	George Lombard (99 Rookie)	.05
29	Chipper Jones (Power Trip)	.50
30	Chipper Jones (Big Play Makers)	.50
31	Greg Maddux	.65
32	Chipper Jones	1.00
33	Javy Lopez	.05
34	Tom Glavine	.10
35	John Smoltz	.10
36	Andruw Jones	.40
37	Brian Jordan	.05
38	Walt Weiss	.05
39	Bret Boone	.10
40	Andres Galarraga	.05
41	Baltimore Orioles (Team Checklist)	.05
42	Ryan Minor (99 Rookie)	.05
43	Jerry Hairston Jr. (99 Rookie)	.05
44	Calvin Pickering (99 Rookie)	.05
45	Cal Ripken Jr. (History in the Making)	.75
46	Cal Ripken Jr.	1.50
47	Charles Johnson	.05
48	Albert Belle	.25
49	Delino DeShields	.05
50	Mike Mussina	.35
51	Scott Erickson	.05
52	Brady Anderson	.05
53	B.J. Surhoff	.05
54	Harold Baines	.05
55	Will Clark	.15
56	Boston Red Sox (Team Checklist)	.05
57	*Shea Hillenbrand* (99 Rookie)	2.50
58	Trot Nixon (99 Rookie)	.10
59	Jin Ho Cho (99 Rookie)	.10
60	Nomar Garciaparra (Power Trip)	.40
61	Nomar Garciaparra (Big Play Makers)	.40
62	Pedro Martinez	.40
63	Nomar Garciaparra	.75
64	Jose Offerman	.05
65	Jason Varitek	.05
66	Darren Lewis	.05
67	Troy O'Leary	.05
68	Donnie Sadler	.05
69	John Valentin	.05
70	Tim Wakefield	.05
71	Bret Saberhagen	.05
72	Chicago Cubs (Team Checklist)	.05
73	*Kyle Farnsworth* (99 Rookie)	.15
74	Sammy Sosa (Power Trip)	.40
75	Sammy Sosa (Big Play Makers)	.40
76	Sammy Sosa (History in the Making)	.40
77	Kerry Wood (History in the Making)	.15
78	Sammy Sosa	.75
79	Mark Grace	.20
80	Kerry Wood	.30
81	Kevin Tapani	.05
82	Benito Santiago	.05
83	Gary Gaetti	.05
84	Mickey Morandini	.05
85	Glenallen Hill	.05
86	Henry Rodriguez	.05
87	Rod Beck	.05
88	Chicago White Sox (Team Checklist)	.05
89	Carlos Lee (99 Rookie)	.05
90	Mark Johnson (99 Rookie)	.05
91	Frank Thomas (Power Trip)	.40
92	Frank Thomas	.75
93	Jim Parque	.05
94	Mike Sirotka	.05
95	Mike Caruso	.05
96	Ray Durham	.05
97	Magglio Ordonez	.10
98	Paul Konerko	.10
99	Bob Howry	.05
100	Brian Simmons	.05
101	Jaime Navarro	.05
102	Cincinnati Reds (Team Checklist)	.05
103	Denny Neagle	.05
104	Pete Harnisch	.05
105	Greg Vaughn	.05
106	Brett Tomko	.05
107	Mike Cameron	.05
108	Sean Casey	.15
109	Aaron Boone	.05
110	Michael Tucker	.05
111	Dmitri Young	.05
112	Barry Larkin	.10
113	Cleveland Indians (Team Checklist)	.05
114	Russ Branyan (99 Rookie)	.05
115	Jim Thome (Power Trip)	.05
116	Manny Ramirez (Power Trip)	.25
117	Manny Ramirez	.40
118	Jim Thome	.05
119	David Justice	.20
120	Sandy Alomar	.05
121	Roberto Alomar	.35
122	Jaret Wright	.05
123	Bartolo Colon	.05
124	Travis Fryman	.05
125	Kenny Lofton	.05
126	Omar Vizquel	.05
127	Colorado Rockies (Team Checklist)	.05
128	Derrick Gibson (99 Rookie)	.05
129	Larry Walker (Big Play Makers)	.10
130	Larry Walker	.20
131	Dante Bichette	.05
132	Todd Helton	.35
133	Neifi Perez	.05
134	Vinny Castilla	.05
135	Darryl Kile	.05
136	Pedro Astacio	.05
137	Darryl Hamilton	.05
138	Mike Lansing	.05
139	Kirt Manwaring	.05
140	Detroit Tigers (Team Checklist)	.05
141	*Jeff Weaver* (99 Rookie)	.50
142	Gabe Kapler (99 Rookie)	.10
143	Tony Clark (Power Trip)	.05
144	Tony Clark	.05
145	Juan Encarnacion	.05
146	Dean Palmer	.05
147	Damion Easley	.05
148	Bobby Higginson	.10
149	Karim Garcia	.05
150	Justin Thompson	.05
151	Matt Anderson	.05
152	Willie Blair	.05
153	Brian Hunter	.05
154	Florida Marlins (Team Checklist)	.05
155	Alex Gonzalez (99 Rookie)	.05
156	Mark Kotsay	.05
157	Livan Hernandez	.05
158	Cliff Floyd	.05
159	Todd Dunwoody	.05
160	Alex Fernandez	.05
161	Mark Mantei	.05
162	Derrek Lee	.05
163	Kevin Orie	.05
164	Craig Counsell	.05
165	Rafael Medina	.05
166	Houston Astros (Team Checklist)	.05
167	Daryle Ward (99 Rookie)	.05
168	Mitch Meluskey (99 Rookie)	.05
169	Jeff Bagwell (Power Trip)	.25
170	Jeff Bagwell	.50
171	Ken Caminiti	.05
172	Craig Biggio	.10
173	Derek Bell	.05
174	Moises Alou	.15
175	Billy Wagner	.05
176	Shane Reynolds	.05
177	Carl Everett	.10
178	Scott Elarton	.05
179	Richard Hidalgo	.10
180	Kansas City Royals (Team Checklist)	.05
181	Carlos Beltran (99 Rookie)	.10
182	Carlos Febles (99 Rookie)	.05
183	Jeremy Giambi (99 Rookie)	.05
184	Johnny Damon	.10
185	Joe Randa	.05
186	Jeff King	.05
187	Hipolito Pichardo	.05
188	Kevin Appier	.05
189	Chad Kreuter	.05
190	Rey Sanchez	.05
191	Larry Sutton	.05
192	Jeff Montgomery	.05
193	Jermaine Dye	.05
194	Los Angeles Dodgers (Team Checklist)	.05
195	Adam Riggs (99 Rookie)	.05
196	Angel Pena (99 Rookie)	.05
197	Todd Hundley	.05
198	Kevin Brown	.10
199	Ismael Valdes	.05
200	Chan Ho Park	.10
201	Adrian Beltre	.10
202	Mark Grudzielanek	.05
203	Raul Mondesi	.15
204	Gary Sheffield	.20
205	Eric Karros	.05
206	Devon White	.05
207	Milwaukee Brewers (Team Checklist)	.05
208	Ron Belliard (99 Rookie)	.05
209	Rafael Roque (99 Rookie)	.05
210	Jeromy Burnitz	.05
211	Fernando Vina	.05
212	Scott Karl	.05
213	Jim Abbott	.05
214	Sean Berry	.05
215	Marquis Grissom	.05
216	Geoff Jenkins	.05
217	Jeff Cirillo	.05
218	Dave Nilsson	.05
219	Jose Valentin	.05
220	Minnesota Twins (Team Checklist)	.05
221	Corey Koskie (99 Rookie)	.05
222	Christian Guzman (99 Rookie)	.05
223	A.J. Pierzynski (99 Rookie)	.05
224	David Ortiz	.05
225	Brad Radke	.05
226	Todd Walker	.05
227	Matt Lawton	.05
228	Rick Aguilera	.05
229	Eric Milton	.05
230	Marty Cordova	.05
231	Torii Hunter	.05
232	Ron Coomer	.05
233	LaTroy Hawkins	.05
234	Montreal Expos (Team Checklist)	.05
235	Fernando Seguignol (99 Rookie)	.05
236	Michael Barrett (99 Rookie)	.10
237	Vladimir Guerrero (Big Play Makers)	.25
238	Vladimir Guerrero	.50
239	Brad Fullmer	.05
240	Rondell White	.10
241	Ugueth Urbina	.05
242	Dustin Hermanson	.10
243	Orlando Cabrerra	.10
244	Wilton Guerrero	.05
245	Carl Pavano	.05
246	Javier Vasquez	.10
247	Chris Widger	.05
248	New York Mets (Team Checklist)	.05
249	Mike Kinkade (99 Rookie)	.05
250	Octavio Dotel (99 Rookie)	.05
251	Mike Piazza (Power Trip)	.50
252	Mike Piazza	1.00
253	Rickey Henderson	.35
254	Edgardo Alfonzo	.05
255	Robin Ventura	.05
256	Al Leiter	.05
257	Brian McRae	.05
258	Rey Ordonez	.05
259	Bobby Bonilla	.05
260	Orel Hershiser	.05
261	John Olerud	.05
262	New York Yankees (Team Checklist)	.10
263	Ricky Ledee (99 Rookie)	.05
264	Bernie Williams (Big Play Makers)	.10
265	Derek Jeter (Big Play Makers)	.50
266	Scott Brosius (History in the Making)	.05
267	Derek Jeter	1.00
268	Roger Clemens	.65
269	Orlando Hernandez	.10
270	Scott Brosius	.05
271	Paul O'Neill	.05
272	Bernie Williams	.20
273	Chuck Knoblauch	.05
274	Tino Martinez	.05
275	Mariano Rivera	.15
276	Jorge Posada	.05
277	Oakland Athletics (Team Checklist)	.05
278	Eric Chavez (99 Rookie)	.15
279	Ben Grieve (History in the Making)	.05
280	Jason Giambi	.30
281	John Jaha	.05
282	Miguel Tejada	.15
283	Ben Grieve	.15
284	Matt Stairs	.05
285	Ryan Christenson	.05
286	A.J. Hinch	.05
287	Kenny Rogers	.05
288	Tom Candiotti	.05
289	Scott Spezio	.05
290	Philadelphia Phillies (Team Checklist)	.05
291	*Pat Burrell* (99 Rookie)	1.50
292	Marlon Anderson (99 Rookie)	.05

293 Scott Rolen (Big Play Makers) .20
294 Scott Rolen .35
295 Doug Glanville .05
296 Rico Brogna .05
297 Ron Gant .05
298 Bobby Abreu .10
299 Desi Relaford .05
300 Curt Schilling .15
301 Chad Ogea .05
302 Kevin Jordan .05
303 Carlton Loewer .05
304 Pittsburgh Pirates (Team Checklist) .05
305 Kris Benson (99 Rookie) .05
306 Brian Giles .05
307 Jason Kendall .05
308 Jose Guillen .05
309 Pat Meares .05
310 Brant Brown .05
311 Kevin Young .05
312 Ed Sprague .05
313 Francisco Cordova .05
314 Aramis Ramirez .05
315 Freddy Garcia .50
316 Saint Louis Cardinals (Team Checklist) .05
317 J.D. Drew (99 Rookie) .40
318 *Chad Hutchinson* (99 Rookie) .25
319 Mark McGwire (Power Trip) .75
320 J.D. Drew (Power Trip) .20
321 Mark McGwire (Big Play Makers) .75
322 Mark McGwire (History in the Making) .75
323 Mark McGwire 1.50
324 Fernando Tatis .05
325 Edgar Renteria .05
326 Ray Lankford .05
327 Willie McGee .05
328 Ricky Bottalico .05
329 Eli Marrero .05
330 Matt Morris .05
331 Eric Davis .05
332 Darren Bragg .05
333 Padres (Team Checklist) .05
334 Matt Clement (99 Rookie) .05
335 Ben Davis (99 Rookie) .05
336 Gary Matthews Jr. (99 Rookie) .05
337 Tony Gwynn (Big Play Makers) .35
338 Tony Gwynn (History in the Making) .35
339 Tony Gwynn .65
340 Reggie Sanders .05
341 Ruben Rivera .05
342 Wally Joyner .05
343 Sterling Hitchcock .05
344 Carlos Hernandez .05
345 Andy Ashby .05
346 Trevor Hoffman .05
347 Chris Gomez .05
348 Jim Leyritz .05
349 San Francisco Giants (Team Checklist) .05
350 Armando Rios (99 Rookie) .05
351 Barry Bonds (Power Trip) .40
352 Barry Bonds (Big Play Makers) .40
353 Barry Bonds (History in the Making) .40
354 Robb Nen .05
355 Bill Mueller .05
356 Barry Bonds .75
357 Jeff Kent .05
358 J.T. Snow .05
359 Ellis Burks .05
360 F.P. Santangelo .05
361 Marvin Benard .05
362 Stan Javier .05
363 Shawn Estes .05
364 Seattle Mariners (Team Checklist) .05
365 Carlos Guillen (99 Rookie) .05
366 Ken Griffey Jr. (Power Trip) .65
367 Alex Rodriguez (Power Trip) .65
368 Ken Griffey Jr. (Big Play Makers) .65
369 Alex Rodriguez (Big Play Makers) .65
370 Ken Griffey Jr. (History in the Making) .65
371 Alex Rodriguez (History in the Making) .65
372 Ken Griffey Jr. 1.25
373 Alex Rodriguez 1.25
374 Jay Buhner .05
375 Edgar Martinez .05
376 Jeff Fassero .05
377 David Bell .05
378 David Segui .05
379 Russ Davis .05
380 Dan Wilson .05
381 Jamie Moyer .05
382 Tampa Bay Devil Rays (Team Checklist) .05
383 Roberto Hernandez .05
384 Bobby Smith .05
385 Wade Boggs .35
386 Fred McGriff .05
387 Rolando Arrojo .05
388 Jose Canseco .35
389 Wilson Alvarez .05
390 Kevin Stocker .05
391 Miguel Cairo .05
392 Quinton McCracken .05
393 Texas Rangers (Team Checklist) .05
394 Ruben Mateo (99 Rookie) .05
395 Cesar King (99 Rookie) .05
396 Juan Gonzalez (Power Trip) .25
397 Juan Gonzalez (Big Play Makers) .25
398 Ivan Rodriguez .35
399 Juan Gonzalez .50
400 Rafael Palmeiro .20
401 Rick Helling .05
402 Aaron Sele .05
403 John Wetteland .05
404 Rusty Greer .05
405 Todd Zeile .05
406 Royce Clayton .05
407 Tom Goodwin .05
408 Toronto Blue Jays (Team Checklist) .05
409 Kevin Witt (99 Rookie .05
410 Roy Halladay (99 Rookie) .05
411 Jose Cruz Jr. .15
412 Carlos Delgado .20
413 Willie Greene .05
414 Shawn Green .20
415 Homer Bush .05
416 Shannon Stewart .10
417 David Wells .10
418 Kelvim Escobar .05
419 Joey Hamilton .05
420 Alex Gonzalez .10
421 Mark McGwire (McGwire Magic) .20
422 Mark McGwire (McGwire Magic) .20
423 Mark McGwire (McGwire Magic) .20
424 Mark McGwire (McGwire Magic) .20
425 Mark McGwire (McGwire Magic) .20
426 Mark McGwire (McGwire Magic) .20
427 Mark McGwire (McGwire Magic) .20
428 Mark McGwire (McGwire Magic) .20
429 Mark McGwire (McGwire Magic) .20
430 Mark McGwire (McGwire Magic) .20
431 Mark McGwire (McGwire Magic) .20
432 Mark McGwire (McGwire Magic) .20
433 Mark McGwire (McGwire Magic) .20
434 Mark McGwire (McGwire Magic) .20
435 Mark McGwire (McGwire Magic) .20
436 Mark McGwire (McGwire Magic) .20
437 Mark McGwire (McGwire Magic) .20
438 Mark McGwire (McGwire Magic) .20
439 Mark McGwire (McGwire Magic) .20
440 Mark McGwire (McGwire Magic) .20
441 Mark McGwire (McGwire Magic) .20
442 Mark McGwire (McGwire Magic) .20
443 Mark McGwire (McGwire Magic) .20
444 Mark McGwire (McGwire Magic) .20
445 Mark McGwire (McGwire Magic) .20
446 Mark McGwire (McGwire Magic) .20
447 Mark McGwire (McGwire Magic) .20
448 Mark McGwire (McGwire Magic) .20
449 Mark McGwire (McGwire Magic) .20
450 Mark McGwire (McGwire Magic) .20
451 Chipper Jones '93 (Rookie Flashback) .50
452 Cal Ripken Jr. '81 (Rookie Flashback) .75
453 Roger Clemens '84 (Rookie Flashback) .35
454 Wade Boggs '82 (Rookie Flashback) .20
455 Greg Maddux '86 (Rookie Flashback) .35
456 Frank Thomas '90 (Rookie Flashback) .40
457 Jeff Bagwell '91 (Rookie Flashback) .25
458 Mike Piazza '92 (Rookie Flashback) .50
459 Randy Johnson '88 (Rookie Flashback) .20
460 Mo Vaughn '91 (Rookie Flashback) .15
461 Mark McGwire '86 (Rookie Flashback) .75
462 Rickey Henderson '79 (Rookie Flashback) .20
463 Barry Bonds '86 (Rookie Flashback) .40
464 Tony Gwynn '82 (Rookie Flashback) .35
465 Ken Griffey Jr. '89 (Rookie Flashback) .65
466 Alex Rodriquez '94 (Rookie Flashback) .65
467 Sammy Sosa '89 (Rookie Flashback) .40
468 Juan Gonzalez '89 (Rookie Flashback) .25
469 Kevin Brown '86 (Rookie Flashback) .05
470 Fred McGriff '86 (Rookie Flashback) .05

1999 UD Ionix

Ionix is a 90-card set that includes a 30-card "Techno" subset that was short-printed (1:4 packs). Packs were sold for $4.99, and contain four cards. The first 60 cards of the set are included in a parallel set in which the photo from the back of the regular card was put on the front of a rainbow-foil Reciprocal card. These cards are sequentially numbered to 750. The remaining 30 cards in the set were also paralleled on a Reciprocal card sequentially numbered to 100. The set also includes 350 Frank Robinson "500 Club Piece of History" bat cards, with a piece of a Robinson game-used bat. Another version of the bat cards includes Robinson's autograph, and are hand-numbered to 20. Insert sets included Hyper, Nitro, Cyber, Warp Zone, and HoloGrFX.

	MT
Complete Set (90):	100.00
Common Player (1-60):	.25
Common Techno (61-90):	.50
Inserted 1:4	
Reciprocals (1-60):	2X
Production 750 sets	
Techno Reciprocals (61-90):	6X
Production 100 sets	
Pack (4):	2.00
Wax Box (20):	35.00

1 Troy Glaus 1.50
2 Darin Erstad .50
3 Travis Lee .25
4 Matt Williams .50
5 Chipper Jones 2.50
6 Greg Maddux 2.00
7 Andruw Jones 1.00
8 Andres Galarraga .25
9 Tom Glavine .25
10 Cal Ripken Jr. 4.00
11 Ryan Minor .25
12 Nomar Garciaparra 2.25
13 Mo Vaughn .75
14 Pedro Martinez .75
15 Sammy Sosa 2.25
16 Kerry Wood .75
17 Albert Belle .60
18 Frank Thomas 2.25
19 Sean Casey .50
20 Kenny Lofton .25
21 Manny Ramirez 1.00
22 Jim Thome .25
23 Bartolo Colon .25
24 Jaret Wright .25
25 Larry Walker .50
26 Tony Clark .25
27 Gabe Kapler .25
28 Edgar Renteria .25
29 Randy Johnson .75
30 Craig Biggio .35
31 Jeff Bagwell 1.00
32 Moises Alou .35
33 Johnny Damon .35
34 Adrian Beltre .50
35 Jeromy Burnitz .25
36 Todd Walker .35
37 Corey Koskie .35
38 Vladimir Guerrero 1.00
39 Mike Piazza 2.50
40 Hideo Nomo .75
41 Derek Jeter 2.50
42 Tino Martinez .25
43 Orlando Hernandez .75
44 Ben Grieve .50
45 Rickey Henderson .75
46 Scott Rolen .75
47 Curt Schilling .35
48 Aramis Ramirez .25
49 Tony Gwynn 2.00
50 Kevin Brown .35

#	Player	MT
51	Barry Bonds	2.25
52	Ken Griffey Jr.	3.00
53	Alex Rodriguez	3.00
54	Mark McGwire	4.00
55	J.D. Drew	.75
56	Rolando Arrojo	.25
57	Ivan Rodriguez	.75
58	Juan Gonzalez	1.00
59	Roger Clemens	2.00
60	Jose Cruz Jr.	.40
61	Travis Lee (Techno)	.50
62	Andres Galarraga (Techno)	.50
63	Andruw Jones (Techno)	1.50
64	Chipper Jones (Techno)	4.00
65	Greg Maddux (Techno)	3.00
66	Cal Ripken Jr. (Techno)	5.00
67	Nomar Garciaparra (Techno)	3.50
68	Mo Vaughn (Techno)	1.00
69	Sammy Sosa (Techno)	3.50
70	Frank Thomas (Techno)	3.50
71	Kerry Wood (Techno)	1.25
72	Kenny Lofton (Techno)	.50
73	Manny Ramirez (Techno)	1.50
74	Larry Walker (Techno)	1.00
75	Jeff Bagwell (Techno)	1.50
76	Randy Johnson (Techno)	1.25
77	Paul Molitor (Techno)	1.25
78	Derek Jeter (Techno)	4.00
79	Tino Martinez (Techno)	.50
80	Mike Piazza (Techno)	4.00
81	Ben Grieve (Techno)	1.00
82	Scott Rolen (Techno)	1.50
83	Mark McGwire (Techno)	5.00
84	Tony Gwynn (Techno)	3.00
85	Barry Bonds (Techno)	3.50
86	Ken Griffey Jr. (Techno)	4.50
87	Alex Rodriguez (Techno)	4.50
88	Juan Gonzalez (Techno)	1.50
89	Roger Clemens (Techno)	3.00
90	J.D. Drew (Techno)	.75
		.75
100	Ken Griffey Jr. (SAMPLE)	3.00

1999 UD Ionix Reciprocal

Reciprocal is a parallel of the Ionix base set in which the front and back photos have been switched. Card numbers carry an "R" prefix. The first 60 Reciprocal parallels were produced in an edition of 750 each; the Techno subset Reciprocals (#61-90) are an edition of just 100 each.

	MT
Common Player (1-60):	1.00
Common Techno (61-90):	3.00
Stars (1-60):	2X
Stars (61-90):	6X

(See 1999 UD Ionix for checklist and base card values.)

1999 UD Ionix Cyber

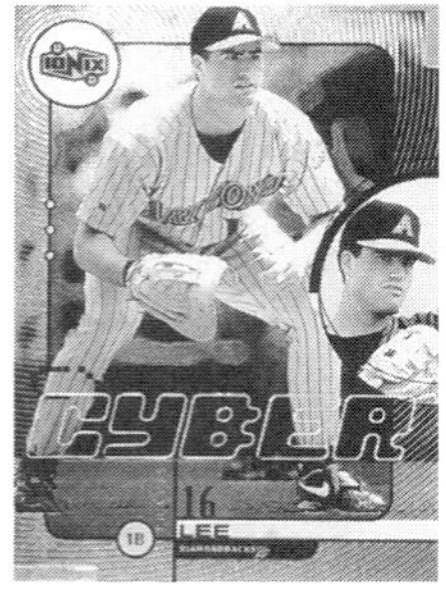

This insert set consisted of 25-cards of baseball's superstars and red-hot rookies. One card was inserted every 53 packs.

		MT
Complete Set (25):		165.00
Common Player:		2.00
C01	Ken Griffey Jr.	15.00
C02	Cal Ripken Jr.	20.00
C03	Frank Thomas	10.00
C04	Greg Maddux	7.50
C05	Mike Piazza	12.50
C06	Alex Rodriguez	15.00
C07	Chipper Jones	12.50
C08	Derek Jeter	12.50
C09	Mark McGwire	20.00
C10	Juan Gonzalez	6.00
C11	Kerry Wood	4.00
C12	Tony Gwynn	7.50
C13	Scott Rolen	4.00
C14	Nomar Garciaparra	10.00
C15	Roger Clemens	7.50
C16	Sammy Sosa	10.00
C17	Travis Lee	2.50
C18	Ben Grieve	3.00
C19	Jeff Bagwell	6.00
C20	Ivan Rodriguez	5.00
C21	Barry Bonds	10.00
C22	J.D. Drew	4.00
C23	Kenny Lofton	2.00
C24	Andruw Jones	6.00
C25	Vladimir Guerrero	6.00

1999 UD Ionix HoloGrFX

This insert set consisted of 10-cards, and featured only the best players in the game. The cards in this set were holographically enhanced. These cards were rare with one card inserted every 1,500 packs.

		MT
Complete Set (10):		425.00
Common Player:		25.00
Inserted 1:1,500		
HG01	Ken Griffey Jr.	60.00
HG02	Cal Ripken Jr.	75.00
HG03	Frank Thomas	45.00
HG04	Greg Maddux	40.00
HG05	Mike Piazza	50.00
HG06	Alex Rodriguez	60.00
HG07	Chipper Jones	50.00
HG08	Derek Jeter	50.00
HG09	Mark McGwire	75.00
HG10	Juan Gonzalez	25.00

1999 UD Ionix Hyper

This insert set featured the top players in baseball, and consisted of 20-cards. Hyper cards were inserted one per nine packs.

		MT
Complete Set (20):		60.00
Common Player:		1.00
Inserted 1:9		
H01	Ken Griffey Jr.	6.00
H02	Cal Ripken Jr.	7.50
H03	Frank Thomas	4.00
H04	Greg Maddux	3.00
H05	Mike Piazza	5.00
H06	Alex Rodriguez	6.00
H07	Chipper Jones	5.00
H08	Derek Jeter	5.00
H09	Mark McGwire	7.50
H10	Juan Gonzalez	2.00
H11	Kerry Wood	1.25
H12	Tony Gwynn	3.00
H13	Scott Rolen	1.50
H14	Nomar Garciaparra	4.00
H15	Roger Clemens	3.00
H16	Sammy Sosa	4.00
H17	Travis Lee	1.00
H18	Ben Grieve	1.25
H19	Jeff Bagwell	2.00
H20	J.D. Drew	1.50

1999 UD Ionix Nitro

Baseball's ten most collectible players are featured in this 10-card insert set. Each card features Ionix technology with rainbow foil and a unique color pattern. Nitro cards were inserted one per 18 packs.

		MT
Complete Set (10):		35.00
Common Player:		1.50
Inserted 1:18		
N01	Ken Griffey Jr.	5.00
N02	Cal Ripken Jr.	6.00
N03	Frank Thomas	3.50
N04	Greg Maddux	3.00
N05	Mike Piazza	4.00
N06	Alex Rodriguez	5.00
N07	Chipper Jones	4.00
N08	Derek Jeter	4.00
N09	Mark McGwire	6.00
N10	J.D. Drew	1.50

1999 UD Ionix Warp Zone

This 15-card insert set contained a special holographic foil enhancement. Warp Zone cards were inserted one per 216 packs.

		MT
Complete Set (15):		200.00
Common Player:		4.00
Inserted 1:216		
WZ1	Ken Griffey Jr.	25.00
WZ2	Cal Ripken Jr.	30.00
WZ3	Frank Thomas	17.50
WZ4	Greg Maddux	15.00
WZ5	Mike Piazza	20.00
WZ6	Alex Rodriguez	25.00
WZ7	Chipper Jones	20.00
WZ8	Derek Jeter	20.00
WZ9	Mark McGwire	30.00
WZ10	Juan Gonzalez	10.00
WZ11	Kerry Wood	4.00
WZ12	Tony Gwynn	15.00
WZ13	Scott Rolen	6.00
WZ14	Nomar Garciaparra	17.50
WZ15	J.D. Drew	5.00

1999 UD Ionix 500 Club Piece of History

These cards feature an actual piece of game-used bat from one of Hall-of-Famer Frank Robinson's Louisville Sluggers. Approximately 350 were made. Robinson also autographed 20 of his Piece of History inserts.

		MT
FR	Frank Robinson (350)	120.00
FRA	Frank Robinson (autographed/20)	650.00

1999 UD Retro

The 110-card base set is comprised of 88 current stars and 22 retired greats. Card fronts have a tan, speckled border while card backs have a year-by-year compilation of the player's stats along with a career note. Retro is packaged in lunchboxes, 24 packs to a box with a SRP of $4.99 per six-card pack.

		MT
Complete Set (110):		15.00
Common Player:		.10
Gold:		10X
Production 250 sets		
Platinum 1/1: VALUES UNDETERMINED		
Wax Pack (6):		2.50
Wax Box (24):		50.00
1	Mo Vaughn	.40
2	Troy Glaus	.50
3	Tim Salmon	.20
4	Randy Johnson	.50
5	Travis Lee	.15
6	Matt Williams	.25
7	Greg Maddux	.85
8	Chipper Jones	1.25
9	Andruw Jones	.75
10	Tom Glavine	.15
11	Javy Lopez	.10
12	Albert Belle	.30
13	Cal Ripken Jr.	2.00
14	Brady Anderson	.10
15	Nomar Garciaparra	1.00
16	Pedro J. Martinez	.60
17	Sammy Sosa	1.00
18	Mark Grace	.30
19	Frank Thomas	1.00
20	Ray Durham	.10
21	Sean Casey	.25
22	Greg Vaughn	.10
23	Barry Larkin	.15
24	Manny Ramirez	.75
25	Jim Thome	.10
26	Jaret Wright	.10
27	Kenny Lofton	.10
28	Larry Walker	.30
29	Todd Helton	.45
30	Vinny Castilla	.10
31	Tony Clark	.10
32	Juan Encarnacion	.10
33	Dean Palmer	.10
34	Mark Kotsay	.10
35	Alex Gonzalez	.10
36	Shane Reynolds	.10
37	Ken Caminiti	.10
38	Jeff Bagwell	.75
39	Craig Biggio	.15
40	Carlos Febles	.10
41	Carlos Beltran	.15
42	Jeremy Giambi	.10
43	Raul Mondesi	.20
44	Adrian Beltre	.20
45	Kevin Brown	.15
46	Jeromy Burnitz	.10
47	Jeff Cirillo	.10
48	Corey Koskie	.10
49	Todd Walker	.10
50	Vladimir Guerrero	.75
51	Michael Barrett	.15
52	Mike Piazza	1.25
53	Robin Ventura	.10
54	Edgardo Alfonzo	.10
55	Derek Jeter	1.25
56	Roger Clemens	.85
57	Tino Martinez	.10
58	Orlando Hernandez	.20
59	Chuck Knoblauch	.10
60	Bernie Williams	.30
61	Eric Chavez	.25
62	Ben Grieve	.25
63	Jason Giambi	.35
64	Scott Rolen	.60
65	Curt Schilling	.25
66	Bobby Abreu	.15
67	Jason Kendall	.10
68	Kevin Young	.15
69	Mark McGwire	2.00
70	J.D. Drew	.35
71	Eric Davis	.10
72	Tony Gwynn	.85
73	Trevor Hoffman	.10
74	Barry Bonds	1.00
75	Robb Nen	.10
76	Ken Griffey Jr.	1.50
77	Alex Rodriguez	1.50
78	Jay Buhner	.10
79	Carlos Guillen	.10
80	Jose Canseco	.50
81	Bobby Smith	.10
82	Juan Gonzalez	.75
83	Ivan Rodriguez	.60
84	Rafael Palmeiro	.30
85	Rick Helling	.10
86	Jose Cruz Jr.	.20
87	David Wells	.15
88	Carlos Delgado	.20
89	Nolan Ryan	2.00
90	George Brett	.75
91	Robin Yount	.50
92	Paul Molitor	.50
93	Dave Winfield	.60
94	Steve Garvey	.15
95	Ozzie Smith	.65
96	Ted Williams	2.00
97	Don Mattingly	1.00
98	Mickey Mantle	3.00
99	Harmon Killebrew	.25
100	Rollie Fingers	.15
101	Kirk Gibson	.10
102	Bucky Dent	.10
103	Willie Mays	1.25
104	Babe Ruth	2.00
105	Gary Carter	.15
106	Reggie Jackson	.65
107	Frank Robinson	.25
108	Ernie Banks	.75
109	Eddie Murray	.35
110	Mike Schmidt	.75

1999 UD Retro Gold/Platinum

This is a 110-card parallel to the base set. Cards have a gold-tone front and are sequentially numbered to 250 sets. A one-of-one Platinum parallel to the base set also is randomly seeded.

	MT
Common Gold:	1.00
Gold Stars:	10X
Platinum 1/1: VALUES UNDETERMINED	

(See 1999 UD Retro for checklist and base card values.)

1999 UD Retro Distant Replay

This 15-card set recounts the most memorable plays from the 1998 season. Card fronts have a black-and-white photo of the player and along the bottom of the photo a date of the memorable play and brief description are given. These are seeded 1:8 packs. A parallel version, Level 2, is also randomly seeded, limited to 100 sequentially numbered sets.

		MT
Complete Set (15):		30.00
Common Player:		1.00
Inserted 1:8		
Level 2:		6X
Production 100 sets		
1	Ken Griffey Jr.	3.00
2	Mark McGwire	4.00
3	Cal Ripken Jr.	4.00
4	Greg Maddux	2.00
5	Nomar Garciaparra	2.25
6	Roger Clemens	2.00
7	Alex Rodriguez	3.00
8	Frank Thomas	2.25
9	Mike Piazza	2.50
10	Chipper Jones	2.50
11	Juan Gonzalez	1.50
12	Tony Gwynn	2.00
13	Barry Bonds	2.25
14	Ivan Rodriguez	1.00
15	Derek Jeter	2.50

1999 UD Retro INKredible

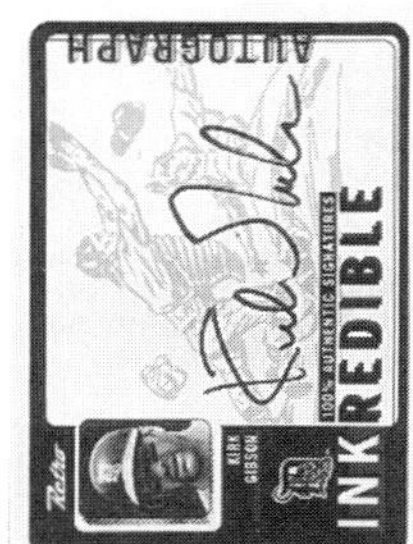

INKredible is an autographed insert set that consists of both current players and retired stars. Card fronts have a small photo in the upper left portion of the featured player and a large signing area. These are seeded 1:23 packs.

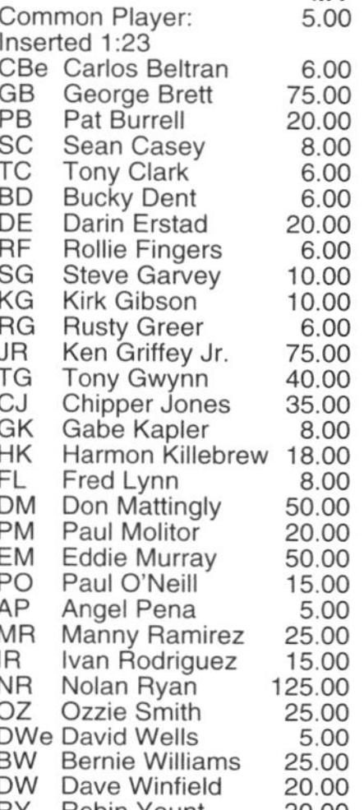

		MT
Common Player:		5.00
Inserted 1:23		
CBe	Carlos Beltran	6.00
GB	George Brett	75.00
PB	Pat Burrell	20.00
SC	Sean Casey	8.00
TC	Tony Clark	6.00
BD	Bucky Dent	6.00
DE	Darin Erstad	20.00
RF	Rollie Fingers	6.00
SG	Steve Garvey	10.00
KG	Kirk Gibson	10.00
RG	Rusty Greer	6.00
JR	Ken Griffey Jr.	75.00
TG	Tony Gwynn	40.00
CJ	Chipper Jones	35.00
GK	Gabe Kapler	8.00
HK	Harmon Killebrew	18.00
FL	Fred Lynn	8.00
DM	Don Mattingly	50.00
PM	Paul Molitor	20.00
EM	Eddie Murray	50.00
PO	Paul O'Neill	15.00
AP	Angel Pena	5.00
MR	Manny Ramirez	25.00
IR	Ivan Rodriguez	15.00
NR	Nolan Ryan	125.00
OZ	Ozzie Smith	25.00
DWe	David Wells	5.00
BW	Bernie Williams	25.00
DW	Dave Winfield	20.00
RY	Robin Yount	30.00

1999 UD Retro INKredible Level 2

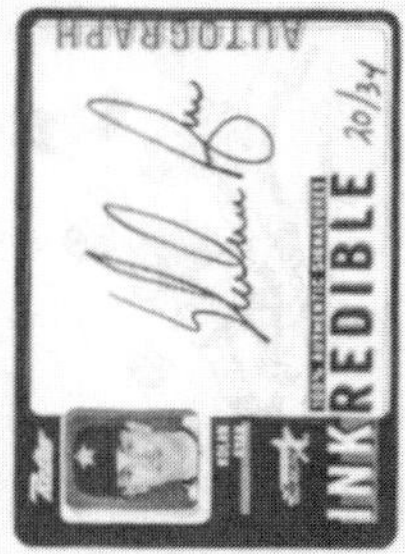

A parallel to INKredible autographed inserts, these are hand-numbered to the featured player's jersey number.

		MT
Common Player:		10.00
Limited to player's jersey #		
CBe	Carlos Beltran (36)	15.00
GB	George Brett (5)	
PB	Pat Burrell (76)	50.00
SC	Sean Casey (21)	40.00
TC	Tony Clark (17)	20.00
BD	Bucky Dent (20)	25.00
DE	Darin Erstad (17)	50.00
RF	Rollie Fingers (34)	20.00
SG	Steve Garvey (6)	
KG	Kirk Gibson (23)	30.00
RG	Rusty Greer (29)	25.00
JR	Ken Griffey Jr. (24)	250.00
TG	Tony Gwynn (19)	150.00
CJ	Chipper Jones (10)	
GK	Gabe Kapler (23)	40.00
HK	Harmon Killebrew (3)	
FL	Fred Lynn (19)	30.00
DM	Don Mattingly (23)	200.00
PM	Paul Molitor (4)	
EM	Eddie Murray (33)	80.00
PO	Paul O'Neill (21)	50.00
AP	Angel Pena (36)	10.00
MR	Manny Ramirez (24)	80.00
IR	Ivan Rodriguez (7)	
NR	Nolan Ryan (34)	400.00

OZ	Ozzie Smith (1)	
DWe	David Wells (33)	25.00
BW	Bernie Williams (51)	40.00
DW	Dave Winfield (31)	60.00
RY	Robin Yount (19)	90.00

1999 UD Retro Lunchbox

Lunchboxes was the packaging for UD Retro. Each lunchbox contains 24 six-card packs and features 17 different current or retired baseball legends including Babe Ruth.

	MT
Complete Set (17):	140.00
Common Lunchbox:	6.00
1 dual-player per case	
Roger Clemens	6.00
Ken Griffey Jr.	8.00
Mickey Mantle	10.00
Mark McGwire	10.00
Mike Piazza	7.50
Alex Rodriguez	8.00
Babe Ruth	10.00
Sammy Sosa	7.50
Ted Williams	10.00
Ken Griffey Jr., Mark McGwire	12.50
Ken Griffey Jr., Babe Ruth	12.50
Ken Griffey Jr., Ted Williams	12.50
Mickey Mantle, Babe Ruth	15.00
Mark McGwire, Mickey Mantle	15.00
Mark McGwire, Babe Ruth	15.00
Mark McGwire, Ted Williams	15.00

1999 UD Retro Old/New School

This 30-card insert set captures 15 Old School players and 15 New School players. Each card is sequentially numbered to 1,000. A parallel version is also randomly seeded and is limited to 50 sequentially numbered sets. Old School cards are basically black-and-white with color graphic highlights on front and back. New School cards have multiple computer-enhanced color photos and silver-foil highlights.

		MT
Complete Set (30):		100.00
Common Player:		1.00
Production 1,000 sets		
Level 2:		5X
Production 50 sets		
1	Ken Griffey Jr.	9.00
2	Alex Rodriguez	9.00
3	Frank Thomas	6.50
4	Cal Ripken Jr.	10.00
5	Chipper Jones	7.50
6	Craig Biggio	1.00
7	Greg Maddux	6.00
8	Jeff Bagwell	4.50
9	Juan Gonzalez	4.50
10	Mark McGwire	10.00
11	Mike Piazza	7.50
12	Mo Vaughn	1.50
13	Roger Clemens	6.00
14	Sammy Sosa	6.50
15	Tony Gwynn	6.00
16	Gabe Kapler	1.50
17	J.D. Drew	2.00
18	Pat Burrell	4.50
19	Roy Halladay	1.00
20	Jeff Weaver	1.00
21	Troy Glaus	3.00
22	Vladimir Guerrero	4.50
23	Michael Barrett	1.00
24	Carlos Beltran	1.00
25	Scott Rolen	3.00
26	Nomar Garciaparra	6.50
27	Warren Morris	1.00
28	Alex Gonzalez	1.00
29	Kyle Farnsworth	1.00
30	Derek Jeter	7.50

1999 UD Retro Piece of History 500 Club

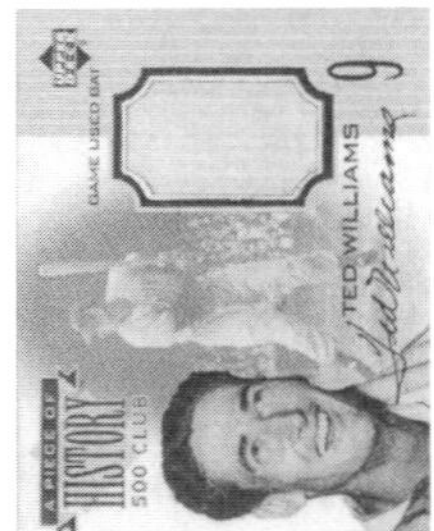

Each one of these inserts features a piece of game-used bat swung by Ted Williams embedded into each card. A total of 350 of these were issued. Williams also autographed nine of the 500 Club Piece of History cards.

		MT
TW	Ted Williams (edition of 350)	350.00
TWA	Ted Williams (autographed/9)	

1999 UD Retro Throwback Attack

This 15-card set has a "Retro" look, borrowing heavily from 1959 Topps. Highlighting top players, the set features card fronts with a circular player photo on a bright orange background. At top in white is, "throwback attack". There is a white border. Backs have a ghosted image of the front photo and career highlights. Cards are attack" across the top and a white border. Card backs are numbered with a "T" prefix and are seeded 1:5 packs. A parallel version is also randomly seeded and limited to 500 numbered sets.

		MT
Complete Set (15):		30.00
Common Player:		.75
Inserted 1:5		
Level 2:		5X
Production 500 sets		
1	Ken Griffey Jr.	4.00
2	Mark McGwire	5.00
3	Sammy Sosa	2.50
4	Roger Clemens	2.00
5	J.D. Drew	1.00
6	Alex Rodriguez	4.00
7	Greg Maddux	2.00
8	Mike Piazza	3.00
9	Juan Gonzalez	1.50
10	Mo Vaughn	.75
11	Cal Ripken Jr.	5.00
12	Frank Thomas	2.50
13	Nomar Garciaparra	2.50
14	Vladimir Guerrero	1.50
15	Tony Gwynn	2.00

2000 Upper Deck

Released in two 270-card series the base cards feature full- bleed fronts with gold foil etching and stamping. Card backs have complete year-by-year statistics.

		MT
Complete Set (540):		80.00
Complete Series I (270):		40.00
Complete Series II (270):		40.00
Common Player:		.15
Common Silver Exclusives:		4.00
Silver Stars:		10X to 20X
Rookies:		5X to 10X
Hobby Pack (10):		3.00
Hobby Box (24):		60.00
1	Rick Ankiel (Star Rookie)	.50
2	Vernon Wells (Star Rookie)	.50
3	Ryan Anderson (Star Rookie)	.40
4	Ed Yarnall (Star Rookie)	.50
5	Brian McNichol (Star Rookie)	.25
6	Ben Petrick (Star Rookie)	.25
7	Kip Wells (Star Rookie)	.25
8	Eric Munson (Star Rookie)	1.50
9	Matt Riley (Star Rookie)	.40
10	Peter Bergeron (Star Rookie)	.40
11	Eric Gagne (Star Rookie)	.25
12	Ramon Ortiz (Star Rookie)	.25
13	Josh Beckett (Star Rookie)	3.00
14	Alfonso Soriano (Star Rookie)	.50
15	Jorge Toca (Star Rookie)	.25
16	Buddy Carlyle (Star Rookie)	.25
17	Chad Hermansen (Star Rookie)	.25
18	Matt Perisho (Star Rookie)	.40
19	*Tomokazu Ohka* (Star Rookie)	.75
20	Jacque Jones (Star Rookie)	.50
21	Josh Paul (Star Rookie)	.40
22	Dermal Brown (Star Rookie)	.50
23	Adam Kennedy (Star Rookie)	.50
24	Chad Harville (Star Rookie)	.40
25	Calvin Murray (Star Rookie)	.40
26	Chad Meyers (Star Rookie)	.40
27	Brian Cooper (Star Rookie)	.40
28	Troy Glaus	.75
29	Ben Molina	.25
30	Troy Percival	.15
31	Ken Hill	.15
32	Chuck Finley	.15
33	Todd Greene	.15
34	Tim Salmon	.25
35	Gary DiSarcina	.15
36	Luis Gonzalez	.15
37	Tony Womack	.15
38	Omar Daal	.15
39	Randy Johnson	.50
40	Erubiel Durazo	.40
41	Jay Bell	.15
42	Steve Finley	.15
43	Travis Lee	.25
44	Greg Maddux	1.50
45	Bret Boone	.15
46	Brian Jordan	.15
47	Kevin Millwood	.25
48	Odalis Perez	.15
49	Javy Lopez	.25
50	John Smoltz	.25
51	Bruce Chen	.25
52	Albert Belle	.60
53	Jerry Hairston Jr.	.15
54	Will Clark	.40
55	Sidney Ponson	.15
56	Charles Johnson	.15
57	Cal Ripken Jr.	2.50
58	Ryan Minor	.25
59	Mike Mussina	.50
60	Tom Gordon	.15
61	Jose Offerman	.15
62	Trot Nixon	.15

No.	Player	Value
63	Pedro Martinez	1.00
64	John Valentin	.15
65	Jason Varitek	.15
66	Juan Pena	.15
67	Troy O'Leary	.15
68	Sammy Sosa	2.00
69	Henry Rodriguez	.15
70	Kyle Farnsworth	.15
71	Glenallen Hill	.15
72	Lance Johnson	.15
73	Mickey Morandini	.15
74	Jon Lieber	.15
75	Kevin Tapani	.15
76	Carlos Lee	.15
77	Ray Durham	.15
78	Jim Parque	.15
79	Bob Howry	.15
80	Magglio Ordonez	.40
81	Paul Konerko	.25
82	Mike Caruso	.15
83	Chris Singleton	.15
84	Sean Casey	.40
85	Barry Larkin	.40
86	Pokey Reese	.15
87	Eddie Taubensee	.15
88	Scott Williamson	.15
89	Jason LaRue	.15
90	Aaron Boone	.15
91	Jeffrey Hammonds	.15
92	Omar Vizquel	.15
93	Manny Ramirez	.75
94	Kenny Lofton	.60
95	Jaret Wright	.20
96	Einar Diaz	.15
97	Charles Nagy	.15
98	David Justice	.25
99	Richie Sexson	.15
100	Steve Karsay	.15
101	Todd Helton	.75
102	Dante Bichette	.25
103	Larry Walker	.50
104	Pedro Astacio	.15
105	Neifi Perez	.15
106	Brian Bohanon	.15
107	Edgard Clemente	.15
108	Dave Veres	.15
109	Gabe Kapler	.25
110	Juan Encarnacion	.15
111	Jeff Weaver	.25
112	Damion Easley	.15
113	Justin Thompson	.15
114	Brad Ausmus	.15
115	Frank Catalanotto	.15
116	Todd Jones	.15
117	Preston Wilson	.15
118	Cliff Floyd	.15
119	Mike Lowell	.15
120	Jorge Fabregas	.15
121	Alex Gonzalez	.15
122	Braden Looper	.15
123	Bruce Aven	.15
124	Richard Hidalgo	.15
125	Mitch Meluskey	.15
126	Jeff Bagwell	.75
127	Jose Lima	.15
128	Derek Bell	.15
129	Billy Wagner	.15
130	Shane Reynolds	.15
131	Moises Alou	.25
132	Carlos Beltran	.25
133	Carlos Febles	.15
134	Jermaine Dye	.15
135	Jeremy Giambi	.15
136	Joe Randa	.15
137	Jose Rosado	.15
138	Chad Kreuter	.15
139	Jose Vizcaino	.15
140	Adrian Beltre	.25
141	Kevin Brown	.25
142	Ismael Valdes	.15
143	Angel Pena	.15
144	Chan Ho Park	.25
145	Mark Grudzielanek	.15
146	Jeff Shaw	.15
147	Geoff Jenkins	.15
148	Jeromy Burnitz	.15
149	Hideo Nomo	.25
150	Ron Belliard	.15
151	Sean Berry	.15
152	Mark Loretta	.15
153	Steve Woodard	.15
154	Joe Mays	.15
155	Eric Milton	.15
156	Corey Koskie	.15
157	Ron Coomer	.15
158	Brad Radke	.15
159	Terry Steinbach	.15
160	Christian Guzman	.15
161	Vladimir Guerrero	1.50
162	Wilton Guerrero	.15
163	Michael Barrett	.25
164	Chris Widger	.15
165	Fernando Seguignol	.25
166	Ugueth Urbina	.15
167	Dustin Hermanson	.15
168	Kenny Rogers	.15
169	Edgardo Alfonzo	.25
170	Orel Hershiser	.15
171	Robin Ventura	.40
172	Octavio Dotel	.15
173	Rickey Henderson	.25
174	Roger Cedeno	.15
175	John Olerud	.30
176	Derek Jeter	2.00
177	Tino Martinez	.40
178	Orlando Hernandez	.25
179	Chuck Knoblauch	.30
180	Bernie Williams	.50
181	Chili Davis	.15
182	David Cone	.25
183	Ricky Ledee	.15
184	Paul O'Neill	.25
185	Jason Giambi	.15
186	Eric Chavez	.15
187	Matt Stairs	.15
188	Miguel Tejada	.15
189	Olmedo Saenz	.15
190	Tim Hudson	.40
191	John Jaha	.15
192	Randy Velarde	.15
193	Rico Brogna	.15
194	Mike Lieberthal	.15
195	Marlon Anderson	.15
196	Bobby Abreu	.15
197	Ron Gant	.15
198	Randy Wolf	.15
199	Desi Relaford	.15
200	Doug Glanville	.15
201	Warren Morris	.15
202	Kris Benson	.15
203	Kevin Young	.15
204	Brian Giles	.15
205	Jason Schmidt	.15
206	Ed Sprague	.15
207	Francisco Cordova	.15
208	Mark McGwire	3.00
209	Jose Jimenez	.15
210	Fernando Tatis	.40
211	Kent Bottenfield	.15
212	Eli Marrero	.15
213	Edgar Renteria	.15
214	Joe McEwing	.15
215	J.D. Drew	.25
216	Tony Gwynn	1.50
217	Gary Matthews Jr.	.15
218	Eric Owens	.15
219	Damian Jackson	.15
220	Reggie Sanders	.15
221	Trevor Hoffman	.15
222	Ben Davis	.15
223	Shawn Estes	.15
224	F.P. Santangelo	.15
225	Livan Hernandez	.15
226	Ellis Burks	.15
227	J.T. Snow	.15
228	Jeff Kent	.15
229	Robb Nen	.15
230	Marvin Benard	.15
231	Ken Griffey Jr.	2.00
232	John Halama	.15
233	Gil Meche	.15
234	David Bell	.15
235	Brian L. Hunter	.15
236	Jay Buhner	.25
237	Edgar Martinez	.25
238	Jose Mesa	.15
239	Wilson Alvarez	.15
240	Wade Boggs	.40
241	Fred McGriff	.25
242	Jose Canseco	.75
243	Kevin Stocker	.15
244	Roberto Hernandez	.15
245	Bubba Trammell	.15
246	John Flaherty	.15
247	Ivan Rodriguez	.75
248	Rusty Greer	.15
249	Rafael Palmeiro	.40
250	Jeff Zimmerman	.15
251	Royce Clayton	.15
252	Todd Zeile	.15
253	John Wetteland	.15
254	Ruben Mateo	.40
255	Kelvim Escobar	.15
256	David Wells	.15
257	Shawn Green	.50
258	Homer Bush	.15
259	Shannon Stewart	.15
260	Carlos Delgado	.50
261	Roy Halladay	.15
262	Fernando Tatis CL	.25
263	Jose Jimenez CL	.15
264	Tony Gwynn CL	.75
265	Wade Boggs CL	.25
266	Cal Ripken Jr. CL	1.00
267	David Cone CL	.15
268	Mark McGwire CL	2.00
269	Pedro Martinez CL	.50
270	Nomar Garciaparra CL	1.00
271	Nick Johnson (Star Rookie)	.75
272	Mark Quinn (Star Rookie)	.15
273	Roosevelt Brown (Star Rookie)	.15
274	Adam Everett (Star Rookie)	.15
275	Jason Marquis (Star Rookie)	.15
276	*Kazuhiro Sasaki* (Star Rookie)	2.00
277	Aaron Myette (Star Rookie)	.15
278	*Danys Baez* (Star Rookie)	.15
279	Travis Dawkins (Star Rookie)	.15
280	Mark Mulder (Star Rookie)	.15
281	Chris Haas (Star Rookie)	.15
282	Milton Bradley (Star Rookie)	.15
283	Brad Penny (Star Rookie)	.15
284	Rafael Furcal (Star Rookie)	.25
285	*Luis Matos* (Star Rookie)	.15
286	Victor Santos (Star Rookie)	.15
287	*Rico Washington* (Star Rookie)	.15
288	Rob Bell (Star Rookie)	.15
289	Joe Crede (Star Rookie)	.15
290	Pablo Ozuna (Star Rookie)	.15
291	*Wascar Serrano* (Star Rookie)	.15
292	*Sang-Hoon Lee* (Star Rookie)	.50
293	Chris Wakeland (Star Rookie)	.15
294	Luis Rivera (Star Rookie)	.15
295	*Mike Lamb* (Star Rookie)	.75
296	Wily Pena (Star Rookie)	1.00
297	*Mike Meyers* (Star Rookie)	.15
298	Mo Vaughn	.50
299	Darin Erstad	.25
300	Garret Anderson	.15
301	Tim Belcher	.15
302	Scott Spiezio	.15
303	Kent Bottenfield	.15
304	Orlando Palmeiro	.15
305	Jason Dickson	.15
306	Matt Williams	.40
307	Brian Anderson	.15
308	Hanley Frias	.15
309	Todd Stottlemyre	.15
310	Matt Mantei	.15
311	David Dellucci	.15
312	Armando Reynoso	.15
313	Bernard Gilkey	.15
314	Chipper Jones	1.50
315	Tom Glavine	.25
316	Quilvio Veras	.15
317	Andruw Jones	.50
318	Bobby Bonilla	.15
319	Reggie Sanders	.15
320	Andres Galarraga	.40
321	George Lombard	.15
322	John Rocker	.15
322	Wally Joyner	.15
324	B.J. Surhoff	.15
325	Scott Erickson	.15
326	Delino DeShields	.15
327	Jeff Conine	.15
328	Mike Timlin	.15
329	Brady Anderson	.20
330	Mike Bordick	.15
331	Harold Baines	.15
332	Nomar Garciaparra	2.00
333	Bret Saberhagen	.15
334	Ramon Martinez	.15
335	Donnie Sadler	.15
336	Wilton Veras	.15
337	Mike Stanley	.15
338	Brian Rose	.15
339	Carl Everett	.15
340	Tim Wakefield	.15
341	Mark Grace	.25
342	Kerry Wood	.30
343	Eric Young	.15
344	Jose Nieves	.15
345	Ismael Valdes	.15
346	Joe Girardi	.15
347	Damon Buford	.15
348	Ricky Gutierrez	.15
349	Frank Thomas	1.00
350	Brian Simmons	.15
351	James Baldwin	.15
352	Brook Fordyce	.15
353	Jose Valentin	.15
354	Mike Sirotka	.15
355	Greg Norton	.15
356	Dante Bichette	.15
357	Deion Sanders	.25
358	Ken Griffey Jr.	2.00
359	Denny Neagle	.15
360	Dmitri Young	.15
361	Pete Harnisch	.15
362	Michael Tucker	.15
363	Roberto Alomar	.50
364	Dave Roberts	.15
365	Jim Thome	.40
366	Bartolo Colon	.15
367	Travis Fryman	.20
368	Chuck Finley	.15
369	Russell Branyan	.20
370	Alex Ramirez	.15
371	Jeff Cirillo	.15
372	Jeffrey Hammonds	.15
373	Scott Karl	.15
374	Brent Mayne	.15
375	Tom Goodwin	.15
376	Jose Jimenez	.15
377	Rolando Arrojo	.15
378	Terry Shumpert	.15
379	Juan Gonzalez	.75
380	Bobby Higginson	.15
381	Tony Clark	.25
382	Dave Mlicki	.15
383	Deivi Cruz	.15
384	Brian Moehler	.15
385	Dean Palmer	.15
386	Luis Castillo	.15
387	Mike Redmond	.15
388	Alex Fernandez	.15
389	Brant Brown	.15
390	Dave Berg	.15
391	A.J. Burnett	.15
392	Mark Kotsay	.15
393	Craig Biggio	.30
394	Daryle Ward	.15
395	Lance Berkman	.15
396	Roger Cedeno	.15
397	Scott Elarton	.15
398	Octavio Dotel	.15
399	Ken Caminiti	.15
400	Johnny Damon	.15
401	Mike Sweeney	.15
402	Jeff Suppan	.15
403	Rey Sanchez	.15
404	Blake Stein	.15
405	Ricky Bottalico	.15
406	Jay Witasick	.15
407	Shawn Green	.50
408	Orel Hershiser	.15
409	Gary Sheffield	.40
410	Todd Hollandsworth	.15
411	Terry Adams	.15
412	Todd Hundley	.15
413	Eric Karros	.15
414	F.P. Santangelo	.15
415	Alex Cora	.15
416	Marquis Grissom	.15
417	Henry Blanco	.15
418	Jose Hernandez	.15

419	Kyle Peterson	.15
420	*John Snyder*	.15
421	Bob Wickman	.15
422	Jamey Wright	.15
423	Chad Allen	.15
424	Todd Walker	.15
425	*J.C. Romero*	.15
426	Butch Huskey	.15
427	Jacque Jones	.15
428	Matt Lawton	.15
429	Rondell White	.25
430	Jose Vidro	.15
431	Hideki Irabu	.15
432	Javier Vazquez	.15
433	Lee Stevens	.15
434	Mike Thurman	.15
435	Geoff Blum	.15
436	Mike Hampton	.15
437	Mike Piazza	2.00
438	Al Leiter	.15
439	Derek Bell	.15
440	Armando Benitez	.15
441	Rey Ordonez	.15
442	Todd Zeile	.15
443	Roger Clemens	1.00
444	Ramiro Mendoza	.15
445	Andy Pettite	.25
446	Scott Brosius	.15
447	Mariano Rivera	.25
448	Jim Leyritz	.15
449	Jorge Posada	.25
450	Omar Olivares	.15
451	Ben Grieve	.25
452	A.J. Hinch	.15
453	Gil Heredia	.15
454	Kevin Appier	.15
455	Ryan Christenson	.15
456	Ramon Hernandez	.15
457	Scott Rolen	.75
458	Alex Arias	.15
459	Andy Ashby	.15
460	(Not issued, see #474)	
460		.15
461	Robert Person	.15
462	Paul Byrd	.15
463	Curt Schilling	.25
464	Mike Jackson	.15
465	Jason Kendall	.15
466	Pat Meares	.15
467	Bruce Aven	.15
468	Todd Ritchie	.15
469	Wil Cordero	.15
470	Aramis Ramirez	.15
471	Andy Benes	.15
472	Ray Lankford	.15
473	Fernando Vina	.15
474a	Jim Edmonds	.25
474b	Kevin Jordan (should be #460)	.15
475	Craig Paquette	.15
476	Pat Hentgen	.15
477	Darryl Kile	.15
478	Sterling Hitchcock	.15
479	Ruben Rivera	.15
480	Ryan Klesko	.15
481	Phil Nevin	.15
482	Woody Williams	.15
483	Carlos Hernandez	.15
484	Brian Meadows	.15
485	Bret Boone	.15
486	Barry Bonds	1.00
487	Russ Ortiz	.15
488	Bobby Estalella	.15
489	Rich Aurilia	.15
490	Bill Mueller	.15
491	Joe Nathan	.15
492	Russ Davis	.15
493	John Olerud	.25
494	Alex Rodriguez	2.50
495	Fred Garcia	.15
496	Carlos Guillen	.15
497	Aaron Sele	.15
498	Brett Tomko	.15
499	Jamie Moyer	.15
500	Mike Cameron	.15
501	Vinny Castilla	.15
502	Gerald Williams	.15
503	Mike DiFelice	.15
504	Ryan Rupe	.15
505	Greg Vaughn	.25
506	Miguel Cairo	.15
507	*Juan Guzman*	.15
508	Jose Guillen	.15
509	Gabe Kapler	.15
510	Rick Helling	.15
511	David Segui	.15
512	Doug Davis	.15
513	Justin Thompson	.15
514	Chad Curtis	.15
515	Tony Batista	.15
516	Billy Koch	.15
517	Raul Mondesi	.25
518	Joey Hamilton	.15
519	Darrin Fletcher	.15
520	Brad Fullmer	.15
521	Jose Cruz Jr.	.15
522	Kevin Witt	.15
523	Mark McGwire (All-UD Team)	1.50
524	Roberto Alomar (All-UD Team)	.25
525	Chipper Jones (All-UD Team)	.75
526	Derek Jeter (All-UD Team)	1.00
527	Ken Griffey Jr. (All-UD Team)	1.00
528	Sammy Sosa (All-UD Team)	1.00
529	Manny Ramirez (All-UD Team)	.40
530	Ivan Rodriguez (All-UD Team)	.40
531	Pedro J. Martinez (All-UD Team)	.40
532	Mariano Rivera (Season Highlights Checklist)	.15
533	Sammy Sosa (Season Highlights Checklist)	1.00
534	Cal Ripken Jr. (Season Highlights Checklist)	1.00
535	Vladimir Guerrero (Season Highlights Checklist)	.75
536	Tony Gwynn (Season Highlights Checklist)	.50
537	Mark McGwire (Season Highlights Checklist)	1.50
538	Bernie Williams (Season Highlights Checklist)	.25
539	Pedro J. Martinez (Season Highlights Checklist)	.40
540	Ken Griffey Jr. (Season Highlights Checklist)	1.00

2000 Upper Deck Exclusives

Labeled "UD Exclusives," these parallel sets were issued in two versions, silvers numbered to 100 each, and golds which were 1-of-1. Except for the appropriately colored foil highlights on front and dot-matrix serial number, the Exclusives are identical to the regular-issue cards. They were inserted exclusively into hobby packs. Because of their rarity and variable demand, the unique gold cards are not priced.

	MT
Common Silver Exclusive:	5.00
Silver Stars/Rookies:	20X

(See 2000 Upper Deck for checklist and base card values.)

2000 Upper Deck Cooperstown Calling

This 12-card set features players deemed by Upper Deck as future Hall of Famers. Card fronts feature silver holo-foil with gold foil stamping. Card backs are numbered with an "CC" prefix and are seeded 1:23 packs.

		MT
Complete Set (15):		120.00
Common Player:		3.00
Inserted 1:23		
1	Roger Clemens	8.00
2	Cal Ripken Jr.	15.00
3	Ken Griffey Jr.	15.00
4	Mike Piazza	12.00
5	Tony Gwynn	8.00
6	Sammy Sosa	12.00
7	Jose Canseco	4.00
8	Larry Walker	3.00
9	Barry Bonds	5.00
10	Greg Maddux	10.00
11	Derek Jeter	12.00
12	Mark McGwire	20.00
13	Randy Johnson	5.00
14	Frank Thomas	8.00
15	Jeff Bagwell	5.00

2000 Upper Deck e-Card

Randomly inserted in series 2 packs, each e-card has an ID number stamped on the card front that can be entered on Upper Deck's website. Collectors then find out if that card "evolves" into a signature card, jersey card or a signed jersey card. They are seeded 1:9 packs and are numbered with an "E" prefix on the card back.

		MT
Complete Set (6):		10.00
Common Player:		1.00
Inserted 1:12		
1	Ken Griffey Jr.	3.00
2	Alex Rodriguez	3.00
3	Cal Ripken Jr.	3.00
4	Jeff Bagwell	1.00
5	Barry Bonds	1.00
6	Manny Ramirez	1.00

2000 Upper Deck eVolve Signature

		MT
Common Player:		40.00
Production 200 sets		
1	Ken Griffey Jr.	85.00
2	Alex Rodriguez	85.00
3	Cal Ripken Jr.	150.00
4	Jeff Bagwell	40.00
5	Barry Bonds	100.00
6	Manny Ramirez	40.00

2000 Upper Deck eVolve Jersey

		MT
Common Player:		15.00
Production 300 sets		
1	Ken Griffey Jr.	40.00
2	Alex Rodriguez	40.00
3	Cal Ripken Jr.	65.00
4	Jeff Bagwell	20.00
5	Barry Bonds	50.00
6	Manny Ramirez	20.00

2000 Upper Deck eVolve Signed Jersey

		MT
Common Player:		80.00
Production 50 sets		
1	Ken Griffey Jr.	185.00
2	Alex Rodriguez	185.00
3	Cal Ripken Jr.	275.00
4	Jeff Bagwell	80.00
5	Barry Bonds	275.00
6	Manny Ramirez	80.00

2000 Upper Deck Faces of the Game

Randomly inserted in series one at a rate of 1:11 packs card fronts feature a close-up photo of the featured player with bronze foil etching and stamping. Backs are numbered with an "F" prefix. Two parallel versions are available, Silvers are serially numbered to 100 and golds limited to one set.

		MT
Complete Set (20):		90.00
Common Player:		1.50
Inserted 1:11		
Silver:		6X to 12X
Production 100 sets		
1	Ken Griffey Jr.	10.00
2	Mark McGwire	12.00
3	Sammy Sosa	8.00
4	Alex Rodriguez	10.00
5	Manny Ramirez	3.00
6	Derek Jeter	8.00
7	Jeff Bagwell	3.00
8	Roger Clemens	4.00
9	Scott Rolen	3.00
10	Tony Gwynn	6.00
11	Nomar Garciaparra	8.00
12	Randy Johnson	2.50
13	Greg Maddux	6.00
14	Mike Piazza	8.00
15	Frank Thomas	3.00
16	Cal Ripken Jr.	8.00
17	Ivan Rodriguez	3.00
18	Mo Vaughn	2.50
19	Chipper Jones	8.00
20	Sean Casey	2.00

2000 Upper Deck Five-Tool Talents

Randomly inserted in series 2 at a rate of 1:11 packs, this 15-card set spotlights players who have "five tools". Card fronts have silver holo-foil throughout with silver foil stamping. Card backs are numbered with an "FT" prefix.

		MT
Complete Set (15):		40.00
Common Player:		1.00
Inserted 1:11		
1	Vladimir Guerrero	3.00
2	Barry Bonds	2.50
3	Jason Kendall	1.00
4	Derek Jeter	6.00
5	Ken Griffey Jr.	8.00
6	Andruw Jones	2.00
7	Bernie Williams	2.00
8	Jose Canseco	2.00
9	Scott Rolen	2.50
10	Shawn Green	2.00
11	Nomar Garciaparra	6.00
12	Jeff Bagwell	2.50
13	Larry Walker	1.50
14	Chipper Jones	5.00
15	Alex Rodriguez	8.00

2000 Upper Deck Game Jersey

These have a piece of game-used jersey from the featured player embedded into the card. This regular version is found both in hobby and retail packs at a rate of 1:2,500 packs.

		MT
Common Player:		15.00
Inserted 1:2,500		
JC	Jose Canseco	20.00
JG	Juan Gonzalez	20.00
VG	Vladimir Guerrero	25.00
TH	Todd Helton	15.00
CJ	Chipper Jones	25.00
GK	Gabe Kapler	15.00
GM	Greg Maddux	35.00
MR	Manny Ramirez	20.00
CR	Cal Ripken Jr.	65.00
GV	Greg Vaughn	15.00

2000 Upper Deck Game Jersey Hobby

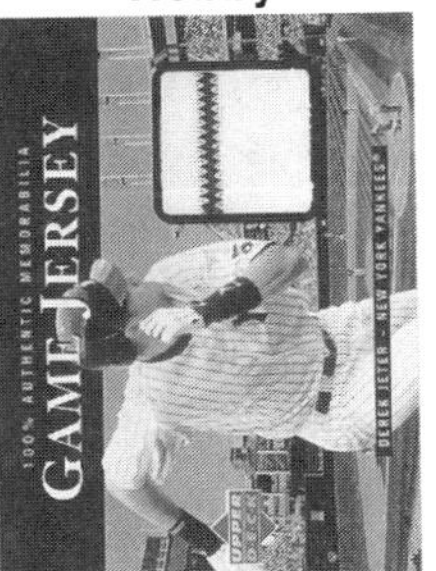

These game-used memorabilia inserts were found exclusively in series 1 packs at a rate of 1:288.

		MT
Common Player:		15.00
Inserted 1:288		50.00
JB	Jeff Bagwell	20.00
TG	Troy Glaus	20.00
CY	Tom Glavine	15.00
Jr.	Ken Griffey Jr.	40.00
DJ	Derek Jeter	50.00
PM	Pedro J. Martinez	25.00
MP	Mike Piazza	40.00
AR	Alex Rodriguez	35.00
FT	Frank Thomas	20.00
LW	Larry Walker	15.00

2000 Upper Deck Game Jersey Patch

Inserted in Series 1 packs at a rate of 1:10,000, these memorabilia inserts have a piece of game-used uniform patch embedded. A 1-of-1 patch of each player was also issued, but cannot be priced due to rarity.

		MT
Common Player:		70.00
Inserted 1:10,000		
JB	Jeff Bagwell	100.00
JC	Jose Canseco	90.00
TG	Troy Glaus	100.00
CY	Tom Glavine	90.00
Jr.	Ken Griffey Jr.	200.00
VG	Vladimir Guerrero	125.00
TH	Todd Helton	90.00
DJ	Derek Jeter	300.00
CJ	Chipper Jones	150.00
GK	Gabe Kapler	70.00
GM	Greg Maddux	175.00
PM	Pedro J. Martinez	150.00
MP	Mike Piazza	200.00
MR	Manny Ramirez	125.00
CR	Cal Ripken Jr.	300.00
AR	Alex Rodriguez	200.00
FT	Frank Thomas	100.00
GV	Greg Vaughn	70.00
LW	Larry Walker	75.00

2000 Upper Deck Game Balls

These inserts feature a piece of game-used baseball embedded into the card from the featured player. Card backs are numbered with the featured player's initials and are found on the average of 1:287 series 2 packs.

		MT
Common Player:		10.00
JB	Jeff Bagwell	15.00
RC	Roger Clemens	35.00
KG	Ken Griffey Jr.	40.00
VG	Vladimir Guerrero	25.00
TG	Tony Gwynn	25.00
DJ	Derek Jeter	50.00
CJ	Chipper Jones	25.00
GM	Greg Maddux	25.00
MM	Mark McGwire	65.00
AR	Alex Rodriguez	40.00
BW	Bernie Williams	10.00

2000 Upper Deck Game Jersey Series 2

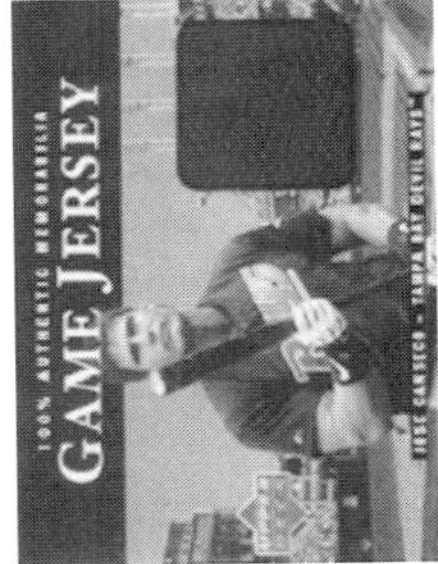

These jersey inserts are found in both hobby and retail packs and are seeded 1:287 packs.

		MT
Common Player:		15.00
AR	Alex Rodriguez	35.00
TG	Tony Gwynn	30.00
FT	Frank Thomas	20.00
MW	Matt Williams	15.00
JT	Jim Thome	25.00
MV	Mo Vaughn	15.00
TGl	Tom Glavine	15.00
BG	Ben Grieve	15.00
TrG	Troy Glaus	20.00
RJ	Randy Johnson	25.00
KM	Kevin Millwood	15.00
KG	Ken Griffey Jr.	40.00
AB	Albert Belle	15.00
DC	David Cone	15.00
MH	Mike Hampton	15.00
EC	Eric Chavez	20.00
EM	Edgar Martinez	15.00
PW	Preston Wilson	15.00
RV	Robin Ventura	15.00

2000 Upper Deck Game Jersey Auto. Hobby Series 2

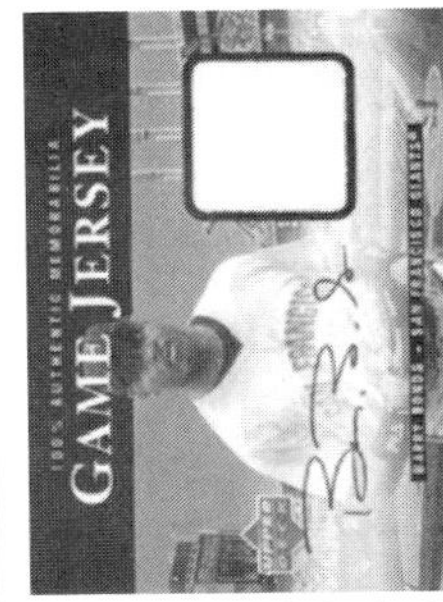

Found exclusively in series 2 packs these autographed game- used memorabilia inserts are found only in hobby packs at a rate of 1:287.

		MT
Common Player:		30.00
H-KG	Ken Griffey Jr.	125.00
H-CR	Cal Ripken Jr.	200.00
H-DJ	Derek Jeter	200.00
H-IR	Ivan Rodriguez	40.00
H-AR	Alex Rodriguez	125.00
H-MR	Manny Ramirez	50.00
H-JC	Jose Canseco	40.00
H-BB	Barry Bonds	150.00
H-SR	Scott Rolen	40.00
H-PO	Paul O'Neill	40.00

H-JK	Jason Kendall	30.00
H-VG	Vladimir Guerrero	65.00
H-JB	Jeff Bagwell	60.00

2000 Upper Deck Game Jersey Patch Series 2

Inserted in Series 2 packs, these memorabilia inserts have a game-used uniform patch embedded and are seeded 1:7,500 packs. A limited one-of-one patch insert for each player is also randomly seeded and are not priced due to their limited nature.

		MT
Common Player:		150.00
JB	Jeff Bagwell	350.00
BB	Barry Bonds	400.00
JC	Jose Canseco	300.00
TGI	Troy Glaus	300.00
KG	Ken Griffey Jr.	800.00
VG	Vladimir Guerrero	400.00
TG	Tony Gwynn	350.00
DJ	Derek Jeter	700.00
RJ	Randy Johnson	450.00
AJ	Andruw Jones	350.00
CJ	Chipper Jones	500.00
GM	Greg Maddux	500.00
PM	Pedro Martinez	500.00
MR	Manny Ramirez	300.00
CR	Cal Ripken Jr.	800.00
SR	Scott Rolen	200.00
AR	Alex Rodriguez	600.00
IR	Ivan Rodriguez	400.00
FT	Frank Thomas	400.00
MV	Mo Vaughn	200.00
MW	Matt Williams	200.00

2000 Upper Deck Hit Brigade

Fifteen of the game's top hitters are featured on a full foiled front with bronze foil stamping. Card backs are numbered with an "H" prefix and are found in series 1 packs at a rate of 1:8. Two parallels are randomly inserted: Silvers are serial numbered to 100 and Golds are limited to one set.

		MT
Complete Set (15):		35.00
Common Player:		.75
Inserted 1:8		
Silver:		10X to 20X
Production 100 sets		
1	Ken Griffey Jr.	5.00
2	Tony Gwynn	3.00
3	Alex Rodriguez	5.00
4	Derek Jeter	4.00
5	Mike Piazza	4.00
6	Sammy Sosa	4.00
7	Juan Gonzalez	1.50
8	Scott Rolen	1.50
9	Nomar Garciaparra	4.00
10	Barry Bonds	2.00
11	Craig Biggio	.75
12	Chipper Jones	4.00
13	Frank Thomas	1.50
14	Larry Walker	1.25
15	Mark McGwire	6.00

2000 Upper Deck Hot Properties

This set spotlights ten rookies and prospects who have a bright future. Card fronts have a horizontal format on a holo-foiled stock with silver foil stamping. Card backs are numbered with an "HP" prefix and are found in series 2 packs at a rate of 1:11.

		MT
Complete Set (15):		20.00
Common Player:		1.00
Inserted 1:11		
1	Carlos Beltran	1.00
2	Rick Ankiel	2.00
3	Sean Casey	1.00
4	Preston Wilson	1.00
5	Vernon Wells	1.00
6	Pat Burrell	4.00
7	Eric Chavez	1.00
8	J.D. Drew	1.00
9	Alfonso Soriano	2.50
10	Gabe Kapler	1.00
11	Rafael Furcal	1.00
12	Ruben Mateo	1.00
13	Corey Koskie	1.00
14	Kip Wells	1.00
15	Ramon Ortiz	1.00

2000 Upper Deck Pennant Driven

This 10-card horizontal set has a holo-foiled card front with silver foil stamping. Card backs are numbered with an "PD" prefix and are seeded 1:4 packs.

		MT
Complete Set (10):		10.00
Common Player:		.50
Inserted 1:4		
1	Derek Jeter	2.00
2	Roberto Alomar	.50
3	Chipper Jones	1.50
4	Jeff Bagwell	.75
5	Roger Clemens	1.00
6	Nomar Garciaparra	2.00
7	Manny Ramirez	.75
8	Mike Piazza	2.00
9	Ivan Rodriguez	.75
10	Randy Johnson	.75

2000 Upper Deck Piece of History-500 Club

This card features a piece of a game-used Louisville Slugger once swung by Aaron. Approximately 350 cards were produced. Also randomly inserted are 44 autographed versions.

		MT
755HR	Hank Aaron	400.00
HAAU	Hank Aaron Auto./44	1000.

2000 Upper Deck Power Deck

Collectors need access to a CD-ROM in order to enjoy these interactive cards. Found exclusively in hobby packs cards 1-8 are seeded 1:23 packs and cards 9-11 are found 1:287 packs.

		MT
Complete Set (11):		50.00
Common Player:		2.00
Inserted 1:23		
1	Ken Griffey Jr.	8.00
2	Cal Ripken Jr.	6.00
3	Mark McGwire	10.00
4	Tony Gwynn	5.00
5	Roger Clemens	4.00
6	Alex Rodriguez	8.00
7	Sammy Sosa	6.00
8	Derek Jeter	6.00
9	Ken Griffey Jr.	35.00
10	Mark McGwire	40.00
11	Reggie Jackson	10.00

2000 Upper Deck Power MARK

		MT
Complete Set (10):		80.00
Common McGwire:		10.00
Inserted 1:23		
Silver:		8X to 15X
Production 100 sets		
1	Mark McGwire	10.00
2	Mark McGwire	10.00
3	Mark McGwire	10.00
4	Mark McGwire	10.00
5	Mark McGwire	10.00
6	Mark McGwire	10.00
7	Mark McGwire	10.00
8	Mark McGwire	10.00
9	Mark McGwire	10.00
10	Mark McGwire	10.00

2000 Upper Deck Power Rally

This 15-card set highlights the top hitters and are numbered with an "P" prefix on the card back. They are found 1:11 packs. Two parallel version are also seeded: Coppers are limited to 100 serial numbered sets and Golds are limited to one set.

		MT
Complete Set (15):		60.00
Common Player:		1.50
Inserted 1:11		
Silver:		8X to 15X
Production 100 sets		
1	Ken Griffey Jr.	8.00
2	Mark McGwire	10.00
3	Sammy Sosa	6.00
4	Jose Canseco	2.50
5	Juan Gonzalez	2.50

6	Bernie Williams	2.00
7	Jeff Bagwell	2.50
8	Chipper Jones	6.00
9	Vladimir Guerrero	4.00
10	Mo Vaughn	2.00
11	Derek Jeter	6.00
12	Mike Piazza	6.00
13	Barry Bonds	3.00
14	Alex Rodriguez	8.00
15	Nomar Garciaparra	6.00

2000 Upper Deck Prime Performers

This 10-card set has a horizontal format on a full holo foiled front, with silver foil etching and stamping. Card backs are numbered with an "PP" prefix and found 1:8 packs.

		MT
Complete Set (10):		15.00
Common Player:		.75
Inserted 1:8		
1	Manny Ramirez	1.00
2	Pedro Martinez	1.00
3	Carlos Delgado	.75
4	Ken Griffey Jr.	3.00
5	Derek Jeter	2.50
6	Chipper Jones	2.00
7	Sean Casey	.75
8	Shawn Green	.75
9	Sammy Sosa	2.50
10	Alex Rodriguez	3.00

2000 Upper Deck STATitude

This 30-card set spotlights the most statistically dominant players on a horizontal format with silver foil stamping. Card backs are numbered with an "S" prefix and are inserted 1:4. Two parallel versions are randomly inserted: Coppers are limited to 100 serial numbered sets and Golds are limited to one set.

		MT
Complete Set (30):		50.00
Common Player:		.50
Inserted 1:4		
Silver:		10X to 20X
Production 100 sets		
1	Mo Vaughn	1.00
2	Matt Williams	.75
3	Travis Lee	.50
4	Chipper Jones	4.00
5	Greg Maddux	4.00
6	Gabe Kapler	.75
7	Cal Ripken Jr.	4.00
8	Nomar Garciaparra	4.00
9	Sammy Sosa	4.00
10	Frank Thomas	1.50
11	Manny Ramirez	1.50
12	Larry Walker	1.25
13	Ivan Rodriguez	1.50
14	Jeff Bagwell	1.50
15	Craig Biggio	.75
16	Vladimir Guerrero	3.00
17	Mike Piazza	4.00
18	Bernie Williams	1.00
19	Derek Jeter	4.00
20	Jose Canseco	1.50
21	Eric Chavez	.50
22	Scott Rolen	1.50
23	Mark McGwire	6.00
24	Tony Gwynn	3.00
25	Barry Bonds	2.00
26	Ken Griffey Jr.	5.00
27	Alex Rodriguez	5.00
28	J.D. Drew	.50
29	Juan Gonzalez	1.50
30	Roger Clemens	2.50

2000 Upper Deck The People's Choice

This 15-card set is printed on a full holo-foiled front with gold foil stamping. Card backs are numbered with an "PC" prefix and are seeded 1:23 packs.

		MT
Complete Set (15):		120.00
Common Player:		3.00
Inserted 1:23		
1	Mark McGwire	20.00
2	Nomar Garciaparra	12.00
3	Derek Jeter	12.00
4	Shawn Green	4.00
5	Manny Ramirez	5.00
6	Pedro Martinez	5.00
7	Ivan Rodriguez	5.00
8	Alex Rodriguez	15.00
9	Juan Gonzalez	5.00
10	Ken Griffey Jr.	15.00
11	Sammy Sosa	12.00
12	Jeff Bagwell	5.00
13	Chipper Jones	10.00
14	Cal Ripken Jr.	15.00
15	Mike Piazza	12.00

2000 Upper Deck 3,000 Hit Club

This continuing series spotlights Hank Aaron. The series includes a Jersey card (350 produced), Bat card (350 produced), Jersey/Bat combo (100 produced) and Autographed Jersey/Bat combo (44 produced).

		MT
HA-B	Hank Aaron bat/350	300.00
HA-JB	Hank Aaron bat/jersey/100	600.00
HA-J	Hank Aaron jersey/350	350.00
HA	Hank Aaron Auto. bat/jersey/44	1000.

2000 Upper Deck Black Diamond

The base set consists of 120-cards, including a 30 card Diamond Debut (91-120) subset that are seeded 1:4 packs. Card fronts are full foiled with silver etching. Card backs have the player's past five years of statistics, a brief career note and small photo.

		MT
Complete Set (120):		100.00
Common Player:		.20
Common Diamond Debut:		1.00
Pack (6):		2.50
Wax Box (24):		45.00
1	Darin Erstad	.40
2	Tim Salmon	.40
3	Mo Vaughn	.40
4	Matt Williams	.25
5	Travis Lee	.20
6	Randy Johnson	.75
7	Tom Glavine	.40
8	Chipper Jones	1.50
9	Greg Maddux	1.50
10	Andruw Jones	.50
11	Brian Jordan	.20
12	Cal Ripken Jr.	2.50
13	Albert Belle	.40
14	Mike Mussina	.50
15	Nomar Garciaparra	2.00
16	Troy O'Leary	.20
17	Pedro J. Martinez	1.00
18	Sammy Sosa	1.50
19	Henry Rodriguez	.20
20	Frank Thomas	1.00
21	Magglio Ordonez	.40
22	Greg Vaughn	.25
23	Barry Larkin	.40
24	Sean Casey	.30
25	Jim Thome	.40
26	Kenny Lofton	.30
27	Roberto Alomar	.60
28	Manny Ramirez	.75
29	Larry Walker	.30
30	Todd Helton	.75
31	Gabe Kapler	.25
32	Tony Clark	.25
33	Dean Palmer	.20
34	Cliff Floyd	.20
35	Alex Gonzalez	.20
36	Moises Alou	.20
37	Jeff Bagwell	.75
38	Craig Biggio	.30
39	Richard Hidalgo	.20
40	Carlos Beltran	.25
41	Johnny Damon	.20
42	Adrian Beltre	.20
43	Gary Sheffield	.40
44	Kevin Brown	.30
45	Jeromy Burnitz	.20
46	Jeff Cirillo	.20
47	Joe Mays	.20
48	Todd Walker	.20
49	Vladimir Guerrero	1.00
50	Michael Barrett	.20
51	Rickey Henderson	.40
52	Mike Piazza	2.00
53	Robin Ventura	.40
54	John Olerud	.40
55	Edgardo Alfonzo	.40
56	Derek Jeter	2.50
57	Orlando Hernandez	.40
58	Tino Martinez	.30
59	Bernie Williams	.50
60	Roger Clemens	1.00
61	Eric Chavez	.20
62	Ben Grieve	.40
63	Jason Giambi	.40
64	Scott Rolen	.50
65	Bobby Abreu	.20
66	Curt Schilling	.30
67	Mike Lieberthal	.20
68	Warren Morris	.20
69	Brian Giles	.20
70	Eric Owens	.20
71	Tony Gwynn	1.00
72	Reggie Sanders	.20
73	Barry Bonds	1.00
74	J.T. Snow	.20
75	Jeff Kent	.20
76	Ken Griffey Jr.	2.00
77	Alex Rodriguez	2.50
78	Edgar Martinez	.20
79	Jay Buhner	.20
80	Mark McGwire	3.00
81	J.D. Drew	.40
82	Eric Davis	.20
83	Fernando Tatis	.20
84	Wade Boggs	.50
85	Fred McGriff	.40
86	Juan Gonzalez	.75
87	Ivan Rodriguez	.75
88	Rafael Palmeiro	.50
89	Shawn Green	.40
90	Carlos Delgado	.60
91	Pat Burrell (Diamond Debut)	3.00
92	Eric Munson (Diamond Debut)	1.00
93	Jorge Toca (Diamond Debut)	1.00
94	Rick Ankiel (Diamond Debut)	2.00
95	Tony Armas Jr. (Diamond Debut)	1.00
96	Byung-Hyun Kim (Diamond Debut)	1.00
97	Alfonso Soriano (Diamond Debut)	5.00
98	Mark Quinn (Diamond Debut)	1.00
99	Ryan Rupe (Diamond Debut)	1.00
100	Adam Kennedy (Diamond Debut)	1.00
101	Jeff Weaver (Diamond Debut)	1.00

102 Ramon Ortiz (Diamond Debut) 1.00
103 Eugene Kingsale (Diamond Debut) 1.00
104 Josh Beckett (Diamond Debut) 2.50
105 Eric Gagne (Diamond Debut) 1.00
106 Peter Bergeron (Diamond Debut) 1.00
107 Erubiel Durazo (Diamond Debut) 1.50
108 Chad Meyers (Diamond Debut) 1.00
109 Kip Wells (Diamond Debut) 1.00
110 Chad Harville (Diamond Debut) 1.00
111 Matt Riley (Diamond Debut) 1.00
112 Ben Petrick (Diamond Debut) 1.00
113 Ed Yarnall (Diamond Debut) 1.00
114 Calvin Murray (Diamond Debut) 1.00
115 Vernon Wells (Diamond Debut) 1.00
116 A.J. Burnett (Diamond Debut) 1.50
117 Jacque Jones (Diamond Debut) 1.00
118 Francisco Cordero (Diamond Debut) 1.00
119 *Tomokazu Ohka* (Diamond Debut) 2.00
120 Julio Ramirez (Diamond Debut) 1.00

2000 Upper Deck Black Diamond Final Cut

A parallel to the 120-card base set the die-cut design can be used to distinguish them from base cards, the card backs are also numbered with an "F" prefix. Each card is serial numbered within an edition of 100 sets.

	MT
Stars (1-90):	15X to 25X
Diamond Debuts:	3X to 5X
Production 100 sets	

(See 2000 UD Black Diamond for checklist and base card values.)

2000 Upper Deck Black Diamond Reciprocal Cut

A parallel to the 120-card base set, the die-cut design can be used to differentiate them from base cards. Card backs are also numbered with an "R" prefix. Cards 1-90 are found 1:7 packs and Diamond Debuts (91-120) are seeded 1:12 packs.

	MT
Stars (1-90):	2X to 5X
Diamond Debuts	1X to 1.5X
1-90 inserted 1:7	
Diamond Debuts inserted 1:12	

(See 2000 UD Black Diamond for checklist and base card values.)

2000 Upper Deck Black Diamond A Piece of History Single

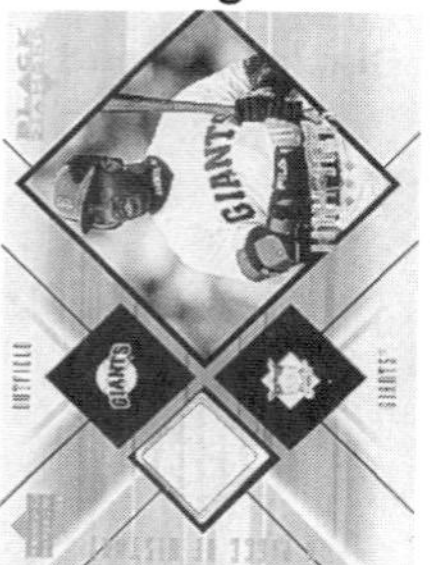

These memorabilia inserts have a piece of game-used bat embedded into the card front and are seeded 1:179 packs.

		MT
Common Player:		10.00
Inserted 1:179		
AB	Albert Belle	10.00
BB	Barry Bonds	40.00
JC	Jose Canseco	15.00
DE	Darin Erstad	10.00
JR	Ken Griffey Jr.	35.00
VG	Vladimir Guerrero	20.00
TG	Tony Gwynn	25.00
TH	Todd Helton	15.00
DJ	Derek Jeter	50.00
AJ	Andruw Jones	10.00
CJ	Chipper Jones	30.00
TL	Travis Lee	10.00
RM	Raul Mondesi	10.00
MP	Mike Piazza	30.00
CAL	Cal Ripken Jr.	50.00
AR	Alex Rodriguez	35.00
IR	Ivan Rodriguez	15.00
SR	Scott Rolen	10.00
MV	Mo Vaughn	10.00

2000 Upper Deck Black Diamond A Piece of History Double

These memorabilia inserts have two pieces of game-used bat embedded into the card front and are a parallel to the single set. They are inserted 1:1,079 packs.

		MT
Common Player:		15.00
Inserted 1:1079		
AB	Albert Belle	15.00
BB	Barry Bonds	75.00
JC	Jose Canseco	40.00
DE	Darin Erstad	20.00
JR	Ken Griffey Jr.	65.00
VG	Vladimir Guerrero	40.00
TG	Tony Gwynn	40.00
TH	Todd Helton	30.00
DJ	Derek Jeter	100.00
AJ	Andruw Jones	30.00
CJ	Chipper Jones	40.00
TL	Travis Lee	15.00
RM	Raul Mondesi	15.00
MP	Mike Piazza	60.00
CAL	Cal Ripken Jr.	100.00
AR	Alex Rodriguez	65.00
IR	Ivan Rodriguez	20.00
SR	Scott Rolen	20.00
MV	Mo Vaughn	15.00

2000 Upper Deck Black Diamond Barrage

This 10-card set features a prismatic background with silver foil stamping. Card backs are numbered with an "B" prefix and are seeded 1:29 packs.

		MT
Complete Set (10):		70.00
Common Player:		3.00
Inserted 1:29		
1	Mark McGwire	15.00
2	Ken Griffey Jr.	12.00
3	Sammy Sosa	10.00
4	Jeff Bagwell	4.00
5	Juan Gonzalez	4.00
6	Alex Rodriguez	10.00
7	Manny Ramirez	4.00
8	Ivan Rodriguez	4.00
9	Chipper Jones	8.00
10	Mike Piazza	10.00

2000 Upper Deck Black Diamond Constant Threat

A ten-card set spotlighting the top hitters in the game. Card backs are numbered with an "T" prefix and are seeded 1:29 packs.

		MT
Complete Set (10):		70.00
Common Player:		3.00
Inserted 1:29		
1	Ken Griffey Jr.	12.00
2	Vladimir Guerrero	6.00
3	Alex Rodriguez	10.00
4	Sammy Sosa	10.00
5	Juan Gonzalez	4.00
6	Derek Jeter	10.00
7	Nomar Garciaparra	10.00
8	Barry Bonds	4.00
9	Chipper Jones	8.00
10	Mike Piazza	10.00

2000 Upper Deck Black Diamond Diamonation

This 10-card set has a holo-foil background with gold foil etching and stamping. Card backs are numbered with an "D" prefix and have an insertion ratio of 1:4 packs.

		MT
Complete Set (10):		15.00
Common Player:		1.00
Inserted 1:4		
1	Ken Griffey Jr.	4.00
2	Randy Johnson	1.00
3	Mark McGwire	5.00
4	Manny Ramirez	1.50
5	Scott Rolen	1.50
6	Bernie Williams	1.00
7	Roger Clemens	2.00
8	Mo Vaughn	1.00
9	Frank Thomas	1.50
10	Sean Casey	1.00

2000 Upper Deck Black Diamond DiamondMight

DiamondMight's have a horizontal format, utilizing holo-foil and gold foil stamping. Card backs are numbered with an "M" prefix and are seeded 1:14 packs.

		MT
Complete Set (10):		40.00
Common Player:		2.50
Inserted 1:14		
1	Ken Griffey Jr.	8.00
2	Mark McGwire	10.00
3	Sammy Sosa	6.00

4	Manny Ramirez	2.50
5	Jeff Bagwell	2.50
6	Frank Thomas	2.50
7	Mike Piazza	6.00
8	Juan Gonzalez	3.00
9	Barry Bonds	3.00
10	Alex Rodriguez	8.00

2000 Upper Deck Black Diamond Diamonds in the Rough

This 10-card set has a horizontal format utilizing holo-foil and gold foil stamping. Card backs are numbered with an "R" prefix and seeded 1:9 packs.

		MT
Complete Set (10):		25.00
Common Player:		1.00
Inserted 1:9		
1	Pat Burrell	5.00
2	Eric Munson	5.00
3	Alfonso Soriano	3.00
4	Ruben Mateo	1.00
5	A.J. Burnett	2.00
6	Ben Davis	1.00
7	Lance Berkman	1.00
8	Ed Yarnall	1.00
9	Rick Ankiel	2.00
10	Ryan Bradley	1.00

2000 Upper Deck Black Diamond Diamond Gallery

This 10-card set spotlights the featured player in a baseball diamond frame with a prismatic background. Gold foil etching and stamping is also used throughout. Card backs are numbered with an "G" prefix and are seeded 1:14 packs.

		MT
Complete Set (10):		60.00
Common Player:		3.00
Inserted 1:14		
1	Derek Jeter	8.00
2	Alex Rodriguez	8.00
3	Nomar Garciaparra	8.00
4	Cal Ripken Jr.	8.00
5	Sammy Sosa	8.00
6	Tony Gwynn	6.00
7	Mark McGwire	12.00
8	Roger Clemens	5.00
9	Greg Maddux	6.00
10	Pedro Martinez	3.00

2000 Upper Deck Black Diamond 500 Club Piece/History

These Reggie Jackson inserts are part of a cross brand insert series paying tribute to baseball's 500 home run club members. These have a piece of Jackson's game-used bat embedded. An autographed version signed to his jersey number (44) are also randomly inserted.

	MT
Reggie Jackson	300.00
Reggie Jackson Autograph/44	750.00

2000 Upper Deck Black Diamond Rookie Edition

		MT
Complete Set (154):		450.00
Common Player:		.15
Common Rookie Gem (91-120):		8.00
Production 1,000		
Rookie Jersey Gems (121-136):		
Inserted 1:24		
USA Authentics (137-154):		
Inserted 1:96		
Golds (1-90):		3-6X
Gold Gems (91-120):		1X
Gold Jerseys (121-136):		1-3X
Pack (6):		2.00
Box (24):		40.00
1	Troy Glaus	.75
2	Mo Vaughn	.40
3	Darin Erstad	.40
4	Jason Giambi	.40
5	Tim Hudson	.25
6	Ben Grieve	.25
7	Eric Chavez	.25
8	Tony Batista	.15
9	Carlos Delgado	.60
10	David Wells	.15
11	Greg Vaughn	.15
12	Fred McGriff	.25
13	Manny Ramirez	.75
14	Roberto Alomar	.60
15	Jim Thome	.40
16	Alex Rodriguez	2.50
17	Edgar Martinez	.15
18	John Olerud	.20
19	Albert Belle	.40
20	Mike Mussina	.40
21	Cal Ripken Jr.	2.50
22	Ivan Rodriguez	.75
23	Rafael Palmeiro	.40
24	Pedro J. Martinez	.75
25	Nomar Garciaparra	2.00
26	Carl Everett	.15
27	Jermaine Dye	.15
28	Mike Sweeney	.15
29	Juan Gonzalez	.75
30	Bobby Higginson	.15
31	Dean Palmer	.15
32	Jacque Jones	.15
33	Eric Milton	.15
34	Matt Lawton	.15
35	Magglio Ordonez	.25
36	Paul Konerko	.15
37	Frank Thomas	1.00
38	Ray Durham	.15
39	Roger Clemens	1.00
40	Derek Jeter	2.50
41	Bernie Williams	.50
42	Jose Canseco	.40
43	Craig Biggio	.25
44	Richard Hidalgo	.15
45	Jeff Bagwell	.75
46	Greg Maddux	1.50
47	Chipper Jones	1.50
48	Rafael Furcal	.25
49	Andruw Jones	.50
50	Geoff Jenkins	.25
51	Jeromy Burnitz	.15
52	Mark McGwire	3.00
53	Rick Ankiel	.50
54	Jim Edmonds	.25
55	Kerry Wood	.25
56	Sammy Sosa	2.00
57	Matt Williams	.25
58	Randy Johnson	.75
59	Steve Finley	.15
60	Curt Schilling	.15
61	Kevin Brown	.15
62	Gary Sheffield	.30
63	Shawn Green	.30
64	Jose Vidro	.15
65	Vladimir Guerrero	1.00
66	Jeff Kent	.15
67	Barry Bonds	1.00
68	Ryan Dempster	.15
69	Cliff Floyd	.15
70	Preston Wilson	.15
71	Mike Piazza	2.00
72	Al Leiter	.15
73	Edgardo Alfonzo	.25
74	Derek Bell	.15
75	Ryan Klesko	.15
76	Tony Gwynn	1.00
77	Bobby Abreu	.15
78	Pat Burrell	.50
79	Scott Rolen	.50
80	Mike Lieberthal	.15
81	Jason Kendall	.15
82	Brian Giles	.25
83	Ken Griffey Jr.	2.00
84	Pokey Reese	.15
85	Dmitri Young	.15
86	Sean Casey	.15
87	Jeff Cirillo	.15
88	Todd Helton	.75
89	Jeffrey Hammonds	.15
90	Larry Walker	.30
91	*Barry Zito*	25.00
92	*Keith Ginter*	10.00
93	*Dane Sardinha*	10.00
94	*Kenny Kelly*	8.00
95	*Ryan Kohlmeier*	8.00
96	*Leo Estrella*	8.00
97	*Danys Baez*	15.00
98	*Paul Rigdon*	8.00
99	*Mike Lamb*	8.00
100	*Aaron McNeal*	10.00
101	*Juan Pierre*	10.00
102	*Rico Washington*	8.00
103	*Luis Matos*	12.00
104	*Adam Bernero*	10.00
105	*Wascar Serrano*	8.00
106	*Chris Richard*	10.00
107	*Justin Miller*	10.00
108	*Julio Zuleta*	8.00
109	*Alex Cabrera*	10.00
110	*Gene Stechschulte*	10.00
111	*Tony Mota*	8.00
112	*Tomokazu Ohka*	10.00
113	*Geraldo Guzman*	8.00
114	*Scott Downs*	8.00
115	*Timoniel Perez*	10.00
116	*Chad Durbin*	10.00
117	*Sun-Woo Kim*	10.00
118	*Tomas de la Rosa*	8.00
119	*Javier Cardona*	10.00
120	*Kazuhiro Sasaki*	15.00
121	*Brad Cresse* (Rookie Jersey Gems)	15.00
122	*Matt Wheatland* (Rookie Jersey Gems)	15.00
123	*Joe Torres* (Rookie Jersey Gems)	15.00
124	*Dave Krynzel* (Rookie Jersey Gems)	10.00
125	*Ben Diggins* (Rookie Jersey Gems)	15.00
126	*Sean Burnett* (Rookie Jersey Gems)	15.00
127	*David Espinosa* (Rookie Jersey Gems)	15.00
128	*Scott Heard* (Rookie Jersey Gems)	15.00
129	*Daylan Holt* (Rookie Jersey Gems)	15.00
130	*Koyie Hill* (Rookie Jersey Gems)	15.00
131	*Mark Buehrle* (Rookie Jersey Gems)	30.00
132	*Xavier Nady* (Rookie Jersey Gems)	20.00
133	*Mike Tonis* (Rookie Jersey Gems)	20.00
134	*Matt Ginter* (Rookie Jersey Gems)	15.00
135	*Lorenzo Barcelo* (Rookie Jersey Gems)	15.00
136	*Cory Vance* (Rookie Jersey Gems)	15.00
137	Sean Burroughs (USA Authentics)	25.00
138	Todd Williams (USA Authentics)	15.00
139	*Brad Wilkerson* (USA Authentics)	15.00
140	*Ben Sheets* (USA Authentics)	25.00
141	*Kurt Ainsworth* (USA Authentics)	15.00
142	Anthony Sanders (USA Authentics)	15.00
143	Ryan Franklin (USA Authentics)	15.00
144	*Shane Heams* (USA Authentics)	15.00
145	*Roy Oswalt* (USA Authentics)	40.00
146	*Jon Rauch* (USA Authentics)	15.00
147	*Brent Abernathy* (USA Authentics)	15.00
148	Ernie Young (USA Authentics)	15.00
149	Chris George (USA Authentics)	15.00
150	Gookie Dawkins (USA Authentics)	15.00
151	Adam Everett (USA Authentics)	15.00
152	*John Cotton* (USA Authentics)	15.00
153	Pat Borders (USA Authentics)	15.00
154	Doug Mientkiewicz (USA Authentics)	15.00

2000 UD Black Diamond Rookie Edition Diamonation

	MT
Complete Set (9):	30.00
Common Player:	1.50

Inserted 1:12

1	Pedro J. Martinez	2.50
2	Derek Jeter	8.00
3	Jason Giambi	1.50
4	Todd Helton	2.50
5	Nomar Garciaparra	6.00
6	Randy Johnson	2.50
7	Jeff Bagwell	2.50
8	Cal Ripken Jr.	8.00
9	Ivan Rodriguez	2.50

2000 UD Black Diamond Rookie Edition Diamond Might

		MT
Complete Set (9):		40.00
Common Player:		1.50
Inserted 1:12		
1	Mark McGwire	10.00
2	Mike Piazza	6.00
3	Frank Thomas	3.00
4	Ken Griffey Jr.	6.00
5	Sammy Sosa	6.00
6	Alex Rodriguez	8.00
7	Carlos Delgado	2.00
8	Vladimir Guerrero	3.00
9	Barry Bonds	2.50

2000 UD Black Diamond Rookie Edition Diamond Skills

		MT
Complete Set (6):		25.00
Common Player:		2.50
Inserted 1:20		
1	Alex Rodriguez	8.00
2	Chipper Jones	5.00
3	Ken Griffey Jr.	6.00
4	Pedro J. Martinez	2.50
5	Ivan Rodriguez	2.50
6	Derek Jeter	8.00

A player's name in *italic* type indicates a rookie card.

2000 UD Black Diamond Rookie Edition Diamond Gallery

		MT
Complete Set (6):		30.00
Common Player:		2.50
Inserted 1:20		
1	Sammy Sosa	6.00
2	Barry Bonds	2.50
3	Vladimir Guerrero	3.00
4	Cal Ripken Jr.	8.00
5	Mike Piazza	6.00
6	Mark McGwire	10.00

2000 Upper Deck Black Diamond Rookie Edition Combos

MT

Random game-used inserts
25 produced of each combo bat
100 produced of combo jersey

DJ-JD Derek Jeter, Joe DiMaggio bat
DJ-MM Derek Jeter, Mickey Mantle bat
JDM Derek Jeter, Joe DiMaggio, Mickey Mantle bat
JWO Derek Jeter, Bernie Williams, Paul O'Neill jersey

2000 Upper Deck Gold Reserve

Gold Reserve is primarily a retail distributed product that has virtually the same design as regular 2000 Upper Deck base cards. The base set consists of 300-cards each with the Upper Deck logo and the featured player's last name stamped in gold foil. Above the player name "Gold Reserve" is stamped in gold foil. The Fantastic Finds subset (268-297) are serial stamped within an edition of 2,500 for each of the subset cards.

		MT
Complete Set (300):		300.00
Common Player:		.15
Common 268-297:		5.00
Production 2,500 sets		
Pack (10):		2.50
Box (24):		45.00
1	Mo Vaughn	.40
2	Darin Erstad	.40
3	Garret Anderson	.25
4	Troy Glaus	.75
5	Troy Percival	.15
6	Kent Bottenfield	.15
7	Orlando Palmeiro	.15
8	Tim Salmon	.25
9	Jason Giambi	.40
10	Eric Chavez	.15
11	Matt Stairs	.15
12	Miguel Tejada	.15
13	Tim Hudson	.25
14	John Jaha	.15
15	Ben Grieve	.25
16	Kevin Appier	.15
17	David Wells	.15
18	Jose Cruz Jr.	.15
19	Homer Bush	.15
20	Shannon Stewart	.15
21	Carlos Delgado	.75
22	Roy Halladay	.15
23	Tony Batista	.25
24	Raul Mondesi	.25
25	Fred McGriff	.25
26	Jose Canseco	.40
27	Roberto Hernandez	.15
28	Vinny Castilla	.15
29	Gerald Williams	.15
30	Ryan Rupe	.15
31	Greg Vaughn	.25
32	Miguel Cairo	.15
33	Roberto Alomar	.50
34	Jim Thome	.30
35	Bartolo Colon	.15
36	Omar Vizquel	.15
37	Manny Ramirez	.75
38	Chuck Finley	.15
39	Travis Fryman	.25
40	Kenny Lofton	.40
41	Richie Sexson	.15
42	Charles Nagy	.15
43	John Halama	.15
44	David Bell	.15
45	Jay Buhner	.15
46	Edgar Martinez	.15
47	Alex Rodriguez	2.50
48	Fred Garcia	.15
49	Aaron Sele	.15
50	Jamie Moyer	.15
51	Mike Cameron	.15
52	Albert Belle	.40
53	Jerry Hairston Jr.	.15
54	Sidney Ponson	.15
55	Cal Ripken Jr.	2.50
56	Mike Mussina	.40
57	B.J. Surhoff	.15
58	Brady Anderson	.25
59	Mike Bordick	.15
60	Ivan Rodriguez	.75
61	Rusty Greer	.15
62	Rafael Palmeiro	.40
63	John Wetteland	.15
64	Ruben Mateo	.15
65	Gabe Kapler	.25
66	David Segui	.15
67	Justin Thompson	.15
68	Rick Helling	.15
69	Jose Offerman	.15
70	Trot Nixon	.15
71	Pedro Martinez	.75
72	Jason Varitek	.15
73	Troy O'Leary	.15
74	Nomar Garciaparra	2.00
75	Carl Everett	.15
76	Wilton Veras	.15
77	Tim Wakefield	.15
78	Ramon Martinez	.15
79	Johnny Damon	.25
80	Mike Sweeney	.15
81	Rey Sanchez	.15
82	Carlos Beltran	.15
83	Carlos Febles	.15
84	Jermaine Dye	.15
85	Joe Randa	.15
86	Jose Rosado	.15
87	Jeff Suppan	.15
88	Juan Encarnacion	.15
89	Damion Easley	.15
90	Brad Ausmus	.15
91	Todd Jones	.15
92	Juan Gonzalez	.75
93	Bobby Higginson	.15
94	Tony Clark	.15
95	Brian Moehler	.15
96	Dean Palmer	.15
97	Joe Mays	.15
98	Eric Milton	.15
99	Corey Koskie	.15
100	Ron Coomer	.15
101	Brad Radke	.15
102	Todd Walker	.15
103	Butch Huskey	.15
104	Jacque Jones	.15
105	Frank Thomas	1.00
106	Mike Sirotka	.15
107	Carlos Lee	.15
108	Ray Durham	.15
109	Bob Howry	.15
110	Magglio Ordonez	.25
111	Paul Konerko	.15
112	Chris Singleton	.15
113	James Baldwin	.15
114	Derek Jeter	2.00
115	Tino Martinez	.25
116	Orlando Hernandez	.25
117	Chuck Knoblauch	.15
118	Bernie Williams	.50
119	David Cone	.25
120	Paul O'Neill	.25
121	Roger Clemens	1.00
122	Mariano Rivera	.25
123	Ricky Ledee	.15
124	Richard Hidalgo	.25
125	Jeff Bagwell	.75
126	Jose Lima	.15
127	Billy Wagner	.15
128	Shane Reynolds	.15
129	Moises Alou	.15
130	Craig Biggio	.30
131	Roger Cedeno	.15
132	Octavio Dotel	.15
133	Greg Maddux	1.50
134	Brian Jordan	.15
135	Kevin Millwood	.25
136	Javy Lopez	.25
137	Bruce Chen	.15
138	Chipper Jones	1.50
139	Tom Glavine	.40
140	Andruw Jones	.40
141	Andres Galarraga	.40
142	Reggie Sanders	.15
143	Geoff Jenkins	.25
144	Jeromy Burnitz	.15
145	Ron Belliard	.15
146	Mark Loretta	.15
147	Steve Woodard	.15
148	Marquis Grissom	.15
149	Bob Wickman	.15
150	Mark McGwire	3.00
151	Fernando Tatis	.15
152	Edgar Renteria	.15
153	J.D. Drew	.15
154	Ray Lankford	.15
155	Fernando Vina	.15
156	Pat Hentgen	.15
157	Jim Edmonds	.25
158	Mark Grace	.25
159	Kerry Wood	.15
160	Eric Young	.15
161	Ismael Valdes	.15
162	Sammy Sosa	2.00
163	Henry Rodriguez	.15
164	Kyle Farnsworth	.15
165	Glenallen Hill	.15
166	Jon Lieber	.15
167	Luis Gonzalez	.15
168	Tony Womack	.15
169	Omar Daal	.15
170	Randy Johnson	.75
171	Erubiel Durazo	.15
172	Jay Bell	.15
173	Steve Finley	.15
174	Travis Lee	.15
175	Matt Williams	.25
176	Matt Mantei	.15
177	Adrian Beltre	.25

178 Kevin Brown .25
179 Chan Ho Park .15
180 Mark Grudzielanek .15
181 Jeff Shaw .15
182 Shawn Green .30
183 Gary Sheffield .40
184 Todd Hundley .15
185 Eric Karros .25
186 Kevin Elster .15
187 Vladimir Guerrero 1.00
188 Michael Barrett .15
189 Chris Widger .15
190 Ugueth Urbina .15
191 Dustin Hermanson .15
192 Rondell White .15
193 Jose Vidro .15
194 Hideki Irabu .15
195 Lee Stevens .15
196 Livan Hernandez .15
197 Ellis Burks .15
198 J.T. Snow .15
199 Jeff Kent .15
200 Robb Nen .15
201 Marvin Benard .15
202 Barry Bonds 1.00
203 Russ Ortiz .15
204 Rich Aurilia .15
205 Joe Nathan .15
206 Preston Wilson .15
207 Cliff Floyd .15
208 Mike Lowell .15
209 Ryan Dempster .15
210 Luis Castillo .15
211 Alex Fernandez .15
212 Mark Kotsay .15
213 Brant Brown .15
214 Edgardo Alfonzo .25
215 Robin Ventura .15
216 Rickey Henderson .25
217 Mike Hampton .15
218 Mike Piazza 2.00
219 Al Leiter .15
220 Derek Bell .15
221 Armando Benitez .15
222 Rey Ordonez .15
223 Todd Zeile .15
224 Tony Gwynn 1.00
225 Eric Owens .15
226 Damian Jackson .15
227 Trevor Hoffman .15
228 Ben Davis .15
229 Sterling Hitchcock .15
230 Ruben Rivera .15
231 Ryan Klesko .15
232 Phil Nevin .15
233 Mike Lieberthal .15
234 Bobby Abreu .25
235 Doug Glanville .15
236 Rico Brogna .15
237 Scott Rolen .60
238 Andy Ashby .15
239 Robert Person .15
240 Curt Schilling .25
241 Mike Jackson .15
242 Warren Morris .15
243 Kris Benson .15
244 Kevin Young .15
245 Brian Giles .15
246 Jason Schmidt .15
247 Jason Kendall .25
248 Todd Ritchie .15
249 Wil Cordero .15
250 Aramis Ramirez .15
251 Sean Casey .25
252 Barry Larkin .40
253 Pokey Reese .15
254 Scott Williamson .15
255 Aaron Boone .15
256 Dante Bichette .25
257 Ken Griffey Jr. 2.00
258 Denny Neagle .15
259 Dmitri Young .15
260 Todd Helton .75
261 Larry Walker .40
262 Pedro Astacio .15
263 Neifi Perez .15
264 Jeff Cirillo .15
265 Jeffrey Hammonds .15
266 Tom Goodwin .15
267 Rolando Arrojo .15
268 Rick Ankiel (Fantastic Finds) 8.00
269 Pat Burrell (Fantastic Finds) 20.00
270 Eric Munson (Fantastic Finds) 8.00
271 Rafael Furcal (Fantastic Finds) 6.00
272 Brad Penny (Fantastic Finds) 5.00
273 Adam Kennedy (Fantastic Finds) 5.00
274 *Mike Lamb* (Fantastic Finds) 8.00
275 Matt Riley (Fantastic Finds) 5.00
276 Eric Gagne (Fantastic Finds) 5.00
277 *Kazuhiro Sasaki* (Fantastic Finds) 20.00
278 Julio Lugo (Fantastic Finds) 5.00
279 Kip Wells (Fantastic Finds) 5.00
280 *Danys Baez* (Fantastic Finds) 8.00
281 Josh Beckett (Fantastic Finds) 10.00
282 Alfonso Soriano (Fantastic Finds) 8.00
283 Vernon Wells (Fantastic Finds) 5.00
284 Nick Johnson (Fantastic Finds) 6.00
285 Ramon Ortiz (Fantastic Finds) 5.00
286 Peter Bergeron (Fantastic Finds) 6.00
287 *Wascar Serrano* (Fantastic Finds) 6.00
288 Josh Paul (Fantastic Finds) 5.00
289 Mark Quinn (Fantastic Finds) 6.00
290 Jason Marquis (Fantastic Finds) 5.00
291 Rob Bell (Fantastic Finds) 5.00
292 Pablo Ozuna (Fantastic Finds) 5.00
293 Milton Bradley (Fantastic Finds) 6.00
294 Roosevelt Brown (Fantastic Finds) 5.00
295 Terrence Long (Fantastic Finds) 5.00
296 *Chad Durbin* (Fantastic Finds) 5.00
297 Matt LeCroy (Fantastic Finds) 5.00
298 Ken Griffey Jr (Checklist) 1.00
299 Mark McGwire (Checklist) 1.50
300 Derek Jeter (Checklist) 1.00

2000 Upper Deck Gold Reserve Game-used Ball

MT

Common Player: 10.00
Inserted 1:480
JB Jeff Bagwell 40.00
BB Barry Bonds 80.00
SC Sean Casey 10.00
RC Roger Clemens 65.00
NG Nomar Garciaparra 65.00
SG Shawn Green 10.00
KG Ken Griffey Jr. 60.00
TG Tony Gwynn 35.00
DJ Derek Jeter 75.00
AJ Andruw Jones 15.00
CJ Chipper Jones 60.00
GM Greg Maddux 50.00
MM Mark McGwire 80.00
MP Mike Piazza 50.00
MR Manny Ramirez 20.00
IR Ivan Rodriguez 20.00
SR Scott Rolen 15.00
GS Gary Sheffield 10.00
SS Sammy Sosa 50.00
BW Bernie Williams 15.00

2000 Upper Deck Gold Reserve Setting the Standard

This 15-card set spotlights the top hitters and are inserted 1:11 packs. Card fronts feature gold foil stamping and card backs are numbered with an "S" prefix.

MT

Complete Set (15): 50.00
Common Player: 1.50
Inserted 1:11
1 Tony Gwynn 3.00
2 Manny Ramirez 2.00
3 Derek Jeter 5.00
4 Cal Ripken Jr. 6.00
5 Mo Vaughn 1.50
6 Jose Canseco 1.50
7 Barry Bonds 2.00
8 Nomar Garciaparra 5.00
9 Juan Gonzalez 2.00
10 Mark McGwire 8.00
11 Alex Rodriguez 6.00
12 Jeff Bagwell 2.00
13 Ken Griffey Jr. 6.00
14 Frank Thomas 3.00
15 Sammy Sosa 5.00

2000 Upper Deck Gold Reserve Solid Gold Gallery

This 12-card set features close-up shots of the featured player accentuated by gold foil stamping. Card backs are numbered with an "G" prefix, these were seeded 1:13 packs.

MT

Complete Set (12): 45.00
Common Player: 1.50
Inserted 1:13
1 Ken Griffey Jr. 6.00
2 Alex Rodriguez 6.00
3 Mike Piazza 5.00
4 Sammy Sosa 5.00
5 Derek Jeter 5.00
6 Jeff Bagwell 2.00
7 Mark McGwire 8.00
8 Cal Ripken Jr. 6.00
9 Pedro Martinez 2.00
10 Chipper Jones 4.00
11 Ivan Rodriguez 2.00
12 Vladimir Guerrero 3.00

2000 Upper Deck Gold Reserve 3,000 Hit Club

This on-going cross brand insert series features Al Kaline. Each card features a piece of Kaline's game-used bat, he also signed six cards.

MT

AK-B Al Kaline bat/400 40.00
AK-BSAl Kaline bat/auto/6

2000 Upper Deck Gold Reserve 24-Karat Gems

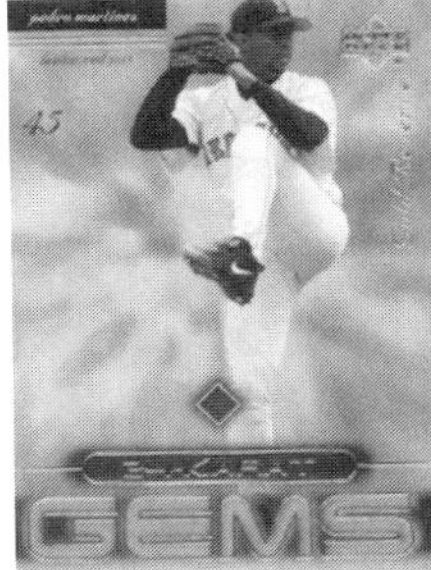

This 15-card set features gold foil stamping on the front and are numbered on the back with an "K" prefix. They are found on the average of 1:7 packs.

MT

Complete Set (15): 20.00
Common Player: 1.00
Inserted 1:7
1 Pedro Martinez 1.50
2 Scott Rolen 1.25
3 Jason Giambi 1.00
4 Jeromy Burnitz 1.00
5 Rafael Palmeiro 1.00
6 Rick Ankiel 1.50
7 Carlos Beltran 1.00
8 Derek Jeter 4.00
9 Jason Kendall 1.00
10 Chipper Jones 3.00
11 Carlos Delgado 1.50
12 Alex Rodriguez 5.00
13 Randy Johnson 1.50
14 Tony Gwynn 2.50
15 Shawn Green 1.00

2000 Upper Deck Gold Reserve UD Authentics

MT

Inserted 1:480
25 Sets Produced
VALUES UNDETERMINED
CB Carlos Beltran
JC Jose Canseco
SG Shawn Green 25.00
KG Ken Griffey Jr.
TG Tony Gwynn 80.00
CJ Chipper Jones 70.00
MR Manny Ramirez

CR	Cal Ripken Jr.	200.00
AR	Alex Rodriguez	125.00
IR	Ivan Rodriguez	

2000 Upper Deck Gold Reserve UD Authentics Gold

		MT
VALUES UNDETERMINED		
CB	Carlos Beltran	
JC	Jose Canseco	
SG	Shawn Green	
KG	Ken Griffey Jr.	
TG	Tony Gwynn	
CJ	Chipper Jones	
MR	Manny Ramirez	
CR	Cal Ripken Jr.	
AR	Alex Rodriguez	
IR	Ivan Rodriguez	

2000 Upper Deck Hitter's Club

The 90-card base set includes only hitters and features past and current stars. The base set consists of 50 regular cards, 25 Why 3K?, and 15 Hitting the Show subset cards. Card backs of the 50 regular cards have complete year-by- year statistics.

		MT
Complete Set (90):		35.00
Common Player:		.15
Pack (5):		2.00
Wax Box (24):		35.00
1	Mo Vaughn	.50
2	Troy Glaus	.75
3	Jeff Bagwell	.75
4	Craig Biggio	.40
5	Jason Giambi	.15
6	Eric Chavez	.25
7	Carlos Delgado	.50
8	Chipper Jones	1.50
9	Andruw Jones	.50
10	Andres Galarraga	.40
11	Jeromy Burnitz	.15
12	Mark McGwire	3.00
13	Mark Grace	.25
14	Sammy Sosa	2.00
15	Jose Canseco	.75
16	Vinny Castilla	.15
17	Matt Williams	.40
18	Gary Sheffield	.25
19	Shawn Green	.50
20	Vladimir Guerrero	1.50
21	Barry Bonds	1.00
22	Manny Ramirez	.75
23	Roberto Alomar	.50
24	Jim Thome	.40
25	Ken Griffey Jr.	2.50
26	Alex Rodriguez	2.50
27	Edgar Martinez	.15
28	Preston Wilson	.15
29	Mike Piazza	2.00
30	Robin Ventura	.25
31	Albert Belle	.50
32	Cal Ripken Jr.	2.50
33	Tony Gwynn	1.50
34	Scott Rolen	.75
35	Bob Abreu	.15
36	Brian Giles	.15
37	Ivan Rodriguez	.75
38	Rafael Palmeiro	.50
39	Nomar Garciaparra	2.00
40	Sean Casey	.40
41	Larry Walker	.50
42	Todd Helton	.75
43	Carlos Beltran	.20
44	Dean Palmer	.15
45	Juan Gonzalez	1.00
46	Corey Koskie	.15
47	Frank Thomas	1.00
48	Magglio Ordonez	.40
49	Derek Jeter	2.00
50	Bernie Williams	.50
51	Paul Waner (Why 3k?)	.40
52	Honus Wagner (Why 3k?)	.50
53	Tris Speaker (Why 3k?)	.40
54	Nap Lajoie (Why 3k?)	.50
55	Eddie Collins (Why 3k?)	.25
56	Roberto Clemente (Why 3k?)	1.50
57	Ty Cobb (Why 3k?)	1.50
58	Cap Anson (Why 3k?)	.50
59	Robin Yount (Why 3k?)	.50
60	Carl Yastrzemski (Why 3k?)	.50
61	Dave Winfield (Why 3k?)	.25
62	Stan Musial (Why 3k?)	1.00
63	Eddie Murray (Why 3k?)	.40
64	Paul Molitor (Why 3k?)	.50
65	Willie Mays (Why 3k?)	2.00
66	Al Kaline (Why 3k?)	.50
67	Tony Gwynn (Why 3k?)	1.50
68	Rod Carew (Why 3k?)	.50
69	Lou Brock (Why 3k?)	.50
70	George Brett (Why 3k?)	1.00
71	Wade Boggs (Why 3k?)	.25
72	Hank Aaron (Why 3k?)	2.00
73	Jorge Luis Toca (Hitting the Show)	.15
74	J.D. Drew (Hitting the Show)	.25
75	Pat Burrell (Hitting the Show)	1.25
76	Vernon Wells (Hitting the Show)	.15
77	Julio Ramirez (Hitting the Show)	.15
78	Gabe Kapler (Hitting the Show)	.25
79	Erubiel Durazo (Hitting the Show)	.25
80	Lance Berkman (Hitting the Show)	.15
81	Peter Bergeron (Hitting the Show)	.15
82	Alfonso Soriano (Hitting the Show)	.25
83	Jacque Jones (Hitting the Show)	.15
84	Ben Petrick (Hitting the Show)	.15
85	Jerry Hairston Jr. (Hitting the Show)	.15
86	Kevin Witt (Hitting the Show)	.15
87	Dermal Brown (Hitting the Show)	.15
88	Chad Hermansen (Hitting the Show)	.15
89	Ruben Mateo (Hitting the Show)	.25
90	Checklist (Ken Griffey Jr.)	.75

2000 Upper Deck Hitter's Club Accolades

These inserts have a full foiled front with gold foil stamping. Card backs are numbered with an "A" prefix and are seeded 1:11 packs.

		MT
Complete Set (10):		40.00
Common Player:		1.50
Inserted 1:11		
1	Robin Yount	2.00
2	Tony Gwynn	4.00
3	Sammy Sosa	5.00
4	Mike Piazza	5.00
5	Cal Ripken Jr.	6.00
6	Mark McGwire	8.00
7	Barry Bonds	2.50
8	Wade Boggs	1.50
9	Ken Griffey Jr.	6.00
10	Willie Mays	5.00

2000 Upper Deck Hitter's Club Autographs

Former and current players are featured in this signature set, which are seeded 1:215 packs. Card backs are numbered with the featured player's initials.

		MT
Common Player:		40.00
Inserted 1:215		
HA	Hank Aaron #44	225.00
WB	Wade Boggs #12	30.00
GB	George Brett #5	90.00
Lou	Lou Brock #20	20.00
Rod	Rod Carew #29	25.00
TG	Tony Gwynn #19	50.00
Al	Al Kaline #6	35.00
WM	Willie Mays #24	180.00
PM	Paul Molitor #4	25.00
EM	Eddie Murray #33	60.00
Man	Stan Musial #6	75.00
Cal	Cal Ripken Jr. #8	200.00
DW	Dave Winfield #31	30.00
Yaz	Carl Yastrzemski #7	80.00
RY	Robin Yount #19	40.00

2000 Upper Deck Hitter's Club Epic Performances

This 10-card set showcases some of baseball's top performances on a full foiled card front with gold foil stamping. Card backs are numbered with an "EP" prefix and are found 1:3 packs.

		MT
Complete Set (10):		20.00
Common Player:		1.00
Inserted 1:3		
1	Mark McGwire	4.00
3	Sammy Sosa	2.50
4	Ken Griffey Jr.	3.00
5	Carl Yastrzemski	1.00
6	Tony Gwynn	2.00
7	Nomar Garciaparra	2.50
8	Cal Ripken Jr.	3.00
9	George Brett	1.50
10	Hank Aaron	2.50
11	Wade Boggs	1.00

2000 Upper Deck Hitter's Club Eternals

These inserts were printed on a full foiled front with the word "Eternals" printed a number of times in the background of the player photo. The player name and Upper Deck logo are stamped in gold foil on the bottom portion of the card. Card backs are numbered with an "E" prefix and are seeded 1:23 packs.

		MT
Complete Set (10):		75.00
Common Player:		3.00
Inserted 1:23		
1	Cal Ripken Jr.	12.00
2	Mark McGwire	15.00
3	Ken Griffey Jr.	12.00

4	Nomar Garciaparra	10.00
5	Tony Gwynn	8.00
6	Derek Jeter	10.00
7	Jose Canseco	4.00
8	Mike Piazza	10.00
9	Alex Rodriguez	10.00
10	Barry Bonds	4.00

2000 Upper Deck Hitter's Club Generations of Excellence

This 10-card insert set features two players who are linked either by team or position, gold foil stamping is used throughout. Card backs are numbered with an "GE" prefix and are seeded 1:6 packs.

		MT
Complete Set (10):		25.00
Common Player:		1.50
Inserted 1:6		
1	Cal Ripken Jr., Eddie Murray	4.00
2	Vladimir Guerrero, Roberto Clemente	2.50
3	George Brett, Robin Yount	2.50
4	Barry Bonds, Willie Mays	4.00
5	Chipper Jones, Hank Aaron	3.00
6	Mark McGwire, Sammy Sosa	5.00
7	Tony Gwynn, Wade Boggs	2.50
8	Rickey Henderson, Lou Brock	1.50
9	Derek Jeter, Nomar Garciaparra	4.00
10	Alex Rodriguez, Ken Griffey Jr.	4.00

2000 Upper Deck Hitter's Club On Target

This 10-card set is printed on a full foiled front with silver foil stamping. Card backs are numbered with an "OT" prefix and are seeded 1:23 packs.

		MT
Complete Set (10):		35.00
Common Player:		1.00
Inserted 1:23		
1	Nomar Garciaparra	8.00
2	Sean Casey	2.00
3	Alex Rodriguez	8.00
4	Troy Glaus	1.50
5	Ivan Rodriguez	3.00
6	Chipper Jones	6.00
7	Manny Ramirez	3.00
8	Derek Jeter	8.00
9	Vladimir Guerrero	5.00
10	Scott Rolen	3.00

2000 Upper Deck Hitter's Club The Hitters' Club

These inserts are seeded 1:95 packs and are numbered on the back with an "HC" prefix.

		MT
Complete Set (10):		150.00
Common Player:		8.00
1	Rod Carew	10.00
2	Alex Rodriguez	30.00
3	Willie Mays	25.00
4	George Brett	20.00
5	Tony Gwynn	25.00
6	Stan Musial	15.00
7	Frank Thomas	15.00
8	Wade Boggs	8.00
9	Larry Walker	10.00
10	Nomar Garciaparra	30.00

2000 Upper Deck Hitter's Club 3,000 Hit Club

Upper Deck's cross brand series pays tribute to players who have reached 3,000 hits. Hitter's Club features Wade Boggs and Tony Gwynn inserts with Bat, Bat and Cap and Autographed versions randomly inserted.

		MT
Common Player:		125.00
WB	Wade Boggs bat/350	40.00
WB	Wade Boggs bat & cap/50	200.00
WB	Wade Boggs AU/12	
TG	Tony Gwynn bat/350	50.00
TG	Tony Gwynn bat & cap/50	300.00
TG	Tony Gwynn AU/19	
GB	Tony Gwynn, Wade Boggs bat/99	150.00

2000 Upper Deck HoloGrFX

The base set consists of 90-cards on a horizontal format. The cards have a holo-foil front utilizing HoloGrFX technology.

		MT
Complete Set (90):		30.00
Common Player:		.20
Pack (4):		2.00
Wax Box (32):		45.00
1	Mo Vaughn	.75
2	Troy Glaus	.75
3	Daryle Ward	.20
4	Jeff Bagwell	1.00
5	Craig Biggio	.50
6	Jose Lima	.20
7	Jason Giambi	.30
8	Eric Chavez	.30
9	Tim Hudson	.40
10	Raul Mondesi	.40
11	Carlos Delgado	.75
12	David Wells	.20
13	Chipper Jones	2.00
14	Greg Maddux	2.00
15	Andruw Jones	.75
16	Brian Jordan	.20
17	Jeromy Burnitz	.40
18	Ron Belliard	.20
19	Mark McGwire	4.00
20	Fernando Tatis	.25
21	J.D. Drew	.25
22	Sammy Sosa	2.50
23	Mark Grace	.40
24	Greg Vaughn	.40
25	Jose Canseco	1.00
26	Vinny Castilla	.30
27	Fred McGriff	.40
28	Matt Williams	.40
29	Randy Johnson	.75
30	Erubiel Durazo	.40
31	Shawn Green	.75
32	Gary Sheffield	.50
33	Kevin Brown	.40
34	Vladimir Guerrero	2.00
35	Michael Barrett	.20
36	Russ Ortiz	.20
37	Barry Bonds	1.00
38	Jeff Kent	.20
39	Kenny Lofton	.75
40	Manny Ramirez	1.00
41	Roberto Alomar	.75
42	Richie Sexson	.20
43	Edgar Martinez	.30
44	Alex Rodriguez	3.00
45	Fred Garcia	.20
46	Preston Wilson	.20
47	Alex Gonzalez	.20
48	Mike Hampton	.20
49	Mike Piazza	2.50
50	Robin Ventura	.40
51	Edgardo Alfonzo	.40
52	Albert Belle	.75
53	Cal Ripken Jr.	3.00
54	B.J. Surhoff	.20
55	Tony Gwynn	2.00
56	Trevor Hoffman	.20
57	Mike Lieberthal	.20
58	Scott Rolen	1.00
59	Bob Abreu	.40
60	Curt Schilling	.40
61	Jason Kendall	.30
62	Brian Giles	.30
63	Kris Benson	.20
64	Rafael Palmeiro	.50
65	Ivan Rodriguez	1.00
66	Gabe Kapler	.40
67	Nomar Garciaparra	2.50
68	Pedro Martinez	1.00
69	Troy O'Leary	.20
70	Barry Larkin	.50
71	Dante Bichette	.40
72	Sean Casey	.50
73	Ken Griffey Jr.	3.00
74	Jeff Cirillo	.40
75	Todd Helton	1.00
76	Larry Walker	.75
77	Carlos Beltran	.25
78	Jermaine Dye	.20
79	Juan Gonzalez	1.00
80	Juan Encarnacion	.20
81	Dean Palmer	.20
82	Corey Koskie	.20
83	Eric Milton	.20
84	Frank Thomas	1.50
85	Magglio Ordonez	.20
86	Carlos Lee	.20
87	Derek Jeter	2.50
88	Tino Martinez	.50
89	Bernie Williams	.75
90	Roger Clemens	1.50

2000 Upper Deck HoloGrFX A Piece of the Series

This inserts have a piece of game-used base from a 1999 World Series game embedded. These were inserted at a rate of 1:215 packs.

		MT
Common Player:		10.00
Inserted 1:215		
1	Derek Jeter	60.00
2	Chipper Jones	30.00
3	Roger Clemens	40.00
4	Greg Maddux	40.00
5	Bernie Williams	15.00
6	Andruw Jones	15.00
7	Tino Martinez	15.00
8	Brian Jordan	10.00
9	Mariano Rivera	15.00
11	Paul O'Neill	15.00
12	Tom Glavine	20.00

2000 Upper Deck HoloGrFX A Piece of Series Autograph

This is an autographed parallel of the Piece of Series insert set that is limited to 25 sets.

		MT
Common Player:		40.00
Production 25 sets		
PSA1	Derek Jeter	500.00
PSA2	Chipper Jones	200.00
PSA3	Roger Clemens	300.00
PSA4	Greg Maddux	400.00
PSA6	Andruw Jones	100.00
PSA7	Tino Martinez	75.00
PSA8	Brian Jordan	40.00
PSA11	Paul O'Neill	90.00
PSA12	Tom Glavine	125.00

2000 Upper Deck HoloGrFX Bomb Squad

This six-card set highlights the top home run hitters. They have a horizontal format with complete holo-foiled fronts. Card backs are numbered with an "BS" prefix and are seeded 1:34 packs.

		MT
Complete Set (6):		
Common Player:		4.00
Inserted 1:34		
1	Ken Griffey Jr.	12.00
2	Mark McGwire	15.00
3	Chipper Jones	8.00
4	Alex Rodriguez	12.00
5	Sammy Sosa	10.00
6	Barry Bonds	4.00

2000 Upper Deck HoloGrFX Future Fame

This six-card set has a horizontal format that is completely holo-foiled with silver foil stamping. Card backs are numbered with an "FF" prefix and seeded 1:34 packs.

		MT
Complete Set (6):		60.00
Common Player:		5.00
Inserted 1:34		
1	Cal Ripken Jr.	12.00
2	Mark McGwire	15.00
3	Greg Maddux	8.00
4	Tony Gwynn	8.00
5	Ken Griffey Jr.	12.00
6	Roger Clemens	6.00

2000 Upper Deck HoloGrFX Longball Legacy

This 15-card set spotlights the top home run hitters on a horizontal format and completely holo-foiled. Card backs are numbered with an "LL" prefix and seeded 1:6 packs.

		MT
Complete Set (15):		40.00
Common Player:		1.00
Inserted 1:6		
1	Mike Piazza	5.00
2	Ivan Rodriguez	2.00
3	Jeff Bagwell	2.00
4	Alex Rodriguez	6.00
5	Jose Canseco	2.00
6	Mark McGwire	8.00
7	Scott Rolen	2.00
8	Carlos Delgado	1.50
9	Mo Vaughn	1.00
10	Manny Ramirez	2.00
11	Matt Williams	1.00
12	Sammy Sosa	5.00
13	Ken Griffey Jr.	6.00
14	Nomar Garciaparra	5.00
15	Larry Walker	1.50

2000 Upper Deck HoloGrFX Stars of the System

This 10-card set features some of baseball's top prospects on a horizontal format. The fronts are completely holo-foiled with silver foil stamping. Card backs are numbered with an "SS" prefix and seeded 1:8 packs.

		MT
Complete Set (10):		20.00
Common Player:		1.00
Inserted 1:8		
1	Rick Ankiel	2.00
2	Alfonso Soriano	3.00
3	Vernon Wells	1.00
4	Ben Petrick	1.00
5	Francisco Cordero	1.00
6	Matt Riley	2.00
7	A.J. Burnett	1.00
8	Pat Burrell	4.00
9	Ed Yarnall	1.00
10	Dermal Brown	1.00

2000 Upper Deck HoloGrFX StarView

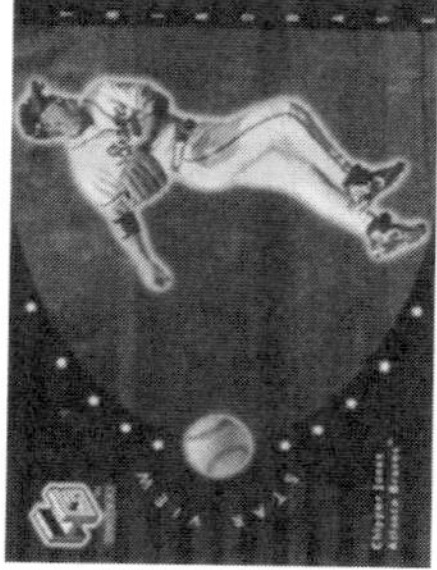

This eight-card set features top stars on a horizontal format. Card backs are numbered with an "SV" prefix and inserted 1:11 packs.

		MT
Complete Set (8):		40.00
Common Player:		2.00
Inserted 1:11		
1	Ken Griffey Jr.	6.00
2	Nomar Garciaparra	5.00
3	Chipper Jones	4.00
4	Mark McGwire	8.00
5	Sammy Sosa	5.00
6	Derek Jeter	5.00
7	Mike Piazza	5.00
8	Alex Rodriguez	6.00

2000 Upper Deck HoloGrFX 3000 Hit Club

Upper Deck pays tribute to members of the 3,000 Hit Club with this cross-brand insert series. Robin Yount and George Brett are featured on a game-used bat card (350 produced), game-used jersey card (350 produced), a bat combo of both players (99 produced) and an autographed combo (10 produced).

		MT
Common Card:		40.00
RY	Robin Yount bat/ 350	40.00
RYJ	Robin Yount jersey/ 350	40.00
GB	George Brett bat/ 350	50.00
GBJ	George Brett jersey/ 350	50.00
BY	George Brett, Robin Yount bat/99	200.00
BYA	George Brett, Robin Yount AU/10	
BYJ	George Brett, Robin Yount jersey/99	200.00

2000 Upper Deck Legends

The 135-card base set consists of 90 regular player cards, 30 20th Century Legends (1:5) and 15 Generation Y2K (1:9). The base cards have a full foiled front with silver foil stamping. Card backs have complete year-by-year statistics.

		MT
Complete Set (135):		150.00
Common Player:		.15
Common Y2K:		1.50
Inserted 1:9		
Common 20th Century Legend		2.00
Inserted 1:5		
Pack (7):		4.00
Box (24):		80.00
1	Darin Erstad	.25
2	Troy Glaus	.75
3	Mo Vaughn	.50
4	Craig Biggio	.25
5	Jeff Bagwell	.75
6	Reggie Jackson	1.00
7	Tim Hudson	.25
8	Jason Giambi	.25
9	Hank Aaron	2.00
10	Greg Maddux	1.50
11	Chipper Jones	1.50
12	Andres Galarraga	.30
13	Robin Yount	.30
14	Jeromy Burnitz	.15
15	Paul Molitor	.40
16	David Wells	.15
17	Carlos Delgado	.75
18	Ernie Banks	.75
19	Sammy Sosa	2.00
20	Kerry Wood	.40
21	Stan Musial	.75
22	Bob Gibson	.50
23	Mark McGwire	3.00
24	Fernando Tatis	.15
25	Randy Johnson	.75
26	Matt Williams	.40

27 Jackie Robinson 2.00
28 Sandy Koufax 1.50
29 Shawn Green .50
30 Kevin Brown .25
31 Gary Sheffield .40
32 Greg Vaughn .15
33 Jose Canseco .50
34 Gary Carter .15
35 Vladimir Guerrero 1.00
36 Willie Mays 2.00
37 Barry Bonds 1.00
38 Jeff Kent .15
39 Bob Feller .40
40 Roberto Alomar .50
41 Jim Thome .30
42 Manny Ramirez .75
43 Alex Rodriguez 2.50
44 Preston Wilson .15
45 Tom Seaver .75
46 Robin Ventura .15
47 Mike Piazza 2.00
48 Mike Hampton .15
49 Brooks Robinson .75
50 Frank Robinson .75
51 Cal Ripken Jr. 2.50
52 Albert Belle .40
53 Eddie Murray .30
54 Tony Gwynn 1.00
55 Roberto Clemente 2.00
56 Willie Stargell .15
57 Brian Giles .15
58 Jason Kendall .15
59 Mike Schmidt .75
60 Bob Abreu .15
61 Scott Rolen .50
62 Curt Schilling .15
63 Johnny Bench .75
64 Sean Casey .15
65 Barry Larkin .40
66 Ken Griffey Jr. 2.50
67 George Brett 1.00
68 Carlos Beltran .15
69 Nolan Ryan 3.00
70 Ivan Rodriguez .75
71 Rafael Palmeiro .40
72 Larry Walker .30
73 Todd Helton .75
74 Jeff Cirillo .15
75 Carl Everett .15
76 Nomar Garciaparra 2.00
77 Pedro Martinez .75
78 Harmon Killebrew .40
79 Corey Koskie .15
80 Ty Cobb 2.00
81 Dean Palmer .15
82 Juan Gonzalez .75
83 Carlton Fisk .15
84 Frank Thomas 1.00
85 Magglio Ordonez .15
86 Lou Gehrig 2.50
87 Babe Ruth 3.00
88 Derek Jeter 2.00
89 Roger Clemens 1.00
90 Bernie Williams .50
91 Rick Ankiel (Generation Y2K) 3.00
92 Kip Wells (Generation Y2K) 1.50
93 Pat Burrell (Generation Y2K) 5.00
94 Mark Quinn (Generation Y2K) 3.00
95 Ruben Mateo (Generation Y2K) .40
96 Adam Kennedy (Generation Y2K) 2.00
97 Brad Penny (Generation Y2K) 1.50
98 *Kazuhiro Sasaki* (Generation Y2K) 2.50
99 Peter Bergeron (Generation Y2K) 2.00
100 Rafael Furcal (Generation Y2K) 2.00
101 Eric Munson (Generation Y2K) 4.00
102 Nick Johnson (Generation Y2K) 4.00
103 Rob Bell (Generation Y2K) 1.50
104 Vernon Wells (Generation Y2K) 2.00
105 Ben Petrick (Generation Y2K) 2.50
106 Babe Ruth (20th Century Legends) 10.00
107 Mark McGwire (20th Century Legends) 10.00
108 Nolan Ryan (20th Century Legends) 10.00
109 Hank Aaron (20th Century Legends) 6.00
110 Barry Bonds (20th Century Legends) 4.00
111 Nomar Garciaparra (20th Century Legends) 6.00
112 Roger Clemens (20th Century Legends) 4.00
113 Johnny Bench (20th Century Legends) 2.50
114 Alex Rodriguez (20th Century Legends) 8.00
115 Cal Ripken Jr. (20th Century Legends) 8.00
116 Willie Mays (20th Century Legends) 6.00
117 Mike Piazza (20th Century Legends) 6.00
118 Reggie Jackson (20th Century Legends) 3.00
119 Tony Gwynn (20th Century Legends) 4.00
120 Cy Young (20th Century Legends) 3.00
121 George Brett (20th Century Legends) 3.00
122 Greg Maddux (20th Century Legends) 5.00
123 Yogi Berra (20th Century Legends) 3.00
124 Sammy Sosa (20th Century Legends) 6.00
125 Randy Johnson (20th Century Legends) 2.50
126 Bob Gibson (20th Century Legends) 2.00
127 Lou Gehrig (20th Century Legends) 8.00
128 Ken Griffey Jr. (20th Century Legends) 8.00
129 Derek Jeter (20th Century Legends) 6.00
130 Mike Schmidt (20th Century Legends) 3.00
131 Pedro Martinez (20th Century Legends) 2.50
132 Jackie Robinson (20th Century Legends) 6.00
133 Jose Canseco (20th Century Legends) 2.00
134 Ty Cobb (20th Century Legends) 5.00
135 Stan Musial (20th Century Legends) 3.00

2000 Upper Deck Legends Commemorative Collection

A metallized photo background on front distinguishes these 1-of-100 inserts from their base-card parallels. Backs have an ink-jetted serial number from within each card's edition of 100.

	MT
Stars (1-90):	10-20X
Y2K:	2-3X
20th Century Legends:	3-6X
Production 100 sets	

(See 2000 Upper Deck Legends for checklist and base card values.)

2000 Upper Deck Legends Defining Moments

This 10-card set highlights the featured player's greatest baseball moment with a date stamped in gold foil on the front and a description of the moment on the back. Card backs are numbered with an "DM" prefix and seeded 1:12 packs.

		MT
Complete Set (10):		35.00
Common Player:		1.00
Inserted 1:12		
1	Reggie Jackson	2.00
2	Hank Aaron	4.00
3	Babe Ruth	6.00
4	Cal Ripken Jr.	6.00
5	Carlton Fisk	1.00
6	Ken Griffey Jr.	3.00
7	Nolan Ryan	6.00
8	Roger Clemens	2.00
9	Willie Mays	4.00
10	Mark McGwire	5.00

2000 Upper Deck Legends Eternal Glory

This six-card set has a full holo-foiled front with gold foil stamping. Card backs are numbered with an "EG" prefix and are inserted 1:24 packs.

		MT
Complete Set (7):		20.00
Common Player:		3.00
Inserted 1:24		
1	Nolan Ryan	8.00
2	Ken Griffey Jr.	4.00
4	Sammy Sosa	4.00
5	Derek Jeter	6.00
6	Willie Mays	5.00
7	Roger Clemens	4.00

2000 Upper Deck Legends Legendary Signatures

These autographed inserts are signed in blue sharpie on the bottom portion and inserted 1:24 packs. A Gold parallel version is also randomly seeded which has gold foil stamping and is individually numbered to 50.

		MT
Common Player:		10.00
Inserted 1:23		
Golds:		1.5-2X
Production 50 sets		
HA	Hank Aaron SP/94	325.00
JB	Johnny Bench	50.00
BB	Bobby Bonds	10.00
LB	Lou Brock	10.00
GB	George Brett	70.00
JC	Jose Canseco	20.00
GC	Gary Carter	10.00
SC	Sean Casey	10.00
RC	Roger Clemens	75.00
DC	Dave Concepcion	10.00
AD	Andre Dawson	15.00
KG	Ken Griffey Jr.	90.00
VG	Vladimir Guerrero	40.00
TG	Tony Gwynn	50.00
RJ	Reggie Jackson	30.00
DJ	Derek Jeter SP/61	400.00
RaJ	Randy Johnson	60.00
CJ	Chipper Jones	50.00
HK	Harmon Killebrew	20.00
FL	Fred Lynn	10.00
DM	Dale Murphy	15.00
SM	Stan Musial	60.00
PN	Phil Niekro	10.00
JP	Jim Palmer	15.00
MP	Mike Piazza	120.00
MR	Manny Ramirez SP/141	100.00
CR	Cal Ripken Jr.	120.00
AR	Alex Rodriguez	65.00
IR	Ivan Rodriguez	15.00
NR	Nolan Ryan	120.00
MS	Mike Schmidt	50.00
TS	Tom Seaver	40.00
OS	Ozzie Smith	30.00
WS	Willie Stargell	35.00
FT	Frank Thomas	20.00
AT	Alan Trammell	10.00
BW	Matt Williams	10.00

2000 Upper Deck Legends Legendary Jerseys

This game-used memorabilia insert set has

a swatch of game- used jersey embedded and were inserted 1:48 packs.

		MT
Common Player:		10.00
Inserted 1:48		
HA	Hank Aaron	50.00
JB	Jeff Bagwell	25.00
JB	Johnny Bench	30.00
WB	Wade Boggs	15.00
BaB	Barry Bonds	60.00
BoB	Bobby Bonds	10.00
GB	George Brett	50.00
LB	Lou Brock	12.00
JC	Jose Canseco	15.00
RC	Roger Clemens	50.00
DC	Dave Concepcion	10.00
DD	Don Drysdale	25.00
RF	Rollie Fingers	10.00
LG	Lou Gehrig pants	275.00
BG	Bob Gibson pants	25.00
KG	Ken Griffey Jr.	40.00
TG	Tony Gwynn	40.00
RJ	Reggie Jackson	20.00
DJ	Derek Jeter	65.00
RaJ	Randy Johnson	40.00
CJ	Chipper Jones	35.00
SK	Sandy Koufax	275.00
SK	Sandy Koufax auto/32	1200.
GM	Greg Maddux	30.00
MM	Mickey Mantle	185.00
RM	Roger Maris pants	65.00
EM	Eddie Mathews	30.00
WM	Willie Mays SP/29	750.00
BM	Bill Mazeroski	10.00
WMc	Willie McCovey	15.00
TM	Thurman Munson	50.00
DM	Dale Murphy	15.00
SM	Stan Musial SP/28	1000.
JP	Jim Palmer	10.00
GP	Gaylord Perry	10.00
MR	Manny Ramirez	15.00
CR	Cal Ripken Jr.	60.00
BR	Brooks Robinson	25.00
FR	Frank Robinson	15.00
AR	Alex Rodriguez	40.00
NR	Nolan Ryan	75.00
MS	Mike Schmidt	35.00
TS	Tom Seaver	30.00
OS	Ozzie Smith	25.00
WS	Willie Stargell	15.00
FT	Frank Thomas	10.00
JT	Joe Torre	15.00
EW	Earl Weaver	10.00
MW	Matt Williams	10.00
MW	Maury Wills	10.00
DW	Dave Winfield	15.00

2000 Upper Deck Legends Ones for the Ages

This seven-card set has a holo-foiled front with gold foil etching and stamping. The player image is in a classic picture framed design. Card backs are numbered with an "O" prefix and seeded 1:24 packs.

		MT
Complete Set (7):		25.00
Common Player:		3.00
Inserted 1:24		
01	Ty Cobb	4.00
02	Cal Ripken Jr.	6.00
03	Babe Ruth	6.00
04	Jackie Robinson	4.00
05	Mark McGwire	5.00
06	Alex Rodriguez	5.00
07	Mike Piazza	4.00

2000 Upper Deck Legends Reflections in Time

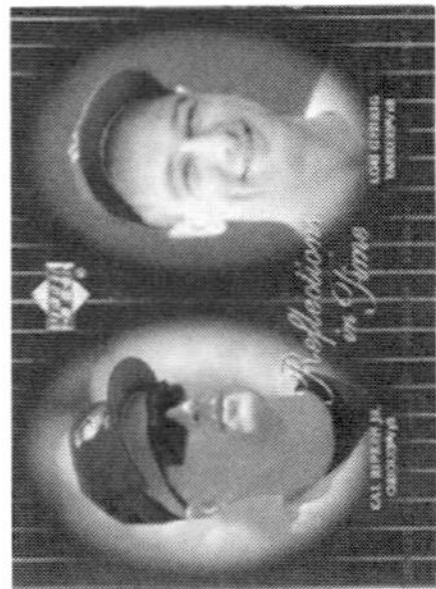

This 10-card horizontal insert set features two players, past and present, linked by significant events or statistics. Card fronts are completely holo-foiled with gold foil stamping. Card backs are numbered with an "R" prefix and inserted 1:12 packs.

		MT
Complete Set (10):		40.00
Common Player:		2.00
Inserted 1:12		
1	Ken Griffey Jr., Hank Aaron	6.00
2	Sammy Sosa, Roberto Clemente	5.00
3	Roger Clemens, Nolan Ryan	8.00
4	Ivan Rodriguez, Johnny Bench	2.00
5	Alex Rodriguez, Ernie Banks	5.00
6	Tony Gwynn, Stan Musial	3.00
7	Barry Bonds, Willie Mays	5.00
8	Cal Ripken Jr., Lou Gehrig	6.00
9	Chipper Jones, Mike Schmidt	4.00
10	Mark McGwire, Babe Ruth	8.00

2000 Upper Deck Legends UD Millenium Team

This nine-card set has a complete holo-foiled front with silver foil stamping. The set is Upper Deck's selections for the all-time 20th century team and are inserted 1:4 packs. Card backs are numbered with an "UD" prefix.

		MT
Complete Set (10):		15.00
Common Player:		1.50
Inserted 1:4		
1	Mark McGwire	2.00
2	Jackie Robinson	2.00
3	Mike Schmidt	1.50
4	Cal Ripken Jr.	3.00
5	Babe Ruth	3.00
7	Willie Mays	2.00
8	Johnny Bench	1.50
9	Nolan Ryan	3.00
10	Ken Griffey Jr.	2.00

2000 Upper Deck Legends 3,000 Hit Club

Upper Deck's continuing series pays tribute to Carl Yastrzemski and Paul Molitor. The series includes 350 Bat cards, 350 Jersey cards, 100 Bat/Jersey combo cards and eight autographed Bat/Jersey combo cards from Yastrzemski and 350 Bat cards from Molitor.

		MT
CY	Carl Yastrzemski bat/350	65.00
CY	Carl Yastrzemski jersey/350	65.00
CY	Carl Yastrzemski bat/jersey/100	200.00
CY	Carl Yastrzemski auto/bat/jersey/8	

2000 Upper Deck MVP

The base set consists of 220-cards with a white bordered design and bronze foil stamping. Card backs have a maximum of 10 year-by-year statistics.

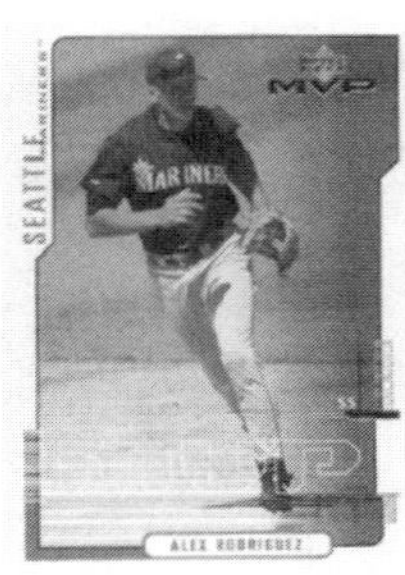

		MT
Complete Set (220):		30.00
Common Player:		.10
Pack (10):		1.50
Wax Box (28):		30.00
1	Garret Anderson	.10
2	Mo Vaughn	.30
3	Tim Salmon	.20
4	Ramon Ortiz	.10
5	Darin Erstad	.20
6	Troy Glaus	.50
7	Troy Percival	.10
8	Jeff Bagwell	.50
9	Ken Caminiti	.10
10	Daryle Ward	.10
11	Craig Biggio	.25
12	Jose Lima	.10
13	Moises Alou	.20
14	Octavio Dotel	.10
15	Ben Grieve	.20
16	Jason Giambi	.20
17	Tim Hudson	.20
18	Eric Chavez	.10
19	Matt Stairs	.10
20	Miguel Tejada	.10
21	John Jaha	.10
22	Chipper Jones	1.00
23	Kevin Millwood	.20
24	Brian Jordan	.10
25	Andruw Jones	.25
26	Andres Galarraga	.40
27	Greg Maddux	1.00
28	Reggie Sanders	.10
29	Javy Lopez	.20
30	Jeromy Burnitz	.20
31	Kevin Barker	.10
32	Jose Hernandez	.10
33	Ron Belliard	.10
34	Henry Blanco	.10
35	Marquis Grissom	.10
36	Geoff Jenkins	.20
37	Carlos Delgado	.50
38	Raul Mondesi	.20
39	Roy Halladay	.10
40	Tony Batista	.20
41	David Wells	.10
42	Shannon Stewart	.10
43	Vernon Wells	.10
44	Sammy Sosa	1.25
45	Ismael Valdes	.10
46	Joe Girardi	.10
47	Mark Grace	.20
48	Henry Rodriguez	.10
49	Kerry Wood	.25
50	Eric Young	.10
51	Mark McGwire	2.00
52	Daryle Kile	.10
53	Fernando Vina	.10
54	Ray Lankford	.10
55	J.D. Drew	.25
56	Fernando Tatis	.20
57	Rick Ankiel	.25
58	Matt Williams	.25
59	Erubiel Durazo	.20
60	Tony Womack	.10
61	Jay Bell	.10
62	Randy Johnson	.50
63	Steve Finley	.10
64	Matt Mantei	.10
65	Luis Gonzalez	.20
66	Gary Sheffield	.25
67	Eric Gagne	.10
68	Adrian Beltre	.20
69	Mark Grudzielanek	.10
70	Kevin Brown	.20
71	Chan Ho Park	.10

72	Shawn Green	.40
73	Vinny Castilla	.20
74	Fred McGriff	.25
75	Wilson Alvarez	.10
76	Greg Vaughn	.20
77	Gerald Williams	.10
78	Ryan Rupe	.10
79	Jose Canseco	.50
80	Vladimir Guerrero	1.00
81	Dustin Hermanson	.10
82	Michael Barrett	.10
83	Rondell White	.20
84	Tony Armas Jr.	.10
85	Wilton Guerrero	.10
86	Jose Vidro	.10
87	Barry Bonds	.75
88	Russ Ortiz	.10
89	Ellis Burks	.10
90	Jeff Kent	.10
91	Russ Davis	.10
92	J.T. Snow	.10
93	Roberto Alomar	.40
94	Manny Ramirez	.50
95	Chuck Finley	.10
96	Kenny Lofton	.40
97	Jim Thome	.40
98	Bartolo Colon	.20
99	Omar Vizquel	.10
100	Richie Sexson	.10
101	Mike Cameron	.10
102	Brett Tomko	.10
103	Edgar Martinez	.20
104	Alex Rodriguez	1.50
105	John Olerud	.20
106	Fred Garcia	.10
107	*Kazuhiro Sasaki*	1.00
108	Preston Wilson	.10
109	Luis Castillo	.10
110	A.J. Burnett	.10
111	Mike Lowell	.10
112	Cliff Floyd	.10
113	Brad Penny	.10
114	Alex Gonzalez	.10
115	Mike Piazza	1.25
116	Derek Bell	.10
117	Edgardo Alfonzo	.20
118	Rickey Henderson	.20
119	Todd Zeile	.10
120	Mike Hampton	.10
121	Al Leiter	.20
122	Robin Ventura	.20
123	Cal Ripken Jr.	1.50
124	Mike Mussina	.40
125	B.J. Surhoff	.10
126	Jerry Hairston Jr.	.10
127	Brady Anderson	.20
128	Albert Belle	.40
129	Sidney Ponson	.10
130	Tony Gwynn	1.00
131	Ryan Klesko	.10
132	Sterling Hitchcock	.10
133	Eric Owens	.10
134	Trevor Hoffman	.10
135	Al Martin	.10
136	Bret Boone	.10
137	Brian Giles	.10
138	Chad Hermansen	.10
139	Kevin Young	.10
140	Kris Benson	.10
141	Warren Morris	.10
142	Jason Kendall	.20
143	Wil Cordero	.10
144	Scott Rolen	.50
145	Curt Schilling	.20
146	Doug Glanville	.10
147	Mike Lieberthal	.10
148	Mike Jackson	.10
149	Rico Brogna	.10
150	Andy Ashby	.10
151	Bob Abreu	.10
152	Sean Casey	.25
153	Pete Harnisch	.10
154	Dante Bichette	.20
155	Pokey Reese	.10
156	Aaron Boone	.10
157	Ken Griffey Jr.	1.50
158	Barry Larkin	.30
159	Scott Williamson	.10
160	Carlos Beltran	.10
161	Jermaine Dye	.10
162	Jose Rosado	.10
163	Joe Randa	.10
164	Johnny Damon	.10
165	Mike Sweeney	.10
166	Mark Quinn	.10
167	Ivan Rodriguez	.50
168	Rusty Greer	.10
169	Ruben Mateo	.10
170	Doug Davis	.10
171	Gabe Kapler	.20
172	Justin Thompson	.10
173	Rafael Palmeiro	.40
174	Larry Walker	.40
175	Neifi Perez	.10
176	Rolando Arrojo	.10
177	Jeffrey Hammonds	.10
178	Todd Helton	.50
179	Pedro Astacio	.10
180	Jeff Cirillo	.10
181	Pedro Martinez	.50
182	Carl Everett	.20
183	Troy O'Leary	.10
184	Nomar Garciaparra	1.25
185	Jose Offerman	.10
186	Bret Saberhagen	.10
187	Trot Nixon	.10
188	Jason Varitek	.10
189	Todd Walker	.10
190	Eric Milton	.10
191	Chad Allen	.10
192	Jacque Jones	.10
193	Brad Radke	.10
194	Corey Koskie	.10
195	Joe Mays	.10
196	Juan Gonzalez	.50
197	Jeff Weaver	.10
198	Juan Encarnacion	.10
199	Deivi Cruz	.10
200	Damion Easley	.10
201	Tony Clark	.10
202	Dean Palmer	.10
203	Frank Thomas	.75
204	Carlos Lee	.10
205	Mike Sirotka	.10
206	Kip Wells	.10
207	Magglio Ordonez	.20
208	Paul Konerko	.20
209	Chris Singleton	.10
210	Derek Jeter	1.25
211	Tino Martinez	.25
212	Mariano Rivera	.20
213	Roger Clemens	.75
214	Nick Johnson	.25
215	Paul O'Neill	.20
216	Bernie Williams	.40
217	David Cone	.20
218	Checklist (Ken Griffey Jr.)	.75
219	Checklist (Sammy Sosa)	.50
220	Checklist (Mark McGwire)	1.00

2000 Upper Deck MVP Silver

A parallel to the 220-card base set. These 1:2 pack inserts can be distinguished from the base cards by the silver foil stamping and a silver foiled facsimile signature of the featured player on the card bottom.

	MT
Stars:	2-3X
Inserted 1:2	

2000 Upper Deck MVP Gold

A parallel to the base set, these can be distinguished from base cards with gold script stamping. Each card is also serial numbered on the card front within an edition of 50 sets.

	MT
Stars:	20-35X
Production 50 sets	

2000 Upper Deck MVP Super

A parallel to the 220-card base set, these inserts can be distinguished from the base cards by the holo-foil stamping used on the Upper Deck logo and the featured player's facsimile signature on the card bottom. The card fronts are also serial numbered within an edition of 25 sets.

	MT
Stars:	40-60X
Production 25 sets	

2000 Upper Deck MVP All-Star Game

		MT
Complete Set (30):		25.00
Common Player:		.50
AS1	Mo Vaughn	.65
AS2	Jeff Bagwell	.75
AS3	Jason Giambi	.65
AS4	Chipper Jones	2.00
AS5	Greg Maddux	1.00
AS6	Tony Batista	.50
AS7	Sammy Sosa	1.50
AS8	Mark McGwire	3.00
AS9	Randy Johnson	.65
AS10	Shawn Green	.50
AS11	Greg Vaughn	.50
AS12	Vladimir Guerrero	.75
AS13	Barry Bonds	1.50
AS14	Manny Ramirez	.75
AS15	Alex Rodriguez	2.50
AS16	Preston Wilson	.50
AS17	Mike Piazza	2.00
AS18	Cal Ripken Jr.	3.00
AS19	Tony Gwynn	1.00
AS20	Scott Rolen	.65
AS21	Ken Griffey Jr.	2.50
AS22	Carlos Beltran	.50
AS23	Ivan Rodriguez	.60
AS24	Larry Walker	.50
AS25	Nomar Garciaparra	1.50
AS26	Pedro Martinez	.75
AS27	Juan Gonzalez	.75
AS28	Frank Thomas	1.50
AS29	Derek Jeter	2.00
AS30	Bernie Williams	.50

2000 Upper Deck MVP Drawing Power

This seven-card set has a holo-foil front with silver foil stamping. Card backs are numbered with an "DP" prefix. They are found on the average of 1:28 packs.

		MT
Complete Set (7):		20.00
Common Player:		1.50
Inserted 1:28		
1	Mark McGwire	5.00
2	Ken Griffey Jr.	4.00
3	Mike Piazza	4.00
4	Chipper Jones	3.00
5	Nomar Garciaparra	4.00
6	Sammy Sosa	4.00
7	Jose Canseco	1.50

2000 Upper Deck MVP Game Used Souvenirs

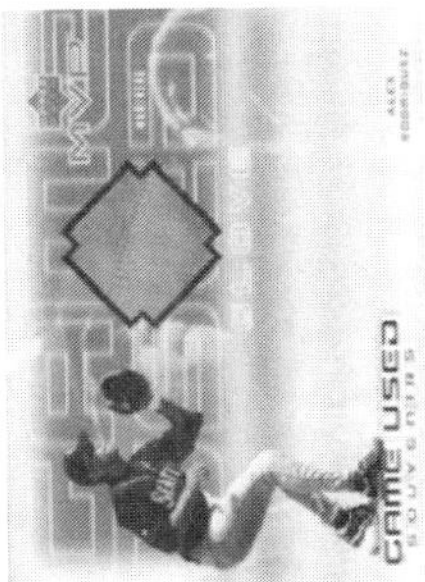

These memorabilia inserts feature a game-used piece of glove embedded and are found exclusively in hobby packs at a rate of 1:130 packs.

		MT
Common Glove:		10.00
Inserted 1:130		
RA	Roberto Alomar	20.00
JB	Jeff Bagwell	35.00
AB	Albert Belle	15.00
BB	Barry Bonds	65.00
JC	Jose Canseco	20.00
WC	Will Clark	25.00
AF	Alex Fernandez	10.00
JG	Jason Giambi	25.00
TGl	Troy Glaus	20.00
AG	Alex Gonzalez	10.00
BG	Ben Grieve	10.00
KG	Ken Griffey Jr.	50.00
VG	Vladimir Guerrero	25.00
TG	Tony Gwynn	40.00
AJ	Andruw Jones	25.00
CJ	Chipper Jones	40.00

KL	Kenny Lofton	10.00
RM	Raul Mondesi	10.00
PO	Paul O'Neill	15.00
RP	Rafael Palmeiro	20.00
MR	Manny Ramirez	20.00
CR	Cal Ripken Jr.	100.00
AR	Alex Rodriguez	65.00
IR	Ivan Rodriguez	15.00
NR	Nolan Ryan	100.00
TS	Tim Salmon	10.00
LW	Larry Walker	10.00
BW	Bernie Williams	15.00
MW	Matt Williams	10.00

2000 Upper Deck MVP Game Used Souvenirs - Bats

These memorabilia inserts have a piece of game-used bat embedded and are seeded exclusively in hobby packs at a rate of 1:130 packs.

		MT
Common Bat:		10.00
Inserted 1:130		
BB	Barry Bonds	40.00
JC	Jose Canseco	15.00
KG	Ken Griffey Jr.	20.00
VG	Vladimir Guerrero	15.00
TG	Tony Gwynn	20.00
CJ	Chipper Jones	15.00
MR	Manny Ramirez	15.00
AR	Alex Rodriguez	20.00
IR	Ivan Rodriguez	10.00
BW	Bernie Williams	15.00

2000 Upper Deck MVP Game Used Souvenirs Autographs

MT

Production 25 sets
VALUES UNDETERMINED

RA	Roberto Alomar
JB	Jeff Bagwell
AB	Albert Belle
BB	Barry Bonds
JC	Jose Canseco
WC	Will Clark
AF	Alex Fernandez
JG	Jason Giambi
TGl	Troy Glaus
AG	Alex Gonzalez
BG	Ben Grieve
KG	Ken Griffey Jr.
VG	Vladimir Guerrero
TG	Tony Gwynn
AJ	Andruw Jones
CJ	Chipper Jones
KL	Kenny Lofton
RM	Raul Mondesi
PO	Paul O'Neill
RP	Rafael Palmeiro
MR	Manny Ramirez
CR	Cal Ripken Jr.
AR	Alex Rodriguez
AR	Alex Rodriguez
IR	Ivan Rodriguez
NR	Nolan Ryan
TS	Tim Salmon
LW	Larry Walker
BW	Bernie Williams
MW	Matt Williams

2000 Upper Deck MVP Prolifics

This seven-card set features a full holo-foiled front with silver foil stamping and are seeded 1:28 packs. Card backs are numbered with an "P" prefix.

		MT
Complete Set (7):		15.00
Common Player:		1.00
Inserted 1:28		
1	Manny Ramirez	1.50
2	Vladimir Guerrero	2.00
3	Derek Jeter	5.00
4	Pedro Martinez	1.50
5	Shawn Green	1.00
6	Alex Rodriguez	4.00
7	Cal Ripken Jr.	5.00

2000 Upper Deck MVP ProSign

These autographed inserts are found exclusively in retail packs at a rate of 1:216.

		MT
Common Player:		8.00
Inserted 1:216 R		
RA	Rick Ankiel	10.00
MB	Michael Barrett	10.00
RB	Rob Bell	8.00
CB	Carlos Beltran	10.00
LB	Lance Berkman	25.00
RB	Rico Brogna	8.00
SC	Sean Casey	12.00
DD	Doug Davis	8.00
ED	Erubiel Durazo	10.00
RF	Robert Fick	10.00
NG	Nomar Garciaparra	100.00
AG	Alex Gonzalez	10.00
KG	Ken Griffey Jr.	100.00
TG	Tony Gwynn	75.00
TH	Tim Hudson	25.00
DJ	Derek Jeter	150.00
CJ	Chipper Jones	80.00
MM	Mike Meyers	8.00
EM	Eric Milton	10.00
JM	Jim Morris	8.00
WM	Warren Morris	8.00
TN	Trot Nixon	10.00
BP	Ben Petrick	8.00
AP	Adam Piatt	10.00
MP	Mike Piazza	100.00
MQ	Mark Quinn	10.00
MR	Manny Ramirez	30.00
RR	Rob Ramsay	8.00
MRe	Mike Redmond	8.00
MRi	Mariano Rivera	15.00
AR	Alex Rodriguez	100.00
MS	Mike Sweeney	12.00
BT	Bubba Trammell	8.00
JV	Jose Vidro	12.00
DW	Daryle Ward	10.00
KW	Kip Wells	10.00
SW	Scott Williamson	8.00
PW	Preston Wilson	12.00
KW	Kevin Witt	8.00
TW	Tony Womack	10.00
EY	Ed Yarnall	8.00
JZ	Jeff Zimmerman	8.00

2000 Upper Deck MVP Pure Grit

These 1:6 pack inserts have a full holo-foiled front with silver foil stamping. Card backs are numbered with an "G" prefix.

		MT
Complete Set (10):		10.00
Common Player:		.50
Inserted 1:6		
1	Derek Jeter	2.50
2	Kevin Brown	.50
3	Craig Biggio	.50
4	Ivan Rodriguez	.75
5	Scott Rolen	.75
6	Carlos Beltran	.50
7	Ken Griffey Jr.	2.00
8	Cal Ripken Jr.	3.00
9	Nomar Garciaparra	2.50
10	Randy Johnson	1.00

2000 Upper Deck MVP Scout's Choice

This ten-card set spotlights some of the best prospects in 2000. The inserts have a full holo-foiled front with silver foil stamping. Card backs are numbered with an "SC" prefix and are seeded 1:14 packs.

		MT
Complete Set (10):		10.00
Common Player:		.50
Inserted 1:14		
1	Rick Ankiel	1.00
2	Vernon Wells	1.00
3	Pat Burrell	3.00
4	Travis Dawkins	.50
5	Eric Munson	.75
6	Nick Johnson	1.50
7	Dermal Brown	.50
8	Alfonso Soriano	3.00
9	Ben Petrick	.50
10	Adam Everett	.50

2000 Upper Deck MVP Second Season Standouts

This 10-card set has a full holo-foiled card front with silver foil stamping. Card backs are numbered with an "SS" prefix and inserted 1:6 packs.

		MT
Complete Set (10):		10.00
Common Player:		.40
Inserted 1:6		
1	Pedro Martinez	1.50
2	Mariano Rivera	.40
3	Orlando Hernandez	.40
4	Ken Caminiti	.40
5	Bernie Williams	.50
6	Jim Thome	.75
7	Nomar Garciaparra	2.00
8	Edgardo Alfonzo	.50
9	Derek Jeter	3.00
10	Kevin Millwood	.50

2000 Upper Deck MVP 3,000 Hit Club

Upper Deck used this cross-brand insert series to salute the players who accomplished 3,000 hits in their career. Stan Musial is featured and offers a game-used memorabilia bat, jersey, jersey/bat combo and combo autograph versions.

		MT
Common Player:		
SM	(Stan Musial jersey-350)	60.00

SM (Stan Musial bat-350) 60.00
SM Stan Musial jersey/bat-100 200.00
SM Stan Musial J/B/Auto-6

2000 Upper Deck Ovation

The base set consists of 90-cards, including a 20-card World Premiere subset and 10-card Superstar Spotlight subset. World Premiere's are found 1:3 packs and Superstar Spotlight's 1:6 packs. Card fronts are embossed, intended to resemble the feel of a baseball and also has silver foil stamping.

	MT
Complete Set (89):	125.00
Common Player:	.25
Common World Prem. (61-80):	2.00
Inserted 1:3	
Common Super. Spot (81-90):	3.00
Inserted 1:6	
Pack (5):	2.75
Wax Box (20):	45.00

1 Mo Vaughn .75
2 Troy Glaus 1.00
3 Jeff Bagwell 1.00
4 Craig Biggio .50
5 Mike Hampton .25
6 Jason Giambi .25
7 Tim Hudson .50
8 Chipper Jones 2.00
9 Greg Maddux 2.00
10 Kevin Millwood .50
11 Brian Jordan .25
12 Jeromy Burnitz .25
13 David Wells .25
14 Carlos Delgado .75
15 Sammy Sosa 2.50
16 Mark McGwire 4.00
17 Matt Williams .50
18 Randy Johnson .75
19 Erubiel Durazo .50
20 Kevin Brown .25
21 Shawn Green .75
22 Gary Sheffield .40
23 Jose Canseco 1.00
24 Vladimir Guerrero 2.00
25 Barry Bonds 3.00
26 Manny Ramirez 1.00
27 Roberto Alomar .75
28 Richie Sexson .25
29 Jim Thome .50
30 Alex Rodriguez 3.00
31 Ken Griffey Jr. 3.00
32 Preston Wilson .25
33 Mike Piazza 2.50
34 Al Leiter .25
35 Robin Ventura .40
36 Cal Ripken Jr. 3.00
37 Albert Belle .75
38 Tony Gwynn 2.00
39 Brian Giles .25
40 Jason Kendall .40
41 Scott Rolen 1.00
42 Bob Abreu .25
43 Ken Griffey Jr. 3.00
44 Sean Casey .40
45 Carlos Beltran .25
46 Gabe Kapler .40
47 Ivan Rodriguez 1.00
48 Rafael Palmeiro .50
49 Larry Walker .75
50 Nomar Garciaparra 2.50
51 Pedro J. Martinez 1.00
52 Eric Milton .25
53 Juan Gonzalez 1.00
54 Tony Clark .25
55 Frank Thomas 1.00
56 Magglio Ordonez .40
57 Roger Clemens 1.50
58 Derek Jeter 2.50
59 Bernie Williams .75
60 Orlando Hernandez .50
61 Rick Ankiel (World Premiere) 3.00
62 Josh Beckett (World Premiere) 10.00
63 Vernon Wells (World Premiere) 3.00
64 Alfonso Soriano (World Premiere) 3.00
65 Pat Burrell (World Premiere) 8.00
66 Eric Munson (World Premiere) 8.00
67 Chad Hutchinson (World Premiere) 3.00
68 Eric Gagne (World Premiere) 2.00
69 Peter Bergeron (World Premiere) 2.00
70 Ryan Anderson (Supposed to have been withdrawn, all known cards have embossed UD racing mark.) 300.00
71 A.J. Burnett (World Premiere) 2.00
72 Jorge Luis Toca (World Premiere) 3.00
73 Matt Riley (World Premiere) 5.00
74 Chad Hermansen (World Premiere) 2.00
75 Doug Davis (World Premiere) 2.00
76 Jim Morris (World Premiere) 2.00
77 Ben Petrick (World Premiere) 3.00
78 Mark Quinn (World Premiere) 3.00
79 Ed Yarnall (World Premiere) 3.00
80 Ramon Ortiz (World Premiere) 3.00
81 Ken Griffey Jr. (Superstar Spotlight) 10.00
82 Mark McGwire (Superstar Spotlight) 12.00
83 Derek Jeter (Superstar Spotlight) 8.00
84 Jeff Bagwell (Superstar Spotlight) 3.00
85 Nomar Garciaparra (Superstar Spotlight) 8.00
86 Sammy Sosa (Superstar Spotlight) 8.00
87 Mike Piazza (Superstar Spotlight) 8.00
88 Alex Rodriguez (Superstar Spotlight) 10.00
89 Cal Ripken Jr. (Superstar Spotlight) 10.00
90 Pedro Martinez (Superstar Spotlight) 3.00

2000 Upper Deck Ovation Standing Ovation

A parallel to the 120-card base set, these are identical to the base cards besides the holographic silver stamping on the card front and the backs serially numbered to 50.

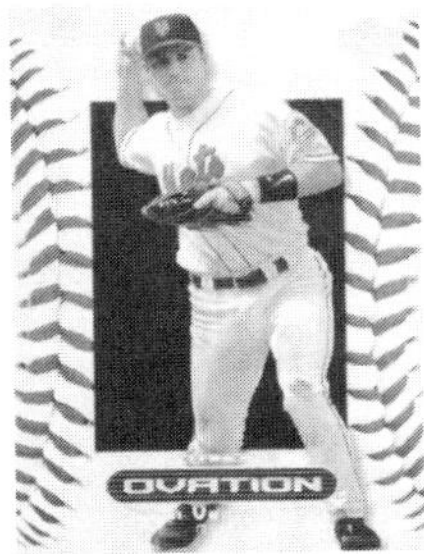

	MT
Stars (1-60):	15X-25X
World Prem. (61-80):	2X-3X
Super. Spot. (81-90):	4X-8X
Production 50 sets	

(See 2000 UD Ovation for checklist and base card values.)

2000 Upper Deck Ovation A Piece of History

These memorabilia inserts feature a piece of game-used bat embedded and are limited to 400 sets produced.

	MT
Common Player:	15.00
Production 400 sets	

JB Jeff Bagwell 25.00
CB Carlos Beltran 10.00
SC Sean Casey 10.00
KG Ken Griffey Jr. 40.00
DJ Derek Jeter 65.00
TG Tony Gwynn 25.00
AJ Andruw Jones 15.00
CJ Chipper Jones 25.00
RP Rafael Palmeiro 15.00
MP Mike Piazza 40.00
MR Manny Ramirez 15.00
CR Cal Ripken Jr. 65.00
AR Alex Rodriguez 40.00
SR Scott Rolen 15.00
SS Sammy Sosa 40.00
FT Frank Thomas 15.00

2000 Upper Deck Ovation Center Stage

Ten of baseball's top performers are highlighted on a card that features gold foil stamping and etching. Card backs are numbered with an "CS" prefix and are seeded 1:9 packs. Two parallels to this insert set are randomly inserted: Golds are found 1:39 packs and Rainbows are seeded 1:99 packs.

	MT
Complete Set (10):	45.00
Common Player:	2.00
Inserted 1:9	
Gold:	2X
Inserted 1:39	
Rainbow:	3X-4X
Inserted 1:99	

1 Jeff Bagwell 2.00
2 Ken Griffey Jr. 5.00
3 Nomar Garciaparra 5.00
4 Mike Piazza 6.00
5 Mark McGwire 6.00
6 Alex Rodriguez 6.00
7 Cal Ripken Jr. 8.00
8 Derek Jeter 8.00
9 Chipper Jones 4.00
10 Sammy Sosa 4.00

2000 Upper Deck Ovation Curtain Calls

This 20-card set features gold foil stamping and highlights some memorable playoff moments. Card backs are numbered with an "CC" prefix and are seeded 1:3 packs.

	MT
Complete Set (20):	25.00
Common Player:	.75
Inserted 1:3	

1 David Cone .75
2 Mark McGwire 3.00
3 Sammy Sosa 2.00
4 Eric Milton .75
5 Bernie Williams 1.00
6 Tony Gwynn 2.00
7 Nomar Garciaparra 3.00
8 Manny Ramirez 1.50
9 Wade Boggs 1.00
10 Randy Johnson 1.50
11 Cal Ripken Jr. 4.00
12 Pedro J. Martinez 1.50
13 Alex Rodriguez 3.00

14	Fernando Tatis	.75
15	Vladimir Guerrero	1.50
16	Robin Ventura	.75
17	Larry Walker	.75
18	Carlos Beltran	1.00
19	Jose Canseco	1.00
20	Ken Griffey Jr.	2.50

2000 Upper Deck Ovation Diamond Futures

This 10-card set highlights some of baseball's top prospects on a full foiled front with silver foil stamping. Card backs are numbered with an "DM" prefix and are seeded 1:6 packs.

		MT
Complete Set (10):		15.00
Common Player:		1.00
Inserted 1:6		
1	J.D. Drew	1.50
2	Alfonso Soriano	3.00
3	Preston Wilson	1.00
4	Erubiel Durazo	3.00
5	Rick Ankiel	1.00
6	Octavio Dotel	1.00
7	A.J. Burnett	1.50
8	Carlos Beltran	1.00
9	Vernon Wells	1.50
10	Troy Glaus	3.00

2000 Upper Deck Ovation Lead Performers

Upper Deck chose 10 players for this set who are thought of as leaders on and off the field. Card fronts have silver foil stamping and card backs are numbered with an "LP" prefix. These are found on the average of 1:19 packs.

		MT
Complete Set (10):		40.00
Common Player:		2.00
Inserted 1:19		
1	Mark McGwire	6.00
2	Derek Jeter	8.00
3	Vladimir Guerrero	3.00
4	Mike Piazza	6.00
5	Cal Ripken Jr.	8.00
6	Sammy Sosa	4.00
7	Jeff Bagwell	2.00
8	Nomar Garciaparra	6.00
9	Chipper Jones	4.00
10	Ken Griffey Jr.	5.00

2000 Upper Deck Ovation Superstar Theatre

This 20-card set is printed on a full foiled card front enhanced by silver foil stamping and etching. Card backs are numbered with an "ST" prefix and seeded 1:19 packs.

		MT
Complete Set (20):		50.00
Common Player:		1.50
Inserted 1:19		
1	Ivan Rodriguez	2.00
2	Brian Giles	2.00
3	Bernie Williams	2.00
4	Greg Maddux	5.00
5	Frank Thomas	2.50
6	Sean Casey	1.50
7	Mo Vaughn	1.50
8	Carlos Delgado	1.50
9	Tony Gwynn	4.00
10	Pedro Martinez	4.00
11	Scott Rolen	2.00
12	Mark McGwire	8.00
13	Manny Ramirez	2.00
14	Rafael Palmeiro	2.00
15	Jose Canseco	2.00
16	Randy Johnson	3.00
17	Gary Sheffield	1.50
18	Larry Walker	1.50
19	Barry Bonds	6.00
20	Roger Clemens	5.00

2000 Upper Deck Ovation Super Signatures

This two-card insert set features Ken Griffey Jr. and Mike Piazza. Spotlighting the autographs of Griffey and Piazza, Super Signatures is issued in three versions: Silver, numbered to 100; Gold, numbered to 50; and Rainbow, numbered to 10.

		MT
Common Card:		
Jr	Ken Griffey Rainbow/10	
KG	Ken Griffey Gold/50	350.00
KG	Ken Griffey Silver/100	200.00
MP	Mike Piazza Rainbow/10	
MP	Mike Piazza Gold/50	400.00
MP	Mike Piazza Silver/100	200.00

2000 Upper Deck Ovation 3,000 Hit Club

Upper Deck's cross brand insert series pays tribute to members of the elite 3,000 Hit Club. Ovation features Willie Mays in the series, which has four versions: Bat card, 300 produced; Jersey card, 350 produced; Bat/Jersey combo, 50 produced; and Bat/Jersey autograph, 24 produced.

		MT
1	Willie Mays (Jersey Card/350)	80.00
2	Willie Mays (Bat Card/300)	80.00
3	Willie Mays (Jersey +Bat Card/50)	400.00
4	Willie Mays (Signed Jersey+Bat Card/24)	1000.

2000 Upper Deck PowerDeck

		MT
Complete Set (12):		55.00
Common Card:		3.00
Pack (1):		4.00
Box:		40.00
1	Sammy Sosa	6.00
2	Ken Griffey Jr.	8.00
3	Mark McGwire	10.00
4	Derek Jeter	6.00
5	Alex Rodriguez	8.00
6	Nomar Garciaparra	6.00
7	Mike Piazza	6.00
8	Cal Ripken Jr.	8.00
9	Ivan Rodriguez	3.00
10	Chipper Jones	5.00
11	Pedro Martinez	3.00
12	Manny Ramirez	3.00

2000 Upper Deck PowerDeck Magical Moments

		MT
Complete Set (2):		20.00
Inserted 1:10 H		
KG	Ken Griffey Jr.	8.00
CR	Cal Ripken Jr.	10.00

2000 Upper Deck PowerDeck Magical Moments Autograph

		MT
Each signed 50 cards		
KG	Ken Griffey Jr.	275.00
CR	Cal Ripken Jr.	275.00

2000 Upper Deck PowerDeck Power Trio

		MT
Complete Set (3):		25.00
Common Player:		30.00
Inserted 1:7		
PT1	Derek Jeter	6.00
PT2	Ken Griffey Jr.	8.00
PT3	Mark McGwire	10.00

2000 Upper Deck Pros and Prospects

The 132-card base set consists of 90 regular player cards, a 30-card Prospective Superstars subset and a 12-card Pro-Fame subset. Prospective Superstars are serially numbered to 1,350 and Pro-Fame are serially numbered to 1,000. Card fronts have a white-bordered design with silver foil stamping. Both subsets are serially numbered on the card front.

		MT
Complete Set (132):		800.00
Common Player (1-90):		.15
Common (91-120):		8.00
Production 1,350 sets		
Common (121-132):		8.00
Production 1,000 sets		
Pack (5):		3.00
Box (24):		55.00
1	Darin Erstad	.40
2	Troy Glaus	.75
3	Mo Vaughn	.50
4	Jason Giambi	.40
5	Tim Hudson	.25
6	Ben Grieve	.25
7	Eric Chavez	.25
8	Shannon Stewart	.15
9	Raul Mondesi	.25
10	Carlos Delgado	.75
11	Jose Canseco	.40
12	Fred McGriff	.25
13	Greg Vaughn	.15
14	Manny Ramirez	.75
15	Roberto Alomar	.60
16	Jim Thome	.40
17	Alex Rodriguez	2.50
18	Fred Garcia	.15
19	John Olerud	.15
20	Cal Ripken Jr.	2.50
21	Albert Belle	.40
22	Mike Mussina	.40
23	Ivan Rodriguez	.75
24	Rafael Palmeiro	.40
25	Ruben Mateo	.15
26	Gabe Kapler	.15
27	Pedro Martinez	.75
28	Nomar Garciaparra	2.00
29	Carl Everett	.15
30	Carlos Beltran	.15
31	Jermaine Dye	.15

32	Johnny Damon	.15
33	Juan Gonzalez	.75
34	Juan Encarnacion	.15
35	Dean Palmer	.15
36	Jacque Jones	.15
37	Matt Lawton	.15
38	Frank Thomas	1.00
39	Paul Konerko	.15
40	Magglio Ordonez	.25
41	Derek Jeter	2.00
42	Bernie Williams	.50
43	Mariano Rivera	.25
44	Roger Clemens	1.00
45	Jeff Bagwell	.75
46	Craig Biggio	.25
47	Richard Hidalgo	.25
48	Chipper Jones	1.50
49	Andres Galarraga	.40
50	Andruw Jones	.50
51	Greg Maddux	1.50
52	Jeromy Burnitz	.15
53	Geoff Jenkins	.25
54	Mark McGwire	3.00
55	Jim Edmonds	.25
56	Fernando Tatis	.15
57	J.D. Drew	.15
58	Sammy Sosa	2.00
59	Kerry Wood	.25
60	Randy Johnson	.75
61	Matt Williams	.25
62	Erubiel Durazo	.15
63	Shawn Green	.25
64	Kevin Brown	.25
65	Gary Sheffield	.25
66	Adrian Beltre	.25
67	Vladimir Guerrero	1.00
68	Jose Vidro	.15
69	Barry Bonds	1.00
70	Jeff Kent	.15
71	Preston Wilson	.15
72	Ryan Dempster	.15
73	Mike Lowell	.15
74	Mike Piazza	2.00
75	Robin Ventura	.15
76	Edgardo Alfonzo	.25
77	Derek Bell	.15
78	Tony Gwynn	1.50
79	Matt Clement	.15
80	Scott Rolen	.75
81	Bobby Abreu	.15
82	Curt Schilling	.15
83	Brian Giles	.15
84	Jason Kendall	.15
85	Kris Benson	.15
86	Ken Griffey Jr.	2.00
87	Sean Casey	.15
88	Pokey Reese	.15
89	Larry Walker	.25
90	Todd Helton	.75
91	Rick Ankiel (Prospective Superstars)	10.00
92	Milton Bradley (Prospective Superstars)	10.00
93	Vernon Wells (Prospective Superstars)	8.00
94	Rafael Furcal (Prospective Superstars)	10.00
95	*Kazuhiro Sasaki* (Prospective Superstars)	25.00
96	*Joe Torres* (Prospective Superstars)	15.00
97	Adam Kennedy (Prospective Superstars)	8.00
98	Adam Piatt (Prospective Superstars)	10.00
99	*Matt Wheatland* (Prospective Superstars)	15.00
100	*Alex Cabrera* (Prospective Superstars)	10.00
101	*Barry Zito* (Prospective Superstars)	40.00
102	*Mike Lamb* (Prospective Superstars)	10.00
103	*Scott Heard* (Prospective Superstars)	15.00
104	*Danys Baez* (Prospective Superstars)	12.00
105	Matt Riley (Prospective Superstars)	8.00
106	Mark Mulder (Prospective Superstars)	8.00
107	*Wilfredo Rodriguez* (Prospective Superstars)	10.00
108	*Luis Matos* (Prospective Superstars)	10.00
109	Alfonso Soriano (Prospective Superstars)	10.00
110	Pat Burrell (Prospective Superstars)	10.00
111	*Mike Tonis* (Prospective Superstars)	15.00
112	*Aaron McNeal* (Prospective Superstars)	10.00
113	*Dave Krynzel* (Prospective Superstars)	15.00
114	Josh Beckett (Prospective Superstars)	20.00
115	*Sean Burnett* (Prospective Superstars)	10.00
116	Eric Munson (Prospective Superstars)	8.00
117	*Scott Downs* (Prospective Superstars)	8.00
118	*Brian Tollberg* (Prospective Superstars)	10.00
119	Nick Johnson (Prospective Superstars)	8.00
120	*Leo Estrella* (Prospective Superstars)	8.00
121	Ken Griffey Jr. (Pro Fame)	20.00
122	Frank Thomas (Pro Fame)	10.00
123	Cal Ripken Jr. (Pro Fame)	25.00
124	Ivan Rodriguez (Pro Fame)	8.00
125	Derek Jeter (Pro Fame)	20.00
126	Mark McGwire (Pro Fame)	30.00
127	Pedro Martinez (Pro Fame)	8.00
128	Chipper Jones (Pro Fame)	15.00
129	Sammy Sosa (Pro Fame)	20.00
130	Alex Rodriguez (Pro Fame)	25.00
131	Vladimir Guerrero (Pro Fame)	10.00
132	Jeff Bagwell (Pro Fame)	8.00

2000 Upper Deck Pros and Prospects Future Forces

This 10-card set highlights top prosects on a card front featuring gold foil stamping and etching. Card backs are numbered with an "F" prefix and are seeded 1:6 packs.

		MT
Complete Set (10):		10.00
Common Player:		.50
Inserted 1:6		
1	Pat Burrell	2.50
2	Brad Penny	.50
3	Rick Ankiel	1.50
4	Adam Kennedy	.50
5	Eric Munson	1.00
6	Rafael Furcal	1.00
7	Mark Mulder	.50
8	Vernon Wells	.50
9	Matt Riley	.50
10	Nick Johnson	1.00

2000 Upper Deck Pros and Prospects ProMotion

This 10-card set spotlights some of baseball's best all- around talents using gold foil stamping. Card backs are numbered with an "P" prefix and are seeded 1:6 packs.

		MT
Complete Set (10):		20.00
Common Player:		.75
Inserted 1:6		
1	Derek Jeter	3.00
2	Mike Piazza	3.00
3	Mark McGwire	5.00
4	Ivan Rodriguez	1.25
5	Kerry Wood	.75
6	Nomar Garciaparra	3.00
7	Sammy Sosa	3.00
8	Alex Rodriguez	4.00
9	Ken Griffey Jr.	3.00
10	Vladimir Guerrero	1.50

2000 Upper Deck Pros and Prospects Rare Breed

Baseball's top performers are spotlighted in this 12-card set on a full foiled silver front with gold foil stamping. Card backs are numbered with an "R" prefix and are inserted 1:12 packs.

		MT
Complete Set (12):		40.00
Common Player:		1.50
Inserted 1:12		
1	Mark McGwire	8.00
2	Frank Thomas	3.00
3	Mike Piazza	5.00
4	Barry Bonds	2.00
5	Manny Ramirez	2.00
6	Ken Griffey Jr.	5.00
7	Nomar Garciaparra	5.00
8	Randy Johnson	2.00
9	Vladimir Guerrero	3.00
10	Jeff Bagwell	2.00
11	Rick Ankiel	1.50
12	Alex Rodriguez	6.00

2000 Upper Deck Pros and Pros. Signed Game-Worn Jerseys

Each of these Game Jersey cards has a piece of jersey swatch and autograph from the featured player. A Level 2 "Gold" version is limited to the player's corresponding uniform number.

		MT
Common Player:		25.00
Inserted 1:96		
BB	Barry Bonds	140.00
JC	Jose Canseco	60.00
JD	J.D. Drew	40.00
TG	Tom Glavine	50.00
LG	Luis Gonzalez	40.00
KG	Ken Griffey Jr.	150.00
TG	Tony Gwynn	60.00
DJ	Derek Jeter	400.00
RJ	Randy Johnson	80.00
CJ	Chipper Jones	80.00
KL	Kenny Lofton	25.00
CR	Cal Ripken Jr.	175.00
AR	Alex Rodriguez	125.00
IR	Ivan Rodriguez	40.00
SR	Scott Rolen	40.00
GS	Gary Sheffield	25.00
FT	Frank Thomas	40.00
MV	Mo Vaughn	30.00
RV	Robin Ventura	25.00
MW	Matt Williams	25.00
PW	Preston Wilson	25.00

2000 Upper Deck Pros and Prospects The Best in the Bigs

This 10-card set spotlights baseball's best performers on a white bordered design with gold foil stamping. Card backs are numbered with an "B" prefix and are inserted 1:12 packs.

		MT
Complete Set (10):		40.00
Common Player:		1.50
Inserted 1:12		
1	Sammy Sosa	5.00
2	Tony Gwynn	3.00
3	Pedro Martinez	2.00
4	Mark McGwire	8.00
5	Chipper Jones	4.00
6	Derek Jeter	5.00
7	Ken Griffey Jr.	5.00
8	Cal Ripken Jr.	6.00
9	Greg Maddux	4.00
10	Ivan Rodriguez	2.00

2000 Upper Deck Pros and Prospects 3,000 Hit Club

Upper Deck's continuing series features Lou Brock and Rod Carew. The series features 350 numbered bat cards, 350 numbered jersey cards and 100 numbered bat/jersey combos. Each player also signed the bat/jersey combos to their jersey number, as Brock signed 20 and Carew 29.

	MT
Lou Brock bat/350	30.00
Lou Brock jersey/350	30.00
Lou Brock bat/jersey/100	75.00
Lou Brock auto./bat/jersey/20	
Rod Carew bat/350	30.00
Rod Carew jersey/350	30.00
Rod Carew bat/jersey/100	75.00
Rod Carew auto./bat/jersey/29	

2000 Upper Deck Ultimate Victory

		MT
Complete Set (120):		600.00
Common Player:		.15
Common Ultimate Rookie (91-120):		6.00
Varying production levels		
1	Mo Vaughn	.40
2	Darin Erstad	.40
3	Troy Glaus	.75
4	Adam Kennedy	.15
5	Jason Giambi	.40
6	Ben Grieve	.25
7	Terrence Long	.15
8	Tim Hudson	.25
9	David Wells	.15
10	Carlos Delgado	.60
11	Shannon Stewart	.15
12	Greg Vaughn	.15
13	Gerald Williams	.15
14	Manny Ramirez	.75
15	Roberto Alomar	.60
16	Jim Thome	.40
17	Edgar Martinez	.15
18	Alex Rodriquez	2.50
19	Matt Riley	.15
20	Cal Ripken Jr.	2.50
21	Mike Mussina	.40
22	Albert Belle	.40
23	Ivan Rodriguez	.75
24	Rafael Palmeiro	.40
25	Nomar Garciaparra	2.00
26	Pedro Martinez	.75
27	Carl Everett	.15
28	*Tomokazu Ohka*	.15
29	Jermaine Dye	.15
30	Johnny Damon	.15
31	Dean Palmer	.15
32	Juan Gonzalez	.75
33	Eric Milton	.15
34	Matt Lawton	.15
35	Frank Thomas	1.00
36	Paul Konerko	.15
37	Magglio Ordonez	.25
38	Jon Garland	.15
39	Derek Jeter	2.50
40	Roger Clemens	1.00
41	Bernie Williams	.50
42	Nick Johnson	.15
43	Julio Lugo	.15
44	Jeff Bagwell	.75
45	Richard Hidalgo	.15
46	Chipper Jones	1.50
47	Greg Maddux	1.50
48	Andruw Jones	.50
49	Andres Galarraga	.25
50	Rafael Furcal	.50
51	Jeromy Burnitz	.15
52	Geoff Jenkins	.25
53	Mark McGwire	3.00
54	Jim Edmonds	.25
55	Rick Ankiel	.50
56	Sammy Sosa	2.00
57	*Julio Zuleta*	.15
58	Kerry Wood	.25
59	Randy Johnson	.75
60	Matt Williams	.25
61	Steve Finley	.15
62	Gary Sheffield	.30
63	Kevin Brown	.15
64	Shawn Green	.25
65	Milton Bradley	.15
66	Vladimir Guerrero	1.00
67	Jose Vidro	.15
68	Barry Bonds	.75
69	Jeff Kent	.15
70	Preston Wilson	.15
71	Mike Lowell	.15
72	Mike Piazza	2.00
73	Robin Ventura	.25
74	Edgardo Alfonzo	.25
75	Jay Payton	.15
76	Tony Gwynn	1.00
77	Adam Eaton	.15
78	Phil Nevin	.15
79	Scott Rolen	.50
80	Bob Abreu	.15
81	Pat Burrell	.50
82	Brian Giles	.25
83	Jason Kendall	.15
84	Kris Benson	.15
85	Gookie Dawkins	.15
86	Ken Griffey Jr.	2.00
87	Barry Larkin	.40
88	Larry Walker	.30
89	Todd Helton	.75
90	Ben Petrick	.15
91	*Alex Cabrera 3,500* (Ultimate Rookie 2000)	8.00
92	*Matt Wheatland 1,000* (Ultimate Rookie 2000)	15.00
93	*Joe Torres 1,000* (Ultimate Rookie 2000)	15.00
94	*Xavier Nady 1,000* (Ultimate Rookie 2000)	30.00
95	*Kenny Kelly 3,500* (Ultimate Rookie 2000)	6.00
96	*Matt Ginter 3,500* (Ultimate Rookie 2000)	6.00
97	*Ben Diggins 1,000* (Ultimate Rookie 2000)	15.00
98	*Danys Baez 3,500* (Ultimate Rookie 2000)	10.00
99	*Daylan Holt 2,500* (Ultimate Rookie 2000)	10.00
100	*Kazuhiro Sasaki 3,500* (Ultimate Rookie 2000)	10.00
101	*Dane Artman 2,500* (Ultimate Rookie 2000)	10.00
102	*Mike Tonis 1,000* (Ultimate Rookie 2000)	20.00
103	*Timoniel Perez 2,500* (Ultimate Rookie 2000)	10.00
104	*Barry Zito 2,500* (Ultimate Rookie 2000)	35.00
105	*Koyie Hill 2,500* (Ultimate Rookie 2000)	8.00
106	*Brad Wilkerson 2,500* (Ultimate Rookie 2000)	10.00
107	*Juan Pierre 3,500* (Ultimate Rookie 2000)	10.00
108	*Aaron McNeal 3,500* (Ultimate Rookie 2000)	8.00
109	*Jay Spurgeon 3,500* (Ultimate Rookie 2000)	8.00
110	*Sean Burnett 1,000* (Ultimate Rookie 2000)	10.00
111	*Luis Matos 3,500* (Ultimate Rookie 2000)	8.00
112	*Dave Krynzel 1,000* (Ultimate Rookie 2000)	15.00
113	*Scott Heard 1,000* (Ultimate Rookie 2000)	15.00
114	*Ben Sheets 2,500* (Ultimate Rookie 2000)	30.00
115	*Dane Sardinha 1,000* (Ultimate Rookie 2000)	15.00
116	*David Espinosa 1,000* (Ultimate Rookie 2000)	15.00
117	*Leo Estrella 3,500* (Ultimate Rookie 2000)	6.00
118	*Kurt Ainsworth 2,500* (Ultimate Rookie 2000)	15.00
119	*Jon Rauch 2,500* (Ultimate Rookie 2000)	20.00
120	Ryan Franklin 2,500 (Ultimate Rookie 2000)	10.00

2000 Upper Deck Ultimate Victory Collection

	MT
Parallel 25 Stars:	20-40X
Rookies (91-120):	2-4X
Production 25 sets	
Parallel 100 Stars:	10-20X
Rookies (91-120):	1-3X
Production 100 sets	
Parallel 250 Stars:	3-6X
Rookies (91-120):	1-2X
Production 250 sets	

2000 Upper Deck Ultimate Victory Diamond Dignitaries

		MT
Complete Set (10):		30.00
Common Player:		1.00
Inserted 1:23		
1	Ken Griffey Jr.	4.00
2	Nomar Garciaparra	4.00
3	Chipper Jones	3.00
4	Ivan Rodriguez	1.00
5	Mark McGwire	5.00
6	Cal Ripken Jr.	6.00
7	Vladimir Guerrero	2.00
8	Alex Rodriguez	5.00
9	Sammy Sosa	4.00
10	Derek Jeter	6.00

2000 Upper Deck Ultimate Victory HOF Game Jersey

		MT
Common Card:		40.00
SA	Sparky Anderson	15.00
CF	Carlton Fisk	25.00
TP	Tony Perez	20.00

2000 Upper Deck Ultimate Victory HOF Game Jersey Combo

		MT
UV-C	Sparky Anderson, Carlton Fisk, Tony Perez	85.00

2000 Upper Deck Ultimate Victory Lasting Impressions

		MT
Complete Set (10):		18.00
Common Player:		1.00
Inserted 1:11		
1	Barry Bonds	3.00

#	Player	MT
2	Mike Piazza	3.00
3	Manny Ramirez	1.50
4	Pedro J. Martinez	1.50
5	Mark McGwire	3.00
6	Ken Griffey Jr.	2.50
7	Ivan Rodriguez	1.00
8	Jeff Bagwell	1.50
9	Randy Johnson	1.50
10	Alex Rodriguez	3.00

2000 Upper Deck Ultimate Victory Starstruck

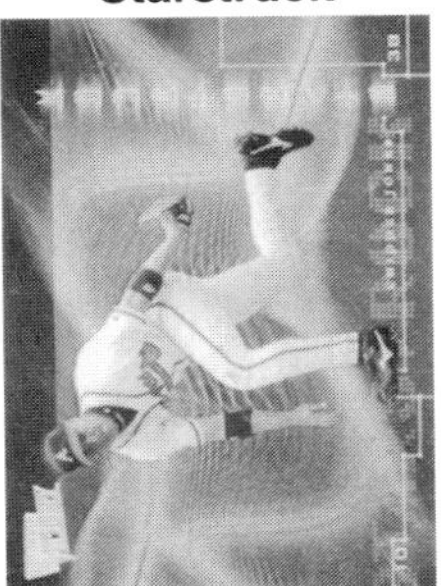

		MT
Complete Set (10):		20.00
Common Player:		1.00
Inserted 1:11		
1	Alex Rodriguez	3.00
2	Frank Thomas	1.00
3	Derek Jeter	4.00
4	Mark McGwire	3.00
5	Nomar Garciaparra	3.00
6	Chipper Jones	2.00
7	Cal Ripken Jr.	4.00
8	Sammy Sosa	2.00
9	Vladimir Guerrero	1.50
10	Ken Griffey Jr.	3.00

2000 Upper Deck Victory

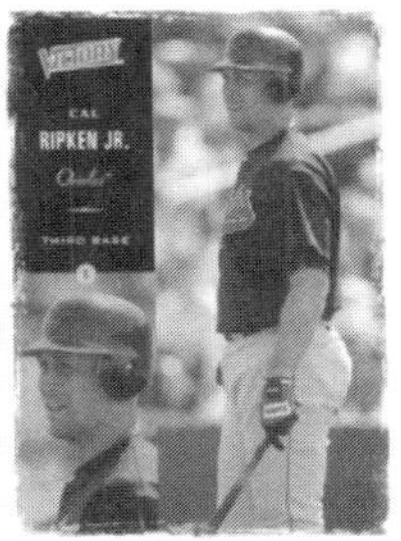

Victory offers no inserts just your standard 440-card base set that features a white bordered design, with two player images on the card front. The base set includes three subsets: Rookie 2000 (331-370); Big Play Makers (371-390) and JUNIOR Circuit (391-440).

		MT
Complete Set (440):		25.00
Complete Factory Set (466):		35.00
Common Player:		.10
Common Griffey (391-440):		.50
Common USA (441-466):		.40
Pack (12):		1.00
Wax Box (36):		25.00
1	Mo Vaughn	.30
2	Garret Anderson	.10
3	Tim Salmon	.20
4	Troy Percival	.10
5	Orlando Palmeiro	.10
6	Darin Erstad	.20
7	Ramon Ortiz	.10
8	Ben Molina	.10
9	Troy Glaus	.40
10	Jim Edmonds	.10
11	Mo Vaughn, Troy Percival	.15
12	Craig Biggio	.25
13	Roger Cedeno	.10
14	Shane Reynolds	.10
15	Jeff Bagwell	.50
16	Octavio Dotel	.10
17	Moises Alou	.15
18	Jose Lima	.10
19	Ken Caminiti	.15
20	Richard Hidalgo	.10
21	Billy Wagner	.10
22	Lance Berkman	.15
23	Jeff Bagwell, Jose Lima	.25
24	Jason Giambi	.10
25	Randy Velarde	.10
26	Miguel Tejada	.10
27	Matt Stairs	.10
28	A.J. Hinch	.10
29	Olmedo Saenz	.10
30	Ben Grieve	.20
31	Ryan Christenson	.10
32	Eric Chavez	.10
33	Tim Hudson	.20
34	John Jaha	.10
35	Jason Giambi, Matt Stairs	.10
36	Raul Mondesi	.20
37	Tony Batista	.10
38	David Wells	.10
39	Homer Bush	.10
40	Carlos Delgado	.40
41	Billy Koch	.10
42	Darrin Fletcher	.10
43	Tony Fernandez	.10
44	Shannon Stewart	.20
45	Roy Halladay	.10
46	Chris Carpenter	.10
47	Carlos Delgado, David Wells	.20
48	Chipper Jones	1.00
49	Greg Maddux	1.00
50	Andruw Jones	.40
51	Andres Galarraga	.30
52	Tom Glavine	.20
53	Brian Jordan	.10
54	John Smoltz	.10
55	John Rocker	.10
56	Javy Lopez	.15
57	Eddie Perez	.10
58	Kevin Millwood	.10
59	Chipper Jones, Greg Maddux	.50
60	Jeromy Burnitz	.20
61	Steve Woodard	.10
62	Ron Belliard	.10
63	Geoff Jenkins	.20
64	Bob Wickman	.10
65	Marquis Grissom	.10
66	Henry Blanco	.10
67	Mark Loretta	.10
68	Alex Ochoa	.10
69	Marquis Grissom, Jeromy Burnitz	.10
70	Mark McGwire	2.00
71	Edgar Renteria	.10
72	Dave Veres	.10
73	Eli Marrero	.10
74	Fernando Tatis	.20
75	J.D. Drew	.20
76	Ray Lankford	.10
77	Daryle Kile	.10
78	Kent Bottenfield	.10
79	Joe McEwing	.10
80	Mark McGwire, Ray Lankford	1.00
81	Sammy Sosa	1.25
82	Jose Nieves	.10
83	Jon Lieber	.10
84	Henry Rodriguez	.10
85	Mark Grace	.20
86	Eric Young	.10
87	Kerry Wood	.25
88	Ismael Valdes	.10
89	Glenallen Hill	.10
90	Sammy Sosa, Mark Grace	.60
91	Greg Vaughn	.20
92	Fred McGriff	.20
93	Ryan Rupe	.10
94	Bubba Trammell	.10
95	Miguel Cairo	.10
96	Roberto Hernandez	.10
97	Jose Canseco	.50
98	Wilson Alvarez	.10
99	John Flaherty	.10
100	Vinny Castilla	.15
101	Jose Canseco, Roberto Hernandez	.25
102	Randy Johnson	.40
103	Matt Williams	.20
104	Matt Mantei	.10
105	Steve Finley	.10
106	Luis Gonzalez	.10
107	Travis Lee	.10
108	Omar Daal	.10
109	Jay Bell	.10
110	Erubiel Durazo	.10
111	Tony Womack	.10
112	Todd Stottlemyre	.10
113	Randy Johnson, Matt Williams	.10
114	Gary Sheffield	.25
115	Adrian Beltre	.10
116	Kevin Brown	.20
117	Todd Hundley	.10
118	Eric Karros	.20
119	Shawn Green	.40
120	Chan Ho Park	.10
121	Mark Grudzielanek	.10
122	Todd Hollandsworth	.10
123	Jeff Shaw	.10
124	Darren Dreifort	.10
125	Gary Sheffield, Kevin Brown	.15
126	Vladimir Guerrero	.75
127	Michael Barrett	.10
128	Dustin Hermanson	.10
129	Jose Vidro	.10
130	Chris Widger	.10
131	Mike Thurman	.10
132	Wilton Guerrero	.10
133	Brad Fullmer	.10
134	Rondell White	.20
135	Ugueth Urbina	.10
136	Vladimir Guerrero, Rondell White	.40
137	Barry Bonds	.60
138	Russ Ortiz	.10
139	J.T. Snow	.10
140	Joe Nathan	.10
141	Rich Aurilia	.10
142	Jeff Kent	.10
143	Armando Rios	.10
144	Ellis Burks	.10
145	Robb Nen	.10
146	Marvin Benard	.10
147	Barry Bonds, Russ Ortiz	.40
148	Manny Ramirez	.50
149	Bartolo Colon	.10
150	Kenny Lofton	.35
151	Sandy Alomar Jr.	.15
152	Travis Fryman	.15
153	Omar Vizquel	.10
154	Roberto Alomar	.40
155	Richie Sexson	.10
156	David Justice	.20
157	Jim Thome	.30
158	Manny Ramirez, Roberto Alomar	.25
159	Ken Griffey Jr.	1.50
160	Edgar Martinez	.15
161	Fred Garcia	.10
162	Alex Rodriguez	1.50
163	John Halama	.10
164	Russ Davis	.10
165	David Bell	.10
166	Gil Meche	.10
167	Jamie Moyer	.10
168	John Olerud	.20
169	Ken Griffey Jr., Fred Garcia	.75
170	Preston Wilson	.10
171	Antonio Alfonseca	.10
172	A.J. Burnett	.10
173	Luis Castillo	.10
174	Mike Lowell	.10
175	Alex Fernandez	.10
176	Mike Redmond	.10
177	Alex Gonzalez	.10
178	Vladimir Nunez	.10
179	Mark Kotsay	.10
180	Preston Wilson, Luis Castillo	.10
181	Mike Piazza	1.25
182	Darryl Hamilton	.10
183	Al Leiter	.20
184	Robin Ventura	.20
185	Rickey Henderson	.20
186	Rey Ordonez	.10
187	Edgardo Alfonzo	.15
188	Derek Bell	.10
189	Mike Hampton	.10
190	Armando Benitez	.10
191	Mike Piazza, Rickey Henderson	.50
192	Cal Ripken Jr.	1.50
193	B.J. Surhoff	.10
194	Mike Mussina	.40
195	Albert Belle	.40
196	Jerry Hairston Jr.	.10
197	Will Clark	.20
198	Sidney Ponson	.10
199	Brady Anderson	.15
200	Scott Erickson	.10
201	Ryan Minor	.10
202	Cal Ripken Jr., Albert Belle	.75
203	Tony Gwynn	1.00
204	Bret Boone	.10
205	Ryan Klesko	.10
206	Ben Davis	.10
207	Matt Clement	.10
208	Eric Owens	.10
209	Trevor Hoffman	.10
210	Sterling Hitchcock	.10
211	Phil Nevin	.10
212	Tony Gwynn, Trevor Hoffman	.50
213	Scott Rolen	.50
214	Bob Abreu	.20
215	Curt Schilling	.20
216	Rico Brogna	.10
217	Robert Person	.10
218	Doug Glanville	.10
219	Mike Lieberthal	.10
220	Andy Ashby	.10
221	Randy Wolf	.10
222	Bob Abreu, Curt Schilling	.15
223	Brian Giles	.20
224	Jason Kendall	.20
225	Kris Benson	.10
226	Warren Morris	.10
227	Kevin Young	.10
228	Al Martin	.10
229	Wil Cordero	.10
230	Bruce Aven	.10
231	Todd Ritchie	.10
232	Jason Kendall, Brian Giles	.10
233	Ivan Rodriguez	.50
234	Rusty Greer	.10
235	Ruben Mateo	.10
236	Justin Thompson	.10
237	Rafael Palmeiro	.25
238	Chad Curtis	.10
239	Royce Clayton	.10
240	Gabe Kapler	.20
241	Jeff Zimmerman	.10
242	John Wetteland	.10
243	Ivan Rodriguez, Rafael Palmeiro	.25
244	Nomar Garciaparra	1.25
245	Pedro Martinez	.50
246	Jose Offerman	.10
247	Jason Varitek	.10
248	Troy O'Leary	.10
249	John Valentin	.10
250	Trot Nixon	.10
251	Carl Everett	.10
252	Wilton Veras	.10
253	Bret Saberhagen	.10
254	Nomar Garciaparra, Pedro J. Martinez	.60
255	Sean Casey	.10
256	Barry Larkin	.25
257	Pokey Reese	.10
258	Pete Harnisch	.10
259	Aaron Boone	.10
260	Dante Bichette	.20
261	Scott Williamson	.10
262	Steve Parris	.10
263	Dmitri Young	.10
264	Mike Cameron	.10
265	Sean Casey, Scott Williamson	.10
266	Larry Walker	.40
267	Rolando Arrojo	.10
268	Pedro Astacio	.10
269	Todd Helton	.50
270	Jeff Cirillo	.10

271 Neifi Perez .10
272 Brian Bohanon .10
273 Jeffrey Hammonds .10
274 Tom Goodwin .10
275 Larry Walker, Todd Helton .25
276 Carlos Beltran .15
277 Jermaine Dye .10
278 Mike Sweeney .10
279 Joe Randa .10
280 Jose Rosado .10
281 Carlos Febles .10
282 Jeff Suppan .10
283 Johnny Damon .10
284 Jeremy Giambi .10
285 Mike Sweeney, Carlos Beltran .10
286 Tony Clark .20
287 Damion Easley .10
288 Jeff Weaver .10
289 Dean Palmer .10
290 Juan Gonzalez .50
291 Juan Encarnacion .10
292 Todd Jones .10
293 Karim Garcia .10
294 Deivi Cruz .10
295 Dean Palmer, Juan Encarnacion .10
296 Corey Koskie .10
297 Brad Radke .10
298 Doug Mientkiewicz .10
299 Ron Coomer .10
300 Joe Mays .10
301 Eric Milton .10
302 Jacque Jones .10
303 Chad Allen .10
304 Cristian Guzman .10
305 Jason Ryan .10
306 Todd Walker .10
307 Corey Koskie, Eric Milton .10
308 Frank Thomas .75
309 Paul Konerko .10
310 Mike Sirotka .10
311 Jim Parque .10
312 Magglio Ordonez .10
313 Bob Howry .10
314 Carlos Lee .10
315 Ray Durham .10
316 Chris Singleton .10
317 Brook Fordyce .10
318 Frank Thomas, Magglio Ordonez .25
319 Derek Jeter 1.25
320 Roger Clemens .75
321 Paul O'Neill .20
322 Bernie Williams .40
323 Mariano Rivera .20
324 Tino Martinez .20
325 David Cone .20
326 Chuck Knoblauch .20
327 Darryl Strawberry .20
328 Orlando Hernandez .10
329 Ricky Ledee .10
330 Derek Jeter, Bernie Williams .50
331 Pat Burrell (Rookie 2000) .60
332 Alfonso Soriano (Rookie 2000) .25
333 Josh Beckett (Rookie 2000) .75
334 Matt Riley (Rookie 2000) .50
335 Brian Cooper (Rookie 2000) .10
336 Eric Munson (Rookie 2000) .75
337 Vernon Wells (Rookie 2000) .10
338 Juan Pena (Rookie 2000) .10
339 Mark DeRosa (Rookie 2000) .10
340 Kip Wells (Rookie 2000) .10
341 Roosevelt Brown (Rookie 2000) .10
342 Jason LaRue (Rookie 2000) .10
343 Ben Petrick (Rookie 2000) .10
344 Mark Quinn (Rookie 2000) .10
345 Julio Ramirez (Rookie 2000) .10
346 Rod Barajas (Rookie 2000) .10
347 Robert Fick (Rookie 2000) .10
348 David Newhan (Rookie 2000) .10
349 Eric Gagne (Rookie 2000) .10
350 Jorge Toca (Rookie 2000) .10
351 Mitch Meluskey (Rookie 2000) .10
352 Ed Yarnall (Rookie 2000) .10
353 Chad Hermansen (Rookie 2000) .10
354 Peter Bergeron (Rookie 2000) .10
355 Dermal Brown (Rookie 2000) .10
356 Adam Kennedy (Rookie 2000) .10
357 Kevin Barker (Rookie 2000) .10
358 Francisco Cordero (Rookie 2000) .10
359 Travis Dawkins (Rookie 2000) .10
360 Jeff Williams (Rookie 2000) .10
361 Chad Hutchinson (Rookie 2000) .10
362 D'Angelo Jimenez (Rookie 2000) .10
363 Derrick Gibson (Rookie 2000) .10
364 Calvin Murray (Rookie 2000) .10
365 Doug Davis (Rookie 2000) .10
366 *Rob Ramsay* (Rookie 2000) .20
367 Mark Redman (Rookie 2000) .10
368 Rick Ankiel (Rookie 2000) .25
369 Domingo Guzman (Rookie 2000) .10
370 Eugene Kingsale (Rookie 2000) .10
371 Nomar Garciaparra (Big Play Makers) .60
372 Ken Griffey Jr. (Big Play Makers) .75
373 Randy Johnson (Big Play Makers) .20
374 Jeff Bagwell (Big Play Makers) .25
375 Ivan Rodriguez (Big Play Makers) .25
376 Derek Jeter (Big Play Makers) .60
377 Carlos Beltran (Big Play Makers) .10
378 Vladimir Guerrero (Big Play Makers) .40
379 Sammy Sosa (Big Play Makers) .60
380 Barry Bonds (Big Play Makers) .40
381 Pedro Martinez (Big Play Makers) .25
382 Chipper Jones (Big Play Makers) .50
383 Mo Vaughn (Big Play Makers) .15
384 Mike Piazza (Big Play Makers) .60
385 Alex Rodriguez (Big Play Makers) .60
386 Manny Ramirez (Big Play Makers) .25
387 Mark McGwire (Big Play Makers) 1.00
388 Tony Gwynn (Big Play Makers) .50
389 Sean Casey (Big Play Makers) .10
390 Cal Ripken Jr. (Big Play Makers) .75
391 Ken Griffey Jr. .40
392 Ken Griffey Jr. .40
393 Ken Griffey Jr. .40
394 Ken Griffey Jr. .40
395 Ken Griffey Jr. .40
396 Ken Griffey Jr. .40
397 Ken Griffey Jr. .40
398 Ken Griffey Jr. .40
399 Ken Griffey Jr. .40
400 Ken Griffey Jr. .40
401 Ken Griffey Jr. .40
402 Ken Griffey Jr. .40
403 Ken Griffey Jr. .40
404 Ken Griffey Jr. .40
405 Ken Griffey Jr. .40
406 Ken Griffey Jr. .40
407 Ken Griffey Jr. .40
408 Ken Griffey Jr. .40
409 Ken Griffey Jr. .40
410 Ken Griffey Jr. .40
411 Ken Griffey Jr. .40
412 Ken Griffey Jr. .40
413 Ken Griffey Jr. .40
414 Ken Griffey Jr. .40
415 Ken Griffey Jr. .40
416 Ken Griffey Jr. .40
417 Ken Griffey Jr. .40
418 Ken Griffey Jr. .40
419 Ken Griffey Jr. .40
420 Ken Griffey Jr. .40
421 Ken Griffey Jr. .40
422 Ken Griffey Jr. .40
423 Ken Griffey Jr. .40
424 Ken Griffey Jr. .40
425 Ken Griffey Jr. .40
426 Ken Griffey Jr. .40
427 Ken Griffey Jr. .40
428 Ken Griffey Jr. .40
429 Ken Griffey Jr. .40
430 Ken Griffey Jr. .40
431 Ken Griffey Jr. .40
432 Ken Griffey Jr. .40
433 Ken Griffey Jr. .40
434 Ken Griffey Jr. .40
435 Ken Griffey Jr. .40
436 Ken Griffey Jr. .40
437 Ken Griffey Jr. .40
438 Ken Griffey Jr. .40
439 Ken Griffey Jr. .40
440 Ken Griffey Jr. .40
441 Tommy Lasorda 1.00
442 Sean Burroughs 1.00
443 Rick Krivda .40
444 *Ben Sheets* 5.00
445 Pat Borders .40
446 *Brent Abernathy* 1.00
447 Tim Young .40
448 Adam Everett .75
449 Anthony Sanders .40
450 Ernie Young .40
451 *Brad Wilkerson* 1.50
452 Kurt Ainsworth 2.00
453 Ryan Franklin .40
454 Todd Williams .40
455 *Jon Rauch* 2.50
456 *Roy Oswalt* 5.00
457 Shane Heams .75
458 Chris George .75
459 Bobby Seay .40
460 Mike Kinkade .40
461 Marcus Jensen .40
462 Travis Dawkins .50
463 Doug Mientkiewicz .40
464 John Cotton .40
465 Mike Neill .40
466 Team Photo USA 2.50

2000 Upper Deck Yankees Legends

	MT
Complete Set (90):	20.00
Common Player:	.15
Pack (5):	4.00
Box (24):	90.00

1 Babe Ruth 2.00
2 Mickey Mantle 2.00
3 Lou Gehrig 2.00
4 Joe DiMaggio 2.00
5 Yogi Berra .75
6 Don Mattingly .75
7 Reggie Jackson 1.00
8 Dave Winfield .40
9 Bill Skowron .15
10 Willie Randolph .15
11 Phil Rizzuto .50
12 Tony Kubek .15
13 Thurman Munson 1.00
14 Roger Maris 1.00
15 Billy Martin .40
16 Elston Howard .15
17 Graig Nettles .15
18 Whitey Ford .50
19 Earl Combes .15
20 Tony Lazzeri .15
21 Bob Meusel .15
22 Joe Gordon .15
23 Jerry Coleman .15
24 Joe Torre .50
25 Bucky Dent .15
26 Don Larsen .40
27 Bobby Richardson .15
28 Ron Guidry .15
29 Bobby Murcer .15
30 Tommy Henrich .15
31 Hank Bauer .15
32 Joe Pepitone .15
33 Clete Boyer .15
34 Chris Chambliss .15
35 Tommy John .15
36 Goose Gossage .15
37 Red Ruffing .15
38 Charlie Keller .15
39 Billy Gardner .15
40 Hector Lopez .15
41 Cliff Johnson .15
42 Oscar Gamble .15
43 Allie Reynolds .15
44 Mickey Rivers .15
45 Bill Dickey .50
46 Dave Righetti .15
47 Mel Stottlemyre .15
48 Waite Hoyt .15
49 Lefty Gomez .15
50 Wade Boggs .50
51 Billy Martin (Magic Numbers) .25
52 Babe Ruth (Magic Numbers) 1.00
53 Lou Gehrig (Magic Numbers) 1.00
54 Joe DiMaggio (Magic Numbers) 1.00
55 Mickey Mantle (Magic Numbers) 1.00
56 Yogi Berra (Magic Numbers) .40
57 Bill Dickey (Magic Numbers) .25
58 Roger Maris (Magic Numbers) .50
59 Phil Rizzuto (Magic Numbers) .25
60 Thurman Munson (Magic Numbers) .50
61 Whitey Ford (Magic Numbers) .25
62 Don Mattingly (Magic Numbers) .40
63 Elston Howard (Magic Numbers) .15
64 Casey Stengel (Magic Numbers) .15
65 Reggie Jackson (Magic Numbers) .50
66 Babe Ruth (1923) (The Championship Years) 1.00
67 Lou Gehrig (1927) (The Championship Years) 1.00
68 Tony Lazzeri (1928) (The Championship Years) .15
69 Babe Ruth (1932) (The Championship Years) 1.00
70 Lou Gehrig (1936) (The Championship Years) 1.00
71 Lefty Gomez (1937) (The Championship Years) .15
72 Bill Dickey (1938) (The Championship Years) .25

73	Tommy Henrich (1939) (The Championship Years)	.15
74	Joe DiMaggio (1941) (The Championship Years)	1.00
75	Spud Chandler (1943) (The Championship Years)	.15
76	Tommy Henrich (1947) (The Championship Years)	.15
77	Phil Rizzuto (1949) (The Championship Years)	.25
78	Whitey Ford (1950) (The Championship Years)	.25
79	Yogi Berra (1951) (The Championship Years)	.40
80	Casey Stengel (1952) (The Championship Years)	.15
81	Billy Martin (1953) (The Championship Years)	.25
82	Don Larsen (1956) (The Championship Years)	.25
83	Elston Howard (1958) (The Championship Years)	.15
84	Roger Maris (1961) (The Championship Years)	.50
85	Mickey Mantle (1962) (The Championship Years)	1.00
86	Reggie Jackson (1977) (The Championship Years)	.50
87	Bucky Dent (1978) (The Championship Years)	.15
88	Wade Boggs (1996) (The Championship Years)	.25
89	Joe Torre (1998) (The Championship Years)	.25
90	Joe Torre (1999) (The Championship Years)	.25
		.15

2000 Upper Deck Yankees Legends Legendary Lumber

		MT
Common Player:		10.00
Inserted 1:23		
HB	Hank Bauer	10.00
YB	Yogi Berra	40.00
PB	Paul Blair	10.00
CB	Clete Boyer	10.00
CC	Chris Chambliss	10.00
JC	Joe Collins	10.00
BD	Bucky Dent	10.00
JD	Joe DiMaggio	200.00
OG	Oscar Gamble	10.00
BG	Billy Gardner	10.00
TH	Tommy Henrich	10.00
RH	Ralph Houk	15.00
EH	Elston Howard	20.00
RJ	Reggie Jackson	25.00
TJ	Tommy John	15.00
CJ	Cliff Johnson	10.00
CK	Charlie Keller	15.00
TK	Tony Kubek	15.00
HL	Hector Lopez	10.00
MM	Mickey Mantle	240.00
RM	Roger Maris	85.00
DM	Don Mattingly	50.00
TM	Thurman Munson	40.00
BM	Bobby Murcer	15.00
GN	Graig Nettles	15.00
JP	Joe Pepitone	15.00
WR	Willie Randolph	15.00
MR	Mickey Rivers	10.00
BR	Babe Ruth	250.00
MS	Moose Skowron	15.00
DW	Dave Winfield	25.00

2000 Upper Deck Yankees Legends Legendary Pinstripes

		MT
Common Player:		20.00
Inserted 1:144		
BD	Bucky Dent	20.00
WF	Whitey Ford	80.00
LG	Lou Gehrig	500.00
GG	Goose Gossage	20.00
RG	Ron Guidry	20.00
TH	Tommy Henrich	20.00
EH	Elston Howard	25.00
RJ	Reggie Jackson	60.00
HL	Hector Lopez	20.00
MM	Mickey Mantle	350.00
RM	Roger Maris	75.00
BM	Billy Martin	65.00
DM	Don Mattingly	150.00
TM	Thurman Munson	120.00
JP	Joe Pepitone	25.00
AR	Allie Reynolds	25.00
BR	Bobby Richardson	20.00
PR	Phil Rizzuto	65.00
DW	Dave Winfield	40.00

2000 Upper Deck Yankees Legends Auto. Legend. Pinstripe

		MT
Common Player:		50.00
BD	Bucky Dent	50.00
WF	Whitey Ford	100.00
GG	Goose Gossage	50.00
RG	Ron Guidry	50.00
TH	Tommy Henrich	50.00
RJ	Reggie Jackson	
HL	Hector Lopez	
GM	Gil MacDougald	60.00
DM	Don Mattingly	225.00
JP	Joe Pepitone	50.00
BR	Bobby Richardson	
PR	Phil Rizzuto	125.00
DW	Dave Winfield	70.00

2000 Upper Deck Yankees Legends Monument Park

		MT
Complete Set (6):		25.00
Common Player:		1.50
Inserted 1:23		2.50
1	Lou Gehrig	6.00
2	Babe Ruth	6.00
3	Mickey Mantle	6.00
4	Joe DiMaggio	6.00
5	Thurman Munson	4.00
6	Elston Howard	1.50

2000 Upper Deck Yankees Legends Murderer's Row

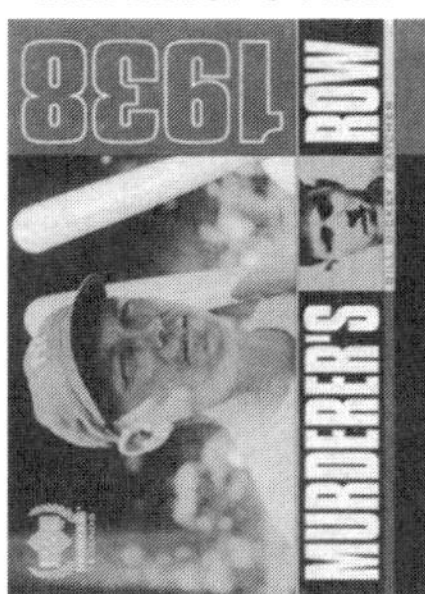

		MT
Complete Set (10):		15.00
Common Player:		1.00
Inserted 1:11		
1	Tony Lazzeri	1.00
2	Babe Ruth	6.00
3	Bob Meusel	1.00
4	Lou Gehrig	6.00
5	Joe Dugan	1.00
6	Bill Dickey	1.50
7	Waite Hoyt	1.00
8	Red Ruffing	1.00
9	Earl Combes	1.00
10	Lefty Gomez	1.00

2000 Upper Deck Yankees Legends Pride of the Pinstripes

		MT
Complete Set (6):		25.00
Common Player:		3.00
Inserted 1:23		
1	Babe Ruth	6.00
2	Mickey Mantle	6.00
3	Joe DiMaggio	6.00
4	Lou Gehrig	6.00
5	Reggie Jackson	3.00
6	Yogi Berra	3.00

Figure values of lower-grade cards from 1981-date as:
Near Mint (NM) 75%
Excellent (EX) 40%
of the listed Mint price

For cards through 1980, values should be figured as:
Excellent (EX) 50%
Very Good (VG) 30%
of the listed
Near Mint price

2000 Upper Deck Yankees Legends The Golden Years

		MT
Complete Set (10):		20.00
Common Player:		1.00
Inserted 1:11		
1	Joe DiMaggio	6.00
2	Phil Rizzuto	1.50
3	Yogi Berra	3.00
4	Billy Martin	1.50
5	Whitey Ford	2.00
6	Roger Maris	4.00
7	Mickey Mantle	6.00
8	Elston Howard	1.00
9	Tommy Henrich	1.00
10	Joe Gordon	1.00

2000 Upper Deck Yankees Legends The New Dynasty

		MT
Complete Set (10):		15.00
Common Player:		1.50
Inserted 1:11		
1	Reggie Jackson	3.00
2	Graig Nettles	1.00
3	Don Mattingly	4.00
4	Goose Gossage	1.00
5	Dave Winfield	2.00
6	Chris Chambliss	1.00
7	Thurman Munson	3.00
8	Willie Randolph	1.00
9	Ron Guidry	1.50
10	Bucky Dent	1.50

2000 UD Ionix

The base set consists of 90 cards, including a 30-card Futuristics subset that were seeded 1:4 packs. A Reciprocal parallel to the base set are also randomly inserted. The cards can distinguished by a holo-foiled front and the number on the back has an "R" prefix. Reciprocals 1-60 are found 1:4

packs, while Futuristics Reciprocals are found on the average of 1:11 packs.

		MT
Complete Set (90):		125.00
Common Player:		.20
Common Futuristic:		2.00
Inserted 1:4		
Reciprocal (1-60):		1.5X-4X
Reciprocal (61-90):		1X-1.5X
Inserted 1:4		
Future Recip. 1:11		
Pack (4):		2.50
Wax Box (24):		50.00
1	Mo Vaughn	.75
2	Troy Glaus	1.00
3	Jeff Bagwell	1.00
4	Craig Biggio	.50
5	Jose Lima	.20
6	Jason Giambi	.20
7	Tim Hudson	.40
8	Shawn Green	.75
9	Carlos Delgado	.75
10	Chipper Jones	2.00
11	Andruw Jones	.75
12	Greg Maddux	2.00
13	Jeromy Burnitz	.20
14	Mark McGwire	4.00
15	J.D. Drew	.40
16	Sammy Sosa	2.50
17	Jose Canseco	1.00
18	Fred McGriff	.50
19	Randy Johnson	.75
20	Matt Williams	.50
21	Kevin Brown	.40
22	Gary Sheffield	.40
23	Vladimir Guerrero	2.00
24	Barry Bonds	1.50
25	Jim Thome	.50
26	Manny Ramirez	1.00
27	Roberto Alomar	.75
28	Kenny Lofton	.75
29	Ken Griffey Jr.	3.00
30	Alex Rodriguez	3.00
31	Alex Gonzalez	.20
32	Preston Wilson	.20
33	Mike Piazza	2.50
34	Robin Ventura	.40
35	Cal Ripken Jr.	2.50
36	Albert Belle	.75
37	Tony Gwynn	2.00
38	Scott Rolen	1.00
39	Curt Schilling	.40
40	Brian Giles	.20
41	Juan Gonzalez	1.00
42	Ivan Rodriguez	1.00
43	Rafael Palmeiro	.60
44	Pedro J. Martinez	1.00
45	Nomar Garciaparra	2.50
46	Sean Casey	.50
47	Aaron Boone	.20
48	Barry Larkin	.50
49	Larry Walker	.75
50	Vinny Castilla	.30
51	Carlos Beltran	.25
52	Gabe Kapler	.40
53	Dean Palmer	.30
54	Eric Milton	.20
55	Corey Koskie	.20
56	Frank Thomas	1.00
57	Magglio Ordonez	.50
58	Roger Clemens	1.50
59	Bernie Williams	.75
60	Derek Jeter	2.50
61	Josh Beckett (Futuristics)	8.00
62	Eric Munson (Futuristics)	8.00
63	Rick Ankiel (Futuristics)	4.00
64	Matt Riley (Futuristics)	5.00
65	Robert Ramsay (Futuristics)	2.00
66	Vernon Wells (Futuristics)	3.00
67	Eric Gagne (Futuristics)	2.00
68	Robert Fick (Futuristics)	2.00
69	Mark Quinn (Futuristics)	4.00
70	Kip Wells (Futuristics)	2.00
71	Peter Bergeron (Futuristics)	2.00
72	Ed Yarnall (Futuristics)	2.00
73	Jorge Luis Toca (Futuristics)	3.00
74	Alfonso Soriano (Futuristics)	3.00
75	Calvin Murray (Futuristics)	2.00
76	Ramon Ortiz (Futuristics)	3.00
77	Chad Meyers (Futuristics)	3.00
78	Jason LaRue (Futuristics)	2.00
79	Pat Burrell (Futuristics)	6.00
80	Chad Hermansen (Futuristics)	2.00
81	Lance Berkman (Futuristics)	2.00
82	Erubiel Durazo (Futuristics)	3.00
83	Juan Pena (Futuristics)	2.00
84	Adam Kennedy (Futuristics)	2.00
85	Ben Petrick (Futuristics)	2.00
86	Kevin Barker (Futuristics)	2.00
87	Bruce Chen (Futuristics)	2.00
88	Jerry Hairston Jr. (Futuristics)	2.00
89	A.J. Burnett (Futuristics)	3.00
90	Gary Matthews Jr. (Futuristics)	2.00

2000 UD Ionix Atomic

This 15-card insert set has a horizontal format on a holo-foil front. Card backs are numbered with an "A" prefix and are found 1:8 packs.

		MT
Complete Set (15):		60.00
Common Player:		2.00
Inserted 1:8		
1	Pedro J. Martinez	2.50
2	Mark McGwire	10.00
3	Ken Griffey Jr.	8.00
4	Jeff Bagwell	2.50
5	Greg Maddux	5.00
6	Derek Jeter	6.00
7	Cal Ripken Jr.	6.00
8	Manny Ramirez	2.50
9	Randy Johnson	2.00
10	Nomar Garciaparra	6.00
11	Tony Gwynn	5.00
12	Bernie Williams	2.00
13	Mike Piazza	6.00
14	Roger Clemens	4.00
15	Alex Rodriguez	8.00

2000 UD Ionix Awesome Powers

A takeoff from the Austin Powers movie which was popular at the time of this release. The cards have a holo-foil front with a "groovin" 70's backdrop. Card backs are numbered with an "AP" prefix and are seeded 1:23 packs.

		MT
Complete Set (15):		150.00
Common Player:		4.00
Inserted 1:23		
1	Ken Griffey Jr.	20.00
2	Mike Piazza	15.00
3	Carlos Delgado	4.00
4	Mark McGwire	25.00
5	Chipper Jones	12.00
6	Scott Rolen	6.00
7	Cal Ripken Jr.	15.00
8	Alex Rodriguez	20.00
9	Larry Walker	5.00
10	Sammy Sosa	15.00
11	Barry Bonds	6.00
12	Nomar Garciaparra	15.00
13	Jose Canseco	6.00
14	Manny Ramirez	6.00
15	Jeff Bagwell	6.00

2000 UD Ionix BIOrhythm

This 15-card set has a holo-foil front and are seeded 1:11 packs. Card backs have a brief career note and are numbered with an "B" prefix.

		MT
Complete Set (15):		75.00
Common Player:		2.00
Inserted 1:11		
1	Randy Johnson	2.50
2	Derek Jeter	8.00
3	Sammy Sosa	8.00
4	Jose Lima	2.00
5	Chipper Jones	6.00
6	Barry Bonds	3.00
7	Ken Griffey Jr.	10.00
8	Nomar Garciaparra	8.00
9	Frank Thomas	3.00
10	Pedro Martinez	3.00
11	Larry Walker	2.50
12	Greg Maddux	6.00
13	Alex Rodriguez	10.00
14	Mark McGwire	12.00
15	Cal Ripken Jr.	8.00

2000 UD Ionix Pyrotechnics

This 15-card set has a holo-foiled front with an insertion ratio of 1:72 packs. Card backs are numbered with an "P" prefix.

		MT
Complete Set (15):		320.00
Common Player:		12.00
Inserted 1:72		
1	Roger Clemens	20.00
2	Chipper Jones	25.00
3	Alex Rodriguez	40.00
4	Jeff Bagwell	12.00
5	Mark McGwire	50.00
6	Pedro Martinez	12.00
7	Manny Ramirez	12.00
8	Cal Ripken Jr.	30.00
9	Mike Piazza	30.00
10	Derek Jeter	30.00
11	Ken Griffey Jr.	40.00
12	Frank Thomas	12.00
13	Sammy Sosa	30.00
14	Nomar Garciaparra	30.00
15	Greg Maddux	25.00

2000 UD Ionix Shockwave

Baseball's top hitters are spotlighted on a holo-foil front. They are found on the average of 1:4 packs and are numbered on the card back with an "S" prefix.

		MT
Complete Set (15):		25.00
Common Player:		.75
Inserted 1:4		
1	Mark McGwire	5.00
2	Sammy Sosa	3.00
3	Manny Ramirez	1.50
4	Ken Griffey Jr.	4.00
5	Vladimir Guerrero	2.50
6	Barry Bonds	2.00
7	Albert Belle	1.00
8	Ivan Rodriguez	1.50
9	Chipper Jones	2.50
10	Mo Vaughn	1.00
11	Jose Canseco	1.50
12	Jeff Bagwell	1.50
13	Matt Williams	.75
14	Alex Rodriguez	4.00
15	Carlos Delgado	.75

2000 UD Ionix Warp Zone

This 15-card set has a holo-foiled front with an insertion ratio of 1:288 packs. Card backs are numbered with an "WZ" prefix.

		MT
Complete Set (15):		425.00
Common Player:		10.00
Inserted 1:288		
1	Cal Ripken Jr.	50.00
2	Barry Bonds	35.00
3	Ken Griffey Jr.	35.00
4	Nomar Garciaparra	35.00
5	Chipper Jones	30.00
6	Ivan Rodriguez	10.00
7	Greg Maddux	30.00
8	Derek Jeter	50.00
9	Mike Piazza	35.00
10	Sammy Sosa	30.00
11	Roger Clemens	25.00
12	Alex Rodriguez	60.00
13	Vladimir Guerrero	15.00
14	Pedro Martinez	15.00
15	Mark McGwire	40.00

2000 UD Ionix UD Authentics

These autographed inserts have a horizontal format and are found on the average of 1:144 packs.

		MT
Common Player:		20.00
Inserted 1:144		
CBE	Carlos Beltran	15.00
AB	Adrian Beltre	20.00
PB	Pat Burrell	30.00
JC	Jose Canseco	30.00
SC	Sean Casey	20.00
BD	Ben Davis	20.00
SG	Shawn Green	20.00
JR	Ken Griffey Jr.	150.00
VG	Vladimir Guerrero	30.00
DJ	Derek Jeter	150.00
GK	Gabe Kapler	20.00
PM	Pedro Martinez	
RM	Ruben Mateo	15.00
RB	Joe McEwing	15.00
MR	Manny Ramirez	30.00
SR	Scott Rolen	25.00
MW	Matt Williams	20.00

2000 UD Ionix 3,000-Hit Club Piece of History

Upper Deck's cross-brand insert series paying tribute to baseball's 3,000 Hit Club members spotlights Roberto Clemente in UD Ionix. Three versions were randomly inserted: A game-used bat card, bat/cut signature card and a cut signature card.

		MT
RC1	Roberto Clemente	120.00
RC2	Roberto Clemente Bat/Cut/5	
RC3	Roberto Clemente Cut/4	

2001 Upper Deck

		MT
Complete Set (450):		100.00
Complete Series 1 (270):		40.00
Complete Series 2 (180):		60.00
Common Player:		.15
Pack (10):		3.00
Box (24):		65.00
1	Jeff DaVanon (Star Rookie)	.15
2	Aubrey Huff (Star Rookie)	.15
3	Pascual Coco (Star Rookie)	.15
4	Barry Zito (Star Rookie)	1.00
5	Augie Ojeda (Star Rookie)	.15
6	Chris Richard (Star Rookie)	.15
7	Josh Phelps (Star Rookie)	.15
8	Kevin Nicholson (Star Rookie)	.15
9	Juan Guzman (Star Rookie)	.15
10	Brandon Kolb (Star Rookie)	.15
11	Johan Santana (Star Rookie)	.15
12	Josh Kalinowski (Star Rookie)	.15
13	Tike Redman (Star Rookie)	.15
14	Ivanon Coffie (Star Rookie)	.15
15	Chad Durbin (Star Rookie)	.15
16	Derrick Turnbow (Star Rookie)	.15
17	Scott Downs (Star Rookie)	.15
18	Jason Grilli (Star Rookie)	.15
19	Mark Buehrle (Star Rookie)	.15
20	Paxton Crawford (Star Rookie)	.15
21	Bronson Arroyo (Star Rookie)	.15
22	Tomas de la Rosa (Star Rookie)	.15
23	Paul Rigdon (Star Rookie)	.15
24	Rob Ramsay (Star Rookie)	.15
25	Damian Rolls (Star Rookie)	.15
26	Jason Conti (Star Rookie)	.15
27	John Parrish (Star Rookie)	.15
28	Geraldo Guzman (Star Rookie)	.15
29	Tony Mota (Star Rookie)	.15
30	Luis Rivas (Star Rookie)	.15
31	Brian Tollberg (Star Rookie)	.15
32	Adam Bernero (Star Rookie)	.15
33	Michael Cuddyer (Star Rookie)	.15
34	Josue Espada (Star Rookie)	.15
35	Joe Lawrence (Star Rookie)	.15
36	Chad Moeller (Star Rookie)	.15
37	Nick Bierbrodt (Star Rookie)	.15
38	Dewayne Wise (Star Rookie)	.15
39	Javier Cardona (Star Rookie)	.15
40	Hiram Bocachica (Star Rookie)	.15
41	Giuseppe Chiaramonte (Star Rookie)	.15
42	Alex Cabrera (Star Rookie)	.15
43	Jimmy Rollins "(Star Rookie)	.15
44	*Pat Flury* (Star Rookie)	.30
45	Leo Estrella (Star Rookie)	.15
46	Darin Erstad	.40
47	Seth Etherton	.15
48	Troy Glaus	.75
49	Brian Cooper	.15
50	Tim Salmon	.25
51	Adam Kennedy	.15
52	Bengie Molina	.15
53	Jason Giambi	.40
54	Miguel Tejada	.15
55	Tim Hudson	.25
56	Eric Chavez	.25
57	Terrence Long	.15
58	Jason Isringhausen	.15
59	Ramon Hernandez	.15
60	Raul Mondesi	.25
61	David Wells	.15
62	Shannon Stewart	.15
63	Tony Batista	.15
64	Brad Fullmer	.15
65	Chris Carpenter	.15
66	Homer Bush	.15
67	Gerald Williams	.15
68	Miguel Cairo	.15
69	Ryan Rupe	.15
70	Greg Vaughn	.25
71	John Flaherty	.15
72	Dan Wheeler	.15
73	Fred McGriff	.30
74	Roberto Alomar	.60
75	Bartolo Colon	.15
76	Kenny Lofton	.40
77	David Segui	.15
78	Omar Vizquel	.15
79	Russ Branyan	.15
80	Chuck Finley	.15
81	Manny Ramirez	.75
82	Alex Rodriguez	2.50
83	John Halama	.15
84	Mike Cameron	.15
85	David Bell	.15
86	Jay Buhner	.15
87	Aaron Sele	.15
88	Rickey Henderson	.30
89	Brook Fordyce	.15
90	Cal Ripken Jr.	2.50
91	Mike Mussina	.40
92	Delino DeShields	.15
93	Melvin Mora	.15
94	Sidney Ponson	.15
95	Brady Anderson	.25
96	Ivan Rodriguez	.75
97	Ricky Ledee	.15
98	Rick Helling	.15
99	Ruben Mateo	.15
100	Luis Alicea	.15
101	John Wetteland	.15
102	Mike Lamb	.15
103	Carl Everett	.15
104	Troy O'Leary	.15
105	Wilton Veras	.15
106	Pedro Martinez	.75
107	Rolando Arrojo	.15
108	Scott Hatteberg	.15
109	Jason Varitek	.15
110	Jose Offerman	.15
111	Carlos Beltran	.15
112	Johnny Damon	.15
113	Mark Quinn	.15
114	Rey Sanchez	.15
115	Mac Suzuki	.15
116	Jermaine Dye	.15
117	Chris Fussell	.15
118	Jeff Weaver	.15
119	Dean Palmer	.15
120	Robert Fick	.15
121	Brian Moehler	.15
122	Damion Easley	.15
123	Juan Encarnacion	.15
124	Tony Clark	.15
125	Cristian Guzman	.15
126	Matt LeCroy	.15
127	Eric Milton	.15
128	Jay Canizaro	.15
129	David Ortiz	.15
130	Brad Radke	.15
131	Jacque Jones	.15
132	Magglio Ordonez	.25
133	Carlos Lee	.15
134	Mike Sirotka	.15
135	Ray Durham	.15
136	Paul Konerko	.15
137	Charles Johnson	.15
138	James Baldwin	.15
139	Jeff Abbott	.15
140	Roger Clemens	1.00
141	Derek Jeter	2.50
142	David Justice	.40
143	Ramiro Mendoza	.15
144	Chuck Knoblauch	.25
145	Orlando Hernandez	.25
146	Alfonso Soriano	.25
147	Jeff Bagwell	.75
148	Julio Lugo	.15
149	Mitch Meluskey	.15
150	Jose Lima	.15
151	Richard Hidalgo	.15
152	Moises Alou	.15
153	Scott Elarton	.15
154	Andruw Jones	.50
155	Quilvio Veras	.15
156	Greg Maddux	1.50
157	Brian Jordan	.15
158	Andres Galarraga	.30
159	Kevin Millwood	.15
160	Rafael Furcal	.20
161	Jeromy Burnitz	.15

162	Jimmy Haynes	.15
163	Mark Loretta	.15
164	Ron Belliard	.15
165	Richie Sexson	.15
166	Kevin Barker	.15
167	Jeff D'Amico	.15
168	Rick Ankiel	.25
169	Mark McGwire	2.50
170	J.D. Drew	.25
171	Eli Marrero	.15
172	Darryl Kile	.15
173	Edgar Renteria	.15
174	Will Clark	.40
175	Eric Young	.15
176	Mark Grace	.30
177	Jon Lieber	.15
178	Damon Buford	.15
179	Kerry Wood	.30
180	Rondell White	.15
181	Joe Girardi	.15
182	Curt Schilling	.15
183	Randy Johnson	.75
184	Steve Finley	.15
185	Kelly Stinnett	.15
186	Jay Bell	.15
187	Matt Mantei	.15
188	Luis Gonzalez	.15
189	Shawn Green	.30
190	Todd Hundley	.15
191	Chan Ho Park	.15
192	Adrian Beltre	.25
193	Mark Grudzielanek	.15
194	Gary Sheffield	.30
195	Tom Goodwin	.15
196	Lee Stevens	.15
197	Javier Vazquez	.15
198	Milton Bradley	.15
199	Vladimir Guerrero	1.00
200	Carl Pavano	.15
201	Orlando Cabrera	.15
202	Tony Armas Jr.	.15
203	Jeff Kent	.15
204	Calvin Murray	.15
205	Ellis Burks	.15
206	Barry Bonds	1.00
207	Russ Ortiz	.15
208	Marvin Benard	.15
209	Joe Nathan	.15
210	Preston Wilson	.15
211	Cliff Floyd	.15
212	Mike Lowell	.15
213	Ryan Dempster	.15
214	Brad Penny	.15
215	Mike Redmond	.15
216	Luis Castillo	.15
217	Derek Bell	.15
218	Mike Hampton	.25
219	Todd Zeile	.15
220	Robin Ventura	.25
221	Mike Piazza	2.00
222	Al Leiter	.25
223	Edgardo Alfonzo	.25
224	Mike Bordick	.15
225	Phil Nevin	.15
226	Ryan Klesko	.25
227	Adam Eaton	.15
228	Eric Owens	.15
229	Tony Gwynn	1.00
230	Matt Clement	.15
231	Wiki Gonzalez	.15
232	Robert Person	.15
233	Doug Glanville	.15
234	Scott Rolen	.40
235	Mike Lieberthal	.15
236	Randy Wolf	.15
237	Bobby Abreu	.25
238	Pat Burrell	.50
239	Bruce Chen	.15
240	Kevin Young	.15
241	Todd Ritchie	.15
242	Adrian Brown	.15
243	Chad Hermansen	.15
244	Warren Morris	.15
245	Kris Benson	.15
246	Jason Kendall	.15
247	Pokey Reese	.15
248	Rob Bell	.15
249	Ken Griffey Jr.	2.00
250	Sean Casey	.15
251	Aaron Boone	.15
252	Pete Harnisch	.15
253	Barry Larkin	.40
254	Dmitri Young	.15
255	Todd Hollandsworth	.15
256	Pedro Astacio	.15
257	Todd Helton	.75
258	Terry Shumpert	.15
259	Neifi Perez	.15
260	Jeffrey Hammonds	.15
261	Ben Petrick	.15
262	Mark McGwire	1.25
263	Derek Jeter	1.25
264	Sammy Sosa	1.00
265	Cal Ripken Jr.	1.25
266	Pedro J. Martinez	.40
267	Barry Bonds	.50
268	Fred McGriff	.20
269	Randy Johnson	.40
270	Darin Erstad	.25
271	*Ichiro Suzuki* (Star Rookie)	12.00
272	*Wilson Betemit* (Star Rookie)	2.00
273	Corey Patterson (Star Rookie)	.25
274	*Sean Douglass* (Star Rookie)	.40
275	*Mike Penney* (Star Rookie)	.40
276	*Nate Teut* (Star Rookie)	.40
277	*Ricardo Rodriguez* (Star Rookie)	.40
278	*Brandon Duckworth* (Star Rookie)	4.00
279	*Rafael Soriano* (Star Rookie)	.40
280	*Juan Diaz* (Star Rookie)	.40
281	*Horacio Ramirez* (Star Rookie)	.50
282	*Tsuyoshi Shinjo* (Star Rookie)	2.00
283	Keith Ginter (Star Rookie)	.15
284	*Esix Snead* (Star Rookie)	.40
285	*Erick Almonte* (Star Rookie)	.60
286	*Travis Hafner* (Star Rookie)	1.00
287	*Jason Smith* (Star Rookie)	.40
288	*Jackson Melian* (Star Rookie)	1.00
289	*Tyler Walker* (Star Rookie)	.50
290	Jason Standridge (Star Rookie)	.15
291	*Juan Uribe* (Star Rookie)	1.00
292	*Adrian Hernandez* (Star Rookie)	.50
293	*Jason Michaels* (Star Rookie)	.40
294	Jason Hart (Star Rookie)	.15
295	*Albert Pujols* (Star Rookie)	10.00
296	*Morgan Ensberg* (Star Rookie)	.75
297	Brandon Inge (Star Rookie)	.15
298	Jesus Colome (Star Rookie)	.15
299	*Kyle Kessel* (Star Rookie)	.40
300	Timo Perez (Star Rookie)	.15
301	Mo Vaughn	.15
302	Ismael Valdes	.15
303	Glenallen Hill	.15
304	Garret Anderson	.15
305	Johnny Damon	.15
306	Jose Ortiz	.15
307	Mark Mulder	.15
308	Adam Piatt	.15
309	Gil Heredia	.15
310	Mike Sirotka	.15
311	Carlos Delgado	.60
312	Alex Gonzalez	.15
313	Jose Cruz Jr.	.15
314	Darrin Fletcher	.15
315	Ben Grieve	.25
316	Vinny Castilla	.15
317	Wilson Alvarez	.15
318	Brent Abernathy	.15
319	Ellis Burks	.15
320	Jim Thome	.25
321	Juan Gonzalez	.75
322	Ed Taubensee	.15
323	Travis Fryman	.15
324	John Olerud	.25
325	Edgar Martinez	.15
326	Fred Garcia	.15
327	Bret Boone	.15
328	Kazuhiro Sasaki	.25
329	Albert Belle	.15
330	Mike Bordick	.15
331	David Segui	.15
332	Pat Hentgen	.15
333	Alex Rodriguez	2.00
334	Andres Galarraga	.25
335	Gabe Kapler	.25
336	Ken Caminiti	.15
337	Rafael Palmeiro	.50
338	Manny Ramirez	.75
339	David Cone	.15
340	Nomar Garciaparra	2.00
341	Trot Nixon	.15
342	Derek Lowe	.15
343	Roberto Hernandez	.15
344	Mike Sweeney	.15
345	Carlos Febles	.15
346	Jeff Suppan	.15
347	Roger Cedeno	.15
348	Bobby Higginson	.15
349	Deivi Cruz	.15
350	Mitch Meluskey	.15
351	Matt Lawton	.15
352	Mark Redman	.15
353	Jay Canizaro	.15
354	Corey Koskie	.15
355	Matt Kinney	.15
356	Frank Thomas	1.00
357	Sandy Alomar Jr.	.15
358	David Wells	.15
359	Jim Parque	.15
360	Chris Singleton	.15
361	Tino Martinez	.15
362	Paul O'Neill	.25
363	Mike Mussina	.40
364	Bernie Williams	.60
365	Andy Pettite	.25
366	Mariano Rivera	.25
367	Brad Ausmus	.15
368	Craig Biggio	.25
369	Lance Berkman	.15
370	Shane Reynolds	.15
371	Chipper Jones	1.50
372	Tom Glavine	.30
373	B.J. Surhoff	.15
374	John Smoltz	.15
375	Rico Brogna	.15
376	Geoff Jenkins	.25
377	Jose Hernandez	.15
378	Tyler Houston	.15
379	Henry Blanco	.15
380	Jeffrey Hammonds	.15
381	Jim Edmonds	.25
382	Fernando Vina	.15
383	Andy Benes	.15
384	Ray Lankford	.15
385	Dustin Hermanson	.15
386	Todd Hundley	.15
387	Sammy Sosa	1.50
388	Tom Gordon	.15
389	Bill Mueller	.15
390	Ron Coomer	.15
391	Matt Stairs	.15
392	Mark Grace	.30
393	Matt Williams	.25
394	Todd Stottlemyre	.15
395	Tony Womack	.15
396	Erubiel Durazo	.15
397	Reggie Sanders	.15
398	Andy Ashby	.15
399	Eric Karros	.15
400	Kevin Brown	.25
401	Darren Dreifort	.15
402	Fernando Tatis	.15
403	Jose Vidro	.15
404	Peter Bergeron	.15
405	Geoff Blum	.15
406	J.T. Snow	.15
407	Livan Hernandez	.15
408	Robb Nen	.15
409	Bobby Estalella	.15
410	Rich Aurilia	.15
411	Eric Davis	.15
412	Charles Johnson	.15
413	Alex Gonzalez	.15
414	A.J. Burnett	.15
415	Antonio Alfonseca	.15
416	Derek Lee	.15
417	Jay Payton	.15
418	Kevin Appier	.15
419	Steve Trachsel	.15
420	Rey Ordonez	.15
421	Darryl Hamilton	.15
422	Ben Davis	.15
423	Damian Jackson	.15
424	Mark Kotsay	.15
425	Trevor Hoffman	.15
426	Travis Lee	.15
427	Omar Daal	.15
428	Paul Byrd	.15
429	Reggie Taylor	.15
430	Brian Giles	.25
431	Derek Bell	.15
432	Francisco Cordova	.15
433	Pat Meares	.15
434	Scott Williamson	.15
435	Jason LaRue	.15
436	Michael Tucker	.15
437	Wilton Guerrero	.15
438	Mike Hampton	.15
439	Ron Gant	.15
440	Jeff Cirillo	.15
441	Denny Neagle	.15
442	Larry Walker	.40
443	Juan Pierre	.15
444	Todd Walker	.15
445	Jason Giambi	.25
446	Jeff Kent	.15
447	Mariano Rivera	.15
448	Edgar Martinez	.15
449	Troy Glaus	.40
450	Alex Rodriguez	1.00

2001 Upper Deck Exclusives

	MT
Silver Stars:	15-25X
Production 100 sets	
Gold Stars:	40-60X
Production 25 sets	

2001 Upper Deck All-Star Heroes Base Cards

		MT
Common Player:		40.00
ASH-DJ	Derek Jeter/ 2000	50.00
ASH-MP	Mike Piazza/ 1996	40.00

2001 Upper Deck All-Star Heroes Jersey Cards

		MT
Common Player:		25.00
RC	Roger Clemens/ 1986	50.00
JD	Joe DiMaggio/36	500.00
TG	Tony Gwynn/1994	35.00
RJ	Randy Johnson/ 1993	25.00
ASH-MM	Mickey Mantle/ 54	500.00
ASH-SS	Sammy Sosa - 2000	50.00

2001 Upper Deck All-Star Heroes Bat Cards

		MT
Common Player:		15.00
ASH-RoC	Roberto Clemente/1961	200.00
ASH-KG	Ken Griffey Jr/ 1992	50.00
ASH-TP	Tony Perez/ 1967	15.00
ASH-CR	Cal Ripken Jr/ 1991	60.00
ASH-AR	Alex Rodriguez/ 1998	35.00
ASH-BR	Babe Ruth/ 1933	300.00

2001 Upper Deck All-Star Salute

		MT
Common Player:		20.00
Inserted 1:288		
AS-HA	Hank Aaron/bat	50.00
AS-HA	Hank Aaron/jersey	50.00
AS-LA	Luis Aparicio/jersey	25.00
AS-JB	Johnny Bench/bat	40.00
AS-JB	Johnny Bench/jersey	75.00
AS-LB	Lou Brock/bat	30.00
AS-RC	Roberto Clemente/jersey	250.00
AS-RJ	Reggie Jackson/jersey	40.00
AS-TM	Thurman Munson/jersey	125.00
AS-BR	Brooks Robinson/bat	40.00
AS-FR	Frank Robinson/jersey	25.00
AS-TS	Tom Seaver/jersey	60.00

2001 Upper Deck Big League Beat

		MT
Complete Set (20):		20.00
Common Player:		.50
Inserted 1:3		
1	Barry Bonds	1.00
2	Nomar Garciaparra	2.00
3	Mark McGwire	3.00
4	Roger Clemens	1.00
5	Chipper Jones	1.50
6	Jeff Bagwell	.75
7	Sammy Sosa	2.00
8	Cal Ripken Jr.	2.50
9	Randy Johnson	.75
10	Carlos Delgado	.75
11	Manny Ramirez	.75
12	Derek Jeter	2.50
13	Tony Gwynn	1.00
14	Pedro J. Martinez	.75
15	Jose Canseco	.50
16	Frank Thomas	1.00
17	Alex Rodriguez	2.50
18	Bernie Williams	.50
19	Greg Maddux	1.50
20	Rafael Palmeiro	.50

2001 Upper Deck Big League Challenge Jerseys

		MT
Common Player:		15.00
Inserted 1:288		
BLC-BB	Barry Bonds	50.00
BLC-JC	Jose Canseco	25.00
BLC-JE	Jim Edmonds	25.00
BLC-TF	Steve Finley	15.00
BLC-TG	Troy Glaus	25.00
BLC-TH	Todd Helton	25.00
BLC-RH	Richard Hidalgo	15.00
BLC-RP	Rafael Palmeiro	25.00
BLC-MP	Mike Piazza	50.00
BLC-GS	Gary Sheffield	15.00
BLC-FT	Frank Thomas	30.00

2001 Upper Deck Classic Midsummer Moments

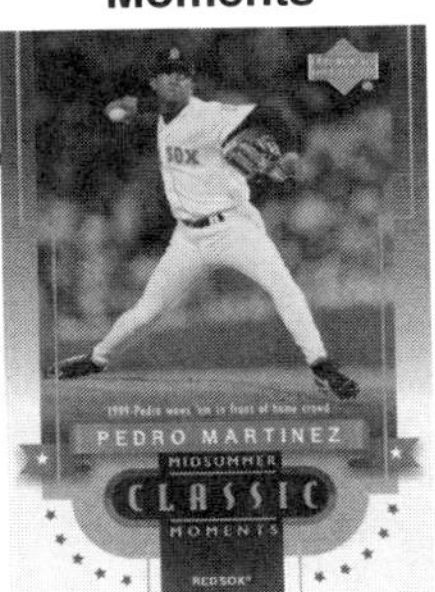

		MT
Complete Set (20):		75.00
Common Player:		1.00
Inserted 1:12		
CM1	Joe DiMaggio - 1936	8.00
CM2	Joe DiMaggio - 1951	8.00
CM3	Mickey Mantle - 1952	8.00
CM4	Mickey Mantle - 1968	8.00
CM5	Roger Clemens - 1986	3.00
CM6	Mark McGwire - 1987	8.00
CM7	Cal Ripken Jr. - 1991	8.00
CM8	Ken Griffey Jr. - 1992	6.00
CM9	Randy Johnson - 1993	2.50
CM10	Tony Gwynn - 1994	3.00
CM11	Fred McGriff - 1994	1.00
CM12	Hideo Nomo - 1995	1.00
CM13	Jeff Conine - 1995	1.00
CM14	Mike Piazza - 1996	6.00
CM15	Sandy Alomar Jr. - 1997	1.00
CM16	Alex Rodriguez - 1998	6.00
CM17	Roberto Alomar - 1998	2.00
CM18	Pedro Martinez - 1999	3.00
CM19	Andres Galarraga - 2000	1.00
CM20	Derek Jeter - 2000	8.00

2001 Upper Deck e-Card

		MT
Complete Set (6):		10.00
Common Player:		1.00
Inserted 1:12		
1	Andruw Jones	1.00
2	Alex Rodriguez	4.00
3	Frank Thomas	2.00
4	Todd Helton	1.50
5	Troy Glaus	1.50
6	Barry Bonds	1.50

2001 Upper Deck eVolve Signature

Because of the addition of Suzuki and Sosa cards after the initial checklist was promulgated by Upper Deck, and the possibility that cards on the initial list may have been deleted, the accuracy of this list cannot be verified. Cards have an "ES-" prefix to their number. Production was reported as 200 of each card.

		MT
Complete Set (8):		750.00
Common Player:		35.00
BB	Barry Bonds	150.00
TG	Troy Glaus	35.00
TH	Todd Helton	35.00
AJ	Andruw Jones	35.00
AR	Alex Rodriguez	75.00
SS	Sammy Sosa	200.00
IS	Ichiro Suzuki	300.00
FT	Frank Thomas	35.00

2001 Upper Deck eVolve Jersey

Because of the addition of Suzuki and Sosa cards after the initial checklist was promulgated by Upper Deck, and the possibility that cards on the initial list may have been deleted, the accuracy of this list cannot be verified. Card numbers have an "EJ-" prefix. Production was reported as 300 of each card.

		MT
Complete Set (8):		225.00
Common Player:		15.00
BB	Barry Bonds	60.00
TG	Troy Glaus	15.00
TH	Todd Helton	15.00
AJ	Andruw Jones	15.00
AR	Alex Rodriguez	40.00
SS	Sammy Sosa	50.00
IS	Ichiro Suzuki	75.00
FT	Frank Thomas	15.00

2001 Upper Deck eVolve Jersey Autograph

Because of the addition of Suzuki and Sosa cards after the initial checklist was promulgated by Upper Deck, and the possibility that cards on the initial list may have been deleted, the accuracy of this list cannot be verified. Cards have an "ESJ-" prefix. The edition is limited to 50 numbered cards each.

		MT
Common Player:		75.00
BB	Barry Bonds	300.00
TG	Troy Glaus	75.00
TH	Todd Helton	75.00
AJ	Andruw Jones	75.00
AR	Alex Rodriguez	150.00
SS	Sammy Sosa	400.00
IS	Ichiro Suzuki	600.00
FT	Frank Thomas	75.00

2001 Upper Deck Game Jersey

		MT
Common Player:		30.00
Inserted 1:288		
KG	Ken Griffey Jr.	150.00
TG	Tony Gwynn	60.00
TH	Todd Helton	60.00
TiH	Tim Hudson	40.00
DJ	Derek Jeter	150.00
AJ	Andruw Jones	50.00
SK	Sandy Koufax	250.00
PO	Paul O'Neill	40.00
MR	Manny Ramirez	40.00
CR	Cal Ripken Jr.	120.00
AR	Alex Rodriguez	80.00
IR	Ivan Rodriguez	50.00
NRa	Nolan Ryan	125.00
NRr	Nolan Ryan	125.00
FT	Fernando Tatis	30.00
RV	Robin Ventura	30.00
BW	Bernie Williams	50.00
MW	Matt Williams	30.00

2001 Upper Deck Game Jersey Autograph

		MT
Common Player:		50.00
Print Runs listed		
KG	Ken Griffey/30	700.00
RA	Rick Ankiel/66	100.00
TG	Tony Gwynn/19	
TH	Todd Helton/17	
TiH	Tim Hudson/15	
AJ	Andruw Jones/25	
SK	Sandy Koufax/32	900.00
PO	Paul O'Neill/21	
JP	Javy Lopez/8	
AR	Alex Rodriguez/3	
IR	Ivan Rodriguez/7	
NRa	Nolan Ryan Mets/30	650.00
NRr	Nolan Ryan Angels/30	650.00
RV	Robin Ventura/4	50.00
MW	Matt Williams/9	375.00

2001 Upper Deck Game Jersey Hobby Autograph

		MT
Common Player:		50.00
Inserted 1:288		
RA	Rick Ankiel	50.00
JB	Jeff Bagwell	80.00
BB	Barry Bonds	150.00
JC	Jose Canseco	80.00
SC	Sean Casey	50.00
JD	J.D. Drew	50.00
JG	Jason Giambi	80.00
SG	Shawn Green	60.00
KG	Ken Griffey Jr.	275.00
MH	Mike Hampton	50.00
RJ	Randy Johnson	100.00
JL	Javy Lopez	50.00
GM	Greg Maddux	140.00
RP	Rafael Palmeiro	60.00
AR	Alex Rodriguez	200.00
NRm	Nolan Ryan	250.00
NRa	Nolan Ryan	250.00
FT	Frank Thomas	125.00

2001 Upper Deck Game Jersey Combo

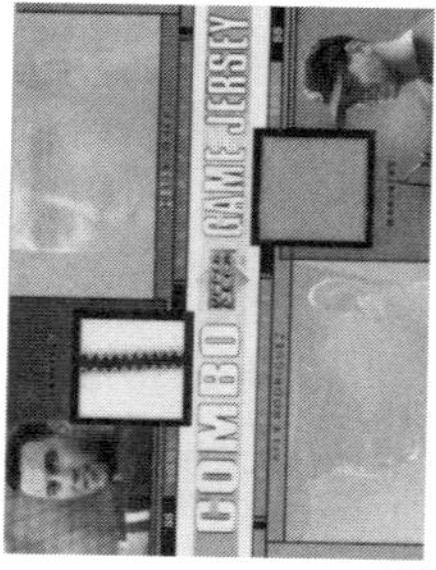

	MT
50 Sets Produced	
BB-KG Barry Bonds, Ken Griffey Jr.	150.00
IR-RP Ivan Rodriguez, Rafael Palmeiro	40.00
DJ-AR Derek Jeter, Alex Rodriguez	215.00
MM-KG Mickey Mantle, Ken Griffey Jr.	600.00
TG-CR Tony Gwynn, Cal Ripken Jr.	100.00
NR-AR Nolan Ryan Astros/Rangers	115.00
NR-MA Nolan Ryan Mets/Astros	115.00
RJ-GM Randy Johnson, Greg Maddux	80.00
VG-MR Vladimir Guerrero, Manny Ramirez	60.00
BB-JC Barry Bonds, Jose Canseco	50.00
FT-JB Frank Thomas, Jeff Bagwell	60.00
AJ-KG Andruw Jones, Ken Griffey Jr.	115.00

2001 Upper Deck Game Jersey Combo Autograph

MT

Production 10 Sets
VALUES UNDETERMINED
BB-KG Barry Bonds, Ken Griffey Jr.
DJ-AR Derek Jeter, Alex Rodriguez
JD-RA J.D. Drew, Rick Ankiel
NR-AR Nolan Ryan
NR-MA Nolan Ryan
BB-JC Barry Bonds, Jose Canseco

2001 Upper Deck Game Jersey Patch

		MT
Common Player:		150.00
Production 25 sets		
RA	Rick Ankiel	100.00
JB	Jeff Bagwell	275.00
BB	Barry Bonds	300.00
JC	Jose Canseco	200.00
JG	Jason Giambi	300.00
KG	Ken Griffey Jr.	650.00
TG	Tony Gwynn	400.00
DJ	Derek Jeter	550.00
RP	Rafael Palmeiro	200.00
CR	Cal Ripken Jr.	675.00
AR	Alex Rodriguez	500.00
IR	Ivan Rodriguez	250.00
NRa	Nolan Ryan	475.00
NRr	Nolan Ryan	475.00
FT	Frank Thomas	250.00

2001 Upper Deck Game Jersey Patch Gold

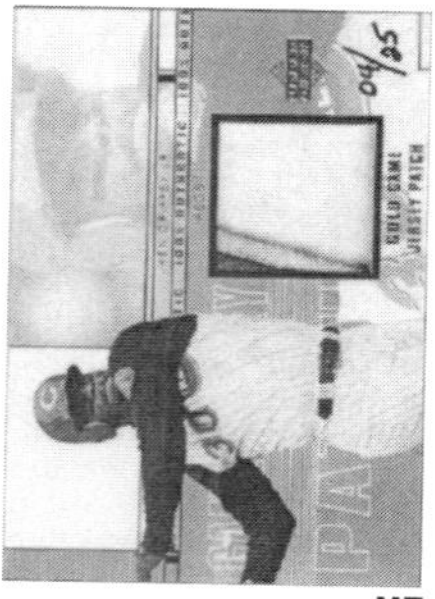

		MT
Common Player:		250.00
Production 25 sets		
BB	Barry Bonds	400.00
JC	Jose Canseco	250.00
JG	Jason Giambi	200.00
KG	Ken Griffey Jr.	700.00
TG	Tony Gwynn	350.00
DJ	Derek Jeter	700.00
CR	Cal Ripken Jr.	700.00
AR	Alex Rodriguez	
NRa	Nolan Ryan	700.00
NRr	Nolan Ryan	700.00
FT	Frank Thomas	300.00

2001 Upper Deck Game Jersey Patch Autograph

		MT
Print Runs listed		
RA	Rick Ankiel /66	150.00
KG	Ken Griffey Jr / 30	850.00
AR	Alex Rodriguez /3	

2001 Upper Deck Game Jersey Auto. Series 2

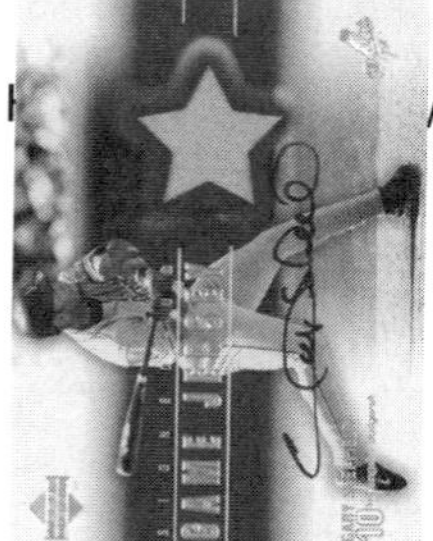

		MT
Common Player:		40.00
Inserted 1:288 H		
JB	Johnny Bench	100.00
BB	Barry Bonds	150.00
JC	Jose Canseco	60.00
RC	Roger Clemens	125.00
TG	Troy Glaus	60.00
KG	Ken Griffey Jr.	200.00
AJ	Andruw Jones	60.00
CJ	Chipper Jones	90.00
CR	Cal Ripken Jr. SP	250.00
AR	Alex Rodriguez	150.00
IR	Ivan Rodriguez SP	100.00
NR	Nolan Ryan	225.00
GS	Gary Sheffield	40.00
SS	Sammy Sosa SP	225.00

2001 Upper Deck Game-Used Ball

		MT
Common Player:		15.00
Production 100 sets		
RA	Rick Ankiel	15.00
JB	Jeff Bagwell	20.00
BB	Barry Bonds	35.00
JG	Jason Giambi	20.00
SG	Shawn Green	15.00
KG	Ken Griffey Jr.	45.00
ToG	Tony Gwynn	30.00
DJ	Derek Jeter	75.00
RJ	Randy Johnson	30.00
AJ	Andruw Jones	20.00
MM	Mark McGwire	100.00
AR	Alex Rodriguez	60.00
IR	Ivan Rodriguez	20.00
SS	Sammy Sosa	50.00

2001 Upper Deck Game-Used Ball Autographs

		MT
Common Player:		60.00
Production 25 Sets		
RA	Rick Ankiel	75.00
JB	Jeff Bagwell	60.00
BB	Barry Bonds	125.00
JG	Jason Giambi	75.00
KG	Ken Griffey Jr.	80.00
SG	Shawn Green	60.00
TH	Todd Helton	60.00
RJ	Randy Johnson	90.00
AR	Alex Rodriguez	80.00

2001 Upper Deck Game-Used Ball Series 2

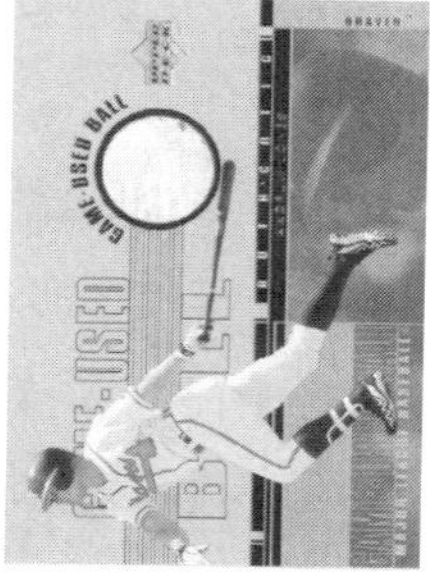

		MT
Common Player:		10.00
Inserted 1:288		
B-JB	Jeff Bagwell	15.00
B-BB	Barry Bonds	20.00
B-RC	Roger Clemens	20.00
B-NG	Nomar Garciaparra	35.00
B-KG	Ken Griffey Jr.	25.00
B-VG	Vladimir Guerrero	15.00
B-DJ	Derek Jeter	35.00
B-AJ	Andruw Jones	15.00
B-CJ	Chipper Jones	20.00
B-JK	Jeff Kent	10.00
B-MM	Mark McGwire	40.00
B-MP	Mike Piazza	30.00
B-CR	Cal Ripken Jr.	25.00
B-MR	Mariano Rivera	15.00
B-AR	Alex Rodriguez	20.00
B-GS	Gary Sheffield	10.00
B-SS	Sammy Sosa	20.00
B-BW	Bernie Williams	10.00

2001 Upper Deck Home Run Explosion

		MT
Complete Set (15):		30.00
Common Player:		.75
Inserted 1:12		
1	Mark McGwire	6.00
2	Chipper Jones	3.00
3	Jeff Bagwell	1.50
4	Carlos Delgado	1.50
5	Barry Bonds	2.00
6	Troy Glaus	1.50
7	Sammy Sosa	4.00
8	Alex Rodriguez	5.00
9	Mike Piazza	4.00
10	Vladimir Guerrero	2.00
11	Ken Griffey Jr.	5.00
12	Frank Thomas	2.00
13	Ivan Rodriguez	1.50
14	Jason Giambi	1.00
15	Carl Everett	.75

2001 Upper Deck Home Run Derby Heroes

		MT
Complete Set (10):		40.00
Common Player:		1.00
Inserted 1:36		
HD1	Mark McGwire - 1999	10.00
HD2	Sammy Sosa - 2000	6.00
HD3	Frank Thomas - 1996	3.00
HD4	Cal Ripken Jr. - 1991	10.00
HD5	Tino Martinez - 1997	1.00
HD6	Ken Griffey Jr. - 1999	8.00
HD7	Barry Bonds - 1996	4.00
HD8	Albert Belle - 1995	1.00
HD9	Mark McGwire - 1992	10.00
HD10	Juan Gonzalez - 1993	3.00

A card number in parentheses ( ) indicates the set is unnumbered.

2001 Upper Deck Midseason Superstar Summit

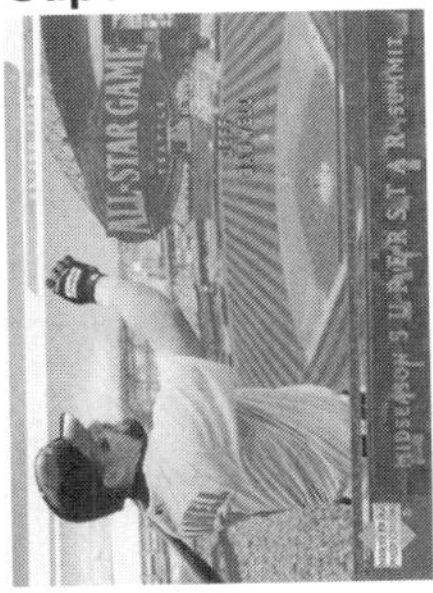

	MT
Complete Set (15):	60.00
Common Player:	1.50
Inserted 1:24	
MS1 Derek Jeter	10.00
MS2 Sammy Sosa	6.00
MS3 Jeff Bagwell	3.00
MS4 Tony Gwynn	4.00
MS5 Alex Rodriguez	8.00
MS6 Greg Maddux	6.00
MS7 Jason Giambi	2.00
MS8 Mark McGwire	10.00
MS9 Barry Bonds	4.00
MS10 Ken Griffey Jr.	8.00
MS11 Carlos Delgado	2.50
MS12 Troy Glaus	3.00
MS13 Todd Helton	3.00
MS14 Manny Ramirez	4.00
MS15 Jeff Kent	1.50

2001 Upper Deck Most Wanted

	MT
Complete Set (15):	30.00
Common Player:	1.00
Inserted 1:14 Series 1	
MW1 Mark McGwire	5.00
MW2 Cal Ripken Jr.	5.00
MW3 Ivan Rodriguez	1.00
MW4 Pedro Martinez	1.00
MW5 Sammy Sosa	2.50
MW6 Tony Gwynn	2.00
MW7 Vladimir Guerrero	1.50
MW8 Derek Jeter	3.00
MW9 Mike Piazza	3.00
MW10 Chipper Jones	3.00
MW11 Alex Rodriguez	4.00
MW12 Barry Bonds	2.50
MW13 Jeff Bagwell	1.50
MW14 Frank Thomas	2.50
MW15 Nomar Garciaparra	2.50

A player's name in *italic* type indicates a rookie card.

2001 Upper Deck Rookie Roundup

		MT
Complete Set (10):		6.00
Common Player:		.50
Inserted 1:6		
1	Rick Ankiel	1.50
2	Adam Kennedy	.50
3	Mike Lamb	.50
4	Adam Eaton	.50
5	Rafael Furcal	.75
6	Pat Burrell	1.50
7	Adam Piatt	.75
8	Eric Munson	.50
9	Brad Penny	.50
10	Mark Mulder	.50

2001 Upper Deck Superstar Summit

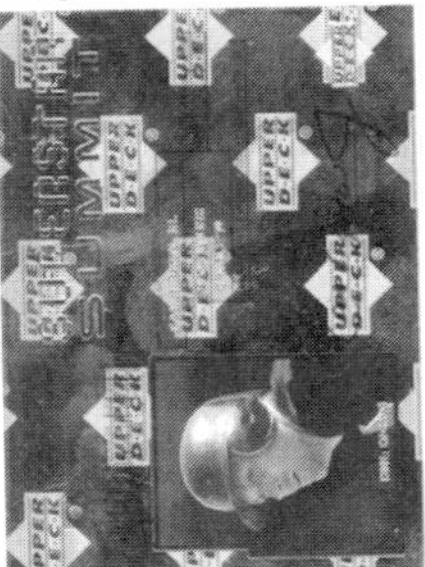

		MT
Complete Set (15):		40.00
Common Player:		1.00
Inserted 1:12		
1	Derek Jeter	5.00
2	Randy Johnson	1.50
3	Barry Bonds	2.00
4	Frank Thomas	2.00
5	Cal Ripken Jr.	5.00
6	Pedro J. Martinez	1.50
7	Ivan Rodriguez	1.50
8	Mike Piazza	4.00
9	Mark McGwire	6.00
10	Manny Ramirez	1.50
11	Ken Griffey Jr.	4.00
12	Sammy Sosa	4.00
13	Alex Rodriguez	5.00
14	Chipper Jones	3.00
15	Nomar Garciaparra	4.00

Figure values of lower-grade cards from 1981-date as:
Near Mint (NM) 75%
Excellent (EX) 40%
of the listed Mint price

For cards through 1980, values should be figured as:
Excellent (EX) 50%
Very Good (VG) 30%
of the listed
Near Mint price

2001 Upper Deck The Franchise

	MT
Complete Set (10):	50.00
Common Player:	2.50
Inserted 1:36	
F1 Frank Thomas	3.00
F2 Mark McGwire	10.00
F3 Ken Griffey Jr.	8.00
F4 Manny Ramirez	4.00
F5 Alex Rodriguez	8.00
F6 Greg Maddux	6.00
F7 Sammy Sosa	6.00
F8 Derek Jeter	10.00
F9 Mike Piazza	8.00
F10 Vladimir Guerrero	4.00

2001 Upper Deck The People's Choice

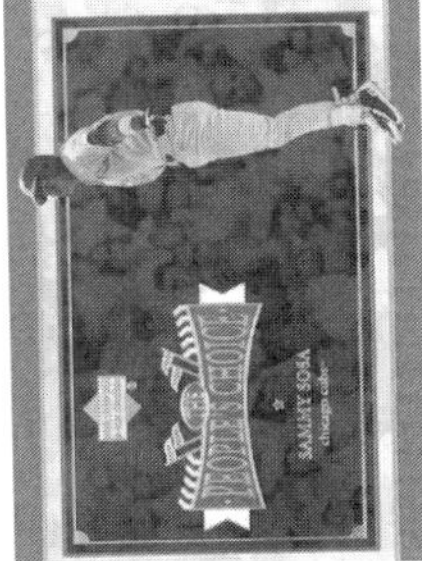

	MT
Complete Set (15):	75.00
Common Player:	2.00
Inserted 1:24	
PC1 Alex Rodriguez	8.00
PC2 Ken Griffey Jr.	8.00
PC3 Mark McGwire	10.00
PC4 Todd Helton	3.00
PC5 Manny Ramirez	4.00
PC6 Mike Piazza	8.00
PC7 Vladimir Guerrero	4.00
PC8 Randy Johnson	3.00
PC9 Cal Ripken Jr.	10.00
PC10 Andruw Jones	2.50
PC11 Sammy Sosa	6.00
PC12 Derek Jeter	10.00
PC13 Pedro Martinez	4.00
PC14 Frank Thomas	3.00
PC15 Nomar Garciaparra	8.00

2001 Upper Deck UD Game-Worn Patch

	MT
Complete Set (9):	700.00
Common Player:	50.00
P-JB Johnny Bench	250.00
P-BB Barry Bonds	125.00
P-KG Ken Griffey Jr.	60.00
P-CJ Chipper Jones	50.00
P-CR Cal Ripken Jr.	75.00
P-AR Alex Rodriguez	75.00
P-IR Ivan Rodriguez	50.00
P-NR Nolan Ryan	75.00
P-SS Sammy Sosa	100.00

2001 Upper Deck Decade

		MT
Complete Set (180):		25.00
Common Player:		.15
Pack (5):		1.50
Box (24):		30.00
1	Nolan Ryan	3.00
2	Don Baylor	.15
3	Bobby Grich	.15
4	Reggie Jackson	.75
5	Jim "Catfish" Hunter	.25
6	Gene Tenace	.15
7	Rollie Fingers	.25
8	Sal Bando	.15
9	Bert Campaneris	.15
10	John Mayberry	.15
11	Rico Carty	.15
12	Gaylord Perry	.15
13	Andre Thornton	.15
14	Buddy Bell	.15
15	Dennis Eckersley	.15
16	Ruppert Jones	.15
17	Brooks Robinson	.75
18	Tommy Davis	.15
19	Eddie Murray	.25
20	Boog Powell	.15
21	Al Oliver	.15
22	Jeff Burroughs	.15
23	Mike Hargrove	.15
24	Dwight Evans	.15
25	Fred Lynn	.15
26	Rico Petrocelli	.15
27	Carlton Fisk	.50
28	Luis Aparicio	.15
29	Amos Otis	.15
30	Hal McRae	.15
31	Jason Thompson	.15
32	Al Kaline	.75
33	Jim Perry	.15
34	Bert Blyleven	.15
35	Harmon Killebrew	1.00
36	Wilbur Wood	.15
37	Jim Kaat	.15
38	Ron Guidry	.15
39	Thurman Munson	1.00
40	Graig Nettles	.15
41	Bobby Murcer	.15
42	Chris Chambliss	.15
43	Roy White	.15
44	J.R. Richard	.15
45	Jose Cruz	.15
46	Hank Aaron	2.00
47	Phil Niekro	.15

48 Bob Horner .15
49 Darryl Evans .15
50 Gorman Thomas .15
51 Don Money .15
52 Robin Yount .75
53 Joe Torre .25
54 Tim McCarver .15
55 Lou Brock .40
56 Keith Hernandez .15
57 Bill Madlock .15
58 Ron Santo .15
59 Billy Williams .15
60 Ferguson Jenkins .25
61 Steve Garvey .15
62 Bill Russell .15
63 Maury Wills .25
64 Ron Cey .15
65 Manny Mota .15
66 Ron Fairly .15
67 Steve Rogers .15
68 Gary Carter .15
69 Andre Dawson .25
70 Bobby Bonds .25
71 Jack Clark .15
72 Willie McCovey .15
73 Tom Seaver 1.00
74 Bud Harrelson .15
75 Dave Kingman .15
76 Jerry Koosman .15
77 Jon Matlack .15
78 Randy Jones .15
79 Ozzie Smith 1.00
80 Garry Maddox .15
81 Mike Schmidt 1.00
82 Greg Luzinski .15
83 Tug McGraw .15
84 Willie Stargell .75
85 Dave Parker .15
86 Roberto Clemente 2.00
87 Johnny Bench 1.50
88 Joe Morgan .40
89 George Foster .15
90 Ken Griffey Sr. .15
91 Carlton Fisk 1972 (1970s Rookie Flashbacks) .50
92 Andre Dawson 1977 (1970s Rookie Flashbacks) .25
93 Fred Lynn 1975 (1970s Rookie Flashbacks) .15
94 Eddie Murray 1977 (1970s Rookie Flashbacks) .25
95 Bob Horner 1978 (1970s Rookie Flashbacks) .15
96 Jon Matlack 1972 (1970s Rookie Flashbacks) .15
97 Mike Hargrove 1974 (1970s Rookie Flashbacks) .15
98 Robin Yount 1974 (1970s Rookie Flashbacks) .50
99 Mike Schmidt 1972 (1970s Rookie Flashbacks) .50
100 Gary Carter 1974 (1970s Rookie Flashbacks) .15
101 Ozzie Smith 1978 (1970s Rookie Flashbacks) .50
102 Paul Molitor 1978 (1970s Rookie Flashbacks) .50
103 Dennis Eckersley 1975 (1970s Rookie Flashbacks) .15
104 Dale Murphy 1976 (1970s Rookie Flashbacks) .15
105 Bert Blyleven 1970 (1970s Rookie Flashbacks) .15
106 Thurman Munson 1970 (1970s Rookie Flashbacks) .75
107 Dave Parker 1973 (1970s Rookie Flashbacks) .15
108 Jack Clark 1975 (1970s Rookie Flashbacks) .15
109 Keith Hernandez 1974 (1970s Rookie Flashbacks) .15
110 Ron Cey 1971 (1970s Rookie Flashbacks) .15
111 Billy Williams 1970 (Decade Dateline) .15
112 Tom Seaver 1970 (Decade Dateline) .75
113 Reggie Jackson 1971 (Decade Dateline) .75
114 Barry Bonds 1971 (Decade Dateline) .15
115 Willie Stargell 1971 (Decade Dateline) .40
116 Harmon Killebrew 1971 (Decade Dateline) .50
117 Roberto Clemente 1972 (Decade Dateline) 1.00
118 Wilbur Wood 1972 (Decade Dateline) .15
119 Billy Williams 1972 (Decade Dateline) .15
120 Nolan Ryan 1973 (Decade Dateline) 1.50
121 Ron Blomberg 1973 (Decade Dateline) .15
122 Hank Aaron 1974 (Decade Dateline) 1.00
123 Lou Brock 1974 (Decade Dateline) .25
124 Al Kaline 1974 (Decade Dateline) .40
125 Brooks Robinson 1975 (Decade Dateline) .40
126 Bill Madlock 1975 (Decade Dateline) .15
127 Rennie Stennett 1975 (Decade Dateline) .15
128 Carlton Fisk 1975 (Decade Dateline) .40
129 Chris Chambliss 1976 (Decade Dateline) .15
130 Ruppert Jones 1977 (Decade Dateline) .15
131 Ron Fairly 1977 (Decade Dateline) .15
132 George Foster 1977 (Decade Dateline) .15
133 Reggie Jackson 1977 (Decade Dateline) .75
134 Ron Guidry 1978 (Decade Dateline) .15
135 Gaylord Perry 1978 (Decade Dateline) .15
136 Bucky Dent 1978 (Decade Dateline) .15
137 Dave Kingman 1979 (Decade Dateline) .15
138 Lou Brock 1979 (Decade Dateline) .15
139 Thurman Munson 1979 (Decade Dateline) .75
140 Willie Stargell 1979 (Decade Dateline) .40
141 Johnny Bench 1970 NL MVP (1970s Award Winners) .75
142 Boog Powell 1970 AL MVP (1970s Award Winners) .15
143 Jim Perry 1970 AL CY (1970s Award Winners) .15
144 Joe Torre 1971 NL MVP (1970s Award Winners) .15
145 Chris Chambliss 1971 AL ROY (1970s Award Winners) .15
146 Ferguson Jenkins 1971 NL CY (1970s Award Winners) .15
147 Carlton Fisk 1972 AL ROY (1970s Award Winners) .40
148 Gaylord Perry 1972 AL CY (1970s Award Winners) .15
149 Johnny Bench 1972 NL MVP (1970s Award Winners) .75
150 Reggie Jackson 1973 AL MVP (1970s Award Winners) .75
151 Tom Seaver 1973 NL CY (1970s Award Winners) .75
152 Thurman Munson 1973 AL GG (1970s Award Winners) .75
153 Steve Garvey 1974 NL MVP (1970s Award Winners) .15
154 Jim "Catfish" Hunter 1974 AL CY (1970s Award Winners) .15
155 Mike Hargrove 1974 AL ROY (1970s Award Winners) .15
156 Joe Morgan 1975 NL MVP (1970s Award Winners) .15
157 Fred Lynn 1975 AL MVP & ROY (1970s Award Winners) .15
158 Tom Seaver 1975 NL CY (1970s Award Winners) .75
159 Thurman Munson 1976 AL MVP (1970s Award Winners) .75
160 Randy Jones 1976 NL CY (1970s Award Winners) .15
161 Joe Morgan 1976 NL ROY (1970s Award Winners) .15
162 George Foster 1977 NL MVP (1970s Award Winners) .15
163 Eddie Murray 1977 AL ROY (1970s Award Winners) .25
164 Andre Dawson 1977 NL ROY (1970s Award Winners) .25
165 Gaylord Perry 1978 NL CY (1970s Award Winners) .15
166 Ron Guidry 1978 AL CY (1970s Award Winners) .15
167 Dave Parker 1978 NL MVP (1970s Award Winners) .15
168 Don Baylor 1979 AL MVP (1970s Award Winners) .15
169 Bruce Sutter 1979 NL CY (1970s Award Winners) .15
170 Willie Stargell 1979 NL co-MVP (1970s Award Winners) .40
171 Brooks Robinson 1970 (1970s World Series Highlights) .50
172 Roberto Clemente 1971 (1970s World Series Highlights) 1.00
173 Gene Tenace 1972 (1970s World Series Highlights) .15
174 Reggie Jackson 1973 (1970s World Series Highlights) .75
175 Rollie Fingers 1974 (1970s World Series Highlights) .15
176 Carlton Fisk 1975 (1970s World Series Highlights) .40
177 Johnny Bench 1976 (1970s World Series Highlights) .75
178 Reggie Jackson 1977 (1970s World Series Highlights) .75
179 Bucky Dent 1978 (1970s World Series Highlights) .15
180 Willie Stargell 1979 (1970s World Series Highlights) .40

2001 Upper Deck Decade Bellbottomed Bashers

		MT
Complete Set (10):		15.00
Common Player:		1.00
Inserted 1:14		
BB1	Reggie Jackson	3.00
BB2	Gorman Thomas	1.00
BB3	Willie McCovey	2.00
BB4	Willie Stargell	2.00
BB5	Mike Schmidt	4.00
BB6	George Foster	1.00
BB7	Johnny Bench	3.00
BB8	Dave Kingman	1.00
BB9	Graig Nettles	1.00
BB10	Steve Garvey	1.00

2001 Upper Deck Decade Decade Dynasties

		MT
Complete Set (10):		20.00
Common Player:		1.00
Inserted 1:14		
D1	Boog Powell	1.00
D2	Johnny Bench	3.00
D3	Willie Stargell	2.00
D4	Jim "Catfish" Hunter	1.00
D5	Steve Garvey	1.00
D6	Carlton Fisk	2.00
D7	Mike Schmidt	4.00
D8	Hal McRae	1.00
D9	Tom Seaver	4.00
D10	Reggie Jackson	3.00

2001 Upper Deck Decade Game-Used Bat

		MT
Common Player:		10.00
Inserted 1:24 H		
B-HA	Hank Aaron	50.00
B-DB	Don Baylor	10.00
B-BB	Bobby Bonds	10.00
B-GC	Gary Carter	15.00
B-JaC	Jack Clark	10.00
B-RC	Roberto Clemente/243	100.00
B-DC	Dave Concepcion	10.00
B-JoC	Jose Cruz	10.00
B-TD	Tommy Davis	10.00
B-AD	Andre Dawson	15.00
B-DaE	Darryl Evans	10.00
B-DwE	Dwight Evans	15.00
B-CF	Carlton Fisk	20.00
B-GF	George Foster	15.00
B-SG	Steve Garvey	15.00
B-BG	Bobby Grich	10.00
B-KG	Ken Griffey Sr.	10.00
B-BH	Bud Harrelson/290	15.00
B-KH	Keith Hernandez/243	40.00
B-RH	Ron Hunt	10.00
B-ReJ	Reggie Jackson	25.00
B-RaJ	Randy Jones	10.00
B-GL	Greg Luzinski	15.00
B-FL	Fred Lynn	15.00
B-GM	Garry Maddox	10.00
B-BiM	Bill Madlock	10.00
B-TiM	Tim McCarver	15.00
B-TuM	Tug McGraw/97	40.00
B-HM	Hal McRae	10.00
B-RM	Rick Monday	10.00
B-WM	Willie Montanez	10.00
B-JM	Joe Morgan	15.00
B-BoM	Bobby Murcer	25.00
B-EM	Eddie Murray	20.00
B-GN	Graig Nettles/219	40.00
B-AO	Al Oliver	10.00
B-DP	Dave Parker	15.00
B-BP	Boog Powell	15.00
B-WR	Willie Randolph	10.00

B-BR	Bill Russell	10.00
B-NR	Nolan Ryan	50.00
B-RS	Ron Santo	20.00
B-ToS	Tom Seaver/121	50.00
B-OS	Ozzie Smith	20.00
B-RW	Roy White	10.00
B-MW	Maury Wills	15.00
B-DW	Dave Winfield	15.00

2001 Upper Deck Decade Game-Used Bat Combo

		MT
Common Card:		40.00
Inserted 1:336		
C-NYY	Reggie Jackson, Graig Nettles, Chris Chambliss, Roy White	80.00
C-LA	Steve Garvey, Ron Cey, Bill Russell, Rick Monday	50.00
C-NYM	Tom Seaver, Bud Harrelson, Ron Hunt, Tug McGraw	80.00
C-CIN	Johnny Bench, George Foster, Ken Griffey Sr., Joe Morgan	90.00
C-ROY	Andre Dawson, Fred Lynn, Carlton Fisk, Eddie Murray	75.00
C-MVPN	Johnny Bench, Steve Garvey, Willie Stargell, George Foster	60.00
C-BAT	Keith Hernandez, Bill Madlock, Fred Lynn, Dave Parker	40.00
C-GGA	Carlton Fisk, Graig Nettles, Bobby Grich, Fred Lynn	40.00
C-GGN	Johnny Bench, Roberto Clemente, Dave Concepcion, Garry Maddox	200.00
C-WS72	Reggie Jackson, Bert Campaneris, Dave Concepcion, Johnny Bench/97	100.00
C-WS73	Reggie Jackson, Bert Campaneris, Tom Seaver, Bud Harrelson	100.00
C-WS74	Reggie Jackson, Bert Campaneris, Steve Garvey, Ron Cey	80.00
C-WS75	Carlton Fisk, Fred Lynn, George Foster, Joe Morgan	60.00
C-WS76	Chris Chambliss, Graig Nettles, Johnny Bench, Ken Griffey Sr/97	100.00
C-WS77	Reggie Jackson, Graig Nettles, Steve Garvey, Ron Cey	80.00
C-WS78	Graig Nettles, Chris Chambliss, Bill Russell, Ron Cey/238	50.00
C-ASMV	Bill Madlock, Joe Morgan, Steve Garvey, Dave Parker	40.00
C-RY	Chris Chambliss, Reggie Jackson, Roy White, Hal McRae/238	75.00
C-RD	George Foster, Joe Morgan, Ron Cey, Bill Russell	40.00

2001 Upper Deck Decade Game-Used Jersey

		MT
Common Player:		10.00
Inserted 1:168		
J-HA	Hank Aaron	40.00
J-LA	Luis Aparicio	15.00
J-SB	Sal Bando/15	
J-JB	Johnny Bench	25.00
J-RC	Roberto Clemente	100.00
J-WD	Willie Davis	10.00
J-RF	Rollie Fingers	20.00
J-CF	Carlton Fisk	25.00
J-KG	Ken Griffey Sr/15	
J-RG	Ron Guidry	20.00
J-BH	Burt Hooton	15.00
L-CH	Jim "Catfish" Hunter	25.00
J-RJ	Reggie Jackson	25.00
J-JKa	Jim Kaat	15.00
J-JKo	Jerry Koosman	20.00
J-BM	Bill Madlock	15.00
J-JM	Jon Matlack	10.00
J-TM	Tug McGraw	15.00
J-BM	Bobby Murcer	25.00
J-JP	Jim Perry	10.00
J-RP	Rico Petrocelli/15	
J-LP	Lou Piniella	20.00
J-WR	Willie Randolph	15.00
J-NR	Nolan Ryan/50	75.00
J-TS	Tom Seaver	40.00
J-WS	Willie Stargell	25.00
J-MW	Maury Wills	15.00

2001 Upper Deck Decade Game-Used Jersey Autograph

		MT
Common Autograph:		25.00
Inserted 1:168 H		
SJ-HA	Hank Aaron/97	
SJ-LA	Luis Aparicio	30.00
SJ-SB	Sal Bando	25.00
SJ-JB	Johnny Bench	70.00
SJ-RF	Rollie Fingers	30.00
SJ-CF	Carlton Fisk/243	
SJ-KG	Ken Griffey Sr.	25.00
SJ-RG	Ron Guidry	40.00
SJ-BH	Burt Hooton	25.00
SJ-RJ	Reggie Jackson/291	
SJ-JKa	Jim Kaat	25.00
SJ-JKo	Jerry Koosman	25.00
SJ-BM	Bill Madlock	25.00
SJ-TM	Tug McGraw	25.00
SJ-BM	Bobby Murcer	50.00
SJ-RP	Rico Petrocelli	40.00
SJ-NR	Nolan Ryan/291	160.00
SJ-MW	Maury Wills	25.00

2001 Upper Deck Decade The Arms Race

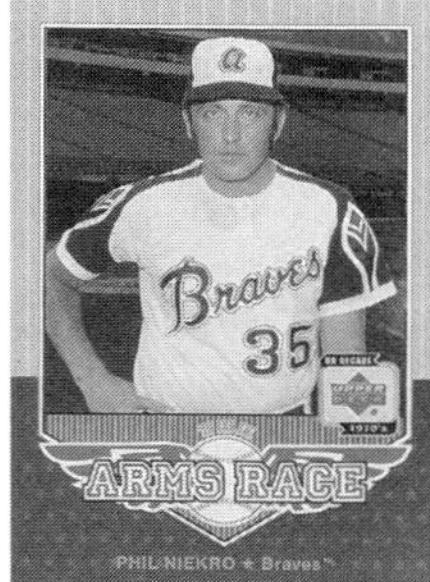

		MT
Complete Set (10):		15.00
Common Player:		1.00
Inserted 1:14		
AR1	Nolan Ryan	8.00
AR2	Ferguson Jenkins	1.00
AR3	Jim "Catfish" Hunter	1.00
AR4	Tom Seaver	4.00
AR5	Randy Jones	1.00
AR6	J.R. Richard	1.00
AR7	Rollie Fingers	1.50
AR8	Gaylord Perry	1.00
AR9	Ron Guidry	1.00
AR10	Phil Niekro	1.00

A player's name in *italic* type indicates a rookie card.

2001 Upper Deck Decade 70s Disco Era Dandies

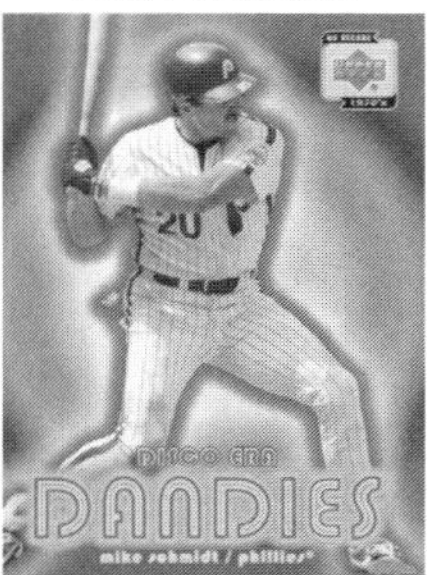

		MT
Complete Set (6):		5.00
Common Player:		.50
Inserted 1:23		
DE1	Mike Schmidt	2.00
DE2	Johnny Bench	1.00
DE3	Lou Brock	.50
DE4	Reggie Jackson	2.00
DE5	Willie Stargell	.50
DE6	Tom Seaver	1.00

2001 Upper Deck Decade 70s Super Powers

		MT
Complete Set (6):		20.00
Common Player:		2.00
Inserted 1:24		
SP1	Reggie Jackson	4.00
SP2	Joe Morgan	2.00
SP3	Willie Stargell	3.00
SP4	Willie McCovey	2.00
SP5	Mike Schmidt	5.00
SP6	Nolan Ryan	8.00

2001 Upper Deck Evolution

		MT
Complete Set (120):		NA
Common Player:		.20
Common SP (91-120):		5.00
Production 2,250		
Pack (5):		2.00
Box (24):		40.00
1	Darin Erstad	.50
2	Troy Glaus	.75
3	Jason Giambi	.75
4	Tim Hudson	.40
5	Jermaine Dye	.20
6	Barry Zito	.40
7	Carlos Delgado	.50
8	Shannon Stewart	.20
9	Jose Cruz Jr.	.20
10	Greg Vaughn	.20
11	Juan Gonzalez	1.00
12	Roberto Alomar	.75
13	Omar Vizquel	.40
14	Jim Thome	.40
15	Edgar Martinez	.20
16	John Olerud	.40
17	Kazuhiro Sasaki	.20
18	Cal Ripken Jr.	3.00
19	Alex Rodriguez	2.50
20	Ivan Rodriguez	1.00
21	Rafael Palmeiro	.75
22	Pedro Martinez	1.00
23	Nomar Garciaparra	2.50
24	Manny Ramirez	1.00
25	Carl Everett	.20
26	Mark Quinn	.20
27	Mike Sweeney	.20
28	Neifi Perez	.20
29	Tony Clark	.20
30	Eric Milton	.20
31	Doug Mientkiewicz	.20
32	Corey Koskie	.20
33	Frank Thomas	1.00
34	David Wells	.20
35	Magglio Ordonez	.20
36	Derek Jeter	3.00
37	Mike Mussina	.75
38	Bernie Williams	.75
39	Roger Clemens	1.50
40	David Justice	.40
41	Jeff Bagwell	1.00
42	Richard Hidalgo	.40
43	Wade Miller	.20
44	Chipper Jones	2.00
45	Greg Maddux	2.00
46	Andruw Jones	.60
47	Rafael Furcal	.40
48	Geoff Jenkins	.40
49	Jeromy Burnitz	.20
50	Ben Sheets	.40
51	Richie Sexson	.20
52	Mark McGwire	3.00
53	Jim Edmonds	.40
54	Darryl Kile	.20
55	J.D. Drew	.50
56	Sammy Sosa	2.00
57	Kerry Wood	.40
58	Randy Johnson	1.00
59	Luis Gonzalez	.75
60	Matt Williams	.40
61	Kevin Brown	.20
62	Gary Sheffield	.40
63	Shawn Green	.40
64	Chan Ho Park	.20
65	Vladimir Guerrero	1.00
66	Jose Vidro	.20
67	Fernando Tatis	.20
68	Barry Bonds	1.50
69	Jeff Kent	.20
70	Russ Ortiz	.20
71	Preston Wilson	.20
72	Ryan Dempster	.20
73	Charles Johnson	.20
74	Mike Piazza	2.50
75	Edgardo Alfonzo	.20
76	Robin Ventura	.40
77	Jay Payton	.20
78	Tony Gwynn	1.25
79	Phil Nevin	.20
80	Pat Burrell	.50
81	Scott Rolen	.50
82	Bob Abreu	.20
83	Brian Giles	.40
84	Jason Kendall	.20
85	Ken Griffey Jr.	2.50
86	Barry Larkin	.50
87	Sean Casey	.40
88	Todd Helton	1.00
89	Larry Walker	.50
90	Mike Hampton	.20
91	*Ichiro Suzuki*	35.00
92	*Albert Pujols*	25.00
93	*Wilson Betemit*	12.00
94	*Jay Gibbons*	15.00
95	*Juan Uribe*	8.00

96 *Morgan Ensberg* 5.00
97 *Christian Parker* 5.00
98 *Tsuyoshi Shinjo* 12.00
99 *Jack Wilson* 5.00
100 *Donaldo Mendez* 5.00
101 *Ryan Freel* 5.00
102 *Juan Diaz* 5.00
103 *Horacio Ramirez* 5.00
104 *Ricardo Rodriguez* 8.00
105 *Erick Almonte* 5.00
106 *Josh Towers* 10.00
107 *Adrian Hernandez* 5.00
108 *Brandon Duckworth* 15.00
109 *Travis Hafner* 8.00
110 *Martin Vargas* 5.00
111 *Kris Keller* 5.00
112 *Brian Lawrence* 5.00
113 *Esix Snead* 5.00
114 *Wilken Ruan* 5.00
115 *Jose Mieses* 5.00
116 *Johnny Estrada* 8.00
117 *Elpidio Guzman* 5.00
118 *Sean Douglass* 5.00
119 *Billy Sylvester* 5.00
120 *Bret Prinz* 5.00

2001 Upper Deck Evolution E-Card UD Classics

MT
Complete Set (15): 40.00
Common Player: 1.00
Prices for unscratched cards
Winners evolve into Game Jersey
Inserted 1:4
EC1 Ken Griffey Jr. 8.00
EC2 Gary Sheffield 1.50
EC3 Randy Johnson 2.50
EC4 Sammy Sosa 4.00
EC5 Carlos Delgado 1.50
EC6 Ichiro Suzuki 15.00
EC7 Andruw Jones 2.00
EC8 Chipper Jones 3.00
EC9 Kazuhiro Sasaki 1.00
EC10Shawn Green 1.00
EC11Alex Rodriguez 4.00
EC12Brian Giles 1.00
EC13J.D. Drew 2.00
EC14Pat Burrell 2.00
EC15Ivan Rodriguez 2.00

2001 Upper Deck Evolution E-Card G-U Bat Cards

MT
Common Player: 10.00
Winners evolve into Bat/Jrsy Auto.
Inserted 1:120
B-RB Russell Branyan 10.00
B-PB Pat Burrell 20.00
B-CD Carlos Delgado 20.00
B-JD J.D. Drew 20.00
B-JaGJason Giambi 20.00
B-KGKen Griffey Jr. 40.00
B-AJ Andruw Jones 20.00
B-JK Jason Kendall 10.00
B-AR Alex Rodriguez 30.00
B-GS Gary Sheffield 10.00

2001 UD Evolution eVolve Signed Bat/Jersey Combo

MT
Common Player: 60.00
JB-RBRussell Branyan 60.00
JB-PBPat Burrell 60.00
JB-CDCarlos Delgado 60.00
JB-JDJ.D. Drew 60.00
JB-JaGJason Giambi 75.00
JB-SGShawn Green 60.00
JB-KGKen Griffey Jr. 100.00
JB-AJAndruw Jones 60.00
JB-CJChipper Jones 75.00
JB-JKJason Kendall 60.00
JB-CRCal Ripken Jr. 75.00
JB-ARAlex Rodriguez 200.00
JB-GSGary Sheffield 60.00
JB-SSSammy Sosa 300.00
JB-ISIchiro Suzuki 600.00

2001 Upper Deck Evolution E-Card UD Classics Jersey

MT
Complete Set (15): 40.00
Common Player: 1.00
Prices for unscratched cards
Winners evolve into Game Jersey
Inserted 1:4
EC1 Ken Griffey Jr. 8.00
EC2 Gary Sheffield 1.50
EC3 Randy Johnson 2.50
EC4 Sammy Sosa 4.00
EC5 Carlos Delgado 1.50
EC6 Ichiro Suzuki 15.00
EC7 Andruw Jones 2.00
EC8 Chipper Jones 3.00
EC9 Kazuhiro Sasaki 1.00
EC10Shawn Green 1.00
EC11Alex Rodriguez 4.00
EC12Brian Giles 1.00
EC13J.D. Drew 2.00
EC14Pat Burrell 2.00
EC15Ivan Rodriguez 2.00

2001 Upper Deck Evolution Ichiro Suzuki All-Star Game

MT
Random inserts
51B Ichiro Suzuki Bronze 15.00
51S Ichiro Suzuki Silver/2001 60.00
51G Ichiro Suzuki Gold/51 300.00
51G Ichiro Suzuki Gold not #'d 25.00

2001 Upper Deck Evolution UD G-U Jersey Cards

MT
Common Player: 15.00
Inserted 1:120
J-RB Russell Branyan 15.00
J-PB Pat Burrell 25.00
J-JD J.D. Drew 25.00
J-JaGJason Giambi 25.00
J-BG Brian Giles 15.00
J-TG Troy Glaus 25.00
J-SG Shawn Green 20.00
J-KG Ken Griffey Jr. 50.00
J-AJ Andruw Jones 25.00
J-CJ Chipper Jones 30.00
J-JK Jason Kendall 15.00
J-CR Cal Ripken Jr. 60.00
J-AR Alex Rodriguez 40.00
J-GS Gary Sheffield 15.00
J-SS Sammy Sosa 40.00

2001 Upper Deck Gold Glove

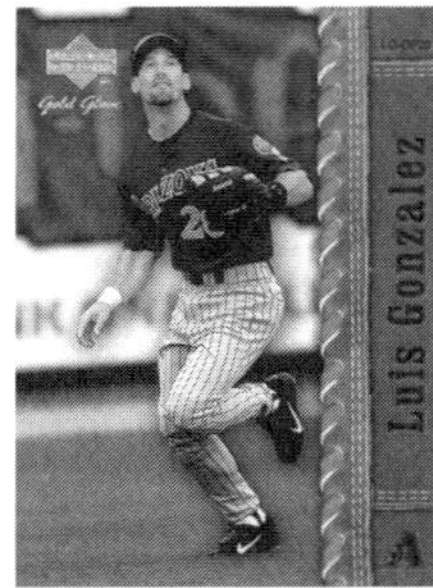

MT
Common Player: .25
Common SP (91-129): 8.00
Production 1,000
Common SP (130-135): 20.00
Production 500
Pack (4): 6.00
Box (20): 100.00
1 Troy Glaus 1.00
2 Darin Erstad .75
3 Jason Giambi 1.00
4 Tim Hudson .50
5 Jermaine Dye .25
6 Raul Mondesi .25
7 Carlos Delgado .75
8 Shannon Stewart .25
9 Greg Vaughn .25
10 Aubrey Huff .25
11 Juan Gonzalez 1.25
12 Roberto Alomar 1.00
13 Omar Vizquel .25
14 Jim Thome .75
15 John Olerud .50
16 Edgar Martinez .25
17 Kazuhiro Sasaki .25
18 Aaron Sele .25
19 Cal Ripken Jr. 4.00
20 Chris Richard .25
21 Ivan Rodriguez 1.25
22 Rafael Palmeiro .75
23 Alex Rodriguez 3.00
24 Pedro Martinez 1.50
25 Nomar Garciaparra 3.00
26 Manny Ramirez 1.50
27 Neifi Perez .25
28 Mike Sweeney .25
29 Bobby Higginson .25
30 Dean Palmer .25
31 Tony Clark .25
32 Doug Mientkiewicz .25
33 Brad Radke .25
34 Joe Mays .25
35 Frank Thomas 1.25
36 Magglio Ordonez .25
37 Carlos Lee .25
38 Bernie Williams 1.00
39 Mike Mussina 1.00
40 Derek Jeter 4.00
41 Roger Clemens 2.00
42 Craig Biggio .40
43 Jeff Bagwell 1.50
44 Lance Berkman .25
45 Andruw Jones .75
46 Greg Maddux 2.50
47 Chipper Jones 2.50
48 Geoff Jenkins .40
49 Ben Sheets .40
50 Jeromy Burnitz .25
51 Jim Edmonds .50
52 Mark McGwire 3.00
53 Mike Matheny .25
54 J.D. Drew .50
55 Sammy Sosa 2.50
56 Kerry Wood .40
57 Fred McGriff .40
58 Randy Johnson 1.25
59 Steve Finley .25
60 Mark Grace .75
61 Matt Williams .50
62 Luis Gonzalez .75
63 Shawn Green .40
64 Kevin Brown .25
65 Gary Sheffield .50
66 Vladimir Guerrero 1.25
67 Tony Armas Jr. .25
68 Barry Bonds 2.00
69 J.T. Snow .25
70 Jeff Kent .25
71 Charles Johnson .25
72 Preston Wilson .25
73 Cliff Floyd .25
74 Robin Ventura .25
75 Mike Piazza 3.00
76 Edgardo Alfonzo .25
77 Tony Gwynn 1.50
78 Ryan Klesko .25
79 Scott Rolen .50
80 Mike Lieberthal .25
81 Pat Burrell .75
82 Jason Kendall .25
83 Brian Giles .50
84 Ken Griffey Jr. 3.00
85 Barry Larkin .50
86 Pokey Reese .25
87 Larry Walker .75
88 Mike Hampton .25
89 Juan Pierre .25
90 Todd Helton 1.25
91 *Mike Penney* 8.00
92 *Wilkin Ruan* 8.00
93 *Greg Miller* 10.00
94 *Johnny Estrada* 10.00
95 *Tsuyoshi Shinjo* 15.00
96 *Josh Towers* 10.00
97 *Horacio Ramirez* 10.00
98 *Ryan Freel* 8.00
99 *Morgan Ensberg* 15.00
100 *Adrian Hernandez* 15.00
101 *Juan Uribe* 8.00
102 *Jose Mieses* 8.00
103 *Jack Wilson* 10.00
104 *Cesar Crespo* 8.00
105 *Bud Smith* 12.00
106 *Erick Almonte* 10.00
107 *Elpidio Guzman* 8.00
108 *Brandon Duckworth* 10.00
109 *Juan Diaz* 8.00
110 *Kris Keller* 10.00
111 *Jason Michaels* 8.00
112 *Bret Prinz* 8.00
113 *Henry Mateo* 8.00
114 *Ricardo Rodriguez* 10.00
115 *Travis Hafner* 8.00
116 *Nate Teut* 8.00
117 *Alexis Gomez* 8.00
118 *Billy Sylvester* 8.00
119 *Adam Pettyjohn* 8.00
120 *Josh Fogg* 12.00
121 *Juan Cruz* 10.00
122 *Carlos Valderrama* 8.00
123 *Jay Gibbons* 15.00
124 *Donaldo Mendez* 8.00
125 *William Ortega* 8.00
126 *Sean Douglass* 10.00
127 *Christian Parker* 8.00
128 *Grant Balfour* 8.00
129 *Joe Kennedy* 8.00
130 *Albert Pujols* 75.00
131 *Wilson Betemit* 20.00
132 *Mark Teixeira* 35.00
133 *Mark Prior* 60.00
134 *Dewon Brazelton* 20.00
135 *Ichiro Suzuki* 90.00

2001 Upper Deck Gold Glove Limited

MT
Common Player: 2.00
Stars (1-90): 10-20X
Rookies (91-135): 1-1.5X
Production 100 sets

2001 Upper Deck Gold Glove Batting Gloves

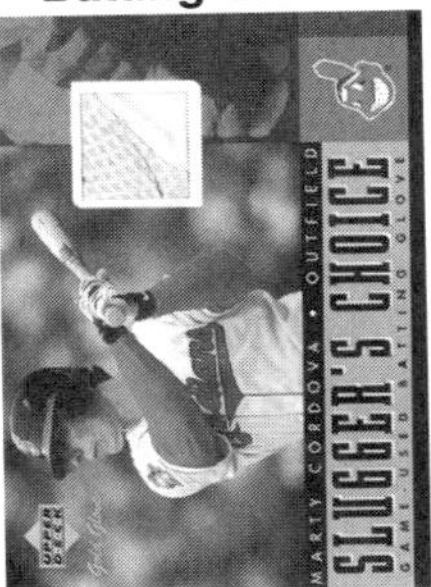

		MT
Common Player:		6.00
Inserted 1:20		
BA	Bobby Abreu	10.00
BA	Brady Anderson	10.00
TB	Tony Batista	8.00
BB	Barry Bonds	30.00
MC	Marty Cordova	8.00
JC	Jose Cruz	10.00
RF	Rafael Furcal	10.00
AG	Andres Galarraga	10.00
JG	Juan Gonzalez	10.00
KGR	Ken Griffey Jr Reds	30.00
KGM	Ken Griffey Jr.	25.00
CJ	Chipper Jones	25.00
EM	Edgar Martinez	20.00
PO	Paul O'Neill	20.00
RP	Rafael Palmeiro	10.00
NP	Neifi Perez	8.00
MR	Manny Ramirez	15.00
ARR	Alex Rodriguez Rangers	25.00
ARM	Alex Rodriguez M's	20.00
HR	Henry Rodriguez	8.00
IR	Ivan Rodriguez	10.00
GS	Gary Sheffield	10.00
SS	Sammy Sosa	25.00
FT	Fernando Tatis	6.00
MT	Miguel Tejada	10.00

2001 Upper Deck Gold Glove Fielder's Gloves

		MT
Common Player:		6.00
Inserted 1:60		
GA	Garret Anderson	8.00
CB	Craig Biggio	25.00
JBi	Johnny Blanchard	15.00
BB	Barry Bonds	50.00
JBu	Jay Buhner	
KC	Ken Caminiti	15.00
RCa	Roy Campanella	50.00
GC	Gary Carter	10.00
RCe	Roger Cedeno	10.00
JD	Johnny Damon	15.00
LD	Leon Day	60.00
OD	Octavio Dotel	
JE	Jim Edmonds	15.00
DE	Dock Ellis	10.00
AF	Alex Fernandez	6.00
CF	Cliff Floyd	10.00
NF	Nellie Fox	60.00
RF	Rafael Furcal	10.00
AG	Alex Gonzalez	6.00
BG	Ben Grieve	8.00
KG	Ken Griffey Jr.	40.00
MG	Marquis Grissom	10.00
LG	Lefty Grove	150.00
THe	Todd Helton	20.00
OH	Orlando Hernandez	
THo	Todd Hollandsworth	8.00
HI	Hideki Irabu	10.00
JI	Jason Isringhausen	15.00
RJ	Reggie Jackson	25.00
CJ	Chipper Jones	40.00
JKa	Jim Kaat	10.00
JKe	Jason Kendall	10.00
RK	Ryan Klesko	8.00
HK	Harvey Kuenn	20.00
CL	Carlos Lee	8.00
KL	Kenny Lofton	20.00
JL	Javy Lopez	10.00
GL	Greg Luzinski	10.00
EM	Edgar Martinez	15.00
PM	Pedro Martinez	25.00
JM	Jose Mesa	
JO	John Olerud	10.00
PO	Paul O'Neill	25.00
RP	Rafael Palmeiro	15.00
CP	Chan Ho Park	25.00
MP	Mike Piazza	40.00
MR	Manny Ramirez	25.00
FR	Frank Robinson	15.00
AR	Alex Rodriguez	40.00
IR	Ivan Rodriguez	
TS	Tim Salmon	
AS	Aaron Sele	6.00
GS	Gary Sheffield	10.00
OS	Ozzie Smith	40.00
SS	Sammy Sosa	35.00
I	Ichiro Suzuki	300.00
FT	Frank Thomas	30.00
OV	Omar Vizquel	20.00
DW	Dave Winfield	25.00
MY	Masato Yoshii	15.00

2001 Upper Deck Gold Glove Fielder's Gloves Autograph

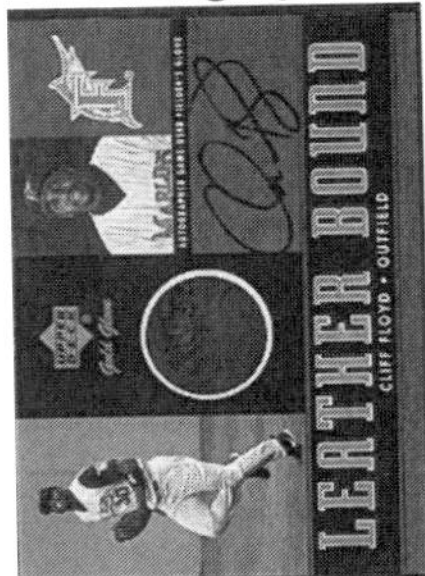

		MT
Common Autograph:		20.00
Inserted 1:240		
BB	Barry Bonds	
JD	Johnny Damon	25.00
JE	Jim Edmonds	
CF	Cliff Floyd	25.00
RF	Rafael Furcal	30.00
RP	Ken Griffey Jr.	250.00
TH	Todd Helton	
RJ	Reggie Jackson	60.00
CJ	Chipper Jones	
JK	Jim Kaat	35.00
JK	Jason Kendall	30.00
RK	Ryan Klesko	25.00
KL	Kenny Lofton	30.00
JL	Javy Lopez	25.00
GL	Greg Luzinski	25.00
EM	Edgar Martinez	60.00
PM	Pedro Martinez	
JO	John Olerud	40.00
PO	Paul O'Neill	60.00
RP	Rafael Palmeiro	
MP	Mike Piazza	
FR	Frank Robinson	50.00
AR	Alex Rodriguez	
IR	Ivan Rodriguez	70.00
AS	Aaron Sele	
GS	Gary Sheffield	
OS	Ozzie Smith	100.00
SS	Sammy Sosa	
I	Ichiro Suzuki	
FT	Frank Thomas	
DW	Dave Winfield	50.00

2001 Upper Deck Gold Glove Game-Used Ball

		MT
Common Player:		6.00
Inserted 1:20		
GC	Ken Griffey Jr., Sean Casey	20.00
RR	Alex Rodriguez, Ivan Rodriguez	25.00
SW	Sammy Sosa, Rondell White	15.00
MP	Mark McGwire, Albert Pujols	75.00
JW	Derek Jeter, Bernie Williams	
RE	Manny Ramirez, Carl Everett	15.00
GE	Troy Glaus, Darin Erstad	15.00
GT	Jason Giambi, Miguel Tejada	15.00
IO	Ichiro Suzuki, John Olerud	60.00
RP	Ivan Rodriguez, Rafael Palmeiro	20.00
GV	Vladimir Guerrero, Jose Vidro	15.00
PS	Mike Piazza, Tsuyoshi Shinjo	30.00
JJ	Chipper Jones, Andruw Jones	20.00
RB	Scott Rolen, Pat Burrell	15.00
WF	Preston Wilson, Cliff Floyd	8.00
JF	Andruw Jones, Rafael Furcal	10.00
BB	Jeff Bagwell, Lance Berkman	20.00
PE	Albert Pujols, Jim Edmonds	30.00
JB	Geoff Jenkins, Jeromy Burnitz	8.00
KG	Jason Kendall, Brian Giles	10.00
BK	Barry Bonds, Jeff Kent	20.00
NK	Phil Nevin, Ryan Klesko	8.00
SG	Gary Sheffield, Shawn Green	8.00
GG	Luis Gonzalez, Mark Grace	20.00
HW	Todd Helton, Larry Walker	15.00
WP	Larry Walker, Juan Pierre	10.00
AG	Roberto Alomar, Juan Gonzalez	20.00
VM	Greg Vaughn, Fred McGriff	
WP	Bernie Williams, Jorge Posada	
RB	Cal Ripken Jr., Tony Batista	30.00
DM	Carlos Delgado, Raul Mondesi	
MG	Doug Mientkiewicz, Cristian Guzman	10.00
TO	Frank Thomas, Magglio Ordonez	20.00
HC	Bobby Higginson, Tony Clark	8.00
SB	Mike Sweeney, Carlos Beltran	8.00
MO	Edgar Martinez, John Olerud	20.00
EA	Darin Erstad, Garret Anderson	10.00
TC	Miguel Tejada, Eric Chavez	15.00
PR	Rafael Palmeiro, Alex Rodriguez	20.00
BA	Pat Burrell, Bobby Abreu	15.00
FJ	Cliff Floyd, Charles Johnson	6.00
VP	Robin Ventura, Mike Piazza	25.00
WS	Kerry Wood, Sammy Sosa	20.00
DP	J.D. Drew, Albert Pujols	40.00
BH	Lance Berkman, Richard Hidalgo	10.00
BS	Jeromy Burnitz, Richie Sexson	6.00
LG	Barry Larkin, Ken Griffey Jr.	35.00
GR	Brian Giles, Aramis Ramirez	10.00
JG	Randy Johnson, Luis Gonzalez	20.00
GB	Shawn Green, Adrian Beltre	8.00
KA	Jeff Kent, Rich Aurilla	10.00
GK	Tony Gwynn, Ryan Klesko	15.00
MJ	Greg Maddux, Chipper Jones	20.00
HH	Mike Hampton, Todd Helton	10.00
SV	Tsuyoshi Shinjo, Robin Ventura	20.00
GJ	Cristian Guzman, Jacque Jones	10.00
CJ	Roger Clemens, Derek Jeter	50.00

2001 Upper Deck Gold Glove Jerseys

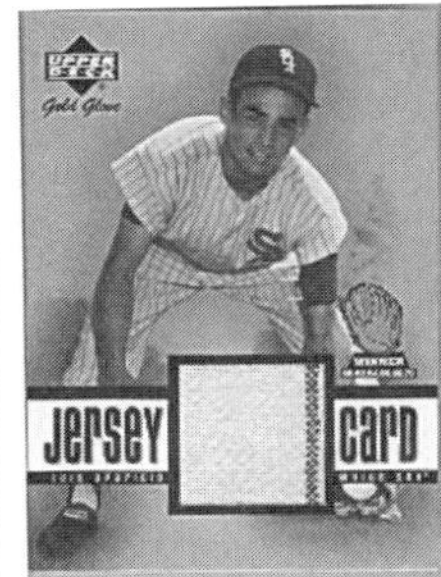

		MT
Common Player:		8.00
Inserted 1:20		
LA	Luis Aparicio	10.00
JB	Jeff Bagwell	20.00
BB	Barry Bonds	25.00
GC	Gary Carter	15.00
CC	Cesar Cedeno	10.00

DE	Darin Erstad	10.00
CF	Carlton Fisk	15.00
MG	Mark Grace	15.00
SG	Shawn Green	8.00
KG	Ken Griffey Jr.	25.00
RG	Ron Guidry	10.00
AJ	Andruw Jones	10.00
JK	Jim Kaat	10.00
GM	Greg Maddux	20.00
MM	Mickey Mantle	200.00
RM	Roger Maris	75.00
DM	Don Mattingly	40.00
TM	Thurman Munson	60.00
MM	Mike Mussina	20.00
RP	Rafael Palmeiro	10.00
BR	Bobby Richardson	20.00
CR	Cal Ripken Jr.	40.00
IR	Ivan Rodriguez	10.00
OS	Ozzie Smith	20.00
IS	Ichiro Suzuki	100.00
OV	Omar Vizquel	10.00
BW	Bernie Williams	20.00

2001 Upper Deck Hall of Famers

		MT
Complete Set (90):		
Common Player:		.15
Hobby Pack (5):		2.50
Box (24):		55.00
1	Reggie Jackson	.75
2	Hank Aaron	1.50
3	Eddie Mathews	.75
4	Warren Spahn	.40
5	Robin Yount	.40
6	Lou Brock	.25
7	Dizzy Dean	.15
8	Bob Gibson	.40
9	Stan Musial	.75
10	Enos Slaughter	.15
11	Rogers Hornsby	.40
12	Ernie Banks	.50
13	Ferguson Jenkins	.15
14	Roy Campanella	.75
15	Pee Wee Reese	.15
16	Jackie Robinson	1.50
17	Juan Marichal	.15
18	Christy Mathewson	.15
19	Willie Mays	1.50
20	Hoyt Wilhelm	.15
21	Buck Leonard	.15
22	Bob Feller	.40
23	Cy Young	.40
24	Satchel Paige	.40
25	Tom Seaver	.50
26	Brooks Robinson	.40
27	Mike Schmidt	.75
28	Roberto Clemente	1.50
29	Ralph Kiner	.15
30	Willie Stargell	.50
31	Honus Wagner	.75
32	Josh Gibson	.40
33	Nolan Ryan	1.50
34	Carlton Fisk	.15
35	Jimmie Foxx	.75
36	Johnny Bench	.75
37	Joe Morgan	.40
38	George Brett	.75
39	Walter Johnson	.40
40	Cool Papa Bell	.15
41	Ty Cobb	1.00
42	Al Kaline	.15
43	Harmon Killebrew	.15
44	Luis Aparicio	.15
45	Yogi Berra	.75
46	Joe DiMaggio	1.50
47	Whitey Ford	.25
48	Lou Gehrig	2.00
49	Mickey Mantle	2.00
50	Babe Ruth	2.00
51	Josh Gibson (Origins of the Game)	.15
52	Honus Wagner (Origins of the Game)	.20
53	Hoyt Wilhelm (Origins of the Game)	.15
54	Cy Young (Origins of the Game)	.20
55	Walter Johnson (Origins of the Game)	.20
56	Satchel Paige (Origins of the Game)	.25
57	Rogers Hornsby (Origins of the Game)	.20
58	Christy Mathewson (Origins of the Game)	.15
59	Tris Speaker (Origins of the Game)	.20
60	Nap Lajoie (Origins of the Game)	.15
61	Mickey Mantle (The National Pastime)	1.00
62	Jackie Robinson (The National Pastime)	.75
63	Nolan Ryan (The National Pastime)	.75
64	Josh Gibson (The National Pastime)	.20
65	Yogi Berra (The National Pastime)	.40
66	Brooks Robinson (The National Pastime)	.20
67	Stan Musial (The National Pastime)	.40
68	Mike Schmidt (The National Pastime)	.40
69	Joe DiMaggio (The National Pastime)	1.00
70	Ernie Banks (The National Pastime)	.25
71	Willie Stargell (The National Pastime)	.25
72	Johnny Bench (The National Pastime)	.40
73	Willie Mays (The National Pastime)	.75
74	Satchel Paige (The National Pastime)	.25
75	Bob Gibson (The National Pastime)	.20
76	Harmon Killebrew (The National Pastime)	.15
77	Al Kaline (The National Pastime)	.15
78	Carlton Fisk (The National Pastime)	.15
79	Tom Seaver (The National Pastime)	.25
80	Reggie Jackson (The National Pastime)	.40
81	Bob Gibson (The Hall of Records)	.20
82	Nolan Ryan (The Hall of Records)	.75
83	Walter Johnson (The Hall of Records)	.20
84	Stan Musial (The Hall of Records)	.40
85	Josh Gibson (The Hall of Records)	.20
86	Cy Young (The Hall of Records)	.20
87	Joe DiMaggio (The Hall of Records)	1.00
88	Hoyt Wilhelm (The Hall of Records)	.15
89	Lou Brock (The Hall of Records)	.15
90	Mickey Mantle (The Hall of Records)	1.00

2001 Upper Deck Hall of Famers Coop. Coll. Game Bat

		MT
Common Player:		20.00
Inserted 1:24		
HA	Hank Aaron	60.00
LA	Luis Aparicio	25.00
EB	Ernie Banks	50.00
JB	Johnny Bench	35.00
YB	Yogi Berra	40.00
JBo	Jim Bottomley	50.00
GB	George Brett	35.00
RC	Roy Campanella	50.00
OC	Orlando Cepeda	20.00
RC	Roberto Clemente SP/409	250.00
JD	Joe DiMaggio	200.00
CF	Carlton Fisk	25.00
RF	Rollie Fingers	20.00
JF	Jimmie Foxx	75.00
HG	Hank Greenberg	60.00
RH	Rogers Hornsby	120.00
RJ	Reggie Jackson	30.00
GK	George Kell	25.00
RK	Ralph Kiner	30.00
MM	Mickey Mantle	200.00
WM	Willie Mays	50.00
JM	Johnny Mize	40.00
JMo	Joe Morgan	20.00
MO	Mel Ott	75.00
JP	Jim Palmer SP/372	90.00
TP	Tony Perez	20.00
BR	Brooks Robinson	30.00
FR	Frank Robinson	30.00
JR	Jackie Robinson SP/371	300.00
BR	Babe Ruth	350.00
NR	Nolan Ryan	100.00
RS	Red Schoendienst	25.00
ES	Enos Slaughter	35.00
DS	Duke Snider	60.00
WS	Willie Stargell	30.00
BW	Billy Williams	25.00
EW	Early Wynn	30.00
RY	Robin Yount	30.00

2001 Upper Deck Hall of Famers Coop. Coll. Game Jersey

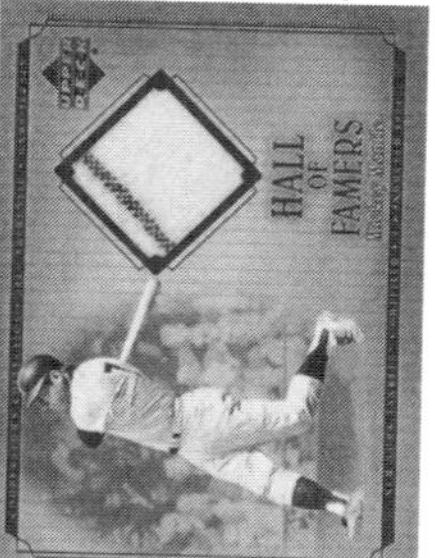

		MT
Common Player:		25.00
Inserted 1:168		
LA	Luis Aparicio	40.00
OC	Orlando Cepeda	30.00
RC	Roberto Clemente	250.00
JD	Joe DiMaggio	200.00
DD	Don Drysdale SP/49	450.00
LG	Lou Gehrig SP/194	550.00
MM	Mickey Mantle SP/216	375.00
WM	Willie Mays	80.00
JM	Joe Morgan	40.00
TP	Tony Perez	40.00
PW	Pee Wee Reese	50.00
BR	Brooks Robinson	50.00
FR	Frank Robinson	50.00
NR	Nolan Ryan	80.00
TS	Tom Seaver	80.00
DS	Duke Snider SP/267	100.00
WS	Willie Stargell	50.00
DSu	Don Sutton	25.00

2001 Upper Deck Hall of Famers Coop. Coll. Jersey Auto.

		MT
Common Autograph:		60.00
Inserted 1:504		
LA	Luis Aparicio	75.00
OC	Orlando Cepeda	80.00
RJ	Reggie Jackson	125.00
EB	Ernie Banks	180.00
JM	Joe Morgan	90.00
TP	Tony Perez	75.00
GB	George Brett	180.00
BR	Brooks Robinson	125.00
FR	Frank Robinson	125.00
NR	Nolan Ryan	200.00
TS	Tom Seaver	180.00
DS	Duke Snider	125.00
WS	Willie Stargell	
DSu	Don Sutton	60.00

2001 Upper Deck Hall of Famers Hall of Fame Gallery

		MT
Complete Set (15):		35.00
Common Player:		1.00
Inserted 1:6		
1	Reggie Jackson	2.00
2	Tom Seaver	1.50
3	Bob Gibson	1.50
4	Jackie Robinson	5.00
5	Joe DiMaggio	6.00
6	Ernie Banks	1.50
7	Mickey Mantle	6.00
8	Willie Mays	5.00
9	Cy Young	1.50
10	Nolan Ryan	6.00
11	Johnny Bench	2.00
12	Yogi Berra	2.00
13	Satchel Paige	1.00
14	George Brett	2.00
15	Stan Musial	2.00

A player's name in *italic* type indicates a rookie card.

2001 Upper Deck Hall of Famers Mantle Pinstripes Excl.

	MT
Complete Set (56):	150.00
Common Mantle:	4.00
One pack/box	

2001 Upper Deck Hall of Famers Mantle Pinstripe Memor.

	MT
Print Runs listed:	
MMBCMickey Mantle bat/cut/7	
MMB Mickey Mantle bat/100	350.00
MMCJMickey Mantle, Joe DiMaggio jsy/50	1000.
MMC Mickey Mantle cut/7	
MMJ Mickey Mantle jsy/100	400.00

2001 Upper Deck Hall of Famers The Class of '36

		MT
Complete Set (5):		12.00
Common Player:		1.50
Inserted 1:17		
1	Ty Cobb	4.00
2	Babe Ruth	6.00
3	Christy Mathewson	1.50
4	Walter Johnson	2.00
5	Honus Wagner	2.00

2001 Upper Deck Hall of Famers The Endless Summer

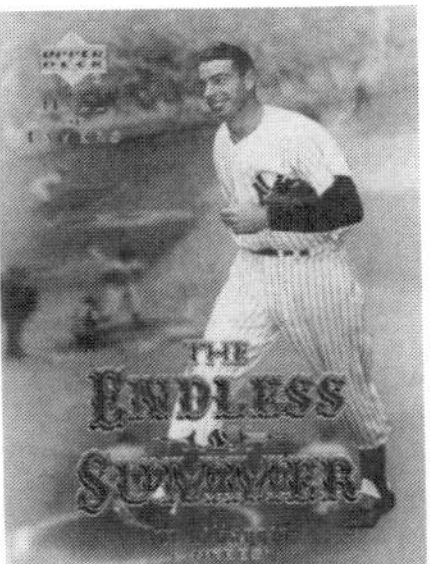

		MT
Complete Set (11):		25.00
Common Player:		1.00
Inserted 1:8		
1	Mickey Mantle	6.00
2	Yogi Berra	2.00
3	Mike Schmidt	2.00
4	Jackie Robinson	5.00
5	Johnny Bench	2.00
6	Tom Seaver	1.50
7	Ernie Banks	1.50
8	Harmon Killebrew	1.00
9	Joe DiMaggio	6.00
10	Willie Mays	5.00
11	Brooks Robinson	1.50

2001 Upper Deck Hall of Famers 20th Century Showcase

		MT
Complete Set (11):		25.00
Common Player:		1.00
Inserted 1:8		
1	Cy Young	1.50
2	Joe DiMaggio	5.00
3	Harmon Killebrew	1.00
4	Stan Musial	2.00
5	Mickey Mantle	6.00
6	Satchel Paige	1.00
7	Nolan Ryan	6.00
8	Bob Gibson	1.50
9	Ernie Banks	1.50
10	Mike Schmidt	2.00
11	Willie Mays	5.00

2001 Upper Deck Legends

		MT
Complete Set (90):		20.00
Common Player:		.20
Pack (5):		3.00
Box (24):		65.00
1	Darin Erstad	.40
2	Troy Glaus	.75
3	Nolan Ryan	3.00
4	Reggie Jackson	.50
5	Jim "Catfish" Hunter	.20
6	Jason Giambi	.50
7	Tim Hudson	.30
8	Miguel Tejada	.30
9	Carlos Delgado	.50
10	Shannon Stewart	.20
11	Greg Vaughn	.20
12	Larry Doby	.20
13	Jim Thome	.40
14	Juan Gonzalez	.75
15	Roberto Alomar	.50
16	Edgar Martinez	.20
17	John Olerud	.40
18	Eddie Murray	.40
19	Cal Ripken Jr.	2.50
20	Alex Rodriguez	2.00
21	Ivan Rodriguez	.75
22	Rafael Palmeiro	.40
23	Jimmie Foxx	.50
24	Cy Young	.50
25	Manny Ramirez	.75
26	Pedro Martinez	1.00
27	Nomar Garciaparra	2.00
28	George Brett	1.00
29	Mike Sweeney	.20
30	Jermaine Dye	.20
31	Ty Cobb	1.50
32	Dean Palmer	.20
33	Harmon Killebrew	.50
34	Matt Lawton	.20
35	Luis Aparicio	.20
36	Frank Thomas	.75
37	Magglio Ordonez	.20
38	David Wells	.20
39	Mickey Mantle	3.00
40	Joe DiMaggio	3.00
41	Roger Maris	.75
42	Babe Ruth	3.00
43	Derek Jeter	2.50
44	Roger Clemens	1.00
45	Bernie Williams	.50
46	Jeff Bagwell	.75
47	Richard Hidalgo	.40
48	Warren Spahn	.40
49	Greg Maddux	1.50
50	Chipper Jones	1.50
51	Andruw Jones	.50
52	Robin Yount	.50
53	Jeromy Burnitz	.20
54	Jeffrey Hammonds	.20
55	Ozzie Smith	.50
56	Stan Musial	1.00
57	Mark McGwire	2.50
58	Jim Edmonds	.30
59	Sammy Sosa	1.50
60	Ernie Banks	.50
61	Kerry Wood	.20
62	Randy Johnson	.75
63	Luis Gonzalez	.40
64	Don Drysdale	.50
65	Jackie Robinson	2.00
66	Gary Sheffield	.20
67	Kevin Brown	.20
68	Vladimir Guerrero	1.00
69	Willie Mays	1.50
70	Mel Ott	.20
71	Jeff Kent	.20
72	Barry Bonds	1.00
73	Preston Wilson	.20
74	Ryan Dempster	.20
75	Tom Seaver	.40
76	Mike Piazza	2.00
77	Robin Ventura	.20
78	Dave Winfield	.40
79	Tony Gwynn	1.00
80	Bob Abreu	.20
81	Scott Rolen	.40
82	Mike Schmidt	.75
83	Roberto Clemente	1.50
84	Brian Giles	.20
85	Ken Griffey Jr.	2.00
86	Frank Robinson	.40
87	Johnny Bench	.75
88	Todd Helton	.75
89	Larry Walker	.40
90	Mike Hampton	.20

2001 Upper Deck Legends Fiorentino Collection

		MT
Complete Set (14):		50.00
Common Player:		2.00
Inserted 1:12		
F1	Babe Ruth	8.00
F2	Satchel Paige	2.00
F3	Joe DiMaggio	6.00
F4	Willie Mays	4.00
F5	Ty Cobb	4.00
F6	Nolan Ryan	8.00
F7	Lou Gehrig	6.00
F8	Jackie Robinson	4.00
F9	Hank Aaron	5.00
F10	Roberto Clemente	5.00
F11	Stan Musial	3.00
F12	Johnny Bench	2.50
F13	Honus Wagner	2.00
F14	Reggie Jackson	2.00

2001 Upper Deck Legends Legendary Cuts

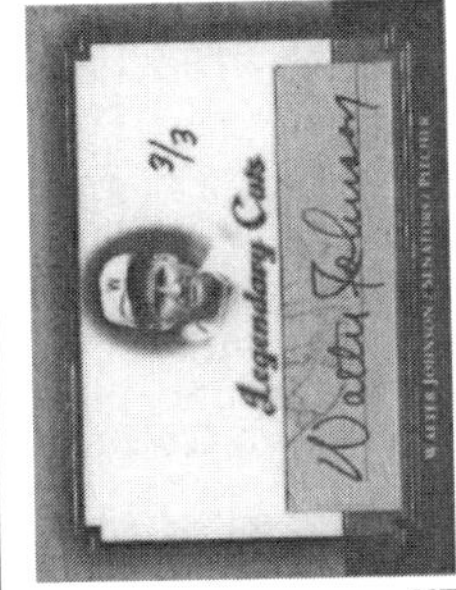

	MT
Complete Set (5):	
Common Player:	
C-TCTy Cobb	
C-WJWalter Johnson (3)	
C-CMChristy Mathewson	
C-BRuBabe Ruth (7)	7500.
C-HWHonus Wagner	

A card number in parentheses ( ) indicates the set is unnumbered.

2001 Upper Deck Legends Legendary Game Jerseys

	MT
Common Player:	10.00
Inserted 1:24	
J-HA Hank Aaron	50.00
J-JB Jeff Bagwell	25.00
J-EB Ernie Banks	40.00
J-YB Yogi Berra	30.00
J-BB Barry Bonds	40.00
J-JC Jose Canseco	15.00
J-RCIRoger Clemens	30.00
J-RoCRoberto Clemente/ 195	170.00
J-JD Joe DiMaggio/ 245	175.00
J-KG Ken Griffey Jr.	40.00
J-TG Tony Gwynn	20.00
J-RJaReggie Jackson	25.00
J-RJoRandy Johnson	20.00
J-CJ Chipper Jones	25.00
J-GMGreg Maddux	25.00
J-MMMickey Mantle/ 245	200.00
J-RM Roger Maris/343	100.00
J-PM Pedro Martinez	30.00
J-WMWillie Mays	40.00
J-SM Stan Musial/490	40.00
J-MP Mike Piazza	50.00
J-MR Manny Ramirez	25.00
J-CR Cal Ripken Jr.	50.00
J-AR Alex Rodriguez	35.00
J-IR Ivan Rodriguez	15.00
J-NR Nolan Ryan	50.00
J-KS Kazuhiro Sasaki	30.00
J-TS Tom Seaver	25.00
J-GS Gary Sheffield	10.00
J-OS Ozzie Smith	20.00
J-SS Sammy Sosa	30.00
J-DWDave Winfield	15.00
J-RY Robin Yount	20.00

2001 Upper Deck Legends Legendary Jerseys Gold

	MT
Common Player:	80.00
Production 25 sets	
GJ-RCIRoger Clemens	175.00
GJ-RoCRoberto Clemente	275.00
GJ-KGKen Griffey Jr.	200.00
GJ-RJReggie Jackson	125.00
GJ-WMWillie Mays	250.00
GJ-ARAlex Rodriguez	150.00
GJ-NRNolan Ryan	275.00
GJ-SSSammy Sosa	175.00
GJ-DWDave Winfield	80.00

2001 Upper Deck Legends Legendary Jerseys Auto.

	MT
Common Player:	60.00
Inserted 1:288	
SJ-EBErnie Banks	75.00
SJ-RCRoger Clemens/ 211	140.00
SJ-KGKen Griffey Jr.	150.00
SJ-RJReggie Jackson/ 224	75.00
SJ-SMStan Musial/ 266	150.00
SJ-ARAlex Rodriguez	120.00
SJ-NRNolan Ryan	175.00
SJ-TSTom Seaver	75.00
SJ-OSOzzie Smith	60.00
SJ-SSSammy Sosa/ 91	175.00

2001 Upper Deck Legends Legendary Jerseys Gold Auto.

	MT
Common Autograph:	180.00
Production 25 sets	
GSJ-EBErnie Banks	250.00
GSJ-RCRoger Clemens	300.00
GSJ-KGKen Griffey Jr.	375.00
GSJ-RJReggie Jackson	250.00
GSJ-ARAlex Rodriguez	275.00
GSJ-NRNolan Ryan	500.00
GSJ-TSTom Seaver	180.00
GSJ-OSOzzie Smith	200.00
GSJ-SSSammy Sosa	375.00

2001 Upper Deck Legends Legendary Lumber

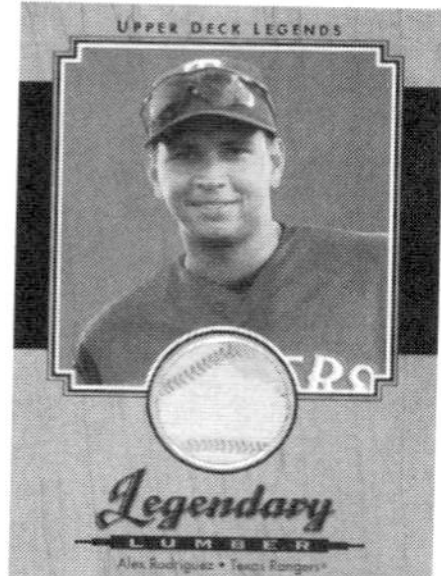

	MT
Common Player:	10.00
Inserted 1:24	
L-HA Hank Aaron	35.00
L-LA Luis Aparicio	10.00
L-EB Ernie Banks/80	70.00
L-JB Johnny Bench	30.00
L-BB Barry Bonds	35.00
L-RCaRoy Campanella/ 335	50.00
L-JC Jose Canseco	15.00
L-RCIRoger Clemens	30.00
L-RoCRoberto Clemente/ 170	150.00
L-JD Joe DiMaggio	125.00
L-JF Jimmie Foxx/351	60.00
L-KG Ken Griffey Jr.	30.00
L-TG Tony Gwynn	20.00
L-RJ Reggie Jackson	20.00
L-RJ Randy Johnson	20.00
L-AJ Andruw Jones	10.00
L-CJ Chipper Jones	25.00
L-MMMickey Mantle	150.00
L-RMRoger Maris	75.00
L-WMWillie Mays	40.00
L-EMEddie Murray	20.00
L-MOMel Ott/355	50.00
L-MPMike Piazza	50.00
L-AP Albert Pujols	75.00
L-MRManny Ramirez	20.00
L-FR Frank Robinson	20.00
L-CR Cal Ripken Jr.	40.00
L-AR Alex Rodriguez	20.00
L-IR Ivan Rodriguez	15.00
L-GS Gary Sheffield	10.00
L-OS Ozzie Smith	15.00
L-SS Sammy Sosa	25.00

2001 Upper Deck Legends Legendary Lumber Gold

	MT
Common Player:	40.00
Production 25 sets	
GL-RCRoger Clemens	90.00
GL-RCRoberto Clemente	300.00
GL-KGKen Griffey Jr.	125.00
GL-RJReggie Jackson	90.00
GL-WMWillie Mays	150.00
GL-PWPee Wee Reese	
GL-ARAlex Rodriguez	100.00
GL-GSGary Sheffield	40.00
GL-SSSammy Sosa	125.00

2001 Upper Deck Legends Legendary Lumber Auto.

	MT
Common Player:	40.00
Inserted 1:288	
SL-LALuis Aparicio	40.00
SL-EBErnie Banks	75.00
SL-RCRoger Clemens/ 227	120.00
SL-KGKen Griffey Jr.	175.00
SL-TGTony Gwynn	75.00
SL-RJReggie Jackson/ 211	75.00
SL-EMEddie Murray	75.00
SL-ARAlex Rodriguez	100.00
SL-SSSammy Sosa/ 66	240.00

2001 Upper Deck Legends Legendary Lumber Gold Auto.

	MT
Common Player:	60.00
Production 25 sets	
GSL-LALuis Aparicio	60.00
GSL-EBErnie Banks	225.00
GSL-RCRoger Clemens	225.00
GSL-KGKen Griffey Jr.	300.00
GSL-TGTony Gwynn	200.00
GSL-RJReggie Jackson	225.00
GSL-EMEddie Murray	140.00
GSL-ARAlex Rodriguez	250.00
GSL-SSSammy Sosa	300.00

2001 Upper Deck Legends Reflections

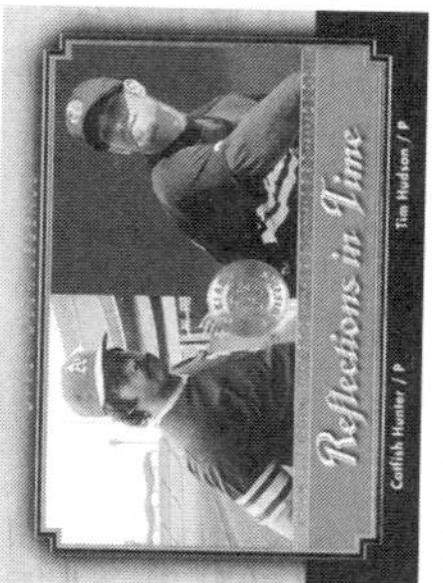

		MT
Complete Set (10):		35.00
Common Player:		2.00
Inserted 1:18		
R1	Bernie Williams, Mickey Mantle	8.00
R2	Pedro Martinez, Cy Young	2.50
R3	Barry Bonds, Willie Mays	5.00
R4	Scott Rolen, Mike Schmidt	3.00
R5	Mark McGwire, Stan Musial	6.00
R6	Ken Griffey Jr., Frank Robinson	5.00
R7	Sammy Sosa, Andre Dawson	4.00
R8	Kevin Brown, Don Drysdale	2.00
R9	Jason Giambi, Reggie Jackson	2.00
R10	Tim Hudson, Jim "Catfish" Hunter	2.00

2001 Upper Deck Legends of New York

The greatest players, teams and events of 20th Century Major League baseball in New York City are featured in this specialty set. The 200-card base set is comprised of a number of different subsets. The front of each card in the base set has an area of flocking in team colors.

		MT
Complete Set (200):		50.00
Common Player:		.20
Pack (5):		2.50
Box (24):		50.00
1	Billy Herman	.20
2	Carl Erskine	.20
3	Burleigh Grimes	.20
4	Don Newcombe	.20
5	Gil Hodges	.75
6	Pee Wee Reese	.75
7	Jackie Robinson	2.00
8	Duke Snider	1.00
9	Jim Gilliam	.20
10	Roy Campanella	1.50
11	Carl Furillo	.20
12	Casey Stengel	.75
13	Casey Stengel	.40
14	Billy Herman	.20
15	Jackie Robinson	1.00
16	Jackie Robinson	1.00
17	Gil Hodges	.40
18	Carl Furillo	.20
19	Roy Campanella	.50
20	Don Newcombe	.40
21	Duke Snider	.75
22	Casey Stengel	.40
23	Burleigh Grimes	.20
24	Pee Wee Reese	.50
25	Jackie Robinson	1.00
26	Jackie Robinson	1.00
27	Carl Erskine	.20
28	Roy Campanella	.75
29	Duke Snider	.75
30	Rube Marquard	.20
31	Ross Youngs	.20
32	Bobby Thomson	.20
33	Christy Mathewson	1.00
34	Carl Hubbell	.20
35	Hoyt Wilhelm	.20
36	Johnny Mize	.40
37	John McGraw	.20

38 Monte Irvin .50
39 Travis Jackson .20
40 Mel Ott 1.00
41 Dusty Rhodes .20
42 Leo Durocher .50
43 John McGraw .20
44 Christy Mathewson .50
45 The Polo Grounds .20
46 Travis Jackson .20
47 Mel Ott .50
48 Johnny Mize .20
49 Leo Durocher .30
50 Bobby Thomson .20
51 Monte Irvin .30
52 Bobby Thomson .20
53 Christy Mathewson .50
54 Christy Mathewson .50
55 Christy Mathewson .50
56 John McGraw .20
57 John McGraw .20
58 John McGraw .20
59 Travis Jackson .20
60 Mel Ott .50
61 Mel Ott .50
62 Carl Hubbell .20
63 Bobby Thomson .20
64 Monte Irvin .20
65 Al Weis .20
66 Donn Clendenon .20
67 Ed Kranepool .20
68 Gary Carter .20
69 Tommie Agee .20
70 Jon Matlack .20
71 Ken Boswell .20
72 Len Dykstra .20
73 Nolan Ryan 3.00
74 Ray Sadecki .20
75 Ron Darling .20
76 Ron Swoboda .20
77 Dwight Gooden .20
78 Tom Seaver 1.00
79 Wayne Garrett .20
80 Casey Stengel .50
81 Tom Seaver .50
82 Tommie Agee .20
83 Tom Seaver .50
84 Yogi Berra .50
85 Yogi Berra .50
86 Tom Seaver .50
87 Dwight Gooden .20
88 Gary Carter .20
89 Ron Darling .20
90 Tommie Agee .20
91 Tom Seaver .50
92 Gary Carter .20
93 Len Dykstra .20
94 Babe Ruth 3.00
95 Bill Dickey .50
96 Rich "Goose" Gossage .20
97 Casey Stengel .50
98 Jim "Catfish" Hunter .75
99 Charlie Keller .20
100 Chris Chambliss .20
101 Don Larsen .40
102 Dave Winfield .75
103 Don Mattingly 2.00
104 Elston Howard .20
105 Frankie Crosetti .20
106 Hank Bauer .20
107 Joe DiMaggio 3.00
108 Graig Nettles .20
109 Lefty Gomez .20
110 Phil Rizzuto 1.00
111 Lou Gehrig 2.00
112 Lou Piniella .20
113 Mickey Mantle 3.00
114 Red Rolfe .20
115 Reggie Jackson 1.00
116 Roger Maris 1.50
117 Ray White .20
118 Thurman Munson 1.50
119 Tom Tresh .20
120 Tommy Henrich .20
121 Waite Hoyt .20
122 Willie Randolph .20
123 Whitey Ford .75
124 Yogi Berra 1.00
125 Babe Ruth 1.50
126 Babe Ruth 1.50
127 Lou Gehrig 1.25
128 Babe Ruth 1.50
129 Joe DiMaggio 1.50
130 Joe DiMaggio 1.50
131 Mickey Mantle 1.50
132 Roger Marris .75
133 Mickey Mantle 1.50
134 Reggie Jackson .75
135 Babe Ruth 1.50
136 Babe Ruth 1.50
137 Babe Ruth 1.50
138 Lefty Gomez .20
139 Lou Gehrig 1.25
140 Lou Gehrig 1.25
141 Joe DiMaggio 1.50
142 Joe DiMaggio 1.50
143 Casey Stengel .40
144 Mickey Mantle 1.50
145 Yogi Berra .50
146 Mickey Mantle 1.50
147 Elston Howard .40
148 Whitey Ford .50
149 Reggie Jackson .50
150 Reggie Jackson .50
151 John McGraw, Babe Ruth 1.00
152 Babe Ruth, John McGraw 1.00
153 Lou Gehrig, Mel Ott .75
154 Joe DiMaggio, Mel Ott 1.00
155 Joe DiMaggio, Billy Herman 1.00
156 Joe DiMaggio, Jackie Robinson 1.50
157 Mickey Mantle, Bobby Thomson 1.00
158 Yogi Berra, Pee Wee Reese .75
159 Roy Campanella, Mickey Mantle 1.00
160 Don Larsen, Duke Snider .50
161 Christy Mathewson .75
162 Christy Mathewson .50
163 Rube Marquard .20
164 Christy Mathewson .50
165 John McGraw .20
166 Burleigh Grimes .20
167 Babe Ruth 1.50
168 Burleigh Grimes .20
169 Babe Ruth 1.50
170 John McGraw .40
171 Lou Gehrig 1.25
172 Babe Ruth 1.50
173 Babe Ruth 1.50
174 Carl Hubbell .20
175 Joe DiMaggio 1.50
176 Lou Gehrig 1.25
177 Leo Durocher .40
178 Mel Ott .50
179 Joe DiMaggio 1.50
180 Jackie Robinson 1.00
181 Babe Ruth 1.50
182 Bobby Thomson .20
183 Joe DiMaggio 1.50
184 Mickey Mantle 1.50
185 Monte Irvin .20
186 Roy Campanella .50
187 Duke Snider .50
188 Dusty Rhodes .20
189 Yogi Berra .50
190 Mickey Mantle 1.50
191 Mickey Mantle 1.50
192 Casey Stengel .40
193 Tom Seaver .50
194 Mickey Mantle 1.50
195 Tommie Agee .20
196 Tom Seaver .50
197 Chris Chambliss .20
198 Reggie Jackson .50
199 Reggie Jackson .50
200 Gary Carter .20

2001 UD Legends of N.Y. Combination Signatures

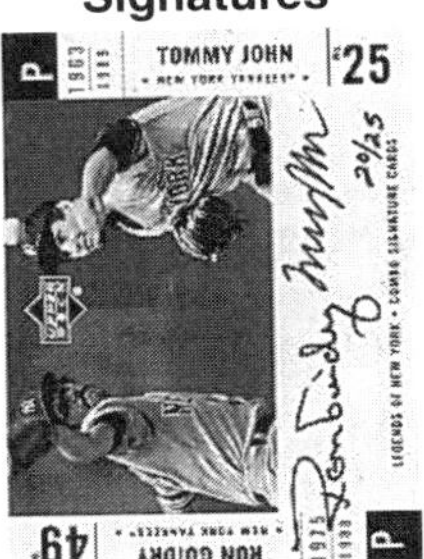

MT
Complete Set (9): 1250.
Common Card: 75.00
S-NP Don Newcombe, Johnny Podres 150.00
S-WM Dave Winfield, Don Mattingly 300.00
S-RS Nolan Ryan, Tom Seaver 500.00
S-LB Don Larsen, Yogi Berra 200.00
S-GJ Ron Guidry, Tommy John 75.00
S-CN Chris Chambliss, Graig Nettles 75.00
S-RD Willie Randolph, Bucky Dent 75.00
S-RW Mickey Rivers, Roy White 75.00
S-WJ Dave Winfield, Reggie Jackson 200.00

2001 UD Legends of N.Y. Legends Cut Signatures

MT
LC-JD Joe DiMaggio (38 issued) 1000.
LC-GH Gil Hodges (1 issued) 3000.
LC-MO Mel Ott (2 issued) 1000.
LC-JR Jackie Robinson (3 issued) 2500.
LC-BR Babe Ruth (5 issued) 5000.

2001 Upper Deck Legends of New York Ebbets Field G-U

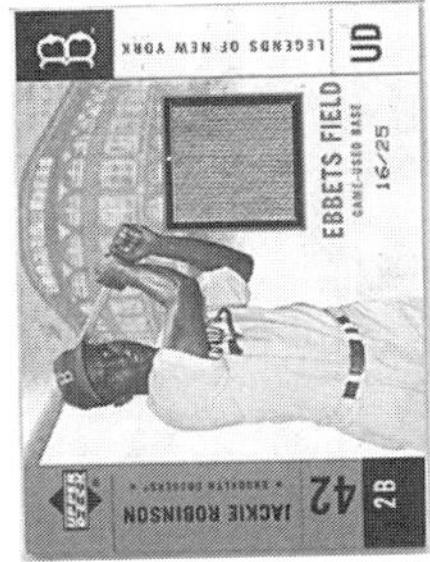

MT
Complete Set (1):
EF-JR Jackie Robinson (100) 55.00

2001 UD Legends of New York Ebbets Field Seat

MT
Complete Set (1):
EFS-JR Jackie Robinson

2001 UD Legends of N.Y. Legendary Dodgers Game Jersey

MT
Common Player: 10.00
Gold Edition of 400: 1.25X
HB Hank Behrman 10.00
CD Chuck Dressen 10.00
CE Carl Erskine 20.00
SJ Spider Jurgenson 10.00
JR Jackie Robinson/126 120.00

2001 UD Legends of N.Y. Legendary Giants Game Jersey

MT
Complete Set (1):
CM Christy Mathewson/63 600.00

2001 UD Legends of N.Y. Legendary Mets Game Jersey

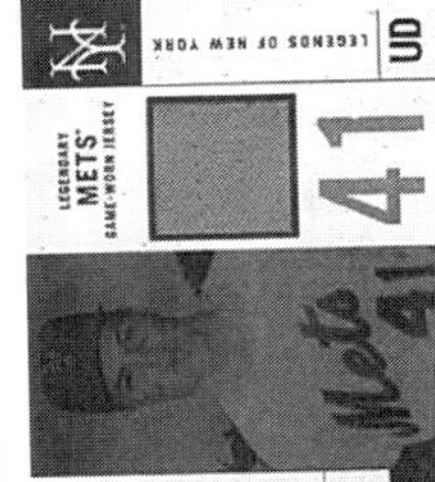

MT
Common Player: 10.00
Gold Edition of 400: 1.25X
RD Ron Darling 35.00
JM Jon Matlack 10.00
RS Ray Sadecki 10.00
TS Tom Seaver 40.00
CS Casey Stengel 30.00
JT Joe Torre 35.00

A card number in parentheses ( ) indicates the set is unnumbered.

2001 UD Legends of N.Y. Legendary Yankees Game Jersey

		MT
Common Player:		
Gold Edition of 400:		1.25X
HB	Hank Bauer	15.00
FC	Frank Crosetti	20.00
JD	Joe DiMaggio/63	
TH	Tommy Henrich	20.00
EH	Elston Howard	15.00
CH	Jim "Catfish" Hunter	25.00
DM	Duke Maas	15.00
MM	Mickey Mantle/63	350.00
RM	Roger Maris/63	
LM	Lindy McDaniel	15.00
TM	Thurman Munson	50.00
GN	Graig Nettles	25.00
PN	Phil Niekro	30.00
JP	Joe Pepitone	15.00
WR	Willie Randolph	15.00
RR	Red Rolfe	15.00
BT	Bob Turley	20.00
DW	Dave Winfield	20.00

2001 UD Legends of N.Y. Legendary Bat Cards

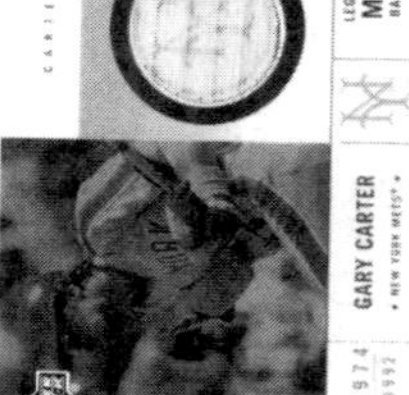

		MT
Common Player:		10.00
Inserted 1:24		
DODGERS		
JG	Jim Gilliam	25.00
BH	Billy Herman	10.00
DN	Don Newcombe/67	50.00
GIANTS		
MO	Mel Ott	
BTh	Bobby Thomson	25.00
METS		
KB	Ken Boswell	10.00
GC	Gary Carter	15.00
DC	Donn Clendenon/60	
LD	Len Dykstra	15.00
WG	Wayne Garrett	10.00
EK	Ed Kranepool	10.00
JM	J.C. Martin	10.00
NR	Nolan Ryan	50.00
TS	Tom Seaver	35.00
RSw	Ron Swoboda	15.00
AW	Al Weis	15.00
YANKEES		
HB	Hank Bauer	15.00
YB	Yogi Berra	50.00
CC	Chris Chambliss/130	15.00
BD	Bill Dickey	25.00
JD	Joe DiMaggio/43	
TH	Tommy Henrich	15.00
EH	Elston Howard	
RJ	Reggie Jackson	30.00
CK	Charlie Keller	20.00
MM	Mickey Mantle/134	200.00
RM	Roger Maris/60	125.00
DM	Don Mattingly	35.00
TM	Thurman Munson	40.00
LP	Lou Piniella	25.00
MR	Mickey Rivers	15.00
BR	Babe Ruth/107	250.00
JT	Joe Torre	
TT	Tom Tresh	25.00
RW	Roy White	
DW	Dave Winfield	15.00

2001 UD Legends of N.Y. Legendary Bat Autograph

		MT
Common Autograph:		
DODGERS		
JG	Jim Gilliam	
DN	Don Newcombe	60.00
METS		
GC	Gary Carter	40.00
DC	Donn Clendenon	30.00
NR	Nolan Ryan/129	200.00
TS	Tom Seaver/89	100.00
RS	Ron Swoboda	
YANKEES		
YB	Yogi Berra	75.00
CC	Chris Chambliss	40.00
RJ	Reggie Jackson/123	75.00
DM	Don Mattingly	150.00
MR	Mickey Rivers	
RW	Roy White	35.00
DW	Dave Winfield/167	

2001 Upper Deck Legends of New York Shea Stadium G-U

	MT
Complete Set (1):	
Gold Edition of 50:	1.25X
SS-TSTom Seaver (100)	55.00

2001 Upper Deck Legends of New York Signed Game Jersey

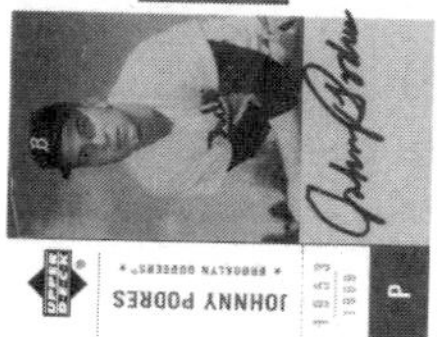

		MT
Common Autograph:		15.00
DODGERS		
CE	Carl Erskine	50.00
JG	Jim Gilliam/49	
JP	Johnny Podres/193	50.00
METS		
GF	George Foster/196	35.00
NR	Nolan Ryan/47	250.00
TS	Tom Seaver/60	
CS	Craig Swan	30.00
YANKEES		
YG	Yogi Berra/73	125.00
BD	Bucky Dent	35.00
RG	Rich Gossage/145	50.00
RG	Ron Guidry	60.00
RJ	Reggie Jackson/47	
TJ	Tommy John	35.00
DL	Don Larsen	80.00
HL	Hector Lopez/195	15.00
SL	Sparky Lyle	70.00
DM	Don Mattingly/72	125.00
PN	Phil Niekro/195	40.00
GN	Graig Nettles	50.00
JP	Joe Pepitone	40.00
WR	Willie Randolph	40.00
DR	Dave Righetti	

2001 UD Legends of New York Yankees Stadium Seat

	MT
Complete Set (1):	
YS-MMMickey Mantle	

2001 UD Legends of N.Y. Triple-Combination Signatures

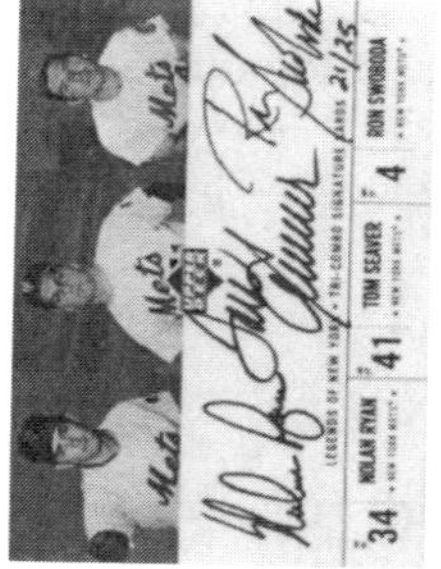

	MT
Complete Set (7):	2000.
Common Player:	150.00
S-NPEDon Newcombe, Johnny Podres, Carl Erskine	400.00
S-WMNDave Winfield, Don Mattingly, Graig Nettles	450.00
S-RSSNolan Ryan, Tom Seaver, Ron Swoboda	550.00
S-LBPDon Larsen, Yogi Berra, Joe Pepitone	250.00
S-GJGRon Guidry, Tommy John, Rich "Goose" Gossage	250.00
S-CNDChris Chambliss, Graig Nettles, Bucky Dent	150.00
S-LRGSparky Lyle, Dave Righetti, Rich "Goose" Gossage	200.00

2001 Upper Deck Legends of New York United We Stand

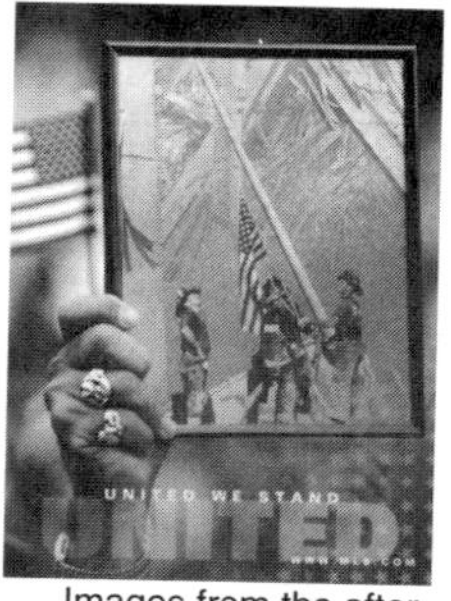

Images from the aftermath of the 9/11/01 terrorist attack on New York's World Trade Center are featured in this insert series found in the UD Legends of New York issue. Red, white and blue stars and stripes are the background on card backs for a message from Upper Deck concerning relief efforts.

	MT
Complete Set (15):	12.50
Common Card:	1.00
Inserted 1:12	
USA1United We Stand	1.00
USA2United We Stand	1.00
USA3United We Stand	1.00
USA4United We Stand	1.00
USA5United We Stand	1.00
USA6United We Stand	1.00
USA7United We Stand	1.00
USA8United We Stand	1.00
USA9United We Stand	1.00
USA10United We Stand	1.00
USA11United We Stand	1.00
USA12United We Stand	1.00
USA13United We Stand	1.00
USA14United We Stand	1.00
USA15United We Stand	1.00

2001 Upper Deck MVP

		MT
Complete Set (330):		35.00
Common Player:		.10
Pack (8):		2.00
Box (24):		45.00
1	Mo Vaughn	.10
2	Troy Percival	.10
3	Adam Kennedy	.10
4	Darin Erstad	.25
5	Tim Salmon	.10
6	Bengie Molina	.10
7	Troy Glaus	.50
8	Garret Anderson	.10
9	Ismael Valdes	.10

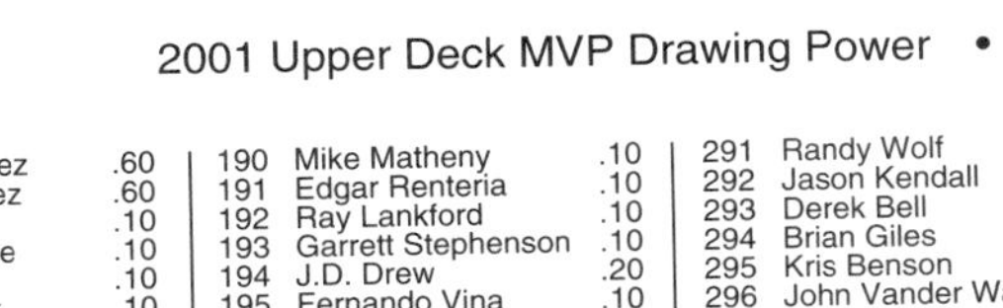

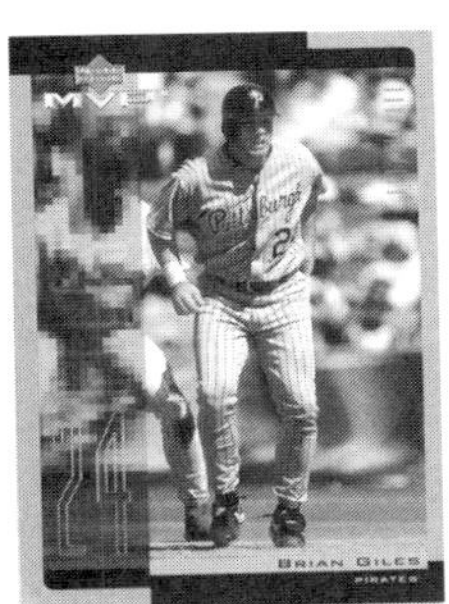

#	Player	MT
10	Glenallen Hill	.10
11	Tim Hudson	.20
12	Eric Chavez	.20
13	Johnny Damon	.10
14	Barry Zito	.40
15	Jason Giambi	.30
16	Terrence Long	.10
17	Jason Hart	.20
18	Jose Ortiz	.25
19	Miguel Tejada	.20
20	Jason Isringhausen	.10
21	Adam Piatt	.10
22	Jeremy Giambi	.10
23	Tony Batista	.10
24	Darrin Fletcher	.10
25	Mike Sirotka	.10
26	Carlos Delgado	.40
27	Billy Koch	.10
28	Shannon Stewart	.10
29	Raul Mondesi	.15
30	Brad Fullmer	.10
31	Jose Cruz Jr.	.10
32	Kelvim Escobar	.10
33	Greg Vaughn	.10
34	Aubrey Huff	.10
35	Albie Lopez	.10
36	Gerald Williams	.10
37	Ben Grieve	.20
38	John Flaherty	.10
39	Fred McGriff	.15
40	Ryan Rupe	.10
41	Travis Harper	.10
42	Steve Cox	.10
43	Roberto Alomar	.40
44	Jim Thome	.20
45	Russell Branyan	.10
46	Bartolo Colon	.10
47	Omar Vizquel	.15
48	Travis Fryman	.15
49	Kenny Lofton	.15
50	Chuck Finley	.10
51	Ellis Burks	.10
52	Eddie Taubensee	.10
53	Juan Gonzalez	.50
54	Edgar Martinez	.10
55	Aaron Sele	.10
56	John Olerud	.20
57	Jay Buhner	.10
58	Mike Cameron	.10
59	John Halama	.10
60	*Ichiro Suzuki*	10.00
61	David Bell	.10
62	Freddy Garcia	.10
63	Carlos Guillen	.10
64	Bret Boone	.10
65	Al Martin	.10
66	Cal Ripken Jr.	1.50
67	Delino DeShields	.10
68	Chris Richard	.10
69	*Sean Douglass*	.25
70	Melvin Mora	.10
71	Luis Matos	.10
72	Sidney Ponson	.10
73	Mike Bordick	.10
74	Brady Anderson	.10
75	David Segui	.10
76	Jeff Conine	.10
77	Alex Rodriguez	1.25
78	Gabe Kapler	.10
79	Ivan Rodriguez	.50
80	Rick Helling	.10
81	Kenny Rogers	.10
82	Andres Galarraga	.15
83	Rusty Greer	.10
84	Justin Thompson	.10
85	Ken Caminiti	.10
86	Rafael Palmeiro	.30
87	Ruben Mateo	.10
88	*Travis Hafner*	.40
89	Manny Ramirez	.60
90	Pedro Martinez	.60
91	Carl Everett	.10
92	Dante Bichette	.10
93	Derek Lowe	.10
94	Jason Varitek	.10
95	Nomar Garciaparra	1.25
96	David Cone	.10
97	Tomokazu Ohka	.10
98	Troy O'Leary	.10
99	Trot Nixon	.10
100	Jermaine Dye	.10
101	Joe Randa	.10
102	Jeff Suppan	.10
103	Roberto Hernandez	.10
104	Mike Sweeney	.10
105	Mac Suzuki	.10
106	Carlos Febles	.10
107	Jose Rosado	.10
108	Mark Quinn	.10
109	Carlos Beltran	.10
110	Dean Palmer	.10
111	Mitch Meluskey	.10
112	Bobby Higginson	.10
113	Brandon Inge	.10
114	Tony Clark	.15
115	Brian Moehler	.10
116	Juan Encarnacion	.10
117	Damion Easley	.10
118	Roger Cedeno	.10
119	Jeff Weaver	.10
120	Matt Lawton	.10
121	Jay Canizaro	.10
122	Eric Milton	.10
123	Corey Koskie	.10
124	Mark Redman	.10
125	Jacque Jones	.10
126	Brad Radke	.10
127	Cristian Guzman	.10
128	Joe Mays	.10
129	Denny Hocking	.10
130	Frank Thomas	.60
131	David Wells	.10
132	Ray Durham	.10
133	Paul Konerko	.10
134	Joe Crede	.10
135	Jim Parque	.10
136	Carlos Lee	.10
137	Magglio Ordonez	.20
138	Sandy Alomar Jr.	.10
139	Chris Singleton	.10
140	Jose Valentin	.10
141	Roger Clemens	.75
142	Derek Jeter	1.50
143	Orlando Hernandez	.20
144	Tino Martinez	.10
145	Bernie Williams	.40
146	Jorge Posada	.20
147	Mariano Rivera	.15
148	David Justice	.20
149	Paul O'Neill	.15
150	Mike Mussina	.25
151	*Christian Parker*	.10
152	Andy Pettite	.15
153	Alfonso Soriano	.25
154	Jeff Bagwell	.50
155	*Morgan Ensberg*	.40
156	Daryle Ward	.10
157	Craig Biggio	.20
158	Richard Hidalgo	.20
159	Shane Reynolds	.10
160	Scott Elarton	.10
161	Julio Lugo	.10
162	Moises Alou	.15
163	Lance Berkman	.20
164	Chipper Jones	1.00
165	Greg Maddux	1.00
166	Javy Lopez	.15
167	Andruw Jones	.40
168	Rafael Furcal	.25
169	Brian Jordan	.10
170	Wes Helms	.10
171	Tom Glavine	.25
172	B.J. Surhoff	.10
173	John Smoltz	.10
174	Quilvio Veras	.10
175	Rico Brogna	.10
176	Jeromy Burnitz	.10
177	Jeff D'Amico	.10
178	Geoff Jenkins	.20
179	Henry Blanco	.10
180	Mark Loretta	.10
181	Richie Sexson	.10
182	Jimmy Haynes	.10
183	Jeffrey Hammonds	.10
184	Ron Belliard	.10
185	Tyler Houston	.10
186	Mark McGwire	1.50
187	Rick Ankiel	.20
188	Darryl Kile	.10
189	Jim Edmonds	.20
190	Mike Matheny	.10
191	Edgar Renteria	.10
192	Ray Lankford	.10
193	Garrett Stephenson	.10
194	J.D. Drew	.20
195	Fernando Vina	.10
196	Dustin Hermanson	.10
197	Sammy Sosa	1.00
198	Corey Patterson	.25
199	Jon Lieber	.10
200	Kerry Wood	.20
201	Todd Hundley	.10
202	Kevin Tapani	.10
203	Rondell White	.10
204	Eric Young	.10
205	Matt Stairs	.10
206	Bill Mueller	.10
207	Randy Johnson	.50
208	Mark Grace	.25
209	Jay Bell	.10
210	Curt Schilling	.20
211	Erubiel Durazo	.10
212	Luis Gonzalez	.20
213	Steve Finley	.10
214	Matt Williams	.20
215	Reggie Sanders	.10
216	Tony Womack	.10
217	Gary Sheffield	.20
218	Kevin Brown	.15
219	Adrian Beltre	.20
220	Shawn Green	.20
221	Darren Dreifort	.10
222	Chan Ho Park	.15
223	Eric Karros	.15
224	Alex Cora	.10
225	Mark Grudzielanek	.10
226	Andy Ashby	.10
227	Vladimir Guerrero	.75
228	Tony Armas Jr.	.10
229	Fernando Tatis	.10
230	Jose Vidro	.10
231	Javier Vazquez	.10
232	Lee Stevens	.10
233	Milton Bradley	.10
234	Carl Pavano	.10
235	Peter Bergeron	.10
236	Wilton Guerrero	.10
237	Ugueth Urbina	.10
238	Barry Bonds	.75
239	Livian Hernandez	.10
240	Jeff Kent	.15
241	Pedro Feliz	.10
242	Bobby Estalella	.10
243	J.T. Snow	.10
244	Shawn Estes	.10
245	Robb Nen	.10
246	Rich Aurilia	.10
247	Russ Ortiz	.10
248	Preston Wilson	.10
249	Brad Penny	.10
250	Cliff Floyd	.10
251	A.J. Burnett	.10
252	Mike Lowell	.10
253	Luis Castillo	.10
254	Ryan Dempster	.10
255	Derrek Lee	.10
256	Charles Johnson	.10
257	Pablo Ozuna	.10
258	Antonio Alfonseca	.10
259	Mike Piazza	1.25
260	Robin Ventura	.10
261	Al Leiter	.15
262	Timoniel Perez	.10
263	Edgardo Alfonzo	.15
264	Jay Payton	.10
265	*Tsuyoshi Shinjo*	1.50
266	Todd Zeile	.10
267	Armando Benitez	.10
268	Glendon Rusch	.10
269	Rey Ordonez	.10
270	Kevin Appier	.10
271	Tony Gwynn	.75
272	Phil Nevin	.10
273	Mark Kotsay	.10
274	Ryan Klesko	.10
275	Adam Eaton	.10
276	Mike Darr	.10
277	Damian Jackson	.10
278	Woody Williams	.10
279	Chris Gomez	.10
280	Trevor Hoffman	.10
281	Xavier Nady	.25
282	Scott Rolen	.25
283	Bruce Chen	.10
284	Pat Burrell	.30
285	Mike Lieberthal	.10
286	*Brandon Duckworth*	.40
287	Travis Lee	.10
288	Bobby Abreu	.10
289	Jimmy Rollins	.10
290	Robert Person	.10
291	Randy Wolf	.10
292	Jason Kendall	.10
293	Derek Bell	.10
294	Brian Giles	.15
295	Kris Benson	.10
296	John Vander Wal	.10
297	Todd Ritchie	.10
298	Warren Morris	.10
299	Kevin Young	.10
300	Francisco Cordova	.10
301	Aramis Ramirez	.10
302	Ken Griffey Jr.	1.25
303	Pete Harnisch	.10
304	Aaron Boone	.10
305	Sean Casey	.20
306	*Jackson Melian*	.75
307	Rob Bell	.10
308	Barry Larkin	.20
309	Dmitri Young	.10
310	Danny Graves	.10
311	Pokey Reese	.10
312	Leo Estrella	.10
313	Todd Helton	.50
314	Mike Hampton	.15
315	Juan Pierre	.10
316	Brent Mayne	.10
317	Larry Walker	.25
318	Denny Neagle	.10
319	Jeff Cirillo	.10
320	Pedro Astacio	.10
321	Todd Hollandsworth	.10
322	Neifi Perez	.10
323	Ron Gant	.10
324	Todd Walker	.10
325	Alex Rodriguez CL	.60
326	Ken Griffey Jr. CL	.60
327	Mark McGwire CL	.75
328	Pedro Martinez CL	.30
329	Derek Jeter CL	.75
330	Mike Piazza CL	.60

2001 Upper Deck MVP Authentic Griffey

Inserted 1:288

		MT
AGS	Ken Griffey Jr. Auto.	125.00
AGJ	Ken Griffey Jr. jersey	50.00
AGC	Ken Griffey Jr. Cap	80.00
AGB	Ken Griffey Jr. bat	35.00
AGU	Ken Griffey Jr. uniform	40.00
AGGS	Ken Griffey Gold Auto/30	400.00
AGGJ	Ken Griffey Jr. Gold jsy/30	250.00
AGGC	Ken Griffey Gold cap/30	250.00
AGGB	Ken Griffey Gold bat/30	250.00
CGR	Ken Griffey Jr., Alex Rodriguez/100	125.00
CGS	Ken Griffey Jr., Sammy Sosa/100	180.00
CGT	Ken Griffey Jr., Frank Thomas/100	100.00

2001 Upper Deck MVP Drawing Power

	MT
Complete Set (10):	35.00
Common Player:	2.00

Inserted 1:12
DP1 Mark McGwire 6.00
DP2 Vladimir Guerrero 2.50
DP3 Manny Ramirez 2.50
DP4 Frank Thomas 2.50
DP5 Ken Griffey Jr. 5.00
DP6 Alex Rodriguez 5.00
DP7 Mike Piazza 5.00
DP8 Derek Jeter 6.00
DP9 Sammy Sosa 4.00
DP10 Todd Helton 2.00

2001 Upper Deck MVP Mantle Pinstripes Exclusive

MT
Complete Set (56): 150.00
Common Mantle: 4.00
One pack/box

2001 Upper Deck MVP Mantle Pinstripes Excl. Memorabilia

MT
Print Runs listed
MMCJ3 Mickey Mantle, Ken Griffey Jr./50 750.00
MMJ3 Mickey Mantle jsy/100 400.00

2001 Upper Deck MVP Souvenirs Two-Player Bat Combo

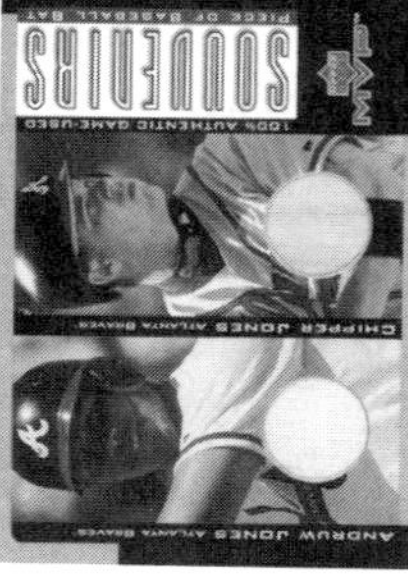

MT
Common Combo: 20.00
Inserted 1:144
B-TS Frank Thomas, Sammy Sosa 30.00
B-RR Alex Rodriguez, Ivan Rodriguez 35.00
B-TG Jim Thome, Ken Griffey Jr. 40.00
B-GS Ken Griffey Jr., Sammy Sosa 50.00
B-WA Kerry Wood, Rick Ankiel 20.00
B-3K Tony Gwynn, Cal Ripken Jr. 60.00
B-DV Carlos Delgado, Jose Vidro 20.00
B-JJ Andruw Jones, Chipper Jones 35.00
B-HR Jose Canseco, Ken Griffey Jr. 40.00
B-JF Chipper Jones, Rafael Furcal 30.00
B-OW Paul O'Neill, Bernie Williams 30.00
B-TO Frank Thomas, Magglio Ordonez 25.00
B-RM Alex Rodriguez, Edgar Martinez 30.00
B-RP Ivan Rodriguez, Rafael Palmeiro 25.00

2001 Upper Deck MVP Souvenirs Three Player Bat Combo

MT
Common Trio: 125.00
Production 25 sets
B-SGR Sammy Sosa, Ken Griffey Jr., Alex Rodriguez 350.00
B-JWO David Justice, Gerald Williams, Paul O'Neill 250.00
B-BGJ Barry Bonds, Ken Griffey Jr., Andruw Jones 350.00
B-CBG Jose Canseco, Barry Bonds, Ken Griffey Jr. 350.00
B-JGC Chipper Jones, Troy Glaus, Eric Chavez 125.00
B-JEG Andruw Jones, Jim Edmonds, Ken Griffey Jr. 275.00

2001 Upper Deck MVP Souvenirs Two-Player Bat Autograph

MT
Common Duo Auto.: 200.00
Production 25 sets
SB-RG Alex Rodriguez, Ken Griffey Jr. 1400.
SB-SG Sammy Sosa, Ken Griffey Jr. 650.00
SB-RR Alex Rodriguez, Ivan Rodriguez 650.00
SB-JG Chipper Jones, Troy Glaus 200.00
SB-TS Frank Thomas, Sammy Sosa 500.00
SB-GD Jason Giambi, Carlos Delgado 200.00
SB-3K Cal Ripken Jr., Tony Gwynn 750.00
SB-TG Frank Thomas, Jason Giambi 240.00
SB-HH Todd Helton, Mike Hampton 200.00

2001 Upper Deck MVP Souvenirs Batting Gloves

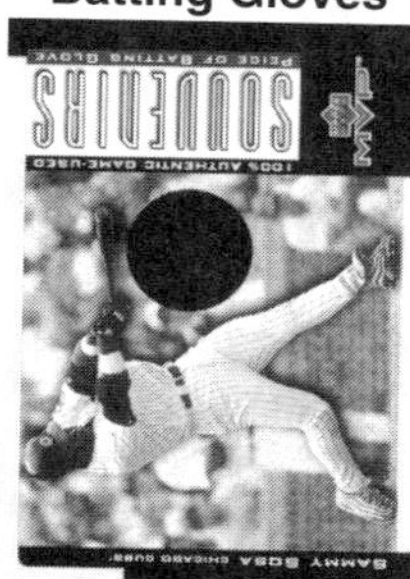

MT
Common Player:
Inserted 1:96 H 20.00
G-BB Barry Bonds 50.00
G-TrG Troy Glaus 20.00
G-JG Juan Gonzalez 25.00
G-KG Ken Griffey Jr. 40.00
G-ToG Tony Gwynn/200 40.00
G-CJ Chipper Jones 35.00
G-JL Javy Lopez 20.00
G-GM Greg Maddux/95 75.00
G-EM Edgar Martinez 20.00
G-FM Fred McGriff 20.00
G-RP Rafael Palmeiro 25.00
G-CR Cal Ripken Jr. 75.00
G-AR Alex Rodriguez 30.00
G-IR Ivan Rodriguez 25.00
G-SS Sammy Sosa 30.00
G-MT Miguel Tejada 20.00
G-FT Frank Thomas 30.00
G-MV Mo Vaughn 20.00

2001 Upper Deck MVP Souvenirs Batting Gloves Autographs

MT
Common Player: 200.00
Production 25 sets
SG-TrG Troy Glaus
SG-KG Ken Griffey Jr. 500.00
SG-ToG Tony Gwynn 250.00
SG-CJ Chipper Jones
SG-CR Cal Ripken Jr. 500.00
SG-AR Alex Rodriguez 350.00
SG-IR Ivan Rodriguez 200.00
SG-SS Sammy Sosa 400.00
SG-FT Frank Thomas 250.00

2001 Upper Deck MVP Super Tools

MT
Complete Set (20): 50.00
Common Player: 1.00
Inserted 1:6
ST1 Ken Griffey Jr. 5.00
ST2 Carlos Delgado 1.50
ST3 Alex Rodriguez 5.00
ST4 Troy Glaus 2.00
ST5 Jeff Bagwell 2.00
ST6 Ichiro Suzuki 12.00
ST7 Derek Jeter 6.00
ST8 Jim Edmonds 1.00
ST9 Vladimir Guerrero 2.50
ST10 Jason Giambi 1.00
ST11 Todd Helton 2.00
ST12 Cal Ripken Jr. 6.00
ST13 Barry Bonds 2.00
ST14 Nomar Garciaparra 5.00
ST15 Randy Johnson 2.00
ST16 Jermaine Dye 1.00
ST17 Andruw Jones 1.50
ST18 Ivan Rodriguez 2.00
ST19 Sammy Sosa 4.00
ST20 Pedro Martinez 2.50

2001 Upper Deck Ovation

MT
Complete Set (90): 300.00
Common Player: .20
Common WP (61-90): 6.00
WP Production 2,000
Pack (5): 4.75
Box (20): 90.00
1 Troy Glaus 1.00
2 Darin Erstad .50
3 Jason Giambi .50
4 Tim Hudson .30
5 Eric Chavez .30
6 Carlos Delgado .75
7 David Wells .20
8 Greg Vaughn .20
9 Omar Vizquel .20
10 Jim Thome .50
11 Roberto Alomar .75
12 John Olerud .30
13 Edgar Martinez .20
14 Cal Ripken Jr. 3.00
15 Alex Rodriguez 2.50
16 Ivan Rodriguez 1.00
17 Manny Ramirez 1.00
18 Nomar Garciaparra 2.50
19 Pedro Martinez 1.25
20 Jermaine Dye .20
21 Juan Gonzalez 1.00
22 Matt Lawton .20
23 Frank Thomas 1.25
24 Maggio Ordonez .20
25 Bernie Williams .75
26 Derek Jeter 3.00
27 Roger Clemens 1.25
28 Jeff Bagwell 1.00
29 Richard Hidalgo .20
30 Chipper Jones 2.00
31 Greg Maddux 2.00
32 Andruw Jones .75
33 Jeromy Burnitz .20
34 Mark McGwire 3.00
35 Jim Edmonds .30
36 Sammy Sosa 2.00
37 Kerry Wood .20
38 Randy Johnson 1.00
39 Steve Finley .20
40 Gary Sheffield .30
41 Kevin Brown .20
42 Shawn Green .30
43 Vladimir Guerrero 1.25
44 Jose Vidro .20
45 Barry Bonds 1.00
46 Jeff Kent .20
47 Preston Wilson .20
48 Luis Castillo .20
49 Mike Piazza 2.50
50 Edgardo Alfonzo .30
51 Tony Gwynn 1.25

52	Ryan Klesko	.20
53	Scott Rolen	.50
54	Bob Abreu	.20
55	Jason Kendall	.20
56	Brian Giles	.30
57	Ken Griffey Jr.	2.50
58	Barry Larkin	.40
59	Todd Helton	1.00
60	Mike Hampton	.20
61	Corey Patterson (World Premiere)	10.00
62	Timoniel Perez (World Premiere)	12.00
63	Toby Hall (World Premiere)	8.00
64	Brandon Inge (World Premiere)	8.00
65	Joe Crede (World Premiere)	12.00
66	Xavier Nady (World Premiere)	15.00
67	*Adam Pettyjohn* (World Premiere)	12.00
68	Keith Ginter (World Premiere)	10.00
69	Brian Cole (World Premiere)	8.00
70	*Tyler Walker* (World Premiere)	12.00
71	*Juan Uribe* (World Premiere)	10.00
72	Alex Hernandez (World Premiere)	10.00
73	Leo Estrella (World Premiere)	8.00
74	Joey Nation (World Premiere)	8.00
75	Aubrey Huff (World Premiere)	8.00
76	*Ichiro Suzuki* (World Premiere)	90.00
77	Jay Spurgeon (World Premiere)	6.00
78	Sun-Woo Kim (World Premiere)	6.00
79	Pedro Feliz (World Premiere)	8.00
80	Pablo Ozuna (World Premiere)	6.00
81	Hiram Bocachica (World Premiere)	6.00
82	Brad Wilkerson (World Premiere)	8.00
83	Rocky Biddle (World ,Premiere)	10.00
84	Aaron McNeal (World Premiere)	6.00
85	Adam Bernero (World Premiere)	6.00
86	Danys Baez (World Premiere)	6.00
87	Dee Brown (World Premiere)	8.00
88	Jimmy Rollins (World Premiere)	10.00
89	Jason Hart (World Premiere)	25.00
90	Ross Gload (World Premiere)	10.00

2001 Upper Deck Ovation A Piece of History

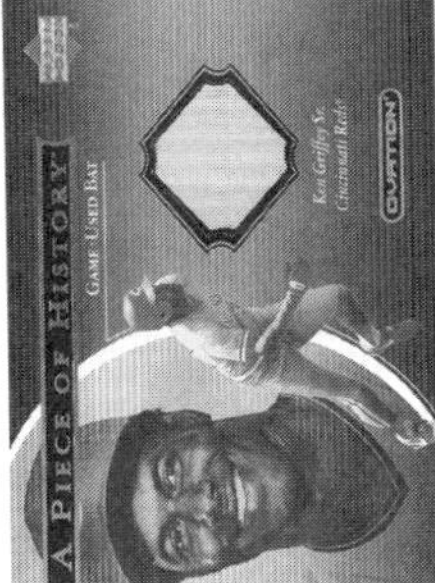

	MT
Common Player:	15.00
Inserted 1:40	

RA	Rick Ankiel	20.00
JB	Johnny Bench	60.00
BB	Barry Bonds	30.00
KB	Kevin Brown	15.00
JC	Jose Canseco	25.00
RC	Roger Clemens	40.00
DC	David Cone	20.00
CD	Carlos Delgado	20.00
JD	Joe DiMaggio	150.00
DD	Don Drysdale SP	60.00
DE	Darin Erstad	25.00
RF	Rollie Fingers SP	25.00
CF	Carlton Fisk	40.00
RF	Rafael Furcal	15.00
TrG	Troy Glaus	25.00
TG	Tom Glavine	20.00
SG	Shawn Green	15.00
KG	Ken Griffey Jr.	50.00
KGs	Ken Griffey Sr.	20.00
MH	Mike Hampton	15.00
RJ	Randy Johnson	25.00
AJ	Andruw Jones	20.00
CJ	Chipper Jones	30.00
GM	Greg Maddux	25.00
MM	Mickey Mantle	200.00
JP	Jim Palmer	40.00
CR	Cal Ripken Jr.	60.00
BR	Brooks Robinson	40.00
AR	Alex Rodriguez	40.00
IR	Ivan Rodriguez	20.00
NR	Nolan Ryan/SP	200.00
TS	Tom Seaver	60.00
GS	Gary Sheffield	15.00
OS	Ozzie Smith SP	60.00
SS	Sammy Sosa	35.00
FT	Frank Thomas	25.00
BW	Bernie Williams	25.00
MW	Matt Williams	15.00
EW	Early Wynn	25.00

2001 Upper Deck Ovation A Piece of History Autograph

MT

Common Player:
VALUES UNDETERMINED

BB	Barry Bonds/25
CD	Carlos Delgado/25
KG	Ken Griffey Jr/30
CJ	Chipper Jones/10
AR	Alex Rodriguez/3
IR	Ivan Rodriguez/7
FT	Frank Thomas/35

2001 Upper Deck Ovation Curtain Calls

		MT
Complete Set (10):		15.00
Common Player:		.75
Inserted 1:7		
1	Sammy Sosa	2.50
2	Darin Erstad	.75
3	Barry Bonds	1.50
4	Todd Helton	1.50
5	Mike Piazza	3.00
6	Ken Griffey Jr.	3.00
7	Nomar Garciaparra	3.00
8	Carlos Delgado	1.00
9	Jason Giambi	.75
10	Alex Rodriguez	3.00

2001 Upper Deck Ovation DiMaggio Pinstripes Exclusive

	MT
Complete Set (56):	150.00
Common DiMaggio:	4.00
One pack/box	

2001 Upper Deck Ovation DiMaggio Pinstripes Memorabilia

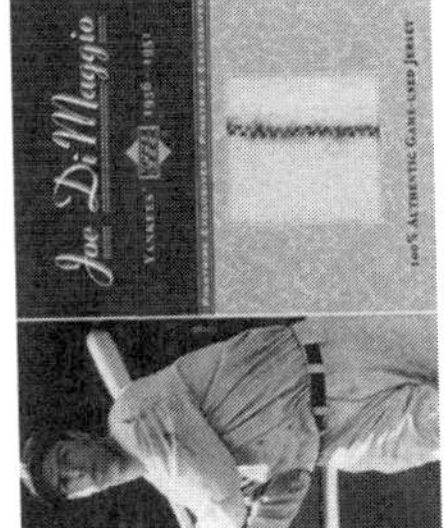

		MT
Print Runs listed:		150.00
JDB	Joe DiMaggio bat/100	250.00
JDBC	Joe DiMaggio bat/cut/5	
JDCJ	Joe DiMaggio, Mickey Mantle jsy/50	1000.
JDJ	Joe DiMaggio jsy/100	300.00

2001 Upper Deck Ovation Lead Performers

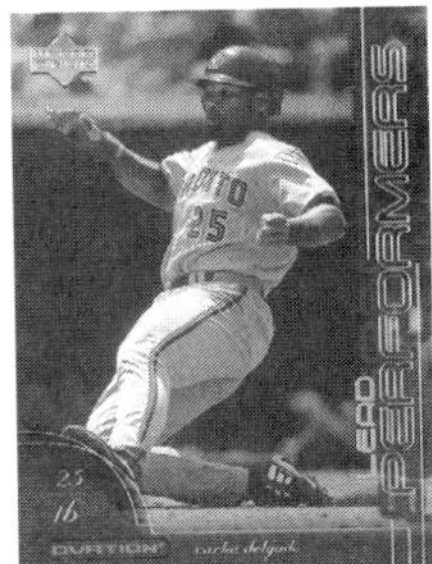

		MT
Complete Set (11):		35.00
Common Player:		1.50
Inserted 1:12		
1	Mark McGwire	6.00
2	Derek Jeter	6.00
3	Alex Rodriguez	5.00
4	Frank Thomas	2.50
5	Sammy Sosa	4.00
6	Mike Piazza	5.00
7	Vladimir Guerrero	2.50
8	Pedro Martinez	2.50
9	Carlos Delgado	1.50
10	Ken Griffey Jr.	5.00
11	Jeff Bagwell	2.00

2001 Upper Deck Ovation Superstar Theatre

		MT
Complete Set (11):		40.00
Common Player:		1.00
Inserted 1:12		
1	Nomar Garciaparra	5.00
2	Ken Griffey Jr.	5.00
3	Frank Thomas	2.50
4	Derek Jeter	6.00
5	Mike Piazza	5.00
6	Sammy Sosa	4.00
7	Barry Bonds	2.50
8	Alex Rodriguez	5.00
9	Todd Helton	2.00
10	Mark McGwire	6.00
11	Jason Giambi	1.00

2001 Upper Deck Prospect Premieres

		MT
Complete Set (90):		25.00
Common Player:		.25
Common Auto. SP (91-102):		25.00
Auto. Production 1,000		
Pack (4):		2.75
Box (18):		45.00
1	*Jeff Mathis*	.50
2	*Jake Woods*	.25
3	*Dallas McPherson*	.50
4	*Steven Shell*	.25
5	*Ryan Budde*	.25
6	*Kirk Saarloos*	.50
7	*Ryan Stegall*	.25
8	*Bobby Crosby*	.50
9	*J.T. Stotts*	.25
10	*Neal Cotts*	.25
11	*Jeremy Bonderman*	.25
12	*Brandon League*	.40
13	*Tyrell Godwin*	.25
14	*Gabe Gross*	1.50

15	*Chris Neylan*	.25
16	*Michael Rouse*	.50
17	*MaCay McBride*	.75
18	*Josh Burrus*	.25
19	*Adam Stern*	.25
20	*Richard Lewis*	.50
21	*Cole Barthel*	.50
22	*Mike Jones*	.25
23	*J.J. Hardy*	.25
24	*Jon Steitz*	.25
25	*Justin Pope*	.75
26	*Dan Haren*	.25
27	*Andy Sisco*	.25
28	*Ryan Theriot*	.25
29	*Ricky Nolasco*	.25
30	*Jon Switzer*	.25
31	*Justin Wechsler*	.25
32	*Mike Gosling*	.25
33	*Scott Hairston*	.75
34	*Brian Pilkington*	.25
35	*Kole Strayhorn*	.50
36	*David Taylor*	.25
37	*Donald Levinski*	.25
38	*Mike Hinckley*	.25
39	*Nick Long*	.25
40	*Brad Hennessey*	.25
41	*Noah Lowry*	.25
42	*Josh Cram*	.25
43	*Jesse Foppert*	1.00
44	*Julian Benavidez*	.75
45	*Daniel Denham*	1.00
46	*Travis Foley*	.75
47	*Mike Conroy*	.25
48	*Jake Dittler*	.25
49	*Rene Rivera*	.25
50	*John Cole*	.25
51	*Lazaro Abreu*	.25
52	*David Wright*	.50
53	*Aaron Heilman*	.50
54	*Lenny DiNardo*	.25
55	*Alhaji Turay*	.25
56	*Chris Smith*	.75
57	*Rommie Lewis*	.25
58	*Bryan Bass*	.75
59	*David Crouthers*	.25
60	*Josh Barfield*	.50
61	*Jacob Peavey*	.50
62	*Ryan Howard*	.25
63	*Gavin Floyd*	1.50
64	*Mike Floyd*	.25
65	*Stefan Bailie*	.25
66	*Jon DeVries*	.25
67	*Steve Kelly*	.50
68	*Alan Moye*	.25
69	*Justin Gillman*	.25
70	*Jayson Nix*	.25
71	*John Draper*	.25
72	*Kenny Baugh*	.75
73	*Michael Woods*	.25
74	*Preston Larrison*	.25
75	*Matt Coenen*	.25
76	*Scott Tyler*	.25
77	*Jose Morales*	.25
78	*Corwin Malone*	1.00
79	*Dennis Ulacia*	.25
80	*Andy Gonzalez*	.25
81	*Kris Honel*	.50
82	*Wyatt Allen*	.25
83	*Ryan Wing*	.25
84	*Sean Henn*	.75
85	*John-Ford Griffin*	1.00
86	*Bronson Sardinha*	1.50
87	*Jon Skaggs*	.25
88	*Shelley Duncan*	.40
89	*Jason Arnold*	.75
90	*Aaron Rifkin*	1.00
91	*Colt Griffin*	25.00
92	*J.D. Martin*	30.00
93	*Justin Wayne*	30.00
94	*John VanBenschotten*	25.00
95	*Chris Burke*	30.00
96	*Casey Kotchman*	60.00
97	*Michael Garciaparra*	40.00
98	*Jake Gautreau*	25.00
99	*Jerome Williams*	25.00
100	*Greg Nash*	25.00
101	*Joe Borchard*	80.00
102	*Mark Prior*	125.00

2001 Upper Deck Prospect Premieres HOB Bat

		MT
Common Player:		8.00
Inserted 1:18		
DB	Don Baylor	8.00
WB	Wade Boggs	15.00
BB	Bill Buckner	8.00
GC	Gary Carter	10.00
DE	Dwight Evans	8.00
SG	Steve Garvey	10.00
KiG	Kirk Gibson	8.00
KeG	Ken Griffey Sr.	8.00
RJ	Reggie Jackson	20.00
DL	Davey Lopes	8.00
FL	Fred Lynn	8.00
BM	Bill Madlock	8.00
TM	Tim McCarver	10.00
JM	Joe Morgan	10.00
MM	Manny Mota	8.00
EM	Eddie Murray	10.00
AO	Al Oliver	8.00
DP	Dave Parker	8.00
TP	Tony Perez	10.00
KP	Kirby Puckett	25.00
OS	Ozzie Smith	15.00
DW	Dave Winfield	15.00

2001 Upper Deck Prospect Premieres HOB Bat Autograph

MT

Complete Set (13):
Common Player:
SB-DBDon Baylor
SB-WBWade Boggs
SB-BBBill Buckner
SB-GCGary Carter
SB-SGSteve Garvey
SB-KiGKirk Gibson
SB-KeGKen Griffey Sr.
SB-JMJoe Morgan
SB-DPDave Parker
SB-TPTony Perez
SB-KPKirby Puckett
SB-OSOzzie Smith
SB-DWDave Winfield

2001 UD Prospect Premieres HOB Dual Combo Jersey

		MT
Common Duo:		15.00
Inserted 1:144		
BH	Bryan Bass, J.J. Hardy	15.00
DG	Shelley Duncan, Tyrell Godwin	15.00
GS	Steve Garvey, Reggie Smith	20.00
HB	Aaron Heilman, Jeremy Bonderman	15.00
JJ	Michael Jordan, Michael Jordan	100.00
SG	Jon Switzer, Mike Gosling	15.00
WP	Dave Winfield, Kirby Puckett	50.00

2001 UD Prospect Premieres HOB Dual Combo Jersey Auto

MT

VALUES UNDETERMINED
SJ-BHBryan Bass, J.J. Hardy
SJ-BKDewon Brazelton, Josh Karp
SJ-BCChris Burke, Bubba Crosby
SJ-GSSteve Garvey, Reggie Smith
SJ-HBAaron Heilman, Jeremy Bonderman
SJ-JJMichael Jordan, Michael Jordan
SJ-MGJoe Morgan, Ken Griffey Sr.
SJ-WPDave Winfield, Kirby Puckett

2001 UD Prospect Premieres HOB Triple Combo Jersey

		MT
Common Card:		
Inserted 1:144		
BKH	Bobby Crosby, Michael Garciaparra, Bronson Sardinha	40.00
BBC	Chris Burke, Bryan Bass, Bubba Crosby	15.00
GGH	Jake Gautreau, Tyrell Godwin, Aaron Heilman	15.00
GMS	Colt Griffin, J.D. Martin, Jon Switzer	15.00
GKB	Gabe Gross, C Kotchmann, Kenny Baugh	20.00
JMD	Michael Jordan, Mickey Mantle, Joe DiMaggio	350.00
JPW	Michael Jordan, Kirby Puckett, Dave Winfield	100.00
MMD	Roger Maris, Mickey Mantle, Joe DiMaggio	700.00
PWC	Kirby Puckett, Dave Winfield, Gary Carter	
VPJ	John VanBenschotten, Mark Prior, Mike Jones	15.00

2001 Upper Deck Prospect Premieres MJ Grandslam Bat

		MT
Complete Set (5):		150.00
Common Card:		30.00
MJ1	Michael Jordan	30.00
MJ2	Michael Jordan	30.00
MJ3	Michael Jordan	30.00
MJ4	Michael Jordan	30.00
MJ5	Michael Jordan (White Sox)	60.00

2001 Upper Deck Prospect Premieres "Tribute to 42"

		MT
Common Robinson:		50.00
Inserted 1:750		
42-B	Jackie Robinson bat	50.00
42-J	Jackie Robinson jersey	90.00
42-C	Jackie Robinson cut	500.00
42-BC	Jackie Robinson bat/cut	
42-JC	Jackie Robinson jsy/cut	
42-B	Jackie Robinson bat/42	150.00
42-J	Jackie Robinson jsy/42	150.00

2001 Upper Deck Pros & Prospects

		MT
Complete Set (141):		
Common Player:		.25
Common (91-135):		6.00
Production 1,250		
Common (136-141):		25.00
Production 500		
Pack (5):		4.00
Box (24):		90.00
1	Troy Glaus	.50
2	Darin Erstad	.40
3	Tim Hudson	.40
4	Jason Giambi	.50
5	Jermaine Dye	.25
6	Barry Zito	.25
7	Carlos Delgado	.50
8	Shannon Stewart	.25
9	Raul Mondesi	.25
10	Greg Vaughn	.25
11	Ben Grieve	.25
12	Roberto Alomar	.60
13	Juan Gonzalez	.75
14	Jim Thome	.50
15	C.C. Sabathia	.25

16	Edgar Martinez	.25
17	Kazuhiro Sasaki	.25
18	Aaron Sele	.25
19	John Olerud	.40
20	Cal Ripken Jr.	3.00
21	Rafael Palmeiro	.50
22	Ivan Rodriguez	.75
23	Alex Rodriguez	2.00
24	Manny Ramirez	.75
25	Pedro Martinez	.75
26	Carl Everett	.25
27	Nomar Garciaparra	2.00
28	Neifi Perez	.25
29	Mike Sweeney	.25
30	Bobby Higginson	.25
31	Tony Clark	.25
32	Doug Mientkiewicz	.25
33	Cristian Guzman	.25
34	Brad Radke	.25
35	Magglio Ordonez	.25
36	Carlos Lee	.25
37	Frank Thomas	.75
38	Roger Clemens	1.00
39	Bernie Williams	.50
40	Derek Jeter	3.00
41	Tino Martinez	.30
42	Wade Miller	.25
43	Jeff Bagwell	.75
44	Lance Berkman	.25
45	Richard Hidalgo	.25
46	Greg Maddux	1.50
47	Andruw Jones	.50
48	Chipper Jones	1.50
49	Rafael Furcal	.25
50	Jeromy Burnitz	.25
51	Geoff Jenkins	.25
52	Ben Sheets	.25
53	Mark McGwire	2.50
54	Jim Edmonds	.25
55	J.D. Drew	.40
56	Fred McGriff	.30
57	Sammy Sosa	1.50
58	Kerry Wood	.40
59	Randy Johnson	.75
60	Luis Gonzalez	.50
61	Curt Schilling	.40
62	Kevin Brown	.25
63	Shawn Green	.25
64	Gary Sheffield	.25
65	Vladimir Guerrero	.75
66	Jose Vidro	.25
67	Barry Bonds	1.50
68	Jeff Kent	.25
69	Rich Aurilia	.25
70	Preston Wilson	.25
71	Charles Johnson	.25
72	Cliff Floyd	.25
73	Mike Piazza	2.00
74	Al Leiter	.40
75	Matt Lawton	.25
76	Tony Gwynn	.75
77	Ryan Klesko	.25
78	Phil Nevin	.25
79	Scott Rolen	.40
80	Pat Burrell	.40
81	Jimmy Rollins	.25
82	Jason Kendall	.25
83	Brian Giles	.25
84	Aramis Ramirez	.25
85	Ken Griffey Jr.	2.00
86	Barry Larkin	.40
87	Sean Casey	.40
88	Larry Walker	.40
89	Todd Helton	.75
90	Mike Hampton	.25
91	*Juan Cruz*	12.00
92	*Brian Lawrence*	8.00
93	*Brandon Lyon*	6.00
94	*Adrian Hernandez*	6.00
95	*Jose Mieses*	6.00
96	Juan Uribe	8.00
97	*Morgan Ensberg*	8.00
98	*Wilson Betemit*	15.00
99	*Ryan Freel*	6.00
100	*Jack Wilson*	6.00
101	*Cesar Crespo*	6.00
102	*Bret Prinz*	6.00
103	*Horacio Ramirez*	6.00
104	*Elpidio Guzman*	6.00
105	*Josh Towers*	10.00
106	*Brandon Duckworth*	10.00
107	*Esix Snead*	6.00
108	*Billy Sylvester*	6.00
109	*Alexis Gomez*	6.00
110	*Johnny Estrada*	8.00
111	*Joe Kennedy*	6.00
112	*Travis Hafner*	6.00
113	*Martin Vargas*	6.00
114	*Jay Gibbons*	10.00
115	*Andres Torres*	6.00
116	*Sean Douglass*	6.00
117	*Juan Diaz*	6.00
118	*Greg Miller*	6.00
119	*Carlos Valderrama*	6.00
120	*William Ortega*	6.00
121	*Josh Fogg*	10.00
122	*Wilken Ruan*	6.00
123	*Kris Keller*	6.00
124	*Erick Almonte*	6.00
125	*Ricardo Rodriguez*	6.00
126	*Grant Balfour*	6.00
127	*Nick Maness*	6.00
128	*Jeremy Owens*	6.00
129	*Doug Nickle*	6.00
130	*Bert Snow*	6.00
131	*Jason Smith*	6.00
132	*Henry Mateo*	6.00
133	*Mike Penney*	6.00
134	*Bud Smith*	20.00
135	*Junior Spivey*	6.00
136	*Ichiro Suzuki*	150.00
137	*Albert Pujols*	80.00
138	*Mark Teixeira*	80.00
139	*Dewon Brazelton*	25.00
140	*Mark Prior*	90.00
141	*Tsuyoshi Shinjo*	40.00

2001 UD Pros & Prospects Franchise Building Blocks

		MT
Complete Set (30):		40.00
Common Player:		1.00
Inserted 1:6		
F1	Darin Erstad, Elpidio Guzman	1.00
F2	Jason Giambi, Jason Hart	1.00
F3	Carlos Delgado, Vernon Wells	1.00
F4	Greg Vaughn, Aubrey Huff	1.00
F5	Jim Thome, C.C. Sabathia	1.00
F6	Edgar Martinez, Ichiro Suzuki	6.00
F7	Cal Ripken Jr., Josh Towers	4.00
F8	Ivan Rodriguez, Carlos Pena	1.00
F9	Nomar Garciaparra, Dernell Stenson	2.50
F10	Mike Sweeney, Dee Brown	1.00
F11	Bobby Higginson, Brandon Inge	1.00
F12	Brad Radke, Adam Johnson	1.00
F13	Frank Thomas, Joe Crede	1.50
F14	Derek Jeter, Nick Johnson	4.00
F15	Jeff Bagwell, Morgan Ensberg	1.50
F16	Chipper Jones, Wilson Betemit	2.00
F17	Jeromy Burnitz, Ben Sheets	1.00
F18	Mark McGwire, Albert Pujols	4.00
F19	Sammy Sosa, Corey Patterson	2.00
F20	Luis Gonzalez, Jack Cust	1.00
F21	Kevin Brown, Luke Prokopec	1.00
F22	Vladimir Guerrero, Wilken Ruan	1.50
F23	Barry Bonds, Carlos Valderrama	2.00
F24	Preston Wilson, Abraham Nunez	1.00
F25	Mike Piazza, Alex Escobar	3.00
F26	Tony Gwynn, Xavier Nady	1.50
F27	Scott Rolen, Jimmy Rollins	1.00
F28	Jason Kendall, Jack Wilson	1.00
F29	Ken Griffey Jr., Adam Dunn	3.00
F30	Todd Helton, Juan Uribe	1.50

2001 Upper Deck Pros & Prospects Ichiro World Tour

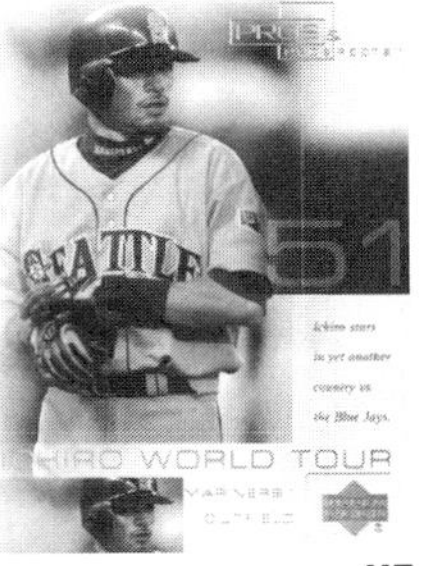

		MT
Complete Set (15):		70.00
Common Ichiro:		5.00
Inserted 1:12		
WT1	Ichiro Suzuki	5.00
WT2	Ichiro Suzuki	5.00
WT3	Ichiro Suzuki	5.00
WT4	Ichiro Suzuki	5.00
WT5	Ichiro Suzuki	5.00
WT6	Ichiro Suzuki	5.00
WT7	Ichiro Suzuki	5.00
WT8	Ichiro Suzuki	5.00
WT9	Ichiro Suzuki	5.00
WT10	Ichiro Suzuki	5.00
WT11	Ichiro Suzuki	5.00
WT12	Ichiro Suzuki	5.00
WT13	Ichiro Suzuki	5.00
WT14	Ichiro Suzuki	5.00
WT15	Ichiro Suzuki	5.00

2001 Upper Deck Pros & Prospects Pros & Prospects Bats

		MT
Common Player:		10.00
Inserted 1:24		
Golds:		3-5X
Production 25 sets		
WI	Bernie Williams, Ichiro Suzuki	75.00
RG	Manny Ramirez, Juan Gonzalez	15.00
RP	Ivan Rodriguez, Mike Piazza	20.00
BT	Jeff Bagwell, Frank Thomas	15.00
GBo	Ken Griffey Jr., Barry Bonds	40.00
SG	Sammy Sosa, Luis Gonzalez	20.00
KA	Jeff Kent, Roberto Alomar	10.00
RF	Alex Rodriguez, Rafael Furcal	20.00
PT	Rafael Palmeiro, Jim Thome	10.00
JP	Chipper Jones, Albert Pujols	35.00
GBu	Shawn Green, Jeromy Burnitz	10.00
JL	Andruw Jones, Kenny Lofton	10.00
MJ	Greg Maddux, Randy Johnson	20.00

2001 Upper Deck Pros & Prospects Pros & Legends Bat

		MT
Common Card:		20.00
Inserted 1:216		
Gold:		3-5X
Production 25 sets		
RF	Manny Ramirez, Carlton Fisk	25.00
BY	Jeromy Burnitz, Robin Yount	20.00
WJ	Bernie Williams, Reggie Jackson	25.00
RG	Cal Ripken Jr., Tony Gwynn	50.00

2001 Upper Deck Pros & Prospects Specialty Jersey

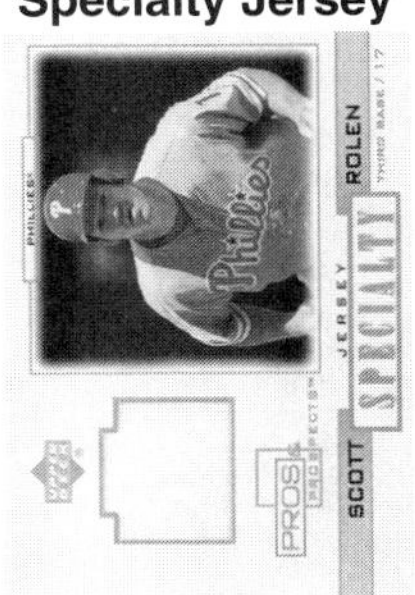

		MT
Common Player:		8.00
Inserted 1:24		
Golds:		3-5X
Production 25 sets		
RA	Roberto Alomar	8.00
BB	Barry Bonds	25.00
JE	Jim Edmonds	8.00
JG	Juan Gonzalez	8.00
SG	Shawn Green	8.00
TG	Tony Gwynn	12.00
RJ	Randy Johnson	15.00
RP	Rafael Palmeiro	8.00
CR	Cal Ripken Jr.	40.00
AR	Alex Rodriguez	20.00
SR	Scott Rolen	8.00
SS	Sammy Sosa	25.00
I	Ichiro	100.00
JT	Jim Thome	8.00
LW	Larry Walker	8.00

2001 Upper Deck Pros & Prospects Then & Now Jersey

		MT
Common Player:		10.00
Inserted 1:24		
Golds:		3-5X
Production 25 sets		
RA	Rick Ankiel	10.00
BB	Barry Bonds	40.00
KB	Kevin Brown	10.00
RC	Roger Clemens	25.00
JE	Jim Edmonds	10.00
FG	Freddy Garcia	10.00
JGi	Jason Giambi	20.00
JGo	Juan Gonzalez	20.00
KG	Ken Griffey Jr.	40.00
RJ	Randy Johnson	15.00
GM	Greg Maddux	25.00
PM	Pedro Martinez	20.00
XN	Xavier Nady	10.00
PN	Phil Nevin	10.00
MP	Mike Piazza	35.00
MR	Manny Ramirez	20.00
AR	Alex Rodriguez	25.00
CS	Curt Schilling	25.00
GS	Gary Sheffield	10.00
RV	Robin Ventura	10.00

2001 UD Pros & Prospects Then & Now Combo Jersey

		MT
NR	Nolan Ryan	125.00

2001 Upper Deck Rookie Update

		MT
Common Player:		.25
Common Rookie:		
Sweet Spot		
Common SP (91-150):		6.00
Production 1,500		
91	Garret Anderson	.25
92	Jermaine Dye	.25
93	Shannon Stewart	.25
94	Ben Grieve	.25
95	Juan Gonzalez	1.00
96	Bret Boone	.25
97	Tony Batista	.25
98	Rafael Palmeiro	.60
99	Carl Everett	.25
100	Mike Sweeney	.25
101	Tony Clark	.25
102	Doug Mientkiewicz	.25
103	Jose Canseco	.50
104	Mike Mussina	.75
105	Lance Berkman	.40
106	Andruw Jones	.60
107	Geoff Jenkins	.40
108	Matt Morris	.25
109	Fred McGriff	.40
110	Luis Gonzalez	.75
111	Kevin Brown	.25
112	Tony Armas Jr.	.25
113	John Vander Wal	.25
114	Cliff Floyd	.25
115	Matt Lawton	.25
116	Phil Nevin	.25
117	Pat Burrell	.50
118	Aramis Ramirez	.25
119	Sean Casey	.40
120	Larry Walker	.50
121	*Albert Pujols*	50.00
122	*Johnny Estrada*	8.00
123	*Wilson Betemit*	20.00
124	*Adrian Hernandez*	8.00
125	*Morgan Ensberg*	8.00
126	*Horacio Ramirez*	6.00
127	*Josh Towers*	8.00
128	*Juan Uribe*	6.00
129	*Wilken Ruan*	8.00
130	*Andres Torres*	6.00
131	*Brian Lawrence*	8.00
132	*Ryan Freel*	6.00
133	*Brandon Duckworth*	12.00
134	*Juan Diaz*	6.00
135	*Rafael Soriano*	8.00
136	*Ricardo Rodriguez*	6.00
137	*Bud Smith*	15.00
138	*Mark Teixeira*	30.00
139	*Mark Prior*	40.00
140	*Jackson Melian*	8.00
141	*Dewon Brazelton*	10.00
142	*Greg Miller*	6.00
143	*Billy Sylvester*	6.00
144	*Elpidio Guzman*	6.00
145	*Jack Wilson*	6.00
146	*Jose Mieses*	6.00
147	*Brandon Lyon*	6.00
148	*Tsuyoshi Shinjo*	15.00
149	*Juan Cruz*	20.00
150	*Jay Gibbons*	12.00
SPx		
Common (181-205)		6.00
Production 1,500		
Cards (206-210) Autographed		
151	Garrett Anderson	.25
152	Jermaine Dye	.25
153	Shannon Stewart	.25
154	Toby Hall	.25
155	C.C. Sabathia	.25
156	Bret Boone	.25
157	Tony Batista	.25
158	Gabe Kapler	.25
159	Carl Everett	.25
160	Mike Sweeney	.25
161	Dean Palmer	.25
162	Doug Mientkiewicz	.25
163	Carlos Lee	.25
164	Mike Mussina	.75
165	Lance Berkman	.40
166	Ken Caminiti	.25
167	Ben Sheets	.40
168	Matt Morris	.25
169	Fred McGriff	.40
170	Curt Schilling	.40
171	Paul LoDuca	.25
172	Javier Vazquez	.25
173	Rich Aurilia	.25
174	A.J. Burnett	.25
175	Al Leiter	.40
176	Mark Kotsay	.25
177	Jimmy Rollins	.25
178	Aramis Ramirez	.25
179	Aaron Boone	.25
180	Jeff Cirillo	.25
181	*Johnny Estrada*	50.00
182	*Dave Williams*	8.00
183	*Donaldo Mendez*	6.00
184	*Junior Spivey*	6.00
185	*Jay Gibbons*	12.00
186	*Kyle Lohse*	8.00
187	*Willie Harris*	8.00
188	*Juan Cruz*	20.00
189	*Joe Kennedy*	8.00
190	*Duaner Sanchez*	8.00
191	*Jorge Julio*	6.00
192	*Cesar Crespo*	8.00
193	*Casey Fossum*	8.00
194	*Brian Roberts*	10.00
195	*Troy Mattes*	6.00
196	*Rob Mackowiak*	6.00
197	*Tsuyoshi Shinjo*	15.00
198	*Nick Punto*	6.00
199	*Wilmy Caceres*	6.00
200	*Jeremy Affeldt*	8.00
201	*Bret Prinz*	8.00
202	*Delvin James*	8.00
203	*Luis Pineda*	8.00
204	*Matt White*	8.00
205	*Brandon Knight*	10.00
206	*Albert Pujols*	120.00
207	*Mark Teixeira*	75.00
208	*Mark Prior*	140.00
209	*Dewon Brazelton*	20.00
210	*Bud Smith*	8.00
SP Authentic		
Common (181-240):		6.00
Production 1,500		
Pack (4):		5.00
Box (18):		85.00
181	Garrett Anderson	.25
182	Jermaine Dye	.25
183	Shannon Stewart	.25
184	Ben Grieve	.25
185	Ellis Burks	.25
186	John Olerud	.50
187	Tony Batista	.25
188	Ruben Sierra	.25
189	Carl Everett	.25
190	Neifi Perez	.25
191	Tony Clark	.25
192	Doug Mientkiewicz	.25
193	Carlos Lee	.25
194	Jorge Posada	.50
195	Lance Berkman	.40
196	Ken Caminiti	.25
197	Ben Sheets	.50
198	Matt Morris	.25
199	Fred McGriff	.40
200	Mark Grace	.50
201	Paul LoDuca	.25
202	Tony Armas, Jr.	.25
203	Andres Galarraga	.40
204	Cliff Floyd	.25
205	Matt Lawton	.25
206	Ryan Klesko	.25
207	Jimmy Rollins	.25
208	Aramis Ramirez	.25
209	Aaron Boone	.25
210	Jose Ortiz	.25
211	*Mark Prior*	55.00
212	*Mark Teixeira*	30.00
213	*Bud Smith*	6.00
214	*Wilmy Caceres*	6.00
215	*Dave Williams*	6.00
216	*Delvin James*	10.00
217	*Endy Chavez*	8.00
218	*Doug Nickle*	10.00
219	*Bret Prinz*	8.00
220	*Troy Mattes*	8.00
221	*Duaner Sanchez*	6.00
222	*Dewon Brazelton*	15.00
223	*Brian Bowles*	8.00
224	*Donaldo Mendez*	8.00
225	*Jorge Julio*	8.00
226	*Matt White*	10.00
227	*Casey Fossum*	15.00
228	*Mike Rivera*	50.00
229	*Joe Kennedy*	6.00
230	*Kyle Lohse*	8.00
231	*Juan Cruz*	8.00
232	*Jeremy Affeldt*	8.00
233	*Brandon Lyon*	8.00
234	*Brian Roberts*	8.00
235	*Willie Harris*	6.00
236	*Pedro Santana*	6.00
237	*Rafael Soriano*	6.00
238	*Steve Green*	75.00
239	*Junior Spivey*	20.00
240	*Rob Mackowiak*	40.00

2001 Upper Deck Rookie Update Ichiro ROY

		MT
Complete Set (51):		40.00
Common Ichiro:		1.00
1	Ichiro Suzuki	1.00
2	Ichiro Suzuki	1.00
3	Ichiro Suzuki	1.00
4	Ichiro Suzuki	1.00
5	Ichiro Suzuki	1.00
6	Ichiro Suzuki	1.00
7	Ichiro Suzuki	1.00
8	Ichiro Suzuki	1.00
9	Ichiro Suzuki	1.00
10	Ichiro Suzuki	1.00
11	Ichiro Suzuki	1.00
12	Ichiro Suzuki	1.00
13	Ichiro Suzuki	1.00
14	Ichiro Suzuki	1.00
15	Ichiro Suzuki	1.00
16	Ichiro Suzuki	1.00
17	Ichiro Suzuki	1.00
18	Ichiro Suzuki	1.00
19	Ichiro Suzuki	1.00
20	Ichiro Suzuki	1.00
21	Ichiro Suzuki	1.00
22	Ichiro Suzuki	1.00
23	Ichiro Suzuki	1.00
24	Ichiro Suzuki	1.00
25	Ichiro Suzuki	1.00
26	Ichiro Suzuki	1.00
27	Ichiro Suzuki	1.00
28	Ichiro Suzuki	1.00
29	Ichiro Suzuki	1.00
30	Ichiro Suzuki	1.00
31	Ichiro Suzuki	1.00
32	Ichiro Suzuki	1.00
33	Ichiro Suzuki	1.00
34	Ichiro Suzuki	1.00
35	Ichiro Suzuki	1.00
36	Ichiro Suzuki	1.00
37	Ichiro Suzuki	1.00
38	Ichiro Suzuki	1.00
39	Ichiro Suzuki	1.00
40	Ichiro Suzuki	1.00
41	Ichiro Suzuki	1.00
42	Ichiro Suzuki	1.00
43	Ichiro Suzuki	1.00
44	Ichiro Suzuki	1.00
45	Ichiro Suzuki	1.00
46	Ichiro Suzuki	1.00
47	Ichiro Suzuki	1.00
48	Ichiro Suzuki	1.00
49	Ichiro Suzuki	1.00
50	Ichiro Suzuki	1.00
51	Checklist (Ichiro Suzuki)	1.00

2001 Upper Deck Rookie Update Ichiro ROY Game Jersey

		MT
Numbers 1-12 production 100		65.00
Numbers 13-17 production 50		85.00
Numbers 18-19 production 25		150.00
J-I1	Ichiro Suzuki	65.00
J-I2	Ichiro Suzuki	65.00
J-I3	Ichiro Suzuki	65.00
J-I4	Ichiro Suzuki	65.00
J-I5	Ichiro Suzuki	65.00
J-I6	Ichiro Suzuki	65.00
J-I7	Ichiro Suzuki	65.00
J-I8	Ichiro Suzuki	65.00
J-I9	Ichiro Suzuki	65.00
J-I10	Ichiro Suzuki	65.00
J-I11	Ichiro Suzuki	65.00
J-I12	Ichiro Suzuki	65.00
J-I13	Ichiro Suzuki	85.00
J-I14	Ichiro Suzuki	85.00
J-I15	Ichiro Suzuki	85.00
J-I16	Ichiro Suzuki	85.00
J-I17	Ichiro Suzuki	85.00
J-I18	Ichiro Suzuki	150.00
J-I19	Ichiro Suzuki	150.00
J-I20	Ichiro Suzuki /1	

2001 Upper Deck Rookie Update Ichiro ROY Game-Used Bat

		MT
Numbers 1-12 production 100		65.00
Numbers 13-17 production 50		85.00

Numbers 18-19
production 25 150.00
B-I1 Ichiro Suzuki 65.00
B-I2 Ichiro Suzuki 65.00
B-I3 Ichiro Suzuki 65.00
B-I4 Ichiro Suzuki 65.00
B-I5 Ichiro Suzuki 65.00
B-I6 Ichiro Suzuki 65.00
B-I7 Ichiro Suzuki 65.00
B-I8 Ichiro Suzuki 65.00
B-I9 Ichiro Suzuki 65.00
B-I10 Ichiro Suzuki 65.00
B-I11 Ichiro Suzuki 65.00
B-I12 Ichiro Suzuki 65.00
B-I13 Ichiro Suzuki 85.00
B-I14 Ichiro Suzuki 85.00
B-I15 Ichiro Suzuki 85.00
B-I16 Ichiro Suzuki 85.00
B-I17 Ichiro Suzuki 85.00
B-I18 Ichiro Suzuki 150.00
B-I19 Ichiro Suzuki 150.00
B-I20 Ichiro Suzuki/1

2001 Upper Deck Rookie Update SP Chirography

MT
Common Autograph: 15.00
LB Lance Berkman/ 100 35.00
KG Ken Griffey Jr/ 250 150.00
TG Tony Gwynn/250 40.00
TG Tony Gwynn/100 50.00
MS Doug Mientkiewicz/ 100 30.00
JP Jorge Posada/250 30.00
JP Jorge Posada/100 40.00
CR Cal Ripken Jr. 100.00
MS Mike Sweeney/ 100 15.00

2001 Upper Deck Rookie Update SP Chirography - Ichiro

Available only as a redemption in UD Rookie Update. Three versions were produced, an unnumbered autographed card, a Silver parallel autograph numbered to 100 and a Gold autograph parallel numbered to 25.

MT
Ichiro (unnumbered)
Ichiro (Silver/100) 550.00
Ichiro (Gold/25)

2001 Upper Deck Rookie Update USA "Touch of Gold"

MT
Common Autograph: 10.00
Production 500 sets
BA Brent Abernathy 15.00
KU Kurt Ainsworth 10.00
PB Pat Borders 10.00
SB Sean Burroughs 25.00
JC John Cotton 10.00
TD Gookie Dawkins 10.00
AE Adam Everett 10.00
RF Ryan Franklin 10.00
CG Chris George 15.00
SH Shane Heams 15.00
MJ Marcus Jensen 10.00
MK Mike Kinkade 10.00
RK Rick Krivda 10.00
DM Doug Mientkiewicz 25.00
MN Mike Neill 10.00
RO Roy Oswalt 40.00
JR Jon Rauch 20.00
AS Anthony Sanders 10.00
BSe Bobby Seay 10.00
BSh Ben Sheets 20.00
BW Brad Wilkerson 10.00
TW Todd Williams 10.00
EY Ernie Young 10.00
TY Tim Young 10.00

2001 UD Rookie Update Winning Materials 2-Player

MT
Common Card: 10.00
Inserted 1:15
CJ-AJ Chipper Jones, Andruw Jones
JK-BB Jeff Kent, Barry Bonds
BB-LG Barry Bonds, Luis Gonzalez 25.00
SS-JG Sammy Sosa, Jason Giambi
JG-BB Jason Giambi, Barry Bonds 25.00
IR-AR Ivan Rodriguez, Alex Rodriguez 25.00
AP-JE Albert Pujols, Jim Edmonds 35.00
GS-SG Gary Sheffield, Shawn Green 15.00
MP-EA Mike Piazza, Edgardo Alfonzo 20.00
LW-TH Larry Walker, Todd Helton 15.00
MR-JG Manny Ramirez, Juan Gonzalez 15.00
TG-CR Tony Gwynn, Cal Ripken Jr. 40.00
SR-BA Scott Rolen, Bobby Abreu 15.00
EM-IS Edgar Martinez, Ichiro Suzuki
JB-CB Jeff Bagwell, Craig Biggio 20.00
KG-SC Ken Griffey Jr., Sean Casey 25.00
EM-JM Eric Milton, Joe Mays 10.00
AP-IS Albert Pujols, Ichiro Suzuki
SH-KS Shigetoshi Hasegawa, Kazuhiro Sasaki
CP-BK Chan Ho Park, Byung-Hyung Kim
HN-SH Hideo Nomo, Shigetoshi Hasegawa
HN-MY Hideo Nomo, Masato Yoshii 20.00
TS-HN Tsuyoshi Shinjo, Hideo Nomo 20.00
CS-RJ Curt Schilling, Randy Johnson 20.00
AS-KS Aaron Sele, Kazuhiro Sasaki 10.00
PM-RJ Pedro Martinez, Randy Johnson 15.00
RC-MP Roger Clemens, Mike Piazza
BW-MR Bernie Williams, Mariano Rivera 15.00
TG-X2 Tony Gwynn 15.00
CR-X2 Cal Ripken Jr. 40.00
JB-RY Jeromy Burnitz, Robin Yount 15.00
CR-EM Cal Ripken Jr., Eddie Murray 30.00
TG-DW Tony Gwynn, Dave Winfield 15.00
FT-MO Frank Thomas, Magglio Ordonez 15.00
PM-GM Pedro Martinez, Greg Maddux 20.00
BW-RJ Bernie Williams, Reggie Jackson 20.00
SS-EB Sammy Sosa, Ernie Banks 40.00
CP-FV Chan Ho Park, Fernando Valenzuela 10.00

2001 UD Rookie Update Winning Materials 3-Player Jersey

MT
Common Card: 10.00
Inserted 1:15
KBA Jeff Kent, Barry Bonds, Rich Aurilia 20.00
JAF Chipper Jones, Andruw Jones, Rafael Furcal 15.00
GZH Jason Giambi, Barry Zito, Tim Hudson 20.00
RRK Alex Rodriguez, Ivan Rodriguez, Gabe Kapler
SKB Gary Sheffield, Eric Karros, Kevin Brown 10.00
SSM Aaron Sele, Ichiro Suzuki, Edgar Martinez 60.00
HDG Todd Helton, Carlos Delgado, Jason Giambi 20.00
VRF Omar Vizquel, Alex Rodriguez, Rafael Furcal 25.00
SYN Kazuhiro Sasaki, Masato Yoshii, Hideo Nomo 20.00
BTD Jeff Bagwell, Frank Thomas, Carlos Delgado 15.00
BGG Barry Bonds, Luis Gonzalez, Ken Griffey Jr. 30.00
RPK Ivan Rodriguez, Mike Piazza, Jason Kendall 20.00
PPV Jay Payton, Mike Piazza, Robin Ventura 15.00
CHN Roger Clemens, Tim Hudson, Hideo Nomo 20.00
PWO Andy Pettite, Bernie Williams, Paul O'Neill 20.00
TDK Frank Thomas, Ray Durham, Paul Konerko 15.00
SJC Curt Schilling, Randy Johnson, Roger Clemens 20.00
DEA J.D. Drew, Jim Edmonds, Bobby Abreu 20.00
DOP Carlos Delgado, Magglio Ordonez, Albert Pujols 20.00
TGA Jim Thome, Juan Gonzalez, Roberto Alomar 15.00
GWS Luis Gonzalez, Matt Williams, Curt Schilling 20.00
MGJ Greg Maddux, Tom Glavine, Andruw Jones 20.00

2001 Upper Deck Sweet Spot

MT
Complete Set (90): 600.00
Common Player: .50
Common Sweet Beginnings: 8.00
(61-90) Production 1,000
Pack (4): 20.00
Box (18): 350.00
1 Troy Glaus 1.50
2 Darin Erstad 1.00
3 Jason Giambi 1.00
4 Tim Hudson .50
5 Ben Grieve .75
6 Carlos Delgado 1.25
7 David Wells .50
8 Greg Vaughn .50
9 Roberto Alomar 1.25
10 Jim Thome .75
11 John Olerud .75
12 Edgar Martinez .50
13 Cal Ripken Jr. 5.00
14 Albert Belle .75
15 Ivan Rodriguez 1.50
16 Alex Rodriguez 4.00
17 Pedro Martinez 2.00
18 Nomar Garciaparra 4.00
19 Manny Ramirez 1.50
20 Jermaine Dye .50
21 Juan Gonzalez 1.50
22 Dean Palmer .50
23 Matt Lawton .50
24 Eric Milton .50
25 Frank Thomas 2.00
26 Magglio Ordonez .75
27 Derek Jeter 5.00
28 Bernie Williams 1.25
29 Roger Clemens 2.00
30 Jeff Bagwell 1.50
31 Richard Hidalgo .75
32 Chipper Jones 3.00
33 Greg Maddux 3.00
34 Richie Sexson .50
35 Jeromy Burnitz .50
36 Mark McGwire 5.00
37 Jim Edmonds .75
38 Sammy Sosa 3.00
39 Randy Johnson 1.50
40 Steve Finley .50
41 Gary Sheffield .75
42 Shawn Green .75
43 Vladimir Guerrero 2.00
44 Jose Vidro .50
45 Barry Bonds 2.00
46 Jeff Kent .75
47 Preston Wilson .50
48 Luis Castillo .50
49 Mike Piazza 4.00
50 Edgardo Alfonzo .75
51 Tony Gwynn 3.00
52 Ryan Klesko .75
53 Scott Rolen 1.00
54 Bob Abreu .50
55 Jason Kendall .50
56 Brian Giles .75
57 Ken Griffey Jr. 4.00
58 Barry Larkin 1.00
59 Todd Helton 1.50
60 Mike Hampton .50
61 Corey Patterson (Sweet Beginnings) 15.00
62 *Ichiro Suzuki* (Sweet Beginnings) 180.00
63 Jason Grilli (Sweet Beginnings) 8.00
64 Brian Cole (Sweet Beginnings) 10.00

65 Juan Pierre (Sweet Beginnings) 10.00
66 Matt Ginter (Sweet Beginnings) 15.00
67 Jimmy Rollins (Sweet Beginnings) 15.00
68 *Jason Smith* (Sweet Beginnings) 15.00
69 Israel Alcantara (Sweet Beginnings) 10.00
70 *Adam Pettyjohn* (Sweet Beginnings) 15.00
71 Luke Prokopec (Sweet Beginnings) 8.00
72 Barry Zito (Sweet Beginnings) 20.00
73 Keith Ginter (Sweet Beginnings) 8.00
74 Sun-Woo Kim (Sweet Beginnings) 10.00
75 Ross Gload (Sweet Beginnings) 15.00
76 Matt Wise (Sweet Beginnings) 10.00
77 Aubrey Huff (Sweet Beginnings) 8.00
78 Ryan Franklin (Sweet Beginnings) 10.00
79 Brandon Inge (Sweet Beginnings) 8.00
80 Wes Helms (Sweet Beginnings) 10.00
81 *Junior Spivey* (Sweet Beginnings) 8.00
82 Ryan Vogelsong (Sweet Beginnings) 15.00
83 John Parrish (Sweet Beginnings) 15.00
84 Joe Crede (Sweet Beginnings) 25.00
85 Damian Rolls (Sweet Beginnings) 8.00
86 *Esix Snead* (Sweet Beginnings) 15.00
87 Rocky Biddle (Sweet Beginnings) 15.00
88 Brady Clark (Sweet Beginnings) 8.00
89 Timoniel Perez (Sweet Beginnings) 20.00
90 Jay Spurgeon (Sweet Beginnings) 10.00

2001 Upper Deck Sweet Spot Big League Challenge

		MT
Complete Set (20):		40.00
Common Player:		1.00
Inserted 1:6		
1	Mark McGwire	6.00
2	Richard Hidalgo	1.00
3	Alex Rodriguez	5.00
4	Shawn Green	1.00
5	Frank Thomas	3.00
6	Chipper Jones	4.00
7	Rafael Palmeiro	1.50
8	Troy Glaus	2.00
9	Mike Piazza	5.00
10	Andruw Jones	1.50
11	Todd Helton	2.00
12	Jason Giambi	1.50
13	Sammy Sosa	4.00
14	Carlos Delgado	1.50
15	Barry Bonds	2.00
16	Jose Canseco	1.50
17	Jim Edmonds	1.00
18	Manny Ramirez	2.00
19	Gary Sheffield	1.00
20	Nomar Garciaparra	5.00

2001 Upper Deck Sweet Spot DiMaggio Pinstripes Excl.

	MT
Complete Set (56):	150.00
Common DiMaggio:	4.00
One pack/box	

2001 Upper Deck Sweet Spot DiMaggio Pinstripes Memor.

		MT
Print Runs listed:		150.00
JDB	Joe DiMaggio bat/100	250.00
JDBC	Joe DiMaggio bat/cut/5	
JDCJ	Joe DiMaggio, Lou Gehrig jsy/50	1100.
JDJ	Joe DiMaggio jsy/100	300.00

2001 Upper Deck Sweet Spot Game-Used Bat

		MT
Common Player:		15.00
Inserted 1:18		
HA	Hank Aaron	100.00
RA	Rick Ankiel	20.00
BB	Barry Bonds	30.00
JC	Jose Canseco	15.00
TC	Ty Cobb	275.00
JD	Joe DiMaggio	200.00
KG	Ken Griffey Jr.	60.00
RJ	Reggie Jackson	30.00
AJ	Andruw Jones	20.00
MM	Mickey Mantle	200.00
WM	Willie Mays	125.00
SM	Stan Musial	75.00
CR	Cal Ripken Jr.	60.00
AR	Alex Rodriguez	40.00
IR	Ivan Rodriguez	20.00
NR	Nolan Ryan	100.00
GS	Gary Sheffield	15.00
SS	Sammy Sosa	30.00
FT	Frank Thomas	30.00

2001 Upper Deck Sweet Spot Game Jerseys

		MT
Common Player:		25.00
Inserted 1:18		
BB	Barry Bonds	35.00
JC	Jose Canseco	25.00
RC	Roger Clemens	40.00
RC	Roberto Clemente	200.00
JD	Joe DiMaggio	200.00
KG	Ken Griffey Jr.	80.00
RJ	Randy Johnson	30.00
AJ	Andruw Jones	20.00
CJ	Chipper Jones	30.00
MM	Mickey Mantle	200.00
WM	Willie Mays	125.00
SM	Stan Musial	75.00
CR	Cal Ripken Jr.	60.00
AR	Alex Rodriguez	40.00
IR	Ivan Rodriguez	25.00
NR	Nolan Ryan	100.00
DS	Duke Snider	60.00
SS	Sammy Sosa	30.00
IS	Ichiro Suzuki	175.00
FT	Frank Thomas	30.00

2001 Upper Deck Sweet Spot S.S. Game-Used Bases Tier 1

		MT
Common Card:		25.00
BH	Barry Bonds, Todd Helton	30.00
MG	Mark McGwire, Ken Griffey Jr.	100.00
JG	Chipper Jones, Nomar Garciaparra	40.00
GD	Vladimir Guerrero, Carlos Delgado	25.00
ST	Sammy Sosa, Frank Thomas	40.00
SR	Gary Sheffield, Alex Rodriguez	30.00
GR	Tony Gwynn, Ivan Rodriguez	30.00
PJ	Mike Piazza, Derek Jeter	50.00
HG	Jeffrey Hammonds, Troy Glaus	20.00
JGi	Randy Johnson, Jason Giambi	25.00
BD	Jeff Bagwell, Jermaine Dye	25.00
RR	Scott Rolen, Cal Ripken Jr.	40.00
GR	Ken Griffey Jr., Manny Ramirez	40.00
RJ	Alex Rodriguez, Derek Jeter	60.00
MP	Mark McGwire, Timoniel Perez	40.00
CP	Roger Clemens, Mike Piazza	40.00

2001 Upper Deck Sweet Spot S.S. Game-Used Bases Tier 2

		MT
Common Card:		50.00
Production 50 sets		
BHK	Barry Bonds, Todd Helton, Jeff Kent	90.00
MGE	Mark McGwire, Ken Griffey Jr., Bobby Edmonds	300.00
JGJ	Chipper Jones, Nomar Garciaparra, Andruw Jones	125.00
GDM	Vladimir Guerrero, Carlos Delgado, Raul Mondesi	60.00
STO	Sammy Sosa, Frank Thomas, Magglio Ordonez	90.00
SRM	Gary Sheffield, Alex Rodriguez, Edgar Martinez	100.00
GRP	Tony Gwynn, Ivan Rodriguez, Rafael Palmeiro	100.00
PJW	Mike Piazza, Derek Jeter, Bernie Williams	150.00
HGH	Jeffrey Hammonds, Troy Glaus, Todd Helton	120.00
JGC	Randy Johnson, Jason Giambi, Eric Chavez	50.00
BDH	Jeff Bagwell, Jermaine Dye, Richard Hidalgo	50.00
RRB	Scott Rolen, Cal Ripken Jr., Albert Belle	120.00
GRT	Ken Griffey Jr., Manny Ramirez, Jim Thome	150.00

2001 Upper Deck Sweet Spot Players Party

		MT
Complete Set (10):		30.00
Common Player:		1.50
Inserted 1:12		
1	Derek Jeter	6.00
2	Randy Johnson	2.00
3	Frank Thomas	3.00
4	Nomar Garciaparra	5.00
5	Ken Griffey Jr.	5.00
6	Carlos Delgado	1.50
7	Mike Piazza	5.00
8	Barry Bonds	2.00
9	Sammy Sosa	4.00
10	Pedro Martinez	2.50

2001 Upper Deck Sweet Spot Signatures

		MT
Common Player:		25.00
RAl	Roberto Alomar	40.00
RAn	Rick Ankiel	30.00
JB	Jeff Bagwell SP/214	150.00
DB	Dusty Baker	30.00
DB	Don Baylor	30.00
BB	Buddy Bell	25.00
AB	Albert Belle	25.00
MB	Milton Bradley	25.00
PB	Pat Burrell	60.00
JC	Jose Canseco	75.00
CB	Chris Chambliss	30.00
RC	Roger Clemens	100.00
TC	Ty Cobb/1	
CD	Carlos Delgado	50.00
JD	Joe DiMaggio SP/150	750.00
DE	Darin Erstad	40.00
RF	Rafael Furcal	50.00
JG	Joe Garagiola	60.00

JG Jason Giambi 50.00
TGl Troy Glaus 60.00
SG Shawn Green 40.00
KG Ken Griffey SP/100 500.00
TGw Tony Gwynn 110.00
AH Art Howe 25.00
TH Tim Hudson 40.00
DJ Davey Johnson 30.00
RJ Randy Johnson 80.00
AJ Andruw Jones 50.00
CJ Chipper Jones 80.00
ML Mike Lamb 25.00
TL Tony LaRussa 40.00
DL Davey Lopes 30.00
BM Bill Madlock 25.00
MM Mickey Mantle SP/10
WM Willie Mays 225.00
HM Hal McRae 25.00
SM Stan Musial 150.00
PO Paul O'Neill 60.00
LP Lou Piniella 40.00
JR Jim Rice 40.00
AR Alex Rodriguez SP/154 275.00
IR Ivan Rodriguez SP/150 140.00
BR Babe Ruth SP/1
NR Nolan Ryan 275.00
GS Gary Sheffield 30.00
SS Sammy Sosa SP/148 375.00
FT Frank Thomas 100.00
AT Alan Trammell 50.00
BV Bobby Valentine 40.00
RV Robin Ventura 40.00
MW Matt Williams 50.00

2001 Upper Deck Ultimate Collection

MT
Common Player: 1.00
Common SP (91-100): 10.00
Production 1,000
Common SP (101-110): 10.00
Production 750
Common (111-120): 25.00
Production 250
Pack (4): 95.00
Box (4): 360.00
1 Troy Glaus 2.50
2 Darin Erstad 1.50
3 Jason Giambi 2.00
4 Barry Zito 1.00
5 Tim Hudson 1.50
6 Miguel Tejada 1.00
7 Carlos Delgado 1.50
8 Shannon Stewart 1.00
9 Greg Vaughn 1.00
10 Toby Hall 1.00
11 Roberto Alomar 2.00
12 Juan Gonzalez 2.50
13 Jim Thome 1.50
14 Edgar Martinez 1.00
15 Freddy Garcia 1.00
16 Bret Boone 1.00
17 Kazuhiro Sasaki 1.00
18 Cal Ripken Jr. 10.00
19 Tim Raines Jr. 1.00
20 Alex Rodriguez 6.00
21 Ivan Rodriguez 2.50
22 Rafael Palmeiro 1.50
23 Pedro Martinez 2.50
24 Nomar Garciaparra 6.00
25 Manny Ramirez 2.50
26 Hideo Nomo 1.50
27 Mike Sweeney 1.00
28 Carlos Beltran 1.00
29 Tony Clark 1.00
30 Dean Palmer 1.00
31 Doug Mientkiewicz 1.00
32 Cristian Guzman 1.00
33 Corey Koskie 1.00
34 Frank Thomas 2.50
35 Magglio Ordonez 1.00
36 Jose Canseco 1.50
37 Roger Clemens 3.00
38 Derek Jeter 10.00
39 Bernie Williams 2.00
40 Mike Mussina 2.00
41 Tino Martinez 1.00
42 Jeff Bagwell 2.50
43 Lance Berkman 1.00
44 Roy Oswalt 1.50
45 Chipper Jones 5.00
46 Greg Maddux 5.00
47 Andruw Jones 1.50
48 Tom Glavine 1.50
49 Richie Sexson 1.00
50 Jeromy Burnitz 1.00
51 Ben Sheets 1.00
52 Mark McGwire 8.00
53 Matt Morris 1.00
54 Jim Edmonds 1.50
55 J.D. Drew 1.50
56 Sammy Sosa 5.00
57 Fred McGriff 1.00
58 Kerry Wood 1.50
59 Randy Johnson 2.50
60 Luis Gonzalez 2.00
61 Curt Schilling 1.50
62 Shawn Green 1.50
63 Kevin Brown 1.00
64 Gary Sheffield 1.50
65 Vladimir Guerrero 2.50
66 Barry Bonds 5.00
67 Jeff Kent 1.00
68 Rich Aurilia 1.00
69 Cliff Floyd 1.00
70 Charles Johnson 1.00
71 Josh Beckett 1.00
72 Mike Piazza 6.00
73 Edgardo Alfonzo 1.00
74 Robin Ventura 1.00
75 Tony Gwynn 2.50
76 Ryan Klesko 1.00
77 Phil Nevin 1.00
78 Scott Rolen 1.50
79 Bobby Abreu 1.00
80 Jimmy Rollins 1.00
81 Brian Giles 1.50
82 Jason Kendall 1.00
83 Aramis Ramirez 1.00
84 Ken Griffey Jr. 6.00
85 Adam Dunn 2.00
86 Sean Casey 1.50
87 Barry Larkin 1.50
88 Larry Walker 1.50
89 Mike Hampton 1.00
90 Todd Helton 2.50
91 Ken Harvey 10.00
92 *William Ortega* 10.00
93 *Juan Diaz* 10.00
94 *Greg Miller* 10.00
95 *Brandon Berger* 20.00
96 *Brandon Lyon* 10.00
97 *Jay Gibbons* 20.00
98 *Rob Mackowiak* 10.00
99 *Erick Almonte* 15.00
100 *Jason Middlebrook* 10.00
101 *Johnny Estrada* 10.00
102 *Juan Uribe* 10.00
103 *Travis Hafner* 15.00
104 *Morgan Ensberg* 20.00
105 *Mike Rivera* 10.00
106 *Josh Towers* 15.00
107 *Adrian Hernandez* 15.00
108 *Rafael Soriano* 10.00
109 *Jackson Melian* 15.00
110 *Wilken Ruan* 10.00
111 *Albert Pujols* 125.00
112 *Tsuyoshi Shinjo* 45.00
113 *Brandon Duckworth* 40.00
114 *Juan Cruz* 75.00
115 *Dewon Brazelton* 25.00
116 *Mark Prior Auto* 320.00
117 *Mark Teixeira Auto* 175.00
118 *Wilson Betemit Auto* 50.00
119 *Bud Smith Auto* 65.00
120 *Ichiro Suzuki Auto* 600.00

2001 Upper Deck Ultimate Collection Game Jersey

MT
Common Player: 15.00
Inserted 1:2
RA Roberto Alomar 30.00
JB Jeff Bagwell 35.00
BB Barry Bonds 50.00
JC Jose Canseco 50.00
RC Roger Clemens 40.00
CD Carlos Delgado 20.00
DE Darin Erstad 20.00
JaG Jason Giambi 25.00
JG Juan Gonzalez 25.00
LG Luis Gonzalez 25.00
SG Shawn Green 25.00
KG Ken Griffey Jr.
TG Tony Gwynn 40.00
TH Todd Helton 40.00
RJ Randy Johnson 25.00
AJ Andruw Jones 25.00
CJ Chipper Jones 30.00
GM Greg Maddux 40.00
MO Magglio Ordonez 20.00
MP Mike Piazza 40.00
AP Albert Pujols 75.00
CR Cal Ripken Jr. 75.00
AR Alex Rodriguez 40.00
IR Ivan Rodriguez 25.00
SR Scott Rolen 25.00
GS Gary Sheffield 15.00
SS Sammy Sosa 50.00
FT Frank Thomas 40.00
LW Larry Walker 20.00
BW Bernie Williams 30.00

2001 Upper Deck Ultimate Collection Ichiro

MT
Pricing not available for all Ichiro's
B-IA Ichiro Suzuki/bat away 80.00
B-IH Ichiro Suzuki/bat home 80.00
B-IS Ichiro Suzuki/bat/250 150.00
B-IG Ichiro Suzuki/bat/200 160.00
SB-I Ichiro Suzuki/bat/auto/50 675.00
J-IA Ichiro Suzuki/jsy/away 80.00
J-IH Ichiro Suzuki/jsy/home 80.00
J-IS Ichiro Suzuki/jsy/250 125.00
J-IG Ichiro Suzuki/jsy/200 150.00
SJ-I Ichiro Suzuki/jsy/auto/50 675.00
UB-I Ichiro Suzuki/base 50.00
UB-ICIchiro Suzuki/base/150 90.00
UB-ISIchiro Suzuki/base/50 150.00
UB-IGIchiro Suzuki/base/25
SUB-IIchiro Suzuki/base/auto/25
BB-I Ichiro Suzuki/ball 60.00
BB-ICIchiro Suzuki/ball/150 100.00
BB-ISIchiro Suzuki/ball/50 150.00
BB-IGIchiro Suzuki/ball/25
SBB-IIchiro Suzuki/ball/auto/25 675.00
C-I Ichiro Suzuki/glove/75 180.00
C-IG Ichiro Suzuki/glove/25
BG-I Ichiro Suzuki/batglove/75 180.00
BG-IGIchiro Suzuki/batglove/25

2001 Upper Deck Ultimate Collection Magic Numbers

MT
Common Player:
Production 150
Coppers #'d to 24 not priced
Silvers #'d to 20 not priced
Golds #'d to 15 not priced
RA Roberto Alomar 35.00
JB Jeff Bagwell 40.00
BB Barry Bonds 60.00
JC Jose Canseco 50.00
RC Roger Clemens 50.00
CD Carlos Delgado 25.00
DE Darin Erstad 25.00
JaG Jason Giambi 30.00
JG Juan Gonzalez 30.00
LG Luis Gonzalez 30.00
SG Shawn Green 30.00
KG Ken Griffey Jr.
TG Tony Gwynn 50.00
TH Todd Helton 50.00
RJ Randy Johnson 30.00
AJ Andruw Jones 30.00
CJ Chipper Jones 40.00
GM Greg Maddux 50.00
MO Magglio Ordonez 25.00
MP Mike Piazza 50.00
AP Albert Pujols 90.00
CR Cal Ripken Jr. 90.00
AR Alex Rodriguez 50.00
IR Ivan Rodriguez 30.00
SR Scott Rolen 30.00
GS Gary Sheffield 20.00
SS Sammy Sosa 60.00
FT Frank Thomas 50.00
LW Larry Walker 25.00
BW Bernie Williams 35.00

2001 Upper Deck Ultimate Collection Ultimate Signatures

MT
Common Autograph: 25.00
Inserted 1:4
Silvers #'d to 24 not priced
Golds #'d to 15 not priced
RA Roberto Alomar 60.00
EB Ernie Banks 80.00
BaB Barry Bonds 150.00
RC Roger Clemens 100.00
CD Carlos Delgado 35.00
CF Carlton Fisk 65.00
JaG Jason Giambi 50.00
TGl Tom Glavine 40.00
LG Luis Gonzalez 40.00
KG Ken Griffey Jr. 200.00
TG Tony Gwynn
RK Ryan Klesko 25.00
SK Sandy Koufax 200.00
EM Edgar Martinez 50.00
HN Hideo Nomo
TP Tony Perez 25.00
KP Kirby Puckett 75.00
CR Cal Ripken Jr. 160.00
AR Alex Rodriguez 100.00
IR Ivan Rodriguez 75.00

TS Tom Seaver 75.00
GS Gary Sheffield 30.00
DS Duke Snider 50.00
SS Sammy Sosa 160.00
FT Frank Thomas
JT Jim Thome 50.00
RY Robin Yount 75.00

2001 Upper Deck Victory

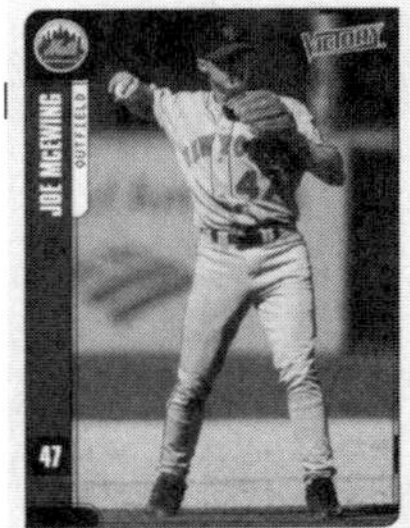

		MT
Complete Set (660):		50.00
Common Player:		.15
1	Troy Glaus	.50
2	Scott Spiezio	.15
3	Gary DiSarcina	.15
4	Darin Erstad	.20
5	Tim Salmon	.20
6	Troy Percival	.15
7	Ramon Ortiz	.15
8	Orlando Palmeiro	.15
9	Tim Belcher	.15
10	Mo Vaughn	.15
11	Bengie Molina	.15
12	Benji Gil	.15
13	Scott Schoeneweis	.15
14	Garret Anderson	.15
15	Matt Wise	.15
16	Adam Kennedy	.15
17	Jarrod Washburn	.15
18	Darin Erstad, Troy Percival	.15
19	Jason Giambi	.20
20	Tim Hudson	.20
21	Ramon Hernandez	.15
22	Eric Chavez	.15
23	Gil Heredia	.15
24	Jason Isringhausen	.15
25	Jeremy Giambi	.15
26	Miguel Tejada	.15
27	Barry Zito	.50
28	Terrence Long	.15
29	Ryan Christenson	.15
30	Mark Mulder	.15
31	Olmedo Saenz	.15
32	Adam Piatt	.15
33	Ben Grieve	.20
34	Omar Olivares	.15
35	John Jaha	.15
36	Jason Giambi, Tim Hudson	.15
37	Carlos Delgado	.40
38	Esteban Loaiza	.15
39	Brad Fullmer	.15
40	David Wells	.15
41	Chris Woodward	.15
42	Billy Koch	.15
43	Shannon Stewart	.15
44	Chris Carpenter	.15
45	Steve Parris	.15
46	Darrin Fletcher	.15
47	Joey Hamilton	.15
48	Jose Cruz Jr.	.15
49	Vernon Wells	.15
50	Raul Mondesi	.15
51	Kelvim Escobar	.15
52	Tony Batista	.15
53	Alex Gonzalez	.15
54	Carlos Delgado, David Wells	.20
55	Greg Vaughn	.15
56	Albie Lopez	.15
57	Randy Winn	.15
58	Ryan Rupe	.15
59	Steve Cox	.15
60	Vinny Castilla	.15
61	Jose Guillen	.15
62	Wilson Alvarez	.15
63	Bryan Rekar	.15
64	Gerald Williams	.15
65	Esteban Yan	.15
66	Felix Martinez	.15
67	Fred McGriff	.20
68	John Flaherty	.15
69	Jason Tyner	.15
70	Russ Johnson	.15
71	Roberto Hernandez	.15
72	Greg Vaughn, Albie Lopez	.15
73	Eddie Taubensee	.15
74	Bob Wickman	.15
75	Ellis Burks	.15
76	Kenny Lofton	.20
77	Einar Diaz	.15
78	Travis Fryman	.15
79	Omar Vizquel	.15
80	Jason Bere	.15
81	Bartolo Colon	.15
82	Jim Thome	.20
83	Roberto Alomar	.40
84	Chuck Finley	.15
85	Steve Woodard	.15
86	Russ Branyan	.15
87	Dave Burba	.15
88	Jaret Wright	.15
89	Jacob Cruz	.15
90	Steve Karsay	.15
91	Manny Ramirez, Bartolo Colon	.20
92	Raul Ibanez	.15
93	Freddy Garcia	.15
94	Edgar Martinez	.15
95	Jay Buhner	.15
96	Jamie Moyer	.15
97	John Olerud	.20
98	Aaron Sele	.15
99	Kazuhiro Sasaki	.20
100	Mike Cameron	.15
101	John Halama	.15
102	David Bell	.15
103	Gil Meche	.15
104	Carlos Guillen	.15
105	Mark McLemore	.15
106	Stan Javier	.15
107	Al Martin	.15
108	Dan Wilson	.15
109	Alex Rodriguez, Kazuhiro Sasaki	.50
110	Cal Ripken Jr.	1.50
111	Delino DeShields	.15
112	Sidney Ponson	.15
113	Albert Belle	.15
114	Jose Mercedes	.15
115	Scott Erickson	.15
116	Jerry Hairston Jr.	.15
117	Brook Fordyce	.15
118	Luis Matos	.15
119	Eugene Kingsale	.15
120	Jeff Conine	.15
121	Chris Richard	.15
122	Fernando Lunar	.15
123	John Parrish	.15
124	Brady Anderson	.15
125	Ryan Kohlmeier	.15
126	Melvin Mora	.15
127	Albert Belle, Jose Mercedes	.15
128	Ivan Rodriguez	.50
129	Justin Thompson	.15
130	Kenny Rogers	.15
131	Rafael Palmeiro	.30
132	Rusty Greer	.15
133	Gabe Kapler	.15
134	John Wetteland	.15
135	Mike Lamb	.15
136	Doug Davis	.15
137	Ruben Mateo	.15
138	Alex Rodriguez	1.25
139	Chad Curtis	.15
140	Rick Helling	.15
141	Ryan Glynn	.15
142	Andres Galarraga	.25
143	Ricky Ledee	.15
144	Frank Catalanotto	.15
145	Rafael Palmeiro, Rick Helling	.20
146	Pedro Martinez	.60
147	Wilton Veras	.15
148	Manny Ramirez	.50
149	Rolando Arrojo	.15
150	Nomar Garciaparra	1.00
151	Darren Lewis	.15
152	Troy O'Leary	.15
153	Tomokazu Ohka	.15
154	Carl Everett	.15
155	Jason Varitek	.15
156	Frank Castillo	.15
157	Pete Schourek	.15
158	Jose Offerman	.15
159	Derek Lowe	.15
160	John Valentin	.15
161	Dante Bichette	.15
162	Trot Nixon	.15
163	Nomar Garciaparra, Pedro Martinez	.25
164	Jermaine Dye	.15
165	Dave McCarty	.15
166	Jose Rosado	.15
167	Mike Sweeney	.15
168	Rey Sanchez	.15
169	Jeff Suppan	.15
170	Chad Durbin	.15
171	Carlos Beltran	.15
172	Brian Meadows	.15
173	Todd Dunwoody	.15
174	Johnny Damon	.15
175	Blake Stein	.15
176	Carlos Febles	.15
177	Joe Randa	.15
178	Makoto Suzuki	.15
179	Mark Quinn	.15
180	Greg Zaun	.15
181	Mike Sweeney, Jeff Suppan	.15
182	Juan Gonzalez	.50
183	Dean Palmer	.15
184	Wendell Magee	.15
185	Todd Jones	.15
186	Bobby Higginson	.15
187	Brian Moehler	.15
188	Juan Encarnacion	.15
189	Tony Clark	.15
190	Rich Becker	.15
191	Roger Cedeno	.15
192	Mitch Meluskey	.15
193	Shane Halter	.15
194	Jeff Weaver	.15
195	Deivi Cruz	.15
196	Damion Easley	.15
197	Robert Fick	.15
198	Matt Anderson	.15
199	Bobby Higginson, Brian Moehler	.15
200	Brad Radke	.15
201	Mark Redman	.15
202	Corey Koskie	.15
203	Matt Lawton	.15
204	Eric Milton	.15
205	Chad Moeller	.15
206	Jacque Jones	.15
207	Matt Kinney	.15
208	Jay Canizaro	.15
209	Torii Hunter	.15
210	Ron Coomer	.15
211	Chad Allen	.15
212	Denny Hocking	.15
213	Cristian Guzman	.15
214	LaTroy Hawkins	.15
215	Joe Mays	.15
216	David Ortiz	.15
217	Matt Lawton, Eric Milton	.15
218	Frank Thomas	.60
219	Jose Valentin	.15
220	Mike Sirotka	.15
221	Kip Wells	.15
222	Magglio Ordonez	.25
223	Herbert Perry	.15
224	James Baldwin	.15
225	Jon Garland	.15
226	Sandy Alomar	.15
227	Chris Singleton	.15
228	Keith Foulke	.15
229	Paul Konerko	.15
230	Jim Parque	.15
231	Greg Norton	.15
232	Carlos Lee	.15
233	Cal Eldred	.15
234	Ray Durham	.15
235	Jeff Abbott	.15
236	Frank Thomas, Mike Sirotka	.20
237	Derek Jeter	1.50
238	Glenallen Hill	.15
239	Roger Clemens	.75
240	Bernie Williams	.40
241	David Justice	.25
242	Luis Sojo	.15
243	Orlando Hernandez	.20
244	Mike Mussina	.25
245	Jorge Posada	.20
246	Andy Pettitte	.20
247	Paul O'Neill	.20
248	Scott Brosius	.15
249	Alfonso Soriano	.25
250	Mariano Rivera	.20
251	Chuck Knoblauch	.20
252	Ramiro Mendoza	.15
253	Tino Martinez	.15
254	David Cone	.15
255	Derek Jeter, Andy Pettitte	.40
256	Jeff Bagwell	.50
257	Lance Berkman	.15
258	Craig Biggio	.20
259	Scott Elarton	.15
260	Bill Spiers	.15
261	Moises Alou	.15
262	Billy Wagner	.15
263	Shane Reynolds	.15
264	Tony Eusebio	.15
265	Julio Lugo	.15
266	Jose Lima	.15
267	Octavio Dotel	.15
268	Brad Ausmus	.15
269	Daryle Ward	.15
270	Glen Barker	.15
271	Wade Miller	.15
272	Richard Hidalgo	.25
273	Chris Truby	.15
274	Jeff Bagwell, Scott Elarton	.25
275	Greg Maddux	1.00
276	Chipper Jones	1.00
277	Tom Glavine	.25
278	Brian Jordan	.15
279	Andruw Jones	.40
280	Kevin Millwood	.15
281	Rico Brogna	.15
282	George Lombard	.15
283	Reggie Sanders	.15
284	John Rocker	.15
285	Rafael Furcal	.25
286	John Smoltz	.15
287	Javy Lopez	.15
288	Walt Weiss	.15
289	Quilvio Veras	.15
290	Eddie Perez	.15
291	B.J. Surhoff	.15
292	Chipper Jones, Tom Glavine	.25
293	Jeromy Burnitz	.15
294	Charlie Hayes	.15
295	Jeff D'Amico	.15
296	Jose Hernandez	.15
297	Richie Sexson	.15
298	Tyler Houston	.15
299	Paul Rigdon	.15
300	Jamey Wright	.15
301	Mark Loretta	.15
302	Geoff Jenkins	.20
303	Luis Lopez	.15
304	John Snyder	.15
305	Henry Blanco	.15
306	Curtis Leskanic	.15
307	Ron Belliard	.15
308	Jimmy Haynes	.15
309	Marquis Grissom	.15
310	Geoff Jenkins, Jeff D'Amico	.15
311	Mark McGwire	1.50
312	Rick Ankiel	.20
313	Dave Veres	.15
314	Carlos Hernandez	.15
315	Jim Edmonds	.20
316	Andy Benes	.15
317	Garrett Stephenson	.15
318	Ray Lankford	.15
319	Dustin Hermanson	.15
320	Steve Kline	.15
321	Mike Matheny	.15
322	Edgar Renteria	.15
323	J.D. Drew	.15
324	Craig Paquette	.15
325	Darryl Kile	.15
326	Fernando Vina	.15
327	Eric Davis	.15
328	Placido Polanco	.15
329	Jim Edmonds, Darryl Kile	.15
330	Sammy Sosa	1.00
331	Rick Aguilera	.15
332	Willie Greene	.15

333 Kerry Wood .20
334 Todd Hundley .15
335 Rondell White .20
336 Julio Zuleta .15
337 Jon Lieber .15
338 Joe Girardi .15
339 Damon Buford .15
340 Kevin Tapani .15
341 Ricky Gutierrez .15
342 Bill Mueller .15
343 Ruben Quevedo .15
344 Eric Young .15
345 Gary Matthews Jr. .15
346 Daniel Garibay .15
347 Sammy Sosa, Jon Lieber .30
348 Randy Johnson .50
349 Matt Williams .20
350 Kelly Stinnett .15
351 Brian Anderson .15
352 Steve Finley .15
353 Curt Schilling .20
354 Erubiel Durazo .15
355 Todd Stottlemyre .15
356 Mark Grace .20
357 Luis Gonzalez .20
358 Danny Bautista .15
359 Matt Mantei .15
360 Tony Womack .15
361 Armando Reynoso .15
362 Greg Colbrunn .15
363 Jay Bell .15
364 Byung-Hyun Kim .15
365 Luis Gonzalez, Randy Johnson .20
366 Gary Sheffield .20
367 Eric Karros .15
368 Jeff Shaw .15
369 Jim Leyritz .15
370 Kevin Brown .20
371 Alex Cora .15
372 Andy Ashby .15
373 Eric Gagne .15
374 Chan Ho Park .15
375 Shawn Green .20
376 Kevin Elster .15
377 Mark Grudzielanek .15
378 Darren Dreifort .15
379 Dave Hansen .15
380 Bruce Aven .15
381 Adrian Beltre .20
382 Tom Goodwin .15
383 Gary Sheffield, Chan Ho Park .15
384 Vladimir Guerrero .60
385 Ugueth Urbina .15
386 Michael Barrett .15
387 Geoff Blum .15
388 Fernando Tatis .15
389 Carl Pavano .15
390 Jose Vidro .15
391 Orlando Cabrera .15
392 Terry Jones .15
393 Mike Thurman .15
394 Lee Stevens .15
395 Tony Armas Jr. .15
396 Wilton Guerrero .15
397 Peter Bergeron .15
398 Milton Bradley .15
399 Javier Vazquez .15
400 Fernando Seguignol .15
401 Vladimir Guerrero, Dustin Hermanson .25
402 Barry Bonds .60
403 Russ Ortiz .15
404 Calvin Murray .15
405 Armando Rios .15
406 Livan Hernandez .15
407 Jeff Kent .20
408 Bobby Estalella .15
409 Felipe Crespo .15
410 Shawn Estes .15
411 J.T. Snow .15
412 Marvin Benard .15
413 Joe Nathan .15
414 Robb Nen .15
415 Shawon Dunston .15
416 Mark Gardner .15
417 Kirk Rueter .15
418 Rich Aurilia .15
419 Doug Mirabelli .15
420 Russ Davis .15
421 Barry Bonds, Livan Hernandez .30
422 Cliff Floyd .15
423 Luis Castillo .15
424 Antonio Alfonseca .15
425 Preston Wilson .15
426 Ryan Dempster .15
427 Jesus Sanchez .15
428 Derrek Lee .15
429 Brad Penny .15
430 Mark Kotsay .15
431 Alex Fernandez .15
432 Mike Lowell .15
433 Chuck Smith .15
434 Alex Gonzalez .15
435 Dave Berg .15
436 A.J. Burnett .15
437 Charles Johnson .15
438 Reid Cornelius .15
439 Mike Redmond .15
440 Preston Wilson, Ryan Dempster .15
441 Mike Piazza 1.00
442 Kevin Appier .15
443 Jay Payton .15
444 Steve Trachsel .15
445 Al Leiter .20
446 Joe McEwing .15
447 Armando Benitez .15
448 Edgardo Alfonzo .15
449 Glendon Rusch .15
450 Mike Bordick .15
451 Lenny Harris .15
452 Matt Franco .15
453 Darryl Hamilton .15
454 Bobby J. Jones .15
455 Robin Ventura .15
456 Todd Zeile .15
457 John Franco .15
458 Mike Piazza, Al Leiter .40
459 Tony Gwynn .75
460 John Mabry .15
461 Trevor Hoffman .15
462 Phil Nevin .15
463 Ryan Klesko .15
464 Wiki Gonzalez .15
465 Matt Clement .15
466 Alex Arias .15
467 Woody Williams .15
468 Ruben Rivera .15
469 Sterling Hitchcock .15
470 Ben Davis .15
471 Bubba Trammell .15
472 Jay Witasick .15
473 Eric Owens .15
474 Damian Jackson .15
475 Adam Eaton .15
476 Mike Darr .15
477 Phil Nevin, Trevor Hoffman .15
478 Scott Rolen .25
479 Robert Person .15
480 Mike Lieberthal .15
481 Reggie Taylor .15
482 Paul Byrd .15
483 Bruce Chen .15
484 Pat Burrell .25
485 Kevin Jordan .15
486 Bobby Abreu .15
487 Randy Wolf .15
488 Kevin Sefcik .15
489 Brian Hunter .15
490 Doug Glanville .15
491 Kent Bottenfield .15
492 Travis Lee .15
493 Jeff Brantley .15
494 Omar Daal .15
495 Bobby Abreu, Randy Wolf .15
496 Jason Kendall .15
497 Adrian Brown .15
498 Warren Morris .15
499 Brian Giles .20
500 Jimmy Anderson .15
501 John Vander Wal .15
502 Mike Williams .15
503 Aramis Ramirez .15
504 Pat Meares .15
505 Jason Schmidt .15
506 Todd Ritchie .15
507 Abraham Nunez .15
508 Jose Silva .15
509 Francisco Cordova .15
510 Kevin Young .15
511 Derek Bell .15
512 Kris Benson .15
513 Brian Giles, Jose Silva .15
514 Ken Griffey Jr. 1.25
515 Scott Williamson .15
516 Dmitri Young .15
517 Sean Casey .20
518 Barry Larkin .25
519 Juan Castro .15
520 Danny Graves .15
521 Aaron Boone .15
522 Pokey Reese .15
523 Elmer Dessens .15
524 Michael Tucker .15
525 Benito Santiago .15
526 Pete Harnisch .15
527 Alex Ochoa .15
528 Gookie Dawkins .15
529 Seth Etherton .15
530 Rob Bell .15
531 Ken Griffey Jr., Steve Parris .50
532 Todd Helton .50
533 Jose Jimenez .15
534 Todd Walker .15
535 Ron Gant .15
536 Neifi Perez .15
537 Butch Huskey .15
538 Pedro Astacio .15
539 Juan Pierre .15
540 Jeff Cirillo .15
541 Ben Petrick .15
542 Brian Bohanon .15
543 Larry Walker .25
544 Masato Yoshii .15
545 Denny Neagle .15
546 Brent Mayne .15
547 Mike Hampton .20
548 Todd Hollandsworth .15
549 Brian Rose .15
550 Todd Helton, Pedro Astacio .20
551 Jason Hart .15
552 Joe Crede .15
553 Timoniel Perez .15
554 Brady Clark .15
555 *Adam Pettyjohn* .15
556 Jason Grilli .15
557 Paxton Crawford .15
558 Jay Spurgeon .15
559 Hector Ortiz .15
560 Vernon Wells .15
561 Aubrey Huff .15
562 Xavier Nady .25
563 Billy McMillon .15
564 *Ichiro Suzuki* 10.00
565 Tomas de la Rosa .15
566 Matt Ginter .15
567 Sun-Woo Kim .15
568 Nick Johnson .15
569 Pablo Ozuna .15
570 Tike Redman .15
571 Brian Cole .15
572 Ross Gload .15
573 Dee Brown .15
574 Tony McKnight .15
575 Allen Levrault .15
576 Lesli Brea .15
577 Adam Bernero .15
578 Tom Davey .15
579 Morgan Burkhart .15
580 Britt Reames .15
581 Dave Coggin .15
582 Trey Moore .15
583 Matt Kinney .15
584 Pedro Feliz .15
585 Brandon Inge .15
586 Alex Hernandez .15
587 Toby Hall .15
588 Grant Roberts .15
589 Brian Sikorski .15
590 Aaron Myette .15
591 Derek Jeter (Big Play Makers) 1.00
592 Ivan Rodriguez (Big Play Makers) .40
593 Alex Rodriguez (Big Play Makers) .75
594 Carlos Delgado (Big Play Makers) .30
595 Mark McGwire (Big Play Makers) 1.00
596 Troy Glaus (Big Play Makers) .40
597 Sammy Sosa (Big Play Makers) .75
598 Vladimir Guerrero (Big Play Makers) .50
599 Manny Ramirez (Big Play Makers) .40
600 Pedro J. Martinez (Big Play Makers) .50
601 Chipper Jones (Big Play Makers) .75
602 Jason Giambi (Big Play Makers) .20
603 Frank Thomas (Big Play Makers) .50
604 Ken Griffey Jr. (Big Play Makers) .75
605 Nomar Garciaparra (Big Play Makers) .75
606 Randy Johnson (Big Play Makers) .40
607 Mike Piazza (Big Play Makers) .75
608 Barry Bonds (Big Play Makers) .50
609 Todd Helton (Big Play Makers) .40
610 Jeff Bagwell (Big Play Makers) .40
611 Ken Griffey Jr. (Victory's Best) .75
612 Carlos Delgado (Victory's Best) .40
613 Jeff Bagwell (Victory's Best) .40
614 Jason Giambi (Victory's Best) .20
615 Cal Ripken Jr. (Victory's Best) 1.00
616 Brian Giles (Victory's Best) .15
617 Bernie Williams (Victory's Best) .30
618 Greg Maddux (Victory's Best) .75
619 Troy Glaus (Victory's Best) .40
620 Greg Vaughn (Victory's Best) .15
621 Sammy Sosa (Victory's Best) .75
622 Pat Burrell (Victory's Best) .20
623 Ivan Rodriguez (Victory's Best) .40
624 Chipper Jones (Victory's Best) .75
625 Barry Bonds (Victory's Best) .50
626 Roger Clemens (Victory's Best) .50
627 Jim Edmonds (Victory's Best) .15
628 Nomar Garciaparra (Victory's Best) .75
629 Frank Thomas (Victory's Best) .50
630 Mike Piazza (Victory's Best) .75
631 Randy Johnson (Victory's Best) .40
632 Andruw Jones (Victory's Best) .30
633 David Wells (Victory's Best) .15
634 Manny Ramirez (Victory's Best) .40
635 Preston Wilson (Victory's Best) .15
636 Todd Helton (Victory's Best) .40
637 Kerry Wood (Victory's Best) .15
638 Albert Belle (Victory's Best) .15
639 Juan Gonzalez (Victory's Best) .40
640 Vladimir Guerrero (Victory's Best) .50
641 Gary Sheffield (Victory's Best) .15
642 Larry Walker (Victory's Best) .15
643 Magglio Ordonez (Victory's Best) .15
644 Jermaine Dye (Victory's Best) .15
645 Scott Rolen (Victory's Best) .20
646 Tony Gwynn (Victory's Best) .50
647 Shawn Green (Victory's Best) .15

648 Roberto Alomar (Victory's Best) .30
649 Eric Milton (Victory's Best) .15
650 Mark McGwire (Victory's Best) 1.00
651 Tim Hudson (Victory's Best) .15
652 Jose Canseco (Victory's Best) .20
653 Tom Glavine (Victory's Best) .20
654 Derek Jeter (Victory's Best) 1.00
655 Alex Rodriguez (Victory's Best) .75
656 Darin Erstad (Victory's Best) .15
657 Jason Kendall (Victory's Best) .15
658 Pedro Martinez (Victory's Best) .50
659 Richie Sexson (Victory's Best) .15
660 Rafael Palmeiro (Victory's Best) .20

2001 Upper Deck Vintage

		MT
Complete Set (400):		45.00
Common Player:		.10
Pack (10):		3.00
Box (24):		65.00
1	Darin Erstad	.40
2	Seth Etherton	.10
3	Troy Glaus	.75
4	Bengie Molina	.10
5	Mo Vaughn	.20
6	Tim Salmon	.25
7	Ramon Ortiz	.10
8	Adam Kennedy	.10
9	Garret Anderson	.10
10	Troy Percival	.10
11	2000 Angels Lineup	.10
12	Jason Giambi	.40
13	Tim Hudson	.10
14	Adam Piatt	.10
15	Miguel Tejada	.20
16	Mark Mulder	.10
17	Eric Chavez	.20
18	Ramon Hernandez	.10
19	Terrence Long	.10
20	Jason Isringhausen	.10
21	Barry Zito	.75
22	Ben Grieve	.25
23	2000 Athletics Lineup	.10
24	David Wells	.10
25	Raul Mondesi	.20
26	Darrin Fletcher	.10
27	Shannon Stewart	.10
28	Kelvim Escobar	.10
29	Tony Batista	.10
30	Carlos Delgado	.50
31	Brad Fullmer	.10
32	Billy Koch	.10
33	Jose Cruz Jr.	.10
34	2000 Blue Jays Lineup	.10
35	Greg Vaughn	.10
36	Roberto Hernandez	.10
37	Vinny Castilla	.10
38	Gerald Williams	.10
39	Aubrey Huff	.10
40	Bryan Rekar	.10
41	Albie Lopez	.10
42	Fred McGriff	.25
43	Miguel Cairo	.10
44	Ryan Rupe	.10
45	2000 Devil Rays Lineup	.10
46	Jim Thome	.25
47	Roberto Alomar	.50
48	Bartolo Colon	.10
49	Omar Vizquel	.20
50	Travis Fryman	.20
51	Manny Ramirez	.75
52	Dave Burba	.10
53	Chuck Finley	.10
54	Russ Branyan	.10
55	Kenny Lofton	.25
56	2000 Indians Lineup	.10
57	Alex Rodriguez	2.00
58	Jay Buhner	.10
59	Aaron Sele	.10
60	Kazuhiro Sasaki	.50
61	Edgar Martinez	.10
62	John Halama	.10
63	Mike Cameron	.10
64	Fred Garcia	.10
65	John Olerud	.20
66	Jamie Moyer	.10
67	Gil Meche	.10
68	2000 Mariners Lineup	.10
69	Cal Ripken Jr.	2.50
70	Sidney Ponson	.10
71	Chris Richard	.10
72	Jose Mercedes	.10
73	Albert Belle	.25
74	Mike Mussina	.50
75	Brady Anderson	.20
76	Delino DeShields	.10
77	Melvin Mora	.10
78	Luis Matos	.10
79	Brook Fordyce	.10
80	2000 Orioles Lineup	.10
81	Rafael Palmeiro	.50
82	Rick Helling	.10
83	Ruben Mateo	.10
84	Rusty Greer	.10
85	Ivan Rodriguez	.75
86	Doug Davis	.10
87	Gabe Kapler	.20
88	Mike Lamb	.10
89	Alex Rodriguez	3.00
90	Kenny Rogers	.10
91	2000 Rangers Lineup	.10
92	Nomar Garciaparra	2.00
93	Trot Nixon	.10
94	Tomokazu Ohka	.10
95	Pedro Martinez	.75
96	Dante Bichette	.20
97	Jason Varitek	.10
98	Rolando Arrojo	.10
99	Carl Everett	.10
100	Derek Lowe	.10
101	Troy O'Leary	.10
102	Tim Wakefield	.10
103	2000 Red Sox Lineup	.10
104	Mike Sweeney	.10
105	Carlos Febles	.10
106	Joe Randa	.10
107	Jeff Suppan	.10
108	Mac Suzuki	.10
109	Jermaine Dye	.10
110	Carlos Beltran	.10
111	Mark Quinn	.10
112	Johnny Damon	.10
113	2000 Royals Lineup	.10
114	Tony Clark	.10
115	Dean Palmer	.10
116	Brian Moehler	.10
117	Brad Ausmus	.10
118	Juan Gonzalez	.75
119	Juan Encarnacion	.10
120	Jeff Weaver	.10
121	Bobby Higginson	.10
122	Todd Jones	.10
123	Deivi Cruz	.10
124	2000 Tigers Lineup	.10
125	Corey Koskie	.10
126	Matt Lawton	.10
127	Mark Redman	.10
128	David Ortiz	.10
129	Jay Canizaro	.10
130	Eric Milton	.10
131	Jacque Jones	.10
132	J.C. Romero	.10
133	Ron Coomer	.10
134	Brad Radke	.10
135	2000 Twins Lineup	.10
136	Carlos Lee	.10
137	Frank Thomas	1.00
138	Mike Sirotka	.10
139	Charles Johnson	.10
140	James Baldwin	.10
141	Magglio Ordonez	.25
142	Jon Garland	.10
143	Paul Konerko	.10
144	Ray Durham	.10
145	Keith Foulke	.10
146	Chris Singleton	.10
147	2000 White Sox Lineup	.10
148	Bernie Williams	.50
149	Orlando Hernandez	.25
150	David Justice	.50
151	Andy Pettite	.25
152	Mariano Rivera	.20
153	Derek Jeter	2.50
154	Jorge Posada	.20
155	Jose Canseco	.50
156	Glenallen Hill	.10
157	Paul O'Neill	.25
158	Denny Neagle	.10
159	Chuck Knoblauch	.20
160	Roger Clemens	1.00
161	2000 Yankees Lineup	.10
162	Jeff Bagwell	.75
163	Moises Alou	.10
164	Lance Berkman	.15
165	Shane Reynolds	.10
166	Ken Caminiti	.10
167	Craig Biggio	.20
168	Jose Lima	.10
169	Octavio Dotel	.10
170	Richard Hidalgo	.20
171	Scott Elarton	.10
172	2000 Astros Lineup	.10
173	Rafael Furcal	.25
174	Greg Maddux	1.50
175	Quilvio Veras	.10
176	Chipper Jones	1.50
177	Andres Galarraga	.30
178	Brian Jordan	.10
179	Tom Glavine	.25
180	Kevin Millwood	.10
181	Javier Lopez	.20
182	B.J. Surhoff	.10
183	Andruw Jones	.50
184	Andy Ashby	.10
185	2000 Braves Lineup	.10
186	Richie Sexson	.10
187	Jeff D'Amico	.10
188	Ron Belliard	.10
189	Jeromy Burnitz	.10
190	Jimmy Haynes	.10
191	Marquis Grissom	.10
192	Jose Hernandez	.10
193	Geoff Jenkins	.20
194	Jamey Wright	.10
195	Mark Loretta	.10
196	2000 Brewers Lineup	.10
197	Rick Ankiel	.50
198	Mark McGwire	2.50
199	Fernando Vina	.10
200	David Renteria	.10
201	Darryl Kile	.10
202	Jim Edmonds	.25
203	Ray Lankford	.10
204	Garrett Stephenson	.10
205	Fernando Tatis	.10
206	Will Clark	.40
207	J.D. Drew	.25
208	2000 Cardinals Lineup	.10
209	Mark Grace	.25
210	Eric Young	.10
211	Sammy Sosa	1.50
212	Jon Lieber	.10
213	Joe Girardi	.10
214	Kevin Tapani	.10
215	Ricky Gutierrez	.10
216	Kerry Wood	.25
217	Rondell White	.20
218	Damon Buford	.10
219	2000 Cubs Lineup	.10
220	Luis Gonzalez	.20
221	Randy Johnson	.75
222	Jay Bell	.10
223	Erubiel Durazo	.10
224	Matt Williams	.30
225	Steve Finley	.10
226	Curt Schilling	.20
227	Todd Stottlemyre	.10
228	Tony Womack	.10
229	Brian Anderson	.10
230	2000 Diamondbacks Lineup	.10
231	Gary Sheffield	.40
232	Adrian Beltre	.25
233	Todd Hundley	.10
234	Chan Ho Park	.20
235	Shawn Green	.25
236	Kevin Brown	.20
237	Tom Goodwin	.10
238	Mark Grudzielanek	.10
239	Ismael Valdes	.10
240	Eric Karros	.10
241	2000 Dodgers Lineup	.10
242	Jose Vidro	.10
243	Javier Vazquez	.10
244	Orlando Cabrera	.10
245	Peter Bergeron	.10
246	Vladimir Guerrero	1.00
247	Dustin Hermanson	.10
248	Tony Armas Jr.	.10
249	Lee Stevens	.10
250	Milton Bradley	.10
251	Carl Pavano	.10
252	2000 Expos Lineup	.10
253	Ellis Burks	.10
254	Robb Nen	.10
255	J.T. Snow	.10
256	Barry Bonds	.75
257	Shawn Estes	.10
258	Jeff Kent	.20
259	Kirk Rueter	.10
260	Bill Mueller	.10
261	Livan Hernandez	.10
262	Rich Aurilia	.10
263	2000 Giants Lineup	.10
264	Ryan Dempster	.10
265	Cliff Floyd	.10
266	Mike Lowell	.10
267	A.J. Burnett	.10
268	Preston Wilson	.10
269	Luis Castillo	.10
270	Henry Rodriguez	.10
271	Antonio Alfonseca	.10
272	Derek Lee	.10
273	Mark Kotsay	.10
274	Brad Penny	.10
275	2000 Marlins Lineup	.10
276	Mike Piazza	2.00
277	Jay Payton	.10
278	Al Leiter	.25
279	Mike Bordick	.10
280	Armando Benitez	.10
281	Todd Zeile	.10
282	Mike Hampton	.20
283	Edgardo Alfonzo	.25
284	Derek Bell	.10
285	Robin Ventura	.20
286	2000 Mets Lineup	.10
287	Tony Gwynn	1.00
288	Trevor Hoffman	.10
289	Ryan Klesko	.10
290	Phil Nevin	.10
291	Matt Clement	.10
292	Ben Davis	.10
293	Ruben Rivera	.10
294	Bret Boone	.10
295	Adam Eaton	.10
296	Eric Owens	.10
297	2000 Padres Lineup	.10
298	Bob Abreu	.10
299	Mike Lieberthal	.10
300	Robert Person	.10
301	Scott Rolen	.50
302	Randy Wolf	.10
303	Bruce Chen	.10
304	Travis Lee	.10
305	Kent Bottenfield	.10
306	Pat Burrell	.50
307	Doug Glanville	.10
308	2000 Phillies Lineup	.10
309	Brian Giles	.25
310	Todd Ritchie	.10
311	Warren Morris	.10
312	John Vander Wal	.10
313	Kris Benson	.10
314	Jason Kendall	.10
315	Kevin Young	.10
316	Francisco Cordova	.10
317	Jimmy Anderson	.10

318 2000 Pirates Lineup .10
319 Ken Griffey Jr. 2.00
320 Pokey Reese .10
321 Chris Stynes .10
322 Barry Larkin .40
323 Steve Parris .10
324 Michael Tucker .10
325 Dmitri Young .10
326 Pete Harnisch .10
327 Adam Graves .10
328 Aaron Boone .10
329 Sean Casey .10
330 2000 Reds Lineup .10
331 Todd Helton .75
332 Pedro Astacio .10
333 Larry Walker .30
334 Ben Petrick .10
335 Brian Bohanon .10
336 Juan Pierre .10
337 Jeffrey Hammonds .10
338 Jeff Cirillo .10
339 Todd Hollandsworth .10
340 2000 Rockies Lineup .10
341 Matt Wise, Keith Luuloa, Derrick Turnbow (Vintage Rookies) .10
342 Jason Hart, Jose Ortiz, Mario Encarnacion (Vintage Rookies) .10
343 Vernon Wells, Pascual Coco, Josh Phelps (Vintage Rookies) .10
344 Travis Harper, Kenny Kelley, Toby Hall (Vintage Rookies) .10
345 Danys Baez, Tim Drew, *Martin Vargas* (Vintage Rookies) .10
346 *Ichiro Suzuki*, Ryan Franklin, Ryan Christianson (Vintage Rookies) 10.00
347 Jay Spurgeon, Lesli Brea, Carlos Casimiro (Vintage Rookies) .10
348 B.J. Waszgis, Brian Sikorski, Joaquin Benoit (Vintage Rookies) .10
349 Sun-Woo Kim, Paxton Crawford, Steve Lomasney (Vintage Rookies) .10
350 Kris Wilson, Orber Moreno, Dee Brown (Vintage Rookies) .10
351 Mark Johnson, Brandon Inge, Adam Bernero (Vintage Rookies) .10
352 Danny Ardoin, Matt Kinney, Jason Ryan (Vintage Rookies) .10
353 Rocky Biddle, Joe Crede, Aaron Myette (Vintage Rookies) .10
354 Nick Johnson, D'Angelo Jimenez, Willi Mo Pena (Vintage Rookies) .10
355 Tony McKnight, Aaron McNeal, Keith Ginter (Vintage Rookies) .10
356 Mark DeRosa, Jason Marquis, Wes Helms (Vintage Rookies) .10
357 Allen Levrault, Horacio Estrada, Santiago Perez (Vintage Rookies) .10
358 Luis Saturria, Gene Stechschulte, Britt Reames (Vintage Rookies) .10
359 Joey Nation, Corey Patterson, Cole Liniak (Vintage Rookies) .25
360 Alex Cabrera, Geraldo Guzman, Nelson Figueroa (Vintage Rookies) .10
361 Hiram Bocachica, Mike Judd, Luke Prokopec (Vintage Rookies) .10
362 Tomas de la Rosa, Yohanny Valera, Talmadge Nunnari (Vintage Rookies) .10
363 Ryan Vogelsong, Juan Melo, Chad Zerbe (Vintage Rookies) .10
364 Jason Grilli, Pablo Ozuna, Ramon Castro (Vintage Rookies) .10
365 Timoniel Perez, Grant Roberts, Brian Cole (Vintage Rookies) .10
366 Tom Davey, Xavier Nady, Dave Maurer (Vintage Rookies) 1.00
367 Jimmy Rollins, Mark Brownson, Reggie Taylor (Vintage Rookies) .10
368 Alex Hernandez, Adam Hyzdu, Tike Redman (Vintage Rookies) .10
369 Brady Clark, John Riedling, Mike Bell (Vintage Rookies) .10
370 Giovanni Carrara, Josh Kalinowski, Elvis Pena (Vintage Rookies) .10
371 Jim Edmonds (Postseason Scrapbook) .10
372 Edgar Martinez (Postseason Scrapbook) .10
373 Rickey Henderson (Postseason Scrapbook) .10
374 Barry Zito (Postseason Scrapbook) .40
375 Tino Martinez (Postseason Scrapbook) .10
376 J.T. Snow (Postseason Scrapbook) .10
377 Bobby Jones (Postseason Scrapbook) .10
378 Alex Rodriguez (Postseason Scrapbook) 1.00
379 Mike Hampton (Postseason Scrapbook) .10
380 Roger Clemens (Postseason Scrapbook) .50
381 Jay Payton (Postseason Scrapbook) .10
382 John Olerud (Postseason Scrapbook) .10
383 David Justice (Postseason Scrapbook) .25
384 Mike Hampton (Postseason Scrapbook) .10
385 Yankees Celebrate (Postseason Scrapbook) .75
386 Jose Vizcaino (Post-season Scrapbook) .10
387 Roger Clemens (Postseason Scrapbook) .50
388 Todd Zeile (Postseason Scrapbook) .10
389 Derek Jeter (Postseason Scrapbook) 1.25
390 Yankees Celebrate (Postseason Scrapbook) .50
391 Nomar Garciaparra - AL Batting (Big League Leaders) .75
392 Todd Helton - NL Batting (Big League Leaders) .40
393 Troy Glaus - AL HR (Big League Leaders) .40
394 Sammy Sosa - NL HR (Big League Leaders) .50
395 Edgar Martinez - AL RBI (Big League Leaders) .10
396 Todd Helton - NL RBI (Big League Leaders) .40
397 Pedro Martinez - AL ERA (Big League Leaders) .40
398 Kevin Brown - NL ERA (Big League Leaders) .10
399 David Wells, Tim Hudson - AL Wins (Big League Leaders) .10
400 Tom Glavine - NL Wins (Big League Leaders) .10

2001 Upper Deck Vintage All-Star Tributes

		MT
Complete Set (10):		40.00
Common Player:		2.00
Inserted 1:23		
1	Derek Jeter	8.00
2	Mike Piazza	6.00
3	Carlos Delgado	2.00
4	Pedro Martinez	2.50
5	Vladimir Guerrero	3.00
6	Mark McGwire	8.00
7	Alex Rodriguez	6.00
8	Barry Bonds	2.50
9	Chipper Jones	5.00
10	Sammy Sosa	5.00

2001 Upper Deck Vintage "Fantasy Outfield" Combo Jersey

MT

Production 25 cards

FO-CJ Joe DiMaggio, Mickey Mantle, Ken Griffey Jr. 1400.

2001 Upper Deck Vintage Glory Days

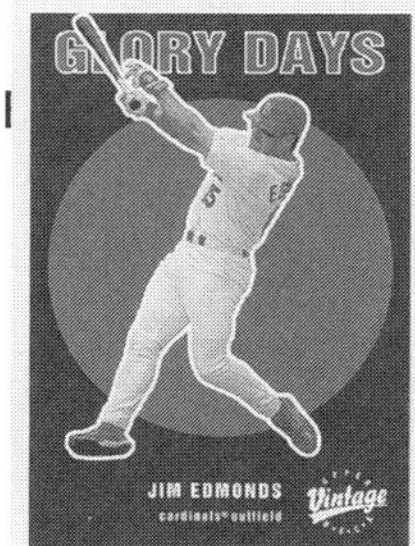

		MT
Complete Set (15):		30.00
Common Player:		1.00
Inserted 1:15		
1	Jermaine Dye	1.00
2	Chipper Jones	5.00
3	Todd Helton	2.50
4	Magglio Ordonez	1.00
5	Tony Gwynn	3.00
6	Jim Edmonds	1.50
7	Rafael Palmeiro	2.00
8	Barry Bonds	2.50
9	Carl Everett	1.00
10	Mike Piazza	6.00
11	Brian Giles	1.50
12	Tony Batista	1.00
13	Jeff Bagwell	2.50
14	Ken Griffey Jr.	6.00
15	Troy Glaus	2.50

2001 Upper Deck Vintage Mantle Pinstripes Memorabilia

MT

Print Runs listed:

MMBC Mickey Mantle bat/cut/7

MMB Mickey Mantle bat/100 350.00

MMCJ Mickey Mantle, Roger Maris jsy/50 750.00

MMC Mickey Mantle cut/7

MMJ Mickey Mantle jsy/100 400.00

2001 Upper Deck Vintage Mantle Pinstripes Exclusive

	MT
Complete Set (56):	150.00
Common Mantle:	4.00
One pack/box	

2001 Upper Deck Vintage Matinee Idols

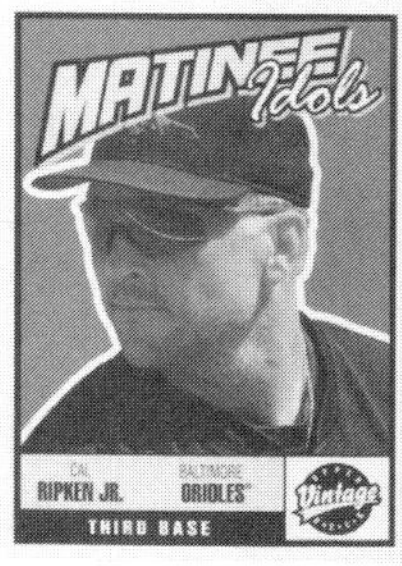

		MT
Complete Set (20):		25.00
Common Player:		.50
Inserted 1:4		
1	Ken Griffey Jr.	2.50
2	Derek Jeter	3.00
3	Barry Bonds	1.00
4	Chipper Jones	2.00
5	Mike Piazza	2.50
6	Todd Helton	1.00
7	Randy Johnson	1.00
8	Alex Rodriguez	2.50
9	Sammy Sosa	2.00
10	Cal Ripken Jr.	3.00
11	Nomar Garciaparra	2.50
12	Carlos Delgado	.75
13	Jason Giambi	.50
14	Ivan Rodriguez	1.00
15	Vladimir Guerrero	1.50
16	Gary Sheffield	.50
17	Frank Thomas	1.50
18	Jeff Bagwell	1.00
19	Pedro Martinez	1.00
20	Mark McGwire	3.00

2001 Upper Deck Vintage Retro Rules

		MT
Complete Set (15):		40.00
Common Player:		1.00
Inserted 1:15		
1	Nomar Garciaparra	6.00
2	Frank Thomas	3.00
3	Jeff Bagwell	2.50
4	Sammy Sosa	5.00
5	Derek Jeter	8.00
6	David Wells	1.00
7	Vladimir Guerrero	3.00

		MT
8	Jim Thome	1.50
9	Mark McGwire	8.00
10	Todd Helton	2.50
11	Tony Gwynn	3.00
12	Bernie Williams	2.00
13	Cal Ripken Jr.	8.00
14	Brian Giles	1.50
15	Jason Giambi	1.50

2001 Upper Deck Vintage "Timeless Teams" Bat

	MT
Common Player:	15.00
Inserted 1:72	
NYY-JDJoe DiMaggio	150.00
NYY-THTommy Henrich	25.00
NYY-CKCharlie Keller	15.00
NYY-BDBill Dickey	40.00
BK-JRJackie Robinson	150.00
BK-RCRoy Campanella	60.00
BK-GHGil Hodges	60.00
BK-DNDon Newcombe	25.00
LA-SGSteve Garvey	20.00
LA-RCRon Cey	20.00
LA-BRBill Russell	15.00
LA-DBDusty Baker	20.00
BA-BPBoog Powell	15.00
BA-BRBrooks Robinson	50.00
BA-FRFrank Robinson	40.00
BA-MBMark Belanger	15.00
PI-RCRoberto Clemente	250.00
PI-WSWillie Stargell	30.00
PI-MSManny Sanguillen	20.00
PI-AOAl Oliver	20.00
OA-RJReggie Jackson	50.00
OA-SBSal Bando	15.00
OA-GTGene Tenace	20.00
OA-JRJoe Rudi	15.00
CI2-JBJohnny Bench	60.00
CI2-TPTony Perez	30.00
CI2-JMJoe Morgan	40.00
CI2-KGKen Griffey Sr.	30.00
NYM-NRNolan Ryan	100.00
NYM-RSRon Swoboda	20.00
NYM-EKEd Kranepool	20.00
NYM-TATommie Agee	20.00

2001 Upper Deck Vintage "Timeless Teams" Jersey

	MT
Common Player:	25.00
Inserted 1:288	
NYY-MMMickey Mantle	225.00
NYY-RMRoger Maris	100.00
NYY-BRBobby Richardson	30.00
CI-DCDave Concepcion	25.00
CI-TPTony Perez	30.00
CI-KGKen Griffey Sr.	30.00
CI-JMJoe Morgan	50.00

2001 Upper Deck Vintage "Timeless Teams" Combo Bat

	MT
Common Player:	100.00
Production 100 sets	
NYY41Joe DiMaggio, Tommy Henrich, Bill Dickey, Charlie Keller	375.00
BKN55Jackie Robinson, Roy Campanella, Gil Hodges, Don Newcombe	475.00
BAL70Frank Robinson, Brooks Robinson, Mark Belanger, Boog Powell	200.00
LA81 Steve Garvey, Ron Cey, Dusty Baker, Bill Russell	100.00
PIT71Roberto Clemente, Willie Stargell, Bill Mazeroski, Al Oliver	475.00
OAK72Reggie Jackson, Sal Bando, Gene Tenace, Joe Rudi	100.00
CIN75Johnny Bench, Tony Perez, Joe Morgan, Ken Griffey Sr.	225.00
NYM69Nolan Ryan, Ron Swoboda, Ed Kranepool, Tommie Agee	275.00

2001 Upper Deck Vintage "Timeless Teams" Combo Jersey

	MT
Production 100 sets	
NYY61Mickey Mantle, Roger Maris, Bobby Richardson	500.00
CIN75Dave Concepcion, Tony Perez, Ken Griffey Sr.	150.00

2001 UD Reserve

		MT
Complete Set (210):		NA
Common Player:		.15
Common SP (181-210):		8.00
Production 2,500		
Pack (5):		2.50
Box (24):		55.00
1	Darin Erstad	.40
2	Tim Salmon	.25
3	Bengie Molina	.15
4	Troy Glaus	.75
5	Glenallen Hill	.15
6	Garret Anderson	.15
7	Jason Giambi	.40
8	Johnny Damon	.15
9	Eric Chavez	.25
10	Tim Hudson	.25
11	Miguel Tejada	.25
12	Barry Zito	.25
13	Jose Ortiz	.15
14	Tony Batista	.15
15	Carlos Delgado	.50
16	Shannon Stewart	.15
17	Raul Mondesi	.15
18	Ben Grieve	.15
19	Aubrey Huff	.15
20	Greg Vaughn	.15
21	Fred McGriff	.25
22	Gerald Williams	.15
23	Bartolo Colon	.15
24	Roberto Alomar	.50
25	Jim Thome	.25
26	Omar Vizquel	.25
27	Juan Gonzalez	.75
28	Ellis Burks	.15
29	Edgar Martinez	.15
30	Aaron Sele	.15
31	Jay Buhner	.15
32	Mike Cameron	.15
33	Kazuhiro Sasaki	.15
34	John Olerud	.25
35	Cal Ripken Jr.	2.50
36	Brady Anderson	.15
37	Pat Hentgen	.15
38	Chris Richard	.15
39	Jerry Hairston Jr.	.15
40	Mike Bordick	.15
41	Ivan Rodriguez	.75
42	Rick Helling	.15
43	Rafael Palmeiro	.50
44	Alex Rodriguez	2.00
45	Andres Galarraga	.25
46	Rusty Greer	.15
47	Ruben Mateo	.15
48	Ken Caminiti	.15
49	Nomar Garciaparra	2.00
50	Pedro Martinez	.75
51	Manny Ramirez	.75
52	Carl Everett	.15
53	Dante Bichette	.25
54	Hideo Nomo	.40
55	Mike Sweeney	.15
56	Carlos Beltran	.15
57	Jeff Suppan	.15
58	Jermaine Dye	.15
59	Mark Quinn	.15
60	Joe Randa	.15
61	Bobby Higginson	.15
62	Tony Clark	.15
63	Brian Moehler	.15
64	Dean Palmer	.15
65	Brandon Inge	.15
66	Damion Easley	.15
67	Brad Radke	.15
68	Corey Koskie	.15
69	Cristian Guzman	.15
70	Eric Milton	.15
71	Jacque Jones	.15
72	Matt Lawton	.15
73	Frank Thomas	.75
74	David Wells	.15
75	Magglio Ordonez	.25
76	Paul Konerko	.15
77	Sandy Alomar Jr.	.15
78	Ray Durham	.15
79	Roger Clemens	1.00
80	Bernie Williams	.50
81	Derek Jeter	2.50
82	David Justice	.40
83	Paul O'Neill	.25
84	Mike Mussina	.40
85	Jorge Posada	.25
86	Jeff Bagwell	.75
87	Richard Hidalgo	.25
88	Craig Biggio	.25
89	Scott Elarton	.15
90	Moises Alou	.25
91	Greg Maddux	1.50
92	Rafael Furcal	.25
93	Andruw Jones	.50
94	Tom Glavine	.25
95	Chipper Jones	1.50
96	Javy Lopez	.15
97	Richie Sexson	.15
98	Jeromy Burnitz	.15
99	Jeff D'Amico	.15
100	Jeffrey Hammonds	.15
101	Geoff Jenkins	.25
102	Ben Sheets	.25
103	Mark McGwire	2.50
104	Rick Ankiel	.25
105	Darryl Kile	.15
106	Edgar Renteria	.15
107	Jim Edmonds	.25
108	J.D. Drew	.25
109	Sammy Sosa	1.50
110	Corey Patterson	.25
111	Kerry Wood	.25
112	Todd Hundley	.15
113	Rondell White	.15
114	Matt Stairs	.15
115	Randy Johnson	.75
116	Mark Grace	.40
117	Steve Finley	.15
118	Luis Gonzalez	.40
119	Matt Williams	.25
120	Curt Schilling	.15
121	Gary Sheffield	.25
122	Kevin Brown	.15
123	Shawn Green	.25
124	Eric Karros	.15
125	Chan Ho Park	.25
126	Adrian Beltre	.25
127	Vladimir Guerrero	1.00
128	Fernando Tatis	.15
129	Lee Stevens	.15
130	Jose Vidro	.15
131	Peter Bergeron	.15
132	Michael Barrett	.15
133	Jeff Kent	.25
134	Russ Ortiz	.15
135	Barry Bonds	1.00
136	J.T. Snow	.15
137	Livan Hernandez	.15
138	Rich Aurilia	.15
139	Preston Wilson	.15
140	Mike Lowell	.15
141	Ryan Dempster	.15
142	Charles Johnson	.15
143	Matt Clement	.15
144	Luis Castillo	.15
145	Mike Piazza	2.00
146	Al Leiter	.15
147	Robin Ventura	.15
148	Jay Payton	.15
149	Todd Zeile	.15
150	Edgardo Alfonzo	.15
151	Tony Gwynn	1.00
152	Ryan Klesko	.15
153	Phil Nevin	.15
154	Mark Kotsay	.15
155	Trevor Hoffman	.15
156	Damian Jackson	.15
157	Scott Rolen	.40

158 Mike Lieberthal .15
159 Bruce Chen .15
160 Bobby Abreu .25
161 Pat Burrell .40
162 Travis Lee .15
163 Jason Kendall .15
164 Derek Bell .15
165 Kris Benson .15
166 Kevin Young .15
167 Brian Giles .25
168 Pat Meares .15
169 Sean Casey .25
170 Pokey Reese .15
171 Pete Harnisch .15
172 Barry Larkin .25
173 Ken Griffey Jr. 2.00
174 Dmitri Young .15
175 Mike Hampton .15
176 Todd Helton .75
177 Jeff Cirillo .15
178 Denny Neagle .15
179 Larry Walker .40
180 Todd Hollandsworth .15
181 *Ichiro Suzuki* (Rookie Reserve) 50.00
182 *Wilson Betemit* (Rookie Reserve) 15.00
183 *Adrian Hernandez* (Rookie Reserve) 8.00
184 *Travis Hafner* (Rookie Reserve) 8.00
185 *Sean Douglass* (Rookie Reserve) 8.00
186 *Juan Diaz* (Rookie Reserve) 8.00
187 *Horacio Ramirez* (Rookie Reserve) 8.00
188 *Morgan Ensberg* (Rookie Reserve) 8.00
189 *Brandon Duckworth* (Rookie Reserve) 10.00
190 *Jack Wilson* (Rookie Reserve) 8.00
191 *Erick Almonte* (Rookie Reserve) 8.00
192 *Ricardo Rodriguez* (Rookie Reserve) 8.00
193 *Elpidio Guzman* (Rookie Reserve) 8.00
194 *Juan Uribe* (Rookie Reserve) 8.00
195 *Ryan Freel* (Rookie Reserve) 8.00
196 *Christian Parker* (Rookie Reserve) 8.00
197 *Jackson Melian* (Rookie Reserve) 8.00
198 *Jose Mieses* (Rookie Reserve) 8.00
199 *Andres Torres* (Rookie Reserve) 8.00
200 *Jason Smith* (Rookie Reserve) 8.00
201 *Johnny Estrada* (Rookie Reserve) 10.00
202 *Cesar Crespo* (Rookie Reserve) 8.00
203 *Carlos Valderrama* (Rookie Reserve) 8.00
204 *Albert Pujols* (Rookie Reserve) 40.00
205 *Wilken Ruan* (Rookie Reserve) 8.00
206 *Josh Fogg* (Rookie Reserve) 10.00
207 *Bert Snow* (Rookie Reserve) 8.00
208 *Brian Lawrence* (Rookie Reserve) 10.00
209 *Esix Snead* (Rookie Reserve) 8.00
210 *Tsuyoshi Shinjo* (Rookie Reserve) 12.00

2001 UD Reserve Big Game Reserve

MT
Complete Set (10): 40.00
Common Player: 1.50
Inserted 1:24
BG1 Alex Rodriguez 6.00
BG2 Ken Griffey Jr. 6.00
BG3 Mark McGwire 8.00
BG4 Derek Jeter 8.00

MT
BG5 Sammy Sosa 5.00
BG6 Pedro Martinez 3.00
BG7 Jason Giambi 1.50
BG8 Todd Helton 2.50
BG9 Carlos Delgado 2.00
BG10 Mike Piazza 6.00

2001 UD Reserve G-U Reserve Base/Ball duo

MT
Common Player: 20.00
Inserted 1:240
B-JR Derek Jeter, Alex Rodriguez 50.00
B-JP Derek Jeter, Mike Piazza 60.00
B-MP Mark McGwire, Mike Piazza 100.00
B-MJ Mark McGwire, Derek Jeter 100.00
B-RM Alex Rodriguez, Mark McGwire 100.00
B-CR Roger Clemens, Alex Rodriguez 40.00
B-ST Sammy Sosa, Frank Thomas 40.00
B-GD Vladimir Guerrero, Carlos Delgado 20.00
B-BH Barry Bonds, Todd Helton 40.00
B-MG Mark McGwire, Ken Griffey Jr. 100.00
B-GS Ken Griffey Jr., Sammy Sosa 50.00
B-GJ Ken Griffey Jr., Derek Jeter 60.00
B-JN Chipper Jones, Nomar Garciaparra 40.00
B-NJ Nomar Garciaparra, Derek Jeter 60.00
B-GR Nomar Garciaparra, Alex Rodriguez 50.00

2001 UD Reserve G-U Reserve Base/Ball trio

MT
Common Card: 50.00
Inserted 1:480
B-JRG Derek Jeter, Alex Rodriguez, Nomar Garciaparra 90.00
B-SGM Sammy Sosa, Ken Griffey Jr., Mark McGwire 125.00
B-PRS Mike Piazza, Alex Rodriguez, Sammy Sosa 75.00
B-GSG Ken Griffey Jr., Sammy Sosa, Vladimir Guerrero 60.00
B-THM Frank Thomas, Todd Helton, Mark McGwire 100.00
B-CMJ Roger Clemens, Pedro Martinez, Derek Jeter 100.00
B-BSH Barry Bonds, Gary Sheffield, Todd Helton 50.00
B-GPJ Vladimir Guerrero, Mike Piazza, Chipper Jones 60.00
B-MJR Mark McGwire, Derek Jeter, Alex Rodriguez 125.00
B-JGS Derek Jeter, Ken Griffey Jr., Sammy Sosa 100.00

2001 UD Reserve G-U Reserve Base/Ball quad

MT
Common Player: 100.00
Production 50 sets
B-SGRM Sammy Sosa, Ken Griffey Jr., Alex Rodriguez, Mark McGwire 325.00
B-GPJG Vladimir Guerrero, Mike Piazza, Chipper Jones, Nomar Garciaparra 100.00
B-THMJ Frank Thomas, Todd Helton, Mark McGwire, Derek Jeter 250.00
B-GBJE Ken Griffey Jr., Barry Bonds, Andruw Jones, Jim Edmonds 175.00
B-PMJR Mike Piazza, Mark McGwire, Derek Jeter, Alex Rodriguez 375.00

2001 UD Reserve Jerseys duo

MT
Common Player: 20.00
Inserted 1:240
J-HG Tim Hudson, Jason Giambi 35.00
J-BK Barry Bonds, Jeff Kent 60.00
J-JJ Andruw Jones, Chipper Jones 40.00
J-GE Troy Glaus, Darin Erstad 35.00
J-WO David Wells, Magglio Ordonez 20.00
J-WE Bernie Williams, Jim Edmonds 25.00
J-DG Carlos Delgado, Jason Giambi 25.00
J-GK Jason Giambi, Jeff Kent 25.00
J-JW Randy Johnson, David Wells 25.00
J-JG Chipper Jones, Troy Glaus 40.00
J-SB Gary Sheffield, Barry Bonds 50.00
J-HE Todd Helton, Darin Erstad 35.00
J-RB Alex Rodriguez, Tony Batista 40.00
J-GW Brian Giles, Bernie Williams 25.00
J-SG Sammy Sosa, Troy Glaus 50.00

2001 UD Reserve Jerseys trio

MT
Common Player: 30.00
Inserted 1:480
J-GHD Jason Giambi, Todd Helton, Carlos Delgado 40.00
J-RSS Alex Rodriguez, Sammy Sosa, Gary Sheffield 75.00
J-WEJ Bernie Williams, Jim Edmonds, Andruw Jones 30.00
J-HJW Tim Hudson, Randy Johnson, David Wells 30.00
J-SOD Sammy Sosa, Magglio Ordonez, Carlos Delgado 60.00
J-GGR Jason Giambi, Troy Glaus, Alex Rodriguez 50.00
J-BWD Tony Batista, Bernie Williams, Carlos Delgado 30.00
J-BSH Barry Bonds, Gary Sheffield, Todd Helton 50.00
J-WSH David Wells, Sammy Sosa, Todd Helton 60.00
J-EKE Darin Erstad, Jeff Kent, Jim Edmonds 30.00

2001 UD Reserve Jerseys quad

MT
Common Player: 40.00
Production 50 sets
J-DRGS Carlos Delgado, Alex Rodriguez, Troy Glaus, Sammy Sosa 100.00
J-GWBG Jason Giambi, Bernie Williams, Barry Bonds, Brian Giles 75.00
J-HKEJ Todd Helton, Jeff Kent, Jim Edmonds, Chipper Jones 60.00
J-HKEJ Gary Sheffield, Magglio Ordonez, Darin Erstad, Tony Batista 40.00
J-JRSB Andruw Jones, Alex Rodriguez, Sammy Sosa, Barry Bonds 150.00

2001 UD Reserve The New Order

MT
Complete Set (10): 40.00
Common Player: 1.50
Inserted 1:24
NO1 Vladimir Guerrero 3.00
NO2 Andruw Jones 2.00
NO3 Corey Patterson 1.50
NO4 Derek Jeter 8.00
NO5 Alex Rodriguez 6.00
NO6 Pat Burrell 1.50
NO7 Ichiro Suzuki 20.00
NO8 Barry Zito 1.50
NO9 Rafael Furcal 1.50
NO10 Troy Glaus 2.50

2001 UD Reserve UD Royalty

MT
Complete Set (10): 50.00
Common Player: 1.50
Inserted 1:24
R1 Ken Griffey Jr. 6.00
R2 Derek Jeter 8.00
R3 Alex Rodriguez 6.00
R4 Sammy Sosa 5.00
R5 Mark McGwire 8.00
R6 Mike Piazza 6.00
R7 Vladimir Guerrero 3.00
R8 Chipper Jones 5.00
R9 Frank Thomas 2.50
R10 Nomar Garciaparra 6.00

2002 Upper Deck

	MT
Complete Set (745):	120.00
Complete Series I (500):	80.00
Complete Series II (245):	40.00
Common Player:	.15
Pack (8):	3.00
Box (24):	70.00

1 Mark Prior (Star Rookie) 6.00
2 Mark Teixeira (Star Rookie) 4.00
3 Brian Roberts (Star Rookie) .15
4 Jason Romano (Star Rookie) .15
5 *Dennis Stark* (Star Rookie) .50
6 Oscar Salazar (Star Rookie) .15
7 John Patterson (Star Rookie) .15
8 Shane Loux (Star Rookie) .15
9 Marcus Giles (Star Rookie) .15
10 Juan Cruz (Star Rookie) .15
11 Jorge Julio (Star Rookie) .15
12 Adam Dunn (Star Rookie) .15
13 Delvin James (Star Rookie) .15
14 Jeremy Affeldt (Star Rookie) .15
15 Tim Raines Jr. (Star Rookie) .15
16 Luke Hudson (Star Rookie) .15
17 Todd Sears (Star Rookie) .15
18 George Perez (Star Rookie) .15
19 Wilmy Caceres (Star Rookie) .15
20 Abraham Nunez (Star Rookie) .15
21 Mike Amrhein (Star Rookie) .50
22 Carlos Hernandez (Star Rookie) .15
23 Scott Hodges (Star Rookie) .15
24 Brandon Knight (Star Rookie) .15
25 Geoff Goetz (Star Rookie) .15
26 Carlos Garcia (Star Rookie) .15
27 Luis Pineda (Star Rookie) .15
28 Chris Gissell (Star Rookie) .15
29 Jae Weong (Star Rookie) .15
30 Paul Phillips (Star Rookie) .15
31 Cory Aldridge (Star Rookie) .15
32 *Aaron Cook* (Star Rookie) .25
33 Rendy Espina (Star Rookie) .15
34 Jason Phillips (Star Rookie) .15
35 Carlos Silva (Star Rookie) .15
36 Ryan Mills (Star Rookie) .15
37 Pedro Santana (Star Rookie) .15
38 John Grabow (Star Rookie) .15
39 Cody Ransom (Star Rookie) .15
40 Orlando Woodlands (Star Rookie) .15
41 Bud Smith (Star Rookie) .15
42 Junior Guerrero (Star Rookie) .15
43 David Brous (Star Rookie) .15
44 Steve Green (Star Rookie) .15
45 Brian Rogers (Star Rookie) .15
46 Juan Figueroa (Star Rookie) .15
47 Nick Punto (Star Rookie) .15
48 Junior Herndon (Star Rookie) .15
49 Justin Kaye (Star Rookie) .15
50 Jason Karnuth (Star Rookie) .15
51 Troy Glaus .75
52 Bengie Molina .15
53 Ramon Ortiz .15
54 Adam Kennedy .15
55 Jarrod Washburn .15
56 Troy Percival .15
57 David Eckstein .15
58 Ben Weber .15
59 Larry Barnes .15
60 Ismael Valdes .15
61 Benji Gil .15
62 Scott Schoeneweis .15
63 Pat Rapp .15
64 Jason Giambi .75
65 Mark Mulder .25
66 Ron Gant .15
67 Johnny Damon .15
68 Adam Piatt .15
69 Jermaine Dye .25
70 Jason Hart .15
71 Eric Chavez .40
72 Jim Mecir .15
73 Barry Zito .40
74 Jason Isringhausen .15
75 Jeremy Giambi .15
76 Olmedo Saenz .15
77 Terrence Long .15
78 Ramon Hernandez .15
79 Chris Carpenter .15
80 Raul Mondesi .15
81 Carlos Delgado .50
82 Billy Koch .15
83 Vernon Wells .15
84 Darrin Fletcher .15
85 Homer Bush .15
86 Pasqual Coco .15
87 Shannon Stewart .15
88 Chris Woodward .15
89 Joe Lawrence .15
90 Esteban Loaiza .15
91 Cesar Izturis .15
92 Kelvim Escobar .15
93 Greg Vaughn .15
94 Brent Abernathy .15
95 Tanyon Sturtze .15
96 Steve Cox .15
97 Aubrey Huff .15
98 Jesus Colome .15
99 Ben Grieve .15
100 Esteban Yan .15
101 Joe Kennedy .15
102 Felix Martinez .15
103 Nick Bierbrodt .15
104 Damian Rolls .15
105 Russ Johnson .15
106 Toby Hall .15
107 Roberto Alomar .75
108 Bartolo Colon .15
109 John Rocker .15
110 Juan Gonzalez 1.00
111 Einar Diaz .15
112 Chuck Finley .15
113 Kenny Lofton .25
114 Danys Baez .15
115 Travis Fryman .25
116 C.C. Sabathia .25
117 Paul Shuey .15
118 Marty Cordova .15
119 Ellis Burks .15
120 Bob Wickman .15
121 Edgar Martinez .25
122 Freddy Garcia .15
123 Ichiro Suzuki 4.00
124 John Olerud .40
125 Gil Meche .15
126 Dan Wilson .15
127 Aaron Sele .15
128 Kazuhiro Sasaki .15
129 Mark McLemore .15
130 Carlos Guillen .15
131 Al Martin .15
132 David Bell .15
133 Jay Buhner .15
134 Stan Javier .15
135 Tony Batista .15
136 Jason Johnson .15
137 Brook Fordyce .15
138 Mike Kinkade .15
139 Willis Roberts .15
140 David Segui .15
141 Josh Towers .15
142 Jeff Conine .15
143 Chris Richard .15
144 Pat Hentgen .15
145 Melvin Mora .15
146 Jerry Hairston Jr. .15
147 Calvin Maduro .15
148 Brady Anderson .15
149 Alex Rodriguez 2.50
150 Kenny Rogers .15
151 Chad Curtis .15
152 Ricky Ledee .15
153 Rafael Palmeiro .50
154 Rob Bell .15
155 Rick Helling .15
156 Doug Davis .15
157 Mike Lamb .15
158 Gabe Kapler .15
159 Jeff Zimmerman .15
160 Bill Haselman .15
161 Tim Crabtree .15
162 Carlos Pena .15
163 Nomar Garciaparra 2.00
164 Shea Hillenbrand .15
165 Hideo Nomo .40
166 Manny Ramirez 1.00
167 Jose Offerman .15
168 Scott Hatteberg .15
169 Trot Nixon .15
170 Darren Lewis .15
171 Derek Lowe .15
172 Troy O'Leary .15
173 Tim Wakefield .15
174 Chris Stynes .15
175 John Valentin .15
176 David Cone .15
177 Neifi Perez .15
178 Brent Mayne .15
179 Dan Reichert .15
180 A.J. Hinch .15
181 Chris George .15
182 Mike Sweeney .15
183 Jeff Suppan .15
184 Roberto Hernandez .15
185 Joe Randa .15
186 Paul Byrd .15
187 Luis Ordaz .15
188 Kris Wilson .15
189 Dee Brown .15
190 Tony Clark .15
191 Matt Anderson .15
192 Robert Fick .15
193 Juan Encarnacion .15
194 Dean Palmer .15
195 Victor Santos .15
196 Damion Easley .15
197 Jose Lima .15
198 Deivi Cruz .15
199 Roger Cedeno .15
200 Jose Macias .15
201 Jeff Weaver .15
202 Brandon Inge .15
203 Brian Moehler .15
204 Brad Radke .15
205 Doug Mientkiewicz .15
206 Cristian Guzman .15
207 Corey Koskie .15
208 LaTroy Hawkins .15
209 J.C. Romero .15
210 Chad Allen .15
211 Torii Hunter .15
212 Travis Miller .15
213 Joe Mays .15
214 Todd Jones .15
215 David Ortiz .15
216 Brian Buchanan .15
217 A.J. Pierzynski .15
218 Carlos Lee .15
219 Gary Glover .15
220 Jose Valentin .15
221 Aaron Rowand .15
222 Sandy Alomar Jr. .15
223 Herbert Perry .15
224 Jon Garland .15
225 Mark Buehrle .15
226 Chris Singleton .15
227 Kip Wells .15
228 Ray Durham .15
229 Joe Crede .15
230 Keith Foulke .15
231 Royce Clayton .15
232 Andy Pettite .40
233 Derek Jeter 3.00
234 Jorge Posada .40
235 Roger Clemens 1.50
236 Paul O'Neill .40
237 Nick Johnson .15
238 Gerald Williams .15
239 Mariano Rivera .25
240 Alfonso Soriano .40
241 Ramiro Mendoza .15
242 Mike Mussina .75
243 Luis Sojo .15
244 Scott Brosius .15
245 David Justice .40
246 Wade Miller .15
247 Brad Ausmus .15
248 Jeff Bagwell 1.00
249 Daryle Ward .15
250 Shane Reynolds .15
251 Chris Truby .15
252 Billy Wagner .15
253 Craig Biggio .25
254 Moises Alou .25
255 Vinny Castilla .15
256 Tim Redding .15
257 Roy Oswalt .40
258 Julio Lugo .15
259 Chipper Jones 2.00
260 Greg Maddux 2.00
261 Ken Caminiti .15
262 Kevin Millwood .15
263 Keith Lockhart .15
264 Rey Sanchez .15
265 Jason Marquis .15
266 Brian Jordan .15
267 Steve Karsay .15
268 Wes Helms .15
269 B.J. Surhoff .15
270 Wilson Betemit .15
271 John Smoltz .15
272 Rafael Furcal .15
273 Jeromy Burnitz .15
274 Jimmy Haynes .15
275 Mark Loretta .15
276 Jose Hernandez .15
277 Paul Rigdon .15
278 Alex Sanchez .15
279 Chad Fox .15
280 Devon White .15
281 Tyler Houston .15
282 Ronnie Belliard .15
283 Luis Lopez .15
284 Ben Sheets .25
285 Curtis Leskanic .15
286 Henry Blanco .15
287 Mark McGwire 2.50
288 Edgar Renteria .15
289 Matt Morris .15
290 Gene Stechschulte .15
291 Dustin Hermanson .15
292 Eli Marrero .15
293 Albert Pujols 1.50
294 Luis Saturria .15
295 Bobby Bonilla .15
296 Garrett Stephenson .15
297 Jim Edmonds .25
298 Rick Ankiel .25
299 Placido Polanco .15
300 Dave Veres .15
301 Sammy Sosa 2.00
302 Eric Young .15
303 Kerry Wood .25
304 Jon Lieber .15
305 Joe Girardi .15
306 Fred McGriff .40

307 Jeff Fassero .15
308 Julio Zuleta .15
309 Kevin Tapani .15
310 Rondell White .15
311 Julian Tavarez .15
312 Tom Gordon .15
313 Corey Patterson .25
314 Bill Mueller .15
315 Randy Johnson 1.00
316 Chad Moeller .15
317 Tony Womack .15
318 Erubiel Durazo .15
319 Luis Gonzalez .75
320 Brian Anderson .15
321 Reggie Sanders .15
322 Greg Colbrunn .15
323 Robert Ellis .15
324 Jack Cust .15
325 Bret Prinz .15
326 Steve Finley .15
327 Byung-Hyun Kim .15
328 Albie Lopez .15
329 Gary Sheffield .40
330 Mark Grudzielanek .15
331 Paul LoDuca .15
332 Tom Goodwin .15
333 Andy Ashby .15
334 Hiram Bocachica .15
335 Dave Hansen .15
336 Kevin Brown .25
337 Marquis Grissom .15
338 Terry Adams .15
339 Chan Ho Park .25
340 Adrian Beltre .25
341 Luke Prokopec .15
342 Jeff Shaw .15
343 Vladimir Guerrero 1.00
344 Orlando Cabrera .15
345 Tony Armas Jr. .15
346 Michael Barrett .15
347 Geoff Blum .15
348 Ryan Minor .15
349 Peter Bergeron .15
350 Graeme Lloyd .15
351 Jose Vidro .15
352 Javier Vazquez .15
353 Matt Blank .15
354 Masato Yoshii .15
355 Carl Pavano .15
356 Barry Bonds 2.00
357 Shawon Dunston .15
358 Livan Hernandez .15
359 Felix Rodriguez .15
360 Pedro Feliz .15
361 Calvin Murray .15
362 Robb Nen .15
363 Marvin Benard .15
364 Russ Ortiz .15
365 Jason Schmidt .15
366 Rich Aurilia .15
367 John Vander Wal .15
368 Benito Santiago .15
369 Ryan Dempster .15
370 Charles Johnson .15
371 Alex Gonzalez .15
372 Luis Castillo .15
373 Mike Lowell .15
374 Antonio Alfonseca .15
375 A.J. Burnett .15
376 Brad Penny .15
377 Jason Grilli .15
378 Derrek Lee .15
379 Matt Clement .15
380 Eric Owens .15
381 Vladimir Nunez .15
382 Cliff Floyd .15
383 Mike Piazza 2.50
384 Lenny Harris .15
385 Glendon Rusch .15
386 Todd Zeile .15
387 Al Leiter .25
388 Armando Benitez .15
389 Alex Escobar .15
390 Kevin Appier .15
391 Matt Lawton .15
392 Bruce Chen .15
393 John Franco .15
394 Tsuyoshi Shinjo .40
395 Rey Ordonez .15
396 Joe McEwing .15
397 Ryan Klesko .15
398 Brian Lawrence .15
399 Kevin Walker .15
400 Phil Nevin .15
401 Bubba Trammell .15
402 Wiki Gonzalez .15
403 D'Angelo Jimenez .15
404 Rickey Henderson .40
405 Mike Darr .15
406 Trevor Hoffman .15
407 Damian Jackson .15
408 Santiago Perez .15
409 Cesar Crespo .15
410 Robert Person .15
411 Travis Lee .15
412 Scott Rolen .40
413 Turk Wendell .15
414 Randy Wolf .15
415 Kevin Jordan .15
416 Jose Mesa .15
417 Mike Lieberthal .15
418 Bobby Abreu .15
419 Tomas Perez .15
420 Doug Glanville .15
421 Reggie Taylor .15
422 Jimmy Rollins .15
423 Brian Giles .25
424 Rob Mackowiak .15
425 Bronson Arroyo .15
426 Kevin Young .15
427 Jack Wilson .15
428 Adam Brown .15
429 Chad Hermansen .15
430 Jimmy Anderson .15
431 Aramis Ramirez .15
432 Todd Ritchie .15
433 Pat Meares .15
434 Warren Morris .15
435 Derek Bell .15
436 Ken Griffey Jr. 2.50
437 Elmer Dessens .15
438 Ruben Rivera .15
439 Jason LaRue .15
440 Sean Casey .25
441 Pete Harnisch .15
442 Danny Graves .15
443 Aaron Boone .15
444 Dmitri Young .15
445 Brandon Larson .15
446 Pokey Reese .15
447 Todd Walker .15
448 Juan Castro .15
449 Todd Helton 1.00
450 Ben Petrick .15
451 Juan Pierre .15
452 Jeff Cirillo .15
453 Juan Uribe .15
454 Brian Bohanon .15
455 Terry Shumpert .15
456 Mike Hampton .15
457 Shawn Chacon .15
458 Adam Melhuse .15
459 Greg Norton .15
460 Gabe White .15
461 Ichiro Suzuki (World Stage) 2.50
462 Carlos Delgado (World Stage) .40
463 Manny Ramirez (World Stage) .50
464 Miguel Tejada (World Stage) .15
465 Tsuyoshi Shinjo (World Stage) .25
466 Bernie Williams (World Stage) .40
467 Juan Gonzalez (World Stage) .50
468 Andruw Jones (World Stage) .40
469 Ivan Rodriguez (World Stage) .50
470 Larry Walker (World Stage) .20
471 Hideo Nomo (World Stage) .20
472 Albert Pujols (World Stage) 1.00
473 Pedro Martinez (World Stage) .75
474 Vladimir Guerrero (World Stage) .50
475 Tony Batista (World Stage) .15
476 Kazuhiro Sasaki (World Stage) .15
477 Richard Hidalgo (World Stage) .15
478 Carlos Lee (World Stage) .15
479 Roberto Alomar (World Stage) .40
480 Rafael Palmeiro (World Stage) .25
481 Ken Griffey Jr. (Griffey Gallery) .75
482 Ken Griffey Jr. (Griffey Gallery) .75
483 Ken Griffey Jr. (Griffey Gallery) .75
484 Ken Griffey Jr. (Griffey Gallery) .75
485 Ken Griffey Jr. (Griffey Gallery) .75
486 Ken Griffey Jr. (Griffey Gallery) .75
487 Ken Griffey Jr. (Griffey Gallery) .75
488 Ken Griffey Jr. (Griffey Gallery) .75
489 Ken Griffey Jr. (Griffey Gallery) .75
490 Ken Griffey Jr. (Griffey Gallery) .75
491 Barry Bonds (Season Highlights Checklist) .50
492 Hideo Nomo (Season Highlights Checklist) .15
493 Ichiro Suzuki (Season Highlights Checklist) .75
494 Cal Ripken Jr. (Season Highlights Checklist) .75
495 Tony Gwynn (Season Highlights Checklist) .40
496 Randy Johnson (Season Highlights Checklist) .40
497 A.J. Burnett (Season Highlights Checklist) .15
498 Rickey Henderson (Season Highlights Checklist) .15
499 Albert Pujols (Season Highlights Checklist) .50
500 Luis Gonzalez (Season Highlights Checklist) .25
501 *Brandon Puffer* .50
502 *Rodrigo Rosario* .75
503 *Tom Shearn* .50
504 *Reed Johnson* .50
505 *Chris Baker* .50
506 *John Ennis* .50
507 *Luis Martinez* .50
508 *So Taguchi* .75
509 *Scotty Layfield* .50
510 *Francis Beltran* .50
511 *Brandon Backe* .50
512 *Doug Devore* .50
513 *Jeremy Ward* .50
514 *Jose Vaverde* .50
515 *P.J. Bevis* .50
516 *Victor Alvarez* .50
517 *Kazuhisa Ishii* 4.00
518 *Jorge Nunez* .50
519 *Eric Good* .50
520 *Ron Calloway* .50
521 Valentino Pasucci .15
522 *Nelson Castro* .50
523 Deivis Santos .15
524 *Luis Ugueto* .50
525 Matt Thornton .15
526 *Hansel Izquierdo* .50
527 *Tyler Yates* .50
528 *Mark Corey* .50
529 *Jaime Cerda* .50
530 *Satoru Komiyama* .50
531 *Steve Bechler* .50
532 *Ben Howard* 1.00
533 *Anderson Machado* .50
534 *Jorge Padilla* .75
535 *Eric Junge* .50
536 *Adrian Burnside* .50
537 *Mike Gonzalez* .50
538 *Josh Hancock* .50
539 *Colin Young* .75
540 *Rene Reyes* .50
541 *Cam Esslinger* .50
542 *Tim Kalita* .50
543 *Kevin Frederick* .50
544 *Kyle Kane* .50
545 *Edwin Almonte* .50
546 Aaron Sele .15
547 Garret Anderson .15
548 Darin Erstad .25
549 Brad Fullmer .15
550 Kevin Appier .15
551 Tim Salmon .25
552 David Justice .25
553 Billy Koch .15
554 Scott Hatteberg .15
555 Tim Hudson .25
556 Miguel Tejada .25
557 Carlos Pena .15
558 Mike Sirotka .15
559 Jose Cruz Jr. .15
560 Josh Phelps .15
561 Brandon Lyon .15
562 Luke Prokopec .15
563 Felipe Lopez .15
564 Jason Standridge .15
565 Chris Gomez .15
566 John Flaherty .15
567 Jason Tyner .15
568 Bobby Smith .15
569 Wilson Alvarez .15
570 Matt Lawton .15
571 Omar Vizquel .25
572 Jim Thome .50
573 Brady Anderson .15
574 Alex Escobar .15
575 Russell Branyan .15
576 Bret Boone .15
577 Ben Davis .15
578 Mike Cameron .15
579 Jamie Moyer .15
580 Ruben Sierra .15
581 Jeff Cirillo .15
582 Marty Cordova .15
583 Mike Bordick .15
584 Brian Roberts .15
585 Luis Matos .15
586 Geronimo Gil .15
587 Jay Gibbons .15
588 Carl Everett .15
589 Ivan Rodriguez .50
590 Chan Ho Park .15
591 Juan Gonzalez .75
592 Hank Blalock .15
593 Todd Van Poppel .15
594 Pedro J. Martinez .75
595 Jason Varitek .15
596 Tony Clark .15
597 Johnny Damon .15
598 Dustin Hermanson .15
599 John Burkett .15
600 Carlos Beltran .15
601 Mark Quinn .15
602 Chuck Knoblauch .15
603 Michael Tucker .15
604 Carlos Febles .15
605 Jose Rosado .15
606 Dmitri Young .15
607 Bobby Higginson .15
608 Craig Paquette .15
609 Mitch Meluskey .15
610 Wendell Magee .15
611 Mike Rivera .15
612 Jacque Jones .15
613 Luis Rivas .15
614 Eric Milton .15
615 Eddie Guardado .15
616 Matt LeCroy .15
617 Mike Jackson .15
618 Magglio Ordonez .25
619 Frank Thomas .75
620 Rocky Biddle .15
621 Paul Konerko .25
622 Todd Ritchie .15
623 Jon Rauch .15
624 John Vander Wal .15
625 Rondell White .15
626 Jason Giambi 1.00
627 Robin Ventura .25
628 David Wells .15
629 Bernie Williams .50
630 Lance Berkman .40
631 Richard Hidalgo .15
632 Greg Zaun .15
633 Jose Vizcaino .15
634 Octavio Dotel .15
635 Morgan Ensberg .15
636 Andruw Jones .50
637 Tom Glavine .40
638 Gary Sheffield .40
639 Vinny Castilla .15
640 Javy Lopez .15
641 Albie Lopez .15
642 Geoff Jenkins .25
643 Jeffrey Hammonds .15
644 Alex Ochoa .15
645 Richie Sexson .25
646 Eric Young .15
647 Glendon Rusch .15
648 Tino Martinez .15
649 Fernando Vina .15

650	J.D. Drew	.25
651	Woody Williams	.15
652	Darryl Kile	.15
653	Jason Isringhausen	.15
654	Moises Alou	.15
655	Alex Gonzalez	.15
656	Delino DeShields	.15
657	Todd Hundley	.15
658	Chris Stynes	.15
659	Jason Bere	.15
660	Curt Schilling	.40
661	Craig Counsell	.15
662	Mark Grace	.40
663	Matt Williams	.25
664	Jay Bell	.15
665	Rick Helling	.15
666	Shawn Green	.40
667	Eric Karros	.15
668	Hideo Nomo	.40
669	Omar Daal	.15
670	Brian Jordan	.15
671	Cesar Izturis	.15
672	Fernando Tatis	.15
673	Lee Stevens	.15
674	Tomokazu Ohka	.15
675	Brian Schneider	.15
676	Brad Wilkerson	.15
677	Bruce Chen	.15
678	Tsuyoshi Shinjo	.25
679	Jeff Kent	.15
680	Kirk Rueter	.15
681	J.T. Snow	.15
682	David Bell	.15
683	Reggie Sanders	.15
684	Preston Wilson	.15
685	Vic Darensbourg	.15
686	Josh Beckett	.25
687	Pablo Ozuna	.15
688	Mike Redmond	.15
689	Scott Strickland	.15
690	Mo Vaughn	.40
691	Roberto Alomar	.50
692	Edgardo Alfonzo	.15
693	Shawn Estes	.15
694	Roger Cedeno	.15
695	Jeromy Burnitz	.15
696	Ray Lankford	.15
697	Mark Kotsay	.15
698	Kevin Jarvis	.15
699	Bobby Jones	.15
700	Sean Burroughs	.15
701	Ramon Vazquez	.15
702	Pat Burrell	.40
703	Marlon Byrd	.15
704	Brandon Duckworth	.15
705	Marlon Anderson	.15
706	Vicente Padilla	.15
707	Kip Wells	.15
708	Jason Kendall	.15
709	Pokey Reese	.15
710	Pat Meares	.15
711	Kris Benson	.15
712	Armando Rios	.15
713	Mike Williams	.15
714	Barry Larkin	.40
715	Adam Dunn	.75
716	Juan Encarnacion	.15
717	Scott Williamson	.15
718	Wilton Guerrero	.15
719	Chris Reitsma	.15
720	Larry Walker	.40
721	Denny Neagle	.15
722	Todd Zeile	.15
723	Jose Ortiz	.15
724	Jason Jennings	.15
725	Tony Eusebio	.15
726	Ichiro Suzuki	1.00
727	Barry Bonds	.75
728	Randy Johnson	.40
729	Albert Pujols	.50
730	Roger Clemens	.50
731	Sammy Sosa	.50
732	Alex Rodriguez	.50
733	Chipper Jones	.50
734	Rickey Henderson	.25
735	Marioners Team Photo	.15
736	Luis Gonzalez	.25
737	Derek Jeter	1.50
738	Ichiro Suzuki	1.00
739	Barry Bonds	.75
740	Curt Schilling	.25
741	Shawn Green	.25
742	Jason Giambi	.50
743	Roberto Alomar	.25
744	Larry Walker	.15
745	Mark McGwire	.75

2002 Upper Deck All-Star Salute Game Jerseys

		MT
Common Player:		10.00
Inserted 1:288		
SA	Sparky Anderson	10.00
LB	Lou Boudreau	15.00
DE	Dennis Eckersley	15.00
NF	Nellie Fox	40.00
KG	Ken Griffey Jr.	35.00
AR	Alex Rodriguez	25.00
DS	Don Sutton	10.00
IS	Ichiro Suzuki	80.00

2002 Upper Deck AL Centennial G-U Jerseys Autograph

		MT
Complete Set (3):		
Common Player:		
SAL-CR	Cal Ripken Jr.	
SAL-IR	Ivan Rodriguez	
SAL-NR	Nolan Ryan	

2002 Upper Deck AL Centennial Jerseys

		MT
Common Player:		15.00
Inserted 1:144		
PM	Pedro Martinez	20.00
CR	Cal Ripken Jr.	40.00
AR	Alex Rodriguez	25.00
IR	Ivan Rodriguez	15.00
NR	Nolan Ryan	40.00
FT	Frank Thomas	15.00

2002 Upper Deck AL Centennial Bats

		MT
Common Player:		100.00
Inserted 1:144		
JD	Joe DiMaggio	125.00
MM	Mickey Mantle	150.00
BR	Babe Ruth	180.00

2002 Upper Deck Big Fly Zone

		MT
Complete Set (10):		20.00
Common Player:		1.00
Inserted 1:14		
Z1	Mark McGwire	4.00
Z2	Ken Griffey Jr.	4.00
Z3	Manny Ramirez	1.50
Z4	Sammy Sosa	3.00
Z5	Todd Helton	1.50
Z6	Barry Bonds	3.00
Z7	Luis Gonzalez	1.00
Z8	Alex Rodriguez	4.00
Z9	Carlos Delgado	1.00
Z10	Chipper Jones	3.00

2002 Upper Deck Breakout Performers

		MT
Complete Set (10):		12.00
Common Player:		.50
Inserted 1:14		
BP1	Ichiro Suzuki	6.00
BP2	Albert Pujols	3.00
BP3	Doug Mientkiewicz	.50
BP4	Lance Berkman	.75
BP5	Tsuyoshi Shinjo	1.00
BP6	Ben Sheets	.75
BP7	Jimmy Rollins	.50
BP8	J.D. Drew	.75
BP9	Bret Boone	.50
BP10	Alfonso Soriano	.75

2002 Upper Deck Championship Caliber

		MT
Complete Set (6):		12.00
Common Player:		1.00
Inserted 1:23		
CC1	Derek Jeter	5.00
CC2	Roberto Alomar	1.25
CC3	Chipper Jones	3.00
CC4	Gary Sheffield	1.00
CC5	Roger Clemens	2.50
CC6	Greg Maddux	3.00

2002 Upper Deck Championship Caliber Swatches

		MT
Common Player:		8.00
Inserted 1:288		
RA	Roberto Alomar/ SP	20.00
KB	Kevin Brown/SP	15.00
CF	Cliff Floyd	10.00
ChJ	Charles Johnson	8.00
RJ	Randy Johnson	20.00
CJo	Chipper Jones/SP	30.00
BL	Barry Larkin	10.00
GM	Greg Maddux/SP	40.00
TM	Tino Martinez	15.00
JO	John Olerud	10.00
AP	Andy Pettite	15.00
JP	Jorge Posada	12.00
CS	Curt Schilling	15.00
BW	Bernie Williams	12.00

2002 Upper Deck Chasing History

		MT
Complete Set (15):		15.00
Common Player:		.75
Inserted 1:11		
CH1	Sammy Sosa	2.50
CH2	Ken Griffey Jr.	3.00
CH3	Roger Clemens	1.50
CH4	Barry Bonds	3.00
CH5	Rafael Palmeiro	1.00
CH6	Andres Galarraga	.75
CH7	Juan Gonzalez	1.00
CH8	Roberto Alomar	1.00
CH9	Randy Johnson	1.50
CH10	Jeff Bagwell	1.25
CH11	Fred McGriff	.75
CH12	Matt Williams	.75
CH13	Greg Maddux	2.50
CH14	Robb Nen	.75
CH15	Kenny Lofton	1.00

2002 Upper Deck Combo Jersey

		MT
Common Player:		15.00
Inserted 1:288		
RS	Alex Rodriguez, Sammy Sosa	40.00
RM	Nolan Ryan, Pedro Martinez	60.00
RC	Nolan Ryan, Roger Clemens	60.00
BS	Barry Bonds, Sammy Sosa	50.00
HK	Shigetoshi Hasegawa, Byung-Hun Kim	15.00

2002 Upper Deck Combo Bat

		MT
Common Combo:		40.00
Inserted 1:288		
CB-RG	Alex Rodriguez, Ken Griffey Jr.	40.00
CB-DM	Joe DiMaggio, Mickey Mantle	275.00

2002 Upper Deck First Timers Jerseys

		MT
Common Player:		10.00
Inserted 1:288		
RB	Russell Branyan	15.00
OD	Omar Daal	10.00
FG	Freddy Garcia	15.00
ML	Matt Lawton	10.00
JM	Joe Mays	15.00
EM	Eric Milton	10.00
CP	Corey Patterson	15.00
AP	Albert Pujols	50.00
SS	Shannon Stewart	10.00

2002 Upper Deck First Timers Jerseys Autograph

		MT
Complete Set (4):		
Common Player:		

SFT-FGFreddy Garcia
SFT-JMJoe Mays
SFT-APAlbert Pujols
SFT-SSShannon Stewart

2002 Upper Deck Game Jerseys

		MT
Common Player:		8.00
Production 350 sets		
Golds:		.75-1.5X
Production 100		
TB	Tony Batista	8.00
AB	Adrian Beltre	8.00
JC	Jeff Cirillo	8.00
KG	Ken Griffey Jr.	30.00
TH	Tim Hudson	10.00
MP	Mike Piazza	20.00
SR	Scott Rolen	15.00
CS	Curt Schilling	15.00
SS	Sammy Sosa	25.00
FT	Frank Thomas	12.00
PW	Preston Wilson	8.00

2002 Upper Deck Game Jersey Autograph

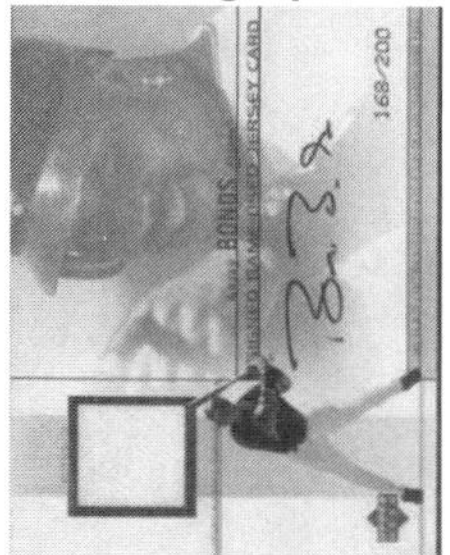

		MT
Common Player:		20.00
Production 200 sets		
BB	Barry Bonds	125.00
CD	Carlos Delgado	125.00
RF	Rafael Furcal	50.00
JGi	Jason Giambi	75.00
KG	Ken Griffey Jr.	225.00
AJ	Andruw Jones	50.00
AP	Albert Pujols	120.00
CR	Cal Ripken Jr.	200.00
NR	Nolan Ryan	140.00
GS	Gary Sheffield	40.00
IS	Ichiro Suzuki	600.00
PW	Preston Wilson	20.00

2002 Upper Deck Game-Used Base

		MT
Common Player:		10.00
Inserted 1:288		
BB	Barry Bonds	20.00
RC	Roger Clemens	20.00
CD	Carlos Delgado	
JG	Jason Giambi	15.00
TG	Troy Glaus	15.00
JG	Juan Gonzalez	15.00
LG	Luis Gonzalez	15.00
SG	Shawn Green	10.00
KG	Ken Griffey Jr.	30.00
DJ	Derek Jeter	40.00
AJ	Andruw Jones	15.00
CJ	Chipper Jones	20.00
MM	Mark McGwire	50.00
MP	Mike Piazza	25.00
CR	Cal Ripken Jr.	40.00
AR	Alex Rodriguez	15.00
IR	Ivan Rodriguez	10.00
KS	Kazuhiro Sasaki	10.00
SS	Sammy Sosa	20.00
IS	Ichiro Suzuki	90.00

2002 Upper Deck Game-Used Base Combo

		MT
Common Combo:		40.00
Inserted 1:288		
RG	Alex Rodriguez, Ken Griffey Jr.	40.00
MJ	Mark McGwire, Derek Jeter	60.00

2002 Upper Deck Game-Used Base Autograph

MT

Complete Set (1):
SB-KGKen Griffey Jr.

2002 Upper Deck Game-Worn Gems

		MT
Common Player:		5.00
Inserted 1:48		
Golds:		1-2X
Production 100 sets		
RA	Roberto Alomar	8.00
EC	Eric Chavez	6.00
CD	Carlos Delgado	8.00
DE	Darin Erstad/SP	10.00
FG	Freddy Garcia/SP	8.00
TG	Tom Glavine	8.00
JG	Juan Gonzalez	8.00
LG	Luis Gonzalez/SP	10.00
MH	Mike Hampton/SP	8.00
CJ	Chipper Jones	20.00
JK	Jason Kendall	5.00
RK	Ryan Klesko/SP	8.00
GM	Greg Maddux	20.00
EM	Edgar Martinez	8.00
PM	Pedro Martinez/SP	15.00
TM	Tino Martinez	8.00
JM	Joe Mays	5.00
EM	Eric Milton	5.00
PN	Phil Nevin	5.00
HN	Hideo Nomo/SP	30.00
JO	John Olerud/SP	8.00
RP	Robert Person	5.00
CR	Cal Ripken Jr.	40.00
IR	Ivan Rodriguez	10.00
SR	Scott Rolen	10.00
CS	Curt Schilling	10.00
AS	Aaron Sele	5.00
GS	Gary Sheffield/SP	8.00
FT	Frank Thomas	10.00
OV	Omar Vizquel/SP	10.00
RY	Robin Yount	25.00

2002 Upper Deck Double Game-Worn Gems

		MT
Common Card:		8.00
Production 450 sets		
Golds:		1-2X
Production 100 sets		
NK	Phil Nevin, Ryan Klesko	8.00
VB	Omar Vizquel, Russell Branyan	15.00
DH	Jermaine Dye, Tim Hudson	10.00
TO	Frank Thomas, Magglio Ordonez	15.00
MI	Edgar Martinez, Ichiro Suzuki/150	80.00
GS	Luis Gonzalez, Curt Schilling	15.00
AP	Roberto Alomar, Mike Piazza	20.00
PL	Robert Person, Mike Lieberthal	8.00
MM	Kevin Millwood, Greg Maddux	20.00
KG	Jason Kendall, Brian Giles	10.00
DF	Carlos Delgado, Shannon Stewart	10.00
PN	Chan Ho Park, Hideo Nomo	35.00

2002 Upper Deck Global Swatch Jerseys

		MT
Common Player:		10.00
Inserted 1:144		
CD	Carlos Delgado	15.00
SH	Shigetoshi Hasegawa	10.00
BK	Byung-Hun Kim	15.00
HN	Hideo Nomo	35.00
CP	Chan Ho Park	15.00
MR	Manny Ramirez	20.00
KS	Kazuhiro Sasaki	15.00
TS	Tsuyoshi Shinjo	20.00
IS	Ichiro Suzuki	120.00
MY	Masato Yoshii	10.00

2002 Upper Deck Global Swatch Jerseys Autograph

MT

Complete Set (2):
Common Player:
SGS-CDCarlos Delgado
SGS-BKByun-Hun Kim

2002 Upper Deck McGwire Memorabilia

		MT
Common Card:		
AM-J	Mark McGwire/ jsy/70	475.00
AM-B	Mark McGwire/ bat/70	550.00
MMc	Mark McGwire/500 HR Club bat/350	550.00
S-MMc	Mark McGwire/ 500 HR Auto./25	
MM-SS	Mark McGwire, Sammy Sosa/25 (combo jersey)	600.00
MM-KG	Mark McGwire, Ken Griffey Jr/25 (combo jersey)	650.00
MM-JG	Mark McGwire, Jason Giambi/25 (combo jersey)	475.00

2002 Upper Deck Return of the Ace

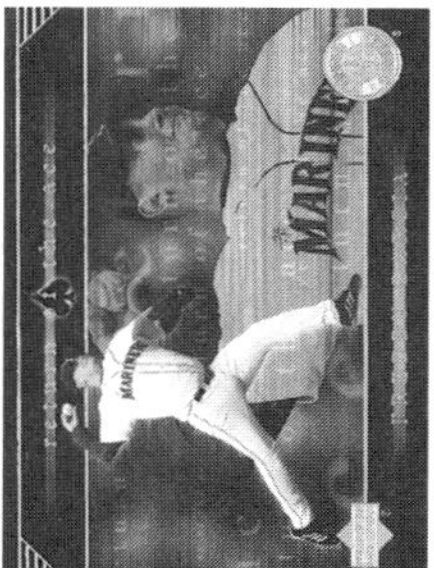

		MT
Complete Set (15):		15.00
Common Player:		1.00
Inserted 1:11		
RA1	Randy Johnson	2.00
RA2	Greg Maddux	3.00
RA3	Pedro Martinez	2.00
RA4	Freddy Garcia	1.00
RA5	Matt Morris	1.00
RA6	Mark Mulder	1.00
RA7	Wade Miller	1.00
RA8	Kevin Brown	1.00
RA9	Roger Clemens	3.00
RA10	Jon Lieber	1.00
RA11	C.C. Sabathia	1.00
RA12	Tim Hudson	1.50
RA13	Curt Schilling	2.00
RA14	Al Leiter	1.00
RA15	Mike Mussina	1.50

2002 Upper Deck Sons of Summer Game Jerseys

		MT
Common Player:		10.00
Inserted 1:288		
RA	Roberto Alomar	10.00
JB	Jeff Bagwell	10.00
RC	Roger Clemens	15.00
JG	Juan Gonzalez	10.00
GM	Greg Maddux	15.00
PM	Pedro Martinez/ SP	15.00
MP	Mike Piazza	15.00
AR	Alex Rodriguez	15.00

2002 Upper Deck Superstar Summit

		MT
Complete Set (6):		15.00
Common Player:		1.50
Inserted 1:23		
SS1	Sammy Sosa	3.00
SS2	Alex Rodriguez	4.00
SS3	Mark McGwire	4.00
SS4	Barry Bonds	3.00
SS5	Mike Piazza	4.00
SS6	Ken Griffey Jr.	4.00

2002 Upper Deck Superstar Summit II

		MT
Complete Set (15):		25.00
Common Player:		1.00
Inserted 1:11		
SS1	Alex Rodriguez	4.00
SS2	Jason Giambi	1.50
SS3	Vladimir Guerrero	1.25
SS4	Randy Johnson	1.25
SS5	Chipper Jones	2.50
SS6	Ichiro Suzuki	4.00
SS7	Sammy Sosa	2.50
SS8	Greg Maddux	2.50
SS9	Ken Griffey Jr.	3.00
SS10	Todd Helton	1.25
SS11	Barry Bonds	3.00
SS12	Derek Jeter	5.00
SS13	Mike Piazza	4.00
SS14	Ivan Rodriguez	1.00
SS15	Frank Thomas	1.25

2002 Upper Deck The People's Choice Game Jerseys

		MT
Common Player:		6.00
Inserted 1:24		
Golds:		1-2X
Production 100 sets		
JBa	Jeff Bagwell	10.00
EB	Ellis Burks/SP	10.00
JBu	Jeromy Burnitz	6.00
OD	Omar Daal	6.00
CD	Carlos Delgado	8.00
RF	Rafael Furcal	6.00
AG	Andres Galarraga/SP	10.00
BG	Brian Giles	10.00
JG	Juan Gonzalez	10.00
KG	Ken Griffey Jr.	20.00
TG	Tony Gwynn	12.00
SH	Sterling Hitchcock	6.00
HI	Hideki Irabu	6.00
CJ	Charles Johnson	6.00
DL	Derek Lowe	8.00
GM	Greg Maddux	15.00
TM	Tino Martinez	10.00
JN	Jeff Nelson	6.00
RO	Rey Ordonez	6.00
RP	Rafael Palmeiro/SP	15.00
RP	Robert Person/SP	10.00
AP	Andy Pettite	10.00
MP	Mike Piazza	20.00
TR	Tim Raines	6.00
MRa	Manny Ramirez	10.00
MRi	Mariano Rivera	8.00
AR	Alex Rodriguez	15.00
TS	Tim Salmon	6.00
CS	Curt Schilling	10.00
TSh	Tsuyoshi Shinjo	10.00
JS	J.T. Snow	6.00
SS	Sammy Sosa	20.00
MS	Mike Stanton	6.00
FT	Frank Thomas	10.00
RV	Robin Ventura	6.00
OV	Omar Vizquel	6.00
DW	David Wells	6.00
BW	Bernie Williams	8.00
MW	Matt Williams/SP	15.00

2002 Upper Deck UD Patch Logo

		MT
Common Player:		60.00
Inserted 1:2,500		
Prices for Stripes & Numbers identical		
BB	Barry Bonds	125.00
JG	Jason Giambi	60.00
KG	Ken Griffey Jr.	200.00
PM	Pedro Martinez	100.00
CR	Cal Ripken Jr.	200.00
AR	Alex Rodriguez	125.00
SS	Sammy Sosa	100.00

2002 Upper Deck UD-Plus

		MT
Common Player:		2.00
Production 1,125 sets		
1 two-card pack per Series 2 H pack		
Comp. Set can be exchanged for Jsy cards		
Redemption Deadline 5-16-03		
UD1	Darin Erstad	3.00
UD2	Troy Glaus	3.00
UD3	Tim Hudson	3.00
UD4	Jermaine Dye	2.00
UD5	Barry Zito	2.00
UD6	Carlos Delgado	3.00
UD7	Shannon Stewart	2.00
UD8	Greg Vaughn	2.00
UD9	Jim Thome	3.00
UD10	C.C. Sabathia	2.00
UD11	Ichiro Suzuki	12.00
UD12	Edgar Martinez	2.00
UD13	Bret Boone	2.00
UD14	Freddy Garcia	2.00
UD15	Matt Thornton	2.00
UD16	Jeff Conine	2.00
UD17	Steve Bechler	2.00
UD18	Rafael Palmeiro	3.00
UD19	Juan Gonzalez	4.00
UD20	Alex Rodriguez	10.00
UD21	Ivan Rodriguez	3.00
UD22	Carl Everett	2.00
UD23	Manny Ramirez	4.00
UD24	Nomar Garciaparra	10.00
UD25	Pedro J. Martinez	4.00
UD26	Mike Sweeney	2.00
UD27	Chuck Knoblauch	2.00
UD28	Dmitri Young	2.00
UD29	Bobby Higginson	2.00
UD30	Dean Palmer	2.00
UD31	Doug Mientkiewicz	2.00
UD32	Corey Koskie	2.00
UD33	Brad Radke	2.00
UD34	Cristian Guzman	2.00
UD35	Frank Thomas	4.00
UD36	Magglio Ordonez	3.00
UD37	Carlos Lee	2.00
UD38	Roger Clemens	6.00
UD39	Bernie Williams	3.00
UD40	Derek Jeter	15.00
UD41	Jason Giambi	5.00
UD42	Mike Mussina	3.00
UD43	Jeff Bagwell	4.00
UD44	Lance Berkman	4.00
UD45	Wade Miller	2.00
UD46	Greg Maddux	8.00
UD47	Chipper Jones	8.00
UD48	Andruw Jones	4.00
UD49	Gary Sheffield	3.00
UD50	Richie Sexson	3.00
UD51	Albert Pujols	8.00
UD52	J.D. Drew	3.00
UD53	Matt Morris	2.00
UD54	Jim Edmonds	3.00
UD55	So Taguchi	3.00
UD56	Sammy Sosa	8.00
UD57	Fred McGriff	3.00
UD58	Kerry Wood	3.00
UD59	Moises Alou	2.00
UD60	Randy Johnson	4.00
UD61	Luis Gonzalez	3.00
UD62	Mark Grace	3.00
UD63	Curt Schilling	4.00
UD64	Matt Williams	2.00
UD65	Kevin Brown	2.00
UD66	Brian Jordan	2.00
UD67	Shawn Green	3.00
UD68	Hideo Nomo	3.00
UD69	Kazuhisa Ishii	20.00
UD70	Vladimir Guerrero	4.00
UD71	Jose Vidro	2.00
UD72	Eric Good	2.00
UD73	Barry Bonds	8.00
UD74	Jeff Kent	3.00
UD75	Rich Aurilia	2.00
UD76	Deivis Santos	2.00
UD77	Preston Wilson	2.00
UD78	Cliff Floyd	2.00
UD79	Josh Beckett	2.00
UD80	Hansel Izquierdo	2.00
UD81	Mike Piazza	10.00
UD82	Roberto Alomar	3.00
UD83	Mo Vaughn	3.00
UD84	Jeromy Burnitz	2.00
UD85	Phil Nevin	2.00
UD86	Ryan Klesko	2.00
UD87	Bobby Abreu	2.00
UD88	Scott Rolen	3.00
UD89	Jimmy Rollins	2.00
UD90	Jason Kendall	2.00
UD91	Brian Giles	3.00
UD92	Aramis Ramirez	2.00
UD93	Ken Griffey Jr.	10.00
UD94	Sean Casey	2.00
UD95	Barry Larkin	3.00
UD96	Adam Dunn	4.00
UD97	Todd Helton	4.00
UD98	Larry Walker	3.00
UD99	Mike Hampton	2.00
UD100	Rene Reyes	2.00

2002 Upper Deck World Series Heroes Base

		MT
Complete Set (1):		
DJ	Derek Jeter	40.00

2002 Upper Deck World Series Heroes Jerseys

		MT
Common Player:		10.00
Inserted 1:288		
JC	Joe Carter	10.00
CF	Carlton Fisk	15.00
DL	Don Larsen	30.00
BM	Bill Mazeroski	15.00

2002 Upper Deck World Series Heroes Bats

		MT
Common Player:		15.00
Inserted 1:288		
JD	Joe DiMaggio	120.00
MM	Mickey Mantle	150.00
KP	Kirby Puckett	30.00
ES	Enos Slaughter	15.00

2002 Upper Deck Yankees Dynasty Jerseys

		MT
Common Combo:		20.00
Inserted 1:288		
PR	Andy Pettite, Mariano Rivera	40.00
BT	Wade Boggs, Joe Torre	30.00
CP	Roger Clemens, Jorge Posada	50.00
DM	Joe DiMaggio, Mickey Mantle	300.00
RK	Willie Randolph, Chuck Knoblauch	20.00
BJ	Scott Brosius, David Justice	30.00
OM	Paul O'Neill, Tino Martinez	40.00
WO	Bernie Williams, Paul O'Neill	40.00
WG	David Wells, Dwight Gooden	25.00
GC	Joe Girardi, David Cone	25.00
KR	Chuck Knoblauch, Tim Raines	25.00

2002 Upper Deck Yankees Dynasty Combo Base

		MT
Common Combo:		50.00
JW	Derek Jeter, Bernie Williams	60.00
CJ	Roger Clemens, Derek Jeter	75.00

2002 Upper Deck 2001 All-Star HR Derby Jerseys

		MT
Common Player:		15.00
Inserted 1:288		
BrB	Bret Boone	15.00
JG	Jason Giambi	20.00
TG	Troy Glaus	
TH	Todd Helton	15.00
AR	Alex Rodriguez	25.00
SS	Sammy Sosa	30.00

2002 Upper Deck 2001's Greatest Hits

		MT
Complete Set (10):		30.00
Common Player:		1.00
Inserted 1:14		
GH1	Barry Bonds	3.00
GH2	Ichiro Suzuki	6.00
GH3	Albert Pujols	3.00
GH4	Mike Piazza	4.00
GH5	Alex Rodriguez	4.00
GH6	Mark McGwire	4.00
GH7	Manny Ramirez	1.50
GH8	Ken Griffey Jr.	4.00
GH9	Sammy Sosa	3.00
GH10	Derek Jeter	5.00

2002 Upper Deck Diamond Connection

MT
Complete Set (550): NA
Common Player: .15
Common Rk (91-200): 4.00
Production 1,500
Common Jersey
(201-270): 5.00
Production 775
Common Jersey
(271-320): 5.00
Production 200
Common Jersey
(321-353): 5.00
Production 150
Common Jersey
(354-368): 6.00
Production 100
Common Bat (369-438): 5.00
Production 775
Common Bat (439-488): 5.00
Production 200
Common Bat (489-521): 5.00
Production 150
Common Bat (522-536): 10.00
Production 100
Pack (5): 6.00
Box (14): 75.00
1 Troy Glaus .50
2 Darin Erstad .40
3 Barry Zito .40
4 Eric Chavez .40
5 Tim Hudson .40
6 Miguel Tejada .40
7 Carlos Delgado .40
8 Shannon Stewart .15
9 Greg Vaughn .15
10 Jim Thome .50
11 C.C. Sabathia .15
12 Ichiro Suzuki 2.50
13 Edgar Martinez .15
14 Bret Boone .15
15 Freddy Garcia .15
16 Jeff Conine .15
17 Alex Rodriguez 2.50
18 Rafael Palmeiro .50
19 Ivan Rodriguez .50
20 Juan Gonzalez .50
21 Pedro J. Martinez 1.00
22 Nomar Garciaparra 2.00
23 Manny Ramirez .75
24 Carlos Beltran .15
25 Mike Sweeney .15
26 Dmitri Young .15
27 Bobby Higginson .15
28 Corey Koskie .15
29 Cristian Guzman .15
30 Doug Mientkiewicz .15
31 Torii Hunter .15
32 Frank Thomas .75
33 Mark Buehrle .15
34 Carlos Lee .15
35 Magglio Ordonez .40
36 Roger Clemens 1.50
37 Bernie Williams .50
38 Jason Giambi 1.50
39 Derek Jeter 3.00
40 Mike Mussina .50
41 Jeff Bagwell .75
42 Richard Hidalgo .15
43 Lance Berkman .75
44 Roy Oswalt .40
45 Chipper Jones 1.50
46 Gary Sheffield .40
47 Andruw Jones .50
48 Greg Maddux 1.50
49 Geoff Jenkins .15
50 Ben Sheets .15
51 Richie Sexson .40
52 Albert Pujols 1.50
53 Matt Morris .15
54 J.D. Drew .40
55 Tino Martinez .25
56 Sammy Sosa 1.50
57 Kerry Wood .50
58 Moises Alou .25
59 Fred McGriff .40
60 Randy Johnson .75
61 Luis Gonzalez .50
62 Curt Schilling .75
63 Kevin Brown .25
64 Shawn Green .40
65 Paul LoDuca .15
66 Vladimir Guerrero 1.00
67 Jose Vidro .15
68 Barry Bonds 2.00
69 Jeff Kent .25
70 Rich Aurilia .15
71 Preston Wilson .15
72 Josh Beckett .15
73 Cliff Floyd .25
74 Mike Piazza 2.00
75 Mo Vaughn .25
76 Roberto Alomar .50
77 Jeromy Burnitz .15
78 Phil Nevin .15
79 Sean Burroughs .15
80 Scott Rolen .40
81 Bobby Abreu .15
82 Pat Burrell .50
83 Brian Giles .40
84 Jason Kendall .15
85 Ken Griffey Jr. 2.00
86 Adam Dunn .75
87 Aaron Boone .15
88 Larry Walker .40
89 Todd Helton .75
90 Mike Hampton .15
91 *Brandon Puffer* 5.00
92 *Rodrigo Rosario* 8.00
93 *Tom Shearn* 4.00
94 Morgan Ensberg 4.00
95 Jason Lane 4.00
96 *Franklyn German* 5.00
97 Carlos Pena 4.00
98 *Joe Orloski* 5.00
99 *Reed Johnson* 5.00
100 *Chris Baker* 5.00
101 *Corey Thurman* 4.00
102 *Gustavo Chacin* 4.00
103 Eric Hinske 8.00
104 *John Foster* 4.00
105 *John Ennis* 5.00
106 *Kevin Gryboski* 4.00
107 Jung Bong 4.00
108 Travis Wilson 4.00
109 *Luis Martinez* 4.00
110 *Brian Mallette* 5.00
111 *Takahito Nomura* 6.00
112 Bill Hall 4.00
113 Jeff Deardorff 4.00
114 Cristian Guerrero 4.00
115 *Scotty Layfield* 4.00
116 *Michael Crudale* 5.00
117 *So Taguchi* 8.00
118 *Jeremy Lambert* 4.00
119 Jimmy Journell 4.00
120 *Francis Beltran* 4.00
121 Mark Prior 10.00
122 Ben Christensen 4.00
123 *Jorge Sosa* 4.00
124 *Brandon Backe* 6.00
125 *Steve Kent* 5.00
126 *Felix Escalona* 4.00
127 *P.J. Bevis* 4.00
128 *Jose Valverde* 4.00
129 *Doug Devore* 6.00
130 *Jeremy Ward* 4.00
131 Mike Koplove 4.00
132 Luis Terrero 4.00
133 John Patterson 4.00
134 *Victor Alvarez* 5.00
135 Kirk Saarloos 4.00
136 *Kazuhisa Ishii* 12.00
137 Steve Colyer 4.00
138 Cesar Izturis 4.00
139 *Ron Calloway* 5.00
140 *Eric Good* 4.00
141 *Jorge Nunez* 4.00
142 Ron Chiavacci 4.00
143 Donnie Bridges 4.00
144 *Nelson Castro* 4.00
145 Deivis Santos 4.00
146 Kurt Ainsworth 4.00
147 Arturo McDowell 4.00
148 *Allan Simpson* 4.00
149 Matt Thornton 4.00
150 *Luis Ugueto* 4.00
151 *J.J. Putz* 4.00
152 *Hansel Izquierdo* 4.00
153 *Oliver Perez* 4.00
154 *Jaime Cerda* 4.00
155 *Mark Corey* 4.00
156 *Tyler Yates* 4.00
157 *Satoru Komiyama* 5.00
158 *Adam Walker* 4.00
159 *Steve Bechler* 6.00
160 Erik Bedard 4.00
161 *Todd Donovan* 4.00
162 *Clifford Bartosh* 4.00
163 *Ben Howard* 8.00
164 *Andy Shibilo* 4.00
165 Dennis Tankersley 4.00
166 Mike Bynum 4.00
167 *Anderson Machado* 4.00
168 *Peter Zamora* 5.00
169 *Eric Junge* 4.00
170 *Elio Serrano* 4.00
171 *Jorge Padilla* 4.00
172 Marlon Byrd 4.00
173 *Adrian Burnside* 4.00
174 *Mike Gonzalez* 4.00
175 J.R. House 4.00
176 Hank Blalock 6.00
177 *Travis Hughes* 4.00
178 Mark Teixeira 6.00
179 *Josh Hancock* 4.00
180 *Anastacio Martinez* 4.00
181 Jorge de la Rosa 4.00
182 Ben Broussard 4.00
183 Austin Kearns 6.00
184 Corky Miller 4.00
185 *Colin Young* 4.00
186 *Cam Esslinger* 4.00
187 *Rene Reyes* 4.00
188 *Aaron Cook* 4.00
189 Alexis Gomez 4.00
190 *Nate Field* 4.00
191 *Miguel Asencio* 4.00
192 Brandon Berger 4.00
193 Fernando Rodney 4.00
194 Andy Van Hekken 4.00
195 *Kevin Frederick* 4.00
196 Todd Sears 4.00
197 *Edwin Almonte* 4.00
198 *Kyle Kane* 8.00
199 *Mitch Wylie* 4.00
200 Mike Porzio 4.00
201 Darin Erstad 6.00
202 Tim Salmon 5.00
203 Jeff Bagwell 10.00
204 Lance Berkman 8.00
205 Eric Chavez 6.00
206 Tim Hudson 6.00
207 Carlos Delgado 8.00
208 Chipper Jones 10.00
209 Gary Sheffield 6.00
210 Greg Maddux 15.00
211 Tom Glavine 6.00
212 Mike Mussina 10.00
213 J.D. Drew 10.00
214 Rick Ankiel 5.00
215 Sammy Sosa 15.00
216 Mike Lieberthal 8.00
217 Fred McGriff 10.00
218 David Wells 5.00
219 Curt Schilling 10.00
220 Luis Gonzalez 8.00
221 Mark Grace 15.00
222 Kevin Brown 5.00
223 Hideo Nomo 25.00
224 Jose Vidro 5.00
225 Jeff Kent 5.00
226 Rich Aurilia 5.00
227 Kenny Lofton 5.00
228 C.C. Sabathia 5.00
229 Edgar Martinez 8.00
230 Freddy Garcia 5.00
231 Cliff Floyd 5.00
232 Preston Wilson 5.00
233 Mike Piazza 10.00
234 Roberto Alomar 8.00
235 Trevor Hoffman 5.00
236 Ryan Klesko 5.00
237 Sean Burroughs 5.00
238 Scott Rolen 8.00
239 Pat Burrell 15.00
240 Edgardo Alfonzo 5.00
241 Brian Giles 8.00
242 Jason Kendall 5.00
243 Alex Rodriguez 15.00
244 Juan Gonzalez 8.00
245 Ivan Rodriguez 6.00
246 Rafael Palmeiro 6.00
247 Ken Griffey Jr. 12.00
248 Adam Dunn 20.00
249 Barry Larkin 5.00
250 Manny Ramirez 10.00
251 Pedro Martinez 10.00
252 Todd Helton 8.00
253 Larry Walker 6.00
254 Randy Johnson 10.00
255 Mike Sweeney 5.00
256 Carlos Beltran 5.00
257 Dmitri Young 8.00
258 Joe Mays 5.00
259 Doug Mientkiewicz 10.00
260 Corey Koskie 5.00
261 Magglio Ordonez 8.00
262 Frank Thomas 8.00
263 Ray Durham 5.00
264 Jason Giambi 15.00
265 Bernie Williams 8.00
266 Roger Clemens 15.00
267 Mariano Rivera 6.00
268 Robin Ventura 6.00
269 Andy Pettite 10.00
270 Jorge Posada 8.00
271 Mike Piazza 15.00
272 Alex Rodriguez 15.00
273 Ken Griffey Jr. 15.00
274 Jason Giambi 20.00
275 Frank Thomas 8.00
276 Greg Maddux 15.00
277 Sammy Sosa 15.00
278 Roger Clemens 15.00
279 Jeff Bagwell 12.00
280 Todd Helton 8.00
281 Ichiro Suzuki 60.00
282 Randy Johnson 10.00
283 Jim Thome 15.00
284 Ivan Rodriguez 8.00
285 Darin Erstad 6.00
286 Eric Chavez 8.00
287 Barry Zito 15.00
288 Carlos Delgado 8.00
289 Omar Vizquel 6.00
290 Edgar Martinez 8.00
291 Manny Ramirez 10.00
292 Mike Sweeney 6.00
293 Tom Glavine 8.00
294 Joe Mays 6.00
295 Eric Milton 6.00
296 Magglio Ordonez 8.00
297 Bernie Williams 8.00
298 Trevor Hoffman 6.00
299 Andruw Jones 8.00
300 Aubrey Huff 5.00
301 Jim Edmonds 8.00
302 Kerry Wood 10.00
303 Luis Gonzalez 8.00
304 Shawn Green 6.00
305 Jose Vidro 5.00
306 Jeff Kent 5.00
307 Edgardo Alfonzo 5.00
308 Preston Wilson 5.00
309 Roberto Alomar 10.00
310 Jeromy Burnitz 5.00
311 Phil Nevin 5.00
312 Ryan Klesko 5.00
313 Bobby Abreu 6.00
314 Scott Rolen 10.00
315 Kazuhiro Sasaki 8.00
316 Jason Kendall 5.00
317 Sean Casey 8.00
318 Larry Walker 8.00
319 Mike Hampton 6.00
320 Juan Gonzalez 8.00
321 Darin Erstad 8.00
322 Tim Hudson 8.00
323 Carlos Delgado 8.00
324 Greg Vaughn 5.00
325 Jim Thome 15.00
326 Ichiro Suzuki 65.00
327 Rafael Palmeiro 8.00
328 Alex Rodriguez 15.00
329 Juan Gonzalez 8.00
330 Manny Ramirez 10.00
331 Carlos Beltran 6.00
332 Eric Milton 6.00
333 Frank Thomas 8.00
334 Roger Clemens 15.00
335 Jason Giambi 20.00
336 Lance Berkman 8.00
337 Greg Maddux 15.00
338 Chipper Jones 10.00
339 Sean Casey 8.00
340 Jim Edmonds 8.00
341 Kerry Wood 10.00
342 Sammy Sosa 15.00
343 Luis Gonzalez 8.00
344 Shawn Green 6.00
345 Jeff Kent 6.00
346 Preston Wilson 6.00
347 Roberto Alomar 10.00
348 Phil Nevin 6.00
349 Scott Rolen 10.00
350 Mike Sweeney 6.00
351 Ken Griffey Jr. 15.00
352 Todd Helton 8.00
353 Larry Walker 6.00
354 Alex Rodriguez 15.00
355 Pedro J. Martinez 10.00
356 Frank Thomas 10.00
357 Jason Giambi 20.00
358 Bernie Williams 10.00
359 Jeff Bagwell 10.00
360 Chipper Jones 12.00
361 Sammy Sosa 20.00
362 Randy Johnson 10.00
363 Shawn Green 6.00
364 Mike Piazza 15.00

#	Player	Price
365	Ichiro Suzuki	85.00
366	Ken Griffey Jr.	15.00
367	Larry Walker	8.00
368	Jim Edmonds	8.00
369	Darin Erstad	8.00
370	Tim Salmon	8.00
371	Mark Kotsay	5.00
372	Craig Biggio	8.00
373	Eric Chavez	10.00
374	David Justice	8.00
375	Carlos Delgado	8.00
376	Chipper Jones	15.00
377	Gary Sheffield	6.00
378	Greg Maddux	10.00
379	Eric Karros	5.00
380	Fred McGriff	8.00
381	J.D. Drew	8.00
382	Rick Ankiel	8.00
383	Sammy Sosa	15.00
384	Moises Alou	5.00
385	Ben Grieve	8.00
386	Greg Vaughn	5.00
387	Jay Payton	5.00
388	Luis Gonzalez	8.00
389	Ray Durham	5.00
390	Shawn Green	8.00
391	Hideo Nomo	20.00
392	Jose Vidro	5.00
393	Jeff Kent	5.00
394	Adrian Beltre	5.00
395	Jim Thome	15.00
396	Bobby Abreu	5.00
397	Edgar Martinez	10.00
398	Carl Everett	5.00
399	Luis Castillo	5.00
400	Preston Wilson	5.00
401	Jermaine Dye	8.00
402	Roberto Alomar	8.00
403	Todd Hundley	5.00
404	Ryan Klesko	8.00
405	Phil Nevin	5.00
406	Scott Rolen	8.00
407	Rafael Furcal	5.00
408	Miguel Tejada	8.00
409	Brian Giles	8.00
410	Jason Kendall	5.00
411	Alex Rodriguez	15.00
412	Juan Gonzalez	8.00
413	Ivan Rodriguez	6.00
414	Rafael Palmeiro	6.00
415	Ken Griffey Jr.	15.00
416	Edgardo Alfonzo	5.00
417	Barry Larkin	8.00
418	Manny Ramirez	8.00
419	Pedro J. Martinez	12.00
420	Todd Helton	8.00
421	Larry Walker	8.00
422	Garrett Anderson	5.00
423	Mike Sweeney	5.00
424	Carlos Beltran	5.00
425	Javier Lopez	5.00
426	J.T. Snow	5.00
427	Doug Mientkiewicz	8.00
428	John Olerud	8.00
429	Magglio Ordonez	6.00
430	Frank Thomas	10.00
431	Kenny Lofton	6.00
432	Al Leiter	5.00
433	Bernie Williams	8.00
434	Roger Clemens	15.00
435	Tom Glavine	10.00
436	Robin Ventura	10.00
437	Chan Ho Park	8.00
438	Jorge Posada	8.00
439	Charles Johnson	5.00
440	Alex Rodriguez	20.00
441	Ken Griffey Jr.	15.00
442	Mark Kotsay	8.00
443	Frank Thomas	12.00
444	Greg Maddux	20.00
445	Sammy Sosa	20.00
446	Tom Glavine	15.00
447	Chipper Jones	20.00
448	Todd Helton	10.00
449	Jeff Cirillo	8.00
450	Steve Finley	10.00
451	Jim Thome	15.00
452	Ivan Rodriguez	8.00
453	Darin Erstad	8.00
454	Eric Chavez	8.00
455	Miguel Tejada	8.00
456	Carlos Delgado	8.00
457	Omar Vizquel	8.00
458	Edgar Martinez	10.00
459	Johnny Damon	8.00
460	Russell Branyan	5.00
461	Kenny Lofton	8.00
462	Jermaine Dye	5.00
463	Ellis Burks	5.00
464	Magglio Ordonez	8.00
465	Bernie Williams	10.00
466	Tim Salmon	6.00
467	Andruw Jones	8.00
468	Jeffrey Hammonds	5.00
469	Jim Edmonds	10.00
470	Kerry Wood	15.00
471	Luis Gonzalez	10.00
472	Shawn Green	8.00
473	Jose Vidro	5.00
474	Jeff Kent	6.00
475	Javier Lopez	5.00
476	Preston Wilson	5.00
477	Roberto Alomar	10.00
478	Robin Ventura	10.00
479	Phil Nevin	5.00
480	Ryan Klesko	8.00
481	Bobby Abreu	6.00
482	Scott Rolen	8.00
483	Brian Giles	8.00
484	Jason Kendall	5.00
485	Tsuyoshi Shinjo	10.00
486	Larry Walker	8.00
487	Mike Lieberthal	8.00
488	Juan Gonzalez	10.00
489	Darin Erstad	8.00
490	Tom Glavine	10.00
491	Carlos Delgado	8.00
492	Greg Vaughn	5.00
493	Jim Thome	15.00
494	Mark Grace	15.00
495	Rafael Palmeiro	8.00
496	Alex Rodriguez	20.00
497	Juan Gonzalez	10.00
498	Miguel Tejada	8.00
499	Carlos Beltran	5.00
500	Andruw Jones	8.00
501	Frank Thomas	12.00
502	Andres Galarraga	5.00
503	Gary Sheffield	8.00
504	Craig Biggio	8.00
505	Greg Maddux	20.00
506	Chipper Jones	20.00
507	Pat Burrell	20.00
508	Jim Edmonds	10.00
509	Kerry Wood	15.00
510	Sammy Sosa	20.00
511	Luis Gonzalez	10.00
512	Shawn Green	8.00
513	Edgardo Alfonzo	5.00
514	Preston Wilson	5.00
515	Roberto Alomar	12.00
516	Phil Nevin	5.00
517	Scott Rolen	10.00
518	Brian Giles	10.00
519	Jorge Posada	10.00
520	Todd Helton	12.00
521	Larry Walker	10.00
522	Alex Rodriguez	25.00
523	Pedro J. Martinez	20.00
524	Frank Thomas	12.00
525	Jason Giambi	20.00
526	Bernie Williams	10.00
527	J.D. Drew	10.00
528	Chipper Jones	25.00
529	Sammy Sosa	25.00
530	Randy Johnson	15.00
531	Shawn Green	10.00
532	Kevin Brown	10.00
533	Brian Giles	12.00
534	Ken Griffey Jr.	20.00
535	Larry Walker	10.00
536	Jim Edmonds	10.00
537	Sean Casey/jsy/775	8.00
538	Ichiro Suzuki/jsy/775	50.00
539	Pat Burrell/jsy/200	15.00
540	Adam Dunn//jsy/200	20.00
541	Lance Berkman/jsy/200	10.00
542	Cliff Floyd/jsy/150	8.00
543	Roger Clemens/jsy/100	20.00
544	Kerry Wood/bat/775	15.00
545	Andruw Jones/bat/775	8.00
546	Manny Ramirez/bat/200	10.00
547	Jorge Posada/bat/200	10.00
548	Fred McGriff/bat/200	10.00
549	Mike Sweeney/bat/150	6.00
550	Todd Helton/bat/100	12.00

2002 Upper Deck Diamond Connection Great Connections

MT

Production 50 sets
No pricing due to scarcity

GC-GR	Jason Giambi, Babe Ruth
GC-MD	Mickey Mantle, Joe DiMaggio
GC-MR	Mark McGwire, Babe Ruth
GC-MS	Mark McGwire, Sammy Sosa
GC-RR	Alex Rodriguez, Nolan Ryan
GC-IG	Ichiro Suzuki, Ken Griffey Jr.

2002 Upper Deck Diamond Connection Mem. Signatures Bat

Varying quantities produced

	Player	MT
JD	Joe DiMaggio/20	950.00
JG	Jason Giambi/49	
KG	Ken Griffey Jr/49	
MMc	Mark McGwire/49	
JM	Joe Morgan/99	35.00
KP	Kirby Puckett/145	
CR	Cal Ripken Jr/145	200.00
AR	Alex Rodriguez/145	
BR	Babe Ruth/3	
NR	Nolan Ryan/99	225.00
SS	Sammy Sosa/99	225.00
IS	Ichiro Suzuki/99	500.00

2002 Upper Deck Diamond Connection Mem. Signatures Jsy

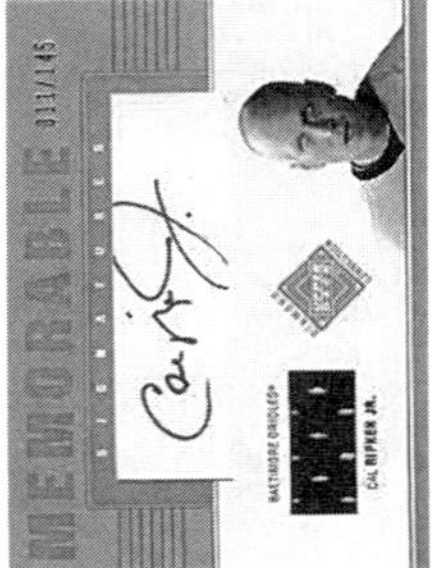

Varying quantities produced

	Player	MT
EB	Ernie Banks/150	
JD	Joe DiMaggio/20	
JG	Jason Giambi/49	
KG	Ken Griffey Jr/49	
SK	Sandy Koufax/150	300.00
MMa	Mickey Mantle/1	
MMc	Mark McGwire/49	
JM	Joe Morgan/99	35.00
CR	Cal Ripken Jr/145	200.00
AR	Alex Rodriguez/145	
BR	Babe Ruth/3	
NR	Nolan Ryan/99	225.00
SS	Sammy Sosa/99	225.00
IS	Ichiro Suzuki/99	500.00

2002 Upper Deck Honor Roll

		MT
Complete Set (100):		25.00
Common Player:		.15
Pack (5):		2.75
Box (24):		55.00
1	Randy Johnson	.50
2	Mike Piazza	1.50
3	Albert Pujols	1.00
4	Roberto Alomar	.40
5	Chipper Jones	1.00
6	Rich Aurilia	.15
7	Barry Bonds	1.00
8	Ken Griffey Jr.	1.50
9	Sammy Sosa	1.00
10	Roger Clemens	.75
11	Ivan Rodriguez	.40
12	Jason Giambi	.50
13	Bret Boone	.15
14	Troy Glaus	.40
15	Alex Rodriguez	1.50
16	Manny Ramirez	.50
17	Bernie Williams	.40
18	Ichiro Suzuki	2.00
19	Matt Thornton	.75
20	*Chris Baker*	.50
21	*Tyler Yates*	.75
22	*Jorge Nunez*	.50
23	*Rene Reyes*	.50
24	*Ben Howard*	2.50
25	*Ron Calloway*	.40
26	Danny Wright	.15
27	*Reed Johnson*	.50
28	Randy Johnson	.25
29	Randy Johnson	.25
30	Randy Johnson	.25
31	Randy Johnson	.25
32	Mike Piazza	.75
33	Mike Piazza	.75
34	Mike Piazza	.75
35	Mike Piazza	.75
36	Albert Pujols	.50
37	Albert Pujols	.50
38	Albert Pujols	.50
39	Albert Pujols	.50
40	Roberto Alomar	.20
41	Roberto Alomar	.20
42	Roberto Alomar	.20
43	Roberto Alomar	.20
44	Chipper Jones	.50
45	Chipper Jones	.50
46	Chipper Jones	.50
47	Chipper Jones	.50
48	Rich Aurilia	.15
49	Rich Aurilia	.15
50	Rich Aurilia	.15
51	Rich Aurilia	.15
52	Barry Bonds	.50
53	Barry Bonds	.50
54	Barry Bonds	.50
55	Barry Bonds	.50

56 Ken Griffey Jr. .75
57 Ken Griffey Jr. .75
58 Ken Griffey Jr. .75
59 Ken Griffey Jr. .75
60 Sammy Sosa .50
61 Sammy Sosa .50
62 Sammy Sosa .50
63 Sammy Sosa .50
64 Roger Clemens .40
65 Roger Clemens .40
66 Roger Clemens .40
67 Roger Clemens .40
68 Ivan Rodriguez .20
69 Ivan Rodriguez .20
70 Ivan Rodriguez .20
71 Ivan Rodriguez .20
72 Jason Giambi .25
73 Jason Giambi .25
74 Jason Giambi .25
75 Jason Giambi .25
76 Bret Boone .15
77 Bret Boone .15
78 Bret Boone .15
79 Bret Boone .15
80 Troy Glaus .20
81 Troy Glaus .20
82 Troy Glaus .20
83 Troy Glaus .20
84 Alex Rodriguez .75
85 Alex Rodriguez .75
86 Alex Rodriguez .75
87 Alex Rodriguez .75
88 Manny Ramirez .25
89 Manny Ramirez .25
90 Manny Ramirez .25
91 Manny Ramirez .25
92 Bernie Williams .20
93 Bernie Williams .20
94 Bernie Williams .20
95 Bernie Williams .20
96 Ichiro Suzuki 1.00
97 Ichiro Suzuki 1.00
98 Ichiro Suzuki 1.00
99 Ichiro Suzuki 1.00
100 Checklist (Original nine players) (Nine team names) .25

2002 Upper Deck Honor Roll Silver

MT
Stars: 10-20X
Production 100 sets
Gold Stars: 25-60X
Production 25 sets

2002 Upper Deck Honor Roll Batting Glove

MT
Numbered to 250
BB Bret Boone/89 20.00
JG Jason Giambi 25.00
KG Ken Griffey Jr. 40.00
AR Alex Rodriguez 25.00
IR1 Ivan Rodriguez 25.00
IR2 Ivan Rodriguez 25.00
SS Sammy Sosa 30.00
I Ichiro Suzuki/46 200.00

2002 Upper Deck Honor Roll Game Jersey

MT
Common Player: 15.00
Inserted 1:90
Golds: 2-3X
Production 99 sets
Each player has multiple versions
BB Bret Boone/SP/45 15.00
RC Roger Clemens 20.00
JG Jason Giambi/SP 20.00
KG Ken Griffey Jr. 25.00
CJ Chipper Jones 20.00
AR Alex Rodriguez 20.00
IR Ivan Rodriguez 15.00
SS Sammy Sosa/SP 25.00
I Ichiro Suzuki/SP 75.00

2002 Upper Deck Honor Roll Game-Used Bat

MT
Common Player: 20.00
Numbered to 99
Each player has multiple versions
BB Bret Boone 20.00
RC Roger Clemens 40.00
JG Jason Giambi 25.00
KG Ken Griffey Jr. 45.00
CJ Chipper Jones 40.00
AR Alex Rodriguez 30.00
IR Ivan Rodriguez 20.00
SS Sammy Sosa 40.00
I Ichiro Suzuki 100.00

2002 Upper Deck Honor Roll Star Swatches Game Jersey

MT
Common Player: 15.00
Inserted 1:90
Golds: 2-5X
Production 24
BB Bret Boone/45 15.00
RC Roger Clemens/29 50.00
JG Jason Giambi 15.00
KG Ken Griffey Jr/SP 35.00
CJ Chipper Jones 20.00
AR Alex Rodriguez 20.00
IR Ivan Rodriguez 15.00
SS Sammy Sosa 20.00
I Ichiro Suzuki/SP 75.00

2002 Upper Deck Honor Roll Stitch of Nine Game Jersey

MT
Common Player: 15.00
Inserted 1:90
Golds: 2-5X
Production 24 sets
BB Bret Boone/45 15.00
RC Roger Clemens 20.00
JG Jason Giambi/SP 20.00
KG Ken Griffey Jr. 25.00
CJ Chipper Jones 20.00
AR Alex Rodriguez 20.00
IR Ivan Rodriguez 15.00
SS Sammy Sosa 20.00
I Ichiro Suzuki/85 75.00

2002 Upper Deck Honor Roll Time Capsule Game Jersey

MT
Common Player: 15.00
Inserted 1:90
Golds: 2-3X
Production 99 sets
BB Bret Boone 15.00
RC Roger Clemens 20.00
JG Jason Giambi/52 25.00
KG Ken Griffey Jr./5
CJ Chipper Jones 20.00
AR Alex Rodriguez 20.00
IR Ivan Rodriguez/SP 20.00
SS Sammy Sosa 20.00
I Ichiro Suzuki 75.00

2002 Upper Deck MVP

MT
Complete Set (300): 20.00
Common Player: .10
Pack (8): 2.00
Box (24): 38.00
1 Darin Erstad .15
2 Ramon Ortiz .10
3 Garret Anderson .10
4 Jarrod Washburn .10
5 Troy Glaus .40
6 *Brendan Donnelly* .10
7 Troy Percival .10

MT
8 Tim Salmon .15
9 Aaron Sele .10
10 Brad Fullmer .10
11 Scott Hatteberg .10
12 Barry Zito .15
13 Tim Hudson .20
14 Miguel Tejada .15
15 Jermaine Dye .10
16 Mark Mulder .10
17 Eric Chavez .15
18 Terrence Long .10
19 Carlos Pena .20
20 David Justice .20
21 Jeremy Giambi .10
22 Shannon Stewart .10
23 Raul Mondesi .15
24 Chris Carpenter .10
25 Carlos Delgado .20
26 Mike Sirotka .10
27 *Reed Johnson* .15
28 Darrin Fletcher .10
29 Jose Cruz Jr. .10
30 Vernon Wells .10
31 Tanyon Sturtze .10
32 Toby Hall .10
33 Brent Abernathy .10
34 Ben Grieve .10
35 Joe Kennedy .10
36 Dewon Brazelton .10
37 Aubrey Huff .10
38 Steve Cox .10
39 Greg Vaughn .10
40 Brady Anderson .10
41 Chuck Finley .10
42 Jim Thome .25
43 Russell Branyan .10
44 C.C. Sabathia .10
45 Matt Lawton .10
46 Omar Vizquel .10
47 Bartolo Colon .15
48 Alex Escobar .10
49 Ellis Burks .10
50 Bret Boone .10
51 John Olerud .20
52 Jeff Cirillo .10
53 Ichiro Suzuki 1.50
54 Kazuhiro Sasaki .10
55 Freddy Garcia .10
56 Edgar Martinez .15
57 Matt Thornton .10
58 Mike Cameron .10
59 Carlos Guillen .10
60 Jeff Conine .10
61 Tony Batista .10
62 Jason Johnson .10
63 Melvin Mora .10
64 Brian Roberts .10
65 Josh Towers .10
66 *Steve Bechler* .10
67 Jerry Hairston Jr. .10
68 Chris Richard .10
69 Alex Rodriguez 1.00
70 Chan Ho Park .10
71 Ivan Rodriguez .30
72 Jeff Zimmerman .10
73 Mark Teixeira .20
74 Gabe Kapler .10
75 Frank Catalanotto .10
76 Rafael Palmeiro .25
77 Doug Davis .10
78 Carl Everett .10
79 Pedro J. Martinez .40
80 Nomar Garciaparra 1.00
81 Tony Clark .10
82 Trot Nixon .10
83 Manny Ramirez .40
84 *Josh Hancock* .10
85 Johnny Damon .10
86 Jose Offerman .10

87 Rich Garces .10
88 Shea Hillenbrand .10
89 Carlos Beltran .10
90 Mike Sweeney .10
91 Jeff Suppan .10
92 Joe Randa .10
93 Chuck Knoblauch .10
94 Mark Quinn .10
95 Neifi Perez .10
96 Carlos Febles .10
97 *Miguel Asencio* .10
98 Michael Tucker .10
99 Dean Palmer .10
100 Jose Lima .10
101 Craig Paquette .10
102 Dmitri Young .10
103 Bobby Higginson .10
104 Jeff Weaver .10
105 Matt Anderson .10
106 Damion Easley .10
107 Eric Milton .10
108 Doug Mientkiewicz .10
109 Cristian Guzman .10
110 Brad Radke .10
111 Torii Hunter .10
112 Corey Koskie .10
113 Joe Mays .10
114 Jacque Jones .10
115 David Ortiz .10
116 *Kevin Frederick* .20
117 Magglio Ordonez .20
118 Ray Durham .10
119 Mark Buehrle .10
120 Jon Garland .10
121 Paul Konerko .10
122 Todd Ritchie .10
123 Frank Thomas .40
124 *Edwin Almonte* .10
125 Carlos Lee .10
126 Kenny Lofton .15
127 Roger Clemens .50
128 Derek Jeter 1.50
129 Jorge Posada .20
130 Bernie Williams .25
131 Mike Mussina .30
132 Alfonso Soriano .40
133 Robin Ventura .15
134 John Vander Wal .10
135 Jason Giambi .40
136 Mariano Rivera .20
137 Rondell White .10
138 Jeff Bagwell .40
139 Wade Miller .10
140 Richard Hidalgo .10
141 Julio Lugo .10
142 Roy Oswalt .20
143 *Rodrigo Rosario* .10
144 Lance Berkman .25
145 Craig Biggio .20
146 Shane Reynolds .10
147 John Smoltz .10
148 Chipper Jones .75
149 Gary Sheffield .20
150 Rafael Furcal .10
151 Greg Maddux .75
152 Tom Glavine .20
153 Andruw Jones .30
154 *John Ennis* .20
155 Vinny Castilla .10
156 Marcus Giles .10
157 Javy Lopez .10
158 Richie Sexson .20
159 Geoff Jenkins .20
160 Jeffrey Hammonds .10
161 Alex Ochoa .10
162 Ben Sheets .20
163 Jose Hernandez .10
164 Eric Young .10
165 Luis Montanez .10
166 Albert Pujols .60
167 Darryl Kile .10
168 *So Taguchi* .75
169 Jim Edmonds .20
170 Fernando Vina .10
171 Matt Morris .10
172 J.D. Drew .20
173 Bud Smith .10
174 Edgar Renteria .10
175 Placido Polanco .10
176 Tino Martinez .10
177 Sammy Sosa .75
178 Moises Alou .15
179 Kerry Wood .25
180 Delino DeShields .10
181 Alex Gonzalez .10
182 Jon Lieber .10
183 Fred McGriff .15
184 Corey Patterson .15
185 Mark Prior .75
186 Tom Gordon .10
187 *Francis Beltran* .10
188 Randy Johnson .40
189 Luis Gonzalez .25
190 Matt Williams .15
191 Mark Grace .25
192 Curt Schilling .25
193 *Doug Devore* .20
194 Erubiel Durazo .10
195 Steve Finley .15
196 Craig Counsell .10
197 Shawn Green .25
198 Kevin Brown .20
199 Paul LoDuca .10
200 Brian Jordan .15
201 Andy Ashby .10
202 Darren Dreifort .10
203 Adrian Beltre .15
204 *Victor Alvarez* .10
205 Eric Karros .10
206 Hideo Nomo .25
207 Vladimir Guerrero .40
208 Javier Vazquez .10
209 Michael Barrett .10
210 Jose Vidro .10
211 Brad Wilkerson .10
212 Tony Armas Jr. .10
213 *Eric Good* .10
214 Orlando Cabrera .10
215 Lee Stevens .10
216 Jeff Kent .10
217 Rich Aurilia .10
218 Robb Nen .10
219 Calvin Murray .10
220 Russ Ortiz .10
221 Deivis Santos .10
222 Marvin Benard .10
223 Jason Schmidt .10
224 Reggie Sanders .10
225 Barry Bonds .75
226 Brad Penny .10
227 Cliff Floyd .10
228 Mike Lowell .10
229 Derrek Lee .10
230 Ryan Dempster .10
231 Josh Beckett .20
232 *Hansel Izquierdo* .10
233 Preston Wilson .10
234 A.J. Burnett .10
235 Charles Johnson .10
236 Mike Piazza 1.00
237 Al Leiter .20
238 Jay Payton .10
239 Roger Cedeno .10
240 Jeromy Burnitz .10
241 Roberto Alomar .30
242 Mo Vaughn .20
243 Shawn Estes .10
244 Armando Benitez .10
245 *Tyler Yates* .10
246 Phil Nevin .10
247 D'Angelo Jimenez .10
248 Ramon Vazquez .10
249 Bubba Trammell .10
250 Trevor Hoffman .10
251 *Ben Howard* .20
252 Mark Kotsay .10
253 Ray Lankford .10
254 Ryan Klesko .10
255 Scott Rolen .20
256 Robert Person .10
257 Jimmy Rollins .10
258 Pat Burrell .20
259 *Anderson Machado* .10
260 Randy Wolf .10
261 Travis Lee .10
262 Mike Lieberthal .10
263 Doug Glanville .10
264 Bobby Abreu .10
265 Brian Giles .15
266 Kris Benson .10
267 Aramis Ramirez .10
268 Kevin Young .10
269 Jack Wilson .10
270 Mike Williams .10
271 Jimmy Anderson .10
272 Jason Kendall .10
273 Pokey Reese .10
274 Robert Mackowiak .10
275 Sean Casey .20
276 Juan Encarnacion .10
277 Austin Kearns .20
278 Danny Graves .10
279 Ken Griffey Jr. 1.00
280 Barry Larkin .20
281 Todd Walker .10
282 Elmer Dessens .10
283 Aaron Boone .10
284 Adam Dunn .40
285 Larry Walker .25
286 *Rene Reyes* .20
287 Juan Uribe .10
288 Mike Hampton .10
289 Todd Helton .40
290 Juan Pierre .10
291 Denny Neagle .10
292 Jose Ortiz .10
293 Todd Zeile .10
294 Ben Petrick .10
295 Ken Griffey Jr. .40
296 Derek Jeter .60
297 Sammy Sosa .30
298 Ichiro Suzuki .60
299 Barry Bonds .30
300 Alex Rodriguez .40

2002 Upper Deck MVP Ichiro - A Season to Remember

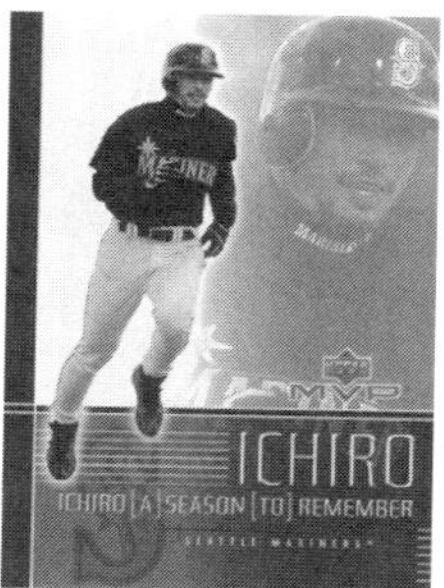

		MT
Complete Set (10):		15.00
Ichiro's (1-10):		2.00
Inserted 1:10		
I1	Ichiro Suzuki	2.50
I2	Ichiro Suzuki	2.50
I3	Ichiro Suzuki	2.50
I4	Ichiro Suzuki	2.50
I5	Ichiro Suzuki	2.50
I6	Ichiro Suzuki	2.50
I7	Ichiro Suzuki	2.50
I8	Ichiro Suzuki	2.50
I9	Ichiro Suzuki	2.50
I10	Ichiro Suzuki	2.50

2002 Upper Deck MVP Souvenirs Bats

		MT
Common Player:		8.00
Inserted 1:144		
RA	Roberto Alomar	20.00
CD	Carlos Delgado	8.00
BG	Brian Giles	8.00
LG	Luis Gonzalez	8.00
SG	Shawn Green	8.00
KG	Ken Griffey Jr.	25.00
TH	Todd Helton	15.00
DJ	David Justice	15.00
JK	Jeff Kent	8.00
RK	Ryan Klesko	10.00
GM	Greg Maddux	20.00
EM	Edgar Martinez	10.00
DM	Doug Mientkiewicz	15.00
MO	Magglio Ordonez	10.00
RP	Rafael Palmeiro/97	18.00
MP	Mike Piazza/97	25.00
AR	Alex Rodriguez	15.00
IR	Ivan Rodriguez	10.00
SR	Scott Rolen	10.00
GS	Gary Sheffield	8.00
SS	Sammy Sosa	20.00
MS	Mike Sweeney	10.00
FT	Frank Thomas/97	25.00
JT	Jim Thome	10.00
GV	Greg Vaughn	8.00
LW	Larry Walker	10.00
BW	Bernie Williams	10.00

2002 Upper Deck MVP Souvenirs Jerseys

		MT
Common Player:		8.00
Inserted 1:48		
RA	Roberto Alomar	10.00
GA	Garret Anderson	10.00
JB	Jeff Bagwell	10.00
AB	Adrian Beltre	10.00
JB	Jeromy Burnitz	10.00
RC	Roger Clemens	15.00
CD	Carlos Delgado	10.00
DE	Darin Erstad	10.00
RF	Rafael Furcal	10.00
JG	Juan Gonzalez	10.00
THo	Trevor Hoffman	10.00
THu	Tim Hudson	12.00
JK	Jeff Kent	8.00
PK	Paul Konerko/SP	20.00
MK	Mark Kotsay	10.00
KL	Kenny Lofton	10.00
EM	Edgar Martinez	10.00
JP	Jay Payton/SP	10.00
MP	Mike Piazza	20.00
AR	Alex Rodriguez	15.00
IR	Ivan Rodriguez	10.00
SR	Scott Rolen	8.00
TS	Tim Salmon	10.00
FT	Frank Thomas	15.00
JT	Jim Thome/SP	15.00
RV	Robin Ventura	10.00
OV	Omar Vizquel	10.00
PW	Preston Wilson	8.00
TZ	Todd Zeile	8.00

2002 Upper Deck MVP Souvenirs Bat/Jersey Combos

		MT
Common Card:		15.00
Inserted 1:144		
EA	Edgardo Alfonzo	15.00
RA	Roberto Alomar	15.00
JB	Jeff Bagwell	20.00
AB	Adrian Beltre	15.00
PB	Pat Burrell/97	
CD	Carlos Delgado	15.00
DE	Darin Erstad	20.00
JG	Jason Giambi	25.00
BG	Brian Giles	20.00
LG	Luis Gonzalez	15.00
SG	Shawn Green	25.00
KG	Ken Griffey Jr.	50.00
TH	Todd Helton	25.00
RJ	Randy Johnson	25.00
CJ	Chipper Jones	25.00
JK	Jeff Kent	15.00
MO	Magglio Ordonez	25.00
RP	Rafael Palmeiro	20.00
MP	Mike Piazza	15.00
AR	Alex Rodriguez	25.00
IR	Ivan Rodriguez	15.00
SR	Scott Rolen	15.00
SS	Sammy Sosa	15.00
JT	Jim Thome	25.00
RV	Robin Ventura	20.00
OV	Omar Vizquel/97	20.00
BW	Bernie Williams/97	25.00
TZ	Todd Zeile	15.00

2002 Upper Deck Ovation

	MT
Complete Set (120):	200.00
Common Player:	.25
Common (61-89,120)	5.00

Production 2,002
Pack (5): 2.75
Box (24): 55.00
1 Troy Glaus .50
2 David Justice .40
3 Tim Hudson .40
4 Jermaine Dye .25
5 Carlos Delgado .40
6 Greg Vaughn .25
7 Jim Thome .50
8 C.C. Sabathia .25
9 Ichiro Suzuki 2.50
10 Edgar Martinez .25
11 Chris Richard .25
12 Rafael Palmeiro .50
13 Alex Rodriguez 2.50
14 Ivan Rodriguez .50
15 Nomar Garciaparra 2.00
16 Manny Ramirez .75
17 Pedro J. Martinez 1.00
18 Mike Sweeney .25
19 Dmitri Young .25
20 Doug Mientkiewicz .25
21 Brad Radke .25
22 Cristian Guzman .25
23 Frank Thomas .75
24 Magglio Ordonez .40
25 Bernie Williams .50
26 Derek Jeter 3.00
27 Jason Giambi 1.50
28 Roger Clemens 1.50
29 Jeff Bagwell .75
30 Lance Berkman .75
31 Chipper Jones 1.50
32 Gary Sheffield .40
33 Greg Maddux 1.50
34 Richie Sexson .40
35 Albert Pujols 1.50
36 Tino Martinez .40
37 J.D. Drew .40
38 Sammy Sosa 1.50
39 Moises Alou .40
40 Randy Johnson .75
41 Luis Gonzalez .50
42 Shawn Green .40
43 Kevin Brown .25
44 Vladimir Guerrero .75
45 Barry Bonds 2.00
46 Jeff Kent .40
47 Cliff Floyd .25
48 Josh Beckett .40
49 Mike Piazza 2.00
50 Mo Vaughn .40
51 Jeromy Burnitz .25
52 Roberto Alomar .50
53 Phil Nevin .25
54 Scott Rolen .50
55 Jimmy Rollins .25
56 Brian Giles .50
57 Ken Griffey Jr. 2.00
58 Sean Casey .40
59 Larry Walker .40
60 Todd Helton .75
61 *Rodrigo Rosario* 10.00
62 *Reed Johnson* 5.00
63 *John Ennis* 5.00
64 *Luis Martinez* 5.00
65 *So Taguchi* 8.00
66 *Brandon Backe* 8.00
67 *Doug Devore* 5.00
68 *Victor Alvarez* 5.00
69 *Kazuhisa Ishii* 15.00
70 *Eric Good* 5.00
71 Deivis Santos 5.00
72 Matt Thornton 5.00
73 *Hansel Izquierdo* 5.00
74 *Tyler Yates* 5.00
75 *Jaime Cerda* 5.00
76 *Satoru Komiyama* 5.00
77 *Steve Bechler* 5.00
78 *Ben Howard* 8.00
79 *Jorge Padilla* 8.00
80 *Eric Junge* 5.00
81 *Anderson Machado* 8.00
82 *Adrian Burnside* 5.00
83 *Josh Hancock* 5.00
84 *Anastacio Martinez* 5.00
85 *Rene Reyes* 5.00
86 *Nate Field* 5.00
87 *Tim Kalita* 5.00
88 *Kevin Frederick* 5.00
89 *Edwin Almonte* 5.00
90 Ichiro Suzuki 1.00
91 Ichiro Suzuki 1.00
92 Ichiro Suzuki 1.00
93 Ichiro Suzuki 1.00
94 Ichiro Suzuki 1.00
95 Ken Griffey Jr. .75
96 Ken Griffey Jr. .75
97 Ken Griffey Jr. .75
98 Ken Griffey Jr. .75
99 Ken Griffey Jr. .75
100 Jason Giambi .50
101 Jason Giambi .50
102 Jason Giambi .50
103 Jason Giambi .50
104 Jason Giambi .50
105 Sammy Sosa .75
106 Sammy Sosa .75
107 Sammy Sosa .75
108 Sammy Sosa .75
109 Sammy Sosa .75
110 Alex Rodriguez .75
111 Alex Rodriguez .75
112 Alex Rodriguez .75
113 Alex Rodriguez .75
114 Alex Rodriguez .75
115 Mark McGwire 1.00
116 Mark McGwire 1.00
117 Mark McGwire 1.00
118 Mark McGwire 1.00
119 Mark McGwire 1.00
120 Alex Rodriguez, Ken Griffey Jr., Mark McGwire, Sammy Sosa, Jason Giambi, Ichiro Suzuki 25.00

2002 Upper Deck Ovation Silver

MT
(1-60): 1-3X
(61-89, 120): .5-1X
(90-119): 2-4X

2002 Upper Deck Ovation Gold

MT
(1-60) print run 25-50: 15-30X
(1-60) p/r 51-75: 8-15X
(1-60) p/r 76-90: 5-10X
(61-120) 25 of each produced
Print runs based on stats

2002 Upper Deck Ovation Authentic McGwire

MT
Varying quantities produced
AM-B Mark McGwire/ bat/70 280.00
AM-BG Mark McGwire/ bat/50 350.00
AM-SB Mark McGwire/ bat/auto/25
AM-J Mark McGwire/ jsy/70 280.00
AM-JG Mark McGwire/ jsy/50 350.00
AM-SJ Mark McGwire/ jsy/auto/25

2002 Upper Deck Ovation Diamond Futures Jersey

MT
Common Player: 6.00
Inserted 1:72
Golds production 25 no pricing
LB Lance Berkman 15.00
RB Russell Branyan 6.00
PB Pat Burrell 15.00
FG Freddy Garcia 10.00
TH Tim Hudson 6.00
JK Jason Kendall 8.00
JP Jorge Posada 10.00
IR Ivan Rodriguez 10.00
JR Jimmy Rollins 10.00
KS Kazuhiro Sasaki 10.00
JV Jose Vidro 6.00
BZ Barry Zito 10.00

2002 Upper Deck Ovation Lead Performer Jersey

MT
Common Player: 6.00
Inserted 1:72
Golds: 25 sets no pricing
JB Jeff Bagwell 8.00
CD Carlos Delgado 6.00
JGi Jason Giambi 18.00
JG Juan Gonzalez 8.00
LG Luis Gonzalez 8.00
KG Ken Griffey Jr/SP 25.00
MP Mike Piazza 15.00
AR Alex Rodriguez 15.00
IR Ivan Rodriguez 8.00
SS Sammy Sosa/SP 15.00
IS Ichiro Suzuki 40.00
FT Frank Thomas 8.00

2002 Upper Deck Ovation Swatches Jersey

MT
Common Player: 6.00
Inserted 1:72
Golds: 25 sets produced no pricing
RA Roberto Alomar/ SP 20.00
EB Ellis Burks 6.00
JB Jeromy Burnitz 6.00
EC Eric Chavez 6.00
CD Carlos Delgado 8.00
DE Darin Erstad 8.00
MG Mark Grace 10.00
CJ Chipper Jones 12.00
GM Greg Maddux 15.00
PM Pedro J. Martinez 10.00
AR Alex Rodriguez 15.00
BW Bernie Williams 10.00

2002 Upper Deck Piece of History

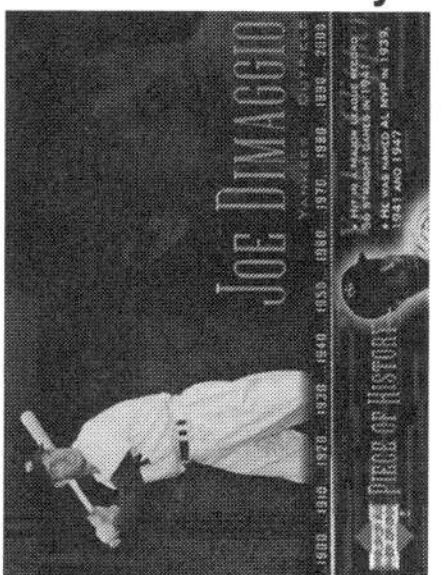

MT
Complete Set (132): 300.00
Common Player: .15
Common SP (91-132): 6.00
Production 625
Pack (5): 2.50
Box (24): 50.00
1 Troy Glaus .60
2 Darin Erstad .25
3 Reggie Jackson .50
4 Miguel Tejada .25
5 Tim Hudson .25
6 Jim "Catfish" Hunter .15
7 Joe Carter .15
8 Carlos Delgado .40
9 Greg Vaughn .15
10 Early Wynn .15
11 Omar Vizquel .15
12 Jim Thome .30
13 Ichiro Suzuki 2.50
14 Edgar Martinez .15
15 Freddy Garcia .15
16 Cal Ripken Jr/SP 20.00
17 Jeff Conine .15
18 Juan Gonzalez .60
19 Nolan Ryan/SP 20.00
20 Alex Rodriguez/ SP 12.00
21 Rafael Palmeiro .40
22 Ivan Rodriguez .50
23 Carlton Fisk .15
24 Wade Boggs .30
25 Pedro J. Martinez .60
26 Nomar Garciaparra 1.50
27 Manny Ramirez .60
28 Mike Sweeney .15
29 Bobby Higginson .15
30 Kirby Puckett .75
31 Doug Mientkiewicz .15
32 Corey Koskie .15
33 Joe Mays .15
34 Frank Thomas .60
35 Magglio Ordonez .25
36 Jason Giambi/SP 10.00
37 Derek Jeter/SP 20.00
38 Mickey Mantle/SP 20.00
39 Joe DiMaggio 2.50
40 Roger Maris 1.00
41 Roger Clemens .75
42 Bernie Williams .50
43 Jeff Bagwell .60
44 Lance Berkman .25
45 Eddie Mathews .50
46 Andruw Jones .40
47 Phil Niekro .15
48 Gary Sheffield .25
49 Chipper Jones 1.25
50 Greg Maddux 1.25
51 Robin Yount .50
52 Richie Sexson .25
53 Jim Edmonds .15
54 J.D. Drew .30
55 Albert Pujols 1.25
56 Andre Dawson .15
57 Billy Williams .15
58 Ernie Banks .60
59 Sammy Sosa/SP 10.00
60 Randy Johnson .60
61 Curt Schilling .25
62 Luis Gonzalez .40
63 Kirk Gibson .15
64 Steve Garvey .15
65 Sandy Koufax/SP 15.00
66 Shawn Green .25
67 Hideo Nomo .25
68 Kevin Brown .15
69 Vladimir Guerrero .60
70 Tim Raines .15
71 Gaylord Perry .15
72 Mel Ott .25
73 Willie McCovey .15
74 Barry Bonds/SP 10.00
75 Jeff Kent .15
76 Cliff Floyd .15
77 Dwight Gooden .15
78 Tom Seaver .60
79 Mike Piazza 1.50
80 Roberto Alomar .50
81 Dave Winfield .25
82 Tony Gwynn .75
83 Scott Rolen .40
84 Bill Mazeroski .15
85 Willie Stargell .25
86 Brian Giles .25
87 Ken Griffey Jr/SP 15.00
88 Sean Casey .25
89 Todd Helton .60
90 Larry Walker .25
91 *Brendan Donnelly* 6.00
92 *Tom Shearn* 6.00
93 *Brandon Puffer* 8.00
94 *Corey Thurman* 6.00
95 *Reed Johnson* 6.00
96 *Gustavo Chacin* 8.00
97 *Chris Baker* 6.00
98 *John Ennis* 8.00
99 *So Taguchi* 20.00
100 *Michael Crudale* 6.00
101 *Francis Beltran* 8.00
102 *Jose Valverde* 10.00
103 *Doug Devore* 6.00
104 *Jeremy Ward* 6.00
105 *P.J. Bevis* 10.00
106 *Steve Kent* 8.00
107 *Brandon Backe* 8.00
108 *Jorge Nunez* 8.00
109 *Kazuhisa Ishii* 50.00
110 *Ron Calloway* 6.00
111 Valentino Pasucci 6.00
112 *J.J. Putz* 8.00
113 Matt Thornton 12.00
114 *Allan Simpson* 6.00
115 *Jaime Cerda* 6.00
116 *Mark Corey* 8.00
117 *Tyler Yates* 8.00
118 *Steve Bechler* 8.00
119 *Ben Howard* 15.00

120	*Clifford Bartosh*	10.00
121	*Todd Donovan*	15.00
122	*Eric Junge*	15.00
123	*Adrian Burnside*	6.00
124	*Andy Pratt*	10.00
125	*Josh Hancock*	8.00
126	*Rene Reyes*	6.00
127	*Cam Esslinger*	6.00
128	*Colin Young*	8.00
129	*Kevin Frederick*	6.00
130	*Kyle Kane*	6.00
131	*Mitch Wylie*	8.00
132	Danny Wright	8.00

2002 Upper Deck Piece of History Batting Champs

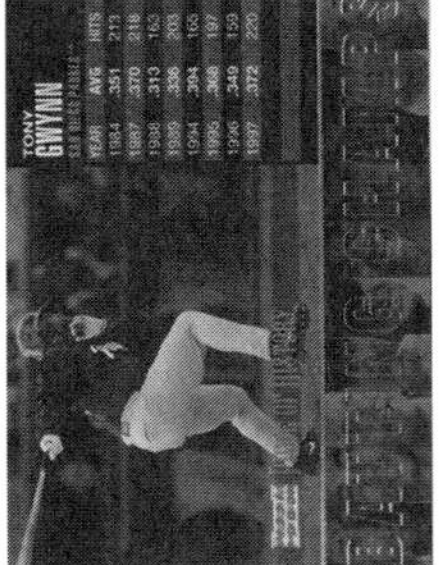

		MT
Complete Set (10):		18.00
Common Player:		1.50
Inserted 1:30		
B1	Tony Gwynn	2.00
B2	Frank Thomas	2.00
B3	Billy Williams	1.50
B4	Edgar Martinez	1.50
B5	Bernie Williams	1.50
B6	Mickey Mantle	6.00
B7	Larry Walker	1.50
B8	Gary Sheffield	1.50
B9	Wade Boggs	1.50
B10	Alex Rodriguez	4.00

2002 Upper Deck Piece of History Batting Champ Jerseys

		MT
Common Player:		8.00
Inserted 1:96		
WB	Wade Boggs	12.00
AG	Andres Galarraga	8.00
TG	Tony Gwynn	15.00
MM	Mickey Mantle/50	200.00
EM	Edgar Martinez	10.00
JO	John Olerud	8.00
PO	Paul O'Neil	12.00
TR	Tim Raines	8.00
AR	Alex Rodriguez	15.00
GS	Gary Sheffield/SP	
FT	Frank Thomas	12.00
LW	Larry Walker/SP	15.00
BeW	Bernie Williams	10.00

2002 UD Piece of History Batting Champ Jerseys Auto.

MT

Complete Set (5):
Common Player:
SBC-TGTony Gwynn Auto/24
SBC-JOJohn Olerud Auto/24
SBC-POPaul O'Neill Auto/24
SBC-ARAlex Rodriguez Auto/24
SBC-FTFrank Thomas Auto/24

2002 Upper Deck Piece of History ERA Leaders

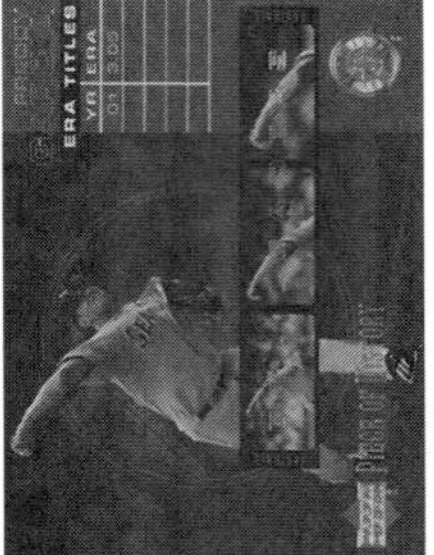

		MT
Complete Set (10):		18.00
Common Player:		1.00
Inserted 1:30		
E1	Greg Maddux	3.00
E2	Pedro J. Martinez	2.00
E3	Freddy Garcia	1.00
E4	Randy Johnson	2.00
E5	Tom Seaver	2.00
E6	Early Wynn	1.00
E7	Dwight Gooden	1.00
E8	Kevin Brown	1.00
E9	Roger Clemens	3.00
E10	Nolan Ryan	6.00

2002 UD Piece of History POH ERA Leaders Jerseys

		MT
Common Player:		8.00
Inserted 1:96		
KB	Kevin Brown	8.00
RC	Roger Clemens	25.00
FG	Freddy Garcia	10.00
DG	Dwight Gooden	10.00
CH	"Catfish" Hunter/SP	15.00
RJ	Randy Johnson	15.00
SK	Sandy Koufax/SP	100.00
GM	Greg Maddux	15.00
PM	Pedro Martinez	15.00
PN	Phil Niekro	10.00
NR	Nolan Ryan/SP	50.00
TS	Tom Seaver	20.00

2002 UD Piece of History ERA Leaders Jerseys Autographs

		MT
production 24 sets		
RC	Roger Clemens	200.00
FG	Freddy Garcia	
SK	Sandy Koufax	750.00

A card number in parentheses ( ) indicates the set is unnumbered.

2002 Upper Deck Piece of History Hitting for the Cycle

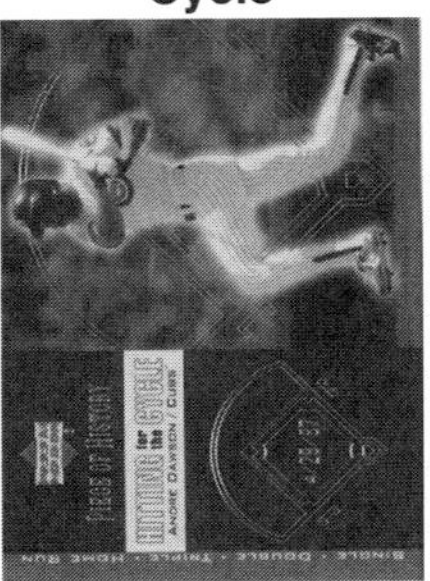

		MT
Complete Set (20):		35.00
Common Player:		1.00
Inserted 1:15		
H1	Alex Rodriguez	4.00
H2	Andre Dawson	1.00
H3	Cal Ripken Jr.	6.00
H4	Carlton Fisk	1.50
H5	Dante Bichette	1.00
H6	Dave Winfield	1.50
H7	Eric Chavez	1.00
H8	Robin Yount	2.00
H9	Jason Kendall	1.00
H10	Jay Buhner	1.00
H11	Jeff Kent	1.00
H12	Joe DiMaggio	6.00
H13	John Olerud	1.00
H14	Kirby Puckett	3.00
H15	Luis Gonzalez	1.50
H16	Mark Grace	1.50
H17	Mickey Mantle	6.00
H18	Miguel Tejada	1.00
H19	Rondell White	1.00
H20	Todd Helton	2.00

2002 UD Piece of History Hitting for the Cycle Bats

		MT
Inserted 1:576		
DB	Dante Bichette	20.00
JB	Jay Buhner	30.00
EC	Eric Chavez	20.00
AD	Andre Dawson	25.00
CF	Carlton Fisk	25.00
LG	Luis Gonzalez	25.00
MM	Mickey Mantle/50	
CR	Cal Ripken Jr/SP	100.00
AR	Alex Rodriguez	35.00
DW	Dave Winfield	25.00

2002 UD Piece of History Hitting for the Cycle Bats Aut

MT

Complete Set (3):
Common Player:
SHC-LGLuis Gonzalez
SHC-CRCal Ripken Jr.
SHC-ARAlex Rodriguez

2002 Upper Deck Piece of History The MVP Club

		MT
Complete Set (14):		30.00
Common Player:		1.00
Inserted 1:22		
M1	Jason Giambi	2.00
M2	Sammy Sosa	3.00
M3	Cal Ripken Jr.	6.00
M4	Robin Yount	2.00
M5	Ken Griffey Jr.	5.00
M6	Kirk Gibson	1.00
M7	Mickey Mantle	6.00
M8	Barry Bonds	3.00
M9	Frank Thomas	2.00
M10	Reggie Jackson	2.00
M11	Jeff Bagwell	2.00
M12	Roger Clemens	3.00
M13	Steve Garvey	1.00
M14	Chipper Jones	3.00

2002 Upper Deck Piece of History MVP Club Jerseys

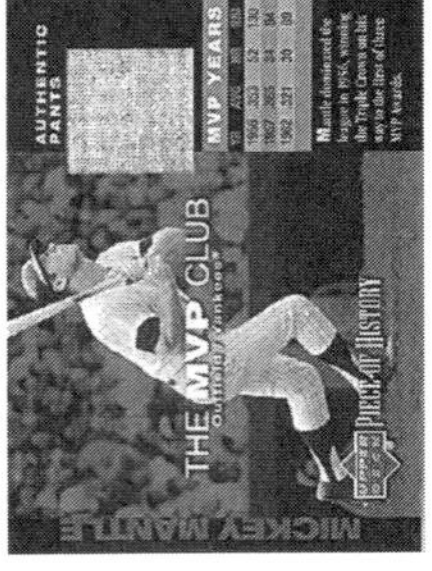

		MT
Common Player:		8.00
Inserted 1:96		
JB	Jeff Bagwell	15.00
RC	Roger Clemens	20.00
SG	Steve Garvey	8.00
JGi	Jason Giambi	15.00
KGi	Kirk Gibson	10.00
JGo	Juan Gonzalez	12.00
KGr	Ken Griffey Jr.	25.00
RJ	Reggie Jackson	15.00
CJ	Chipper Jones	15.00
JK	Jeff Kent	8.00
BL	Barry Larkin/SP	25.00
MM	Mickey Mantle/50	250.00
RM	Roger Maris/50	110.00
CR	Cal Ripken Jr.	35.00
IR	Ivan Rodriguez	10.00
SS	Sammy Sosa	20.00
FT	Frank Thomas	12.00
RY	Robin Yount/SP	40.00

2002 Upper Deck Piece of History MVP Club Jerseys Auto.

	MT
Complete Set (3):	
Common Player:	
SM-KG Ken Griffey Jr.	
SM-CR Cal Ripken Jr.	
SM-SS Sammy Sosa	

2002 Upper Deck Piece of History Tape Measure Heroes

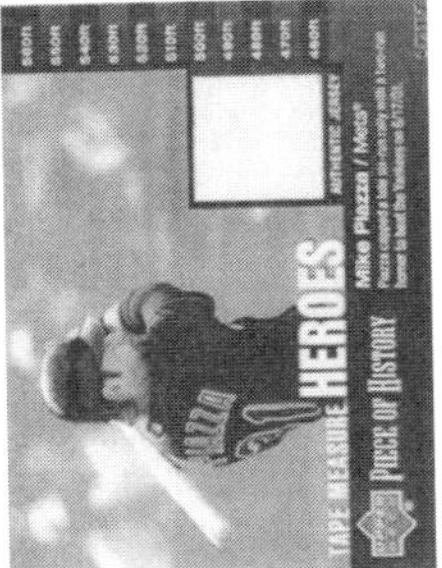

	MT
Complete Set (30):	50.00
Common Player:	1.00
Inserted 1:10	
TM1 Joe Carter	1.00
TM2 Cal Ripken Jr.	6.00
TM3 Mike Piazza	4.00
TM4 Shawn Green	1.25
TM5 Mark McGwire	5.00
TM6 Reggie Jackson	1.50
TM7 Mickey Mantle	6.00
TM8 Manny Ramirez	2.00
TM9 Mo Vaughn	1.00
TM10 Jeff Bagwell	2.00
TM11 Sammy Sosa	3.00
TM12 Tony Gwynn	2.00
TM13 Bill Mazeroski	1.00
TM14 Jose Canseco	1.50
TM15 Brian Giles	1.00
TM16 Kirk Gibson	1.00
TM17 Kirby Puckett	3.00
TM18 Wade Boggs	1.50
TM19 Albert Pujols	3.00
TM20 David Justice	1.00
TM21 Steve Garvey	1.00
TM22 Luis Gonzalez	1.50
TM23 Derek Jeter	6.00
TM24 Robin Yount	2.00
TM25 Barry Bonds	3.00
TM26 Alex Rodriguez	4.00
TM27 Willie Stargell	1.50
TM28 Carlton Fisk	1.50
TM29 Carlos Delgado	1.50
TM30 Ken Griffey Jr.	5.00

2002 UD Piece of History Tape Measure Heroes Jerseys

	MT
Common Player:	8.00
Inserted 1:96	
JB Jeff Bagwell	12.00
WB Wade Boggs	15.00
JCa Jose Canseco	30.00
JoC Joe Carter	8.00
CD Carlos Delgado	8.00
CF Carlton Fisk	15.00
SGa Steve Garvey	8.00
KGi Kirk Gibson	12.00
BG Brian Giles	12.00
SGr Shawn Green	8.00
KGr Ken Griffey Jr/90	50.00
TG Tony Gwynn/SP	
RJ Reggie Jackson/23	
MMa Mickey Mantle/50	275.00
RM Roger Maris/50	120.00
BM Bill Mazeroski	15.00
MP Mike Piazza	20.00
MR Manny Ramirez	15.00
CR Cal Ripken Jr.	30.00
AR Alex Rodriguez	15.00
SS Sammy Sosa	20.00
WS Willie Stargell	15.00
RY Robin Yount	40.00

2002 Upper Deck Piece of History The 500 Home Run Club

	MT
Complete Set (9):	25.00
Common Player:	1.50
Inserted 1:9	
HR1 Harmon Killebrew	3.00
HR2 Jimmie Foxx	3.00
HR3 Reggie Jackson	3.00
HR4 Mickey Mantle	8.00
HR5 Ernie Banks	3.00
HR6 Eddie Mathews	3.00
HR7 Mark McGwire	6.00
HR8 Willie McCovey	1.50
HR9 Mel Ott	3.00

2002 UD Piece of History POH 500 HR Club Jerseys

	MT
Inserted 1:336	
HA Hank Aaron	40.00
EB Ernie Banks/SP	50.00
JF Jimmie Foxx	60.00
RJ Reggie Jackson	25.00
MM Mickey Mantle/50	300.00
EM Eddie Mathews	30.00
WM Willie McCovey	25.00
MO Mel Ott	40.00

2002 UD Piece of History 500 HR Club Jerseys Auto.

	MT
Complete Set (2):	
Common Player:	
SHR-EB Ernie Banks	
SHR-RJ Reggie Jackson	

2002 Upper Deck Piece of History 300 Game Winners

	MT
Complete Set (6):	12.00
Common Player:	1.00
Inserted 1:50	
GW1 Nolan Ryan	6.00
GW2 Tom Seaver	3.00
GW3 Cy Young	3.00
GW4 Gaylord Perry	1.00
GW5 Early Wynn	1.00
GW6 Phil Niekro	1.00

2002 UD Piece of History 300 Game Winners Jerseys

	MT
Common Player:	15.00
Inserted 1:576	
PN Phil Niekro	15.00
GP Gaylord Perry	15.00
NR Nolan Ryan/SP	65.00
TS Tom Seaver/SP	30.00

2002 Upper Deck Prospect Premieres

	MT
Complete Set (109):	
Common Player (1-60):	.40
Common (61-85):	5.00
Inserted 1:18	
Common (86-97):	10.00
Inserted 1:18	
Pack (4):	2.75
Box (18):	45.00
1 *Josh Rupe*	.40

	MT
2 *Blair Johnson*	.40
3 *Jason Pridie*	.75
4 *Tim Gilhooly*	.40
5 *Kennard Jones*	.40
6 *Darrell Rasner*	.40
7 *Adam Donachie*	.75
8 *Josh Murray*	.40
9 *Brian Dopirak*	.40
10 *Jason Cooper*	2.00
11 *Zach Hammes*	.40
12 *Jon Lester*	.40
13 *Kevin Jepsen*	.40
14 *Curtis Granderson*	.75
15 *David Bush*	.40
16 *Joel Guzman*	.50
17 *Matt Pender*	.40
18 *Derick Grigsby*	.40
19 *Jeremy Reed*	.40
20 *Jonathan Broxton*	.40
21 *Jesse Crain*	.40
22 *Justin Jones*	1.50
23 *Brian Slocum*	1.00
24 *Brian McCann*	.75
25 *Francisco Liriano*	.40
26 *Fred Lewis*	.50
27 *Steve Stanley*	.40
28 *Chris Snyder*	.40
29 *Daniel Cevette*	1.50
30 *Kiel Fisher*	.40
31 *Brandon Wheeder*	.40
32 *Pat Osborn*	.40
33 *Taber Lee*	.40
34 *Dan Ortmeyer*	.50
35 *Josh Johnson*	.40
36 *Val Majewski*	.50
37 *Larry Broadway*	.40
38 *Joey Gomes*	.75
39 *Eric Thomas*	.40
40 *James Loney*	2.00
41 *Charlie Morton*	.40
42 Mark McLemore	.40
43 *Matt Craig*	.40
44 *Ryan Rodriguez*	.40
45 *Rich Hill*	.40
46 *Bob Malek*	.40
47 *Justin Maureau*	.40
48 *Randy Braun*	.40
49 *Brian Grant*	.50
50 *Tyler Davidson*	.40
51 *Travis Hanson*	.50
52 *Kyle Boyer*	.40
53 *James Holcomb*	.40
54 *Ryan Williams*	.40
55 *Ben Crockett*	.40
56 *Adam Greenberg*	.40
57 *John Baker*	.40
58 *Matt Carson*	.40
59 *Jonathan George*	.40
60 *David Jensen*	.40
61 *Nick Swisher*	12.00
62 *Brent Cleven*	8.00
63 *Royce Ring*	8.00
64 *Mike Nixon*	5.00
65 *Ricky Barrett*	5.00
66 *Russ Adams*	8.00
67 *Joe Mauer*	15.00
68 *Jeff Francoeur*	35.00
69 *Joseph Blanton*	5.00
70 *Micah Schilling*	8.00
71 *John McCurdy*	5.00
72 *Sergio Santos*	15.00
73 *Josh Womack*	5.00
74 *Jared Doyle*	5.00
75 *Ben Fritz*	8.00
76 Greg Miller	5.00
77 *Luke Hagerty*	10.00
78 *Matt Whitney*	10.00
79 *Dan Meyer*	5.00
80 *Bill Murphy*	5.00
81 *Zach Segovia*	8.00
82 *Steve Obenchain*	8.00
83 *Matt Clanton*	8.00
84 *Mark Teahen*	8.00
85 *Kyle Pawelczyk*	8.00
86 *Khalil Greene/auto*	30.00
87 *Joe Saunders/auto*	10.00
88 *Jeremy Hermida/auto*	15.00
89 *Drew Meyer/auto*	12.00
90 *Jeff Francis/auto*	10.00
91 *Scott Moore/auto*	20.00
92 *Prince Fielder/auto*	40.00
93 *Zack Greinke/auto*	12.00
94 *Chris Gruler/auto*	12.00
95 *Scott Kazmir/auto*	75.00
96 *B.J. Upton/auto*	35.00
97 *Clint Everts/auto*	10.00
98 Cal Ripken Jr.	1.00
99 Cal Ripken Jr.	1.00
100 Mark McGwire	1.00
101 Mark McGwire	1.00
102 Mark McGwire	1.00
103 Mark McGwire	1.00
104 Mark McGwire	1.00
105 Joe DiMaggio	1.00
106 Joe DiMaggio	1.00
107 Joe DiMaggio	1.00
108 Joe DiMaggio	1.00
109 Joe DiMaggio	1.00

2002 Upper Deck Prospect Premieres Future Gems Quads

MT

Common Card: 4.00
Inserted 1:box

1 David Bush, Matt Craig, Blair Johnson, Brian McCann 4.00
2 Jason Cooper, Jonathan George, Larry Broadway, Joel Guzman 4.00
3 Matt Craig, Josh Murray, Brian McCann, Jason Pridie 4.00
4 Jesse Crain, Brian Grant, Curtis Granderson, Joey Gomes 4.00
5 Tyler Davidson, Val Majewski, Kennard Jones, Daniel Cevette 4.00
6 Joe DiMaggio, Jon Lester, Mac, Mark McLemore 4.00
7 Jonathan George, Jeremy Reed, Adam Donachie, Matt Carson 4.00
8 Jonathan George, Eric Thomas, Joel Guzman, Kiel Fisher 4.00
9 Tim Gilhooly, Brandon Wheeder, Brian Slocum, Brian Dopirak 4.00
10 Brian Grant, Rich Hill, Joey Gomes, Joe DiMaggio 4.00
11 Derick Grigsby, Bob Malek, James Loney, Fred Lewis 4.00
12 Zach Hammes, James Holcomb, Cal Ripken Jr., Kennard Jones 4.00
13 Rich Hill, Mark McGwire, Brian Grant, Matt Carson 4.00
14 James Holcomb, David Jensen, Kennard Jones, Ryan Williams 4.00
15 David Jensen, Francisco Liriano, Ryan Williams, Travis Hanson 4.00
16 Blair Johnson, Jesse Crain, Adam Greenberg, Curtis Granderson 4.00
17 Jon Lester, Jonathan George, Adam Donachie, Mark McLemore 4.00
18 Francisco Liriano, Mark McGwire, Travis Hanson, Taber Lee 4.00
19 Val Majewski, Charlie Morton, Daniel Cevette, Joey Gomes 4.00
20 Bob Malek, Zach Hammes, Fred Lewis, Cal Ripken Jr. 4.00
21 Justin Maureau, Joe DiMaggio, Chris Snyder, Mark McGwire 4.00
22 Mark McGwire, Bob Malek, Joe DiMaggio, Kyle Boyer 4.00
23 Charlie Morton, David Bush, Joey Gomes, Blair Johnson 4.00
24 Josh Murray, Mark McGwire, Jason Pridie, Joe DiMaggio 4.00
25 Matt Pender, Mark McGwire, Mark McLemore, Ryan Rodriguez 4.00
26 Jason Pridie, Josh Murray, Matt Craig, Brian McCann 4.00
27 Jeremy Reed, Blair Johnson, Matt Carson, Adam Greenberg 4.00
28 Cal Ripken Jr., Jason Cooper, Matt Carson, Larry Broadway 4.00
29 Ryan Rodriguez, Eric Thomas, Pat Osborn, Randy Braun 4.00
30 Josh Rupe, Tyler Davidson, John Baker, Kennard Jones 4.00
31 Eric Thomas, Derick Grigsby, Randy Braun, James Loney 4.00
32 Eric Thomas, Matt Pender, Kiel Fisher, Mark McLemore 4.00
33 Brandon Wheeder, Rich Hill, Brian Dopirak, Brian Grant 4.00

2002 UD Prospect Premieres Heroes of Baseball Quads

MT

Common Quad: 10.00
Production 85 sets

1 Joe DiMaggio, Tony Gwynn 15.00
2 Joe DiMaggio, Tony Gwynn, Cal Ripken Jr. 20.00
3 Joe DiMaggio, Mickey Mantle, Willie Stargell 20.00
4 Tony Gwynn, Ozzie Smith, Willie Stargell 10.00
5 Tony Gwynn, Willie Stargell, Joe DiMaggio, Joe Morgan 15.00
6 Tony Gwynn, Willie Stargell, Cal Ripken Jr., Ozzie Smith 15.00
7 Mickey Mantle, Mark McGwire, Joe Morgan, Tom Seaver 20.00
8 Mickey Mantle, Tom Seaver 20.00
9 Mark McGwire, Joe Morgan 20.00
10 Mark McGwire, Cal Ripken Jr., Tony Gwynn, Joe DiMaggio 25.00
11 Mark McGwire, Tom Seaver, Joe Morgan, Ozzie Smith 15.00
12 Joe Morgan, Tony Gwynn 10.00
13 Joe Morgan, Joe DiMaggio, Mickey Mantle, Cal Ripken Jr. 25.00
14 Joe Morgan, Joe DiMaggio, Willie Stargell, Tony Gwynn 15.00
15 Ozzie Smith, Joe DiMaggio, Ozzie Smith, Willie Stargell 15.00
16 Ozzie Smith, Mark McGwire, Willie Stargell, Tony Gwynn 15.00
17 Ozzie Smith, Tom Seaver, Mark McGwire 15.00
18 Cal Ripken Jr., Mickey Mantle, Joe DiMaggio, Joe Morgan 20.00
19 Cal Ripken Jr., Mark McGwire, Cal Ripken Jr. 20.00
20 Tom Seaver, Joe DiMaggio, Tom Seaver, Joe DiMaggio 15.00
21 Tom Seaver, Joe Morgan, Ozzie Smith, Willie Stargell 10.00
22 Tom Seaver, Cal Ripken Jr., Mark McGwire, Mickey Mantle 20.00
23 Willie Stargell, Ozzie Smith 10.00
24 Willie Stargell, Ozzie Smith, Tom Seaver, Joe Morgan 10.00

2002 UD Prospect Premieres UD Heroes of Baseball

MT

Complete Ripken set (10): 15.00
Common Ripken: 2.00
Complete Morgan set (10): 4.00
Common Morgan: .50
Complete Stargell set (10): 5.00
Common Stargell: .50
Complete Seaver set (10): 10.00
Common Seaver: 1.25
Complete Mantle set (10): 15.00
Common Mantle: 2.00
Complete DiMaggio set (10): 12.00
Common DiMaggio: 1.50
Complete Gwynn set (10): 10.00
Common Gwynn: 1.25
Complete McGwire set (10): 12.00
Common McGwire: 1.50
Complete Ozzie Smith (10): 8.00
Com mon Ozzie: 1.00
Sets include Headers
Inserted 1:1

2002 Upper Deck Sweet Spot

MT

Complete Set (175): NA
Common Player: .40
Common (91-130): 5.00
Production 1,300
Common Auto. (131-145): 15.00
Production 750 or 100
Common Game Faces (146-175): 4.00
Inserted 1:24
Parallel (146-175): 1.5X-3X
Production 100
Pack (4): 9.00
Box (12): 95.00

1 Troy Glaus .75
2 Darin Erstad .75
3 Tim Hudson .75
4 Eric Chavez .75
5 Barry Zito .75
6 Miguel Tejada 1.00
7 Carlos Delgado .60
8 Eric Hinske .40
9 Ben Grieve .40
10 Jim Thome 1.00
11 C.C. Sabathia .40
12 Omar Vizquel .60
13 Ichiro Suzuki 3.00
14 Edgar Martinez .40
15 Bret Boone .40
16 Freddy Garcia .40
17 Tony Batista .40
18 Geronimo Gil .40
19 Alex Rodriguez 3.00
20 Rafael Palmeiro .75
21 Ivan Rodriguez .75
22 Hank Blalock .40
23 Juan Gonzalez .75
24 Nomar Garciaparra 2.50
25 Pedro J. Martinez 1.50
26 Manny Ramirez 1.00
27 Mike Sweeney .40
28 Carlos Beltran .40
29 Dmitri Young .40
30 Torii Hunter .40
31 Eric Milton .40
32 Corey Koskie .40
33 Frank Thomas 1.00
34 Mark Buehrle .40
35 Magglio Ordonez .75
36 Roger Clemens 2.00
37 Derek Jeter 4.00
38 Jason Giambi 2.00
39 Alfonso Soriano 3.00
40 Bernie Williams .75
41 Jeff Bagwell 1.00
42 Roy Oswalt .75
43 Lance Berkman .75
44 Greg Maddux 2.00
45 Chipper Jones 2.00
46 Gary Sheffield .60
47 Andruw Jones .75
48 Richie Sexson .75
49 Ben Sheets .40
50 Albert Pujols 2.00
51 Matt Morris .40
52 J.D. Drew .75
53 Sammy Sosa 2.00
54 Kerry Wood .75
55 Mark Prior 1.00
56 Moises Alou .40
57 Corey Patterson .40
58 Randy Johnson 1.00
59 Luis Gonzalez .75
60 Curt Schilling 1.00
61 Shawn Green .60
62 Kevin Brown .40
63 Paul LoDuca .40
64 Adrian Beltre .40
65 Vladimir Guerrero 1.25
66 Jose Vidro .40
67 Javier Vazquez .40
68 Barry Bonds 3.00
69 Jeff Kent .60
70 Rich Aurilia .40
71 Mike Lowell .40
72 Josh Beckett .40
73 Brad Penny .40
74 Roberto Alomar .75
75 Mike Piazza 3.00
76 Jeromy Burnitz .40
77 Mo Vaughn .40
78 Phil Nevin .40
79 Sean Burroughs .40
80 Jeremy Giambi .40
81 Bobby Abreu .60
82 Jimmy Rollins .40
83 Pat Burrell .75
84 Brian Giles .75
85 Aramis Ramirez .40
86 Ken Griffey Jr. 2.50
87 Adam Dunn 1.00

88 Austin Kearns .75
89 Todd Helton .75
90 Larry Walker .60
91 *Earl Snyder* 5.00
92 *Jorge Padilla* 6.00
93 *Felix Escalona* 5.00
94 *John Foster* 15.00
95 *Brandon Puffer* 5.00
96 *Steve Bechler* 6.00
97 *Hansel Izquierdo* 5.00
98 *Chris Baker* 5.00
99 *Jeremy Ward* 5.00
100 *Kevin Frederick* 5.00
101 *Josh Hancock* 5.00
102 *Allan Simpson* 8.00
103 *Mitch Wylie* 5.00
104 *Mark Corey* 5.00
105 *Victor Alvarez* 5.00
106 *Todd Donovan* 5.00
107 *Nelson Castro* 5.00
108 *Chris Booker* 5.00
109 *Corey Thurman* 5.00
110 Kirk Saarloos 10.00
111 *Michael Crudale* 5.00
112 *Jason Simontacchi* 15.00
113 *Ron Calloway* 5.00
114 *Brandon Backe* 5.00
115 *Tom Shearn* 5.00
116 *Oliver Perez* 15.00
117 *Kyle Kane* 5.00
118 *Francis Beltran* 5.00
119 *So Taguchi* 10.00
120 *Doug Devore* 8.00
121 *Juan Brito* 5.00
122 *Clifford Bartosh* 5.00
123 *Eric Junge* 5.00
124 *Joe Orloski* 5.00
125 *Scotty Layfield* 5.00
126 *Jorge Sosa* 5.00
127 *Satoru Komiyama* 5.00
128 *Edwin Almonte* 5.00
129 *Takahito Nomura* 5.00
130 *John Ennis* 8.00
131 *Kazuhisa Ishii/ Auto/100* 110.00
132 *Ben Howard/ Auto/100* 35.00
133 *Aaron Cook/ Auto/750* 15.00
134 *Anderson Machado/ Auto/750* 15.00
135 *Luis Ugueto/ Auto/750* 25.00
136 *Tyler Yates/ Auto/750* 20.00
137 *Rodrigo Rosario/ Auto/750* 15.00
138 *Jaime Cerda/ Auto/750* 15.00
139 *Luis Martinez/ Auto/750* 15.00
140 *Rene Reyes/ Auto/750* 15.00
141 *Eric Good/Auto/750* 15.00
142 Matt Thornton/ Auto/100 30.00
143 *Steve Kent/ Auto/750* 15.00
144 *Jose Valverde/ Auto/750* 15.00
145 *Adrian Burnside/ Auto/750* 15.00
146 Barry Bonds 12.00
147 Ken Griffey Jr. 10.00
148 Alex Rodriguez 12.00
149 Jason Giambi 8.00
150 Chipper Jones 10.00
151 Nomar Garciaparra 12.00
152 Mike Piazza 12.00
153 Sammy Sosa 10.00
154 Derek Jeter 18.00
155 Jeff Bagwell 6.00
156 Albert Pujols 10.00
157 Ichiro Suzuki 12.00
158 Randy Johnson 6.00
159 Frank Thomas 6.00
160 Greg Maddux 10.00
161 Jim Thome 6.00
162 Scott Rolen 6.00
163 Shawn Green 4.00
164 Vladimir Guerrero 6.00
165 Troy Glaus 6.00
166 Carlos Delgado 4.00
167 Luis Gonzalez 4.00
168 Roger Clemens 8.00
169 Todd Helton 5.00
170 Eric Chavez 6.00
171 Rafael Palmeiro 5.00
172 Pedro J. Martinez 8.00
173 Lance Berkman 6.00
174 Josh Beckett 4.00
175 Sean Burroughs 4.00

2002 Upper Deck Sweet Spot Bat Barrels

MT

Complete Set (28):
Common Player:
100 Total Produced
B-RA Roberto Alomar
B-MA Moises Alou
B-RAn Rick Ankiel
B-RC Roger Clemens
B-JD J.D. Drew
B-BG Brian Giles
B-TG Tom Glavine
B-JGo Juan Gonzalez
B-LG Luis Gonzalez
B-SG Shawn Green
B-KG Ken Griffey Jr.
B-TH Todd Helton
B-AJ Andruw Jones
B-CJ Chipper Jones
B-GM Greg Maddux
B-MC Mark McGwire
B-MO Magglio Ordonez
B-RP Rafael Palmeiro
B-AR Alex Rodriguez
B-IR Ivan Rodriguez
B-GS Gary Sheffield
B-SS Sammy Sosa
B-IS Ichiro Suzuki
B-FT Frank Thomas
B-JT Jim Thome
B-LW Larry Walker
B-BW Bernie Williams
B-PW Preston Wilson

2002 Upper Deck Sweet Spot Legendary Signatures

MT

Common Autograph: 20.00
Inserted 1:72
LA Luis Aparicio/485 25.00
JD Joe DiMaggio/50
RF Rollie Fingers/866 20.00
SG Steve Garvey/871 20.00
KH Keith Hernandez/ 906 20.00
FJ Ferguson Jenkins/ 857 20.00
AK Al Kaline/835 40.00
SK Sandy Koufax/ 485 240.00
FL Fred Lynn/853 20.00
MM Mark McGwire/ 90 750.00
PM Paul Molitor/852 30.00
GP Gaylord Perry/921 25.00
BP Boog Powell/944 20.00
CR Cal Ripken Jr./ 194 175.00
BR Brooks Robinson 35.00
AT Alan Trammell/ 843 35.00

2002 UD Sweet Spot Mark McGwire Priority Signing Redem.

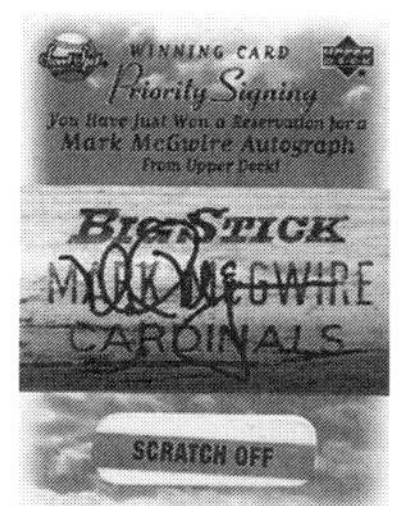

MT

100 Produced
MM Mark McGwire 1000.

2002 Upper Deck Sweet Spot Signatures

MT

Common Autograph: 25.00
Inserted 1:72
LB Lance Berkman/ 291 55.00
HB Hank Blalock/291 30.00
BB Barry Bonds/380 275.00
JB Jeromy Burnitz/ 291 25.00
SB Sean Burroughs/ 291 30.00
RC Roger Clemens/ 194 125.00
CD Carlos Delgado/ 291 25.00
AD Adam Dunn/291 50.00
FG Freddy Garcia/ 145 30.00
JG Jason Giambi/291 85.00
BG Brian Giles/291 30.00
TG Tom Glavine/291 40.00
LG Luis Gonzalez/ 291 35.00
KG Ken Griffey Jr./ 291 160.00
AJ Andruw Jones/ 291 45.00
RO Roy Oswalt/291 40.00
MPr Mark Prior/291 75.00
AR Alex Rodriguez/ 291 160.00
SR Scott Rolen/291 40.00
SS Sammy Sosa/ 145 280.00
MS Mike Sweeney/ 291 30.00
IS Ichiro Suzuki/145 600.00
FT Frank Thomas/ 291 50.00
JT Jim Thome/291 55.00
BZ Barry Zito/291 50.00

2002 Upper Deck Sweet Spot Sweet Swatches

MT

Common Player: 6.00
Inserted 1:12
JBa Jeff Bagwell 10.00
JBe Josh Beckett 6.00
SB Sean Burroughs 6.00
EC Eric Chavez 6.00
JE Jim Edmonds 8.00
DE Darin Erstad 8.00
JGi Jason Giambi 12.00
BG Brian Giles 8.00
JGo Juan Gonzalez 6.00
LG Luis Gonzalez 8.00
SG Shawn Green 6.00
KG Ken Griffey Jr. 15.00
KI Kazuhisa Ishii 10.00
CJ Chipper Jones 12.00
GM Greg Maddux 12.00
PM Pedro J. Martinez 10.00
MP Mike Piazza 15.00
AR Alex Rodriguez 15.00
IR Ivan Rodriguez 8.00
SR Scott Rolen 6.00
SS Sammy Sosa 15.00
IS Ichiro Suzuki 40.00
FT Frank Thomas 8.00
OV Omar Vizquel 8.00
BW Bernie Williams 10.00

2002 Upper Deck Sweet Spot USA Jerseys

MT

Common Player: 6.00
Inserted 1:12
BA Brent Abernathy 6.00
TB Taggert Bozied 10.00
DB Dewon Brazelton 6.00
AE Adam Everett 6.00
DG Danny Graves 6.00
JG Jake Gautreau 8.00
JK Josh Karp 8.00
AK Adam Kennedy 10.00
JM Joe Mauer 20.00
DM Doug Mientkiewicz 10.00
EM Eric Munson 6.00
XN Xavier Nady 6.00
RO Roy Oswalt 10.00
MP Mark Prior 18.00
JR Jon Rauch 6.00
MT Mark Teixeira 10.00
JW Justin Wayne 8.00

2002 Upper Deck Sweet Spot Classics

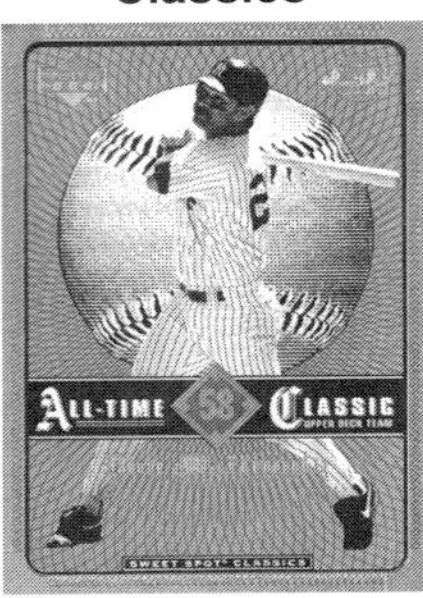

		MT
Complete Set (90):		40.00
Common Player:		.40
Pack (4):		14.00
Box (12):		160.00
1	Mickey Mantle	3.00
2	Joe DiMaggio	3.00
3	Babe Ruth	3.00
4	Ty Cobb	1.50
5	Nolan Ryan	3.00
6	Sandy Koufax	2.00
7	Cy Young	1.00
8	Roberto Clemente	2.00
9	Lefty Grove	.50
10	Lou Gehrig	2.50
11	Walter Johnson	1.00
12	Honus Wagner	1.00
13	Christy Mathewson	.75
14	Jackie Robinson	1.50
15	Joe Morgan	.50
16	Reggie Jackson	.75
17	Eddie Collins	.40
18	Cal Ripken Jr.	3.00
19	Hank Greenberg	.40
20	Harmon Killebrew	.75
21	Johnny Bench	1.00
22	Ernie Banks	1.00
23	Willie McCovey	.40
24	Mel Ott	.40
25	Tom Seaver	1.00
26	Tony Gwynn	.75
27	Dave Winfield	.50
28	Willie Stargell	.40
29	Mark McGwire	2.00
30	Al Kaline	.75
31	Jimmie Foxx	.75
32	Satchel Paige	1.50
33	Eddie Murray	.40
34	Lou Boudreau	.40
35	"Shoeless" Joe Jackson	1.50
36	Luke Appling	.40
37	Ralph Kiner	.40
38	Robin Yount	.75
39	Paul Molitor	.75
40	Juan Marichal	.40
41	Brooks Robinson	.75
42	Wade Boggs	.50
43	Kirby Puckett	1.00
44	Yogi Berra	1.00
45	George Sisler	.40
46	Buck Leonard	.40
47	Billy Williams	.40
48	Duke Snider	.75
49	Don Drysdale	.60
50	Bill Mazeroski	.40
51	Tony Oliva	.40
52	Luis Aparicio	.40
53	Carlton Fisk	.40
54	Kirk Gibson	.40
55	Jim "Catfish" Hunter	.40
56	Joe Carter	.40
57	Gaylord Perry	.40
58	Don Mattingly	2.00
59	Eddie Mathews	1.25
60	Ferguson Jenkins	.40
61	Roy Campanella	1.00
62	Orlando Cepeda	.40
63	Tony Perez	.40
64	Dave Parker	.40
65	Richie Ashburn	.40
66	Andre Dawson	.40
67	Dwight Evans	.40
68	Rollie Fingers	.40
69	Dale Murphy	.40
70	Ron Santo	.40
71	Steve Garvey	.40
72	Monte Irvin	.40
73	Alan Trammell	.40
74	Ryne Sandberg	1.00
75	Gary Carter	.40
76	Fred Lynn	.40
77	Maury Wills	.40
78	Ozzie Smith	1.00
79	Bobby Bonds	.40
80	Mickey Cochrane	.60
81	Dizzy Dean	.60
82	Graig Nettles	.40
83	Keith Hernandez	.40
84	Boog Powell	.40
85	Jack Clark	.40
86	Dave Stewart	.40
87	Tommy Lasorda	.40
88	Dennis Eckersley	.40
89	Ken Griffey Sr.	.40
90	Bucky Dent	.40

2002 Upper Deck Sweet Spot Classics Bat Barrels

MT

VALUES UNDETERMINED DUE TO SCARCITY

JB	Johnny Bench/5
YB	Yogi Berra/3
WB	Wade Boggs/2
BBo	Bob Boone/2
GC	Gary Carter/1
RC	Roberto Clemente/1
JD	Joe DiMaggio/5
DE	Dwight Evans/1
SG	Steve Garvey/1
HG	Hank Greenberg/1
KG	Ken Griffey Sr/3
TG	Tony Gwynn/12
RJ	Reggie Jackson/13
FJ	Ferguson Jenkins/1
AK	Al Kaline/4
FL	Fred Lynn/2
BM	Bill Madlock/1
DM	Don Mattingly/1
PM	Paul Molitor/4
TM	Thurman Munson/1
GN	Graig Nettles/2
DP	Dave Parker/4
KP	Kirby Puckett/4
CR	Cal Ripken Jr/5
BR	Brooks Robinson/2
BaR	Babe Ruth/1
NR	Nolan Ryan/4
BW	Billy Williams/2
DW	Dave Winfield/1

2002 Upper Deck Sweet Spot Classics Game Jersey

		MT
Common Player:		8.00
Inserted 1:8		
WB	Wade Boggs	12.00
GC	Gary Carter	10.00
JC	Joe Carter	8.00
JD	Joe DiMaggio/53	260.00
RF	Rollie Fingers	10.00
SG	Steve Garvey	10.00
TG	Tony Gwynn	15.00
RJ	Reggie Jackson	15.00
SK	Sandy Koufax /SP	160.00
BM	Bill Madlock	10.00
MM	Mickey Mantle/ 53	320.00
JMa	Juan Marichal	15.00
DM	Don Mattingly	40.00
PM	Paul Molitor	15.00
EM	Eddie Murray	15.00
GN	Graig Nettles	15.00
DP	Dave Parker	10.00
CR	Cal Ripken Jr.	30.00
NR	Nolan Ryan	40.00
RS	Ryne Sandberg	20.00
TS	Tom Seaver	20.00
OS	Ozzie Smith	25.00
DSn	Duke Snider/53	125.00
WS	Willie Stargell	20.00
DSt	Dave Stewart	8.00
BW	Billy Williams	15.00
RY	Robin Yount	15.00

2002 Upper Deck Sweet Spot Classics Game Jersey Gold

The game-jersey cards in Sweet Spot Classics were paralleled in a special Gold Edition, with each player's swatch cards numbered within an edition of 25 each.

		MT
Common Player:		45.00
WB	Wade Boggs	125.00
GC	Gary Carter	60.00
JC	Joe Carter	45.00
JD	Joe DiMaggio	325.00
RF	Rollie Fingers	60.00
SG	Steve Garvey	60.00
TG	Tony Gwynn	160.00
RJ	Reggie Jackson	250.00
SK	Sandy Koufax	300.00
BM	Bill Madlock	45.00
MM	Mickey Mantle	400.00
JMa	Juan Marichal	60.00
DM	Don Mattingly	225.00
PM	Paul Molitor	60.00
EM	Eddie Murray	60.00
GN	Graig Nettles	45.00
DP	Dave Parker	45.00
CR	Cal Ripken Jr.	250.00
NR	Nolan Ryan	250.00
RS	Ryne Sandberg	150.00
TS	Tom Seaver	200.00
OS	Ozzie Smith	225.00
DSn	Duke Snider	150.00
WS	Willie Stargell	60.00
DSt	Dave Stewart	45.00
BW	Billy Williams	60.00
RY	Robin Yount	60.00

2002 Upper Deck Sweet Spot Classics Game-Used Bats

		MT
Common Player:		5.00
Inserted 1:8		
JB	Johnny Bench	20.00
YB	Yogi Berra	30.00
WB	Wade Boggs	12.00
BBo	Bob Boone	10.00
BBu	Bill Buckner	5.00
GC	Gary Carter	10.00
RC	Roberto Clemente	65.00
BD	Bucky Dent	12.00
JD	Joe DiMaggio/40	300.00
DE	Dwight Evans	10.00
SG	Steve Garvey	10.00
HG	Hank Greenberg/ SP	70.00
KG	Ken Griffey Sr.	10.00
TG	Tony Gwynn	15.00
RJ	Reggie Jackson	15.00
FJ	Ferguson Jenkins	10.00
AK	Al Kaline	20.00
FL	Fred Lynn	10.00
BM	Bill Madlock	10.00
DM	Don Mattingly	35.00
PM	Paul Molitor	15.00
TM	Thurman Munson	50.00
GN	Graig Nettles	15.00
DP	Dave Parker	10.00
KP	Kirby Puckett	25.00
CR	Cal Ripken Jr.	40.00
BR	Brooks Robinson	15.00
NR	Nolan Ryan	50.00
BW	Billy Williams	12.00
DW	Dave Winfield	10.00

Figure values of lower-grade cards from 1981-date as:
Near Mint (NM) 75%
Excellent (EX) 40%
of the listed Mint price

For cards through 1980, values should be figured as:
Excellent (EX) 50%
Very Good (VG) 30%
of the listed
Near Mint price

2002 Upper Deck Sweet Spot Classics Game-Used Bats Gold

Each of the Game-Used Bats cards in Sweet Spot Classics can also be found in a Gold Edition, numbered to just 25 for each player.

		MT
Common Player:		25.00
JB	Johnny Bench	100.00
YB	Yogi Berra	125.00
WB	Wade Boggs	100.00
BBo	Bob Boone	40.00
BBu	Bill Buckner	35.00
GC	Gary Carter	40.00
RC	Roberto Clemente	250.00
BD	Bucky Dent	25.00
JD	Joe DiMaggio	250.00
DE	Dwight Evans	25.00
SG	Steve Garvey	35.00
HG	Hank Greenberg	125.00
KG	Ken Griffey Sr.	25.00
TG	Tony Gwynn	150.00
RJ	Reggie Jackson	150.00
FJ	Ferguson Jenkins	45.00
AK	Al Kaline	75.00
FL	Fred Lynn	25.00
BM	Bill Madlock	25.00
DM	Don Mattingly	125.00
PM	Paul Molitor	40.00
TM	Thurman Munson	150.00
GN	Graig Nettles	25.00
DP	Dave Parker	25.00
KP	Kirby Puckett	125.00
CR	Cal Ripken Jr.	225.00
BR	Brooks Robinson	75.00
NR	Nolan Ryan	175.00
BW	Billy Williams	45.00
DW	Dave Winfield	45.00

2002 UD Sweet Spot Classics Sweet Spot Signatures

		MT
Common Autograph:		25.00
Inserted 1:24		
EB	Ernie Banks	80.00
JB	Johnny Bench	80.00
YB	Yogi Berra/100	220.00
AD	Andre Dawson/100	130.00
BD	Bucky Dent	25.00
DeE	Dennis Eckersley	40.00
RF	Rollie Fingers	30.00
CF	Carlton Fisk/100	160.00
SG	Steve Garvey	35.00
KG	Kirk Gibson/SP	75.00
KH	Keith Hernandez	35.00
RJ	Reggie Jackson/SP	140.00
FJ	Ferguson Jenkins	30.00
AK	Al Kaline	50.00
SK	Sandy Koufax/SP	400.00
TL	Tommy Lasorda	50.00
FL	Fred Lynn	40.00
DoM	Don Mattingly	140.00
BM	Bill Mazeroski	40.00
WM	Willie McCovey/SP	75.00
PM	Paul Molitor	40.00
JM	Joe Morgan	50.00
DaM	Dale Murphy	50.00
GP	Gaylord Perry	30.00
BP	Boog Powell	35.00
KP	Kirby Puckett	240.00
CR	Cal Ripken Jr.	200.00
BR	Brooks Robinson	50.00
NR	Nolan Ryan/74	400.00
TS	Tom Seaver	70.00
OS	Ozzie Smith/137	250.00
DaS	Dave Stewart	25.00
AT	Alan Trammell	30.00
DW	Dave Winfield/70	200.00

2002 UD Sweet Spot Classics Sweet Spot Signatures Gold

Each of the Sweet Spot Signatures autographed ball-panel cards was also made in a Gold Edition numbered to just 25 of each player.

		MT
Common Card:		60.00
EB	Ernie Banks	350.00
JB	Johnny Bench	250.00
YB	Yogi Berra	350.00
AD	Andre Dawson	75.00
BD	Bucky Dent	60.00
DeE	Dennis Eckersley	60.00
RF	Rollie Fingers	75.00
CF	Carlton Fisk	225.00
SG	Steve Garvey	125.00
KG	Kirk Gibson	75.00
KH	Keith Hernandez	75.00
RJ	Reggie Jackson	300.00
FJ	Ferguson Jenkins	100.00
AK	Al Kaline	150.00
SK	Sandy Koufax	550.00
TL	Tommy Lasorda	150.00
FL	Fred Lynn	125.00
DoM	Don Mattingly	250.00
BM	Bill Mazeroski	175.00
WM	Willie McCovey	200.00
PM	Paul Molitor	250.00
JM	Joe Morgan	200.00
DaM	Dale Murphy	225.00
GP	Gaylord Perry	100.00
BP	Boog Powell	100.00
KP	Kirby Puckett	200.00
CR	Cal Ripken Jr.	450.00
BR	Brooks Robinson	150.00
NR	Nolan Ryan	850.00
TS	Tom Seaver	210.00
OS	Ozzie Smith	250.00
DaS	Dave Stewart	100.00
AT	Alan Trammell	100.00
DW	Dave Winfield	200.00

2002 Upper Deck Victory

		MT
Complete Set (550):		40.00
Common Player:		.10
Pack (10):		1.00
Box (36):		32.00
1	Troy Glaus	.30
2	Tim Salmon	.20
3	Troy Percival	.10
4	Darin Erstad	.25
5	Adam Kennedy	.10
6	Scott Spiezio	.10
7	Ramon Ortiz	.10
8	Ismael Valdes	.10
9	Jarrod Washburn	.10
10	Garrett Anderson	.10
11	David Eckstein	.10
12	Mo Vaughn	.25
13	Benji Gil	.10
14	Bengie Molina	.10
15	Scott Schoeneweis	.10
16	Troy Glaus, Ramon Ortiz	.20
17	David Justice	.25
18	Jermaine Dye	.10
19	Eric Chavez	.25
20	Jeremy Giambi	.10
21	Terrence Long	.10
22	Miguel Tejada	.20
23	Johnny Damon	.10
24	Jason Hart	.10
25	Adam Piatt	.10
26	Billy Koch	.10
27	Ramon Hernandez	.10
28	Eric Byrnes	.10
29	Olmedo Saenz	.10
30	Barry Zito	.20
31	Tim Hudson	.25
32	Mark Mulder	.20
33	Jason Giambi, Mark Mulder	.25
34	Carlos Delgado	.40
35	Shannon Stewart	.10
36	Vernon Wells	.10
37	Homer Bush	.10
38	Brad Fullmer	.10
39	Jose Cruz	.10
40	Felipe Lopez	.10
41	Raul Mondesi	.20
42	Esteban Loaiza	.10
43	Darrin Fletcher	.10
44	Mike Sirotka	.10
45	Luke Prokopec	.10
46	Chris Carpenter	.10
47	Roy Halladay	.10
48	Kelvim Escobar	.10
49	Carlos Delgado, Billy Koch	.20
50	Nick Bierbrodt	.10
51	Greg Vaughn	.10
52	Ben Grieve	.10
53	Damian Rolls	.10
54	Russ Johnson	.10
55	Brent Abernathy	.10
56	Steve Cox	.10
57	Aubrey Huff	.10
58	Randy Winn	.10
59	Jason Tyner	.10
60	Tanyon Sturtze	.10
61	Joe Kennedy	.10
62	Jared Sandberg	.10
63	Esteban Yan	.10
64	Ryan Rupe	.10
65	Toby Hall	.10
66	Greg Vaughn, Tanyon Sturtze	.10
67	Matt Lawton	.10
68	Juan Gonzalez	.40
69	Jim Thome	.25
70	Einar Diaz	.10
71	Ellis Burks	.10
72	Kenny Lofton	.10
73	Omar Vizquel	.10
74	Russell Branyan	.10
75	Brady Anderson	.10
76	John Rocker	.10
77	Travis Fryman	.10
78	Wil Cordero	.10
79	Chuck Finley	.10
80	C.C. Sabathia	.10
81	Bartolo Colon	.10
82	Bob Wickman	.10
83	Roberto Alomar, C.C. Sabathia	.20
84	Ichiro Suzuki	1.50
85	Edgar Martinez	.10
86	Aaron Sele	.10
87	Carlos Guillen	.10
88	Bret Boone	.10
89	John Olerud	.20
90	Jamie Moyer	.10
91	Ben Davis	.10
92	Dan Wilson	.10
93	Jeff Cirillo	.10
94	John Halama	.10
95	Freddy Garcia	.10
96	Kazuhiro Sasaki	.10
97	Mike Cameron	.10
98	Paul Abbott	.10
99	Mark McLemore	.10
100	Ichiro Suzuki, Freddy Garcia	.50
101	Jeff Conine	.10
102	David Segui	.10
103	Marty Cordova	.10
104	Tony Batista	.10
105	Chris Richard	.10
106	Willis Roberts	.10
107	Melvin Mora	.10
108	Mike Bordick	.10
109	Jay Gibbons	.10
110	Mike Kinkade	.10
111	Brian Roberts	.10
112	Jerry Hairston Jr.	.10
113	Jason Johnson	.10
114	Josh Towers	.10
115	Calvin Maduro	.10
116	Sidney Ponson	.10
117	Jeff Conine, Jason Johnson	.10
118	Alex Rodriguez	1.00
119	Ivan Rodriguez	.40
120	Frank Catalanotto	.10
121	Mike Lamb	.10
122	Ruben Sierra	.10
123	Rusty Greer	.10
124	Rafael Palmeiro	.20
125	Gabe Kapler	.15
126	Aaron Myette	.10
127	Kenny Rogers	.10
128	Carl Everett	.10
129	Rick Helling	.10
130	Ricky Ledee	.10
131	Michael Young	.10
132	Doug Davis	.10
133	Jeff Zimmerman	.10
134	Alex Rodriguez, Rick Helling	.40
135	Manny Ramirez	.40
136	Nomar Garciaparra	1.00
137	Jason Varitek	.10
138	Dante Bichette	.10
139	Tony Clark	.10
140	Scott Hatteberg	.10
141	Trot Nixon	.10
142	Hideo Nomo	.25
143	Dustin Hermanson	.10
144	Chris Stynes	.10

145 Jose Offerman .10
146 Pedro Martinez .50
147 Shea Hillenbrand .10
148 Tim Wakefield .10
149 Troy O'Leary .10
150 Ugueth Urbina .10
151 Manny Ramirez, Hideo Nomo .25
152 Carlos Beltran .10
153 Dee Brown .10
154 Mike Sweeney .10
155 Luis Alicea .10
156 Raul Ibanez .10
157 Mark Quinn .10
158 Joe Randa .10
159 Roberto Hernandez .10
160 Neifi Perez .10
161 Carlos Febles .10
162 Jeff Suppan .10
163 Dave McCarty .10
164 Blake Stein .10
165 Chad Durbin .10
166 Paul Byrd .10
167 Carlos Beltran, Jeff Suppan .10
168 Craig Paquette .10
169 Dean Palmer .10
170 Shane Halter .10
171 Bobby Higginson .10
172 Robert Fick .10
173 Jose Macias .10
174 Deivi Cruz .10
175 Damion Easley .10
176 Brandon Inge .10
177 Mark Redman .10
178 Dmitri Young .10
179 Steve Sparks .10
180 Jeff Weaver .10
181 Victor Santos .10
182 Jose Lima .10
183 Matt Anderson .10
184 Roger Cedeno, Steve Sparks .10
185 Doug Mientkiewicz .10
186 Cristian Guzman .10
187 Torii Hunter .10
188 Matt LeCroy .10
189 Corey Koskie .10
190 Jacque Jones .10
191 Luis Rivas .10
192 David Ortiz .10
193 A.J. Pierzynski .10
194 Brian Buchanan .10
195 Joe Mays .10
196 Brad Radke .10
197 Denny Hocking .10
198 Eric Milton .10
199 LaTroy Hawkins .10
200 Doug Mientkiewicz, Joe Mays .10
201 Magglio Ordonez .20
202 Jose Valentin .10
203 Chris Singleton .10
204 Aaron Rowand .10
205 Paul Konerko .10
206 Carlos Lee .10
207 Ray Durham .10
208 Keith Foulke .10
209 Todd Ritchie .10
210 Royce Clayton .10
211 Jose Canseco .20
212 Frank Thomas .40
213 David Wells .10
214 Mark Buehrle .10
215 Jon Garland .10
216 Magglio Ordonez, Mark Buehrle .15
217 Derek Jeter 1.50
218 Bernie Williams .30
219 Rondell White .10
220 Jorge Posada .20
221 Alfonso Soriano .25
222 Ramiro Mendoza .10
223 Jason Giambi .75
224 John Vander Wal .10
225 Steve Karsay .10
226 Nick Johnson .10
227 Mariano Rivera .20
228 Orlando Hernandez .10
229 Andy Pettitte .20
230 Robin Ventura .10
231 Roger Clemens .60
232 Mike Mussina .40
233 Derek Jeter, Roger Clemens .50
234 Moises Alou .20
235 Lance Berkman .20
236 Craig Biggio .20
237 Octavio Dotel .10
238 Jeff Bagwell .40
239 Richard Hidalgo .10
240 Morgan Ensberg .10
241 Julio Lugo .10
242 Daryle Ward .10
243 Roy Oswalt .20
244 Billy Wagner .10
245 Brad Ausmus .10
246 Jose Vizcaino .10
247 Wade Miller .10
248 Shane Reynolds .10
249 Jeff Bagwell, Wade Miller .20
250 Chipper Jones .75
251 Brian Jordan .10
252 B.J. Surhoff .10
253 Rafael Furcal .10
254 Julio Franco .10
255 Javy Lopez .10
256 John Burkett .10
257 Andruw Jones .20
258 Marcus Giles .10
259 Wes Helms .10
260 Greg Maddux .75
261 John Smoltz .10
262 Tom Glavine .20
263 Vinny Castilla .10
264 Kevin Millwood .10
265 Jason Marquis .10
266 Chipper Jones, Greg Maddux .40
267 Tyler Houston .10
268 Mark Loretta .10
269 Richie Sexson .20
270 Jeromy Burnitz .10
271 Jimmy Haynes .10
272 Geoff Jenkins .20
273 Ron Belliard .10
274 Jose Hernandez .10
275 Jeffrey Hammonds .10
276 Curtis Leskanic .10
277 Devon White .10
278 Ben Sheets .20
279 Henry Blanco .10
280 Jamey Wright .10
281 Allen Levrault .10
282 Jeff D'Amico .10
283 Richie Sexson, Jimmy Haynes .10
284 Albert Pujols .75
285 Jason Isringhausen .10
286 J.D. Drew .25
287 Placido Polanco .10
288 Jim Edmonds .20
289 Fernando Vina .10
290 Edgar Renteria .10
291 Mike Matheny .10
292 Bud Smith .10
293 Mike Defelice .10
294 Woody Williams .10
295 Eli Marrero .10
296 Matt Morris .10
297 Darryl Kile .10
298 Kerry Robinson .10
299 Luis Saturria .10
300 Albert Pujols, Matt Morris .40
301 Sammy Sosa .75
302 Michael Tucker .10
303 Bill Mueller .10
304 Ricky Gutierrez .10
305 Fred McGriff .20
306 Eric Young .10
307 Corey Patterson .10
308 Alex Gonzalez .10
309 Ron Coomer .10
310 Kerry Wood .20
311 Delino DeShields .10
312 Jon Lieber .10
313 Tom Gordon .10
314 Todd Hundley .10
315 Jason Bere .10
316 Kevin Tapani .10
317 Sammy Sosa, Jon Lieber .40
318 Steve Finley .10
319 Luis Gonzalez .25
320 Mark Grace .25
321 Craig Counsell .10
322 Matt Williams .20
323 Tony Womack .10
324 Junior Spivey .10
325 David Dellucci .10
326 Jay Bell .10
327 Curt Schilling .25
328 Randy Johnson .40
329 Danny Bautista .10
330 Miguel Batista .10
331 Erubiel Durazo .10
332 Brian Anderson .10
333 Byung-Hyun Kim .10
334 Luis Gonzalez, Curt Schilling .20
335 Paul LoDuca .10
336 Gary Sheffield .20
337 Shawn Green .25
338 Adrian Beltre .20
339 Darren Dreifort .10
340 Mark Grudzielanek .10
341 Eric Karros .10
342 Cesar Izturis .10
343 Tom Goodwin .10
344 Marquis Grissom .10
345 Kevin Brown .20
346 James Baldwin .10
347 Terry Adams .10
348 Alex Cora .10
349 Andy Ashby .10
350 Chan Ho Park .20
351 Shawn Green, Chan Ho Park .20
352 Jose Vidro .10
353 Vladimir Guerrero .40
354 Orlando Cabrera .10
355 Fernando Tatis .10
356 Michael Barrett .10
357 Lee Stevens .10
358 Geoff Blum .10
359 Brad Wilkerson .10
360 Peter Bergeron .10
361 Javier Vazquez .10
362 Tony Armas Jr. .10
363 Tomokazu Ohka .10
364 Scott Strickland .10
365 Vladimir Guerrero, Javier Vazquez .20
366 Barry Bonds .75
367 Rich Aurilia .10
368 Jeff Kent .10
369 Andres Galarraga .20
370 Desi Relaford .10
371 Shawon Dunston .10
372 Benito Santiago .10
373 Tsuyoshi Shinjo .10
374 Calvin Murray .10
375 Marvin Benard .10
376 J.T. Snow .10
377 Livan Hernandez .10
378 Russ Ortiz .10
379 Robb Nen .10
380 Jason Schmidt .10
381 Barry Bonds, Russ Ortiz .30
382 Cliff Floyd .10
383 Antonio Alfonseca .10
384 Mike Redmond .10
385 Mike Lowell .10
386 Derrek Lee .10
387 Preston Wilson .10
388 Luis Castillo .10
389 Charles Johnson .10
390 Eric Owens .10
391 Alex Gonzalez .10
392 Josh Beckett .10
393 Brad Penny .10
394 Ryan Dempster .10
395 Matt Clement .10
396 A.J. Burnett .10
397 Cliff Floyd, Ryan Dempster .10
398 Mike Piazza 1.00
399 Joe McEwing .10
400 Todd Zeile .10
401 Jay Payton .10
402 Roger Cedeno .10
403 Rey Ordonez .10
404 Edgardo Alfonzo .10
405 Roberto Alomar .30
406 Glendon Rusch .10
407 Timo Perez .10
408 Al Leiter .15
409 Lenny Harris .10
410 Shawn Estes .10
411 Armando Benitez .10
412 Kevin Appier .10
413 Bruce Chen .10
414 Mike Piazza, Al Leiter .40
415 Phil Nevin .10
416 Ryan Klesko .10
417 Mark Kotsay .10
418 Ray Lankford .10
419 Mike Darr .10
420 D'Angelo Jimenez .10
421 Bubba Trammell .10
422 Adam Eaton .10
423 Ramon Vazquez .10
424 Cesar Crespo .10
425 Trevor Hoffman .10
426 Kevin Jarvis .10
427 Wiki Gonzalez .10
428 Damian Jackson .10
429 Brian Lawrence .10
430 Phil Nevin, Trevor Hoffman .10
431 Scott Rolen .25
432 Marlon Anderson .10
433 Bobby Abreu .10
434 Jimmy Rollins .10
435 Doug Glanville .10
436 Travis Lee .10
437 Brandon Duckworth .10
438 Pat Burrell .25
439 Kevin Jordan .10
440 Robert Person .10
441 Johnny Estrada .10
442 Randy Wolf .10
443 Jose Mesa .10
444 Mike Lieberthal .10
445 Bobby Abreu, Robert Person .10
446 Brian Giles .20
447 Jason Kendall .10
448 Aramis Ramirez .10
449 Rob Mackowiak .10
450 Abraham Nunez .10
451 Pat Meares .10
452 Craig Wilson .10
453 Jack Wilson .10
454 Gary Matthews Jr. .10
455 Kevin Young .10
456 Derek Bell .10
457 Kip Wells .10
458 Jimmy Anderson .10
459 Kris Benson .10
460 Brian Giles, Todd Ritchie .10
461 Sean Casey .20
462 Wilton Guerrero .10
463 Jason LaRue .10
464 Juan Encarnacion .10
465 Todd Walker .10
466 Aaron Boone .10
467 Pete Harnisch .10
468 Ken Griffey Jr. 1.00
469 Adam Dunn .40
470 Barry Larkin .20
471 Kelly Stinnett .10
472 Pokey Reese .10
473 Brady Clark .10
474 Scott Williamson .10
475 Danny Graves .10
476 Ken Griffey Jr., Elmer Dessens .10
477 Larry Walker .25
478 Todd Helton .40
479 Juan Pierre .10
480 Juan Uribe .10
481 Mario Encarnacion .10
482 Jose Ortiz .10
483 Todd Hollandsworth .10
484 Alex Ochoa .10
485 Mike Hampton .10
486 Terry Shumpert .10
487 Denny Neagle .10
488 Jose Jimenez .10
489 Jason Jennings .10
490 Todd Helton, Mike Hampton .20
491 Tim Redding .10
492 Mark Teixeira 2.00
493 Alex Cintron .10
494 Tim Raines Jr. .10
495 Juan Cruz .20
496 Joe Crede .10
497 Steve Green .10
498 Mike Rivera .10
499 Mark Prior 1.50
500 Ken Harvey .10
501 Tim Spooneybarger .10
502 Adam Everett .10
503 Jason Standridge .10
504 Nick Neugebauer .10
505 Adam Johnson .10
506 Sean Douglass .10
507 Brandon Berger .10
508 Alex Escobar .10
509 Doug Nickle .10
510 Jason Middlebrook .10

511 Dewon Brazelton .10
512 Yorvit Torrealba .10
513 Henry Mateo .10
514 Dennis Tankersley .10
515 Marlon Byrd .75
516 Andy Barkett .10
517 Orlando Hudson .10
518 Josh Fogg .10
519 Ryan Drese .10
520 Mike MacDougal .10
521 Luis Pineda .10
522 Jack Cust .10
523 Kurt Ainsworth .10
524 Bart Miadich .10
525 Dernell Stenson .10
526 Carlos Zambrano .10
527 Austin Kearns .50
528 Larry Barnes .10
529 Mike Cuddyer .10
530 Carlos Pena .75
531 Derek Jeter 1.00
532 Ken Griffey Jr. .75
533 Manny Ramirez .25
534 Luis Gonzalez .20
535 Sammy Sosa .50
536 Roger Clemens .40
537 Phil Nevin .10
538 Mike Piazza .75
539 Alex Rodriguez .75
540 Jason Giambi .50
541 Randy Johnson .25
542 Albert Pujols .50
543 Jeff Bagwell .25
544 Shawn Green .15
545 Carlos Delgado .15
546 Pedro Martinez .25
547 Todd Helton .25
548 Roberto Alomar .20
549 Barry Bonds .40
550 Ichiro Suzuki 1.00

2002 Upper Deck Victory Gold

	MT
Stars:	3-6X
Inserted 1:2	

2002 Upper Deck Vintage

	MT
Complete Set (300):	30.00
Common Player:	.10

1 Darin Erstad .20
2 Mo Vaughn .20
3 Ramon Ortiz .10
4 Garret Anderson .10
5 Troy Glaus .50
6 Troy Percival .10
7 Tim Salmon .10
8 Wilmy Caceres, Elpidio Guzman .10
9 2001 Anaheim Angels .10
10 Jason Giambi .50
11 Mark Mulder .20
12 Jermaine Dye .10
13 Miguel Tejada .20
14 Tim Hudson .25
15 Eric Chavez .20
16 Barry Zito .10
17 Oscar Salazar, Juan Pena .10
18 2001 Oakland Athletics .10
19 Carlos Delgado .40
20 Raul Mondesi .15
21 Chris Carpenter .10
22 Jose Cruz Jr. .10
23 Alex Gonzalez .10
24 Brad Fullmer .10
25 Shannon Stewart .10
26 Brandon Lyon, Vernon Wells .10
27 2001 Toronto Blue Jays .10
28 Greg Vaughn .10
29 Toby Hall .10
30 Ben Grieve .10
31 Aubrey Huff .10
32 Tanyon Sturtze .10
33 Brent Abernathy .10
34 Dewon Brazelton, Delvin James .10
35 2001 Tampa Bay Devil Rays .10
36 Roberto Alomar .50
37 Juan Gonzalez .60
38 Bartolo Colon .20
39 C.C. Sabathia .10
40 Jim Thome .40
41 Omar Vizquel .20
42 Russell Branyan .10
43 Ryan Drese, Roy Smith .10
44 2001 Cleveland Indians .10
45 Edgar Martinez .20
46 Bret Boone .10
47 Freddy Garcia .10
48 John Olerud .25
49 Kazuhiro Sasaki .10
50 Ichiro Suzuki 2.50
51 Mike Cameron .10
52 Rafael Soriano, Dennis Stark .10
53 2001 Seattle Mariners .10
54 Tony Batista .10
55 Jeff Conine .10
56 Jason Johnson .10
57 Jay Gibbons .10
58 Chris Richard .10
59 Josh Towers .10
60 Jerry Hairston Jr. .10
61 Sean Douglass, Tim Raines Jr. .10
62 2001 Baltimore Orioles .10
63 Alex Rodriguez 1.50
64 Ruben Sierra .10
65 Ivan Rodriguez .60
66 Gabe Kapler .20
67 Rafael Palmeiro .30
68 Frank Catalanotto .10
69 Mark Teixeira, Carlos Pena .75
70 2001 Texas Rangers .10
71 Nomar Garciaparra 1.50
72 Pedro Martinez .60
73 Trot Nixon .10
74 Dante Bichette .10
75 Manny Ramirez .60
76 Carl Everett .10
77 Hideo Nomo .40
78 Dernell Stenson, Juan Diaz .10
79 2001 Boston Red Sox .10
80 Mike Sweeney .10
81 Carlos Febles .10
82 Dee Brown .10
83 Neifi Perez .10
84 Mark Quinn .10
85 Carlos Beltran .10
86 Joe Randa .10
87 Ken Harvey, Mike MacDougal .10
88 2001 Kansas City Royals .10
89 Dean Palmer .10
90 Jeff Weaver .10
91 Jose Lima .10
92 Tony Clark .10
93 Damion Easley .10
94 Bobby Higginson .10
95 Robert Fick .10
96 Pedro Santana, Mike Rivera .10
97 2001 Detroit Tigers .10
98 Doug Mientkiewicz .10
99 David Ortiz .10
100 Joe Mays .10
101 Corey Koskie .10
102 Eric Milton .10
103 Cristian Guzman .10
104 Brad Radke .10
105 Adam Johnson, Juan Rincon .10
106 2001 Minnesota Twins .10
107 Frank Thomas .60
108 Carlos Lee .10
109 Mark Buehrle .10
110 Jose Canseco .30
111 Magglio Ordonez .10
112 Jon Garland .10
113 Ray Durham .10
114 Joe Crede, Josh Fogg .10
115 2001 Chicago White Sox .10
116 Derek Jeter 2.50
117 Roger Clemens 1.00
118 Alfonso Soriano .40
119 Paul O'Neill .25
120 Jorge Posada .25
121 Bernie Williams .50
122 Mariano Rivera .25
123 Tino Martinez .20
124 Mike Mussina .50
125 Nick Johnson, Erick Almonte .10
126 2001 New York Yankees .10
127 Jeff Bagwell .60
128 Wade Miller .10
129 Lance Berkman .20
130 Moises Alou .15
131 Craig Biggio .20
132 Roy Oswalt .20
133 Richard Hidalgo .15
134 Morgan Ensberg, Tim Redding .10
135 2001 Houston Astros .10
136 Greg Maddux 1.25
137 Chipper Jones 1.25
138 Brian Jordan .10
139 Marcus Giles .10
140 Andruw Jones .40
141 Tom Glavine .40
142 Rafael Furcal .25
143 Wilson Betemit, Horacio Ramirez .25
144 2001 Atlanta Braves .10
145 Jeromy Burnitz .10
146 Ben Sheets .10
147 Geoff Jenkins .20
148 Devon White .10
149 Jimmy Haynes .10
150 Richie Sexson .10
151 Jose Hernandez .10
152 Jose Mieses, Alex Sanchez .10
153 2001 Milwaukee Brewers .10
154 Mark McGwire 2.00
155 Albert Pujols 1.00
156 Matt Morris .10
157 J.D. Drew .25
158 Jim Edmonds .20
159 Bud Smith .25
160 Darryl Kile .10
161 William Ortega, Luis Saturria .10
162 2001 St. Louis Cardinals .10
163 Sammy Sosa 1.25
164 Jon Lieber .10
165 Eric Young .10
166 Kerry Wood .25
167 Fred McGriff .25
168 Corey Patterson .20
169 Rondell White .15
170 Juan Cruz, Mark Prior 1.00
171 2001 Chicago Cubs .10
172 Luis Gonzalez .40
173 Randy Johnson .60
174 Matt Williams .25
175 Mark Grace .25
176 Steve Finley .10
177 Reggie Sanders .10
178 Curt Schilling .25
179 Alex Cintron, Jack Cust .10
180 2001 Arizona Diamondbacks .10
181 Gary Sheffield .25
182 Paul LoDuca .10
183 Chan Ho Park .25
184 Shawn Green .25
185 Eric Karros .15
186 Adrian Beltre .15
187 Kevin Brown .20
188 Ricardo Rodriguez, Carlos Garcia .10
189 2001 Los Angeles Dodgers .10
190 Vladimir Guerrero .60
191 Javier Vazquez .10
192 Jose Vidro .10
193 Fernando Tatis .10
194 Orlando Cabrera .10
195 Lee Stevens .10
196 Tony Armas Jr. .10
197 Donnie Bridges, Henry Mateo .10
198 2001 Montreal Expos .10
199 Barry Bonds 1.00
200 Rich Aurilia .10
201 Russ Ortiz .10
202 Jeff Kent .15
203 Jason Schmidt .10
204 John Vander Wal .10
205 Robb Nen .10
206 Yorvit Torrealba, Kurt Ainsworth .10
207 2001 San Francisco Giants .10
208 Preston Wilson .10
209 Brad Penny .10
210 Cliff Floyd .10
211 Luis Castillo .10
212 Ryan Dempster .10
213 Charles Johnson .10
214 A.J. Burnett .10
215 Abraham Nunez, Josh Beckett .10
216 2001 Florida Marlins .10
217 Mike Piazza 1.50
218 Al Leiter .20
219 Edgardo Alfonzo .10
220 Tsuyoshi Shinjo .20
221 Matt Lawton .10
222 Robin Ventura .15
223 Jay Payton .10
224 Alex Escobar, Jae Weong Seo .10
225 2001 New York Mets .10
226 Ryan Klesko .10
227 D'Angelo Jimenez .10
228 Trevor Hoffman .10
229 Phil Nevin .10
230 Mark Kotsay .10
231 Brian Lawrence .10
232 Bubba Trammell .10
233 Jason Middlebrook, Xavier Nady .10
234 2001 San Diego Padres .10
235 Scott Rolen .20
236 Jimmy Rollins .10
237 Mike Lieberthal .10
238 Bobby Abreu .10
239 Brandon Duckworth .10
240 Robert Person .10
241 Pat Burrell .20
242 Nick Punto, Carlos Silva .10
243 2001 Philadelphia Phillies .10
244 Brian Giles .25

245 Jack Wilson .10
246 Kris Benson .10
247 Jason Kendall .10
248 Aramis Ramirez .15
249 Todd Ritchie .10
250 Robert Mackowiak .10
251 John Grabow, Humberto Cota .10
252 2001 Pittsburgh Pirates .10
253 Ken Griffey Jr. 2.00
254 Barry Larkin .25
255 Sean Casey .25
256 Aaron Boone .10
257 Dmitri Young .10
258 Pokey Reese .10
259 Adam Dunn .40
260 David Espinosa, Dane Sardinha .10
261 2001 Cincinnati Reds .10
262 Todd Helton .60
263 Mike Hampton .20
264 Juan Pierre .10
265 Larry Walker .25
266 Juan Uribe .10
267 Jose Ortiz .10
268 Jeff Cirillo .10
269 Jason Jennings, Luke Hudson .10
270 2001 Colorado Rockies .10
271 Ichiro Suzuki 1.50
272 Larry Walker .20
273 Alex Rodriguez .75
274 Barry Bonds .50
275 Roger Clemens .50
276 Curt Schilling .15
277 Freddy Garcia .10
278 Randy Johnson .25
279 Mariano Rivera .15
280 Robb Nen .10
281 Jason Giambi .25
282 Jorge Posada .15
283 Jim Thome .20
284 Edgar Martinez .10
285 Andruw Jones .20
286 Chipper Jones .50
287 Matt Williams .15
288 Curt Schilling .20
289 Derek Jeter 1.00
290 Mike Mussina .25
291 Bret Boone .10
292 Alfonso Soriano .20
293 Randy Johnson .25
294 Tom Glavine .20
295 Curt Schilling .20
296 Randy Johnson .25
297 Derek Jeter 1.00
298 Tino Martinez .10
299 Curt Schilling .20
300 Luis Gonzalez .20

2002 Upper Deck Vintage Day at the Park

MT
Complete Set (6): 20.00
Common Player: 1.50
Inserted 1:23
DP1 Ichiro Suzuki 6.00
DP2 Derek Jeter 6.00
DP3 Alex Rodriguez 4.00
DP4 Mark McGwire 5.00
DP5 Barry Bonds 3.00
DP6 Sammy Sosa 3.00

2002 Upper Deck Vintage Night-Gamers

MT
Complete Set (12): 10.00
Common Player: .75
Inserted 1:11
NG1 Todd Helton .75
NG2 Manny Ramirez .75
NG3 Ivan Rodriguez .50
NG4 Albert Pujols 1.50
NG5 Greg Maddux 1.50
NG6 Carlos Delgado .50
NG7 Frank Thomas .75
NG8 Derek Jeter 3.00
NG9 Troy Glaus .50
NG10 Jeff Bagwell .75
NG11 Juan Gonzalez .75
NG12 Randy Johnson 1.00

2002 Upper Deck Vintage Sandlot Stars

MT
Complete Set (12): 25.00
Common Player: .75
Inserted 1:11
SS1 Ken Griffey Jr. 3.00
SS2 Derek Jeter 4.00
SS3 Ichiro Suzuki 4.00
SS4 Nomar Garciaparra 2.50
SS5 Sammy Sosa 2.00
SS6 Chipper Jones 2.00
SS7 Jason Giambi .75
SS8 Alex Rodriguez 2.50
SS9 Mark McGwire 3.00
SS10 Barry Bonds 2.00
SS11 Mike Piazza 2.50
SS12 Vladimir Guerrero 1.00

2002 Upper Deck Vintage Special Collection Jerseys

MT
Common Player: 8.00
Inserted 1:144
StB Stan Bahnsen 8.00
SaB Sal Bando 12.00
BC Bert Campaneris 15.00
AD Andre Dawson 15.00
RF Rollie Fingers 15.00
MG Mark Grace 25.00
MH Mike Hegan 8.00
CH "Catfish" Hunter 20.00
RJ Reggie Jackson 25.00
FJ Ferguson Jenkins 15.00
PL Paul Linblad 8.00
JR Joe Rudi 15.00
RS Ryne Sandberg 50.00
SS Sammy Sosa 40.00
BW Billy Williams 25.00

2002 Upper Deck Vintage Timeless Teams Bat

MT
Inserted 1:288
SEA Ichiro Suzuki, Edgar Martinez, John Olerud, Bret Boone 125.00
NYY Mariano Rivera, Bernie Williams, Paul O'Neill, Jorge Posada 40.00
ATL Tom Glavine, Greg Maddux, Chipper Jones, Andruw Jones 45.00
CLE Juan Gonzalez, Jim Thome, Roberto Alomar, Kenny Lofton 45.00
OAK Jose Canseco, Ricky Henderson, Dave Parker, Don Baylor 50.00
OF Mickey Mantle, Joe DiMaggio, Reggie Jackson, Babe Ruth
1B Willie McCovey, Frank Thomas, Hank Greenberg, Eddie Murray 40.00
OF Ken Griffey Jr., Barry Bonds, Ricky Henderson, Tony Gwynn 100.00

2002 Upper Deck Vintage Timeless Teams Jerseys

MT
Common Player: 10.00
Inserted 1:144
JB Johnny Bench 25.00
DE Dwight Evans 15.00
RF Rollie Fingers 15.00
CH "Catfish" Hunter 20.00
RJ Reggie Jackson 30.00
AJ Andruw Jones 15.00
CJ Chipper Jones 25.00
FL Fred Lynn 15.00
GM Greg Maddux SP
EMa Edgar Martinez 15.00
WM Willie McCovey 20.00
EMu Eddie Murray 15.00
KS Kazuhiro Sasaki 20.00
IS Ichiro Suzuki SP

2002 Upper Deck Vintage Timeless Teams Combo Jerseys

MT
Inserted 1:288
NYY00 Roger Clemens, Mariano Rivera, Bernie Williams 40.00
ATL96 Greg Maddux, Chipper Jones, Andruw Jones 40.00
OAK74 Rollie Fingers, Jim "Catfish" Hunter, Reggie Jackson 40.00
HOF36 Ty Cobb, Babe Ruth, Honus Wagner

2002 Upper Deck Vintage Vintage Aces Jerseys

MT
Common Player: 8.00
Inserted 1:144
RC Roger Clemens SP
JD John Denny 8.00
TH Tim Hudson 15.00
FJ Ferguson Jenkins 15.00
RJ Randy Johnson 20.00
GM Greg Maddux 40.00
JM Juan Marichal 15.00
MMa Mike Marshall 10.00
PM Pedro Martinez 20.00
MMu Mike Mussina 25.00
HN Hideo Nomo 30.00
NR Nolan Ryan 100.00
JS Johnny Sain 20.00
MT Mike Torrez 10.00

2002 Upper Deck Vintage Vintage Signature Combos

MT
Common Player:
Production 100 sets
VS-FB Carlton Fisk, Johnny Bench
VS-JM Reggie Jackson, Willie McCovey
VS-SD Ryne Sandberg, Andre Dawson
VS-BR Sal Bando, Joe Rudi
VS-EL Dwight Evans, Fred Lynn
VS-AT Roberto Alomar, Jim Thome
VS-BB Yogi Berra, Johnny Bench
VS-GR Ken Griffey Jr., Alex Rodriguez
VS-JO Edgar Martinez, John Olerud

2002 Upper Deck World Series Heroes

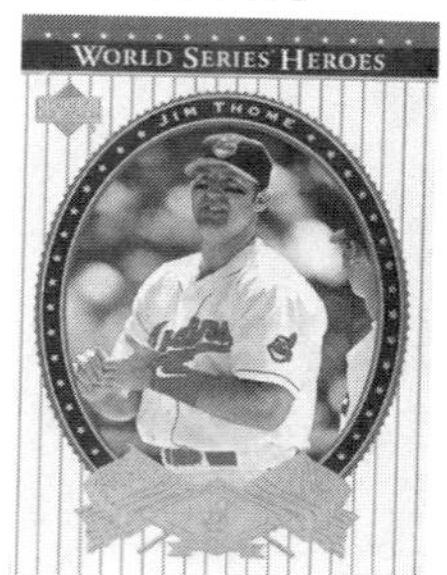

MT
Complete Set (180): 120.00
Common Player: .15
Common RC (91-135): 1.50
Common (136-180): 1.00
Inserted 1:10
Pack (5):
Box (24): 60.00
1 Jim "Catfish" Hunter .15
2 Jimmie Foxx .50
3 Mark McGwire 2.00
4 Rollie Fingers .15
5 Rickey Henderson .40
6 Joe Carter .15
7 John Olerud .25
8 Roberto Alomar .50
9 Pat Hentgen .15
10 Devon White .15
11 Eddie Mathews .50
12 Greg Maddux 1.25
13 Chipper Jones 1.25
14 Tom Glavine .25
15 Andruw Jones .40
16 David Justice .25
17 Fred McGriff .15
18 Ryan Klesko .15
19 John Smoltz .15
20 Javy Lopez .15
21 Marquis Grissom .15
22 Robin Yount .75
23 Ozzie Smith .75
24 Frankie Frisch .15

25 Stan Musial 1.00
26 Randy Johnson .75
27 Luis Gonzalez .40
28 Matt Williams .15
29 Steve Finley .15
30 Sandy Koufax 2.00
31 Duke Snider .50
32 Kirk Gibson .15
33 Steve Garvey .15
34 Jackie Robinson 1.50
35 Don Drysdale .50
36 Juan Marichal .50
37 Mel Ott .50
38 Orlando Cepeda .15
39 Jim Thome .50
40 Manny Ramirez .75
41 Omar Vizquel .15
42 Lou Boudreau .15
43 Gary Sheffield .15
44 Moises Alou .15
45 Livan Hernandez .15
46 Edgar Renteria .15
47 Al Leiter .15
48 Tom Seaver .75
49 Gary Carter .15
50 Mike Piazza 1.50
51 Nolan Ryan 2.50
52 Robin Ventura .15
53 Mike Hampton .15
54 Jesse Orosco .15
55 Cal Ripken Jr. 2.50
56 Brooks Robinson .75
57 Tony Gwynn .75
58 Kevin Brown .15
59 Curt Schilling .50
60 Cy Young .50
61 Honus Wagner .75
62 Willie Stargell .40
63 Wade Boggs .40
64 Carlton Fisk .40
65 Ken Griffey Sr. .15
66 Joe Morgan .15
67 Johnny Bench 1.00
68 Barry Larkin .40
69 Jose Rijo .15
70 Ty Cobb 1.50
71 Kirby Puckett 1.50
72 Chuck Knoblauch .15
73 Harmon Killebrew .50
74 Mickey Mantle 2.50
75 Joe DiMaggio 2.00
76 Don Larsen .40
77 Thurman Munson .75
78 Roger Maris 1.50
79 Phil Rizzuto .50
80 Babe Ruth 2.50
81 Lou Gehrig 2.00
82 Billy Martin .40
83 Derek Jeter 2.50
84 Roger Clemens 1.25
85 Tino Martinez .15
86 Bernie Williams .50
87 Mariano Rivera .25
88 Andy Pettitte .40
89 David Wells .15
90 Jorge Posada .25
91 *Rodrigo Rosario* 1.50
92 *Brandon Puffer* 1.50
93 *Franklyn German* 1.50
94 *Reed Johnson* 1.50
95 *Chris Baker* 1.50
96 *John Ennis* 1.50
97 *Luis Martinez* 1.50
98 *Takaki Nomura* 2.00
99 *So Taguchi* 4.00
100 *Michael Crudale* 1.50
101 *Francis Beltran* 1.50
102 *Steve Kent* 1.50
103 *Jorge Sosa* 1.50
104 *Felix Escalona* 1.50
105 *Jose Valverde* 1.50
106 *Doug Devore* 2.00
107 *Kazuhisa Ishii* 5.00
108 *Victor Alvarez* 1.50
109 *Eric Good* 1.50
110 *Jorge Nunez* 1.50
111 *Ron Calloway* 1.50
112 *Nelson Castro* 1.50
113 Matt Thornton 1.50
114 *Luis Ugueto* 1.50
115 *Hansel Izquierdo* 1.50
116 *Jamie Cerda* 1.50
117 *Mark Corey* 1.50
118 *Tyler Yates* 1.50
119 *Satoru Komiyama* 1.50
120 *Steve Bechler* 1.50
121 *Ben Howard* 2.00
122 *Anderson Machado* 1.50
123 *Jorge Padilla* 1.50
124 *Eric Junge* 1.50
125 *Adrian Burnside* 1.50
126 *Mike Gonzalez* 1.50
127 *Anastacio Martinez* 1.50
128 *Josh Hancock* 1.50
129 *Rene Reyes* 1.50
130 *Aaron Cook* 1.50
131 *Cam Esslinger* 1.50
132 *Juan Brito* 1.50
133 *Miguel Ascencio* 1.50
134 *Kevin Frederick* 1.50
135 *Edwin Almonte* 1.50
136 Troy Glaus 1.00
137 Darin Erstad 1.00
138 Jeff Bagwell 1.50
139 Lance Berkman 1.50
140 Tim Hudson 1.25
141 Eric Chavez 1.25
142 Barry Zito 1.50
143 Carlos Delgado 1.00
144 Richie Sexson 1.00
145 Albert Pujols 3.00
146 Sammy Sosa 3.00
147 Kerry Wood 1.50
148 Greg Vaughn 1.00
149 Shawn Green 1.00
150 Vladimir Guerrero 2.00
151 Barry Bonds 5.00
152 C.C. Sabathia 1.00
153 Ichiro Suzuki 5.00
154 Freddy Garcia 1.00
155 Edgar Martinez 1.00
156 Josh Beckett 1.00
157 Cliff Floyd 1.00
158 Mo Vaughn 1.00
159 Jeromy Burnitz 1.00
160 Sean Burroughs 1.00
161 Phil Nevin 1.00
162 Scott Rolen 1.25
163 Brian Giles 1.25
164 Alex Rodriguez 5.00
165 Ivan Rodriguez 1.25
166 Juan Gonzalez 1.25
167 Rafael Palmeiro 1.25
168 Nomar Garciaparra 4.00
169 Pedro J. Martinez 2.00
170 Ken Griffey Jr. 4.00
171 Adam Dunn 1.50
172 Todd Helton 1.25
173 Mike Sweeney 1.00
174 Carlos Beltran 1.00
175 Dmitri Young 1.00
176 Doug Mientkiewicz 1.00
177 Torii Hunter 1.00
178 Frank Thomas 1.50
179 Maggio Ordonez 1.00
180 Jason Giambi 3.00

2002 UD World Series Heroes Match-Ups Memorabilia

MT
Common Card: 8.00
Inserted 1:24
MU00Mike Piazza, Roger Clemens 20.00
MU00aAndy Pettitte, Mike Piazza 20.00
MU00bAl Leiter, Derek Jeter 20.00
MU00dEdgardo Alfonzo, Mariano Rivera 8.00
MU00eJohn Franco, Derek Jeter 10.00
MU00cRobin Ventura, Roger Clemens 8.00
MU01Mariano Rivera, Luis Gonzalez 8.00
MU01aPaul O'Neill, Curt Schilling 8.00
MU01bBernie Williams, Randy Johnson 8.00
MU01cDavid Justice, Curt Schilling
MU01dRandy Johnson, Bernie Williams 8.00
MU01eCurt Schilling, Tino Martinez 8.00
MU01fRoger Clemens, Luis Gonzalez 15.00
MU01gPaul O'Neill, Byung-Hyun Kim 10.00
MU01hLuis Gonzalez, Mariano Rivera/97 12.00
MU03Honus Wagner, Cy Young 200.00
MU09Ty Cobb, Honus Wagner/SP 250.00
MU30Jimmie Foxx 25.00
MU36Joe DiMaggio, Mel Ott/SP 80.00
MU49Duke Snider, Joe DiMaggio 25.00
MU53Jackie Robinson, Billy Martin 25.00
MU55Mickey Mantle, Jackie Robinson 110.00
MU56Don Larsen, Duke Snider 25.00
MU56aDon Larsen, Jackie Robinson 20.00
MU57Eddie Mathews, Yogi Berra 15.00
MU58Yogi Berra, Eddie Mathews 12.00
MU62Roger Maris, Juan Marichal 40.00
MU63Sandy Koufax, Mickey Mantle 100.00
MU66Don Drysdale, Brooks Robinson/SP 40.00
MU69Nolan Ryan, Brooks Robinson 50.00
MU72Joe Morgan, Jim "Catfish" Hunter 8.00
MU72aRollie Fingers, Johnny Bench 10.00
MU73Tom Seaver, "Catfish" Hunter 15.00
MU74Jim "Catfish" Hunter, Steve Garvey 8.00
MU74aDavey Lopes, Jim "Catfish" Hunter 8.00
MU76Ken Griffey Sr., Thurman Munson 12.00
MU76aThurman Munson, Johnny Bench 20.00
MU78Thurman Munson, Steve Garvey 12.00
MU78aBill Russell, Thurman Munson 12.00
MU81Steve Garvey, Dave Winfield 8.00
MU82Robin Yount, Ozzie Smith 15.00
MU83Cal Ripken Jr., Joe Morgan
MU84Jack Morris, Tony Gwynn 12.00
MU86Jesse Orosco, Roger Clemens 15.00
MU87Ozzie Smith, Kirby Puckett 35.00
MU88Mark McGwire, Kirk Gibson/SP
MU90Barry Larkin, Mark McGwire/SP 25.00
MU91Tom Glavine, Kirby Puckett 20.00
MU93Joe Carter, Curt Schilling 8.00
MU95Dennis Martinez, David Justice 8.00
MU96Andruw Jones, Andy Pettitte 8.00
MU96aTim Raines, Tom Glavine 10.00
MU96bKenny Rogers, Chipper Jones 8.00
MU95aKenny Lofton, John Smoltz 8.00
MU97Jim Thome, Kevin Brown 10.00
MU98Tony Gwynn, Bernie Williams 10.00
MU98aTrevor Hoffman, Bernie Williams/SP 8.00
MU99Jorge Posada, Greg Maddux 15.00
MU99aGreg Maddux, Derek Jeter 40.00
MU99bPaul O'Neill, John Smoltz 8.00
MU99cChipper Jones, Mariano Rivera 15.00

2002 Upper Deck World Series Heroes Patch Collection

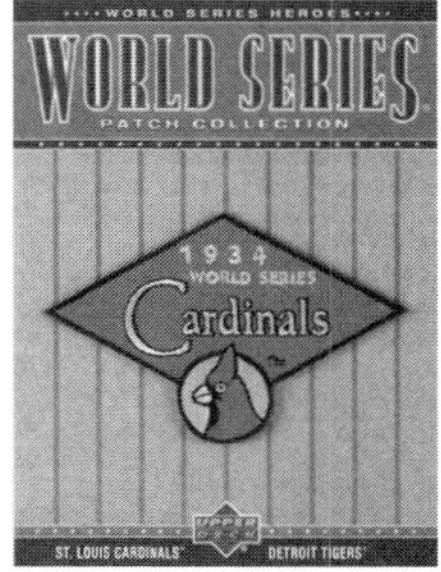

MT
Common Patch: 15.00
Inserted 1:hobby box
WS031903 World Series25.00
WS051905 World Series25.00
WS061906 World Series20.00
WS071907 World Series20.00
WS081908 World Series25.00
WS091909 World Series20.00
WS101910 World Series20.00
WS111911 World Series20.00
WS121912 World Series30.00
WS131913 World Series20.00
WS141914 World Series25.00
WS151915 World Series20.00
WS161916 World Series25.00
WS171917 World Series20.00
WS181918 World Series30.00
WS191919 World Series25.00
WS201920 World Series20.00
WS211921 World Series15.00
WS221922 World Series20.00
WS231923 World Series20.00
WS241924 World Series20.00
WS251925 World Series25.00
WS261926 World Series25.00
WS271927 World Series25.00
WS281928 World Series25.00
WS291929 World Series20.00
WS301930 World Series20.00
WS311931 World Series25.00
WS321932 World Series30.00
WS331933 World Series20.00
WS341934 World Series20.00
WS351935 World Series20.00
WS361936 World Series20.00
WS371937 World Series20.00
WS381938 World Series25.00
WS391939 World Series20.00
WS401940 World Series20.00
WS411941 World Series20.00
WS421942 World Series20.00
WS431943 World Series20.00
WS441944 World Series30.00
WS451945 World Series20.00
WS461946 World Series25.00
WS471947 World Series25.00
WS481948 World Series25.00
WS491949 World Series25.00
WS501950 World Series25.00
WS511951 World Series25.00
WS521952 World Series25.00
WS531953 World Series25.00
WS541954 World Series15.00
WS551955 World Series35.00
WS561956 World Series25.00
WS571957 World Series25.00
WS581958 World Series20.00
WS591959 World Series20.00
WS601960 World Series20.00
WS611961 World Series35.00

WS621962 World Series25.00
WS631963 World Series25.00
WS641964 World Series20.00
WS651965 World Series20.00
WS661966 World Series25.00
WS671967 World Series20.00
WS681968 World Series30.00
WS691969 World Series35.00
WS701970 World Series20.00
WS711971 World Series20.00
WS721972 World Series20.00
WS731973 World Series25.00
WS741974 World Series20.00
WS751975 World Series30.00
WS761976 World Series30.00
WS771977 World Series20.00
WS781978 World Series20.00
WS791979 World Series20.00
WS801980 World Series20.00
WS811981 World Series30.00
WS821982 World Series20.00
WS831983 World Series30.00
WS841984 World Series20.00
WS851985 World Series25.00
WS861986 World Series25.00
WS871987 World Series20.00
WS881988 World Series25.00
WS891989 World Series20.00
WS901990 World Series20.00
WS911991 World Series20.00
WS921992 World Series20.00
WS931993 World Series20.00
WS951995 World Series20.00
WS961996 World Series20.00
WS971997 World Series20.00
WS981998 World Series15.00
WS991999 World Series20.00
WS002000 World Series
WS012001 World Series20.00

2002 UD World Series Heroes Patch Collection Autographs

MT
Inserted 1:336
WS93Joe Carter 50.00
WS99Roger Clemens 95.00
WS74Rollie Fingers 30.00
WS75Carlton Fisk 50.00
WS81Steve Garvey 35.00
WS65Sandy Koufax 250.00
WS56Don Larsen 80.00
WS89Mark McGwire 650.00
WS76Joe Morgan 50.00
WS91Kirby Puckett 90.00
WS83Cal Ripken Jr. 160.00
WS70Brooks Robinson 80.00
WS69Nolan Ryan 260.00
WS73Tom Seaver 65.00
WS55Duke Snider 65.00
WS82Ozzie Smith 90.00

2002 Upper Deck 40-Man

MT
Complete Set (1182): 240.00
Common Player: .15
Silvers: 2-4X
Inserted 1:4
Rainbows: 6-10X
Production 40 sets
Hobby Pack (10): 2.50
Hobby Box (24): 40.00
1 Darin Erstad .40
2 Kevin Appier .15
3 Scott Schoeneweis .15
4 Bengie Molina .15
5 Troy Glaus .75
6 Adam Kennedy .15
7 Aaron Sele .15
8 Garret Anderson .25
9 Ramon Ortiz .15
10 Dennis Cook .15
11 Scott Spiezio .15
12 Orlando Palmeiro .15
13 Troy Percival .15
14 David Eckstein .15
15 Jarrod Washburn .40
16 Nathan Haynes .15
17 Benji Gil .15
18 Alfredo Amezega .15
19 Ben Weber .15
20 Al Levine .15
21 Brad Fullmer .15
22 Elpidio Guzman .15
23 Tim Salmon .25
24 Jose Nieves .15
25 Shawn Wooten .15
26 Lou Pote .15
27 Mickey Callaway .15
28 Steve Green .15
29 John Lackey .15
30 Mark Lukasiewicz .15
31 Jorge Fabregas .15
32 Jeff Da Vanon .15
33 Elvin Nina .15
34 Donne Wall .15
35 Eric Chavez .50
36 Jermaine Dye .15
37 Scott Hatteberg .15
38 Mark Mulder .50
39 Ramon Hernandez .15
40 Jim Mecir .15
41 Barry Zito .50
42 Greg Myers .15
43 David Justice .50
44 Mike Magnante .15
45 Terrence Long .15
46 Tim Hudson .50
47 Olmedo Saenz .15
48 Billy Koch .15
49 Carlos Pena .50
50 Mike Venafro .15
51 Mark Ellis .15
52 Randy Velarde .15
53 Jeremy Giambi .15
54 Mike Colagelo .15
55 Mike Holtz .15
56 Chad Bradford .15
57 Miguel Tejada .50
58 Mike Fyhrie .15
59 Eric Hiljus .15
60 Juan Pena .15
61 Mario Valdez .15
62 *Franklyn German* .50
63 Carlos Delgado .75
64 Orlando Hudson .15
65 Chris Carpenter .15
66 Kelvim Escobar .15
67 Felipe Lopez .15
68 Brandon Lyon .15
69 Jose Cruz Jr. .15
70 Luke Prokopec .15
71 Darrin Fletcher .15
72 Bob File .15
73 Felix Heredia .15
74 Mike Sirotka .15
75 Shannon Stewart .15
76 Joe Lawrence .15
77 Chris Woodward .15
78 Dan Plesac .15
79 Pedro Borbon .15
80 Roy Halladay .40
81 Raul Mondesi .40
82 Steve Parris .15
83 Homer Bush .15
84 Esteban Loaiza .15
85 Vernon Wells .15
86 Justin Miller .15
87 Scott Eyre .15
88 Dave Berg .15
89 *Gustavo Chacin* .15
90 *Joe Orloski* .40
91 *Corey Thurman* .15
92 Tom Wilson .15
93 Eric Hinske .50
94 *Chris Baker* .40
95 *Reed Johnson* .40
96 Greg Vaughn .15
97 Toby Hall .15
98 Brent Abernathy .15
99 Bobby Smith .15
100 Tanyon Sturtze .15
101 Chris Gomez .15
102 Joe Kennedy .15
103 Ben Grieve .15
104 Aubrey Huff .15
105 Jesus Colome .15
106 *Felix Escalona* .40
107 Paul Wilson .15
108 Ryan Rupe .15
109 Jason Tyner .15
110 Esteban Yan .15
111 Russ Johnson .15
112 Randy Winn .15
113 Wilson Alvarez .15
114 Wilmy Caceres .15
115 Steve Cox .15
116 Dewon Brazelton .15
117 Doug Creek .15
118 Jason Conti .15
119 John Flaherty .15
120 Delvin James .15
121 *Steve Kent* .15
122 Kevin McGlinchy .15
123 Travis Phelps .15
124 Bobby Seay .15
125 Travis Harper .15
126 Victor Zambrano .15
127 Jace Brewer .15
128 Jason Smith .15
129 Ramon Soler .15
130 *Brandon Backe* 2.00
131 *Jorge Sosa* .25
132 Jim Thome 1.00
133 Brady Anderson .15
134 C.C. Sabathia .15
135 Einar Diaz .15
136 Ricky Gutierrez .15
137 Danys Baez .15
138 Bob Wickman .15
139 Milton Bradley .15
140 Bartolo Colon .40
141 Jolbert Cabrera .15
142 Eddie Taubensee .15
143 Ellis Burks .15
144 Omar Vizquel .40
145 Eddie Perez .15
146 Jaret Wright .15
147 Chuck Finley .15
148 Paul Shuey .15
149 Travis Fryman .15
150 Wil Cordero .15
151 Ricardo Rincon .15
152 Victor Martinez .15
153 Charles Nagy .15
154 Alex Escobar .15
155 Russell Branyan .15
156 Matt Lawton .15
157 Ryan Drese .15
158 Jerrod Riggan .15
159 David Riske .15
160 Jake Westbrook .15
161 Mark Wohlers .15
162 John McDonald .15
163 Ichiro Suzuki 3.00
164 Freddy Garcia .15
165 Edgar Martinez .15
166 Ben Davis .15
167 Shigetoshi Hasegawa .15
168 Carlos Guillen .15
169 Ruben Sierra .15
170 Joel Pineiro .15
171 Norm Charlton .15
172 Bret Boone .15
173 Jamie Moyer .15
174 Jeff Nelson .15
175 Kazuhiro Sasaki .50
176 Jeff Cirillo .15
177 Mark McLemore .15
178 Paul Abbott .15
179 Mike Cameron .15
180 Dan Wilson .15
181 John Olerud .50
182 Arthur Rhodes .15
183 Desi Relaford .15
184 John Halama .15
185 Antonio Perez .15
186 Ryan Anderson .15
187 James Baldwin .15
188 Ryan Franklin .15
189 Justin Kaye .15
190 *J.J. Putz* .40
191 *Allan Simpson* .40
192 Matt Thornton .15
193 *Luis Ugueto* .40
194 Chris Richard .15
195 Sidney Ponson .15
196 Brook Fordyce .15
197 Luis Matos .15
198 Josh Towers .15
199 David Segui .15
200 Chris Brock .15
201 Tony Batista .15
202 Erik Bedard .15
203 Marty Cordova .15
204 Jerry Hairston Jr. .15
205 Jason Johnson .15
206 Buddy Groom .15
207 Mike Bordick .15
208 Melvin Mora .15
209 Calvin Maduro .15
210 Jeff Conine .15
211 Luis Rivera .15
212 Jay Gibbons .15
213 B.J. Ryan .15
214 Sean Douglass .15
215 Rodrigo Lopez .15
216 Rick Bauer .15
217 Scott Erickson .15
218 Jorge Julio .15
219 Willis Roberts .15
220 John Stephens .15
221 Geronimo Gil .15
222 Chris Singleton .15
223 Mike Paradis .15
224 John Parrish .15
225 *Steve Bechler* .50
226 *Mike Moriarty* .15
227 Luis Garcia .15
228 Alex Rodriguez 3.00
229 Mark Teixeira .50
230 Chan Ho Park .15
231 Todd Van Poppel .15
232 Mike Young .15
233 Kenny Rogers .15
234 Rusty Greer .15
235 Rafael Palmeiro .75
236 Francisco Cordero .15
237 John Rocker .15
238 Dave Burba .15
239 Travis Hafner .15
240 Kevin Mench .15
241 Carl Everett .15
242 Ivan Rodriguez .75
243 Jeff Zimmerman .15
244 Juan Gonzalez 1.00
245 Herbert Perry .15
246 Rob Bell .15
247 Doug Davis .15
248 Frank Catalanotto .15
249 Jay Powell .15
250 Gabe Kapler .15
251 Joaquin Benoit .15
252 Jovanny Cedeno .15
253 Hideki Irabu .15
254 Dan Miceli .15
255 Danny Kolb .15
256 Colby Lewis .15
257 Rich Rodriguez .15
258 Ismael Valdes .15
259 Bill Haselman .15
260 Jason Hart .15
261 Rudy Seanez .15
262 *Travis Hughes* .40
263 Hank Blalock .50
264 Steve Woodard .15
265 Nomar Garciaparra 3.00
266 Pedro J. Martinez 1.50
267 Frank Castillo .15
268 Johnny Damon .15
269 Doug Mirabelli .15
270 Derek Lowe .40
271 Shea Hillenbrand .50
272 Paxton Crawford .15
273 Tony Clark .15
274 Dustin Hermanson .15
275 Trot Nixon .15
276 John Burkett .15
277 Rich Garces .15
278 *Josh Hancock* .15
279 Michael Coleman .15
280 Darren Oliver .15
281 Jason Varitek .15
282 Jose Offerman .15
283 Tim Wakefield .15
284 Rolando Arrojo .15
285 Rickey Henderson .75
286 Ugueth Urbina .15
287 Casey Fossum .15
288 Manny Ramirez 1.00
289 Sun-Woo Kim .15

290 Juan Diaz .15
291 Willie Banks .15
292 *Jorge De La Rosa* .50
293 Juan Pena .15
294 Jeff Wallace .15
295 Calvin Pickering .15
296 *Anastacio Martinez* .40
297 Carlos Baerga .15
298 Rey Sanchez .15
299 Mike Sweeney .15
300 Jeff Suppan .15
301 Brent Mayne .15
302 Chad Durbin .15
303 Dan Reichert .15
304 Raul Ibanez .15
305 Joe Randa .15
306 Chris George .15
307 Michael Tucker .15
308 Paul Byrd .15
309 Kris Wilson .15
310 Luis Alicea .15
311 Neifi Perez .15
312 Brian Shouse .15
313 Chuck Knoblauch .15
314 Dave McCarty .15
315 Blake Stein .15
316 Alexis Gomez .15
317 Mark Quinn .15
318 A.J. Hinch .15
319 Carlos Febles .15
320 Roberto Hernandez .15
321 Brandon Berger .15
322 *Jeff Austin* .40
323 Corey Bailey .15
324 Tony Cogan .15
325 *Nate Field* .40
326 Jason Grimsley .15
327 Darrell May .15
328 Donnie Sadler .15
329 Carlos Beltran .15
330 *Miguel Asencio* .40
331 Jeff Weaver .15
332 Bobby Higginson .15
333 Mike Rivera .15
334 Matt Anderson .15
335 Craig Paquette .15
336 Jose Lima .15
337 Juan Acevedo .15
338 Danny Patterson .15
339 Andres Torres .15
340 Dean Palmer .15
341 Randall Simon .15
342 Craig Monroe .15
343 Damion Easley .15
344 Robert Fick .15
345 Steve Sparks .15
346 Dmitri Young .15
347 Nate Cornejo .15
348 Matt Miller .15
349 Wendell Magee .15
350 Shane Halter .15
351 Brian Moehler .15
352 Mitch Meluskey .15
353 Jose Macias .15
354 Mark Redman .15
355 Jeff Farnsworth .15
356 Kris Keller .15
357 Adam Pettyjohn .15
358 Fernando Rodney .15
359 Andy Van Hekken .15
360 Damian Jackson .15
361 Jose Paniagua .15
362 Jacob Cruz .15
363 Doug Mientkiewicz .15
364 Torii Hunter .15
365 Brad Radke .15
366 Denny Hocking .15
367 Mike Jackson .15
368 Eddie Guardado .15
369 Jacque Jones .15
370 Joe Mays .15
371 Matt Kinney .15
372 Kyle Lohse .15
373 David Ortiz .15
374 Luis Rivas .15
375 Jay Canizaro .15
376 Dustan Mohr .15
377 LaTroy Hawkins .15
378 Warren Morris .15
379 A.J. Pierzynski .15
380 Eric Milton .15
381 Bob Wells .15
382 Cristian Guzman .15
383 Brian Buchanan .15
384 Bobby Kielty .15
385 Corey Koskie .15
386 J.C. Romero .15
387 Jack Cressend .15
388 Mike Duvall .15
389 Tony Fiore .15
390 Tom Prince .15
391 Todd Sears .15
392 *Kevin Frederick* .40
393 Frank Thomas 1.00
394 Mark Buehrle .15
395 Jon Garland .15
396 Jeff Liefer .15
397 Maggio Ordonez .50
398 Rocky Biddle .15
399 Lorenzo Barcelo .15
400 Ray Durham .15
401 Bob Howry .15
402 Aaron Rowand .15
403 Keith Foulke .15
404 Paul Konerko .50
405 Sandy Alomar Jr. .15
406 Mark Johnson .15
407 Carlos Lee .15
408 Jose Valentin .15
409 Jon Rauch .15
410 Royce Clayton .15
411 Kenny Lofton .40
412 Tony Graffanino .15
413 Todd Ritchie .15
414 Antonio Osuna .15
415 Gary Glover .15
416 Mike Porzio .15
417 Danny Wright .15
418 Kelly Wunsch .15
419 Miguel Olivo .15
420 *Edwin Almonte* .15
421 *Kyle Kane* .50
422 *Mitch Wylie* .15
423 Derek Jeter 4.00
424 Jason Giambi 1.50
425 Roger Clemens 1.50
426 Enrique Wilson .15
427 David Wells .15
428 Mike Mussina .75
429 Bernie Williams .75
430 Mike Stanton .15
431 Sterling Hitchcock .15
432 Alex Graman .15
433 Robin Ventura .50
434 Mariano Rivera .50
435 Jay Tessmer .15
436 Andy Pettite .50
437 John Vander Wal .15
438 Adrian Hernandez .15
439 Alberto Castillo .15
440 Steve Karsay .15
441 Alfonso Soriano 2.50
442 Rondell White .15
443 Nick Johnson .50
444 Jorge Posada .50
445 Ramiro Mendoza .15
446 Gerald Williams .15
447 Orlando Hernandez .15
448 Randy Choate .15
449 Randy Keisler .15
450 Ted Lilly .15
451 Christian Parker .15
452 Ron Coomer .15
453 Marcus Thames .15
454 Drew Henson .50
455 Jeff Bagwell 1.00
456 Wade Miller .15
457 Lance Berkman 1.50
458 Julio Lugo .15
459 Roy Oswalt .75
460 Nelson Cruz .15
461 Morgan Ensberg .15
462 Geoff Blum .15
463 *Ryan Jamison* .50
464 Billy Wagner .15
465 Dave Mlicki .15
466 Brad Ausmus .15
467 Jose Vizcaino .15
468 Craig Biggio .50
469 Shane Reynolds .15
470 Gregg Zaun .15
471 Octavio Dotel .15
472 Carlos Hernandez .15
473 Richard Hidalgo .15
474 Daryle Ward .15
475 Orlando Merced .15
476 John Buck .15
477 Adam Everett .15
478 Doug Brocail .15
479 Brad Lidge .15
480 Scott Linebrink .15
481 T.J. Mathews .15
482 Greg Miller .15
483 Hipolito Pichardo .15
484 *Brandon Puffer* .15
485 Ricky Stone .15
486 Jason Lane .15
487 Brian L. Hunter .15
488 *Rodrigo Rosario* .50
489 *Tom Shearn* .50
490 Gary Sheffield .75
491 Tom Glavine .75
492 Mike Remlinger .15
493 Henry Blanco .15
494 Vinny Castilla .15
495 Chris Hammond .15
496 Kevin Millwood .50
497 Darren Holmes .15
498 Cory Aldridge .15
499 Tim Spooneybarger .15
500 Rafael Furcal .50
501 Albie Lopez .15
502 Javy Lopez .40
503 Greg Maddux 2.50
504 Andruw Jones .75
505 Steve Torrealba .15
506 George Lombard .15
507 B.J. Surhoff .15
508 Marcus Giles .15
509 Derrick Lewis .15
510 Wes Helms .15
511 John Smoltz .50
512 Chipper Jones 2.50
513 Jason Marquis .15
514 Mark DeRosa .15
515 Jung Bong .15
516 *Kevin Gryboski* .15
517 Damian Moss .15
518 Horacio Ramirez .15
519 Scott Sobkowiak .15
520 Billy Sylvester .15
521 Nick Green .15
522 Travis Wilson .15
523 Ryan Langerhans .15
524 *John Ennis* 1.00
525 *John Foster* .15
526 Keith Lockhart .15
527 Julio Franco .15
528 Richie Sexson .75
529 Jeffrey Hammonds .15
530 Ben Sheets .50
531 Mike DeJean .15
532 Mark Loretta .15
533 Alex Ochoa .15
534 Jamey Wright .15
535 Jose Hernandez .15
536 Glendon Rusch .15
537 Geoff Jenkins .50
538 Luis S. Lopez .15
539 Curtis Leskanic .15
540 Chad Fox .15
541 Tyler Houston .15
542 Nick Neugebauer .15
543 Matt Stairs .15
544 Paul Rigdon .15
545 Bill Hall .15
546 Luis Vizcaino .15
547 Lenny Harris .15
548 Alex Sanchez .15
549 Raul Casanova .15
550 Eric Young .15
551 Jeff Deardorff .15
552 Nelson Figueroa .15
553 Ron Belliard .15
554 Mike Buddie .15
555 Jose Cabrera .15
556 J.M. Gold .15
557 Ray King .15
558 Jose Mieses .15
559 *Takahito Nomura* .50
560 Ruben Quevedo .15
561 Jackson Melian .15
562 Cristian Guerrero .15
563 Paul Bako .15
564 *Luis Martinez* .50
565 *Brian Mallette* .50
566 Matt Morris .50
567 Tino Martinez .40
568 Fernando Vina .15
569 Gene Stechschulte .15
570 Andy Benes .15
571 Placido Polanco .15
572 Luis Garcia .15
573 Jim Edmonds .50
574 Bud Smith .15
575 Mike Matheny .15
576 Garrett Stephenson .15
577 Miguel Cairo .15
578 Darryl Kile .15
579 Mike Timlin .15
580 Rick Ankiel .15
581 Jason Isringhausen .15
582 Albert Pujols 2.50
583 Eli Marrero .15
584 Steve Kline .15
585 J.D. Drew .50
586 Mike DiFelice .15
587 Dave Veres .15
588 Kerry Robinson .15
589 Edgar Renteria .15
590 Woody Williams .15
591 Chance Caple .15
592 *Michael Crudale* .15
593 Luther Hackman .15
594 Josh Pearce .15
595 Kevin Joseph .15
596 Jimmy Journell .15
597 *Jeremy Lambert* .40
598 Mike Matthews .15
599 Les Walrond .15
600 Keith McDonald .15
601 William Ortega .15
602 *Scotty Layfield* .50
603 *So Taguchi* 2.00
604 Eduardo Perez .15
605 Sammy Sosa 2.50
606 Kerry Wood .75
607 Kyle Farnsworth .15
608 Alex Gonzalez .15
609 Tom Gordon .15
610 Carlos Zambrano .15
611 Roosevelt Brown .15
612 Bill Mueller .15
613 Mark Prior 2.50
614 Darren Lewis .15
615 Joe Girardi .15
616 Fred McGriff .50
617 Jon Lieber .15
618 Robert Machado .15
619 Corey Patterson .50
620 Joe Borowski .15
621 Todd Hundley .15
622 Jason Bere .15
623 Moises Alou .40
624 Jeff Fassero .15
625 Jesus Sanchez .15
626 Chris Stynes .15
627 Delino DeShields .15
628 Augie Ojeda .15
629 Juan Cruz .15
630 Ben Christensen .15
631 Mike Meyers .15
632 Will Ohman .15
633 Steve Smyth .15
634 Mark Bellhorn .15
635 Nate Frese .15
636 David Kelton .15
637 *Francis Beltran* .40
638 Antonio Alfonseca .15
639 Donovan Osborne .15
640 Shawn Sonnier .15
641 Matt Clement .15
642 Luis Gonzalez .75
643 Brian Anderson .15
644 Randy Johnson 1.50
645 Mark Grace .75
646 Danny Bautista .15
647 Junior Spivey .15
648 Jay Bell .15
649 Miguel Batista .15
650 Tony Womack .15
651 Byung-Hyun Kim .15
652 Steve Finley .40
653 Rick Helling .15
654 Curt Schilling 1.00
655 Erubiel Durazo .15
656 Chris Donnels .15
657 Greg Colbrunn .15
658 Mike Morgan .15
659 Jose Guillen .15
660 Matt Williams .50
661 Craig Counsell .15
662 Greg Swindell .15
663 Rod Barajas .15
664 David Dellucci .15
665 Todd Stottlemyre .15
666 *P.J. Bevis* .15
667 Mike Koplove .15
668 Mike Myers .15
669 John Patterson .15
670 Bret Prinz .15
671 *Jeremy Ward* .50
672 Danny Klassen .15
673 Luis Terrero .15
674 *Jose Valverde* .50
675 *Doug Devore* .50
676 Quinton McCracken .15
677 Paul LoDuca .15

No.	Player	Price
678	Mark Grudzielanek	.15
679	Kevin Brown	.50
680	Paul Quantrill	.15
681	Shawn Green	.75
682	Hideo Nomo	.75
683	Eric Gagne	.15
684	Giovanni Carrara	.15
685	Marquis Grissom	.15
686	Hiram Bocachica	.15
687	Guillermo Mota	.15
688	Alex Cora	.15
689	Odalis Perez	.15
690	Brian Jordan	.15
691	Andy Ashby	.15
692	Eric Karros	.40
693	Chad Krueter	.15
694	Dave Roberts	.15
695	Omar Daal	.15
696	Dave Hansen	.15
697	Adrian Beltre	.50
698	Terry Mulholland	.15
699	Cesar Izturis	.15
700	Steve Colyer	.15
701	Carlos Garcia	.15
702	Ricardo Rodriguez	.15
703	Darren Dreifort	.15
704	Jeff Reboulet	.15
705	*Victor Alvarez*	.50
706	*Kazuhisa Ishii*	5.00
707	Jose Vidro	.15
708	Henry Mateo	.15
709	Tony Armas Jr.	.15
710	Carl Pavano	.15
711	Peter Bergeron	.15
712	Bruce Chen	.15
713	Orlando Cabrera	.15
714	Britt Reames	.15
715	Masato Yoshii	.15
716	Fernando Tatis	.15
717	Graeme Lloyd	.15
718	Scott Stewart	.15
719	Lou Collier	.15
720	Michael Barrett	.15
721	Vladimir Guerrero	1.50
722	Troy Mattes	.15
723	Brian Schneider	.15
724	Lee Stevens	.15
725	Javier Vazquez	.15
726	Brad Wilkerson	.15
727	Zach Day	.15
728	Ed Vosberg	.15
729	Tomokazu Ohka	.15
730	Mike Mordecai	.15
731	Donnie Bridges	.15
732	Ron Chiavacci	.15
733	T.J. Tucker	.15
734	Scott Hodges	.15
735	Valentino Pascucci	.15
736	Andres Galarraga	.15
737	Scott Downs	.15
738	*Eric Good*	.15
739	*Ron Calloway*	.50
740	*Jorge Nunez*	.15
741	Henry Rodriguez	.15
742	Jeff Kent	.15
743	Russ Ortiz	.15
744	Felix Rodriguez	.15
745	Benito Santiago	.15
746	Tsuyoshi Shinjo	.50
747	Tim Worrell	.15
748	Marvin Benard	.15
749	Kurt Ainsworth	.15
750	Edwards Guzman	.15
751	J.T. Snow	.15
752	Jason Christiansen	.15
753	Robb Nen	.15
754	Barry Bonds	3.00
755	Shawon Dunston	.15
756	Chad Zerbe	.15
757	Ramon E. Martinez	.15
758	Calvin Murray	.15
759	Pedro Feliz	.15
760	Jason Schmidt	.15
761	Damon Minor	.15
762	Reggie Sanders	.15
763	Rich Aurilia	.15
764	Kirk Rueter	.15
765	David Bell	.15
766	Yorvit Torrealba	.15
767	Livan Hernandez	.15
768	Felix Diaz	.15
769	Aaron Fultz	.15
770	Ryan Jensen	.15
771	Arturo McDowell	.15
772	Carlos Valderrama	.15
773	*Nelson Castro*	.50
774	Jay Witasick	.15
775	Deivis Santos	.15
776	Josh Beckett	.15
777	Charles Johnson	.15
778	Derrek Lee	.15
779	A.J. Burnett	.15
780	Vic Darensbourg	.15
781	Cliff Floyd	.50
782	Jose Cueto	.15
783	Nate Teut	.15
784	Alex Gonzalez	.15
785	Brad Penny	.15
786	Kevin Olsen	.15
787	Mike Lowell	.15
788	Mike Redmond	.15
789	Braden Looper	.15
790	Eric Owens	.15
791	Andy Fox	.15
792	Vladimir Nunez	.15
793	Luis Castillo	.15
794	Ryan Dempster	.15
795	Armando Almanza	.15
796	Preston Wilson	.15
797	Pablo Ozuna	.15
798	Gary Knotts	.15
799	Ramon Castro	.15
800	Benito Baez	.15
801	Michael Tejera	.15
802	Claudio Vargas	.15
803	Chip Ambres	.15
804	*Hansel Izquierdo*	.50
805	Tim Raines	.15
806	Marty Malloy	.15
807	Julian Tavarez	.15
808	Roberto Alomar	.75
809	Al Leiter	.50
810	Jeromy Burnitz	.15
811	John Franco	.15
812	Edgardo Alfonzo	.15
813	Mike Piazza	3.00
814	Shawn Estes	.15
815	Joe McEwing	.15
816	David Weathers	.15
817	Pedro Astacio	.15
818	Timoniel Perez	.15
819	Grant Roberts	.15
820	Rey Ordonez	.15
821	Steve Trachsel	.15
822	Roger Cedeno	.15
823	Mark Johnson	.15
824	Armando Benitez	.15
825	Vance Wilson	.15
826	Jay Payton	.15
827	Mo Vaughn	.50
828	Scott Strickland	.15
829	Mark Guthrie	.15
830	Jeff D'Amico	.15
831	*Mark Corey*	.50
832	Kane Davis	.15
833	Jae Weong Seo	.15
834	Pat Strange	.15
835	*Adam Walker*	.15
836	Tyler Walker	.15
837	Gary Matthews Jr.	.15
838	*Jaime Cerda*	.25
839	*Satoru Komiyama*	.50
840	*Tyler Yates*	.50
841	John Valentin	.15
842	Ryan Klesko	.40
843	Wiki Gonzalez	.15
844	Trevor Hoffman	.15
845	Sean Burroughs	.40
846	Alan Embree	.15
847	Dennis Tankersley	.15
848	D'Angelo Jimenez	.15
849	Kevin Jarvis	.15
850	Mark Kotsay	.15
851	Phil Nevin	.25
852	Jeremy Fikac	.15
853	Brett Tomko	.15
854	Brian Lawrence	.15
855	Steve Reed	.15
856	Bubba Trammell	.15
857	Tom Davey	.15
858	Ramon Vazquez	.15
859	Tom Lampkin	.15
860	Bobby Jones	.15
861	Ray Lankford	.15
862	Mark Sweeney	.15
863	Adam Eaton	.15
864	Trenidad Hubbard	.15
865	Jason Boyd	.15
866	Javier Cardona	.15
867	*Clifford Bartosh*	.50
868	Mike Bynum	.15
869	*Eric Cyr*	.50
870	Jose Nunez	.15
871	Ron Gant	.15
872	Deivi Cruz	.15
873	*Ben Howard*	1.50
874	*Todd Donovan*	.25
875	*Andy Shibilo*	.15
876	Scott Rolen	.75
877	Jose Mesa	.15
878	Rheal Cormier	.15
879	Travis Lee	.15
880	Mike Lieberthal	.15
881	Brandon Duckworth	.15
882	David Coggin	.15
883	Bobby Abreu	.50
884	Turk Wendell	.15
885	Marlon Byrd	.15
886	Jason Michaels	.15
887	Robert Person	.15
888	Tomas Perez	.15
889	Jimmy Rollins	.15
890	Vicente Padilla	.15
891	Pat Burrell	.75
892	Dave Hollins	.15
893	Randy Wolf	.15
894	Jose Santiago	.15
895	Doug Glanville	.15
896	Cliff Politte	.15
897	Marlon Anderson	.15
898	Ricky Bottalico	.15
899	Terry Adams	.15
900	Brad Baisley	.15
901	Hector Mercado	.15
902	*Elio Serrano*	.50
903	Todd Pratt	.15
904	*Peter Zamora*	.50
905	Nick Punto	.15
906	Ricky Ledee	.15
907	*Eric Junge*	.15
908	*Anderson Machado*	.50
909	*Jorge Padilla*	.50
910	John Mabry	.15
911	Brian Giles	.75
912	Jason Kendall	.40
913	Jack Wilson	.15
914	Kris Benson	.15
915	Aramis Ramirez	.15
916	Mike Fetters	.15
917	Adrian Brown	.15
918	Pokey Reese	.15
919	Dave Williams	.15
920	Mike Benjamin	.15
921	Kip Wells	.15
922	Mike Williams	.15
923	Pat Meares	.15
924	Ron Villone	.15
925	Armando Rios	.15
926	Jimmy Anderson	.15
927	Robert Mackowiak	.15
928	Kevin Young	.15
929	Brian Boehringer	.15
930	Joe Beimel	.15
931	Chad Hermansen	.15
932	Scott Sauerbeck	.15
933	Josh Fogg	.15
934	*Mike Gonzalez*	.15
935	Mike Lincoln	.15
936	Sean Lowe	.15
937	Matt Guerrier	.15
938	Ryan Vogelsong	.15
939	J.R. House	.15
940	Craig Wilson	.15
941	Tony Alvarez	.15
942	J.J. Davis	.15
943	Abraham Nunez	.15
944	*Adrian Burnside*	.50
945	Ken Griffey Jr.	2.50
946	Jimmy Haynes	.15
947	Juan Castro	.15
948	Jose Rijo	.15
949	Corky Miller	.15
950	Elmer Dessens	.15
951	Aaron Boone	.15
952	Juan Encarnacion	.15
953	Chris Reitsma	.15
954	Wilton Guerrero	.15
955	Danny Graves	.15
956	Jim Brower	.15
957	Barry Larkin	.50
958	Todd Walker	.15
959	Gabe White	.15
960	Adam Dunn	1.00
961	Jason LaRue	.15
962	Reggie Taylor	.15
963	Sean Casey	.40
964	Scott Williamson	.15
965	Austin Kearns	.75
966	Kelly Stinnett	.15
967	Jose Acevedo	.15
968	Gookie Dawkins	.15
969	Brady Clark	.15
970	Scott Sullivan	.15
971	Ricardo Aramboles	.15
972	Lance Davis	.15
973	Seth Etherton	.15
974	Luke Hudson	.15
975	Joey Hamilton	.15
976	Luis Pineda	.15
977	John Riedling	.15
978	Jose Silva	.15
979	Dane Sardinha	.15
980	Ben Broussard	.15
981	David Espinosa	.15
982	Ruben Mateo	.15
983	Larry Walker	.50
984	Juan Uribe	.15
985	Mike Hampton	.15
986	*Aaron Cook*	.15
987	Jose Ortiz	.15
988	Todd Jones	.15
989	Todd Helton	1.00
990	Shawn Chacon	.15
991	Jason Jennings	.15
992	Todd Zeile	.15
993	Ben Petrick	.15
994	Denny Neagle	.15
995	Jose Jimenez	.15
996	Juan Pierre	.15
997	Todd Hollandsworth	.15
998	Kent Mercker	.15
999	Greg Norton	.15
1000	Terry Shumpert	.15
1001	Mark Little	.15
1002	Gary Bennett	.15
1003	Dennys Reyes	.15
1004	Justin Speier	.15
1005	John Thomson	.15
1006	Rick White	.15
1007	*Colin Young*	.40
1008	*Cam Esslinger*	.50
1009	*Rene Reyes*	.50
1010	Mike James	.15
1011	Morgan Ensberg	.15
1012	Adam Everett	.15
1013	Rodrigo Rosario	.15
1014	Carlos Pena	.15
1015	Eric Hinske	.50
1016	Orlando Hudson	.15
1017	Reed Johnson	.15
1018	Jung Bong	.15
1019	Bill Hall	.15
1020	Mark Prior	1.50
1021	Francis Beltran	.15
1022	David Kelton	.15
1023	Felix Escalona	.15
1024	Jorge Sosa	.15
1025	Dewon Brazelton	.15
1026	Jose Valverde	.15
1027	Luis Terrero	.15
1028	Kazuhisa Ishii	2.00
1029	Cesar Izturis	.15
1030	Ryan Jensen	.15
1031	Matt Thornton	.15
1032	Hansel Izquierdo	.15
1033	Jaime Cerda	.15
1034	Erik Bedard	.15
1035	Sean Burroughs	.15
1036	Ben Howard	.15
1037	Ramon Vazquez	.15
1038	Marlon Byrd	.15
1039	Josh Fogg	.15
1040	Hank Blalock	.50
1041	Mark Teixeira	.50
1042	Kevin Mench	.15
1043	Dane Sardinha	.15
1044	Austin Kearns	.50
1045	Anastacio Martinez	.15
1046	Eric Munson	.15
1047	Jon Rauch	.15
1048	Nick Johnson	.50
1049	Alex Graman	.15
1050	Drew Henson	.50
1051	Darin Erstad	.50
1052	Garret Anderson	.15
1053	Craig Biggio	.50
1054	Lance Berkman	.50
1055	Jeff Bagwell	1.00
1056	Shannon Stewart	.15
1057	Chipper Jones	2.00
1058	J.D. Drew	.50
1059	Moises Alou	.15
1060	Mark Grace	.50
1061	Jose Vidro Expos	.15
1062	Vladimir Guerrero	1.00
1063	Matt Lawton	.15
1064	Ichiro Suzuki	2.50
1065	Edgar Martinez	.15

1066 John Olerud .50
1067 Jeff Cirillo .15
1068 Mike Lowell .15
1069 Mike Piazza 2.50
1070 Roberto Alomar .75
1071 Bobby Abreu .15
1072 Jason Kendall .15
1073 Brian Giles .50
1074 Rafael Palmeiro .50
1075 Ivan Rodriguez .50
1076 Alex Rodriguez 2.50
1077 Juan Gonzalez .75
1078 Nomar Garciaparra 2.00
1079 Manny Ramirez 1.00
1080 Sean Casey .25
1081 Barry Larkin .25
1082 Larry Walker .40
1083 Carlos Beltran .15
1084 Corey Koskie .15
1085 Magglio Ordonez .25
1086 Frank Thomas .75
1087 Kenny Lofton .25
1088 Derek Jeter 3.00
1089 Bernie Williams .50
1090 Jason Giambi 1.00
1091 Troy Glaus .50
1092 Jeff Bagwell .75
1093 Lance Berkman .50
1094 David Justice .25
1095 Eric Chavez .25
1096 Carlos Delgado .40
1097 Gary Sheffield .40
1098 Chipper Jones 1.50
1099 Andruw Jones .50
1100 Richie Sexson .40
1101 Albert Pujols 1.50
1102 Sammy Sosa 1.50
1103 Fred McGriff .40
1104 Greg Vaughn .15
1105 Matt Williams .25
1106 Luis Gonzalez .40
1107 Shawn Green .40
1108 Andres Galarraga .15
1109 Vladimir Guerrero .75
1110 Barry Bonds 2.00
1111 Rich Aurilia .15
1112 Ellis Burks .15
1113 Jim Thome .50
1114 Bret Boone .15
1115 Cliff Floyd .15
1116 Mike Piazza 2.00
1117 Jeromy Burnitz .15
1118 Phil Nevin .15
1119 Brian Giles .50
1120 Rafael Palmeiro .50
1121 Juan Gonzalez .75
1122 Alex Rodriguez 2.50
1123 Manny Ramirez .75
1124 Ken Griffey Jr. 2.00
1125 Larry Walker .40
1126 Todd Helton .50
1127 Mike Sweeney .15
1128 Frank Thomas .75
1129 Paul Konerko .40
1130 Jason Giambi .75
1131 Aaron Sele .15
1132 Roy Oswalt .40
1133 Wade Miller .15
1134 Tim Hudson .40
1135 Barry Zito .40
1136 Mark Mulder .25
1137 Greg Maddux 1.50
1138 Tom Glavine .40
1139 Ben Sheets .40
1140 Darryl Kile .15
1141 Matt Morris .15
1142 Kerry Wood .40
1143 Jon Lieber .15
1144 Juan Cruz .15
1145 Randy Johnson .75
1146 Curt Schilling .75
1147 Kevin Brown .15
1148 Javier Vazquez .15
1149 Russ Ortiz .15
1150 C.C. Sabathia .15
1151 Bartolo Colon .15
1152 Freddy Garcia .15
1153 Jamie Moyer .15
1154 Josh Beckett .50
1155 Brad Penny .15
1156 Al Leiter .40
1157 Brandon Duckworth .15
1158 Robert Person .15
1159 Kris Benson .15
1160 Chan Ho Park .15
1161 Pedro J. Martinez .75
1162 Mike Hampton .15
1163 Jeff Weaver .15
1164 Joe Mays .15
1165 Brad Radke .15
1166 Eric Milton .15
1167 Roger Clemens 1.00
1168 Mike Mussina .50
1169 Andy Pettite .50
1170 David Wells .15
1171 Ken Griffey Jr. 1.00
1172 Ichiro Suzuki 1.25
1173 Jason Giambi .50
1174 Alex Rodriguez 1.00
1175 Sammy Sosa .75
1176 Nomar Garciaparra 1.00
1177 Barry Bonds 1.00
1178 Mike Piazza 1.00
1179 Derek Jeter 1.50
1180 Randy Johnson .40
1181 Jeff Bagwell .40
1182 Albert Pujols .75

2002 Upper Deck 40-Man Gargantuan Gear

MT
Complete Set (25):
Common Player:
G-JB James Baldwin
G-BC Bruce Chen
G-JD Jermaine Dye
G-JG Juan Gonzalez
G-BG Ben Grieve
G-KG Ken Griffey Jr.
G-TH Tim Hudson
G-AJ Andruw Jones
G-JK Jeff Kent
G-ML Mike Lieberthal
G-TM Tino Martinez
G-JO John Olerud
G-MO Magglio Ordonez
G-MP Mike Piazza
G-JP Jorge Posada
G-AP Andy Pettite
G-BR Brad Radke
G-AR Alex Rodriguez
G-SR Scott Rolen
G-CS Curt Schilling
G-AS Aaron Sele
G-IS Ichiro Suzuki
G-BW Bernie Williams
G-DY Dmitri Young
G-TZ Todd Zeile

2002 Upper Deck 40-Man Looming Large Jerseys

MT
Common Player: 8.00
Production 250 sets
LBa Jeff Bagwell 15.00
LB Lance Berkman 15.00
JBu John Burkett 8.00
SC Sean Casey 10.00
TC Tony Clark 8.00
RC Roger Clemens 20.00
JC Jeff Cirillo 8.00
JD J.D. Drew 10.00
CE Carl Everett 8.00
CF Chuck Finley 10.00
TF Travis Fryman 8.00
JGi Jason Giambi 20.00
BG Brian Giles 10.00
TG Tom Glavine 10.00
JGo Juan Gonzalez 12.00
KG Ken Griffey Jr. 25.00
TH Todd Helton 15.00
RJ Randy Johnson 15.00
DK Darryl Kile 40.00
AL Al Leiter 8.00
ML Mike Lieberthal 10.00
KL Kenny Lofton 8.00
GM Greg Maddux 20.00
EM Edgar Martinez 10.00
FM Fred McGriff 10.00
MO Magglio Ordonez 8.00
HN Hideo Nomo 50.00
RP Rafael Palmeiro 10.00
JP Jorge Posada 15.00
SR Shane Reynolds 8.00
AR Alex Rodriguez 15.00
JR Jimmy Rollins 20.00
KS Kazuhiro Sasaki 15.00
CS Curt Schilling 12.00
JS J.T. Snow 8.00
SS Sammy Sosa 20.00
FT Frank Thomas 10.00
IV Ismael Valdes 8.00
RV Randy Velarde 8.00
RV Ron Villone 8.00
BZ Barry Zito 10.00

2002 Upper Deck 40-Man Lumber Yard

MT
Common Player: 10.00
Inserted 1:168
LY1 Chipper Jones 15.00
LY2 Joe DiMaggio 40.00
LY3 Albert Pujols 20.00
LY4 Mark McGwire 35.00
LY5 Sammy Sosa 15.00
LY6 Vladimir Guerrero 15.00
LY7 Barry Bonds 25.00
LY8 Mickey Mantle 50.00
LY9 Mike Piazza 20.00
LY10 Alex Rodriguez 15.00
LY11 Nomar Garciaparra 35.00
LY12 Ken Griffey Jr. 30.00
LY13 Frank Thomas 10.00
LY14 Jason Giambi 25.00
LY15 Derek Jeter 35.00
LY16 Luis Gonzalez 10.00
LY17 Jeff Bagwell 10.00
LY18 Todd Helton 10.00

2002 Upper Deck 40-Man Mark McGwire Flashbacks

MT
Complete Set (40): 120.00
Common McGwire: 4.00
Inserted 1:24
MM1 Mark McGwire 4.00
MM2 Mark McGwire 4.00
MM3 Mark McGwire 4.00
MM4 Mark McGwire 4.00
MM5 Mark McGwire 4.00
MM6 Mark McGwire 4.00
MM7 Mark McGwire 4.00
MM8 Mark McGwire 4.00
MM9 Mark McGwire 4.00
MM10 Mark McGwire 4.00
MM11 Mark McGwire 4.00
MM12 Mark McGwire 4.00
MM13 Mark McGwire 4.00
MM14 Mark McGwire 4.00
MM15 Mark McGwire 4.00
MM16 Mark McGwire 4.00
MM17 Mark McGwire 4.00
MM18 Mark McGwire 4.00
MM19 Mark McGwire 4.00
MM20 Mark McGwire 4.00
MM21 Mark McGwire 4.00
MM22 Mark McGwire 4.00
MM23 Mark McGwire 4.00
MM24 Mark McGwire 4.00
MM25 Mark McGwire 4.00
MM26 Mark McGwire 4.00
MM27 Mark McGwire 4.00
MM28 Mark McGwire 4.00
MM29 Mark McGwire 4.00
MM30 Mark McGwire 4.00
MM31 Mark McGwire 4.00
MM32 Mark McGwire 4.00
MM33 Mark McGwire 4.00
MM34 Mark McGwire 4.00
MM35 Mark McGwire 4.00
MM36 Mark McGwire 4.00
MM37 Mark McGwire 4.00
MM38 Mark McGwire 4.00
MM39 Mark McGwire 4.00
MM40 Mark McGwire 4.00

2002 Upper Deck 40-Man Super Swatches

MT
Common Player: 6.00
Production 250 sets
EA Edgardo Alfonzo 6.00
RA Rich Aurilia 8.00
JB Jeff Bagwell 15.00
SC Sean Casey 10.00
CD Carlos Delgado 8.00
RD Ray Durham 6.00
DE Darin Erstad 15.00
JG Juan Gonzalez 12.00
MG Mark Grace 12.00
SG Shawn Green 10.00
KG Ken Griffey Jr. 25.00
TG Tony Gwynn 25.00
MH Mike Hampton 6.00
TH Trevor Hoffman 10.00
CJ Chipper Jones 15.00
DJ David Justice 8.00
KL Kenny Lofton 6.00
JM Joe Mays 6.00
EM Eric Milton 10.00
MM Matt Morris 10.00
HN Hideo Nomo 50.00
JP Jorge Posada 15.00
MR Manny Ramirez 12.00
MR Mariano Rivera 12.00
AR Alex Rodriguez 15.00
IR Ivan Rodriguez 10.00
KS Kazuhiro Sasaki 15.00
CS Curt Schilling 10.00
BS Ben Sheets 8.00
SS Sammy Sosa 20.00
IS Ichiro Suzuki 65.00
MS Mike Sweeney 6.00
FT Frank Thomas 10.00
GV Greg Vaughn 6.00
JV Jose Vidro 6.00
DW David Wells 10.00
MY Masato Yoshii 12.00

2002 UD Authentics

MT
Complete Set (200): 80.00
Common Player: .25
Reversed Negatives: 1-2.5X
Inserted 1:9
Pack (5): 4.00
Box (18): 65.00
1 Brad Fullmer .25
2 Garret Anderson .25
3 Darin Erstad .40
4 Jarrod Washburn .25
5 Troy Glaus .75
6 Barry Zito .50

7 David Justice .40
8 Eric Chavez .40
9 Tim Hudson .50
10 Miguel Tejada .25
11 Jermaine Dye .25
12 Mark Mulder .40
13 Carlos Delgado .75
14 Jose Cruz Jr. .25
16 Shannon Stewart .25
17 Raul Mondesi .25
18 Tanyon Sturtze .25
19 Toby Hall .25
20 Greg Vaughn .25
21 Aubrey Huff .25
22 Ben Grieve .25
23 Brent Abernathy .25
24 Jim Thome .50
25 C.C. Sabathia .25
26 Matt Lawton .25
27 Omar Vizquel .25
28 Ellis Burks .25
29 Russ Branyan .25
30 Bartolo Colon .25
31 Ichiro Suzuki 4.00
32 John Olerud .50
33 Freddy Garcia .25
34 Mike Cameron .25
35 Jeff Cirillo .25
36 Kazuhiro Sasaki .40
37 Edgar Martinez .25
38 Bret Boone .25
39 Jeff Conine .25
40 Melvin Mora .25
41 Jason Johnson .25
42 Chris Richard .25
43 Tony Batista .25
44 Ivan Rodriguez .75
45 Gabe Kapler .25
46 Rafael Palmeiro .60
47 Alex Rodriguez 2.50
48 Juan Gonzalez 1.00
49 Carl Everett .25
50 Nomar Garciaparra 2.50
51 Trot Nixon .25
52 Manny Ramirez 1.00
53 Pedro J. Martinez 1.00
54 Johnny Damon .25
55 Shea Hillenbrand .25
56 Mike Sweeney .25
57 Mark Quinn .25
58 Joe Randa .25
59 Carlos Beltran .25
60 Chuck Knoblauch .25
61 Robert Fick .25
62 Jeff Weaver .25
63 Bobby Higginson .25
64 Dean Palmer .25
65 Dmitri Young .25
66 Corey Koskie .25
67 Doug Mientkiewicz .25
68 Joe Mays .25
69 Torii Hunter .25
70 Cristian Guzman .25
71 Jacque Jones .25
72 Magglio Ordonez .25
73 Paul Konerko .25
74 Carlos Lee .25
75 Mark Buehrle .25
76 Jose Canseco .50
77 Frank Thomas 1.00
78 Roger Clemens 1.50
79 Derek Jeter 4.00
80 Jason Giambi 1.00
81 Rondell White .25
82 Bernie Williams .75
83 Jorge Posada .50
84 Mike Mussina .75
85 Alfonso Soriano .50
86 Wade Miller .25
87 Jeff Bagwell 1.00
88 Craig Biggio .40
89 Roy Oswalt .50
90 Lance Berkman .75
91 Daryle Ward .25
92 Chipper Jones 2.00
93 Greg Maddux 2.00
94 Marcus Giles .25
95 Gary Sheffield .50
96 Tom Glavine .50
97 Andruw Jones .50
98 Rafael Furcal .25
99 Richie Sexson .40
100 Ben Sheets .50
101 Jose Hernandez .25
102 Geoff Jenkins .40
103 Jeffrey Hammonds .25
104 Edgar Renteria .25
105 Matt Morris .40
106 Tino Martinez .25
107 Jim Edmonds .40
108 Albert Pujols 2.00
109 J.D. Drew .50
110 Fernando Vina .25
111 Darryl Kile .25
112 Sammy Sosa 2.00
113 Fred McGriff .50
114 Kerry Wood .75
115 Moises Alou .40
116 Jon Lieber .25
117 Mark Grace .50
118 Randy Johnson 1.00
119 Curt Schilling .50
120 Luis Gonzalez .75
121 Steve Finley .25
122 Matt Williams .50
123 Shawn Green .50
124 Kevin Brown .40
125 Adrian Beltre .50
126 Paul LoDuca .25
127 Hideo Nomo .50
128 Brian Jordan .25
129 Vladimir Guerrero 1.00
130 Javier Vazquez .25
131 Jose Vidro .25
132 Orlando Cabrera .25
133 Jeff Kent .25
134 Rich Aurilla .25
135 Russ Ortiz .25
136 Barry Bonds 2.00
137 Preston Wilson .25
138 Ryan Dempster .25
139 Cliff Floyd .25
140 Josh Beckett .50
141 Mike Lowell .25
142 Mike Piazza 3.00
143 Roberto Alomar .75
144 Al Leiter .40
145 Edgardo Alfonzo .25
146 Roger Cedeno .25
147 Jeromy Burnitz .25
148 Phil Nevin .25
149 Mark Kotsay .25
150 Ryan Klesko .25
151 Trevor Hoffman .25
152 Bobby Abreu .25
153 Scott Rolen .75
154 Jimmy Rollins .25
155 Robert Person .25
156 Pat Burrell .50
157 Randy Wolf .25
158 Brian Giles .50
159 Aramis Ramirez .25
160 Kris Benson .25
161 Jason Kendall .25
162 Ken Griffey Jr. 3.00
163 Sean Casey .50
164 Adam Dunn .75
165 Barry Larkin .50
166 Todd Helton 1.00
167 Mike Hampton .25
168 Larry Walker .50
169 Juan Pierre .25
170 Juan Uribe .25
171 *So Taguchi* 6.00
172 *Brendan Donnelly* .75
173 *Chris Baker* .50
174 *John Ennis* 3.00
175 *Francis Beltran* .75
176 Danny Wright .50
177 *Brandon Backe* .75
178 *Mark Corey* 1.00
179 *Kazuhisa Ishii* 10.00
180 *Ron Calloway* .50
181 *Kevin Frederick* .75
182 *Jaime Cerda* .75
183 *Doug Devore* .50
184 *Brandon Puffer* 3.00
185 *Andy Pratt* 1.00
186 *Adrian Burnside* 1.00
187 *Josh Hancock* .75
188 *Jorge Nunez* .50
189 *Tyler Yates* .75
190 *Kyle Kane* .75
191 *Jose Valverde* .50
192 Matt Thornton .50
193 *Ben Howard* 5.00
194 *Reed Johnson* .75
195 *Rene Reyes* .50
196 *Jeremy Ward* .50
197 *Steve Bechler* .50
198 *Cam Esslinger* .50
199 *Michael Crudale* .50
200 *Todd Donovan* 1.00

2002 UD Authentics Retro UD Jerseys

		MT
Common Player:		8.00
Inserted 1:16		
Golds:		1-2X
Production 275 sets		
Reverse Neg.:		1-2X
Production 350 sets		
JB	Jeff Bagwell	15.00
KB	Kevin Brown	8.00
EC	Eric Chavez	8.00
RC	Roger Clemens/SP	25.00
CD	Carlos Delgado	8.00
JD	J.D. Drew	10.00
JE	Jim Edmonds	8.00
DE	Darin Erstad	8.00
RF	Rafael Furcal	10.00
JG	Jason Giambi	15.00
TG	Tom Glavine	10.00
LG	Luis Gonzalez	8.00
KG	Ken Griffey Jr.	25.00
TH	Todd Helton	12.00
RJ	Randy Johnson	12.00
AJ	Andruw Jones	8.00
CJ	Chipper Jones	15.00
GM	Greg Maddux	15.00
TM	Tino Martinez/SP/25	
MP	Mike Piazza	20.00
MR	Manny Ramirez	12.00
AR	Alex Rodriguez	20.00
IR	Ivan Rodriguez	12.00
SR	Scott Rolen/SP/25	
SS	Sammy Sosa/SP	20.00
MS	Mike Sweeney	8.00
FT	Frank Thomas	12.00
BW	Bernie Williams	10.00
BZ	Barry Zito	8.00

2002 UD Authentics Retro UD Star Rookie Jerseys

		MT
Common Player:		8.00
Inserted 1:16		
Golds:		1-2X
Production 275 sets		
CB	Craig Biggio	8.00
PB	Pat Burrell	10.00
BG	Brian Giles	12.00
JG	Juan Gonzalez	12.00
LG	Luis Gonzalez	8.00
SG	Shawn Green	8.00
KG	Ken Griffey Jr.	25.00
RJ	Randy Johnson	12.00
CJ	Chipper Jones	15.00
DJ	David Justice	8.00
GK	Gabe Kapler/SP	
RK	Ryan Klesko	8.00
KL	Kenny Lofton	8.00
PM	Pedro J. Martinez	15.00
HN	Hideo Nomo	20.00
JO	John Olerud	8.00
MO	Magglio Ordonez	12.00
RP	Robert Person	8.00
AP	Albert Pujols	20.00
MR	Manny Ramirez/SP	15.00
AR	Alex Rodriguez	20.00
IR	Ivan Rodriguez	10.00
KS	Kazuhiro Sasaki	12.00
GS	Gary Sheffield	8.00
SS	Sammy Sosa/SP	20.00
I	Ichiro Suzuki	50.00
JT	Jim Thome	12.00
LW	Larry Walker	8.00

2002 UD Authentics Signed Retro UD Star Rookie Jerseys

	MT
Complete Set (3):	
Common Player:	
SSR-KG Ken Griffey Jr.	
SSR-AR Alex Rodriguez	
SSR-JT Jim Thome	

2002 UD Authentics Signed UD Heroes of Baseball

		MT
Random Inserts:		
G	Ken Griffey Jr/185	140.00
R	Alex Rodriguez/185	90.00
I	Ichiro Suzuki/125	400.00

2002 UD Authentics Stars of '89 Jersey Cards

		MT
Common Player:		8.00
Inserted 1:16		
RA	Roberto Alomar	10.00
KB	Kevin Brown	8.00
EB	Ellis Burks	8.00
JC	Jose Canseco	10.00
RC	Roger Clemens	15.00
DC	David Cone	8.00
AG	Andres Galarraga	8.00
TG	Tom Glavine	10.00
JG	Juan Gonzalez	12.00
MG	Mark Grace	8.00
KG	Ken Griffey Jr.	25.00
RH	Rickey Henderson	20.00
RJ	Randy Johnson	12.00
DJ	David Justice	8.00
BL	Barry Larkin/SP	20.00
AL	Al Leiter	8.00
GM	Greg Maddux	15.00
EM	Edgar Martinez	8.00
FM	Fred McGriff	8.00
JO	John Olerud	8.00
PO	Paul O'Neill	8.00
RP	Rafael Palmeiro	8.00
CS	Curt Schilling	8.00
GS	Gary Sheffield	8.00
SS	Sammy Sosa	20.00
RV	Robin Ventura	8.00
LW	Larry Walker	8.00
MW	Matt Williams	8.00

2002 UD Authentics UD Heroes of Baseball

	MT
Complete Set (30):	220.00
Ichiro:	12.00
Griffey Jr.:	10.00
Alex Rodriguez:	8.00
Production 1,989 sets	
HB-I1 Ichiro Suzuki	12.00
HB-I2 Ichiro Suzuki	12.00
HB-I3 Ichiro Suzuki	12.00
HB-I4 Ichiro Suzuki	12.00
HB-I5 Ichiro Suzuki	12.00
HB-I6 Ichiro Suzuki	12.00
HB-I7 Ichiro Suzuki	12.00
HB-I8 Ichiro Suzuki	12.00
HB-I9 Ichiro Suzuki	12.00
HB-I10 Ichiro Suzuki	12.00
HB-G1 Ken Griffey Jr.	10.00
HB-G2 Ken Griffey Jr.	10.00
HB-G3 Ken Griffey Jr.	10.00
HB-G4 Ken Griffey Jr.	10.00
HB-G5 Ken Griffey Jr.	10.00
HB-G6 Ken Griffey Jr.	10.00
HB-G7 Ken Griffey Jr.	10.00
HB-G8 Ken Griffey Jr.	10.00
HB-G9 Ken Griffey Jr.	10.00
HB-G10 Ken Griffey Jr.	10.00
HB-R1 Alex Rodriguez	8.00
HB-R2 Alex Rodriguez	8.00
HB-R3 Alex Rodriguez	8.00
HB-R4 Alex Rodriguez	8.00
HB-R5 Alex Rodriguez	8.00
HB-R6 Alex Rodriguez	8.00
HB-R7 Alex Rodriguez	8.00
HB-R8 Alex Rodriguez	8.00
HB-R9 Alex Rodriguez	8.00
HB-R10 Alex Rodriguez	8.00

2002 UD Authentics 1989 Flashbacks

		MT
Complete Set (12):		30.00
Common Player:		1.50
Production 4,225 sets		
F1	Ken Griffey Jr.	8.00
F2	Gary Sheffield	1.50
F3	Randy Johnson	3.00
F4	Roger Clemens	4.00
F5	Greg Maddux	5.00
F6	Mark Grace	2.00
F7	Barry Bonds	5.00
F8	Roberto Alomar	2.00
F9	Sammy Sosa	5.00
F10	Rafael Palmeiro	2.00
F11	Edgar Martinez	1.50
F12	Jose Canseco	2.00

2003 Upper Deck

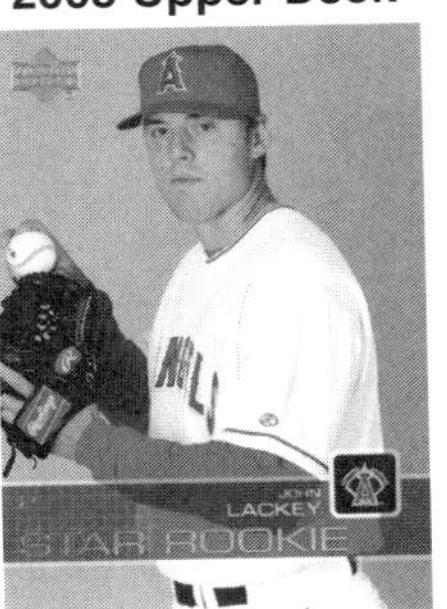

		MT
Complete Set (270):		40.00
Common Player:		.15
Pack (8):		3.00
Box (24):		60.00
1	John Lackey	.15
2	Alex Cintron	.15
3	Jose Leon	.15
4	Bobby Hill	.15
5	Brandon Larson	.15
6	Raul Gonzalez	.15
7	Ben Broussard	.15
8	Earl Snyder	.15
9	Ramon Santiago	.15
10	Jason Lane	.15
11	Keith Ginter	.15
12	Kirk Saarloos	.15
13	Juan Brito	.15
14	Runelvys Hernandez	.15
15	Shawn Sedlacek	.15
16	Jayson Durocher	.15
17	Kevin Frederick	.15
18	Zach Day	.15
20	Marcus Thames	.15
21	Esteban German	.15
22	Brett Myers	.15
23	Oliver Perez	.15
24	Dennis Tankersley	.15
25	Julius Matos	.15
26	Jake Peavy	.15
27	Eric Cyr	.15
28	Mike Crudale	.15
29	Josh Pearce	.15
30	Carl Crawford	.15
31	Tim Salmon	.25
32	Troy Glaus	.60
33	Adam Kennedy	.15
34	David Eckstein	.15
35	Bengie Molina	.15
36	Jarrod Washburn	.15
37	Ramon Ortiz	.15
38	Eric Chavez	.40
39	Miguel Tejada	.50
40	Adam Piatt	.15
41	Jermaine Dye	.15
42	Olmedo Saenz	.15
43	Tim Hudson	.25
44	Barry Zito	.25
45	Billy Koch	.15
46	Shannon Stewart	.15
47	Kelvim Escobar	.15
48	Jose Cruz Jr.	.15
49	Vernon Wells	.15
50	Roy Halladay	.15
51	Esteban Loaiza	.15
52	Eric Hinske	.15
53	Steve Cox	.15
54	Brent Abernathy	.15
55	Ben Grieve	.15
56	Aubrey Huff	.15
57	Jared Sandberg	.15
58	Paul Wilson	.15
59	Tanyon Sturtze	.15
60	Jim Thome	.60
61	Omar Vizquel	.25
62	C.C. Sabathia	.15
63	Chris Magruder	.15
64	Ricky Gutierrez	.15
65	Einar Diaz	.15
66	Danys Baez	.15
67	Ichiro Suzuki	2.00
68	Ruben Sierra	.15
69	Carlos Guillen	.15
70	Mark McLemore	.15
71	Dan Wilson	.15
72	Jamie Moyer	.15
73	Joel Pineiro	.15
74	Edgar Martinez	.15
75	Tony Batista	.15
76	Jay Gibbons	.15
77	Chris Singleton	.15
78	Melvin Mora	.15
79	Geronimo Gil	.15
80	Rodrigo Lopez	.15
81	Jorge Julio	.15
82	Rafael Palmeiro	.50
83	Juan Gonzalez	.50
84	Mike Young	.15
85	Hideki Irabu	.15
86	Chan Ho Park	.15
87	Kevin Mench	.15
88	Doug Davis	.15
89	Pedro Martinez	.75
90	Shea Hillenbrand	.15
91	Derek Lowe	.15
92	Jason Varitek	.15
93	Tony Clark	.15
94	John Burkett	.15
95	Frank Castillo	.15
96	Nomar Garciaparra	2.00
97	Rickey Henderson	.40
98	Mike Sweeney	.15
99	Carlos Febles	.15
100	Mark Quinn	.15
101	Raul Ibanez	.15
102	A.J. Hinch	.15
103	Paul Byrd	.15
104	Chuck Knoblauch	.15
105	Dmitri Young	.15
106	Randall Simon	.15
107	Brandon Inge	.15
108	Damion Easley	.15
109	Carlos Pena	.15
110	George Lombard	.15
111	Juan Acevedo	.15
112	Torii Hunter	.15
113	Doug Mientkiewicz	.15
114	David Ortiz	.15
115	Eric Milton	.15
116	Eddie Guardado	.15
117	Cristian Guzman	.15
118	Corey Koskie	.15
119	Magglio Ordonez	.25
120	Mark Buehrle	.15
121	Todd Ritchie	.15
122	Jose Valentin	.15
123	Paul Konerko	.25
124	Carlos Lee	.15
125	Jon Garland	.15
126	Jason Giambi	1.25
127	Derek Jeter	2.50
128	Roger Clemens	1.00
129	Raul Mondesi	.15
130	Jorge Posada	.25
131	Rondell White	.15
132	Robin Ventura	.25
133	Mike Mussina	.50
134	Jeff Bagwell	.60
135	Craig Biggio	.25
136	Morgan Ensberg	.15
137	Richard Hidalgo	.15
138	Brad Ausmus	.15
139	Roy Oswalt	.25
140	Carlos Hernandez	.15
141	Shane Reynolds	.15
142	Gary Sheffield	.25
143	Andruw Jones	.50
144	Tom Glavine	.40
145	Rafael Furcal	.15
146	Javy Lopez	.15
147	Vinny Castilla	.15
148	Marcus Giles	.15
149	Kevin Millwood	.15
150	Jason Marquis	.15
151	Ruben Quevedo	.15
152	Ben Sheets	.15
153	Geoff Jenkins	.15
154	Jose Hernandez	.15
155	Glendon Rusch	.15
156	Jeffrey Hammonds	.15
157	Alex Sanchez	.15
158	Jim Edmonds	.25
159	Tino Martinez	.25
160	Albert Pujols	.75
161	Eli Marrero	.15
162	Woody Williams	.15
163	Fernando Vina	.15
164	Jason Isringhausen	.15
165	Jason Simontacchi	.15
166	Kerry Robinson	.15
167	Sammy Sosa	1.25
168	Juan Cruz	.15
169	Fred McGriff	.25
170	Antonio Alfonseca	.15
171	Jon Lieber	.15
172	Mark Prior	.40
173	Moises Alou	.15
174	Matt Clement	.15
175	Mark Bellhorn	.15
176	Randy Johnson	.75
177	Luis Gonzalez	.25
178	Tony Womack	.15
179	Mark Grace	.30
180	Junior Spivey	.15
181	Byung-Hyun Kim	.15
182	Danny Bautista	.15
183	Brian Anderson	.15
184	Shawn Green	.25
185	Brian Jordan	.15
186	Eric Karros	.15
187	Andy Ashby	.15
188	Cesar Izturis	.15
189	Dave Roberts	.15
190	Eric Gagne	.15
191	Kazuhisa Ishii	.15
192	Adrian Beltre	.15
193	Vladimir Guerrero	.75
194	Tony Armas Jr.	.15
195	Bartolo Colon	.15
196	Troy O'Leary	.15
197	Tomokazu Ohka	.15
198	Brad Wilkerson	.15
199	Orlando Cabrera	.15
200	Barry Bonds	2.00
201	David Bell	.15
202	Tsuyoshi Shinjo	.15
203	Benito Santiago	.15
204	Livan Hernandez	.15
205	Jason Schmidt	.15
206	Kirk Reuter	.15
207	Ramon E. Martinez	.15
208	Mike Lowell	.15
209	Luis Castillo	.15
210	Derrek Lee	.15
211	Andy Fox	.15
212	Eric Owens	.15
213	Charles Johnson	.15
214	Brad Penny	.15
215	A.J. Burnett	.15
216	Edgardo Alfonzo	.15
217	Roberto Alomar	.50
218	Rey Ordonez	.15
219	Al Leiter	.15
220	Roger Cedeno	.15
221	Timoniel Perez	.15
222	Jeromy Burnitz	.15
223	Pedro Astacio	.15
224	Joe McEwing	.15
225	Ryan Klesko	.15
226	Ramon Vazquez	.15
227	Mark Kotsay	.15
228	Bubba Trammell	.15
229	Wiki Gonzalez	.15
230	Trevor Hoffman	.15
231	Ron Gant	.15
232	Bobby Abreu	.15
233	Marlon Anderson	.15
234	Jeremy Giambi	.15
235	Jimmy Rollins	.15
236	Mike Lieberthal	.15
237	Vicente Padilla	.15
238	Randy Wolf	.15
239	Pokey Reese	.15
240	Brian Giles	.25
241	Jack Wilson	.15
242	Mike Williams	.15
243	Kip Wells	.15
244	Robert Mackowiak	.15
245	Craig Wilson	.15
246	Adam Dunn	.60
247	Sean Casey	.15
248	Todd Walker	.15
249	Corky Miller	.15
250	Ryan Dempster	.15
251	Reggie Taylor	.15
252	Aaron Boone	.15
253	Larry Walker	.30
254	Jose Ortiz	.15
255	Todd Zeile	.15
256	Bobby Estalella	.15
257	Juan Pierre	.15
258	Terry Shumpert	.15
259	Mike Hampton	.15
260	Denny Stark	.15
261	Shawn Green	.25
262	Derek Lowe	.15

263	Barry Bonds	1.00
264	Mike Cameron	.15
265	Luis Castillo	.15
266	Vladimir Guerrero	.40
267	Jason Giambi	.60
268	Eric Gagne	.15
269	Magglio Ordonez	.20
270	Jim Thome	.30

2003 Upper Deck Big League Breakdown

		MT
Complete Set (15):		25.00
Common Player:		.50
Inserted 1:8		
BL1	Troy Glaus	1.00
BL2	Miguel Tejada	.75
BL3	Chipper Jones	2.50
BL4	Torii Hunter	.50
BL5	Nomar Garciaparra	3.00
BL6	Sammy Sosa	2.50
BL7	Todd Helton	1.00
BL8	Lance Berkman	.75
BL9	Shawn Green	.75
BL10	Vladimir Guerrero	1.50
BL11	Jason Giambi	2.50
BL12	Derek Jeter	5.00
BL13	Barry Bonds	4.00
BL14	Ichiro Suzuki	3.00
BL15	Alex Rodriguez	4.00

2003 Upper Deck Game Swatches Hobby

		MT
Common Player:		5.00
Inserted 1:72		
SB	Sean Burroughs/SP	8.00
CD	Carlos Delgado/SP	8.00
GM	Greg Maddux	12.00
MM	Mike Mussina	10.00
MO	Magglio Ordonez	5.00
CP	Carlos Pena	5.00
MP	Mike Piazza/SP	15.00
AR	Alex Rodriguez	15.00
CC	C.C. Sabathia	5.00
CS	Curt Schilling/100	10.00
SS	Sammy Sosa	15.00
BW	Bernie Williams	10.00

2003 Upper Deck Game Jersey Autograph

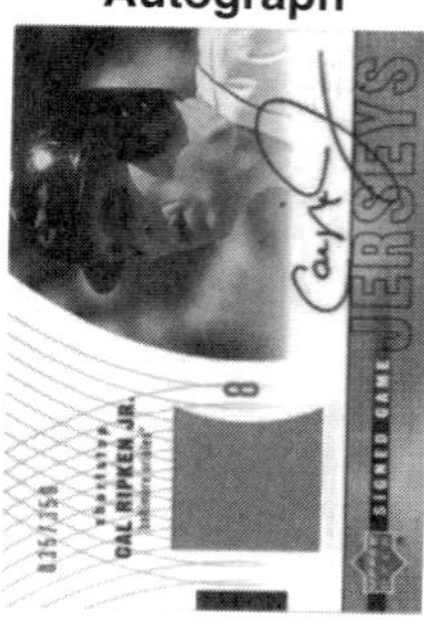

		MT
Golds:		1.5-2X
Production 25 or 75		
RC	Roger Clemens/350	90.00
JG	Jason Giambi/350	65.00
KG	Ken Griffey Jr/350	110.00
MM	Mark McGwire/150	350.00
CR	Cal Ripken Jr/350	140.00
AR	Alex Rodriguez/350	120.00
SS	Sammy Sosa/150	180.00

2003 Upper Deck Lineup Time Jerseys

		MT
Common Player:		6.00
Inserted 1:96		
RC	Roger Clemens/SP	15.00
CD	Carlos Delgado	8.00
JD	J.D. Drew	6.00
SG	Shawn Green	8.00
TH	Todd Helton	8.00
RJ	Randy Johnson/SP	12.00
GM	Greg Maddux	12.00
IS	Ichiro Suzuki	45.00
JT	Jim Thome	12.00
BW	Bernie Williams	10.00

2003 Upper Deck Mark of Greatness

		MT
400 Total cards produced		
MoG	Mark McGwire	350.00
MoG	Mark McGwire/Gold/25	
MoG	Mark McGwire/Silver/70	400.00

2003 Upper Deck Mid-Summer Stars

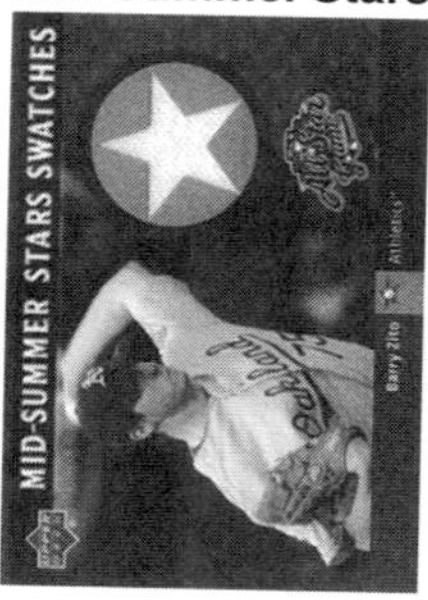

		MT
Common Player:		5.00
Inserted 1:72		
RC	Roger Clemens	12.00
CD	Carlos Delgado	8.00
JE	Jim Edmonds	8.00
DE	Darin Erstad	8.00
FG	Freddy Garcia	5.00
TG	Tom Glavine	8.00
JG	Juan Gonzalez	8.00
SG	Shawn Green/SP	8.00
RJ	Randy Johnson	10.00
AJ	Andruw Jones	6.00
EM	Edgar Martinez	10.00
HN	Hideo Nomo	30.00
MP	Mike Piazza	15.00
MR	Manny Ramirez	8.00
AR	Alex Rodriguez	15.00
KS	Kazuhiro Sasaki	8.00
CS	Curt Schilling	10.00
SS	Sammy Sosa	15.00
IS	Ichiro Suzuki/SP	40.00
FT	Frank Thomas	8.00
RV	Robin Ventura	8.00
DW	David Wells	5.00
BZ	Barry Zito	10.00

2003 Upper Deck NL All-Star Swatch

		MT
Common Player:		5.00
Inserted 1:72		
SC	Sean Casey	5.00
CF	Cliff Floyd	5.00
TGl	Tom Glavine	8.00
TGw	Tony Gwynn	12.00
MH	Mike Hampton	5.00
TH	Trevor Hoffman	5.00
RK	Ryan Klesko	5.00
AL	Al Leiter	5.00
FM	Fred McGriff	5.00
MM	Matt Morris	8.00
CS	Curt Schilling	8.00
JV	Jose Vidro	5.00

2003 Upper Deck Patch Logo

MT

Quantity produced listed
PL-JBJeff Bagwell/41
PLE-RCRoger Clemens/34
PLE-JDJoe DiMaggio/9
PLE-JGJason Giambi/34
PLE-KGKen Griffey Jr./50
PL-THTodd Helton/41
PL-KIKazuhisa Ishii/54
PL-RJRandy Johnson/50
PL-CJChipper Jones/52
PL-GMGreg Maddux/50
PLE-MMMickey Mantle/10
PLE-MGMark McGwire/43
PLE-MPMike Piazza/61
PLE-ARAlex Rodriguez/34
PLE-SSSammy Sosa/60
PLE-ISIchiro Suzuki/46
PL-FTFrank Thomas/52
PL-BWBernie Williams/42

2003 Upper Deck Patch Number

MT

Common Player:
Quantity produced listed
PNE-JGJason Giambi/68
PNE-KGKen Griffey Jr./97
PN-THTodd Helton/27
PN-KIKazuhisa Ishii/63
PN-RJRandy Johnson/90
PN-CJChipper Jones/44
PNE-MGMark McGwire/60
PNE-ARAlex Rodriguez/56
PNE-SSSammy Sosa/100
PN-FTFrank Thomas/91
PN-BWBernie Williams/66

2003 Upper Deck Patch Stripes

MT

Common Player:
Quantity produced listed
PS-JBJeff Bagwell/73
PSE-JGJason Giambi/66
PSE-KGKen Griffey Jr./63
PS-THTodd Helton/43
PS-KIKazuhisa Ishii/58
PS-RJRandy Johnson/58
PS-CJChipper Jones/58
PSE-MGMark McGwire/63
PSE-ARAlex Rodriguez/63
PSE-SSSammy Sosa/63
PSE-ISIchiro Suzuki/63
PS-FTFrank Thomas/58
PS-BWBernie Williams/58

2003 Upper Deck Slammin' Sammy Tribute Jersey

		MT
384 Total produced		
SST	Sammy Sosa	175.00
SST	Sammy Sosa/Gold/25	290.00
SST	Sammy Sosa/Silver/66	240.00

2003 Upper Deck Star-Spangled Swatches

		MT
Common Player:		5.00
Inserted 1:72		
MA	Michael Aubrey	8.00
KB	Kyle Bakker	15.00
CC	Chad Cordero	5.00
SC	Shane Costa	12.00
AH	Aaron Hill	5.00
PH	Philip Humber	6.00
CJ	Conor Jackson	8.00
GJ	Grant Johnson	5.00
EP	Eric Patterson	8.00
DP	Dustin Pedroia	15.00
LP	Landon Powell	12.00
CQ	Carlos Quentin	5.00
KS	Kyle Sleeth	12.00
HS	Huston Street	12.00
BS	Brad Sullivan	5.00
RW	Rickie Weeks	8.00

2003 Upper Deck Superstar Slam Jerseys

		MT
Common Player:		4.00
Inserted 1:48		
JB	Jeff Bagwell	8.00
JG	Jason Giambi	10.00
JGo	Juan Gonzalez	6.00
LG	Luis Gonzalez	4.00
KG	Ken Griffey Jr.	15.00
CJ	Chipper Jones	10.00
MP	Mike Piazza	12.00
AR	Alex Rodriguez	15.00
SS	Sammy Sosa	15.00
FT	Frank Thomas	8.00

2003 Upper Deck The Chase for 755

		MT
Complete Set (15):		18.00
Common Player:		.75
Inserted 1:8		
C1	Troy Glaus	1.00
C2	Andruw Jones	1.00
C3	Manny Ramirez	1.25
C4	Sammy Sosa	2.50
C5	Ken Griffey Jr.	3.00
C6	Adam Dunn	1.25
C7	Todd Helton	1.00
C8	Lance Berkman	.75
C9	Jeff Bagwell	1.25
C10	Shawn Green	.75
C11	Vladimir Guerrero	1.50
C12	Barry Bonds	4.00
C13	Alex Rodriguez	4.00
C14	Juan Gonzalez	1.00
C15	Carlos Delgado	.75

2003 Upper Deck Triple Game Jersey

		MT
Quantity produced listed		
Golds:		1.5-2X
Production 50, 25 or 10		
ARZ	Randy Johnson, Curt Schilling, Luis Gonzalez/150	40.00
CIN	Ken Griffey Jr., Sean Casey, Adam Dunn/150	45.00
HOU	Jeff Bagwell, Lance Berkman, Craig Biggio/150	40.00
TEX	Rafael Palmeiro, Alex Rodriguez, Juan Gonzalez/150	
ATL	Chipper Jones, Greg Maddux, Gary Sheffield/75	
CHC	Sammy Sosa, Moises Alou, Kerry Wood/75	65.00
NYM	Mike Piazza, Roberto Alomar, Mo Vaughn/75	
SEA	Ichiro Suzuki, Freddy Garcia, Bret Boone/75	80.00
NYY	Roger Clemens, Jason Giambi, Bernie Williams/75	

Z

1995 Zenith

At the top of the pyramid of Pinnacle's baseball card lines for 1995 was Zenith, a super-premium brand utilizing all-foil metallized printing technology on double-thick 24-point cardboard stock to emphasize the quality look and feel. Six-card packs carried a retail price of $3.99. Two styles comprise the 150-card base set. The 110 veteran player cards are curiously arranged in alphabetical order according to the player's first names (with the exception of card #48, a special Japanese-language card of Hideo Nomo). These cards have a color player action photo on a black and gold background that is a view of a pyramid from its pinnacle. One the horizontal back, a portrait photo of the player in a partly-cloudy blue sky overlooks a playing field which offers his hit location preferences versus righty and lefty pitching. A scoreboard has his 1994 and career stats. The Pinnacle anti-counterfeiting optical-variable bar is in the lower-right corner. The rookie cards which comprise the final 40 cards in the set have a color photo at center with a gold-tone version of the same picture in the background. A large gold "ROOKIE" is vertically at right. Backs are similar to those on the verterans' cards except they have a scouting report in place of the hit-location chart.

		MT
Complete Set (150):		20.00
Common Player:		.15
Pack (6):		1.50
Wax Box (24):		24.00
1	Albert Belle	.35
2	Alex Fernandez	.15
3	Andy Benes	.15
4	Barry Larkin	.20
5	Barry Bonds	1.50
6	Ben McDonald	.15
7	Bernard Gilkey	.15
8	Billy Ashley	.15
9	Bobby Bonilla	.15
10	Bret Saberhagen	.15
11	Brian Jordan	.15
12	Cal Ripken Jr.	2.50
13	Carlos Baerga	.15
14	Carlos Delgado	.35
15	Cecil Fielder	.15
16	Chili Davis	.15
17	Chuck Knoblauch	.15
18	Craig Biggio	.35
19	Danny Tartabull	.15
20	Dante Bichette	.15
21	Darren Daulton	.15
22	Dave Justice	.35
23	Dave Winfield	.60
24	David Cone	.15
25	Dean Palmer	.15
26	Deion Sanders	.20
27	Dennis Eckersley	.15
28	Derek Bell	.15
29	Don Mattingly	1.50
30	Edgar Martinez	.15
31	Eric Karros	.15
32	Erik Hanson	.15
33	Frank Thomas	1.50
34	Fred McGriff	.15
35	Gary Sheffield	.35
36	Gary Gaetti	.15
37	Greg Maddux	1.25
38	Gregg Jefferies	.15
39	Ivan Rodriguez	.75
40	Kenny Rogers	.15
41	J.T. Snow	.15
42	Hal Morris	.15
43	Eddie Murray (3,000 hit)	.45
44	Javier Lopez	.15
45	Jay Bell	.15
46	Jeff Conine	.15
47	Jeff Bagwell	1.00
48	*Hideo Nomo*	1.25
49	Jeff Kent	.15
50	Jeff King	.15
51	Jim Thome	.15
52	Jimmy Key	.15
53	Joe Carter	.15
54	John Valentin	.15
55	John Olerud	.15
56	Jose Canseco	.60
57	Jose Rijo	.15
58	Jose Offerman	.15
59	Juan Gonzalez	1.00
60	Ken Caminiti	.15
61	Ken Griffey Jr.	2.00
62	Kenny Lofton	.15
63	Kevin Appier	.15
64	Kevin Seitzer	.15
65	Kirby Puckett	1.25
66	Kirk Gibson	.15
67	Larry Walker	.35
68	Lenny Dykstra	.15
69	Manny Ramirez	1.00
70	Mark Grace	.30
71	Mark McGwire	2.50
72	Marquis Grissom	.15
73	Jim Edmonds	.15
74	Matt Williams	.30
75	Mike Mussina	.60
76	Mike Piazza	1.75
77	Mo Vaughn	.40
78	Moises Alou	.25
79	Ozzie Smith	1.25
80	Paul O'Neill	.15
81	Paul Molitor	.75
82	Rafael Palmeiro	.35
83	Randy Johnson	.65
84	Raul Mondesi	.25
85	Ray Lankford	.15
86	Reggie Sanders	.15
87	Rickey Henderson	.65
88	Rico Brogna	.15
89	Roberto Alomar	.50
90	Robin Ventura	.15
91	Roger Clemens	1.25
92	Ron Gant	.25
93	Rondell White	.25
94	Royce Clayton	.15
95	Ruben Sierra	.15
96	Rusty Greer	.15
97	Ryan Klesko	.15
98	Sammy Sosa	1.50
99	Shawon Dunston	.15
100	Steve Ontiveros	.15
101	Tim Naehring	.15
102	Tim Salmon	.30
103	Tino Martinez	.15
104	Tony Gwynn	1.25
105	Travis Fryman	.15
106	Vinny Castilla	.15
107	Wade Boggs	.60
108	Wally Joyner	.15
109	Wil Cordero	.15
110	Will Clark	.30
111	Chipper Jones	1.75
112	C.J. Nitkowski	.15
113	Curtis Goodwin	.15
114	Tim Unroe	.15
115	Vaughn Eshelman	.15
116	Marty Cordova	.15
117	Dustin Hermanson	.15
118	Rich Becker	.15
119	Ray Durham	.15
120	Shane Andrews	.15
121	Scott Ruffcorn	.15
122	*Mark Grudzielanek*	.45
123	James Baldwin	.15
124	*Carlos Perez*	.15
125	Julian Tavarez	.15
126	Joe Vitiello	.15
127	Jason Bates	.15
128	Edgardo Alfonzo	.15
129	Juan Acevedo	.15
130	Bill Pulsipher	.15
131	*Bob Higginson*	1.00
132	Russ Davis	.15
133	Charles Johnson	.15
134	Derek Jeter	1.75
135	Phil Nevin	.25
136	LaTroy Hawkins	.15
137	Brian Hunter	.15
138	Roberto Petagine	.15
139	Jim Pittsley	.15
140	Garret Anderon	.15
141	Ugueth Urbina	.15
142	Antonio Osuna	.15
143	Michael Tucker	.15
144	Benji Gil	.15
145	Jon Nunnally	.15
146	Alex Rodriguez	2.00
147	Todd Hollandworth	.15
148	Alex Gonzalez	.20
149	*Hideo Nomo*	1.25
150	Shawn Green	.45
---	Numeric checklist	.15
---	Chase program checklist	.15

1995 Zenith All-Star Salute

The most common of the Zenith inserts is a series of 18 All-Star Salute cards. Fronts have action photos printed on foil. Backs have the 1995 All-Star Game logo and a large photo of the player taken at the game, with a few words about his All-Star history. The Salute cards are seeded at the rate of one per six packs, on average.

		MT
Complete Set (19):		18.00
Common Player:		.50
1	Cal Ripken Jr.	3.00
2	Frank Thomas	1.25
3	Mike Piazza	2.00
4	Kirby Puckett	1.50
5	Manny Ramirez	1.00
6	Tony Gwynn	1.50
7	Hideo Nomo	.75
8	Matt Williams	.50
9	Randy Johnson	.75
10	Raul Mondesi	.60
11	Albert Belle	.60
12	Ivan Rodriguez	.75
13	Barry Bonds	1.25
14	Carlos Baerga	.50
15	Ken Griffey Jr.	2.50
16	Jeff Conine	.50
17	Frank Thomas	1.25
18	Cal Ripken Jr., Barry Bonds	2.00

1995 Zenith Rookie Roll Call

Dufex foil printing technology on both front and back is featured on this insert set. Fronts have a large and a small player photo on a green background dominated by a large star. Backs have another photo on a green and gold background. A prestigious black and gold box at left in the horizontally formatted design has a few good words about the prospect. Stated odds of finding a Rookie Roll Call card are one per 24 packs, on average.

		MT
Complete Set (18):		40.00
Common Player:		1.00
1	Alex Rodriguez	9.00
2	Derek Jeter	8.00
3	Chipper Jones	8.00
4	Shawn Green	2.50
5	Todd Hollandsworth	1.00
6	Bill Pulsipher	1.00
7	Hideo Nomo	2.50
8	Ray Durham	1.00
9	Curtis Goodwin	1.00
10	Brian Hunter	1.00
11	Julian Tavarez	1.00
12	Marty Cordova	1.00
13	Michael Tucker	1.00
14	Edgardo Alfonzo	1.50
15	LaTroy Hawkins	1.00
16	Carlos Perez	1.00
17	Charles Johnson	1.50
18	Benji Gil	1.00

1995 Zenith Z-Team

The scarcest of the Zenith insert cards are those of 18 "living legends" profiled in the Z-Team series. Found at an average rate of only one per 72 packs, the cards are printed in technology Pinnacle calls 3-D Dufex.

		MT
Complete Set (18):		130.00
Common Player:		2.50
1	Cal Ripken Jr.	20.00
2	Ken Griffey Jr.	17.50
3	Frank Thomas	13.50
4	Matt Williams	5.00
5	Mike Piazza	15.00
6	Barry Bonds	13.50
7	Raul Mondesi	2.50
8	Greg Maddux	12.00
9	Jeff Bagwell	10.00
10	Manny Ramirez	10.00
11	Larry Walker	5.00
12	Tony Gwynn	12.00
13	Will Clark	5.00
14	Albert Belle	4.00
15	Kenny Lofton	2.50
16	Rafael Palmeiro	5.00
17	Don Mattingly	13.50
18	Carlos Baerga	2.50

1996 Zenith

Pinnacle's 1996 Zenith set has 150 cards in the regular set, including 30 Rookies, 20 Honor roll and two checklist cards. Each card in the set has a parallel Artist's Proof version (seeded one per every 35 packs). Insert sets include Z Team, Mozaics and two versions of Diamond Club. Normal Dufex versions of Diamond Club appear one every 24 packs; parallel versions, which have an actual diamond chip incorporated into the card design, were seeded one per every 350 packs.

		MT
Complete Set (150):		30.00
Common Player:		.15
Common Artist's Proofs:		2.00
Star Artist's Proofs:		12X
Pack (6):		2.50
Wax Box (24):		40.00
1	Ken Griffey Jr.	2.50
2	Ozzie Smith	1.50
3	Greg Maddux	1.50
4	Rondell White	.30
5	Mark McGwire	3.00
6	Jim Thome	.15
7	Ivan Rodriguez	1.00
8	Marc Newfield	.15
9	Travis Fryman	.15
10	Fred McGriff	.15
11	Shawn Green	.45
12	Mike Piazza	2.00
13	Dante Bichette	.15
14	Tino Martinez	.15
15	Sterling Hitchcock	.15
16	Ryne Sandberg	1.00
17	Rico Brogna	.15
18	Roberto Alomar	.65
19	Barry Larkin	.25
20	Bernie Williams	.35
21	Gary Sheffield	.35
22	Frank Thomas	1.75
23	Gregg Jefferies	.15
24	Jeff Bagwell	1.25
25	Marty Cordova	.15
26	Jim Edmonds	.15
27	Jay Bell	.15
28	Ben McDonald	.15
29	Barry Bonds	1.75
30	Mo Vaughn	.60
31	Johnny Damon	.25
32	Dean Palmer	.15
33	Ismael Valdes	.15
34	Manny Ramirez	1.00
35	Edgar Martinez	.15
36	Cecil Fielder	.15
37	Ryan Klesko	.15
38	Ray Lankford	.15
39	Tim Salmon	.30
40	Joe Carter	.15
41	Jason Isringhausen	.15
42	Rickey Henderson	.75
43	Lenny Dykstra	.15
44	Andre Dawson	.40
45	Paul O'Neill	.15
46	Ray Durham	.15
47	Raul Mondesi	.25
48	Jay Buhner	.15
49	Eddie Murray	.65
50	Henry Rodriguez	.15
51	Hal Morris	.15
52	Mike Mussina	.75
53	Wally Joyner	.15
54	Will Clark	.40
55	Chipper Jones	2.00
56	Brian Jordan	.15
57	Larry Walker	.30
58	Wade Boggs	.75
59	Melvin Nieves	.15
60	Charles Johnson	.15
61	Juan Gonzalez	1.00
62	Carlos Delgado	.35
63	Reggie Sanders	.15
64	Brian Hunter	.15
65	Edgardo Alfonzo	.15
66	Kenny Lofton	.15
67	Paul Molitor	.75
68	Mike Bordick	.15
69	Garret Anderson	.15
70	Orlando Merced	.15
71	Craig Biggio	.25
72	Chuck Knoblauch	.15
73	Mark Grace	.40
74	Jack McDowell	.15
75	Randy Johnson	.75
76	Cal Ripken Jr.	3.00
77	Matt Williams	.40
78	Benji Gil	.15
79	Moises Alou	.30
80	Robin Ventura	.15
81	Greg Vaughn	.15
82	Carlos Baerga	.15
83	Roger Clemens	1.50
84	Hideo Nomo	.60
85	Pedro Martinez	1.00
86	John Valentin	.15
87	Andres Galarraga	.15
88	Andy Pettitte	.35
89	Derek Bell	.15
90	Kirby Puckett	1.50
91	Tony Gwynn	1.50
92	Brady Anderson	.15
93	Derek Jeter	2.00
94	Michael Tucker	.15
95	Albert Belle	.35
96	David Cone	.15
97	J.T. Snow	.15
98	Tom Glavine	.25
99	Alex Rodriguez	2.50
100	Sammy Sosa	1.75
101	Karim Garcia	.25
102	Alan Benes	.15
103	Chad Mottola	.15
104	*Robin Jennings*	.15
105	Bob Abreu	.25
106	Tony Clark	.15
107	George Arias	.15
108	Jermaine Dye	.15
109	Jeff Suppan	.15
110	*Ralph Milliard*	.15
111	Ruben Rivera	.15
112	Billy Wagner	.15
113	Jason Kendall	.15
114	*Mike Grace*	.15
115	Edgar Renteria	.15
116	Jason Schmidt	.15
117	Paul Wilson	.15
118	Rey Ordonez	.15
119	*Rocky Coppinger*	.15
120	*Wilton Guerrero*	.30
121	Brooks Kieschnick	.15
122	Raul Casanova	.15
123	Alex Ochoa	.15
124	Chan Ho Park	.30
125	John Wasdin	.15
126	Eric Owens	.15
127	Justin Thompson	.15
128	Chris Snopek	.15
129	Terrell Wade	.15
130	*Darin Erstad*	3.00
131	Albert Belle (Honor Roll)	.20
132	Cal Ripken Jr. (Honor Roll)	1.50
133	Frank Thomas (Honor Roll)	.90
134	Greg Maddux (Honor Roll)	.75
135	Ken Griffey Jr. (Honor Roll)	1.25
136	Mo Vaughn (Honor Roll)	.30
137	Chipper Jones (Honor Roll)	1.00
138	Mike Piazza (Honor Roll)	1.00
139	Ryan Klesko (Honor Roll)	.15
140	Hideo Nomo (Honor Roll)	.25
141	Roberto Alomar (Honor Roll)	.30
142	Manny Ramirez (Honor Roll)	.50
143	Gary Sheffield (Honor Roll)	.15
144	Barry Bonds (Honor Roll)	.90
145	Matt Williams (Honor Roll)	.15
146	Jim Edmonds (Honor Roll)	.15
147	Derek Jeter (Honor Roll)	1.50
148	Sammy Sosa (Honor Roll)	.90
149	Kirby Puckett (Honor Roll)	.75
150	Tony Gwynn (Honor Roll)	.75

1996 Zenith Artist's Proofs

Each card in the '96 Zenith base set can also be found in a specially marked Artist's Proof version. The AP cards were found on average of once per 35 packs.

		MT
Common Player:		2.00
Stars:		12X

(See 1996 Zenith for checklist and base card values.)

1996 Zenith Diamond Club

Twenty different players are featured on these two 1996 Pinnacle Zenith insert cards. Normal Dufex versions are inserted one per every 24 packs. Parallel versions of these cards, containing an actual diamond chip incorporated into the design, were seeded one per every 350 packs.

		MT
Complete Set (20):		60.00
Common Player:		1.50
Diamond Versions:		12X
1	Albert Belle	2.50
2	Mo Vaughn	2.50
3	Ken Griffey Jr.	7.50
4	Mike Piazza	6.00
5	Cal Ripken Jr.	9.00
6	Jermaine Dye	1.50
7	Jeff Bagwell	3.50
8	Frank Thomas	4.50
9	Alex Rodriguez	7.50
10	Ryan Klesko	1.50
11	Roberto Alomar	3.00
12	Sammy Sosa	4.50
13	Matt Williams	2.00
14	Gary Sheffield	2.00
15	Ruben Rivera	1.50
16	Darin Erstad	3.00
17	Randy Johnson	3.00
18	Greg Maddux	4.00
19	Karim Garcia	1.50
20	Chipper Jones	6.00

1996 Zenith Mozaics

Each of these 1996 Pinnacle Zenith cards contains multiple player images for the team represented on the card. The cards were inserted one per every 10 packs.

		MT
Complete Set (25):		60.00
Common Player:		.75
1	Greg Maddux, Chipper Jones, Ryan Klesko	5.00
2	Juan Gonzalez, Will Clark, Ivan Rodriguez	3.00
3	Frank Thomas, Robin Ventura, Ray Durham	3.50
4	Matt Williams, Barry Bonds, Osvaldo Fern	
5	Randy Johnson, Alex Rodriguez	9.00
6	Sammy Sosa, Ryne Sandberg, Mark Grace	6.00
7	Jim Edmonds, Tim Salmon, Garret Anderson	1.00
8	Cal Ripken Jr., Roberto Alomar, Mike Mussina	7.50
9	Mo Vaughn, Roger Clemens, John Valentin	4.50
10	Barry Larkin, Reggie Sanders, Hal Morris	1.00
11	Ray Lankford, Brian Jordan, Ozzie Smith	3.00
12	Dante Bichette, Larry Walker, Andres Galarraga	1.00
13	Mike Piazza, Hideo Nomo, Raul Mondesi	6.00
14	Ben McDonald, Greg Vaughn, Kevin Seitzer	.75
15	Joe Carter, Carlos Delgado, Alex Gonzalez	.75
16	Gary Sheffield, Charles Johnson, Jeff Conine	1.00
17	Rondell White, Moises Alou, Henry Rodriguez	.75
18	Albert Belle, Manny Ramirez, Carlos Baerga	3.00
19	Kirby Puckett, Paul Molitor, Chuck Knoblauch	3.00
20	Tony Gwynn, Rickey Henderson, Wally Joyner	4.50
21	Mark McGwire, Mike Bordick, Scott Brosius	7.50
22	Paul O'Neill, Bernie Williams, Wade Boggs	1.50
23	Jay Bell, Orlando Merced, Jason Kendall	.75
24	Rico Brogna, Paul Wilson, Jason Isringhausen	.75
25	Jeff Bagwell, Craig Biggio, Derek Bell	3.00

1996 Zenith Z-Team

Pinnacle's 1996 Zenith baseball continues the Z Team insert concept with a new clear plastic treatment that is micro-etched for a see-through design that allows light to shine through etched highlights and a green baseball field background. The 18 cards were seeded one per every 72 packs.

		MT
Complete Set (18):		100.00
Common Player:		2.00
1	Ken Griffey Jr.	12.50
2	Albert Belle	3.50
3	Cal Ripken Jr.	15.00
4	Frank Thomas	9.00
5	Greg Maddux	8.00
6	Mo Vaughn	3.00
7	Chipper Jones	10.00
8	Mike Piazza	10.00
9	Ryan Klesko	2.00
10	Hideo Nomo	5.00
11	Roberto Alomar	5.00
12	Manny Ramirez	6.00
13	Gary Sheffield	2.50
14	Barry Bonds	9.00
15	Matt Williams	2.00
16	Jim Edmonds	2.00
17	Kirby Puckett	8.00
18	Sammy Sosa	9.00

1997 Zenith

This set combines standard size trading cards with cards in an 8" x 10" format. The standard size set consists of 60 cards. Card fronts feature full-bleed photos and the word "Zenith", but no reference to the player's name or team is found on the fronts. Backs have another player photo, a hit location chart and 1996/career stats. There are four inserts in the set, all of which are printed on the larger size format - 8" x 10", 8" x 10" Dufex, 8" x 10" V-2, and Z-Team. Each sale unit contained one pack of five standard-size cards and two larger size cards for a suggested retail price of $9.99.

		MT
Complete Set (50):		24.00
Common Player:		.15
Pack 5 (cards) 2 (8x10):		3.00
Wax Box (12):		35.00
1	Frank Thomas	1.25
2	Tony Gwynn	1.00
3	Jeff Bagwell	.75
4	Paul Molitor	.65
5	Roberto Alomar	.60
6	Mike Piazza	1.50
7	Albert Belle	.35
8	Greg Maddux	1.00
9	Barry Larkin	.25
10	Tony Clark	.15
11	Larry Walker	.35
12	Chipper Jones	1.50
13	Juan Gonzalez	.75
14	Barry Bonds	1.25
15	Ivan Rodriguez	.60
16	Sammy Sosa	1.25
17	Derek Jeter	1.50
18	Hideo Nomo	.45
19	Roger Clemens	1.00
20	Ken Griffey Jr.	1.75
21	Andy Pettitte	.35
22	Alex Rodriguez	1.75
23	Tino Martinez	.15
24	Bernie Williams	.35
25	Ken Caminiti	.15
26	John Smoltz	.25
27	Javier Lopez	.15
28	Mark McGwire	2.00
29	Gary Sheffield	.35
30	David Justice	.35
30p	David Justice (marked SAMPLE)	1.50
31	Randy Johnson	.65
32	Chuck Knoblauch	.15
33	Mike Mussina	.55
34	Deion Sanders	.25
35	Cal Ripken Jr.	2.00
36	Darin Erstad	.50
37	Kenny Lofton	.15
38	Jay Buhner	.15
39	Brady Anderson	.15
40	Edgar Martinez	.15
41	Mo Vaughn	.45
42	Ryne Sandberg	.75
43	Andruw Jones	.75
44	Nomar Garciaparra	1.25
45	*Hideki Irabu*	.45
46	Wilton Guerrero	.15
47	*Jose Cruz Jr.*	.45
48	Vladimir Guerrero	.75
49	Scott Rolen	.60
50	Jose Guillen	.15

1997 Zenith V-2

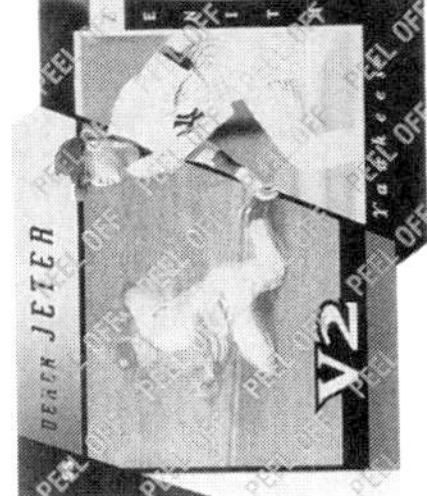

This eight-card die-cut insert utilizes motion technology as well as foil printing to create a very high-tech 8" x 10" card. Cards were inserted 1:47 packs.

		MT
Complete Set (8):		60.00
Common Player:		6.00
1	Ken Griffey Jr.	12.00
2	Andruw Jones	6.00
3	Frank Thomas	7.50
4	Mike Piazza	9.00
5	Alex Rodriguez	12.00
6	Cal Ripken Jr.	15.00
7	Derek Jeter	9.00
8	Vladimir Guerrero	6.00

1997 Zenith Z-Team

This nine-card 8" x 10" insert is printed on a mirror gold mylar foil stock with each card sequentially numbered to 1,000.

		MT
Complete Set (9):		95.00
Common Player:		5.00
1	Ken Griffey Jr.	17.50
2	Larry Walker	5.00
3	Frank Thomas	12.00
4	Alex Rodriguez	17.50
5	Mike Piazza	15.00
6	Cal Ripken Jr.	20.00
7	Derek Jeter	15.00
8	Andruw Jones	7.50
9	Roger Clemens	10.00

1997 Zenith 8x10 and 8x10 Dufex

This 24-card insert takes select cards from the standard set and blows them up to an 8" x 10" format. Cards were inserted one per pack. A Dufex version of each 8" x 10" insert card was also available at a rate of one per pack (except in packs which contained either a Z-Team or V-2 card).

		MT
Complete Set (24):		35.00
Common Player:		.75
Dufex versions:		1X
1	Frank Thomas	2.50
2	Tony Gwynn	2.00
3	Jeff Bagwell	1.50
4	Ken Griffey Jr.	3.50
5	Mike Piazza	3.00
6	Greg Maddux	2.00
7	Ken Caminiti	.75
8	Albert Belle	.75
9	Ivan Rodriguez	1.00
10	Sammy Sosa	2.50
11	Mark McGwire	4.00
12	Roger Clemens	2.00
13	Alex Rodriguez	3.50
14	Chipper Jones	3.00
15	Juan Gonzalez	1.50
16	Barry Bonds	2.50
17	Derek Jeter	3.00
18	Hideo Nomo	1.50
19	Cal Ripken Jr.	4.00
20	Hideki Irabu	.75
21	Andruw Jones	1.50
22	Nomar Garciaparra	2.50
23	Vladimir Guerrero	1.50
24	Scott Rolen	1.00

1998 Zenith

Zenith Baseball was part of Pinnacle's "Dare to Tear" program. Sold in three-card packs, the set consisted of 5"-x-7" cards, each with a standard-size card inside. Collectors had to decide whether to keep the large cards or tear them open to get the smaller card inside. Eighty 5"-x-7" cards and 100 regular cards made up the set. The regular, or Z2, cards were paralleled twice - Z-Silver (1:7) and Z-Gold (numbered to 100). The large cards also had two parallels - Impulse (1:7) and Gold Impulse (numbered to 100). Inserts include Raising the Bar, Rookie Thrills, Epix, 5x7 Z Team, Z Team, Gold Z Team, Rookie Z Team and Gold Rookie Z Team.

		MT
Complete Set (100):		36.00
Common Player:		.15
Silvers:		2X
Inserted 1:7		
Pack (3):		4.00
Wax Box (18):		60.00
1	Larry Walker	.35
2	Ken Griffey Jr.	2.50
3	Cal Ripken Jr.	3.00
4	Sammy Sosa	2.00
5	Andruw Jones	1.25
6	Frank Thomas	2.00
7	Tony Gwynn	1.75
8	Rafael Palmeiro	.35
9	Tim Salmon	.35
10	Randy Johnson	1.00
11	Juan Gonzalez	1.25
12	Greg Maddux	1.75
13	Vladimir Guerrero	1.25
14	Mike Piazza	2.25
15	Andres Galarraga	.15
16	Alex Rodriguez	2.50
17	Derek Jeter	2.25
18	Nomar Garciaparra	2.00
19	Ivan Rodriguez	1.00
20	Chipper Jones	2.25
21	Barry Larkin	.25
22	Mo Vaughn	.50
23	Albert Belle	.35
24	Scott Rolen	1.00
25	Sandy Alomar Jr.	.15
26	Roberto Alomar	.60
27	Andy Pettitte	.35
28	Chuck Knoblauch	.15
29	Jeff Bagwell	1.25
30	Mike Mussina	.60
31	Fred McGriff	.15
32	Roger Clemens	1.75
33	Rusty Greer	.15
34	Edgar Martinez	.15
35	Paul Molitor	1.00
36	Mark Grace	.35
37	Darin Erstad	.45
38	Kenny Lofton	.15
39	Tom Glavine	.25
40	Javier Lopez	.15
41	Will Clark	.35
42	Tino Martinez	.15
43	Raul Mondesi	.25
44	Brady Anderson	.15
45	Chan Ho Park	.25
46	Jason Giambi	.45
47	Manny Ramirez	1.25
48	Jay Buhner	.15
49	Dante Bichette	.15
50	Jose Cruz Jr.	.25
51	Charles Johnson	.15
52	Bernard Gilkey	.15
53	Johnny Damon	.25
54	David Justice	.35
55	Justin Thompson	.15
56	Bobby Higginson	.25
57	Todd Hundley	.15
58	Gary Sheffield	.35
59	Barry Bonds	2.00
60	Mark McGwire	3.00
61	John Smoltz	.25
62	Tony Clark	.15
63	Brian Jordan	.15
64	Jason Kendall	.15
65	Mariano Rivera	.25
66	Pedro Martinez	1.00
67	Jim Thome	.15
68	Neifi Perez	.15
69	Kevin Brown	.25
70	Hideo Nomo	.55
71	Craig Biggio	.25
72	Bernie Williams	.35
73	Jose Guillen	.15
74	Ken Caminiti	.15
75	Livan Hernandez	.15
76	Ray Lankford	.15
77	Jim Edmonds	.15
78	Matt Williams	.35
79	Mark Kotsay	.15
80	Moises Alou	.25
81	Antone Williamson	.15
82	Jaret Wright	.15
83	Jacob Cruz	.15
84	Abraham Nunez	.15
85	Raul Ibanez	.15
86	Miguel Tejada	.25
87	Derek Lee	.15
88	Juan Encarnacion	.15
89	Todd Helton	.45
90	Travis Lee	.25
91	Ben Grieve	.35
92	Ryan McGuire	.15
93	Richard Hidalgo	.25
94	Paul Konerko	.25
95	Shannon Stewart	.15
96	Homer Bush	.15
97	Lou Collier	.15
98	Jeff Abbott	.15
99	Brett Tomko	.15
100	Fernando Tatis	.15

1998 Zenith Silver

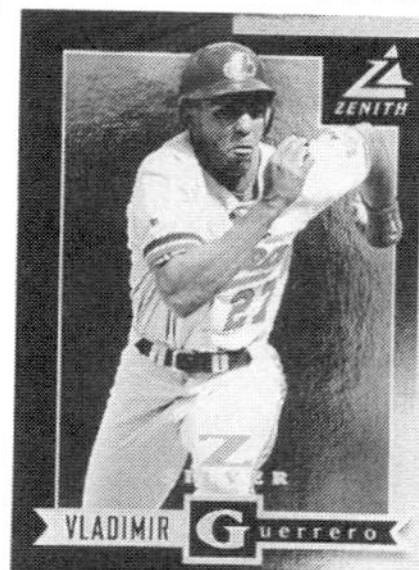

This parallel set reprinted all 100 standard sized cards in Zenith on silver foilboard, with a "Z-Silver" logo across the bottom center. Z-Silvers were inserted one per seven packs.

	MT
Common Player:	1.00
Stars/RCs:	2X
Inserted 1:7	

(See 1998 Zenith for checklist and base card values.)

1998 Zenith Z-Gold

	MT
Common Player:	5.00
Stars/Rookies 20X	
Production 100 sets	

(See 1998 Zenith for checklist and base card values.)

1998 Zenith Epix

Epix is a cross-brand insert. The set honors the top Plays, Games, Seasons and Moments in the careers of top baseball players. Epix consisted of 24 cards in Zenith, inserted 1:11. The cards have orange, purple and emerald versions.

		MT
Complete Set (24):		130.00
Common Card:		2.00
Purples:		1X
Emeralds:		2X
1	Ken Griffey Jr. S	12.00
2	Juan Gonzalez S	6.00
3	Jeff Bagwell S	6.00
4	Ivan Rodriguez S	4.00
5	Nomar Garciaparra S	8.50
6	Ryne Sandberg S	5.00
7	Frank Thomas M	8.50
8	Derek Jeter M	10.00
9	Tony Gwynn M	7.50
10	Albert Belle M	3.00
11	Scott Rolen M	4.00
12	Barry Larkin M	2.00
13	Alex Rodriguez P	12.00
14	Cal Ripken Jr. P	15.00
15	Chipper Jones P	10.00
16	Roger Clemens P	7.50
17	Mo Vaughn P	2.50
18	Mark McGwire P	15.00
19	Mike Piazza G	10.00
20	Andruw Jones G	6.00
21	Greg Maddux G	7.50
22	Barry Bonds G	8.50
23	Paul Molitor G	2.50
24	Eddie Murray G	2.00

1998 Zenith Raising the Bar

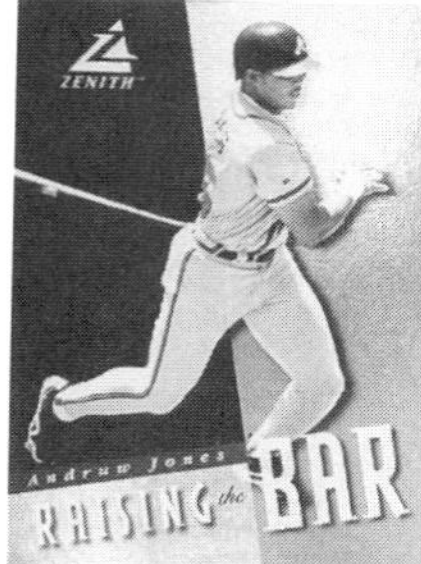

Raising the Bar is a 15-card insert seeded 1:25. The set features players who have set high standards for other players to follow.

		MT
Complete Set (15):		80.00
Common Player:		3.00
Inserted 1:25		
1	Ken Griffey Jr.	10.00
2	Frank Thomas	6.50
3	Alex Rodriguez	10.00
4	Tony Gwynn	5.00
5	Mike Piazza	7.50
6	Ivan Rodriguez	3.00
7	Cal Ripken Jr.	12.50
8	Greg Maddux	5.00
9	Hideo Nomo	3.00
10	Mark McGwire	12.50
11	Juan Gonzalez	3.50
12	Andruw Jones	3.50
13	Jeff Bagwell	3.50
14	Chipper Jones	7.50
15	Nomar Garciaparra	6.50

1998 Zenith Rookie Thrills

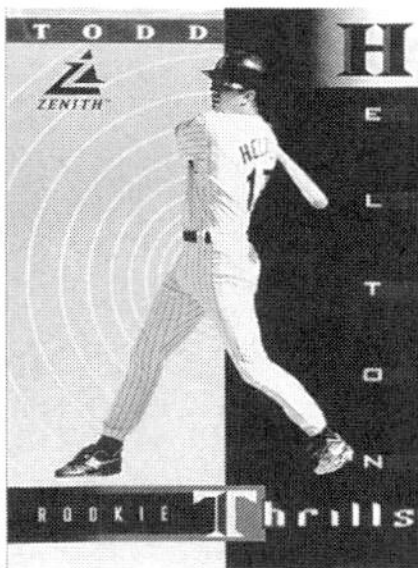

Rookie Thrills is a 15-card insert seeded 1:25. The set features many of the top rookies of 1998 in action photos printed on a silver-foil background. Backs have a few words about the player's career to that point.

		MT
Complete Set (15):		30.00
Common Player:		2.00
Inserted 1:25		
1	Travis Lee	2.50
2	Juan Encarnacion	2.00
3	Derrek Lee	2.00
4	Raul Ibanez	2.00
5	Ryan McGuire	2.00
6	Todd Helton	4.00
7	Jacob Cruz	2.00
8	Abraham Nunez	2.50
9	Paul Konerko	2.50
10	Ben Grieve	3.00
11	Jeff Abbott	2.00
12	Richard Hidalgo	2.50
13	Jaret Wright	2.00
14	Lou Collier	2.00
15	Miguel Tejada	3.00

1998 Zenith Z-Team

The Z Team insert was created in 5x7 and standard-size versions, each inserted at a 1:35 pack rate. The nine Rookie Z Team cards were seeded 1:58 and gold versions of both were found 1:175.

		MT
Complete Set (18):		100.00
Common Player:		3.00
Golds:		2X
Inserted 1:175		
1	Frank Thomas	7.50
2	Ken Griffey Jr.	12.50
3	Mike Piazza	10.00
4	Cal Ripken Jr.	15.00
5	Alex Rodriguez	12.50
6	Greg Maddux	6.00
7	Derek Jeter	10.00
8	Chipper Jones	10.00
9	Roger Clemens	6.00
10	Ben Grieve	3.00
11	Derrek Lee	3.00
12	Jose Cruz Jr.	3.00
13	Nomar Garciaparra	7.50
14	Travis Lee	3.00
15	Todd Helton	4.50
16	Paul Konerko	3.00
17	Miguel Tejada	3.00
18	Scott Rolen	4.50

1998 Zenith Z-Team 5x7

The 5x7 Z Team insert is a nine-card set seeded one per 35 packs.

		MT
Complete Set (9):		75.00
Common Player:		7.50
Inserted 1:35		
1	Frank Thomas	8.50
2	Ken Griffey Jr.	12.50
3	Mike Piazza	10.00
4	Cal Ripken Jr.	15.00
5	Alex Rodriguez	12.50
6	Greg Maddux	7.50
7	Derek Jeter	10.00
8	Chipper Jones	10.00
9	Roger Clemens	7.50

1998 Zenith 5x7

The 80 Zenith 5x7 cards all contained a regular-size card. Collectors could tear open the 5x7 to get at the smaller card inside. The set has two parallels: 5x7 Impulse (1:7) and 5x7 Gold Impulse (1:43).

		MT
Complete Set (80):		37.00
Common Player:		.25
Impulse Silvers:		2X
Inserted 1:7		
1	Nomar Garciaparra	2.25
2	Andres Galarraga	.25
3	Greg Maddux	2.00
4	Frank Thomas	2.25
5	Mark McGwire	4.00
6	Rafael Palmeiro	.40
7	John Smoltz	.35
8	Jeff Bagwell	1.50
9	Andruw Jones	1.50
10	Rusty Greer	.25
11	Paul Molitor	1.00
12	Bernie Williams	.40
13	Kenny Lofton	.25
14	Alex Rodriguez	3.00
15	Derek Jeter	2.50
15s	Derek Jeter ("SAMPLE" overprint on back)	1.75
16	Scott Rolen	1.00
17	Albert Belle	.50
18	Mo Vaughn	.75
19	Chipper Jones	2.50
20	Chuck Knoblauch	.25
21	Mike Piazza	2.50
22	Tony Gwynn	2.00
22s	Tony Gwynn ("SAMPLE" overprint on back)	1.25
23	Juan Gonzalez	1.50
24	Andy Pettitte	.40
25	Tim Salmon	.40
26	Brady Anderson	.25
27	Mike Mussina	.75
28	Edgar Martinez	.25
29	Jose Guillen	.25
30	Hideo Nomo	.75
31	Jim Thome	.25
32	Mark Grace	.40
33	Darin Erstad	.50
34	Bobby Higginson	.35
35	Ivan Rodriguez	1.00
36	Todd Hundley	.25
37	Sandy Alomar Jr.	.25
38	Gary Sheffield	.40
39	David Justice	.40
40	Ken Griffey Jr.	3.00
40s	Ken Griffey Jr. ("SAMPLE" overprint on back)	1.50
41	Vladimir Guerrero	1.50
42	Larry Walker	.40
43	Barry Bonds	2.25
44	Randy Johnson	1.00
45	Roger Clemens	2.00
46	Raul Mondesi	.35
47	Tino Martinez	.25
48	Jason Giambi	.60
49	Matt Williams	.40
50	Cal Ripken Jr.	4.00
51	Barry Larkin	.35
52	Jim Edmonds	.25
53	Ken Caminiti	.25
54	Sammy Sosa	2.25
55	Tony Clark	.25
56	Manny Ramirez	1.50
57	Bernard Gilkey	.25
58	Jose Cruz Jr.	.35
59	Brian Jordan	.25
60	Kevin Brown	.35
61	Craig Biggio	.35
62	Javier Lopez	.25
63	Jay Buhner	.25
64	Roberto Alomar	.75
65	Justin Thompson	.25
66	Todd Helton	.65
67	Travis Lee	.35
68	Paul Konerko	.35
69	Jaret Wright	.25
70	Ben Grieve	.50
71	Juan Encarnacion	.25
72	Ryan McGuire	.25
73	Derrek Lee	.25
74	Abraham Nunez	.25
75	Richard Hidalgo	.25
76	Miguel Tejada	.35
77	Jacob Cruz	.25
78	Homer Bush	.25
79	Jeff Abbott	.25
80	Lou Collier	.25
	Checklist	.10

1998 Zenith 5x7 Impulse Silver

These silver parallels reprinted each of the 80 cards in the 5" x 7" set. Cards were called Impulse and carried that logo on the front and were inserted one per seven packs. Since these cards contained other cards inside them, they are condition sensitive and only worth full price if left in mint condition and not cut open.

	MT
Common Player:	2.00
Stars/RCs:	2X
Inserted 1:7	

(See 1998 Zenith 5x7 for checklist and base card values.)

Late Additions

2002 Bowman Draft Picks & Prospects

	MT
Complete Set (165):	40.00
Common Player:	.15
Common RC:	.25
Pack 4 Bowman + 2 Chrome:	4.00
Box (24):	90.00
BDP1 *Clint Everts*	.50
BDP2 *Fred Lewis*	.40
BDP3 *Jonathan Broxton*	.15
BDP4 *Jason Anderson*	.15
BDP5 *Mike Eusebio*	.15
BDP6 *Zack Greinke*	.60
BDP7 *Joe Blanton*	.15
BDP8 *Sergio Santos*	1.00
BDP9 *Jason Cooper*	.40
BDP10 *Delwyn Young*	.50
BDP11 *Jeremy Hermida*	1.00
BDP12 *Dan Ortmeyer*	.40
BDP13 *Kevin Jepsen*	.15
BDP14 *Russ Adams*	.50
BDP15 *Mike Nixon*	.40
BDP16 *Nick Swisher*	.50
BDP17 *Cole Hamels*	.50
BDP18 *Brian Dopirak*	.75
BDP19 *James Loney*	2.00
BDP20 *Denard Span*	.50
BDP21 *Billy Petrick*	.15
BDP22 *Jared Doyle*	.15
BDP23 *Jeff Francoeur*	3.00
BDP24 *Nick Bourgeois*	.15
BDP25 *Matt Cain*	.15
BDP26 *John McCurdy*	.40
BDP27 *Mark Kiger*	.15
BDP28 *Bill Murphy*	.15
BDP29 *Matt Craig*	.15
BDP30 *Mike Megrew*	.15
BDP31 *Ben Crockett*	.15
BDP32 *Luke Hagerty*	.50
BDP33 *Matt Whitney*	1.00
BDP34 *Dan Meyer*	.15
BDP35 *Jeremy Brown*	.40
BDP36 *Doug Johnson*	.15
BDP37 *Steve Obenchain*	.15
BDP38 *Matt Clanton*	.40
BDP39 *Mark Teahen*	.15
BDP40 *Thomas Carrow*	.15
BDP41 *Micah Schilling*	.50
BDP42 *Blair Johnson*	.15
BDP43 *Jason Pridie*	1.00
BDP44 *Joey Votto*	.50
BDP45 *Taber Lee*	.15
BDP46 *Adam Peterson*	.15
BDP47 *Adam Donachie*	.15
BDP48 *Josh Murray*	.15
BDP49 *Brent Clevlen*	.50
BDP50 *Chad Pleiness*	.40
BDP51 *Zach Hammes*	.50
BDP52 *Chris Snyder*	.15
BDP53 Chris Smith	.15
BDP54 *Justin Maureau*	.15
BDP55 *David Bush*	.15
BDP56 *Tim Gilhooly*	.15
BDP57 *Blair Barbier*	.15
BDP58 *Zach Segovia*	.40
BDP59 *Jeremy Reed*	.50
BDP60 *Matt Pender*	.15
BDP61 *Eric Thomas*	.15
BDP62 *Justin Jones*	.75
BDP63 *Brian Slocum*	.40
BDP64 *Larry Broadway*	.40
BDP65 *Bo Flowers*	.15
BDP66 *Scott White*	.75
BDP67 *Steve Stanley*	.15
BDP68 *Alex Merricks*	.15
BDP69 *Josh Womack*	.15
BDP70 *Dave Jensen*	.15
BDP71 *Curtis Granderson*	.50
BDP72 *Pat Osborn*	.40
BDP73 *Nic Carter*	.15
BDP74 *Mitch Talbot*	.15
BDP75 *Don Murphy*	.15
BDP76 *Val Majewski*	.40
BDP77 *Javy Rodriguez*	.15
BDP78 *Fernando Pacheco*	.40
BDP79 *Steve Russell*	.15
BDP80 *Jon Slack*	.15
BDP81 *John Baker*	.15
BDP82 *Aaron Coonrod*	.15
BDP83 *Josh Johnson*	.15
BDP84 *Jake Blalock*	1.00
BDP85 *Alex Hart*	.15
BDP86 *Wes Bankston*	2.00
BDP87 *Josh Rupe*	.15
BDP88 *Dan Cevette*	.50
BDP89 *Kiel Fisher*	.40
BDP90 *Alan Rick*	.15
BDP91 *Charlie Morton*	.40
BDP92 *Chad Spann*	.15
BDP93 *Kyle Boyer*	.15
BDP94 *Bob Malek*	.15
BDP95 *Ryan Rodriguez*	.15
BDP96 *Jordan Renz*	.15
BDP97 *Randy Frye*	.15
BDP98 *Rich Hill*	.15
BDP99 *B.J. Upton*	2.50
BDP100 *Dan Christensen*	.15
BDP101 Casey Kotchman	2.00
BDP102 *Eric Good*	.15
BDP103 *Mike Fontenot*	.40
BDP104 *John Webb*	.15
BDP105 *Jason Dubois*	.15
BDP106 *Ryan Kibler*	.15
BDP107 *John Peralta*	.40
BDP108 Kirk Saarloos	.75
BDP109 *Rhett Parrott*	.15
BDP110 *Jason Grove*	.15
BDP111 Colt Griffin	1.00
BDP112 Dallas McPherson	.40
BDP113 *Oliver Perez*	1.00
BDP114 *Marshall McDougall*	.15
BDP115 *Mike Wood*	.15
BDP116 Scott Hairston	.75
BDP117 *Jason Simontacchi*	.75
BDP118 *Taggert Bozied*	2.00
BDP119 Shelly Duncan	.15
BDP120 *Dontrelle Willis*	.75
BDP121 Sean Burnett	.15
BDP122 *Aaron Cook*	.15
BPD123 Brett Evert	.15
BDP124 Jimmy Journell	.15
BDP125 Brett Myers	.15
BDP126 Brad Baker	.15
BDP127 Billy Traber	.50
BDP128 Adam Wainwright	.15
BDP129 *Jason Young*	.40
BDP130 John Buck	.15
BDP131 *Kevin Cash*	.15
BDP132 *Jason Stokes*	3.00
BDP133 Drew Henson	.25
BDP134 *Chad Tracy*	.50
BDP135 Orlando Hudson	.15
BDP136 Brandon Phillips	.15
BDP137 Joe Borchard	.15
BDP138 Marlon Byrd	.15
BDP139 Carl Crawford	.15
BDP140 Michael Restovich	.15
BDP141 *Corey Hart*	.75
BDP142 Edwin Almonte	.15
BDP143 *Francis Beltran*	.15
BDP144 *Jorge De La Rosa*	.15
BDP145 *Gerardo Garcia*	.15
BDP146 *Franklyn German*	.15
BDP147 Francisco Liriano	.15
BDP148 Francisco Rodriguez	.50
BDP149 Ricardo Rodriguez	.15
BDP150 Seung Jun Song	.15
BDP151 John Stephens	.15
BDP152 *Justin Huber*	.75
BDP153 Victor Martinez	.40
BDP154 Hee Seop Choi	.15
BDP155 Justin Morneau	.15
BDP156 Miguel Cabrera	.15
BDP157 *Victor Diaz*	.50
BDP158 Jose Reyes	.40
BDP159 *Omar Infante*	.15
BDP160 Angel Berroa	.15
BDP161 Tony Alvarez	.15
BDP162 *Shin-Soo Choo*	1.00
BDP163 Wily Mo Pena	.15
BDP164 Andres Torres	.15
BDP165 *Jose Lopez*	1.50

2002 Bowman Draft Picks & Prospects Fabric of Future

		MT
Common Player:		5.00
Inserted 1:55		
EA	Edwin Almonte	5.00
TA	Tony Alvarez	5.00
FB	Francis Beltran	5.00
AB	Angel Berroa	5.00
SB	Sean Burnett	6.00
KC	Kevin Cash	6.00
HC	Hee Seop Choi	10.00
SC	Shin-Soo Choo	10.00
CC	Carl Crawford	8.00
JR	Jorge de la Rosa	5.00
VD	Victor Diaz	5.00
GG	Gerardo Garcia	5.00
FG	Franklyn German	5.00
CH	Corey Hart	6.00
DH	Drew Henson	12.00
JH	Justin Huber	10.00
JK	Josh Karp	8.00
FL	Francisco Liriano	5.00
JL	Jose Lopez	10.00
BM	Brett Meyers	8.00
WP	Wily Mo Pena	10.00
MR	Michael Restovich	6.00
JS	John Stephens	5.00
JS	Jason Stokes	12.00
AT	Andres Torres	5.00
BT	Billy Traber	10.00
CT	Chad Tracy	12.00
AW	Adam Wainwright	6.00

2002 Bowman Draft Picks & Prospects Freshman Fiber

		MT
Common Player:		4.00
Bat inserted 1:605		
Jersey 1:45		
BA	Brent Abernathy	4.00
DB	Dewon Brazelton	4.00
MB	Marlon Byrd/bat	10.00
TH	Toby Hall	4.00
JH	Josh Hamilton	6.00
AH	Aubrey Huff	4.00
AK	Austin Kearns/bat	12.00
JK	Joe Kennedy	4.00
JS	Jared Sandberg	4.00
JWS	Jason Standridge	4.00
MT	Mark Teixeira/bat	10.00
JV	John Van Benschoten	4.00

2002 Bowman Draft Picks & Prospects Signs of the Future

		MT
Common Autograph:		5.00
EB	Erik Bedard	8.00
LB	Larry Bigbie	5.00
TB	Taylor Buchholz	8.00
DD	Daniel Denham	8.00
ME	Morgan Ensberg	8.00
MF	Mike Fontenot	8.00
KH	Kris Honel	8.00
BI	Brandon Inge	5.00
NJ	Nic Jackson	10.00
MJ	Mitch Jones	5.00
BK	Bob Keppel	8.00
TL	Todd Linden	15.00
JM	Jake Mauer	8.00
JEM	Justin Morneau	10.00
LN	Lance Niekro	8.00
CP	Christian Parra	5.00
BP	Brandon Phillips	5.00
JR	Juan Rivera	8.00
BS	Bud Smith	10.00
AT	Chad Tracy	20.00
JW	Jerome Williams	8.00

2002 Bowman Chrome Draft Picks & Prospects

	MT
Complete Set (175):	275.00
Common Player:	.25
Common RC:	.75
1-165 two per pack	
Common Auto (166-175):	12.00
Auto's inserted 1:45	
BDP1 *Clint Everts*	1.50
BDP2 *Fred Lewis*	1.00
BDP3 *Jonathan Broxton*	.25
BDP4 *Jason Anderson*	.25
BDP5 *Mike Eusebio*	.25
BDP6 *Zack Greinke*	1.50
BDP7 *Joe Blanton*	.25
BDP8 *Sergio Santos*	2.50
BDP9 *Jason Cooper*	1.00
BDP10 *Delwyn Young*	1.50
BDP11 *Jeremy Hermida*	2.50
BDP12 *Dan Ortmeyer*	1.00
BDP13 *Kevin Jepsen*	.25
BDP14 *Russ Adams*	1.00
BDP15 *Mike Nixon*	1.00
BDP16 *Nick Swisher*	1.25
BDP17 *Cole Hamels*	1.50
BDP18 *Brian Dopirak*	2.00
BDP19 *James Loney*	5.00
BDP20 *Denard Span*	1.00
BDP21 *Billy Petrick*	.25
BDP22 *Jared Doyle*	.25
BDP23 *Jeff Francoeur*	8.00
BDP24 *Nick Bourgeois*	.25
BDP25 *Matt Cain*	.25
BDP26 *John McCurdy*	1.00
BDP27 *Mark Kiger*	.25
BDP28 *Bill Murphy*	.25
BDP29 *Matt Craig*	.25
BDP30 *Mike Megrew*	.25
BDP31 *Ben Crockett*	.25
BDP32 *Luke Hagerty*	1.00
BDP33 *Matt Whitney*	2.50
BDP34 *Dan Meyer*	.25
BDP35 *Jeremy Brown*	1.00
BDP36 *Doug Johnson*	.25
BDP37 *Steve Obenchain*	.25
BDP38 *Matt Clanton*	1.00
BDP39 *Mark Teahen*	.25
BDP40 *Thomas Carrow*	.25
BDP41 *Micah Schilling*	1.50
BDP42 *Blair Johnson*	.25
BDP43 *Jason Pridie*	2.50
BDP44 *Joey Votto*	1.00
BDP45 *Taber Lee*	.25
BDP46 *Adam Peterson*	.25
BDP47 *Adam Donachie*	.25
BDP48 *Josh Murray*	.25
BDP49 *Brent Clevlen*	1.50
BDP50 *Chad Pleiness*	1.00
BDP51 *Zach Hammes*	1.50
BDP52 *Chris Snyder*	.25
BDP53 Chris Smith	.25
BDP54 *Justin Maureau*	.25
BDP55 *David Bush*	.25
BDP56 *Tim Gilhooly*	.25
BDP57 *Blair Barbier*	.25
BDP58 *Zach Segovia*	1.00
BDP59 *Jeremy Reed*	1.00
BDP60 *Matt Pender*	.25
BDP61 *Eric Thomas*	.25
BDP62 *Justin Jones*	2.00
BDP63 *Brian Slocum*	1.00
BDP64 *Larry Broadway*	1.00
BDP65 *Bo Flowers*	.25
BDP66 *Scott White*	2.00
BDP67 *Steve Stanley*	.25
BDP68 *Alex Merricks*	.25

BDP69*Josh Womack* .25
BDP70*Dave Jensen* .25
BDP71*Curtis Granderson* 1.50
BDP72*Pat Osborn* 1.00
BDP73*Nic Carter* .25
BDP74*Mitch Talbot* .25
BDP75*Don Murphy* .25
BDP76*Val Majewski* 1.00
BDP77*Javy Rodriguez* .25
BDP78*Fernando Pacheco* 1.00
BDP79*Steve Russell* .25
BDP80*Jon Slack* .25
BDP81*John Baker* .25
BDP82*Aaron Coonrod* .25
BDP83*Josh Johnson* .25
BDP84*Jake Blalock* 3.00
BDP85*Alex Hart* .25
BDP86*Wes Bankston* 5.00
BDP87*Josh Rupe* .25
BDP88*Dan Cevette* 1.50
BDP89*Kiel Fisher* 1.00
BDP90*Alan Rick* .25
BDP91*Charlie Morton* 1.00
BDP92*Chad Spann* .25
BDP93*Kyle Boyer* .25
BDP94*Bob Malek* .25
BDP95*Ryan Rodriguez* .25
BDP96*Jordan Renz* .25
BDP97*Randy Frye* .25
BDP98*Rich Hill* .25
BDP99*B.J. Upton* 6.00
BDP100*Dan Christensen* .25
BDP101Casey Kotchman 5.00
BDP102*Eric Good* .25
BDP103*Mike Fontenot* 1.00
BDP104*John Webb* .25
BDP105*Jason Dubois* .25
BDP106*Ryan Kibler* .25
BDP107*John Peralta* 1.00
BDP108Kirk Saarloos 2.00
BDP109*Rhett Parrott* .25
BDP110*Jason Grove* .25
BDP111Colt Griffin 2.00
BDP112Dallas McPherson 1.00
BDP113*Oliver Perez* 2.50
BDP114*Marshall McDougall* .25
BDP115*Mike Wood* .25
BDP116Scott Hairston 2.00
BDP117*Jason Simontacchi* 2.00
BDP118*Taggert Bozied* 5.00
BDP119Shelly Duncan .25
BDP120*Dontrelle Willis* 2.00
BDP121Sean Burnett .25
BDP122*Aaron Cook* .25
BPD123Brett Evert .25
BDP124Jimmy Journell .25
BDP125Brett Myers .25
BDP126Brad Baker .25
BDP127Billy Traber 1.50
BDP128Adam Wainwright .25
BDP129Jason Young 1.00
BDP130John Buck .25
BDP131Kevin Cash .25
BDP132*Jason Stokes* 7.00
BDP133Drew Henson .50
BDP134*Chad Tracy* 1.50
BDP135Orlando Hudson .25
BDP136Brandon Phillips .25
BDP137Joe Borchard .25
BDP138Marlon Byrd .25
BDP139Carl Crawford .25
BDP140Michael Restovich .25
BDP141*Corey Hart* 2.00
BDP142Edwin Almonte .25
BDP143*Francis Beltran* .25
BDP144*Jorge De La Rosa* .25
BDP145*Gerardo Garcia* .25
BDP146*Franklyn German* .25
BDP147Francisco Liriano .25
BDP148Francisco Rodriguez 1.00
BDP149Ricardo Rodriguez .25
BDP150Seung Jun Song .25
BDP151John Stephens .25
BDP152Justin Huber 2.00
BDP153Victor Martinez 1.00
BDP154Hee Seop Choi .25
BDP155Justin Morneau .25
BDP156Miguel Cabrera .25
BDP157*Victor Diaz* 1.25
BDP158Jose Reyes .75
BDP159*Omar Infante* .25
BDP160Angel Berroa .25
BDP161Tony Alvarez .25
BDP162*Shin-Soo Choo* 2.50
BDP163Wily Mo Pena .25
BDP164Andres Torres .25
BDP165*Jose Lopez* 4.00
BDP166*Scott Moore/auto* 25.00
BDP167*Chris Gruler/auto* 15.00
BDP168*Joe Saunders/auto* 12.00
BDP169*Jeff Francis/auto* 15.00
BDP170*Royce Ring/auto* 15.00
BDP171Greg Miller/auto 15.00
BDP172*Brandon Weeden/auto* 15.00
BDP173*Drew Meyer/auto* 20.00
BDP174*Khalil Greene/auto* 40.00
BDP175*Mark Schramek/auto* 18.00

2002 Bowman Chrome Draft Picks & Prospects Refractor

	MT
Cards 1-165:	2-4X
Rookies 1-175:	.75-1.5X

1-165 production 300 sets
166-175 inserted 1:154

2002 Bowman Chrome Draft Picks & Prospects Gold Refract

	MT
Cards 1-165:	8-15X
Rookies 1-165:	4-10X

1-165 production 50 sets
166-175 no pricing

2002 Bowman Chrome Draft Picks & Prospects X-Fractor

	MT
Cards 1-165:	2-5X
Rookies 1-165:	2-3X
Rookies 166-175:	.75-2X

1-165 production 150 sets
166-175 inserted 1:309

2002 Donruss The Rookies

	MT
Complete Set (110):	25.00
Common Player:	.15
Common Rookie:	.25
Pack (5):	3.00
Box (24):	60.00

1 *Kazuhisa Ishii* 1.00
2 *P.J. Bevis* .25
3 *Jason Simontacchi* .75
4 John Lackey .15
5 *Travis Driskill* .25
6 *Carl Sadler* .25
7 *Tim Kalita* .25
8 *Nelson Castro* .25
9 *Francis Beltran* .25
10 *So Taguchi* .50
11 *Ryan Bukvich* .25
12 Brian Fitzgerald .15
13 *Kevin Frederick* .25
14 *Chone Figgins* .25
15 Marlon Byrd .15
16 *Ron Calloway* .25
17 Jason Lane .15
18 *Satoru Komiyama* .25
19 *John Ennis* .25
20 *Juan Brito* .25
21 *Gustavo Chacin* .25
22 *Josh Bard* .50
23 Brett Myers .15
24 *Mike Smith* .25
25 Eric Hinske .15
26 Jake Peavy .15
27 *Todd Donovan* .25
28 *Luis Ugueto* .25
29 *Corey Thurman* .25
30 *Takahito Nomura* .25
31 *Andy Shibilo* .25
32 *Mike Crudale* .25
33 *Earl Snyder* .25
34 Brian Tallet .75
35 *Miguel Asencio* .25
36 *Felix Escalona* .25
37 Drew Henson .40
38 *Steve Kent* .25
39 *Rene Reyes* .25
40 *Edwin Almonte* .25
41 *Chris Snelling* 1.00
42 *Franklyn German* .25
43 *Jeriome Robertson* .25
44 *Colin Young* .25
45 *Jeremy Lambert* .25
46 Kirk Saarloos .75
47 *Matt Childers* .25
48 Justin Wayne .15
49 *Jose Valverde* .25
50 Wily Mo Pena .15
51 *Victor Alvarez* .25
52 *Julius Matos* .25
53 *Aaron Cook* .40
54 *Jeff Austin* .25
55 *Adrian Burnside* .25
56 *Brandon Puffer* .25
57 *Jeremy Hill* .25
58 *Jaime Cerda* .25
59 *Aaron Guiel* .25
60 Ron Chiavacci .15
61 *Kevin Cash* .25
62 Elio Serrano .15
63 *Julio Mateo* .25
64 *Cam Esslinger* .25
65 *Ken Huckaby* .25
66 *Wiki Nieves* .25
67 *Luis Martinez* .25
68 *Scotty Layfield* .25
69 *Jeremy Guthrie* 1.50
70 *Hansel Izquierdo* .25
71 *Shane Nance* .25
72 *Jeff Baker* 2.00
73 *Clifford Bartosh* .25
74 *Mitch Wylie* .25
75 *Oliver Perez* 1.00
76 Matt Thornton .15
77 *John Foster* .25
78 Joe Borchard .15
79 *Eric Junge* .25
80 *Jorge Sosa* .25
81 *Runelvys Hernandez* .25
82 Kevin Mench .15
83 *Ben Kozlowski* .50
84 *Trey Hodges* .40
85 *Reed Johnson* .25
86 *Eric Eckenstahler* .25
87 *Franklin Nunez* .25
88 Victor Martinez .50
89 *Kevin Gryboski* .25
90 Jason Jennings .15
91 *Jim Rushford* .25
92 *Jeremy Ward* .25
93 *Adam Walker* .25
94 *Freddy Sanchez* .25
95 *Wilson Valdez* .25
96 Lee Gardner .15
97 *Eric Good* .25
98 Hank Blalock .50
99 Mark Corey .15
100 *Jason Davis* .25
101 *Mike Gonzalez* .25
102 *David Ross* .25
103 *Tyler Yates* .15
104 *Cliff Lee* .50
105 *Mike Moriarty* .25
106 *Josh Hancock* .25
107 *Jason Beverlin* .25
108 *Clay Condrey* .25
109 *Shawn Sedlacek* .25
110 Sean Burroughs .15

Donruss Originals
401 *Runelvys Hernandez* .25
402 *Wilson Valdez* .25
403 Brian Tallet 1.50
404 *Chone Figgins* .25
405 *Jeriome Robertson* .25
406 *Shane Nance* .25
407 *Aaron Cook* .75
408 *Trey Hodges* .75
409 *Matt Childers* .25
410 *Mitch Wylie* .25
411 *Rene Reyes* .25
412 Mike Smith .25
413 *Jason Simontacchi* 1.50
414 Luis Martinez .25
415 *Kevin Cash* .25
416 Todd Donovan .25
417 Scotty Layfield .25
418 Joe Borchard .25
419 Adrian Burnside .25

Donruss Studio
Common Studio RC: 4.00
Production 1,500
251 *Freddy Sanchez* 6.00
252 *Josh Bard* .25
253 *Trey Hodges* 6.00
254 *Jorge Sosa* 4.00
255 *Ben Kozlowski* 8.00
256 *Eric Good* 4.00
257 Brian Tallet 8.00
258 *P.J. Bevis* 4.00
259 *Rodrigo Rosario* 4.00
260 Kirk Saarloos 8.00
261 *Runelvys Hernandez* 4.00
262 *Josh Hancock* 4.00
263 *Tim Kalita* 4.00
264 *Jason Simontacchi* 8.00
265 *Clay Condrey* 4.00
266 *Cliff Lee* 8.00
267 *Aaron Guiel* 4.00
268 *Andy Pratt* 4.00
269 *Wilson Valdez* 4.00
270 *Oliver Perez* 10.00
271 Joe Borchard 10.00
272 *Jeriome Robertson* 4.00
273 *Aaron Cook* 6.00
274 *Kevin Cash* 4.00
275 *Chone Figgins* 4.00

Best of Fan Club
Common Best of Fan Club RC: 5.00
Production 1,350
Best of Fan Club Spotlights: 1.5-3X
Production 100 sets
201 Kirk Saarloos 6.00
202 *Oliver Perez* 8.00
203 *So Taguchi* 6.00
204 *Runelvys Hernandez* 5.00
205 *Freddy Sanchez* 6.00
206 *Cliff Lee* 8.00
207 *Kazuhisa Ishii* 8.00
208 *Kevin Cash* 5.00
209 *Trey Hodges* 6.00
210 *Wilson Valdez* 5.00
211 *Satoru Komiyama* 5.00
212 *Luis Ugueto* 5.00
213 Joe Borchard 10.00
214 Brian Tallet 8.00
215 *Jeriome Robertson* 5.00
216 *Eric Junge* 5.00
217 *Aaron Cook* 6.00
218 *Jason Simontacchi* 6.00
219 *Miguel Asencio* 5.00
220 *Josh Bard* 6.00
221 *Earl Snyder* 5.00
222 *Felix Escalona* 5.00
223 *Rene Reyes* 5.00
224 *Chone Figgins* 5.00
225 *Chris Snelling* 8.00

Fan Club
Inserted 1:4 Retail
201 Kirk Saarloos 3.00
202 *Oliver Perez* 4.00
203 *So Taguchi* 3.00
204 *Runelvys Hernandez* 1.50
205 *Freddy Sanchez* 2.00
206 Cliff Lee 3.00
207 *Kazuhisa Ishii* 4.00
208 Kevin Cash 1.50
209 Trey Hodges 1.50
210 Wilson Valdez 1.50
211 *Satoru Komiyama* 1.50
212 *Luis Ugueto* 1.50
213 Joe Borchard 4.00
214 Brian Tallet 3.00
215 *Jeriome Robertson* 1.50
216 Eric Junge 1.50
217 Aaron Cook 1.50
218 Jason Simontacchi 3.00
219 Miguel Asencio 1.50
220 Josh Bard 2.00
221 *Earl Snyder* 1.50
222 Felix Escalona 1.50
223 Rene Reyes 1.50
224 Chone Figgins 1.50
225 *Chris Snelling* 4.00

Elite
Common Elite RC: 5.00
Production 1,000
Elite Turn of the Century: 1-2.5X

Production 100 sets
201 *Chris Snelling* 10.00
202 *Satoru Komiyama* 5.00
203 *Jason Simontacchi* 10.00
204 *Tim Kalita* 4.00
205 *Runelvys Hernandez* 5.00
206 Kirk Saarloos 4.00
207 *Aaron Cook* 8.00
208 *Luis Ugueto* 5.00
209 *Gustavo Chacin* .25
210 *Francis Beltran* .25
211 *Takahito Nomura* 5.00
212 *Oliver Perez* 5.00
213 *Miguel Asencio* 4.00
214 *Rene Reyes* 5.00
215 *Jeff Baker* 50.00
216 *Jon Adkins* 5.00
217 *Carlos Rivera* 10.00
218 *Corey Thurman* 5.00
219 *Earl Snyder* 5.00
220 *Felix Escalona* 5.00
221 *Jeremy Guthrie* 40.00
222 *Josh Hancock* 5.00
223 *Ben Kozlowski* 10.00
224 *Eric Good* 5.00
225 *Eric Junge* 6.00
226 *Andy Pratt* 5.00
227 Matt Thornton 5.00
228 *Jorge Sosa* 5.00
229 Mike Smith 5.00
230 *Mitch Wylie* 5.00
231 *John Ennis* 5.00
232 *Reed Johnson* 5.00
233 Joe Borchard 15.00
234 *Ron Calloway* 5.00
235 Brian Tallet 10.00
236 *Chris Baker* 5.00
237 *Cliff Lee* 12.00
238 *Matt Childers* 5.00
239 *Freddy Sanchez* 6.00
240 *Chone Figgins* 5.00
241 *Kevin Cash* 5.00
242 *Josh Bard* 6.00
243 *Jeriome Robertson* 5.00
244 *Jeremy Hill* 5.00
245 *Shane Nance* 5.00
246 *Wes Obermueller* 5.00
247 *Trey Hodges* 8.00
248 *Eric Eckenstahler* 5.00
249 *Jim Rushford* 5.00
250 *Jose Castillo* 40.00
251 *Garrett Atkins* 15.00
252 *Alexis Rios* 10.00
253 *Ryan Church* 15.00
254 *Jimmy Gobble* 10.00
255 Corwin Malone 6.00
257 *Nic Jackson* 10.00
258 *Tommy Whiteman* 10.00
259 Mario Ramos 5.00
260 *Rob Bowen* 8.00
261 *Josh Wilson* 5.00
262 *Tim Hummel* 5.00
264 *Gerald Laird* 8.00
265 *Vinny Chulk* 5.00
266 *Jesus Medrano* 5.00
272 *Adam LaRoche* 35.00
273 *Adam Morrissey* 10.00
274 *Henri Stanley* 10.00
275 *Walter Young* 50.00
Donruss Classics
Common Classics RC: 5.00
Production 1,500
Classics Timeless Tributes: 1.5-3X
Production 100 sets
201 *Oliver Perez* .25
202 *Aaron Cook* .25
203 *Eric Junge* 6.00
204 *Freddy Sanchez* .25
205 *Cliff Lee* .25
206 *Runelvys Hernandez* .25
207 *Chone Figgins* 5.00
208 *Rodrigo Rosario* .75
209 *Kevin Cash* 6.00
210 *Josh Bard* 5.00
211 *Felix Escalona* 4.00
212 *Jeriome Robertson* 5.00
213 *Jason Simontacchi* 8.00
214 *Shane Nance* 8.00
215 *Ben Kozlowski* 5.00
216 Brian Tallet 5.00
217 *Earl Snyder* 5.00
218 *Andy Pratt* 4.00
219 *Trey Hodges* 5.00
220 Kirk Saarloos 5.00
221 *Rene Reyes* 5.00
222 Joe Borchard 5.00
223 *Wilson Valdez* 10.00
224 *Miguel Asencio* 5.00
225 *Chris Snelling* 6.00
Diamond Kings
Common DK RC: 3.00
Inserted 1:10
151 *Chris Snelling* 10.00
152 *Satoru Komiyama* 6.00
153 *Oliver Perez* 10.00
154 Kirk Saarloos 5.00
155 *Rene Reyes* 3.00
156 *Runelvys Hernandez* 3.00
157 *Rodrigo Rosario* 8.00
158 *Jason Simontacchi* .75
159 *Miguel Asencio* 4.00
160 *Aaron Cook* 4.00

2002 Donruss The Rookies Autographs

MT
Common Autograph: 8.00
Print runs listed
1 Kazuhisa Ishii/25
2 P.J. Bevis/50
7 Tim Kalita/25
9 Francis Beltran/100 10.00
10 So Taguchi/15
13 Kevin Frederick/100 10.00
14 Chone Figgins/100 8.00
15 Marlon Byrd/100 20.00
17 Jason Lane/100 10.00
18 Satoru Komiyama/25
19 John Ennis/100 10.00
22 Josh Bard/100 15.00
25 Eric Hinske/100 20.00
28 Luis Ugueto/100 8.00
29 Corey Thurman/100 8.00
30 Takahito Nomura/100 40.00
33 Earl Snyder/100 10.00
34 Brian Tallet/100 15.00
36 Felix Escalona/25
37 Drew Henson/50 35.00
39 Rene Reyes/50
40 Edwin Almonte/50
41 Chris Snelling/50
42 Franklyn German/100 10.00
45 Jeremy Lambert/100 10.00
46 Kirk Saarloos/50
47 Matt Childers/100 8.00
50 Wily Mo Pena/100 18.00
51 Victor Alvarez/100 10.00
61 Kevin Cash/100 10.00
62 Elio Serrano/100 10.00
64 Cam Esslinger/100 10.00
69 Jeremy Guthrie/100 55.00
71 Shane Nance/100 10.00
72 Jeff Baker/100 25.00
75 Oliver Perez/25
76 Matt Thornton/100 10.00
78 Joe Borchard/100 40.00
79 Eric Junge/25
82 Kevin Mench/100 10.00
83 Ben Kozlowski/100
84 Trey Hodges/100 10.00
85 Reed Johnson/100 10.00
88 Victor Martinez/100
90 Jason Jennings/100 12.00
95 Wilson Valdez/100 10.00
97 Eric Good/100 10.00
98 Hank Blalock/100
104 Cliff Lee/100 25.00
110 Sean Burroughs/50 25.00

2002 Donruss The Rookies Rookie Crusade

MT
Common Player: 3.00
Production 1,500 sets
1 Corky Miller 3.00
2 Jack Cust 3.00
3 Erik Bedard 3.00
4 Andres Torres 3.00
5 Geronimo Gil 3.00
6 Rafael Soriano 3.00
7 Johnny Estrada 3.00
8 Steve Bechler 3.00
9 Adam Johnson 3.00
10 So Taguchi 5.00
11 Dee Brown 3.00
12 Kevin Frederick 3.00
13 Allan Simpson 3.00
14 Ricardo Rodriguez 3.00
15 Jason Hart 3.00
16 Matt Childers 3.00
17 Jason Jennings 3.00
18 Anderson Machado 3.00
19 Fernando Rodney 3.00
20 Brandon Larson 3.00
21 Satoru Komiyama 3.00
22 Francis Beltran 3.00
23 Joe Thurston 3.00
24 Josh Pearce 3.00
25 Carlos Hernandez 3.00
26 Ben Howard 3.00
27 Wilson Valdez 3.00
28 Victor Alvarez 3.00
29 Cesar Izturis 3.00
30 Endy Chavez 3.00
31 Michael Cuddyer 4.00
32 Bobby Hill 4.00
33 Willie Harris 3.00
34 Joe Crede 3.00
35 Jorge Padilla 3.00
36 Brandon Backe 3.00
37 Franklyn German 3.00
38 Xavier Nady 3.00
39 Raul Chavez 3.00
40 Shane Nance 3.00
41 Brandon Claussen 3.00
42 Tom Shearn 3.00
43 Freddy Sanchez 3.00
44 Chone Figgins 3.00
45 Cliff Lee 3.00
46 Brian Mallette 3.00
47 Mike Rivera 3.00
48 Elio Serrano 3.00
49 Rodrigo Rosario 3.00
50 Earl Snyder 4.00

2002 Donruss The Rookies Rookie Crusade Autograph

MT
Common Autograph: 6.00
Print runs listed
1 Corky Miller/500 8.00
2 Jack Cust/500 10.00
3 Erik Bedard/100 10.00
4 Andres Torres/500 8.00
5 Geronimo Gil/500 6.00
6 Rafael Soriano/500 12.00
7 Johnny Estrada/400 6.00
8 Steve Bechler/500 6.00
9 Adam Johnson/500 8.00
10 So Taguchi/15
11 Dee Brown/500 8.00
12 Kevin Frederick/150 12.00
13 Allan Simpson/150 8.00
14 Ricardo Rodriguez/500 6.00
15 Jason Hart/500 8.00
16 Matt Childers/150 12.00
17 Jason Jennings/500 12.00
18 Anderson Machado/500 10.00
19 Fernando Rodney/500 6.00
20 Brandon Larson/400 10.00
21 Satoru Komiyama/25
22 Francis Beltran/500 8.00
23 Joe Thurston/500 10.00
24 Josh Pearce/500 6.00
25 Carlos Hernandez/500 8.00
26 Ben Howard/500 6.00
27 Wilson Valdez/500 6.00
28 Victor Alvarez/500 8.00
29 Cesar Izturis/500 8.00
30 Endy Chavez/500 6.00
31 Michael Cuddyer/375 15.00
32 Bobby Hill/250 15.00
33 Willie Harris/300 8.00
34 Joe Crede/100 12.00
35 Jorge Padilla/475 10.00
36 Brandon Backe/350 8.00
37 Franklyn German/500 8.00
38 Xavier Nady/500 10.00
39 Raul Chavez/500 6.00
40 Shane Nance/500 6.00
41 Brandon Claussen/150 12.00
42 Tom Shearn/500 6.00
44 Chone Figgins/500 8.00
45 Cliff Lee/500 18.00
46 Brian Mallette/150 8.00
47 Mike Rivera/400 8.00
48 Elio Serrano/500 6.00
49 Rodrigo Rosario/100 10.00
50 Earl Snyder/100 10.00

2002 Donruss The Rookies Best of Fan Club Autograph

MT
Common Autograph:
Print Runs listed
201 Kirk Saarloos/100 30.00
202 Oliver Perez/25
203 So Taguchi/10
206 Cliff Lee/50
207 Kazuhisa Ishii/15
208 Kevin Cash/50 10.00
209 Trey Hodges/100 15.00
210 Wilson Valdez/50 10.00
211 Satoru Komiyama/25
212 Luis Ugueto/75 12.00
213 Joe Borchard/50 40.00
214 Brian Tallet/50 20.00
216 Eric Junge/25
220 Josh Bard/50 15.00
221 Earl Snyder/100 12.00
222 Felix Escalona/25
223 Rene Reyes/50 10.00
224 Chone Figgins/100 10.00
225 Chris Snelling/50 30.00

2002 Donruss The Rookies Donruss Classics Signatures

MT
Common Autograph:
Print Runs listed
201 Oliver Perez/50
203 Eric Junge/50 12.00
205 Cliff Lee/100 30.00
207 Chone Figgins/100 10.00
208 Rodrigo Rosario/250 10.00
209 Kevin Cash/100 10.00
210 Josh Bard/100 15.00
211 Felix Escalona/25
214 Shane Nance/200 10.00
215 Ben Kozlowski/200 20.00
216 Brian Tallet/100 18.00
217 Earl Snyder/100 10.00
218 Andy Pratt/250 10.00
219 Trey Hodges/250 15.00
220 Kirk Saarloos/100 30.00
221 Rene Reyes/50 10.00
222 Joe Borchard/100 30.00
223 Wilson Valdez/100 10.00
225 Chris Snelling/100 25.00

2002 Donruss The Rookies Donruss Studio Private Signing

MT
Print Runs listed
252 Josh Bard/100 15.00

253 Trey Hodges/250 15.00
255 Ben Kozlowski/200 20.00
257 Brian Tallet/100 20.00
258 P.J. Bevis/50
260 Kirk Saarloos/100 30.00
266 Cliff Lee/100 25.00
271 Joe Borchard/100 35.00

2002 Donruss The Rookies Elite Turn of the Cent. Auto.

MT

Common Autograph:
Print Runs listed
201 Chris Snelling/50
202 Satoru Komiyama/25
204 Tim Kalita/25
206 Kirk Saarloos/50
208 Luis Ugueto/25
210 Francis Beltran/25
211 Takahito Nomura/25
212 Oliver Perez/25
214 Rene Reyes/25
215 Jeff Baker/100
216 Jon Adkins/100 10.00
217 Carlos Rivera/100
218 Corey Thurman/25
219 Earl Snyder/25
220 Felix Escalona/25
221 Jeremy Guthrie/100 80.00
223 Ben Kozlowski/100
224 Eric Good/100 10.00
225 Eric Junge/25
226 Andy Pratt/25
227 Matt Thornton/25
231 John Ennis/25
232 Reed Johnson/25
233 Joe Borchard/25
235 Brian Tallet/25
236 Chris Baker/25
237 Cliff Lee/25
238 Matt Childers/25
240 Chone Figgins/100 12.00
241 Kevin Cash/100 10.00
242 Josh Bard/25
245 Shane Nance/25
247 Trey Hodges/100 20.00
251 Garrett Atkins/100
253 Ryan Church/100
254 Jimmy Gobble/100 30.00
255 Corwin Malone/100 18.00
258 Tom Whiteman/10 30.00
259 Mario Ramos/100 10.00
260 Rob Bowen/100 20.00
261 Josh Wilson/100 10.00
262 Tim Hummel/100 10.00
264 Gerald Laird/100 35.00
266 Jesus Medrano/100 10.00
272 Adam LaRoche/100
273 Adam Morrissey/100 18.00
274 Henri Stanley/100 35.00

2002 Donruss The Rookies Phenoms

MT

Common Player: 3.00
Production 1,000 sets
1 Kazuhisa Ishii 6.00
2 Eric Hinske 4.00
3 Jason Lane 3.00
4 Victor Martinez 6.00
5 Mark Prior 8.00
6 Antonio Perez 3.00
7 John Buck 3.00
8 Joe Borchard 3.00
9 Alexis Gomez 3.00
10 Sean Burroughs 3.00
11 Carlos Pena 3.00
12 Bill Hall 3.00
13 Alfredo Amezaga 3.00
14 Ed Rogers 3.00
15 Mark Teixeira 5.00
16 Chris Snelling 5.00
17 Nick Johnson 3.00
18 Angel Berroa 3.00
19 Orlando Hudson 3.00
20 Drew Henson 4.00
21 Austin Kearns 6.00
22 Dewon Brazelton 3.00
23 Dennis Tankersley 3.00
24 Josh Beckett 3.00
25 Marlon Byrd 4.00

2002 Donruss The Rookies Phenoms Autographs

MT

Common Autograph: 8.00
Print runs listed
1 Kazuhisa Ishii/25
2 Eric Hinske/500 15.00
3 Jason Lane/500 10.00
4 Victor Martinez/225 20.00
5 Mark Prior/100
6 Antonio Perez/500 8.00
7 John Buck/100 10.00
8 Joe Borchard/100 40.00
9 Alexis Gomez/400 10.00
10 Sean Burroughs/15 15.00
11 Carlos Pena/150 12.00
12 Bill Hall/200 8.00
13 Alfredo Amezaga/500 8.00
14 Ed Rogers/500 8.00
15 Mark Teixeira/100 30.00
16 Chris Snelling/100 30.00
17 Nick Johnson/250 15.00
18 Angel Berroa/500 8.00
19 Orlando Hudson/400 10.00
20 Drew Henson/500 25.00
21 Austin Kearns/75 40.00
22 Dewon Brazelton/350 10.00
23 Dennis Tankersley/100 10.00
24 Josh Beckett/125
25 Marlon Byrd/500 15.00

2002 Upper Deck Ballpark Idols

MT

Complete Set (245):
Common Player: .15
Common (201-245): 4.00
Production 1,750
Pack (5): 2.50
Box (24 + bobber): 60.00
1 Troy Glaus .75
2 Kevin Appier .15
3 Darin Erstad .25
4 Garret Anderson .25
5 Brad Fullmer .15
6 Tim Salmon .25
7 Eric Chavez .25
8 Tim Hudson .25
9 David Justice .25
10 Barry Zito .25
11 Miguel Tejada .40
12 Mark Mulder .15
13 Jermaine Dye .15
14 Carlos Delgado .40
15 Jose Cruz Jr. .15
16 Brandon Lyon .15
17 Shannon Stewart .15
18 Eric Hinske .25
19 Chris Carpenter .15
20 Greg Vaughn .15
21 Tanyon Sturtze .15
22 Jason Tyner .15
23 Toby Hall .15
24 Ben Grieve .15
25 Jim Thome .75
26 Omar Vizquel .25
27 Ricky Gutierrez .15
28 C.C. Sabathia .15
29 Ellis Burks .15
30 Matt Lawton .15
31 Milton Bradley .15
32 Edgar Martinez .15
33 Ichiro Suzuki 1.50
34 Bret Boone .15
35 Freddy Garcia .15
36 Mike Cameron .15
37 John Olerud .25
38 Kazuhiro Sasaki .15
39 Jeff Cirillo .15
40 Jeff Conine .15
41 Marty Cordova .15
42 Tony Batista .15
43 Jerry Hairston Jr. .15
44 Jason Johnson .15
45 David Segui .15
46 Alex Rodriguez 2.00
47 Rafael Palmeiro .40
48 Carl Everett .15
49 Chan Ho Park .15
50 Ivan Rodriguez .50
51 Juan Gonzalez .60
52 Hank Blalock .25
53 Manny Ramirez .60
54 Pedro J. Martinez .75
55 Tony Clark .15
56 Nomar Garciaparra 1.50
57 Johnny Damon .15
58 Trot Nixon .15
59 Rickey Henderson .50
60 Mike Sweeney .15
61 Neifi Perez .15
62 Joe Randa .15
63 Carlos Beltran .15
64 Chuck Knoblauch .15
65 Michael Tucker .15
66 Dean Palmer .15
67 Bobby Higginson .15
68 Dmitri Young .15
69 Randall Simon .15
70 Mitch Meluskey .15
71 Damion Easley .15
72 Joe Mays .15
73 Doug Mientkiewicz .15
74 Corey Koskie .15
75 Brad Radke .15
76 Cristian Guzman .15
77 Torii Hunter .15
78 Eric Milton .15
79 Frank Thomas .60
80 Paul Konerko .25
81 Mark Buehrle .15
82 Magglio Ordonez .25
83 Carlos Lee .15
84 Joe Crede .15
85 Derek Jeter 2.50
86 Bernie Williams .50
87 Mike Mussina .50
88 Jorge Posada .25
89 Roger Clemens 1.25
90 Jason Giambi 1.25
91 Alfonso Soriano 1.25
92 Rondell White .15
93 Jeff Bagwell .60
94 Lance Berkman .50
95 Roy Oswalt .25
96 Richard Hidalgo .15
97 Wade Miller .15
98 Craig Biggio .25
99 Greg Maddux 1.25
100 Chipper Jones 1.25
101 Gary Sheffield .40
102 Rafael Furcal .15
103 Andruw Jones .50
104 Vinny Castilla .15
105 Marcus Giles .15
106 Tom Glavine .40
107 Richie Sexson .40
108 Geoff Jenkins .15
109 Glendon Rusch .15
110 Eric Young .15
111 Ben Sheets .15
112 Alex Sanchez .15
113 Albert Pujols 1.00
114 J.D. Drew .25
115 Matt Morris .15
116 Jim Edmonds .25
117 Tino Martinez .15
118 Scott Rolen .50
119 Edgar Renteria .15
120 Sammy Sosa 1.25
121 Kerry Wood .25
122 Moises Alou .15
123 Jon Lieber .15
124 Fred McGriff .25
125 Juan Cruz .15
126 Alex Gonzalez .15
127 Corey Patterson .15
128 Randy Johnson .75
129 Luis Gonzalez .25
130 Steve Finley .15
131 Matt Williams .15
132 Curt Schilling .50
133 Mark Grace .40
134 Craig Counsell .15
135 Shawn Green .25
136 Kevin Brown .15
137 Hideo Nomo .40
138 Paul LoDuca .15
139 Brian Jordan .15
140 Eric Karros .15
141 Adrian Beltre .15
142 Vladimir Guerrero .75
143 Fernando Tatis .15
144 Javier Vazquez .15
145 Orlando Cabrera .15
146 Tony Armas Jr. .15
147 Jose Vidro .15
148 Barry Bonds 2.00
149 Rich Aurilia .15
150 Tsuyoshi Shinjo .15
151 Jeff Kent .25
152 Russ Ortiz .15
153 Jason Schmidt .15
154 Reggie Sanders .15
155 Preston Wilson .15
156 Luis Castillo .15
157 Charles Johnson .15
158 Josh Beckett .15
159 Derrek Lee .15
160 Mike Lowell .15
161 Mike Piazza 2.00
162 Roberto Alomar .40
163 Al Leiter .15
164 Mo Vaughn .25
165 Jeromy Burnitz .15
166 Edgardo Alfonzo .15
167 Roger Cedeno .15
168 Ryan Klesko .25
169 Brian Lawrence .15
170 Sean Burroughs .15
171 Phil Nevin .15
172 Ramon Vazquez .15
173 Mark Kotsay .15
174 Marlon Anderson .15
175 Mike Lieberthal .15
176 Bobby Abreu .15
177 Pat Burrell .50
178 Robert Person .15
179 Brandon Duckworth .15
180 Jimmy Rollins .15
181 Brian Giles .30
182 Pokey Reese .15
183 Kris Benson .15
184 Aramis Ramirez .15
185 Jason Kendall .15
186 Kip Wells .15
187 Ken Griffey Jr. 1.50
188 Adam Dunn .50
189 Barry Larkin .40
190 Sean Casey .15
191 Austin Kearns .40
192 Aaron Boone .15
193 Todd Helton .40
194 Juan Pierre .15
195 Mike Hampton .15
196 Jose Ortiz .15
197 Larry Walker .25
198 Juan Uribe .15
199 Ichiro Suzuki (Checklist) .75
200 Jason Giambi (Checklist) .50
201 *Franklyn German* 4.00
202 *Rodrigo Rosario* 4.00
203 *Brandon Puffer* 4.00
204 Kirk Saarloos 8.00
205 *Chris Baker* 4.00
206 *John Ennis* 4.00
207 *Luis Martinez* 4.00
208 *So Taguchi* 6.00
209 *Michael Crudale* 4.00
210 *Francis Beltran* 4.00
211 *Brandon Backe* 4.00
212 *Felix Escalona* 4.00
213 *Jose Valverde* 4.00
214 *Doug Devore* 4.00
215 *Kazuhisa Ishii* 10.00
216 *Victor Alvarez* 4.00
217 *Ron Calloway* 4.00
218 *Eric Good* 4.00
219 Jorge Nunez 4.00
220 Deivis Santos 4.00
221 *Nelson Castro* 4.00
222 Matt Thornton 4.00
223 *Jason Simontacchi* 8.00
224 *Hansel Izquierdo* 4.00
225 *Tyler Yates* 4.00
226 *Jaime Cerda* 4.00

227 *Satoru Komiyama* 5.00
228 *Steve Bechler* 4.00
229 *Ben Howard* 4.00
230 *Todd Donovan* 4.00
231 *Jorge Padilla* 5.00
232 *Eric Junge* 4.00
233 *Anderson Machado* 4.00
234 *Adrian Burnside* 4.00
235 *Mike Gonzalez* 4.00
236 *Josh Hancock* 4.00
237 *Anastacio Martinez* 4.00
238 *Chris Booker* 4.00
239 *Rene Reyes* 4.00
240 *Cam Esslinger* 4.00
241 *Oliver Perez* 10.00
242 *Tim Kalita* 4.00
243 *Kevin Frederick* 4.00
244 *Mitch Wylie* 4.00
245 *Edwin Almonte* 4.00

2002 Upper Deck Ballpark Idols Bronze

MT
Stars (1-200): 8-15X
SP's (201-245): .75-1.5X
Production 100 sets

2002 Upper Deck Ballpark Idols Gold

MT
No Pricing due to scarcity
Production 25 sets

2002 Upper Deck Ballpark Idols Bobbers

MT
Common Player:
Inserted 1:box
Roberto Alomar 15.00
Roberto Alomar/SP/Home
Jeff Bagwell 20.00
Josh Beckett 12.00
Josh Beckett/SP/Home
Barry Bonds 30.00
Barry Bonds/SP/Home
Sean Burroughs 12.00
Sean Burroughs/SP/Home
Roger Clemens/SP/Red Sox
Roger Clemens 20.00
Roger Clemens/SP/Yanks Home
Joe DiMaggio/555/Away 40.00
Joe DiMaggio/361/Home 50.00
Nomar Garciaparra 20.00
Nomar Garciaparra/SP/Home
Jason Giambi 20.00
Jason Giambi/SP/Home
Luis Gonzalez 15.00
Luis Gonzalez/SP/Home
Ken Griffey Jr./SP/M's
Ken Griffey Jr. 25.00
Ken Griffey Jr./SP/Home
Vladimir Guerrero 20.00
Kazuhisa Ishii 12.00
Kazuhisa Ishii/SP/Home
Derek Jeter/SP/Away 40.00
Derek Jeter/SP/Home
Randy Johnson/D'backs 15.00
Randy Johnson/Expos 15.00
Chipper Jones 20.00
Greg Maddux 20.00
Mickey Mantle/777/Away 50.00
Mickey Mantle/536/Home 60.00
Mark McGwire/SP/A's
Mark McGwire/Cards 35.00
Mark McGwire/SP/Cards/Home
Mike Piazza/SP/Dodgers
Mike Piazza/Mets 25.00
Mark Prior 20.00
Mark Prior/SP/Home
Albert Pujols 20.00
Albert Pujols/SP
Alex Rodriguez 20.00
Alex Rodriguez/SP/Home
Ivan Rodriguez 15.00
Ivan Rodriguez/SP/Home
Curt Schilling/D'backs 15.00
Curt Schilling/SP/Orioles
Sammy Sosa/Cubs/Away 25.00
Sammy Sosa/SP/Cubs/Home
Sammy Sosa/SP/Rangers
Ichiro Suzuki/SP/Away 30.00
Ichiro Suzuki/SP/Home
Frank Thomas 15.00
Frank Thomas/SP/Home
Jim Thome 20.00
Jim Thome/SP/Home

2002 Upper Deck Ballpark Idols Bobbers Gold

MT
Amount produced listed
Joe DiMaggio/56/Away 100.00
Joe DiMaggio/41/Home 125.00
Mickey Mantle/77/Away 140.00
Mickey Mantle/61/Home 125.00

2002 Upper Deck Ballpark Idols Field Garb Jerseys

MT
Common Player: 6.00
Inserted 1:72
TB Tony Batista 6.00
BG Brian Giles 6.00
RJ Randy Johnson 12.00
JK Jeff Kent 6.00
TM Tino Martinez 6.00
JO John Olerud 6.00
AR Alex Rodriguez 12.00
IR Ivan Rodriguez 6.00
MS Mike Sweeney 6.00
RV Robin Ventura 6.00
LW Larry Walker 6.00
BZ Barry Zito 8.00

2002 Upper Deck Ballpark Idols Figure Heads

MT
Complete Set (10): 25.00
Common Player: 2.00
Inserted 1:12
F1 Ichiro Suzuki 3.00
F2 Sammy Sosa 2.50
F3 Alex Rodriguez 4.00
F4 Jason Giambi 2.50
F5 Barry Bonds 4.00
F6 Chipper Jones 2.50
F7 Mike Piazza 4.00
F8 Derek Jeter 5.00
F9 Nomar Garciaparra 3.00
F10 Ken Griffey Jr. 3.00

2002 Upper Deck Ballpark Idols Player's Club Jerseys

MT
Common Player: 6.00
Inserted 1:72
KB Kevin Brown 6.00
DE Darin Erstad 8.00
RF Rafael Furcal 6.00
TH Tim Hudson 6.00
AJ Andruw Jones 8.00
JK Jason Kendall 6.00
MM Mark McGwire/SP 70.00
PN Phil Nevin 6.00
HN Hideo Nomo 20.00
MO Magglio Ordonez 6.00
CS Curt Schilling 8.00
IS Ichiro Suzuki/SP 40.00
JT Jim Thome 12.00

2002 Upper Deck Ballpark Idols Playmakers 2002

MT
Complete Set (20): 35.00
Common Player: .75
Inserted 1:6
P1 Ken Griffey Jr. 3.00
P2 Alex Rodriguez 4.00
P3 Sammy Sosa 2.50
P4 Derek Jeter 5.00
P5 Mike Piazza 4.00
P6 Jason Giambi 2.50
P7 Barry Bonds 4.00
P8 Frank Thomas 1.25
P9 Randy Johnson 1.50
P10 Chipper Jones 2.50
P11 Jeff Bagwell 1.25
P12 Vladimir Guerrero 1.50
P13 Albert Pujols 2.00
P14 Nomar Garciaparra 3.00
P15 Ichiro Suzuki 3.00
P16 Troy Glaus 1.00
P17 Ivan Rodriguez 1.00
P18 Carlos Delgado .75
P19 Greg Maddux 2.50
P20 Todd Helton 1.00

2002 Upper Deck Ballpark Idols Uniform Sluggers

MT
Common Player: 6.00
Inserted 1:72
JB Jeff Bagwell 8.00
JGi Jason Giambi 15.00
JGo Juan Gonzalez 8.00
SG Shawn Green 6.00
KG Ken Griffey Jr./SP 25.00
TH Todd Helton 8.00
CJ Chipper Jones 12.00
MM Mickey Mantle/SP 100.00
MP Mike Piazza 15.00
AR Alex Rodriguez 12.00
SS Sammy Sosa/95
BW Bernie Williams 8.00

2002 Upper Deck Ultimate Collection

MT
Complete Set (120): N/A
Common Player (1-60): 2.00
Production 799
Common Player (61-110, 114-120): 10.00
Production 550
Common (111-113): 25.00
Production 330
Pack (4): 100.00
Box (4): 375.00
1 Troy Glaus 2.50
2 Luis Gonzalez 2.00
3 Curt Schilling 2.50
4 Randy Johnson 4.00
5 Andruw Jones 2.50
6 Greg Maddux 6.00
7 Chipper Jones 6.00
8 Gary Sheffield 2.00
9 Cal Ripken Jr. 12.00
10 Manny Ramirez 3.00
11 Pedro J. Martinez 4.00
12 Nomar Garciaparra 8.00
13 Sammy Sosa 6.00
14 Kerry Wood 2.00
15 Mark Prior 2.00
16 Magglio Ordonez 2.00
17 Frank Thomas 3.00
18 Adam Dunn 3.00
19 Ken Griffey Jr. 8.00
20 Jim Thome 3.00
21 Larry Walker 2.00
22 Todd Helton 2.00
23 Nolan Ryan 12.00
24 Jeff Bagwell 3.00
25 Roy Oswalt 2.00
26 Lance Berkman 2.00
27 Mike Sweeney 2.00
28 Shawn Green 2.00
29 Hideo Nomo 2.00
30 Torii Hunter 2.00
31 Vladimir Guerrero 4.00
32 Tom Seaver 4.00
33 Mike Piazza 10.00
34 Roberto Alomar 2.00
35 Derek Jeter 12.00
36 Alfonso Soriano 6.00
37 Jason Giambi 6.00
38 Roger Clemens 6.00
39 Mike Mussina 2.50
40 Bernie Williams 2.50
41 Joe DiMaggio 10.00
42 Mickey Mantle 15.00
43 Miguel Tejada 2.50
44 Eric Chavez 2.00
45 Barry Zito 2.00
46 Pat Burrell 2.50
47 Jason Kendall 2.00
48 Brian Giles 2.00
49 Barry Bonds 10.00
50 Ichiro Suzuki 8.00
51 Stan Musial 8.00
52 J.D. Drew 2.00
53 Scott Rolen 2.50
54 Albert Pujols 4.00
55 Mark McGwire 10.00
56 Alex Rodriguez 10.00
57 Ivan Rodriguez 2.50
58 Juan Gonzalez 2.50
59 Rafael Palmeiro 2.00
60 Carlos Delgado 2.00
61 *Jose Valverde* 10.00
62 *Doug Devore* 10.00
63 *John Ennis* 10.00
64 Joey Dawley 10.00
65 *Trey Hodges* 12.00
66 Mike Mahoney 10.00
67 *Aaron Cook* 12.00
68 *Rene Reyes* 10.00
69 Mark Corey 10.00
70 *Hansel Izquierdo* 10.00
71 *Brandon Puffer* 10.00
72 *Jeriome Robertson* 10.00
73 Jose Diaz 10.00
74 David Ross 10.00
75 *Jayson Durocher* 10.00
76 *Eric Good* 10.00
77 *Satoru Komiyama* 10.00
78 *Tyler Yates* 10.00
79 *Eric Junge* 10.00
80 *Anderson Machado* 12.00
81 *Adrian Burnside* 10.00
82 *Ben Howard* 10.00
83 *Clay Condrey* 10.00
84 *Nelson Castro* 10.00
85 *So Taguchi* 15.00
86 *Mike Crudale* 10.00
87 Scotty Layfield 10.00
88 *Steve Bechler* 10.00
89 *Travis Driskill* 10.00
90 *Howie Clark* 10.00
91 *Josh Hancock* 10.00
92 *Jorge De La Rosa* 10.00
93 *Anastacio Martinez* 10.00
94 Brian Tallet 12.00
95 *Carl Sadler* 10.00
96 *Cliff Lee* 15.00
97 *Josh Bard* 12.00
98 *Wes Obermueller* 10.00
99 Juan Brito 10.00

100 *Aaron Guiel* 10.00
101 *Jeremy Hill* 10.00
102 *Kevin Frederick* 10.00
103 *Nate Field* 10.00
104 *Julio Mateo* 10.00
105 *Chris Snelling* 15.00
106 *Felix Escalona* 10.00
107 *Reynaldo Garcia* 10.00
108 *Mike Smith* 10.00
109 *Ken Huckaby* 10.00
110 *Kevin Cash* 10.00
111 *Kazuhisa Ishii/auto* 50.00
112 *Freddy Sanchez/auto* 30.00
113 *Jason Simontacchi/auto* 25.00
114 *Jorge Padilla/auto* 15.00
115 Kirk Saarloos/auto 25.00
116 *Rodrigo Rosario/auto* 15.00
117 *Oliver Perez/auto* 35.00
118 *Miguel Asencio/auto* 15.00
119 *Franklyn German/auto* 15.00
120 *Jaime Cerda/auto* 15.00

2002 Upper Deck Ultimate Collection Double Barrel

MT
Quantity produced listed
DB-BRManny Ramirez, Jeff Bagwell/1
DB-DGJoe DiMaggio, Ken Griffey Jr./5
DB-DJCarlos Delgado, Jason Giambi/2
DB-GHTodd Helton, Shawn Green/2
DB-GIKen Griffey Jr., Ichiro Suzuki/3
DB-GJLuis Gonzalez, Randy Johnson/1
DB-GPJuan Gonzalez, Rafael Palmeiro/3
DB-IMEdgar Martinez, Ichiro Suzuki/1
DB-JJAndruw Jones, Chipper Jones/2
DB-JMChipper Jones, Greg Maddux/1
DB-RIIvan Rodriguez, Alex Rodriguez/5 2225.
DB-RMAlex Rodriguez, Miguel Tejada/2
DB-RRCal Ripken Jr., Alex Rodriguez/9 1625.
DB-RSSammy Sosa, Manny Ramirez/3
DB-SCSammy Sosa, Fred McGriff/3
DB-SMMark McGwire, Sammy Sosa/1
DB-TDCarlos Delgado, Jim Thome/3
DB-TOMaggio Ordonez, Frank Thomas/4 950.00

2002 Upper Deck Ultimate Collection Jerseys Tier 1

MT
Common Player: 12.00
Production 99 sets
Golds: .75-1.5X
Production 50 sets
RC Roger Clemens 25.00
JD Joe DiMaggio 100.00
AD Adam Dunn 20.00
JG Jason Giambi 20.00
KG Ken Griffey Jr. 30.00
KI Kazuhisa Ishii 12.00
RJ Randy Johnson 20.00
AJ Andruw Jones 12.00
CJ Chipper Jones 20.00
MM Mickey Mantle 125.00
PM Pedro J. Martinez 15.00
MC Mark McGwire 60.00
MP Mike Piazza 25.00
PR Mark Prior 30.00
MR Manny Ramirez 12.00
CR Cal Ripken Jr. 45.00
AR Alex Rodriguez 30.00
IR Ivan Rodriguez 15.00
AS Alfonso Soriano 30.00
SS Sammy Sosa 40.00
IS Ichiro Suzuki 45.00

2002 Upper Deck Ultimate Collection Jerseys Tier 3

MT
Common Player: 8.00
Stars: .4-.6X Tier 1 price
Production 199 sets

2002 Upper Deck Ultimate Collection Jerseys Tier 2

MT
Same price as Tier 1
Production 99 sets
Golds: 1.5-2X
Production 25 sets

2002 Upper Deck Ultimate Collection Jerseys Tier 4

MT
Common Player: 8.00
Stars: .4-.6X Tier 1 price
Production 199 sets

2002 Upper Deck Ultimate Collection Patch

MT
Common Player: 30.00
Production 100 sets
LG Luis Gonzalez 30.00
SG Shawn Green 30.00
TH Todd Helton 30.00
KI Kazuhisa Ishii 50.00
CJ Chipper Jones 40.00
MM Mark McGwire 180.00
MP Mark Prior 45.00
IR Ivan Rodriguez 35.00
SS Sammy Sosa 65.00
IS Ichiro Suzuki 200.00

2002 Upper Deck Ultimate Collection Double Patches

MT
Common Card: 40.00
Production 100 sets
Golds: .75-1.5X
Production 50 sets
DE J.D. Drew, Jim Edmonds 75.00
GC Jason Giambi, Roger Clemens 100.00
IG Ken Griffey Jr., Ichiro Suzuki 220.00
JS Randy Johnson, Curt Schilling 75.00
MG Tom Glavine, Greg Maddux 75.00
MS Sammy Sosa, Mark McGwire 250.00
PA Mike Piazza, Roberto Alomar 110.00
RG Alex Rodriguez, Juan Gonzalez 80.00
RM Manny Ramirez, PedroJ. Martinez 40.00

2002 Upper Deck Ultimate Collection Signatures Tier 1

MT
Common Autograph: 20.00
Quantity produced listed
Golds: No Pricing
Production 25 sets
RA1 Roberto Alomar/155 45.00
LB1 Lance Berkman/179 25.00
PB1 Pat Burrell/95 50.00
RC1 Roger Clemens/320 80.00
CD1 Carlos Delgado/95 30.00
JD1 J.D. Drew/220 25.00
AD1 Adam Dunn/125 45.00
JG1 Jason Giambi/295 50.00
BG1 Brian Giles/220 25.00
LG1 Luis Gonzalez/199 25.00
KG1 Ken Griffey Jr./195 125.00
JK1 Jason Kendall/220 20.00
MP1 Mark Prior/160 50.00
CR1 Cal Ripken Jr./75 165.00
AR1 Alex Rodriguez/329 100.00
SR1 Scott Rolen/160 25.00
GS1 Gary Sheffield/95 20.00
JT1 Jim Thome/95 65.00
BZ1 Barry Zito/199 50.00

2002 Upper Deck Ultimate Collection Signatures Tier 2

MT
Quantity produced listed
Golds: No Pricing
Production 10 sets
JB2 Jeff Bagwell/51 55.00
LB2 Lance Berkman/85 45.00
JG2 Jason Giambi/50 75.00
LG2 Luis Gonzalez/70 30.00
KG2 Ken Griffey Jr./30
TG2 Tony Gwynn/51 75.00
TH2 Todd Helton/51 60.00
AJ2 Andruw Jones/51 50.00
MP2 Mark Prior/60 70.00
KP2 Kirby Puckett/75 85.00
AR2 Alex Rodriguez/75 100.00
SR2 Scott Rolen/60 50.00
DS2 Duke Snider/51 75.00
FT2 Frank Thomas/51 65.00
KW2 Kerry Wood/51
BZ2 Barry Zito/70 50.00

2002 Upper Deck Ultimate Collection Signed Excellence

MT
Quantity produced listed
Golds: No Pricing
Production 1 set
I1 Ichiro Suzuki/56 375.00
I2 Ichiro Suzuki/51 375.00
I3 Ichiro Suzuki/23
I4 Ichiro Suzuki/12
I5 Ichiro Suzuki/batting 300.00
I6 Ichiro Suzuki/throwing 300.00
MM1 Mark McGwire/70 275.00
MM2 Mark McGwire/65 275.00
MM3 Mark McGwire/49 300.00
MM4 Mark McGwire/25
MM5 Mark McGwire/standing 220.00
MM6 Mark McGwire/waving 220.00
MM7 Mark McGwire/fielding 220.00
SS1 Sammy Sosa/66 175.00
SS2 Sammy Sosa/64 175.00
SS3 Sammy Sosa/54 175.00
SS4 Sammy Sosa/21
SS5 Sammy Sosa/running 150.00
SS6 Sammy Sosa/holding bat 150.00
SS7 Sammy Sosa/150 150.00

2003 Donruss

MT
Complete Set (400): 40.00
Common Player: .15
Pack (13): 2.25
Box (24): 45.00
1 Vladimir Guerrero .75
2 Derek Jeter 2.50
3 Adam Dunn .60
4 Greg Maddux 1.25
5 Lance Berkman .40
6 Ichiro Suzuki 2.00
7 Mike Piazza 2.00
8 Alex Rodriguez 2.00
9 Tom Glavine .25
10 Randy Johnson .75
11 Nomar Garciaparra 1.50
12 Jason Giambi 1.25
13 Sammy Sosa 1.25
14 Barry Zito .25
15 Chipper Jones 1.25
16 Magglio Ordonez .25
17 Larry Walker .25
18 Alfonso Soriano 1.50
19 Curt Schilling .50
20 Barry Bonds 2.00
21 Joe Borchard .15
22 Chris Snelling .25
23 Brian Tallet .15
24 Cliff Lee .15
25 Freddy Sanchez .15
26 Chone Figgins .15
27 Kevin Cash .15
28 Josh Bard .15
29 Jeriome Robertson .15
30 Jeremy Hill .15
31 Shane Nance .15
32 Jake Peavy Padres .15
33 Trey Hodges .15
34 Eric Eckenstahler .15
35 Jim Rushford .15
36 Oliver Perez .15
37 Kirk Saarloos .15
38 Hank Blalock .50
39 Francisco Rodriguez .25
40 Runelvys Hernandez .15
41 Aaron Cook .15
42 Josh Hancock .15
43 P.J. Bevis .15
44 Jon Adkins .15
45 Tim Kalita .15
46 Nelson Castro .15
47 Colin Young .15
48 Adrian Burnside .15
49 Luis Martinez .15
50 Peter Zamora .15
51 Todd Donovan .15
52 Jeremy Ward .15
53 Wilson Valdez .15
54 Eric Good .15
55 Jeff Baker .15
56 Mitch Wylie .15
57 Ron Calloway .15
58 Jose Valverde .15
59 Jason Davis .15
60 Scotty Layfield .15
61 Matt Thornton .15
62 Adam Walker .15
63 Gustavo Chacin .15
64 Ron Chiavacci .15
65 Wiki Nieves .15
66 Clifford Bartosh .15
67 Mike Gonzalez .15
68 Justin Wayne .15

69 Eric Junge .15
70 Ben Kozlowski .15
71 Darin Erstad .40
72 Garret Anderson .40
73 Troy Glaus .60
74 David Eckstein .15
75 Adam Kennedy .15
76 Kevin Appier .15
77 Jarrod Washburn .15
78 Scott Spiezio .15
79 Tim Salmon .25
80 Ramon Ortiz .15
81 Bengie Molina .15
82 Brad Fullmer .15
83 Troy Percival .15
84 David Segui .15
85 Jay Gibbons .15
86 Tony Batista .15
87 Scott Erickson .15
88 Jeff Conine .15
89 Melvin Mora .15
90 Buddy Groom .15
91 Rodrigo Lopez .15
92 Marty Cordova .15
93 Geronimo Gil .15
94 Kenny Lofton .15
95 Shea Hillenbrand .15
96 Manny Ramirez .60
97 Pedro Martinez .75
98 Nomar Garciaparra 1.50
99 Rickey Henderson .40
100 Johnny Damon .15
101 Trot Nixon .15
102 Derek Lowe .15
103 Hee Seop Choi .15
104 Mark Teixeira .40
105 Tim Wakefield .15
106 Jason Varitek .15
107 Frank Thomas .60
108 Joe Crede .15
109 Magglio Ordonez .30
110 Ray Durham .15
111 Mark Buehrle .15
112 Paul Konerko .25
113 Jose Valentin .15
114 Carlos Lee .15
115 Royce Clayton .15
116 C.C. Sabathia .15
117 Ellis Burks .15
118 Omar Vizquel .25
119 Jim Thome .75
120 Matt Lawton .15
121 Travis Fryman .15
122 Earl Snyder .15
123 Ricky Gutierrez .15
124 Einar Diaz .15
125 Danys Baez .15
126 Robert Fick .15
127 Bobby Higginson .15
128 Steve Sparks .15
129 Mike Rivera .15
130 Wendell Magee .15
131 Randall Simon .15
132 Carlos Pena .15
133 Mark Redman .15
134 Juan Acevedo .15
135 Mike Sweeney .15
136 Aaron Guiel .15
137 Carlos Beltran .15
138 Joe Randa .15
139 Paul Byrd .15
140 Shawn Sedlacek .15
141 Raul Ibanez .15
142 Michael Tucker .15
143 Torii Hunter .40
144 Jacque Jones .15
145 David Ortiz .15
146 Corey Koskie .15
147 Brad Radke .15
148 Doug Mientkiewicz .15
149 A.J. Pierzynski .15
150 Dustan Mohr .15
151 Michael Cuddyer .15
152 Eddie Guardado .15
153 Cristian Guzman .15
154 Derek Jeter 2.50
155 Bernie Williams .50
156 Roger Clemens 1.25
157 Mike Mussina .50
158 Jorge Posada .40
159 Alfonso Soriano 1.50
160 Jason Giambi 1.25
161 Robin Ventura .25
162 Andy Pettitte .25
163 David Wells .15
164 Nick Johnson .15
165 Jeff Weaver .15
166 Raul Mondesi .15
167 Rondell White .15
168 Tim Hudson .25
169 Barry Zito .40
170 Mark Mulder .25
171 Miguel Tejada .40
172 Eric Chavez .25
173 Billy Koch .15
174 Jermaine Dye .15
175 Scott Hatteberg .15
176 Terrence Long .15
177 David Justice .25
178 Ramon Hernandez .15
179 Ted Lilly .15
180 Ichiro Suzuki 2.00
181 Edgar Martinez .15
182 Mike Cameron .15
183 John Olerud .25
184 Bret Boone .15
185 Dan Wilson .15
186 Freddy Garcia .15
187 Jamie Moyer .15
188 Carlos Guillen .15
189 Ruben Sierra .15
190 Kazuhiro Sasaki .15
191 Mark McLemore .15
192 Chris Snelling .15
193 Joel Pineiro .15
194 Jeff Cirillo .15
195 Rafael Soriano .15
196 Ben Grieve .15
197 Aubrey Huff .15
198 Steve Cox .15
199 Toby Hall .15
200 Randy Winn .15
201 Brent Abernathy .15
202 Chris Gomez .15
203 John Flaherty .15
204 Paul Wilson .15
205 Chan Ho Park .15
206 Alex Rodriguez 2.00
207 Juan Gonzalez .50
208 Rafael Palmeiro .40
209 Ivan Rodriguez .50
210 Rusty Greer .15
211 Kenny Rogers .15
212 Ismael Valdes .15
213 Frank Catalanotto .15
214 Hank Blalock .40
215 Michael Young .15
216 Kevin Mench .15
217 Herbert Perry .15
218 Gabe Kapler .15
219 Carlos Delgado .25
220 Shannon Stewart .15
221 Eric Hinske .15
222 Roy Halladay .15
223 Felipe Lopez .15
224 Vernon Wells .15
225 Josh Phelps .15
226 Jose Cruz .15
227 Curt Schilling .50
228 Randy Johnson .75
229 Luis Gonzalez .25
230 Mark Grace .40
231 Junior Spivey .15
232 Tony Womack .15
233 Matt Williams .25
234 Steve Finley .15
235 Byung-Hyun Kim .15
236 Craig Counsell .15
237 Greg Maddux 1.25
238 Tom Glavine .40
239 John Smoltz .15
240 Chipper Jones 1.25
241 Gary Sheffield .25
242 Andruw Jones .40
243 Vinny Castilla .15
244 Damian Moss .15
245 Rafael Furcal .15
246 Javy Lopez .15
247 Kevin Millwood .15
248 Kerry Wood .40
249 Fred McGriff .25
250 Sammy Sosa 1.25
251 Alex Gonzalez .15
252 Corey Patterson .15
253 Moises Alou .15
254 Juan Cruz .15
255 Jon Lieber .15
256 Matt Clement .15
257 Mark Prior .40
258 Ken Griffey Jr. 1.50
259 Barry Larkin .25
260 Adam Dunn .60
261 Sean Casey .15
262 Jose Rijo .15
263 Elmer Dessens .15
264 Austin Kearns .40
265 Corky Miller .15
266 Todd Walker .15
267 Chris Reitsma .15
268 Ryan Dempster .15
269 Aaron Boone .15
270 Danny Graves .15
271 Brandon Larson .15
272 Larry Walker .40
273 Todd Helton .40
274 Juan Uribe .15
275 Juan Pierre .15
276 Mike Hampton .15
277 Todd Zeile .15
278 Todd Hollandsworth .15
279 Jason Jennings .15
280 Josh Beckett .15
281 Mike Lowell .15
282 Derrek Lee .15
283 A.J. Burnett .15
284 Luis Castillo .15
285 Tim Raines .15
286 Preston Wilson .15
287 Juan Encarnacion .15
288 Charles Johnson .15
289 Jeff Bagwell .60
290 Craig Biggio .25
291 Lance Berkman .40
292 Daryle Ward .15
293 Roy Oswalt .40
294 Richard Hidalgo .15
295 Octavio Dotel .15
296 Wade Miller .15
297 Julio Lugo .15
298 Billy Wagner .15
299 Shawn Green .40
300 Adrian Beltre .25
301 Paul LoDuca .15
302 Eric Karros .15
303 Kevin Brown .15
304 Hideo Nomo .40
305 Odalis Perez .15
306 Eric Gagne .15
307 Brian Jordan .15
308 Cesar Izturis .15
309 Mark Grudzielanek .15
310 Kazuhisa Ishii .15
311 Geoff Jenkins .15
312 Richie Sexson .40
313 Jose Hernandez .15
314 Ben Sheets .15
315 Ruben Quevedo .15
316 Jeffrey Hammonds .15
317 Alex Sanchez .15
318 Eric Young .15
319 Takahito Nomura .15
320 Vladimir Guerrero .75
321 Jose Vidro .15
322 Orlando Cabrera .15
323 Michael Barrett .15
324 Javier Vazquez .15
325 Tony Armas Jr. .15
326 Andres Galarraga .15
327 Tomokazu Ohka .15
328 Bartolo Colon .15
329 Fernando Tatis .15
330 Brad Wilkerson .15
331 Masato Yoshii .15
332 Mike Piazza 2.00
333 Jeromy Burnitz .15
334 Roberto Alomar .50
335 Mo Vaughn .25
336 Al Leiter .25
337 Pedro Astacio .15
338 Edgardo Alfonzo .15
339 Armando Benitez .15
340 Timoniel Perez .15
341 Jay Payton .15
342 Roger Cedeno .15
343 Rey Ordonez .15
344 Steve Trachsel .15
345 Satoru Komiyama .15
346 Scott Rolen .40
347 Pat Burrell .50
348 Bobby Abreu .25
349 Mike Lieberthal .15
350 Brandon Duckworth .15
351 Jimmy Rollins .15
352 Marlon Anderson .15
353 Travis Lee .15
354 Vicente Padilla .15
355 Randy Wolf .15
356 Jason Kendall .15
357 Brian Giles .40
358 Aramis Ramirez .15
359 Pokey Reese .15
360 Kip Wells .15
361 Josh Fogg .15
362 Mike Williams .15
363 Jack Wilson .15
364 Craig Wilson .15
365 Kevin Young .15
366 Ryan Klesko .15
367 Phil Nevin .15
368 Brian Lawrence .15
369 Mark Kotsay .15
370 Brett Tomko .15
371 Trevor Hoffman .15
372 Deivi Cruz .15
373 Bubba Trammell .15
374 Sean Burroughs .15
375 Barry Bonds 2.00
376 Jeff Kent .25
377 Rich Aurilia .15
378 Tsuyoshi Shinjo .15
379 Benito Santiago .15
380 Kirk Rueter .15
381 Livan Hernandez .15
382 Russ Ortiz .15
383 David Bell .15
384 Jason Schmidt .15
385 Reggie Sanders .15
386 J.T. Snow .15
387 Robb Nen .15
388 Ryan Jensen .15
389 Jim Edmonds .25
390 J.D. Drew .25
391 Albert Pujols 1.00
392 Fernando Vina .15
393 Tino Martinez .15
394 Edgar Renteria .15
395 Matt Morris .15
396 Woody Williams .15
397 Jason Isringhausen .15
398 Placido Polanco .15
399 Eli Marrero .15
400 Jason Simontacchi .15

2003 Donruss Stat Line Career

MT
Cards serial numbered
251-400: 3-6X
Print run 151-250: 4-8X
Print run 101-150: 5-10X
Print run 61-100: 8-15X
Print run 31-60: 10-20X
Numbered to career stat

2003 Donruss Stat Line Season

MT
Cards serial numbered
151-200: 4-8X
Print run 101-150: 5-10X
Print run 61-100: 8-15X
Print run 31-60: 10-20X
Numbered to 2002 stat

2003 Donruss All-Stars

MT
Complete Set (10): 40.00
Common Player: 2.00
Retail only
1 Ichiro Suzuki 8.00
2 Alex Rodriguez 8.00
3 Nomar Garciaparra 6.00
4 Derek Jeter 10.00
5 Manny Ramirez 2.50
6 Barry Bonds 8.00
7 Adam Dunn 2.00
8 Mike Piazza 8.00
9 Sammy Sosa 5.00
10 Todd Helton 2.00

2003 Donruss Anniversary 1983

MT
Complete Set (20): 50.00
Common Player: 1.50
Inserted 1:12
1 Dale Murphy 2.00
2 Jim Palmer 2.00

3 Nolan Ryan 8.00
4 Ozzie Smith 4.00
5 Tom Seaver 4.00
6 Mike Schmidt 5.00
7 Steve Carlton 2.00
8 Robin Yount 3.00
9 Ryne Sandberg 4.00
10 Cal Ripken Jr. 8.00
11 Fernando Valenzuela 1.50
12 Andre Dawson 2.00
13 George Brett 6.00
14 Eddie Murray 3.00
15 Dave Winfield 2.00
16 Johnny Bench 5.00
17 Wade Boggs 2.00
18 Tony Gwynn 4.00
19 San Diego Chicken 1.50
20 Ty Cobb 5.00

2003 Donruss Bat Kings

MT
Common Player: 10.00
Studio Series: 1.5-3X
Production 25 or 50
1 Scott Rolen/250 20.00
2 Frank Thomas/250 15.00
3 Chipper Jones/250 25.00
4 Ivan Rodriguez/250 15.00
5 Stan Musial/100 40.00
6 Nomar Garciaparra/250 30.00
7 Vladimir Guerrero/250 15.00
8 Adam Dunn/250 15.00
9 Lance Berkman/250 10.00
10 Magglio Ordonez/250 12.00
11 Ernie Banks/50 40.00
12 Manny Ramirez/100 25.00
13 Mike Piazza/100 40.00
14 Alex Rodriguez/100 25.00
15 Todd Helton/100 20.00
16 Andre Dawson/100 20.00
17 Cal Ripken Jr/100 60.00
18 Tony Gwynn/100 35.00
19 Don Mattingly/100 60.00
20 Ryne Sandberg/100 40.00

2003 Donruss Diamond Kings

MT
Complete Set (20): 120.00
Common Player: 2.00
Production 2,500 sets
Studio Series: 1.5-3X
Production 250 sets
1 Vladimir Guerrero 5.00
2 Derek Jeter 15.00
3 Adam Dunn 5.00
4 Greg Maddux 8.00
5 Lance Berkman 3.00
6 Ichiro Suzuki 10.00
7 Mike Piazza 10.00
8 Alex Rodriguez 10.00
9 Tom Glavine 3.00
10 Randy Johnson 5.00
11 Nomar Garciaparra 10.00
12 Jason Giambi 8.00
13 Sammy Sosa 8.00
14 Barry Zito 3.00
15 Chipper Jones 8.00
16 Magglio Ordonez 2.00
17 Larry Walker 2.00
18 Alfonso Soriano 10.00
19 Curt Schilling 4.00
20 Barry Bonds 10.00

2003 Donruss Elite Series

MT
Complete Set (15): 60.00
Common Player: 2.00
Production 2,500 sets
Dominators production 25 sets not priced
1 Alex Rodriguez 8.00
2 Barry Bonds 10.00
3 Ichiro Suzuki 8.00
4 Vladimir Guerrero 4.00
5 Randy Johnson 4.00
6 Pedro Martinez 4.00
7 Adam Dunn 3.00
8 Sammy Sosa 6.00
9 Jim Edmonds 2.00
10 Greg Maddux 6.00
11 Kazuhisa Ishii 2.00
12 Jason Giambi 6.00
13 Nomar Garciaparra 8.00
14 Tom Glavine 2.00
15 Todd Helton 2.50

2003 Donruss Elite Dominators

MT
No Pricing 25 sets produced
1 Alex Rodriguez
2 Barry Bonds
3 Ichiro Suzuki
4 Vladimir Guerrero
5 Randy Johnson
6 Pedro Martinez
7 Adam Dunn
8 Sammy Sosa
9 Jim Edmonds
10 Greg Maddux
11 Kazuhisa Ishii
12 Jason Giambi
13 Nomar Garciaparra
14 Tom Glavine
15 Todd Helton

2003 Donruss Jersey Kings

MT
Common Player: 10.00
Studio Series: 1.5-3X
Production 25 or 50
1 Juan Gonzalez/250 15.00
2 Greg Maddux/250 30.00
3 Nomar Garciaparra/250 30.00
4 Troy Glaus/250 20.00
5 Reggie Jackson/100 20.00
6 Alex Rodriguez/250 25.00
7 Alfonso Soriano/250 25.00
8 Curt Schilling/250 12.00
9 Vladimir Guerrero/250 20.00
10 Adam Dunn/250 15.00
11 Mark Grace/100 25.00
12 Roger Clemens/100 30.00
13 Jeff Bagwell/100 25.00
14 Tom Glavine/100 20.00
15 Mike Piazza/100 50.00
16 Rod Carew/100 30.00
17 Rickey Henderson/100 35.00
18 Mike Schmidt/100 50.00
19 Cal Ripken Jr/100 60.00
20 Dale Murphy/100 15.00

2003 Donruss Longball Leaders

MT
Complete Set (10): 35.00
Common Player: 1.50
Production 1,000 sets
Seasonal Sum: 4-8X
Numbered to 2002 HR total
1 Alex Rodriguez 6.00
2 Alfonso Soriano 6.00
3 Rafael Palmeiro 1.50
4 Jim Thome 3.00
5 Jason Giambi 5.00
6 Sammy Sosa 5.00
7 Barry Bonds 8.00
8 Lance Berkman 2.00
9 Shawn Green 1.50
10 Vladimir Guerrero 4.00

2003 Donruss Production Line

MT
Complete Set (30): 120.00
Common Player: 2.00
Numbered to selected stat
Die-Cuts: 1-3X
Production 100 sets
1 Alex Rodriguez/1,015 6.00
2 Jim Thome/1,122 3.00
3 Lance Berkman/982 2.00
4 Barry Bonds/1,381 8.00
5 Sammy Sosa/993 5.00
6 Vladimir Guerrero/1,01 3.00
7 Barry Bonds/582 10.00
8 Jason Giambi/435 6.00
9 Vladimir Guerrero/417 4.00
10 Adam Dunn/400 3.00
11 Chipper Jones/435 6.00
12 Todd Helton/429 3.00
13 Rafael Palmeiro/571 2.00
14 Sammy Sosa/594 6.00
15 Alex Rodriguez/623 8.00
16 Larry Walker/602 2.00
17 Lance Berkman/578 2.00
18 Alfonso Soriano/547 6.00
19 Ichiro Suzuki/321 8.00
20 Mike Sweeney/340 2.00
21 Manny Ramirez/349 4.00
22 Larry Walker/338 2.00
23 Barry Bonds/370 12.00
24 Jim Edmonds/311 2.00
25 Alfonso Soriano/300 8.00
26 Jason Giambi/335 6.00
27 Miguel Tejada/336 4.00
28 Brian Giles/309 3.00
29 Vladimir Guerrero/364 5.00
30 Pat Burrell/319 8.00

2003 Donruss Timber and Threads

MT
Common Player: 6.00
1 Al Kaline/bat/125 60.00
2 Alex Rodriguez/bat/350 20.00
3 Carlos Delgado/bat/250 8.00
4 Cliff Floyd/bat/250 8.00
5 Eddie Mathews/bat/125 35.00
6 Edgar Martinez/bat/125 10.00
7 Ernie Banks/bat/50 40.00
8 Ivan Rodriguez/bat/125 15.00
9 J.D. Drew/bat/125 8.00
10 Jorge Posada/bat/300 10.00
11 Lou Brock/bat/125 20.00
12 Mike Piazza/bat/125 35.00
13 Mike Schmidt/bat/125 50.00
14 Reggie Jackson/bat/125 20.00
15 Rickey Henderson/bat/125 25.00
16 Robin Yount/bat/125 35.00
17 Rod Carew/bat/125 35.00
18 Scott Rolen/bat/125 20.00
19 Shawn Green/bat/200 8.00
20 Willie Stargell/bat/125 15.00
21 Alex Rodriguez/jsy/175 20.00
22 Andruw Jones/jsy/275 8.00
23 Brooks Robinson/jsy/150 25.00
24 Chipper Jones/jsy/150 30.00
25 Greg Maddux/jsy/175 35.00
26 Hideo Nomo/jsy/300 45.00
27 Ivan Rodriguez/jsy/225 8.00
28 Jack Morris/jsy/150 8.00
29 J.D. Drew/jsy/150 8.00
30 Jeff Bagwell/jsy/500 15.00
31 Jim Thome/jsy/200 20.00
32 John Smoltz/jsy/175 8.00
33 John Olerud/jsy/450 8.00
34 Kerry Wood/jsy/200 15.00
35 Harmon Killebrew/jsy/50 60.00
36 Larry Walker/jsy/500 6.00
37 Magglio Ordonez/jsy/150 10.00
38 Manny Ramirez/jsy/500 10.00
39 Mike Piazza/jsy/300 25.00
40 Mike Sweeney/jsy/200 8.00
41 Nomar Garciaparra/jsy/200 25.00
42 Paul Konerko/jsy/500 12.00
43 Pedro Martinez/jsy/175 20.00
44 Randy Johnson/jsy/175 20.00
45 Roger Clemens/jsy/350 20.00
46 Shawn Green/jsy/250 8.00
47 Todd Helton/jsy/175 8.00
48 Tom Glavine/jsy/225 12.00
49 Tony Gwynn/jsy/150 30.00
50 Vladimir Guerrero/jsy/450 20.00

2003 Donruss Team Heroes

Each issue of the Feb., 2003, Beckett Baseball Card Monthly included a sample 2003 Donruss Team Heroes card rubber-cemented inside. The cards differ from the issued version only in the appearance on back of a (usually) silver-foil "SAMPLE" notation. Some cards were produced with the overprint in gold-foil, in much more limited quantities. The number of different players' cards involved in the promotion is unknown.

MT
Complete Set (540): 55.00
Common Player: .15
Pack (13): 2.50
Box (24): 55.00
1 Adam Kennedy .15
2 Steve Green .15
3 Rod Carew .40
4 Alfredo Amezaga .15

No.	Player	Price
5	Reggie Jackson	.50
6	Jarrod Washburn	.15
7	Nolan Ryan	3.00
8	Tim Salmon	.25
9	Garret Anderson	.25
10	Darin Erstad	.25
11	Elpidio Guzman	.15
12	David Eckstein	.15
13	Troy Percival	.15
14	Troy Glaus	.75
15	Doug Devore	.15
16	Tony Womack	.15
17	Matt Williams	.25
18	Junior Spivey	.15
19	Mark Grace	.50
20	Curt Schilling	.75
21	Erubiel Durazo	.15
22	Craig Counsell	.15
23	Byung-Hyun Kim	.15
24	Randy Johnson	1.00
25	Luis Gonzalez	.40
26	John Smoltz	.15
27	Tim Spooneybarger	.15
28	Dale Murphy	.50
29	Warren Spahn	.50
30	Jason Marquis	.15
31	Kevin Millwood	.15
32	Javy Lopez	.15
33	Vinny Castilla	.15
34	Julio Franco	.15
35	Trey Hodges	.15
36	Chipper Jones	1.50
37	Gary Sheffield	.25
38	Billy Sylvester	.15
39	Tom Glavine	.40
40	Rafael Furcal	.15
41	Cory Aldridge	.15
42	Greg Maddux	1.50
43	John Ennis	.15
44	Wes Helms	.15
45	Horacio Ramirez	.15
46	Derrick Lewis	.15
47	Marcus Giles	.15
48	Eddie Mathews	.75
49	Wilson Betemit	.15
50	Andruw Jones	.50
51	Josh Towers	.15
52	Ed Rogers	.15
53	Kris Foster	.15
54	Brooks Robinson	.75
55	Cal Ripken Jr.	3.00
56	Brian Roberts	.15
57	Luis Rivera	.15
58	Rodrigo Lopez	.15
59	Geronimo Gil	.15
60	Erik Bedard	.15
61	Jim Palmer	.40
62	Jay Gibbons	.15
63	Travis Driskill	.15
64	Larry Bigbie	.15
65	Eddie Murray	.40
66	Hoyt Wilhelm	.15
67	Bobby Doerr	.15
68	Pedro J. Martinez	1.00
69	Roger Clemens	1.50
70	Nomar Garciaparra	2.00
71	Trot Nixon	.15
72	Dennis Eckersley	.15
73	John Burkett	.15
74	Tim Wakefield	.15
75	Wade Boggs	.40
76	Cliff Floyd	.15
77	Casey Fossum	.15
78	Johnny Damon	.15
79	Fred Lynn	.15
80	Rickey Henderson	.40
81	Juan Diaz	.15
82	Manny Ramirez	.75
83	Carlton Fisk	.50
84	Jorge De La Rosa	.15
85	Shea Hillenbrand	.15
86	Derek Lowe	.15
87	Jason Varitek	.15
88	Carlos Baerga	.15
89	Freddy Sanchez	.15
90	Ugueth Urbina	.15
91	Rey Sanchez	.15
92	Josh Hancock	.15
93	Tony Clark	.15
94	Dustin Hermanson	.15
95	Ryne Sandberg	1.50
96	Fred McGriff	.25
97	Alex Gonzalez	.15
98	Mark Belhorn	.15
99	Fergie Jenkins	.25
100	Jon Lieber	.15
101	Francis Beltran	.15
102	Greg Maddux	1.50
103	Nate Frese	.15
104	Andre Dawson	.25
105	Carlos Zambrano	.15
106	Steve Smyth	.15
107	Ernie Banks	1.00
108	Will Ohman	.15
109	Kerry Wood	.50
110	Bobby Hill	.15
111	Moises Alou	.15
112	Hee Seop Choi	.15
113	Corey Patterson	.15
114	Sammy Sosa	1.50
115	Mark Prior	.50
116	Juan Cruz	.15
117	Ron Santo	.15
118	Billy Williams	.15
119	Antonio Alfonseca	.15
120	Matt Clement	.15
121	Carlton Fisk	.50
122	Joe Crede	.15
123	Magglio Ordonez	.40
124	Frank Thomas	.75
125	Joe Borchard	.15
126	Royce Clayton	.15
127	Luis Aparicio	.15
128	Willie Harris	.15
129	Kyle Kane	.15
130	Paul Konerko	.25
131	Matt Ginter	.15
132	Carlos Lee	.15
133	Mark Buehrle	.15
134	Adam Dunn	.75
135	Eric Davis	.15
136	Johnny Bench	1.00
137	Joe Morgan	.25
138	Austin Kearns	.40
139	Barry Larkin	.40
140	Ken Griffey Jr.	2.00
141	Luis Pineda	.15
142	Corky Miller	.15
143	Brandon Larson	.15
144	Wily Mo Pena	.15
145	Lance Davis	.15
146	Tom Seaver	1.00
147	Luke Hudson	.15
148	Sean Casey	.15
149	Tony Perez	.15
150	Todd Walker	.15
151	Aaron Boone	.15
152	Jose Rijo	.15
153	Ryan Dempster	.15
154	Danny Graves	.15
155	Matt Lawton	.15
156	Cliff Lee	.15
157	Ryan Drese	.15
158	Danys Baez	.15
159	Einar Diaz	.15
160	Milton Bradley	.15
161	Earl Snyder	.15
162	Ellis Burks	.15
163	Lou Boudreau	.15
164	Bob Feller	.15
165	Ricardo Rodriguez	.15
166	Victor Martinez	.15
167	Alex Herrera	.15
168	Omar Vizquel	.15
169	David Elder	.15
170	C.C. Sabathia	.15
171	Alex Escobar	.15
172	Brian Tallet	.15
173	Jim Thome	.75
174	Rene Reyes	.15
175	Juan Uribe	.15
176	Jason Romano	.15
177	Juan Pierre	.15
178	Jason Jennings	.15
179	Jose Ortiz	.15
180	Larry Walker	.25
181	Cam Esslinger	.15
182	Todd Helton	.50
183	Aaron Cook	.15
184	Jack Cust	.15
185	Jack Morris	.15
186	Mike Rivera	.15
187	Bobby Higginson	.15
188	Fernando Rodney	.15
189	Al Kaline	1.00
190	Carlos Pena	.15
191	Alan Trammell	.15
192	Mike Maroth	.15
193	Adam Pettyjohn	.15
194	David Espinosa	.15
195	Adam Bernero	.15
196	Franklyn German	.15
197	Robert Fick	.15
198	Andres Torres	.15
199	Luis Castillo	.15
200	Preston Wilson	.15
201	Pablo Ozuna	.15
202	Brad Penny	.15
203	Josh Beckett	.15
204	Charles Johnson	.15
205	Wilson Valdez	.15
206	A.J. Burnett	.15
207	Abraham Nunez	.15
208	Mike Lowell	.15
209	Jose Cueto	.15
210	Jeriome Robertson	.15
211	Jeff Bagwell	.75
212	Kirk Saarloos	.15
213	Craig Biggio	.25
214	Rodrigo Rosario	.15
215	Roy Oswalt	.25
216	John Buck	.15
217	Tim Redding	.15
218	Morgan Ensberg	.15
219	Richard Hidalgo	.15
220	Wade Miller	.15
221	Lance Berkman	.50
222	Raul Chavez	.15
223	Carlos Hernandez	.15
224	Greg Miller	.15
225	Tom Shearn	.15
226	Jason Lane	.15
227	Nolan Ryan	3.00
228	Billy Wagner	.15
229	Octavio Dotel	.15
230	Shane Reynolds	.15
231	Julio Lugo	.15
232	Daryle Ward	.15
233	Mike Sweeney	.15
234	Angel Berroa	.15
235	George Brett	1.50
236	Brad Voyles	.15
237	Brandon Berger	.15
238	Chad Durbin	.15
239	Alexis Gomez	.15
240	Jeremy Affeldt	.15
241	Bo Jackson	.75
242	Dee Brown	.15
243	Tony Cogan	.15
244	Carlos Beltran	.15
245	Joe Randa	.15
246	Pee Wee Reese	.25
247	Andy Ashby	.15
248	Cesar Izturis	.15
249	Duke Snider	.50
250	Mark Grudzielanek	.15
251	Chin-Feng Chen	.15
252	Brian Jordan	.15
253	Steve Garvey	.15
254	Odalis Perez	.15
255	Hideo Nomo	.50
256	Kevin Brown	.15
257	Eric Karros	.15
258	Joe Thurston	.15
259	Carlos Garcia	.15
260	Shawn Green	.40
261	Paul LoDuca	.15
262	Kazuhisa Ishii	.15
263	Victor Alvarez	.15
264	Eric Gagne	.15
265	Don Sutton	.15
266	Orel Hershiser	.15
267	Dave Roberts	.15
268	Adrian Beltre	.15
269	Don Drysdale	.50
270	Jackie Robinson	1.50
271	Tyler Houston	.15
272	Omar Daal	.15
273	Marquis Grissom	.15
274	Paul Quantrill	.15
275	Paul Molitor	.50
276	Jose Hernandez	.15
277	Takahito Nomura	.15
278	Nick Neugebauer	.15
279	Jose Mieses	.15
280	Richie Sexson	.40
281	Matt Childers	.15
282	Bill Hall	.15
283	Ben Sheets	.15
284	Brian Mallette	.15
285	Geoff Jenkins	.15
286	Robin Yount	.75
287	Jeff Deardorff	.15
288	Luis Rivas	.15
289	Harmon Killebrew	.50
290	Michael Cuddyer	.15
291	Torii Hunter	.15
292	Kevin Frederick	.15
293	Adam Johnson	.15
294	Jack Morris	.15
295	Rod Carew	.40
296	Kirby Puckett	1.50
297	Joe Mays	.15
298	Jacque Jones	.15
299	Cristian Guzman	.15
300	Kyle Lohse	.15
301	Eric Milton	.15
302	Brad Radke	.15
303	Doug Mientkiewicz	.15
304	Corey Koskie	.15
305	Jose Vidro	.15
306	Claudio Vargas	.15
307	Gary Carter	.15
308	Andre Dawson	.25
309	Henry Mateo	.15
310	Andres Galarraga	.15
311	Zach Day	.15
312	Bartolo Colon	.15
313	Endy Chavez	.15
314	Javier Vazquez	.15
315	Michael Barrett	.15
316	Vladimir Guerrero	1.00
317	Orlando Cabrera	.15
318	Al Leiter	.15
319	Timoniel Perez	.15
320	Rey Ordonez	.15
321	Gary Carter	.15
322	Armando Benitez	.15
323	Dwight Gooden	.15
324	Pedro Astacio	.15
325	Roberto Alomar	.50
326	Edgardo Alfonzo	.15
327	Nolan Ryan	3.00
328	Mo Vaughn	.25
329	Ryan Jamison	.15
330	Satoru Komiyama	.15
331	Mike Piazza	2.50
332	Tom Seaver	1.00
333	Jorge Posada	.40
334	Derek Jeter	2.50
335	Babe Ruth	3.00
336	Lou Gehrig	2.50
337	Andy Pettitte	.40
338	Mariano Rivera	.25
339	Robin Ventura	.15
340	Yogi Berra	1.00
341	Phil Rizzuto	.50
342	Bernie Williams	.50
343	Alfonso Soriano	1.50
344	Drew Henson	.15
345	Erick Almonte	.15
346	Rondell White	.15
347	Christian Parker	.15
348	Joe Torre	.25
349	Nick Johnson	.15
350	Raul Mondesi	.15
351	Brandon Claussen	.15
352	Reggie Jackson	.50
353	Roger Clemens	1.50
354	Don Mattingly	2.00
355	Jason Giambi	1.50
356	Adrian Hernandez	.15
357	Jeff Weaver	.15
358	Mike Mussina	.50
359	Brett Jodie	.15
360	David Wells	.15
361	Enos Slaughter	.15
362	Whitey Ford	.50
363	Eric Chavez	.25
364	Miguel Tejada	.40
365	Barry Zito	.25
366	Bert Snow	.15
367	Rickey Henderson	.50
368	Juan A. Pena	.15
369	Terrence Long	.15
370	Dennis Eckersley	.15
371	Mark Ellis	.15
372	Tim Hudson	.25
373	Jose Canseco	.50
374	Reggie Jackson	.50
375	Mark Mulder	.15
376	David Justice	.25
377	Jermaine Dye	.15
378	Brett Myers	.15
379	Lenny Dykstra	.15
380	Vicente Padilla	.15
381	Bobby Abreu	.15
382	Pat Burrell	.50
383	Jorge Padilla	.15
384	Jeremy Giambi	.15
385	Mike Lieberthal	.15
386	Anderson Machado	.15
387	Marlon Byrd	.15